The International Who's Who 1989-90

The International Who's Who 1989-90

FIFTY-THIRD EDITION

EUROPA PUBLICATIONS LIMITED

Fifty-third Edition 1989

© **Europa Publications Limited 1989**
18 Bedford Square, London WC1B 3JN, England

Australia and New Zealand
James Bennett (Collaroy) Pty. Ltd., 4 Collaroy Street,
Collaroy, N.S.W. 2097, Australia

India
UBS Publishers' Distributors Ltd.,
P.O.B. 7015, 5 Ansari Road, New Delhi 110002

Japan
Maruzen Co. Ltd., P.O.B. 5050, Tokyo International 100–31

ISBN 0-946653-50-X

Library of Congress Catalog Card Number 35-10257

Printed and bound in England by
Staples Printers Rochester Limited,
Love Lane, Rochester, Kent.

FOREWORD TO THE 53rd EDITION

This is the 53rd edition of THE INTERNATIONAL WHO'S WHO. Since the appearance of the first edition in 1935 the book has grown to encompass almost every field of human activity, and now contains over 19,000 biographies. Until the 1960s few personal details were given, but during that decade the entries were expanded to include details of place of birth, parentage, marriage, children and leisure interests. This has resulted in a more interesting and lively book, which answers the needs of readers seeking information on the lives of our most famous and influential contemporaries.

Very few countries have their own Who's Whos, and few national Who's Whos appear annually. THE INTERNATIONAL WHO'S WHO contains in one volume biographical information from almost every country, most of it unavailable in any other annual reference book. More than 1,500 biographies appear in this edition for the first time, and the existing entries have, of course, been revised and updated by the Editor and the Europa team of experienced Assistant Editors.

May 1989.

ABBREVIATIONS

A.A.A.	Agricultural Adjustment Administration
A.A.A.S.	American Association for the Advancement of Science
A.A.F.	Army Air Force
A.A.S.A.	Associate of the Australian Society of Accountants
A.B.	Bachelor of Arts
A.B.A.	American Bar Association
AB	Aktiebolag
A.C.	Companion of the Order of Australia
A.C.A.	Associate of the Institute of Chartered Accountants
A.C.C.A.	Associate of the Association of Certified Accountants
Acad.	Academy, Académie
Accad.	Accademia
Accred.	Accredited
A.C.I.S.	Associate of the Chartered Institute of Secretaries
A.C.P.	American College of Physicians
A.C.S.	American Chemical Society
A.C.T.	Australian Capital Territory
ADC	Aide-de-camp
Admin.	Administrative, Administration, Administrator
Adm.	Admiral
A.E.	Air Efficiency Award
A.E.R.E.	Atomic Energy Research Establishment
A.F.	Air Force
A.F.C.	Air Force Cross
AfDB	African Development Bank
affil.	affiliated
AFL	American Federation of Labor
A.F.M.	Air Force Medal
AG	Aktiengesellschaft (Joint Stock Company)
Agric.	Agriculture
a.i.	ad interim
A.I.A.	Associate of Institute of Actuaries; American Institute of Architects
A.I.A.A.	American Institute of Aeronautics and Astronautics
A.I.B.	Associate of the Institute of Bankers
AICC	All-India Congress Committee
A.I.C.E.	Associate of the Institute of Civil Engineers
A.I.Ch.E.	American Institute of Chemical Engineers
AIDS	Acquired Immune Deficiency Syndrome
A.I.E.E.	American Institute of Electrical Engineers
A.I.M.E.	American Institute of Mining Engineers; Associate of the Institution of Mining Engineers
A.I.Mech.E.	Associate of the Institution of Mechanical Engineers
A.I.R.	All-India Radio
Akad.	Akademie
Ala.	Alabama
A.L.S.	Associate of the Linnaean Society
Alt.	Alternate
A.M.	Master of Arts; Alpes Maritimes; Albert Medal; Member of the Order of Australia
Amb.	Ambassador
A.M.I.C.E.	Associate Member of the Institution of Civil Engineers
A.M.I.E.E.	Associate Member of the Institution of Electrical Engineers
A.M.I.Mech.E.	Associate Member of the Institution of Mechanical Engineers
A.N.U.	Australian National University
A.O.	Officer of the Order of Australia
A.P.	Andhra Pradesh
Apdo	Apartado
approx.	approximately
Apptd.	Appointed
A.R.A.	Associate of the Royal Academy
A.R.A.M.	Associate of the Royal Academy of Music
ARC	Agriculture Research Council
A.R.C.A.	Associate of the Royal College of Art
A.R.C.M.	Associate of the Royal College of Music
A.R.C.O.	Associate Royal College of Organists
A.R.C.S.	Associate of the Royal College of Science
A.R.I.B.A.	Associate of the Royal Institute of British Architects
Ariz.	Arizona
Ark.	Arkansas
A.R.S.A.	Associate of the Royal Scottish Academy; Associate of the Royal Society of Arts
A.S.L.I.B.	Association of Special Libraries and Information Bureaux
A.S.M.E.	American Society of Mechanical Engineers
Asoc.	Asociación
Ass.	Assembly
Asscn.	Association
Assoc.	Associate
A.S.S.R.	Autonomous Soviet Socialist Republic
Asst.	Assistant
ATV	Associated Television
Aug.	August
b.	born
B.A.	Bachelor of Arts; British Airways
B.A.A.S.	British Association for the Advancement of Science
B.A.F.T.A.	British Academy of Film and Television Awards
B.Agr.	Bachelor of Agriculture
B.A.O.	Bachelor of Obstetrics
B.Arch.	Bachelor of Architecture
Bart.	Baronet
B.A.S.	Bachelor in Agricultural Science
BBC	British Broadcasting Corporation
B.C.	British Columbia
B.C.C.	British Council of Churches
B.C.E.	Bachelor of Civil Engineering
B.Ch., B.Chir.	Bachelor of Surgery
B.C.L.	Bachelor of Civil Law; Bachelor of Canon Law
B.Com(m).	Bachelor of Commerce
B.C.S.	Bachelor of Commercial Sciences
B.D.	Bachelor of Divinity
Bd.	Board
B.D.S.	Bachelor of Dental Surgery
B.E.	Bachelor of Engineering; Bachelor of Education
BEA	British European Airways
B.Econs.	Bachelor of Economics
B.Ed.	Bachelor of Education
Beds.	Bedfordshire
B.E.E.	Bachelor of Electrical Engineering
B.E.M.	British Empire Medal
B.Eng.	Bachelor of Engineering
Berks.	Berkshire
B.F.A.	Bachelor of Fine Arts
B.F.I.	British Film Institute
B.I.M.	British Institute of Management
biog.	biography
BIS	Bank for International Settlements
B.L.	Bachelor of Laws
Bldg.	Building
B.Lit(t).	Bachelor of Letters
B.LL.	Bachelor of Laws
B.L.S.	Bachelor in Library Science
blvd.	boulevard
B.M.	Bachelor of Medicine
B.M.A.	British Medical Association
B.Mus.	Bachelor of Music
Bn.	Battalion
BNOC	British National Oil Corporation
BOAC	British Overseas Airways Corporation
B.P.A.	Bachelor of Public Administration
Brig.	Brigadier
B.S.	Bachelor of Science; Bachelor of Surgery
B.S.A.	Bachelor of Scientific Agriculture
B.Sc.	Bachelor of Science
Bt.	Baronet
Bucks.	Buckinghamshire
c.	child, children
C.A.	Chartered Accountant
Calif.	California
Cambs.	Cambridgeshire
Cand.	Candidate, Candidature
Cantab.	Of Cambridge University
Capt.	Captain
Cards.	Cardiganshire
C.B.	Companion of the (Order of the) Bath
CBC	Canadian Broadcasting Corporation
C.B.E.	Commander of (the Order of) the British Empire
CBI	Confederation of British Industry
C.B.I.M.	Companion of British Institute of Management

ABBREVIATIONS

CBS	Columbia Broadcasting System	D.C.	District of Columbia
C.C.	Companion of Order of Canada	D.C.L.	Doctor of Civil Law
CCP	Chinese Communist Party	D.C.M.	Distinguished Conduct Medal
C.D.	Canadian Forces Decoration	D.C.M.G.	Dame Commander of (the Order of) St. Michael and St. George
Cdre.	Commodore		
CDU	Christlich-Demokratische Union	D.Cn.L.	Doctor of Canon Law
C.E.	Civil Engineer, Chartered Engineer	D.Comm.	Doctor of Commerce
CEAO	Communauté Economique de l'Afrique de l'Ouest	D.C.S.	Doctor of Commercial Sciences
Cen.	Central	D.C.T.	Doctor of Christian Theology
C.Eng.	Chartered Engineer	D.C.V.O.	Dame Commander of the Royal Victorian Order
CENTO	Central Treaty Organization	D.D.	Doctor of Divinity
C.E.O.	Chief Executive Officer	D.D.R.	Deutsche Demokratische Republik (German Democratic Republic)
C.E.R.N.	Conseil (now Organisation) Européen(ne) pour la Recherche Nucléaire		
		D.D.S.	Doctor of Dental Surgery
C.F.R.	Commander of the Federal Republic of Nigeria	Dec.	December
C.G.M.	Conspicuous Gallantry Medal	D.Econ.	Doctor of Economics
CGT	Confédération Général du Travail	Del.	Delegate, delegation, Delaware
C.H.	Companion of Honour	Denbighs.	Denbighshire
Chair.	Chairman, Chairwoman, Chairperson	D. en D.	Docteur en Droit
Ch.B.	Bachelor of Surgery	D. en Med.	Docteur en Medicine
C.Chem.	Chartered Chemist	D.Eng.	Doctor of Engineering
Chem.	Chemistry	Dept.	Department
Ch.M	Master of Surgery	D.E.S.	Department of Education and Science
C.I.	Channel Islands	Desig.	Designate
CIA	Central Intelligence Agency	D. ès L.	Docteur ès Lettres
Cía.	Compañía (Company)	D. ès Sc.	Docteur ès Sciences
Cia.	Compagnia (Company)	Devt.	Development
CID	Criminal Investigation Department	D.F.	Distrito Federal
C.I.E.	Companion of (the Order of) the Indian Empire	D.F.A.	Doctor of Fine Arts
Cie.	Compagnie (Company)	D.F.C.	Distinguished Flying Cross
C.I.E.E.	Companion of the Institution of Electrical Engineers	D.F.M.	Distinguished Flying Medal
		D.H.	Doctor of Humanities
C.-in-C.	Commander-in-Chief	D.Hist.	Doctor of History
CIO	Congress of Industrial Organizations	D.H.L.	Doctor of Hebrew Literature
C.L.D.	Doctor of Civil Law (U.S.A.)	D.Hum.Litt.	Doctor of Humane Letters
C.Lit.	Companion of Literature	D.I.C.	Diploma of Imperial College
C.M.	Canada Medal; Master in Surgery	Dip.A.D.	Diploma in Art and Design
CMEA	Council for Mutual Economic Assistance	Dip.Agr.	Diploma in Agriculture
C.M.G.	Companion of (the Order of) St. Michael and St. George	Dip.Ed.	Diploma in Education
		Dip(l).Eng.	Diploma in Engineering
C.N.A.A.	Council for National Academic Awards	Dir.	Director
C.N.R.S.	Centre National de la Recherche Scientifique	Dist.	District
Co.	Company; County	D.Iur.	Doctor of Law
C.O.	Commanding Officer	D. Iur. Utr.	Doctor of both Civil and Canon Law
COI	Central Office of Information	Div.	Division; Divisional
Col.	Colonel	D.Jur.	Doctor of Law
Coll.	College	D.K.	Most Esteemed Family (Malaysia)
Colo.	Colorado	D.L.	Deputy Lieutenant
COMECON	Council for Mutual Economic Assistance	D.Lit(t).	Doctor of Letters; Doctor of Literature
Comm.	Commission	D.L.S.	Doctor of Library Science
Commdg.	Commanding	D.M.	Doctor of Medicine (Oxford)
Commdr.	Commander, Commandeur	D.M.D.	Doctor of Dental Medicine
Commdt.	Commandant	D.M.S.	Director of Medical Services
Commr.	Commissioner	D. Min. Sci.	Doctor of Municipal Science
Conf.	Conference	D.Mus.	Doctor of Music
Confed.	Confederation	D.M.V.	Doctor of Veterinary Medicine
Conn.	Connecticut	D.O.	Doctor of Ophthalmology
Contrib.	Contributor; contribution	D.P.H.	Diploma in Public Health
C.O.O.	Chief Operating Officer	D.P.M.	Diploma in Psychological Medicine
Corp.	Corporate	D.Phil.	Doctor of Philosophy
Corpn.	Corporation	Dr. Agr.	Doctor of Agriculture
Corresp.	Correspondent; Corresponding	Dr.Ing.	Doctor of Engineering
CP	Communist Party; Caixa Postal (Post Office Box)	Dr.Iur.	Doctor of Laws
CPA	Commonwealth Parliamentary Association	D(r).Med.	Doctor of Medicine
C.P.A.	Certified Public Accountant	Dr.Oec.(Publ.)	Doctor of (Public) Economy
C.Phys.	Chartered Physicist	Dr.rer.nat.	Doctor of Natural Sciences
CPP	Convention People's Party (Ghana)	Dr.rer.Pol.	Doctor of Political Science
CPPCC	Chinese People's Political Consultative Conference	Dr.SC.	Doctor of Sciences
CPSU	Communist Party of the Soviet Union	Dr.Sc.Nat.	Doctor of Natural Sciences
cr.	created	D.S.	Doctor of Science
C.Sc.	Candidate of Sciences	D.S.C.	Distinguished Service Cross
CSCE	Conference on Security and Co-operation in Europe	D.Sc.	Doctor of Science
C.S.I.	Companion of (the Order of) the Star of India	D.Sc.S.	Doctor of Social Science
CSIRO	Commonwealth Scientific and Industrial Research Organization	D.S.M.	Distinguished Service Medal
		D.S.O.	Companion of the Distinguished Service Order
C.S.S.R.	Czechoslovak Socialist Republic	D.S.T.	Doctor of Sacred Theology
C.St.J.	Commander of (the Order of) St. John of Jerusalem	D.Tech.	Doctor of Technology
Cttee.	Committee	D.Theol.	Doctor of Theology
C.V.	Commanditaire Vennootschap	D.T.M.(& H.)	Diploma in Tropical Medicine (and Hygiene)
C.V.O.	Commander of the Royal Victorian Order	D.U.P.	Diploma of the University of Paris
d.	daughter(s)		
D.Arch	Doctor of Architecture	E.	East
D.B.	Bachelor of Divinity	ECA	Economic Co-operation Administration; Economic Commission for Africa
D.B.A.	Doctor of Business Administration		
D.B.E.	Dame Commander of (the Order of) the British Empire	ECAFE	Economic Commission for Asia and the Far East
		ECE	Economic Commission for Europe

ABBREVIATIONS

ECLA	Economic Commission for Latin America
Econ(s).	Economic(s)
ECOSOC	Economic and Social Council
ECSC	European Coal and Steel Community
ECWA	Economic Commission for Western Asia
ed.	educated; editor; edited
Ed.D.	Doctor of Education
Ed.M.	Master of Education
E.D.	Efficiency Decoration; Doctor of Engineering (U.S.A.)
Ed.	Editor
Edin.	Edinburgh
Edn.	Edition
Educ.	Education
EEC	European Economic Community
EFTA	European Free Trade Association
e.h.	Ehrenhalben (Honorary)
EIB	European Investment Bank
E.M.	Edward Medal; Master of Engineering (U.S.A.)
Emer.	Emeritus
Eng.	Engineering
Eng.D.	Doctor of Engineering
ESCAP	Economic and Social Commission for Asia and the Pacific
est.	established
ETH	Eidgenössische Technische Hochschule (Swiss Federal Institute of Technology)
Ets.	Etablissements
EURATOM	European Atomic Energy Community
Exec.	Executive
Exhbn.	Exhibition
Ext.	Extension
f.	founded
F.A.A.	Fellow of Australian Academy of Science
F.A.A.T.S.	Fellow Australian Academy of Technological Sciences
F.A.C.C.	Fellow of the American College of Cardiology
F.A.C.C.A.	Fellow of the Association of Certified and Corporate Accountants
F.A.C.E.	Fellow of the Australian College of Education
F.A.C.P.	Fellow of American College of Physicians
F.A.C.S.	Fellow of the American College of Surgeons
F.A.H.A.	Fellow Australian Academy of the Humanities
F.A.I.A.	Fellow of the American Institute of Architects
F.A.I.A.S.	Fellow of the Australian Institute of Agricultural Science
F.A.I.M.	Fellow of the Australian Institute of Management
FAO	Food and Agriculture Organization
F.A.S.E.	Fellow of Antiquarian Society, Edinburgh
F.A.S.S.A.	Fellow Academy of Social Sciences of Australia
F.B.A.	Fellow of the British Academy
FBI	Federal Bureau of Investigation
F.B.I.M.	Fellow of the British Institute of Management
F.B.I.P.	Fellow of the British Institute of Physics
F.C.A.	Fellow of the Institute of Chartered Accountants
F.C.A.E.	Fellow Canadian Academy of Engineering
F.C.G.I.	Fellow of the City and Guilds of London Institute
F.C.I.A.	Fellow Chartered Institute of Arbitrators
F.C.I.B.	Fellow Chartered Institute of Bankers
F.C.I.C.	Fellow of the Chemical Institute of Canada
F.C.I.S.	Fellow of the Chartered Institute of Secretaries
FCO	Foreign and Commonwealth Office
F.C.S.D.	Fellow Chartered Society of Designers
F.C.T.	Federal Capital Territory
F.C.W.A.	Fellow of the Institute of Cost and Works Accountants
FDGB	Freier Deutscher Gewerkschaftsbund
FDP	Freier Demokratische Partei
Feb.	February
Fed.	Federation; Federal
F.Eng.	Fellow, Fellowship of Engineering
F.F.C.M.	Fellow of Faculty of Community Medicine
F.G.S.	Fellow of the Geological Society
F.G.S.M.	Fellow of the Guildhall School of Music
F.I.A.	Fellow of the Institute of Actuaries
F.I.A.L.	Fellow of the International Institute of Arts and Letters
F.I.A.M.	Fellow of the International Academy of Management
F.I.A.M.S.	Fellow of the Indian Academy of Medical Sciences
F.I.Arb.	Fellow of the Institute of Arbitrators
F.I.B.	Fellow of the Institute of Bankers
F.I.B.A.	Fellow of the Institute of Banking Associations
F.I.C.E.	Fellow of the Institution of Civil Engineers
F.I.Chem.E.	Fellow of the Institute of Chemical Engineers
F.I.D.	Fellow of the Institute of Directors
F.I.E.	Fellow of the Institute of Engineers
F.I.E.E.	Fellow of the Institution of Electrical Engineers
F.I.E.E.E.	Fellow of the Institute of Electrical and Electronics Engineers
F.I.J.	Fellow of the Institute of Journalists
Fil.Lic.	Licentiate in Philosophy
F.I.M.	Fellow of the Institute of Metallurgists
F.I.M.E.	Fellow of the Institute of Mining Engineers
F.I.Mech.E.	Fellow of the Institute of Mechanical Engineers
F.I.M.I.	Fellow of the Institute of the Motor Industry
F.Inst.F.	Fellow of the Institute of Fuel
F.Inst.M.	Fellow of the Institute of Marketing
F.Inst.P.	Fellow of the Institute of Physics
F.Inst.Pet.	Fellow of the Institute of Petroleum
F.I.P.M.	Fellow of the Institute of Personnel Management
F.I.R.E.	Fellow of the Institution of Radio Engineers
Fla.	Florida
F.L.A.	Fellow of the Library Association
FLN	Front de Libération Nationale
F.L.S.	Fellow of the Linnaean Society
fmr.	former
fmrly.	formerly
F.N.I.	Fellow of the National Institute of Sciences of India
F.N.Z.I.A.	Fellow of the New Zealand Institute of Architects
F.R.A.C.P.	Fellow of the Royal Australasian College of Physicians
F.R.A.C.S.	Fellow of the Royal Australasian College of Surgeons
F.R.A.I.	Fellow of the Royal Anthropological Institute
F.R.A.I.A.	Fellow of the Royal Australian Institute of Architects
F.R.A.I.C.	Fellow of the Royal Architectural Institute of Canada
F.R.A.M.	Fellow of the Royal Academy of Music
F.R.A.S.	Fellow of the Royal Astronomical Society; Fellow of the Royal Asiatic Society
F.R.Ae.S.	Fellow of the Royal Aeronautical Society
F.R.B.S.	Fellow of the Royal Society of British Sculptors
F.R.C.M.	Fellow of the Royal College of Music
F.R.C.O.	Fellow of the Royal College of Organists
F.R.C.O.G.	Fellow of the Royal College of Obstetricians and Gynaecologists
F.R.C.P. (U.K.)	Fellow of the Royal College of Physicians (United Kingdom)
F.R.C.P.(E.)	Fellow of the Royal College of Physicians (Edinburgh)
F.R.C.S.(E.)	Fellow of the Royal College of Surgeons (Edinburgh)
F.R.Econ.S.	Fellow of the Royal Economic Society
F.R.E.S.	Fellow of the Royal Entomological Society
F.R.F.P.S.	Fellow of the Royal Faculty of Physicians and Surgeons
F.R.G.	Federal Republic of Germany
F.R.G.S.	Fellow of the Royal Geographical Society
F.R.Hist.S.	Fellow of the Royal Historical Society
F.R.Hort.S.	Fellow of the Royal Horticultural Society
F.R.I.B.A.	Fellow of the Royal Institute of British Architects
F.R.I.C.	Fellow of the Royal Institute of Chemists
F.R.I.C.S.	Fellow of the Royal Institute of Chartered Surveyors
F.R.Met.Soc.	Fellow of the Royal Meteorological Society
F.R.P.S.	Fellow of the Royal Photographic Society
F.R.S.	Fellow of the Royal Society
F.R.S.A.	Fellow of the Royal Society of Arts
F.R.S.A.M.D.	Fellow of the Royal Scottish Academy of Music and Drama
F.R.S.C.	Fellow of the Royal Society of Canada; Fellow of the Royal Society of Chemistry
F.R.S.E.	Fellow of the Royal Society of Edinburgh
F.R.S.L.	Fellow of the Royal Society of Literature
F.R.S.M.	Fellow of the Royal Society of Medicine
F.R.S.S.	Fellow of the Royal Statistical Society
F.R.S.S.A.	Fellow of the Royal Society of South Africa
F.S.A.	Fellow of the Society of Antiquaries
F.S.I.A.D.	Fellow of the Society of Industrial Artists and Designers
F.T.I.	Fellow of the Textile Institute
F.T.S.	Fellow of Technological Sciences
F.Z.S.	Fellow of the Zoological Society
Ga.	Georgia
GATT	General Agreement on Tariffs and Trade
G.B.	Great Britain
G.B.E.	Knight (or Dame) Grand Cross of (the Order of) the British Empire
G.C.	George Cross
G.C.B.	Knight Grand Cross of (the Order of) the Bath
G.C.I.E.	Knight Grand Commander of (the Order of) the Indian Empire
G.C.M.G.	Knight (or Dame) Grand Cross of (the Order of) St. Michael and St. George
G.C.S.I.	Knight Grand Commander of (the Order of) the Star of India

ABBREVIATIONS

G.C.V.O.	Knight (or Dame) Grand Cross of the Royal Victorian Order
G.D.R.	German Democratic Republic
Gen.	General
GHQ	General Headquarters
Glam.	Glamorganshire
GLC	Greater London Council
Glos.	Gloucestershire
G.M.	George Medal
GmbH	Gesellschaft mit beschränkter Haftung (Limited Liability Company)
G.O.C. (in C)	General Officer Commanding (in Chief)
Gov.	Governor
Govt.	Government
GPO	General Post Office
Grad.	Graduate
G.R.S.M.	Graduate of the Royal School of Music
G.S.O.	General Staff Officer
Hants.	Hampshire
h.c.	honoris causa
H.E.	His Eminence; His (or Her) Excellency
Herefords.	Herefordshire
Herts.	Hertfordshire
H.H.	His (or Her) Highness
H.L.D.	Doctor of Humane Letters
H.M.	His (or Her) Majesty
H.M.S.	His (or Her) Majesty's Ship
Hon.	Honourable; Honorary
Hons.	Honours
Hosp.	Hospital
HQ	Headquarters
H.R.H.	His (or Her) Royal Highness
HSWP	Hungarian Socialist Workers' Party
Hunts.	Huntingdonshire
Ia.	Iowa
IAEA	International Atomic Energy Agency
IATA	International Air Transport Association
IBA	Independent Broadcasting Authority
IBRD	International Bank for Reconstruction and Development (World Bank)
ICAO	International Civil Aviation Organization
ICC	International Chamber of Commerce
ICE	Institution of Civil Engineers
ICEM	Intergovernmental Committee for European Migration
ICFTU	International Confederation of Free Trade Unions
ICI	Imperial Chemical Industries
ICOM	International Council of Museums
ICS	Indian Civil Service
ICSID	International Centre for Settlement of Investment Disputes
Ida.	Idaho
IDA	International Development Association
IDB	Inter-American Development Bank
I.E.E.	Institution of Electrical Engineers
I.E.E.E.	Institution of Electrical and Electronic Engineers
IFAD	International Fund for Agricultural Development
IFC	International Finance Corporation
Ill.	Illinois
ILO	International Labour Organization
IMCO	Inter-Governmental Maritime Consultative Organization
I.Mech.E.	Institution of Mechanical Engineers
IMF	International Monetary Fund
Inc.	Incorporated
Ind.	Indiana; Independent
Insp.	Inspector
Inst.	Institute; Institution
Int.	International
INTUC	Indian National Trades Union Congress
IOC	International Olympic Committee
IPU	Inter-Parliamentary Union
I.S.O.	Companion of the Imperial Service Order
ITA	Independent Television Authority
ITU	International Telecommunications Union
ITV	Independent Television
IUPAC	International Union of Pure and Applied Chemistry
IUPAP	International Union of Pure and Applied Physics
Jan.	January
J.C.B.	Bachelor of Canon Law
J.C.D.	Doctor of Canon Law
J.D.	Doctor of Jurisprudence
J.M.K.	Johan Mangku Negara (Malaysia)

J.P.	Justice of the Peace
Jr.	Junior
Jt.	Joint
J.U.D.	Juris utriusque Doctor (Doctor of both Civil and Canon Law)
Ju.D.	Doctor of Law
J.U.Dr.	Juris utriusque Doctor (Doctor of both Civil and Canon Law), Doctor of Law
Kan.	Kansas
K.B.E.	Knight Commander of (the Order of) the British Empire
K.C.	King's Counsel
K.C.B.	Knight Commander of (the Order of) the Bath
K.C.I.E.	Knight Commander of (the Order of) the Indian Empire
K.C.M.G.	Knight Commander of (the Order of) St. Michael and St. George
K.C.S.I.	Knight Commander of (the Order of) the Star of India
K.C.V.O.	Knight Commander of the Royal Victorian Order
K.G.	Knight of (the Order of) the Garter
KGB	Committee of State Security (U.S.S.R.)
K.K.	Kaien Kaisha
KLM	Koninklijke Luchtvaart Maatschappij (Royal Dutch Airlines)
K.P.	Knight of (the Order of) St. Patrick
K.St.J.	Knight of (the Order of) St. John of Jerusalem
K.T.	Knight of (the Order of) the Thistle
Kt.	Knight
Ky.	Kentucky
La.	Louisiana
L.A.	Los Angeles
Lab.	Laboratory
Lancs.	Lancashire
L.D.S.	Licentiate in Dental Surgery
Legis.	Legislative
Leics.	Leicestershire
L. en D.	Licencié en Droit
L. ès L.	Licencié ès Lettres
L. ès Sc.	Licencié ès Sciences
L.H.D.	Doctor of Humane Letters
L.I.	Long Island
Lic. en Der.	Licenciado en Derecho
Lic. en Fil.	Licenciado en Filosofía
Lic.Med.	Licentiate in Medicine
Lieut.	Lieutenant
Lincs.	Lincolnshire
Litt.D.	Doctor of Letters
LL.B.	Bachelor of Laws
LL.D.	Doctor of Laws
LL.L.	Licentiate of Laws
LL.M.	Master of Laws
L.M.	Licentiate of Medicine; or Midwifery
L.N.	League of Nations
L.Ph.	Licentiate of Philosophy
L.R.A.M.	Licentiate of the Royal Academy of Music
L.R.C.P.	Licentiate of the Royal College of Physicians
L.S.E.	London School of Economics
Ltd(a).	Limited; Limitada
L.Th.	Licentiate in Theology
m.	married; marriage; metre(s)
M.A.	Master of Arts
M.Agr.	Master of Agriculture (U.S.A.)
Maj.	Major
Man.	Manager, Managing, Management; Manitoba
M.Arch.	Master of Architecture
Mass.	Massachusetts
Math.	Mathematics, Mathematical
M.B.	Bachelor of Medicine
M.B.A.	Master of Business Administration
M.B.E.	Member of (the Order of) the British Empire
M.C.	Military Cross
M.C.E.	Master of Civil Engineering
MCC	Marylebone Cricket Club
M.Ch.	Master of Surgery
M.Ch.D.	Master of Dental Surgery
M.C.L.	Master of Civil Law
M.Com(m).	Master of Commerce
Md.	Maryland
M.D.	Doctor of Medicine
M.Div.	Master of Divinity
M.D.S.	Master of Dental Surgery
Me.	Maine
mem.	member
M.Eng.	Master of Engineering (Dublin)

ABBREVIATIONS

M.F.A.	Master of Fine Arts
Mfg.	Manufacturing
Mfrs.	Manufacturers
Mgr.	Monseigneur; Monsignor
M.I.	Marshall Islands
M.I.A.	Master of International Affairs
M.I.C.E.	Member of the Institution of Civil Engineers
M.I.Chem.E.	Member of the Institution of Chemical Engineers
Mich.	Michigan
Middx.	Middlesex
M.I.E.E.	Member of the Institution of Electrical Engineers
Mil.	Military
M.I.Mar.E.	Member of the Institute of Marine Engineers
M.I.Mech.E.	Member of the Institution of Mechanical Engineers
M.I.Min.E.	Member of the Institution of Mining Engineers
Minn.	Minnesota
M.Inst.T.	Member of the Institute of Transport
Miss.	Mississippi
M.I.Struct.E.	Member of the Institution of Structural Engineers
M.I.T.	Massachusetts Institute of Technology
M.J.	Master of Jurisprudence
M.L.A.	Member of the Legislative Assembly
M.L.C.	Member of the Legislative Council
M.M.	Military Medal
Mo.	Missouri
M.O.H.	Medical Officer of Health
Mon.	Monmouthshire
Mont.	Montana
Movt.	Movement
M.P.	Member of Parliament; Madhya Pradesh (India)
M.P.A.	Master of Public Administration (Harvard)
M.Ph.	Master of Philosophy (U.S.A.)
M.P.P.	Member of Provincial Parliament (Canada)
M.R.A.S.	Member of the Royal Asiatic Society
MRC	Medical Research Council
M.R.C.P. (U.K.)	Member of the Royal College of Physicians (United Kingdom)
M.R.C.P.(E.)	Member of the Royal College of Physicians (Edinburgh)
M.R.C.S.(E.)	Member of the Royal College of Surgeons (Edinburgh)
M.R.C.V.S.	Member of the Royal College of Veterinary Surgeons
M.R.I.	Member of the Royal Institution
M.R.I.A.	Member of the Royal Irish Academy
M.R.I.C.	Member of the Royal Institute of Chemistry
MRP	Mouvement Républicain Populaire
M.S.	Master of Science; Master of Surgery
M.Sc.	Master of Science
M. Sc. S.	Master of Social Science
M.T.S.	Master of Theological Studies
MU.Dr.	Doctor of Medicine
Mus.Bac. or B.	Bachelor of Music
Mus.Doc. or D.	Doctor of Music
Mus.M.	Master of Music (Cambridge)
M.V.D.	Master of Veterinary Medicine
M.V.O.	Member of the Royal Victorian Order
M.W.	Master of Wine
N.	North
N.A.S.	National Academy of Sciences (U.S.A.)
NASA	National Aeronautical and Space Administration
Nat.	National
NATO	North Atlantic Treaty Organization
Naz.	Nazionale
N.B.	New Brunswick
NBC	National Broadcasting Corporation
N.C.	North Carolina
N.D.	North Dakota
N.E.	North East, Near East
Neb.	Nebraska
NEDC	National Economic Development Council
Nev.	Nevada
N.H.	New Hampshire
N.I.H.	National Institute of Health
N.J.	New Jersey
N.M.	New Mexico
Northants.	Northamptonshire
Notts.	Nottinghamshire
Nov.	November
NPC	National People's Congress
nr.	near
NRC	Nuclear Research Council
N.S.	Nova Scotia
N.S.F.	National Science Foundation
N.S.W.	New South Wales
N.T.	Northern Territory
NV	Naamloze Vennootschap
N.W.	North West
N.W.T.	North West Territories
N.Y.	New York
N.Z.	New Zealand
N.Z.I.C.	New Zealand Institute of Chemistry
O.	Ohio
OAS	Organization of American States
OAU	Organization of African Unity
O.B.E.	Officer of (the Order of) the British Empire
O.C.	Officer of the Order of Canada
Oct.	October
OECD	Organization for Economic Co-operation and Development
OEEC	Organization for European Economic Co-operation
O.F.S.	Orange Free State
Okla.	Oklahoma
O.M.	Member of the Order of Merit
Ont.	Ontario
O.P.	Ordo Praedicatorum (Dominicans)
OPEC	Organization of the Petroleum Exporting Countries
O.P.M.	Office of Production Management
Ore.	Oregon
Org.	Organization
O.S.B.	Order of St. Benedict
Oxon.	Of Oxford University; Oxfordshire
Pa.	Pennsylvania
Parl.	Parliament; Parliamentary
P.C.	Privy Councillor
PCC	Provincial Congress Committee
Pd.B	Bachelor of Pedagogy
Pd.D.	Doctor of Pedagogy
Pd.M.	Master of Pedagogy
P.E.I.	Prince Edward Island
Pembs.	Pembrokeshire
PEN	Poets, Playwright, Essayists, Editors and Novelists (Club)
Perm.	Permanent
Ph.B.	Bachelor of Philosophy
Ph.D.	Doctor of Philosophy
Ph.Dr.	Doctor of Philosophy
Pharm.D.	Docteur en Pharmacie
Phila.	Philadelphia
Ph.L.	Licentiate of Philosophy
PLA	People's Liberation Army; Port of London Authority
PLC	Public Limited Company
P.O.(B.)	Post Office (Box)
P.O.W.	Prisoner of War
PPR	Polish Workers' Party
P.P.R.A.	Past President of the Royal Academy
P.Q.	Province of Quebec
P.R.A.	President of the Royal Academy
Pref.	Prefecture
Prep.	Preparatory
Pres.	President
P.R.I.	President of the Royal Institute (of Painters in Water Colours)
P.R.I.B.A.	President of the Royal Institute of British Architects
Prin.	Principal
Priv. Doz.	Privat Dozent (recognized teacher not on the regular staff)
P.R.O.	Public Relations Officer
Proc.	Proceedings
Prof.	Professor
Propr.	Proprietor
Prov.	Province, Provincial
P.R.S.	President of the Royal Society
P.R.S.A.	President of the Royal Scottish Academy
P.S.M.	Panglima Setia Mahota
Pty.	Proprietary
Publ(s).	Publication(s)
Publr.	Publisher
Pvt.	Private
PZPR	Polish United Workers' Party
Q.C.	Queen's Counsel
q.v.	quod vide (which see)
Q.S.O.	Queen's Service Order
R.A.	Royal Academy; Royal Academician; Royal Artillery
R.A.A.F.	Royal Australian Air Force
R.A.C.	Royal Armoured Corps
R.A.C.P.	Royal Australasian College of Physicians
R.A.F.	Royal Air Force
R.A.F.V.R.	Royal Air Force Volunteer Reserve
R.A.M.	Royal Academy of Music

ABBREVIATIONS

R.A.M.C.	Royal Army Medical Corps		Tech.	Technical, Technology
R.A.O.C.	Royal Army Ordnance Corps		Temp.	Temporary
R.E.M.E.	Royal Electric and Mechanical Engineers		Tenn.	Tennessee
R.C.	Roman Catholic		Tex.	Texas
R.C.A.	Royal College of Art; Royal Canadian Academy; Radio Corporation of America		Th.B.	Bachelor of Theology
			Th.D.	Doctor of Theology
R.C.A.F.	Royal Canadian Air Force		TH.Dr.	Doctor of Theology
RCP	Romanian Communist Party		Th.M.	Master of Theology
Regt.	Regiment		Trans.	Translation; translator
Rep.	Representative; Represented		Treas.	Treasurer
Repub.	Republic		TU(C)	Trades Union (Congress)
resgnd.	resigned		TV	Television
retd.	retired			
Rev.	Reverend		U.A.E.	United Arab Emirates
R.I.	Rhode Island		U.A.R.	United Arab Republic
R.I.B.A.	Royal Institute of British Architects		UDEAC	L'Union Douanière et Economique de l'Afrique Centrale
R.M.A.	Royal Military Academy			
R.N.	Royal Navy		UDR	Union des Démocrates pour la République
R.N.R.	Royal Naval Reserve		U.E.D.	University Education Diploma
R.N.V.R.	Royal Naval Volunteer Reserve		U.K.	United Kingdom (of Great Britain and Northern Ireland)
R.N.Z.A.F.	Royal New Zealand Air Force			
R.P.	Member Royal Society of Portrait Painters		UKAEA	United Kingdom Atomic Energy Authority
R.P.R.	Rassemblement pour la République		UMIST	University of Manchester Institute of Science and Technology
R.S.A.	Royal Scottish Academy; Royal Society of Arts			
R.S.C.	Royal Shakespeare Company		UMNO	United Malays National Organization
RS.Dr.	Doctor of Social Sciences		UN(O)	United Nations (Organization)
R.S.F.S.R.	Russian Soviet Federative Socialist Republic		UNA	United Nations Association
R.S.L.	Royal Society of Literature		UNCTAD	United Nations Conference on Trade and Development
Rt. Hon.	Right Honourable			
Rt. Rev.	Right Reverend		UNDP	United Nations Development Programme
R.V.O.	Royal Victorian Order		UNDRO	United Nations Disaster Relief Office
R.W.S.	Royal Society of Painters in Water Colours		UNEF	United Nations Emergency Force
			UNEP	United Nations Environment Programme
s.	son(s)		UNESCO	United Nations Educational, Scientific and Cultural Organisation
S.	South			
S.A.	South Africa; Société Anonyme, Sociedad Anónima		UNHCR	United Nations High Commissioner for Refugees
S.A.E.	Society of Aeronautical Engineers		UNICEF	United Nations International Children's Emergency Fund
Salop	Shropshire			
S.A.L.T.	Strategic Arms Limitation Treaty		UNIDO	United Nations Industrial Development Organization
Sask.	Saskatchewan		UNITAR	United Nations Institute for Training and Research
S.B.	Bachelor of Science (U.S.A.)		Univ.	University
S.C.	South Carolina; Senior Counsel		UNKRA	United Nations Korean Relief Administration
SCAP	Supreme Command Allied Powers		UNRRA	United Nations Relief and Rehabilitation Administration
Sc.B.	Bachelor of Science			
Sc.D.	Doctor of Science		UNRWA	United Nations Relief and Works Agency
S.Dak.	South Dakota		U.P.	United Provinces, Uttar Pradesh (India)
SDLP	Social and Democratic Liberal Party		UPU	Universal Postal Union
SDP	Social Democratic Party		U.S.A.	United States of America
S.E.	South East		U.S.A.A.F.	United States Army Air Force
SEATO	South East Asia Treaty Organization		U.S.A.F.	United States Air Force
Sec.	Secretary		U.S.N.	United States Navy
SEC	Securities and Exchange Commission		U.S.N.R.	United States Navy Reserve
Secr.	Secretariat		U.S.S.	United States Ship
SED	Sozialistische Einheitspartei Deutschlands (Socialist Unity Party of the German Democratic Republic)		U.S.S.R.	Union of Soviet Socialist Republics
			Va.	Virginia
Sept.	September		V.C.	Victoria Cross
S.-et-O.	Seine-et-Oise		Vic.	Victoria
SHAEF	Supreme Headquarters Allied Expeditionary Force		Vol(s).	Volume(s)
SHAPE	Supreme Headquarters Allied Powers in Europe		Vt.	Vermont
S.J.	Society of Jesus (Jesuits)			
S.J.D.	Doctor of Juristic Science		W.	West
S.M.	Master of Science		W.A.	Western Australia
S.O.A.S.	School of Oriental and African Studies		Warwicks.	Warwickshire
Soc.	Society, Société		Wash.	Washington (State)
S.p.A.	Società per Azioni		WCC	World Council of Churches
SPD	Sozialdemokratische Partei Deutschlands		WCT	World Championship Tennis
Sr.	Senior		WEU	Western European Union
S.R.C.	Science Research Council		WFTU	World Federation of Trade Unions
S.S.M.	Seria Seta Mahkota (Malaysia)		WHO	World Health Organization
S.S.R.	Soviet Socialist Republic		Wilts.	Wiltshire
St.	Saint		WIPO	World Intellectual Property Organization
Staffs.	Staffordshire		Wis.	Wisconsin
S.T.B.	Bachelor of Sacred Theology		WMO	World Meteorological Organization
S.T.D.	Doctor of Sacred Theology		Worcs.	Worcestershire
S.T.L.	Licentiate of Sacred Theology		W.R.A.C.	Women's Royal Army Corps
S.T.M.	Master of Sacred Theology		W.R.N.S.	Women's Royal Naval Service
str.	strasse		W.Va.	West Virginia
Supt.	Superintendent		Wyo.	Wyoming
S.W.	South West			
			YMCA	Young Men's Christian Association
T.A.	Territorial Army		Yorks.	Yorkshire
T.D.	Territorial Decoration; Teachta Dála (mem. of the Dáil)		YWCA	Young Women's Christian Association

REIGNING ROYAL FAMILIES

Biographical entries of most of the reigning monarchs and of certain other members of the reigning royal families will be found in their appropriate alphabetical order in the biographical section of this book

BAHRAIN
Reigning Amir
SHEIKH ISA BIN SULMAN AL-KHALIFA; b. 3 July 1933; succeeded as Ruler of Bahrain on the death of his father, Sheikh Sulman bin Hamad al-Khalifa, November 1961; assumed the title of Amir, August 1971.

Crown Prince
Sheikh Hamad bin Isa al-Khalifa; b. 28 January 1950; married 1968, Shaikha bint Ebrahim Al-Khalifa; three sons.

BELGIUM
Reigning King
KING BAUDOUIN ALBERT CHARLES LÉOPOLD AXEL MARIE GUSTAVE; b. 7 September 1930; succeeded to the throne 17 July 1951, after abdication of his father, King Léopold III; married 15 December 1960, Doña Fabiola Mora y Aragón (b. 11 June 1928).

Father of the King
King Léopold III; b. 3 November 1901, died 25 September 1983; married (1) 4 November 1926, Princess Astrid of Sweden (b. 17 November 1905, died 29 August 1935); (2) 11 September 1941, Mlle Mary Lilian Baels (three children).

Brother of the King
Prince Albert, Prince of Liège; b. 6 June 1934; married 2 July 1959, Donna Paola Ruffo di Calabria (two sons, one daughter).

Sister of the King
Joséphine Charlotte, Princess of Belgium; b. 11 October 1927; married 9 April 1953, Prince Jean of Luxembourg (b. 5 January 1921) (five children).

BHUTAN
Reigning King
THE DRUK GYALPO JIGME SINGHYE WANGCHUK, King of Bhutan; b. 11 November 1955; succeeded to the throne 24 July 1972, on the death of his father, the Druk Gyalpo Jigme Dorji Wangchuk; crowned 2 June 1974.

Brother of the King
H.R.H. Namgyel Wangchuk.

Sisters of the King
H.R.H. Ashi Sonam Chhoden Wangchuk.

H.R.H. Ashi Dechen Wangmo Wangchuk.

Parents of the King
The Druk Gyalpo Jigme Dorji Wangchuk; b. 1928; married 1953, Queen Ashi Kesang Wangchuk; succeeded to the throne 28 October 1952; died 21 July 1972.

BRUNEI
Reigning Sultan and Yang di-Pertuan
H.M. Sultan Haji HASSANAL BOLKIAH; b. 15 July 1946; succeeded his father Sir Omar 'Ali Saifuddin II as 29th Sultan 5 October 1967, crowned 1 August 1968; married RAJA ISTERI ANAK SALEHA, two sons, four daughters; also married PENGIRAN ISTERI HAJJAH MARIAM 1981, one son, two daughters.

Brothers of the Sultan
H.R.H. Prince Mohammed Bolkiah.

H.R.H. Prince Haji Sufri Bolkiah.

H.R.H. Prince Haji Jefri Bolkiah.

DENMARK
Reigning Queen
QUEEN MARGRETHE II; b. 16 April 1940; succeeded to the throne 14 January 1972, on the death of her father, King Frederik IX; married 10 June 1967, Count Henri de Laborde de Monpezat (Prince Henrik) (b. 11 June 1934).

Children of the Queen
Prince Frederik André Henrik Christian (heir-apparent); b. 26 May 1968.

Prince Joachim Holger Waldemar Christian; b. 7 June 1969.

Parents of the Queen
King Frederik IX; b. 11 March 1899; died 14 January 1972; son of King Christian X and Queen Alexandrine; married 24 May 1935, Princess Ingrid of Sweden (b. 28 March 1910).

Sisters of the Queen
Princess Benedikte; b. 29 April 1944; married 3 February 1968, Prince Richard zu Sayn-Wittgenstein-Berleburg; son Prince Gustav, b. 12 January 1969; daughter Princess Alexandra, b. 20 November 1970; daughter Princess Nathalie, b. 2 May 1975.

Queen Anne-Marie of the Hellenes; b. 30 August 1946; married 18 September 1964, King Constantine II of the Hellenes; sons Prince Paul, b. 20 May 1967, Prince Nicholaos, b. 1 October 1969, Prince Filippos, b. 26 April 1986; daughters Princess Alexia, b. 10 July 1965, Princess Theodora, b. 9 June 1983.

JAPAN
Reigning Emperor
EMPEROR AKIHITO; b. 23 December 1933; succeeded his father January 1989; married 10 April 1959, PRINCESS MICHIKO SHODA.

Children of the Emperor
Prince Naruhito (Hironomiya), b. 23 February 1960.

Prince Fumihito (Ayanomiya), b. 30 November 1965.

Princess Sayako (Norinomiya), b. 18 April 1969.

Parents of the Emperor
Emperor Hirohito; b. 29 April 1901; married 26 January 1924, died 7 January 1989; Princess Nagako Kuni (b. 6 March 1903), daughter of Prince Kuni.

JORDAN
Reigning King
KING HUSSEIN IBN TALAL; b. 14 November 1935; succeeded to the throne on the abdication of his father, August 1952; ascended the throne 2 May 1953; married 19 April 1955, PRINCESS DINA, daughter of Abd-el-Hamid al Aoun (now divorced); married 25 May 1961, Miss Antoinette Gardner, PRINCESS MUNA AL-HUSSEIN (divorced 1972); married 24 December 1972, ALIA' BAHA' EDDIN TOUKAN (Queen Alia Al-Hussein, died 10 February 1977); married 15 June 1978, Miss ELIZABETH HALABI (Queen Noor Al-Hussein).

Children of the King
Princess Alia; b. 13 February 1956; married Nasser Wasfi Mirza 1977 (divorced 1983); married Mohammed Farid Al-Saleh; son b. 1981.

Prince Abdullah; b. 30 January 1962.

Prince Feisal; b. 11 October 1963; married August 1987, Alia al-Tabba.

Princess Zein; b. 26 April 1968.

Princess Ayeshia; b. 26 April 1968.

Princess Haya; b. 3 May 1974.

Prince Ali; b. 23 December 1975.

Prince Hamzeh; b. 29 March 1980.

Prince Hashem; b. 10 June 1981.

Princess Iman; b. 24 April 1983.

Princess Rayah; b. 9 February 1986.

Parents of the King

King Talal ibn Abdullah; b. 26 February 1907, died 8 July 1972; married 27 November 1933, Queen Zein Al Sharaf.

Brothers and Sister of the King

H.R.H. Prince Mohammed; married 9 January 1964, Princess Firyal (divorced 1976); sons Prince Talal, b. 26 July 1965 and Prince Ghazi, b. 15 October 1966 married 22 April 1981, Taghrid Al-Majali.

H.R.H. Prince Hassan (named as Crown Prince, 1 April 1965); married Princess Tharwat; daughters Princess Rahma, Princess Sumaya, Princess Badia; son Prince Rashid.

H.R.H. Princess Basmah; married 2 April 1970, Lt. Timor al-Daghistani (divorced 1980); daughter, Princess Farah, b. 25 March 1971; son, Prince Ghazi, b. 15 October 1974 married 1980 Waleed Kurdi, son Sa'ad al Kurdi, b. 8 November 1982.

KUWAIT

Reigning Amir

SHEIKH JABER AL-AHMAD AL-JABER AL-SABAH; b. 29 June 1926; succeeded his uncle, Sheikh Sabah al-Salim al-Sabah, 31 December 1977.

Crown Prince

SHEIKH SAAD AL-ABDULLAH AL-SALEM AL-SABAH; proclaimed Crown Prince 31 January 1978.

LESOTHO

Reigning King

KING MOSHOESHOE II; b. 2 May 1938; married 23 August 1962, PRINCESS TABITHA 'MASENTLE; became King when Lesotho gained independence, 1966.

Children of the King

Prince Letsie David Mohato; b. 17 July 1963.

Prince Seeiso Simeone; b. 16 April 1966.

Princess Constance Christina Sebueng Maseeiso; b. 24 December 1969.

Parents of the King

Seeiso Griffith, late Paramount Chief of Basutoland (b. 1905) and the late 'Ma-Bereng.

LIECHTENSTEIN

Reigning Prince

FRANZ JOSEF II; b. 16 August 1906; succeeded his great-uncle, 26 July 1938; married 7 March 1943, COUNTESS GINA VON WILCZEK (PRINCESS GEORGINE) (b. 24 October 1921).

Children of the Prince

Hereditary-Prince Hans Adam Pius; b. 14 February 1945; married 30 July 1967, Countess Marie Kinsky; sons, Prince Alois, b. 11 June 1968; Prince Maximilian, b. 16 May 1969; Prince Constantin, b. 15 March 1972; daughter Princess Tatjana, b. 10 April 1973.

Prince Philipp Erasmus; b. 19 August 1946; married 11 September 1971, Mademoiselle Isabelle de l'Arbre de Malander; sons, Prince Alexander, b. 19 May 1972; Prince Wenzeslaus, b. 12 May 1974; Prince Rudolf, b. 7 September 1975.

Prince Nicolaus; b. 24 October 1947; married 20 March 1982, Princess Margaretha of Luxembourg; daughters, Princess Maria-Anunciata, b. 12 May 1985, Princess Marie-Astrid, b. 26 June 1987.

Princess Nora Elisabeth; b. 31 October 1950; married 11 June 1988, Vicente Marques de Mariño.

Prince Franz Josef Wenzel; b. 19 November 1962.

Brothers and Sisters of the Prince

Princess Maria Theresia (Countess Strachwitz); b. 14 January 1908; died 30 September 1973.

Prince Karl Alfred; b. 16 August 1910; died 17 November 1985.

Prince Georg Hartmann; b. 11 November 1911.

Prince Ulrich; b. 29 August 1913; died 13 October 1978.

Princess Maria Henriette (Countess zu Eltz); b. 6 November 1914.

Prince Alois; b. 20 December 1917; died 14 February 1967.

Prince Heinrich Hartneid; b. 21 October 1920.

LUXEMBOURG

Reigning Monarch

GRAND DUKE JEAN; b. 5 January 1921; succeeded 12 November 1964, on the abdication of his mother, Grand Duchess Charlotte; married 9 April 1953, JOSEPHINE CHARLOTTE, PRINCESS OF BELGIUM (b. 11 October 1927).

Children of the Grand Duke

Princess Marie-Astrid; b. 17 February 1954; married 6 February 1982, Carl Christian of Hapsburg Lorraine, Archduke of Austria; daughter Marie-Christine Anne Astrid Zita Charlotte of Hapsburg Lorraine, b. 31 July 1983, son Prince Imre, b. 8 December 1985, son Prince Christophe, b. 2 February 1988.

Prince Henri; b. 16 April 1955; married 14 February 1981, Maria-Teresa Mestre; sons, Guillaume Jean Joseph Marie, b. 11 November 1981, Félix Léopold Marie Guillaume, b. 3 June 1984, Louis Xavier Marie Guillaume, b. 3 August 1986.

Prince Jean; b. 15 May 1957.

Princess Margaretha; b. 15 May 1957; married 20 March 1982, Prince Nicolaus of Liechtenstein; daughter, Princess Maria Annunciata, b. 12 May 1985, daughter Princess Marie-Astrid, b. 6 July 1987.

Prince Guillaume; b. 1 May 1963.

Parents of the Grand Duke

Grand Duchess Charlotte, Duchess of Nassau; b. 23 January 1896, died 9 July 1985; succeeded 15 January 1919; abdicated in favour of her son, Grand Duke Jean, 12 November 1964; married 6 November 1919, Prince Félix of Bourbon Parma (b. 28 September 1893, died 8 April 1970).

Brother and Sisters of the Grand Duke

Princess Elisabeth; b. 22 December 1922; married 9 May 1956, Prince François Ferdinand of Hohenberg (b. 13 September 1927, died 15 August 1977); two d.

Princess Marie-Adelaide; b. 21 May 1924; married 10 April 1958, Count Charles Joseph Henckel de Donnersmarck (b. 7 November 1928); three s. one d.

Princess Marie-Gabrielle; b. 2 August 1925; married 6 November 1951, Count Knud de Holstein-Ledreborg (b. 2 October 1919); seven d.

Prince Charles; b. 7 August 1927; married 1 March 1967, Joan Douglas Dillon; one s. one d.; died 26 July 1977.

Princess Alix; b. 24 August 1929; married 17 August 1950, H.H. Prince Antoine de Ligne (b. 8 March 1925); three s. three d.

MALAYSIA

Supreme Head of State (Yang di-Pertuan Agong)*

SULTAN AZLAN MUHIBBUDDIN SHAH IBNI AL-MARHUM SULTAN YUSSUF GHAFARULLAHU-LAHU SHAH; Sultan of Perak; b. 19 April 1928; installed as ninth Yang di-Pertuan Agong 26 April 1989; married Tuanku Bainun Mohamed Ali 1954; two sons, three daughters.

* Reign ends in 1994.

MONACO

PRINCE RAINIER III; b. 31 May 1923; succeeded his grandfather, Prince Louis II, 9 May 1949; married 18 April 1956, Miss GRACE PATRICIA KELLY, daughter of the late Mr. John Brendan Kelly and Mrs. Margaret Kelly, of Philadelphia, U.S.A., b. 12 November 1929, died 14 September 1982.

Children of the Prince

Princess Caroline Louise Marguerite; b. 23 January 1957; married 1st Philippe Junot, 28 June 1978 (divorced 1980); married 2nd Stefano Casiraghi, 29 December 1983; son, Andrea Albert, b. 8 June 1984; daughter, Charlotte, b. 3 August 1986.

Prince Albert Alexandre Louis Pierre; b. 14 March 1958.

Princess Stéphanie Marie Elisabeth; b. 1 February 1965.

Parents of the Prince

Princess Charlotte, Duchess of Valentinois (b. 30 September 1898; died 16 November 1977); married 19 March 1920, Comte Pierre de Polignac, who thus became Prince Pierre of Monaco; he died 10 November 1964.

MOROCCO
Reigning King

KING HASSAN II (formerly Crown Prince Moulay Hassan); b. 9 July 1929; son of King Mohammed V (died 26 February 1961); became King of Morocco when he succeeded his father, 3 March 1961.

Children of the King

Princess Lalla Myriam; b. 26 August 1962; m. Fouad Fillali September 1984.

Prince Sidi Mohamed (Crown Prince); b. 21 August 1963.

Princess Lalla Asma; b. 1965; m. Khalid Bouchentouf 7 June 1987.

Princess Lalla Hasna; b. 1967.

Prince Moulay Rachid; b. July 1970.

Brother and Sisters of the King

Prince Moulay Abdullah (deceased); married Lamia Solh.

Princess Lalla Aicha.

Princess Lalla Malika.

Princess Lalla Nezha (deceased).

Princess Lalla Amina.

Princess Lalla Fatima Zohra.

NEPAL
Reigning King

KING BIRENDRA BIR BIKRAM SHAH DEV; b. 28 December 1945; succeeded to the throne, 31 January 1972, on the death of his father King Mahendra; crowned 24 February 1975; married 1970, PRINCESS AISHWARYA RAJYA LAXMI DEVI RANA.

Children of the King

Crown Prince Deependra Bir Bikram Shah Dev; b. 27 June 1971.

Princess Shruti Rajya Laxmi Devi Shah; b. 16 October 1976.

Prince Nirajan Bir Bikram Shah; b. 6 November 1978.

NETHERLANDS
Reigning Queen

QUEEN BEATRIX WILHELMINA ARMGARD; b. 31 January 1938; succeeded to the throne on the abdication of her mother, 30 April 1980; married 10 March 1966, PRINCE CLAUS GEORGE WILLEM OTTO FREDERIK GEERT OF THE NETHERLANDS, Jonkheer van Amsberg (b. 6 September 1926).

Children of the Queen

Prince Willem-Alexander Claus George Ferdinand, Prince of Orange-Nassau; b. 27 April 1967.

Prince Johan Friso Bernhard Christiaan David; b. 25 September 1968.

Prince Constantijn Christof Frederik Aschwin; b. 11 October 1969.

Sisters of the Queen

Princess Irene Emma Elisabeth; b. 5 August 1939; married 29 April 1964, Prince Carlos Hugo of Bourbon Parma (divorced 1981); sons Prince Carlos Xavier Bernardo, b. 27 January 1970, Prince Jaime Bernardo, b. 13 October 1972; daughters Princess Margarita Maria Beatriz, b. 13 October 1972, Princess Maria Carolina Christina, b. 23 June 1974.

Princess Margriet Francisca; b. 19 January 1943; married 10 January 1967, Pieter van Vollenhoven; sons, Prince Maurits Willem Pieter Hendrik van Orange Nassau van Vollenhoven, b. 17 April 1968, Prince Bernhard Lucas Emmanuel, b. 25 December 1969, Prince Pieter-Christiaan Michiel, b. 22 March 1972, Prince Floris Frederik Martyn, b. 10 April 1975.

Princess Maria Christina; b. 18 February 1947; married 28 June 1975, Jorge Guillermo; sons Bernardo Federico Tomás, b. 17 June 1977, Nicolas Daniel Mauricio, b. 6 July 1979; daughter, Princess Juliana Edenia Antonia, b. 8 October 1981.

Parents of the Queen

Princess Juliana (Louise Emma Marie Wilhelmina) of the Netherlands, Princess of Orange Nassau, Duchess of Mecklenburg; Princess of Lippe-Biesterfeld, etc.; b. 30 April 1909; succeeded to the throne on the abdication of her mother, 4 September 1948; inaugurated 6 September 1948; abdicated 30 April 1980; married 7 January 1937, Prince Bernhard Leopold Frederik Everhard Julius Coert Karel Godfried Pieter of the Netherlands, Prince of Lippe-Biesterfeld (b. 29 June 1911).

NORWAY
Reigning King

KING OLAV V; b. 2 July 1903; succeeded to the throne on the death of his father, King Haakon VII, 21 September 1957; married 21 March 1929, Princess Märtha of Sweden (b. 28 March 1901, died 5 April 1954), daughter of Prince Carl (third son of King Oscar II of Norway and Sweden).

Children of the King

Crown Prince Harald; b. 21 February 1937; married 29 August 1968, Miss Sonja Haraldsen (now Crown Princess Sonja), daughter Princess Märtha Louise, b. 22 September 1971; son Prince Haakon Magnus, b. 20 July 1973.

Princess Ragnhild Alexandra; b. 9 June 1930; married 15 May 1953, Hr. Erling Lorentzen; three children.

Princess Astrid Maud Ingeborg; b. 12 February 1932; married 12 January 1961, Hr. Johan Martin Ferner; five children.

Parents of the King

King Haakon VII of Norway; b. 3 August 1872, died 21 September 1957; elected King of Norway by the Storting, 18 November 1905; married 22 July 1896, Princess Maud (b. 26 November 1869, died 20 November 1938), third daughter of King Edward VII of Great Britain.

OMAN
Reigning Sultan

SULTAN QABOOS BIN SAID; b. 18 November 1940; succeeded to the throne on the abdication of his father, Sultan Said bin Taimur (1910–72), 23 July 1970.

QATAR
Reigning Amir

SHEIKH KHALIFA BIN HAMAD AL-THANI; b. 1932; succeeded his cousin, Sheikh Ahmad bin Ali al-Thani, 22 February 1972.

SAUDI ARABIA
Reigning King

KING FAHD IBN ABDUL AZIZ; b. 1920; succeeded to the throne on the death of his brother, King Khalid, 13 June 1982.

Brothers of the King include

King Saud ibn Abdul Aziz; b. 15 January 1902; proclaimed King 12 November 1953, following the death of his father, King Abdul Aziz (Ibn Saud); relinquished the throne 1 November 1964; died 23 February 1969.

King Faisal ibn Abdul Aziz; b. 9 April 1906; acceded 1 November 1964; died 24 March 1975.

Amir Mohammed; b. 1912; died 1988.

King Khalid ibn Abdul Aziz; b. 1913; acceded 25 March 1975; died 13 June 1982.

Crown Prince Abdullah ibn Abdul Aziz; b. August 1921.

Amir Sultan; b. 1922.

SPAIN
Reigning King

KING JUAN CARLOS I; b. 5 January 1938; succeeded to the throne 22 November 1975; married 14 May 1962, Princess Sophia of Greece (b. 2 November 1938), daughter of the late King Paul of the Hellenes and Queen Frederica.

Children of the King

Princess Elena; b. 20 December 1963.

Princess Cristina; b. 13 June 1965.

Prince Felipe; b. 30 January 1968.

Parents of the King

Don Juan de Borbón y Battenberg, Count of Barcelona; b. 20 June 1913; married 1935, Doña María de las Mercedes de Borbón y Orleans.

SWAZILAND
Reigning Monarch

KING MSWATI III; installed as constitutional ruler 1986.

Father of the King

King Sobhuza II; b. 22 July 1899, died 21 August 1982.

SWEDEN
Reigning King

KING CARL XVI GUSTAF; b. 30 April 1946; succeeded to the throne 19 September 1973, on the death of his grandfather King Gustaf VI Adolf; married 19 June 1976, Silvia Renate Sommerlath (b. 23 December 1943); daughter, Victoria Ingrid Alice Désirée, b. 14 July 1977; son, Carl Philip Edmund Bertil, b. 13 May 1979; daughter, Madeleine Thérèse Amelie Josephine, b. 10 June 1982.

Parents of the King

Prince Gustaf Adolf, Duke of Västerbotten; b. 22 April 1906, died 26 January 1947; married 20 October 1932, Sibylla, Princess of Saxe-Coburg and Gotha (b. 18 January 1908, died 28 November 1972).

Sisters of the King

Princess Margaretha; b. 31 October 1934; married 30 June 1964, Mr. John Ambler; daughter, Sibylla Louise, b. 14 April 1965; sons, Charles Edward, b. 14 July 1966; James Patrick, b. 10 June 1969.

Princess Birgitta; b. 19 January 1937; married 25 May 1961, Prince of Hohenzollern Johann Georg; sons, Carl Christian, b. 5 April 1962; Hubertus, b. 9 June 1966; daughter, Desirée, b. 27 November 1963.

Princess Désirée; b. 2 June 1938; married 5 June 1964, Baron Niclas Silfverschiöld; son, Carl Otto Edmund, b. 22 March 1965; daughters, Christina Louise Madeleine, b. 29 September 1966, Hélène, b. 20 September 1968.

Princess Christina; b. 3 August 1943; married 15 June 1974, Tord Magnuson; sons, Carl Gustaf Victor, b. 8 August 1975, Tord Oscar Fredrik, b. 20 June 1977, Victor Edmund Lennart, b. 10 September 1980.

THAILAND
Reigning King

KING BHUMIBOL ADULYADEJ; b. 5 December 1927; succeeded to the throne on the death of his brother, King Ananda Mahidol, 9 June 1946; married 28 April 1950, MOM RAJAWONG SIRIKIT KITIYAKARA (b. 12 August 1932), daughter of H.H. Prince Nakkhatra Mongkol Kitiyakara, Krommuen Chandaburi Suranat.

Children of the King

Princess Ubol Ratana; b. 5 April 1951; married August 1972, Peter Ladd Jensen (relinquished Royal claims); daughter, Khun Ploy Pailin, b. May 1981, son, Khun Bhumi, b. August 1983, Khun Sirikitiya, b. 1985.

Crown Prince Vajiralongkorn; b. 28 July 1952; proclaimed Crown Prince December 1972; married 3 January 1977, Mom Luang Somsawalee Kitiyakara; daughter, Princess Bhajara Kitiyabha, b. 7 December 1978.

Princess Maha Chakri Sirindhorn; b. 2 April 1955.

Princess Chulabhorn; b. 4 July 1957; married 7 January 1982, Squadron Leader Virayuth Didyasarin; daughter, Princess Siribha Chutabhorn, b. 8 October 1982, daughter, Princess Aphithayadhorn Kittikhun, b. 6 May 1984.

Parents of the King

Prince Mahidol of Songkhla and Princess Sri Sangwalya.

Sister of the King

Princess Kalyani Vadhana.

TONGA
Reigning King

KING TAUFA'AHAU TUPOU IV; b. 4 July 1918; succeeded to the throne 15 December 1965, on the death of his mother, Queen Salote Tupou III; married 1947, Princess Halaevalu Mata'aho 'Ahome'e (b. 1926), (now Queen Halaevalu Mata'aho).

Mother of the King

Queen Salote Tupou III; b. 13 March 1900; married 1917, Prince Viliami Tungi (Prince Consort); died 15 December 1965.

Children of the King

Prince Tupouto'a (Crown Prince); b. 4 May 1948.

Princess Salote Mafile'o Pilolevu Tuku'aho Tuita; b. 17 November 1951; married 21 July 1976, Captain Ma'ulupekotofa Tuita.

Prince Fatafehi Alaivahamama'o Tuku'aho (known as Honorable Maátu); b. 17 December 1954.

Prince Lavaka Ata' Ulukalala (fmrly. known as 'Aho'eitu' Unuaki'otonga Tuku'aho); b. 12 July 1959; married 11 December 1982, Nanasipau'u Vaea (now Princess Nanasipau'u).

UNITED ARAB EMIRATES
Reigning Rulers

Ruler of Sharjah: Sheikh SULTAN BIN MUHAMMAD AL-QASIMI; succeeded to the throne 1972.

Ruler of Ras al Khaimah: Sheikh SAQR BIN MUHAMMAD AL-QASIMI; succeeded to the throne 1948.

Ruler of Umm al Quwain: Sheikh RASHID BIN AHMED AL-MU'ALLA; succeeded to the throne 1981.

Ruler of Ajman: Sheikh HUMAID BIN RASHID AL-NUAMI; succeeded to the throne 1981.

Ruler of Dubai: Sheikh RASHID BIN SAID AL-MAKTOUM; succeeded to the throne 1958.

Ruler of Abu Dhabi: Sheikh ZAYED BIN SULTAN AL-NAHAYAN; succeeded to the throne 1966.

Ruler of Fujairah: Sheikh HAMAD BIN MUHAMMAD AL-SHARQI; succeeded to the throne 1974.

UNITED KINGDOM
Reigning Queen

QUEEN ELIZABETH II; b. 21 April 1926; succeeded to the throne 6 February 1952, on the death of her father, King George VI; crowned 2 June 1953; married 20 November 1947, H.R.H. The Prince Philip, DUKE OF EDINBURGH, K.G. (b. 10 June 1921), son of Prince Andrew of Greece and Princess Alice of Battenberg (Mountbatten).

Children of the Queen

Prince Charles Philip Arthur George, Prince of Wales, Duke of Cornwall and Rothesay, Earl of Chester and Carrick, Baron of Renfrew, Lord of the Isles and Great Steward of Scotland, K.G. (heir-apparent); b. 14 November 1948; married 29 July 1981, Lady Diana Frances Spencer; sons, Prince William Arthur Philip Louis, b. 21 June 1982; Prince Henry Charles Albert David, b. 15 September 1984.

Princess Anne Elizabeth Alice Louise, The Princess Royal; b. 15 August 1950; married 14 November 1973, Captain Mark Phillips; son, Peter Mark Andrew, b. 15 November 1977; daughter, Zara Anne Elizabeth, b. 15 May 1981.

Prince Andrew Albert Christian Edward, Duke of York; b. 19 February 1960; married Miss Sarah Ferguson 23 July 1986; daughter, Princess Beatrice Elizabeth Mary, b. 9 August 1988.

Prince Edward Antony Richard Louis; b. 10 March 1964.

Parents of the Queen

King George VI; b. 14 December 1895; son of King George V and Queen Mary; married 26 April 1923, Lady Elizabeth Angela Marguerite Bowes-Lyon (b. 4 August 1900); succeeded to the throne 11 December 1936; died 6 February 1952.

Sister of the Queen

Princess Margaret Rose; b. 21 August 1930; married 6 May 1960, Antony Armstrong-Jones, later the Earl of Snowdon, G.C.V.O. (divorced 1978); son, David Albert Charles, Viscount Linley, b. 3 November 1961; daughter, Lady Sarah Frances Elizabeth Armstrong-Jones; b. 1 May 1964.

The full titles of Queen Elizabeth II are as follows:

United Kingdom

"Elizabeth the Second, by the Grace of God, of the United Kingdom of Great Britain and Northern Ireland and of Her other Realms and Territories Queen, Head of the Commonwealth, Defender of the Faith."

Canada

"Elizabeth the Second, by the Grace of God, of the United Kingdom, Canada and Her other Realms and Territories Queen, Head of the Commonwealth, Defender of the Faith."

Australia

"Elizabeth the Second, by the Grace of God Queen of Australia and Her other Realms and Territories, Head of the Commonwealth."

New Zealand

"Elizabeth the Second, by the Grace of God, Queen of New Zealand and Her Other Realms and Territories, Head of the Commonwealth, Defender of the Faith."

Jamaica

"Elizabeth the Second, by the Grace of God, of Jamaica and of Her other Realms and Territories Queen, Head of the Commonwealth."

Barbados

"Elizabeth the Second, by the Grace of God, Queen of Barbados and of Her other Realms and Territories, Head of the Commonwealth."

Mauritius

"Elizabeth the Second, Queen of Mauritius and of Her other Realms and Territories, Head of the Commonwealth."

The Bahamas

"Elizabeth the Second, by the Grace of God, Queen of the Commonwealth of The Bahamas and of Her other Realms and Territories, Head of the Commonwealth."

Grenada

"Elizabeth the Second, by the Grace of God, Queen of the United Kingdom of Great Britain and Northern Ireland and of Grenada and Her other Realms and Territories, Head of the Commonwealth."

Papua New Guinea

"Elizabeth the Second, Queen of Papua New Guinea and of Her other Realms and Territories, Head of the Commonwealth."

Solomon Islands

"Elizabeth the Second, by the Grace of God Queen of the Solomon Islands and of Her other Realms and Territories, Head of the Commonwealth."

Tuvalu

"Elizabeth the Second, by the Grace of God Queen of Tuvalu and of Her other Realms and Territories, Head of the Commonwealth."

Saint Lucia

"Elizabeth the Second, by the Grace of God, Queen of Saint Lucia and of Her other Realms and Territories, Head of the Commonwealth."

Saint Vincent and the Grenadines

"Elizabeth the Second, by the Grace of God, Queen of Saint Vincent and the Grenadines and of Her other Realms and Territories, Head of the Commonwealth."

Belize

"Elizabeth The Second, by the Grace of God, Queen of Belize and of Her Other Realms and Territories, Head of the Commonwealth."

Antigua and Barbuda

"Elizabeth the Second, by the Grace of God, Queen of Antigua and Barbuda and of Her other Realms and Territories, Head of the Commonwealth."

Saint Christopher and Nevis

"Elizabeth the Second, by the Grace of God, Queen of Saint Christopher and Nevis and of Her other Realms and Territories, Head of the Commonwealth."

The Republics of India, Ghana, Cyprus, Tanzania, Uganda, Kenya, Zambia, Malawi, Nigeria, Singapore, Botswana, Guyana, Nauru, The Gambia, Sierra Leone, Bangladesh, Sri Lanka, Malta, Trinidad and Tobago, Seychelles, Dominica, Kiribati, Zimbabwe, Vanuatu and Maldives, together with the Federation of Malaysia, the Kingdom of Lesotho, the Kingdom of Swaziland, the Kingdom of Tonga, the Independent State of Western Samoa and the Sultanate of Brunei, recognize the Queen as "Head of the Commonwealth".

OBITUARY

* The biographies of some of those whose deaths were noted after the preparation of copy for this edition (completed in May 1989) still appear in the text. Their names are marked with an asterisk in the following list.

Adams, John Frank	7 Jan. 1989
Addams, Charles Samuel	29 Sept. 1988
Aleksandrowicz, Julian	18 Oct. 1988
Allott, Gordon Llewellyn	17 Jan. 1989
Alvarez, Luis Walter	1 Sept. 1988
Anchiskin, Aleksandr Ivanovich	Deceased
Anderson, Herbert L.	16 July 1988
Andreadis, Stratis G.	14 Feb. 1989
Andrewes, Sir Christopher Howard	31 Dec. 1988
*Andrews, Harry (Fleetwood)	6 March 1989
Annigoni, Pietro	28 Oct. 1988
Arias Madrid, Arnulfo	10 Aug. 1988
Ashton, Sir Frederick	18 Aug. 1988
*Bahuguna, Hemavati Nandan	17 March 1989
Ball, Alan Hugh	5 Oct. 1987
*Ball, Lucille	26 April 1989
*Barlow, Harold Everard Monteagle	20 April 1989
Barrie, Sir Walter	8 Dec. 1988
Beach, Frank Ambrose	15 June 1988
*Bechtel, Stephen Davison	14 March 1989
Bellisario, Marisa	4 Aug. 1988
*Beniuc, Mihai	24 April 1988
*Benjamin, Hilde	20 April 1989
Bhattacharya, Bhabani	Oct. 1988
Birrenbach, Kurt	Deceased
Blessing, Werner	Deceased
Blunt, Christopher Evelyn	20 Nov. 1987
Boldizsar, Ivan	22 Dec. 1988
Bonvoisin, Baron Pierre de	1982
Bourbon, H.R.H. Prince Alfonso de	30 Jan. 1989
Bourne, Geoffrey Howard	19 July 1988
Bradshaw, Thornton F.	6 Dec. 1988
Braunshteyn, Aleksandr Yevseyevich	1 July 1986
Brewster, Kingman	8 Nov. 1988
Breycha-Vauthier, Arthur	Deceased
Broda, Christian	Deceased
*Brodal, Alf	29 Feb. 1988
*Brodie, Bernard Beryl	27 Feb. 1989
Brooks, John Wood	4 Jan. 1989
Burns, Arthur Edward	15 Dec. 1986
Bustamante Y Rivero, Jose Luis	Jan. 1988
*Calvert, Pierre Louis	12 March 1989
Campbell, Roald F.	Deceased
Cao Jinghua	July 1987
Cardin, Hon. Luis-Joseph-Lucien	13 June 1988
Carlsson, Bernt	21 Dec. 1988
*Carter, Hon. Sir Douglas Julian	7 Nov. 1988
Casamayor, Serge Fuster	29 Oct. 1988
Cassavetes, John	3 Feb. 1989
Castle, Norman Henry	11 July 1988
Cepede, Michel	26 Nov. 1988
Cerulli, Enrico	19 Sept. 1988
Chen Shixiang	25 Jan. 1988
*Chen Zizhuang	Deceased
Christensen, Christian	Deceased
Chrysler, Walter P., Jr.	17 Sept. 1988
*Ciupe, Aurel	7 July 1988
*Civil, Alan	19 March 1989
Clark, Col. Charles Willoughby	1 March 1988
Collar, (Arthur) Roderick	28 Dec. 1986
Colombani, Ignace Jean Aristide	19 Aug. 1988
Cook, Arthur Herbert	26 July 1988
Cooray, H.E. Cardinal Thomas Benjamin	29 Oct. 1988
Couch, John Nathaniel	Deceased
*Cowley, Malcolm	28 March 1989
Cyrankiewicz, Jozef	20 Jan. 1989
Dali, Salvador, Marquis of Pubol	23 Jan. 1989
*Dalrymple, Ian Murray	28 April 1989
Dart, Raymond Arthur	22 Nov. 1988
Dearden, H.E. Cardinal John	1 Aug. 1988
de Ferranti, Basil Reginald Vincent Ziani	24 Sept. 1988
Degan, Constante	1988
De Geer, Jan Gustaf Gerard	Deceased

Deng Jiaxian	29 July 1986
De Young, Russell	25 May 1988
Dietl, Jaroslav	29 June 1985
Ding Xiangqi	8 March 1989
*Diori, Hamani	23 April 1989
Dixon, Malcolm	7 Dec. 1985
Dobrzanski, Bohdan	16 Sept. 1987
Doko, Toshiwo	4 Aug. 1988
Dorati, Antal	13 Nov. 1988
*Dorrance, John Thompson, Jr.	9 Sept. 1989
*du Maurier, Dame Daphne	19 March 1989
Dunckel, Wallis Bleecker	21 Jan. 1988
*Du Plessis, Frederick Johannes	April 1989
Edwards, Gordon	Deceased
Elliot, Sir John	18 Sept. 1988
Elstub, Sir John (de Holt)	24 Jan. 1989
Enters, Angna	25 Feb. 1989
*Evans, Maurice	15 March 1989
Evans, (William) Charles	24 July 1988
Fadiga, Abdoulaye	11 Oct. 1988
Felfe, Werner	7 Sept. 1988
Fergusson, Francis	Deceased
Ferrari, Enzo	14 Aug. 1988
Festinger, Leon	11 Feb. 1989
Fieldhouse, William	16 Jan. 1988
Fornasetti, Piero	9 Oct. 1988
Francis, Sir Frank Charlton	15 Sept. 1988
Fraser of Tulleybelton, Baron; Walter Ian Reid Fraser	17 Feb. 1989
Frey-Wyssling, Albert	30 Aug. 1988
Furstenburg, H.E. Cardinal Maximilian de	22 Sept. 1988
Georges-Picot, Jacques Marie Charles	6 Feb. 1987
Gibson, James Douglas	Deceased
Glushko, Valentin Petrovich	10 Jan. 1989
Goldstein, Sydney	Deceased
Gordy, Walter	Deceased
Graham, Gerald Sandford	5 July 1988
*Graur, Alexandru	9 July 1988
Grendys, Michal	27 July 1987
Grimes, William Francis	25 Dec. 1988
Guden, Hilde	Sept. 1988
*Gumede, Josiah	28 March 1989
Gutowski, Armin Ferdinand	Deceased
Halkin, Shimon (Simon)	19 Nov. 1987
Hamengkubuwono IX, H.R.H. Sultan Dorodjatun	2 Oct. 1988
Hamilton, Patrick John Sinclair	12 June 1988
Hancock, Sir (William) Keith	13 Aug. 1988
Harding of Petherton, Baron; Field Marshal John Harding	20 Jan. 1989
Harrison, Francis Llewelyn	29 Dec. 1987
Harwood, Raymond Charles	20 June 1987
Haydon, Denis Arthur	29 Nov. 1988
He Changgong	Dec. 1987
Hinz, Werner	Deceased
Hirohito, Emperor of Japan	7 Jan. 1989
Holmes, John Wendell	13 Aug. 1988
Houseman, John	31 Oct. 1988
Hryniewiecki, Jerzy	31 Aug. 1988
*Hu Yaobang	15 April 1989
Hua Luogeng	12 June 1985
Hulton, Sir Edward George Warris	8 Oct. 1988
Hunt, Gen. Sir Peter Mervyn	4 Oct. 1988
Huriaux, Charles	14 Dec. 1988
Huxley, Sir Leonard George Holden	4 Sept. 1988
Ihnatowicz, Zbigniew	Deceased
Iskowitz, Gershon	Jan. 1988
Issigonis, Sir Alec Arnold Constantine	3 Oct. 1988
Jagvaral, Nyamyn	19 Sept. 1987
Jeffreys, Sir Harold	18 March 1989
Jepson, Selwyn	10 March 1989

OBITUARY

Ji Dengkui	13 July 1988
Jiang Nanxiang	3 May 1988
Johanesson, Olafur	Deceased
Jones, Francis Edgar	10 April 1988
Kairamo, Kari Antero Oswald	11 Dec. 1988
Kaverin, Venyamin Aleksandrovich	May 1989
Kawasaki, Kunio	7 April 1988
Kerby, William Frederick	19 March 1989
Kinzel, Augustus Braun	Deceased
Kirkley, Sir (Howard) Leslie	9 Jan. 1989
Kirst, Hans Hellmut	23 Feb. 1989
*Kolosov, Mikhail Nikolayevich	Deceased
Krogman, Wilton	Deceased
Krwawicz, Tadeusz Jan	17 Aug. 1988
Kulisiewicz, Tadeusz	18 Aug. 1988
*Kuraishi, Tadao	Deceased
Lacoste, Robert	9 March 1989
Laufberger, Vilem	29 Dec. 1986
Lazarus, Ralph	19 June 1988
Leach, Sir Edmund	6 Jan. 1989
Lederer, Edgar	23 Oct. 1988
Lemnitzer, Gen. Lyman L.	12 Nov. 1988
*Leone, Sergio	30 April 1989
Lepine, Pierre Raphael	20 March 1989
Lewy, Hans	23 Aug. 1988
Li Shu	9 Dec. 1988
Li Zhimin	July 1987
*Liepa, Maris-Rudolf Eduardovich	25 March 1989
Lillie, Beatrice	20 Jan. 1989
Liu Simu	21 Feb. 1985
Livingston, (M.) Stanley	Deceased
Llewellyn, Sir Frederick John	15 Nov. 1988
Logan, Joshua	12 Aug. 1988
Lohse, Richard Paul	Deceased
Lorenz, Konrad	27 Feb. 1989
Losev, Sergei A.	3 March 1988
Luke, Sir Stephen Elliot Vyvyan	27 Feb. 1988
McCann, Hugh James	Deceased
McCloy, John Jay	11 March 1989
McConnell, Thomas Raymond	16 Jan. 1989
McCracken, James	Deceased
McFall, David Bernard	18 Sept. 1988
Maddock, Sir Ieuan	29 Dec. 1988
*Maegraith, Brian Gilmore	2 April 1989
Mallabar, Sir John	20 Aug. 1988
Mallea, Eduardo	Deceased
Mapplethorpe, Robert	9 March 1989
Marai, Sandor	Deceased
Marchand, Jean	28 Aug. 1988
Margerit, Robert	June 1988
Marshall, Rt. Hon. Sir John Ross	30 Aug. 1988
Masson, Marcel	10 Aug. 1988
Matsumoto, Shigeharu	10 Jan. 1989
*Matsushita, Konosuke	27 April 1989
Matthews, Denis	24 Dec. 1988
Mayneord, William Valentine	10 Aug. 1988
Melen, Ferit	3 Sept. 1988
Melentiyev, Lev Aleksandrovich	Deceased
Mendez Manfredini, Augusto	26 June 1988
Menen, (Salvator) Aubrey Clarence	13 Feb. 1989
Merrison, Sir Alexander Walter	19 Feb. 1989
Meynell, Laurence W.	14 April 1989
Michel, Hans A.	2 Jan. 1989
Miki, Takeo	14 Nov. 1988
Mitchell, John Newton	9 Nov. 1988
*Mo Yingfeng	17 Feb. 1989
Møller-Christensen, Peter Vilhelm	15 Nov. 1988
Moran, Patrick Alfred Pierce	19 Sept. 1988
Morris, Bede	July 1988
Mundia, Nalumino	11 Aug. 1988
Murphy, William Parry	9 Oct. 1987
Nasalli Rocca Di Corneliano, H.E. Cardinal Mario	11 Sept. 1988
Navarra, Andre	31 July 1988
Nef, John Ulric	25 Dec. 1988
Nian Dexiang	5 Oct. 1986
Noguchi, Isamu	30 Dec. 1988
Norstad, Gen. Lauris	12 Sept. 1988
*Ochab, Edward	1 May 1989
Ollennu, Nii Amaa	19 Dec. 1986
Ooka, Shohei	25 Dec. 1988
Pan Shuh	26 March 1988
Panchen Lama (Bainqen Erdini Qoigyu Gyaincain)	28 Jan. 1989
Parmar, Yeshwant Singh	3 May 1981
Parnicki, Teodor	5 Dec. 1988
Peart, Baron; (Thomas) Frederick Peart	26 Aug. 1988
Perowne, Stewart Henry	10 May 1989
Plettner, Bernhard	April 1988
Ponge, Francis	6 Aug. 1988
Presser, Jackie	9 July 1988
Probst, Gerald Graham	15 Jan. 1989
Qian Changzhao	14 Oct. 1988
Qian Junrui	25 May 1988
Radwan, Abdel Hamid	1 Nov. 1987
Ranki, Gyorgy	21 Feb. 1988
Rao Bin	Sept. 1987
Reed, Philip Dunham	10 March 1989
Richter, Curt Paul	24 Dec. 1988
Roberthall, Baron; Robert Lowe Hall	17 Sept. 1988
*Robertson, Alan	25 April 1989
Ross of Marnock, Baron; William Ross	10 June 1988
Rota, Francesco	24 July 1985
Russell, Francis Henry	31 March 1989
Sadykov, Abid Sadykovich	22 July 1987
Saragat, Giuseppe	11 June 1988
Sargant, William Walters	31 Aug. 1988
Sasaki, Tadashi	July 1988
Schelsky, Helmut	24 Feb. 1984
Schiotz, Frederik Axel	Feb. 1989
Schwedhelm, Karl	9 March 1988
Scott, Michael	25 Jan. 1989
Seefried, Irmgard	24 Nov. 1988
Seereekissoon, Rameshchand	28 March 1987
*Segre, Emilio	22 April 1989
Shann, Sir Keith Charles Owen	Aug. 1988
Shannon, William Vincent	27 Sept. 1988
Shepley, James Robinson	2 Nov. 1988
Sieghart, Paul	12 Dec. 1988
Silkin of Dulwich, Baron; Samuel Charles Silkin	17 Aug. 1988
Singh, Nagendra	11 Dec. 1988
*Siri, H.E. Cardinal Giuseppe	2 May 1989
Sitwell, Sir Sacheverell	1 Oct. 1988
Skryabin, Georgiy Konstantinovich	26 March 1989
Smirnov, Vladimir Ivanovich	16 June 1988
Smith, Sir Thomas Broun	15 Oct. 1988
Sobolev, Sergey Lvovich	3 Jan. 1989
Solh, Takieddine	27 Nov. 1988
Sopwith, Sir Thomas	27 Jan. 1989
Soter, Istvan	7 Oct. 1988
Spitsyn, Victor	Deceased
Staiger, Emil	28 April 1987
Stazewski, Henryk	10 June 1988
Stewart, Sir Herbert Ray	3 Feb. 1989
Stone, Marshall Harvey	9 Jan. 1989
Stratton, Sir Richard (James)	26 July 1988
Strauss, Franz Josef	3 Oct. 1988
Stuckenschmidt, Hans Heinz	15 Aug. 1988
Sugar, Rezso	21 Sept. 1988
Swiderski, Jan	18 Oct. 1988
Szentkuthy, Miklos	19 July 1988
Taktashvili, Otar Vasilyevich	1989
Tamaki, Kazuo	Jan. 1987
Tan Zhenlin	30 Sept. 1983
Taranczewski, Wacław	11 Feb. 1987
Taylor, Edward Plunket	14 May 1989
Thomas, Very Rev. Francis Gerard	25 Dec. 1988
Thorley, Sir Gerald Bowers	Deceased
Tinbergen, Nikolaas	24 Dec. 1988
*Tishler, Max	18 March 1989
*Tjibaou, Jean-Marie	4 May 1989
Tompe, Istvan	14 Dec. 1988
Trench, Sir David	3 March 1988
Truong Chinh	30 Sept. 1988
Tuchman, Barbara W.	8 Feb. 1989
Ulanhu, Gen.	8 Dec. 1988
Ulrich, Franz	Deceased
Vallentin, Maxim	2 Sept. 1987
Virally, Michel	27 Jan. 1989
Volk, H.E. Cardinal Hermann	1 July 1988
Volobuyev, Vladimir Rodyonovich	Deceased

xix

OBITUARY

Wallich, Henry Christopher	15 Sept. 1988	Xiao Jingguang	29 March 1989
Walsh, William Henry	7 April 1986	Xu Dixin	10 Feb. 1988
Wankel, Felix	9 Oct. 1988		
Warner, John Christian	12 April 1989		
Weeks, Edward A.	11 March 1989	Yang Chengzhong	Dec. 1987
Wei Wenbo	Nov. 1987	Yates, Alden Perry	12 April 1989
Welham, David R.	27 Feb. 1989	Ye Qing	July 1987
Weores, Sandor	22 Jan. 1989	Young, Sir Frank George	20 Sept. 1988
*Whitney, Hassler	10 May 1989		
Wiarda, Gerard J.	12 June 1988		
Willing, Victor Arthur James	1 June 1988	Zeman, Karel	5 April 1989
Wingfield Digby, George	11 Jan. 1989	Zhu Yunqian	March 1989
Wolman, Abel	22 Feb. 1989	Zia Ul-Haq, Gen. Mohammad	17 Aug. 1988
Wootton, Baroness Barbara Frances	11 July 1988	Zobell, Claude E.	14 March 1989
Wu Zhongchao	7 Oct. 1984	Zolotukhin, Grigoriy Sergeyevich	20 Sept. 1988

THE INTERNATIONAL WHO'S WHO

1989-90

A

AAKVAAG, Torvild; Norwegian business executive; b. 18 Jan. 1927, Baerum; s. of Torvild Aakvaag and Dagny Rivertz; m. Dagen Dahl 1952; trained as lawyer; attached to Norwegian Ministry of Foreign Affairs 1951-56; joined legal dept., Norsk Hydro 1956, Head of legal dept. 1967-70; Gen. Man. Petroleum Div. Norsk Hydro 1970-75, Exec. Vice-Pres. 1975, Deputy Pres. 1977, Pres. March 1984-. *Address:* Norsk Hydro, P.O. Box 2594 Solli, N-Oslo 2, Norway. *Telephone:* 47 2 43 21 00.

AALBERSE, Petrus Josephus Mattheus; Netherlands lawyer and politician; b. 1910, Leiden; m. Augusta I. Housz 1939; three s. three d.; ed. Gymnasium St. Aloysius and Univ. of Leiden; Sec. Building Industry Asscn. 1942-47; Adviser, social orgs. 1947-62; mem. Wassenaar Town Council 1945-54; Sec. and later Pres. Landelijk Comité Rechtszekerheid 1947-52; Sec. Catholic Social Advice and "Raad van Overleg" 1955-62; Pres. Catholic People's Party 1962-68; mem. Second Chamber of States-Gen. 1963-69; mem. State Council 1969-; Commdr. Order of Gregory the Great, Commdr. Order of Orange Nassau. *Leisure interests:* books, television, golf. *Address:* Ruychrocklaan 370, The Hague, Netherlands. *Telephone:* 070-248677.

AARS, Knut; Norwegian diplomatist (retd.); b. 14 July 1918, Oslo; s. of Jacob and Anna (née Broedsgaard) Aars; m. Gerd Sandvik 1943; one s. one d.; ed. Oslo Univ.; Lawyer, Deputy Judge 1941-44; Norwegian Legation, Stockholm 1944-45, Lisbon 1948-50; Sec. Ministry of Foreign Affairs 1945-48; Washington 1950-52; Chief, Div. for NATO Affairs, Ministry of Foreign Affairs 1952-55; Deputy Perm. Rep. to North Atlantic Council 1955-58; Counsellor, London 1958-62; Amb. to Iran and Pakistan 1962-65, also accred. to Afghanistan 1964-66; Special Adviser to Ministry of Foreign Affairs 1966-70; Perm. Rep. of Norway to North Atlantic Council 1970-71; mem. Norwegian Inst. of Int. Affairs 1972-73; Ministry of Foreign Affairs 1973-74; Amb. to Argentina, Paraguay and Uruguay 1974-80, to Israel 1980-84. *Address:* Oscars gate 71, Oslo 2, Norway.

AARVIK, Egil; Norwegian politician; b. 12 Dec. 1912, Borsa; s. of Julius and Louise (née Lie) Aarvik; m. Anna C. Grove-Nielsen 1938; three s. one d.; Sec. Norwegian Lutheran Inner Mission 1934-37, Danish Inner Mission 1937, Stavanger Inner Mission 1940-46; journalist on daily newspaper Dagsavisa, Trondheim 1947-50, Ed. 1950-55; Ed. Folkets Framtid (organ of Christian People's Party) 1948-65; mem. Nat. Bd. of Norwegian Blue Cross 1958-, Chair. 1960-; mem. Strinda Municipal Council 1952-56; mem. Storting for Oslo 1961-65, 1969-, Chair. Social Affairs Cttee. 1961-65; Minister of Social Affairs 1965-70; Pres. Lagting 1974-; Vice-Chair. Norwegian Nobel Cttee. 1974-81, Chair. 1981-; Christian People's Party. *Address:* Korsnebbv. 3, 3140 Borgheim, Norway. *Telephone:* 22000 (Home).

ABAKANOWICZ, Magdalena; Polish artist, weaver and sculptor; b. 20 June 1930, Falenty, nr. Warsaw; d. of Konstanty and Helena Abakanowicz; m. Jan Kosmowski 1956; ed. Warsaw Acad. of Fine Arts; mem. of ZAIKS Asscn. of authors; work includes monumental space forms of woven fibres, cycles of figurative sculptures of burlap, wood and clay, cast metal, stone, drawings, paintings with collage and gouache; head of weaving studio at Acad. of Fine Arts, Poznań 1979, Prof. 1979; Dr. h.c (R.C.A.), London 1974; Minister of Culture and Art Prize (1st Class) 1965; Gold Medal VIII Int. Biennale of Arts, São Paulo 1965; State Prize 1972; Gottfried von Herder Prize 1979; Alfred Jurzykowski Foundation Prize 1982, Chevalier, Ordre des Arts et d'Lettres, Paris 1985; Order of Polonia Restituta and others. *Works:* Relief woven composition for North Brabant Provincial Building, Netherlands; sculpture for Elbląg, Poland; one-woman exhbns.: Zachęta State Gallery, Warsaw 1965, 1975, Kunsthaus Zürich 1968, Nat. Museum Stockholm 1970, Pasadena Art Museum 1971, Düsseldorf Kunsthalle 1972, Henie-Onstad Foundation, Oslo 1977, Muzeum Sztuki, Łódź 1978, Whitechapel Art Gallery, London 1975, Art Gallery of New South Wales, Sydney, Nat. Gallery of Victoria, Melbourne 1976, Musée d'Art Moderne de la Ville de Paris 1982, Museum of Contemporary Art, Chicago 1982, Musée d'Art Modern, Montreal 1983 and others; Biennale: Biennale de Lausanne 1962-79; Biennale of Art, São Paulo 1965, 1979, Venice Biennale 1968, 1980, ROSC, Dublin 1980, Nat. Gallery, Berlin 1982, Museum of Ateneum, Helsinki 1983. *Collections:* Muzeum Sztuki, Łódź and Wrocław; Museum of Modern Art, New York; Metropolitan Museum, New York; Museum of Modern Art, Kyoto; Stedelijk Museum, Amsterdam; Australian Nat. Collection, Canberra; Centre Georges Pompidou, Paris; Museu de Arte Contemporaneo, São Paulo; Nat. Museum, Stockholm; Frans Hals Museum, Haarlem; Henie-Onstad Foundation, Oslo; Museum

Bellerive, Zurich; Museum of Contemporary Art, Chicago; Spazi d'Arte G. Gori Collection, Italy; Israel Museum, Jerusalem; Muzeum Narodowe, Warsaw, and others. *Leisure interests:* swimming, walking in the countryside and forests. *Address:* Ul. Bzowa 1, 02-708 Warsaw, Poland.

ABALKHAIL, Mohamed Ali, B.A.; Saudi Arabian government official and financial executive; b. 1935, Buraida; m. 1966; two s. two d.; ed. Cairo Univ.; began career as Asst. Dir. of Office of Minister of Communications, later Dir.; Dir.-Gen. of Inst. of Public Admin.; Deputy Minister of Finance and Nat. Econ., then Vice-Minister, Minister of State, Minister for Finance and Nat. Econ. 1975-; Chair. of Bd., Saudi Int. Bank, London, Public Investments Fund, Inst. of Public Admin.; Chair. Saudi Devt. Fund (overseas devt. assistance fund); mem. Supreme Consultative Council of Petroleum and Minerals, Royal Comm. on Jubail and Yanbu Industrial Estates; mem. Bd., Saudia-Saudi Airlines Corpn.; decorations from Belgium, Egypt, France, Niger, Pakistan, Saudi Arabia, Sudan. *Leisure interests:* reading, some sports. *Address:* Ministry of Finance and National Economy, Airport Rd, Riyadh, Saudi Arabia. *Telephone:* 404-3380.

ABALKIN, Leonid; Soviet political adviser; b. 1930; ed. Inst. of Nat. Econ.; Deputy Head Acad. of Social Sciences of the Central Cttee. 1976, Head Faculty of Political Econ. 1978; Dir. Inst. of the Econ., Acad. of Sciences 1986-; Corresp. mem. Acad. of Sciences 1987-; Columnist Trud. *Publications:* numerous articles in Soviet press. *Address:* Institute of the Econ., Academy of Sciences of the USSR, Moscow V-71, Leninsky Pr. 14, U.S.S.R. *Telephone:* 234 21 53.

ABASHIDZE, Grigor Grigorevich; Soviet (Georgian) author and poet; b. 1 Aug. 1913, Chyatura, Georgia; ed. Tbilisi Univ.; mem. CPSU 1944-; cand. mem. Cen. Cttee. Georgian CP 1964-71, mem. 1971-; First Sec. and Chair. Georgian Branch of Union of Soviet Writers 1967-; Sec. U.S.S.R. Writers' Union 1970-; Stalin Prize; Hero of Socialist Labour 1974; two Orders and various medals. *Publications include:* Enemies 1941, Tank Duel 1941; verse cycles: Lenin in Samgori, On the Southern Border 1949; poems: George the Sixth 1942, About the First Men of Tbilisi 1959, The Long Night 1963, Lasharela 1965 and others.

ABASHIDZE, Irakliy Vissarionovich; Soviet (Georgian) poet; b. 1909, Khoni (Kutaisi), Georgia; ed. State Univ., Georgia; mem. CPSU 1939-; Man. Ed. several periodicals 1930-53; First Sec., later Pres. Writers' Union of Georgian S.S.R. 1953-64, 1964-67; mem. Cen. Cttee. of Georgian CP 1954-71, 1981-, cand. mem. 1971-81; mem. Georgian Acad. of Sciences 1960-, Vice-Pres. 1970-76; Deputy to and Chair. Supreme Soviet of the Georgian S.S.R. 1971-; Order of Lenin (twice), and three others. *Publications include:*Verse 1932, New Verse 1938, Colours 1962, Palestine, Palestine 1966, I am the Earth 1965, Rapprochement 1966. *Address:* c/o Georgian Communist Party, Tbilisi, U.S.S.R.

ABAZA, Mohamed Maher O.; Egyptian engineer and politician; b. 1930; ed. Faculty of Eng. and postgraduate studies in Fed. Repub. of Germany and Sweden; worked on Aswan Dam project; participated in laying down of High Dam electric power grids; fmr. head of electricity authority; First Under-Sec. Ministry of Electricity 1974-82; Minister of Electricity and Energy 1982-. *Address:* Ministry of Electricity and Energy, Cairo, Egypt. *Telephone:* 831204.

ABBADO, Claudio; Italian conductor; b. 26 June 1933, Milan; s. of Michelangelo Abbado and Maria Carmela Savagnone; m. Gabriella Cantaluppi; two s. one d.; ed. Conservatorio Giuseppe Verdi, Milan, and Musical Acad. in Vienna; guest conductor of principal orchestras in Europe and America; conductor at principal festivals and opera houses since 1961; Musical Dir. Scala Theatre, Milan 1968-86; Prin. Conductor Vienna Philharmonic Orchestra 1971-; Prin. Guest Conductor London Symphony Orchestra 1979, Prin. Conductor 1979-83, Music Dir. 1983-88; Music Dir. European Community Youth Orchestra 1977-, Vienna State Opera 1987-; Principal Guest Conductor Chicago Symphony Orchestra 1982-; numerous guest appearances; Sergei Koussevitsky Prize, Tanglewood 1958, Dmitri Mitropoulos Prize, New York 1963, Mozart-Medaille of the Mozart Gemeinde, Vienna 1973; since 1965 yearly recipient of int. prizes for recordings (Diapason, Deutscher Schallplattenpreis, Grand Prix du Disque, Grammy Award, etc.). *Leisure interests:* literature, painting, theatre, sports. *Address:* Piazzetta Bossi 1, 20121 Milan, Italy.

ABBOUD, A. Robert, M.B.A., LL.B.; American banker; b. 29 May 1929, Boston, Mass.; s. of Alfred and Victoria Abboud; m. Joan Grover Abboud

1955; one s. two d.; ed. Harvard Coll., Harvard Law School, Harvard Business School; Asst. Cashier, Int. Dept., First Nat. Bank of Chicago 1960, Asst. Vice-Pres. Int. 1962, Vice-Pres. 1964, Sr. Vice-Pres. 1969, Exec. Vice-Pres. 1972, Vice-Chair. 1973, Deputy Chair. of Bd. 1974–75, Chair. of Bd. 1975–80; Pres., C.O.O. and Dir. Occidental Petroleum Corpn. 1980–84; Pres. A. Robert Abboud and Co., Fox Grove, Ill., Chair. Braeburn Inc.; fmr. Dir. of numerous cos.; Dir. Cities Service 1982–; Hart, Schaffner and Marx, AAR Corpn., ICN Biomedicals and ICN Pharmaceuticals, Inland Steel Co.; Head First City Bancorp 1987–. *Publications:* Introduction of U.S. Commercial Paper in Foreign Markets—Premature and Perilous? 1970, A Proposed Course for U.S. Trade and Investment Policies 1971, A Proposal to Help Reverse the Narrowing Balance in the U.S. Balance of Trade 1971, The Outlook for a New Monetary System 1971, Opportunities for Foreign Banks in Singapore 1971, The International Competitiveness of U.S. Banks and the U.S. Economy 1972, Money in the Bank: How Safe is it? 1988. *Address:* First City Bancorporation of Texas, Inc., P.O.B. 2387, Houston, Tex. (Office); High Point Farm, Route 1, Box 209, Algonquin, Ill. 60102, U.S.A. (Home). *Telephone:* (713) 658-6109 (Office); (312) 658-4808 (Home).

ABBOUD, Robert (see Abboud, A. Robert).

ABDALLA, Sayed Abdel Rahman, M.B.A.; Sudanese politician and diplomat; b. 1933, Abu Hamad; ed. Khartoum Univ. Coll. and School of Admin. and New York Univ.; joined govt. service as admin. for Eastern, Southern and Cen. Sudan 1954–63; Dir. Sudan Inst. of Public Service 1963–65; Dir. UN Africa Training and Research Cen. Admin. for Devt., Tangier, Morocco 1965; served UN as Project Man. for Nat. Inst. of Public Admin., Libya; fmr. Chair. of Sudan Public Service Council; fmr. Chair. of Bd. Kenana Sugar Project; fmr. mem. of Sudan Supreme Judicial Council of Sudan Comm. of resettlement of population made homeless by the Aswan Dam; mem. of Cen. Cttee. of Sudan Socialist Union Political Bureau 1971–78; Deputy Minister of Local Govt. 1971; Minister of Public Service and Admin. Reform 1971–77; Minister of Industry 1977–78; Minister of Transport 1978; Asst. Sec.-Gen. Sudan Socialist Union 1978–79; Deputy Dir. and Officer in Charge of Div. of Devt. Admin. of UN Dept. of Tech. Co-operation, New York 1979–80; Perm. Rep. to UN 1980–84. *Address:* c/o Ministry of Foreign Affairs, Khartoum, Sudan.

ABDALLAH ABDEREMANE, Ahmed; Comoros politician; b. c. 1919; former businessman; Rep. of the Comoros in French Senate 1959–72; fmr. Rep. of Anjouan in Comoros Chamber of Deputies; Pres. of Govt. Council 1972–73, of Govt. 1973–75; Leader of Union démocratique des Comores 1974, Parti pour l'Indépendance et l'Unité des Comores 1974–75; elected Head of State July 1975; Pres. of the Comoros July-Aug. 1975, concurrently Minister of Justice, Keeper of the Seals; overthrown in coup Aug. 1975; after fall of Govt. of Ali Soilih in coup May 1978, became Pres. of Fed. and Islamic Repub. of the Comoros; also Pres. of Politico-Military Directory, Minister of Defence; Minister of Justice and the Civil Service 1978–82; dissolved Council of Ministers and Fed. Assembly Jan. 1982; announced new govt. Feb. 1982. *Address:* Office du Président, Moroni, Grand-Comore, République des Comores.

ABDALLAH, Ahmedou Ould; Mauritanian diplomatist and politician; b. 1940, El Birié par Aioun-El-Atrouss; ed. Coll. du Rosso, Lycée Van Vollenhoven, Dakar, Senegal, Univs. of Grenoble and Paris; appointed Director, Ministry of Industrialization 1968, Admin., Soc. Minière de Mauritanie 1969; Minister of Commerce and Transport 1971–72; Amb. to U.S.A. 1972–76, to Belgium 1976–78; with UN. *Publication:* Investir en Mauritanie 1970. *Address:* c/o Delegation of Mauritania to United Nations, United Nations, New York, N.Y. 10021, U.S.A.

ABDEL-GHANI, Abdul Aziz, M.A. (ECON.); Yemeni economist and politician; b. 4 July 1939, Haifan, Yemen Arab Repub.; s. of Abdulghani Saleh and Tohfa Moqbel; m. Aceya Hamza 1966; four s. one d.; ed. Colorado Coll. and Colorado Univ., U.S.A.; Minister of Health 1967–68, of Economy 1968–69, 1970–71; Chair. Tech. Office, Bd. of Planning 1969–70; fmr. Minister of the Interior; Gov. Cen. Bank of Yemen 1971–75; Prime Minister 1975–80, 1983–; Vice-Chair. Cttee. for Second Five-Year Plan April 1981–. *Leisure interests:* swimming, hiking. *Address:* Office of the Prime Minister, Sana'a, Yemen Arab Republic. *Telephone:* 2116.

ABDEL HALIM ABU-GHAZALA, Marshal Mohamed, M.SC.(ECON.); Egyptian army officer and politician; b. 1 Jan. 1930, El Behaira; m. 1953; two s. three d.; ed. War Coll., Egypt, U.S. Army War Coll.; fought in Palestine War 1948, Suez War 1956, Wars of June 1967 and Oct. 1973; rank of Major 1958, Col. 1966, Major-Gen. 1974, Lieut.-Gen. 1980, Marshal 1982; Commdr. of an Artillery Brigade 1968, an Artillery Div. 1969–71; Commdr. 2nd Field Army Artillery 1971 and 1973; Chief of Staff, Artillery Corps 1972 and 1973; Dir. Mil. Intelligence and Reconnaissance Dept. 1974–76; Defence Attaché, Embassy, U.S.A. 1976–80; Chief of Staff, Armed Forces 1980–81, C.-in-C. March 1981–; also Minister of Defence and Mil. Production March 1980–; Deputy Prime Minister 1982–; numerous awards and medals. *Publications include:* Soviet Military Strategy, History of Art of War (five vols.), The Guns Opened Fire at Noon (October War), Mathematics and Warfare, and 17 books on military affairs. *Leisure interests:* reading, chess, tennis, basketball, soccer. *Address:* Ministry of Defence and Military Production, 5 Sharia Ismail Abaza, Kasr el-Eini, Cairo, Egypt. *Telephone:* 600 736, 829 785.

ABDEL MEGUID, Abdel Razzaq, PH.D.(ECONS.); Egyptian politician; b. 4 May 1931, Alexandria; s. of Mohamed Fahmy Abdel Meguid and Naguiba J. Nadouri; ed. faculty of Commerce, Alexandria Univ., Univs. of Birmingham and Oxford; Dir. of Regional Planning, Aswan Governorate 1960–62; Visiting Prof., Texas Univ. 1962; Dir. Research Dept., Bank of Alexandria 1963; Chief Expert, Ministry of Planning; Minister of Planning April-Oct. 1977, 1978–80; Dir.-Gen. Authority for Foreign Investments and Free Zones (GAFIFZ) 1977–; Asst. Sec.-Gen. UN, Developing Countries Div. Dec. 1977; Deputy Prime Minister for the Economy 1980–82; f. International Arbitration Centre in Cairo. *Publications include:* numerous books on the social and economic aspects of the Egyptian governorates, on economic planning and development and banking in the Middle East. *Address:* c/o Council of Ministers, Cairo, Egypt.

ABDEL MEGUID, Ahmed Esmat, PH.D.; Egyptian diplomatist; b. 22 March 1923, Alexandria; m. Eglal Abou-Hamda 1950; three s.; ed. Faculty of Law, Alexandria Univ. and Univ. of Paris; Attaché and Sec., Embassy, London 1950–54; Head British Desk, Ministry of Foreign Affairs 1954–56, Asst. Dir. Legal Dept. 1961–63, Head Cultural and Tech. Assistance Dept. 1967–68; Counsellor, Perm. Mission to European Office of UN, Geneva 1957–61; Minister Counsellor, Embassy, Paris 1963–67; Official Spokesman of Govt. and Head Information Dept. 1968–69; Amb. to France 1969–70; Minister of State for Cabinet Affairs 1970–72; Head, Perm. Del. to UN 1972–82; Minister of Foreign Affairs 1984–; Deputy Prime Minister 1985–; Chair. Cairo Preparatory Conf. for Geneva Peace Conf. 1977–; mem. Politbureau, Nat. Democratic Party, Int. Law Asscn., took part in UN confs. on the Law of the Sea 1959, on Consular Relations 1963 and on the Law of Treaties 1969; ordre nat. du Mérite 1967, Grand Croix 1971, 1st Class Decoration, Arab Repub. of Egypt 1970, and numerous foreign decorations. *Publications:* several articles in Revue égyptienne de droit international. *Address:* 78 El Nile Street, Apt. 23, Giza, Cairo, Egypt (Home).

ABDEL-RAHMAN, Aisha, PH.D. (pen name **Bint el-Shati**); Egyptian writer and university professor; ed. Cairo Univ.; Asst. Lecturer, Cairo Univ. 1939–; Literary Critic Al Ahram 1942–; Inspector in Arabic Languages and Literature, Ministry of Educ. 1942–; Lecturer in Arabic, Ain Shams Univ. 1950–57, Asst. Prof. 1957–62, Prof. of Arabic Literature and Chair., Univ. Coll. for Women 1962–; mem. Higher Council of Arts and Letters 1960–; State Prize 1936, Acad. of Arabic Language Award for Textual Studies 1950, for Short Story 1954. *Publications:* Rissalet el Ghofram by Abul Ala'a 1950, New Values in Arabic Literature 1961, The Koran: Literary Interpretation 1962, Ibn Seeda's Arabic Dictionary 1962, Contemporary Arab Women Poets 1963; six books on illustrious women of Islam; two novels; four vols. of short stories. *Address:* 13 Agam Street, Heliopolis, Cairo, Egypt.

ABDEL-RAHMAN, Ibrahim Helmi, PH.D.; Egyptian United Nations official; b. 5 Jan. 1919; ed. Univs. of Cairo, London, Edinburgh, Cambridge and Leiden; Lecturer in Astronomy and Astrophysics, later Asst. Prof., Cairo Univ. 1942–53; Sec.-Gen. Council of Ministers 1953–58; Dir. Egyptian Atomic Energy Comm. 1954–59; mem. and Sec.-Gen. Nat. Science Council 1956–58; mem. Nat. Planning Comm. 1957–60; Dir. Inst. of Nat. Planning 1960–63; UN Commr. for Industrial Devt. 1963–66; Exec. Dir. UN Industrial Devt. Org. (UNIDO) 1967–74; Sr. Adviser to Prime Minister 1975, 1978; Minister of Nat. Planning and Admin. Reform 1975–76; Adviser to the Prime Minister for Planning and Econ. Affairs 1976; mem. Egyptian Del. UNESCO Gen. Conf. 1948, 1952, 1954; mem. Egyptian Acad. of Science and Institut d'Egypte. *Address:* c/o Council of Ministers, Cairo, Egypt.

ABDEL WAHAB, Mohamed Mahmoud F.; Egyptian engineer and politician; b. 1932; m.; two c.; ed. Ain Shams Univ.; held various posts in mil. factories; Chair. El Nasr Automotive Co. 1984; Minister of Industry 1985–. *Address:* Ministry of Industry, 2 Sharia Latin America, Cairo, Egypt. *Telephone:* (02) 3543600.

ABDELLAH, Faye Glenn, B.S., M.A., ED.D.; American nurse and psychologist; ed. Teachers' Coll., Columbia Univ.; first woman to be apptd. Deputy Surgeon General, U.S. Public Health Service 1981–; 36 academic and professional awards including six hon. degrees. *Publications:* Better Patient Care through Nursing Research (with E. Levine) 1986; more than 135 publs. (books, monographs and articles). *Leisure interests:* piano and swimming. *Address:* 3713 Chanel Road, Annandale, Va. 22003, U.S.A. *Telephone:* (301) 443-4000.

ABDELLAOUI, Aissa; Algerian politician; b. 15 Dec. 1941, Charef; m.; four c.; Dir. Agriculture, willaya d'Oran 1967–68; Warden, The Oranie forests 1968–69; Dir.-Gen. Inst. de tech. agricole de Mostaganem 1969–70, ONTF 1971–75; Dir. of Forests, Ministry of Agric. 1975–79; Sec. Gen. to Sec. of State for Forests 1981–84; Deputy Minister of Forestry and the Environment 1984–88, Minister of Public Works 1988–. *Address:* 135 rue Didouche Mourad, Algiers, Algeria. *Telephone:* (2) 59-00-29.

ABDESSALAM, Belaid, B.A.; Algerian politician; b. July 1928, Dehemcha; m.; four s. two d.; ed. Grenoble Univ.; fmr. Hon. Pres. Union Générale des Etudiants Musulmans Algériens (UGEMA); Instructor Front de Libération Nationale (FLN) School, Oujda; Political Adviser in Cabinet of M. Ben Khedda 1961; in charge of Econ. Affairs, FLN Provisional Exec. 1962;

Pres., Dir.-Gen. Soc. Nat. pour la Recherche, la Production, le Transport, la Transformation et la Commercialisation des Hydrocarbures (SON-ATRACH) 1964-66; Minister of Industry and Energy 1966-77 (retaining SONATRACH post 1965-66), of Light Industry 1977-84; Pres. of Special Econ. Comm. of Cen. Cttee. of FLN 1979-81; Chair. Council Org. of Arab Petroleum Exporting Countries 1974. *Address:* c/o Front de Libération Nationale, place Emir Abdelkader, Algiers, Algeria.

ABDNOR, James, B.A.; American politician; b. 13 Feb. 1923, Kennebec, S.D.; s. of Samuel J. and Mary (Wehby) Abdnor; ed. Univ. of Nebraska; teacher, coach, Presho, S.D. 1950-51; farmer, rancher, Kennebec 1945-; mem. 93rd-96th Congresses from S.D.; Chair. S.D. Young Republicans 1953-55; mem. S.D. Senate 1956-69, Pres. a.i. 1967-68; Lieut.-Gov. S.D. 1969-70; Senator from S. Dakota 1981-87; Admin. Small Business Administration, Wash. 1987-. *Address:* Kennebec, S.D. 57544, U.S.A.

ABDOH, Djalal, LL.D.; Iranian diplomatist; b. 1909, Teheran; s. of Mohamad and Batool Abdoh; m. Sedighe Etemad 1938; three d.; ed. Teheran and Paris Univs.; Asst. Dir. Ministry of Justice 1937-39; Public Prosecutor, Court of Govt. Employees, Teheran 1941-43; Dir.-Gen. Ministry of Justice 1943-44; mem. Parl. 1944-49; mem. Iranian Del. to UN 1946-53, 1954-59; Deputy Perm. Rep. Iranian Mission to UN 1949-53; Dir.-Gen. of Political Affairs, Ministry of Foreign Affairs 1954-55; Amb. and Perm. Rep. to UN 1955-59; Minister of Foreign Affairs 1959; UN Plebiscite Commr., British Cameroons 1959-61; Roving Amb. of Iran 1961-62; Prof. Int. Law and Political Science, Teheran Univ. 1961; Admin. UN Temporary Exec. Authority (UNTEA, West New Guinea) Oct. 1962-May 1963; Amb. to India 1965-68, to Italy 1968-72; Man. Dir. Iranian Bankers' Assen. 1972-78; mem. Currency and Credit Council 1972-78, Perm. Court of Arbitration 1946-78; Pres. Iranian Assen. for the UN 1972, Int. Law Assen. Iranian Branch 1973. *Publications:* Civil Procedure of Iran, Comparative Law, International Private Law, Eléments psychologiques dans les contrats, Le ministère public, Le régime pénitentiaire en Iran, The Political Situation in the Middle East (Persian), The Political Situation in Africa (Persian).

ABDOUN, Amin Magzoub, B.A.; Sudanese diplomatist; b. 22 Aug. 1930, Berber; s. of Magzoub Abdoun and Khadija Maharam; m. Raga Abdoun 1956; two d.; ed. Univ. of Khartoum; Consul Gen. Asmara, Eritrea 1961-63; Head Political Section Sudan MFA 1965-68; Amb. to India 1968-70, to Cen. African Repub. 1970-72, to U.A.E. 1972-73, to Czechoslovakia 1973-74; Perm. Rep. to U.N. 1986-. *Leisure interests:* reading, walking. *Address:* 210 E. 49th Street, New York, N.Y. 10017, U.S.A. *Telephone:* (212) 421-2680.

ABDRASHITOV, Vadim; Soviet film director; b. 1950; graduated VGIK, Moscow 1974. *Films include:* Witness for the Defence (U.S.S.R. Riga Prize) 1977, The Turning 1978, Foxhunting 1981, The Train has Stopped 1982 (scripts by Alexander Mindadze), The Servant 1988.

ABDUL BAQI, Murtada Said; Iraqi politician; b. 1941, Ramadi; ed. Higher Teachers' Training Inst. and Univ. of Baghdad, Coll. of Law and Politics; School teacher, Fallouja 1966-67; mem. Revolutionary Command Council 1968; Chair. Kurdish Affairs Bureau and Peace Cttee. 1968; mem. World Peace Cttee.; Minister of Labour 1970-71, of the Economy June-Oct. 1971, of Foreign Affairs 1971-74; Amb. to U.S.S.R. 1974-75.

ABDUL JAMIL BIN ABDUL RAIS, Tan Sri, P.M.N., P.J.K.; Malaysian diplomatist; b. 14 Jan. 1912, Kuala Kangsar, Perak; s. of Abdul and Saodah Rais; m. Norhimah Abdul Jamil 1936; four s. seven d.; ed. Clifford School and Oxford Univ., England; joined Admin. Service 1932; State Sec., Perlis 1951-52; State Financial Officer, Selangor 1954-55, State Sec. 1956; Chief Minister, State of Selangor 1957-59; Deputy Sec. to the Treasury 1959-61; Sec. to the Treasury (Federal) 1961-64; Chief Sec. to Malaysian Govt., Head of Home and Foreign Service, Sec. to the Cabinet 1964-67; High Commr. for Malaysia in U.K. 1967-1971, concurrently Amb. to Ireland; Chair. Penang Port Comm. 1971-, Nat. Family Planning Bd.; Nat. Vice-Chair. Malaysian Red Crescent Soc.; fmr. Chair. Malaysian Boy Scout Assen.; fmr. Pres. Malaysian Lawn Tennis Assen. and other sports assens. *Leisure interests:* reading, walking. *Address:* 16 Ayer Rajah Road, Penang, Malaysia.

ABDUL LATIF, Haji Java bin; Brunei diplomatist; b. 1939; m.; six c.; ed. Manchester Univ.; Govt. Deputy Agent, London 1981-82; Commr. to Malaysia 1982-84, High Commr. 1984-86; Amb. to the Philippines Oct. 1986-87; Perm Rep. of Brunei Darussalam to the UN 1987-; Pres. Brunei State Youth Council 1977-80; fmr. mem. World Assembly of Youth, World Assembly of Muslim Youth and Asian Youth Council. *Address:* Permanent Mission of Brunei Darussalam, 866 United Nations Plaza, 2nd Floor, Room 248, New York, NY 10017, U.S.A. *Telephone:* (212) 838-1600.

ABDUL RAHMAN PUTRA, Tunku (Prince), D.M.N., C.H.; Malaysian politician; b. 8 Feb. 1903; m. 3rd Puan Sharifah Rodziah binti Syed Alwi Barakbah 1939; one s. one d. (both by 1st wife); one s. three d. (all adopted); ed. Alor Star, Bangkok, Penang, St. Catharine's Coll., Cambridge, and Inner Temple, London; joined Kedah State Civil Service 1931, Dist. Officer; appointed to Exec. and Legis. Councils, Malaya, as unofficial mem. 1952; Leader Fed. Legis. Council; Chief Minister and Minister for Home Affairs 1955; first Prime Minister and Minister of External Affairs, Malaya 1957-63, Malaysia 1963-70, Minister of Information and Broadcasting 1963-64,

also Minister of Culture, Youth and Sports at various times; leader United Malay Nat. Org. 1952-70; Chancellor, Univ. of Malaya 1962; Sec.-Gen. Islamic Conf. 1963-71; Chair. Star Publs., Penang, Muslim Welfare Org. (PERKIM); Vice-Pres. (for life) Commonwealth Soc.; Order of Nat. Crown of Malaysia, Kedah Order of Merit and several hon. degrees and foreign decorations, including U.S. Sports Acad. Distinguished Service Award 1981. *Publications:* Mahsuri (play about Malaya) 1941, (filmed 1958); Raja Bersiong (a story of his ancestors) (filmed 1966), Looking Back 1977, Viewpoints 1978, Lest We Forget, Political Awakening 1986. *Leisure interests:* golf, football, walking, swimming, racing, motor-boating, photography, collecting ancient weapons, particularly the Malay Kris. *Address:* 16 Ayer Road, Penang, Malaysia. *Telephone:* 65970 (Home).

ABDULAH, Frank, M.A.; Trinidad and Tobago diplomatist (retd.); b. 8 Nov. 1928, Trinidad; s. of late Walter and Mildred Abdulah; m. 1st Norma Miller 1954 (divorced); four d.; m. 2nd Marie-Germaine Musso 1988; ed. Queen's Royal, Port of Spain, and Magdalen Coll., Oxford; Asst. Sec. Ministry of External Affairs 1962-63; First Sec., Kingston, Jamaica 1963-64; First Sec., Counsellor, London 1964-68; Counsellor, Ottawa 1968-70; Deputy Perm. Rep. to UN 1970-73, Amb. and Perm. Rep. 1975-82; Perm. Sec., Ministry of External Affairs 1973-75; High Commr. in U.K. 1983-85; Perm. Sec., Ministry of External Affairs 1985-88. *Leisure interests:* music, sport. *Address:* 70 Ariadita Avenue, Port of Spain, Trinidad and Tobago.

ABDULAI, Yesufu Seyyid Momoh; Nigerian economist; b. 19 June 1940, Auchi; s. of Momoh Abdulai and Haijia Fatimah Abdulai; m. Zene Makonnen Abdulai 1982; three s. one d.; ed. Mount Allison Univ. and McGill Univ.; Tech. Asst. to Exec. Dir. for African Group 1, World Bank Group, Washington 1971-73, Advisor to Exec. Dir. 1973-78, Alternate Exec. Dir. for Africa Group 1 1978-80, Exec. Dir. 1980-82, Vice-Chair. Jt. Audit Cttee. Exec. Bd. 1980-82; Chair. Jt. Secr. African Exec. Dirs. of the World Bank Group and the IMF 1975-77; Man. Dir. and C.E.O. Fed. Mortgage Bank of Nigeria Jan. 1982-83; Dir. Gen. and C.E.O. OPEC Fund for Int. Devt. 1983-. *Leisure interests:* sport, reading, photography, listening to music. *Address:* OPEC Fund for International Development, Parkring 8, P.O. Box 995, 1011 Vienna, Austria. *Telephone:* 51564-166.

ABDULGANI, Roeslan; Indonesian diplomatist, civil servant and politician (retd.); b. 1914, Surabaya, East Java; s. of Mr. Abdulgani and Siti Murad; m. Sihwati Nawangwulan 1938; two s. three d.; ed. Teacher Training Coll., Surabaya; active in Nat. Youth Movement seeking independence from Dutch; active in anti-Japanese underground during Japanese occupation; Ed. Bakti, East Java 1945; Sec.-Gen. Ministry of Information 1947-53; Sec.-Gen. Ministry of Foreign Affairs 1953-56; Del. to UN 1951, 1956, 1966; Sec.-Gen. Afro-Asian Conf., Bandung 1955; headed del. to Suez Conf. 1956; Minister of Foreign Affairs 1956-57; mem. Constituent Assembly 1957; Vice-Chair. Nat. Council 1957-59; Vice-Chair. Supreme Advisory Council 1959-62; Co-ordinating Minister and Minister of Information 1963-65; Deputy Prime Minister for Political Institutions 1966; Perm. Rep. to UN 1967-71; Lecturer Monash Univ. and other Australian univs. 1972; Research Fellow Prince Bernhard Fund, Netherlands, U.K. 1973; Vice-Pres. 24th UN Gen. Ass. 1969; Consultant, Nat. Defence and Security Council of Indonesia; Consultant on problems of mass media, UNESCO, Paris 1977; Chair. Team of advisers to Pres. on State Ideology Pancasila, 1978; several hon. degrees; Indonesian medals; mem. PNI (Indonesian Nat. Party). *Publications:* In Search of Indonesian Identity, The Bandung Spirit, Indonesian and Asian-African Nationalism, Pantjasila: The Prime Mover of the Indonesian Revolution, Hero's Day: In Memory of the Fighting in Surabaya on 10 November 1945, The Hundred Days in Surabaya that Shook Indonesia, Impact of Utopian-Scientific and Religious Socialism on Indonesian Socialism, 25 Years: Indonesia in the UN, Personal Experiences During the Japanese Occupation, and others. *Leisure interests:* walking, reading, classical music. *Address:* 11 Jalan Diponegoro, Jakarta, Indonesia.

ABDULLA OSMAN DAAR, Aden; Somali businessman and politician; b. 1908, Beledwin; ed. Govt. School, Somalia; served in Italian Admin. 1929-41; joined Somali Youth League 1944, Leader 1953, Pres. 1954-56, 1958-59; Pres. Nat. Ass. 1956-60, Constituent Ass. 1960; Pres. Somali Repub. 1961-67; Deputy to Nat. Ass. 1967-69; detained following coup 1969, released 1973. *Address:* c/o Government Offices, Mogadishu, Somalia.

ABDULLAH, Farooq, M.B.; Indian politician; b. 21 Oct. 1937, Srinagar, Kashmir; s. of Sheikh Mohammad Abdullah; m. Mollie Abdullah 1968; one s. three d.; Chief Minister, Jammu and Kashmir 1982-84; Pres. State Centre Labour Union, Jammu and Kashmir Nat. Conf.; Chair. Jammu & Kashmir Muslim Auquaf Trust, Sher-i-Kashmir Nat. Medical Inst. Trust; mem. of Parl. *Leisure interests:* golf, photography, walking. *Address:* 40 Gupkar Road, Srinagar; Residency Road, Jammu, Tawi, India. *Telephone:* 78484, 74020; 5252, 46943.

ABDULLAH BIN ALI, Datuk; Malaysian diplomatist; b. 31 Aug. 1922, Johore; m. Datin Badariah binti Haji Abdul Aziz; two s. two d.; ed. Raffles Coll., Singapore, Australian Nat. Univ., Canberra; Johore civil service 1954-56, Malayan civil service 1956; joined foreign service 1957; served in India, Switzerland, Australia, Thailand, Ethiopia, Morocco; between overseas appointments served as Nat. Sec. of Assen. of S.E. Asia, Chief of Protocol and Deputy Sec.-Gen. (Admin. and Gen. Affairs) in Foreign Ministry; attended numerous int. confs. as mem. of Malaysian dels., incl.

Gen. Ass. of UN in New York; High Commr. to Singapore 1971-75; Amb. to Fed. Repub. of Germany 1975; High Commr. to U.K. 1975-79; Dir. Guthrie Ropel Berhad 1979-; Dato Paduka Mahkota Johore (Order of Crown of Johore), Kesatria Mangku Negara (Officer grade of Order of Chivalry of Malaysia), Order of Sacred Heart (Japan), Bintang Jasa (Indonesia). *Leisure interests:* tennis, golf, swimming, ornithology. *Address:* Ministry of Foreign Affairs, Kuala Lumpur, Malaysia.

ABDULLAH BIN MOHD SALLEH, Tan Sri, B.A.; Malaysian petroleum executive and fmr. civil servant; b. 24 June 1926, Malacca; s. of Mohd. Salleh; m. Mahani Abdul Razak; two s. one d.; ed. High School, Malacca, Malay Coll., Kuala Kangsar, Univ. of Malaya in Singapore; posts in Admin. and Diplomatic Service 1955-71; Sec.-Gen. Ministry of Agric. and Fisheries 1972; Dir.-Gen. Public Service Dept. 1974; Chief Sec. to Govt. of Malaysia, Sec. to the Cabinet, Head of the Civil Service 1976-78; Chair. and Chief Exec. PETRONAS (Nat. Petroleum Co. of Malaysia) 1979-83, Pres. 1984-87. *Leisure interest:* golf. *Address:* PETRONAS, Dayabumi, Kuala Lumpur (Office); 21 Jalan Setiajaya, Damansara Heights, Kuala Lumpur, Malaysia (Home). *Telephone:* 03-2550915 (Home).

ABDULLAH IBN ABDUL AZIZ, H.R.H. Crown Prince; Saudi Arabian prince, army officer and politician; b. Aug. 1921; s. of the late King Abdul Aziz ibn Saud; brother of H.M. King Fahd (q.v.); Commdr. Nat. Guard 1962-; Second Deputy Prime Minister 1975-82, First Deputy Prime Minister June 1982-; became Crown Prince June 1982. *Leisure interests:* hunting, horse racing. *Address:* Council of Ministers, Jeddah, Saudi Arabia.

ABDURAZAKOV, Bakhodir Abbasovich; Soviet official; mem. of Auditing Comm. of Uzbek CP 1966-71, 1981-; Head of Dept. of Science and Educational Inst. of Cen. Cttee. Uzbek CP 1978-80; Head of Dept. of Propaganda 1980-; mem. Cen. Cttee., Uzbek CP 1981. *Address:* Central Committee of the Uzbek Communist Party, Tashkent, Uzbek S.S.R., U.S.S.R.

ABE, Isao, B.A.; Japanese diplomatist; b. 22 Nov. 1914, Tokyo; s. of Tadashi Abe; m. Tessie Yasuko Miyazaki 1948; one d.; ed. Tokyo Imperial Univ.; joined Diplomatic Service 1940; Lecturer, Tokyo Univ. 1953-56; served Embassies in Italy 1956-58, Switzerland 1958-61; mem. Perm. Mission to UN 1965-70; Amb. to Belgium and Luxembourg and Perm. Rep. to EEC 1971-76; Perm. Rep. to UN 1976-79; Grand Master of Ceremonies, Imperial Household of Japan. *Address:* Kunaicho, 1-1, Chiyoda, Chiyoda-ku, Tokyo, Japan.

ABE, Kobo; Japanese novelist and playwright; b. 7 March 1924, Tokyo; s. of Asakichi and Yorimi Abe; m. Machiko Yamada 1947; one d.; ed. Tokyo Univ; Post-War Literature Prize 1950, 25th Akutagawa Prize 1951, Kishida Prize for Drama 1958, Yomiuri Literary Prize 1962. *Publications:* Owarishi Michino Shirubeni (The Road Sign at the End of the Road), Akai Mayu (Red Cocoon) 1949, Kabe-S. Karumashi No Hanzai (The Crimes of S. Karma, Esq.) 1951, Kiga Domei (Hunger Union) 1954, Seifuku and other plays (The Uniform) 1955, Doreigari (Hunt for a Slave) 1955, Kemonotachi wa Kokyo o Mezasu (Animals are Forwarding to Their Natives) 1957, Dai Yon Kanpyoki (The Fourth Unglacial Period) 1959, Yurei wa Kokoniiru (Here is a Ghost) 1959, Ishi no Me (Eyes of Stone) 1960, Suna no Onna (The Woman in the Dunes) 1962, Tanin no Kao (The Face of Another) 1964, Omaenimo Tsumi Ga Aru (You are Guilty, Too) 1965, Enomoto Buyo 1965, Moetsukita Chiza (The Ruined Map) 1969, Bo ni natta otoko (The Man Who Became a Stick) 1969, Inter Ice Age 4 1970, Mihitsu no Koi (Premeditated Act of Uncertain Consequences) 1971, Gaido Book (Guide Book) 1971, Hoako otoko (The Box Man) 1973, Ai no Megane wa iromegane (Love's Spectacles Are Coloured Glass) 1973, Midoriiro no stocking (Green Stocking) 1974, Ue 1975, Warau Thuki (Smiling Moon) 1975, Mikkai (Secret Rendezvous) 1977, Kozo wa Shinda (The Little Elephant is Dead) 1979, Hakobune Sakuramaru (Ark Sakuramaru) 1984. *Leisure interests:* photography, driving. *Address:* 1-22-10, Wakabacho, Chofu City, Tokyo, Japan. *Telephone:* 03-300-3833.

ABE, Shintaro; Japanese journalist and politician; b. 29 April 1924, Yamaguchi Pref.; s. of Kan and Shizuko Abe; m. Yoko Abe 1951; two s.; ed. Tokyo Univ.; mem. House of Reps. 1958-; Private Sec. to Prime Minister Nobusuke Kishi; fmr. Deputy Sec.-Gen. Liberal-Democratic Party, Sec.-Gen. 1987-; Chair. Diet Policy Cttee., LDP 1976-77, Policy Affairs Research Council 1979-81; Minister of Agric. and Forestry 1974-76, of Int. Trade and Industry 1981-82, of Foreign Affairs 1982-86; Chair. Gen. Council Liberal Democratic Party (LDP) 1986-, Sec.-Gen. LDP; Chief Cabinet Sec. 1977-78. *Address:* Liberal Democratic Party, 1-11-23, Nagatacho, Chiyoda-ku, Tokyo 100 (Office); 30-29, 1-chome, Tomigaya, Shibuya-ku, Tokyo, Japan (Home). *Telephone:* 467-8000 (Home).

ABELA, Wistin, M.P.; Maltese politician; b. 19 Oct. 1933, Zejtun; s. of late Carmelo and Felicia (née Abela) Abela; m. Catherine (née Abela) Abela; one s. two d.; ed. Lyceum, Royal Univ. of Malta; fmr. Section Leader (Clerks) Malta Drydocks, Pres. of Labour League of Youth, Zejtun; Auditor of Malta Labour Party, M.P. 1966-; Parl. Sec. Ministry of Finance and Customs and at Office of Prime Minister 1971-74, Minister of Devt. 1974-76, Minister of Devt., Energy, Port and Telecommunications 1976-81, Deputy Prime Minister and Minister of Econ. Devt. 1981-83, Minister of Finance and Customs 1983-87; Labour. *Address:* c/o Ministry of Finance and Customs, Auberge de Castille, Valletta, Malta.

ABELSON, Philip Hauge, PH.D.; American physicist and editor; b. 27 April 1913, Tacoma, Wash.; s. of Ole Andrew and Ellen Hauge Abelson; m. Neva Martin 1936; one d.; ed. Washington State Coll. and Univ. of California at Berkeley; Asst. Physicist, Dept. of Terrestrial Magnetism, Carnegie Inst. of Washington 1939-41, Staff mem. (of Dept.) 1946-53, Dir. Geophysical Lab. 1953-71; Pres. Carnegie Inst. of Washington 1971-78; Principal Physicist and Civilian-in-Charge, Naval Research Lab. Branch, Navy Yard, Philadelphia 1941-46; Co-Ed., Journal of Geophysical Research 1959-65; Ed., Science 1962-85; Resident Fellow Resources for the Future Inc. 1985-; mem. Nat. Insts. of Health Biophysics and Biophysical Chemistry Study Section 1956-59, Gen. Advisory Cttee., to Atomic Energy Comm. 1960-63, Cttee. on Science and Public Policy of Nat. Acad. of Sciences 1962-63; Consultant to Nat. Aeronautics and Space Admin. 1960-63; mem. N.A.S., A.A.A.S., American Philosophical Soc. and many other learned socs.; Pres. American Geophysical Union 1972-74, Int. Union of Geological Sciences 1972-76; Hon. D.Sc. (Yale) 1964, (Southern Methodist Univ.) 1969, (Tufts Univ.) 1976; D.H.L. (Univ. of Puget Sound) 1968; U.S. Navy Distinguished Civilian Service Medal 1945, Physical Sciences Award, Washington Acad. of Sciences 1950, Distinguished Alumnus Award, Washington State Univ. 1962, Hillebrand Award, Chemical Soc. of Washington 1962, Modern Medicine Award 1967, Joseph Priestley Award 1973, Kalinga Prize for Popularization of Science 1973, American Medical Asscn. Scientific Achievement Award 1974; work includes identification of uranium fission products 1939-40, co-discovery of Neptunium 1940, separation of uranium isotopes 1943, biosynthesis in micro-organisms 1953, amino acids in fossils 1955, fatty acids in rocks 1956. *Publications:* author: Energy for Tomorrow 1975, Enough of Pessimism 1985; co-author: Studies in Biochemistry in Escherichia coli 1955; editor: Research in Geochemistry vols. 1 and 2 1959, 1967, Energy: Use, Conservation and Supply 1974, Food: Politics, Economics, Nutrition, and Research 1975, Materials: Renewable and Nonrenewable 1976, Electronics: The Continuing Revolution 1977. *Address:* Resources for the Future Inc., 1616 P Street, N.W., Washington, D.C. 20036, U.S.A.

ABERCONWAY, 3rd Baron, of Bodnant; Charles Melville McLaren; British business executive; b. 16 April 1913; s. of 2nd Baron Aberconway, C.B.E. and of the late Christabel Aberconway; m. 1st Deirdre Knewstub 1941 (dissolved 1949), one s. two d.; m. 2nd Ann Lindsay Bullard 1949, one s.; ed. Eton Coll., and New Coll., Oxford; Barrister, Middle Temple 1937; Army service 1939-45; Chair. John Brown & Co. Ltd. 1953-78, Pres. July 1978-84; Chair. English China Clays Ltd. 1963-84, Pres. 1984-; fmr Deputy Chair. Westland Aircraft Ltd. and Sun Alliance; Pres. Royal Horticultural Soc. 1961-84, Pres. Emer. 1984-; Commr. Gen. Int. Garden Festival, Liverpool 1984. *Leisure interests:* gardening, travel, motoring. *Address:* 25 Egerton Terrace, London, S.W.3, England; and Bodnant, Tal-y-cafn, Colwyn Bay, Clwyd, North Wales.

ABERKANE, Abdelhamid; Algerian politician; b. 30 July 1945, Khroub; m.; three c.; Prof. Medical Sciences, CHU, Constantine; Dean and Dir. Faculté de médecine de Constantine 1970-74; Pres. Conseil médical de Constantine 1976-80; Rector Univ. de Constantine; Minister of Higher Educ. 1988-. *Address:* 1 rue Bachir Attar, Palais du 1er Mai, Algiers, Algeria. *Telephone:* (2) 66-33-61.

ABERNATHY, Rev. Ralph David; American clergyman and civil rights leader; b. 11 March 1926, Linden, Ala.; m. Juanita Odessa Jones 1952; four c.; ed. Alabama State Univ. and Atlanta Univ.; Army service during Second World War; Pastor, First Baptist Church of Montgomery 1951-61; organized Montgomery Improvement Asscn. 1955; helped organize Southern Christian Leadership Conf., Atlanta 1957, became Sec.-Treas., Vice-Pres. 1965-68, Pres. 1968-77, Pres. Emer. 1977-; Pastor, West Hunter Street Baptist Church, Atlanta 1961-; mem. Nat. Asscn. for Advancement of Colored People (NAACP); jailed numerous times with late Dr. Martin Luther King; Chair. Comm. on Racism and Apartheid; Hon. LL.D. (Allen Univ.) 1960, (Long Island Univ.) 1969, (Alabama State Univ.) 1974, Hon. D.D. (Morehouse Coll.) 1971, (Kalamazoo Coll.) 1978; Peace Medallion (German Democratic Repub.) 1971. *Address:* 1040 Gordon Street, S.W. Atlanta, Ga. 30310, U.S.A.

ABIKO, Tokichi; Japanese politician; b. 22 Feb. 1904, Yamagata Pref.; ed. Tokyo Univ.; with Agric. and Forestry Ministry 1929-52; Gov. Yamagata Pref. 1955-73; mem. House of Councillors 1974-; Chair. Standing Cttee. on Foreign Affairs 1977; Minister of Home Affairs 1980-81. *Publication:* book of essays on local government and politics. *Address:* c/o Liberal-Democratic Party, 7, 2-chome, Hirakawacho, Chiyoda-ku, Tokyo, Japan.

ABIRACHED, Robert, D. ES L.; French professor and writer; b. 25 August, 1930, Beirut, Lebanon; m. Marie-France de Bailliencourt 1974; one s. one d.; ed. Lycée Louis-le-Grand and Ecole Normale Supérieure, Paris; Attaché C.N.R.S. 1960-64; Drama Critic Nouvel Observateur 1964-66; Literary and Drama Critic La Nouvelle Revue Française 1956-72; Lecturer, later Prof. Univ. of Caen, Prof. and Dir. Dept. of Drama, Univ. of Paris X Oct. 1988-; Dir. Theatre and Exhibitions, Ministry of Culture 1981-88; Chevalier Légion d'honneur, Officier du Mérite, Commandeur des Arts et Lettres; Prix Sainte-Beuve. *Publications:* Casanova ou la dissipation (essay) 1961, l'Emerveillée (novel) 1963, Tu connais la musique? (play), La Crise du personnage dans le théâtre moderne (essay) 1978. *Address:* Université de

Paris, 200 avenue de la Republique, 92001 Nanterre; 4 rue Robert-Turquan, 75016 Paris, France (Home).

ABISINITO, Kiatro Ottao, M.A.; Papua New Guinea diplomatist; ed. Papua New Guinea Univ. and the Fletcher School of Law and Diplomacy, Mass.; officer, Int. Relations Branch, Papua New Guinea Foreign Ministry, then Asst. Sec.; Exec. Officer, Nat. Exec. Council of Papua New Guinea; Second Sec. Papua New Guinea Embassy, Jakarta; Perm. Rep. to UN 1986-87, also accred. to U.S.A. *Address:* c/o Ministry for Foreign Affairs, Kumul Avenue, Waigani, Papua New Guinea.

ABLON, Ralph E.; American business executive; b. 1916, Tupelo, Miss.; m.; four c.; ed. Ohio State Univ.; Teacher, Ohio State Univ. 1938-39; worked for Luria Brothers and Co. 1939-62, Dir. 1962-; served in U.S. Navy during Second World War; Exec. Vice-Pres. Luria Brothers 1948-55, Pres. 1955-62; Chair. and C.E.O. Ogden Corpn. 1962-, Pres. 1972-86. *Address:* Ogden Corporation, 2 Pennsylvania Plaza, New York, N.Y. 10021, U.S.A.

ABOUREZK, James G.; American lawyer and politician; b. 24 Feb. 1931, Wood, S. Dak.; s. of Charles and Lena Mickel Abourezk; m. 1st Mary Ann Houlton 1952, two s. one d.; m. 2nd Margaret Bethea 1982; ed. South Dakota School of Mines, Univ. of South Dakota School of Law; served U.S. Navy 1948-52; fmr. partner, law firm of LaFleur and Abourezk; mem. House of Reps. 1971-73; Senator from S. Dakota 1973-79; partner, Abourezk, Sobol and Trister, Washington 1979-; Democrat. *Leisure interests:* writing, photography, guitar, jazz.

ABRAGAM, Anatole, D.PHIL.; French physicist; b. 15 Dec. 1914, Griva-Semgallen, Russia; s. of Simon Abragam and Anna Maimin; m. Suzanne Lequesme 1944; ed. Lycée Janson, Sorbonne, Oxford Univ.; Research Assoc., Centre Nat. de la Recherche Scientifique 1946; joined French Atomic Energy Comm. 1947, Physicist, later Sr. Physicist 1947-55, Head of Magnetic Resonance Lab. 1955-58, Head of Solid State Physics and Nuclear Physics Dept. 1959-65, Dir. of Physics 1965-70, Dir. of Research 1971-80; Prof. of Nuclear Magnetism, Coll. de France 1960-; Pres. French Physical Soc. 1967; mem. Acad. of Sciences 1973-; Hon. Fellow, American Acad. of Arts and Sciences, Merton and Jesus Colleges, Oxford 1976; Foreign mem. U.S. N.A.S., Royal Soc.; mem. Pontifical Acad. of Sciences; Dr. h.c. (Kent) 1968, (Oxford) 1976, and others; Holweck Prize, London Physical Soc. 1958, Grand Prix Cognac-Jay, Acad. of Sciences 1970, and others, Grand Officier, ordre nat. du Mérite, Commandeur, Légion d'honneur, Lorentz Medal 1982. *Publications:* Discovery of Anomalous Hyperfine Structure in Solids 1950, Dynamic Polarization in Solids 1957, The Principles of Nuclear Magnetism 1961, Nuclear Anti-ferromagnetism 1969, Electron Paramagnetic Resonance of Transition Elements (with B. Bleaney) 1970, Nuclear Pseudomagnetism 1971, Nuclear Ferromagnetism 1973, Nuclear Magnetism: Order and Disorder (with M. Goldman) 1982, Reflexions of a Physicist 1985, De la physique avant toute chose 1987. *Leisure interest:* English and Russian literature. *Address:* Collège de France, 3 rue d'Ulm, 75005 Paris (Office); 33 rue Croulebarbe, 75013 Paris, France (Home). *Telephone:* 4707 62 57 (Home).

ÁBRAHÁM, Dr. Ambrus; Hungarian neuro-histologist; b. 20 Nov. 1893, Tusnád, Transylvania (now Romania); s. of István Ábrahám and Teréz Koródy; ed. Budapest Univ.; Asst. lecturer, Budapest Univ. 1917, senior lecturer 1926, titular extraordinary Prof. 1936; Prof. Zoology at Teacher's Training Coll. of Szeged 1934-39, Dir. 1939-40; Prof. and Dir. of Inst. of Comparative Anatomy, Histology, Physiology and Biology, Univ. of Szeged 1940-67; Senior mem. Hungarian Acad. of Sciences; mem. Hungarian Soc. of Biology, Hungarian Soc. of Anatomists, Histologists and Embryologists, Hungarian Soc. of Pathologists; Fellow, Acad. of Zoology, Agra, India; Assoc. Fellow, Royal Soc. of Medicine; mem. World Fed. of Neurology; Charter mem. European Soc. for Comparative Endocrinology (Manchester) 1963; Kossuth Prize 2nd Class, Labour Order of Merit, Golden Degree. *Publications:* Anatomy, Biology, Hygienics (co-author) 1958, Die mikroskopische Innervation des Herzens und Blutgefässe von Vertebraten 1964 (in English 1968), Összehasonlító állatszervezettan (Comparative animal anatomy) 1964, Iconography of Sensory Nerve Endings 1981, scientific articles in Hungarian and int. periodicals. *Leisure interests:* microscopy, music. *Address:* József Attila Tudományegyetem, Állattani Tanszék Szeged, Egyetem-utca 2, Hungary.

ABRAHAM, Sir Edward Penley, Kt., C.B.E., D.PHIL., F.R.S.; British biochemist; b. 10 June 1913, Southampton; s. of Albert Penley Abraham and Mary Hearn; m. Asbjörg Harung 1939; one s.; ed. Queen's Coll., Oxford; Fellow of Lincoln Coll., Oxford 1948-80; Reader in Chemical Pathology, Oxford Univ. 1960-64, Prof. of Chemical Pathology 1964-80; Rockefeller Foundation Travelling Fellow at Univ. of Stockholm 1939, Univ. of Calif. 1948; CIBA Lecturer at Rutgers Univ., N.J. 1957; Guest Lecturer, Univ. of Sydney 1960; Rennebohm Lecturer, Univ. of Wis. 1967; L. P. Garrod Lecturer, London 1986; Hon. mem. American Acad. of Pharmaceutical Sciences 1967; Squibb Lecturer, Rutgers Univ., N.J. 1972; Hon. Fellow Queen's Coll. 1973, Linacre Coll. 1976, Lady Margaret Hall, Oxford 1978, Green Coll. 1981, Lincoln Coll. 1981, Wolfson Coll. 1982 and St. Peter's Coll. 1983; Foreign Hon. mem. American Acad. Arts and Sciences 1983; Hon. D.Sc. (Exeter) 1980, (Oxford) 1984; Royal Soc. Royal Medal 1973, Scheele Medal (Sweden) 1975, Chem. Soc. Award in Medicinal Chemistry 1976, Royal Soc. Mullard Medal 1980, Int. Soc. of Chemotherapy Award

1983. *Publications:* Biochemistry of Some Peptide and Steroid Antibiotics; part-author: Antibiotics, The Chemistry of Penicillin, General Pathology, Biosynthesis and Enzymic Hydrolysis of Penicillins and Cephalosporins; scientific papers on the penicillins and cephalosporins and other antibiotics. *Leisure interests:* walking, skiing. *Address:* Badgers Wood, Bedwell Heath, Boars Hill, Oxford, England (Home). *Telephone:* 735395 (Home).

ABRAHAM, F. Murray; American actor; b. 24 Oct. 1939, Pittsburgh; ed. Texas Univ.; Prof. Brooklyn Coll. 1985-; Dir. No Smoking Please; numerous Broadway plays, musicals, TV appearances and films: *Films:* Amadeus 1985, The Name of the Rose 1987; narrator Herman Melville, Damned in Paradise 1985; Obie Award (for Uncle Vanya) 1984; Golden Globe Award 1985; Los Angeles Film Critics Award 1985; Acad. Award (for Amadeus) 1985.

ÁBRAHÁM, Dr. Kálmán; Hungarian politician and engineer; b. 27 June 1931, Budapest; s. of Kálmán Ábrahám and Mária Bodnár; m. Mária Földi 1953; one d.; ed. Budapest Tech. Univ., Tech. Univ. of Building and Communications; Chief Eng., Tech. Dir. Road and Railway Planning Co., Budapest 1958-70; Head Public Roads Dept., Ministry of Transport and Communications 1970-74; Sec. of State 1974-77; Minister of Building and Urban Devt. 1977-84; Pres. Nat. Authority for Environment Protection and Nature Conservation 1984-88; Sec. of State Ministry of Environmental and Water Affairs 1987-; mem. Hungarian Socialist Workers' Party 1951; Chair. Exec. Cttee. for Devt. of Lake Balaton Area; Order of Labour, Golden Grade 1977. *Publications:* Környezetünk jövője (The Future of Our Environment) 1986; numerous tech. books and articles. *Leisure interests:* tennis, reading, swimming. *Address:* Ministry of Environmental and Water Affairs, Budapest, Hungary.

ABRAHAMS, Ivor; British sculptor and painter; b. 10 Jan. 1935, Lancs.; s. of Harry Abrahams and Rachel Kalisky; m. 1st Victoria Taylor (divorced 1974), one s.; m. 2nd Evelyne Horvais, one s.; ed. Wigan Grammar School, Lancs., St. Martin's School of Art and Camberwell School of Art, London; part-time Lecturer in Sculpture and Drawing, Birmingham Coll. of Art 1960-64, Coventry Coll. of Art 1964-68; Visiting Lecturer, R.C.A., Slade School of Fine Art and Goldsmith's Coll. of Art 1970-80; many one-man and group exhbns. in Europe and U.S.A. since 1962; works in numerous public collections including Victoria and Albert Museum and Tate Gallery, London, Wedgwood Museum, Stoke-on-Trent, Walker Art Gallery, Liverpool, Arnolfini Gallery, Bristol, Nat. Gallery of Australia, Canberra, Bibliothèque Nationale, Paris, Museum of Modern Art and Metropolitan Museum of Modern Art, New York, Denver Museum, Colo., Fort Lauderdale Museum, Fla. Buymans Museum, Rotterdam, British Council and Arts Council of G.B. *Leisure interests:* books, postcards and golf. *Address:* 67 Bathurst Gardens, London, NW2 5JH, England. *Telephone:* 01-969 2505.

ABRAHAMSON, Gen. James A.; American air force officer and defence official; b. 19 May 1933, Williston, N.D.; s. of Norval S. Abrahamson and Thelma B. Helle; m. Barbara Jean Northcott 1959 (died 1985); one s. one d.; ed. M.I.T. and Univ. of Oklahoma; commissioned U.S.A.F. 1955, Lieut. Gen. 1982, Gen. 1987; Flight Instructor Bryan A.F. Base, Tex. 1957-59; Spacecraft Project Officer Vela Nuclear Detection Satellite Programme, L.A.A.F. Station 1961-64; Fighter Pilot Tactical Air Command 1964; Astronaut U.S.A.F. Manned Orbiting Lab. 1967-69; mem. staff Nat. Aeronautics and Space Council, White House 1969-71; Commdr. 4950th Test Wing U.S.A.F. 1973-74; Insp. Gen. A.F. Systems Command 1974-76; Dir. F-16 Fighter Programme 1976-80; Deputy Chief of Staff for Systems Andrews A.F. Base, Md. 1980-81; Assoc. Admin. for Space Transportation System, NASA HQ 1981-84; Dir. Strategic Defence Initiative Org. 1984-89; numerous awards and medals. *Leisure interests:* sports, music and poetry. *Address:* 4782 Command Lane, Andrews A.F. Base, Md. 20335 (Home); OSD/SDIO, Pentagon, Washington D.C. 20301-7100, U.S.A.

ABRAHAMSSON, Bo Axel; Swedish company executive; b. 20 July 1931, Stockholm; s. of Axel and Viola (née Ek) Abrahamsson; m. 1st Lili-Christine Engdahl 1959, 2nd Helène Westerlundh 1985; two s. three d.; ed. Royal Inst. of Tech., Stockholm; mem. of Bd. of Dirs. Gränges AB, Lamco, LIO, Platzer Bygg AB, Cominvest AB, Industri-Matematik AB, Fredells Trävaru AB, PIAB, Stena AB, Concordia Maritime AB, AB Forssjö Bruk; Pres. Motivation Bo, Abrahamsson AB, Stockholm 1982-; mem. Industrial Cttee., Royal Swedish Acad. of Eng. Sciences. *Leisure interests:* golf, tennis, hunting, skiing. *Address:* c/o Gränges AB, Birger Jarlsgatan 52, Stockholm 10326, Sweden.

ABRAMOV, Grigoriy Grigoriyevich; Soviet politician; b. 10 Jan. 1908, Karandeevka, Ryazan; ed. Bauman Tech. Inst., Moscow; Engineer 1941-47; party work 1947-49; Second Sec. Mytishchi Town Cttee., Communist Party, First Sec. Shchelkovsk Town Cttee. 1949-55; Section Leader, Moscow Region Party Cttee. 1955-59, Second Sec. 1959-60, First Sec. 1960-63; First Deputy Chair. Econ. Council 1963-65; Deputy Minister Chemical and Oil Machine Building 1965-; mem. Central Cttee. CPSU 1961-66; Deputy to U.S.S.R. Supreme Soviet 1962-66; mem. Presidium of Supreme Soviet 1962-66; Order of Red Banner of Labour (four times). *Address:* Ministry of Chemical and Oil Machine Building, 25 Bezbozhny pereulok, Moscow, U.S.S.R.

ABRAMOVITZ, Max, M.S.; American architect; b. 23 May 1908, Chicago; s. of Benjamin Abramovitz and Sophia Maimon; m. 1st Anne Marie Causey

1937 (divorced), 2nd Anita Brooks 1964; one s. one d.; ed. Illinois and Columbia Univs., Ecole des Beaux Arts, Paris; mem. of Harrison, Fouilhoux & Abramovitz 1941–45, Harrison & Abramovitz 1945–76; Abramovitz-Harris-Kingsland 1976–85, Abramovitz, Kingsland, Schiff, New York 1985; U.S. Army (Corps of Engineers) 1942–45; Deputy Dir. of Planning, UN, New York 1947–52; U.S. Air Force (Colonel) 1950–52; Fellow, American Inst. of Architects; mem. Architectural League of New York, American Soc. of Civil Engineers, Century Assocn.; fmr. Dir. Regional Plan Assocn. Inc.; Trustee, Mount Sinai Hospital; Legion of Merit 1945; Hon. Dr. of Fine Arts, (Pittsburgh and Ill.); Award of Achievement, Univ. of Ill. Alumni Assocn. 1963; Fellow, Brandeis Univ. 1963. *Works include:* Jewish Chapel, U.S. Mil. Acad. (New York), Corning Glass Center (Corning, N.Y.) 1951, U.S. Steel Building, Alcoa Building (Pittsburgh), U.S. Embassy (Rio de Janeiro) 1952, U.S. Embassy (Havana) 1953, Three Chapels at Brandeis Univ. 1955, Corning Glass Building (New York) 1959, Philharmonic Hall, Lincoln Center for the Performing Arts (New York), Columbia Univ. Law School and Library (New York) 1962, Univ. of Illinois Assembly Hall (Champaign, Ill.) 1963, Phoenix Mutual Life Insurance Bldg. (Hartford, Conn.) 1964, Hilles Library, Radcliffe Coll., Cambridge, Mass. 1966, Beth Zion Temple, Buffalo, N.Y. 1967, Krannert Center for the Performing Arts, Urbana, Ill., Nationwide Insurance Co., Columbus, Ohio 1977, Tour GAN, La Défense, Paris 1977, La Banque Rothschild, Paris, Owens-Ill. World HQ, Toledo 1984. *Address:* 930 Fifth Avenue, New York, N.Y. 10021, U.S.A.

ABRAMS, Herbert Leroy, M.D.; American professor of radiology; b. 16 Aug. 1920, New York; s. of Morris Abrams and Freda (née Sugarman) Abrams; m. Marilyn Spitz 1942; one s. one d.; ed. Cornell Univ., State Univ. of New York; began medical practice Stanford Univ., faculty mem. School of Medicine 1951–67, Dir. Div. Diagnostic Roentgenology 1961–67, Prof. of Radiology 1962–67; Philip H. Cook Prof. of Radiology, Harvard Univ. 1967–85, Chair. Dept. of Radiology 1967–80; Radiologist-in-Chief, Peter Bent Brigham Hosp., Boston 1967–80; Chair. Dept. of Radiology, Brigham & Women's Hosp., Boston 1981–85; Radiologist-in-Chief, Sidney Farber Cancer Inst., Boston 1974–85; Prof. of Radiology, Stanford Univ. Medical School 1985–; Clinical Prof. Univ. of California Medical School 1986–; Ed.-in-Chief Postgraduate Radiology 1982–, Cardiovascular and Interventional Radiology 1978–85; R.H. Nimmo Visiting Prof., Univ. of Adelaide 1976; Hon. Fellow Royal Coll. of Radiology, Royal Coll. of Surgeons (Ireland). *Publications:* Congenital Heart Disease 1965, Coronary Arteriography: A Practical Approach 1983, Ed. Abrams Angiography 1983. *Leisure interests:* English and American Literature, tennis, music. *Address:* Stanford University School of Medicine, Room S-056, Stanford, Calif. 94305 (Office); 714 Alvarado Row, Stanford, Calif. 94305, U.S.A. (Home). *Telephone:* 415-723 6258 (Office); 415-424 8552 (Home).

ABRASSIMOV, Pyotr Andreyevich; Soviet diplomatist; b. 16 May 1912, Bogushevskoe, Byelorussia; ed. Byelorussian State Univ.; Electrician 1928–31; Soviet Army 1941–42; mem. CPSU 1940–, Party work 1942–46, 1950–52, 1955–56; Perm. Rep. Byelorussian S.S.R. Council of Ministers at U.S.S.R. Council of Ministers 1946–48; First Vice-Chair. Byelorussian S.S.R. Council of Ministers 1948–50, 1952–55; Minister-Counsellor, Soviet Embassy, Peking 1956–57; Amb. to Poland 1957–61, to the German Democratic Republic 1962–71, 1975–83, to France 1971–73, concurrently to Madagascar 1972–73, to Japan 1985–87; Head Dept. for Liaison with Communist Parties of Socialist Countries 1973–75; Chair. State Cttee. for Foreign Tourism 1983–85; First Sec. Smolensk Regional Cttee. of CPSU 1961–62; mem. Cen. Cttee. CPSU 1961–; Deputy to Supreme Soviet of U.S.S.R.; Order of Lenin (twice), Red Banner, Red Banner of Labour, October Revolution. *Address:* Ministry of Foreign Affairs, Moscow, U.S.S.R.

ABRASZEWSKI, Andrzej, M.A., LL.D.; Polish diplomatist; b. 4 Jan. 1938; ed. Cen. School for Foreign Service, Warsaw, and Copernicus Univ., Toruń; researcher, Polish Inst. for Int. Affairs, Warsaw 1962–71; Sec. Polish Nat. Cttee. on the 25th anniversary of the UN 1970; Counsellor to the Minister for Foreign Affairs, Dept. of Int. Orgs., Ministry of Foreign Affairs, Warsaw 1971–; mem. Polish del. to Gen. Ass. of the UN 1971–82, mem. Ad Hoc Working Group on UN's programme and budget machinery 1975, mem. Advisory Cttee. on Admin. and Budgetary Questions 1977–84, mem. Fifth Cttee. (Admin. and Budgetary) of Gen. Ass. 1979–84, Chair. 1982–84, Adviser to Minister of Foreign Affairs 1984–. *Publications:* various papers on UN affairs. *Address:* Ministerstwo Spraw Zagranicznych, 00-580 Warsaw, al. I Armii Wojska Polskiego 23, Poland.

ABRIKOSOV, Aleksey Alekseyevich; Soviet physicist; b. 25 June 1928, Moscow; s. of Aleksey Ivanovich Abrikosov and Fanny Davidovna Vulf; m. Svetlana Yuriyevna Bun'kova 1977; two s. one d.; ed. Moscow Univ.; Postgraduate Research Assoc., Research Worker, Inst. of Physical Problems, U.S.S.R. Acad. of Sciences 1948–65; Head of Dept., Inst. of Theoretical Physics, U.S.S.R. Acad. of Sciences 1965–88, Dir. Inst. of High Pressure Physics 1988–; Research Assoc., Asst. Prof., Prof. Moscow Univ. 1951–68, Prof. Gorky Univ. 1971–72, Prof. Moscow Physical Eng. Inst. 1974–75, Head Chair. Theoretical Physics, Moscow Inst. of Steel and Alloys 1976–; Corresp. mem. U.S.S.R. Acad. of Sciences 1964–; Dr. h.c. (Moscow) 1955; D.S. h.c. (Lausanne) 1975; Lenin Prize 1966, Fritz London Award 1972, U.S.S.R. State Prize 1982. *Publications:* Quantum Field Theory Methods in Statistical Physics 1962, Introduction to the Theory of Normal

Metals 1972, Fundamentals of Metal Theory 1987, and works on plasma physics, quantum electro-dynamics, theory of superconductors, magnetism, astro-physics, quantum liquids and semimetals. *Leisure interests:* skiing, mountaineering. *Address:* Landau Institute of High Pressure Physics, Troitsk, Moscow 142092, U.S.S.R.

ABRIL MARTORELI, Fernando, DR. AGRIC. ENG.; Spanish politician; b. 1936, Valencia; m.; studied rural econ. and agricultural engineering; fmr. Pres. of Diputación (city council) of Segovia; fmr. Dir.-Gen. FORPPA; fmr. Dir.-Gen. of Agricultural Production; now mem. Higher Agrarian Council; Chair. Spanish Dairying Fed.; mem. Cortes (Parl.); Minister of Agriculture 1976–77; Deputy Prime Minister 1977–80 (responsibility for Political Affairs 1977–78, for Economic Affairs 1978–80); various nat. decorations. *Address:* c/o Oficina del Primer Ministro, Madrid, Spain.

ABS, Hermann J.; German banker; b. 15 Oct. 1901; ed. part-time studies, Univs. of Bonn and Cologne; joined staff of Delbrück Schickler & Co., bankers, Berlin 1929, Partner 1935–37; mem. Management Bd. Deutsche Bank, Berlin 1937; mem. Management Bd. Kreditanstalt für Wiederaufbau, Frankfurt 1948–59, Chair. 1959, now Hon. Chair.; Head, German Del. on German External Debts 1951–53; mem. Man. Bd. Süddeutsche Bank A.G. 1952–67, now Hon. Pres. Deutsche Bank A.G., Frankfurt; Chair. Supervisory Bd. Dahlbusch Verwaltungs-AG, Gelsenkirchen, Prym Verwaltungsgesellschaft mbH, Stolberg; Hon. mem. Supervisory Bd. Hoesch Werke AG, Dortmund; Hon. Chair. and mem. Supervisory Bd. Deutsche Lufthansa AG, Cologne; Hon. Chair. Supervisory Bd. Daimler-Benz AG, Stuttgart, Enka AG, Wuppertal-Elberfeld, Flachglas AG, Gelsenkirchen, Deutsche Solvay-Werke GmbH, Solingen-Ohligs, Philipp Holzmann AG, Frankfurt, PWA Papierwerke Waldhof-Aschaffenburg AG, Munich, Rheinisch-Westfälisches Elektrizitätswerk AG, Essen, Salamander AG, Kornwestheim, Süddeutsche Zucker-AG Mannheim, Kreditanstalt für Wiederaufbau, Frankfurt; Dr. rer. pol. h.c. (Univ. of Göttingen, Wirtschaftshochschule, Mannheim, etc.). *Address:* Taunusanlage 12, Frankfurt/Main 6000, Federal Republic of Germany.

ABSE, Dannie, M.R.C.S., L.R.C.P., F.R.S.L.; British physician and author; b. 22 Sept. 1923, Cardiff, Wales; s. of Rudolph Abse and Kate Shepherd; m. Joan Mercer 1951; one s. two d.; ed. St. Illtyd's Coll. Cardiff, Univ. Coll. Cardiff, King's Coll. London and Westminster Hosp., London; first book of poems published while still a medical student 1948; qualified as doctor 1950; Squadron-Leader R.A.F. 1951–55; doctor in charge of chest clinic at Cen. Medical Establishment, Cleveland St., London until 1981, part-time and freelance writer 1981–; Writer in Residence, Princeton Univ., N.J., U.S.A. 1973–74; Pres. Poetry Soc.; Welsh Arts Council Literature Prize; Jewish Chronicle Award; Cholmondeley Award 1983. *Publications:* Collected Poems 1948–1977, Pythagoras (a play), Ash on a Young Man's Sleeve 1954, Way Out in the Centre 1981, Ask the Bloody Horse 1986, Journals from the Ant Heap 1986, White Coat, Purple Coat 1989 and many others. *Address:* 85 Hodford Road, London, N.W.11; Green Hollows, Craig-yr-Eos Road, Ogmore-by-Sea, Glamorgan, South Wales.

ABSHIRE, David Manker, PH.D.; American diplomatist and administrator; b. 4 Nov. 1926, Chattanooga, Tenn.; s. of James Ernest and Phyllis Patten Abshire; m. Carolyn Sample Abshire 1957; one s. four d.; ed. Baylor School, Chattanooga, U.S. Mil. Acad., West Point, N.Y., Georgetown Univ., Washington, D.C.; Exec. Dir., Center for Strategic and Int. Studies, Georgetown Univ. 1962–70, Chair. 1973–82, Pres. 1982–83; Asst. Sec. of State for Congressional Relations 1970–73; Perm. Rep. to NATO 1983–87; Special Counsellor to Pres. Jan.-April 1987; Chancellor Center for Strategic and Int. Studies (CSIS) April–Dec. 1987, Pres. 1988–; Co-ed. Washington Quarterly 1977–83; Chair., U.S. Bd. for Int. Broadcasting 1974–77; Dir., Nat. Security Group, Transition Office of Pres.-elect Reagan 1980–81; mem. Congressional Cttee. on the Org. of Govt.; for the Conduct of Foreign Policy 1973–75; mem. Bd. Procter and Gamble, Ogden Corpn., BP American Advisory Cttee.; Order of Crown (Belgium), Commdr. Ordre de Leopold (Belgium). *Publications:* International Broadcasting: A New Dimension of Western Diplomacy 1976, Foreign Policy Makers: President vs. Congress 1979, The Growing Power of Congress 1981. *Leisure interest:* historical literature. *Address:* CSIS, Suite 400, 1800 K Street, N.W., Washington, D.C. 20006, U.S.A. *Telephone:* 202-775-3212.

ABU BASHA, Hassan, B.SC.; Egyptian politician; b. 1923; m. (wife deceased); three c.; ed. Police Acad.; held various posts in police force; Deputy Dir. of State Security Investigation Dept. 1971, Dir. 1975; First Asst. to Minister of Interior 1978; Minister of Interior 1982, of Local Govt. 1985–86; mem. Political Bureau, Nat. Democratic Party. *Address:* c/o Ministry of Local Government, Cairo, Egypt.

ABU-GHAZALA, Marshal Mohamed Abdel Halim (see Abdel Halim, Abu-Ghazala, Marshal Mohamed).

ABULADZE, Tengiz; Soviet film director; b. 1933, Georgia; grad. Georgian Inst. of Cinema, Tbilisi 1953; Lenin Prize for Art 1988; Films include: Magdana's Donkey 1956 (together with R. Chkheidze) (First Prize Cannes Film Festival), Other People's Children 1959, Grandmother, Iliko and Ilarion and Me 1963, The Prayer 1968, Molba 1973, The Wishing Tree 1978, Repentance 1986.

ABUL NOUR, Mohamed El Ahmadi, M.A., PH.D.; Egyptian politician; b. 1932; ed. Theological Faculty, Al-Azhar Univ.; teacher Al-Azhar Insts.

1957-63, Reader, Theological Faculty 1963, teacher and head of Al-Tafsir section of Faculty for Girls 1973, Prof. of Al-Hadith 1981, later Dean, Faculty for Girls; Vice-Pres. Muslim Youth Socs.; Minister of Wakfs 1985-86. *Publications:* several works on Al-Tafsir and Al-Hadith. *Address:* c/o Ministry of Wakfs, Sharia Sabri Abu Alam, Ean El Luk, Cairo, Egypt.

ABUSHADI, Mohamed Mahmoud, PH.D., A.C.I.P.; Egyptian banker; b. 15 Aug. 1913, Fayoum; s. of Mahmoud and Seddika (Hashad) Abu Shadi; m. Colleen Althea Bennet 1947; two s. two d.; ed. Cairo Univ., Chartered Inst. of Patent Agents, and American Univ., Washington; Controller-Gen., Insurance Dept., Ministry of Finance 1949-52; Dir.-Gen. Govt. Insurance and Provident Funds 1953; Chair. and Man. Dir. Devt. and Popular Housing Co. 1954-55; Sub-Gov. Nat. Bank of Egypt 1955-60, Man. Dir. 1960-67, Chair. and Man. Dir. 1967-70; Chair. Union de Banques Arabes et Françaises (UBAF), Paris 1970-87, UBAF Bank Ltd., London 1971-; Chair. Social Insurance Org. 1956-57; Chair. and Man. Dir. Cairo Insurance Co. 1956-57; Man. Dir. Cairo Bank 1956-57; Pres. Int. Bankers' Asscn. 1976-; Order of the Repub., (2nd Class), Order of Merit, (1st Class), Commdr., Officier, Légion d'honneur. *Publications:* The Art of Central Banking and its Application in Egypt 1962, Central Banking in Egypt 1952, Will New York Attract Arab Capital? 1974, The Experience of the Arab-French Banks 1974, Oil Funds: The Search for Supplementary Recycling Mechanisms 1975, The Role of Finance in Promoting Arab European Business Cooperation 1976. *Leisure interests:* swimming, tennis, art. *Address:* Union de Banques Arabes et Françaises, 190 avenue Charles de Gaulle, 92200 Neuilly sur Seine (Office); 52 avenue Foch, 75016 Paris, France (Home). *Telephone:* 47 38 01 01 (Office).

ABU TALEB, Sufi Hassan, D. EN DROIT; Egyptian professor and politician; b. 27 Jan. 1925, Fayoum; ed. Cairo Univ. Law School, Faculty of Law, Paris and Rome Univs.; Prof. of Law Cairo Univ. 1952-58, Chair. History and Philosophy of Law Dept. 1958-65; Legal Adviser, Univ. of Assiut (Asyut) 1965, Univ. of Cairo 1967; joined Arab Socialist Union 1962, Sec.-Gen. 1964; lecturer in law, Beirut Arab Univ. 1970-72; Prof. of Law, Cairo Univ. 1972, appointed Vice-Pres. 1973, Pres. 1975-78; elected mem. for Fayoum, People's Ass. Oct. 1976; joined Arab Socialist Party Nov. 1976; a founder of Nat. Democratic Party 1978; mem. Higher Ministerial Cttee. for Egyptian-Sudanese Political and Econ. Fed.; elected Speaker, People's Ass. 1978-84; mem. Bd. of Dirs., Islamic Studies Inst., Cairo, Conf. on Islamic Educ., Mecca (Makkah); has lectured at several American Univs. *Publications:* Arab Society 1965, Studies in Arab Nationalism, The Legal Status of Women in the Arab Countries (in French) and many others. *Address:* The People's Assembly, Cairo, Egypt.

ABUZEID, Salah; Jordanian diplomatist and fmr. politician; b. 21 April 1925, Irbid; m.; ed. Law Coll. of Syrian Univ., Damascus, and Syracuse Univ., U.S.A.; Government Official 1950-58; Dir. Amman Radio Station 1958-59; Asst. Dir.-Gen. Hashemite Broadcasting Service 1959-62, Dir.-Gen. of Hashemite Broadcasting Service and Chief of Nat. Guidance 1962-64; Minister of Information 1964-65, 1967, of Culture and Information 1967-68; Amb. to U.K. 1969, 1976-78; Minister of Culture and Information 1969-70; Special Adviser to H.M. The King 1970-72; Minister of Foreign Affairs 1972-73; mem. Senate, Head of Foreign Relations Cttee. 1974-76; Adviser to H.M. The King 1976; sentenced to 3 years' imprisonment (commuted to six months) for misusing funds April 1979; numerous decorations. *Publication:* Al Hussein bin Talal 1958. *Address:* c/o Ministry of Foreign Affairs, Amman, Jordan.

ABZUG, Bella Savitzky, LL.B.; American lawyer and politician; b. 24 July 1920, New York; d. of Emanuel and Esther Savitzky; m. Maurice M. Abzug 1944; two d.; ed. Bronx public schools, Hunter Coll., Univ. of New York; admitted to New York bar 1947, practised in New York 1944-70, 1980-; mem. House of Reps. from 19th District, New York, then 20th District, New York 1970-76; Writer, Ms. Magazine, New York 1979-; mem. House Public Works Cttee., Government Operations Cttee. (Chair. Sub-Cttee. on Govt. Information and Individual Rights); co-author Freedom of Information and Privacy Acts; mem. Pres.'s Comm. on Observance of Int. Women's Year (IWY), Congressional Adviser to IWY Int. Conf., Mexico City 1975; spokeswoman for peace, full employment, job-producing public works programmes, federalization of welfare, openness in govt., equal rights, consumer and environmental protection, aid to cities, programmes for sr. citizens, aid to Israel; mem. Women Strike for Peace (founder and Nat. Legis. Dir. 1961-70), Women's Prison Asscn., Nat. Org. for Women until 1979, Nat. Women's Political Caucus (founder and fmr. Chair.), American Civil Liberties Union, Democratic Study Group, Congress for Peace through Law, Hadassah, UN Asscn., B'nai B'rith, Hunter Coll. Hall of Fame; Hon. D. Iur. (New York); Democrat-Liberal. *Publications:* Bella! Ms. Abzug Goes to Washington 1972; Gender Gap: Bella Abzug's Guide to Political Power for American Women 1984; numerous articles for magazines, contributor to numerous anthologies on women's movement.

ACCARDO, Salvatore; Italian violinist; b. 26 Sept. 1941, Turin; s. of Vincenzo and Ines Nea Accardo; m. Resy Corsi 1973; ed. Conservatorio S. Pietro a Majella, Naples and Accademia Musicale Chigiana, Siena; first professional recital 1954; won 1st prize Geneva Competition at age 15 and 1st prize Paganini Competition at age 17; repertoire includes concertos by Bartók, Beethoven, Berg, Brahms, Bruch, Paganini, Penderecki, Prokofiev,

Saint-Saëns, Sibelius, Stravinsky and Tchaikovsky; plays with world's leading conductors and orchestras including Amsterdam Concertgebouw, Berlin Philharmonic, Boston Symphony, Chicago Symphony, Cleveland, La Scala, Milan, Santa Cecilia, Rome, BBC Symphony, London Symphony and Philharmonia; also appears as soloist/dir. with the English, Scottish and Netherlands Chamber Orchestras; Artistic Dir. Naples Festival. *Recordings include:* the Paganini Concertos and Caprices (Deutsche Grammophon), concerts by Beethoven and Brahms, complete works for violin and orchestra by Bruch, concertos by Mendelssohn, Dvořák, Sibelius and Tchaikovsky (Philips/Phonogram); Cavaliere di gran Croce 1982; numerous music prizes include Caecilia Prize (Brussels) and Italian Critics' Prize for recording of the Six Paganini Concertos and Diapuson d'Or for recording of the Sibelius Concerto. *Publications:* edn. Paganini Sixth Concerto, Paganini: Variations on "Carmagnola". *Leisure interests:* Hi Fi, electronics, sport and cooking. *Address:* c/o Robert Leslie, 53 Bedford Road, London, SW4, England.

ACEVES PARRA, Salvador; Mexican doctor and politician; b. 4 April 1904, Michoacán; s. of José M. Aceves and María Parra de Aceves; m. Carmen G. C. de Aceves 1934; two s. two d.; ed. Nat. Preparatory School, Mexico City, and Faculty of Medicine, Univ. Nacional Autónoma de México; Asst. at Propadeutic Medical Clinic, Faculty of Medicine, Univ. Nacional Autónoma de México 1933-36, Prof. of Medical Pathology 1936-44, Prof. of Medical Clinic 1944-68; Prof. of Graduate Course in Cardiology 1935-68; Asst. Prof., later Prof., at Graduate School; Intern Doctor, Gen. Hospital 1933-36, attached to Intern Medical Service 1936-38, Head of Medical Service, Gen. Hospital 1938-44; Head, Nat. Inst. of Cardiology Service 1944-61; Dir. Nat. Inst. of Cardiology 1961-65; Under-Sec., Secr. of Public Health and Welfare 1965-68, Sec. 1968-70; Hon. mem. Council of Seminaries of Mexican Culture 1960-; mem. Nat. Acad. of Medicine, Pres. 1951, 1952; Pres. Mexican Cardiology Soc. 1947-49, 1956-58; mem. Govt. Council, Nat. Univ. of Mexico; mem. numerous American and Latin American medical socs.; Commdr., Order of Merit (Italy) 1964, Decoration for Medical Merit (Brazil) 1967. *Leisure interests:* reading, horse-riding. *Address:* Nuevo León 66, 3°, México, D.F. (Office); B. Traven No. 166, México 13, D.F., Mexico (Home). *Telephone:* 528-68-38 (Office); 524-16-84 (Home).

ACHEBE, Chinua, B.A., F.R.S.L.; Nigerian writer; b. 16 Nov. 1930, Ogidi, Anambra State; s. of late Isaiah O. and Janet N. Achebe; m. Christie C. Okoli 1961; two s. two d.; ed. Government Coll., Umuahia, and Univ. Coll., Ibadan; Producer, Nigerian Broadcasting Corpn., Lagos 1954-58, Regional Controller, Enugu 1958-61, Dir. Voice of Nigeria, Lagos 1961-66; Sr. Research Fellow, Univ. of Nigeria, Nsukka 1967-72; Rockefeller Fellowship 1960-61; UNESCO Fellowship 1963; Foundation mem. Soc. of Nigerian Authors 1982-; mem. Gov. Council, Lagos Univ. 1966, mem. E. Cen. State Library Bd. 1971-72; Founding Ed., Okike 1971-; Prof. of English, Univ. of Mass. 1972-75, Univ. of Conn. 1975-76, Univ. of Nigeria, Nsukka 1976-81; Prof. Emer. Nsukka 1985-; Pro-Chancellor and Chair. of Council, Anambra State Univ. of Tech., Enugu, Nigeria 1986-; Regents Lecturer, Univ. of Calif., Los Angeles 1984; Founding Ed. African Writers' Series (Heinemann) 1962-72; Dir. Heinemann Educational Books (Nigeria) Ltd., Nwamife (Publishers), Enugu; Pres. Assen. of Nigerian Authors 1981-; mem. Tokyo Colloquium 1981; Hon. mem. American Acad. of Arts and Letters 1982; Gov. Newsconcern Int. Foundation 1983; Hon. Fellow, Modern Language Assen. of America 1974; Neil Gunn Int. Fellow 1975; Fellow, Ghana Assen. of Writers 1975; Hon. D.Univ.; Hon. D.Litt. (eight times); Hon. D.H.L. (Mass.); Hon. LL.D. (P.E.I.); Margaret Wrong Memorial Prize 1959, Nigerian Nat. Trophy 1960, Jock Campbell New Statesman Award 1965, Commonwealth Poetry Prize 1972, The Lotus Prize (Afro-Asian writers) 1975, Order of the Federal Republic (Nigeria) 1979, Nigerian Nat. Merit Award 1979. *Publications:* Things Fall Apart 1958, No Longer at Ease 1960, Arrow of God 1964, A Man of the People 1966, Chike and the River 1966, Poems 1971, Girls at War 1972, Beware Soul Brother 1972, How the Leopard Got His Claws 1973, Morning Yet on Creation Day 1975, The Flute 1978, The Drum 1978, Anthills of the Savannah 1987, Nigerian Topics (Essays) 1988, Hopes and Impediments—Selected Essays 1965-87 1988. *Leisure interest:* music. *Address:* P.O. Box 53, Nsukka, Anambra State, Nigeria.

ACHILLE, Jean-Claude; French public administrator; b. 6 June 1926, Agen; m. Lise-Rose Rame 1961; one s.; ed. Ecole Polytechnique and Ecole des Mines, Paris; Engineer, coal mining, Bassin de Blanzy 1950-51; Engineer of Mines, Valenciennes, then Asst. to Chief Engineer, Douai Mines 1951-56; Tech. Councillor and Dir. of Offices at Ministry of Industry and Commerce 1956-59; Asst. Dir.-Gen. Gaz de France 1959-63; Dir.-Gen. Charbonnages de France 1963-68; Dir. Houillères du bassin du Nord et du Pas-de-Calais, Houillères du bassin de Lorraine 1963-68; mem. Econ. and Social Cttee. European Community 1963-68; mem. Bd. of Dirs. and Dir.-Gen. Rhône-Poulenc, S.A. 1968-76, Vice-Pres. 1975-77; mem. Advisory Council Banque de France 1975-; Pres. Union des Industries Chimiques 1977; Chair. Fed. Industries Engrais; Dir. numerous other companies; Officier, Légion d'honneur et des Palmes académiques, Officier du Mérite. *Address:* 64 avenue Marceau, 75008, Paris, France (Office). *Telephone:* 47-20-56-03.

ACHOUR, Habib; Tunisian trade union leader and politician; b. 1913; joined Néo-Destour party 1934; f. Union Générale Tunisienne de Travail (UGTT) with Farhat Hached 1946; arrested for inciting strikes 1947, 1952; elected Sec.-Gen. UGTT 1963-66; mem. Political Bureau, Parti Socialiste

Destourien (PSD) 1947-66; imprisoned March-Sept. 1966; elected mem. Nat. Ass. 1969; readmitted to Political Bureau 1970 (-Jan. 1978) and re-elected Sec.-Gen. UGTT 1970 (-March 1978); sentenced to 10 years' hard labour following severe anti-govt. rioting Jan. 1978, later pardoned but remained under house arrest 1979; pardoned and released Nov. 1981; appointed Pres. UGTT 1981. *Address:* Union Générale Tunisienne du Travail, 29 Place M'Hamed Ali, Tunis, Tunisia.

ACKER, Sven Hermann; Danish public servant, b. 27 Feb. 1911, Copenhagen; s. of Fr. Acker and Karen Frisenette; m. Drude Kvalsund 1940; ed. Ordrup Gymnasium and Københavns Universitet; Sec. to Minister of Public Works 1946-48; Del. UN Transport Cttee., Geneva 1947-50, 1952-56; Chair. UN Cttee. on Road Transport, Geneva 1954-56; Dir.-Gen. Nat. Travel Asscn. of Denmark 1957-67, Danish Tourist Bd. 1967-69; Chair. Regional Comm. for Europe, Int. Union of Official Travel Orgs. 1964-67; Chair. European Travel Comm. 1971-73; Vice-Pres. Acad. Int. du Tourisme 1977; mem. Exec. Cttee. for Preservation of Natural Amenities in Denmark 1957-59; mem. Exec. Cttee., Europa Nostra; Vice-Chair. Cttee. Royal Danish Music and Ballet Festival 1957-68; Knight 1st Class Order of Dannebrog, Commdr. Icelandic Order of the Falcon; Danish Tourist Board Medal. *Leisure interest:* Danish history. *Address:* Hostrups Have I, 1954 Copenhagen V (Home); Nordre Strandvej 408, 3100 Hornbaek, Denmark.

ACKEREN, Robert Van; West German film maker, screenplay writer and producer; b. 22 Dec. 1946, Berlin; s. of Max and Hildegard Van Ackeren; ed. in film studies, Berlin; German Film Prize, Ernst Lubitsch Prize, Federal Film Prize (Fed. Repub. of Germany), Prix Celuloide, Premio Incontri Int., Prix L'âge d'or and other awards. *Films:* Blondie's No. 1 1971, Küss mich, Fremder 1972, Harlis 1973, Der letzte Schrei 1975, Belcanto 1977, Das andere Lächeln 1978, Die Reinheit des Herzens 1980, Deutschland Privat 1981, Die flambierte Frau 1983, Die Tigerin 1985, Der Venusfalle 1987. *Address:* Kurfürstendamm 132A, D-1000 Berlin 31, Federal Republic of Germany. *Telephone:* (30) 891 33 55.

ACKLEY, (Hugh) Gardner, PH.D.; American educationist, economist and diplomatist; b. 30 June 1915, Indianapolis, Ind.; s. of Hugh M. and Margaret (McKenzie) Ackley; m. Bonnie A. Lowry 1937; two s.; ed. Western State Teachers Coll. and Univ. of Michigan; Instructor, Ohio State Univ. 1939-40, Univ. of Mich. 1940-41; Office of Price Administration, Washington 1941-43, 1944-46; Office of Strategic Services 1943-44; Asst. Prof. Univ. of Mich. 1946-47; Assoc. Prof. 1947-52, Prof. 1952-68; Econ. Adviser and Asst. Dir. Office of Price Stabilization 1951-52; mem. Bd. of Editors, American Economic Review 1953-56; Dir. Social Science Research Council 1959-62; mem. Council of Econ. Advisers, Exec. Office of the Pres. of U.S. 1962-68, Chair. 1964-68; Amb. to Italy 1968-69; Henry Carter Adams Univ. Prof. of Political Economy, Univ. of Mich. 1969-83, Emer. 1984-; Consultant, Baker, Weeks & Co. 1970-74; Dir. Nat. Bureau of Econ. Research 1971-79, Banco di Roma (Chicago) 1973-86; mem. American Philosophical Society; Trustee, Joint Council on Econ. Educ. 1971-77; Assoc. Staff mem. Brookings Inst. 1976-80; mem. Advisory Council on Social Security 1978-79; mem. Research Advisory Bd., Cttee. for Econ. Devt. 1979-82; Pres. American Econ. Asscn. 1983; mem. Trilateral Comm. 1979-83; Fellow American Acad. of Arts and Sciences; Hon. LL.D. (Western Mich.) 1964, (Kalamazoo Coll.) 1967; Cavaliere del Gran Croce, Ordine al Merito della Repubblica Italiana. *Publications:* Macroeconomic Theory 1961, Un Modello Econometrico dello Sviluppo Italiano nel Dopoguerra 1963, Stemming World Inflation 1971, Macroeconomics: Theory and Policy 1978; columnist Dun's Business Month (1971-84); numerous articles, reviews, contributions to symposia, etc. *Address:* Department of Economics, University of Michigan, Ann Arbor, Mich. 48104 (Office); 907 Berkshire Road, Ann Arbor, Mich. 48104, U.S.A. (Home). *Telephone:* 313-665-8770.

ACKNER, Rt. Hon. Sir Desmond (James Conrad), KT., P.C.; British judge; b. 18 Sept. 1920; s. of Conrad and Rhoda Ackner; m. Joan Evans 1946; one s. one d.; ed. Highgate School, Clare Coll., Cambridge; served in R.A. 1941-42, Admiralty Naval Branch 1942-45; called to Bar, Middle Temple 1945; Q.C. 1961; Recorder of Swindon 1962-71; Judge of Courts of Appeal of Jersey and Guernsey 1967-71; a Judge of the High Court of Justice, Queen's Bench Div. 1971-80; presiding Judge, Western Circuit 1976-79; mem. Gen Council of Bar 1957-61, 1963-70, Hon Treas.1964-66, Vice-Chair. 1966-68, Chair. 1968-70; Bencher, Middle Temple 1965, Deputy Treas. 1983, Treas. 1984; mem. Senate of the Four Inns of Court 1966-70, Vice-Pres. 1968-70; Pres. Senate of the Inns of Court and the Bar 1980-82; Lord Justice of Appeal 1980-86; Lord of Appeal in Ordinary 1986-; Chair. Law Advisory Cttee, British Council 1980-; Hon. mem. Canadian Bar Asscn. 1973-. *Leisure interests:* swimming, sailing, gardening, theatre. *Address:* 7 Rivermill, 151 Grosvenor Road, London, S.W.1; Browns House, Sutton, nr. Pulborough, West Sussex, England. *Telephone:* 01-821 8068; (079) 87 206.

ACKROYD, Norman, A.R.A., A.R.C.A.; British artist; b. 26 March 1938, Leeds; s. of Albert Ackroyd and Clara Briggs; m. 1st Sylvia Buckland 1963 (dissolved 1975) two d.; m. 2nd Penelope Hughes Stanton, one s. one d.; ed. Cockburn High School, Leeds, Leeds Coll. of Art, Royal Coll. of Art; Visiting Tutor in Etching, Central School of Art and Design 1965-; Prof. of Etching, Univ. of Indiana 1970; exhbns. at Mickelson Gallery, Wash. 1973, 1977, 1979, 1982, 1984, 1988, Anderson Oday Gallery, London 1979, 1988, Dolan Maxwell Gallery, Phila. 1981, 1983, 1985, 1987, 1989; British Int. Print Biennale Prize 1974, 1982. *Publications:* Landscapes and Figures, Etchings (with William McIllvannry) 1973, The Pictish Coast (with Douglas Dunn) 1988. *Leisure interests:* British history, archaeology, cricket. *Address:* c/o Royal Academy of Arts, Piccadilly, London W.1, England.

ACKROYD, Peter, M.A., F.R.S.L.; British writer; b. 5 Oct. 1949; s. of Graham Ackroyd and Audrey Whiteside; ed. St. Benedict's School, Ealing, Clare Coll., Cambridge and Yale Univ.; Literary Ed. The Spectator 1973-77, Jt. Man. Ed. 1978-82; Chief Book Reviewer The Times 1986-; Mellon Fellow Yale Univ. *Publications: poetry:* London Lickpenny 1973, Country Life 1978, The Diversions of Purley 1987; *novels:* The Great Fire of London 1982, The Last Testament of Oscar Wilde 1983 (Somerset Maugham Prize 1984), Hawksmoor 1985 (Whitbread Award; Guardian Fiction Prize), Chatterton 1987, First Light 1989; *non-fiction:* Notes for a New Culture 1976, Dressing Up 1979, Ezra Pound and his World 1980, T.S. Eliot 1984 (Whitbread Award; Heinemann Awards). *Address:* Anthony Sheil Associates Ltd., 43 Doughty Street, London, WC1N 2LF, England. *Telephone:* 01-405 9351.

ACLAND, Sir Antony (Arthur), G.C.M.G., K.C.V.O.; British diplomatist; b. 12 March 1930; s. of Brig. P. B. E. Acland; m. 1st Clare Anne Verdon 1956 (died 1984), two s. one d.; m. 2nd Jennifer McGougan (née Dyke) 1987; ed. Eton Coll., Christ Church, Oxford; joined diplomatic service 1953; at Middle East Centre for Arab Studies 1954; served in Dubai 1955, Kuwait 1956; Foreign Office 1958-62; Asst. Pvt. Sec. to Sec. of State 1959-62; mem. U.K. Mission to UN 1962-66; Head of Chancery, U.K. Mission, Geneva 1966-68; F.C.O. 1968-, Head of Arabian Dept. 1970-72; Prin. Pvt. Sec. to Foreign and Commonwealth Sec. 1972-75; Amb. to Luxembourg 1975-77, to Spain 1977-79; Deputy Under-Sec. of State, FCO 1980-82, Perm. Under-Sec. of State and Head of Diplomatic Service 1982-86; Amb. to U.S.A. 1986-. *Address:* c/o Foreign and Commonwealth Office, London, S.W.1, England.

ACZÉL, György; Hungarian politician; b. 1917, Budapest; m. Zsuzsa Csato (died 1986); joined Workers' Movement 1933; mem. CP 1935-; Party Sec., Zemplén and Baranya after 1945; First Deputy Minister of Educ. 1958-67; mem. Cen. Cttee. Hungarian Socialist Workers' Party 1956-, Sec. Cen. Cttee. 1967-74, 1982-85, mem. Political Cttee. 1970-88; mem. Parl., Deputy Prime Minister 1974-82; Gen. Dir. HSWP Inst. of Social Sciences 1985-; Order of Merit of the Hungarian People's Repub., Order of the Socialist Fatherland, Worker-Peasant Power Memorial Medal. *Publications:* Eszménk erejével (By Strength of our Idea) 1970, Szocialista kulturaközösségi ember (Socialist Culture-Community Man) 1975, Elmaradt vita helyett (In Lieu of an Omitted Debate) 1975, A szabadság jelene és jövője a szocializmusban (Freedom Today and Tomorrow within Socialism) 1977, A kor amelyben élünk (The Age we are Living In) 1978, A szabadság rendjéért (For the Order of Freedom) 1979, Folytatás és megujulás (Continuation and Renewal) 1980, Attila József 1980, Bartók utjai (Bartok's Roads) 1981, Beszélgetések Magyarországról, szocializmusról (Dialogues on Hungary, on Socialism) 1982, Szocializmus, nemzet, kultura (Socialism, Nation, Culture) 1985, Jövőt mutató elődök (Foregoers as Pilots of Tomorrow) 1986. *Address:* Hungarian Socialist Workers' Party Institute of Social Sciences, Benczur utca 33, 1068 Budapest, Hungary. *Telephone:* 214-830.

ACZEL, Janos D., F.R.S.C., PH.D.; Canadian (b. Hungarian) mathematician; b. 26 Dec. 1924, Budapest; s. of Pezso Aczel and Iren Aczel; m. Susan Kende 1946; two d.; ed. D. Berzsenyi High School, Univ. of Budapest; Teaching Asst., Univ. of Budapest 1946-48; Statistician, Metal Workers' Trade Union, Budapest 1948; Asst. Prof., Univ. of Szeged 1948-50; Assoc. Prof. and Dept. Head, Tech. Univ., Miskolc 1950-52; Dept. Head, Assoc. Prof. then Prof., L. Kossuth Univ., Debrecen 1952-65; Prof., Univ. of Waterloo, Ont., Canada 1965-; many visiting professorships and fellowships, N. America, Europe, Africa, Asia and Australia 1963-; Ed. several math. journals; mem. Council, cttees. of Royal Soc. of Canada (Convener Math. Div. 1974-75, Chair. Acad. of Science Editorial Cttee. 1977-78); Chair. Int. Symposia on Functional Equations 1962-; donor L. Fejer Scholarship, Univ. of Waterloo; mem. Canadian Math. Soc., American Math. Soc., Austrian Math. Soc., New York Acad. of Science; M. Beke Award (L. Bolyai Math. Soc.) 1961, Award of Hungarian Acad. of Sciences 1962, Distinguished Prof., Univ. of Waterloo 1969, F.R.S.C. 1971, Cajal Medal (Nat. Research Council of Spain) 1988. *Publications:* over 210 articles and nine books, including A Short Course on Functional Equations Based upon Recent Applications to the Social and Behavioral Sciences 1986, Functional Equations in Several Variables (with J. Dhombres) 1988; Ed.-in-Chief Aequationes Math; Ed. series Encyclopedia of Mathematics and Its Applications; Theory and Decision, Series B. *Leisure interests:* reading swimming. *Address:* Department of Pure Mathematics, University of Waterloo, Waterloo, Ont., N2L 3G1 (Office); 97 McCarron Crescent, Waterloo, Ont., N2L 5M9, Canada (Home).

ADA, Prof. Gordon Leslie, D.SC.; Australian research scientist; b. 6 Dec. 1922, Sydney; s. of W. L. Ada and Erica Flower; m. Jean MacPherson 1946; three s. one d.; ed. Fort Street Boy's High School, Sydney and Univ. of Sydney; Research Scientist Nat. Inst. for Medical Research, London 1946-48, Walter and Eliza Hall Inst., Melbourne 1948-68; mem. and Chair. Scientific Council, Int. Agency for Research on Cancer, Lyon; mem. Scientific and Tech. Advisory Cttee. WHO, UNDP and World Bank

Special Programme on Tropical Diseases; mem. Global Advisory Council for Medical Research, WHO 1981-84; Chair. WHO Programme on Vaccine Devt. 1984-; Consultant WHO 1988-; Visiting Prof. John Hopkins School of Hygiene and Public Health, Baltimore 1988-; Fellow, Australian Acad. of Science. *Publications:* Antigens, Lymphoid Cells and the Immune Response (with G. J. V. Nossal) 1971; about 180 scientific papers on virology and immunology. *Leisure interests:* sailing, music, walking. *Address:* Microbiology Department, John Curtin School of Medical Research, P.O. Box 334, Canberra, A.C.T. 2601 (Office); 71 Parkhill Street, Pearce, A.C.T. 2607, Australia (Home). *Telephone:* (062) 49-2596 (Office); (062) 86-2044 (Home).

ADACHIBARA, Akifumi, B.L.; Japanese business executive; b. 3 Nov. 1924, Kanagawa; m. Sumiko Yamamoto 1954; one s.; ed. Tokyo Univ.; joined Topy Industries Ltd. 1950, Dir. Corp. Planning Div. 1973, Man. Dir. 1976, Sr. Man. Dir. 1980, Exec. Vice-Pres. 1982, Pres. June 1983-; Dir. KEIDANREN (Japan Fed. of Econ. Org.) July 1983, Japan Auto Parts Industries Asscn. July 1983, Exec. Cttee. Japan Iron and Steel Fed. July 1983; Decorated Ranju Hosho May 1988. *Publication:* Kentucky Colonel 1985. *Leisure interest:* kouta (old-fashioned Japanese song). *Address:* 1-6-9 Sanno Ohta-ku, Tokyo 143, Japan. *Telephone:* (03) 776-6673.

ADAM, Encik Mohamed Adib Haji Mohamed; Malaysian politician; b. 1941, Kesang Tua; ed. Univ. of Malaya and Lincoln's Inn, London; former civil servant; attaché, Malaysian Embassy, The Hague 1975; Exec. Sec. United Malay Nat. Org. 1977-78; mem. Parl. 1978-; Chief Minister of Melaka 1978-82; Minister of Information 1982, of Land and Regional Devt. 1984-86. *Address:* c/o House of Representatives, Kuala Lumpur, Malaysia.

ADAM, Robert (Robin) Wilson: British petroleum executive; b. 21 May 1923, Aberdeen; s. of Robert Ross Adam and Agnes Wilson Adam; m. Marion Nancy Scott 1957; ed. Fettes Coll., Edinburgh; war service in India and Burma; joined Anglo-Iranian Oil Co. (later The British Petroleum Co.) as chartered accountant 1950, Asst. Chief Accountant 1959-64, with Cen. Planning Dept. 1964-67, Gen. Man. 1966-67; Dir. BP Chemicals 1966-68, Gen. Man. Finance and Planning Dept. 1967-69; Pres. BP North America Inc. 1969-72; Dir. BP Trading Ltd. 1973-75; Dir. Standard Oil Co. Inc. (SOHIO) 1972-76 and 1978-83; Man. Dir. The British Petroleum Co. PLC 1975-83, Deputy Chair. 1981-83; Dir. BP Canada (Inc.) 1972-84, Chair. 1981-82, BP (Southern Africa) Pty. Ltd. 1984; Dir. Gen. Accident Fire and Life Assurance Corpn. 1980-; Dir. MEPC PLC 1982-, Chair. 1984-88; Dir. London and Scottish Marine Oil Co. 1984-, Chair. 1985-88; Dir. Dunlop PLC 1985-; mem. Council, Stock Exchange 1983-. *Leisure interest:* golf. *Address:* 25 Onslow Square, London, S.W.7; Brook House, 113 Park Lane, London, W1Y 4AY, England.

ADAM, Theo; German concert singer; b. 1 Aug. 1926, Dresden; s. of Johannes Adam and Lisbeth (née Dernstorf); m. Eleonore Adam 1949; two s. one d.; ed. Gymnasium and Conservatory; engagements with Dresden State Opera 1949, Bayreuth Festival 1952-79, Salzburg Festival 1969, 1971, 1980-83; mem. Deutsche Staatsoper, Berlin 1953-; has appeared with Vienna and Munich State Operas since 1967; Pres. of Curatorium Oper, Dresden 1985-; numerous recordings; Österreichischer Kammersänger, Bayerischer Kammersänger; Nat. Prize (First Class) of G.D.R. *Publications:* Seht, hier ist Tinte, Feder, Papier 1980, Die 100 Rolle. *Leisure interest:* swimming. *Address:* Schillerstrasse 14, 8054 Dresden, German Democratic Republic. *Telephone:* 003751/36997.

ADAMEC, Ladislav; Czechoslovak politician; b. 10 Sept. 1926, Frenstat pod Radhostem, N. Moravia; ed. Vocational School of Econs. and Czechoslovak CP Coll. of Political Studies; mem. CP of Czechoslovakia (CPCZ) 1946-; fmr. Dir. Mez plant, Frenstat; Deputy Chair. N. Moravian Regional Nat. Cttee.; Deputy, Czech Nat. Council 1969-; Deputy Premier, Czech Govt. 1969, First Deputy Premier 1986, Premier 1987; Deputy Premier, Fed. Govt. of Czechoslovakia 1987-88, Premier Oct. 1988-; mem. CPCZ Cen. Cttee. 1966-, mem. Presidium 1987-; mem. CPCZ Nat. Econ. Comm. 1971-. *Address:* Government Presidium of C.S.S.R., Prague 1, nábř. kpt. Jaroše 4, Czechoslovakia.

ADAMI, Edward Fenech (see Fenech Adami, Edward).

ADAMKIEWICZ, Franciszek, D.SC. TECH; Polish politician; b. 28 Sept. 1919, Germany; ed. Tech. Univ., Poznań; worked in H. Cegielski metal works, Poznań 1946-71; posts in econs., investments and tech. sections; Tech. Dir. 1965-67, Gen. Dir. 1967-71; First Deputy Minister of Heavy Industry 1971-76; Minister of Heavy and Agricultural Machine Industries March 1976-80; Amb. to Austria 1980-83; mem. Polish United Workers' Party (PZPR); Order of Banner of Labour (1st class) and other decorations. *Address:* c/o Ministerstwo Spraw Zagranicznych, Al. I Armii Wojska Polskiego 23, 00-580 Warsaw, Poland.

ADAMS, Brockman, LL.B; American lawyer and politician; b. 13 Jan. 1927, Atlanta, Ga.; s. of Charles Leslie Adams and Vera Eleanor (née Beemer); m. Mary Elizabeth Scott 1952; two s. two d.; ed. Washington Univ. and Harvard Law School; served U.S. Navy 1944-46; law practice 1952-61; U.S. Attorney for W. District of Wash. 1961-64; mem. House of Reps. 1965-76, mem. Interstate and Foreign Commerce Cttee. and Transportation sub-cttee., Chair. Budget Cttee. 1975-76; U.S. Sec. for Transportation 1977-79; U.S. Senator for Wash. Jan. 1987-; partner Garvey, Schubert, Adams and Barer 1979-86; Instructor, American Inst. of Banking 1955-60;

Chair. Presidential Campaign of J. F. Kennedy in W. Wash, 1960; mem. Dist. of Columbia, Wash. State and American Bar Asscns. *Address:* U.S. Senate, 513 Hart Senate Office Bldg., Washington, D.C. 20510 (Office); 717B Federal Avenue East, Seattle, Wash. 98102, U.S.A. (Home).

ADAMS, Charles Francis, A.B.; American industrialist; b 2 May 1910, Boston, Mass.; s. of Charles Adams and Frances Lovering; m. 1st Margaret Stockton (died 1972), one s. two d.; m. 2nd Beatrice D. Penati 1973; ed. St. Mark's School and Harvard Univ.; joined Paine, Webber, Jackson & Curtis (Investment Banking) 1934, Partner 1938; served with U.S. Navy (Commdr.) 1940-46; with Paine, Webber, Jackson & Curtis 1946-47; Exec. Vice-Pres. Raytheon Mfg. Co. (now Raytheon Co.) 1947, Pres. 1948-60, 1962, Chair. 1964-75, Chair. Finance Cttee. 1975-; Dir. Liberty Mutual Insurance Co. 1953-, Liberty Mutual Fire Insurance Co. 1968-, Pan American World Airways Inc. 1967-, First Nat. Bank of Boston 1959-75, The Gillette Co. 1960-, A. C. Cossor Ltd. 1961-; hon. degrees, Bates Coll., Northeastern and Suffolk Univs. *Address:* Raytheon Company, 141 Spring Street, Lexington, Mass. 02173, (office); 195 Dedham Street, Dover, Mass. 02030, U.S.A. (Home). *Telephone:* 617-862-6600 (Office).

ADAMS, Douglas (Noel); British author; b. 1952; radio producer, BBC, London 1978; script ed. Doctor Who, BBC TV 1978-80. *Publications:* The Hitch Hiker's Guide to the Galaxy 1978, The Restaurant at the End of the Universe 1980, Life, The Universe and Everything 1982, The Meaning of Liff (with J. Lloyd) 1983, So Long and Thanks for All the Fish 1985, The Utterly, Utterly Merry (ed.) 1986, Comic Relief Christmas Book (co-author) 1986, Long Dark Tea-time of the Soul 1988. *Address:* c/o Ed Victor Ltd., 162 Wardour Street, London, W.1, England.

ADAMS, Léonie, B.A., D.LITT.; American poet and teacher; b. 9 Dec. 1899, Brooklyn, New York; d. of Charles Frederick Adams and Henrietta Rozier (Adams); m. William Troy 1933 (died 1961); ed. Barnard Coll.; editorial work, Wilson Publishing Co., Metropolitan Museum of Art and others 1922-28; Guggenheim Fellowship for Creative Writing 1928-30; Instructor in Literature, New York Univ. 1930-32, Sarah Lawrence Coll. 1933-34, in Literature and Writing, Bennington Coll. 1935-37, 1941-44, in Writing, New Jersey Coll. for Women 1946-48, Columbia Univ. 1947-68; Visiting Prof. Univ. of Wash. 1960, 1968-69, Purdue Univ. 1971-72; Consultant in Poetry, Library of Congress 1948-49; Fellow in American Letters, Library of Congress 1948-55; mem. Nat. Inst. of Arts and Letters (Award 1949, Sec. 1959-61); Fellowship Acad. American Poets 1974; Hon. D.Litt. (New Jersey Coll. for Women) 1950; Harriet Monroe Award 1954; Shelley Memorial Award 1954; Bollingen Prize in Poetry 1955 (jointly); Acad. of American Poets Award 1959; Fulbright Lecturer in American Studies, France 1955-56; Sabbatical Grant, Nat. Council on the Arts 1966-67; Brandeis Univ. Poetry Medal and Award 1969; Mark Rothke Foundation Award 1973; Distinguished Alumna Medal, Barnard Coll. 1974. *Publications:* Those Not Elect (and other poems) 1925, High Falcon 1929, Lyrics of François Villon (edited, with translation) 1933, Poems, A Selection 1954. *Leisure interest:* gardening. *Address:* Candlewood Valley Care Center, 30 Park Lane East, New Milford, Conn. 06776, U.S.A. *Telephone:* (203) 355 0971.

ADAMS, Prof. Norman, R.A., A.R.C.A., F.R.S.A.; British painter and professor of fine art; b. 9 Feb. 1927, London; s. of Albert Henry Adams and Winifred Elizabeth Rose; m. Anna Teresa Butt 1947; two s.; ed. Newcastle upon Tyne Univ., Harrow School of Art, Royal Coll. of Art, London; first exhbn. Young Contemporaries 1950; numerous solo exhbns. in London, N. England, Scotland and U.S.A.; exhbns. with British Council 1954-55; teacher at St. Albans, Maidstone, Hammersmith Art Schools and Royal Acad. Schools 1956; Head of Painting, Manchester Coll. of Art and Design 1962-71; elected Assoc. of Royal Acad. 1967; Visiting Tutor, Leeds Univ. 1973-76; Prof. of Fine Art and Dir. of King Edward VII Coll. Univ. of Newcastle upon Tyne 1981-; Prof. of Painting and Keeper, Royal Acad. of Arts, London 1986-. *Public collections include:* Tate Gallery, London, Scottish Nat. Gallery of Modern Art, Edinburgh, Ulster Museum, Belfast, Nat. Gallery of New Zealand, Wellington. *Publications:* Alibis and Convictions 1978, A Decade of Painting 1971-81 1981. *Leisure interests:* art, music, literature. *Address:* Royal Academy of Arts, Piccadilly, London (Office); Butts, Horton-in-Ribblesdale, Settle, N. Yorks, England (Home). *Telephone:* 01-734 9052 (Office); (07296) 284 (Home).

ADAMS, Sir Philip George Doyne, K.C.M.G.; British diplomatist (retd.); b. 17 Dec. 1915, Wellington, New Zealand; s. of the late George Basil Doyne Adams and Arline Maud (née Dodgson) Adams; m. Hon. Mary Elizabeth Lawrence 1954; two s. two d.; ed. Lancing and Christ Church, Oxford; Vice-Consul, Beirut 1939-41; war service 1941; Third Sec., Cairo 1944-45; Second Sec., Jeddah 1945-47; Foreign Office, London 1947-51; First Sec., Vienna 1951-54; Trade Commr., Khartoum 1954-56; Regional Information Officer, Beirut 1956-59; Foreign Office, London 1959-63; Consul-Gen., Chicago 1963-65; Amb. to Jordan 1966-70; Asst. Under-Sec. FCO 1970; Deputy Sec. Cabinet Office 1971-72; Amb. to Egypt 1973-75; Dir. Ditchley Foundation 1977-82; mem. Bd. British Council 1977-82, Marshall Aid Commemoration Comm. 1979-88. *Address:* The Malt House, Ditchley, Enstone, Oxon.; 78 Sussex Square, London, W.2, England (Home).

ADAMS, Richard George, M.A.; British novelist; b. 9 May 1920, Newbury, Berks.; s. of Dr. E. G. B. Adams, F.R.C.S., and Lilian Rosa (Button) Adams; m. Barbara Elizabeth Acland 1949; two d.; ed. Bradfield Coll., Berks., and Worcester Coll., Oxford; army service 1940-46; Home Civil Service 1948-

74; Pres. Royal Society for the Prevention of Cruelty to Animals 1980–82; Writer-in-Residence, Univ. of Florida, 1975, Hollins Coll., Va. 1976; F.R.S.L.; Carnegie Medal 1972, Guardian Award for Children's Literature 1972, Medal of California Young Readers' Asscn. 1977. *Publications:* Watership Down 1972, Shardik 1974, Nature Through the Seasons, The Tyger Voyage 1976, The Plague Dogs 1977, The Ship's Cat 1977, Nature Day and Night 1978, The Girl in a Swing 1980, The Unbroken Web (The Iron Wolf) 1980, Voyage through the Antarctic 1982, Maia 1984, The Bureaucats 1985, A Nature Diary 1985, Occasional Poets: anthology (ed. and contributor) 1986, The Legend of Te Tuna 1986, Traveller 1988. *Leisure interests:* chess, ornithology, folk-song, country walking. *Address:* Benwell's, 26 Church Street, Whitchurch, Hants., RG28 7AR, England.

ADAMS, Robert McCormick, Jr., PH.D.; American anthropologist; b. 23 July 1926, Chicago, Ill.; s. of Robert McCormick and Janet (Lawrence) Adams; m. Ruth S. Skinner 1953; one d.; ed. Univ. of Chicago; Instructor, Univ. of Chicago 1955–57, Asst. Prof. 1957–61, Assoc. Prof. 1961–62, Prof. 1962–, Dir. Oriental Inst. 1962–68, 1981–83, Prof. of Anthropology 1963–, Dean of Social Sciences 1970–74, 1979–80, Univ. Provost 1982–84; Sec. Smithsonian Inst. 1984–; Chair. Ass. of Behavioral and Social Sciences, Nat. Research Council 1973–76; Visiting Prof., Harvard 1962, 1977, Univ. of Calif. (Berkeley) 1963; Annual Prof., Baghdad School, American Schools of Oriental Research 1966–67; field research in Iraq, Iran, Mexico, Saudi Arabia and Syria; Lewis Henry Morgan Prof., Univ. of Rochester 1965; Councillor, N.A.S. 1981–; mem. American Acad. of Arts and Sciences, American Anthropological Asscn., American Assc. for the Advancement of Science, Middle East Studies Assc., American Philosophical Soc., German Archaeological Inst.; Trustee, National Opinion Research Center 1970–, Nat. Humanities Center 1976–, Russell Sage Foundation 1978–. *Publications:* Land behind Baghdad: a History of Settlement on the Diyala Plains 1965, The Evolution of Urban Society: Early Mesopotamia and Prehispanic Mexico 1966, (with H. J. Nissen) The Uruk Countryside 1972, Heartland of Cities 1981, (with N. J. Smelser and D. J. Treiman) Behavioral and Social Science Research: A National Resource (2 Vols.) 1982. *Leisure interests:* skiing, mountaineering. *Address:* Smithsonian Institution, Washington, D.C. 20560 (Office); 2810 31st Street, N.W., Washington, D.C.; P.O. Box ZZ, Basalt, Colo. 81621, U.S.A. *Telephone:* 202-357-1846 (Office); 202-965-0456; 303-927-3380 (Homes).

ADAMS, William James, C.M.G., M.A.; British diplomatist; b. 30 April 1932, Wolverhampton; s. of late William Adams and Norah Walker; m. Donatella Pais-Tarsilia 1961; two s. one d.; ed. Wolverhampton Grammar School, Shrewsbury School and Queen's Coll. Oxford; Royal Artillery 1950–51; entered Foreign Office 1954; Middle East Centre Arabic Studies (Lebanon) 1955; British Political Residency, Bahrain 1955–57; Asst. Political Agent, Trucial States 1957–58; British Embassy, Manila 1960–63; British Embassy, Paris 1965–69; Econ. Comm. for Africa, Addis Ababa 1972–73; Counsellor, British Representation to European Communities, Brussels 1973–77; British Embassy, Rome 1977–80; Asst. Under-Sec. FCO 1980–84; Amb. to Tunisia 1984–87, to Egypt 1987–; Hon. Order of the Star of Honour (Ethiopia); Hon. Order of the Two Niles (Sudan). *Leisure interests:* family life, reading, travel. *Address:* c/o Foreign and Commonwealth Office, London, SW1A 2AH, England.

ADAMS-SCHNEIDER, Hon. Sir Lance Raymond, K.C.M.G.; New Zealand politician and diplomatist; b. 1919, Wellington; s. of A. A. Adams; m. Shirley Lois Brunton 1945; two s. one d.; ed. Mt. Albert Grammar School; Man. Taumarunui dept. store; served in Second World War, N.Z. Medical Corps; Vice-Chair. Nat. Party in Waitomo electorate; mem. S. Auckland Div. Exec.; M.P. for Hamilton 1959–69, for Waikato 1969–81; Minister of Broadcasting, Minister Asst. to Minister of Customs 1969; Minister of Customs, Asst. Minister of Industries and Commerce 1969–72; Minister of Health, Social Security and Social Welfare Feb.–Nov 1972; Opposition Spokesman on Health and Social Welfare 1972–75, on Industry, Commerce and Customs 1974–75; Minister of Trade and Industry 1975–81; Amb. to U.S.A. 1982–84. *Address:* 41 Kanpur Road, Broadmeadows, Wellington 4, New Zealand.

ADAMSON, Sir (William Owen) Campbell, Kt.; British economist and business executive; b. 26 June 1922, Glasgow, Scotland; s. of John and Elsie (née Glendinning) Adamson; m. 1st Gilvray Allan 1945 (dissolved), two s. two d.; m. 2nd Josephine Lloyd Chandler; ed. Rugby School and Corpus Christi Coll., Cambridge; joined Baldwins Ltd. 1945; various posts in Steel Co. of Wales and Richard Thomas & Baldwins after mergers 1951–67, Dir. 1959; mem. Iron and Steel Fed. team visiting U.S.S.R. 1956; Industrial Adviser, Dept. of Econ. Affairs 1967, Senior Industrial Adviser 1967, Deputy Under Sec. of State 1968; Dir.-Gen. Confed. of British Industry 1969–76; Dir. Imperial Group 1976–86; Chair. Revertex Chemicals Jan. 1978–80; Chair. Barclays Tozer Ltd. (B.T.L.) 1977–81; Chair. Abbey National Building Soc. 1978–; Dir. Lazard Bros. and Co. 1977–87, Tarmac Ltd. 1980–; Chair. Renold PLC 1982–86; founder mem. Social Science Research Council; mem. BBC Gen. Advisory Cttee.; mem. Council of Iron and Steel Inst. 1960–72; mem. Council, Industrial Soc.; Visiting Fellow, Lancaster Univ. 1970, Nuffield Coll., Oxford 1971–79; Gov. Rugby School 1980–; Vice-Pres. Inst. & Manpower Studies 1982–. *Leisure interests:* music, swimming, tennis. *Address:* Abbey House, Baker Street, London, N.W.1, England. *Telephone:* 01-486 5555.

ADDISON, Cyril Clifford, PH.D., F.R.S., F.INST.P., F.R.S.C.; British professor of chemistry; b. 28 Nov. 1913; s. of Edward Thomas Addison and Olive Clifford; m. Marjorie Whineray Thompson 1939; one s. one d.; ed. Workington and Millom Grammar Schools, Cumberland, Univ. of Durham (Hatfield Coll.); Scientific Officer, British Launderers' Research Assc. 1936–38; Lecturer, Harris Inst., Preston 1938–39; Ministry of Supply, Chemical Inspection Dept. 1939–45; Chemical Defence Research Establishment 1945; Lecturer, Univ. of Nottingham 1946, Reader in Inorganic Chem. 1952; Prof. of Inorganic Chem., Univ. of Nottingham 1960–78, Dean of Faculty of Pure Science 1968–71, Leverhulme Emer. Fellow 1978; Distinguished Visiting Prof., Auburn Univ., Alabama, U.S.A. 1979–80; mem. Chemical Soc. Council 1954–57 (Pres. 1976–77), Inst. of Chem. Council 1948–51, 1962–65 (Vice-Pres. 1965–67); Hon. D.Sc. (Durham). *Publications:* The Chemistry of the Liquid Alkali Metals 1984; numerous papers in scientific journals. *Leisure interests:* mountain walking, gardening. *Address:* Department of Chemistry, The University, Nottingham, England. *Telephone:* Nottingham 484848.

ADDISON, John; American composer of film music; b. March 1920; composer of music for numerous films, TV dramas etc. since 1948. *Films include:* School for Scoundrels, The Entertainer, A French Mistress, A Taste of Honey, Go to Blazes, The Loneliness of the Long Distance Runner, Tom Jones, Girl with Green Eyes, Guns at Batasi, The Amorous Adventures of Moll Flanders, I Was Happy Here, A Fine Madness, The Charge of the Light Brigade, Mr Forbush and the Penguins, Sleuth, Luther, Swashbuckler, The Seven Per Cent Solution, A Bridge Too Far, Strange Invaders, Codename Emerald.

ADEBO, Simeon Olaosebikan, C.M.G., the Okanlomo of Itoko and of Egbaland; Nigerian lawyer and diplomatist; b. 5 Oct. 1913, Abeokuta, Nigeria; s. of Chief Adebo, the Okanlomo of Itoko, and Fowotade; m. Regina Abimbola Majekodunmi 1941; three s. one d.; ed. King's Coll., Lagos, London Univ. and Gray's Inn, London; Perm. Sec. to Ministry of Finance, W. Nigeria 1957–59, to Treasury 1959–60; Head of Civil Service and Chief Sec. to Govt. of W. Nigeria 1961–62; Perm. Rep. of Nigeria to the United Nations 1962–67; UN Under-Sec.-Gen. and Exec. Dir. of UN Inst. for Training and Research 1968–72; Pres. Soc. for Int. Devt. 1966–67, 1967–68; Vice-Pres. World Assc. of World Federalists; Chair. Nat. Univs. Comm. of Nigeria 1975–77; Chair. Nat. Inst. for Policy and Strategic Studies 1979–82; Chancellor, Univ. of Ife 1982–84; Commdr. Fed. Repub. of Nigeria; thirteen hon. degrees. *Publications:* Report on the Nigerianization of the Nigerian Civil Service (with Sir Sydney Phillipson) 1953, Memoir: Our Unforgettable Years 1984. *Leisure interests:* tennis and reading. *Address:* Abimbola Lodge, P.O. Box 139, Abeokuta, Nigeria. *Telephone:* (039) 230605.

ADEDEJI, Adebayo, B.SC. (ECON.), M.P.A., PH.D.; Nigerian economist; b. 21 Dec 1930, Ijebu-Ode; s. of Mr. and Mrs. L. S. Adedeji; m. Susan Aderinola Ogun 1957; four s. two d.; ed. Ijebu-Ode Grammar School, Univ. Coll., Ibadan, Univ. Coll., Leicester and Harvard Univ.; Asst. Sec., Ministry of Econ. Planning, W. Nigeria 1958–61, Principal Asst. Sec. (Finance) 1962–63; Deputy Dir. Inst. of Admin., Univ. of Ife 1963–66, Dir. 1967– (on leave of absence 1971–); Prof. of Public Admin., Univ. of Ife 1968– (leave of absence 1971–); Nat. Manpower Bd. 1967–71; Fed. Commr. for Econ. Devt. and Reconstruction 1971–75; Chair. Directorate, Nigerian Youth Services Corps 1973–75; UN Under-Sec.-Gen and Exec. Sec. UN Econ. Comm. for Africa June 1975–; Chair. Senate of UN Inst. for Namibia 1975–; founder and editor, Quarterly Journal of Administration 1967–75; Fellow, Nigerian Inst. of Management; Pres. Nigerian Econ. Soc. 1971–72; Pres. African Assc. for Public Admin. and Management 1974–83; Vice-Chair. Assc. of Schools and Inst. of Admin. of Int. Inst. of Admin. Sciences 1970–; numerous awards, including Hon. D.Litt., Hon. LL.D. (Dalhousie Univ., Univ. of Zambia); and numerous foreign decorations. *Publications:* A Survey of Highway Development in Western ·Nigeria 1960, Nigerian Administration and its Political Setting (Ed.) 1969, Nigerian Federal Finance: Its Development, Problems and Prospects 1969, Local Government Finance in Nigeria: Problems and Prospects (Co-ed.) 1972, Management Problems and Rapid Urbanisation in Nigeria (Co-ed.) 1973, The Tanzania Civil Service, a Decade after Independence 1974, Developing Research on African Administration: Some Methodological Issues (co-editor) 1974, Africa, The Third World and the Search for a New Economic Order 1977, Africa and the New International Economic Order: A Reassessment 1979, The Indigenization of the African Economy 1981, Economic Crisis in Africa: African Perspectives on Development Problems and Potentials (Co.-Ed.) 1985, Towards the Dawn of the Third Millenium and the Beginning of the Twenty-First Century 1986. *Leisure interests:* photography, lawn tennis, golf, walking. *Address:* United Nations Economic Commission for Africa, P.O. Box 60072, Addis Ababa, Ethiopia (Office); Asiwaju Court, G.R.A. Erunwon Road, P.O. Box 203, Ijebu-Ode, Nigeria. *Telephone:* 44-58-04 (Office); 18-05-00 (Home).

ADELMAN, Irma Glicman, PH.D.; American (b. Romanian) professor of economics; b. 14 March 1930, Romania; d. of the late Jacob Max Glicman and Raissa Etinger; m. Frank Louis Adelman 1950 (divorced 1979); one s.; ed. Univ. of Calif. at Berkeley; Asst. Prof., Stanford Univ. 1960–62; Assoc. Prof., Johns Hopkins Univ. 1962–66; Prof. of Econs., Northwestern Univ. 1967–72; Sr. Economist, Devt. Research Cen., IBRD 1971–72; Prof. of Econs., Univ. of Md. 1972–79; Consultant, U.S. Dept. of State 1963–, IBRD

1968-, ILO, Geneva 1973-; Fellow, Netherlands Inst. of Advanced Study, Cleveringa Chair Leiden Univ. 1977-78; Prof. of Econs. and Agric. and Resource Econs., Univ. of Calif. at Berkeley 1979-; Vice-Pres. American Econ. Asscn.; Fellow, American Acad. of Arts and Sciences, Econometric Soc.; Order of the Bronze Tower (South Korea). *Publications:* Theories of Economic Growth and Development 1964, Society, Politics and Economic Development (with C. T. Morris) 1967, Economic Growth and Social Equity in Developing Countries (with C. T. Morris) 1973, Income Distribution Planning (with Sherman Robinson) 1978, Comparative Patterns of Economic Development: 1850-1914 (with C.T. Morris) 1987. *Leisure interests:* art, theatre, music. *Address:* 207 Gianninni Hall, University of California at Berkeley, Calif. 94720 (Office); 10 Rosemont Avenue, Berkeley, Calif. 94708, U.S.A. (Home). *Telephone:* 415 642-6417 (Office); 415 527-5280 (Home).

ADELMAN, Kenneth Lee, PH.D.; American government official; b. 9 June 1946, Chicago, Ill.; s. of Harry Adelman and Corinne Unger; m. Carol Craigle 1971; two d.; ed. Grinnell Coll., Georgetown Univ.; with U.S Dept. of Commerce 1968-70; Special Asst. VISTA, Washington, D.C. 1970-72; Liaison Officer, AID 1975-76; Asst. to Sec. of Defense 1976-77; Sr. Political Scientist, Stanford Research Inst. Arlington, Va. 1977-81; Amb. and Deputy Perm. Rep. to UN 1981-83; Dir. Arms Control and Disarmament Agency (ACDA) 1983-; Instructor in Shakespeare, Georgetown Univ. 1977-79. *Publications:* articles in newspapers, magazines and professional journals. *Address:* Arms Control and Disarmament Agency, 320 21st Street, N.W., Washington, D.C. 20451, U.S.A.

ADELSOHN, Ulf, LL.B.; Swedish politician; b. 4 Oct. 1941, Stockholm; s. of Oskar and Margareta Adelsohn; m. Lena Liljeroth 1981; one d.; ed. legal adviser, Real Estate Co., Stockholm City 1968-70; Man.'s Asst., Swedish Confederation of Professional Asscns. 1970-73; Commr., Street and Traffic Dept., Stockholm City Admin. 1973-76; Finance Commr. 1976-79; Minister for Transport and Communications 1979-81; mem. Riksdagen (Parl.) 1982-; Chair. Moderata Samlingspartiet (Conservative Party) 1981-86. *Publications:* Torsten Kreuger, Sanningen pa väg (Torsten Kreuger, Truth on its Way) 1972, Kommunalmän: Hur skulle ne göra om det vore era egna pengar? (Local Politicians: What would you do if it was your money?) 1978, Ulf Adelsohn Partiledare 1981-86 (Chair. of the Party 1981-86) 1987. *Leisure interests:* hockey, tennis. *Address:* Strandvägen 35, 114 56 Stockholm, Sweden.

ADEMOLA, Rt. Hon. Sir Adetokunbo Adegboyega, P.C., K.B.E., C.F.R.; Nigerian lawyer; b. 1 Feb. 1906, Abeokuta; s. of late Sir Ladapo Ademola, Paramount Ruler of Egbaland; m. Kofo Moore 1939; three s. two d.; ed. St. Gregory's Grammar School, Lagos, King's Coll., Lagos, Cambridge Univ. and Middle Temple, London; in Crown Law Office, Lagos 1934-35; Admin. officer, Enugu 1935; in private practice as barrister and solicitor, Lagos 1936-39; Magistrate in Nigeria 1939-49; Puisne Judge, Nigeria 1949-55; Chief Justice, Western Region 1955-58; Chief Justice, Supreme Court 1958-72; Chair. Census Board 1972-75; Chancellor, Univ. of Nigeria 1975-; Chair. Commonwealth Foundation Jan 1978-; hon. mem. Int. Comm. of Jurists; mem. Int. Olympic Cttee. 1963-; mem. Comm. of experts advising ILO on Convention; Hon. Bencher, Middle Temple 1959; Grand Commdr. Order of Niger 1972; Hon. LL.D., Hon. D.Sc. *Leisure interest:* golf. *Address:* Office of the Chancellor, University of Nigeria, Nsukka Anambra State (Office); 1 The Close, Adetokunbo Ademola Street, Victoria Island, P.O. Box 6967, Lagos, Nigeria (Home). *Telephone:* 613249 (Home).

ADERS, Robert O., J.D.; American lawyer and retail executive; b. 21 April 1927, Bridgeton, Ind.; s. of Oral Aders and Frieda Howell; m. 1st Marguerite Herschede 1951; one s. four d.; m. 2nd Tabitha Simpson 1975; ed. Miami, Oxford, Ohio and Indiana Univs.; with U.S.N.R. 1944-46, 1952-54; served in U.S. Dept. of Justice; joined The Kroger Co. 1957, Gen. Attorney 1962, Vice-Pres. and Gen. Counsel 1964, Vice-Pres. and Sec. 1966, Vice-Chair. 1970, Chair. of Bd. 1970-74; mem. Nat. Business Council for Consumer Affairs 1972-; Advisor to Cost of Living Council 1972-74; Under-Sec. Dept. of Labor 1975-76; Pres. Food Marketing Inst. 1976-; Dir. Ranco Inc.; mem. Bd. of Trustees, Ohio Wesleyan Univ.; mem. various civic orgs., etc. *Address:* 1750 K Street N.W., Washington, D.C. 20006, U.S.A. (Office).

ADEWOYE, Dr. Omoniyi; Nigerian university lecturer and politician; b. 27 Oct. 1939, Inisha, Oyo State; m.; three c.; ed. Kiriji Memorial Coll., Igbajo, Univ. of Ibadan and Columbia Univ., New York; Lecturer in History, Univ. of Ibadan 1968-75, Sr. Lecturer 1975; Commr. for Econ. Devt., Western State 1975-76; Commr. for Finance and Econ. Devt., Oyo State 1976-77; Fed. Commr. for Econ. Devt. 1977-79; First Chair. Council of Ministers, Econ. Community of West African States 1977-78; Chair. Council of Ministers, Nigerian-Niger Jt. Comm. 1977-78; Hon. Treas. Historical Soc. of Nigeria 1972-77; Woodrow Wilson Dissertation Scholarship (Columbia Univ.) 1967, Afgrad Fellowship (U.S.A.) 1964-68. *Publications:* The Legal Profession in Nigeria 1865-1962, 1977, The Judicial System in Southern Nigeria, 1854-1954, 1977. *Leisure interests:* gardening, reading, writing, music. *Address:* P.O. Box 37, Inisha Town, Via Oshogbo, Nigeria (Home).

ADISESHIAH, Malcolm Sathianathan, M.A., PH.D.; Indian educationalist; b. 18 April 1910, Madras; s. of Veranaci P. Adiseshiah and Nessammah Adiseshiah; m. Elizabeth Adiseshiah 1952; ed. Madras, London and Cambridge Univs.; Lecturer of Econs. St. Paul's Coll., Calcutta Univ. 1930-36;

Prof. of Econs. Madras Christian Coll. 1940-46; Assoc. Gen. Sec. Int. Student Service 1946-48; Dep. Dir. Exchange of Persons Service, UNESCO 1948-50; Dir. Dept. of Tech. Assistance, UNESCO 1950-54; Asst. Dir.-Gen. UNESCO 1955-63, Deputy Dir.-Gen. 1963-70; Chair. UNESCO Int. Inst. for Educ. Planning 1981-; Chair. Madras Inst. of Devt. Studies; Vice-Chancellor, Madras Univ. 1975-78, mem. Rajya Sabha 1978-; Pres. Tamil Nadu State Council for Science and Tech., Govt. of Tamil Nadu, Madras. *Publications:* Demand for Money 1938, Agricultural Economic Development 1941, Handicraft Industries 1942, Rural Credit 1943, Planning Industrial Development 1944, Restless Nations 1962, War on Poverty 1963, Non-political UN 1964, Welfare and Wisdom 1965, Economics of Indian Natural Resources 1966, Education and National Development 1967, Adult Education 1968, Some Thoughts on Unesco in the Second Development Decade 1969, Brain Drain from the Arab World 1969, Let My Country Awake 1970, Madras Development Seminar Series 1971, It is Time to Begin 1972, Techniques of Perspective Planning 1973, Plan Implementation: Problems and Prospects for the Fifth Plan 1974, Towards a Learning Society 1974, Science in the Battle against Poverty 1975, Literacy Discussion 1976, Towards a Functional Learning Society 1976, Mid-Term Review of the Economy 1976, Backdrop to Learning Society 1978, Educational Perspectives in Tamil Nadu: 1976-86 1978, Mid-Year Review of the Economy 1977-83, Economics of Non-Formal Education 1979, Adult Education Faces Inequality 1981, Mid-Term Review of the Sixth Plan 1982, Some Thoughts on the Seventh Five Year Plan 1985, Seventh Plan Perspectives 1985, Shaping National Events: The Economy as seen in Parliamentary Statements 1985, Entrepreneurship Development for Tamil Nadu 1985, Monetary Policy: Review of the Chakravarty Report 1986, Fiscal Policy: Review of the Proposal for a Long-Term Fiscal Policy 1986, Role of Foreign Trade in Indian Economy 1986, Mid-Year Review of the Economy 1986, Tax Policy-Proposals for Direct Tax Reform 1987, Price Policy-Analysis of Administered and Support Prices 1987. *Address:* Madras Institute of Development Studies, 79 II Main Road, Gandhi Nagar, Madras 600 020, India. *Telephone:* 412589.

ADJANI, Isabelle; French actress; b. 27 June 1955; one s.; ed. Lycée de Courbevoie; Pres. Comm. d'avances sur recettes 1986-. *Films:* Faustine ou le bel été 1972, la Gifle 1974, l'Histoire d' Adèle H. 1975 (Best Actress, New York Critics 1976), le Locataire 1976, Barocco 1977, Violette et François 1977, Driver 1977, Nosferatu 1978, les Soeurs Brontë 1979, Possession 1980 (Best Actress, Cannes 1981), Clara et les chics types 1980, Quartet 1981 (Best Actress, Cannes 1982), l'Année prochaine si tout va bien 1981, Antonieta 1982, l'Eté meurtrier 1983 (Best Actress César 1984), Mortelle randonné 1983, Subway 1985, Ishtar 1987, Camille Claudel 1988 (Best Actress César 1989). *Theatre:* la Maison de Bernarda 1970, 1974, l'Avare 1972-73, l'Ecole des femmes 1973, Port-Royal 1973, Ondine 1974. *TV appearances include:* le Petit bougnat 1969, le Secret des flamands 1972, l'Ecole des femmes 1973, Top à Sacha Distel 1974. *Address:* c/o Irène Murroni, 33 rue Marbeuf, 75008 Paris; Secrétariat de la Commission d'avances sur recettes, 11 rue Galilée, 75116 Paris, France.

ADKISSON, Perry Lee, PH.D.; American entomologist; b. 11 March 1929, Hickman, Arkansas; s. of Robert L. and Imogene (Perry) Adkisson; m. Frances Rozelle 1956; one d.; ed. Univ. of Arkansas, Kansas State Univ. and Harvard Univ.; Asst. Prof. of Entomology Univ. of Missouri 1956-58; Assoc. Prof. of Entomology Texas A&M Univ. 1958-63, Prof. of Entomology 1963-67, Head, Dept. of Entomology 1967-78, Distinguished Prof. of Entomology 1979-, Vice-Pres. for Agric. and Renewable Resources 1978-80, Deputy Chancellor for Agric. 1980-83, Deputy Chancellor 1983-86, Chancellor 1986-; Consultant Int. AEC, Vienna 1969-74; Chair. Texas Pesticide Advisory Comm. 1972; mem. panel on integrated pest control FAO, Rome 1971-78; mem. N.A.S., mem. Governing Bd. Int. Crop Research Inst. for Semi-Arid Tropics 1982-, Standing Cttee. for Int. Plant Protection Congresses 1984-, Texas Science and Tech. Council 1986-, Advisory Cttee., Export-Import Bank of the U.S. 1987; Alexander Von Humboldt Award 1980, Distinguished Service Award, American Inst. of Biological Sciences 1987 and numerous others. *Publications:* Controlling Cotton's Insect Pests: A New System 1982; several papers on insect diapause and other entomological topics. *Leisure interests:* gardening, fishing. *Address:* Office of the Chancellor, The Texas A&M University System, College Station, Tex. 77843; The Reed House, 1 Reed Dr., College Station, Tex. 77843, U.S.A. (Home).

ADLER, Julius, PH.D.; American biologist and biochemist; b. 30 April 1930, Edelfingen, Germany; s. of Adolf Adler and Irma Stern; m. Hildegard Wohl 1963; one s. one d.; ed. Harvard Univ. and Univ. of Wisconsin; emigrated to U.S.A. 1938, naturalized U.S. citizen 1943; Postdoctoral Fellow, Wash. Univ., St. Louis 1957-59, Stanford Univ. 1959-60; Asst Prof., Depts. of Biochemistry and Genetics, Univ. of Wis. 1960-63, Assoc. Prof. 1963-66, Prof. 1966-, Edwin Bret Hart Prof. 1972-; Steenbock Prof. of Microbiological Sciences 1982-; Dr. h.c. (Tübingen) 1987; mem. American Acad. of Arts and Sciences, N.A.S.; Selman A. Waksman Microbiology Award, N.A.S. 1980, Otto-Warburg medal, German Soc. of Biological Chemistry 1986, Hilldale Award, Univ. of Wisconsin 1988, R.H. Wright Award, Simon Fraser Univ. 1988. *Publications:* research papers on the behaviour of simple organisms, especially bacteria. *Address:* Department of Biochemistry, University of Wisconsin-Madison, Madison, Wis. 53706, U.S.A.

ADLER, Larry (Lawrence Cecil); American mouth organist; b. 10 Feb. 1914; s. of Louis Adler and Sadie Hack; m. 1st Eileen Walser 1938 (dissolved 1961), one s. two d.; m. 2nd Sally Cline 1969 (dissolved 1977), one d.; ed. Baltimore City Coll.; won Maryland Harmonica Championship 1927; first stage appearance, New York 1928; first British appearance in C. B. Cochran's Streamline revue 1934; first appearance as soloist with symphony orchestra, Sydney, Australia 1939; jt. recital tours with dancer Paul Draper, U.S. 1941-49; soloist with New York Philharmonic and other major U.S. orchestras and orchestras in England, Japan and Europe; war tours for Allied Troops 1943, 1944, 1945, Germany 1947, 1949, Korea (British Commonwealth Div.) 1951, Israel (Six-Day War) 1967, (Yom Kippur War) 1973; numerous one-man TV shows; soloist, first performance of unpublished George Gershwin quartet (MS gift to Adler from Ira Gershwin) Edinburgh Festival 1963; works composed for him by Ralph Vaughan Williams, Malcolm Arnold, Darius Milhaud, Arthur Benjamin, Gordon Jacob and others. *Compositions include:* film scores for Genevieve, King and Country, High Wind in Jamaica, The Great Chase etc.; TV scores for BBC serial Midnight Men, various TV plays and documentaries; music for TV commercials, children's records, stage plays etc.; concert music, Theme and Variations, Camera III; one-man show, From Hand to Mouth, Edinburgh Festival 1965, other festivals 1965-. *Publications:* How I Play 1937, Larry Adler's Own Arrangements 1960, Jokes and How to Tell Them 1963. *Leisure interests:* tennis, journalism, cycling, conversation. *Address:* c/o Michael Bakewell, 118 Tottenham Court Road, London, W.1, England.

ADLERCREUTZ, (Carl) Herman (Thomas), M.D., PH.D.; Finnish professor of clinical chemistry; b. 10 April 1932, Helsinki; s. of Erik and Elisabeth Adlercreutz; m. 1st Marie-Louise Gräsbeck 1956 (divorced 1974), 2nd Sirkka T. Neva 1976; one s. two d.; ed. Univ. of Helsinki; Research Fellow, Hormone Lab. Dept. of Obstetrics & Gynaecology, Karolinska Hosp. Stockholm 1958-61; Resident in Internal Medicine, Univ. of Helsinki 1961-64, Acting Asst. Prof. of Internal Medicine 1964-65, Assoc. Prof. of Clinical Chem. 1965-69, Acting Prof. of Clinical Chem. 1967-69, Prof. of Clinical Chem. 1969-; Chief Physician, Central Lab. Helsinki Univ. Central Hosp. 1965-; Research Prof. Acad. of Finland 1983-88; mem. fourteen foreign socs.; Finnish White Rose Order of Knighthood and other awards and distinctions. *Publications:* about 500 publications mainly in the fields of steroid hormones, endocrinology, nutrition and cancer. *Leisure interests:* gardening, fishing, sport. *Address:* Department of Clinical Chemistry, University of Helsinki, Meilahti Hospital, Haartmanikatu 4, 00290 Helsinki (Office); Riskutie 13, 00950 Helsinki, Finland (Home). *Telephone:* 358-0-4711/2569 (Office); 358-0-320258 (Home).

ADNI, Daniel; Israeli concert pianist; b. 6 Dec. 1951, Haifa; ed. High Schools in Haifa and Tel-Aviv, Conservatoire of Music in Paris; first Recital in Haifa 1963; professional debut, London 1970; New York debut 1976; has played at most musical centres in the world incl. U.K., Fed. Repub. of Germany, Israel, U.S.A., Japan, South Africa, Switzerland, Norway, Netherlands, Romania; made over 20 records for EMI-His Master's Voice; First Prize, Paris Conservatoire; First Prize, Young Concert Artists' Auditions, New York. *Leisure interests:* cinema, theatre, bridge, walks, sightseeing. *Address:* c/o Ibbs and Tillett, 18b Pindock Mews, Little Venice, London, W9 2PY, England.

ADO, Andrey Dmitriyevich; Soviet physiologist; b. 12 Jan. 1909, Kazan; ed. Kazan Medical Inst.; mem. CPSU 1943-; Assoc., Prof., Head of Chair, Kazan Medical Inst. 1931-52, Head of Chair, Second Moscow Medical Inst. 1952-; Corresp. mem. U.S.S.R. Acad. of Medical Sciences 1945-65, mem. 1965-; Dir. Research Allergological Lab., U.S.S.R. Acad. of Medical Sciences 1961-; Vice-Chair. Bd. U.S.S.R. and Moscow Socs. of Pathophysiologists; Asst. Ed., Patologicheskaya fiziologiya; Chair. Problem Comm. on Allergy; Order of Lenin, Badge of Honour, etc. *Publications:* over 200 works on inflammation, allergy and immunity. *Address:* Allergological Laboratory, U.S.S.R. Academy of Medical Sciences, 10 Leninsky Prospekt, Moscow, U.S.S.R.

ADOUKI, Martin, D.JUR.; Congo diplomatist; b. 8 April 1942, Makoua; ed. Bordeaux and Paris Univs. and the Int. Inst. of Public Admin., Paris; Information Officer for the Group of African, Caribbean and Pacific Countries (ACP) in Brussels and attended negotiations between the ACP and the EEC; fmrly. Lecturer in Law at the Marien Ngouabi Univ., Brazzaville and later Special Adviser to the Prime Minister of the Congo; Perm. Rep. of the Congo to the UN 1985-. *Address:* 14 East 65th Street, New York, N.Y. 10021, U.S.A. *Telephone:* (212) 744-7840.

ADRIAN, 2nd Baron (cr. 1955), of Cambridge; Richard Hume Adrian, M.D., F.R.S.; British physiologist; b. 16 Oct. 1927; s. of 1st Baron Adrian and Hester Agnes Pinsent; m. Lucy Caroe 1967; ed. Swarthmore High School, U.S.A., Westminster School, Trinity Coll., Cambridge; nat. service, R.A.M.C. 1952-54; G. H. Lewes Student, Physiology Lab., Univ. of Cambridge 1954; Univ. Demonstrator 1956; Fellow, Corpus Christi Coll. 1956; Univ. Lecturer 1961; Reader in Experimental Biophysics 1968; Prof. of Cell Physiology, Univ. of Cambridge 1978-; Master of Pembroke Coll., Cambridge 1981-; Vice-Chancellor, Cambridge Univ. 1985-87; Fellow, Churchill Coll., Cambridge 1961-81; Trustee British Museum 1979-; Hon. Fellow Darwin Coll., Cambridge 1987-; Dr. h.c. (Poitiers) 1975. *Publications:* articles in Journal of Physiology. *Leisure interests:* sailing, skiing.

Address: The Master's Lodge, Pembroke College, Cambridge, CB2 1RF, England. *Telephone:* Cambridge 338127.

ADVANI, Lal K.; Indian politician, fmr. journalist and social worker; b. 8 Nov. 1927, Karachi (now in Pakistan); s. of Kishinchand Advani and Gyani Advani; m. Kamala Jagtiani 1965; one s. one d.; ed. St. Patrick's High School, Karachi, D.G. Nat. Coll., Hyderabad, Sind, Govt. Law Coll., Bombay; joined Rashtriya Swayam Sevak Sangh (RSS, social work org.) 1942, Sec. of Karachi branch 1947; joined Bharatiya Jana Sangh (BJS) 1951; party work in Rajasthan until 1958, Sec. of Delhi State Jana Sangh 1958-63, Vice-Pres. 1965-67; mem. Cen. Exec. of BJS 1966; Joint Ed. of BJS paper Organizer 1960-67; mem. interim Metropolitan Council, Delhi 1966, leader of Jana Sangh Gp. 1966; Chair. of Metropolitan Council 1967; mem. Rajya Sabha 1970-, head of Jana Sangh parl. gp. 1970; Pres. Bharatiya Jana Sangh 1973-77 (incorp. in Janata); detained during emergency 1975-77; Gen. Sec. Janata Party Jan.-May 1977; Minister of Information and Broadcasting 1977-79; Gen. Sec. Bharatiya Janata Party 1980-86, Pres. 1986-. *Publications:* A Prisoner's Scrap-Book, The People Betrayed. *Leisure interests:* theatre, cinema, books. *Address:* C-1/6, Pandara Park, New Delhi, India. *Telephone:* 384397 (Home).

ADYAA, Gelegiyn; Mongolian politician; b. 1934; ed. Trade Tech. School, Faculty of Foreign Languages and Literature, Mongolian State Univ.; journalist on newspaper Unen 1957-60; journalist, Ed. Information and Radio Directorate of Council of Ministers 1960-64; Duty Ed. and head of a dept., State Cttee. for Information and Radio 1964-68; Deputy Chair. State Cttee. for Information, Radio and TV 1968-71; Head of Party Orgs. Dept. Mongolian People's Revolutionary Party (MPRP) Cen. Cttee. 1972-79; mem. MPRP Cen. Cttee. 1976-83, a Sec. 1979-85; Deputy to People's Great Hural (Ass.) 1973-. *Address:* c/o Central Committee of the Mongolian People's Revolutionary Party, Ulan Bator, Mongolia.

ADYRKHAEVA, Svetlana Dzantemirovna; Soviet ballerina; b. 1938; ed. Leningrad Choreographic School; danced with Glinka Theatre of Opera and Ballet, Chelyabinsk 1955-58; with Odessa Opera and Ballet 1958-60; teacher at U.S.S.R. State Acad. of Ballet and Theatre 1960-. U.S.S.R. People's Artist 1980. *Main roles include:* Odette-Odile, Princess Florine, Woman of the Bronze Mountain (Prokofiev's Stone Flower), Zarema (Asafiev's Fountain of Bakhchisaray), Mehmene Banu (Melikov's Legend of Love), Aegina (Khatchachurian's Spartacus), Kitri (Minkus's Don Quixote). *Address:* U.S.S.R. State Academy of Ballet and Theatre, Moscow, U.S.S.R.

AEPPLI, Oswald, DR.IUR.; Swiss banker (retd.); b. 13 May 1916, Zürich; m.; one d.; ed. Cantonal High School, Zürich, Law Faculty of Zürich Univ.; admitted to bar, Zürich; joined Crédit Suisse 1944, Legal Adviser 1950, Man. 1963, Gen. Man 1969, Chair. Bd. 1977-83, mem. Bd. 1983-. *Address:* c/o Crédit Suisse, P.O. Box 590, 8021 Zürich, Switzerland.

AFANASIYEV, Georgiy Dmitriyevich; Soviet geologist; b. 17 March 1906, Novorossiysk; ed. Leningrad State Univ.; Research work, Inst. of Petrology 1930; mem. CPSU 1948-; Head of Dept. of Gen. Petrography, U.S.S.R. Acad. of Sciences Inst. of Geology of Ore Deposits, Petrography, Mineralogy and Geochemistry 1950; Sr. Scientific Assoc., Inst. of Geological Sciences of U.S.S.R. Acad. of Sciences 1937-56, Inst. of the Geology of Ore Deposits, Petrography, Mineralogy and Geochemistry of U.S.S.R. Acad. of Sciences 1956-; Scientific Sec., Dept. of Geological and Geographical Sciences, U.S.S.R. Acad. of Sciences 1948-53; Corresp. mem. U.S.S.R. Acad. of Sciences 1953-78; Deputy Chief Scientific Sec., U.S.S.R. Acad. of Sciences 1958-78; Asst. to Chief Ed. of Proceedings of the U.S.S.R. Acad. of Sciences, Geological Series 1954-59, Chief Ed. 1959-76; Vice-Pres. Comm. for Absolute Dating of Geological Formations 1962-63, Pres. 1963-; Pres. of the Petrographic Cttee. 1962-; Order of Lenin, Order of Red Banner of Labour, Badge of Honour, Order of Patriotic War. *Address:* U.S.S.R. Academy of Sciences, 14 Leninsky Prospekt, Moscow, U.S.S.R.

AFANASIYEV, Sergey Aleksandrovich; Soviet politician; b. 30 Aug. 1918, Novorossiysk, Krasnodar Territory; ed. Bauman Tech. Inst., Moscow; Engineer, Ministry of Armaments 1941-46; Dep. Head Dept. Ministry of Armaments of U.S.S.R. 1946-53; Head of Technological Bd. U.S.S.R. Ministry of Defence Industries 1953-57; Deputy Chair., then Chair. Leningrad Council of Nat. Economy 1958-61; Chair. of R.S.F.S.R. Council of Nat. Economy, Deputy Chair. Council of Ministers R.S.F.S.R. 1961-65; U.S.S.R. Minister of Gen. Machine Bldg. 1965-83, of Heavy and Transport Eng. April 1983-88; mem. Cen. Cttee. CPSU 1961-; Deputy to U.S.S.R. Supreme Soviet 1962-; U.S.S.R. State Prize, Order of Lenin (four times) and other decorations. *Address:* Ministry of Heavy and Transport Engineering, Moscow, U.S.S.R.

AFANASIYEV, Viktor Grigorevich, PH.D.; Soviet journalist; b. 18 Nov. 1922, Aktamysh, Tatar, A.S.S.R.; ed. Chita Pedagogical Inst.; mem. CPSU 1943-; in Soviet Army 1940-53; Deputy Dir. Chelyabinsk Pedagogical Inst. 1953-59; Head, Dept. of Scientific Communism, Acad. of Social Sciences, of the Cen. Cttee., CPSU 1960-68; Corresp. mem. of the U.S.S.R. Acad. of Sciences 1972-; Deputy Ed.-in-Chief, then first Deputy Ed.-in-Chief, Pravda, 1968-74, Ed.-in-Chief April 1976-; Ed.-in-Chief, Kommunist (organ of the Cen. Cttee., CPSU) 1974-76; Chair. U.S.S.R. Union of Journalists April 1976-; mem. of the Cen. Cttee., CPSU 1976-; Order of October Revolution and other decorations. *Publications:* Scientific Management of Society (2nd ed. 1973), Social Information and the Management of Society

1975, The Foundations of Philosophy (10th ed. 1977). *Address:* Pravda, Ul. Pravdy 24, Moscow, U.S.S.R. (Office).

AFFANDI, Achmad; Indonesian politician; b. 27 Oct. 1927, Kuningan, W. Java; ed. Univ. of Indonesia, Bogor, Army Staff and Command Coll., Bandung and Univ. of Kentucky; teacher, Sr. High School and Teachers' Coll., Bogor 1953–57; Asst. Faculty of Agric., Bogor 1957–58, Asst. Lecturer 1959–60; Jr. Lecturer, Inst. of Agric., Bogor 1960–62, Lecturer 1962–64; Head, Bureau for Equipment and Campus Devt., Dept. of Higher Educ. and Science 1962–64; sr. official, Dept. of Defence and Security 1965–67; Dir. of Animal Husbandry, Bimas (Mass Guidance) poultry farming 1968–69; Agric. Attaché, The Hague 1969–71; Sec. Bimas Supervisory Body, Dept. of Agric. 1971–73; Insp.-Gen. Dept. of Agric. 1973–74; Dir.-Gen. of Food Crops, Dept. of Agric. 1974; Jr. Minister for Food Production 1978–83; Minister of Agric. 1983–. *Address:* Ministry of Agriculture, Jln. Salemba Raya 16, Jakarta, Indonesia.

AFFLECK, James G., PH.D. American business executive; b. 1923; m.; ed. Princeton Univ.; joined American Cyanamid Co. 1947; successively research chemist, chemist, tech. rep., Man. New York New Products Office 1947–57; Man. Rubber Chem. Dept. 1957–61; Asst. Gen. Man. Commercial Devt. Div. 1961–64; Consumer Products 1964–65, Int. Divs. 1965–67; Gen. Man. Agricultural Div. 1967–71; Corporate Vice-Pres. 1971–72, Pres. 1972–76; Chair., Pres. and C.E.O. American Cyanamid 1976–82, Chair. 1982–; Dir. Potlatch Corpn., N.J. Bell, Prudential Insurance Co.; Trustee, Foundation of Coll. of Medicine and Dentistry, N.J., American Enterprise Inst., Jt. Council on Econ. Educ., Fairleigh Dickinson Univ.; mem. Bd. of Dirs. Pharmaceutical Mfrs. Asscn., Nat. Asscn. of Mfrs. *Address:* Office of the Chairman, American Cyanamid Co., Wayne, N.J. 07470, U.S.A.

AFFLECK, Raymond Tait, B. ARCH.; Canadian architect; b. 20 Nov. 1922, Penticton, B.C.; s. of Dr. John Earnest Affleck and Barbara (Tait) Affleck; m. Betty Ann Henley 1951; four s. one d.; ed. McGill Univ.; practising architect, Montreal 1955–; Partner Arcop Assocs., Montreal and Toronto; Consultant, Nat. Capital Comm., Ottawa 1967–76, Wascana Centre Authority, Regina 1979–; Visiting Prof. McGill Univ. 1965–; mem. Royal Canadian Acad.; Fellow, Royal Architectural Inst. of Canada; Hon. LL.D. (Calgary) 1972; Dr. h.c. (N.S. Tech. Coll., Halifax) 1976, Hon. D.Sc. (McGill Univ., Montreal) 1984, LL.D. h.c. (Concordia Univ., Montreal) 1988; Canadian Centennial Medal 1967, Massey Medals in Architecture; Médaille d'honneur, ordre des Architectes du Québec 1983, and others. *Publications:* Exhibitions and International Fairs as a Means of Mass Communications 1968, and several articles. *Leisure interests:* gardening, skiing, travel. *Address:* 1440 St. Catherine Street W., Suite 612, Montreal, P.Q., Canada (Office); *Telephone:* 878-3941; 488-1461.

AFLAK, Michel, LL.D.; Syrian politician and journalist; b. 1910, Damascus; ed. Greek-Orthodox Lyceum, Damascus, Univ. of Paris. Teacher in schools, Damascus; Founder Baath Arab Socialist Renaissance Party, Pres. 1940; f. Al Baath party newspaper 1946; Minister of Educ. 1954; emigrated to Lebanon 1966. *Publication:* Fi Sabil Al Baath 1959. *Address:* Raouché, Beirut, Lebanon.

AFONIN, Venyamin Georgievich; Soviet government official; First Sec. Nevinnomysk Gorkom CPSU (Stavropol Region) 1979–80; Sec. Stavropol Dist. Cttee. CPSU 1981–83; Head of Dept. of Chemical Industry of Cen. Cttee. CPSU 1983–; Deputy to R.S.F.S.R. Supreme Soviet 1983–; cand. mem. Cen. Cttee. CPSU 1986–. *Address:* Central Committee of the Communist Party of the Soviet Union, Staraya pl. 4, Moscow, U.S.S.R.

AFRAH, Maj.-Gen. Hussein Kulmia; Somali army officer and politician; b. 1920, Margeh; ed. Italian Secondary School, Mogadishu, and Italian Officers' Acad., Rome; shopkeeper until 1943; joined Police Force 1945; criminal investigation training in Kenya 1945; then instructor and translator, Police Training School Mogadishu; at Italian Secondary School Mogadishu 1950–54, Italian Officers' Acad. 1954–55; ADC to fmr. Pres. Osman 1960; mem. Supreme Revolutionary Council 1970–76, Vice-Pres. 1973–76; Chair. Econ. Cttee. 1973; Sec. of State for the Interior 1970–74; Deputy Head of State 1976–80, mem. Political Bureau, Somali Socialist Revolutionary Party 1976–; Pres. Adviser on Govt. Affairs 1980–84. *Address:* Somali Socialist Revolutionary Party Headquarters, Mogadishu, Somalia.

AGA KHAN IV, H.H. Prince Karim, B.A.; Spiritual leader and Imam of Ismaili Muslims; b. 13 Dec. 1936, Creux-de-Genthod, Geneva; s. of late Prince Aly Salomon Khan and of Princess Joan Aly Khan (née Yarde-Buller); m. Sarah Frances Croker-Poole 1969; two s. one d.; ed. Le Rosey, Switzerland, Harvard Univ., U.S.A.; became Aga Khan on the death of his grandfather Sir Sultan Mohamed Shah, Aga Khan III, G.C.S.I., G.C.I.E., G.C.V.O., 1957; granted title of His Highness by Queen Elizabeth II 1957, of His Royal Highness by the Shah of Iran 1959; founder Pres. Aga Khan Foundation 1967, Aga Khan Award for Architecture 1976, Inst. of Ismaili Studies 1977, Aga Khan Trust for Culture 1988; f. and Chancellor Aga Khan Univ., Pakistan 1983; Commdr. ordre du Mérite Mauritanien 1960; Grand Croix, ordre du Prince Henry du Gouvernement Portugais 1960, ordre Nat. de la Côte d'Ivoire 1965, de la Haute-Volta 1965, ordre Malgache 1966, ordre du Croissant Vert des Comores 1966; Grand Cordon ordre du Tadj de l'Empire d'Iran 1967, Nishan-I-Imtiaz, Pakistan 1970; Cavaliere di Gran Croce dell'Ordine al Merito della Repubblica (Italy) 1977; Grand Officier de l'ordre Nat. du Lion (Sénégal) 1982, Nishan-e-Pakistan, Pakistan

1983, Grand Cordon of Ouissam-al Arch (Morocco) 1986; Cavaliere del Lavoro (Italy) 1988; Hon. LL.D. (Peshawar Univ.) 1967, (Univ. of Sind) 1970, (McGill Univ., Montreal) 1983. *Leisure interests:* breeding race-horses, yachting, golf, skiing. *Address:* Aiglemont, 60270 Gouvieux, France.

AGA KHAN, Prince Sadruddin; Iranian UN official; b. 1933, Paris; s. of Sultan Mohammed Shah, Aga Khan III and Andrée Josephine Carron; m. 1st Nina Sheila Dyer 1957, 2nd Catherine Sursock 1972; ed. Harvard Univ. and Harvard Univ. Graduate School for Arts and Sciences; UNESCO Consultant for Afro-Asian Projects 1958; Head of Mission and Adviser to UN High Commr. for Refugees 1959–60; UNESCO Special Consultant to Dir.-Gen. 1961; Exec. Sec. Int. Action Cttee. for Preservation of Nubian Monuments 1961; UN Deputy High Commr. for Refugees 1962–65, High Commr. 1965–77; Consultant to Sec.-Gen. of UN 1978–; Chair. and founding mem. Independent Comm. on Internal Humanitarian Issues 1983–; UN Co-ordinator for Econ. and Humanitarian Programmes in Afghanistan 1988–; Publr. the Paris Review; Founder and Sec. Harvard Islamic Assocn.; Chair. Consortium Costa Smeralda; Pres. Council on Islamic Affairs, New York City; mem. Inst. of Differing Civilizations, Brussels; founder mem. and Pres. Groupe de Bellerive; Vice-Pres. World Wildlife Fund Int.; Commdr.'s Cross with Star of Order of Merit (Poland); Order of St. Sylvester The Pope; Order of Star of the Nile (Sudan); Order of Homayoun First Class (Iran); UN Human Rights Award 1978; Commdr., Légion d'honneur (France) 1979; German UN Assocn. Dag-Hammarskjöld hon. medal 1979; Co-winner Olympia Prize, Alexander Onassis Foundation 1982; Commdr. of the Golden Ark (Netherlands) 1985. *Publications:* Lectures on Refugee Problems. *Leisure interests:* Islamic art, primitive art, photography, sailing. *Address:* Château de Bellerive, 1245 Collonge-Bellerive, Geneva, Switzerland. *Telephone:* (022) 468866.

AGAM, Yaacoy; Israeli artist; b. 1928, Rishon Le-zion; m. Clila Agam 1954; two s. one d.; ed. Bezalel School of Art, Jerusalem, Atelier d'art abstrait, Paris; one-man exhbns. in Galerie Craven, Paris 1953, Galerie Denise René, Paris 1956, 1958, Palais des Beaux-Arts, Brussels 1958, Tel-Aviv Museum 1958, Suzanne Bollag Gallery, Zürich 1959, 1962, Drian Gallery, London 1959, Marlborough Gerson Gallery, New York 1966, Galerie Denise René, New York 1971, Guggenheim Museum, New York 1980; travelling retrospective exhbn. Paris (Nat. Museum of Modern Art), Amsterdam, Düsseldorf, Tel-Aviv 1972–73; numerous group exhbns. 1954–. *Works include:* Transformes Musicales 1961, Double Metamorphosis, Shalom Liner 1964, Sculptures in the City, Reims 1970, sculpture and mural, President's mansion, Israel 1971, Water-Fire fountain, St. Louis 1971, Pompidou room, Elysée Palace 1972, environment, Elysée Palace, Paris 1972, mobile wall, School of Science, Montpellier 1972, design and realization of a square in defence quarter, Paris, incl. water fountain and monumental sculpture 1973, Villa Regina, Miami (biggest painting in the world, at 300,000 sq. ft.) 1984, Homage to Mondrian (a whole building), L.A. 1984; films produced incl. Recherches et inventions 1956, Le désert chante, 1957. *Publications:* 36 books covering his non-verbal visual learning method (visual alphabet). *Address:* 26 rue Boulard, Paris, France. *Telephone:* 322-00-88.

AGAMIRZYAN, Ruben Sergeyevich; Soviet film director; b. 1922, Armenia; served in Soviet Army 1942–46; ed. Directors' Faculty of Leningrad Inst. of Theatre, Music and Cinema; mem. CPSU 1948–; Actor and Dir. of Chekhov Russian Theatre, Moldavia 1946–48; Dir. of Pushkin Theatre, Leningrad 1953–61; perm. Dir. at Gorky Theatre, Leningrad 1961–66; prin. Dir. at Komissarzhevskaya Theatre, Leningrad; teacher at Leningrad Inst. of Theatre, Music and Cinema; U.S.S.R. People's Artist 1983. *Address:* Leningrad Institute of Theatre, Music and Cinematography, Ul. Mokhovaya 34, Leningrad, U.S.S.R.

AGANBEGYAN, Abel; Soviet (Armenian) economist; b. 8 Oct. 1932, Tbilisi, Georgia; m. Zoya V. Kupriyanova 1953; one s. one d.; ed. Moscow State Econ. Inst.; Economist, Gen. Econ. Dept., State Cttee. for Labour and Wages 1955–61; Head of Lab., Inst. of Econs. and Industrial Eng., Siberian Branch of U.S.S.R. Acad. of Sciences 1961–67, Dir. Inst. of Econs. and Industrial Eng. 1967–; Prof. of Econs., Novosibirsk State Univ.; mem. U.S.S.R. Acad. of Sciences; Fellow, Econometric Soc.; Order of Lenin, of Red Banner of Labour; Dr. h.c. (Łódź, Poland). *Publications:* Wages and Salaries in the U.S.S.R. 1959, On the Application of Mathematics and Electronic Machinery in Planning 1961, Some Questions of Monopoly Price Theory with Reference to the U.S.A. 1961, Economical-Mathematical Analysis of Input-Output Tables in U.S.S.R. 1968, System of Models of National Economy Planning 1972, Management of the Socialist Enterprises 1979, Management and Efficiency: U.S.S.R. Economy in 1981–85 1981, Siberia—not by Hearsay (with Z. Ibragimova) 1981. *Address:* Prospekt Lavrentjeva 17, Novosibirsk 90, 630090, U.S.S.R. *Telephone:* 65 05 36.

AGEE, William McReynolds, M.B.A.; American company executive; b. 5 Jan. 1938, Boise, Ida.; s. of Harold J. and Suzanne (McReynolds) Agee; m. 1st Diane Weaver 1957, one s. two d.; m. 2nd Mary Cunningham 1982, one d.; ed. Stanford Univ., Boise Junior Coll., Univ. of Idaho, Harvard Univ.; with Boise Cascade Corpn. 1963–72; Sr. Vice-Pres. and Chief Financial Officer, Bendix Corpn. 1972–76, Pres. and C.O.O. 1976–77, Chair. and C.E.O. 1977–83, Pres. 1977–79; Chair. C.E.O. Morrison Knudsen Corpn. 1988–; Dir. ASARCO Inc., Equitable Life Assurance Soc. of U.S., Dow Jones & Co. Inc., Econ. Club of Detroit, Detroit Renaissance Inc.,

Nat. Council for U.S.-China Trade, Gen. Foods Corpn., Detroit Econ. Growth Corpn. 1978-, United Foundation, Nat. Council for U.S.-China Trade; mem. Conf. Bd., Council on Foreign Relations, Business Round-table, American and other insts. of CPAs, Board of Dirs., Assocs. of Harvard Business School Feb. 1977-, United Negroes Coll. Fund Feb. 1977-; Chair. Gov's. Higher Educ. Capital Investment Advisory Cttee., Pres's. Industrial Advisory Sub-cttee. on Econ. and Trade Policy 1978-79, Advisory Council Cranbrook Educational Community Aug. 1978-, Trustee 1978-; Trustee Urban Inst., Cttee. for Econ. Devt. May 1977-, Citizen Research Council, Mich. March 1977-; Hon. Dr. (Lawrence Inst. of Tech.) 1977, Hon. D.Sc. (Nathaniel Hawthorne Coll.) 1977, Univ. of Idaho Alumni Hall of Fame 1978, Hon. D.C.S. (Eastern Mich. Univ.) 1978, Hon. LL.D. (Univ. of Detroit) 1980, Hon. D.B.A. (Bryant Coll.), (R.I.) 1980, (Cleary Coll., Mich.) 1980. *Leisure interests:* tennis, golf, swimming.

AGEYEV, Gen. Geniy Yevgenevich; b. 1929; Soviet state official; ed. Irkutsk Mining and Metallurgical Inst.; Komsomol work 1952-55; Deputy Sec. of Party Cttee. of Bratsk Hydro-Electric Station 1955-61; Deputy Dir. of Irkutsk State Cttee. of CPSU 1961-63; First Sec. of Kirov Regional Cttee. of CPSU, Second Sec. of Irkutsk State Cttee. of CPSU 1963-65; Deputy Dir., Dir. of Ukrainian KGB 1965-73; Managing Dir., Sec. of Party Cttee., Corresp. Member of USSR KGB 1973-83; Deputy Pres. of USSR KGB 1983-85; Gen.-Col. 1986; Cand. Mem. of Cen. Cttee. of CPSU 1986. *Address:* The Kremlin, Moscow, U.S.S.R.

AGEYEV, Nikolay Vladimirovich, D.SC.; Soviet physical chemist; b. 30 June 1903, Tbilisi; ed. Leningrad Polytechnical Inst., Kaiser Wilhelm-Inst. für Metallforschung (Berlin-Dahlem); Docent, Leningrad Polytechnical Inst. 1930-38; Head of Lab., Inst. of Gen. and Inorganic Chem., U.S.S.R. Acad. of Sciences 1938-51; Prof. Gen. Chem. 1940-; mem. CPSU 1944-; Deputy Dir. Baikov Inst. of Metallurgy, U.S.S.R. Acad. of Sciences 1951-71, Dir. 1971-75; Head of Lab., Baikov Inst. of Metallurgy 1975-; Corresp. mem. U.S.S.R. Acad. of Sciences 1946-68, Academician 1968-; Pres. Scientific Council of Physical Chemical Bases of Metallurgical Processes, U.S.S.R. Acad. of Sciences; mem. Inst. of Metals (London) 1929-48, corresp. mem. to Council 1944-48; mem. Canadian Inst. Mining and Metallurgy 1973-; Hon. mem. Iron and Steel Inst. of Japan 1975-; Ed.-in-Chief, Problems of Contemporaneous Metallurgy 1951-62, Metallurgical Abstract 1953-, Phase Diagrams of Metallic Systems 1959-, U.S.S.R. Acad. of Sciences, Bulletin-Metals 1965-; Order of Lenin (twice), Order of October Revolution, Order of Red Banner (three times) and other decorations. *Publications:* X-Ray Metallography 1932, Thermal Analysis of Metals and Alloys 1936, The Chemistry of Metallic Alloys 1941, The Nature of Chemical Bond in Metallic Alloys 1947, and other works on metals and alloys. *Address:* A. A. Baikov Institute of Metallurgy, U.S.S.R. Academy of Sciences, Leninsky Prospekt 49, Moscow 117334, U.S.S.R. *Telephone:* 135-65-72.

AGIUS, George; Maltese diplomatist; b. 14 Nov. 1924; m.; one s.; ed. Oxford Univ.; Gen. Sec. Malta Labour Party 1955-57; Sec. Gen., Gen. Workers' Union of Malta 1971; attended Int. Labour Conf. 1972-76; mem. Exec. Bd. European TU Confed. 1973-76; Amb. to various Western European countries 1977-78; Perm. Rep. of Malta to the UN 1985-87. *Address:* c/o Ministry of Foreign Affairs, Valletta, Malta.

AGNELLI, Giovanni, DR.JUR.; Italian industrialist; b. 12 March 1921, Turin; s. of Edoardo Agnelli and Princess Virginia Bourbon del Monte; brother of Umberto Agnelli (q.v.); m. Princess Marella Caracciolo di Castagneto 1953; one s. one d.; grandson of Giovanni Agnelli, founder of F.I.A.T. (mfrs of land, sea and air engines and vehicles); Vice-Chair. Fiat 1945-63, Man. Dir. 1963-66, Chair. 1966-; Chair. Istituto Finanziario Industriale (IFI), IFI Int., Fondazione Giovanni Agnelli; Vice-Chair. Assoc. for the Monetary Union of Europe; mem. Exec. Bd. Confederation of Italian Industry, mem. Bd. Turin Industrial Asscn., Italian Stock Compan-ies Asscn., Eurafrance (Paris), Credito Italiano, Mediobanca; mem. Int. Advisory Cttee. Chase Manhattan Bank, Atlantic Advisory Council United Technologies Corpn., Advisory Bd. Petrofina, Int. Industrial Conf. of San Francisco; Gov. Atlantic Inst. for Int. Affairs; mem. Exec. Cttee. Trilateral Comm., Paris; mem. Groupe des Présidents de Grandes Entreprises Euro-péennes (Brussels); mem. Advisory Bd. Bilderberg Meetings, The Hague; Pres. La Stampa (newspaper); Cross for Military Valour. *Address:* Fiat S.p.A., 10 Corso Marconi, Turin (Office); Villa Frescot, Strada di San Vito, 256-Turin, Italy (Home). *Telephone:* 65651.

AGNELLI, Umberto, DR.JUR.; Italian motor executive; b. 1 Nov. 1934, Lausanne, Switzerland; s. of Edoardo Agnelli and Princess Virginia Bour-bon del Monte; brother of Giovanni Agnelli (q.v.); m. Allegra Caracciolo 1974; three s.; ed. Univ. Turin; Pres. Federazione Nazionale Calcio 1959; Pres. and Man. Dir. Società Assicuratrice Industriale (SAI) 1962-71; Pres., Chair. Fiat-France 1965-80; Pres. Piaggio & Co. 1965-; Man. Dir. Fiat SpA 1970-76, Vice-Pres. 1976-79, 1980-, Vice-Pres. and Man. Dir. 1979-80; Pres. Fiat Auto SpA 1980; Pres. TEXSID 1978-80; Dir. RIV-SKF 1962-79; Dir. Banco di Roma 1983-; Vice-Pres. and Man. Dir. IFI 1981; Vice-Pres. and mem. Bd. Fondazione Agnelli; Pres. CCMC; mem. Senate (CD) 1976-79; mem. Confederazione Generale dell'Industria Italiana, Chambre Syndicale des Constructeurs d'Automobiles, Advisory Cttee., Allianz Ver-sicherungs AG, European Advisory Council to A.T.T., American and European Communities Asscn., Advisory Cttee. First Nat. Bank of Chicago

1978; Grand Officer Order of Merit (Italy). *Publications:* numerous articles in journals and econ. reviews. *Address:* Fiat S.p.A., Corso Marconi 10, Turin, Italy. *Telephone:* 65651.

AGNEW, Harold Melvin, PH.D.; American physicist; b. 28 March 1921, Denver, Colo.; s. of Sam E. and Agusta (Jacobs) Agnew; m. Beverly Jackson 1942; one s. one d.; ed. Univs. of Denver and Chicago; Los Alamos Scientific Lab. 1943-46, Alt. Div. Leader 1949-61, Leader Weapons Div. 1964-70, Dir. Los Alamos Scientific Lab. 1970-79; Pres. GA Technologies Inc. 1979-85, Dir. 1985-; New Mexico State Senator 1955-61; Scientific Adviser, Supreme Allied Commdr. in Europe, Paris 1961-64; Chair. Army Scientific Advisory Panel 1965-70, mem. 1970-74; Chair. Gen. Advisory Cttee. U.S. Arms Control and Disarmament Agency 1972-76, mem. 1976-80; mem. Aircraft Panel, President's Scientific Advisory Cttee. 1965-73, U.S.A.F. Scientific Advisory Bd. 1957-69, Defense Scientific Bd. 1965-70, Govt. of N.M. Radiation Advisory Council 1959-61; Sec. N.M. Health and Social Services 1971-73; mem. Aerospace Safety Advisory Panel, NASA 1968-74, 1986-; White House Science Council 1982-; Woodrow Wilson Nat. Fellowship Foundation 1973-; Fellow, American Physical Soc.; mem. N.A.S., Nat. Acad. of Eng.; Ernest Orlando Lawrence Award 1966; Enrico Fermi Award, Dept. of Energy 1978. *Address:* 322 Punta Baja Drive, Solana Beach, Calif. 92075, U.S.A. *Telephone:* 619-481-8908.

AGNEW, Rudolph Ion Joseph, F.R.S.A.; British business executive; b. 12 March 1934; s. of Rudolph John and Pamela Geraldine (née Campbell) Agnew; m. Whitney Warren 1980; ed. Downside School; Commissioned Officer 8th King's Royal Irish Hussars 1953-57; joined Consolidated Gold Fields 1957; worked in South Africa, U.S.A., Canada and Australia; Chief Exec. Amey Roadstone Corpn. 1974-78, Chair. 1974-77; Exec. Dir. Consoli-dated Gold Fields PLC 1973-, Deputy Chair. 1978-82, Group Chief Exec. 1978-, Chair. 1983-, mem. Cttee. of Man. Dirs. 1986-; Fellow, Game Conservancy. *Leisure interest:* shooting. *Address:* Consolidated Gold Fields PLC, 31 Charles II Street, St. James's Square, London, SW1P 3HS, England. *Telephone:* 01-606 1020.

AGNEW, Spiro Theodore, LL.B.; American lawyer and politician; b. 9 Nov. 1918, Baltimore, Md.; s. of Theodore Spiro Agnew and Margaret Akers Agnew (family name was Anagnostopoulos); m. Elinor Isabel Judefind 1942; one s. three d.; ed. Baltimore public schools, Johns Hopkins Univ. and Univ. of Baltimore; army officer, served France and Germany, Second World War; legal studies 1947; Mil. service, Korean War; joined private law firm 1952, later established own law office in Baltimore; Chief Exec., Baltimore County 1962-66; Gov. of Maryland 1967-69; Vice-Pres. of the United States 1969-73, resgnd; with Pathlite Inc., Crofton, Md. 1974-; int. trade consultant; Republican. *Publications:* The Canfield Decision 1976, Go Quietly . . . Or Else 1980. *Leisure interests:* tennis, golf, reading, music.

AGO, Roberto, C.B.E., LL.D., P.S.D.; Italian university professor; b. 26 May 1907, Vigevano, Pavia; s. of late Gen. Pietro Ago and Maria Marini; m. Luciana Cova 1936; three s. two d.; ed. Univ. of Naples. Lecturer in Int. Law, Univ. of Cagliari 1930-33, Univ. of Messina 1933-34; Prof. of Int. Law, Univ. of Catania 1934, Univ. of Genoa 1935, Milan Univ. 1938, Rome Univ. 1956, Prof. Emer. 1983-; Pres. Italian Soc. for Int. Org.; Italian Del. to ILO Conf. 1946-, to UNESCO 1949-50, Law of Sea Conf. 1958-60, Vienna Conf. on Diplomatic Relations 1961; Pres. Vienna Conf. Law of Treaties 1968-69; mem. Comm. for drafting European Constitution 1952; Chair. Gov. Bd. ILO 1954-55, 1967-68; mem. and fmr. Pres. Int. Law Comm. of UN 1957-79; mem. Perm. Court of Arbitration 1957-; Hon. Pres. World Fed. of UN Asscns.; Judge *ad hoc*, Int. Court of Justice 1959-60, Judge 1979-; Pres. Court's Chamber for Gulf of Maine Dispute; Pres. Curatorium Hague Acad. of Int. Law, Arbitration Tribunal France-Germany, France-U.S.A.; mem. and Pres. numerous other int. tribunals and conciliation comms.; mem. and First Vice-Pres. Inst. de Droit Int.; mem. American Acad. of Political and Social Sciences, Inst. Hellénique Droit Int., Accademia dei Lincei, Société Royale de Belgique; Hon. mem. Indian Soc. Int. Law, American Soc. Int. Law; Grand Cross, Order of Merit (Italy), Order of Merit (Fed. Germany); Officier, Légion d'honneur, Hon. C.B.E.; Order of St. Gregory the Great; Dr. h.c. (Geneva, Nancy, Nice, Paris, Toulouse). *Publications:* Teoria del diritto internazionale pri-vato 1934, Il requisito dell'effettività dell'occupazione in diritto internazion-ale 1934, Règles générales des conflits de lois 1936, La responsabilità indiretta in diritto internazionale 1936, Lezioni di diritto internazionale privato 1939, Le délit international 1939, Lezioni di diritto internazionale 1943, Scienza giuridica e diritto internazionale 1950, Diritto positivo e diritto internazionale 1956, International Organisations and their Functions in the Field of Internal Activities of States 1957, Positive Law and International Law 1957, Il Trattato istitutivo dell' Euratom 1961, The State and International Organisation 1963, La qualité de l'état pour agir en matière de protection diplomatique des sociétés 1964, Le Nazioni Unite per il diritto internazionale 1965, La coopération internationale dans le domaine du droit international public 1966, La codification du droit inter-national et les problèmes de sa réalisation 1968, Sur la protection diploma-tique des personnes morales 1969, La fase conclusiva dell'opera di codificazione del diritto internazionale 1969, Premier, deuxième, troisième, quatrième, cinquième, sixième, septième et huitième rapport à la C.D.I. sur la responsabilité des Etats 1969-79, Nazioni Unite: venticinque anni dopo 1970, Droit des traités à la lumière de la Convention de Vienne 1971, Caratteri generali della comunità internazionale e del suo diritto 1974-75,

Eccezioni "non esclusivamente preliminari" 1975, Il pluralismo della comunità internazionale alle sue origini 1977, Pluralism and the Origins of International Community 1978, Scritti sulla responsabilita internazionale degli stati 1978, 1986, Les premières collectivités interétatiques méditerranéennes 1981, The First International Communities in the Mediterranean World 1983, Le Droit International dans la Conception de Grotius 1983, Positivism (International Law) 1985, I quaranta anni delle Nationi Unite 1985. *Leisure interests:* collecting modern paintings, gardening. *Address:* 143 Via della Mendola, 00100 Rome, Italy. *Telephone:* 328-42-31.

AGOSHKOV, Mikhail Ivanovich; Soviet mining specialist; b. 12 Nov. 1905, Petrovsk-Zabaikalsky, Chita Region; ed. Far East Polytechnic Inst., Vladivostock; Lecturer, Far East Polytechnic Inst. 1931–33; Dean, North Caucasian Inst. of Mines and Metallurgy 1933–41; Asst. Dir. Inst. of Mines, U.S.S.R. Acad. of Sciences 1941–58; mem. CPSU 1943–; Head, Lab. of Mining Inst., U.S.S.R. Acad. of Sciences 1954–; Prof. Inst. of Nonferrous Metals 1951–; Deputy Chief Learned Sec., U.S.S.R. Acad. of Sciences 1957; Corresp. mem. U.S.S.R. Acad. of Sciences 1953–; four Orders; State prizewinner 1951. *Publications:* Mining of Ore Deposits 1945, Methods of Estimating Output of Metal Mines 1949, Research of Technological Processes of Underground Mining 1959, Mining Methods of Vein Type Deposits 1960, Mining of Ore and Placer Deposits 1962, Underground Working of Ore Deposits 1966. *Address:* U.S.S.R. Academy of Sciences, 14 Leninsky Prospekt, Moscow, U.S.S.R.

AGRANAT, Simon, LL.D.; Israeli judge; b. 1906, U.S.A.; ed. Chicago Univ.; settled in Palestine 1930; law practice 1931–40; Magistrate 1940–48; Pres. District Court, Haifa 1948–50; Judge Supreme Court 1950–76, Deputy Pres. 1961–66, Pres. 1966–76; mem. Perm. Court of Arbitration (The Hague) 1962–68; Chair. Inquiry Comm., Yom Kippur War 1974. *Address:* 62b American-Canadian Quarter, Jerusalem, Israel.

AGRAWAL, Prabhu Lal; Indian engineer and business executive; b. 22 Oct. 1926, Udaipur, Rajasthan; s. of Shri Tilok Chand Agrawal and Narayan Devi Agrawal (deceased); m. Pushpa Devi 1948; one s. one d.; ed. Banaras Hindu Univ. and Univ. of Sheffield; Lecturer, College of Mining and Metallurgy, Banaras Hindu Univ., then Asst. Prof., 1947–56; Tech. Officer Rourkela Steel Plant, then Sr. Fuel Engineer, then Asst. Chief Fuel Engineer, then Supt. Energy & Economy Dept., then Chief Supt., 1965–66, Asst. Gen. Supt. 1966–69, Gen. Man. 1971–76, Man. Dir. 1976–78; Gen. Supt. Alloy Steels Plant 1969–70; Gen. Supt. Bokaro Steel Ltd. 1970–71; Chair. Steel Authority of India 1978–80; Tech. Adviser PT Krakatan Steel, Jakarta 1980–; Hon. mem. Indian Inst. of Metals 1980; Holker Fellow, Banaras Hindu Univ.; Uttar Pradesh Prize for Audyogik Indhan; Nat. Metallurgists Day Award; Verdienstkreuz (1st Class); FIE Foundation Award, India 1980; Tata Gold Medal, Indian Inst. of Metals 1981. *Publications:* Audyogik Indhan (Hindi); several technical papers and reports. *Leisure interest:* reading. *Address:* C-441, Defence Colony, New Delhi 110024, India (Home). *Telephone:* 622906 (Home).

AGRAWALA, Vasudeva Sharan, PH.D., D.LITT.; Indian university professor and writer; b. Aug. 1904; ed. Banaras Hindu Univ. and Lucknow Univ.; Curator, Mathura Museum 1931–39, Lucknow Museum 1940–45; Supt. Nat. Museum and Nat. Museum Branch of Archaeological Survey of India, New Delhi 1946–51; Prof. and Head of Dept. of Art and Architecture, Coll. of Indology, Banaras Hindu Univ. 1951; fmr. Pres. Museums Assçn. of India and other historical assçns.; Pres. All-India Prakrit Text Soc. 1964–. *Publications:* A Revised Catalogue of Mathura Museum 1950, India as Known to Panini 1953, Paninikalina Bharatavarsha 1955, Jayasi's Padamavata 1955, Kadambari: A Cultural Study 1958, Prithiviputra, or Essays on Indian Culture 1960, Sparks from the Vedic Fire 1962, The Thousand-Syllabled Speech of Vedic Symbolism, Vol. I 1963, Vidyapati's Kirtilata 1962, Matsya Purana: A Study 1963, Devi Mahatmya: Glorification of the Great Goddess 1963, Solar Symbolism of the Boar 1963, Vedic Lectures 1963, Harshacharita: A Cultural Commentary 1964, Vamana Purana: A Study 1964, Bharata Savitri, Vol. I 1957, Vol. II 1964, Chakradhvaja: The Wheel Flag of India 1964, Ancient Indian Folk-Cults 1964, Divyavadana 1965, Indian Art 1965, Heritage of Indian Art 1971. *Address:* Department of Art and Architecture, College of Indology, Banaras Hindu University, Banaras 5, India.

AGT, Andries A. M. van; Netherlands politician; b. 2 Feb. 1931, Geldrop; s. of Frans van Agt and Anna Frencken; m. Eugenie Krekelberg 1958; one s. two d.; ed. Catholic Univ., Nijmegen. Worked at Ministry of Agric. and Fisheries, then Ministry of Justice 1958–68; Prof. of Penal Law, Univ. of Nijmegen 1968–; Minister of Justice 1971–77; Deputy Prime Minister 1973–77; Prime Minister and Minister of Gen. Affairs 1977–82; Minister of Foreign Affairs 1982; M.P. 1983; Gov. Prov. of Noord-Brabant 1983–87; Amb., Head Del. of European Communities, Tokyo 1987–. *Address:* Europahouse, 9-15 Sanbancho, Chiyoda-ku, Tokyo 102, Japan.

AGUILAR MAWDSLEY, Andrés; Venezuelan diplomatist and lawyer; b. 10 July 1924, Caracas; ed. Univ. Central de Venezuela, Caracas and McGill Univ., Montreal; Teacher of Civil Law, Univ. Cen. de Venezuela 1948, Prof. of Law 1958–; Teacher of Civil Law, Univ. Católica Andrés Bello, Caracas 1954, Prof. 1958, Vice-Rector 1962–63; legal adviser to Venezuela Chamber of Building 1957–58; mem. Gov. Bd., Banco Industrial de Venezuela 1958–59; Minister of Justice until 1963; Perm. Rep. to European

Office of the UN, Geneva 1963–65; mem. several ILO cttees. and Pres. ILO Conf. 1964; Pres. of Council of ICEM 1964–65; Head of Venezuelan Del. to Int. Conf. on Human Rights, Teheran 1968; Pres. Nat. Gov. Bd. of Caritas 1966–69; mem. Gov. Bd. Inst. of Higher Studies in Admin. 1966; Chair. Nat. Council of Int. Council on Social Welfare 1968; Pres. Venezuelan Asscn. for UN 1967–68; mem. UN Comm. of Inquiry (Iran) 1980; has held posts in several orgs. concerned with social welfare and educ.; Perm. Rep. to UN 1969–72; Amb. to U.S.A. 1972–74; mem. Inter-American Comm. on Human Rights 1972– (fmr. Chair.); Pres. Int. Comm. of Jurists 1986–; mem. Panel of Legal Experts of INTELSAT 1974. *Publications:* Possession in the Civil Law of the Province of Quebec (in French), La responsabilidad contractual del arquitecto y del empresario por vicios y defectos de la obra, Protectión familiar, La delincuencia en Venezuela: Su prevención, La obligación de alimentos en derecho venezolano; articles on legal subjects published in specialized journals. *Address:* c/o Ministerio de Relaciones Exteriores, Casa Amarilla, esq. Principal, Caracas, Venezuela.

AGUIRRE OBARRIO, Eduardo Enrique, DR. EN DERECHO; Argentine lawyer and politician; b. 14 May 1923, Berlin, Germany; s. of Luis M. Aguirre and Analía María Obarrio de Aguirre; m. Diana María Braceras Santamarina; two s. two d.; ed. Univ. de Buenos Aires; Adviser/Consultant, Ministry of Interior 1955, Gen. Assessor 1955–57 and Deputy Departmental Dir. 1957; Deputy Sec. of Nat. Defence 1962; majority leader in the Senate 1963–65; Pvt. Sec. to Minister of Justice 1967–70; Under-Sec. of Justice 1970–71; Pres. of Caja Fed. de Ahorro y Préstamo para la Vivienda (Fed. Housing Savings and Lending Bank) 1972; Minister of Defence 1972–73; Prof. of Criminal Law, Univ. de Buenos Aires 1956–; Gran Cruz del Condor de los Andes (Bolivia). *Publications:* various legal publications. *Leisure interests:* tennis, chess, bridge, piano. *Address:* Sánchez de Bustamante 2657/59, 1°, Buenos Aires, Argentina. *Telephone:* 83-4858.

AGUIRRE VELÁZQUEZ, Ramón; Mexican politician; b. Sept. 1935, San Felipe, Guanajuato; ed. Nat. Univ. of Mexico and postgraduate courses abroad; taught at Nat. School of Commerce and Admin., Nat. Univ. of Mexico and Nat. Inst. of Public Admin.; Judge Advocate on Taxation, Ministry of Finance; Asst. Dir., then Under-Sec. of Expenditure; Dir.-Gen. Mexican Mortgage Soc.; Vice-Pres. of Planning and Finance, Somex Bank; Under-Sec. of Budget, Ministry of Planning and Budget; mem. Nat. Univ. of Public Accountants (Pres. 1980–82); Mayor of Mexico City Dec. 1982–; mem. PRI (Institutional Revolutionary Party). *Address:* Departamento del Distrito Federal, Plaza de la Constitución y Pino Suárez, México 1, D.F., Mexico.

AGUTTER, Jenny; British actress and dancer; b. 20 Dec. 1952, Taunton; ed. Elmhurst Ballet School; film debut in East of Sudan 1964; has appeared in numerous TV films, dramas and series and on stage with RSC and Nat. Theatre; *Plays include:* Tempest, Spring Awakening, Hedda Gabler, Betrayal. *Films include:* Ballerina, I Start Counting, The Railway Children, Walkabout, Logan's Run, The Eagle Has Landed, Equus, Man in the Iron Mask, Riddle of the Sands, Sweet William, The Survivor, Amy, An American Werewolf in London, Secret Places, Dark Tower. *Publication:* Snap 1983. *Address:* c/o William Morris Agency, 31 Soho Square, London, W.1, England.

AHDE, Matti Allan; Finnish politician; b. 23 Dec. 1945, Oulu; s. of Risto Ahde and Lalya Ahde; m. Hilkka Riikonen; two s. one d.; worked as electrician and civil servant; M.P. 1970–; Chair. State Youth Council 1970–74; mem. Exec. Finnish S.D.P. 1972–, Oulu City Council 1972–84; Chair. State Sports Council 1975–77, Pres. Workers' Sports Fed. 1978–; Vice-Pres. Finnish Olympic Cttee. 1978–, Finnish Nat. Opera 1980–; Chair. Bd. Trustees Royal Opera House Foundation 1980–; First Minister of the Interior 1982–83, Minister of the Environment 1983–87; Second Vice-Pres. of Finnish S.D.P. 1984–87, First Vice-Pres. 1987–; Speaker of Parl. 1987–. *Leisure interests:* sports, music. *Address:* Parliament, SF-00102 Helsinki, Finland. *Telephone:* 4321.

AHERN, Bertie; Irish politician; b. 12 Sept. 1951, Dublin; m. Miriam P. Kelly; two d.; ed. Rathmines Coll. of Commerce, Dublin and Univ. Coll., Dublin; formerly accountant, Mater Hosp., Dublin; mem. Dail 1977–; mem. Dublin City Council 1979–, Lord Mayor 1986–87; Minister of State, Dept. of Taoiseach and of Defence March-Nov. 1982; Minister for Labour 1987–; Fianna Fail. *Address:* Ministry of Labour, Davitt House, 50–60 Mespil Road, Dublin 4; 25 Church Avenue, Drumcondra, Dublin 9, Republic of Ireland (Home). *Telephone:* 01 374267 (Home); 01 374129 (Office).

AHIDJO, Ahmadou; Cameroonian politician; b. 24 Aug. 1924, Garoua; ed. Ecole Supérieure d'Administration, Yaoundé; began career in radio admin.; elected as Rep. to Representative Ass. of Cameroon 1947; fmr. Sec. of Ass., Pres. Admin. Affairs Comm., Vice-Pres.; Counsellor Ass. of the French Union 1955–58, fmr. Sec.; Pres. Territorial Ass. of Cameroon 1956–57; Minister of the Interior 1957–59; Deputy Prime Minister 1957–58; Prime Minister 1958–59; Prime Minister and Minister of the Interior, independent state of Cameroon Jan.-May 1960; Pres. Repub. of Cameroon May 1960–61, of the Fed. Repub. of Cameroon 1961–72, United Repub. of Cameroon 1972–82; Pres. Union Nationale Camerounaise (UNC) 1966–83; in exile in France July 1983–; Chair. OAU Ass. of Heads of State 1969, Pres. UDEAC Council of Heads of State 1970, 1978; Grand Croix, Légion d'honneur, Grand Insignia, Order of the Star of Africa, Knight Order of the Black Star of Benin.

AHLFORS, Lars Valerian, PH.D., LL.D.; American professor of mathematics; b. 18 April 1907, Helsinki, Finland; s. of Karl Ahlfors and Sieva Helander; m. Erna Lehnert 1933; three d.; ed. Univ. of Helsinki; Lecturer, Harvard Univ. 1935-38; Prof., Univ. of Helsinki 1939-44, Univ. of Zürich 1945-46; Prof. of Math., Harvard Univ. 1946-77, W. C. Graustein Prof. 1964-77, Prof. Emer. 1977-; mem. N.A.S.; Fields Medal for Math., Wolf Prize, Vihuri Int. Prize. *Publications:* Complex Analysis 1953, Riemann Surfaces (with L. Sario) 1960, Quasiconformal Mappings 1966, Conformal Invariants 1973, and many articles on mathematical analysis. *Address:* Department of Mathematics, Harvard University, Cambridge, Mass. 02138; 160 Commonwealth Avenue, Boston, Mass. 02116, U.S.A. (Home). *Telephone:* 617-262-0974.

AHLMARK, Per, B.A.; Swedish fmr. politician, journalist and poet; b. 15 Jan. 1939, Stockholm; s. of Prof. Axel Ahlmark; m. (divorced), one s. one d.; m. 2nd Bibi Andersson (q.v.) 1978 (divorced); Leader of Young Liberals 1960-62; journalist for Expressen; mem. Parl. 1967-78; Deputy Chair. Swedish-Israeli Friendship Org. 1970-; mem. Council of Europe 1971-76; mem. Royal Comms. on Literature, Human Rights, etc. in the 70s; Leader, Folkpartiet (Liberal Party) 1975-78; Deputy Prime Minister and Minister of Labour 1976-78; Deputy Chair. Martin Luther King Fund 1968-73; Chair. Swedish Film Inst. 1978-81; Deputy Chair. Swedish Comm. Against Antisemitism 1983-; Adviser to Elie Wiesel Foundation for Humanity, New York 1987-; Defender of Jerusalem Award 1986. *Publications:* several political books and numerous articles, three books of poetry. *Leisure interests:* films, books, theatre. *Address:* Folkungag 61, 11622 Stockholm, Sweden.

AHLSEN, Leopold; German author; b. 12 Jan. 1927, Munich; m. Ruth Gehwald 1964; one s. one d.; Gerhart Hauptmann Prize; Schiller-Förderungspreis; Goldener Bildschirm; Hörspielpreis der Kriegsblinden; Silver Nymph of Monaco and other awards. *Publications:* 8 plays, 23 radio plays, 34 television plays, 4 novels. *Leisure interest:* joinery. *Address:* Waldschulstrasse 58, 8000 Munich 82, Federal Republic of Germany. *Telephone:* 089/4301466.

AHLSTRÖM, Krister Harry, M.SC.; Finnish business executive; b. 29 Aug. 1940, Helsinki; s. of Harry F. and Asta A. (née Seege) Ahlström; m. Anja I. Artto 1974; one s. three d.; ed. Helsinki Univ. of Technology; Product Eng., Gen. Man. and mem. Bd. of Man. Oy Wärtsilä Ab 1966-81; Dir. and mem. Exec. Bd. A. Ahlström Corpn. 1981-82, Pres. and C.E.O. 1982-. *Leisure interest:* sailing. *Address:* A. Ahlström Corporation, P.O. Box 329, 00101 Helsinki (Office); Itäinen Puistotie 2, 00140 Helsinki, Finland (Home). *Telephone:* 358 0 16231 (Office); 358 0 605423 (Home).

AHMAD, Datuk Abdul Ajib bin; Malaysian politician; b. 13 Sept. 1947, Segamat, Johore; ed. Malay Coll. Kuala Kangsar, Perak, Mara Inst. of Tech. and Univ. of Malaya; formerly served with Ministry of Foreign Affairs; later Exec., Shell Oil Co., Kuala Lumpur; Press Sec. to Dato Musa Hitam (Minister of Primary Industries, later Deputy Prime Minister) 1975-82; mem. State Ass. for Endau 1982-86; apptd. Menteri Besar Johor 1982; mem. Parl. 1986-; Minister, Prime Minister's Dept. Aug 1986-; mem. UMNO Supreme Council 1984-. *Leisure interests:* sport, reading. *Address:* Prime Minister's Department, Kuala Lumpur, Malaysa.

AHMAD, Awang Mohammed Yussof, B.A.; Brunei diplomatist; b. 1944, Brunei; m.; two c.; ed. Western Australia and Manchester Univs.; Admin. Officer, Brunei Educ. Dept. 1972-75; Acting Dist. Officer of Belait Dist. and Chair. Belait and Seria Municipal Bd. 1975-76; Acting Sec. Public Service Comm. and Deputy Controller, Customs and Excise 1976; Sr. Admin. Officer, Office of the Gen. Adviser to the Sultan of Brunei Darussalam 1980-81; Deputy Dir. of the Establishment Dept. 1981; Dist. Officer, Tutong Dist. 1983-84; Amb. to the Philippines 1984-86; Perm. Rep. to the UN 1986-87. *Address:* c/o Ministry of Foreign Affairs, Bandar Seri Begawan, Brunei.

AHMAD, Othman Ibrahim al-, M.B.A.; Saudi Arabian civil servant; b. 12 Dec. 1942, Saudi Arabia; with Inst. of Public Admin. 1968-71, Dir.-Gen. Bd. of Employment and Examination, Civil Service Bureau 1971-76, Asst. Vice-Pres. Gen. Bureau, Civil Service 1976-78, Vice-Pres. 1978-81; Asst. Sec.-Gen. for Organizational Affairs, League of Arab States 1981-; Vice-Pres. Civil Service Bureau 1984-. *Publications:* Employment Policy in Saudi Arabia 1971, Workforce in the Government Sector and Employment Problems 1975, Methods of Assessment of the Needs for Government Employment 1977, Problems and Policies in Planning Government Employment 1979. *Address:* League of Arab States, Avenue Khéreddine Pacha, Tunis, Tunisia; P.O. Box 1222, Riyadh, Saudi Arabia. *Telephone:* (Riyadh) 402-7452.

AHMADU-SUKA, Osman; Nigerian diplomatist; b. 22 Sept. 1926, Wara, Sokoto; ed. Achimota Coll., Ghana, Loughborough Training Coll., England, Univs. of London and Columbia; Education Service, Sokoto Native Authority and Govt. of Northern Nigeria 1946-59; Premier's Office, Kaduna 1960-62; First Sec. (Educ.), High Comm., U.K. 1962-64; Counsellor and Head of Chancery, Embassy, U.S.A. 1964-66; Consul-Gen. in New York 1966-68; Amb. to Egypt 1968-73, to Netherlands 1973-75; High Commr. to U.K. 1975-76; Rep., Commonwealth Liaison Cttee. 1962-64; alt. Perm. Rep. to UNESCO 1962-64. *Address:* c/o Ministry of Foreign Affairs, Lagos, Nigeria.

AHMED, Fakhruddin, M.A.; Bangladesh diplomatist; b. 1 April 1931; s. of late A. A. F. Mohi; m. Helen Ahmed 1963 (died 1984); one s. one d.; ed. Dhaka Univ., Fletcher School of Law and Diplomacy, Boston, U.S.A.; with Foreign Service of Pakistan 1954-71, Junior Diplomatist, Saudi Arabia 1957-59, Vice-Consul, U.S.A. 1959-63, Second Sec., Iran 1963-65, First Sec., then Acting High Commr., Ghana 1967-68, served Ministry of Foreign Affairs 1968-71, Dir. 1968-70, Dir.-Gen. 1971; with Foreign Service of Bangladesh 1972, Additional Sec., then Foreign Sec., Ministry of Foreign Affairs 1972-76, Amb. to Italy (also to accred. to Switzerland), Perm. Rep. to FAO 1976-78, Amb. to Yugoslavia (also accred. to Greece, Albania) 1978-82, High Commr. in U.K. 1982-86 (also Amb. to Portugal 1983-86); Foreign Sec., Ministry of Foreign Affairs June 1986-. *Leisure interests:* reading, walking, photography. *Address:* Ministry of Foreign Affairs, 23/6 Mirpur Road, Topkhana Road, Dhaka, Bangladesh.

AHMED, Kazi Zafar, B.A.; Bangladesh politician; b. 1 July 1940, Cheora; s. of Kazi Ahmed Ali; m.; three d.; ed. Dhaka Univ.; Office Sec. East Pakistan Students Union Cen. Cttee. 1957, Office Sec. 1957-62, Gen. Sec. 1962-63; imprisoned several times for political activities between 1963 and 1965; Pres. Bangla Sramik Fed. 1967; actively participated in struggle for independence 1971; Sec.-Gen. Cen. Cttee. Nat. Awami Party 1972-74; f. United People's Party 1974, Sec. Gen. 1974, Chair. Cen. Cttee. 1979-; mem. Nationalist Front 1978; Ed. Nayajug; Minister of Educ. 1978, Deputy Prime Minister, also in charge of Ports, Shipping and River Transport 1986-87, Political Adviser to the Pres. and Minister of Information 1988-. *Address:* c/o Ministry of Information, Bangladesh Secretariat, Bhaban 4, 2nd 9-Storey Building, 6th Floor, Dhaka, Bangladesh.

AHMED, Khandakar Moshtaque; Bangladesh lawyer and politician; b. 1918; ed. Dacca Univ.; joined Quit India movement 1942; imprisoned 1946; collaborated with Sheikh Mujibur Rahman in Bengali language movement, later in Awami League; imprisoned several times by Pakistan authorities; Minister of Foreign Affairs, Law and Parliamentary Affairs in Govt. of Bangladesh April-Dec. 1971 (in exile in India), of Law, Parliamentary Affairs and Land Revenue 1971-72, of Power, Irrigation and Flood Control 1972-74, of Trade and Commerce 1974-75; Pres. of Bangladesh, also Minister of Defence and Home Affairs Aug.-Nov. 1975; detained Nov. 1976; sentenced to 5 years' imprisonment Feb. 1977, to additional 3 years for corruption and abuse of power March 1977; released March 1980.

AHMED, Maj.-Gen. Mohamed el-Baghir; Sudanese army officer and politician; b. 1927, El Sofi; m.; four s. one d.; ed. Commercial Secondary School, Khartoum, Military Coll. and Cairo Univ.; commissioned 1950; Chief of Staff, Southern Command 1958; Mil. Gov. Upper Nile Province 1959; Mil. Attaché, London 1960-67; Dir. of Training and Chief of Staff, Southern Command 1968; Commdr. Mil. Coll. 1968-69; Under-Sec. Ministry of Defence June-Dec. 1969; First Deputy Chief of Staff of Armed Forces 1969-70, Chief of Staff 1970-71; Minister of the Interior 1971-73, Jan.-Aug. 1975; First Vice-Pres. of Sudan 1972-77; mem. Exec. Bureau, Sudanese Socialist Union; mem. Council, Univ. of Khartoum; del. to several int. confs.; several decorations. *Address:* c/o Office of the Executive Bureau, Sudanese Socialist Union, P.O. Box 1850, Khartoum, Sudan.

AHMED, Moudud, M.A.; Bangladesh politician; b. 1940, Noakhali; s. of the late Bara Moulana; m. Hasna Jasimuddin; two s.; ed. Dhaka Univ.; fmr. Gen. Sec. East Pakistan House, England; took an active part in struggle for independence, organising External Publicity Div. of Bangladesh Govt. in exile; Ed. Bangladesh (weekly); Lawyer, Bangladesh Supreme Court 1972-74; Gen. Sec. Cttee. for Civil Liberties Legal Aid 1974; imprisoned during State of Emergency 1974; Head, Bangladesh delegation to 32nd Session UN Gen. Ass. 1977; Adviser to Pres. 1977; Minister of Communications 1985-86, Deputy Prime Minister in charge of Ministry of Industries July 1986-88, Prime Minister and Minister of Industry 1988-. *Publications:* Bangladesh Contemporary Events and Documents, Bangladesh Constitutional Quest for Autonomy 1974; *Address:* Ministry of Commerce and Industries, Shilpa Bhaban, Motijheel C/A, Dhaka, Bangladesh.

AHOMADEGBÉ, Justin Tometin; Benin politician; b. 1917; ed. William Ponty School, Dakar, and School of Medicine, Dakar; medical work, Cotonou, Porto-Novo 1944-47; mem. Gen. Council, Dahomey 1947, Sec.-Gen. Bloc Populaire Africain; Sec.-Gen. Union Démocratique Dahoméenne (UDD) 1956; mem. Grand Council, A.O.F. 1957; mem. Dahomey Legis. Ass. 1959, Pres. 1959-60; medical work 1960-61; imprisoned 1961-62; Minister of Health, Public Works and Nat. Education 1963; Vice-Pres. of Dahomey, Pres. of Council of Ministers and Minister in Charge of Interior, Defence, Security and Information 1964-65, also in charge of the Plan 1965; mem. Presidential Council 1970-72; Head of State May-Oct. 1972; imprisoned 1972 released April 1981. *Address:* c/o Ministry of Justice, Cotonou, Benin.

AHRENDS, Peter, A.A.DIPL. (HONS.), A.R.I.B.A.; British architect; b. 30 April 1933, Berlin, Germany; s. of Steffen Bruno Ahrends and Margerete Maria Sophie Visino; m. Elizabeth Robertson 1954; two d.; ed. King Edward VII School, Johannesburg, Architectural Assocn., London; Research into decoration in Islamic Architecture 1956; Teacher (part-time) Architectural Assocn. School of Architecture 1960-61; f. architectural practice Ahrends, Burton and Koralek 1961-; commissions include Trinity Coll. Library, Dublin, variety of educational, commercial, industrial and museum bldgs. 1961-; Prof. of Architecture, Bartlett School of Architecture and Planning

Oct. 1986–; exhbns. at R.I.B.A. Heinz Gallery 1980, Royal Inst. of Architects of Ireland 1981, Museum of Finnish Architecture, Helsinki 1982, Alvar Aalto Museum, Jyvaskyla 1982, Architectural Asscn., Oslo 1983; won competition with project for Nat. Gallery Hampton Site Extension; Visiting Prof. of Architecture, Kingston Polytechnic 1983–84; Structural Steel Design Award 1980, R.I.B.A. Good Design in Housing award 1977, R.I.B.A. Architecture Award 1978. *Address:* 16 Rochester Road, London, NW1 9JH (Home); 7 Chalcot Road, London, NW1 8LH, England. *Telephone:* 01-485 7570 (Home); 01-586 3311 (Office).

AHRENS, Joseph; German composer; b. 17 April 1904, Sommersell, Westphalia; s. of Robert and Elisabeth Ahrens; m. Gisela Schroeder 1931; one s. one d.; ed. Staatliche Akad. für Kirchen- und Schulmusik, Berlin; asst. teacher in high schools until 1934; cathedral organist, St. Hedwig's Cathedral, Berlin 1934–45; Lecturer, Staatliche Akad. 1928–45, Prof. 1936; Prof. Staatliche Hochschule für Musik, Berlin 1945; Prof. Emer. Hochschule der Künste, Berlin 1972–; Kunstpreis der Stadt Berlin 1955; Equitem Ordinis Sancti Gregorii Magni, Rome; Silver Pontifical Medal. *Works include:* 29 works for organ and vocal music. *Publications:* Die Formprinzipien des Gregorianischen Chorals und mein Orgelstil 1977, Von den modi zur Dodekaphonie 1979. *Address:* Hüningerstrasse 26, 1000 Berlin 33, Federal Republic of Germany. *Telephone:* (030) 832 53 90.

AHRLAND, Karin Margareta, LL.B.; Swedish politician; b. 20 July 1931, Torshälla; d. of Valfrid and Greta (née Myhlén) Andersson; m. 1st Hans F. Petersson 1958 (dissolved 1962); m. 2nd Nils Ahrland 1964; one s.; ed. Univ. of Lund; chief lawyer, County of Malmöhus 1971–76; mem. Riksdag (Parl.) 1976–; Minister for Public Health and Medical Services 1981–82; Del. UN Comm. of Status of Women 1976–79; Chair. Nat. Cttee. for Equality between Men and Women 1979–81; Chair. Nat. Arts Council 1980; Liberal. *Address:* Fredriksbergsgatan 2, S 212 11 Malmö, Sweden.

AHRONOVITCH, Yuri (George); Israeli (Soviet-born) conductor; b. 13 May 1932, Leningrad; s. of Michael Ahronovitch and Anna Eskina; m. Tamar Sakson 1973; ed. Leningrad Conservatorium, studied conducting with Kurt Sanderling and Nathan Rachlin; Conductor Saratov Philharmonic Orchestra 1956–57, Yaroslav Symphony Orchestra 1957–64; Chief Conductor Moscow Radio Symphony Orchestra 1964–72; left U.S.S.R. to settle in Israel 1972; opera début in Europe, Cologne 1973; début Royal Opera House Covent Garden (Boris Godunov) 1974; Chief Conductor Gürzenich Orchestra, Cologne 1975–, Stockholm Philharmonic Orchestra 1982–. *Address:* Stockholm Philharmonic Orchestra, Hotorget 8, Stockholm, Sweden.

AHRWEILER, Hélène, D. ES L.; French professor; b. 28 Aug. 1926, Athens, Greece; d. of Nicolas Glykatzi and Calliroe Psaltides; m. Jacques Ahrweiler 1958; one d.; ed. Univ. of Athens; Research Worker C.N.R.S. 1955–67, Head of Research 1964–67; Prof. Univ. of Paris-Sorbonne 1967–; Pres. Univ. de Paris 1976–81; Rector Acad., Chancellor Univs. of Paris 1982–89; Sec.-Gen. Int. Cttee. of Historical Sciences 1980–; Vice-Pres. conseil d'orientation du Centre Georges Pompidou 1975, conseil supérieur de l'Education Nationale 1983–; Pres. Centre Georges Pompidou Feb. 1989–; mem. Greek, British, Belgian, German and Bulgarian Acads. *Publications:* Byzance et la Mer 1966, Etudes sur les structures administratives et sociales de Byzance 1971, l'idéologie politique de l'empire byzantin 1975, Byzance: les pays et les territoires 1976. *Leisure interests:* tennis, swimming. *Address:* 17 rue de la Sorbonne, 75005 Paris (Univ.); 28 rue Guynemer, 75006 Paris, France (Home).

AI QING (see Jiang Haicheng).

AI ZHISHENG; Chinese government official; b. 1929, Hanyang Co., Hubei Prov.; ed. Beijing Qinghua Univ.; Vice-Pres., Qinghua Univ. 1982–83; Deputy Sec. State Council 1983–85; Minister of Radio and TV 1985–; alt. mem. 12th Cen. Cttee. CCP 1985–; mem. 13th Cen. Cttee. CCP 1988–. *Address:* Ministry of Radio and Television, P.O. Box 4501, Beijing, People's Republic of China.

AICHINGER, Ilse; Austrian writer; b. 1 Nov. 1921, Vienna; m. Günter Eich (died 1972); ed. high school and Universität Wien; formerly worked with Inge Scholl at Hochschule für Gestaltung, Ulm; later worked as a reader for S. Fischer (publishers), Frankfurt and Vienna; Förderungspreis des Österreichischen Staatspreises 1952, Preis der Gruppe 47 1952, Literaturpreis der Freien und Hansestadt Bremen 1954, Immermannpreis der Stadt Düsseldorf 1955, Literaturpreis der Bayerischen Akademie 1961, Ny-ell Sachs-Preis, Dortmund 1971, City of Vienna Literature Prize 1974, Georg Trackle Prize 1979, Petrarca Prize 1982. *Publications:* Die Grössere Hoffnung (novel) 1948, Knöpfe (radio play) 1952, Der Gefesselte (short stories) 1953, Zu keiner Stunde (dialogues) 1957, Besuch im Pfarrhaus (radio play) 1961, Wo ich wohne (stories, dialogues, poems) 1963, Eliza, Eliza (stories) 1965, Nachricht von Tag (stories) 1970.

AIGRAIN, Pierre Raoul Roger, D. ÉS SC.; French physicist; b. 28 Sept. 1924, Poitiers; s. of Marius and Germaine (née Ligault) Aigrain; m. Francine Bogard 1947; three s.; ed. secondary schools in Metz, Poitiers, Nancy, Annecy, Lycée Saint Louis, Paris, Naval School, Carnegie Inst. of Tech., Pittsburgh and Faculté des Sciences, Paris; Attaché, Research and Study Centre, French Navy 1948–50; Asst. Collège de France 1950–51; Engineer Atomic Energy Comm. 1951–52; Head of physics lectures, Faculté des Sciences, Lille 1952; mem. council and Nat. Sec. French Physics Soc. 1953,

Sec.-Gen. 1959–; Head of lectures Faculté des Sciences, Paris 1954, Titular Prof. gen. electrotechnology 1958–63, energy 1963–65; Vice-Pres. consultative cttee. for scientific and tech. research 1958–61; Scientific Dir. in charge of research and experimentation, Army ministry 1961–65; Dir. Higher Ed. Ministry of Nat. Ed. 1965–67, Gen. Del. for scientific and tech. research 1968–73; Prof. M.I.T. 1973–74; Gen. Tech. Dir. Thomson Group 1974–78; Admin. Fondation pour l'Innovation 1973–; Pres. Admin. Council Institut des hautes études scientifiques 1977–78; Sec. of State in Charge of Research, Prime Minister's Office 1978–81; Dir.-Gen. (scientific and tech.) Thomson Brandt and Thomson C.S.F. 1981–83, Scientific Adviser to Pres. Thomson group 1983–; Pres. Cttee. of Econ. and Industrial Co-operation between French and Chinese Business, Conseil nat. du Patronat Francais 1984–; Pres. de la Soc. française de physique; mem. Atomic Energy Cttee. 1968–. American Acad. of Arts and Science; Foreign mem. Royal Swedish Acad. of Science; Assoc. mem. American Acad. of Sciences 1974–; Fellow Inst. of Electrical and Electronic Engineers; Foreign Assoc. Nat. Acad. of Eng. 1976–; Officier, Légion d'honneur, Commdr., ordre nat. du Mérite and Palmes academiques, Chevalier du Mérite agricole; Commdr. Nat. Order of Senegal, Order of Merit (Fed. Rep. Germany); Médaille de l'aéronautique; prix Robin (Soc. Française de Physique) 1974. *Address:* 8 square Henry-Paté, 75016 Paris (Home); Thomson, 173 boulevard Haussmann, 75379 Paris cedex 08, France (Office).

AIKEN, Linda H., PH.D.; American nurse sociologist; b. 29 July 1943, Roanoke; ed. Univ. of Florida, Gainesville, Univ. of Texas, Austin, Univ. of Wisconsin, Madison; nurse, Univ. of Fla. Medical Center 1964–65; Instructor, Coll. of Nursing, Univ. of Fla. 1966–67; Instructor, School of Nursing, Univ. of Miss. 1967–70, Clinical Nurse Specialist 1967–70; lecturer, School of Nursing, Univ. of Wis. 1973–74; Program Officer, Robert Wood Johnson Foundation 1974–76, Dir. of Research 1976–79, Asst. Vice-Pres. 1979–81, Vice-Pres. 1981–87; Prof. of Nursing and Sociology, Dir. for Nursing Affairs, Univ. of Pennsylvania 1988–; Assoc. Ed. Journal of Health and Social Behaviour 1979–81; Jessie M. Scott Award, American Nurses Asscn. 1984. *Publications:* Nursing in the 1980s': Crises, Challenges, Opportunities (Ed.) 1982, Evaluation Studies Review Annual 1985 (Co-Ed. with B. Kehrer) 1985, Applications of Social Science to Clinical Medicine and Health Policy (co-ed. with D. Mechanic) 1986. *Address:* University of Pennsylvania, School of Nursing, Nursing Education Building, Philadelphia, Pa. 19104-6096, U.S.A.

AILES, Stephen; American lawyer; b. 25 March 1912, Romney, W. Va.; s. of Eugene E. Ailes and Sallie Cornwell Ailes; m. Helen Wales 1939; three s. one d.; ed. Episcopal High School, Alexandria, Va., Princeton Univ., and West Virginia Univ. Law School; Asst. Prof. of Law, W. Va. Univ. 1937–40; pvt. legal practice 1940–42; Legal Staff, Office of Price Admin. 1942–46; partner in law firm Steptoe & Johnson, Washington, D.C. 1948–, (excepting leave of absence); Counsel, American Econ. Mission to Greece 1947; Under-Sec. of Army 1961–64; Sec. of the Army 1964–65; Pres. and C.E.O. Asscn. of American Railroads 1971–77. *Address:* 4550 N Park Avenue, Chevy Chase, Md. 20815, U.S.A. (Home).

AILLERET, Pierre Marie Jean; French engineer; b. 10 March 1900, Vienne en Arthies (S. et O.); s. of Amédée Ailleret and Angèle Devaine; m. Denise Nodé-Langlois 1935; three s. three d.; ed. Lycée Carnot, Ecole Polytechnique, Paris; Prof. Ecole Nationale des Ponts et Chaussées 1938–70; Dir. Studies and Research, Electricité de France 1946–59, Asst. Dir.-Gen. 1959–66, Scientific and Tech. Counsellor 1967–70; Pres. Training Council, Conservatoire nationale des arts et métiers 1963–75; mem. Atomic Energy Cttee. 1951–67; Pres. Union technique de l'électricité 1958–75, Hon. Pres. 1975–; Pres. Int. Electrotechnical Comm. 1967–70; fmr. Vice-Pres. Asscn. Française de normalisation, Hon. Pres. 1976–; Admin. Sociedad hispano-francesa de energía nuclear; Pres. Société française des électriciens 1948, Soc. des ingénieurs civils de France 1957; fmr. Vice-Pres. Comité technique de l'électricité; Commdr. Légion d'honneur. *Publications:* Ed. Essai de théorie de la normalisation eyrolles 1982; Dimensional Standardisation 1985, Dimensional Standardisation and Modular Coordination 1986. *Address:* 12 place des Etats-Unis, 75116 Paris (Office); 34 rue des Vignes, 75016, Paris, France (Home).

AINI, Mohsen Ahmed al-; Yemeni politician and diplomatist; b. 20 Oct. 1932, Bani Bahloul, N. Yemen; m. Aziza Abulahom 1962; two s. two d.; ed. Faculty of Law, Cairo Univ. and the Sorbonne, Paris; school-teacher, Aden 1958–60; Int. Confederation of Arab Trade Unions 1960–62; Minister of Foreign Affairs, Yemeni Repub. Sept.–Dec. 1962, 1974–80; Perm. Rep. to UN 1962–65, 1965–66, 1967–69; Minister of Foreign Affairs May–July 1965; Prime Minister Nov.–Dec. 1967, 1974–80; Amb. to U.S.S.R. 1968–70; Prime Minister, Minister of Foreign Affairs Feb. 1970–Feb. 1971, Sept. 1971–Dec. 1972, June 1974–Jan. 1975; Amb. to France Aug.–Sept. 1971, 1975–76, to U.K. 1973–74, to Fed. Repub. of Germany 1981–84, to U.S.A. 1984–; Perm. Rep. to UN 1980–81. *Address:* Embassy of the Yemen Arab Republic, 600 New Hampshire Avenue, N.W. Washington D.C. 20037, U.S.A.

AINO, Koichiro; Japanese politician; b. 1928; former Vice-Minister of Foreign Affairs; Minister of State and Dir.-Gen. of the Econ. Planning Agency Jan. 1989–. *Address:* 3-1, Kasumigaseki, Chiyoda-ku, Tokyo, Japan. *Telephone:* (3) 581 0261.

AIPA, Rt. Rev. Benson Nathaniel; Malawi ecclesiastic; b. 27 May 1937, Malindi Mangochi; s. of Ernest Aipa and Maria Aipa; m. Mtendere Chiwaya 1964; five s. three d.; ed. Zomba Secondary School, St. Michael's Coll., St. John's Seminary, Lusaka, West Hill Coll., Birmingham and Ecumenical Inst. Geneva; tutor, Chilema 1969-74; Vicar-Gen. 1974; Archdeacon of Mangochi West 1978-80, of Blantyre 1985-87; Vicar-Gen. 1986-87; Canon 1986; Bishop of S. Malawi 1987-. *Leisure interests:* football, athletics, gardening. *Address:* Diocese of S. Malawi, P.O. Chilema, Zomba, Malawi.

AIREY, Sir Lawrence, K.C.B., M.A.; British government administrator; b. 10 March 1926, Co. Durham; s. of Lawrence Clark Airey and Isabella Marshall Airey (née Pearson); m. Patricia Anne Williams 1953; two s. one d.; ed. Newcastle Royal Grammar School, Peterhouse, Cambridge, Nuffield Coll., Oxford; entered Civil Service 1949; Gen. Register Office 1949-56; Cabinet Office 1956-58; with H.M. Treasury 1958-80; Under-Sec. 1969-73, Deputy Sec. 1973-77; Second Perm. Sec. (Domestic Econ.) H.M. Treasury 1977; Chair. Bd. of Inland Revenue 1980-86; non-exec. Dir. Standard Life Assurance Co. 1987-, Deputy Chair. 1988-; Consultant Drivers Jonas Partners 1986-; Research Fellow, Nuffield Coll., Oxford, 1961-62; mem. Bd. British Nat. Oil Corpn. 1976-77. *Leisure interest:* book collecting. *Address:* Lions House, Berwick-upon-Tweed, Northumberland, England.

AIRLIE, 13th Earl of, **David George Patrick Coke Ogilvy,** K.T., G.C.V.O., P.C., D.L.; British business executive; b. 17 May 1926, London; s. of 12th Earl of Airlie, K.T., G.C.V.O., M.C., and Lady Alexandra Marie Bridget Coke; m. Virginia Fortune Ryan 1952; three s. three d.; ed. Eton Coll.; Chair. Schroders PLC. 1977-84, Ashdown Investment Trust Ltd. 1968-84, J. Henry Schroder Bank AG (Switzerland) 1977-84; Chair. Gen. Accident Fire and Life Assurance Corpn. PLC 1987-; Dir. J. Henry Schroder Wagg & Co. Ltd. 1961-84, Schroder, Darling and Co. Holdings Ltd. (Australia) 1977-84, Schroders Inc. (U.S.A.) 1977-84, Schroder Int. Ltd. 1973-84, Scottish & Newcastle Breweries PLC 1969-83; Dir. Royal Bank of Scotland Group PLC 1983-; Lord Chamberlain of the Queen's Household 1984-; Gov. Nuffield Hosps. *Address:* 5 Swan Walk, London, SW3 4JJ; Lord Chamberlain's Office, Buckingham Palace, London, S.W.1; Cortachy Castle, by Kirriemuir, Angus, Scotland. *Telephone:* 01-930 4832.

AISIN GHIORROH PUJIE, Chinese politician; b. 1907, Beijing; younger brother of Aisin Ghirroh Pu Yi, China's last emperor of Qing dynasty, who reigned in 1908-11; m. Iroko Sage; two d.; convicted of war crimes and jailed 1945-59; released from prison 1959; Deputy, 5th NPC 1978-83; mem. Chinese friendship del. to Japan 1980; Deputy, 6th NPC 1983-88; mem. Standing Cttee. 6th NPC 1983-88; Vice-Pres. Soc. for Sino-Japanese Relations 1984-; Advisor, Assen. for Int. Friendly Contacts 1984-; Deputy, 7th NPC 1988-; mem. Standing Cttee. 7th NPC 1988-. *Address:* Standing Committee, National People's Congress, Tian An Men Square, Beijing, People's Republic of China.

AITCHISON, Craigie, A.R.A.M.; British artist; b. 13 Jan. 1926, Scotland; s. of the late Rt. Hon. Lord Aitchison and of Lady Aitchison; ed. Slade School of Fine Art, London; British Council/Italian Govt. Scholarship for Painting 1955; Edwin Austin Abbey Premier Scholarship 1970; Arts Council Bursary 1976; one-man exhbns. at Beaux Arts Gallery, Marlborough Fine Art, Rutland Gallery, Serpentine Gallery, 12 Duke Street Gallery and others, London, Compass Gallery, Glasgow, Scottish Arts Council, Edin., Kettle's Yard, Cambridge, Artis, Monte Carlo and others; many mixed exhbns. in U.K., Italy, Japan, France and India; works in public collections including Tate Gallery, Arts Council of G.B., Contemporary Art Soc., London, Scottish Nat. Gallery of Modern Art, Scottish Arts Council, Walker Art Gallery, Liverpool and Newcastle Region Art Gallery, N.S.W., Australia; Prizewinner John Moores Liverpool Exhbn. 1974-75; Johnson's Wax Award for Best Painting at R.A. Summer Exhbn. 1982. *Address:* 32 St. Mary's Gardens, London, S.E.11, England. *Telephone:* 01-582 3708.

AITKEN, Donald Hector, I.S.O., B.E.; Australian civil engineer; b. 8 Jan. 1925, Perth; s. of Hector G. and Ivy F. Aitken; m. Margaret E. Wiseman 1954; three s. one d.; ed. Guildford Grammar School and Univ. of W. Australia; civil eng. Main Roads Dept. of W. Australia 1946-57, Sr. Div. Eng. 1957-64, Chief Eng. 1964, Commr. of Main Roads 1965-67; Pro-Chancellor, Univ. of W. Australia 1975-81, Chancellor 1981-; Dir. Western Mining Corpn. 1987; Hon. Fellow, Inst. of Engs., Australia; Hon. mem. The Road Eng. Assen. of Asia and Australasia; Fellow Australian Acad. of Technological Sciences and Eng.; Companion of Imperial Services Order, Queen's Jubilee Medal 1977 and other awards. *Publications:* numerous technical papers for major int. confs. and eng. publs. *Leisure interests:* golf, theatre, music. *Address:* Main Roads Department, Waterloo Crescent, East Perth 6000, Western Australia (Office); 34 Glengarriff Drive, Floreat Park 6014, Western Australia (Home). *Telephone:* (09) 387 3163 (Home).

AITKEN, Martin Jim, D.PHIL., F.R.S.; British physicist; b. 11 March 1922, Stamford, Lincs.; s. of Percy Aitken and Ethel Brittain; m. Joan Killick; `one s. four d.; ed. Stamford School, Lincs., Wadham Coll., Oxford; war service as Radar Officer, R.A.F., Far East 1942-46; Research in Nuclear Physics, Clarendon Lab., Oxford 1949-56; Deputy Dir., Research Lab. for Archaeology and the History of Art, Oxford Univ. 1957-; Prof. of Archaeometry, Oxford Univ. 1985-; Fellow of Linacre Coll., Oxford 1965-, Soc. of Antiquaries 1962-. *Publications:* Physics and Archaeology 1961, Archaeological Involvements of Physics (in Physics Reports, Vol. 40C) 1978, Thermoluminescence Dating 1985, Science-based Dating in Archae-

ology 1989. *Leisure interest:* sailing-dinghy racing. *Address:* White Cottage, Islip, Oxford, OX5 2SY, England. *Telephone:* (08675) 3377.

AITKEN, Sir Robert Stevenson, M.D., D.PHIL., F.R.C.P., F.R.C.P.E., F.R.A.C.P.; British physician; b. 16 April 1901, Wyndham, N.Z.; m. Margaret G. Kane 1929; one s. two d.; ed. N.Z. schools, Univs. of Otago and Oxford; London Hosp. 1926-34; Reader in Medicine, British Postgraduate Medical School, Univ. of London 1935-38; Regius Prof. of Medicine Univ. of Aberdeen 1939-48; Vice-Chancellor, Univ. of Otago, N.Z. 1948-53; Vice-Chancellor Univ. of Birmingham 1953-68; Deputy Chair. Univ. Grants Cttee. 1968-73; Chair. Birmingham Repertory Theatre 1961-74; Hon. LL.D. (Dalhousie, Melbourne, Panjab, McGill, Pennsylvania, Aberdeen, Newfoundland, Leicester, Birmingham, Otago), Hon. D.C.L. (Oxon.), Hon. D.Sc. (Sydney, Liverpool). *Address:* 6 Hintlesham Avenue, Birmingham B15 2PH, England.

AITMATOV, Chingiz Torekulovich; Soviet writer; b. 12 Dec. 1928, Sheker Village, Kirghizia; s. of Torokul Aitmatov and Nagima Aitmatov; m. Maria Urmatova 1974; three s. one d.; ed. Kirghiz Agricultural Inst.; writer 1952-; fmrly. Corresp. for Pravda; mem. CPSU 1959-; First Sec. of Cinema Union of Kirghiz S.S.R. 1964-69, Chair. 1969-86; Chair. of Union of Writers of Kirghiz S.S.R. 1986-; Cand. mem. Cen. Cttee. of CP of Kirghiz S.S.R. 1969-71, mem. 1971-; People's Writer of Kirghiz S.S.R. 1968; Vice-Chair. Cttee. of Solidarity with Peoples of Asian and African Countries; mem. Comm. for Foreign Affairs of Soviet of Nationalities, U.S.S.R. Supreme Soviet 1974-; Deputy to U.S.S.R. Supreme Soviet; mem. European Academy of Arts, Science and Humanity 1983, World Academy of Art and Science 1987; Chair. Issyk-Kul Forum 1986-; Order of Red Banner of Labour (twice); Lenin Prize for Tales of the Hills and the Steppes 1963; State prizewinner 1968, Hero of Socialist Labour 1978, State Prize in Literature 1983. *Publications include:* stories: Face to Face, Short Stories, Melody 1961, Tales of the Hills and the Steppes 1963; Stories 1967; novels: Djamilya 1959, My Poplar in a Red Kerchief 1960, Camel's Eye, The First Teacher, Farewell Gulsary, Masher's Field 1963, The White Steamship (English trans. 1972), The Lament of the Migrating Bird (English trans. 1972), The Ascent of Mount Fuji (with Muhamegjanov) 1973, co-author of Earth and Water 1978, Works (3 vols.) 1978, Early Storks 1979, Stories 1979, Piebald Dog, Running Along the Sea Shore, The Day Lasts More Than a Hundred Years 1980, Executioner's block (English trans. 1987) 1986, The Place of the Skull. *Leisure interest:* skiing. *Address:* Union of Writers of Kirghiz S.S.R., Ulitsa Pervomajskaja 59, Frunze, U.S.S.R. (Office); Ulitsa Toktogula 98, Frunze, U.S.S.R. (Home).

AJMANI, Jagdish Chand, B.A.; Indian diplomatist; b. 4 April 1930, Shimla; s. of the late Dip Chand and Radha Ajmani; m. Asha Ajmani 1955; two s. two d.; ed. Modern School and MB Higher Secondary School, Delhi, St. Stephen's Coll., Delhi Univ. and Brasenose Coll., Oxford; joined Foreign service 1952; Third Sec. and Second Sec., Cairo 1955-57; Official Sec., Canberra 1957-60; First Sec., Baghdad 1960-63; Dir., Ministry of External Affairs 1963-67; Counsellor Tokyo 1967-69; attended Nat. Defence Coll., New Delhi 1970; Consul-Gen., Berlin and later Amb. to German Democratic Repub. 1974-77, to Fed. Repub. of Germany 1986-; High Commr. in Australia 1977-80; Amb. to Italy 1980-84; Perm. Rep. to FAO 1980-84. *Leisure interests:* golf, yoga. *Address:* Indian Embassy, 5300 Bonn 1, Adenauerallee 262-264, Federal Republic of Germany.

AJOSE-ADEOGUN, Mobolaji, J.P., F.C.I.S.; Nigerian government official and fmr. petroleum executive; b. 12 May 1927, Lagos; ed. C.M.S. Grammar School, Lagos, Univ. Coll. and S.O.A.S., Univ. of London; Barclays Bank, D.C.O., Lagos 1947-50; Transport Man., General Motors Ltd., Leyton, London 1954; Higher Clerical Officer, Hackney Borough Council, London 1955; joined Shell Nigeria Ltd. 1955, Dir. 1971-75, Admin. Man. 1971-75; Fed. Commr. for Co-operatives and Supply 1975-76; Fed. Commr. on Special Duty, Chair. Fed. Capital Devt. Authority March 1976-79; J.P., Lagos State 1975; mem. Inst. of Personnel Man., London, Inst. of Public Relations, London, Nigerian Inst. of Man. 1966, Nigerian Inst. of Int. Affairs 1967. *Address:* c/o Federal Capital Development Authority, Lagos, Nigeria.

AKAMA, Yoshihiro; Japanese banker; b. 2 Dec. 1916, Tokyo; s. of Nobuyoshi and Midori (Nannichi) Akama; m. Hiroko Nitta 1945; one s. three d.; ed. Tokyo Univ.; Man. Dir. Mitsubishi Trust & Banking Corpn. 1965-69, Sr. Man. Dir. 1969-70, Deputy Pres. 1970-71, Pres. 1971-78, Chair. 1978-82, Counsellor 1982-; Blue Ribbon Medal 1977. *Leisure interests:* Igo, fishing. *Address:* Mitsubishi Trust & Banking Corporation, 4-5, Marunouchi 1-chome, Chiyoda-ku, Tokyo 100 (Office); 4-15-22 Komagome Toshima-ku, Tokyo, Japan (Home). *Telephone:* 03-917-5755.

AKASHI, Toshio; Japanese banker; b. 24 Aug. 1915, Fukuoka Prefecture; m.; two s. one d.; ed. Tokyo Univ.; joined Sanwa Bank 1942, Chief Sec. 1958, Gen. Man. of Shimbashi Branch 1960, of Tokyo Govt. and Municipal Business Dept. 1962, of Tokyo Business Promotion Dept. 1963, of Fukuoka Branch 1964, of Personnel Dept. 1966, Dir. 1967, Man. Dir. 1968, Senior Man. Dir. 1972, Deputy Pres. 1973, Pres. Sanwa Bank 1976-83. *Leisure interests:* reading, golf. *Address:* c/o Sanwa Bank Ltd., 4-10, Fushimi-cho, Higashi-ku, Osaka, Japan.

AKASHI, Yasushi; Japanese diplomatist; b. 19 Jan. 1931, Akita; m.; two c.; ed. Univ. of Tokyo, Univ. of Virginia, Fletcher School of Law and

Diplomacy and Columbia Univ.; Political Affairs Officer UN Secr. 1957-74; Chair. Univ. Seminar on Modern East Asia 1963-64; Amb. at Perm. Mission to UN, New York 1974-79; UN Under-Sec.-Gen. for Public Information 1979-87, for Disarmament Affairs 1987-; has represented Japan in Gen. Ass. and numerous UN confs. and organs; Chair. Budget and Finance Cttee. Governing Council UNDP 1978; mem. Advisory Cttee. on Admin. and Budgetary Questions 1974, 1977; Assoc. Columbia Univ. Seminars, Chair. Conf. of Mid-Career Asian Leaders on Devt. 1967; Dir. Int. Peace Acad., Better World Soc.; Sec. Founding Cttee. UN Univ.; fmr. Visiting Lecturer Univ. of Tokyo, Int. Christian Univ., Tokyo and Sophia Univ. *Publications:* The United Nations 1965, From the Windows of the United Nations 1984, The Lights and Shadows of the United Nations 1985, and numerous articles. *Address:* United Nations Plaza, New York, N.Y. 10017, U.S.A. *Telephone:* (212) 963 1234.

AKATANI, Genichi; Japanese United Nations official; b. 29 Sept. 1917, Taipei; ed. Univ. of Oxford and Sophia Univ., Tokyo; joined Japanese Foreign Service 1945; Second Sec., Paris 1954, First Sec. 1955; Head, East-West Trade Div., Econ. Affairs Bureau, Ministry of Foreign Affairs 1958; Counsellor, Washington, D.C. 1961-66; Counsellor, Public Information Bureau, Ministry of Foreign Affairs 1966-72; Amb. at Large, Ministry of Foreign Affairs 1972; Asst. Sec.-Gen. for Public Information, UN 1972-77, Under Sec.-Gen. 1978-79; del. to several sessions of UN Gen. Ass. *Address:* c/o Ministry of Foreign Affairs, 2-2-1 Kasumigaseki, Chiyoda-ku, Tokyo, Japan.

AKBULUT, Yildirim; Turkish politician; b. 1935, Erzincan; m.; three c.; ed. Univ. of Istanbul; fmr. practising lawyer; Deputy for Erzincan 1983-; mem. Motherland Party; fmr. Deputy Speaker of Parl., Speaker Dec. 1987-; Minister of Interior 1986-87. *Address:* The National Assembly, Ankara, Turkey.

AKE, Siméon; Ivory Coast lawyer and diplomatist; b. 4 Jan. 1932, Binger-ville; m. Aune Maud Bonful, 1958; five c.; ed. Univs. of Dakar and Grenoble; Chef de Cabinet to Minister of Public Service, Ivory Coast 1959-61; First Counsellor, Ivory Coast Mission to UN 1961-63; Dir. of Protocol, Ministry of Foreign Affairs 1963-64; Amb. to U.K., Sweden, Denmark and Norway 1964-66; Perm. Rep. of Ivory Coast to UN 1966-77; Minister of Foreign Affairs July 1977-; mem. Guiding Cttee., Parti démocratique de la Côte d'Ivoire (PDCI-RDA) Oct. 1975-; Commdr. ordre Nat. de la République de la Côte d'Ivoire, de l'ordre de St. Grégoire; Grand Officer, Légion d'honneur; distinctions from Belgium, Brazil, Spain, Cameroun. *Address:* 01 Boite Postale V. 109, Abidjan, Ivory Coast. *Telephone:* 225-320888.

AKENSON, Donald Harman, PH.D., F.R.S.A., F.R.S.C.; Canadian professor of history; ed. Yale Coll. and Harvard Univ.; Allston Burr Sr. Tutor, Dunster House, Harvard Coll. 1966-67; Asst. Prof. of History, Queen's Univ., Kingston, Ont. 1970-74, Prof. 1974-; Guggenheim Fellow 1984-85; Chalmers Prize 1985; Landon Prize 1987 and many other awards and distinctions. *Publications:* The Irish Education Experiment 1970, The Church of Ireland: Ecclesiastical Reform and Revolution 1800-1885 1971, Education and Enmity: The Control of Schooling in Northern Ireland 1920-50 1973, The United States and Ireland 1973, A Mirror to Kathleen's Face: Education in Independent Ireland 1922-60 1975, Local Poets and Social History: James Orr, Bard of Ballycarry 1977, Between Two Revolutions: Island-magee, Co. Antrim 1798-1920 1979, A Protestant in Purgatory: Richard Whately: Archbishop of Dublin 1981, The Irish in Ontario: A Study of Rural History 1984, Being Had: Historians, Evidence and the Irish in North America 1985. Novels: The Lazar House Notebooks 1981, Brotherhood Week in Belfast 1984, The Orangeman: The Life and Times of Ogle Gowan 1986, The Edgerston Audit 1987; occasional papers and reviews. *Address:* Department of History, Queen's University, Kingston, Ont., K7L 3N6, Canada.

ÅKERMAN, Johan, M.B.A.; Swedish business executive; b. 19 Sept. 1925, Lund; s. of Prof. Gustaf Åkerman and Anna-Lisa Ekelund; m. Gunilla Bergenstråhle 1953 (divorced 1975); one s. two d.; ed. Stockholm School of Econs. and Univ. of California; with Stockholms Enskilda Bank, Stockholm 1947, World Bank (IBRD), Washington 1953, Electro-Invest 1955; joined the Grängesberg Co. (now Gränges A.B.) 1960, Pres. 1971-77. *Leisure interests:* skiing, skating, sailing, golf. *Address:* Urdavagen 14, 18264 Djurskolm, Sweden.

ÅKERMAN, (Knut Lennart) Alf, M.S.; Swedish business executive; b. 24 Feb. 1923, Lund; s. of Åke Åkerman and Hildur Åkerman (née Sonesson); m. Gun Widding 1953; three s. one d.; ed. Massachusetts Inst. of Tech., U.S.A.; Head Research and Devt. Dept., Reymersholms Gamla Ind. AB 1956-58; Head Tech. and Devt. Dept. AB Marabou 1959-61, Deputy Man. Dir. 1961-67; Man. Dir. Skandinaviska Banken, Stockholm 1968-71; Man. Dir. Skandinaviska Enskilda Banken, Gothenburg 1972-84; Chair. Trygg Hansa Ins. (mem. 1972-) 1985-, Perstorp AB 1974-, AB Catena 1984-, Victor Hasselblad AB 1979-, BASF Svenska AB 1981-, Svenska BP AB 1984-, Scandinavian Heart Center 1983-, SSPA Maritime Consulting AB 1984-, Safe Offshore AB 1985, Findus AB, Databolin AB, STUF-Eng. Research Council of STU; mem. Bd. of Dirs. AB SKF, AB Papyrus, Nordstjernan AB, Gadelius AB, KabiVitrum AB, Volvo Finance S.A., Geneva, Johnson Line AB; mem. and Deputy Chair. Royal Swedish Acad. of Eng. Sciences; mem. Bd. Fed. of Swedish Industries, World Wildlife Fund etc.; Kt. Commdr. Royal Order of Wasa; Hon. D.Eng. (Chalmers

Univ. of Tech., Gothenburg) 1985. *Leisure interests:* biochemistry, wildlife, archaeology, music. *Address:* Skandinaviska Enskilda Banken, S 405 04 Göteborg (Office); Södra Box 76, S 43041 Kullavik, Sweden (Home). *Telephone:* 031-62 22 05 (Office); 031-93 16 74 (Home).

AKERS, John Fellows, B.S.; American business executive; b. 28 Dec 1934, Boston, Mass.; s. of Kenneth Fellows and Mary Joan (Reed) Akers; m. Susan Davis 1960; one s. two d.; ed. Yale Univ.; served U.S.N.R. 1956-60; joined IBM Corpn. as a Sales Trainee 1960, Vice-Pres., Asst. Group Exec. 1976-78, Vice-Pres., Group Exec. 1978-82, Sr. Vice-Pres., Group Exec. 1982-83; Pres. 1983-, C.E.O. 1984-, Chair. 1986-; mem. Bd. New York Times Co.; Co-Chair. of Business Round Table; mem. Bd. of Trustees Calif. Inst. of Tech., Metropolitan Museum of Art; mem. Advisory Bd. Yale School of Org. and Man.; mem. Bd. of Govs. United Way of America. *Address:* IBM Corporation, Old Orchard Road, Armonk, N.Y. 10504, U.S.A.

AKERS-JONES, Sir David, K.B.E., C.M.G., M.A.; British civil servant; b. 14 April 1927; s. of Walter George Jones and Dorothy Jones; m. Jane Spickernell 1951; one s. (deceased) one d.; ed. Worthing High School and Brasenose Coll. Oxford; with British India Steam Navigation Co. 1945-49; Malayan Civil Service 1954-57; Hong Kong Civil Service 1957-, Sec. for New Territories and for District Admin., Hong Kong Govt. 1973-85, Chief Sec. 1985-86; Acting Gov. Hong Kong 1986-87; Chair. Hong Kong Housing Authority 1988-; Vice-Pres. Hong Kong Football Asscn. 1967-. *Leisure interests:* painting, gardening, walking and music. *Address:* Dragonview, Lot 93 DD399, Castle Peak Road, Hong Kong.

AKERT, Konrad, M.D.; Swiss professor of physiology; b. 21 May 1919, Zürich; m. Ruth Giger, 1947; three s. one d.; ed. Literarygymnasium Zürich, Medical School of the Univ. of Zürich; Instructor of Physiology at Johns Hopkins Univ., Baltimore, U.S.A. 1952; Asst. Prof. of Physiology, Univ. of Wisconsin, Madison 1953, Assoc. Prof. of Physiology 1955, Prof. of Anatomy and Physiology 1960; Prof. of Neurophysiology and Dir. of Brain Research Inst., Univ. of Zürich 1961-83, Dean of Faculty of Medicine 1974-76, Dir. of Physiology and Brain Research Insts. 1979-83, Rector 1984-; Founder and Ed.-in-Chief of journal Brain Research 1966-76; Robert Bing Prize 1960, Otto Naegeli Prize 1969; Dr. h.c. (Geneva) 1976; Hon. Research prof. (Academia Sinica Peking) 1980. *Publications:* about 340 scientific publications. *Leisure interests:* history, politics, mountaineering. *Address:* University of Zürich, Kunstlergasse 1, CH-8001, Zürich; Bächtold-strasse 1, CH-8044, Zürich, Switzerland. *Telephone:* 1/257 2218 (Office); 1/47 40 44 (Home).

AKHMADULINA, Bella Akhatovna; Soviet poet; b. 10 April 1937, Moscow; d. of Ahat and Nadya (née Lazareva) Akhmadulin; m. 1st Yevgeniy Yevtushenko (q.v.) 1960; m. 2nd Yuriy Nagibin; m. 3rd Boris Messerer 1974; ed. Gorky Inst. of Literature; Hon. mem. American Acad. of Arts and Letters 1977. *Poems include:* The String 1962, The Rain 1963, My Ancestry 1964, Summer Leaves 1968, The Lessons of Music 1969, Fever and Other New Poems (trans. into English) 1970, Tenerezza 1971, The Rain 1974, Poems 1975, The Dreams about Georgia 1977, The Candle 1978, The Snowstorm 1978, Dreams of Georgia 1979 and translations from Georgian. *Address:* U.S.S.R. Union of Writers, Ulitsa Vorovskogo 20, Moscow G-69, U.S.S.R.

AKHMEDOV, Fikrat Gamidovich; Soviet official; cand. mem. Cen. Cttee. of Azerbaidzhan CP 1971-76, mem. 1976-; Head of Dept. of Science and Educational Insts. Cen. Cttee. of Azerbaidzhan CP 1976-80; Deputy Chair. Council of Ministers, Azerbaidzhan S.S.R, 1980-. *Address:* Council of Ministers, Baku, Azerbaidzhan S.S.R., U.S.S.R.

AKHROMEYEV, Marshal Sergey Fyodorovich; Soviet army officer; b. 1923; ed. Mil. Acad. of Tank Troops and Mil. Acad. of Gen. Staff; mem. CPSU 1943-; entered Soviet Army 1940, command posts at the front 1941-45; Regt. Commdr., then Div. Commdr. 1946-64; command posts 1964-72; Head of a Section in U.S.S.R. Ministry of Defence 1974-79; First Deputy Chief of Gen. Staff of U.S.S.R. Armed Forces 1979-84, Chief of Staff 1984-88; cand. mem. Cen. Cttee., CPSU 1981-. Lenin Prize. *Address:* c/o Ministry of Defence, 34 Naberezhnaya M. Thoreza, Moscow, U.S.S.R.

AKHTAR, Muhammad, M.SC., PH.D., F.R.S.; British/Pakistani professor of biochemistry; b. 23 Feb. 1933, Punjab, India; s. of Muhammad Azeem Chaudhry; m. Monika E. Schürmann 1963; two s.; ed. Univ. of Punjab and Imperial Coll., London; research scientist, Research Inst. for Medicine and Chem., Cambridge, Mass. 1959-63; Lecturer in Biochem. Univ. of Southampton 1963-66, Sr. Lecturer 1966-68, Reader 1968-73, Prof. 1973-, Head Dept. of Biochem. 1978-, Chair. School of Biochemical and Physiological Sciences 1983-87; Founding Fellow Third World Acad. of Sciences; mem. Council Royal Soc. 1983-85; Biochemical Soc. Cttee. 1983-86; Sitara-I-Imtiaz (Pakistan). *Publications:* numerous articles in biochemical and chemical journals. *Address:* Department of Biochemistry, University of Southampton, Bassett Crescent East, Southampton, SO9 3TU (Office).

AKHUND, Iqbal Ahmad; Pakistani diplomatist; b. 1924, Hyderabad, Sind; s. of Abdullah Shaffimohammed and Maryam Shaikh; m. Yolanda Gombert 1955; three s. one d.; ed. Bombay Univ.; served in diplomatic missions in Canada, Spain, Netherlands, Saudi Arabia, Malaysia and the Perm. Mission to the UN in New York 1949-56; Private Sec. to the Foreign Minister 1956-58; Dir. Foreign Office 1964-66, Dir.-Gen. 1966-68; Amb. to Egypt 1968-71; Amb. to Yugoslavia 1971-72; Perm. Rep. to the UN 1972-78;

Vice-Pres. UN Econ. and Social Council 1974, Pres. 1975; Chair. Ad Hoc Cttee. on Sanctions against Rhodesia 1976; Pres. UN Security Council 1976; Chair. "Group of 77" 1976–77; Vice-Pres. Cttee. of the Whole July 1978; mem. Inter-Governmental group of Experts on Devt. and Disarmament; mem. Int. Cttee. of Inst. on Man and Science; Amb. to France (also accred. to Ireland) 1978–80; UN Resident Co-ordinator and Special Rep. of Sec.-Gen. in Lebanon 1979–84; Asst. Sec.-Gen. UN Centre Against Apartheid 1984–86; Special Adviser, Aspen Inst. for Humanistic Studies; founding assoc. John J. MacCloy Int. Center, New York. *Leisure interests:* reading, music, golf, photography. *Address:* c/o United Nations, New York, N.Y. 10017, U.S.A.

AKI, Keiiti, PH.D.; American academic; b. 3 March 1930, Yokohama, Japan; s. of Koichi Aki and Fumiko Kojima; m. Haruko Uyeda 1956; two s.; ed. Univ. of Tokyo, Geophysical Inst.; Research Fellow, Calif. Inst. of Tech., U.S.A. 1958–60; Research Fellow and Assoc. Prof., Univ. of Tokyo 1960–66; Prof. of Geophysics, M.I.T. 1966–84, R. R. Schrock Prof. of Earth and Planetary Sciences 1982–84; W. M. Keck Foundation Prof. of Geological Sciences, Univ. of Southern Calif., U.S.A. 1984–; Distinguished Visiting Prof., Univ. of Alaska 1981–; Fellow A.A.A.S.; mem. N.A.S.; medal of the Seismological Society of America 1987; Hon. Foreign Fellow European Union of Geosciences 1987. *Publications:* (Co-author) Quantitative Seismology (Vol. I and II) 1980, Orogeny 1983. *Leisure interests:* swimming, skiing, sailing, surfing. *Address:* Department of Geological Sciences, University of Southern California, Los Angeles, Calif. 90089-0741, U.S.A. *Telephone:* (213) 743-3510.

AKILANDAM, Perungalur Vaithialingam (pseudonym Akilon); Indian Tamil writer; b. 27 June 1922, Perungalur; s. of M. Vaithialingam and V. Amirdhammal; ed. Maharaja's Coll., Pudukkottai; writer 1940–; in Indian Post & Telegraph Dept. 1945–58; freelance writer 1958–; Sec. Tamil Writers' Assen., Tiruchy 1953–57; Sec.-Gen. Fed. of All-India Tamil Writers 1962– (Vice-Pres. 1977–); Dir. Tamil Writers' Co-op. Soc. 1963–; mem. Tamil Advisory Bd., Sahitya Akademi 1964–; Producer, Spoken Word in Tamil, All-India Radio, Madras 1965–; Pres. Tamil Writers' Assen. 1967 (Vice-Pres. 1977–); Kalai Majai Prize for Penn 1946, Tamil Akademi Award for Nenjin Alaigai 1953, Sahitya Akademi Award for Vengaiyin Maindan 1963, Tamilnadu Govt. Award for Kayalvizhi 1968, for Erimalai 1973, Nehru Award for Soviet Land 1978. *Publications include:* novels: Penn 1946, Snehithi 1950, Nenjin Alaigai 1953, Pavai Vilakku 1958, Vengaiyin Maindan 1961, Ponmalar 1964, Kayalvizhi 1964, Chittirap Paavai 1967; short stories: Sakthival 1947, Nilavinilay 1950, Vazhi Pirandhadu 1952, Sahodarar Andro? 1963, Nellore Arisi 1967, Erimalai 1971. *Leisure interests:* reading and short travels. *Address:* 13 Kustian Beach Street, Santhome, Madras 600004, India. *Telephone:* 751173.

AKIMAN, Nazmi; Turkish diplomatist; b. 1929; m. İleri Zarbun 1957; two s.; ed. Istanbul and Columbia Univs.; joined Turkish Ministry of Foreign Affairs 1957; First Sec. Turkish Mission to UN, New York 1959–64; Chief of Cabinet, Ankara 1964–66; Counsellor, Turkish Mission to NATO 1966–70; Deputy Sec.-Gen. CENTO, Ankara 1970–74; Deputy Perm. Rep. to UN 1975–80; Amb. to Cuba 1980–81, to Greece 1984–; decorations from Spain, Iran and Saudi Arabia. *Publication:* Yeni Eylüller (poems) *Address:* Turkish Embassy, 8 King George II Street, 106 74 Athens, Greece.

AKINKUGBE, Oladipo Olujimi, M.D., D.PHIL., D.T.M. & H., F.R.C.P.; Nigerian professor of medicine; b. 17 July 1933, Ondo; s. of Chief Odofin David Akinkugbe and Chief (Mrs.) Grace Akinkugbe; m. Dr. Folasade Dina 1965; two s.; ed. Govt. Coll., Ibadan, Univ. Coll., Ibadan, Univs. of London, Liverpool and Oxford; Lecturer in Medicine, Univ. of Ibadan 1964–66, Sr. Lecturer 1966–68, Prof. 1968, Dean of Medicine 1970–74, Chair. of Cttee. of Deans 1972–74, mem. Council 1971–74; Visiting Prof. Medicine, Harvard Univ. 1974–75; Principal, Univ. Coll., Ilorin 1975–77; Vice-Chancellor Univ. of Ilorin 1977–78, Ahmadu Bello Univ. 1978–79; Pro-Chancellor and Chair. Council, Port Harcourt Univ. 1986–; Pres. Nigerian Assen. of Nephrology 1987–89; mem. Scientific Advisory Panel CIBA Foundation, Council of Int Soc. of Hypertension, WHO Expert Cttees. on Cardiovascular Diseases, Smoking Control, Professional and Tech. Educ. of Medical and Auxiliary Personnel, Sr. Consultant 1983–84; Visiting Fellow, Balliol Coll., Oxford 1981–82; Commdr. Noble Order of the Niger 1979, Officier, ordre Nat. de la République de Côte d'Ivoire; Hon. D.Sc. (Ilorin) 1982, Fellow Nigerian Acad. of Science. *Publications:* High Blood Pressure in the African 1972, Priorities in National Health Planning 1974 (Ed.), Hypertension in Africa (Ed.) 1975, Cardiovascular Diseases in Africa (Ed.) 1976, Clinical Medicine in the Tropics—Cardiovascular Disease 1986, many papers on hypertension and renal disease. *Leisure interests:* music, squash, gardening. *Address:* c/o Department of Medicine, University of Ibadan, Ibadan (Office); Summit, Olubadan Aleshinloye Way, Iyaganku, Ibadan, Nigeria (Home).

AKINS, James E.; American diplomatist, writer and lecturer; b. 15 Oct. 1926, Akron, Ohio; s. of Bernice Bixler and Quay Akins; m. Marjorie Abbott 1954; one s. one d.; ed. Akron Univ.; U.S. Navy 1945–46; undertook relief work with non-profit org. 1948–50; taught in Lebanon 1951–52; Asst. Ed. with research org. 1953–54; entered Foreign Service 1954; held numerous diplomatic posts in Paris 1954–55, Strasbourg 1955–56, Damascus 1956–57, Kuwait 1958–60, Baghdad 1961–64; with Secr., Washington, D.C. 1965–67, Dir. Fuels and Energy Office 1968–72; Amb. to Saudi Arabia 1973–75; mem. Council on Foreign Relations, American Archeology Soc.,

Assen. of Political and Social Scientists; Hon. D. Hum. Litt. (Wittenberg) 1979. *Publications:* numerous articles on oil and energy policy and the Middle East. *Leisure interests:* opera, archaeology. *Address:* 2904 Garfield Terrace, Washington, D.C. 20008, U.S.A. *Telephone:* 202-234-9119 (Office); 202-234-9152 (Home).

AKIRA, Yeiri; Japanese business executive; b. 15 April 1928; ed. Univ. of Tokyo; joined Bridgestone Corpn. 1953, Pres. Thailand Operations 1969, Gen. Man. Osaka Br. 1972, Dir. and Gen. Man. 1974, Dir. and Gen. Man. of Corporate Personnel Div. 1975, Man. Dir. Corporate Planning and Personnel Operations 1977, also Gen. Man. Office of Pres. 1978, Sr. Man. Dir. Office of the Pres. and Personnel Operations 1980, Sr. Man. Dir. Tire Sales Operations 1981, also Int. Operations 1982, Exec. Vice-Pres. Bridgestone Corpn. 1984, Pres. 1985–. *Address:* Bridgestone Corporation 10-1 Kyobashi 1-Chome, Chuo-ku, Tokyo 104, Japan.

AKIYA, Einosuke: Japanese religious leader; b. 15 July 1930, Tokyo; s. of late Jubei Akiya and of Yuki Akiya; m. Akiko Ishida 1957; two s.; ed. Waseda Univ.; with Soka Gakkai 1951–, Young Men's Div. Chief 1956–59, Youth Div. Chief 1959–61, Dir. 1961–62, Vice-Gen. Dir. 1962–67, Exec. Dir. 1967–70; Vice-Pres. 1970–81, Pres. 1981–; Gen. Ed. Seikyo Shimbun 1970–75, Rep. Dir. 1975–, Chair. Cen. Council Soka Gakkai 1979–, Gen. Dir. Soka Gakkai Int. 1981–. *Leisure interests:* reading, music. *Address:* Soka Gakkai Headquarters, 32 Shinano-machi, Shinjuku-ku, Tokyo 160 (Office). *Telephone:* 03-353-7111.

AKO, Ernest, C.V., D.S.O.; Ghanaian police official; joined Ghana Police Force 1941, Insp. 1954, Asst. Commr. 1967, Commr. 1973, Insp.-Gen. 1974–78; Commr. for Internal Affairs, Nat. Redemption Council 1974–77; mem. Supreme Mil. Council Oct. 1975–78; Companion of the Order of Ghana. *Address:* c/o Police Headquarters, Accra, Ghana.

AKPORODE CLARK, B.; Nigerian diplomatist; b. 16 April 1934; m. Lillian Clarke; three s. two d.; ed. Govt. Coll., Ughelli and Univ. of Ibadan; Admin. Officer, Public Service of Western Region and served Ministries of Econ. Devt., Health and Social Welfare, Trade, Finance and Establishment, Agric. and Natural Resources, and Office of the Premier 1957–61; First Sec., Ministry of Foreign Affairs 1961; First Sec. and Head of Chancery, Liberia and Guinea 1961–62, India 1962–63; First Sec. in charge of OAU matters, Africa Div., Ministry of Foreign Affairs 1963–64, Head, Africa Div. 1964–65; Counsellor and Head of Chancery, Perm. Mission to UN, New York 1965–69; Under-Sec. on special duties, Ministry of External Affairs Jan.-Dec. 1969, Deputy Perm. Sec. 1970–73, Dir.-Gen. 1981–84; Perm. Rep. to UN at Geneva and Amb. to Switzerland, Austria and Turkey 1973–77; Amb. to Ethiopia 1977–79; Perm. Rep. to UN, New York 1979–81; Regional Rep. for Africa, Office of UN Commr. for Namibia, Zambia 1984–. *Address:* P.O. Box 34550, Lusaka, Zambia.

AKRITIDIS, Nicolaos; Greek politician; b. 1935, Kataha, Pieria Pref.; ed. Univ. of Thessalonika; fmr. lecturer in physics and surveying, Univ. of Thessalonika; helped found Prometheus Tech. School, Thessalonika 1966; joined Pasok 1974; Alderman of Thessalonika 1975; Deputy to Parl. 1977–; Minister for Communications 1981–84, of Commerce 1984–86, Sept. 1987–89. *Address:* c/o Ministry of Commerce, Kanningos Square, Athens, Greece. *Telephone:* 923.3941.

AKSYONOV, Aleksandr Nikiforovich; Soviet politician; b. 1924, Byelorussia; ed. Party Higher School of Cen. Cttee. CPSU; worked on collective farm 1941–42; Soviet Army 1942–43; Prin. of an elementary school 1943–44; Sec. of Chkalov Dist. Komsomol and mem. CPSU 1945–; First Sec. Byelorussian Komsomol 1944–57; mem. Cen. Cttee. Byelorussian CP 1956–; Cand. mem. Politburo 1956–57; Sec. Politburo of Cen. Cttee., Byelorussian Komsomol 1957–60; Minister of the Interior, Byelorussian SSR 1960–62; Minister for Maintenance of Public Order 1962–65; Deputy to U.S.S.R. Supreme Soviet 1966–; First Sec. Vitebsk Dist. Cttee. of Byelorussian CP 1966–71; Second Sec. and mem. Politburo, Cen. Cttee. of Byelorussian CP 1971–78; Chair. Council of Ministers of Byelorussian SSR 1978–82; Amb. to Poland 1982–85; Pres. U.S.S.R. State Cttee. on Radio and Television Broadcasting 1985–; mem. Cen. Cttee. CPSU 1976–. *Address:* State Committee on Radio and Television Broadcasting, Moscow, U.S.S.R.

AKSYONOV, Vasiliy Pavlovich; Soviet writer; b. 20 Aug. 1932, Kazan; s. of Pavel V. Aksyonov and Yevgeniya Ginzburg; m. Kira L. Mendeleva 1957; one s.; ed. Leningrad Medical Inst.; Physician 1956–60, Moscow Tubercular Dispensary 1960–; professional writer 1960–; fmr. mem. Union of Soviet Writers; mem. Editorial Board Yunost. *Publications:* novels: Colleagues 1960, Starry Ticket 1961, 1970, Oranges from Morocco 1963, Time, My Friend, Time 1964, The Empty Barrels 1968, Love of Electricity 1971, My Grandpa is a Monument 1972, The Box Inside Which Something Knocks (children's book) 1976, Our Golden Ironware 1980, The Burn 1980, The Island of Crimea 1981, An Aristopheana 1981, Paper Landscape 1983, The Right to the Island 1983, Say 'Cheese' 1985, In Search of a Genre 1986, In Search of Melancholy Baby 1987; collected stories: Catapult 1964, Half-Way to the Moon 1966, Wish You Were Here 1969; screenplay for films: Colleague, My Young Friend, When They Raise the Bridges, Travelling 1967, The Murmar House 1972; play: On Sale 1965; travel: An Unusual Journey 1963, Twenty-Four Hours Non-Stop 1976, The Steel Bird and Other Stories 1978; joint ed. Metropol 1979, Four Temperaments (comedy)

1979. *Leisure interests:* music, travelling, running. *Address:* c/o Random House Inc., 201 East 50th Street, New York, N.Y. 10022, U.S.A.

AKURGAL, Ekrem, PH.D.; Turkish archaeologist; b. 30 March 1911, Istanbul; ed. Germany; Prof. Univ. of Ankara 1941–81; has conducted excavations at Sinope, Phokaia, Daskyleion, Pitane and Erythrai 1953–, at Izmir 1967–; Visiting Prof., Princeton Univ. 1961–62, W. Berlin 1971–72, Vienna 1980–81; mem. Turkish Historical Soc. (Sec.-Gen. 1951–61), Turkish High Comm. for Ancient Monuments; mem. British, Austrian, Danish, French and Swedish Acads.; Hon. mem. Soc. for Promotion of Hellenic Studies, London, German, Austrian, American Inst. of Archaeology; Dr. h.c. (Bordeaux) 1961; Goethe Medal (Fed. Repub. of Germany) 1979; Grand Prize, Turkish Ministry of Culture 1981. *Publications:* Griechische Reliefs aus Lykien 1942, Remarques stylistiques sur les reliefs de Malatya 1946, Späthethitische Bildkunst 1949, Phrygische Kunst 1955, Die Kunst Anatoliens von Homer bis Alexander 1961, Die Kunst der Hethiter 1961, Orient und Okzident 1966, Treasures of Turkey (with Mango and Ettinghausen) 1966, Urartäische und Altiranische Kunstzentren 1968, The Art and Architecture of Turkey 1981, Alt-Smyrna 1983, Ancient Civilizations and Ruins of Turkey (5th edn.) 1983. *Address:* Türk Tarih, Kurumu Kizilay Sok. 1, Ankara (Office); Cinnah cad. 90/5 çankaya, Ankara, Turkey (Home).

AKWAA', Brig. Mohamed Ali al-; Yemeni army officer; b. 1933, Sana'a; m.; five c.; ed. secondary school, Mil. Coll., Sana'a; participated in the movts. against last three Imams of Yemen, Free Yemenis Revolution 1948, attempted coup 1955, Revolution of 26 Sept. 1962; leading figure in movt. which ousted Pres. al-Sallal 1967; has held several posts in mil. and civil service including Asst. Mil. Commdr. Taiz District, Head Criminal Investigation Dept., Head Nat. Security (Intelligence) Dept.; Chief of Staff, Army Operations, Head S. Yemen Relief Office attached to Presidency; Minister of the Interior 1973–74. *Address:* Bir Al-Azab, Sana'a, Yemen Arab Republic.

AKWEI, Richard Maximilian; Ghanaian diplomatist; b. 27 Nov. 1923, Accra; s. of Richard Mabuo Akwei and Martha Akwei; m. Josephine Akosua Afram 1956; two s. one d.; ed. Achimota Coll., Accra, London Univ. and Christ Church, Oxford; Administration Officer, Ghana Civil Service 1950–56; Ghana Diplomatic Service 1956–; attached to U.K. High Comm., Ottawa 1956–57; First Sec., Washington 1957–60; Dir. W. European and E. European Depts. Ministry of Foreign Affairs, Accra 1960–64; Amb. to Mexico 1964–65; Perm. Rep. to UN, Geneva, and Amb. to Switzerland 1965–67; Perm. Rep. to UN, New York 1967–72; Amb. to People's Repub. of China 1972–76; Sr. Prin. Sec. Ministry of Foreign Affairs 1976–78, Vice-Chair. Int. Civil Service Comm., UN 1978, Acting Chair. 1979, Chair. 1980; Franklin Peace Medal 1970. *Leisure interests:* tennis, music, photography, reading.

ALAIN, Marie-Claire; French organist; b. 10 Aug. 1926, Saint-Germain-en-Laye; d. of Albert and Madeleine (Alberty) Alain; m. Jacques Gommier 1950; one s. one d.; ed. Institut Notre Dame, Sainte-Germain-en-Laye, Conservatoire Nat. Supérieur de Musique, Paris; organ teacher, Conservatoire de Musique de Rueil-Malmaison; Lecturer, Summer Acad. for organists, Haarlem, Netherlands 1956–; numerous concerts throughout world 1955–; lecturer at numerous univs. throughout world; expert on organology to Minister of Culture; Hon. D.Hum.Litt. (Colorado State Univ.); Hon. D.Mus. (Southern Methodist Univ., Dallas); numerous prizes for recordings and performances including Buxtehudepreis (Lübeck, Fed. Repub. of Germany); Prix Léonie Sonning, Copenhagen: Prix Franz Liszt, Budapest; Officier Légion d'Honneur, Ordre du Mérite, Arts et Lettres. *Recordings:* over 200 records, including complete works of J. Alain, C. P. E. Bach, J. S. Bach, C. Balbastre, G. Böhm, N. Bruhns, D. Buxtehude, L. N. Clérambault, F. Couperin, L. C. Daquin, C. Frank, N. de Grigny, J. A. Guilain, G. F. Handel, J. Haydn, F. Mendelssohn, A. Vivaldi, etc. *Address:* 1 ave. Jean-Jaurès, 78580 Maule, France.

ALAMI, Sa'd Eddin, B.A.; Jordanian religious leader; b. 1911, Jerusalem; s. of Jalal Eddin and Fatmeh Alami; m. 1st Ismat Nuseibeh 1937 (died 1983), 2nd Nuzhah Khalidy 1985; three s. four d.; ed. Fraires Coll. Jerusalem and Azhar Univ. Cairo; teacher, Dar el-Ulum, Jaffa 1932, Orphanage School, Jerusalem 1935–36; Chief Cleric, Shari'ah Courts 1937–45; Qadi in Tiberias 1946–47, in Nazareth 1948, in Ramallah 1949–50, in Nablus 1951–52; Mufti of Jerusalem 1953–; Qadi in Jerusalem 1974–82; Head of Waqf, Chief Justice, Mufti of Jerusalem, Chair. Higher Islamic Council 1982–; Pres. Jerusalem Univ. 1984–; mem. League of Islamic World, Mecca 1984–. *Publication:* Book of the Higher Islamic Council 1985. *Leisure interests:* reading and study. *Address:* 6 Hariri Street, Jerusalem; P.O. Box 19859, Jerusalem, Israel. *Telephone:* Jerusalem 283528 (Home).

ALAMUDDIN, Najib Salim, B.A.; Lebanese airline executive; b. 9 March 1909, Baakline; s. of Wadad and Salim Alamuddin; m. Dr. Ida Kunzler Alamuddin 1940; two s. one d.; ed. American Univ. of Beirut and Coll. of South West, Exeter, England; Teacher of Eng. and Math., American Univ. of Beirut 1930–33; Insp. of Math., Educ. Dept., Govt. of Trans-Jordan 1933–36; Insp.-Gen. of Customs, Trade and Industry, Trans-Jordan 1939–40; Chief Sec. Govt. of Trans-Jordan 1940–42; founded Near East Resources Co. 1942; Gen. Man. Middle East Airlines 1952–56, Chair. and Pres. 1956–77, Hon. Chair. 1977–; Minister of Tourism and Information 1965, of Public Works and Transport 1966, 1973; mem. Exec. Cttee. of Int. Air Transport Asscn.; Hon. mem. Bd. of Trustees, American Univ. of Beirut;

Dir. Inst. du Transport Aérien, and several Lebanese cos.; Hon. C.B.E. and several foreign decorations. *Leisure interest:* farming. *Address:* c/o Middle East Airlines Airliban, MEA Buildings, Airport Boulevard, P.O. Box 206, Beirut, Lebanon.

ALARCÓN DE QUESADA, Ricardo; Cuban diplomatist; b. 21 May 1937; ed. Univ. de Habana; Head of Student Section, Provincial Office of 26 July Revolutionary Movement 1957–59; Pres. Univ. Students' Fed., Sec. Union of Young Communists; Dir. for Regional Policies (Latin America), Ministry of Foreign Affairs 1962–66; mem. Governing Council of Inst. for Int. Politics, Ministry of Foreign Affairs, Deputy Minister of Foreign Affairs 1978, mem. Tech. Advisory Council 1980; Perm. Rep. of Cuba to the UN 1966–78; Pres. UNDP 1976–77; Alt. mem. Cen. Cttee. of CP of Cuba 1980–. *Address:* c/o Ministry of Foreign Affairs, Havana, Cuba.

ALATAS, Ali; Indonesian diplomat; b. 4 Nov. 1932, Jakarta; s. of Abdullah Alatas; m. Yunisa Alatas 1956; three d.; ed. Acad. for Foreign Affairs and School of Law, Univ. of Indonesia; Financial and Econ. Ed. P.I.A. Nat. news agency, Jakarta; joined Ministry of Foreign Affairs 1954; Second Sec. (later First Sec.), Bangkok, Thailand 1956–69; Dir. Information and Cultural Affairs, Jakarta 1960–65, Dir. 1965–66, 1970–72; Counsellor (later Minister Counsellor), Washington, D.C. 1966–70; Sec. Directorate Gen. for Political Affairs, Jakarta, Chef de Cabinet to Minister of Foreign Affairs 1972–75; Perm. Rep. to UN 1976–78, 1982–84, 1985–87; Sec. to the Vice-Pres. of Indonesia 1978–82; Chair. First Cttee., 40th U.N. Gen. Ass. 1985; Indonesian Order of Merit. *Leisure interests:* golf, reading, music, swimming. *Address:* Permanent Mission of Indonesia to the United Nations, 325 East 38th Street, New York, N.Y. 10016, U.S.A. *Telephone:* (212) 972-8333.

ALBA, H.R.H., the Duke of; Jesus, D.PHIL.; Spanish philosopher; b. 9 June 1934, Madrid; m. the Duchess of Alba; five s. one d.; author of seven books; mem. Royal Spanish Academy. *Publications:* essays, poems, short stories, memoirs, art and poetry criticisms. *Address:* Palacio di Linia, 28008 Madrid, Spain.

ALBAN-HANSEN, Erik; Danish civil servant; b. 29 July 1920, Copenhagen; s. of Ejler Vilhelm Hansen and Vilhelmine Hansen (née Lorentzen); m. Vibeke Poulson 1943; one s. two d.; ed. Univ. of Copenhagen; Prin., Prices and Monopoly Control 1943; Prin., Dept. of Customs and Excise 1944–47, Head of Section 1947–62, Asst. Sec. 1962–65, Deputy Sec. 1965–73; Fed. of Danish Industries 1946–59; Dir.-Gen. of Financial Insts. and Fiscal Matters, Comm. of European Communities 1973–77. *Leisure interest:* music. *Address:* Bymosevej 69, 3200 Hensinge, Denmark.

ALBEE, Edward Franklin; American playwright; b. 12 March 1928; ed. Lawrenceville and Choate Schools, Washington, and Columbia Univ.; Comm. Chair. Brandeis Univ. Creative Arts Awards 1983, 1984; mem. Nat. Inst. of Arts and Letters; Gold Medal, American Acad. and Inst. of Arts and Letters 1980; inducted, Theatre Hall of Fame 1985; has written a number of plays, including: The Death of Bessie Smith, The American Dream, The Sand Box 1961, Zoo Story 1961, Who's Afraid of Virginia Woolf 1962, stage adaptation of The Ballad of the Sad Café (Carson McCullers) 1963, Tiny Alice 1964, Malcolm (from novel by James Purdy) 1966, A Delicate Balance (Pulitzer Prize 1967) 1966, Everything in the Garden (after a play by Giles Cooper) 1967, Box, Quotations from Chairman Mao Tse-tung 1968, All Over 1971, Seascape (Pulitzer Prize 1975) 1975, Listening 1975, Counting the Ways 1976, The Lady from Dubuque 1977, Lolita (adapted from Vladimir Nabokov) 1979, The Man Who Had Three Arms 1981, Finding the Sun 1982, Walking 1984, Marriage 1986–87. *Leisure interest:* collecting art. *Address:* 14 Harrison Street, New York, N.Y. 10013, U.S.A.

ALBERS, Hans, DR. RER. NAT.; German business executive; b. 4 March 1925, Lingen; joined BASF, 1953, Deputy Chair. Man.Bd. until 1982, Chair. 1983–; Chair. Verband der Chemischen Industrie eV 1986–. *Address:* BASF AG, Postfach, 6700 Ludwigshafen, Federal Republic of Germany.

ALBERT, Adrien, A.O., D.SC., PH.D., F.A.A.; Australian professor of medical chemistry; b. 19 Nov. 1907, Sydney; s. of Jacques Albert and Blanche Albert; ed. The Scots College, Sydney, Sydney Univ., London Univ., U.K.; research and teaching staffs of Sydney Univ. 1938–47; Adviser on Medical Chem. to Army Medical Directorate 1942–46; Research Fellow, Wellcome Research Inst., London 1947–48; Foundation Prof. and Head Dept. of Medical Chem., John Curtin School of Medical Research, Australian Nat. Univ., Canberra 1949–73, Prof. Emer. 1973–; Prof. Emer. State Univ. of New York 1973–; Smissman Award, American Chemical Soc. 1981. *Publications:* The Acridines, Heterocyclic Chemistry, Ionization Constants (with E. P. Serjeant), Selective Toxicity, Xenobiosis 1987. *Leisure interests:* Australian wildflowers, classical music. *Address:* Chemistry School, Faculty of Science, Australian National University, Canberra, 2601 Australia. *Telephone:* (062) 49-3071.

ALBERT, Calvin; American sculptor; b. 19 Nov. 1918, Grand Rapids, Mich.; s. of Philip and Ethel Albert; m. Martha Neff 1941; one d.; ed. Inst. of Design, Chicago, Art Inst. of Chicago and Archipenko School of Sculpture; Teacher, New York Univ. 1949–52, Brooklyn Coll. 1947–49, Inst. of Design 1942–46; Prof. of Art, Pratt Inst. 1949–85, Prof. Emer. 1985–; 31 one-man exhbns. including Landmark, Stable and Borgenicht Galleries, New York, Palace of Legion of Honor, San Francisco, Art. Inst. of Chicago; retrospective exhbn. at Guildhall Museum, East Hampton, N.Y. 1979; other exhbns. in the U.S. and Galleria George Lester, Rome; sculpture and drawings in collections of Whitney Museum, Metropolitan Museum, Jewish Museum, Art Inst. of Chicago, Detroit Inst. of Arts, Univ. of Nebraska, Chrysler Museum of Art and Nelson-Atkins Museum of Art; Fulbright Advanced Research Grant to Italy 1961; Tiffany Grants 1963, 1965; Guggenheim Fellowship 1966; Nat. Inst. of Arts and Letters Award 1975. *Publication:* Figure Drawing Comes to Life (with Dorothy Seckler) 1987. *Leisure interest:* boating. *Address:* 325 West 16th Street, New York, N.Y. 10011 (Office); 114 Three Mile Harbour, Hog Creek Road, East Hampton, N.Y. 11937, U.S.A. (Home). *Telephone:* (516) 324-4566 (Home).

ALBERT, Carl Bert, B.C.L., LL.D.; American lawyer and politician; b. 10 May 1908; s. of Ernest H. Albert and Leona Scott; m. Mary Harmon 1942; one s. one d.; ed. Univ. of Oklahoma and Oxford Univ.; admitted to Oklahoma Bar 1936; Legal Clerk, Federal Housing Admin. 1935-37; practised law, Oklahoma City 1937; attorney and accountant Sayre Oil Co. 1937-38; law practice, Mattoon, Ill. 1938-39; legal dept., Ohio Oil Co. 1939-40; served army 1941-46; practised law, McAlester, Oklahoma 1946-47; mem. House of Reps. 1947-79, Democratic Whip 1955; Majority Leader 1962-71; Speaker of House of Reps. 1971-76; Bronze Star. *Address:* Route 2, McAlester, Okla. 74501, U.S.A.

ALBERTY, Robert Arnold, PH.D.; American professor of chemistry; b. 21 June 1921, Winfield, Kan.; s. of Luman H. and Mattie Arnold Alberty; m. Lillian Jane Wind 1944; one s. two d.; ed. Lincoln High School, Lincoln, Neb., Univ. of Nebraska and Univ. of Wisconsin; Instructor, Chemistry Dept., Univ. of Wis. 1947-48, Asst. Prof. 1948-50, Assoc. Prof. 1950-56, Prof. 1956-57, Assoc. Dean of Letters and Science 1962-63, Dean of Graduate School 1963-67; Prof. of Chemistry M.I.T. 1967-; Dean, School of Science 1967-82; mem. N.A.S. 1965-, American Acad. of Arts and Sciences 1968-, Inst. of Medicine 1973-; Chair. Comm. on Human Resources, Nat. Research Council 1971-77; Fellow, AAAS 1976-; Dir. Colt Industries 1978-; Dir. Inst. for Defense Analysis 1980-86; Chair. Cttee. on Chemistry and Public Affairs, American Chemical Soc. 1980; Eli Lilly Award for research in enzyme kinetics 1956; Hon. Dr. (Nebraska) 1967, (Lawrence) 1967. *Publications:* Physical Chemistry (co-author) 5th edn. 1979, Experimental Physical Chemistry (with others) 1962. *Leisure interest:* designing and building a summer cabin. *Address:* School of Science, Massachusetts Institute of Technology, Cambridge, Mass. 02139 (Office); 7 Old Dee Road, Cambridge, Mass. 02138, U.S.A. (Home).

ALBERTZ, Heinrich; German politician and ecclesiastic; b. 22 Jan. 1915; ed. theological studies in Berlin, Halle and Breslau; Curate in Berlin 1937, arrested during Second World War as active member of Protestant Church; Head of Refugee Office, City of Celle 1946; mem. Social Democrat Party (SPD) 1946-; Rep. for Refugees, Lower Saxony Landtag 1947; mem. Refugee Council, Exec. Cttee. of SPD 1947; Dir. of Senate Cttee. for People's Welfare, W. Berlin 1955-59; Head of Senate Chancellery, W. Berlin 1961-63; Senator for Internal Affairs, W. Berlin 1961-63; Deputy Mayor and Senator for Internal Affairs 1965-66; Mayor of W. Berlin Dec. 1966-67; Protestant Priest in W. Berlin 1968-; Niedersächsische Landesmedaille, Grosses Verdienstkreuz mit Stern und Schulterband. *Address:* 28 Bremen 1, Riekestr. 2, Federal Republic of Germany.

ALBRECHT, Ernst Carl Julius, DR.RER.POL.; German economist and politician; b. 29 June 1930, Heidelberg; s. of Carl Albrecht, M.D., and Dr. Adda Albrecht (née Berg); m. Dr. Heidi Adele Stromeyer 1953; five s. two d.; ed. Univs. of Tübingen, Cornell, Basle, Bonn; Attaché to Council of Ministers, ECSC 1954; Head of Common Market section of Brussels conf. for preparation of Treaties of Rome 1956; C.E.O. to EEC Commr. Hans von der Groeben 1958; Deputy Head of Comm. del. at negotiations with Denmark, Ireland, Norway and U.K. for accession to EEC 1961-63; Dir.-Gen. for Competition, EEC Comm. 1967-70; Financial Dir. Bahlsens Keksfabrik, biscuit mfrs. 1971-76; mem. Land (Parl.) for Lower Saxony 1970-, Minister-Pres. of Lower Saxony Feb. 1976-; Grosses Bundesverdienstkreuz 1983; Christlich-Demokratische Union (CDU). *Publication:* Der Staat—Idee und Wirklichkeit (The State—Ideal and Reality) 1976. *Address:* Am Brink 2B, 3167 Burgdorf OT Beinhorn, Federal Republic of Germany. *Telephone:* (05136) 82141.

ALBUQUERQUE, José Osório da Gama e Castro Saraiva de, LIC. EM DIR.; Portuguese judge; b. 3 Aug. 1910, Fornos de Algodres; s. of Conselheiro Luis Osório and Margarida de Albuquerque Osório; m. Zilia de Serpa Brandão 1934; six s. five d.; ed. Universidade de Coimbra; Asst. to Procurator of Repub. 1934-42; Judge 1942-57; Procurator, Appeal Court, Oporto district 1942-44; Deputy Procurator-Gen. of Repub. 1946-54; Procurator-Gen. of the Repub. 1954-57; Appeal Court Judge 1957-61; Supreme Court Judge 1961; Pres. of the Supreme Court of Justice 1966; Gran Cruz de Ordem de Cristo. *Leisure interest:* gardening. *Address:* Rua do Francisco de Almeida 63, Lisbon 3, Portugal. *Telephone:* 61 07 74.

ALBY, Pierre; French mining engineer; b. 23 Nov. 1921, Paris; s. of Henry and Yvonne (née Nicoletis) Alby; m. Marine Amet 1948; two s. five d.; ed. Lycées Carnot and St. Louis, Paris, Lycée Blaise Pascal, Clermont-Ferrand, Ecole Polytechnique, Paris, Ecole des Mines, Paris; mining engineer, Bethune 1945-49; Chief of War Economy Dept., Defence Secr. 1949-53; Asst. Sec.-Gen. Interministerial Cttee. on European Econ. Co-operation 1953-57; Dir. of Mines, Ministry of Industry 1957-64; Asst. Gen.

Man. Gaz de France 1964-69, Gen. Man. 1969-79, Pres. 1979-86, Hon. Pres. 1986-; Vice-Pres. Megal 1976-78; Pres. ERAP 1980-82; Dir. Petrofigaz 1973; Vice-Pres. Council of Mines 1982-87; Pres. Int. Group of Liquefied Natural Gas Importers 1987-; Dir. Gazocéan 1982-85; Commdr., Légion d'honneur, Commdr., ordre national du Mérite, ordre du Mérite commercial, Italian Order of Merit, ordre de Saint-Charles (Monaco). *Address:* 62 rue de Courcelles, 75008 Paris; 8 rue Guy de Maupassant, 75116 Paris, France. *Telephone:* 47 54 21 02 (Office); 45 04 19 40 (Home).

ALCONADA ARAMBURU, Carlos Roman Santiago, DR.; Argentine lawyer; b. 25 July 1920, La Plata; m. Balbina Maria Mogliano; nine s.; ed. Nat. Univ. La Plata; Law Prof.; Minister of Interior 1957-58, of Educ. and Justice 1963-66, 1983-86. *Address:* c/o Ministerio de Educacion y Justicia, Marcelo T. de Alvear 1650, C.P. 1060, Buenos Aires, Argentina.

ALCORN, (Hugh) Meade, Jr., LL.B.; American politician; b. 20 Oct. 1907, Suffield, Conn.; s. of late Hugh M. and Cora W. Alcorn; m. 1st Janet Hoffer 1933 (deceased), one s. (deceased) one d.; m. 2nd Marcia Powell 1955; ed. Dartmouth Coll. and Yale Univ.; admitted to Connecticut Bar 1933; Partner Tyler, Cooper and Alcorn Hartford 1933-; Asst. State's Attorney, Hartford County, 1935-42, State's Attorney 1942-48; mem. Connecticut House of Reps. 1937, 1939 and 1941, Majority Leader 1939, Speaker 1941; Republican Chair. Suffield, Conn. 1938-53; del. Republican Nat. Convention 1940, 1948, 1952, 1956 (Chair.), alt. del. 1944; Seventh District Committeeman; Nat. Committeeman from Conn. 1953-61; Vice-Chair. Cttee. on Arrangements for 1956 Republican Nat. Convention 1956; Chair. Republican Nat. Cttee. 1957-59; mem. Hartford County, Conn. State (Pres. 1950-51) and American Bar Asscns., American Judicature Soc.; Fellow, American Coll. of Trial Lawyers; Dir. United Bank & Trust Co., Hartford, Conn.; Hon. LL.D. (Hartford) 1974. *Leisure interests:* fishing, hunting. *Address:* 49 Russell Avenue, Suffield, Conn. 06078, U.S.A. (Home). *Telephone:* 668-7306 (Home).

ALDA, Alan, B.S.; American actor; b. 28 Jan. 1936, New York; s. of Robert Alda and Joan Browne; m. Arlene Weiss; ed. Fordham Univ.; performed with Second City 1963; Broadway roles in The Owl and the Pussycat, Purlie Victorious, Fair Game for Lovers, The Apple Tree, etc. *Films include:* Gone are the Days 1963, Paper Lion 1968, The Extraordinary Seaman 1968, The Moonshine War 1970, Jenny 1970, The Mephisto Waltz 1971, To Kill a Clown 1972, California Suite 1978, Same Time Next Year 1978, The Seduction of Joe Tynan (also wrote screenplay) 1979, actor, dir., writer of films: The Four Seasons 1981, Sweet Liberty 1986. *TV includes:* The Glass House 1972, M*A*S*H 1972-83, Tune in America 1975, Kill Me If You Can (film) 1977; devised series We'll Get By 1975; Theatre World Award for Fair Game for Lovers; Emmy Award (Best Actor in Comedy Series) for M*A*S*H. *Address:* c/o Martin Bregman Productions, 641 Lexington Avenue, New York, N.Y. 10022, U.S.A.

ALDER, Berni Julian, PH.D.; American theoretical physicist; b. 9 Sept. 1925, Duisburg, Germany; s. of Ludwig Alder and Ottilie Gottschalk; m. Esther Romella Berger 1956; two s. one d.; ed. Univ. of California (Berkeley), and California Inst. of Technology; Instructor, Univ. of Calif. (Berkeley) 1951-54; Theoretical Physicist, Univ. of Calif. Lawrence Radiation Lab. 1955-; Prof. of Applied Science, Univ. of California at Davis 1987-; Nat. Science Foundation Sr. Post Doctoral Fellow, Weizman Inst. (Israel) and Univ. of Rome 1963-64; Van der Waals Prof., Univ. of Amsterdam 1971; Guggenheim Fellow, Cambridge (U.K.) and Leiden (Netherlands) 1954-55; Assoc. Prof., Univ. of Paris 1976-; Hinshelwood Prof., Oxford Univ. 1986; Ed. Journal of Computational Physics; mem. N.A.S.; Hildebrand Award, American Chem. Soc. 1985. *Publications:* many chapters in books and articles in journals. *Leisure interests:* hiking, skiing. *Address:* Lawrence Livermore National Laboratory, P.O. Box 808, Livermore, Calif. 94550, U.S.A.

ALDINGTON, 1st Baron (cr. 1962); **Toby (Austin Richard William) Low,** P.C., K.C.M.G., C.B.E., F.R.S.A., D.S.O., T.D.; British banker and industrialist; b. 25 May 1914, London; s. of Col. Stuart Low, D.S.O. and Hon. Lucy Gwen, d. of Lord Atkin; m. Araminta, d. of Sir Harold MacMichael, G.C.M.G., D.S.O., 1947; one s. two d.; called to Bar 1939; Army Service 1939-45; Conservative M.P. 1945-62; Parl. Sec. to Ministry of Supply 1951-54; Minister of State, Bd. of Trade 1954-57; Deputy Chair. Conservative Party Org. 1959-63; Chair. Grindlays Bank Ltd. (fmrly. Nat. and Grindlays) 1963-76, Port of London Authority 1971-77, Gen. Advisory Council of BBC 1971-77; Chair. Sun Alliance and London Insurance Group 1971-85, Westland PLC 1977-85 (Pres. 1985), Man. Cttee. Inst. of Neurology (1961-79), Independent Schools Jt. Council 1986-; Deputy Chair. Gen. Electric PLC 1968-84; Dir. Lloyds Bank PLC 1967-85, Citicorp N.A. (U.S.A.) 1969-84; Pres. British Standards Inst. 1986-; Hon. Fellow New Coll., Oxford; Warden of Winchester Coll. 1979-87; Chair. Leeds Castle Foundation 1984-. *Leisure interests:* golf, gardening. *Address:* Knoll Farm, Aldington, nr. Ashford, Kent, England. *Telephone:* 02-3372 292.

ALDISS, Brian Wilson; British writer; b. 18 Aug. 1925, Norfolk; m. 2nd Margaret Manson 1965; two s. two d.; ed. Framlingham Coll. and West Buckland School; fmrly. soldier, draughtsman, bookseller and film critic; Literary Ed. Oxford Mail 1957-69; Pres. British Science Fiction Asscn. 1960-65; Joint-Pres. European Science Fiction Cttees. 1976-80; Chair. John W. Campbell Memorial Award 1976-77; Chair. Cttee. of Man. Soc. of Authors 1977-78; mem. Literature Advisory Panel, Arts Council 1978-80;

Chair. Cultural Exchanges Cttee. of Authors 1978; Judge, Booker McConnell Prize 1981; Pres. World SF 1982–; Vice-Pres. Soc. for Anglo-Chinese Understanding; Hugo Award for Hothouse 1962, Nebula Award for The Saliva Tree 1965, Ditmar Award for World's Best Contemporary Science Fiction Writer 1969, British Science Fiction Asscn. Award for The Moment of Eclipse 1972, Eurocon III Merit Award for Billion Year Spree 1976, Jules Verne Award for Non-Stop 1977, 1st James Blish Award for Excellence in Criticism 1977, Pilgrim Award 1978, John W. Campbell Award 1983, Kurt Lasswitz Award 1984, I.A.F.A. Distinguished Scholarship Award 1986, J. Lloyd Eaton Award 1988. *Publications:* The Brightfount Diaries 1955, Space, Time & Nathaniel 1957, Non-Stop 1958, The Male Response 1959, Hothouse 1962, The Airs of Earth 1963, The Dark Light Years 1964, Greybeard 1964, Earthworks 1965, Best Science Fiction Stories of Brian W. Aldiss 1965, Cities and Stones: A Traveller's Jugoslavia 1966, Report on Probability A 1968, Barefoot in the Head 1969, Intangibles Inc., 1969, A Brian Aldiss Omnibus 1969, The Hand-Reared Boy 1970, The Shape of Further Things 1970, A Soldier Erect 1971, The Moment of Eclipse 1971, Brian Aldiss Omnibus 2 1971, Penguin Science Fiction Omnibus (ed.) 1973, Comic Inferno 1973, Billion Year Spree 1973, Frankenstein Unbound 1973, The Eighty-Minute Hour 1974, Hell's Cartographers (editor) 1975, Space Odysseys, Evil Earths, Science Fiction Art 1975, The Malacia Tapestry, Galactic Empires (2 vols.) 1976, Last Orders, Brothers of the Head 1977, Perilous Planets, A Rude Awakening 1978, Enemies of the System 1978, This World and Nearer Ones 1979, Pile 1979, New Arrivals, Old Encounters 1979, Moreau's Other Island 1980, Life in the West 1980, An Island called Moreau 1981, Foreign Bodies 1981, Helliconia Spring 1982, Science Fiction Quiz 1983, Helliconia Summer 1983, Seasons in Flight 1984, Helliconia Winter 1985, The Pale Shadow of Science 1985, . . . And the Lurid Glare of the Comet 1986, Trillion Year Spree 1986 (Hugo Award 1987), Ruins 1987, Forgotten Life 1988, Science Fiction Blues 1988. *Leisure interests:* the past, the future. *Address:* Woodlands, Foxcombe Road, Boars Hill, Oxford, England. *Telephone:* 0865 735744.

ALDRICH, Hulbert Stratton, PH.B.; American banker; b. 3 April 1907, Fall River, Mass.; s. of Stanley Alden Aldrich and Jane Stratton (Pratt) Aldrich; m. Amy Durfee 1934; two d.; ed. Phillips Acad. and Yale Univ.; joined New York Trust Co. 1930, Asst. Treas. 1939–43, Vice-Pres. 1943–52, Pres. 1952–59 (co. merged with Chemical Corn Exchange Bank to form Chemical Bank New York Trust Co.); Vice-Chair. Chemical Bank 1959–72; Chair. Hill Samuel Inc. 1972–; Dir. numerous other companies. *Leisure interest:* tennis. *Address:* 30 Rockefeller Plaza, New York, N.Y. 10112 (Office); 1088 Park Avenue, New York, N.Y. 10028, U.S.A. (Home).

ALDRIDGE, (Harold Edward) James; British author and journalist; b. 10 July 1918; s. of William Thomas Aldridge and Edith Quayle Aldridge; m. Dina Mitchnik 1942; two s.; with Herald and Sun, Melbourne, Australia 1937–38, Daily Sketch and Sunday Dispatch, London 1939; with Australian Newspaper Service and North American Newspaper Alliance (as war correspondent), Finland, Norway, Middle East, Greece, U.S.S.R. 1939–45; correspondent for Time and Life, Teheran 1944; Rhys Memorial Award 1945; Lenin Peace Prize 1972. *Publications:* Signed With Their Honour 1942, The Sea Eagle 1944, Of Many Men 1946, The Diplomat 1950, The Hunter 1951, Heroes of the Empty View 1954, Underwater Hunting for Inexperienced Englishmen 1955, I Wish He Would Not Die 1958, Gold and Sand (short stories) 1960, The Last Exile 1961, A Captive in the Land 1962, The Statesman's Game 1966, My Brother Tom 1966, The Flying 19 1966, Living Egypt (with Paul Strand) 1969, Cairo: Biography of a City 1970, A Sporting Proposition 1973, The Marvellous Mongolian 1974, Mockery in Arms 1974, The Untouchable Juli 1975, One Last Glimpse 1977, Goodbye Un-America 1979, The Broken Saddle 1982, The True Story of Lilli Stubek 1984, The True Story of Spit Mac Phee 1985. *Leisure interests:* underwater, trout fishing, hunting. *Address:* 21 Kersley Street, London, S.W.11, England.

ALDRIN, Edwin Eugene (Buzz), Jr., D.SC.; American astronaut; b. 20 Jan. 1930, Montclair, N.J.; s. of late Col. Edwin E. Aldrin and late Marion M. Aldrin; divorced 1978; two s. one d.; ed. U.S. Military Acad. and Massachusetts Inst. of Technology; fmr. mem. U.S. Air Force; completed pilot training 1952; flew combat missions during Korean War; later became aerial gunnery instructor, Nellis Air Force Base, Nev.; attended Squadron Officers' School at Air Univ., Maxwell Air Force Base, Ala.; later Flight Commdr. 36th Tactical Fighter Wing, Bitburg, Germany; completed astronautics studies at M.I.T. 1963; selected by NASA as astronaut 1963; Gemini Target Office, Air Force Space Systems Div., L.A., Calif. 1963; later assigned to Manned Spacecraft Center, Houston, Tex.; pilot of backup crew for Gemini IX mission 1966; pilot for Gemini XII 1966; backup command module pilot for Apollo VIII; lunar module pilot for Apollo XI, landed on the moon 20 July 1969; Commdt. Aerospace Research Pilot School 1971–72; Scientific Consultant, Beverly Hills Oil Co., L.A.; Fellow, American Inst. of Aeronautics and Astronautics; Hon. mem. Royal Aeronautical Soc.; several honorary degrees and numerous decorations and awards; retd. from U.S.A.F. 1972; Pres. Research & Eng. Consultants Inc. 1972–; consultant to JRW, Jet Propulsion Lab. *Publications:* First on the Moon: A Voyage with Neil Armstrong (with Michael Collins) 1970, Return to Earth 1973. *Leisure interest:* scuba diving. *Address:* Center for Aerospace Sciences, University of North Dakota, Box 8216, University Station, Grand Forks, N.D. 58202, U.S.A.

ALEBUA, Rt. Hon. Ezekiel, P.C.; Solomon Islands politician; fmr. Deputy Prime Minister; Prime Minister of the Solomon Is. Dec. 1986–; mem. Solomon Is. United Party (SIUPA). *Address:* Office of the Prime Minister, Honiara, Solomon Islands.

ALEKPEROV, Aziz Aga-Aga-baba; Soviet foreign trade official; b. 1 Jan. 1916; ed. Inst. of Foreign Trade, Moscow; has worked in foreign trade 1938–; various posts in All Union Vostokintorg (Eastern Foreign Trade) Asscn., Chair. 1965–87. *Address:* c/o All Union Vostokintorg Association, 32-34 Smolenskaya-Sennaya Ploshchad, 121200 Moscow, U.S.S.R.

ALEKSANDROV, Aleksandr Danilovich; Soviet mathematician; b. 4 Aug. 1912, Volyn, Ryazan Region; ed. Leningrad Univ.; Lecturer Leningrad Univ. 1952, Rector 1952–64; mem. CPSU 1951–; specialized in subject of convex bodies and general surfaces in geometry; corresp. mem. Acad. of Sciences of U.S.S.R. 1946–64, mem. 1964–; Head of Dept., Inst. of Math., Siberian Br. U.S.S.R. Acad. of Sciences 1964–; U.S.S.R. Master of Sport in Mountaineering 1949; Lobachevsky Int. Prize 1951, Alexander Karpinsky Prize 1984, State prizewinner; Order of Lenin and other decorations. *Publications:* The Internal Geometry of Convex Surfaces 1948, Convex Polyhedrons 1950. *Address:* Akademgorodok, Institute of Mathematics, Novosibirsk, U.S.S.R.

ALEKSANDROV, Aleksandr Pavlovich; Soviet pilot and cosmonaut; b. 1943, Moscow; ed. Baumann Tech. Inst., Moscow; mem. CPSU 1970–; after service in Soviet Army started work with Space Programme 1964–; took part in elaboration of control system of space-craft, Cosmonaut since 1978, participated in Soyuz-T and Salyut programmes; successfully completed 148-day flight to Salyut-7 orbital station with V. A. Lyakhov (q.v.) and effected space-walk, June 1984; Hero of Soviet Union 1983.

ALEKSANDROV, Anatoliy Petrovich, D.SC.; Soviet physicist; b. 13 Feb. 1903, Tarashcha, Kiev Region, Ukraine; ed. Kiev Univ.; work devoted to physics of dielectrics, mechanical and electrical properties of high polymeric compounds; developed widely-used static theory of strength of solids; invented relaxation theory of elasticity in polymers, etc.; invented an anti-mine defence for ships during Second World War 1941–45; Corresp. mem. U.S.S.R. Acad. of Sciences 1943–53, mem. 1953–, Pres. 1976–86; Dir. Inst. of Physical Problems, U.S.S.R. Acad. of Sciences 1946–55, Dir. Kurchatov Inst. of Atomic Energy 1960–; mem. CPSU 1962–; Deputy to U.S.S.R. Supreme Soviet 1962–70; mem. Cen. Cttee. CPSU 1966–; Chair. Cttee. for Lenin Prizes and State Prizes in Science and Tech. of U.S.S.R. Council of Ministers 1978–; Lenin Prize 1959, U.S.S.R. State Prize 1942, 1949, 1951, 1953; Order of Lenin (six times), Hero of Socialist Labour (twice), Gold Star of Friendship Between Peoples 1983 and other decorations. *Address:* I. V. Kurchatov Atomic Energy Institute, Ul. Kurchatova 46, Moscow; U.S.S.R. Academy of Sciences, Leninsky Prospekt 14, Moscow, U.S.S.R.

ALEKSANKIN, Aleksandr Vasilevich; Soviet politician; b. 1929; ed. Byelorussian Agric. Acad.; mem. CPSU 1956–; Management of Min. of Agric. of Byelorussian SSR; Deputy Min., Min. of Water Supply for Byelorussian SSR 1959–71; First Deputy Min. of Water Supply for U.S.S.R. 1971–74; Deputy Pres. of RSFSR Council of Mins. 1974–; Mem. of Cen. Auditing Comm. of CPSU 1974; reconfirmed 1986. *Address:* The Kremlin, Moscow, U.S.S.R.

ALEKSEY (b. A. M. Ridiger); Russian Orthodox clergyman; b. 23 Feb. 1929, Tallinn, Estonia; ed. Leningrad Theological Seminary; Chair. Tartu Cathedral; Bishop of Tallinn and Estonia 1961; Vice-Chair. Dept. of External Affairs, Moscow Patriarchate 1962–; Archbishop, Admin. Manager of Moscow Patriarchy, perm. mem. of Holy Synod, Chair. Teaching Cttee. of Moscow Patriarchate 1964–68; Metropolitan of Tallinn and Estonia 1968–; Chair. Conf. of European Churches 1972–. *Address:* Metropolitanate of Tallinn and Estonia, Tallinn, Estonian S.S.R., U.S.S.R.

ALEKSEYEV, Aleksandr Ivanovich; Soviet diplomatist and journalist (retd.); b. 3 Aug. 1913, Moscow; ed. Moscow Univ.; Diplomatic Service 1941–; First Sec. Buenos Aires 1954–58; Head of Dept. for Latin American Countries, State Cttee. of U.S.S.R. Council of Ministers for Cultural Relations with Foreign Countries 1959–60; Counsellor, Havana 1960–62, Amb. to Cuba 1962–67; at staff of Ministry of Foreign Affairs 1967–68; Vice-Chair. Bd. of Novosti Press Agency 1969–74; Amb. to Madagascar 1974–80; Order of Red Banner of Labour (three times), Badge of Honour. *Address:* c/o Ministry of Foreign Affairs, Moscow, U.S.S.R.

ALEKSEYEV, Dmitri; Soviet pianist; b. Aug. 1947, Moscow; m. Tatiana Sarkissova; ed. Cen. School of Moscow Conservatoire: studied under Dmitri Bashkirov; winner Int. Tchaikovsky Competition, Moscow 1974, 5th Leeds Int. Piano Competition 1975 and other int. competitions; performs regularly in the U.S.S.R., in U.K. and throughout Europe and U.S.A. and has toured Japan, Australia etc.; recordings in U.S.S.R. and for EMI include works by Brahms, Prokofiev, Rachmaninov, Shostakovich and Chopin. *Address:* c/o Harold Holt Ltd., 31 Sinclair Road, London, W14 ONS, England. *Telephone:* 01-603 4600.

ALEKSEYEV, Pyotr Fyodorovich; Soviet journalist; b. 8 July 1913, Sergeyevka, Kustanai Region, Kazakh S.S.R.; ed. Tashkent Pedagogical Inst. and Higher Party School of the CPSU; Young Communist League Official, Uzbek S.S.R. 1931–32; journalistic work 1932–62; Ed.-in-Chief

Selskaya Zhizn (Country Life) 1962-71; Ed.-in-Chief Sovietskaya Rossia 1971-75; Ed., Izvestia 1975-83; mem. CPSU 1940-; mem. Cen. Auditing Comm. of the CPSU 1966-71, Cand. mem. Cen. Cttee. CPSU 1971-76, mem. Cen. Cttee. CPSU 1976-. *Address:* c/o Izvestia, Pushkinskaya pl. 5, Moscow, U.S.S.R.

ALEMANN, Dr. Roberto Teodoro; Argentine politician and economist; b. 22 Dec. 1922, Buenos Aires; m.; four c.; ed. Nat. Coll. of Buenos Aires, Buenos Aires Univ., Bern Univ., Switzerland; positions include Financial Counsellor to Argentine Embassy in London; Dir. Finance and Economy, Ministry of Finance 1958; Adviser to Minister of Economy 1958-59; Under-Sec. of Economy 1959; Financial Counsellor in Washington 1959-61; Minister of Economy 1961-62; Amb. to U.S.A. 1962-63; Ed. for Alemann S.R.L. of Argentinisches Tageblatt (Argentine daily newspaper); Pres. Bd. of Dirs. Ciba Geigy Argentina 1964-81; Consultant to Union Bank of Switzerland, Zürich 1964-81; Minister of Economy 1981-82. *Publications:* Economic Systems, How to Find a Solution to the Present Economic Crisis?, Towards an Argentine Policy on Investment 1956. *Address:* c/o Ministry of Economy, Buenos Aires, Argentina.

ALESHIN, Georgiy Vasilevich; Soviet politician; b. 1931; ed. Tomsk Electro-mechanical Inst. of Engineering and Railways; worked with railway Dir. of Western Siberia 1954-56; Second, First Sec. of First of May ('Pervomaysky') Regional Cttee. 1956-58; Deputy Sec., Sec. of Party Cttee. of locomotive depôt of Insk Western Siberian railway 1958-62; Second Sec. 1962-64, First Sec. of First of May Regional Cttee. of Novosibirsk CPSU 1964-73; Second Sec., 1973-79; First Sec. of Novosibirsk CPSU State Comm. 1979-85; worked for CPSU Cen. Cttee. 1985; Second Sec. of Estonian CP Cen. Cttee. 1985-; Cand. Mem. of CPSU Cen. Cttee. 1986-. *Address:* The Kremlin, Moscow, U.S.S.R.

ALEXANDER, Sir Alex (Sandor), Kt.; British business executive; b. 21 Nov. 1916; m. Margaret Irma 1946; two s. two d.; ed. Charles Univ., Prague; Founder, Westwick Frosted Products (merged with Ross Group Ltd. 1954); Dir. Ross Group 1954-69, Chair. Ross Frozen Food Div. 1954-61, Poultry Div. 1961-68; Man. Dir. and Chief Exec. Ross Group Ltd. 1967-69, Chair. 1969; Dir. Imperial Group Ltd. (fmrly. Imperial Tobacco Group) 1969-79; Chair. Imperial Foods Ltd. 1969-79; Chair. and C.E.O. J. Lyons and Co. 1979-July 1989; Vice-Chair. Allied Lyons PLC 1982-88; Pres. Nat. Assen. of Frozen Food Producers 1957, 1971; Chair. Pea Growers' Research Org. 1959-61, Nat. Assen. of Poultry Packers 1965, Fed. of British Poultry Industries 1966-68; Dir. Royal Opera House 1987-, Chair. Royal Opera House Trust 1987-; Dir. British United Trawlers Ltd. 1969-81, Deputy Chair. 1972-80; Dir. Nat. Westminster Bank Ltd., Eastern Region 1973-84; Dir. Ransomes, Sims and Jefferies Ltd. 1974-83, March-wiel 1978-, Inchcape Insurance Holdings Ltd. 1978-86, Allied Breweries Ltd. (now Allied Lyons) 1978- (Vice-Chair. 1982-), London Wall Holdings PLC 1986-, Hiram Walter-Gooderham and Worts 1987-; Dir. Tate and Lyle (non exec.), Unigate (non exec.); Gov. British Nutrition Foundation 1975-79, Royal Ballet 1985-; mem. Court, Univ. of E. Anglia 1961, Agriculture Econ. Devt. Cttee. 1974-78; Chair. Theatre Royal (Norwich) Trust Ltd. 1969-84; Trustee and Vice-Chair. Glyndebourne Arts Trust 1975-; Pres. British Food Export Council 1973-76; Fellow, Royal Soc. of Arts, Inst. of Man., Inst. of Grocery Distribution 1975; High Sheriff of Norfolk 1976-77; Trustee, Charities Aid Foundation 1979-86; Pres. Processors and Growers Research Org. 1978-82; mem. Eastern Gas Bd. 1963-72; Chair Appeals Cttee. of the British Red Cross Soc. (Norfolk Branch) 1958-74; Friend, Royal Coll. of Physicians 1982-. *Leisure interests:* shooting, tennis, painting, theatre, opera. *Address:* Westwick Hall, Westwick, Norwich, Norfolk, NR10 5BW (Home); Almed House, 156 St. John Street, London EC1P 1AR, England (Office). *Telephone:* 01-253 9911 (Office); Swanton Abbott 664 (Home).

ALEXANDER, Clifford L., LL.D.; American lawyer and government official; b. 21 Sept. 1933, Harlem, New York; s. of Clifford and Edith (née McAllister) Alexander; m. Adele Logan 1959; one s. one d.; ed. Harvard Univ., Yale Univ.; practised as lawyer in New York, partner in Verner, Liipfert, Bernhard, McPherson and Alexander, law firm; Foreign Affairs Officer, Nat. Security Council Staff 1963-64; Deputy Special Asst., later Deputy Special Counsel to Pres. Lyndon Johnson 1964-67; Chair. Equal Employment Opportunity Comm. 1967-69, resigned; mem. Comm. for the Observance of Human Rights 1968; Special Amb. to Swaziland 1968; Partner in Arnold & Porter, law firm; news commentator and host, Cliff Alexander—Black on White TV programme 1971-74; Prof. of Law, Howard Univ. 1973-74; U.S. Sec. of the Army 1977-81; Pres. Alexander & Assocs. Inc. 1981-; mem. Bd. of Dirs. Pennsylvania Power & Light Co.; Adjunct Prof., Georgetown Univ.; Prof. Howard Univ., Washington; mem. Bd. of Dirs. Mexican-American Legal Defense and Educ. Fund, Dreyfus Third Century Fund Inc., MCI Corpn., Dreyfus Common Stock Fund, Dreyfus Tax Exempt Fund; mem. American and D.C. Bar Assens.; fmr. mem. Bd. Overseers Harvard Univ.; Trustee, Atlanta Univ.; Hon. LL.D. (Univ. of Maryland, Atlanta Univ.); Frederick Douglass Award and other decorations. *Address:* Alexander & Assocs. Inc., 400 C Street, N.E., Washington, D.C. 20002; 512 A Street, S.E., Washington, D.C. 20003, U.S.A. (Home). *Telephone:* (202) 546 0111 (Office).

ALEXANDER, Sir Darnley Arthur Raymond, Kt., C.B.E., LL.B., Q.C.; Nigerian lawyer; b. 28 Jan. 1920, Castries, St. Lucia, West Indies; s. of the late Pamphile Joseph Alexander, M.B.E., and Lucy Alexander; m. Mildred Margaret King 1943 (died 1980); one s. one d.; ed. St. Mary's Coll., St. Lucia, Univ. Coll., London; Middle Temple 1938, called to bar 1942; legal service in Jamaica and Turks and Caicos Islands 1944-57, Western Nigeria 1957-63, Solicitor-Gen. 1960, Q.C. 1961; Judge, High Court of Lagos (later Lagos State) 1964-69; Chief Justice of South-Eastern State 1969-75, of Fed. Repub. of Nigeria 1975-79; mem. Nigerian Soc. of Int. Law 1968-, Nigerian Inst. of Int. Affairs 1979-88, Nigeria-Britain Assen. 1986-; Chair. Kiribati Constitutional Review Comm. 1985; fmr Chair., now Life mem. Body of Benchers of the Nigerian Bar; Chair. Nigerian Law Reform Comm. 1979-; Commdr. of the Order of the Fed. Repub. of Nigeria; Grand Commdr. of the Order of the Niger; Patron Nigerian-W. Indian Assen. 1979-. *Leisure interests:* music, reading. *Address:* c/o Nigerian Law Reform Commission, Secretariat Complex, Ikoyi, P.O. Box 60008, Lagos (Office); 18 Osborne Road, Ikoyi, Nigeria (Office). *Telephone:* 681080.

ALEXANDER, Donald Crichton, LL.B.; American lawyer and government official; b. 22 May 1921, Pine Bluff, Ark.; s. of William Crichton and Ella Temple (née Fox); m. Margaret Louise Savage 1946; two s.; ed. Yale Univ. and Harvard Law School; Assoc. Covington and Burling, law firm 1948-54; Assoc., Taft, Stettinius and Hollister, Ohio, law firm 1954-56, Partner 1956-66; Partner, Dinsmore, Shohl, Coates and Deupree, law firm 1966-73; Commr. of Internal Revenue 1973-77; mem. Comm. on Fed. Paperwork 1975-77; Partner, Morgan, Lewis and Bockius, law firm 1979-85; Partner, Cadwalader, Wickersham and Taft (law firm) 1985-; Commr., Interior Dept. Comm. for Federal Coal Leasing 1983-84; Dir. U.S. Chamber of Commerce 1984-; Chair. Internal Revenue Service Exempt Orgs. Advisory Group 1987-. *Publications:* The Arkansas Plantation 1943, numerous articles on federal taxation. *Address:* 1333 New Hampshire Avenue, N.W., Washington, D.C. 20036 (Office); 2801 New Mexico Avenue, N.W., Washington, D.C. 20007, U.S.A. (Home). *Telephone:* 202-862 2200 (Office).

ALEXANDER, Sir (John) Lindsay, Kt., M.A.; British banker; b. 12 Sept. 1920, Gloucester; s. of Ernest Daniel Alexander and Florence Mary Mainsmith; m. Maud Lilian Collard 1944; two s. one d.; ed. Alleyn's School and Brasenose Coll., Oxford; Man. Dir. Ocean Transport and Trading Ltd. 1955-71, Chair. 1971-80; Chair. Liverpool Port Employers' Assen. 1964-67; Vice-Chair. Nat. Assen. of Port Employers 1965-69; Chair. Cttee. of European Nat. Shipowners' Assens. 1971-73; Vice-Pres. Chamber of Shipping of U.K. 1973-74, Pres. 1974-75; Dir. Lloyds Bank 1970- (Deputy Chair. 1980-88), Lloyds Bank Int. 1975-85 (Deputy Chair. 1979-80, Chair. 1980-85, Vice-Chair. Lloyds Bank U.K. Man. 1981-85), British Petroleum Co. Ltd. 1975-; Dir. Hawker Siddeley Group 1981-, Jebsen's Drilling PLC 1981-86; Dir. Wellington Underwriting Holdings Ltd. 1986-; Dir. Britoil plc 1988-; Dir. Abbey Life Group 1989; former Deputy Chair. Lloyds Merchant Bank Holdings Ltd., Lloyds Bank Canada; Fellow, Chartred Inst. of T.P.T. 1971; Hon. Fellow Brasenose Coll.; Companion, Inst. of Man. 1972; Commdr. Royal Order of St. Olav (Norway); Hon. mem. Master Mariners Co. 1974-. *Leisure interests:* gardening, music, photography. *Address:* c/o Lloyds Bank PLC, 71 Lombard Street, London, EC3P 3BS, England. *Telephone:* 01-626 1500.

ALEXANDER, Jonathan James Graham, D.PHIL., F.B.A., F.S.A.; British reader in history of art; b. 20 Aug. 1935, London; s. of Arthur Ronald Brown and Frederica Emma Graham (who m. 2nd Boyd Alexander); m. Mary Davey 1974; one s.; ed. Magdalen Coll. Oxford; Asst., Dept. of Western Manuscripts, Bodleian Library, Oxford 1963-71; Lecturer, History of Art Dept., Univ. of Manchester 1971-73, Reader 1973-87; Prof. of Fine Arts Inst. of Fine Arts, New York Univ. 1988-; Lyell Reader in Bibliography, Oxford Univ. 1982-83; Sandars Lecturer, Cambridge Univ. 1984-85. *Publications:* Illuminated Manuscripts in the Bodleian Library, Oxford (with Otto Pächt) (3 vols.) 1966, 1970, 1973, Italian Illuminated Manuscripts in the library of Major J. R. Abbey (with A. C. de la Mare) 1969, Norman Illumination at Mont St. Michel c. 966-1100 1970, The Master of Mary of Burgundy, A Book of Hours 1970, Italian Renaissance Illuminations 1977, Insular Manuscripts 6th-9th Century 1978, The Decorated Letter 1978, Illuminated Manuscripts in Oxford College Libraries, The University Archives and the Taylor Institution (with E. Temple) 1986, Age of Chivalry (Jt. Ed.) 1987; articles in Burlington Magazine, Arte Veneta, Pantheon etc. *Leisure interest:* gardening. *Address:* Institute of Fine Arts, 1 East 78th Street, New York, N.Y. 10021, U.S.A. *Telephone:* (212) 772-5800.

ALEXANDER, Sir Michael O'Donel Bjarne, K.C.M.G.; British diplomatist; b. 19 June 1936; s. of Conel Hugh O'Donel Alexander and Enid Constance Alexander (née Neate); m. Traute Anna Krohn 1960; two s. one d.; ed. St. Paul's School, King's Coll. Cambridge and Yale Univ., U.S.A. (Harkness Fellow); served R.N. 1956-57; joined H.M. Foreign (later Diplomatic) Service 1962; served Moscow 1963-65, Singapore 1965-68, London 1968-74 (Asst. Private Sec. to Sir Alec Douglas-Home and James Callaghan 1972-74), Geneva 1974-77; Deputy Head, later Head, of Personnel Operations Dept., F.C.O. 1977-79; Private Sec. (Overseas Affairs) to Prime Minister Margaret Thatcher 1979-81; Amb. to Austria 1982-86; Leader of U.K. Del. to Negotiations on Mutual Force Reductions in Cen. Europe 1985-86, Perm. Rep. on the N. Atlantic Council, Brussels 1986-. *Leisure interests:* reading and sport. *Address:* c/o Foreign and Commonwealth Office, King Charles Street, London, S.W.1, England.

24

ALEXANDER, (Padimjarethalakkal) Cherian, M.LITT., D.LITT.; Indian diplomatist; b. 10 March 1921; m. Ackama Alexander 1942; two s. two d.; ed. India and U.K.; Indian Admin. Service, Kerala Cadre 1948; Devt. Commr. Small Scale Industries 1960–63; Sr. Adviser, Centre for Industrial Devt., UN, New York 1963–66; Chief UN Project on Small Industries and Chief Adviser to Govt. of Iran 1970–73; Devt. Commr. Small Scale Industries 1973–75; Sec. Foreign Trade, later Commerce Sec. 1975–78; Sr. Adviser, later Exec. Dir. and Asst. Sec.-Gen. Int. Trade Centre, UNCTAD-GATT, Geneva 1978–81; Prin. Sec. to Prime Minister of India 1981–85; High Commr. in U.K. 1985–88; Gov., Tamil Nadu 1988–. *Publications:* The Dutch in Malabar, Buddhism in Kerala, Industrial Estates in India. *Address:* Raj Bhavan, Madras, Tamil Nadu, India.

ALEXANDER, Robert McNeill, M.A., PH.D., D.SC., F.R.S.; British professor of zoology; b. 7 July 1934, Lisburn, N. Ireland; s. of Robert Priestley Alexander and Janet (née McNeill) Alexander; m. Ann Elizabeth Coulton 1961; one s. one d.; ed. Tonbridge School and Cambridge Univ.; lecturer Univ. Coll. of N.Wales, Bangor 1958–69; Prof. of Zoology Univ. of Leeds 1969–; Hon. mem. American Soc. of Zoologists 1986; Scientific Medal (Zoological Soc. of London) 1969, Linnean Medal for Zoology (Linnean Soc. of London) 1979. *Publications:* Functional Design in Fishes 1967, Animal Mechanics 1968, Size and Shape 1971, The Chordates 1975, The Invertebrates 1979, Locomotion of Animals 1982, Optima for Animals 1982, Elastic Mechanisms in Animal Movement 1988, Dynamics of dinosaurs and other extinct giants 1989, and many scientific papers. *Leisure interests:* local history and history of natural history. *Address:* Department of Pure and Applied Biology, University of Leeds, Leeds, LS2 9JT, England (Office); 14 Moor Park Mount, Leeds, LS6 4BU, England (Home). *Telephone:* (0532) 332911 (Office); (0532) 759218 (Home).

ALEXANDRA, H.R.H. Princess (see Ogilvy, the Hon. Mrs. Angus).

ALEXANDRIS, Efstathios (Stathis); Greek politician; b. Amphassa; joined EAM resistance org. during Nazi occupation; after liberation, exiled to island of Makronisos for 2 years; practised as lawyer, taking part in several political trials during mil. dictatorship; joined PASOK after fall of dictatorship; M.P. for Second Athens Dist. 1977–; mem. Cen. Cttee., then main speaker for Parl. Working Group on Justice, Domestic Matters and Premiership; Minister for Merchant Marine 1986–88. *Address:* Ministry of Merchant Marine, Odos Vas. Sophias 150, Piraeus, Greece. *Telephone:* (21) 412 1211.

ALEXANDROV (see Aleksandrov).

ALEXANDRU, Constantin; Romanian wrestler; b. 15 Dec. 1953, Constanţa; s. of Nicolae and Tinca Alexandru; m.; one s.; office worker; world champion for juniors, Miami Beach 1973; European champion, Madrid 1974, Ludwigshafen 1975, Bursa 1977, Oslo 1978, Bucharest 1979; Silver Medal World Championship, Katowice 1974, European Championship, Leningrad 1976, Olympic Games, Moscow 1980; World University Games, Bucharest 1981; World Champion Mexico City 1978, San Diego 1979; Champion of Romania's Int. Wrestling Tour 1981. *Address:* Clubul sportiv Steaua, Calea Plevnei 114, Bucharest, Romania. *Telephone:* 49-33-90.

ALEXEYEV (see Alekseyev).

ALEXIADIS, George; Greek lawyer and public official; b. 18 Dec. 1911, Tropea, Arcadia; s. of Dr. Stavros Alexiadis and Panagiota Giannakopoylos; m. Katherine Tsarpalis 1967; ed. Athens Univ.; practising lawyer 1933–; Legal Adviser to Nat. Bank of Greece 1940; head of a resistance org. and pubr. of an underground newspaper 1941–45; Counsellor to Athens Muncipality 1950; fmr. Dir.-Gen. Hellenic Nat. Broadcasting Inst.; Minister of Employment Oct.–Nov. 1973; mem. of European Parl. 1982–; mem. Cen. Cttee. of Hellenic Red Cross 1987; Editorial writer for Vesta; Medal of Nat. Resistance; Gold Medal of Athens Municipality 1987; Progressive Party. *Publications include:* Legal and Social Aspects of the Idea of the State 1939, Introduction to Land Allotment 1941, Geo-Economy and Geo-Policy of Greek Countries 1945 and 1946, The Reform of Criminal Law in Soviet Russia 1957, Perspective 1960, Political History of Modern Greece 1960–63, The First Balkan Alliance of 1867-1868 1971, The Origins of the Greek-Italian War 1973, A Strange Theory About the French Revolution 1975, Territorial Sea—Continental Shelf and the Turkish Pretensions on the Aegean 1976, The Revelation of a Myth—The Greek-Turkish "Friendship" 1977, NATO 1978, Panslavism 1979, The First Greek Legislator 1979, The Law of Ancient Sparta 1987. *Leisure interests:* stamps, gardening. *Address:* 41 Levidou Street, Kiphissia, Greece (Home). *Telephone:* 8083006 (Home).

ALEXIS, Francis, PH.D., LL.M.; Grenada lawyer and politician; b. 3 Oct. 1947, Grenada; s. of John Everest Alexis and Anastasia Omega Alexis; m. Margaret de Bique 1973; two d.; ed. Grenada Boys' Secondary School, Univ. of West Indies, Hugh Wooding Law School and Univ. of Cambridge; fmr. clerk, Jonas Brown & Hubbards Ltd., Grenada; later civil servant, Grenada; Sr. Lecturer in Law, and Deputy Dean, Faculty of Law, Univ. of West Indies; Barrister-at-Law, Grenada; mem. Parl. 1984–; Minister of Labour, Cooperatives, Social Security and Local Govt. 1984–87; Attorney-Gen. and Minister of Legal Affairs and Labour 1987; Opposition M.P. 1987; founder mem. and Deputy Leader New Nat. Party 1986, Nat. Democratic Congress 1987–. *Publications:* Commonwealth Caribbean Legal Essays 1981, Changing Caribbean Constitutions 1983, H. Aubrey Fraser: Eminent

Caribbean Jurist 1985; articles in law journals. *Leisure interests:* reading, writing, music. *Address:* Church Street, St. George's (Office); St. Paul's, St. George's, Grenada (Home). *Telephone:* 809440 1825 (Office); 809 440-2378 (Home).

ALFIDJA, Abderrahmane; Niger politician and financial official; b. 1942; ed. Univs. of Dijon and Paris; Section Chief Trade and Transportation, Research and Programmes Dept., Gen. Devt. Commissariat, Chief of Dept. 1965; Economist, Research Div. UNECE, Geneva 1968–70; Dir. of Research and Programmes 1970, subsequently of Planning, Ministry of Devt. and Co-operation; Sec. of State for Foreign Affairs and Int. Co-operation 1974; Minister of Econ. Affairs, Trade and Industry 1975–78; Alt. Exec. Dir. IMF 1978–82, Exec. Dir. 1982–86. *Address:* c/o Ministry of Foreign Affairs, Niamey, Niger.

ALFONSÍN FOULKES, Dr. Raúl: Argentine lawyer and politician; b. 13 March 1926, Chascomus; m. María Barreneche; three s. three d.; ed. Liceo Militar General San Martín, Nat. Univ. of La Plata; journalist, Chascomus; f. El Imparcial newspaper; joined Movimiento de Intransigencia y Renovación 1944; mem. Unión Cívica Radical (Pres. July 1983–); Municipal Councillor, Chascomus 1950; mem. Buenos Aires Prov. Legislature 1952; imprisoned 1953; mem. Chamber of Deputies 1963–66, 1973–76; f. Movimiento de Renovación y Cambio 1966; Pres. of Argentina Dec. 1983–89; Dr. h.c. (Univ. of New Mexico) 1985, (Santiago de Compostela) 1988; Principe de Asturias Prize 1985, Shared Human Rights Prize of Council of Europe 1986. *Address:* Oficina del Presidente, Casa Rosada, Buenos Aires, Argentina.

ALFONZO-RAVARD, Brig.-Gen. Rafael; Venezuelan petroleum executive and retd. army officer; b. Caracas; s. of Santiago Alfonzo-Rivas and Isabel Ravard de Alfonzo; m. Corina Wallis de Alfonzo 1956; ed. Mil. Acad., Cen. Univ., Mass. Inst. of Tech., U.S.A., Ecole Supérieure de Guerre, France; commissioned Lieut. Venezuelan army 1940; Pres. Comm. on Hydro-electric Devt. of Caroní River 1953, Venezuelan Devt. Corpn. 1958; Acting Minister of Devt. 1958; Gov. for Venezuela, World Bank 1958–74; Pres. Venezuelan Guyana Corpn. 1960–74; Brig.-Gen. 1965; retd. from army 1972; fmr. Pres. Petróleos de Venezuela, S.A.; Pres. Venezuelan Nat. Cttee. World Power/Energy Conf. 1956–; mem. Venezuelan Nat. Acad. of Science 1973; various nat. and foreign mil. and other decorations. *Publications:* Thirty-five Years in the Development of Infrastructure for the Production and Consumption of Energy in Venezuela 1981, 7 Años de una Gestion (speeches) 1982. *Address:* c/o Petroleos de Venezuela, S.A., Edif. Creole, Bello Monte, Aptdo. 169, Caracas 1010, Venezuela.

ALFVÉN, Hannes Olof Gösta, PH.D.; Swedish professor of plasma physics; b. 30 May 1908, Norrköping; s. of Johannes Alfvén and Anna-Clara Alfvén; m. Kerstin Erikson 1935; one s. four d.; ed. Univ. of Uppsala; Prof. of Theory of Electricity, Royal Inst. of Tech., Stockholm 1940–45, of Electronics 1945–63, of Plasma Physics 1963–73; mem. Swedish Acad. of Sciences; Foreign Assoc. U.S. Acad. of Sciences; Foreign mem. USSR Acad. of Sciences, Royal Soc.; mem. other foreign Acads.; Gold Medal, Royal Astronomical Soc. (U.K.) 1967; Nobel Prize for Physics 1970; Lomonosov Gold Medal, U.S.S.R. Acad. of Sciences 1971. *Publications:* papers in physics and astrophysics and: Cosmical Electrodynamics 1950, On the Origin of the Solar System 1954, Cosmical Electrodynamics: Fundamental Principles (with C.-G. Fälthammar) 1963, Worlds-Antiworlds 1966, Cosmic Plasma (monograph) 1981. *Address:* c/o Department of Plasma Physics, Royal Institute of Technology, S-100 44 Stockholm, Sweden; EE & CS, Code 014, University of California, San Diego, La Jolla, Calif. 92093, U.S.A. *Telephone:* (8) 7907691; (619) 5342700.

ALGABID, Hamid; Niger politician; fmr. Minister of State for Planning, Commerce and Transportation; fmr. Minister del. for Finance; Prime Minister of Niger Nov. 1983–. *Address:* Office du Premier Ministre, Niamey, Niger.

ÅLGÅRD, Ole, CAND.JUR.; Norwegian diplomatist; b. 9 Sept. 1921; s. of Gabriel and Bertha Ålgård; m. Rigmor Braathe; one s. one d.; ed. Univ. of Oslo; joined Ministry of Foreign Affairs 1946; Sec., Moscow 1947–50; Chargé d'Affaires, Vienna 1951–56; Ministry of Foreign Affairs, Chief of Section 1956–71; Deputy Perm. Rep. to UN 1961–64; Counsellor, Norwegian Embassy, Brussels and Perm. Rep. to Council of Europe 1964–66; Amb. to People's Repub. of China 1966–71; del. to UN Gen. Ass. 1970–71; Perm. Rep. to UN 1972–82; Amb. to Denmark 1982–. *Leisure interests:* history, fishing, coin and stamp collecting. *Address:* Trondhjems Plads 4, DK-2100 Copenhagen, Denmark. *Telephone:* (45) (1) 38 89 85.

ALGAYER, Jaromir; Czechoslovak politician; b. 1935, Puste Ulany, Galanta District; mem. CP of Czechoslovakia (CPCZ) 1959–; Dir. Regional Agric. Bd. Bratislava 1975–86; Chair. W. Slovak Regional Nat. Cttee. 1986; mem. Cen. Cttee. CP of Slovakia (CPSL); mem. Presidium, West Slovak Regional CPSL Cttee.; Deputy, Slovak Nat. Council 1986–; Minister of Agriculture and Food Oct. 1988–. *Address:* Ministry of Agriculture and Food, Prague, Czechoslovakia.

ALHEGELAN, Sheikh Faisal Abdul Aziz al-; Saudi Arabian diplomatist; b. 7 Oct. 1929, Riyadh; s. of Sheikh Abdul Aziz Al-Hegelan and Fatima Al-Eissa; m. Nouha Tarazi 1961; three s.; ed. Faculty of Law, Fouad Univ., Cairo; Ministry of Foreign Affairs 1952–54; served Embassy in Washington, D.C. 1954–58; Chief of Protocol in Ministry 1958–60; Political Adviser to

H.M. King Sa'ud 1960–61; Amb. to Spain 1961–68, to Venezuela and Argentina 1968–75, to Denmark 1975–76, to U.K. 1976–79, to U.S.A. 1979–83; Minister of State and mem. Council of Ministers (Saudi Arabia) April–Sept. 1984, of Health Sept. 1984–; Chair. Bd. of Dirs., Saudi Red Crescent Soc. 1984–; Order of King Abdulaziz, Gran Cruz Cordon of King Abdul Aziz, Order of Isabela la Católica (Spain), Gran Cordon, Orden de Libertador (Venezuela), Grande Oficial, Orden Riobranco (Brazil). *Leisure interests:* bridge, golf. *Address:* c/o Ministry of Health, Riyadh, Saudi Arabia.

ALI, Ahmad Mohamed, LL.B., D.P.A.; Saudi Arabian development banker; b. 13 April 1932, Medina; s. of Mohamed Ali and Amina Ali; m. Ghada Mahmood Masri 1968; one s. three d.; ed. Cairo Univ., Univ. of Michigan, New York State Univ.; Vice-Chancellor, King Abdul Aziz Univ., Jeddah 1967–72; Deputy Minister for Tech. Affairs, Ministry of Educ. 1972–75; Pres. Islamic Devt. Bank 1975–; mem. Bd. King Saud Univ., Riyadh, King Abdul Aziz Univ., Jeddah; mem. Admin. Bd. Saudi Credit Bank. *Leisure interests:* cycling, walking. *Address:* Islamic Development Bank, P.O. Box 5925, Jeddah 21432, Saudi Arabia. *Telephone:* (1) 33994, (1) 33995.

ALI, Fathi Mohamed, PH.D.; Egyptian politician; Deputy Dean, Faculty of Commerce, Ain Shams Univ. 1978; mem. of Bd. of several banks; Adviser, Cen. Bank of Egypt 1978–; Minister for Higher Educ. 1985–87. *Publications:* many studies in the field of higher educ. *Address:* c/o Ministry for Higher Education, 4 Sharia Ibrahim Nagiv, Cairo (Garden City), Egypt.

ALI, H. A. Mukti; Indonesian comparative religion specialist; b. 1923, Central Java; m.; two s. one d.; ed. Indonesia, Pakistan, Canada; Vice-Chancellor, IAIN "Sunan Kalijaga", Yogjakarta 1964–71; Minister of Religious Affairs 1971–78; mem. Supreme Advisory Council 1978–83; Adviser to UNESCO on Islamic Culture 1979–; mem. Akademi Jakarta 1979–, Advisory Bd. for the Establishment of Parl. of Religions, New York 1984–, Nat. Hijra Council, Islamabad 1986–. *Publications:* Modernization of Islamic Schools, Comparative Religion, its Method and System, Religion and Development in Indonesia etc. *Leisure interest:* reading novels. *Address:* Iain Sunan, Kalijaga, Yogyakarta (Office); Sagan GkI/100, Yogyakarta, Indonesia (Home).

ALI, Lieut.-Gen. Kamal Hassan; Egyptian army officer and politician; b. 18 Sept. 1921, Cairo; m. Amal Khairy; one s. two d.; ed. secondary school, Mil. Acad., British Armoured School, Staff Coll., Festrel Acad., U.S.S.R., Nasser Higher Mil. Acad.; career in Army from graduation at Mil. Acad. 1942; promoted Lieut. 1942, First Lieut. 1946, Capt. 1948; Senior Instructor, Armour School 1953; Major 1954; Staff Officer, 2nd Armoured Operational Group 1956; Lieut.-Col. 1957; Commdr. 70th Brigade 1960; Instructor, Staff Coll. 1961; Brigadier 1965, Commdr. 2nd Armoured Brigade 1966; Chief of Staff, 21st Armoured Div. 1968, Commdr. 1969; Chief of Operational Branch, Operations Dept. 1970; Major-Gen. and Chief of Staff of Armoured Corps 1971; Dir. 1972; Asst. Minister of War 1975; Chief of Gen. Intelligence 1975; Minister of Defence and War Production, C.-in-C. of Armed Forces, Lieut.-Gen. 1978–80; Deputy Prime Minister and Minister of Foreign Affairs 1980–84, Prime Minister of Egypt 1984–85; Chair. Egyptian Gulf Bank 1987–; Liberation Order 1952, Memorial Order 1958; many ribbons and medals. *Address:* El Orman Plaza Building, 8, 10 Ahmed Nessim Street, Giza; 110 Amar Ibn Yasser, Misr El Gadida, Egypt. *Telephone:* 2442700.

ALI, Lieut.-Gen. Mir Shawkat; Bangladesh diplomatist; b. 19 Jan. 1938, Dhaka; s. of Mir Mahboob Ali and Begum Shahajadi; m. Begum Tahmina Shawkat 1963; one s. three d.; ed. Mil. Acad., Kakul and Command and Staff Coll., Quetta; held posts in Bangladesh Army of Chief of Gen. Staff, and Prin. Staff Officer to Supreme Commdr. of Armed Forces; Commdr. two Brigades and two Infantry Divs.; retd. from Army 1981 with rank of Lieut.-Gen.; Amb. to Egypt 1981 (also accred. to Sudan and Ethiopia), then to Fed. Repub. of Germany (also accred. to Austria), High Commr. to U.K. (also accred. to Portugal) 1986–87; Bir Uttam 1971; Pres. Gold Medal (twice). *Leisure interests:* reading, cuisine, outdoor sports. *Address:* c/o Ministry of Foreign Affairs, Dhaka, Bangladesh.

ALI, Muhammad; American boxer; b. (as Cassius Marcellus Clay) 17 Jan. 1942, Louisville, Ky.; s. of Cassius Marcellus Clay Sr. and Odetta Lee Grady; m. 1st Sonje Roi (dissolved 1966); m. 2nd Belinda Boyd (Khalilah Toloria) 1967 (divorced 1977); four c.; m. 3rd Veronica Porche 1977, one c.; m. 4th Yolanda Williams; ed. Louisville; amateur boxer 1954–60, Olympic Games light-heavyweight champion 1960; professional boxer 1960–, won world heavyweight title Feb. 1964, defeating Sonny Liston; adopted name Muhammad Ali 1964; stripped of title after refusing to be drafted into U.S. Army 1967, won case in U.S. Supreme Court and returned to professional boxing 1970; regained world heavyweight title Oct. 1974, defeating George Foreman in Zaire; lost title to Leon Spinks 1978, regained title from Spinks 1978; 56 victories in 61 fights up to Dec. 1981; lost to Larry Holmes Oct. 1980; mem. of U.S. Black Muslim movement; Special Envoy of President Carter to Africa 1980 (to urge boycott of Olympic Games); fmr. mem. Peace Corps Advisory Council; acted in films The Greatest 1976, Freedom Road 1980 and in Freedom Road (television) 1978; Hon. Consul-Gen. for Bangladesh in Chicago Feb. 1978–. *Publications:* The Greatest: My Own Story (autobiography) 1975. *Address:* P.O. Box 76972, Los Angeles, Calif. 90076, U.S.A.

ALI, Sadiq, B.A.; Indian politician; b. 1910, Udaipur, Rajasthan; s. of Shri Tahir Ali; m. Shrimati Shanti Sadiq Ali 1951; ed. Allahabad Univ; Gen. Sec. Indian Nat. Congress, New Delhi, Perm. Sec. All-India Congress Cttee. 1938–47; mem. Lok Sabha 1951–52, Rajya Sabha 1958–70; Gen. Sec. Indian Nat. Congress 1958–64, 1966–69; Pres. Opposition Congress Party 1971–73; Chief Ed. AICC Econ. Review 1960–69; Chair. Gandhi Smarak Sangrahalaya Samiti 1966–77; Gov. of Maharashtra 1977–80, of Tamil Nadu 1980–82; associated with Indian freedom movement 1930; Chair. Gandhi Nat. Museum and Library, New Delhi 1965–. *Publications:* Know Your Country, Congress Ideology and Programme, Culture of India, General Election 1957, Towards Socialist Thinking in Congress, Campaign Against Nuclear Arms. *Address:* c/o Raj Bhavan, Madras 22, Tamil Nadu, India.

ALI, Salah Omar Al-; Iraqi politician and diplomatist; b. 1 July 1937; m.; three c.; ed. Univ. of Baghdad; fmr. Minister of Information; mem. Revolutionary Command Council of Iraq 1968–70, of Baath Socialist Party; Ed.-in-Chief Al-Thawra 1969; Amb. to Sweden 1972–76, to Spain 1976–78; Permanent Rep. of Iraq to UN 1978–82. *Address:* c/o Ministry of Foreign Affairs, Baghdad, Iraq.

ALI, Saleh Ahmad al-; D.PHIL.; Iraqi professor of history; b. 1918, Mosul; m. Aida al-Ali 1954; two s. five d.; ed. High Teachers' Coll., Baghdad, Univs. of Cairo and Oxford; lecturer, then Asst. Prof., then Prof. 1949–; Head, Dept. of History, Coll. of Arts, Baghdad 1956–58; Dean, Inst. of Higher Islamic Studies, Baghdad 1964–68; Chief, Centre of Arabic Heritage Studies, Baghdad 1979–82; Pres. Iraqi Acad. 1978–; Fuad Jalal Prize (Cairo). *Publications:* Social and Economic Organization in Basrah, Lectures on Arabic History, Extension of the Arabs, Studies in the Development of Arabic Thought and numerous articles. *Address:* Iraqi Academy, Waziriyah, Baghdad, Iraq. *Telephone:* 25026 (Baghdad); 5511385.

ALI, Sultan Abu, PH.D.; Egyptian politician; b. Nov. 1937; ed. Harvard Univ.; worked at stock exchange, Alexandria 1955–65; Fellow, Inst. of Nat. Planning 1965–67; Kuwaiti Fund for Devt. 1973–79; Deputy Chair. Investment Authority July 1984–; Minister of Economy and Foreign Trade 1985–86. *Address:* c/o Ministry of the Economy, 8 Sharia Adly, Cairo, Egypt.

ALI, Zine El Abidene ben; Tunisian politician; b. 3 Sept. 1936, Hammam Sousse; m.; three c.; ed. as graduate in electronics, Saint-Cyr Military Acad. (France), Chalons-sur-Marne School of Artillery (France), Special School of Intelligence and Security (U.S.A.); Head of Mil. Security 1958–74; Mil. and Naval Attaché, Rabat, Morocco 1974–77; mem. of Cabinet for Minister of Nat. Defence, Dir.-Gen. Nat. Security 1977–80; Amb. to Poland 1980–84; Sec. of State for Nat. Security 1984–85, Minister of the Interior 1986–87, Minister of State for the Interior May-Nov. 1987, Pres. of Tunisia Nov. 1987–; mem. politbureau of Parti Socialiste Destourien (PSD) 1986, Sec.-Gen. PSD 1986; Order of Merit of Bourguiba, Order of Independence, Order of the Repub., several foreign orders. *Address:* Présidence de la République, Tunis, Tunisia.

ALI SAMATER, Gen. Mohammed; Somali army officer and politician; b. 1931, Chisimaio; ed. Intermediate School, Mogadishu, Mil. Acad., Rome, Mil. Acad., Moscow; Commdt. Somali Police 1956, Maj.-Adjutant 1958–65; Brig.-Gen. Nat. Army 1967, Maj.-Gen. 1973; Sec. of State for Defence 1971–76, C.-in-C. Armed Forces 1971–78; fmr. Vice-Pres. Political Bureau, Somali Socialist Revolutionary Party; Minister of Defence 1976–81, 1982–; First Vice-Pres. Supreme Revolutionary Council (now Council of Ministers) 1982–; Prime Minister of Somalia 1987–; Chair. Defence and Security Cttee., Supreme Council of the Revolution 1980–82, Vice-Pres. of Council 1981–82. *Address:* Office of the Prime Minister, Mogadishu, Somalia.

ALIA, Ramiz; Albanian politician; b. 1925, Shkodër; m. Semiram Alia; active in 1939–45 war; mem. of political shock 7th brigade; political leader 2nd Div.; fought in Yugoslavia at Kosova, Metohia, Sandjak, Political Commissar of the 5th Div.; First Sec. Cen. Cttee. Communist Youth –1955; Minister of Educ.; mem. of the Cen. Cttee. CP since the 1st Congress; since 4th Congress mem. of the Politburo, Sec. Cen. Cttee. CP, First Sec. April 1985–; Vice-Chair. of the Gen. Council of the Democratic Front of Albania; Deputy to People's Ass. from 2nd Legislature; Chair. Presidium of People's Ass. (Head of State) Nov. 1982–. *Address:* Office of the President, Tirana, Albania.

ALIER, Abel, LL.B., LL.M.; Sudanese politician; b. 1933, Bor District, Upper Nile Province; s. of Kwai and Anaai Alier; m. Siama Fatma Bilal 1970; one s. two d.; ed. Univs. of Khartoum and Yale; former advocate; District Judge in El Obeid, Wad Medani and Khartoum until 1965; participant in Round Table Conf. and mem. Twelve Man Cttee. to Study the Southern problem 1965; mem. Constitution Comms. 1966–67, 1968; fmr. mem. Law Reform Comm. and Southern Front; Minister of Supply and Internal Trade 1969–70; Minister of Works 1970–71; Minister of Southern Affairs 1971–72, of Construction and Public Works 1983–85; Vice-Pres. 1971–82; Pres. Supreme Exec. Council for the South 1972–78, 1980–81; mem. Political Bureau, Sudanese Socialist Union, Bd. of Dirs., Industrial Planning Corpn.; mem. Nat. Scholarship Bd.; Hon. LL.D. (Khartoum) 1978. *Leisure interests:* tennis, athletics, reading, history and literature. *Address:* c/o Ministry of Construction and Public Works, Sudan.

ALIEVA, Fazu; Soviet Avar poet; b. 1932, Ginichutl, Daghestan A.S.S.R.; mem. CPSU 1965–; ed. Moscow Gorky Inst.; People's Poet of Daghestan

1969, Order of the Badge of Honour. *Works include:* Native Village 1959, The Blue Road 1959, On the Sea-Shore 1961, Spring Wind 1962, I Give Out Rainbows 1963, In the Heart of Every Person is Ilyich 1965, Fate (novel) 1964, The Carving on the Stone 1966, The Wind Won't Carry Away the Clod of Earth (novel) 1967, The Eighteenth Spring 1968. *Address:* U.S.S.R. Union of Writers, Ulitsa Vorovskogo 52, Moscow, U.S.S.R.

ALIGER, Margarita Iosifovna; Soviet poetess; b. 7 Oct. 1915, Odessa; m. Konstantin Makarov-Rakitin 1936 (died 1941); two d.; ed. Gorky Literary Inst.; mem. C.P.S.U. 1942–; State prizewinner 1943; Order of Red Banner of Labour 1965; Badge of Honour; Order of Friendship of the Peoples 1975, Stalin Prize. *Publications:* Year of Birth 1938, The Railway 1939, Stones and Grasses 1940, To the Memory of the Brave 1942, Zoya 1942, Lyrics 1943, Your Victory 1946, Selected Poems 1947, A Tale of Truth 1947, First Thunder 1947, First Signs 1948, The Lenin Hills 1953, The Beautiful Metcha-River 1953, Man on His Way 1954, Lyrics 1955, From a Notebook 1957, Lyrics and Poems 1959, A Few Steps 1964, Poetry 1967, The Blue Hour 1970, Poems in 2 vols. 1970, Verse and Prose (2 vols.) 1975; Essays: Chilean Summer 1965, Return to Chile 1966; trans. poems of Aragon, Pablo Neruda, Bagriana, etc. 1968, A Path Through the Rye, Essays and Memoirs 1980, Quarter of a Century Poetry 1981. *Address:* 17 Lavrushinsky per. app. 41, Moscow 109017, U.S.S.R. *Telephone:* 2315894.

ALIMARIN, Ivan Pavlovich; Soviet chemist; b. 11 Sept. 1903, Moscow; s. of Pavel and Maria Alimarin; m. Zoya Alimarina 1936; one s. one d.; ed. Moscow Univ.; at All-Union Research Inst. of Mineral Raw Materials 1923–53; Prof. Moscow Inst. of Fine Chemical Tech. 1950–1953, Moscow Univ. 1953–; at Inst. of Geochemistry and Analytical Chem., U.S.S.R. Acad. of Sciences 1949–; Corresp. mem. U.S.S.R. Acad. of Sciences 1953–66, mem. 1966–; Hon. mem. Analytical Chem. Soc., England 1968–; Acad. of Science, Finland 1974–, Chemical Soc. of the German Democratic Repub.; Hon. D.Phil. (Polytechnical Univ., Budapest) 1971, (Göteborg) 1973, D.Sc. (Birmingham, U.K.); State Prize; Order of Lenin (four times), Hero of Socialist Labour and other decorations. *Publications:* Qualitative Poly-microanalysis 1952, Inorganic Ultramicroanalysis 1960, Qualitative Micro-analysis of Minerals and Ores 1961. *Leisure interests:* photography, fishing. *Address:* V.I. Vernadsky Institute of Geochemistry and Analytical Chemistry, 19 Kosygin Str., 117334 Moscow, U.S.S.R.

ALIMOV, Aleksandr Nikolayevich; Soviet economist; b. 30 Sept. 1923, Donetsk; s. of Nikolag Alimov and Yevdokiya Alimova; m. Olga Amosovna Alimova 1944; two s.; ed. Union Financial Inst.; served in Soviet Army 1941–47; mem. CPSU 1943–; active in various trusts 1949–53; student, Moscow Mining Inst. 1953–57; Section Chief in Dept. of Mining Econ. at Coal Research Inst., Donetsk, later Chief of Inst. 1957–64; Deputy Dir. Inst. of Econs. at Acad. of Sciences of Ukrainian S.S.R. 1965–, Section Chief 1984–; Corresp. mem. Ukrainian S.S.R. Acad. of Sciences 1966–, mem. 1973–; Order of Red Banner (twice), Order of Fatherland War (1st class), Order of Alexander Nevsky, several medals. *Leisure interest:* motorcar enthusiast. *Publications:* over 300 scientific works. *Address:* Institute of Economics, Academy of Sciences of Ukrainian S.S.R., Ul. P. Myrnogo 26, Kiev, U.S.S.R.

ALIMOV, Timur Agzamovich; Soviet politician; b. 1936; ed. Tashkent Inst. of Irrigation Engineering and Agric. Mechanisation; engineer on construction of channel in Afghanistan 1960–62; senior engineer, Uzgipro-vodkhoz 1962–65; senior engineer, Dir. of Tashkent reservoir div. 1965–67; mem. of CPSU 1967–; Head of section of water supply and irrigation with Uzbek SSR Council of Mins. 1967–75; Man., Uzbek SSR Council of Ministers 1975–78; Pres. of Tashkent Exec. Cttee. of Uzbek CP. 1978–85; First Sec. of Tashkent Exec. Cttee. of Uzbek CP. 1985–; Cand. mem. of CPSU Cen. Cttee. 1986–. *Address:* Uzbek SSR Council of Ministers, Tashkent, Uzbekistan, U.S.S.R.

ALIOTO, Joseph Lawrence; American lawyer and politician; b. 1916, San Francisco, Calif.; s. of Giuseppe and Domenica (Lazio) Alioto; m. Angelina Genaro 1941 (divorced 1977); m. 2nd Kathleen Sullivan Alioto; six s. one d.; ed. Roman Catholic coll.; fmr. govt. lawyer, Washington, specializing in anti-trust cases; returned to private practice in Calif.; Sec. Rice Growers' Asscn. of Calif.; Mayor of San Francisco 1968–76; Democrat. *Leisure interests:* music, reading, golf. *Address:* City Hall, San Francisco, Calif. 94102, U.S.A.

ALIREZA, Ali A.; Saudi Arabian diplomatist; m.; ed. Falah School, Victoria Coll., Alexandria, Univ. of California, Berkeley; attached to del. to UN, San Francisco 1945; Adviser to H.R.H. Prince Faisal 1946; Minister Plenipotentiary 1947; del. to UN 1947–53; Minister of State attached to Office of Prince Faisal 1955; del. to Bandung Conf. Indonesia 1955; mem. Bd. of Dirs., Saudi Arabian Monetary Agency 1970–; Amb. to U.S.A., also accred. to Mexico 1975–79. *Address:* c/o Ministry of Foreign Affairs, Jeddah, Saudi Arabia.

ALIYEV, Geidar Ali Rza Ogly; Soviet politician; b. 10 May 1923, Baku, Azerbaizhan; ed. Azerbaizhan State Univ.; official of security forces and mem. Council of Ministers of Nakhichevan Autonomous Repub. 1941–49; student 1949–50; leading official of Ministry of Internal Affairs and Cttee. of State Security (KGB) of Azerbaizhan S.S.R.; Deputy Chair. KGB, Azerbaizhan S.S.R. 1964–67, Chair. 1967–69, rank of Maj.-Gen.; cand. mem. Cen. Cttee. of Communist Party of Azerbaizhan (CPA) 1966–69, mem.

Cen. Cttee. CPA 1969–, mem. Bureau of CPA 1969–, First Sec. Cen. Cttee. of CPA 1969–82; mem. CPSU 1945–, mem. Cen. Cttee. CPSU 1971–, cand. mem. Politburo of Cen. Cttee. CPSU 1976–82, mem. 1983–87; Deputy to U.S.S.R. Supreme Soviet 1970–74; Vice-Chair. Soviet of the Union 1974; First Deputy Chair. U.S.S.R. Council of Ministers 1982–87; Order of Lenin (three times) and other decorations, including Hammer and Sickle Gold Medal, Hero of Socialist Labour (twice). *Address:* c/o Council of Ministers, The Kremlin, Moscow, U.S.S.R.

ALKHIMOV, Vladimir Sergeyevich; Soviet foreign trade official and banker; b. 25 Oct. 1919; s. of Sergei Alkhimov; m. Antonia Alkhimov 1946; two d.; ed. Leningrad Financial and Economic Inst., and Acad. of Foreign Trade; mem. CPSU 1942–; Chief of Dept., later Deputy Dir., Research Inst. of World Markets 1950–57; Commercial Counsellor, U.S.A. 1957–60; Deputy Chief, later Chief of Dept., Ministry of Foreign Trade 1961–67; Deputy Minister of Foreign Trade 1967–76; Chair. of the Bd., U.S.S.R. State Bank 1976–86; Deputy to U.S.S.R. Supreme Soviet 1977–; cand. mem. Cen. Cttee. CPSU 1981–82, mem. 1982–; State Prize 1982, Hero of Soviet Union, Order of Lenin (three times), Gold Star Medal, Order of the Red Banner and other decorations. *Address:* c/o State Bank of the U.S.S.R., 12 Neglinnaya ulitsa, Moscow 103016, U.S.S.R.

ALLADAYE, Maj. Michel; Benin army officer; b. 1940, Abomey; m.; five c.; ed. Lycée Victor Ballot, Ecole Mil. de Saint-Cyr, Ecole Supérieure Technique du Génie, Versailles; Commdr. 1st Eng. Corps, Dahomey Armed Forces, Kandi 1963–67; promoted to rank of Capt. 1967; worked successively in Eng. Unit, Army Gen. Staff Command, Services Battalion Command; Commdr., Dir. Mil. Engs.; Minister of Foreign Affairs 1972–80, of Co-operation 1976–80, of Legislation and Social Affairs 1980–82, of Justice 1980–83; Chevalier, Légion d'honneur. *Address:* c/o Ministère de Justice, Cotonou, Benin.

ALLAIS, Maurice; French economist and engineer; b. 31 May 1911, Paris; s. of Maurice and Louise (Caubet) Allais; m. Jacqueline Bouteloup 1960; one d.; ed. Ecole Polytechnique and Ecole Nat. Supérieure des Mines de Paris; Dept. of Mines and Quarries 1937–43; Dir. Bureau de Documentation Minière 1943–48; econ. research 1948–; Prof. of Economic Analysis, Ecole Nat. Supérieure des Mines de Paris 1944–; Prof. of Econ. Theory, Inst. of Statistics, Univ. of Paris 1947–68; Dir. of Research, Centre Nat. de la Recherche Scientifique 1954–; Dir. Centre for Econ. Analysis 1946–; Prof. Graduate Inst. of Int. Studies, Geneva 1967–70; Dir. Séminaire Clément Juglar d'Analyse Monétaire, Univ. of Paris-X (Nanterre) 1970–; Dr. h.c. (Groningen); Lanchester Prize, American Soc. for Operations Research, Gold Medal, Société d'Encouragement pour l'Industrie Nationale, Gold Medal, Centre National de la Recherche Scientifique, Prix Robert Blanché, Grand Prix Zerilli Marumó, Académie des Sciences Morales et Politiques, Nobel Prize for Econs. 1988 and other awards; Hon. Ingénieur Général au Corps des Mines; Officier Légion d'honneur, Officier Palmes académiques, Chevalier Ordre de l'Economie Nationale. *Publications:* A la Recherche d'un Discipline Economique 1943, Abondance ou misère 1946, Economie et intérêt 1947, Traité d'économie pure 1952, La gestion des houillères nationalisées et la théorie économique 1953, Les fondements comptables de la macroéconomie 1954, Le pendule paraconique 1957–59, Manifeste pour une société libre 1958, L'Europe unie, route de la prospérité 1960, Le Tiers-Monde au carrefour—Centralisation autoritaire ou planification concurrentielle 1962, L'Algérie d'Evian 1962, The Role of Capital in Economic Development 1963, Reformulation de la théorie quantitative de la monnaie 1965, L'Impôt sur le capital 1966, The Conditions of the Efficiency in the Economy 1967, Growth without Inflation 1968, Growth and Inflation 1969, La libéralisation des relations économiques internationales 1970, Les théories de l'équilibre économique général et de l'efficacité maximale 1971, Forgetfulness and Interest 1972, The General Theory of Surplus and Pareto's Fundamental Contribution 1973, Inequality and Civilization 1973, La création de monnaie et de pouvoir d'achat par le mécanisme du crédit 1974, The Psychological Rate of Interest 1974, L'inflation française et la croissance 1974, Classes sociales et civilisations 1974, Taux d'expansion de la dépense globale et vitesse de circulation de la monnaie 1975, Inflation répartition des revenus et indexation 1976, L'impôt sur le capital et la réforme monétaire 1977, Expected Utility Hypotheses and the Allais Paradox 1979, La théorie générale des surplus 1980, Frequency, Probability and Chance 1982, The Foundations of the Theory of Utility and Risk 1984, Determination of Cardinal Utility 1985, The Concepts of Surplus and Loss and the Reformulation of the Theories of Stable General Economic Equilibrium and Maximum Efficiency 1985, The Empirical Approaches of the Hereditary and Relativistic Theory of the Demand for Money 1985. *Leisure interests:* history, physics, swimming, skiing. *Address:* 62 boulevard Saint Michel, 75006 Paris (Office); 15 rue des Gâte-Ceps, 92210 Saint-Cloud, France (Home). *Telephone:* 46 02 53 35 (Home).

ALLAN, Sir Colin Hamilton, K.C.M.G., O.B.E., M.A., F.R.A.I.; British overseas administrator (retd.); b. 23 Oct. 1921, Wellington, New Zealand; s. of John Calder Allan and Mabel Eastwood; m. Betty Dorothy Evans 1955; three s.; ed. Hamilton High School, Canterbury Univ., Magdalene Coll., Cambridge Univ.; Cadet, Admin. Service, British Solomon Islands 1945; District Commr., Western Solomons 1946–49, Malaita 1949–52; Special Lands Commr. 1953–57; Sr. Asst. Sec. Western Pacific High Comm. 1957–58; Asst. Resident Commr. New Hebrides 1959–66, Resident Commr. 1966–73;

Gov. and C.-in-C. Seychelles, Commr. British Indian Ocean Territory 1973-76; Gov. Solomon Islands and High Commr. for Western Pacific 1976-78; Visiting Fellow Australian Nat. Univ.; mem. Leprosy Trust Bd., N.Z.; mem. N.Z. Advisory Council to Archbishop, Prov. of Melanesia 1982; Trustee, Ranfurly Library Service, N.Z. 1984- (Chair. 1986); Visiting Lecturer Auckland Univ., Univ. of N.S.W.; Commdr. l'ordre Nat. du Mérite 1966. *Publications:* Customary Land Tenure in the British Solomon Islands Protectorate 1958; articles on overseas admin., anthropology, etc. *Leisure interests:* reading The Times, visiting art galleries. *Address:* Glen Rowan, 17 Sale Street, Howick, Auckland, New Zealand (Home). *Telephone:* 535 6462.

ALLAN, James Nicholas, C.B.E., B.SC.ECON.; British diplomatist; b. 22 May 1932, London; s. of Morris Allan and the late Joan Bach; m. Helena Susara Crouse 1961; one s. one d.; ed. Gresham's School, Holt, Norfolk, London School of Econs.; mil. service 1950-53; Asst. Prin., Commonwealth Relations Office (CRO) 1956-58; Third, then Second Sec., High Commission, S. Africa 1958-59; Private Sec. to Parliamentary Under-Sec. 1959-61; First Sec., High Comm., Sierra Leone 1961-64, Cyprus 1964; CRO, then FCO 1964-68; Head of Chancery, Embassy, People's Repub. of China 1969-71, Luxembourg 1971-73; Northern Ireland Office, Belfast 1973-75; Counsellor, FCO 1976; Head of Overseas Information Dept., FCO 1978-81; Gov.'s Staff, Salisbury, S. Rhodesia 1979-80; High Commr. in Mauritius 1981-85, also Amb. to Fed. Islamic Repub. of Comoros 1984-85; Amb. to Mozambique 1986-. *Address:* c/o Foreign and Commonwealth Office, King Charles Street, London, S.W.1, England.

ALLAN, John Dykes, B.A.SC.; Canadian industrialist; b. 31 July 1925, Vancouver; s. of William Allan; m. Marjorie Alice Pearson 1949; ed. Lord Byng High School, Vancouver, and Univ. of British Columbia; Pres. and C.E.O. Stelco (Steel Co. of Canada) Inc.; Dir. Stelco Inc., Royal Trustco Ltd., Toronto Dominion Bank, Rockwell Int. of Canada Ltd., C-I-L Inc., Gulf Canada Ltd.; mem. American Iron and Steel Inst., Int. Iron and Steel Inst., Canadian Mfrs. Asscn. *Leisure interests:* golf, cross-country skiing. *Address:* 2238 Shardawn Mews, Mississauga, Ont., L5C 1W5 (Home); Toronto-Dominion Centre, P.O. Box 205, Toronto, Ont., M5K 1J4, Cananda (Office).

ALLARDT, Erik Anders, M.A., PH.D.; Finnish professor of sociology; b. 9 Aug. 1925, Helsinki; m. Sagi Nylander 1947; one s. two d.; ed. Univ. of Helsinki; Prof. of Sociology, Univ. of Helsinki 1958-85, Dean of the Faculty of Social Sciences 1969-70; Pres. Acad. of Finland 1986-; Fellow, Woodrow Int. Center for Scholars 1978-79; Visiting Prof. numerous countries and univs.; Hon. Dr. (Stockholm) 1978, (Åbo Akademi) 1978, (Uppsala) 1984. *Publications:* (with Rokkan) Mass Politics: Studies in Political Sociology 1970, Implications of the Ethnic Revival in Modern, Industrialized Society 1979, (with Lysgaard and Sørensen) Sociologin i Sverige, vetenskap, miljö och organisation 1988. *Address:* The Academy of Finland, P.O. Box 57, SF-00551 Helsinki, Finland. *Telephone:* 358-0-77581.

ALLCHIN, Frank Raymond, PH.D., F.B.A., F.S.A.; British university lecturer; b. 9 July 1923, Harrow; s. of Frank MacDonald Allchin and Louise Maude Wright; m. Bridget Gordon 1951; one s. one d.; ed. Regent Street Polytechnic School of Architecture and S.O.A.S., London; Lecturer in Indian Archaeology, S.O.A.S. 1954-59; Lecturer in Indian Studies, Cambridge 1959-72, Reader 1972-; Fellow of Churchill Coll., Cambridge 1963-. *Publications:* Co-author: The Birth of Indian Civilization 1968, The Rise of Civilization in India and Pakistan 1982. *Leisure interests:* walking, gardening. *Address:* Westgate House, 3 Orwell Road, Barrington, Cambridge, CB2 5SE, England.

ALLÈGRE, Maurice Marie, L. EN D.; French research co-ordinator; b. 16 Feb. 1933, Antibes; s. of Guy Allègre and Renée-Lise Bermond; m. Catherine Pierre 1962; one s. one d.; ed. Ecole Polytechnique, Ecole nat. supérieure des Mines and Ecole nat. supérieure du pétrole et des moteurs; Researcher Direction des Carburants, Ministry of Industry 1957-62; Dir. Mines de l'Organisme Saharien 1962-64; Tech. Adviser to Ministry of Finance and Econ. Affairs 1965-67; Pres. Inst. de Recherche d'informatique et d'automatique 1968-74; Chief of Mission to New Caledonia 1975; Asst. Dir.-Gen. Inst. Français du Pétrole 1976-81; Pres. and Dir.-Gen. ISIS 1976-81; Pres. FRANLAB, COFLEXIP 1976-81; Dir. Scientific and Tech. Devt., Ministry of Research and Tech. 1982-84; Pres. Agence nat. de valorisation et de la Recherche 1982-84; Dir.-Gen. Bureau de Recherches Géologiques et Minières 1984-88, Pres. Oct. 1988-. *Leisure interests:* photography, skiing, sailing. *Address:* Bureau de Recherches Géologiques et Minières, Tour Mirabeau, 39-43 Quai André Citroën, 75739 Paris Cedex 15, France. *Telephone:* (33) 1 45 78 33 33.

ALLEN, Sir Douglas Albert Vivian, G.C.B. (see Croham, Baron).

ALLEN, Gary James, B.COM., F.C.M.A.; British business executive; b. 30 Sept. 1944, Birmingham; s. of Alfred Allen; m. Judith A. Nattrass 1966; three s.; ed. King Edward VI Grammar School, Aston, Birmingham and Liverpool Univ.; Man. Dir. IMI Range Ltd. 1973-77; Dir. IMI PLC 1978-, Man. Dir. 1986-; Dir. N. V. Bekaert SA, Belgium 1987-; Chair. Optilon Ltd. 1979-84, Eley Ltd. 1981-85, IMI Components Ltd. 1981-85; mem. Nat. Council CBI 1986-; mem. Council, Birmingham Chamber of Industry and Commerce 1983- (Chair. Industrial Affairs Cttee. 1985-88); mem. Council Univ. of Birmingham 1985- and Hon. Life mem. Court 1984-.

Leisure interests: sport, reading, gardening. *Address:* IMI PLC, P.O. Box 216, Birmingham, B6 7BA (Office). *Telephone:* 021-356 4848 (Office).

ALLEN, Sir Geoffrey, Kt., PH.D., F.R.S., F.INST.P., F.P.R.I.; British polymer scientist and administrator; b. 29 Oct. 1928, Clay Cross, Derbyshire; s. of John James and Marjorie Allen; m. Valerie Frances Duckworth 1972; one d.; ed. Clay Cross Tupton Hall Grammar School, Univ. of Leeds; Postdoctoral Fellow, Nat. Research Council, Canada 1952-54; Lecturer, Univ. of Manchester 1955-65, Prof. of Chemical Physics 1965-75; Prof. of Polymer Science, Imperial Coll. of Science and Tech., Univ. of London 1975-76, of Chemical Tech. 1976-81, Fellow Imperial Coll. 1986-; Chair. Science Research Council 1977-81; Head, Unilever Research Oct. 1981-, Dir. of Unilever responsible for Research and Eng. 1982-; Visiting Fellow, Robinson Coll., Cambridge 1980-; Hon. M.Sc. (Manchester); Dr h.c. (Open Univ.); Hon. D.Sc. (Durham) 1984, (Bath, Bradford, Keele, Loughborough) 1985, (Essex, Leeds) 1986, (Cranfield) 1988. *Leisure interests:* walking, talking, eating.

ALLEN, John Frank, M.SC., M.A., PH.D., F.R.S., F.R.S.E; British professor of physics; b. 6 May 1908, Winnipeg, Canada; s. of Prof. Frank Allen and Sarah (née Harper) Allen; m. Elfriede Hiebert 1933 (divorced 1947); one adopted s.; ed. Univ. of Manitoba, Univ. of Toronto, Calif. Inst. of Tech. Univ. of Cambridge; with Ministry of Supply 1939-44; Lecturer and Fellow, St. John's Coll., Cambridge 1938-47; Prof. of Natural Philosophy, Univ. of St. Andrews 1947-78, Prof. Emer. 1978-. *Films:* Superfluid Helium 1983, The Meissner Effect 1985, The Standing Soliton 1986. *Publications:* numerous articles on low temperature research. *Leisure interests:* golf, film making. *Address:* 2 Shorehead, St. Andrews, KY16 9RG, Scotland. *Telephone:* (0334) 72717.

ALLEN, John Robert Lawrence, D.SC., F.R.S., F.G.S.; British professor of geology; b. 25 Oct. 1932; s. of George Eustace Allen and Alice Josephine (née Formby); m. Jean Mary Wood 1960; four s. one d.; ed. St. Philip's Grammar School, Birmingham, Univ. of Sheffield; mem. staff, Univ. of Reading 1959-, Prof. of Geology 1972-; Lyell Medal, Geological Soc. 1980, David Linton Award, British Geomorphological Research Group 1983, Twenhofel Medal, Soc. of Econ. Paleontologists and Minerologists 1987. *Publications:* Current Ripples 1968, Physical Processes of Sedimentation 1970, Sedimentary Structures 1982, Principles of Physical Sedimentology 1985; numerous contribs. to professional journals. *Leisure interests:* music, opera. *Address:* 17c Whiteknights Road, Reading, Berks., RG6 2BY, England. *Telephone:* Reading 64621.

ALLEN, John Walter, M.A., F.R.S.E.; British physicist; b. 7 March 1928, Birmingham; s. of Walter Allen and Beryl Parsons; m. 1st Mavis Williamson 1956 (died 1972), 2nd Hania Szawelska 1981; one s.; ed. King Edward's School, Birmingham and Sidney Sussex Coll., Cambridge; R.A.F. Educ. Br. 1949-51; staff scientist, Ericsson Telephones, Nottingham 1951-56; Royal Naval Scientific Service, Services Electronics Research Lab. 1956-68; Visiting Prof. Stanford Univ. 1964-66; Tullis Russell Fellow, Univ. of St. Andrews 1968-72, Reader in Physics, Dir. of Wolfson Inst. of Luminescence 1972-81, Prof. of Solid State Physics 1981-. *Publications:* some 80 papers in scientific journals including the first account of a practical light-emitting diode. *Leisure interests:* archaeology, traditional dance. *Address:* Department of Physics, University of St. Andrews, North Haugh, St. Andrews, Fife, Scotland. *Telephone:* 0334-76-161.

ALLEN, Gen. Lew, Jr., M.S., PH.D.; American air force officer; b. 30 Sept. 1925, Miami, Dade, Fla.; s. of the late Lew Allen and Zella Holman; m. Barbara McKelden Frink 1949; two s. three d.; ed. Gainesville Junior Coll., U.S. Mil. Acad. West Point, Air Tactical School Tyndall, Univ. of Illinois; Pilot, Carswell Air Force Base, Tex. 1946-50; Physicist, Los Alamos Scientific Laboratory, N.M. 1954-57; various posts Kirkland Air Force Base, N.M. 1957-61; Space Tech. Office and OSD, Washington, D.C. 1961-65; OSAF, Los Angeles, Calif. 1965-68; OSAF Washington, D.C. 1968-70; OSAF, Los Angeles, Calif. 1970-71; SAMSO, Los Angeles, Calif. 1971-73; c/s, HQ AFSC, Andrews Air Force Base, Md. 1973; Deputy to Dir. of Cen. Intelligence for the Intelligence Community 1973; Dir. NSA and Chief of Cen. Security Service, Fort Meade, Md. 1973-77; Commdr., AFSC, Andrews Air Force Base 1977-78; Vice-Chief of Staff USAF April-June 1978, Chief of Staff USAF 1978-82; Dir. Jet Propulsion Lab., Pasadena, Calif. 1982-; mem. Nat. Acad. of Eng. 1977-; Defense Distinguished Service Medal, Distinguished Service Medal of the Air Force, Legion of Merit with 2 Oak Leaf Clusters, Joint Service Commendation and various other U.S. awards and medals, Order of Nat. Security (Repub. of Korea). *Leisure interests:* racquet ball, scuba diving, jogging. *Address:* Jet Propulsion Laboratory, California Institute of Technology, 4800 Oak Grove Drive, Pasadena, Calif. 91109, U.S.A. *Telephone:* (818) 354-3405.

ALLEN, Percival, PH.D., F.R.S.; British geologist; b. 15 March 1917, Brede, Sussex; s. of the late Norman Williams Allen and Mildred Kathleen Allen (née Hoad); m. Frances Margaret Hepworth 1941; three s. one d.; ed. Rye Grammar School, Univ. of Reading; served in R.A.F. 1941-42; Asst. Lecturer Univ. of Reading 1945-46; Univ. Demonstrator, Univ. of Cambridge 1946-47, Lecturer 1947-52; Prof. of Geology, Univ. of Reading 1952-82, Emer. Prof. of Geology 1982-; Sec. Philpots Quarry Ltd.; Dean of Science Faculty, Univ. of Reading 1963-66; Visiting Prof., Univ. of Kuwait 1970; a Vice-Pres. Royal Soc. 1977-79; Pres. Geological Soc. 1978-80; Adviser UNDP Nile Delta Project 1972-75; Geology Consultant, India, for UNESCO/UNDP 1976–77; Algerian Sahara Glacials Expedition 1970; Tibet Geotraverse Follow-up 1986; Chair. Int. Confs. Organizing Cttees. of Seventh Int. Sedimentology Congress 1967, First European Earth and Planetary Physics Colloquium 1971, First Meeting European Geological Socs. 1975; Sec.-Gen. Int. Assoc. of Sedimentologists 1967–71; Chair. Royal Soc. Expeditions Cttee. 1974–84; Royal Soc. Assessor to NERC 1977–80; Chair. British Nat. Cttee. for Geology 1982–; Hon. mem. of Bulgarian Geological Soc., of Geological Assen. and of Int. Assen. of Sedimentologists; Council mem. Natural Environment Research Council 1971–74; Fellow, Indian Natural Sciences Acad.; Lyell Medal, Geological Soc. of London 1971. *Publications:* Papers on Wealden (Lower Cretaceous) and Torridonian (Proterozoic) Sedimentary in various scientific journals from 1938 onwards. *Leisure interests:* chess, natural history, gardening. *Address:* Sedimentary Research Laboratory, Dept. of Geology, University of Reading, Reading, RG6 2AB; Orchard End, Hazeley Bottom, Hartley Wintney, Hampshire, RG27 8LU, England. *Telephone:* Reading 875123, ext. 7803 (Office); Hartley Wintney 2229 (Home).

ALLEN, Sir Peter Christopher, Kt., M.A., B.SC.; British industrial chemist and business executive; b. 8 Sept. 1905, Ashtead, Surrey; s. of the late Sir Ernest King Allen and Florence Mary (née Gellatly); m. 1st Violet Sylvester Wingate-Saul 1931 (died 1951), two d.; m. 2nd Consuelo Maria Linares Rivas; ed. Harrow School and Trinity Coll., Oxford; joined Brunner, Mond and Co. (now Mond Div. of I.C.I.) 1928; Man. Dir. Plastics Div., Imperial Chemical Industries (I.C.I.) 1942–48, Chair. Plastics Div. 1948–51, Dir. of I.C.I. 1951–71, Deputy Chair. 1963–68, Chair. 1968–71; Pres. Canadian Industries Ltd. 1959–62, Chair. 1962–68; Pres. and Chair. I.C.I. of Canada Ltd. 1961–68; Dir. Royal Trust Co., Canada 1961–64; mem. Export Council for Europe 1962–65; Vice-Chair. of Assen. of British Chemical Mfrs. 1963–65; Pres. British Plastics Fed. 1963–65; mem. Iron & Steel Holding and Realisation Agency 1963–67; mem. British Nat. Export Council (Chair. 1970–73), Chair. Cttee. for Exports to Canada 1964–67; mem. Nat. Econ. Devt. Cttee. for Chemical Industry 1964–67; Commonwealth Export Council 1964–67; Pres. Chemical Industries Assen. Ltd. 1965–67; mem. Council of Confederation of British Industry 1965–67; Deputy Chair. African Explosives & Chemical Industries Ltd. 1968–71; Dir. ICIANZ 1968–71, Bank of Montreal 1968–75, British Insulated Callender's Cables (BICC) 1971–81; Pres. Univ. of Manchester Inst. of Science and Tech. 1968–71; Vice-Pres. British Assen. for Commercial and Industrial Educ. 1969–; mem. Industrial Policy Group 1969–72; mem. British Overseas Trade Bd. 1972–75, Hon. mem. Canadian Chemical Producers Assen. 1962–; Advisory Dir. New Perspective Fund 1973–85; Fellow, British Inst. of Man., Inst. of Dirs.; Hon. D.Tech. (Loughborough); Hon. Fellow, Trinity Coll., Oxford; Freeman, City of London 1978; Gov. Harrow School 1969–82. *Publications:* The Railways of the Isle of Wight 1928, Locomotives of Many Lands 1954, On the Old Lines 1957, Narrow Gauge Railways of Europe (with P.B. Whitehouse) 1959, Steam on the Sierra (with R.A. Wheeler) 1960, Round the World on the Narrow Gauge (with P.B. Whitehouse) 1966, The Curve of Earth's Shoulder (with Consuelo Allen) 1966, Rails in the Isle of Wight (with A. B. MacLeod) 1967, Famous Fairways 1968, Play the Best Courses 1973, Narrow Gauge the World Over (with P. B. Whitehouse) 1976, The 91 Before Lindbergh 1985. *Leisure interests:* foreign travel, railways, golf, writing, philately. *Address:* Telham Hill House, Battle, Sussex, England.

ALLEN, Richard V.; American international business consultant; b. 1 Jan. 1936, Collingswood, N.J.; s. of C. Carroll Allen Sr. and Magdalen Buchman; m. Patricia Ann Mason 1957; seven c.; ed. Notre Dame Univ. and Univ. of Munich; helped found Cen. for Strategic and Int. Studies, Georgetown Univ. 1962; Consultant and fmr. Prof. Hoover Inst., Stanford Univ.; with Nat. Security Council 1968–69; int. business consultant; mem. Ronald Reagan's staff, campaigns 1976–, Bd. Govs. Ronald Reagan Presidential Foundation 1985–; Pres. Richard V. Allen Co., Washington 1982–; Head Nat. Security Council and Nat. Security Adviser 1981–82 (resgnd.); Sr. Council for Foreign Policy and Nat. Security Affairs, Repub. Nat. Cttee. 1982–; Distinguished Fellow and Chair. Asian Studies Center, The Heritage Foundation 1982–; Chair. German-American Tricentennial Foundation 1983–; Founding mem. U.S. Nat. Cttee. for Pacific Basin 1984; Sr. Fellow, Hoover Inst.; Hon. degrees (Hanover Coll.) 1981, (Korea Univ.) 1982; Order of Diplomatic Merit Ganghwa (Repub. of Korea) 1982, Kt. Commdr.'s Cross (Fed. Repub. of Germany) 1983, Order of Brilliant Star (Repub. of China) 1986, Sovereign Mil. Order of Kts. of Malta 1987. *Address:* 905 16th Street, N.W., Washington, D.C. 20006, U.S.A.

ALLEN, Thomas, C.B.E., F.R.C.M., A.R.C.M.; British opera and concert singer; b. 10 Sept. 1944, Seaham, Co. Durham; s. of Thomas Boaz and Florence Allen; m. 1st Margaret Holley 1968 (divorced 1986); one s.; m. 2nd Jeannie Gordon Lascelles 1988; ed. Robert Richardson Grammar School, Ryhope, Royal Coll. of Music, London; prin. baritone, Welsh Nat. Opera 1969–72, Royal Opera House, Covent Garden 1972–78, Glyndebourne Opera 1973–, singing in Die Zauberflöte 1973, Le Nozze di Figaro 1974, Così fan Tutte 1975, Don Giovanni 1977, The Cunning Little Vixen 1977 and Simon Boccanegra, Billy Budd, La Bohème, L'Elisir d'Amore, Faust, Albert Herring, Die Fledermaus, etc.; Queen's Prize 1967, Gulbenkian Fellow 1968; R.A.M. (Hon.) 1988; Hon. M.A. (Newcastle) 1984, Hon. D.Mus. (Durham) 1988. *Leisure interests:* golf, gardening, sailing, ornithology, walking. *Address:* c/o John Coast Ltd., Manfield House, 376/379 Strand, London, WC2 0LR, England.

ALLEN, Walter Ernest, B.A., F.R.S.L.; British author and professor of English (retd.); b. 23 Feb. 1911, Birmingham; s. of Charles Henry Allen and Annie Maria Allen; m. Peggy Yorke Joy; two s. two d.; ed. King Edward's Grammar School and Birmingham Univ.; freelance author and broadcaster; Visiting Prof.of English,Coe Coll., Iowa 1955–56, Vassar Coll., U.S.A. 1963–64, Univ. of Kansas 1967; Literary Editor New Statesman 1959–61; Prof. of English Studies, New Univ. of Ulster 1968–73; Berg Prof. of English, New York Univ. 1970–71; Visiting Prof. of English, Dalhousie Univ., Canada 1973–74; C. P. Miles Prof. of English, Virginia Polytechnic Inst. and State Univ., U.S.A. 1974–75. *Publications:* novels: Innocence is Drowned 1938, Blind Man's Ditch 1939, Living Space 1940, Rogue Elephant 1946, Dead Man Over All 1950, Get Out Early 1986; literary criticism: The English Novel 1954, Six Great Novelists 1955, Tradition and Dream 1964, George Eliot 1964, The Urgent West 1969, Transatlantic Crossing 1971, The Short Story in English 1981, As I Walked Down New Grub Street 1981. *Address:* 4B Alwyne Road, London, N.1, England. *Telephone:* 01-226 7085.

ALLEN, William Clifford, M.B.A.; Bahamian economist and financial analyst; b. 15 March 1937, Nassau; m. Aloma Munnings 1960; three s. one d.; ed. St. Augustine's Coll., Coll. of City of New York, New York Univ.; Research Man. Bahamas Monetary Authority 1970–74; Chair. Bd. Bahamasair Holdings Ltd. 1973–80, Deputy Chair. 1980–; Deputy Gov. Cen. Bank of the Bahamas 1974–80, Gov. and Chair. 1980–87. *Leisure interest:* tennis. *Address:* P.O. Box 2490, Prospect Ridge Road, Nassau, Bahamas.

ALLEN, William Sidney, PH.D., F.B.A.; British professor of philology; b. 18 March 1918, London; s. of W. P. Allen and Ethel Allen (née Pearce); m. Aenea McCallum 1955; ed. Christ's Hosp. and Trinity Coll. Cambridge; war service in Royal Tank Regt. and Gen. Staff (Intelligence) 1939–45, mentioned in despatches; Lecturer in Phonetics and in Comparative Linguistics, S.O.A.S., Univ. of London 1948–55; Prof. of Comparative Philology, Univ. of Cambridge 1955–82, Prof. Emer. 1982–, Fellow of Trinity Coll. 1955–; Pres. The Philological Soc. 1965–67; Ed. Lingua 1963–85; Porson Scholar, Cambridge 1939. *Publications:* Phonetics in Ancient India 1953, Sandhi 1962, Vox Latina 1965, Vox Graeca 1968, Accent and Rhythm 1973. *Leisure interests:* gardening and travel. *Address:* Trinity College, Cambridge, CB2 1TQ; 24 Sherlock Road, Cambridge, CB3 0HR, England (Home). *Telephone:* (0223) 356739.

ALLEN, Woody (Allen Stewart Konigsberg); American actor, writer, producer and director; b. 1 Dec. 1935, Brooklyn, New York; s. of Martin and Nettie (née Cherry) Konigsberg; m. 1st. Harlene Rosen, divorced; 2nd. Louise Lasser 1966, divorced 1969; one s. by Mia Farrow; ed. City Coll. of New York and New York Univ.; made his debut as a performer in 1961 at the Duplex in Greenwich Village; has performed in a variety of nightclubs across the U.S.; produced the play Don't Drink the Water at the Morosco Theater 1966, and at the Broadhurst Theatre 1969; made his Broadway début as Allan Felix in Play it Again, Sam, which he also wrote; play: The Floating Light Bulb 1981. *Films include:* What's New Pussycat? 1965, Casino Royale 1967, What's Up, Tiger Lily? 1967, Take the Money and Run 1969, Bananas 1971, Everything You Always Wanted to Know About Sex 1972, Play it Again, Sam 1972, Sleeper 1973, Love and Death 1976, The Front 1976, Annie Hall 1977, Interiors 1978, Manhattan 1979, Stardust Memories 1980, A Midsummer Night's Sex Comedy 1982, Zelig 1983, Broadway Danny Rose 1984, The Purple Rose of Cairo 1985, Hannah and her Sisters 1985, Radio Days 1987, September 1987, Another Woman 1988, Oedipus Wrecks 1989; during the 1950s wrote for television performers Herb Shriner 1953, Sid Caesar 1957, Art Carney 1958–59, Jack Parr and Carol Channing. Also wrote for the Tonight Show and the Gary Moore Show. Academy Award for Best Director, and Best Writer for Annie Hall. *Publications:* Getting Even 1971, Without Feathers 1975, Side Effects 1980, has also contributed to Playboy and New Yorker. *Leisure interests:* chocolate milk shakes, poker, chess and baseball; also a noted clarinettist. *Address:* 930 Fifth Avenue, New York, N.Y. 10021, U.S.A.

ALLER, Lawrence Hugh, M.A., PH.D.; American astronomer; b. 24 Sept. 1913, Tacoma, Wash.; s. of late Leslie E. Aller and late Lena B. Aller; m. Rosalind Duncan Hall 1941; two s. one d.; ed. Univ. of California, Berkeley, and Harvard Univ. Soc. of Fellows, Harvard Univ. 1939–42; Asst. Prof. Indiana Univ. 1945–48; Assoc. Prof. Univ. of Michigan 1948–54, Prof. 1954–62; Prof. of Astronomy, Univ. of Calif., Los Angeles 1962–84, Prof. Emer. 1984–; Visiting Prof. Australian Nat. Univ. 1960–61, Univ. of Toronto 1961–62, Univ. of Sydney 1968, Univ. of Tasmania 1969, Univ. of Queensland 1977–78, Raman Inst., Bangalore 1978, Int. School of Advanced Studies, Trieste 1981, Univ. of S. Calif. 1983–84; Guest Investigator, Mount Wilson Observatory 1946–82; mem. N.A.S.; Fellow, American Acad. of Arts and Sciences. *Publications:* Atoms, Stars and Nebulae (with Leo Goldberg) 1942 and 1971 (sole author), Atmospheres of Sun and Stars 1953, 1963, Nuclear Transformations, Stellar Interiors and Nebulae 1954, Gaseous Nebulae 1956, Abundance of Elements 1961, Atmospheres of the Stars and Suns 1963, Physics of Thermal Gaseous Nebulae 1984. *Leisure interests:* photography, travel. *Address:* Astronomy Department, University of California, Los Angeles, Calif. 90024 (Office); 18118 W. Kingsport Drive, Malibu, Calif. 90265, U.S.A. (Home). *Telephone:* (213) 825-3515 (Office); (213) 454-7498.

ALLERSLEV JENSEN, Erik; Danish library director; b. 22 May 1911, Holstebro; s. of Sigurd Jensen and Meta Hansen; m. Gudrun Franck 1938 (died 1956); two d.; ed. Danish Library School; Asst. Librarian, Frederiksberg Public Library 1933–37; Head of Dept. of Printed Catalogue Cards, State Inspection of Public Libraries 1937–42; Dir. Danish Library Bureau 1942–46; Deputy Dir. State Inspection of Public Libraries 1946–59, Dir. State Inspection of Public Libraries 1960–75, (retd.) 1975; Dir. Danish Library School 1946–56; Dir. Nordic School of Advanced Library Studies, Gothenburg 1958–68; Chair. Public Libraries Section of Int. Fed. of Library Assens. (I.F.L.A.) 1965–69, mem. exec. bd. I.F.L.A. 1967–73. *Publications:* Dansk Bogfortegnelse (The Danish Nat. Bibliography) 1935–60, Decimal-Klassedeling (Decimal Classification), 4th Edition, 1954, Lærebog i Biblioteksteknik (Manual of Library Economy), 4th Edition, 1959, Dansk biblioteksslitteratur (Danish Library Literature: A Bibliography) 1950, Biblioteker og Løesning (Libraries and Reading) 7 vols. 1956–64, Skrifter udsendt af den Nordiske Fortsœttelsesskole for Bibliotekarer (Publs. from the Nordic Library School in Gothenburg) 4 vols. 1960–62, Biblioteksstudier (Library Studies) 7 vols. 1963–70, Biblioteksscentralens Forhistorie og Første År (History of the Danish Library Bureau) 1979, Til Biblioteks-sagens Fremme Traek af Bibliotekstilsynets Virksomhed indtil 1970 (History of the Danish State Inspection of Public Libraries until 1970) 1985, Georg Krogh-Jensen 1987; Editor Reol (Scandinavian Library Journal) 1962–67; Editor Scandinavian (Public Library Quarterly) 1968–69. *Address:* DK-1820 Frederiksberg Allé 66, Frederiksberg C, Denmark. *Telephone:* 01-31-15 63.

ALLEST, Frédéric Jean Pierre d'; French engineer; b. 1 Sept. 1940, Marseilles; s. of Pierre and Luce d'Allest; m. Anne-Marie Morel 1963; three s.; ed. Ecole Saint Joseph and Lycée Thiers, Marseilles, Ecole Polytechnique and Ecole Nat. supérieure d'aéronautique; Centre National d'Etudes Spatiales (CNES) 1966–70, 1973–, Head of Ariane project 1973–76, Dir. Ariane Programme 1976–82, Dir.-Gen. CNES 1982–89; with Europa III project, European Launcher Devt. Org. 1970–72; Pres. Soc. Arianespace 1980–; Chevalier, Légion d'honneur, Officier ordre national du Mérite; Prix de l'aéronautique. *Leisure interests:* sport, alpinism; *Address:* CNES, 2 place Maurice Quentin, 75035 Paris Cédex 01 (Office); 6 rue Marcel Allegot, 92190 Meudon, France (Home). *Telephone:* 508-75-00 (Office).

ALLEY, Col. Alphonse; Benin army officer and politician; b. 9 April 1930, Bassila; s. of Amadou Alley and Amina Akim; m.; six c.; ed. primary schools at Lomé, Togo, secondary school in Senegal, and military colls. in France and Ivory Coast; joined 5th Senegalese Rifle Regt., Dakar; served in Indo-China 1950–53, Morocco 1955–56, Algeria 1959–61; returned to Dahomey 1961; Second-Lieut. Dahomeyan Army 1961, Capt. 1962, Major 1964, Lieut.-Col. 1967, Chief of Staff 1967; Pres. of Dahomey Dec. 1967–68; Sec.-Gen. for Nat. Defence 1970–72; arrested Feb. 1973, sentenced to twenty years' detention. *Leisure interests:* all forms of sport. *Address:* Carré 181-182, B.P. 48, Cotonou, Benin.

ALLEY, William J.; American lawyer and business executive; b. 27 Dec. 1929, Vernon, Tex.; s. of Willie H. and Opal C. Alley; m. Deborah Bunn 1979; one s. four d.; ed. Durant High School, Northeastern Agricultural and Mechanical Coll., Univ. of Oklahoma; attorney, Oklahoma State Insurance Bd. 1956–57; Asst. Vice-Pres. Pioneer American Insurance Co. 1957–59, Vice-Pres. 1959–60, Vice-Pres. and Agency Dir. 1960–66, Dir. 1961–67, Sr. Vice-Pres. Marketing 1966–67; Vice-Pres., Franklin Life Insurance Co., 1967–69, Sr. Vice-Pres. Agency 1969–74, Exec. Vice-Pres. 1974–76, Pres. and C.E.O. 1976–77, Chair., Pres. and C.E.O. 1977–86, Chair. 1986–87; Sr. Vice-Pres. Strategic Planning, American Brands Inc. 1983–85, Sr. Vice-Pres. and Chief Financial Officer 1985–86, Vice-Chair. 1986–87, C.O.O. 1987, Chair. of Bd. and C.E.O. 1987–, Dir. 1979–. *Leisure interests:* hunting, fishing, tennis, flying. *Address:* 194 Greenley Road, New Canaan, Conn. 06840 (Home); American Brands Inc., 1700 East Putnam Avenue, Old Greenwich, Conn., 06870-0819, U.S.A. (Office). *Telephone:* (203) 698-5100 (Office).

ALLIALI, Camille; Ivory Coast lawyer and diplomatist; b. 23 Nov. 1926; m.; five c.; ed. Dakar Lycée and Lycée Champollion, Grenoble; fmr. Advocate, Court of Appeal, Abidjan; Press Sec. Parti Démocratique de la Côte d'Ivoire 1959–, Deputy 1958–60; Vice-Pres. Nat. Ass., Ivory Coast 1957–60; Senator of French Community 1959–61; Amb. to France 1961–63; Perm. Del. UNESCO 1961–63; Minister of Foreign Affairs 1963–66; Minister of Justice 1966–83, Minister of State 1983–; mem. Cen. Cttee. of Parti démocratique de la Côte d'Ivoire (PDCI); PDCI Press Sec. 1959–; Commdr., Légion d'honneur and many other decorations. *Address:* Office of the Prime Minister, Abidjan, Ivory Coast.

ALLIBONE, Thomas Edward, C.B.E., PH.D., D.SC., D.ENG., F.AM.I.E.E., F.R.S., F.ENG.; British scientist; b. 11 Nov. 1903, Sheffield; s. of Henry James and Eliza Allibone; m. Dorothy Margery Boulden, L.R.A.M., A.R.C.M. 1931; two d.; ed. Sheffield and Cambridge Univs; High Voltage Lab. Metropolitan Vickers Co. 1930–44; Univ. of Calif. (British team, Atomic Bomb) 1944–45; Dir. Research Lab., Assoc. Electrical Industries, Aldermaston 1946–63; Scientific Adviser to A.E.I. Ltd. 1963; Dir. Assoc. Electrical Industries (Woolwich) Ltd. 1950–63; Chief Scientist, Central Electricity Generating Bd. 1963–70; External Prof. of Electrical Eng., Leeds Univ. 1967–79, Emer. Prof. 1979–; Robert Kitchin (Sadlers') Research Prof. City Univ. 1971–, First Poynton Visiting Prof. 1984–; Vice-Pres. Inst. Physics 1948–52;

Chair. Research Cttee., Electrical Research Assen. 1955–62; Vice-Pres. Royal Inst. 1955–57, 1969–72; mem. Council, Physical Soc. 1953–57, Council of Inst. of Electrical Engineers 1937–53, Advisory Council, Royal Mil. Coll., Shrivenham; Pres. Section A British Assen. 1958, Inst. of Information Scientists 1967–69; Trustee, British Museum 1968–75; Hon. F.I.E.E., Hon. D.Sc., Hon. D.Eng.; Röntgen Medal, British Inst. of Radiology; Thornton and Cooper Hill Medals, Inst. of Electrical Engineers; Melchett Medal, Inst. of Fuel. *Publications:* High Voltage Electrical Phenomena and Thermonuclear Reactions, Release and Use of Atomic Energy, Rutherford, the Father of Nuclear Energy, The Royal Society and its Dining Clubs; contribution to Lightning and Lightning Protection, Cockcroft and the Atom 1984, Cambridge Physics in the Thirties 1984, The Making of Physicists 1987. *Leisure interests:* history, archaeology, gardening, handicrafts. *Address:* York Cottage, Lovel Road, Winkfield, Windsor, England. *Telephone:* Winkfield Row 88 4501.

ALLIMADI, E. Otema; Ugandan diplomatist and politician; b. 11 Feb. 1929, Kitgum; s. of the late Saulo Allimadi and of Susan (née Layado) Allimadi; m. Alice Lamunu 1954; six s. three d.; ed. in Uganda; N.C.O. in E. African Army Medical Corps. 1947–53; mem. Uganda Nat. Congress 1953, Nat. Admin. and Organizing Sec. 1956–59, Sec.-Gen. 1959, later Vice-Chair. Uganda People's Congress; Deputy Perm. Rep. to UN 1964–66; Amb. to U.S.A. 1966–71, concurrently Perm. Rep. to UN 1967–71; Minister of Foreign Affairs 1979–80; Prime Minister 1980–85.

ALLINSON, Sir Walter Leonard, K.C.V.O., C.M.G., M.A.; British diplomatist (retd.); b. 1 May 1926, London; s. of Walter and Alice Frances (Cassidy) Allinson; m. Margaret Patricia Watts 1951; three d.; ed. Friern Barnet Grammar School, Merton Coll., Oxford, Royal Coll. of Defence Studies; Asst. Prin., Petroleum Div., Ministry of Fuel and Power 1947–48; Asst. Prin., later Prin., Ministry of Educ. 1948–58 (Asst. Private Sec. to Minister 1953–54); First Sec., Commonwealth Relations Office 1958–60; served in Lahore and Karachi, Pakistan 1960–62, Madras and Delhi, India 1963–66; Deputy, later Head of Perm. Under-Sec.'s Dept., FCO 1968–70; Counsellor and Head of Chancery, later Deputy High Commr., Nairobi, Kenya 1970–73; Deputy High Commr. and Minister, Delhi, India 1975–78; British High Commr., Lusaka, Zambia 1978–80; Asst. Under-Sec. of State (Africa) 1980–82; High Commr. in Kenya and Amb. to UN Environment Programme 1982–86; Vice-Pres. Royal Africa Soc. 1982–; mem. Governing Council, British Inst. in Eastern Africa 1986–; Kenya Scouts Medal of Merit 1973. *Leisure interests:* rough gardening, walking, reading. *Address:* c/o National Westminster Bank PLC, 6 Tothill Street, London, SW1H 9ND, England.

ALLIS, William Phelps; American physicist; b. 15 Nov. 1901, Menton, France; s. of Edward Phelps Allis, Jr. and Amédine (Sgrena) Allis; m. Nancy Olive Morison 1935; two s. one d.; ed. Massachusetts Inst. of Tech., Univ. of Nancy (France), Princeton Univ. and Univ. of Munich; mem. of Physics Faculty, Massachusetts Inst. of Technology 1925–; Prof. of Physics 1950–67, Prof. Emer. 1967–; on staff, Radiation Lab., Office of Scientific Research and Devt. 1940–42; Consultant, Los Alamos Scientific Lab. 1952–76; Asst. Sec.-Gen. for Scientific Affairs, NATO 1962–64; Vice-Pres. American Acad. of Arts and Sciences 1960–62; U.S. Army 1942–45, rank of Lieut.-Col.; Visiting Prof., Harvard Univ. 1960; Visiting Fellow, Oxford Univ. 1968; Exchange Prof., Univ. de Paris-Sud intermittently 1969–84; Chair. Gaseous Electronics Conf. 1949–62, Hon. Chair. 1966–; Visiting Prof., Middle East Tech. Univ. 1970, Univ. of South Florida 1971, Instituto Técnico de Electrónica, Lisbon, Univ. of Western Ontario 1973; Fulbright Sr. Lecturer Univ. of Innsbruck, Austria 1974–75; Consultant, Office Nat. d'Etudes et de Recherches Aerospatiales 1972, 1974, 1976, 1977, 1983; Fellow, American Physical Soc., American Assen. for the Advancement of Science, American Acad. of Arts and Sciences, Inst. of Physics (London), Royal Soc. of Arts, Visiting Fellow, Joint Inst. for Lab. Astrophysics 1979–80; Legion of Merit (U.S.A.) 1945; Officier, Légion d'honneur 1976; Dr. h.c. (Paris-Sud) 1976. *Publications:* Thermodynamics and Statistical Mechanics 1952, Handbuch der Physik (vol. 21) 1956), Nuclear Fusion 1960, Waves in Anisotropic Plasmas 1963, Electrons, Ions and Waves 1967. *Leisure interests:* climbing, skiing, canoeing, opera. *Address:* Massachusetts Institute of Technology, Cambridge, Mass. 02139 (Office); 33 Reservoir Street, Cambridge, Mass. 02138, U.S.A. (Home). *Telephone:* 617-876-7535.

ALLISON, Richard Clark, B.A., LL.B.; American judge; b. 10 July 1924, New York; s. of Albert F. and Anice (née Clark) Allison; m. Anne Elizabeth Johnston 1950; two s. one d.; ed. Univ. of Virginia; called to New York Bar 1948; practised in New York City 1948–52, 1954–55, 1955–; partner law firm Reid & Priest 1961–87; mem. Iran-U.S. Claims Tribunal, The Hague 1988–; mem. A.B.A. (Chair. Cttee. Latin American Law 1964–68, Int. Law Section 1976–77, Nat. Inst. on Doing Business in Far East 1972, Int. Legal Exchange Program 1981–85), Int. Bar Assen. (Chair. Conf. 1986, Ethics Cttee. 1986–); mem. Société Int. des Avocats, Inter-American Bar Assen., American Foreign Law Assen., American Arbitration Assen. (Nat. Panel), Southwestern Legal Foundation (Advisory Bd.), American Soc. of Int. Law, Council on Foreign Relations, American Bar Foundation, Assen. of Bar of City of New York (Int. Law Cttee.), Raven Soc., SAR, St. Andrew's Soc., New York. *Publications:* Protecting Against the Expropriation Risk in Investing Abroad 1988; legal articles. *Address:* Iran-U.S. Claims Tribunal, Parkweg 13, 2585 JH The Hague (Office); Nassau Odijck-straat 55, 2596 AG The Hague, The Netherlands (Home). *Telephone:* (31) (70) 52.00.64 (Office).

ALLISON, Rt. Rev. Sherard Falkner, D.D., LL.D.; British ecclesiastic; b. 19 Jan. 1907; s. of Rev. W. S. Allison; m. Ruth Hills 1936; one s. (and one s. deceased) two d.; ed. Jesus Coll. and Ridley Hall, Cambridge; Curate, St. James's, Tunbridge Wells 1931-34; Chaplain, Ridley Hall, Cambridge 1934-36; Vicar, Rodbourne Cheney, Swindon 1936-40, Erith 1940-45; Prin., Ridley Hall 1945-50; Bishop of Chelmsford 1951-61, of Winchester and Prelate of the Order of the Garter 1961-74. *Leisure interests:* sailing, water-colour sketching, bird-watching. *Address:* Winton Lodge, Aldeburgh, Suffolk, England. *Telephone:* Aldeburgh 2485.

ALLMAND, Warren, B.A., B.C.L.; Canadian politician; b. 19 Sept. 1932, Montreal; s. of Harold W. Allmand and Rose McMorrow; m. Patricia Burns 1966 (separated); one s. two d.; ed. Loyola Coll., St. Francis Xavier, McGill and Paris Univ.; admitted to Quebec Bar 1958; practised law 1958-66; part-time Lecturer in Political Science and Commercial Law 1962-65; mem. Parl. for Notre-Dame-de-Grâce 1965-; mem. several Parl. Standing Cttees.; Solicitor-Gen. 1972-75; Minister of Indian Affairs and Northern Devt. 1976-77, of Consumer and Corporate Affairs 1977-79; Liberal. *Leisure interests:* running, skiing, tennis, hockey, music, theatre. *Address:* 2525 Cavendish Boulevard, Suite 232, Montreal, Quebec H4B 2Y6, Canada.

ALLOUACHE, Merzak; Algerian film director; b. 6 Oct. 1944, Algiers; s. of Omar and Fatma Allouache; m. Lazib Anissa 1962; one d.; worked in Nat. Inst. of Cinema, Algiers, later in Inst. of Film, Paris; after return to Algeria worked as Adviser, Ministry of Culture; Silver Prize, Moscow Festival; Tanit D'Or Prize, Carthage 1979. *Films include;* Our Agrarian Revolution (documentary) 1973, Omar Gatlato, Les aventures d'un héros, L'homme qui regardait les Fenêtres 1982. *Address:* Cité des Asphodeles, Bt D15, 183 Ben Aknoun, Algiers, Algeria. *Telephone:* 79 33 60.

ALMEYDA MEDINA, Clodomiro; Chilean professor and politician; b. 1923, Santiago; m. Irma Cáceres; three c.; ed. Alemán High School and Faculty of Law, Univ. de Chile; joined Socialist party 1941; held various posts rising to Under Sec.-Gen.; Prof. of Philosophy, Teacher Training Inst., Univ. de Chile 1952; Prof. of Philosophy, Univ. Popular Valentín Latelier; Prof. of Rural Econ., Univ. de Chile; Dir. School of Sociology, Univ. de Chile 1966, Prof. of Political Sciences, Schools of Law and Political and Admin. Studies; Prof. of Dialectical Materialism, School of Sociology; mem. Cen. Cttee. Socialist Party; Minister of Labour 1952-53, of Mines 1953-61; Deputy 1961-65; mem. Chilean del. to UN Gen. Ass. 1970; Minister of Foreign Affairs 1970-73, of Defence 1973; imprisoned Sept. 1973, released Jan. 1975, granted political asylum in Romania; returned to Chile 1987; convicted of charges of propagating violence and entering Chile illegally, imprisoned 1987-88, released Oct. 1988.

ALMODÓVAR, Pedro; Spanish film director; b. 1949, Calzada de Calatrava; fronted a rock band; worked at Telefónica for ten years; started career with full-length super-8 films; made 16mm. short films, including Salome 1978-83; *films include:* Pepe, Luci, Bom y otras montón, Laberinto de pasiones 1980, Dark Habits 1983, What Have I Done to Deserve This? 1985, Matador 1986, Law of Desire 1987, Women on the Verge of a Nervous Breakdown 1988 (Felix Award 1988); Cambio 16 Man of the Year 1989. *Publication:* Fuego en las entrañas 1982.

ALMOGI, Yosef; Israeli politician; b. 4 May 1910, Poland; s. of Zevi and Hanna Almogi; m. Shifra Weinblatt 1934; two s.; settled in Israel 1930; mem. Kibbutz Hakovesh 1930; mem. Hagana Command 1933-39; with British Army 1939-40; in German captivity 1941-45; Gen. Sec. Haifa Labour Council, mem. Exec. Cttee. Histadrut 1947-59; elected to Parl. 1955; Gen. Sec. Mapai 1959-61; Minister without Portfolio 1961-62; Minister of Devt. and Housing 1962-64; Minister of Labour 1968-73; Mayor of Haifa 1973-76; Chair. Jewish Agency for Israel 1976-77. *Address:* 120 Arlozorov Street, Haifa, Israel. *Telephone:* 04-640775.

ALMOND, Gabriel Abraham; American educator; b. 12 Jan. 1911, Rock Island, Ill.; s. of the late David and Lisa Almond; m. Dorothea Kaufmann 1937; three c.; ed. Univ. of Chicago; Fellow, Social Science Research Council 1935-36, 1946; Instructor, Political Science, Brooklyn Coll. 1939-42; Office of War Information, Washington 1942-45, War Dept., European Theatre of Operations 1945; Research Assoc. Inst. of Int. Studies, Yale Univ. 1947-49, Assoc. Prof. of Political Science 1949-51; Assoc. Prof. of Int. Affairs, Princeton Univ. 1951-54, Prof. 1954-57, Prof. of Politics 1957-59; Prof. of Political Science, Yale 1959-63; Prof. of Political Science, Stanford Univ. 1963, Exec. Head, Dept of Political Science, Stanford Univ. 1964-69; Fulbright Lecturer Kiev State Univ. 1989; Consultant, Air Univ. 1948, Dept. of State 1950, Office of Naval Research 1951, Science Advisory Bd., U.S. Air Force 1960-61; Fellow, American Acad. of Arts and Sciences; Pres. American Political Science Assn. 1965-66; mem. Social Science Research Council 1956-, American Philosophical Soc.; Fellow, Nat. Endowment for Humanities; N.A.S.; Overseas Fellowship, Churchill Coll., Cambridge 1972-73; Visiting Fellow A.N.U. 1983. *Publications:* The American People and Foreign Policy 1950, The Appeals of Communism 1954; editor The Struggle for Democracy in Germany 1949, The Politics of the Developing Areas 1960; co-author The Civic Culture 1963; Comparative Politics: A Developmental Approach 1966, Political Development 1970, Crisis, Choice and Change 1973, Comparative Politics; System, Process, Policy 1978, The Civic Culture Revisited 1980, Progress and its Discontents 1981, Comparative Politics Today 1988. *Leisure interests:* carpentry, swimming,

bird-watching. *Address:* 4135 Old Trace Road, Palo Alto, Calif., U.S.A. (Home).

ALMUNIA AMANN, Joaquín; Spanish politician; b. 1948, Bilbao; m.; two c.; ed. Univ. of Deusto; economist, various Spanish chambers of commerce in mem. countries of EEC; econ. adviser to Exec. Cttee., Unión General de Trabajo; Sec. for trade union relations, then head of Dept. of Research and Planning, then head of Perm. Cttee. for Political Man., Partido Socialista Obrero Español 1981; Minister of Labour and Social Security 1982-86; Minister of Public Admin. 1987-. *Address:* Ministro para las Administraciones Públicas, P° Castellana, 3, 28046 Madrid, Spain (Office).

ALONEFTIS, Andreas P., M.B.A.; Cypriot politician and bank official; b. 1945, Nicosia; m. Nedi Georghiades; one s. one d.; ed. New York Inst. of Finance Coll. of New York Stock Exchange, Southern Methodist Univ., Dallas, Tex., U.S.A.; served Nat. Guard 1964-66; studied finance and accountancy in U.K.; served 16 years in Cyprus Devt. Bank; Gen. Man. and First Exec. Officer, Cyprus Investment and Securities Corpn. Ltd. (CISCO) 1982-88; Gen. Man. Lombard-NatWest Bank, Nicosia 1988-; Minister of Defence 1988-. *Address:* Ministry of Defence, Nicosia, Cyprus.

ALONSO, Dámaso, PH.D.; Spanish university professor and writer; b. 1898, Madrid; m. Eulalia Galvarriato (novelist) 1929; ed. Univ. of Madrid; fmr. Lecturer in Spanish at Univs. of Berlin, Cambridge, Stanford, California, Hunter College, New York, Inst. of Int. Education, New York, at Columbia Univ. New York; Visiting Prof. at Yale, Johns Hopkins Univ., Harvard; Prof. at Centre of Historical Studies, Madrid 1923-36; Prof. of Spanish Language and Literature, Valencia Univ. 1933-39; Prof. of Romance Philology, Madrid Univ. 1939-68; mem. Royal Spanish Acad. (Dir.), Royal Acad. of History, Madrid, Modern Humanities Research Asscn. (Pres. 1960); foreign mem. Arcadia and Lincei (Rome), Crusca (Florence), American Philosophical Soc.; Corresp. mem. British Acad.; Pres. Int. Asscn. of Hispanists 1962-65; Dr. h.c. (Lima, Bordeaux, Rome, Hamburg, Oxford, Freiburg, Massachusetts, Leeds, Costa Rica and Lisbon). *Publications:* Criticism: Temas gongorinos 1927, La Lengua poética de Góngora 1935, 1950, 1961, La Poesía de San Juan de la Cruz 1946, 1958, 1967 (Italian trans.), Ensayos sobre Poesía española 1944, Vida y obra de Medrano 1948, Pt. II (with S. Reckert) 1958, Poesía Española 1950, Seis calas en la expresión literaria española (co-author) 1951, Poetas españoles contemporáneos 1952, La Primitiva Epica francesa a la luz de una "Nota Emilianense" 1945, Estudios y Ensayos gongorinos 1955, Menéndez Pelayo, Crítico literario, De los siglos oscuros al de oro 1958, Primavera temprana de la literatura europea 1961, Góngora y el Polifemo 1960, Dos españoles del Siglo de Oro 1960, Cuatro poetas españoles 1962, Del Siglo de Oro a este Siglo de siglas 1962, En Torno a Lope 1972; Poetry: Poemas Puros 1921, Oscura Noticia 1944, Hijos de la Ira 1944, Hombre y Dios 1955, Poemas escogidos 1969; Obras Completas I-IV 1971-75; trans. of James Joyce, G. M. Hopkins and von Wartburg into Spanish. *Address:* Avenida A. Alcocer 23, Madrid 16, Spain.

ALPER, Howard, PH.D., F.R.S.C.; Canadian professor of chemistry; b. 17 Oct. 1941, Montreal; s. of Max Alper and Frema Alper; m. Anne Fairhurst 1966; two d.; ed. Sir George Williams Univ., and McGill Univ.; NATO Postdoctoral Fellow, Princeton Univ. 1967-68; Asst. Prof. State Univ. of New York at Binghamton 1968-71, Assoc. Prof. 1971-74; Assoc. Prof. Univ. of Ottawa 1975-77, Prof. 1978-, Chair. Dept. of Chem. 1982-85; Guggenheim Fellowship 1985-86; Killam Research Fellow 1986-88; Chemical Inst. of Canada Inorganic Chem. Award 1980, Catalysis Award 1984. *Publications:* more than 225 papers and 15 patents in the area of organometallic chemistry and catalysis. *Address:* Department of Chemistry, University of Ottawa, Ottawa, Ont. K1N 9B4, Canada. *Telephone:* 613-564-2214.

ALPERT, Joseph Stephen, M.D.; American professor of medicine; b. 1 Feb. 1942, New Haven, Conn.; s. of Zelly C. Alpert and Beatrice A. Kopsofsky; m. Helle Mathiasen 1965; one s. one d.; ed. Yale and Harvard Univs.; Instructor in Medicine, Peter Bent Brigham Hosp., Harvard Univ. 1973-74; Lieut-Commdr. U.S. Navy, Dir Coronary Care Unit, San Diego Naval Hospital and Asst. Prof. of Medicine, Univ. of Calif., San Diego 1974-76; Dir. Levine Cardiac Unit and Asst. Prof. of Medicine, Peter Bent Brigham Hospital and Harvard Univ. 1976-78; Dir. Div. of Cardiovascular Medicine and Prof. of Medicine, Univ. of Mass. Medical School 1978-; Fulbright Fellow, Copenhagen 1963-64; U.S. Public Health Service Fellow, Harvard and Copenhagen 1966-67; Nat. Inst. of Health Special Fellow, Harvard 1972-74; Fellow, American Coll. of Physicians, American Coll. of Cardiology, American Heart Asscn., American Coll. of Chest Physicians; Gold Medal of Univ. of Copenhagen and other awards. *Publications:* The Heart Attack Handbook 1978, Physiopathology of the Cardiovascular System 1984; co-author of other books and author of more than 200 articles in scientific journals. *Leisure interests:* poetry, music, swimming, running, cooking, travel. *Address:* 55 Lake Avenue North, Worcester, Mass. 01605 (Office); 55 Nathan Road, Newton Centre, Mass. 02159, U.S.A. (Home). *Telephone:* 617-856-3191 (Office); 617-965-3236 (Home).

ALPHAND, Hervé; French economist and diplomatist (retd.); b. 31 May 1907; m. Nicole Merenda Alphand (died 1979); ed. Lycée Janson de Sailly and Ecole des Sciences Politiques; Insp. of Finances and Dir. Trade Agreements Div., Ministry of Commerce 1937-38; Sec.-Gen. Ministerial Cttee. of Nat. Economy 1938; Financial Counsellor to Embassy, Washington 1940-41; Dir. of Econ. Affairs, French Nat. Cttee. 1941-44; Dir.-Gen.

French Foreign Office 1945; French Amb. to OEEC; Deputy to Atlantic Council 1950; mem. NATO Perm. Council 1952-54; Amb. to UN 1955, to U.S.A. 1956-65; Sec.-Gen. French Foreign Office 1965-72; mem Conseil de l'ordre de la Légion d'honneur 1973-; Grand Officier, Légion d'honneur, Grand Croix, ordre nat. du Mérite. *Publication:* The Astonishment of Being 1977. *Address:* 122 rue de Grenelle, 75007 Paris, France. *Telephone:* 45 51-44-59.

ALPORT, 1st Baron, cr. 1961, of Colchester; **Cuthbert James McCall Alport,** P.C., T.D., D.L.; British politician; b. 22 March 1912, Johannesburg, South Africa; s. of Prof. A. C. Alport, F.R.C.P. and Janet McCall; m. Rachel Cecilia Bingham 1945 (died 1983); one s. two d.; ed. Haileybury, Cambridge Univ.; Pres. Cambridge Union Soc. 1935; Tutor Ashridge Coll. 1935-37; called to Bar; War Service 1939-45; Dir. Conservative Political Centre 1945-50; Conservative M.P. for Colchester 1950-61; Chair. Joint East and Central African Board 1953-55; Asst. Postmaster-Gen. 1955-57; Parl. Under-Sec. of State, Commonwealth Relations Office 1957-59, Minister of State 1959-61; High Commr. to Fed. of Rhodesia and Nyasaland 1961-63; U.K. Del. to Council of Europe, Strasbourg 1964-65; Prime Minister's Special Envoy to Rhodesia 1967; Deputy Speaker, House of Lords 1971-82, 1983-; Adviser to Home Sec. 1973-82; Pro-Chancellor, City Univ. 1972-79; High Steward of Colchester 1967-; Patron, Mercury Theatre, Colchester; Master Skinners Co. 1969-70, 1982-83; Deputy Lieut. of County of Essex 1974; Pres. Minories Art Gallery, Colchester 1977-; Hon. D.C.L.(City Univ.) 1979. *Publications:* Kingdom in Partnership 1937, Hope in Africa 1952, The Sudden Assignment 1965. *Leisure interests:* preservation and development of Colchester; family and home. *Address:* The Cross House, Layer de la Haye, Colchester, Essex, England. *Telephone:* Layer de la Haye 217.

ALPTEMOÇİN, Ahmet Kurtcebe, M.E.; Turkish politician; b. 1940, Istanbul; s. of Ali Riza and Zekiye Alptemocin; m. Gulseren Susler 1966; one s.; ed. Middle East Tech. Univ.; army service 1962-64; engineer in design office Ministry of Public Works 1964-65; engineer design Demag Bagger U. Kram GmbH, Dusseldorf 1965-68; Dir. of production Turkish Tractor Factory 1968-69; Dir. of foundations Taysan Co. Bursa 1969-78; Dir. Gen. Kapsan Co. Bursa 1978; Chair. Form Fleks Co. 1978-33; Minister Finance and Customs 1984-; mem. Parl. for Bursa 1983; mem. Chamber Asscn. Mechanical Engineers, Industrialists and Businessmen of Bursa. *Address:* Ministry of Finance, Maliye ve Gunuruk Bakanliği, Ankara, Turkey.

ALSOGARAY, Alvaro C.; Argentinian politician; fmr. Minister of Industry, of Employment, of the Economy; fmr. Amb. to U.S.A.; Chair. Unión del Centro Democrático; Deputy, Congreso de la Nación; mem. Academia Nacional de Ciencias Económicas, Sociedad Liberal Internacional Mont Pélerin; Chair. Instituto de la Economia Social de Mercado. *Publications:* Politica y Economia en Latinoamérica, Bases para la Acción Futura, Teoría y Práctica en la Acción Económica; numerous articles. *Address:* c/o Unión del Centro Democrático, Buenos Aires, Argentina.

ALSOP, Joseph Wright, Jr., B.A.; American journalist and author; b. 11 Oct. 1910, Avon, Conn.; s. of Joseph W. and Corinne D. (Robinson) Alsop; m. Mrs. Susan M. J. Patten 1961 (divorced 1978); ed. Groton School and Harvard Univ.; mem. New York Herald Tribune staff, New York 1932-35, Washington 1936-37; author (with Robert Kintner) of syndicated column The Capital Parade (North American Newspaper Alliance) 1937-40; Lieut.-Commdr. U.S. Navy 1940, later jointed Volunteer Air Force as aide to Gen. Chennault; captured by Japanese at Hong Kong, exchanged and returned to U.S.; Dir. Lend-Lease Mission to China, Chungking 1942; author (with brother Stewart Alsop) of column Matter of Fact (New York Herald Tribune Syndicate) 1946-58, sole author (Los Angeles Times Syndicate) 1958-74; Mellon Lecturer, Nat. Gallery of Art 1978; Legion of Merit, Order of Cloud Banner (China). *Publications:* The 168 Days (with Turner Catledge), Men Around the President (with Robert Kintner) 1938, The American White Paper (with Robert Kintner) 1940, We Accuse (with Stewart Alsop) 1955, The Reporter's Trade (with Stewart Alsop) 1958, From the Silent Earth 1964, The Life and Times of Franklin D. Roosevelt—FDR 1982, The Rare Art Traditions 1982. *Address:* 2806 N Street, N.W., Washington, D.C. 20007, U.S.A.

ALSTON, Robert John, B.A., C.M.G.; British diplomatist; b. 10 Feb. 1938; s. of Arthur William Alston and Rita Alston; m. Patricia Claire Essex 1969; one s. one d.; ed. Ardingly Coll., New Coll., Oxford; joined H.M. Diplomatic Service 1961, Third Sec. Kabul 1963, Eastern Dept. Foreign Office 1966, Head of Computer Study Team FCO 1969, First Sec., Econ., Paris 1971, First Sec. and Head of Chancery, Tehran 1974, Asst. Head, Energy, Science and Space Dept., FCO 1977, Head, Jt. Nuclear Unit, FCO 1978, Political Counsellor, U.K. Del. to NATO 1981, Head of Defence Dept., FCO 1984; Amb. to Oman 1986-. *Leisure interests:* gardening, reading, listening to music. *Address:* Foreign and Commonwealth Office, King Charles Street, London, SW1A 2AH, England.

ALTANGEREL, Bat-Ochiryn; Mongolian politician; b. 10 Feb. 1934; ed. Inst. USSR; Chief Engineer, Ulaanbaatar Meat Factory 1958-61; Minister of Food Industry 1961-63; Deputy Chair. Council of Ministers 1987-; First Sec. Ulaanbaatar Cttee., Mongolian People's Revolutionary Party (MPRP) 1963-87; Alt. mem. Political Bureau, MPRP Cen. Cttee. 1973-81, mem. 1981-; Deputy to Great People's Hural, Chair. 1981-87; awarded Mongolian orders and medals. *Address:* Government Palace, Ulaanbaatar, Mongolia.

ALTES, Frederik Korthals; Netherlands politician; b. 1931, Amsterdam; ed. Leiden Univ.; practised as barrister; mem. First Chamber, States-Gen. 1981-; Minister of Justice Nov. 1982-; Chair. Volkspartij voor Vrijheid en Democratie (VVD) 1975-81. *Address:* Volkspartij voor Vrijheid en Democratie, Koninginnegracht 57, 2514 AE The Hague, Netherlands.

ALTMAN, Robert; American writer, director and producer; b. 20 Feb. 1925, Kansas City; m. Kathryn Reed; two s.; (also two s. one d. from two previous marriages); ed. Univ. of Missouri; Television work includes Bonanza, Kraft Theatre, Bus Stop, Combat, Cannes Film Festival Grand Prize for M*A*S*H; mem. Dirs. Guild of America. *Films include:* The Delinquents 1955, The James Dean Story 1957, Nightmare in Chicago 1964, Countdown 1968, That Cold Day in the Park 1969, M*A*S*H 1970, Brewster McCloud 1971, McCabe and Mrs. Miller 1972, Images 1972, The Long Goodbye 1973, Thieves Like us 1973, California Split 1974, Nashville 1975, Buffalo Bill and the Indians 1976, Welcome to LA 1977, The Late Show 1977, Three Women 1977, A Wedding 1979, Remember My Name 1979, Quintet 1979, A Perfect Couple 1979, Rich Kids 1979, Popeye 1980, Health 1980, The Easter Egg Hunt 1981, Come Back to the Five and Dime, Jimmy Dean, Jimmy Dean 1982, Secret Honor 1984, Fool for Love 1986, Aria (Segment) 1987, Beyond Therapy 1987, Tanner '88 (Dir. with Garry Trudeau, q.v.).

ALTMAN, Stuart Harold, PH.D.; American professor of health; b 8 Aug. 1937, Bronx, New York; s. of Sidney Altman and Florence Altman; m. Diane Kleinberg; three d.; ed. City Coll. of New York and Univ. of California, Los Angeles; Labor Market Economist, Fed. Reserve Bd. 1962-64; Econ. Consultant and Manpower Economist, Office of Asst. Sec. of Defense, Washington, D.C. 1964-66; Asst Prof. of Econs., Brown Univ. 1966-68, Assoc. Prof. 1968-70; Univ. Fellow and Dir. of Health Studies, Urban Inst. 1970-71; Deputy Admin., Office of Health, Cost of Living Council, Dept. of Health, Educ. and Welfare 1973-74, Deputy Asst. Sec. for Planning and Evaluation (Health) 1971-76; Visiting Lecturer, Graduate School of Public Policy, Univ. of Calif., Berkeley 1976-77; Dean and Sol C. Chaikin Prof. of Nat. Health Policy, Heller School, Brandeis Univ. 1977-; Chair. Prospective Payment Assessment Comm., U.S. Congress 1983-86, 1986-89; mem. Inst. of Medicine (mem. Governing Council 1982-83), Bd., Robert Wood Johnson Clinical Scholars. *Publications:* The Growing Physician Surplus: Will it Benefit or Bankrupt the U.S. Health System 1982, Ambulatory Care: Problems of Cost and Access (with others) 1985, Will the Medicare Prospective Payment System Succeed? Technical Adjustments Can Make the Difference 1986 and other publs. *Leisure interests:* sailing, cross-country skiing, boating and tennis. *Address:* Heller Graduate School, Brandeis University, Waltham, Mass. 02254; 11 Bakers Hill Road, Weston, Mass. 02193, U.S.A. (Home). *Telephone:* (617) 736-3803 (Office); (617) 988-9144 (Home).

ALTUNIN, Aleksandr Terentevich; Soviet army officer and politician; b. 14 Aug. 1921, Steklyanka, Omsk Dist.; ed. School for Infantry training, Frunze Mil. Acad. 1945-48; accountant, sec. of a rural soviet 1937-39; served in Soviet Army 1939-45; mem. CPSU 1943-; chief of an operational unit 1948-52; Chief-of-Staff of a div. 1952-56; at Mil. Acad. of Gen. Staff 1956-57; Deputy Commdr., Commdr. of a div., sr. posts in Gen. Staff 1958-68; Commdr. of unit, Baltic Mil. Dist. 1966-68; Deputy to R.S.F.S.R. Supreme Soviet 1967-71; Commdr. North Caucasian Mil. Dist. 1968-70; Head of main Admin. of cadres, U.S.S.R. Ministry of Defence 1970-72; Deputy to Council of Nationalities, U.S.S.R. Supreme Soviet 1970-; Head of U.S.S.R. Civil Defence, U.S.S.R. Deputy Minister of Defence 1972-, mem. Gen. Inspectorate 1986-; mem. Cen. Cttee. CPSU 1976-; Army Gen. 1977-; Enrico Fermi Award 1987; Hero of Soviet Union 1944, Order of Red Banner (twice), Order of Alexander Nevsky, Order of Red Star, Mongolian Order 1972, Order of Lenin 1978, 1981, many other medals. *Publications include:* papers on nat. security and books about Second World War experiences. *Address:* The Kremlin, Moscow, U.S.S.R.

ALVA, Dinker, B.SC. (TECH.); Indian industrialist; b. 2 July 1933, Mangalore; s. of the late Shanker Alva and Kamala Alva; m. Shashikala Alva 1960; one s. one d.; ed. Madras Univ.; employed by Delhi Cloth and Gen. Mills Ltd. 1954-58; Industrial Consultant IBCON Pvt. Ltd. 1958-60; Sales Dir. The Bombay Dyeing and Mfg. Co. Ltd. 1960-66, Gen. Man. (Sales) 1969-74, Dir. 1974-79, Pres. 1979-; Gen. Man. Anglo-French Textiles Ltd. 1966-69; Pres.-Dir. P.T. Five Star Industries Ltd. Indonesia 1981-; Chair. Naperol Investments Pvt. Ltd. 1980-, Macrofil Investments Ltd. 1985-; mem. Governing Bd., Bombay Textile Research Asscn. *Leisure interests:* music, reading, tennis. *Address:* 426 Samudra Mahal, Dr. Annie Besant Road, Worli, Bombay 400 018, India. *Telephone:* 263853/268071 (Office); 4925531/4927008 (Home).

ALVA CASTRO, Luis; Peruvian politician and economist; b. Trujillo; ed. Universidad Nacional de Trujillo; fmr. Dir. Corporación de Desarollo Económico y Social de la Libertad; Deputy for Libertad; has held various posts in Partido Aprista Peruano including Sec.-Gen. of Northern Regional Org., mem. Political Comm. and Nat. Sec. for Electoral Matters; Chair. Nat Planning Comm. of Partido Aprista Peruano; Second Vice-Pres. of Repub., Pres. Council of Ministers (Prime Minister) and Minister of Economy and Finance 1985-87. *Publications:* La Necesidad del Cambio, Manejo Presupuestal del Perú, En Defensa del Pueblo, Endeudamiento Externo del Perú, Deuda Externa: Un reto para los Latinoamericanos and other books and essays. *Address:* c/o Ministry of Economy and Finance, Cuadra Avenida Abancay 5, Lima, Peru.

ALVAREZ, Mario Roberto; Argentine architect; b. 14 Nov. 1913, Buenos Aires; m. Jorgelina Ortiz de Rosas 1953; one s. one d.; ed. Colegio Nacional, Buenos Aires, and Univ. of Buenos Aires; in private practice, Buenos Aires 1937–, as Mario Roberto Alvarez and Assocs. 1947–; architect, Ministry of Public Works 1937–42; municipal architect, Avellaneda 1942–47; adviser, Secr. of Public Works, City of Buenos Aires 1958–62; Sec. to World Football Cup Stadium Comm., Buenos Aires 1972–78; Vice-Pres. Cen. Soc. of Architects 1953–55; exhibited, Sťao Paulo Bienal 1957 and several other exhbns. of Argentine architecture in Buenos Aires and abroad; prizewinner in numerous int. architectural competitions; Hon. Fellow, American Inst. of Architects; Dr. h.c. (La Plata) 1982; Great Prize of the Nat. Fund of Arts 1976; Hon. mem. Inst. of City Planning, Peru 1979. *Address:* Mario Roberto Alvarez y Asociados, Solis 370, Buenos Aires, Argentina.

ALVAREZ ALVAREZ, José Luis, D.JUR.; Spanish politician; b. 1930, Madrid; m. Mercedes Royo Villanueva Payá; five c.; ed. Univ. Complutense de Madrid; lecturer of Law, Complutense Univ., Madrid 1967–72; f. Tacito Group; Chair. Bd. FEDISA; co-founder Popular Party 1976; elected UCD Deputy, Madrid 1977; Mayor of Madrid 1978–79; fmrly. Councillor, Madrid City Council, Chair. Educ. Cttee., Monitoring Cttee. for Spanish Radio and Television, Congress of Deputies; Minister for Transport and Communications 1980–82, for Agric., Fisheries and Food 1981–82; Vice-Pres. PDP –1986. *Publication:* España desde el Centro.

ALVAREZ ARMELLINO, Gen. Gregorio Conrado; Uruguayan army officer and politician; b. 26 Nov. 1925, Montevideo; s. of Gen. Gregorio Alvarez Lezama and Bianca Armellino de Alvarez Lezama; m. María del Rosario Flores 1978; one d.; ed. José Pedro Varela High School and Uruguay Mil. Coll.; Officer, Cavalry Regt. 1946–59; Head of Cavalry Operations Training, Mil. Coll. 1960–62; Chief of Republican Guard 1962–79; promoted to Gen. 1971; Joint Chief of Staff 1971–79; First Sec. Council of Nat. Security 1973–74; 4th Div. Army Commander 1974–78; C.-in-C. of the Army 1978–79; retd. from armed forces 1979; Pres. of Uruguay 1981–84; various military decorations. *Leisure interests:* horse-riding, fishing, hunting. *Address:* c/o Oficina del Presidente, Montevideo, Uruguay.

ALVAREZ RENDUELES, José Ramón, PH.D., LL.M.; Spanish central banker; b. 17 June 1940, Gijón; s. of Ramón Alvarez Medina; m. Eugenia Villar 1964; four s. one d; State Economist 1964; rank of Full Prof. in Public Finance 1973; Head of Econ. Studies in Planning Comm. 1969; Dir. Inst. of Econ. Devt. 1973; Tech. Sec.-Gen. Ministry of Finance 1973–75, Under-Sec. for Econ. 1975–76; Sec. of State for Econ. Affairs 1977–78; Gov. Bank of Spain 1978–84; Chair. Banco Zaragozano COFIR and Productos Pirelli 1986–. *Publications:* Valoración actual de la imposición sobre consumo 1971, La Hacienda pública y el medio ambiente 1973. *Leisure interests:* golf, music, literature, lawn tennis. *Address:* La Masó 21, Madrid 28034 (Mirasierra), Spain (Home).

ALVERNY, Marie-Thérèse d', DR.PHIL.; French palaeographical archivist; b. 25 Jan. 1903, Boën sur Lignon, Loire; d. of André d'Alverny and Magdeleine des Colombiers de Boismarmin; ed. Univ. de Strasbourg and Univ. de Paris à la Sorbonne, Ecole nat. des Chartes and Ecole pratique des Hautes Etudes, Paris; Librarian Bibliothèque nat. 1928, Asst. Keeper of MSS. 1947–62; Prof. Centre of Higher Studies of Medieval Civilization, Univ. of Poitiers 1957–; Maître de Recherche, Centre nat. de la Recherche scientifique (CNRS) 1963–66, Dir. of Research 1967–73, Hon. Dir. 1973–; Visiting Fellow, Inst. for Advanced Study, Princeton 1961, 1971, Harvard Univ. 1977; Visiting Prof. Barnard Coll. and Columbia Univ. 1968–69, Calif. Univ. 1974, 1981; Co-Dir. Archives d'Histoire doctrinale et littéraire du Moyen-Age 1954–; mem. Editorial Cttee. Scriptorium 1966–, Manuscripta 1968–, Vivarium 1974; mem. Soc. of Ecole Nat. des Chartes (Pres. 1965–66), Comité des Travaux Historiques et Scientifiques, Soc. of Latin Studies and Int. Cttee. of Palaeography, Int. Acad. of History of Science; Corresp. mem. Mediaeval Acad. of America, American Philosophical Soc., American Acad. of Arts and Sciences, Acad. of Humanities of Barcelona and British Acad., Bayerische Akademie der Wissenschaften; Hon. Fellow St. Hilda's Coll., Oxford; Chevalier, Légion d'honneur; Red Cross War Medal; Dr. h.c. (Oxford, Smith Coll., Pontifical Inst. of Medieval Studies, Toronto), (Padova Univ.), Médaille de Guerre de la croix rouge. *Publications:* La sagesse et ses sept filles: Recherches sur les allégories de la philosophie et des arts libéraux IXe-XIIe siècle 1946, Catalogue général des manuscrits latins de la Bibliothèque nationale, vols. III 1952, IV 1958, V 1968, Catalogue des manuscrits datés en écriture latine, vols. II 1962, III 1974 and IV 1981, Deux traductions latines du Coran au Moyen Age 1948, Marc de Tolède, traducteur d'Ibn Tumart 1950–51, Avicenna latinus in vols. 1961–72, Alain de Lille, Textes inédits, avec une introduction sur sa vie et ses oeuvres 1965, Al-Kindi, De Radiis 1975, L'Homme comme symbole, Le microcosme 1976 and many articles on medieval history. *Leisure interest:* gardening. *Address:* Centre National de la Recherche Scientifique, 40 avenue d'Iéna, Paris 75116 (Office); 58 rue de Vaugirard, Paris 75006; and Clairac, par Meyrannes (Gard), France (Homes). *Telephone:* 45-48-09-03 (Paris home).

ALVEY, John, C.B., B.SC. (ENG.), F.I.E.E., F.ENG.; British engineer; b. 19 June 1925; s. of G.C.V. Alvey and H.E. Pellat; m. Celia E. Marson 1955; three s.; ed. Reeds School and Northampton Eng. Coll. (now City Univ.); Stock Exchange, London 1941–43; Service with R.N. 1943–46; Defence Science 1950–80; Dir. Admiralty Surface Weapons Establishment 1976–77; Chief Scientist, R.A.F. 1977–80; Sr. Dir. of Tech., British Telecom 1980–83, Man. Dir. for Procurement and Eng.-in-Chief 1983–86; Chair. SIRA 1987–; Hon. Fellow, Queen Mary Coll. 1988; Hon. D.Sc. (City Univ.). *Publication:* The Alvey Committee Report 1982. *Leisure interests:* skiing, watching rugby, walking, reading, music, theatre. *Address:* 81 Newgate Street, London, EC1A 7AJ (Office); 9a St. Omer Road, Guildford, Surrey, GU1 2DA, England (Home). *Telephone:* 01-356 5320 (Office); (0483) 63859 (Home).

ALWAN, Hamia; Iraqi politician and former journalist; b. 1930, Babylon Governorate; ed. American Univ. in Beirut; served Ministry of Finance for several years; arrested several times for political activity; Editor-in-Chief and Publisher Al-Shaab newspaper; served in State Org. of Commerce; Dir.-Gen. of Information 1968; Minister of State for Presidential Affairs 1968; Minister of Culture and Information 1969, of Youth 1970; Head of Iraqi-German Friendship Asscn. 1972; Minister of Information 1972; Head of Exec. Bureau, Gen. Fed. of Iraqi Youth 1974; Minister of State 1974–76; Head of Bureau of Vice-Chair. of Revolutionary Command Council with rank of Minister 1976–77; Minister of State for Foreign Affairs 1977. *Address:* c/o Ministry of Foreign Affairs, Karradat Mariam, Baghdad, Iraq.

ALZAMORA, Carlos; Peruvian diplomatist; b. 20 May 1926, Lima; s. of Carlos and María Pía Alzamora; m. Juana Leguía 1959; joined Ministry of Foreign Affairs 1943, Foreign Service 1949, served in missions to Bolivia, Brazil, Ecuador, Italy, OAS, Paraguay, U.S.A.; Under-Sec. for Econ. and Integration Affairs, Ministry of Foreign Affairs 1969–71; Head of first trade mission to China 1971; Amb. and Perm. Rep. to UN Office in Geneva 1972–75, to UN, New York 1975–78, 1979–80; Perm. Sec. Latin American Econ. System 1979–84; mem. dels. to several sessions of Gen. Ass. including sixth and seventh special sessions, to ECOSOC, Conf. of Cttee. on Disarmament, UNCTAD III and IV; head of dels. to various int. confs. on devt., of Group of 77 (Sec.-Gen. of second ministerial meeting 1971), and on non-alignment, GATT, ILO and UNDP; Amb. in special missions on econ. co-operation to France, U.S.A. and Germany; negotiator of Andean Integration Agreement 1969–71; Vice-Pres. Gen. Assembly of UN 1975, 1977; Alt. Exec. Dir. World Bank Bd. 1971. *Address:* Ministry of Foreign Affairs, 820 Second Avenue, Suite 1600, New York, N.Y. 10017, U.S.A.

AMAD, Hani Subhi al-, M.A., PH.D.; Jordanian librarian; b. 1938, Salt; s. of Subhi al-Amad and Suhaila al-Amad; m. Intesar Bashiti 1968; two s. two d.; ed. Salt Secondary School, Cairo Univ. and in U.S.A.; Librarian, Univ. of Jordan Library 1963–73, Dir. 1983–; Librarian, Faculty of Arts & Human Sciences, Univ. of Moh. V, Rabat 1974–76; Dir.-Gen. Culture and Arts Dept., Amman 1977–78; Asst. Prof. Faculty of Arts, Univ. of Jordan 1979–, Asst. Dean 1981–83; Pres. Jordan Library Asscn. 1984–85; Jordanian Writers' Union 1987–. *Publications:* Jordan Folk Songs 1969, Jordan Folk Proverbs 1978, Cultural Policy in Jordan 1980, Studies in Biographical Sources 1981, Jordan Folk Elegies: Lamentation 1984, Directory of Notables in the Southern Region of Bilad Ash-Sham 1985, Literature of Writing and Authorship among Arabs: A General View 1986, Principles of Methodology in Arabic authorship extracted from Introductions 1987, Arab Character in the Biography of Princess That al-Himmah 1988. *Leisure interest:* reading and doing research. *Address:* The Library, University of Jordan, Amman, Jordan. *Telephone:* 843555/3135.

AMADO, Jorge; Brazilian novelist; b. 10 Aug. 1912, Itabuna, Bahia; s. of João Amado de Faria and Eulalia Leal Amado; m. Zelia Gattai 1945; one s. one d.; Calouste Gulbenkian Prize, Acad. du Monde Latin 1971; Nat. Literary Prize (Brazil); Nonnino Literary Prize (Italy); Commdr., Légion d'Honneur, France. *Publications include:* Mar Morto, Jubiabá, The Violent Land, São Jorge dos Ilheus, Cacau, Suor, Capitães da Areia, ABC de Castro Alves, Bahia de Todos os Santos, O Amor do Soldado, Seara Vermelha, O Cavaleiro da Esperança, O Mundo da Paz, Os subterrâneos da Liberdade, Gabriela Cravo e Canela, Os velhos marinheiros, Os pastores da noite, Dona Flor e seus dois maridos! Tenda dos Milagres, Teresa Bautista Cansada de Guerra, Tieta do Agreste e Farda, Fardão, Camisola de Dormir, O Menino Grapiúna, Tocaia Grande. *Leisure interests:* reading, gardening, cats, poker. *Address:* Rua Alagoinhas 33, Rio Vermelho-Salvador, Bahia, Brazil. *Telephone:* 247-2165.

AMALDI, Edoardo, PH.D.; Italian physicist; b. 5 Sept. 1908, Carpanetov; s. of Ugo Amaldi and Luisa Basini; m. Ginestra Giovene 1933; two s. one d.; ed. Rome Univ.; fmr. Prof. Gen. Physics, Rome Univ.; mem. Accademia Naz. dei Lincei, Foreign mem. Royal Soc. of Sciences of Uppsala, U.S.S.R. Acad. of Sciences; Hon. mem. Royal Inst. of Great Britain, Nat. Acad. of Sciences of U.S.A., Royal Soc. (U.K.); Hon. D.Sc. (Glasgow and Oxford), Commandeur Ordre Couronne (Belgium), Fregene Prize 1984. *Publications:* various papers on atomic and nuclear problems. *Address:* Accademia Nazionale dei Lincei, Palazzo Corsini, Via della Lungara 10, 00165 Rome, Italy.

ÅMAN, Karl E., M.B.A.; Swedish business executive; b. 6 Oct. 1928, Härnösand; s. of Erik and Therese Åman; m. Berit Lundgren 1951; two s.; in banking until 1970; Man. Dir. AB Alfort & Cronholm paint industry 1970–73; Deputy Man. Dir. Svenska Handelsbanken 1973–75; Man. Dir. ICA AB (food retailing and food industry) 1975–82; Man. Dir. Statsföretag

AB 1982-84; Chair. of Bd. Investment AB Procordia, Statsföretag International AB, Svenska Tobaks AB; mem. Bd. of Dirs. Liber Grafiska AB, Försäkringsbolaget Pensionsgaranti, Arbetsmarknadsförsäkringar, Cadbury Slotts AB, ICC Sweden, Skandia, SARA AB, Svenska Finans, Allmänna Bevaknings AB, BS Konsult AB, AB Eiser, Saxylle-Kilsund AB, Svenska Handelsbanken. *Leisure interest:* golf. *Address:* Trebackavägen 4, S-182 65 Djursholm, Sweden.

AMANDRY, Pierre, D. ÈS L.; French academic; b. 31 Dec. 1912, Troyes; s. of Albert Amandry and Marguerite Philippon; m. Angélique Pavlidi 1944; one s. one d.; ed. Ecole Normale Supérieure and Univ. of Paris/Sorbonne; Sec.-Gen. French Archaeological School, Athens 1942-49, Dir. 1969-81; Asst. Prof. Univ. of Paris 1949-50; Prof. Univ. of Strasbourg 1951-69; mem. Inst. de France (Acad. des Inscriptions et Belles Lettres); Assoc. mem. Acad. Royale de Belgique; foreign mem. Athens Acad.; Corresp. Fellow British Acad.; Hon. mem. British Soc. for Promotion of Hellenic Studies, Archaeological Inst. of America; Hon. Vice-Pres. Archaeological Soc. of Athens 1987; Officier, Légion d'honneur, decorations from Greece and Belgium. *Publications:* La mantique apollinienne à Delphes 1950, La colonne du Sphinx des Naxiens et le Portique des Athéniens à Delphes 1953, Collection Hélène Stathatos I. les bijoux antiques 1953, Collection Hélène Stathatos III. Objets antiques et byzantins 1963, and 130 articles in various periodicals. *Address:* 54 boulevard Saint Jacques, 75014 Paris, France. *Telephone:* 45.87.17.07.

AMANO, Kosei; Japanese politician; b. 1905; previous posts include Dir.-Gen. Nat. Land Agency; Chair. Cttee. on Construction, on Discipline and on Budget, House of Reps.; Chair. Liberal Democratic Party (LDP) Comm. on Highways; Minister of Construction 1986-87; Liberal Democratic Party. *Address:* Ministry of Construction, 1-3 Kasumigaseki 2-chome, Chiyoda-ku, Tokyo, Japan.

AMARASINGHE, N.; Sri Lankan librarian; b. 4 July 1935; m. Padma Edirisinghe 1970; one s. one d.; ed. Nugawela Cen. Coll., Univ. of Ceylon, Peradeniya and School of Librarianship and Archives, Univ. Coll. London; Asst. Govt. Archivist, Dept. of Nat. Archives 1961-63; Ed., Ceylon Nat. Bibliography 1963-68; Head, Dept. of Library Science, Junior Univ. Coll. 1968-69; Asst. Librarian (Research), Univ. of Ceylon, Peradeniya 1969-73; Head of Dept. of Library Science, Univ. of Ceylon, Vidyalankara 1973-76; Educ. Officer, Sri Lanka Library Asscn. 1975-79; Dir. Nat Library of Sri Lanka 1976-, Sec. Ceylon Nat. Library Services Bd. 1976-; Admin. ISBN Agency, Sri Lanka 1984-; Visiting Lecturer in Library and Information Science, Colombo Univ. 1984-; Chair. 3rd Int. Conf. of Dirs. of Nat. Libraries of Asia and Oceania 1985-87. *Address:* No. 74, 3rd Lane, Model Town, Ratmalana, Sri Lanka. *Telephone:* 598847, 95200, 95199 (Office); 507206 (Home).

AMARO DA COSTA, Adelino; Portuguese politician and journalist; b. 1943, Lisbon; taught at Higher Inst. of Tech.; Head of Office of Studies and Planning, Ministry of Educ.; mem. Constituent Ass. for Braga 1975-76; mem. Nat. Ass. for Oporto, re-elected Dec. 1979-; Minister of Defence 1980-81; Chair. Centrist Political Cttee. Jan. 1979-; Co-Founder Centre Democratic Party (CDS); Founder and Ed. university newspaper Tempo, Ed. newspaper Madrid, Spain. *Address:* c/o Ministerio da Defesa Nacional, Praça do Comércio, Lisbon-2, Portugal.

AMATO, Giuliano; Italian politician; b. 13 May 1938, Turin; joined Italian Socialist Party (PSI) 1958, mem. Cen. Cttee. 1978-; elected Deputy for Turin-Novara-Vercelli 1983, 1987; fmr. Under-Sec. of State, Presidency of Council of Ministers; Vice-Pres. Council of Ministers and Minister of the Treasury 1987-; Prof. of Italian and Comparative Constitutional Law, Univ. of Rome. *Address:* Camera dei Deputati, Rome, Italy.

AMBARTSUMIAN, Sergey Aleksandrovich; Soviet scientist and state official; Vice-Pres. of Armenian Acad. of Sciences 1975-; Chair. of Exec. Cttee. of Armenian S.S.R. 1975-. *Address:* Academy of Sciences of Armenian S.S.R., Yerevan, U.S.S.R.

AMBARTSUMYAN, Victor Amazaspovich; Soviet astrophysicist; b. 18 Sept. 1908, Tbilisi; m. Vera Ambartsumyan 1931; two s. two d.; ed. Leningrad Univ. and Pulkovo Observatory; Lecturer and research worker Leningrad Univ. 1931-43; Prof. Astrophysics Erevan Univ. 1947-; Corresp. mem. U.S.S.R. Acad. of Sciences 1939-53, mem. 1953-; mem. CPSU 1940-; founder and Dir. Byurakan Astrophysics Observatory 1945-; mem. Armenian Acad. of Sciences 1943-, Pres. 1947-; Vice-Pres. Int. Astronomical Union 1948-55, Pres. 1961-64; Past Pres. Int. Council of Scientific Unions (ICSU) 1969; Deputy Supreme Soviet U.S.S.R. 1950-; mem. Foreign Affairs Comm., Soviet of Union; mem. Cen. Cttee. Communist Party of Armenia; specialist on problems of theoretical astrophysics; Corresp. mem. French Acad. of Sciences, German Acad. of Sciences (Berlin); Hon. mem. American Acad. of Arts and Sciences; Foreign Assoc. N.A.S. (U.S.A.) 1959; Foreign mem. Royal Soc. 1969, Acad. des Sciences 1978-; mem. Indian Nat. Acad. of Sciences; State Prize 1946, 1950; Hero of Socialist Labour twice, Hammer and Sickle Gold Medal, five Orders of Lenin, two Orders of Red Banner of Labour, Order of the October Revolution 1983. *Publications:* Teoretischeskaya astrofizika 1939, Evolyutsiya zvezd i astrofizika 1947, Novyi sposob rascheta rasseyania sveta v mutnoi srede 1942, O rasseyaniys sveta atmosferami planet 1942, K voprosu o diffusnom otrazheniy sveta mutnoi sredoi 1943, Nauchnye Trudy (2 vols.) 1960,

Problemy Vnegalktricheskikh Issledovaniy in Voprosy Kosmogoniy, Vol. 8 1962, Problemy Evolyutsiy v selennoy 1968. *Address:* Academy of Sciences of Armenian S.S.R., 24 Marshal Bagramian Avenue, Erevan, U.S.S.R.

AMBLER, Eric, O.B.E.; British writer; b. 28 June 1909; s. of Alfred Percy and Amy Madeleine Ambler; m. 1st Louise Crombie 1939, 2nd Joan Harrison 1958; ed. Colfe's Grammar School and London Univ.; engineering apprentice 1927-28; advertising copywriter 1929-35; professional writer 1936-; served World War II; Lieut.-Col. 1944; Asst. Dir. of Army Kinematography, War Office 1944-46; wrote and produced film The October Man 1947. *Screenplays include:* The Way Ahead 1944, The October Man 1947, The Passionate Friends 1948, Highly Dangerous 1950, The Magic Box 1951, Gigolo and Gigolette (in Encore) 1952, The Card 1952, Rough Shoot 1953, The Cruel Sea 1953, Lease of Life 1954, The Purple Plain 1954, Yangtse Incident 1957, A Night to Remember 1958, Wreck of the Mary Deare 1959, Love Hate Love 1970. *Publications:* The Dark Frontier 1936, Uncommon Danger 1937, Epitaph for a Spy 1938, Cause for Alarm 1938, The Mask of Dimitrios 1939, Journey into Fear 1940, Judgement on Deltchev 1951, The Schirmer Inheritance 1953, The Night-comers 1956, Passage of Arms 1959, The Light of Day 1962, The Ability to Kill (essays) 1963, To Catch a Spy (ed. and introduced) 1964, A Kind of Anger (Edgar Allan Poe Award 1964) 1964, Dirty Story 1967, The Intercom Conspiracy 1969, The Levanter (Golden Dagger Award 1973) 1972, Doctor Frigo (MWA Grand Master Award 1975) 1974, Send No More Roses 1977, The Care of Time 1981, Here Lies (autobiog.) 1985 (Diamond Dagger Award 1986). *Address:* c/o Campbell Thomson and Mc Laughlin Ltd., 31 Newington Green, London, N16 9PU, England.

AMBRASEYS, Nicholas, PH.D., F.I.C.E., F.ENG.; British professor of engineering seismology; b. 19 Jan. 1929, Athens, Greece; s. of Neocles Ambraseys and Cleopatra Ambraseys; m. Xeni Stavrou 1955; ed. Univ. of Athens and Imperial Coll. of Science and Tech., Univ. of London; Prof. of Hydrodynamics, Nat. Tech. Univ. of Athens 1963-64; Lecturer in Soil Mechanics, Imperial Coll., London 1965-68, Reader in Eng. Seismology 1968-73, Prof. 1973, Head of Eng. Seismology Section 1969-; led UN/UNESCO earthquake reconnaissance missions to Yugoslavia, Iran, Turkey, Pakistan, Romania, Algeria, Italy, E. Africa, Nicaragua and Cen. Africa 1963-81; mem. UN Advisory Bd. for reconstruction of Skopje 1964-69; Chair. British Nat. Cttee. for Earthquake Eng., ICE 1966-71; Vice-Pres. European Asscn. of Earthquake Eng. 1967-75; mem. and Chair. UNESCO Advisory Cttee. on Earthquake Risk 1971-81; Busk Medal for Scientific Discovery (Royal Geographical Soc.) 1975. *Publications;* A History of Persian Earthquakes (with G. Melville) 1982 and over 100 papers in scientific and eng. journals. *Leisure interests;* historical geography, archaeology, travel. *Address:* Department of Civil Engineering, Imperial College of Science and Technology, London, SW7 2BU; 19 Bede House, Manor Fields, London, SW15 3LT, England (Home). *Telephone:* 01-589 5111 (College); 01-788 4219 (Home).

AMBRIÉRE, Francis; French writer and journalist; b. 27 Sept. 1907, Paris; m. Suzanne Rannou 1931; two c.; m. 2nd Madeleine Fargeaud 1979; two c.; ed. Univs. of Dijon and Paris; before Second World War was Ed. Nouvelles Littéraires and dramatic critic Mercure de France; served in French Army in Second World War; prisoner in Germany and Poland; Dir. of Guides Bleus 1945-72; Prés.-Dir. Gén. of L'Université des Annales 1947-72; dramatic critic of monthly Les Annales; mem. Jury, Prix Théophraste Renaudot 1945-; Vice-Pres. of Jury, Prix Albert-Londres 1972-; Officier, Légion d'honneur, Commdr. des Arts et Lettres, Officer Order of Cedar (Lebanon), Order Polonia Restituta. *Publications:* La vie secrète des Grands Magasins 1932, Le favori de François Ier 1936, Les Grandes vacances (Prix Goncourt 1946), Le solitaire de La Cervara 1947, La galérie dramatique 1949, Le Maroc 1952, Le Siècle des Valmore 1987. *Address:* 15 rue Sainte-Genevieve, Cauvigny, 60730 Sainte-Geneviève, France. *Telephone:* 44 07 38 21.

AMELING, Elly; Netherlands opera singer; b. (as Elisabeth Sara Ameling) 1938, Rotterdam; studied singing with Jo Bollekamp, with Jacoba and Sam Dresden, and with Bodi Rapp; studied French art song with Pierre Bernac; has given recitals in Europe, S. Africa, Japan; début in U.S.A. 1968, annual tours of U.S.A. and Canada 1968-; has sung with Concertgebouw, New Philharmonic Orchestra, BBC Symphony Orchestra, Berlin Philharmonic, Cincinnati Symphony, San Francisco Symphony, Toronto Symphony, Chicago Symphony; has appeared in Mozart Festival, Washington, D.C. 1974, Caramoor Festival 1974, Art Song Festival, Princeton, N.J. 1974; major recordings, Mozart Concert, Handel Concert, Cantatas (Bach), Mörike Lieder (Wolf), Aimez-vous Handel?, Aimez-vous Mozart?, Christmas Oratorio (Bach), Symphony No. 2 (Mahler), Te Deum (Bruckner), Italienisches Liederbuch (Wolf); First Prize, Concours Int. de Musique, Geneva; Grand Prix du Disque, Edison Prize, Preis der Deutschen Schallplattenkritik, Stereo Review Record of the Year Award; Knight Order of Orange-Nassau.

AMELKO, Admiral Nikolay Nikolayevich; Soviet naval officer; b. 22 Nov. 1914, Leningrad; ed. Frunze Higher Naval School and Acad. of General Staff. Naval service 1933-; Commdr. of ships, Baltic Fleet 1937-41; Commdr. of ship formation 1941-46; Chief of Staff, Pacific Fleet 1956-62; Commdr. Pacific Fleet 1962-69; Deputy C.-in-C. of U.S.S.R. Navy 1969-;

mem. CPSU 1944–, Cand. mem. Central Cttee. of CPSU 1966–71; Deputy to U.S.S.R. Supreme Soviet 1966–; Order of Lenin (three times), Order of Red Flag (twice) and other decorations. *Address:* U.S.S.R. Ministry of Defence, 34 Naberezhnaya M. Thoreza, Moscow, U.S.S.R.

AMERASINGHE, Chittharanjan Felix, B.A., LL.B., PH.D., LL.D.; Sri Lankan international lawyer; b. 2 March 1933, Colombo; s. of Samson Felix Amerasinghe, O.B.E. and Mary Victorine Abeyesundere; m. Wimala Nalini Pieris 1964; one s. two d.; ed. Royal Coll., Colombo, Trinity Hall, Cambridge Univ., Harvard Univ. Law School; lecturer in Law, Univ. of Ceylon 1962–65, Sr. Lecturer 1965–68, Reader 1968–69, Second Prof. of Law 1969–71; Counsel, World Bank 1970–75, Sr. Counsel 1975–81, Exec. Sec. World Bank Admin. Tribunal 1981–; Consultant in Int. Law, Govt. of Ceylon 1963–70; mem. Ceylon Govt. Comm. on Local Govt. 1969; Exec. Council mem. American Soc. of Int. Law 1980–83; Assoc. mem. Inst. de Droit Int. 1981–87, mem. 1987–; mem. Int. Law Asscn. 1986–; Henry Arthur Thomas Classical Award, Cambridge Univ. 1953, Angus Classical Prize 1953, Clement Davies Prize for Law 1955, Trinity Hall Studentship 1956–58, Yorke Prize 1964, Research Fellowship, Harvard Univ. Law School 1957. *Publications:* Some Aspects of the Actio Iniuriarum in Roman-Dutch Law 1966, Defamation and Other Injuries in Roman-Dutch Law 1968, State Responsibility for Injuries to Aliens 1967, Studies in International Law 1969, The Doctrines of Sovereignty and Separation of Powers in the Law of Ceylon 1970, The Law of the International Civil Service (2 vols) 1988, Documents on International Administrative Tribunals 1989, Case Law of the World Bank Administrative Tribunal 1989; articles in leading law and int. law journals. *Leisure interests:* religious reflection, classical and jazz music, art, artifacts, philately, photography, walking. *Address:* The World Bank, 1818 H Street NW, Washington, D.C. 20433 (Office); 6100 Robinwood Road, Bethesda, Md. 20817, U.S.A. (Home). *Telephone:* (202) 477-5031 (Office); (301) 229-2766 (Home).

AMERY, Carl (see Christian Mayer).

AMERY, Rt. Hon. Julian, M.P.; British politician; b. 27 March 1919; s. of the late Rt. Hon. Leopold Amery; m. Catherine, d. of Rt. Hon. Harold Macmillan (q.v.), 1950; one s. three d.; ed. Eton and Oxford Univ.; War Corresp., Spanish Civil War 1938–39; Attaché H.M. Legation, Belgrade, and on special missions 1939–40; Sgt. R.A.F. 1940–41; commissioned and transferred to Army; active service, Egypt, Palestine, Adriatic 1941–42; liaison officer to Albanian Resistance 1944; on the staff of Sir Winston Churchill's personal mission to Generalissimo Chiang Kai-shek 1945; M.P. 1950–66, 1969–; Under-Sec. of State for War 1957–58, for Colonies 1958–60; Sec. of State for Air 1960–62; Minister for Aviation 1962–64; Minister of Public Building and Works June-Oct. 1970; Minister for Housing and Construction 1970–72; Minister of State, Foreign and Commonwealth Office 1972–74; Dir. Vaal Reefs Exploration and Mining Co., Western Deepderels Ltd.; Consultant Sedgwick Forbes Overseas Group Ltd; Adviser Bank of Credit and Commerce Int.; Kt. Commdr. of the Phoenix, Order of Oman (1st Class), Order of Skanderbeg; Conservative. *Publications:* Sons of the Eagle, The Life of Joseph Chamberlain, Joseph Chamberlain and the Tariff Reform Campaign 1969, Approach March 1973. *Leisure interests:* skiing, travel. *Address:* 112 Eaton Square, London, S.W.1, England. *Telephone:* 01-235 1543.

AMES, Bruce Nathan, PH.D.; American professor of biochemistry; b. 16 Dec. 1928, New York; s. of Dr. M. U. and Dorothy Andres Ames; m. Dr. Giovanna Ferro-Luzzi 1960; two c.; ed. Cornell Univ. and California Inst. of Tech.; Postdoctoral Fellow, Nat. Insts. of Health 1953–54, Biochemist 1954–60; Nat. Science Foundation Fellow, Labs. of F. C. Crick, Cambridge and F. Jacob, Paris 1961; Chief Section of Microbial Genetics, Lab. of Molecular Biology, Nat. Insts. of Health 1962–67; Prof. of Biochemistry, Univ. of Calif., Berkeley 1968–, Chair. Dept. of Biochemistry 1983–; mem. Nat. Cancer Advisory Bd. 1976–82, N.A.S., American Acad. of Arts and Sciences; Fellow, American Asscn. for the Advancement of Science; Eli Lilly Award, American Chem. Soc. 1964; Arthur Flemming Award 1966, Rosenstiel Award 1976, Fed. of American Socs. for Experimental Biology Award 1976, Wankel Award 1978, John Scott Medal 1979, Bolton L. Corson Medal 1980, New Brunswick Lectureship Award of American Soc. for Microbiology 1980, Gen. Motors Cancer Research Fund Charles S. Mott Prize 1983, Gairdner Foundation Award 1983, Tyler Prize for Environmental Achievement 1985. *Publications:* scientific papers in areas of operons, biochemical genetics, histidine biosynthesis, mutagenesis, detection of environmental carcinogens and mutagens, oxygen radicals as a cause of aging and degenerative diseases, anti-carcinogens. *Address:* University of California, Department of Biochemistry, Berkeley, Calif. 94720 (Office); 1324 Spruce Street, Berkeley, Calif. 94709, U.S.A. (Home). *Telephone:* (415) 642-5165 (Office).

AMES, Michael McClean, PH.D., F.R.S.C.; Canadian professor of anthropology; b. 19 June 1933, Vancouver; s. of Ernest O. F. Ames and Elsie McClean; m. (separated); one s. one d.; ed. Univ of British Columbia and Harvard Univ.; Asst. Prof. of Sociology, McMaster Univ. 1962–64; Asst. Prof. Univ. of B.C. 1964, now Prof. of Anthropology; Dir. Museum of Anthropology, Univ. of B.C. 1974–; consultant to various museums and projects since 1976; Guggenheim Fellowship 1970–71. *Publications:* Manlike Monsters on Trial 1980, Museums, The Public and Anthropology 1986; articles in academic and museum journals. *Leisure interests:* hiking,

photography. *Address:* Museum of Anthropology, The University of British Columbia, 6393 N.W. Marine Drive, Vancouver, B.C. V6T 1W5 (Office); Suite 21, 1348 Nelson Street, Vancouver, B.C., V6E 1J9, Canada (Home).

AMIES, (Edwin) Hardy, C.V.O., F.R.S.A.; British couturier; b. 17 July 1909; s. of late Herbert William Amies and of Mary Hardy; ed. Brentwood School; Trainee, W. & T. Avery, Birmingham 1930–34; Man. Designer Lachasse, Farm Street, London, W.1 1934–39; Intelligence Corps 1939–45; Man. Dir. Hardy Amies Ltd. 1946–; opened Hardy Amies Boutique Ltd. 1950; Dressmaker to the Queen 1955–; Design Consultant to Alexandra Overalls Ltd., Cambridge Clothing Co. Ltd. (New Zealand), Coppley Noyes & Randall Ltd. (Canada), Daito Woollen Spinning & Weaving Co. Ltd. (Japan), T. Lipson & Sons Ltd. (Canada), Michelsons Ltd., Currie Neckwear Co. (Canada), Berkley Shirt Co. (U.S.A.), and numerous other companies; Chair. Inc. Soc. of London Fashion Designers 1959–60; Officier de l'Ordre de la Couronne (Belgium) 1946; Royal Designer for Industry 1964, British Knitting and Clothing Export Council Award; numerous design awards. *Publications:* Just So Far 1954, ABC of Men's Fashion 1964, Still Here 1984. *Leisure interests:* lawn tennis, gardening and opera. *Address:* Hardy Amies Ltd., 14 Savile Row, London, W.1, England (Office); 29 Cornwall Gardens, London, S.W.7, England (Home). *Telephone:* 01-734 2436 (Office).

AMIN, Mahmoud, PH.D.; Egyptian petroleum geologist; b. 30 April 1920, Cairo; m. 1945; two s. one d.; ed. Cairo and London Univs. Deputy Gen. Man. of Exploration and Production, Egyptian Petroleum Corpn. 1958–68; Chair. Western Desert Petroleum Corpn. 1968–75; Asst. Sec.-Gen. OAPEC 1975–79, Petroleum Consultant 1979–. *Publications:* Economics of Petroleum Resources, about 25 scientific papers on geology and petroleum, about 100 articles on petroleum. *Address:* 20 Mohamed Hassan Street, Heliopolis, Cairo (Office); 391 Horyia Street, Apart. 802, Alexandria, Egypt (Home). *Telephone:* 836212/828266 (Office); 44958 (Home).

AMIN, Mirza Ruhul; Bangladesh politician; b. Feb. 1922, Panchagarh Dist.; ed. Calcutta Univ.; mem. Dinajpur (now Panchagarh) Zilla Bd. 1956, 1960; f. Sec. Thakurgaon Girls High School 1957–68; Commr. Thakurgaon Pourashava 1958; Chair. Thakurgaon Municipal Cttee. 1960, 1964, 1977; mem. East Pakistan Provincial Ass. 1962, 1965; f. Sec. Thakurgaon Mahila Coll. 1977–85; mem. Rajshahi Div. Devt. Bd. 1977–80; mem. Parl. 1979–, Minister of Land Admin. and Land Reforms 1986, Minister of Agric. 1986–87, of Fisheries and Livestock 1987–88. *Address:* c/o Ministry of Agriculture, Bhaban 4, 2nd Storey, Dhaka, Bangladesh.

AMIN, Mostafa, M.A.; Egyptian journalist; b. 21 Feb. 1914, Cairo; s. of Mohamed Amin Youssef and Ratibah Zagloul; ed. American Univ. of Cairo and Georgetown Univ., U.S.A.; began his career publishing and writing for magazines, incl. El Raghaeb, Rose el Youssef 1928; Deputy Chief Ed. Akher Saa weekly magazine 1934, Ed.-in-Chief 1938; City Ed. Al Ahram daily 1939–44, Diplomatic Ed. 1940; Ed.-in-Chief Al Isnain weekly 1941–44; founder Akhbar el Yom weekly newspaper and publishing house, jointly with his brother Ali Amin 1944; mem. House of Reps. 1944; purchased Akher Saa weekly magazine 1946; founded Akher Lahza, El Guil 1951, weekly magazines; arrested 26 times for editorial policies during 1951; founded Al-Akhbar daily 1952; published Al Mokhtar for Reader's Digest 1956–67; Vice-Chair. Press Bd. 1960, dismissed by Pres. Gamal Abdul Nasser 1960; Chair. of Bd., Dar al Hilal Publrs. 1961; Chair. of Bd., Akhbar el Yom Publishers 1962–64, Editorial Man. 1964–65; arrested 1965, sentenced to life imprisonment 1966, reprieved by Pres. Anwar Sadat 1974; Ed.-in-Chief Akhbar el Yom 1974–76, staff writer 1976–. *Publications:* Laughing America 1943, First Year in Prison. *Address:* Dar Akhbar el Yom, 6 Sharia al-Safaha, Cairo, Egypt.

AMIN, Samir, D.ECON.; Egyptian economist; b. 4 Sept. 1931, Cairo; s. of Farid and Odette Amin; m. Isabelle Eynard 1957; no c.; ed. Univ. of Paris; Sr. Economist, Econ. Devt. Org., Cairo 1957–60; Tech. Adviser for Planning to Govt. of Mali 1960–63; Prof. of Econs., Univs. of Poiters, Paris and Dakar; Dir. UN African Inst. for Econ. Devt. and Planning 1970–. *Publications:* Trois expériences africaines de développement, Mali, Guinée, Ghana 1965, L'économie du Maghreb (2 vols.) 1967, Le développement du capitalisme en Côte d'Ivoire 1968, Le monde des affaires sénégalaises 1968, Maghreb in the Modern World 1970, L'accumulation à l'échelle mondiale 1970, L'Afrique de l'ouest bloquée 1971, Le développement inégal 1973, The Arab Nation 1978, Class and Nation 1980. *Leisure interest:* history. *Address:* Forum du Tiers Monde, B.P. 3501, Dakar, Senegal.

AMIN DADA, Field-Marshal Idi; Ugandan army officer and fmr. Head of State; b. 1925, Kakwa Region, West Nile; s. of late Amin Dada; joined King's African Rifles 1946; rank of Corporal 1949, Major 1963, Col. 1964; Deputy Commdr. of the Army 1964; Commdr. of the Army and Air Force 1966–70; rank of Brig.-Gen. 1967, Maj.-Gen. 1968, promoted Field-Marshal July 1975; leader of mil. coup d'état which deposed Pres. Milton Obote Jan. 1971; Pres. and Chief of Armed Forces 1971–79 (Life Pres. 1976–79 overthrown in Tanzanian invasion, fled Uganda); Minister of Defence 1971–75; Chair. Defence Council 1972–79; Minister of Internal Affairs 1973, of Information and Broadcasting 1973, of Foreign Affairs Nov. 1974–Jan. 1975, of Health 1977–79, of Foreign Affairs 1978, of Information, Broadcasting and Tourism, Game and Wildlife 1978–79, of Internal Affairs 1978–79; Chief of Staff of the Army 1974–79; Chair. OAU Ass. of Heads of State 1975–76, presided over Kampala Summit 1975, Addis Ababa Summit 1976; Heavyweight Boxing Champion of Uganda 1951–60; awarded eight highest mil. decorations of Uganda; Hon. LL.D. (Kampala) 1976; resident in Libya 1979–80; in exile in Jeddah, Saudi Arabia 1980–.

AMINI, Ali, D.ECON. ET IUR.; Iranian politician; b. 1905, Teheran; s. of Mohsen and Achraf Amini; m. Baloul Voosough 1932; one s.; ed. Ecole de Droit, Grenoble, and Faculté de Droit, Paris, France; Alternate Judge, Court of First Instance, and Penal Branch, Court of Appeal, Teheran 1931; fmr. Dir.-Gen. Dept. of Customs and Monopolies 1933, Econ. Section, Ministry of Finance 1939; Asst. Prime Minister 1940; fmr. Dir. Foreign Exchange Comm.; fmr. Deputy, 15th Legislative Session of the Majlis; fmr. Head of Narcotics Del. to Geneva and U.S.A.; Minister of Nat. Economy; fmr. Head of Iranian Trade Del. to Germany and France; Minister of Econ. 1952; Minister of Finance 1953, of Justice 1955; Amb. to U.S.A. 1956–58; Leader of Independents in general election 1960; Prime Minister 1961–62. *Publication:* L'institution du monopole de commerce extérieur en Perse.

AMIR MACHMUD, Lieut.-Gen.; Indonesian army officer and politician; b. 21 Feb. 1923, Cimahi, West Java; ed. Technical School, Army Staff Coll. (SSKAD); several army posts 1943–65, including Deputy Chief of Staff Dwikora Command i 1961, Commdr. Mil. Territory X, Lambung Mangkurat, S. Kalimantan 1962–65, Commdr. Mil. Territory V/Djaja 1965; promoted to rank of Lieut.-Col. 1957, Col. 61, Brig.-Gen. 1964, Maj.-Gen. 1966, Lieut.-Gen. 1970; Minister of Home Affairs, Pembangunan (Devt.) Cabinet 1969; Chair. of govt. body for the implementation of Act of Free Choice in W. Irian (now Irian Jaya) according to New York Agreement on Irian Jaya 1969; implemented gen. elections 1971; Minister of Home Affairs, 2nd Pembangunan Cabinet 1973–82; Chair. Majlis Permusyawaratan Rakyat (People's Consultative Ass.) Oct. 1982–. *Address:* Department of Home Affairs, Jalan Veteran, Jakarta, Indonesia.

AMIRTHALINGAM, Appapillai, B.A.; Ceylonese (Tamil) lawyer and politician; b. 26 Aug. 1927, Jaffna; s. of S. Appapillai and A. Valliammai; m. Mangayakarasi Vallipuram 1954; two s.; ed. Univ. of Ceylon, Ceylon Law Coll.; called to the bar 1952; mem. House of Reps. 1956–70, Nat. State Ass. July 1977–; in political detention 1958, 1959, 1961, 1976; founder mem. Ilankai Tamil Arasu Kadchi (Ceylon Fed. Party) 1949, Gen. Sec. 1964–72, Pres. 1973–; Sec.-Gen. Tamil United Liberation Front 1973–; Leader of Opposition 1977–83. *Publications:* (in Tamil) Our Objective 1954, Lessons of Bangladesh 1972, Racial Segregation in Ceylon 1973. *Address:* Moolai, Chulipuram; and Sravasti, Colombo, Sri Lanka. *Telephone:* Vaddukoddai 235 (Chulipuram); 91078 (Colombo).

AMIS, Kingsley, C.B.E., M.A.; British author; b. 16 April 1922, London; s. of William Robert and Rosa Annie (née Lucas) Amis; m. 1st Hilary A. Bardwell 1948, two s. one d.; m. 2nd Elizabeth Jane Howard 1965 (divorced 1983); ed. City of London School, St. John's Coll., Oxford. Lecturer in English, Univ. Coll. of Swansea 1949–61; Fellow of Peterhouse, Cambridge 1961–63; Visiting Fellow in Creative Writing, Princeton Univ. 1958–59; Visiting Prof. of English Vanderbilt Univ. 1967–68; Booker-McConnell Prize for The Old Devils 1986; Somerset Maugham Award, John W. Campbell Memorial Award; Hon. Fellow, Univ. Coll., Swansea. *Publications:* A Frame of Mind 1953, Lucky Jim 1954, That Uncertain Feeling 1955, A Case of Samples 1956, I Like it Here 1958, New Maps of Hell 1960, Take a Girl Like You 1960, My Enemy's Enemy 1962, One Fat Englishman 1963, The James Bond Dossier 1965, The Egyptologists (with Robert Conquest) 1965, The Anti-Death League 1966, A Look Around the Estate (poems 1957–1967) 1967, Colonel Sun 1968 (as Robert Markham), I Want it Now 1968, The Green Man 1969, What Became of Jane Austen? 1970, Girl, 20 1971, On Drink 1972, The Riverside Villas Murder 1973, Ending Up 1974, Rudyard Kipling and His World 1975, The Alteration 1976, Jake's Thing 1978, Collected Poems 1944–1979 1979, Russian Hide-and-Seek 1980, Collected Short Stories 1980, Every Day Drinking 1983, Stanley and the Women 1984, How's your Glass 1984, The Old Devils 1986, The Great British Songbook (with James Cochrane) 1986, Difficulties with Girls 1988, The Amis Anthology: A Personal Choice of English Verse 1988; edited New Oxford Book of Light Verse 1978, Faber Popular Reciter 1978, The Golden Age of Science Fiction 1981. *Leisure interests:* classical music, thrillers, television. *Address:* Jonathan Clowes and Co., 22 Prince Albert Road, London, N.W.1, England

AMIS, Martin Louis, B.A.; British author; b. 25 Aug. 1949; s. of Kingsley Amis (q.v.) and Hilary Bardwell; ed. Exeter Coll. Oxford; Fiction and poetry Ed. Times Literary Supplement 1974; Literary Ed. New Statesman 1977–79; special writer for The Observer newspaper 1980–; Somerset Maugham Award (for The Rachel Papers) 1974. *Publications:* The Rachel Papers 1973, Dead Babies 1975, Success 1978, Other People: a mystery story 1981, Money 1984, The Moronic Inferno: and other visits to America 1986, Einstein's Monsters (five stories) 1987. *Leisure interests:* tennis, chess, snooker. *Address:* c/o A. D. Peters, 10 Buckingham Street, London, W.C.2, England. *Telephone:* 01-839 2556.

AMIT, Maj.-Gen. Meir, M.B.A.; Israeli business executive and politician; b. 17 March 1921, Tiberias; s. of Simon and Chaya Slutsky; m. Yona Kelman 1941; three d.; ed. Columbia Univ., New York; mem. Kibbutz Alonim 1939; served in Israeli Defence Forces 1948–68, fmr. Head of Mil. Intelligence and Head of Israeli Security Service; Pres. Koor Industries 1968–77; Minister of Transport and Communication 1977; mem. of Knesset 1977–81; management consultant 1982; Chair. MA'OF 1982–85; Dir. Zim

Lines, Israel Corpn. 1985; Chair. Navot Technology, Gen. Satellite Corpn., etc. *Leisure interests:* photography, collecting dolls and educational games. *Address:* 55, Atlazorof Street, Ramat-Gan, Israel.

AMITSUR, Shimshon Avraham, M.A., PH.D.; Israeli mathematician; b. 26 Aug. 1921, Jerusalem; m. Sarah Frenkiel 1948; one s. two d.; ed. Hebrew Univ.; served British Army and Jewish Brigade 1942–46, Israel Army 1948–49; mem. Inst. for Advanced Studies, Princeton, N.J. 1952–54; Lecturer, Hebrew Univ. 1954–56, Assoc. Prof. 1956–60, Prof. 1960–; Man. Project on High School Math. 1960–; mem. Israel Acad. of Sciences and Humanities (Chair. Science Section 1980–86); Israel Prize for Exact Science (with J. Levitzky 1953); Rothschild Prize for Math. 1969. *Publications:* about 100 scientific papers. *Address:* 43 Harlap Street, Jerusalem, Israel 92341. *Telephone:* (02)-63 69 65.

AMMAR, Mohamed Ali; Algerian politician; b. 1937; m.; six c.; ed. Univ. of Algiers; militant Nat. Liberation Front 1954–; Head Algerian Gen. Worker's Union 1962–63; Divisional Inspector of Labour; Head Dept. Etudes et Conception du Parti; Pres. Comm. Volontariat, Comm. for Educ. and Training; Amb. to Libya; mem. Cen. Cttee. Nat. Liberation Front 1979–; Minister of Information and Culture 1988–. *Address:* 11 chemin Doudon Mokhtar Ben-Aknoun, Algiers, Algeria. *Telephone:* 79-23-23.

AMMON, Günter Karl-Johannes, DR.MED.; German psychiatrist, neurologist and psychoanalyst; b. 9 May 1918, Berlin; s. of Paul Ammon and Lucia Ammon nee Kühn; m. Gisela Kutz 1965; one d.; ed. Univs. of Greifswald, Heidelberg, Humbold and Free Univ. Berlin; Psychiatrist, Psychoanalyst and Lecturer, Menninger Foundation, Menninger School of Psychiatry, Topeka State Hosp. and C.F. Menninger Memorial Hosp., Topeka, Kansas, U.S.A., Consultant for the Psychiatric State Hosps. for Kansas, Veterans Admin. and Family Service Center, Topeka, Psychotherapy and Group Psychotherapy Supervisor, Trainer of Group Dynamic Self-Experience Groups 1956–65; Training-Analyst and Lecturer, Psychoanalytic Berlin Institute 1965–69; Lecturer on Psychosomatic Medicine, Seminar on Death and Dying, Free Univ., Berlin 1974–76; Dir. Berlin Inst. for Dynamic Psychiatry and Group Dynamics 1969–; Chief Consultant Dynamic Psychiatric Hosps. in Bavaria 1981–; private psychoanalytic and psychiatric practice in West Berlin, training analyst 1981–; has carried out research and taught in many countries; Pres. World Asscn. for Dynamic Psychiatry 1981–; Pres. German Asscn. for Dynamic Psychiatry 1981–; mem. Nat. Inst. for Care of the Seriously Ill and Dying; Corresp. Fellow, American Psychiatric Asscn.; Founder, German Asscn. for Psychosomatic Medicine and German Acad. for Psychoanalysis; mem. numerous asscns. including World Fed. for Mental Health and World Asscn. for Social Psychiatry; Grand Cross of the Constantin Order, Grand Officer of the Order of the Most Holy Saviour. *Publications:* Milieutherapie 1959, Gruppendynamik der Agression 1970, Dynamische Psychiatrie 1973, Gruppenpsychotherapie 1973, Psychoanalyse und Psychosomatik 1974, Psychotherapie des Psychosen 1975, Handbuch der dynamischen Psychiatrie 1979, 1982; Ed. and Co-ed. various publs. *Leisure interests:* dance, painting, travelling, archaeological collecting, riding. *Address:* Wielandstr. 27/28, 1000 Berlin 15, Federal Republic of Germany. *Telephone:* 883-49-81.

AMOUZEGAR, Jamshid, B.C.E., M.S., PH.D.; Iranian politician; b. 25 June 1923; s. of Turan and Habibollah Amouzegar; m. Ulrike Amouzegar 1951; ed. Univs. of Teheran, Cornell, Washington; UN Expert, Mission to Iran 1951; Chief, Eng. Dept 1952–55; Deputy Minister of Health 1955–58; Minister of Labour 1958–59, of Agriculture 1959–60; Consulting Eng. 1960–64; Chair. Int. Civil Service Advisory Bd. of UN 1962–67; Minister of Health 1964–65, of Finance 1965–74, of Interior and Employment 1974–76; Minister of State 1976–77; Sec.-Gen. Rastakhiz Party 1976–77, Jan.-Aug. 1978; Prime Minister of Iran 1977–78; Pres. OPEC 1974; fmr. Chief Oil Negotiator to Shah; First Order of the Taj. *Leisure interests:* listening to music, reading poetry.

AMOYAL, Pierre Alain Wilfred; French violinist; b. 22 June 1949, Paris; s. of Dr. Wilfred and Vera (Popravka) Amoyal; m. Susan Moses 1973; one s.; ed. Cours d'Etat, Vanves, Conservatoire Nat. Supérieur de Musique, Paris, Univ. of Southern California, U.S.A. (studied with Jascha Heifetz, q.v.); invited by Sir Georg Solti to perform Berg's violin concerto with Orchestre de Paris 1971; invited by Pierre Boulez to perform Schoenberg's Concerto with Orchestre de Paris 1977; Prof. of Violin, Conservatoire Nat. Supérieur de Musique, Paris 1977; Lausanne Conservatory 1977–; numerous performances throughout world with orchestras including Royal Philharmonic, New Philarmonia, l'Orchestre Nat. de France, Residentie-Orkest, The Hague; First Prize, Conservatoire de Versailles 1960, Conservatoire Nat. Supérieur de Musique, Paris 1962, for chamber music, Conservatoire Nat. Supérieur de Musique; Prix Ginette Neveu; Prix Paganini; Prix Enesco 1970; Grand Prix du Disque 1974, 1977. *Numerous recordings including:* Symphonie espagnole (Lalo); Violin Concerto (Mendelssohn); Concertos Nos. 1 and 2 and 2 Sonatas (Prokofiev); Tartini's concertos; Third Concerto, Havanaise, and Rondo capriccioso (Saint-Saëns); Concerto No. 1 (Bruch); Concerto (Glazunov); Sonatas (Faure); Horn Trio (Brahms); Concertos (Mozart); Concerto (Sibelius); Concerto (Tchaikovsky). *Leisure interests:* photography, literature, sport. *Address:* 11 Route de Saint Cergue, 1268 Begnins, Switzerland.

AMRI SUED, Ismail; Rwandan government official; b. 1942, Ruhengeri; m. Nadia Musabeyezu 1975; one s. one d.; ed. Collège du Saint Esprit,

Bujumbura, Collège Christ-Roi, Nyanza and Catholic Univ., Louvain, Belgium; Research Asst. N.V. Philips (Eindhoven) 1969–70; Chief of Div. Ministry of Foreign Affairs 1973; Dir. Nat. Broadcasting Corpn. 1973–74; Adviser to Pres. on Foreign Policy 1974–79; Sec.-Gen. Organisation Commune Africaine et Mauricienne (OCAM) 1979–85; Amb. to Kenya 1985–; Commdr., Ordre Léopold II (Belgium), Ordre nat. de Mauritanie, Ordre nat. du Zaire, Ordre nat. du Mérite (France), Chevalier de la Reconnaissance Centrafricaine, Officier de l'Ordre Nat. de la Paix (Rwanda). *Publication:* L'adaption du travailleur africain à l'entreprise industrielle: cas de la Tanzanie 1971. *Address:* Rwandan Embassy, Mama Ngina Street, IHL Bldg., 12th Floor, Nairobi, Kenya. *Telephone:* 334341, 336365.

AMRITANAND, Rt. Rev. Joseph; Indian ecclesiastic; b. 17 Feb. 1917; ed. Forman Christian Coll., Lahore and Bishop's Coll.; Ordained Deacon 1941, Priest 1943; Bishop of Assam 1949–62; Bishop of Lucknow 1962–70; Bishop of Calcutta 1970–82, also of Durgapur 1972–74. *Address:* 2B Church Lane, Allahabad, 211002, Uttar Pradesh, India.

AMSTERDAM, Gustave G.; American financier; b. 25 Aug. 1908, Philadelphia; s. of Benjamin Amsterdam and Anna Feld; m. Valla Abel 1933; one s.; ed. Univ. of Pennsylvania; Vice-Pres. Albert M. Greenfield & Co. 1938–56; Vice-Pres. Bankers' Securities Corpn. 1946–51, Exec. Vice-Pres. 1951–55, Pres. 1955–70, Chair. 1959–; Chair. City Stores Co., Diversified Stores Co. Inc.; Pres. Benjamin Franklin Hotel Corpn., Albert M. Greenfield Foundation; Vice-Pres. Bankers' Realty Corpn., Lit Bros. Foundation; mem. of bd. of numerous other cos.; Trustee, Univ. of Pa. *Address:* 5209 Woodbine Avenue, Philadelphia, Pa. 19131, U.S.A. (Home).

AMUDUN NIYAZ; Chinese party and government official; b. 1932; First Sec. Urumqi Municipality CCP 1977–79; Vice-Chair. Govt. of Xinjiang Uygur Autonomous Region 1979–83; Chair. Standing Cttee. of Xinjiang Uygur Autonomous Region People's Congress 1985–; Deputy Sec., Xingjiang Uygur Autonomous Region Cttee. CCP 1985–. *Address:* Standing Committee of Xinjiang Uygur Autonomous Region People's Congress, Urumqi, People's Republic of China.

AN GANG; Chinese party journalist; Corresp. People's Daily 1953; Sec. Journalists' Asscn. 1960–66; Deputy Ed.-in-Chief People's Daily 1960–66, 1976–; Ed.-in-Chief Econ. Daily 1983–86; Dir. of Inst. of Journalism; mem. 6th CPPCC Standing Cttee. *Address:* The Economic Daily, Wang Fujing Street 277, Beijing, People's Republic of China.

AN MIN (Wang, An Min); Chinese university professor; b. 15 March 1922, Shandong; s. of Wang Jing Xuan and Zhou Al-Lian; m. Wu Pei (Wu Guang Rui) 1951; one s. one d.; ed. Ming Hsien High School and Nat. Cen. Univ.; mem. Friends Ambulance Unit 1941–49; mem. Faculty Beijing Agric. Univ. 1949–, Head Dept. Animal Science 1979–82, Pres. Univ. 1982–87; Vice-Chair. Scientific and Tech. Cttee. Ministry of Agric., Animal Husbandry and Fisheries 1983–87; Head Animal Science Section Nat. Academic Degree Cttee. 1984–; Pres. Domestic Animal and Poultry Information Centre 1984–87; Dir. Int. Goat Asscn. 1982–87, China Int. Conf. Centre for Science and Tech. 1984–; Vice-Chair. Chinese Asscn. of Agricultural Science 1983–87; Chief Ed. Chinese Journal of Animal Science 1980–84. *Leisure interests:* music, theatre and travel. *Address:* 303 Building 15, Beijing Agricultural University, Beijing 100094, China. *Telephone:* 285831 (Ext. 670).

AN PINGSHENG; Chinese politician; b. 1912, Jiangxi; m. Chen Ying; Provincial Cadre in Guangdong 1955, Vice-Gov. Guangdong 1956–61; Sec. Guangxi CCP Cttee. 1961–67, 1971–75, First Sec. 1975–77; Vice-Chair. Guangxi Revolutionary Cttee. 1968–75, Chair. 1975–77; Chair. Yunnan Revolutionary Cttee. 1977–, Yunnan Prov. Revolutionary Cttee. 1977–79, Yunnan Prov. People's Congress 1979–83, First Sec. Yunnan CCP Cttee. 1977–; First Political Commissar Yunnan Mil. Region 1977–; mem. 10th Cen. Cttee. 1973, 11th Cen. Cttee. 1977, 12th Cen. Cttee. 1982–87; Chair. Guiding Cttee. for Party Consolidation, Yunnan CCP Cttee. 1983–; mem. Cen. Advisory Cttee. 1987–. *Address:* People's Republic of China.

AN SHIWEI (Imam al-Haj Salah); Chinese politician; mem. Presidium 6th CPPCC 1983–; Deputy Head Work Group for Religion, CPPCC 1983–. *Address:* Chinese People's Political Consultative Council, Beijing, People's Republic of China.

AN ZHENDONG; Chinese government official; b. 1931; Chief Engineer 2nd Light Industry Bureau 1982; Vice-Chair. 7th Cen. Cttee. Jiusan Society, 1983–; Vice-Gov. Heilongjiang 1983–; *Address:* Heilongjiang Provincial People's Government, Harbin, People's Republic of China.

AN ZHIWEN; Chinese politician; b. 1919, Shanxi; Deputy Dir. Research Office, N.E. China Bureau 1950; mem. Cultural and Educational Cttee., N.E. China People's Govt. 1950–52; Deputy Dir. Industry Dept., N.E. China People's Govt. 1950–52; mem. State Planning Comm., GAC 1952–54; Vice-Chair. State Construction Comm., State Council 1954–58; State Planning Comm. 1958; mem. Standing Cttee., 3rd CPPCC 1958–65; Vice-Chair. Jilin Provincial Revolutionary Cttee. 1977–79; Minister, 6th Ministry of Machine-Building 1981–82; Vice-Minister, State Comm. for Restructuring Econ. System 1982–; Alt. mem. 12th Cen. Cttee, CCP 1982–87; mem. Cen. Advisory Cttee. 1987–. *Address:* c/o State Council, Beijing, People's Republic of China.

AN ZHIYUAN; Chinese diplomatist; b. 1921; official in Ministry of Railways 1963–64; Chargé d'Affaires in Embassy, U.S.S.R. 1965–71; mem.

PRC del. to UN 1971; Dir. Dept. for Int. Orgs., Ministry of Foreign Affairs, Geneva 1972–75; Perm. Rep. to UN 1975–80; Amb. to Bulgaria 1978–83, to Fed. Repub. of Germany 1983–85. *Address:* c/o Ministry of Foreign Affairs, Beijing, People's Republic of China.

ANAND, Bal Krishan, M.B., B.S., M.D.; Indian physiologist; b. 19 Sept. 1917, Lahore; s. of V. D. Anand and Saraswati Anand; m. Kamla Puri 1942; one s. two d.; ed. Government Coll. and K.E. Medical Coll., Lahore; Prof. of Physiology, Lady Hardinge Medical Coll., New Delhi 1949–57, All India Inst. of Medical Sciences, New Delhi 1957–74, Prof. Emer. 1977–; Pres. XXVI Int. Congress of Physiological Sciences, New Delhi 1974; Asst. Dir. WHO. (S.E. Asia) 1974–77; Dir. Inst. of Medical Sciences, Srinagar 1982–85; Vice-Chancellor, Banaras Hindu Univ., Varanasi 1978; Pres. Indian Nat. Acad. of Medical Sciences; Pres. Nat. Bd. of Examinations 1979; Pres. Asscn. for Advancement of Medical Educ. 1984–86; Chair. Post-graduate Cttee. of Medical Council of India 1985–; Hon. D.Sc. (Banaras) 1983; Rockefeller Foundation Fellow at Yale Univ. School of Medicine 1950–51; Fellow Indian Acad. of Medical Sciences, Nat. Inst. of Sciences (F.N.I.); Indian Council of Medical Research Sr. Research Award 1962; Watumull Foundation Award in Medicine 1961; Sir Shanti Swaroof Bhatnagar Memorial Award for Scientific Research in Medicine 1963; Padma Shri 1969; Medical Council of India Silver Jubilee Research Award 1969; Dr. B. C. Roy Award for Eminent Medical Man 1984. *Leisure interests:* literature, photography, tennis, hiking. *Address:* B9/21, Vasant Vihar, New Delhi, India. *Telephone:* 672949.

ANAND, Mulk Raj, PH.D.; Indian writer and critic; b. 12 Dec. 1905, Peshawar; s. of Lalchand Anand and Ishwar Kaur; m. 1st Kathleen van Gelder 1939 (divorced 1948), m. 2nd Shirin Vajifdar 1950; one d.; ed. Punjab and London Univs.; active in Nationalist and Gandhi movements; lecturer, London County Council; BBC broadcaster, film script writer, British Ministry of Information; edited (1956) various magazines; Leverhulme Fellow for Research in Hindustani literature; fmr. Editor Marg magazine, India; mem. Indian Nat. Acad. of Letters, Indian Nat. Acad. of Arts, Indian Nat. Book Trust; fmr. Tagore Prof. of Art and Literature, Punjab Univ., Chandigarh; Fellow, Nat. Acad. of Art, New Delhi; Padma Bhushan 1967; D.Litt. h.c. (Delhi, Benares, Andhra, Patiala, Shantiniketan). *Publications:* Novels: The Bubble, Morning Face, Private Life of an Indian Prince, The Big Heart, The Sword and the Sickle, Across the Black Waters, Untouchable, Coolie, The Barbers' Trade Union, Seven Summers, etc.; Essays: Apology for Heroism, Seven Little Known Birds of the Inner Eye, etc. *Leisure interests:* gardening, walking, travel. *Address:* Jassim House, 25 Cuffe Parade, Colaba, Bombay 5, India. *Telephone:* Bombay 211371.

ANANEV, Anatoliy Andreyevich; Soviet author; b. 18 July 1925, Dzhambul, Kazakhstan; ed. Dept. of Philology, Kazakh State Univ.; mem. CPSU 1950–; ed. Oktyabr 1984–. *Publications:* Tales of Vernensk 1958, Small Cover 1959, The Shadow of Jesus 1961, The Trump Cards of the Monk Grigorii 1964, Years Without War 1984. *Address:* U.S.S.R. Union of Writers, 52, ul. Vorovskogo, Moscow, U.S.S.R.

ANASTASATU, Constantin, PH.D.; Romanian phthisiologist; b. 2 Sept. 1917, Corabia; s. of Dumitru and Ana Anastasatu; m. Dr. Lia Pascu 1950; ed. Colls. of Medicine in Bucharest 1937–42, Cluj, and Sibiu 1942–43; Asst. Prof. Phthisiology Faculty of Medicine, Cluj 1945–56; Assoc. Prof. Inst. of Medicine, Timişoara 1956–62; Prof. Inst. of Medicine and Pharmacy, Bucharest 1962–87, Rector 1970–74, Consultant Prof. 1987–; Dir. Tuberculosis Research Inst. 1970–; corresp. mem. Romanian Acad. 1974–, Pneumology Socs. France, Portugal, Bulgaria, Czechoslovakia; mem. Acad. of Medical Sciences 1969–; Pres. Soc. of Pneumology and Phthisiology 1960–; Pres. Int. Union against Tuberculosis, Europe 1977–80; Hon. mem. U.S.S.R. Phthisiologists Asscn. 1986–; C. Forlanini Gold Medal, Italian Fed. of Tuberculosis 1967; and many other Romanian and foreign awards. *Publications:* Chimioterapia şi chimioprofilaxia tuberculozei (Chemotherapy and Chemoprophylaxis of Tuberculosis) 1964, Pneumologie (Pneumology) 1965, Scintigrafia pulmonară (Pulmonary Scanning) 1970, Ftiziologia clinică (Clinical Phthisiology), 2 vols. (co-author) 1972, 1975, Terapia tuberculozei pulmonare (The Therapy of Pulmonary Tuberculosis) 1973, Pneumoftiziologie Clinica (Clinical Pneumophthisiology), 2 vols. (ed.) 1978, 1981, Riscurile Fumatului (Smoking Risks) 1982, Aparatul respirator (Pulmonary diseases) Vol. I. (ed.) 1983, Cancerul bronhopulmonar (Bronchopulmonary Cancer) 1986, Sindroame respiratorii post-tuberculoase (Respiratory post-tuberculosis syndromes) 1987. *Leisure interest:* music. *Address:* c/o Tuberculosis Research Institute, Sos Viilor 90, Bucharest 75239, Romania. *Telephone:* 23 98 01.

ANCHISHKIN, Aleksandr Ivanovich, D.ECON.; Soviet economist and academic; b. 1933; ed. Moscow State Univ. 1956; mem. CPSU 1963–; asst. 1956–66, sr. research worker with U.S.S.R. Gosplan Econ. Inst. 1966–70; Head of Dept. Cen. Econ.-Math. Inst. of Acad. of Sciences 1970–81, Prof. 1977; Head of Dept. of U.S.S.R. Gosplan 1981–82; Prof. of Planning of National Econ., Moscow State Univ. 1982–85; Dir. Acad. of Sciences, Inst. of Econ. Planning and Prognosis of Scientific and Tech. Progress 1985–; mem. U.S.S.R. Acad. of Sciences 1984–; specialist in the theory of widespread production, macro-modelling and prognosis of national economy. [*Deceased.*]

ANCLAM, Kurt; German politician; b. 7 May 1918, Kowanz; m.; one c.; ed. elementary school; baker's apprentice, rising to master baker 1932-51; mem. Schwerin Liberal Democratic Party Council 1949-54; mem. Central Cttee. 1957-, mem. Political Sub-Cttee. of Central Cttee. 1967-; correspondence course at ASR Potsdam-Babelsberg—qualified as lawyer 1953-59; Personal Adviser to Deputy Chair. of Council of Ministers 1957-66; Chair. Halle District Asscn. of Liberal Democratic Party 1966-85; Deputy to People's Chamber 1954-63 and 1967-; Deputy Chair. sub-cttee. supervising elections 1967-71, mem. Council of State 1971-86; Vaterländischer Verdienstorden (in Gold, Silver and Bronze) and other decorations. *Address:* Staatsrat, 1020 Berlin, Marx-Engels-Platz, German Democratic Republic.

ANDENAES, Johannes, DR.JUR.; Norwegian professor of law; b. 7 Sept. 1912, Innvik; s. of Mads and Signe (née Mydland) Andenaes; m. Ida Rören 1939; two s. two d.; ed. Univ. of Oslo; Asst. judge 1936-37; Asst. Prof., Univ. of Oslo 1939, Prof. 1945-82, Dean, School of Law 1959-60, 1968-69; Rector 1970-72; Pres. Norwegian Acad. of Science and Letters 1977-81; Visiting Prof., Univ. of Pa. 1963, Chicago 1968, Minn. 1974; Visiting Fellow, All Souls Coll., Oxford 1971; Dr. jur. h.c. (Copenhagen, Uppsala); Sellin-Glueck Award, American Soc. of Criminology 1979; Nordic Prize for legal scholarship 1981. *Publications:* Alminnelig Strafferett, Norsk straffeprosess, Statsforfatningen in Norge, Punishment and Deterrence, Norway and the Second World War, Det vanskelige oppgjöret, Spesiell Strafferett, Et liv blant paragrafer. *Address:* University of Oslo, Karl Johansgate 47, Oslo 1; Generallunden 23, 0381 Oslo 3, Norway (Home). *Telephone:* 02-429010 (Office); 02-524127 (Home).

ANDERS, Edward, PH.D., M.A.; American professor of chemistry; b. 21 June 1926, Liepaja Latvia; s. of Adolph Alperovitch and Erica Leventals; m. Joan Elizabeth Fleming 1955; one s. one d.; ed. Univ. of Munich, Columbia Univ.; Instructor in Chem., Univ. of Ill. at Urbana 1954-55; Asst. Prof. of Chem. Univ. of Chicago 1955-60, Assoc. Prof. 1960-62, Prof. 1960-73, Horace B. Horton Prof. of Physical Sciences 1973-; Visiting Prof. Calif. Inst. of Tech. 1960, Univ. of Berne 1963-64, 1970, 1978, 1980-81, 1983, 1987-88; Research Assoc. Field Museum of Natural History 1968-; Fellow American Acad. of Arts and Sciences 1973-; mem. N.A.S. 1974-; Assoc. Royal Astronomical Soc., U.K. 1974-; Cleveland Prize, A.A.A.S. 1959; Smith Medal, N.A.S. 1971, Leonard Medal, Meteoritical Soc. 1974. *Publications:* about 200 articles in scientific journals. *Leisure interests:* classical music, hiking, photography. *Address:* The Enrico Fermi Institute, The University of Chicago, 5640 S. Ellis Avenue, Chicago, Ill. 60637, U.S.A. *Telephone:* (312) 702-7108.

ANDERS, William Alison, M.SC.; American government official and fmr. astronaut; b. 17 Oct. 1933, Hong Kong; s. of Commdr. and Mrs. Arthur F. Anders; m. Valerie Hoard; four s. one d.; ed. U.S. Naval Acad. and Air Force Inst. of Tech., Wright-Patterson Air Force Base, Ohio; Commissioned in the Air Force and received flight training; fighter pilot, Air Defense Command; nuclear eng. and instructor pilot, Air Force Weapons Lab., Kirtland Air Force Base, New Mexico; selected as astronaut by NASA 1963; backup pilot for the Gemini XI mission 1966; lunar module pilot for the maiden voyage to the moon on Apollo VIII Dec. 1968; backup command module pilot on Apollo XI mission 1969; Exec. Sec. Nat. Aeronautics and Space Council 1969-73; Commr. Atomic Energy Comm. 1973-74; Chair. Nuclear Regulatory Comm. 1974-76; Major-Gen. U.S.A.F. Reserves 1983-; Sr. Exec. Vice-Pres. Textron Inc., Rhode Island 1984-. *Address:* Textron Inc., 40 Westminster Street, Providence, R.I. 02903, U.S.A.

ANDERSEN, Anders; Danish farmer and politician; b. 1 Oct. 1912, Voldby; s. of Jens and Astrid Andersen; m. Karen Margrethe Bilde Sørensen 1937; one s. three d.; ed. Askov Folk High School, Ladelund Farmers' School; mem. Folketing 1953-79, 1981-; Pres. Agric. Council 1960-73; Minister of Finance 1973-75, of Econ. Affairs and of Taxation, Customs and Excise 1978-79, of Econ. Affairs 1982-87. *Address:* Benzonslyst, Sangstrupvej 50, 8500 Grenå, Denmark. *Telephone:* (06) 332108.

ANDERSEN, Hans George, LL.M.; Icelandic diplomatist; b. 1919, Winnipeg, Canada; s. of F. A. Andersen, C.P.A. and Thora Andersen; m. Astridur Helgadóttir 1945; one s. one d.; ed. Univ. of Iceland and Harvard Univ.; Legal Adviser, Ministry of Foreign Affairs, Lecturer, Univ. of Iceland 1948-54; Amb. to NATO 1954-62, to OEEC 1956-62, to France 1961-62, to Sweden 1962-63, to Norway 1969-; Legal Adviser, Ministry for Foreign Affairs 1969-; Amb. to U.S.A. 1976-87, to the UN 1986-; Chair. Icelandic del. to Third UN Conf. on the Law of the Sea; Commdr. of the Order of the Falcon (with Star); Grand Cross St. Olav (Norway), Grand Cross, Order of Merit (Italy). *Leisure interests:* reading, swimming. *Address:* Ministry of Foreign Affairs, Hverfisgotu 115, 150 Reykjavik, Iceland.

ANDERSEN, Ib; Danish ballet dancer; b. 14 Dec. 1954, Copenhagen; s. of Ingolf and Anna Andersen; ed. with Royal Danish Ballet; ballet dancer, Royal Danish Ballet 1973, Prin. Dancer 1975; Prin. Dancer, New York City Ballet 1980-; Nijinsky Prize. *Address:* New York State Theater, New York, N.Y. 10023, U.S.A.

ANDERSEN, Mogens; Danish painter; b. 8 Aug. 1916, Copenhagen; s. of late Einar F. T. Andersen and late Erna Ingeborg, née Andersen; m.

Inger Therkildsen 1947; one s. one d.; ed. in Copenhagen under art master P. Rostrup Boyesen; art teacher Copenhagen 1952-59, Académie de la Grande Chaumière, Paris 1963; mem. cttee. Danish Art Exhbn. Arrangement 1956-58; Pres. Danish State Art Foundation 1977-80; mem. Royal Acad. of Fine Arts 1956, Prof. 1970-72; mem. PEN Club; Eckersberg Medal 1949, Thorvaldsen Medal 1984, Chevalier, Légion d'honneur, Kt. of Dannebrog, and other awards. *Exhibitions:* Copenhagen 1935-40, 1942-50, 1953-66, 1967; Paris 1950-74, 1981. *Private Exhbns.:* Copenhagen 1953, 1963, 1966, 1968, 1969, 1976 (retrospective), Alborg (Denmark) 1954, 1972, Lund (Sweden) 1959, Paris 1954, 1959, 1963, 1966, 1967, 1973, 1975, 1981, Warsaw 1973, Belgrade 1973, Zagreb, Randers 1981, Aarhus 1982, Budapest 1983, 1984; group exhbns. in Europe and the U.S.A.; Venice Biennale 1968, retrospective Copenhagen 1988; paintings hung in Modern Museum, Skopje 1965, Bridgestone Museum, Tokyo, Kunstmuseum, Malmø, and many other museums in Denmark, Sweden, Norway, Poland and U.S.A. *Major works:* Composition in Niels Bohr Inst., Copenhagen 1955, Mural, Central Library, Copenhagen 1958-59, Composition in Central Library, Århus 1964, October, State Art Museum 1964, Mural, Gentofte Town Hall 1971, Restaurante Copenhagen, Paris 1973, Handelsbanken, Copenhagen 1975, Northern Feather Inst., Danmarks Tekniske Højskole 1979, Panum-institutet, Copenhagen 1981, Kunstmuseum, Bochum 1981, Musikhuset, Aarhus 1982, Metalskolen, Holstebro, Skäfogaard, Mörke konstmuseum, Lund. *Publications:* Moderne fransk malerkunst 1948, Omkring Kilderne 1967, Nødigt, Men Dog Gerne 1976, Ungdomsrjesen 1979, Om Kunst og Samfund 1980, Huset 1986. *Address:* Strandagervej 28, 2900 Hellerup, Copenhagen, Denmark. *Telephone:* (31) 62 02 66.

ANDERSEN, Ronald Max, M.S., PH.D.; American sociologist; b. 15 Feb. 1939, Omaha, Neb.; m.; one c.; ed. Univ. of Santa Clara and Purdue Univ.; Research Assoc. Purdue Farm Cardiac Project, Dept. of Sociology, Purdue Univ. 1962-63; Assoc. Study Dir. Nat. Opinion Research Center, Univ. of Chicago 1963-66, Research Assoc. Center for Health Admin. Studies 1963-77; Instructor Grad. School of Business, Univ of Chicago 1966-68, Asst. Prof. 1968-72, Asst. Prof. Dept. of Sociology 1970-72, Assoc. Prof. Grad. School of Business and Dept. of Sociology 1972-74, 1974-77, Prof. 1977-; Assoc. Dir. Center for Health Admin. Studies 1977-80, Dir. and Dir. Grad. Program in Health Admin. 1980-; mem. numerous cttees., advisory panels etc.; mem. American Sociological Assen., American Statistical Assen., American Public Health Assen. *Publications:* author and co-author of numerous books, monographs, book chapters and articles in professional journals. *Address:* Center for Health Administration Studies, Graduate School of Business, The University of Chicago, 1101 East 58th Street, Walker 111H, Chicago, Ill. 60637, U.S.A. *Telephone:* (312) 702-7104.

ANDERSEN, Svend, M.POL.ECON.; Danish banker (retd.); b. 26 Sept. 1915, Copenhagen; s. of Christen Andersen and Paula Ingrid (née Nielsen); m. Alice Elkiaer Hansen 1942; three s.; ed. Københavns Universitet; Economist, Nat. Bank of Denmark 1940, Chief of Secr. 1950-61, Man. 1961-62, Deputy Gov. 1962-63, mem. Bd. of Govs. 1963-82; Economist, Int. Bank for Reconstruction and Devt. (World Bank) 1946-50; mem. Bd., Deputy Chair. The Ship Credit Fund of Denmark 1963-82, War Risk Insurance of Danish Ships of Copenhagen and Danish War Risk Cargo Insurance of Copenhagen 1963-85, Nat. Econ. Soc. 1966-72, Chair. 1979-83; Chair. Bd. of Copenhagen Stock Exchange 1982-86; mem. Nordic Cttee. for Financial Matters 1966-82, Chair. 1966-74; mem. Lauritz Andersens Fund 1970-82, Monetary Cttee. of EEC 1973-82, Vice-Chair. 1976-79; Commdr.'s Cross (Denmark). *Publications:* papers on economic policy, especially monetary affairs. *Leisure interest:* modern history. *Address:* Esperance Allé 6A, DK 2920 Charlottenlund, Denmark. *Telephone:* (01) 624007.

ANDERSEN, Torkild, M.SC., DR.PHIL.; Danish professor of physics; b. 19 June 1934, Randers; m. Inger Bloch-Petersen 1957; one s. one d.; ed. Tech. Univ. Copenhagen; industrial chemist 1958-59; Asst. and Assoc. Prof. of Chem., Univ. of Aarhus 1958-71, Prof. of Physics (Atomic Physics) 1971-; Postdoctoral Fellow, Univ. of Cambridge 1961-63; Visiting Prof. Univ. of Colo. 1984-85, Flinders Univ. S. Australia 1988; mem. Royal Danish Acad. of Science; N. Bjerrum Prize 1972. *Publications:* 125 scientific contribs. to chemistry of physics journals. *Address:* Institute of Physics, University of Aarhus, 8000 Aarhus C (Office); 37 Klokkerbakken, 8210 Aarhus V, Denmark (Home).

ANDERSON, Campbell McCheyne, B.ECON., A.A.S.A.; Australian business executive; b. 17 Sept. 1941, Sydney; s. of Allen Taylor Anderson and Ethel Catherine Rundle; m. Sandra Maclean Harper 1965; two s. one d.; ed. Armidale School, N.S.W., Univ. of Sydney; audit clerk, Priestley and Morris 1958-59; with Boral Ltd. 1962-69; then Reef Oil Ltd. and Basin Oil Ltd. 1969-72; with Burmah Oil Australia Ltd. 1972-73, New York 1973-74, Div. Dir., then Chief Financial Officer, Burmah Oil Trading Ltd., U.K. 1974-75, Dir. 1975-76, Exec. Dir. Burmah Oil Co. Ltd. 1976-82, Man. Dir. Burmah Oil PLC 1982-85; Man. Dir. Renison Goldfields Consolidated Ltd. 1985-, Man. Dir. and C.E.O. 1986-; Dir. Consolidated Gold Fields PLC 1985-; Chair., Man. Dir. and Dir. of numerous cos. in U.K. and overseas. *Leisure interests:* golf, shooting, horse-racing, swimming. *Address:* 77 Drumalbyn Road, Bellevue Hill, N.S.W. 2023 (Home); Gold Fields House, 1 Alfred Street, Sydney, N.S.W. 2000, Australia (Office). *Telephone:* (02) 327 5507 (Home); (02) 20512 (Office).

ANDERSON, Carl David, PH.D., SC.D., LL.D.; American physicist; b. 3 Sept. 1905; ed. California Inst. of Technology; Teaching Fellow in Physics 1927–30, Research Fellow 1930–33, Asst. Prof. of Physics 1933–37, Assoc. Prof. Calif. Inst. of Tech. 1937–39, Prof. 1939–76, Emer. 1976–; Chair. Div. of Physics, Mathematics and Astronomy 1962–70; awarded Gold Medal of American Inst. 1935, Nobel Prize for Physics 1936, Elliott Cresson Medal of Franklin Inst. 1937; John Ericsson Medal of American Soc. of Swedish Engineers 1960; engaged in research on gamma rays and cosmic rays 1930–; mem. N.A.S., American Acad. of Arts and Sciences and American Philosophical Soc. *Address:* c/o Department of Physics, California Institute of Technology, Pasadena, Calif. 91109, U.S.A.

ANDERSON, Charles Alfred, PH.D., D.SC.; American research geologist (retd.); b. 6 June 1902, Bloomington, Calif.; s. of Amel A. Anderson and Mary Lyman; m. Helen Argall 1927; one s.; ed. Pomona Coll. and Univ. of California (Berkeley); Instructor, Univ. of Calif. 1928–30, Asst. Prof. 1930–38, Assoc. Prof. 1938–42; U.S. Geological Survey, Washington, D.C. 1942–72, Chief of Mineral Deposits Branch 1953–58, Chief Geologist 1959–64, Research Geologist 1964–72; Pres. Soc. Econ. Geologists 1968; mem. Emer. N.A.S., American Acad. of Arts and Sciences; Fellow, Geological Soc. of America, Mineral Soc. of America, American Geophysical Union; Distinguished Service Award 1960, Penrose Medal, Soc. of Econ. Geologists 1974. *Publications:* Tuscan Formation of Northern California 1933, Volcanoes of Medicine Lake Highland, California 1941, Reconnaissance Survey of Roberts Mountains, Nevada 1942, Geology of Islands and Neighbouring Land Areas, Gulf of California 1950, Geology and Ore Deposits of Jerome Area, Arizona 1958, Massive Sulfide Deposits and Volcanism 1969. *Leisure interests:* bird watching, photography. *Address:* 900 E. Harrison, L50 Pomona, Calif. 91676, U.S.A.

ANDERSON, Christopher, B. ECONS.; Australian journalist; b. 9 Dec. 1944; s. of C. F. and L. A. Anderson; m. Gabriella Douglas 1969; one s. one d.; ed. Picton High School, N.S.W., Univ. of Sydney; journalist and political commentator 1962–76; Deputy Ed., later Ed., The Sun-Herald 1976–79; Deputy Ed., later Ed., The Sydney Morning Herald 1980–83, Ed.-in-Chief 1983–88; Group Ed. Dir. John Fairfax Ltd. 1988–. *Address:* John Fairfax Ltd., P.O. Box 506, Sydney 2001, Australia. *Telephone:* (02) 282 2830.

ANDERSON, Don L., PH.D.; American geophysicist; b. 5 March 1933, Frederick, Md.; m. Nancy Lois Ruth 1956; one s. one d.; ed. Rensselaer Polytechnic Inst. and California Inst. of Tech.; Geophysicist, Chevron Oil Co. 1955–56; Geophysicist, Geophysics Research Directorate, Air Force Cambridge Research Center 1956–58; Research Fellow, Calif. Inst. of Tech. 1962–63, Asst. Prof. 1963–64, Assoc. Prof. 1964–68, Prof. 1968–, Dir. Seismological Lab. 1967–; Ed. Physics of the Earth and Planetary Interiors 1977–; Assoc. Ed. Tectonophysics, Physics and Chemistry of the Earth, Journal of Geodynamics etc.; mem. Space Science Bd., Geophysics Research Forum (Chair. 1983–), Bd. on Earth Sciences of N.A.S. and several other cttees. and bds.; Fellow American Geophysical Union (Pres. 1986–88), A.A.A.S., Geological Soc. of America, N.A.S., Royal Astronomical Soc.; Hon. Foreign Fellow, European Union of Geosciences; mem. Seismological Soc. of America; Sloan Foundation Fellow 1964–67; J.B. Macelwane Award, American Geophysical Union 1966; Sr. Fulbright-Hays Award (Australia) 1975, Newcomb Cleveland Prize (A.A.A.S.) 1976–77, NASA Distinguished Scientific Achievement Award 1977, Emil Wiechert Medal, German Geophysical Soc. 1986, Arthur L. Day Medal, Geological Soc. of America 1987. *Address:* Seismological Laboratory, California Institute of Technology, 1201 East California Boulevard, Pasadena, Calif. 91125 (Office); 669E Alameda Street, Altadena, Calif. 91001, U.S.A. (Home). *Telephone:* (818) 356-6901 (Office); (818) 797-7426 (Home).

ANDERSON, Donald Thomas, A.O., D.SC., F.R.S.; Australian (naturalized) professor of biology; b. 29 Dec. 1931, Eton, England; s. of Thomas and Flora Anderson; m. Joanne T. Claridge 1960; one s.; ed. King's Coll., London; Lecturer in Zoology, Univ. of Sydney, Australia 1958, Sr. Lecturer 1963, Reader 1968, Prof. 1972, Challis Prof. of Biology 1984–; Visiting Prof., King's Coll., London 1970. *Publication:* Embryology and Phylogeny in Annelids and Arthropods 1973. *Leisure interests:* photography, gardening. *Address:* Zoology Building, AO8, School of Biological Sciences, University of Sydney, Sydney, N.S.W. 2006 (Office); 52 Spruson Street, Neutral Bay, Sydney, N.S.W. 2089, Australia (Home). *Telephone:* 02-692-2438 (Office); 02-929-7583 (Home).

ANDERSON, Ephraim Saul, C.B.E., M.D., F.R.C.P., F.R.S.; British medical scientist; b. 1911; s. of Benjamin Anderson and Ada Anderson; m. Carol Jean Thompson 1959 (divorced); three s.; ed. Rutherford Coll. and King's Coll. Medical School, Univ. of Durham, Newcastle upon Tyne; gen. practitioner 1935–39; served R.A.M.C. 1940–46; Pathologist 1943–46; Registrar in Bacteriology, Postgraduate Medical School 1946–47; mem. staff, Enteric Reference Lab., Public Health Lab. Service 1947–52, Deputy Dir. 1952–54, Dir. 1954–78; WHO Fellow 1953; Chair. Int. Fed. for Enteric Phage Typing, Int. Union of Microbiological Socs. 1966– (Jt. Chair. 1958–66); Dir. Int. Reference Lab. for Enteric Phage Typing, Int. Fed. for Enteric Phage Typing 1954–78; Dir. Collab. Centre for Phage Typing and Resistance of Enterobacteria of WHO 1960–78; mem. WHO Expert Advisory Panel for Enteric Diseases; Fellow Inst. of Biology; Hon. D.Sc. (Newcastle) 1975. *Publications:* contribs. to The Bacteriophages 1959, The World Problem of Salmonellosis 1964; numerous articles on bacteriophage typing and its

genetic basis, microbial ecology, transferable drug resistance, its evolution, and epidemiology. *Leisure interests:* music, photography. *Address:* 10 Rosecroft Avenue, London, NW3 7QB, England.

ANDERSON, Eugenie Moore; American diplomatist; b. 26 May 1909, Adair, Iowa; d. of E. A. Moore and Flora McMillen Moore; m. John Pierce Anderson 1930; one s. one d.; ed. Stephens Coll., Simpson Coll., Carleton Coll., Inst. of Musical Art, New York City; Amb. to Denmark 1949–53; Chair. Minnesota State Comm. for Fair Employment Practices 1955–60; mem. Bd., U.S. Cttee. for Refugees 1959–60; mem. Democratic Nat. Advisory Cttee. on Foreign Policy 1957–60; mem. Bd. of Dirs. American Asscn. for the UN 1959–61; Vice-Chair. Citizens' Cttee. for Int. Devt. 1961–62; Trustee, American Freedom from Hunger Foundation 1962; Minister to Bulgaria 1962–65; U.S. Rep. to UN Trusteeship Council and mem. U.S. Del. to UN as Amb. 1965–68; Dir. First Nat. Bank of Minn. 1971–74; Trustee Minn. Soc. of Fine Arts 1975–. *Leisure interests:* music, reading, art, travel. *Address:* Tower View, Red Wing, Minn. 55066, U.S.A. *Telephone:* 612-388-6553.

ANDERSON, George Wishart, M.A., D.D., D. THEOL., F.B.A., F.R.S.E.; British academic; b. 25 Jan. 1913, Arbroath, Scotland; s. of George Anderson and Margaret Gordon Wishart; m. 1st Edith Joyce Marjorie Walter 1941 (deceased); m. 2nd Anne Phyllis Walter 1959; one s. one d.; ed. Arbroath High School, St. Andrews, Cambridge and Lund Univs.; Asst. Tutor Richmond Coll., Surrey 1939–41; R.A.F. Chaplain 1941–46; Lecturer in Old Testament Languages and Literature, Handsworth Coll. Birmingham 1946–56; Lecturer in Old Testament Literature and Theology, Univ. of St. Andrews 1956–58; Prof. of Old Testament Studies, Univ. of Durham 1958–62; Prof. of Old Testament Literature and Theology, Univ. of Edin. 1962–68, of Hebrew and Old Testament Studies 1968–82; Speaker's Lecturer in Biblical Studies, Univ. of Oxford 1976–80; Prof. Emer. 1982–; Burkitt Medal for Biblical Studies (British Acad.). *Publications:* A Critical Introduction to the Old Testament 1958, The History and Religion of Israel 1966; translated He That Cometh (S. Mowinckel) 1956, The Ras Shamra Discoveries and Old Testament (A.S. Kapelrud) 1963, 1965; Ed. A Decade of Bible Bibliography 1967, Tradition and Interpretation 1979. *Leisure interests:* reading, music. *Address:* 51 Fountainhall Road, Edinburgh, EH9 2LH, Scotland. *Telephone:* 031-667-2945.

ANDERSON, Gerry; British puppeteer and film maker; b. 1929; m. Sylvia Anderson (divorced). *Television series include:* Adventures of Twizzle (52 shows) 1956, Torchy the Battery Boy (26 shows) 1957, Four Feather Falls (52 shows) 1958, Supercar (39 shows) 1959, Fireball XL5 (39 shows) 1961, Stingray (39 shows) 1962–63, Thunderbirds (32 shows screened in 20 countries) 1964–66 (Royal Television Soc. Silver Medal), Captain Scarlet (32 shows) 1967, Joe 90 (30 shows) 1968, The Secret Service (13 shows) 1968, UFO (26 shows) 1969–70, The Protectors (52 shows) 1971–72, Space 1999 (48 shows) 1973–76, Terrahawks (39 shows) 1982–83, Dick Spanner (26 shows) 1987; numerous television commercials; Silver Arrow Award. *Films:* Thunderbirds are Go 1966, Thunderbird 6 1968, Doppelganger 1969. *Address:* c/o The Official Gerry Anderson Magazine, S.I.G., 332 Lytham Road, South Shore, Blackpool, FY4 1DW, England.

ANDERSON, Harold David, A.O., O.B.E., B.A.; Australian diplomatist; b. 6 Sept. 1923, Adelaide; s. of Axel Harold Anderson and Dorothy Eldridge Anderson (née Long); m. Annabel Bessie Johnston 1952; two d.; served with Australian military forces in Second World War; joined Australian Foreign Service 1945; served in Paris, Karachi, Noumea; Chargé d'Affaires, Phnom Penh 1955–57; First Sec. Tokyo 1957–58; Counsellor Dept. of External Affairs 1959; Imperial Defence Coll. 1963; Amb. to Viet-Nam 1964–66; Australian Observer Viet-Nam Peace Negotiations 1968–70; Amb. to France and Permanent Rep. to UNESCO 1973–78; Perm. Rep. of Australia to UN 1978–82; Amb. to European Communities, Belgium and Luxembourg 1983–87. *Leisure interest:* squash. *Address:* c/o Ministry of Foreign Affairs, Administrative Building, Parkes, A.C.T. 2600, Australia.

ANDERSON, Sir (James) Norman (Dalrymple), Kt., O.B.E., Q.C., M.A., LL.D., F.B.A.; British educationalist; b. 29 Sept. 1908, Aldeburgh, Suffolk; s. of William Anderson and Lilian Cohen; m. Patricia Hope Givan 1933; one s. two d. (deceased); ed. St. Lawrence Coll., Trinity Coll., Cambridge (Sr. Scholar); Missionary, Egypt Gen. Mission 1932–40; Capt. Libyan Arab Force 1940–41; Major (Political Officer for Sanusi Affairs) 1941; Lieut.-Col. (Sec. for Arab Affairs, Civil Affairs Branch, G.H.Q., M.E. 1943, Political Sec. 1943); Col. (Chief Sec., Civil Affairs Branch) 1944–46; lectured on Islamic Law in Cambridge 1947–50; Lecturer in Islamic Law, School of Oriental and African Studies, Univ. of London 1947; Reader in Oriental Laws, Univ. of London 1951; Prof. of Oriental Laws Univ. of London 1953–75, Prof. Emer. 1975–; Head of Dept. of Law, School of Oriental and African Studies 1953–71; Lecturer in Mohammedan Law, Council of Legal Educ. 1953–71; Visiting Prof., Princeton Univ. and New York Univ. Law School 1958, Harvard Law School 1966; Chair. U.K. National Comm. of Comparative Law 1957–59; Dir. Inst. of Advanced Legal Studies, Univ. of London 1959–76; Dean, Faculty of Law, Univ. of London 1965–69; Pres. Soc. of Public Teachers of Law 1969–70; Chair. House of Laity, Gen. Synod of Church of England 1970–79; mem. Panel of Advisory Jurists to Northern Nigerian Govt. 1958, 1962; Vice-Pres. Int. African Law Assn.; mem. Int. Cttee. of Comparative Law 1963–67; Hon. D.D. (St. Andrews) 1974; Hon. Litt.D. (Wheaton Coll.) 1980; Libyan Order of Independence, Class II.

Publications: The World's Religions (Gen. Editor) 1950, Islamic Law in Africa 1954, Islamic Law in the Modern World 1959, Changing Law in Developing Countries (Editor) 1963, Family Law in Asia and Africa (Editor) 1968, Into the World: The need and limits of Christian involvement 1968, Christianity: the Witness of History 1969, Christianity and Comparative Religion 1970, Morality, Law and Grace 1972, A Lawyer among the Theologians 1973, Law Reform in the Muslim World 1976, Issues of Life and Death 1976, Liberty, Law and Justice 1978, The Mystery of the Incarnation 1978, God's Law and God's Love 1980, God's Word for God's World 1981, The Teaching of Jesus 1983, Christianity and World Religions: The Challenge of Pluralism 1984, Jesus Christ: the Witness of History 1985, An Adopted Son: The Story of my Life 1985, Freedom under Law 1988; contributions on Islamic Law, etc., to various learned journals. *Leisure interest:* reading; *Address:* 9 Larchfield, Gough Way, Cambridge, England. *Telephone:* Cambridge 358778.

ANDERSON, John Bayard, J.D., LL.M.; American politician; b. 15 Feb. 1922, Rockford, Ill.; s. of E. Albin Anderson and the late Mabel Ring; m. Keke Machakos 1953; one s. four d.; ed. Univ. of Illinois, Harvard Law School; admitted to Ill. Bar 1946; practiced law, Rockford, Ill. 1946-48, 1950-52, 1955-56; Instructor, Northeastern Univ. Law School 1948-49; State Dept. Career Diplomatic Service 1952-55; Winnebago County, Ill., State's Attorney 1956-60; Congressman, 16th Dist., Ill. Nov. 1960-79; mem. U.S. House of Reps. 1960-79; Chair. House Republican Conf. 1979; Ind. cand. for U.S. Pres. 1980; Chair. Nat. Unity Party; Political Comment-ator WLS-TV, Chicago 1981-; Visiting Prof. of Politics Brandeis Univ. 1980-, Oregon State Univ. 1980-, Univ. of Massachussetts 1980-; Lecturer in Political Science, Bryn Mawr Coll. 1980-, Nova Univ. Cen. for Study of Law 1987-; Trustee, Trinity Coll., Deerfield, Ill.; Hon. LL.D. (Ill., Wheaton Coll., Shimer Coll., Biola Coll., Geneva Coll., North Park Coll., Houghton Coll., Trinity Coll.). *Publications:* Between Two Worlds: A Congressman's Choice 1970, Vision and Betrayal in America 1975, Congress and Con-science (Ed.) 1970, The American Economy We Need But Won't Get. *Address:* 2711 Highcrest Road, Rockford, Ill. 61107 and 5616 Ogden Road, Bethesda, Md. 20016, U.S.A. (Homes).

ANDERSON, John Stuart, PH.D., M.A., F.R.S., F.A.A.; British chemist; b. 9 Jan. 1908, London; s. of John Anderson and Emma Sarah Pitt; m. Joan Habershon Taylor 1935; one s. three d.; ed. Imperial Coll. of Science and Technology and Heidelberg Univ.; Asst. Lecturer, Imperial Coll. of Science 1932-38; Sr. Lecturer, Univ. of Melbourne 1938-47, Prof. and Head of Chem. Dept. 1954-59; Deputy Chief Scientific Officer, Atomic Energy Research Establishment, Harwell 1947-53; Dir. Nat. Chemical Lab. (U.K.) 1959-63; Prof. of Inorganic Chem., Oxford Univ. 1963-75, now Emer.; Hon. Professorial Fellow, Univ. Coll. of Wales, Aberystwyth 1975-; Treas. Australian Acad. of Science 1956-59; Hon. Fellow Indian Acad. of Sciences; Hon. D.Sc.(Bath) 1979; Davy Medal (Royal Soc.) 1973, Longstaff Medal (Chemical Soc.) 1975. *Publications:* numerous papers in scientific journals. *Leisure interests:* reading, painting, photography. *Address:* The Cottage, Abermagwr, Dyfed, Wales (Home).

ANDERSON, Dame Judith, D.B.E.; Australian actress; b. 10 Feb. 1898, Adelaide; m. 1st Prof. B. H. Lehmann 1937 (divorced 1939); m. 2nd Luther Greene 1946 (divorced 1950); ed. Norwood High School; stage debut in A Royal Divorce, Theatre Royal, Sydney 1915; went to New York 1918; *Stage appearances have included:* The Dove, Behold the Bridegroom, Strange Interlude, Mourning becomes Electra, Come of Age, The Old Maid, Hamlet, Macbeth, Family Portrait, Tower Beyond, Three Sisters, Medea, The Seagull, The Oresteia. *Films:* Rebecca, Edge of Darkness, Laura, King's Row, Spectre of the Rose, The Red House, Pursued, Tycoon, Cat on a Hot Tin Roof, Macbeth, Don't Bother to Knock, A Man Called Horse, The Chinese Prime Minister (TV) 1974, Star Trek III. *Address:* 808 San Ysidro Lane, Santa Barbara, Calif. 93103, U.S.A. (Home).

ANDERSON, Lindsay Gordon, M.A.; British film and theatre director; b. 17 April 1923, Bangalore, S. India; s. of Maj.-Gen. A. V. Anderson and Mrs. Estelle Bell Sleigh; ed. St. Ronan's School, Cheltenham Coll., and Wadham Coll., Oxford; Co-Founder and Editor *Film Review Sequence* 1947-52; Co-Founder Free Cinema Group, Nat. Film Theatre 1956-59; Pres. Jury, Canadian Nat. Film Festival 1963; Jury mem. Int. Festivals Delhi 1965, Venice 1966, Pres. of Jury, Delhi 1983; Assoc. Dir. Royal Court Theatre 1969-75. *Films directed:* Wakefield Express 1953, Thursday's Children (with Guy Brenton) 1954, O Dreamland 1954, Every Day Except Christmas 1957, This Sporting Life 1963, The White Bus 1965/66, Raz, Dwa, Trzy (The Singing Lesson) for Documentary Studio, Warsaw 1967, If ... 1968, O Lucky Man! 1973, In Celebration 1974, Britannia Hospital 1982, If You Were There ... 1985, The Whales of August 1987, Glory! Glory! 1988. *Stage productions:* The Long and the Short and the Tall 1959, Serjeant Musgrave's Dance 1959, The Lily White Boys 1960, Billy Liar 1960, The Fire Raisers 1961, The Diary of a Madman 1963, Andorra 1964, Julius Caesar 1964, The Cherry Orchard 1966; directed Polish production of Inadmissible Evidence (Nie Do Obrony), Teatr Wspolczesny, Warsaw 1966; In Celebration 1969, The Contractor 1969, Home (London and Broadway) 1970, The Changing Room 1971, The Farm 1973, Life Class 1974, What the Butler Saw 1975, The Seagull 1975, The Bed before Yesterday 1975, The Kingfisher 1977, Alice's Boys 1978, Early Days 1980, Hamlet 1981, The Holly and the Ivy 1982, The Cherry Orchard 1983, The Playboy of the Western World 1985, In Celebration (New York) 1985,

Hamlet (Washington, D.C.) 1986, Holiday 1987; television debut The Old Crowd 1979. *Publications:* Making a Film 1962, About John Ford 1981. *Leisure interests:* photography, video-recording. *Address:* c/o Maggie Parker, Al Parker Ltd., 55 Park Lane, London, W.1., England.

ANDERSON, Marian; American singer; b. 27 Feb. 1902; ed. Philadelphia public school; studied with Agnes Reifsneider, Giuseppe Boghetti and Frank La Forge; concerts in U.S.A., Europe, Africa, S. America, Japan and W. Indies 1926-53; U.S. del. to UN 1958; U.S. Presidential Medal of Freedom award 1962, Congressional Medal of Honor, Nat. Medal of Arts 1986, and numerous American and overseas awards. *Publications:* My Lord, What a Morning! (autobiography) 1956. *Address:* Danbury, Conn. 06810, U.S.A.

ANDERSON, Michael; British film director; b. 30 Jan. 1920, London; ed. in France; Co-Dir. Private Angelo (with Peter Ustinov) 1949; Dir. Water-front 1950, Hell is Sold Out 1952, Night Was Our Friend, Dial 17, Will Any Gentleman?, The House of The Arrow 1952, The Dam Busters 1954, Around the World in Eighty Days 1956, Yangtse Incident 1957, Chase a Crooked Shadow 1957, Shake Hands with the Devil 1958, Wreck of the Mary Deare 1959-60, All the Fine Young Cannibals 1960, The Naked Edge 1961, Flight from Ashiya (in Japan) 1962, Operation Crossbow 1964, The Quiller Memorandum 1966, Shoes of The Fisherman 1969, Pope Joan 1970-71, Doc Savage (in Hollywood) 1973, Conduct Unbecoming 1974, Logan's Run (M.G.M. Hollywood) 1975, Orca—Killer Whale 1976, Domi-nique 1977, The Martian Chronicles 1978, Bells 1979-80. *Address:* c/o Film Rights Ltd., 113-117 Wardour Street, London, W.1, England.

ANDERSON, Odin Waldemar, PH.D.; American educator; b. 5 July 1914, Minneapolis, Minn.; s. of Edwin Anderson and Anna Ormbreck; m. Helen Hay 1939; one s. one d.; ed. Univs. of Wisconsin-Madison and Michigan, Ann Arbor; Instructor, School of Public Health, Univ of Mich. 1945-49; Assoc. Prof., Faculty of Medicine, Univ. of Western Ont., London, Ont., Canada 1949-52; Research Dir., Health Information Foundation, New York 1952-62; Adjunct Assoc. Prof., Graduate School, New York Univ. 1953-57; Adjunct Assoc. Prof., School of Public Health, Columbia Univ., New York 1957-62; Assoc. Prof., Graduate School of Business and Dept. of Sociology, Univ. of Chicago 1962-64, Prof. 1964-80, Emer. Prof., and re-appointed part-time 1980-, Dir. Center for Health Admin. Studies 1972-80; Prof. of Sociology, Univ. of Wis.-Madison 1980-; Dr. h.c. (Uppsala, Sweden) 1977; Eminent Medical Sociologist, American Sociological Assen. 1980, Distin-guished Health Services Researcher, Assen. of Health Services Research 1985. *Publications:* Health Care: can there be Equity: the U.S., Sweden and England 1972, Health Services in the U.S.; a Growth Enterprise since 1875 1985, HMO Development, Patterns and Prospects: A Comparative Analysis of HMOs 1985, Cross-National Comparisons of Health Services in Seven Countries: Observations and Generalizations 1989. *Leisure interests:* music, jogging, hiking. *Address:* Department of Sociology, University of Wisconsin-Madison, Social Science Building, Madison, Wis. 53706; 2105 Kendall Avenue, Madison, Wis. 53705, U.S.A. (Home). *Telephone:* (608) 262-2133 (Office); (608) 233-6055 (Home).

ANDERSON, Philip W., PH.D.; American physicist; b. 13 Dec. 1923, Indianapolis, Ind.; s. of Prof. H. W. Anderson and Elsie Osborne Anderson; m. Joyce Gothwaite 1947; one d.; ed. Univ. High School, Urbana, Ill., and Harvard Univ.; Naval Research Laboratory 1943-45; mem. Technical Staff Bell Telephone Laboratories 1949-84, Chair Theoretical Physics Dept. 1959-61, Asst. Dir. Physical Research Laboratory 1974-76, Consulting Dir. 1976-84; Visiting Lecturer, Univ. of Tokyo 1953-54; Overseas Fellow, Churchill Coll., Cambridge 1961-62; Editor Physics 1964-68; Visiting Prof. of Theoretical Physics, Cambridge Univ. 1967-75; Prof. Princeton Univ. 1975-; mem. Nat. Acad. of Sciences 1967-, mem. Council 1976-79, American Acad. of Arts and Sciences 1966-; mem. Japanese Physical Soc., Inst. of Physics and Physical Soc.; Foreign mem. Royal Soc.; Foreign Assoc. Accademia dei Lincei 1985; Fellow, American Physical Soc., American Assen. for the Advancement of Science; Hon. Fellow, Jesus Coll., Cam-bridge; Hon. D.Sc. (Univ. of Illinois); Nobel Prize for Physics 1977, O. E. Buckley Prize, American Physical Soc., Dannie Heineman Prize, Acad. of Sciences, Göttingen; Guthrie Medal, Inst. of Physics, U.K., Golden Plate Award, American Acad. of Achievement June 1978, Nat. Medal of Science 1982. *Publications:* Concepts in Solids 1963, Basic Notions in Condensed Matter Physics 1984; review articles and book chapters on exchange in insulators, Josephson effect and quantum coherence, hard superconductors, localized moments, resonances in transition metals, etc.; approx. 268 research papers on spectral line broadening, magnetism, superconductivity, many-body theory, quantum chemistry, nuclear physics, etc.; presented Cherwell-Simon Memorial lecture at Oxford Univ. 1980. *Leisure interests:* hiking, Go (rank shodan), gardening and ecology, studying social and biological sciences, Romanesque architecture. *Address:* Princeton Univer-sity, Princeton, N.J. 08540, U.S.A.

ANDERSON, Robert, M.A.E.; American business executive; b. 2 Nov. 1920, Columbus, Neb.; s. of late Robert Anderson and of Lillian Anderson Bays; m. 1st Constance Anderson (divorced 1972), one s. one d.; m. 2nd Diane Clark Lowe 1973; ed. Fairfax High School, Los Angeles, Colorado State Univ. and Chrysler Inst. of Engineering; with Chrysler Corpn. 1946-68, Vice-Pres. and Gen. Man. Chrysler-Plymouth Div. 1965, subsequently Vice-Pres. Product Planning and Devt.; Dir. Commercial Products Group, North

American Rockwell Corpn. 1968–, Pres. 1968; Exec. Vice-Pres. North American Rockwell Corpn. 1969–70, Pres. and C.O.O. (now Rockwell Int. Corpn.) 1970–74, Pres., Chief Exec. Officer 1974–79, Chair. and C.E.O. 1979–87, Chair. 1987–; Dir. Hospital Corpn. of America, Celanese Corpn., Security Pacific Nat. Bank, Security Pacific Corpn., Owens-Illinois, Inc.; mem. Bd. of Trustees, Calif. Inst. of Tech. 1975–, Carnegie-Mellon Univ. 1978–; Hon. Alumnus Award and Hon. LL.D. (Colorado State). *Leisure interests:* golf, tennis. *Address:* Rockwell International Corporation, 600 Grant Street, Pittsburgh, Pa. 15219, U.S.A.

ANDERSON, Robert Bernerd; American lawyer and public servant; b. 4 June 1910, Burleson, Texas; s. of Robert Lee and Elizabeth (Haskew) Anderson; m. Ollie Mae Rawlings Anderson 1935; two s.; ed. Godley High School, Weatherford Coll. and Univ. of Texas; taught in Burleson High School 1927–30; studied Univ. of Texas Law School 1930–32, was meanwhile elected to the Texas legislature; practised law 1932; Asst. Attorney-Gen. of Texas and Prof. of Law at Univ. of Texas 1933; State Tax Commr. 1934–37, and Chair. and Exec. Dir. Texas Unemployment Comm. 1936; Gen. Counsel for the Waggoner Estate (oil and ranching empire) 1937, Gen. Man. 1941–53; U.S. Sec. of Navy 1953–54; Deputy Sec. of Defense 1954–55; Sec. of Treasury 1957–61; Special Envoy of U.S. Pres. to U.A.R. Oct. 1967; served as Pres. of Texas Board of Educ., Dir. of the Reserve Bank of Texas and on many other public bodies; fmr. Pres. Ventures Ltd., Chair. Robert B. Anderson and Co. Ltd. *Address:* Robert B. Anderson and Co. Ltd., 518 Fifth Avenue-7th Floor, New York, N.Y. 10036, U.S.A. (Office).

ANDERSON, Robert Orville, B.A.; American cattle rancher and business exec.; b. 13 April 1917, Chicago, Ill.; s. of Hugo A. and Hilda Nelson Anderson; m. Barbara Herrick Phelps 1939; two s. five d.; ed. Univ. of Chicago; founder and Pres. Hondo Oil and Gas Co. (fmrly. Malco Refineries Inc.) 1941–63; Founder and Owner, Lincoln County Livestock Co., New Mexico; Chair. Federal Reserve Bank of Dallas 1959–65; Dir. Northern Natural Gas Co. 1960–63; Chair. of Exec. Cttee. and Dir. The Atlantic Refining Co. 1963–65 (now ARCO), Chair. of Board 1965–85, C.E.O. 1965–82; Chair. The Observer Ltd. 1981–83, Deputy Chair. July 1983–; Chair. of Bd., Diamond A. Cattle Co., Roswell, New Mexico; mem. Nat. Petroleum Council 1954–; Chair. Aspen Inst. for Humanistic Studies 1959–; Chair. Lovelace Foundation 1962–; Trustee of Bd. Eisenhower Exchange Fellowships, Univ. of Chicago 1963–, Calif. Inst. of Technology; mem. Washington Inst. for Foreign Affairs 1963–; official of numerous civic and business orgs. *Address:* P. O. Box 1000, Roswell, N.M., 88201, U.S.A. (Office). *Telephone:* 505-622-3140.

ANDERSON, Roger E., B.S.; American banker; b. 29 July 1921, Chicago, Ill.; s. of Elmer and June Anderson; m. 1st Marilyn Spence 1949 (deceased); two s.; m. 2nd Linda Kohler 1985; ed. Northwestern Univ.; joined Continental Illinois Nat. Bank 1946, Commercial Dept. 1947–48, Asst. Cashier 1949, successively Second Vice-Pres., Vice-Pres., Senior Vice-Pres. of Int. Banking 1959–68, Exec. Vice-Pres., Dir. 1968–73, Vice-Chair. 1971; Corpn. Dir. S. C. Johnson and Son Inc. 1970–84, Amsted Industries Inc. 1971–; Chair. of Bd. of Dirs. of Continental Illinois Corpn. and Continental Illinois Nat. Bank 1973–84; Corpn. Dir. Eastman Kodak Co. 1976–; Trustee Savings and Profit Sharing Fund of Sears Employees 1980–84; Dir. Lloyd A. Fry Foundation. *Leisure interests:* fishing, photography. *Address:* 135 S. LaSalle St., Suite 1100, Chicago, Ill. 60603, U.S.A.

ANDERSON, Roy Arnold, M.B.A.; American financial executive; b. 15 Dec. 1920, Ripon, Calif.; s. of Carl Gustav Anderson and Esther Marie Johnson; m. Betty Leona Boehme 1948; two s. two d.; ed. Ripon Union High School, Humphrey's School of Business, Stanford Univ.; Man., Factory Accounting, Westinghouse Electric Corpn. 1952–56; Man., Accounting and Finance, also Dir., Management Controls, Lockheed Missiles and Space Co. 1956–65; Dir. of Finance, Lockheed Georgia Co. 1965–68; Asst. Treas. Lockheed Aircraft Corpn. (now Lockheed Corpn.) 1968–69, Vice-Pres. and Controller 1969–71, Senior Vice-Pres., Finance 1971–75, Vice-Chair. of Bd., Chief Financial and Admin. Officer 1975–77, Chair. and C.E.O. 1977–85, Dir., Chair. Exec. Cttee. and Consultant 1985–88, Chair. Emer. Jan. 1989–. *Leisure interest:* tennis. *Address:* Lockheed Corporation, 4500 Park Granada Boulevard, Calabasas, Calif. 91503, U.S.A. *Telephone:* (213) 847-6452.

ANDERSON, Roy Malcolm, PH.D., A.R.C.S., D.I.C., F.R.S.; British university professor of biology; b. 12 April 1947, Herts.; s. of James Anderson and Betty Watson-Weatherborn; m. Dr. Mary Joan Mitchell 1975; ed. Duncombe School, Bengeo, Richard Hale School, Hertford, Imperial Coll., Univ. of London; IBM Research Fellow, Oxford Univ. 1971–73; Lecturer, King's Coll., Univ. of London 1973–77; Lecturer, Imperial Coll. 1977–80, Reader 1980–82, Prof. of Parasite Ecology 1982–, Head of Dept. of Pure and Applied Biology 1984–; Chair. Terrestrial Life Sciences Cttee., Nat. Environment Research Council; Patron Virgin Health Care Foundation, Tropical Medicine and Infectious Diseases Panel for Wellcome Trust 1986–; Council mem. Nat. Environment Research Council 1988–, Zoological Soc. 1988–; mem. Bd. of Dirs., AIDS Policy Unit 1988–; Fellow Inst. of Biology; Zoological Soc. Scientific Medal 1982, Huxley Memorial Medal 1983, C.A. Wright Memorial Medal 1986, David Starr Jordan Prize 1986, Chalmers Medal 1988. *Publications:* Population Dynamics of Infectious Disease Agents: Theory and Applications (Ed.) 1982, Population Biology of Infect-

ious Diseases (Jt. Ed. with R. M. May) 1982. *Leisure interests:* hill walking, croquet, natural history, photography. *Address:* 64 Kew Green, Kew, Richmond, Surrey, TW9 3AP, England.

ANDERSON, Theodore Wilbur, PH.D.; American professor of statistics and economics; b. 5 June 1918, Minneapolis, Minn.; s. of Theodore Wilbur Anderson and Evelynn Johnson Anderson; m. Dorothy Fisher 1950; one s. two d.; ed. North Park Coll., Northwestern Univ., Princeton Univ.; Research Assoc. Cowles Comm. for Research in Econs., Univ. of Chicago 1945–46; at Columbia Univ. 1946–67, Instructor in Math. Statistics 1946–47, Asst. Prof. in Math. Statistics 1947–50, Assoc. Prof. 1950–56, Prof. 1956–67, Acting Chair. 1950–51, 1963, Chair. of Dept. 1956–60, 1964–65; Prof. of Statistics and Econs., Stanford Univ. 1967–, Prin. Investigator Nat. Science Foundation Project Dept. of Econs. 1969–83, Prin. Investigator Army Research Office Project Dept. of Statistics 1982–; Guggenheim Fellow, Univs. of Stockholm and Cambridge 1947–48; Academic Visitor, Imperial Coll. of Science and Tech., U.K., Univ. of London, Visiting Prof. of Math., Univ. of Moscow, Visiting Prof. of Statistics, Univ. of Paris 1967–68; Academic Visitor, L.S.E. 1974–75; Research Consultant, Cowles Foundation for Research in Econs. 1946–60; Consultant, Rand Corpn. 1949–66; Fellow, Center for Advanced Study in the Behavioral Sciences 1957–58, Visiting Scholar 1972–73, 1980; Distinguished Scholar, Calif. Inst. of Tech. 1980; Visiting Prof. of Econs., Columbia Univ. 1983–84, New York Univ. 1983–84; Sabbaticant, IBM Systems Research Inst. 1984; Research Assoc. Naval Postgraduate School 1986–87; Fellow Acad. of Arts and Sciences 1974–; mem. N.A.S. 1976–; Pres. Inst. of Mathematical Statistics 1963, mem. Council; Vice-Pres. American Statistical Soc. 1971–73; mem. Econometric Soc., Inst. of Math. Statistics (mem. Council); Royal Statistical Soc., U.K.; American Math. Soc., Bernoulli Soc. for Math. Statistics and Probability, Indian Statistical Inst., Int. Statistical Inst., Statistical Soc. of Canada; Hon. D.Lit. (North Park Coll.) 1988; R. A. Fisher Award (Cttee. of Pres. of Statistical Socs.) 1985, Distinguished Alumnus Award, North Park Coll. 1987, Samuel S. Wilks Memorial Medal, American Statistical Asscn. 1988. *Publications:* An Introduction to Multivariate Statistical Analysis 1958, 1984, The Statistical Analysis of Time Series 1971, A Bibliography of Multivariate Statistical Analysis (with S. D. Gupta and G. Styan) 1972, Introductory Statistical Analysis (with S. Sclove) 1974, An Introduction to the Statistical Analysis of Data (with S. Sclove) 1978, 1986, A Guide to MINITAB for the Statistical Analysis of Data (with B. Eynon) 1986 and some 115 articles in statistical journals; Ed. and fmr. Ed. of numerous specialist journals. *Leisure interests:* tennis, swimming, travelling. *Address:* Department of Statistics, Sequoia Hall, Stanford University, Stanford, Calif. 94305-4065; 746 Santa Ynez Street, Stanford, Calif. 94305, U.S.A. (Home). *Telephone:* (415) 723-4732; (415) 327-5204 (Home).

ANDERSON, Thomas Foxen, PH.D.; American biologist; b. 7 Feb. 1911, Manitowoc, Wis.; s. of late Anton Anderson and Mabel Foxen; m. Wilma Fay Ecton 1937; one s. one d.; ed. Calif. Inst. of Technology and Univ. of Munich; Instructor in Chemistry, Univ. of Chicago 1936–37; Investigator in Botany, Univ. of Wis. 1937–39, Instructor in Physical Chemistry 1939–40; R.C.A. Fellow of Nat. Research Council 1940–42; Assoc. Johnson Foundation Univ. of Pennsylvania 1942–46, mem. of Faculty 1946–, Prof. of Biophysics 1958–78; Sr. mem. Inst. for Cancer Research 1958–, Sr. mem. Emer. 1983–; Fulbright and Guggenheim Fellow, Inst. Pasteur, Paris 1955–57; mem. N.A.S., Chair. Genetics Section 1985–88; Electron Microscope Soc. of America (Pres. 1955), Int. Fed. of Electron Microscope Socs. (Pres. 1960–64), Biophysical Soc. (Pres. 1965), American Soc. of Naturalists, A.A.A.S., American Soc. of Microbiology, Deutsche Gesellschaft für Elektronenmikroscopie, Soc. Française de Microscopie Electronique (Hon. mem.); mem. Int. Cttee. on Nomenclature of Viruses 1968–72; Silver Medal of Inst. Pasteur 1957; Distinguished Award (Int. Fed. of Electron Microscope Socs.) 1978. *Publications:* The Reactions of Bacterial Viruses with Their Host Cells (Botanical Review 15) 1949, Bacteriophages (Annual Review of Microbiology 4) 1950, Recombination and Segregation in Escherichia coli (Cold Spring Harbor Symposium on Quantitative Biology 23) 1958, The Molecular Organization of Virus Particles (Molecular Organization and Biological Function editor John M. Allen) 1967, Some Personal Memories of Research (Annual Review of Microbiology) 1975, Reflections on Phage Genetics (Annual Review of Genetics) 1981. *Leisure interests:* golf, travel, water-colour painting. *Address:* The Institute for Cancer Research, 7701 Burholme Avenue, Philadelphia, Pa. 19111, U.S.A. *Telephone:* (215) 728-2481.

ANDERSON, Warren M., LL.B.; American business executive; b. 29 Nov. 1921, Brooklyn, New York; s. of John M. and Ida Peterson Anderson; m. Lillian Christensen 1947; ed. Colgate Univ., Western Reserve Univ.; joined Union Carbide Corpn. 1945; engaged in chemicals, plastics, gases, metals and carbons industries; responsible for operations in U.S.A., Europe, Latin America, Africa, Middle East; Vice-Pres. of Corpn. 1969, Exec. Vice-Pres. 1973–77, mem. Bd. of Dirs. 1974–, now of Exec. Cttee. of Bds.; Pres. and C.O.O., Union Carbide Corpn. 1977–82, Chair. and C.E.O. 1982–86. *Address:* 270 Park Avenue, New York, N.Y. 10017, U.S.A. *Telephone:* (212) 551-4158.

ANDERSON, Wendell Richard, B.A., LL.B.; American politician; b. 1 Feb. 1933, St. Paul, Minn.; s. of Theodore M. Anderson and Gladys Nord; m. Mary C. McKee 1963; one s. two d.; ed. Univ. of Minn.; mem. Minnesota House of Reps. 1958–62; elected to Minn. Senate 1962, re-elected 1966;

Gov. of Minnesota 1971–76; Senator from Minnesota 1976–79; Democratic Farmer Labour Party. *Leisure interests:* hockey, golf.

ANDERSON, Capt. William R.; American naval officer; b. 17 June 1921, Bakerville, Tenn.; s. of Mr. and Mrs. D. H. Anderson; m. Yvonne Etzel 1943; two s.; ed. Columbia Military Acad. and U.S. Naval Acad.; commissioned 1942; service in submarines 1942–59; Idaho Univ. Inst. of Naval Tactics 1951; Naval Reactors Branch, Atomic Energy Comm. 1956–57, 1959; Commdr. Nautilus, the world's first atomic submarine 1957–59 (in which he achieved the first totally submerged transit of the North Pole and N.W. Passage 1958); Freedoms Foundation 1962–64; mem. U.S. House of Reps. 1964–72; Computer Corporate Exec. 1972–; Bronze Star Combat "V", Legion of Merit 1958, Christopher Columbus Int. Medal (Italy) 1958, Patron's Medal, Royal Geographical Soc. 1959, Freedom Leadership Award 1960, various war and campaign medals; Democrat. *Publications:* Nautilus 90 North 1959, First under the North Pole 1959, The Useful Atom 1966. *Address:* 2700 Virginia Avenue, N.W., Washington, D.C. 20037, U.S.A. *Telephone:* 202-333-3938.

ANDERSON, William Summers, A.A.S.A.; British business executive; b. 29 March 1919, Hankow, China; s. of William G. and Mabel Anderson; m. Janice Elizabeth Robb 1947; three d.; ed. Public and Thomas Hanbury School, Shanghai; Internal Auditor Hongkong and Shanghai Hotels Ltd. 1938–39; auditor Linstead and Davis 1940–41; war service 1941–45; Nat. Cash Register Corpn. (NCR) (U.K.) 1945, Man. NCR Hong Kong 1946–59, Vice-Pres. Far East and Chair. NCR Japan 1959–72, Corporate Pres. and Dir. 1972–, Chief Exec. Officer 1973–83, Chair. and Pres. 1974–76, Chair. 1976–84. *Leisure interests:* sailing, golf. *Address:* 895 West Rahn Road, Dayton, Ohio 45429, U.S.A. (Home). *Telephone:* 513-449-2250.

ANDERSON-IMBERT, Enrique, PH.D.; Argentine university professor; b. 12 Feb. 1910, Argentina; s. of José Enrique Anderson and Honorina Imbert; m. Margot Di Clerico 1934; one s. one d.; ed. Univ. Nacional de Buenos Aires; Prof., Univ. Nacional de Cuyo, Argentina 1940–41, Univ. Tucumán, Argentina 1941–46, Univ. of Michigan 1947–65; First Victor S. Thomas Prof. of Hispanic American Literature, Harvard Univ. 1965–; mem. American Acad. of Arts and Sciences 1967, Academia Argentina de Letras, 1978; City of Buenos Aires prize for novel Vigilia 1934. *Publications:* Vigilia 1934, El arte de la prosa en Juan Montalvo 1948, Historia de la literatura hispanoamericana 1954, El grimorio 1961, Vigilia-Fuga 1963, El gato de Cheshire 1965, Genio y figura de Sarmiento 1967, La originalidad de Rubén Darío 1967, La sandía y otros cuentos 1969, Una aventura de Sarmiento en Chicago 1969, La locura juega al ajedrez 1971, La flecha en el aire 1972, Los domingos del profesor 1972, Estudios sobre letras hispánicas 1974, La Botella de Klein 1975, Los primeros cuentos del mundo 1977, Victoria 1977, El realismo magico 1978, Teoria y técnica del cuento 1979, En el telar del tiempo: Dos mujeres y un Julián 1982, La prosa 1984, La crítica literaria 1984, El tamaño de las brujas 1986, Nuevos estudios sobre letvas hispanas 1986. *Address:* 20 Elizabeth Road, Belmont, Mass. 02178, U.S.A.

ANDERSSON, Bibi; Swedish actress; b. 11 Nov. 1935; d. of Josef and Karin Andersson; m. 1st Kjell Grede 1960; one d.; m. 2nd Per Ahlmark (q.v.) 1979 (divorced); ed. Terserus Drama School and Royal Dramatic Theatre School, Stockholm; Malmö Theatre 1956–59, Royal Dramatic Theatre, Stockholm 1959–; appearances at Uppsala Theatre 1962–; *Plays acted in include:* Erik XIV 1956, Tre systrar 1961, King John 1961, Le balcon 1961, La grotte 1962, Uncle Vanya 1962, Who's Afraid of Virginia Woolf 1963, As You Like It 1964, After the Fall 1964–65, The Full Circle 1973, Twelfth Night 1975, The Night of the Tribades 1977, Twelfth Night 1980, Antigone 1981, A Streetcar Named Desire 1981, 1983, L'oiseau bleu 1981, Prisoners of Altona 1982, The Creditors 1984–85, Ett gästabud i Pestens tid 1986; *Films acted in include:* Sjunde inseglet (Seventh Seal) 1956, Smultronstället (Wild Strawberries) 1957, Nära livet (The Brink of Life) 1958, Sommarnöje Sökes (Summer House Wanted) 1958, Djävulens öga (Eye of the Devil) 1961, Älskarinnen (The Mistress) 1962, För att inte tala om alla dessa kvinnor (All Those Women) 1964, Juninatt (June Night) 1965, Ön (The Island) 1965, Syskonbädd (My Sister, My Love) 1966, Persona 1966, Duel at Diablo 1966, Story of a Woman 1968, The Girls 1969, The Kremlin Letter 1970, A Passion, The Touch 1971, Scenes from a Marriage 1974, I Never Promised you a Rose Garden, La rivale 1976, An Enemy of the People 1976, Quintet 1979, Svarte Fugler 1982, Berget på månens baksida 1982. *Address:* Tykövägen 28, Lidingö 18161, Sweden; c/o Royal Dramatic Theatre, Stockholm, Sweden. *Telephone:* Stockholm 656100, 7664616.

ANDERSSON, Börje; Swedish politician; b. 26 June 1930, Borlänge; journalist on Social Democratic newspaper Dala-Demokraten 1948–53; elementary school teacher, Borlänge 1955–67; Municipal Commr., Borlänge 1967; mem. Exec. Cttee. Social Democratic Labour Party, Borlänge branch 1957, Dalarna Dist. 1957 (Chair. 1972); Chair. Municipal Bd., Borlänge 1968; mem. Bd. Social Democratic Labour Party 1975; Minister of Defence 1982–83; County Councillor 1963–; Chair. Leisure Amenities Council, Swedish Assen. of Local Authorities 1967–; mem. Bd. Nat. Road Admin. 1976–, Swedish State Power Bd. 1981–. *Address:* c/o Ministry of Defence, Stockholm, Sweden.

ANDERSSON, Harriet; Swedish actress; b. 1932, Stockholm; theatre career commenced in chorus at Oscars Theatre; subsequently appeared in

reviews and then started serious dramatic career at Malmö City Theatre 1953; now appears regularly at Kunigliga Dramatiska Teatern, Stockholm; best-known stage appearances include performances of Anne Frank in The Diary of Anne Frank, Ophelia in Hamlet, in The Beggar's Opera and in plays by Chekhov; numerous film appearances including several by Ingmar Bergman (q.v.): Summer with Monica 1953, Sawdust and Tinsel 1953, Women's Dreams 1955, Dreams of a Summer Night 1955, Through a Glass Darkly 1961, All Those Women 1964, Cries and Whispers 1973; films directed by Jörn Donner (q.v.): One Sunday in September 1963, To Love 1964, Adventure Starts Here 1965, Stimulantia 1965–66, Rooftree 1966, Anna 1970; other films include: Siska 1962, Dream of Happiness 1963, Loving Couples 1964, For the Sake of Friendship 1965, Vine Bridge 1965, The Serpent 1966, The Deadly Affair 1967, The Girls 1968, The Stake; German Film Critics' Grand Prize for Through a Glass Darkly; Swedish Film Assen. plaque; Best Actress Award, Venice Film Festival 1964 (for To Love). *Address:* c/o Sandrew Film & Theater AB, Box 5612, 114 86 Stockholm, Sweden.

ANDERSSON, Sten; Swedish politician; b. 1923, Stockholm; teacher and guide, Workers' Educ. Assen.; mem. Social Democratic Youth League, later Branch Chair.; elected to Stockholm County Council 1950, mem. City Exec., Finance Cttee. and Real Estate Cttee.; Dist. Organizing Sec. Stockholm branch, Socialdemokratiska Arbetarepartiet (Social Democratic Labour Party—SAP) 1953, Branch Sec. 1958, Branch Chair. 1975; Sec. SAP 1962; Minister of Health and Social Affairs 1982–85, of Foreign Affairs Oct. 1985–. *Address:* Utrikesdepartementet, Gustav Adolfs torg 1, S-103 23 Stockholm, Sweden.

ANDRE, Carl; American sculptor; b. 16 Sept. 1935, Quincy, Mass.; s. of George H. Andre and Margaret M. (Johnson) Andre; ed. Phillips Acad., Andover, Mass., served U.S. Army 1955–56; went to New York 1957; worked as freight brakeman and conductor of Pa. Railroad 1960–64; first public exhbn. 1964. *Address:* c/o Paula Cooper, 155 Wooster Street, New York, N.Y. 10012, U.S.A.; Konrad Fischer, Platanestrasse 7, 4 Düsseldorf, Federal Republic of Germany. *Telephone:* (212) 674-0766 (New York); (211) 68-59-08 (Düsseldorf).

ANDRÉ, Harvie, P.C., PH.D.; Canadian politician and engineer; b. 27 July 1940, Edmonton, Alberta; m. Joan Smith 1965; one s. two d.; ed. Univ. of Alberta, Calif. Inst. of Tech.; fmrly. Prof. of Eng., Univ. of Alberta and Consultant Engineer; elected M.P. 1972, fmrly. Caucus spokesperson on Nat. Defence, fmr. spokesperson on Energy, on Econ. Devt., on Treasury Bd., on Science and Tech., on Youth; fmr. mem. Standing Cttee. on External Affairs, on Nat. Defence, on Natural Resources and Public Works, on Finance, Trade and Econ. Affairs, fmr. mem. Special Jt. Cttee. on Senate Reform; Minister of Supply and Services 1984–85, Minister for Consumer and Corporate Affairs 1986–89, of Regional Industrial Expansion, Science and Tech. Jan. 1989–. *Address:* Room 558, Confederation Bldg., House of Commons, Ottawa, Ont., K1A OA2, Canada.

ANDRÉ, Maurice; French trumpeter; b. 21 May 1933, Alès, Gard; s. of Marcel André and Fabienne Volpelière; m. Lilianne Arnoult 1956; four c.; ed. Conservatoire national supérieur de musique, Paris; apprenticed as coal miner before formal music studies; won Prix d'honneur for trumpet; joined Paris Radio Orchestra; subsequently First Trumpet, Lamoureur Orchestra and other orchestras; played in jazz groups and chamber orchestras; now soloist with world's leading orchestras; specialises in baroque and contemporary music; Prof. of Trumpet, Paris Conservatoire 1967–; has made about 260 recordings, including 30 trumpet concertos; Chevalier de la Légion d'honneur; commdr. des Arts et des Lettres; First Prize, Geneva Int. Competition 1955, Munich Int. Competition 1963, Schallplattenpreis, Berlin 1970. *Leisure interests:* pen and ink drawing, gardening, swimming. *Address:* 77137 Presles-en-Brie, France.

ANDREI, Ştefan; Romanian politician; b. 29 March 1931, Podari-Livezi, Dolj County; ed. Inst. of Civil Eng., Bucharest; Asst. Prof. Inst. of Civil Eng. and Inst. of Oil, Gas and Geology, Bucharest 1956–63; mem. Union of Communist Youth (UCY) 1949–54; joined student movement 1951; mem. Exec. Cttee. Union of Student Assens. 1958–62; mem. Bureau Cen. Cttee. UCY 1962–65; mem. Romanian Communist Party (RCP) 1954–; alt. mem. Cen. Cttee. RCP 1969–72, mem. 1972–; First Deputy Head of Int. Section Cen. Cttee. 1966–72; Sec. Cen. Cttee. 1972–78; alt. mem. Exec. Political Cttee. 1974–; mem. Perm. Bureau, Exec. Political Cttee. 1974–84; Minister for Foreign Affairs 1978–85; Secr. Cen. Cttee. 1985–87; Deputy Prime Minister Oct. 1987–; mem. Grand Nat. Assembly 1975–; mem. Nat. Council Front of Socialist Democracy and Unity 1980–; several Romanian orders and medals. *Address:* c/o Central Committee of the Romanian Communist Party, Bucharest, Romania. *Telephone:* 15-02-00.

ANDRÉN, Carl-Gustaf, D.D.; Swedish university administrator; b. 7 July 1922, Slättåkra; s. of Rev. Victor and Andréa (née Johanson) Andrén; m. Karin E. Tengwall 1949; three s.; Asst. Prof. of Practical Theology, Lund Univ. 1957-64, Head of Admin. of Educ. 1964–67, Prof. of Practical Theology and Church Law 1967–80, Rector 1977–80; Chancellor of univs. and colls. in Sweden 1980–; mem. several scientific socs. in Sweden. *Publication:* De septem sacramentis 1963. *Address:* National Board of Universities and Colleges in Sweden, Box 45501, S-104 30 Stockholm; Jakob Westinsgatan 1A, S-112 20 Stockholm, Sweden.

ANDREOLI, Kathleen Gainor; American university administrator; b. 22 Sept. 1935, Albany, New York; d. of John Edward Gainor and Edmunda Ringelmann Gainor; m. Thomas Eugene Andreoli 1960; one s. two d.; ed. Georgetown Univ. and Vanderbilt Schools of Nursing and Univ. of Ala. School of Nursing, Birmingham; Staff Nurse, Albany Hosp. Medical Center, New York 1957; Instructor, various schools of nursing 1957-70; Educational Dir., Physician Asst. Program, Dept. of Medicine, School of Medicine, Univ. of Ala. 1970-75, subsequently Asst. then Assoc. of Nursing 1970-79, Prof. of Nursing 1979; various admin. positions, Univ. of Texas Health Science Center, Houston 1979-, Prof. of Nursing 1982-, Vice-Pres. for Educational Services, Interprofessional Educ. and Int. Programs 1984-87; Vice-Pres. Nursing Affairs and John L. and Helen Kellogg Dean of Coll. of Nursing Rush Univ., Chicago 1987-. *Leisure interests:* music, art, reading, bicycling, travelling. *Address:* 1653 West Congress Parkway, Chicago, Ill. 60612, U.S.A. (Office). *Telephone:* (312) 942-7117.

ANDREOTTI, Giulio; Italian journalist and politician; b. 14 Jan. 1919, Rome; s. of Philip Andreotti; m. Livia Danese 1945; two s. two d.; ed. Univ. of Rome; Pres., Fed. of Catholic Univs. in Italy 1942-45; Deputy to the Constituent Assembly 1945 and to Parl. 1947-; Under-Sec. in the Govts. of De Gasperi and Pella 1947-53; Minister for the Interior in Fanfani Govt. 1954; Minister of Finance 1955-58, of Treasury 1958-59, of Defence 1959-60, 1960-66, March-Oct. 1974, of Industry and Commerce 1966-68, for the Budget, and Econ. Planning and in charge of Southern Devt. Fund 1974-76, Chair. Christian Democratic Parl. Party in Chamber of Deputies 1948-72; Prime Minister 1972-73, 1976-79; Chair. Foreign Affairs Cttee., Chamber of Deputies; Minister of Foreign Affairs Aug. 1983-. *Publications:* Editor of Concretezza 1954-76, A Ogni morte di Papa 1980, Visti da vicino 1983, Diari 1976-79. *Address:* 326 Corso Vittorio Emanuele, Rome, Italy.

ANDRETTI, Mario Gabriele; American racing driver; b. 29 Feb. 1940, Montona, Italy; m. Dee Ann Hoch 1961; three c.; began midget car racing in United States, graduating to United States Auto Club Nat. Formula; USAC Champion 1965, 1966 and 1969; winner of Indianapolis 500 Miles 1969, 1981; winner of Daytona 500 Miles NASCAR stock car race 1967; began Formula 1 racing in 1968; World Champion 1978, third 1977; Pres. Andretti Racing Enterprises, Nazareth 1968-. *Grand Prix wins:* 1971 South African (Ferrari), 1976 Japanese (Lotus-Ford), 1977 (United States West (Lotus-Ford), 1977 Spanish (Lotus-Ford), 1977 French (Lotus-Ford), 1977 Italian (Lotus-Ford), 1978 Argentine (Lotus-Ford), 1978 Belgian (Lotus-Ford), 1978 Spanish (Lotus-Ford), 1978 French (Lotus-Ford), 1978 German (Lotus-Ford), 1978 Dutch (Lotus-Ford). *Leisure interests:* music, especially opera. *Address:* 53 Victory Lane, Nazareth, Pa. 18064, U.S.A.

ANDREW, Ludmilla; Canadian soprano opera singer; b. Canada, of Russian parentage; operatic début in Vancouver as Donna Elvira; British déebut as Madam Butterfly with Sadler's Wells Opera; noted for Russian song repertoire; has given many broadcasts of French, German and Russian song repertoire with Geoffrey Parsons; many recital tours; now appears regularly at world's leading opera houses and at maj. int. music festivals; roles include Aida, Anna Bolena, Leonore, Norma, Senta, Sieglinde and Turandot. *Address:* c/o Performing Arts, 1 Hinde Street, London, W1M 5RH, England.

ANDREW, Sydney Percy Smith, M.A., F.R.S., F.ENG., F.I.CHEM.E., M.I.MECH.E; British chemical engineer; b. 16 May 1926; s. of Harold C. Andrew and Kathleen M. Andrew (née Smith); m. Ruth Harrison Kenyon 1986; ed. Barnard Castle School, King's Coll., Durham Univ., Trinity Hall, Cambridge; joined ICI, Billingham Div. 1950, Chemical Eng. Research 1951, Plant Engineer 1953, Section Man. Reactor Research 1955, Process Design 1959, Sr. Research Assoc., Group Man. Catalysts and Chemicals Research 1963-76; Consulting Chemical Engineer; Visiting Prof. Univ. of Bath; Hon. D.Sc. (Leeds) 1979. *Publications:* Catalyst Handbook 1970; papers on chemical eng., applied chem. and crop growth. *Leisure interests:* archaeology, ancient and medieval history. *Address:* 1 The Wynd, Stainton in Cleveland, Middlesbrough, TS8 9BP, England. *Telephone:* (0642) 596348.

ANDREWARTHA, Herbert George, M.AGR.SC., D.SC., F.A.A.; Australian professor of zoology (retd); b. Dec. 1907, Perth; s. of George Andrewartha and Elise M. Morgan; m. Hattie V. Steele 1936 (died 1984); one s. one d.; ed. Perth Modern School, Univs. of W. Australia, Melbourne, Adelaide, Cambridge, N. Carolina and Duke Univ.; Entomologist, Waite Agric. Research Inst. Univ. of Adelaide 1946-50, Sr. Entomologist 1950-55; Reader in Animal Ecology, Dept. of Zoology, Univ. of Adelaide 1955-62, Prof. 1962-72; Hon. Visiting Research Fellow, Waite Agric. Research Inst. 1975-(89). *Publications:* The Distribution and Abundance of Animals (with L. C. Birch) 1954, Introduction to the Study of Animal Populations 1961, The Ecological Web: More on the Distribution and Abundance of Animals 1984; more than 50 papers in scientific journals. *Leisure interests:* reading, gardening, tennis. *Address:* 37 Claremont Avenue, Netherby, South Australia 5062. *Telephone:* (08) 793962.

ANDREWS, Anthony; British actor; b. 1948, Hampstead, London; m. Georgina Simpson; one s. one d.; ed. Royal Masonic Public School; started acting 1967. *TV appearances include:* Doomwatch, Woodstock 1972, A Day Out, Follyfoot, Fortunes of Nigel 1973, The Pallisers, David Copperfield 1974, Upstairs, Downstairs 1975, French Without Tears, The Country Wife, Much Ado About Nothing 1977, Danger UXB 1978, Romeo and Juliet 1979, Brideshead Revisited 1980, Ivanhoe 1982, The Scarlet Pimper-

nel 1983. *Films Include:* A War of the Children, Take Me High 1973, Operation Daybreak 1975, Les Adolescentes 1976, The Holcroft Covenant 1986, Second Victory 1987, Woman He Loved 1988, The Lighthorsemen 1988. *Play:* One of Us 1986. *Address:* International Creative Management, 388-396 Oxford Street, London W.1, England.

ANDREWS, David Roger Griffith, C.B.E., M.A., C.B.I.M., A.C.M.A.; British company executive; b. 27 March 1933, Hamilton, Ont., Canada; s. of C. and G.M. Andrews; m. Dorothy Ann Campbell 1963; two s. one d.; ed. Abingdon School and Pembroke Coll., Oxford; Assistant Controller, Ford of Europe 1968; Controller, British Leyland Motor Corpn. Ltd. 1969; Finance Dir., Austin Morris Ltd. 1970; Man. Dir. Power and Transmission Div. BLMC Ltd. 1973; Man. Dir. Leyland Int. 1975; Exec. Vice-Chair. B.L. Ltd. 1977-82, Dir. 1982-86; Chair. Leyland Group 1981-82, Landrover Group 1981-82, Chair. and C.E.O. Landrover-Leyland Group 1982-, Rover Group 1986-; Dir. Elvich Ltd., Clarges Pharmaceutical Trustees Ltd. *Address:* Gainford, Mill Lane, Gerrards Cross, Bucks., SL9 8BA, England. *Telephone:* 0753-884310.

ANDREWS, Harry (Fleetwood), C.B.E.; British actor; b. 10 Nov. 1911; s. of Arthur Andrews and Amy Andrews; ed. Tonbridge and Wrekin Coll.; with Liverpool Repertory 1933-35; Horatio in Hamlet, New York 1936; John Gielgud's Season 1937; served World War II; with Old Vic 1945-49. *Stage roles include:* Bolingbroke, Mirabel, Warwick in St. Joan, Shakespeare Memorial Theatre; Wolsey, Macduff, Brutus, Bolingbroke in Henry IV (Parts I and II) 1949-51; Enobarbus, Buckingham, Kent 1953; Othello, Claudius 1956; Menenius in Coriolanus 1959; Casanova in Camino Real, Phoenix Theatre 1957; Henry VIII, Old Vic 1958; Allenby in Ross, Haymarket 1960; Rockhart in The Lizard on the Rock, Phoenix 1962; Ekhart in Baal, Phoenix 1963; Crampton in You Never Can Tell, Haymarket 1966; King Lear, Royal Court 1971; Ivan in The Family, Haymarket 1978; Uncle Vanya, Haymarket 1982, A Patriot for Me, Chichester and Haymarket 1983, L.A. 1984. *Films include:* The Red Beret 1952, Helen of Troy, Alexander the Great 1956, A Hill in Korea 1956, Moby Dick 1956, Saint Joan 1957, Dreyfus, Ice Cold in Alex 1958, Solomon and Sheba 1959, Question of Larceny, Circle of Deception 1960, The Best of Enemies 1962, The Inspector, Barabbas, Reach for Glory, Nine Hours to Rama, 55 Days at Peking 1962, The Snout, The Best of Everything, The Hill 1965, The Agony and the Ecstasy, Sands of the Kalahari 1965, Modesty Blaise 1966, The Deadly Affair 1966, The Jokers 1967, The Long Duel, A Dandy in Aspic, The Charge of the Light Brigade 1968, The Night They Raided Minsky's 1968, The Southern Star, The Seagull 1968, A Nice Girl Like Me 1969, Too Late the Hero, The Gaunt Woman, Entertaining Mr. Sloane 1970, Country Dance 1970, Wuthering Heights 1970, Burke and Hare 1971, Nicholas and Alexandra 1971, I Want What I Want 1971, The Nightcomers, The Ruling Class 1972, Man of La Mancha 1972, Theatre of Blood 1973, The Mackintosh Man 1974, Man at the Top 1974, Jacob and Esau, The Bluebird 1976, Sky Riders, The Passover Plot, The Prince and The Pauper, Equus, The Four Feathers, Superman, The Titanic, The Captain, The Curse of King Tutankhamen. *TV appearances include:* Leo Tolstoy, An Affair of Honour, Edward VII, Clayhanger, The Garth People, Valley Forge, Two Gentle People, A Question of Faith, A Question of Guilt, Constance Kent, Closing Ranks, Dynasty, LENT, Inside Story, All Passion Spent, Cause Célèbre, Clowns 1989. *Leisure interests:* riding, sailing, gardening.
[Died 6 March 1989.]

ANDREWS, Henry Nathaniel Jr., M.S., PH.D.; American palaeobotanist; b. 15 June 1910, Melrose, Mass.; s. of Henry N. Andrews Sr. and Florence C. M. Hollings; m. Elisabeth C. Ham 1939; two s. one d.; ed. M.I.T., Washington Univ., St. Louis, Miss., Cambridge Univ.; Asst. to Full Prof., Washington Univ., St. Louis, Miss. 1939-64; Palaeobotanist and Asst. to Dir., Miss. Botanical Garden 1941-64; mem. part-time staff, U.S. Geological Survey 1950-60; Prof. and Head of Botany Dept., Univ. of Conn. 1964-75, Prof. Emer. 1975-; mem. N.A.S. Merit Award, Botanical Soc. of America. *Publications:* numerous articles, chiefly on palaeobotany; Ancient Plants 1947, Studies in Paleobotany 1961, Index of Generic names of Fossil Plants 1955, Traité de Paléobotanique, Vol. IV (jt. author), The Fossil Hunters 1980, Plant Life in the Devonian (with P. Gensel) 1984. *Leisure interests:* hiking, natural history in general, walking on beaches, art, boat restorations. *Address:* RFD 1, Box 146, Laconia, N.H. 03246, U.S.A. *Telephone:* 603-524 1288.

ANDREWS, John Hamilton, A.O., F.T.S., M.ARCH.; Australian architect; b. 29 Oct. 1933; s. of the late K. Andrews; m. Rosemary Randall 1958; four s.; ed. N. Sydney Boys' High School, Univ. of Sydney, Harvard Univ.; private practice, Toronto, Canada 1962, Sydney 1970-; mem. Staff, Univ. of Toronto School of Architecture 1962-67, Chair. and Prof. of Architecture 1967-69; mem. Visual Arts Bd., Australia Council 1977-80; Chair. Architecture and Design Comm., Australia Council 1980-, Founding Chair. Design Arts Bd., 1983-88; Architectural Juror, Australian Archives Nat. Headquarters Building 1979, Parl. House Competition 1979-80; mem. R.I.B.A., Bd., Australia Council 1988-; Assoc. N.Z. Inst. of Architects; Fellow, Royal Architectural Inst. of Canada; Life Fellow, Royal Australian Inst. of Architects; Hon. Fellow, American Inst. of Architects; Centennial Medal (Canada) 1967; Massey Medal (Canada) 1967; Arnold Brunner Award, U.S. Acad. of Arts and Letters 1971; American Inst. of Architects Honour Award 1973; Gold Medal, Royal Australian Inst. of Architects 1980,

Advance Australia Award 1982. *Principal works:* Scarborough Coll., Toronto, Harvard Graduate School of Design, Harvard Univ., Cameron Offices, Canberra, American Express Tower, Sydney, Intelsat Headquarters Building, Washington, D.C., Hyatt Hotel, Perth, Convention Centre Darling Harbour, Sydney, Convention Centre and Hyatt Hotel, Adelaide, World Congress Centre and Eden on the Yarra Hotel, Melbourne. *Publication:* Architecture: A Performing Art 1982. *Leisure interests:* fishing, surfing. *Address:* John Andrews International Pty. Ltd., 1017 Barrenjoey Road, Palm Beach, N.S.W. 2108 (Office); 32 Florida Road, Palm Beach, N.S.W. 2108, Australia (Home). *Telephone:* 9195455 (Office).

ANDREWS, Julie; British actress and singer; b. 1 Oct. 1935, Walton-on-Thames, Surrey, m. 1st Tony Walton 1959 (dissolved 1968), one d.; m. 2nd Blake Edwards 1969; first stage appearance at the age of twelve as singer, London Hippodrome; played in revues and concert tours; appeared in pantomime Cinderella, London Palladium; played leading parts in The Boy Friend, New York 1954, My Fair Lady 1959-60, Camelot, New York 1960-62; television play High Tor; several television shows including The Julie Andrews Hour 1972-73; Academy Award (Oscar) Best Actress 1964; three Golden Globe Awards, Emmy Award 1987. *Films:* Mary Poppins 1963, The Americanization of Emily 1964, The Sound of Music 1964, Hawaii 1965, Torn Curtain 1966, Thoroughly Modern Millie 1966, Star! 1967, Darling Lili 1970, The Tamarind Seed 1973, 10 1979, Little Miss Marker 1980, S.O.B. 1980, Victor/Victoria 1981, The Man Who Loved Women 1983, That's Life 1986, Duet For One 1986, The Sound of Christmas (TV) 1987. *Publication:* Mandy, The Last of the Really Great Wangdoogles 1973. *Address:* Triad Artists, 10100 Santa Monica Boulevard, 16th Floor, Los Angeles, Calif. 90067, U.S.A. *Telephone:* (213) 556-2727.

ANDREWS, Kenneth Raymond, PH.D., F.B.A.; British professor of history; b. 26 Aug. 1921, London; s. of Arthur Andrews and Marion Andrews; m. Ottilie Kalman 1969; two step-s.; ed. Henry Thornton School, Clapham, London and King's Coll., London; Southend Polytechnic 1954-56; Chiswick Polytechnic 1956-63; Univ. of Liverpool 1963-64; Univ. of Hull 1964-86; Prof. of History 1979-, part time 1986-88, Emer. 1988-. *Publications:* Elizabethan Privateering 1964, Drake's Voyages 1967, The Spanish Caribbean 1978, Trade, Plunder and Settlement 1984. *Leisure interests:* chess, tennis, cooking. *Address:* The University, Hull, Yorks., England. *Telephone:* (0482) 46311.

ANDREWS, Mark, B.S., LL.D.; American farmer and politician; b. 19 May 1926, Fargo, N.D.; s. of Mark and Lilian (Hoyler) Andrews; m. Mary Willming 1949; one s. two d.; ed. Univ. of North Dakota; farmer, Mapleton, N.D. 1949-; mem. Congress from 1st Dist., N.D., 1963-73, at large 1973-81, mem. Appropriations Cttee.; Senator from North Dakota 1981-87; Chair. Andrews Assocs. Inc. 1987-; del. to FAO Conf., Rome 1975; Republican. *Address:* Mapleton, N.D. 58059, U.S.A. (Home).

ANDREYEV, Aleksandr Fyodorovich, DR. PHYS. SC.; Soviet physicist; b. 1939; ed. Moscow Inst. of Tech. Physics; junior, senior scientific asst., 1964-79; Prof. 1979; Corresp. mem. of U.S.S.R. Acad. of Sciences 1981-; Deputy Dir. of U.S.S.R. Acad. of Sciences Vavilov Inst. for Study of Physics 1984-; mem. CPSU 1985-; Lenin Prize for Work on 'The Tunnel Transfer of Matter and Quantity Crystallisation', publ. 1972-84. *Address:* U.S.S.R. Acad. of Sciences Vavilov Inst. for Study of Physics, Moscow, U.S.S.R.

ANDREYEV, Vladimir Alekseyevich; Soviet actor and stage director; b. 1930; m.; one s. one d.; ed. State Inst. of Theatre Arts Cinema (GITIS); actor with Yermolova Theatre Moscow 1952-70, chief dir. 1970-85; mem. CPSU 1962-; Chief. Dir. of Maly Theatre, Moscow 1985-; teaches concurrently at GITIS, Prof. 1978-; U.S.S.R. People's Artist 1985; Stanislavsky State Prize 1980; *Roles include:* Aleksey in M. Rozov's It's High Time!, Vasilkov in Ostrovsky's Crazy Money, Golubkov in Bulgakov's Flight, Sattarov in Valeyev's I Give You Life. *Productions include:* Vampilov's plays: Last Summer in Chulimsk, and The Duck Hunt; Money for Mary (based on a work by V. Rasputin), The Shore (based on Yuriy Bondarev's novel), Challenge (by G. Markov and E. Shim), Uncle Vanya. *Address:* Maly Theatre, Sverdlov Square, Moscow, U.S.S.R.

ANDRIAMAHAZO, Brig.-Gen. Gilles; Malagasy army officer; b. 1919, Fort-Dauphin, Tuléar Prov.; ed. Ecole Supérieure de Guerre, Paris; promoted to rank of Col.; then Inspector of Infantry and Artillery, Gen. Staff Headquarters at the Presidency; Brig.-Gen., Inspector-Gen. of the Armed Forces 1970; Mil. Gov. of Tananarive 1972; Minister of Territorial Admin. 1972-75; Chair. Mil. Directorate Feb.-June 1975; fmr. Head of Mil. Cttee. for Devt. *Address:* c/o Supreme Revolutionary Council, Antananarivo, Madagascar.

ANDRIASHEV, Anatoliy Petrovich; Soviet zoologist; b. 19 Aug. 1910, Montpellier, France; s. of P. E. Waitashevsky and N. Y. Andriasheva; m. Nina N. Savelyeva 1934; two d.; ed. Leningrad Univ.; Postgraduate, Research Assoc., Asst. Prof. Leningrad Univ. 1933-39; Sebastopol Biological Scientific Station 1939-44; Chief, Antarctic Research Div., Inst. of Zoology, U.S.S.R. Acad. of Sciences 1944-, Prof. 1970-; Vice-Pres. European Ichthyological Union 1979-82, Hon. mem. 1982-; Arctic and Bering Sea expeditions 1932, 1936, 1937, 1946, 1951; Antarctic expeditions 1955-58, 1971-72, 1975-76; Corresp. mem. U.S.S.R. Acad. of Sciences 1966-; Hon. Arctic explorer of the U.S.S.R. 1947-; Hon. Foreign mem. of American

Soc. of Ichthyologists and Herpetologists; State prizewinner 1971. Ed.-in-Chief Ichthyology 1977-. *Publications:* works on ichthyology, marine zoogeography and Antarctic biology. *Leisure interests:* skiing, photography, the French Impressionists. *Address:* Zoological Institute, Universiteskaya Nab. 1, Academy of Sciences, Leningrad 164, U.S.S.R.

ANDRIESSEN, Franciscus H. J. J.; Netherlands politician; b. 1929; ed. Univ. of Utrecht; mem. of Second Chamber, States-Gen. (Parl.) 1967-; Minister of Finance 1977-80; Commr. for Competition Policy and Relations with the European Parl., Comm. of European Communities 1981-84; for Agric. and Fisheries 1984-85, for Agric. and Forestry 1986-89, for External Relations and Trade Policy Jan. 1989-; mem. Catholic People's Party, Christian Democratic Appeal. *Address:* Commission of the European Communities, 200 rue de la Loi, 1049 Brussels, Belgium.

ANDRIESSEN, Jacobus Eije, M.A., PH.D.; Netherlands economist and business executive; b. 25 July 1928, Rotterdam; m. Josephina Hoogeweij 1952; ed. Erasmus Univ., Rotterdam and Amsterdam Free Univ.; Dir. Dept. of Gen. Econ. Policy, Ministry of Econ. Affairs 1955-59; Prof., Law Faculty, Univ. of Amsterdam 1959-63; mem. Econ. and Social Cttee. of European Econ. Community (EEC), Netherlands Social and Econ. Council 1959-63; Minister of Econ. Affairs 1963-65; Chair. of Exec. Bd. Royal Packaging Industries Van Leer B. V. 1965-87; Chair. Bd. of Dirs. Ballast-Nedam, Bd. of Dirs. Postbank NV; Chair. Cen. Cttee. of Statistics, Dutch Christian Employers Asscn., Foundation of Modern Art. *Publications:* Development of Modern Price Theory 1955, The Theory of Economic Policy (co-editor) 1962, Economics in a Mirror 1964, Social-economic Administration in the Netherlands (co-editor) 1987, Riding the Wave (co-editor) 1987, Economics in Theory and Practice 1987. *Leisure interests:* modern literature, painting and films, golf. *Address:* Waldeck Pyrmontlaan 16, Wassenaar, Netherlands. *Telephone:* 01751-79019.

ANDRIEU, René Gabriel, B.P., L.-ès-L.; French journalist; b. 24 March 1920, Beauregard (Lot); s. of Alphonse Andrieu and Esther Vernhet; m. Janine Vigié 1947; one d.; ed. Toulouse Univ.; Diplomatic Editor le Soir 1946-58; Chief Editor L'Humanité 1958-; Croix de guerre, Médaille de la Résistance, Légion d'honneur; mem. Central Cttee. French Communist Party 1961-. *Publications:* Les communistes et la révolution 1968, En feuilletant l'Histoire de France (with Jean Effel) 1969, Du bonheur et rien d'autre 1975, Lettre ouverte à ceux qui se réclament du socialisme 1978, Choses dites 1979, Stendhal ou le bal masqué 1983. *Address:* 5 rue du Faubourg Poissonnière, 75440 Paris, France.

ANDROSCH, Dr. Hannes; Austrian economist and politician; b. 18 April 1938, Vienna; m. Brigitte Schärf; two c.; ed. Hochschule für Welthandel, Vienna; Asst. auditor, Fed. Ministry of Finance 1956-66; Sec. Econ. Affairs Section, Socialist Parl. Party 1963-66, Vice-Chair. 1974-85; mem. Nationalrat (Nat. Council) 1967-85; Minister of Finance 1970-81, Vice-Chancellor 1976-81; Chair. and Gen. Man. Creditanstalt-Bankverein 1981-87; Chair. Österreichische Kontrolbank AG 1985-86; Grand Gold Medal of Honour. *Address:* c/o Creditanstalt-Bankverein, Schottengasse 6, 1011 Vienna, Austria.

ANDROUTSOPOULOS, Adamantios, LL.B., LL.M., J.D.; Greek politician; b. 1919, Psari, Greece, ed. Athens Univ., John Marshall Law School, Chicago, U.S.A., Chicago Univ.; Lawyer 1947; Prof. of Law, Chicago Industrial School; Scientific collaborator at Roosevelt Univ., Mundelein Coll., John Marshall Law School, Fengen Coll.; returned to Greece 1967; Minister of Finance 1967-71, of Interior 1971-73; Prime Minister 1973-74; mem. Athens Lawyers' Union, American Judicature Soc., American Business Law Asscn. *Publications:* State Distributions and National Economy, The Problem of Causation in Maritime Law, Legal Terminology of the Greek-American Dictionary. *Address:* 63 Academias Street, Athens, Greece.

ANDRUS, Cecil D.; American politician; b. 25 Aug. 1931, Hood River, Ore.; s. of Hal S. and Dorothy (Johnson) Andrus; m. Carol M. May 1949; three d.; ed. Oregon State Univ.; served U.S. Navy 1951-55; mem. Idaho Senate 1961-66, 1960-70; State Gen. Man. Paul Revere Life Insurance Co. 1969-70; Gov. of Idaho 1971-77, Jan. 1987-; Chair. Nat. Govs. Conf. 1976; Sec. of Interior 1977-81; Dir. Bekar Industries Corpn. 1981-; Hon. LL.D. (Gonzaga Univ., Spokane, Wash.) 1975; Democrat. *Address:* 1280 Candleridge Drive, Boise, Ida. 83712, U.S.A.

ANDRUSZKIEWICZ, Zdzisław Antoni, M.A.; Polish publisher and politician; b. 28 Feb. 1928, Cukrownia Żytyńska; m.; one c.; ed. Maria Curie-Skłodowska Univ., Lublin; active in youth movement, Lublin and Warsaw 1954-64; Ed.-in-Chief, Walka Młodych, Warsaw 1965-72; Deputy Head later Head, Dept. for Sports and Tourism Orgs. of Cen. Cttee. of Polish United Workers' Party (PZPR) 1972-78; Pres. Workers' Publishing Co-operative "Prasa-Książka-Ruch", Warsaw 1978-85; mem. PZPR 1953-; mem. PZPR Cen. Revisional Comm. 1980-81; mem. Polish Journalists' Asscn. 1971-82, Vice-Chair. Main Bd. 1974-77; Vice-Chair. Main Bd. of Polish-Soviet Friendship Soc. 1979-84, Presidium mem. 1984-; Officer's Cross of Order of Polonia Restituta, Bronze, Silver and Gold Cross of Merit and other decorations. *Publications:* articles in Walka Młodych, Nowe Drogi, Ideologia i Polityka. *Leisure interests:* reading, gardening. *Address:* ul. Madalińskiego 55 m. 2, 02-544 Warsaw, Poland. *Telephone:* 28-01-79 (Office).

ANDZHAPARIDZE, Georgiy; Soviet publisher and literary critic; b. 1943, Moscow; ed. Moscow Univ.; started publishing 1968; series of articles on foreign literature in periodic press; Chief Ed. of Raduga (publishing-house for foreign literature). *Works include:* On the Way to a Hero 1979, Consumer! Rebel! Fighter! 1982. *Address:* Raduga Publishing House, Moscow, U.S.S.R.

ANFINSEN, Christian Boehmer, PH.D.; American biochemist; b. 26 March 1916, Monessen, Pa.; s. of late Christian Boehmer Anfinsen and Sophie née Rasmussen; m. 1st Florence Bernice Kenenger 1941 (divorced 1978), one s. two d.; m. 2nd Libby Esther Shulman Ely 1979; ed. Swarthmore Coll., Univ. of Pennsylvania, Harvard Medical School; Asst. instructor in organic chem. Univ. of Pennsylvania 1938–39; Fellow, American Scandinavian Foundation, visiting investigator Carlsberg laboratory, Copenhagen, Denmark 1939–40; Fellow, Harvard Univ. 1941–43, Instructor in Biological Chem., Harvard Medical School 1943–45; Civilian with Office of Scientific Research and Devt. CMR 1944–46; Assoc. in Biological Chem., Harvard Medical School 1945–48; Senior Fellow, American Cancer Soc., Visiting Investigator, Medical Noble Inst. with Prof. Hugo Theorell 1947–48; Markle Scholar and Asst. Prof. Biological Chem., Harvard Medical School, also consultant in research anaesthesia, Mass. Gen. Hosp. 1948–50; Chief, Laboratory of Cellular Physiology, Nat. Heart Inst. 1950–52; Chief, Laboratory of Cellular Physiology and Metabolism, Nat. Heart Inst. 1952–62; Prof. Dept. of Biological Chem., Harvard Medical School 1962–63; Chief, Laboratory of Chemical Biology Nat. Inst. of Arthritis, Metabolism and Digestive Diseases 1963–81; Prof. of Biology, Johns Hopkins Univ. 1982–; mem. Bd. of Govs., Weizmann Inst. of Science, Rehovot, Israel; mem. American Soc. of Biological Chemists (Pres. 1971–72), N.A.S., Royal Danish Acad., Pontifical Acad. of Sciences 1981–; Rockefeller Foundation Public Service Award 1954; Hon. D.Sc. (Swarthmore Coll.) 1965; Harvey Lecturer 1966; Hon. D.Sc. (Georgetown) 1967; Hon. D.Sc. (New York Medical Coll.) 1969; Hon. Fellow, Weizmann Inst. of Science 1969; EMBO Lecturer for Sweden 1970; Visiting Fellow, All Souls Coll. Oxford 1970; Jubilee Lecturer 1972; Hon. D.Sc. (Univ. of Pa.) 1973; Mathers Lectures (Indiana Univ.) 1974; Hon. D.Sc. (Gustavus Adolphus Coll.), Kempner Lectureship (Univ. of Texas, Galveston) 1975; Naff Lectures (Univ. of Kentucky); Hon. D.Sc. (Brandeis) 1977; Hon. D.Sc. (Providence Coll.) 1978; Hon. D.Sc. (Naples), (Yeshiva) 1982, (Adelphi) 1987; Nobel Prize for Chem. 1972. *Publications:* The Molecular Basis of Evolution 1959; numerous articles in learned journals on protein structure, enzyme functions and properties, and allied subjects. *Leisure interests:* sailing, music. *Address:* Department of Biology, Johns Hopkins University, 34th and Charles Street, Baltimore, Md. 21218, U.S.A. *Telephone:* 301-338 8552.

ANGELINI, Arnaldo M.; Italian university professor in electrical and nuclear engineering; b. 2 Feb. 1909, Force, Ascoli Piceno Prov.; s. of Licinio and Anita Lucangeli; m. Livia Rossi 1937; two s. one d.; Man. Dir., Gen. Man. Terni Co.; Gen. Man. ENEL 1963–73, Chair. 1973–79, Hon. Pres. and Consultant 1979–; Pres. SIR Finanziaria S.p.A. and SIR Consorzio Industriale S.p.A. 1979–80; Prof. Electrical Eng., Univ. of Rome, Dir. Electric Eng. Inst.; Hon. Prof., Polytechnic Inst. of New York 1975–; fmrly. Vice-Pres.; Comitato Nazionale per le Ricerche Nucleari; mem. Council Italian Forum for Nuclear Energy (FIEN), Pres. 1959–60; mem. Steering Cttee. Comitato Nazionale per l'Energia Nucleare 1960–73; mem. Scientific and Technical Cttee. EURATOM, Pres. 1961, Vice-Pres. 1964; mem. del. to Conf. on Peaceful Uses of Nuclear Energy, Geneva 1955, 1958, 1964, 1971; Hon. Exec. Vice-Pres. World Energy Conf.; Chair. Gen. Assembly, Org. of Nuclear Energy Producers (OPEN) 1976–79; New Acad. of Sciences 1981–; Pres. Associazione Elettrotecnica ed Elettronica Italiana (AEI) 1959–61, now Emer. mem. Gen. Presidency; Pres. Int. Union of Electric Energy Producers and Distributors (UNIPEDE) 1979–81; Fellow and Life mem. Inst. of Electrical and Electronic Eng.; National mem. Accad. Nazionale dei Lincei; Foreign Assoc., Nat. Acad. of Eng. of the U.S.A.; Fellow American Nuclear Soc.; mem. Soc. Française des Electriciens, and other socs.; Pugno Vanoni, Jona and Castellani Prizes, AEI, Simon Ramo Prize. *Address:* 5 Via Francesco Coletti, 00191 Rome, Italy (Home).

ANGELL, Wayne D., PH.D.; American economist; b. 1930, Kansas; m.; four c.; ed. Univ. of Kansas; Prof. Ottawa Univ. 1956–, Dean 1969–72; mem. Kansas House of Reps 1961–67; Dir. Fed. Reserve Bank, Kansas City 1979–; mem. of Fed. Reserve Bd. *Leisure interest:* tennis. *Address:* Federal Reserve System, 20th Street and Constitutional Avenue, N.W., Washington, D.C. 20551, U.S.A.

ANGELOU, Maya; American authoress; b. 4 April 1928, St. Louis; d. of Bailey Johnson and Vivian Baxter; one s.; Woman of Year in Communications 1976; TV appearances include: The Richard Pryor Special and Roots. *Publications:* I Know Why the Caged Bird Sings 1970, Just Give Me A Cool Drink of Water 'Fore I Die 1971, Georgia, Georgia 1972, Gather Together In My Name 1974, Oh Pray My Wings Are Gonna Fit Me Well 1975, Singin' and Swingin' and Gettin' Merry Like Christmas 1976, And Still I Rise 1976, The Heart of a Woman 1986, All God's Children Need Travelling Shoes 1987, Now Sheba Sings the Song 1987. *Address:* c/o Dave Le Camera Lordly and Dame Inc., 51 Church Street, Boston, Mass. 02116, U.S.A.

ANGELOZ, Eduardo César; Argentinian politician; b. 18 Oct. 1931, Rio Tercero, Córdoba; m. Marta Marin; three c.; ed. Universidad Nacional de Córdoba; active mem. Unión Civica Radical 1953–; Sec. Ministry of Public Works, Prov. of Córdoba 1955; Sec. Gen. Prov. Energy Corp., Córdoba 1956; Prov. Senator 1963; Nat. Senator, Sec. Comm. on Energy and Fuels, Nat. Senate 1973; mem. staff, OAS 1976; Gov. Prov. of Córdoba 1983–87, 1987–; candidate in presidential elections 1989. *Publications:* El Tiempo de los Argentinos, Tiempo de la Transición; numerous essays and articles. *Address:* c/o Unión Civica Radical, Buenos Aires, Argentina.

ANGENOT, Marc, D.PHIL., F.R.S.C.; Canadian professor of French and comparative literature; b. 21 Dec. 1941, Brussels; s. of Marcel Angenot and Zoé-Martha DeClercq; m. 1st Joséphine Brock 1966 (divorced 1976), one s. one d.; m. 2nd Nadia Khouri 1981, one d.; ed. Univ. Libre de Bruxelles; Prof. of French and Comparative Literature, McGill Univ. 1967–; Assoc. Dir Ecole des Hautes Etudes en Sciences Sociales, France 1985; Killam Fellowship 1987; Prix Biguet (Acad. Française) 1983. *Publications:* Le Roman populaire 1975, Les Champions des femmes 1977, Glossaire pratique de la critique contemporaine 1979, La Parole pamphlétaire 1982, Critique de la raison sémiotique 1985, Le Cru et le faisandé 1986; numerous articles and contributions in literary theory and discourse analysis. *Address:* 4572 Harvard Avenue, Montreal, H4A 2X2, Canada. *Telephone:* (514) 488-1388.

ANGERER, Paul; Austrian composer, conductor and instrumentalist; b. 16 May 1927, Vienna; s. of Otto and Elisabeth Angerer; m. Anita Rosser 1952; two s. two d.; ed. Hochschule für Musik und darstellende Kunst, Vienna; viola player, Vienna Symphony 1947, leading solo viola player 1953–57; viola player, Tonhaile Zürich 1948, Suisse Romande Orch., Geneva 1949; Dir. and Chief Conductor, Chamber Orch. of Wiener Konzerthausgesellschaft 1956–63; composer and conductor, Burgtheater, Vienna and Salzburg and Bregenz festivals 1960–; perm. guest conductor, Orchestra sinfonica di Bolzano e Trento "Haydn" 1964–; first conductor, Bonn city theatre 1964–66; music dir. Ulm theatre 1966–68; Chief of opera, Salzburger Landestheater 1967–72; Dir. S.W. German Chamber Orch., Pforzheim 1971–82; Prof. Hochschule, Vienna 1983–; leader of Concilium Musicum; several prizes including Austrian State Prize 1956, Theodor Körner Prize 1958, Vienna Cultural Prize 1983. *Works include:* orchestral pieces, chamber works, viola and piano concertos, a dramatic cantata, television opera, works for organ, harp, viola, harpsichord, etc.; numerous recordings both as soloist and conductor. *Address:* Esteplatz 3/26, A-1030 Vienna; Unternalb 21, A-2070 Retz, Austria. *Telephone:* 0222/75 12 71; 02942/ 25 85.

ANGREMY, Jean-Pierre (Pierre-Jean Rémy); French diplomatist; b. 21 March 1937; ed. Institut d'études politiques, Paris; served Hong Kong 1963–64, Beijing 1964–66, London 1966–71, 1975–79; Cultural, Scientific and Tech. Relations, Paris 1971–72; seconded to ORTF 1972–75; seconded to Ministry of Culture and Communication 1979–84; Consul, Florence 1984–87; Dir.-Gen. Cultural, Scientific and Tech. Relations 1987–. *Publications:* 25 novels and other publs. *Address:* Ministère des Affaires Etrangères, Quai d'Orsay, 75700 Paris, France. *Telephone:* (1) 45 55 95 40.

ANGUIANO, Raúl; Mexican painter; b. 26 Feb. 1915, Guadalajara, Jalisco; s. of José Anguiano and Abigail V. de Anguiano; one s. two d.; m. 2nd Brigita Anderson 1977; studied under José Vizcarra and Ixca Farias; concerned in Modern Art movement, Mexico 1934; founder mem. Taller de Gráfica Popular; studied at Art Students' League, New York 1941; one-man exhbns. in Mexico, Paris 1952, 1965, 1967, San Francisco 1953–65, Havana 1956, Chile 1960, Moscow 1962, Rome 1965–67, Miami 1965, San Antonio (Texas) 1966, Quito 1971, Mexico City 1972, Palm Springs, Calif. 1974; has exhibited in collective exhbns. in London, Warsaw, Tokyo, Berlin, Prague, Peking, Lille, Los Angeles, Lugano, etc.; works include murals for the Hormona Laboratories, Onyx-Mex industries and the Nat. Museum of Anthropology, Mexico City; has completed series of works about lacandones of Lacandona Jungle; retrospective exhbn. Salón de la Plástica Mexicana, Mexico 1969; guest teacher, lecturer and invited to exhibit works at Univ. of W. Indies, Kingston, Jamaica 1970; painted mural at Olympia Hotel, Kingston; numerous prizes; decoration granted by Italian Govt. 1977. *Leisure interests:* music, reading, writing. *Address:* Anaxágoras 1326, Colonia Narvarte, Mexico 13, D.F. Mexico. *Telephone:* 575-07 56, 575-14 54.

ANGUS, Michael Richardson, B.SC., C.B.I.M.; British company director; b. 5 May 1930, Ashford, Kent; s. of William Richardson Angus and Doris Margaret Breach; m. Eileen Isabel May Elliott 1952; two s. one d.; ed. Marling School, Stroud, Bristol Univ.; served in R.A.F. 1951–54; joined Unilever PLC 1954, Marketing Dir. Thibaud Gibbs, Paris 1962–65, Man. Dir. Research Bureau 1965–67, Sales Dir. Lever Brothers, U.K. 1967–70, Dir. Unilever PLC and Unilever N.V. May 1970–, Toilet Preparations Co-ordinator 1970–76, Chemicals Co-ordinator 1976–80, Regional Dir. N. America 1979–84, Chair. and C.E.O. Unilever United States Inc., New York 1980–84, Chair. and C.E.O. Lever Brothers Co., New York 1980–84, Vice-Chair. Unilever PLC 1984–86, Chair. May 1986–; Gov. Ashridge Man. Coll. 1974–; Jt. Chair. Netherlands-British Chamber of Commerce 1984–; Non-Exec. Dir. Whitbread and Co. PLC 1986–, Thorn EMI PLC 1988–, British Airways PLC 1988–; Trustee, Leverhulme Trust 1984–. *Leisure* *interests:* countryside, wine and puzzles. *Address:* Unilever PLC, P.O. Box 68, Unilever House, London, EC4P 4BQ, England. *Telephone:* 01-822 5252.

ANGYAL, Stephen John, O.B.E., PH.D., D.SC., F.A.A.; Australian (b. Hungarian) professor of organic chemistry; b. 21 Nov. 1914, Budapest; s. of Charles Engel and Maria Szanto; m. Helga Ellen Steininger 1941; one s. one d.; ed. Pazmany Peter Univ., Budapest; Research Chemist, Chinoin Pharmaceutical Works, Budapest 1937–40; Research Chemist, Nicholas Pty. Ltd., Melbourne, Australia 1941–46; Lecturer, Univ. of Sydney 1946–52; Nuffield Dominion Travelling Fellow 1952; Assoc. Prof. of Organic Chem., Univ. of N.S.W. 1953–60, Prof. 1960–80, Dean of Science 1970–79; H.G. Smith Memorial Medal, Royal Australian Chem. Inst. 1958, Haworth Medal and Lectureship, Royal Soc. of Chem. 1980, Hudson Award, American Chemical Soc. 1987. *Publications:* Conformational Analysis (with others) 1965; about 200 research publs. in chemical journals. *Leisure interests:* swimming, skiing, bushwalking, music. *Address:* 304 Sailors Bay Road, Northbridge, N.S.W. 2063, Australia. *Telephone:* (02) 958-7209.

ANIKST, Aleksandr Abramovich; Soviet literary critic, Shakespeare specialist and theatre critic; b. 1910, Zürich; mem. CPSU 1942–; first works published 1930. *Publications include:* History of English Literature 1956, Six Stories about American Theatre 1963, The Theatre of Shakespeare's Time 1965, The Theory of Drama from Aristotle to Lessing 1967, The Theory of Drama in Russia from Pushkin to Chekhov 1972, Shakespeare: The Playwright's Craft 1974, The First Editions of Shakespeare 1974.

ANIN, Patrick Dankwa, M.A., LL.B.; Ghanaian judge; b. 27 July 1928, Bekwai, Ashanti; m. Doris Marian Dadzie 1958; two s. two d.; ed. Achimota Coll., Selwyn Coll., Cambridge, and London School of Economics.; called to Bar, Middle Temple 1956, Called to Gold Coast Bar 1956; fmr. Dir. Bank of Ghana; mem. Electoral Comm. 1966–67; Commr. for Communications 1967–68, Commr. for External Affairs 1968–69; Justice of Appeal, Ghana Court of Appeal 1969–; Chair. Bribery and Corruption Comm. 1971–74; Chair. Council of Univ. of Ghana, Legon 1976–78; Justice of Appeal, Court of Appeal of The Gambia, Nov. 1978–. *Leisure interests:* reading, tennis. *Address:* Justice of Appeal's Chambers, Court of Appeal, Supreme Court, P.O. Box 119, Accra, Ghana.

ANISHCHEV, Vladimir Petrovich; Soviet politician; b. 1935; mem. CPSU 1961–; ed. Voronezh Inst. of Contruction Engineering; Komsomol work 1954, 1957–65; served in Soviet Army 1954–56; party work 1965–; deputy, head of section of Voronezh CPSU State Comm. 1970–72; deputy head of section of Voronezh District Cttee. of CPSU 1972–74; first sec. of Voronezh CPSU Regional Cttee. 1974–78; Pres. of Voronezh City Exec. Cttee. of CPSU 1978–80, first sec. 1980–85; work for CPSU Cen. Cttee. 1985–; sec. 1985–86, second sec. of Cen. Cttee. of Uzbek CP 1986–; mem. of Cen. Cttee. of CPSU 1986–; Deputy to U.S.S.R. Supreme Soviet. *Address:* Cen. Cttee. of Uzbek CP, Tashkent, U.S.S.R.

ANISIMOV, Anatoly Vasilevich; Soviet diplomatist; b. 1919; mem. diplomatic service 1946–; Counsellor, Iran Embassy 1961–65; mem. of Apparat of Ministry of Foreign Affairs 1965–68, 1972–77; Amb. to Jordan 1968–72, to Libya 1977–86. *Address:* Ministry of Foreign Affairs, The Kremlin, Moscow, U.S.S.R.

ANISIMOV, Pavel Petrovich; Soviet official; b. 1928; ed. Aeronautical Inst., Kazan; mem. CPSU 1952–; engineer, Sec. of Komsomol Cttee. 1952–55; Sec. Party Cttee., Zhdanov Works, Leningrad 1955–61; sr. posts in Leningrad CPSU 1961–64; City Sec. of CPSU, Leningrad 1964–68; Deputy Head of Party Org.; work with Cen. Cttee., CPSU 1968–73; Second Sec. and mem. Politburo, Cen. Cttee. of Armenian CP 1973–79; mem. Cen. Cttee., Armenian CP 1976–81; cand. mem. Cen. Cttee. CPSU 1976–81; cand. mem. Cen. Cttee. CPSU 1976–; Deputy Chair. State Planning Cttee. (Gosplan) of U.S.S.R. 1979–; Order of October Revolution. *Address:* State Planning Committee, Prospekt Marksa 12, Moscow, U.S.S.R. *Telephone:* (095) 292-80-00.

ANKERSMIT, Franklin Rudolf, PH.D.; Netherlands lecturer; b. 20 march 1945, Diepenveen; s. of R. Ankersmit and C.M. Ankersmit-Dekker; Assoc. Prof. History Dept., Groningen Univ. 1975, Sr. Lecturer in Intellectual History and Philosophy of History 1984–; mem. Royal Acad. of Sciences 1986. *Publications:* Narrative logic. A semantic analysis of the historian's language 1983, Denken over geschiedenis, een overzicht van moderne geschiedfilosofische opvattingen 1984, The reality effect in the writing of history. On art and history 1989. *Leisure interest:* music. *Address:* History Department, Groningen University, Grote Rozenstraat 38, 9712 TJ Groningen (Univ.); Oosterweg 65, 9751 PC Haren (Gn), The Netherlands (Home). *Telephone:* (0) 50-635984 (Univ.); (0) 50-348975 (Home).

ANKRAH, Gen. Joseph Arthur; Ghanaian army officer; b. 18 Aug. 1915, Accra; s. of Samuel P. K. Ankrah and Beatrice A. Quaynor; m. 1st Elizabeth Oyoe 1939, 2nd Felicia Kailey 1953, 3rd Mildred C. Akosua 1962; seven s. eleven d.; ed. Wesley Methodist School, Accra and Accra Acad.; comes from Ga tribe, S. Ghana; Warrant Officer II, Infantry and Staff, Second World War; commissioned 1947; Battalion Commdr., later Brigadier, Kasai Prov. Congo 1960–61, awarded Ghana Mil. Cross; Deputy Chief of Defence Staff, Ghana 1961–65; Chief of Defence Staff and Chair. Nat. Liberation Council, Ghana, 1966–69; Officer Order of the Volta, Grand Cordon Most Venerable Order of Knighthood of the Pioneers (Liberia).

Leisure interests: sport, horse racing, gardening, reading. *Address:* c/o House D594/3 Asylum Down, Accra, Ghana. *Telephone:* Accra 24583.

ANKUM, Hans (Johan Albert), D.JUR.; Netherlands professor of Roman Law; b. 23 July 1930, Amsterdam; s. of Lecndert and Johanna (née Van Kuykhof) Ankum; m. 1st Joke Houwink 1957 (divorced 1970); m. 2nd Pelline van Es 1970; one s. three d.; ed. Zaanlands Lyceum, Zaandam, Univ. of Amsterdam, Univ. of Paris; Asst. Roman Law and Juridical Papyrology, Univ. of Amsterdam 1956–60; Lecturer in Roman Law and Legal History, Univ. of Leyden 1960–63, Prof. 1965–69; Prof. of Roman Law, Legal History and Juridical Papyrology, Univ. of Amsterdam 1965–; mem. Royal Dutch Acad. of Sciences 1986–; Winkler Prins award; Dr. h.c. (Amsterdam). *Publications:* Die geschiedenis der 'Actio Pantiana'; numerous books and articles in Roman law and legal history. *Leisure interests:* classical music, history of art, travel. *Address:* Faculty of Law, University of Amsterdam, Oudezÿds Achterburgwal, NL-1012 DL Amsterdam 217-219 (Office); Zonnebloemlaan 8, NL-2111ZG Aerdenhout, The Netherlands (Home). *Telephone:* (20)-5253408 (Office); (23)-243036 (Home).

ANLYAN, William, B.S., M.D.; American professor of surgery and medical consultant; b. 14 Oct. 1925, Alexandria, Egypt; ed. Yale Univ. and Duke Univ. Hosp.; Instructor in Surgery Duke Univ. School of Medicine 1950–51, Assoc. 1951–53, Asst. Prof. of Surgery 1953–58, Assoc. Prof. 1958–61, Prof. 1961–, Assoc. Dean 1963–64, Dean 1964–69; Assoc. Provost Duke Univ. 1969, Vice-Pres. for Health Affairs 1969–83, Chancellor for Health Affairs 1983–, Exec. Vice-Pres. 1987–, Chancellor 1988–; numerous exec. posts Assccn. of American Medical Colls. 1965–, Distinguished Service Mem. 1974–, American Medical Assccn. 1971–74, American Surgical Assccn. 1970–; mem. Bd. of Dirs. Assccn. for Acad. Health Centers 1971–, Pres. 1974–75; mem. Research Strengthening Group for Special Programme for Research and Training in Tropical Diseases, WHO 1981–85, Chair. Univ. Council's Cttee. on Medical Affairs (WHO), Yale Univ. 1987–; mem. Council Govt.-Univ.-Industry Research Roundtable 1984–86; mem. several advisory and research cttees., N.C. 1965–; Consultant Gen. Surgery, Durham Veterans' Hosp. 1955–73; mem. U.S. dels. consulting on health and medical educ., China, Poland, Israel, Egypt, Saudi Arabia, Japan etc.; mem. Bd. of Regents Nat. Library of Medicine 1968–71, Chair. 1971–72, Consultant 1972–; mem. Bd. of Dirs. Wachovia Bank 1970–, G.D. Searle and Co. 1974–85, Pearle Health Services Inc. 1983–, N.C. Inst. of Medicine 1983–, Durham Chamber of Commerce Jan. 1988–; mem. Bds. of Visitors and Trustees numerous univs.; mem. numerous professional socs.; mem. Editorial Bd. The Pharos 1968–; Hon. D.S. (Rush Medical Coll.) 1973; Modern Medicine Award for Distinguished Achievement 1974, Gov.'s Award for Distinguished Meritorious Service 1978, Distinguished Surgeon Alumnus 1979, Yale Univ. School of Medicine, The Abraham Flexner Award, Asscn. of American Medical Colls. 1980, Civic Honor Award, Durham Chamber of Commerce 1981, Award of Merit, Duke Univ. Hosp. and Health Admin. Alumni Asscn. 1987. *Publications:* contrib. and ed. several books; over 100 articles in professional journals on health and surgical topics. *Address:* Duke University Medical Center (Box 3701), Durham, N.C. 27710 (Office); 1516 Pinecrest Road, Durham, N.C. 27705 U.S.A. (Home). *Telephone:* (919) 684-3438 (Office); (919) 489-3196 (Home).

ANN-MARGRET; American actress, singer and dancer; b. 1941, Stockholm, Sweden; m. Roger Smith 1967; film début in Pocketful of Miracles 1961. *Films include:* State Fair, Bye Bye Birdie, Once A Thief, The Cincinnati Kid, Stagecoach, Murderer's Row, C.C. & Co., Carnal Knowledge, RPM, The Train Robbers, Tommy, The Twist, Joseph Andrews, Last Remake of Beau Geste, Magic, Middle Age Crazy, Return of the Soldier, I Ought to Be in Pictures, Looking to Get Out, Twice in a Lifetime, 52 Pick-Up 1987, New Life 1988; also appears in cabaret and on TV. *Address:* Career Artists International, 11030 Ventura Blvd., Suite 3, Studio City, Calif., U.S.A.

ANNAKIN, Kenneth; British film director and writer; b. Beverley, Yorks. *Films include:* Across the Bridge, Swiss Family Robinson, Very Important Person, The Longest Day (British segment), The Fast Lady, The Informers, Those Magnificent Men in Their Flying Machines, Battle of the Bulge, The Long Duel, Monte Carlo or Bust, Call of the Wild, Paper Tiger, The Fifth Musketeer, The Pirate, Cheaper to Keep Her, The Pirate Movie, Pippi Longstocking. *Address:* c/o William Morris, 31 Soho Square, London, W.1, England.

ANNAN, Baron (Life Peer) cr. 1965, of Royal Burgh of Annan; **Noel Gilroy Annan,** O.B.E., M.A.; British university official; b. 25 Dec. 1916, London; s. of late James Gilroy Annan and Fannie Quinn; m. Gabriele Ullstein 1950; two d.; ed. Stowe School, King's Coll., Cambridge.; served in War Office, War Cabinet Offices and Mil. Intelligence 1940–44, France and Germany 1944–46; Gen. Staff Officer, Political Division, British Control Comm. 1945–46; Fellow, King's Coll., Cambridge 1944–56, 1966, Asst. Tutor 1947, Lecturer in Politics 1948–66, Provost 1956–66; Provost of Univ. Coll., London 1966–78; Vice-Chancellor, Univ. of London 1978–81; Gov. of Stowe School 1945–66, Queen Mary Coll. 1956–60; Senior Fellow, Eton Coll. 1956–66; mem. Gulbenkian Cttee. for Art in U.K. 1957–64, Chair. Educ. Cttee. 1971–76; mem. Academic Planning Board, Univ. of East Anglia 1960; Chair. Academic Planning Board, Univ. of Essex 1962; mem. Academic Advisory Board Brunel Univ. 1964; mem. Public Schools Comm. 1966–70; Chair. Cttee. on Future of Broadcasting 1974–77; Trustee, British

Museum 1963-78, Nat. Gallery 1978- (Chair. 1980-); Dir. Royal Opera House, Covent Garden 1966-78; F.R.Hist.S.; Fellow, Berkeley Coll., Yale 1963; Hon. Fellow, Univ. Coll., London 1968; Emer. Fellow, Leverhulme Trust 1984; Hon. D.Litt. (York, Ontario, New York Univ.); D.Univ. (Essex); Hon. D.Laws (Univ. of Pennsylvania); Foreign Hon. mem. American Acad. of Arts and Sciences; Le Bas Prize 1948, James Tait Black Memorial Prize 1951, Clark Kerr Medal (Univ. of Calif., Berkeley) 1985. *Publications:* Leslie Stephen: His Thought and Character in Relation to His Time 1951, The Intellectual Aristocracy (in Studies in Social History, edited by J. H. Plumb) 1956, The Curious Strength of Positivism in English Political Thought 1959, Kipling's Place in the History of Ideas (in Kipling's Mind and Art) 1964, Roxburgh of Stowe 1965, Annan Report on the Future of Broadcasting 1977, and articles in Victorian Studies and other periodicals. *Leisure interest:* writing English prose. *Address:* 16 St. John's Wood Road, London, NW8 8RE, England. *Telephone:* 01-289 2555.

ANNE, H.R.H. The Princess (see Royal, H.R.H. The Princess.)

ANNENBERG, Walter H.; American publisher and diplomatist; b. 13 March 1908, Milwaukee, Wis.; s. of M. L. Annenberg; m. 1st Veronica Dunkelman (divorced), one d.; m. 2nd Leonore Cohn 1951; Pres. Triangle Publications Inc., Pa.; publishes TV Guide; Pres. M. L. Annenberg Foundation, Annenberg Fund; Amb. to U.K. 1969-75; Founder of Annenberg School of Communications at Univ. of Pa. and Univ. of S. Calif.; Trustee Nat. Trust for Historic Preservation, Univ. of Pa.; Emer. Trustee, Eisenhower Medical Center; several hon. degrees; Officier, Légion d'honneur; Commdr., Orders of Lion of Finland, Crown of Italy; Commdr. Order of Merit (Italy); Hon. K.B.E.; Presidential Medal of Freedom 1986. *Address:* 250 King of Prussia Road, Radnor, Pa. 19088 (Office); Llanfair Road, Wynnewood, Pa. 19096, U.S.A. (Home).

ANNESLEY, Hugh; British police officer; b. 1939, Dublin; m.; two c.; joined Metropolitan Police 1958; Asst. Chief Constable of Sussex with special responsibility for personnel and training 1976; Deputy Asst. Commr., Metropolitan Police 1981, Asst. Commr. 1985; Head Operations Dept., Scotland Yard 1987-89; Chief Constable of the Royal Ulster Constabulary June 1989-; Queen's Police Medal 1986. *Address:* Brooklyn, Knock Road, Belfast, BT5 6LE, N. Ireland. *Telephone:* Belfast 652062.

ANNIS, Francesca; British actress; d. of Anthony Annis and Mariquita Annis; unmarried, one s. two d. by Patrick Wiseman; with R.S.C. 1975-78. *Plays include:* The Tempest, The Passion Flower Hotel, Hamlet, Troilus and Cressida, Comedy of Errors, The Heretic. *Films include:* Cleopatra, Saturday Night Out, Murder Most Foul, The Pleasure Girls, Run With the Wind, The Sky Pirates, The Walking Stick, Penny Gold, Macbeth, Krull, Dune, Under the Cherry Moon, Golden River, El Rio de Oro. *Television includes:* Great Expectations, Children in Uniform, Love Story, Danger Man, The Human Jungle, Lily Langtry (role of Lily), Madame Bovary, Partners in Crime, Coming Out of Ice, Why Didn't They Ask Evans?, Magnum P.I., Inside Story. *Address:* c/o Dennis Sellinger, ICM, 388-396 Oxford Street, London, W.1., England.

ANNORKWEI II, Nene, Q.M.C.; Ghanaian chief; b. 1900; ed. Wesleyan School, Accra; entered Nigerian civil service as Treasury Clerk 1919; transferred to Gold Coast 1930; promoted to Accountant 1944; elected Manche of Prampram 1948; appointed Treas. of Provincial Council, Eastern Province, and mem. Council's Standing Cttee. 1948; later Pres. Joint Provincial Council of Chiefs (representing Eastern and Western Regions); Chair. Ghana Museum and Monuments Board 1957-; Queen's Medal for Chiefs 1956. *Address:* Manche of Prampram, Prampram, Ghana.

ANSELL, Barbara Mary, C.B.E., M.D., F.R.C.S., F.R.C.P.; British doctor; b. 30 Aug. 1923, Warwick; d. of Herbert Joseph Ansell and Annie Olivia Ansell; m. Angus Harold Weston; ed. King's High School for Girls, Warwick, Birmingham Medical School; Research Fellow, Research and Educ. Hosp., Chicago, U.S.A. 1953-54; Consultant Physician (Rheumatology), Canadian Red Cross Memorial Hosp., Taplow, Bucks. 1962; Head, Div. of Rheumatology, Clinical Research Centre, Northwick Park Hosp., Harrow, Middx. 1976-88; Queen's Prize, Birmingham Univ. 1944. *Publications:* Surgical Management of Juvenile Chronic Polyarthritis (with G.P. Arden) 1978, Rheumatic Disorders in Childhood 1980, Inflammatory Disorders in Muscle: in Clinics in Rheumatic Diseases 1984. *Leisure interests:* opera, travel, food, wine. *Address:* The Consulting Rooms, 9 Beaumont Road, Windsor, Berks.; Dumgoyne, Templewood Lane, Stoke Poges, Bucks., SL2 4BG, England.

ANSELL, Graham Keith, B.A. (HONS.); New Zealand diplomatist; b. 2 March 1931, Lower Hutt, New Zealand; m. Mary Diana Wilson 1953; three s. one d.; ed. Horowhenua Coll., Palmerston North Boys' School and Victoria Univ., Wellington. Dept. of Industries and Commerce 1948-51, of External Affairs 1951-56; Second Sec., High Comm. to Ottawa 1956-59; Asst., then Acting Head, Econ. and Social Affairs Div., Dept. of External Affairs 1959-62; Deputy High Commr., Apia 1962-64, Canberra 1964-68; Head, Econ. Div., Ministry of Foreign Affairs 1968-71; Minister, N.Z. Embassy, Tokyo 1971-73; High Commr. in Fiji 1973-76, in Nauru 1974-76; Amb. to Belgium, Luxembourg and the European Communities (also accred. to Denmark) 1977-81; Dir. N.Z. Planning Council 1981-82; Amb. to Japan 1983-84; Deputy Sec. Ministry of Foreign Affairs 1984-85; High Commr. in Australia 1985-89. *Leisure interests:* music, walking, horticul-

ture. *Address:* New Zealand High Commission, Commonwealth Avenue, Canberra, A.C.T. 2600 (Office); 21 Mugga Way, Red Hill, Canberra, A.C.T., Australia (Home).

ANSELMI, Tina; Italian politician; b. 25 March 1927, Castelfranco Veneto; worked for the resistance with Cesare Battisti Brigade; mem. Democrazia Cristiana (DC) 1944-; concerned mainly with questions of family affairs and industrial relations; fmr. Vice-Pres. European Feminist Union; mem. Parl. 1968-; fmr. Under-Sec. in Ministry of Labour; Minister of Labour 1976-78, of Health 1978-79. *Address:* Castelfranco Veneto, Italy (Home).

ANSI, Saud bin Salim al-, B.A.; Omani diplomatist; b. 23 Dec. 1949, Salalah; m.; four c.; ed. Beirut Univ.; Ministry of Information and Culture and of Diwan Affairs 1974-75; Dir. Dept. of Research and Studies 1976-78; First Sec. Embassy, Tunis 1975-76, Consul-Gen., Karachi 1978-80, Amb. to Djibouti 1980-82, to Kuwait 1982-84; Perm. Rep. to the UN 1984-88. *Address:* c/o Permanent Mission of Oman to the United Nations, 866 United Nations Plaza, Suite 540, New York, N.Y. 10017, U.S.A. *Telephone:* 355-3505.

ANSIMOV, Georgiy Pavlovich; Soviet theatre director; b. 1922; ed. Lunacharsky State Inst. of Theatre, Art and Cinema (under B.A. Pokrovsky); Artistic Dir. of GABT 1955-64, 1980-; Artistic Dir. and main producer, Moscow Operetta Theatre 1964-76; main productions: Story of a Real Man (Prokofiev); Carmen, The Tale of Tsar Sultan (Rimsky Korsakov), West Side Story, Orpheus in the Underworld, War and Peace (Prokofiev); Bethrothal in the Monastery (Prokofiev). Teaches at Lunacharsky Inst., Professor 1977-; U.S.S.R State Artist 1986. *Address:* Lunacharsky Institute, Moscow, U.S.S.R.

ANSON, John, C.B., M.A.; British civil servant; b. 3 Aug. 1930, Yeovil; s. of late Sir Edward R. Anson and of the Dowager Lady Anson; m. Myrica Fergie-Woods 1957; two s. two d.; ed. Winchester Coll., and Magdalene Coll., Cambridge; served H.M. Treasury 1954-68; Financial Counsellor, British Embassy, Paris 1968-70; Asst. Sec. Cabinet Office 1971-72, Under-Sec. 1972-74; Under-Sec. H.M. Treasury 1974-77, Deputy Sec. 1977-87; Head, Treasury Del. and Econ. Minister, British Embassy, Washington, D.C., and U.K. Exec. Dir. IMF and IBRD (World Bank) 1983-; Second Perm. Sec. (Public Expenditure), H.M. Treasury 1987-; Smith's Prize, Cambridge Univ. 1954. *Address:* c/o H.M. Treasury, Parliament Street, London, SW1P 3AG, England. *Telephone:* 01-270 3000.

ANSON, Malcolm Allinson, M.A.; British business executive; b. 23 April 1924, Bristol; s. of Sir (George) Wilfrid Anson and Dinah Maud Lilian Anson (née Bourne); m. Isabel Alison Valerie Lothian 1950; three s. one d.; ed. Winchester and Trinity Coll., Oxford; Royal Horse Artillery, Europe and India 1943-46; joined Imperial Group; W. A. & A. C. Churchman 1948-50, W. D. & H. O. Wills 1950-67; Imperial Tobacco Ltd. HQ 1967; Asst. Man. Dir. ITL 1973-77; Deputy Chief Exec. Imperial Group 1978-79, Deputy Chair. 1979, Chair. 1980-81; Dir. Nat. Westminster Bank 1981-85; Chair. Wessex Water Authority 1982-87, Careers Advisory Bd., Bristol Univ. 1971-, mem. Univ. Council; High Sheriff of Avon 1977-78; Vice-Chair. Clifton Coll. Council 1978-; Master Soc. of Merchant Venturers, Bristol 1979-80. *Leisure interests:* skiing, sailing, golf, shooting. *Address:* Hill Court, Congresbury, Bristol, BS19 5AD, England (Home). *Telephone:* Yatton 832117 (Home).

ANSTEE, Margaret Joan, M.A., B.SC. (ECON.); British United Nations official; b. 25 June 1926; d. of Edward C. Anstee and Anne A. Mills; ed. Chelmsford Co. High School for Girls, Newham Coll. Cambridge and Univ. of London; Lecturer in Spanish, Queen's Univ. Belfast 1947-48; Third Sec. Foreign Office 1948-52; UN Tech. Assistance Bd. Manila 1952-54; Spanish Supervisor, Univ. of Cambridge 1955-56; UN Tech. Assistance Bd. Bogotá 1956-57, Uruguay 1957-59, Bolivia 1960-65; Resident Rep. UNDP Ethiopia and UNDP Liaison Officer with ECA 1965-67; Sr. Econ. Adviser, Office of Prime Minister, London 1967-68; Sr. Asst. to Commr. in charge of study of Capacity of UN Devt. System 1968-69; Resident Rep. UNDP, Morocco 1969-72, Chile (also UNDP Liaison Officer with ECLA) 1972-74; Deputy to UN Under Sec.-Gen. in charge of UN Relief Operation to Bangladesh and Deputy Co-ordinator of UN Emergency Assistance to Zambia 1973; with UNDP, New York 1974-78; Asst. Sec.-Gen. of UN (Dept. of Tech. Co-operation for Devt.) 1978-85; Under Sec.-Gen., Dir-Gen. of UN office at Vienna, Head of Centre for Social Devt. and Humanitarian Affairs, June 1987-; Special Rep. of Sec.-Gen. to Bolivia 1982-85, for co-ordination of earthquake relief assistance to Mexico 1985-87; Co-ordinator of UN Drug Control Related Activities June 1987-; decorations from Mexico and Bolivia. *Publications:* The Administration of International Development Aid 1969, Gate of the Sun: A Prospect of Bolivia 1970, Africa and the World (ed. with R. K. A. Gardiner and C. Patterson) 1970. *Leisure interests:* writing, gardening, hill-walking (preferably in the Andes), birdwatching, swimming. *Address:* Vienna International Centre, P.O. Box 500, A-1400, Vienna, Austria.

ANTES, Horst; German painter and sculptor; b. 28 Oct. 1936, Heppenheim a.d.B.; s. of Valentin Antes and Erika Antes; m. Dorothea Grossmann 1961; one s. one d.; ed. State Acad. of Fine Arts, Karlsruhe; worked in Florence, then Rome; Prof. at State Acad. of Fine Arts, Karlsruhe 1965-71, 1984-; mem. Acad. der Künste, Berlin, now living in Berlin, Karlsruhe and Tuscany, Italy; Villa Romana Prize, Florence 1962; Villa Massimo

Prize, Rome 1963; UNESCO Prize, Venice Biennale 1966. One-man shows: Troisième Biennale de Paris, Museum Ulm, Städtische Galerie Munich 1964; Gallery Stangl Munich 1965, 1968, 1972, 1975; Galerie Defet, Nuremberg 1966, 1972, 1976, 1978, 1984, 1988; Galerie Krohn, Badenweiler 1964, 1967, 1977, 1984; Gimpel and Hanover Gallery, Zürich and London 1967, 1970, 1973, 1976, 1980; Lefèbre Gallery, New York 1967, 1969, 1972, 1974, 1976, 1978, 1980, 1982, 1984, 1985, 1986; 10th Biennale São Paulo 1969, Staatliche Kunsthalle Baden-Baden, Kunsthalle Bern, Kunsthalle Bremen, Frankfurter Kunstverein 1971–72; Badischer Kunstverein Karlsruhe 1978; Galerie Gunzenhauser, Munich 1979, 1981, 1983, 1986, 1987, Galerie Brusberg, Hanover 1979, 1982, 1983; Brühl, Schloss Augustenburg 1980; Galerie Valentien, Stuttgart 1966, 1970, 1981, Nishimura Gallery, Tokyo 1981, 1984; Galerie Der Spiegel, Cologne 1960, 1963, 1965, 1982, 1984, 1987; Kunsthalle, Bremen 1983, Sprengel Museum, Hannover 1983, Wilh-Hack Museum, Ludwigshafen 1982; Guggenheim Museum, New York 1984; Galerie Neumann, Düsseldorf 1985; Städt. Galerie, Villingen-Schwerringen u. Kunstverein Hochrhein, Bad Säckingen 1987; Galerie Levy, Hamburg 1988; Freie Akad. der Künste, Hamburg 1988; Galerie Bernd Lutze, Friedrichshaffen 1988; Group exhbns.: Pittsburgh Int. Exhbn. 1961, 1964, 1970, 1977; Dokumenta, Kassel 1964, 1968, 1977; Europalia, Brussels 1977; Im Namen des Volkes, Duisburg, Remscheid, Vienna, Sculptures Européennes, Brussels 1979; Skulptur im 20. Jahrhundert, Basel Wenkenpark 1980; Meridian House International, Washington, D.C., Deweer Art Gallery, Belgien, Galerie Der Spiegel, Cologne, Grosse Kunstausstellung, Munich, Triennale für Kleinplastik, Budapest 1981, Nat. Museum, Seoul, Goethe Inst., London 1983, Athens 1984; Neue Darmstädter Sezession, Darmstadt, Staatsgalerie, Stuttgart 1982; Nationalgalerie, Berlin 1985, Taimer Gallery, Tokyo 1986, Positionen-Malerei aas der BRD, Berlin, Dresden 1986, Hannover 1987; Interfacies 1986; Palma de Mallorca 1986; Intergrafik D.D.R., Berlin 1987; Int. Art Show for End of World Hunger, Minn. etc. 1987; Guggenheim Museum, New York 1987; Aalborg 1988, Toledo Museum of Art, Ohio 1988; Catalogues: Catalog of Etchings 1962–66 (G. Gercken) 1968, Catalog of Books (W. Euler) 1968, Catalog of Steel Sculptures (H. G. Sperlich) 1976, Catalog of Lithographs (B. Lutze) 1976, 25 Votive (1983/84). *Address:* Hohenbergstrasse 11, 7500 Karlsruhe 41 (Wolfartsweier), Federal Republic of Germany. *Telephone:* (0721) 491621.

ANTHONY, Rt. Hon. (John) Douglas, P.C., C.H.; Australian farmer, business executive and fmr. politician; b. 31 Dec. 1929, Murwillumbah; s. of Hubert Lawrence and Jessie (née Stirling) Anthony; m. Margot Macdonald Budd 1957; two s. one d.; ed. Murwillumbah High School, The King's School, Paramatta, and Queensland Agricultural Coll.; mem. House of Reps. 1957–84, Exec. Council 1963–72, 1975–, Minister for the Interior 1964–67, of Primary Industry 1967–71, for Trade and Industry 1971–72, for Overseas Trade 1975–77, for Minerals and Energy Nov.-Dec. 1975, for Nat. Resources 1975–77, for Trade and Resources 1977–83; Deputy Prime Minister Feb. 1971-Dec. 1972, 1975–83; Deputy Leader Nat. Country Party of Australia (now Nat. Party of Australia) 1966–71, Leader 1971–84; Dir. numerous cos. *Leisure interests:* golf, tennis, swimming. *Address:* Sunnymeadows, Muruillumbah, N.S.W. 2484, Australia.

ANTICO, Sir Tristan, Kt., A.C.; Australian business executive; b. 25 March 1923; m. Dorothy Bridget Shields 1950; three s. four d.; ed. Sydney Boys' High School; Co. Sec. Melocco Bros. Pty. Ltd.; f. A & C Concrete (now Pioneer Int. Ltd.) 1959, Chair. 1959–; Chair. Ampol Ltd, Ampol Exploration Ltd.; Dir. Qantas Airways Ltd., Giant Resources Ltd.; Trustee Art Gallery N.S.W. Foundation, Randwick Racecourse; former Chair. St. Vincent's Hosp., Dir. Exec. Bd., AMCHAM, Pres. Italian Chamber of Commerce; former mem. Export Devt. Advisory Council, numerous advisory Bds.; Commendatore-Dell'Ordine Della Stella Della Solidarieta Italiana. *Leisure interests:* horse-racing, horse-breeding, swimming, boating. *Address:* 11th Floor, 55 Macquarie Street, Sydney, N.S.W. 2000 (Office); 161 Raglan Street, Mosman, Sydney, N.S.W. 2088, Australia (Home). *Telephone:* 279231 (Office); 9694070 (Home).

ANTON, Ioan, DR.ENG.; Romanian professor of fluid flow machinery; b. 18 July 1924, Vintere; s. of Mihai Anton; m. Viorica Flueraş 1949; one s. one d.; ed. Polytech. Inst. of Timişoara; Assoc. Prof. 1951, Prof. 1962; Dean, Faculty of Mech. Eng., Polytech. Inst. of Timişoara 1961–63, Head, Fluid Flow Machine Dept. 1962–73, 1982, Rector 1971–81; Dir. Tech. Research Centre, Timişoara, Romanian Acad. 1969–70; Dir. Research Lab. for Hydraulic Machines, Timişoara 1970–74; Vice-Pres. Nat. Council for Science and Tech. 1973–79; Vice-Pres. Romanian Acad. 1974–; State Prize 1953, Aurel Vlaicu Prize, Romanian Acad. 1958. *Publications:* Experimental Testing of Fluid Flow Machines (with A. Bărglăzan) 1952, Hydraulic Turbines 1979, Cavitation, Vol. 1 1984, Vol. 2 1985, Hydrodynamics of Bulb Type Turbines and Bold Type Pump-Turbines (with V. Cîmpeanu and I. Carte) 1988 and over 175 papers on hydraulic machines, cavitation and boiling, and magnetic fluids. *Address:* 1900 Timişoara, Bd. Mihai Viteazul nr. 1, Romania. *Telephone:* 961-12496.

ANTONAKAKIS, Dimitris; Greek architect; b. 22 Dec. 1933, Chania, Crete; m. Suzana Maria (née Kolokytha) Antonakakis (q.v.) 1961; one s. one d.; ed. School of Architecture, Nat. Tech. Univ. Athens; partnership with Suzana Antonakakis (q.v.), Athens 1959–; Asst. Instructor in Architecture 1959–64; Founder and Prin. (with S. Antonakakis) Atelier 66 1965; Instructor Architecture, Nat. Tech. Univ., Athens 1964–78, Lecturer 1978–; mem. and Treas. Admin. Cttee., Greek Architectural Asscn. 1962–63; Pres.

Asscn. of Assts. and Instructors, Nat. Tech. Univ. 1975–77; Vice-Pres. Cen. Admin. Cttee., Asscn. of Assts. and Instructors of Greek Univs. 1976–77; numerous awards and prizes. *Works include:* Archaeological Museum, Chios 1965–66, Hotel Hydra Beach, Hermionis 1965–69, vertical additions, House in Port Phaliron 1967–72, miners' housing complex, Distomo 1969, apartment bldg., Em. Benaki 118, Athens 1973–74, holiday house, Spata 1973–75, Hotel Lyttos, Heraclion, Crete 1973–82, Zannas House, Philopapos Hill, Athens 1980–82. *Publications:* numerous architectural articles. *Address:* Atelier 66, Em. Benaki 118, Athens 114-73, Greece. *Telephone:* 3617-768, 3634-451.

ANTONAKAKIS, Suzana Maria; Greek architect; b. 25 June 1935, Athens; m. Dimitris Antonakakis (q.v.) 1961; one s. one d.; ed. School of Architecture, Nat. Tech. Univ., Athens; partnership with Dimitris Antonakakis, Athens 1959–; Founder and Co-Prin. (with Dimitris Antonakakis) Atelier 66 1965–; mem. Admin. Cttee. Greek Architects Asscn. 1971–72; Pres. Dept. of Architecture, Tech. Chamber of Greece 1982–83; numerous awards and prizes. *Works include:* Archaeological Museum, Chios 1965–66, Hotel Hydra Beach, Hermionis 1965–69, vertical additions, House in Port Phaliron 1967–72, miners' housing complex, Distomo 1969, apartment bldg., Em. Benaki 118, Athens 1973–74, holiday house, Spata 1973–75, Hotel Lyttos, Heraclion, Crete 1973–82, Zannas House, Philopapos Hill, Athens 1980–82. *Publications:* numerous architectural articles; trans. Entretien (Le Corbusier) 1971. *Address:* Atelier 66, Em. Benaki 118, Athens 114-73, Greece. *Telephone:* 3617-768, 3634-451.

ANTOÑANZAS, Juan Miguel, D.ENG.; Spanish engineer and business executive; b. 4 Oct. 1932, San Sebastián; s. of Adolfo Antoñanzas and Ana Pérez Egea; m. Pilar Toledo 1957; eight s. two d.; ed. Colegio del Pilar, Madrid, Madrid Univ.; Commercial Gen. Man., Barreiros 1959–62; Operations Gen. Man., Barreiros-Chrysler 1962–69; Gen. Man. Marconi Española (ITT) 1969–74; Asst. to Pres. Instituto Nacional de Industria 1974–75, Chair. and Exec. Pres. 1977–79; Chair. and Exec. Pres., SEAT, S.A. 1977–84; Vice-Chair. Tecnicas Reunidas 1984–87; Exec. Dir. Russell Reynolds Assocs. 1988; dir. of numerous corpns.; Victor de Plata; Gran Cruz del Mérito Militar; Gran Cruz de Mauritania. *Leisure interests:* reading, art, theatre, outdoor living. *Address:* Doctor Arce, 20, Madrid-2, Spain (Home).

ANTONELLI, H.E. Cardinal Ferdinando Giuseppe; Italian ecclesiastic; b. 14 July 1896, Subbiano, Arezzo; ordained priest 1922; Titular Archbishop of Idicra 1966; cr. Cardinal 1973; Deacon of Church of S. Sebastiano al Palatino, Rome –1984. *Address:* 00153 Roma, Piazza S. Calisto 16, Italy. *Telephone:* 698.71.24.

ANTONIO (Antonio Ruiz Soler); Spanish dancer; b. 4 Nov. 1921, Seville; s. of Francisco and Maria Dolores Soler; danced with Rosario under name Los Chavalillos Sevillanos, later Rosario and Antonia until 1952; with own company, Antonio, Ballet Español 1952– and Antonio y sus Ballets de Madrid 1964; Dir. Spanish Nat. Ballet 1980–; Cross of Isabel la Católica; Gold Medal of Swedish Dance Acad.; Medal of Ministry of Information 1963; Cross of Commdr. of Civil Merit; Gold Plate of Spanish Artists Syndicate; Silver Plate of Ministry of Information to First Dancer of Spain; Gold Medal, Spanish Inst. of New York 1979; Medal of Work and numerous other medals and decorations. *Address:* Coslada 7, Madrid, Spain. *Telephone:* Madrid 256-24-01.

ANTONIONI, Michelangelo, L. ECON. AND COMM.; Italian film director; b. 29 Sept. 1912, Ferrara; s. of Carlo and Elisabetta Antonioni; m. 1st Letizia Balboni 1942; m. 2nd Enrica Fico 1986; ed. Univ. of Bologna; Film critic Corriere Padano and L'Italia Libera; City of Munich Prize 1968. *Films:* Gente del Po 1943–47, Amorosa Menzogna 1949, N.U. 1948, Sette Canne un Vestito, La Villa dei Mostri, Superstizione 1949 (documentaries); Cronaca di un Amore 1950, La Signora Senza Camelie 1951–52, I Vinti 1952, Amore in Città 1953, Le Amiche 1955, Il Grido 1957, L'Avventura 1959 (Critics' Award, Cannes 1960), La Notte 1961 (Silver Bear, Berlin Film Festival 1961), L'Eclisse 1962, Il Deserto Rosso 1964 (Golden Lion, XXV Venice Film Festival 1964), Blow Up 1966 (Golden Palm, Cannes Film Festival 1967; Best Dir., Annual Awards of the Nat. Soc. of Film Critics), Zabriskie Point 1970, Chung Kuo-China 1972, The Passenger 1974, Il Mistero di Oberwald 1979, Identificazione di una Donna 1982 (Grand Prix, Cannes Film Festival 1982). *Leisure interests:* tennis, ping-pong. *Address:* Via Vincenzo Tiberio 18, 00191 Rome, Italy.

ANTONIY, Metropolitan (Anatoly Melnikov), D.THEOL.; Soviet ecclesiastic; b. 19 Feb. 1924, Moscow; unmarried; ed. Moscow Theol. Inst., Moscow Theol. Acad.; ordained Russian Orthodox Priest 1950; Asst. Rector, Odessa Theol. Seminary 1950–52, Saratov Theol. Seminary 1952–56; elevated to rank of Archimandrite 1956; Rector, Minsk Theol. Seminary and Dean, Gyrovitsi Dormition Monastery 1956–63; Rector, Odessa Theol. Seminary 1963–65; Bishop of Belgorod-Dnestrovsky, Vicar of Odessa Diocese 1964; Bishop of Minsk 1965, Archbishop of Minsk 1965, Metropolitan of Minsk and Byelorussia 1975–78 of Leningrad and Novgorod 1978–; Perm mem. Holy Synod of Moscow Patriarchate; Chair. Leningrad Section, Dept. of External Church Affairs; Ed. The Theological Magazine; Hon. mem. Moscow Theol. Acad., Leningrad Theol. Acad. 1979. *Publications:* Pastoral Observance according to St. John Chrysostom 1950, The Cyrovitsi Monastery in the History of Western Russian Dioceses 1470-1956 1963, publs. in theol. journals. *Leisure interests:* scientific and theological books. *Address:* Obvodny 17, Leningrad, C-167, U.S.S.R.

ANTONOV, Alexei Konstantinovich; Soviet politician; b. 8 June 1912; ed. Leningrad Polytechnic Inst. Engineer, later Chief Factory Engineer 1935-37; econ. work, Leningrad Regional Econ. Cttee. 1957-59, Deputy Chair. Leningrad Regional Econ. Cttee. 1959-61, Chair. 1961-65; mem. CPSU 1940-; Cand. mem. Cen. Cttee. of CPSU 1961-72, mem. 1972-; Minister of Electro-Tech. Industry (U.S.S.R.) 1965-80; a Vice-Chair. Council of Ministers Dec. 1980-; Perm. Rep. to COMECON (CMEA) Nov. 1985-; Deputy to U.S.S.R. Supreme Soviet 1962-; U.S.S.R. State Prize, Order of Lenin (twice) and other decorations. *Address:* c/o Council for Mutual Economic Assistance, Prospekt Kalinina 56, Moscow 121205, U.S.S.R.

ANTONOV, Sergei Fyodorovich; Soviet engineer, diplomatist and politician; b. 25 Sept. 1911, Pokrovskoe, Tyumen Oblast; ed. Leningrad Inst. of Engineers for Dairy Products Industry and Higher Party School of Cen. Cttee.; worked fmrly. in agencies and ministries of meat and milk industry; Minister of Milk and Dairy Products Industry 1954-57; Envoy-Counsellor, Embassy to People's Repub. of China 1958-60; Amb. to Afghanistan 1960-65; Minister of Meat and Milk Industry 1965-84; Deputy U.S.S.R. Supreme Soviet 1966-; mem CPSU 1937-, mem. Central Auditing Comm. CPSU 1966-76; mem. Cen. Cttee. CPSU 1976-; Order of Lenin, Order of October Revolution and other decorations. *Address:* c/o Ministry of Meat and Milk Industry, Moscow, U.S.S.R.

ANTONOV, Sergei Petrovich; Soviet writer and critic; b. 1915, Petrograd; m.; 4 c.; ed. Leningrad Highway Inst.; writer 1947-; State Prize 1951. *Publications include:* novels and stories: Lena 1948, Rains 1951, The Penkovo Affair 1956, Empty Journey 1960, Alenka 1960, Torn Rouble Note 1966, Silver Wedding 1972, The Three Warrior-Knights 1973; Vaska 1987, Ravines 1988; *criticism:* Letters about the Short-Story 1964, First-Person Narrative 1973, The Word 1974. *Address:* Ul. W. Ulbricht 16, ap. 72, 125252, Moscow, U.S.S.R.

ANUSZKIEWICZ, Richard Joseph, M.F.A., B.S.; American artist; b. 23 May 1930, Erie, Pa.; s. of Adam Jacob Anuszkiewicz and Victoria Jankowski; m. Sarah Feeney 1960; one s. one d.; ed. Cleveland Inst. of Art, Yale Univ., Kent State Univ.; one-man exhbns. at Butler Art Inst., Youngstown, Ohio 1955, The Contemporaries, New York 1960, 1961, 1963, Sidney Janis Gallery, New York 1965-67, Cleveland Museum of Art 1967, Kent State Univ. 1968, Andrew Crispo Gallery, New York 1975, 1977, La Jolla Museum of Contemporary Art, Calif. 1976, Univ. Art Museum, Berkeley, Calif. 1977, Columbus Gallery of Fine Arts, Ohio 1977; represented in numerous group exhbns. including Museum of Modern Art 1960-61, 1963, 1965, Washington Gallery of Modern Art 1963, Tate Gallery, London 1964, Art Fair, Cologne 1967, etc.; represented in perm. collections at Museum of Modern Art, Whitney Museum of American Art, Albright-Knox Art Gallery, Butler Art Inst., Yale Art Gallery, Chicago Art Inst., Fogg Art Museum, Harvard Univ., etc.; artist-in-residence Dartmouth 1967, Univ. of Wis. 1968, Cornell Univ. 1968, Kent State Univ. 1968. *Publications:* articles in learned journals. *Address:* c/o Crispo Gallery, 41 East 57th Street, New York, N.Y. 10022, U.S.A.

ANWAR SANI, Chaidir; Indonesian diplomatist; b. 19 Feb. 1918, Padang; m.; six c.; ed. Univ. of Leyden, Netherlands; First Sec., Indonesian Embassy, Paris 1950-52; Ministry of Foreign Affairs, Djakarta, Chief Asian Div. 1952-55, Deputy Head Asian and Pacific Directorate 1957-60, Head Directorate of Int. Orgs. 1965-66, Chef de Cabinet 1966 and Dir.-Gen. of Political Affairs 1966-70; Counsellor, Embassy, Cairo 1955 and Peking 1955-57; Minister Counsellor, Embassy, New Delhi 1960-64; Amb. to Belgium and Luxembourg and Head Indonesian Mission to the EEC 1970-72; Perm. Rep. to UN 1972-79; Amb. to Trinidad and Tobago 1974-79, to the Bahamas 1977-79; Dir.-Gen. Political Affairs 1979-. *Address:* 6 Penjambon, Jakarta, Indonesia.

ANYAOKU, Eleazar Chukwuemeka (Emeka), Ndichie Chief Adazie of Obosi, B.A.; Nigerian diplomatist; b. 18 Jan. 1933, Obosi; s. of the late Emmanuel Chukwuemeka Anyaoku, Ononupo of Okpuno Ire and Cecilia Adiba (née Ogbogu); m. Ebunola Olubunmi 1962; three s. one d.; ed. Merchants of Light School, Oba, Univ. of Ibadan; Commonwealth Devt. Corpn., London and Lagos 1959-62; joined Nigerian Diplomatic Service 1962, mem. Nigerian Perm. Mission to UN, New York 1963-66; seconded to Commonwealth Secr., Asst. Dir. Int. Affairs Div. 1966-71, Dir. 1971-75, Asst. Sec.-Gen. of the Commonwealth 1975-77, elected Deputy Sec.-Gen. (Political) Dec. 1977, re-elected 1983, 1984; Minister of External Affairs, Nigeria Nov.-Dec. 1983; Sec. Review Cttee. on Commonwealth Inter-governmental Orgs. June-Aug. 1966; Commonwealth Observer Team for Gibraltar Referendum Aug.-Sept. 1967; mem. Anguilla Comm., West Indies Jan.-Sept. 1970; Deputy Conf. Sec., meeting of Commonwealth Heads of Govt., London 1969, Singapore 1971, Conf. Sec., Ottawa 1973, Kingston, Jamaica 1975; Leader, Commonwealth Mission to Mozambique 1975; Commonwealth Observer, Zimbabwe Talks, Geneva Oct.-Dec. 1976; Vice-Pres. Royal Commonwealth Soc. 1975- (Deputy Chair. 1972); Chair. Africa Centre, London 1977-82 (Dir. 1971-77); mem. Cttee. of Man., Inst. of Commonwealth Studies, London Univ. 1972-; mem. Council of Overseas Devt. Inst. 1979-, Council of the Selly Oak Colls., Birmingham 1980-86, Council, Save the Children Fund 1984-; Council of Int. Inst. for Strategic

Studies, London 1987-; Commdr. of the Order of the Niger (Nigeria). *Publication:* The Racial Factor in International Politics 1977. *Leisure interests:* tennis, athletics, swimming, reading. *Address:* Commonwealth Secretariat, Marlborough House, Pall Mall, London, S.W.1, England; Orimili, Obosi, Nigeria. *Telephone:* 01-839 3411. (London).

APANG, Gegong; Indian politician; b. 1 Nov. 1945, Karko, E. Siang Dist., Arunachal Pradesh; s. of Emi Apang; m.; four s. two d.; ed. J. N. Coll., Pasighat; mem. Arunachal Pradesh Council 1972-78; mem. First Provisional Legis. Ass. 1975-78; Minister of Agric. 1977; mem. First Legis. Ass. of Arunachal Pradesh 1978, Minister of Agric. etc. 1978; Chief Minister of Arunachal Pradesh 1980-; mem. Congress 1980-, Leader, Congress (I) Legis. Party, Arunachal Pradesh; Chair. Arunachal Pradesh Voluntary Service Corps, Yingkiong Co-operative Soc. Ltd., State Forest Corpn., State Sports Council, State Welfare (Charitable) Soc.; founder and Chair. Boum Kakir Mission for orphans, Boleng, E. Siang Dist., and Donyi Polo Vidhya Bhavan Mission Soc., New Itanagar. *Leisure interests:* games and sports, gardening and rearing poultry. *Address:* Chief Minister's Office, Arunachal Pradesh, New Itanagar 791 111, India. *Telephone:* Itanagar 456 (Office); Itanager 341, 543 (Home).

APEL, Hans Eberhard, DR.RER.POL.; German economist and politician; b. 25 Feb. 1932, Hamburg; m. Ingrid Schwingel 1956; two d.; ed. Hamburg Univ.; Apprentice, Hamburg export and import business 1951-54; Sec. Socialist Group in European Parl. 1958-61, Head, Econ., Finance and Transport Dept. 1962-65; mem. Bundestag 1965-, Chair. Transport Cttee. 1969-72; Deputy Chair. Social Democratic Group in Bundestag 1969-72; mem. Nat. Exec., then Deputy Chair. Social-Democratic Party (SPD) 1970-; Parl. Sec. of State, Fed. Ministry of Foreign Affairs 1972-74; Fed. Minister of Finance 1974-78, of Defence 1978-82; Dir. World Bank 1974. *Publications:* Edwin Cannan und seine Schüler 1961, Raumordnung in der Bundesrepublik 1964, Europas neue Grenzen 1964, Der deutsche Parlamentarismus 1968, Bonn, den ... Tagebuch eines Abgeordneten 1972, 100 Antworten auf 100 Anfragen 1975. *Leisure interests:* music, sailing, soccer. *Address:* Rögenfeld 42c, 2000 Hamburg 67, Federal Republic of Germany.

APEL, Willi, DR.PHIL.; American (b. German) musicologist; b. 1893, Konitz, W. Prussia (now Chojnice, Poland); s. of Max and Ida Apel (née Schoenlank); m. Ursula Siemering 1928; ed. Univs. of Bonn, Munich, Berlin; Piano studies with Leonid Kreutzer, Edwin Fischer; lecturer on music 1926-36; went to U.S.A. 1936; taught at Longy School of Music 1936-43, Harvard Univ. and Radcliffe Coll. 1938-42, Boston Center for Adult Education 1937-50; Prof. of Music, Indiana Univ. 1950-63, Emeritus Prof. 1964-; Fellow, Medieval Acad. of America; Hon. Ph.D. (Univ. of Pavia) 1982; Gold Medal, Monteverdi Festival, Venice 1968. *Publications:* The Notation of Polyphonic Music 800-1600 1942, Harvard Dictionary of Music 1944 (rev. 1969), Historical Anthology of Music (with A. T. Davison, 2 vols.) 1946, 1950, Masters of the Keyboard 1947, French Secular Music of the Late 14th Century 1950, Gregorian Chant 1958, Harvard Brief Dictionary of Music 1960, Geschichte der Orgel- und Klaviermusik bis 1700 1967, French Secular Compositions of the 14th Century, 3 vols. 1969-72, Keyboard Music of the 14th and 15th Centuries 1963, Marco Facoli, Collected Works 1963, Constanzo Antegnati, L'Antegnata Intravolatura 1963, Spanish Organ Masters after Antonio de Cabezon 1967, Pieter Cornet, Collected Keyboard Works 1969, The Tablature of Celle 1971, Delphin Strunck and Peter Mohrhardt, Original Compositions for Organ 1973, Joseph Jimenez, Collected Organ Compositions 1975. *Address:* Franz-Joseph-Strasse 7A, 8000 Munich 40, Federal Republic of Germany. *Telephone:* 341844.

APITHY, Sourou Migan; Benin politician; b. 8 April 1913; ed. Ecole Libre des Sciences Politiques, Ecole Nat. d'Organisation Economique et Sociale. Deputy of Dahomey to French Constituent Assemblies 1945-46; mem. Nat. Assembly 1946-58; del. to seventh and eighth sessions UN 1953; mem. Grand Council French West Africa 1947-57; Pres. Gen. Council Dahomey 1955-57; Prime Minister Provisional Govt. 1958-59; Minister without Portfolio 1960; Vice-Pres. and Minister of the Plan and Devt. 1960; Amb. of Dahomey to France, U.K., and Switzerland to 1963; Minister of Finance, Economy and the Plan 1963-64; Pres. of the Repub. of Dahomey 1964-65; mem. Pres. Council 1970-72; detained following coup 1972; released April 1981; Commdr. de la Grande-Comore. *Publication:* Au Service de mon Pays. *Address:* c/o Ministry of Justice, Cotonou, Benin.

APONTE MARTÍNEZ, H.E. Cardinal Luis; American (Puerto Rican) ecclesiastic; b. 4 Aug. 1922, Lajas; s. of Santiago Evangelista Aponte and Rosa Martinez; ed. St. Ildefonso Seminary, San Juan and St. John's Seminary, Boston, Mass., U.S.A.; ordained priest 1950; Curate, Patillas, then Pastor of Santa Isabel; Sec. to Bishop McManus, Vice-Chancellor of Diocese of Ponce 1955-57; Pastor of Aibonito 1957-60; Chaplain to Nat. Guard 1957-60; Auxiliary Bishop of Ponce and Titular Bishop of Lares 1960-63; Bishop of Ponce 1963-64; Archbishop of San Juan 1964-; created Cardinal by Pope Paul VI 1973; Dir. of Devt. for Catholic Univ. of Puerto Rico 1960-63, fmr. Chancellor; Pres. Puerto Rican Episcopal Conf. 1966-; Hon. LL.D. (Fordham) 1966; Hon. S.T.D. (Inter-American Univ. of Puerto Rico) 1969. *Address:* Arzobispado, Calle San Jorge 201, Santurce, Puerto Rico 00912. *Telephone:* 727-7273.

APPEL, André, D.D., L.H.D., LL.D.; French ecclesiastic; b. 20 Dec. 1921, Strasbourg; s. of Georges Appel and Erna Meyer; m. Marjorie Pedersen 1950; three s. one d.; ed. Collège de Saverne, Univs. of Strasbourg, Paris and Tübingen; fmr. Chaplain Univ. of Paris; Sec.-Gen. French Protestant Fed. 1956-64; Pastor Temple Neuf, Strasbourg 1964-65; Sec.-Gen. Lutheran World Fed. 1966-74; Pres. Lutheran Church, Alsace and Lorraine 1974-; Pres. Conf. des Eglises européennes 1974-, also Pres. Nat. Alliance of French Lutheran Churches 1983-.

APPEL, Karel Christian; Netherlands painter; b. 25 April 1921, Amsterdam; ed. Rijksakademie van Beeldende Kunsten, Amsterdam; began career as artist 1938; exhibitions in Europe, America and Japan 1950-; has executed murals in Amsterdam, The Hague, Rotterdam, Brussels and Paris; UNESCO Prize, Venice Biennale 1953; Lissone Prize, Italy 1958; Acquisition Prize, São Paulo Bienal 1959; Graphique Int. Prize, Ljubljana, Yugoslavia 1959; Guggenheim Nat. Prize, Netherlands 1951; Guggenheim Int. Prize 1961. *Address:* c/o Galerie Statler, 51 rue de Seine, Paris, France (Office).

APPIAH, Joe; Ghanaian lawyer and politician; b. 16 Nov. 1918, Kumasi; m. Peggy Cripps 1953; ed. Mfantisipim Secondary School, Cape Coast; worked as lawyer, later politician; mem. Convention People's Party; formed Opposition Nat. Liberation Movement Feb. 1955; imprisoned 1960-62; mem. Political Cttee. July 1966-69; goodwill Amb. to U.S.A. and U.K. Sept. 1966; Leader, Nationalist Party with M.K. Apaloo May 1969, merged to form United Nat. Party (UNP) July 1969; defeated in elections Aug. 1969; Pres. Ghana Bar Asscn.; Chair. opposition Justice Party Oct. 1970-72; Roving Amb. for Nat. Redemption Council and Vice-Chair. Cttee. to guide Ghana's return to civilian rule 1972-77; Perm. Rep. to UN 1977-78; leader, Methodist Church, Kumasi, and local preacher. *Address:* Ekuona Chambers, P.O. Box 829, Kumasi, Ghana.

APPLETON, Rt. Rev. George, C.M.G., M.A., M.B.E.; British ecclesiastic; b. 20 Feb. 1902, Windsor; s. of Thomas George and Lily Appleton; m. Marjorie A. Barrett 1929; one s. two d.; ed. County Boys' School, Maidenhead, Selwyn Coll., Cambridge and St. Augustine's Coll., Canterbury; ordained deacon 1925, priest 1926; Curate, Stepney Parish Church 1925-27; Missionary in charge Soc. for the Propagation of the Gospel Mission, Irrawaddy Delta 1927-33; Warden, Coll. of Holy Cross, Rangoon 1933-41; Archdeacon of Rangoon 1943-46; Dir. of Public Relations, Govt. of Burma 1945-46; Vicar of Headstone 1947-50; Sec. Conf. of British Missionary Socs. 1950-57; Rector, St. Botolph, Aldgate, London 1957-62; Archdeacon of London and Canon of St. Paul's Cathedral 1962-63; Archbishop of Perth (Australia) 1963-69; Anglican Archbishop in Jerusalem 1969-74; retd. 1974; Buber-Rosenzweig Medal, Council of Christians and Jews 1975. *Publications:* John's Witness to Jesus 1955, In His Name 1956, Glad Encounter 1959, On the Eightfold Path 1961, Daily Prayer and Praise 1962, Acts of Devotion 1963, One Man's Prayers 1967, Jerusalem Prayers for the World Today 1973, Journey for a Soul 1974, The Word is the Seed 1976, The Practice of Prayer 1979, Praying with the Bible 1981, Glimpses of Faith 1982, Prayers from a Troubled Heart 1983, The Quiet Heart 1984, (ed.) The Oxford Book of Prayer 1985, Understanding the Psalms 1987, 100 Personal Prayers 1988, Prayer in a Troubled World 1988, Paul Misunderstood 1989. *Address:* 112A St. Mary's Road, Oxford, OX4 1QF, England. *Telephone:* 0865-248272.

APPLEYARD, Sir Raymond K., K.B.E., PH.D.; British scientist; b. 5 Oct. 1922, Birtley; m.; one s. two d.; ed. Rugby School, Trinity Coll., Cambridge; Instructor in Physics and Biophysics, Yale Univ. 1949-51; Fellow in Natural Sciences, Rockefeller Foundation 1951-53; Assoc. Research Officer, Atomic Energy of Canada Ltd. 1953-56; Sec. UN Scientific Cttee. on the Effects of Atomic Radiation 1957-61; Dir. Biology Services, European Atomic Energy Community (EURATOM) 1961-73; Exec. Sec. European Molecular Biology Org. 1965-73; Sec. European Molecular Biology Conf. 1969-73; Dir.-Gen. Scientific and Tech. Information and Information Management, Comm. of European Communities 1973-81, for Information Market and Innovation 1981-86; Hon. Dr. Med. (Ulm) 1977. *Address:* c/o Directorate-General for Information Market and Innovation, Bâtiment Jean Monnet, Luxembourg-Kirchberg, Luxembourg; 120 rue de la Loi, Brussels, Belgium.

APRAHAMIAN, Felix; British music critic, writer and broadcaster; b. 5 June 1914, London; ed. Tollington School; contributor to musical press 1931-, national press 1937-; broadcaster 1942-; Asst. Sec. and Concert Dir. London Philharmonic Orchestra 1940-46; Consultant, United Music Publishers Ltd. 1946-64; Deputy Music critic Sunday Times 1948-; Music editor The Listener 1966-67; Lecturer Richmond Adult Coll. 1969-, Stanford Univ. in U.K. 1969-83, City Literary Inst. 1973-; Morley Coll. 1975-82; Hon. Sec. The Organ Music Soc. 1935-70; Hon. mem. R.C.O. 1973, BBC Cen. Music Advisory Cttee. 1958-61; Co-founder and organizer, Concerts de Musique Française 1942-64; Adviser, Delius Trust 1961-; mem. and Pres. Int. Music Juries, Geneva and Montreux 1963-. *Publications:* (Ed.) Ernest Newman's Essays from the World of Music 1956; More Essays from the World of Music 1958; Essays on Music from The Listener 1967-. *Leisure interests:* horticulture, bibliophily. *Address:* 8 Methuen Park, London, N10 2JS, England.

APRÓ, Antal; Hungarian politician (retd.); b. 8 Feb. 1913, Szeged; joined Communist Party 1931; Pres. of Building Workers' Asscn. 1945; Gen. Sec. Trade Union Council 1948-51; Minister of Building Materials Industry 1952-53; Deputy Prime Minister 1953-56, 1961-71; Minister of Industry 1956-57; First Deputy Prime Minister 1957-61; Perm. Rep. to Council for Mutual Econ. Aid 1959-71; Pres. Nat. Council, Patriotic People's Front

1956-57; Pres. of Nat. Ass. 1971-84; Chair. Hungarian-Soviet Friendship Soc. 1971-; mem. Political Cttee., Socialist Workers' Party 1971-80, Cen. Cttee. 1980-88. *Address:* Hungarian-Soviet Friendship Society, 1071 Budapest, Gorkij fasor 45, Hungary. *Telephone:* 426-950.

AQUARONE, Stanislas Raoul Adrien, PH.D.; Australian international civil servant; b. 13 Nov. 1915, Melbourne; m. 1941; two s. two d.; ed. Univ. of Toronto Schools, Univ. of Toronto and Columbia Univ., N.Y.; fmr. teacher of French language and literature, Hamilton Coll. and in Columbia, Panama and Toronto Univs.; Sec. Int. Court of Justice 1948-51, First Sec. 1951-60, Deputy Registrar 1960-66; Registrar 1966-80. *Publication:* The Life and Works of Emile Littré (1801-1881) 1958.

AQUINO, (Maria) Corazon (Cory), B.A.; Philippine politician; b. 25 Jan. 1933, Tarlac Prov.; d. of José Cojuangco; m. Benigno S. Aquino, Jr. 1956 (assassinated 1983); one s. four d.; ed. Raven Hill Acad., Philadelphia, Notre Dame School, New York, Mount St. Vincent Coll., New York; in exile in U.S.A. with her husband 1980-83; mem. United Nationalist Democratic Org. (UNIDO) 1985-; President of the Philippines (after overthrow of régime of Ferdinand Marcos q.v.) Feb. 1986-. *Address:* Office of the President, Manila, Philippines.

AQUINO, Francisco, M.P.A.; Salvadorian agricultural engineer and economist; b. 12 Sept. 1919; s. of Francisco Aquino and Lucila Herrera; m. María Dalila Negro 1946; three s. one d.; ed. Coll. for Agronomic Studies, San Salvador and Harvard Univ., U.S.A. Land Appraiser, Mortgage Bank, San Salvador 1942; Analyst, Nat. Planning Asscn., Washington, D.C. 1943; Man. Fed. of Rural Credit Co-operatives, San Salvador 1944; Adviser to Minister of Economy, Guatemala 1946-47; Dir. Econs. Research Dept., Ministry of Agriculture, San Salvador 1947-48; Economist, Econ. Comm. for Latin America (ECLA) 1948-56; Chief, Cereals Section, Food and Agricultural Org. (FAO), Rome 1956-59; Dir. ECLA-FAO Econs. Div., Santiago de Chile 1959-61; Minister of Agriculture, El Salvador April-June 1961; Pres. Banco Central de Reserva de El Salvador, and concurrently, Gov. for El Salvador, in Int. Monetary Fund (IMF), in Int. Bank for Reconstruction and Devt. (IBRD—World Bank) and Affiliate in Cen. American Bank for Econ. Integration, also mem. Nat. Planning Council and Pres. Cen. American Monetary Council 1961-66; Technical Man. Inter-American Devt. Bank, Washington, D.C. 1967-68; Exec. Dir. UN-FAO World Food Programme 1968-76; Amb. to U.S.A. 1980; Chair. Joint Bd. of Govs. IMF-IBRD 1964; Order of Christopher Columbus. *Leisure interests:* music and wild-life. *Address:* c/o Ministerio des Asuntos Exteriores, San Salvador, El Salvador.

ARAFAT, Yasser (pseudonym of Mohammed Abed Ar'ouf Arafat); Palestinian resistance leader; b. 24 Aug. 1929, Jerusalem; ed. Cairo Univ.; joined League of Palestinian Students 1944, mem. Exec. Cttee. 1950, Pres. 1952-56; formed, with others, Al Fatah movt. 1956; engineer in Egypt 1956, Kuwait 1957-65; Pres. Exec. Cttee. of Palestine Nat. Liberation Movement (Al Fatah) June 1968-; Chair. Exec. Cttee. Palestine Liberation Org. 1968-, Pres. Cen. Cttee., Head, Political Dept. 1973-; Gen. Commdr. Palestinian Revolutionary Forces; addressed UN Gen. Assembly Nov. 1974; Joliot-Curie Gold Medal, World Peace Council Sept. 1975. *Address:* c/o Palestine Liberation Organization, Tunis, Tunisia.

ARAIN, Shafiq, M.P.; Ugandan politician and diplomatist; b. 20 Nov. 1933; s. of the late Din Mohd. Arain; m. Maria Leana Godinho 1966; one s. two d.; ed. Govt. School, Kampala, Regent's Polytechnic, London and Nottingham Univ.; M.P. (U.P.C.) 1962-71; mem. E. African Legis. Assembly 1963-71; E. African Minister for Common Market and Econ. Affairs, later E. African Minister for Communications, Research and Social Services; Chair. Minimum Wages Comm. 1964, Statutory Comm. on Co-operative Movt. 1967; del. to UN Gen. Assembly 1965-66; leader del. to Canada and Commonwealth Parl. Asscn. (CPA) Conf., Trinidad and Tobago 1969; mem. Gov. Council, Univ. of Dar es Salaam 1967-68; Chair. Uganda Branch, CPA 1969-70; in exile, London 1971-79; Minister without Portfolio, President's Office, and High Commr. to U.K. 1980-85. *Leisure interests:* golf, reading, walking. *Address:* Blanton House, Kennel Avenue, Ascot, Berks., SL5 7PB, England. *Telephone:* Ascot 26660.

ARAIZA, Francisco; Mexican opera singer; b. 4 Oct. 1950, Mexico City; s. of José Araiza and Guadalupe Araiza; m. Vivian Jaffray; one s. one d.; ed. Univ. of Mexico City, Mexico City and Munich Acads of Music; first engagement as lyric tenor in Karlsruhe, Fed. Repub. of Germany 1974; debut as Ferrando in Così fan Tutte 1975; debut at Zurich Opera House with Almaviva 1976; has become one of the leading tenors worldwide, performing at all the most important opera houses, specialising in recitals accompanied by piano or orchestra; has participated in festivals of Salzburg, Hohenems, Bayreuth, Edin., Aix-en-Provence; recent roles as: Leicester in Maria Stuarda, Zurich 1984, Duca in Rigoletto, Zurich 1985, title role in Faust, Vienna 1985, Alfredo in La Traviata, Houston 1985, Rodolfo in La Bohème, Percy/Anna in Bolena, Hoffman in Contes d'Hoffmann, Pinkerton in Madame Butterfly, Arturo in I Puritoni, Riccardo in Un ballo in maschera; Deutscher Schallplatten Prize 1984; Orphée d'Or 1984. *Recordings:* Magic Flute, Falstaff, The Creation (with Karajan), Cosi fan tutte (with Muti), Barbieri di Siviglia, Don Pasquale, La Cenerentola, Italiana in Algeri, Lied von der Erde (Giulini), Album with Arias, Schubert Lieder, Die schöne Müllerin. *Address:* c/o Rita Schütz, Artists Management, Rütistrasse 52, CH-8044, Zurich-Gockhausen, Switzerland.

ARAKI, Yoshiro; Japanese banker; b. 9 July 1921, Aichi Pref.; s. of Danzo and Mitsuyo Araki; m. Kimiko Ando 1952; one s. one d.; ed. Kyoto Univ.; joined Yasuda Bank (Fuji Bank 1948-) 1945; Chief Man. Honjo Branch 1966-68, Hiroshima Branch 1968-70, of Business Devt. Div. 1970; Dir. and Chief Man. Business Div. 1970-72, Head Office Business Div. 1972-73; Man. Dir. 1973-75, Deputy Pres. 1975-81, Pres. Fuji Bank 1981-87, Chair. 1987-; Dir. Japanese Fed. of Bankers' Asscns. 1981-87, Chair. 1982-83, 1986-87; Vice-Chair. Tokyo Bankers' Asscn. 1981-82, 1985-86; Vice-Chair. Japanese Asscn. of Corp. Execs. 1982-. *Leisure interest:* golf. *Address:* The Fuji Bank Ltd., 5-5, Otemachi 1-chome, Chiyoda-ku, Tokyo (Office); 26-5, Utsukushigaoka 3-chome, Midori-ku, Yokohama, Japan (Home). *Telephone:* (03) 216-2211 (Office).

ARAL, H. Cahit; Turkish politician; b. 1927, Elaziğ; ed. Istanbul Tech. Univ.; mechanical eng. with State Directorate of Highways; active in establishment of six industrial complexes; Minister for Industry and Commerce 1983-87. *Address:* c/o Sanayi ve Ticaret Bakanliği, Ankara, Turkey.

ARAÑA OSORIO, Gen. Carlos Manuel; Guatemalan army officer and politician; b. 17 July 1918; fmr. Commdr. Zacapa Brigade, Guatemala Army; fmr. Amb. to Nicaragua; mem. Movimiento de Liberación Nacional (MLN); Pres. of Guatemala 1970-74. *Address:* c/o Oficina del Presidente, Guatemala City, Guatemala.

ARANGIO-RUIZ, Gaetano; Italian professor of law; b. 10 July 1919, Milan; s. of Vincenzo and Ester Mauri Arangio-Ruiz; ed. Univ. of Naples; Prof. Int. Law 1952-, Univ. of Padua 1955-67, Univ. of Bologna 1968-74, Univ. of Rome 1974-; Visiting Prof. European Cen., Johns Hopkins School of Advanced Int. Studies 1967-75; Lecturer, Hague Acad. of Int. Law 1962, 1972, 1977, 1984; mem. UN Int. Law Comm. 1985-. *Publications:* Rapporti contrattuali fra Stati e organizzazione internaz. 1950, Gli enti soggetti 1951, Su la dinamica della base sociale 1954, L'Etat dans le sens du droit des gens et la notion du droit international, 'Oesterreichische Zeitschrift für Oeffentliches Recht' 1975-76, Human Rights and Non-Intervention in the Helsinki Final Act (Hague Acad. Recueil) 1977, The UN Declaration on Friendly Relations and the System of the Sources of International Law (Sijthoff) 1979, Le Domaine reservé 1987, Gen. Course in Int. Law, Hague Acad. 1984. *Address:* Corso Trieste 51, 00198 Rome, Italy (Home). *Telephone:* 4958201 (Office); (06) 869720 and (0564) 812171 (Home).

ARÁNGUIZ DONOSO, Horacio: Chilean politician; b. 29 Mar. 1942, Santiago; s. of Horacio Aránguiz and Clemencia Donoso; m. Ana María Pinto; three s. one d.; ed. Colegio de los Sagrados Corazones and Univ. of Chile; fmr. Dean, Faculty of History and Geography and Political Sciences, Universidad Católica de Chile; Minister of Educ. 1983-86. *Address:* c/o Ministerio de Educación, Avda. Libertador Bernardo O'Higgins 1371, 7° Piso, Santiago, Chile. *Telephone:* 710292.

ARAPOV, Boris Aleksandrovich; Soviet composer; b. 12 Sept. 1905, St. Petersburg (now Leningrad); s. of Aleksandr Borisovich Arapov and Yelizaveta Ivanovna Arapova; m. Tatiana Todorova 1933; two d.; ed. Leningrad Conservatoire; teacher at Leningrad Conservatoire 1930-; Prof. 1940-, Head of Dept. Composition; Sec. of Bd. Leningrad Section, Soviet Composers' Union; People's Artist of R.S.F.S.R. 1976-; awards include Honoured Worker of Arts of Uzbek S.S.R. 1944, of R.S.F.S.R. 1957, Order of Red Banner of Labour 1953. *Major compositions:* (works for opera and ballet) Hodja Nasreddin (Uzbek comic opera) 1944, Frigate "Victory" (opera) 1957, Rain (chamber opera) 1965, Portrait of Dorian Gray (ballet) 1971; (orchestral works) Tadzhik Suite 1938, Russian Suite 1951, Free China (symphonic poem) 1959, Symphony No. 3 1962, Concerto for Violin and Orchestra 1964, Concerto for Full Symphony Orchestra 1969, Concerto for Violin, Piano, Percussion and Chamber Orchestra (In Memory of I. Stravinsky) 1973, Symphony No. 4 for Reciter, Baritone, Mezzo-Soprano, 2 Mixed Choirs and Full Symphony Orchestra (after verses by V. Briusov, B. Mayakovsky, S. Orlov, S. Shchipachev, M. Vloshin) 1975; (vocal orchestral works) Vocal Cycle for Tenor, Baritone and Orchestra (on verses by A. Pushkin) 1937, Vocal Cycle for Soprano, Tenor, and Nonet: "Four Times of Year" (on verses by Japanese Chokku) 1977; (orchestral chamber works) Humoresque for Piano 1937, 3 Pieces on Mongol Themes for Clarinet, Violin and Piano 1943, 6 Pieces on Chinese Themes for Piano 1955, Etude-Scherzo for Piano 1967, Sonata for Piano 1970, 3 Pieces for Piano 1970; (vocal chamber works) 4 Romances for Soprano and Piano (on verses by A. Blok) 1947-63, Negro Protest Songs for Voice and Jazz Orchestra 1940, Four Songs for Voice and Piano 1949, "Monologue" for Baritone, Tuba, Percussion and Piano (after verses by A. Voznesensky) 1969, Four Sonnets by Petrarch for Mezzo-Soprano and Piano 1975, Second Sonata for Piano 1976, Sonata for Violin and Piano 1978, two Monologues for Baritone and Piano (on verses by B. Pasternak) 1980, Symphony No. 5 1981, Symphony No. 6 1983, Choreographic Poem on Oscar Wilde's novel The Picture of Dorian Grey 1983. *Leisure interests:* travel, Western European painting, oriental decorative art. *Address:* Prospekt Y. Gagarina 35, kv. 65, Leningrad 196135, U.S.S.R. *Telephone:* 293-82-63.

ARASHI, Qadi Abdul Karim al-; Yemeni politician; fmr. Minister for Local Govt. and the Treasury; Speaker of the Constituent People's Ass. Feb. 1978-; Chair. Provisional Presidential Council June-July 1978; Vice-Pres. Yemen Arab Republic July 1978-. *Address:* Constituent People's Assembly, Sana'a, Yemen Arab Republic.

ARASKOG, Rand Vincent: American business executive; b. 30 Oct. 1931, Fergus Falls, Minn.; s. of Randolph Victor and Hilfred Mathilda Araskog; m. Jessie Marie Gustafson 1956; ed. U.S. Mil. Acad. and Harvard Univ.; special asst. to Dir., Dept. of Defense, Washington, D.C. 1954-59; Dir. Marketing, aeronautical div., Honeywell Inc., Minneapolis 1960-66; Vice-Pres. ITT, Group Exec. ITT Aerospace Electronics, Components and Energy Group, Nutley, N.J. 1971-76; Pres. 1979-85, C.E.O. ITT Corpn., New York 1979-, Chair. Bd. and Exec. and Policy Comms. 1980-, also Dir.; Chair. Nat. Security Telecommunications Advisory Cttee. 1983-; mem. Bd. of Govs., Aerospace Industries Asscn., Exec. Council, Air Force Asscn. *Address:* ITT World Headquarters, 320 Park Ave., New York, N.Y. 10022, U.S.A.

ARAÚJO, José Emílio Gonçalves, DR.AGRON.; Brazilian soil scientist; b. 8 Sept. 1922, Rio de Janeiro; s. of Antônio Araújo Fernández and Emerenciana Gonçalves; m. Laurinda Lopez 1946; one s. two d.; ed. Universidade Rural do Brasil, Rio de Janeiro, Universidade Federal Rural do Sul, Pelotas, Cornell Univ., N.Y., U.S.A.; acting Prof., Coll. of Agriculture, Universidade Federal de Pelotas 1946-48, Prof. 1948-65; Prof. Escola Agrotécnica Visconde de Graça, Pelotas 1952-60; Natural Resources Expert, Inter-American Inst. of Agricultural Sciences, OAS 1965, Dir.-Gen. 1970-76, re-elected 1976; Dir. Inter-American Program for Rural Devt. and Agrarian Reform of the Secretariat of the OAS 1965-70; Chief, Soils Section, Instituto Agronômico do Sul 1947-50, Dir. 1952-53, mem. Perm. Technical Council on Soils 1958-61; mem. Brazilian Soc. for Soil Science, Brazilian Geological Soc., Brazilian Soc. for the Advancement of Science, American Soc. of Agronomy, Latin-American Soc. of Soil Science, Int. Soil Science Asscn., etc.; Officer, Orden del Mérito Agrícola (Colombia) 1970, Commdr. Orden Mérito Agrícola (Peru) 1973, Isabel La Católica Award (Spain), and other awards. *Publications:* more than 35 formal papers and two books on agricultural soil research, agrarian reform and other related subjects. *Address:* Inter-American Institute for Cooperation on Agriculture, Apartado Postal 55, 2200 Coronado, San José, Costa Rica. *Telephone:* 29-02-22.

ARAÚJO SALES, H.E. Cardinal Eugénio de; Brazilian ecclesiastic; b. 8 Nov. 1920, Acari, Rio Grande do Norte; s. of Celso Dantas and D. Josefa de Araujo Sales; ordained 1943; Bishop 1954; Apostolic Administrator, See of São Salvador da Bahia until 1968; Archbishop of São Sebastião do Rio de Janeiro 1971-; cr. Cardinal 1969. *Leisure interest:* reading. *Address:* Palácio São Joaquim, Rua da Glória 446, 20241 Rio de Janeiro, RJ, Brazil. *Telephone:* 292-3132; 222-2308.

ARBATOV, Georgiy Arkadevich; DR. HIST. SC.; Soviet academician, administrator and party official; b. 1923, Kherson; s. of Arkady Michailovich Arbatov and Anna Vasilievna Arbota; m. Svetlana Pavlovna Goriacheva 1948; one s.; ed. Moscow Inst. for Int. Relations; Soviet Army 1941-44; mem. CPSU 1943-; Ed. of publishing house for foreign literature and periodicals (Voprosy filosofii, Novoe vremya, Kommunist) 1949-60; Columnist Problems of Peace and Socialism 1960-62; Section Chief at Inst. of World Econ. and Int. Relations of U.S.S.R. Acad. of Sciences 1962-64; Worked for CPSU Cen. Cttee. 1964-67; Dir. Inst. of U.S. and Canadian Studies, U.S.S.R. Acad. of Sciences 1967-; Deputy U.S.S.R. Supreme Soviet 1974-; mem. Presidium 1988-; Academician 1974; mem. Palme Comm. 1980-; mem. Cen. Auditing Comm. of CPSU 1971-76; cand. mem. and mem. CPSU Cen. Cttee. 1976-; Order of the Red Star 1943, Badge of Honour 1962, Red Banner of Labour 1967, 1983, Order of Lenin 1975, 1983, Order of the Great Patriotic War, 1st Rank 1985. *Address:* 2/3 Khlebny per., Moscow G-69, 121814, U.S.S.R. *Telephone:* 2905875.

ARBEID, Murray; British fashion designer; b. 30 May 1935, London; ed. Quintin School, London; apprenticed to Michael Sherard 1952; opened own business 1954-; designer and design consultant, Norman Hartnell 1988-. *Leisure interests:* music, literature, art. *Address:* Castle House, 75-76 Wells Street, London, W1P 3RE, England.

ARBELI-ALMOZLINO, Shoshana; Israeli politician; b. 1926, Mosul, Iraq; d. of Shmuel Arbeli and Sapira Chai; m. Nathan Almozlino 1965; ed. Baghdad Higher Seminary for Teachers; active in underground Zionist movement 1946-47; moved to Israel 1947; mem. Kibbutz Neveh Or 1947-51; worked in Immigration Absorption 1950-52; worked in Histadrut (Gen. Labour Fed.) and Labour Bureau Service 1952-59; with Fed. of Working Women Volunteers, Naamat 1959-66; Labour Party mem. Knesset (Parl.) 1966-; Chair. Labour Cttee. 1969-74, 1974-77; Deputy Chair. Knesset 1977-81; Chair. Interior and Environmental Quality Cttee. 1981-84; Deputy Minister of Health 1984-86, Minister 1986-; several recognition awards from Histadrut and voluntary socs. *Publications:* articles in popular journals. *Leisure interests:* swimming, watching football. *Address:* 29 Herzog Street, Givataim, Tel Aviv, Israel. *Telephone:* (03) 748744.

ARBER, Werner, PH.D.; Swiss microbiologist; b. 1929, Gränichen, Aargau; m.; two c; ed. Aargau Gymnasium, Eidgenössische Technische Hochschule, Zürich; Asst. at Laboratory of Biophysics, Univ. of Geneva 1953-58, Dozent then Extraordinary Prof. Molecular Genetics 1962-70; Research Assoc., Dept. of Microbiology, Univ. of Southern Calif. 1958-59; Visiting Investigator, Dept. of Molecular Biology Univ. of Calif., Berkeley 1970-71; Prof. of Microbiology, Univ. of Basel 1971-; Joint Winner Nobel Prize for Physiology or Medicine 1978. *Address:* Biozentrum der Universität, Basel,

70 Klingelbergstrasse, CH-4056 Basel, Switzerland (Office). *Telephone:* (061) 253880.

ARBULÚ GALLIANI, Gen. Guillermo; Peruvian army officer and government official; b. Trujillo; m. Bertha Tanaka de Azcárate; one s. two d.; ed. Chorillos Mil. Acad.; Sub-Lieut., Eng. Corps 1943, Lieut. 1946, Capt. 1949, Major 1955, Lieut.-Col.1959, Col. 1964, Brig.-Gen. 1971, Div. Gen. 1975-; fmr. Chief of Staff, 1st Light Div.; fmr. Dir. of Logistics; fmr. Chief of Operations, Armed Forces Gen. Staff; fmr. Dir. of Mil. Eng. Coll.; fmr. Instructor, Higher War Coll.; fmr. Adviser to Ministries of Mining and Fisheries; fmr. Pres. Empresa Pública de Servicios Pesqueros (State Fishing Corpn.); Pres. Joint Armed Forces Command; Prime Minister and Minister of Defence 1976-78, Amb. to Chile 1978-79, to Spain 1979-80; del. to Latin American Conf. of Ministers of Labour; rep. of Ministry of Foreign Affairs to negotiations for Andean Pact; rep. to 11th American Mil. Congress; Commdr. Mil. Order of Ayacucho; Jorge Chávez Award; Grand Officer of Peruvian Crosses of Aeronautical Merit, Naval Merit; Grand Cross, Peruvian Order of Mil. Merit; Grand Officer, Mayo Cross of Mil. Merit (Argentina). *Address:* c/o Ministry of Foreign Affairs, Lima, Peru.

ARBUZOV, Boris Aleksandrovich; Soviet chemist; b. 4 Nov. 1903, Novaya Aleksandriya; s. of Aleksandr Arbuzov and Yekaterina Arbuzova; m. Olga Mikhailova 1926; one d.; ed. Inst. of Agriculture and Forestry, Kazan, and Univ. of Kazan; Docent Professor, Institute of Chemical Technology, Kazan 1930-38; Prof. Organic Chem., Univ. of Kazan 1938-67, Dean Chem. Div. 1940-50; Dir. Inst. Organic Chem. in Kazan, U.S.S.R. Acad. of Sciences 1958-65; Dir. A. M. Butlerov Chemical Inst., Univ. of Kazan 1960-88; Dir. Arbuzov Inst. Organic and Physical Chem. 1965-71; corresp. mem. U.S.S.R. Acad. of Sciences 1943-53, mem. 1953-; Deputy to U.S.S.R. Supreme Soviet 1966-89; awards include U.S.S.R. State Prize 1951, Lenin Prize 1978, Hero of Socialist Labour, five Orders of Lenin, Order of Red Banner of Labour (twice), Order of October Revolution, Order of People's Friendship, Hammer and Sickle Gold Medal. *Publications include:* Investigations in the Field of Isomeric Rearrangements of Bicyclic Terpens and their Epoxydes 1936, The Arbuzov Transformation; Organophosphorus compounds, a structural study of organic compounds by physical methods. *Address:* Arbuzov Institute of Organic and Physical Chemistry, Kazan; 5 Shkolny Pereulok, fl. 4, Kazan 420012, U.S.S.R. *Telephone:* 32-37-90.

ARCHAMBAULT, Pierre; French journalist; b. 24 June 1912, Tours; s. of Alexandre Archambault and Augustine Bégaud; m. 2nd Claude Frère 1970; Préfet (Acting) Indre-et-Loire 1944; Dir.-Gen. La Nouvelle République du Centre-Ouest 1944-72, Vice-Pres. du Directoire, Tours 1973-, Président d'Honneur; Pres. Syndicat Nat. de la Presse Quotidienne Régionale 1951-71, later Man.; Pres. Confédération de la Presse Française 1970-; mem. Council, Agence France-Presse 1957-69, 1971-; mem. Man. Council Office de Radiodiffusion-Télévision Française (ORTF) 1964-72; mem. Haut Conseil de l'Audiovisuel; Pres. Inter France Quotidiens 1975-78; mem. Commission de la Qualité; Commdr. de la Légion d'honneur, Officier des Palmes académiques and several war decorations and other awards. *Address:* 4-18 rue de la Préfecture, 37000 Tours (Office); 71 blvd. Béranger, 37000 Tours, France (Home). *Telephone:* (47) 61.81.46 (Office).

ARCHER, Jeffrey Howard, F.R.S.A.; British author and politician; b. 15 April 1940; s. of William and Lola (née Cook) Archer; m. Mary Weeden 1966; two s.; ed. Wellington School and Brasenose Coll., Oxford; mem. GLC for Havering 1966-70; mem. Parl. for Louth (Conservative) 1969-74; Deputy Chair. Conservative Party 1985-86; mem. Exec. British Theatre Museum. *Publications:* Not a Penny More, Not a Penny Less 1975, Shall we tell the President? 1977, Kane and Abel 1979, A Quiver Full of Arrows 1980, The Prodigal Daughter 1982, First Among Equals 1984, A Matter of Honour 1985, Beyond Reasonable Doubt (play) 1987, A Twist in the Tale 1988. *Leisure interests:* theatre, cinema, cricket. *Address:* 93 Albert Embankment, London, S.E.1; The Old Vicarage, Grantchester, Cambridge, England.

ARCHIBALD, George Christopher, M.A., B.SC. (ECON.), F.R.S.C.; professor of economics; b. 30 Dec. 1926; s. of late 1st Baron Archibald, and Dorothy H. Edwards; disclaimed peerage for life 1975; m. 1st Liliana Barou 1951 (divorced 1965), 2nd Daphne M. Vincent 1971; ed. Phillips Exeter Acad. U.S.A., King's Coll. Cambridge and L.S.E.; served Army 1945-48; formerly lecturer in Econs., Otago Univ., New Zealand and London School of Econs.; Prof. of Econs. Univ. of Essex; Prof. of Econs., Univ. of British Columbia 1970-; Fellow, Econometric Soc. *Publications:* Theory of the Firm (Ed.) 1971, Introduction to a Mathematical Treatment of Economics 1973. *Address:* Department of Economics, University of British Columbia, Vancouver, B.C. V6T 1W5, Canada.

ARCINIEGAS, Germán, D.L.; Colombian writer and diplomatist; b. 6 Dec. 1900, Bogotá; s. of Rafael Arciniegas and Aurora Angueyra; m. Gabriela Vieira 1926; two d.; ed. Univ. Nacional, Bogotá; Vice-Consul, London 1929; Chargé d'affaires, Buenos Aires 1940; Minister of Education, Republic of Colombia 1942-46; Visiting Prof. Univ. of Chicago 1944, Univ. of Calif. 1945, Columbia Univ. 1947; Prof. Columbia Univ. 1954-59; Amb. to Italy 1959-62, to Venezuela 1967-70, to Vatican City 1976-78; Dean, Faculty of Philosophy and Letters, Universidad de los Andes, Bogotá 1979-81; Pres. Acad. Colombiana de Historia 1980-; Ed. Cuadernos, Paris 1962-65,

Amérique Latine, a monthly section of Revue des deux Mondes 1974-; Ed. Correo de los Andes 1979; mem. Acad. of History and Letters of Colombia; corresp. mem. acads. in Spain, Argentina, Mexico, Cuba, etc.; Hammarsjköld Prize 1967. *Publications:* El Estudiante de la Mesa Redonda 1932, América Tierra Firme 1937, Los Comuneros 1938, The Knight of El Dorado 1942, Germans in the Conquest of America 1943, The Green Continent 1944, Este Pueblo de América 1945, Caribbean, Sea of the New World 1946, The State of Latin America 1952, Amerigo and the New World 1955, Italia, Guía para Vagabundos 1959, América Mágica 1959, América Mágica II 1961, Cosas del Pueblo 1962, El Mundo de la Bella Simoneta 1962, Entre el Mar Rojo y el Mar Muerto 1964, Latin America: A Cultural History 1966, Genio y Figura de Jorge Isaacs 1967, Medio Mundo Entre un Zapato 1969, Nuevo Diario de Noé 1969, Colombia Itinerario y Espíritu de la Independencia 1969, Roma Secretísima 1972, América en Europa 1975, Fernando Botero 1978, El revés de la Historia 1979, Los Pinos Nuevos 1982, Bolívar y la Revolución 1984, OEA La Suerte de una Institución Regional 1985, De Pio XII a Juan Pablo II 1986, Bolivar, de San Jacinto a Santa Maria. *Address:* Academia Colombiana de Historia, Calle 92 10-21 Bogotá, Colombia. *Telephone:* 2363175.

ARCULUS, Sir Ronald, K.C.M.G., K.C.V.O., M.A., F.B.I.M.; British diplomatist (retd.); b. 11 Feb. 1923, Birmingham; s. of the late Cecil Arculus, M.C., and Ethel Lilian Arculus; m. Sheila Mary Faux 1953; one s. one d.; ed. Solihull School, Exeter Coll., Oxford and Imperial Defence Coll.; served in Fourth Queen's Own Hussars 1942-45 (attained rank of Capt.); Foreign Office 1947; San Francisco 1948-50; La Paz 1950; Ankara 1953-56; Foreign Office 1957-60; First Sec. (Commercial), Washington 1961-65; Dir. of Trade Devt., New York 1965-68; Imperial Defence Coll. 1969; Head of Science and Technology Dept., FCO 1970-73; Minister (Economic), Paris 1973-77; Amb. to Law of Sea Conference 1977-79; Amb. to Italy 1979-83; Special Adviser to Government on Channel Tunnel trains 1987; Dir. Glaxo Holdings PLC 1983-; Dir. of Appeals King's Medical Research Trust 1984-88; Freeman of the City of London; Gov. British Inst., Florence; Consultant London and Continental Bankers Ltd. 1985-, Trusthouse Forte 1983-86. *Leisure interests:* travel, fine arts, music. *Address:* 20 Kensington Court Gardens, London, W8 5QF, England. *Telephone:* 01-938 1594.

ARDEN, John; British playwright; b. 26 Oct. 1930, Barnsley; s. of Charles Alwyn Arden and Annie Elizabeth Layland; m. Margaretta Ruth D'Arcy 1957; five s. (one deceased); ed. Sedbergh School, King's Coll., Cambridge, and Edin. Coll. of Art; Fellow in Playwriting, Bristol Univ. 1959-60; Visiting Lecturer (Politics and Drama), New York Univ. 1967; Regent's Lecturer, Univ. of California, Davis 1973; Writer in Residence, Univ. of New England, Australia 1975; mem. Corrandulla Arts and Entertainment Club 1973, Entertainment Club 1973, Galway Theatre Workshop 1975. *Plays:* All Fall Down 1955, The Life of Man 1956, The Waters of Babylon 1957, Live Like Pigs 1958, Sergeant Musgrave's Dance 1959, Soldier, Soldier 1960, The Happy Haven (with Margaretta D'Arcy) 1960, The Business of Good Government (with Margaretta D'Arcy) 1960, Wet Fish 1962, The Workhouse Donkey 1963, Ironhand 1963, Ars Longa Vita Brevis (with Margaretta D'Arcy) 1964, Armstrong's Last Goodnight 1964, Left Handed Liberty 1965, Friday's Hiding (with Margaretta D'Arcy) 1966, The Royal Pardon (with Margaretta D'Arcy) 1966, Muggins is a Martyr (with Margaretta D'Arcy and C.A.S.T.) 1968, The Hero Rises Up (musical with Margaretta D'Arcy) 1968, two autobiographical plays 1972, The Ballygombeen Bequest (with Margaretta D'Arcy) 1972, The Island of the Mighty (with Margaretta D'Arcy) 1972, Keep These People Moving (with Margaretta D'Arcy) 1972, The Non-Stop Connolly Show (with Margaretta D'Arcy) 1975, Pearl 1977, Vandaleur's Folly (with Margaretta D'Arcy) 1978, The Little Gray Home in the West (with Margaretta D'Arcy) 1978, The Making of Muswell Hill (with Margaretta D'Arcy) 1979, The Ingenious Gentleman, Don Quixote de la Mancha (adapted from Cervantes) 1980, Garland for a Hoar Head 1982, The Old Man Sleeps Alone 1982, The Manchester Enthusiasts (with Margaretta D'Arcy) 1984, Whose Is The Kingdom? (with Margaretta D'Arcy) 1986. Television documentary: Profile of Sean O'Casey (with Margaretta D'Arcy) 1973. Essays: To Present the Pretence 1977; Novel: Silence Among the Weapons 1982. *Address:* c/o Margaret Ramsay Ltd., 14A Goodwin's Court, London, W.C.2, England.

ARDWICK, Baron (Life Peer), cr. 1970, of Barnes in the London Borough of Richmond-upon-Thames; **John Cowburn Beavan;** British journalist and politician; b. 1910; ed. Manchester Grammar School; with Evening Chronicle, Manchester 1928-30, Manchester Evening News 1930-40; Diarist, Leader Writer Evening Standard 1940-42; News Ed. and Chief Sub-Ed., The Observer 1942-43; Ed., Manchester Evening News; Dir. Manchester Guardian and Evening News Ltd., 1943-55; London Ed., Manchester Guardian 1946-55; Asst. Dir. Nuffield Foundation 1955-60; Ed., Daily Herald Oct. 1960-62; Political Adviser, Daily Mirror Group 1962-75; mem. Ed. Bd. The Political Quarterly 1978-; Chair. Press Freedom Cttee., Commonwealth Press Union 1980-; Chair. Industrial Sponsors 1975-, Back Bencher's Co-ordinating Cttee. 1986-; mem. European Parl. 1975-79. *Address:* 10 Chester Close, London, S.W.13, England.

AREF, Maj.-Gen. Abdul Rahman Mohammed (brother of late President Abdul Salam Aref); Iraqi army officer and politician; b. 1916; ed. Baghdad Military Acad.; Head of Armoured Corps until 1962; Commdr. 5th Div. Feb. 1963-Nov. 1963; assisted in overthrow of Gen. Kassem 1963; mem. Regency Council 1965; Asst. Chief of Staff Iraqi Armed Forces Dec.

1963-64; Acting Chief of Staff 1964, Chief of Staff 1964-68; Pres. of Iraq April 1966-July 1968, also Prime Minister May-July 1967.

AREILZA, José Maria de, Count of Motrico; Spanish diplomatist and politician; b. 3 Aug. 1909, Bilbao; s. of Enrique de Areilza and Countess de Rodas; m. Mercedes de Churruca, Countess Motrico 1932; three s. two d.; ed. Bilbao Univ. and Univ. of Salamanca; Mayor of Bilbao 1937; Dir.-Gen. of Industry, Franco Cabinet 1938-40; mem. Cortes 1943-47; Amb. to Argentina 1947-50; industrial and banking activities 1950-54; Amb. to U.S.A. 1954-60, to France 1960-64; Sec.-Gen. Monarchist Party 1966-69; Nat. Econ. Counsellor; mem. Nat. Council and Political Junta of Falange; mem. Federación de Estudios Independientes (Fedisa); Minister of Foreign Affairs 1975-76, co-founder and Leader, Partido Popular 1976; Pres. Assembly, Council of Europe 1981-83; Grand Cross of Carlos III, of Isabel la Católica, Merito Civil; Légion d'honneur; Orden del Libertador (Argentina). *Publications:* Reivindicaciones de España 1941, Embajadores sobre Espana 1946, Escritos Políticos 1968, Cien Artículos 1971, Figuras y Pareceres 1973, Así los he visto 1974, Diario de un Ministro de la Monarquía 1978. *Leisure interests:* books, travel, engravings. *Address:* Fuente del Rey, 11 Aravaca, Spain (Home). *Telephone:* 207 02 59 (Home).

ARENDT, Walter; German politician; b. 17 Jan. 1925, Hessen; m. Erna Arendt 1948; one s.; ed. Akad. der Arbeit, Frankfurt and Akad. für Gemeinschaft, Hamburg; Miner in Hessen 1939-47; Ed. IG Bergbau und Energie, Bochum 1948, mem. Man. Bd. 1955, Chair. 1964-69; mem. Bundestag (SPD) 1961-83, mem. European Parl. 1961-69; mem. Presidium, SPD 1973; Pres. Int. Union of Miners 1967-69; Minister for Labour and Social Welfare 1969-76; Grosses Bundesverdienstkreuz 1975.

ARENS, Moshe, M.K.; Israeli politician, professor and diplomatist; b. 7 Dec. 1925, Lithuania; ed. Massachusetts and California Insts. of Technology, U.S.A.; Assoc. Prof. of Aeronautical Eng. Technion (Israel Inst. of Tech.), Haifa; Deputy Dir. Israel Aircraft Industries, Lod; Amb. to U.S.A. 1982-83; Minister of Defence 1983-84, without Portfolio -1987, of Foreign Affairs Dec. 1988-; elected to Knesset, mem. Knesset Finance Cttee. 1973; Israel Defence Prize 1971; Assoc. Fellow, A.I.A.A. *Publications:* several books on propulsion and flight mechanics. *Address:* Ministry of Foreign Affairs, Jerusalem; 49 Hagderot, Savyon, Israel (Home).

ARES, Rev. Richard, O.C., PH.D., F.R.S.C.; Canadian ecclesiastic; b. 7 Jan. 1910, Marieville, P.Q.; s. of Georges Ares and Dorila Théberge; ed. Séminaire St. Hyacinthe, Univ. of Montreal, Scholasticat Immaculée-Conception, Inst. Catholique, Paris and Univ. of Paris; mem. Royal Comm. on Constitutional Problems, Québec 1953-56; mem. Acad. des Sciences morales et politiques du Québec; Pres. Semaines sociales du Canada; Dir Relations (review) 1956-69. *Publications:* Notre question nationale 1945, L'Eglise et la société internationale 1949, La Confédération, Pacte ou Loi? 1949, Pour un Québec fort 1963, Le role de l'Etat dans un Québec fort 1962, Dossier sur le Pacte fédératif de 1867 1967, Les positions—ethniques, linguistiques et réligieuses—des Canadiens français à la suite du recensement de 1971 1975, L'Eglise dans le monde d'aujourd'hui 1977. *Address:* 25 ouest, rue Jarry, Montreal, P.Q. H2P 1S6, Canada.

ARESPACOCHAGA Y FELIPE, Juan de; Spanish civil engineer and economist; b. 1920, Madrid; s. of Nicolás de Arespacochaga; m. Marta Llopiz 1949; one s. eight d.; ed. Univ. of Madrid; Pres. of Popular Group in the Senate; fmr. Lord Mayor of Madrid; Senator by royal nomination; fmr. Dir.-Gen. for Tourist Promotion; Chair. Acad. Internationale de Tourisme, Empresa Nacional de Turismo, Nat. Asscn. of Spanish Roads; Chair. Civil Eng. Asscn., mem. Nat. Coll. of Economists, Nat. Coll. of Civil Engineers, etc.; Grand Cross of Civil Merit and Orders from Italy, Portugal, Mexico, Tunisia and Lebanon. *Publications:* Las Obras Hidráulicas y la decadencia económica de España 1948, El aceite de Oliva, moneda mediterránea 1949, El multiplicador económico en las obras de riego 1956, Los transportes españoles y la integración europea 1959, Las inversiones de O.P. en la Plan Nacional 1979, Alcalde sólo. *Leisure interests:* yacht, golf, winter sports. *Address:* Alberto Alcocer 13, Madrid 16, Spain. *Telephone:* 250-31-16.

ARGAN, Giulio Carlo; Italian professor of art; b. 17 May 1909, Turin; s. of Valerio and Libera Roncaroli; m. Anna Maria Mazzucchelli 1939; one d.; ed. Univ. of Turin; Supt. of State Museums and Galleries 1933, later Cen. Dir. of State Museums and Galleries until 1955; Prof. of Modern Art, Univ. of Rome 1959-80; Mayor of Rome (independent Communist candidate) 1976-79; mem. Senate 1983-; Founder, Dir. Storia dell' Arte review, Co-Dir. L'Arte review; mem. Lincei Acad., San Luca Acad., Turin Acad. of Sciences, Palermo Acad. of Sciences and Letters, Bologna Acad. Clementina; Feltrinelli Prize for art criticism, Ulysses Prize for architecture criticism. *Publications:* L'Architettura preromanica e romanica in Italia 1936, L'Architettura del duecento e del trecento in Italia 1937, 1943, Arturo Tosi 1938, Giacomo Manzù 1942, Henry Moore 1948, Walter Gropius e la Bauhaus 1951, Borromini 1952, La Scultura di Picasso 1953, Studi e Note 1955, Fra Angelico 1955, Breuer 1955, Botticelli 1956, Brunelleschi 1955, Arturo Martini 1956, L'Architettura barocca in Italia 1957, Salvezza e caduta nell'arte moderna 1964, L'Europa delle capitali 1964, Progetto e destino 1965, Capogrossi 1967, Storia dell'arte italiana (3 vols.) 1968, The Renaissance City 1969, Studi e note: dal Bramante al Canova 1970, L'arte moderna 1770-1970 1970, Man Ray 1970, Mastroianni 1971, Henry Moore 1972, Die Kunst des 20 Jahrhunderts 1880-1940, 1977 and numerous articles.

Address: Via Gaetano Sacchi 20, 00153 Rome (Office); Via Filippo Casini 16, 00153 Rome, Italy (Home). *Telephone:* 5810112.

ARGAÑA, Luis Maria; Paraguayan politician; fmr. Amb. to the UN; Pres. Supreme Court 1983-88 (resgnd.); Minister of Foreign Affairs Feb. 1989-. *Address:* Ministry of Foreign Affairs, Palacio de Gobierno, Asuncion, Paraguay.

ARGERICH, Martha; Argentinian pianist; b. 5 June 1941, Buenos Aires; studied with V. Scaramuzzo, Friedrich Gulda, Nikita Magaloff, Madeleine Lipatti and Arturo Benedetto Michaelangeli; début Buenos Aires 1949; London début 1964; soloist with world's leading orchestras; First Prize Busoni Contest and Geneva Int. Music Competition 1957, Int. Chopin Competition, Warsaw 1965. *Address:* c/o Reinhard Paulsen, Goette Konzert Direktion, Colonnaden 70, 2000 Hamburg 36, Federal Republic of Germany. *Telephone:* 346018.

ARGOV, Shlomo, M.SC.(ECON.); Israeli diplomatist; b. 14 Dec. 1929, Jerusalem; m.; one s. two d.; ed. Georgetown Univ., Washington D.C., L.S.E.; Nat. Military Service 1947-50; Prime Minister's Office, Jerusalem 1955-59; Consul-Gen. of Israel, Lagos, Nigeria 1959-60; Counsellor, Embassy, Ghana 1960-61; Consul, New York 1961-64; Deputy Dir., U.S. Div., Ministry for Foreign Affairs, Jerusalem 1965-68, Asst. Dir.-Gen. (Dir. of Israel Information Services) 1974-77; Minister, Embassy of Israel, Washington D.C. 1968-71; Amb. to Mexico 1971-74, to the Netherlands 1977-79, to U.K. 1979-82. *Address:* c/o Foreign Ministry, Jerusalem, Israel.

ARGUETA, Manlio; El Salvadorean writer; has lived in exile in Costa Rica since 1973; won the Univ. of Central America prize for his novel One Day of Life 1980. *Publications:* One Day of Life 1980 (trans. into English 1984), Cuscatlan (novel) 1987. *Address:* c/o Chatto and Windus, Publishers, 30 Bedford Sq., London WC1B 3RP, England.

ARGYRIS, John, D.SC.ENG., F.R.S., F.R.AE.S.; British professor of aeronautical structures; b. 19 Aug. 1916; s. of Nicolas Argyris and Lucie Argyris; m. Inga-Lisa Johansson 1953; one s.; ed. Technical Univs. in Athens, Munich and Zürich; research, J. Gollnow u. Sohn, Stettin; Research and Tech. Officer, Royal Aeronautical Soc. 1943-49; Sr. Lecturer, Dept. of Aeronautics, Imperial Coll. London 1949, Reader in Theory of Aeronautical Structures 1950, Prof. 1955-75, Visiting Prof. 1975-78, now Prof. Emer.; Dir. Inst. for Statics and Dynamics, Stuttgart 1959-84, Inst. for Computer Applications, Stuttgart 1984-; Royal Medal, Royal Soc. 1985; Grosses Bundesverdienstkreuz (Fed. Germany); numerous other honours and awards. *Publications:* Handbook of Aeronautics (Vol. I) 1952, Energy Theorems and Structural Analysis 1960, Modern Fuselage Analysis and the Elastic Aircraft 1963, Recent Advances in Matrix Methods of Structural Analysis 1964, Introduction into the Finite Element Method (Vols. I, II and III) 1986; more than 330 articles in professional journals etc. *Leisure interests:* reading, music, hiking, archaeology. *Address:* Institute for Computer Applications, 27 Pfaffenwaldring, D-7000 Stuttgart 80, Federal Republic of Germany.

ARIARAJAH, Wesley, TH.M., M.PHIL., PH.D.; Sri Lankan ecclesiastic; b. 2 Dec. 1941, Jaffna; s. of Ponniah David Seevaratnam and Grace Annalukshmi (née Sinnapu); m. Christine Shyamala Chinniah 1974; three d.; ed. Madras Christian Coll., United Theological Coll., Bangalore, Princeton (N.Y.) Seminary, Univ. of London; ordained in Methodist Church; Minister Methodist Church of Sri Lanka, Jaffna 1966-68; Lecturer Theological Coll. Lanka, Pilimatalawa 1969-71; Chair. North and East Dist., Methodist Church, Jaffna 1974-81; staff WCC programme on Dialogue with People of Living Faiths, Geneva 1981-83, Dir. 1983-; delivered Sixth Lambeth Interfaith Lecture 1987. *Publications:* Dialogue 1980, The Bible and People of Other Faiths 1986; Contrib. articles to specialist journals. *Leisure interest:* reading. *Address:* World Council of Churches, Dialogue with People of Living Faiths, 150 route de Ferney, CH-1211 Geneva 20 (Office); 16 Avenue des Amazones, CH-1224 Chêne-Bougeries, Geneva, Switzerland (Home). *Telephone:* (022) 91 63 28 (Office); (022) 48 51 41 (Home).

ARIAS, Dame Margot Fonteyn de, D.B.E. (wife of Roberto Arias, q.v.); British ballerina; b. (as Margaret Hookham) 18 May 1919; ed. U.S.A. and China; as prima ballerina of the Royal Ballet Company, London, has danced all principal classical roles as well as leading roles in many modern ballets, and has appeared in many countries all over the world; *films include* I am a Dancer 1972; introduced and narrated B.B.C. TV series The Magic of Dance 1979; Pres. Royal Acad. of Dancing 1954-; Chancellor, Durham Univ. 1982-; Benjamin Franklin Medal 1973, Anglo-German Shakespeare Prize 1977; several hon. degrees, including Hon. Dr. (Durham) 1982, Order of Finnish Lion, Order of Estacio de Sa (Brazil) 1973, Chevalier Ordre of Merit of Duarte, Sanchez and Mella (Dominican Repub.) 1975. *Publications:* Margot Fonteyn (autobiog.) 1975, A Dancer's World 1978, The Magic of Dance 1980, Pavlova Impressions 1984. *Address:* c/o Royal Opera House, Covent Garden, London, W.C.2, England.

ARIAS, Roberto Emilio, B.A.; Panamanian lawyer, editor and diplomatist; b. 26 Oct. 1918; s. of Harmodio Arias and Rosario Guardia de Arias; m. 1st Querube Solis 1946, one s. two d.; m. 2nd Dame Margot Fonteyn (de Arias q.v.) 1955; ed. Peddie School, New Jersey, and St. John's Coll. Cambridge, Sorbonne Univ. and Columbia Univ.; called to Panamanian Bar 1939; Ed. El Panamá-América 1942-48; Publisher La Hora 1948-68; Del. to UN Ass. 1953; Amb. to U.K. 1955-58, 1960-62; Deputy to Nat.

Ass. of Panama 1964-68; paralysed in assassination attempt 1964. *Address:* P.O. Box 6-1140, El Dorado, Panama City, Panama.

ARIAS E., Ricardo M.; Panamanian diplomatist, politician and businessman; b. 1912, in Embassy of Panama, Washington, D.C., U.S.A.; s. of Francisco Arias Paredes and Carmen Espinosa de Arias; m. Olga Arias; two s. two d.; ed. Colegio La Salle, Panama, Shenandoah Valley Acad., Va., Georgetown Univ., Washington, D.C., U.S.A. and Univ. Católica de Chile; mem. Nat. Electoral Jury 1944-48; Minister of Agric., Commerce and Industries 1949-51, of Labour, Health and Social Welfare 1952-55; Second Vice-Pres. of the Republic 1952-55, Acting Pres. Sept. 1954; Minister of Foreign Affairs Jan. 1955; Pres. of the Republic of Panama 1955-56; fmr. Amb. to U.S.A. and to OAS; Rep. to Int. Bank for Reconstruction and Development 1956; defeated candidate, Presidential election May 1960; Amb. to U.S.A. 1964-68; Exec. Vice-Pres. DISA, S.A. 1968-; Leader, Coalición Patriótica Nacional; Pres. Sociedad Ganadera (Cattle Asscn.), Cía. Panameña de Aviación; Hon. LL.D. (Rockhurst Coll.); numerous Panamanian and foreign orders. *Leisure interest:* golf. *Address:* Apdo. 4549, Panama City, Panama.

ARIAS NAVARRO, Carlos; Spanish lawyer and politician; b. 11 Dec. 1908; Legal Asst., Ministry of Justice; Public Prosecutions Dept., Supreme Court; Civil Gov. León Prov. 1944-49, Navarre 1949; Dir.-Gen. of Security 1957; Mayor of Madrid 1965-73; Minister of Interior June-Dec. 1973; Prime Minister 1974-76; mem. Popular Alliance Party. *Address:* c/o Oficina del Presidente del Gobierno, Madrid, Spain.

ARIAS-SALGADO Y MONTALVO, Fernando; Spanish diplomatist; b. 3 May 1938, Valladolid; s. of Gabriel Arias-Salgado y Cubas; m. María Isabel Garrigues López-Chicheri 1969; one s. one d.; ed. Univ. of Madrid, Coll. of Lawyers, Madrid; entered Diplomatic School 1963; Sec. Perm. Del. of Spain to UN 1966-68; Adviser, UN Security Council 1968-69; Asst. Dir.-Gen. Promotion of Research, Ministry of Educ. and Science 1971, Asst. Dir.-Gen. of Int. Co-operation, Ministry of Educ. and Science 1972; Legal Adviser, Legal Dept. (Int. Affairs), Ministry of Foreign Affairs 1973-75, Dir. 1983-85; Counsellor, Spanish Del. to Int. Court of Justice 1975; Tech. Sec.-Gen. Ministry of Foreign Affairs 1976; Dir.-Gen. Radiotelevisión Española 1977-81; Amb. to U.K. Jan. 1981-83.

ARIAS SÁNCHEZ, Oscar, PH.D.; Costa Rican politician; b. 13 Sept. 1941; m.; ed. Univ. of Costa Rica, L.S.E. and Univ. of Essex; Prof. School of Political Sciences Univ. of Costa Rica 1969-72; Financial Adviser to Pres. of Repub. 1970-72; Minister of Nat. Planning and Econs. Policy 1972-77; Int. Sec. Liberación Nacional Party 1975, Gen. Sec. 1979-83, 1983-; Congressman in Legis. Ass. 1978-82; Pres. of Costa Rica Feb. 1986-; mem. Bd. Cen. Bank 1972-77, Vice-Pres. 1970-72; ad hoc Comm. mem. Heredia's Nat. Univ. 1972-75; mem. Bd. Tech. Inst. 1974-77; mem. Rector's Nat. Council 1974-77; mem. Bd. Int. Univ. Exchange Fund, Geneva 1976; mem. N.-S. Roundtable 1977; has participated in numerous int. meetings and socialist conventions; instrumental in formulating the Cen. American Peace Agreement 1986-87; Nobel Peace Price 1987; Dr. h.c. (Oviedo) 1988. *Publications:* Pressure Groups in Costa Rica 1970 (Essay's Nat. Award 1971), Who Governs in Costa Rica? 1976, Latin American Democracy, Independence and Society 1977, Roads for Costa Rica's Development 1977, New Ways for Costa Rican Development 1980, and several articles in newspapers and in nat. and foreign magazines. *Address:* Casa Presidencial, Apdo 10.176, San José, Costa Rica.

ARIAS STELLA, Dr. Javier; Peruvian politician and pathologist; b. 2 Aug. 1924, Lima; m. Nancy Castillo; four c.; ed. San Luis School, Universidad Nacional Mayor de San Marcos and San Fernando Medical School; lectured in univs. in England, U.S.A., Argentina, Mexico and Brazil; work on pathology now known as the "Arias Stella Reaction or Phenomenon" published 1954; Nat. Sec.-Gen. Acción Popular (political party) 1959-; Minister of Public Health 1963-65, 1967-68; in exile, Argentina 1973, Venezuela 1974; Minister for Foreign Affairs 1980-83; Perm. Rep. to the UN 1984-86; Hipolito Unanue (Peru), Premio Roussel Perú and numerous decorations. *Publications:* nearly 100 works on pathology. *Address:* Ministry of Foreign Affairs, Ucayali 363, Lima, Peru.

ARIDOR, Yoram, M.JUR.; Israeli lawyer and politician; b. 24 Oct. 1933, Tel-Aviv; m.; three c.; ed. Hebrew Univ. of Jerusalem; mem. Knesset 1969-88, Chair. Cttee. for Interior and Environmental Affairs 1975-77, Chair. Sub-Cttee. for Constitutional Law 1975-77, mem. Cttee. for Legislation and Justice 1969-81, Deputy Minister in P.M.'s office 1977-81; Minister of Finance 1981-83, also of Communications Jan.-July 1981; Chair. Herut (Freedom) Movt. in Histradrut (Gen. Fed. of Labour) 1972-77, mem. Cen. Cttee. Herut Movt. 1961-, Chair. Secr. 1979-87; fmr. Gov. IMF. *Address:* 38 Haoranim Street, Ramat-Efal, Israel.

ARIE, Thomas Harry David, M.A., B.M., D.P.M., F.R.C.P., F.R.C.PSYCH., F.F.C.M.; British psychiatrist; b. 9 Aug. 1933, Prague, Czechoslovakia; s. of late Dr. O. M. Arie and Mrs. H. Arie; m. Dr. Eleanor Aitken 1963; one s. two d.; ed. Balliol Coll., Oxford; Sr. Lecturer in Social Medicine, London Hosp. Medical Coll. 1962-68; Consultant Psychiatrist for Old People, Goodmayes Hosp. 1969-77; Foundation Prof. and Head, Dept. of Health Care of the Elderly, Nottingham Univ. 1977-; Consultant Psychiatrist to Nottingham Health Authority 1977-; Vice-Pres. Royal Coll. of Psychiatrists 1984-86, Chair. Specialist Section on Old Age 1981-86; Sec., Geriatric Psychiatry

Section, World Psychiatric Asscn. 1983-. *Publications:* Ed. Health Care of the Elderly 1981, Recent Advances in Psychogeriatrics 1985; papers on the care of the aged, old age psychiatry, epidemiology and educ. *Address:* Department of Health Care of the Elderly, Medical School, Queen's Medical Centre, Nottingham, NG7 2UH, England. *Telephone:* (0602) 421421, Ext. 3166.

ARIFIN, Bustanil; Indonesian politician; b. 10 Oct. 1925, Padang Panjang, W. Sumatra; ed. Faculty of Law, Univ. of Pajajaran, Bandung; commissioned into army 1946; active service during first and second Dutch Mil. Action 1946-48; Deputy Head, Bureau of Training for Army Supply, Cimahi 1954; Instr. and later Head of Educ. Bureau, Training Course in Army Supply 1961-65; staff mem. Devt. Command in border territories 1965-67; Asst. Supervisor, Nat. Logistics Command 1967-69; Deputy Head of Supply and Distribution Div. Inst. of Logistics (BULOG) 1969; Consul-Gen. New York 1972; Head, Inst. of Logistics 1973; Jr. Minister for Co-operatives 1978-83; Minister of Co-operatives 1983-. *Address:* Ministry of Co-operatives, Jln. Moh. Ihkwan Rais 5, Jakarta Pusat, Indonesia.

ARIKAN, Vural; Turkish politician; b. 1929, Akkoy; m.; ed. Faculty of Political Sciences and Law, Istanbul Univ.; admin. in industrial establishments and specialist in tax law; Minister of Finance and Customs 1983-84. *Address:* c/o Maliye ve gumruk Bakanliği, Ankara, Turkey.

ARIKPO, Okoi, PH.D.; Nigerian politician; b. 1916, Ugep, E. Nigeria; ed. Nigeria, and Univ. of London; teacher, Univ. of London 1949-51; mem. E. Nigeria House of Assembly 1952, later mem. Fed. House of Reps. until 1954; later Minister of Lands and Mines; scientist and teacher 1961-67; Fed. Commr. for Trade June 1967-Sept. 1968; Fed. Commr. for External Affairs Sept. 1968-75; Sec. Nigerian Univ. Comm. *Address:* c/o Federal Ministry for External Affairs, Lagos, Nigeria.

ARINZE, H.E. Cardinal Francis A.; Nigerian ecclesiastic; b. 1 Nov. 1932, Eziowelle, Onitsha; s. of Joseph Arinze Nwankwu and Bernadette M. Arinze; ordained 1958; consecrated Bishop (Titular Church of Fissiana) 1965; Archbishop of Onitsha 1967; elevated to Cardinal 1985; Pres. Secr. for Non-Christians. *Publication:* Alone with God 1987. *Leisure interests:* tennis, reading. *Address:* Secretariat for Non-Christians, 00120 Vatican City, Italy. *Telephone:* (698) 3648, (698) 4321.

ARISAWA, Hiromi, DR.ECON.; Japanese professor of economics and statistics; b. 16 Feb. 1896, Kochi Pref.; s. of Mototaro and Hide Arisawa; m. Shizuko Arisawa 1930; two s. two d.; ed. Univ. of Tokyo; Assoc. Prof. Univ. of Tokyo 1924-45, Prof. 1945-56, Prof. Emer. 1956-; Pres. Hosei Univ. 1959-62; Chair. Japan Atomic Industrial Forum 1973-; Pres. Japan Acad. 1980-; Person of Cultural Merits (Japan); Officier, Légion d'honneur. *Publications:* Analytical Studies on the Control of Industries in Japan 1937, Some Problems on Inflation and Socialization 1948. *Leisure interest:* the game of Go. *Address:* 1-31-10 Minami Asagaya, Suginami-ku, Tokyo, 166, Japan. *Telephone:* (03) 311-2777.

ARISTOV, Boris Ivanovich; Soviet politician; b. 1925; ed. Ulyanov Electrotechnical Inst., Leningrad; war service 1942-45; electrical assembler, engineer, chief technologist Svetlana Factory, Leningrad 1947-52; mem. CPSU 1945-; State and party official 1952-; Deputy Chair. Leningrad City Soviet exec. cttee. 1969-71, First Sec. 1971-78; Amb. to Poland 1978-83, Deputy Foreign Minister 1983-85, Minister for Foreign Trade Oct. 1985-; mem. Cen. Cttee. CPSU 1971-; Deputy to Supreme Soviet of the U.S.S.R.; various decorations. *Address:* c/o Ministry of Foreign Trade, Moscow, U.S.S.R.

ARIYOSHI, George Ryoichi, JU.D.; American politician; b. 12 March 1926, Honolulu, Hawaii; s. of Ryozo Ariyoshi and Mitsue (Yoshikawa) Ariyoshi; m. Jean Miya Hayashi 1955; two s. one d.; ed. McKinley High School, Honolulu, Michigan State Univ. and Univ. of Michigan Law School; private law practice, Honolulu 1953-70; mem. Territorial House of Reps. 1954-58, of Territorial Senate 1959, of State Senate 1960-70; Lieut. Gov. 1970-74, Gov. of State of Hawaii 1974-87; Chair. Western Govs.' Conf. 1977-78, 1984-; Pres. Pacific Basin Devt. Council 1980-81; Dir. First Hawaiian Bank 1962-70, Pacific Resources 1964-70; Hawaiian Insurance and Guaranty 1965-70; Distinguished Alumni Awards, Univ. of Hawaii and Michigan State Univ.; Hon. LL.D. (Univ. of the Philippines), (Guam, Mich. State); Hon. D.H. (Visayas), (Soka) 1984. *Leisure interest:* sports. *Address:* Executive Chambers, State Capitol, Honolulu, Hawaii 96813, U.S.A. *Telephone:* (808) 548-5420.

ARJONA PÉREZ, Marta María; Cuban sculptor and ceramic artist; b. 4 May 1923, Havana; d. of Ernesto and Norak Arjona Pérez; unmarried; ed. San Alejandro Nat. School of Beaux Arts and Paris; various exhbns. in Cuba and overseas 1945-52; Dir. Nuestro Tiempo Soc. Gallery 1953-59; Nat. Dir. of Plastic Arts, then Museums and Monuments 1959-77, Dir. of Cultural Heritage 1977-; Pres. Cuban Cttee., Int. Council of Museums; Medal, then Order of Raúl Gómez García 1975, 1982. *Works on view* include ceramic murals at the Palacio de la Revolución (with René Portocarrero) and Escuela V. I. Lenin (with Mariano Rodríguez). *Publications:* various articles in specialist periodicals. *Address:* Quinta B, no. 8605 entre 86 y 88, Miramar, Playa (Home); Calle A, no. 608 entre 25 y 27, Vedado, Havana, Cuba (Office). *Telephone:* 2-8155 (Home).

ARKADIEV, Georgiy Petrovich; Soviet diplomatist; b. 5 Feb. 1905, Pokhvistnevo Village, Kuibyshev Region; ed. Economic and Diplomatic

Inst; publishing and pedagogical activities 1919–36; joined Soviet diplomatic service 1936; People's Commissariat for Foreign Affairs 1937–44; Ministry of Foreign Affairs 1944–47; Soviet Mil. Administration, Germany 1947–49; Counsellor, U.S.S.R. Diplomatic Mission to G.D.R. 1949–51; Foreign Ministry U.S.S.R. 1951–52, Chief U.S.A. Dept. 1952–53; Ambassador to Norway 1954–56; Deputy Perm. U.S.S.R. Rep. to UN 1956–60; Under-Sec. UN, Head Dept. of Political and Security Council Affairs 1960–61, resigned 1962; Head, Dept. of Int. Econ. Orgs. of Ministry of Foreign Affairs 1962–66; Perm. Rep. of U.S.S.R. to IAEA, Vienna 1966; Perm. U.S.S.R. Rep. at Int. Orgs. in Vienna 1968–75. *Address:* c/o Ministry of Foreign Affairs, Moscow, U.S.S.R.

ARKELL, John Heward, C.B.E., T.D., M.A., C.B.I.M.; British business executive; b. 20 May 1909, Tytherington, Glos.; s. of Rev. H.H. Arkell, M.A. and Gertrude M. (née Heward) Arkell; m. 1st Helen B. Huitfeldt 1940, 2nd Meta B. Grundtvig (diss.); three s. one d.; ed. Dragon School, Oxford, Radley Coll. and Christ Church, Oxford; Sec. Sir Max Michaelis (Investment) Trust 1931–37; Asst. Sec. Council for the Protection of Rural England 1937–39; army service 1939–45; Personnel Man., J. Lyons & Co. Ltd. 1945–49; Controller of Staff Admin., BBC 1949–58, Dir. 1958–60; Dir. of Admin. BBC 1960–70; Chair. Air Transport and Travel Industry Training Bd. 1970–80; Sr. Assoc. Leo Kramer Int. 1980–86; Lay mem. Nat. Industrial Relations Court 1971–74; Dir. Boots Co. Ltd. 1970–79, The Coates Group of Companies 1970–76, U.K. Provident Inst. 1971–80; mem. Council for Industry Man. Educ. 1971–; Chair. British Inst. of Management 1972–74; mem. Council of CBI 1972–74; Fellow, Royal Soc. of Arts 1973; Visiting Fellow, Admin. Staff Coll., Henley-on-Thames 1971–; Vice-Pres. Council for Protection of Rural England 1975–; Fellow Inst. of Personnel Man. 1974–; mem. Final Selection Bd., Civil Service Comm. 1978–81; mem. Council, Nat. Trust 1971–84; Gov. Radley Coll. 1965–70; Founder (now Jt. Pres.) Christ Church (Oxford) United Clubs 1931–; musical compositions (publr. EMI): Bless Them Lord, The Leander Waltz, Seringa, Candlelight. *Leisure interests:* walking, sailing, swimming, composing light music. *Address:* Pinnocks, Fawley, Henley-on-Thames, Oxon, England. *Telephone:* Henley 573017.

ARKHIPOV, Ivan Vasiliyevich; Soviet politician; b. 1 May 1907, Kaluga; ed. Moscow Instrument Building Inst.; engineer 1921–38; mem. Cen. Cttee. CPSU 1932–; First Deputy People's Commissar, then First Deputy Minister of Non-Ferrous Metallurgy of U.S.S.R. 1943–58; Deputy Chair. State Cttee. for Foreign Econ. Relations, Council of Ministers of U.S.S.R. 1958–59, First Deputy Chair. 1959–74; Vice-Chair. Council of Ministers of U.S.S.R. 1974–80, First Vice-Chair. 1980–86; Deputy to Supreme Soviet; Hero of Socialist Labour, Order of Ho Chi Minh and other decorations. *Address:* c/o Council of Ministers, The Kremlin, Moscow, U.S.S.R.

ARKHIPOVA, Irina Konstantinovna; Soviet mezzo-soprano; b. 2 Jan. 1925, Moscow; attended vocal classes at Inst. of Architecture, Moscow, from which graduated, 1948; entered Moscow Conservatoire 1953 (pupil of L. Savransky); stage début as soloist (Carmen) with Bolshoi Theatre, 1956; People's Artist of U.S.S.R. 1966; mem. CPSU 1963–; mem. U.S.S.R. Supreme Soviet; opera and song recitals since 1956 at Milan, Vienna, Paris, London and in U.S.A.; also performs French and Italian repertoire, roles include Carmen, Amneris in Aida, Hélène in War and Peace; People's Artist of the U.S.S.R.

ARKIN, Alan Wolf; American actor and director; b. 26 March 1934; s. of David and Beatrice Arkin; m. 2nd Barbara Dana, one s; two s. from first marriage; ed. Los Angeles City Coll., Los Angeles State Coll., Bennington Coll.; made professional theatre début with the Compass Players, St. Louis 1959; later joined Second City group, Chicago 1960; made New York début at Royal, in revue From the Second City 1961; played David Kolvitz in Enter Laughing 1963–64 (Tony Award 1963), appeared in revue A View Under The Bridge, 1964; Harry Berline in Luv; dir. Eh? at the Circle in the Square, 1966; Hail Scrawdyke 1966, Little Murders, 1969, White House Murder Case 1970; dir. The Sunshine Boys 1972; dir. Molly 1973, Joan Lorraine 1974. *Films include:* The Russians Are Coming, the Russians Are Coming 1966, Women Times Seven 1967, Wait Until Dark 1967, Inspector Clouseau 1968, The Heart is a Lonely Hunter 1968, Popi 1969, Catch 22 1970, Little Murders (also dir.) 1971, Last of the Red Hot Lovers 1972, Freebie and the Bean 1974, Rafferty and the Gold Dust Twins 1975, Hearts of the West 1975, The In-Laws 1979, The Magician of Lublin 1979, Simon 1980, Chu Chu and the Philly Flash 1981, Improper Channels 1981, The Last Unicorn 1982, Joshua Then and Now (also dir.) 1985. *TV appearances include:* The Love Song of Barney Kempinski 1966, The Other Side of Hell 1978, The Defection of Simas Kudirka 1978, Captain Kangaroo, A Deadly Business 1986; Theatre World Award 1964 for Enter Laughing. New York Film Critics; Award Best Supporting Actor for Hearts of the West and for Heart is a Lonely Hunter. *Publications:* Tony's Hard Work Day, The Lemming Condition, Halfway Through the Door, The Clearing 1986.

ARLETTY (see Leonie Bathiat).

ARLMAN, Paul, M.A.; Netherlands banker and international civil servant; b. 7 Nov. 1946, Bussum; s. of Evert Arlman and Corrie Jacobs; m. Kieke Wijs 1971; one s. one d.; ed. Hilversum Grammar School, Rotterdam Econ. Univ. and Peace Research Inst., Groningen; served in the Treasury, The

Hague 1970–74, as Treasury Rep. to the Netherlands Embassy, Washington D.C. 1974–78; Div. Chief Treasury, The Hague 1978–81, Dir. and Deputy Asst. Sec. Int. Affairs 1981–86; Exec. Dir. IBRD, IDA, IFC, MIGA 1986–; mem. Bd. of Dirs., EIB 1981–86, Chair. Bd. Policy Cttee. 1983–84. *Leisure interests:* literature, tennis, skiing, outdoor sports. *Address:* 1818 H Street N.W., Suite 1306, Washington D.C. 20433 (Office); 7005 Beechwood Drive, Chevy Chase, MD 20815, U.S.A. (Home). *Telephone:* (202) 477-5286; (301) 654-3944.

ARLOTT, (Leslie Thomas) John, O.B.E.; British journalist, author and broadcaster; b. 25 Feb. 1914, Basingstoke; s. of late William John and Nellie Jenvey Arlott; m. 1st Dawn Rees, two s. (one deceased); m. 2nd Valerie France (died 1976), one s. (one d. deceased); m. 3rd Patricia Hoare 1977; ed. Queen Mary's School, Basingstoke; clerk in mental hospital 1930–34; Detective Sgt., police force, 1934–45; Producer, BBC 1945–50; Gen. Instructor, BBC Staff Training School 1951–53; contested (Liberal) Epping Div., Gen. Election 1955 and 1959; fmr. cricket commentator for BBC; wine corresp. and general writer The Guardian; Pres. Hants. Schools Cricket Asscn. 1966–80, Cricketers Asscn. 1968–; Sports Journalist of 1979 (British Press Award), Sports Personality of 1980 (Soc. of Authors' Pye Radio Award), Sports Presenter of the Year 1980 (TV and Radio Industries Award); Hon. Life mem. MCC 1980; Hon. M.A. (Southampton) 1973; Hon. D.Univ. (Open Univ.) 1981. *Publications:* Landmarks (with G. R. Hamilton) 1943, Of Period and Place (poems) 1944, Clausentum (poems) 1945, First time In America (anthology) 1949, Concerning Cricket 1949, How to Watch Cricket 1949, Maurice Tate 1951, Concerning Soccer 1952, Cricket (Pleasures of Life series) (Ed.) 1953, The Picture of Cricket 1955, English Cheeses of the South and West 1956, Jubilee History of Cricket 1965, Vintage Summer 1967, The Noblest Game (with Sir Neville Cardus) 1969, Fred: portrait of a fast bowler 1971, The Ashes 1972, Island Camera: the Isles of Scilly in the photography of the Gibson family 1973, The Snuff Shop 1974, The Oxford Companion to Sports and Games (Ed.) 1975, Burgundy Vines and Wines (with Christopher Fielden) 1976, Krug: House of Champagne 1977, An Eye for Cricket (with Patrick Eagar) 1979, Jack Hobbs: a Profile of the Master 1981, A Word from Arlott (ed. David Allen) 1983, Wine (ed.) 1984, Arlott on Cricket 1985, Another Word from Arlott (with D. Allen) 1985, Botham (with Eagan) 1985, Arlott in Conversation with Mike Brearley 1986, John Arlott's 100 Greatest Batsmen 1986, Arlott on Wine 1986. *Address:* c/o The Guardian, 119 Farringdon Road, London, EC1R 3ER, England.

ARMACOST, Michael Hayden, M.A., PH.D. (brother of Samuel Henry Armacost q.v.); government official and politician; b. 15 April 1937; s. of George H. and Verda Gay (Hayden) Armacost; m. Roberta June Bray 1959; three s.; ed. Carleton Coll., Friedrich Wilhelms Univ., Columbia Univ.; Assoc. Prof. Govt., Pomona Coll., Claremont, Calif. 1962–70; Wig Distinguished Prof. 1966; Special Asst. to Amb., American Embassy, Tokyo 1972–74, Amb. (desig.) to Japan 1989–; mem. Policy Planning, Staff Dept., Washington 1974–77; Sr. Staff mem., Nat. Security Council, Washington 1977–78; Dep. Asst. Sec. Defence, Int. Security Affairs Defence Dept., Washington 1978–79; Principal Deputy Asst. Sec. E. Asian and Pacific Affairs 1980–81; Amb. to Philippines 1982–84; Undersec. Political Affairs 1984–89; mem. Council on Foreign Relations; Visiting Prof. Int. Relations, Int. Christian Univ., Tokyo 1968–69; Superior Honour Award, State Dept. 1976; Distinguished Civilian Service Award, Defence Dept. 1980; Presidential Meritorious Award; White House Distinguished Fellow 1969–70. *Publications:* The Politics of Weapons Innovation 1969, The Foreign Relations of United States 1969. *Address:* Department of State, 2210 C Street, N.W., Washington, D.C. 20520, U.S.A.

ARMACOST, Samuel Henry, (brother of Michael Hayden Armacost, q.v.); American banker; b. 1939, Newport News, Va.; m. Mary Jane Armacost 1962; two d.; ed. Denison Univ., Granville, Ohio, Stanford Univ.; joined Bank of America as credit trainee 1961; London branch 1969–71; State Dept. Office of Monetary Affairs (executive exchange programme) 1971–72; Head Europe, Middle East and Africa Div., London 1977–79; Cashier Bank of America and Treasurer of its Holding Co. Bank-America Corpn. 1979–80; Pres. and C.E.O. Bank of America and Bank-America Corpn. 1981–86, Chair. and C.E.O. 1986 (resgnd); Investment Banker Merrill Lynch and Co. 1987; Man. Dir. Merrill Lynch Capital Markets 1988–. *Address:* Bank of America, P.O. Box 3700, San Francisco, Calif. 94137, U.S.A.

ARMANI, Giorgio; Italian fashion designer; b. 11 July 1934, Piacenza; s. of late Ugo Armani and of Maria Raimondi; ed. Liceo School, Piacenza and Univ. of Milan; window dresser, then asst. buyer La Rinascente, Milan 1957–64; Designer and Product Developer Hitman (menswear co. of Cerruti group) 1964–70; freelance designer for several firms 1970; founded Giorgio Armani SpA with Sergio Galeotti 1975, achieved particular success with unconstructed jackets of mannish cut for women, trademarks also in babywear, underwear, accessories, perfume; appeared on cover of Time 1982; numerous awards including Cutty Sark 1980, 1981, 1984, 1986, 1987, (First Designer Laureate 1985), Ambrogino D'Oro, Milan 1982, Int. Designer Award, Council of Fashion Designers of America 1983, L'Occhio D'Oro 1984, 1986, 1987, 1988, L'Occhiolino D'Oro 1986, 1987, Grand 'Ufficiale dell'ordineal merito 1986, Gran Cavaliere 1987, Time-Life Achievement Award 1987, Cristobal Balenciaga Award 1988. *Leisure interest:* tennis. *Address:* Via Borgonuovo 21, 20121 Milano, Italy. *Telephone:* 02-801481.

ARMATRADING, Joan; British singer and songwriter; b. 9 Dec. 1950, St. Kitts, West Indies; moved to Birmingham, U.K. 1958; began professional career in collaboration with lyric-writer Pam Nestor 1972. *Recordings include:* Whatever's For Us 1973, Back To The Night 1975, Joan Armatrading 1976, Show Some Emotion 1977, My, Myself, I 1980, Walk Under Ladders 1981, The Key 1983, Secret Secrets 1985, The Shouting Stage 1988.

ARMITAGE, Kenneth, C.B.E.; British sculptor; b. 18 July 1916, Leeds; ed. Leeds Coll. of Art and Slade School, London; teacher of Sculpture, Bath Acad. of Art 1947–56; Gregory Fellowship, Leeds Univ. 1953; British Council Visitor in Sculpture to Venezuela 1963–64; One-man exhbns. London 1952, 1957, 1962, 1965, New York 1954, 1956, 1958, 1962, Retrospective exhbn. Whitechapel Art Gallery, London 1959, Sala Mendoza, Caracas, Venezuela 1982; represented at Venice Biennale 1958; Guest Artist, City of Berlin 1967–69; Hakone Open-Air Sculpture, Japan 1969, one-man exhbn. touring Tokyo, Osaka, Nagoya 1978; retrospective exhbn., Paris 1985; sculpture Comm., new British Embassy, Brasilia 1985–86; many groups exhbns. in America and Europe; works in major public collections throughout the world; David Bright Prize Venice Biennale 1958. *Address:* 22A Avonmore Road, London, W14 8RR, England.

ARMSTRONG, Mrs. Anne Legendre, B.A.; American company director, politician and diplomatist; b. 27 Dec. 1927, New Orleans, La.; d. of Armant and Olive Legendre; m. Tobin Armstrong 1950; three s. two d.; ed. Foxcroft School, Middleburg, Va., and Vassar Coll.; Republican Nat. Committee woman from Texas 1968–73; Republican Nat. Comm. Co-Chair. 1971–73; Counsellor to Pres. Nixon with cabinet rank 1973–74; Counsellor to Pres. Ford with cabinet rank 1974; resigned from govt. service 1974; Amb. to U.K. 1976–77; Lecturer in Diplomacy, Georgetown Univ. 1977–; Dir. Halliburton, Gen. Motors, Boise Cascade 1977–; Dir. American Express Co. 1983–; Chair. English-Speaking Union of U.S. 1977–80; Chair. Pres.'s Foreign Intelligence Advisory Bd. 1981–; Chair. Bd. of Trustees Center for Strategic and Int. Studies, Washington, D.C. 1987–; Co-Chair. Reagan-Bush Campaign 1980; Chair. Texas Women's Alliance 1985–; mem. Visiting Cttee. JFK School of Govt., Harvard Univ. 1978–82, Comm. on Integrated Long-Term Strategy 1987; mem. Bd. of Regents, Smithsonian Inst., 1978–; Trustee American Assocs. of R.A., of TRUST 1985–; Pres. Blair House Restoration Fund 1985–; Hon. LL.D. (Bristol, U.K.) 1976, (Washington and Lee) 1976, (Williams Coll., Mass.) 1977, (St. Mary's) 1978, (Tulane) 1978; Republican Woman of the Year Award 1979, Texan of the Year Award 1981, Texas Women's Hall of Fame 1986, Presidential Medal of Freedom 1987. *Address:* Armstrong Ranch, Armstrong, Tex. 78338, U.S.A.

ARMSTRONG, David Malet, B.PHIL., PH.D.; Australian professor of philosophy; b. 8 July 1926, Melbourne; s. of Capt. J. M. Armstrong and Philippa Suzanne Marett; m. Jennifer Mary de Bohun Clark 1982; ed. Dragon School, Oxford, England, Geelong Grammar School, Sydney and Oxford Univs.; Asst. Lecturer in Philosophy, Birkbeck Coll., London Univ. 1954–55; lecturer, Sr. Lecturer in Philosophy, Univ. of Melbourne 1956–63; Challis Prof. of Philosophy, Univ. of Sydney 1964–; Fellow Australian Acad. of Humanities. *Publications:* Berkeley's Theory of Vision 1961, Perception and the Physical World 1962, A Materialist Theory of the Mind 1968, Belief, Truth and Knowledge 1973, Universals and Scientific Realism 1978, The Nature of the Mind, and Other Essays 1983, What is a Law of Nature? 1983, Consciousness and Causality (with Norman Malcolm) 1984, A Combinatorial Theory of Possibility 1988. *Address:* Department of Traditional and Modern Philosophy, Sydney University, Sydney, N.S.W. 2006; 206 Glebe Point Road, Glebe, N.S.W. 2037, Australia. *Telephone:* 692 2466 (Office); 660 1435 (Home).

ARMSTRONG, John Archibald, O.C., B.SC.; Canadian oil company executive (retd.); b. 24 March 1917, Dauphin, Man.; s. of Herbert Humphrey and Louisa Isabella (née McDonald) Armstrong; m. June Keith 1943 (died 1987); three s.; ed. Univ. of Manitoba, Queen's Univ.; joined Imperial Oil Ltd. as geologist 1940, Exploration Geophysicist 1940–49, Exploration Man., Edmonton 1951, Asst. Regional Man., Producing Dept., Calgary 1954, Gen. Man. Toronto 1960, Dir. Imperial Oil Ltd. 1961, Exec. Vice-Pres. 1966, Pres. 1970–82, C.E.O. 1973–81, Chair. of the Bd. 1974–82; Man. Consultant DSBARJCO Inc. 1982–; Pres. Ds Oro Resources Inc.; Life mem. Fraser Inst.; fmr. Vice-Chair. and fmr. Dir., Export Devt. Corpn.; Finance Chair. Gov. Gen. Canadian Study Conf. 1987, Trustee Duke of Edinburgh Commonwealth Study Confs.; fmr. Dir. Royal Bank of Canada; Hon. LL.D. (Winnipeg, Calgary). *Address:* 65 Harbour Square, Suite 2604, Toronto, Ont. M5J 2L4, Canada (Home).

ARMSTRONG, Neil A.; American astronaut and professor of engineering; b. 5 Aug. 1930, Wapakoneta, Ohio; m. Janet Shearon; two s.; ed. Purdue Univ. and Univ. of Southern California; naval aviator 1949–52, flew combat missions during Korean War; joined NASA Lewis Flight Propulsion Laboratory 1955, later transferred to NASA High Speed Flight Station, Edwards, Calif., as aeronautical research pilot; was X-15 project pilot flying to over 200,000 ft. and at approx. 4,000 m.p.h.; other flight test work included X-1 rocket research plane, F-100, F-101, F-104, F5D, B-47 and the paraglider; selected as astronaut by NASA Sept. 1962; command pilot for Gemini VIII 1966; backup pilot for Gemini V 1965, Gemini XI 1966; flew to the moon in Apollo XI July 1969, first man to set foot on the moon 20 July 1969; Chair. Peace Corps Nat. Advisory Council 1969; Deputy Assoc. Admin. for Aeronautics, NASA, Washington 1970–71; Prof. of Engineering, Univ. of Cincinnati 1971–79; Chair. Cardwell Int. Ltd. 1979–81; Chair. CTA Inc. 1982–; Dir. numerous cos.; mem. Pres's Comm. on Space Shuttle 1986, Nat. Comm. on Space 1985–86; mem. Nat. Acad. of Engineering; Fellow, Soc. of Experimental Test Pilots, American Inst. of Aeronautics and Astronautics, Royal Aeronautical Soc.; hon. mem. Int. Acad. of Astronautics; Hon. Fellow, Int. Astron. Fed.; numerous decorations and awards from 17 countries including Presidential Medal of Freedom, NASA Exceptional Service Award, Royal Geographical Soc. Gold Medal and Harmon Int. Aviation Trophy 1970. *Address:* P.O. Box 436, Lebanon, Ohio 45036, U.S.A.

ARMSTRONG, Robert Douglas, F.C.A.; Canadian business executive (retd.); b. 25 April 1916, Ottawa; s. of William Allan Armstrong and Jennie Berry; m. Dorothea C. Fairleigh 1939; three s. one d.; formerly with Imperial Oil Ltd., Sarnia, Calgary and Toronto; Dir. of Finance and Admin. A. V. Roe Canada Ltd. (Hawker-Siddeley); Vice-Pres. Accounting and Finance, Canadian National Railway; Vice-Pres. Corporate Planning, Chrysler Canada Ltd., Windsor; Asst. Gen. Man. Chrysler Plymouth Div. for U.S.A.; Pres. Chrysler Leasing Corpn., Canadian Foundation Ltd.; Pres. and Chief Exec. Rio Algom Ltd., Chair., Dir. and Chief Exec. 1975–81. *Leisure interests:* golf, skiing, swimming. *Address:* 30 Glenorchy Drive, Don Mills, Ont. M3C 2P9, Canada.

ARMSTRONG, Robin Louis, B.A., PH.D., F.R.S.C.; Canadian professor of physics; b. 14 May 1935, Galt, Ont.; s. of Robert Dockstader Armstrong and Beatrice Jenny (née Grill) Armstrong; m. Karen Elisabeth Hansen 1960; two s.; ed. Preston High School, Univs. of Toronto and Oxford; Asst. Prof. of Physics Univ. of Toronto 1962–68, Assoc. Prof. 1968–71, Prof. 1971–; Assoc. Chair. Physics Univ. of Toronto 1969–74, Chair. 1974–82, Dean Faculty Arts and Science 1982–; Pres. Canadian Inst. for Neutron Scattering 1986–; Dir. Canadian Inst. for Advanced Research 1981–82, Huntsman Marine Lab. 1983–87, Rutherford Memorial Fellowship (Royal Soc. Canada) 1961; Herzberg Medal 1973. *Publications:* over 130 research articles on condensed matter physics in numerous journals. *Leisure interests:* jogging and skiing. *Address:* Office of the Dean, Faculty of Arts and Science, University of Toronto, 100 George Street, Toronto, Ont. M5S 1A1 (Office); 540 Huron Street, Toronto, Ont., M5R 2R7, Canada (Home). *Telephone:* 416-978 3383 (Office); 416-323 3870 (Home).

ARMSTRONG, Sheila Ann, F.R.A.M.; British concert and opera singer; b. 13 Aug. 1942, England; d. of William R. and Janet Armstrong; m. David E. Cooper 1980; no c.; ed. Hirst Park Girls' School, Ashington, Northumberland and Royal Acad. of Music; recipient of Mozart and Kathleen Ferrier Awards 1965; since then has appeared in opera at Glyndebourne, Scottish National Opera, Sadlers Wells, English Nat. Opera North and Royal Opera House, Covent Garden as well as giving recitals around the world with most of the maj. orchestras; has made extensive recordings; Hon, M.A. (Newcastle), Mozart Prize, Kathleen Ferrier Memorial Award. *Leisure interests:* collecting keys, interior decoration and design, flower-arranging, sewing. *Address:* Bradgate, Tilford Road, Hindhead, Surrey, GU26 6ST, England.

ARMSTRONG, Sir Thomas Henry Wait, Kt., M.A., D.MUS., F.R.C.M.; British musician; b. 15 June 1898; s. of A. E. Armstrong; m. Hester Draper 1926 (died 1982); one s. one d.; ed. Keble Coll., Oxford and Royal Coll. of Music. Organist Thorney Abbey 1914; Sub-Organist, Peterborough Cathedral 1915; served R.G.A. 1917–19; Sub-Organist, Manchester Cathedral 1922; Organist, St. Peter's, Eaton Square 1923; Organist, Exeter Cathedral 1928; Cramb Lecturer in Music, Univ. of Glasgow 1949; Student of Christ Church, Oxford 1939–55; Student Emeritus 1955–81; Hon. Student 1981–; Choragus of the Univ. and Lecturer in Music 1937–54; Conductor of Oxford Bach Choir and Oxford Orchestral Soc.; Organist, Christ Church, Oxford 1953–55; Principal, Royal Acad. of Music 1955–68; Chair. Henry Wood Nat. Memorial Trust 1980–; Hon. F.R.C.O., F.R.A.M. *Address:* 1 East Street, Olney, Bucks MK46 4AP, England.

ARMSTRONG OF ILMINSTER, Baron (Life Peer) cr. 1988, of Ashill in the County of Somerset; **Robert Temple Armstrong,** G.C.B., C.V.O., M.A.; British civil servant; b. 30 March 1927, Oxford; s. of Sir Thomas Armstrong (q.v.) and of Lady Armstrong (née Draper); m. 1st Serena Mary Benedicta Chance 1953 (divorced 1985); two d.; m. 2nd Mary Patricia Carlow 1985; ed. Eton Coll. and Christ Church, Oxford; Asst. Prin. Treasury 1950–55, Private Sec. to Economic Sec. 1953–54; Private Sec. to Chancellor of the Exchequer (Rt. Hon. R. A. Butler) 1954–55; Prin. Treasury 1955–64; Asst. Sec. Cabinet Office 1964–66; Asst. Sec. Treasury 1966–68; Prin. Private Sec. to Chancellor of the Exchequer (Rt. Hon. Roy Jenkins, q.v.) 1968; Under-Sec. Treasury 1968–70; Prin. Private Sec. to the Prime Minister 1970–75; Deputy Under-Sec. of State, Home Office 1975–77, Perm. Under-Sec. of State 1977–79; Sec. of the Cabinet 1979–87; Perm. Sec. Man. and Personnel Office 1981–87; Head, Home Civil Service 1981–87; Sec. Radcliffe Cttee. on Monetary System 1957–59; Sec. to the Dirs., Royal Opera House, Covent Garden 1968–87, Dir. Jan. 1988–; Dir. Bristol and West Bldg. Soc. 1988–; Chair. Bd. of Trustees, Victoria and Albert Museum 1988–; mem. Rhodes Trust 1975–; Fellow, Eton Coll. 1979–; Hon. Student, Christ

Church 1985. *Leisure interests:* music, gardening. *Address:* c/o Holt's, 22 Whitehall, London, SW1A 2EB, England.

ARNALL, Ellis Gibbs; American politician and lawyer; b. 20 March 1907, Newnan, Ga.; s. of Joseph Gibbs and Bessie Ellis Arnall; m. 1st Mildred Delaney Slemons 1935 (died 1980), one s. one d.; m. 2nd Ruby Hamilton McCord 1981; ed. Mercer Univ., Univ. of the South (Sewanee), and Georgia Univ.; mem. Georgia legislature; Asst. Attorney-Gen. 1937–39; Attorney-Gen. 1939–43; Gov. of Georgia 1943–47; Pres. Soc. of Ind. Motion Picture Producers 1943–67; Senior Partner Law Firm Arnall, Golden and Gregory; mem. U.S. Del. to 4th annual conf. UNESCO, Paris 1949; U.S. Del. Anglo-American Film Conf., London 1950; Trustee Univ. of the South, Mercer Univ.; Dir. U.S. Office of Price Stabilization 1952; Pres. Ind. Film Producers' Export Asscn. 1956–; Chair. Bd. of Dirs. Nat. Asscn. of Life Insurance Companies; Chair. Bd. of Dir. Coastal States Life Insurance 1956–; Vice-Chair. Sun Life Group of America 1979–; Dir. First Nat. Bank; Dir. of numerous other companies; mem. U.S. Nat. Comm. for UNESCO 1963–72. *Publications:* The Shore Dimly Seen 1946, What the People Want 1947. *Address:* Arnall, Golden & Gregory, 55 Park Place, Atlanta, Ga. 30335 (Office); 3 Muscogee Way N.W., Atlanta, Ga. 30305, U.S.A. (Home). *Telephone:* 404-577 5100 (Office).

ÁRNASON, Tómas; Icelandic politician; b. 21 July 1923, Seydisfjördur; s. of Árni Vilhjálmsson and Gudrun (née Thorvardardóttir) Árnason; m. Thora Kristín Eiríksdóttir 1949; four s.; ed. Univ. of Iceland, Harvard Law School. Advocate at Akureyri 1949–51 and 1952–53; Advocate, Supreme Court 1964–72; Chief, Div. of Defence Affairs, Ministry of Foreign Affairs 1953–60; mem. of Parl. 1956, 1958, 1959, 1968–73, 1974–85; Minister of Finance 1978–80, of Trade and Commerce 1980–83; a Gov. Cen. Bank of Iceland 1985–; Man. Dir. of newspaper Tíminn 1960–64; Man. Dir. Econ. Devt. Inst. 1972–78; mem. del. to UN; mem. del. to North Atlantic Ass. 1974–78, 1983–84; mem. Central Cttee. of Progressive Party, Cashier 1968, Sec. 1978–83; mem. Bd. Nordic Investment Bank. *Leisure interests:* golf, fishing. *Address:* Sedlabanki Íslands, Hafnarstraeti 10, P.O. Box 160, 121 Reykjavík; Hraunbraut 20, 200 Kópavogur, Iceland (Home). *Telephone:* 40972 (Home).

ARNAUD, Claude, L. ÈS L., L. EN D.; French diplomatist; b. 9 Nov. 1919, Voiteur (Jura); s. of Dr. Paul Arnaud, M.D.; m. 1st Sonia Larrain Beutner 1962 (deceased); m. 2nd Christiane Guida 1972, one s. one d.; ed. Univs. of Dijon, Lyon and Paris (Sorbonne); Attaché, Washington, 1945–46; Office of Resident-Gen. in Morocco 1946–51; First Sec. Bonn 1952–55; Econ. Dept., Foreign Office, Paris 1955–59; Counsellor, Chargé d'affaires, Belgrade 1959–62; Minister-Counsellor, Perm. Mission to UN 1962–65; Amb. to Laos Jan. 1966–68, to Kenya 1968–69; Dir. European Dept., Ministry of Foreign Affairs 1969–72, Deputy Dir. for Political Affairs 1972–75; Amb. to People's Repub. of China 1975–79, to U.S.S.R. 1981–85, to Mongolia 1984–85; Amb. of France 1985–; Diplomatic Counsellor, Ministry of Foreign Affairs 1985–; Perm. Rep. to NATO Council, Brussels 1979–81; Officier Légion d'honneur, Croix de guerre 1939–45, Commdr., Ordre nationale du Mérite. *Address:* 5 avenue Alphand, 75016 Paris, France (Home).

ARNAUSKAS, Leonas Semenovich; Soviet architect; b. 1921, Lithuania; ed. Moscow Architecture Inst.; worked on Novye Cheryomushki residential scheme, Moscow 1950s–60s, Krasnaya Presna complex, Moscow, also Olympic Village, 1970s; now chief architect on Mosproyekt-2; U.S.S.R. Council of Ministers' Prize 1972, Lenin Prize (for Olympic Village) 1982.

ARNDT, Otto; German building mechanic, railway engineer and politician; b. 19 July 1920, Aschersleben; Gen. Man. Deutsche Reichsbahn (G.D.R. Railways), Berlin 1961–64 and 1971–; Deputy Minister of Transport 1964–70, Minister 1971–; mem. German Communist Party (KPD) 1945; mem. Cen. Cttee. Socialist Unity Party of Germany (SED) 1971–; decorations include Vaterländischer Verdienstorden in Gold, Orden Banner der Arbeit. *Address:* Ministerium für Verkehr, 1086 Berlin, Voss Strasse 33, German Democratic Republic.

ARNDT, Ulrich W., F.R.S.; British research physicist; b. 23 April 1924, Berlin, Germany; s. of E. J. and C. M. Arndt; m. Valerie Hilton-Sergeant 1958; three d.; ed. Dulwich Coll., London, King Edward VI High School, Birmingham and Emmanuel Coll. Cambridge; Research Fellow, Birmingham Univ. 1948–49; mem. Research Staff, Royal Inst., London 1950–63, Dewar Research Fellow 1954–59; Research Assoc., Univ. of Wis., U.S.A. 1956–58; mem. Scientific Staff, MRC Lab. of Molecular Biology, Cambridge 1963–. *Publications:* Single Crystal Diffractometry (with B. T. M. Willis) 1966, The Rotation Method in Crystallography (with A. J. Wonacott) 1978 and over 100 papers in scientific journals. *Leisure interests:* reading, walking and history. *Address:* 28 Barrow Road, Cambridge, CB2 2AS, England. *Telephone:* (0223) 350660.

ARNEDO ORBANANOS, Miguel Angel, B.L., B.ECONS.; Spanish banker; Economist, Research Dept., Banco de Espana 1969; specialist in Int. Econ. 1973–; Deputy Dir. Monetary and Statistical Research 1981, Deputy Dir. for Foreign Relations 1984; mem. Cttee. on Capital Movts. and Invisible Transactions, OECD 1981–86; Vice-Pres. EIB 1986–. *Address:* European Investment Bank, 100 boulevard Konrad Adenauer, Luxembourg-Kirchberg, 2950 Luxembourg.

ARNELL, Richard Anthony Sayer; British composer, conductor and film producer; b. 15 Sept. 1917, London; s. of late Richard Sayer Arnell and Helène Marie Sherf; m. Audrey Millar Paul 1982; three d.; ed. University Coll. School and Royal Coll. of Music; Music consultant, BBC North American Service 1943–46; Lecturer, Trinity Coll. of Music, London 1948–87; Lecturer, Royal Ballet School 1958–59; Ed. "The Composer" 1961–64; Visiting lecturer (Fulbright exchange), Bowdoin Coll., Maine, U.S.A. 1967–68; Visiting Prof., Hofstra Univ., N.Y. 1968–70; Music dir. and mem. Bd. London Int. Film School 1975–; Chair. Composers' Guild of G.B. 1974–75, 1977–79, Young Musicians' Symphony Orch. Soc. 1973–75, 1977–79; Music. dir. Ram Filming Ltd. 1980–; Dir. A plus A Ltd. 1984–; Chair. London Int. Film School Trust 1981–; Chair. Friends of London Int. Film School 1982–87, Vice-Pres. 1987–; Chair. Friends of Trinity Coll. of Music Jr. Dept. 1986–87, Vice-Pres. 1987–; Composer of the Year 1966 (Music Teachers' Asscn. Award). *Compositions include:* Opera: Love in Transit, Moonflowers, Gesualdo 1988; Ballet scores: Punch and the Child 1947, Harlequin in April 1951, the Great Detective 1953, The Angels 1957, Giselle (reorchestrated) 1965; Film scores: The Land 1941, The Third Secret 1963, The Visit 1964, The Man Outside 1966, Topsail Schooner 1966, Bequest for a Village 1969, Second Best 1972, Stained Glass 1973, Wires Over the Border 1974, Black Panther 1977, Antagonist 1980, Dilemma 1981, Toulouse Lautrec 1984, Light of the World 1988; other works: Symphonic Portrait, Lord Byron, for Sir Thomas Beecham 1953, Landscapes and Figures 1956, Petrified Princess, puppet operetta for BBC 1959; Robert Flaherty, Impression for Radio Eireann 1960, Musica Pacifica for Edward Benjamin 1963, Festival Flourish, for Salvation Army 1965, Piano Concerto for RPO 1967, Overture, Food of Love, for Portland Symphony Orch. 1968, My Ladye Greene Sleeves, for Hofstra Univ. 1968, Nocturne 1968, I Think of all Soft Limbs 1971, Astronaut One 1973, Life Boat Voluntary, for Royal Nat. Lifeboat Inst. 1974, Call, for LSO 1980, RVW's Almanac 1984, Six Lawrence Poems 1985, Ode to Beecham, for RPO 1986, Brass Symphony (6) 1987; also six symphonies, two violin concertos, harpsichord concerto, two piano concertos, six string quartets, two quintets, organ works, music for string orch., wind ensembles, brass ensembles, song cycles and electronic music. *Leisure interests:* cooking, travel. *Address:* 5 Wharfe Bank Terrace, Tadcaster, N. Yorkshire, LS24 9BA, England. *Telephone:* 0937-834493.

ARNETT, Edward McCollin, PH.D.; American professor of chemistry; b. 25 Sept. 1922, Philadelphia; s. of John Hancock Arnett and Katherine McCollin; m. 1st Mary H. Flounders 1951 (divorced 1970), two s.; m. 2nd Sylvia Gettmann 1970, three step s.; ed. Germantown Friends School, Univ. of Pennsylvania, Harvard Univ.; Research Dir. Max Levy and Co., Philadelphia 1949–53; Assoc. Prof. Western Maryland Coll. 1953–55; Research Fellow, Harvard Univ. 1955–57; Asst. Prof., then Prof. Univ. of Pittsburgh 1957–80; R. J. Reynolds Industries Prof. of Chem., Duke Univ. 1980–; mem. N.A.S. 1983; Pittsburgh Award 1976, James Flack Norris Award 1977, American Chem. Soc. Petroleum Chem. Soc. Award 1984, Allen R. Day Award (Philadelphia) 1986. *Publications:* 160 scientific articles in physical organic chemistry. *Address:* Gross Laboratory, Duke University, Durham, N.C. 27706 (Office); 2529 Perkins Road, Durham, N.C., U.S.A. (Home). *Telephone:* (919) 684-2874 (Office); (919) 489-4133 (Home).

ARNOLD, Armin, PH.D., F.R.S.C.; Swiss/Canadian professor, writer and critic; b. 1 Sept. 1931, Zug, Switzerland; ed. Univs. of Fribourg, London and Zürich; Asst. Prof. of German, Univ. of Alberta 1959–61, McGill Univ. 1961–64, Assoc. Prof. 1964–68, Prof. 1968–84, Auxiliary Prof. 1984–; Dozent, Höhere Wirtschafts- und Verwaltungsschule, Olten 1984–. *Publications:* D. H. Lawrence and America 1958, James Joyce 1963, Die Literatur des Expressionismus 1966, Friedrich Dürrenmatt 1969, Prosa des Expressionismus 1972, Kriminalroman-führer 1978, etc. *Address:* Staadstrasse 39, CH-2540 Grenchen, Switzerland.

ARNOLD, Daryl; American business executive and diplomatist; b. 12 Nov. 1924, Calif.; s. of Laurence F. Arnold and Etta Emma Coe; m. Shirley Ann Haymore 1946; two s. one d.; ed. Univ. of S. Calif. and Midshipman School, N.Y.; rank of Lieutenant U.S.N. 1943–46; worked on family farm 1946–51; Owner Ocean View Farms and Cee Dee Ranch Co. 1951–70; Man. Northern Div., Freshpict Foods Inc. 1969–70; Pres. Free Marketing Council 1970–71; Pres. and C.E.O. Western Growers Asscn. 1971–87; Amb. to Singapore 1987–; Apptd. to U.S./Japan Advisory Comm. 1983–84, Bd. for Int. Food and Agricultural Devt. 1982–83; Produce Man of the Year 1978. *Leisure interests:* golf, hunting. *Address:* American Embassy, 30 Hill Street, Singapore 0617. *Telephone:* (65) 338-0251.

ARNOLD, Hans Redlef, PH.D.; German diplomatist; b. 14 Aug. 1923, Munich; s. of Karl Arnold and Anne-Dora Volquardsen; m. Karin Baroness von Egloffstein 1954; three d.; ed. Univ. of Munich; joined Foreign Service, Fed. Repub. of Germany; served Embassy, Paris 1952–55, Foreign Office, Bonn 1955–57, Embassy, Washington 1957–61, Foreign Office 1961–68; Amb. to Netherlands 1968–72; Head, Cultural Dept., Foreign Office 1972–77; Amb. to Italy 1977–81; Insp.-Gen. German Foreign Service 1981–82; Amb. and Perm. Rep. to UN and Int. Orgs., Geneva 1982–86; several nat. and foreign decorations. *Publications:* Cultural Export as Policy? 1976, Foreign Cultural Policy 1980. *Leisure interests:* mountaineering, skiing, travelling. *Address:* Heft, 8201 Riedering/Obb., Federal Republic of Germany. *Telephone:* (08032) 5255, (089) 3617603.

ARNOLD, James R., M.A., PH.D.; American professor of chemistry and space scientist; b. 5 May 1923, Metuchen, N.J.; s. of Abraham S. and Julia J. Arnold; m. Louise C. Arnold 1952; three s.; ed. Princeton Univ.; Asst. Princeton 1943, Manhattan Project 1943–46; Fellow, Inst. of Nuclear Studies, Univ. of Chicago 1946; Nat. Research Fellow, Harvard 1955–57; Assoc. Prof., Dept. of Chem., Univ. of Calif., San Diego 1958–60, Prof. 1960–, Harold C. Urey Prof. 1983–; Dir. Calif. Space Inst. (S.I.O.), Univ. of Calif., San Diego 1980–; recipient of lunar samples from missions of Apollo XI, XII, XIV, XV; member of N.A.S., A.A.A.S., A.C.S., American Acad. of Arts and Sciences; Nat. Council of World Federalists 1970–72; Guggenheim Fellow, India 1972–73; specialized in field of cosmic-ray produced nuclides, meteorites, lunar samples and cosmochemistry. *Publications:* over fifty articles in scientific reviews and journals. *Address:* Department of Chemistry, University of California, San Diego, La Jolla, Calif. 92037, U.S.A. *Telephone:* 714-452 2908.

ARNOLD, Malcolm, C.B.E., F.R.C.M.; British composer; b. 21 Oct. 1921, Northampton; s. of William and Annie Arnold; two s. one d.; ed. Royal Coll. of Music, London; Principal Trumpet, London Philharmonic Orchestra 1942–44 and 1946–48; served army 1944–46; full-time composer and conductor 1948–; awarded Cobbett Prize 1941, Mendelssohn Scholarship 1948; Hon. D.Mus. (Exeter) 1969, (Durham) 1982, (Leicester) 1984; Hon. R.A.M.; Bard of the Cornish Gorsedd. *Works include:* Beckus the Dandipratt (overture) 1943, and 8 other overtures; 1st Symphony 1949, 2nd Symphony 1953, 3rd Symphony 1957, 4th Symphony 1960, 5th Symphony 1961, 6th Symphony 1967, 7th Symphony 1973; 8th Symphony 1978; 14 concertos; Homage to the Queen, Coronation Ballet performed at Covent Garden 1953, and 4 other ballets; chamber music, vocal music, brass band music; film music Bridge on the River Kwai 1958 (Hollywood Oscar), Inn of the Sixth Happiness (Ivor Novello Award) 1959. *Leisure interests:* reading and conversation. *Address:* c/o Faber Music Ltd., 3 Queen Square, London, WC1N 3AU, England. *Telephone:* 01-278 6881.

ARNON, Daniel I(srael), PH.D.; American biochemist; b. 14 Nov. 1910, Poland; s. of Leon and Rachel (Chodes) Arnon; m. Lucile Jane Soule 1940; two s. three d.; ed. Univ. of California, Berkeley; Instructor to Asst. Prof., Univ. of Calif., Berkeley 1936–43; Lieut. to Major U.S. Army and Air Corps. 1943–46; Assoc. Prof., Berkeley 1946–50; Guggenheim Fellow, Cambridge Univ. 1947–48; Prof. of Plant Physiology, Univ. of Calif., Berkeley 1950–60, Prof. of Cell Physiology 1961–78, Prof. Emer. 1978–; Research Biochemist 1978–, Founding Chair. Dept. of Cell Physiology 1961–78, Biochemist in Calif. Agric. Experimental Station 1958–78; Guggenheim Fellow, Cambridge 1947–48; Lecturer Belgian-American Foundation, Univ. of Liege 1948; Fulbright Guest Investigator, Max-Planck Inst. für Zellphysiologie, Berlin-Dahlem 1955–56; Guggenheim Fellow 1962–63; mem. N.A.S., Fellow A.A.A.S., American Acad. of Arts and Sciences; mem. A.C.S., American Soc. Photobiology, American Soc. Biological Chem., Biochem. Soc. (London), American Soc. Plant Physiology (Pres. 1952–53), Scandinavian Soc. Plant Physiology; Foreign mem. Royal Swedish Acad. of Sciences, Acad. d'Agriculture de France, Deutsche Akademie der Naturforscher Leopoldina; Hon. mem. Spanish Biochemical Society 1975–; Charles F. Kettering Research Award, Kettering Foundation and N.A.S.-Nat. Research Council; Newcomb Cleveland Prize; Gold Medal, Univ. of Pisa; Stephen Hales Prize, Charles Reid Barnes Life-Membership Award; Kettering Award in Photosynthesis, American Soc. of Plant Physiologists; Nat. Medal of Science (U.S.A.) 1973; Dr. h.c. Bordeaux 1975, Finsen Medal, Asscn. Int. de Photobiologie 1988. *Publications:* about 300 articles on photosynthesis and related subjects. *Leisure interests:* swimming, classical music. *Address:* Division of Molecular Plant Biology, Hilgard Hall, University of California, Berkeley, Calif. 94720 (Office); 28 Norwood Avenue, Berkeley, Calif. 94707, U.S.A. (Home). *Telephone:* 415-642-8642 (Office); 415-526-5575 (Home).

ARNOUL, Françoise (Françoise Gautsch); French actress; b. 9 June 1931, Constantine, Algeria; d. of Gen. Arnoul Gautsch and Jeanne Gradwohl; m. Georges Cravenne (divorced); ed. Lycée de Rabat, Lycée Molière (Paris) and Paris Conservatoire; Officier des Arts et des Lettres; *films include:* Nous irons à Paris, La maison Bonnadieu, Le désir et l'amour, La plus belle fille du monde, Les compagnons de la nuit, Les amants du Tage, French-Cancan, Des gens sans importance, Thérèse Etienne, La chatte, Asphalte, La bête à l'affût, Le bal des espions, La chatte sort ses griffes, La morte-saison des amours, Le testament d'Orphée, Les Parisiennes, Dimanche de la vie, Le Congrès s'amuse, Españolas en Paris 1970, Van der Valk 1972, Dialogue d'exiles 1975, Dernière sortie avant Roissy 1977, Ronde de Nuit 1984; numerous TV roles; theatre debut in Les Justes (Camus), Versailles 1966. *Leisure interest:* dancing. *Address:* 53 rue Censier, 75005 Paris, France (Home).

ARNS, H.E. Cardinal Paulo Evaristo; Brazilian ecclesiastic; b. 14 Sept. 1921, Forquilhinha, Criciúma, Santa Catarina; s. of Gabriel and Helena Steiner Arns; ed. Univ. de Paris and Ecole des Hautes Etudes, Paris; taught theology and french, Univ. Católica de Petrópolis; pastoral work in Petrópolis; Aux. Bishop of São Paulo 1966; Archbishop of São Paulo, 1970–; Grand Chancellor of Pontificia Univ. Católica de São Paulo; mem. Sacred Congregation for the Sacraments (Vatican); mem. UN Int. Independent Comm. on Humanitarian Issues; cr. Cardinal by Pope Paul VI 1973; Nansen Prize (UN) 1985; Hon. LL.D. (Notre Dame, Ind., U.S.A.). *Publications:*

numerous works and translations on religious and racial topics, including A Quem iremos, Senhor? 1968, Comunidade: União e Ação 1972, Sê Fiel 1977, Em Defesa dos Direitos Humanos 1978, Convite para Rezar 1978, Presença e Força do Cristão 1978, Discutindo o Papel da Igreja 1980, Os Ministérios na Igreja 1980, O que é Igreja 1981, Meditações para o Dia-a-Dia (vols. 1–4) 1981–83, Pensamentos 1982, Olhando o Mundo com São Francisco 1982, A Violencia em nossos Dias 1983, Para Ser Jovem Hoje 1983, Santos e Heróis do Povo 1984. *Address:* Avenida Higienopolis, 890, 01238 São Paulo, S.P., Brazil. *Telephone:* (011) 826-0133.

AROSEMENA MONROY, Carlos Julio, D.IUR.; Ecuadorean politician; b. 1920; Counsellor, Ecuadorean Embassy, Washington 1946–52; Chair. Chamber of Deputies 1952; Minister of Defence 1952–53; Vice-Pres. 1960–61; Pres. of Ecuador 1961–63. *Address:* c/o Ministerio de Asuntos Exteriores, Quito, Ecuador.

AROUNA, Mounkella; Niger diplomatist; b. 1938, Quallan; m.; six c.; ed. Univ. of Dakar and African Inst. for Econ. Devt., Dakar, Senegal; Head Rural Devt. Unit, Dept. of Devt. 1967–70, Head Research and Monitoring Unit 1970–72; Dir. Int. Co-operation, Ministry of Devt. and Co-operation 1972–74; Sec. of State for Devt. 1974–75, for Foreign Affairs 1975–76; Minister of Mining and Water Supply 1976–80, of Mining 1980–81; Amb. to France 1981–83; Perm. Rep. of Niger to the UN 1984–85. *Address:* c/o Ministry of Foreign Affairs, Niamey, Niger.

ARQUETTE, Rosanna; American actress; m. 1st (divorced); m. 2nd James N. Howard; *films include:* Gorp, Off the Wall, S.O.B., Baby, It's You, The Aviator, Desperately Seeking Susan, 8 Million Ways to Die, After Hours, Nobody's Tool, The Big Blue, Life Lessons; *TV films include:* Harvest Home, The Wall, The Long Way Home, The Executioner's Song, One Cooks, the Other Doesn't, The Parade.

ARRABAL, Fernando; Spanish writer; b. 11 Aug. 1932, Melilla, Morocco; m. Luce Moreau; one s. one d; political prisoner in Spain 1967; now lives in Paris; founder "Panique" movt. with Topor, Jodorowsky, etc.; Grand Prix du Théâtre 1967, Grand Prix Humour Noir 1968, Premio Nadal (Spain) 1983, World's Theater Prize 1984. *Publications:* plays: 49 plays including Le cimetière des voitures, Guernica, Le grand cérémonial, L'architecte et l'Empereur d'Assyrie, Le jardin des délices, Et ils Passerent des menottes aux fleurs, Le ciel et la merde, Bella ciao, La Tour de Babel, L'extravagante réussite de Jésus-Christ, Les délices de la chair, La traversée de l'empire; novels: Baal Babylone 1959, L'enterrement de la sardine 1962, Fêtes et rites de la confusion 1965, La tour prend garde, La reverdie, La vierge rouge, Bréviaire d'amour d'un haltérophile; poetry: La pierre de la folie 1963, 100 sonnets 1966, Humbles paradis; essays: numerous, including Le 'Panique', Le New York d'Arrabal, Lettre au Général Franco. *Films:* directed and written: Viva la Muerte, J'irai comme un cheval fou, L'arbre de Guernica, L'odyssée de la Pacific, Le cimetière des voitures. *Leisure interest:* chess. *Address:* 22 rue Jouffroy, Paris 75017, France. *Telephone:* 42673695.

ARRAU, Claudio; concert pianist; b. 6 Feb. 1903, Chillán, Chile; s. of Carlos and Lucretia Arrau; m. Ruth Schneider 1938; ed. privately; gave first concert at age of five in Santiago; Buenos Aires debut at age of seven; studied in Berlin with Martin Krause (pupil of Liszt) 1912–18; int. concert debut, Berlin 1915; London debut 1920; first American concerts 1923, returned 1941 and annual tours since; world tours include Russia 1929, 1930, 1968, Australia 1947, 1952, 1958, 1968, 1974, South Africa 1949, 1952, 1956, Israel 1951, 1953, 1962, 1970, India, Sri Lanka and Singapore 1955, 1956, Japan 1965, 1970, 1972, 1982, 1987; frequent tours of South America; annual U.S. and European tours; awarded Liszt and Ibach prizes 1912, 1916 and 1917; First Prize Concours International des Pianistes de Genève 1927; Order of the Aztec Eagle 1982; Commdr. Légion d'honneur, Nat. Arts Prize (Chile) 1983, Int. UNESCO Music Award 1983; decorations from several countries. *Publications:* Beethoven Piano Sonatas Vol. I 1974, Vol. II 1975. *Leisure interests:* books, gardening, art, antiques. *Address:* c/o International Creative Management Artists, 40 West 57th Street, New York, N.Y. 10019, U.S.A.

ARREAZA ARREAZA, Julio César, PH.D.; Venezuelan oil executive; b. 28 Feb. 1923; s. of the late Julio Arreaza Matute and Carmen Arreaza de Arreaza; m. Beatriz Bustamante de Arreaza 1949; three s. two d.; ed. Cen. Univ. of Venezuela; Lawyer 1948–59; Legal Adviser to Ministry of Mines and Hydrocarbons 1959–63; Dir.-Gen. Ministry of Mines and Hydrocarbons (frequently acting Minister) 1963–69; mem. Presidential Comm. for Oil Reversion, Head Legal Sub-Comm.; mem. High Level Comm. on aspects of nationalization of Oil Industry; First Vice-Pres. Designate Petróleos de Venezuela, S.A. 1975, confirmed as Vice-Pres. 1979, 1981; Comendador, Orden del Libertador, Orden Francisco Miranda (First Class), Mérito al Trabajo (First Class). *Address:* Avenida El Paseo, Quinta Marisela, Urb. Prados del Este, Caracas 1080. *Telephone:* 771061.

ARRIAGA, General Kaúlza de; Portuguese army officer; b. 18 Jan. 1915, Oporto; ed. Univ. of Oporto, Portuguese Mil. Acad. and Portuguese Inst. for Higher Mil. Studies. Instructor, Field School for Mil. Engineers 1939–45; attended Gen. Staff Course 1945–49; Lisbon Mil. H.Q. and Army Gen. Staff 1949–50; at Ministry for Nat. Defence and Rep. of Minister of Defence in Tech. Comm. for External Econ. Co-operation 1950–53; Head of Office of Minister of Nat. Defence and Min. of Defence Rep. at Tech. Comm. for External Co-operation and Atomic Energy Bd. 1954–55; Under-Sec. of State for Aeronautics, later Sec. 1955–62; High Command Course 1963–64; Brig. 1964; Prof. of Strategy and Tactics, Inst. for High Mil. Studies 1964–66; Chair. Atomic Energy Bd. 1967; Gen. 1968; Commdr. all Portuguese Ground Forces in Mozambique 1969–70; C.-in-C. Portuguese Forces in Mozambique 1970–73; retd. May 1974; arrested Sept. 1974, released Jan. 1976; mem. Overseas Council 1965–69; Chair. Exec. Cttee. Soc. Portuguesa de Exploração de Petróleos (ANGOL) 1966–69; Pres. Equestrian Fed. 1968; several Portuguese and foreign decorations. *Publications include:* works on engineering, atomic energy and military affairs. *Address:* c/o Junta de Energia Nuclear, Rua de S. Pedro de Alcântara 79, Lisbon, Portugal.

ARRIGHI DE CASANOVA, Emile, D.IUR.; French civil servant and financial executive; b. 21 Oct. 1920, Bastia, Corsica; s. of Pierre and Catherine (Paoli) Arrighi de Casanova; m. Geneviève Barthelemy 1946; four c.; ed. Lycée Mignet, Univ. of Aix-en-Provence; Dir. of Internal Trade, Ministry of Industry and Trade 1951–59; Dir. of Industrial Expansion, Ministry of Industry 1959–65; Dir.-Gen. Chamber of Commerce and Industry of Paris 1965–77; Chair. Econ. and Social Cttee. for Corsica 1974–83; Conseiller d'Etat en Service extraordinaire 1976–79; Chair. Soc. du Marché d'Interêt national de Rungis 1977–81; Pres. Palais des congrès, Paris 1977–84, Institut du développement 1984–; mem. Corsican Ass. 1986–; mem. Econ. and Social Council 1979; Commdr. de la Légion d'honneur; Commdr. Ordre nat. du Mérite. *Address:* CES, Palais d'Iéna, 75775 Paris cedex 16 (Office); 7 rue Molitor, 75016 Paris, France.

ARRILLAGA, Josu, PH.D., D.SC., F.R.S.(N.Z.); Spanish professor of electrical engineering; b. 21 Jan. 1934; s. of Jose Maria and Maria Mercedes Arrillaga; m. Greta Robinson 1968; two s. two d.; ed. in Spain and Univ. of Manchester Inst. of Science and Tech.; Industrial Engineer, ISOLUX, Spain 1955–59; A.E.J. Engineer, Manchester 1959–61; Research student UMIST 1961–66; Lecturer Salford Univ. 1966–67; Lecturer and Sr. Lecturer, UMIST 1967–75, Head Power Systems and High Voltage 1970–75; Prof. of Electrical Eng., Univ. of Canterbury, N.Z. 1975–, Head Dept. of Electrical and Electronic Eng. 1986–; John Hopkins prize, I.E.E. 1975. *Publications:* Computer Modelling of Power Systems, Power System Harmonics, HVDC Transmission; 140 technical articles. *Leisure interest:* gardening. *Address:* 11 Chilcombe Street, Christchurch 4, New Zealand. *Telephone:* Christchurch 517627.

ARRINDELL, Sir Clement Athelston, G.C.M.G., G.C.V.O., Q.C.; St. Kitts-Nevis lawyer and civil servant; b. 16 April 1932, St. Christopher, West Indies; s. of George E. Arrindell and Hilda I. Arrindell; m. Evelyn Eugenia O'Loughlin 1967; ed. St. Kitts-Nevis Grammar School (Island Scholar 1948) and Lincoln's Inn, London; practising barrister-at-law 1959–66; Dist. Magistrate 1966–74; Chief Magistrate 1975–77; Puisne Judge 1978–81; Gov. 1981–83, Gov.-Gen. of St. Kitts-Nevis 1983–. *Leisure interests:* gardening, piano playing, classical music. *Address:* Government House, St. Kitts, West Indies. *Telephone:* 2315 and 2260.

ARRON, Henck Alphonsus Eugène; Suriname politician; b. 25 April 1936, Paramaribo; s. of J. S. Arron and Mrs. J. Arron-Halfhide; m. Antoinette Emelie Francis Leeuwin 1963; worked at Bank of Amsterdam, Netherlands; joined staff of Vervuurts (now Hakrin) Bank, Surinam; mem. Parl. 1963–80; Chair. Nationale Partij Surinam 1970–80; Minister of Finance in pre-independence govt. 1973–77; Prime Minister and Minister of Gen. Affairs and Foreign Affairs 1973–80 (deposed in coup); mem. Supreme Council 1985–87; Vice-Pres. Jan. 1988–; arrested Aug. 1980, released 1981; Man. Dir. Surinaamse Volkscredietbank 1982–. *Leisure interests:* fishing, reading, music, pottery. *Address:* Office of the Vice-President, Paramaribo, Suriname.

ARROW, Kenneth J., PH.D.; American professor of economics; b. 23 Aug. 1921, New York; s. of Harry I. and Lillian Arrow; m. Selma Schweitzer 1947; two s.; ed. The City College, Columbia Univ.; Capt. U.S. A.A.F. 1942–46; Research Assoc. Cowles Comm. for Research in Econ., Univ. of Chicago 1947–49; Asst. Assoc. and Prof. of Econs., Statistics and Operations Research, Stanford Univ., 1949–68; Prof. of Econs. Harvard Univ., 1968–79; Prof. of Econs. and Operations Research, Stanford Univ., 1979–; mem. N.A.S., American Acad. of Arts and Sciences, American Phil. Soc., Finnish Acad. of Sciences, British Acad., Inst. of Medicine; Pres. Int. Soc. for Inventory Research 1983–; Dir. various cos.; Hon. LL.D. (City Univ., Univ. of Chicago); Hon. Dr. of Social and Econ. Sciences (Vienna); Hon. Sc.D. (Columbia Univ.) 1973; D.Soc.-Sci. (Yale) 1974; Hon. Dr. (Univ. René Descartes) 1974; Hon. LL.D. (Hebrew Univ. Jerusalem) 1975, Hon. D. Pol. Sci. (Helsinki) 1976, Dr. h.c. (Univ. Aix-Marseille III) 1985, D.Litt. (Cambridge) 1985; Nobel Memorial Prize in Econ. Science 1972; Order of the Rising Sun (Japan). *Publications:* Social Choice and Individual Values 1951, 1963, Studies in the Mathematical Theory of Inventory and Production (with S. Karlin and H. Scarf) 1958, Studies in Linear and Nonlinear Programming (with L. Hurwicz and H. Uzawa) 1958, A Time Series Analysis of Inter-industry Demands (with M. Hoffenberg) 1959, Public Investment, The Rate of Return and Optimal Fiscal Policy (with M. Kurz) 1970, Essays in the Theory of Risk-Bearing 1971, General Competitive Analysis (with F. H. Hahn) 1971, The Limits of Organization 1973, Studies

in Resource Allocation Processes (with L. Hurwicz) 1977, Collected Papers 1983–85, Social Choice and Multicriterion Decision Making (with others) 1985; about 160 articles in learned journals. *Leisure interests:* walking, music. *Address:* Department of Economics, Stanford Univ., Stanford, Calif. 94305 (Office); 580 Constanzo Street, Stanford, Calif. 94305, U.S.A. (Home). *Telephone:* 415-723 9165 (Office).

ARRUPE, Father Pedro, S.J.; Spanish ecclesiastic; b. 14 Nov. 1907, Bilbao; s. of Marcelino and Dolores Gondra Arrupe; ed. with Fathers of Escuelas Pías, Bilbao, Univ. of Madrid (Medicine), and Jesuit studies in Spain, Belgium, Netherlands and U.S.A.; entered Society of Jesus 1927; in Japan 1938–65, engaged in parish ministries, training of Novices; was in Hiroshima when first atomic bomb exploded; Provincial Superior 1954–65; Superior-Gen. of Soc. of Jesus 1965–83. *Publications:* eight spiritual books (Japanese) Este Japón increíble—Memorias del P. Arrupe, Escala en España, Nuestra vida consagrada, Ante un mundo en cambio (Spanish), Witnessing to Justice (English, Italian, Spanish), Men for Others (English, Italian), Jesuit General in the Philippines, A Planet to Heal, La vida religiosa ante un reto histórico 1978, Hambre de pan y de Evangelico 1978, Challenge to Religious Life Today 1979, Justice with Faith Today 1980, Intentidad del Jesuita en Nuestros Tiempos 1980, Cartas del Padre Arrupe 1980, L'Espérance ne trompe pas 1981, La Iglesia de Hoy y del Futuro 1981, Hombres para los demás 1983, Enél sólo la Esperanza 1984. *Address:* Superiore Generale della Compagnia di Gesù, Borgo Santo Spirito 5, C.P. 6139, 00195 Rome, Italy.

ARSENIS, Gerasimos; Greek economist and politician; b. 1931, Cephalonia; ed. Univ. of Athens and Mass. Inst. of Tech.; worked for United Nations 1960; Dir. Dept. of Econ. Studies, OECD Research Centre 1964–66; Sr. Official, Prebisch Group, UN 1966–73; Dir. UNCTAD 1973; Gov. Bank of Greece 1981–84; Alt. Minister of Nat. Economy 1982–84; Minister of Finance and Nat. Economy 1984–85, of Merchant Marine June–July 1985; expelled from PASOK 1986; f. Democratic Initiative Party 1987, Leader 1987–. *Address:* Democratic Initiative Party, Athens, Greece.

ARTEH GHALIB, Omar; Somali politician; b. 1930, Hargeisa; m.; seven c.; ed. St. Paul's Coll., Cheltenham, U.K. and Univ. of Bristol; Teacher 1946–49; Headmaster, various elementary schools 1949–54; Vice-Principal, Intermediate School, Sheikh, Somalia 1954–56; Principal, Intermediate School, Gabileh 1958; Officer in charge of Adult Educ. 1959; District Commr. in Public Admin. 1960–61; First Sec. Somali Embassy, Moscow 1961–62; Rapporteur, Special Cttee. on South-West Africa, UN 1962–63; Counsellor, Perm. Mission of Somalia at UN 1964; Amb. to Ethiopia 1965–68; mem. Somali Nat. Assembly 1969; Sec. of State for Foreign Affairs 1969–76; Minister of Culture and Higher Education 1976–78, in the President's Office 1978–80; mem. Cttee. for Social and Political Thought 1976–; Speaker, People's Ass. 1982–; attended most OAU Summit and Ministerial Confs. *Publications include:* Back from the Lion of Judah. *Address:* People's Assembly, Mogadishu, Somalia.

ARTHUR, James Greig, PH.D., F.R.S.C.; Canadian professor of mathematics; b. 18 May 1944, Hamilton; s. of John G. Arthur and Katherine (née Scott) Arthur; m. Dorothy P. Helm 1972; two s.; ed. Univ. of Toronto, Yale Univ.; Instructor Princeton Univ. 1970–72; Asst. Prof. Yale Univ. 1972–76; Prof. Duke Univ. 1976–79, Univ. of Toronto 1979–; Sloan Fellow 1975–77, Stracie Memorial Fellowship 1982–84; Synge Award in Math. 1987. *Publications:* numerous scientific papers and articles. *Leisure interests:* tennis, squash, golf. *Address:* 23 Woodlawn Avenue, W. Toronto, Ont., M4V 1G6, Canada.

ARTHUR, James Stanley, C.M.G., B.SC.; British diplomatist (retd.); b. 3 Feb. 1923, Aberdeen; s. of Laurence and Catherine Arthur; m. Marion North 1950; two s. two d.; ed. Anderson Educ. Inst., Shetland Isles, Trinity Acad., Edinburgh and Liverpool Univs.; Ministry of Education (later Dept. of Educ. and Science) 1947–66, Private Sec. to Parl. Sec. 1948–50, Principal Private Sec. to Minister 1960–62; Foreign Office 1966–67; Counsellor, High Comm., Nairobi 1967–70; Deputy High Commr., Malta 1970–73; High Commr., Fiji 1974–78 (also accred. to Nauru); High Commr., Barbados 1978–82, Dominica 1978–82, Saint Lucia 1979–82, Saint Vincent and the Grenadines 1979–82, Grenada (non-resident) 1980–82, Antigua and Barbuda 1981–82; U.K. Govt. Rep. to (now fmr.) West Indies Associated States 1978–82; mem. Court Liverpool Univ. 1987, Cen. Council, Royal Commonwealth Soc. 1988–. *Leisure interests:* golf, music. *Address:* Moreton House, Longborough, Moreton-in-Marsh, Glos., GL56 0QQ, England. *Telephone:* Cotswold 30774.

ARTHURS, Harry William, F.R.S.C., LL.M.; Canadian barrister, professor of law and academic; b. 9 May 1935, Toronto; s. of Leon Arthurs and Ellen H. (Dworkin) Arthurs; m. Penelope Geraldine Ann Milnes 1974; two s.; ed. Univ. of Toronto, Harvard Univ., U.S.A.; Asst., Assoc. then full Prof. of Law, Osgoode Hall Law School, York Univ., Ont. 1961–, Dean of Law School 1972–77, Pres. York Univ. 1985–; mediator and arbitrator in labour disputes 1961–; author, lecturer 1961–; Bencher, Law Soc. of Upper Canada 1979–83; mem. Econ Council of Canada 1978–81; Chair. Consultative Group, Research and Educ. in Law 1980–84; Chair. Council of Ont. Univs. 1987–; Hon. LL.D. (W. Sherbrooke and Brock Univs., Law Soc. of Upper Canada). *Publications:* Industrial Relations and Labour Law in Canada (with H. Glasbeek and D. Carter) 1984, Law and Learning (Report on Legal

Research and Education in Canada) 1984, Without the Law: Administrative Justice and Legal Pluralism in Nineteenth Century England 1985. *Address:* Office of the President, Ross Building, Room S949, York University, North York, Ont., M3J 1P3, Canada. *Telephone:* (416) 736 5200.

ARTSCHWAGER, Richard Ernst; American artist; b. 26 Dec. 1923, Washington, D.C.; m. 1st Catherine Kord, 2nd Molly O'Gorman; two d.; ed. Cornell Univ.; studied with Amedee Ozenfant, New York 1949–50; baby photographer 1950–53; cabinet-maker 1953–65; has exhibited with Richard Bellamy and Leo Castelli also many group and one-man shows in U.S.A. and Europe 1963–. *Publication:* The Hydraulic Door Check 1967. *Address:* 158 S. Oxford Street, Brooklyn, N.Y. 11217, U.S.A.

ARTZT, Alice Josephine, B.A.; American classical guitarist; b. 16 March 1943, Philadelphia, Pa.; d. of Harriett Green Artzt and Maurice G. Artzt; ed. Columbia Univ. and studied composition with Darius Milhaud and guitar with Julian Bream, Ida Presti and Alexandre Lagoya; taught at Mannes Coll. of Music 1966–69, Trenton State Univ. 1977–80; now teaches privately; concert performances world-wide. *Publications:* The Art of Practicing, The International GFA Guitarists' Cookbook (Ed.); numerous articles in guitar and music periodicals. *Leisure interests:* hi-fi, travel, Chaplin movies. *Address:* 180 Claremont Avenue, Apt. 31, New York, N.Y. 10027, U.S.A.

ARYAL, Krishna Raj, M.ED., M.A.; Nepali politician; b. Dec. 1928, Kathmandu; ed. Durbar High School, Tri-Chandra Coll., Allahabad Univ., India, Univ. of Oregon, U.S.A. Lecturer, Nat. Teachers' Training Centre 1954–56; Prof. of Educ., Coll. of Educ. 1956–59; Ed. Education Quarterly 1956–59, Nabin Shikshya 1956–59; Founder, Admin. and Principal Shri Ratna Rajya Laxmi Girls' Coll. 1961–71; Asst. Minister for Educ. 1971–72, Minister of State for Educ. 1972–73, Minister of Educ. 1973–75, concurrently Pro-Chancellor, Tribhuvan Univ. 1973–75; Minister of Foreign Affairs 1975–79; Amb. to France 1979–85; Gorakha Dakhinbahu (2nd Class); Grand Officer of Yugoslav Star (2nd Class); Grand Cordon of Yugoslav Star (1st Class); Order of the Million Elephants (Laos); Order of the Rising Sun, First Class (Japan). *Publications:* Monarchy in the Making of Nepal (in English), Education for Development of Nepal (in English), Facts of Interest (series in Nepali), Science of Education (Nepali). *Address:* Gaihiri Dhara, Kathmandu, Nepal (Home).

ASADA, Shizuo; Japanese aviation official; b. 13 Oct. 1911, Osaka; s. of Eijiro and Tama Asada; m. Hisako Tinako 1940; one s. two d.; ed. Law Dept., Tokyo Imperial Univ. (now Tokyo Univ.). Dir. Bureau of Shipping, Ministry of Transport 1958–61; Admin. Vice-Minister of Transport 1961–63; Sr. Vice-Pres. Japan Air Lines 1963–69, Exec. Vice-Pres. 1969–71, Pres. 1971–81, Counsellor, Dir. 1981–; Exec. Dir. Japan Fed. of Employers' Assens.; Dir. Fed. of Econ. Orgs., Japan Aeronautic Assen., Japan Econ. Research Center, Transportation Econ. Research Center; mem. Exec. Cttee. Int. Air Transport Assen., Japan Nat. Tourist Org.; mem. Aircraft Industry Council, Council for Civil Aviation, Invisible Trade Council, Shipping and Shipbuilding Rationalization Council. *Leisure interests:* golf, go, calligraphy. *Address:* Japan Air Lines, 7-3, Marunouchi 2-chome, Chiyoda-ku, Tokyo 100 (Office); 1-45 Tokiwadai, Hodogaya-ku, Yokohama City, Kanagawa Prefecture, Japan (Home). *Telephone:* 045-333-1355.

ASADOV, Eduard Arkadevich; Soviet poet; b. 1923, Merv, Turkmen S.S.R.; secondary schooling in Moscow; Red Army 1941, seriously wounded and lost sight 1945; started publishing 1948; ed. Gorky Inst. of World Literature Moscow. *Publications:* Again into the Line (Verse) 1984, Bright Roads 1951, Snowy Evening 1956, The Soldiers Have Returned from the War 1957, Galina 1960, Lyrical Limits 1962, I Love Forever 1965, Be Happy, Dreamers 1966, Isle of Romance 1969, Goodness 1972. *Address:* U.S.S.R. Union of Writers, Ul. Vorovskogo 52, Moscow, U.S.S.R.

ASANGONO, Evuna Owono; Equatorial Guinean diplomatist; b. 23 May 1944, Nkumekien-Yebecon; m.; two s. three d.; ed. School of Admin., then School of Diplomacy, Santa Isabel (now Malabo); served as Admin. Officer in Ministry of Interior 1966 and 1969–71, also Ministry of Education 1967–68; First Sec. Permanent Mission to UN. 1972–74; Amb. to Ethiopia 1975; Roving Amb. and Envoy 1976–77; Perm. Rep. to UN 1977–80; Amb. to Spain 1980–81. *Address:* c/o Ministry of Foreign Affairs, Malabo, Equatorial Guinea.

ASANO, Teiji; Japanese business executive; b. 1906; ed. Tohoku Imperial Univ.; joined shipbuilding dept., Mitsui & Co. 1930; entered Tamano Shipyard Ltd. (predecessor of Mitsui Shipbuilding & Eng. Co. Ltd.) 1948; Man. Dir. Mitsui Shipbuilding & Eng. Co. 1958, Man. Dir. 1965, Vice-Pres. 1968, fmr. Chair. of Bd., Dir. and Counsellor 1973–76, Counsellor 1976–; Pres. Showa Aircraft Industry Co. Ltd. 1973–79, Chair. 1979–. *Address:* c/o Mitsui Shipbuilding & Engineering Co. Ltd., 6-4, Tsukiji 5-chome, Chuo-ku, Tokyo, Japan. *Telephone:* 544-3000.

ASANTE, Samuel Kwadwo Boaten, LL.B., LL.M., J.S.D.; Ghanaian lawyer and international official; b. 11 May 1933, Asokore; s. of Daniel Y. Asante and Mary Baafi; m. Philomena Margaret Aidoo 1961; two s. three d.; ed. Achimota School, Univs. of Nottingham and London, and Yale Univ. Law School; State Attorney in the Ministry of Justice of Ghana 1960–61; Lecturer in Law and Acting Head of Law Dept., Univ. of Ghana 1961–65; Lecturer, Leeds Univ., U.K. 1965–66; Attorney World Bank, Washington,

D.C. 1966–69; Adjunct Prof. of Law, Howard Univ. Law School, Washington, D.C. 1967–69; Solicitor-Gen. of Ghana 1969–74; mem. Arbitration Panel, Int. Cen. for Settlement of Investment Disputes, Washington, D.C. 1971–; Chair. Public Agreements Review Cttee. of Ghana 1972–77; Deputy Attorney-Gen. of Ghana 1974–77; Chief Legal Adviser, UN Comm. on Transnational Corpns., New York Aug. 1977–83, Dir. 1983–; Dir. Int. Third World Legal Studies Assen., New York; mem. Bd. Dirs. Int. Devt. Law Inst., Rome; Taylor Lecturer, Lagos Univ. 1978; mem. Law Faculty, Cambridge 1978–79, Life mem.; Consultant, Commonwealth Secr., African Devt. Bank and UNITAR; Guest Lecturer numerous univs. and institutions worldwide; Guest Fellow, Berkeley Coll., Yale Univ. 1964–65; fmr. Sterling, Fulbright and Aggrey Fellow; Fellow of World Acad. of Arts and Sciences 1975, Ghana Acad. of Arts and Sciences 1976; Visiting Fellow of Clare Hall, Cambridge 1978–79, Life mem.; Visiting Prof. of Temple Univ. Law School, Philadelphia 1979; mem. Exec. Council, American Soc. of Int. Law 1979, mem. Gen. Legal Council, Ghana; mem. Advisory Bd., Foreign Investment Law Journal-ICSID Review; Ghana Book Award. *Publications:* Property Law and Social Goals in Ghana 1976, Transnational Investment Law and National Development 1979, and various articles in law journals. *Leisure interests:* tennis, golf, reading biographies. *Address:* United Nations Centre on Transnational Corporations, 2 United Nations Plaza, New York, N.Y. 10017, U.S.A. (Office); 412 Pinebrook Boulevard, New Rochelle, New York, N.Y. 10804, U.S.A. (Home).

ASCHOFF, Jürgen Walter Ludwig, DR.MED.; German physiologist; b. 25 Jan. 1913, Freiburg im Breisgau; s. of Ludwig Aschoff and Clara Dieterichs; m. Hilde W. Jung 1942; three s. three d.; ed. Univs. of Bonn and Freiburg i. Br.; Research Assoc. Inst. of Physiology, Göttingen 1939–47; Lecturer in Physiology, Univ. of Würzburg 1948–49; Assoc. Prof. Max-Planck-Inst. für medizinische Forschung, Heidelberg 1950–61; Scientific mem. Max-Planck-Gesellschaft 1958; Dir. Max-Planck-Inst. für Verhaltensphysiologie, Seewiesen and Andechs 1961–81, retd.; Dr.phil.h.c. (Umea, Sweden) 1977; Dr.med.h.c. (Giessen); mem. Deutsche Akad. der Naturforscher Leopoldina; Feldberg Prize 1983. *Address:* Jacobistr. 29, 7800 Freiburg/Breisgau, Federal Republic of Germany. *Telephone:* (0761) 37295.

ASENSIO-WUNDERLICH, Julio; Guatemalan diplomatist; b. 5 Nov. 1911, Guatemala City; s. of Dr. José Luis Asensio and Mrs. Beatrix Wunderlich de Asensio; m. Elena Aguirre-Wyld 1938; four s. one d.; ed. Univ. de San Carlos de Guatemala and Loyola Coll., Montreal; Deputy Minister of Foreign Relations, Guatemala 1954, Minister-Counsellor, Embassy of Guatemala, Washington, D.C. 1955–58; Legal Counsellor, Foreign Office, Guatemala 1958–64; Amb. to U.S.A. 1970–78; mem. Del. to UN Gen. Assembly 1954–55, Perm. Rep. to UN 1976–78; Orden del Mérito Civil (Spain), Caballero de San Silvestre (Vatican). *Leisure interests:* reading, coffee growing. *Address:* c/o Ministerio de Relaciones Exteriores, Guatemala City, Guatemala.

ÁSGRÍMSSON, Halldór; Icelandic politician; b. 1947; m. Sigurjóna Sigurdardóttir; three d.; ed. Co-operative's Commercial Coll. and commercial univs. in Bergen and Copenhagen; Lecturer in Auditing and Accounting, Univ. of Iceland 1973–75; mem. Parl. 1974–78, 1979–; mem. Bd. Cen. Bank of Iceland 1976–81, Chair. 1981–83; mem. Nordic Council 1977–78, 1979–83, Chair. 1982–83; Chair. Icelandic Del. 1982–83; Minister of Fisheries 1983–88, of Justice and Ecclesiastical Affairs Sept. 1988–; Vice-Chair. Progressive Party. *Address:* Ministry of Justice and Ecclesiastical Affairs, Arnarhvàli, 150 Reykjavík, Iceland.

ASH, Eric Albert, C.B.E., PH.D., F.R.S., F.C.G.I., F.I.E.E., F.I.E.E.E., F.INST.P., F.ENG.; British university rector; b. 31 Jan. 1928, Berlin, Germany; s. of Walter and Dorothea Ash; m. Clare Babb 1954; five d.; ed. Univ. Coll. School and Imperial Coll., London; Research Fellow, Stanford Univ. 1952–54; Research Asst., Queen Mary Coll., London 1954–55; Research Engineer, Standard Telecommunications Labs. Ltd. 1955–63; Sr. Lecturer, Univ. Coll, London 1963–65, Reader 1965–67, Prof. of Electrical Eng. 1967-80, Pender Prof., and Head, Dept. of Electronic and Electrical Eng. 1980–85; Rector, Imperial Coll., London 1985–; Non-Exec. Dir. British Telecom 1987–; Hon. D. Sc. (Leicester) 1987; Royal Medal (Royal Soc.) 1986. *Publications:* papers on topics of physical electronics in various eng. and physics journals. *Leisure interests:* music, skiing, swimming. *Address:* Rector's Office, Imperial College, London, SW7 2AZ, England.

ASH, Roy Lawrence, M.B.A.; American industrialist; b. 20 Oct. 1918, Los Angeles, Calif.; s. of Charles K. and Fay (Dickinson) Ash m. Lila M. Hornbek 1943; three s. two d.; ed. Harvard Univ. Bank of America 1936–42, 1947–49; Private to Capt., U.S. A.F. 1942–46; Chief Financial Officer, Hughes Aircraft Co. 1949–53; Co-founder and Dir., Litton Industries Inc. 1953–72; Pres. 1961–72; mem. Bd. of Dirs. Bankamerica Corpn. 1968–72, 1976–, Bank of America N.T. and S.A. 1964–72, 1978–, Global Marine Inc. 1965–72, 1975–81, Pacific Mutual Life Insurance Co. 1965–72, Los Angeles World Affairs Council 1968–72, (Pres. 1970–72), 1978–; Chair. President's Advisory Council on Exec. Org. 1969–71; Asst. to the Pres. of the U.S.A. for Exec. Man. 1972–74; Dir. U.S. Office of Man. and Budget 1973–75; Chair. and Chief Exec. Officer, AM Int. 1976–81; Co-Chair. Japan-California Assen. 1965–72, 1980–81; Vice-Chair. Los Angeles Olympic Organizing Cttee. 1979–84; mem. Bd. and Pres. L.A. Music Center Opera 1987–; Dir. Sara Lee Corpn. 1979–; mem. The Business Roundtable 1977–81, The Conference Bd. 1977–, Bd. of U.S. Chamber of Commerce 1979–85; mem.

Bd. of Trustees, California Inst. of Tech. 1967-72; Trustee, Cttee. for Econ. Devt. 1970-72, 1975-; Hon. LL.D. (Pepperdine) 1976; Kt. of Malta; Horatio Alger Award 1966. *Address:* 1900 Avenue of the Stars, Los Angeles, Calif. 90067 (Office); 655 Funchal Road, Los Angeles, Calif, 90077, U.S.A. (Home).

ASHBERY, John Lawrence, M.A.; American author and critic; b. 28 July 1927, Rochester, N.Y.; s. of Chester F. and Helen L. Ashbery; ed. Deerfield Acad., Mass., Harvard Coll., Columbia and New York Univs.; copywriter, Oxford Univ. Press, New York 1951-54, McGraw-Hill Book Co. 1954-55; lived in France 1955-57, 1958-65; art critic European edn. New York Herald Tribune 1960-65; Paris corresp. Art News, N.Y. 1964-65, Exec. Ed. 1965-72; art critic, Art International, Lugano 1961-64; ed. Locus Solus 1960-62, Art and Literature, Paris 1963-66; Prof. of English and co-dir. MFA program in Creative Writing, Brooklyn Coll., N.Y. 1974-; Poetry ed. Partisan Review, New York 1976-80; art critic, New York (magazine) 1978-80, Newsweek 1980-85; recipient of numerous awards and honours, including MacArthur Award 1985. *Publications:* non-fiction: Fairfield Porter 1983, R. B. Kitaj (with others) 1983; novel: A Nest of Ninnies (with J. Schuyler) 1969; plays: Three Plays 1978; numerous volumes of verse. *Address:* c/o Georges Borchardt Inc., 136 East 57th Street, New York, N.Y. 10022, U.S.A.

ASHBY, Baron (Life Peer), cr. 1973, of Brandon, Suffolk; **Eric Ashby,** Kt., F.R.S., D.SC., M.A., D.I.C.; British botanist and university administrator; b. 24 Aug. 1904, London; s. of Herbert C. Ashby and Helena M. Chater; m. Elizabeth H. Farries 1931; two s.; ed. City of London School, Imperial Coll. of Science, London, and Univ. of Chicago; Commonwealth Fund Fellow, U.S.A. 1929-31; lecturer in Botany, Imperial Coll. 1931-35; Reader in Botany, Univ. of Bristol 1935-37; Prof. of Botany, Univ of Sydney, Australia 1938-46; Harrison Prof. of Botany, Manchester Univ. 1946-50; Pres. and Vice-Chancellor, The Queen's Univ. Belfast 1950-59; Counsellor and Chargé d'affaires Australian Legation, Moscow 1945; mem. Exec. Council Scientific and Industrial Research 1956-60; Master of Clare Coll., Cambridge 1958-75; Fellow of Clare Coll. Cambridge 1958, Life Fellow 1975; Chair. Int. Comm. on Higher Educ. in Nigeria 1959-61; Vice-Chair. Asscn. of Univs. of British Commonwealth 1959-61; Vice-Chair. Commonwealth Scholarships Comm. 1959-62; mem. Univ. Grants Cttee. 1960-67; Chair. Cttee. of Award, Commonwealth Fund of N.Y. 1963-69; Hon. Adviser, Nigerian Nat. Univ. Comm. 1962-65; Pres. British Asscn. for Advancement of Science 1963; Council Royal Soc. 1964-65; Trustee Ciba Foundation 1966-79; mem. Cen. Advisory Council for Science and Technology 1967-69; Vice-Chancellor, Univ. of Cambridge 1967-69; Chair. Royal Comm. on Pollution 1970-73; Chancellor, Queen's Univ. Belfast 1970-84; Visiting Prof., Univ. of Michigan 1976-78; Trustee, British Museum 1969-77; Tanner Lecturer 1979; Order of Andrés Bello 1st Class (Venezuela) 1974; Dr. h.c. several univs. *Publications:* Environment and Plant Development 1931, English-German Botanical Terminology 1938, Challenge to Education 1946, Scientist in Russia 1947, Science and the People 1953, Technology and the Academics 1958, Community of Universities 1963, African Universities and Western Tradition 1964, Universities, British, Indian, African 1966, The Rise of the Student Estate in Britain 1970, Masters and Scholars 1970, Any Person, Any Study 1971, Portrait of Haldane 1974, Adapting Universities to a Technological Society 1974, Reconciling Man with the Environment 1978, The Politics of Clean Air (with Mary Anderson) 1981. *Address:* c/o Clare College, Cambridge, England.

ASHBY, Michael Farries, PH.D., F.R.S.; British professor of engineering materials; b. 20 Nov. 1935; s. of Lord Ashby and Elizabeth Helen Farries; m. Maureen Ashby 1962; two s. one d.; ed. Campbell Coll., Belfast, Queens' Coll., Cambridge; Asst., Univ. of Göttingen, Fed. Repub. of Germany 1962-65; Asst. Prof., Harvard Univ., U.S.A. 1965-69, Prof. of Metallurgy 1969-73; Prof. of Eng. Materials, Univ. of Cambridge 1973-; Ed. Acta Metallurgica 1974-; mem. Akad. der Wissenschaften zu Göttingen 1980; Hon. M.A. (Harvard) 1969. *Leisure interests:* music, design. *Address:* 51 Maids Causeway, Cambridge, CB5 8DE, England. *Telephone:* Cambridge 64741.

ASHCROFT, John, J.D.; American state governor; b. Chicago; m.; three c.; ed. Yale Univ. and Univ. of Chicago; admitted, Missouri State Bar, U.S. Supreme Court Bar; Assoc. Prof. S.W. Missouri State Univ. Springfield; legal practice, Springfield, Mo. until 1973; State Auditor, Missouri 1973-75, Asst. Attorney-Gen. 1975-77, Attorney-Gen. 1977-84; Gov. of Missouri 1985-; recordings as gospel singer; Republican. *Publications:* College Law for Business (with wife), It's the Law 1979. *Address:* Office of the Governor, State Capitol, Jefferson City, Mo. 65102, U.S.A.

ASHCROFT, Dame Peggy (Dame Edith Margaret Emily Hutchinson), D.B.E.; British actress; b. 22 Dec. 1907; d. of William Worsley Ashcroft and Violet Maud Bernheim; m. 1st Rupert Hart-Davis 1929 (dissolved); m. 2nd Theodore Komisarjevsky 1934 (dissolved); m. 3rd Jeremy Hutchinson 1940 (dissolved 1966); one s. one d.; ed. Croydon and Central School of Speech Training, Albert Hall, London; first appeared at Birmingham Repertory Theatre 1926; Hon. D.Litt. (Oxford) 1961, (Leicester) 1964, (Reading) 1986, (Bristol) 1986; Hon. D.Lit. (London) 1965, (Cambridge) 1972; Hon. D. Univ. (Open Univ.) 1986; King's Gold Medal (Norway); *roles include:* Constance Neville (She Stoops to Conquer), Naomi (Jew Süss) 1929, Desdemona (with Paul Robeson) 1930, Irina (The Three Sisters) 1937-38, Cecily Cardew

(The Importance of Being Ernest) 1939-40, 1942, Catherine (The Dark River) 1943, Haymarket Repertory Season 1944-45, Evelyn Holt (Edward My Son) 1947, Catherine Sloper (The Heiress) 1949, Hester Collyer (The Deep Blue Sea) 1952, Hedda Gabler 1954, Miss Madrigal (The Chalk Garden), Shen Te (The Good Woman of Setzuan) 1956, Rebecca West (Rosmersholm) 1959, title role Duchess of Malfi 1961, Madame Ranevsky (The Cherry Orchard) 1962, and numerous Shakespearian performances at The Old Vic, London, and as mem. Royal Shakespeare Company (RSC), Stratford and London 1960-64, Dir. RSC 1968-; has appeared in London in The Seagull 1964, Days in the Trees 1966, Ghosts 1967, Delicate Balance 1968, Landscape 1969, Katherine of Aragon in Henry VIII (Stratford-on-Avon), The Plebeians 1970, The Lovers of Viorne (Evening Standard Best Actress Award 1972) 1971, Lloyd George Knew My Father 1972, Old Times 1972, John Gabriel Borkman 1975, Happy Days 1975, Old World 1976, Watch on the Rhine 1980, Family Voices 1981, All's Well that Ends Well 1981; films incl. The Wandering Jew, Thirty-Nine Steps, The Nun's Story, Sunday Bloody Sunday, Three into Two Won't Go, Passage to India 1984 (Acad. Award 1984), When the Wind Blows (voice in animated film) 1987, A Perfect Spy 1987, Madame Sousatza; *TV appearances include:* Cream in my Coffee, Caught on a Train 1980, The Jewel in the Crown 1984. *Address:* Manor Lodge, Frognal Lane, London, N.W.3, England.

ASHDOWN, Jeremy John Durham (Paddy Ashdown); British politician; b. 27 Feb. 1941; s. of John W. R. D. Ashdown and Lois A. Ashdown; m. Jane Courtenay 1961; ed. Bedford School; served R.N. 1959-71, Captain R.M.; joined Diplomatic Service, First Sec. Mission to U.N., Geneva 1971-76; Commercial Man.'s Dept., Westland Group 1976-78; Senior Man., Morlands Ltd. 1978-81; employee Dorset Co. Council 1982-83; Parl. spokesman for Trade and Industry 1983-86; Liberal/SDP Alliance spokesman on Education and Science 1987; M.P. Yeovil (Liberal) 1983-88; Leader of the Social and Liberal Democrats 1988-. *Leisure interests:* walking, gardening, wine making. *Address:* Vane Cottage, Norton sub Hamdon, Somerset, TA14 6SG, England. *Telephone:* Chiselborough 491.

ASHE, Arthur Robert, B.S.; American professional lawn tennis player; b. 10 July 1943, Richmond, Va; s. of Arthur R. and Mattie Cordell (Cunningham) Ashe; m. Jeanne-Marie Moutoussamy 1977; ed. Univ. of California; Pres. Asscn. of Tennis Professionals 1974-76; adviser to United Negro Coll. Fund 1975-, African Student Aid Fund 1973-; Vice-Pres. (U.S.A.) Le Coq Sportif Tenniswear; Chair. Advisory Staff of AMF-Head Racket Co.; Tennis Dir. Doral County Club, Miami, Fla.; Sports Commentator, ABC Television 1977-; U.S. Army Lieut. 1967-69; U.S. Men's Hard Court Singles Champion 1963, U.S. Men's Clay Court Champion 1967, U.S. Amateur Champion 1968, U.S. Open Champion 1968, Australian Open Champion 1970, French Open Doubles Champion 1972, Wimbledon Singles Champion 1975, Australian Open Doubles Champion 1977; Capt. U.S. Davis Cup Team 1981-85; U.S. Jaycees T.O.Y.M. 1968; Consultant and mem. Bd. Aetna Life and Casualty Co.; Sports Commentator HBO; Hon. Doctorates from Princeton, Dartmouth Coll., Trinity (Hartford), Bryant Coll., Va. Union, Le Moyne Coll. *Publications:* Arthur Ashe: Portrait in Motion 1974, Off the Court, Arthur Ashe's Tennis Clinic 1982. *Leisure interests:* music, reading, golf. *Address:* 888 17 Street N.W. 1200, Washington, D.C. 20006, U.S.A. *Telephone:* (202) 457-8823.

ASHE, Sir Derick Rosslyn, K.C.M.G., M.A. (OXON.); British diplomatist (retd.); b. 20 Jan. 1919, Guildford, Surrey; s. of Frederick Allen and Rosalind Ashe (née Mitchell); m. Rissa Guinness (née Parker) 1957; one s. one d.; ed. Bradfield Coll., Trinity Coll., Oxford; served in H.M. Forces 1940-46, mentioned in despatches 1945; Second Sec. Control Comm. for Germany 1947-49; Private Sec. to Perm. Under-Sec. of State for German Section, Foreign Office 1950-53; First Sec. La Paz 1953-55; Foreign Office 1955-57; First Sec. Information, Madrid 1957-61; Foreign Office 1961-62; Counsellor, Head of Chancery, Addis Ababa 1962-64; Havana 1964-66; Head of Security Dept., Foreign and Commonwealth Office 1966-69; Minister, Tokyo 1969-71; Amb. to Romania 1972-75, to Argentina 1975-77 (withdrawn Jan. 1976); alternate leader of U.K. del. to Disarmament Conf., Geneva 1977-79, to UN Special Session on Disarmament, New York 1977-78; Kt. Order of Orange-Nassau. *Leisure interests:* gardening, antiques. *Address:* Dalton House, Hurstbourne Tarrant, Andover, Hampshire, England. *Telephone:* Hurstbourne Tarrant 276.

ASHER, Jane; British actress; b. 5 April 1946; m. Gerald Scarfe (q.v.); has appeared in numerous films, on TV and the London stage. *Films include:* Greengage Summer, Masque of the Red Death, Alfie, Deep End, Henry the Eighth and his Six Wives, Success is the Best Revenge, Dreamchild. *Plays include:* Henceforward. *Address:* c/o Chatto & Linnit, Ltd., Prince of Wales Theatre, Coventry Street, London, W.1, England.

ASHFORD, William Stanton, O.B.E.; British diplomatist (retd.); b. 4 July 1924; m. Rosalind Anne Collett 1957; two s.; ed. Winchester Coll., Balliol Coll., Oxford; served in R.A.F. 1943-47; Air Ministry 1948; First Sec. (Information) and Dir. British Information Service (B.I.S.), Freetown, Sierra Leone 1961; First Sec. (Information) and Dir. B.I.S., Accra, Ghana 1962; Acting Consul.-Gen., Tangier, Morocco 1965; First Sec. (Information), Bombay, India 1966; Regional Information Officer, Montreal 1967; on loan to Northern Ireland Office 1972; Foreign and Commonwealth Office 1974; Consul-Gen., Adelaide, Australia 1976-80; High Commr. in Vanuatu 1980-

82. *Address:* c/o Lloyds Bank Ltd., Fore Street, Bodmin, Cornwall, PL31 2HP, England. *Telephone:* Bodmin 3434.

ASHIHARA, Yoshinobu, B.A., M.ARCH., D.ENG.; Japanese architect; b. 7 July 1918, Tokyo; s. of Dr. Nobuyuki Ashihara and Kikuko Fujita; m. Hatsuko Takahashi 1945; one s. one d.; ed. Univ. of Tokyo and Harvard Univ. Graduate School; worked in architectural firms, Tokyo 1946-52; in Marcel Breuer's firm, New York 1953; visited Europe on Rockefeller Travel Grant 1954; Head, Yoshinobu Ashihara and Assocs. 1955-; Lecturer in Architecture, Hosei Univ., Tokyo 1955-59, Prof. of Architecture 1959-65; Prof. of Architecture, Musashino Art Univ., Tokyo 1964-70; Visiting Prof., School of Architecture and Building, Univ. of New South Wales, Australia 1966, Dept. of Architecture, Univ. of Hawaii 1969; Prof. of Architecture, Univ. of Tokyo 1970-79; Pres. Japan Architects' Assen. 1980-82; Architectural Inst. of Japan 1985-87; Award of Architectural Inst. of Japan for Chuo-Koron Building 1960; Special Award of Architectural Inst. of Japan for Komazawa Olympic Gymnasium 1965; Ministry of Educ. Award for Japan Pavilion, Expo 1967, Montreal; NSID Golden Triangle Award (U.S.A.) 1970, Commendatore, Ordine al Merito (Italy) 1970, Order of Commdr. of Lion (Finland) 1985, Japan Acad. of Arts Award 1984; Hon. F.A.I.A. 1979; Hon. Fellow Royal Australian Inst. of Architects 1987. *Works include:* Chuo-Koron Building, Sony Building, Komazawa Olympic Gymnasium 1965, Japanese Pavilion, Expo 67, Montreal, Fuji Film Bldg. 1969. *Publications:* Exterior Design in Architecture 1969, The Aesthetic Townscape 1983. *Leisure interests:* sauna, travelling. *Address:* Y. Ashihara, Architect and Associates, Sumitomo Seimei Building, 31-15 Sakuragaoka-cho, Shibuya-ku, Tokyo 150 (Office); 47 Nishihara-3, Shibuya-ku, Tokyo 151, Japan (Home). *Telephone:* 463-7461 (Office); 465-2661 (Home).

ASHIMOV, Baiken Ashimovich; Soviet politician; b. 10 Aug. 1917, Shabakbai, Kochetav oblast, Kazakhstan; ed. Leningrad Zoological Inst. and CPSU Higher Party School; mem. CPSU 1940-; army service 1938-41, 1942-45; party and local work, Kokchetav Region, Kazakh S.S.R. 1945-60; Chair. Karaganda Regional Exec. Cttee. 1961-63, 1964-68; First Sec. Karaganda Regional Agric. Cttee., CP Kazakhstan 1963-64; First Sec. Taldy-Kurgan Regional Cttee., CP Kazakhstan 1968-70; mem. Cen. Cttee. Kazakhstan 1961-; mem. Bureau of Cen. Cttee. CP Kazakhstan 1970-; Chair. Kazakh S.S.R. Council of Ministers 1970-84; Deputy to U.S.S.R. Supreme Soviet 1970-; mem. Cen. Cttee. CPSU 1971-; Order of Lenin (four times), Hero of Socialist Labour 1977 and numerous decorations. *Address:* c/o Council of Ministers of the Kazakh S.S.R., Alma-Ata, U.S.S.R.

ASHKENAZY, Vladimir; Russian-born concert pianist and conductor; b. 6 July 1937, Gorky, U.S.S.R.; s. of David Ashkenazy and Evstolia (née Plotnova); m. Thorunn Sofia Johannsdottir 1961; two s. three d.; ed. Central Music School, Moscow, and Moscow Conservatoire; Second Prize, Int. Chopin Competition, Warsaw 1955; Gold Medal, Queen Elizabeth Int. Piano Competition, Brussels 1956; Joint winner (with John Ogdon, q.v.) Int. Tchaikovsky Piano Competition, Moscow 1962; Prin. Guest Conductor, Philharmonia Orchestra 1982-83; Music Dir. Royal Philharmonic 1987-; Hon. R.A.M.; Icelandic Order of the Falcon; concerts worldwide; many recordings. *Address:* Sonnenhof 4, 6004 Lucerne, Switzerland.

ASHMORE, Admiral of the Fleet Sir Edward (Beckwith), G.C.B., D.S.C.; British naval officer; b. 11 Dec. 1919, Queenstown, Eire; s. of Vice-Adm. L. H. Ashmore, C.B., D.S.O., and T. V. Shutt; m. Elizabeth Mary Doveton Sturdee 1942; one s. one d.; ed. Royal Naval Coll., Dartmouth; Served H.M.S. Birmingham, Jupiter, Middleton 1938-42; Staff, C.-in-C. Home Fleet 1944-45; mentioned in despatches 1946; Asst. Naval Attaché, British Embassy, Moscow 1946-47; Squadron Communications Officer 3rd Aircraft Carrier Squadron 50; Commdr. 1950; H.M.S. Alert 1952-53; Capt. 1955; Capt. (F) 6th Frigate Squadron, Commdg. Officer H.M.S. Blackpool 1958; Dir. of Plans, Admiralty and Ministry of Defence 1960-62; Commdr. British Forces Caribbean Area 1963-64; Rear-Adm. 1965; Asst. Chief of Defence Staff, Signals 1965-67; Flag Officer, Second-in-Command, Far East Fleet 1967-68; Vice-Adm. 1968; Vice-Chief Naval Staff 1969-71; Adm. 1970; C.-in-C. Western Fleet Sept.-Oct. 1971; C.-in-C. Fleet 1971-73; Chief of Naval Staff and First Sea Lord 1974-77; Chief of Defence Staff Feb.-Aug. 1977; First and Principal Naval ADC to Her Majesty the Queen 1974-77; Adm. of the Fleet 1977; Dir. Racal Electronics Ltd. 1978-; Gov. Sutton's Hospital in Charterhouse 1975, Charterhouse School 1984; mem. Council of the Soc. of British Aerospace Cos. Ltd. 1982-. *Address:* c/o National Westminster Bank Limited, 26 Haymarket, London, S.W.1, England.

ASHTAL, Abdalla Saleh al-, M.A.; Yemeni diplomatist; b. 5 Oct. 1940, Addis Ababa, Ethiopia; m. Vivian Eshoo al-Ashtal; one s. one d.; ed. Menelik II Secondary School, American Univ. of Beirut and New York Univ.; Asst. Dir. Yemeni Bank for Reconstruction Devt., Sanaa 1966-67; mem. Supreme People's Council, Hadramout Province 1967-68, Gen. Command Yemeni Nat. Liberation Front 1968-70; Political Adviser, Perm. Mission to UN 1970-72, Sr. Counsellor 1972-73, Perm. Rep. 1973-; Non-Resident Amb. to Canada 1974-, to Mexico 1975-79, to Brazil 1985-. *Address:* Permanent Mission of the People's Democratic Repub. of Yemen to the United Nations, 413 East 51st Street, New York, N.Y. 10022, U.S.A.

ASHTON, Norman Henry, C.B.E., D.SC., F.R.C.P., F.R.C.S., F.R.C.PATH., F.R.S.; British university professor; b. 11 Sept. 1913; s. of Henry James Ashton and Margaret Ann Ashton; ed. West Kensington School, King's Coll. and Westminster Hosp. Medical School, London Univ.; Asst. Pathologist, Princess Beatrice Hosp. 1939; House Surgeon, House Physician, Sr. Casualty Officer 1939-41; Dir. Pathology, Kent and Canterbury Hosp. 1941; Lieut. Col. R.A.M.C. 1946; Pathologist Gordon Hosp. 1947; Dir., Dept. of Pathology, Inst. of Ophthalmology 1948-78; Reader in Pathology, London Univ. 1953, Prof. 1957-78, Prof. Emer. 1978-; Visiting Prof., Johns Hopkins Hosp. 1959; Consultant Pathologist, Moorfields Eye Hosp. 1948-78, mem. Bd. of Govs. 1963-66, 1975-78; Chair. British Diabetes Assen. Cttee. on Blindness in Diabetes 1967-70; mem. Bd. of Govs., Royal Nat. Coll. for the Blind 1977-; Life Pres., European Ophthalmic Pathology Soc.; Hon. mem., British Div., Int. Acad. of Pathology; Pres. Ophthalmological Soc. of the United Kingdom 1979-81; Master, Soc. of Apothecaries of London 1984-85; Freeman of City of London; Proctor Medal for Research in Ophthalmology (U.S.A.) 1957; Doyne Medal (Oxford) 1960; Bowman Medal 1965; Gonin Gold Medal 1978; 1st Jules Stein Award (U.S.A.) 1981. *Publications:* numerous articles in scientific journals. *Leisure interests:* painting, gardening. *Address:* 4 Bloomfield Road, Little Venice, London, W9 1AH, England. *Telephone:* 01-286 5536.

ASHWORTH, John Michael, PH.D., D.SC.; British biologist; b. 27 Nov. 1938, Luton; s. of Jack Ashworth and Mary Ousman; m. Ann Knight 1963 (died 1985); one s. three d.; ed. Exeter Coll., Oxford, Leicester Univ., Brandeis Univ., U.S.A., Univ. of California, San Diego; Harkness Fellow, Commonwealth Fund, New York, N.Y. 1965-67; Lecturer, Biochemistry Dept., Univ. of Leicester 1967-71, Reader 1971-73; Prof., Biology Dept., Univ. of Essex 1973-79; Chief Scientist, Cen. Policy Review Staff, Cabinet Office 1976-81; Under-Sec. Cabinet Office 1979-81; Vice-Chancellor, Univ. of Salford Sept. 1981-; Chair. Bd. Nat. Computer Centre 1983-, Nat. Accreditation Council for Certification Bodies, Chair. Tech. Advisory Cttee., Jaguar Cars PLC; mem. Bd. of Granada TV 1986-; Colworth Medal of Biochemical Soc. 1972. *Publications:* editor: Outline Studies in Biology; author: Cell Differentiation 1973, The Slime Moulds (with J. Dee) 1976, over 50 papers on biological and biochemical topics in scientific journals. *Address:* University of Salford, Salford, M5 4WT, England.

ASIMAKOPULOS, Athanasios, M.A. PH.D., F.R.S.C.; Canadian professor of economics; b. 28 May 1930, Montreal; s. of Antonios Asimakopulos and Paraskevi Sepentzie; m. Marika Salamis 1961; two d.; ed. McGill Univ. and Univ. of Cambridge; Asst. Prof. Royal Mil. Coll., Kingston, Ont. 1957-59, of Econs. McGill Univ. 1959-63, Assoc. Prof. 1963-66, Prof. 1966-87, Dow Prof. of Political Econ. 1988-; Chair. Dept. of Econs. 1974-78; mem. research staff Royal Comm. on Govt. Org. 1961, on Banking and Finance 1962; Man. Ed. Canadian Journal of Econs. 1968-72. *Publications:* The Reliability of Selected Price Indexes as Measures of Price Trends 1964, An Introduction to Economic Theory: Microeconomics 1978, The Nature of Public Pension Plans: Intergenerational Equity, Funding and Saving 1980, Theories of Income Distribution (Ed.) 1988, Investment, Employment and Income Distribution 1988. *Leisure interest:* reading. *Address:* Department of Economics, McGill University, 855 Sherbrooke Street West, Montreal, P.Q., H3A 2T7 (Office); 3230 The Boulevard, Westmount, P.Q., H3Y 1S3, Canada (Home). *Telephone:* (514) 931-5355.

ASIMOV, Isaac PH.D.; American biochemist and science fiction writer; b. 2 Jan. 1920, Petrovichi, U.S.S.R.; s. of Judah Asimov and Anna Rachel (Berman) Asimov; m. 1st Gertrude Blugerman 1942, one s. one d.; m. 2nd Janet O. Jeppson 1973; ed. Columbia Univ.; Instructor in Biochemistry, Boston Univ. School of Medicine 1949-51, Asst. Prof. 1951-55, Assoc. Prof. 1955-79, Prof. 1979-; professional writer 1938-; numerous awards. *Publications:* 357 books including The Human Body 1963, The Human Brain 1964, New Intelligent Man's Guide to Science 1965, Asimov's Biographical Encyclopedia of Science and Technology 1964, Understanding Physics 1966, The Universe 1966, Is Anyone There? 1967, Asimov's Guide to the Bible 1968, Photosynthesis 1969, Shaping of England 1969, Opus 100 1969, Solar System and Back 1970, The Gods Themselves, Ed. Nebula Award Stories 1973, The Tragedy of the Moon (essays) 1974, Words of Science 1974, Our Federal Union 1975, Eyes on the Universe 1975, The Ends of the Earth 1975, Murder at the ABA 1976, The Bicentennial Man 1976, Familiar Poems Annotated 1976, The Collapsing Universe 1977, Mars, the Red Planet 1977, The Golden Door 1977, Quasar, Quasar, Burning Bright 1978, Animals of the Bible 1978, Life and Time 1978, In Memory Yet Green 1979, Opus 200 1979, Extraterrestrial Civilizations 1979, A Choice of Catastrophes 1979, Isaac Asimov's Book of Facts 1979, Casebook of the Black Widowers 1980, In Joy Still Felt 1980, The Annotated Gulliver's Travels 1980, In the Beginning 1981, Asimov on Science Fiction 1981, Venus: Near Neighbour of the Sun 1981, The Sun Shines Bright 1981, The Complete Robot 1982, Exploring the Earth and the Cosmos 1982, Foundation's Edge 1982, Counting the Eons 1983, The Winds of Change and Other Stories 1983, The Roving Mind 1983, The Measure of the Universe 1983, The Union Club Mysteries 1983, Norby, the Mixed-Up Robot 1983, The Robots of Dawn 1983, Banquets of the Black Widowers 1984, Opus 300 1984, Asimov's New Guide to Science 1984, Asimov's Guide to Halley's Comet 1985, Exploding Suns 1985, Robots 1985, The Subatomic Monster 1985, Robots and Empire 1985, Norby and the Invaders 1985, The Alternate Asimovs 1986, The Dangers of Intelligence 1986, Foundation and Earth 1986, Norby and the Queen's Necklace 1986, Far as Human Eye Could See 1987, Past, Present and Future 1987, How to Enjoy Writing

1987, Norby finds a Villain 1987, Fantastic Voyage II 1987, Prelude to Foundation 1988, The Mammoth Book of Classic Science Fiction 1988, guides and children's books. *Leisure interests:* no leisure. *Address:* 10 West 66th Street, Apt. 33A, New York, N.Y. 10023, U.S.A.

ASIMOV, Mukhamed Saifitdinovich; Soviet philosopher and politician; b. 1 Sept. 1920, Leninabad; m. Monand Asimova 1923; two s. three d.; ed. Uzbek State Univ., Samarkand, and Acad. of Social Sciences. Army Service 1941–46; mem. CPSU 1945–; Senior Lecturer, Leninabad Pedagogical Inst. 1946–54; Postgraduate student, Acad. of Social Sciences 1954–55; Rector, Dushanbe Polytechnic Inst. 1956–62; Minister of Educ. of Tajik S.S.R. 1962–65; mem. Cen. Cttee. CP of Tajikistan 1962–; mem. Presidium, Sec. Cen. Cttee. of CP of Tajikistan, Chair. Party and State Control Cttee., Tajik S.S.R., Deputy Chair. Council of Ministers of Tajik S.S.R. 1962–65; Pres. Acad. of Sciences of Tajik S.S.R. 1965–; Deputy to U.S.S.R. Supreme Soviet 1966–; mem. Cen. Cttee. CP of Tajikistan; Corresp. mem. U.S.S.R. Acad. of Sciences; decorations including Order of Lenin. *Publications:* Asari barchastai filosofiya i marxist 1960, Materiya ba tasviri fizikii olam 1966, Paidoish ba inkishofi taffakuri falsafi 1970. *Leisure interest:* chess. *Address:* Academy of Sciences, Lenin Street 33, Dushanbe 26, Tajikistan, U.S.S.R. *Telephone:* 22-50-83.

ASKEW, Reubin O'Donovan, LL.B.; American lawyer and politician; b. 11 Sept. 1928, Muskogee, Okla.; s. of Leo G. Askew and Alberta N. O'Donovan; m. Donna L. Harper 1956; one s. one d.; ed. Escambia County Public School System, Florida State Univ., Univ. of Florida Coll. of Law and Denver Univ.; Partner in law firm, Pensacola, Florida 1958–70; Asst. County Solicitor, Escambia Co., Florida 1956–58; mem. State of Florida House of Reps. 1958–62; State Senate 1962–70; Gov. of Florida 1971–79; U.S. Trade Rep. 1979–81; Dir in law firm, Miami 1981–88; Chair. Education Commission of U.S.A. 1973; Chair. Southern Govs. Conf. 1974–78, Chair. Nat. Dem. Govs. Conference 1976, Nat. Govs. Conference 1976–77; Chair. Presidential Advisory Bd. on Ambassadorial Appointments 1977–79, Select Comm. on Immigration and Refugee Policy 1979; Visiting Fellow, Inst. of Politics, Harvard Univ. 1979; Chubb Fellow, Yale Univ.; Hon. degrees Univ. of Notre Dame, Stetson Univ., Rollins Coll., Eckerd Coll., Florida Southern Coll., Saint Leo Coll., Miami Univ., Bethune-Cookman Coll., Univ. of West Fla., Barry Univ., Univ. of Florida, Univ. of Tampa, Belmont Abbey Coll.; John F. Kennedy Award, Nat. Council of Jewish Women 1973, Hubert Harley Award (American Judicature Soc.) 1973, Nat. Wildlife Fed. Award 1972, Outstanding Conservationist of Year Award, Florida Audubon Soc. 1972, Herbert H. Lehman Ethics Award 1973, Salvation Army Gen. William Booth Award 1973, Distinguished Community Service Award, Brandeis Univ., Ethics and Govt. Award, Common Cause; Order of COIF (Hon.) Coll. of Law, Univ. of Fla., Albert Einstein Distinguished Achievement Award, Yeshiva Univ.; Democrat; Presbyterian. *Publications:* Trade Services and the World Econ. 1983, Opinion: Public Welfare 1984. *Address:* Akerman, Senterfitt and Edison, P.O. Box 321, Orlando, Fla. 32802, U.S.A. (Office). *Telephone:* (407) 843-7860 (Office).

ASKONAS, Brigitte Alice, PH.D., F.R.S.; British immunologist; b. 1 April 1923; d. of the late Charles F. Askonas and Rose Askonas; ed. McGill Univ., Montreal, Canada and Univ. of Cambridge, England; Research Student, School of Biochemistry, Univ. of Cambridge 1949–52; Immunology Div., Nat. Inst. for Medical Research, London 1953–, Head 1977–88; Dept. of Bacteriology and Immunology, Harvard Medical School, Boston, Mass., U.S.A. 1961–62; Basel Inst. for Immunology, Switzerland 1971–72; Attached to Molecular Immunology Group, Inst. of Molecular Medicine, John Radcliffe Hosp. 1989–; Hon. mem. American Soc. of Immunology, Société française d'Immunologie, British Soc. of Immunology; Hon. D.Sc. (McGill Univ.). *Publications:* scientific papers in various biochemical and immunological journals and books. *Leisure interests:* art, travel. *Address:* c/o Molecular Immunology Group, Institute of Molecular Medicine, John Radcliffe Hospital, Headington, Oxford OX3 9DU; 23 Hillside Gardens, London, N6 5SU, England. *Telephone:* 01-348 6792.

ÅSLING, Nils Gunnar, B.SC.; Swedish politician and banker; b. 15 Dec. 1927, Åse; m. Karin Asling; twin s. one d.; ed. Schools of Agriculture, Torsta and Sånga-Säby, Stockholm School of Social Studies and Stockholm Univ.; mem. Riksdag 1969–88, Cttee. on Finance 1973–76; Minister of Industry 1976–78, 1979–82; mem. Exec. Centre Party; Chair. Swedish Asscn. of Co-operative Banks; Chair. Banking Co. of Swedish Co-operative Banks; mem. bd. Fed. of Swedish Farmers, Industrifonden, Aktiefrämjandet, Camfore group of cos., Svenska Rymdaktriebolaget (Spacecorpn.). *Publications:* The New Era 1955, Per Olof Sundman, a Portrait 1970, Ideas and Realities 1970, The Crisis and Reformation of Swedish Industry: The Perspective of Industrial Policies for the 1980s 1979, Struggle for Power or Collaboration 1983. *Leisure interests:* art, literature. *Address:* Foreningsbankernas Bank, P.O. Box 5844, 10248 Stockholm (Office); Åse, 83047 Trångsviken, Sweden (Home).

ASMODI, Herbert; German playwright; b. 30 March 1923, Heilbronn; m. T. Katja; ed. Ruprecht-Karl Universität, Heidelberg; war service 1942–45; studied 1947–52; freelance writer, Munich 1952–; mem. PEN; Gerhart Hauptmann-Preis der Freien Volksbühne Berlin 1954, Tukan Prize, Munich 1971, Bayerischer Verdienstorden. *Publications include:* plays: Jenseits vom Paradies 1954, Pardon wird nicht gegeben 1956, Tierjagt 1957, Die Menschenfresser 1959, Nachsaison 1970, Mohrenwäsche, Dichtung und

Wahrheit 1969, Stirb und Werde 1965, Nasrin oder Die Kunst zu Träumen 1970, Marie von Brinvilliers 1971, Geld 1973; Poems: Jokers Gala 1975, Jokers Farewell 1977. *Address:* Wiedenmayer Strasse 42, 8000 Munich 22, Federal Republic of Germany.

ASP, Eero Rafael; Finnish monetary official; b. 24 Feb. 1922, Helsinki; s. of Einar Walfrid Asp and Eva Elisabet Tynell; m. Sisko Oili Karstila 1953; one d.; ed. Helsinki Univ.; Bank of Finland, Helsinki 1948, Sec. Bank of Finland 1955–58, 1960–62; Alt. mem. Bd. of Govs. IMF 1957–58, 1961–62, mem. Bd. of Dirs. 1958–60, 1968–70; Man. Dir. Export Guarantee Bd., Helsinki 1962–71, Finnish Export Credit Ltd., Helsinki 1963–82; Alt. mem. Bd. of Govs., Asian Devt. Bank 1966–82; Chair., Bd. of Dirs Postipankki (U.K.) Ltd. 1982–; mem. Admin. Council Banque Indosuez (Finland) S.A. 1982–. *Leisure interest:* golf. *Address:* Lyokkiniemi 7, 02160 Espoo, Finland. *Telephone:* Helsinki 427786.

ASPER, Israel Harold, Q.C., LL.M.; Canadian lawyer and business executive; b. 11 Aug. 1932, Minnedosa, Manitoba; s. of Leon and Cecilia Asper; m. Ruth M. Bernstein 1956; two s. one d.; ed. Kelvin High School, Winnipeg, and Univ. of Manitoba; with Drache, Meltzer, Essers, Gold & Asper 1957–59; f. Asper & Co. (now Buchwald, Asper & Co.), law firm, Winnipeg 1959, Sr. Partner Asper & Co. 1959–70; Sr. Partner Buchwald, Asper, Henteleff 1970–77; fmr. mem. Legis Ass.; Man. fmr. Leader Liberal Party; Chair. of Bd. Global Television Network and Canwest Broadcasting Ltd.; Chair. and C.E.O. CanWest Capital Corpn. 1977–; Chair. Bd. Can-West Trust Co. of Canada, Canadian Surety Co. of Canada, Western Approaches Ltd., SaskWest TV Ltd, CPTV Inc.; mem. Bd. numerous cos. and orgs. *Publications:* The Benson Iceberg: A Critical Analysis of The White Paper on Tax Reform in Canada 1970; weekly newspaper column in Toronto Globe & Mail 1966–77. *Address:* 6th Floor, 1 Lombard Place, Winnipeg, Man., R3B 0X3, Canada; 1063 Wellington Crescent, Winnipeg, Man. R3N 0A1, Canada (Home). *Telephone:* (204) 956-2025 (Office); (204) 284-2407 (Home).

ASRI BIN HAJI MUDA, Datuk Haji Mohamed, S.P.M.K.; Malaysian politician; b. 10 Oct. 1923; fmr. teacher; acting Sec.-Gen. Pan-Malayan Islamic Party 1949–54, Commr., Kelantan 1954–61, Vice-Pres. 1961–64, Pres. 1964–82; mem. Kelantan State Assembly 1959–68, Speaker 1964–68; M.P. 1959–68; mem. Nat. Unity Council 1969–; Minister of Land Devt., Mines and Special Functions 1972–76, of Land, Mines and Regional Devt. 1976–77; Nat. M.P. –1978, Deputy Chair. Nat. Council for Islamic Affairs 1973–. *Address:* Pan-Malayan Islamic Party, 214-1A Jalan Pahang, Kuala Lumpur, Malaysia.

ASSAD, Lieut.-Gen. Hafiz al-; Syrian army officer and politician; b. 1928; m.; four s. one d.; ed. Military Coll., Aviation Coll; mem. Baath Party 1946–; formed Baathist Mil. Cttee. when in Egypt; dismissed from the army, rejoined 1963, promoted Gen. of Air Force 1964; Minister of Defence and Commdr. of Air Force 1966–70; Prime Minister 1970–71; Sec. Baath Party Nov. 1970–; Pres. of Syria March 1971–; mem. Pres. Council, Fed. of Arab Repubs. 1971; Pres. Syrian Nat. Progressive Front 1972–; Dr. h.c. (Damascus) 1972. *Address:* Office of the President, Damascus, Syria.

ASSAD, Nassir El-Din El-, M.A., PH.D.; Jordanian scholar; b. 1923, Aqaba; s. of Ahmed Jamil and Amina El-Assad; m. Awatif Hafez 1946; three s. one d.; ed. Univ. of Cairo; Dean, Faculty of Arts and Educ., Univ. of Libya 1959–61; Dean, Faculty of Arts, also Pres. of Univ., Univ. of Jordan 1962–68, Pres. 1978–80; Asst. Dir.-Gen. ALECSO 1970–77; Amb. to Saudi Arabia 1977–78; Pres. Royal Acad. for Islamic Civilization Research (Al Albait Foundation) 1980–; Minister of Higher Educ. 1985–; King Faisal Int. Prize (Arabic Literature) 1981. *Publications:* 32 works including: Recent Literary Trends in Palestine and Jordan 1957, Modern Poetry in Palestine and Jordan 1961, Singing and Singing Girls in Pre-Islamic Arabia 1968, The Sources of Pre-Islamic Poetry 1982. *Address:* c/o University of Jordan, P.O. Box 1682, Amman, Jordan.

ASSENMACHER, Ivan, M.D., D.SC.; French professor of physiology; b. 17 May 1927, Erstein; s. of Ivan Assenmacher and Mary (née Wetzel) Assenmacher; m. Violette Rochedieu 1952; two s.; ed. Univs. of Strasbourg and Paris; Asst. Faculty of Medicine Univ. of Strasbourg 1950–53, Asst. Prof. 1953–57; Sub-Dir. Histophysiology Lab., Coll. de France, Paris 1957–59; Assoc. Prof. Univ. of Montpellier 1959–62, Prof. Physiology 1962–; Head of Neuroendocrinology Lab., C.N.R.S., Montpellier 1967–; Exchange Prof. Physiology, Univ. of Calif., Berkeley 1976, 1982; mem. Acad. des Sciences 1982–; mem. Consultative Cttee. for Univs., Paris 1967–80, 1986–, Nat. Cttee. for Scientific Research, Paris 1967–75, 1980–86, Gutachtergruppe für Neuroendokrinologie 1975–85, and Neuropeptide 1985–, Deutsche Forschungsgemeinschaft, Bonn; Chevalier Ordre Nat. du Mérite; Officier Ordre Palmes Académiques, Médaille des Réfractaires 1944–45. *Publications:* Photorégulation de la Reproduction (with J. Benoit) 1970, Environmental Endocrinology (with D. S. Farner) 1978, Endocrine Regulations as Adaptive Mechanisms to the Environment (with J. Boissin) 1987. *Address:* Laboratory of Neuroendocrinology, UA-1197-C.N.R.S., Department of Physiology, University of Montpellier II, F-34060 Montpellier (Office); 419 Avenue d'Occitanie, F-34090 Montpellier, France (Home). *Telephone:* 67.63.91.44 (Office); 67.63.22.20 (Home).

ASTACIO, Dr. Julio Ernesto; Salvadorian politician, physician and surgeon; b. 1932, San Salvador; m. Marta de Astacio; two s. one d.; ed.

Univ. de El Salvador; specialized at Lady of Lourdes Hosp., Univ. of Pennsylvania, Walter Reed Hosp., Washington, D.C., U.S.A.; postgraduate studies in radiology, Saint Christopher's Children's Hosp., Philadelphia, Univs. of Munich and Erlange, Germany; fmr. Prof. of Radiology, Radiological Anatomy, Physiology and Pediatric Radiology, Univ. de El Salvador; fmr. Head of Radiology Dept., Benjamin Bloom's Children's Hosp., San Salvador and physician at the Mil. Hosp.; Vascular Radiologist, Salvadorian Inst. of Social Security Hosp.; Vice-Pres. of El Salvador 1977–79. *Address:* San Salvador, El Salvador.

ASTAFIEV, Viktor Petrovich; Soviet writer; b. 1 May 1924, Ovsyanka Village, Krasnoyarsk District; brought up in orphanage, served in World War II; writer 1951–; State prizewinner 1978. *Publications include:* novels: Till Next Spring 1953, The Snows are Melting 1958, Shooting Star 1962, Vasyutkin Lake 1962, Stories: Theft. Somewhere the War is Droning 1968, Blue Dusk 1968; Tales 1969; The Horse With the Pink Mane and Other Siberian Stories (Eng. trans.) 1970, The Last Bow 1971; The Light Afternoon and Other Tales 1973; Shepherd & Shepherdess 1973; The King-Fish (State Prize) 1978, Collected Works (4 vols.) 1979, The Sad Detective 1986. *Address:* U.S.S.R. Union of Writers, Ulitsa Vorovskogo 52, Moscow, U.S.S.R.

ASTON, James William, B.S.; American banker; b. 6 Oct. 1911, Farmersville, Tex.; s. of Joseph A. and Jimmie G. J. Aston; m. Sarah C. Orth 1935; one s.; ed. Texas A. & M. Univ.; served U.S.A.A.F. 1941–45; Vice-Pres. Repub. Nat. Bank (now NCNB Texas) of Dallas 1945–55, Exec. Vice-Pres. 1955–57, Pres. 1957–61, Pres. and Chief Exec. Officer 1961–65, Chair. and Chief Exec. Officer 1965–74, Dir. 1957–77, Chair. Exec. Comm. 1977–87, Consultant 1987–; Chair. and C.E.O. RepublicBank Corpn. (multi-bank holding co.) 1974–77, Dir. 1974–87; official of numerous civic and philanthropic orgs. *Leisure interests:* golf, hunting. *Address:* NCNB Texas, P.O. Box 660020, Dallas, Tex. 75266-0020 (Office); 5000 Royal Lane, Dallas, Tex. 75229, U.S.A. (Home).

ASTOR, Hon. (Francis) David Langhorne; British journalist; b. 5 March 1912, London; s. of 2nd Viscount Astor; m. 1st Melanie Hauser 1945, one d.; m. 2nd Bridget Aphra Wreford 1952, two s. three d.; ed. Eton and Balliol Coll., Oxford; staff, Yorkshire Post 1936; served Second World War 1939–45; Foreign Ed. The Observer 1946–48, Ed. 1948–75, Dir. 1976–81; mem. Council Royal Inst. of Int. Affairs 1977–; Croix de guerre. *Publication:* Peace in the Middle East: Super Powers and Security Guarantees (with V. Yorke) 1978. *Address:* 9 Cavendish Avenue, St. John's Wood, London, NW8 9JD; and Manor House, Sutton Courtenay, Berks., England. *Telephone:* 01-286 0223/4 (London); Abingdon 848-221.

ÅSTRÖM Carl Sverker, B.A., LL.B.; Swedish diplomatist; b. 30 Dec. 1915, Uppsala; s. of John and Brita Åström; joined diplomatic service 1939; Attaché, Moscow 1940–43; at Ministry of Foreign Affairs 1943–46, 1948–53; Sec. Washington, D.C. 1946–48; Counsellor, London 1953–56; Dir. Political Dept., Ministry of Foreign Affairs 1956–63; Perm. Rep. to UN 1964–70; Head of Del. for negotiations with EEC 1970–72; Sec.-Gen. Ministry of Foreign Affairs 1972–78; Amb. to France 1978–82. *Address:* c/o Ministry of Foreign Affairs, Stockholm, Sweden.

ASUKATA, Ichio; Japanese politician; b. 1915. Mayor of Yokohama 1963; Head Nat. Asscn. of Progressive Mayors; fmr. mem. House of Councillors; Chair. Socialist Party of Japan 1977–84. *Address:* c/o Nippon Shakaito, 1-8-1 Nagata-cho, Chiyoda-ku, Tokyo, Japan.

ATALA NAZZAL, César; Peruvian banker and politician; b. 10 June 1917, Huancavelica; ed. Universidad Nacional Mayor de San Marcos; fmr. exec. Vidrios Peruanos S.A., Productos de Hielo Seco y Gas Carbónico S.A., Aguas Minerales Viso y San Mateo S.A. and other cos.; on staff of OAS 1962–64; with IDB from 1971, elected Alternate Dir. of IDB for Peru and Colombia 1980, elected Exec. Dir. 1981; Man. and Founder, Banco Exterior de España y de los Andes in Peru and Dir. representing Banco Exterior de España; active in Partido Aprista Peruano since his youth, imprisoned in 1932, Party's Nat. Sec. for Economy 1956; elected Nat. Deputy 1962; fmr. Chair. of Bd. of La Tribuna, Lima; Minister of Industry, Tourism and Integration 1985–86. *Address:* Ministry of Industry, Tourism and Integration, Calle 1 Oueste, Corpac, San Isidro, Lima 27, Peru. *Telephone:* 407120.

ATANASOV, Georgi; Bulgarian politician; b. Plovdid; ed. Sofia Univ.; mem. Politburo, Cen. Cttee. CP.; Chair. Council of Ministers March 1986–. *Address:* Council of Ministers, Blvd. Dondukov 1, Sofia 1000, Bulgaria.

ATASOY, Veysel; Turkish politician; b. 1947, Zonguldak; unmarried; ed. schools in Devrek, Istanbul Kabatas, High School and School of Political Science, Istanbul; deputy local official, Alanya, Akyazi, Menemen and Yeşilova townships; local admin. Kaynarca, Varto and Karayazi townships; Sec.-Gen. State Personnel Office 1980; Adviser, State Planning Org. 1981; mem. Parl. from Zonguldak; Minister of Transportation and Communications 1986–87, Minister of State for Environment and Mining 1987–88. *Address:* c/o Ministry of Environment, Ankara, Turkey.

ATASSI, Nureddin, M.D.; Syrian politician; b. 1929; ed. Damascus Univ. Minister of the Interior Aug. 1963; Deputy Prime Minister Oct. 1964; mem. Syrian Presidential Council May 1964–Dec. 1965; Pres. of Syria 1966–70,

also Prime Minister 1968–70; Sec.-Gen. Syrian Baath Party 1966–70; in exile in Libya.

ATHANASSIADES, Panos; Greek newspaper proprietor; b. 17 March 1899, Kydonias; ed. Commercial School of Chalke, Athens Univ.; Propr. Delpa, maritime agency 1920–; Publr. of Bulletin Maritime de Constantinople, daily 1922–24, Index Maritime de Constantinople 1923–24, Naftemboriki, daily journal of finance, commerce, shipping and industry 1924; Lecturer, School of Industry, Piraeus 1959–62; Publr. Vradyni, daily 1962–; Pres. Org. of Port of Piraeus 1960–64; Int. Union of Transport 1955; mem. Council Nat. Org. of Tourism 1956–59; Knight of Dannebrog (Denmark). *Publications:* numerous articles. *Address:* 132 Patission Street, Athens 802, Greece.

ATHERTON, Alfred Leroy Jr., B.SC., M.A.; American diplomatist; b. 22 Nov. 1921, Pittsburgh; s. of Alfred Leroy and Joan (née Reed) Leroy; m. Betty Wylie Kittredge 1946; two s. one d.; ed. Harvard Univ.; joined Foreign Service 1947; Vice-Consul, Stuttgart and Bonn 1947–52; Second Sec., U.S. Embassy, Syria 1953–56; Consul, Aleppo, Syria 1957–58, Calcutta, India 1962–65; Int. Relations Officer, Bureau of Near Eastern and S. Asian Affairs, State Dept. 1959–61, Deputy Dir. 1965–66, Country Dir. (Iraq, Jordan, Lebanon, Syria) 1966–67, (Israel and Arab-Israeli Affairs) 1967–70; Deputy Asst. Sec. of State 1970–74, Asst Sec. of State 1974–78; Amb. at Large with Special Responsibility for Middle East Peace Negotiations 1978–79; Amb. to Egypt 1979–83; Dir.-Gen., Foreign Service, State Dept. 1983–85; mem. Reform Bd. Dept. of State 1983–; Dir. The Harkness Fellowships 1985–; Chair. New York-Cairo Sister City Cttee. 1986–; mem. Bd. Dirs., US N.Z. Council 1987–; Trustee, the Una Chapman Cox Foundation 1985–87, Exec. Dir. 1989–; Pres. Distinguished Service Award 1983. *Leisure interests:* photography, travel. *Address:* 4301 Massachusetts Avenue, N.W., Apt. 5003, Washington, D.C. 20016, U.S.A. (Home). *Telephone:* (202) 244 1060 (Home); (212) 535 0400 (Office).

ATHERTON, David, M.A. (CANTAB), L.R.A.M., L.T.C.L., L.G.S.M.; British conductor; b. 3 Jan. 1944, Blackpool; s. of Robert and Lavinia Atherton; m. Ann Gianetta Drake 1970; one s. two d.; ed. Cambridge Univ.; Répétiteur, Royal Opera House, Covent Garden 1967–68; Founder, London Sinfonietta, Musical Dir. 1967–73; Resident Conductor, Royal Opera House 1968–79; Artistic Dir. and Conductor, London Stravinsky Festival 1979–82, Ravel/Varese Festival 1983–84; début La Scala, Milan 1976, San Francisco Opera 1978; youngest-ever conductor at Henry Wood Promenade Concerts, London 1968; début Royal Festival Hall, London 1969; has conducted performances in Europe, Middle East, Far East, Australasia, N. America 1970–; Music Dir. and Prin. Conductor San Diego Symphony Orchestra 1980–87; Prin. Conductor and Artistic Adviser Royal Liverpool Philharmonic Orchestra 1980–83, Prin. Guest Conductor 1983–86; Prin. Guest Conductor BBC Symphony Orchestra; Conductor of the Year Award, Composers' Guild of G.B. 1971, Edison Award 1973, Grand Prix du Disque Award 1977, Koussevitzky Award 1981, Int. Record Critics Award 1982, Prix Caecilia 1982. *Publications:* The Complete Instrumental and Chamber Music of Arnold Schoenberg and Roberto Gerhard (Ed.) 1973, Pandora and Don Quixote Suites by Roberto Gerhard (Ed.) 1973; Contrib. to The Musical Companion 1978, The New Grove Dictionary 1981. *Leisure interests:* travel, squash, theatre. *Address:* c/o Harold Holt Ltd., 31 Sinclair Road, London, W14 0NS. England. *Telephone:* 01-603 4600.

ATHFIELD, Ian Charles, DIP.ARCH.; New Zealand architect; b. 15 July 1940, Christchurch; s. of Charles Leonard Athfield and Ella Agnes Taylor; m. Nancy Clare Cookson 1962; two s.; ed. Christchurch Boys High School, Auckland Univ. School of Architecture; a Principal of Structon Group Architects, Wellington 1965–68; own practice 1968–; winner Int. Design Competition for Housing, Manila, Philippines 1976; numerous awards include N.Z.I.A. Silver Medal 1970, Bronze Medal 1975, Gold Medal 1982; AA Award 1968, 1972; N.Z. Tourist and Publicity Design Award 1975; joint winner Design Competition for Low Cost Housing, Fiji 1978; AAA Monier Design Award 1983, N.Z.I.A. Branch Award 1984. *Leisure interests:* building, gardening. *Address:* P.O. Box 3364, Wellington (Office); 105 Amritsar Street, Khandallah, Wellington, New Zealand (Home). *Telephone:* 792-119 (Office); 793-832 (Home).

ATIQI, Abdel-Rahman Salim al-; Kuwaiti diplomatist and politician; b. 5 April 1928; ed. High School, Kuwait; Sec.-Gen. Police Dept., Kuwait 1949–59; Dir.-Gen. Health Dept. 1959–61; Del. to UN 1960–61, to WHO, Geneva 1961, to UN Gen. Assembly 1961; Amb. to U.S.A. 1962–63; Under-Sec. Ministry of Foreign Affairs 1963–67; Minister of Finance 1967–81, of Oil Affairs 1967–75; Chair. Kuwait Fund for Arab Econ. Devt., Public Inst. for Social Security 1977–80; Adviser to the Amir with rank of Minister Aug. 1981–; Gov. for Kuwait, Islamic Devt. Bank. *Address:* Kuwait Fund for Arab Economic Development, P.O. Box 2921, Kuwait City, Kuwait.

ATIYA, Aziz Suryal, M.A., PH.D., LITT.D., LL.D., D.HUM.LITT.; Egyptian historian and writer; b. 7 July 1898; ed. Univs. of Liverpool and London; Charles Beard Fellow and Univ. Fellow, Univ. of Liverpool 1930–32; History Tutor, School of Oriental Studies, Univ. of London 1933–34; Prof. of Medieval and Oriental History, Univ. of Bonn 1935–38; Prof. Medieval History, Cairo 1938–42, Alexandria 1942–54; consultant to Library of Congress, Washington, D.C. 1950–51; visiting lecturer U.S. univs., Univ. of Zürich and Swiss Inst. of Int. Affairs 1950–51; Pres. Inst. of Coptic

Studies, Cairo 1954–56; Medieval Acad. Visiting Prof. of Islamic Studies, Univ. of Michigan, Ann Arbor 1955–56; Luce Prof. of World Christianity, Union Theological Seminary, and Visiting Prof. of History, Columbia Univ., New York 1956–57; Visiting Prof. of Arabic and Islamic History, Princeton Univ. 1957–58; mem. Inst. for Advanced Study, Princeton 1958–59; Dir., Middle East Center, Utah Univ. 1959–67; Distinguished Prof. of History, Utah 1967–; corresp. mem. UNESCO Int. Comm. for the Scientific and Cultural History of Mankind; corresp. mem. Coptic Archaeological Soc.; mem. Medieval Acad. of America, Mediterranean Acad., Rome; Hon. D.H.L. *Publications:* The Crusade of Nicopolis 1934, The Crusade in the Later Middle Ages 1938, Egypt and Aragon—Embassies and Diplomatic Correspondence between 1300 and 1330 1938, Kitab Qawanin al-Dawawin by Saladin's Wazir ibn Mammati 1943, History of the Patriarchs of the Egyptian Church (2 vols.) 1948–59, Monastery of St. Catherine in Mt. Sinai 1949, The Mt. Sinai Arabic Microfilms 1954, Coptic Music 1960, Crusade, Commerce and Culture 1962, The Crusades—Historiography and Bibliography 1962, History of Eastern Christianity 1968, Kitab al-Ilman by al-Nuwairy (7 vols.) 1968–76, etc. (all books in either English or Arabic). *Address:* 1335 Perry Avenue, Salt Lake City, Utah 84103, U.S.A. *Telephone:* Salt Lake City 328-3339.

ATIYAH, Sir Michael Francis, Kt., PH.D., F.R.S.; British mathematician; b. 22 April 1929, London; s. of Edward Selim Atiyah and Jean (Levens) Atiyah; m. Lily Brown 1955; three s.; ed. Victoria Coll., Egypt, Manchester Grammar School and Trinity Coll. Cambridge; Research Fellow, Trinity Coll., Cambridge 1954–58, Hon. Fellow 1976–; Fellow, Pembroke Coll., Cambridge 1958–61 (Hon. Fellow 1983), Univ. Lecturer 1957–61; Reader, Oxford Univ., and Fellow, St. Catherine's Coll., Oxford 1961–63; Savilian Prof. of Geometry, Oxford Univ., and Fellow of New Coll., Oxford 1963–69; Prof. of Mathematics, Inst. for Advanced Study, Princeton, N.J. 1969–72; Royal Soc. Research Prof., Oxford Univ. 1973–; Fellow, St. Catherine's Coll. 1973–; Pres. London Mathematical Soc. 1974–76; Pres. Mathematical Asscn. 1981; mem. Science and Eng. Research Council 1984–, Council Royal Soc. 1984–85; Fields Medal, Int. Congress of Mathematicians, Moscow 1966; Royal Medal of Royal Soc. (U.K.) 1968; De Morgan Medal, London Mathematical Soc. 1980; Feltrinelli Prize, Accademia Nazionale dei Lincei 1981, King Faisal Int. Prize for Science 1987; Hon. D.Sc. (Bonn, Warwick, Durham, St. Andrews, Dublin, Chicago, Edinburgh, Cambridge, Essex, London, Sussex, Ghent); Foreign mem. American Acad. of Arts and Sciences, Swedish Acad. of Sciences, Leopoldina Acad. (G.D.R.), N.A.S., Acad. des Sciences (France), Royal Irish Acad. *Publications:* K-Theory 1966, Commutative Algebra 1969, Geometry and Dynamics of Magnetic Monopoles 1988. *Leisure interests:* gardening, music. *Address:* Mathematical Institute, 24–29 St. Giles, Oxford, OX1 3LB (Office); Shotover Mound, Headington, Oxford, England (Home). *Telephone:* Oxford 62359.

ATIYEH, Victor G.; American politician; b. 20 Feb. 1923, Portland, Ore.; s. of George and Linda Asley Atiyeh; m. Dolores Hewitt 1944; one s. one d.; ed. Washington High School, Portland and Univ. of Oregon, Eugene; State Rep., Oregon 1959–65, State Senator 1965–78; Gov. of Oregon 1979–87; Republican. *Leisure interests:* antique gun collector, fly fishing, golf. *Address:* Victor Atiyeh and Co., 519 S.W. Park, Suite 208, Portland, Ore. 97205, U.S.A. *Telephone:* (503) 222-2244.

ATKINS, Rt. Hon. Sir Humphrey Edward (see Colnbrook).

ATKINS, Orin Ellsworth, LL.B.; American oil executive; b. 6 June 1924, Pittsburgh, Pa.; s. of Orin E. Atkins and Dorothy Whittaker Atkins; m. Kathryn Agee Atkins 1950; two s.; ed. Marshall Coll., Huntington, W. Va., Univs. of Pennsylvania and Virginia; admitted to W. Va. Bar 1950, Ky. Bar 1952; with Ashland Oil Inc. (Ky.) 1950–, Exec. Asst. 1956–59, Admin. Vice-Pres. 1959–65, Dir. 1962–, Pres. and Chief Exec. Officer 1965–72, Chair. of Bd. and Chief Exec. Officer 1972–81; Hon. LL.D. (Marshall Univ.) 1970, (Transylvania Univ.) 1980. *Address:* c/o 1409 Winchester Avenue, Ashland, Ky. 41101, U.S.A. (Office).

ATKINSON, Anthony Barnes, M.A., F.B.A.; British professor of economics; b. 4 Sept. 1944, Caerleon; m. Judith Mary Mandeville 1965; two s. one d.; ed. Cranbrook School, Kent and Churchill Coll., Cambridge; Prof. of Econs., Univ. of Essex 1970–76; Head Dept. of Political Economy, Univ. Coll. London 1976–79; Prof. of Econs. L.S.E. 1980–; Ed. Journal of Public Economics 1972–; mem. Royal Comm. on Distribution of Income and Wealth 1978–79, Retail Prices Index Advisory Cttee. 1984–; Fellow, St. John's Coll., Cambridge 1967–70; Fellow, Econometric Soc. 1984, Pres. 1988; Vice-Pres. British Acad. 1988–90; Pres. of the European Econ. Asscn. 1989, Hon. mem. American Econ. Asscn. 1985; Hon. Dr. rer. Pol., D.SC.; UAP Prix Scientifique 1986. *Publications:* Poverty in Britain and the Reform of Social Security 1969, Unequal Shares 1972, The Economics of Inequality 1975, Distribution of Personal Wealth in Britain (with A. Harrison) 1978, Lectures on Public Economics (with J. E. Stiglitz) 1980, Social Justice and Public Policy 1983, Parents and Children (with A. Maynard and C. Trinder), Poverty and Social Security 1989. *Address:* 33 Hurst Green, Brightlingsea, Colchester, Essex, England.

ATKINSON, Conrad; British artist; b. 15 June 1940, Cleator Moor, Cumbria; m. Margaret Harrison 1967; two d.; ed. Whitehaven Grammar School, Carlisle and Liverpool Colls. of Art and Royal Acad. Schools, London; Granada Fellow in Fine Art 1967–68; Churchill Fellow in Fine Art 1972; Fellow in Fine Art, Northern Arts 1974–76; Lecturer, Slade School of Fine Art 1976–79; Visual Art Adviser to GLC 1982–86; Power Lecturer, Univ. of Sydney 1983; Artist-in-Residence, London Borough of Lewisham 1984–86, Edin. Univ. 1986–87; Adviser Labour Party 1985–86 (Visual Arts Policy); exhbns. include Strike at Brannans, ICA 1972, Work, Wages and Prices, ICA 1974, A Shade of Green on Orange Edge, Arts Council of N.I. Gallery, Belfast, Material, Ronald Feldman Fine Arts, New York, At the Heart of the Matter, ICA 1982, Ronald Feldman Fine Arts "Goldfish", New York 1985. *Leisure interest:* rock and roll music. *Address:* 172 Erlanger Road, London, S.E.14, England. *Telephone:* 01-639 0308.

ATKINSON, Sir Frederick John, K.C.B., M.A.; British economist; b. 7 Dec. 1919, London; s. of George E. Atkinson and Elizabeth S. Cooper; m. Margaret Grace Gibson 1947; two d.; ed. Jesus Coll., Oxford Univ.; Lecturer, Jesus and Trinity Colls., Oxford 1947–49; Econ. Adviser, Cabinet Office 1949–51, at Embassy, Washington 1951–54 and at Treasury 1955–69; Chief Econ. Adviser, Dept. of Trade and Industry 1970–73; Asst. Sec.-Gen. OECD 1973–75; Deputy Sec. Chief Econ. Adviser, Dept. of Energy 1975–77; Chief Econ. Adviser, Treasury 1977–79; Hon. Fellow, Jesus Coll., Oxford 1979–. *Publication:* (jt. author) Oil and the British Economy 1983. *Leisure interest:* reading. *Address:* 26 Lee Terrace, London, S.E.3; Tickner Cottage, Church Lane, Aldington, Kent, England. *Telephone:* 01-852 1040; Aldington 514.

ATKINSON, Harry Hindmarsh, PH.D.; British physicist; b. 5 Aug. 1929, Wellington, New Zealand; s. of late Harry Temple Hindmarsh and Constance Hindmarsh Shields; m. Anne Judith Barrett 1958; two s. one d.; ed. Canterbury Univ. Coll., N.Z., Corpus Christi Coll. and Cavendish Lab., Univ. of Cambridge; Asst. Lecturer of Physics, Canterbury Univ. Coll., N.Z. 1952–53; Research Asst., Cornell Univ., U.S.A. 1954–55; Sr. Research Fellow, A.E.R.E., Harwell 1958–61; Head, General Physics Group, Rutherford Lab. 1961–69; Staff Chief Scientific Adviser to U.K. Govt., Cabinet Office 1969–72; Head, Astronomy, Space and Radio Div., Science Research Council 1972–78, Under Sec. and Dir., Astronomy, Space and Nuclear Physics 1983–86; Under Sec. and Dir. of Science, Science and Eng. Research Council 1983–88, Under Sec. and Dir. (Special Responsibilities) 1988–; Chair. Anglo-Dutch Astronomy Cttee. 1981–, Steering Cttee., Inst. Laue Langevin (ILL), Grenoble 1984–88; Vice-Chair. Council, European Space Agency 1981–84, Chair. 1984–87; U.K. del. Intergovernmental Panel on High Energy Physics 1983–, Council of European Synchrotron Radiation Facility 1985–88; U.K. mem. Anglo-Australian Telescope Bd. 1979–88. *Address:* Science and Engineering Research Council, Polaris House, North Star Avenue, Swindon, Wilts., SN2 1ET, England. *Telephone:* (0793) 26222.

ATKINSON, John Dunstan, O.B.E., M.AGR.SC., D.SC.; British agricultural scientist (retd.); b. 3 March 1909, Wellington, N.Z.; m. Ethel Mary Thorp 1934; two s.; ed. Wanganui Collegiate School and Massey Agricultural Coll.; joined Dept. of Scientific and Industrial Research (DSIR) 1932, discovered boron deficiency of apples 1934, Dir. Fruit and Research Div. 1948, combined Fruit Research and Plant Diseases Div. 1969–74; 5 years war service to rank of maj.; mem. Council Auckland Inst. and Museum 1960–80. *Publications:* Diseases of Tree Fruits 1971, D.S.I.R.'s First Fifty Years 1976. *Leisure interests:* reading, fishing. *Address:* Apt. 323, Northbridge, Akoranga Drive, Northcote, Auckland 9, New Zealand. *Telephone:* 493805.

ATKINSON, Maj.-Gen. Sir Leonard Henry, K.B.E., B.SC., C.ENG.; British army officer, engineer and company director; b. 4 Dec. 1910, Hale, Cheshire; s. of Arnold Henry and Catherine Mary (Cook) Atkinson; m. Jean Eileen Atchley 1939; three d. one s.; ed. Wellington Coll., Berks., Univ. Coll., London; apprentice with Satchwell Controls, Gen. Electric Co. (GEC), Slough 1932–36; Commissioned Lieut., Royal Electrical and Mech. Engs. (REME); on active service, H.Q. Guards Armoured Div. in Europe, H.Q. Airborne Corps India, later Europe, Far East, Australia, New Zealand, U.S.A., Canada, Ministry of Defence; retd. as Dir. Electrical and Mech. Eng., Army, Ministry of Defence 1966; Col. Commdt. REME 1967–72; Dir. Harland Engineering 1966–69, WEIR 1969–72, United Gas Industries 1972–76, C. W. Walker 1973–75, Equity and General PLC 1978–; Chair. C. Gold Assocs. 1976–87; Chair. Technology Transfer Assocs. Ltd. 1980–88; Man. Dir. Harland Simon 1969–72; Chair. Council of Eng. Insts. 1974; Chair. Dept. of Industry Terotechnology 1970–75, Cen. Berks. Training Ltd. 1984–88; Vice-Chair. Southern Regional Council for Further Educ. 1978–85; Fellow Univ. Coll., London 1977; Fellow, Inst. of Mech. Engs., Inst. of Electrical Engs., Inst. of the Motor Industry, Inst. of Gas Engs., Inst. of Electronic and Radio Engs. (Pres. 1968–69); Hon. mem. Plant Engs.; Gov. Reading Coll. of Techn. 1968–85; Wakefield Gold Medal 1976. *Leisure interests:* livery company (Master, Worshipful Co. of Turners 1987); philately, photography. *Address:* Fair Oak, Ashford Hill, Nr. Newbury, Berks., RG15 8BJ, England. *Telephone:* (07356) 4845.

ATKINSON, Sir Robert, Kt., D.S.C., R.D., F.ENG., F.I.MECH., B.SC.ENG.; British business executive; b. 7 March 1916, Tynemouth, Northumberland; s. of Nicholas and Margaret Atkinson; m. 1st Joyce Forster 1941 (died 1973), one s. one d.; m. 2nd Margaret Hazel Walker 1977; ed. Christ Church School, Tynemouth Grammar School, Univ. of London; served World War II (D.S.C. and two bars; mentioned in despatches); Man. Dir. William Doxford 1957–61; Tube Investments 1961–67; Unicorn Industries 1967–72;

Chair. Aurora Holdings 1972–; Chair. and Chief Exec. British Shipbuilders 1980–; non-Exec. Dir. Stag Furniture Holdings 1973. *Publications:* The Design and Operating Experience of an Ore Carrier Built Abroad 1957, Some Crankshaft Failures: Investigations into Causes and Remedies 1960, The Manufacture of Crankshafts (North East Coast of Engineers and Shipbuilders Gold Medal) 1961, British Shipbuilders' Offshore Division 1962, Productivity Improvement in Ship Design and Construction 1983. *Leisure interest:* salmon fishing. *Address:* Southwood House, Itchen Abbas, Hants., SO21 1AT, England. *Telephone:* 096-278-610 (Home).

ATRASH, Muhammad al-, PH.D.; Syrian international official; b. 13 Nov. 1934, Tartous; s. of Hassan Sayed al-Atrash and Aziza Sayed al-Atrash; m. Felicia al-Atrash 1958; two s. one d.; ed. American Univ., Beirut, Lebanon, American Univ., Washington, D.C., U.S.A., London School of Econs.; joined Cen. Bank of Syria 1963, Research Dept. 1963, Head of Credit Dept. 1966–70; Alt. Exec. Dir. IMF 1970–73; Deputy Gov. Cen. Bank of Syria 1974; Exec. Dir. IBRD 1974–76, IMF 1976–78; del. to Second Cttee. of UN Gen. Assembly, to UNCTAD and other int. econ. confs. 1963–70; part-time Lecturer, Univ. of Damascus 1963–70; mem. Deputies of IMF Interim Cttee. of the Bd. of Govs. on Reform of Int. Monetary System 1972–74; Assoc. mem. IMF Interim Cttee. 1974–76, *ex officio* mem. 1976–78; Minister of Economy and Foreign Trade 1980–82. *Publications:* articles in Al-Abhath (Quarterly of the American Univ. of Beirut) 1963, 1964, 1966. *Leisure interests:* swimming, walking, reading books on history and literature. *Address:* c/o Ministry of Economy and Foreign Trade, Damascus, Syria.

ATTALI, Bernard; French business executive; b. 1 Nov. 1943, Algiers; s. of Simon Attali and Fernande Abecassis; m. Hélène Scebat 1974; ed. Lycée Gauthier, Algiers, Lycée Janson-de-Sailly, Paris, Faculté de Droit, Paris, Inst. d'Etudes Politiques, Paris and Ecole Nat. d'Admin.; auditor, Cour des Comptes 1968, adviser 1974; on secondment to Commissariat Général du Plan d'Equipement et de la Productivité 1972–74; Délégation à l'Aménagement du Térritoire et à l'Action Regionale (Datar) 1974–80, 1981–84; Finance Dir. Soc. Club Méditérranée 1980–81; Pres. Regional Cttee. of EEC 1982–; Pres. Groupe des Assurances Nationales (Gan) 1984–86; Pres. Banque pour l'Industrie Française 1984–86; Adviser on European Affairs, Commercial Union Assurance 1986–; Pres. Supervisory Council, Sociétés Epargne de France 1986–, Commercial Union lard 1986–; Ordre Nat. du Mérite. *Address:* Commercial Union lard, 104 avenue Richelieu, 75002 Paris (Office); 12 avenue Pierre 1er de Serbie, 75016 Paris, France (Home).

ATTALLAH, Naim Ibrahim; British publisher and financial adviser; b. 1 May 1931, Haifa, Palestine; s. of Ibrahim Attallah and Genevieve Attallah; m. Maria Nykolyn 1957; one s.; ed. Coll. des Frères, Haifa and Battersea Polytechnic, London; Propr. Quartet Books 1976–, Women's Press 1977–, Robin Clark 1980–, Pipeline Books 1978–, The Literary Review 1981–, Apollo (with Algy Cluff) 1984–, The Wire 1984–; Financial Dir. Asprey PLC 1979–; Chair. Namara Group of cos. 1973–, launched Parfums Namara 1985. *Films produced:* The Slipper and the Rose (with David Frost q.v.) 1975, Brimstone and Treacle (Exec. Producer) 1982, and several TV documentaries. *Theatre:* Happy End (Co-Presenter) 1975, The Beastly Beatitudes of Balthazar B. (Presenter and Producer) 1981, Trafford Tanzi (Co-Producer) 1982. *Publication:* Women 1987. *Leisure interests:* classical music, opera, theatre, cinema, photography and fine arts. *Address:* Namara House, 45-46 Poland Street, London, W1V 4AU. *Telephone:* 01-439 6750.

ATTAR, Mohamed Said al-; Yemeni economist; b. 26 Nov. 1927; m.; two c.; ed. Ecole Pratique des Hautes Etudes à la Sorbonne, Inst. d'Etude du Développement Econ. et Social (I.E.D.E.S.), Univ. de Paris; research I.E.D.E.S. 1960–62; Dir.-Gen. Yemen Bank for Reconstruction and Devt. 1962–65; Minister of Econ. March-Aug. 1965; Pres. Econ. Comm. Oct. 1965–Feb. 1966; Pres. Bd. Yemen Bank and Pres. of Econ. High Comm. March 1966–68; Perm. Rep. to UN 1968–71, 1973–74; Deputy Premier for Financial Affairs and Minister of Economy Aug.-Sept. 1971; Exec. Sec. UN Econ. Comm. for W. Asia 1974–85, Special Adviser to govt. on econ. plan 1981. *Publications:* L'industrie du gant en France 1961, L'épicerie à Paris 1961, Etude sur la croissance économique de l'Afrique Occidentale 1962, Le marché industriel et les projets de l'Arabie Saoudite 1962, Le sous-développement économique et social du Yémen (Perspectives de la révolution Yémenite) 1964, Arabic edition 1965.

ATTAS, Haydar Abu Bakr al-; Yemeni politician; fmr. Minister of Construction; Prime Minister of People's Democratic Repub. of Yemen 1985–86; President (following overthrow of govt. of Ali Nasser Mohammed q.v.) Feb. 1986–. *Address:* Office of the President, Aden, People's Democratic Republic of Yemen.

ATTASSI, Lt.-Gen. Louai; Syrian army officer and politician; b. 1926; ed. Syrian Military Acad., and Staff Officers' Coll., Homs.; took part in Palestinian war 1948; opposed Syrian break with Egypt 1961; Garrison Commdr., Aleppo April 1962; Mil. Attaché, Syrian Embassy, Washington 1962–63; C.-in-C. of Syrian Armed Forces and Pres. of Revolutionary Council March-July 1963. *Address:* Damascus, Syrian Arab Republic.

ATTENBOROUGH, Sir David Frederick, Kt., C.B.E., M.A., F.R.S.; British broadcaster and writer; b. 8 May 1926, London; s. of Frederick and Mary Attenborough; brother of Sir Richard Attenborough (q.v.); m. Jane Elizabeth Ebsworth Oriel 1950; one s. one d.; ed. Wyggeston Grammar School, Leicester, and Clare Coll., Cambridge; Royal Navy 1947–49; Ed. Asst. in publishing house 1949–52; with BBC Television 1952–73, Trainee Producer BBC TV 1952–54, Producer of zoological, archaeological, travel, political and other programmes 1954–64, Dir. of Programmes, TV 1969–73; mem. Man. Bd., BBC 1969–73; freelance broadcaster and writer 1973–; mem. Nature Conservancy Council 1975–82; Goodwill Amb. for UNICEF 1987–; Fellow, Soc. of Film and Television Arts 1980; Hon. Fellow, Clare Coll., Cambridge 1980, U.M.I.S.T. 1980; Int. Trustee, World Wild Life Fund 1981–; Trustee, British Museum 1980–, Science Museum 1984–87; Hon. D.Litt. (Leicester, London, Birmingham and City Univs.), Hon. D.Sc. (Liverpool, Ulster, Sussex, Bath, Durham, Keele and Heriot-Watt), Hon. LL.D. (Bristol and Glasgow) 1977, Hon. D.Univ. (Open Univ.) 1980, (Essex) 1987; Special Award, Guild of TV Producers 1961, Silver Medal, Royal TV Soc. 1966, Silver Medal, Zoological Soc. of London 1966, Desmond Davis Award, Soc. of Film and TV Arts 1970, Cherry Kearton Award, Royal Geographical Soc. 1972, UNESCO Kalinga Prize 1982, Medallist, Acad. of Natural Sciences, Philadelphia 1982, Encyclopedia Britannica Award 1987. *Publications:* Zoo Quest to Guiana 1956, Zoo Quest for a Dragon 1957, Zoo Quest in Paraguay 1959, Quest in Paradise 1960, Zoo Quest to Madagascar 1961, Quest under Capricorn 1963, The Tribal Eye 1976, Life on Earth 1979, The Zoo Quest Expeditions 1982; The Living Planet 1984, The First Eden, The Mediterranean World and Man 1987. *Leisure interests:* music, tribal art, natural history. *Address:* 5 Park Road, Richmond, Surrey, England.

ATTENBOROUGH, Philip John; British publisher; b. 3 June 1936; s. of John Attenborough and Barbara née Sandle; m. Rosemary Littler 1963; one s. one d.; ed. Rugby, Trinity Coll., Oxford; joined Hodder & Stoughton 1957, Dir. 1963, Sales Dir. 1969; Chair. Hodder & Stoughton Ltd. and Hodder & Stoughton Holdings Ltd. 1975–, Lancet Ltd. 1977–; mem. Council, Publishers' Assen. 1976–, Pres. 1983–85. *Leisure interests:* trout fishing, playing golf and tennis, watching cricket. *Address:* Coldhanger, Seal Chart, Sevenoaks, Kent, England. *Telephone:* Sevenoaks 61516.

ATTENBOROUGH, Sir Richard Samuel, Kt., C.B.E.; British actor, producer and director; b. 29 Aug. 1923; s. of Frederick and Mary Attenborough; brother of Sir David Attenborough (q.v.); m. Sheila Sim; one s. two d.; ed. Wyggeston Grammar School, Leics., and Royal Acad. of Dramatic Art, London; first stage appearance in Ah! Wilderness, Palmers Green 1941; West End debut in Awake and Sing 1942; first film appearance In Which We Serve 1942; R.A.F. 1943, seconded to R.A.F. Film Unit 1944–46; returned to stage 1949; formed Beaver Films with Bryan Forbes (q.v.), appearing in and co-producing The Angry Silence 1959; formed Allied Film Makers 1960; produced Whistle Down the Wind 1961, The L-Shaped Room 1962, Seance on a Wet Afternoon 1963; Chair. Royal Acad. of Dramatic Art (RADA); Pro-Chancellor, Sussex Univ. 1970–; Gov. Nat. Film School 1970–; Chair. Capital Radio 1973–; Deputy Chair. Channel Four TV Co. 1980–87, Chair. 1987–; Gov. and Chair. British Film Inst. Jan. 1982–; mem. Cinematograph Films Council 1967–73, Arts Council of Great Britain 1970–72; Trustee, Tate Gallery 1976–82; Chair. Goldcrest Films 1981–, of Goldcrest Films and TV 1985–; Chair. British Screen Advisory Council 1987–; work for UNICEF as Goodwill Amb. 1987–; Best Actor Award, San Sebastian 1964, British Film Acad. 1964; Hollywood Golden Globe Awards 1966, 1967, 1969, 1983; First of Cinematograph Exhibitors Assen. annual awards for Distinguished Service to British Cinema 1967; Hon. D.Litt. (Leicester), (Kent) 1981, (Sussex) 1987; Hon. D.C.L. (Newcastle); Martin Luther King Jr. Non Violent Peace Prize 1983, European Film Award 1988; Pres. Richmond and Twickenham SDP Area Party 1982–; Padma Bhushan (India) 1982. *Stage appearances include:* The Little Foxes 1942, Brighton Rock 1943, The Way Back 1949, To Dorothy a Son 1950–51, Sweet Madness 1952, The Mousetrap 1952–54, Double Image 1956–57, The Rape of the Belt 1957–58. *Film appearances include:* School for Secrets, The Man Within, Dancing with Crime, Brighton Rock, London Belongs to Me, The Guinea Pig, Morning Departure, Hell is Sold Out, The Magic Box, Gift Horse, Eight O'Clock Walk, The Ship that Died of Shame, Private's Progress, The Baby and the Battleship, Brothers in Law, Dunkirk, The Man Upstairs, Sea of Sand, Danger Within, I'm All Right Jack, Jet Storm, S.O.S. Pacific, The Angry Silence, The League of Gentlemen, Only Two Can Play, All Night Long, The Dock Brief, The Great Escape, Seance on a Wet Afternoon, The Third Secret, The Guns of Batasi, The Flight of the Phoenix, The Sand Pebbles, Dr. Dolittle, The Bliss of Mrs. Blossom, The Last Grenade, A Severed Head, David Copperfield, Loot, 10 Rillington Place, Ten Little Indians, Brannigan, Rosebud, Conduct Unbecoming, The Chess Players, The Human Factor; *Director:* Magic, Oh What a Lovely War!, Young Winston, A Bridge Too Far, Chorus Line, Gandhi, Cry Freedom. *Publications:* In Search of Gandhi 1982, Richard Attenborough's Cry Freedom 1987. *Leisure interests:* collecting 20th-century painting and Picasso ceramics, gramophone records, Chelsea Football Club. *Address:* Old Friars, Richmond Green, Surrey, England.

ATTERSEE; Austrian artist; b. (as Christian Ludwig) 28 Aug. 1942, Vienna; s. of Christian and Susanne Ludwig; unmarried; ed. Akademie für Angewandte Kunst, Vienna; has worked as an artist since 1963; more than 100 one-man exhbns. in Germany, France, Netherlands, Italy, Austria and Switzerland, including Venice Biennale. *Publications:* Attersee Werksquer 1962–82, Attersee, Biennale Venedig 1984. *Leisure interest:* sailing.

Address: Seilerstätte 5/14, 1010 Vienna, Austria. *Telephone:* (0222) 513-2177.

ATTEYA, Ahmad Mamdouh, B.A.; Egyptian politician; b. 1923; ed. studies in law and Islamic sharia (jurisprudence); held various posts in Office of Public Prosecutor and the judiciary; apptd. judge 1952, then counsellor in Court of Appeals; Head, Public Prosecutor's Office, Kuwait 1968; Pres. Supreme Constitutional Court 1968; mem. legis. cttee. which unified laws in Libya; Minister of Justice 1977, 1982-87. *Address:* Ministry of Justice, Justice Building, Cairo (Lazoughli) Egypt. *Telephone:* 31176.

ATTIGA, Ali Ahmad, PH.D.; Libyan economist; b. Oct. 1931, Misratah; one s. five d.; ed. Univs. of Wisconsin and Calif.; Asst. Econ. Adviser, Nat. Bank of Libya 1959-60, Head, Econ. Research Dept. and Chief Ed. Economic Bulletin 1960-64, 1966-68; mem. Joint Planning Cttee., Nat. Planning Council 1963-66; Under-Sec. Ministry of Planning and Devt. 1964-66; mem. Supreme Petroleum Council 1964-66; Chair. Energy Cttee., Nat. Planning Council 1965-66; Minister of Planning and Devt. 1968-69, of Econ. 1969; Gen. Man. Libya Insurance Co. 1970-73, Chair. 1973; Chair. and Founder, Nat. Investment Co. 1971-73; Chair. Libyan Hotels and Tourist Co. 1971-73; Dir. Arab Re-insurance Co., Beirut 1971-73; Sec.-Gen. Org. of Arab Petroleum Exporting Countries 1973-79; mem. Bd. of Dirs., Coll. of Advanced Technology 1964-66. *Publication:* The Impact of Oil on the Libyan Economy 1956-1969 1974. *Address:* c/o Ministry of Foreign Affairs, Tripoli, Libya.

ATWOOD, John Leland, A.B., B.S.; American engineer; b. 26 Oct. 1904; ed. Hardin Simmons Univ. and Univ. of Texas; Junior Engineer, Army Air Corps, Wright Field, Ohio 1928; Design Engineer, Douglas Aircraft Co. 1930-34; Vice-Pres. and Chief Engineer, North American Aviation Inc. (became North American Rockwell, now Rockwell Int. Corpn.) 1934, Pres. 1948-70, Chief Exec. Officer 1960, Chair. of the Bd. 1962, Senior Consultant and Dir. 1970-78; numerous awards and prizes, including Hon. Fellow, American Inst. of Aeronautics and Astronautics, Pres. 1954; Nat. Aeronautic Assen. Wright Brothers Memorial Trophy 1983-; mem. Soc. Automotive Engineers. *Address:* P.O.B. 1587, Vista, Calif. 92083,U.S.A.

ATWOOD, Margaret, C.C., A.M.; Canadian author; b. 18 November 1939, Ottawa; ed. Univ. of Toronto and Harvard Univ.; taught at Univ. of British Columbia 1964-65, Sir George Williams Univ. 1967-68, Univ. of Alberta 1969-70, York Univ. 1971; Writer-in-residence, Univ. of Toronto 1972-73; Guggenheim Fellowship 1981; several awards for poetry and fiction, including Commonwealth Literary Prize 1987; Hon. D.Litt. (Trent) 1973, (Concordia) 1980, (Trent Univ.), (Smith Coll.) 1982, (Univ. of Toronto) 1983, (Mount Holyoke) 1985, (Univ. of Waterloo) 1985, (Univ. of Guelph) 1985, Hon. LL.D. (Queen's Univ.) 1974. *Publications:* poetry: The Circle Game 1966, The Animals in that Country 1969, The Journals of Susanna Moodie 1970, Procedures for Underground 1970, Power Politics 1971, You Are Happy 1974, Selected Poems 1976, Two Headed Poems 1978, True Stories 1981, Snake Poems 1983, Interlunar 1984; fiction: The Edible Woman 1969, Surfacing 1972, Lady Oracle 1973, Dancing Girls 1977, Life Before Man 1979, Bodily Harm 1981, Encounters With the Element Man 1982, Murder in the Dark 1983, Bluebeard's Egg (short stories) 1983, Unearthing Suite 1983, The Handmaid's Tale 1986, Cat's Eye 1988; non-fiction: Survival: a Thematic Guide to Canadian Literature 1972, Second Words: Selected Critical Prose 1982, (ed.) The Oxford Book of Canadian Verse in English 1982, The Oxford Book of Canadian Short Stories in English (ed.) 1987, Interlunar 1988; children's books: Up in the Tree 1978, Anna's Pet 1980; reviews and critical articles. *Address:* McClelland and Stewart, 481 University Avenue, Suite 900, Toronto, Ont., M5G 2E9, Canada.

ATZMON, Moshe; Israeli conductor; b. 30 July 1931, Budapest, Hungary; m. 1954; two d.; ed. Tel-Aviv Acad. of Music, Guildhall School of Music, London; left Hungary for Israel 1944; played the horn professionally in various orchestras for several years; second prize Dimitri Mitropoulos Competition for Conductors, New York 1963; Leonard Bernstein Prize 1963; First Prize, Int. Conductors Competition, Liverpool, England 1964; has conducted in Israel, England, Australia, Germany, Sweden, Norway, Switzerland, Spain, Finland, Italy, Austria, Turkey and U.S.A.; Chief Conductor, Sydney Symphony Orchestra 1969-71; Chief Conductor, North German Symphony Orchestra 1972; Musical Dir. Basel Symphony Orchestra 1972. *Leisure interests:* reading, travelling. *Address:* 16 Canfield Gardens, London, N.W.6, England. *Telephone:* 01-624 6322.

AUBERGER, Bernard, ING. CIVIL, L. EN D., DIPL.; French banker; b. 5 Dec. 1937, Gennevilliers; s. of Paul Auberger and Jeanne (née Geny) Auberger; m. Christine Baraduc 1963; three s. one d.; ed. Ecole des Mines, Paris, Inst. d'Etudes Politiques, Paris, Ecole Nat. d'Admin., Paris; Investigating Officer French Ministry of Finance 1966-70; Adviser to Gen. Man. Crédit Nat., Paris 1970-72; Financial Attaché French Embassy, New York 1972-74; Dir. of Cabinet for Under Sec. for Finance 1974; attached to Industrial Relations Cttee. 1974-75; Dir. Production and Trade, French Ministry of Agric. 1975-80; Man. Société Générale 1981, Cen. Man. 1982-; mem. Econ. and Social Council 1982-; Gen. Man. Caisse Nat. de Crédit Agricole 1986-88; Chevalier Ordre Nat. du Mérite, Chevalier du Mérite Agricole, Chevalier, Légion d'honneur. *Address:* 13 rue du Bois-Joli, Meudon 92190, France (Home). *Telephone:* 45.34.08.78 (Home).

AUBERT, Maurice, D.JUR.; Swiss lawyer; b. 26 Dec. 1924, Geneva; m. Suzanne Boissier 1950; two s. three d.; ed. Univ. of Geneva and London School of Econs.; Man. legal dept. and partner, MM. Hentsch & Cie (bankers), Geneva 1956-63; mem. and Pres. Geneva Municipal Council 1957-68; mem. and Pres. Parl. of Canton of Geneva 1968-80; Pres. Univ. Inst. for Devt. Studies; mem. Int. Cttee. of Red Cross 1978, Vice-Pres. 1984-. *Publications:* books and articles on legal matters. *Leisure interests:* jogging, cross-country skiing. *Address:* International Committee of the Red Cross, 17 avenue de la Paix, CH 1211 Geneva, Switzerland. *Telephone:* (022) 34 60 01.

AUBERT, Pierre; Swiss politician and lawyer; b. 3 March 1927, La Chaux-de-Fonds; s. of the late Alfred and Henriette Erni Aubert; m. Anne-Lise Borel 1953; one s. one d.; ed. Univ. of Neuchatel; mem. of local Assembly, La Chaux-de-Fonds 1960-68, Pres. 1967-68; mem. Legislative Assembly of Canton of Neuchâtel 1961-75, Pres. 1969-70; Labour mem. Council of States (upper house of Fed. Assembly) 1971-77; mem. Fed. Council (Govt.) 1978-87, Vice-Pres. Jan.-Dec. 1982; Pres. of Switzerland Jan.-Dec. 1983, Jan.-Dec. 1987; Head of Fed. Foreign Affairs Dept. 1978-87. *Leisure interests:* camping, boxing, skiing, cycling, theatre, watches. *Address:* c/o Federal Department of Foreign Affairs, Palais Fédéral, 3003 Berne, Switzerland.

AUBOUIN, Jean Armand, D. ÈS SC.; French academic; b. 5 May 1928, Evreux; m. Françoise Delpouget 1953; two d.; ed. Lycées Buffon and St.-Louis, Ecole Normale Supérieure and Univ. of Paris; Asst. Univ. of Paris 1952-62, Prof. 1962-; mem. Acad. of Sciences Inst. of France 1981-, Vice-Pres. 1986-88, Pres. 1989-; Pres. Société Géologique de France 1976; Scientific Advisory Bds. of Bureau de Recherches Géologiques et Minières 1984, and Inst. Française de Recherche pour l'Exploitation de la Mer 1985; mem. Planning Cttee. Int. Programme of Ocean Drilling 1980; mem. Scientific Advisory Bds. of various geology-related programmes; Foreign mem. Academia dei Lincei, Italy 1974, Acad. of Sciences, U.S.S.R. 1976; Acad. of Athens, Greece 1980; Hon. Fellow Geological Soc. of London 1976, of America 1980; C.N.R.S. Medal 1959, Museo de la Plata Medal 1977, Ville de Paris Medal 1980; Prize Viquesnel (Soc. Géologique de France) 1962, Prize Charles Jacob (Acad. des Scienses) 1976, Chevalier Ordre des Palmes académiques, Chevalier Ordre Nat. du Mérite. *Publications:* Géologie de la Grèce septentrionale 1959, Geosynclines 1965, Manuel de Cartographie (Co.Ed.) 1970, Précis de Géologie (Co-Ed.) 1968, numerous papers on geological topics. *Leisure interests:* reading, mountain walking and swimming at sea. *Address:* Université P. et M. Curie, Département de Géotectonique, Tour 26-0, 1er Etage, 4 Place Jussieu, 75252 Paris Cédex 05, France (Office); 22 Rue des Chêneaux, 92330 Sceaux, France (Home). *Telephone:* 43 29 35 12 (Office); 47 02 63 71 (Home).

AUBRUN, Charles Vincent; French professor of Spanish; b. 4 April 1906, Clichy, Paris; s. of Charles F. and Suzanne (née Miraucourt) Aubrun; m. Hilda Grace Donnelly 1929; ed. Univ. of Paris; Prof., Univ. of Poitiers 1942-45, Univ. of Bordeaux 1945-51, Univ. of Paris 1951-72, Dir. Centre of Hispanic Studies 1953-72, Univ. of Nice 1972-78; Guest Prof. Univ. of Texas, Austin, Columbia Univ., U.C. Santa Barbara, Cornell, Stanford, Bloomington, San José de Costa Rica, U.C. Los Angeles; Officier Légion d'honneur, Commander Palmes académiques. *Publications:* Bolivar: choix de lettres, discours, proclamation 1934, Lope de Vega, Peribáñez 1943, Le chansonnier espagnol d'Herberay des Essarts, 15e siècle 1951, L'Amérique Centrale 1952-74, Histoire des lettres hispano-américaines 1954, Calderón, La estatua de Prometeo 1961, Calderón, Eco y Narciso 1961, Bolívar, Cuatro cartas y una memoria 1961, Lope de Vega, La Circe 1962, Histoire du théâtre espagnol 1965, 1968, La comédie espagnole (1600-1680) 1966, L'espagnol à l'Université (2 vols.) 1967, 1970, L'Espagne au siècle d'or 1971, La littérature espagnole 1977, 1982, French Homage 1977, Les vieux romances espagnols (1440-1550) 1986, International Festschrift (Berlin, New York) 1986 and articles on Calderón and European ballads in the 15th and 16th centuries. *Leisure interest:* writing my memoirs. *Address:* Mennetou-sur-Cher 41320, Loir-et-Cher, France (Home). *Telephone:* 54 98 12 46.

AUCHINCLOSS, Louis Stanton, LL.B., D.LITT.; American lawyer and author; b. 27 Sept. 1917; s. of Joseph Howland and Priscilla (née Stanton) Auchincloss; m. Adele Lawrence 1957; three s.; ed. Groton School, Yale Univ. and Univ. of Virginia; admitted to New York Bar 1941, Assoc. Sullivan and Cromwell 1941-51, Hawkins, Delafield and Wood, New York 1954-58, partner 1958-; Lieut. U.S. Navy 1941-45; Pres. Museum of the City of New York; mem. Nat. Inst. of Arts and Letters. *Publications:* The Indifferent Children 1947, The Injustice Collectors 1950, Sybil 1952, A Law for the Lion 1953, The Romantic Egoists 1954, The Great World and Timothy Colt 1956, Venus in Sparta 1958, Pursuit of the Prodigal 1959, House of Five Talents 1960, Reflections of a Jacobite 1961, Portrait in Brownstone 1962, Powers of Attorney 1963, The Rector of Justin 1964, Pioneers and Caretakers 1965, The Embezzler 1966, Tales of Manhattan 1967, A World of Profit 1969, Motiveless Malignity 1969, Edith Wharton: A Woman in Her Time 1971, I Come as a Thief 1972, Richelieu 1972, The Partners 1974, A Winter's Capital 1974, Reading Henry James 1975, The Winthrop Covenant 1976, The Dark Lady 1977, The Country Cousin 1978, Persons of Consequence 1979, Life, Law and Letters 1979, The House of the Prophet 1980, The Cat and the King 1981, Watchfires 1982, Exit Lady

Masham 1983, The Book Class 1984, Honorable Men 1985, Diary of a Yuppie 1986, Skinny Island 1987, The Golden Calves 1988. *Address:* 67 Wall Street, New York, N.Y. 10005 (Office); 1111 Park Avenue, New York, N.Y. 10028, U.S.A. (Home).

AUCOTT, George William, B.S.; American company executive; b. 24 Aug. 1934, Philadelphia; s. of George William and Clara Anna (Nagel) Aucott; m. Ruth Tonetta Heller 1956; one s. two d.; ed. Ursinus Coll., Collegeville, Pa. and Harvard Univ.; served U.S. army 1957–60; joined Firestone Tire & Rubber Co. 1956, Pres. Firestone Industrial Products Co. 1978, Firestone Canada Inc. 1978–80, Vice-Pres. Mfg. parent co., Akron, Ohio 1980; Pres. and C.O.O. Firestone Int. 1982–, mem. Bd. of Dirs. and Exec. Vice-Pres. of Corpn. 1986–; Bd. Dirs. Akron United Way, 1968–73; Pres. and Dir. Akron YMCA 1969–73; mem. Bd. of Dirs. Rubber Mfrs. Asscn., Rubber Asscn. *Address:* 1200 Firestone Parkway, Akron, Ohio 44317 (Office).

AUDERSKA, Halina; Polish writer; b. 3 July 1904, Odessa; d. of Roman and Helena Auderska; ed. Warsaw Univ.; literary and lexicographical activity 1924–; secondary school teacher 1926–39; underground teaching activity during German occupation, soldier in Home Army, editor Operation "N", military press corresp. in Warsaw Rising 1944; Head Publishing House Trzaska, Evert i Michalski 1946–50; Head Lexicographical Dept., co-ordinator, Deputy Ed.-in-Chief Dictionary of Polish Language (11 vols.), Polish Acad. of Sciences 1950–69; mem. Editorial Bd. Concise Dictionary of Polish Language 1969; mem. Editoral Cttee. Encyclopedia of Warsaw, Polish PEN Club; co-f., Sec. of Dialog (monthly) 1956–59; mem. Parl. 1980–; Pres. newly created Polish Writers' Asscn. 1983–86, Hon. Pres. 1986–; mem. Nat. Council of Culture; The City of Warsaw Prize 1971, Prime Minister Prize 1975, Minister of Culture and Art Prize 1977, Prime Nat. Prize 1984, Homo Varsoviensis 1986, Meritorious Order for Nat. Culture 1986, and many other awards and prizes; Commdr's., Officer's and Kt.'s Cross Order of Polonia Restituta, Order of Banner of Labour (1st and 2nd Class), Cross of Valour (twice), Cross of Warsaw Rising. *Publications: novels:* Poczwarki wielkiej parady 1935, Jabłko granatu 1971, Ptasi gościniec 1973, Babie lato 1974, Miecz Syreny 1980, Zwyczajnie człowiek 1980, Smok w herbie: królowa Bona 1983, Zabiè strach 1985; *plays:* Zbiegowie 1952, Rzeczpospolita zapłaci 1954, Spotkanie w ciemnościach 1961; *stories:* Szmaragdowe oczy 1977, Bratek 1977, Koń, 1985, and over 80 radio plays, vol. of radio plays Kwartet wokalny 1977. *Leisure interest:* gardening. *Address:* ul. Kopernika 11 m. 11, 00-359 Warsaw, Poland. *Telephone:* 26-35-14.

AUDRAIN, Paul André Marie; French business executive; b. 17 May 1945, Chambéry, Savoie; s. of Jean Audrain and Margueritte Gubian; m. Danièle Pons 1967; two s.; ed. Lycée d'Etat de Chambéry, Lycée du Parc Lyon, Ecole Supérieure des Sciences Economiques et Commerciales, Paris; Engineer, IBM France 1969–70; Financial and Admin. Dir. Aiglon, Angers 1970–74; Financial Dir. Christian Dior 1974–79, then Sec. Gen., Financial and Admin. Dir. 1979–84, Chair. and C.E.O. 1984–85, Pres. 1985–86; Int. Dir. Financière Agache 1986–87; Chair. and C.E.O. Christian Lacroix 1987–88, Pierre Balmain 1988–89. *Leisure interests:* collecting 19th century canes, skiing, tennis, sailing, golf, motor-cycling. *Address:* 1 rue Frederic Sauton, 75005 Paris (Home); 27 rue du Phare, Port Navalo, 56 640 Arzon (Home); c/o Pierre Balmain, 44 rue François-1er, 75008 Paris, France (Office).

AUDRAN, Stéphane (see Colette Dacheville).

AUDRY, Colette; French writer; b. 6 July 1906, Orange; d. of Charles and Inès (née Combe) Audry; m. Robert Minder (divorced); one. s.; ed. Ecole Normale Supérieure, Sèvres; Prof. of Literature, Lycée Molière, Paris 1945–65; Literary Critic Les Temps Modernes 1945–55; on staff Editions Denoël 1963–; mem. Exec. Cttee. Parti Socialiste 1971–; film-set designer and scriptwriter; Prix Medicis for Derrière la baignoire 1962, Officier des Arts et des Lettres. *Publications include:* On joue perdant, Aux yeux du souvenir, Léon Blum ou la politique du juste, Connaissance de Sartre, Sartre ou la réalité humaine 1966, Derrière la baignoire, L'autre planète 1972, Les militants et leurs morales 1976, La statue 1983, L'héritage 1984, Françoise l'ascendante 1986; screen-plays: Les malheurs de Sophie, La bataille du rail, Olivia, Absence, Liberté surveillée, Fruits amers, Le Socrate; play: Soledad. *Address:* Résidence du Val (3b), 91120 Palaiseau, France.

AUERBACH, Charlotte, D.SC., PH.D., F.R.S., F.R.S.E.; British geneticist; b. 14 May 1899, Crefeld, Germany; ed. Univs. of Würzburg, Freiburg, Berlin and Edinburgh; left Germany 1933; Asst., Inst. of Animal Genetics, Univ. of Edinburgh, Lecturer 1946, Reader 1957, Prof. 1967, Prof. Emer. 1969–; Visiting Prof. Oak Ridge Nat. Laboratory, U.S.A. 1958; mem. Japan Genetics Soc., Danish Acad. of Sciences; Foreign Assoc. N.A.S., U.S.A. 1970; Hon. D.Sc. Leiden (Netherlands) 1975, Cambridge 1977, Dublin 1977; Darwin Medal (Royal Soc.) 1976; research on the chemical induction of mutations. *Publications include:* Adventures with Rosalind (children's book) 1945; Genetics in the Atomic Age 1956, 1965, The Science of Genetics 1962, 1969, Mutation 1962, Heredity 1965, Mutation Research 1976. *Leisure interests:* literature, music, hiking, gardening. *Address:* Institute of Animal Genetics, The University, West Mains Road, Edinburgh, EH9 1SN; 31 Upper Gray Street, Edinburgh, EH9 1SN, Scotland.

AUERBACH, Frank; British artist; b. 29 April 1931, Berlin; s. of Max and Charlotte Auerbach; m. Julia Wolstenholme 1958; one s.; ed. St. Martin's School of Art, London, Royal Coll. of Art; one-man exhbns. at Beaux-Arts Gallery, London 1956, 1959, 1961, 1962, 1963, Marlborough Fine Art, London 1965, 1967, 1971, 1974, 1983, 1987, Marlborough Gallery Inc., New York 1969, Villiers Art Gallery, Sydney 1972, Univ. of Essex, Colchester 1973, Galleria Bergamini, Milan 1973, Marlborough, Zurich 1976, Retrospective Exhbn., Arts Council, Hayward Gallery, London, Fruit Market Gallery, Edinburgh 1978, Bernard Jacobson, New York 1979, Marlborough Gallery, New York 1982, Anne Berthoud, London 1983, Kunstverein, Hamburg 1986, Museum Folkwang, Essen, Centro de Arte Reina Sofia, Madrid 1987; group exhbns. at Tooths Gallery, London 1958, 1971, N.Y. Foundation, Rome 1958, Carnegie Int. Exhbn., Pittsburg 1958, 1961, Dunn Int. Exhbn., London 1963, Gulbenkian Exhbn., London 1964, Peter Stuyvesant Foundation Collection, London 1967, Vienna 1970, Palazzo dell' Accad. and Palazzo Reale, Genoa 1972; Los Angeles County Museum 1975, New Spirit in Painting, London 1981, Westkunst, Cologne 1981, Eight Figurative Painters, Yale Centre for British Art, Santa Barbara Museum 1981–82, Venice Biennale 1982, Mona, New York 1984, Tate Gallery, London 1984, Venice Biennale 1986 (Golden Lion Award), R.A., London 1987, MOMA, Oxford 1987, Kunstnernes Hus, Oslo 1987; works in public collections in U.K., Australia, Brazil, U.S.A., Mexico, Israel; Silver Medal for Painting, Royal Coll. of Art. *Address:* c/o Marlborough Fine Art, 6 Albemarle Street, London, W1X 3HF, England.

AUERBACH, Stanley Irving, M.S., PH.D.; American ecologist; b. 21 May 1921, Chicago, Ill.; s. of Abraham and Carrie Friedman Auerbach; m. Dawn Patricia Davey 1954; two s. two d.; ed. Univ. of Illinois and Northwestern Univ.; Second Lieut. U.S. Army 1942–44; instructor, then Asst. Prof., Roosevelt Univ., Chicago 1950–54; Assoc. scientist, then scientist, Health Physics Div., Oak Ridge Nat. Laboratory 1954–59, Senior Scientist, Section Leader 1959–70, Dir. Ecological Sciences Div. 1970–72, Environmental Sciences Div. 1972–86, Sr. Staff Adviser 1986–; Visiting Research Prof. Radiation Ecology, Univ. of Georgia, Athens, Ga. 1964–; Adjunct Prof., Dept. Ecology, Univ. of Tenn., Knoxville 1965–; mem. U.S. Cttee. Int. Biological Program; Dir. Eastern Deciduous Forest Biome Project 1968–76–; mem. Special Comm. on Biological Water Quality of Ohio River Valley Sanitation Comm. 1971–81, Bd. Environmental Consultants for Tenn.-Tombigbee Waterway, U.S. Army Corps of Engineers 1975–82, Energy Research and Devt. Admin. (ERDA) Ad Hoc Cttee. on Shallow Land Burial of Transuranic Waste 1976–80, Pres.'s Cttee. on Health and Ecological Effects on Increased Coal Utilization 1977–78, Research Advisory Cttee., Resources for the future 1978–; mem. Bd. of Trustees, Inst. of Ecology 1971–74, N.A.S.—NRC Bd. on Energy Studies, Bd. of Govs. American Inst. of Biological Sciences 1965–66, Ecological Soc. of America, Scientific Research Soc. of America (Pres. Oak Ridge Br. 1972–73), Cttee. on Energy and the Environment, N.A.S. Comms. on Physical Sciences, Nat. Resources (Chair. Environmental Studies Bd. 1983–), Exec. Cttee. Science Advisory Bd., U.S. Environmental Protection Agency 1986–(88); mem. British Ecological Soc., Nature Conservancy, Health Physics Soc., Soc. of Systematic Zoology; Radiation Research (A.A.A.S.); Leader, Interdisciplinary Review Group, Corps of Engineers, Tennessee-Tombigbee, Waterway project 1982–. *Publications:* miscellaneous publications in ecology and radioecology. *Address:* P.O. Box X, Bldg. 1505, Oak Ridge, Tenn. 37831-6035 (Office); 24 Wildwood Drive, Oak Ridge, Tenn. 37830, U.S.A. (Home).

AUGER, Arleen, B.A.; American soprano; b. 13 Sept 1939, Los Angeles; d. of Everett N. Auger and Doris (Moody) Auger; ed. California State Univ., Long Beach, and studied with Ralph Errolle, Chicago; music teacher, Los Angeles, Denver, Chicago 1963–67; début Vienna State Opera (Queen of the Night in Die Zauberflöte) 1967, mem. Opera 1967–74; freelance 1974–; début La Scala, Milan (in Ravel's L'enfant et les sortilèges) 1975, Metropolitan Opera, New York (in Beethoven's Fidelio) 1978; first American to sing at a British Royal Wedding-Prince Andrew and Sarah Ferguson 1986; has made opera, concert and recital appearances in major European and N. American centres; Prof. of Music for Voice Univ. of Frankfurt 1975–87; First Prize, I. Victor Fuchs Competition, L.A. 1967 and numerous prizes for recordings. *Leisure interests:* cooking, reading, theology, philosophy, swimming and the fine arts. *Address:* c/o IMG Artists, 22 E 71st Street, New York, N.Y. 10021, U.S.A. *Telephone:* 914-428-4342.

AUGER, Pierre Victor, D. ÈS S., F.R.S.A.; French physicist and university professor; b. 14 May 1899; s. of Victor and Eugénie Auger; m. Suzanne Motteau 1927; two d.; ed. Ecole Normale Supérieure, and Univ. of Paris; Asst., Faculty of Sciences, Univ. of Paris 1927, Dir. of Studies 1932, Prof. 1937–; Research Assoc. Univ. of Chicago 1941–44; Dir. of Higher Educ., Ministry of Educ., Paris 1945–48; Dir. Dept. of Natural Sciences UNESCO 1948–59; Chair. French Cttee for Space Research 1959–62; mem. Anglo-Canadian team on Atomic Energy, Canada 1942–44; French del. to UN Atomic Energy Comm. 1946–48; Dir.-Gen. European Space Research Org. 1962–67; mem. French Acad. of Sciences 1977; Grand Officier, Légion d'honneur, Commandeur des Palmes académiques; Int. Feltrinelli Prize 1961, Kalinga Prize 1972, Gaede Langmuir Award 1978. *Publications:* Les rayons cosmiques 1941, What are Cosmic Rays? 1944, L'homme microscopique 1952, Main Trends in Scientific Research 1961, De ça de là (poetry) 1983. *Leisure interests:* popularization of science through the media, sculpture, poetry. *Address:* 12 rue Emile Faguet, Paris 75014, France. *Telephone:* 540-96-34 (Home).

AUGSTEIN, Rudolf; German magazine publisher; b. 5 Nov. 1923, Hannover; s. of Friedrich Augstein and Gertrude (née Staaden); m.; four c.; ed. High School; Lieut., Second World War; Publr. Der Spiegel (weekly) 1947–; under arrest (for alleged political offence) Oct. 1962–Feb. 1963, elected Bundestag Nov. 1972, resigned Jan. 1973; mem. German PEN 1965–; FDP; Dr. h.c. (Bath) 1983, (Wuppertal) 1987. *Publications:* Spiegelungen 1964, Konrad Adenauer 1964, Preussens Friedrich und die Deutschen 1968, Jesus Menschensohn 1972, Liberlebensgross Herr Strauss 1980. *Address:* Spiegel-Verlag Rudolf Augstein GmbH & Co., Brandstwiete 19, 2000, Hamburg 11, Federal Republic of Germany. *Telephone:* 040-3-00-71.

AUGUSTE, Yves L.; Haitian diplomatist; practised Law, Port-au-Prince 1946–50, 1959–65; served as 1st Sec. Haitian Embassies, Madrid and Washington D.C. 1950–57; Adviser on Trade to the OAS 1957–58; Teacher of Literature and Languages, Zaire 1965–69, Headmaster Bukavu Secondary School 1967–68; Prof. of French and Int. Relations, Lincoln Univ., Pa. 1970–75; Prof. of Haitian Culture, New York Univ. 1975; Prof. Seton Hall Univ., N.J. 1984–85; Deputy Perm. Rep. to the UN 1986–April 1987, Perm. Rep. 1987–. *Publications include:* two books on Haiti and the United States from 1804–62 and 1862–1900. *Address:* Permanent Mission of Haiti, 801 Second Ave, Room 300, New York, N.Y., U.S.A. *Telephone:* (212) 370-4840.

AUJALEU, Eugène Jean Yves; French physician; b. 29 Oct. 1903, Negrepelisse, Tarn et Garonne; s. of Eugène Henri Aujaleu (Dr. Med.) and Clare Pailler; m. Blanche Dumas 1937; two d. (one deceased); ed. Toulouse Faculty of Medicine; taught at mil. school of medicine 1936; Inspector-Gen. of Health 1941; Dir. Health Service, Free French Govt. Algiers 1942–44; Dir. of Social Hygiene, Ministry of Health 1945; Dir.-Gen. of Public Health 1956–64; Dir.-Gen. Nat. Inst. of Health and Medical Research 1964–69, Hon. Dir.-Gen.; Councillor of State 1966–70; Chair. WHO Exec. Bd. 1959–60; Pres. 21st World Health Assembly 1968, Int. Centre for Cancer Research, Lyons 1965–71, Mental Health Assen. 1967–, Conseil supérieur d'hygiène publique 1976–80; Conseil d'administration du Centre Int. de l'Enfance 1978–83. *Leisure interests:* music, gardening. *Address:* 144 boulevard du Montparnasse, Paris 75014, France. *Telephone:* 4 322 5930.

AUKIN, David, B.A.; British theatrical producer and solicitor; b. 12 Feb. 1942, Harrow; s. of Charles Aukin and Regina Aukin; m. Nancy Meckler 1969; two s.; ed. St. Paul's School, London and St. Edmund Hall, Oxford; founder of Foco Novo and Jt. Stock Theatre cos. and admin. producer for various fringe theatre groups 1970–75; Admin. Dir. Hampstead Theatre 1975–79, Dir. 1979–84; Dir. Leicester Haymarket Theatre 1984–86; now Exec. Dir. Royal Nat. Theatre of Great Britain; Pres. Soc. of West End Theatres 1988–. *Address:* National Theatre, South Bank, London, SE1 9PX, England. *Telephone:* 01-928 2033.

AULBEKOV, Erkin Nurzhanovich; Soviet politician; b. 1930; ed. Timiryazev Agric. Acad., Moscow; senior agronomist, mem. CPSU 1952; dir. of a state collective farm in N. Kazakhstan 1953–61; First Deputy Pres., Second Sec., Pres. of N. Kazakhstan District Exec. Cttee. 1961–65; First Deputy Min. of Agric. for Kazakhstan SSR 1965–67; Min. for Cereal Production and Fodder Industry of Kazakhstan SSR 1967–68; First Sec. of various district cttees. of Kazakhstan CP 1968–; mem. of Cen. Cttee. of CPSU 1976–; Deputy to U.S.S.R. Supreme Soviet; mem. of Cen. Cttee. of CPSU 1986. *Address:* The Kremlin, Moscow, U.S.S.R.

AUMALE, Christian d', L. EN D.; French diplomatist; b. 23 May 1918, Lausanne, Switzerland; s. of Jacques and Elisabeth (née Le Bon de la Pointe) Aumale; m. Claude Darasse 1940; one s. one d.; ed. Lycée Condorcet, Faculté de Droit, Paris, London School of Econs. and Consular Acad., Vienna; Ministry of Foreign Affairs 1943–45, 1948–53, 1956–62; Second Sec., Copenhagen 1945–48; Counsellor, Tokyo 1953–56; Counsellor, then Minister, Bonn 1964; Asst. Dir. Econ. and Financial Affairs, Ministry of Foreign Affairs 1968; Amb. and Head of French Del. to OECD 1978–82; Ambassadeur de France 1982; Pres. of Electricity and Water, Madagascar 1982–; Officier, Légion d'honneur, Croix de guerre, Commdr. Ordre national du Mérite, Officier du Mérite agricole. *Address:* 52 rue de Lisbonne, 75008 Paris (Office); 6 rue Yvon Villarceau, 75016 Paris, France (Home).

AUMONS, Jean-Pierre (see Salomons, Jean-Pierre).

AUNE, Leif Jørgen; Norwegian politician; b. 7 June 1925, Bodø. Consultant, Industrial Devt. Assen. for N. Norway 1951; Sec. Office for Regional Planning, Nordland 1951; Consultant, Devt. Fund for N. Norway 1954; Deputy Dir.-Gen. Regional Devt. Fund 1961; Exec. Dir. of Finance, Tromso 1970–73; Under-Sec. of State, Ministry of Local Govt. and Labour 1971–72; Minister of Local Govt. and Labour 1973–78; Man. Dir. Regional Devt. Fund 1978–; Dir. Krisiania Banhz Kreditkasse; Chair. Norwegian Refge Secretariate; Norwegian Tax Comm.; Labour. *Address:* c/o Regional Development Fund, Oslo-Dep, Oslo 1, Norway.

AURA, Matti Ilmari, LL.M.; Finnish business executive; b. 18 June 1943, Helsinki; s. of Teuvo Ensio Aura and Kielo Kaina Kivekäs; m. Marja H. Hiippala 1967; two s.; ed. Munkkiniemi High School and Univ. of Helsinki; lawyer, Finnish Export Credit Ltd. 1968–69, Confed. of Finnish Industries

1970–71; Man. Dir. Cen. Bd. of Finnish Wholesale and Retail Assen. 1972–85; Man. Dir. Cen. Chamber of Commerce of Finland 1986–. *Address:* P.O. Box 1000, 00101 Helsinki (Office); Louhentie 1 H 25, 02130 Espoo, Finland (Home). *Telephone:* (358) 650133 (Office); (358) 465610 (Home).

AURA, Teuvo Ensio, LL.M.; Finnish politician; b. 28 Dec. 1912, Ruskeala; s. of Jalo Aura and Aino Sofia Kolehmainen; m. 1st Kaino Kielo Kivekäs 1939 (died 1970), two s. one d. (deceased); m. 2nd Sirkka Annikki Wiik 1976; ed. Univ. of Helsinki; worked for Bd. of Supply 1940–41, Chair. 1942; Dir. Post Office Savings Bank 1942–43, Dir.-Gen. 1943–68; Chair. Econ. Council 1946–47, 1951–56; mem. Joint Del. of Credit Inst. 1949–68; Minister of Commerce and Industry 1950–51, 1953–54, 1957; Minister of Justice 1951; Chair. numerous bds. and cttees. include: Admin. Bd. of Industrialization Fund 1954–60; mem. Finance Bd. 1953; mem. Bd., Mutual Life Insurance Co., Salama 1950–71, Insurance Co. Pohjola 1955–81, Helsinki Chamber of Commerce 1958–81; mem. of Admin. Bd., Rauma, Repola and Kemira Oy 1961–72; Chair. Admin. Bd., Aluma Oy, IBM in Finland, Finnish Fair Corpn., L. M. Ericsson in Finland Oy, Teräsbetoni Oy, Helsingin Seudun Lämpövoima Oy and Mankala Oy; mem. Bourse of Helsinki, Union of the Finnish Lawyer; Lord Mayor of Helsinki 1968–79; Prime Minister May–July 1970, Oct. 1971–72; Commdr., First Class, Order of the White Rose, Order of the Cross of Liberty, Commdr. Order of the Lion of Finland and many other honours. *Publications:* Talous ja yhteiskunta (Economy and Society); several articles on political economy and communal politics in various publications. *Leisure interests:* literature and art. *Address:* Rauhankatu 2 a D 86, 00170 Helsinki 17, Finland. *Telephone:* 635-563.

AUROUX, Jean; French politician; b. 19 Sept. 1942, Thizy, Rhône; s. of Louis and Jeanne (née Masson) Auroux; m. Lucienne Sabadie 1967; one s. one d.; ed. Lycée Jean Puy, Roanne, Faculté de Lyon; City Councillor, Roanne 1976–, Mayor 1977–; mem., then Vice-Pres. Departmental Assembly of Rhône-Alpes 1977–81; Parti Socialiste Nat. Del. for Housing 1978; mem. Nat. Assembly 1978–81, 1986–, mem. Finance Cttee.; Minister of Labour 1981–82, Minister Del. attached to Social Affairs Ministry, in charge of Labour Affairs 1982–83, Sec. of State at Ministry of Industry and Research in charge of Energy 1983–84, at Ministry of Urban Planning, Housing and Transport 1984–85, Minister 1985–86. *Publication:* Géographie économique à usage scolaire. *Address:* Assemblée Nationale, 75355 Paris (Office); Mairie, 42300 Roanne (Office); 83 rue Claude Bochard, 42300 Roanne, France (Home).

AUSTAD, Tore; Norwegian teacher and politician; b. 8 April 1935, Strømmen; ed. Univ. of Oslo and Naval Defence Coll.; Lieut., Norwegian Navy 1955–58; secondary school teacher 1961–; Prof. of Norwegian Language and Literature; Univ. of Chicago 1964–66; mem. Storting (Parl.) 1977–; Minister for Church and Educ. Oct. 1981–83. *Address:* The Royal Ministry of Church and Education, Akersgaten 42, Pb 8119 Dep, Oslo, Norway. *Telephone:* (02) 11 90 90.

AUSTEN, K(arl) Frank, M.D.; American professor of medicine; b. 14 March 1928, Akron, Ohio; s. of Karl and Bertle J. Arnstein; m. Jocelyn Chapman 1959; two s. two d.; ed. Amherst Coll. and Harvard Medical School; Intern in Medicine, Mass. Gen. Hosp. 1954–55, Asst. Resident 1955–56, Sr. Resident 1958–59, Chief Resident 1961–62, Asst. in Medicine 1962–63, Asst. Physician 1963–66; Physician-in-Chief, Robert B. Brigham Hosp. Boston 1966–80; Physician, Peter Bent Brigham Hosp. Boston 1966–; Chief Rheumatology Div. Beth Israel Hosp., Boston 1980–; Asst. in Medicine, Harvard Medical School 1961, Instr. 1962, Assoc. 1962–64, Asst. Prof. 1965–66, Assoc. Prof. 1966–68, Prof. 1969–72, Theodore Bevier Bayles Prof. of Medicine 1972–; Chief Rheumatology Div., Beth Israel Hosp.; numerous Cttee. assignments, guest lectureships, etc.; mem. numerous professional orgs. and recipient of numerous prizes and awards. *Publications:* numerous publications on immunology, etc. *Leisure interests:* coaching youth soccer, jogging, gardening. *Address:* Brigham and Women's Hospital Tower, 16B, 75 Francis Street, Boston, Mass 02115, U.S.A.; The Seeley G. Mudd Building, Room 604, 250 Longwood Avenue, Boston, Mass. 02115, U.S.A. *Telephone:* 617-732-1995.

AUSTIN, Colin François Lloyd, D.PHIL., F.B.A.; British classical scholar; b. 26 July 1941, Melbourne, Australia; s. of Lloyd James Austin; m. Mishtu Mazumdar 1967; one s. one d.; ed. Lycée Lakanal, Paris, Manchester Grammar School, Jesus Coll. Cambridge (Scholar), Christ Church Oxford (Sr. Scholar) and Freie Universität, West Berlin; Research Fellow, Trinity Hall, Cambridge Univ. 1965–69, Dir. of Studies in Classics 1965–; Asst. Lecturer in Classics, Cambridge Univ. 1969–72, Lecturer 1973–88, Reader in Greek Language and Literature 1988–; Hallam Prize 1961, Browne Medal 1961, Porson Prize 1962. *Publications:* Nova Fragmenta Euripidea 1968, Menandri Aspis et Samia 1969–70, Comicorum Graecorum Fragmenta in papyris reperta 1973, Poetae Comici Graeci (with R. Kassel): vol. III 2 Aristophanes, Testimonia et Fragmenta 1984, vol. IV Aristophon–Crobylus 1983, vol. V Damoxenus–Magnes 1986, vol. VII Menecrates-Xenophon 1989. *Leisure interests:* cycling, philately, wine tasting. *Address:* Trinity Hall, Cambridge, CB2 1TJ (Office); 7 Park Terrace, Cambridge, CB1 1JH, England (Home). *Telephone:* Cambridge 332520 (Office); Cambridge 62732 (Home).

AUSTREGÉSILO DE ATHAYDE, Belarmino Maria; Brazilian journalist; b. 25 Sept. 1898, Caruarú, Pernambuco; s. of José Feliciano Augusto de Athayde and Constância Adelaide Austregésilo de Athayde; m. Maria José de Queiroz; two s. one d.; ed. Seminário de Prainha, Fortaleza, Liceu do Ceará and Univ. do Rio de Janeiro; teacher 1917–18; Dir. Sec. A Tribuna 1918–21; on staff of Correio da Manhã 1921; Dir. O Jornal (with Diários Associados) 1924–32; exiled for political reasons 1932; Dir. Diàrio da Noite; Ed.-in-Chief O Jornal; mem. Brazilian Del. UN Gen. Assembly, Paris 1948; mem. Brazilian Acad. of Letters 1931–, Pres. 1959–80, 1986–; Ordem do Mérito Naval Aeronáutico 1957, Militar 1963, Jornalístico 1965; numerous foreign decorations. *Publications:* Histórias Amargas 1921, Quando as Hortencias Florescem 1921, A Influência Espiritual Americana 1938, Fora da Imprensa 1948, Mestre de Liberismo 1952, Na Academia 1953, Discurso de recepção a José Lins do Rego 1956, Vanaverba 1966, Epistola aos Contemporâneos 1967, Conversas na Barbearia Sol 1971. *Address:* c/o Academia Brasileira de Letras, Avenida Presidente Wilson 203, Rio de Janeiro, RJ (Office); Rua Cosme Velho 599, Rio de Janeiro, RJ, Brazil (Home). *Telephone:* 225-4368 (Home).

AUSTRIAN, Robert, M.D.; American physician and professor of medicine; b. 12 April 1916, Baltimore, Md.; ed. Johns Hopkins Univ.; numerous hosp. appts. at Johns Hopkins and other hosps. 1941–86; Consultant in Medicine, Veterans Admin. Hosp., Pa. 1968–; Visiting Physician, Hosp. of the Univ. of Pa. 1962–; teaching appts. at Johns Hopkins Univ. School of Medicine, New York Univ. Coll. of Medicine, State Univ. of New York Coll. of Medicine 1942–86; John Herr Musser Prof. of Medicine 1962– (Chair. of Dept. of Research Medicine, Univ. of Pa. School of Medicine 1962–86), Prof. Emer. 1986–, Prof. of Medicine 1962–; Visiting Scientist, Dept. of Microbial Genetics, Pasteur Inst., Paris, France 1960–61; Dir. WHO Collaborating Centre for Reference and Research on Pneumococci, Univ. of Pa. School of Medicine 1978–; mem. WHO Expert Advisory Panel on Acute Bacterial Disease 1979–; mem. Editorial Bd. Antimicrobial Agents and Chemotherapy, Review of Infectious Diseases, Vaccine; mem. Scientific Advisory Cttee., The Wistar Inst., mem. American Philosophical Soc. 1987–; Fellow A.A.A.S., American Acad. of Microbiology; Master, American Coll. of Physicians; mem. N.A.S. and numerous socs.; Hon. D.Sc. (Pennsylvania) 1987; numerous awards. *Publications:* Life with the Pneumococcus: Notes from the Bedside, Laboratory and Library 1985; 165 scientific articles in medical journals. *Address:* Department of Research Medicine, University of Pennsylvania Medical Center, The School of Medicine, 36th Street and Hamilton Walk G3, Philadelphia, Pa. 19104, U.S.A. *Telephone:* (215) 662-3186.

AUTANT-LARA, Claude; French film director and author; b. 5 Aug. 1901, Luzarches; s. of Edouard and Louise (née Larapidie de L'Isle) Autant-Lara; m. Ghislaine Auboin (deceased); ed. Lycée Janson de Sailly, Mill Hill School, London, Ecole des Arts Décoratifs, and Ecole des Beaux-Arts; entered French film industry 1919; directed first short picture Faits-Divers 1923; Pres. Syndicat des Techniciens du Cinéma Français 1948–55, then Hon. Pres.; Pres. Fédération Nationale du Spectacle 1957–63, then Hon. Pres.; mem. Acad. des Beaux-Arts; Grand Prix de la Critique internationale 1947, and many other prizes; Chevalier de la Légion d'honneur; Officier ordre nat. du Mérite; Commandeur des Arts et des Lettres. *Principal films:* Le mariage de chiffon, Sylvie et le fantôme, Occupe-toi d'Amélie, Le diable au corps, Douce, The Red Inn, Game of Love, Le rouge et le noir, Seven Sins, Marguerite de la nuit, la traversée de Paris, En cas de malheur, La jument verte, Le bois des amants, Tu ne tueras poi꞉.., Vive Henri-IV, Vive l'amour, Le Comte de Monte-Cristo, Le meurtrier, Le magot de Joséfa, Le journal d'une femme en blanc, Le nouveau journal d'une femme en blanc, Le plus vieux métier du monde 1967, Le franciscain de Bourges 1968, Les patates, Lucien Leuwen (TV serial) 1973, Gloria. *Publications:* Télémafia, La rage dans la coeur, Hollywood Cake Walk. *Address:* 66 rue Lepic, 75018 Paris, France; La Poterie, 7 Calade St.-Roch, 06410 Biot, France.

AUTIN, Jean Georges, D. EN. D., L. ES. L.; French public servant; b. 31 Dec. 1921, Paris; s. of Emmanuel Autin and Marie-Thérèse Lubin; m. Hélène Maud Aulagnon 1946; two d.; ed. Lycée Louis-le-Grand, Paris, Ecole Libre des Sciences Politiques, Ecole nationale des langues orientales vivantes; Admin. overseas finance 1944–55, Inspector 1955–68; Prof. des Sciences Financières, Inst. Int. d'Admin. Publique 1956–78; Financial and Admin. Dir., Ministry of Aid and Cooperation 1959–60; Dir. Gen. Admin. Ministry of Culture 1960–66, Dir. Antiquities and Excavations 1963–66; Insp.-Gen. Finances 1968–; Prof. at Univs. Panthéon-Sorbonne and Paris-Dauphine 1981–; mem. Bd. of Dirs. ORTF, Pres. Financial Cttee. 1972–74; Pres., Dir.-Gen. Sofratev 1973–75; Pres. Télé-Diffusion de France 1975–81, Inst. Régional d'Admin., Lyon 1971–85, Union Européenne de Radiodiffusion 1978–83, Ecole normale de musique 1981–, Organismes financiers de radio-télévision 1983–; mem. Higher Authority of Audio-Visual Communications 1982–; Acad. d'architecture 1983; du conseil de l'institut d'étude de la Défense nat. 1986–, Comm. nat. de la communication et des libertés 1986; prix de l'institut de France 1984; Commandeur, Légion d'honneur, Ordre nat. du Mérite, des Arts et Lettres, Officier des Palmes Académiques, du Mérite agricole. *Publications:* Initiation aux finances publiques 1971, Vingt ans de politique financière 1972, La France des bâtisseurs—vingt siècles d'architecture 1978, Louis XIV architecte 1981, Prosper Mérimée 1983, Rencontres du Palais Royal sur Mérimée 1983, Les Frères Pereïre, Sept défis audiovisuels 1984, Savorgnan de Brazza 1985, Jules Romains 1985. *Leisure interests:* music, archaeology, architecture, painting. *Address:* 21

rue Barbès, Montrouge 92120, Paris (Office); 19 avenue du Président Wilson, 75116 Paris, France (Home). *Telephone:* 657-11-15 (Office); 227-86-17 (Home).

AUTRUM, Hansjochem, DR.PHIL.; German academic; b. 6 Feb. 1907, Bromberg; s. of the late Otto Autrum and Olga Goerges; m. Ilse Bredow 1935 (deceased); one d.; ed. Univ. of Berlin; Asst. in Zoology, Univ. of Berlin 1935; Asst. and Asst. Prof. Inst. of Zoology, Göttingen 1945; Prof. and Head of Dept. Univ. of Würzburg 1952, Univ. of Munich 1958–75, now Prof. Emer.; Vice-Pres. Bavarian Acad. of Sciences 1977–85; Dr. rer.nat. h.c.; Dr.phil. h.c.; Feldberg Prize; Carus Medal (Akad. Leopoldina). *Publications:* several books, book chapters and 200 scientific papers. *Leisure interests:* music, African art. *Address:* Maximilianstrasse 46, 8000 Munich 22, Federal Republic of Germany. *Telephone:* (089) 29 98 12.

AVEDON, Richard; American photographer; b. 15 May 1923, New York; s. of Jack Avedon and Anna Polonsky; m. 1st Dorcas Nowell 1944, 2nd Evelyn Franklin 1951; one s.; ed. Columbia; staff photographer Harper's Bazaar 1945–65, mem. editorial staff Theatre Arts Magazine 1952, Vogue magazine 1966–; one man exhbns. Smithsonian Inst. 62, Minneapolis Inst. of Arts 70, Museum of Modern Art 74, Marlborough Gallery, New York 75, Metropolitan Museum of Art, New York 1978, Univ. Art Museum, Berkeley, Calif. 1980, Amon Carter Museum, Fort Worth, Texas 1985, and American tour; his work is represented in collections of many major museums and in private collections; Fellow Timothy Dwight Coll. Yale Univ. 1975–; Pres.'s Fellow Rhode Island School of Design 1978; Highest Achievement Medal Awards, Art Dirs. Show 1950; Popular Photography World's 10 Greatest Photographers 1958; Nat. Magazine Award for Visual Excellence 1976; Citation of Dedication to Fashion Photography, Pratt Inst. 1976; Chancellor's Citation, Univ. of Calif., Berkeley 1980; Art Dirs. Club Hall of Fame 1982, American Soc. of Magazine Photographers Photographer of the Year 1985, Best Photographic Book of the Year Award, Maine Photographic Workshop 1985, Dir. of the Year, Adweek magazine 1985. *Publications:* Observations 1959, Nothing Personal 1964, Ed. Diary of a Century (photographs by Jacques Henri Lartigue, q.v.) 1970, Alice in Wonderland 1973, Portraits 1976, Rolling Stone Magazine, "The Family" 1976, Avedon: Photographs 1947–77 1978, In the American West 1985. *Address:* 407 East 75th Street, New York, N.Y. 10021, U.S.A. *Telephone:* (212) 879-6325.

AVELINE, Claude; French writer and painter; b. 19 July 1901, Paris; only s. of Georges Avtsine and Cecile Tchernomordik; m. Jeanne Barusseaud 1964; one adopted s.; Hon. Pres. Soc. Anatole France; Pres. of Jury for Prix Jean-Vigo (Cinema) 1950–75; exhbns. of fibre-tip colour paintings in Paris 1972, 1974, 1978, 1980, 1984, Ljubljana 1973, Brussels 1975, Zagreb 1976, Belgrade 1976; Officier de la Légion d'honneur; Médaille de la Résistance (with rosette), Commdr. des Arts et des Lettres, etc.; Grand Prix Société des Gens de Lettres 1952; Prix Italia 1956; Prix de la Radio de la Société des Auteurs Dramatiques 1976; Grand Prix Poncetton 1978; Prix Int. de la Société Européenne de Culture 1986. *Publications:* Novels: Le Point du Jour 1928, La vie de Philippe Denis (Madame Maillart 1930, Les amours et les haines 1952, Philippe 1955), Le prisonnier 1936, Le temps mort 1944, Suite policière (La double mort de Frédéric Belot 1932, Voiture 7 place 15 1937, L'Abonné de la ligne U 1947, Le jet d'eau 1947, L'oeil-de-chat 1970), Pour l'amour de la nuit 1959, Le poids du feu 1959, Le bestiaire inattendu 1959, C'est vrai mais il ne faut pas le croire 1960, Hoffmann Canada 1977, Par le silence et par la voix 1987; Essays and Travel Books: La merveilleuse légende du Bouddha 1928, Routes de la Catalogne ou Le livre de l'amitié 1932, La promenade égyptienne 1934, Les devoirs de l'esprit 1945, Et tout le reste n'est rien (La Religieuse portugaise) 1951, Les mots de la fin 1957, Le code des jeux 1961, Avec toi-même et caetera 1963, Les réflexions de Monsieur F.A.T. 1963, Célébration du lit 1967; Le haut mal des créateurs 1973; De fil en aiguille aux apprêts de l'Après 1987, Anatole France le vivant 1987, Plus vrais que soi (Le romancier et ses personnages) 1988, Moi par un autre (Chronique d'une enfance et d'une adolescence dans les XX premières années du siècle) 1988; Children's Books: Baba Diène et Morceau-de-Sucre 1937, De quoi encore? 1946, L'Arbre Tic-Tac 1950; Play: L'as de coeur (ballet, music by Henri Sauguet) 1961, Brouart et le désordre 1964, La parade de la rengaine 1967; Poetry: Io Hymen suivi de Chants funèbres 1925 (new version 1980), Portrait de l'Oiseau-Qui-N'existe-Pas 1970, De 1968, Monologue pour un disparu 1973. *Address:* Ty Guennic, 56780 Ile-aux-Moines; 12 rue Theophraste-Renaudot, 75015 Paris, France.

AVEROFF-TOSSIZZA, Evangelos, LL.D., PH.D.; Greek economist, journalist and politician; b. 1910, Trikala, Thessaly; s. of Anastassios and Efthymia Averoff-Tossizza; m. Dina Lykiardopoulo; two d.; ed. Univ. of Lausanne; began career as journalist, worked in Switzerland and Greece; Gov. of Corfu 1941; active in resistance movement during 1941–44 war, imprisoned in Northern Italy, later escaped and continued resistance work until end of war; Lieut. 1944, assigned to Hellenic Mil. Mission, Rome; mem. of Parl. 1946–; fmr. Minister of Supply, National Economy and Commerce, and Under-Sec. for Foreign Affairs; Minister of Agriculture Feb.-May 1956, 1967, of Foreign Affairs 1956–63; joined National Radical Union 1956; during 1967–74 dictatorship sentenced to five years' imprisonment Aug. 1967; imprisoned July 1973 for his part as political adviser in the Mutiny of the Navy; Minister of Nat. Defence 1974–81; Deputy Prime Minister

June–Oct. 1981; Leader, New Democracy Party 1981–84; Grand Cross, Order of the Phoenix (Greece), and decorations from other countries. *Publications:* include Non-Fiction: The Population Problem of Greece 1939 (Prize of the Acad. of Athens), Freedom or Death 1945, The Foreign Policy of Greece 1960, Lost Opportunities: The Cyprus Question, 1950–63 1987; Fiction: The Cry of the Land 1964, The Land of Sorrow 1966, The Delphic Land 1968, When the Gods Used to Forget 1969, When the Gods Used to Bless 1971; Play: Return to Mycenae 1973. *Address:* 33 Pentelis Street, Kifissia, Athens, Greece (Home).

AVERY, Mary Ellen, A.B., M.D.; American physician; b. 6 May 1927, New Jersey; d. of William Clarence Avery and Mary Catherine Miller; ed. Wheaton Coll., Mass., Johns Hopkins School of Medicine; Eudowood Assoc. Prof. of Pediatrics, Johns Hopkins Univ. 1966–69; Prof. and Chairman, Pediatrics, Faculty of Medicine, McGill Univ., Physician-in-Chief, Montreal Children's Hosp. 1969–74; Thomas Morgan Rotch Prof. of Pediatrics, Harvard Medical School 1974–; Physician-in-Chief, Children's Hosp., Boston 1974–85; John and Mary Markle Scholar 1961–66; Trudeau Medal, American Thoracic Soc.; numerous honorary degrees. *Publications:* The Lung and its Disorders in the Newborn Infant 1981, Born Early 1983, Diseases of the Newborn 1984, Pediatric Medicine 1989. *Address:* Children's Hospital, 300 Longwood Avenue, Boston, Mass. 02115, U.S.A. *Telephone:* (617) 566 4832.

AVERY, William Hinckley, A.M., PH.D.; American physicist; b. 25 July 1912, Fort Collins, Colo.; s. of Edgar Delano Avery and Mabel A. Gordon; m. Helen W. Palmer 1937; one s. one d.; ed. Pomona Coll. and Harvard Univ.; Postdoctoral Research Asst. Infrared Spectroscopy, Harvard 1937–39; Research Chemist, Shell Oil Co., St. Louis, Houston 1939–43; Head, Propulsion Div. Allegany Ballistics Lab. Cumberland, Md. 1943–46; Consultant in Physics and Chem. Arthur D. Little Co., Cambridge, Mass. 1946–47; Professional staff mem. Applied Physics Lab. Johns Hopkins Univ. 1947–73, Asst. Dir. Exploratory Devt. 1973–78, Dir. Ocean Energy Programs 1978–; mem. various Govt. Advisory panels etc.; mem. Nat. Acad. of Eng., N.A.S., American Chem. Soc.; Fellow, American Inst. of Aeronautics and Astronautics; Presidential Certificate of Merit 1948, Sir Alfred Egerton Award 1972, IR 100 Award 1979 and other awards and distinctions. *Address:* Johns Hopkins Road, Laurel, Md. 20707 (Office); 724 Guilford Court, Silver Spring, Md. 20901, U.S.A.

AVICE, Edwige, L. ÈS L.; French politician; b. 13 April 1945, Nevers; d. of Edmond Bertrand and Hélène Guyot; m. Etienne Avice 1970; ed. Cours Fénelon, Nevers, Lycée Pothier, Orléans, Univ. of Paris; worked for Nat. Cttee. for Housing Improvement 1970; Int. Dept., Crédit Lyonnais 1970–73; on staff of Dir.-Gen. of Paris Hospitals 1973–78; mem. Parti Socialiste (P.S.) 1972–, mem. Exec. Bureau 1977–, P.S. Nat. Del. for Nat. Service; mem. Nat. Assembly 1978–81; Minister-Del. for Free Time, Youth and Sports 1981–84; Sec. of State attached to the Minister of Defence 1984–86; Minister-Del. attached to the Minister for Foreign Affairs May 1988–. Conseillère de Paris 1983–; re-elected Socialist deputy 1986. *Leisure interests:* travelling, music, swimming, walking, fencing. *Address:* Assemblée nationale, 75355 Paris; Ministry of Foreign Affairs, 37 quai d'Orsay, 75700 Paris; c/o Parti Socialiste, 10 rue de Solférino, 75333 Paris, France.

AVIDOM (MAHLER-KALKSTEIN), Menahem, B.A.; Israeli composer; b. 6 Jan. 1908, Stanislau (fmrly. Austria, now U.S.S.R.); s. of Isaac Kalkstein and Helena Mahler; m. Suzanne Soumis-Lyonnais 1935; two d.; ed. American Univ., Beirut, and in Paris; Lecturer on theory of music, Hebrew Conservatoire of Music, Tel-Aviv 1936–, and Music Teachers' Training Coll. Tel-Aviv 1945–; Sec.-Gen. Israel Philharmonic Orchestra 1945–; Vice-Pres. Bd. of Dirs. Acum (Composers and Authors Assen.), Dir.-Gen. 1955–80; Dir. Arts Dept. Jerusalem Convention Centre 1952; Art Adviser, Govt. Tourist Centre, Ministry of Commerce and Industry 1954–; Pres. League of Composers 1958, Hon. Pres. 1983; mem. Nat. Arts Council 1962; Fellow Int. Inst. of Arts and Letters 1958; Israel State Prize 1961, Tel Aviv Municipality Prize 1948, 1956; Israel Philharmonic Prize 1953; Authors' and Composers' Assen. Prize 1962, Prize for Life-Work 1982. *Compositions include:* First woodwind Quartet 1937, Polyphonic Suite for strings 1938, A Folk Symphony 1947, Symphony No. 2 David 1948, Sinfonietta 1951, 2 Piano Sonatinas 1949, Concertino for violinist Jascha Heifetz, Concertino for cellist Gregor Piatigorsky 1951, Alexandra Hashmonaïth (opera in 3 acts) 1952, Jubilee Suite, Triptyque Symphonique, concerto for strings and flute, music for strings, symphonies 3, 4, 5 and 6, psalms and cantatas, 12 Preludes Variés for piano, Metamorphoses for string quartet 1960, Symphony No. 7 (25th anniversary of Israel Philharmonic Orchestra), Enigma, septet for 5 wood instruments, piano and percussion, Quartet for brass, Reflexions for 2 flutes, Triptyque for Solo violin, "B-A-C-H" Suite for Chamber Orchestra, Festival Sinfonietta (Symphony No. 8) 1966, The Crook (comic opera) 1966/67, Symphonie Variée (Symphony No. 9) for Chamber Orchestra 1968, Concertino for Violin and Chamber Orchestra 1968, The Farewell (Chamber Opera in one act) 1970, Spring-Overture for Symphony Orchestra 1972, 6 Inventions for Piano in Homage and on the Name of Arthur Rubinstein 1973, Passacaglia for Piano 1973, Piece on the Name of SCHoENBERG for Piano 1974, The Emperor's New Clothes (comic opera in one act) for Israel Festival 1976, Twelve Hills (cantata) for Testimonium 1976, Five Psalms for Jerusalem Foundation 1976, Beyond (cantata for voice and three instruments), Yodfat's Cave (musical drama)

1977, Once Upon a Time (five short tales for piano) 1978, The End of King Og (children's opera) 1979, Movements for String Quartet (or String Orchestra) 1979, The First Sin (satirical opera in four scenes) 1980, Elegie, At Rachel's Tomb, The Voice of Rovina (three vocal compositions) 1980, Sinfonia Brevis (Symphony No. 10) 1981, Monothema (sonatina for string quartet) 1982, Woodwind quintet 1983, quartet 1984, Bach'ianas for brass quintet, chamber orchestra, piano, Triptyque for piano, Trialogue for piano, violin and cello 1985, Chaconne for piano, flute and oboe 1986, Dialogues for oboe and bassoon 1986, Trio for piano, violin and cello 1986, six epigrams for piano 1987, Jerusalem Songs for children's choir 1987, Movement for four horns 1987, Clarinet Sonata 1988. *Leisure interests:* painting, chess, music reviews. *Address:* ACUM House, Rothschild Boulevard 118, Tel-Aviv (Office); 30 Samadar Street, Ramat-Gan, Israel (Home). *Telephone:* 240110 (Office); 795512 (Home).

AVILA, Rev. Fernando Bastos de; Brazilian ecclesiastic and sociologist; b. 17 March 1918; ed. Univ. do Nova Friburgo (Brazil), Univ. de Louvain and Gregorian Univ., Rome; Prof. of Sociology, Pontificia Univ. Católica do Rio de Janeiro 1957–; Social Dir. Nat. Catholic Immigration Comm. 1954–; mem. Council, Nat. Fed. of Trade 1960–; Dir. Inst. Brasileiro de Desenvolvimento (IBRADES). *Publications:* Economic Impacts of Immigration 1956, L'immigration au Brésil 1957, Introdução a Sociologia 1962, Solidarismo 1965, Pequena Enciclopédia de Moral Ecivismo 1967. *Address:* 115 rua Bambina-Botatogo, Rio de Janeiro, RJ, Brazil.

AVINERI, Shlomo; Israeli professor of political science; b. 20 Aug. 1933, Bielsko, Poland; s. of Michael Avineri and Erna Groner; m. Dvora Nadler 1957; one d.; ed. Shalva Secondary School, Tel-Aviv, Hebrew Univ., Jerusalem, and London School of Econs.; has lived in Israel since 1939; Prof. of Political Science, Hebrew Univ. Jerusalem 1971–, Dir. Eshkol Research Inst. 1971–74, Dean of Faculty of Social Sciences 1974–76; Dir.-Gen. Ministry of Foreign Affairs 1976–77; visiting appointments at Yale Univ. 1966–67, Wesleyan Univ., Middletown, Conn. 1971–72, Research School of Social Sciences, Australian Nat. Univ. 1972, Cornell Univ. 1973, Univ. of Calif. 1979; mem. Int. Inst. of Philosophy 1980–; Fellow, Woodrow Wilson Centre, Washington, D.C. 1983–84; British Council Scholarship 1961; Rubin Prize in the Social Sciences 1968; Naphtali Prize for study of Hegel 1977; Present Tense Award for Study of Zionism 1982. *Publications:* The Social and Political Thought of Karl Marx 1968, Karl Marx on Colonialism and Modernization 1968, Israel and the Palestinians 1971, Marx' Socialism 1972, Hegel's Theory of the Modern State 1973, Varieties of Marxism 1977, The Making of Modern Zionism 1981, Moses Hess—Prophet of Communism and Zionism 1985. *Address:* Department of Political Science, The Hebrew University, Jerusalem (Office); 10 Hagedud Ha-ivri Street, Jerusalem, Israel (Home).

AVNER, Yehuda; Israeli diplomatist; b. 30 Dec. 1928, Manchester, England; m. Miriam Avner; one s. three d.; ed. Manchester High School, London School of Journalism; emigrated to Israel; Ed. of Publs., The Jewish Agency, Jerusalem 1956–64; with Ministry of Foreign Affairs 1964–67, Ed. of Political Publs. 1964–67, Dir. of Foreign Press Bureau 1972–74, Asst. to Prime Minister 1964–67, 1972–74; First Sec., then Counsellor, Embassy, Washington, D.C. 1968–72; seconded to Prime Minister's bureau 1974–77, Adviser to Prime Minister 1974–77, 1977–83; Amb. to U.K. July 1983–88. *Publication:* "The Young Inheritors": A Portrait of Israeli Youth. *Address:* c/o Ministry of Foreign Affairs, Hakirya, Romema, Jerusalem, Israel. *Telephone:* 02-303111.

AVRIL, Pierre; French professor; b. 18 Nov. 1930, Pau; s. of Stanislas Avril and Geneviève Camion; m. Marie-Louise Hillion; one s.; Asst. Pierre Mendès France 1955–62, Ed.-in-Chief Cahiers de la Répub. 1960–62; sub.-ed. Soc. Gen. de Presse 1962–69; Prof. Faculté de Droit de Poitiers 1972–79, Univ. de Paris X 1979–88, Univ. de Droit de Paris 1988–. *Publications:* Le Régime politique de la Ve République 1964, Un président pour quoi faire? 1965, Essais sur les partis 1986, La Ve République—histoire politique et constitutionnelle 1987, Droit parlementaire (with others) 1988. *Address:* 48 rue Gay-Lussac, 75005 Paris, France (Home). *Telephone:* (1) 43 26 36 43 (Home).

AVRIL, Brig.-Gen. Prosper; Haitian army officer and politician; ed. Mil. Acad. Haiti and Univ. of Haiti Law School; fmr. adviser to deposed Pres. Jean-Claude Duvalier; adviser to mil.-civilian junta headed by Gen. Namphy and mem. Nat. Governing Council 1986; Commdr. Presidential Guard 1988; maj. participant in June 1988 coup which overthrew civilian govt. of Leslie Manigat; leader of coup which deposed regime of Gen. Namphy (q.v.) Sept. 1988; Pres. of Haiti Sept. 1988–. *Address:* Office of the President, Port-au-Prince, Haiti.

AVTSYN, Aleksandr Pavlovich; Soviet pathologist; b. 13 Sept. 1908, Moscow; s. of Pavel Ivanovich and Maria Aleksandrovna Avtsyn; ed. First Moscow Medical Inst. Assoc., Inst. of Neuropsychiatric Prophylaxis 1933–38; Asst. Prof. Third Moscow Medical Inst. 1937–41; Asst. Prof. First Moscow Medical Inst. 1942–43; Army Pathologist 1943–46; Head of Dept., Inst. of Normal and Pathological Morphology, U.S.S.R. Acad. of Medical Sciences 1945–61; Corresp. mem. U.S.S.R. Acad. of Medical Sciences 1961–65, mem. U.S.S.R. Acad. of Medical Sciences 1965–; Dir. Inst. of Human Morphology, U.S.S.R. Acad. of Medical Sciences 1961–; Vice-Chair. Moscow Soc. of Pathologicoanatomists, Vice-Chair, U.S.S.R. Soc. of

Pathologicoanatomists; mem. Ed. Bd. Arkhiv patologii, Co-Ed. Big Medical Encyclopaedia; Order of Lenin (twice), Order of Red Banner of Labour and Bulgarian Red Banner of Labour; U.S.S.R. State Prize in Medicine/Geographical Pathology 1982. *Publications:* Over 200 works on pathological anatomy of cerebral tumours, geographical pathology, pathology of cells, infectious diseases and military pathology. *Address:* Institute of Human Morphology, U.S.S.R. Academy of Medical Sciences, 3 Ulitsa Tsurupi, Moscow, U.S.S.R.

AVVEDUTO, Saverio, D.PHIL.; Italian government official; b. 29 Jan. 1924, Ispica; s. of Pietro and Carmela Luca; m. Cannata Clelia 1951; one d.; Chief Ed. Review Dialogos; mem. Scientific Comm. of Inst. for Italian Encyclopaedia; Dir. of Sociology of Educ., Univ. of Rome; now Dir-Gen. Ministry of Educ.; Hon. Fellow, Coll. of Preceptors, Univ. of London; Ordre des Palmes Académiques, Univ. of Paris. *Publications:* L'Uomo in Quanto Ricchezza 1968, La Societá Scientifica 1969, Rapporto Sulla Scienza 1972, Il Neon e le Lucerne 1974, La Scuola in Europa 1982, L'Universitá Italiana 1984, Prossimi 6,000 Giorni 1985. *Address:* Dialogos, C.P. 30098, Rome 47 (Office); Via G. Carini, Rome 71, Italy.

AWAD, Muhammad Hadi; Yemeni diplomatist; b. 5 May 1934; m. Adelah Moh'd Hadi Awad 1956; one s. three d.; ed. Murray House Coll. of Educ.; teacher 1953–59; Educ. Officer 1960–62; Chief Insp. of Schools 1963–65; Vice-Principal As-Shaab Coll. 1965–67; Perm. Rep. to Arab League 1968–70, concurrently Amb. to U.A.R., also accred. to Sudan, Lebanon, Libya and Iraq; Perm. Sec. Ministry of Foreign Affairs 1970–73; Amb. to U.K. 1973–80, concurrently to Spain and Sweden 1974–80, to Denmark, Portugal, the Netherlands 1975–80; Amb. to Tunisia and Perm. Rep. to the Arab League 1980–. *Leisure interest:* photography. *Address:* P.O. Box 68, Elmanzan, Tunis, Tunisia. *Telephone:* 237 327, 237 317.

AWADALLAH, Babikir; Sudanese jurist and politician; b. 1917, El Citaina, Blue Nile Province; ed. School of Law, Gordon Coll., Khartoum; District Judge 1947–54; resigned to become Speaker of Sudanese House of Reps. 1954–57; Judge of the Supreme Court 1957, Chief Justice 1964–69; Prime Minister and Minister of Foreign Affairs May-Oct. 1969; Deputy Chair. Revolutionary Council, Minister of Foreign Affairs 1969–70, Minister of Justice 1969–71, Deputy Prime Minister 1970–71; fmr. Chair. Dept. of English and Dean of Faculty of Arts, Univ. of Cape Coast; Sec.-Gen. Action Congress Party; Amb. to Brazil 1984–; Adjunct Prof., Univ. of Fla., Gainesville; Contributing Ed., Transition and Alcheringa; Gurrey Prize for Poetry, Nat. Book Council Award for Poetry 1979; Longmans and Fairfield fellowships. First Vice-Pres. of Sudan 1971–72. *Address:* c/o Sudanese Socialist Union, Khartoum, Sudan.

AWOONOR, Kofi Nyidevu, PH.D.; Ghanaian writer, teacher and diplomatist; b. 13 March 1935; s. of Kosiwo and Atsu Awoonor; m.; four s. one d.; ed. Univ. of Ghana, Univ. Coll., London, and State Univ. of N.Y.; Research Fellow, Inst. of African Studies; Man. Dir. Film Corpn., Accra; Longmans Fellow, Univ. of London; Asst. Prof. and later Chair. Comparative Literature Program, State Univ. of N.Y., Stony Brook; Visiting Prof., Univ. of Texas, Austin and New School of Social Research, N.Y.; fmrly. Prof. of Comparative Literature, State Univ. of N.Y., Stony Brook; detained in Ghana for allegedly harbouring leader of coup 1975; on trial 1976, sentenced to one year's imprisonment Oct. 1976, pardoned Oct. 1976; fmr. Chair. Dept. of English and Dean of Faculty of Arts, Univ. of Cape Coast; Sec.-Gen. Action Congress Party; Amb. to Brazil 1984–; Adjunct Prof., Univ. of Fla., Gainesville; Contributing Ed., Transition and Alcheringa; Gurrey Prize for Poetry, Nat. Book Council Award for Poetry 1979; Longmans and Fairfield fellowships. *Publications:* poetry: Rediscovery 1964, Messages 1970, Night of My Blood 1971, House by the Sea 1978; prose: This Earth My Brother 1971, Guardians of the Sacred Word 1973, Ride Me Memory 1973, Breast of the Earth 1974 (history of African literature), Traditional African Literature (Series, Ed.), Alien Corn (novel) 1974, Where is the Mississippi Panorama 1974, Fire in the Valley: Folktales of the Ewes 1980, Until the Morning After (collected poems), The Ghana Revolution. *Leisure interests:* jazz, tennis, hunting. *Address:* Embassy of Ghana, Q110, Conj. 8, Casa 2, Brasília, Brazil.

AX, Emanuel, B.A.; American pianist (b. Polish); b. 8 June 1949, Lwów; s. of Joachim Ax and Hellen (Kurtz) Ax; m. Yoko Nozaki 1974; one s. one d.; went to Canada 1959, to U.S.A. 1961; naturalized 1970; ed. Columbia Univ. and Juillard School of Music; concert tour S. America 1969; New York début, Alice Tully Hall 1973; appearances with major orchestras including New York Philharmonic, Phila., Chicago Symphony, Los Angeles, London Philharmonic, Berlin Philharmonic, BBC Symphony, Vienna Philharmonic, Israel Philharmonic and Cleveland orchestras; extensive concert and recital tours; many recordings; First Prize Artur Rubenstein Int. Competition 1974, Record of the Year Award, Stereo Review 1977, One of Five Best Records of the Year Award, Time Magazine 1977, Avery Fisher Award 1979, four Grammy awards. *Address:* c/o ICM Artists Ltd., 40 West 57th Street, New York, N.Y. 10019, U.S.A.

AXELROD, Julius, PH.D.; American biochemical pharmacologist; b. 30 May 1912, New York; s. of Isadore and Molly (Leichtling) Axelrod; m. Sally Taub Axelrod 1938; two s.; ed. Coll. of the City of New York, New York Univ. and George Washington Univ. Lab.; Asst., Dept. of Bacteriology, New York Univ. Medical School 1933–35; Chemist, Laboratory of Industrial Hygiene 1935–46; Research Assoc., Third New York Univ. Research Div., Goldwater Memorial Hosp. 1946–49; Assoc. Chemist, Nat. Heart Inst., Nat. Inst. of Health 1949–50, Chemist 1950–53, Sr. Chemist 1953–55; Chief, Section on Pharmacology, Lab. of Chemical

Science, Nat. Inst. of Mental Health, Health Services and Mental Health Admin., Dept. of Health, Educ. and Welfare 1955–84; Guest Worker, Nat. Inst. of Mental Health 1984–; mem. Scientific Advisory Bd., Nat. Foundation, Brookhaven Nat. Lab., Center for Biomedical Educ., and many others; mem. Int. Brain Research Organization; Senior mem. Inst. of Medicine; Foreign mem. Royal Society; Fellow, American Coll. of Neuropsychopharmacology (mem. Council 1966–69); mem. A.C.S., American Soc. of Pharmacology and Experimental Therapeutics, American Soc. of Biological Chemists, A.A.A.S.; Fellow, American Acad. of Arts and Sciences, N.A.S.; corresp. mem. German Pharmacological Soc.; Foreign mem. Acad. der Naturforcher DDR; Hon. Sc.D. (Univ. of Chicago, Medical Coll. of Wisconsin, New York Univ, Medical Coll. of Pa. Univ. of Pa.); Hon. LL.D. (George Washington Univ.); Dr. h.c. (Univ. of Panama); Hon. LL.D. (Coll. of the City of New York), etc.; Gairdner Foundation Award 1967; Distinguished Achievement Award, George Washington Univ. 1968, Dept. of Health, Educ. and Welfare 1970, Modern Medicine Magazine 1970; Claude Bernard Medal, Univ. of Montreal 1969, Nobel Prize for Medicine or Physiology 1970, Albert Einstein Achievement Award, Yeshiva Univ. 1971, Torald Sollmann Award in Pharmacology 1973, Paul Hoch Award, American Psychopathological Assen. 1975, etc.; several research awards, memorial lectureships etc. *Publications:* 450 articles in professional journals, also abstracts and press articles. *Leisure interests:* music, reading. *Address:* 10401 Grosvenor Place, Rockville, Md. 20852, U.S.A. (Home). *Telephone:* (301) 493-6376.

AXEN, Hermann; German party official; b. 6 March 1916, Leipzig; m.; two d.; mem. Communist Youth League 1932; emigrated to France 1938–40; imprisoned in concentration camps 1940–45; mem. Communist Party 1942–; Sec. Central Council of Free German Youth 1946–49; mem. Cen. Cttee. Socialist Unity Party (SED) 1950, Sec. 1966; Chief Ed. Neues Deutschland 1956–66; Candidate mem. of Politburo of Cen. Cttee. of Socialist Unity Party 1963–70, mem. 1970–; mem. Volkskammer 1954–; Chair. Foreign Cttee., Volkskammer; decorations include Karl-Marx-Orden, Silver and Gold Medal Vaterländischer Verdienstorden, Banner der Arbeit. *Address:* Sozialistische Einheitspartei Deutschlands, 102 Berlin, Am Marx-Engels-Platz 2, German Democratic Republic.

AXER, Erwin; Polish theatre producer and director; b. 1 Jan. 1917, Vienna, Austria; s. of Dr. Maurycy Axer and Fryderyka Schuster; m. Bronisława Kreczmar 1945 (died 1973); two s.; ed. Lwów, and Nat. Acad. of Theatrical Art, Warsaw; Asst. Producer, Nat. Theatre, Warsaw 1938–39; Actor-Producer, Polish Drama Theatre, U.S.S.R. 1939–41; Artistic Dir., Teatr Kameralny, Łódź 1946–49; Dir. and producer Teatr Współczesny (Contemporary Theatre) Warsaw 1949–81; Dir. and Chief Producer, Nat. Theatre, Warsaw 1955–57; Asst. Prof. Producers' Dept., State Higher Theatrical School, Łódź 1946–49, Warsaw 1949–57, Extraordinary Prof. 1957–66, Prof. Ordinary 1966–81, Prof. Emer. 1981–; State Prizes for Artistic Achievement 1951, 1953, 1955, 1962, Nagroda Krytyki im. Boya-Żeleńskiego (Critics Award) 1960; Commdr. Cross of Polonia Restituta; Order of Banner of Labour (1st Class); other awards and prizes. *Productions include:* Major Barbara (Shaw) 1947, Niemcy (Kruczkowski) 1955, Kordian (Słowacki) 1956, Pierwszy dzień wolności 1959, Iphigenia in Tauris 1961, Kariera Arturo Ui (Brecht) Warsaw 1962, Leningrad 1963, Three Sisters (Chekhov) 1963, Düsseldorf 1967, Androcles and the Lion (Shaw), Warsaw 1964, Tango (Mrożek), Warsaw 1965, Düsseldorf 1966, Die Ermittlung (Weiss), Warsaw 1966, Le Piéton de l'Air (Ionesco), Warsaw 1967, Maria Stuart (Schiller), Warsaw 1969, Dwa Teatry (Szaniawski), Leningrad 1969, Matka (Witkiewicz) Warsaw 1970, Porträt eines Planeten, Düsseldorf 1970, Old Times and Macbeth, Warsaw 1972, Uncle Vanya, Munich 1972, Ein Fest für Boris, Vienna (Kainz Award) 1973, King Lear (Bond), Warsaw, 1974, Endgame (Beckett), Vienna 1976, Kordian Warsaw 1977, Seagull (Chekhov), Vienna 1977, Biedermann und die Brandstifter (Max Frisch), Zürich 1978, Krawiec (Tailor by Mrożek), Warsaw 1979, Wesele (Wyspiański) New York 1962, Our Town, Leningrad 1979, John Gabriel Borkman, Zürich 1979, Triptychon (Frisch), Warsaw 1980, Die Schwärmer (Musil), Vienna 1980, Amphitryon (Kleist), Vienna 1982, Till Damascus (Strindberg), Munich 1983, Reigen (Schnizler), Vienna 1983, Vinzenz (Musil), Vienna 1985, Am Ziel (Bernhard Berlin) 1987, Nachtasyl (Gorki Berlin) 1987. *Publications include:* Listy ze sceny I (Letters from the Stage) 1955, Listy ze sceny II 1957, Sprawy Teatralne (Things Theatrical) 1966, Ćwiczenia Pamięci (Exercises of the Memory) 1984, essays, serial, articles on theatre. *Address:* Ul. Odyńca 27 m. 11, 02-606 Warsaw, Poland. *Telephone:* 44-01-16.

AXFORD, David Norman, M.A., M.SC.(ELEC.), PH.D., C.ENG., F.I.E.E.; British meteorologist; b. 14 June 1934, London; s. of Norman Axford and Joy A. (Williams) Axford; m. 1st Elizabeth A. Stiles 1962 (divorced 1980); one s. two d.; m. 2nd Diana Bufton 1980; three step-s. one step-d.; ed. Merchant Taylors School, Plymouth Coll., St. John's Coll. Cambridge and Southampton Univ.; Scientific Officer, Kew Observatory 1960–62; Sr. Scientific Officer, various R.A.F. stations 1962–68; Prin. Scientific Officer, Meteorological Research Flight, Royal Aircraft Establishment, Farnborough 1968–76; Asst. Dir. (SPSO) Operation Instrumentation Branch 1976–80; Asst. Dir. (SPSO), Telecommunications 1980–82; Deputy Dir. Observational Services 1982–84; Dir. of Services and Deputy to Dir.-Gen. Meteorological Office 1984–; Pres. N. Atlantic Ocean Station Bd. 1982–85; Chair. Cttee. of Operational World Weather Watch System Evaluations—N. Atlantic

(CONA) 1985–; Hon. Sec. Royal Meteorological Soc. 1983–88; Groves Award 1972. *Publications:* articles in professional journals. *Leisure interests:* home and garden, food and wine. *Address:* Rudgewick Cottage, Binfield Heath, Henley-on-Thames, Oxon., England (Home). *Telephone:* (0344) 420242 (Office).

AYALA, Francisco Jose, PH.D.; American (naturalized) professor of genetics; b. 12 March 1934, Madrid, Spain; s. of Francisco and Soledad (née Pereda) Ayala; m. Hana Lostakova 1985; two s.; ed. Univ. of Madrid and Columbia Univ.; Research Assoc. Rockefeller Univ., New York 1964–65, Asst. Prof. 1967–71; Asst. Prof. Providence Coll., R.I. 1965–67; Assoc. Prof., later Prof. of Genetics Univ. of Calif., Davis 1971–87, Dir. Inst. of Ecology 1977–81, Assoc. Dean of Environmental Studies 1977–81; Distinguished Prof. of Biology Univ. of Calif., Irvine 1987–; mem. N.A.S., American Acad. of Arts and Sciences, American Philosophical Soc.; Dr. h.c. (León) 1982, (Madrid) 1986, (Barcelona) 1986. *Publications:* Studies in the Philosophy of Biology 1974, Molecular Evolution 1976, Evolution 1977, Evolving: The Theory and Processes of Organic Evolution 1979, Population and Evolutionary Genetics 1982, Modern Genetics 1984 and more than 300 scientific articles. *Leisure interests:* skiing, tennis, travel. *Address:* Department of Ecology and Evolutionary Biology, University of California, Irvine, Calif., 92717, U.S.A. (Office); 12 Locke Court, Irvine, Calif. 92715, U.S.A. (Home). *Telephone:* (714) 856-8293 (Office).

AYALON, David, M.A., PH.D.; Israeli professor of the history of the Islamic peoples; b. 17 May 1914, Haifa; s. of Michael and Rela Ayalon; m. Myriam Ayalon 1965; ed. Reali High School, Haifa and Hebrew Univ. of Jerusalem; Political Dept. Jewish Agency 1938–48; Ministry of Foreign Affairs 1948–49; Founder and Dir. Dept. of Middle East in Modern Times, Hebrew Univ. of Jerusalem 1949–63, Dir. Inst. of Asian and African Studies 1963–67; Visiting Prof. Princeton Univ. and Univ. of Calif. Berkeley 1967–68; mem. Inst. for Advanced Study, Princeton 1976–77; mem. Israeli Acad. of Sciences and Humanities 1961–, Emer. 1983–; Rockefeller Fellow 1952–59; Israel Prize for the Humanities 1972; Rothschild Prize for the Humanities 1975. *Publications:* Arabic-Hebrew Dictionary of Modern Arabic (with P. Shinar) 1947, Gunpowder and Firearms in the Mamluk Kingdom: A Challenge to a Medieval Society 1956, The Great Yasa of Chingiz Khan—A Reexamination 1971–73, Studies on the Mamluks of Egypt 1977, The Mamluk Military Society 1979, Outsiders in the Lands of Islam 1988. *Address:* Institute of Asian and African Studies, Hebrew University of Jerusalem, 7 Kikar Magnes, Jerusalem 92304, Israel (Home). *Telephone:* (02) 633306 (Home).

AYANDHO, Bernard Christian; Central African Republic politician; b. 15 Dec. 1930; Prime Minister of Cen. African Repub. Sept. 1979–Aug. 1980; later rep. for Air Afrique, Equatorial Region; Pres. Chamber of Commerce and Industry. *Address:* Chambre de Commerce, d'Industrie, des Mines et de l'Artisanat, BP 813, Bangui, Central African Republic. *Telephone:* 61-42-55.

AYARI, Chedli, L. EN D., D. ÈS SC.(ECON.); Tunisian economist, diplomatist and politician; b. 24 Aug. 1933, Tunis; s. of Sadok and Fatouma Chedly; m. Elaine Vatteau 1959; three c.; ed. Collège Sadiki and Inst. de Hautes Etudes; with Société Tunisienne de Banque 1958; Asst. Faculté de Droit et des Sciences Economiques et Politiques, Tunis 1959; Econ. Counsellor, Perm. Mission of Tunis at UN 1960–64; Exec. Dir. IBRD 1964–65; Dean, Faculté de Droit, Tunis 1965–67; Dir. C.E.R.E.S. 1967–69; Sec. of State in charge of Plan 1969–70; Minister of Nat. Educ., Youth and Sport 1970–71; Amb. to Belgium Feb.-March 1972; Minister of Nat. Economy 1972–74, of Planning 1974–75; Chair. of Bd. and Gen. Man. Arab Bank for Econ. Devt. in Africa March 1975–; Prof. of Economics, Agrégé de Sciences Economiques, Tunis; Assoc. Prof. Univ. of Aix-Marseilles, Feb. 1989–; mem. UN Cttee. of Planning for Devt.; Dr. h.c. (Aix-Marseilles) 1972; Grand Officier Legion d'honneur, Grand Cordon, Ordre de la République. *Publications:* numerous books and articles on economic and monetary problems. *Leisure interest:* music. *Address:* Rue Tanit, Gammarth, La Marsa, Tunis, Tunisia (Home). *Telephone:* 270-038 (Home).

AYCKBOURN, Alan, C.B.E.; British playwright and theatre director; b. 12 April 1939, London; s. of Horace Ayckbourn and Irene Maud (née Worley); m. Christine Helen (née Roland) 1959; two s.; ed. Haileybury; went straight into the theatre on leaving school as stage manager and actor with various repertory cos. in England; founder mem. Victoria Theatre Co., Stoke-on-Trent 1962–64; Drama Producer, BBC Radio 1964–70; Artistic Dir., Stephen Joseph Theatre in the Round, Scarborough 1971–; Assoc. Dir. Bedroom Farce (Nat. Theatre) 1977, Sisterly Feelings (Nat. Theatre) 1980; Dir. Ten Times Table (West End) 1978, Joking Apart (West End) 1979, Season's Greetings (West End) 1980, Way Upstream (Nat. Theatre) 1982, Intimate Exchanges 1984, A Chorus of Disapproval (Nat. Theatre) 1985, Women in Mind (West End) 1986, Tons of Money (Nat. Theatre) 1986, A View from the Bridge (Nat. Theatre) 1987, A Small Family Business (Nat. Theatre) 1987, 'Tis Pity She's a Whore (Nat. Theatre) 1988; Hon. D.Litt. (Hull) 1981, (Keele, Leeds) 1987; Evening Standard Award for Best New Comedy for Absurd Person Singular 1973, for Best New Play for The Norman Conquests 1974, for Best New Play for Just Between Ourselves 1977; Plays and Players Award for Best New Play for The Norman Conquests 1974; Variety Club of Great Britain Playwright of the Year 1974, Plays and Players Award for Best New

Comedy for Joking Apart 1979, London Evening Standard Award, Olivier Award and Drama Award for Best Comedy for A Chorus of Disapproval 1985, London Evening Standard Award for Best New Play for A Small Family Business 1987, Plays and Players Director of the Year Award for a View from the Bridge 1987. *Plays:* Relatively Speaking 1965, The Sparrow 1967, How the Other Half Loves 1969, Family Circles 1970, Time and Time Again 1971, Absurd Person Singular 1972, The Norman Conquests 1973, Jeeves (book and lyrics for Andrew Lloyd Webber musical) 1975, Absent Friends 1974, Confusions 1974, Bedroom Farce 1975, Just Between Ourselves 1976, Ten Times Table 1977, Men on Women on Men (revue with music by Paul Todd) 1978, Joking Apart 1978, Sisterly Feelings 1979, Taking Steps 1979, Suburban Strains (musical play with music by Paul Todd) 1980, Season's Greetings 1980, Making Tracks (with Paul Todd) 1981, Way Upstream 1981, Intimate Exchanges 1982, Incidental Music (with Paul Todd) 1983, A Chorus of Disapproval 1984 (film 1988), The Westwoods 1984, Woman in Mind 1985, Mere Soup Songs (with Paul Todd) 1986, A Small Family Business 1986, Henceforward 1987, Man of the Moment 1988. *Publications:* The Norman Conquests 1975, Three Plays 1977, Joking Apart and other plays 1979, Sisterly Feelings and Taking Steps 1981, A Chorus of Disapproval, Woman in Mind, A Small Family Business, Henceforward. *Leisure interests:* music, cricket, astronomy. *Address:* c/o Margaret Ramsay Ltd., 14A Goodwin's Court, St. Martin's Lane, London WC2N 4LL, England. *Telephone:* 01-240 0691.

AYDALOT, Maurice, D. EN D.; French judge; b. 22 June 1905; s. of Joseph Aydalot and Marguerite Rieumajou; m. Madeleine de Casabianca 1933; two s.; ed. Faculté de Droit de Paris; Magistrat, Ministry of Justice 1930; Deputy Public Prosecutor, Paris 1947, Public Prosecutor 1951, Prosecutor-Gen., Court of Appeal, Paris 1957–62, Pres. of Chamber 1985–; Prosecutor-Gen., Court of Cassation 1962–67; First Pres. Court of Cassation 1967–75, Hon. Pres. 1975–; Counsellor, Court of Appeal, Paris 1976–; Vice-Pres. Assen. nationale des docteurs en droit 1970, Pres. 1974–79; Grand Croix, Légion d'honneur, Ordre nationale du Mérite, Commdr. Ordre des Arts et des Lettres. *Publications:* Le délit d'atteinte au crédit de l'état, L'expertise comptable judiciaire, Législation pénale en matière commerciale, Magistrat 1976. *Address:* 165 avenue de Wagram, 75017 Paris, France (Home).

AYDELOTTE, William Osgood, PH.D.; American university professor; b. 1 Sept. 1910, Bloomington, Ind.; s. of Frank Aydelotte and Marie Osgood Aydelotte; m. Myrtle Elizabeth Kitchell 1956; two s.; ed. William Penn Charter School, Harvard Coll. and Univ. of Cambridge; Asst., Chair.'s Office, Fed. Home Loan Bank Bd., Washington, D.C. 1934–36; Instructor, then Asst. Prof., Trinity Coll., Hartford, Conn. 1937–43; Visiting Lecturer, Smith Coll., Northampton, Mass. 1943–45; Visiting Lecturer, Princeton Univ. 1945–47; Asst. Prof., Univ. of Iowa 1947–49, Assoc. Prof. 1949–50, Prof. 1950–78, Emer. Prof. 1978–; Chair. History Dept. 1947–59, 1965–68, Roy J. Carver Prof. 1976–78; Visiting Prof., Harvard Univ. 1966; Visiting Prof., Univ. of Leicester, England 1971; Fellow, Center for Advanced Study in the Behavioral Sciences 1976–77; Hon. O.B.E. 1961; mem. N.A.S. *Publications:* Bismarck and British Colonial Policy 1937, The Dimensions of Quantitative Research in History (Jt. Ed.) 1972, Quantification in History 1971, The History of Parliamentary Behavior (Ed.) 1977, numerous articles. *Leisure interests:* walking, swimming and sailing. *Address:* 201 North First Avenue, Iowa City, Iowa 52230, U.S.A.; 149 Oswegatchie Road, Waterford, Conn. 96385, U.S.A. *Telephone:* (319) 338-1791; (203) 443-7123.

AYDIN, Mehmet; Turkish politician; b. 1928, Samsun; m.; three c.; ed. Samsun Lycée, Dept. of Political Science and Finance, Istanbul Univ.; Georgetown Univ., Washington, D.C., U.S.A.; civil servant 1950–; studied devt. of land and water resources for OECD in U.S.A., economic planning in Netherlands 1963; Gen. Dir in Ministry of Commerce 1967–70; worked for Ginia Frintas Companies; Sr. Dir. of Food, Ministry of Agric.; Minister of Health and Social Welfare 1983–86. *Publications:* 20 books in Turkish and English. *Address:* Saglik ve Sosyal Yardim Bakanligi, Yenisehir, Ankara, Turkey. *Telephone:* (41) 258238.

AYER, Sir Alfred Jules, Kt., M.A., F.B.A.; British university professor; b. 29 Oct. 1910, London; s. of late Jules L.C. and Reine (née Citroen) Ayer; m. 1st Grace I. R. Lees 1932, one s. one d.; m. 2nd Alberta C. Chapman 1960, one s.; m. 3rd Vanessa M. A. Lawson 1983 (died 1985); ed. Eton Coll. and Christ Church, Oxford; Lecturer in Philosophy, Christ Church, Oxford 1932–35, Research Student of Christ Church 1935–44; Fellow of Wadham Coll. Oxford 1944–46, Dean of Wadham 1945–46; Grote Prof. of the Philosophy of Mind and Logic, Univ. of London 1946–59; Wykeham Prof. of Logic, Oxford 1959–78; served in Welsh Guards and on Intelligence Duties during Second World War; Attaché British Embassy, Paris 1945; Fellow of New Coll., Oxford 1959–78, Emer. Fellow 1978–80; Fellow of Wolfson Coll., Oxford 1978–83; Pres. Soc. for Applied Philosophy 1982–85; Chevalier, Légion d'honneur 1977; Hon. Fellow of Wadham Coll., Oxford 1957–, Univ. Coll. London, New Coll., Oxford; Hon. Student of Christ Church, Oxford; Hon. mem. American Acad. of Arts and Sciences 1963; Foreign mem. Royal Danish Acad. of Sciences and Letters 1976; Dr. h. c. (Univ. of Brussels) 1962, Hon. D. Litt. (Univ. of East Anglia, Univ. of London, Univ. Trent, Canada, Bard Univ., U.S.A., Univ. of Durham). *Publications:* Language, Truth and Logic 1936, The Foundations of Empirical Knowledge 1940, Thinking and Meaning 1947, British Empirical Philosophers (editor, with Raymond Winch) 1952, Philosophical Essays 1954, The Problem of Knowledge 1956, Privacy 1960, Philosophy and Language 1960, Logical Positivism (Ed.) 1960, Concept of a Person and Other Essays 1963, The Origins of Pragmatism 1968, Metaphysics and Common Sense 1969, Russell and Moore: The Analytical Heritage 1971, Probability and Evidence 1972, Russell 1972, Bertrand Russell as a Philosopher 1972, The Central Questions of Philosophy 1973, Part of My Life 1977, Perception and Identity 1979, Hume 1980, Philosophy in the 20th Century 1982, Freedom and Morality 1984, More of My Life 1984, Wittgenstein 1985, Voltaire 1986, Thomas Paine 1988; numerous articles in philosophical and literary journals. *Address:* 51 York Street, London, W.1, England. *Telephone:* 01-402 0235.

AYERS, Thomas G.; American business executive; b. 16 Feb. 1915, Detroit, Mich.; m. Mary Andrew; four s. one d.; ed. Univ. of Mich.; joined Public Service Co. of Northern Illinois (fmrly. a div. of Commonwealth Edison) 1938, Man. of Industrial Relations 1948; Asst. Vice-Pres. of Industrial Relations, Commonwealth Edison Co. 1952, Vice-Pres. 1953, Exec. Vice-Pres. 1962-64, Pres. 1964-73, Dir. 1965-, Chair., C.E.O. 1973-80, Pres. 1973-77; Dir. First Nat. Bank of Chicago, Gen. Dynamics Corpn., Zenith Radio Corpn.; Dir. and fmr. Pres. Chicago Asscn. of Commerce and Industry; Chair. Breeder Reactor Corpn.; Exec. Nat. Electric Reliability Council; Dir. Edison Electric Inst.; Trustee, North-western Univ.; Hon. LL.D. (Elmhurst Coll.). *Address:* 199 Montclair Avenue, Glen Ellyn, Ill. 60137, U.S.A. (Home).

AYGI, Gennadi Nikolaevich; Soviet poet; b. 1934, Shfimurzino, Chuvash S.S.R.; ed. Gorky Literary Inst., Moscow; started writing in Russian rather than Chuvash 1960-; worked in Mayakovsky Museum, Moscow 1961-71; trans. and writer 1971-. *Publications include:* Poetry 1954-71, Munich 1975; A Celebrated Winter, Paris 1982; Prix Paul Desfeuilles 1968 (for trans. of French poetry into Chuvash). *Address:* U.S.S.R. Union of Writers, 52 ul. Vorovskogo, Moscow, U.S.S.R.

AYLESTONE, Baron (Life Peer), cr. 1967, of Aylestone in the City of Leicester; **Herbert William Bowden,** P.C., C.H., C.B.E.; British politician and television executive; b. 20 Jan. 1905; m. Louisa G. Brown 1928; one d.; Pres. Leicester Labour Party 1938; M.P. 1945-67; Parl. Private Sec. to Postmaster-Gen. and Minister of Pensions 1946-47; Asst. Govt. Whip 1947-50, Deputy Opposition Whip 1950-55, Chief Opposition Whip 1955-64; Lord Pres. of the Council 1964-66; Leader House of Commons 1964-66; Sec. of State for Commonwealth Affairs 1966-67; Chair. Independent Broadcasting Authority (IBA) 1967-75; Leader Social Democratic Party, House of Lords 1981-83, Deputy Speaker; Gold Medal, Royal TV Soc. 1975. *Address:* House of Lords, London, SW1A 0AA, England.

AYLMER, Gerald Edward, D.PHIL., F.B.A.; British historian; b. 30 April 1926, near Ludlow, Shropshire; s. of E. A. Aylmer and G. P. Aylmer née Evans; m. Ursula Adelaide Nixon 1955; one s. one d.; ed. Winchester Coll. and Balliol Coll. Oxford; J. E. Procter Visiting Fellow, Princeton Univ., U.S.A. 1950-51; Jr. Research Fellow, Balliol Coll. 1951-54; Asst. Lecturer, Modern History Dept., Univ. of Manchester 1954-57, Lecturer 1957-62; Prof. of History and Head of Dept., Univ. of York 1963-78; Visiting mem. of Inst. for Advanced Study, Princeton 1975; Master of St. Peter's Coll. Oxford 1978-; Pres. Royal Historical Soc. 1984-88. *Publications:* The King's Servants 1961, The Struggle for the Constitution 1963 (U.S. edn.: A Short History of 17th Century England), The Interregnum (Ed.) 1972, The State's Servants 1973, A History of York Minster (Ed. with R. Cant) 1977, The Levellers in the English Revolution 1975, Rebellion or Revolution? England 1640-60 1986. *Address:* Canal House, St. Peter's College, Oxford, OX1 2DL, England. *Telephone:* (0865) 240554; (0865) 278862.

AYOOLA, Emmanuel Olayinka, B.A., LL.B.; Nigerian judge; b. 27 Oct. 1933, Ilesha; s. of Chief E.O. Ayoola and Chief Dorcas O. Ayoola; ed. Ilesha Grammar School, Univ. of London (external) and Lincoln Coll., Oxford; called to Bar, Lincoln's Inn, London 1958; enrolled as barrister and solicitor, Supreme Court of Nigeria 1959; legal practice, Ayoola & Co. 1959-76; Judge, High Court of Oyo State of Nigeria 1976; Judge, The Gambia Court of Appeal 1980; Chief Justice of the Gambia 1983-. *Leisure interests:* music, gardening, walking. *Address:* Chief Justice's Chambers, Supreme Court, Banjul (Office); 36 Atlantic Road, Fajara, The Gambia (Home). *Telephone:* 27380 (Office); 95347 (Home).

AYYOUBI, Mahmoud Ben Saleh al-; Syrian politician; b. 1932; fmr. Dir.-Gen. for Admin. Affairs, Euphrates Dept.; Minister of Educ. 1969-71; Deputy Premier 1970-71; Vice-Pres. 1971-75; Prime Minister 1972-76; mem. Baath Party Regional Command 1971-75, Jan. 1980-. *Address:* c/o Office of the Prime Minister, Damascus, Syria.

AZARNOFF, Daniel L(ester), M.S., M.D.; American physician and business executive; b. 4 Aug. 1926, Brooklyn, New York; s. of Samuel J. and Kate (Asarnow) Azarnoff; m. Joanne Stokes 1951; two s. one d.; ed. Rutgers Univ. and Univ. of Kansas; Instructor in Anatomy, Univ. of Kansas 1949-50, Research Fellow 1950-52, Intern 1955-56, Nat. Heart Inst. Resident Research Fellow 1956-58, Asst. Prof. of Medicine 1962-64, Assoc. Prof. 1964-68, Dir. Clinical Pharmacology Study Unit 1964-68, Assoc. Prof. of Pharmacology 1965-68, Prof. of Medicine and Pharmacology 1968, Dir. Clinical Pharmacology-Toxicology Center 1967-68, Distinguished Prof.

1973-78; Asst. Prof. of Medicine St. Louis Univ. 1960-62; Visiting Scientist, Fulbright Scholar, Karolinska Inst., Stockholm, Sweden 1968; Sr. Vice-Pres. Worldwide Research and Devt., G. D. Searle & Co., Chicago 1978, Pres. Searle Research and Devt., Skokie, Ill. 1979-85; Pres. D. L. Azarnoff Assocs., Inc. 1986-; Prof. of Pathology and Clinical Prof. of Pharmacology, Northwestern Univ. 1978-85; Chair. Cttee. on Problems of Drug Safety, N.A.S. 1972-76; Consultant to numerous govt. agencies; mem. Nat. Comm. on Orphan Diseases, Dept. of Health and Human Services; Ed. Review of Drug Interactions 1974-77, Yearbook of Drug Therapy 1977-79; Series Ed. Monographs in Clinical Pharmacology 1977-; Fellow, American Coll. of Physicians, New York Acad. of Scientists; mem. American Soc. of Clinical Nutrition, American Nutrition Inst., American Fed. of Clinical Research, British Pharmacological Soc. American Medical Asscn., Royal Soc. for the Promotion of Health, Inst. of Medicine (N.A.S.) and others; Ciba Award for gerontological research 1958, Rector's Medal (Univ. of Helsinki) 1968, Burroughs Wellcome Scholar 1964. *Address:* 400 Oyster Point Boulevard, Suite 325, 80 San Francisco, Calif. 94080, U.S.A. (Office); 210 Robin Road, Hillsborough, Calif. 94010, U.S.A. (Home). *Telephone:* (415) 588-9187 (Office); (415) 340-9048 (Home).

AZCONA DEL HOYO, José; Honduran engineer and politician; b. 26 Jan. 1927, La Ceiba; s. of José Simón Azcona Velez and Carmen Hoyo Perez de Azcona; m. Miriam Bocock Selva; two s. one d.; ed. Universidad Nacional Autónoma de Honduras and Instituto Tecnológico de Estudios Superiores de Monterrey, Mexico; civil engineer, with special interest in low-cost housing, planning and urban devt.; Gen. Man. Federación Hondureña de Cooperativas de Vivienda Limitada 1973-82; started political activities when a student; Liberal cand. in 1963 gen. elections (interrupted by coup d'état); apptd. Sec. for Org. and Propaganda, Movimiento Liberal Rodista 1975; mem. Exec. Council 1977-, Sec. Gen. 1981-; Deputy to Congreso Nacional 1982-86; Minister of Communications, Public Works and Transport 1982-83; fmr. Pres. Liberal Party Cen. Exec. Council; Pres. of Honduras Nov. 1985-. *Address:* Casa Presidencial, 6a Avda, 1a Calle, Tegucigalpa, Honduras.

AZEREDO DA SILVEIRA, Antônio Francisco; Brazilian diplomatist; b. 22 Sept. 1917, Rio de Janeiro; s. of Flavio and Lea Maria Azeredo da Silveira; m. May Paranhos Azeredo da Silveira 1943; four c.; ed. Instituto Rio-Branco; joined foreign service 1945, served in Havana, Buenos Aires, Florence, Madrid and Rome, Consul-Gen. Paris 1961-63; Perm. Rep. to Office of UN at Geneva 1966-68; Amb. to Argentina 1968-74; Minister of Foreign Relations 1974-79; Amb. to U.S.A. 1979-83; del. to several confs. of OAS, GATT and UNCTAD, ICEM etc.; decorations from Fed. Repub. of Germany, Italy, Ecuador, Peru, Chile, Netherlands, Austria, Spain and Malta. *Address:* Avenida Vieira Souto, 408-apto, 401, Rio de Janeiro, RJ, Brazil (Home).

AZEVEDO, Carlos de, M.A., F.R.S.A.; Portuguese museum administrator; b. 1918, Lisbon; s. of António Martins de Azevedo and Delfina M. de Azevedo; m. Maria Teresa Falcão 1940; three s.; ed. Lisbon Univ.; Lecturer in Portuguese, Oxford Univ. 1945-47; Visiting Lecturer in Art History, Miami Univ., Oxford, Ohio 1976-83; at Lisbon Museum of Ancient Art 1948-50; carried out official survey of Portuguese monuments in India 1951; Curator, Lisbon Museum of Contemporary Art 1955-60; Exec. Sec. Fulbright Comm. in Portugal 1960-73; Head Div. of Foreign Cultural Relations, Ministry of Educ. 1973-74, Dir. Internal Cultural Relations 1974-; rep. of The Connoisseur in Portugal 1954-76; Lecturer in Art History, Miami Univ., Ohio 1976-83; Sec. Portuguese Cttee. Int. Council of Museums (ICOM) 1967-74; Corresp. mem. Lisbon Nat. Acad. of Fine Arts. *Publications:* Portuguese Country Houses, Churches of Portugal, two books on Portuguese colonial architecture, one on old Portuguese organ-cases, various studies and articles. *Leisure interests:* old organs, playing the harpsichord. *Address:* Rua Custódio Vieira, 2-3°-Dt°., 1200 Lisbon, Portugal. *Telephone:* 68-34-25.

AZIKIWE, Rt. Hon. Nnamdi, P.C., M.A., M.SC., LL.D., D.LITT. (Ndichie Chief Owelle of Onitsha); Nigerian politician (retd.); b. 16 Nov. 1904, Zungeru; s. of Obed Edom Chukwuemeka and Rachel Ogbenyeanu Azikiwe; three s. one d.; ed. Lincoln and Pennsylvania Univs.; fmr. Instructor in History and Political Science Lincoln Univ., Pa.; fmr. Gov. Dir. African Continental Bank Ltd.; fmr. Chair. Associated Newspapers of Nigeria Ltd., African Book Co. Ltd.; Pres. Nat. Council of Nigeria and the Cameroons 1946-60; Vice-Pres. Nigerian Nat. Democratic Party; elected mem. of Legislative Council of Nigeria 1947-51; mem. Brooke Arbitration Tribunal 1944, Nigerianisation Comm. 1948, MacDonald Arbitration Tribunal 1948; mem. Western House of Assembly 1952-53, Eastern House 1954-59; fmr. Minister of Local Govt., Eastern Region, and Minister of Internal Affairs 1955-57; Premier, Eastern Nigeria 1954-59; Pres. Fed. Senate 1960; Gov.-Gen. and C.-in-C. Fed. of Nigeria 1960-63, President of Nigeria 1963-66; Leader Nigeria People's Party (NPP) 1979- (political parties banned 1984); NPP candidate in Presidential election, August 1979; retd. from politics 1986; Fellow, Inst. of Journalists 1961-; Chancellor and Chair. Council of the Univ. of Nigeria 1961-66; Joint Pres. Anti-Slavery Soc. for Human Rights 1970-; Chancellor, Univ. of Lagos 1972-76. *Publications:* Liberia in World Politics 1934, Renascent Africa 1937, The African in Ancient and Medieval History 1938, Land Tenure in Northern Nigeria 1942, Political Blueprint of Nigeria 1943, Economic Reconstruction of Nigeria 1943, Economic

Rehabilitation of Eastern Nigeria 1955, Zik: a Selection of Speeches 1961, Military Revolution in Nigeria 1972, Meditations: A Collection of Poems 1965, Dialogue on a New Capital for Nigeria 1974. *Leisure interests:* walking, swimming, research in my private library. *Address:* Onuiyi Haven, P.O. Box 7, Nsukka, Nigeria.

AZIMOV, Sarvar Alimadjanovich, DR.PHIL.SC.; Soviet philologist and diplomatist; b. 20 May 1923, Djizak Village, Uzbekistan; ed. Middle Asian State Univ.; First Sec. Bd. of Uzbek Writers' Union 1956-57; Minister of Culture, Uzbek S.S.R. 1957-59; Deputy Chair. Council of Ministers, and Minister of Foreign Affairs, Uzbek S.S.R. 1959-69; Amb. to Lebanon 1969-74, to Pakistan 1974-80. *Publications:* many works on Middle Asian and Near Eastern Literature problems. *Address:* c/o Ministry of Foreign Affairs, Moscow, U.S.S.R.

AZIZ, Datin Paduka Rafidah, M.ECONS.; Malaysian politician; b. 4 Nov. 1943, Selama Perak; m. Mohammed Basir bin Ahmad; three c.; ed. Univ. of Malaya; tutor, Asst. Lecturer, Lecturer and Chair. Rural Devt. Div. Faculty of Econs. Univ. of Malaya 1966-76; mem. Parl. 1978-; Deputy Minister of Finance 1977-80; Minister of Public Enterprise 1980-88, of Trade and Industry March 1988-; mem. UMNO Supreme Council 1975-; holder of many other public appts. and del. to numerous int. confs.; Ahli Mangku Negara, Datuk Paduka Mahkota Selangor. *Leisure interests:* reading, decoration, music, squash. *Address:* Ministry of Trade and Industry, Block 10, Government Offices Complex, Jalan Duta, 50622 Kuala Lumpur, Malaysia.

AZIZ, Ungku Abdul, D.ECONS.; Malaysian professor and university administrator; b. 28 Jan. 1922, London, U.K.; m. Sharifah Azah Aziz; one d.; ed. Raffles Coll. and Univ. of Malaya in Singapore, Waseda Univ., Tokyo, Johore State Civil Service; Lecturer in Econs., Univ. of Malaya in Singapore till 1952; Head, Dept. of Econs., Univ. of Malaya, Kuala Lumpur 1952-61, Dean of Faculty 1961-65, Vice-Chancellor 1968-88, Royal Prof. of Econs. 1978-; Pres. Nat. Co-operative Movement (ANGKASA) 1971, Asscn. of S.E. Asian Institutions of Higher Learning (ASAIHL) 1973-75; Chair. Asscn. of Commonwealth Univs. 1974-75, Malaysian Nat. Council for ASAIHL, Malaysian Examinations Council 1980-; mem. United Nations Univ. Council; Corresp. mem. of Advisory Bd., Modern Asian Studies 1973-75; mem. Econ. Asscn. of Malaysia, Int. Asscn. of Agricultural Economists, Joint Advisory Cttee. of FAO, UNESCO and ILO; mem. Nat. Consultative Council and Nat. Unity Advisory Council, Govt. of Malaysia; Fellow, World Acad. of Arts and Sciences 1965-; Tun Abdul Razak Foundation Award 1978, Japan Foundation Award 1981; Ordre des Arts et des Lettres (France) 1965; Hon. D.Hum.Litt. (Univ. of Pittsburgh); Hon. Ed. D. (Chulalongkorn Univ.) Thailand 1977; Hon. D.Jur. (Waseda Univ.) Japan 1982; Hon. LL.D. (Buckingham) 1987. *Leisure interests:* jogging, reading and photography. *Address:* Chancellery, University of Malaya, Kuala Lumpur 22-11 Malaysia. *Telephone:* Kuala Lumpur 568400.

AZKOUL, Karim, PH.D.; Lebanese diplomatist and writer; b. 15 July 1915, Rachaya; s. of Najeeb Azkoul and Latifah Assaly; m. Eva Corey 1947; one s. one d.; ed. Jesuit Univ. of St. Joseph, Beirut, and Univs. of Paris, Berlin, Bonn and Munich. Prof. of History, Arab and French Literature, and Philosophy in various colls. in Lebanon 1939-46; Dir. of an Arabic publishing house and monthly Arabic review The Arab World, Beirut 1943-45; mem. Lebanese Del. to UN, New York 1947-50, Acting Perm. Del. to UN 1950-53; Head of UN Affairs Dept., Ministry of Foreign Affairs 1953-57; Head, Perm. Del. to UN 1957-59, Rapporteur Cttee. on Genocide 1948, Humanitarian, Cultural and Social Cttee. of Gen. Ass. 1951, Cttee. on Freedom of Information 1951; First Vice-Chair. Human Rights Comm. 1958; Chair. Negotiating Cttee. for Extra Budgetary Funds 1952-54; Consul-Gen. in Australia and New Zealand 1959-61; Amb. to Ghana, Guinea

and Mali 1961-64, to Iran and Afghanistan 1964-66; Journalist 1966-68; Prof. of Philosophy, Beirut Coll. for Women 1968-72, Lebanese Univ. 1970-72; Chief Ed. The Joy of Knowledge, Arabic Encyclopedia (10 vols.) 1978-; mem. PEN, Emergency World Council, Hague 1971-; mem. Bd. of Trustees, Bd. of Management of Theological School of Balamand, Lebanon, Cttee. for Defence of Human Rights in Lebanon; Order of Cedar (Lebanon), Order of Holy Sepulchre (Jerusalem), Order of St. Marc (Alexandria), Order of the Brilliant Star (Republic of China), Order of Southern Star (Brazil), Order of St. Peter and Paul (Damascus). *Publications:* Reason and Faith in Islam (in German) 1938, Reason in Islam (in Arabic) 1946, Freedom (co-author) 1956, Freedom of Association (UN) 1968; trans. into Arabic Consciencism (Nkrumah) 1964; Arab Thought in the Liberal Age (Albert Hourani) 1969. *Leisure interests:* reading and writing. *Address:* 6 rue René Blanc, 74100 Annemasse, France. *Telephone:* 50 92 6467.

AZNAVOURIAN, Varenagh (pseudonym Charles Aznavour); French singer and film star; b. 22 May 1924; ed. Ecole centrale de T.S.F., Centre de spectacle, Paris; with Jean Dasté Company 1941; with Pierre Roche in Les fâcheux and Arlequin 1944; numerous song recitals in Europe and U.S.A.; Chevalier Légion d'honneur, des Arts et des Lettres; several prizes. *Films include:* La tête contre les murs 1959, Ne tirez pas sur le pianiste 1960, Un taxi pour Tobrouk, Le testament d'Orphée, Le diable et les dix commandements, Haute-infidélité 1964, La métamorphose des cloportes 1965, Paris au mois d'août 1966, Le facteur s'en va-t-en guerre 1966, Le diable par le queue 1968, Candy 1969, Les intrus 1973, Sky Riders, Intervention Delta, Folies bourgeoises, Dix petits nègres 1976, The Twist 1976, The Tin Drum 1979, Qu'est-ce qui a fait courir David? 1982, Les fantômes du chapelier 1982, La montagne magique 1983, Vive la vie 1984. Film music includes: Soupe au lait, L'île du bout du monde, Ces dames préfèrent le mambo, Le cercle vicieux, De quoi tu te mêles Daniela, Douce violence, Les Parisiennes; also author and singer of numerous songs; composer of operetta Monsieur Carnaval 1965. *Leisure interests:* photography, do-it-yourself. *Address:* 12 rue de Penthièvre, 75008 Paris (Office); 4 avenue du Lieutel, Galluis, 78490 Montfort l'Amaury, France (Home).

AZUELA, Arturo; Mexican writer; b. 1938; fmr. mathematician and violinist in various symphony orchestras; published first novel 1973; mem. Academia Mexicana de la Lengua 1986-. *Publications:* El tamaño del infierno, La casa de las 1,000 vírgenes, Manifestacion de silencios. *Address:* c/o Academia Mexicana de la Lengua, Donceles 66, 06010 México, D.F. Mexico.

AZUMA, Hiroshi, PH.D.; Japanese professor of education; b. 3 Feb. 1926, Tokyo; s. of Toshiro and Setsuko Azuma; m. Yasuko Azuma 1950; one s. one d.; ed. First High School of Japan, Univ. of Tokyo, Univ. of Illinois; Instructor in Psychology and Educational Psychology 1951-57; Research Assoc., Bureau of Educational Research, Univ. of Ill. 1960-62; Assoc. Prof. of Child Study, Japan Women's Univ. 1962-65; fmr. Prof. Faculty of Educ., Univ. of Tokyo; fmr. Prof. of Educational Psychology and Methods of Instruction, and fmr. Dean of Faculty of Educ., Univ. of Tokyo. *Leisure interest:* travelling. *Address:* 3-13-2, Tamagawa Gakuen, Machida-shi, Tokyo, Japan 194.

AZZATO, Louis E., B.S.; American business executive; b. 8 Oct. 1930, New York; s. of John Azzato and Margaret Ronca; m. Margaret J. McCarthy 1955; one s. three d.; ed. City Coll. of New York; with Foster Wheeler Corpn. 1952-74, 1978-; Vice-Pres. Foster Wheeler Italiana, Milan 1967-74; Chair. and C.E.O. Glitsch Inc., Dallas 1974-78; Sr. Vice-Pres. Foster Wheeler Corpn. 1978-80, Exec. Vice-Pres. 1980-81; Pres. and C.E.O. Foster Wheeler Italiana 1981-; Dir. First Fidelity Bancorp., N.J. *Address:* 22 Lord William Penn Drive, Morristown, N.J. 07960, U.S.A.

B

BA, Babacar, L. ÈS SC.; Senegalese politician; b. 14 June 1930, Kaolack; ed. Univ. of Dakar; Gov. Oriental Province 1960-61; Principal Private Sec. to the Presidency 1961-62, 1968-70; District Commr. 1963-66; Counsellor in charge of EEC affairs, Embassy in Brussels 1966-68; Principal Private Sec. to Minister of Foreign Affairs 1968; Sec.-Gen. at the Presidency 1970-71; Minister of State of Finance and Econ. Affairs 1971-78, of Foreign Affairs March-Sept. 1978; Sec. for Int. Relations Feb.-Sept. 1978; Pres. Advisory Bd. Kaolack 1978-; fmr. Pres. Banque Centrale des Etats de l'Afrique de l'Ouest. *Address:* Conseil municipal, Kaolack, Senegal.

BA JIN (LI YAOTANG); Chinese writer and journalist; b. 25 Nov. 1904, Chengdu, Sichuan Prov.; m. Xiao Shan 1944 (died 1972); one s. one d.; ed. Foreign Language School, Chengdu; studied in France and adopted name Ba Jin (taken from first syllable of Bakunin and the last of Kropotkin) 1926; Ed. fortnightly provincial Ban Yue 1928; writer and translator, Shanghai 1929; visited Japan 1934; Chief Ed. Shanghai Cultural Life Publishing House 1935; joined Lu Xun's China Literary Work Soc. 1936; Co-Ed. (with Mao Dun) Shouting Weekly and Bonfire Weekly 1937; Vice-Chair. Union of Chinese Writers 1953 (now Chair.); Deputy to NPC 1954; Chief. Ed. People's Literature 1957-58; Vice-Chair. China Fed. of Literary and Art Circles 1960; Chief Ed. Shanghai Literature 1961; in disgrace 1968-77; Vice-Chair. 5th Municipal CPPCC Cttee., Shanghai 1977-; mem. Presidium 6th Nat. CPPCC Cttee. 1983-; Exec. Council, China Welfare Inst. 1978-; Vice-Chair. China Fed. of Literary and Art Circles 1978-; Pres. China PEN Centre 1980-, Nat. Literary Foundation 1986-; Hon. Pres. Fiction Soc. 1984-; Hon. Chair. China Shakespeare Research Foundation 1984-; Hon. mem. A.A.A.S. 1985. *Publications include:* Extinction 1928, The Family 1931, Trilogy of Love 1932-33, The History of the Nihilist Movement 1936, Spring 1937, Autumn 1940, Festival Day of Warsaw 1950, Living Among Heroes 1953, Three Comrades 1962, Essays by the Sickbed 1984. *Address:* c/o China PEN, Shatan Beijie 2, Beijing, People's Republic of China.

BABA, Encik Abdul Ghafar Bin; Malaysian politician; b. 18 Feb. 1925, Kuala Pilah, Negeri Sembilan; ed. Sultan Idris Teachers' Training Coll., Tanjong Malim; school teacher 1944-55; mem. Fed. Legis. Council 1955; Chief Minister of Malacca 1955-67; Chair. MARA 1967; Senator and Minister without Portfolio 1967; Minister of Nat. and Rural Devt. 1969-74; Minister of Agric. and Rural Devt. 1974; Chair. Kompleks Kewangan Bd., Pegi Malaysia Bhd., Dunlop Estates Bhd. 1976-86; Deputy Prime Minister and Minister of Nat. and Rural Devt. May 1986-, Acting Prime Minister Jan. 1989-; Vice-Pres. UMNO 1974. *Leisure interest:* golf. *Address:* Ministry of National and Rural Development, 1st Floor, Bangunan Bank Rakyat, Jalan Tangsi, Kuala Lumpur, Malaysia.

BABA, Corneliu; Romanian artist; b. 18 Nov. 1906, Craiova; ed. Bucharest Univ. and Inst. of Fine Arts, Iaşi; Prof. Inst. of Fine Arts, Iaşi, and N. Grigorescu Inst. of Fine Arts, Bucharest; First exhbn. 1941; numerous official exhbns. in Romania, Moscow, Venice, Vienna, Prague, Warsaw, Rome, Sofia, etc. 1944-; one-man exhbns. Brussels 1964, Berlin 1964, New York 1970; Vice-Pres. Romanian Nat. Peace Cttee.; Hon. mem. U.S.S.R. Acad. of Art 1958-; Corresp. mem. Acad. Socialist Republic of Romania 1963-; mem. Acad. of Arts, Berlin 1964-; People's Artist 1962. *Major works:* Odihna la Cîmp (Resting in the Fields) 1954, Ţăranii (Peasants) 1958, Oţelari (Steelworkers) 1960, portraits of M. Sadoveanu, Lucia Sturdza Bulandra, Tudor Arghezi, and book illustrations. *Address:* Uniunea Artiştilor Plastici, Str. Nicolae Iorga 42, Bucharest, Romania. *Telephone:* 50.73.80.

BABADZHAN, Ramz (b. Babadzhanov, Ramz Nasyrovich); Soviet author, b, 1921, Uzbekistan; ed. Pedagogical Inst., Tashkent; Deputy Chair. Uzbek Writers' Union; mem. CPSU 1951-; Chair. Uzbek Republican Cttee. on Relations with African and Asian Writers; first works published 1935; U.S.S.R. State Prize 1972. *Publications include:* Dear Friends, Thank You, My Dear, The Heart Never Sleeps, Selected Poetry, A Poet Lives Twice, Living Water; over 20 works in Uzbek and 5 in Russian. *Address:* Uzbek Writers' Union, Tashkent, U.S.S.R.

BABANGIDA, Maj.-Gen. Ibrahim; Nigerian army officer and Head of State; ed. Niger provincial secondary school, Bida, Kaduna Mil. Training Coll. and Indian Mil. Acad.; commissioned 1963, Lieut. 1966; training with R.A.C., U.K. 1966; C.O. during Biafran civil war; Co Commdr. and Instructor, Nigerian Defence Acad. 1970-72; rank of Maj. then Lieut.-Col Armoured Corps 1974; trained at U.S. Army Armoury School 1974; promoted to Maj.-Gen., Dir. of Army Duties and Plans 1983; took part in overthrow of Pres. Shehu Shagari 1983; mem. Supreme Mil. Council and Chief Army Staff 1983-85; Pres. of Nigeria following coup overthrowing Maj.-Gen. Muhammadu Buhari (q.v.) Aug. 1985; Pres. Police Council 1989-. *Address:* Office of the President, Lagos, Nigeria.

BABAYEV, Agadzhan Geldevich, DR. GEOG. SC.; Soviet geographer; b. 1929, Turkmenistan; s. of Geldy Babayev and Ogulbek Babayev; m. Dunyagozel Babayeva 1951; two s. six d.; ed. State Pedagogical Inst., Ashkhabad; mem. CPSU 1954-; Dir. Inst. of Sand Areas Devt. and Pedology 1959-62; Prof., Inst. for Desert Research, Acad. of Sciences of Turkmen S.S.R. 1959-, Dir. 1962-75, 1981-; mem. Acad. of Sciences, Turkmen S.S.R. 1976-, then Pres.; Corresp. mem. Acad. of Sciences of the U.S.S.R. 1976-; Chair. Turkmen Geographical Soc. 1959-86; Chief Ed. journal Problems of Desert Devt. 1967-; author of over 200 scientific papers on problems of developing deserts in U.S.S.R. *Address:* Desert Institute, 15 Gogol Street, Ashkhabad, 744000 Turkmen S.S.R.; Academy of Sciences, Ul. Gogolya 15, Ashkhabad, Turkmen S.S.R., U.S.S.R.

BABAYEVSKY, Semyon Petrovich; Soviet writer; b. 6 June 1909, Kunye village, Kharkov Region, Ukraine; m. 1929; two s.; ed. Moscow Literary Inst.; mem. CPSU 1939-; war corresp. 1941-45; Deputy to Supreme Soviet of U.S.S.R. 1950-58; mem. Bd. U.S.S.R. Union of Writers'; State Prizewinner 1948, 1949, 1950; Order of Red Banner of Labour 1959, 1969. *Publications:* Novels: Cavalier of the Golden Star, Geese Island 1947, Light over the Earth 1949, Well-Spring Grove 1956, White Mosque, Sukhaya Buivola 1958, Along Paths and Roads 1958, Son's Mutiny 1961, Native Land, The Whole World, Native Country 1969, Selected Works (2 vols.) 1971, Contemporaries 1972, 1974; On Verbor Farm, Stories 1973, Stanitsa 1976, Privolje 1978, Selected Works (5 vols.) 1979-80, How to Live 1984. *Address:* 27 Ulitsa Krasnoarmeiskaya kv. 87, Moscow 125319, U.S.S.R.

BABB, Albert Leslie, PH.D.; American (b. Canadian) biomedical engineer; b. 7 Nov. 1925, Vancouver; s. of Clarence Stanley and Mildred (Gutteridge) Babb; m. Marion A. McDougall; two s. one d.; ed. Univ. of British Columbia, Canada and Univ. of Illinois, U.S.A.; Chemical Engineer, Nat. Research Council of Canada 1948; Research Engineer, Rayonier Inc. 1951-52; mem. Faculty, Univ. of Wash., Seattle 1952-, Chair. Nuclear Eng. Group 1957-65, Prof. of Chemical Eng. 1960-, Dir. of Nuclear Reactor Labs. 1962-72, Prof. of Nuclear Eng. 1965-, Chair. Dept. of Nuclear Eng. 1965-81, Acting Chair. 1984-, Acting Chair. of Chemical Eng. 1985, Prof. of Bioengineering 1985-; Visiting Lecturer in many countries; Fellow, American Inst. of Chemists; mem. American Nuclear Soc., American Chemical Soc., American Inst. of Chemical Engineers, Engineers' Jt. Council, Nat. Acad. of Eng., American Nephrology Soc., American Soc. for Artificial Internal Organs, Int. Soc. for Artificial Organs, European Dialysis and Transplantation Asscn., Inst. of Medicine, N.A.S.; co-inventor of artificial kidney systems, techniques for early diagnosis of cystic fibrosis using a nuclear reactor, extracorporeal system for treatment of sickle cell anaemia, computerized wearable insulin pump for diabetics; Nat. Kidney Foundation Pioneer Award 1982 and other awards. *Address:* 3237 Lakewood Avenue South, Seattle, Wash. 98144; c/o College of Engineering, University of Washington, Seattle, Washington 98195, U.S.A.

BABBITT, Milton Byron, D.MUS., M.F.A.; American composer; b. 10 May 1916, Philadelphia; s. of Albert E. Babbitt and Sarah Potamkin; m. Sylvia Miller 1939; one d.; ed. New York and Princeton Univs.; Music Faculty, Princeton Univ. 1938-, Math. Faculty 1943-45, Bicentennial Preceptor 1953-56, Prof. of Music 1966-84, Prof. Emer. 1984-; Dir. Columbia-Princeton Electronic Music Center; Nat. Inst. Arts and Letters Award 1959; Guggenheim Fellow 1960-61; MacArthur Fellow 1986-91; Hon. D. Mus. (Glasgow); Gold Medal, Brandeis Univ. 1970; Pulitzer Prize 1982; mem. American Acad. of Arts and Sciences and Nat. Inst. of Arts and Letters. *Works include:* Music for the Mass 1940, Composition for Four Instruments 1948, Woodwind Quartet 1953, All Set 1957, Vision and Prayer 1961, Philomel 1964, Tableaux 1972, Reflections 1975, Solo Requiem 1977, Paraphrases 1979, Ars Combinatoria 1981, Melismata 1982, Canonic Form 1983, Transfigured Noted 1986, The Joy of More Sextets 1986, Whirled Series 1987. *Publication:* The Function of Set Structure in the Twelve Tone System 1946. *Leisure interest:* philosophy. *Address:* 222 Western Way, Princeton, N.J. 08540, U.S.A. *Telephone:* (609) 921-9548.

BABCOCK, Horace W., PH.D.; American astronomer; b. 13 Sept. 1912, Pasadena, Calif.; s. of Harold D. Babcock and Mary G. (Henderson); m. 1st M. B. Anderson 1940, one s. one d.; m. 2nd Elizabeth M. Aubrey 1958; one s.; ed. California Inst. of Tech. and Univ. of California; Instructor, Yerkes and McDonald Observatories 1939-41; Staff mem. Radiation Lab., Mass. Inst. of Tech. 1941-42; Staff mem. Rocket Project, Calif. Inst. of Tech. 1942-45; Staff mem. Mount Wilson and Palomar Observatories 1946-, Asst. Dir. 1957-64, Dir. 1964-78; mem. N.A.S. (Draper Medal 1957), Council mem. 1973-76; founding Dir. Las Campanas Observatory (Chile) of Carnegie Inst. of Washington; mem. American Philosophical Soc., American Acad. of Arts and Sciences; Assoc. Royal Astronomical Soc.; Hon. Sc.D. (Newcastle) 1965; Eddington Medal, Royal Astronomical Soc. 1957, Gold Medal 1970; Bruce Medal, Astronomical Soc. of Pacific; U.S. Navy Bureau of Ordnance Devt. Award. *Publications:* Articles in scientific and technical journals, mainly on magnetic fields of the sun and stars, theory of the sun's magnetic field, rotation and mass distribution of the spiral galaxy in Andromeda, ruling of diffraction gratings, astronomical instrumentation, observatory devt. in southern hemisphere. *Address:* Mount Wilson and

Las Campanas Observatories, 813 Santa Barbara Street, Pasadena, Calif. 91101 (Office); 2189 N. Altadena Drive, Altadena, Calif. 91001, U.S.A. (Home). *Telephone:* 213-577-1122 (Office).

BABENKO, Alexander Alexandrovich; Soviet politician; b. 1935; ed. as constructional engineer; worked in construction, to head of combine; mem. CPSU 1961–; First Deputy Minister of Construction of Heavy Industry Enterprises of U.S.S.R. 1977; Minister of Construction in Areas of the Far East and Trans-Baikal of U.S.S.R.; Prize, U.S.S.R. Council of Ministers. *Address:* Council of Ministers, The Kremlin, Moscow, U.S.S.R.

BABENKO, Hector; Argentinian film director; b. 7 Feb. 1946, Buenos Aires; eight years in Europe as writer, house painter, door to door salesman, film extra etc. *Films:* Rei Da Nolte 1976, Lucio Flavio—Passageiro Da Agonia 1978, Pixote 1980, Kiss of the Spider Woman 1985, Ironweed 1987. Best Foreign Film Award for Pixote (New York Film Critics). *Address:* São Paulo, Brazil.

BABICS, Antal, DR. MED.; Hungarian surgeon and urologist; b. 4 Aug. 1902, Lovászpatona; s. of Endre Babics and Róza Moór; m. Ilona Esterházy 1940; Lecturer, Urological Clinic, Budapest Medical Univ. 1940, Prof. and Dir. of Clinic 1945–74; Corresp. mem. Hungarian Acad. of Sciences 1949–50, full mem. 1950–, Sec. Medical Dept., Hungarian Acad. of Sciences; mem. Presidium Int. Urological Soc.; Hon. mem. Soviet Soc. of Surgeons, Urological Socs. of Italy, Germany, Austria and Romania, Purkinje Soc. of Czechoslovakia, Soviet Medical Acad.; Kossuth Prize 1951; Labour Order of Merit, golden degree 1951, 1955, 1970, Banner Order of Hungarian Repub., Trade Union Gold Medals 1962, 1972, 1974, 1977; Patriotic People's Front award of merit 1975, Banner Order of Hungarian Repub. (decorated with rubies) 1982. *Publications include:* Urology 1952, 1972, The Theory and Clinical Aspects of Kidney Necrosis 1952, The Lymphatic System of the Kidney 1957, Haematurie 1959, Clinical and Theoretical Pictures of some Renal Diseases 1964, Early Diagnosis of Cancer in the Urological System 1971, Anuria: The Therapeutic Experiences 1972, Intraoperative Diagnosis of Misleading Cases in Urology 1977. *Leisure interests:* angling, walking, dogs, natural science books. *Address:* H-1026 Budapest II, Pór Bertalan utca 5, Hungary. *Telephone:* 559-981 (Home).

BABIKIAN, Khatchik Diran; Lebanese lawyer and politician; b. 1924, Cyprus; m. 1956; five d.; ed. Collège Italien, Beirut, Faculté Française de Droit, Beirut, Faculté de Paris, Univ. of London; Barrister; Deputy for Beirut 1957, 1960, 1964, 1968, 1972; mem. Parl. Comm. on Justice; Pres. Traffic Comm., Parl. Comm. on Planning, Lebanese Management Asscn. 1972; Minister for Admin. Reform 1960–61; Minister of Public Health 1968–69; Minister of Tourism 1969–70, of Information 1972–73, of Planning 1973, of Justice 1980–81, 1982; Pres. Armenian Nat. Assembly 1972, 1976; Vice-Pres. World Asscn. of French-Speaking Parliamentarians 1982–; Dir. Banque du Crédit Populaire SAL; Officier Légion d'honneur 1986. *Address:* Place de l'Etoile, Beirut (Office); Rue Abrine, Achrafié, Beirut, Lebanon (Home). *Telephone:* 335773 (Office); 322013 (Home).

BABIUCH, Edward, M.ECON.; Polish politician (retd.); b. 28 Dec. 1927, Grabocin, Będzin District, Katowice Voivodship; ed. Silesian Technical Scientific Establishment Main School of Planning and Statistics, Warsaw and Central Party School, Warsaw; mem. Polish United Workers' Party (PZPR) 1948–81 (expelled); functions in Voivodship Bd., Katowice 1949 and subsequently in Cen. Bd. of Polish Youth Union: worked at Cen. Cttee. of PZPR 1955–59; Sec. PZPR Warsaw Voivodship Cttee. 1959–63; Deputy Head, Organization Dept., Cen. Cttee. 1963–65, Head 1965–70; Ed.-in-Chief, Życie Partii 1963–65; Deputy to Seym 1969–80; mem. Cen. Cttee. PZPR 1964–80, mem. Politburo 1970–80; Sec. Cen. Cttee. 1970–80; Chair. Seym Comm. of Nat. Defence 1971–72, PZPR Deputies to Seym Club 1972–80; mem. Presidium, All-Polish Cttee. of Nat. Unity Front 1971; mem. State Council 1972–80, Deputy Chair. 1976–80; Chair. Council of Ministers Feb.–Aug. 1980; interned 1981–82; Order of Banner of Labour (1st and 2nd Class), Officer's and Knight's Cross of Order of Polonia Restituta, Order of Yugoslav Star with Ribbon 1973, Medal of 30th Anniversary of People's Poland, Order of Builders of People's Poland 1977, and numerous foreign awards.

BACALL, Lauren (Betty Joan Perske); American actress; b. 16 Sept. 1924; m. 1st Humphrey Bogart 1945 (died 1957), 2nd Jason Robards 1961 (divorced); two s. one d. *Films include:* To Have and Have Not, The Big Sleep, Confidential Agent, Dark Passage, Key Largo, Young Man with a Horn, Bright Leaf, How to Marry a Millionaire, Woman's World, The Cobweb, Blood Alley, Written on the Wind, Designing Woman, The Gift of Love, Flame over India, Sex and the Single Girl, Harper, Murder on the Orient Express 1974, The Shootist 1976, Health 1980, The Fan 1981, Appointment with Death 1988, Mr North 1988, Tree of Hands 1989; plays: Goodbye Charlie 1960, Cactus Flower 1966, Applause 1970 (Tony Award, Best Actress in a Musical 1970) (London 1972), Woman of the Year 1981 (Tony Award 1981), Sweet Bird of Youth (London) 1985. *Publications:* Lauren Bacall By Myself 1978. *Address:* c/o Johnnie Planco William Morris Agency, 1350 Avenue of the Americas, New York, N.Y. 10019; Dakota, Central Park West, New York, U.S.A. (Home).

BACCHETTI, Fausto, LL.D.; Italian diplomatist; b. 12 May 1917, Chieti; s. of Tito and Teresa (née Vescovali) Bacchetti; m. Amata Martorelli 1950; one d.; ed. Univ. of Rome; Private Secretary to Deputy Prime Minister 1944–46; entered Foreign Service 1948, served in Embassy, London 1951–56, del. to NATO 1952–64, Embassy, Paris 1964–65; Dir. of Cabinet of Sec.-Gen., NATO 1965–71; Deputy Dir.-Gen. for Co-operation, Rome 1971–74; Amb. to Israel 1974–78; Italian Rep. to OECD 1978–80; Amb. to Austria 1980–83; mem. Bd. of Dirs. Toro Insurance SpA, Turin; Cavaliere di Gran Croce al merito della Repubblica; Officier, Légion d'honneur; Order of Merit, Fed. Repub. of Germany. *Publications:* La Strategia Nucleare 1964, Memoirs 1988. *Leisure interests:* tennis, golf, skiing. *Address:* Via Gramsci 34, 00197 Rome, Italy.

BACCOUCHE, Hedi; Tunisian politician; b. 1930; active mem. Tunisian Independence Movt.; Pres. Fed. des étudiants destouriens; detained by French authorities 1952; Dir. PSD Political Bureau –1987; Minister of Social Affairs April–Nov. 1987; Prime Minister Nov. 1987–. *Address:* Office of the Prime Minister, Tunis, Tunisia.

BACHER, Robert Fox, B.S., PH.D.; American physicist; b. 31 Aug. 1905, Loudonville, Ohio; s. of Harry and Byrl (née Fox) Bacher; m. Jean Dow 1930; one s. one d.; ed. Univ. of Michigan; Nat. Research Fellow Physics, Calif. Inst. of Technology 1930–31, M.I.T. 1931–32; Alfred Lloyd Fellow, Univ. of Michigan 1932–33; Instructor, Columbia Univ. 1934–35; Instructor to Prof., Cornell Univ. 1935–49; Radiation Laboratory, M.I.T. 1940–45 (on leave 1943–45); Los Alamos Laboratory, Atomic Bomb Project 1943–46; Dir. of Laboratory of Nuclear Studies, Cornell Univ. 1946; mem. U.S. Atomic Energy Comm. 1946–49; Prof. of Physics, Calif. Inst. of Technology 1949–76, Prof. Emer. 1976–, Chair. Div. of Physics, Mathematics and Astronomy 1949–62, Provost 1962–70; mem. President's Science Advisory Cttee. 1953–55, 1957–60; Trustee, Carnegie Corpn. 1959–76, Claremont Graduate School 1971–, Universities Research Assen. 1965–75 (Chair. 1969–73, Pres. 1973–74), Rand Corpn. 1950–60; Pres. Int. Union of Pure and Applied Physics 1969–72; mem. N.A.S., American Philosophical Soc., American Acad. of Arts and Sciences, American Physical Soc. (Pres. 1964), A.A.A.S.; awarded Medal for Merit by Pres. Truman Jan. 1946. *Publications:* Atomic Energy States (with S. Goudsmit) 1932. *Address:* California Institute of Technology, Pasadena, Calif. 91125 (Office); 1300 Hot Springs Road, Monceito, Calif. 93108, U.S.A. (Home).

BACHI, Roberto, D. IUR.; Israeli professor emeritus of statistics and demography; b. 16 Jan. 1909, Rome, Italy; s. of Riccardo Bachi and Clelia Lampronti; m. Vera Colombo 1934; one s. three d.; ed. Faculty of Law, Univ. of Rome; Prof. of Statistics, Univ. of Sassari 1935–36, Univ. of Genoa 1937–38; Prof. of Statistics and Demography, Hebrew Univ. of Jerusalem 1945–77, Prof. Emer. 1977–, Dean Faculty of Social Sciences 1953–54, Pro-Rector 1959–60; Govt. Statistician of Israel 1948–71; Chair. Public Statistical Advisory Bd. 1962–; Bublick Prize (Hebrew Univ.) 1972, Rothschild Prize 1978, Israel Prize, Demography 1982. *Publications:* include some 10 books and monographs and 200 papers on various aspects of demography. *Address:* Hovevei Zion Street 19, Jerusalem 92225, Israel. *Telephone:* 632 410.

BACHMANN, Kurt; German journalist and politician; b. 1909; fmr. leatherworker; joined C.P. of Germany 1932, worked underground in Cologne; fled to France 1938, joined Resistance Movement 1940; arrested in S. France 1942, imprisoned in seven concentration camps; helped found Assen. of Victims of Nazi Persecution 1945, and helped publish Volksstimme (Communist newspaper), Cologne; mem. Exec. C.P. of Germany 1950–56 (party banned 1956); later became Bonn corresp. for Die Tat (weekly of Assen. of Victims of Nazi Persecution); mem. Fed. Organizing Cttee., German C.P. 1968; Chair. of German C.P. 1969–73. *Address:* German Communist Party, Düsseldorf, Federal Republic of Germany.

BACHRACH, Howard L., PH.D.; American biochemist; b. 21 May 1920, Faribault, Minn.; m. Shirley F. Lichterman 1943; one s. one d.; ed. Univ. of Minnesota; Chemist, Jos. Seagram & Co., Lawrenceberg, Ind. 1942; Research Asst., Explosives Research Lab., Carnegie Inst. of Tech. 1942–45; Research Asst., Univ. of Minn. 1945–49; Biochemist, Foot-and-Mouth Disease Research Mission, U.S. Dept. of Agric., Denmark 1949–50; Research Biochemist, Biochemistry and Virus Lab., Univ. of Calif., Berkeley 1950–53; Chief Scientist and Head, Biochemical and Physical Investigations, Plum Island Animal Disease Center, U.S. Dept. of Agric. 1953–81, Research Chemist 1981–89, Consultant-Collaborator 1985–89; developed unifying strategies of animal virus replication 1978; first purification and visualization of polio virus 1953, and of foot-and-mouth virus 1958; first immunization of livestock with protein isolated from foot-and-mouth disease virus 1975; first production through gene splicing of an effective vaccine against disease of animals or humans; mem. N.A.S.; Fellow, New York Acad. of Sciences; Hon. mem. American Coll. of Veterinary Microbiology; many awards, including U.S. Presidential Citation 1965, A.A.A.S.-Newcomb Cleveland Prize 1982, American Chem. Soc. Spencer Medal 1983, Nat. Medal of Science 1983, Nat. Award for Agricultural Excellence 1983 and Alexander von Humboldt Award 1983. *Publications:* 150 publs.; patents on molecular virology and vaccines. *Address:* U.S. Department of Agriculture, Plum Island Animal Disease Center, P.O. Box 848, Greenport, N.Y. 11944; 295 Dayton Road, P.O. Box 1054, Southold, N.Y. 11971, U.S.A. (Home).

BACHYNSKI, Morrel Paul, PH.D., F.R.S.C., F.I.E.E.E.; Canadian physicist; b. 19 July 1930, Bienfait, Sask.; m. Slava Krkovic 1959; two d.; ed. Univ. of

Saskatchewan and McGill Univ.; Lab. Dir., Microwave and Plasma Physics, RCA Ltd. 1960–65, Dir. Research 1965–75, Vice-Pres. Research and Devt. 1975–76; Pres. MPB Technologies Inc. 1977–; mem. Canadian Assen. of Physicists (Pres. 1968), Assen. of Scientific, Eng. and Tech. Community of Canada (Pres. 1974–75), Nat. Research Council of Canada (Chair. on Fusion 1977–87), Science Council of Canada; Fellow Canadian Aeronautics and Space Inst., American Physical Soc.; Prix Scientifique de Québec 1973, Canada Enterprise Award 1977, Queen's Silver Jubilee Medal 1977, Canadian Assen. of Physicists Medal of Achievement 1984, Canadian Research Man. Medal of Achievement 1988. *Publications:* The Particle Kinetics of Plasma (Co-Author) 1968; more than 80 publs. in scientific and eng. journals. *Leisure interest:* tennis. *Address:* 78 Thurlow Road, Montreal, H3X 3G9, Quebec, Canada.

BACKE, John David, M.B.A.; American communications executive; b. 5 July 1932, Akron, Ohio; s. of John and Ellen (née Enyedy) Backe; m. Katherine Elliott 1955; one s. one d.; ed. Miami Univ., Ohio, and Xavier Univ., Ohio; various engineering, financial and marketing positions in General Electric Co. 1957–66; Vice-Pres. and Dir. of Marketing, Silver Burdett Co. 1966–68, Pres. 1968–69; Exec. Vice-Pres. General Learning Corpn. 1969, Pres. and Chief Exec. Officer 1969–73; Pres. of Publishing Group, CBS Inc. 1973–76, of CBS Inc. (also C.E.O.) 1976–80, Tomorrow Entertainment, Inc. (also C.E.O.) 1981–84, Chair. 1984–; Dir. of Business Marketing, Corpn. of New York 1978–; Cinema Products, Los Angeles 1988–; Chair., C.E.O., Backe Group Inc. 1984–; Station WDKY-TV, Lexington 1985–; Gulfshore Publ. Co., Naples 1986–; Special Del. to UNESCO Conf. on publishing for Arabic-speaking countries 1972; mem. Nat. Advisory Cttee. for Illinois Univ. Inst. for Aviation; Hon. LL.D. (Miami and Xavier). *Leisure interest:* multi-engine piloting. *Address:* 327 East 50th Street, New York, N.Y. 10022 (Office); 10 Glenwood Drive, Saddle River, N.J. 07450, U.S.A. (Home).

BACKENSTOSS, Gerhard, PH.D.; German university professor and physicist; b. 28 Oct. 1924, Lörrach; s. of Karl Backenstoss and Martha Straub; m. Margret Frankenbusch 1961; one s. three d.; ed. Univs. of Freiburg and Basel; Research Physicist, Bell Telephone Laboratories, N.J. 1955–57; Research Asst. Carnegie Inst. of Tech., Pittsburgh, Pa. 1957–58; Research Leader, CERN, Geneva 1959–66; Research Leader and Prof. Univ. of Karlsruhe 1966–74; Prof. and Dir. Inst. of Physics, Univ. of Basel 1974–; discovered antiprotonic and sigma-hyperonic atoms 1970; work on exotic atoms, pion absorption, proton-antiproton interaction; Röntgen Prize, Giessen 1970. *Publications:* numerous articles on nuclear and elementary particle physics. *Leisure interests:* history, music. *Address:* Binsenacker-strasse 3, CH-4125 Riehen, Basel, Switzerland.

BACKSTRÖM, Sven; Swedish architect; b. 20 Jan. 1903, Havdhem, Gotland; s. of Victor Backström and Josefina Thomasson; m. Gunvor Homgren 1937; three s. one d.; ed. Högre Allmänna Läroverket, Visby and Royal Tech. Univ., Stockholm; own architectural practice in partnership with Leif Reinius 1936; architect SAR, Svenska Arkitekters Riksförbund 1936–; architect, Royal Palace, Strömsholm 1951–78; mem. Royal Acad. of Free Arts; SAR Kasper Salin Award for Åhlén dept. store 1967; Prince Eugen Medal 1970; Kt. Commdr., Royal Order of Vasa 1973; Master Builder Olle Engkvist Medal 1973. *Publications:* articles in architectural reviews. *Address:* Storgatan 11, S-114 44 Stockholm, Sweden. *Telephone:* 08-60 91 47.

BACKUS, George Edward, S.M., PH.D., F.R.S.A.; American theoretical geophysicist; b. 24 May 1930, Chicago, Ill.; s. of late Milo Morlan Backus and of Dora (née Dare) Backus; m. 1st Elizabeth E. Allen 1961, two s. one d.; m. 2nd Marianne McDonald 1971; m. 3rd Varda Peller; ed. Thornton Township High School, Harvey, Ill. and Univ. of Chicago; Asst. Examiner, Univ. of Chicago 1949–50; Junior Mathematician, Inst. for Air Weapons Research, Univ. of Chicago 1950–54; Physicist, Project Matterhorn, Princeton Univ. 1957–58; Asst. Prof. of Mathematics, M.I.T. 1958–60; Assoc. Prof. of Geophysics, Univ. of Calif. (La Jolla) 1960–62, Prof. 1962–; mem. Scientific Advisory Cttee. to NASA on jt. NASA/CNES Magnetic Satellites; Co.-Chair. Int. Working Group on Magnetic Field Satellites 1983–; mem. Visiting Cttee. Inst. de Physique du Globe de Paris 1987–; Guggenheim Fellowship 1963, 1971; Fellow American Geophysical Union, American Acad. of Arts and Sciences, R.S.A., Royal Astronomical Soc.; mem. N.A.S.; Gold Medal, Royal Astronomical Soc. 1986, John Adam Fleming Medal, American Geophysical Union 1986. *Publications:* Self-Sustaining Dissipative Kinematic Fluid Dynamo 1958, Rotational Splitting of the Free Oscillations of the Earth 1961, Propagation of Short Waves on a Slowly Rotating Earth 1962, Magnetic Anomalies over Oceanic Ridges 1964, Possible Forms of Seismic Anistropy 1962, 1965, 1970, Potentials for Tangent Tensor Fields on Spheroids 1966, Inversion of Seismic Normal Mode Data (with F. Gilbert) 1966, Geomagnetic Data and Core Motions 1967, Inversion of Earth Normal Mode Data (with F. Gilbert) 1968, 1969, 1970, Inference from Inaccurate and Inadequate Data 1971, 1972, Mathematical Representation of Seismic Sources 1976, Computing Extrema of Multidimensional Polynomials 1980, Relative Importance of Tectonic Plate-Driving Forces 1981, Construction of Geomagnetic Field Models 1982, Mantle Filters 1983, Geostrophic and Steady Core Flows 1985, Modelling Ionospheric Currents 1986, The 1969 Magnetic Impulse 1986. *Leisure interests:* hiking, swimming, history, reading, disciplined fiction,

flying, skiing. *Address:* Institute of Geophysics and Planetary Physics, University of California, San Diego, A-025, La Jolla, Calif. 92093 (Office); 9362 La Jolla Farms Road, La Jolla, Calif. 92037, U.S.A. (Home). *Telephone:* 619-534-2468 (Office); 619-455-8972 (Home).

BACKUS, John, A.M.; American computer scientist; b. 3 Dec. 1924, Philadelphia; s. of Cecil Franklin Backus and Elizabeth Edsall; m. 2nd Una Stannard 1968; two d.; ed. Columbia Univ.; Research Staff mem., Thomas J. Watson Research Center 1959–63; IBM Fellow, IBM Almaden Research Center, San José, Calif. 1963–; Visiting Prof., Univ. of California, Berkeley 1980; Fellow American Acad. of Arts and Sciences; mem. Assen. for Computing Machinery, American Mathematical Soc., N.A.S., Nat. Acad. Eng., European Assen. for Theoretical Computer Science; numerous awards include National Medal of Science 1975, A. M. Turing Award, Assen. for Computing Machinery 1977, D. Univ. (York, England) 1985. *Publications:* Systems Design of the IBM 704 Computer (with G. M. Amdahl) 1954, The Fortran Automatic Coding System (with others) 1957, The Syntax and Semantics of the Proposed International Algebraic Language of the Zürich ACM-GAMM Conference 1959, Report on the Algorithmic Language ALGOL 60 (with others) 1960, Can Programming Be Liberated from the von Neumann Style? A Functional Style and Its Algebra of Programs, (Communications of the Assen. for Computing Machinery) 1978, Is Computer Science Based on the Wrong Fundamental Concept of Program? An Extended Concept in Algorithmic Languages (Holland) 1981. *Address:* IBM Almaden Research Center, K53/803, 650 Harry Road, San José, Calif. 95120-6099 (Office); 91 St. Germain Avenue, San Francisco, Calif. 94114, U.S.A. (Home). *Telephone:* (415) 545-2060, (408) 927-1848 (Office).

BACON, Edmund Norwood, B.ARCH.; American architect and planner; b. 2 May 1910, Philadelphia; s. of Ellis W. and Helen Comly Bacon; m. Ruth Holmes 1938; two s. four d.; ed. Cornell Univ. and Cranbrook Acad.; Architectural Designer, Shanghai, China 1934; housing projects for W. Pope Barney, Architect, Philadelphia 1935; Supervisor of City Planning, Flint (Michigan) Inst. of Research and Planning; Man. Dir. Philadelphia Housing Assen. 1940–43; Co-Designer Better Philadelphia Exhibition and Senior Land Planner, Philadelphia City Planning Comm.; Exec. Dir. Philadelphia City Planning Comm. 1949–70; Adjunct Prof., Univ. of Pa. 1950–; Professional Adviser, Franklin Delano Roosevelt Memorial Competition 1959; mem. President's Citizens' Advisory Cttee. on Environmental Quality 1970; numerous awards. *Publication:* Design of Cities 1967 (revised 1974). *Films:* has produced/directed five films on architecture. *Address:* 2117 Locust Street, Philadelphia, Pa. 19103, U.S.A. (Home). *Telephone:* (215) 567-0693.

BACON, Francis; British artist; b. 28 Oct. 1909, Dublin; self-taught; exhibited furniture and rugs of his own design, Queensbury Mews studio; began painting 1929; destroyed nearly all earlier works 1941–44; Rep. G.B. with Ben Nicholson and Lucian Freud 27th Venice Biennale 1954. *One-man exhibitions:* Hanover Gall., London, 1949, 1950, 1951, 1952, 1954, 1957, 1959; Durlacher Bros., N.Y. 1953, ICA, London 1955; Galerie Rive Droite, Paris 1957; Galleria Galatea, Turin 1958, 1970; Marlborough Fine Art, London 1960, 1963, 1965, 1967, 1983, 1985; Tate Gall., London 1962 (retrospective) (travelled to Mannheim, Turin, Zürich, Amsterdam 1962–63), 1985 (retrospective) (travelled to Stuttgart, Berlin 1985–86); Solomon R. Guggenheim Museum, N.Y. 1963 (retrospective); Kunsthalle, Hamburg 1965 (retrospective); Galerie Maeght, Paris 1966, 1984, (Lelong) 1987; Oberes Schloss, Siegen 1967, Marlborough, N.Y. 1968, 1980, 1984, 1987; Grand Palais, Paris 1971 (retrospective); Metropolitan Museum of Art, N.Y. 1975; Galerie Claude Bernard, Paris 1977; Musée de Arte Moderno, Mexico 1977; Fundación Juan March, Madrid; Fundación Joan Miró, Barcelona 1978; Nat. Museum of Modern Art, Tokyo 1983 (retrospective); Galerie Beyeler, Basle 1987, Central House of the Union of Artists, Moscow 1988; Marlborough Gallery, Tokyo 1988–89, Hirshhorn Museum, Washington 1988–89 (retrospective). *Important works include:* triptychs: Three Studies for Figures at the Base of Crucifixion 1944, Three Studies for a Crucifixion 1962, Three Figures in a Room 1964, Crucifixion 1965, Sweeney Agonistes 1967, Oresteia 1981, Triptych 1970, 1972, 1973, 1976, 1985–86, 1987, single oils: Painting 1946, Study after Velasquez's Portrait of Pope Innocent X 1953, Two Figures 1953, Study for Portrait of Van Gogh VI 1957, Portrait of Isabel Rawsthorne Standing in a Street in Soho 1967, Landscape 1978, Jet of Water 1979, Study of the Human Body 1982; paintings acquired by maj. museum collections throughout the world; Rubens Prize 1967, Painting Award, Pittsburgh Int., Carnegie Institute 1967. *Address:* c/o Marlborough Fine Art, 6 Albemarle Street, London, W1X 4BY, England.

BACON, Francis Thomas, O.B.E., F.R.S., M.A., F.ENG., M.I.MECH.E., C.ENG.; British mechanical engineer; b. 21 Dec. 1904, Billericay; s. of Mr. and Mrs. T. W. Bacon; m. Barbara Winifred Papillon 1934; one s. one d.; ed. Eton and Trinity Coll., Cambridge; with C. A. Parsons & Co., Newcastle upon Tyne 1925–40; anti-submarine work for Admiralty in Second World War; research on Hydrox Fuel Cell, Cambridge Univ. 1946–56; consultant to Nat. Research Development Corpn. on development of Hydrox Fuel Cells, Cambridge 1957–62; consultant to Energy Conversion Ltd. 1962–71, to Fuel Cells Ltd. 1972–73, to Johnson Matthey 1984–; Hon. D.Sc. (Newcastle upon Tyne) 1980; S. G. Brown Award (Royal Soc.) 1965, British Silver Medal (Royal Aeronautical Soc.) 1969, Churchill Gold Medal Award (Soc.

of Engineers) 1972, Melchett Medal (Inst. of Fuel) 1972, Bruno Breyer Memorial Medal (Royal Australian Chemical Inst.) 1976, Vittorio de Nora Diamond Shamrock Award and Prize (Electrochemical Soc.) 1978. *Publications:* numerous papers on fuel cells and several book chapters. *Leisure interests:* walking in the hills, gardening. *Address:* Trees, 34 High Street, Little Shelford, Cambridge, CB2 5ES, England. *Telephone:* Cambridge 843116.

BACON, Paul; French politician; b. 1 Nov. 1907, Paris; s. of Laurent Bacon and Maria Baradat; m. Marthe Rajaud 1932; two s.; ed. Ecole Professionnelle de Pau; began career as furniture designer 1923–27; mem. Gen. Secrétariat Jeunesse Ouvrière Chrétienne 1927–37; Chief Ed. of Monde Ouvrier 1937–39; served French Army 1939–40; mem. Assemblée Nationale Consultative 1944–45 (Groupe Résistance ouvrière); Dir. of Syndicalisme (organ of Confédération Française des Travailleurs Chrétiens) 1945; Deputy (M.R.P.), Vice-Pres. Assemblée Nat. Constituante 1946–; Sec. to Presidency of Council 1949–50; Minister of Labour and Social Security, Bidault, Queuille, Pleven, Faure Cabinets 1950–52, Mayer Cabinet 1953, Laniel Cabinet 1953–54, Faure Cabinet 1955–56, Gaillard Cabinet 1957–58; Minister without Portfolio, subsequently Minister of Labour, de Gaulle Cabinet 1958; Minister of Labour, Debré Cabinet 1959–May 1962, Pompidou Cabinet 1962; mem. Conseil Economique et Social 1963; Dir. Turin Int. Centre for Advanced Technical and Vocational Training, Int. Labour Org. (ILO) 1964–67; Chair. Centre d'Etude des Revenus et des Coûts (Commissariat-Gén du Plan) 1967–77; mem. Conseil National de la Statistique 1973–77; Société Archéologique, Historique et Scientifique de Gascogne 1982–; Député honoraire, Officier, Légion d'honneur; Commdr., Mérite social, Santé publique. *Publications:* La naissance de la classe ouvrière, Vers la réforme de l'entreprise capitaliste, La democratie économique et sociale. *Leisure interest:* painting. *Address:* Chemin du Courdé, 32200 Gimont (Office); 23 avenue Balzac, 94210 La Varenne-St.-Hilaire (Val de Marne), France (Home). *Telephone:* (62) 67-72-89 (Office); (48) 83-15-58 (Home).

BACQUIER, Gabriel; French (baritone) opera singer; b. 17 May 1924, Béziers; s. of Augustin Bacquier and Fernande Severac; m. 1st Simone Teisseire 1943, 2nd Mauricette Bénard 1958; two s.; ed. Paris Conservatoire; debut at Théâtre Royal de la Monnaie, Brussels 1953; joined Opéra de Paris 1956; debut at Carnegie Hall 1960, Metropolitan Opera, New York 1961; now appears regularly at the Vienna State Opera, Covent Garden, La Scala, Opéra de Paris and most leading opera houses. Repertoire includes Otello, Don Giovanni, Pelléas et Mélisande, Damnation de Faust, Tosca, Falstaff; several recordings; Prix national du disque français 1964, and other prizes; Chevalier, Légion d'honneur, Officier, ordre nationale du Mérite, Officier des Arts et des Lettres. *Leisure interests:* painting, drawing. *Address:* 141 rue de Rome, 75017 Paris, France. *Telephone:* 227-33-84.

BÁCS, Ludovic; Romanian conductor and composer; b. 19 Jan. 1930, Petrila; s. of Ludovic Bács and Iuliana Bács (Venczel); m. Ecse Gyöngyver, 1952; two s.; ed. Dima Gh. Conservatory, Cluj-Napoca Tchaikovski Conservatory, Moscow, Cluj-Napoca Coll. of Philosophy 1948–49; began career as conductor Symphonic Orchestra of Romanian Radio, also Artistic Dir. 1964–; Prof. Bucharest Conservatory 1960–66; f. Musica rediviva 1966, the first group of performers to render ancient Romanian music; he conducted concerts in U.S.S.R., Poland, Czechoslovakia, Hungary, Bulgaria, the G.D.R., West Berlin, Fed. Germany, Holland, Switzerland, Spain; mem. Romanian Composers' Union; Cultural Merit Award, the Medal of Labour, Prize of the Theatre and Music Assen. *Works include:* orchestration of Bach's Art of the Fugue (on record), numerous adaptations from 15th-18th century music: Bach, Monteverdi, Backfarg, from Codex Caioni a.o. *Address:* Nuferilor 63-64, Bucharest (Office); D. Golescu 31, ap.87, Bucharest 1, Romania (Home).

BADAWI, Abdel Halim; Egyptian diplomatist; b. 26 July 1930, m.; two s.; ed. Cairo Univ.; joined Egyptian Foreign Service 1951; posts at Egyptian Embassies in London and Yaoundé, Cameroon 1953–61, Minister Counsellor, London 1974–76; Counsellor Egyptian Mission to UN, New York 1966–71, Deputy Perm. Rep. 1976–78, Perm. Rep. 1986–; fmr. Amb. to Portugal; Asst. to Minister of Foreign Affairs, Cairo 1982–86. *Address:* Permanent Mission of Egypt to United Nations, 36 East 67th Street, New York, N.Y. 10021, U.S.A. *Telephone:* (212) 879-6300.

BADAWI, Datuk Abdullah Bin Haj, B.A.; Malaysian politician; b. 26 Nov. 1939, Pulau Pinang; m. Datin Endon bint Datuk Mahmud; ed. Univ. of Malaya; Asst. Sec. Public Service Dept. 1964; Asst. Sec. MAGERAN 1969; Asst. Sec. Nat. Security Council 1971; Dir. (Youth), Ministry of Sport, Youth and Culture 1971–74, Deputy Sec.-Gen. 1974–78; Minister without Portfolio, Prime Minister's Dept. 1982; Minister of Educ. 1984–86, of Defence May 1986–87; mem. UMNO Supreme Council 1982–; many other public appts.; recipient of four awards. *Address:* Ministry of Defence, Jalan Padang Tembak, Kuala Lumpur 15-03, Malaysia.

BADDILEY, Sir James, Kt., M.A., PH.D., D.SC., SC.D., F.R.S.E., F.R.S.; British professor of chemical microbiology; b. 15 May 1918, Manchester; s. of the late James Baddiley and Ivy (Cato) Baddiley; m. Hazel M. Townsend 1944; one s.; ed. Manchester Grammar School and Univ. of Manchester; Beyer Fellow 1983–84; ICI Fellow, Univ. of Cambridge 1944–49; Fellow, Swedish

Medical Research Council, Stockholm 1947–49; mem. of staff Dept. of Biochemistry, Lister Inst., London 1949–54; Prof. of Organic Chem., Univ. of Durham, Kings Coll. 1955–63; Prof. of Organic Chem., Univ. of Newcastle upon Tyne 1963–77, Head of the School of Chem. 1968–78, Prof. of Chem. Microbiology 1977–83; Science and Engineering Research Council Sr. Fellow, Univ. of Cambridge 1981–83; Hon. Dir. Microbiological Chem. Research Lab. 1968–83; mem. Science Research Council 1979–81; Fellow, Pembroke Coll., Cambridge; Hon. mem. American Soc. for Biochemistry and Molecular Biology; Rockefeller Fellow, Harvard Medical School 1954; Tilden Lecturer, Chemical Soc. 1959, Karl Folkers Prof., Univ. of Illinois 1962, Leeuwenhoek Lecturer, Royal Soc. 1967, Pedler Lecturer, Chem. Soc. 1978, Bose Endowment Lecturer, Bose Inst., Calcutta 1980; Meldola Medal, Royal Inst. of Chem. 1947, Corday-Morgan Medal and Prize, Chem. Soc. 1952, Davy Medal, Royal Soc. 1974; Hon. D.Sc. (Heriot-Watt) 1978, (Bath) 1986. *Publications:* Numerous publications in bio-chem. and microbiological chem. *Leisure interests:* gardening, music, photography. *Address:* Department of Biochemistry, Tennis Court Road, Cambridge, CB2 1QW (Office); Hill Top Cottage, Hildersham, Cambridge, CB1 6DA, England (Home). *Telephone:* Cambridge 333600 (Office); Cambridge 893055 (Home).

BADER, Richard Frederick William, PH.D., F.R.S.C.; Canadian professor of chemistry; b. 15 Oct. 1931, Kitchener, Ont.; s. of Albert Bader and Alvina Gerloff; m. Pamela L. Kozenof 1958; three d.; ed. McMaster Univ. and Mass. Inst. of Technology; Postdoctoral Fellowship, Univ. of Cambridge 1958–59; Asst. Prof. Univ. of Ottawa 1959–62, Assoc. Prof. 1962–63; Assoc. Prof. McMaster Univ. 1963–66, Prof. of Chem. 1966–; A.P. Sloan Research Fellowship 1964–66; Steacie Memorial Fellowship 1967–69; Guggenheim Memorial Fellowship 1979–80. *Publications:* articles in professional journals. *Address:* Department of Chemistry, McMaster University, Hamilton, Ont., L8S 4M1 (Office); 126 Birrett Drive, Burlington, Ont., L7L 2T1, Canada (Home). *Telephone:* (416) 525-9140 Ext. 3499 (Office).

BADGER, Sir Geoffrey Malcolm, Kt., A.O., PH.D.; Australian scientist; b. 10 Oct. 1916, Port Augusta, South Australia; s. of John McDougall Badger and Laura Mary Badger née Brooker; m. Edith Maud Chevis 1941; no c.; ed. Geelong Coll., Gordon Inst. of Tech., Univs. of Melbourne, London and Glasgow; Finney-Howell Research Fellow, London 1939, 1940; Research Chemist, ICI Dyestuffs Ltd., Manchester 1941–43; Instructor Lieut., R.N. 1943–46; ICI Research Fellow, Univ. of Glasgow 1946–49; Sr. Lecturer, then Reader, then Prof. of Organic Chem., Univ. of Adelaide 1949–64, Prof. Emer. 1964–, Deputy Vice-Chancellor 1966–67, Vice-Chancellor 1967–77; mem. Exec., CSIRO (Canberra) 1964–65; Research Prof. 1977–79; Chair. Australian Science and Tech. Council, Canberra 1979–82; H.G. Smith Medal 1951, A.E. Leighton Medal 1971, ANZAAS Medal 1981. *Publications:* six books and more than 200 scientific papers. *Leisure interests:* reading, writing, walking. *Address:* 1 Anna Court, Delfin Island, West Lakes, South Australia 5021.

BADHAM, Leonard, C.B.I.M.; British business executive; b. 10 June 1923, London; m. Joyce R. Lowrie 1944; two d.; ed. Wandsworth Grammar School; war service 1943–47; Man. Trainee, J. Lyons & Co., Ltd. 1939, mem. Bd. of Dirs. 1965–, Chief Comptroller 1965, Tech. and Commercial Co-ordinator 1967, Exec. Dir. Finance and Admin. 1970, Asst. Group Man. Dir. 1971, Deputy Group Man. Dir. 1975, Man. Dir. 1977, Vice-Chair. 1984–; Dir. Allied-Lyons PLC 1978–; Fellow Hotel Catering and Industrial Man. Assen. *Leisure interests:* bridge, gardening. *Address:* 26 Vicarage Drive, East Sheen, London, SW14 8RX, England. *Telephone:* 01-876 4373.

BADIAN, Ernst, M.A., LIT.D., D.PHIL., F.B.A.; Professor of history; b. 8 Aug. 1925; s. of Joseph and Sally (née Horinger) Badian; m. Nathalie A. Wimsett 1950; one s. one d.; ed. Christchurch Boys' High School, Canterbury Univ. Coll., Christchurch, N.Z. and Univ. Coll., Oxford; Asst. Lecturer in Classics, Victoria Univ. Coll., Wellington 1947–48; Rome Scholar in Classics, British School at Rome 1950–52; Asst. Lecturer in Classics and Ancient History, Univ. of Sheffield 1952–54; Lecturer in Classics, Univ. of Durham 1954–65; Prof. of Ancient History, Univ. of Leeds 1965–69; Prof. of Classics and History, State Univ. of N.Y. at Buffalo 1969–71; Prof. of History, Harvard Univ. 1971–82, John Moors Cabot Prof. 1982–; Fellow, American Acad. of Arts and Sciences, American Numismatic Soc.; corresp. mem. Austrian Acad. of Sciences, German Archaeological Inst.; foreign mem. Finnish Acad. of Sciences; Visiting Prof. and lecturer at many univs. in U.S.A., Canada, Australia, S. Africa, Europe etc.; Hon. Fellow Univ. Coll., Oxford; Hon. mem. Soc. for Roman Studies. *Publications:* Foreign Clientelae (264–70 BC) 1958, Studies in Greek and Roman History 1964, Polybius 1966, Roman Imperialism in the Late Republic 1967, Publicans and Sinners 1972; articles in classical and historical journals. *Leisure interests:* travel, reading. *Address:* Department of History, Harvard University, Cambridge, Mass. 02138, U.S.A.

BADINGS, Prof. Henk, DR.ENG.; Netherlands composer; b. 17 Jan. 1907, Bandoeng, Indonesia (fmrly. Dutch East Indies); s. of Herman Louis Johan Badings and Maria Susanna Polvliet; m. Jeannette Tukke 1946; one d.; ed. Tech. Univ., Delft; Asst. in Palaeontology, Tech. Univ., Delft 1931–34; first symphony performed by the Concertgebouw-Orchestra in Amsterdam 1930; Prof. of Composition, Rotterdam Conservatoire 1934–35; Prof. of Composition, Musical Lyceum, Amsterdam 1935–37, Co-Dir. 1937–41; Dir. State Conservatoire, The Hague 1941–45; free-lance composer 1945–; Dir.

Electronic Music Studio, Univ. of Utrecht 1961-64, Prof. of Acoustics and Information Theory 1962-77; Guest Prof., Adelaide Univ. (Australia) 1962-63; Prof. of Musical Composition, Musikhochschule, Stuttgart (Germany) 1962-72; mem. Royal Flemish Acad. of Art; Hon. Citizen of New Martinsville, W. Va., U.S.A.; Paganini Prize 1953, Italia Prize 1954, Marzotto Prize 1964, Rai-Italia Prize 1971, Sweelink Prize 1972, Medal, Acad. Française 1981. *Compositions:* sixteen symphonies and other symphonic music, chamber music, music for amateurs, choral works, operas, etc., as well as electronic music. *Leisure interests:* geology, plastic arts, literature, travelling. *Address:* Hugten 5, 6026 RG, Maarheeze, Netherlands. *Telephone:* 04957-327.

BADINTER, Robert, LL.D., A.M.; French lawyer and professor of law; b. 30 March 1928, Paris; s. of Simon Badinter and Charlotte Rosenberg; m. 1st Anne Vernon 1957, 2nd Elisabeth Bleustein-Blanchet 1966; two s. one d.; ed. Lycées Janson-de-Sailly, Ampère and Carnot, Paris, Univ. of Paris, Columbia Univ., New York; Lawyer, Paris Court of Appeal 1951; Tutor, Univ. of Paris 1954-58; Prof. of Law, Univs. of Dijon 1966, Besançon, Amiens 1969, Paris I (Sorbonne) 1974-81; Minister of Justice and Keeper of the Seals June 1981-86; Head Constitutional Council Feb. 1986-. *Publications:* L'exécution 1973, Liberté, libertés 1976. *Address:* Conseil constitutionnel, 2 rue de Montpensier, 75001 Paris (Office): 38 rue Guynemer, 75006 Paris, France (Home).

BADRAN, Mudar, B.A.; Jordanian politician and civil servant; b. 1934, Jerash; ed. Univ. of Damascus, Syria; Lieutenant and Legal Consultant, Jordanian armed forces 1957, Maj. and Legal Adviser to the Armed Forces Treasury 1962; Asst. Chief, Jordanian Foreign Intelligence 1965; Deputy Chief of Gen. Intelligence 1966, Chief 1968; Retd. Maj.-Gen. 1970; Chief Chamberlain of the Royal Court 1970, Sec.-Gen.; Nat. Security Adviser to H.M. King Hussein (q.v.) 1970; Minister in the Royal Court 1972; Nat. Security Adviser to King Hussein 1973; Minister of Educ. 1973-74; Chief of the Royal Court 1974-76; Minister of Defence and of Foreign Affairs 1976-79; Prime Minister 1976-79, 1980-84; also Minister of Defence 1980-84; mem. Nat. Consultative Council 1979-; fmr. mem. Exec. Council of the Arab Nat. Union. *Address:* c/o Office of the Prime Minister, Amman; Shmaisani, Amman, Jordan.

BADURA-SKODA, Paul; Austrian pianist; b. 6 Oct. 1927; s. of Ludwig Badura and Margarete Badura (née Winter); m. Eva Badura-Skoda (née Halfar); two s. two d.; ed. Realgymnasium courses in conducting and piano, Konservatorium der Stadt Wien, and Edwin Fischer's Master Class in Lucerne; regular concerts since 1948; tours all over the world as soloist and with leading orchestras; conductor of chamber orchestra 1960-; yearly master classes fmrly. in Edinburgh, Salzburg and Vienna Festival 1958-63; artist in residence, Univ. of Wisconsin, master classes in Madison, Wisconsin 1966-71; recorded over 100 L.P. records including complete Beethoven and Schubert sonatas; First Prize Austrian Music Competition 1947; Austrian Cross of Honour for Science and Arts (1st Order) 1976, Bösendorfer-Ring 1978. *Compositions:* Mass in D, Cadenzas to Piano and Violin Concertos by Mozart and Haydn, completion of 5 unfinished Piano Sonatas by Schubert 1976, and of unfinished Larghetto and Allegro for 2 Pianos by Mozart, Elegy for Piano 1980, Sonatine Romantique for Violin and Piano 1980. *Publications:* Co-author Interpreting Mozart on the Keyboard (with Eva Badura-Skoda), Die Klaviersonaten von Beethoven (with Jörg Demus) 1970; Editions of Schubert, Mozart, Chopin; numerous articles. *Leisure interest:* chess. *Address:* Zuckerkandlgass 14, Vienna 1190, Austria.

BAEZ, Joan; American folk singer; b. 9 Jan. 1941, Staten Island, N.Y.; d. of Albert V. and Joan (Bridge) Baez; m. David Harris 1968 (divorced 1973); one s.; ed. School of Fine and Applied Arts, Boston Univ.; began career as singer in coffee houses, appeared at Ballad Room, Club 47 1958-68, Gate of Horn, Chicago 1958, Newport, R.I., Folk Festival 1959-69, Town Hall and Carnegie Hall, New York 1962, 1967, 1968; gave concerts in black colls. in southern U.S.A. 1963; toured Europe 1970, 1971, 1972, 1977 (U.K.), 1980, 1983, 1984, U.S.A. 1970, 1971, 1972, 1973, 1976, 1982, 1983, 1984, Democratic Repub. of Viet-Nam 1972, Australia 1985; recordings with Vanguard Records 1960-72, A & M Record Co. 1972-76, Portrait Records 1977-80, Gold Castle Records 1987-; awarded eight gold albums, one gold single; many TV appearances; began refusing payment of war taxes 1964; detained for civil disobedience opposing conscription 1967; speaking tour of U.S.A. and Canada for draft resistance 1967-68; Founder, Vice-Pres. Inst. for Study of Non-Violence 1965; mem. Nat. Advisory Council, Amnesty Int. 1974-; Founder, Humanitas Int. Human Rights Comm. Feb. 1979-; Gandhi Memorial Int. Foundation Award 1988; Chevalier, Légion d'Honneur. *Publications:* Joan Baez Songbook 1964, Daybreak 1968, Coming Out (with David Harris) 1971, And then I wrote . . . (songbook) 1979, And a Voice to Sing With 1987. *Address:* Diamonds and Rust Productions, P.O. Box 1026, Menlo Park, Calif. 94026; Humanitas/International Human Rights Committee, P.O. Box 818, Menlo Park, Calif. 94026, U.S.A. *Telephone:* (415) 328-0266; (415) 324-9077.

BAFFI, Paolo; Italian banker and economist; b. 5 Aug. 1911, Broni, Pavia; s. of Giovanni and Giuseppina Lolla; m. Maria A. Dalla Torre; two s.; ed. Bocconi Univ. of Milan; joined Banca d'Italia 1936, Research Dept. 1936-56, Econ. Adviser 1956-60, Dir.-Gen. 1960-75, Gov. 1975-79, Hon. Gov. 1979-; Econ. Adviser, BIS 1956-60, mem. Bd. of Dirs. 1975; Visiting Prof. Cornell

Univ. 1959-60; Prof. Monetary History and Policy, Rome Univ. 1970-80; Chair. Ufficio Italiano dei Cambi 1975-79; Gov. for Italy, IBRD (World Bank) 1975-79; mem. Cttee. of Central Bank Govs., EEC 1975-79; mem. Bd. of Dirs. Consiglio Nazionale delle Ricerche 1975-79; Dir. BIS 1980-; Alt. Gov. for Italy, IMF 1979-80; mem. Accad. Naz. dei Lincei; Cavaliere di Gran Croce; Commdr. Légion d'honneur (France). *Publications:* The Dollar and Gold 1953, Monetary Developments in Italy from the War Economy to Limited Convertibility 1935-1956 1958, Studi Sulla Moneta 1965, Nuovi studi sulla Moneta 1973, Saving in Italy today 1974, Italy's Narrow Path 1975, Alla ricercadi un valore perduto, la moneta 1980, Credito e sotto sviluppo 1981. *Address:* c/o Banca d'Italia, Via Nazionale 91, 00184 Rome, Italy (Office). *Telephone:* 4672.

BAFIA, Jerzy, D.JUR.; Polish judge and politician; b. 5 May 1926, Płociczno, Suwałki District; s. of Franciszek and Maria Bafia; m. Stanisława Bafia 1950; one s.; ed. Jagellonian Univ., Cracow; Judge, District Court of Justice, then Voivodship Court of Justice, Cracow 1950-53; with Supreme Court of Justice 1953-54; with Ministry of Justice 1954-69, Dir. Dept. of Codification 1958-69; Doctor of Legal Sciences, Warsaw Univ. 1961-64, Asst. Prof. 1964-70, Prof. Extraordinary 1970-78, Ordinary Prof. in Penal Law Inst. 1978-; Head, Criminology Research Centre 1971-; Asst. Prof. Silesian Univ. 1969-70; Head Chancellery, Seym (Parl.) 1969-72; First Chief Justice of Supreme Court 1972-76; Deputy to Seym 1972-80; Minister of Justice 1976-81; Sec.-Gen. Polish Lawyers' Asscn. 1964-72, mem. Codifying Cttee., Sec. of Cttee. Presidium 1964-69; Chair. Scientific Council, Inst. of State and Law, Polish Acad. of Sciences (fmr. Inst. of Legal Sciences); Vice-Pres. Int. Union of Lawyers (Democrats) 1968-72; mem. Legis. Council attached to Council of Ministers 1973-, Polish United Workers' Party, Cen. Comm. of Party Control 1976-81; ed.-in-chief monthly "Nowe Prawo" 1984-; decorations include Commdr.'s Cross with Star, Knight Cross Order of Polonia Restituta, Order of Banner of Labour (1st class). *Publications:* The Changes of Legal Qualification 1964, Commentary of Penal Law Code 1971, The Problems of Criminology 1978, Principles of Law Creation 1980, Penal Financial Law 1980, Press-Control Law 1983, The Rule of Law 1985. *Leisure interests:* tennis, gardening. *Address:* ul. Sułkowicka 6 m. 3, 00-396 Warsaw, Poland (Home). *Telephone:* 41-87-97 (Home).

BAFILE, H.E. Cardinal Corrado; fmr. Prefect of the S.C. for the Causes of Saints; b. 4 July 1903; s. of Vincenzo and Maddalena Tedeschini; ed. State Univ., Rome, and Lateran Univ., Rome; ordained priest 1936; Vatican Secretariat of State 1939-; Privy Chamberlain to Pope John XXIII 1958-60; Papal Nuncio to Germany 1960-75; Titular Archbishop of Antiochia in Pisidia 1960-76; cr. Cardinal 1976, now Cardinal Deacon. *Address:* Vatican City, Rome, Italy. *Telephone:* 698 42 43.

BAGAZA, Col. Jean-Baptiste; Burundi army officer and politician; b. 29 Aug. 1946, Rutovu, Bururi Prov.; m. Fausta Bagaza; four c.; ed. Ecole des Cadets, Brussels, and the Belgian Mil. School, Arlon; fmr. Asst. to Gen. Ndabemeye; Chief of Staff of the Armed Forces, rank of Lt.-Col.; led coup to overthrow Pres. Micombero Nov. 1976; Pres. of the Repub. of Burundi 1976-87, also Minister of Defence; Pres. Union pour le progrès national (UPRONA) 1976-87; promoted to Col. 1977; in Belgium 1987-88, reported to be in Libya 1989.

BAGBENI ADEITO NZENGEYA; Zaïre diplomatist; b. Jan. 1941, Stanleyville (now Kisangani); m.; five c.; ed. Inst. of Higher Overseas Studies, Paris, Univ. of Paris/Sorbonne, Int. Law Acad., The Hague and Int. Relations Inst., Geneva; held various posts in Dept. of Foreign Affairs of Zaïre; Amb. to the Netherlands 1971-72, to Ethiopia and OAU 1972-75; Dir.-Gen. Dept. of Foreign Affairs and Int. Co-operation 1975-76; Pres. Perm. Comm. of Public Admin. 1976-80; Perm. Rep. to UN, Geneva 1980-83; Amb. to India, Indonesia, Sri Lanka and Singapore 1983-85; Perm. Rep. to UN 1985-; Chair. First Cttee. (Political and Security), UN 1987-. *Address:* Permanent Mission of Zaïre, 767 Third Avenue, 25th Floor, United Nations, New York, N.Y. 10017, U.S.A.

BAGGE, Povl, PH.D.; Danish retired professor of history; b. 30 Nov. 1902, Frederiksberg; s. of Jacob and Gertrud K. Bagge; m. Gudrun Ørsted Thiele 1945; one s. one d.; ed. Askov Folk High School, Technical Univ. of Copenhagen and Univ. of Copenhagen; school teacher, Rødding 1927-29; sub-editor, Dansk biografisk leksikon 1931-44; Archivist, Provincial Archives, Copenhagen 1937-46; Keeper, Provincial Archives, Odense 1946-50; Prof. of History, Univ. of Copenhagen 1951-73; mem. (now retd.), Det Kgl. danske Videnskabernes Selskab, The Clara Lachmann Foundation, The Sonning Foundation, Royal Soc. for Danish History, Soc. for Publishing Modern Danish History, The Arhus Learned Soc.; fmr. mem. Bd. The Danish Acad. in Rome. *Publications:* Studier over D.G. Monrads Statstankeri 1936, J.N. Madvigs levned og politiske virksomhed 1955. *Leisure interest:* detective novels. *Address:* Sortedams Dosseringen 69, 4, 2100 Copenhagen Ø, Denmark. *Telephone:* 01 423079.

BAGGETT, Adm. Lee, Jr.; American naval officer; b. 11 Jan. 1927, Oxford, Miss.; s. of late Lee Baggett and Estelle Brown Baggett; m. Doris Simmons 1954; ed. Univ. of Mississippi, U.S. Naval Acad., U.S. Navy Postgrad. School and U.S. Naval War Coll.; Ensign, U.S. Navy 1950; Commdr. U.S.S. Courlan 1953-55, U.S.S. Firm 1960-61; Nuclear Test Plans Officer, Defense Atomic Support Agency 1962-64; Commdr. U.S.S. Decatur 1966-68; Dir. Guided Missile Div. Bureau of Naval Ordnance

1970–72; Commdr. U.S.S. Reeves 1972–73; Chief of Staff, U.S. Sixth Fleet 1973–75; ASW Systems Project Officer and Dir. ASW Warfare Div. OPNAV 1975–77; Commdr. Naval Surface Group Mid-Pacific 1977–79; Commdr. Naval Surface Force Pacific Fleet 1979–82; Dir. Naval Warfare, OPNAV 1982–85; Commdr. Allied Forces Southern Europe and Commdr. U.S. Naval Forces Europe 1985; rank of Adm. 1985; Supreme Allied Commdr. Atlantic and C.-in-C. U.S. Atlantic Command 1985–; Distinguished Service Medal with Gold Star, Legion of Merit, Bronze Star Medal with Gold Star, Meritorious Service Medal, Combat Action Ribbon, Royal Norwegian Order of Merit, Repub. of Vietnam Navy Distinguished Serving Order. *Leisure interest:* golf. *Address:* Supreme Allied Commander Atlantic/Commander-in-Chief, U.S. Atlantic Command, Norfolk, Va. 23511-5100, U.S.A. *Telephone:* (804) 445-5911.

BAGGIO, H.E. Cardinal Sebastiano; Vatican ecclesiastic; b. 16 May 1913, Rosà, Italy; s. of Giovanni Battista and Pierina Baggio; ed. Seminario Vescovile di Vicenza, Pontificia Università Gregoriana, Pontificia Accademia Ecclesiastica and Scuola di Paleografia e Biblioteconomia at the Vatican library; ordained priest 1935; Sec. Nunciatures in El Salvador, Bolivia, Venezuela 1938–46; with Secr. of State 1946–48; Chargé d'affaires, Colombia 1948–50; Sacra Congregazione Concistoriale 1950–53; Titular Archbishop of Ephesus 1953–; Apostolic Nuncio, Chile 1953–59; Apostolic Del., Canada 1959–64; Apostolic Nuncio, Brazil 1964–69; cr. Cardinal April 1969; Archbishop of Cagliari 1969–73; Prefect, Sacred Congregation for the Bishops 1973–84; Cardinal-Bishop of Velletri 1974–; Pres. Pontifical Comm. for the Vatican City State 1984–; Chamberlain of the High Roman Church 1985; Hon. mem. Rotary Int. 1980–; orders from Bolivia, Brazil, Chile, Colombia, Ecuador, Malta, Portugal and Venezuela. *Address:* Piazza della Città Leonina 9, 00193 Rome, Italy. *Telephone:* 65-40-137.

BAGIROV, Kyamran Mamed ogly; Soviet official; b. 1933, Azerbaidzhan; ed. Azerbaidzhan Polytechnic Inst., Baku and Higher Party School of Cen. Cttee. of CPSU; teacher 1957–63; mem. CPSU 1961–; sr. posts in construction industry 1963–68; mem. Council of Ministers of Azerbaidzhan S.S.R. 1968–71; deputy chief of a section of Cen. Cttee. of Azerbaidzhan CP 1971–74; First Sec. of a City Cttee. of CP in Azerbaidzhan 1974–78; Sec. and mem. Politburo, Cen. Cttee. of Azerbaidzhan CP 1978–, First Sec. Dec. 1982–88; mem. CPSU Cen. Cttee. 1986–, Supreme Soviet of U.S.S.R. *Address:* Central Committee of the Azerbaidzhan Communist Party, Baku, Azerbaidzhan, U.S.S.R.

BAGLI, Ibrahim Taher al-; Kuwaiti government official; b. 1942, Kuwait; m. 1969; one s. three d.; Dir. Antiquities and Museums Dept., Ministry of Information. *Publication:* A Comprehensive Report on the Archaeological Excavation in Failaka Island. *Leisure intrests:* travel and tours. *Address:* Ministry of Information, Kuwait National Museum, Department of Antiquities and Museums, P.O. Box 193, 13002 Safat, Kuwait. *Telephone:* 432020 (Office); 633415 (Home).

BAGNALL, Field Marshal Sir Nigel (Thomas), G.C.B., C.V.O., M.C.; British army officer; b. 10 Feb. 1927; s. of Lieut.-Col. Harry S. and Marjory M. Bagnall; m. Anna C. Church 1959; two d.; ed. Wellington Coll.; joined army 1945; commissioned into Green Howards 1946; 6th Airborne Div., Palestine 1946–48; Green Howards, Malaya 1949–53; Dir. of Borneo Operations, Gen. Staff Officer (Intelligence) 1966–67; command, 4/7 Royal Dragoon Guards, N. Ireland and British Army of the Rhine (BAOR) 1967–69; Sr. Directing Staff (Army), Joint Services Staff Coll. 1970; command, Royal Armoured Corps HQ 1 (Branch) Corps 1970–72; Defence Fellow, Balliol Coll., Oxford 1972–73; Sec. Chief of Staff Cttee. 1973–75; Gen. Officer Commanding 4th Div. 1975–77; Asst. Chief of Defence Staff (Policy), Ministry of Defence 1978–80; Commdr. 1st British Corps 1981–83; Col. Comdt., Army Physical Training Corps 1981–85, Chief of Gen. Staff 1985–88; Commdr.-in-Chief BAOR and Commdr. Northern Army Group 1983–85; Aide-de-Camp Gen. to the Queen 1985–; Hon. Fellow Balliol Coll., Oxford 1986. *Leisure interests:* country pursuits. *Address:* c/o Williams and Glyn's, Kirkland House, London, S.W.1, England.

BAGNALL, Richard Maurice, M.B.E.; British business executive (retd.); b. 20 Nov. 1917, Ealing; s. of Francis Edward and Edith Bagnall; m. Irene Pickford 1946; one s. one d.; ed. Repton; served in Royal Artillery, Shropshire Yeomanry (mentioned in despatches) 1939–43, Brigade Major 6th Army Group, R.A., Italy 1944–45; joined Tube Investments Ltd. 1938, Dir. 1969–81, a Man. Dir. 1974–81, Deputy Chair. 1976–81; Dir. Round Oak Steel Works 1974–81, Alt. Chair. 1976–81; Council Mem. British Nat. Cttee., Int. Chamber of Commerce 1975–81; Bronze Star (U.S.A.) 1945. *Leisure interests:* golf, gardening, photography. *Address:* Vila da Chypre, Carvoeiro, 8400 Lagoa, Algarve, Portugal.

BAGNOLD, Brigadier Ralph Alger, O.B.E., F.R.S.; British geologist, explorer and fmr. army officer; b. 3 April 1896; s. of Col. A. H. Bagnold; m. Dorothy Alice Plank 1946; one s. one d; ed. Malvern Coll., Royal Mil. Acad., Woolwich and Gonville and Caius Coll., Cambridge; Commission Royal Engs. 1915, Capt. 1918, transferred to Royal Corps of Signals 1920, Maj. 1927, retd. 1935; called up to 1939, raised and commanded Long Range Desert Group in Middle E. 1940–41, Deputy Signal Officer-in-Chief, Middle E. 1943–44; organized and led numerous explorations in Libyan Desert and elsewhere 1925–32; Consultant on movement of sediments by wind and water 1956–; Fellow Imperial Coll., Univ. of London 1971–;

Founder's Medal of Royal Geographical Soc. 1935, G. K. Warren Prize, U.S. Acad. of Sciences 1969, Penrose Medal, Geological Soc. of America 1970, Wollaston Medal, Geological Soc. of London 1971, Sorby Medal, Int. Asscn. of Sedimentologists 1978. *Publications:* Libyan Sands 1935, Physics of Blown Sand and Desert Dunes 1941; papers and other publs. on deserts, hydraulics, beach formation and random distrubutions. *Leisure interests:* exploration, research. *Address:* 7 Manor Way, Blackheath, London, SE3 9EF, England. *Telephone:* 01-852 1210.

BAGSHAWE, Kenneth Dawson, M.D., F.R.C.P., F.R.C.O.G.; British physician and medical oncologist; b. 17 Aug. 1925, Marple, Cheshire; s. of Harry Bagshawe and Gladys Bagshawe; m. 1st Ann A. Kelly 1946, 2nd Sylvia D. Lawler (née Corben) 1977; one s. one d.; ed. Harrow Co. School, London School of Econs. and St. Mary's Hosp. Medical School, Univ. of London; served R.N. 1943–46; Research Fellow, Johns Hopkins Hosp. 1955–56; Sr. Registrar, St. Mary's Hosp. 1956–60; Sr. Lecturer in Medicine, Charing Cross Hosp. Medical School 1961–63; Consultant Physician and Dir. Dept. of Medical Oncology 1961–; Prof. of Medical Oncology, Charing Cross Hosp. Medical School 1974–; Chair. Scientific Cttee. Cancer Research Campaign 1983–; mem. various cancer research cttees. etc.; Fellow. Royal Coll. of Radiologists; Hamilton Fairley Lectureship 1982; Krug Award for Excellence in Medicine 1980; Edgar Gentilli Prize (R.C.O.G.) 1980. *Publications:* Choriocarcinoma 1969, Medical Oncology 1976, Germ Cell Tumours 1983, and articles in professional journals. *Leisure interests:* travel, walking, demolition and conservation. *Address:* Department of Medical Oncology, Charing Cross Hospital, London, W6 8RF (Office); 115 George Street, London, W1H T5A; Hatfield Lodge, Chilham, nr. Canterbury, Kent. England (Home). *Telephone:* 01-748 9625 (Office); 01-262 6033 (London); (0227) 730258 (Kent).

BAHADUR K.C., Kaisher; Nepalese educationist and diplomatist; b. 28 Jan. 1907, Kathmandu; s. of Maj. Dan Bahadur and Kumari Khattri Chettri; m. Home Kumari 1923; one s. one d.; ed. St. Paul's Mission School, St. Xavier's Coll., Calcutta, and Univ. Coll., Calcutta; Trans. and Lecturer, Tri-Chandra Coll. 1930–32; research in MSS., inscriptions and sculpture, Nepal 1932–45; Nepalese Resident in Tibet 1946–49; Sec. Ministry of Educ., Health and Local Self Govt. 1956–61; Del. to UN 1956–57, UNESCO 1960; Amb. to People's Repub. of China, concurrently to Mongolian People's Repub. and Burma 1961–65, also to Repub. of Indonesia and Kingdom of Laos 1962–65; Chair. Nepal Public Service Comm. 1966–70; Chief Ed., Civil Service Journal of Nepal; awarded Italian Order of Merit 1953; Order of the Gurkhas (1st Class) of King Mahendra 1962; Recipient of Coral Casket and Bowl from Govt. of People's Republic of China on Nepal-China work 1974. *Publications:* Countries of the World 1935, Ancient and Modern Nepal 1953, Materials for the Study of Nepalese History and Culture 1958, Judicial Customs of Nepal, Part I 1958, Part II 1965, Eroticism in Nepalese Art 1960, Introduction to Kathmandu and Patan 1961, Universal Value of Nepalese Aesthetics, Parts I and II 1961–62, trans. of Kirataruniye, Nepal and her Neighbours 1974, Nepal after the Revolution of 1950 1975, Memoirs of My Four Years and Three Months in the People's Republic of China and South-East Asia, trans. of Nepalese inscriptions, Ensemble of the Stone Sculpture and Licchavi Inscriptions of Nepal 1980–85. *Leisure interest:* researching. *Address:* 636 Kamal Pokhari, Kathmandu, Nepal. *Telephone:* 11696.

BAHADUR, Raj, B.SC., M.A., LL.B.; Indian lawyer and politician; b. 21 Aug. 1912; s. of Sunder Lal; m. Vidyawati Srivastava 1936; four s. one d.; ed. Maharaja's Coll., Jaipur, Agra Coll. and St. John's Coll., Agra; mem. Cen. Advisory Cttee. Bharatpur State 1939–42, Municipal Comm. 1941–42; resigned from these posts in connection with "Quit India" Movement; mem. Rep. Assembly 1943; imprisoned for participation in freedom struggle 1945 and 1947; Sec. Assembly Praja Parishad Party 1943–48, Gen. Sec. Matsya Union Congress Cttee. 1948–49; Pres. Bharatpur Bar Asscn. 1948–51; elected to Constituent Assembly of India 1948–50; mem. Union Parl. 1950–67, 1971–77; Sec. Congress Party in Parl. 1950–52; Deputy Minister, later Minister of State for Communications 1951–56; led Indian Del. to 10th Session of Int. Civil Aviation Org., Caracas; Minister of Communications 1956–57; Minister of State for Transport and Communications 1957–62; Minister of State for Transport 1962–63, Minister of Transport 1963–65, and of Civil Aviation 1965; Minister of Information and Broadcasting 1966–67; Advocate, Supreme Court of India 1967; Amb. to Nepal 1968–71; Minister of Parl. Affairs, Shipping and Transport 1971–73, of Communications 1973–74, of Tourism and Civil Aviation 1973–76; mem. Rajasthan P.C.C. and All-India Congress Cttee. 1956–82; mem. Rajasthan State Legis. Ass. June 1980–, Leader Congress (S) group; awarded Tamrapatra 1974. *Leisure interest:* collecting books. *Address:* 3 Hospital Road, Jaipur, Rajasthan; N-33 Panchshila Park, New Delhi 110017, India. *Telephone:* 72458; 651577.

BAHAR, Abdul Aziz Ahmed al-, B.A.ECONS.; Kuwaiti businessman; b. 1929, Kuwait; s. of Ahmed al-Bahar and Aisha al-Hamad; m. Mariam al-Rifai 1954; two s. three d.; ed. American Univ., Beirut; Dir.-Gen. of Housing Dept., Ministry of Finance 1956–61, of Kuwait Fund for Arab Econ. Devt. 1961–62; Hon. Consul, Repub. of Costa Rica 1963–81; Chair. Kuwait Nat. Industries 1963–65, Kuwait Insurance Co. 1965–67, Kuwait Foreign Trading Contracting and Investment Co. 1965–73, Commercial Bank of Kuwait 1965–78, of Arab European Financial Man. Co. 1978–79; Dir.

Kuwait Chamber of Commerce and Industry 1962–72, Kuwait Metal Pipe Industries 1965–67, Rifbank 1967–74, Arab Trust 1975–78, United Bank of Kuwait Ltd., London 1970–75, Cen. Bank of Kuwait 1980–; Deputy Chair. Commercial Bank of Dubai 1970–78; fmr. Chair. Kuwait Investment Co.; mem. Kuwait Economists Soc., Kuwaiti Graduate Soc. 1960–66; Trustee, Kuwait Univ. 1966–70. *Leisure interests:* reading, swimming, fishing. *Address:* P.O. Box 460, Safat, Kuwait. *Telephone:* 819592.

BAHCALL, John Norris, PH.D.; American professor of astrophysics; b. 30 Dec. 1934, Shreveport, Los Angeles; s. of Malcolm and Mildred Bahcall; m. Neta Asaf; two s. one d.; ed. Harvard Univ.; Asst. Prof., Calif. Inst. of Tech. 1965–67, Assoc. Prof. 1967–70; mem. Inst. for Advanced Study, Princeton, N.J. 1968–71, Prof. 1971–; Visiting Lecturer, Astronomy Dept., Princeton Univ. 1971–; Helen B. Warner Prize, American Astronomical Soc. 1970; Sloan Foundation Fellowship 1968. *Publications:* numerous scientific publs. *Leisure interests:* tennis, swimming and reading. *Address:* Institute for Advanced Study, School of Natural Sciences, Princeton, N.J. 08540, U.S.A. *Telephone:* (609) 734-8054.

BAHNINI, Hadj M'Hammed, L. EN D., L. ÉS L.; Moroccan politican; b. 1914, Fez; ed. Lycée Gouraud (now Lyceé Hassan II), Rabat; Sec., Royal Palace; Magistrate, Haut Tribunal Chérifien; Instructor, Collège Impérial and Private Tutor to H.R.H. Crown Prince Moulay El Hassan, Prince Moulay Abdallah, Princess Lalla Aïcha and Princess Lalla Malika; Dir. of the Imperial Cabinet 1950–51; Del. Judge, Meknès 1951; exiled Dec. 1952–July 1954; Sec.-Gen. of the Cabinet 1955–72; Minister of Justice 1958–65; Minister of Admin. Affairs 1965–70; Minister of Nat. Defence 1970–71; Minister of Justice, Sec.-Gen. of Govt. 1971–72, also Deputy Prime Minister April–Nov. 1972; Minister of State for Culture 1972–81; Minister of State Without Portfolio 1981–. *Address:* c/o Ministry of State, Royal Palace, Rabat, Morocco.

BAHR, Egon; German government official and journalist; b. 18 March 1922, Treffurt; m. Dorothea Grob 1945; one s. one d.; journalist 1945–, Contributor Die Neue Zeitung 1948–59, Das Tagesspiegel 1950; Chief Commentator RIAS (Rundfunk im amerikanischen Sektor Berlins) 1950–60; Dir. Press and Information Office of Berlin 1960–66; promoted to rank of Amb. in diplomatic service 1967; Dir. of Planning Staff, Diplomatic Service 1967–68; Ministerial Dir. 1968–69; State Sec., Bundeskanzleramt and Plenipotentiary of the Fed. Govt. in Berlin 1969–72; mem. of Parl. (Bundestag) 1972; Fed. Minister without Portfolio attached to the Fed. Chancellor's Office 1972–74, for Overseas Devt. Aid (Econ. Co-operation) 1974–76; Dir. Institut für Friedensforschung und Sicherheitspolitik Sept. 1984–; mem. PEN 1974–, Ind. Comm. on Disarmament and Security 1980–; Theodor-Heuss-Preis 1976; Gustav-Heinemann-Bürgerpreis 1982. *Publication:* Was wird aus den Deutschen? 1982. *Address:* Bundeshaus, 5300 Bonn 1, Federal Republic of Germany. *Telephone:* 02221-5321.

BAHUGUNA, Hemavati Nandan, B.A.; Indian politician; b. 25 April 1919, Bughani, Garhwal; s. of late Shri Rewati Nandan Bahuguna; m. Kamala Bahuguna 1946; two s. one d.; ed. D.A.V. Coll., Dehradun, and Allahabad Univ.; active in Independence Movement whilst a student; participated in Quit India Movement 1942; trade union organizer under Indian Nat. TUC, Allahabad; formed Mazdoor Sabha trade union org., Allahabad, mem. 1948–57; mem. Uttar Pradesh Legis. Assembly 1952–69; Parl. Sec. to State Minister of Labour and Social Welfare 1957–58, Deputy Minister of Labour and Industry 1958–60; State Minister of Labour 1962–67, of Finance and Transport 1967–69; Gen. Sec. All-India Congress Cttee. 1969–71; mem. from Allahabad, Lok Sabha 1971–73; Union Minister of Communications 1971–73; Leader of Congress Legislative Party in Uttar Pradesh 1973; Chief Minister of Uttar Pradesh 1973–75, resigned; resigned from Congress Party Feb. 1977; Gen. Sec. Congress for Democracy Feb.–May 1977; Minister of Fertilizers, Petroleum and Chemicals 1977–79, of Finance July–Oct. 1979; mem. Janata Party 1977–79; fmr. Sec.-Gen. Indian Nat. Congress (I); mem. Lok Sabha from Lucknow March 1977–81 (resgnd. from Congress Party and gave up seat in Lok Sabha); won by-election for seat in Lok Sabha, Garhwal-In-Up Hills May 1982; Pres. Lok Dal 1987–; Pres. Democratic Socialist Party 1982–84; has established several schools and travelled extensively. *Leisure interests:* gardening, social service, writing, studies. *Address:* 81 Lodi Estate, New Delhi, India (Home). *Telephone:* 694323 (Home).

BAI DONGCAI; Chinese politician; Sec. District CCP Cttee., Nanchang 1949; Political Comm., Nanchang Mil. District, Jiangxi 1949; mem. Jiangxi Section, CPPCC 1951; Dir. Party School, Nanchang District 1952; mem. CCP Cttee., Jiangxi 1953; Council mem. People's Govt., Jiangxi 1953; Sec. District CCP Cttee., Nanchang, Jiangxi 1955–56; mem. People's Govt., Jiangxi 1955; Sec. CCP Cttee., Jiangxi 1956 Cultural Revolution; Chancellor, Industrial Work Univ., Jiangxi 1960 Cultural Revolution; disappeared during Cultural Revolution; Vice-Chair. Provincial Revolutionary Cttee., Jiangxi 1970; Deputy Sec., Secr. CCP Cttee., Jiangxi 1970–73; Sec. CCP Cttee., Jiangxi 1973–82, 1982–; mem. 11th Cen. Cttee. of CCP 1977–; Vice-Chair. Provincial Revolutionary Cttee., Jiangxi 1978–79; Gov. Jiangxi 1979–82; mem. of 12th Cen. Cttee. of CCP 1982–85; mem. Advisory Comm. (Cen. Cttee. of CCP) 1985–; First Sec. Jiangxi CCP Cttee. 1982–; First Political Commissar Jiangxi Mil. Dist. 1983–. *Address:* c/o Chinese Communist Party Committee, Jiangxi, People's Republic of China.

BAI HUA; Chinese writer; b. 20 Nov. 1930, Hsin Yang City, He Nan Province; m. Wang Pei 1956; one s.; wrote screen play for film Bitter Love; winner, Nat. Poetry Award 1981 for Spring Tide in Sight. *Publications include:* Little Birds Don't Understand What Big Trees Sing (novel); Chinese Scholartree's Song (play). *Leisure interests:* travel, music, swimming. *Address:* c/o China PEN Centre, Shatan Beijie 2, Beijing; Room 706, 4 Lane 83, Jiangning Road, Shanghai, People's Republic of China. *Telephone:* 535727.

BAI JIEFU; Chinese government official; Deputy Head China-Cape Verde Friendship Asscn. 1986–; Vice-Pres. China Asscn. for Int. Friendship 1985; Chair. 6th Beijing CPPCC Municipal Cttee. 1986–. *Address:* Beijing Chinese People's Political Consultative Council, Beijing, People's Republic of China.

BAI JINIAN; Chinese party official; Sec. CCP Cttee., Shaanxi 1984–; mem. 12th Cen. Cttee. CCP 1985–87. *Address:* Shaanxi Provincial Chinese Communist Party, Xian, Shaanxi, People's Republic of China.

BAI LICHEN; Chinese government official; mem. Standing Cttee. CCP Prov. Cttee. Liaoning 1985–; Vice-Gov. Liaoning 1985–; mem. 13th Cen. Cttee. CCP 1987–; Chair. Ningxia Hui. *Address:* Liaoning Provincial People's Government, Shenyang, People's Republic of China.

BAI RUBING; Chinese party official; b. 1906, Shaanxi; Dir. Cen. Admin. of Handicraft Industry, State Council 1954–58; Sec. CCP Shandong 1958–67; Vice-Gov. of Shandong 1958–63, Gov. 1963–67; criticized and removed from office during Cultural Revolution 1967; Vice-Chair. Shandong Revolutionary Cttee. 1971; Deputy Sec. CCP Shandong 1971; First Political Commissar Jinan Mil. Region, PLA 1974–80; Second Sec. CCP Shandong 1974, First Sec. 1974–82; mem. 10th Cen. Cttee. of CCP 1973, 11th Cen. Cttee. 1977–82, Cen. Advisory Cttee. 1982–. *Address:* c/o CCP, Shandong, People's Republic of China.

BAI SHANGWU; Chinese party official; mem. Standing Cttee. CCP Prov. Cttee. Sichuan 1983–; Chair. Sichuan Prov. Political Science and Law Cttee. 1983–; Political Commissar Sichuan Prov. People's Govt. 1983–. *Address:* Sichuan Provincial People's Government, Chengdu, People's Republic of China.

BAI SHOUYI (Djamal al-Din); Chinese historian; b. 1909; Dir. History Dept. of Beijing Teachers Coll. 1963–66; in disgrace during Cultural Revolution 1966–76; mem. China's NPC del. to Iran and Kuwait 1976; Dir. History Dept. of Beijing Teachers Univ. 1978–; Vice-Chair. Nationalities Cttee. 5th NPC 1979–83; Vice-Chair. China's Islamic Asscn. 1980–; mem. 6th NPC 1983–88; mem. 7th NPC 1988–. *Publications:* An Outline History of China 1983. *Address:* Beijing Teachers University, Xizhimenwai Street, Beijing, People's Republic of China.

BAI XUESHI; Chinese artist; b. 1915, Beijing; studied under Liang Shunian; Assoc. Prof. Cen. Inst. of Applied Arts, Beijing. *Works include:* Myriad Peaks Contending, Riverside Village, Riverboats in Springtime. *Address:* Central Institute of Applied Arts, Beijing, People's Republic of China.

BAI YANG (YANG CHENGFANG); Chinese actress; b. 22 April 1920, Beijing; m. Jiang Junchao; one s. one d.; ed. Beijing Drama School; actress, Star Film Studio, Shanghai 1936–37, Chongqing 1938–45; actress, Shanghai Film Studio 1949–; won Best Film Actress Award in China 1957; was branded a 'counter-revolutionary' during the Cultural Revolution 1966–77; rehabilitated 1978; Pres. Asscn. of Chinese Film 1981–; acted in Crisscross Streets 1936, Chu Yuan 1942, 1953, Zhufu (New Year's Sacrifice) 1957, and others. *Address:* 978 Huashan Road, Shanghai, People's Republic of China. *Telephone:* 523248 (Shanghai).

BAIBAKOV, Nikolay Konstantinovich; Soviet politician; b. 7 March 1911; ed. Azerbaijan Industrial Inst.; oil-mining engineer in Azerbaijan oil field 1932–37; Chief Engineer and Man. of Leninneft Oil Trust in Baku 1937; Dir. Vostokneft in Soviet East 1938–39; Dir. Cen. Management Bd. for oil extraction in Eastern districts of the People's Commissariat of Oil Industry 1939–40; Deputy People's Commissar and People's Commissar of the Oil Industry to U.S.S.R. 1940–46; Minister of Oil Industry of U.S.S.R. 1948–55; Deputy to U.S.S.R. Supreme Soviet 1946–50, 1954–62, 1966–; Chair. of U.S.S.R. State Planning Cttee. 1955–58, 1965–86; first Deputy Chair. of Council of Ministers of R.S.F.S.R. and Chair. of State Planning Cttee. of R.S.F.S.R. 1957; Vice-Chair. U.S.S.R. Council of Ministers 1965–85; Chair. State Cttee. of the Chemical and Oil Industry 1963–66; mem. Cen. Cttee. of CPSU 1952–61, 1966–; Chair. State Planning Cttee. of U.S.S.R. 1983–85; Order of Lenin (five times), Order of Red Banner (twice), Hero of Socialist Labour, Lenin Prize, and medals. *Address:* c/o State Planning Committee, 4 1st Dyakovsky pereulok, Moscow, U.S.S.R.

BAILAR, Benjamin Franklin, B.A., M.B.A.; American government official and business executive; b. 21 April 1934, Champaign, Ill.; s. of Dr. John C. Bailar, Jr. and the late Florence (née Catherwood) Bailar; m. Anne Tveit 1958; one s. one d.; ed. Univ. of Colorado and Harvard Graduate School of Business Admin.; Continental Oil Co. 1959–62; American Can Co. 1962–72, Vice-Pres. 1967–72; Senior Asst. Postmaster-Gen. U.S. Postal Service 1972–74, Deputy Postmaster-Gen. 1974–75, Postmaster-Gen. 1975–78; Exec. Vice-Pres., Dir. U.S. Gypsum Co., Chicago 1978–82; Pres. and

C.E.O. Scott Publishing Co. 1983-85; Dir. Dana Corpn., Toledo, Ohio 1980-, U.S. Can, Oakbrook, Ill., Transco Energy Co. 1988-, Proler Industries 1988-, CF and I Steel 1988-; Dean, Prof. of Admin., Jones Graduate School of Admin., Univ. of Houston 1987-; mem. Advisory Cttee., Control Risk Group Ltd., London; Trustee Adler Planetarium, Chicago. *Address:* 2121 Kirby Drive, #141, Houston, Texas 77019, U.S.A. *Telephone:* (713) 524 0276.

BAILEY, Sir Alan Marshall, K.C.B., M.A., B.PHIL.; British civil servant; b. 26 June 1931; s. of John Marshall Bailey and Muriel May Bailey; m. 1st Stella Mary Scott 1959 (divorced 1981), three s.; m. 2nd Shirley Jane Barrett 1981; ed. Bedford School, St. John's and Merton Colls. Oxford; Harkness Commonwealth Fellowship, U.S.A. 1963-64; Prin. Private Sec. to Chancellor of the Exchequer 1971-73; Under-Sec., H.M. Treasury 1973-78, Deputy Sec. 1978-83; mem. Cen. Policy Review Staff, Cabinet Office 1981-82; Second Perm. Sec., Public Services, H.M. Treasury 1983-85; Perm. Sec., Dept. of Transport 1986-. *Address:* 11 Park Row, London, S.E.10, England. *Telephone:* 01-858 3015.

BAILEY, David, F.R.P.S., F.S.I.A.D.; British photographer and film director; b. 2 Jan. 1938, London; s. of Herbert William Bailey and Gladys Agnes Bailey; m. 1st Rosemary Bramble 1960, m. 2nd Catherine Deneuve (q.v.) 1965, m. 3rd Marie Helvin (divorced 1985), m. 4th Catherine Dyer 1986; one d.; self-taught; Photographer for Vogue, U.K., U.S.A., France, Italy and advertising photography 1959-; Dir. Commercials 1966-; Dir. and Producer TV documentaries 1968-; Exhbn. Nat. Portrait Gallery 1971; Photographers' Gallery 1973, Olympus Gallery 1980, 1982, 1983, Victoria and Albert Museum 1983; Int. Centre of Photography, New York 1984. *Publications:* Box of Pinups 1964, Goodbye Baby and Amen 1969, Warhol 1974, Beady Minces 1974, Mixed Moments 1976, Trouble and Strife 1980, N.W.1 1982, Black and White Memories 1983, Nudes 1981-84 1984, Imagine 1985, The Naked Eye: Great photographs of the nude (with Martin Harrison) 1988. *Leisure interests:* photography, aviculture, travel, painting. *Address:* c/o Camera Eye Ltd., 24-26 Brownlow Mews, London, WC1N 2LA, England. *Telephone:* 01-242 5734.

BAILEY, D(avid) R(oy) Shackleton, LITT.D., F.B.A.; British academic; b. 12 Oct. 1917, Lancaster; s. of John Henry Shackleton Bailey and Rosamund Maud Giles; ed. Gonville and Caius Coll. Cambridge; Fellow, Gonville and Caius Coll. 1944-55, Praelector 1954-55, Deputy Bursar 1964, Sr. Bursar 1965-68, Univ. Lecturer in Tibetan 1948-68; Fellow, Dir. of Studies in Classics, Jesus Coll. Cambridge 1955-64; Visiting Lecturer in Classics, Harvard Univ., U.S.A. 1963, Prof. of Greek and Latin 1975-82, Pope Prof. of Latin Language and Literature 1982-88; Prof. of Latin, Univ. of Mich., Ann Arbor 1968-75; Fellow, American Acad. of Arts and Sciences; mem. American Philosophical Soc.; Hon. D.Litt. (Dublin) 1984; Charles J. Goodwin Award of Merit 1978; Nat. Endowment for Humanities Fellow 1980-81; Kenyon Medal, British Acad. 1985. *Publications:* The Satapancasatka of Matrceta 1951, Propertiana 1956, Cicero's Letters, 10 vols. 1965-81, Cicero 1971, Profile of Horace 1982, Anthologia Latina I 1982, Horatius 1985, Cicero's Philippics 1986, Lucanus 1988 and others; Harvard Studies in Classical Philology (Ed.) 1978-85; articles on oriental and classical subjects in professional journals. *Address:* 303 North Division, Ann Arbor, Mich. 48104, U.S.A.

BAILEY, Sir Harold Walter, Kt., D.PHIL., M.A., F.B.A.; British oriental scholar; b. 16 Dec. 1899, Devizes, Wilts.; s. of Frederick C. Bailey and Emma J. Reichart; ed. Univ. of West Australia and Oxford Univ.; Lecturer in Iranian Studies, School of Oriental Studies, London Univ. 1929-36; Prof. of Sanskrit, Cambridge Univ. 36-67, Emeritus Prof. 1967-; Corresp. mem. Danish Acad. 1946, Norwegian Acad. 1947, Acad. of History and Antiquities, Sweden; mem. Inst. de France (Acad. des Inscriptions et Belleslettres) 1968; Fellow, Australian Acad. of the Humanities 1970; Hon. Fellow, School of Oriental and African Studies, London 1963, St. Catherine's Coll., Oxford 1976; Hon. D.Litt. (Univ. of W. Australia, Australian Nat. Univ., Oxford Univ.); Hon. D.D. (Manchester Univ.) 1979. *Publications:* Zoroastrian Problems in the Ninth Century Books 1943, Khotanese Texts I-VII 1945-85, Khotanese Buddhist Texts 1951, Saka documents I-IV 1960-67, Saka Documents Text Volume 1968, Dictionary of Khotan Saka 1979; The Culture of the Sakas in Ancient Iranian Khotan, The Columbia Lectures on Iranian Studies no. 1 1982 and many articles in learned periodicals. *Address:* Queens' College, Cambridge; 23 Brooklands Avenue, Cambridge, CB2 2BG, England. *Telephone:* (0223) 356841.

BAILEY, Norman Stanley, C.B.E., B.MUS.; British operatic and concert singer; b. 23 March 1933, Birmingham; s. of Stanley Ernest and Agnes Train (Gale) Bailey; m. 1st Doreen Evelyn Simpson 1957 (divorced 1983); two s. one d.; m. 2nd Kristine Ciesinski 1985; ed. East Barnet Grammar School, England, Boksburg High School, South Africa, Prince Edward School, Rhodesia, Rhodes Univ., South Africa, Akad. für Musik und Darstéllende Kunst, Vienna; engaged full time at Linz Landestheater, Austria 1960-63, Wuppertaler Bühnen 1963-64, Deutsche Oper am Rhein, Düsseldorf and Duisburg 1964-67; Prin. Baritone English Nat. Opera, Sadler's Wells 1967-71; freelance 1971-; debut at La Scala, Milan 1967, Royal Opera House, Covent Garden 1969, Bayreuth Festival 1969, Paris Opera 1973, Vienna State Opera 1976, Metropolitan Opera, New York 1976; appearances Paris Opera, Edin. Festival, Hamburg State Opera, Munich State Opera; Prof. of Voice, Royal Coll. of Music, London. *Major recordings and TV films include:* Der fliegende Holländer (The Flying

Dutchman), Die Meistersinger von Nürnberg (The Mastersingers of Nuremberg), King Priam, Der Ring des Nibelungen (The Nibelung's Ring), Macbeth, La Traviata, Falstaff; D. Mus. h.c. (Rhodes) 1986; awarded Hon. R.A.M. 1981, Sir Charles Santley Memorial Prize 1977. *Leisure interests:* golf, chess, micro-computing, mem. Bahá'í World Faith. *Address:* c/o Music International, 13 Ardilaun Road, Highbury, London, N5 2QR; 84 Warham Road, South Croydon, Surrey, CR2 6LB, England (Home). *Telephone:* 01-688 9742 (Home).

BAILEY, Paul, F.R.S.L.; British freelance writer; b. 16 Feb. 1937; s. of Arthur Oswald Bailey and Helen Maud Burgess; ed. Sir Walter St. John's School, London; Actor 1956-64, appearing in The Sport of My Mad Mother 1958 and Epitaph for George Dillon 1958; Literary Fellow at Univs. of Newcastle and Durham 1972-74; Bicentennial Fellowship 1976; Visiting Lecturer in English Literature, North Dakota State Univ. 1977-79; Somerset Maugham Award 1968; E. M. Forster Award 1978; George Orwell Memorial Prize 1978. *Publications:* At the Jerusalem 1967, Trespasses 1970, A Distant Likeness 1973, Peter Smart's Confessions 1977, Old Soldiers 1980, An English Madam 1982, Gabriel's Lament 1986. *Leisure interests:* visiting churches, opera, watching tennis. *Address:* 79 Davisville Road, London, W12 9SH, England. *Telephone:* 01-749 2279.

BAILEY, Ralph E., B.S.; American business executive; b. 23 March 1924, Pike County, Ind.; s. of Enos M. Bailey and Gertie L. Taylor; m.; one s. three d.; ed. Purdue Univ.; with Northern Ill. Coal Corpn. 1949-50, Sinclair Coal Co. 1950-55; Peabody Coal Co. 1955-65, Vice-Pres. in charge of Mining Operations 1963-64, Exec. Vice-Pres. Operations 1964-65; Vice-Pres. Consolidation Coal Co., Pittsburgh, Pa. 1965-68, Sr. Vice-Pres. 1968-70, Exec. Vice-Pres. 1970-74, Pres. 1974-, Chair. -1977; Vice-Chair. Continental Oil Co. (now Conoco Inc.) 1975-77, Pres. 1977-, Chair. 1979-87, C.E.O. 1979-; Chair. and C.E.O. Meridian Energy Corpn. 1987-, American Bailey Corpn. 1987-. *Address:* Conoco Inc., 1007 Market Street, Wilmington, Del. 19898, U.S.A.

BAILLIE, Alastair Turner, B.A.; British diplomatist; b. 24 Dec. 1932; s. of Archibald Turner Baillie and Margaret Pinkerton Baillie; m. 1st Wilma Noreen Armstrong 1965 (divorced 1974), one s.; m. 2nd Irena Maria Gregor 1977, one step s. one step d.; ed. Dame Allan's School, Newcastle upon Tyne and Christ's Coll. Cambridge; Nat. Service, commissioned Queen's Own Cameron Highlanders 1951-53; with Overseas Civil Service in North Borneo (subsequently Sabah, Malaysia) 1957-67; joined Diplomatic Service 1967; at FCO 1967-73; Consul (Commercial), Karachi, Pakistan 1973-77; First Sec. and Head of Chancery, Manila, Philippines 1977-80; Counsellor, Addis Ababa, Ethiopia 1980-81; Counsellor (Commercial), Caracas, Venezuela 1981-83; Gov. of Anguilla 1983-87; Deputy High Commr. in Calcutta 1987-. *Leisure interests:* sport, reading and travelling. *Address:* c/o Foreign and Commonwealth Office, London, SW1A 2AH, England.

BAILLY, Jean Paul Marie Henri; French industrialist; b. 5 June 1921, Orléans; s. of Paul M. E. Bailly and Maria J. L. Julien; m. Hélène V. Vienot 1946; one s. one d.; ed. Prytanée Militaire de La Flèche (Sarthe) and Ecole Polytechnique; engineer at collieries in Bassin du Nord and Pas de Calais 1946-54; Asst. Dir.-Gen., then Dir.-Gen. Mines de Zellidja and Fonderie de Penarroya 1954-61; Asst. Dir.-Gen. Société des Ciments Lafarge 1961-66, Dir.-Gen. 1966-74; Pres. Dir.-Gen. Lafarge Coppée 1983-84, Hon. Pres. 1984-; Pres. Conseil d'admin. de la Société de l'industrie minérale 1984-; Officier, Légion d'honneur. *Address:* 28 rue Emile-Menier, 75116 Paris (Office); 13 rue des Pyramides, 75001 Paris, France (Home).

BAILYN, Bernard, PH.D.; American historian; b. 10 Sept. 1922, Hartford, Conn.; s. of Charles Manuel Bailyn and Esther Schloss; m. Lotte Lazarsfeld 1952; two s.; ed. Williams Coll. and Harvard Univ.; mem. Faculty, Harvard Univ. 1953-, Prof. of History 1961-66, Winthrop Prof. of History 1966-81, Adams Univ. Prof. 1981-; Dir. Charles Warren Center for Studies in American History 1983-; Ed.-in-Chief John Harvard Library 1962-70; Trevelyan Lecturer, Cambridge Univ. 1971; mem. American Historical Asscn. (Pres. 1981), American Acad. of Arts and Sciences, Nat. Acad. of Educ., American Philosophical Soc., Royal Historical Soc., Mass. Historical Soc., Mexican Acad. of History and Geography; Robert H. Lord Award, Emmanual Coll. 1967; 8 hon. degrees. *Publications:* New England Merchants in the 17th Century 1955, Massachusetts Shipping 1697-1714: A Statistical Study 1959, Education in the Forming of American Society 1960, Pamphlets of the American Revolution 1750-1776, Vol. I 1965, The Ideological Origins of the American Revolution (Pulitzer and Bancroft Prizes 1968) 1967, The Origins of American Politics 1968, The Ordeal of Thomas Hutchinson (Nat. Book Award 1975) 1974, The Great Republic (co-author) 1977, Voyagers to the West (Pulitzer Prize 1986) 1986; co-ed.: The Intellectual Migration 1930-1960 1969, Law in American History 1972, Perspectives in American History 1967-77, The Press and the American Revolution 1980. *Address:* 170 Clifton Street, Belmont, Mass. 02178, U.S.A.

BAINBRIDGE, Beryl, F.R.S.L.; British actress and writer; b. 21 Nov. 1934; d. of Richard and Winifred (née Baines) Bainbridge; m. Austin Davies 1954 (dissolved); one s. two d.; ed. Merchant Taylor's School, Liverpool, Arts Educational Schools, Tring; Guardian Fiction Award for The Bottle Factory Outing, Whitbread Award for Injury Time; acted in plays: Tiptoe Through the Tulips 1976, The Warriors Return 1977, It's a Lovely Day Tomorrow 1977, Journal of Bridget Hitler 1981, Somewhere More Central (TV) 1981,

Evensong (TV) 1986. *Publications:* A Weekend with Claude 1967, Another Part of the Wood 1968, Harriet Said . . . 1972, The Dressmaker 1973, The Bottle Factory Outing 1974, Sweet William 1975 (film 1980), A Quiet Life 1976, Injury Time 1977, Young Adolf 1978, Winter Garden 1980, English Journey (TV series) 1984, Watson's Apology 1984, Mum and Mr. Armitage 1985, Forever England 1986 (TV series 1986), Filthy Lucre 1986, An Awfully Big Adventure 1989. *Address:* 42 Albert Street, London, NW1 7NU, England. *Telephone:* 01-387 3113.

BAINBRIDGE, Kenneth Tompkins, M.S., M.A., PH.D.; American physicist; b. 27 July 1904, Coopers-town, N.Y.; s. of William Warin and Mae (née Tompkins) Bainbridge; m. 1st Margaret Pitkin 1931 (died 1967), one s. two d.; m. 2nd Helen Brinkley King 1969; ed. Massachusetts Inst. of Technology and Princeton Univ.; Nat. Research Council Fellow 1929-31; Bartol Research Foundation Fellow 1931-33, Guggenheim Memorial Foundation Fellow 1933-34; Asst. Prof. Harvard Univ. 1934-38, Assoc. Prof. 1938-46, Prof. of Physics 1946, Chair. Dept. of Physics 1953-56; George Vasmer Leverett Prof. of Physics, Harvard 1961-74, Emer. Prof. 1975-; now design consultant to linear direct current motors; Div. Leader, Nat. Defense Research Cttee., Radiation Laboratory 1940-43; Group and Division Leader, Los Alamos Laboratory 1943-46; awarded Levy Medal, Franklin Inst. 1933; elected American Acad. Arts and Sciences 1938, N.A.S. 1946; Dir. first atomic bomb "Trinity" test Feb.-Sept. 1945; awarded Presidential Certificate of Merit for war research work on radar 1948; Trustee Assoc. Univs. Inc. 1958-59. *Leisure interests:* painting, photography, travel. *Address:* 5 Nobscot Road, Weston, Mass. 02193, U.S.A.

BAIRD, Charles Fitz, A.B.; American business executive (retd.); b. 4 Sept. 1922, Southampton, N.Y.; s. of George White and Julia (Fitz) Baird; m. Norma Adele White 1947; two s. two d.; ed. Middlebury Coll., New York Univ. and Harvard Univ.; served as Captain, U.S. Marine Corps Reserve 1943-46, 1951-52; with Standard Oil Co., N.J. 1948-65, Deputy European Financial Rep., London 1955-58, Asst. Treas. 1958-62, Dir. Esso Standard S.A. Française 1962-65; Asst. Sec. Financial Man., U.S. Navy 1965-67, Under-Sec. 1967-69; Vice-Pres. Finance, Int. Nickel Co. of Canada Ltd. (Inco Ltd.) 1969-72, Sr. Vice-Pres. 1972-76, Dir. 1974-; Vice-Chair. 1976-77, Pres. 1977-80, Chair. and CEO 1980-87; Dir. Bank of Montreal, ICI Americas N. America Advisory Bd., Aetna Life and Casualty Co.; mem. Pres.'s Comm. Marine Science, Eng. and Resources 1967-69, Nat. Advisory Comm. on Ocean and Atmosphere 1972-74, Bd. of Advisers Naval War Coll. 1970-74, Council on Foreign Relations; mem. Bd., Bucknell Univ.; Hon. LL.D.; U.S. Navy Distinguished Civilian Service Award 1969. *Address:* c/o Inco Limited, Royal Trust Tower, Toronto Dominion Centre, P.O. Box 44, Toronto, Ont., M5K 1N4, Canada.

BAIRD, Dugald Euan, B.A.; American business executive; b. 16 Sept. 1937, Aberdeen, Scotland; s. of Dugald Baird and Matilda D. Tennant; m. Angelica Hartz 1961; two c.; ed. Univs. of Aberdeen and Cambridge; Field engineer, Schlumberger, Europe, Asia, Africa 1960-69; Asst. Regional Man. Schlumberger Overseas, Singapore 1969-72; Divisional Man. South Gulf Div. Schlumberger Overseas, Dubai 1972-74; Personnel Man. Schlumberger Technical Services, Paris 1975-76; Exec. Vice-Pres. Schlumberger Ltd., New York 1976-86, Chair., Pres. and C.E.O. 1986-. *Address:* Schlumberger Ltd., 277 Park Avenue, New York, N.Y. 10172, U.S.A.

BAIRD, Joseph Edward; American banker and company executive; b. 18 March 1934, Columbus, Ohio; s. of Judge Edward Graham Baird and Alice Hoover Baird; m. Anne Marie Baird 1958; one s. two d.; ed. Yale Univ.; Chase Manhattan Bank 1959-66; Smith, Barney & Co. Inc. 1966-67; Man. Dir., Chief Exec. Western American Bank (Europe) Ltd., London 1968-73; Pres., Chief Operating Officer, Occidental Petroleum Corpn. 1973-78. *Leisure interest:* sailing. *Address:* c/o Occidental Petroleum Corporation, 10889 Wilshire Boulevard, Suite 1500, Los Angeles, Calif. 90024, U.S.A.

BAJAJ, Rahul, LL.B., M.B.A.; Indian industrialist; b. 10 June 1938, Calcutta; m. Rupa Bajaj 1961; two s. one d.; ed. St. Stephen's Coll., Delhi, Govt. Law Coll., Bombay, Harvard Univ.; Dir. Bajaj Auto Ltd. 1956-60, Chair. and Man. Dir. 1972-; Chair. Maharashtra Scooters Ltd. 1975-, Indian Airlines 1986-; Pres. Asscn. of Indian Automobile Mfrs. 1976-78, Mahratta Chamber of Commerce and Industries 1983-85, Confed. of Eng. Industry 1979-80; Chair. Devt. Council for Automobiles and Allied Industries 1975-77; mem. Exec. Cttee. Confed. of Eng. Industry 1978-, Governing Council, Automotive Research Asscn of India 1972-, Devt. Council for Automobiles and Allied Industries 1987-, World Econ. Forum's Advisory Council 1984-; Man of the Year Award (Nat. Inst. of Quality Assurance) 1975, Business Man of the Year Award (Business India Magazine) 1985. *Address:* Bajaj Auto Ltd., Bombay-Poona Road, Akurdi, Pune 411 035, India (Office). *Telephone:* 0212-86250/83399 (Office); 0212-82857 (Home).

BAJAJ, Ramkrishna; Indian business executive; b. 22 Sept. 1923, Wardha, Maharashtra; s. of late Jamnalal Bajaj and Janakidevi Bajaj; m. Vimla Bajaj 1947; three s.; Chair. and Man. Dir. The Hindustan Sugar Mills Ltd.; Chair. Bachraj & Co., Ltd., Bajaj Int. Pvt. Ltd., Hercules Hoists Ltd.; Vice-Chair. Mukand Iron & Steel Works Ltd.; Dir. Andhra Valley & Power Supply Co., Ltd., Hind Lamps Ltd., etc.; fmr. Pres. Fed. of Indian Chambers of Commerce and Industry, Indian Nat. Cttee. of ICC, Indian Merchants' Chamber etc.; Indian Merchants' Chamber Award 1985; Shiromani Award (Pres. of India) 1986. *Publications:* in English: The Young Russia 1960, Social Role of Business 1970, Challenges to Trade and

Industry 1982, Indian Economy: Emerging Perspectives 1986; in Hindi: Japan Ki Sair, Rusi Yuvakon Ke Beech, Atlantic Ke Uspar. *Leisure interests:* badminton, swimming. *Address:* Bajaj Bhawan, Jamnalal Bajaj Marg, 226 Nariman Point, Bombay 400021 (Office); Mount Unique, 13th Floor, 62A Peddar Road, Bombay 400 021, India (Home). *Telephone:* 2023626 (Office); 367154 (Home).

BAJPAI, Rajendra Kumari, D.PHIL.; Indian politician; b. 8 Feb. 1925, Bhagalpur; d. of Krishna Mishra; m. D. N. Bajpai; one s. one d.; mem. Legis. Ass., Uttar Pradesh 1962-77, Minister of Educ. 1970, Minister of Health 1971, Minister of Food and Civil Supplies 1973-75, Minister of Power and Labour 1976-77, Pres. Uttar Pradesh Congress Cttee. 1971-72; mem. Lok Sabha 1980; Gen. Soc. All India Congress Cttee. 1980-85; Union Minister of State for Welfare Sept. 1985-; Delegate to UNO 1980; Head, Indian Del. to Int. Conf. on Social Welfare 1986. *Publications:* articles on social, political and econ. issues. *Leisure interests:* reading books on politics and econs. *Address:* c/o Lok Sabha, New Delhi, India.

BAJSZCZAK, Jerzy, M.ENG.; Polish politician; b. 18 Feb. 1936, Warsaw; s. of Stanislaw Bajszczak and Helena Bajszczak; m. Maria Bajszczak 1962; one d.; ed. Cracow Tech. Univ.; Bldg. supervisor, Industrial Kilns Construction Enterprise, Warsaw 1960; Head of Dept., Chemical Plants Bldg. Union, Warsaw 1960-70; Dir., Kujawy Industrial Bldg. Enterprise, Włocławek 1971-73; Deputy Dir. of Dept. of Industrial Bldg. 1973-74, then Dir. Dept. of Science, Tech. and Design 1974-80 in Ministry of Bldg. and Bldg. Materials Industry; Gen. Dir. Bistyp Research and Design Centre of Industrial Bldg. 1980-; Minister of Bldg, Local and Municipal Econ. 1986-87; mem. Polish United Workers' Party (PZPR); mem. Council of Bldg. and Bldg. Materials Industry, Scientific Council of Inst. of Org., Man. and Econs. of Bldg. Industry; Officer's Cross of Order of Polonia Restituta and other decorations. *Leisure interests:* gardening, reading, theatre. *Address:* 4110 Melsztynska Street, Flat 22, 02-537 Warsaw, Poland.

BAJT, Aleksander, D.ECONS.; Yugoslavian professor of economics; b. 27 Feb. 1921, Ljubljana; s. of Aleš Bajt and Franja Bajt-Lukač; m. Dragica Zupanič 1946; ed. Law School, Univ. of Ljubljana; Dir. Slovenian Textile Ind. 1946-50; Asst. Prof. of Econs., Law School, Univ. of Ljubljana 1951-65, Prof. 1965-; Visiting Prof. Univ. of Va. 1968-69; f. Econs. Inst. of Law Faculty 1963, Ind. Inst. 1971-; Ed. Privredna kretanja Jugoslavije, Gospodarska gibanja 1971-; mem. Slovenian Acad. of Arts and Sciences 1987-; Corresp. mem. Slovenian Acad. of Arts and Sciences 1981-. *Publications:* Marxov zakon vrednosti 1953, Political Economy 1958, Introduction to Political Economy 1965, Principles of Economics (in Serbocroat) 1967, Principles of Economic Analysis and Policy 1979, Alternative Economic Policy 1986, and over 200 papers on economic subjects. *Address:* Pleteršnikova 32, Ljubljana, Yugoslavia. *Telephone:* 218-704 (Office); 312-160 (Home).

BAKA, Władysław, D.ECON.SC.; Polish economist and politician; b. 24 March 1936, Boksycka; ed. Warsaw Univ.; staff of Warsaw Univ. 1959-, Asst. Prof. 1971-77, Head, Research Centre of Planning and Econ. Policy 1971-73, Extraordinary Prof. 1977-; Deputy Head, Econ. Dept. of Cen Cttee. of Polish United Workers' Party (PZPR) 1973-81; Sec. Comm. for Econ. Reform 1980-85, Deputy Chair. 1986-; Minister Plenipotentiary for Econ. Reform, mem. Presidium of Govt. 1981-85; Pres. Nat. Bank of Poland 1985-88; mem. Presidium, Econ. Sciences Cttee. of Polish Acad. of Sciences 1975-81; mem. Consultative Council attached to Chair. Council of State 1986-; mem. PZPR 1955-, Political Bureau and Sec. Cen. Cttee. 1988-; Gov. representing Poland in IBRD 1986-; Commdr.'s and Kt.'s Cross of Order of Polonia Restituta. *Publications:* numerous works on planning and econ. policy including Programowanie rozwoju gałęzi przemysłu 1971, Rachunek ekonomiczny w gospodarce socjalistycznej (co-author) 1973, Planowanie gospodarki narodowej (co-author) 1975, Strategia rozwoju społeczno-gospodarczego Polski Ludowej 1980, Polska reforma gospodarcza 1982. *Address:* Komitet Centralny PZPR, ul. Nowy Świat 6, 00-497 Warszawa, Poland.

BAKER, Alan, PH.D., F.R.S.; British mathematician; b. 19 Aug. 1939, London; s. of Barnet and Bessie Baker; ed. Stratford Grammar School, University Coll., London, and Trinity Coll., Cambridge; Fellow, Trinity Coll., Cambridge 1964-, Research Fellow 1964-68, Dir. of Studies in Math. 1968-74; Prof. of Pure Math. Univ. of Cambridge 1974-; Visiting Prof. Stanford Univ. 1974 and other univs. in U.S.A.; Fields Medal 1970, Adams Prize 1972; Hon. Fellow, Indian Nat. Science Acad. *Publications:* Transcendental Number Theory 1975, A Concise Introduction to the Theory of Numbers 1984; papers in scientific journals. *Leisure interests:* travel, photography, theatre. *Address:* Department of Pure Mathematics and Mathematical Statistics, 16 Mill Lane, Cambridge, CB2 1SB; Trinity College, Cambridge, CB2 1TQ, England. *Telephone:* (0223) 337999; (0223) 338400.

BAKER, Carroll; American actress; b. 1931, Johnstown, Pa.; d. of William W. Baker and Virginia Duffy; m. 1st Jack Garfein 1955 (divorced); one s. one d.; m. 2nd Donald Burton 1982; ed. St. Petersburg Jr. Coll., Florida; Broadway appearances include All Summer Long 1954, Come on Strong 1962; toured Vietnam with Bob Hope q.v. 1966; mem. Acad. of Motion Picture Arts and Sciences; several acting awards. *Films include:* Giant 1956, Baby Doll 1957, The Big Country 1958, But Not for Me 1959, The

Miracle 1959, Bridge to the Sun 1960, Something Wild 1961, How the West Was Won 1962, Station Six Sahara 1962, Carpetbaggers 1963, Cheyenne Autumn 1963, Mr Moses 1964, Sylvia 1964, Harlow 1965, The Harem 1967, Honeymoon 1968, The Sweet Body of Deborah 1968, Captain Apache 1971, Bad 1977, Watcher in the Woods 1980, Red Monarch 1983, The Secret Diary of Sigmund Freud 1983, Star 80 1983, Ironweed 1987. *Publications:* Baby Doll (autobiog.), A Roman Tale. *Address:* c/o Creative Management, 8899 Beverly Boulevard, Los Angeles, Calif. 90048, U.S.A.

BAKER, Frederick William George, B.SC.; British administrator and author; b. 24 March 1928, Wallington; s. of Edward Baker and Sarah Pedder; m. Jacqueline Laclavère 1962; one s. one d.; ed. Univ. of Manchester, Ecole des Hautes Etudes en Sciences Sociales, Paris; Asst. Ed., Research and Journal of Tropical Agric. 1955-56; Asst. to Sec.-Gen., IGY Cttee. 1957, 1960; Gen. Ed., IGY Annals 1962-65; Exec. Sec., Int. Biological Programme 1963-66, Int. Council of Scientific Unions 1966-; Fellow, World Acad. of Arts and Sciences. *Publications:* Annals of the International Year (Ed.), Approaches to Earth Survey Problems through Use of Space Techniques (Ed.), Ecology in Practice (Ed.), ICSU: A Brief Review. *Leisure interests:* history of science, polar exploration, gardening. *Address:* 51, boulevard de Montmorency, Paris 75016, France. *Telephone:* (33) 1-45250329.

BAKER, George Pierce, A.M., PH.D.; American educationist; b. 1 Nov. 1903, Cambridge, Mass.; s. of Geo P. and Christina H. Baker; m. 1st Ruth Bremer 1926, 2nd Mary E. Osher 1978; one s. three d.; ed. Harvard Univ.; Instructor in Econs. and Tutor in Div. of Econ. History and Govt., Harvard Coll. 1928-36; Asst. Prof. of Transportation, Harvard Business School 1936-39, Assoc. Prof. 1939-46, James J. Hill Prof. 1946-63, Prof. Emer. 1970-, George Fisher Baker Prof. of Admin. 1963-70, Dean of Faculty 1962-69; mem. of Civil Aeronautics Bd. 1940-42, Vice-Chair. 1942; Lieut.-Col. Quartermaster Corps 1942, Col.-Gen. Staff Corps 1943-45; Dir. Office of Transport and Communications Policy, State Dept. 1945-46; U.S. mem. UN Transport and Communications Comm. 1945-56; Prof. of Int. Transport and Communications, Fletcher School of Law and Diplomacy 1946-47; mem. American Soc. Traffic and Transport, Transport Asscn. of America, Pres. 1954-62, Chair. of Bd. 1962-68; Fellow, American Acad. of Arts and Sciences; Trustee Penn Cen. Transportation Co. 1970-74; Hon. LL.D. (Harvard Univ.) 1969 and seven other hon. degrees; Legion of Merit; Transport Man of Year Award 1959; Harry E. Salzberg Medal, Syracuse Univ. 1958, Seley Transport Award 1967. *Publications:* The Formation of the New England Railroad Systems 1937, Case Problems in Transportation Management (with G. E. Germane) 1957. *Address:* 4075 East Campbell Avenue, Phoenix, Ariz. 85018, U.S.A. *Telephone:* 602-956-9537.

BAKER, Howard Henry, Jr., LL.B.; American politician and attorney; b. 15 Nov. 1925, Huntsville, Tenn.; s. of Howard H. Baker and Dora Ladd; m. Joy Dirksen 1951; one s. one d.; ed. The McCallie School, Chattanooga, Univ. of the South, Sewanee, Tennessee, Tulane Univ. of New Orleans, and Univ. of Tennessee Coll. of Law; U.S. Naval Reserve 1943-46; fmr. partner in Baker, Worthington, Barnett & Crossley, Knoxville, Tenn.; fmr. Chair. Bd. First Nat. Bank, Oneida, Tenn.; Senator from Tennessee 1967-85; Minority Leader in the Senate 1977-81, Majority Leader 1981-85; White House Chief of Staff Feb. 1987-Dec. 1988; mem. law firm Vinson and Elkins 1984; Medal of Freedom 1984; Republican. *Leisure interests:* tennis, photography. *Address:* c/o The White House Office of the Chief of Staff, Washington, D.C. 20500, U.S.A.

BAKER, James Addison, III, LL.B.; American lawyer and government official; b. 28 April 1930, Texas; s. of James A. Baker, Jr., and Bonner Means; m. Susan Garrett; eight c.; ed. Princeton Univ. and Univ. of Texas Law School; served U.S. Marine Corps 1952-54; with law firm Andrews, Kurth, Campbell and Jones, Houston, Texas 1957-75; Under-Sec. of Commerce under Pres. Ford 1975; Nat. Chair. Ford's presidential campaign 1976; Campaign Dir. for George Bush in primary campaign 1980, later joined Reagan campaign; White House Chief of Staff and on Nat. Security Council 1981-85; Trustee, Woodrow Wilson Int. Center for Scholars, Smithsonian Inst. 1977-; Sec. of the Treasury 1985-88, nominated Sec. of State Dec. 1988; Co-Chair. Campaign to elect Bush as Pres. *Leisure interests:* jogging, tennis, hunting. *Address:* Office of the Secretary of State, 2210 C Street, N.W., Washington, D.C. 20520, U.S.A.

BAKER, Dame Janet, D.B.E., F.R.S.A.; British mezzo-soprano; b. 21 Aug. 1933, Hatfield, Yorks.; d. of Robert Abbott and May (née Pollard) Baker; m. James Keith Shelley 1957; ed. York Coll. for Girls, Wintringham, Grimsby; Pres. Royal Scottish Acad. of Music and Drama 1983-; Pres. London Sinfonia 1986-; retd. from operatic stage July 1982, continues to give concert performances; Kathleen Ferrier Memorial Prize 1956; Queen's Prize 1959; Shakespeare Prize, F.v.S. Foundation of Hamburg; Hon. D.Mus. (Birmingham) 1968, (Leicester) 1974, (London) 1974, (Hull) 1975, (Oxford) 1975, (Leeds) 1980, (Lancaster) 1983, (York) 1984, (Cambridge) 1984; Hon. LL.D. (Aberdeen) 1980; Hon. D.Litt. (Bradford) 1983; Hon. Fellow, St. Anne's Coll., Oxford 1975, Downing Coll., Cambridge 1985; Grand Prix, French Nat. Acad. of Lyric Recordings 1975, Leonie Sonning Prize (Denmark) 1979. *Publication:* Full Circle (autobiog.) 1982. *Leisure interest:* reading. *Address:* c/o Ibbs and Tillett, 450-452 Edgware Road, London, W2 1EG, England.

BAKER, Rt. Rev. John Austin, M.A., M. LITT.; British ecclesiastic; b. 11 Jan. 1928, Birmingham; s. of George Austin Baker and Grace Edna Baker; m. Gillian Mary Leach 1974; ed. Marlborough Coll., Oriel Coll., Oxford and Cuddesdon Theological Coll.; ordained 1954; Official Fellow, Chaplain and Lecturer in Divinity Corpus Christi Coll., Oxford 1959-73; Lecturer in Theology Brasenose and Lincoln Colls., Oxford; Dorrance Visiting Prof. Trinity Coll., Hartford, Conn. 1967; Canon of Westminster 1973-82; Visiting Prof., King's Coll., London 1974-76; Sub-Dean of Westminster and Lector Theologiae 1978-82; Rector of St. Margaret's, Westminster 1978-82; Chaplain to Speaker of House of Commons 1978-82; Bishop of Salisbury 1982-; mem. Church of England Doctrine Comm. 1967-81, 1984-87, Chair. 1985-87; mem. Standing Comm., WCC Faith and Order Comm. 1984-87; Emer. Fellow, Corpus Christi Coll., Oxford 1977-. *Publications:* The Foolishness of God 1970, Travels in Oudamovia 1976, The Whole Family of God 1981, numerous theological articles and trans. *Address:* South Canonry, 71 The Close, Salisbury, Wilts., SP1 2ER, England. *Telephone:* (0722) 334031.

BAKER, John Hamilton, PH.D., LL.D., F.B.A., F.R.HIST.S.; British barrister, legal historian and law teacher; b. 10 April 1944, Sheffield; s. of Kenneth Lee Vincent Baker and Marjorie Bagshaw; m. Veronica Margaret Lloyd 1968; two d.; ed. King Edward VI Grammar School, Chelmsford and Univ. Coll. London; Asst. Lecturer in Law, Univ. Coll. London 1965-67, Lecturer 1967-70; Barrister Inner Temple, London 1966; Librarian, Squire Law Library, Cambridge 1971-73; Lecturer in Law, Cambridge Univ. 1973-83, Reader in English Legal History 1983-88, Prof. 1988-, Fellow of St. Catharine's Coll. 1971-; Hon. Bencher, Inner Temple, London 1988; Jt. Literary Dir. Selden Soc. 1981-; Yorke Prize (Cambridge) 1975; Ames Prize (Harvard Law School) 1985. *Publications:* An Introduction to English Legal History 1971, The Reports of Sir John Spelman 1977, Manual of Law French 1979, The Order of Serjeants at Law 1984, English Legal MSS in the U.S.A. 1985, The Legal Profession and the Common Law 1986, Sources of English Legal History (with S. F. C. Milsom) 1986, The Notebook of Sir John Port 1987. *Address:* St. Catharine's College, Cambridge, CB2 1RL: 75 Hurst Park Avenue, Cambridge, CB4 2AB, England (Home). *Telephone:* Cambridge 338317 (Coll.); Cambridge 62251 (Home).

BAKER, John William; British business executive; b. 5 Dec. 1937; s. of Reginald Baker and Wilhelmina Baker; m. 1st Pauline Moore 1962, one s.; m. 2nd Gillian Bullen; ed. Harrow Weald Co. Grammar School and Oriel Coll., Oxford; served army 1959-61, Ministry of Transport 1961-70, Dept. of Environment 1970-74; Deputy C.E.O. Housing Corpn. 1974-78; Sec. Cen. Electricity Generating Bd. 1979-80, Bd. mem. 1980, Jt. Man. Dir. 1986-; C.E.O. Nat. Power Co. *Leisure interests:* tennis, squash, bridge, music, theatre. *Address:* Central Electricity Generating Board, Sudbury House, 15 Newgate Street, London, EC1 7AU, England. *Telephone:* 01-634-7039.

BAKER, Rt. Hon. Kenneth (Wilfred), P.C., M.P.; British politician; b. 3 Nov. 1934; s. of W. M. Baker; m. Mary Elizabeth Gray-Muir 1963; one s. two d.; ed. St. Paul's School and Magdalen Coll. Oxford; nat. service 1953-55; served Twickenham Borough Council 1960-62; as Conservative candidate contested Poplar 1964, Acton 1966; Conservative M.P. for Acton 1968-70; Parl. Sec. Civil Service Dept. 1972-74, Parl. Pvt. Sec. to Leader of Opposition 1974-75; Minister of State and Minister for Information Tech., Dept. of Trade and Industry 1981-84; Sec. of State for the Environment 1985-86, for Educ. and Science 1986-; mem. Public Accounts Cttee. 1969-70; mem. Exec. 1922 Cttee. 1978-81; Chair. Hansard Soc. 1978-81; Sec. Gen. UN Conf. of Parliamentarians on World Population and Devt. 1978. *Publications:* I Have No Gun But I Can Spit 1980, London Lines (Ed.) 1982, 1984, The Faber Book of English History in Verse 1988. *Leisure interest:* collecting books. *Address:* House of Commons, London, S.W.1, England.

BAKER, Paul T., PH.D.; American professor of anthropology; b. 28 Feb. 1927, Burlington, Ia.; s. of Palmer Ward Baker and Viola (née Thornell) Laughlin; m. Thelma M. Shoher 1949; one s. three d.; ed. Univ. of New Mexico and Harvard Univ.; Research Scientist, U.S. Army Climatic Research Lab. 1952-57; Asst. Prof. of Anthropology, Penn. State Univ. 1957-61, Assoc. Prof. 1961-64, Prof. 1965-81, Head Dept. of Anthropology 1980-85, Evan Pugh Prof. of Anthropology 1981-87, Evan Pugh Prof. Emer. 1987-; Pres. Int. Asscn. of Human Biologists, American Asscn. of Physical Anthropologists 1969-71, Human Biology Council 1974-77; Chair. U.S. Man and Biosphere Program 1983-85; mem. N.A.S.; Huxley Medal (Royal Anthropological Soc., London) 1982, Gorjanovic-Krambergeri Medal (Croatian Anthropological Soc.) 1985. *Publications:* The Biology of Human Adaptability (Co.Ed.) 1966, Man in the Andes: A Multidisciplinary Study of High Altitude Quechua 1976, The Biology of High Altitude Peoples (Ed.) 1978, The Changing Samoans: Behavior and Health in Transition 1986, Human Biology (co-author) 1987. *Leisure interest:* sailing. *Address:* 47-450 Lulani Street, Kaneohe, Hawaii 96744, U.S.A. *Telephone:* (808) 239 8228.

BAKER, Russell Wayne, D.LITT.; American journalist and author; b. 14 Aug. 1925, London Co., Va.; s. of Benjamin R. Baker and Lucy E. Robinson; m. Miriam E. Nash 1950; two s. one d.; ed. Johns Hopkins Univ.; served U.S.N.R. 1943-45; with Baltimore Sun 1947-64; mem. Washington Bureau, New York Times 1954-62; author-columnist, editorial page,

Observer 1962–; mem. American Acad., Inst. of Arts and Letters; Pulitzer Prize for distinguished commentary 1979; Pulitzer Prize for Biography 1983 and other awards; several hon. degrees. *Publications:* American in Washington 1961, No Cause for Panic 1964, All Things Considered 1965, Our Next President 1968, Poor Russell's Almanac 1972, The Upside Down Man 1977, Home Again, Home Again 1979, So This is Depravity 1980, Growing Up 1982, The Rescue of Miss Yaskell and Other Pipe Dreams 1983. *Address:* 229 West 43rd Street, New York, N.Y. 10036, U.S.A. (Office).

BAKER, William Oliver, B.S., PH.D.; American research chemist; b. 15 July 1915, Chestertown, Md.; s. of Harold M. and Helen (Stokes) Baker; m. Frances Burrill 1941; one s.; ed. Washington Coll., Maryland, and Princeton Univ.; with Bell Telephone Labs. 1939–, in charge of polymer research and devt. 1948-51, Asst. Dir. of Chemical and Metallurgical Research 1951-54, Dir. of Research, Physical Sciences 1954-55, Vice-Pres. Research 1955-73, Pres. 1973-79, Chair. of the Bd. 1979-80; mem. N.A.S., Nat. Acad. of Engineering, Inst. of Medicine, American Philosophical Soc., American Acad. of Arts and Sciences, Nat. Comm. on Jobs and Small Business 1985–, Nat. Comm. on Role and Future of State Colls. and Univs. 1985–, Comm. on Science and Tech. of New Jersey 1985–; numerous awards include Perkin Medal 1963; Priestley Medal 1966; Edgar Marburg Award 1967; A.S.T.M. Award to Executives 1967; Industrial Research Institute Medal 1970; Frederik Philips Award (Inst. of Elec. and Electronics Engineers) 1972; Industrial Research Man of the Year Award 1973; James Madison Medal, Princeton Univ. 1975; Gold Medal, American Inst. of Chemists 1975; Mellon Inst. Award 1975; American Chemical Soc. Parsons Award 1976; Franklin Inst. Delmer S. Fahrney Medal 1977; J. Willard Gibbs Medal, American Chemical Soc. 1978, Madison Marshall Award 1980; von Hippel Award, Materials Research Soc. 1978; Bush Medal, Nat. Science Foundation 1982; and 24 hon. degrees. *Publications:* Rheology, Vol. III 1960, Listen to Leaders in Engineering 1965, Perspectives in Polymer Science 1966, Science: The Achievement and the Promise 1968, 1942-1967, Twenty-five Years at RCA Laboratories: Materials Science and Engineering in the United States 1970, The Technological Catch and Society 1975, Science and Technology in America—An Assessment 1977, Resources of Organic Matter for the Future—Perspectives and Recommendations 1978; contributions to many symposia and publs.; about 95 research papers in journals and holder of 13 patents. *Address:* AT & T Bell Laboratories, 600 Mountain Avenue, Murray Hill, N.J. 07974, U.S.A. (Office). *Telephone:* 201-582-3423.

BAKER, Wilson, M.A., PH.D., D.SC., F.R.S., F.R.S.C; British professor of organic chemistry (retd.); b. 24 Jan. 1900, Runcorn; s. of Harry Baker and Mary Baker; m. Juliet Elizabeth Glaisyer 1927; one s. two d.; ed. Liverpool Coll. Upper School, Victoria Univ. of Manchester; Asst. Lecturer in Chem., Univ. of Manchester 1924-27; Tutor in Chem., Dalton Hall, Manchester 1926-27; Univ. Lecturer and Demonstrator in Chem., Univ. of Oxford 1937-44; Alfred Capper Pass Prof. of Organic Chem., Univ. of Bristol 1945-65, Dean of Faculty of Science 1948-51, Emer. Prof. 1965–; Vice-Pres. Chemical Soc. 1957-60. *Publications:* numerous papers on organic chem., dealing chiefly with synthesis of natural products, devt. of synthetical processes, compounds of abnormal aromatic type, organic inclusion compounds, and the preparation of large-ring compounds, and the chem. of penicillin, publ. mainly in Journal of the Chemical Soc.; 2nd edn. of Sidgwick's The Organic Chemistry of Nitrogen (with T.W.J. Taylor) 1937. *Leisure interests:* walking, gardening, music, mineralogy. *Address:* Lane's End, 54 Church Road, Winscombe, Avon, England. *Telephone:* Winscombe 3112.

BAKHRAKH, Lev Davidovich; Soviet physicist; b. 22 July 1921, Rostov-on-Don; ed. Zhukovsky Air Force Engineering Acad.; Research Assoc. Inst. of Instrument-making 1945–, Radio-engineering Inst., Moscow 1947–; mem. CPSU 1947–; Corresp. mem. of U.S.S.R. Acad. of Sciences 1966–; State Prize 1951; Lenin Prize 1961. *Publications:* Works on radiophysics and radio engineering. *Address:* c/o U.S.S.R. Academy of Sciences, 14 Leninsky Prospekt, Moscow, U.S.S.R.

BAKHT, Sikander; Indian politician; b. 24 Aug. 1918, Delhi; s. of Hafiz Mohd Yusuf and N. Yusuf; m. Raj Sharma 1952; two s.; ed. Delhi Univ.; mem. of Indian Nat. Congress until 1969; mem. All-India Congress Cttee. (Org.), also mem. Working Cttee. 1969-77; mem. Delhi Metropolitan Council for 10 years; detained for 18 months during emergency 1975-76; mem. for Chandni Chowk, Lok Sabha March 1977–; Minister of Works, Housing, Supply and Rehabilitation 1977-80; mem. and Gen. Sec. Janata Party 1977; Gen. Sec. Bharatiya Janata Party (BJP) 1980-82, now Vice-Pres. *Leisure interests:* sports, music. *Address:* B-34/1, East Kallash, New Delhi 110001, India. *Telephone:* 638198.

BAKHTIAR, Shapour; Iranian lawyer and politician; b. 1916; ed. in Paris and Beirut; supporter of Nat. Front opposition to Govt. of Shah Mohammad Reza Pahlavi; Deputy Minister during Nat. Front Govt. of Dr. Mossadeq 1951-53; imprisoned several times during reign of Shah; Deputy Leader of Nat. Front –1979; Chair. Regency Council and Prime Minister Jan.–Feb. 1979; resigned after return of Ayatollah Khomeini (q.v.) Feb. 1979; Leader Nat. Movt. of Iranian Resistance. *Address:* Suresnes, Paris, France.

BAKI, Boulaem; Algerian politician; b. 1922, El-Bayadh; Head People's Party of Algeria for the South Oran Dist. 1945-48; Deputy, Movt. for the

Triumph of Democratic Liberties 1948; rejoined the underground forces as Zonal Political Commr. 1956; Deputy, Nat. People's Ass. 1977; mem. Comité Cen., Minister of Religious Affairs 1979 and 1986–; Minister of Justice 1986. *Address:* 2 ave Timgad, Hydra, Algiers, Algeria. *Telephone:* (2) 60-85-55.

BAKKE, Hallvard, B.COMM.; Norwegian journalist and politician; b. 4 Feb. 1943, Flesberg; s. of Bjarne K. Bakke and Anne Ranvik Bakke; m. Inger Karine Skaanes 1969; one s. one d.; mem. of Bergen Municipal Council 1967–; Norwegian School of Econs. and Business Admin. 1968; Alt. Rep. to Parl. 1969–; Admin. Man. Den Nationale Scene, Bergen 1969-76; Chair. Hordaland County Org., Labour Party 1974–; Minister of Commerce and Shipping 1976-79, of Culture and Scientific Affairs May 1986–. *Address:* Kolstirusten 4, 5030 Landås, Bergen, Norway (Home). *Telephone:* 05/28-37-71 (Home).

BAKKEN, Anne-Lise; Norwegian politician; b. 30 March 1952, Eidskog; m.; mem. Storting 1977; mem. Nat. Youth Council 1977–; mem. Exec. Bd. of AUF (Norwegian Labour Youth League), Vice-Chair. 1977-81; Minister of Consumer Affairs and Govt. Admin. 1986-88; Chair. Crime Prevention Council 1980–. *Address:* c/o Ministry of Consumer Affairs and Government Administration., P.O. Box 8004, Dep., Oslo 1, Norway. *Telephone:* (2) 11-90-90.

BAKKENKIST, Siebrand Cornelis; Netherlands business executive; b. 23 Sept. 1914, Amsterdam; m. Elisabeth Wegenaar; two s.; ed. Univ. of Amsterdam; Founder and Man. Bakkenkist, Spits & Co. (consultancy firm) 1942-64; mem. Bd. of dirs. Zwanenberg-Organon (now part of AKZO N.V.) 1964; mem. Bd. of Dirs. AKZO N.V. 1967-85; Deputy Pres. Man. Bd., AKZO N.V. 1969; fmr. Chair. VMF-STORK –1985; fmr. Pres. Verband von Nederlandsche Ondernemingen (Fed. of Netherlands Industry); Officer, Order of Orange-Nassau. *Address:* VMF-STORK, fmr. Vlaardingenlaan 11, P.O. Box 9251, Amsterdam 1017, Netherlands.

BAKLANOV, Grigoriy Yakovlevich; Soviet author; b. 1923, Voronezh; ed. Gorky Inst. of Literature, Moscow; mem. CPSU 1942–; first works published 1950. *Publications include:* In Snegiri 1954, Nine Days 1958, The Dead Are Not Ashamed 1961, and many others. *Address:* U.S.S.R. Union of Writers, 52 ul. Vorovskogo, Moscow, U.S.S.R.

BAKLANOV, Oleg Dmitrievich; Soviet politician; b. 1932; ed. All-Union Inst. of Energetics; engineer, senior engineer, dir. of Kharkov technical appliances plant 1950-55; mem. CPSU 1953–; gen. dir. of production unit 1975-76; Deputy Min. of Gen. Machine Construction in U.S.S.R. 1981-83, First Deputy Min. 1983-86, Min. 1986; mem. of CPSU Cen. Cttee. 1986–; Deputy to Supreme Soviet; Hero of Socialist Labour; Lenin Prize. *Address:* The Kremlin, Moscow, U.S.S.R.

BAKR, Rashid El Tahir; Sudanese politician; b. 1930, Karkoj; ed. Univ. of Khartoum; fmr. advocate; imprisoned for opposition to the regime of Gen. Ibrahim Abboud 1958-64; Minister of Animal Resources and Justice 1965; Amb. to Libya 1972-74; apptd. mem. Political Bureau, Sudanese Socialist Union (SSU) and Sec. Farmers' Union in the SSU 1972; Asst. Sec.-Gen. Sectoral Orgs., SSU 1974; Speaker, People's Nat. Assembly 1974-76, 1980-81; Second Vice-Pres. of Sudan 1976-80; Prime Minister 1976-77; Minister of Foreign Affairs 1977-80; Chair. OAU Council of Ministers 1978-79; Attorney-Gen. 1983-84; mem. group of 41 set up to revitalize policy-making organs of SSU Jan. 1982.

BALAFREJ, Ahmed; Moroccan politican; b. 1908; ed. Univs. of Paris and Cairo; Sec.-Gen. in Istiqlal (Independence) Party 1944; later exiled by French, returned to Morocco 1955; Minister of Foreign Affairs 1955-58; Prime Minister May-Dec. 1958; Amb.-at-Large 1960-61; Deputy Prime Minister June 1961; Minister of Foreign Affairs 1961-63; Personal Rep. of King with rank of Minister 1963-72. *Address:* Rabat, Morocco.

BALAGUER, Joaquín; Dominican diplomatist and politician; b. 1 Sept. 1907, Villa Bisonó; s. of Joaquín Balaguer Lespier and Carmen Celia Ricardo Vda. Balaguer; ed. Univ. de Santo Domingo and Univ. de París à la Sorbonne; served Madrid 1932-35; Under-Sec. of Foreign Affairs 1936-40; Minister to Colombia 1940-46; Alt. Rep. to UN 1947; Minister of Foreign Affairs 1954-55, of Educ. and Arts 1955-57; Vice-Pres. of Dominican Repub. 1957-60, Pres. of the Dominican Repub. 1960, 1966-78, Aug. 1986–; voluntary exile in U.S.A. 1962-65; Founder-Leader Partido Reformista 1962–. *Address:* Oficina del Presidente, Santo Domingo, D.N., Dominican Republic.

BĂLĂIŢĂ, George; Romanian writer; b. 17 April 1935, Bacău; s. of Gheorghe Bălăiţă and Constantina Popa Bălăiţă; m. Lucia Gavril 1959; one s.; ed. Coll. of Philology; Ed. of cultural review Ateneu (Bacău) 1964-78; Dir. Cartea Românească publishing house, Bucharest 1982–; Vice-Pres. of the Romanian Writers' Union; Prize of the Romanian Acad. 1978; Prize of the Romanian Writers' Union 1975; Fulbright stipendiate 1980. *Major works:* novels: Lumea în două zile (The World in Two Days) 1967, Ucenicul neascultător (The Disobedient Apprentice) 1978; essays: A Provincial's Nights 1982. *Address:* 24-26 Bd. Ana Ipătescu, Bucharest, Romania.

BALANDIN, Anatoliy Nikiforovich; Soviet government official and agricultural specialist; b. 14 July 1927; ed. Orenburg Agric. Inst. 1952; chief agronomist, then dir. of a machine-tractor station, Orenburg Dist. 1952-57;

mem. CPSU 1954–; Instructor, Dept. of Agric, Orenburg Dist. CPSU 1957–62; Dir. of Sorochinsk Collective and State Farm Production Admin., Orenburg Dist. Cttee. CPSU 1962–64; Sec. (responsible for agric.), Orenburg Dist. Cttee CPSU 1964–66; Chair., Exec. Cttee., Orenburg Dist, Workers' Soviet 1966–80; Deputy to the Council of the Union, U.S.S.R. Supreme Soviet 1966–; First Sec., Orenburg Dist. Cttee. CPSU and mem of Mil. Council, Volga Mil. Dist. 1980–; mem. Cen. Cttee. CPSU 1981–. *Address:* Central Committee of the Communist Party of the Soviet Union, Staraya pl. 4, Moscow, U.S.S.R.

BALANDIN, Yuriy Nikolayevich; Soviet official; b. 1925; ed. Timiryazev Agric. Acad., Moscow; served in Soviet Army 1943–46; mem. CPSU 1944–; senior agronomist, Moscow district; senior scientific asst. at Inst. of Potato Agric. 1955–58; work for Moscow District Cttee. of CPSU 1959–61; for CPSU Cen. Cttee. 1961–71; First Sec. of Kostroma CPSU District Cttee. 1971–86; mem. CPSU Cen. Cttee. 1976–; deputy pres. of Gosagroprom (State Agric. Industries Board of U.S.S.R.) 1986–; mem. of CPSU Cen. Cttee. 1986–. *Address:* State Agricultural Industries Board of U.S.S.R., Moscow, U.S.S.R.

BALASSA, Bela; American (b. Hungarian) economist and educator; b. 6 April 1928, Budapest, Hungary; s. of George and Charlotte (Andreics) Balassa; m. Carol Ann Levy 1960; one s. one d.; ed. Univ. of Budapest, Acad. of Foreign Trade, Budapest and Yale Univ.; arrived U.S.A. 1957; naturalized 1962; Asst. later Assoc. Prof. Yale Univ. 1959–67; Adviser, later Consultant Econs. Dept. IBRD 1966–; Prof. of Political Econ. Johns Hopkins Univ. 1967–; Visiting Prof. Univ. of California at Berkeley, 1961–62, Columbia Univ. 1963–64; econ. adviser to int. orgs. and foreign govts., consultant to govt. and industry 1963–; Rockefeller Fellow 1957–58; Relm Foundation grantee 1958; Ford Foundation Dissertation Fellow 1958–59; Social Science Research Council grantee 1963; Nat. Science Foundation grantee 1970–74; Pres. Assen. of Comparative Econ. Studies 1979–80; mem. American Econ. Assen., Econometric Soc., Royal Econ. Soc.; Lauréat de l'Institut de France 1980, Bernhard Harms Prize in Int. Econs. 1984, V. K. Ramaswami Memorial Lecture 1986. *Publications:* The Hungarian Experience in Economic Planning 1959, The Theory of Economic Integration 1961, Trade Prospects for Developing Countries 1964, Economic Development and Integration 1965, Trade Liberalization among Industrial Countries: Objectives and Alternatives 1967, Studies in Trade Liberalization 1967, The Structure of Protection in Developing Countries 1971, European Economic Integration 1975, Policy Reform in Developing Countries 1977, Development Strategies in Semi-Industrial Countries 1981, The Newly-Industrializing Countries in the World Economy 1981; Turkey: Industrialization and Trade Strategy 1982; Morocco: Industrial Incentives and Export Promotion 1984, Change and Challenge in the World Economy 1985, Towards Renewed Economic Growth in Latin America 1986, Adjusting to Success: Balance of Payments Policy in East Asia 1987; contributing Ed.: Changing Patterns in Foreign Trade and Payments 1964, Economic Progress, Private Values and Public Policy: Essays in Honor of William Fellner 1977. *Leisure interests:* opera, swimming. *Address:* 1818 H Street, N.W., Washington, D.C. 20433 (Office); 2134 Wyoming Avenue, N.W., Washington, D.C. 20008, U.S.A. (Home).

BALASSA, Iván; Hungarian ethnographer; b. 5 Oct. 1917, Báránd; s. of József Balassa and Edit Szabó; m. Éva Márton 1942; one s. one d.; ed. Univ. of Arts and Sciences, Debrecen; Scientific Advisor Hungarian Agricultural Museum; Pres. editorial Cttee, Ethnographia; Pres. Hungarian Ethnographic Soc. 1982–; Titular Univ. Prof; hon. mem. Royal Acad. of Sciences of Denmark 1975–; Hon. mem. Royal Gustavus Adolphus Acad. of Sweden 1983–; holder of Herder Prize 1980. *Publications:* A magyar kukorica (The maize of Hungary) 1960, Karcsai mondák (Folk Tales of Karcsa) 1963, Földmüvelés a Hegyközben (Farming in the Hegyköz) 1964, Az eke és a szántás története Magyarországon (The History of the Plough and Ploughing in Hungary) 1973, Jankó János 1975, Magyar néprajz—in co-authorship with Gyula Ortutay (Hungarian Ethnography) 1979, Az arató munkások Magyarországon 1848–1944 (Hired harvesters in Hungary) 1985, Hungarian Ethnography and Folklore 1985, Báránd története és néprajza (History and Ethnography of the Village of Báránd) 1985, A magyar parasztemetök (Hungarian Peasant Cemeteries) 1989, A szomszédos országok magyarjainak néprajza (Ethnography of Hungarians in the Neighbouring Countries) 1989, Csüry Bálint 1988; about 500 studies in Hungarian and foreign journals. *Leisure interest:* gardening. *Address:* 1015 Budapest, Batthyány utca 3. *Telephone:* (1) 356-700.

BALASSA, Sándor; Hungarian composer; b. 20 Jan. 1935, Budapest; s. of János Balassa and Eszter Bora; m. Irén Balogh; one s. one d.; ed. Budapest Conservatory and Music Acad. of Budapest; began career as a mechanic; entered Budapest Conservatory at age 17; studied composition under Endre Szervánszky at Budapest Music Acad., obtained diploma 1965; music dir. Hungarian Radio 1964–80; Teacher of instrumentation, Music. Acad. Budapest 1981; Erkel Prize 1972, Critics' Prize (Hungarian Radio) 1972, 1974, Listeners' Prize (Hungarian Radio) 1976, Distinction for Best Work of the Year, Paris Int. Tribune of Composers 1972, Merited Artist of the Hungarian People's Repub. 1978, Kossuth Prize 1983. *Compositions:* vocal: Legenda 1967, Antinomia 1968, Requiem for Lajos Kassák 1969, Cantata Y 1970, Motetta 1973, Tresses 1979, Kyrie for female choir 1981, The Third Planet, opera-cantata 1986; opera: Az ajtón kivül (The Man Outside)

1976; instrumental: Dimensioni 1966, Quartetto per percussioni 1969, Xenia 1970, Tabulae 1972, The Last Shepherd 1978, Quintet for Brass 1979, The Flowers of Hajta 1984; orchestral: Lupercalia 1971, Iris 1972, Chant of Glarus 1978, The Island of Everlasting Youth 1979, Calls and Cries 1980, A Daydreamer's Diary 1983, Three Phantasias 1984, Little Grape and Little Fish 1987. *Leisure interest:* nature. *Address:* Szölö utca 33, 1034 Budapest, V.4. Hungary.

BALASURIYA, Stanislaus Tissa, B.A., S.T.L.; Ceylonese ecclesiastic; b. 29 Aug. 1924, Kahatagasdigililia; s. of William Balasuriya and Victoria Balasuriya; ed. Univ. of Ceylon, Gregorian Univ., Rome, Oxford Univ., Maris Stella Coll., Negombo, St. Patrick's Coll., Jaffna and St. Joseph's Coll., Colombo; helped found Aquinas Univ. with Friar Pillai Jan. 1954, Rector 1964–; f. Centre for Soc. and Religion, Colombo Aug. 1971, Dir. 1971–; Ed. Logos, Quest, Voices of the Third World, Social Justice; Khan Memorial Gold Medal for Econs. *Publications:* Jesus Christ and Human Liberation, Eucharist & Human Liberation, Catastrophe July '83, Planetary Theology. *Leisure interest:* writing. *Address:* Centre for Society and Religion, 281 Deans Road, Colombo 10, Sri Lanka. *Telephone:* 595425.

BALAYAN, Roman Gurgenovich; Soviet film director; b. 15 April 1941; ed. Kiev Theatre Inst. *Films include:* The Romashkin Effect, 1973, Chestnut 1976, The Kiss 1983, Dream and Waking Flights 1983, Keep Me Safe, My Talisman 1985.

BALCER, Łukasz, M.A.; Polish lawyer and politician; b. 21 July 1935, Sieraków, Poznań Voivodship; m.; two c.; ed. Law Faculty of Adam Mickiewicz Univ., Poznań 1957; employed wiht District Court, Lębork 1959–60; Barrister, mem. Barristers' Group, Puck 1963–65; Deputy Chair., Municipal Nat. Council, Gdynia 1965–69; Deputy Chair., Voivodship Nat. Council, Gdańsk 1969–73; mem. Democratic Party (SD) 1962–, Sec. SD Voivodship Cttee., Gdańsk 1974–81; Pres. of Gdańsk Centre of the Chief Admin. Court 1981–82; Vice-Voivode of Gdańsk Voivodship 1982–86; Under-Sec. of State, Office for Environmental Protection and Water Economy 1986–87, Ministry of Environmental Protection and Natural Resources 1987–88; Minister of Justice 1988–; Deputy to Seym (Parl.) 1980–85, Deputy Chair. Seym Comm. of Economic Plan, Budget and Finance 1980–84, mem. Seym Comm. of Admin., Internal Affairs and Jurisdiction 1981; Deputy Chair. Seym Comm. of Constitutional Responsibility 1982, Deputy Chair. Seym Comm. of Legis. Work 1983–84, Chair. Seym Comm. of Culture 1984–85; Knight's and Officer's Cross of Polonia Restituta Order, other decorations. *Leisure interests:* yachting, excursions, walking, theatre, books, sport, medal engraving. *Address:* Ministerstwo Sprawiedliwości, Al. Ujazdowskie 11, 00-950 Warsaw, Poland.

BALDERSTONE, Sir James Schofield; Australian business executive; b. 2 May 1921, Melbourne; s. of late J. S. Balderstone; m. Mary Tyree 1946; two s. two d.; ed. Scotch Coll., Melbourne; Gen. Man. and Dir. for Australia, Thomas Borthwick and Sons (Australia) 1953–67; Man. Dir. Stanbroke Pastoral Co. Pty. Ltd. 1964–81, Chair. 1982–; Chair. Squatting Investment Co. 1966–73; Dir. Commercial Bank of Australia (merged to become Westpac Banking Corpn.) 1970–82; Dir. The Broken Hill Proprietary Co. Ltd. 1971–, Chair. 1984–89; Pres. Inst. of Public Affairs (Vic.) 1981–84; Chair. Commonwealth Govt. Policy Discussion Group on Agric. 1981–82; Dir. Victorian Branch Bd., Australian Mutual Provident Soc. 1962–, Deputy Chair. 1977–84, Chair. 1984–, mem., Prin. Bd. 1979–; Dir. Woodside Petroleum Ltd. 1976–83; Dir. N.W. Shelf Devt. 1976–83; Dir. ICI Australia Ltd. 1981–84, Chase-AMP Bank 1985–. *Leisure interests:* farming, reading, watching sport. *Address:* The Broken Hill Proprietary Co. Ltd., 140 William Street, Melbourne 3000, Vic. (Office); 115 Mont Albert Road, Canterbury 3126, Vic. Australia (Home). *Telephone:* 609 3883 (Office); 836-3137 (Home).

BALDESCHWIELER, John Dickson, PH.D.; American professor of chemistry; b. 14 Nov. 1933, Elizabeth, N.J.; s. of Emile L. Baldeschwieler and Isobel M. Dickson; m. Marcia Ewing; two s. one d.; ed. Cornell Univ. and Univ. of Calif., Berkeley; Asst. Prof. Harvard Univ. 1962–65; Assoc. Prof. Stanford Univ. 1965–67, Prof. of Chem. 1967–73; Deputy Dir. Office of Science and Tech. Exec. Office of Pres. of U.S.A. 1971–73; Prof. of Chem. Calif. Inst. of Tech. 1973–, Chair. Div. of Chem. and Chem. Eng. 1973–78; Chair. Bd. of Dirs. Vestar Research Inc. 1981–; mem. numerous advisory cttees. and comms.; Alfred P. Sloan Foundation Fellow 1962–65; American Chem. Soc. Award in Pure Chem. 1967. *Publications:* numerous articles in professional journals. *Leisure interests:* hiking, skiing, photography, music, travel. *Address:* Division of Chemistry and Chemical Engineering, California Institute of Technology, 1201 E. California Road, Pasadena, Calif. 91125 (Office); 619 S. Hill Avenue, Pasadena, Calif. 91106, U.S.A. (Home).

BALDIN, Aleksandr Mikhailovich; Soviet physicist; b. 1926; ed. Moscow Engineering-Physical Inst.; on staff of U.S.S.R. Acad. of Sciences Physics Inst. 1949–68; Asst. Prof. at Moscow Univ. 1955–60, Prof. 1965; Chief of a group from various insts. researching into nuclear physics 1961–68; Dir. of Lab. of Higher Energies of United Inst. of Nuclear Research 1968–; Prof. of Moscow Physical Eng. Inst. 1971–; State Prize 1973; mem. of U.S.S.R. Acad. of Sciences 1981–. *Address:* U.S.S.R. Academy of Sciences, Institute of Nuclear Physics, Profsoyuznaya 7a, Moscow, U.S.S.R.

BALDWIN, Jack Edward, PH.D., F.R.S.; British professor of chemistry; b. 8 Aug. 1938, London; s. of Frederick C. Baldwin and Olive F. Headland; m. Christine L. Franchi 1977; ed. Lewes County Grammar School and Imperial Coll., London; Asst. Lecturer in Chem., Imperial Coll. 1963, Lecturer 1966; Asst. Prof. Penn. State Univ. 1967, Assoc. Prof. 1969; Assoc. Prof. M.I.T. 1970, Prof. 1972; Daniell Prof. of Chem. King's Coll., London 1972; Prof. of Chem. M.I.T. 1972–78; Waynflete Prof. of Chem., Univ. of Oxford, and Head, Dyson Perrins Lab. 1978–; Hon. D.Sc. (Warwick) 1988; Corday Morgan Medal, Chem. Soc. 1975; Karrer Medal, Univ. of Zürich 1984; Dr. P. Janssen Prize (Belgium) 1988. *Publications:* papers in organic and biorganic chem. in Journal of American Chem. Soc. and Journal of Chem. Soc. *Address:* Dyson Perrins Laboratory, University of Oxford, South Parks Road, Oxford, England. *Telephone:* Oxford 57809.

BALDWIN, Robert Roy, PH.D.; British university professor (retd.); b. 9 Feb. 1920, Widnes; m. Valerie Aucutt 1947; two d.; ed. Wallasey Grammar School and Emmanuel Coll., Cambridge; Physical Chemist, Thornton Research Centre, Shell Research Ltd 1941–47; Lecturer in Physical Chemistry, Hull Univ. 1947–57, Sr. Lecturer 1957–63, Reader 1963–66, Prof. 1966–84, Head, Chemistry Dept. 1982–84, Prof. Emer. 1984–; Royal Chemical Soc. 1985 Award for "Reaction Kinetics." *Publications:* over 100 scientific research papers. *Leisure interests:* fell walking, music, photography, badminton. *Address:* Chemistry Department, University of Hull, Cottingham Road, Hull, Nth. Humberside, HU6 7RX, England. *Telephone:* 0482-465590.

BALEVSKI, Angel Tonchev, D.SC.; Bulgarian engineer; b. 15 April 1910, Troyan; s. of Toncho Angelov Balevski and Penka Kalcheva Balevska; m. Laura Todorova Kamedulska 1938; one s. one d.; ed. Brno, Czechoslovakia; Prof. of Metals and Technology of Metals, Higher Inst. of Mechanical and Electrical Engineering 1945–68, Rector 1966–68; Vice-Pres. State Cttee. for Science and Technological Progress 1960–61; Dir. Dept. of Engineering, Bulgarian Acad. of Sciences 1960–68; Vice-Pres. Presidium of Union of Scientific Workers 1964–; Dir. Inst. of Metals and Technology of Metals 1967–; Ed.-in-Chief Techničeska Misăl (Technical Thought); mem. Cen. Cttee., Bulgarian Communist Party 1966–, Nat. Assembly 1969–, State Council 1971–; Chair. Bulgarian-Czechoslovak Friendship Soc.; Corresp. mem. Bulgarian Acad. of Sciences 1952–66, mem. 1966, Pres. 1968–88, Hon. Pres. 1988; Foreign mem. Acad. of Sciences, U.S.S.R. 1971; Hon. mem. Acad. of Science of Hungary 1970, Poland 1971; Foreign mem. Acad. of Science of Czechoslovakia 1973, German Democratic Repub. 1974, Mongolian People's Repub. 1974, Acad. of Athens 1977; Hon. mem. Polish Soc. of Theoretical and Applied Mechanics; mem. Standing Cttee. of Pugwash Movt. 1971–; Hon. D.Eng., Higher Technological School, Ilmenau (G.D.R.) 1973; Hon. Ph.D. (Karlovy Univ.) 1980; numerous prizes and awards including Dimitrov Prize Laureate 1951, 1969; Merited Scientist 1966; People's Scientist 1971; Int. prize of CIAK (Italy) 1979; Order of Red Banner of Labour 1959; Order of Georgi Dimitrov 1970, 1975; Order of Cyril and Methodius (1st and 2nd Class) 1957, 1963; Gold Medal, French Soc. for the Promotion of Scientific Research and Invention Activities 1970, for Scientific and Humanitarian Merits, Acad. of Science, Czechoslovakia 1979, Univ. of Hamburg, Fed. Repub. of Germany 1980, Czechoslovak Soc. for Int. Relations 1980, Slovakian Acad. of Sciences 1980, Tech. Univ., Brno 1981, Purkyne Univ., Brno 1981; Hon. Medal, Kliment Ohridski Univ., Sofia 1980; Hon. medal "Marin Drinov" of Bulgarian Acad. of Sciences 1980; Gold Star of Friendship of Peoples (G.D.R.) 1978; Order of Friendship Among Peoples, U.S.S.R. 1980; Palmes Académiques, France 1979; Special Nicholas Copernicus Medal of Poland 1973; M. V. Lomonosov Gold Medal, U.S.S.R. Acad. of Sciences 1975; Hero of Socialist Labour 1975, 1980; Order of Georgi Dimitrov 1985; Order for Peace and Friendship (Hungary) 1985; Förderpreis für die Europaïsche Wissenschaft, Körber-Preis für die Europeische Wissenschaft (Hamburg) 1985. *Publications:* several articles in learned journals. *Leisure interests:* history and literature. *Address:* Bulgarian Academy of Sciences, 7 Noemvri 1, 1040 Sofia (Office); 31 Asparouh Street, 1463 Sofia, Bulgaria (Home). *Telephone:* 80-30-15 (Office); 80-30-44 (Home).

BALHAJAV, Tserenpiliin; Mongolian politician; b. 20 Dec. 1928; ed. Higher Party School of Mongolian People's Revolutionary Party Cen. Cttee., Moscow State Univ. and Acad. of Social Sciences of CPSU Cen. Cttee.; lecturer, Higher Party School of MPRP Cen. Cttee. 1952–55; research worker, Head of section, Dept., Inst. of Party History of MPRP Cen. Cttee. 1955–72; Head of Dept. MPRP Cen. Cttee. 1972–84; a Sec. of MPRP Cen. Cttee. 1984–; Deputy to the Great People's Hural (Ass.); awarded Mongolian orders and medals. *Address:* Central Committee of the Mongolian People's Revolutionary Party, Ulan Bator, Mongolian People's Republic.

BALICKI, Zdzisław, M.ECON.SC.; Polish politician and journalist; b. 27 Oct. 1930, Niemenczyn; m.; ed. Higher School of Econs., Wrocław; worked in Communal Office, Koźminek, Chief of Financial Dept., Machines Repair Establishment, Jodłownik 1952–55; worked in District Cttees. of PZPR in Dzierżoniów, Lubań, Śląski and Jelenia Góra 1955–63; Head of Organizational Dept. of PZPR Voivodship Cttee., Wrocław 1963–64; First Sec. Town and District Cttee. PZPR, Wałbrzych 1964–73; Ed.-in-Chief, daily newspaper Gazeta Robotnicza, Wrocław 1973–80, 1982–83; Chair. Cttee. for Radio and TV Polskie Radio i Telewizja 1980–81; Presidium mem. of Gen. Bd. of Journalists Asscn. of Polish People's Republic 1983–87; Deputy mem. PZPR Cen. Cttee. Oct. 1980, 1988–; mem. Cen. Cttee. 1986–; First Sec. to PZPR Voivodship Cttee., Wrocław 1983–; deputy to Seym 1965–80 and 1985–; Officer's Cross, Order of Polonia Restituta; Order of Banner of Labour (2nd class). *Leisure interests:* browsing through encyclopaedias and picking mushrooms. *Address:* Komitet Wojewódzki PZPR, Pl. Dąbrowszczaków 38, 50-204 Wrocław, Poland. *Telephone:* 48-2500 (Home).

BALILES, Gerald L., J.D.; American state governor; b. 8 July 1940, Stuart, Va.; ed. Wesleyan Univ. and Univ. of Va.; admitted Va. Bar 1967, U.S. Supreme Court Bar 1971; Asst. Attorney-Gen. of Virginia 1967–72, Deputy Attorney-Gen. 1972–75, Attorney-Gen. 1982–86; mem. Va. House of Dels. 1976–82; fmr. Partner, Lacy & Baliles, Richmond; Gov. of Virginia 1986–; Democrat. *Address:* Office of the Governor, Capitol Building, 3rd Floor, Richmond, Va. 23219, U.S.A.

BALL, Sir Christopher John Elinger, Kt., M.A.; British academic; b. 22 April 1935; s. of the late Laurence Elinger Ball and Christine Florence Mary (née Howe) Ball; m. Wendy Ruth Colyer 1958; three s. three d.; ed. St. George's School, Harpenden, Merton Coll., Oxford; Second Lieut. Parachute Regt. 1955–56; Lecturer in Comparative Linguistics, School of Oriental and African Studies (Univ. of London) 1961–64; Fellow and Tutor in English Language, Lincoln Coll., Oxford 1964–69, Senior Tutor and Tutor for Admissions 1971–72, Bursar 1972–79; Warden, Keble Coll., Oxford 1980–88; Jt. Founding Ed. Toronto Dictionary of Old English 1970; mem. General Bd. of the Faculties 1979–82, Hebdomadal Council 1985–, Council and Exec., Templeton Coll., Oxford 1981–, Editorial Bd., Oxford Review of Educ. 1984–; Chair. Bd. of Nat. Advisory Body for Public Sector Higher Educ. in England 1982–88, Oxford Univ. English Bd. 1977–79, Jt. Standing Cttee. for Linguistics 1979–83, Conf. of Colls. Fees Cttee. 1979–85, Higher Educ. Information Services Trust 1987, Educ.-Industry Forum 1988–; Sec. Linguistics Asscn. G.B. 1964–67; Publications Sec. Philological Soc. 1969–75; Gov. St. George's School, Harpenden 1985–, Centre for Medieval Studies, Oxford 1987, Brathay Hall Trust 1988–, Manchester Polytechnic 1989; Founding Fellow in Kellogg Forum for Continuing Education, Oxford Univ. 1988–89, Hon. Fellow (Lincoln Coll., Oxford) 1981, (Keble College, Oxford) 1989, (Manchester Polytechnic) 1988. *Publications:* Fitness For Purpose 1985, various contribs. to philological, linguistic and educ. journals. *Address:* 45 Richmond Road, Oxford, OX1 2JJ. *Telephone:* 310800.

BALL, Christopher John Watkins, B.IUR., M.A.(ECON.); South African banker; b. 2 Nov.1939, Johannesburg; s. of Clifford G.W. Ball and Cynthia L. Brayshaw; m. Susan Anne Nellist 1968; one s. two d.; ed. Univs. of Witwatersrand and Cambridge; Baring Bros. & Co., London 1968–73; Barclays Nat. Merchant Bank, Johannesburg 1973–76; Man. Dir. Barclays Western Bank Ltd., Johannesburg 1978–80; Regional Gen. Man. Barclays Bank PLC, London 1980–83; Man. Dir. First Nat. Bank of Southern Africa Ltd. 1984–89. *Leisure interests:* golf, tennis, squash, gardening. *Address:* 84 Market Street, Johannesburg, P.O. Box 1153, Johannesburg 2000, South Africa. *Telephone:* 632 9111.

BALL, George Wildman; American lawyer and government official; b. 21 Dec. 1909; ed. Northwestern Univ.; admitted to Illinois Bar 1934, D.C. Bar 1946; law practice Chicago 1935–42, Washington 1946–61; Assoc. Gen. Counsel Lend-Lease Admin. 1942–43, Foreign Econs. Admin. 1943–44; Dir. U.S. Strategic Bombing Survey, London 1944–45; Political Adviser to Adlai Stevenson; Under-Sec. of State for Econ. Affairs Feb.-Dec. 1961; Under-Sec. of State 1961–1966; Counsel, Cleary, Gottlieb, Steen and Hamilton 1966–68, 1969–; Pres. of Bd. of Dirs. of Lehmann Brothers Int. Ltd. 1966–68; Perm. Rep. to UN June-Sept. 1968; Sr. Partner, Lehman Brothers Int. Jan.-May 1968, 1969–82; Hon. LL.D. (Northwestern Univ.); Officier, Légion d'honneur (France); Grand Cross, Order of the Crown (Belgium); Grand Official, Order of Merit (Italy); Medal of Freedom (U.S.A.); Democrat. *Publications:* The Discipline of Power 1968, Diplomacy for a Crowded World: An American Foreign Policy 1976, The Past Has Another Pattern (memoirs) 1982, Error and Betrayal in Lebanon 1984. *Address:* 107 Library Place, Princeton, N.J. 08540, U.S.A.

BALL, James (see Ball, Sir (Robert) James).

BALL, Lucille; American actress; b. 6 Aug. 1911, Jamestown, N.Y.; m. 1st Desi Arnaz 1940 (divorced 1960); one s. one d.; m. 2nd Gary Morton 1961; film actress 1934–; TV actress; Pres. Desilu Productions Inc. 1962–67; Lucille Ball Productions 1967–; Kennedy Center Honor 1986; Emmy Award 1952, 1955, 1967, 1968. *Films include:* Roberta, Chatterbox, Follow the Fleet, Stage Door, Having a Wonderful Time, Affairs of Annabell, Room Service, Valley of the Sun, Seven Days Leave, DuBarry was a Lady, Best Foot Forward, Meet the People, Thousands Cheer, Without Love, Love from a Stranger, Her Husband's Affairs, Forever Darling, Facts of Life, Mame 1974; TV Shows: I Love Lucy 1951–60, The Lucy Show 1962–68, Here's Lucy 1968–74. *Address:* 1041 North Formosa Avenue, Los Angeles, Calif. 90046; Lucille Ball Productions, 9200 Sunset Boulevard, #916, Los Angeles, Calif. 90069, U.S.A.

BALL, Sir (Robert) James, Kt., PH.D.; British professor of economics; b. 15 July 1933, Saffron Walden; s. of Arnold James Hector Ball; m. 1st Patricia Mary Hart Davies 1954, 2nd Lindsay Jackson (née Wonnacott) 1970; one s. three d. one step-s.; ed. St. Marylebone Grammar School,

Queen's Coll., Oxford, Univ. of Pennsylvania; Research Officer, Oxford Univ. Inst. of Statistics 1957-58; IBM Fellow, Univ. of Pa. 1958-60; Lecturer Univ. of Manchester 1960-63, Sr. Lecturer 1963-65; Prof. of Econs., London Business School 1965-, Deputy Prin. 1971-72, Prin. 1972-84; Dir. Barclays Bank Trust Co. Ltd. 1973-86, IBM U.K. Ltd. 1979-; Chair. Legal and General Group PLC. 1980-; Dir. London and Scottish Marine Oil 1988-; mem. Council British-N. American Cttee. 1985-, Research Asscn. 1985-, Marshall Aid Commemoration Comm. 1987-; Econ. Adviser, Touche Ross & Co. 1984-; Trustee Foulkes Foundation 1984-, Civic Trust 1986-, Economist 1987-; Hon. D.Sc. (Aston) 1987, Hon. D.Soc.Sc. (Manchester) 1988; Freeman of City of London 1987. *Leisure interests:* chess, fishing, gardening. *Address:* Sussex Place, Regent's Park, London, NW1 4SA, England (Office).

BALL, William, A.B., M.A.; American actor and theatrical director; b. 1931, Evanston, Ill.; s. of Catherine and Russell Ball; ed. Fordham Univ. and Carnegie Inst. of Technology; Oregon Shakespearian Festival 1950-53; Antioch Shakespeare Festival 1954; Group 20 Players 1956; San Diego Shakespeare Festival 1955; Arena Stage, Washington, D.C. 1957-58; Back to Methuselah, Broadway, New York and tour 1958; Six Characters in Search of an Author, Così Fan Tutte 1959, The Inspector General 1960, Porgy and Bess 1961, Midsummer Night's Dream 1963; New York City Center Opera Co. off-Broadway: The Misanthrope, The Lady's Not for Burning, The Country Wife, Ivanov, A Month In The Country 1956-58, Under Milk Wood 1956-61, Six Characters In Search of an Author 1963, The Tempest, Stratford, Conn., Shakespeare Festival; Yeoman of the Guard (Stratford, Canada) 1964; Librettist and Dir. Natalia Petrovna (New York City Center Opera Co.) 1964; Tartuffe (Lincoln Center Repertory Co.) 1965; Founder and Gen. Dir. American Conservatory Theater (A.C.T.) initiated at Pittsburgh Playhouse in 1965 with a 16-play double repertory theatre; Gen. Dir. American Conservatory Theater 1965-; resident in San Francisco 1967-; Fulbright Scholarship to Great Britain, NBC/RCA Fellowship to Carnegie Inst. of Technology, Ford Foundation Director's Grant 1959, Ford Foundation Comm. for opera libretto Natalia Petrovna; Hon. Ph.D. four American colls. and univs., including Carnegie-Mellon Univ. 1979; Tony Award 1979. *Publication:* A Sense of Direction. *Leisure interests:* meditation, photography, films, travel. *Address:* 450 Geary Street, San Francisco, Calif. 94102, U.S.A.

BALLADUR, Edouard, L. EN D.; French politician; b. 2 May 1929, Smyrna, Turkey; s. of Pierre Balladur and Emilie Latour; m. Marie-Josèphe Delacour 1957; four s.; ed. Lycée Thiers, Marseilles, Faculté de Droit, Aix-en-Provence, Inst. d'Etudes Politiques, Paris and Ecole Nationale d'Admin.; auditor, Conseil d'Etat 1957, Maître des requêtes 1963; adviser to Dir.-Gen. of ORTF 1962-63; mem. Admin. Council of ORTF 1967-68; Tech. Adviser, Office of Prime Minister Georges Pompidou 1966-68; Pres. French soc. for bldg. and devt. of road tunnel under Mont Blanc 1968-81; mem. Admin. Council, Nat. Forestry Office 1968-73; Asst. Sec.-Gen. Presidency of Repub. 1969, Sec.-Gen. 1974; Pres. Dir.-Gen. Générale de Service Informatique 1977-86; Pres. Compagnie Europééne d'Accumulateurs 1980-86; mem. Conseil d'Etat 1984; Minister of the Econ., of Finance and Privatization 1986-88; Chevalier, Légion d'honneur. *Publication:* l'Arbre de mai 1979.

BALLANTINE, Duncan Smith A.B., PH.D.; American administrator; b. 5 Nov. 1912, Garden City, N.Y.; s. of Raymond and Amy Smith Ballantine; m. 1st Margarette Torbert 1941, 2nd Saffeti Acele 1962; one s. two d.; ed. Amherst Coll. (Massachusetts), and Harvard Univ.; held various teaching appointments 1936-42; served with U.S.N.R. 1942-46; Assoc. Prof. History, Mass. Inst. Technology 1947-52; Pres. Reed Coll. 1952-55; Pres. Robert Coll. 1955-61; Research Assoc. Harvard Univ. Center for Int. Affairs 1962; Dir. Educ. Dept., Int. Bank for Reconstruction and Devt. (World Bank), then consultant to IBRD 1977-; mem. Soc. for Int. Devt., Middle East Inst.; Hon. LL.D. *Publications:* U.S. Naval Logistics in the Second World War 1947. *Leisure interests:* tennis, gardening, fishing, art. *Address:* International Bank for Reconstruction & Development (World Bank), 1818 H Street, N.W., Washington, D.C. (Office); 5107 Saugapore Road, Bethesda, Md. 20816, U.S.A. (Home). *Telephone:* 229-7596 (Home).

BALLANTINE, Ian, B.A.; American publisher; b. 15 Feb. 1916, New York; s. of Edward James Ballantine and Stella Ballantine; m. Elizabeth Nora Jones 1939; one s.; ed. Columbia Univ. and L.S.E.; Pres. Penguin Books Inc. 1939-45; Bantam Books Inc. 1945-52, Ballantine Books 1952-72; Vice-Pres. Rufus Publs. 1972-. *Leisure interest:* skiing. *Address:* Bantam Books, 666 Fifth Avenue, New York, N.Y. 10103, U.S.A. (Office).

BALLARD, James Graham; British novelist and short story writer; b. 15 Nov. 1930; s. of James Ballard and Edna Ballard (née Johnstone); m. Helen Mary Matthews 1954 (died 1964); one s. two d.; ed. Leys School, Cambridge and King's Coll. Cambridge. *Publications:* The Drowned World 1963, The 4-Dimensional Nightmare 1963, The Terminal Beach 1964, The Drought 1965, The Crystal World 1966, The Disaster Area 1967, The Atrocity Exhibition 1970, Crash 1973, Vermilion Sands 1973, Concrete Island 1974, High Rise 1975, Low-Flying Aircraft 1976, The Unlimited Dream Company 1979, Myths of the Near Future 1982, Empire of the Sun 1984, The Venus Hunters 1986, The Day of Creation 1987, Running Wild 1988, Memories of the Space Age 1988. *Address:* 36 Old Charlton Road, Shepperton, Middx., England. *Telephone:* Walton-on-Thames 225692.

BALLE, Francis, D. ÈS L.; French professor; b. 15 June 1939, Fourmies; s. of Marcel Balle and Madeleine (née Leprohon) Balle; m. Marie Derieux 1972; three d.; ed. Inst. d'Etudes Politiques; philosophy teacher Ecole Normale d'Oran 1963-65; Asst. Lecturer Faculté des Lettres, Ecole de Journalisme, Algiers 1965-67, Univ. de Paris-Sorbonne 1967-70, Univ. René Descartes, Univ. Paris VI 1970-72; Lecturer Univ. de Droit, d'Econ. et de Sciences Sociales 1972, Prof. 1978-; Dir. Inst. Français de Presse 1976-86, Inst. de Recherche et d'Etudes sur la Communication 1986-; Vice-Chancellor Univs. de Paris July 1986-; Visiting Prof. Univ. of Stanford, Calif. 1981-83; Chevalier Ordre National de la Légion d'Honneur, Palmes Académiques. *Publications:* The Media Revolution in America and Western Europe 1984, Les nouveaux médias (with Gerard Eymery) 1987, Et si la Presse n'existait pas 1987, Médias et Sociétés 1988. *Leisure interests:* music, painting. *Address:* 47 rue des Ecoles, 75005 Paris (Office); 18 rue Greuze, 75116 Paris, France (Home). *Telephone:* (1) 40 46 20 17 (Office); (1) 47 27 78 31 (Home).

BALLESTEROS SOTA, Severiano; Spanish golfer; b. 9 April 1957, Pedreña, Santander; s. of Baldomero Ballesteros and Carmen Sota Ocejo; m. Carmen Botin Suáz 1988; professional 1974-; won Spanish Young Professional title 1974; 55 int. titles; won Dutch Open and two major European tournaments and, with Manuel Pinero, World Cup; won Opens of France, Switzerland and Japan, four other major tournaments in Europe, Japan and New Zealand, and World Cup, with Antonio Garrido 1977; won Opens of Japan, Germany, Kenya, Scandinavia and Switzerland and tournament in U.S.A. 1978; British Open Champion (youngest this century) 1979, 1984, 1988; second European and youngest ever winner U.S. Masters 1980; World Matchplay Title 1981, 1982, 1984, 1985; winner U.S. Masters 1980, 1983, Henry Vardon Trophy 1976, 1977, 1978, 1986, Ryder Cup 1979, 1983, 1985, 1987; acted in film Escape to Paradise 1987. *Leisure interests:* ping-pong, chess, fitness, shooting, reading, music. *Address:* Fairway, S.A., Ruiz Zorilla, 16-2°J 39009 Santander, Spain.

BALLESTRERO, H.E. Cardinal Anastasio Alberto; Italian ecclesiastic; b. 3 Oct. 1913, Genoa; ordained priest 1936; Bishop of Bari 1974-77; Archbishop of Turin 1977-; cr. Cardinal 1979; mem. Sacred Congregation for Religious Orders and Secular Insts.; mem. Sacra Congregazione dei Vescovi e per gli Affari Pubblici della Chiesa; entitled S. Maria sopra Minerva. *Address:* Via Arcivescovado 12, 10121 Torino, Italy. *Telephone:* (011) 545 234.

BALLMER, Ray Wayne, M.SC.; American mining executive; b. 6 May 1926, Santa Rita, New Mexico; s. of Gerald Jacob and Martha (Wilhelmson) Ballmer; m. Doris Greer 1945; one s. one d.; ed. N.M. School of Mines, Massachusetts Inst. of Technology; held senior posts with Kennecott Copper Corpn., U.S.A., with responsibilities in Ariz. and Bingham Canyon, Utah operations; later Man. Dir. Bougainville Copper Ltd., responsible for design, construction and commissioning of Bougainville copper operation; Exec. Vice-Pres., Pres. Amoco Minerals Co. 1975-82; Pres., C.O.O. and Dir. Rio Algom Ltd., Toronto 1982-88, Vice-Chair. and Dir. 1988-. *Leisure interests:* boating, golf, skiing. *Address* Rio Algom Ltd., 120 Adelaide Street W., Toronto, Ont., M5H 1W5 (Office); 228 Glen Road, Toronto, Ont., M4W 2X3, Canada (Home).

BALLOU, Clinton Edward, PH.D.; American professor of biochemistry; b. 18 June 1923, Idaho; s. of William Clinton Ballou and Mollie Bernt; m. Dorothy Lun Wu 1949; one s. one d.; ed. Oregon State Coll. and Univ. of Wisconsin, Madison; Nat. Inst. of Health Postdoctoral Fellow, Univ. of Edin., Scotland 1950-51, Univ. of Calif., Berkeley 1951-53, Research Biochemist 1953-55, Asst. Prof. of Biochemistry 1955-57, Assoc. Prof. 1957-62, Prof. 1962-; Guggenheim Memorial Fellow 1968; mem. N.A.S.; Claude Hudson Award, American Coll. of Surgeons 1981. *Publications:* over 180 publs. in major scientific journals dealing with biochemistry of complex carbohydrates and microbial cell surfaces. *Leisure interests:* travel, reading, fly fishing, gardening, sports, star-gazing. *Address:* Department of Biochemistry, University of California, Berkeley, Calif. 94720, U.S.A. *Telephone:* (415) 642-5494.

BALMONT, Boris Vladimirovich; Soviet politician; b. 1927; ed. Bauman Inst. Moscow; mem. CPSU 1956-; various posts in factory man., Dir. of plant 1952-65; Dean of Bauman Inst. 1965-; Head of Section, U.S.S.R. Ministry of General Machine Construction 1965-73; Deputy Minister of Machine Tool and Precision Instruments Industry 1976-81; Minister 1981-87; cand. mem. Cen. Cttee. CPSU 1981-, mem. 1986-; Hero of Socialist Labour 1978. *Address:* Ministry of Machine Tool and Precision Instruments Industry, Kremlin, Moscow, U.S.S.R.

BALOGUN, Kolawole, Chief Jagun of Otan, LL.B., PH.D.; Nigerian lawyer, politician and diplomatist; b. 1926; s. of Moses and Marian Balogun; ed. Govt. Coll., Ibadan; on staff of Nigerian Advocate, later radio announcer, then Asst. Ed. West African Pilot; legal studies in London 1948-51, called to the Bar 1951; Sec. London branch National Council of Nigeria and the Cameroons (NCNC) 1951; Nat. Sec. NCNC 1951-57; mem. of Fed. Parl. 1954; Fed. Minister without Portfolio 1955, of Information 1955-58; resigned from Govt. 1958; Nigerian Commr. in Ghana 1959-60, High Commr. 1960-61; fmr. mem. of Ministry of Foreign Affairs; Chair, Nigerian Nat. Shipping Line 1962-65; Commr. for Econ. Planning and Social Devt., Mil. Govt. of W. Nigeria 1967; Commr. for Educ. 1968-70. *Publication:*

Government in Old Oyo Empire 1985. *Address:* Maye Lodge, P.O. Box 50, Osogbo, Nigeria.

BALSAM, Martin Henry; American actor; b. 4 Nov. 1919, New York; s. of Albert and Lillian (née Weinstein) Balsam; m. 1st Pearl L. Somner 1952 (divorced 1954); m. 2nd Joyce Van Patten 1959 (divorced 1962), one d.; m. 3rd Irene Miller 1963; ed. New School of Social Research; acting debut in The Play's the Thing, Locust Valley, N.Y. 1941; New York debut in Ghost for Sale 1941. *Stage appearances include:* Lamp at Midnight 1947, The Wanhope Building, High Tor, A Sound of Hunting, Macbeth 1948, Sundown Beach 1948, The Closing Door 1949, You Know I Can't Hear You When the Water's Running (Tony Award) 1967, Cold Storage, Three Men on a Horse, A View from the Bridge, The Iceman Cometh. *Films include:* On the Waterfront 1954, Twelve Angry Men 1957, Marjorie Morningstar 1957, Al Capone 1959, Middle of the Night 1959, Psycho 1960, All at Home 1960, Breakfast at Tiffany's 1961, Ada 1961, Cape Fear 1962, The Captive City 1962, Who's Sleeping in My Bed 1963, Seven Days in May 1963, The Carpetbaggers 1963, 1,000 Clowns (Acad. Award) 1964, Bedford Incident, Harlow, After the Fox 1965, Hombre 1966, Among the Paths to Eden 1967, Me, Natalie, Good Guys and Bad Guys, 2001: A Space Odyssey 1968, Catch 22, Tora Tora Tora, Little Big Man 1969, The Anderson Tapes, The Commissioner 1970, The Sentinel 1977, Silver Bears 1978, Cuba 1979, There Goes the Bride 1980, St. Elmo's Fire 1985, The Goodbye People 1986; numerous nightclub and TV appearances; regular in TV series Archie Bunker's Place 1979; mem. Actors' Equity Asscn., American Fed. of TV and Radio Artists, Screen Actors' Guild, Actors' Studio. *Address:* c/o Don Buchwald and Associates, 10 East 44th Street, New York, N.Y. 10017, U.S.A.

BALSEMÃO, Francisco Pinto (see Pinto Balsemão).

BALSTAD, Jan; Norwegian politician; b. 16 Nov. 1937; m.; apptd. Sec. Norwegian Union of Iron and Metalworkers 1968, Norwegian Fed. of Trade Unions 1981; Minister of Trade and Shipping 1988–; fmr. mem. Bd., Norsk Jernverk, Norwegian Industrial Fund, Demokratisk Arbeidslivsutvikling, Royal Norwegian Council for Scientific and Industrial Research. *Address:* Ministry of Trade and Shipping, Victoria Terrasse 7, P.O.B. 8113 Dep., 0032 Oslo 1, Norway. *Telephone:* (2) 31-40-50.

BALTHUS (see Klossowski de Rola, Comte Balthasar).

BALTIMORE, David, PH.D.; American biologist; b. 7 March 1938, New York, N.Y.; s. of Mr. and Mrs. Richard Baltimore; m. Alice Huang 1968; one d.; ed. Swarthmore Coll. and Rockefeller Univ.; Postdoctoral Fellow, Mass. Inst. of Technology (M.I.T.) 1963-64, Albert Einstein Coll. of Medicine, New York 1964-65; Research Assoc., Salk Inst., La Jolla, Calif. 1965-68; Assoc. Prof., M.I.T. 1968-72, Prof. of Microbiology 1972–; American Cancer Soc. Prof. of Microbiology 1973-83; Dir. Whitehead Inst. for Biomedical Research 1982–; Eli Lilly Award in Microbiology and Immunology 1971; U.S. Steel Foundation Award in Molecular Biology 1974; Nobel Prize 1975. *Address:* Whitehead Institute, 9 Cambridge Center, Cambridge, Mass. 02142 (Office); 26 Reservoir Road, Cambridge, Mass. 02138, U.S.A. (Home).

BALTSA, Agnes; Greek opera singer; b. Lefkas; ed. Acad. of Music, Athens and in Munich (Maria Callas Scholarship); opera debut as Cherubino, Frankfurt 1968;debut at Vienna State Opera (Octavian) 1970, Salzburg Festival 1970, La Scala, Milan (Dorabella) 1976, Paris Opera and Covent Garden, London (Cherubino) 1976, Metropolitan Opera, New York (Octavian) 1980; mem. Deutsche Oper Berlin 1973–; performs at all major opera houses in world and has given concerts in Europe, U.S.A. and Japan with Karajan, Böhm, Bernstein, Muti, etc.; Österreichische Kammersängerin 1980, Deutscher Schallplattenpreis 1983, Prix Prestige Lyrique (French Ministry of Culture) 1984; has made about 30 operatic recordings. *Leisure interests:* swimming, fashion. *Address:* c/o Management Rita Schültz, Rütistrasse 52, CH-8044, Zürich-Gockhausen, Switzerland.

BALTL, Dr. Hermann Josef; Austrian professor of law; b. 2 Feb. 1918, Graz; s. of Josef Baltl and Melaure Baltl; m. Anneliese Presinger 1950; one d.; Assoc. Prof. of Law and Legal History, Graz 1965, Prof. 1971–; lectures in int. law; Ed. Grazer Rechts-und-Staatswissenschaftliche Studien; mem. Austrian Acad. of Sciences; numerous awards and prizes. *Publications:* several books. *Address:* 8010 Graz, Harrachgasse 28, Austria.

BAM, Arvind Shankar, B.SC.; Indian civil servant and United Nations official; b. 12 March 1918; m. Mrinal Coomarie 1945; one s. two d.; ed. Fergusson Coll., Poona, and King's Coll., London; entered Civil Service 1941, Asst. Collector, Dharwar 1942-44; Special Officer, Civil Supplies, Darjeeling 1944-45; District Controller of Civil Supplies, Jalpaiguri 1945-46; Asst. Collector, Broach 1946-47; Under-Sec., Home Dept., Govt. of Bombay April-Aug. 1947, Deputy Sec. 1947-49; First Collector and District Magistrate, Kolhapur 1949-52; Deputy Sec. Ministry of Rehabilitation, Calcutta 1952-57; Controller for Iron and Steel 1957-61; Chair. Tea Bd., Govt. of India 1961-65; Gen. Man. Indian Airlines Corpn. 1965-66, Chair. and Gen. Man. 1966-67; Resident Rep. of UN Devt. Programme in Yugoslavia 1967-74, in Liberia 1974-77; Regional Adviser, U.N. Devt. Programme, New York 1977–; Leader, Indian Steel Del. to ECAFE 1960. *Address:* UN Development Programme, 1 United Nations Plaza, New York, N.Y. 10017, U.S.A. (Office).

BAMFORD, Clement Henry, PH.D., SC.D., D.SC., F.R.S.C., F.R.S.; British academic; b. 10 Oct. 1912, Stafford; s. of Frederic Jesse and Catherine Mary (née Shelley) Bamford; m. Daphne Ailsa Stephan 1938; one s. one d.; ed. King Edward VI School, Stafford, Trinity Coll., Cambridge; Fellow Trinity Coll., Cambridge 1937-41; with Special Operations Exec. 1942-45; with Fundamental Research Lab., Courtaulds Ltd., Maidenhead 1945-62; Dir. 1947-62; Campbell Brown Prof. of Ind. Chemistry, Univ. of Liverpool 1962-80, Prof. Emer. 1980–, Hon. Research Fellow, Inst. of Medical and Dental Bio-engineering 1981–, Dean, Faculty of Science 1965-68, Pro-Vice-Chancellor 1972-75, Head of Dept., Inorganic, Physical and Ind. Chemistry 1973-78; Pres., Macromolecular Div. of Int. Union of Pure and Applied Chemistry 1981-85; Life mem. Soc. of Chemical Ind., Royal Soc. of Chem.; Meldola Medal, Royal Inst. of Chemistry 1941, Award in Macromolecules and Polymers, Royal Soc. of Chemistry 1977; Hon. D.Sc. (Univ. of Bradford) 1980, (Univ. of Lancaster) 1988. *Publications:* Synthetic Polypeptides (with others) 1956, Kinetics of Vinyl Polymerization by Radical Mechanisms (with others) 1958, Jt. Editor of series: Comprehensive Chemical Kinetics 1969-85, many scientific papers. *Leisure interests:* violin playing, gardening. *Address:* The Institute of Medical and Dental Bioengineering, University of Liverpool, P.O. Box 147, Liverpool, L69 3BX (Office); Broom Bank, Tower Road, Prenton, Birkenhead, Merseyside, L42 8LH, England (Home). *Telephone:* 051 709 0141 ext. 2718 (Office); 051 608 3979 (Home).

BANANA, Rev. Dr. Canaan Sodindo, B.A., M.T.S.; Zimbabwean ecclesiastic and nationalist leader; b. 5 March 1936, Esiphezini, Matabeleland; m. Janet Mbuyazwe 1961; three s. one d.; ed. Tegwani Training Inst., Epworth Theological Coll., Kansai Industrial Centre, Japan, Wesley Theological Seminary, U.S.A., Univ. of S.A.; Chaplain, Tegwani High School 1965-66; ordained Methodist at Epworth 1966; Prin. Matjinke Boarding School 1966; Chair. Bulawayo Council of Churches 1969-70, Southern Africa Urban Industrial Mission 1970-73; founder mem. and Vice-Pres. African Nat. Council (ANC) 1971-73; ANC rep. in U.S.A. and UN 1973-75; Chaplain American Univ. 1974-75; detained 1975-76; Press Spokesman for ANC 1976; attended Geneva Conf. on Rhodesia 1976–; founder mem. and publicity sec. People's Movt. 1976; in detention several times and publs. banned in Rhodesia; Pres. Repub. of Zimbabwe 1980-87; f. Mushandira Pamure Project 1980; f. Kushinga-Phikelela Agric. Inst. 1981; Chancellor of Univ. of Zimbabwe 1983-87; Hon. LL.D. (American Univ., Univ. of Zimbabwe). *Publications:* The Zimbabwe Exodus, The Gospel According to the Ghetto, Theology of Promise, The Woman of My Imagination, The Ethos of Socialism 1987. *Leisure interests:* soccer, table tennis, lawn tennis. *Address:* c/o State House, Harare, Zimbabwe.

BANBURY, (Frederick Harold) Frith; British theatrical director, actor and manager; b. 4 May 1912, Plymouth; s. of Rear Admiral Frederick Arthur Frith Banbury and Winifred Fink; ed. Stowe School, Oxford Univ. and Royal Acad. Dramatic Art; made first stage appearance 1933 and appeared on the London stage, in plays and on television until 1947; has since concentrated on direction. *Plays directed include:* Dark Summer 1947, The Holly and the Ivy 1950, Waters of the Moon 1951, The Deep Blue Sea 1951, Morosco (New York) 1952, A Question Of Fact 1953, Marching Song 1954, Love's Labours Lost, (Old Vic) 1954, The Diary of Anne Frank 1956, A Dead Secret 1957, Flowering Cherry 1957, A Touch of the Sun 1958, The Ring of Truth 1959, The Tiger and the Horse 1960, The Wings of the Dove 1963, The Right Honourable Gentleman (New York) 1965, Howards End 1967, Dear Octopus 1967, Enter a Free Man 1968, My Darling Daisy 1970, The Winslow Boy 1970, Captain Brassbound's Conversion 1971, Reunion in Vienna 1972, The Day After the Fair 1972, In U.S.A. 1973, Glasstown 1973, Ardèle 1975, Family Matter 1976, On Approval 1977, Motherdear 1980, Dear Liar 1982, The Aspern Papers 1984, The Corn is Green 1985, The Admirable Crichton 1988, and others in New York, Paris, Tel Aviv, Toronto, Hong Kong, Johannesburg, Nairobi, Sydney, Melbourne. *Leisure interest:* playing the piano. *Address:* 18 Park Saint James, Prince Albert Road, London, NW8 7LE, England. *Telephone:* 01-722 8481.

BANCROFT, Baron (Life Peer), cr. 1982, of Coatham in the County of Cleveland; **Ian Powell Bancroft,** G.C.B., M.A.; British fmr. civil servant; b. 23 Dec. 1922, Barrow-in-Furness, Lancs. (now Cumbria); s. of A. E. and L. Bancroft; m. Jean Swaine 1950; two s. one d.; ed. Coatham School, Balliol Coll., Oxford; served in Rifle Brigade 1942-45; entered H.M. Treasury 1947; Private Sec. to Sir Henry Wilson Smith 1948-50, to Chancellor of the Exchequer 1953-55 to Lord Privy Seal 1955-57; Cabinet Office 1957-59; Principal Private Sec. to successive Chancellors of the Exchequer 1964-66; Under-Sec. H.M. Treasury 1966-68; Civil Service Dept. 1968-70; Deputy Sec., Dir.-Gen. of Org. and Establishments, Dept. of the Environment 1970-72; Commr. of Customs and Excise and Deputy Chair. of Bd. 1972-73; Second Perm. Sec. Civil Service Dept. 1973-75; Perm. Sec. Dept. of the Environment 1975-77; Head of Home Civil Service and Perm. Sec. Civil Service Dept. 1978-81; Dir. Bass PLC 1982–, Rugby Group PLC 1982–, Sun Life Assurance PLC 1983- (Deputy Chair. 1986-), Bass Leisure Ltd. 1984–, Grindlays Bank PLC 1987–, ANZ Merchant Bank 1987; Chair. Royal Hospital and Home, Putney; Pres. Bldg. Centre Trust 1987–; Vice-Pres. Building Socs. Assen.; Chair. of Council, Mansfield Coll., Oxford; Gov., Cranleigh School; Visiting Fellow, Nuffield Coll., Oxford 1973-81; Hon. Fellow Balliol Coll., Oxford. *Address:* House of Lords, Westminster, London, S.W.1, England.

BANCROFT, Anne; American actress; b. 17 Sept. 1931, New York; d. of Michael and Mildred (née DiNapoli) Italiano; m. 2nd Mel Brooks (q.v.) 1964; one s.; ed. Christopher Colombus High School, New York. *Theatre:* Broadway debut in Two for the Seesaw 1958, played Anne Sullivan in The Miracle Worker 1959-60; The Devils 1965, The Little Foxes 1967, A Cry of Players 1968, Golda 1977. *Films:* The Miracle Worker, Don't Bother to Knock, Tonight We Sing, Demetrius and the Gladiators, The Pumpkin Eater, Seven Women, The Graduate 1968, Young Winston 1971, The Prisoner of Second Avenue 1974, The Hindenberg 1975, Lipstick 1976, Silent Movie 1976, The Turning Point 1977, Golda 1977, Silent Movie, The Elephant Man 1980, To Be or Not to Be 1984, Torch Song Trilogy 1989; wrote, directed and acted in Fatso. Numerous TV appearances including Mother Courage and her Children, Annie, the Woman in the Life of a Man, Jesus of Nazareth 1977, Marco Polo 1981, Agnes of God 1985, 84 Charing Cross Road 1986, 'Night Mother 1986; Academy Award for film The Miracle Worker 1962; Golden Globe Award 1968; Emmy Award for Annie, the Woman in the Life of a Man 1970. *Address:* c/o 20th Century Fox Studios, P.O. Box 900, Beverly Hills, Calif. 90213, U.S.A. (Office).

BANCROFT, Harding Foster; American newspaper executive; b. 29 Dec. 1910, New York; s. of Francis Sidney Bancroft and Beatrice F. Jordan; m. 1st Jane Northrop 1936; two s. two d.; m. 2nd Edith Merrill 1986; ed. Williams Coll. and Harvard Law School; Lawyer 1936-41; Office of Price Admin., Washington 1941-43; Lend-Lease Admin. 1943; U.S. Navy 1943-45; Chief Div. UN Political Affairs, Dept. of State 1945; U.S. Deputy Rep., UN Collective Measures Comm. 1950-53; Legal Adviser, Int. Labour Org. (ILO), Geneva 1953-56; Sec. The New York Times 1957-63, Dir. 1961-76, Exec. Vice-Pres. 1963-74, Vice-Chair. 1974-76; mem. U.S. Del. UN Gen. Assembly 1966; Dir. Gaspesia Pulp & Paper Co., Foreign Policy Asscn.; Trustee, Clark Art Inst., mem. Int. Council Museum of Modern Art, Council on Foreign Relations, Century Asscn.; mem. Bd. of Dirs. UN Asscn. of the U.S.A., Greer Children's Community. *Address:* Verbank Road, Millbrook, N.Y. 12545, U.S.A. (Home). *Telephone:* 212R-H4-3485.

BANDA, Aleke Kadonaphani; Malawi journalist and politician; b. 19 Sept. 1939, Livingstone, Zambia; s. of Eliazar G. Banda and Lilian Phiri; m. Mbumba M. Kahumbe 1961; two s. one d.; ed. United Missionary School, Que Que and Inyati School, Bulawayo; Sec. Nyasaland African Contress (N.A.C.), Que Que Branch 1954; Gen. Sec. S. Rhodesia African Students Asscn. 1957-59; arrested and detained in Rhodesia 1959, deported to Nyasaland; Founder-mem. Malawi Congress Party (MCP), Sec.-Gen. 1959-73, mem. 1974-; Ed. Nyasaland TUC newspaper Ntendere Pa Nchito and mem. TUC Council 1959-60; Personal Political Sec. to Dr. Hastings Banda 1960-73; Sec. MCP Del. to Lancaster House Conf. resulting in self-govt. for Malawi 1960; Sec. to subsequent confs. 1960, 1962; Man. Ed. Malawi News 1959-66; Dir. Malawi Press Ltd. 1960; Dir.-Gen. Malawi Broadcasting Corpn. 1964-66; Nat. Chair. League of Malawi Youth and Commdr. Malawi Young Pioneers 1963-73; Dir. Reserve Bank of Malawi 1965-66; Minister of Devt. and Planning 1966-67, of Econ. Affairs (incorporating Natural Resources, Trade and Industry, and Devt. and Planning), and Minister of Works and Supplies 1967-68, of Trade and Industry (incorporating Tourism, Information and Broadcasting) 1968-69, of Finance and of Information and Tourism 1969-72, of Trade, Industry and Tourism 1972-73; dismissed from Cabinet posts and party 1973, reinstated as mem. party 1974; fmr. Chair. Nat. Bank of Malawi. *Leisure interest:* tennis. *Address:* c/o Malawi Congress Party, P.O. Box 5250, Limbe, Malawi.

BANDA, Hastings Kamuzu, PH.B., B.SC., M.B., CH.B., M.D., L.R.C.S.; Malawi doctor and politician; b. 14 May 1906; ed. mission school, Edinburgh Univ. and in U.S.A.; worked in gold mine; spent twelve years in U.S. in study and medical practice; medical practice in Willesden, England, until 1954, in Kumasi, Ghana 1954-58; returned to Nyasaland to take up leadership of Malawi Congress Party 1958-; detained during declared state of emergency March 1959-April 1960; Minister of Natural Resources, Survey and Local Govt. 1961-63; Prime Minister of Nyasaland 1963-64, of Malawi 1964-66, Pres. of Repub. of Malawi July 1966- (named Pres. for Life 1971); Pres. of Malawi Congress Party 1966- (named Pres. for Life 1971); also Minister of External Affairs, Justice, Works and Supplies, Agriculture and C.-in-C. of Armed Forces; Chancellor, Univ. of Malawi 1965-. *Address:* Office of the President, Private Bag 388, Capital City, Lilongwe 3, Malawi.

BANDA, Rupiah Bwezani, B.A.; Zambian diplomatist; b. 19 Feb. 1937, Gwanda, S. Rhodesia; s. of Bwezani and Sara Zulu Banda; m. Hope Mwansa Makulu 1966; five s.; ed. Secondary School, Munali, Zambia, Univ. of Ethiopia, Lund Univ., Sweden, Wolfson Coll., Cambridge; Rep. of United Nat. Independence Party (UNIP) in N. Europe 1960-64; First Sec. for Int. Affairs, Nat. Union of N. Rhodesia Students; Amb. to United Arab Repub. 1965-67, to U.S.A. 1967-69; Exec. Chair. Rural Devt. Corpn. 1970-71; Gen. Man. Nat. Marketing Bd. of Zambia 1971-74; Perm. Rep. to UN 1974-75; Minister of Foreign Affairs 1975-76; Pres. UN Council for Namibia 1974-75; Chair. Chipoza Holdings, Robert Hudson Ltd., Allenwest and Chiparamba Enterprises; elected M.P. Munali constituency 1978. *Leisure interests:* tennis, reading politics, football. *Address:* Robert Hudson (Zambia) Ltd., P.O. Box R.W. 48, Lusaka, Zambia. *Telephone:* 212559, 211371, 215087.

BANDAR IBN SULTAN IBN ABDULAZIZ AL-SAUD, M.A.; Saudi Arabian diplomatist and army officer; b. 2 March 1949, Taif; s. of H.R.H. Prince Sultan ibn Abdulaziz al-Saud; m. H.R.H. Princess Haifa bint Faisal ibn Abdulaziz al-Saud; two s. three d.; ed. R.A.F. Coll., Cranwell, U.S.A.F. Advanced Program and Johns Hopkins Univ.; fighter pilot, Royal Saudi Air Force 1969-82; in charge of special Saudi Arabian liaison mission to U.S.A. for purchase of AWACS and other defence equipment 1981; Defence and Mil. Attaché, Saudi Arabian Mil. Mission to U.S.A. 1982-83; Amb. to U.S.A. 1983-. *Leisure interests:* flying, racquetball, reading. *Address:* Royal Embassy of Saudi Arabia, 601 New Hampshire Avenue, N.W., Washington, D.C. 20037, U.S.A. *Telephone:* (202) 342-3800.

BANDARANAIKE, Sirimavo Ratwatte Dias; Ceylonese politician; b. 17 April 1916, Ratnapura, Sabaragamuwa Prov.; d. of Barnes Ratwatte and Rosemund Mahawalatenne Ratwatte; ed. St. Bridget's Convent, Colombo; m. S. W. R. D. Bandaranaike (Prime Minister of Ceylon 1956-59) 1940; one. s. two d.; Pres. of Sri Lanka Freedom Party 1960-; Prime Minister, Minister of Defence and External Affairs 1960-65; mem. Senate until 1965; Leader of Opposition 1965-70; Prime Minister, Minister of Defence and Foreign Affairs, Planning, Econ. Affairs and Plan Implementation 1970-77; Pres. Sri Lanka Nidahas Sewaka Sangamaya. *Leisure interests:* gardening, reading, cooking. *Address:* 65 Rosmead Place, Colombo 7, Sri Lanka. *Telephone:* 94539.

BANDEEN, Robert Angus, O.C., PH.D.; Canadian company executive; b. 29 Oct. 1930, Rodney, Ont.; s. of John Robert and Jessie Marie (Thomson) Bandeen; m. Mona Helen Blair 1958; four s.; ed. Univ. of Western Ontario and Duke Univ., U.S.A.; joined Canadian Nat. Railways 1955, Research and Devt. Dept. 1955-66, Dir. of Corporate Planning 1966-68, Vice-Pres. Corporate Planning and Finance 1968-71, Vice-Pres. Great Lakes Region, Toronto 1971-72, Exec. Vice-Pres. Finance and Admin. 1972-74, Pres. 1974-82, C.E.O. 1974-82; Pres. and Chair., Crown Life Insurance Co. 1982-84, Chair. and C.E.O. 1984-85; Pres. Crownx Inc. 1984-85; Pres. and C.E.O. Cluny Corpn. 1986-; Dir. numerous cos.; Chair. Counsel Life Insurance Co., Cytex Inc.; fmr. Chancellor Bishop's Univ., Lennoxville, Quebec; Vice-Pres. Art Gallery of Ontario; Gov. Olympic Trust of Canada; mem. British-N. American Cttee.; Senator Stratford Shakespearian Festival Foundation; Hon. LL.D. (W. Ont.) 1975, (Dalhousie) 1978, (Bishops) 1978, (Queens) 1982; Kt. St. J. 1980; Salzberg Medal (Syracuse Univ.) 1982. *Leisure interests:* squash, tennis, skiing. *Address:* 57 Cluny Drive, Toronto, Ont., M4W 2R1, Canada. *Telephone:* (416) 368 9606 (Office).

BANDEIRA DE MELLO, Lydio Machado, DR.JUR.; Brazilian university professor emeritus; b. 19 July 1901, Abaete, Minas Gerais; s. of Dr. Lydio Alerano and Adélia Machado Bandeira de Mello; m. Amália Introcaso Bandeira de Mello 1928; two s. two d.; ed. Univ. of Brazil; Prof. of Criminal Law, Univ. of Minas Gerais 1952-71, Comparative Criminal Law 1959-71, Prof. Emer. 1972-. *Publications:* O Problema do Mal 1935, A Procura de Deus 1938, Responsabilidade Penal 1941, Prova Matemática da Existência de Deus 1942, Teoria do Destino 1944, Metafísica do Número 1946, A Predestinação Para O Bem 1948, Tabu, Pecado e Crime 1949, Dezessete Aventuras no Reino de Deus 1952, O Real e o Possível 1953, Manual de Direito Penal (Vols. 1-4) 1953-58, A Origem dos Sexos 1955, Filosofia do Direito 1957, Ontologia e Lógica da Contradição 1959, Metafísica do Tempo 1961, O Direito Penal Hispano-Luso Medievo (2 vols.) 1961, Tratado de Direito Penal, Crime e Exclusão de Criminalidade 1962, Da Responsabilidade Penal e Da Isenção de Pena 1962, Da Capitulação dos Crimes e da Fixação das Penas 1963, Metafísica da Gravitação 1963, Memória Espaço e Tempo (2 vols.) 1963, Cosmologia do Movimento 1965, Teologia Matemática 1965, Metafísica do Espaço 1966, A Pluralidade de Consciências 1967, Crítica Cosmológica de Física Quántica 1968, Fórmulas Gerais da Distribuição de Probabilidades 1968, Evangelho para Bacharéis 1969, O Criminoso, O Crime e a Pena 1970, Trabalhos de Algoritmia (Aritmética e Algebra) Superior 1971, A Existéncia e a Imortalidade da Alma 1972, As Credenciais da Razão 1973, Teoria Algébrica das Permutações Condicionadas 1972, Crítica do Principio da Razão Suficiente 1974, A Falibilidade da Indução 1974, A Conquista do Reino de Deus (2 vols.) 1975, O Possível Puro 1975, Cosmologia Científica 1976, Metafísica da Sensação 1977, A Matemática do Universo e a Matemática Dos Homens 1978, Voluntariedade da Vinda dos Homens para a Terra (A Genética Experimental 1979) 1980, Deus e cada Homem 1980, Sem Angústia Diante de Deus 1982, O Universo Físico Feito 1982, Para Receber Homens Livres 1982, Universos Abstratos em Possível Expansão Ilimitável 1983, Jesus meu Mestre 1984. *Leisure interests:* walking, cinema-going, philately. *Address:* Rua Rodrigues Caldas, 703 Belo Horizonte, Minas Gerais, Brazil. *Telephone:* 3370198.

BANDLER, John William, PH.D., F.I.E.E., F.R.S.C.; Canadian professor of electrical and computer engineering; b. 9 Nov. 1941, Jerusalem; ed. Imperial Coll. London; Mullard Research Labs., Redhill, Surrey 1966; Univ. of Man. 1967-69; McMaster Univ. 1969, Prof. 1973; fmr. Chair. Dept. of Electrical Eng., McMaster Univ.; now Dir. of Research, Simulation Optimization Systems Research Lab. *Publications:* more than 220 papers in journals and books and book chapters. *Address:* Department of Electrical and Computer Engineering, McMaster University, Hamilton, Ont., L8S 4L7, Canada.

BANERJI, Asoka Nath, B.SC., LL.B.; Indian politician; b. 19 Dec. 1917, Banaras; ed. Patna and Calcutta Univs.; served in army 1941-46; joined Indian Admin. Service 1947; various posts 1947-56; Deputy Gen. Man. Durgapur Steel Project 1956-61; Iron and Steel Controller for India

1961–63; Gen. Man. Rourkela Steel Plant 1964–67; Deputy Chair. Hindustan Steel Ltd. 1967–69; Dir.-Gen. Bureau of Public Enterprises 1969–73; Special Sec., Ministry of Industrial Devt. 1973–74; Sec., Ministry of Works and Housing 1974–76; Adviser to Gov. of Gujarat, Chair. Public Enterprises Selection Bd., Chair. Banking Service Comm. 1976; started legal practice in Supreme Court and Delhi High Court 1977–81; Gov. Himachal Pradesh 1981–83; Gov. Karnataka 1983–Feb. 1988. *Address:* c/o Raj Bhavan, Bangalore, Karnataka, India.

BANERJI, Shishir Kumar, B.A.; Indian diplomatist and administrator; b. 21 Oct. 1913, Uttarpara; s. of Mr. and Mrs. A. D. Banerji; m. Gauri Chatterjee 1939; two s. two d.; ed. Univ. of Allahabad and New Coll., Oxford; joined ICS 1937; Deputy Commr. Central Provinces 1937–46; Sec. Civil Supplies, Cen. Provs. Govt. 1946–47; First Sec., Chargé d'affaires, Teheran 1947–49; Deputy Sec. Ministry of External Affairs 1949–51; Deputy High Commr., Lahore 1951–54; Consul-Gen. San Francisco 1954–56; Chair. UN Visiting Mission to British and French Togoland 1955; Envoy to Syria 1956, Amb. 1957–58; High Commr. to Malaya and Commr. to Singapore, Sarawak, Brunei and North Borneo 1958–59; Joint Sec., Ministry of External Affairs 1960–61; Chief of Protocol 1961–64; Chief Inspector of Indian Missions abroad 1964; Amb. to Fed. Repub. of Germany 1964–67, to Japan 1967–70; Sec. Ministry of External Affairs 1970–72; Lieut. Gov. Goa 1972–78; mem. Asscn. of Indian Diplomats India Int. Centre, New Delhi, Indian Nat. Trust for Art and Cultural Heritage (Adviser, Legislation and Constitution); mem. Exec. Bd. of Indian Nat. Cttee. of Int. Council of Monuments and Sites (ICOMOS). *Publication:* From Dependence to Non-alignment: Experiences of an Indian Administrator and Diplomat. *Leisure interest:* Indian art and heritage, environment and int. affairs. *Address:* 3 Vasant Marg, New Delhi 110057, India.

BANGEMANN, Martin, D.JUR.; German politician and lawyer; b. 15 Nov. 1934, Wanzleben; s. of Martin Bangemann and Lotte Telge; m. Renate Bauer 1962; three s. one d.; ed. secondary school, Emden and Univs. of Tübingen and Munich; mem. Freie Demokratische Partei (FDP) 1963–, Deputy 1969, mem. Regional Exec. Baden-Württemberg FDP 1973–78 (resgnd.), mem. Nat. Exec. 1969– (resgnd. as Gen. Sec. 1975), Chair. FDP Feb. 1985–; mem. Bundestag 1973–79, European Parl. 1979–84; Minister of Econs. 1984–88; EEC Commr. for Internal Market, Industry, relations with European Parl. Jan. 1989. *Leisure interests:* philosophy, horticulture. *Address:* Sannentalstrasse 9, 7418 Metzingen, Württemberg, Federal Republic of Germany.

BANGERTER, Hans Ernst; Swiss sports official; b. 10 June 1924, Studen, Bienne; m. Hedy Tanner 1948; one s. two d.; ed. Technical Coll., Bienne; Asst. Sec. Int. Fed. of Association Football (FIFA), Zürich 1953–59; Sec.-Gen. European Union of Asscn. Football (UEFA), Berne 1960–. *Leisure interests:* gardening, golf, skiing, walking, mountaineering. *Address:* UEFA, P.O. Box 16, Berne 15, Switzerland (Office); Hubelgasse 25, 3065 Bolligen, BE, Switzerland (Home). *Telephone:* 031 32 1735 (Office).

BANGERTER, Norman Howard; American politician; b. 4 Jan. 1933, Granger, Utah; s. of William H. and Isabelle (Bawden) Bangerter; m. Colleen Monson 1953; four s. two d. one foster s.; ed. Univ. of Utah and Brigham Young Univ.; Vice-Pres. B and H Real Estate Co. 1970–; Pres. Bangerter Hendrickson Co. 1970, NHB Construction Co. 1983–; mem. Utah House of Reps. 1974–84, Speaker 1981–84; Gov. of Utah Jan. 1985–; Vice-Chair., Western Govs. Asscn. 1985–86; Vice-Chair., School Facilities Sub-cttee. Educ. 1991 Project, Nat. Gov.'s Assn.; Republican. *Leisure interests:* golf, basketball, waterskiing, reading. *Address:* Office of the Governor, 210 State Capital, Salt Lake City, Utah 84114, U.S.A.

BANHAM, John Michael Middlecott, M.A., L.L.D.; British business executive; b. 22 Aug. 1940; s. of Terence Middlecott Banham and Belinda Joan Banham; m. Frances Favell 1965; one s. two d.; ed. Charterhouse, Queens' Coll., Cambridge; with H.M. Foreign Service 1962–64; Dir. of Marketing, Wallcoverings Div., Reed Int. 1965–69; with McKinsey & Co. Inc. 1969, Assoc. 1969–75, Prin. 1975–80, Dir. 1980–83; Controller Audit Comm. for Local Authorities in England and Wales 1983–87; Dir.-Gen. CBI March 1987–. *Publications:* Future of the British Car Industry 1975, Realising the Promise of a National Health Service 1977, and numerous reports for Audit Comm. on educ., social services, housing, etc. 1984–87. *Address:* Penberth, St. Buryan, nr. Penzance, Cornwall.

BANHARN SILPAARCHA, Nai; Thai politician; b. 20 July 1932, Suphan Buri; m. Nang Jamsai; one s. two d.; ed. Bangkok Business Coll.; mem. Municipal Ass. Suphan Buri 1974; subsequently mem. Nat. Legis. Ass.; mem. Senate 1975; Deputy Sec.-Gen. Chat Thai Party; M.P. for Suphan Buri 1976–; Deputy Minister of Industry 1976–86; Minister of Communications Aug. 1986–88. *Address:* c/o Ministry of Communications, Rajdamnern Nok Avenue, Bangkok 10100, Thailand.

BANI-SADR, Abolhasan; Iranian politician; b. 1933, Hamadan, W. Iran; s. of the Ayatollah Sayed Nasrollah Bani-Sadr; ed. Sorbonne and Teheran Univs.; supporter of Mossadeq (Prime Minister of Iran 1951–53); joined underground anti-Shah movement 1953; imprisoned after riots over Shah's land reforms 1963; in exile in Paris 1963–79; taught at the Sorbonne; close associate of the Ayatollah Ruhollah Khomeini (q.v.), and returned to Iran after overthrow of Shah; Minister of Econ. and Financial Affairs 1979–80; Acting Foreign Minister Nov. 1979 (dismissed); President of Iran 1980–81;

mem. Supervisory Bd. of Cen. Bank of Iran 1979; mem. Revolutionary Council 1979–81 (Pres. 1980–81); fled to France 1981, subsequently formed Nat. Council of Resistance to oppose the Govt. (in alliance with Massoud Rajavi, Leader of Mujaheddin Kalq, and Abdel-Rahman Ghassemlov, Leader of Democratic Party of Kurdistan, Nat. Democratic Front and other resistance groups), Chair. 1981–84. *Publications:* The Economics of Divine Unity, Oil and Violence, L'espérance trahie 1982, and numerous articles and pamphlets on economics and politics.

BANK-ANTHONY, Sir Mobolaji, K.B.E.; Nigerian business executive; b. 11 June 1907; ed. Methodist Boys' High School, Lagos, Church Missionary Society Grammar School, Lagos, Ibeju-Ode Grammar School; Postal Clerk, Nigerian Post and Telegraph Dept. 24; later built up palm oil business and after Second World War built up construction, haulage and cinema companies; fmr. Chair. Nigerian Stock Exchange; Fellow Inst. of Directors, London, Royal Commonwealth Soc. *Address:* Executive House, 2A Oil Mill Street, P.O. Box 75, Lagos, Nigeria (Office).

BANNEN, Ian; British actor; b. Airdrie, Scotland; s. of John James Bannen and Clare Galloway; m. Marilyn Salisbury 1978; film début in Carlton Browne of the F.O. 1958; with the R.S.C. 1961–62. *Films include:* Station Six Sahara 1963, The Hill 1964, Flight of the Phoenix 1965, Penelope 1966, Lock up Your Daughters 1968, The Deserter 1970, Doomwatch 1972, The Mackintosh Man 1973, The Offence 1973, The Driver's Seat 1974, Bite the Bullet 1975, The Sweeney 1977, Darkness into Darkness 1977, Watcher in the Woods 1979, Eye of the Needle 1980, Night Crossing 1980, Gandhi 1982, The Prodigal 1982, Gorky Park 1983, Lamb 1985, Defence of the Realm 1985, Attack on the Pope 1985, Hope and Glory 1987, The Courier 1987, Ghost Story, Circles In A Forest, Dangerous Love, The Gamble, Witch Story, George's Island 1988. *TV appearances include:* Tinker, Tailor, Soldier, Spy 1979, The Hard World 1982, Tickets for the Titanic 1986, Bookie 1987. *Leisure interests:* reading, walking, swimming, photography. *Address:* c/o Jean Diamond, London Management, 235 Regent Street, London, W.1, England. *Telephone:* 01-493 1610.

BANNISTER, Sir Roger G., K.B.E., D.M., F.R.C.P.; British consultant physician, neurologist, university administrator and athlete; b. 23 March 1929, London; s. of the late Ralph and of Alice Bannister; m. Moyra Elver Jacobsson; two s. two d.; ed. City of Bath Boys' School, Univ. Coll. School, Exeter and Merton Colls., Oxford, St. Mary's Hosp. Medical School, London; winner, Oxford and Cambridge Mile 1947–50; Pres. Oxford Univ. Athletic Club 1948; British Mile Champion 1951, 1953, 1954; world record one mile 1954, first sub-four minute mile 1954; Master Pembroke College, Oxford 1985–; Consultant Neurologist, Nat. Hosp. for Nervous Diseases, London; Hon. LL.D. (Liverpool) 1972, Hon. D.Sc. (Sheffield) 1978, Hon. D.Sc. (Bath) 1984, (Rochester) 1986, (Williams) 1987, Hon. M.D. (Pavia) 1986; Hon. Fellow UMIST 1974; Hans-Heinrich Siegbert Prize 1977. *Publications:* First Four Minutes 1955, Ed. Brain's Clinical Neurology, various medical articles on physiology and neurology, Ed. Autonomic Failure 1988. *Address:* Master's Lodgings, Pembroke College, Oxford, OX1 1DW, England. *Telephone:* (0865) 276403.

BANNON, Hon. John Charles, B.A., LL.B.; Australian politician; s. of C. Bannon; m. 1st, one d.; m. 2nd. Angela Bannon 1982; ed. St. Peter's Coll., Univ. of Adelaide; Industrial Advocate AWU 1969–73; Adviser to Commonwealth Minister of Labour and Immigration 1973–75; Asst. Dir. S. Australian Dept. of Labour and Industry 1975–77; mem. House Ass. 1977–; Minister for Community Devt., Minister for Local Govt., Minister for Recreation and Sport 1978–79; Leader of the Opposition 1979–82; Premier of S. Australia, Minister of State Devt., and Minister for the Arts 1982–85; Premier of S. Australia and Minister for the Arts 1985–; Labor. *Address:* Shop 43, North Park Shopping Centre, Prospect 5082, South Australia.

BANSAL, Ghamandi Lal, M.A., LL.B.; Indian commercial executive; b. 3 Dec. 1914, Ranikhet, U.P.; s. of Musaddi Lal; m. Mrs. Shanti Bansal 1941; three s. two d.; ed. A.V. Mission School, Ranikhet, Government Intermediate Coll., Almora, and Lucknow Univ.; fmr. mem. Indian Parl. 1952–57; Dir. State Bank of India; Sec.-Gen. Fed. of Indian Chambers of Commerce and Industry, All-India Organization of Industrial Employers, Indian Nat. Cttee. of Int. Chamber of Commerce 1954–75; Vice-Pres. Indian Council of World Affairs; Chair. Nat. Cttee. for the Devt. of Backward Areas; Chair. Governing Body of Shri Ram Coll. of Commerce; Treas. Helen Keller Trust for the Blind, Deaf and Dumb; Vice-Pres. Indian Inst. of Foreign Trade; Sec. Indian Council for Child Welfare Trust; Trustee Prime Minister's Students Fund Trust; mem. G.B. Pant Centenary Celebrations Cttee.; Dir.-Gen. Econ. Research Div., Birla Inst. of Scientific Research. *Publications:* India and Pakistan—An Analysis of Economic, Agricultural and Mineral Resources. *Leisure interests:* reading, golf. *Address:* A/37 Kailash Colony, New Delhi 110048, India. *Telephone:* 805-3146, 3707, 3708 (Office); 6417398, 6431052, 6432498 (Home).

BANTADTAN, Banyat; Thai politician; b. 15 May 1942, Sarat Thani; unmarried; ed. Thammasart Univ.; joined Accelerated Rural Devt. Office 1969, fmr. Asst. Chief of Planning Section –1974; M.P. 1975–; Sec. to Minister of Interior; then Deputy Minister of Interior in first, second and third Prem govts.; Minister in Prime Minister's Office 1979–86; Minister of Science and Tech. Aug. 1986–88. *Address:* Ministry of Science and

Technology, 6th and 7th Floors, Department of Science Service Building, Yothi Road, Phyathai, Bangkok 10400, Thailand.

BANZER SUÁREZ, Gen. Hugo; Bolivian army officer and politician; b. 10 May 1926, Santa Cruz; s. of César Banzer and Luisa Suárez; m. Yolanda G. Prada 1962; two s. three d.; ed. Colegio Militar, La Paz; Commdr. Bolivian 4th Cavalry Regiment; Minister of Educ. and Culture 1964–66; Mil. Attaché Washington, D.C. 1967–69; Dir. Colegio Militar 1969–71; in exile Jan.-Aug. 1971; Pres. of Bolivia 1971–78; overthrown in coup July 1978; Leader Acción Democrática Nacionalista 1980–; in exile, Argentina, then Pres. cand. 1985; Order of Mil. Merit (U.S.A.), and other national and foreign decorations.

BAO CONG; Chinese government official; Vice-Chair. Heilongjiang Prov. People's Govt. 1983–. *Address:* Heilongjiang Provincial People's Government, Harbin, People's Republic of China.

BAO TONG; Chinese government official; Vice-Minister for Restructuring Economic System 1984–; Sr. Official, Premier's Office 1985–; mem. 13th Cen. Cttee. CCP 1987–. *Address:* Premier's Office, State Council, Zhongnan Hai, Beijing, People's Republic of China.

BAO TONGZHI; Chinese government official; Deputy Dir. Cinema Bureau 1986–. *Address:* Cinema Bureau, Ministry of Radio, Cinema and Television, Beijing, People's Republic of China.

BAO WENKUI; Chinese agronomist; b. 8 May 1916; ed. in U.S.A.; Prof. Chinese Acad. of Agricultural Sciences; Deputy, 5th NPC 1978–83; Dir. Inst. of Crop Breeding and Cultivation, Beijing 1981–; Deputy, 6th NPC 1983–88; mem. Dept. of Biology, Academia Sinica 1985–. *Address:* Chinese Academy of Agricultural Sciences, Baishiqiao Road, Beijing, People's Republic of China.

BARABANOV, Yevgeniy Viktorovich; Soviet art critic; b. 1943, Leningrad; ed. Moscow School of Art, Faculty of History of Art, Moscow Univ.; mem. editorial bd. of journal Decorative Art; worked in Museum of Fine Art, Moscow; mem. of editorial bd. of Iskusstvo Publishing House –1973; mem. Orthodox Church 1960–; published in samizdat and abroad numerous articles on philosophy and religion 1973–; wrote letter in defence of Solzhenitsyn 1974; *Publications include:* Early Christian Aesthetics 1976–77 (Paris), The Moral Pre-Requisite of Christian Unity (Russkaya mysl') 1974; The Fate of Christian Culture (Kontinent) 1976.

BARAKAT, Gamal Eddin, LL.B., B.LITT.; Egyptian diplomatist; b. 18 Feb. 1921, Cairo; s. of late Mohamed Barakat; m. Elham Amber 1955; one s. two d.; ed. Helwan Secondary School, Cairo Univ., Hague Acad. of Int. Law, Oriel Coll., Oxford; Third Sec., Egyptian Embassy, London 1950–52; with Political Dept., Ministry of Foreign Affairs 1953–55; Secr., Anglo-Egyptian Treaty negotiations 1954; Consul-Gen., Aleppo, Syria 1955–58; Counsellor, Washington, D.C. 1958–60; Head of In-Service Training Dept., Ministry of Foreign Affairs 1961–63; mem. OAU Experts Cttee., Addis Ababa 1963–64; Amb. to Uganda 1964–68, also to Burundi 1968, to Finland 1968–73; Asst. to the President's Adviser on Nat. Security 1973–74; Head of Cultural Relations and Tech. Co-operation Dept., Ministry of Foreign Affairs 1975; Amb. to Iraq 1976–77; Dir. Foreign Service Inst., Ministry of Foreign Affairs 1979–80; Adviser to Ministry of Finance 1980–82; UN Consultant, Inst. of Diplomatic Studies, Saudi Arabian Foreign Ministry 1984–87; Order of the Repub. 1954, 1964, Order of Merit (Egypt) 1958, 1973, Order of Merit (Syria) 1958, Order of the Lion (Finland) 1973. *Publications:* Status of Aliens in Egypt 1949, Diplomatic Terminology (in English and Arabic) 1982, Diplomacy Past, Present and Future 1985. *Leisure interest:* angling. *Address:* 55 Hegaz Street, Heliopolis, Cairo, Egypt. *Telephone:* 2432487.

BARANOV, Vasiliy Gavrilovich, Soviet endocrinologist; b. 25 Dec. 1899, Gatchina, Leningrad Region; s. of Gavril Petrovich Baranov and Julia Ivanovna Baranova; m. Maria Mikhailovna Tushinskaya 1952; ed. Leningrad Military Medical Acad; army therapeutist; Intern 1925–29; Senior Assoc. Inst. of Experimental Medicine 1932–40; Head of Dept., First Leningrad Medical Inst. 1938–41, 1945–46; Senior Research Assoc. 1946–54; Head of Laboratory, Inst. of Physiology 1954–, Prof. 1954; Corresp. mem. U.S.S.R. Acad. of Medical Sciences 1952–60, mem. 1960–; mem. Bd. U.S.S.R. Soc. of Therapeutists; Chair. All-Union Soc. of Endocrinologists, Leningrad Soc. of Endocrinologists; Orders of Lenin, Red Banner of Labour and Red Star and other decorations. *Publications:* Over 135 works on endocrinology, including pathogenesis and treatment of toxic goitre, diabetes mellitus, physiology and pathology of ageing and climax. *Leisure interests:* holidays at country house and travelling, boating, walking, thinking over scientific problems. *Address:* Pavlov Institute of Physiology, U.S.S.R. Academy of Sciences, 6 Naberezhnaya Makarova, Leningrad, U.S.S.R.

BARBARA, Agatha; Maltese politician; b. 11 March 1923, Zabbar; d. of late Joseph and Antonia (née Agius) Barbara; ed. Govt. Grammar School, Valletta; school teacher; mem. Labour Party 1946–; Malta's first female M.P.; M.P. 1947–82; Minister of Educ. 1955–58, 1971–74, of Labour, Culture and Welfare 1974–81; Pres. of Repub. of Malta Feb. 1982-Feb. 1987; fmr. mem. ARP (World War II), later supervisor Victory Kitchens Army Munitions Depts.; fmr. Man. Advertising Dept. Freedom Press; mem. St. John Alliance (UK), Int. Social Democratic Women; Pres. Malta Labour

Party Women's Club; Chair. Exec. Cttee. Malta Labour Party Women's Movement; Hon. Pres. St. Michael's Band Club, Maltese Settlers' Club (Australia); Hon. D.Phil. (Beijing); Stara Planina, 1st Degree (Bulgaria) 1983, Order of Nat. Flag, 1st Class (Democratic People's Repub. of Korea), Hishau (Pakistan). *Leisure interests:* philately, classical and modern music. *Address:* The Palace, Valletta (Office); The Palace, St. Anton, Malta (Official Residence). *Telephone:* 21221 (Office).

BARBENEL, Joseph Cyril, PH.D., F.R.S.E.; British bioengineer; b. 2 Jan. 1937, London; m. Lesley Mary Hyde Jowett 1964; two s. one d.; ed. Hackney Downs Grammar School, London, London Hosp. Dental School, Univ. of London, Queen's Coll., Univ. of St. Andrews, Univ. of Strathclyde, Glasgow; Dental House Surgeon, London Hosp. 1960; Royal Army Dental Corps 1960–62; gen. dental practice, London 1963; Lecturer, Dental Prosthetics, Univ. of Dundee 1967–69, Univ. of Strathclyde 1970, Sr. Lecturer, Bioeng. Unit 1970–82, Reader 1982–85, Prof. 1985–; Consulting Prof., Chongqing Univ., China; Visiting Prof. Tech. Univ. of Vienna; Pres. Biological Eng. Soc. (mem. Council, Chair. Professional Cttee.), Int. Soc. for Bioeng. and the Skin (mem. Cttee., Sec. for Standardization), Royal Soc. of Medicine (mem. Steering Cttee., Forum on Clinical Haemorheology); Pres. The Soc. for Tissue Viability; Chief Examiner, Clinical Eng., Inst. of Physical Sciences in Medicine; mem. Admin. Cttee., Int. Fed. of Medical and Biological Eng.; Nuffield Foundation Award 1963–66. *Publications:* Clinical Aspects of Blood Rheology (with Lowe and Forbes) 1981, Pressure Sores (with Lowe and Forbes) 1983, Blood flow in Artificial Organs and Cardiovascular Prostheses (with co-eds.) 1988, Blood flow in the Brain (with co-eds.) 1988, numerous scientific papers. *Leisure interests:* music, theatre, reading. *Address:* University of Strathclyde Bioengineering Unit, Wolfson Centre, 106 Rottenrow, Glasgow, G4 0NW; 151 Maxwell Drive, Glasgow, G41, Scotland (Home). *Telephone:* (041) 552 4400 Ext. 3221 (Office); (041) 427 0765 (Home).

BARBER, Baron (Life Peer), cr. 1974, of Wentbridge in West Yorkshire; **Anthony Perrinot Lysberg Barber,** P.C., T.D.; British banker and fmr. politician; b. 4 July 1920, Hull; s. of John Barber, C.B.E., and Katy Lysberg; m. Jean Patricia Asquith 1950 (died 1983); two d.; ed. Retford School and Oriel Coll., Oxford; army service 1939–40, Royal Air Force 1940–45; mem. Parl. 1951–64, 1965–74; Parl. Private Sec., Air Ministry 1952–54; Govt. Whip 1955–57; Lord Commissioner of the Treasury 1957–58; Parl. Private Sec. to Prime Minister 1958–59; Econ. Sec. to the Treasury 1959–62; Financial Sec. to the Treasury 1962–63; Minister of Health 1963–64; Chair. Conservative Party 1967–70; Chancellor of Duchy of Lancaster June-July 1970; Chancellor of Exchequer 1970–74; Dir. British Ropes (now Bridon) 1964–70, 1974–83, several banks incl. Chartered Bank 1966–70, British Petroleum 1979–88; Chair. Redfearn Nat. Glass 1967, Standard Chartered Bank 1974–87; mem. Cttee. of Inquiry into events leading to Argentine invasion of the Falkland Islands 1982, Commonwealth Group on S. Africa 1985; Hon. Fellow, Oriel Coll., Oxford 1971. *Address:* House of Lords, London, S.W.1, England. *Telephone:* 01-280 7001.

BARBER, Clarence Lyle, O.C., PH.D., F.R.S.C.; Canadian professor of economics; b. 5 May 1917, Wolseley, Sask.; s. of Richard Edward Barber and Lulu Pearl Lyons; m. Barbara Anne Patchet 1947; four s.; ed. Wolseley High School, Univ. of Saskatchewan, Clark Univ., Univ. of Minnesota, U.S.A.; served R.C.A.F. 1943–45; Statistician, Statistics Canada 1945–48; Asst. Prof., McMaster Univ. 1948–49; Assoc. Prof., Univ. of Manitoba 1949–65, Prof. 1956–83, Distinguished Prof. 1982–, Prof. Emer. 1985–; Dir. of Research, Royal Comm. on Flood Cost-Benefit, Man. 1957–59; Adviser on Nat. Income, Govt. of Philippines 1959–60; Commr. Royal Comm. on Farm Machinery 1966–70, on Welfare, Man. 1972, Nat. Comm. on Inflation 1979, Royal Comm. on the Econ. Union and Devt. Prospects for Canada 1982–85; Pres. Canadian Asscn. of Univ. Teachers 1958–59, Canadian Econ. Asscn. 1972–73; Hon. LL.D. (Univ. of Guelph) 1988. *Publications:* Inventories and the Business Cycle 1952, Theory of Fiscal Policy Applied to a Province 1966, Collected Economic Papers 1982, Unemployment and Inflation 1980 and Controlling Inflation 1982 (both with J. C. P. McCallum); On the Origins of the Great Depression 1978. *Address:* 766 Richmond Avenue, Victoria, B.C. V8S 3Z1, Canada. *Telephone:* (1) 604-595-6891.

BARBER, John Norman Romney; British business executive; b. 22 April 1919, Leigh-on-Sea, Essex; s. of George Ernest and Gladys Eleanor Barber; m. Babette Chalu 1941; one s.; Principal, Cen. Finance Dept., Ministry of Supply 1946–55; with Ford Motor Co. Ltd. 1955–65, Dir. of Finance 1962–65, Founder, Chair. Ford Motor Credit Co. 1963; Dir. of Finance, AEI Ltd. 1966; Finance Dir. Leyland Motor Corpn. 1967, Dir. of Finance and Planning, British Leyland Motor Corpn. 1968, Deputy Man. Dir. 1971, Deputy Chair. 1973–74; Deputy Chair. John E. Wiltshier Gp. Ltd. 1979–; Chair. Aberhurst Ltd. 1976–, A. C. Edwards Eng. Ltd. 1976–81; Dir. Acrow PLC 1977–85, Good Relations Group PLC 1980–, Cox & Kings Holdings Ltd. 1980–81, Spear and Jackson Int. PLC 1980–, C & K Consulting Group 1982–, Cox & Kings Financial Services Ltd 1980–85, C & K Exec. Search Ltd 1981–85, Twinprint Ltd. 1981–, Economists Advisory Group Ltd. 1981–, C & K Marketing Ltd. 1982–; Past Chair. Bd. of Trade Investments Grants Advisory Cttee.; fmr. mem. Royal Comm. on Medical Educ.; fmr. mem. Advisory Cttee. on Energy Conservation to Ministry of Energy; fmr. Vice-Pres., Soc. of Motor Mfrs. and Traders; Companion, British Inst. of Management. *Leisure interests:* motor sport, photography, reading, music, forestry. *Address:* Balcary, Earleswood, Fairmile Lane, Cobham, Surrey, KT11 2BZ, England.

BARBER, Norman Frederick, D.SC., F.R.S.N.Z.; British physicist; b. 31 Dec. 1909, Castleford, Yorks.; s. of Benjamin Teal Barber and Sarah Jane Wilkinson; m. 1st Hilda Brearley 1934 (died 1955), 2nd Ruth Enid Dowden 1956; one s. one d.; ed. Castleford Secondary School, Lees Univ.; school teacher St. Helens and Bradford 1933–37; Research Physicist, R.N. Scientific Pool, Prin. Scientific Officer 1946–50; Research Physicist, N.Z. DSIR 1950–64; Prof. of Theoretical Physics, Victoria Univ., Wellington, N.Z. 1964–76; now teaches part-time; Admiralty ex-gratia award for war work 1951, Winstone Art Award (sculpture) 1985, Award "for outstanding contrib. to Marine Science in N.Z." 1985, Exhibiting mem. N.Z. Acad. of Fine Arts 1987. *Publications:* Generation and Propagation of Ocean Waves and Swell (with F. Ursell) 1948, Experimental Correlograms and Fourier Transforms 1961, Wind Waves 1969; author and ed. high school physics textbooks. *Leisure interests:* art work and physics teaching. *Address:* Flat 7, 147 Ohiro Road, Brooklyn, Wellington 2, New Zealand. *Telephone:* Wellington 850-346.

BARBERIS, Pierre Georges; French banker; b. 29 May 1942, Grenoble; m. Sabine Heitzmann 1965; one s. one d.; ed. École Polytechnique; Caisse des Dépôts et Consignations 1964–68; Crédit Lyonnais 1969–79; Chair. Trigano 1979–83; Gen. Man. Crédit du Nord 1985–86; Adviser to Pres. of Mutuelles unies Axa 1987–; mem. Institut des Actuaires Français. *Leisure interests:* skiing, squash and cycling. *Address:* Axa, Rouen Belbeuf 3037x, 76029 Rouen Cedex (Office); 82 rue Charles Laffitte, 92200 Neuilly et La Grangeat, 74700 Combloux, France (Home).

BARBIERI, Fedora; Italian singer; b. 4 June 1919; ed. Trieste High School and Conservatoire; scholarship to Teatro Lirico, Florence 1940; debut as Fidalma in Cimarosa's The Secret Marriage, Teatro Comunale, Florence 1940; has appeared in leading roles at La Scala, Milan 1942–, Teatro Colón, Buenos Aires 1947–, Metropolitan Opera House, New York and Royal Opera House, Covent Garden, London 1950–; has also appeared at numerous important festivals and opera seasons in Italy, Germany, U.S.A., France, Spain, Portugal, Brazil, Austria, etc.; has sung leading roles in recordings of Aida, Il Trovatore, Requiem, Falstaff, Un Ballo in Maschera (Verdi), La Gioconda (Ponchielli), La Favorita and Linda di Chamonix (Donizetti), Suor Angelica (Puccini). *Address:* Viale Belfiore 9, Florence, Italy.

BARBIERI, Lázaro; Argentine university professor; b. 1911; ed. Univ. Nacional de Tucumán; fmr. Prof. of Sociology, Univ. Nacional de Tucumán; Prof of Argentine History and Social Thought, Univ. Nacional de Tucumán; Gov. of Tucumán Province. *Publications:* La Integración de Latinoamérica—Su Problemática Sociológica, La Reforma Religiosa y la Formación de la Conciencia Moderna, Sociología de la Educación y la Problemática del Sistema Educativo. *Address:* Universidad Nacional de Tucumán, Ayacucho 482, San Miguel de Tucumán, Argentina.

BARBOT, Ivan, L. ès L.; French police commissioner; b. 5 Jan. 1937, Ploeuc; s. of Pierre Barbot and Anne (née Le Calvez) Barbot; m. Roselyne de Lestrange 1971; three c.; ed. Lycée de Saint-Brieuc, Univ. of Paris; Prin. Pvt. Sec. to Chief Commr., Tarn-et-Garonne 1961; Prin. Pvt. Sec., later Dir. of Staff to Chief Commr., Haute-Savoie 1962; Dir. of Staff, Paris Region Pref. 1967; Deputy Chief Commr., Etampes 1969; Deputy Chief Commr. without portfolio, Official Rep. to the Cabinet 1974; Tech. Adviser to the Cabinet 1974–77; Sec.-Gen. Seine-Saint-Denis 1977–82; Chief Commr. and Superintendent, Dept. de la Charente 1982–85, du Var 1985–87; Dir.-Gen. Police nat. 1987–; Pres. Interpol 1988–; Officier ordre nationale du Mérite, Mérite agricole, Chevalier Légion d'honneur, Palmes Académiques, Arts et Lettres; Médaille de la jeunesse et des sports. *Address:* Direction générale de la Police nationale, 11 rue des Saussaies, 75008 Paris, France (Office).

BARBOUR, Very Rev. Robert Alexander Stewart, M.C., M.A., B.D., S.T.M., D.D.; British university professor and ecclesiastic (retd.); b. 11 May 1921, Edinburgh; s. of George F. Barbour and Helen V. Hepburne-Scott; m. Margaret Pigot 1950; three s. one d.; ed. Rugby School, Balliol Coll. Oxford, Univ. of St. Andrews and Yale Univ.; mil. service 1940–45; Lecturer and Sr. Lecturer in New Testament, New Coll. Univ. of Edin. 1955–71; Prof. of New Testament Exegesis, Univ. of Aberdeen 1971–85; Master, Christ's Coll. Aberdeen 1977–82; Chaplain-in-Ordinary to H.M. The Queen 1976–; Dean, Chapel Royal in Scotland 1981–; Prelate of Priory of Scotland of Order of St. John 1977–; Moderator, Gen. Ass. of Church of Scotland 1979–80; Chair. Scottish Churches Council 1982–86; Hon. D.D. *Publications:* The Scottish Horse 1939–45 1950, Traditio-Historical Criticism of the Gospels 1972, What is the Church For? 1973. *Leisure interests:* music, forestry, walking. *Address:* Fincastle, Pitlochry PH16 5RJ, Scotland. *Telephone:* 0796 3209.

BARBOZA, Julio, LL.M.; Argentine diplomatist and lawyer; b. 17 March 1926, Argentina; s. of Frederico B. and Matilde C. Barboza; m. 1st Nora M. Feigin 1959 (divorced 1972), one s. one d.; m. 2nd Laura S. Guzzetti 1974, two s.; ed. Univ. of Buenos Aires, Southern Methodist Univ., Dallas, Tex., U.S.A., The Hague Acad. of Int. Law, Inst. for the Foreign Service, Buenos Aires, and Colombia Univ., New York; Prof. of Law, Southern Methodist Univ. 1959–60, School of Diplomacy, Catholic Univ., Cordoba

1968–69, Inst. of Foreign Service, Argentina 1970; El Salvador Univ. 1978; Legal Adviser, Ministry of Foreign Affairs 1970–72; Argentine Agent, Beagle Channel Affair (arbitration with Chile) 1970–77; Amb. to Poland 1979–84; Prof. of Int. Law, Univ. of Buenos Aires; mem. UN Int. Law Comm.; decorations from Brazil, Colombia, Chile, Ecuador, Peru. *Publications:* numerous articles on law and international relations in Argentinian and foreign publications. *Leisure interests:* reading history and philosophy, tennis and skiing. *Address:* Ministry of Foreign Affairs, Reconquista 1088, 1033 Buenos Aires, Argentina.

BARCIKOWSKI, Kazimierz, D.ECON.; Polish politician; b. 22 March 1927, Zglechów, Mińsk Mazowiecki Dist.; m.; ed. Higher School of Farming, Łódź, and Higher School of Social Sciences, Warsaw; during Second World War combatant in Home Army; active mem. Rural Youth Union ("Wici") 1946–48; posts in Polish Youth Union, Łódź 1948–49, mem. Gen. Bd. 1950–56, Sec. 1956; Vice-Chair. Gen. Bd. Rural Youth Union 1957–62, subsequently Chair. 1962–65; Sub-Ed., State Publishing House "Iskry", Warsaw 1954–56; mem. Polish United Workers' Party (PZPR) 1953–; Deputy Head, Organizational Dept. Cen. Cttee. PZPR 1964–68; Ed.-in-Chief Życie Partii (Party Life) 1965–68; Deputy mem. Cen. Cttee. PZPR 1964–68, mem. 1968–, Sec. 1970–74, 1980–85, alt. mem. Politburo 1971–81, mem. 1981–, First Sec. Voivodship Cttee. PZPR, Poznań 1968–71, Cracow 1977–80, Chair. Presidium of Nat. Council of City of Cracow 1977–80, Deputy to Seym 1965–; Minister of Agric. and mem. Presidium of Govt. 1974–77; Deputy Chair. Council of Ministers Feb.–Oct. 1980; Chair. Govt. Cttee. for talks with Interfactory Strike Cttee., Szczecin 1980; Co. Chair. Joint Govt. and Episcopate Cttee. 1980–; mem. Council of State 1980–85, Deputy Chair. Council of State 1985–; Chair. Comm. of Social Policy and Health Protection of PZPR Cen. Cttee. 1986–; Order of Banner of Labour (1st and 2nd Class), Order of Builders of People's Poland 1977. *Address:* Kancelaria Rady Państwa, ul. Wiejska 4/6, 00-902 Warsaw, Poland.

BARCLAY, Sir Roderick Edward, G.C.V.O., K.C.M.G.; British diplomatist (retd.); b. 22 Feb. 1909, Kobe, Japan; s. of J. G. and Mrs. Barclay; m. Jean Gladstone 1934; one s. three d.; ed. Harrow School and Trinity Coll., Cambridge; entered Foreign Service 1932; served Brussels, Paris and Washington; Principal Private Sec. to Sec. of State for Foreign Affairs 1949–51; Asst. Under-Sec. of State 1951, Deputy Under-Sec. of State 1953; Amb. to Denmark 1956–60; Deputy Under-Sec. of State for Foreign Affairs 1960–63; Amb. to Belgium 1963–69; Dir. Barclays Bank S.A. 1969–79, Chair. 1970–74; Dir. Slough Estates Ltd. 1969–84, Barclays Bank Int. Ltd. 1971–77, Banque Bruxelles Lambert 1971–77. *Publications:* Ernest Bevin and the Foreign Office 1932–69. *Leisure interests:* shooting, fishing, travel. *Address:* Great White End, Latimer, Bucks., England. *Telephone:* Little Chalfont 2050.

BARCO VARGAS, Virgilio, M.SC.S., PH.D.; Colombian diplomatist and politician; b. 1921, Cúcuta; m. Caroline Isakson de Barco; ed. Univ. Nacional, Bogotá, M.I.T., Boston Univ.; Councillor and Pres. of Municipal Council in Durania, Northern Santander, later in Bogotá; fmr. Sec. Gen. and Acting Minister of Communications, mem. House of Reps., Senator; fmr. Minister of Public Works; fmr. Amb. to U.K.; fmr. Minister of Agric.; fmr. Mayor of Bogotá; Exec. Dir. IBRD 1968, 1970–74; then mem. of Foreign Affairs Advisory Cttee., Amb. to U.S.A. and Bahamas; Presidential Cand. and Nat. Dir. Liberal Party 1985; Pres. of Colombia Aug. 1986–. *Address:* The Presidential Palace, Bogotá, Colombia.

BARCROFT, Henry, M.D., F.R.C.P., F.R.S.; British physiologist; b. 18 Oct. 1904, Cambridge; s. of the late Sir Joseph Barcroft and Mary A. Ball; m. Bridget M. Ramsey 1933; three s. one d.; ed. Marlborough Coll., King's Coll., Cambridge and St. Mary's Hospital, London; Lecturer in Physiology, University Coll., London 1932–35; Dunville Prof. of Physiology, Queen's Univ., Belfast 1935–48; Prof. of Physiology, St. Thomas's Hospital Medical School, Univ. of London 1948–71, Emer. (Hon. Consultant) 1971–; Sir Henry Wellcome Trustee 1966–74; Chair. Research Defence Soc. 1969–72, Sec. 1972–77, Vice Pres. 1978–, Hon. D.Sc. (W. Australia, Queen's Univ., Belfast), Hon. M.D. (Innsbruck); Hon. mem. Soc. Française d'Angiologie; Pro meritis médaille in silver, Karl Franzens Univ., Graz. *Publications:* Sympathetic Control of Human Blood Vessels (with H. J. C. Swan) 1952; papers in Journal of Physiology and other scientific journals. *Leisure interests:* sailing, golf. *Address:* 73 Erskine Hill, London, NW11 6EY, England. *Telephone:* 01-458 1066.

BARCS, Sándor; Hungarian journalist; b. 10 Nov. 1912; s. of Sándor Barcs Sr. and M. Wack; m. 1st Maria Molnár 1945, 2nd Marta Kenéz 1962, 3rd Magdolna Szabó 1970; two s. two d.; Ed., Hungarian News Agency 1945–50, Gen. Man. 1950–80; mem. Council Patriotic People's Front, Parl. and Presidential Council 1953–75, 1978–; Chair. Hungarian Football Asscn. 1949–63; Vice-Pres. European Football Union (UEFA) 1962–78, Acting Chair. 1972–73; mem. Parl., mem. Council Interparliamentary Union 1963–; Chair. Nat. Fed. of Hungarian Journalists 1965–74; Labour Order of Merit, golden degree 1970, Order of the Red Banner 1972, Great Silver Medal of Honour (Austria) 1979, Banner Order of the Hungarian People's Repub. *Leisure interests:* angling, soccer. *Address:* 1025 Budapest, Görgényi u. 14, Hungary. *Telephone:* 767-986.

BARD, Allen J., PH.D.; American professor of chemistry; b. 18 Dec. 1933, New York; ed. City Coll. of New York and Harvard Univ.; Thayer

Scholarship 1955–56; Nat. Science Foundation Postdoctoral Fellowship 1956–58; joined chem. staff of Univ. of Tex., Austin 1958, Prof. of Chem. 1967–, Jack S. Josey Prof. 1980–82, Norman Hackerman Prof. 1982–85, Hackerman-Welch Prof. 1985–; consultant to several labs. including E.I. duPont, Texas Instruments and several govt. agencies; research interests in application of electrochemical methods to study of chemical problems; Vice-Chair. Nat. Research Council; Ed.-in-Chief Journal of American Chemical Soc. 1982–; Fellow A.A.A.S.; mem. American Chemical Soc., Electrochemical Soc.; Ward Medal in Chem. 1955, Harrison Howe Award, American Chemical Soc. 1980, Carl Wagner Memorial Award, Electrochemical Soc. 1981, Bruno Breyer Memorial Medal, Royal Australian Chem. Inst. 1984, Fisher Award in Analytical Chem., American Chemical Soc. 1984, Charles N. Reilley Award, Soc. of Electroanalytical Chem. 1984; Dr. h.c. (Paris) 1986, New York Acad. of Sciences Award in Math. and Physical Sciences 1986, Willard Gibbs Award, American Chem. Soc. 1987, Olin-Palladium Award, Electrochem. Soc. 1987. *Publications:* Chemical Equilibrium 1966, Electrochemical Methods (with L. R. Faulkner) 1980; approx. 400 papers and book chapters; Ed. Electroanalytical Chemistry (15 vols.) 1966–, The Encyclopedia of the Electrochemistry of the Elements, 16 vols. 1973–82. *Address:* Department of Chemistry, University of Texas, Austin, Tex. 78712; 6202 Mountainclimb Drive, Austin, Tex. 78731, U.S.A. (Home).

BARDECHE, Maurice, D. ÈS L.; French professor (retd.) and author; b. 1 Oct. 1907, Dun-sur-Auron; m. Suzanne Brasillach 1934; four s. one d.; ed. Lycée de Bourges, Lycée Louis-le-Grand and Ecole Normale Supérieure; Prof. of French Literature, Univ. of Lille 1942–45, Coll. de Normandie 1954–60; f. and Dir. Défense de l'Occident 1952–82, Editions des Sept Couleurs 1948–78; Jt. Pres. European Social Movt. 1952–59; Prix de la Critique littéraire 1972. *Publications:* Histoire du cinéma 1935, Balzac romancier 1940, Stendhal romancier 1946, Lettre à François Mauriac 1947, Nuremberg ou la Terre promise 1948, l'Oeuvre de Flaubert 1954, Marcel Proust romancier 1971, Céline 1987. *Leisure interest:* rugby. *Address:* B.P. 184, 75228 Paris cedex 05, France (Office).

BARDEEN, John, PH.D., D.SC.; American physicist; b. 23 May 1908, Madison, Wis.; s. of Charles Russell Bardeen and Althea Harmer; m. Jane Maxwell 1938; two s. one d.; ed. Univs. of Wisconsin and Princeton; Geophysicist with Gulf Research and Devt. Corpn. 1930–33; Junior Fellow, Harvard Univ. 1935–38; Asst. Prof. of Physics, Univ. of Minnesota 1938–41; Physicist at U.S. Naval Ordnance Laboratory 1941–45; Research Physicist, Bell Telephone Laboratory 1945–51; Prof. of Electrical Engineering and Physics, Univ of Illinois 1951–75, Prof. Emer. 1975–; mem. President's Science Advisory Cttee. 1959–62; mem. American Acad. Arts and Sciences, American Phil. Soc.; Foreign mem. Royal Soc. Great Britain, Indian Nat. Science Acad., Pakistan Acad. of Science, Hungarian Acad. of Science, Acad. of Sciences U.S.S.R.; Hon. mem. Japan Acad.; Hon. Dr. (Venezuelan Acad.); Fellow, American Physical Soc., Pres. 1968–69; Ballantine Medal, Franklin Inst. 1952; Buckley Prize, American Physical Soc. 1954; John Scott Medal, Philadelphia 1955; Nobel Prize for Physics for research leading to the invention of the transistor (with W. Shockley and W. H. Brattain) 1956; Fritz London Award 1962; Vincent Bendix Award 1964; Nat. Medal of Science 1966; Morley Award 1968; Nobel Prize for Physics (with L.N. Cooper, q.v., and J. R. Schrieffer, q.v.) 1972; Franklin Medal 1975; Presidential Medal of Freedom 1977, Founders Award, Nat. Acad. of Eng. 1984, Lomosonov Gold Medal 1988. *Address:* 55 Greencroft, Champaign, Ill. 61820, U.S.A. *Telephone:* 217-352-6497.

BARDINI, Adolfo, DR.ING.; Italian industrial executive; b. 9 April 1915, Genoa; s. of the late Emilio Bardini and Eugenia Baltuzzi; m. 1st Ernestina Zampaglione 1939, two d.; m. 2nd Mirella Noli Parmeggiani 1972; ed. Naples Univ.; Gen. Man. Fabbrica Macchine Industriali, Naples 1952–55; Dir. and Gen. Man. Nuova San Giorgio, Genoa 1955–62; Dir. and Gen. Man. Alfa Romeo S.p.A. 1962–74; Chair. Autodelta S.p.A. 1962–74, ANFIA (Italian Assen. of Motor Vehicle Mfrs.) 1975–78, Turin Int. Motor Show 1975–78; Dir. C.M.I. S.p.A., Genoa 1975–82; Pres. C.L.C.A. (Comité de Liaison de la Construction Automobile pour les Pays de la Communauté Economique Européenne) 1978–80, Elettronica San Giorgio S.p.A. ELSAG, Genoa 1979–84, Hon. Chair. 1984–. *Address:* ELSAG, Via Puccini 2, 16154 Genova-Sestri (Office); Corso Monforte 36, 20122 Milan, Italy (Home). *Telephone:* Genoa 60011 (Office).

BARDINI, Aleksander; Polish theatre and opera director, actor and professor; b. 17 Nov. 1913, Łódź; m.; one d.; ed. State Inst. of Theatrical Art, Warsaw; teacher, Warsaw State Higher School of Theatrical Arts 1950–65, Prof. 1966–78, Prof. Emer. 1978–; developed contemporary style of musical interpretation; numerous awards include State Prize (3rd class) 1953, Collective State Prize (2nd class) 1955; Knight's, Officer's and Commdr.'s Cross, Order of Polonia Restituta; Minister of Culture and Arts Prize (1st class) 1965, 1976, Nat. Educ. Comm. Medal 1976, Gold Screen Prize (Ekran) 1977, City of Warsaw Prize, 1982. *Productions:* operas; Jutro (Baird), Electra 1971, Boris Godunov, Otello, Cosi fan tutte, The Queen of Spades, Samson and Delilah, Prisoner, Bluebeard's Castle; plays: Dziady (Mickiewicz), Midsummer Night's Dream, Henry IV, Measure for Measure, A Streetcar Named Desire, The Night of the Iguana, Tango (Mrożek), Uncle Vanya, John Gabriel Borkman, Three Sisters, The Barbarians, Cabale und Liebe, films: The Gorgonowa Case (Sprawa Gorgonowej), The Office (Urząd), Endlessly (Bezkońca), The Last Manuscript; series of

TV programmes: Rendez-vous with A. Bardini; writer of musical spectacles; has performed numerous oratorios of Schönberg, Penderecki, Wiechowicz etc. *Leisure interest:* music, reading. *Address:* Ul. Mokotowska 17 m. 21, 00-640 Warsaw, Poland. *Telephone:* 25-21-22.

BARDONNET, Daniel, D.JUR., DR.RER.POL.; French international lawyer; b. 18 May 1931, Moulins; s. of Louis Bardonnet and Marguerite Dory; m. Geneviève Paintaud-Briand 1958; two s.; ed. Lycée Banville, Moulins and Faculty of Law, Univ. of Paris; Prof. Faculty of Law, Univ. of Tananarive, Madagascar 1960–66, Univ. of Rabat, Morocco 1966–72; Fellow, Woodrow Wilson Int. Center for Scholars, Washington, D.C. 1972–73; Prof. Faculty of Law, Univ. of Paris XII 1973–77; Prof. Inst. d'Etudes Politiques de Paris 1975–84; legal adviser, French del. to Law of Sea Conf. 1976–82; Ed. Annuaire Français de Droit International 1977–; Prof. Faculty of Law, Paris Univ. of Law, Econ. and Social Sciences 1977–; Sec.-Gen. Hague Acad. of Int. Law 1985–; mem. Scientific Council of Inst. du Droit Econ. de la Mer, Monaco 1985–; Assoc. of Inst. of Int. Law 1987–; Prix Léon Juillot de la Morandière (Inst. de France) 1972, Chevalier Légion d'Honneur. *Publications:* Le Tribunal des Conflits, juge du fond 1959, L'évolution de la structure du Parti radical 1960, La Succession d'Etats à Madagascar 1970, Les frontières terrestres et la relativité de leur tracé 1976; articles in legal journals. *Leisure interests:* sea, forest, literature, 18th-century art. *Address:* 5 rue des Eaux, 75016, Paris, France. *Telephone:* (1) 45.20.95.80.

BARDOT, Brigitte; French actress; b. 28 Sept. 1934; d. of Louis and Anne-Marie (Mücel) Bardot; m. 1st Roger Vadim (q.v.), 2nd Jacques Charrier, 3rd Gunther Sachs (dissolved 1969); one s.; ed. Paris Conservatoire; stage and film career 1952–; Étoile de Cristal from Acad. of Cinema 1966; Chevalier, Legion d'honneur 1985; films include Manina: la fille sans voile, Le fils de Caroline chérie, Futures vedettes, Les grandes manoeuvres, La lumière d'en face, Cette sacrée gamine, La mariée est trop belle, Et Dieu créa la femme, En effeuillant la marguerite, Une parisienne, Les bijoutiers du clair de lune, En cas de malheur, La femme et le pantin, Babette s'en va-t-en guerre, Voulez-vous danser avec moi?, La vérité, Please not now?, Le mépris, Le repos du guerrier, Une ravissante idiote, Viva Maria, A coeur joie 1967, Two weeks in September 1967, Shalako 1968, Les femmes 1969, Les novices 1970, Boulevard du rhum 1971, Les pétroleuses 1971, Don Juan 1973, L'Histoire très bonne et très joyeuse de Colinot trousse-chemise 1973, Noonah, le petit phoque blanc. *Leisure interest:* swimming. *Address:* La Madrague, 83990 Saint-Tropez (Var), France.

BARECKI, Józef, M.A.; Polish journalist and politician; b. 22 Nov. 1926, Cracow; m.; two c.; ed. Higher School of Social Sciences, Warsaw; Ed., daily newspaper Głos Szczeciński, Szczecin 1947–52, Ed.-in-Chief 1956–66; Sub-Ed. Kurier Szczeciński 1952–55; Sub-Ed. Trybuna Ludu (daily), Warsaw 1966–72, Ed.-in-Chief 1972–80; fmr. mem. Polish Journalists' Assen. (SDP), fmr. Chair. Bd. of SDP Warsaw Branch, Chair. Gen. Bd. of SDP 1978–80; Deputy Chair. Int. Journalists' Org.; Chair. Cttee. for Radio and TV (Polskie Radio i Telewizja) Aug.–Sept. 1980; Govt. Press Spokesman 1980–81; Ed.-in-Chief Polish Govt. Rzeczpospolita (daily) 1981–86; mem. PZPR, deputy mem. PZPR Cen. Cttee. 1971–75, mem. Cen. Cttee. 1975–81; Deputy to Seym 1976–; Head, Propaganda Dept., PZPR Cen. Cttee. 1986–87; Ed-in-Chief Nowe Drogi (monthly) 1987–; Order of Banner of Labour (1st class), Commdr.'s, Officer's and Kt.'s Cross, Order of Polonia Restituta and other decorations. *Address:* Redakcja Nowe Drogi, ul. Maszyńskiego 18, 00-485 Warsaw, Poland (Office); ul. Walecznych 28 m. 7, 03-916 Warsaw, Poland. *Telephone:* 28-09-61 (Office); 17-55.97.

BARENBOIM, Daniel, F.R.C.M.; Israeli concert pianist and conductor; b. 15 Nov. 1942, Buenos Aires, Argentina; s. of Prof. Enrique and Aida (née Schuster) Barenboim; m. Jacqueline du Pré 1967 (died 1987); ed. Santa Cecilia Acad., Rome; studied piano with his father and other musical subjects with Nadia Boulanger, Edwin Fischer and Igor Markevitch; début in Buenos Aires at age of seven; played Bach D Minor Concerto with orchestra at Salzburg Mozarteum at age of nine; has played in Europe regularly 1954–; yearly tours of U.S.A. 1957–; has toured Japan, Australia and S. America; has played with or conducted London Philharmonic, Philharmonia Orchestra, London Symphony Orchestra, Royal Philharmonic, Chicago Symphony Orchestra, New York Philharmonic, Philadelphia Orchestra, Israel Philharmonic, Vienna Philharmonic, Berlin Philharmonic; frequently tours with English Chamber Orchestra and with them records for E.M.I. (projects include complete Mozart Piano Concertos and late Symphonies); other recording projects include complete Beethoven Sonatas and Beethoven Concertos (with New Philharmonia Orchestra conducted by Klemperer); has appeared in series of Master-classes on BBC television; presented Festival of Summer Music on South Bank, London 1968, 1969; leading role in Brighton Festival 1967–69; appears regularly at Edinburgh Festival; conductor, Edinburgh Festival Opera 1973; Musical Dir. Orchestre de Paris 1975–89, Chicago Symphony Orchestra 1989–; Beethoven Medal 1958; Paderewski Medal 1963; Beethoven Soc. Medal 1982. *Address:* c/o Harold Holt Ltd., 31 Sinclair Road, London, W.14, England.

BARGHOORN, Frederick Charles, PH.D.; American university professor; b. 4 July 1911; ed. Amherst Coll. and Harvard Univ.; Press Attaché, American Embassy, Moscow 1943–47; Dept. of Political Science, Yale Univ. 1947–85, Prof. of Political Science 1956–85. *Publications:* The Soviet Image of the United States 1950, Soviet Russian Nationalism 1956, The Soviet

Cultural Offensive 1960, Soviet Foreign Propaganda 1964, Politics in the U.S.S.R. 1966. *Address:* Department of Political Science, Yale University, New Haven, Connecticut, U.S.A. (Office).

BARING, Hon. Sir John Francis Harcourt, Kt., C.V.O., M.A., F.I.B.; British merchant banker; b. 2 Nov. 1928, London; s. of 6th Baron Ashburton and Hon. Doris Mary Therese Harcourt; m. Susan Mary Renwick 1955 (dissolved 1984), two s. two d.; 2nd Sarah Crewe 1987; ed. Eton Coll. and Trinity Coll., Oxford; Dir. Baring Bros. & Co. Ltd. 1955–, Chair. 1974–, Chair. Barings PLC 1985–; Dir. Royal Insurance Co. Ltd. 1964–82, Deputy Chair. 1975–82, Trafford Park Estates Ltd. 1964–77, Dir. Outwich Investment Trust Ltd. 1965–87, Chair. 1967–87, Pye Holdings Ltd. 1966–79, Outwich Ltd. (Johannesburg) 1967–77, British Petroleum Co. 1982–; mem. British Transport Docks Bd. 1966–72; mem. Gen. Council of British Bankers Asscn. 1975–, Vice-Pres. 1977–81; mem. Pres.'s Cttee. CBI 1976–79, Gen. Council CBI 1976–80; Chair. Accepting Houses Cttee. 1977–81, NEDC Cttee. on Finance for Industry 1980–87; Pres. Overseas Bankers Club 1977–78; Rhodes Trustee 1970–, Chair. 1987–, Trustee Nat. Gallery 1981–87; mem. Council Baring Foundation 1971–, Chair. 1987–; Dir. Dunlop Holdings 1981–84, Bank of England 1983–, Stratton Investment Trust PLC 1986–, Chair. 1986–; Receiver-Gen. Duchy of Cornwall 1974–; Fellow, Eton Coll. 1982; Hon. Fellow, Hertford Coll., Oxford 1979. *Address:* Baring Bros. & Co. Ltd., 8 Bishopsgate, London, EC2N 4AE, England (Office). *Telephone:* 01-283 8833.

BARKAUSKAS, Antanas Stasevich; Soviet government official; b. 20 Jan. 1917, Paparchiai, Lithuania; m. Zoya Yarashunaite 1961; one s. one d.; ed. Higher Communist Party School, Moscow, and Acad. of Social Sciences; mem. of Lithuanian Young Komsomol League 1940; Soviet official in Kaunas 1940–41; served in 16th Lithuanian Div. 1942–44; mem. CPSU 1942–, party official in Kaunas during post-war period; Sec. Vilnius (later Kaunas) Regional Cttee. of Lithuanian C.P. 1950–53; Teacher, Head of Dept., Kaunas Polytechnic Inst. 1953–55; Head of Dept., Cen. Cttee. of Lithuanian C.P. 1959–60, mem. Cen. Cttee. 1960–, Sec. of Cen. Cttee. 1961–75, mem. Secr. 1961–, mem. Politburo 1962–66; Deputy to Supreme Soviet of Lithuania 1959–, Chair. of Presidium of Supreme Soviet of Lithuanian S.S.R. 1959–75, Pres. of Presidium 1975–86; Deputy to Supreme Soviet of U.S.S.R. 1974–, Vice-Chair. of Presidium 1976–86; mem. Cen. Inspection Cttee. of CPSU 1976–; Cand. mem. Cen. Cttee., CPSU 1981–; Honoured Cultural Worker of Lithuanian S.S.R. 1967, Order of October Revolution 1971, Order of Red Banner of Labour 1965, 1973, Order of Red Star 1947, six medals. *Publications:* Country, Culture, Rural Life 1967, Culture and Society 1975, Lithuanian Countryside: Past, Present and Future (in English, French, German, Hungarian and Arabic) 1976. *Leisure interests:* fiction, travelling, sport. *Address:* c/o Presidium of Lithuanian Supreme Soviet, 53 Lenin pr., Vilnius, Lithuanian S.S.R., U.S.S.R.

BARKE, (James) Allen; British motor executive; b. 16 April 1903; s. of James E. Barke and Emma Livsey; m. 1st Doris Marian Bayne 1937 (died 1952), two s. one d.; m. 2nd Marguerite Amy Sutcliffe (née Williams) 1953 (died 1968); ed. technical school; gen. engineering 1922–32; Ford Motor Co. 1932–; Chaser, Purchase Dept. 1933–38; Buyer, Purchase Dept. 1939–47; Chief Buyer (Tractors) 1947–48; Man. Leamington Foundry 1948–53; Exec. Dir. and Gen. Man. Briggs Motor Bodies Ltd. 1953–59; Dir. Product Divs. Ford Motor Co. 1959–61; Asst. Man. Dir. 1961–62, Man. Dir. 1962–63, Chief Exec. Officer and Man. Dir. 1963–65, Vice-Chair. 1965–68; Dir. De La Rue Co. 1970–73, Falcon Engineering Co. 1972–. *Address:* Thurlestone, Mill Green, Ingatestone, Essex, England. *Telephone:* Ingatestone 352949.

BARKELEY, Norman A., B.A.; American business executive; ed. Michigan State Univ.; Instrument Div. Lear Siegler, Inc., Grand Rapids, Mich. 1956–73; Vice-Pres. (Operations Exec.) Automotive Operations 1978, Corp. Vice-Pres. 1979; Corp. Vice-Pres. Aerospace Group 1980–83, Exec. Vice-Pres. 1983–85; Pres. and mem. Bd. of Dirs. Lear Siegler, Inc. 1985–, Chair. and C.E.O. 1986–; Pres. and C.E.O. Ducommun Inc. 1988–; Dir. Marshall Univ. Soc. of Yeager Scholars. *Address:* Lear Siegler, Inc., 2850 Ocean Park Blvd., P.O. Box 2158, Santa Monica, Calif. 90406, U.S.A. *Telephone:* (213) 452-8885.

BARKER, Edmund William, M.A., LL.B.; Singapore politician; b. 1 Dec. 1920, Singapore; s. of Clarence Barker and Dorothy Evelyne Paterson; m. Gloria Hyacinth Quintal 1948; one s. three d.; ed. Raffles Coll., Singapore, St. Catharine's Coll., Cambridge and Inner Temple, London; practised law in Singapore 1952–64; elected M.P. Tanglin constituency 1963–; Speaker of Singapore Legislative Assembly 1963–64; Minister for Law 1964–88, for Nat. Devt. 1965–75, for Home Affairs 1972, for the Environment July 1975–79, for Science and Technology 1977–81; Pres., Singapore National Olympic Council; Award for Distinguished Service, U.S. Sports Acad. *Address:* 3rd Floor, City Hall, St. Andrew's Road, Singapore 0617. *Telephone:* 3378191.

BARKER, George Granville; British writer; b. 26 Feb. 1913, Loughton, Essex; s. of George Barker and Marion Frances Taaffe; m. Elspeth Cameron Langlands 1964; two s. two d.; ed. Marlborough Road School, Chelsea, London; Prof. of English Literature, Imperial Tohoku Univ., Japan 1939–41; lived in America 1941–43; returned to England 1944; in Rome 1960–65; Visiting Prof. New York State Univ. 1965; Visiting Prof. of Literature, Univ. of Wis. 1971–72, Florida Int. Univ. 1974; Arts Fellow,

York Univ. 1966–67. *Publications:* Poems 1933, Alanna Autumnal 1933, Calamiterror, Janus 1935, Lament and Triumph 1940, News of the World, The True Confession of George Barker 1950, Collected Poems 1957, Two Plays, The View from a Blind I 1962, The New Confession 1963, Dreams of Summer Night 1965, The Golden Chains 1968, Essays 1968, Essays 1969, Poems for Children 1969, To Aylsham Fair 1970, At Thurgarton Church 1970, Poems of Places and People 1971, The Alphabetical Zoo 1972, In Memory of David Archer 1973, Dialogues etc. 1976, Villa Stellar 1978, Anno Domini 1983, Collected Poems 1987. *Leisure interests:* painting, admiring architecture. *Address:* c/o Faber and Faber, 3 Queen Square, London, W.C.1 (Office); Bintry House, Itteringham, Aylsham, Norfolk, England (Home). *Telephone:* Saxthorpe 240 (Home).

BARKER, Horace Albert, PH.D., D.SC.; American professor of biochemistry; b. 29 Nov. 1907, Oakland, Calif.; s. of A. C. Barker and Nettie Barker; m. Margaret D. McDowell 1933; one s. two d.; ed. Stanford Univ.; Nat. Research Council Fellow in Biological Sciences, Hopkins Marine Station 1933–35; Gen. Educ. Bd. Fellow, Technical Univ., Delft, Holland 1935–36; Instructor in Soil Microbiology, Div. of Plant Nutrition, and Junior Soil Microbiologist in Agric. Experiment Station, Univ. of Calif. 1936–40, Asst. Prof. and Assoc. Soil Microbiologist 1940–45, Assoc. Prof. and Assoc. Soil Microbiologist 1945–46, Prof. and Soil Microbiologist 1946–50, Prof. of Plant Biochemistry and Microbiologist 1950–57, Prof. of Microbial Biochemistry and Microbiologist 1957–59, Prof. of Biochemistry and Microbiologist 1959–75, Emer. Prof. 1975–; Chair. Dept. of Plant Nutrition 1949–50, Dept. of Plant Biochemistry 1950–53, Vice-Chair. Dept. of Agric. Biochemistry 1958–59, Chair. Dept. of Biochemistry 1962–64; on editorial boards of various scientific journals; mem. N.A.S., American Acad. of Arts and Sciences and other socs.; numerous awards including Gowland Hopkins Medal, Biochemistry Soc., London 1967, Nat. Medal of Science 1968. *Publications:* Bacterial Fermentations 1956; over 230 papers; research into various aspects of bacterial metabolism, including the synthesis and oxidation of fatty acids, fermentation of amino acids and purines, carbohydrate transformation and methane formation; isolation, structure and function of cobamide coenzymes; bacterial enzymes. *Leisure interests:* fishing and mountaineering. *Address:* Department of Biochemistry, Biochemistry Building, University of California, Berkeley, Calif. 94720, U.S.A. (Office); 561 Santa Clara Avenue, Berkeley, Calif. 94707, U.S.A. (Home). *Telephone:* 415-642-5688 (Office).

BARLETTA, Nicolás Ardito, PH.D., M.S.; Panamanian politician and economist; b. 21 Aug. 1938, Aguadulce, Coclé; s. of Nicolás Ardito Barletta and Leticia de Ardito Barletta; m. Maria Consuelode Barletta; two s. one d.; ed. Univ. of Chicago and N. Carolina State Univ.; Cabinet mem. and Dir. Planning 1968–70; Dir. Econ. Affairs Org. of American States 1970–73; Minister of Planning 1973–78; Negotiator of econ. aspects of Panama Canal Treaties 1976–77; Vice-Pres. World Bank for Latin America and Caribbean 1978–84; founder and first Pres. World Bank for Latin America and Caribbean 1978–84; founder and first Pres. Latin American Export Bank 1978; Pres. Latin American Econ. System (SELA) Constituent Ass.; Pres. of Panama 1984–85; Int. Consultant 1986. *Publications:* numerous Latin American and Panamanian devt. studies. *Leisure interests:* tennis and music. *Address:* P.O. Box 4339, Panamá 5, Republic of Panama. *Telephone:* 63-6766 (Office); 26-0255 (Home).

BAR-LEV, Lieut.-Gen. Haim; Israeli soldier; b. 1924, Austria; m.; one s. one d.; ed. Mikhev Israel Agricultural School, Columbia Univ. School of Econs. and Admin., U.S.A.; joined Palmach Units 1942; Platoon Commdr., Beith-Ha'Arava 1944; Commdr. D Co., Yesreel 1945–46; Commdr. Palmach non-commdg. officer's course and C.O. Eight Regt., Negev Brigade 1947, Operations Officer 1948; Commdr. Armoured Units 1948; Instructor and later Commdr., Bn. Commdrs. course 1949–52; Chief of Staff, Northern Command 1952–53; C.O. Givati Brigade 1954–55; Dir. G.H.Q. Training Div. 1956; Commdr. Armoured Brigade during Sinai campaign; Commdr. Armoured Corps 1957–61; made study tour of armoured corps of Western European countries and U.S.A. 1961; after obtaining M.A., Columbia Univ., visited U.S. army installations and the armies of the Philippines, Japan, Thailand and S. Vietnam; Dir. Gen. Staff (Operations) Branch 1964–66; Deputy Chief of Staff Israel Defence Forces 1967, Chief of Staff 1968–72; Minister of Commerce and Industry 1972–77, of Police Affairs Sept. 1984–; elected to Knesset June 1977; Sec.-Gen. Israel Labour Party 1978–. *Address:* Israel Labour Party, P.O. Box 3263, Tel-Aviv, Israel.

BARLOG, Boleslaw; German theatre director and producer; b. 28 March 1906, Breslau (now Wrocław); m. Herta Barlog 1939; ed. Oberrealschule, Berlin; Asst. Producer, Volksbühne, Berlin 1930–33; Asst. Dir. UFA and TERRA films 1935–39, Dir. 1939–45; Dir.-Gen. Berlin Municipal Theatres 1945–72 (Schlosspark Theatre 1945–72, Schiller Theatre 1951–72, Schiller-Theatre Workshop 1959–72); Dir.-Gen. Carl-Zuckmayer Gesellschaft 1972–75, now Hon. Pres.; Hon. Prof. h.c.; mem. Acad. of Arts, Berlin; Grand Order of Merit with Star (Fed. Germany) 1950; Ordre National de l'Art et des Lettres. *Address:* Spindelmühler Weg 7, 1000 Berlin 45, Federal Republic of Germany. *Telephone:* 8117314.

BARLOW, Harold Everard Monteagle, PH.D., F.R.S., F.ENG.; British electrical engineer; b. 15 Nov. 1899, London; s. of Leonard Barlow, M.I.E.E. and Katherine Barlow (née Monteagle); m. Janet Hastings Eastwood 1931; three s. one d.; ed. City and Guilds Engineering Coll., London, and Univ.

Coll., London; Sub-Lieut. R.N.V.R. 1917–18; East Surrey Ironworks Ltd. 1923; Barlow & Young Ltd. 1923–24; war service 1939–45; Supt. Radio Dept., Royal Aircraft Establishment, Farnborough 1939–45; Academic Staff, Univ. Coll. London 1924–67; Emer. Prof. of Electrical Engineering, Univ. of London 1967–; Dir. Marconi Instrument Co. Ltd. 1967–; Chair. British Nat. Cttee. of Int. Radio Union 1967–; Chair. High Frequency Measurements Cttee., and mem. Council, British Calibration Service, Ministry of Technology (now Dept. of Trade and Industry), London 1967–; mem. Nat. Electronics Council 1967–; Hon. Research Fellow, Univ. Coll. London 1967–; Royal Medal Royal Soc. London 1988. *Publications:* Microwaves and Waveguides 1950, Microwave Measurements (with A. L. Cullen) 1952, Radio Surface Waves (with J. Brown) 1961, about 50 scientific papers. *Leisure interests:* travel, walking, sailing. *Address:* 13 Hookfield, Epsom, Surrey, England (Home). *Telephone:* Epsom 21586.

BARLOW, Horace B., SC.D., M.D., F.R.S.; British physiologist; b. 8 Dec. 1921, Chesham Bois; s. of James A. Barlow and Emma N. Darwin; m. 1st Ruth Salaman 1954 (divorced 1970); four d.; m. 2nd Miranda Smith 1980; one s. one d.; ed. Trinity Coll., Cambridge, Harvard Medical School and Univ. Coll. Hospital; Fellow, Trinity Coll., Cambridge 1950–53, 1973–; Fellow and Lecturer, King's Coll., and Demonstrator, Physiological Lab. 1953–64; Prof. of Physiological Optics and Physiology, Univ. of Calif., Berkeley 1964–73; Royal Soc. Research Prof., Physiological Laboratory, Cambridge 1973–. *Publications:* 8 Papers on the neurophysiology of vision in The Journal of Physiology. *Leisure interests:* walking, music, skiing. *Address:* Physiological Laboratory, Cambridge, CB2 3EG (Office); Trinity College, Cambridge, CB2 1TQ, England.

BARLOW, Thomas James, B.S.; American business executive; b. 22 June 1922, Houston, Tex.; s. of Thomas J. Barlow and Dorothy James; m. Billye Louise Sears 1944; one s. one d.; ed. Texas A & M Univ. and Harvard Univ.; served U.S.N.R. (rank of Lieut.) WWII; trainee, Western Cottonoil Co., Abilene, Tex. 1946–47, Asst. Gen. Man. 1948–49; construction engineer, San Joaquin Cottonoil Co., Bakersfield, Calif. 1948; Supt. Western Cotton Products Co. Phoenix 1949–50; Production Man. Nile Ginning Co., Minia, Egypt 1950–56; Production Engineer, Anderson, Clayton & Co., Houston 1956–57, Vice-Pres. 1961–66, Pres. and C.E.O. 1966–76, Chair. of Bd. and Chair. Exec. Cttee. 1976–, C.E.O. 1976–85; Dir. Cen. S.W. Corpn., Hughes Tool Co. *Address:* Anderson, Clayton & Co., First International Plaza, Box 2538, 1100 Louisiana, Houston, Tex. 77252, U.S.A.

BARLOW, Sir William, Kt., D.SC., F.ENG., F.I.E.E., F.I.MECH.E.; British engineer; b. 8 June 1924, Oldham; s. of Albert Edward and Annice Barlow; m. Elaine Mary Atherton Adamson 1948; one s. one d.; ed. Manchester Grammar School and Manchester Univ.; English Electric Co. Ltd. 1947–68; Man. Dir. English Electric Computers 1967–68; Chief Exec. Ransome Hoffmann Pollard Ltd. 1969–77, Chair. 1971–77; Chair. Post Office Corpn. 1977–80; Dir. Thorn EMI PLC 1980–, Chair. of Eng. Group 1980–84; Dir. BICC PLC 1981–; Chair. 1985–; Chair. Design Council 1980–86, Metal Industries Ltd. 1980–84, Eng. Council 1988; Dir. Racal Telecommunications PLC 1988; Gov. London Business School 1979–; Pres. British Electrotechnical and Allied Mfrs. Assen (BEAMA) 1986–87; Hon. D.Sc. (Cranfield Inst. of Tech.) 1979, (Bath) 1986, (Aston) 1988, D.Tech. (Liverpool Polytechnic) 1988; Vice-Pres., Fellowship of Eng. *Leisure interest:* golf. *Address:* BICC PLC, Devonshire House, Mayfair Place, London, W1X 5FH, England (Office). *Telephone:* 01-629 6622 (Office).

BARLTROP, Roger Arnold Rowlandson, C.M.G., C.V.O., M.A.; British diplomatist; b. 19 Jan. 1930, Leeds; s. of E. W. Barltrop and E. A. L. Barltrop (née Baker); m. Penelope P. Dalton 1962; two s. two d.; ed. Solihull School, Leeds Grammar School and Exeter Coll., Oxford; Second Sec., British High Comm., New Delhi 1956–57; First Sec., Nigeria 1960–62, Rhodesia 1962–65, Turkey 1969–70; Deputy British Govt. Rep. W. Indies Assoc. States 1971–73; Counsellor, Addis Ababa 1973–77; Head, Commonwealth Co-ordination Dept., F.C.O. 1978–82; High Commr., later Amb., in Fiji (also accred. to Nauru and Tuvalu) 1982–. *Leisure interests:* sailing, family history, opera. *Address:* c/o Foreign and Commonwealth Office, King Charles Street, London, SW1A 2AH, England.

BÄRLUND, Kaj-Ole Johannes, M.SC. (ECON.); Finnish politician; b. 9 Nov. 1945, Porvoo; m. Eeva-Kaisa Oksama 1972; journalist, Finnish Broadcasting Co. 1967–71; Public Relations Officer, Cen. Org. of Finnish Trade Unions 1971–72; Legis. Sec. Ministry of Justice 1972–79; mem. Parl. 1979–; Chair. Porvoo City Council 1979–87; Chair. Swedish Labour Union of Finland 1983–; Minister of the Environment 1987–; Social Democratic Party. *Address:* Ministry of the Environment, P.O. Box 399, 00121, Helsinki, Finland. *Telephone:* (90) 19911.

BARNABY, Charles Frank, PH.D.; British physicist; b. 27 Sept. 1927, Andover, Hants.; s. of Charles H. Barnaby and Lilian Sainsbury; m. Wendy Elizabeth Field 1972; one s. one d.; ed. Andover Grammar School and Univ. of London; Physicist, U.K. Atomic Energy Authority 1950–57; mem. Senior Scientific Staff, Medical Research Council, Univ. Coll. Medical School 1957–68; Exec. Sec. Pugwash Confs. on Science and World Affairs 1968–70; Dir. Stockholm Int. Peace Research Inst. (SIPRI) 1971–81; Prof. of Peace Studies, Free Univ., Amsterdam 1981–85; Dir. World Disarmament Campaign (U.K.) 1982–; Co-Dir. Just Defence 1982–. *Publications:* Man and the Atom 1971, Ed. Preventing the Spread of Nuclear Weapons 1971,

Co-editor Anti-ballistic Missile Systems 1971, Disarmament and Arms Control 1973, The Nuclear Age 1976, Prospects for Peace 1980, Future Warfare (ed. and co-author) 1983, Space Weapons 1984, The Automated Battlefield 1986, The Invisible Bomb 1989; articles in scientific journals. *Leisure interests:* natural history. *Address:* Brandreth, Chilbolton, Stockbridge, Hants., England. *Telephone:* Chilbolton 423 (Home).

BARNALA, Surjit Singh, LL.B.; Indian lawyer and politician; b. 21 Oct. 1925, Ateli, Gurgaon Dist. (now in Haryana); ed. Lucknow Univ.; Shiromani Akali Dal M.P. for Barnala 1967–; Union Agric. and Irrigation Minister in Janata Govt. 1977–80; mem. Lok Sabha for Barnala 1980–; elected Acting Pres. Shiromani Akali Dal 1985; Leader Akali Legislature Party 1985; Chief Minister of Punjab 1986–87; practises law in Punjab and Haryana High Court. *Leisure interest:* painting. *Address:* Raj Bhavan, Chandigarh, Punjab, India.

BARNARD, Christiaan Neethling, M.MED., M.D., M.S., PH.D., F.A.C.C.; South African heart surgeon (retd.) and farmer; b. 8 Oct. 1922, Beaufort West, Cape Province; s. of Adam Hendrik Barnard and Maria Elisabeth de Swart; m. 1st Aletta Gertruida Louw 1948 (divorced 1970), one s. (deceased) one d.; m. 2nd Barbara M. Zoellner 1970 (divorced 1982), two s.; m. 3rd Karin Setzkorn 1987; one s.; ed. Univ. of Cape Town; graduated as doctor 1946; intern, Groote Schuur Hospital, Cape Town 1947; then spent two years in general practice in Ceres; then Senior Resident Medical Officer, City Fever Hospital, Cape Town; returned to Groote Schuur Hospital; then Charles Adams Memorial Scholar, Univ. of Minnesota, concentrating on cardiothoracic surgery; on return to Groote Schuur Hospital concentrated on open-heart operations and cardiac research; Surgery of Common Congenital Cardiac Malformations (with V. Sehrire) 1968; Head of Cardiac Research and Surgery, Univ. of Cape Town 1968–83, Prof. Emer. 1984–; Sr. Consultant and Scientist in Residence, Okla. Heart Centre at Baptist Medical Centre, Okla. City 1985–; developed the Barnard Valve, for use in open-heart surgery; performed first successful open-heart operation in South Africa; performed first successful heart transplant operation in world 1967, first successful double heart transplant operation 1974; Hon. D.Sc. (Univ. of Cape Town). *Publications:* One Life (autobiography, with C. B. Pepper) 1970, Heart Attack: All You Have To Know About It 1971, The Unwanted (with S. Stander) 1974, South Africa: Sharp Dissection 1977, In the Night Season (with S. Stander) 1977, Best Medicine 1979, Good Life—Good Death 1980, The Body Machine 1981, The Living Body (with Karl Sabbagh) 1984, The Arthritis Handbook (jtly) 1984. *Leisure interests:* power-boats, water skiing, fishing, flying. *Address:* P.O. Box 988, Cape Town 8000, South Africa. *Telephone:* 953-2194.

BARNARD, Eric Albert, PH.D., F.R.S.; British biochemist; b. 2 July 1927; m. Penelope J. Hennessy 1956; two s. two d.; ed. Davenant Foundation School, King's Coll., Univ. of London; Nuffield Foundation Fellow, King's Coll. 1956–59, Asst. Lecturer 1959–60, Lecturer 1960–64; Assoc. Prof. of Biochemical Pharmacology, State Univ. of New York 1964–65, Prof. of Biochemistry 1965–76, Head Biochemistry Dept. 1969–76; Rank Prof. of Physiological Biochemistry, Imperial Coll. of Science and Tech., London 1976–85, Chair. Div. of Life Sciences 1977–85, Head Dept. of Biochemistry 1979–85; Dir. MRC Molecular Neurobiology Unit, Cambridge 1985–; Rockefeller Fellow, Univ. of Calif., Berkeley 1960–61; Guggenheim Fellow, MRC Lab. of Molecular Biology, Cambridge 1971; Visiting Prof., Univ. of Marburg, Fed. Rep. of Germany 1965; Visiting Scientist, Inst. Pasteur, France 1973; mem. American Soc. of Biological Chemists, Int. Soc. of Neurochemistry; Cttee. mem. MRC; Josiah Macy Faculty Scholar Award, U.S.A. 1975, Medal of Polish Acad. of Sciences 1980, Ciba Medal and Prize 1985. *Publications:* Ed. of five scientific books; mem. editorial bd. four scientific journals; numerous papers in learned journals. *Leisure interest:* the pursuit of good claret. *Address:* Medical Research Council Molecular Neurobiology Unit, Medical Research Council Centre, University of Cambridge, Hills Road, Cambridge, CB2 2QH, England. *Telephone:* Cambridge 245133.

BARNARD, Lance Herbert, A.O.; Australian politician and diplomatist (retd.); b. 1 May 1919, Launceston, Tasmania; m. 2nd Jill Newton; one s. four d. (one deceased); ed. Launceston Tech. Coll.; mil. service in Second World War 1940–45, Australian Cadet Corps, with rank of Captain 1945–54; M.P. 1954–75; mem. Jt. Public Accounts Cttee. 1956–58; Fed. Parl. Labor Party Exec. 1958–61; State Pres. Tasmanian Branch, Australian Labor Party 1963–66; 1970–72, Joint Parl. Cttee. on Foreign Affairs 1967–69; Deputy Leader Parl. Labor Party 1967–75; Joint Select Cttee. on Defence Forces Retirement Benefits Legislation 1970–71; Deputy Prime Minister 1972–74; Minister for Defence 1972–75; Amb. to Sweden, Finland and Norway 1975–78; Dir. Office of Australian War Graves 1981–83. *Publications:* Australian Defence—Policy and Programmes. *Address:* 6 Bertland Court, Launceston, Tasmania 7250, Australia.

BARNARD, Lukas Daniel, M.A., D.PHIL.; South African university professor and intelligence officer; b. 14 June 1949, Otjiwarongo; s. of Nicolaas Evehardus Barnard and Magdalena Catharina Beukes; m. Engela Brand 1971; three s.; ed. Otjiwarongo High School, Univ. of O.F.S.; Senior Lecturer Univ. of O.F.S. 1976, Prof. and Head, Dept. of Political Science 1978; Dir.-Gen. Nat. Intelligence Service (fmrly. Dept. of Nat. Security) 1980–; S. African Police Star for Outstanding Service 1985, Order of the Star of S. Africa (Class 1), Gold 1987. *Leisure interests:* tennis, angling, squash, jogging. *Address:* c/o National Intelligence Service, Private Bag X9A7, Pretoria 0001, South Africa. *Telephone:* 3228133.

BARNDORFF-NIELSEN, Ole Eiler, SC.D.; Danish professor of mathematical statistics; b. 18 March 1935, Copenhagen; m. Bente Jensen-Storch 1956; two s. two d.; ed. Univ. of Copenhagen and Aarhus Univ.; Prof. of Mathematical Statistics, Inst. of Mathematics, Aarhus Univ. 1973–; mem. Royal Danish Acad. of Sciences and Letters 1980–. *Publications:* Information and Exponential Families in Statistical Theory 1978, Parametric Statistical Models and Likelihood 1988, Asymptotic Techniques for use in Statistics (with D. R. Cox) 1989, numerous scientific papers. *Leisure interests:* biography, blown sands, opera, tennis. *Address:* Department of Theoretical Statistics, Institute of Mathematics, Aarhus University, 8000 Aarhus (Inst.); Dalvangen 48, 8270 Højbjerg, Denmark (Home). *Telephone:* (06) 127188 (Inst.); (06) 271442 (Home).

BARNES, Dame (Alice) Josephine (Mary Taylor), D.B.E., M.A., D.M., F.R.C.P., F.R.C.S., F.R.C.O.G.; British obstetrician and gynaecologist; b. 18 Aug. 1912, Sheringham; d. of Rev. Walter Wharton Barnes and Alice Mary Ibbetson; m. Sir Brian Warren (divorced 1964); one s. two d.; ed. Oxford High School, Lady Margaret Hall, Oxford and Univ. Coll. Hospital; Consulting Obstetrician and Gynaecologist Elizabeth Garrett Anderson Hospital 1947–, Charing Cross Hospital 1954–; Surgeon Marie Curie Hospital 1947–67; appointments at Univ. Coll. Hospital, Samaritan Hospital, Queen Charlotte's Hospital, Radcliffe Infirmary; Pres. Medical Women Fed. 1966–; Vice-Pres. Royal Coll. of Obstetricians and Gynaecologists 1975–78; Pres. Union Professionelle Int. de Gynécologie et d'Obstetrique 1977–79; Pres. Women's Nat. Cancer Control Campaign 1974–, Nat. Asscn. of Family Planning Doctors 1976–; Asscn. of Chartered Physiotherapists in Obstetrics and Gynaecology, British Medical Assn. 1979–80, Royal Medical Benevolent Fund 1982–; Fellow, Kings Coll., London 1985, mem. Council 1985–; Fellow, Royal Holloway and Bedford New Coll. 1986; Hon. F.R.C.P.I. 1977; Hon. Fellow, Lady Margaret Hall, Oxford 1980; Hon. M.D. (Liverpool) 1979; Hon. D.Sc. (Leicester) 1980; Hon. D.M. (Southampton) 1981; Commdr. du Bontemps de Médoc et des Graves 1986; Suckling Prize, F. T. Roberts Prize; Tuke Medal, Fellowes Medal. *Publications:* Gynaecological Histology 1948, The Care of the Expectant Mother 1954, Lecture Notes on Gynaecology 1966, Scientific Foundations of Obstetrics and Gynaecology (Ed. jointly) 1970, Essentials of Family Planning 1976; numerous contributions to medical literature. *Leisure interests:* music, gastronomy, motoring, foreign travel. *Address:* 8 Aubrey Walk, London, W8 7JG, England. *Telephone:* 01-727 9832.

BARNES, Christopher Richard, B.SC., PH.D., F.R.S.C.; Canadian geologist; b. 20 April 1940, Nottingham, England; m. Susan M. Miller 1961; three d.; ed. Univs. of Birmingham and Ottawa; NATO Research Fellow Univ. of Wales, Swansea 1964–65; Asst. Prof. Univ. of Waterloo 1965–70, Assoc. Prof. 1970–76, Prof. and Chair. 1976–81, Biology Dept. 1973–81, Adjunct Prof. 1981–82; Sr. Research Fellow Univ. of Southampton, U.K. 1971–72; Univ. of Cambridge 1980–81; Prof. and Head Memorial Univ. of Newfoundland 1981–87; Acting Dir. Centre for Earth Resources Research 1984–87; Dir.-Gen. Sedimentary and Marine Geosciences, Geological Survey of Canada 1987–; Bancroft Award 1982; Geological Assn. of Canada Nat. Lecturer 1978, Past-Pres's Medal 1977. *Publications:* over 70 scientific works in geological journals. *Address:* Energy, Mines and Resources Canada, Room 2054, 20th Floor, 580 Booth Street, Ottawa, Ont., Canada, K1A OE4. *Telephone:* (613) 992-5265.

BARNES, Clive Alexander, C.B.E.; British journalist, dance and theatre critic; b. 13 May 1927, London; m.; two c.; ed. King's Coll., London and Oxford Univ.; served R.A.F. 1946–48; Admin. officer, Town Planning Dept., London County Council 1952–61; also active as freelance journalist contributing articles, reviews and criticisms on music, dance, theatre, films and television to the New Statesman, The Spectator, The Daily Express, The New York Times, etc.; Chief dance critic, the Times, London 1961–65; Exec. Ed., Dance and Dancers, Music and Musicians, Plays and Players 1961–65; Dance Critic. The New York Times 1965–78, also Drama Critic (weekdays only) 1967–77; Assoc. Ed., Chief Drama and Dance Critic, New York Post 1977–; a New York Corresp. of The Times 1970–; Kt. Order of the Dannebrog (Denmark). *Publications:* Ballet in Britain Since the War, Frederick Ashton and His Ballet, Ballet Here and Now, Dance As It Happened, Dance in the Twentieth Century, Dance Scene: U.S.A.; Ed. Nureyev 1983. *Address:* 45 W. 60th Street, Apt. 8A, New York, N.Y. 10023, U.S.A.

BARNES, Edward Larrabee, M.ARCH.; American architect; b. 22 April 1915, Chicago Ill.; s. of Cecil and Margaret H. (Ayer) Barnes; m. Mary E. Coss 1944; one s.; ed. Milton Acad., Harvard Univ. and Graduate School of Design; Sheldon Travelling Fellowship 1942; architectural practice in New York 1949–; Critic of Architectural Design, Pratt Inst., Brooklyn 1954–59, Yale School of Architecture 1957–64, Eliot Noyes Critic, Harvard Graduate School of Design 1979; Jefferson Prof., Univ. of Virginia 1980; work exhibited at Museum of Modern Art (New York), Carnegie Inst. (Pittsburgh, Pa.), Whitney Museum, New York and published in architectural magazines; Dir. Municipal Art Soc. of New York 1960; Fellow, American Inst. of Architects; Trustee, American Acad. in Rome 1963–78, Vice-Pres. 1973, First Vice-Chair. 1975; Trustee, Museum of Modern Art, New York, 1975–; Assoc. Nat. Acad. of Design 1969, Academician 1974–;

Fellow, American Acad. of Arts and Sciences 1978–; Yale Award for Distinction in the Arts 1959, Arnold Brunner Prize, Nat. Inst. of Arts and Letters 1959, Silver Medal, Architectural League, (New York) 1960, A.I.A. Medal of Hon. (New York chapter) 1971, A.I.A. Collaborative Achievement in Architecture 1972, Hon. Award 1972, 1977, 1986, Harleston Parker Award, Boston Soc. of Architects 1972, Louis Sullivan Award 1979, Honor Award, Connecticut Soc. of Architects 1980, A.I.A. Architectural Firm Award 1980, Thomas Jefferson Award 1981 (Univ. of Virginia), Honor Award, New Mexico Soc. of Architects 1983, Excellence in Design award, N.Y. State Asscn. of Architects 1984, Harvard Univ. 350th Anniversary Medal 1986, and other awards; Hon. Dr. of Fine Arts (Rhode Island School of Design) 1983, Hon. D.Hum.Litt. (Amherst Coll.) 1984. *Works include:* pre-fabricated house, private houses, camps, academic buildings and master plans, office bldgs. and corporate head-quarters, museums and botanical gardens including Haystack Mountain School of Arts and Crafts, Maine; master plans for State Univ. of New York at Purchase and Potsdam; office bldgs. for New England Merchants Nat. Bank, Boston, IBM headquarters in New York City and Mt. Pleasant, New York; master plan and office/retail complex, Crown Center, Kansas City; Walker Art Gallery, Minneapolis, Minn.; Sarah Scaife Gallery, Pittsburgh, Pa.; Chicago Botanic Garden, Dallas Museum of Art, etc. *Leisure interests:* music, piano, sailing, climbing. *Address:* 320 West 13th Street, New York, N.Y. 10014 (Office); Wood Road, Mount Kisco, N.Y. 10549, U.S.A. (Home). *Telephone:* 212-929-3131.

BARNES, Harry George, Jr., M.A.; American diplomatist; b. 5 June 1926, St. Paul, Minn.; s. of Harry George and Bertha Pauline (Blaul) Barnes; m. Elizabeth Ann Sibley 1948; one s. three d.; ed. Amherst Coll. and Columbia Univ.; served with A.U.S 1944–46; Vice-Consul, Bombay 1951–53; Consular Officer, Prague 1953–55; Russian Area and Language Trainee, Oberammergau, Germany 1955–56; Second Sec., Consul, Moscow 1956–69; Office of Soviet Union Affairs, Dept. of State 1959–62; Nat. War Coll. 1962–63; Deputy Chief of Mission, American Embassy, Nepal 1963–67, Romania 1968–71; Office of Personnel, Dept. of State 1971–72; Deputy Exec. Sec., Dept. of State 1972–74; Amb. to Romania 1974–77, to India 1981–85, to Chile 1985–88; Dir.-Gen. of the Foreign Service and Dir. of Personnel, Dept. of State 1977–81; retd. from U.S. Foreign Service 1988; present Exec. Dir. Critical Languages and Area Studies Consortium. *Leisure interest:* trekking. *Address:* Hapenny Road, Peachum, U.T. 05862, U.S.A.

BARNES, Sir (Ernest) John (Ward), K.C.M.G., M.B.E. (MIL.); British diplomatist (retd.); b. 22 June 1917, London; s. of Rt. Rev. E. W. Barnes (3rd Bishop of Birmingham) and Adelaide Ward; m. Cynthia M. R. Stewart 1948; two s. three d.; ed. Winchester Coll. and Trinity Coll., Cambridge; served in Royal Artillery 1939–46; joined diplomatic service 1946; postings to Washington, Beirut and Bonn; Amb. to Israel 1969–72, to the Netherlands 1972–77; Dir. Alliance Investment Ltd. 1977–87; Dir. Whiteaway, Laidlaw Ltd. 1979–88; Chair. Sussex Rural Community Council 1982–87, Govs. Hurstpierpoint Coll. 1982–87; mem. of Council, Univ. of Sussex 1981–85 (Vice-Chair. 1982–84). *Publication:* Ahead of His Age 1979. *Address:* Hampton Lodge, Hurstpierpoint, Sussex, BN6 9QN, England (Home); 20 Thurloe Place Mews, London, SW7 2HL, England. *Telephone:* 0273-833247; 01-584 9652.

BARNES, John Arundel, D.S.C., M.A., D.PHIL., F.B.A.; British sociologist; b. 9 Sept. 1918, Reading, Berks.; s. of Thomas D. Barnes and Grace M. Barnes; m. Helen F. Bastable 1942; three s. one d.; ed. Christ's Hosp., St. John's Coll. Cambridge, Univ. of Cape Town and Balliol Coll. Oxford; served RN 1940–46; Research Officer, Rhodes-Livingstone Inst. N. Rhodesia 1946–49; Lecturer, Dept. of Anthropology, Univ. Coll. London 1949–51; Fellow, St. John's Coll. Cambridge 1950–53; Simon Research Fellow, Univ. of Manchester 1951–53; Reader in Anthropology, London School of Econs. 1954–56; Prof. of Anthropology, Univ. of Sydney 1956–58, Australian Nat. Univ. 1958–69; Fellow, Churchill Coll. Cambridge 1965–66, 1969–; Prof. of Sociology, Univ. of Cambridge 1969–82; Visiting Fellow, Australian Nat. Univ. 1985–; Fellow, Acad. of Social Sciences, Australia; Wellcome Medal 1950, Rivers Medal 1959, Royal Anthropological Inst. *Publications:* Marriage in a Changing Society 1951, Politics in a Changing Society 1954, Three Styles in the Study of Kinship 1971, The Ethics of Inquiry in Social Science 1977, Who Should Know What? 1979. *Address:* Department of Sociology, Research School of Social Sciences, Australian National University, G.P.O. Box 4, Canberra, A.C.T. 2601, Australia. *Telephone:* (062) 49 4037.

BARNES, Robert Henry, B.S., M.D.; American psychiatrist; b. 4 Nov. 1921, Worcester, Mass.; s. of Harry Elmer Barnes and Grace Stone Barnes; m. Beverly R. Feingold 1967; one s. one d. and one stepson; ed. Union Coll. Schenectady, New York, Duke Univ. and Univ. of Colorado; Instructor, Psychosomatic Medicine, Univ. of Colorado 1952–53, Asst. Prof. of Psychiatry, Duke Univ. 1953–56; Assoc. Prof., Prof. and Chair., Dept. of Psychiatry, Univ. of Missouri in Kansas City 1956–68; Exec. Dir Greater Kansas City Mental Health Foundation 1956–68; Acting Dir. Epidemiological Field Station, Kansas City, Missouri 1967–68; Prof. of Psychiatry, Univ. of Texas School of Medicine, San Antonio 1968–72; Prof. and Chair. Dept. of Chemistry, Texas Technical Univ. School of Medicine 1972–; Fellow, American Psychiatric Assn.; Consultant Nat. Inst. of Mental Health in Community Mental Health Programs and Epidemiology 1962–.

Publications: A Community Concern (with Epps and McPartland) 1965; and 30 articles on geriatrics, psychosomatic medicine, electroencephalography, cerebral circulation, psychiatric education, and group therapy. *Leisure interests:* private flying, hunting, fishing, cooking. *Address:* Texas Technical University, School of Medicine, Lubbock, Tex. 79409, U.S.A. (Office) *Telephone:* 806-742-5273.

BARNES, Zane E., B.S.; American business executive; b. 2 Dec. 1921, Marietta, Ohio; s. of Emmett and Frances Barnes; two d. one s.; ed. Marietta Coll., Bowling Green State Univ., Univ. of Notre Dame, Ind.; Vice-Pres./Gen. Man. Pacific Northwest Bell Telephone Co. 1964-65, Vice-Pres. Personnel Ohio Bell Telephone Co. 1965-67, Vice-Pres. Operations Pacific Northwest Bell Telephone Co. 1967-70, Pres. 1970-73; Pres. Southwestern Bell Telephone Co. 1973-74, Pres. and C.E.O. 1974-86, Chair. Bd., Pres. and C.E.O. Southwestern Bell Corpn. 1983-; Dir. various cos.; Americanism Award of the Anti-Defamation League of B'nai B'rith 1980, Downtown St. Louis, Inc. Levee Stone Award 1984, Man of the Year, St. Louis Variety Club 1985. *Leisure interests:* golf, tennis. *Address:* Southwestern Bell Corporation, One Bell Center, Suite 4200, St. Louis, Mo. 63101, U.S.A. *Telephone:* 314 235 9800.

BARNETT, Baron (Life Peer), cr. 1983, of Heywood and Royton in Greater Manchester; **Joel Barnett,** P.C., J.P.; British politician; b. 14 Oct. 1923; s. of Louis and Ettie Barnett; m. Lillian Goldstone 1949; one d.; ed. Derby Street Jewish School, Manchester Central High School; Certified Accountant 1974; Sr. Partner accountancy practice, Manchester 1953-74, 1979-80; served Royal Army Service Corps and British Mil. Govt. in Germany; mem. Borough Council, Prestwich, Lancs. 1956-59; Hon. Treas. Manchester Fabian Soc. 1953-65; Labour Cand. for Runcorn Div. of Cheshire 1959; M.P. for Heywood and Royton Div. of Lancashire 1964-83, mem. House of Commons Public Accounts Cttee. 1965-71, Chair. 1979-83; mem. Public Expenditure Cttee. 1971-74, Select. Cttee. on Tax Credits 1973-74; Vice-Chair. Parl. Labour Party Econ. and Finance Group 1966-67, Chair. 1967-70, 1972-74; Opposition Spokesman on Treas. Matters 1970-74; Chief Sec. to the Treas. 1974-79, mem. Cabinet 1977-79; mem. Halle Cttee. 1982-; Vice-Chair. Bd. of Govs., BBC Aug. 1986-; Chair., Dir., consultant to a number of cos.; Chair. British Screen Finance 1985-; Hansard Soc. for Parl. Govt.; Children's Medical Charity Trust PLC; Trustee Victoria and Albert Museum 1983-; Gov. Birkbeck Coll., London Univ; Hon. Visiting Fellow, Univ. of Strathclyde 1980-; Hon. LL.D. (Strathclyde) 1983. *Publication:* Inside the Treasury 1982. *Leisure interests:* walking, conversation, reading, good food. *Address:* Flat 92, 24 John Islip Street, London, S.W.1; 7 Hillingdon Road, Whitefield, Manchester, M25 7QQ, Lancs., England (Homes). *Telephone:* (061) 766 3634.

BARNETT, Correlli Douglas, M.A.; British military historian; b. 28 June 1927, London; s. of Douglas A. Barnett and Kathleen M. Barnett; m. Ruth Murby 1950; two d.; ed. Trinity School, Croydon and Exeter Coll. Oxford; Intelligence Corps 1945-48; North Thames Gas Bd. 1952-57; public relations 1957-63; Keeper of Archives, Churchill Coll. Cambridge 1977-; Defence Lecturer, Univ. of Cambridge 1980-83; Fellow Churchill Coll., Cambridge 1977-; mem. Cttee. London Library 1977-79, 1982-84; Screenwriters' Guild Award for Best British TV Documentary (The Great War) 1964; F.R.S.L. Award for Britain and Her Army 1971; Winston Churchill Memorial Lecturer, Switzerland 1982. *Publications:* The Hump Organisation 1957, The Channel Tunnel (with Humphrey Slater) 1958, The Desert Generals 1960, The Swordbearers 1963, Britain and Her Army 1970, The Collapse of British Power 1972, Marlborough 1974, Bonaparte 1978, The Great War 1979, The Audit of War 1986, Hitler's Generals 1988. *Leisure interests:* gardening, interior decorating, eating, idling, mole-hunting. *Address:* Churchill College, Cambridge; Catbridge House, East Carleton, Norwich, Norfolk, NR14 8JX, England. *Telephone:* (0223) 336175 Cambridge; Mulbarton 410.

BARNETT, Lloyd M.H.; Jamaican diplomatist; b. 6 Jan. 1930; m.; ed. London School of Econs., Univ. of Madrid, Fletcher School of Law and Diplomacy and American Univ., Washington D.C.; joined Jamaican Foreign Service 1962; post at Embassy in Washington D.C. 1962-65; post in Perm. Mission to UN, New York 1965-69, Perm. Rep. 1984-; Deputy Perm. Rep. to O.A.S. 1970-74; Amb. to Cuba and Peru 1974/75, to Venezuela, accred. to Brazil, Colombia, Ecuador 1975-78; Dir. Political Div. in Ministry of Foreign Affairs, Jamaica 1978-84. *Address:* Permanent Mission of Jamaica to United Nations, 866 Second Ave., 15th Floor, 2 Dag Hammarskjöld Plaza, New York, N.Y. 10017, U.S.A. *Telephone:* (212) 688-7040.

BARNETT, Peter Leonard; Australian journalist, broadcaster and administrator; b. 21 July 1930, Albany, Western Australia; s. of Leonard Stewart and Ruby Barnett; m. Siti Nuraini Jatim 1970; one s.; ed. Guildford Grammar School, Western Australia, Univ. of Western Australia; Canberra Rep. and Columnist, The Western Australian 1953-57; South-East Asia Corresp., Australian Broadcasting Comm. 1961, 1963, 1964, Jakarta Rep. 1962, New York and UN Corresp. 1964-67, Washington Corresp. 1967-70; News Ed., Radio Australia, Melbourne 1971-72, Washington Corresp. 1972-80, Controller, Melbourne 1980-84, Dir. 1984-; Exec. Dir. Australian Broadcasting Corpn. 1984-; Gov. Dir. The Australasian Acad. of Broadcasting Arts and Sciences. *Leisure interests:* swimming, gardening, literature, musical composition. *Address:* Radio Australia, 699 Highbury Road, East Burwood, Melbourne 3151 (Office); 63 Lum Road, Wheelers Hill, Melbourne 3150, Australia (Home). *Telephone:* (03) 235-2266 (Office).

BARNEVIK, Percy Nils, M.B.A.; Swedish business executive; b. 13 Feb. 1941, Simrishamn; s. of Einar and Anna Barnevik; m. Aina Orvarsson 1963; two s. one d.; ed. Gothenburg School of Econs., Stanford Univ., U.S.A.; Man. Admin. Devt., Group Controller, Sandvik AB 1969-75, Pres. U.S. subsidiary 1975-79, Exec. Vice-Pres. parent co. 1979-80, Chair. Sandvik AB Oct. 1983-; Pres. and Chief Exec. ASEA, Västerås 1980. *Address:* ASEA AB, S-721 83 Västerås, Sweden. *Telephone:* 021-137020.

BARON, Franklin Andrew; Dominican business executive, politician and diplomatist; b. 19 Jan. 1923, Dominica; s. of Alexander and O. M. Baron; m. Sybil Baron 1973; ed. Dominica Grammar School; owner A. A. Baron & Co. (gen. merchants) 1945-; mem. Dominica Legis. Council 1948-61, Exec. Council 1955-61; Political Leader, Dominica United People's Party 1954-66; Minister of Trade and Production 1956-60; Chief Minister 1960-61; Chair. Dominica Tourist Bd. 1970-72; Adviser, Barclays Bank Int. 1975-; Dir. Dominica Electricity Services 1981-; Perm. Rep. to UN and OAS 1982-; Amb. to U.S.A. 1982-86; High Commr. to London 1986-. *Leisure interests:* gardening, reading. *Address:* P.O. Box 57, Cork Street, Roseau, Dominica (Office); Syb Bar Aerie, Champs Fleurs, Eggleston, Dominica (Home). *Telephone:* 2445 (Office); 3014 (Home).

BARON, Jean-Jacques; French engineer; b. 11 May 1909, Angerville L'Orcher, Seine Maritime; s. of Charles and Marie (née Noual) Baron; m. Germaine Lilly Labarthe 1939; three s.; ed. Ecole Centrale des Arts et Manufactures, Paris; Engineer, later Technical Dir. L'Aluminium Français 1933-57; Dir. Compagnie Péchiney Ugine Kuhlmann (fmrly. Péchiney) 1958-74; Dir., Adviser, Nuclear Section, Soc. Péchiney 1971-85; Dir. Ecole Centrale des Arts et Manufactures, Paris 1967-78; Pres. Conseil Nat. des Ingénieurs Français 1978-82; Commandeur Ordre national du Mérite, Officier Légion d'honneur, Commandeur Ordre des palmes académiques; Fellow, Imperial Coll. of Science and Technology, London. *Address:* 21 rue Cassette, 75006, Paris (Office); 7 avenue Bosquet, 75007 Paris, France (Home). *Telephone:* 42223550 (Office); 45550971 (Home).

BARÓN CRESPO, Enrique; Spanish politician; b. 1944, Madrid; m.; three d.; ed. Calasancio de las Escuelas Pías Coll., Instituto Católico de Dirección de Empresas, Ecole Supérieure des Sciences Economiques et Commerdiales, Paris; mem. Federación Universitaria Democrática Española; mem. Unión Sindical Obrero 1964; ran legal and econ. consultancy with Agapito Ramos; mem. Convergencia Socialista and Federación de Partidos Socialistas (FPS); negotiated electoral coalition of FPS with the Partido Socialista Obrero Español (PSOE); mem. Congress of Deputies 1977-, PSOE spokesman for econ. affairs, public finance and the budget 1977-82; Minister of Transport and Tourism 1982-85; mem. European Parl. 1986-. *Leisure interests:* jazz, painting, walking, skiing. *Address:* Centre Européen, Plateau de Kirchberg, BP2929, Luxembourg (Office).

BAROOAH, Dev Kanta, LL.B.; Indian politician; b. 22 Feb. 1914, Dibrugarh (Assam); s. of late Nilkanta Barooah; m. Priyalata Barooah; one s.; ed. Nowgong Govt. School and Banaras Hindu Univ.; Sec., Assam P.C.C. 1938-45; Ed. Dainik, Assamiya and Natun Asamiya (daily newspapers); mem. Constituent Ass. 1949-51, Lok Sabha, 1952-57; mem. Legislative Ass. of Assam 1957-60, Speaker 1960; Chair. Oil Refinery 1960; mem. Assam Legis. Assembly 1962-66, 1967, Minister of Educ. and Co-operation 1962; Chair. Oil India 1968; Gov. of Bihar 1971-73; Minister of Petroleum and Chemicals 1973-74; Pres. Indian Nat. Congress Party 1974-77. *Publication:* a volume of poetry in Assamese. *Leisure interests:* gardening, reading. *Address:* 5 Dr. Rajendra Prasad Road, New Delhi; 23 Tughlak Road, New Delhi, India. *Telephone:* 615117, 72120.

BAROYAN, Organes Vagarshakovich; Soviet health official; b.24 Dec. 1906, Erevan; ed. First Medical Inst. of Moscow; Prof. of Epidemiology and Microbiology; Dir., Dept. of Epidemiology, Ivanovski Virology Inst. of Acad. of Medical Sciences; Dir. Gamalei Inst. of Epidemiology and Microbiology, Acad. of Medical Sciences 1964; Asst. Dir.-Gen. World Health Organization, Geneva 1961-64; Prof. and Academician Acad. of Medical Sciences of U.S.S.R. 1965-; mem. Int. Epidemiological Asscn.; Hon. mem. Soc. of Czechoslovak Epidemiologists and Microbiologists, of Purkyně Medical Soc. of Czechoslovakia; State Prize, Order of Red Star (twice), Order of Red Banner of Labour; Badge of Honour, Iranian orders. *Publications:* about 200 on epidemiology of virus infections. *Address:* c/o N. F. Gamalei Institute of Epidemiology and Microbiology, 18 Ulitsa Gamalei, Moscow, U.S.S.R.

BARR, James, M.A., D.D., D.THEOL., F.B.A., F.R.A.S.; British university professor; b. 20 March 1924, Glasgow, Scotland; s. of Prof. and Mrs. Allan Barr; m. Jane J. S. Hepburn 1950; two s. one d.; ed. Daniel Stewart's Coll., Edinburgh, Univ. of Edinburgh; Minister, Church of Scotland, Tiberias, Israel 1951-53; Prof. of New Testament, Presbyterian Coll., Montreal, Canada 1953-55; Prof. of Old Testament, Univ. of Edinburgh 1955-61, Princeton Theological Seminary (N.J.) 1961-65; Prof. of Semitic Languages and Literatures, Univ. of Manchester 1965-76; Oriel Prof. of Interpretation of Holy Scripture, Univ. of Oxford 1976-78; Regius Prof. of Hebrew, Oxford 1978-; mem. governing body SOAS 1980-85; Visiting Prof., Hebrew Univ. of Jerusalem 1973, Univ. of Chicago, Ill. 1975, 1981, Univ. de Strasbourg, France 1975-76, Brown Univ. Rhode Island 1985,

Univ. of Otago 1986, Univ. of S.A. 1986; Vanderbilt Univ., Nashville, Tenn. 1987–88; Currie Lecturer, Austin Theological Seminary, Tex. 1964; Guggenheim Memorial Fellowship for study in biblical semantics 1965; Cadbury Lecturer, Univ. of Birmingham 1969; F.B.A. 1969; Croall Lecturer, Univ. of Edinburgh 1970; Grinfield Lecturer on the Septuagint, Univ. of Oxford 1974–78; Firth Lecturer, Univ. of Nottingham 1978; Sprunt Lecturer, Univ. of Virginia. 1982; mem. Inst. for Advanced Study, Princeton, N.J. 1985; Schweich Lectures, British Acad. 1986; Corresp. mem. Göttingen Acad. of Sciences, Fed. Repub. of Germany 1976, Norwegian Acad. 1977; Hon. mem. Soc. of Biblical Literature, U.S.A. 1983; D.D. Oxford Univ. 1981; Hon. D.D., Knox Coll., Toronto, Canada 1964, Univ. of Dubuque, Iowa 1974, Univ. of St. Andrews 1974, Univ. of Edinburgh 1983; Hon. D. Theol. (Univ. of S.A.) 1986, (Paris, France) 1988; Hon. D.D. (Univ. of Toronto, Canada) 1988; Hon. Fellow, School of Oriental and African Studies, London 1975, Oriel Coll., Oxford 1980. *Publications:* The Semantics of Biblical Language 1961, Biblical Words for Time 1962, Old and New in Interpretation 1966, Comparative Philology and the Text of the Old Testament 1968, The Bible in the Modern World 1973, Fundamentalism 1977, Explorations in Theology 1980; Holy Scripture: Canon, Authority, Criticism 1983, Escaping from Fundamentalism 1984, The Variable Spellings of the Hebrew Bible 1988; editor: Oxford Hebrew Dictionary 1974–80. *Address:* Christ Church, Oxford; Oriental Institute, Oxford (Office); 6 Fitzherbert Close, Iffley, Oxford, OX4 4EN, England (Home). *Telephone:* Oxford 772741 (Home).

BARR, Joseph Walker; M.A.; American business executive; b. 17 Jan. 1918, Vincennes, Ind.; s. of Oscar Lynn Barr and Stella F. Walker; m. Beth A. Williston 1939; one s. four d.; ed. DePauw Univ. and Harvard Univ.; fmr. Exec. Vice-Pres. Merz Engineering, Indianapolis; fmr. Sec.-Treas. Barr Devt. Corpn., Indianapolis; fmr. mem. U.S. House of Reps., mem. Banking and Currency Comm.; Asst. to Sec. (Congressional Relations), Dept. of Treasury 1961–64; Chair. Bd. Fed. Deposit Insurance Corpn. 1964–65; Under-Sec. of Treasury 1965–68, Sec. 1968–69; Pres. American Security and Trust Co. 1969–72, Chair. of the Bd. 1973–74; Partner J & J Co. 1976–; Chair. Federal Home Loan Bank, Atlanta, Ga.; Dir. 3M Co., Burlington Industries, Commercial Credit Co., Student Loan Marketing Asscn., Washington Gas Light Co., Control Data Corpn., Manor Care Inc., Fed. Home Loan Bank, Atlanta, Ga., CONRAIL; mem. Bd. of Regents, Georgetown Univ.; Hon. LL.D. Vincennes Univ. 1966, DePauw Univ. 1967. *Address:* Suite 422, 2111 Jefferson Davis Highway, N. Arlington, Va. 22202 (Office); Houyhnhnm Farm, Hume, Va. 22639, U.S.A. (Home). *Telephone:* (202) 638-7676 (Office).

BARR, Morris Alfred, LL.D.; Australian international administrator and business executive; b. 23 Dec. 1922, Melbourne; s. of Benjamin Alfred Barr and Margaret Bell; m. Shirley Frances Deacon 1957; ed. Scotch Coll., Melbourne Univ. and Melbourne Conservatorium of Music; mem. editorial staff Melbourne Argus; served with Australian Imperial Forces and Far Eastern Liaison Office; Head, Melbourne Conservatorium of Music 1948; with English-Speaking Union 1951–, Dir. of Programmes 1959–64, Dir.-Gen. 1964–69; Part-time lecturer in int. affairs to British Armed Services 1953–64; Int. Co-ordinator Winston Churchill Memorial Trust 1960–65; Chair. and Man. Dir. Associated Consultants (Construction) Ltd. 1969–; Trustee, Univ. of Louisville (Humphrey Centenary Scholarship Trust); Trustee and Cttee. mem., Britain-Australia vocational exchange 1974–; Chair. Australian Musical Asscn. 1974–; Deputy Chair. Victoria (Australia) Promotion Cttee. 1978–80, Jt. Chair. 1983–, Victoria Econ. Devt. Corpn. 1981–83, Victoria Cttee. 1984–; Deputy Chair. Latchway Ltd. 1983–; Hon. D.H., Univ. of Louisville 1979–. *Leisure interests:* music, swimming, golf. *Address:* 88 Baker Street, London, W1M 1DL (Office); 52 Rosebank Holyport Road, London, SW6 6LY, England (Home).

BARR, Murray Llewellyn, O.C., M.D., F.R.S.; Canadian professor emeritus of anatomy; b. 20 June 1908, Belmont, Ont.; s. of William L. Barr and Margaret (McLellan) Barr; m. Ruth V. King 1934; three s. one d.; ed. Univ. of Western Ontario; intern at Hamot Hosp., Erie, Pa.; general practice, London, Ont. 1934–36; Instructor, Dept. of Anatomy, Univ. of W. Ont. 1936–39; medical branch, Royal Canadian Air Force 1939–45; Assoc. Prof. Dept. of Anatomy, Univ. of W. Ont. 1945–50, Prof. 1950–73, Prof. Emer. 1973–; Gairdner Foundation Award of Merit; several hon. degrees and other awards. *Publications:* A Century of Medicine at Western 1977, The Human Nervous System: An Anatomical Viewpoint 1979; more than 100 scientific articles, mostly on some aspect of human cytogenetics. *Leisure interest:* medical history. *Address:* 452 Old Wonderland Road, London, Ont., N6K 3R2, Canada. *Telephone:* (519) 471-5618.

BARRAN, Sir David Haven, Kt.; British oil executive; b. 23 May 1912, London; s. of John N. Barran, Bt., and Alice M. Parks; m. Jane Lechmere Macaskie 1944; four s. three d.; ed. Winchester Coll. and Trinity Coll., Cambridge; Asiatic Petroleum Co. 1934–61, served Egypt, Sudan, Red Sea, India, London 1934–58, Pres. Asiatic Petroleum Corpn., New York 1958–61; Man. Dir. The Shell Petroleum Co., Shell Int. Petroleum Co. 1961–72; Principal Dir. Bataafse Petroleum Mij. N.V. 1961–72; Dir. Shell Transport and Trading Co. Ltd. 1961–83, Deputy Chair. 1964–67; Man. Dir. 1967–72, Chair 1967–72; Dir. Shell Oil Co. 1964–72, Chair. 1970–72; Dir. Midland Bank 1972–82, Deputy Chair. 1976–80, Chair. 1980–82; Dir. City Investment Co. of N.Y. 1972–84, Glaxo 1972–82, Gen. Accident

Insurance 1972–83, Canadian Imperial Bank 1972–80, B.I.C.C. 1972–83, Standard Chartered Bank 1977–79. *Leisure interests:* gardening, shooting, golf, embroidery, (Pres. Embroiderers' Guild 1982–87). *Address:* Brent Eleigh Hall, Sudbury, Suffolk, England (Home). *Telephone:* Lavenham 247202.

BARRATT-BOYES, Sir Brian Gerald, K.B.E., M.D., CH.M., F.R.A.C.S., F.R.S.N.Z.; New Zealand cardiothoracic and vascular surgeon; b. 13 Jan. 1924, Wellington; s. of Gerald Boyes and Edna (Boyes) Barratt; m. 1st Norma Thompson (divorced 1986); five s.; m. 2nd Sara Monester 1986; ed. Wellington Coll. and Univ. of Otago; Fellowship, Cardiothoracic Surgery, Mayo Clinic 1953–55; N.Z. Nuffield Travelling Fellow, Univ. of Bristol, U.K. 1956; Sr. Thoracic Surgeon, Green Lane Hosp. Auckland 1957–65, Surgeon in Charge, Cardiothoracic Surgical Unit 1965–88; pvt. practice, Mater Misericordiae Hosp., Epsom, Auckland 1966–; R.T. Hall Prize Cardiology Soc. of Australia and N.Z. 1966; Hon. F.A.C.S.; Hon. F.R.C.S. 1985; Hon. D.Sc. 1985. *Publications:* Heart Disease in Infancy: Diagnosis and Surgical Treatment 1973, Textbook of Cardiac Surgery (with J.W. Kirklin) 1986. *Leisure interests:* farming, fishing, golf. *Address:* Greenhills, P.O. Box 51, Waiwera, Hibiscus Coast, New Zealand (Home).

BARRAUD, Henry; French composer and author; b. 23 April 1900, Bordeaux; m. Geneviève Bertrand 1936; one s. three d.; staff mem. Int. Exhbn. 1935–38; Dir. Nat. Programme Radio-diffusion Française 1944–65, Lecturer in Music 1966–84; Grand Prix Nat. de la Musique, Grand Prix de la Sacem; Officier Légion d'honneur, Commandeur ordre national du Mérite. *Major works include:* le Mystère des saints innocents (oratorio) 1945, Te Deum, Pange Lingua, La Divine Comédie, 3 symphonies, 5 operas, 2 ballets, 3 concertos and 2 rhapsodies for orchestra. *Publications:* Hector Berlioz, La France et la Musique occidentale, Pour comprendre les musiques d'aujourd'hui, les Cinq Grand Opéras. *Address:* 1 Chemin de Presles, 94410 Saint-Maurice, France (Home). *Telephone:* 42 83 95 90 (Home).

BARRAULT, Jean-Louis; French actor and producer; b. 8 Sept. 1910, Vésinet; s. of Jules Barrault and Marcelle Hélène Vallette; m. Madeleine Renaud (q.v.) 1940; ed. Collège Chaptal; Master at Collège Chaptal 1931; began stage career in role of servant in Volpone 1931; produced and acted in a number of plays, including: Autour d'une mère 1935; Hamlet, Tandis que j'agonise, Numance 1937, La faim; with the Comédie-Française, 1940–47: Antoine et Cléopâtre, Le soulier de satin; founded Compagnie M. Renaud-J.-L. Barrault 1947: Les nuits de la colère, Les fausses confidences, Amphitryon, Baptiste, Occupe-toi d'Amélie, Le procès, Partage de midi, Le bossu, Christophe Colomb, Pour Lucrèce, La cerisaie 1954, Le songe des prisonniers 1955, (Théâtre Marigny) Le personnage combattant, Madame Sans-Gêne, La vie Parisienne 1958, Rabelais 1969, Jarry sur la butte 1970, Harold et Maude 1973, Zarathustra (dir., actor) 1974; Dir. Théâtre de France (fmr. Odéon) 1959–68, Théâtre des Nations 1965–67, 1972–74; Founder and Dir. Théâtre d'Orsay 1974–81; Officier, Légion d'honneur; Commdr. Ordre des Arts et des Lettres; *films include:* Les beaux jours, Hélène 1936, Mademoiselle Docteur, Drôle de drame, Un grand amour de Beethoven, Le puritain 1937, L'or dans la montagne 1939, La symphonie fantastique 1942, Les enfants du paradis 1944, Le cocu magnifique 1946, La ronde 1950, Versailles 1955, That Night at Varennes 1982; Dir. Odéon Théâtre de France 1959–68, Théâtre des Nations 1965–67, 1972–74. *Publications:* Réflexions sur le théâtre 1949, Nouvelles réflexions sur le théâtre 1959, Journal de bord 1961, Souvenirs pour demain 1972, Comme je le pense 1975, Saisir le présent 1984; Ed. Cahiers de la Compagnie M. Renaud-J.-L. Barrault. *Leisure interest:* swimming. *Address:* 18 avenue du Président Wilson, 75116 Paris, France.

BARRE, Raymond; French international civil servant and politician; b. 12 April 1924, Saint-Denis, Réunion; s. of René and Charlotte (née Déramond) Barre; m. Eve Hegedüs 1954; two s.; ed. Faculté de Droit, Paris, and Inst. d'Etudes Politiques, Paris; Prof. at Inst. des Hautes Etudes, Tunis 1951–54; Prof. at Faculté de Droit et de Sciences économiques, Caen 1954–63; Prof. Inst. d'Etudes politiques, Paris 1961, 1982–, Faculté de Droit et Sciences économiques, Paris 1962; Dir. du Cabinet to Minister of Industry 1959–62; mem. Cttee. of Experts (Comité Lorain) studying financing of investments in France 1963–64; mem. Comm. of Gen. Econ. and Financing of Fifth Plan and other govt. cttees.; Vice-Pres. of Comm. of European Communities responsible for Econ. and Financial Affairs 1967–72; mem. Gen. Council, Banque de France 1973; Minister of Foreign Trade Jan.-Aug. 1976; Prime Minister 1976–78, 1978–81, also Minister of Economy and Finance 1976–78; mem. for Rhône, Nat. Assembly 1978–. *Publications:* Economie politique 1956, Une politique pour l'avenir 1982, Réflexions pour demain 1982. *Address:* Assemblée Nationale, 75355 Paris (Office); 4-6 avenue Emile-Acollas, 75007 Paris, France (Home).

BARREAS ARRECHEA, Ricardo Alfredo, DR. MED.; Argentinian physician and politician; b. 3 July 1934, Posadas; m. María Marta Preuciano; four c.; ed. Univ. de la Ciudad de Buenos Aires; Head, Dept. of Surgery, Hosp. Cen. de Posadas; Prin. Surgeon Sanatorio Nosiglia; fmr. mem. Juventud Radical Metropolitana; Vice-Pres. Dist. Misiones de la Unión Cívica Radical; Del. to Nat. Cttee., now Second Vice-Pres. Conducción Nacional U.C.R.; cand. for Gov., Prov. de Misiones 1973, 1975, Gov. 1983–87; Minister of Health and Social Affairs 1987–; mem. Soc. Argentina de Gastroenterología, Soc. de Proctología, Soc. Argentina de Cirugía. *Address:* Ministerio de Salud y Acción Social, Buenos Aires, Argentina.

BARRENECHEA, Norberto M., P.H.D.; Argentine business executive and diplomatist; b. 20 Aug. 1924, Buenos Aires; s. of Juan Carlos and Maria Elena Torres; m. Elisabeth M. Duhalde 1949; two s. two d.; ed. Univ. de Buenos Aires; Pres. of Bd. of Dirs. and Gen. Attorney Pedro D. Duhalde y Cía. S.A. (agricultural firm) 1958–84; Gen. Attorney El Grillo S.A., Don Pedro Dionisio S.A., Hasparren S.A., Inaga S.A., Barrenechea Igarreta S.R.L.; mem. Council Banco Sudameris; Amb. of Argentina in U.S.A. 1964–66; Technical mem. Comm. for Promotion of Econ. Devt. in Argentina; mem. American-Argentine Univ. Asscn., Corporación Argentina de Aberdeen Angus, Jockey Club. *Publications:* Treatise on Auditing, Treatise on Financial Mathematics. *Leisure interest:* collecting bulls. *Address:* Sarmiento 329, Buenos Aires, Argentina. *Telephone:* 783-3900; 311-3074/5.

BARRER, Richard Maling, D.SC., PH.D., F.R.S.; New Zealand scientist and university professor; b. 16 June 1910, Wellington; s. of T. R. and N. A. R. Barrer; m. Helen Frances Yule 1939; one s. three d.; ed. Canterbury Coll., Univ. of New Zealand and Clare Coll., Univ. of Cambridge; Research Fellow, Clare Coll., Cambridge 1937–39; Head. Dept. of Chem., Tech. Coll., Bradford 1939–46; Reader in Chem., Bedford Coll., Univ. of London 1946–48; Prof. of Chem., Univ. of Aberdeen 1948–54; Prof. of Physical Chem., Imperial Coll., Univ. of London 1954–77, Head, Chem. Dept. 1956–76, Dean, Royal Coll. of Science 1963–66, Prof. Emer. and Sr. Research Fellow 1977–; Gov. Chelsea Coll., Univ. of London 1960–81; Hon. Assoc. Royal Coll. of Science 1959; Hon. Fellow, Royal Soc. of N.Z. 1965, N.Z. Inst. of Chem. 1987; Hon. D.Sc. (Bradford Univ.) 1967, (Aberdeen Univ.) 1984. *Publications:* Diffusion In and Through Solids 1941, 1951, Zeolites and Clay Minerals as Sorbents and Molecular Sieves 1978, Hydrothermal Chemistry of Zeolites 1982; contrib. chapters to books, and numerous research papers. *Leisure interests:* gardening, tennis. *Address:* Department of Chemistry, Imperial College, London, SW7 2AY, England. *Telephone:* 01-589 5111.

BARRETT, Charles Kingsley, D.D., F.B.A.; British professor of divinity (retd.); b. 4 May 1917, Salford, Lancs.; s. of Rev. F. Barrett and Clara Barrett née Seed; m. Margaret E. Heap 1944; one s. one d.; ed. Shebbear Coll., Pembroke Coll. Cambridge and Wesley House, Cambridge; Lecturer in Theology, Durham Univ. 1945–58, Prof. of Divinity 1958–82; Visiting Lecturer and Prof. in various European countries, U.S.A., Canada, Australia and N.Z.; Pres. Studiorum Novi Testamenti Societas 1973–74; Dr. h.c. (Hull, Aberdeen, Hamburg); Burkitt Medal for Biblical Study 1966; von Humboldt Forschungspreis 1988. *Publications:* The Holy Spirit and the Gospel Tradition 1947, The Gospel according to St. John 1955, 1978, From First Adam to Last 1962, Jesus and the Gospel Tradition 1967, The Epistles to the Corinthians 1968, 1973, The Signs of an Apostle 1970, Essays on Paul 1982, Essays on John 1982; Freedom and Obligation 1985; Church, Ministry and Sacraments in the New Testament 1985; several other books and many articles in learned journals and symposia. *Address:* 8 Prince's Street, Durham, DH1 4RP, England. *Telephone:* (091) 386 1340.

BARRETT, Charles S., PH.D.; American physicist, crystallographer and metallurgist; b. 28 Sept. 1902, Vermillion, S. Dakota; s. of Charles H. and Laura D. Barrett; m. Dorothy Adams 1928; one d.; ed. Univs. of S. Dakota and Chicago; Div. of Physical Metallurgy, Naval Research Laboratory, Anacostia, D.C. 1928–32; Metals Research Laboratory and Dept. of Metallurgy, Carnegie Inst. of Technology, Pittsburgh 1932–46; Prof., James Franck Inst., Univ. of Chicago 1946–70, Emer. 1970–; Adjunct Prof. of Physics and Research Prof., Univ. of Denver 1970–; Eastman Visiting Prof., Oxford Univ. 1965–66; Ed. Metals and Alloys Section of Structure Reports for Int. Union of Crystallography 1949–51; Pres. American Soc. for X-ray and Electron Diffraction 1947; mem. Exec. Cttee. American Inst. for Mining and Metallurgical Engineers 1954–57 (Mathewson Medal 1934, 1944, 1950, Hume- Rothery Award 1976), Fellow 1965–; mem. Nat. Acad. of Sciences 1967–; Hon. mem. American Soc. of Metals (Howe Medal 1939); mem. Ship Steel Cttee. of Nat. Research Council 1948–62, Advisory Cttee., Office of Ordnance Research 1956–59; Fellow, American Physical Soc., American Crystallographic Asscn., Inst. of Metals, U.S.A. Nat. Cttee of Int. Union of Crystallography 1950–55; Clamer Medal of Franklin Inst. 1950; Heyn Medal of Deutsche Gesellschaft für Metallkunde, gold médals of American Soc. for Metals and Japan Inst. of Metals and Acta Metallurgica. *Publications:* Structure of Metals 1943, 1953, 1966; over 180 papers on research in metallurgy, crystallography and physics. *Leisure interests:* painting watercolours, scientific writing, and golf. *Address:* Engineering Dept., University of Denver, Denver, Colo. 80208, U.S.A.

BARRETT, David, B.A., M.S.W.; Canadian politician; b. 2 Oct. 1930, Vancouver, B.C.; s. of Samuel Barrett and Rose Hyatt; m. Shirley Hackman 1953; two s. one d.; ed. Seattle and St. Louis Univs.; Social Worker, Probation Officer, St. Louis Co. Juvenile Court, St. Louis, Mo.; Supervisor of Social Training, Haney Correctional Inst.; Personnel and Staff Training Officer; Supervisor of Counselling Services, John Howard Soc. of B.C., Vancouver; mem. B. C. Legis. Ass. 1960–; Leader of the Opposition 1969, 1976–84; Premier of B.C., Minister of Finance 1972–75; Public Affairs Broadcaster C.J.O.R. Va. 1985–; New Democratic Party. *Address:* c/o C.J.O.R., 1401 W. 8th Street, Vancouver, B.C. V6H 1C9, Canada.

BARRETT, Edward Ware, A.B.; American journalist; b. 3 July 1910, Birmingham, Ala.; s. of Edward Ware and Lewis R. (Butt) Barrett; m. Mason Daniel 1939; two d.; ed. Princeton Univ. and Univ. of Dijon; on staff of Birmingham (Ala.) News 1929 and 1931; with Columbia Broadcasting System 1932–33; with Newsweek 1933–50, Washington Corresp. 1934–35, Nat. Affairs Ed. 1935–40, Assoc. Ed. 1940–42, Ed. Dir. 1946–50; with Office of War Information 1942–43, with Psychological Warfare Branch of Allied Force H.Q. 1943–44; Exec. Dir. of O.W.I. overseas operations, then Dir. of overseas branch 1944–45; U.S. Asst. Sec. of State for Public Affairs 1950–52; Ed., Consultant, New York 1952–54; Pres. Edward W. Barrett and Assocs. 1952–56; Exec. Vice-Pres. Hill and Knowlton 1953–56; Dean, Graduate School of Journalism, Columbia Univ. 1956–68; Dir. Communications Inst., Acad. for Educational Devt. 1969–; Trustee Inst. of Int. Educ. 1952–60, Atlantic Council of the U.S. 1957–; Dir. UN Asscn. 1960–70; Pres. Asscn. for Educ. in Journalism 1966–67; Dir. Race Relations Information Center 1969–74, Chair. 1973–74; Dir. Foreign Policy Asscn. 1974–. *Publications:* Truth is Our Weapon 1953, Educational T.V.—Who Should Pay? 1968; Ed. This is Our Challenge 1958, Journalists in Action 1963. *Address:* Hawkwood Lane, Greenwich, Conn. 06830 U.S.A. (Home).

BARRETT, Tom Hans, M.B.A.; American business executive; b. 13 Aug. 1930, Topeka, Kan.; s. of William and Myrtle (Huss) Barrett; m. Marilyn E. Dunn 1956; three d.; ed. Kansas State Univ. and Mass. Inst. of Technology; Vice-Pres. the Goodyear Tire & Rubber Co. 1976–78, Exec. Vice-Pres. 1978–81, Group Exec. Vice-Pres. 1981–83, Pres. and C.O.O. 1983–, C.E.O. Jan. 1989–; mem. Bd. of Dirs., A. O. Smith Corpn., Rubbermaid Inc.; mem. Exec. Cttee., Nat. Asscn. of Mfrs. *Leisure interest:* golf. *Address:* The Goodyear Tire & Rubber Company, 1144 East Market Street, Akron, Ohio 44316; 2135 Stockbridge Road, Akron, Ohio 44313, U.S.A. (Home). *Telephone:* (216) 796-4014 (Office).

BARRIE, George Napier, B.A., LL.B., LL.D.; South African professor and advocate; b. 9 Oct. 1940, Pietersburg; m. Marie Howell 1970; two s. one d.; ed. Pretoria Univ., Univ. of S.A. and Univ. Coll. London; State advocate Supreme Court 1964–69; Sr. Law Adviser Dept. of Foreign Affairs 1970–80; Prof. of Int. and Constitutional Law, Rand Afrikaans Univ. 1981–; Leader of S.A. Del. to numerous int. confs.; mem. S.A. Del. to Int. Bar Asscn. Conf. 1984, 1986. *Publications include:* Topical International Law 1979 and numerous works and articles on int. and constitutional law; co-author: Nuclear Non-Proliferation: The Why and the Wherefore 1985, Constitutions of Southern Africa 1985, Law of South Africa 1986, Law of the Sea 1987. *Leisure interest:* long distance running. *Address:* Faculty of Law, Rand Afrikaans University, P.O. Box 524, Johannesburg, South Africa.

BARRINGTON, Nicholas John, C.V.O., C.M.G., F.R.S.A.; British diplomatist; b. 23 July 1934; s. of late Eric A. Barrington and Mildred Bill; ed. Repton School and Clare Coll. Cambridge; joined H.M. Diplomatic Service 1957; served Kabul 1959, U.K. Del. to European Communities, Brussels 1963, Rawalpindi 1965, Tokyo 1972–75, Cairo 1978–81; Minister and Head, British Interests Section, Teheran 1981–83; Asst. Under-Sec. of State, FCO 1984–87; Amb. to Pakistan 1987–; Order of the Sacred Treasure, Japan 1975. *Leisure interests:* theatre, drawing, tennis, prosopography. *Address:* c/o Foreign and Commonwealth Office, London, S.W.1, England.

BARRINGTON-WARD, Rt. Rev. Simon, M.A., D.D.; British ecclesiastic; b. 27 May 1930, London; s. of Robert McGowan Barrington-Ward and Margaret A. Radice; m. Dr. Jean Barrington-Ward; two d.; ed. Eton Coll., Magdalene Coll. Cambridge and Westcott House, Cambridge; ordained, diocese of Ely 1956; Chaplain, Magdalene Coll. Cambridge 1956–60; Lecturer, Ibadan Univ. Nigeria 1960–63; Fellow and Dean of Chapel, Magdalene Coll. Cambridge 1963–69; Principal Church Missionary Soc. Coll. Selly Oak, Birmingham 1969–74; Gen. Sec. Church Missionary Soc. 1974–85; Canon, Derby Cathedral 1975–85; Chaplain to H.M. The Queen 1983–85; Bishop of Coventry 1985–; Hon. D.D. (Wycliffe Coll. Toronto) 1983. *Publications:* Love Will Out 1988; articles and book chapters. *Leisure interests:* hill walking, music, cycling, calligraphy. *Address:* The Bishop's House, Davenport Road, Coventry, West Midlands, CV5 6PW, England. *Telephone:* 0203-72244.

BARRIONUEVO, Hugo Mario; Argentine union leader; b. 24 Dec. 1931, Cordoba; m. Nydia Nilda Davalos; three s.; ed. Arts and Skills School, Rufino; Head Union of the Food Manufacturing Union, 1963–83; workers Del. to the Int. Labour Org.; Minister of Labour and Social Security 1984–87. *Address:* Ministerio de Trabajo y Seguridad Social, Avenida Julio A, Roca 609 C.P. 1067, Buenos Aires, Argentina.

BARRIONUEVO PEÑA, José; Spanish politician; b. 13 March 1942, Berja; m.; three c.; mem. Agrupación de Estudiantes Tradicionalistas; held posts in Sindicato Español Universitaria; became journalist; mem. Convergencia Socialista; town councillor, Madrid; Inspector de trabajo, Madrid 1971; Asst. Dir.-Gen. Ministry of Labour until 1979; socialist cand. in elections for Mayor of Madrid 1979; Minister of Interior 1982–88, of Transport, Tourism and Communications July 1988–. *Address:* Minister of Transport, Tourism and Communications, Nuevos Ministerios, Plaza San Juan de la Cruz, Madrid 3, Spain.

BARRON, Sir Donald James, Kt., D.L., B.COM., C.A.; British businessman; b. 17 March 1921, Edinburgh; s. of Albert Gibson Barron and Elizabeth Macdonald; m. Gillian Mary Saville 1956; three s. two d.; ed. George

Heriot's School, Edinburgh, Univ. of Edinburgh; joined Rowntree & Co. Ltd. 1952, Dir. 1961, Vice-Chair. 1965; Chair. Rowntree Mackintosh Ltd. 1966–81; Vice-Chair. Midland Bank PLC 1981–82 (Dir. 1972–), Chair: 1982–87; mem. Bd. of Banking Supervision 1987–; Vice-Chair. Canada Life Assurance Co. of Great Britain 1983 (Dir. 1980–); Dir. Investors in Industry Group PLC 1980–, Canada Life Unit Trust Mans. 1980–; mem. Council of C.B.I. 1966–81, Soc. Science Research Council 1971–72, Univ. Grants Cttee. 1972–81, Council Inst. of Chartered Accountants of Scotland 1980–81, Council of British Inst. of Management 1979–80; Trustee, Joseph Rowntree Memorial Trust 1966–, Chair. 1981–; mem. NEDC 1983–85; Dir. Clydesdale Bank 1986–87; Gov. London Business School 1982–88; Treas. Univ. of York 1966–72, a Pro-Chancellor 1982–; Hon. Dr. (Loughborough 1982, Heriot-Watt 1983, Council for Nat. Academic Awards 1983, Edinburgh 1984, Nottingham 1985, York 1986). *Leisure interests:* golf, tennis, gardening. *Address:* Greenfield, Sim Balk Lane, Bishopthorpe, York, YO2 1QH, England (Home). *Telephone:* York 705675.

BARROW, Gen. Robert Hilliard, B.S.; American marine officer; b. 5 Feb. 1922, Baton Rouge, La.; s. of Robert E. Barrow and Mary M. Haralson; m. Patricia A. C. Pulliam 1953; two s. three d.; ed. Louisiana State Univ., Univ. of Md., Tulane Univ., Amphibious Warfare School, Quantico, Va., and Nat. War Coll., Washington; commissioned U.S. Marine Corps 1943, General 1978; served China 1944–46; Aide to Commdg. Gen. Fleet Marine Force, Atlantic 1946–48; Commdg. Officer, Company A, 1st Bn., 2nd Marines, and Company A, 1st Bn., 1st Marines, also staff assignments, Marine Corps HQ 1948–56; Bn. Exec. Officer, 2nd Bn., 6th Marines 1956–57; Marine Officer Instructor, Tulane Univ. 1957–60; staff assignments, Marine Corps. Educ. Center, Quantico, Va. 1960–63; Asst. Chief of Staff, G-3, Task Force 79/III Marine Amphibious Force 1963–64; Asst. G-3 Plans Officer, G-3, Fleet Marine Force, Pacific 1964–68; Regimental Commdr., 9th Marines 1968–69; Commdg. Gen., Marine Corps Base, Camp Smedley D. Butler, Deputy Commdr., Marine Corps Bases, Pacific (Forward) 1969–72; Commdg. Gen., Marine Corps Recruit Depot, Parris Island, S.C. 1972–75; Deputy Chief of Staff, Manpower, Marine Corps HQ 1975–76; Commdg. Gen., Fleet Marine Force, Atlantic, 1976–78; Asst. Commdt. Marine Corps 1978–79, Commdt. 1979–; numerous mil. decorations incl. Navy Cross, Distinguished Service Cross (Army), Silver Star Medal, Legion of Merit, Bronze Star Medal, Joint Service Commendation Medal. *Leisure interest:* golf. *Address:* Commandant of the Marine Corps (Code CMC), Washington, D.C. 20380; The Commandant's House, Marine Barracks, 8th and I Streets, S.E., Washington, D.C. 20390, U.S.A. *Telephone:* (202) 694-2500.

BARROW, Dame Ruth Nita, B.SC.; Barbadian diplomatist; ed. Columbia Univ., New York, Univ. of Toronto and Edinburgh Univ.; various staff, teaching and admin. posts in nursing and public health, Barbados and Jamaica 1940–56; Prin. Nursing Officer, Jamaica 1956–62; Nursing Adviser Pan American Health Org. 1967–71; Assoc. Dir of Christian Medical Comm. of WCC, Geneva 1971–75, Dir. 1975–80; Health Consultant WHO 1981–86; Perm. Rep. of Barbados to UN 1986–; Pres. World YWCA 1975–83, Int. Council for Adult Educ. 1982; a Pres. of WCC 1983; participated in numerous int. confs. on population, health and women; mem. Commonwealth Group Eminent Persons (EPG) on S.A. 1986. *Address:* Permanent Mission of Barbados to United Nations, 800 Second Ave., 18th Floor, New York, N.Y. 10017, U.S.A. *Telephone:* (212) 867-8431.

BARROWCLOUGH, Anthony Richard, Q.C.; British lawyer and civil servant; b. 24 June 1924; m. Mary Agnes Pery-Knox-Gore 1949; one s. one d.; ed. Stowe School and New Coll. Oxford; served war service as R.N.V.R. 1943–46; called to Bar, Inner Temple 1949, Bencher 1982; Recorder 1972–84; part-time mem. Monopolies Comm. 1966–69; mem. Council on Tribunals 1985–; Parl. Commr. for Admin. and Health Service Commr. for England, Wales and Scotland 1985–. *Address:* 60 Ladbroke Grove, London, W.11; The Old Vicarage, Winsford, near Minehead, Somerset, England.

BARRY, Marion Shepilov, Jr.; American politician; b. 6 March 1936, Itta Bena, Miss.; s. of Marion S. Barry and Mattie Barry; m. Effi Barry 1978; one s.; ed. LeMoyne Coll., Fisk Univ., Univs. of Kansas and Tennessee; Dir. of Operations, Pride Inc., Washington, D.C. 1967; co-founder, Chair. and Dir. Pride Econ. Enterprises, Inc., Washington, D.C. 1968; mem. Washington D.C. School Bd. 1971–74; mem. Washington City Council 1974–78; Mayor of Washington 1979–. *Address:* Office of the Mayor, District Building, 14th and East Streets, N.W., Washington, D.C. 20004, U.S.A.

BARRY, Peter; Irish politician; b. 1928, Cork; s. of Anthony and Rita Barry; m. Margaret O'Mullane 1957; four s. two d.; Man. Dir. of a tea firm; mem. of the Dáil 1969–; fmr. Chair. Oireachtas Cttee., Fine Gael Party; fmr. Lord Mayor of Cork and Chair. Cork and Kerry Regional Devt. Bd.; Fine Gael Spokesman on Labour and the Public Service 1972–73; Minister for Transport and Power 1973–76, for Educ. 1976–77; Fine Gael Spokesman on Finance and Econ. Affairs 1977–81; Minister for the Environment 1981–82; Fine Gael Spokesman on the Environment 1982; Minister for Foreign Affairs 1982–87; Opposition Spokesman on Foreign Affairs 1987–. *Address:* "Sherwood", Blackrock Road, Cork, Ireland.

BARSCHALL, Henry Herman, PH.D.; American physicist; b. 29 April 1915, Berlin, Germany; m. Eleanor Folsom 1955; one s. one d.; ed. Princeton Univ.; Asst. Prof. Univ. of Wis. 1946–47, Assoc. Prof. 1947–50, Prof. 1950;

Chair. Dept. of Physics 1951, 1954, 1956–57, 1963–64, Bascom Prof. of Physics and Nuclear Eng. 1973–87; Visiting Prof. Univ. of Calif. 1971–73; Assoc. Div. Leader Lawrence Livermore Lab., Univ. of Calif. 1971–73; Councillor-at-Large, American Physical Soc. 1983–86; Ed. Physical Review C 1972–; Fellow American Acad. of Arts and Sciences; Hon. Dr. (Marburg, Fed. Repub. of Germany) 1982; Bonner Prize American Physical Soc.; mem. N.A.S., Chair. Physics Section 1980–83; mem. Governing Bd. American Inst. of Physics 1983–88. *Address:* 1150 University Avenue, Madison, Wis. 53706 (Office); 1110 Tumalo Trail, Madison, Wis. 53711, U.S.A. (Home). *Telephone:* 608-262-9569 (Office); 608-233-6920 (Home).

BARSHAI, Rudolf Borisovich; Soviet conductor; b. 28 Sept. 1924, Labinskaya, Krasnodar Territory; s. of Boris and Maria Barshai; ed. Moscow Conservatoire; performed in chamber ensembles with Shostakovich, Richter, Oistrakh, Rostropovich; founded Moscow Chamber Orchestra 1955; Prin. Conductor and Artistic Adviser, Bournemouth Symphony Orchestra Sept. 1982–; numerous tours abroad; composer of orchestrations and arrangements for chamber orchestra of old and contemporary music. Living in Israel.

BARSTOW, Josephine Clare, C.B.E., B.A.(HONS.); British opera singer; b. 27 Sept. 1940, Sheffield; d. of Harold Barstow and Clara Barstow; m. 1st Terry Hands 1964 (divorced 1968), 2nd Ande Anderson 1969; ed. Birmingham Univ.; taught English in London area for two years; début in operatic profession with Opera for All 1964; for short time co. mem. Welsh Nat. Opera, then English Nat. Opera; now freelance singer in all nat. opera houses in G.B. and in Paris, Vienna, Salzburg, Zürich, Geneva, Turin, Florence, Cologne, E. Berlin, U.S.S.R., Chicago, San Francisco, New York, Houston and many other American opera houses; chief roles: Violetta (Traviata), Leonora (Forza del Destino), Elisabeth (Don Carlos), Lady Macbeth, Leonore (Fidelio), Sieglinde, Arabella, Salome, The Marshallin, Tosca, Mimi, Manon Lescaut, Emilia Marty, Jenůfa, Katya Kabanova, Medea, Renata (The Fiery Angel), Katerina Ismailova; world premières of Tippet, Henze and Penderecki; Verdi Recital Record with English National Opera Orchestra and Mark Elder; Hon. D.Mus. (Birmingham). *Leisure interests:* farming (cattle) and breeding Arabian horses. *Address:* c/o John Coast, Manfield House, 376/9 Strand, Covent Garden, London, WC2R 0LR, England. *Telephone:* 01-379 0022.

BART, Lionel; British composer and lyricist; b. 1 Aug. 1930; *Principal works:* lyrics for Lock Up Your Daughters 1959, music and lyrics for Fings Ain't Wot They Used T'be 1959, music, lyrics and book for Oliver! 1960 (film 1968), music, lyrics and direction of Blitz! 1962, music and lyrics of Maggie May 1964, Winnie 1988; film scores include: Serious Charge, In the Nick, Heart of a Man, Let's Get Married, Light Up the Sky, The Tommy Steele Story, The Duke Wore Jeans, Tommy the Toreador, Sparrers Can't Sing, From Russia with Love, Man in the Middle; many individual hit songs; Ivor Novello Awards as song writer 1957 (three), 1959 (four), 1960 (two); Variety Club Silver Heart as Show Business Personality of the Year, Broadway, U.S.A. 1960; Antoinette Perry Award (Tony) for Oliver! 1962; Gold disc for soundtrack of Oliver! 1969. *Address:* c/o Patricia MacNaughton, MLR, 200 Fulham Road, London, S.W.10, England.

BARTELSKI, Leslaw, LL.M.; Polish writer; b. 8 Sept. 1920, Warsaw; s. of Zygmunt and Zofia Ulanowska; m. Maria Zembrzuska 1947; one s. one d.; ed. Univ. of Warsaw; mem. of resistance movement 1939–44; mem. Sztuka i Naród (Art and Nation) 1942–44; Co-Ed. Nowiny Literackie 1947–48, Nowa Kultura 1953–63, Kultura 1963–72; mem. Presidium of Gen. Council, Union of Fighters for Freedom and Democracy 1969–79, Deputy Pres. 1979–; mem. PEN; Chair. Warsaw Branch, Polish Writers' Assen. 1972–78, mem. Polish Writers' Assen. 1983–; Visiting Prof., Univ. of Warsaw 1970–71, 1977–78; Vice-Pres. Warsaw City Council 1973–80; State Prize (3rd class) 1951, Prize of Minister of Defence (2nd class) 1969, Pietrzak Prize 1969 and 1985, Warsaw Prize 1969, Prize of Minister of Culture and Art 1977 (1st class); Commdr.'s Cross, Order of Polonia Restituta, Order of Cyril and Methodius (1st class) Bulgaria, Cross of Valour, Warsaw Insurgent Cross. *Publications:* novels include Ludzie zza rzeki 1951, Pejzaż dwukrotny 1958, Wodorosty 1964, Mickiewicz na wschodzie 1966, Dialog z cieniem 1968, Niedziela bez dzwonów 1973, Krwawe skrzydła 1975, Rajski ogród 1978; essays: Genealogia ocalonych 1963, Jeździec z Madary 1963, Powstanie Warszawskie 1965, Walcząca Warszawa 1968, Mokotów 1944, 1971, Z głową na karabinie 1974, Pamięć żywa 1977, Polscy pisarze współcześni 1944–74 (biographical dictionary) 1977, Kusociński 1979, Cień wojny 1983; monograph: Pieśñ niepodlegla 1987. *Leisure interests:* history of the Second World War, sport. *Address:* Ul. Joliot Curie 17 m.1, 02-646 Warsaw, Poland. *Telephone:* 44-31-10.

BARTH, Else M.; Norwegian/Netherlands professor of logic and analytical philosophy; b. 3 Aug. 1928, Strinda, Norway; m. Hendrik A. J. F. Misset 1953; ed. Univs. of Oslo, Trondheim, Amsterdam and Leyden; Reader in Logic, Utrecht Univ. 1971–77; Prof. of Analytical Philosophy, Groningen Univ. 1977–87, of Logic and Analytical Philosophy 1987–; Pres. Evert Willem Beth Foundation 1976–; mem. Royal Netherlands Soc. of Sciences, Norwegian Soc. of Sciences. *Publications:* The Logic of the Articles in Traditional Philosophy. A Contribution to the Study of Conceptual Structures 1974, Perspectives on Analytic Philosophy, in Mededeolingen der Koninklijke Nederlandse Akademie van Wetenschappen, afd. Letterkunde,

Nieuwe Reeks 1979, From Axiom to Dialogue—A philosophical study of logics and argumentation (with E. C. W. Krabbe) 1982, Argumentation: Approaches to Theory Formation. Containing the Contributions to the Groningen Conference on the Theory of Argumentation, October 1978 (Ed., with J. L. Martens) 1982, Problems, Functions, and Semantic Roles—A Pragmatist's Analysis of Montague's Theory of Sentence Meaning (with R. T. P. Wiche) 1986; numerous contribs. to learned journals and published lectures. *Leisure interests:* music, cultural and political philosophy, literature, skiing. *Address:* Filosofisch Institut, University of Groningen, Westersingel 19, 9718 CA Groningen (Office); Kamperfoelieweg 16, 9765 HK Paterswolde; Nachtegaallaan 26, 2224 JH Katwijk aan Zee, The Netherlands (Home). *Telephone:* (050) 636146, 636148 (Office); (05907) 4315 (Paterswolde); (01718) 13353 (Katwijk aan Zee).

BARTH, John, M.A.; American novelist and professor of English; b. 27 May 1930, Cambridge, Md.; s. of John J. Barth and Georgia Simmons; m. 1st Harriette Anne Strickland 1950, two s. one d.; m. 2nd Shelly Rosenberg 1970; ed. Johns Hopkins Univ.; Instructor Pennsylvania State Univ. 1953, Assoc. Prof. until 1965; Prof. of English, State Univ. of New York at Buffalo 1965-73, Johns Hopkins Univ. 1973-; Nat. Acad. of Arts and Letters Award; Nat. Book Award 1973; Rockefeller Foundation Grant; Brandeis Univ. Citation in Literature; Hon. Litt.D. (Univ. of Maryland). *Publications:* Novels: The Floating Opera 1956, The End of the Road 1958, The Sot-Weed Factor 1960, Giles Goat-Boy 1966; Lost in the Funhouse (stories) 1968, Chimera 1972, Letters 1979, Sabbatical (novel) 1982, The Friday Book (essays) 1984, The Tidewater Tales: A Novel 1987. *Address:* Johns Hopkins University, Baltimore, Md. 21218, U.S.A.

BARTHA, Dénes (Dennis R.), DR. PHIL. HABIL.; Hungarian musicologist; b. 2 Oct. 1908, Budapest; s. of Richard Bartha and Paula Imling; m. Susan Bartha 1939; two s. one d.; ed. High School of Music, Budapest, and Berlin Univ.; Librarian, Music Dept. Nat. Library 1930; joined staff Budapest High School of Music 1935-42, Prof. of Musicology 1942 (Deputy Chair. 1951-); Music Critic Pester Lloyd 1939-44; Ed. monthly journal Magyar Zenei Szemle 1941-44; Music Adviser to Budapest Municipal Orchestra 1947-48; Ed. Zenei Szemle 1947-48, Zenetudományi Tanulmányok (with B. Szabolcsi) (Vols. 1-10) 1953-62; Studia Musicologica (with B. Szabolcsi) 1961-; mem. Directorium Int. Soc. of Musicology, American Musical Soc.; Neilson Prof. Smith Coll., Northampton, Mass. 1964: Visiting Prof. Harvard Univ. 1964-65, Cornell Univ. 1965-66, Univ. of Illinois 1966, Univ. Coll. Santa Barbara 1971, 1973; A. Mellon Prof. Univ. of Pittsburgh 1966-67, 1969-79; Brechemin Prof. Univ. of Wash. 1980-81; Dent Medal 1963, Erkel Prize 1969; Banner Order of the Hungarian People's Repub. 1983; Hungarian State Prize 1988. *Publications:* include Egyetemes Zenetörténet (General History of Music) (2 vols.) 1935, Musik, Musikgeschichte, Musikleben in Ungarn 1940, Die ungarische Musik (with Zoltán Kodály) 1943, A Zenetörténet Antológiája 1948, 1970, Ötödfélszáz Énekek 1953, The Nine Symphonies of Beethoven 1956, 1958, 1970, J. S. Bach 1956, 1960, Haydn als Opernkapellmeister 1960, J. Haydn, Ges. Briefe und Dokumente Krit. Ausgabe 1965, Zenei Lexikon (3 vols.) 1965; Ed. of La Canterina 1959, L'Infedeltà delusa 1964, Le Pescatrici 1972 (Haydn operas). *Leisure interests:* alpinism, chess. *Address:* 1012 Budapest, I. Attila-ut. 87, Hungary. *Telephone:* 753-462.

BARTHA, Tibor; Hungarian ecclesiastic; b. 13 July 1912, Magyarkapud; s. of Lajos Bartha and Ida Demény; m. Szende G. Szabó; one s. one d.; ed. Univs. of Debrecen, Halle, Marburg and Basel; Prof. Theological Acad. Debrecen 1953-58; Bishop Transtibiscan Reformed Diocese 1958-86; Chair. Reformed Church Synod of Hungary 1962-86; Chair. Oecumenical Church Council of Hungary 1959-86; mem. Cen. Bd. of World Council of Churches 1958-83; mem. Reformed World Fed. Exec. Cttee. 1961-77; Vice-Pres. Christian Peace Conf. 1964-78, Hon. Pres. 1978-86; Pres. Oecumenical Peace Cttee. of Hungary's Nat. Peace Council 1983-86; Bd. mem. Nat. Peace Council 1958-, World Peace Council 1968-86; Vice-Pres. Nat. Cttee. for European Security and Co-operation 1974-; M.P. 1958-86; mem. Pres. Council 1963-86; Dr. h.c. Evangelic Lutheran Theology Seminary of Budapest and United Theology Seminary of Kolozsvár, Cluj, Romania; Labour Order of Merit, Banner Order of Hungarian People's Repub., St. Vladimir Order (Russian). *Publications:* Az Isten igéje és igehirdetésünk (The Word of God and our Preaching it) 1938, Chair. drafting cttee.: Studia et Acta Historiae Ecclesiasticae in four vols. 1965-84, Heritage and Obligation (Synodial Teaching) 1967, Jubilee Commentaries 1967, Ige, egyház, nép (Logos, Church, People) (Vols. I-II) 1972, Diaconal Manual 1980, Divine Service Procedural Order 1985; Pres. Oecumenical Cttee. for the new complete Hungarian Bible translation. *Address:* General Synod of the Reformed Church in Hungary, 1146 Budapest, Abonyi utca 21, Hungary. *Telephone:* 227-870.

BARTHELME, Donald; American author; b. 1931, Philadelphia; s. of Donald Barthelme and Helen Bechtold; m. Marion Knox 1978; two d.; mem. Authors Guild, American PEN, American Acad. and Inst. of Arts and Letters; Guggenheim Fellow 1966; Nat. Book Award 1972; Nat. Inst. of Arts and Letters Award 1972; Rea Award 1988. *Publications:* Snow White 1967, Come Back, Dr. Caligari (short stories) 1964, Unspeakable Practices, Unnatural Acts 1968, City Life 1970, Sadness 1972, Guilty Pleasures (stories) 1974, The Dead Father (novel) 1975, Amateurs (stories) 1976, Great Days 1979, Sixty Stories 1981, Overnight to Many Distant Cities 1983, Paradise 1986, Forty Stories 1987. *Address:* c/o New Yorker Magazine, 25 W 43rd Street, New York, N.Y. 10036, U.S.A.

BARTHELMEH, Hans Adolf, DIPL. KFM; German business executive (retd.); b. 19 Sept. 1923, Cologne; s. of Johann and Gertrud (née Weiler) Barthelmeh; m. Helene Fries 1950; one s.; ed. Univ. of Cologne; Internal Auditor (taxes), Fed. Financial Admin., Cologne 1950-52; with Ford-Werke AG, Cologne 1952-; first, Head, Tax Dept., then Head depts., Finance Div. 1955-63; Chief Controller, Operations 1963-66; mem. Bd. of Man. (Finance) 1966-68, (Sales) 1968-71; Pres. and Chair. Man. Bd., Ford-Werke AG, Cologne, 1966-73; Gen. Man. Ford Motor GmbH, Salzburg, Austria 1957-59; Chair. Rank Xerox GmbH, Düsseldorf 1980-83; Chair. Bd. of Dirs. Ford-Credit AG, Cologne; mem. Man. Bd., Verband der Deutschen Automobilindustrie e.V., Frankfurt; fmr. mem. Bd. of Dirs. American Chamber of Commerce, Fed. Repub. of Germany; mem. Industry Cttee. Chamber of Industry and Commerce, Cologne; mem. Regional Council Deutsche Bank AG, Bd. of Dirs., Deutsche Automobil-Treuhand GmbH until 1973; Pres. and Chair. Man. Bd. Gildemeister AG, Bielefeld 1974-78; mem. Advisory Bd., Deutsche Bank AG, Düsseldorf, Supervisory Bd., Rank Xerox Austria; fmr. mem. Bd. of Dirs. Gildemeister Italiana S.p.A., Ponte S. Pietro, Gildemeister Maquinas Operatrizes S.A., Brazil. *Leisure interests:* swimming, walking, books on futurology, philosophy, psychology and history, playing the piano. *Address:* Herrenstrunder Strasse 2a, 5000 Cologne 80, Federal Republic of Germany.

BARTLETT, Boyd C., B.S.; American business executive; b. 21 Oct. 1925, Cameron, Wis.; s. of Roy M. Bartlett and Verna E. Boortz; m. Joyce M. Samborn 1946; two s. one d.; ed. Univ. of Wisconsin; joined Deere & Co. 1952, Vice-Pres. Farm Equipment and Consumer Products Marketing 1972-79, Sr. Vice-Pres. 1979-83, Exec. Vice-Pres. Operations 1983-85, Pres. and C.O.O. 1985-87; Dir. Quad City Devt. Group, Rock Island, Ill. 1979-85; mem. Farm and Industrial Equipment Inst., Farm Foundation. *Address:* c/o Deere & Co., John Deere Road, Moline, Ill. 61265, U.S.A.

BARTLETT, John Vernon, C.B.E., M.A., F.ENG., F.I.C.E., F.I.E.Aust., F.A.S.C.E.; British consulting engineer; b. 18 June 1927, London; s. of late Vernon F. Bartlett and of Olga (née Testrup) Bartlett; m. Gillian Hoffman 1951; four s.; ed. Stowe School and Trinity Coll., Cambridge; Engineer, John Mowlem & Co., Ltd. 1951-57; joined Mott Hay & Anderson 1957, Partner 1966, Chair. 1973-88; Chair. British Tunnelling Soc, 1977-79; Pres. Inst. of Civil Engs. 1982-83; Telford Gold Medals 1971, 1973; S. G. Brown Medal, Royal Soc. 1973. *Publications:* Tunnels: Planning, Design and Construction (with T. M. Megaw) 1981; various professional papers. *Leisure interests:* sailing, maritime history. *Address:* Mott Hay & Anderson, 20/26 Wellesley Road, Croydon, CR9 2UL (Office); 6 Cottenham Park Road, Wimbledon, London, SW20 0RZ, England (Home). *Telephone:* 01-686 5041 (Office); 01-946 9576 (Home).

BARTLETT, Neil, B.SC., PH.D., F.R.S.; British chemist; b. 15 Sept. 1932, Newcastle upon Tyne; s. of Norman and Ann Willins (née Vock) Bartlett; m. Christina Isabel Cross 1957; three s. one d.; ed. Heaton Grammar School, Newcastle upon Tyne, King's Coll., Durham Univ.; Sr. Chemistry Master, The Duke's School, Alnwick, Northumberland 1957-58; Faculty mem. Dept. of Chem., Univ. of B.C., Canada 1958-66; Prof. of Chem. Princeton Univ., N.J., U.S.A. 1966-69; Scientist, Bell Telephone Labs., Murray Hill, N.J. 1966-69; Prof. of Chem. and Prin. Investigator Lawrence Berkeley Lab., Univ. of Calif., Berkeley 1969-; Brotherton Visiting Prof., Chemistry Dept., Leeds Univ. 1981; Erskine, Visiting Fellow, Univ. of Canterbury, N.Z. 1983; Visiting Fellow, All Souls Coll., Oxford Univ. 1984; Assoc. of Inst. of Jozef Stefan, Yugoslavia; mem. Leopoldina Acad., Halle 1969; Corresp. mem. Göttingen Acad. 1977, Nat. Acad. of Sciences 1979; Research Corpn. Award 1965; Dannie Heineman Prize 1971; Robert A. Welch Award 1976, W. H. Nichols Medal, U.S.A. 1983, Moissan Fluorine Centennial Medal, Paris 1986, Prix Moissan 1988. *Publications:* The Chemistry of the Monatomic Gases (with F. O. Sladky, A. H. Cockett and K. C. Smith) 1973, Noble-Gas Compounds (with D. T. Hawkins and W. E. Falconer) 1978; more than 100 scientific papers including reports on the first preparation of the oxidised oxygen cation O_2^+ and the first true compound of a noble gas. *Leisure interests:* water-colour painting, antique silver. *Address:* Department of Chemistry, University of California, Berkeley, Calif. 94720; 6 Oak Drive, Orinda, Calif. 94563, U.S.A. (Home). *Telephone:* (415) 642-7259 (Office).

BARTLETT, Paul Doughty; American professor of chemistry; b. 14 Aug. 1907, Ann Arbor, Mich.; s. of George Miller and Mary L. (Doughty) Bartlett; m. Mary Lula Court 1931; one s. two d.; ed. Amherst Coll. and Harvard Univ.; Nat. Research Fellow, Rockefeller Inst. 1931-32; Instructor Univ. of Minnesota 1932-34, Harvard Univ. 1934-37; Asst. Prof. Harvard Univ. 1937-40, Assoc. Prof. 1940-46, Prof. 1946-48, Erving Prof. of Chem. 1948-75, Emer. 1975-; Robert A. Welch Research Prof., Texas Christian Univ. 1974-85, Emer. 1985-; guest lecturer at many American and European Univs.; exchange visitor Univ. of Leningrad 1961; Centenary Lecturer 1969, Ingold Lecturer, Chemical Soc., London 1974; Chair. Organic Division American Chemical Soc. 1948, North-eastern Section 1953-54; Pres. Organic Division Int. Union of Pure and Applied Chem. 1967-69; Chair U.S. Nat. Cttee. for Int. Union of Pure and Applied Chem. 1969; Program Chair. 23rd Int. Congress of Pure and Applied Chem. 1971; fmr. mem. editorial boards of The Journal of the American Chemical

Society, Journal of Organic Chemistry, Journal of Polymer Science and mem. editorial advisory board of Tetrahedron; Guggenheim and Fulbright Fellow 1957; mem. N.A.S., American Acad. of Arts and Sciences, Deutsche Akademie der Naturforscher Leopoldina, American Philosophical Soc.; Hon. Fellow, Royal Soc. of Chem. (London); Hon. mem. Swiss Chemical Soc. 1972-, Japan Chem. Soc. 1978-; Hon. Sc.D. (Amherst Coll. and Univ. of Chicago), Dr. h.c. (Paris, Munich and Montpellier); many awards including American Chem. Soc. Award in Pure Chem. 1938, August Wilhelm von Hofmann Medal of Gesellschaft Deutscher Chemiker 1962, Willard Gibbs Medal (American Chem. Soc.) 1963, Roger Adams Award (A.C.S.) 1963, President's Nat. Medal of Science 1968, James Flack Norris Award in Physical Organic Chem. (American Chem. Soc.) 1969, John Price Wetherill Medal (Franklin Inst.) 1970, Linus Pauling Medal 1976, Nichols Medal 1976, Alexander v. Humboldt Sr. Scientist Award (Freiburg Univ.) 1976, (Munich Univ.) 1977, Guggenheim Fellowship 1971-72, James Flack Norris Award in Teaching of Chemistry 1978, Wilfred T. Doherty Award 1980, Max Tishler Award (Harvard) 1981, Robert A. Welch Award 1981, S. W. Regional Award (American Chem. Soc.) 1984. *Publications:* Nonclassical Ions and about 250 research papers in chemical journals on reaction mechanisms. *Address:* Department of Chemistry, Harvard University, 12 Oxford Street, Cambridge, Mass. 02138, U.S.A. (Office).

BARTLETT DÍAZ, Manuel; Mexican politician; b. Feb. 1936, Puebla; ed. Nat. Univ. of Mexico, Univs. of Paris and Manchester; Adviser, Cen. Office of Credit, Ministry of Finance 1962-64; Asst. to Sec.-Gen., Nat. Fed. of Rural Workers 1963-64; Asst. Sec. PRI (Institutional Revolutionary Party) 1964-68; Prof. of Gen. Theory of the State, Nat. Univ. of Mexico 1968; various posts at Ministry of Interior 1969-76; Sec. Fed. Electoral Comm. 1970-76; Sec. Admin. Bd. Nat. Bank of Co-operative Devt. and Dir. of Political Affairs, Ministry of Foreign Affairs 1976-79; Adviser to Minister of Programming and Budget 1979; Sec.-Gen. Nat. Exec. Cttee. of PRI 1981; Minister of the Interior 1982-88, of Educ. 1988-. *Address:* Secretaria de Gobernacion, Bucareli No. 99, México, D.F., Mexico.

BARTON, Anne, PH.D.; professor of English; b. 9 May 1933; d. of Oscar Charles Rosen and Blanche Godfrey (née Williams) Barton; m. 1st William Harvey Righter 1957; 2nd John Bernard Adie Barton 1969; ed. Bryn Mawr Coll. and Cambridge Univ.; Lecturer History of Art, Ithaca Coll., N.Y. 1958-59; Rosalind Carlisle Research Fellow, Girton Coll. Cambridge 1960-62, Official Fellow in English 1962-72; Hildred Carlisle Prof. of English and Head Dept. of English, Bedford Coll., London 1972-74; Fellow and Tutor in English, New Coll., Oxford and Common Univ. Fund Lecturer 1974-84; Prof. of English, Cambridge Univ. 1984-; Fellow of Trinity Coll., Cambridge 1986-; mem. Editorial Bds. Shakespeare Survey 1972-, Shakespeare Quarterly 1981-, Studies in English Literature 1976-; Hon. Fellow, Shakespeare Inst., Univ. of Birmingham. *Publications:* Shakespeare and the Idea of the Play 1962; Ben Jonson, Dramatist 1984, numerous essays in journals. *Leisure interests:* opera, travel, fine-arts. *Address:* Trinity College, Cambridge, CB2 1TQ, England.

BARTON, Sir Derek Harold Richard, Kt., F.R.S., F.R.S.E.; British organic chemist; b. 8 Sept. 1918; s. of William Thomas and Maude Henrietta Barton; m. 1st Jeanne Kate Wilkins 1944, one s.; m. 2nd Christiane Cognet; ed. Tonbridge School and Imperial Coll., Univ. of London; Lecturer, Imperial Coll. 1945-59; Visiting Prof., Harvard Univ. 1949-50; Reader in Organic Chemistry, Birkbeck Coll., Univ. of London 1950-53, Prof. 1953-55; Regius Prof. of Chemistry, Glasgow Univ. 1955-57; Hoffman Prof. of Organic Chemistry, Imperial Coll. of Science and Technology, Univ. of London 1970-78 (Prof. 1957-70); Dir. Inst. de Chimie des Substances Naturelles, Gif-sur-Yvette 1978-1986; Distinguished Prof. Texas A and M Univ. 1986-; Pedler Lecturer, Chem. Soc. 1967; Hon. Fellow, Deutsche Akad. der Naturforscher Leopoldina 1967; Hon. D.Sc. (Univ. of Montpellier) 1962, (Univ. of Dublin) 1964, (St. Andrews, Colombia, New York) 1970, (Coimbra Univ.) 1971, (Oxford Univ., Manchester Univ.) 1972, (Univ. of South Africa) 1973; (City Univ.) 1974, (London) 1984; Hon. Dr. numerous other univs.; Nobel Prize for Chem. 1969; Foreign Assoc. U.S. Nat. Sciences 1970-; Royal Medal, Royal Soc. 1972; Copley Medal, Royal Soc. 1980; Officier Légion d'honneur; numerous other medals. *Address:* Department of Chemistry, Texas A and M University, College Station, Texas 77843, U.S.A.

BARTON, John Bernard Adie, C.B.E., M.A.; British drama director and adaptor; b. 26 Nov. 1928, London; s. of Sir Harold Montagu Barton and Lady Joyce Barton (née Wale); m. Anne Righter 1968; ed. Eton Coll. and King's Coll., Cambridge; Drama Lecturer, Univ. of Berkeley, Calif. 1953-54; Fellow, King's Coll. Cambridge 1954-59; Asst. Dir. (to Peter Hall) Royal Shakespeare Co. 1959; Assoc. Dir. 1964-. *Productions for R.S.C. include:* The Wars of the Roses (adapted, edited, co-directed) 1963, Love's Labour's Lost 1965, 1978, All's Well That Ends Well, Julius Caesar, Troilus and Cressida 1968-69, Twelfth Night, When Thou Art King 1969-70, Othello, Richard II, Henry V 1971, Richard II 1973, Dr. Faustus, King John (co-dir.), Cymbeline (co-dir.) 1974-75, Much Ado About Nothing, Troilus and Cressida, The Winter's Tale, King Lear, A Midsummer Night's Dream, Pillars of the Community 1976, The Way of the World 1978, The Merchant of Venice, Love's Labour's Lost 1978, The Greeks 1980, Hamlet 1980, Merchant of Venice, Two Gentlemen of Verona 1981, Titus Andronicus 1981, La Ronde 1982, Life's a Dream 1984, The Devils 1984, Waste

1985, Dream Play 1985, The Rover 1986, The Three Sisters 1988; also School for Scandal, Norway 1983, For Triumph Apollo 1983, The Vikings 1983. *Television productions:* Playing Shakespeare 1982, Mallory's Morte d'Arthur 1983. *Publications:* The Hollow Crown, The Wars of the Roses, The Greeks, La Ronde. *Address:* 14 De Walden Court, 85 New Cavendish Street, London, W.1, England. *Telephone:* 01-636 7031.

BARTON, William Hickson; Canadian diplomatist (retd.); b. 10 Dec. 1917, Winnipeg, Man.; s. of Ernest J. and Norah M. (née Hickson) Barton; m. Jeanie Robinson 1947; one s.; ed. Univ. of British Columbia; Canadian Army 1940-46; Sec. Defence Research Bd. of Canada 1946-52; joined Dept. of External Affairs, Ottawa 1952; Counsellor, Canadian Embassy, Vienna 1956; Minister, Canadian Mission at UN, New York 1961; Dir.-Gen. UN Bureau, Dept. of External Affairs 1964; Asst. Under-Sec. of State for External Affairs 1970; Amb. and Perm. Rep. to Office of UN, Geneva 1972-76, New York 1976-80; Special Adviser to Under-Sec. of State for External Affairs 1980; Chair. Canadian Inst. for Int. Peace and Security 1984-; mem. Refugee Status Advisory Cttee. 1981-88; Dir. Klöckner Stadler Hunter Ltd. 1980-; Hon. LL.D. (Mt. Allison) 1978. *Address:* 13 Kilbarry Crescent, Ottawa, Canada (Home).

BARTOSHEVICH, Gennadiy Georgievich; Soviet politician; b. 1934; ed. Byelorussian Polytechnical Inst.; Higher Party School of CPSU Cen. Cttee.; on cttee. for radio-information, Min. of Culture of Byelorussian SSR 1952-54; served in Soviet Army 1954-57; mem. CPSU 1957-; sec. of party cttee. of Minsk factory 1962-; party work 1967-; Second Sec. of Frunze, then Central Regional Cttees. of CP (Minsk), First Sec. of Molodechnensky State Comm. of the Party 1969-73; First Sec. of Frunze Regional Cttee. of Minsk 1974-77; Pres., First Sec. of Minsk City Exec. Cttee. 1977-83; Second Sec. of Cen. Cttee. of CP of Byelorussia 1983-87; mem. of CPSU Cen. Cttee. 1986-; Deputy of U.S.S.R. Supreme Soviet. *Address:* Central Committee of CP of Byelorussia, Minsk, U.S.S.R.

BARTOSIEWICZ, Zbigniew, M.ENG.; Polish politician; b. 24 Sept. 1932, Czestochowa; ed. Faculty of Mechanics, Gdánsk Technical Univ.; worked in machine-industry 1952-76; Chief of Production, motor-lorries works, Lublin 1960-67, Tech. Dir. 1967-69; Dir. gear-box factory, Tczew 1969-72; Gen. Dir. Zamech Machine Works, Elblag 1972-76; Under-Sec. of State, Ministry of Heavy and Agricultural Machines Industry 1976-79; Minister of Energetics and Atomic Energy 1979-81; mem. Polish United Workers' Party (PZPR) 1954-, Deputy mem. Cen. Cttee. 1980-81; Officer's Cross of Order Polonia Restituta and other decorations.

BARTUREN DUEÑAS; Peruvian politician and civil servant; b. 5 Nov. 1936, Lima; ed. Universidad Nacional Mayor de San Marcos; taught at Graduate Business Admin. School 1965-66, subsequently at Public Admin. School; specialist in preparation and evaluation of investment projects, Interamerican Devt. Bank 1972-73; Head, Planning Office, Nat. Fisheries Co. 1970-73; Deputy Finance Dir. Centromin Perú 1979-84; Minister of Agric. 1985-86. *Address:* Avenida Salaverry s/n, Edificio M. de Trabajo, Lima, Peru. *Telephone:* 324040.

BARWICK, Rt. Hon. Sir Garfield Edward John, P.C., G.C.M.G., A.K., B.A., LL.B.; Australian lawyer and politician; b. 22 June 1903, Sydney; s. of Jabez Edward Barwick and Lily Grace Barwick (née Ellicot); m. Norma Mountier Symons 1929; one s. one d.; ed. Fort St. Boys' High School Sydney, Sydney Univ.; admitted to N.S.W. Bar 1927, Victoria Bar 1945, Queensland Bar 1958; Pres. N.S.W. Bar Asscn. 1950-52, 1955-56, Law Council of Australia 1952-54; mem. Fed. House of Reps. for Parramatta 1958-64; Attorney-Gen. 1958-64; Acting Minister for External Affairs March-April, Aug.-Nov. 1959, April-June 1960, Minister for External Affairs 1961-64; Chief Justice of Australia 1964-81; Chancellor Macquarie Univ., Sydney, 1967-78; Pres. Australian Inst. of Int. Affairs 1972-83; Judge *ad hoc,* Int. Court of Justice 1973-74; Pres. Royal N.S.W. Inst. for Deaf and Blind Children 1976-; Leader, Australian Del. SEATO Council, Bangkok 1961, Paris 1963; UN Del. 1960, 1962-64; Australian Del. to ECAFE, Manila 1963; Australian Del. ANZUS, Canberra 1962, Wellington 1963; Hon. LL.D. (Sydney). *Leisure interests:* gardening, fishing, yachting. *Address:* 71 The Cotswolds, Curagul and Bobbin Head Roads, North Turramurra, N.S.W. 2074, Australia.

BARYŁA, Gen. Józef, H.H.D.; Polish army officer and politician; b. 21 Nov. 1924, Zawiercie, Katowice Voivodship; m.; one d.; ed. Officer's Artillery Coll. and Mil. Political Acad.; worker in glass works during German occupation; mem. Polish People's Army 1945-; took part in fighting against armed underground Orgs. 1945-47; mem. Polish Workers' Party 1946-48, Polish United Workers' Party (PZPR) 1948-; Man. posts in political apparatus of Polish Army, including Deputy Commdt. of Officer's Motor Coll. 1953-55, Second-in-Command of Artillery Div. 1955-60, Deputy Chief of Propaganda Bd. of Main Political Bd. of Polish Army 1960-67, Chief 1967-68; Deputy Commdr. of Pomeranian Mil. Dist. 1968-72; Maj.-Gen. 1970; First Deputy Chief of Main Political Bd. of Polish Army 1972-80, Chief 1980-86; Deputy Minister of Nat. Defence 1980-86; Lieut.-Gen. 1974, Gen. 1983; mem. Mil. Council of Nat. Salvation 1981-83; alt. mem. PZPR Cen. Cttee. 1975-80, 1982-85, mem. 1980-81, 1985-, Sec. 1985-88, mem. Political Bureau of PZPR Cent. Cttee. 1986-88; Chair. Editorial Council, Życie Partii 1986-; Deputy of Seym (Parl.) 1985-; Order of Builders of People's Poland, Commdr.'s Cross with Star, Commdr.'s Cross of Order of Polonia Restituta, Order of Banner of Labour (1st Class) and other decorations. *Address:* Komitet Centralny PZPR, ul. Nowy Świat 6, 00-497 Warsaw, Poland.

BARYSHNIKOV, Mikhail; fmrly. Soviet ballet dancer; b. 28 Jan. 1948, Riga, Latvia; s. of Nikolay and Aleksandra (née Kisselov) Baryshnikov; ed. Riga Ballet School and Kirov Ballet School, Leningrad; mem. Kirov Ballet Co. 1969-74; guest artist with many leading ballet cos. including American Ballet Theatre, Nat. Ballet of Canada, Royal Ballet, Hamburg Ballet, Fed. Repub. of Germany, Ballet Victoria, Australia, Stuttgart Ballet, Fed. Repub. of Germany, Alvin Ailey Co., U.S.A. 1974-; joined New York City Ballet Co. 1978, resigned 1979; Artistic Dir., American Ballet Theatre Sept. 1980-; Gold Medal, Varna Competition, Bulgaria 1966, First Int. Ballet Competition, Moscow, U.S.S.R. 1968; Nijinsky Prize, First Int. Ballet Competition, Paris Acad. de Danse 1968. *Ballets (world premières):* Vestris 1969, Medea 1975, Push Comes to Shove 1976, Hamlet Connotations 1976, Other Dances 1976, Pas de Duke 1976, La Dame De Pique 1978, L'Après-midi d'un Faune 1978, Santa Fe Saga 1978, Opus 19 1979, Rhapsody 1980. *Films:* The Turning Point 1977, White Nights 1985, Giselle 1987, Dancers 1987. *Choreography:* Nutcracker 1976, Don Quixote 1978, Cinderella 1984. *Publication:* Baryshnikov at Work 1977. *Address:* c/o American Ballet Theater, 890 Broadway, New York, N.Y. 10003, U.S.A.

BARZEL, Rainer, DR. IUR.; German civil servant and politician; b. 20 June 1924, Braunsberg, East Prussia; s. of Dr. Candidus Barzel and Maria née Skibowski; m. 1st Kriemhild Schumacher 1948 (died 1980); one d. (deceased); m. 2nd Helga Henselder 1982; ed. Gymnasium, Braunsberg (East Prussia), Berlin, and Univ. of Cologne; Air Force, Second World War; Civil Service, North Rhine-Westphalia, Ministry for Fed. Affairs 1949-56, resigned 1956; mem. Bundestag 1957-87, Pres. 1983-84; Fed. Minister for All-German Affairs 1962-63; mem. Christian Democrat Party (CDU), Deputy and Acting Chair. CDU/CSU Parl. Group in Bundestag 1963-64, Chair. 1964-73; Chair. CDU 1971-73, Chair. Econ. Affairs Cttee. of Bundestag 1977-79, resigned 1979, Chair. Foreign Affairs Cttee. 1980-82; Co-ordinator for French-German Affairs 1980, 1986-; Fed. Minister for Inter-German Affairs 1982-83; Pres. German-French Inst., Ludwigsburg 1980-83. *Publications:* Die geistigen Grundlagen der politischen Parteien 1947, Souveränität und Freiheit 1950, Die deutschen Parteien 1951, Gesichtspunkte eines Deutschen 1968, Es ist noch nicht zu spät 1976, Auf dem Drahtseil 1978, Das Formular 1979, Unterwegs—Woher und Wohin? 1982, Im Streit und umstritten 1986. *Leisure interests:* skating, curling, archaeology. *Address:* Görresstrasse Bundeshaus, 5300 Bonn 1, Federal Republic of Germany. *Telephone:* 0228-16-2109.

BARZUN, Jacques, PH.D.; American university professor and writer; b. 30 Nov. 1907, Créteil, France; s. of Henri Martin and Anna-Rose Barzun; m. 1st Mariana Lowell 1936 (died 1979); m. 2nd Marguerite Lee Davenport 1980; two s. one d.; ed. Lycée Janson de Sailly and Columbia Univ.; Instructor in History, Columbia Univ. 1929, Asst. Prof. 1938, Assoc. Prof. 1942, Prof. 1945-, Dean of Graduate Faculties 1955-58, Dean of Faculties and Provost 1958-67, Seth Low Prof. 1960, Univ. Prof. 1967-75; Prof. Emer. 1975-; Literary Adviser, Scribner's 1975-; mem. Acad. Delphinale (Grenoble), American Acad. and Inst. of Arts and Letters (Pres. 1972-75, 1977-78), American Historical Asscn., Royal Soc. of Arts, American Arbitration Assen.; fmr. Dir. Council for Basic Educ., New York Soc. Library, Open Court Publications Inc., Peabody Inst.; mem. Advisory Council, Univ. Coll. at Buckingham, Editorial Bd. Encyclopedia Britannica 1979-, American Philosophical Soc.; Chevalier de la Légion d'honneur; Extraordinary Fellow, Churchill Coll., Cambridge 1961. *Publications:* The French Race 1932, Race: A Study in Modern Superstition 1937, Of Human Freedom 1939, Darwin, Marx, Wagner 1941, Teacher in America 1945, Berlioz and the Romantic Century 1950, God's Country and Mine 1954, The Energies of Art 1956, Music in American Life 1956, The Modern Researcher 1957 (with H. Graff), The House of Intellect 1959, Classic, Romantic and Modern 1961, Science, the Glorious Entertainment 1964, The American University 1968, A Catalogue of Crime (with W. Taylor) 1971, On Writing, Editing and Publishing 1971, The Use and Abuse of Art 1974, Clio and the Doctors 1974, Simple and Direct 1975, Critical Questions 1982, A Stroll with William James 1983, A Word or Two Before You Go 1986; Ed. Pleasures of Music 1951, The Selected Letters of Lord Byron 1953, New Letters of Berlioz (and trans.) 1954, The Selected Writings of John Jay Chapman 1957, Modern American Usage (with others); Trans.: Diderot: Rameau's Nephew 1952, Flaubert's Dictionary of Accepted Ideas 1954, Evenings with the Orchestra 1956, Courteline: A Rule is a Rule 1960, Beaumarchais: The Marriage of Figaro 1961. *Address:* Charles Scribners, 115 Fifth Avenue, New York, N.Y. 10003, U.S.A. *Telephone:* (212) 614-1337.

BASALDELLA, Afro; Italian painter; b. 1912; ed. Acad. of Fine Arts, Venice; works under the name of Afro; represented in the most important museums of U.S.A. and Europe; executed design for Ritratto di Don Chisciotte Rome 1957; first prize Venice Biennale 1956, second prize Pittsburgh Int. 1959, UNESCO Award, Paris. *Address:* Via Nicolo Tartaglia 3, Rome, Italy.

BASANG; Chinese party official; b. 1938, Lang, Tibet; ed. Tibetan Minorities Inst. 1956; served as a slave to the Landlord of Chika 1947-56; joined the CCP 1959; Vice-Chair. Tibet Autonomous Region Revolutionary Cttee. 1968-79; Sec. Secr. CCP Cttee. Tibet 1971-77; Chair. Women's Fed.

of Tibet 1973; mem. 10th CCP Cen. Cttee. 1973; Chair. Langxian Co. Revolutionary Cttee. 1974; mem. Standing Cttee. 4th NPC 1975; 5th NPC 1978; Deputy Head Leading Group for Party Consolidation CCP Cttee. Tibet 1977-; mem. CCP 11th Cen. Cttee. 1977; Deputy for Tibet to 5th NPC 1978; mem. Pres. 1979; Vice-Chair. People's Govt. of Tibet 1979-83; mem. 12th CCP Cen. Cttee. 1982-86. *Address:* Chinese Communist Party Tibet Autonomous Region, Lhasa, People's Republic of China.

BASENDWAH, Mohamed Salem; Yemeni diplomatist; b. 18 Jan. 1935, Aden; m.; five c.; Minister of Labour, Social Welfare and Youth 1974, of State, and Political Adviser to the Pres. 1975, fmr. Minister of Devt. and Chair. Cen. Planning Org., of Information and Culture 1978-79; Adviser to the Pres. and Deputy Prime Minister 1979-; Perm. Rep. to UN 1985-. *Address:* Permanent Mission of the Yemen Arab Republic to the United Nations, 747 Third Avenue, 8th Floor, New York, N.Y. 10017, U.S.A. *Telephone:* 355-1730, 1731.

BASFORD, Hon. (Stanley) Ronald, P.C., B.A., LL.B., Q.C., Canadian politician; b. 22 April 1932, Winnipeg, Man.; s. of Douglas and Elizabeth Basford; m. Madeleine Kirk Nelson 1967; one s. one d.; ed. Univ. of British Columbia; practised in Vancouver law firm; mem. of Parl. for Vancouver 1963-79; observer to many Int. confs.; Co-Chair. Joint Commons-Senate Cttee. on Consumer Credit and Cost of Living 1967; Minister of Consumer and Corporate Affairs 1968, of Urban Affairs 1972, of Nat. Revenue 1974, of Justice and Attorney-General 1975-78 (retd.); Partner, Davis & Co., Barristers & Solicitors 1979-; Dir. ITT Industries of Canada Ltd., Gendis Inc., Alltrans Group of Canada Ltd. (fmrly), Vancouver Public Aquarium Assen., North East Coal Devt. Project 1981-84; Dir. and mem. of Exec. Cttee. of Canadian Imperial Bank of Commerce; Liberal. *Leisure interest:* fishing. *Address:* 2800 Park Place, 666 Burrard Street, Vancouver, B.C. V6C 2Z7 (Office); 1870 West 43rd Avenue, Vancouver, B.C. V6M 2C5, Canada (Home).

BASHILOV, Sergei Vasilievich; Soviet politician and engineer; b. 1923; railway construction engineer, then site chief, then sector head, then chief engineer and admin. of trust, Tyumen Region; headed org. of U.S.S.R. Ministry of Heavy Construction; worked as Head of Dept. of Bldg. and Bldg. Industry of U.S.S.R. Gosplan 1979; mem. CPSU 1947-; Minister for Bldg. in Areas of the Far East and Trans-Baikal 1979, then Minister for the Construction of Heavy Industry Enterprises 1986-; fmr. Chair. of U.S.S.R. State Cttee. for Construction; cand. mem. Cen. Cttee. of CPSU 1981-, mem. 1986-. *Address:* The Kremlin, Moscow, U.S.S.R.

BASINSKI, Zbigniew Stanislaw, O.C., D.PHIL., D.SC., F.R.S.(C), F.R.S.; Canadian scientist; b. 28 April 1928, Wolkowysk, Poland; s. of Antoni and Maria Zofia Anna (née Hilferding) Basinski; m. Sylvia Joy Pugh 1952; two s.; ed. Lyceum of Krzemieniec, Poland, Univ. of Oxford; Research Asst., Univ. of Oxford 1951-54; staff mem. Dept. of Mechanical Eng. (Cryogenic Lab.), Massachusetts Inst. of Tech. 1954-56; Prin. Research Officer, Head of Materials Physics, Div. of Physics, Nat. Research Council of Canada 1956-87; Research Prof. Inst. for Materials Research, Dept. of Materials Science and Eng., McMaster Univ., Hamilton 1987-; Ford Distinguished Visiting Prof., Carnegie Inst. of Tech., Pittsburgh, Penn. 1964-65; Commonwealth Visiting Prof., Univ. of Oxford (Fellow of Wolfson Coll.) 1969-70; Overseas Fellow, Churchill Coll., Cambridge 1980-81. *Publications:* numerous research papers, mainly on crystal defects and mechanical properties of metals. *Address:* Institute for Materials Research, 1280 Main Street West, Hamilton, Ont. L8S 4M1, Canada (Office); 98 Bluebell Crescent, Ancaster, Ont. L9K 1G1, Canada (Home). *Telephone:* (416) 525-9140 Ext. 3498 (Office); (416) 648-5435 (Home).

BASIR, Ismail; Malaysian banker; b. 1927, Taiping, Perak State; ed. Serdang Agricultural Coll. and Durham Univ.; Lecturer, Universiti Pertanian Malaysia; Asst. Agricultural Officer Serdang Agricultural Coll.; Dir. Agric. Dept., Dir.-Gen. Agric., later Exec. Dir. Johore State Devt. Corpn.; Chair. Nat. Padi and Rice Authority 1981-, Food Industries Malaysia 1981-; Exec. Chair. Bank Bumiputra Malaysia Bhd. Jan. 1985-; Head BMF, Kewangan Bumiputra, Bumiputra Merchant Bankers Jan. 1985-; Dir. Bank Negara 1981-, and of several other cos. *Address:* Bank Bumiputra Malaysia Berhad, Menara Bumiputra, Jalan Melaka, Kuala Lumpur 01-18, Malaysia. *Telephone:* (03) 988011.

BASKAKOV, Vladimir Yvtikhianovich, PH.D.; Soviet academician; b. 20 July 1921; ed. Leningrad Univ.; mem. CPSU 1945-; started publishing 1952; First Deputy Chair. of U.S.S.R. Goskino 1962-74; teacher at All-Union Inst. of Cinema (VGIK) 1964-; Prof. 1981; Dir. of All-Union Inst. of Film Studies (V.N.I.I.) 1974-; Sec. of Admin. of U.S.S.R. Union of Cinema Artists 1981-. *Publications include:* Screen and Time 1974, The Contradictory Screen 1980, The Rhythm of Time: Cinema Today 1983, The Militant Screen 1984. *Address:* c/o Vsesoyuzny Institut Kinomatografii, Moscow, U.S.S.R.

BASOLO, Fred, PH.D.; American professor of chemistry; b. 11 Feb. 1920, Coello, Ill.; s. of John and Catherine Basolo; m. Mary P. Basolo 1947; one s. three d.; ed. Southern Illinois Normal Univ. and Univ. of Illinois; Research Chemist, Rohm & Haas Chemical Co. 1943-46; Instructor, subsequently Asst. Prof., Assoc. Prof. and Prof. of Chem., Northwestern Univ. 1946-, Chair. of Chem. Dept. 1969-72, Morrison Prof. of Chem. 1980-; NATO Distinguished Prof., Tech. Univ. of Munich 1969; NATO Sr. Scientist Fellow, Italy 1981; mem. Editorial Bd. Inorganica Chemica Acta 1967–, Inorganica Chemica Acta Letters 1977– and other publs.; Hon. D.Sc. (Southern Ill.) 1984; Hon. Prof. Lanzhou Univ., China 1985; Fellow A.A.A.S. (Chair. Chem. Section 1979); mem. American Chemical Soc. (mem. Bd. of Dirs. 1982–84, Pres. 1983), N.A.S., Chemical Soc. (London); Hon. mem. Italian Chemical Soc.; Foreign mem. Accademia Naz. dei Lincei, Italy; Guggenheim Fellow, Copenhagen 1954–55; Sr. Nat. Research Foundation Fellow, Rome 1962–63; American Chemical Soc. Award for Research in Inorganic Chem. 1964, Award for Distinguished Service in Inorganic Chem. 1975; Dwyer Medal Award 1976. *Publications:* Mechanisms of Inorganic Reactions (with R. G. Pearson), Co-ordination Chemistry (with R. C. Johnson—several edns. in trans.); more than 300 scientific publs. *Address:* Department of Chemistry, Northwestern University, Evanston, Ill. 60201, U.S.A.

BASOV, Aleksandr Vasiliyevich, M.SC.; Soviet politician and diplomatist; b. 20 March 1912, Stanitsa Baklanovskaya, Tsimlaynsk district, Rostov region; ed. Vologda Agricultural Inst.; Veterinary Inst. 1930–42; teacher 1942–54; Sec. Rostov Regional Cttee., CPSU 1954–55; Chair. Rostov District Exec. Cttee. 1955–60; First Sec. Rostov District Cttee., CPSU 1960–62; mem. Cen. Cttee, CPSU 1961–76; Counsellor, Cuba 1962–65; Minister of Agriculture of R.S.F.S.R. 1965; Amb. to Romania 1965–71, to Chile 1971–73, to Australia and Fiji 1974–79; Order of Lenin (twice). *Address:* c/o Ministry of Foreign Affairs, Moscow, U.S.S.R.

BASOV, Nikolai Gennadiievich; Soviet physicist; b. 14 Dec. 1922, Voronezh; s. of Prof. Gennadiy Fedorovich Basov and Zinaida Andreievna Molchanova; m. Kseniya Tikhonovna Nazarova 1950; two s.; ed. Moscow Inst. of Physical Engineers; P. N. Lebedev Physical Inst. 1950–; Vice-Dir. 1958–73, Dir. 1973–; founded Laboratory of Quantum Radio-physics 1963–; Prof. Moscow Inst. of Physical Engs. 1963–; Deputy of U.S.S.R. Supreme Soviet 1974–, mem. Presidium 1982; mem. CPSU 1951–; Corresp. mem. U.S.S.R. Acad. of Sciences 1962–66, Academician 1966–, mem. Presidium 1967–; fellow Optical Soc. of America, Indian Nat. Acad. of Sciences, mem. Akad. der Wissenschaften der DDR, Berlin, Deutsche Akad. der Naturforscher Leopoldina, Bulgarian Acad. of Sciences, Polish Acad. of Sciences, Czechoslovak Acad. of Sciences, Royal Swedish Acad. of Eng. Sciences, Prague Polytechnic Inst., Polish Military-Tech. Acad., Jena Univ., Pavia Univ., Italy, Madrid Polytechnic Univ.; Vice-Chair. Exec. Council of World Fed. of Scientific Workers 1976–83, Vice-Pres. of World Fed. of Research Workers 1983–, Chair. of Bd., All-Union Soc. Znanie, U.S.S.R. 1978; Ed. Priroda (Nature) popular science magazine 1967–, Soviet Journal of Quantum Electronics; Hon. Dr. (Prague Polytechnic Inst.); Lenin Prize 1959, Nobel Prize for Physics 1964, Order of Lenin 1967, 1969, 1972, 1975, 1982, Hero of Socialist Labour 1969, 1982, Gold Medal of Czechoslovak Acad. of Sciences 1975, A. Volta Gold Medal 1977; E. Henkel Gold Medal (G.D.R.) 1986, Order of Kirill and Methodii (Bulgaria) 1981, Commdr.'s Cross Order of Merit (Poland) 1986, Kalinga Prize, UNESCO 1986, Gold Medal Slovak Acad. of Sciences 1988. *Leisure interests:* photography, skiing. *Address:* P. N. Lebedev Physical Institute of the Academy of Sciences, 53 Leninsky Prospect, Moscow, U.S.S.R. (Office).

BASOV, Vladimir Pavlovich; Soviet actor and film director; b. 1923; ed. Directors' School of Moscow All-Union Inst. of Cinema (under guidance of Yutkevich and Romm) 1952; mem. CPSU 1948–; worked with Mosfilm studios 1953–; People's Artist of U.S.S.R. 1983. *Films include:* The Fall of the Emirate, Battle on the Road, Silence, The Shield and Sword, Dangerous Turn (after J. B. Priestley), Facts of Yesterday (R.S.F.S.R. State Prize 1982). *Principal roles include:* Poloter in Strolling Round Moscow, Luzhin in Crime and Punishment, the Landowner in Flight, and many others.

BASSANI, Giorgio; Italian writer; b. 1916; ed. Univ. of Bologna; Chief Ed. Botteghe Oscure 1948–60, Dir. of Literary Series with Feltrinelli including Il Gattopardo, G. di Lampedusa 1957–63; Teacher History of Theatre, Acad. d'Arte Drammatica 1957–68; Vice-Pres. Radio Televisione Italiana 1964–65; mem. Italia Nostra 1955– (Pres. 1966–); Strega Prize 1956, Viareggio Prize 1962, Campiello Prize 1969, Nelly Sachs Prize 1969. *Publications:* Cinque storie ferraresi 1956, Gli occhiali d'oro (novel) 1958, Il giardino dei Finzi-Contini (novel) 1962, L'alba ai vetri (poems) 1963, Dietro la porta (novel) 1964, Le parole preparate (essays) 1966, L'airone (novel) 1968, Heron 1970, Epitaffio (poems) 1974. *Address:* Via G. B. De Rossi 33, Rome, Italy.

BASSANI, Giuseppe Franco, DR.SC.; Italian professor of physics; b. 29 Oct. 1929, Milan; s. of Luigi Bassani and Claretta Riccadonna; m. Serenella Figini 1959; one s. one d.; ed. Univs. of Pavia and Illinois; research physicist, Argonne Nat. Lab. 1960–65; Prof. of Physics, Univ. of Pisa 1965–70, Univ. of Rome 1970–80, Scuola Normale Superiore, Pisa 1980–; corresp. mem. Accad. dei Lincei; Dr.h.c. (Toulouse), (Lausanne) 1986. *Publications:* Electronic States and Optical Transitions in Solids (co-author) 1975 and articles in professional journals. *Leisure interest:* history. *Address:* Scuola Normale Superiore, Pisa 56100, Italy. *Telephone:* 050-597111 (Office); 050-26073 (Home).

BASSET, Michail Edward Rainton, PH.D., M.P.; New Zealand politician; b. 1938, Auckland; m.; two c.; ed. Owairaka, Dilworth and Mount Albert Grammar Schools, Auckland Univ.; Sr. Lecturer in History, Auckland

Univ., Sr. Tutor 1977; mem. Auckland City Council 1971; M.P. for Waitemata 1972–75; for Te Atatu 1978–; Minister of Health and of Local Govt. 1984–87, of Internal Affairs, of Local Govt., of Civil Defence, of Arts and Culture Aug. 1987–; mem. Parl. Select Cttee. on local Bills and on the Library; Labour. *Leisure interests:* table tennis, boating and fishing. *Address:* House of Representatives, Wellington, New Zealand.

BASSOLE, Bazomboué Léandre, M.A.; Burkina Faso diplomatist; b. 21 Sept. 1946, Koudougou; m.; two s. one d.; ed. Higher Educ. Centre, Ouagadougou, Univ. of Bordeaux and Int. Inst. for Public Admin., Paris; Counsellor State Protocol Dept., Legal Affairs and Claims Dept. and Int. Co-operation Dept. of Ministry of Foreign Affairs 1975–76, Dir. for Admin. and Consular Affairs 1976–77; Second Counsellor, later First Counsellor, Upper Volta Embassy, Paris 1977–81; First Counsellor, Perm. Mission of Upper Volta to the UN 1981–82, Chargé d'affaires 1982–83, Perm. Rep. of Upper Volta (now Burkina Faso) to the UN 1983–86. *Address:* c/o Ministry of Foreign Affairs, Ouagadougou, Burkina Faso.

BASTID, Suzanne; French lawyer; b. 15 Aug. 1906, Rennes; d. of Jules Basdevant and Renée Mallarmé; m. 1937; three d.; ed. Lycée de Grenoble, Lycée de Fénelon, Paris, and Faculty of Law, Univ. de Paris; Prof., Faculty of Law, Lyon 1933–46, Paris 1946–77; Prof. Inst. d'Etudes Politiques, Univ. de Paris 1946–78; Pres. Admin. Tribunal, UN 1952–68, Vice-Pres. 1969–79, 1981–82, Pres. 1979–81; Sec.-Gen. Inst. of Law 1963–69, First Vice-Pres. 1969–71; Pres. Soc. Française pour le Droit International; mem. French Del. to UN Gen. Assembly (4th to 13th Sessions); mem. French Del. 20th and 22nd UNESCO Conf.; mem. Acad. des Sciences Morales et Politiques, Pres. 1982; mem. Conseil de l'ordre de la Légion d'honneur 1983–; Commdr. Légion d'honneur, Commdr. Royal Order of Sahametri (Cambodia). *Publications include:* Les fonctionnaires internationaux, Jurisprudence de la Cour internationale de justice, Les tribunaux administratifs internationaux et leur jurisprudence, Les questions territoriales devant la C.I.J., Les traités dans la vie internationale; Ed. Annuaire français de droit international 1955–. *Leisure interest:* gardening. *Address:* 88 rue de Grenelle, 75007 Paris, France; 71550 Anost, France (Home). *Telephone:* 45-48 63 34; 85-827165.

BASTIDE, François-Régis; French author and diplomatist; b. 1 July 1926, Biarritz; s. of Edouard Bastide and Suzanne Canton; m. 1st Monica Sjöholm (divorced), one s. one d.; m. 2nd J. Huguenin 1966, one d.; ed. Coll. Saint-Louis-de-Gonzague and Lycée de Bayonne; Information Officer, Mil. Govt. of Sarre 1945; Sec.-Gen. Centre Culturel de Royaumont 1947; Maison Descartes, Amsterdam 1950; Literary Adviser, Editions du Seuil 1953–; Producer of literary and drama programmes, ORTF 1949–; mem. reading panel, Comédie Française 1968–75; Municipal Councillor, Biarritz 1978; Nat. Del. of Párti Socialiste 1978; del. to many confs., advisory appts. etc.; Amb. to Denmark 1982–85, to Austria 1985–88; Amb. and Perm. Del. of France at Unesco 1989–; Prix de Régnier (Acad. Française) 1981; Officier, Légion d'honneur, Ordre Nat. du Mérite; Commdr. des Arts et des Lettres; Grand Cross, Order of Dannebrog. *Publications:* Lettre de Bavière, La Troisième Personne, La Jeune Fille et la Mort, Saint-Simon par lui-même (Grand Prix de la Critique) 1953, Suède, les Adieux (Prix Fémina) 1956, Flora d'Amsterdam 1957, La Vie rêvée 1962, Le Troisième Concerto (Grand Prix de la Télévision) 1963, Zodiaque 1963, La Palmeraie 1967, La Forêt noire 1968, Au théâtre, certains soirs 1973, La Fantaisie du voyageur 1976, Siegfried 78 1978, L'Enchanteur et nous 1981; adaptation and animation for television. *Address:* Permanent Delegation of France, 1 rue Miollis, 75015 Paris, France.

BASU, Jyoti, B.A.; Indian politician and lawyer; b. 1914; ed. Loreto Day School, St. Xavier's School, St. Xavier's Coll.; went to England, called to Middle Temple Bar; during stay in England actively associated with India League and Fed. of Indian Students in England, Sec. of London Majlis, and came in contact with CP of Great Britain; returned to Calcutta 1940; a leader of fmr. Eastern Bengal Railroad Workers' Union; elected to Bengal Legis. Council 1946; after Partition remained a mem. of W. Bengal Legis. Ass.; arrested for membership of CP after party was banned 1948, but released on orders of High Court; became Chair. Editorial Bd. Swadhinata; mem. W. Bengal Legis. Ass. 1952–72; fmr. Sec. Prov. Cttee. of CP, mem. Nat. Council, Cen. Exec. Cttee. and Nat. Secr. until CP split 1963; subsequently mem. Politbureau, CP of India (Marxist); imprisoned 1948, 1949, 1953, 1955, 1963, 1965; Deputy Chief Minister and Minister in Charge of Finance in first United Front Govt. 1967, Deputy Chief Minister in second United Front Govt.; M.P. for Satgachia 1977; subsequently Leader of Left Front Legislature Party; Chief Minister of W. Bengal 1982–. *Address:* Raj Bhavan, Calcutta, W. Bengal, India.

BATA, Thomas John, C.C.; Canadian shoe executive; b. 17 Sept. 1914, Prague, Czechoslovakia; s. of the late Thomas Bata and Marie Bata; m. Sonja Ingrid Wettstein; one s. three d.; ed. privately and Acad. of Commerce, Uherske Hradiste; Chair. Bata Ltd.; Chair. of Bata Shoe Co. of Canada Ltd. 1939–, British Bata Shoe Co. Ltd. 1946–, Bata Industries Ltd. Dir. and officer of several cos. connected with Bata Group; fmr. Dir. Toronto and Canadian Pacific Airlines; fmr. Dir. and mem. Exec. Cttee., IBM World Trade Corpn., U.S.A., IBM Canada Ltd.; Dir. American Management Asscn. 1958–61, Canadian Council Int. Chamber of Commerce, mem. Exec. Cttee., ICC, Canadian Exec. Service Overseas; Chair. Comm. on Multinational Enterprises; Chair. Cttee. on Devt. of the Business and Industry Advisory Cttee., OECD; mem. Bd. of Govs. Canadian Export Asscn., Toronto Arts Foundation, Stratford Shakespearean Festival Foundation; Founding mem. and mem. Planning Council, The President's Professional Asscn. (U.S.A.) 1961; Fellow, Int. Acad. of Man.; Dir. French Chamber of Commerce, Canada; Hon. Gov. Trent Univ.; Founder and fmr. Dir. Young President's Asscn.; mem. Chief Execs. Forum, Canadian Inst. of Int. Affairs; Special Adviser, UN Cttee. on Transnat. Corpns.; Bd. of Dirs. Nat. Ballet Guild of Canada; Chair. Bd. of Govs., Trent Univ. *Leisure interests:* tennis, scuba diving. *Address:* 59 Wynford Drive, Don Mills, Ont. M3C 1K3 (Office); 44 Park Lane Circle, Don Mills, Ont. M3C 2N2, Canada.

BATALIN, Yuriy Petrovich; Soviet politician; b. 28 July 1927; ed. Ural Polytech. Inst., Sverdlovsk; foreman of trust, Bashkir A.S.S.R. 1950-52; construction engineer on coal, energy and petrol plants in Bashkir A.S.S.R. 1952-57; chief engineer of various trusts 1957-70; mem. CPSU 1956-; chief engineer and deputy head of admin. for construction of petroleum and gas enterprises in Tyumen 1965-70; U.S.S.R. Deputy Minister for Gas Industry 1970-72, for Construction of Petroleum and Gas Enterprises 1972-73; U.S.S.R. First Deputy Minister for Construction of Petroleum and Gas Enterprises 1973-83; Chair., U.S.S.R. State Cttee. for Labour and Social Problems; mem. U.S.S.R. Council of Ministers 1983-85; Deputy to Council of Nationalities, U.S.S.R. Supreme Soviet 1984-; Deputy Chair., U.S.S.R. Council of Ministers 1985-; mem. Presidium of U.S.S.R. Council of Ministers 1985-, Cen. Cttee. of CPSU 1986-; Pres. of U.S.S.R. State Comm. on Construction 1986-; Order of Lenin 1973, Order of Red Banner 1977, Lenin Prize 1980. *Address:* Council of Ministers, The Kremlin, Moscow, U.S.S.R.

BATALOV, Aleksey Vladimirovich; Soviet film actor and director; b. 1928, Vladimir; ed. Moscow Arts Theatre Studio; actor with Cen. Theatre of Soviet Army 1950-53; with Moscow Art Academic Theatre 1953-56; film début 1954; Order of Lenin, People's Artist of R.S.F.S.R. 1969. *Roles include:* Aleksei Zhurbin in A Large Family 1954, Sasha in The Rumyantsev Case 1956, Boris in The Cranes Are Flying 1957, Gusev in Nine Days in One Year 1962, Pavel Vlasov in Mother 1964, Gurov in The Lady with the Lap-dog 1965; Directed The Overcoat 1960, The Three Fat Men 1966.

BATBEDAT, Jean, LL.B.; French diplomatist; b. 15 Feb. 1926, Paris; s. of Bernard Batbedat and Jeanne (née Laborde) Batbedat; m. Suzanne Magnier 1956; one s. one d.; ed. Paris Univ., Nat. School of Oriental Languages, Paris; Vice-Consul, French Consulate Gen., Calcutta 1953-55; First Sec. French Embassy, New Delhi 1959-61; Inst. des Hautes Etudes de Défense Nat., Paris 1962; Counsellor, French Embassy, Tunis 1962-66, Moscow 1966-69; Jt. Dir., Direction du Personnel 1974; Jt. Dir.-Gen., Dir.-Gen. des Relations Culturelles 1981; French Amb. to Ireland, Dublin 1982-85, Dir. Diplomatic Archives and Documentation, Ministry of Foreign Affairs, Paris 1985-; Officier, Ordre de la Légion d'Honneur; Officier, Ordre Nat. du Mérite. *Publications:* La Petite Marche du Telengana 1968, Le Dieu Assassiné 1974, Roman de la Begum Sombre 1980, etc. *Address:* 15 Rue des Beaux Arts, 75006 Paris, France.

BATCHELOR, George Keith, PH.D., F.R.S.; British professor of applied mathematics; b. 8 March 1920, Melbourne, Australia; s. of George C. Batchelor and Ivy C. Berneye; m. Wilma M. Rätz 1944; three d.; ed. Essendon High School, Melbourne Boys' High School, Univs. of Melbourne and Cambridge; Research Officer, Div. of Aeronautics, Commonwealth Council for Scientific and Industrial Research, Melbourne 1941-44; Fellow, Trinity Coll., Cambridge 1947-; ed. Journal of Fluid Mechanics 1956-; Lecturer, Univ. of Cambridge 1948-59, Reader in Fluid Dynamics 1959-64, Head, Dept. of Applied Mathematics and Theoretical Physics 1959-83, Prof. of Applied Math. 1964-83, Prof. Emer. 1983-; Chair. European Mechanics Cttee. 1964-87, U.K. Nat. Cttee. for Theoretical and Applied Mechanics 1967-73; mem. Royal Soc. of Sciences of Uppsala, Sweden; Foreign mem. Polish Acad. of Sciences, American Acad. of Arts and Sciences, Foreign assoc. French Acad. of Sciences; Hon. D.Sc. (Grenoble) 1959, (Tech. Univ. of Denmark) 1974, (McGill Univ., Montreal) 1986, Adams Prize, Cambridge Univ. 1951, Agostinelli Prize, Accademia dei Lincei 1986, Royal Medal, Royal Soc. 1988, Timoshenko Medal, A.S.M.E. 1988. *Publications:* The Theory of Homogenous Turbulence 1953, An Introduction to Fluid Dynamics 1967. *Address:* Department of Applied Mathematics and Theoretical Physics, University of Cambridge, Cambridge (Office); Cobbers, Conduit Head Road, Cambridge, England (Home). *Telephone:* 0223-337915 (Office); 0223-356387 (Home).

BATEMAN, Leslie Clifford, C.M.G., D.SC., PH.D., F.R.S.; British scientist; b. 21 March 1915, Yiewsley; s. of Charles Samuel Bateman and Florence Skinner; m. 1st Marie Pakes 1945 (died 1967); two s.; m. 2nd Eileen Jones 1973, one step-s. one step-d.; ed. Univ. Coll., London, and Oriel Coll., Oxford; Chemist, Natural Rubber Producers' Research Asscn., England 1941-53, Dir. of Research 1953-62; Controller of Rubber Research, Malaysia 1962-74; Special Adviser, Malaysian Rubber Research and Devt. Bd. 1974-75; Sec.-Gen. Int. Rubber Study Group 1976-83; Jubilee Foundation Lecturer 1971, Inst. of the Rubber Industry; Hon. D.Sc. (Malaya) 1968, (Aston) 1972; Fellow, Univ. Coll., London 1974; Colwyn Medal 1962, Panglima Setia Makhota, Malaysia 1974. *Publications:* Ed. and contributor to The Chemistry and Physics of Rubber-like Substances 1963; numerous publs. in Journal of Chemical Society, etc. and on the techno-economic

position of the natural rubber industry. *Leisure interests:* outdoor activities, particularly cricket and golf.

BATEMAN, Sir Ralph (Melton), K.B.E., M.A., F.C.I.S.; British business executive; b. 15 May 1910, Rochdale, Lancs.; s. of the late Dr. and Mrs. W. H. Bateman; m. Barbara Yvonne Litton 1935; two s. two d.; ed. Epsom Coll. and Univ. Coll., Oxford; Turner and Newall Ltd. 1931-, Dir. 1957-, Deputy Chair. and Joint Man. Dir. 1959-67, Chair. 1967-76; Pres. of Confed. of British Industry 1974-76; Chair. Stothert and Pitt 1977-85; Deputy Chair. Furness, Withy and Co. to 1984, Rea Brothers to 1985; mem. Nat. Econ. Devt. Council 1973-76; Companion British Inst. of Man.; Fellow, Chartered Inst. of Secs., Royal Soc. of Arts; mem. Court, Manchester Univ., Univ. of Salford; fmr. Chair. (currently Vice-Pres.) Bd. of Govs., Ashridge Coll. of Management; Hon. D.Sc. (Univ. of Salford) 1969, (Univ. of Buckingham) 1983. *Leisure interests:* family and social affairs. *Address:* 2 Bollin Court, Macclesfield Road, Wilmslow, Cheshire, SK9 2AP, England (Home). *Telephone:* (0625) 530437 (Home).

BATEMAN, Robert McLellan, B.A., LL.D., O.C.; Canadian artist; b. 24 May 1930, Toronto; s. of Joseph W. and Anne McLellan Bateman; m. 1st Suzanne Bowermann 1960; m. 2nd Birgit Freybe 1975; four s. one d.; ed. Forest Hill Collegiate, Toronto and Univ. of Toronto; high school art teacher for 20 years; began full-time painting 1976, numerous museum exhbns. between 1959 and 1988; mem. Niagara Escarpment Comm. 1970-85; Master Artist, Leigh Yawkey Woodson Museum 1982; Hon. life mem. Fed. of Canadian Artists, Canadian Wildlife Fed., Audubon Soc., World Wildlife Fund Int. etc.; several hon. degrees; Queen Elizabeth II Jubilee Medal 1977, Officer Order of Canada 1983, Medal of Honour, World Wildlife Fund 1985. *Publications:* The Art of Robert Bateman 1981, The World of Robert Bateman 1985. *Leisure interests:* hiking, snorkelling, cross-country skiing, guitar, birdwatching. *Address:* Box 115, Fulford Harbour, B.C. V0S 1C0, Canada.

BATENBURG, Andries, DR. ECON.; Netherlands banker; b. 11 Oct. 1922, Rotterdam; s. of A. Batenburg and C. C. Keller; m. Margaretha Hartman 1949; two d.; ed. Netherlands Econ. Univ.; joined Nederlandsche Handel-Maatschappij N.V. 1948; Man. Dir. Algemene Bank Nederland N.V. 1966, mem. Presidium 1970, Chair. Managing Bd. 1974-84; Chair. VMF Stork (Netherlands) May 1985-. *Publications:* Enkele Hoofdlijnen van de Monetaire Politiek (Some Principal Aspects of Monetary Policy). *Address:* c/o VMF Stork, Amsterdam, Netherlands (Office).

BATES, Alan; British actor; b. 17 Feb. 1934, Allestree, Derbys.; s. of Harold A. Bates and Florence M. Wheatcroft; m. Victoria Ward 1970; twin s.; ed. Belper Grammar School and Royal Acad. of Dramatic Art (RADA); spent one year with Midland Repertory Co., Coventry; *subsequent stage appearances in London include roles in* The Mulberry Bush, Look Back in Anger (also in Moscow and New York), The Country Wife, In Celebration, Long Day's Journey into Night (also at Edinburgh Festival), The Caretaker (also in New York), The Four Seasons, Hamlet (also in Nottingham), Butley (also in New York, Los Angeles and San Francisco), Life Class, Otherwise Engaged 1975-76, The Seagull 1976, Stage Struck; has also appeared at Canadian Shakespeare Festival, Stratford, Ont. in title role of Richard III and as Ford in The Merry Wives of Windsor; also in Poor Richard (New York), Venice Preserved (Bristol), The Taming of the Shrew (Stratford-upon-Avon), A Patriot for Me (London and Chichester) 1983, Dance of Death 1985, Yonadab 1985, Melon 1987, Ivanov 1989. *Films:* The Entertainer 1960, Whistle Down the Wind 1961, A Kind of Loving 1962, The Running Man 1962, The Caretaker 1963, Nothing but the Best 1964, Zorba the Greek 1965, Georgy Girl 1965, King of Hearts 1966, Far from the Madding Crowd 1966, The Fixer 1967, Women in Love 1968, The Three Sisters 1969, The Go-Between 1971, A Day in the Death of Joe Egg 1972, Butley 1973, The Impossible Object 1973, In Celebration 1974, Royal Flash 1974, An Unmarried Woman 1977, The Shout 1977, The Rose 1978, Nijinsky 1979, The Trespasser 1980, Quartet 1981, The Return of the Soldier 1982, The Wicked Lady 1982, Duet for One 1987, Prayer for the Dying 1987, The Lair of the White Worm. *T.V.:* Two Sundays, Plaintiff and Dependant, The Collection, The Mayor of Casterbridge, Very Like a Whale, A Voyage Round my Father 1982, An Englishman Abroad 1983, Dr. Fischer of Geneva or the Bomb Party 1984, Pack of Lies 1988; received Tony Award for Butley, Broadway, New York 1973, Variety Club Award for Otherwise Engaged 1975, An Englishman Abroad, Separate Tables 1983. *Leisure interests:* squash, swimming, tennis, driving, travelling, reading. *Address:* c/o Michael Linnit, Chatto & Linnit Ltd., Globe Theatre, Shaftesbury Avenue, London, W.1, England.

BATES, Sir David Robert, Kt., D.SC., F.R.S.; British physicist; b. 18 Nov. 1916, Omagh, N. Ireland; s. of late Walter V. Bates and Mary O. Bates (née Shera); m. Barbara B. Morris 1956; one s. one d.; ed. Royal Belfast Academical Inst., Queen's Univ., Belfast and Univ. Coll., London; Admiralty Research Lab. Teddington 1939-41; Mine Design Dept. H.M.S. Vernon 1941-45; Lecturer in Math., Univ. Coll., London 1945-50; Consultant, US Naval Ordnance Test Station, Inyttern, Calif. 1950; Reader in Physics, Univ. Coll., London 1951; Prof. of Applied Math., Queen's Univ., Belfast 1951-68, of Theoretical Physics 1968-74, Special Research Chair. 1968-82, now Emer.; Smithsonian Regent's Fellow, Center for Astrophysics, Cambridge, Mass., and Research Assoc. Harvard Univ. 1982-83; Foreign Assoc. N.A.S., and Royal Acad. of Belgium; foreign mem. A.A.A.S. and other learned socs.; Hughes Medal (Royal Soc.), Gold Medal (Royal Astronomical Soc.), Chree Medal (Inst. of Physics), Fleming Medal (American Geophysical Union). *Leisure interests:* radio, walking. *Address:* 1 Newforge Grange, Belfast, BT9 5QB, Northern Ireland. *Telephone:* 0232-665640.

BATES, David Vincent, M.D., F.R.C.P., F.R.C.P.C., F.A.C.P., F.R.S.C.; Canadian physician; b. 20 May 1922, Kent, England; s. of Dr. John V. Bates and Alice E. Dickins; m. Gwendolyn M. Sutton 1948; one s. two d.; ed. Rugby School, Penbroke Coll., Cambridge and St. Bartholomew's Hospital, London; served R.A.M.C., Far East 1945-48; Beit Memorial Research Fellow 1949-52; First Asst. Prof. Medical Unit, St. Bartholomew's Hosp. 1954-56; Assoc. Prof. of Medicine, McGill Univ. 1956, Prof. of Experimental Medicine 1967, Chair. Dept. of Physiology 1967-72; Dean, Faculty of Medicine, Univ. of British Columbia 1972-77, Prof. of Medicine and Head Respiratory Div., Dept. of Medicine 1978-81, Prof. Emer. 1987-; mem. Science Council of Canada 1973-79; mem. Bd. of Environmental Studies, N.A.S. 1987-; Robert Cooke Medal, American Acad. of Allergy 1966; Ramazzini Medal, Italy 1985. *Publications:* Respiratory Function in Disease (with R. V. Christie) 1964, A Citizen's Guide to Air Pollution 1973; 180 scientific papers on lung disease and lung physiology; five papers on science policy. *Leisure interests:* poetry, gardening, sailing. *Address:* Department of Health Care and Epidemiology, Mather Building, University of British Columbia, Vancouver, V6T 1W5; 4891 College High Road, Vancouver, B.C., V6T 1G6, Canada. *Telephone:* (604) 228-4925; (604) 228-0484 (Home).

BATES, Richard Heaton Tunstall, D.SC., F.I.E.E.E., F.ENG.; British-New Zealand scientist and university professor; b. 8 July 1929, Sheffield; s. of Lieut.-Col. William N. Bates and Mary H. Bates (née Wilkinson); m. Philippa Harding 1954; three s. one d.; ed. Wellington Coll. and University Coll., Univ. of London; Design Engineer, Vickers-Armstrong, Weybridge, Surrey 1952-55, Decca Radar, Tolworth, Surrey 1955-57; Advisory Engineer, Canadian Westinghouse, Hamilton, Ont., Canada 1957-59; Systems Engineer, Nat. Co., Malden, Mass., U.S.A. 1960-62; Staff mem., Mitre Corpn., Bedford, Mass. 1962-65, Sperry Rand Research Center, Sudbury, Mass. 1965-66; Sr. Lecturer, Eng. School, Univ. of Canterbury, Christchurch, N.Z. 1967-69, Reader 1969-75, Prof. (Personal Chair) 1975-; Pres. Australasian Coll. of Physical Scientists in Medicine 1981-83; Fellow Royal Soc. of N.Z., Optical Soc. of America; Cooper Prize, Royal Soc. of N.Z. 1980, Mechaelis Prize, Otago Univ. 1980, Snell Premium LEE 1987. *Publications:* Image Restoration and Reconstruction (with M. J. McDonnell) 1986; about 300 publs. (scientific papers, book chapters, conf. papers and reviews) 1956-. *Leisure interests:* walking, fly-fishing, watching rugby and cricket, concert and theatre-going. *Address:* Electrical and Electronic Engineering Department, University of Canterbury, Christchurch, New Zealand. *Telephone:* (03) 482009 ext. 7278.

BATESON, Paul Patrick Gordon, PH.D., F.R.S.; British university professor; b. 31 March 1938, Chinnor Hill, Oxon.; s. of Richard Gordon Bateson and Solvi Helene Berg; m. Dusha Matthews 1963; two d.; ed. Westminster School, Univ. of Cambridge; Stanford Medical Centre, Univ. of Calif.; Sr. Asst. in Research Sub-Dept. of Animal Behaviour, Univ. of Cambridge 1965-69, Dir. 1976-80, Lecturer in Zoology 1969-78, Reader in Sub-Dept. of Animal Behaviour 1978-84, Prof. of Ethology 1984-; Provost of King's Coll. Cambridge 1988-; Scientific Medal (Zoological Soc. of London) 1976. *Publications:* (with others) Defended to Death 1983, Ed. Perspectives in Ethology 1973, Growing Points in Ethology 1976, Mate Choice 1983. *Address:* Sub-Department of Animal Behaviour, University of Cambridge, Madingley, Cambridge, CB3 8AA (Office); 37 Panton Street, Cambridge, CB2 1HL, England (Home). *Telephone:* 0954-210301 (Office); 0223-62977 (Home).

BATHIAT, Leonie (pseudonym Arletty): French actress; b. 15 May 1898, Courbevoie; d. of Michel Bathiat and Marie (née Dautreix) Bathiat; on stage has played in Le bonheur mesdames, Fric-frac and Un tramway nommé Désir, La descente d'Orphée (Tennessee Williams) 1959, Un otage at Théâtre de France 1962, L'étouffe chrétien 1962, Les monstres sacrés 1966; played title role in Phèdre on radio; has made a number of films including Le chien rapporte 1931, Hôtel du nord 1938, Tempête 1939, Le jour se lève 1939, Fric-frac 1939, Circonstances atténuantes 1939, Madame Sans-Gêne 1941, Les visiteurs du soir 1942, Les enfants du paradis 1944, Maxime 1959, Huis clos 1959, La gamberge 1961, Le jour le plus long 1961, Tempo di Roma 1962, Le voyage à Biarritz 1962, Gibier de potence. *Publication:* La défense 1971. *Address:* 14 rue de Rémusat, 75016 Paris, France.

BATIFFOL, Henri; French lawyer and university professor; b. 16 Feb. 1905, Paris; s. of Louis Batiffol and Suzanne Genets; m. Suzanne Lot 1932 (died 1983); two s. two d.; ed. Lycées Buffon and Louis-le-Grand, Paris, Univ. of Paris; Prof. Faculty of Law, Lille 1931-50, Dean 1947-50; Prof. Faculty of Law and Economic Sciences, Paris 1950-76, Hon. Prof. 1976-; Ed.-in-Chief later Dir., Revue critique de droit international privé 1948-; Del. to Pvt. Int. Law Conf., The Hague 1951-; Assoc. then mem. Inst. of Int. Law 1948-; mem. Curatorium, Acad. of Int. Law, The Hague 1962-84; mem. Inst. (Acad. Moral and Political Sciences); Officier, Légion d'honneur, Commdr., l'Ordre nat. du Mérite, l'Ordre d'Orange Nassau. *Publications:* Les conflits de lois en matière de contrats 1938, Traité de droit international privé 1949 (7th ed. with Paul Lagarde (q.v.) 1983), Aspects philosophiques

du droit international privé 1956, La philosophie du droit 1960, Problèmes de base de philosophie du droit 1979. *Address:* 44 ave. Marceau, Paris 75008, France. *Telephone:* (1) 47 23 94 02.

BATIZ CAMPBELL, Enrique; Mexican conductor; b. 4 May 1942, Mexico, D.F.; s. of José Luis Bátiz and Maria Elena Campbell; m. 1st Eva Maria Zuk 1965 (divorced 1983); one s. one d.; m. 2nd Elena Campbell Lombardo; ed. Centro Universitario México, Julliard School of Music, New York, and private studies in Warsaw; f. and Gen. Music Dir. Symphony Orchestra of State of Mexico 1971-83; Conductor and Artistic Dir. Philharmonic Orchestra of Mexico City 1983-; Guest Conductor, Royal Philharmonic Orchestra, London 1984; numerous honours and awards; 71 recordings published worldwide; Order of Rio Branco (Brazil) 1986. *Leisure interests:* swimming, listening to classical music. *Address:* Cerrada Rancho los Colorines No. 11, Col AMSA, Delegación Tlalpan, México, D.F. 14000; Periferico Sur 5141, Col. Isidro Fabela, Delegación Tlalpan, México, D.F. 14030, Mexico. *Telephone:* 655-2582; 655-2569.

BATLINER, Gerard, DR.IUR.; Liechtenstein lawyer; b. 9 Dec. 1928, Eschen; s. of Andreas and Karolina Batliner; m. Christina Negele 1965; two s.; ed. Grammar School, Schwyz, Switzerland, and Univs. of Zürich, Fribourg, Paris, and Freiburg im Breisgau; practice at County Court of Principality of Liechtenstein 1954-55; Lawyer, Vaduz 1956-62, 1970-; Vice-Pres. Progressive Burgher Party 1958-62; Vice-Mayor of Eschen 1960-62; Head of Govt. of Principality of Liechtenstein 1962-70; Pres. Liechtenstein Parl. 1974-78, Vice-Pres. 1978-82; Head of Liechtenstein Parl. Del. to the Council of Europe 1978-82; a Vice-Pres Parl. Assembly, Council of Europe, session 1981-82; mem. European Comm. on Human Rights 1983-; Ed.-in-Chief Liechtenstein Politische Schriften (Liechtenstein Political Publications); Dr. h.c. (Univ. of Basel) 1988; Fürstlicher Justizrat 1970; Grand Cross of the Liechtenstein Order of Merit, Grand Silver Cross of Honour (Austria). *Address:* Am Schrägen Weg 2, FL-9490 Vaduz, Liechtenstein.

BATMUNH, Jambyn; Mongolian politician; b. 10 March 1926; ed. Mongolian State Univ. and Acad. of Social Sciences of CPSU Central Cttee., U.S.S.R.; Lecturer, Mongolian State Univ. and Pedagogical Inst. 1951-52; lecturer, Vice-Rector, Higher Party School of Mongolian People's Revolutionary Party (MPRP) Cen. Cttee. 1952-58; Head of Dept., Vice-Rector, Rector, Higher School of Econs. 1962-67; Vice-Rector, Mongolian State Univ. 1967-73; Head of Science and Educ. Dept., MPRP Cen. Cttee. 1973-74; Deputy Chair. Council of Ministers May-June 1974, Chair. 1974-84; Chair. Presidium of People's Great Hural (Assembly) Dec. 1984-; alt. mem. MPRP Cen. Cttee. 1971-76, mem. Cen. Cttee. 1976-, mem. Political Bureau, MPRP Cen. Cttee. 1974-, Gen. Sec. Cen. Cttee. Aug. 1984-; Deputy to the Great People's Hural 1973-; various State orders and medals. *Address:* Central Committee of the Mongolian People's Revolutionary Party, Ulaanbaatar, Mongolia.

BATSANOV, Boris Terentevich; Soviet official; b. 1927; ed. Inst. of Foreign Trade, Moscow, and U.S.S.R. Foreign Ministry Higher School; mem. CPSU 1951-; Second Sec. Embassy in Fed. Repub. of Germany 1955-58; Sr. positions in Ministry of Foreign Affairs 1961-67; mem. of Council of Ministers 1967-74; mem. of CPSU Cen. Auditing Comm. 1976-86; Head of Secr. of Pres. of Council of Ministers 1974-; mem. of Cen. Cttee. CPSU 1976-. *Address:* The Kremlin, Moscow, U.S.S.R.

BATT, Neil Leonard Charles, B.A.(HONS); Australian politician; b. 14 June 1937, Hobart; s. of Clyde Wilfred Luke and Miriam (née Wilkie) Batt; m. Anne Cameron Teniswood 1962; three d.; ed. Hobart High School, Univ. of Tasmania; Secondary School teacher 1960-61 and 1964-66; mem., House of Ass., Tasmanian Parl. 1969-80; Minister of Transport and Chief Sec. 1972-74, Minister for Educ. 1974-77, Deputy Premier and Treasurer 1977-80, Minister for Forests 1978-80, Minister for Finance 1979-82; Nat. Pres. Australian Labor Party 1978-80; Dir. TNT Group of Cos. for Vic. and Tasmania 1982-86, Resident Dir. TNT Man. Pty. Ltd. 1982-; mem. Jackson Cttee.; Trustee, Nat. Gallery of Vic. 1983-, Treas. 1984-; Commr. of Commonwealth Serum Labs. 1983-, Chair. 1984-; mem. Bd. of Australian Opera 1984-. *Leisure interests:* swimming, yachting. *Publications:* The Great Depression in Australia 1970, The Role of the University Today 1977, Information Power 1977. *Address:* 81 York Street, Sandy Bay, Tasmania 7005, Australia.

BATTEN, Alan Henry, PH.D., D.SC., F.R.S.C.; Canadian astronomer; b. 21 Jan. 1933, Whitstable, England; s. of George Cuthbert Batten and Gladys (Greenwood) Batten; m. Lois Eleanor Dewis 1960; one s. one d.; ed. Wolverhampton Grammar School, Univs. of St. Andrews and Manchester; Research Asst., Univ. of Manchester and Jr. Tutor, St. Anselm Hall of Residence 1958-59; Post-doctoral Fellow, Dominion Astrophysical Observatory, Victoria, B.C., Canada 1959-61, staff mem. 1961-, Sr. Research Officer 1967-; Vice-Pres. Astronomical Soc. of Pacific 1974-76; Pres. Canadian Astronomical Soc. 1974-76, Royal Astronomical Soc. of Canada 1977-78, Comm. 30 of Int. Astronomical Union 1976-79, Comm. 42 1982-85; Vice-Pres. Int. Astronomical Union 1985-; Queen's Silver Jubilee Medal 1977. *Publications:* The Determination of Radial Velocities and their Applications (Co-Ed.) 1967, Extended Atmospheres and Circumstellar Matter in Close Binary Systems (Ed.) 1973, Binary and Multiple Systems of Stars 1973, Resolute and Undertaking Characters: The Lives of Wilhelm and Otto Struve 1988; about 100 scientific papers. *Leisure interest:* campanology. *Address:* Dominion Astrophysical Observatory, 5071 West Saanich Road, Victoria, B.C., V8X 4M6 (Office); 2987 Westdowne Road, Victoria, B.C., V8R 5G1, Canada (Home). *Telephone:* (604) 388 0001 (Office); (604) 592-1720 (Home).

BATTEN, Sir John Charles, K.C.V.O., M.D., F.R.C.P.; British physician; b. 11 March 1924; s. of the late Raymond Wallis Batten and of Gladys Charles; m. Anne Margaret Oriel 1950; one s. two d. (and one d. deceased); ed. Mill Hill School, St. Bartholomew's Medical School; jr. appointments, St. George's Hospital and Brompton Hospital 1946–58; Surgeon Capt., Royal Horse Guards 1947–49; Physician, St. George's Hospital 1958–79, Brompton Hospital 1959–86, King Edward VII Hospital for Officers 1968–, King Edward VII Hospital, Midhurst 1969–; Physician to H.M. Royal Household 1970–74, Physician to H.M. the Queen 1974–, Head H.M. Medical Household 1982–; Dorothy Temple Cross Research Fellow, Cornell Univ. Medical Coll., New York 1954–55; Deputy Chief Medical Referee, Confederation Life Asscn. of Canada 1958–74, Chief Medical Referee 1974–; Examiner in Medicine, London Univ. 1968; Marc Daniels Lecturer, Royal Coll. of Physicians 1969; mem. Bd. of Govs., Brompton Hospital 1966–69, Medical School Council, St. George's Hospital 1969, Man. Cttee., King Edward VII Hospital Fund, Council, Royal Soc. of Medicine 1970; Censor, Royal Coll. of Physicians 1977–78, Sr. Censor 1980–81, Vice-Pres. 1980–81; Hon. Physician to St. Dunstan's 1960–, St. George's Hospital 1980–, Brompton Hosp. 1986–; Consultant to King Edward VII Convalescent Home, Isle of Wight 1975–85. *Publications:* articles in medical books and journals. *Address:* 7 Lion Gate Gardens, Richmond, Surrey, England. *Telephone:* 01-940 3282.

BATTEN, William Milfred, B.S.; American business executive; b. 4 June 1909, Reedy, W. Va.; s. of Lewis A. Batten and Gurry Goff; m. Kathryn Pherabe Clark 1935; one s. one d.; ed. Parkersburg High School, W. Va. and Ohio State Univ.; Salesman, Section Man., Asst. Man., J. C. Penney Co. store, Lansing, Mich. 1935–40; Training Dir. Personnel Dept. J. C. Penney Co., New York 1940–42; consultant in Organization Planning & Control Div. Office of Q.M.G., Washington 1942; military service, Office of Q.M.G., U.S. Army as Lieut.-Col. 1942–45; Zone Personnel Rep. (Eastern Zone), J. C. Penney Co., New York 1945–51, Asst. to Pres. 1951–58, Vice-Pres. 1953–58, Pres. 1958–64, Chair. of Bd. 1964–74; Dir. New York Stock Exchange 1972–76, Chair. 1976–84; Chair. Business Council 1971–72; Pres. Econ. Club of New York 1967–68; mem. The White House Preservation Fund, Nat. Humanities Center Bd., Nat. Comm. on Fraudulent Financial Reporting 1985–; Hon. LL.D. (Alderson-Broaddus Coll.; Morris Harvey Coll. and W. Va. Univ., W. Va. Wesleyan Coll.), Hon. L.H.D. (Marietta Coll., Ohio State Univ.). *Address:* 11 Wall Street, New York, N.Y. 10005 (Office); Locust Valley, Long Island, N.Y. 11560, U.S.A. (Home).

BATTERSBY, Alan Rushton, PH.D., D.SC., SC.D., F.R.S.; British chemist; b. 4 March 1925, Leigh; s. of William and Hilda Battersby; m. Margaret Ruth Hart 1949; two s.; ed. Leigh Grammar School, Manchester Univ., St. Andrews Univ.; Lecturer in Chem., St. Andrews Univ. 1948–53, Bristol Univ. 1954–62; Prof. of Organic Chem., Liverpool Univ. 1962–69; Cambridge Univ. 1969–; Hon. D.Sc. (Rockefeller Univ.) 1977, Hon. LL.D. (St. Andrew's Univ.) 1977; Corday-Morgan Medal and Prize 1961, Tilden Lectureship and Medal 1963, Hugo Müller Lectureship and Medal 1972, Flintoff Medal 1975, Paul Karrer Medal and Lecture 1977, Davy Medal 1977, Max Tishler Award and Lectureship (Harvard) 1978, W. von Hofmann Award and Lectureship 1979, Medal for Chemistry of Natural Products 1979, Pedlar Lectureship and Medal 1980, Roger Adams Award and Medal, American Chemical Soc. 1983, Davy Medal, Royal Soc. 1984, Baker Lectureship, Cornell Univ. 1984, Havinga Medal 1984, Longstaff Medal 1984, Royal Medal 1984, Robert Robinson Lectureship 1985, Antonio Feltrinelli Int. Prize for Chemistry, Accademia Nazionale dei Lincei, Italy 1986, Varro Tyler Award, Purdue, U.S.A. 1987, Medal of Société Royale de Chimie, Belgium 1987; Adolf Windaus Medal and Lectureship German Chem. Soc. 1987, Marvel Lectureship, Illinois, U.S.A. 1989, Gilman Lectureship, Iowa, U.S.A. 1989; Wolf Foundation Chemistry Prize 1989. *Publications:* original papers in the major chemical journals. *Leisure interests:* trout fishing, hiking, gardening, classical music. *Address:* University Chemical Laboratory, Lensfield Road, Cambridge, CB2 1EW (Office); 20 Barrow Road, Cambridge, CB2 2AS, England (Home). *Telephone:* 0223-336400 (Office); 0223-63799 (Home).

BATTISTA, Orlando Aloysius; American business executive; b. 20 June 1917, Cornwall, Canada; s. of James L. and Carmella Battista; m. Helen Battista; one s. one d.; ed. McGill Univ.; with American Viscose Corpn. 1940–63; Asst. Dir. Corpn. Research 1961–63; Asst Dir. Cen. Research Dept., FMC Corpn. 1964–70; Vice-Pres. Science and Tech. Avicon Inc., Fort Worth, Tex. 1971–74; Adjunct Prof. of Chemistry, Univ. of Texas, Arlington 1979–; Chair., Pres. and C.E.O. Research Services Org., World Olympiads of Knowledge 1977–; Pres. O. A. Battista Research Inst.; Founder-Ed. Knowledge Magazine 1976–; Pres. American Inst. of Chemists 1977–79; Chair. and Pres. Fastcrete Corpn. 1985, the O.A. Battista Research Inst. 1985, Knowledge Inc. 1986; Founder and Pres. Knowledge Olympics; Fellow N.Y. Acad. of Sciences; D.Sc. h.c. (St. Vincent Coll.) 1955; Hon. D.Sc. (Clarkson Univ.) 1985; major awards of American Chemical Soc., James Grady Gold Medal 1973, Creative Invention Gold Medal 1983, Anseline Payen Medal 1985, Applied Polymer Science Award 1987, Napo-

leon Hill Gold Medal Award for Creative Achievement 1986. *Publications:* over 20 books, numerous articles and scientific papers. *Leisure interest:* increasing knowledge. *Address:* World Headquarters, Knowledge Olympics, 3863 South West Loop 820, Suite 100, Fort Worth, Tex. 76133-2076, U.S.A.

BATTLE, Kathleen, M.MUS.; American opera singer; d. of Ollie Layne Battle and Grady Battle; ed. Coll.-Conservatory of Music, Univ. of Cincinnati; professional début in Brahms Requiem, Cincinnati May Festival, then Spoleto Festival, Italy 1972; début Metropolitan Opera, New York as shepherd in Wagner's Tannhäuser 1977; regular guest with orchestras of New York, Chicago, Boston, Philadelphia, Cleveland, L.A., San Francisco, Vienna, Paris and Berlin, at Salzburg, Tanglewood and other festivals, and at the major opera houses including Metropolitan, New York, Covent Garden, London, Paris and Vienna; appearances in 1985/86 season include Sophie in Der Rosenkavalier and Susanna in Figaro, Metropolitan New York, U.S. première parts of Messiaen's St. Francis of Assisi with Boston Symphony Orchestra and recitals U.S.A. and in Toronto, Paris, Vienna and Florence; appearances in 1986/87 season include Zerbinetta in Ariadne auf Naxos and Adina in L'Elisir d'amore, Metropolitan New York and recitals in Japan, London, Salzburg and Vienna; recordings include Brahms Requiem and Songs, Mozart Requiem, Don Giovanni, Seraglio and concert arias, Verdi's Un Ballo in Maschera and Berg's Lulu Suite; New Year's Eve Gala, Vienna; planned recordings include Fauré Requiem; Dr. h.c. (Cincinnati and Westminster Choir Coll., Princeton), Grammy Award 1987. *Leisure interests:* gardening, cooking, sewing, piano, dance. *Address:* c/o Columbia Artist Management Inc., 165 West 57th Street, New York, N.Y. 10019, U.S.A.

BATTLE, Lucius Durham, A.B., LL.B.; American educationist; b. 1 June 1918, Dawson, Ga.; s. of Warren L. Battle and Jewel B. Durham; m. Betty Davis 1949; two s. two d.; ed. Univ. of Florida; Man. of student staff, Univ. of Florida Library 1940–42; Assoc. Admin. Analyst, War Dept. 1942–43; U.S. Naval Reserve 1943–46; Foreign Affairs Specialist, Dept. of State, Washington 1946–49; Special Asst. to Sec. of State 1949–53, 1961–64, also Exec. Sec. Dept. of State 1961–62; First Sec., Copenhagen 1953–55; Deputy Exec. Sec. NATO, Paris 1955–56; Asst. Sec. of State for Educational and Cultural Affairs 1962–64; Amb. to United Arab Repub. 1964–67; Asst. Sec. of State for Near Eastern and S. Asian Affairs, Washington 1967–68; Vice-Pres. for Corporate Affairs, Communications Satellite Corpn., Washington, D.C. 1968–73, Senior Vice-Pres. for Corporate Affairs 1974–80; Pres. Middle East Inst., Washington, D.C., 1973–74, 1986–; Lucius D. Battle Associates 1984–86; mem. Advisory Council, Center for U.S.-European Middle East Co-operation 1981–; Chair. UNESCO Gen. Conf., Paris 1962; Adviser, Foundation for Middle East Peace 1981–; mem. Bd. of Dirs. World Affairs Council, Washington, D.C. 1980–; mem. Nat. Bd. Smithsonian Assocs. 1981–; Vice-Pres. Colonial Williamsburg Inc., Williamsburg Restoration Inc. 1956–61; Pres. Bacon House Foundation; Trustee, Meridan House Int., American Univ. Cairo, The Jordan Soc. 1982–; mem. Bd. of Dirs. Foreign Policy Assen., School of Advanced Int. Studies, Middle East Inst., George C. Marshall Research Foundation, First American Bank, N.A. Dec. 1982–; mem. Bd. Nat. Defense Univ. Foundation 1982–; mem. Founders' Council, Inst. for Study of Diplomacy, Georgetown Univ. 1978–; mem. Advisory Bd. Faith and Hope, WAFA WAL AMAL, Center for Contemporary Arab Studies, Georgetown Univ., Inst. for Psychiatry and Foreign Affairs; mem. American Foreign Service Assen. (Pres. 1962–63), Nat. Study Comm. on Records and Documents of Federal Officials, Dept. of State Fine Arts Cttee.; Communications exec. Dir. COMSAT Gen. Corpn.; Chair. Nat. Cttee. to honour the 14th Centennial of Islam 1979–; Chair. The Johns Hopkins Foreign Policy Inst., School for Advanced Int. Studies, The Johns Hopkins Univ., Washington, D.C. 1980–84; Lucius D. Battle and Assocs. 1984–; Order of Republic (1st class), Egypt 1978. *Address:* 4856 Rockwood Parkway, N.W. Washington, D.C. 20016, U.S.A. (Home). *Telephone:* 202-785-1141.

BATTS, Warren Leighton; American business executive; b. 4 Sept. 1932, Norfolk, Va.; s. of John Leighton and Allie Belle (née Johnson) Batts; m. Eloise Pitts 1957; one d.; Georgia Inst. of Tech., Harvard; with Kendall Co. 1963–64; Exec. Vice-Pres. Fashion Devt. Co. 1964–66; Vice-Pres., Douglas Williams Assocs. 1966–67; Founder, Triangle Corpn. 1967, Pres. and Chief Exec. Officer 1967–71; Vice-Pres., Mead Corpn. 1971–73, Pres. 1973–, Chief Exec. Officer 1978–80; Pres. Dart Industries 1980–81, Pres. Dart & Kraft 1981–86; Chair. and C.E.O. Premark Int. Inc. 1986–. *Address:* Premark International Inc., 1717 Deerfield Road, Illinois 60015, U.S.A. *Telephone:* (312) 405-6300.

BATTY, Sir William (Bradshaw), Kt.; British motor executive (retd.); b. 15 May 1913, Manchester; s. of Rowland and Nellie Batty; m. Jean Ella Brice 1946; one s. one d.; ed. Hulme Grammar School, Manchester; apprentice toolmaker, Ford Motor Co. Ltd. 1930, company trainee 1933; Man. Tractor Div. 1955; Gen. Man. Tractor Group 1961; Dir. of Car and Truck Group 1964; Exec. Dir. Ford Motor Co. Ltd. 1963, Man. Dir. 1967–73, Chair. 1972–76; Dir. Henry Ford and Son Ltd., Cork 1965–76; Chair. Ford Motor Credit Co. Ltd. 1968–76, Automotive Finance Ltd. 1970–76; Dir. Ford Lusitana SARL, Portugal 1973–76; Pres. Soc. of Motor Mfrs. and Traders 1975–76, Vice-Pres. 1976–. *Leisure interests:* golf, sailing, gardening. *Address:* Glenhaven Cottage, Riverside Road West, Newton Ferrers, Plymouth, Devon, England. *Telephone:* Plymouth 872415.

BATU BAGEN; Chinese party and government official; Deputy for Inner Mongolia, 5th NPC; Vice-Chair. Autonomous Regional Government, Inner Mongolia 1979–83; alt. mem. Cen. Cttee. CCP 1982–; Chair. Autonomous Regional People's Congress, Inner Mongolia 1983–; Deputy Sec. CCP Cttee., Inner Mongolia Autonomous Region 1983–; mem. Presidium, 6th NPC 1986–. *Address:* Autonomous Regional People's Congress, Hohhot, Nei Monggol, People's Republic of China.

BAUCUS, Max, LL.B.; American senator; b. 11 Dec. 1941, Helena, Mont.; m.; one s.; ed. Helena High School, Stanford Univ. and Stanford Law School; staff attorney, Civil Aeronautics Bd., Washington, D.C. 1967–69; legal staff, Securities and Exchange Comm. 1969–71; legal asst. to Chair. S.E.C. 1970–71; private law practice, Missoula, Mont. 1971; Acting Exec. Dir. and Cttee. Coordinator, Mont. Constitutional Convention; elected to Montana State Legislature 1972; two terms in U.S. House of Reps. for Mont. Western Dist., mem. House Appropriations Cttee. and Deputy Whip; Senator from Montana Nov. 1978–; mem. Senate Finance Cttee., Environment and Public Works Cttee. and Select Cttee. on Small Business; several other sub-cttees.; Democrat. *Address:* 706 Hart, Senate Office Building, Washington, D.C. 20510, U.S.A.

BAUDO, Serge; French conductor; b. 16 July 1927, Marseilles; s. of Etienne Baudo and Geneviève Tortelier; m. Madeleine Reties 1947; one s. one d.; ed. Conservatoire national supérieur de musique, Paris; Music Dir. Radio Nice 1957–59; Conductor Paris Opera Orchestra 1962–66; titular Conductor and Orchestral Dir. a.i. Orchestre de Paris 1968–70; Music Dir. Opéra de Lyon 1969–71, Orchestre Nat. de Lyon 1971–87; has conducted many of world's leading orchestras; Founder Berlioz Festival, Lyons 1979–; Chevalier ordre national du mérite; Officier des Arts et des Lettres; de la Légion d'Honneur; numerous prix du disque. *Address:* Musicaglotz, 11 rue le verrier, Paris, France (Office); 143 rue Duguesclin, 69006 Lyon, France (Home).

BAUDOUIN I; King of the Belgians; Baudouin Albert Charles Léopold Axel Marie Gustave; b. 7 Sept. 1930; s. of King Léopold III and Queen Astrid; m. Doña Fabiola Mora y Aragón (b. 11 June 1928) 1960; no c.; ed. privately; Prince Royal 1950; succeeded his father on his abdication 17 July 1951. *Address:* The Royal Palace, Brussels, Belgium.

BAUDOUIN, Jean-Louis, B.A., B.C.L., PH.D.; Canadian lawyer and professor of law; b. 8 Aug. 1938, Boulogne, France; s. of Louis Baudouin and Marguerite Guerin; m. Renée Lescop 1966; four d.; ed. Univ. of Paris, McGill Univ., Montreal, Canada; admitted to Bar of Quebec 1959; Prof. of Law, Univ. of Montreal 1963–; Commr., Law Reform Comm. of Canada 1976–78, Vice-Chair. 1978–80; mem. Royal Soc. of Canada. *Publications:* Les Obligations 1970, 1983, La Responsabilité Civile 1973, Le Secret Professionnel 1964, Produire l'Homme: de quel Droit? 1987. *Leisure interests:* windsurfing, fishing, wine-tasting. *Address:* Faculté de Droit, 3101 chemin de la Tour, C.P. 6128 Succ.A, Montreal H3C 3J7 (Office); 186 Bloomfield, Montreal, Quebec, H2V 3R4, Canada (Home).

BAUDRIER, Jaqueline; French journalist and diplomatist; b. 16 March 1922, Beaufai; m. 1st Maurice Baudrier (divorced), 2nd Roger Perriard 1957; ed. Univ. of Paris; political reporter, Actualités de Paris news programme, and foreign news reporter and presenter on various news programmes, Radiodiffusion-Télévision Française 1950–60; Sec.-Gen. Soutien fraternel des journalistes 1955–; Ed.-in-Chief of news programmes, Office de Radiodiffusion-Télévision Française (ORTF) 1963–66, in charge of main news programme 1966–68; Asst. Dir. of radio broadcasting, in charge of information 1968–69; Dir. of Information, 2nd TV channel (A2) 1969–72; Dir. 1st TV channel network (TF1) 1972–74; Chair. Radio-France (nat. radio broadcasting co.) 1975–81; mem. Bd. of Dirs. Télédiffusion de France (nat. TV broadcasting co.) 1975–81; Pres. Communauté radiophonique des programmes de langue française 1977–79; Vice-Chair. Programming Comm. Union européenne de radiodiffusion 1978, re-elected 1980; Perm. Rep. of France to UNESCO 1981–85; mem. Exec. Cttee., UNESCO 1984–85, Comm. nat. de la Communication et des Libertés 1986–; prix Maurice Bourdet 1960, prix Ondes 1969; Chevalier, Légion d'honneur, Officier, Ordre nationale du Mérite. *Address:* 60 quai Louis Blériot, 75016 Paris (Home); C.N.C.L., 56 rue Jacob, 75006 Paris, France (Office).

BAUER, Ludwig; Austrian business executive; b. 23 Sept. 1908, Hadersdorf-Weidlingau; s. of Ludwig and Margarethe (née Marno) Bauer; m. Helene Arcon 1977; ed. Realschule and Handelsakademie; with Vacuum Oil Co. 1928–38, AG der Kohlenwertstoffverbände, Gruppe Benzin-Benzol 1938–; "Martha" Erdöl G.m.b.H. 1946, Man. 1955, Gen. Dir. 1960; Chair. Man. Bd. ÖMV Aktiengesellschaft 1966–80; Hon. Senator Montanistischen Hochschule, Leoben; Grosses Ehrenzeichen für Verdienste um die Republik Österreich, Silbernes Komturkreuz des Ehrenzeichens für Verdienste um das Bundesland Niederösterreich, Grosses Silbernes Ehrenzeichen des Landes Wien, Goldenes Ehrenzeichen des Landes Oberösterreich, Goldenes Ehrenzeichen des Landes Salzburg (Austria), Ordine al Merito (Italy). *Leisure interests:* literature, music, art. *Address:* Otto-Wagner-Platz 5, 1091 Vienna, Austria. *Telephone:* 42-36-21.

BAUER, Baron (Life Peer), cr. 1983, of Market Ward in the City of Cambridge, **Peter Thomas Bauer,** M.A., F.B.A.; British economist; b. 6 Nov. 1915, Budapest, Hungary; ed. Scholae Piae (Budapest) and Gonville and

Caius Coll., Cambridge; Fellow Gonville and Caius Coll. Cambridge 1946–60, 1968–; Reader, Agricultural Econ. Univ. of London 1947–48; Univ. Lecturer in Econ., Cambridge Univ. 1948–56, Smuts Reader in Commonwealth Studies 1956–60; Prof. of Econ. (with special reference to econ. devt. and underdeveloped countries), Univ. of London 1960–83, Prof. Emer. 1983–. *Publications:* The Rubber Industry 1948, West African Trade 1954, The Economics of Under-developed Countries (with B. S. Yamey) 1957, Economic Analysis and Policy in Under-developed Countries 1958, Indian Economic Policy and Development 1961, Markets, Market Control and Marketing Reform (Selected Papers, with B. S. Yamey) 1969, Dissent on Development: Studies and Debates in Development Economics 1972, Equality, The Third World and Economic Delusion 1981, Reality and Rhetoric: Studies in the Economics of Development 1984; numerous articles on economic subjects. *Address:* House of Lords, Westminster, London, S.W.1, England (Office).

BAUGH, Kenneth Lee O'Neil, M.B., B.S., F.R.C.S.; Jamaican consultant surgeon and politician; b. 24 Feb. 1941, Montego Bay; s. of Kenneth and Lilieth (née King) Baugh; m. Vilma Douglas; two s. one d.; ed. Cornwall Coll., Univ. of the West Indies and postgraduate studies in U.K.; intern, Univ. Hosp., Univ. of the West Indies 1968–72; Consultant, Univ. of the West Indies 1974–76; Consultant Surgeon, Cornwall Regional Hosp. 1976, Sr. Medical Officer 1978–80; mem. Parl. 1980–; Minister of Health 1980–89.

BAUM, Bernard René, PH.D., F.R.S.C.; Canadian scientist; b. 14 Feb. 1937, Paris, France; s. of Kurt Baum and Marta Berl; m. Danielle Habib 1961; one d.; ed. Hebrew Univ., Jerusalem; Research Scientist, Plant Research Inst., Dept. of Agric., Ottawa, Canada 1966–74; Sr. Research Scientist, Biosystematics Research Inst., Agric. Canada, Ottawa 1974–80, Prin. Research Scientist, Biosystematics Research Centre 1980–, Section Chief, Cultivated Crops Section 1973–77, Section Head, Vascular Plants Section 1982–87, Acting Dir., Geostrategy Div., Devt. Policy Directorate 1981–82; mem. Acad. of Sciences (Royal Soc. of Canada), Botanical Soc. of America, Societé Botanique de France, Int. Asscn. for Plant Taxonomy and other socs.; Founder mem. Hennig Soc.; Fellow Linnean Soc., London; George Lawson Medal, Canadian Botanical Asscn. 1979. *Publications:* Material of an International Oat Register 1973, Oats: wild and cultivated. A monograph of the genus Avena 1977, The Genus Tamarix 1978, Barley Register 1985; 130 scientific publs. *Leisure interests:* swimming long distance, classical music. *Address:* Biosystematics Research Centre, Agriculture Canada, Central Experimental Farm, Ottawa, Ont., K1A 0C6 (Office); 15 Murray Street No. 408, Ottawa, Ont., K1N 9M5, Canada (Home). *Telephone:* (613) 996 1665 (Office); (613) 237 2918 (Home).

BAUM, Warren C., PH.D.; American international finance official; b. 2 Sept. 1922, New York; s. of William and Elsie Baum; m. Jessie Scullen 1946; two d.; ed. Columbia Coll. and Harvard Univ.; with Office of Strategic Services 1942–46; Economic Co-operation Admin. 1949–51; Mutual Security Agency 1952–53; Economist, RAND Corpn. 1953–56; Chief, Office of Network Study, Fed. Communications Comm. 1956–59; Economist, European Dept. World Bank 1959–62; Div. Chief, European Dept. 1962–64; Asst. Dir. in charge of Transportation, Projects Dept. 1964–68; Deputy Dir., Projects Dept. July 1968; Assoc. Dir., Projects Nov. 1968–72; Vice-Pres. Projects Staff 1972–83, Vice-Pres. 1983–; Chair. Consultative Group on Int. Agricultural Research 1974–83, Chair. Emer. 1984–. *Publications:* The Marshall Plan and French Foreign Trade 1951, The French Economy and the State 1956, Investing in Development 1985. *Address:* 1818 H. Street, N.W., Washington, D.C. 20433, U.S.A..

BAUM, H.E. Cardinal William Wakefield, S.T.D., S.T.L.; American ecclesiastic; b. 21 Nov. 1926, Dallas, Tex.; s. of Harold E. and Mary Leona (Hayes) White, step-father Jerome C. Baum; ed. Kenrick Seminary, St. Louis and Univ. of St. Thomas Aquinas, Rome; ordained to priesthood 1951; Assoc. Pastor, St. Aloysius, St. Therese's and St. Peter's parishes, Kan. City, Mo. 1951–56; Instructor and Prof., Avila Coll., Kan. City 1954–56; 1958–63; Admin. St. Cyril's Parish, Sugar Creek, Mo. 1960–61; Hon. Chaplain of His Holiness the Pope 1961; Peritus (Expert Adviser), Second Vatican Council 1962–65; First Exec. Dir. Bishops' Comm. for Ecumenical and Interreligious Affairs, Washington 1964–67, Chair. 1972; mem. Jt. Working Group of reps. of Catholic Church and World Council of Churches 1965–69; mem. Mixed Comm. of reps. of Catholic Church and Lutheran World Fed. 1965–66; Chancellor, Diocese of Kan. City, St. Joseph 1967–70; Hon. Prelate of His Holiness the Pope 1968; Pastor, St. James Parish, Kan. City 1968–70; Bishop, Diocese of Springfield-Cape Girardeau 1970; mem. Synod of Bishops 1971; Archbishop of Washington 1973–80; Chancellor of the Catholic Univ. 1973–; Cardinal 1976–; Prefect, Sacred Congregation for Catholic Educ. Jan. 1980–; Permanent Observer-Consultant for Vatican Secretariat for Promoting Christian Unity; Chair. USCC-NCCB Doctrine Cttee., Cttee. for Pastoral Research and Practices; mem. Secretariat for Non-Christians; Hon. D.D., Muhlenberg Coll., Allentown, Pa. 1967, Georgetown Univ., Wash., St. John's Univ., Brooklyn, N.Y. *Leisure interests:* reading, music. *Publications:* The Teaching of Cardinal Cajetan on the Sacrifice of the Mass 1958, Considerations Toward the Theology on the Presbyterate 1961. *Address:* Piazza della Città Leonina 9, 00193 Rome, Italy.

BAUMANN, Herbert Karl Wilhelm; German composer and conductor; b. 31 July 1925, Berlin; s. of Wilhelm and Elfriede (née Bade) Baumann; m.

Marianne Brose 1951; two s.; ed. Berlin Classical High School, Schillergymnasium and Int. Music Inst.; conductor, Tchaikovsky Symphony Orch. 1947; composer and conductor, Deutsches Theater, Berlin 1947–53, Staatliche Berliner Bühnen: Schillertheater and Schlossparktheater 1953–70, Bayerisches Staatsschauspiel: Residenztheater, Munich 1971–79; freelance composer 1979–. *Works include:* stage music (Ballets: Alice in Wonderland, Rumpelstilzchen), music for radio, cinema and television, orchestral, chamber and choral works, several suites for plucked instruments and works for organ. *Leisure interests:* travelling and wandering, reading, especially books on fine arts. *Address:* Franziskanerstrasse 16, Apt. 1419, D-8000 Munich 80, Federal Republic of Germany. *Telephone:* 089-48 97 45.

BAUMEL, Jacques; French politician; b. 6 March 1918, Marseille; m.; two d.; Deputy for Hauts-de-Seine (R.P.R.); Mayor of Rueil-Malmaison; Councillor, Hautes-de-Seine; Vice-Pres. Comm. on National Defence and the Armed Forces; Chair. Political Comm., Parl. Ass., Council of Europe; fmr. govt. minister and senator; Pres. Académie Diplomatique Internationale, Fondation du Futur; Chair Ass. Nationale de Téléspectateurs français; Chevalier, Légion d'honneur; Compagnon de la Libération; Croix de guerre; Médaille de la Résistance. *Publication:* Une Certaine Idée de la France 1985. *Address:* C.P., Palais-Bourbon, 75355 Paris; Rassemblement pour la République, 123 rue de Lille, 75007 Paris; Mairie, 92501 Rueil-Malmaison Cedex, France. *Telephone:* 49.63.67.88 (Palais-Bourbon); 47.08.41.18 (Rueil-Malmaison).

BAUMGARTNER, Ferdinand, DR.THEOL.; Austrian librarian; b. 1 May 1931; s. of Ferdinand Baumgartner and Grete Tomek; m. Johanna Wania; one s. one d.; ed. Univ. of Vienna; Head of Directorate, Univ. of Vienna Library 1968–72; Head of Dept. Fed. Ministry of Science and Research 1979; now Dir. Univ. of Vienna Library; Pres. Assen. of Austrian Librarians 1981–; Editor, Biblos and Biblos-Schriften; Gold Badge of Honour, Repub. of Austria. *Address:* Dr Karl Lueger Ring 1, A-1010 Vienna (Office); Freisingerstrasse 11, A-3400 Klosterneuburg, Austria (Home). *Telephone:* 43002371 (Office); 2800 (Home).

BAUMOL, William Jack, PH.D.; American professor of economics; b. 26 Feb. 1922, New York; s. of Solomon and Lillian Baumol; m. Hilda Missel; one s. one d.; ed. Coll. of City of New York and Univ. of London; junior economist, U.S. Dept. of Agriculture 1942–43, 1946; Asst. Lecturer, London School of Econs. 1947–49; Dept. of Econs., Princeton Univ. 1949–, Prof. of Econs. 1954–; Dir. C.V. Starr Centre for Applied Econs., New York Univ. 1984–; Prof. of Econs. New York Univ. 1971–; Pres. Eastern Econ. Assen. 1978–79, Assen. of Environmental and Resource Economists 1979, American Econ. Assen. 1981; Pres. Atlantic Econ. Soc. 1985–; mem. Nat. Acad. of Sciences 1987–; Hon. Fellow, L.S.E.; Hon. doctorates, Stockholm School of Econs., Univ. of Basle, etc.; Frank E. Seidman Award, Political Econ. 1987. *Publications:* 20 books including: Economic Dynamics 1951, Business Behavior, Value and Growth 1959, Economic Theory and Operations Analysis 1961, Performing Arts: The Economic Dilemma (with W. G. Bowen) 1966, Theory of Environmental Policy (with W. E. Oates) 1975, Economics, Environmental Policy, and The Quality of Life (with W. E. Oates and S. B. Blackman) 1979, Economics: Principles and Policy (with A. S. Blinder) 1979, Contestable Markets and the Theory of Industry Structure (with J. C. Panzar and R. D. Willig) 1982, Productivity Growth and U.S. Competitiveness (ed. with K. McLennan) 1985, Superfairness: Application and Theory 1986 (Best Book in Business, Man. and Econs., Assen. American Publishers), Microtheory: Applications and Origins 1986, Productivity and American Leadership: The Long View (with S. A. Batey Blackman and E. N. Wolff) 1989. *Leisure interests:* woodcarving, painting. *Address:* Department of Economics, Princeton University, Princeton, N.J. 08544; Department of Economics, New York University, 269 Mercer Street, New York, N.Y. 10003 (Offices); P.O. Box 1502, Princeton, N.J. 08542; 100 Bleecker Street, Apt. 29A, New York, N.Y. 10012, U.S.A. (Homes). *Telephone:* 609-452-4033 (Princeton Univ.); (212) 998-8943 (New York Univ.).

BAUNSGAARD, Hilmar Tormod Ingolf, Danish businessman and politician; b. 26 Feb. 1920, Slagelse; m. Egone Baunsgaard; one d.; ed. commercial schools; Deputy Man. grocery firm 1944–47; Business Man. Købmaendenes Indkøbscentral A/S HOKI, Odense 1947–61; Marketing Man. at WA Reklame-Marketing S/I 1964–68; Pres. Social-Liberal Party Youth 1948–50; mem. Exec. Social-Liberal Party 1948–57, Vice-Pres. 1954–57; mem. of Folketing (Parl.) 1957–77; Minister of Commerce 1961–64; Prime Minister 1968–71; mem. Bd. Nat. Bank of Denmark 1960–61, 1966–68, 1971–75; mem. Bd. Politiken (newspaper) 1975, Chair. Bd. 1976. *Leisure interests:* gardening, painting. *Address:* Blidahpark 34, 2900 Hellerup, Denmark.

BAUTIER, Robert-Henri; French professor of diplomacy; b. 19 April 1922, Paris; s. of the late Edgar Bautier and Suzanne Voyer; m. Anne-Marie Regnier 1948; one d.; ed. Ecole des Chartes, Sorbonne and Ecole des Hautes Etudes; archivist, Nat. Archives 1943; Head Archivist, Archives départementales de la Creuse 1944; mem. Ecole Française de Rome 1945; Keeper, Archives de France 1948; Prof. Ecole Nat. des Chartes 1961–; Pres. Comm. Int. de Diplomatique 1980–; mem. Inst. de France (Acad. des Inscriptions et Belles Lettres); Assoc. Fellow, British Acad.; Fellow, Medieval Acad. of America; Assoc. mem. Belgian Acad. etc.; Chevalier, Légion d'Honneur, Commdr. des Palmes Académiques, des Arts et Lettres

and other distinctions. *Publications:* numerous books and more than 200 articles in learned journals. *Address:* 13 rue de Sévigné, 75004 Paris; Les Rabuteloires, 45360 Chatillon-sur-Loire, France. *Telephone:* 48.87.23.38; 38 31 47 05.

BAVARIA, Duke of; Albrecht Luitpold Ferdinand Michael; b. 3 May 1905, Munich, Germany; s. of the late Rupprecht Kronprinz von Bayern and Marie Gabriele Herzogin in Bayern; m. 1st Marie Gräfin Draskovich von Trakostjan 1930 (died 1969), 2nd Marie-Jenke Gräfin Keglevich von Buzin (died 1983); two s. two d.; ed. Wittelsbacher Gymnasium, Munich, Ettal monastery and Univ. of Munich; succeeded his father as head of Royal House of Bavaria (House of Wittelsbach) 1955; Hon. Senator and Dr.med.vet. h.c., Univ. of Munich. *Publications:* Uber Rehe in einem Steirischen Gebirgsrevier 1975. *Address:* Schloss Nymphenburg, D-8000 Munich 19, Federal Republic of Germany. *Telephone:* 089-17 22 25.

BAVIN, Rt. Rev. Timothy John, M.A.; British bishop; b. 17 Sept. 1935, Northwood, England; s. of Edward and Marjorie Bavin; ed. St. George School, Windsor, Brighton Coll., Worcester Coll., Oxford Univ., Cuddesdon Coll.; Asst. Priest, St. Alban's Cathedral, Pretoria 1961–64; Chaplain, St. Alban's Coll., Pretoria 1964–69; Asst. Priest, Uckfield, Sussex, England 1969–71; Vicar, Church of the Good Shepherd, Brighton 1971–73; Dean of Johannesburg 1973–74; Bishop Nov. 1974–84; Bishop of Portsmouth, England 1985–; mem. Oratory of the Good Shepherd 1987–. *Leisure interests:* music, walking, gardening, Victoriana. *Address:* Bishopswood, Fareham, Hampshire, PO14 1NT, England. *Telephone:* 0329-280247.

BAWDEN, Edward, C.B.E., R.A., R.D.I.; British artist; b. 1903; m. Charlotte Epton 1932; one s. one d.; ed. Cambridge School of Art and Royal Coll. of Art; fmr. Tutor of Graphic Design, Royal Coll. of Art; Official War Artist, Middle East 1940–45; work represented in Tate Gallery, London, and in other London, provincial and Commonwealth galleries; Trustee, Tate Gallery 1951–58. *Address:* 2 Park Lane, Saffron Walden, Essex, England.

BAWDEN, Nina Mary, M.A., J.P., F.R.S.L.; English novelist; b. 19 Jan. 1925, London; d. of Charles Mabey and Ellalaine Ursula May Mabey; m. 1st H. W. Bawden 1947, two s. (one deceased) one d.; m. 2nd Austen S. Kark (q.v.) 1954, two step-d.; ed. Ilford County High School, Somerville Coll., Oxford; Asst., Town and Country Planning Assen. 1946–47; J.P., Surrey 1968; Pres. Soc. of Women Writers and Journalists 1981–; Guardian Prize for Children's Literature 1975; Yorkshire Post Novel of the Year Award 1976. *Publications:* The Birds on the Trees 1970, Anna Apparent 1972, George Beneath a Paper Moon 1974, Afternoon of a Good Woman 1976, Familiar Passions 1979, Walking Naked 1981, The Ice House 1983, Circles of Deceit 1987; for children: Carrie's War, The Peppermint Pig, The Runaway Summer, The Finding 1985, Princess Alice 1985, Keeping Henry 1988. *Leisure interests:* theatre, cinema, travel, croquet. *Address:* 22 Noel Road, London, N1 8HA, England.

BAWN, Cecil Edwin Henry, C.B.E., PH.D., F.R.S.; British professor of physical chemistry; b. 6 Nov. 1908; m. Winifred Mabel Jackson 1934; two s. one d.; ed. Cotham Grammar School, Bristol, Univ. of Bristol; Asst. Lecturer in Chem., Univ. of Manchester 1931–34, Lecturer 1934–38; during Second World War was in charge of a Physico-Chemical Section in Armament Research Dept., Ministry of Supply; Lecturer in Physical Chem., Univ. of Bristol 1938–45, Reader 1945–49, Grant-Brunner Prof. of Inorganic and Physical Chem. 1948–69, Brunner Prof. of Physical Chem. 1969–73, Emer. Prof. 1973–; mem. Univ. Grants Cttee. 1965–74; Hon. D.Sc. (Bradford) 1966, (Birmingham) 1968, (Bristol) 1974; Swinburne Gold Medal 1966. *Publications:* The Chemistry of High Polymers 1948; papers in chemical journals. *Address:* Springfields, Stoodleigh, nr. Tiverton, Devon, EX16 9PT, England. *Telephone:* Oakford 220.

BAXANDALL, Michael David Kighley, M.A., F.B.A.; British historian; b. 18 Aug. 1933, Cardiff; s. of David K. Baxandall and Sarah I.M. Thomas; m. Katharina D. Simon 1964; one s. one d.; ed. Manchester Grammar School, Downing Coll. Cambridge, and Univs. of Pavia and Munich; Asst. Keeper, Dept. of Sculpture, Victoria & Albert Museum, London 1961–65; Lecturer in Renaissance Studies, Warburg Inst. Univ. of London 1965–72, Reader in History of the Classical Tradition 1973–80, Prof. of History of the Classical Tradition 1980–; Slade Prof. of Fine Art, Univ. of Oxford 1974–75; A.D. White Prof.-at-Large, Cornell Univ. 1982–; Prof. of Art History, Univ. of Calif. Berkeley 1986–; Mitchell Prize for History of Art 1980; Prix Vasari de l'Essai Etranger 1986. *Publications:* Giotto and the Orators 1971, Painting and Experience in 15th Century Italy 1972, The Limewood Sculptors of Renaissance Germany 1980, Patterns of Intention 1985. *Address:* Warburg Institute, University of London, Woburn Square, London, WC1H 0AB, England. *Telephone:* 01-580 9663.

BAXENDELL, Sir Peter Brian, Kt., C.B.E., B.SC., A.R.S.M., F.ENG.; British petroleum engineer; b. 28 Feb. 1925, Runcorn; s. of Lesley Wilfred Baxendell and Evelyn Gaskin; m. Rosemary Lacey 1949; two s. two d.; ed. St. Francis Xavier's Coll., Liverpool, Royal School of Mines, Imperial Coll., London; with Royal Dutch/Shell Group 1946–; Anglo-Egyptian Oilfields 1947–50; Compania Shell de Venezuela 1950–63; Tech. Dir. Shell-BP Nigeria 1963–66, Man. Dir. 1969–72; Shell Int. London, Eastern Region 1966–69; Chair. Shell U.K. 1973–79; Man. Dir. Royal Dutch/Shell Group 1973–85; Vice-Chair. Cttee. of Man. Dirs. 1979–82, Chair. 1982–85; Chair. Shell Transport and Trading 1979–85, Dir. 1973–; Dir. Hawker Siddeley

Group 1984–, Chair. May 1986–; Dir. Inchcape PLC 1986–; Dir. Sun Life Assurance Co. of Canada 1986–; mem. Univ. Grants Cttee. 1983–, Univs. Funding Council 1989–; Fellow, Imperial Coll. Science and Tech., London 1983; Hon. D.Sc. (Herriot-Watt) 1982, (Queen's, Belfast) 1986, (London) 1986, (Loughborough) 1987. *Leisure interests:* fishing, tennis. *Address:* c/o Royal Dutch/Shell Group, Shell Centre, London, S.E.1, England (Office). *Telephone:* 01-934 2772.

BAXTER, Glen; British artist; b. 4 March 1944, Leeds; s. of Charles and Florence Baxter; one s. one d.; ed. Cockburn Grammar School, Leeds and Leeds Coll. of Art; has exhibited his drawings in New York, San Francisco, Venice, Amsterdam and Paris and represented U.K. at the Sydney Biennale 1986; major retrospective at Musée de l'Abbaye Sainte-Croix, Les Sables d'Olonne, France 1987; illustrated Charlie Malarkey and the Belly Button Machine 1986. *Publications:* The Impending Gleam 1981, Atlas 1982 and Glen Baxter: His Life: The Years of Struggle 1983, Jodhpurs in the Quantocks 1986. *Address:* c/o Aitken and Stone, 29 Fernshaw Road, London, SW10 0TG.

BAXTER, Sir John Philip, K.B.E., PH.D., M.I.CHEM.E., F.R.A.C.I., M.I.E. (Aust.), F.A.A.; Australian chemical engineer and educationist; b. 7 May 1905; m. Lilian May Baxter 1931; three s. one d.; ed. Hereford, and Birmingham Univ.; Research Dir.-Gen. Chemicals Division I.C.I. and Dir. Thorium Ltd. 1949; Prof. of Chemical Engineering N.S.W. Univ. of Technology 1949–53, Dir. 1953–54, Vice-Chancellor (now Univ. of New South Wales) 1955–69; Chair. Atomic Energy Comm. 1957–72; Chair. Sydney Opera House Trust 1969–75; Fellow, Australian Acad. of Science; Hon. LL.D. (Montreal) 1958; Hon. D.Sc. (Newcastle, Queensland); Hon. D.Tech. (Loughborough) 1969; Kernot Medal 1970. *Leisure interest:* lawn tennis. *Address:* 1 Kelso Street, Enfield, N.S.W. 2136, Australia. *Telephone:* 7474261.

BAXTER, Rodney James, SC.D., F.A.A., F.R.S.; Australian professor of physics; b. 8 Feb. 1940, London, England; s. of Thomas J. Baxter and Florence Baxter; m. Elizabeth A. Phillips 1968; one s. one d.; ed. Bancroft's School, Essex, Trinity Coll., Cambridge and Australian Nat. Univ.; Reservoir Engineer, Iraq Petroleum Co. 1964–65; Research Fellow, Australian Nat. Univ. 1965–68; Asst. Prof. Mass. Inst. of Tech. 1968–70; Fellow, Australian Nat. Univ. 1971–81, Prof. Dept. of Theoretical Physics 1981–; Pawsey Medal, Australian Acad. of Science 1975, Boltzmann Medal, Int. Union of Pure and Applied Physics 1980, Dannie Heineman Prize, American Inst. of Physics 1987. *Publication:* Exactly Solved Models in Statistical Mechanics 1982. *Leisure interest:* theatre. *Address:* Department of Theoretical Physics, Australian National University, G.P.O. Box 4, Canberra 2601, Australia.

BAYER, Oswald; German ecclesiastic and professor of theology; b. 30 Sept. 1939, Nagold; s. of Emil and Hermine Bayer; m. Eva Bayer 1966; ed. Tübingen, Bonn and Rome; Vicar, Evangelische Landeskirche, Württemberg 1964; Asst. Univ. of Tübingen 1965–68; Evangelical Monastery, Tübingen 1968–71; Priest, Taebingen 1972–74; Prof. of Systematic Theology, Univ. of Bochum 1974–79, Univ. of Tübingen 1979–, Dir. Inst. of Christian Sociology 1979–. *Publications:* several books on theological topics. *Address:* Evangelisch-theologische Fakultät der Universität Tübingen, Institut für Christliche Gesellschaftslehre, Hölderlinstrasse 16, 7400 Tübingen (Office); Am unteren Herrlesberg 36, 7400 Tübingen, Federal Republic of Germany (Home). *Telephone:* 07071-292591 (Office); 07071-81897 (Home).

BAYERO, Alhaji Ado; Nigerian administrator; b. 1930, Kano; s. of Alhaji Abdullahi Bayer, Emir of Kano; ed. Kano Middle School; clerk, Bank of W. Africa; M.P., N. House of Ass. 1955–57; Chief of Kano Native Authority Police 1957–62; Amb. to Senegal 1962–63; Emir of Kano 1963–; Chancellor, Univ. of Nigeria, Nsukka, E. Nigeria 1966–75, Chancellor Univ. of Ibadan 1975–85. *Leisure interests:* photography, riding, reading. *Address:* c/o University of Ibadan, Ibadan, Nigeria.

BAYEV, Aleksandr Aleksandrovich, D.SC.; Soviet biochemist; b. 10 Jan. 1904, Chita; s. of Alexander Bayev and Manefa Baeva; m. Ecaterina Kosyakina 1944; one s. one d.; ed. Kazan State Univ.; Physician 1927–30; Lecturer, Kazan Medical Inst. 1930–35; Sr. Research Worker, Bakh Inst. of Biochem., U.S.S.R. Acad. of Sciences 1935–59; Head of Lab., Inst. of Molecular Biology 1959–; mem. CPSU 1964–; corresp. mem. U.S.S.R. Acad. of Sciences 1968–70, mem. 1970–, mem. Inst. Molecular Biology; mem. Acads. of Poland, Bulgaria, Hungary, G.D.R., and Leopoldina Acad.; Pres. Int. Union of Biochemistry 1976–79; U.S.S.R. State Award 1969; Order of Lenin 1974, 1981; Hero of Socialist Labour 1981; Order of Oct. Revolution 1984. *Publications:* works on primary structure of nucleic acids and molecular genetics. *Address:* Institute of Molecular Biology, 117984 Moscow, 334 Ulitsa Vavilova, U.S.S.R. *Telephone:* 35 23 31.

BAYH, Birch Evans, Jr.; American lawyer, farmer and politician; b. 22 Jan. 1928, Terre Haute, Ind.; s. of Birch and Leah (Hollingsworth) Evans; m. Marvella Hern 1952; one s.; ed. Purdue Univ. and Indiana Univ; farmer, Terre Haute 1952–57; admitted to Ind. Bar 1961; mem. Indiana House of Reps. 1955–62, Minority Leader 1957–58, 1961–62, Speaker 1959–60; U.S. Senator from Indiana 1963–81; Sr. Partner Bayh, Tabber & Capehart, Indianapolis and Washington, then Partner Rivkin, Radler, Dunne and Bough; Democrat. *Address:* Suite 1025, 1575 1st Street, N.W., Washington, D.C. 20005, U.S.A. (Office).

BAYH, Evan, B.S., J.D.; American politician; b. 26 Dec. 1955, Terre Haute, Ind.; s. of Birch Evans Bayh Jr. (q.v.) and Marvella Hern; m.; ed. Indiana Univ. and Univ. of Virginia; Sec. of State of Indiana 1987–89; Gov. of Indiana 1989–; Democrat. *Address:* Office of the Governor, State Capitol, Indianapolis, Ind., U.S.A.

BAYI, Filbert; Tanzanian athlete; b. 22 June 1953, Karatu Mbulu Dist.; joined Air Transport Battalion (TPDF), Dar es Salaam; beat Tanzanian Nat. Champion over 1,500 m., Dar es Salaam 1972; 1,500 m. Gold Medal Nat. Championships, Dar es Salaam 1972, All African Games, Lagos, Nigeria (record time) 1973; first competed Europe June 1973; 1,500 m. Gold Medal (world record), Commonwealth Games, Christchurch, New Zealand 1974; has competed on all five continents. *Address:* c/o Ministry of Information, Dar es Salaam, Tanzania.

BAYKARA, Zeyyad; Turkish politician; b. 1918, Kamaliye; ed. Faculty of Political Sciences, Ankara Univ.; posts held include: Dir.-Gen. State Treasury, Under-Sec., Prime Minister's Office and Ministry of Finance; Minister of State, of Justice and Deputy Prime Minister in various Turkish govts.; Deputy Prime Minister and Minister of State 1980–83. *Address:* c/o Office of the Deputy Prime Minister, Başbakanlık, Bakanlıklar, Ankara, Turkey.

BAYLE, Henry Robert Auguste, B.A.; French diplomatist; b. 30 Nov. 1915, Sainte Adresse; s. of Auguste and Margueritte (née Bricka) Bayle; m. 1st Nicoletta La Torre, two s. two d.; m. 2nd Jutta Hansen 1962; ed. Ecole Normale Supérieure; served in World War II 1939–41; joined Ministry of Foreign Affairs 1944; Press and Information Service 1944–46; Rome 1946, The Hague 1947, High Comm., Bonn, Fed. Repub. of Germany 1949–55; Asst. Dir. Far East Dept. of Ministry of Foreign Affairs 1955–58; Rio de Janeiro 1958–60; Ministry 1960–62; Amb. to Trinidad and Tobago 1962–66, to Cuba 1966–72, to Pakistan 1972–76, to German Democratic Repub. 1976–80; Chair. Comm. for Protection of the Rhine against Pollution 1981–83; Officier, Légion d'honneur, Commdr. ordre nat. du Mérite, Médaille militaire, Croix de guerre. *Leisure interests:* golf, history, travel. *Address:* 46 rue Pergolèse, 75116 Paris, France and Villa L'Alma, Avenue A. Daudet, 06 Mougins. *Telephone:* (45) 00 08 66 (Paris).

BAYLET, Jean-Michel; French journalist and politician; b. 17 Nov. 1946, Toulouse; s. of Jean Baylet and Evelyne Issac; m. Marie-France Marchand 1985; studied law; ed. and Dir. La Dépêche du Midi 1975–; Nat. Sec. Mouvement des Radicaux de Gauche 1973, Vice-Chair. 1978, Chair. 1983; mem. of Parl. for Tarn et Garonne 1978; Sec. of State, Ministry of Foreign Affairs 1984–86; Chair. Tarn et Garonne Council 1985–; elected Senator from Tarn-et-Garonne 1986. *Publication:* La nouvelle alliance 1985. *Leisure interests:* squash, moto-cross, jazz. *Address:* Palais du Luxembourg, 75291 Paris Cedex 06 (Office); avenue Jean Baylet, 31300 Toulouse, 14 rue des Prêtres, 31000 Toulouse, France.

BAYLEY, John Oliver, M.A.; British professor of English literature; b. 27 March 1925; s. of F. J. Bayley; m. (Jean) Iris Murdoch (q.v.) 1956; ed. Eton and New Coll. Oxford; served in army 1943–47; mem. St. Antony's and Magdalen Colls. Oxford 1951–55; Fellow and Tutor in English, New Coll. Oxford 1955–74; Warton Prof. of English Literature and Fellow, St. Catherine's Coll. Oxford 1974–. *Publications:* In Another Country (novel) 1954, The Romantic Survival: A Study in Poetic Evolution 1956, The Characters of Love 1961, Tolstoy and the Novel 1966, Pushkin: A Comparative Commentary 1971, The Uses of Division: unity and disharmony in literature 1976, An Essay on Hardy 1978, Shakespeare and Tragedy 1981, The Order of Battle at Trafalgar 1987, The Short Story: Henry James to Elizabeth Bowen 1988. *Address:* St. Catherine's College, Oxford, England.

BAYLISS, Sir Noel Stanley, Kt., C.B.E., PH.D., F.A.A.; Australian retired professor of chemistry; b. 19 Dec. 1906, Brisbane; s. of Henry Bayliss and Nelly Stothers; m. Nellie E. Banks 1933; two s.; ed. Coburg High School, Melbourne High School, Melbourne and Oxford Univs. and Univ. of Calif. Berkeley; Sr. Lecturer in Chem. Univ. of Melbourne 1933–37; Prof. of Chem. Univ. of W. Australia 1938–71; Pres. Royal Australian Chem. Inst. (R.A.C.I.) 1955–56, A.N.Z.A.A.S. 1962; mem. Australian Univs. Comm. 1959–70 and other public bodies; Hon. Fellow, Australian Coll. of Educ.; H. G. Smith Memorial Medal (R.A.C.I.); Leighton Memorial Medal (R.A.C.I.); Hon. D.Sc. (Univ. of W. Australia); Hon. D. Univ. (Murdoch Univ.). *Publications:* over 80 papers in scientific journals. *Leisure interests:* music, golf. *Address:* 104 Thomas Street, Nedlands, Western Australia 6009, Australia. *Telephone:* (09) 386 1453.

BAYLISS, Sir Richard Ian Samuel, K.C.V.O., M.D., F.R.C.P.; British physician; b. 2 Jan. 1917, Tettenhall; s. of the late Frederick William and Muryel Anne Bayliss; m. 1st Margaret Joan Hardman Lawson (dissolved 1956); m. 2nd Constance Ellen Frey 1957 (dissolved 1979); m. 3rd Marina Audrey Felicité Rankin (née de Borchgrave d'Altena) 1979; one s. three d.; ed. Rugby School, Clare Coll. Cambridge, St. Thomas's Hosp. London, Columbia Univ. New York; Casualty Officer, House Physician, Registrar, Resident Asst. Physician, St. Thomas's Hosp. 1941–44; Officer in Charge, Medical Div., Royal Army Medical Corps India 1944–48; Lecturer in Medicine, Hammersmith Hosp. and Physician, Royal Postgraduate Medical School 1948–54; Rockefeller Fellow, Columbia Univ. 1950–51; Physician, Westminster Hosp. 1954–81; Dean, Westminster Medical School 1960–64; Physician, King Edward VII Hosp. for Officers 1964–87; Physician to H. M. Household 1964–70, to H.M. The Queen 1970–82, Head of H.M. Medical

Household 1973–82; Medical Dir. Swiss Reassurance Co. 1970–85; Dir. and Vice-Chair. Patients Provident Asscn. 1979–89; Deputy Dir., Research Unit, Royal Coll. of Physicians 1982–. *Publications:* various publications in textbooks and medical journals on endocrine, metabolic and cardiovascular diseases. *Leisure interests:* skiing, music. *Address:* Flat 7, 61 Onslow Square, London, SW7 3LS, England. *Telephone:* 01-589 3087.

BAYM, Gordon Alan, A.M., PH.D.; American physicist and educator; b. 1 July 1935, New York; s. of Louis and Lillian Baym; m. Lillian Hartmann; two s. two d.; ed. Cornell Univ., Harvard Univ.; Fellow, Universitetets Institut for Teoretisk Fysik, Copenhagen 1960–62; Lecturer, Univ. of Calif., Berkeley 1962–63; Prof. of Physics, Univ. of Ill., Urbana 1963–; Visiting Prof., Univs. of Tokyo and Kyoto 1968, Nordita, Copenhagen 1970, 1976, Niels Bohr Inst. 1976, Univ. of Nagoya 1979; Visiting Scientist, Academia Sinica, Beijing 1979; mem. Advisory Bd. Inst. of Theoretical Physics, Santa Barbara, Calif. 1978–83; mem. sub-cttee. on theoretical physics, physics advisory cttee., Nat. Scientific Foundation (NSF) 1980–81, mem. Physics Advisory Cttee. 1982–85; mem. Nuclear Science Advisory Cttee., Dept. of Energy/NSF 1982–; Fellow, A.A.A.S., American Acad. of Arts and Sciences, American Physical Soc.; Research Fellow, Alfred P. Sloan Foundation 1965–68; NSF postdoctoral fellow 1960–62; Trustee, Assoc. Univs. Inc.; mem. American Astronomical Soc., Int. Astronomical Union, N.A.S.; Sr. U.S. Scientist Award, Alexander von Humboldt Foundation 1983. *Publications:* Quantum Statistical Mechanics (jt. author) 1962, Lectures on Quantum Mechanics 1969, Neutron Stars 1970, Neutron Stars and the Properties of Matter at High Density 1977. *Leisure interests:* photography and mountains. *Address:* Loomis Laboratory of Physics, University of Illinois, 1110 West Green Street, Urbana, Ill. 61801, U.S.A. *Telephone:* 217-333-4363.

BAYNE, Nicholas Peter, C.M.G., M.A., D.PHIL.; British diplomatist; b. 15 Feb. 1937, London; s. of the late Capt. Ronald Bayne, R.N. and of Elizabeth (née Ashcroft) Bayne; m. Diana Wilde 1961; three s.; ed. Eton Coll. and Christ Church, Oxford; joined H.M. Diplomatic Service 1961; served Manila 1963–66, Bonn 1969–72; seconded to H.M. Treasury 1974–75; Financial Counsellor, Paris 1975–79; Head of Econ. Relations Dept., FCO 1979–82; Royal Inst. of Int. Affairs 1982–83; Amb. to Zaire, also accred. to Congo, Rwanda, Burundi 1983–84; Amb. and Perm. Rep. to OECD 1985–88. *Publication:* Hanging Together: the Seven-Power Summits (with R. Putnam) 1984. *Leisure interests:* reading, sightseeing. *Address:* c/o Foreign and Commonwealth Office, King Charles Street, London, SW1, England.

BAYRAMOĞLU, Fuat; Turkish diplomatist; b. 1912, Ankara; s. of Mehmet Tayyip and Hüsniye Bayramoğlu; m. Nesteren Bayramoğlu; ed. School of Political and Administrative Sciences, Istanbul, and Univ. of Liège; entered Diplomatic Service 1939; mem. Gen. Directorate of Press and Publication Cttee. 1943; Head of Secretariat Prime Minister's Office 1944–46; Chair. Press Dept. Cttee. 1946; Dir. in Foreign Ministry 1948; Consul, Cyprus 1949; Consul Gen., Jerusalem 1951–53; Dir.-Gen. Consular and Claims Dept., Ministry of Foreign Affairs, Ankara 1953–57; Amb. to Norway 1957–59, to Iraq 1959–60, to Iran 1960–62, to Italy 1962–63; Sec.-Gen. Ministry of Foreign Affairs 1963–65; Amb. to Belgium 1965–67, to Italy 1967–69, to U.S.S.R. 1969–71; Chair. Inspection Corps 1971–72; Sec.-Gen. of the Presidency 1972–77; Homayoun Order of Iran 1962, Grand Croix de Mérite Civil Espagnol 1963, Grande Croce all'Ordine del Merito della Repubblica Italiana 1969, Presidential Distinguished Service Award 1973, Foreign Ministry Distinguished Service Award 1973, Gold Medal of Iqbal Birth Centenary (Pakistan) 1979. *Publications:* Turkish version of The Rubaiyat of H. G. Nakhai 1967, 1974, Rubailer (Book of quatrains with trans. into Persian) 1974, 1976, Türk Cam Sanati ve Beykoz İşleri 1974, English edn. Turkish Glass Art and Beykoz Ware 1976, Tezhipli ve Padişah Onayli Fermanlar 1976, Haci Bayram-ı Veli, yaşamı, soyu, vakfı 1983, and several legal and sociological articles. *Leisure interests:* philately, clock and watch collection. *Address:* Kandilli, Cadessi No. 60, Istanbul, Turkey. *Telephone:* 3320663.

BAYS, Karl, B.S., M.B.A.; American business executive; b. 23 Dec. 1933, Loyall, Ky.; s. of James K. Bays and Myrtle (Criscillis) Bays; m. Billie Joan White 1955; one s. one d.; ed. Eastern Kentucky Univ., Indiana Univ.; Pres. American Hosp. Supply Corpn. 1970–74, C.E.O. 1971–85, Chair. 1974–85; Chair. Baxter Int. 1985–87; Chair. and C.E.O. Whitman Corpn. 1987–; Hon. L.L.D. (Eastern Ky.) 1977, Hon D.H.L. (Cumberland Coll.) 1981; Horatio Alger Award 1979. *Leisure interests:* golf, tennis. *Address:* Whitman Corporation, 111 East Wacker Drive, Chicago, Ill. 60601, U.S.A. *Telephone:* (312) 565-3005.

BAYÜLKEN, Ümit Halük; Turkish diplomatist; b. 7 July 1921, Istanbul; s. of Staff Officer H. Hüsnü Bayülken and Mrs. Melek Bayülken; m. Mrs. Valihe Salci 1952; one s. one d.; ed. Lycée of Haydarpasa, Istanbul, and Univ. of Ankara (Political Sciences); Ministry of Foreign Affairs 1944–; Reserve Officer in Army 1945–47; Vice-Consul, Frankfurt (Main) 1947–49; First Sec., Bonn 1950–51; Ministry of Foreign Affairs 1951–53; First Sec. Turkish Perm. Mission to UN 1953–57, Counsellor 1957–59; Turkish Rep. to London Joint Cttee. on Cyprus 1959–60; Dir.-Gen., Policy Planning Group, Ankara 1960–63, Deputy Sec.-Gen. for Political Affairs 1963–64, Sec.-Gen. 1964–66; Amb. to U.K. 1966–69, concurrently accred. to Malta May 1968–July 1969; Perm. Rep. of Turkey to UN 1969–71; Minister of

Foreign Affairs 1971–74; Sec.-Gen. CENTO 1975–77; Sec.-Gen. of the Presidency 1977–; Minister of Defence 1980–83; M.P. from Antalya 1983–87; Pres. Atlantic Treaty Asscn. (Turkey) 1984; Hon. G.C.V.O. (U.K.), Order of Isabel la Católica (Spain), Grosses Bundesverdienstkreuz (Fed. Repub. of Germany), numerous other int. awards; Hon. mem. Mexican Acad. Int. Law, etc. *Publications:* lectures, articles, studies and essays on minorities, Cyprus, principles of foreign policy, int. relations and disputes, including the Cyprus Question in the UN 1975, Collective Security and Defence Organizations in Changing World Conditions 1976. *Leisure interests:* music, painting, reading. *Address:* Nergiz Sokak 15/20 Cankaya, Ankara, Turkey. *Telephone:* 127-0858.

BAZAINE, Jean, L. ès L.; French painter; b. 21 Dec. 1904, Paris; s. of Léon Bazaine and Clémence Temblaire; executed stained glass windows for church at Assy 1946, at Saint Séverin, Paris 1966, ceramic mural and windows at Audincourt 1951–54, ceramic mural at UNESCO 1960, and Maison de la Radio, Paris 1963; exhibited Galerie Carré, Galerie Maeght, Paris; Retrospective Exhbns., Berne 1958, Eindhoven 1959, Hanover 1963, Zürich 1963, Oslo 1963, Paris 1965; Rep. at Biennali of Venice, São Paulo and Carnegie; Grand Prix Nat. des Arts 1964; Commdr. ordre des Arts et des Lettres 1979; paintings in most of the leading museums in U.S.A. and Europe. *Publications:* Notes sur la peinture d'aujourd'hui 1948, Exercice de la peinture 1973. *Address:* Galerie Adrien Maeght, 42 rue du Bac, 75006 Paris (Office); 36 rue Pierre Brossolette, 92140 Clamart, France (Home).

BAZARGAN, Mehdi; Iranian university professor, engineer and politician; b. Sept. 1907, Teheran; s. of Abbasagholi and Sedigheh Bazargan; m. Malak Tabatabai 1939; two s. three d.; ed. Ecole Centrale des Arts et Manufactures de Paris; Asst. Prof. Teheran Univ., then Prof., then Dean; fmr. Man. Dir. Nat. Oil Co. of Iran during Prime Minister Mossadeq's rule; founding mem. of Iranian Soc. of Engs. 1944, Nat. Resistance Movement of Iran 1953; arrested 1955, 1957, 1962 and 1978 for anti-Shah activities; Man. Dir. YAD Consulting Engs.; Safyad Air Conditioning Equipment Mfg. Co.; Leader Freedom of Iran Movement (affiliated with Nat. Front of Mossadegh); mem. Islamic Revolutionary Council 1979–81; apptd. Prime Minister by Ayatollah Khomeini (q.v.); assumed office after overthrow of Dr. Bakhtiar's govt. Feb.–Nov. 1979; resgnd. over internal disputes; M.P. Teheran 1981–84. *Publications:* over 60 books and pamphlets on engineering, industry, science, thermodynamics theory, social studies, with emphasis on Iranian struggles until the revolutionary victory in 1979, the history of the Islamic Repub. of Iran, research on Holy Koran. *Leisure interests:* family gatherings, mountain-climbing, studying and writing books. *Address:* YAD Building, Ghazali Avenue, Teheran, Iran. *Telephone:* 678870.

BAZELON, David Lionel; American judge; b. 3 Sept. 1909, Superior, Wis.; m. Miriam Kellner 1936; two s.; ed. Univ. of Illinois and Northwestern Univ.; private practice, Ill. 1932–35; Asst. U.S. Attorney, Northern District of Ill. 1935–40; sr. mem. Gottlieb and Schwartz 1940–46; Asst. Attorney-Gen. U.S. Lands Div. 1946–47, Office of Alien Property 1947–49; Judge, U.S. Court of Appeals, Dist. of Columbia circuit 1949–, Chief Judge 1962–78, Sr. Circuit Judge 1979–86; Lecturer in Psychiatry, The Johns Hopkins Univ. School of Medicine 1964–; Clinical Prof. of Psychiatry (Socio-legal aspects), George Washington Univ. 1966; Chair. Task Force on Law, President's Panel on Mental Retardation 1961–62; mem. Bd. of Dirs. American Orthopsychiatric Asscn. 1965–72, Pres. 1969–70; mem. Bd. of Dirs. Joint Comm. on Mental Health of Children Inc. 1965–70; mem. Harvard Univ. Program on Technology and Soc. Advisory Cttee. 1966–71, Nat. Advisory Mental Health Council, Public Health Service 1967–71; mem. Bd. of Trustees, Salk Inst. for Biological Studies 1961–, Alcohol Research Center 1979; mem. U.S. Mission on Mental Health to U.S.S.R. 1967; Sr. mem. Inst. of Medicine, N.A.S. 1977; . John F. Kennedy Center for Research on Educ. and Human Devt. Nat. Advisory Cttee. 1968–77, Battelle-Northwest Behavioral and Social Science Consulting Panel 1970–72, Advisory Cttee. on Child Devt., Nat. Research Council 1971–78, Advisory Bd., Div. on the Legal, Ethical and Educational Aspects of Medicine, N.A.S. 1977–78, UN Assocn. Panel on Human Rights and U.S. Foreign Policy 1978–79; American Assocn. for the Advancement of Science, Cttee. on Science, Freedom and Responsibility 1980–; Chair. Advisory Bd., Boston Univ. Center for Law and Life Sciences 1970; Fellow, American Acad. of Arts and Sciences, Boston, Mass. 1970–; Isaac Ray Award, American Psychiatric Assocn. 1960–61, Hon. Fellow 1962, Distinguished Service Award 1975; Hon. Fellow, American Coll. of Legal Medicine 1975; Hon. LL.D. (Colby Coll.) 1966, Boston Univ. Law School 1969, Albert Einstein Coll. of Medicine, Yeshiva Univ. 1972, Northwestern Univ. 1974; Univ. of S. Calif. 1977, Syracuse Univ. 1980, Georgetown Univ. Law Center 1980, Univ. of Santa Clara 1982; numerous other univs. *Address:* 2700 Virginia Avenue, N.W., Apartment 1207, Washington, D.C. 20037, U.S.A. (Home). *Telephone:* 535-3385.

BAZIN, Germain (René Michel), D. ÈS L., L. EN D.; French museum curator and university professor; b. Suresnes; s. of Ch. Bazin and J. Laurence Mounier-Pouthôt; m. Suzanne Heller 1947; ed. Institution de Ste. Croix, Neuilly, Coll. Ste. Croix, Orléans, Coll. de Pont Levoy and Univ. de Paris; Prof., Brussels Free Univ. 1934; began Museum career in Dept. of Drawings, Ecole des Beaux Arts; Keeper of Paintings, Louvre 1937, Dir. of Paintings and Drawings 1951–65, Dir. of Restoration, Paintings of

French Museums 1965–70; Prof. of Museum Studies at Ecole du Louvre 1941–70; now Hon. Curator-in-Chief, Museum of Louvre and Research Prof. York Univ., Toronto; Infantry Capt. 1939–45; active work in protection of French art treasures 1940–45; organized over 30 exhbns. in France and abroad; has frequently lectured in Europe, U.S.A., S. America; has made film on Impressionism; Art Adviser for film The Louvre (N.B.C., New York); Del. to numerous UNESCO Cttees; mem. Inst. de France (Acad. des Beaux-Arts), Central Inst. of Conservation, Rome, Conservateur, Musée Condé Chantilly 1982, numerous acads.; Officier Légion d'honneur, Commdr. ordre des Arts et des Lettres, Grand Officier de l'Ordre de Léopold (Belgium), Commdr. de la Couronne (Belgium), Commdr. Ordre du Mérite (Italy) and Orders from Italy, Portugal, Sweden and Brazil; Dr. h.c. Univ. do Brazil and D.H., Villanova Univ., Pennsylvania; books translated into twenty languages. *Publications:* Le Mont St. Michel 1932, Le Louvre 1933, Les trésors de la peinture française 1941, Fra Angelico 1943, Corot 1943, L'époque impressionniste 1944, Le crépuscule des images 1946, Les grands maîtres hollandais 1949, Histoire générale de l'art (de la préhistoire à nos jours) 1953, L'art religieux baroque au Brésil 1956, Les trésors de la peinture au Louvre 1958, Les maîtres des écoles étrangères au Musée de l'Ermitage 1960, Gallery of Flowers 1960, Les trésors du Musée du Jeu de Paume 1961, L'Aleijadinho 1963, Le message de l'absolu 1964, Baroque et rococo 1965, Le temps des musées 1967, Avant-garde de la peinture, Sculpture mondiale, Destins du baroque 1970, Manet 1972, Le langage des styles 1976, Les palais de la foi 1980, L'Univers impressionniste 1982, La fleur et les peintres 1984, Histoire de l'histoire de l'art de Vasari à nos jours 1986. *Address:* 23 Quai Conti, 75006 Paris, France.

BAZIN, Hervé (see Hervé-Bazin, Jean-Pierre Marie).

BAZIN, Marc Louis, L. EN D.; Haitian politician; b. 6 March 1932, Saint-Marc; s. of Louis Bazin and Simone St. Vil; m. Marie Yolène Sam 1981; ed. Lycée Petion, Port-au-Prince, Univ. of Paris, Solvay Inst. Brussels and American Univ. Washington, D.C.; Admin. Asst. Ministry of Foreign Affairs 1950; Prof. of Civic Educ. Lycée Petion, Haiti 1951; Legal Adviser, Cabinet Rivière (real estate agency), Paris 1958; Lecturer in Commercial Law, Paris 1960; Tech. Adviser, Treasury Dept., Rabat, Morocco 1962, Deputy Gen. Counsel 1964; Technical Adviser, Ministry of Finance, Rabat 1965; Sr. Loan Officer, IBRD, Washington, D.C. 1968; Deputy Chief IBRD Mission in West Africa, Ivory Coast 1970; Div. Chief, IBRD, Washington, D.C. 1972; Dir. Riverblindness Program, WHO, Upper Volta 1976; Man. Dir. Industrial Devt. Fund, Port-au-Prince 1980; Minister of Finance and Econ. Affairs 1982; Special rep. of IBRD at UN 1982; Div. Chief for int. orgs. IBRD 1986; Pres. Mouvement pour l'Instauration de la Démocratie en Haiti (MIDH) 1986–; Officer, Order of the Ouissam Alaouite (Morocco); Knight of Nat. Order of Merit (Burkina Faso). *Address:* 152 rue des Miracles, Port-au-Prince (Office); 2e avenue du Travail, No. 8, Port-au-Prince, Haiti.

BEACH, Morrison H.; American insurance executive; b. 10 Jan. 1917, Winsted, Conn.; s. of Howard Edmund and Edith (Morrison) Beach; m. Evelyn R. Harris 1942; one s. two d.; ed. Williams Coll., Massachusetts Inst. of Technology, Connecticut Univ. Law School; with Travelers Insurance Co. 1939–, Actuary 1950, Assoc. Actuary 1954, Actuary 1957, Second Vice-Pres. and Actuary 1959, Second Vice-Pres. Exec. Dept. 1962, Vice-Pres. 1964, Sr. Vice-Pres. 1965, Exec. Vice-Pres. 1970, Pres. 1971–73, Chair. and C.E.O. 1973–81, Chair. Bd. 1981–82; Chair. Conn. Higher Educ. Loan Authority; mem. Conn. Bar Asscn.; Chair. of numerous business and philanthropic concerns; Fellow, Soc. of Actuaries; mem. American Acad. of Actuaries. *Leisure interests:* golf, music. *Address:* c/o The Travelers Insurance Companies, One Tower Square, Hartford, Conn. 06115, U.S.A. (Office).

BEADLE, George Wells, PH.D.; American biologist; b. 22 Oct. 1903, Nebraska; s. of Chauncey and Hattie Beadle; m. 1st Marion D. Hill 1928 (divorced 1953); m. 2nd Muriel M. Barnett 1953; two s.; ed. Univ. of Nebraska and Cornell Univ.; Nat. Research Fellow, Calif. Inst. of Technology 1931–33, Research Fellow and Instructor 1933–36; Asst. Prof. of Genetics, Harvard Univ. 1936–37; Prof. of Biology, Stanford Univ. 1937–46; Prof. of Biology and Chair. Div. of Biology, Calif. Inst. of Technology 1946–61; Pres. American Asscn. for the Advancement of Science 1956–57; Eastman Visiting Prof., Oxford 1958–59; Pres. Univ. of Chicago 1961–69; Dir. American Medical Asscn. and Inst. for Biomedical Research 1968–70; Prof. of Biology, Univ. of Chicago 1961–68, Prof. Emer., William E. Wrather Distinguished Service Prof., Hon. Trustee 1969–; mem. Advisory Bd. Robert A. Welch Found. 1971–; mem. N.A.S., American Acad. of Arts and Sciences, Royal Soc., Danish Royal Soc., Nat. Science Acad. India, Ist. Lombardo di Lettere, Milan, Japan Acad., Indian Nat. Science Acad; Lasker Award 1950, Dyer Award 1951, Emil C. Hansen Prize 1953, Nobel Prize for Medicine (with Lederberg and Tatum) 1958, Albert Einstein Award 1958, Nat. Award, American Cancer Soc. 1959, Kimber Genetics Award, N.A.S. 1960; D.Sc. (Hon.) Yale, Nebraska, North-western, Rutgers, Kenyon, Wesleyan, Oxford, Birmingham, and numerous others. *Publications:* An Introduction to Genetics (jointly) 1939, Genetics and Modern Biology 1963, The Language of Life (with Muriel Beadle) 1966. *Leisure interests:* photography, mountaineering. *Address:* 900 E. Harrison D-33, Pomona, Calif. 91767, U.S.A. (Home).

BEALE, Geoffrey Herbert, M.B.E., PH.D., F.R.S., F.R.S.E.; British research scientist; b. 11 June 1913, London; s. of Herbert Walter and Elsie Beale; m. Betty Brydon McCallum 1949 (dissolved 1969); three s.; ed. Imperial Coll., Univ. of London; mem. Research Staff, John Innes Horticultural Inst. 1935–40; Intelligence Corps (war service) 1940–45; with Carnegie Inst., Cold Spring Harbor, New York 1946–47; Rockefeller Fellow, Indiana Univ. 1947–48; Lecturer in Genetics, Edinburgh Univ. 1948–63, Royal Soc. Research Prof. 1963–78, Hon. Research Prof. 1978–; Visiting Research Worker, Chulalongkorn Univ., Bangkok. *Publications:* Genetics of Paramecium aurelia 1954, Extranuclear Genetics (with Jonathan Knowles) 1978. *Leisure interests:* music, languages (especially Thai). *Address:* 23 Royal Terrace, Edinburgh, EH7 5AH, Scotland. *Telephone:* (031) 557-1329.

BEALL, Donald Ray, B.S., M.B.A.; American business executive; b. 29 Nov. 1938, Beaumont, Calif.; s. of Ray C. and Margaret (née Murray) Beall; m. Joan Frances Lange 1961; two s.; ed. San Jose State Coll. and Univ. of Pittsburgh; various financial and management positions, Ford Motor Co., Newport Beach, Calif., Philadelphia and Palo Alto, Calif. 1961–68; Exec. Dir. Corporate Financial Planning, Rockwell Int., El Segundo, Calif. 1968–69, Exec. Vice-Pres. Electronics Group 1969–71; Exec. Vice-Pres. Collins Radio Co., Dallas 1971–74; Pres. Collins Radio Group, Dallas, Rockwell Int. 1974–76, Pres. Electronics Operations 1976–77, Exec. Vice-Pres. 1977–79, Dir. 1978–; Pres. Rockwell Int. 1979–, C.O.O. 1979–88, Chair. and C.E.O. Feb. 1988–; mem. Pres.'s Export Council 1981–85. *Leisure interests:* tennis and boating. *Address:* Rockwell International Corporation, 2230 East Imperial Highway, El Segundo, Calif. 90245, U.S.A. *Telephone:* (213) 647-5000.

BEAME, Abraham David, C.P.A.; American local government official; b. 20 March 1906, London, England; s. of Philip and Esther (Goldfarb) Beame; m. Mary Ingerman 1928; two s.; ed. City Coll., New York; Partner Beame-Greidinger (Accountants), New York 1925–45; Asst. Budget Dir., New York City 1946–52, Budget Dir. 1952–61, Comptroller 1962–65, 1969–73, Mayor 1974–77; Chair. Advisory Comm. Intergovernmental Relations, Washington 1978–; Commentator on Urban Affairs, WNBC-TV, New York 1978–; numerous awards from charitable, religious and civic orgs. *Publications:* various articles, mostly concerning govt. and financial topics. *Address:* Advisory Commission on Intergovernmental Relations, 1111 20th Street, N.W., Washington, D.C. 20575, U.S.A.

BEAMENT, Brigadier George Edwin, O.B.E., C.M., E.D., C.D., Q.C., LL.D., B.A.SC. (retd.); Canadian officer and lawyer; b. 12 April 1908, Ottawa, Ont; s. of Thomas Arthur Beament, Q.C. and Edith Louise Beament (née Belford); m. Brenda Yvonne Mary Thoms 1941; one s. one d.; ed. Royal Military Coll., Kingston, Toronto Univ., Osgoode Hall Law School, Staff Coll., Camberley; called to Ontario Bar 1934; Partner Beament and Beament, Ottawa 1937; mobilized 2nd Field Battery R.C.A., Major 1939; proceeded to England in command 2/14 Field Battery R.C.A. 1940; Brigade Major 1st Canadian Armoured Brigade 1941; C.O. 6 Canadian Field Regiment R.C.A., Lieut.-Col. 1942; Col., Gen. Staff First Canadian Army 1943; Brig.-Gen. Staff First Canadian Army 1945; mentioned in despatches; Pres. Khaki Univ. of Canada in the U.K. 1945–46; now Counsel Beament, Green, Barristers and Solicitors; Pres. Royal Mil. Coll. Club of Canada 1953–54; Pres. Ottawa Community Chests 1953–55; Pres. United Services Inst. 1955–56; Pres. Ottawa Y.M.C.A. 1958–60; Gov. Carleton Univ. 1956–73; mem. Nat. Capital Comm. 1960–66; Bencher Law Soc. Upper Canada 1964–75, Life mem. 1984, Hon. Col. 30th Field Regiment R.C.A. 1968–78; Hon. Pres. Ottawa YM-YWCA 1969–72; Hon. mem. Corps of Commissionaires (Ottawa); awarded Croix de guerre avec palme, Order of the White Lion (3rd Class), Czechoslovak Military Cross, Chancellor, Ven. Order of St. John (Canada) 1975–78, Knight of Grace, Ven. Order of St. John 1964, Knight of Justice, Ven. Order of St. John 1975; mem. O.C. 1986; LL.D. (h.c.) (Royal Mil. Coll. of Canada) 1984; L.S.M. Medal, Law Soc. of Upper Canada 1987. *Leisure interests:* travel, historical research, reading. *Address:* 14th Floor, 155 Queen Street, Ottawa, Ontario K1P 6L1 (Office); Snowberry, North Road, Old Chelsea, P.Q. J0X 2N0, Canada (Home). *Telephone:* 238-2229 (Office); 827-2150 (Home).

BEAMENT, Sir James (William Longman), Kt., PH.D., F.R.S.; British professor of agriculture and science; b. 17 Nov. 1921, Crewkerne, Somerset; s. of Tom Beament and Elizabeth Munden; m. Sara Juliet Barker 1962; two s.; ed. Crewkerne Grammar School, Queens' Coll., Cambridge, London School of Tropical Medicine; Research Officer, Agric. Research Council 1948–61; Lecturer, Univ. of Cambridge 1961–67, Fellow and Tutor, Queens' Coll. 1962–67, Chair. Faculty of Biology 1962–72, 1982–84; Prof. of Agric. and Head, Dept. of Applied Biology 1969–; mem. Gen. Bd. Cambridge Univ. Press 1963–67, Reader 1967–69, Syndic. 1969–79; mem. Natural Environment Research Council 1970–83, Chair, 1976–80; Vice-Pres. Queens' Coll., Cambridge 1981–; Scientific Medal, Zoological Soc. of London. *Publications:* numerous scientific papers; Ed. Soc. Experimental Biology Symposia, Ed.-in-Chief Journal of Agric. Science. *Leisure interests:* composing music, playing jazz, building maintenance. *Address:* Department of Applied Biology, Pembroke Street, Cambridge, CB2 3DX; Queens' College, Cambridge (Offices); 19 Sedley Taylor Road, Cambridge, CB2 2PW, England (Home). *Telephone:* 0223-334433, 336611 (Offices); 0223-246045 (Home).

BEAN, William Bennett, M.D.; American physician; b. 8 Nov. 1909, Manila, Philippines; s. of Robert Bennett and Adelaide Leiper (Martin) Bean; two s. one d.; ed. Univ. of Virginia; Intern, Johns Hopkins Univ. Hosp. 1935–36; Asst. Resident Physician, Boston City Hosp. 1936–37; Sr. Medical Resident, Cincinnati Gen. Hosp. 1937–38, Asst. Attending Physician 1941–46, Clinician, Out-Patient Dept. 1946–48, Attending Physician 1946–48; Dir. Heat Research, Clinical testing of rations, Armored Medical Research Laboratory 1942–45, Commdg. Officer; Asst. Prof. Univ. of Cincinnati Medical Coll. 1940–47, Assoc. Prof. 1947–48; Prof. Head Dept. of Internal Medicine, Univ. of Iowa Medical Coll. 1948–70; Physician-in-Chief Univ. Hosps. 1948–70; Sir William Osler Prof. 1970–80, Prof. Emer. 1980–; Kempner Prof. and Dir. Inst. for Medical Humanities, Univ. of Tex. Medical Branch 1974–80, Acting Chair. Dept. of Dermatology 1977–78; Groedel Lecturer, Alan Gregg Lecturer, Garland Lecturer, Fielding Garrison Lecturer; mem. New York Acad. of Sciences, World Medical Assen., Royal Soc. of Medicine, Pan American Medical Assen., American Clinical and Climatological Assen., Horseshoe Soc., and many other socs.; Corresp. mem. Mexican Soc. for Philosophy and Medicine; John Horsley Memorial Prize, Univ. of Virginia 1944; Groedel Medal 1961; U.S.Army Commendation Medal, American Coll. of Cardiology Medal. *Publications:* Sir William Osler; Aphorisms from his Bedside Teachings and Writings (3rd edn.) 1968, Vascular Spiders and Related Lesions of the Skin 1958, Aphorisms from Latham 1962, Rare Diseases and Lesions; their Contribution to Clinical Medicine 1967. Ed. Monographs in Medicine 1951–52; Book Review Ed. Archives of Internal Medicine 1955–61, Ed.-in-Chief 1962–66; Ed. Consultant Modern Medicine 1964–67, Stedman's Medical Dictionary, Familiar Medical Quotations; Ed. Current Medical Dialog 1967–75; Ed.-in-Chief Texas Reports on Biology and Medicine 1977–80, Walter Reed: A Biography 1982; specialist articles. *Address:* 11 Rowland Ct., Iowa City, Iowa 52240, U.S.A. *Telephone:* 319/356-2569.

BEARN, Alexander Gordon, M.D., F.A.C.P.; American (b. British) pharmaceutical executive and professor of medicine; b. 29 March 1923, Cheam, England; s. of Edward Gordon Bearn and Rose Kay; m. Margaret Slocum 1952; one s. one d.; ed. Epsom Coll. and Guy's Hospital, Univ. of London; Postgraduate Medical School, London 1949–51; Asst. to Prof., Rockefeller Univ., New York, U.S.A. 1951–64, Prof. 1964–66; Prof. and Chair. Dept. of Medicine, Cornell Univ. Medical Coll. 1966–77; Physician-in-Chief New York Hosp. 1966–77; Stanton Griffis Distinguished Medical Prof. 1976–80; Prof. of Medicine, Cornell Univ. Medical Coll. 1966–; Sr. Vice-Pres., Medical and Scientific Affairs, Merck Sharp & Dohme Int. 1979–; mem. N.A.S., Amercian Philosophical Soc.; Pres. American Soc. of Human Genetics 1971; Lowell Lecture, Harvard Univ. 1958; Alfred Benzon Prize (Denmark); Hon. M.D. (Catholic Univ., Korea), Dr. h.c. (René Descartes, Paris). *Publications:* Progress in Medical Genetics (Ed.) 1962–85, Cecil Loeb Textbook of Medicine (Assoc. Ed.) 1963, 1967, 1971, 1975, numerous articles in medical and scientific journals. *Leisure interests:* biographies and travel. *Address:* Merck Sharp & Dohme International, P.O. Box 2000, Rahway, N.J. 07065 (Office); 1225 Park Avenue, New York, N.Y. 10028, U.S.A. (Home). *Telephone:* (201) 574-6833 (Office); (212) 534-2495 (Home).

BEATER, Bernard Edwin, M.A., D.PHIL., D.SC., F.R.S.C., F.R.S.S.A.; South African soil scientist; b. 8 June 1908, Durban, S. Africa; s. of George E. Beater and Margaret T. Thompson; m. Evelyn F. Mitchell 1938 (died 1972); one s. one d.; ed. Durban High School, Natal Univ., Durban-Westville Univ. and Pretoria Univ.; research, Soil Science Dept. S. African Sugar Assen. Experiment Station 1934–68. *Publications:* five books including: Soil Series of the Natal Sugar Belt 1970, Founding of the South African Sugar Experiment Station and the Development of Research over the First Fifty Years 1925–75 1989; 69 technical papers. *Leisure interest:* tennis. *Address:* 5 Sandown Gardens, Umgeni Park, Durban North, Natal, South Africa 4051.

BEATON, William Henry, B.ENG.; Canadian consulting engineer; b. 4 May 1921, Montreal; s. of William A. Beaton and Catherine Direen; m. Annah Jean Meikle 1951; one s. two d.; ed. McGill Univ., Montreal; with Stadler Hurter & Co. (consulting engs.) 1947; J. A. Beauchemin & Assocs. (consulting engs.), Assoc. 1954; Partner, Beauchemin-Beaton-Lapointe (consulting engs.) 1956, Sr. Partner 1972–; Chair. of Bd. Cansult Ltd. (Beauchemin-Beaton-Lapointe affiliate devoted to overseas projects) 1975–82, Deputy Chair. 1982–86. *Publications:* miscellaneous technical articles. *Leisure interests:* reading, music. *Address:* 79 Lakeshore Road, Beaconsfield, Quebec, H91V 4H7, Canada. *Telephone:* (514) 694-7191.

BEATRIX, Queen of the Netherlands; **Beatrix Wilhelmina Armgard;** b. 31 Jan. 1938, Baarn; d. of Queen Juliana (q.v.) and Bernhard, Prince of the Netherlands (q.v.); succeeded to the throne on abdication of her mother 30 April 1980; m. Claus George Willem Otto Frederik Geert von Amsberg 10 March 1966; children: Prince Willem-Alexander Claus George Ferdinand, Prince of Orange, b. 27 April 1967; Prince Johan Friso Bernhard Christiaan David, b. 25 Sept. 1968; Prince Constantijn Christof Frederik Aschwin, b. 11 Oct. 1969; ed. Baarn Grammar School, Leiden State Univ. *Address:* c/o Government Information Service, Press and Publicity Department, Binnen Hof 19, 2513 AA The Hague, Netherlands. *Telephone:* 070-564136.

BEATTIE, Hon. Sir David Stuart, G.C.M.G., G.C.V.O., LL.D., Q.C., Q.S.O.; New Zealand lawyer and administrator; b. 29 Feb. 1924, Sydney, Australia; m. Norma Macdonald 1950; three s. four d.; ed. Dilworth School and Univ.;

Naval Officer, Second World War; barrister and solicitor; Judge of Supreme Court 1969–80; Gov.-Gen. of New Zealand Oct 1980–85; Chair. N.Z. Meat Industry Assen. Inc.; Pres. Auckland District Law Soc. 1964; N.Z. Services rugby 1944–45; Chair. Royal Comm. on Courts 1977–79, Winston Churchill Trust 1976–80, Admiralty Reform Cttee. 1973; Chair. of Trustees, N.Z. Sports Foundation 1977–80; several directorships 1986. *Address:* 18 Golf Road, Heretaunga, Upper Hutt, Wellington, New Zealand (Home).

BEATTY, Perrin, B.A.; Canadian politician; b. 1 June 1950, Toronto; s. of Martha Beatty; m. Julia Kenny 1974; one s.; ed. Upper Canada Coll., Univ. of Western Ont.; Special Asst. to Minister of Health, Ont.; mem. House of Commons 1972–; Minister of State for Treasury Bd. 1979; Minister of Nat. Revenue 1984–85; Solicitor-Gen. for Canada 1985–86, Acting Solicitor-Gen. Jan. 1989–; Minister of Defence 1986–89, of Nat. Health and Welfare Jan. 1989–; mem. Special Jt. Cttee. on Constitution 1978, Chair. Progressive Conservative Caucus Cttee. on Supply and Services, Spokesperson on Communications; Co-chair. of Standing Jt. Cttee. on Regulations and other Statutory Instruments; Caucus spokesperson on Revenue Canada; Chair. of Caucus Cttee. on Fed. Prov. Relations and of Progressive Conservative Task Force on Revenue Canada 1983. *Leisure interests:* music, woodwork and reading. *Address:* Department of National Health and Welfare, Brooke Claxton Building, Tunney's Pasture, Ottawa, Ont. K1A 0K9, Canada.

BEATTY, Warren, American actor; b. 30 March 1937, Richmond, Virginia; s. of Ira Beatty and Kathlyn Maclean; ed. Stella Adler Theatre School. *Film appearances include:* Splendor in the Grass 1961, Roman Spring of Mrs. Stone 1961, All Fall Down 1962, Lilith, 1965, Mickey One 1965, Promise Her Anything 1966, Kaleidoscope 1966, Bonnie and Clyde 1967, The Only Game in Town 1969, McCabe and Mrs. Miller 1971, Dollars 1972, The Parallax View 1974, Shampoo (producer and co-screenwriter) 1975, The Fortune 1976, Heaven Can Wait (producer, co-dir. and co-screenwriter) 1978, Reds (producer, dir., Acad. Award for Best Dir. 1981) 1981, Ishtar 1987. *TV appearances include:* Studio One and Playhouse 90; theatre roles include: A Loss of Roses 1960. *Address:* c/o Directors Guild of America, 7950 Sunset Boulevard, Hollywood, Calif. 90046, U.S.A.

BEAUDOIN, Gérald-A., O.C., Q.C., M.A., LL.L.; Canadian lawyer and university professor; b. 15 April 1929, Montreal; s. of Armand Beaudoin and Aldéa St.-Arnaud; m. Renée Desmarais 1954; four d.; ed. Univs. of Montreal, Toronto, Ottawa; pvt. practice with Paul Gerin-Lajoie Q.C. in Montreal 1955–56; mem. Advisory Council, Dept. of Justice, Ottawa 1956–65; Asst. Parl. Counsel, House of Commons 1965–69; Prof. of Constitutional Law, Univ. of Ottawa 1969–, Dean of Law 1969–79, Assoc. Dir., Human Rights Center 1981–86, Dir. 1986–; mem. Pépin-Robarts Royal Comm. (Task Force on Canadian Unity) 1977–79; mem. Académie canadienne-française, Royal Soc. of Canada; Titular mem. Int. Acad. of Comparative Law; Prix du doyen 1953, Medal of ACFAS 1987. *Publications:* Essais sur la Constitution 1979, Le partage des pouvoirs, 3rd edn. 1983; Ed. The Supreme Court of Canada 1986, Charter Cases 1987; Co-Ed. Canadian Charter of Rights and Freedoms 1982, Perspectives canadiennes et euro-péennes des droits de la personne 1986; 70 articles on the Canadian Constitution. *Leisure interests:* reading, travels. *Address:* Faculty of Law, Civil Law Section, 57 Copernicus, University of Ottawa, Ottawa, Ont., K1N 6N5 (Office); 4 St.-Thomas, Hull, Quebec, J8Y 1L4, Canada (Home). *Telephone:* (613) 564-4951 (Office); (819) 771-4742 (Home).

BEAUJEU-GARNIER, Jacqueline; French professor; b. 1 May 1917, Aiguilhe; d. of Jacques Garnier and Marthe (née Perrin) Garnier; m. Jean Beaujeu 1942 (divorced 1967); one s.; ed. Lycées de Roanne et du Mans, Univ. of Paris-Sorbonne; Asst. Lecturer Paris-Sorbonne 1942–46, Prof. 1960–87; Lecturer Univ. of Poitiers 1947–48; Prof. Univ. of Lille 1948–60, Hon. Prof. 1961–; Sec.-Gen. Information Géographique 1940–; Jt. Dir. Annales de Géographie; Pres. Soc. de Géographie 1983, CREPIF 1986–; Officier Légion d'honneur, Commandeur ordre national du Mérite, Palmes académiques; Médaille d'Argent de la Soc. de Géographie de Paris 1963, Assen. of American Geographers Medal 1984, American Geographical Soc. Medal 1985, Research Award (Royal Scottish Soc. of Geography) 1988, Grande Médaille de Vermeil de la Ville de Paris 1988. *Publications:* Le Morvan et sa bordure 1948, l'Économie de l'Amérique latine, l'Économie du Moyen-Orient, Géographie de la Population, 2 Vols. 1956–58, l'Europe du Nord et du Nord-Ouest (with others) 1958–63, Traité de Géographie urbaine 1963, Trois milliards d'hommes 1965, La Population française 1969, Les Régions des Etats-Unis 1970, La Géographie: méthodes et perspectives 1971, France 1975, Géographie du Commerce 1977, Atlas et Géographie de Paris et de l'Ile de France 1977, Géographie urbaine 1980. *Address:* 6 rue Pierre et Marie Curie, 75005 Paris, France (Home).

BEAULNE, Joseph-Charles-Léonard Yvon; Canadian diplomatist; b. 22 Feb. 1919, Ottawa; s. of Leonard Beaulne and Yvonne Daoust; m. Thérèse Pratte 1946; five c.; ed. Univ. of Ottawa; served with Canadian Army in U.K., N. Africa, Italy and N.W. Europe; joined Canadian Dept. of External Affairs 1948, served Rome, Buenos Aires and Havana 1948–61; Amb. to Venezuela 1961–64; Minister in Washington 1964–67; Amb. to Brazil 1967–69; Perm. Rep. to UN 1969–72; Asst. Sec. of State 1972–74; Dir.-Gen. Bureau of African and Middle Eastern Affairs, Dept. of External Affairs 1974–76; Perm. Del. to UNESCO 1976–79; Rep. of Canada to UN Human Rights Comm. 1976–; Amb. to Holy See. 1979–84. *Address:* c/o Ministry of

External Affairs, Lester B. Pearson Building, Ottawa, Ont., K1A 0G2, Canada.

BEAUMONT, Sir Richard Ashton, K.C.M.G., O.B.E.; British diplomatist (retd.); b. 29 Dec. 1912; s. of Arthur R. Beaumont and Evelyn Rendle; m. 1st A. Lou Camran 1942 (died 1985); one d.; m. 2nd Melanie Anns 1989; ed. Repton and Oriel Coll., Oxford; entered Consular Service 1936, served Beirut 1936, Damascus 1938; war service 1941–44; joined Foreign Office 1945, served Mosul 1946–47; Chargé d'affaires, Damascus 1947; Consul, Jerusalem 1948–49, Caracas 1949–53, Baghdad 1953–57; Imperial Defence Coll. 1958; Head of Arabian Dept. Foreign Office 1959–61; Amb. to Morocco 1961–65, to Iraq 1965–67; at Foreign Office 1967–69; Amb. to Egypt 1969–72; Dir.-Gen. Middle East Assoc. 1973–78; Gov. S.O.A.S. 1973–78; Trustee, Thomson Foundation 1974–; Chair. Bd. Arab-British Chamber of Commerce 1980–; Chair. Anglo-Arab Assoc. 1979–. *Leisure interest:* gardening. *Address:* 14 Cadogan Square, London, SW1X 0JU, England.

BEAVEN, Peter Jamieson, DIP.ARCH., A.R.I.B.A., F.N.Z.I.A.; New Zealand architect; b. 13 Aug. 1925, Christchurch; s. of Eric Tamate Beaven and Maria Joan Jamieson; m. Anne Mary Beaglehole 1952; one s. two d.; ed. Christ's Coll., Christchurch, Univ. Coll., Auckland; Sub-Lieut. Royal Naval Volunteer Reserve, Far East; practised in Christchurch for twenty years; founded first N.Z. Civic Trust; Chair. Environment Advisory Cttee., Christchurch City Council; Principal, Beaven Hunt Assocs.; Gold Medal, N.Z. Inst. of Architects 1966, various merit awards in N.Z. architecture. *Leisure interests:* yachting, sketching, painting, walking, reading. *Publications:* Urban Renewal Report (N.Z. Govt.), co-author New Zealand Architecture 1840-1970 1973. *Address:* Beaven Hunt Associates, P.O. Box 1766, Christchurch (Office); 22 Salisbury Street, Christchurch 1, New Zealand (Home).

BEAZLEY, Kim Christian, M.A., M.PHIL.; Australian politician; b. 14 Dec. 1948, Perth; s. of Kim Edward Beazley; m. Mary Beazley; two d.; ed. Univ. of Western Australia, Oxford Univ.; fmr. Lecturer in Social and Political Theory, Murdoch Univ. Perth; M.P. for Swan 1980–; Minister for Aviation 1983–84, for Defence Dec. 1984–, Special Minister of State 1983–84; Labor Party. *Address:* Department of Defence, Russell Offices, Canberra, A.C.T. 2600, Australia. *Telephone:* (062) 659111.

BĘBENEK, Stanisław, M.A.; Polish editor and journalist; b. 19 July 1920, Wołowice, Cracow Voivodship; widower; two s.; ed. Acad. of Political Sciences, Warsaw; Dir. and Ed.-in-Chief, State Agricultural and Forestry Publrs. Warsaw 1958–64; Dir. for Programme Matters, Warsaw TV 1964–67; Dir. State Publishing Inst., Warsaw 1968–71; Dir. Theatre, Music and Concert Dept. of Ministry of Culture and Art 1971–73; adviser to Chair. of Council of Ministers 1973–75; Pres. and Ed.-in-Chief, Czytelnik Publrs. 1975–; Pres. Polish Soc. of Book Publrs. 1980–; mem. Polish Workers' Party 1943–48, Polish United Workers' Party (PZPR) 1948–; Officer's and Commdr.'s Cross of Order of Polonia Restituta, Order of Banner of Labour (2nd Class) and other decorations. *Leisure interest:* travel. *Address:* Al. Wyzwolenia 12a, 00-570 Warsaw, Poland. *Telephone:* 21-68-51 (Home); 28-31-78 (Office).

BECHER, Ulrich; Austrian-Swiss writer; b. 2 Jan. 1910, Berlin, Germany; s. of Richard Becher and Elisa Ulrich von Rickenbach; m. Dana Roda 1934; one s.; ed. Werner-Siemens-Gymnasium, Berlin, Freie Schulgemeinde Wickersdorf, and Univs. of Geneva, Berlin and Leipzig; fmr. mem. George Grosz circle, Berlin; went to Vienna 1933; newspaper corresp. Paris and Switzerland; escaped to Zürich 1938; in Rio de Janeiro 1941–43, Brazilian interior 1944, New York City 1945–48, Basle 1949–; Drama Prize, German Stage Club, Cologne for Mademoiselle Löwenzorn 1955, Swiss Schiller Foundation Prize 1976. *Publications:* Männer machen Fehler (short stories) 1932, Die Eroberer (short stories) 1936, Nachtigall will zum Vater fliegen (novel) 1950, Kurz nach 4 (novel) 1957, Männer machen Fehler, Geschichten der Windrose (collected short stories) 1958, Das Herz des Hais (novel) 1960, Brasilianischer Romanzero 1962; plays: Niemand 1934, Der Bockerer (with Peter Preses) 1948, Der Pfeifer von Wien (with P. Preses) 1950, Samba 1951, Feuerwasser 1952, Mademoiselle Löwenzorn 1954, Die Kleinen und die Grossen 1957, Der Herr kommt aus Bahia 1958, Makumba 1965, Biene gib mir Honig 1972; Murmeljagd (novel in 5 vols.) (American edn. Woodchuckhunt): Tote Zeit, Licht im See, Geisterbahn I, Geisterbahn 11, Die Strasse über San Gian 1969, Der schwarze Hut 1972, Das Profil (novel) 1973, William's Ex-Casino (novel) 1974, SIFF (Selective Identification of Friend and Foe) (essays) 1978. *Address:* Spalenring 95, Basle, Switzerland. *Telephone:* 22-51-70.

BECHERER, Hans Walter, M.B.A.; American business executive; b. 19 April 1935, Detroit, Mich.; s. of Max Becherer and Mariele Specht; m. Michele Beigbeder 1959; one s. one d.; ed. Trinity Coll., Hartford, Conn. and Munich and Harvard Univs.; Exec. Asst. Office of Chair. Deere & Co., Moline, Ill. 1966–69; Gen. Man. John Deere Export, Mannheim, Germany 1969–73; Dir. Export Marketing, Deere & Co., Moline, Ill. 1973–77, Vice-Pres. 1977–83, Sr. Vice-Pres. 1983–86, Exec. Vice-Pres. 1986–87, Pres. and C.O.O. 1987–. *Address:* Deere & Company, John Deere Road, Moline, Ill. 61265 (Office); 788 25th Avenue Court, Moline, Ill. 61265, U.S.A. (Home). *Telephone:* 309-765-4449 (Office).

BECHERT, Heinz, D.PHIL.; German professor of Indology; b. 26 June 1932, Munich; s. of Rudolf Bechert and Herta Bechert; m. Marianne

Würzburger 1963; ed. Univs. of Munich and Hamburg; Research Asst. Univ. of Saarbrücken 1956–61; Univ. of Mainz 1961–64; Prof. of Indology Univ. of Göttingen 1965–. *Publications:* author and editor of 25 books and 150 contribs. in academic journals. *Address:* Seminar für Indologie und Buddhismuskunde, Universität Göttingen, Hainbundstr. 21, D-3400 Göttingen, Federal Republic of Germany. *Telephone:* (0551) 57068.

BECHTEL, Stephen Davison; American engineer-constructor; b. 24 Sept. 1900, Aurora, Ind.; s. of Warren A. and Clara (West) Bechtel; m. Laura Adaline Peart 1923; one s. one d.; ed. Univ. of California; joined W.A. Bechtel Co., Vice-Pres. 1925–36, Pres. 1936–46; First Vice-Pres. Six Companies Inc. (constructors of Hoover Dam) 1931–36; Dir. Bechtel-McCone Corpn. 1937–49; during Second World War Chair. Calif. Shipbuilding Corpn.; now Senior Dir. The Bechtel Group.; mem. and fmr. mem. numerous orgs. and socs.; Dir. Stanford Research Inst. 1949, now Emer.; Pres. Lakeside Corpn.; Trustee Ford Foundation 1960–70; mem. Business Advisory Council U.S. Dept. of Commerce 1950–60 (Chair. 1958–59); Hon. mem. The Business Council 1961–; Hon. LL.D. numerous univs. 1954, 1958, 1976, 1982, Hon. D.Eng. (Univ. of Pacific) 1966, (Washington Univ.) 1976, Dr. h.c. (Univ. of San Francisco) 1982; John Fritz Medal 1961, Nat. Defense Transportation Award 1960, Order of Cedar (Lebanon), Kt. Order of St. Sylvester (Holy See), Kt. Commdr. Court of Honour and numerous awards and decorations.
[*Died 14 March 1989.*]

BECHTEL, Stephen Davison, Jr., B.SC., M.B.A.; American business executive; b. 10 May 1925, Oakland, Calif.; s. of Stephen Davison Bechtel (q.v.) and Laura (Peart) Bechtel; m. Elizabeth Mead Hogan 1946; two s. three d.; ed. Univ. of Colorado, Purdue Univ., Stanford Univ.; eng. and management positions with cos. in Bechtel Group, Inc. 1941–60, Pres. 1960–73, Chair. 1973–80, Chair. Bechtel Group Inc. 1980–; Dir. IBM Corpn., Southern Pacific Co.; mem. and fmr. Vice-Chair. Business Council; Chair. Nat. Acad. of Eng.; mem. American Inst. of Mining, Metallurgical and Petroleum Engineers, Fellow, American Soc. of Civil Engineers; Hon. Fellow, Inst. Chemical Engineers (U.K.); Hon. D.Eng. (Purdue) 1972; Hon. D.Sc. (Univ. of Colorado); Officier, Légion d'honneur; Distinguished Alumnus Award, Purdue Univ. 1964; Ernest C. Arbuckle Distinguished Alumnus Award, Stanford Univ. 1974; Outstanding Achievement in Construction Award, Moles 1977; Distinguished Engineering Alumnus Award, Univ. of Colorado 1979; Herbert Hoover Medal 1981, Chairs'. Award, American Assoc. of Eng. Socs. 1982; Washington Award (Nat. Eng. Soc.) 1985; American Soc. of Civil Engineers Pres.'s Award 1985. *Leisure interests:* golf, shooting, tennis, flyfishing, backpacking, photography. *Address:* Bechtel Group Inc., P.O. Box 3965, San Francisco, Calif. 94119 (Office); P.O. Box 3809, San Francisco, Calif. 94119, U.S.A. (Home). *Telephone:* (415) 768-7600 (Office).

BECK, Béatrix Marie; Swiss writer; b. 30 July 1914; ed. Lycée de St. Germain-en-Laye and Université de Grenoble; fmr. Sec. to André Gide; journalist; mem. Jury, Prix Fémina; Prix Goncourt for Léon Morin, prêtre; Prix Félix Fénéon; Prix Fondation Delmas 1979. *Publications:* Barny, Une mort irrégulière, Léon Morin, prêtre, Des accommodements avec le ciel, Le premier mai, Abram Krol, Le muet, Cou coupé court toujours.

BECK, Brian Edgar, M.A.; British ecclesiastic; b. 27 Sept. 1933, London; s. of A. G. Beck and of the late C. A. Beck; m. Margaret Ludlow 1958; three d.; ed. City of London School, Corpus Christi Coll., Cambridge and Wesley House, Cambridge; Asst. Tutor Handsworth Coll. 1957–59; ordained Methodist Minister 1960; Circuit Minister, Suffolk 1959–62; St. Paul's United Theological Coll., Limuru, Kenya 1962–68; Tutor Wesley House, Cambridge 1968–80, Prin. 1980–84; Sec. Methodist Conf. of G.B. 1984–; Co.-Chair. Oxford Inst. of Methodist Theological Studies 1976–; Sec. E. African Church Union Consultation Worship and Liturgy Cttee. 1963–68; mem. World Methodist Council 1966–71, 1981–. *Publications:* (contrib. to) Christian Belief, A Catholic-Methodist Statement 1970, Unity the Next Step? 1972, Suffering and Martyrdom in the New Testament 1981, Reading the New Testament Today 1977, and articles in theological journals. *Leisure interests:* walking and DIY. *Address:* 1 Central Buildings, Westminster, London, SW1H 9NH (Office); 76 Beaumont Road, Purley, Surrey, CR2 2EG, England (Home). *Telephone:* 01-222 8010 (Office); 01-645 9162 (Home).

BECK, Conrad; Swiss composer; b. 16 June 1901, Lohn, Schaffhausen; m. Friedel Ehrsam 1941; two s.; ed. Konservatorium, Zürich; further musical studies in Paris with Ibert, Honegger and Roussel 1923–32; Ludwig Spohr Prize, City of Brunswick, Composers Prize of Assen. of Swiss composers, Kunstpreis, City of Basel; Commdr. Order of Cultural Merit, Monaco 1973. *Principal works:* seven symphonies, many other symphonic works, concertos, two oratorios, cantatas, chamber music, etc., including Der Tod zu Basel (Miserère), Die Sonnenfinsternis, Elegie. *Leisure interest:* mountaineering. *Address:* St. Johann Vorstadt 82, Basel, Switzerland. *Telephone:* 570309.

BECK, Sir Edgar (Charles), Kt., C.B.E., F.ENG., F.I.C.E.; British engineer; b. 11 May 1911; s. of Edgar Bee and Nellie Stollard (née Osborne) Beck; m. Mary Agnes Sorapure 1933 (divorced 1972), three s. two d.; m. 2nd Anne Teresa Corbould 1972; ed. Lancing Coll., Jesus Coll., Cambridge; joined John Mowlem & Co. Ltd. as engineer 1933, Dir. 1940, Man. Dir.

1958, Chair. 1961-79, Pres. 1981-; Dir. Scaffolding G.B. Ltd. 1942 (Chair. 1958-78), Builders' Insurance Ltd. 1959 (Deputy Chair. 1969); mem. Export Credits Guarantee Dept. Advisory Council 1964-69; Pres. Fed. of Civil Eng. Contractors 1971-75; Chair. Export Group for the Constructional Industries 1959-63; British Hospitals Export Council 1964-75; Underwriting mem. Lloyd's 1955-. *Leisure interests:* golf, salmon fishing. *Address:* 13 Eaton Place, London, S.W.1, England. *Telephone:* 01-235 7455.

BECK, John C., M.D.; American professor of medicine; b. 4 Jan. 1924, Audubon, Ia.; s. of Wilhelm and Marie Beck; one s.; ed. McGill Univ.; Physician-in-Chief, Royal Victoria Hospital 1964-74, Sr. Physician, Dept. of Medicine 1974-81; Prof. of Medicine, Univ. of Calif., San Francisco 1974-79; Visiting Prof. U.C.L.A. 1978-79, Dir. Multicampus Div. of Geriatric Medicine, School of Medicine, U.C.L.A. and Prof. of Medicine, U.C.L.A. 1979-; numerous other professional appts. *Publications:* articles in professional journals. *Address:* U.C.L.A. School of Medicine, Division of Geriatric Medicine, 32-144 CHS, Los Angeles, Calif. 90024, U.S.A.

BECK, Robert A.; American insurance executive; b. 6 Oct. 1925, New York, N.Y.; s. of Arthur C. and Alma (Wickware) Beck; m. Frances Kenny 1948; three s. two d.; ed. Bronx High School of Science, Syracuse Univ., Syracuse, N.Y; joined The Prudential Insurance Co. of America as Special Agent 1951, Pres. 1974-78; Chair. and C.E.O. Sept. 1978-87, Chair. Emer. 1987-; Chair. Business Roundtable 1984-86; Dir. Prudential Insurance Co. of America, Campbell Soup Co., Xerox Corpn.; mem. Nat. Comm. Social Security Reform, Exec. Cttee. of Pres. Reagan's Private Sector Survey on Cost Control; Chair. Nat. Center for State Courts, United Way of America, the American Coll.; Kt. of Malta. *Leisure interests:* golf, fishing, scuba diving, sailing, jogging, squash, paddle ball, the arts. *Address:* The Prudential Insurance Company of America, Prudential Plaza, Newark, N.J. 07101 (Office); 8 Somerset Drive, Rumson, N.J. 07760, U.S.A. (Home).

BECK, T. Mihály; Hungarian chemist; b. 14 Nov. 1929, Szöreg; s. of Dezső Beck and Rózsi Weisz; m.Piroska Ébrey; two s.; ed. Univ. of Szeged; Head Hungarian Acad. of Sciences research dept. for reaction kinetics 1952-68; corresp. mem. Hungarian Acad. of Sciences 1973, mem. 1979, mem. of Presidium 1985-; Prof. of Physical Chemistry and Head of Dept. Univ. of Debrecen 1968-; mem. Bureau of IUPAC; hon. mem. Finnish Acad. of Sciences, Akademie der Wissenschaften GDR; Editorial Bd. mem. numerous Hungarian and other journals; Labour Order of Merit 1965; State Prize 1985. *Publications:* Komplex egyensulyok kémiája 1965, Tudományáltudomány (Science and Pseudoscience) 1977, 1978. *Leisure interests:* history and sociology of science, numismatics, tennis. *Address:* Kossuth Lajos Tudományegyetem, Debrecen 4010, P.O. Box 7, Hungary. *Telephone:* (36/52) 16-666.

BECK, Tamás, PH.D.; Hungarian engineer; b. 1929, Budapest; m. Ilona Beck; ed. studies in mechanical eng., Princeton Univ.; Ministry of Industry, Budapest 1952-63; Hungarian Hemp Industries 1963-70; Man. Dir. Budaflax Hungarian Linen Industries; Pres. Hungarian Chamber of Econ. (formerly Commerce) 1982-; Minister of Trade 1988-; mem. Comms. for Fibre Tech. and Econs., Hungarian Acad. of Sciences; Prof. Tech. Univ. of Budapest, Tech. Coll. for Light Industry; consultant, Nat. Comm. for Tech. Devt.; mem. State Technical Devt. Cttee. 1973-, Hungarian Acad. of Sciences, Fibres and Econ. Cttee. 1975-, Cen. Cttee., Hungarian Socialist Worker's Party 1987-, Hungarian Technical and Scientific Assen. for the Textile Industry; several awards and decorations including Eötvos Prize 1980, State Prize 1985. *Publications:* many books and papers on numerous topics. *Address:* 1121-Budapest, Méra u. 5/7; Budapest V.Vigadó utca 6, Hungary. *Telephone:* 124-826 (Office).

BECKENBAUER, Franz; German footballer; b. 11 Sept. 1945; s. of the late Franz Beckenbauer Sr. and of Antonia Beckenbauer; m. Brigitte Wittmann; three s.; ed. Northern Coll. of Insurance Studies; played for Bayern Munich and New York Cosmos football clubs; won West German Cup (with Bayern Munich) 1966, 1967, 1969, 1971, West German Championship 1972, 1974, European Cup Winners 1967, European Cup 1974-76, World Club Championship 1976; won European Nations Cup (with West German Nat. Team) 1972, World Cup 1974; won North American Championship (with New York Cosmos) 1977, 1978-80; European Footballer of the Year 1972, 1976, West German Footballer of the Year 1980; Professional Football Man. 1977-, Man. West German Nat. Team 1984-; f. Franz Beckenbauer Foundation 1982; Bayern Verdienstorden 1982; Order of FIFA (Int. Football Fed.) 1984. *Publication:* Einer wie ich (Someone like Me). *Address:* DFB, Otto-Fleck-Schneise 6, 6000 Frankfurt/Main 71, Federal Republic of Germany. *Telephone:* 0611 - 71 04 05.

BECKER, Aharon; Israeli labour official; b. 1906, Brest-Litovsk, Russia; m. Cyla Selzer 1930; one s. two d.; went from Russia to Israel 1924; mem. Kibbutz 1925; building worker 1925-28; Sec. Ramat Gan Labour Council 1929-32; Sec. Union of Textile Workers 1933-34; mem. Exec. of Labour Council in Tel-Aviv 1934-43; Man. Dir. Industrial Dept., Co-operative Wholesale Soc. 1943-47; Head of Supply Mission, Ministry of Defence 1948-49; Head of Trade Union Dept. and mem. Exec. Bureau, Histadrut 1949-60, Sec.-Gen. 1961-69; Deputy mem. Governing Body of ILO 1956-70; mem. Knesset; mem. Secr. of Israel Labour Party; mem. Council of Dirs, Bank of Israel. *Publications:* numerous articles in Hebrew and British

press; various booklets and publications on economic and labour problems. *Address:* 66 Keren Kayemet Boulevard, Tel-Aviv, Israel.

BECKER, Boris; German tennis player; b. 22 Nov. 1967, Leimen, near Heidelberg; s. of Karl-Heinz and Elvira Becker; started playing tennis at Blau-Weiss Club, Leimen; coached by Gunther Bosch, West German Tennis Fed.; won West German Jr. Championship 1983; subsequently runner-up U.S. Jr. Championship; coached by Ion Tiriac since 1984; quarter-finalist Australian Championship, winner Young Masters Tournament, Birmingham, England 1985; Grand Prix Tournament, Queen's 1985; won Men's Singles Championship, Wimbledon 1985 (youngest ever winner and finalist; beat Kevin Curren), also won 1986, finalist 1988; finalist Benson and Hedges Championship, Wembley, London 1985; Sportsman of the Year 1985, Hon Citizen Leimen 1986. *Address:* Nusslocher Strasse 51, 6906 Leimen, Baden, Federal Republic of Germany.

BECKER, Carl Johan; Danish archaeologist; b. 3 Sept. 1915, Copenhagen; s. of Carl and Henny Becker (née Döcker); m. Birgit Hilbert 1949; three d.; ed. Metropolitanskolen, Københavns Universitet; Asst., Nat. Museum 1934-41, Asst.-Keeper 1941-52; Prof. of Prehistoric Archaeology, Univ. of Copenhagen 1952-85, Dean Faculty of Arts 1963-64, mem. Konsistorium 1964-70; Chief Ed. Acta Archaeologica 1948-84; mem. Royal Danish Acad. of Sciences and Letters, Danish Research Council for the Humanities 1968-75; Corresp. Fellow, British Acad.; mem. Cttee. of Thai-Danish Archaeological Expedition and numerous European Prehistoric and Archaeological societies; Knight First Class Order of Danebrog. *Publications:* Enkeltgravkulturen på de danske Øer 1936, Mosefundne Lerkar fra Yngre Stenalder 1948, Die Mittel-Neolithischen Kulturen in Südskandinavien 1955, 1971, Förromersk Jernalder i Syd-og Midtjylland 1961, Studies in Northern Coinages of the Eleventh Century 1981. *Leisure interest:* numismatics. *Address:* 23 Egernvej, DK-2000-Frederiksberg, Denmark. *Telephone:* 01-86-57-11.

BECKER, Gary Stanley, PH.D.; American economics educator; b. 2 Dec. 1930, Pottsville, Pa.; s. of Louis William and Anna Siskind Becker; m. Guity Nashat 1979; two s. two d.; ed. Princeton Univ., Univ. of Chicago; Asst. Prof., Univ. of Chicago 1954-57; Asst. and Assoc. Prof. of Econs. Columbia Univ. 1957-60, Prof. of Econs. 1960, Arthur Lehman Prof. of Econs. 1968-69; Ford Foundation Visiting Prof. of Econs., Univ. of Chicago 1969-70, Univ. Prof., Dept. of Econs, 1970-83, Depts. of Econs. and Sociology 1983-, Chair. Dept. of Econs. 1984-85; Research Assoc., Econs. Research Center, N.O.R.C. 1980-; mem. N.A.S., Int. Union for the Scientific Study of Population, American Philosophical Soc. and American Econ. Assen. (Pres. 1987), Mont Pelerin Soc. (Dir. 1985); Fellow, American Statistical Assen., Econometric Soc., Nat. Acad. of Educ., American Acad. of Arts and Sciences, Univ. of Illinois, Chicago 1988; Hon. degrees Hebrew Univ. of Jerusalem 1985, Knox Coll., Galesburg, Ill. 1985; W. S. Woytinsky Award (Univ. of Mich.) 1964, John Bates Clark Medal (American Econ. Assen.) 1967, Frank E. Seidman Distinguished Award in Political Econ. 1985, Award of Merit (Nat. Insts. of Health) 1986. *Publications:* The Economics of Discrimination 1957, Human Capital 1964, Human Capital and the Personal Distribution of Income: Analytical Approach 1967, Economic Theory 1971, Essays in the Economics of Crime and Punishment (ed., with William M. Landes) 1974, The Allocation of Time and Goods over the Life Cycle (with Gilbert Ghez) 1975, The Economic Approach to Human Behavior 1976, A Treatise on the Family 1981, columnist Business Week 1985-, numerous articles in professional journals. *Address:* Department of Economics, 1126 East 59th Street, Chicago, Ill. 60637, U.S.A. *Telephone:* (312) 702-8168.

BECKER, Gert; German company executive; b. 21 Aug. 1933, Kronberg; s. of Otto Becker and Henriette (née Syring); m. Margrit Bruns 1960; one s. one d.; ed. Akademie für Welthandel, Frankfurt; Sales Dept., Degussa, Frankfurt 1956; with rep. office in Teheran, Iran 1960, with subsidiary in São Paolo, Brazil 1963, Div. Man., Frankfurt 1966, Dir. 1971, Man. Dir. Degussa, Frankfurt 1977-, Pres. and C.E.O. *Leisure interests:* literature, book collecting, golf. *Address:* Friedrichstrasse 100, 6242 Kronberg/Ts., Federal Republic of Germany. *Telephone:* 4456.

BECKER, Hans Detlev; German publisher and journalist; b. 11 June 1921, Freiburg, Elbe; s. of Albert and Hildegard Becker; m. Elisabeth Burkhard 1953; ed. Univ. of Münster; Ed. Der Spiegel 1947-49; Man. Ed. 1950-58, Chief Ed. 1959-61, Publr. 1962-83, Consulting Partner 1984-. *Leisure interest:* golf. *Address:* Postfach 30 0641, D-2000, Hamburg 36, Federal Republic of Germany.

BECKER, Horst Carl E., D.JUR.; German diplomatist; b. 16 May 1924, Cologne; m. Verena Countess zu Münster 1965 (divorced 1969); two d.; ed. Univs. of Freiburg and Bonn; admitted to the Bar 1951; Political Dept., Foreign Office 1955; Embassy, London 1958; served in Perm. Mission to NATO 1961; Embassy, The Hague 1968; Amb. to Somalia 1974; mem. Gen. Secr. NATO, Brussels 1977; Amb. to New Zealand 1985-; Order of Merit, Commander Order of Orange. *Leisure interests:* painting, drawing, golf, tennis. *Address:* 96, Park Road, Tudor House, Belmont, Wellington, New Zealand. *Telephone:* 651 845.

BECKER, Isidore A., B.A.; American company executive; b. 10 May 1926, New York, N.Y.; s. of Max and Eva (née Chester) Becker; m. Adele Sandler 1947; one s. one d.; ed. Brooklyn Coll; partner, Herbert D. Silver

& Co. 1956-63; Dir. Rapid-American Corpn. 1964-82, Financial Vice-Pres. and Chair. Financial Cttee. 1964-72, Vice-Chair. of Bd. 1967-72, 1976-82, Pres. 1972-76; Treas. and Chief Financial Officer, McCrory Corpn. 1964-70, Dir. 1964-; Vice-Chair. and Dir., Glen Alden Corpn. 1964-72; Chair. of Bd., Schenley Industries 1968-82, Shaw-Ross Int. Importers Inc. 1983-, Sauthene Wine and Spirits 1983-. *Address:* 126 East 56th Street, New York, N.Y. 10022 (Office); 215 East 68th Street, New York, N.Y. 10021, U.S.A. (Home).

BECKER, Jurek; German author; b. 30 Sept. 1937, Łódź, Poland; s. of Max and Hanna Becker; m. Christine Harsch-Niemeyer 1986; two s. (by previous m.); ed. Humboldt Univ., Berlin, and Filmhochschule, Potsdam-Babelsberg; freelance author 1961-; mem. PEN 1971-; writer-in-residence, Oberlin Coll., Ohio 1978; Guest Prof., Univ. of Essen 1979, Augsburg 1981; mem. Deutsche Akademie für Sprache und Dichtung 1983-; Heinrich-Mann-Preis (G.D.R.) 1971, Charles Veillon Prize (Switzerland) 1972, Bremen Literature Prize 1974, Nat. Prize of G.D.R. 1975, Adolf-Grimme Prize 1987; City author, Bergen-Enkheim (Fed. Repub. of Germany) 1982. *Publications:* novels: Jakob der Lügner 1969, Irreführung der Behörden 1973, Der Boxer 1975, Schlaflose Tage 1978, Aller Welt Freund 1982, Bronstein's Kinder 1986; short stories: Nach der ersten Zukunft 1980; several screen-plays, including for TV Liebling, Kreuzberg 1986. *Address:* c/o Suhrkamp Verlag, P.O. Box 4229, 6000 Frankfurt 1, Federal Republic of Germany. *Telephone:* 069-75 60 10.

BECKER, Jürgen; German writer and editor; b. 10 July 1932, Cologne; s. of Robert and Else (née Schuchardt) Becker; m. 1st Marie Becker 1954 (dissolved 1965), one s.; m. 2nd Rango Bohne 1965, one step s. one step d.; ed. Univ. of Cologne; various jobs until 1959; freelance writer and contributor to W. German Radio 1959-64; Reader at Rowohlt Verlag 1964-65; freelance writer; living in Cologne, Berlin, Hamburg and Rome; Dir. Suhrkamp-Theaterverlag 1974; now Head of Drama Dept., Deutschlandfunk Köln; mem. Akademie der Künste Berlin, Deutsche Akademie für Sprache und Dichtung Darmstadt, PEN Club; Förderpreis des Landes Niedersachsen 1964, Stipendium Deutsche Akad. Villa Massimo, Rome 1965, 1966, Group 47 Prize 1967, Literaturpreis der Stadt Köln 1968, Literaturpreis, Bavarian Acad. of Arts 1980, Kritikerpreis 1981, Bremer Literaturpreis 1986. *Publications:* Phasen (Text and Typogramme with Wolf Vostell) 1960, Felder (short stories) 1964; Ränder (short stories) 1968, Bilder, Häuser (Radio Play) 1969, Umgebungen (short stories) 1970, Schnee (poems) 1971, Das Ende der Landschaftsmalerei (poems) 1974, Erzähl mir nichts vom Kreig (poems) 1977, In der verbleibenden Zeit (Poetry) 1979, Erzählen bis Ostende (short stories) 1981, Gedichte 1965-1980 (collected poems) 1981; Ed. Happenings (documentary with Wolf Vostell) 1965. *Address:* Am Klausenberg 84, 5000 Köln-Brück, Federal Republic of Germany. *Telephone:* 8411-39.

BECKETT, John Michael, M.A., F.R.S.A., C.B.I.M.; British lawyer and business executive; b. 22 June 1929; s. of late H. N. Beckett and C. L. Beckett (née Allsop); brother of Sir Terence Beckett (q.v.); m. Joan Mary Rogerson 1955; five d.; ed. Wolverhampton Grammar School, Magdalen Coll., Oxford; called to bar, Gray's Inn 1954-55; with Tootal Ltd. 1955-58; with Tarmac Ltd. 1958-75, Dir. 1963-82, (non-exec. 1975-82); Chief Exec. British Sugar Corpn. Ltd. 1975-82; Chair. British Sugar Bureau 1978-81; Chair. UK Sugar Industries Asscn. 1978-81; Chair. Woolworth Holdings PLC 1982-86; Chair. British Slag Fed. 1967-69; Chair. Asphalt and Coated Macadam Asscn. 1971-73; Dir. Johnson Matthey 1985-86; mem. Transport and Road Research Advisory Cttee. 1972-80, Chair. 1977-80; Hon. Fellow Inst. of Quarrying. *Address:* c/o Woolworth House, 242-246 Marylebone Road, London, NW1 6JL, England (Office). *Telephone:* 01-262 1222.

BECKETT, Samuel, M.A.; Irish author in French and English languages; b. 13 April 1906; ed. Portora Royal School and Trinity Coll., Dublin; lecturer Ecole Normale Supérieure, Paris, 1928-30, Trinity Coll., Dublin 1930-32; now lives in Paris; Foreign Hon. mem. American Acad. of Arts and Sciences 1968; Prix Formentor 1961, Nobel Prize for Literature 1969, C.Lit. 1984; Croix de Guerre. *Publications:* Verse: Whoroscope 1930, Echo's Bones 1935; Novels: Murphy 1938, Watt 1944, Mercier et Camier 1946, Molloy 1951, Malone meurt 1952, L'Innommable 1953, Comment c'est, Imagination Dead Imagine 1966, Ill Seen, Ill Said 1982, Collected Poems in English and French 1977; Short Stories: More Pricks than Kicks 1934, Nouvelles et textes pour rien 1955, Le Dépeupleur 1971 (English Version The Lost Ones 1972), Four Novellas 1977, Company 1980; Stage Plays: En attendant Godot 1952 (English version Waiting for Godot), Fin de partie 1957 (English version Endgame), Krapp's Last Tape 1959, Happy Days 1960, Play 1963, Not I 1973, Rockaby 1981; Radio Plays: All that Fall 1957, Embers 1959, Words and Music 1961, Cascando 1964, Ends and Odds 1977, Stirrings Still 1989, Nohow On (novellas). TV Plays: Ghost Trio and ... But the Clouds 1977, Essay: Proust 1965; No's Knife; Collected Shorter Prose 1945-66 1977, Collected Poems in English and French 1977, Collected Poems (1930-78) 1984, Collected Shorter Plays 1984, Complete Dramatic Works 1986. *Address:* c/o Faber & Faber Ltd., 3 Queen Square, London, WC1, England.

BECKETT, Sir Terence (Norman), Kt., K.B.E., B.SC., F.ENG., C.ENG., F.I.MECH.E., F.B.I.M., F.I.M.I., F.R.S.A.; British business executive; b. 13 Dec. 1923, Walsall, Staffs.; s. of Horace Norman and Clarice Lillian (née Allsop) Beckett, brother of John Beckett (q.v.); m. Sylvia Gladys Asprey 1950;

one d.; ed. Wolverhampton and S. Staffs. Tech. Coll., London School of Econs.; Capt. Royal Electrical and Mechnical Eng., served in Britain, India and Malaya 1945-48; joined Ford Motor Co. as Man. Trainee 1950, Styling Man., Briggs Motor Bodies Ltd. (Ford subsidiary) 1954, Admin. Man., Engineer, then Man. Product Staff 1955, Gen. Planning Man., Product Planning Staff 1961, Man. Marketing Staff 1963, Dir., Car Div., Ford Motor Co. Ltd. 1964, Exec. Dir. 1966, Dir. of Sales 1968, Vice-Pres. European and Overseas Sales Operations, Ford of Europe 1969-73; Man. Dir., Chief Exec., Ford Motor Co. Ltd. 1974-80, Chair. 1976-80; fmr. Chair. Ford Motor Credit Co. Ltd.; Dir. (non-exec.) CEGB 1987-; Chair. and Pro-Chancellor Univ. of Essex Oct. 1989-; fmr. Dir. ICI, Ford Nederland N.V., Ford Lusitana S.A.RL., Portugal, Henry Ford & Son Ltd., Ireland, Ford Motor Co. A/S, Denmark, Ford Motor Co. AB, Sweden, Automotive Finance Ltd.; fmr. mem. of Council CBI, Dir.-Gen. 1980-87, mem. Council and Exec. Cttee. Soc. of Motor Mfrs. and Traders; mem. NEDC 1980-; mem. Court and Council Essex Univ. 1985-, Top Salaries Review Body 1987-; Fellow, Fellowship of Eng. 1980; Chair. Governing Body of London Business School, London Business School Trust Co. Ltd. 1979-86, Council of Motor Cycle Trades Benevolent Fund; Gov., Cranfield Inst. of Tech., Nat. Inst. of Econ. and Social Research, London School of Econs.; Patron, Manpower Services Comm. Award Scheme for Disabled People; Hon. Fellow, Sidney Sussex Coll., Cambridge 1981-; Hon. D.Sc. (Cranfield Inst. of Tech.) 1977, (Heriot-Watt) 1981, Hon. D.Sc.Econ. (London) 1982; Hambro Businessman of the Year Award 1978; BIM Gold Medal 1980. *Leisure interests:* ornithology, music. *Address:* c/o Barclays Bank PLC, 74 High Street, Ingatestone, Essex, England.

BECKH, Harald J. von, M.D.; Argentine medical scientist; b. 17 Nov. 1917, Vienna, Austria; s. of Johannes A. and Elisabeth von Beckh (née Flach-Hillé); ed. Theresianum High School, Vienna and Vienna Univ.; career devoted to aviation and later to space medicine, and in particular to weightlessness and its effects on living organisms; Lecturer Aeromedical Acad. Berlin 1941, Buenos Aires Nat. Inst. of Aviation Medicine 1947; joined staff of U.S. Air Force Aeromedical Field Laboratory, Holloman Air Force Base, N.M. 1956, Scientific Dir. Oct. 1958-64; Chief Scientist 1964-70; Dir. of Research Aerospace Medical Research Dept., Naval Air Devt. Center 1970-; Prof. of Human Physiology, New Mexico State Univ. 1959-70; mem. Armed Forces/Nat. Research Council Cttee. on Bio-Astronautics 1958-61; mem. Space Medicine Cttee. of Int. Astronautical Fed. 1961-, Int. Acad. of Astronautics; hon. mem. German Rocket Soc., Medical Asscn. of Armed Forces of Argentina, Portuguese Centre of Astronautical Studies, Spanish Soc. of Aerospace Medicine, Austrian Astronautical Soc.; Fellow, British Interplanetary Soc., Aerospace Medical Asscn. (Pres. Space Medicine Branch 1978-79); Assoc. Fellow, American Inst. of Aeronautics and Astronautics; Sr. mem. American Rocket Soc. (Pres. Holloman Section 1959-61); mem. Int. Acad. of Aviation Medicine; Arnold D. Tuttle Award of the Aerospace Medical Asscn. 1972, Melbourne W. Boynton Award of the American Astronautical Soc. 1972, Hermann Oberth Honor Ring, Hermann Oberth Soc. 1975, Hubertus Strughold Award of Aerospace Medical Asscn. 1976, Jeffries Medical Research Award of American Inst. of Aeronautics and Astronautics 1977. *Publications:* Fisiología de Vuelo 1955, Basic Principles of Aerospace Medicine 1960; numerous papers in Journal of Aviation Medicine and Journal of the British Interplanetary Society and other aeronautical and aeromedical journals in U.S.A., Great Britain, Germany, Argentina and Spain. *Leisure interests:* French and Spanish literature, flying. *Address:* P.O. Box 1220, Warminster, Pa. 18974, U.S.A. *Telephone:* (215) 441-2530 (Office); (215) 672-4455 (Home).

BECKINGHAM, Charles Fraser, M.A., F.B.A.; British professor of Islamic Studies; b. 18 Feb. 1914, Houghton, Hunts.; s. of Arthur Beckingham and Alice Beckingham; m. Margery Ansell 1946 (died 1966); one d.; ed. The Grammar School, Huntingdon and Queens' Coll. Cambridge; Prof. of Islamic Studies, Univ. of Manchester 1958-65; Prof. of Islamic Studies, Univ. of London 1965-81, Emer. Prof. 1981-; Pres. Hakluyt Soc. 1969-72; Int. Dir., Fontes Historiae Africanae Project, Union Académique Int. 1986-; Jt. Ed. Journal of Semitic Studies 1959-64, Ed. 1964-65; Ed. Journal of the Royal Asiatic Soc. 1984-87. *Publications:* Some Records of Ethiopia 1954 and The Prester John of the Indies 1961 (both with G. W. B. Huntingford), The Hebrew Letters of Prester John (with E. Ullendorff, q.v.) 1982, Between Islam and Christendom 1983, The Itinerario of Jeronimo Lobo (with M. G. da Costa and D. M. Lockhart) 1984; articles in acad. journals. *Address:* 3 Pipe Passage, Lewes, East Sussex, BN7 1YG, England.

BECKWITH, Athelstan Laurence Johnson, D.PHIL., F.A.A.; Australian professor of organic chemistry; b. 20 Feb. 1930, Perth, W.A.; s. of Laurence A. and Doris G. Beckwith; m. Phyllis Kaye Marshall 1953; one s. two d.; ed. Univ. of Western Australia and Balliol Coll., Oxford Univ.; Research Scientist, CSIRO, Melbourne 1957-58; Lecturer in Chem., Univ. of Adelaide 1958-62, Prof. of Organic Chem., 1965-81; Lecturer, Imperial Coll., Univ. of London 1962-63; Visiting Prof., Univ. of York 1968; Prof. of Organic Chem., A.N.U. 1981-, Dean 1989-; Pres. Royal Australian Chemical Inst. 1984-85; Vice-Pres. Australian Acad. of Science 1985-86; Syntex Pacific Coast Lecturer 1986; Rennie Memorial Medal 1960; Carnegie Fellow 1968; H. G. Smith Memorial Medal 1980. *Publications:* numerous scientific papers and reviews in chemistry journals, etc. *Leisure interests:* reading, performing music, model-making, golf. *Address:* Research School of Chemistry, Australian National University, G.P.O. Box 4, Canberra, A.C.T. 2601 (Office); 2/14 Currie Crescent, Kingston, A.C.T. 2604, Australia (Home). *Telephone:* (062) 494012 (Office); (062) 953694 (Home).

BEDBROOK, Sir George Montario, Kt., O.B.E., M.B., M.S., F.R.A.C.S., F.R.C.S.; Australian orthopaedic surgeon; b. 8 Nov. 1921, Melbourne, Vic.; s. of Arthur Ernest Bedbrook and Ethel Bedbrook (née Prince); m. Jessie Violet Page 1946; two s. three d.; ed. State School, Coburg, Victoria, Univ. High School, Melbourne, Medical School, Univ. of Melbourne; Resident Medical Officer, Royal Melbourne Hosp. 1944–45; Lecturer in Anatomy, Univ. of Melbourne 1946–50; Resident Medical Officer, Nat. Orthopaedic Hosp., England 1951; Registrar, Orthopaedic Dept., Croydon Group Hosps., England 1951–53; started in pvt. practice in Perth, W.A. 1953; joined Orthopaedic Dept., Royal Perth Hosp. 1953, joined Paraplegic Service 1954, Head Dept. of Paraplegia, Royal Perth Hosp. and Royal Perth Rehabilitation Hosp. 1954–72, Sr. Surgeon 1972–81, Emer. Orthopaedic Surgeon 1981–, Head Dept. of Orthopaedic Surgery 1965–75, Chair. 1975–79; Vice-Chair. Nat. Advisory Council for the Handicapped 1975–83, Australian Council for Rehabilitation of the Disabled 1970–80; Pres. Australian Orthopaedic Assen. 1977, Int. Medical Soc. of Paraplegia 1981–84; Councillor Western Pacific Orthopaedic Assen.; mem. Rehabilitation Int., Int. Assen. for the Study of Pain, Scoliosis Research Soc., Australian Medical Assen., Australian Assen. of Surgeons, College of Rehabilitation Medicine, Advisory Body on Rehabilitation Medicine (Fed. Govt.) and many other assens. and cttees.; Hon. M.D. (W.A.) 1973, Hon. D.Tech. (W.A. Inst. of Tech.) 1974, Hon. F.R.C.S. (Edin.) 1981; Betts' Medal, Australian Orthopaedic Assen. 1972, Medal of Honour, (Int. Medical Soc. of Paraplegia) 1978, Lawrence Poole Prize and Lecturer, Univ. of Edin. 1981 and other prizes. *Publications:* The Care and Management of Spinal Cord Injuries, Lifetime Care of the Paraplegic Patient; over 117 scientific papers and publs. *Address:* 13 Colin Grove, West Perth, W.A. 6005, Australia.

BEDDOME, John MacDonald; Canadian oil executive; b. 20 Sept. 1930, Vernon, B.C.; one s. one d.; ed. Univ. of British Columbia; with Gulf Oil Canada 1952–71; with Dome Petroleum Ltd. 1971–, Pres. and C.O.O. 1983–88; Chair. & Dir. TransCanada Pipelines 1979–83; Dir. PanArctic Oils Ltd., Encor Energy Corpn. Ltd., Ipsco Inc., Canadian Petroleum Assen. *Address:* P.O. Box 200, Calgary, Alberta T2P 2H8, Canada. *Telephone:* (403) 234-4911.

BEDELL, Ralph Clairon, A.M., PH.D.; American university professor and public servant; b. 4 June 1904, Hale, Mo.; s. of Charles Edward Bedell and Jennie Eaton Bedell; m. 1st Stella Virginia Bales 1929 (deceased), 2nd Ann Barclay Sorency 1968 (deceased), 3rd Myra Jervey Hoyle 1976; ed. Central Missouri State Univ. and Univ. of Missouri-Columbia; Prof. of Educational Psychology, Northeast Mo. State Univ. 1933–37; Dean of Faculty, Cen. Mo. State Univ. 1937; Prof. of Educational Psychology and Measurements, Univ. of Nebraska 1938–50; served Navy 1942–45; Prof. of Psychology and Educ., The American Univ., Washington, D.C. 1950–52; with U.S. Office of Educ., Dept. of Health, Educ. and Welfare 1952–66; on leave 1955–58; Sec.-Gen. S. Pacific Comm. Nouméa, New Caledonia 1955–58; Prof. of Educ., Univ. of Missouri-Columbia 1967–74; Emer. Prof. 1974–, Consultant and Research Assoc. 1974–75; Consultant, Stephens Coll. 1975–76; Consultant, Lincoln Univ. of Missouri 1976–77; Consultant, Mo. Co-ordinating Bd. for Higher Ed. 1976–78; Consultant on Teacher Education, Prince of Songkla Univ., Pattani, Thailand 1980–86. *Publications:* General Science for To-day (co-author) 1936, Pre-Flight Aeronautics (co-author) 1942, Basic Guidance for Nebraska Schools (Ed.) 1948, Teacher Immortal (jtly.) 1984. *Address:* 106 South Ann, Columbia, Mo. 65201, U.S.A. *Telephone:* (314) 443-3006.

BEDFORD, David, A.R.A.M.; British composer; b. 4 Aug. 1937, London; s. of L. H. Bedford and L. F. K. Duff; m. 1st M. Parsonage 1958 (divorced), two d.; m. 2nd S. Pilgrim 1969 (divorced), two d.; ed. Lancing Coll. and R.A.M.; teacher of Music, Whitefield School, Hendon, London 1966–69, Queen's Coll., Harley Street, London 1969–80; Assoc. Visiting Composer, Gordonstoun School 1980–; Youth Music Dir. English Sinfonia 1986–; Patron Barnet Schools Music Assen. 1987; since 1980 freelance composer and arranger; compositions: Music for Albion Moonlight 1965, Star Clusters 1971, The Golden Wine 1974, Star's End 1974, The Rime of the Ancient Mariner 1978, The Death of Baldur 1979, Sun Paints Rainbows 1982, Symphony No. 1 1983, Symphony No. 2 1985, some music for film The Killing Fields 1984, Absolute Beginners 1985, The Mission 1986, Into Thy Wondrous House 1986, Ma non Sempere 1987, Gere Curam Mei Nobis (for Katherine) 1987; Licentiate of Trinity Coll. of Music. *Leisure interests:* squash, film and cricket. *Address:* 39 Shakespeare Road, Mill Hill, London, NW7 4BA, England. *Telephone:* 01-959 3165.

BEDFORD, Steuart John Rudolf, B.A., F.R.C.O., F.R.A.M.; British conductor; b. 31 July 1939, London; s. of L. H. and Lesley (Duff) Bedford; m. 1st Norma Burrowes (q.v.) 1969 (divorced 1980); m. 2nd Celia Harding 1980; two d.; ed. Lancing Coll., Sussex, Oxford Univ., Royal Acad. of Music.; operatic training as repetiteur, asst. conductor, Glyndebourne Festival 1965–67; English Opera Group (later English Music Theatre), Aldeburgh and London 1967–73; Artistic Dir. and Resident Conductor, English Music Theatre and Aldeburgh Festival 1975–; Musical Dir. English Sinfonia 1982–; freelance conductor, numerous performances with English Opera Group, Welsh Nat. Opera, Metropolitan Opera, New York (operas include

Death in Venice, The Marriage of Figaro), Royal Danish Opera; also at Royal Opera House, Covent Garden (operas include Owen Wingrave, Death in Venice, Così fan tutte) Santa Fe Opera, Teatro Colón, Buenos Aires, Brussels, Lyon etc.; conductor for BBC, Netherlands Radio, Belgian Radio; Medal of the Worshipful Co. of Musicians. *Leisure interests:* golf, skiing. *Address:* c/o Harrison-Parrott Ltd., 12 Penzance Place, London, W11 4PA, England.

BEDI, Bishan Singh, B.A.; Indian cricketer; b. 25 Sept. 1946, Amritsar; s. of late Gyan Singh Bedi and Rajinder Kaur Bedi; m. 1st Glenith Jill Bedi 1969, one s. one d.; m. 2nd Inderjit Bedi 1980; ed. Punjab Univ.; employed by Steel Authority of India, New Delhi; slow left-arm bowler; has played for India in 53 tests 1966–, captained India in 14 Tests; has captained Delhi in Ranji Trophy and North Zone in Duleep Trophy; played for Northants. 1972–77; Hon. Life mem. M.C.C. 1981, nat. selector; Padma Shri 1969; Arjuna Award 1971. *Leisure interests:* reading, photography, swimming and letter-writing. *Address:* Ispat Bhawan, Lodhi Rd, New Delhi 3, India. *Telephone:* 43133.

BÉDIÉ, Henri Konan, L. EN D., D. ÈS SC.; Côte d'Ivoire economist and politician; b. 1934, Dadiékro; m. Henriette Koizan 1958; two s. two d.; ed. Poitiers Univ., France; worked as civil servant in France 1959–60; Counsellor at French Embassy, Washington, D.C. May-Aug. 1960; founded Ivory Coast mission to the UN 1960; Chargé d'affaires for Ivory Coast to U.S.A. 1960, Amb. 1960–66; Amb. to Canada 1963–66; Minister of Econ. and Finance 1966–77; Special Adviser for African affairs to Int. Finance Corpn. 1978–80; Pres. Nat. Ass. 1980–; mem. Bureau Politique, Parti Démocratique de la Côte d'Ivoire (PDCI) 1965–; Pres. OAMPI (Office africain et malgache de la propriété industrielle); Pres. BOAD (Banque ouest-africaine de développement); Admin. UNESCO Int. Cultural Funds; Grand Officier de l'ordre nat. (Côte d'Ivoire), Commdr. Légion d'honneur, Grand Officier ordre nat. du Mérite and other orders and decorations. *Address:* Palais de l'Assemblée, B.P. 1381, Abidjan, Côte d'Ivoire.

BEDJAOUI, Mohammed; Algerian lawyer; b. 21 Sept. 1929, Sidi-Bel-Abbès; s. of Benali Bedjaoui and Fatima Oukili; m. Leila Francis 1962; two d.; ed. Univ. of Grenoble and Institut d'Etudes Politiques, Grenoble; Lawyer, Court of Appeal, Grenoble 1951; research worker at Centre Nat. de la Recherche Scientifique (CNRS) Paris 1955; Legal Counsellor of the Arab League in Geneva 1959–62; Legal Counsellor Provisional Republican Govt. of Algeria in Exile 1958–61; Dir. Office of the Pres. of Nat. Constituent Ass. 1962; mem. Del. to UN 1957, 1962, 1977, 1978–82; Sec.-Gen. Council of Ministers, Algiers 1962–63; Pres. Soc. Nat. des Chemins de Fer Algériens (SNCFA) 1964; Dean of the Faculty of Law, Algiers Univ. 1964; Minister of Justice and Keeper of the Seals 1964–70; mem., special reporter, Int. Law Comm. 1965–82; Amb. to France 1970–79; Perm. Rep. to UNESCO 1971–79, to UN 1979–82; Vice-Pres. UN Council on Namibia 1979–82; mem. UN Comm. of Inquiry (Iran) 1980; Pres. Group of 77 1981–82; Judge Int. Court of Justice March 1982–88; Head Algerian del. to UN Conf. on Law of the Sea 1976–80; mem. Int. Inst. of Law; Carnegie Endowment for Int. Peace 1956; ordre du Mérite Alaouite, Morocco; Order of the Repub., Egypt; Commdr. Légion d'Honneur (France), ordre de la Résistance (Algeria). *Publications:* International Civil Service 1956, Fonction publique internationale et influences nationales 1958, La révolution algérienne et le droit 1961, Succession d'états 1970, Terra nullius, droits historiques et autodetermination 1975, Non-alignment et droit international 1976, Pour un nouvel ordre économique international 1979. *Address:* International Court of Justice, Peace Palace, 2517 KJ, The Hague, Netherlands; 39 rue des Pins, Hydra, Algiers, Algeria. *Telephone:* 92 44 41; 60-30-89.

BEDNARSKI, Henryk; Polish educator and politician; b. 22 June 1934, Małkinia Górna; m. 1960; one s.; ed. Pedagogical Coll., Gdańsk, Nicolaus Copernicus Univ., Toruń, Adam Mickiewicz Univ., Poznań; supplementary studies Party Coll. of Cen. Cttee. CPSU, Moscow; Dir. Inst. of Social Sciences Pedagogical Coll., Bydgoszcz 1973–78, Pro-rector Pedagogical Coll. 1978–80; Head Dept. of Science and Educ. PZPR; of Voivodship Cttee., Bydgoszcz 1973–78, First Sec. 1980–83; mem. PZPR Cen. Cttee. Nov. 1983–, Sec. Cen. Cttee. Nov. 1983–87, Head, Ideological Comm. of PZPR Cen. Cttee. 1986–88; Minister of Nat. Educ. 1987–88; Chair. Editorial Council, Ideologia i Polityka 1986–; Officer's and Kt.'s Cross Order of Polonia Restituta and other distinctions. *Publications:* about 100 works on sociology of educ. in rural environment.

BEDNORZ, George, PH.D.; German physicist; b. 16 May 1950; ed. Swiss Federal Inst. of Tech., Zürich; with IBM Research Lab., Rüschlikon, Zürich 1982–; shared Nobel Prize for Physics for discovery of new superconducting materials 1987. *Address:* IBM Zürich Research Laboratory, Säumerstrasse 4, CH-8803 Rüschlikon, Zürich, Switzerland. *Telephone:* 41-1-72 48 111.

BEDOYA VELEZ, Luis; Peruvian politician and civil engineer; b. 10 May 1920, Lima; ed. Antigua Eng. School and Univs. of Mexico and Guadalajara; became involved with Partido Aprista Peruano 1935; deported to Panama, then went to Mexico to complete studies 1941; returned to Peru, Nat. Organizing Sec. of the party 1945–46; subsequently arrested and after release returned to professional activity as builder 1948–85; organized 13th Congress of the party in Trujillo 1980; mem. Electoral Comm., Municipal Elections 1983, Gen. Elections 1985; Minister of Housing 1985–. *Address:*

Ministry of Housing, D. Cueto 120, Jesús Maria, Lima, Peru. *Telephone:* 716070.

BEDSER, Alec Victor, C.B.E.; British cricketer and company director; b. 4 July 1918, Reading; s. of the late Arthur and Florence Beatrice Bedser; ed. Monument Hill Secondary School, Woking; joined professional staff of Surrey County Cricket Club 1938; served R.A.F. 1939–46; selected for England v. India June 1946; played in 51 Test Matches; as bowler, took record number of Test wickets (236, since beaten) including 104 v. Australia. retd. from 1st class cricket 1960; mem. England Cricket Selection Cttee. of Test and County Cricket Bd. 1962–83, Chair. 1968–81; Asst. Man. (to the late Duke of Norfolk) MCC tour to Australia 1962–63, Man. MCC tour to Australia 1974–75, to Australia and India 1979–80; mem. MCC Cttee., Cricket Cttee. of Test and County Cricket Bd.; Pres. Surrey C.C.C. 1987–88, fmr. Vice-Pres. and cttee. mem.; started office equipment firm in partnership with twin brother, Eric A. Bedser 1955; now consultant, Industrial Services and Cleaning Group. *Publications:* Our Cricket Story (with Eric A. Bedser) 1951, Bowling 1952, Following On (with Eric A. Bedser) 1954, May's Men in Australia 1959, Cricket Choice 1981, Twin Ambitions (autobiog. with Alex Bannister) 1986. *Leisure interests:* cricket, golf, gardening, charities. *Address:* c/o Initial Contract Services Ltd., 1/5 Bermondsey Street, London, SE1 2ER, England. *Telephone:* 01-403 3566.

BEEBY, Clarence Edward, C.M.G., PH.D.; New Zealand educationist and administrator; b. 16 June 1902, Leeds, England; s. of Anthonv Beeby and Alice Beeby (née Rhodes); m. Beatrice Eleanor Newnham 1926; one s. one d.; ed. Christchurch Boy's High School, Canterbury Coll., Univ. of New Zealand, Univ. Coll., London, and Univ. of Manchester; Lecturer in Philosophy and Educ., Canterbury Univ. Coll., Univ. of N.Z. 1923–34; Dir. N.Z. Council for Educational Research 1934–38; Asst. Dir. of Educ., Educ. Dept., N.Z. 1938–40, Dir. of Education 1940–60 (on leave of absence 1948–49); Asst. Dir.-Gen. of UNESCO 1948–49; Amb. to France 1960–63; leader N.Z. Dels. to Gen. Confs. of UNESCO 1946, 1947, 1950, 1953, 1954, 1956, 1958, 1960, 1963; Hon. Counsellor of UNESCO 1950; mem. of UNESCO Exec. Bd. 1960–63, Chair. 1963; Research Fellow, Harvard Univ. 1963–67; Chair. UNESCO Evaluation Panel for World Functional Literacy Projects 1967–70; Commonwealth Visiting Prof., Univ. of London 1967–68; Consultant to Australian Govt. on educ. in Papua and New Guinea 1969–; Consultant to Ford Foundation in Indonesia 1970–77; UNDP Consultant to Ministry of Educ., Malaysia 1976; Consultant to Univ. of Papua New Guinea 1982–; mem. Council of Consultant Fellows, Int. Inst. for Educ. Planning 1972–78; Foreign Assoc. U.S. Nat. Acad. of Educ. 1981–; Consultant to World Bank Educ. Dept. 1983, to Aga Khan Foundation in Tanzania 1987; Grand Cross Order of St. Gregory; Hon. LL.D. (Otago), Hon. Lit.D. (Wellington); Mackie Medal (ANZAAS) 1971. *Publications:* The Intermediate Schools of New Zealand 1938, Entrance to University (with W. Thomas and M.H. Oram) 1939, The Quality of Education in Developing Countries 1966, Qualitative Aspects of Educational Planning (editor) 1969, Assessment of Indonesian Education: A Guide in Planning 1979. *Leisure interests:* cabinet making, trout fishing, gardening. *Address:* 73 Barnard Street, Wellington, New Zealand (Home). *Telephone:* 557-939 (Office); 725-088 (Home).

BEELEY, Sir Harold, K.C.M.G., C.B.E., M.A.; British diplomatist; b. 15 Feb. 1909, London; s. of Frank Arthur Beeley; m. Karen Brett-Smith (née Shields) 1958; one step s. three d., two step d.; ed. Highgate School and Queen's Coll., Oxford; lecturer at Univs. of Sheffield, London, Oxford and Leicester 1930–39; entered Foreign Service 1946; Counsellor, Copenhagen 1949–50, Baghdad 1950–53, Washington 1953–55; Amb. to Saudi Arabia 1955; Asst. Under-Sec. Foreign Office 1956–58; Deputy Perm. Rep. to UN 1958–61; Amb. to United Arab Republic 1961–64, 1967–69; Perm. Rep. of U.K. to Disarmament Conf., Geneva 1964–67; retired from Diplomatic Service 1969; lecturer, Queen Mary Coll., London 1969–75; Pres. Egypt Exploration Soc. 1969–; Chair. World of Islam Festival Trust 1973–; Chair. Arab-British Centre 1977–81, Egyptian-British Chamber of Commerce 1981–; mem. Bd. Arab-British Chamber of Commerce 1979–81. *Publication:* Disraeli 1936. *Address:* 38 Slaidburn Street, London, S.W.10, England.

BEER, Otto F., DR. PHIL.; Austrian writer, journalist and professor; b. 8 Sept. 1910, Vienna; s. of Leopold J. and Emma (née Pabst) Beer; m. Gerty Mothwurf 1949; ed. Univ. of Vienna; Ed. Neues Wiener Journal and Neues Wiener Tagblatt until 1939; Chief Ed. Salzburger Nachrichten 1945; Drama Critic, Welt am Abend 1946–48, Der Standpunkt, Merano 1948–52, Neues Österreich, Vienna 1952–67, Österreichischer Rundfunk 1967–, Süddeutsche Zeitung 1967–. *Publications:* Zehnte Symphonie 1952, Wiedersehen in Meran 1952, Ich-Rodolfo-Magier 1965, Christin-Theres 1967; comedies: Man ist nur zweimal jung 1955, Operette 1960, Die Eintagsfliege 1961, Bummel durch Wien 1971, Der Fenstergucker 1974, Einladung nach Wien 1977. *Leisure interest:* music. *Address:* Lederergasse 27, Vienna VIII, Austria. *Telephone:* 42-04-84.

BEER, Samuel Hutchison, PH.D.; American university professor; b. 28 June 1911, Bucyrus, Ohio; s. of William Cameron and Jesse Blanche (née Hutchison) Beer; m. Roberta Frances Reed 1935; one s. two d.; ed. Staunton Military Acad., Univ. of Michigan, and Oxford and Harvard Univs.; writer, Resettlement Admin. and Democratic Nat. Cttee. 1935–36; Reporter New York Post 1936–37; Fortune magazine 1937–38; Instructor in Govt., Harvard Univ. 1938–42, Asst. Prof. 1946–48, Assoc. Prof. 1948–53,

Prof. of Govt. 1953–87, Chair. Dept. of Govt. 1954–58, Eaton Prof. of Science of Govt. 1971–87; Nat. Chair. Americans for Democratic Action 1959–62; U.S. Army 1942–45. *Publications:* The City of Reason 1949, Treasury Control: The Coordination of Financial and Economic Policy in Great Britain 1956, Patterns of Government: Major Political Systems of Europe (co-author) 1958 (3rd edn. 1973), Modern British Politics 1965, The State and the Poor 1970, Britain against Itself, the Political Contradictions of Collectivism 1982. *Address:* 87 Lakeview Avenue, Cambridge, Mass. 02138, U.S.A.

BEERING, Steven Claus, M.D.; American university president; b. 20 Aug. 1932, Berlin, Germany; s. of Steven and Alice Friedrick Beering; m. Jane Pickering 1956; three s.; ed. Univ. of Pittsburgh; Prof. of Medicine 1969–; Asst. Dean, Indiana Univ. School of Medicine 1969–70, Assoc. Dean 1970–74, Dean 1974–83, Dir. Indiana Univ. Medical Center 1974–83; Pres. Purdue Univ. 1983–; numerous awards and prizes. *Publications:* numerous articles in professional journals. *Leisure interests:* music, photography, reading, travel. *Address:* Purdue University, West Lafayette, Ind. (Office); 575 McCormick Road, West Lafayette, Ind. 47906, U.S.A. (Home). *Telephone:* 317-494-9708 (Office); 317-743-9933 (Home).

BEERS, William O.; American food company executive; b. 26 May 1914, Lena, Ill.; s. of Ernest and Rose (Binz) Beers; m. 1st Mary E. Holmes (deceased), 2nd Frances L. Miller 1954; two s. three d.; ed. Univ. of Wisconsin.; joined Kraft, Inc. 1937, Dir. 1965–, Pres. 1968–73, Chair. 1972–79; Pres. Kraft Foods Div. 1965–68; Dir. A.M.R. Corpn., American Airlines, Northern Telecom Ltd.; mem. Business Council, Alumni Foundation, Univ. of Wis.; Hon. mem. Business Council; Hon. LL.D. (Univ. of Wis.). *Address:* Suite 2530, One First National Plaza, Chicago, Ill. 60603, U.S.A. (Office).

BEETHAM, Bruce Craig, Q.S.O., M.PHIL., M.P.; New Zealand politician; b. 16. Feb 1936, New Plymouth; s. of Stanley De Velle and Frances Agnes (née Watts) Beetham; m. 1st Raewyn Natalie Mitchell 1965, three s. one d; m. 2nd Beverley May Clark 1980, two step. s.; ed. New Plymouth Boys' School and Univ. of Auckland and Waikato; taught at New Plymouth Boys' High School 1959–63, and at Taupo Coll. 1964–65; Sr. Secondary Asst., Pio Pio District High School 1966; Lecturer in History, Hamilton Teachers Coll. 1967–77; fmr. Asst. Secretary N.Z. Teachers Asscn.; Research Chair. N.Z. Social Credit Party 1970, Pres. and Leader 1972–85, 1988–; leader N.Z. Democratic Party 1985–86; M.P. for Rangitikei 1978–84; mem. Parl. Statutes Revision Cttee. 1978–80; mem. Electoral Law Cttee. 1980–84; Mayor of Hamilton 1976–77, Deputy Mayor Marton 1986–; Deputy Chair. Wanganui Area Health Bd., 1986–; mem. Council of Univ. of Waikato; Exec. mem. of Hamilton Regional Planning Authority; Group Controller Hamilton Civil Defence Org. *Leisure interests:* tennis, rugby. *Address:* Lindenhall, 14 Skerman Street, Marton, New Zealand. *Telephone:* 0652 2899.

BEETHAM, Marshal of the R.A.F. Sir Michael (James), G.C.B., C.B.E., D.F.C., A.F.C., F.R.S.A., F.R.AE.S.; British air force officer; b. 17 May 1923, London; s. of Major G. C. Beetham; m. Patricia E. Lane 1956; one s. one d.; ed. St. Marylebone Grammar School, London; joined R.A.F. 1941; served 35, 50, 57 Squadrons, Bomber Command 1943–46; HQ Staff 1947–49; 82 (RECCE) Squadron, E. Africa 1949–51; Staff Coll. 1952; Directorate of Operational Requirements, Air Ministry 1953–56; C.O. 214 (Valiant) Squadron, R.A.F. Marham 1958–60; Group Captain, Operations, HQ Bomber Command 1962–64; C.O. R.A.F. Khormaksar, Aden 1964–66; Imperial Defence Coll. 1967; Ministry of Defence Dir. of Operations (R.A.F.) 1968–70; Commdt. R.A.F. Staff Coll. 1970–72; Asst. Chief of Staff (Plans and Policy) SHAPE 1972–75; Deputy C.-in-C. Strike Command 1975–76; C.-in-C. R.A.F. Germany and Commdr. 2nd Allied Tactical Air Force 1976–77; Chief of the Air Staff, Royal Air Force 1977–82; Air ADC to H.M. the Queen 1977–82; Dir. Brixton Estate PLC 1983, GEC Avionics Ltd. 1984–, (Chair. 1986–); Chair. Trustees R.A.F. Museum 1983–; Hon. Liveryman, Guild of Air Pilots and Air Navigators 1984–. *Leisure interests:* golf, tennis. *Address:* c/o R.A.F. Club, 128 Picadilly, London, SW1, England.

BEETZ, The Hon. Mr Justice Jean, M.A., LL.D., F.R.S.C.; Canadian puisne judge (retd.); b. 27 March 1927, Montreal, Quebec; ed. Univs. of Montreal, Oxford, U.K.; called to Quebec Bar 1950; Asst. Prof., Faculty of Law, Univ. of Montreal 1953–59, Assoc. Prof. 1959–66, Prof. 1966–73, Dean of Law 1968–70; created Q.C. 1965; Asst. Sec. to Cabinet 1966–68; Special Counsel to Prime Minister on constitutional matters 1968–71; Puisne Judge, Quebec Court of Queen's Bench 1973, of Supreme Court of Canada Jan. 1974–88; several hon. degrees. *Address:* 400 Stewart Street, Apartment 2405 Ottawa, Ont., K1N 6L2, Canada.

BEEVERS, Harry, PH.D.; American biologist; b. 10 Jan. 1924, Shildon, England; s. of Norman and Olive Beevers; m. Jean Sykes 1949; one s.; ed. Univ. of Durham; post-doctoral research, Univ. of Oxford 1946–50; Asst. Prof. of Biology, Purdue Univ. 1950–53, Assoc. Prof. 1953–58, Prof. 1958–69; Prof. of Biology, Univ. of Calif., Santa Cruz 1969–; Pres. American Soc. of Plant Physiologists 1961; Sr. U.S. Scientist, Alexander von Humboldt Foundation 1986; mem. N.A.S.; Fellow American Acad. of Arts and Sciences 1973; mem. Deutsche Botanische Gesellschaft 1982; Sigma Xi Research Award, Purdue Univ. 1958; McCoy Research Award 1968, Stephen Hales Award, American Society of Plant Physiologists 1970; Hon.

D.Sc. (Purdue Univ.) 1971, (Univ. of Newcastle upon Tyne) 1974, (Nagoga Univ.) 1986. *Publications:* Respiratory Metabolism in Plants 1961; 150 articles on plant metabolism in scientific journals. *Leisure interest:* gardening. *Address:* Biology Department, University of California, Santa Cruz, Calif. 95060 (Office); 46 South Circle Drive, Santa Cruz, Calif. 95060, U.S.A. (Home). *Telephone:* (408) 429-2046 (Office); (408) 458-9295 (Home).

BEFFA, Jean-Louis Guy Henri; French business executive; b. 11 Aug. 1941, Nice; s. of Edmond Beffa and Marguerite Feursinger; m. Marie-Madeleine Brunel-Grasset 1967; two s. one d.; ed. Lycée Masséna, Nice, Ecole Nat. Supérieure des Mines and Inst. d'Etudes Politiques, Paris; Mining Engineer Clermont-Ferrand 1967; motor fuel man. 1967-74; head of refinery service 1970-73; Asst. to Dir. 1973-74; Chief Mining Eng. 1974; Dir. of Planning, Cie. de Saint-Gobain-Pont-à-Mousson 1975-77; Dir.-Gen. Société Pont-à-Mousson 1978, Pres. Dir.-Gen. 1979-82; Deputy Dir. (Pipelines) Saint-Gobain-Pont-à-Mousson 1978, Dir 1979-82; Dir.-Gen. Cie. de Saint-Gobain 1982-86, Pres. Dir.-Gen. 1986-; mem. int. consultative cttee. Chemical Bank 1986-. *Leisure interests:* swimming, golf. *Address:* Les miroirs, 18 avenue d'Alsace, 92400 Courbevoie, France (Office).

BEGG, Admiral of the Fleet Sir Varyl, G.C.B., D.S.O., D.S.C., K.ST.J., P.M.N. (Malaysia); British naval officer; b. 1 Oct. 1908, London; s. of F. C. Begg and M. C. Robinson; m. Rosemary Cowan 1943; two s.; ed. St Andrews School, Eastbourne, Malvern Coll., Naval Staff Coll. and Imperial Defence Coll.; Royal Navy 1926, Gunnery Officer 1933, H.M.S. Glasgow 1939-40, H.M.S. Warspite 1940-43; commanded H.M. Gunnery School, Chatham 1948-50, 8th Destroyer Flotilla 1950-52, H.M.S. Excellent 1952-54, H.M.S. Triumph 1955-56, Chief of Staff to C.-in-C. Portsmouth 1957-58; Flag Officer Commanding Fifth Cruiser Squadron and Flag Officer, Second-in-Command, Far East Station 1958-60; a Lord Commr. of Admiralty and Vice-Chief of Naval Staff 1961-63; C.-in-C. British Forces in Far East and U.K.; Mil. Adviser to SEATO 1963-65; C.-in-C. Portsmouth and Allied C.-in-C. Channel 1965-66; Chief of Naval Staff and First Sea Lord 1966-68; Gov. and C.-in-C. Gibraltar 1969-73. *Leisure interests:* fishing, gardening. *Address:* Copyhold Cottage, Chilbolton, Stockbridge, Hants., England. *Telephone:* Chilbolton 320.

BEGGS, James Montgomery, M.B.A.; American business executive; b. 9 Jan. 1926, Pittsburgh, Pa.; s. of the late James A. and Elizabeth M. Beggs; m. Mary Elizabeth Harrison 1953; two s. three d.; ed. U.S. Naval Acad., Harvard Grad. School of Business Admin.; with U.S. Navy 1947-54; Gen. Man. Underseas Div., Westinghouse Electric Corpn. 1955-60, Gen. Man. Systems Operating Div. 1960-63, Vice-Pres. Defense and Space Cen. and Gen. Man. Surface Div. 1963-67, Corpn. Dir. Purchases and Traffic 1967-68; Assoc. Admin. Office of Advanced Research and Tech., NASA 1968-69, Admin. 1981-85; Under-Sec. U.S. Dept. of Transport 1969-73; Man. Dir. Operations, Summa Corpn. 1973-74; Exec. Vice-Pres. Aerospace, Gen. Dynamics Corpn. 1974-81; Chair. Space Lab. 1988-; numerous honorary degrees. *Leisure interests:* golf, hunting. *Address:* 5408 Falmouth Road, Bethesda, Md. 20814, U.S.A. (Home). *Telephone:* 301-229-9372 (Home).

BEGIN, Menachem, M.J.; Israeli lawyer and politician; b. 16 Aug. 1913, Brest-Litovsk, Russia; s. of Zeev-Dov and Hassia Begin; m. Aliza Arnold (died 1982); one s. two d.; ed. Mizrachi Hebrew School, Univ. of Warsaw; Head of Betar Zionist Youth Movement in Poland 1939-; arrested and held in concentration camp in Siberia 1940-41; C.-in-C. of Irgun Zvai Leumi in Israel 1942; founded (now Chair.) Herut (Freedom) Movement in Israel 1948; mem. Knesset (Parl.); Minister without Portfolio 1967-70; Prime Minister 1977-83, Minister of Defence 1980-81; Jt. Chair. Likud (Unity) Party 1973-84; Hon. Dir. (Bar Ilan Univ.); Hon. D. Litt. (Yeshiva Univ., N.Y.) 1978; Nobel Prize for Peace (shared with Pres. Sadat) 1978. *Publications:* The Revolt: Personal Memoirs of the Commander of Irgun Zvai Leumi 1949, White Nights 1957, 1977, In the Underground (writings and documents) 1978. *Address:* Herut Movement Headquarters, Beit Jabotinsky, 38 King George Street, Tel Aviv, Israel.

BEGOUGNE DE JUNIAC, Gontran; French diplomatist; b. 28 July 1908, Limoges; s. of Octave Begougne de Juniac and Madeleine Desgranges; m. Myriam des Moutis 1959; one s.; ed. Ecole Montalembert, Limoges, Ecole Libre des Sciences Politiques, Paris, and Univ. de Paris à la Sorbonne; Deputy Consul 1935; Sec. of Embassy, Berlin 1936-37, Moscow 1937-41; Ministry of Foreign Affairs 1941; Sec. of Embassy, Dublin 1945-47; Div. of Cultural Relations, Ministry of Foreign Affairs 1947-49, Sec.-Gen. of Four Powers Conf. 1949; Counsellor, Washington 1949-55; Minister and Minister-Counsellor, London 1955-60; Amb. to Ethiopia 1960-65, to Turkey 1965-70, to Belgium 1970-73; Commdr. Légion d'honneur, Commdr. ordre nat. du Mérite, Grand-Croix de l'ordre de Léopold et de l'ordre de la Couronne de Belgique. *Publications:* Le dernier roi des rois; articles in Revue des Deux Mondes. *Address:* 11 boulevard du Général Koenig, Neuilly/Seine, France. *Telephone:* 624-07-60 (Home).

BÉGUIN, Bernard, L. ÈS L.; Swiss journalist; b. 14 Feb. 1923, Sion, Valais; s. of Bernard Béguin and Clemence Welten; m. Antoinette Waelbroeck 1948; two s. two d.; ed. Geneva High School, Geneva Univ. and Graduate Inst. of Int. Studies; Swiss Sec. World Student Relief 1945-46; corresp. at U.N. European Headquarters; Journal de Genève 1946-70, Foreign Ed. 1947, Ed.-in-Chief 1959-70; Diplomatic Commentator, Swiss Broadcasting System 1954-59, Swiss T.V. 1959-70; Head of Programmes, Swiss French-

speaking TV 1970-73; Deputy Dir. Radio and T.V. 1973-86; Cen. Pres. Swiss Press Asscn. 1958-60, Hon. mem. 1974-; Visiting Prof. in Professional Ethics, Univ. of Neuchâtel 1984-88; Pres., Swiss Press Council 1985-; mem. Fed. Comm. on Cartels 1964-80; mem. Bd., Swiss Telegraphic Agency 1968-71. *Leisure interests:* sailing, camping. *Address:* 41 avenue de Budé, 1202 Geneva 1, Switzerland. *Telephone:* 33-75-30.

BEHREND, Hilde, PH.D., B.SC.(ECON.); British economist; b. 13 Aug. 1917, Berlin, Germany; d. of Dr. F. W. Behrend and Marie Behrend (née Zöllner); ed. Grammar School, Berlin and London School of Economics; came to Britain 1936; teaching and secretarial posts 1938-42; Grammar School teacher of German and French 1944-49; Asst. Lecturer and Research Fellow, Faculty of Commerce and Social Science, Univ. of Birmingham 1949-54; lecturer, Edinburgh Univ. 1954-64, Sr. lecturer 1964-72, Reader 1972-73, Personal Chair. in Industrial Relations 1973-82, Prof. Emer., Hon. Fellow; mem. of various research bodies on incomes, etc.; mem. Manpower Services Comm., Lothian (Dist.) Manpower Cttee. 1976-79. *Publications:* Absence Under Full Employment 1951, A National Survey of Attitudes to Inflation and Incomes Policy 1966 (with Harriet Lynch and Jean Davies), Incomes Policy and the Individual (with Harriet Lynch, Howard Thomas and Jean Davies) 1967, Views on Pay Increases, Fringe Benefits and Low Pay 1970, Views on Income Differentials and the Economic Situation 1970, Incomes Policy, Equity and Pay Increase Differentials 1973, Attitudes to Price Increases and Pay Claims 1974, How to Monitor Absence from Work: from Head-Count to Computer 1978, Problems of Labour and Inflation 1984, Information and Government (Ed. Davidson and White) (contrib.) 1988, and numerous articles in academic journals. *Leisure interests:* walking, sketching, indoor plants.

BEHREND, Siegfried; German professor of music, guitarist, conductor and composer; b. 19 Nov. 1933, Berlin; s. of Karl Behrend and Cornelia Apin; m. Claudia Brodzinska; ed. Klindworth Schwarenka Conservatoire, Berlin; debut, Leipzig 1953 and has since appeared in most of world's major concert halls; has made numerous radio recordings and music for 200 films; has published 400 compositions; hon. life mem. American Guitar Foundation, Japan and New Zealand Guitar Asscns.; Bundesverdienstkreuz. *Address:* D-8151 Wall in Bayern, Alter Pfarrhof, Haus No 1, Federal Republic of Germany.

BEHRENS, Hildegard; German opera singer; b. Oldenburg; ed. Freiburg Music Conservatory; opera debut, Freiburg 1971; resident mem. Deutsche Oper am Rhein, Düsseldorf; has appeared with Frankfurt Opera, Teatro Nacional de San Carlo, Lisbon, Vienna State Opera, Metropolitan Opera, New York; soloist, Chicago Symphony Orchestra 1984. *Address:* c/o Columbia Artists Management Inc., 165 W 57th Street, New York, N.Y. 10019, U.S.A.

BEHRMAN, Richard Elliot, M.D., J.D.; American professor of pediatrics; b. 13 Dec. 1931, Philadelphia, Pa.; s. of Robert Behrman and Vivian Keegan; m. Ann Nelson 1954; one s. three d.; ed. Amherst Coll., Harvard Univ., Univ. of Rochester and Johns Hopkins Univ.; Oregon Regional Primate Research Center and Univ. of Oregon Medical School 1965-68; Prof. of Pediatrics and Dir. Neonatal Intensive Care Unit and Nurseries, Univ. of Ill. Coll. of Medicine 1968-71; Prof. and Chair. Dept. of Pediatrics and Dir. Babies Hospital, Columbia Univ. Coll. of Physicians and Surgeons 1971-76; Prof. and Chair. Dept. of Pediatrics and Dir. Dept. of Pediatrics, Rainbow Babies and Children's Hosp. Case Western Reserve Univ. School of Medicine 1976-82; Dean, School of Medicine, Case Western Reserve Univ. 1980-, Vice-Pres. Medical Affairs 1987-. *Address:* School of Medicine, Case Western Reserve University, Cleveland, Ohio 44106, U.S.A. *Telephone:* 216-368-2820 (Office); 216-423-0675 (Home).

BEI DAO; Chinese poet; b. 2 Aug. 1949, Beijing; m. Shao Fei; one d.; experimental poet who first achieved prominence during Democracy Movement 1978-79 through the unofficial literary magazine Today. *Publications:* Waves 1985, Collected Poems of Bei Dao 1986. *Address:* Flat 504, Building 1, Beijing Art Studio, Tuanjiehu, Beijing, People's Republic of China.

BEI SHIZHANG, DR. RER. NAT.; Chinese biologist, university professor and institute director; b. 10 Oct. 1903, Ningpo; s. of Bei Qingyang and Chen Ahua; m. Cheng Ihming 1931; two s. two d.; ed. Tongji Medical and Eng. School, Shanghai and Univ. of Freiburg i. Breisgau, Univ. of München, Univ. of Tübingen; Asst. Inst. of Zoology, Univ. Tübingen 1928-29; returned home 1929; Assoc. Prof., Prof. and Chair. of Dept. of Biology, Univ. of Zhejiang 1930-50, Dean of Science Faculty 1949-50; Dir. Inst. of Experimental Biology, Chinese Acad. of Sciences 1950-58, Science Sec. 1953-58; Chair. Dept. of Biophysics, Univ. of Science and Tech., China 1958-64, Dept. of Biology 1978-82; Dir. Inst. of Biophysics, Chinese Acad. of Sciences 1958-83, Hon. Dir. 1985-; Pres. Chinese Zoological Soc. 1978-83, Chinese Biophysical Soc. 1980-83, (Hon. Pres. 1983-86); Deputy Ed.-in-Chief Scientia Sinica 1958-83, Encyclopedia of China 1984-; Ed.-in-Chief Acta Biophysica Sinica 1985-; mem. Div. of Biological Sciences, Chinese Acad. of Sciences; mem. 1st 1954, 2nd 1959, 3rd 1964, 4th 1975, 5th 1978 and 6th 1983 NPC. *Publications:* include studies on cell reformation, chromatin, DNA and histories in yolk granules; several articles in Science Record and Scientia Sinica. *Address:* Institute of Biophysics, Chinese

Academy of Sciences, Beijing, People's Republic of China. *Telephone:* 28-1064.

BEICKLER, Ferdinand; German automobile executive; b. 2 Nov. 1922, Mainz; m.; two s.; joined Adam Opel AG, Rüsselsheim, as apprentice toolmaker 1937, studied mechanical eng.; Tech. Dir. Bochum plant 1964, Chief of operations, Bochum 1966-70, Mfg. Dir. and mem. Bd. of Mans. 1970-82, Chair. Bd., Man. Dir. 1982-87; Chair. Supervisory Bd. Adam Opel 1987-; Vice-Pres. Gen. Motors Corpn. 1986-87; Man. Dir. Vauxhall Motors Ltd., Luton, U.K. 1979; German Fed. Service Cross 1975. *Leisure interests:* classical music, golf. *Address:* c/o Adam Opel AG, Rüsselsheim, Federal Republic of Germany.

BEIER, Friedrich-Karl, DR.IUR.; German professor of law and consultant; b. 9 April 1926, Berlin; s. of Gustav Beier and Johanna (née Taube) Beier; m. Judith Mertens 1951; three s.; ed. Univ. of Berlin, Berlin Court of Appeals, Univ. of Munich; mem. Exec. Cttee. Int. Asscn. for the Protection of Industrial Property 1958-; Vice-Pres. Deutsche Vereinigung für gewerblichen Rechtsschutz und Urheberrecht 1965; at Munich Univ. 1960-, Scientific Counsel Inst. Industrial Property and Copyright Law 1960-65, Co.-Dir. 1965-, Prof. of Law 1965-; with Max-Planck-Inst. for Foreign and Int. Patent, Copyright and Competition Law 1966-, Dir. 1971-73, Man. Dir. 1973-; Legal Adviser EEC Commission 1974-79; Pres. Programme Cttee. Int. Asscn. for Protection of Industrial Property; Dr. h.c. (Uppsala), (Poznań); mem. Acad. of Science and Art 1983-; mem. Int. Acad. of Comparative Law 1984-. *Publications:* several books and numerous articles on intellectual property law. *Leisure interests:* swimming, sailing, skiing, wandering. *Address:* Lärchenstrasse 1, D-8033 Krailling (Home); Max-Planck-Institut fur Ausländisches und Internationales Patent-, Urheber- und Wettbewerbsrecht, Siebertstrasse 3, D-8000 München 80, Federal Republic of Germany.

BEIL, Gerhard, DR.RER.POL.; German politician; b. 28 May 1926, Leipzig; ed. Berlin Coll. of Econs., Berlin Humboldt Univ. and Potsdam-Babelsberg Acad. of Political and Legal Studies; fmr. trainee steel fitter; mem. Sozialistische Einheitspartei Deutschlands (SED) 1953, cand. mem. of Cen. Cttee. 1976-81, mem. 1981-; Trade Rep. G.D.R. Embassy, Vienna 1958-62; Dir. Gen. of Trade in W. Europe 1962-65; Deputy Minister of Trade 1965-68; State Sec. and First Deputy Minister of Foreign Trade 1968-86, Minister of Foreign Trade 1986-; mem. G.D.R. Council of Ministers 1977-; Dr. h.c. (Kepler Univ., Austria). *Address:* Sozialistische Einheitspartei Deutschlands, Am Marx-Engels-Platz 2, 1020 Berlin, German Democratic Republic.

BEINECKE, William Sperry; American lawyer and business executive; b. 22 May 1914, New York; s. of Frederick William and Carrie (née Sperry) Beinecke; m. Elizabeth Barrett Gillespie 1941; two s. two d.; ed. Phillips Acad., Andover, Westminster School, Connecticut, Yale Univ. and Columbia Univ., New York; admitted to New York Bar 1941; Assoc. Chadbourne, Wallace, Parke and Whiteside 1940-41, 1946-48; U.S. Navy 1941-45; Partner, Casey, Beinecke and Chase 1948-51; Gen. Counsel, The Sperry and Hutchinson Co. 1952-54, Gen. Counsel and Vice-Pres. 1954-60, Pres. 1960-67, C.E.O. 1967-80, now Trustee, Consolidated Edison Co. of New York; Dir., Antaeus Enterprises, Inc.; several hon. degrees. *Address:* 420 Lexington Avenue, New York, N.Y. 10170 (Office); 21 East 79th Street, New York, N.Y. 10021, U.S.A. (Home).

BEISE, S. Clark, B.S.; American banker; b. 13 Oct. 1898, Windom, Minn.; s. of Dr. Henry C. and Blanche (Johnson) Beise; m. Virginia Carter 1934; one s. one d.; ed. Univ. of Minnesota School of Business; regimental supply sergeant in First World War; worked with Minneapolis Trust Co. 1922-24, with Nat. Bank Examiners Minneapolis office (covering Ninth Fed. Reserve District) 1924-27; with People's Nat. Bank Jackson (Mich.) rising to Vice-Pres. 1927-33; Nat. Bank, Jackson 1930-33; Nat. Bank Examiner, Twelfth Fed. Reserve District 1933-36; Vice-Pres. Bank of America 1936-45, Exec. Vice-Pres. 1945-51, Sr. Vice-Pres. 1951-54, Pres. 1954-63, Chair. Exec. Cttee. 1963-69, Hon. Dir. 1969-; fmr. mem. Cttee. for Econ. Devt., Conf. Bd.; fmr. Dir. Stanford Research Inst., Walt Disney Productions; fmr. Chair. San Francisco Foundation, Distribution Cttee.; fmr. mem. Business Council; fmr. mem. Bd. Fruehauf Corpn., Georgia-Pacific Corpn.; Hon. Chair. Golden Gate Chapter, American Red Cross; fmr. mem. Advisory Council, San Francisco Planning and Urban Renewal Asscn.; Hon. LL.D. St. Mary's Coll. of Calif. 1960; Ordine del Merito della Repubblica Italiana 1957; nominated Calif. Industrialist of the Year 1963 (Calif. Museum of Science and Industry, Los Angeles). *Address:* Bank of America Center, San Francisco, Calif. 94137 (Office); 420 El Cerrito Avenue, Hillsborough, Calif. 94010, U.S.A. (Home).

BEIT-ARIÉ, Malachi, M.A., M.L.S., PH.D.; Israeli university professor and palaeographer; b. 20 May 1937, Petah-Tiqva; s. of Meir Beit-Arié and Esther (née Elpiner) Beit-Arié; m. Dalia Mamut 1958; one s. two d.; ed. Hebrew Univ., Jerusalem; Dir. The Hebrew Palaeography Project, Israel Acad. of Sciences and Humanities 1965-, Inst. of Microfilmed Hebrew Manuscripts 1970-78; Sr. Lecturer in Codicology and Palaeography, Hebrew Univ. 1975-78, Assoc. Prof. 1979-83, Prof. 1984-; Dir. Nat. and Univ. Library 1979-; Visiting Fellow Wolfson Coll., Oxford 1984-85; Anne Frank Awards for poetry 1961. *Publications:* These Streets, Those Mountains (lyrics) 1963, The Hills of Jerusalem and All the Pain (poems) 1967,

Manuscrits médiévaux en caractères hébraiques (with C. Sirat), Parts I-III 1972-86, Hebrew Codicology 1977, The Only Dated Medieval MS Written in England 1985, Medieval Specimens of Hebrew Scripts 1987. *Leisure interest:* classical music. *Address:* P.O. Box 503, Jerusalem 91-004 (Office); 9 Bustanai Street, Jerusalem 93229, Israel (Home). *Telephone:* (02) 660351 (Office); (02) 633940 (Home).

BEITH, Sir John Greville Stanley, K.C.M.G.; British diplomatist (retd.); b. 4 April 1914, London; s. of William Beith and Margaret Stanley; m. Diana Gregory-Hood (née Gilmour); one s. one d.; one step s. one step d.; ed. Eton and King's Coll., Cambridge; Diplomatic Service 1937-74, Athens, Buenos Aires; Foreign Office 1940-49; Head of U.K. Del. to UN, Geneva 1949-53; First Sec. and Head of Chancery, Prague 1953-54; Counsellor and Head of Chancery, Paris 1954-59; Head of Levant Dept. Foreign Office 1959-61, North and East African Dept. 1961-63; Amb. to Israel 1963-66; Asst. Sec.-Gen. NATO 1966-67; Under-Sec. Foreign and Commonwealth Office 1967-69; Amb. to Belgium 1969-74. *Leisure interests:* music, racing, books. *Address:* Dean Farm House, Sparsholt, Winchester, Hants., England. *Telephone:* Sparsholt 326.

BEITZ, Berthold; German industrialist; b. 26 Sept. 1913; m. Else Hochheim 1939; three d.; ed. secondary school; bank apprentice; employment in Shell, Hamburg; in charge of the Galician oilfields, Poland 1939-44; Deputy Chair. British Zonal Insurance Control Dept. 1946; Dir.-Gen. Iduna Germania Insurance Co. 1949-53; General-bevollmächtigter Dr. Alfried Krupp von Bohlen and Halbach 1953-67; Chair. Bd. of Curators, Alfried Krupp von Bohlen und Halbach-Stiftung; Chair. Supervisory Bd., Fried. Krupp G.m.b.H., Essen, Grundig AG; mem. Supervisory Bd., Gelsenberg AG; Chair. Cttee. of the Max-Grundig Foundation; mem. Bd. Sophia-Jacoba trade union; Hon. mem. Int. Olympic Cttee; mem. Nat. Olympic Cttee. Presidium; Chair. Bd., Ruhr Cultural Foundation (Kulturstiftung Ruhr); mem. 'pro ruhrgebiet' Cttee.; Direktoriums der Univ. Witten-Herdecke; Yad Vashem Medal (Israel), Grosses Bundesverdienstkreuz mit Stern und Schulterband, Grosskreuz des Verdienstordens der Bundesrepublik Deutschland, Commandorium with Star of Order of Merit (Poland), First Class Order of Madara Reiter (Bulgaria); Freeman of the City of Essen; Hon. Dr. (Greifswald Univ.); hon. mem. Univ. of Essen; and numerous decorations. *Leisure interests:* yachting, hunting, jazz, modern painting. *Address:* Hügel 15, 4300 Essen 1, Federal Republic of Germany. *Telephone:* 188-4810.

BÉJART, Maurice Jean, (b. Maurice Berger); French dancer, choreographer and stage director; b. 1 Jan. 1927, Marseilles; s. of Gaston Berger; ed. Lycée in Marseilles; with Marseilles Opera and Royal Opera, Stockholm, before founding Ballet de l'Etoile, Paris 1954, Dir. 1954-57; Dir., Ballet Théâtre de Paris 1957-59; Dir. Ballet du XXe Siècle, Brussels 1960-, Brussels Opera, Théâtre Royal de la Monnaie; Dir. Asscn. Mudra (Dancing School), Brussels 1972-; Grand Prix de la Musique 1970; Chevalier de l'ordre des Arts et des Lettres, Grand Officier Order of the Crown (Belgium), Médaille de l'ordre du Soleil levant (Japan). *Productions include:* Orphée, Le voyage, Le sacre du printemps, Les noces, Don Juan, Boléro, Symphonie pour un homme seul, Nijinsky, Clown of God (ballets); The Merry Widow, Tales of Hoffmann, Ode à la Joie (9th Symphony), La damnation de Faust, Messe pour le temps présent, Romeo et Juliette, Prospective, Baudelaire, Ni fleurs—ni couronnes, La tentation de St-Antoine, A la recherche de ..., Le marteau sans maître, La Traviata, Per la Dolce Memoria di quel Giorno 1974, Ce que l'amour me dit 1974, Chants d'amour et de guerre 1975, Notre Faust 1975, Petrushka 1977, Don Giovanni 1980, Messe pour le temps futur 1983, Le Martyr de Saint Sébastien 1986. *Publications:* Mathilde ou le temps perdu (novel) 1963, L'autre chant de la danse 1974, La Reine verte (play). *Address:* Théâtre royal de la Monnaie, 4 rue Léopold, Brussels (Office); Mudra, 103 rue Bara, Brussels, Belgium (Home).

BEJGER, Stanisław, M.ECON.SC.; Polish politician; b. 12 Nov. 1929, Piątkowo; s. of Leon Bejger and Janina Bejger; m. Teresa Bejger 1954; one s. one d.; ed. Higher School of Maritime Trade, Sopot, Higher School of Econs., Sopot, Higher School of Social Sciences of Cen. Cttee. of Polish United Workers' Party (PZPR), Warsaw; Sr. Counsellor, Ministry of Shipping 1958-59; Dir. Operation Div. of Polish Ocean Lines (PLO) 1963-66, Dir.-Gen. PLO 1966-76; commercial counsellor at Embassy in Finland 1976-80; Dir. Div. of Asian and Australian Lines, PLO 1980-81; Minister of Maritime Economy Office 1981-82; First Sec. of Voivodship Cttee. of PZPR, Gdańsk 1982-88; mem. PZPR 1948-, mem. PZPR Cen. Cttee. 1982-88, alt. mem. Political Bureau of PZPR Cen. Cttee. 1982-88, Chair. Maritime Cttee. of Cen. Cttee. 1982-88; Deputy to Seym 1985-; Amb. to Austria 1988-; Kt.'s Cross of Order of Polonia Restituta, Order of Banner of Labour (1st Class), Gold Cross of Merit. *Address:* Botschaft der Volksrepublik Polen, Hietziner Hauptstrasse 42c, P.O. Box 17, 1BO Wien XIII, Austria.

BEJM, Tadeusz; Polish politician; b. 27 April 1929, Kuźnica Stara nr. Kłobuck; ed. Higher Econ. School, Sopot; mem. Polish Youth Union 1948-55, Meat Industry Cen. Bd., Katowice 1950; army and navy service 1950-53; Polish Ocean Lines, Gdynia 1953-58; mem. Polish United Workers' Party (PZPR) 1953-, First Sec. Gdańsk-Portowa District Cttee. 1958-59, Propaganda Sec. Gdańsk Town Cttee. 1959-63; Chair. Presidium of Gdańsk Town Nat. Council 1963-69, of Gdańsk Voivodship Nat. Council 1969-71;

First Sec. Gdańsk Voivod Cttee., PZPR 1971-75; Minister of Admin., Local Economy and Environmental Protection 1975-76, of Transport 1976-77, Minister-mem. Council of Ministers 1977-80, Deputy Chair. Supreme Chamber of Control 1977-85; mem. Cen. Cttee., PZPR 1971-81; Deputy to Seym 1972-76; Knight's Cross, Order of Polonia Restituta 1969, Order of Banner of Labour, 2nd Class 1974. *Address:* PZPR, 00-920 Warsaw, Novy Swiat 6, Poland.

BEK, Wiesław Marian, M.SC.; Polish journalist and publisher; b. 2 Dec. 1929, Łódź; m.; one s.; ed. Łódź Univ.; Man. ed., later Sub-ed., daily Głos Robotniczy, Łódź 1949-64; Sec. Voivodship Cttee. of Polish United Workers' Party (PZPR), Łódź 1964-68; Deputy Head, later Head of Press Bureau of PZPR Cen. Cttee. 1968-72; Pres. Książka i Wiedza Publrs., Warsaw 1972-73; First Vice-Pres. Workers' Publishing Co-operative "Prasa-Książka-Ruch", Warsaw 1973-78; First Vice-Minister of Culture and Art 1978-80; Head of Dept. for Ideology and Educ. of PZPR Cen. Cttee. 1980; Ed.-in-Chief Trybuna Ludu, daily of PZPR Cen. Cttee. 1980-85; Amb. to Bulgaria 1986-; mem. PZPR 1954-, deputy mem. PZPR Cen. Cttee. 1971-75, mem. Cen. Party Control Comm. 1975-81; Pres. Polish-Mongolian Soc.; Commdr.'s and Officer's Cross of Order of Polonia Restituta, Order of Banner of Labour (1st Class) and other decorations. *Leisure interests:* reading, gardening. *Address:* Embassy of the Polish People's Republic, Car Krum 46, Sofia, Bulgaria. *Telephone:* 885161.

BEKHTEREVA, Natalya Petrovna, DR. MED. SCI.; Soviet physiologist; b. 1924, Leningrad; ed. Leningrad Medical Inst., mem. CPSU 1959-; Bekhterev Inst. for Research into the Brain; junior research worker at U.S.S.R. Acad. of Medical Sciences Inst. of Experimental Medicine 1950-54; on staff of Neuro-surgical Inst. of Ministry of Health 1954-62; on staff of Inst. of Experimental Medicine (Head of lab., deputy Dir.) 1962-, Dir. 1970-; mem. of U.S.S.R. Acad. of Sciences 1981-. *Address:* U.S.S.R. Academy of Sciences, Leninsky Pr. 14, Moscow V-71, U.S.S.R.

BELAFONTE, Harry; American singer; b. 1 March 1927, New York; s. of Harold George Belafonte Sr. and Malvene Love Wright; m. 2nd Julie Robinson 1957; one s. three d.; ed. George Washington High School, New York.; in Jamaica 1935-39; service with U.S. Navy 1943-45; American Negro Theater; student at Manhattan New School for Social Research Dramatic Workshop 1946-48; first engagement at the Vanguard, Greenwich Village; European tours 1958, 1976, 1981, 1983; Pres. Belafonte Enterprises Inc.; Goodwill Amb. for UNICEF 1987; Host Nelson Mandela Birthday Concert, Wembley 1988; Broadway appearances in Three For Tonight, Almanac, Belafonte At The Palace, and in films Bright Road, Carmen Jones 1952, Island in the Sun 1957, The World, the Flesh and the Devil 1958, Odds Against Tomorrow 1959, The Angel Levine (also producer) 1969, Grambling's White Tiger 1981; produced with Sidney Poitier Buck and the Preacher 1971 (also acted), Uptown Saturday Night 1974; Emmy Television Award for Tonight with Belafonte 1960; Producer Strolling 20's 1965, A Time for Laughter 1967, Harry and Lena 1970, Beat Street 1984; Hon. D.Hum. (Park Coll., Mo.) 1968, Hon. D.Arts, New School of Social Research, New York 1968; numerous recordings. *Leisure interests:* photography, water skiing, recording. *Address:* c/o Belafonte Enterprises Inc., 157 West 57th St., New York, N.Y. 10019, U.S.A.

BÉLANGER, Gerard, M.A., M.SOC.SC.; Canadian professor of economics; b. 23 Oct. 1940, St. Hyacinthe; s. of Georges Bélanger and Cécile Girard; m. Michèle Potvin 1964; one d.; ed. Princeton and Laval Univs.; Prof. Dept. of Econs. Laval Univ. 1967-, Prof. of Econs. 1977-; Research Co-ordinator, Howe Inst. Montreal 1977-79; mem. Task Force on Urbanization, Govt. of Quebec 1974-76; Sec. Acad. of Letters and Social Sciences, Royal Soc. of Canada 1985-88; Woodrow Wilson Fellow. *Publications:* The Price of Health 1972, Le financement municipal au Québec 1976, Taxes and Expenditures in Québec and Ontario 1978, Le prix du transport au Québec 1978, L'économique du secteur public 1981, Croissance du Secteur Public et Fédéralisme 1988. *Address:* Department of Economics, Université Laval, Québec, G1K 7P4 (Office); 3384 Gaspareau, Ste-Foy, Québec, G1W 2N2, Canada (Home). *Telephone:* (418) 656-6776 (Office); (418) 653-9084 (Home).

BELANGER, Michel; Canadian civil servant and banker; b. 10 Sept. 1929, Levis, Quebec; m.; six c.; ed. Laval Univ;. Quebec, McGill Univ., Montreal; Dept. of Finance, Canadian Govt., Ottawa 1954-60, Quebec City 1960-72; Asst. Deputy Minister of Natural Resources 1961-65, Deputy Minister of Industry and Commerce 1966-69; Econ. Adviser to Exec. Council 1969-71; Sec. Treasury Bd. 1971-73; Pres. and C.E.O. Montreal Stock Exchange 1973-76; Pres. Provincial Bank of Canada 1976-77; Chair. Nat. Bank of Canada Nov. 1979-, C.E.O. 1979-89; Dir. Canadian Int. Paper Co., MICC Investments Ltd., Simpsons-Sears Ltd.; mem. "Régie de la Place des Arts"; Dir. Clinical Research Inst., Montreal, C. D. Howe Inst. *Address:* National Bank of Canada, 600 de la Gauchetière Street, W., Montreal, Quebec H3B 4L2, Canada.

BELAÚNDE TERRY, Fernando; Peruvian architect and politician; b. 7 Oct. 1913; ed. France and U.S.A.; mem. Chamber of Deputies 1945-48; Dean in School of Architecture, Lima 1948-56; Leader Acción Popular (AP) 1956-; Presidential Candidate 1956, 1962; Pres. of Peru 1963-68 (deposed by military coup); fled to New York Oct. 1968; lecturing at Harvard Univ. Nov. 1968; returned to Peru briefly Dec. 1970, deported at end of month, returned Jan. 1976; Pres. of Peru July 1980-85. *Publications:*

Peru's Own Conquest (autobiog.). *Address:* Oficina del Presidente, Lima, Peru.

BELCHIOR, Murillo, M.D.; Brazilian physician; b. 26 April 1913, Rio de Janeiro; s. of Carlos de Britto Bayma Belchior and Laura Bastos Belchior; m. Jean Shafer Belchior 1945; two d.; ed. Colégio Santo Inàcio, Univs. of Brazil and Michigan and Harvard Univ.; Chief, Clinical Dept., Santa Casa Hosp. 1942-; Dir. for int. health, Ministry of Health 1963-69; Pres. Fed. Council of Medicine 1968, Council of Int. Org. of Medical Sciences 1979-, U.S.-Brazil Cultural Inst. 1974-; mem. New York Acad. of Sciences; Fellow, Royal Soc. of Medicine (U.K.); Eisenhower Fellow. *Leisure interests:* cultural matters. *Address:* Rua Bolivar, 7 apto. 6 (Copacabana), 20.061 Rio de Janeiro, Brazil. *Telephone:* 236.6429.

BELFRAGE, Leif Axel Lorentz, LL.D.; Swedish diplomatist; b. 1 Feb. 1910; m. Greta Jering 1937; one s. three d.; ed. Stockholm Univ.; practised law at Stockholm Magistrates Court 1933, subsequently joined Ministry of Commerce; Dir. Swedish Clearing Office 1940; Dir. Swedish Trade Comm. 1943-45; entered Foreign Office 1945, Head of Section in Commercial Dept. 1945-46; Commercial Counsellor, Washington 1946-49; Head of Commercial Dept., Foreign Office, Stockholm 1949-53; Asst. Under-Sec. of State at Foreign Office 1953-56, Perm. Under-Sec. of State 1956-67; Amb. to U.K. 1967-72; Amb. and Rep. to OECD and UNESCO 1972-76; Jt. adviser PKbanken, Stockholm 1976-; Hon. G.B.E. (U.K.) *Address:* PKbanken, Hamngatan 12, 10571, Stockholm, Sweden.

BELGIUM, King Baudouin I of (see Baudouin).

BELIARD, Jean; French diplomatist; b. 22 March 1919, Colmar; m. 1st Diana J. Mowrer 1950, one s. (deceased) one d.; m. 2nd Denise Leboulleux 1967, two s.; ed. Faculté des Sciences Politiques and Faculté de Droit, Paris; attaché, Washington 1945-48; Deputy Dir. NATO Inf. Service 1951-53; Consul-Gen., Detroit 1954-56, Chicago 1958-64; Dir.-Gen. Radio Monte Carlo 1966-68; Consul-Gen., New York 1968-69; Dir. Press and Information Service, Ministry of Foreign Affairs 1970-73; Amb. to Mexico 1973-77, to Brazil 1977-81, to Canada 1981-84; Sec.-Gen. Atlantic Treaty Asscn. Jan. 1985-; Pres. France-Amérique 1985-; Croix de Guerre, Commdr. Légion d'honneur, Commdr. ordre du Mérite, Bronze Star (U.S.A.). *Publications:* Vertige en eau profonde 1964, Meurtre à l'alpe d'Huez 1968. *Leisure interests:* tennis, gardening, old books. *Address:* 96 ter rue de Longchamp, Neuilly 92200, France.

BELIGAN, Radu; Romanian actor; b. 14 Dec. 1918, Galbeni, Bacău County; ed. Bucharest Conservatoire; started career at Muncă şi Lumină (Work and Light) Theatre in Bucharest, then played at Alhambra and Nat. Theatre; Prof. Inst. of Drama and Film Art Bucharest 1960-68; Merited Artist 1953, People's Artist 1962; Dir. Teatrul de Comedie 1960-68; Dir. Nat. Theatre 1969-; Chair. Int. Theatre Inst.; mem. Cen. Cttee. Romanian CP 1969-; mem. Exec. Bureau Nat. Council Front of Socialist Democracy and Unity 1980-; performances in classic and modern Romanian plays and Int. repertoire (Shakespeare, Gogol, Chekhov, Albee, Dürrenmatt and others). *Publications:* Pretexte şi subtexte (Pretexts and Understatements), essays, 1968; Luni, marţi, miercuri (Monday, Tuesday, Wednesday), Memoirs 1978. *Address:* Teatrul Naţional, Bd. Nicolae Bălcescu 2, Bucharest, Romania. *Telephone:* 15 15 02.

BELIKOV, Gen. Valeriy Aleksandrovich; Soviet army officer; ed. Mil. Acad. of Armoured Car Forces, Mil. Acad. of GHQ; served in Soviet Army 1942-; served in a series of responsible posts in tank divs. 1945-; mem. CPSU 1949-; C.O. tank regiment, deputy commdr. of tank division 1956-68; various posts of command 1968-; Commdr. of N. Caucasian Forces 1976-, of Cis-Carpathian Mil. Districts 1979-; C.-in-C. Soviet Forces in Germany 1979-; Cand. mem. of CPSU Cen. Cttee. 1986; Deputy to U.S.S.R. Supreme Soviet. *Address:* c/o Ministry of Defence, Moscow, U.S.S.R.

BELIN, Roger, D.IUR.; French civil servant; b. 21 March 1916; m. Christiane Bressac 1961; ed. Univ. of Paris Law Faculty, Paris School of Political Sciences; Auditeur Conseil d'Etat 1943; Chargé de Mission, Présidence du Conseil 1944; Maître des Requêtes, Conseil d'Etat 1949; mem. Atomic Energy Cttee. 1951; Dir. Présidence du Conseil 1955; Sec.-Gen. of the Govt. 1958; Pres. Régie autonome des transports parisiens 1964-81; Hon. Conseiller d'Etat 1981; Pres. Union Int. des Transports Publics 1973-79; Man. Dir. of newspaper Le Parisien Libéré 1982-84; Chargé de Mission to Edouard Balladeur (Minister of State, of Economy, of Finance, of Privatisation) 1986-88; Commdr. Légion d'honneur. *Address:* Ministère de l'Economie et des Finances, 93 rue de Rivoli, 75056 Paris (Office); 9 boulevard Flandrin, 75116 Paris, France (Home).

BELKAID, Aboubakr; Algerian politician; b. 19 March 1934; m.; three c.; mem. secr. de l'Amicale des Algériens en France; Head Suport Network for Prisoners; arrested at Franco-Belgian frontier 1961, imprisoned Fresnes 1961-62; Head of Rural Animation at the Office for Education and Training 1963-64; Deputy to the Minister of Social Affairs 1964-65; Dir. l'Institut nat. de la formation professionale 1965-71, of training and selection, Expansial 1971-73; Dir. of Studies at Presidency of Republic 1973-77; Sec. Gen. MUCH 1977-80; Deputy Minister of Construction 1984-86; Minister of Labour 1986-87, of Higher Educ. 1987-88, the Interior and Local Communication 1988-; mem. UNESCO Consultative Cttee. for Educ.

and Training 1968–72. *Address:* Palais du Governement, Algiers, Algeria. *Telephone:* (2) 63-23-40.

BELKHODJA, Mohamed Moncef; Tunisian banker; b. 12 Feb. 1932, Bizerte; s. of Ahmed and Om héni Belkhodja; m. Michelle Rivière; two d.; Admin. and Chair. and Man. Dir. Banque de Développement Economique de Tunisie; fmr. Chair. and Man. Dir. Banque Nationale de Tunisie; fmr. Exec. Dir. IBRD; fmr. Dir of Credit and Banks, Banque Centrale de Tunisie, Gov. July 1980–86; Pres., Asscn. of African Cen. Banks 1985–. *Address:* Association of African Central Banks, 15 Boulevard Franklin Roosevelt, B.P. 1791, Dakar, Senegal. *Telephone:* 21-38-21.

BELL, David Elliott; American economist; b. 20 Jan. 1919, Jamestown, N.D.; s. of Reginald Bell and Florence Boise Bell; m. Mary Barry 1943; one s. one d.; ed. Pomona Coll., and Harvard Univ.; joined Budget Bureau 1941; served U.S. Marine Corps, Second World War; Budget Bureau 1945–47; Asst. in White House 1947–51; Admin. Asst. to Pres. Truman 1951–53; Head, Harvard Univ. Econ. Advisory Group to Pakistan 1954–57; lecturer in Econs., Littauer Center (Harvard Graduate School of Public Admin.) 1957, Sec. (Chief Admin. Officer) 1959–61; Dir. U.S. Budget Bureau 1961–62; Admin., Agency for Int. Devt. 1962–66; Vice-Pres. (Int. Activities), Ford Foundation 1966–69, Exec. Vice-Pres. 1969–81; Clarence Gamble Prof. of Population Sciences and Int. Health, Chair. Dept. of Population Sciences and Dir. Harvard Center for Population Studies, Harvard School of Public Health 1981–. *Address:* 1 Waterhouse Street, Cambridge, Mass. 02138, U.S.A. *Telephone:* (617) 497-9672.

BELL, (Ernest) Arthur, C.B., PH.D., C.CHEM., F.L.S., F.R.S.C.; British scientist; b. 20 June 1926, Gosforth, Northumberland; s. of Albert and Rachel Enid (née Williams) Bell; m. Jean Swinton Ogilivie 1952; two s. one d.; ed. Dame Allan's School, Newcastle upon Tyne, King's Coll., Newcastle, Univ. of Durham, Trinity Coll., Univ. of Dublin; Research Chemist, ICI 1946–47, Demonstrator and holder of Sarah Purser Research Award, Trinity Coll., Dublin 1947–49, Asst. to Prof. of Biochemistry 1949–53; Lecturer in Biochemistry, King's Coll., London 1953–64, Reader 1964–68, Prof. of Biology and Head of Dept. of Plant Sciences 1972–81, Dean of Natural Science 1980–81; Prof. of Botany, Univ. of Texas at Austin 1968–72; Dir. Royal Botanic Gardens, Kew Nov. 1981–88; Consultant Dir. CAB Int. Mycological Inst. 1982–88; mem. Working Party on Naturally Occurring Toxicants in Foods 1983–; Sr. Foreign Scientist and Fellow of Natural Science Foundation of U.S.A.; Visiting Prof. Univ. of Kansas 1964, Univ. of Sierra Leone 1977, King's Coll., London 1982–; Reading 1982–88; Sr. Visiting Fellow, Australia 1980; Cecil H. and Ida Green Visiting Prof. Univ. of British Columbia 1987; Visitng Prof. Univ. of Texas at Austin 1988–; scientific Dir., Texas Botanical Garden Soc. 1988–; Fellow, King's Coll., London 1982; Vice-Pres. Linnean Soc. of London 1982; Pres., Plant Biology Section, British Asscn. for the Advancement of Science 1985–86; Hon. mem. Phytochemical Soc. of Europe 1985–; Visiting Fellow, Japan Soc. for the Promotion of Science 1986; Pres. King's Coll. London Asscn. 1986–88; *Publications:* over 120 publications on plant biochemistry, chemotaxonomy and chemical ecology. *Leisure interests:* walking, travel, rugby football. *Address:* 3, Hillview, Wimbledon, London SW20 0TA, England. *Telephone:* 01-946 2626.

BELL, Geoffrey Lakin, B.SC.ECON.; British international banker; b. 8 Nov. 1939, Grimsby; s. of late Walter Lakin Bell and of Anne Bell; m. Joan Rosine Abel 1973; one c.; ed. Grimsby Tech. High School and London School of Econs.; H.M. Treasury 1961–63; Visiting Economist Federal Reserve System 1963–64; H.M. Treasury and Lecturer, L.S.E. 1964–66; Adviser British Embassy, Washington 1966–69; joined J. Henry Schroder Wagg and Co. Ltd. 1969, Asst. to Chair. 1969–72; Dir. and Exec. Vice-Pres. Schroder Int. Ltd.; Dir. Schroder Bermuda Ltd.; Exec. Sec. Group of Thirty; Pres. Geoffrey Bell and Co. Ltd. Aug. 1982–. *Publication:* The Euro-Dollar Market and the International Financial System 1973, contrib. The Times and numerous academic and other publications. *Address:* 300 East 56th Street, Apt. 7J, New York, N.Y. 10022, U.S.A.; 17 Abbotsbury House, Abbotsbury Road, London, W14 8EN, England. *Telephone:* 212-838-1193 (U.S.A.); 01-603 9408 (England).

BELL, George Douglas Hutton, C.B.E., PH.D., F.R.S.; British agricultural scientist; b. 18 Oct. 1905, Swansea; s. of George H. Bell and Lilian M. Hutton; m. Eileen G. Wright 1934; two d.; ed. Bishop Gore's Grammar School, Swansea, Univ. Coll. of N. Wales, and Univ. of Cambridge; Research Officer, Plant Breeding Inst. 1931, Univ. Demonstrator, Cambridge 1933, Lecturer 1944; Fellow, Selwyn Coll., Cambridge 1944–54, Hon. Fellow 1965; Dir. Plant Breeding Inst., Cambridge 1947–71; Fellow, Royal Soc. 1965, Vice-Pres. 1976–78; Research Medal, Royal Agric. Soc. of England 1956; Mullard Medal, Royal Soc. 1967; Hon. D.Sc. (Univs. of Reading, Wales and Liverpool), Hon.Sc.D. (Cambridge); Massey Ferguson Nat. Award 1973. *Publications:* Cultivated Plants of the Farm 1948, The Breeding of Barley Varieties in Barley and Malt 1962, Cereal Breeding in Vistas in Botany Vol. II 1963, Phylogeny of Temperate Cereals in Crop Plant Evolution 1965; papers on barley and breeding in Journal of Agricultural Science, etc. *Leisure interests:* music, theatre, natural history, sport, gardening. *Address:* 6 Worts Causeway, Cambridge, CB1 4RL, England. *Telephone:* 0223-247449.

BELL, Sir (George) Raymond, K.C.M.G., C.B.; British financial official; b. 13 March 1916; m. Joan Elizabeth Coltham 1944; four c.; ed. Bradford

Grammar School, St. John's Coll., Cambridge.; entered Civil Service, Asst. Prin. 1938; Ministry of Health 1938; H.M. Treasury 1939; war service Royal Navy, Lieut. R.N.V.R. 1941–44; Prin. Civil Service 1945, Sec. (Finance), Office of High Commr. in Canada 1945–48; Asst. Sec. 1951; Counsellor, U.K. Perm. Del. to OEEC/NATO, Paris 1953–56; Prin. Pvt. Sec. to Chancellor of Exchequer 1958–60; Under Sec. 1960; mem. U.K. Del. to Brussels Conf. 1961–62, 1970–72, Deputy Sec. 1966; Deputy Sec. H.M. Treasury 1966–72; Vice-Pres. European Investment Bank (EIB) 1973–78, Hon. Vice-Pres. 1978–. *Leisure interests:* music, reading, travel. *Address:* Quartier des Bories, Aouste-sur-Sye, 26400 Crest (Drôme), France. *Telephone:* 75 25 26 94.

BELL, Griffin Boyette, LL.B.; American government official and fmr. judge; b. 31 Oct. 1918, Americus, Ga.; s. of A. C. and Thelma (née Pilcher) Bell; m. Mary Foy Powell 1943; one s.; ed. Georgia Southwestern Coll. and Mercer Univ.; served U.S. Army (Maj.) 1941–46; admitted to Ga. Bar 1947; practice in Savannah and Rome, Ga. 1947–53; Partner, King and Spalding, Atlanta 1953–59, Man. Partner 1959–61; Sr. Partner 1979–; U.S. Judge, 5th Circuit Court of Appeals 1961–76; U.S. Attorney-Gen. 1977–79; Chair. Atlanta Comm. on Crime and Delinquency 1965–66; Chair. American Del., Conf. on Security and Co-operation in Europe, Madrid 1980; mem. Bd. of Dirs., Fed. Judicial Centre 1974–76; Pres. American Coll. of Trial Lawyers 1985–86; mem. Sec. of State's Advisory Cttee. on S.A. 1986; mem. American Law Inst., American Coll. of Trial Lawyers, American Bar Assn.; Hon. LL.D. (Mercer Univ.) 1967 and several other colls. and univs.; Thomas Jefferson Memorial Foundation Award for excellence in law 1974. *Address:* King and Spalding, 2500 Trust Company Tower, Atlanta, Ga. 30303 (Office); 206 Townsend Place, N.W., Atlanta, Ga. 30327, U.S.A. (Home).

BELL, James Dunbar, PH.D.; American fmr. diplomatist; b. 1 July 1911, Lebanon, New Hampshire; s. of Frank U. Bell and Louise Dunbar; m. Stephanie Anne Matthews 1961; three s. two d.; ed. Univs. of Chicago and New Mexico; reporter Albuquerque Journal, New Mexico 1933–34; Chief Statistician, New Mexico Dept. of Public Welfare 1936–37; Instructor Gary Coll. 1939–41; Analyst, Office of Co-ordinator, Inter-American Affairs 1941–42; Special Asst., Dept. of Justice 1943–44; Prof. Hamilton Coll. 1946–47; Dept. of State 1944–70, Bogotá, Santiago, Manila 1944–52; Officer-in-Charge, Philippine Affairs, Washington 1953–54; Deputy Dir. Philippine and Southeast Asian Affairs 1954–55; Dir. Office of Southwest Pacific Affairs 1956–57, 1960–64; Deputy Chief of Mission and Counsellor, Jakarta 1957–59; Amb. to Malaysia 1964–69; lecturer Merrill Coll., Univ. of Calif., Santa Cruz 1970–71; Acting Dir. Center for South Pacific Studies, Univ. of Calif., Santa Cruz 1973–74; Fellow of Merrill Coll. 1969–. *Leisure interests:* gold, politics. *Address:* 14 Kite Hill Road, Santa Cruz, Calif. 95060, U.S.A.

BELL, John Alexander Gordon; Canadian business executive; b. 16 Aug. 1929, Rivers, Manitoba; s. of John Edwin Bell, D.D. and Mary MacDonald (McIlraith) Bell; m. Charlene Elizabeth McCabe 1959; one s. one d.; ed. primary and secondary schools in Man., Newfoundland and Ont.; with The Bank of Nova Scotia 1948–; at Queen and Church Branch, Toronto 1948; at Gen. Office on Inspection Staff 1953; Special Rep., London 1955; Man., West End, London 1957; Asst. Man. Toronto Branch 1959, Man., Halifax 1962, Ottawa 1964, Kingston, Jamaica 1965, Asst. Gen. Man. Kingston 1966, Man. Dir. The Bank of Nova Scotia Jamaica Ltd. 1967, Gen. Man. Metropolitan Toronto Branches 1968, Deputy Chief Gen. Man. 1969, Exec. Vice-Pres. and Chief Gen. Man. 1972–79, Pres. and C.O.O. 1979–82, Deputy Chair., Pres. and C.O.O. 1982–; Dir. Bank of Nova Scotia and numerous cos. *Address:* The Bank of Nova Scotia, 44 King Street W., Toronto, Ontario, Canada (Office). *Telephone:* 866-6161.

BELL, John Milton, O.C., PH.D., F.R.S.C.; Canadian animal nutritionist and agrologist; b. 16 Jan. 1922, Islay, Alberta; s. of Milton Wilfred Bell and Elsie J. Larmour; m. E. M. Joan Smith 1944; three s. two d.; ed. Univ.of Alberta, McGill and Cornell Univs.; Asst. Prof. Coll. of Agric. Univ. of Saskatchewan 1948–52, Assoc. Prof. 1952–53, Prof. and Head of Animal Science 1954–75, Assoc. Dean (Research) 1975–80, Burford Hooke Prof. of Agricultural Science 1980–84, now Prof. of Animal Science, Dept. of Animal and Poultry Science; Fellow, Agricultural Inst. of Canada; Borden Award 1962 and other awards. *Publications:* more than 150 publs. in research journals, book chapters etc. *Leisure interest:* photography. *Address:* University of Saskatchewan, Department of Animal and Poultry Science, Saskatoon, Sask., S7N 0W0 (Office); 1530 Jackson Avenue, Saskatoon, Sask., S7H 2N2, Canada (Home). *Telephone:* (306) 966-4130 (Office); (306) 343-9017 (Home).

BELL, John Stewart, PH.D., F.R.S.; British physicist; b. 28 July 1928, Belfast, Northern Ireland; s. of Annie and John Bell; m. Mary Ross 1954; ed. Tech. High School, Belfast, Queen's Univ. Belfast and Univ. of Birmingham; with Atomic Energy Research Establishment, Harwell 1949–60; C.E.R.N., Geneva, Switzerland 1960–. *Publications:* papers on electromagnetic, nuclear and quantum theory, especially elementary particle physics. *Address:* CERN-TH, 1211 Geneva 23, Switzerland. *Telephone:* 83 24 39.

BELL, Sir Raymond (see Bell, Sir George Raymond).

BELL, Robert Edward, C.C., PH.D., F.R.S., F.R.S.C.; Canadian physicist; b. 29 Nov. 1918, England; s. of Edward R. Bell and Edith E. Rich; m. Jeanne Atkinson 1947; one d.; ed. elementary and high school, Ladner, B.C., Univ. of British Columbia and McGill Univ.; Physicist, Nat. Research Council of Canada, Ottawa 1941–45; Physicist, Chalk River Nuclear Labs. 1946–56, on loan to McGill Univ. 1952–56; Assoc. Prof. of Physics, McGill Univ. 1956–60, Rutherford Prof. 1960–83, and Dir. Foster Radiation Lab. 1960–69, Dean of Graduate Studies and Research 1969–70; Prin. and Vice-Chancellor, McGill Univ. 1970–79; Dir. Arts, Sciences and Technology Centre, Vancouver 1983–85; Pres. Canadian Asscn. of Physicists 1965–66; Pres. Royal Soc. of Canada 1978–81; Canadian Centennial Medal 1967, Medal for Achievement in Physics, Canadian Asscn. of Physicists 1968; Companion of the Order, Canada 1971. *Publications:* over 50 articles in scientific journals and contributions to books. *Leisure interests:* reading, amateur carpentry. *Address:* 822 Tsawwassen Beach, Delta, B.C., Canada V4M 2J3. *Telephone:* (604) 943-0667.

BELL, Ronald Percy, M.A., LL.D., D.SC., D.TECH., F.R.S., F.R.S.E., F.R.I.C.; British professor of chemistry; b. 24 Nov. 1907, Maidenhead, Berks.; s. of Edwin Alfred Bell and Beatrice Annie Ash; m. Margery Mary West 1931; one s.; ed. Maidenhead County Boys' School and Balliol Coll., Oxford; Fellow, Balliol Coll., Oxford 1933–67, Vice-Master 1965–66, Hon. Fellow 1967; Univ. Reader in Physical Chem., Oxford 1955–66; Prof. of Chem., Univ. of Stirling, Scotland 1967–75, Emer. 75–; Hon. Research Prof., Univ. of Leeds 1976–; Chemical Soc. Liversidge Lecturer 1973–74; Spiers Memorial Lecturer 1975; Foreign mem. Royal Danish Acad. of Arts and Sciences 1962; Foreign Assoc. U.S. N.A.S. 1972–; Foreign Hon. mem. American Acad. Arts and Sciences 1974; Leverhulme Emer. Fellow 1976; Hon. LL.D., (Ill. Inst. of Technology) 1964, Hon. D. Tech., Tech. Univ. of Denmark 1969; Hon. D.Sc. (Kent); Hon. D. Univ., (Stirling); Meldola Medal 1936, Chem. Soc. Award in Kinetics and Mechanism 1974. *Publications:* Acid-Base Catalysis 1941, Acids and Bases 1952, The Proton in Chemistry 1959, The Tunnel Effect in Chemistry 1980. *Leisure interest:* music. *Address:* 5 Park Villa Court, Leeds LS8 1EB, England. *Telephone:* Leeds 664236.

BELL, Terrel Howard, B.A., ED.D.; American educationalist and politician; b. 11 Nov. 1921, Lava Hot Springs, Idaho; s. of Willard Dewain and Alta (Martin) Bell; m. Betty Ruth Fitzgerald 1957; four s.; ed. Southern Idaho Coll. of Educ. and Utah Univ.; High School Teacher chem. and physics, Eden, Ohio 1946–47; Supt. Schools, Rockland (Idaho) Valley Schools 1947–54, Star Valley School Dist., Afton, Wyoming 1955–57, Weber Cty. (Utah) School Dist. 1957–62; Prof. of School Admin., Utah State Univ. 1962–63; Supt. Public Instruction, State of Utah 1963–70; Assoc. Commr. Regional Office Coordination, U.S. Office of Educ., Dept. of Health, Educ. and Welfare, and Acting Commr. 1970, Deputy Commr. School Systems 1971, Commr. Educ. 1974–76; Supt. Granite School System, Utah 1971–74; Commr. Educ., State of Utah, Salt Lake City 1976–80; U.S. Sec. of Educ. 1981–85; Prof. Utah Univ. 1985–; Chair. Utah Textbook Comm., Utah Course Study Comm; Exec. Officer Utah Bd. of Educ.; mem. American Asscn. of School Administrators, Council Chief State School Officers. *Publications:* The Prodigal Pedagogue (novel) 1956, Effective Teaching: How to Recognize and Reward Competence 1962, A Philosophy of Education for the Space Age 1963, Your Child's Intellect—A Guide to Home-Based Pre-school Education 1972, A Performance Accountability System for School Administrators 1974, Active Parent Concern 1976, The 13th Man: A Reagan Cabinet Memoir 1988. *Address:* University of Utah, Salt Lake City, Utah 84112, U.S.A.

BELL, Thomas Johnston, M.C., C.D., LL.D.; Canadian business executive; b. 26 June 1914, Southampton, Ont.; s. of Charles M. and Hazel Bell; m. Edna Gertrude Harshman McGregor 1948; two s. four d.; ed. Ridley Coll. and Univ. of Toronto; associated with Fed. Wire and Cable Co. Ltd., Guelph, Ont. 1936–55; Pres. Fiberglas Canada Ltd., Toronto 1956–67; Pres. and C.E.O., Abitibi Paper Co. Ltd., Toronto 1967, Chair. and C.E.O. 1973; Chair. Abitibi-Price Inc. 1979–83, Dir. 1983–; Dir. Matthews Group Ltd., Fiberglas Canada Inc. *Address:* 175 Teddington Park, Toronto, Ont. M4N 2C7, Canada.

BELL, William Edwin, C.B.E., B.SC.; British oil industry executive; b. 4 Aug. 1926, Leicester; s. of Cuthbert Edwin Bell and Winifred Mary Simpson; m. Angela Josephine Vaughan 1952; two s. two d.; ed. Birmingham Univ. and Royal School of Mines, Imperial Coll. of Science and Tech., London; joined Royal Dutch Shell Group 1948; Dir. Shell U.K. Ltd. and Gen. Man. Shell U.K. Exploration and Production 1973; Man. Dir. Shell U.K. Ltd. 1976–79; Dir. Shell Int. Petroleum Co. Ltd. and Middle E. Regional Co-ordinator 1980–84; Chair. Enterprise Oil PLC 1984–; Pres. U.K. Offshore Operators' Asscn. 1975–76; Dir. Costain Group PLC 1982–; mem. Advisory Bd., Brown and Root (U.K.) Ltd. 1983–. *Leisure interests:* yachting and golf. *Address:* Fordcombe Manor, Fordcombe, nr. Tunbridge Wells, Kent, TN3 0SE, England. *Telephone:* (0892) 74214.

BELLAMY, David James, PH.D., F.L.S.; British botanist, writer and broadcaster; b. 18 Jan. 1933; s. of Thomas Bellamy and Winifred (née Green); m. Rosemary Froy 1959; two s. three d.; ed. Chelsea Coll. of Science and Tech. and Bedford Coll., London Univ.; Lecturer, then Sr. Lecturer, Dept. of Botany, Univ. of Durham 1960–80, Hon. Prof. of Adult and Continuing Educ. 1980–; Visiting Prof. Massey Univ., N.Z. 1988–89; Special Prof. of

Botany Nottingham Univ.; TV and radio presenter and scriptwriter; series include: Life in Our Sea 1970, Bellamy on Botany 1973, Bellamy's Britain 1975, Bellamy's Europe 1977, Botanic Man 1978, Up a Gum Tree 1980, Backyard Safari 1981, The Great Seasons 1982, Bellamy's New World 1983, End of the Rainbow Show 1986, S.W.A.L.L.O.W. 1986, Turning the Tide 1986, Bellamy's Bugle 1986, 1987, 1988, Bellamy on Top of the World 1987, Bellamy's Journey to the Centre of the World 1987, Bellamy's Bird's Eye View 1988, Bellamy on the Book 1988; Founder Dir. Conservation Foundation; Pres. WATCH 1982–; Pres. Youth Hostels Asscn. 1983; Pres. Population Concern 1987. *Publications include:* Peatlands 1974, Life Giving Sea 1977, Half of Paradise 1979, The Great Seasons 1981, Discovering the Countryside with David Bellamy (Vols. I, II) 1982, (Vols. III, IV) 1983, The Mouse Book 1983, The Queen's Hidden Garden 1984, Bellamy's Ireland 1986, Bellamy's Changing Countryside (4 vols.) 1988 and books connected with TV series. *Leisure interests:* children and ballet. *Address:* Mill House, Bedburn, Bishop Auckland, Co. Durham, England.

BELLET, Pierre Rémy; French lawyer (retd.); b. 7 Sept. 1911, Maisons-Laffitte; s. of Daniel Bellet and Lilly Bourgeois; m. Annette Hirchberg 1946; three s.; ed. Lycée Janson-de-Sailly, Univ. of Paris, Ecole des Sciences Politiques; trainee lawyer, Paris Court of Appeal 1933–35, Pres. of Chamber 1964–65; 1st Vice-Pres. Seine Tribunal de Grande Instance 1965–68, Pres. 1968–72; Councillor, Court of Cassation 1968, Pres. of Chamber 1972–77, First Pres. 1977–80; Vice-Pres. Cttee. of Int. Private Law 1965–71, Pres. 1971–; Pres. Admin. Council, Ecole Nat. de la Magistrature; Pres. Comm. Nat. de l'informatique et des libertés 1978–79; Chair. 2nd Chamber, Iran-U.S.A. Arbitration Tribunal 1981–83; Pres. Council of Int. Arbitration Franco-Arab Chamber of Commerce 1983–; Vice-Pres. Juristes européens; Dr. h.c. (Glasgow, Geneva); Prize, Paris Faculty of Law; Grand Officier, Légion d'honneur, Commdr. ordre nat. du Mérite. *Leisure interests:* sailing, painting. *Address:* 15 avenue du Président Wilson, 75116 Paris, France. *Telephone:* 723-50-61 (Home).

BELLMON, Henry, B.S.; American farmer and politician; b. 3 Sept. 1921, Tonkawa, Okla.; m. Shirley Osborn 1947; three d.; ed. Oklahoma State Univ.; U.S. Marine Corps 1942–46; mem. Okla. Legis. 1946–48; farmer 1945–; State Chair. Republican Party 1960–62; Gov. of Oklahoma 1963–67; Chair. Nixon for Pres. Cttee. 1968; Senator from Okla. 1969–80. *Address:* Route One, Red Rock, Okla., U.S.A.

BELLOW, Saul, B.S.; American writer; b. 10 June 1915, Quebec, Canada; s. of Abraham and Liza (née Gordon) Bellow; m. 4th Alexandra Bagdasar (divorced); three s.; ed. Northwestern Univ.; Professor, Univ. of Minn. 1946–48; Prof. Princeton Univ. 1952–53; Prof. Univ. of Chicago 1964–; mem. Comm. on Social Thought 1963–; Nat. Book Award, Inst. of Arts and Letters 1953, Ford Foundation Grant 1959, Prix Int. de Littérature 1965, U.S. Nat. Book Award for The Adventures of Augie March 1954, Herzog 1965, Mr. Sammler's Planet 1971, Pulitzer Prize for Humboldt's Gift 1976, Nobel Prize for Literature 1976; Fellow, American Acad. of Arts and Sciences, Commandeur, Légion d'Honneur; Malaparte Literary Award 1984, Nat. Medal of Arts 1988. *Publications:* include contributions to numerous magazines and journals; also Dangling Man 1944, The Victim 1947, The Adventures of Augie March 1953, Seize the Day 1956, Henderson the Rain King 1959, Herzog 1964, Mosby's Memoirs and Other Stories 1968, Mr. Sammler's Planet 1969, Humboldt's Gift 1975, To Jerusalem and Back: A Personal Account (non-fiction) 1976, The Dean's December 1981, Him with His Foot in His Mouth and Other Stories 1984, More Die of Heartbreak 1987. *Address:* c/o Committee on Social Thought, University of Chicago, 1126 East 59th Street, Chicago, Ill. 60637, U.S.A.

BELLUGI, Piero; Italian conductor; b. 14 July 1924, Florence; s. of Mario Bellugi and Giulia Favilli; m. 1st Ursula Herzberger 1954 (divorced), 2nd Margherita Vivian 1960; five c.; ed. Conservatorio Cherubini, Florence, Accademia Chigiana, Siena, Akad. des Mozarteums, Salzburg, and Tanglewood, Mass., U.S.A.; Musical Dir. Oakland (Calif.) and Portland (Ore.) Symphony Orchs. 1955–61; Perm. conductor, Radio Symphony Orch., Turin 1967; Prof. courses for orchestral players and conductor, Italian Youth Orchestra 1981–; guest conductor, La Scala, Milan (début 1961), Vienna State Opera, Rome Opera, Aix-en-Provence Festival, Berlin Radio, Paris, Rome S. Cecilia, Chicago, San Francisco Operas, etc.; Hon. mem. Nat. Acad. Luigi Cherubini of Music, Letters and Arts. *Address:* 50027 Strada in Chianti, Florence, Italy. *Telephone:* (55) 858116, 858556.

BELLUSCHI, Pietro, DOTT.ING.; American architect; b. 18 Aug. 1899, Ancona, Italy; s. of Guido Belluschi and Camilla Dogliani; m. 1st Helen Hemila 1934 (deceased), 2nd Marjorie Bruckner 1965; two s.; ed. Univ. of Rome and Cornell Univ.; Draftsman for A. E. Doyle, Architect, Portland, Ore. 1925–28; chief designer A. E. Doyle & Assoc. 1928–33, partner 1933–43; own architectural practice 1943–; Dean, School of Architecture and Planning, M.I.T. 1951–65; Fellow, American Acad. of Arts and Sciences, Royal Acad. of Fine Arts, Copenhagen; mem. Nat. Acad. of Design; life mem. Nat. Inst. of Arts and Letters; Gold Medal, Italian Charitable Soc.; Commendatore della Repubblica Italiana; Gold Medal, American Inst. of Architects 1972; numerous honorary degrees and other distinctions. *Principal works:* Portland Art Museum, Equitable Building, Oregonian Publishing Plant (all Portland, Ore.); Library for Bennington Coll., Vt. 1959; Juilliard School, Lincoln Center for the Performing Arts, N.Y. City 1969; Bank of America World Headquarters Building (San Francisco); many churches and temples in U.S.A. *Address:* 700 N.W. Rapidan Terrace, Portland, Ore. 97210, U.S.A. *Telephone:* (503) 225 0131.

BELMONDO, Jean-Paul; French actor, b. 9 April 1933, Paris; s. of Paul Belmondo; m. 1952, divorced 1967; one s. two d.; ed. Ecole Alsacienne, Paris, Cours Pascal and Conservatoire nat. d'art dramatique; started career on the stage; mainly film actor since 1957; Pres. French Union of Actors 1963–66; Prix Citron 1972; Chevalier, Légion d'honneur; Chevalier, ordre nat. du Mérite, Arts et des Lettres. *Plays acted in include:* L'hôtel du libre-échange, Oscar, Trésor-Party, Médée, La mégère apprivoisée, Kean, ou Désordre et Génie 1987. *Films acted in include:* Sois belle et tais-toi, A pied, à cheval et en voiture, les Tricheurs, Charlotte et son Jules, Drôle de dimanche 1958, Les Copains du dimanche, Mademoiselle Ange, A double tour, Classe tous risques, Au bout de souffle, L'Amour, La Novice, La Ciociara, Moderato Cantabile, Léon Morin Prêtre, Le Doulos 1962, Dragées au poivre, L'Aîné des Ferchaux, Peau de banane, 100,000 dollars au soleil 1963, Two Women, The Man From Rio, Echappement libre 1964, Les tribulations d'un Chinois en Chine, Pierrot le Fou 1965, Paris, brûle-t-il? 1966, Le Voleur 1966, Casino Royale 1967, The Brain 1969, La Sirène du Mississippi 1969, Un Homme qui me plaît 1970, Borsalino 1970, The Burglars 1972, La Scoumoune 1972, L'Héritier 1972, Le Magnifique 1973, Stavisky 1974, Peur sur la ville 1975, L'Incorrigible 1975, L'Alpageur, Le corps de mon ennemi 1976, L'Animal 1977, Flic ou Voyou 1979, L'As de as (also produced) 1982, Le Marginal 1983, Joyeuses Pâques, Les Morfalous 1984, Hold-up 1985, Itinéraire d'un enfant gâté; Chevalier de la Legion d'honneur, des Arts et des Lettres, Officier ordre nat. du Mérite. *Publications:* 30 Ans et 25 Films (autobiog.) 1963. *Address:* Cerito Films, 5 rue Clément Marot, 75008 Paris, France (Office).

BELOFF, Baron (Life Peer), cr. 1981, of Wolvercote in the County of Oxfordshire; **Max Beloff,** Kt., M.A., D.LITT., F.B.A., F.R.HIST.S., F.R.S.A.; British historian; b. 2 July 1913, London; s. of S. and M. Beloff; m. Helen Dobrin 1938; two s.; ed. St. Paul's School, Corpus Christi Coll. and Magdalen Coll., Oxford; Asst. Lecturer in History, Manchester Univ. 1939–46; Nuffield Reader in Comparative Study of Institutions, Oxford Univ. 1946–56; Fellow of Nuffield Coll. 1947–57; Gladstone Prof. of Govt. and Public Admin., Univ. of Oxford, Fellow of All Souls Coll. 1957–74; Prin., Univ. Coll. at Buckingham 1974–79; Fellow of St. Antony's Coll., Oxford 1975–84; Chair. Advisory Bd., Conservative Research Dept. 1982–87; Hon. D.C.L. (Bishop's Univ.); Hon. LL.D. (Univ. of Pittsburgh), (Univ. of Manchester) 1989; Hon. D.Litt. (Bowdoin Coll.), (Buckingham) 1983; Hon. Dr. Univ. (Aix-Marseille); Emer. Fellow, All Souls Coll., Oxford 1980–. *Publications:* Public Order and Popular Disturbances 1660-1714 1938, The Foreign Policy of Soviet Russia 1947–49, Thomas Jefferson and American Democracy 1948, Soviet Policy in the Far East 1944–51 1953, The Age of Absolutism 1660-1815 1954, Foreign Policy and the Democratic Process 1955, Europe and the Europeans 1957, The Great Powers 1959, The American Federal Government 1959, New Dimensions in Foreign Policy 1961, The United States and the Unity of Europe 1963, Europe du XIX et XX Siècle 1960–66 (Jt. Ed.), The Balance of Power 1968, The Future of British Foreign Policy 1969, Imperial Sunset, Vol. I 1969, Vol. II 1989, The Intellectual in Politics 1970, The Government of the United Kingdom (Jt. Author) 1980, 1985, Wars and Welfare 1914–45 1984. *Leisure interests:* cricket, opera. *Address:* House of Lords, London, S.W.1; Flat 9, 22 Lewes Crescent, Brighton, England. *Telephone:* 01-219 6669; (0273) 688622.

BELONOGOV, Aleksandr M.; Soviet diplomatist; b. 1931; m.; two c.; ed. Soviet Inst. of Int. Relations; entered Ministry of Foreign Affairs 1954, staff mem. Legal Dept. and Dept. of Int. Econ. Orgs. 1954–62, Sr. Counsellor, then Head of Unit, then Deputy Head Dept. of Int. Policy Planning 1973–84; Second, then First Sec. at Soviet Embassy, London 1962–67; Amb. to Egypt 1984–86; Perm. Rep. of U.S.S.R. to UN 1986–; holds various govt. orders and medals. *Address:* Permanent Mission of U.S.S.R. to United Nations, 136 East 67th Street, New York, N.Y. 10021, U.S.A. *Telephone:* (212) 861-4900.

BELOUSOV, Igor Sergeyevich; Soviet politician; b. 1928; mem. CPSU 1955; worked as foreman, then chief engineer of shipbuilding yard; Deputy Minister of Shipbuilding 1969, First Deputy Minister 1976; Minister of Shipbuilding of U.S.S.R. Jan. 1984–; mem. of CPSU Cen. Cttee 1986–; Hero of Socialist Labour; State Prize. *Address:* Ministry of Shipbuilding, Sadovaya-Kudrinskaya ul. 11, Moscow, U.S.S.R.

BELOUSOV, Vladimir Vladimirovich, D.SC.; Soviet geologist; b. 30 Oct. 1907, Moscow; s. of Vladimir and Xenia Belousov; m. Natalia Gourvitch 1931; one s.; ed. Moscow Univ.; Consultant, Council for Research of Productive Resources under U.S.S.R. Acad. of Sciences 1931–32; geologist, Cen. Research Inst. of Prospecting 1932–38; Sr. Scientific Assoc., U.S.S.R. Acad. of Sciences 1938–44; Head of Dept., Moscow Inst. for Prospecting 1942–49; Prof. 1940; Head of Geology Dept., Inst. of Physics of the Earth of U.S.S.R. Acad. of Sciences 1944–; Vice-Chair. Tech. Council, U.S.S.R. Ministry of Geology 1947–56; Prof., Moscow State Univ. 1953–; Corresp. mem. U.S.S.R. Acad. of Sciences 1953–; Chair. Soviet Geophysical Cttee. 1960–; Vice-Chair. Int. Geophysics Cttee. 1960–64; Pres. Int. Cttee. for Upper Mantle of the Earth Projects 1964–70; Head of Planetary and Marine Geophysics Dept., Inst. of Physics of the U.S.S.R. Acad. of Sciences 1975–; mem. Swedish, Indian and N.Y. Acads. of Sciences; Hon. mem. Geological Socs. of U.S.A., Belgium, India, France and U.K. *Publications:*

Basic Problems in Geotectonics 1962, Crust and Upper Mantle of Continents 1966, Crust and Upper Mantle of Oceans 1968, Principles of Geotectonics 1975, and several articles in professional journals; principal work in problems of structure and development of the Earth's crust, relationship between deep and geological processes, tectonophysics. *Leisure interests:* skiing, tourism. *Address:* Soviet Geophysical Committee, Molodejnaia 3, Moscow 296, U.S.S.R.

BELOV, Marshal Andrei Ivanovich; Soviet army officer; b. 19 Aug. 1917, Pskov; joined CPSU 1941; served in Soviet army 1938–; Mil. Electro-Technical Acad.; fought in Finno-Soviet War of 1939–40; tank signals engineer July 1940–; Chief of signals of mechanized corps on Southern, 1st Ukranian, 3rd Byelorussian, 2nd Baltic Fronts 1942–45; Chief of signals of mechanized corps of 1st Far Eastern Front Aug.–Sept. 1945; Sr. lecturer, head of faculty, Mil. Signals Acad. 1945–57; Chief of army signals of Turkestan Mil. Dist. 1957–60, of Strategic Rocket Forces 1960–68; First Deputy Chief, Army Signals, Ministry of Defence 1968–70, Chief. 1970–77; rank of Marshal (Signals) 1973; Deputy Chief of Staff of Soviet Forces Oct. 1977–; Order of Lenin, Order of Red Banner, Order of Red Star (three times) and other decorations. *Address:* c/o Ministry of Defence, Moscow, U.S.S.R.

BELOV, Vasiliy Ivanovich; Soviet writer; b. 23 Oct. 1932, Timonikha, Vologda; mem. CPSU and U.S.S.R. Union of Writers; worked on kolkhoz, received industrial training at a FZO school, then as a joiner and mechanic; served in Soviet Army; staff writer on regional newspaper 'Kommunar' in Gryazovets (Vologda) 1950s; secondary ed. (evening classes) 1956–59; mem. Literary Inst. of Union of Writers 1959–64. *Publications include:* My Village in the Forest 1961, Hot Summer 1963, Tisha and Grisha 1966, Carpenter Stories 1968 (English trans. 1969), An Ordinary Affair 1969, Village Tales 1971, Day after Day 1972, The Hills 1973, Looks can Kiss 1975. *Address:* c/o U.S.S.R. Union of Writers, Moscow, U.S.S.R.

BELSHAW, Cyril Shirley, PH.D., F.R.S.C.; Canadian anthropologist and writer; b. 3 Dec. 1921, Waddington, N.Z.; s. of Horace Belshaw and Marion L. S. (née McHardie) Belshaw; m. Betty J. Sweetman 1943 (deceased); one s. one d.; ed. Auckland Univ. Coll. and Victoria Coll., Wellington (Univ. of New Zealand), London School of Econs.; Dist. Officer and Deputy Commr. for Western Pacific, British Solomon Islands 1943–46; Sr. Research Fellow, Australian Nat. Univ. 1950–53; Prof. Univ. of British Columbia 1953–86, Prof. Emer. 1986–; Dir. Regional Training Centre for UN Fellows, Van. 1961–62; Ed. Current Anthropology 1974–84; mem. numerous UNESCO comms., working parties and consultancy groups; Pres. Int. Union of Anthropological and Ethnological Sciences 1978–83, XIth Int. Congress of Anthropological and Ethnological Sciences 1983; Exec. American Anthropological Assoc. 1969–70; Chair. Standing Cttee. Social Sciences and Humanities Pacific Science Assen. 1968–76; Hon. Life mem. Royal Anthropological Inst. 1978, Pacific Science Assen. 1981. *Publications:* Island Administration in the South West Pacific 1950, Changing Melanesia 1954, In Search of Wealth 1955, The Great Village 1957, The Indians of British Columbia (with others) 1958, Under the Ivi Tree 1964, Anatomy of a University 1964, Traditional Exchange and Modern Markets (eds. in 5 languages) 1965, The Conditions of Social Performance 1970, Towers Besieged 1974, The Sorcerer's Apprentice 1976, The Complete Good Dining Guide to Restaurants in Greater Vancouver 1984. *Leisure interests:* gardening, photography, travel, restaurants. *Address:* 1224 Island Park Walk, Vancouver B.C., V6H 3T4, Canada. *Telephone:* 604-732-1720.

BELSKY, Igor Dmitriyevich; Soviet choreographer; b. 28 March 1925; ed. Leningrad Ballet School; Dancer with Leningrad Kirov Theatre of Opera and Ballet 1943–62; teacher of folk character dance at Leningrad Choreography School 1946–; Producer and Choreographer, Leningrad Kirov Theatre of Opera and Ballet 1959–62, Chief Choreographer 1962–; People's Artist of the R.S.F.S.R. *Principal roles:* Rotbart (Swan Lake), Nurali (Fountain of Bakhchiserai), Tybalt (Romeo and Juliet), Shurale (Yarushllin's Shurale), Severyan (Prokofiev's Stone Flower), Mako (Karayev's Thunder Road). *Chief productions:* Shores of Hope (Petrov) 1959, Leningrad Symphony (Shostakovich) 1961, Humpbacked Horse (Shchedrin) 1963. *Address:* Leningrad Kirov Theatre of Opera and Ballet, Ploshchad Iskusstva I, Leningrad, U.S.S.R.

BELSTEAD, 2nd Baron (cr. 1938); **John Julian Ganzoni,** Bt., P.C., J.P., M.A.; British government official; b. 30 Sept. 1932; s. of 1st Baron Belstead and of late Gwendolen Gertrude Turner; ed. Eton Coll. and Christ Church, Oxford; Parl. Under-Sec. of State Dept. of Educ. and Science 1970–73, N. Ireland Office 1973–74, Home Office 1979–82, Minister of State FCO 1982–83, Ministry of Agric., Fisheries and Food 1983–87, Dept. of Environment 1987–88; Lord Privy Seal and Leader of the House of Lords 1988–; Chair. Assen. Governing Bodies of Public Schools 1974–79; J.P., Borough of Ipswich 1962; D.L., Suffolk 1979. *Address:* The Old Rectory, Great Bealings, nr. Woodbridge, Suffolk, England. *Telephone:* Grundisburgh 278.

BELTRÁN, Washington; Uruguayan newspaper executive and former politician; b. 6 April 1914, Montevideo; s. of Washington Beltrán and Elena Mullin de Beltrán; m. Esther Storace Arrosa de Beltrán 1943; three s. three d.; ed. Univ. de la República; joined El País 1939, Sub-Dir. 1949–61, Co-Dir. 1961–; mem. House of Reps. 1946, 1955; founded Reconstrucción Blanca and Union Blanca Democrática groups, both within Partido

Nacional; elected Senator 1959, 1967, 1971; mem. Consejo Nacional de Gobierno 1962-67, Pres. of Uruguay 1965-66; proscribed by mil. govt. 1973-80; since 1980 has dedicated most of time to journalism, especially editorials (collected in a book 1985); attended UNICEF World Conf. 1982; Amb. Plenipotentiary to Vatican and companion to Pope on his visit to Uruguay 1987; Pres. Sino-Uruguayan Foundation; Círculo de Tennis de Montevideo; numerous decorations from many countries. *Address:* El País, Zelmar Michelini 1287, P.3., Montevideo, Uruguay. *Telephone:* 91.95.56.

BELTRÃO, Alexandre Fontana; Brazilian coffee executive; b. 28 April 1924, Curitiba, Paraná; s. of Alexandre Beltrão and late Zilda Fontana Beltrão; m. Anna Emilia Beltrão 1964; two c.; ed. Instituto Santa Maria, Curitiba, Univ. de São Paulo, Escola Nacional de Engenharia, Rio de Janeiro; asst. engineer 1944; army officer 1945-46; asst. engineer, Dept. of Soil Mechanics, Inst. de Pesquisas Tecnológicas, São Paulo 1948; trained in regional planning at Inst. Nat. d'Aerophotogrametrie, Ministère de la Reconstruction, Paris and at Ministry of Works, London 1950-51; founder and Dir. of SPL (Planning Services Ltd.) 1954-; observer, Govt. of State of Paraná to UN Int. Coffee Conf. 1962; special adviser to Pres. Brazilian Coffee Inst. 1964; Chief Brazilian Coffee Inst. Bureau, N.Y. 1965-67; Pres. World Coffee Promotion Cttee. of Int. Coffee Org. 1965-67; Exec. Dir. Int. Coffee Org. May 1968-; Commdr. Order of Rio Branco. *Publications:* Paraná and the Coffee Economy 1963, essay on Economy of States of Paraná, Pará and Ceará (Brazil) 1958. *Address:* International Coffee Organization, 22 Berners Street, London, W.1, England. *Telephone:* 01-580 8591 (London); 287-0051 (Rio).

BELTRÃO, Helio Marcos Penna, F.I.A.M.; Brazilian lawyer, economist and management consultant; b. 15 Oct. 1916, Rio de Janeiro; s. of Heitor Beltrão and Christianna Penna Beltrão; m. Maria Cotuinho Beltrão 1966; one s. two d.; ed. Faculdade Nacional de Direito and New York Univ.; Dir. and Pres. of Social Security Agency (IPASE, IAPI) 1941-46; Pres. Brazilian Petroleum Inst. 1954-56; Dir. of Petrobrás S.A. (Govt. Oil Co.) 1954-56; Sec. of Planning, State of Guanabara 1960-61; mem. Bd. Nat. Bank of Econ. Devt. 1961-62, 1972-79, Itaipu Binacional 1974-79; mem. Cttee. on Fed. Admin. Reorganization 1964-67; Minister of Planning and Gen. Co-ordination 1967-69; Dir. and Vice-Pres. Mesbla S.A. (chain of dept. stores), Rio de Janeiro 1962-71; Pres. Ultra Group of Cos 1969-79, mem. Bd. 1986-; Pres. Getec-Guanabara Química Industrial 1970-79; mem. Bd. 1986-; Dir. and Vice-Pres. Paraíso Cement Co. 1970-73; Pres. Brazilian Acad. of Science and Admin. 1975-79; mem. Bd. Companhia Siderúrgica Nacional 1978-79; Minister for Debureaucratization 1979-83; Minister for Social Security 1982-83; mem. Bd. Brazilian Petroleum Inst. 1983-; Pres. of Petrobrás S.A. 1985-86. *Leisure interest:* popular music. *Address:* Rua Prudente de Moraes, 1179, Ipanema, Rio de Janeiro, R.J. Brazil.

BELYAK, Konstantin Nikitovich; Soviet government official; b. 1916, Tomsk, R.S.F.S.R.; mem. CPSU 1942-; graduated Tomsk Polytechnic Inst. 1936; locksmith, technologist, dept. head of a plant 1930-48; Dir. of factories in Kuybyshev, Komsomolsk-na-Amure and Voronezh 1948-57; Chair. of Voronezh Econ. Council 1957-63; Chair. of Econ. Council of Cen. Black Earth (Chernozem) Zone 1963-64; Deputy to U.S.S.R. Supreme Soviet 1962-66; First Deputy U.S.S.R. Minister for Tractor and Agricultural Machine Construction 1966-73; U.S.S.R. Minister for Machine Construction for Cattle Industry and Fodder Production 1973-85; cand. mem. of Cen. Cttee. of CPSU 1976, now mem.; Hero of Socialist Labour 1981. *Address:* Ministry of Machine Construction for the Cattle Industry and Fodder Production, Lesnaya ul. 43, Moscow, U.S.S.R.

BELYAKOV, Oleg Sergeyevich; Soviet official; b. 1933; ed. Dzerzhinsky Higher Naval Eng. Inst.; mem. CPSU 1961; engineer 1958-64; party work, Leningrad 1964-; work for CPSU Cen. Cttee 1972-; Deputy Head Dept. of Defence Industry of Cen. Cttee. CPSU 1982-85; Head of Dept. 1985-; Asst. to Sec. of CPSU Cen. Cttee. 1983-85; mem. Cen. Cttee. CPSU 1986-. *Address:* Central Committee of the Communist Party of the Soviet Union, Staraya pl. 4. Moscow, U.S.S.R.

BELYAKOV, Rostislav Appolonovich, DR.TECH.SCI.; Soviet mechanical scientist; b. 1919; ed. Ordzhonikidze Aviation Inst., Moscow; mem. CPSU 1944-; leading positions as engineer and designer 1941-; corresp. mem. of U.S.S.R. Acad. of Sciences 1974, mem. 1981-; Hero of Socialist Labour 1971, 1982, U.S.S.R. State Prize 1952, Lenin Prize 1972; Deputy to U.S.S.R. Supreme Soviet. *Address:* U.S.S.R. Academy of Sciences, Leninsky Pr. 14, Moscow V-71, U.S.S.R.

BELYAYEV, Albert Andreyevich, DR. PHIL. SC.; Soviet politician; b. 1928; ed. Archangel Nautical School and Archangel Pedagogical Inst.; mem. CPSU 1950-; UN div. of CPSU Cen. Cttee.; navigator on Arctic vessels 1950-53; komsomol work, First Sec. of Murmansk State Cttee. 1953-55; Second, First Sec. of Murmansk District Cttee. 1955-62; work for CPSU Cen. Cttee. 1962-73; Deputy Head of Section of CPSU Cen. Cttee. 1973-79; mem. of Praesidium of Cttee. on State prizes, U.S.S.R. Council of Mins. 1979-86; Editor-in-Chief of Soviet Culture 1986-; mem. of CPSU Cen. Auditing Comm. 1986-. *Address:* Soverskaya Kultura, ul. Pravda 24, Moscow, U.S.S.R.

BELYAYEV, Spartak Timofeyevich, DR.SC.; Soviet physicist; b. 27 Oct. 1923, Moscow; ed. Moscow State Univ.; junior research worker, senior research worker, Head of Laboratory, I. Kurchatov Inst. of Nuclear

Physics 1952-62; Siberian Dept., Acad. of Sciences 1962-; Prof., Rector, Novosibirsk State Univ. 1965; Corresp. mem. U.S.S.R. Acad. of Sciences 1964-68, Academician 1968-; mem. CPSU 1943-; Order of Lenin, Red Star, Order of October Revolution and medals. *Publications:* Scientific works in field of theory of atomic nucleus, particle movement in cyclotron, physics of relativistic plasma, statistic physics of quantum, many body systems. *Address:* c/o Academy of Sciences of U.S.S.R., Leninsky Prospekt 14, Moscow V-71, U.S.S.R.

BEN ABBES, Youssef, M.D.; Moroccan physician, diplomatist and politician; b. 15 Aug. 1921, Rabat; m. Marie Ben Abbes; two c.; ed. Marrakesh, Medical Coll. of Algiers and Paris; joined Public Health Service 1949, Dir. several hosps., then Insp. of Public Health; Minister of Health 1958-62, of Health and Educ. 1961, of Educ., Youth and Sport 1961-65, of Foreign Affairs 1970-71; Mayor of Marrakesh and Pres. Provincial Council; Amb. to U.A.R. 1965-66, to Italy and Greece 1967-68, to Algeria 1969-70, to Spain 1971-72, to France and UNESCO 1972-, to the Vatican 1976; Commdr. de l'ordre nationale du Trone (Morocco), Commdr. de l'ordre nationale du Mérite and other orders and decorations. *Address:* Embassy of Morocco, 3-5 rue Le Tasse, 75016 Paris, France.

BEN ABDALLAH, Moncef, L. ÈS SC.; Tunisian economist; b. 21 Oct. 1946, Tunis; ed. Ecole Centrale, Paris; Engineer, Chief of Production, Soc. Tunisienne d'Electricité et du Gaz 1972-75; Chargé de mission, Office of Minister of Nat. Econ. 1975-76; Deputy Dir. state petroleum co. (ETAP) 1978-79; Dir. of Industry, Ministry of Industry, Mines and Energy 1979; Chef de Cabinet, Ministry of Nat. Econ. 1980; Pres.-Dir.-Gen. Agence de Promotion des Investissements 1980-85; Commdr., ordre de la République. *Address:* Agence de Promotion des Investissements, 7 rue du Royaume de l'Arabie Saoudite, Tunis, Tunisia.

BEN BELLA, Mohammed; Algerian politician; b. 1916; Warrant Officer in Moroccan regiment during Second World War (decorated); Chief O.A.S. rebel military group in Algeria 1947; imprisoned 1949-52 (escaped); directed Algerian nat. movement from exile in Libya 1952-56; arrested Oct. 1956; held in France 1959-62; Vice-Premier, Algerian Nationalist Provisional Govt., Tunis 1962, Leader, Algerian Political Bureau, Algeria 1962, Premier of Algeria Sept. 1962-65. Pres. of Algeria Sept. 1963-65; detained 1965-80; restricted residence, Msila 1979-80; freed 1981; Chair. Int. Islamic Comm. for Human Rights, London 1982-; Lenin Peace Prize 1964. *Address:* Paris, France.

BEN-DAVID, Zadok; Israeli sculptor; b. 1949, Yemen; s. of Moshe and Hana Ben-David; ed. Acad. of Art and Design, Jerusalem, Reading Univ. 1974-75 and St. Martin's School of Art, London 1975-76; Sculpture teacher at St. Martin's School of Art 1977-82, Ravensbourne Coll. of Art and Design, Bromley 1982-85; first one man show at Air Gallery, London 1980; Exhbns. at 121 Gallery, Antwerp 1984, Benjamin Rhodes Gallery, London 1985, Albert Totam Gallery N.Y. 1987; represented Israel in the Biennale di Venezia, Italy 1988. *Publications:* (catalogues) Zadok Ben-David 1987, The Israeli Pavilion—The Venice Biennale 1988, From Two Worlds. *Leisure interests:* cinema, modern literature. *Address:* 36 Brecknock Road, London N7 ODD, (Home); 72, King George Street, Greenwich, London, SE10, England (Office). *Telephone:* (01) 607-1596 (Home); (01) 858-7315 (Office).

BEN-NATAN, Asher; Israeli diplomatist; b. 15 Feb. 1921, Vienna; s. of Nahum Ben-Natan and Bertha Ben-Natan; m. Erika Frudt 1940; one s. one d.; ed. Z. P. Hayut Hebrew Coll., Vienna and Institut des Hautes Etudes Internationales, Geneva; co-founder and mem. Kibbutz Mederot-Zeraim 1938-44, latterly Sec. and Treas.; Political Dept., Jewish Agency 1944-45; on mission to Europe to organize rescue of Jews and illegal immigration to Palestine: attached to office of Head of Jewish Agency 1945-47; Ministry of Foreign Affairs 1948-51; studies in Geneva 1951-53; Govt. Rep. on Bd. of Red Sea Inkodeh Co. 1953-56, Gen. Man. 1955-56; Rep. of Ministry of Defence in Europe 1956-58; Dir.-Gen. Ministry of Defence 1959-65; Amb. to Fed. Repub. of Germany 1965-70, to France 1970-75; Political Adviser to Minister of Defence 1975-78; Chair. Ben-Gurion Foundation 1983-; Adviser to Prime Minister on Special Affairs 1985-; Pres. Israel-German Assen. 1973-; Officier Légion d'honneur; Commdr. ordre nat. (Ivory Coast); Commdr. ordre de l'Etoile equatoriale (Gabon); Louis Waiss Peace Prize 1974. *Publications:* Briefe an den Botschafter 1970, Dialogue avec des Allemands 1973. *Address:* 89 University Street, Tel-Aviv, Israel. *Telephone:* 413398.

BENACERRAF, Baruj; American (b. Venezuelan) professor of pathology; b. 29 Oct. 1920, Caracas, Venezuela; m. Annette Dreyfus 1943; one d.; ed. Lycée Janson, Paris, Columbia Univ., New York, Medical Coll. of Virginia; Internship, Queens General Hospital, New York 1945-46; army service 1946-48; Research Fellow Dept. of Microbiology, Coll. of Physicians and Surgeons, Columbia Univ., N.Y. 1948-50; Chargé de Recherches, CNRS, Hôpital Broussais, Paris 1950-56; Asst. Prof. of Pathology, New York Univ. School of Medicine 1956-58, Assoc. Prof. of Pathology 1958-60, Prof. of Pathology 1960-68; Chief, Lab. of Immunology, Nat. Inst. of Allergy and Infectious Diseases, Nat. Insts. of Health, Bethesda, Md. 1968-70; Fabyan Prof. of Comparative Pathology and Chair. Dept. of Pathology, Harvard Medical School, Boston, Mass. 1970-; Assoc. Ed. American Journal of Pathology, Journal of Experimental Medicine; mem. Immunology "A" Study Section, Nat. Insts. of Health 1965-69; Scientific Advisor World

Health Org. for Immunology; Trustee and mem. Scientific Advisory Bd., Trudeau Foundation 1970–77; mem. Scientific Advisory Bd. Mass. General Hospital 1971–74; mem. Bd. of Govs. Weizmann Inst. of Science; Chair. Scientific Advisory Cttee., Centre d'Immunologie de Marseille, CNRS-INSERM; Pres. American Assen. of Immunologists 1973–74; Pres. Fed. of American Socs. for Experimental Biology 1974–75; Pres. Dana-Farber Cancer Inst., Boston, Mass. 1980; Pres. Int. Union of Immurological Socs.; Fellow, American Acad. of Arts and Sciences; mem. American Assen. of Immunologists, American Assen. of Pathologists and Bacteriologists, American Soc. for Experimental Pathology, Soc. for Experimental Biology and Medicine, British Assen. for Immunology, French Soc. of Biological Chemistry, Harvey Soc., New York Acad. of Sciences, American Acad. of Sciences, Inst. of Medicine; Rabbi Shai Shacknai Prize in Immunology and Cancer Research (Hebrew Univ. of Jerusalem) 1974, T. Duckett Jones Memorial Award, Helen Hay Whitney Foundation 1976, Nobel Prize for Physiology or Medicine 1980. *Address:* Dana-Farber Cancer Institute, 44, Binney Street, Boston, Mass. D2115, U.S.A.

BENACHENHOU, Mouroud, M.ECON., D.SOC.; Algerian economist; b. 30 July 1938, Tlemecen; s. of late Mohammed Benachenhou and Rostane Hiba; m. Norya Berbar 1962; two s. one d.; ed. Univ. D'Alger, Univ. de Bordeaux; Officer Nat. Liberation Army 1956–62; Adviser, Ministry of Agric. 1965–66; Dir. Nat. Agronomic Inst., Algiers 1966–78; Dir. Higher Ed. 1971–78; Dir. Centre of Research on Agronomy 1976–82; Perm. Sec. Ministry of Finance 1982–; Exec. Dir. World Bank 1982–85; Medaille de la Resistance. *Publications:* The Future of the University 1979, Higher Education in Algeria 1976. *Leisure interests:* tennis, chess. *Address:* c/o Ministry of Finance, Palais du Gouvernement, Algiers, Algeria.

BÉNARD, André Pierre Jacques; French business executive; b. 19 Aug. 1922, Draveil, Essone; s. of Marcel Bénard and Lucie Thalmann; m. Jacqueline Preiss 1946; one s.; ed. Lycée Janson-de-Sailly, Lycée Georges Clémenceau, Nantes, Lycée Thiers, Marseilles, Ecole Polytechnique, Paris; joined Royal Dutch/Shell Group 1946; with Société Anonyme des Pétroles Jupiter 1946–49; Shell Petroleum Co. Ltd., London 1949–50; Head of Bitumen services, Société des Pétroles Shell Berre 1950–58, Head Nat. Activities Dept. 1958–59; Asst. Dir.-Gen. Société pour l'Utilisation Rationnelle des Gaz 1960–61, Pres. Dir.-Gen. 1962–64; Marketing Man. Shell Française 1964–67, Pres. Man. Dir. 1967–70; Regional Co-ordinator Europe 1970; Dir. Shell Petroleum N.V. 1970; Dir. The Shell Petroleum Co. Ltd. 1970; Man. Dir. Royal Dutch Petroleum Co. 1971–83, mem. Supervisory Bd. 1983–; Hon. Pres., French Chamber of Commerce and Industry, in the Netherlands 1980–; Jt. Chair. Eurotunnel 1986–; Prix Descartes 1982; Médaille des Evadés; Médaille de la Résistance; Chevalier de l'ordre nat. du Mérite, Officier Légion d'honneur, Commdr. Order of Orange Nassau, Chevalier du Mérite agricole. *Leisure interest:* golf. *Address:* Eurotunnel SA, Tour Franklin, cedex 11, 92081 Paris-La-Défense 8, France.

BÉNARD, Jean Pierre, L. ÈS L.; French diplomatist (retd.); b. 29 Feb. 1908; s. of Georges Bénard and Reine Say; m. Yvonne Mamet 1928 (died 1983); ed. Lycée Janson de Sailly and Univ. de Paris à la Sorbonne; Journalist, Agence Havas, Washington 1934–36, Chief, News Service, Middle East and Cairo 1936–39; Diplomatic Service 1945–72, Counsellor, U.S.A. 1945–54; Deputy Dir. NATO Information Div. 1955–57; Minister, Tunisia 1957–60; Amb. to Fed. Republic of Cameroon 1960–65, Ethiopia 1965–71; Dir. Cabinet of the Sec. of State for Foreign Affairs 1971–72; Pres. GERDAT (Study and Research Group for Devt. of Tropical Agronomy) 1972–80; Officier, Légion d'honneur. *Address:* 61 rue Caulaincourt, 75018 Paris, France.

BENAUD, Richard (Richie), O.B.E.; Australian fmr. cricketer; b. 6 Oct. 1930; s. of Louis Richard and Irene Benaud; m. Daphne Elizabeth Surfleet 1967; two s. by previous marriage; ed. Parramatta High School; represented Australia in 63 Test Matches, 28 as Captain (including three tours of England 1953, 1956, 1961); int. sports consultant; TV Commentator, BBC 1960–,–Channel Nine 1977–. *Publications:* Way of Cricket 1960, Tale of Two Tests 1962, Spin Me a Spinner 1963, The New Champions 1965, Willow Patterns 1972, Benaud on Reflection 1984. *Leisure interests:* golf, physical fitness. *Address:* 19/178 Beach Street, Coogee, New South Wales 2034, Australia. *Telephone:* Sydney 665-6464.

BENAVIDES ESCOBAR, Lieutenant-General César Raúl; Chilean army officer and politician; b. 12 March 1920, Santiago; m. María del Carmen Montero Marín; one d.; ed. Mil. School, Mil. Eng. School, Acad. of War, Signal School, Fort Monmouth, U.S.A., Acad. of Nat. Defence; Commdr. 8th "Membrillar" Telecommunications Regt. 1963; Dir. School of Telecommunications 1966; Mil., Naval and Air Force Attaché, Chilean Embassy in Ecuador 1967; Head of Army Telecommunications 1970; Dir. Acad. of War 1971; Dir. Army Operations 1972; Dir. of Army Instruction 1972; Commdr. Mil. Insts. 1973; C.-in-C. V-Div. of Army and Quartermaster Gen., Prov. of Magallanes 1974; Minister of State, Ministry of Interior 1974, of Nat. Defence 1978; Minister of Transport and Telecommunications April 1978–87; numerous mil. decorations. *Address:* Ministry of Transport and Telecommunications, Amunátegui 139, Santiago, Chile. *Telephone:* 726503.

BENAWA, Abdul Raouf; Afghan writer and administrator; b. 1913; ed. Ganj Public School, Kandahar; mem. Language Dept. Afghan Acad. 1939;

mem. Words Dept. Afghan Acad. and Asst. Information Dept. 1940; Dir. Publication Dept. Afghan Acad. 1941; Gen. Dir. Pushtu Tolana; Sec. Afghan Acad. and Dir. Kabul magazine; proprietor of weekly magazine Hewad; mem. History Dept. 1950, Dir. Internal Publ. Dept. 1951, Gen. Dir. 1952; Press Attaché India 1953–56; Pres. Radio Kabul 1956–63; Press and Cultural Counsellor, Cairo 1963. *Publications:* Women in Afghanistan, Mir Wiess Neeka, Literary Sciences, Pushtu Songs, De Ghanamo Wazhai, Pushtoonistan, A Survey of Pushtoonistan, Rahman Baba, Pir mohammad-Kakar, Khosh-hal Khan se Wai, Pushtoo Killi, Vol. 4, Kazim Khan-e-Shaida; translations: Mosa-fir Iqbal, Geetan-Jali Tagoor, Da Darmistatar Pushtoo Seerane, Leaders of Pashtoonistan, History of Hootaki, Preshana afkar (poem), Da zra khwala, Pashto writers today (2 vols.), Pashto reader for schools, Pachakhan (A leader of Pashtoni), Landei (public poems); plays: I-Zoor gonahgar (Old criminal), Ishtebah (confusion), Kari bar asal, Aash-yanae aqab, Zarang Chaoki der khater, Hakoomat baidar.

BENDA, Ernst; German lawyer and politician; b. 15 Jan. 1925, Berlin; s. of Rudolf and Margarete (née Marsmann) Benda; m. Waltraut Vorbau 1956; one s. one d.; ed. Kant-Gymnasium, Berlin-Spandau, Humboldt Univ., Freie Univ. Berlin, Univ. of Wisconsin; war service; prisoner-of-war; Humboldt Univ. 1946–48; Freie Univ., Berlin 1948–51; Univ. of Wis. 1949–55; Dist. appointment, Spandau 1951–54; mem. Berlin House of Reps. 1955–57, Bundestag 1957–71; in practice as lawyer 1956–71; Chair. Berlin Christian Democratic Union Youth Dept. 1952–54; mem. Fed. Govt. 1966; Under-Sec. in Interior Ministry; Minister of the Interior 1968–69; Pres. Fed. Constitutional Court, Karlsruhe 1971–83; Prof. Constitutional Law Univ. of Freiburg 1983–; Hon. Prof., Law Faculty, Trier Univ. 1977; Hon. D.Jur. (Würzburg Univ.) 1974; Pipe Smoker of the Year 1979. *Publications:* Notstandsverfassung und Arbeitskampf 1963, Rechtsstaat und Verjährung 1965, Industrielle Herrschaft und sozialer Staat 1966, Die Notstandsverfassung 1966, Der Rechtsstaat in der Krise 1971. *Leisure interests:* fishing, sailing. *Address:* 75 Karlsruhe 41, Käthe Kollwitz Strasse 46, Federal Republic of Germany.

BENDER, Arnold Eric, PH.D.; British nutrition scientist; b. 24 July 1918, Liverpool; m.; two s.; ed. Liverpool Institute, Univs. of Liverpool and Sheffield; Research Chemist, British Drug Houses 1940–45; Nuffield Research Fellow, Univ. of Sheffield 1945–47, Asst. Lecturer 1947–49; Head of Nutrition Team, Crookes Labs. 1949–54; Head of Research, Bovril Ltd. 1954–61; Head of Research and Devt., Farley's Infant Foods Ltd. 1961–64; Sr. Lecturer (later Reader) Queen Elizabeth Coll., Univ. of London 1965–71, Prof. of Nutrition 1971–78, Prof. of Nutrition and Dietetics, and Head of Dept. of Food Science and Nutrition 1978–83; Chair. of Council Royal Soc. of Health 1987–88; Pres. Inst. of Food Science and Tech. 1989–; mem. Exec. Cttee., Int. Union of Food Science and Technology 1979–83, Vice-Pres. 1983–(87); Hon. mem. American Public Health Assen. 1987; Hon. Fellow Royal Soc. of Health 1988; Hon. D.Sc. (Complutense, Madrid) 1983. *Publications:* Dictionary of Nutrition and Food Technology 1960, Nutrition and Dietetic Foods 1967, Value of Food 1970, Facts of Food 1976, Food Processing and Nutrition 1978, Pocket Guide to Calories and Nutrition 1979, Nutrition for Medical Students (with Dr. D. A. Bender) 1982, Health or Hoax 1985, Food Tables (with D. A. Bender) 1986; research papers and review articles in scientific journals. *Leisure interests:* gardening, filming, lecturing. *Address:* 2 Willow Vale, Fetcham, Leatherhead, Surrey, KT22 9TE, England.

BENDER, Myron L(ee), PH.D.; American chemist and educator; b. 20 May 1924, St. Louis; s. of Averam Burton and Fannie Leventhal Bender; m. Muriel B. Schulman 1952; three s.; ed. Purdue Univ.; Chemist, Eastman Kodak Co. 1944–45; Postdoctoral student, Harvard 1948–49; AEC Fellow, Univ. of Chicago 1949–50; Instructor, Univ. of Connecticut 1950–51; Instructor to Assoc. Prof. Ill. Inst. of Technology 1951–60; mem. Faculty Northwestern Univ. 1960–, Prof. of Chemistry 1962–85, Prof. of Biochemistry 1974–85, Prof. Emer. 1985–; Consultant to govt. and industry 1959–; Sloan Fellow 1959–63; mem. N.A.S., American Chem. Soc. and other Socs.; Visiting Fellow, Merton Coll., Oxford Univ.; Visiting Fulbright Prof., Univ. of Zagreb, Yugoslavia 1977, Visiting Prof., Japan Soc. for the Promotion of Science 1974, Univ. of Queensland, Australia 1979, Nankai Univ., Tianjin, People's Repub. of China 1982, Kyoto Univ., Japan 1982; Midwest Award of the ACS; D.Sc., Purdue Univ. *Publications:* 5 books, 17 monographs, 203 tech. articles. *Address:* Northwestern University, Evanston, Ill. 60201 (Office); 2514 Sheridan Road, Evanston, Ill. 60201, U.S.A. (Home). *Telephone:* 492-7675 (Office); 869-6307 (Home).

BENDETSEN, Karl Robin, A.B., J.S.D., LL.D., D.M.S.; American lawyer and business executive; b. 11 Oct. 1907, Aberdeen, Wash.; s. of Albert M. and Ann (Bentson) Bendetsen; m. 1st Billie McIntosh 1938, 2nd Maxine Bosworth 1947, 3rd Gladys Ponton de Arce 1972; one s. one d.; ed. Leland Stanford Univ.; Law practice 1932–40, 1947–48; U.S. Army 1940–45; Man. Counsel 1946–47; Special Asst. to Sec. of Defense 1948; Asst. and Under-Sec. of Army 1948–52; Chair. Bd. Panama Canal Co. 1950–54; Dir.-Gen. U.S. Railroads 1950–52; Champion Paper and Fiber Co. (later Champion Papers) 1952; Pres., Chair., C.E.O. Champion Papers (later Champion Int.) 1960–72, Chair. Exec. Cttee. 1972–75; Dir. Champion Int., Westinghouse, New York Stock Exchange; Special Rep. with rank of Amb. to Fed. Rep. of Germany and Philippines 1956; Chair. Cttee. on Non-Mil. Instruction, Office of Sec. of Defense 1962; Vice-Chair. Defense Manpower Comm.

1974–76; Officier, Légion d'honneur, Croix de guerre, D.S.M. with Oak Leaf Cluster, Silver Star, Legion of Merit with three clusters, Bronze Star Medal, Medal of Freedom, Hon. O.B.E., Distinguished Civilian Service Medal. *Address:* 2918 Garfield Terrace, N.W., Washington, D.C. 20008 (Home); 1850 K Street, N.W., Washington, D.C. 20006, U.S.A. (Office).

BENDITT, Earl Philip, M.D.; American pathologist; b. 15 April 1916, Philadelphia, Pa.; s. of Milton Benditt and Sarah (Schoenfeld) Benditt; m. Marcella Wexler 1945; four s.; ed. Swarthmore Coll., Harvard Medical School and Univ. of Chicago; Instructor in Pathology, Univ. of Chicago 1944–47, Asst. Prof. 1947–52, Assoc. Prof. 1952–57; Prof. and Chair. Dept. of Pathology, Univ. of Wash., Seattle 1957–81, Prof. of Pathology 1981–86, Prof. Emer. 1986–; Distinguished Physician, Seattle Veterans' Admin. Hosp. 1988–; Visiting Scholar, Sir William Dunn School of Pathology, Univ. of Oxford 1979–80; Welcome Foundation Visiting Prof. Cornell Univ. Medical School 1987; Fellow, N.A.S., A.A.A.S. *Publications:* 230 papers on pathology and related subjects. *Leisure interests:* sailing, art. *Address:* 3717 East Prospect Street, Seattle, Wash. 98112, U.S.A. *Telephone:* (206) 322-5731.

BENDJEDID, Col. Chadli (see Chadli, Col. Bendjedid).

BENEDETTI, Mario; Uruguayan writer; b. 14 Sept. 1920, Paso de los Toros, Tacuarembo; s. of Brenno Benedetti and Matilde Farrugia; m. Luz López; ed. Colegio Alemán; Journalist on Marcha (weekly) and Literary, Film and Theatre Critic on El Diario, Tribuna Popular and La Mañana; visited Europe 1957, 1966–67. *Publications:* Fiction: Esta mañana 1949, El último viaje y otros cuentos 1951, Quién de nosotros 1953, Montevideanos 1959, La Tregua 1963, Gracias por el Fuego 1965, La muerte y otras sorpresas 1968; Plays: Ustedes por ejemplo 1953, El Reportaje 1958, Ida y Vuelta 1958; Poetry: La víspera indeleble 1945, Sólo mientras tanto 1950, Poemas de la Oficina 1956, Poemas del Hoyporhoy 1965, Inventario 1965, Contra los puentes levadizos 1966, A ras de sueño 1967; Essays: Peripecia y novela 1948, Marcel Proust y otros ensayos 1951, Literatura uruguaya siglo XX 1963, Letras del continente mestizo 1967, Sobre artes y oficios 1968.

BENEDICT, Manson, PH.D.; American engineer; b. 9 Oct. 1907, Lake Linden, Mich.; s. of C. Harry and Lena Manson Benedict; m. Marjorie Oliver Allen 1935; two d.; ed. Cornell Univ. and Massachusetts Inst. of Technology; Nat. Research Fellow, Harvard Univ. 1935–36, Research Assoc. in Geophysics 1936–37; Research Chemist, M. W. Kellogg Co. 1938–43; in charge of Process Design Uranium-235 Gaseous Diffusion Plant, Kellex Corpn. 1943–46; Dir. Process Devt., Hydrocarbon Research Inc. 1946–51; Prof. of Nuclear Eng., M.I.T. 1951–73, Head of Nuclear Eng. Dept. 1958–71, Inst. Prof. 1969–73, Inst. Prof. Emer. 1973–; Scientific Adviser, Nat. Research Corpn. 1951–57, Dir. 1960–66; mem. Gen. Advisory Cttee. U.S. Atomic Energy Comm. 1958–68, Chair. 1962–64; Dir. Atomic Industrial Forum 1967–72; Dir. Burns and Roe Inc. 1979–85; mem. N.A.S., Nat. Acad. of Eng.; Perkin Medal of Soc. of Chemical Industry, American Section; Nat. Medal of Science. *Publications:* Engineering Development in the Gaseous Diffusion Process (Co-Ed.), Nuclear Chemical Engineering (Co-Author) 1981. *Leisure interest:* golf. *Address:* Room 24109, Massachusetts Institute of Technology, Cambridge, Mass. (Office); 108 Moorings Park Drive, Naples, Fla. 33942, U.S.A. (Home).

BENEDICTO, Roberto S., A.A., LL.B., LL.M.; Philippine lawyer, banker and diplomatist; b. 17 April 1917, La Carlota, Negros Occidental; m. Julita Campos; one d.; ed. Univ. of the Philippines, George Washington Univ., U.S.A.; Major in the Philippines Armed Forces 1941–45; Acting Provincial Fiscal, Negros Occidental 1945; Prof. Commercial Law, Far Eastern Univ. 1948–55; Gov. Devt. Bank of the Philippines 1957–59; Exec. Vice-Pres. Treas. Philippine Commercial and Industrial Bank 1962–65; Pres., Vice-Chair. Philippine Nat. Bank; mem. Monetary Bd., Cen. Bank of the Philippines; alt. Gov. IMF, IBRD 1966–70; Amb. to Japan 1972–78; mem. Cabinet Exec. Cttee. Aug. 1982–; Pres. Nat. Sugar Trading Corpn.; Chair., Philippine Sugar Comm.; Pres. Nat. Sugar Trading Corpn.; Chair. Republic Planters Bank 1978–80; Vice-Chair., Kilusan ng Bagong Lipunan, Region VI 1978–81; mem. Bd. of Regents, Univ. of Philippines 1982; Pres. Boy Scouts of Philippines 1982; Philippine Legion of Merit, Philippine Defense Medal, Philippine American Defense Medal, Asiatic Pacific Theatre Medal, Philippine Liberation Medal (First Class), Order of the Rising Sun, Outstanding Citizen of Manila. *Address:* Kanlaon Towers, Roxas Boulevard, Metro Manila, Philippines (Home).

BENEDIKTSSON, Einar, M.A.; Icelandic diplomatist; b. 30 April 1931, Reykjavík; s. of Stefan M. Benediktsson and Sigridur Oddsdóttir; m. Elsa Petursdóttir 1956; three s. two d.; ed. Colgate Univ., N.Y., Fletcher School of Law and Diplomacy, Mass., London School of Econs., Inst. des Etudes Européennes, Turin, Italy; with Org. for European Econ. Co-operation, Paris 1956–60; Head of Section, Ministries of Econ. Affairs and Commerce 1960–64, Ministry of Foreign Affairs 1964, 1968–70; Counsellor, Icelandic Embassy, Paris 1964–68; Perm. Rep. to Int. Orgs., Geneva 1970–76; Chair. EFTA Council 1975; Amb. to France 1976–82 (also accred. to Spain, Portugal and Cape Verde, Perm. Rep. to OECD and UNESCO), to U.K. 1982–86 (also accred. to Netherlands, Ireland and Nigeria), to Belgium 1986– (also accred. to EEC); Perm. Rep. to NATO 1986–; Commdr. Order of Falcon (Iceland), various foreign decorations. *Address:* Icelandic

Delegation to EEC, 5 rue Archimèdes, 1040 Brussels; 19 ave. des Lauriers, 1050 Brussels, Belgium. *Telephone:* 231.03.95 (Office); 731.11.87 (Home).

BENEDIKTSSON, Jakob, PH.D., D.LITT.; Icelandic philologist; b. 20 July 1907, Fjall; s. of Benedikt Sigurdsson and Sigurlaug Sigurdardóttir; m. Grethe Kyhl 1936; ed. Univ. of Copenhagen; Assistant Prof. Old-Icelandic Dictionary (Copenhagen) 1939–46; Librarian Univ. of Copenhagen 1943–46; Ed.-in-Chief Icelandic Dictionary Univ. of Iceland 1948–77; foreign mem. Royal Danish Acad. of Sciences and Letters, Norwegian Acad. of Sciences and Letters, Swedish Acad. *Publications:* Gísli Magnússon 1939, Chronologie de deux listes des prêtres kamiréens 1940, Jardabók Árna Magnussonar og Páls Vídalíns (vols. VII, X, XI) 1940–43, Skardsbók (Corpus codicum Islandicorum XVI) 1943, Two Treatises on Iceland 1943, Veraldar saga 1944, Ferdabók Tómasar S≃mundssonar 1947, Ole Worm's Correspondence with Icelanders 1948, G. Andrésson, Deilurit 1948, Persius rimur 1949, Arngrimi Jonae Opera I-IV 1950–57, Arngrímur Jónsson and his Works 1957, Skardsárbók 1958, Sturlunga Saga (Early Icelandic Manuscript I) 1958, Islenzk-dönsk ordabók, Vidbaetir 1963, Islendingabók, Landnámabók 1968, Landnámabók 1974, Rómverjasaga (Early Icelandic Manuscript XIII) 1980, Arngrímur Jonsson Crymogaea 1985, Lærdómslistir 1987. *Address:* 2 Stigahlíd, Reykjavík, Iceland. *Telephone:* 30987.

BENDRYSHEV, Vladimir Nikolaevich; Soviet diplomatist; b. 1920; mem. of diplomatic service 1946–; U.S.S.R. Adviser 1962–66, Perm. Rep. at UN, Geneva 1966–68; mem. of staff of Ministry of Foreign Affairs 1968–73; Amb. to Malaysia 1973–78. *Address:* c/o Ministry of Foreign Affairs, Smolenskaya-Sennaya pl. 32/34, Moscow, U.S.S.R.

BENEDYKTOWICZ, Witold; Polish theologian; b. 25 June 1921, Cracow; s. of Zbigniew Benedyktowicz and Klotyda Benedyktowicz; three s.; ed. Faculty of Evangelical Theology, Warsaw Univ.; clergyman Methodist Church in Poland 1943–; custodian Warsaw Univ. Library 1956–67; lecturer and researcher Christian Theology Acad., Warsaw 1967–, Head Systematic Theology Dept. 1967–, Asst. Prof. 1967–72, Extraordinary Prof. 1972–80, Ordinary Prof. 1980–; Chief Supt. Methodist Church in Poland 1969–83; Pres. Polish Ecumenical Council 1975–83, Hon. Pres. 1983–; mem. Working Cttee. Int. Christian Peace Conference, Prague 1968–; mem. Churches Comm. for Int. Matters, Geneva 1969–; mem. Consultative Council attached to Chair. of Council of State 1986–; Commdr.'s, Officer's and Kt.'s Cross Order of Polonia Restituta, Gold Cross of Merit and other decorations. *Publications include:* Próba irenologii chrześcijańskiej. Dōświadczenia praskie 1965, Bemerkungen zur Theorie und Praxis der christlichen Friedensarbeit in: Friedensforschung und Friedensdienst 1972, Die Interpretation des Neuen Testaments in Konfrontation mit dem Sozialismus in: Begegnung mit Polen 1974, Co powinniśmy czynić. Zarys ewangelickiej etyki teologicznej 1975, Ekumenia, pokój, pojednanie 1988. *Leisure interests:* reading novels and memoirs, and opera. *Address:* ul. Mokotowska 12, 00-561 Warsaw, Poland. *Telephone:* (29) 74-25 (Home); (28) 53-28 (Office).

BENFLIS, Ali; Algerian politician; b. 8 Sept. 1944, Batna; m.; four c.; ed. Univ. of Algiers; Deputy Dir. Cttee. on Infant Delinquancy, Ministry of Justice 1969; Public Prosecutor, Batna 1970; Procurator Gen., Constantine 1971–74; Pres. of the Bar, East Algeria 1983; Founding mem. of Algerian League for Human Rights 1987; Pres. of the Bar, Batna 1987; Pres. Eastern Region, Algerian League for Human Rights 1987; Minister of Justice 1988–. *Address:* 8 rue de Khartoum, el-Biar, Algiers, Algeria. *Telephone:* (2) 78-20-90.

BENFREHA, Ahmed; Algerian politician; b. 1940, Mascara; m.; three c.; ed. Inst. Abdelhamid Ben Badis, Constantine, Univ. de la Zitouna and Univ. of Algiers; research worker Agronomie-Inst. de recherches; chargé de mission, Ministry of Agric.; Cen. Dir. Ministry of Agric.; Head of Student Cell, Nat. Liberation Front, Tunis; Deputy Nat. Popular Assembly; Sec. of State for Fishing 1980–82, Fishing and Maritime Transport 1982–84; Minister of Public Works 1984–88, Hydraulics and Forests 1988–; mem. Central Cttee. Nat. Liberation Front 1979–. *Address:* le Grand Seminaire, Kouba, Algiers, Algeria. *Telephone:* (2) 59-95-00.

BENGELLOUN, Ahmed Majid, L. EN D.; Moroccan lawyer and politician; b. 27 Dec. 1927, Fez; ed. Inst. of Political Science, Paris; Public Prosecutor, Marrakesh 1956, later Public Prosecutor of Mil. Tribunal, Meknés, Gen. Counsel, Supreme Court; Public Prosecutor Court of Appeal 1960–64; Minister of Information 1965–67, 1972–74; Sec.-Gen. Ministry of Justice 1967; Minister at the Royal Cabinet 1967–71, of Civil Service 1971–72, of Information 1972–74; Prosecutor-Gen. 1974; fmr. Prof. Inst. des Hautes Etudes Juridiques; Dean, Faculty of Law and Econs., Univ. of Rabat, Ecole Marocaine d'Admin.; mem. Comm. for the Drafting of the Penal Code and Penal Procedure Code; has attended numerous int. judicial confs.; Order of the Throne, and several foreign decorations. *Address:* Faculty of Law and Economics, P.O. Box 721, Avenue des Nations Unies, Rabat, Morocco.

BENGTSON, Hermann, DR.PHIL.; German professor of ancient history; b. 2 July 1909, Ratzeburg; s. of Hermann Bengtson and Margarete Käselau; m. Luise Rambold 1940; one d.; ed. Gymnasium Ratzeburg, Univs. of Hamburg, Munich and Pisa; Privatdozent, Heidelberg 1940; Acting Prof. Jena 1942–45; Prof. of Ancient History, Univ. of Würzburg 1952, Univ. of Tübingen 1963, Univ. of Munich 1966–78, Prof. Emer. 1978–; mem. Bavarian Acad. of Sciences; Hon. mem. Soc. for Promotion of Hellenic Studies;

Bavarian Order of Merit. *Publications:* Einführung in die Alte Geschichte 1949, Griechische Geschichte 1950, Römische Geschichte 1967, Marcus Antonius 1977, Kaiser Augustus 1981, Die Diadochen 1987, Die hellenistische Weltkultur 1988. *Address:* 8000 Munich 50, Im Eichgehölz 4, Federal Republic of Germany. *Telephone:* (089) 8 11 42 45.

BENGTSON, Torsten Stanley; Swedish politician; b. 10 Jan. 1914, Halmstad; s. of Otto Alexander and Alma Desideria Bengtson; two s. one d.; ed. privately; member of Riksdag (Parl.) 1950-82, First Deputy Speaker 1970-79; Pres. Riksbanken (Central Bank of Sweden) 1976-82; Del. to UN Gen. Ass. for 25 years; Deputy Chair. Int. Council of Parliamentarians on Alcohol and Drug Policy 1975-; Commdr. Order of North Star, First Class. *Leisure interests:* music, sports. *Address:* P.O. Box 4036, 550 04 Jönköping, Sweden. *Telephone:* 036/12-48-44.

BENGTSSON, Ingemund; Swedish politician; b. 1919, Veddinge, Halland; ed. County Coll; formerly Man. Halland County Labour Exchange; mem. of Parl. 1951-; consultant to Ministry for Health and Welfare 1954-65; mem. Bd. Social Democrat Party, fmrly. Vice-Pres. Social Democrat Party Member's Council; mem. Swedish del. to UN Gen. Ass. 1963-67; Pres. UN Cttee. on the Human Environment 1972-74; Minister of Agric. 1969-73, of Labour 1973-76; Speaker of the Parl. 1979-. *Address:* c/o Riksdag, S-100 12 Stockholm, Sweden.

BENGZON, Cesar, B.A., LL.B.; Philippine judge; b. 29 May 1896; ed. Ateneo de Manila and Univ. of the Philippines; Law Clerk, Bureau of Justice 1919, Special Attorney, then Asst. Attorney 1920, Solicitor-Gen. 1931; Dean and Prof. of Law, Univ. of Manila 1928-32; Under-Sec. of Justice and Chair. Bd. of Pardons 1933; Assoc. Justice, Court of Appeals 1936; Assoc. Justice, Supreme Court 1945; Prof. of Law, Univ. of Santo Tomás and Philippine Law School 1948-54; Chair. Senate Electoral Tribunal 1950-57; Chief Justice Supreme Court 1961; Judge, Int. Court of Justice, The Hague 1966-76; mem. Philippine Acad. of Sciences and Humanities 1964-; Pres. Philippine Section, Int. Comm. of Jurists 1964, 1966; mem. Nat. Research Council 1964-, American Judicature Soc. 1965, Philippine Soc. of Int. Law 1965-; LL.D. h.c. Univ. of Manila 1957, Ateneo de Manila Univ. 1964, Univ. of the Philippines 1964. *Address:* c/o National Research Council of the Philippines, University of the Philippines, Diliman, Rizal, The Philippines.

BENHAMOUDA, Boualem; Algerian politician; b. 8 March 1933, Cherchell; m.; two s. one d.; Minister of Ex-Combattants 1965-70, of Justice 1970-77, of Public Works 1977-80, of the Interior 1980-82, of Finance 1982-86; mem. Political Bureau of Nat. Liberation Front (FLN) 1979-; Chair. FLN Cttee. on Educ. Training and Culture 1979-80; responsible for the Inst. of Global Studies of Strategy (political and econ. matters). *Leisure interests:* reading, studying, cultural travel. *Address:* Council of Ministers, Algiers, Algeria.

BENHIMA, Mohamed, M.D.; Moroccan physician and politician; b. 25 June 1924, Safi; s. of Tayeb Benhima and Ben Hida; m.; four c.; ed. Faculté de Médecine de Nancy, France; Chief Medical Officer, Had Court District 1954-56; Chief of Cen. Service for Urban and Rural Hygiene 1956-57; Head of Personal Office of Minister of Public Health 1957-60; Sec.-Gen. Ministry of Public Health Jan.-June 1960; Gov. of Provinces of Agadir and Tarfaya 1960-61; Minister of Public Works 1961-62, 1963-65, 1967-72, of Commerce, Industry, Mines, Handicrafts and Merchant Marine 1962-63, of Nat. Educ. 1965-67; Prime Minister 1967-69; Minister of State for Agric. and Agrarian Reform 1969-70; Minister of Health 1969-72, of Internal Affairs 1972-73; Minister of State for Co-operation and Training 1973-77, for the Interior 1977-79; decorations from Govts. of Belgium, Morocco, Sweden, Ethiopia, Tunisia, Liberia, France, Italy, Niger, Libya, Ivory Coast, Cameroon and United Arab Republic. *Address:* Km. 5.5, Route des Zaërs, Rabat, Morocco.

BENICHOU, Jacques, L. ÈS SC.; French engineer and business executive; b. 12 May 1922, Constantine, Algeria; s. of Joseph Benichou and Jeanne (née Moatti) Benichou; m. Suzanne Granvaux 1951; three c.; ed. Lycée d'Alger, Algiers, Faculté des Sciences de Paris, Ecole Polytechnique and Ecole Nat. Supérieure de l'Aéronautique; Air Eng., Service Tech. de l'Aéronautique 1948-52; Principal Air Eng., Circonscription Aéronautique Régionale de Paris 1952-56; Chief Air Eng., Service des Marchés et la de Production Aéronautique 1956-60; Ministerial Del. for Armaments 1960-64; Chief Air Eng., Cadre de Réserve 1964; Sec.-Gen. Société Messier 1964, Dir.-Gen. 1969-71; Admin.-Dir.-Gen. Messier Hispano Bugatti (M.H.B.) 1971, Pres.-Dir.-Gen. 1973-82; mem. Bd. Groupement des industries françaises aéronautiques et spatiales 1974, Vice-Pres. 1982; Pres.-Dir.-Gen. Société nat. d'étude et de construction de moteurs d'aviation 1982-; Pres. GIFAS (Groupement des Industries Aéronautiques et Spatiales) 1985, Hon. Pres. 1987-; Admin. SNECMA, Aerospatiale, SOGEPA; Commdr. Légion d'honneur; Officier, Ordre nat. du Mérite; Médaille de l'Aéronautique. *Publications:* articles in professional journals. *Leisure interests:* tennis, swimming, golf. *Address:* 43 boulevard Exelmans, 75016 Paris, France. (Home).

BENÍTEZ, Jaime, LL.D.; Puerto Rican educator and government official; b. 29 Oct. 1908, Vieques; s. of Don Luis Benítez and Doña Cándida Rexach Benítez; m. Luz A. Martínez 1941; one s. two d.; ed. Georgetown Univ.

and Univ. of Chicago; Instructor in Political Science, Univ. of Puerto Rico 1931-41, Assoc. Prof. 1941-42, Chancellor of Univ. 1942-66, Pres. 1966-71; Res. Commr. from Puerto Rico in the U.S. 1972-76; mem. House of Reps. Cttee. on Educ. and Labour 1972; Head Hearings Officer, Nat. War Labor Bd., Washington; Del. to UNESCO Conf., Paris 1951; mem. U.S. Nat. Comm. UNESCO 1951-55; Pres. Cttee. of Bill of Rights, Puerto Rico Constitutional Convention 1951; mem. Housing Cttee., U.S. Fed. Housing Agency 1957; U.S. Del., Conf. of Univs., Utrecht, Holland 1948; Fellow American Acad. of Arts and Sciences, American Acad. of Political and Social Sciences, Federal Bar Asscn., Nat. Asscn. of State Univs. (Pres. 1958), Colegio de Abogados de Puerto Rico; Hon. LL.D. (Inter-American, San German, New York, Fairleigh Dickinson Univs. and Catholic Univ. of Puerto Rico). *Publications:* The Concept of the Family in Roman and Common Law Jurisprudence 1931, Political and Philosophical Theories of José Ortega y Gasset 1939, Reflexiones Sobre el Presente 1950, La Iniciación Universitaria y las Ciencias Sociales 1952, The United States, Cuba, and Latin America 1961, Junto a la Torre 1963, Discurso en Salamanca 1965, Sobre el Futuro Cultural y Político de Puerto Rico 1965. *Leisure interest:* flying kites.

BENIUC, Mihai, D.PHIL.; Romanian writer and scientist; b. 20 Nov. 1907, Sebiş-Arad; s. of Atanasie and Veselina Beniuc; m. 1st Emma-Sylvia Friedmann 1945 (died 1978); m. 2nd Anastasia Nitelea 1981; two s.; ed. Sebiş, Cluj Univ. and in Germany; Prof. Psychology, Cluj and Bucharest Univ.; mem. Grand Nat. Ass. 1957-65; Chair. Writers' Union 1958-65; mem. Philology, Literature and Arts Section, Romanian Acad. 1955-; State Prizes 1951 and 1954; Hero of Socialist Labour 1971; Union of Writer's Great Poetry Prize 1982. *Publications:* Verse: Songs of Desolation 1938, New Songs 1940, Poems 1943, The Lost City 1943, A Man is Waiting for the Sunrise 1946, Banners 1952, The Apple Tree near the Road 1954, Durability 1955, The Heart of Old Vesuvius, Journeys Through Constellations 1957, An Hour before Sunset 1959, Songs of the Heart 1961, The Matter and the Dreams 1961, Colours of the Autumn 1962, Strings of Time 1963, Headlights 1964, Rock Flowers 1965, Day by Day 1965, Other Ways 1967, Lights at Dusk 1970, Watchtower 1972, Autumn Fires 1974, Night Patrol 1975, The Voice of Rocks 1978, I Leave You as Leaves 1978, Elegies 1978, Struggling against Time 1980, 75 Poems 1982 (many translated), The Golden Vein 1984, The Winter of the Magnolia 1984, The Stake of Poetry 1985, At the Will of the Wind 1987, My Own Vlasia 1987; Dramatic poem: Horea 1987; Non-fiction: Learning and Intelligence in Animals 1934, The Roundabout Path of the Fighting Fish 1938, Animal Psychology 1970; Fiction: Personal Hate, On the Edge of the Knife 1959, An Ordinary Man has Disappeared 1964; Plays: In the Cucu Valley 1949, The Return 1960; Criticism: Our Poetry 1956, Mason Manole 1957. *Leisure interests:* philosophy, psychology, ecology and protection of animals. *Address:* Strada Gradina Bordei 51, Bucharest, Romania. *Telephone:* 33-12-33.

BENJAMIN, Hilde; German lawyer and politician; b. (as Hilde Lange) 5 Feb. 1902; m. Georg Benjamin 1926; studied law; practising lawyer until 1933; joined Communist Party 1927; commercial employment during Nazi regime; State lawyer in Berlin 1945; joined Sozialistische Einheitspartei Deutschlands (S.E.D.) 1946; Vice-Pres. Supreme Court 1949-53; Minister of Justice 1953-67; Prof. of History of Admin. of Justice, Deutsche Akad. für Staats- und Rechtswissenschaft 1967-; mem. Cen. Cttee. S.E.D. 1954; mem. Volkskammer 1949-67; Clara-Zetkin Medal, two Distinguished Service Orders, Order of the Banner of Labour, Medal for Fighters against Fascism, Order of Merit (Gold); Dr. h.c. *Address:* Deutsche Akademie für Staats- und Rechtswissenschaft, 1502 Potsdam-Babelsberg, August-Bebel Strasse 89, German Democratic Republic.

BENJAMIN, (Thomas) Brooke, M.A., PH.D., F.R.S., M.ENG.; British scientist; b. 15 April 1929; s. of Thomas Joseph Benjamin and Ethel Mary Benjamin (née Brooke); m. 1st Helen Gilda-Marie Rakower Ginsburg 1956 (divorced 1974), one s. two d.; m. 2nd Natalia Marie-Thérèse Court 1978, one d.; ed. Wallasey Grammar School, Univ. of Liverpool, Yale Univ., U.S.A., Univ. of Cambridge; Fellow of King's Coll., Cambridge 1955-64; Asst. Dir. of Research, Univ. of Cambridge 1958-67, Reader in Hydrodynamics 1967-70; Prof. of Math. and Dir., Fluid Mechanics' Research Inst., Essex Univ. 1970-78; Sedleian Prof. of Natural Philosophy, and Fellow of The Queen's Coll., Oxford 1979-; Visiting Prof. Univ. of Wis., U.S.A. 1980-81, of Houston, U.S.A. 1985, of Calif., Berkeley 1986; Chair. Math. Cttee., S.R.C. 1975-78; Jt. Royal Soc. Inst. of Maths. Educ. Cttee. 1979-85; Ed. Journal of Fluid Mechanics 1960-65; Consultant to English Electric Co. 1956-67; William Hopkins Prize, Cambridge Philosophical Soc. 1969. *Publications:* various papers on theoretical and experimental fluid mechanics. *Leisure interest:* music. *Address:* Mathematical Institute, 24-29 St. Giles, Oxford, OX1 3LB (Office); 8 Hernes Road, Oxford, OX2 7PU, England (Home). *Telephone:* Oxford 273525 (Office); Oxford 54439 (Home).

BENJELLOUN, Tahar; Moroccan writer; b. 1944, Fes; m. 1986; one d.; ed. Lycée Regnault de Tanger, Faculté de Lettres de Rabat and Univ. of Paris; columnist Le Monde 1973-; Chevalier des Arts et des Lettres, Légion d'honneur; Médaille du Mérite national (Morocco); Prix Goncourt 1987. *Publications:* Harrouda 1973, la Reclusion solitaire 1976, les Amandiers sont morts de leurs blessures (poems) 1976, Moha le fou, Moha le sage 1978, la Prière de l'absent 1980, l'Enfant de sable 1985, la Nuit sacrée

1987. *Address:* Editions du Seuil, BP 80, 27 rue Jacob, 75261 Paris cedex 06, France (Office).

BENJENK, Munir P.; American (Turkish-born) international finance official; b. 12 June 1924, Istanbul; s. of Pertev Benjenk and Stella Habib; ed. Robert Coll., Istanbul and London School of Econs.; with BBC 1949–51; with Org. for Econ. Co-operation and Devt. (OECD) Paris 1953–63, Dir. Tech. Assistance Programme, OECD; joined World Bank 1963, Chief of N. Africa Div. 1965–67, Deputy Dir. Middle East and N. Africa Dept. 1967–68, Europe, Middle East and N. Africa Dept. 1968–70, Dir. 1970–72, Vice-Pres. for Europe, Middle East and N. Africa 1972–75, 1976–80; Vice-Pres. External Relations 1980–84, mem. Man. Cttee. 1981–84; Sr. Int. Adviser Standard Chartered Bank PLC (London) 1984–88; Visiting Fellow, St. Antony's Coll., Oxford Univ. 1975–76; Fellow, Johns Hopkins Univ. Foreign Policy Inst. 1986–88; Order of Merit of the Italian Repub. 1960; Order of Cedars of Lebanon. *Leisure interests:* classical music, history. *Address:* 1308 28th Street, N.W., Washington, D.C. 20007, U.S.A.; 73 Cadogan Square, London, S.W.1, England.

BENKE, Mrs. Valéria; Hungarian politician; b. 26 June 1920, Gyönk; ed. teacher training; joined Communist Party 1941; Trade Union Sec., Szeged 1944; Teacher, Party Acad. 1945–46; party worker, Budapest 1946–48; Budapest Sec., Women's Fed. 1948–50; Sec. Nat. Peace Council 1950–54; Pres. Hungarian Radio and Television 1954–58; Minister of Public Educ. 1958–61; M.P. 1949–71; mem. Cen. Cttee. of Hungarian Socialist Workers' Party 1957–, Presidential Council 1967–71, Political Cttee. 1970–85; Ed.-in-Chief, Társadalmi Szemle; Order of Merit of the People's Republic (three times), Red Banner Order of Labour, Labour Order of Merit; Medal of Socialist Fatherland. *Address:* Hungarian Socialist Workers' Party, Budapest V, Széchenyi rakpart 19, Hungary. *Telephone:* 111-400.

BENKEI, András; Hungarian politician; b. 11 Sept. 1923, Nyiregyháza; s. of István Benkei; m. Erzsébet Habony 1949; two d.; former mechanic; Sec. Szabolcs-Szatmár County Cttee. of Food Industry Trade Union 1949; Head, Industrial Dept., Szabolcs-Szatmár County Party Cttee. 1951–54; First Sec. Nyiregyháza Municipal Cttee., Hungarian Socialist Workers Party 1954–56; First Sec. Szabolcs-Szatmár County Party Cttee. 1956–63; Minister of Internal Affairs 1963–80; mem. Cen. Cttee. Hungarian Socialist Workers Party; M.P.; Pres. Nat. Council for Traffic Security 1973–; Red Banner Order of Labour. *Leisure interests:* literature, sport. *Address:* National Council for Traffic Security, 1051 Budapest, Zrinyi-utca 4, Hungary. *Telephone:* 121-710.

BENMAATI, Nadir; Algerian politician; b. 1944; m.; two c.; civil servant for construction and housing 1970–; business devt. 1970–77; Cen. Dir., Dir-Gen., Sec. Gen. Union of Algerian Sociologists and Economists 1983–88; Minister of Construction, Housing and Regional Development 1988–. *Address:* route des 4 Canons, Tagarins, Algiers, Algeria. *Telephone:* (2) 61-20-14.

BENN, Rt. Hon. Tony, P.C., M.A., M.P.; British politician; b. 3 April 1925, London; s. of William Wedgwood Benn (1st Viscount Stansgate), P.C. and Margaret Eadie (Holmes); m. Caroline de Camp 1949; three s. one d.; ed. Westminster School and New Coll., Oxford; R.A.F. Pilot 1943–45; Oxford Univ. 1946–49; Producer, BBC 1949–50; Labour M.P. for Bristol S.E. 1950–60, compelled to leave House of Commons on inheriting peerage 1960, re-elected and unseated 1961, renounced peerage and re-elected 1963, contested and lost Bristol East seat in 1983, re-elected as mem. for Chesterfield March 1984–; Nat. Exec. Labour Party 1959–; Chair. Fabian Soc. 1964; Postmaster-Gen. 1964–66; Minister of Technology 1966–70, of Power 1969–70; Shadow Minister of Trade and Industry 1970–74; Sec. of State for Industry and Minister of Posts and Telecommunications 1974–75; Sec. of State for Energy 1975–79; Vice-Chair. Labour Party 1970, Chair. 1971–72; Chair. Labour Party Home Policy Cttee. 1974–82; Cand. for Leadership of Labour Party 1976, for Deputy Leadership 1971, 1981; Pres. EEC Energy Council 1977; fmr. mem. Bureau Confed. of Socialist Parties of the European Community; Hon. LL.D. (Strathclyde Univ.), Hon. LL.D. (Williams Coll., U.S.A.), Hon. D.Tech. (Bradford), Hon. D.Sc. (Aston). *Publications:* The Privy Council as a Second Chamber 1957, The Regeneration of Britain 1964, The New Politics 1970, Speeches by Tony Benn 1974, Arguments for Socialism 1979, Arguments for Democracy 1981, Parliament, People and Power 1982, The Sizewell Syndrome 1984, Writings on the Wall 1984, Out of the Wilderness: Diaries 1963–67, 1987, Office without Power: Diaries 1968–72, 1988. *Address:* House of Commons, Westminster, London, S.W.1, England.

BENNET, Douglas J., Jr., PH.D.; American public administrator; b. 23 June 1938, Orange, N.J.; s. of Douglas and Phoebe Bennet; m. Susanne Klejman 1959; two s. one d.; ed. Wesleyan Univ., Middletown, Conn., Univ. of Calif. (Berkeley) and Harvard Univ.; Asst. to Econ. Adviser (Dr. C. E. Lindblom), Agency for Int. Devt., New Delhi 1963–64; Special Asst. to Amb. Chester Bowles, U.S. Embassy, New Delhi 1964–66; Asst. to Vice-Pres. Hubert Humphrey 1967–69; Admin. Asst. to Senator T. F. Eagleton 1969–73, to Senator A. Ribicoff 1973–74; Staff Dir. Senate Budget Cttee. 1974–77; Asst. Sec. of State, Congressional Relations 1977–79; Admin. U.S. Agency for Int. Devt. 1979–81; Pres. Roosevelt Center for American Policy Studies 1981–83; Pres. Nat. Public Radio (NPR) 1983–; mem. Council of Foreign Relations, North South Round Table, Soc. for

Int. Devt., Carnegie Endowment Study on Organizing Int. Financial Co-operation in 1980s; Dir. Overseas Educ. Fund, KTI Corpn. *Publications:* articles in newspapers and journals. *Leisure interests:* sailing, skiing. *Address:* 3206 Klingle Road, N.W., Washington, D.C. 20008; Selden Road, Hadlyme, Conn. 06439, U.S.A. (Homes). *Telephone:* (202) 822-2010 (Office); (202) 337-4424; (203) 526-3388 (Homes).

BENNETT, Alan; British playwright and actor; b. 9 May 1934; s. of Walter Bennett and Lilian Mary Peel; unmarried; ed. Leeds Modern School, Exeter Coll., Oxford; Jr. Lecturer, Modern History, Magdalen Coll., Oxford 1960–62; co-author and actor Beyond the Fringe, Edin. 1960, London 1961, New York 1962; author and actor On the Margin (television series) 1966, Forty Years On (play) 1968; *Plays:* Getting On 1971, Habeas Corpus 1973, The Old Country 1977, Enjoy 1980, Kafka's Dick 1986, Single Spies 1988. *Television scripts:* A Day Out (film) 1972, Sunset Across the Bay (TV film) 1975, A Little Outing, A Visit from Miss Prothero (plays) 1977, Doris and Doreen, The Old Crowd, Me! I'm Afraid of Virginia Woolf, All Day on the Sands, Afternoon Off, One Fine Day 1978–79, Intensive Care, Our Winnie, A Woman of No Importance, Rolling Home, Marks, Say Something Happened, An Englishman Abroad 1982, The Insurance Man 1986, Talking Heads. *Films:* A Private Function 1984, Prick Up Your Ears 1987. *Publications:* Beyond the Fringe (with Peter Cook, Jonathan Miller and Dudley Moore, qq.v.) 1962, Forty Years On 1969, Getting On 1972, Habeas Corpus 1973, The Old Country 1978, Enjoy 1980, Office Suite 1981, Objects of Affection 1982, The Writer in Disguise 1985, Two Kafka Plays 1987, Talking Heads 1988, Single Spies 1989; regular contrib. to London Review of Books. *Address:* c/o A.D. Peters and Co. Ltd., Fifth Floor, The Chambers, Chelsea Harbour, Lots Road, London SW10 0XF, England. *Telephone:* (01) 376-7676.

BENNETT, Lt.-Col. Sir Charles Moihi To Arawaka, Kt., D.S.O., M.A., DIP.ED., DIP.SOC.SC.; New Zealand diplomatist; b. 1913; ed. Univ. of N.Z. and Exeter Coll., Oxford; Schoolmaster 1937; Staff mem. N.Z. Broadcasting Service 1938–39; service with N.Z. Army in U.K., Greece, Crete, N. Africa, commanding Maori Battalion from Alamein to Tunis 1939–46; Staff mem. War Histories Section, Internal Affairs Dept., mem. Ngarimu Scholarship Fund Bd. 1947–50; Asst. Controller Maori Welfare Div., Maori Affairs Dept. 1951–57, Dir. 1957–58; mem. State Literary Advisory Cttee., N.Z. Parole Bd. 1951; N.Z. High Commr. to Malaya (the first Maori to lead an overseas Mission) 1959–63; Asst. Sec. Dept. of Maori Affairs, Wellington 1963–69; Vice-Pres. N.Z. Labour Party 1970–72, Pres. 1973–76; Hon. LL.D. Univ. Canterbury, N.Z. *Address:* Otimi Street, Maketu, Bay of Plenty, New Zealand. *Telephone:* Te Puke 32010.

BENNETT, Emmett Leslie, PH.D.; American classical scholar; b. 12 July 1918, Minneapolis, Minn.; s. of Emmett L. Bennett and Mary C. Buzzelle; m. Marja Adams 1942; five c.; ed. Univ. of Cincinnati; Research analyst, U.S. War Dept. 1942–45; taught in Dept. of Classics, Yale Univ. 1947–58; Fulbright Research Scholar, Athens 1953–54, Cambridge 1965; mem. Inst. for Advanced Study, Guggenheim Fellow, Visiting Lecturer in Greek, Bryn Mawr Coll. 1955–56; Dept. of Classical Languages, Univ. of Texas 1958–59; Univ. of Wis. Inst. for Research Humanities 1959–, Acting Dir. 1968–69, 1972–75; Dept. of Classics 1960–, Moses S. Slaughter Prof. of Classical Studies 1978–88, Emer. 1988–; Visiting Prof. Univ. of Colorado 1967, of Cincinnati 1972; Elizabeth A. Whitehead Prof., American School of Classical Studies 1986–87; corresp. mem. German Archaeological Inst.; Hon. Councillor Archaeological Soc. of Athens; mem. Comité Int. Permanent des Etudes Mycéniennes, Archaeological Inst. of America, American Philological Asscn. *Publications:* The Pylos Tablets 1951 and 1956, The Mycenae Tablets 1953 and 1958, Mycenaean Studies 1964, Ed., Nestor 1957–77, etc. *Address:* 1401 Observatory Drive, University of Wisconsin, Madison, Wis. 53706, U.S.A. *Telephone:* (608) 257-3162.

BENNETT, Frederick Onslow Alexander Godwyn, B.A.(CANTAB.), T.D.; British business executive; b. 21 Dec. 1913, Shenley; s. of Alfred Bennett and Marjorie Muir Bremner; m. Rosemary Perks 1942; one s. four d.; ed. Winchester Coll., Trinity Coll., Cambridge; joined Whitbread & Co. as pupil brewer 1935; mil. service, mentioned in despatches 1939–45; Man. Dir. Whitbread & Co. Ltd. 1949, Deputy Chair. 1959, Chief Exec. 1968–74, Chair. 1972–78; Chair. Whitbread Investment Co. Ltd. 1978–88; Master of Brewers' Co. 1963–64; Chair. Brewers' Soc. 1972–74; U.S. Bronze Star 1944. *Leisure interests:* shooting, racing. *Address:* Grove House, Selling, Faversham, Kent, ME13 9RN, England. *Telephone:* Selling 250.

BENNETT, Hywel; British actor and director; b. 8 April 1944, Garnant, South Wales; s. of Gorden Bennett and Sarah Gwen Lewis; m. Cathy McGowan 1970; one d.; ed. Henry Thornton Grammar School, Clapham, London, and Royal Acad. of Dramatic Art; London stage debut as Ophelia in Youth Theatre's Hamlet, Queen's Theatre 1959; played in repertory, Salisbury and Leatherhead 1965. *Stage roles include:* Puck in A Midsummer Night's Dream, Edin. Festival 1967; Prince Hal in Henry IV (Parts I and II), Mermaid 1970; Antony in Julius Caesar, Young Vic 1972; Stanley in The Birthday Party, Gardner Cen., Brighton 1973; Hamlet (touring S. Africa) 1974; Danny in Night Must Fall, Sherman, Cardiff 1974 and Shaw, 1975; Jimmy Porter in Look Back in Anger, Belgrade, Coventry 1974; Konstantin in the Seagull (on tour), Birmingham Repertory Co. 1974, Otherwise Engaged, Comedy Theatre 1978, Terra Nova, Chichester 1979, The Case of the Oily Levantine, Her Majesty's 1980, She Stoops to

Conquer, Nat. Theatre 1984-85; has directed several plays including Rosencrantz and Guildenstern are Dead, Leatherhead 1975, A Man for All Seasons, Birmingham 1976, I Have Been Here Before, Sherman Theatre, Cardiff 1976, Otherwise Engaged, Library Theatre, Manchester 1978, What the Butler Saw, Theatre of Wales, Cardiff 1980, Fly Away Home (also producer), Hammersmith 1983, The Three Sisters, Albery Theatre 1986. *Films include:* The Family Way 1966, Twisted Nerve 1968, The Virgin Soldiers 1969, Loot 1970, Percy 1971, Alice in Wonderland 1972, Endless Night 1972, Murder Elite, War Zone, Frankie and Johnnie 1985. *TV appearances include:* Romeo and Juliet, The Idiot, Unman, Wittering and Zigo, A Month in the Country, Malice Aforethought (serial), Shelley (two series), Tinker, Tailor, Soldier, Spy (serial) 1979, Coming Out, Pennies From Heaven, Artemis '81, The Critic, The Consultant, Absent Friends, Checkpoint Chiswick, The Secret Agent, many voice-overs and narrations; radio plays. *Leisure interests:* fishing, cooking, golf, painting, walking, swimming and reading. *Address:* c/o James Sharkey Associates, 15 Golden Square, London, W1R 3AG, England.

BENNETT, Ivan Loveridge, Jr., A.B., M.D., L.H.D.; American physician and teacher; b. 4 March 1922, Washington, D.C.; s. of Ivan and Ruby Bennett; m. Martha Rhodes 1944; two s. two d.; ed. Emory Coll., Emory Univ. Medical School, Johns Hopkins and Duke Univs.; U.S. Navy Medical Corps 1947-49; Asst. Prof. of Medicine, Yale Univ. 1952-54; Assoc. Prof. of Medicine, Johns Hopkins Univ. 1954-57, Prof. 1957-58, Baxley Prof. of Pathology 1958-69; Pathologist-in-Chief, Johns Hopkins Hosp. 1958-69; Deputy Dir. and Acting Dir. Office of Science and Tech., The White House 1966-69; Dean of Medical School, New York Univ. 1969-81, Vice-Pres. for Health Affairs 1969-73, Exec. Vice-Pres. 1973-81, Acting Pres. 1979-81, Prof. of Medicine 1970-; Consultant to numerous U.S. agencies; Dir. Technicon Corpn. 1971-79, Prudential Insurance Co. 1980-; mem. Inst. of Medicine, Nat. Acad. of Sciences and numerous science and medical asscns. *Publications:* more than 300 scientific reports. *Address:* New York University Medical Center, 550 First Avenue, MSB 138, New York, N.Y. 10016, U.S.A. *Telephone:* 212-340-5959.

BENNETT, Jack Franklin, PH.D.; American economist; b. 17 Jan. 1924, Macon, Ga.; s. of Andrew Jackson Bennett and Mary Eloise Franklin Bennett; m. Shirley Elizabeth Goodwin 1949; three s. one d.; ed. Woodrow Wilson High School, Washington, D.C., Yale and Harvard Univs.; Communications Officer, U.S. Navy 1944-46; Joint U.S./U.K. Export-Import Agency, Berlin 1946; Econ. Co-operation Admin. 1950; Special Asst. to Admin., Tech. Co-operation Admin. 1951-53; Sr. Economist, Presidential Comm. on Foreign Econ. Policy 1953-54; Foreign Exchange Analyst, Standard Oil Co. (N.J.) 1955; Presidential Citizens' Cttee. on Mutual Security 1956-57: European Financial Rep., Standard Oil (N.J.) 1958-60, Asst. Treas., Exec. Asst. to Chair. 1961-64, Chief Economist, Man. Co-ordination and Planning 1965-66, Gen. Man. Supply Dept. Humble Oil 1967-69, Dir. and Vice-Pres. Esso Int. 1969-71, Sr. Vice-Pres. and Dir. Exxon 1975-; Deputy Under-Sec. for Monetary Affairs U.S. Treasury Dept. 1971-74, Under-Sec. March-July 1974, Under-Sec. for Monetary Affairs 1974-75; Alexander Hamilton Award 1974. *Publications:* articles in Foreign Affairs, Journal of Finance, Economia Internazionale. *Leisure interests:* swimming, tennis, inventing. *Address:* c/o Exxon Corporation, 1251 Avenue of the Americas, New York, N.Y. 10020, U.S.A. *Telephone:* (212) 333-6820 (Office).

BENNETT, Jill; British actress; b. 24 Dec. 1932, Penang; d. of Randle and Nora Bennett; m. 1st Willis Hall 1962 (dissolved 1965), 2nd John Osborne (q.v.) 1968 (dissolved 1977); ed. Tortington Park and Priors Field, Stratford-upon-Avon; first London appearance in Captain Carvallo, St. James's Theatre 1950; has since appeared in productions of classical and contemporary plays in London (especially at Royal Court Theatre), Chichester, Nottingham, Edinburgh Festival etc.; Co-founder Off The Avenue 1986; Evening Standard Award and Variety Club's Best Actress for Pamela in Osborne's Time Present 1968; *films include:* Lust for Life, The Nanny, The Criminal, The Charge of the Light Brigade, Inadmissible Evidence, Julius Caesar, I Want What I Want, Quilp, Full Circle, For Your Eyes Only, Britannia Hospital, Lady Jane, Hawks. *TV:* Paradise Postponed and numerous other appearances. *Publication:* Godfrey: A Special Time Remembered 1983. *Leisure interests:* riding, water skiing, art. *Address:* James Sharkey Associates, 15 Golden Square, London, W.1, England.

BENNETT, John Coleman, D.D., S.T.D.; American theologian (retd.); b. 22 July 1902, Kingston, Canada; s. of William Russell and Charlotte Coleman Bennett; m. Anne McGrew Bennett 1931; two s. one d.; ed. Phillips Exeter Acad., Williams Coll., Oxford Univ. and Union Theological Seminary; mem. of Faculty, Auburn Theological Seminary 1930-38; Prof. of Theology, Pacific School of Religion 1938-43; Prof. of Christian Theology and Ethics, Union Theological Seminary 1943-, Dean of Faculty 1955-63, William E. Dodge Jr. Prof. of Applied Christianity 1957-61, Reinhold Niebuhr Prof. of Social Ethics 1961-70, Pres. 1963-70; Visiting Prof. Christian Ethics, Pacific School of Religion 1970-77; Adjunct Prof., Univ. of Calif.; Lecturer, Claremont School of Theology 1980-81; Pres. American Theological Soc. 1954, American Soc. for Christian Social Ethics 1961; Co-Ed. Christianity and Crisis; 22 hon. degrees, mainly D.D. *Publications:* Social Salvation 1935, Christian Realism 1941, Christian Ethics and Social Policy 1946,

Christianity and Communism 1948 (new ed. Christianity and Communism Today 1960), Christians and the State 1958, Nuclear Weapons and the Conflict of Conscience 1962 (ed.), Foreign Policy in Christian Perspective 1966, The Radical Imperative 1975, U.S. Foreign Policy and Christian Ethics (Co-author) 1977. *Address:* 620 Plymouth Road, Claremont, Calif. 91711, U.S.A. *Telephone:* 714-624-3752.

BENNETT, Maxwell Richard, B.ENG., PH.D., F.A.A.; Australian professor of physiology; b. 19 Feb. 1939, Melbourne; s. of Herman Adler Bennett (Bercovici) and Ivy G. Arthur; m. Gillian R. Bennett 1965; one s. one d.; ed. Christian Brothers Coll., St Kilda, Melbourne and Univ. of Melbourne; John & Alan Gilmour Research Fellow, Univ. of Melbourne 1965; lecturer in Physiology, Univ. of Sydney 1969, Reader 1973, Prof. of Physiology 1983-, Dir. Neurobiology Research Centre 1982-. *Publications:* Autonomic Neuromuscular Transmission 1972, Development of Neuromuscular Synapses 1983. *Address:* Neurobiology Research Centre, University of Sydney, N.S.W. 2006, Australia. *Telephone:* 629 2034.

BENNETT, Michael Vander Laan, B.S., D.PHIL.; American professor of neuroscience; b. 7 Jan. 1931, Madison, Wis.; s. of Martin Toscan Bennett and Cornelia Vander Laan Bennett; m. Ruth Berman 1963; one s. one d.; ed. Yale Univ. and Oxford Univ., England; research worker, Dept. of Neurology, Coll. of Physicians and Surgeons, Columbia Univ. 1957-58, Research Assoc. 1958-59; Asst. Prof. of Neurology, Columbia Univ. 1959-61, Assoc. Prof. 1961-66; Prof. of Anatomy, Albert Einstein Coll. of Medicine 1967-74; Co-Dir. Neurobiology Course, Marine Biological Lab. 1970-74; Prof. of Neuroscience, Albert Einstein Coll. of Medicine 1974-, Dir. Div. of Cellular Neurobiology 1974-, Chair. Dept. of Neuroscience 1982-, Sylvia and Robert S. Olnick Prof. 1986-; Rhodes Scholar 1952; Sr. Research Fellowship, Nat. Inst. of Health 1960-62; Fellow, Nat. Neurological Research Foundation 1958-60, A.A.A.S., New York Acad. of Sciences; mem. N.A.S., American Assen. of Anatomists, American Physiological Soc., American Soc. for Cell Biology, American Soc. of Zoologists, Biophysical Soc., Soc. for Neuroscience, Soc. of Gen. Physiologists; mem. Editorial Bds. Brain Research 1975-, Journal of Cell Biology 1983-85, Journal of Neurobiology 1969- (Assoc. Ed. 1979-), Journal of Neurocytology 1980-82, Journal of Neuroscience. *Publications:* over 160 papers in scholarly journals and books. *Leisure interests:* running, hiking, skiing and scuba. *Address:* Albert Einstein College of Medicine, Department of Neuroscience, Bronx, N.Y. 10461 (Office); 10 Alderbrook Road, Riverdale, N.Y. 10471, U.S.A. (Home). *Telephone:* (212) 430-2536 (Office); (212) 796 1810 (Home).

BENNETT, Richard Rodney, C.B.E., A.R.A.M., F.R.A.M.; British composer; b. 29 March 1936, Broadstairs, Kent; s. of H. Rodney Bennett and Joan Esther Bennett; ed. Leighton Park School, Reading, Royal Acad. of Music, London and under Pierre Boulez, Paris; commissioned to write two operas by Sadler's Wells 1962; Prof. of Composition, Royal Acad. of Music 1963-65; Vice-Pres. Royal Coll. of Music 1983-; mem. Gen. Council, Performing Right Soc. 1975-; Arnold Bax Soc. Prize for Commonwealth Composers 1964; Anthony Asquith Memorial Award for Murder on the Orient Express film music, Soc. of Film and TV Awards 1974. *Compositions:* The Approaches of Sleep 1959, Journal, Calendar, Winter Music 1960, The Ledge, Suite Française, Oboe Sonata 1961, Nocturnes, London Pastoral, Fantasy 1962, Aubade, Jazz Calendar, String Quartet No. Four, Five Studies 1964, Symphony No. 1 1965, Epithalamion 1966, Symphony No. 2 1967, Wind Quintet, Piano Concerto 1968, Jazz Pastoral 1969, Oboe Concerto 1970, Guitar Concerto 1971, Viola Concerto 1973, Commedia I-IV 1972-73, Spells (choral) 1975, Serenade for Youth Orchestra 1977; Opera: The Mines of Sulphur 1964, A Penny for a Song 1966, Victory 1969, All the King's Men (children's opera) 1969; Isadora (ballet) 1981; Film Music: Indiscreet, Devil's Disciple, Blind Date, The Mark, Only Two Can Play, Wrong Arm of the Law, Heavens Above, Billy Liar, One Way Pendulum, The Nanny, The Witches, Far from the Madding Crowd, Billion Dollar Brain, The Buttercup Chain, Secret Ceremony, Figures in a Landscape, Nicholas and Alexandra, Lady Caroline Lamb, Voices, Murder on the Orient Express, Equus, Sherlock Holmes in New York, L'Imprecateur, The Brinks Job, Yanks, Return of the Soldier; TV music for series Hereward the Wake, The Christians. *Leisure interests:* cinema, modern jazz. *Address:* c/o Mrs Keys, London Management, Regent House, 235 Regent Street, London, W.1, England.

BENNETT, Robert Frederick, J.D.; American lawyer and politician; b. 23 May 1927, Kansas City, Mo.; s. of Otto F. and Dorothy Bess Dodds Bennett; m. Olivia Fisher 1971; one s. three d.; ed. Shawnee Mission North High School and Univ. of Kansas; served U.S. Marine Corps 1945-47, 1950-51; Sr. Partner, Bennett, Lytle, Wetzler, Winn and Martin, law firm 1952-74, 1979-; City Councilman, City of Prairie Village 1955-57, Mayor 1957-65; mem. Kansas State Senate 1965-75, Pres. 1973-75; Gov. of State of Kansas 1975-79; Chair. Nat. Republican Govs.' Assen. 1976; mem. Policy Cttee. Nat. Govs.' Assen. 1977; Chair. Interstate Oil Compact Comm. 1978; fmr. Chair. Kan. League of Municipalities; fmr. Sec.-Treas. Kan. Bar Assen.; fmr. Chair. several Senate and jt. cttees.; admitted to practise law in state and fed. courts of Kan., Mo. Supreme Court, U.S. Supreme Court; various awards. *Publications:* Legislative articles for Kansas Law Review. *Leisure interests:* reading, hunting, fishing. *Address:* 5000 West 95th Street, Suite 300, Prairie Village, Kansas 66207 (Office); 5315 West 96th

Street, Overland Park, Kansas 66207, U.S.A. (Home). *Telephone:* (913) 642-7300 (Office).

BENNETT, Roy Frederick, F.C.A.; Canadian business executive; b. 18 March 1928, Winnipeg, Man.; s. of Charles William Bennett (deceased) and Gladys Mabel Matthews; m. Gail Cook Bennett 1978; two s. two d.; ed. Collegiate Inst., N. Toronto and Inst. of Chartered Accountants; Ford Motor Co. of Canada Ltd., Asst. Controller 1960-62, Dir. Vehicle Marketing 1962-63, Dir. Corporate Planning 1963-64, Gen. Marketing Man. 1964-65, Vice-Pres. Finance 1965-70, Dir. 1966-, Pres. and C.E.O. 1970-81, Chair. and C.E.O. 1981-82; Pres. Bennecon Ltd. 1982-; Dir. BP Canada Inc.; Jannock Ltd.; Inglis Ltd.; Bell Canada Inc.; Chair. Niagara Inst.; mem. Business Council on Nat. Issues. *Leisure interests:* golf, squash, tennis, skiing. *Address:* Bennecon Ltd., Toronto-Dominion Tower, Suite 2810, Toronto, Ont., M5K 1E7, Canada.

BENNETT, William John, PH.D., J.D.; American administrator and politician; b. 31 July 1943, Brooklyn; m. Mary Glover 1982; Asst. to Pres., Boston Univ. 1972-76; Exec. Dir. Nat. Humanities Center, N.C. 1976-79, Pres. 1979-81; Assoc. Prof. N.C. State Univ., Raleigh 1979-81, Univ. of N.C. 1979-81; Pres. Nat. Endowment for Humanities 1981; Sec. for Educ. 1985-88; Dir. Nat. Drug Policy Jan. 1989-; fmr. Democrat, joined Republican Party 1986. *Address:* Office of National Drug Policy, Old Executive Office Bldg., Washington, D.C. 20506, U.S.A.

BENNETT, William Richards; Canadian politician and businessman; b. 14 April 1932, Kelowna, B.C.; s. of the late William Andrew Cecil Bennett (Premier of B.C. 1952-72) and of Annie Elizabeth May (Richards) Bennett; m. Audrey Lyne James 1955; four s.; ed. Kelowna High School; established business including 17 companies, starting with retail furniture and appliance stores in B.C.; mem. B.C. Legis. Ass. for Okanagan S. Sept. 1973-; Leader Social Credit Party in B.C. Nov. 1973-; Premier of B.C. Dec. 1975-86 (resgnd.). *Leisure interests:* tennis, skiing, jogging. *Address:* R.R. No. 1, Pritchard Drive, Westbank, B.C., Canada. *Telephone:* (604) 387-1715.

BENNETT, William Tapley, Jr., J.D., D.C.L., American diplomatist, university professor and consultant; b. 1 April 1917, Griffin, Ga.; s. of William Tapley and Annie Mem Little Bennett; m. Margaret Rutherfurd White 1945; two s. three d.; ed. Univ. of Georgia, Univ. of Freiburg, Germany, and George Washington Univ.; Instructor in Political Science, Univ. of Ga. 1937; with Nat. Inst. of Public Affairs 1939-40; Dept. of Agric. 1940; Asst. to Co-ordinator, Office of Defense Housing 1940-41; with State Dept. 1941-85, served in U.S. Army 1944-46; Officer in charge Cen. American and Panama Affairs 1949-51, Caribbean Affairs 1951, Deputy Dir. S. American Affairs 1951-54; Nat. War Coll. 1954-55; Special Asst. to Deputy Under-Sec. of State 1955-57; Counsellor, Vienna 1957-61, Rome 1961; Counsellor (with rank of Minister), Athens 1961-64; Amb. to Dominican Repub. 1964-66, to Portugal 1966-69; State Dept. Rep. to Air Force Univ. 1969-71; Deputy U.S. Rep. and Amb. UN Security Council 1971-77; U.S. Rep. to 26th-31st UN Gen. Assemblies 1971-76; Pres. UN Trusteeship Council 1972-73; Perm. Rep. to NATO 1977-83; Asst. Sec. of State for Congressional Relations 1983-85; Adjunct Prof. of Int. Relations, Ga. Univ. 1985-; Consultant, Inst. of Foreign Policy Analysis, Tufts Univ.; Sr. Fellow Inst. of Higher Defense Studies; Gov. Foreign Policy Asscn.; Dir. Atlantic Council U.N. Assscn., Meridian House; mem. Bd. of Visitors, Air Force Univ. 1986-; American Acad. of Diplomacy; Council on Foreign Relations; medals for distinguished service from U.S. State and Defense Depts. *Leisure interests:* sailing, skiing, photography, travel, golf. *Address:* 2500 Virginia Avenue, N.W., Washington D.C., 20037, U.S.A. *Telephone:* (202) 337-3415.

BENNIGSEN-FOERDER, Rudolf von; German business executive; b. 2 July 1926, Berlin; s. of Rudolf and Margarethe (née Welt) v. Bennigsen-Foerder; m. Johanna Wirmer 1955; no c.; ed. Univs. of Erlangen, Bonn and Geneva; with Ministry of Finance 1957-59; joined VEBA AG 1959, Chair. Man. Bd. 1971-; Chair. Supervisory Bd. Major Co. Veba Group; Ruhrkohle AG; Bewag AG; Hapag-Lloyd AG; mem. Supervisory Bd. several cos.; mem. Bd. Nat. Union of German Employers' Asscns.; Confed. of German Industry; Hon. Consul-Gen. of Norway; Hon. D.Eng. (Essen); several honours and distinctions. *Address:* 4 Düsseldorf 30, Karl-Arnold-Platz 3, Federal Republic of Germany. *Telephone:* (0211) 45791.

BEŇO, Mikuláš, C.S.C.; Czechoslovak politician; b. 12 Nov. 1930, Nová Bošáca, Trenčín district; ed. Coll. of Politics, Cen. Cttee. of CP of Czechoslovakia, and Acad. of Social Sciences of CPSU, Moscow; held several tech., econ. and political posts in clothing factory 1947-56; Official, Regional Cttee., CP of Slovakia, Žilina 1956-57, Sec. Regional Cttee. of Czechoslovak Union of Youth 1957-59; Regional Cttee. CP of Slovakia, Banská Bystrica 1962-65, Sec. 1969-70; Official, Cen. Cttee. of CP of Slovakia 1968-69; Deputy Head, Propaganda and Agitation Dept., CP of Czechoslovakia 1970-71; Deputy Head, Secr. of Gen. Sec. of Cen. Cttee. of CP of Czechoslovakia 1971-73, Head 1973-77; mem. Cen. Cttee. of CP of Czechoslovakia 1976-89, Sec. and mem. Secr. 1977-89; Deputy to House of the People, Fed. Ass. 1978-; Order of Merit in Construction, Order of the Republic 1980. *Address:* Ústřední výbor KSČ, Prague 1, nábřeží Ludvíka Svobody 12, Czechoslovakia.

BENOÎT, Henri, D. ÈS SC.; French scientist; b. 11 July 1921, Montpellier; s. of Jean-Daniel and Henriette (née Bois) Benoît; m. Marie-Thérèse Bigand 1946; two s. one d.; ed. Ecole Normale Supérieure de Paris and Univ. of Strasbourg; Research Asst. Harvard Univ. 1952-53; Prof. Univ. of Strasbourg (Dir. Physics and Chemistry Research Unit) 1954-, Inst. Charles Sandron 1985; Dir. Centre for Macromolecular Research, C.N.R.S. 1967-78; mem. Nat. Cttee., C.N.R.S. 1967-75; Pres. Div. of Macromolecular Chem., IUPAC 1971-; Dr. h.c. (Uppsala) 1971, (Aberdeen) 1973 (Lodz) 1977; mem. French Physical Soc.; Corresp. mem. Acad. des Sciences 1983-; Hon. mem. Spanish Chem. Soc.; Von Humboldt Stiftung, American Physical Soc. (Polymer Physics Div.) and American Chemical Soc. (Polymer Chem. Div.) Prizes. *Address:* 13 rue de Seltz, 67000 Strasbourg, France.

BENSLIMANE, Abdelkader; Moroccan politician; b. 1932; ed. Toulouse Univ., France; joined Ministry of Finance 1957; Amb. to France 1961-63; attached to Maghreb Consultative Comm., Ministry of Finance; Amb. to Belgium 1972; Minister of Trade, Industry, Mines and Merchant Marine 1972-74; of Finance 1974-77; fmr. Chair. and Gen. Man. Banque Nationale pour le Développement Economique, Rabat; Amb. to Fed. Rep. of Germany 1984-86. *Address:* Place des Alaouites, B.P. 407, Rabat, Morocco.

BENSON, Baron (Life Peer), cr. 1980, of Drovers in the county of West Sussex; **Henry Alexander Benson,** G.B.E., F.C.A.; British chartered accountant; b. 2 Aug. 1909, Johannesburg; s. of Alexander S. and Florence (née Cooper) Benson; m. Virginia Macleod 1939; two s. one d.; ed. South Africa; commissioned Grenadier Guards 1940-45; Dir. Royal Ordnance Factories 1943-44; Controller of Building Materials Ministry of Works 1945; Adviser on housing production, Ministry of Health 1945; Dir. Hudson's Bay Co. 1953-62, Deputy Gov. 1955-62; Dir. Finance Corpn. for Industry 1953-79; mem. Council, Inst. of Chartered Accountants 1956-75, Pres. 1966; Investigator Ulster Transport Authority 1961, shipping services in N.Z. trade 1962, turnover tax cttee. 1963; Joint Commr. on formation of CBI 1963; Joint Insp. Rolls Razor Affair 1964; Chair. Iron and Steel Fed. Devt. Cttee. 1966; Trustee, Times Trust 1967-81; mem. Perm. Joint Hops Cttee. 1967-73; Chair. Nat. Trust Inquiry Cttee.; Racing Industry Inquiry Cttee. 1967; Vice-Pres. UEC 1969-70; mem. Ministry of Defence Admin. Cttee. 1969-71, Dockyard Policy Bd. 1970-75; Sr. Partner, Coopers and Lybrand 1947-75; mem. CBI Co. Affairs Cttee. 1972-73; Chair. Int. Accounting Standards Cttee. 1973-76, Royal Comm. on Legal Services 1976-79; Chair. Exec. Cttee. of Accountants' Joint Disciplinary Scheme 1979-86; Dir. Finance for Industry Ltd. 1974-79; Industrial and Commercial Finance Corpn. 1974-79; Non-Exec. Dir. Hawker Siddeley 1975-81; mem. Govs.' City Liaison Cttee. 1974-75; Treas. Open Univ. 1975-79; Adviser to the Gov. of Bank of England 1975-83; Hon. Master of the Bench, Inner Temple 1983-; mem. Roskill Cttee. on Fraud Trials 1984-85. *Leisure interests:* shooting, sailing, golf. *Address:* 9 Durward House, 31 Kensington Court, London, W.8, England (Home). *Telephone:* 01-937 4850.

BENSON, Andrew Alm, PH.D.; American biochemist and plant physiologist; b. 24 Sept. 1917, Modesto, Calif.; s. of Carl B. Benson and Emma C. Alm; m. 1st Ruth Carkeek 1942, 2nd Dorothy Dorgan 1971; one s. three d. (two deceased); ed. Modesto High School, Univ. of Calif., Berkeley and Calif. Inst. of Tech.; Instructor, Univ. of Calif., Berkeley 1942-43; Research Assoc. Stanford Univ. 1944-45; Asst. Dir. Bioorganic Group, Radiation Lab., Univ. of Calif., Berkeley 1946-54; Assoc. Prof. of Agricultural Biological Chemistry Pennsylvania State Univ. 1955-60, Prof. 1960-61; Prof.-in-Residence, Physiological Chem. and Biophysics, U.C.L.A. 1961-62; Prof. Scripps Inst. of Oceanography, Univ. of Calif., San Diego 1962-, Asst. Dir. 1966-; mem. N.A.S., A.A.A.S.; Dr. h.c. (Oslo, Paris) and other awards and distinctions. *Publications:* Path of Carbon in Photosynthesis 1947-55, Wax in Oceanic Food Chains 1975, Arsenic Metabolism, a Way of Life in the Sea 1984; 250 articles in scientific journals. *Address:* Marine Biology Research Division A-002, Scripps Institution of Oceanography, La Jolla, Calif. 92093 (Office); 6044 Folsom Drive, La Jolla, Calif. 92037, U.S.A. (Home). *Telephone:* 619-534-4300 (Office); 619-459-1010 (Home).

BENSON, Sir Christopher John, Kt., F.R.I.C.S.; British chartered surveyor; b. 20 July 1933, Wheaton Aston; m. Margaret Josephine Bundy 1960; two s.; ed. Worcester Cathedral King's School, Thames Nautical Training Coll.; Dir. MEPC PLC 1974-, Man. Dir. 1976-, Vice-Chair. 1977-; Chair. London Docklands Devt. Corpn. 1984-, Reedpack Jan. 1989-; Dir. House of Fraser 1982, Royal Opera House Covent Garden 1984; Trustee, Civic Trust; Pres. British Property Fed.; Hon. Bencher of Middle Temple, London. *Leisure interests:* aviation, opera, swimming. *Address:* Brook House, 113 Park Lane, London, W1Y 4AY (Office); Pauls Dene House, Castle Road, Salisbury, Wilts., SP1 3RY, England (Home). *Telephone:* Salisbury 22187.

BENSON, Hon. Edgar John, P.C., B.COM.(M.), LL.D., F.C.A.; Canadian chartered accountant and politician; b. 1923; ed. Queen's Univ., Kingston, Ontario; joined firm England, Leonard and Macpherson (chartered accountants), Kingston, Ont. 1952; Asst. Prof. of Commerce, Queen's Univ., Kingston 1952-62; M.P. 1962-72; Parl. Sec. to Minister of Finance 1963-64; Minister of Nat. Revenue 1965-68; Pres. of Treasury Bd. 1965-68; Minister of Finance 1968-72, also Receiver-Gen. 1968-72; Minister responsible for Cen. Mortgage and Housing Corpn. 1968-72; Minister of Nat. Defence Jan.-Oct. 1972; Pres. Canadian Transport Comm. 1972-82; Amb. to Ireland 1982-86; Liberal. *Address:* Canadian Embassy, 65 St. Stephen's Green, Dublin 2, Ireland.

BENSON, Ezra Taft, M.S.; American agriculturist and religious leader; b. 4 Aug. 1899; ed. Brigham Young Univ., Iowa State Coll., and Univ. of California; missionary of Church of Jesus Christ of Latter-day Saints in U.K. 1921-23; County Agricultural Agent, Univ. of Idaho Extension Service 1929, Extension Economist and Marketing Specialist 1930-39, Head Dept. of Agricultural Econs. and Marketing 1931; Sec. Idaho Co-operative Council 1933-38; Exec. Sec. Nat. Council of Farmer Co-operatives 1939-43; served on several advisory cttees. and nat. boards in field of agric. 1939-; mem. Exec. Cttee. American Inst. of Co-operation 1942-52, Chair. Bd. of Trustees 1952; mem. Farm Foundation 1946, 1950; mem. Nat. Agricultural Advisory Cttee. during Second World War, mem. Nat. Farm Credit Cttee. 1940-43; U.S. del. Int. Conf. of Farm Orgs., London 1946; U.S. Sec. of Agric. 1953-61; Dir. Corn Products Inc. 1961-; mem. Council of Twelve, Church of Jesus Christ of Latter-day Saints 1943-, Pres. Mormon Church European Mission 1963; Leader, Mormon Church Nov. 1985-; Republican. *Address:* Church of Jesus Christ Latter Day Saints, 50 E.N. Temple Street, Salt Lake City, Utah 84150, U.S.A.

BENSON, Sidney William, PH.D.; American professor of chemistry; b. 26 Sept. 1918, New York; one s. one d.; ed. Stuyvesant High School, Columbia Coll. and Harvard Univ.; Postdoctoral Research Fellow, Harvard Univ. 1941-42; Instructor in Chem., Coll. of City of New York 1942-43; Asst. Prof., Univ. of Southern Calif. 1943-48, Assoc. Prof. 1948-51, Prof. of Chemistry 1951-64, 1976-; Scientific Co-Director, Loker Hydrocarbon Research Inst. 1978-; Chair. Dept. of Kinetics and Thermochemistry, Stanford Research Inst. 1963-76; mem. Int. Editorial Bd., Elsevier Publishing Co., Amsterdam, Netherlands 1965-; Ed.-in-Chief Int. Journal of Chemical Kinetics 1967-83, Ed. Emer. 1983-; mem. Editorial Bd. Journal of Physical Chem. 1981-84; Fellow, A.A.A.S., American Physical Soc.; mem. American Chemical Soc., N.A.S.; Guggenheim Fellow, Chemical Kinetics and Fulbright Fellow to France 1950-51; American Chemical Soc. Award in Petroleum Chem. 1977; Fellowship Award of the Japanese Soc. for Promotion of Science 1980; Irving Langmuir Award in Chemical Physics, American Chemical Soc. 1986; Polanyi Medal for Work in Chemical Kinetics (Royal Soc.) 1986, American Chemical Soc. Award, Orange Co. 1986, U.S.C. Award, Presidential Medallion 1986. *Leisure interests:* skiing, swimming and tennis. *Address:* Loker Hydrocarbon Research Institute, University of Southern California, University Park, Los Angeles, Calif. 90089-1661; 1110 North Bundy Drive, Los Angeles, Calif. 90049, U.S.A. (Home). *Telephone:* (213) 743-2030 (Office); (213) 471-5841 (Home).

BENSON, Sir (William) Jeffrey, Kt., F.I.B.; British banker; b. 15 July 1922, Leeds; s. of Herbert and Lilian (Goodson) Benson; m. Audrey Winifred Parsons 1947; two s.; ed. West Leeds High School; joined Nat. Provincial Bank Ltd. 1939; served R.A.F. 1941-46; Asst. Gen. Man. Nat. Provincial Bank 1965-68; Regional Exec. Dir. Nat. Westminster Bank Ltd. 1968-73, Gen. Man. of Man. Services Div. 1973-75, Deputy Chief Exec. 1975-77, Group Chief Exec. 1978-82, Deputy Chair. 1983-87; Chair. Export Guarantees Advisory Council 1982-87; Dir. Nat. Westminster Bank U.S.A. 1982-87; Dir. (non-exec.) Curry's Group 1983-84 (resgnd.); Pres. Inst. of Bankers 1983-84; Non-Exec. Dir. The 600 Group PLC 1983, Vice-Chair. 1985-87, Chair. 1987-. *Leisure interests:* golf, swimming. *Address:* Hythe End House, Chertsey Lane, Staines, Middx., TW18 3EL, England; Auben, 24 Spencer Walk, Rickmansworth, Herts., WD3 4EE, England (Home). *Telephone:* 0784-61545; 09237 78260 (Home).

BENTELE, Raymond F., B.S.; American business executive; b. 1936; m.; ed. N.E. Missouri State Coll.; accountant, S.D. Leidesdorf & Co. 1960-65; Treasurer, Controller, Germania Savings and Loan Assen. 1965-67; joined Mallinckrodt, Inc. 1967, Asst. Controller 1969-71, Controller 1971-74, Vice-Pres. 1974-76, Vice-Pres. Finance and Admin. 1976-77, Vice-Pres. Int. Group 1977-78, Sr. Vice-Pres., Group Exec. 1978-79, Pres. and C.E.O. 1979-86; Sr. Vice-Pres. Int. Minerals & Chemical Corpn. 1986-. *Address:* c/o Mallinckrodt, Inc., 675 McDonnell Boulevard, St. Louis, Mo. 63134, U.S.A.

BENTHAM, Richard Walker, B.A., LL.B., F.R.S.A.; British professor of law; b. 26 June 1930; s. of Richard H. Bentham and Ellen W. Fisher; m. Stella W. Matthews 1957; one d.; ed. Trinity Coll. Dublin and Middle Temple, London; called to Bar 1955; Lecturer in Law, Univ. of Tasmania 1955-57, Univ. of Sydney 1957-61; Legal Dept. British Petroleum Co. PLC 1961-83, Deputy Legal Adviser 1979-83; Prof. of Petroleum and Mineral Law and Dir. Centre for Petroleum and Mineral Law Studies, Univ. of Dundee 1983-; mem. Int. Law Assen., Int. Bar Assen. *Publications:* publications in learned journals in the U.K. and overseas. *Leisure interests:* cricket, military history. *Address:* West Bryans, 87 Dundee Road, West Ferry, Dundee, DD5 1LZ, Scotland. *Telephone:* 0382 23181 (Office); 0382 77100 (Home).

BENTLEY, (Charles) Fred, M.SC., PH.D., F.R.S.C.; Canadian professor of soil science; b. 14 March 1914, Mass., U.S.A.; s. of Charles F. Bentley and Lavina A. (née MacKenzie) Bentley; m. Helen S. Petersen 1943; one s. one d.; ed. Univ. of Alberta and Minnesota; Instructor in Soil Science Univ. of Minn. 1942-43; Instructor and Asst. Prof. Soil Science Univ. of Sask. 1943-46; Faculty mem. Soil Science Univ. of Alberta 1946-79, Dean Faculty of Agric. 1959-68, Prof. Emer. 1979-; Special Adviser, Agric., Canadian Int. Devt. Agency 1968-69; mem. Bd. of Govs. Int. Devt. Research Centre 1970-74; Chair. of Bd. Int. Crops Research Inst. for

Semi-Arid Tropics, Hyderabad, India 1972-82, Int. Bd. for Soil Research and Man., Bangkok, Thailand 1983-87; Consulting Agrologist, Int. Devt. Volunteer 1979-; Hon. D.Sc. (Guelph) 1984; Fellow American Assen. for Advancement of Science 1962, Agric. Inst. of Canada, Canadian Soc. of Soil Science, American Soc. of Soil Science, American Soc. of Agronomy; Pres. Int. Soc. of Soil Science 1975; Queen's Silver Jubilee Medal; numerous other awards and distinctions. *Publications:* over 100 scientific reports and papers. *Leisure interests:* world development, international affairs, agriculture and human welfare. *Address:* 13103-66 Avenue, Edmonton, Alberta, T6H 1Y6, Canada. *Telephone:* (403) 435-6523.

BENTLEY, Gerald Eades, Jr., D.PHIL., D.LITT., F.R.S.C.; American-Canadian scholar and professor of English; b. 23 Aug. 1930, Chicago, Ill.; s. of Gerald Eades Bentley and Esther Felt Bentley; m. Elizabeth Budd 1952; two d.; ed. Princeton Univ. and Oxford Univ., U.K.; Instructor, Univ. of Chicago Dept. of English 1956-60; Asst., later full Prof. of English, Univ. of Toronto, Canada 1960-; Fulbright Lecturer, Univ. of Algiers 1967-68, Univ. of Poona, India 1975-76, Fudan Univ., Shanghai, People's Repub. of China 1982-83; Guggenheim Fellow, London 1958-59; Fellow of Canada Council and successor Social Science and Humanities Research Council of Canada 1970-71, 1977-78, 1984-85; Co-founder Conf. on Editorial Problems 1964-, currently Chair.; Jenkins Award for Bibliography. *Publications:* Ed. William Blake, Vala, or The Four Zoas 1963, Ed. William Blake's Writings, 2 vols. 1978, Blake Records 1969, Blake Books 1977, Blake Records Supplement 1988; The Early Engravings of Flaxman's Classical Designs 1964, A Bibliography of George Cumberland 1975, Ed. Editing Eighteenth Century Novelists 1975. *Leisure interests:* book collecting, travel. *Address:* University College, University of Toronto, Toronto, Ont., M5S 1A1 (Office); 246 MacPherson Avenue, Toronto, Ont., M4V 1A2, Canada (Home). *Telephone:* (416) 978-4004 (Office); (416) 922-5163 (Home).

BENTLEY, Helen Delich; American government official, journalist and television and film producer; b. Ruth, Nev.; d. of Michael and Mary (Kovich) Delich; m. William Roy Bentley 1959; ed. Univ. of Nevada, George Washington Univ. and Univ. of Missouri; Reporter, Ely Record, Nev. 1940-42: Political Campaign Man. for Senator James G. Scrugham, White Pine Co., Nev. 1942; Bureau Man. United Press, Fort Wayne, Ind. 1944-45; Reporter Baltimore Sun 1945-53, Maritime Ed. 1953-69; Television Producer, world trade and maritime shows 1950-64; Public Relations Adviser, American Assen. Port Authorities 1958-62, 1964-67; Chair. Fed. Maritime Comm. 1969-75; Chair. American Bi-centennial Fleet Inc. 1973-76; Pres. and C.E.O. HDB Int. 1975-85; Pres. Int. Resources and Devt. Corpn., Washington 1976-77; Columnist and Shipping Ed. World Ports Magazine 1981-85; elected to Congress 1984-; mem. numerous govt. cttees.; many prizes and awards; Republican. *Address:* P.O.B. 10619, Towson, Md. 21204 (Office); 408 Chapelwood Lane, Lutherville, Md. 21093, U.S.A. (Home).

BENTLEY, Sir William, K.C.M.G.; British diplomatist (retd.); b. 15 Feb. 1927, Bury; s. of Lawrence and Elsie Jane Bentley; m. Karen Ellen Christensen 1950; two s. three d.; ed. Bury High School, Victoria Univ. of Manchester, Wadham Coll., Oxford, Coll. of Europe, Bruges; mil. service 1945-48; Foreign Office (FO, now FCO) 1952; Third Sec., later Second Sec., Tokyo 1952-57; UN Dept., FO 1957-60; First Sec. Perm. Mission to UN, New York 1960-63; Far East Dept., FO 1963-65; Head of Chancery, Kuala Lumpur 1965-69; Deputy Commr.-Gen. British Pavilion, Expo 70, Osaka 1969-70; Counsellor, Belgrade 1970-73; Head of Perm. Under-Sec.'s Dept., FCO 1973-74; Head, Far East Dept., FCO 1974-76; Amb. to Philippines 1976-81; High Commr. in Malaysia 1981-83; Amb. to Norway 1983-87; Chair. Soc. of Pension Consultants, Coflexip (U.K.) Ltd., Roehampton Inst. of Higher Educ.; Deputy Chair. Protech. Int. (U.K.) Ltd.; mem. various bds. *Leisure interests:* golf, skiing, fishing, shooting. *Address:* 48 Bathgate Road, London, SW19 5PJ, England. *Telephone:* 01-949 7330.

BENTON, Peter Faulkner, M.A., C.B.I.M.; British administrative official; b. 6 Oct. 1934, London; s. of S. Faulkner Benton and Hilda Benton; m. Ruth S. Cobb 1959; two s. three d.; ed. Oundle School and Queen's Coll. Cambridge; jr. man. positions in Unilever, Shell Chemicals and Berger, Jenson and Nicholson 1959-64; consultant, McKinsey & Co., London and Chicago 1964-71; Dir. Gallaher Ltd. 1971-77; Man. Dir. Post Office Telecommunications 1978-81; Deputy Chair. British Telecom 1981-83; Chair. European Practice, Nolan, Norton & Co. 1984-87; Dir. Singer & Friedlander Ltd. 1983-, Tandata Holdings PLC. 1983-, Turing Inst. 1985-; Dir. Gen. British Inst. of Man. 1987-. *Leisure interests:* reading, fishing, golf. *Address:* Northgate House, Highgate Hill, London, N6 5HD, England. *Telephone:* 01-341 1133.

BENTOV, Mordechai; Israeli journalist and politician; b. 28 March 1900, Warsaw, Poland; s. of Joseph and Helen Bentov; m. Zipora Redlich 1926; two d.; ed. Inst. of Technology, Warsaw Univ. and Jerusalem Law Classes; settled in Palestine 1920; Founder and Chief Ed. Al Hamishvar 1943-48 and 1949-55; signed Declaration of Independence of Israel 1948; mem. Knesset 1949-; Minister of Labour and Reconstruction, Provisional Govt. 1948-49; Minister of Devt. 1955-61; mem. Jewish Agency Del. to UN, Lake Success 1947; Del. to Zionist Congresses, Round Table Conf. London 1939, World Jewish Congress, U.S.A. 1944, Geneva 1953; mem. Secr. United Workers Party (MAPAM); Chair. Econ. Affairs Cttee. of the Knesset 1951-55; Minister of Housing 1966-70; mem. World Exec. Hashomer Hatzair, Exec. Histadrut and Zionist Action Cttee.; mem. Exec.

World Jewish Congress. *Publications:* The Case for Bi-National Palestine 1946, Israel's Economy at the Crossroads 1965, Israel, the Palestinians and the Left 1971, Bentov's Report on Policy for Diminishing Social and Economic Gaps 1974, The End to Social Immobilism 1981, Memoirs 1983. *Leisure interests:* photography, filming. *Address:* Kibbutz Mishmar Haemek 19236, Israel. *Telephone:* 04-994162.

BENTSEN, Lloyd Millard, Jr., LL.B.; American politician; b. 11 Feb. 1921, Mission, Tex.; s. of the late Lloyd M. Bentsen and of Edna Ruth (Colbath) Bentsen; m. Beryl A. Longino 1943; two s. one d.; ed. Univ. of Texas, Austin; served U.S. Army 1942-45; County Judge, Hidalgo County, Tex. 1946-48; mem. House of Reps. 1948-54; Pres. Lincoln Consolidated, Houston, until 1970; U.S. Senator from Tex. 1971-; cand. for U.S. Vice-Pres. (with Michael Dukakis, q.v.) in 1988 presidential election; Chair. Finance Sub-Cttee. on Private Pensions, Public Works Sub-Cttee. on Transportation, Jt. Econ. Sub-Cttee. on Econ. Growth; mem. Senate Finance Cttee., Chair. 1988-, Senate Environment and Public Works Cttee., Jt. Econ. Cttee.; Distinguished Flying Cross; Air Medal with Three Oak Leaf Clusters; Democrat. *Address:* Office of the Senate Care of Postmaster, Washington, D.C. 20515; 4026 Federal Building, 515 Rusk Street, Houston, Tex. 77002; 912 Federal Building, Austin, Tex. 78701, U.S.A.

BENTZON, Niels Viggo; Danish composer; b. 24 Aug. 1919; s. of the late Viggo and Karen Emma (née Hartmann) Bentzon; ed. Danish Royal Conservatory; musical works: thirteen symphonies, six piano concertos, opera: Faust, choral works, five ballets, concertos for flute and harmonica, pieces for chamber orchestra, string quartet and piano. *Address:* Egernvej 39, 2000 Copenhagen, Denmark.

BENYA, Anton; Austrian trade union official: b. 1912; ed. occupational school; electromechanic, shop steward; mem. Exec. Cttee. Metal Workers and Miners Union 1948, Chair. 1962-77; Sec. Austrian Trade Union Fed. 1948, Vice-Pres. 1959, Pres. 1963-87; M.P. 1956-87; Pres. Nationalrat 1971-87. *Address:* Elisabethallee 83, 1130 Vienna XIII, Austria.

BENZER, Seymour, PH.D.; American biologist; b. 15 Oct. 1921, New York; s. of Mayer Benzer and Eva Naidorf; m. 1st Dorothy Vlosky 1942 (died 1978), two c.; m. 2nd Carol Miller 1980, one c.; ed. Brooklyn Coll. and Purdue Univ.; Asst. Prof. of Physics Purdue Univ. 1947-53, Assoc. Prof. of Biophysics 1953-58, Prof. 1958-61, Stuart Distinguished Prof. 1961-67; Biophysicist Oak Ridge Nat. Laboratory 1948-49; Research Fellow Calif. Inst. of Technology 1949-51, Visiting Assoc. 1965-67, Prof. of Biology 1967-75, Boswell Prof. of Neuroscience 1975-; Fulbright Research Scholar, Pasteur Inst., Paris 1951-52; Senior Nat. Science Foundation Research Fellow Cambridge 1957-58; Fellow, American Asscn. for the Advancement of Science; mem. N.A.S., Harvey Soc., Biophysical Soc., American Acad. of Arts and Sciences, American Philosophical Soc., Foreign mem. Royal Soc. London; awards include Sigma Xi Research Award 1957, Ricketts Award, Univ. of Chicago, Lasker Award 1971, Prix Charles-Leopold Mayer, French Acad. of Sciences 1975; Harvey Prize, Technion, Israel 1977; Warren Triennial Prize, Mass. General Hosp. 1977; Dickson Prize, Carnegie-Mellon Univ. 1978; Nat. Medal of Science (U.S.A.) 1983; Rosenstiel Award, Brandeis Univ. 1986; T. H. Morgan Medal, Genetics Soc. of America 1986; Lashley Award, American Philosophical Soc. 1988; Dr. h.c. (Purdue) 1968, (Columbia) 1974, (Yale) 1977, (Brandeis) 1978, (City Univ. of New York) 1978, (Univ. of Paris) 1983. *Publications:* The Elementary Units of Heredity 1957, Induction of Specific Mutations with 5-bromouracil 1958, Topology of the Genetic Fine Structure 1959, Topography of the Genetic Fine Structure 1961, A Change from Nonsense to Sense in the Genetic Code 1962, On the Role of Soluble Ribonucleic Acid in Coding for Amino Acids 1962, A Physical Basis for Degeneracy in the Genetic Code 1962, Adventures in the rII Region 1966, Isolation of Behavioral Mutants of Drosophila by countercurrent Distribution 1967, Genetic Dissection of the Drosophila Nervous System by means of Mosaics 1970, Mapping of Behavior in Drosophila Mosaics 1972, Genetic Dissection of Behavior 1973, Dunce, a Mutant of Drosophila Deficient in Learning 1976, Monoclonal Antibodies against the Drosophila Nervous System 1982, Antigenic Cross-Reaction between Drosophila and Human Brain 1983, Neuronal Development in the Drosophila Retina, Monoclonal Antibodies as Molecular Probes 1984, from Monoclonal Antibody to Gene for a Neuron-Specific Glycoprotein in Drosophila 1985. *Address:* Division of Biology, California Institute of Technology, Pasadena, Calif. 91125 (Office); 2075 Robin Road, San Marino, Calif. 91108, U.S.A. (Home). *Telephone:* (213) 356-4963 (Office).

BENZI, Roberto; Italian/French conductor; b. 12 Dec. 1937, Marseille; s. of Giuseppe Benzi and Maria Pastorino; m. Jane Rhodes 1968; studied conducting with Andre Cluytens; début as conductor, Bayenne, France 1948; tours in Europe and S. America 1949-52; opera conducting debut 1954; conducted Carmen, Paris Opera 1959; guest conductor Europe, Japan, U.S.A. and main music festivals; Music Dir. Bordeaux-Aquitaine Orchestra 1973-87; Chevalier, Légion d'honneur, Ordre National du Mérite and des Palmes Académiques. *Publications:* orchestrations of Brahms op. 23 Schumann Variations 1970, Brahms op. 24 Variations and Fugue on a theme by Handel 1973, Rossini Thème et Variations 1978, Erik Satie Je te veux, valse 1987. *Leisure interests:* wildlife, astronomy, cycling. *Address:* 12 Villa Sainte Foy, 92200 Neuilly-sur-Seine, France. *Telephone:* 46.24.27.85.

BÉRARD, Armand; French diplomatist; b. 2 May 1904; s. of Victor Bérard and Alice Colin; m. Isabelle de Savignac 1945; two d.; ed. Ecole Normale Supérieure, Paris, Heidelberg Univ., and French School for Advanced Spanish Studies, Madrid; served Berlin 1931, Office of Under-Sec., Foreign Affairs 1936, Office of Foreign Minister 1936-37, Washington 1938, Rome (Quirinal) 1939; mem. French Del. to Armistice Comm. Wiesbaden 1940-42; mem. Underground Foreign Affairs Study Bureau 1942; escaped to Algiers 1944; Minister-Counsellor, Wash. 1945; Deputy High Commr. in Germany 1949; Diplomatic Adviser to Prime Minister 1955; Amb. to Japan 1956-59; Perm. Rep. to UN 1959-62; Amb. to Italy 1962-67; Perm. Rep. to UN 1967-70; Gov. Fondation européenne de la Culture; mem. Comm. des archives diplomatiques 1975-, Fondation pour le développement culturel Japonais en France; Grand Officer, Légion d'honneur. *Publications:* L'Allemagne et la réorganisation de l'Europe 1944, Au temps du danger Allemand 1976, Washington et Bonn 1978, L'ONU Oui ou Non 1979, Une ambassade au Japon 1981, Cinq années au palais Farnèse 1982. *Address:* 25 rue du Bois de Boulogne, 92200 Neuilly-sur-Seine, France. *Telephone:* 46-24-35-44.

BERARD, Maurice Robert Georges; French banker; b. 17 March 1891, Paris; s. of Philippe Berard; m. Yolande de Loys-Chandieu 1918 (deceased); two s. (deceased), one d.; ed. Paris Univ.; Hon. Pres. Bank of Syria and Lebanon; Hon. Pres. Friends of Nat. Museum of Modern Art; Vice-Pres. Friends of the Louvre; Hon. Pres. Asscn. Léonard de Vinci; Gold Medal Aero Club of America and Aero Club of France; Officier Légion d'honneur; Croix de guerre 1914-18; D.C.M.; Mérite agricole. *Publications:* Renoir à Wargemont, Une Famille du Dauphiné. *Leisure interests:* art, archaeology, agriculture. *Address:* 7 rue Alfred Dehodencq, 75016 Paris, France. *Telephone:* 520.16.94.

BERAS ROJAS, H.E. Cardinal Octavio Antonio; Dominican ecclesiastic; b. 16 Nov. 1906, El Sybo; s. of Octavio Beras and Teresa Rojas; ed. Colegio de Santo Tomás, Seminario de Santo Tomás, Colegio Pío Latino-americano, Rome and Gregorian Univ., Rome; f. Accíon Católica, Santiago de los Cab. 1933; Sec.-Gen. Archdiocese of Santo Domingo 1935; Dir. Seminario Verdad Católica and Dir. Emisora Católica; Pres. Ecclesiastical Tribunal, Organizer of Synod; Auxiliary Archbishop of Santo Domingo cum iure successionis 1945; Metropolitan Archbishop of Santo Domingo and Primate of the West Indies 1961-81; Sec.-Gen. First Conf. of Latin-American Episcopate 1955; Pres. Dominican Episcopal Conf. 1963-75; cr. Cardinal 1976; Dr. h.c. (Santo Domingo and Univ. Catolica "Madre y Maestra"). *Leisure interests:* camping, nature. *Address:* c/o Arzobispade, Cayetano Rodríguez 22, Santo Domingo, Dominican Republic. *Telephone:* 685-3141.

BERCOT, Pierre, D. EN D.; French businessman; b. 12 July 1903, Paris; m. Vivaldine Pinchon 1938; three c.; ed. Lycée Henri IV, Faculté de Droit, Paris, Ecole Nationale des Langues Orientales; Pres., Gen. Man. Soc. Anonyme André Citroën (Citroën, S.A. since 1968) 1958-70, Hon. Pres. 1971-76; Pres. Comobil, S.A., Geneva 1966-79; Hon. Pres. Comotor, S.A., Luxembourg 1967-78. *Leisure interests:* music, yachting. *Address:* 24 bis Parc de Montretout, 92210 Saint-Cloud, France.

BERECZ, Frigyes; Hungarian politician; b. 1933, Budapest; apprentice school; joined the army 1949; joined the HSWP 1962, mem. Cent. Cttee 1980; electrical engineer; started as electrician, later worked consecutively as works man., dept. leader and Dir. in Beloiannis Telecommunications Works, post of Gen. Man. 1981; Vice-Premier of Council of Ministers 1987; Minister of Industry 1987-. *Address:* Ministry of Industry, 1024 Budapest, Martirok utja 85, Hungary. *Telephone:* 326-570.

BERECZ, János, PH.D.; Hungarian politician and historian; b. 18 Sept. 1930, Ibrány; three c.; ed. Lenin Inst., Budapest, Acad. of Social Sciences, Moscow; departmental head Communist Youth League 1955-63; postgrad. researcher Acad. of Social Sciences, Moscow 1963-66; Sec. party Cttee. Ministry of Foreign Affairs 1966-72; Deputy Leader 1972-74, head Foreign Dept. HSWP Cen. Cttee. 1974-82; Ed.-in-Chief of daily Népszabadság 1982-85; Sec. HSWP Cen. Cttee. 1985-; head Agitation and Propaganda Bd. attached to HSWP Cen. Cttee. 1985-; M.P. 1985-; mem. Political Cttee. HSWP 1987-; Pres. Foreign Affairs Section Soc. for Political Sciences 1982-86; Hon. Prof. Karl Marx Univ. of Econ., Budapest 1983. *Publications:* Ellenforradalom tollal és fegyverrel (Counter-revolution with Pen and Arms) 1969, Baráti szövetségben (In fraternal Alliance) 1972, 1986, A szociáldemokrácia és a nemzetközi kommunista mozgalom (Social Democracy and the International Communist Movement) 1978, Harc és együttműködés (Struggle and Cooperation) 1979, Vitáink és egységünk (Debates and Unity) 1981, Kihívások, válaszok (Challenges, Replies) 1983, Folyamatosság és megujulás az MSZMP politikájában (Continuity and Renewal in the HSWP Policy) 1985. *Address:* Hungarian Socialist Workers Party Central Committee, 1358 Budapest, Széchenyi rakpart 19, Hungary. *Telephone:* 111-400.

BEREGOVOY, Georgiy Timofeyevich; Soviet cosmonaut; b. 15 April 1921, Fedorovka, Poltava Dist.; ed. Mil. Aviation School, Lugansk, and Mil. Flying Acad.; pilot; cosmonaut 1964-; Maj.-Gen. in Soviet Air Force 1968-; earth orbit in 'Soyuz 3', 1968, and several manoeuvres, including two rendezvous with 'Soyuz 2'; Order of Lenin (twice), Order of Red Banner (twice), Order of Alexander Nevsky, Order of Red Star (twice) and many others.

BÉRÉGOVOY, Pierre Eugene; French politician; b. 23 Dec. 1925, Déville-les-Rouen; s. of Adrien and Irène (née Baudelin) Bérégovoy; m. Gilberte Bonnet 1948; one s. two d.; ed. Ecole primaire supérieure, Elbeuf, Inst. du travail, Faculté de droit, Strasbourg; Head of Sub-div., then Asst. to Dir. Société pour le développement de l'industrie du gaz (S.D.I.G.); Chargé de mission, Gaz de France 1978-81; mem. Econ. and Social Council 1979-81; Sec.-Gen. to Presidency 1981-82, Minister of Social Affairs and Nat. Solidarity 1982-84, of Economy, Finance and Budget 1984-86,of State for Economy, Finance and the Budget May 1988-; founder-mem. Parti Socialist Autonome 1958; Socialist deputy 1986-88; Maire de la Nièvre 1983-; mem. Secr. Parti Socialiste Unifié 1963-67; mem. Man. Cttee. and Exec. Bd. Parti Socialiste 1969, Nat. Sec. for Social Affairs 1973-75, in charge of Foreign Affairs 1975-81; responsible for party to Liaison Cttee. of the Left; f. club, Socialisme moderne 1967. *Leisure interests:* rural antiquities, football, cycling, cross-country running. *Address:* Ministry of Economy, Finance and the Budget, 246 blvd. St.-Germain, 75700 Paris; Mairie, 58000 Nevers; 69 rue de Varenne, 75007 Paris, France (Home).

BERENBLUM, Isaac, M.D., M.SC.; Israeli pathologist and experimental biologist; b. 26 Aug. 1903, Bialystok, Poland; s. of Paul and Michle Berenblum; m. Doris L. Bernstein 1928; two d.; ed. Bristol Grammar School and Leeds Univ.; Riley-Smith Research Fellow, Dept. Experimental Pathology and Cancer Research, Leeds Univ. Medical School 1927-36; Beit Memorial Research Fellow, Dunn School of Pathology, Oxford Univ. 1936-40; Departmental and Univ. Demonstrator in Pathology, Oxford Univ. 1940-48; in charge of Oxford Univ. Research Centre of British Empire Cancer Campaign 1940-48; Special Research Fellow, Nat. Cancer Inst., Bethesda, Md., U.S.A. 1948-50; Visiting Prof. of Oncology, Hebrew Univ., Jerusalem 1951-57; Jack Cotton Prof. of Cancer Research, Head of Dept. of Experimental Biology, The Weizmann Inst. of Science, Rehovot, Israel 1950-71, Emeritus Prof. 1971-; Scholar-in-Residence, Fogarty Int. Center, Nat. Inst. of Health, Bethesda, Md. 1971; Hon. Life mem. New York Acad. of Sciences 1958, American Assen. for Cancer Research, European Assen. for Cancer Research, mem. Israel Nat. Acad. Sciences and Humanities, World Acad. Arts and Sciences; Israel Prize for Biology 1975, Bertner Award and Medal for Cancer Research (Univ. of Texas) 1978, Sloan Award and Medal, Gen. Motors Cancer Research Foundation, Washington, D.C. 1980. *Publications:* Science versus Cancer 1946, Man against Cancer 1952, Cancer Research Today 1967, Carcinogenesis as a Biological Problem 1974. *Leisure interests:* chess, writing, listening to music. *Address:* Weizmann Institute of Science, Rehovot, Israel. *Telephone:* (08) 483511.

BEREND, T. Iván; Hungarian economic historian; b. 11 Dec. 1930, Budapest; s. of Mihály Berend and Elvira Gellei; m. Rózsa Berger 1953; two d.; ed. Univ. of Economy and Univ. of Sciences, Budapest; Asst. lecturer, Karl Marx Univ. of Economy 1953, sr. lecturer 1960, Prof. of Econ. History 1964-, Head of Dept. 1967, Rector 1973-79; Gen. Sec. Hungarian Historical Soc. 1966-72, Pres. 1975-79; mem. H.S.W.P. Cen. Cttee.; Corresp. mem. Hungarian Acad. of Sciences 1973-79, mem. 1979-85, Pres. 1985-; Fellowship, Ford Foundation, New York 1966-67; Visiting Fellow, St. Antony's Coll., Oxford 1972-73; Visiting Prof. Univ. of Calif., Berkeley 1978; Visiting Fellow, All Souls Coll., Oxford 1980; Fellow, Woodrow Wilson Int. Center for Scholars, Washington 1982-83; Co-Chair. Bd. of Dirs. Inst. for E.-W. Security Studies; mem. Int. Fed. of Social Sciences (IFSO); mem. Exec. Cttee. of Int. Econ. Soc. 1982-86, Vice-Pres. 1986-; Corresp. mem. Royal Historical Soc. 1981; Kossuth Prize 1961, State Prize 1985. *Publications:* (with György Ránki): Magyarország gyáripara 1900-1914 1955, Magyarország gyáripara a II. világháboru előtt és a háboru időszakában 1933-1944 1958, Magyarország a fasiszta Németország "életerében" 1960, Magyarország gazdasága az I. világháboru után 1919-1929 1966, Economic Development in East-Central Europe in the 19th and 20th Centuries 1974, Hungary—A Century of Economic Development, Underdevelopment and Economic Growth, The European Periphery and Industrialization 1780-1914 1982, The Hungarian Economy in the Twentieth Century 1985, The European Economy in the Nineteenth Century 1987; (as sole author): Ujjáépités és a nagytőke elleni harc Magyarországon 1945-1948 1962, Gazdaságpolitika az első ötéves terv megindításáor 1948-1950 1964, Öt előadás gazdaságról és oktatásról 1978, Napjaink a történelemben 1980, Válságos évtizedek 1982, Gazdasági utkeresés 1983, The Crisis Zone of Europe 1986, Szocializmus és reform 1986. *Address:* Hungarian Academy of Sciences, 1361 Budapest, Roosevelt tér 9, Hungary. *Telephone:* 327-176.

BERENDONCK, Gerd; German diplomatist; b. 5 March 1924, Solingen; s. of Gerhard Hubert and Regina (née Rauh) Berendonck; m. Friedel Darius 1953; two d.; ed. schools in Untrecht, Solingen, Baden and Vienna and Univs. of Passau, Bonn and Regensburg; Lieut. German Navy 1942-46; joined foreign service 1952; served Bogotá 1954-56, Bangkok 1956-61, Beijing 1975-77, Moscow 1977-80; Ministry of Foreign Affairs, Bonn 1962-64, 1969-75; Amb. to Cambodia 1964-69, to Algeria 1980-84, to Pakistan 1984-89. *Address:* Steinweg 1, D-5307 Wachtberg-Villip, Federal Republic of Germany.

BÉRENGER, Paul Raymond, B.A.; Mauritian politician; b. 26 March 1945, Quatre Bornes; m. Arline Perrier 1971; one s. one d.; ed. Collège du Saint Esprit, Univ. of Wales and Sorbonne, Paris; Gen. Sec. Mouvement Militant Mauricien 1969-82; Minister of Finance 1982-83, M.P. 1982-83; Gov. IMF,

African Devt. Bank/African Devt. Fund. *Leisure interests:* reading, swimming. *Address:* Wellington Street, Quatre Bornes, Mauritius (Home). *Telephone:* 54-1998 (Home).

BERESFORD, Bruce; Australian film director; b. 16 Aug 1940, Sydney; s. of Leslie Beresford and Lona Beresford; m. Rhoisin Beresford 1965; two s. one d.; ed. Univ. of Sydney; worked in advertising; worked for Australian Broadcasting Comm.; went to England 1961; odd jobs including teaching; film ed. Nigeria 1964-66; Sec. to British Film Inst.'s Production Bd. 1966; feature film dir. 1971-; directed many short films 1960-75. *Directed feature films:* The Adventures of Barry Mackenzie 1972, Barry Mackenzie Holds His Own 1974, Side by Side 1975, Don's Party 1976, The Getting of Wisdom 1977, Money Movers 1979, Breaker Morant 1980, Puberty Blues 1981, The Club 1981, Tender Mercies 1983, King David 1984, Crimes of the Heart 1986, Fringe Dwellers 1986, Aria (segment) 1987, Her Alibi 1988. *Address:* c/o William Morris, 31 Soho Square, London, W.1, England.

BERESFORD, Dennis Robert, B.S., C.P.A.; American accountant; b. 23 Nov. 1938, Los Angeles; s. of Robert Melvin Beresford and Florence Elaine (Smith) Beresford; m. Marian Sweeny 1961; one s. one d.; ed. Univ. of Southern California, Los Angeles; joined L.A. office of Ernst & Whinney 1961, Nat. Office, Cleveland 1971, partner and Nat. Dir. of Accounting Standards 1972-86; Chair. Financial Accounting Standards Bd. 1987-; mem. Bd. of Advisers, Univ. of Southern Calif. School of Accounting 1980-, Exec. Cttee. SEC and Financial Reporting Inst. 1982-, Editorial Bd. American Accounting Assen.'s Accounting Horizons 1986-; Price Waterhouse Award for Outstanding Graduate at Univ. of Southern Calif. 1961; Outstanding Article Award of Journal of Accountancy. *Publication:* Accounting for Income Taxes (research study) 1983. *Leisure interests:* golf, reading. *Address:* Financial Accounting Standards Board, 401 Merritt Seven, Norwalk, Conn. 06851 (Office); 15 Heather Drive, Stamford, Conn. 06903, U.S.A. (Home).

BERESFORD, Meg, B.A.; British campaign organiser; b. 5 Sept. 1937, Birmingham; d. of John Tristram Beresford and Anne Isobel Northcroft (née Stuart Wortley); two s.; ed. Sherborne School for Girls, Dorset and Univ. of Warwick; Founder mem. and Co-ordinator, Campaign Atom, Oxford 1980-81; elected to Nat. Council Campaign for Nuclear Disarmament (CND) 1980; Organising Sec. European Nuclear Disarmament 1981-83; Vice-Chair. CND 1983-85, Gen. Sec. 1985-. *Leisure interests:* walking, the environment, reading and art. *Address:* Campaign for Nuclear Disarmament, 22-24 Underwood Street, London, N1 7JG (Office); 48 Stratford Street, Oxford, England. *Telephone:* 01-250 4010 (Office); (0865) 247429.

BERETTA, David; American chemical engineer; b. 16 July 1928, Cranston, R.I.; m. Serena Shuebruk; two s. one d.; ed. Univ. of Rhode Island, Rhode Island Coll. and Univ. of Connecticut; with Fram Corpn. of E. Providence 1949-51; service with U.S. Army Chemical Corps, Korean War; joined Chemical Div., Uniroyal Inc. 1953, Factory Man. Naugatuck Plant 1965, Vice-Pres. Chemical Operations, Uniroyal Ltd., Canada 1966, Vice-Pres. Marketing 1968-70, Pres. Uniroyal Chemical 1970, Group Vice-Pres. 1972-73, Dir. 1974-, C.O.O. 1974, Chair. 1974-82, C.E.O. 1974-81, Pres. 1974-77; Pres. Executive Consultants Inc. 1983-; fmr. Dir., Chair., Chief Exec., Rubber Mfrs. Assen.; mem. American Inst. of Chemical Engs., Rhode Island Professional Engs., Business Advisory Council, Rhode Island Univ. Coll. of Business Admin.; Trustee Cttee. for Economic Devt. *Address:* c/o American Institute of Chemical Engineers, 345 East 47th Street, New York, N.Y. 10017, U.S.A.

BERG, Adrian, M.A., A.R.C.A.; British artist; b. 12 March 1929, London; s. of Charles Berg and Sarah (née Sarby) Berg; ed. Charterhouse, Gonville and Caius Coll., Cambridge, Trinity Coll. Dublin, St. Martin's and Chelsea Schools of Art and Royal Coll. of Art; one-man exhbns. in London, Florence, Düsseldorf, Montreal, Toronto and Chicago since 1964; Arts Council Serpentine Gallery, Paintings 1977-86; several prizes including Gold Medal, Florence Biennale 1973, Maj. Prize, Tolly Cobbold Eastern Arts Assen. Exhbn. 1981 and Third Prize, John Moores Liverpool Exhbn. 1982-83, Nat. Trust Foundation for Art Award 1987. *Address:* The Picadilly Gallery, 16 Cork Street, London, W1X 1PF, England.

BERG, Bernard; Luxembourg politician; b. 14 Sept. 1931, Dudelange; m. Christine Schaffner 1957; one s.; ed. State Industrial School, Labour High School; Sec. of Labour Del. of Arbed steel works at Dudelange; then Vice-Chair. Cen. Labour Del. of Arbed Steel Corpn; then Chair. of Cen. Labour Del. of Arbed Corpn. and Chair. of Labour Del. of Arbed works at Dudelange; mem. Cen. Cttee. of Luxembourg Workers' Trade Union, later Vice-Chair., then Chair.; mem. Council of Gen. Confed. of Labour; mem. Chamber of Deputies 1968-74; Minister of Labour and Social Security, also of Family, Housing and Social Welfare 1974-79, Vice-Pres. of Govt. (Deputy Prime Minister) 1976-79; Deputy Chair. Parl. Group 1979-84; Minister of Health and Social Security June 1984-; Socialist. *Address:* Ministry of Social Security, 26, rue Zithe, 2763 Luxembourg. *Telephone:* (49) 92-11.

BERG, Christian, D.PHIL.; Danish professor of mathematics; b. 2 June 1944, Haarslev; m. Margrete Vergmann 1967; one s. one d.; ed. Univ. of Copenhagen; Assoc. Prof., Univ. of Copenhagen 1972, Prof. of Math. 1978-; mem. Danish Natural Sciences Research Council 1985, Royal Danish Acad.

of Sciences and Letters 1982; Gold Medal Univ. of Copenhagen 1970. *Publications:* Research monographs: Potential theory on locally compact abelian groups (with Forst) 1975, Harmonic Analysis on Semigroups (with Maserick and Christensen) 1984, numerous papers on potential theory. *Address:* Department of Mathematics, Universitetsparken 5, 2100 Copenhagen Ø, Denmark. *Telephone:* (01) 353133.

BERG, Eivinn; Norwegian diplomatist; b. 31 July 1931, Sandefjord; s. of Morten Berg and Ester Christoffersen; m. Unni Berg 1957; one s. two d.; ed. Norwegian Coll. of Econs. and Business Admin., Bergen, Norway; entered Foreign Service 1957; Attaché and Vice-Consul, Chicago 1957–60; Ministry of Foreign Affairs 1960–63, 1968–70; First Sec. Norwegian Perm. Del. to EFTA/GATT, UN Office, Geneva 1963–66, Head of Dept., EFTA 1966–68; Counsellor of Embassy, Brussels, and Norway's Mission to EEC 1970–73; Dir. Int. Affairs Norwegian Shipowners Asscn., Oslo 1973–78; Deputy Dir.-Gen. Ministry of Foreign Affairs (Dept. of External Econ. Affairs) 1978–80, Dir.-Gen. 1980–81, State Sec. 1984–88; Amb. and Perm. Rep. of Norway to NATO 1984–88, to EEC 1989–; Commdr., Order of the Crown, Belgium 1974, Commdr., Henrique Infante, Portugal 1980, Caballero Gran Cruz al Merite Civil, Spain 1982, Grand Lion Order of the Lion, Finland 1983, Grand Officier, Order Nat. du Mérite, France 1984, Commdr., Royal Order of St. Olav, Norway 1987. *Leisure interests:* tennis, golf, sailing, painting. *Address:* Permanent Mission of Norway to the European Communities, Rue Archimède 17, 1040 Brussels (Office); Avenue Jules César, 1150 Brussels, Belgium (Home).

BERG, Knut, M.A., D.PHIL.; Norwegian art historian; b. 4 Aug. 1925, Oslo; s. of Arno and Signe (née Mowinckel-Larsen) Berg; m. Marcia W. Robinson 1953; two s. one d.; ed. Univ. of Oslo; research scholar, Univ. of Oslo 1953–65; curator, Dept. of Prints and Drawings, Nasjonalgalleriet 1965–73, Dir. Nasjonalgalleriet 1973–; mem. Norwegian Acad. of Science and the Humanities, Norwegian Cultural Council; Chair. State Cttee. for Cultural Exchanges with Foreign Countries 1981, Soc. for Benefit of City of Oslo 1980; mem. numerous other bds. and cttees.; Hon. mem. Norwegian Soc. of Art Historians. *Publications:* Studies in Tuscan Twelfth Century Illumination 1968, King Magnus Haakonson's Laws of Norway 1983; ed. History of Norwegian Art (Vol. 1–7) 1981–83, Dictionary of Norwegian Artists 1981–86. *Address:* Nasjonalgalleriet, Universitetsgaten 13, Oslo 1; Haakon den Godes vei 18, Norway. *Telephone:* 14 28 04.

BERG, Paul, B.S., PH.D.; American biochemist; b. 30 June 1926, New York; s. of Harry Berg and Sarah Brodsky; m. Mildred Levy 1947; one s.; ed. Pennsylvania State Univ. and Western Reserve Univ.; Postdoctoral Fellow, Copenhagen Univ., Denmark 1952–53; Postdoctoral Fellow, Wash. Univ., St. Louis, Mo. 1953–54, Scholar in Cancer Research 1954–57, Asst. to Assoc. Prof. of Microbiology 1955–59; Prof. of Biochemistry, Stanford Univ. School of Medicine, Stanford, Calif. 1959–, Chair Dept. of Biochemistry 1969–74, Dir. Center for Molecular and Genetic Medicine 1984–; Sr. Post-Doctoral Fellow of Material Science Foundation 1961–68; Pres. American Soc. of Biological Chemists 1975–76; mem. N.A.S. 1966–; Eli Lilly Prize in Biochemistry 1959, Calif. Scientist of the Year 1963, V. D. Mattia Award 1972, shared Nobel Prize for Chem. 1980, Nat. Medal of Science. *Publications:* 70 publs. in fields of biochemistry and microbiology. *Leisure interests:* travel, art, and sports. *Address:* Stanford University School of Medicine, 838 Santa Fé Avenue, Stanford, Calif. 94305, U.S.A. (Office). *Telephone:* (415) 723-6170 (Office).

BERGANZA, Teresa; Spanish mezzo-soprano singer; b. 16 March 1935, Madrid; d. of Guillermo and Ascension Berganza; m. Felix Lavilla 1957; one s. two d; debut in Aix-en-Provence 1957, in England, Glyndebourne 1958; has sung at La Scala, Milan, Opera Roma, Metropolitan, New York, Chicago Opera House, San Francisco Opera, Covent Garden, etc.; has appeared at festivals in Edinburgh, Holland, Glyndebourne; concerts in France, Belgium, Holland, Italy, Germany, Spain, Austria, Portugal, Scandinavia, Israel, Mexico, Buenos Aires, U.S.A., Canada, etc.; appeared as Rosina in Il Barbiere di Siviglia, Covent Garden 1967; Premio Lucrezia Arana; Premio extraordinario del Conservatorio de Madrid; Grande Cruz, Isabel la Católica; Harriet Cohen Award; Commdr., Ordre des Arts et des Lettres. *Film:* Don Giovanni. *Publication:* Flor de Soledad y Silencio 1984. *Leisure interests:* art, music, reading. *Address:* c/o Lies Askonas, 19A Air Street, Regent Street, London, W.1, England; San Lorenzo del Escorial, Madrid; Cafeto No. 5, Madrid 7, Spain. *Telephone:* 01-734 5459 (London); 251 30 27 (Madrid).

BERGE, Gunnar; Norwegian politician; b. 29 Aug. 1940, Etne; m.; sheet metal worker; mem. Stavanger City Council 1963–67; Chair. Rogaland Co. AUF (Norwegian Labour Youth League) 1965–66; mem. Storting 1969, Chair. Standing Cttee. on Finance 1978–81, Vice-Chair. 1981–; Minister of Finance May 1986–; fmr. Vice-Pres. of Lagting. *Address:* Ministry of Finance, P.O. Box 8008, Dep., 0030 Oslo 1, Norway. *Telephone:* (2) 11-90-90.

BERGÉ, Pierre Vital Georges; French business executive; b. 14 Nov. 1930, l'Ile d'Oléron; s. of Pierre Bergé and Christiane (née Sicard) Bergé; ed. Lycée Eugène-Fromentin, La Rochelle; Dir. and Ed.-in-Chief la Patrie mondiale 1949–61; f. and Dir.-Gen. Yves Saint Laurent 1961–, Pres. 1971–; Pres. Yves Saint Laurent of America Inc., New York 1971–; Chair. Asscn. of Theatres of the Paris Opera Sept. 1988–; Pres. Chambre syndicale du prêt-à-porter des couturiers et des créateurs de mode 1974–; Dir. Lundis musicaux de l'Athénée 1977–; Admin. Cttee. for the Devt. and Promotion of Textile and Design, Fondation Cartier Parsons School of Design 1985–; Pres. Inst. français de la mode 1985–; Chevalier Légion d'honneur. *Publications:* Bernard Buffet 1957, studies on Pierre Mac-Orlan, Henry de Montherlant, Jean Anouilh, Francis Carco and Jean Giono. *Leisure interest:* modern art. *Address:* 5 avenue Marceau, 75116 Paris (Office); 55 rue de Babylone, 75007 Paris, France (Home).

BERGEN, Candice Patricia; American actress and photo-journalist; b. 19 May 1946, Beverly Hills; d. of Edgar and Frances (née Westerman) Bergen; m. Louis Malle (q.v.) 1980; one d.; ed. Westlake School for Girls, Univ. of Pa.; *Films include:* The Group 1966, The Sand Pebbles 1966, The Day the Fish Came Out 1967, Vivre Pour Vivre 1967, The Magus 1968, Getting Straight 1970, Soldier Blue 1970, The Adventurers 1970, Carnal Knowledge 1971, The Hunting Party 1971, T. R. Baskin 1972, 11 Harrowhouse 1974, Bite the Bullet 1975, The Wind and the Lion 1976, The Domino Principle 1977, A Night Full of Rain 1977, Oliver's Story, 1978, Starting Over 1979, Rich and Famous 1981, Gandhi 1982, Stick 1985, Au Revoir les Enfants (co-Dir) 1987; photojournalist work has appeared in Vogue, Cosmopolitan, Life and Esquire. *Publications:* The Freezer, (in Best Short Plays of 1968), Knock Wood (autobiog.) 1984. *Address:* c/o William Morris Agency, 151 El Camino, Beverly Hills, Calif. 90212, U.S.A.

BERGEN, William Benjamin, B.S., AERO.E.; American aerospace engineer and business executive; b. 29 March 1915; s. of Oldfield and Hazel Bergen; m. 1st Gertrude Catherine Coxon 1943, 2nd Eleanor Mae Page 1968; one s. one d.; ed. Mass. Inst. of Technology; Glenn L. Martin Co., Baltimore, Md. (now Martin Co.) 1937–, Chief Engineer 1949–51, Vice-Pres. Engineering 1951–53, Exec. Vice-Pres. 1953–55, Pres. 1959; Rockwell Int. (fmrly. N. American Rockwell) Pres. Space Div. 1967–70, Pres. Aerospace Operations 1971–, Corporate Vice-Pres. Aerospace 1974–; Dir. Calif. State Chamber of Commerce; mem. S.A.E., Holland Soc.; Fellow A.I.A.A.; Lawrence Sperry Award 1943. *Leisure interests:* flying, golf, hunting, tennis. *Address:* c/o Aerospatiale, 37 boulevard de Montmorency, Paris 16e, France.

BERGENSTRÖM, Stig Gullmar, LL.D.; Swedish administrator; b. 3 Dec. 1909, Cannes, France; m. Hélène Renfer 1958; one s. one d. and six c. from previous marriages; ed. Univ. of Uppsala; judiciary service at Court of Justice 1934–37; Sec.-Gen. Group of the Swedish Employers' Confed. 1937, Asst. Dir. 1941, Vice-Dir. 1944, Dir. 1949–79; mem. Employers' Group of Governing Body of ILO 1950–79; Vice-Pres. Exec. Cttee. of Int. Org. of Employers 1952–62, Pres. Exec. Cttee. 1963–79, Hon. Pres. 1980–; Chair. Int. Council of Danish, Finnish, Norwegian and Swedish Employers' Confederations; Vice-Chair. Governing Body ILO 1969–79. *Leisure interests:* sailing, philately. *Address:* 26 Chemin Colladon, 1209 Geneva, Switzerland.

BERGER, John; British author and art critic; b. 5 Nov. 1926, London; s. of late S.J.D. Berger and Miriam Berger (née Branson); ed. Cen. School of Art and Chelsea School of Art, London; began career as painter and teacher of drawing; exhbns. at Wildenstein, Redfern and Leicester Galleries, London; Art Critic Tribune, New Statesman; numerous TV appearances including Monitor, two series for Granada; Scenario: La Salamandre (with Alain Tanner), Le Milieu du Monde, Jonas (New York Critics Prize for Best Scenario of Year 1976); George Orwell Memorial Prize 1977. *Publications:* fiction: A Painter of Our Time 1958, The Foot of Clive 1962, Corker's Freedom 1964, G (Booker Prize, James Tait Black Memorial Prize) 1972, Pig Earth 1979, Once in Europa 1987, theatre: Question of Geography (with Nella Bielski) 1984 (staged in Marseille, Paris and by R.S.C., Stratford); non-fiction: Marcel Frishman 1958, Permanent Red 1960, The Success and Failure of Picasso 1965, A Fortunate Man: the story of a country doctor (with J. Mohr) 1967, Art and Revolution, Moments of Cubism and Other Essays 1969, The Look of Things, Ways of Seeing 1972, The Seventh Man 1975 (Prize for Best Reportage, Union of Journalists and Writers, Paris 1977), About Looking 1980, Another Way of Telling (with J. Mohr) 1982, And Our Faces, My Heart, Brief as Photos 1984, The White Bird 1985 (U.S.A. as The Sense of Sight 1985); translations: (with A. Bostock): Poems on the Theatre by B. Brecht 1960, Return to My Native Land by Aime Cesaire 1969; (with Lisa Appignanesi): Oranges for the Son of Alexander Levy by Nella Bielski 1982. *Address:* Quincy, Mieussy, 74440 Taninges, France.

BERGER, Wilhelm Georg; Romanian composer and musicologist; b. 4 Dec. 1929, Rupea, Brașov; studied violin at Bucharest Conservatoire; member of Bucharest Philharmonic Orchestra 1948–58; mem. Composers' Union Quartet 1953–57; Sec. Romanian Composers' Union 1968–; "Prince Rainier III of Monaco" Prize, Monte Carlo, 1964, Concours international de composition d'oeuvres pour quatuor à cordes Prize, Liège, 1965, "Reine Elisabeth de Belgique" Int. Musical Contest Prize 1966, "George Enescu" Prize of Romanian Acad. 1966, Composers' Union Prize 1969. *Compositions:* Fourteen symphonies, numerous concerts for soloist instruments (violin, viola, cello, clarinet) and orchestra, lieder, chamber music (15 string quartets, sonatas, etc.). *Publications:* Studies: Moduri și proprtii; Structuri sonore si aspectele lor armonice (Modes and proportions; Sonorous structures and their harmonic aspects), articles and lectures; Ghid pentru muzica instrumentală de cameră (Guidebook for instrumental chamber music) 1965; Muzica simfonică (Baroque-Classical 1967, Romantic

1972, Modern 1974, Contemporary 1976); Quartetul de coarde de la Haydn la Debussy (The string quartet from Haydn to Debussy) 1970. *Address:* Uniunea Compozitorilor, Str. Constantin Exarcu 2, Bucharest, Romania. *Telephone:* 15 98 98.

BERGERON, André Louis; French printer and trade unionist; b. 1 Jan. 1922, Suarce; s. of Louis and Marie (née Voëlin) Bergeron; m. Georgette Monnier 1954; ed. Tech. Coll., Belfort; printer 1936–48; Sec.-Gen. of Typographical Union, Belfort 1946–47; Force-Ouvrière 1947–48, Perm. Sec. Belfort Area 1948; Sec.-Gen. Fédération Force Ouvrière du Livre 1948–50; Regional Del. Force Ouvrière and mem. Exec. Cttee. 1950–56, mem. Bureau de la Confédération 1956–63, Sec.-Gen. Force Ouvrière 1963–; Pres. admin. council régime nat. d'assurance chômage 1958–86, Vice-Pres. 1986–. *Publications:* Lettre ouverte á un syndiqué 1975, Ma route et mes combats 1976, Quinze cents jours 1984. *Address:* Force Ouvrière, 198 avenue du Maine, 75014 Paris (Office); 14 rue du Stade-Buffalo, 92120 Montrouge, France (Home). *Telephone:* 539-22-03 (Office).

BERGERSEN, Fraser John, M.SC., D.SC., F.R.S., F.A.A.; Australian research scientist; b. 26 May 1929, New Zealand; s. of Victor E. and Arabel H. (Young) Bergersen; m. Gladys I. Heather 1952; two s. one d.; ed. Hamilton High School, New Zealand, Univs. of Otago and New Zealand; Assoc., Bacteriology Dept., Univ. of Otago 1952–54; Div. of Plant Industry, CSIRO 1954–, Chief Research Scientist 1972–; Australian Acad. of Science Council 1987–; Foreign Sec. 1989–; Research Assoc. Univ. of Wisconsin 1958–59; Royal Soc. Commonwealth Fund Fellow, Univ. of Sussex 1973; David Rivett Medal, CSIRO 1968. *Publications:* Methods for Evaluating Biological Nitrogen Fixation 1980, Root Nodules of Legumes: Structure and Functions 1982; more than 140 papers on microbiology and biological nitrogen fixation. *Leisure interests:* music, gardening. *Address:* CSIRO Division of Plant Industry, G.P.O. Box 1600, Canberra, A.C.T. 2601 (Office); 13 Ferdinand Street, Campbell, Canberra, A.C.T. 2601, Australia (Home). *Telephone:* (062) 46 5098 (Office); (062) 477413 (Home).

BERGGREN, Bo Erik Gunnar; Swedish company executive; b. 11 Aug. 1936, Falun; s. of Tage Berggren and Elsa Höglund; m. Gunbritt Haglund 1962; two s. two d.; ed. Royal Inst. of Tech.; metallurgical research and devt., Stora Kopparbergs Bergslags AB (now Stora), Domnarvet 1962–68, Mill Man., Söderfors 1968–74, Vice-Pres., Falun 1975–78, Pres., Man. Dir., C.E.O. 1984–; Pres. Incentive AB, Stockholm 1978–84. *Address:* Stora Kopparbergs Bergslags AB, S-791 80 Falun, Sweden. *Telephone:* 023-80000.

BERGGREN, Thommy; Swedish actor; b. 1937; ed. The Pickwick Club (private dramatic school), Atelieteatern, Stockholm, and Gothenburg Theatre; Gothenburg Theatre 1959–63; Royal Dramatic Theatre, Stockholm 1963–; *plays acted in include:* Gengangaren (Ibsen) 1962, Romeo and Juliet 1962, Chembalo 1962, Who's Afraid of Virginia Woolf 1964. *Films acted in include:* Pärlemor 1961, Barnvagnen (The Pram) 1962, Kvarteret Korpen (Ravens End) 1963, En söndag i september (A Sunday in September) 1963, Karlek 65 (Love 65) 1965, Elvira Madigan 1967, The Black Palm Trees 1969, The Ballad of Joe Hill 1971. *Address:* c/o Svenska Filminstitutet, Kungsgatan 48, Stockholm C., Sweden.

BERGHAUS, Ruth; German theatre director; b. 2 July 1927, Dresden; m. Paul Dessau (died 1979); choreographer of the Paluccaschule, Dresden, and the Theater der Freundschaft 1951–64; joined Berliner Ensemble 1964, Deputy Dir. 1970–71, Dir. 1971–77; Dir. Staatsoper 1977–79. *Productions at Berliner Ensemble include:* Viet Nam Diskurs (Peter Weiss), Im Dickicht der Städte (Bertolt Brecht) 1971, Die Gewehre der Frau Carrar 1971, Omphale (Peter Hacks) 1972, Zement (Heiner Müller) 1973, Die Mutter 1974; also responsible for several productions at the State Opera, Berlin, including works by R. Strauss, Rossini, Weber and Dessau; The Trojans, Frankfurt 1986, Tristan and Isolde, Hamburg 1988; mem. Berlin City Parliament 1971–; extraordinary mem. Deutsche Akad. der Künste. *Address:* c/o Deutsche Staatsoper, Unter den Linden 7, Box 1300, 108 Berlin, German Democratic Republic.

BERGLAND, Robert Selmer; American farmer and politician; b. 22 July 1928, Roseau, Minn.; s. of Selmer and Mabel (Evans) Bergland; m. Helen Grahn 1950; four s. two d.; ed. Univ. of Minnesota School of Agric.; rep. of Minn. Farmers' Union 1948–50; farmer 1950–; Sec. Roseau County Democratic Farmer-Labor Party, Minn. 1951–52, Chair. 1953–54; Chair. Minn. Agricultural Stabilization and Conservation Service Cttee.. 1961–63, Dir. of Service for Midwest 1963–68; mem. House of Reps. 1971–76, served House Agric. Cttee.; Agricultural Adviser to Senator W. Mondale (fmr. U.S. Vice-Pres.) 1977; U.S. Sec. for Agric. 1977–81; mem. Minn. Farmers' Union, Nat. Farmers' Org.; Gold Letter Award, Univ. of Minn. *Address:* Route 3, Roseau, Minn. 56751, U.S.A. (Home).

BERGLUND, Paavo Allan Engelbert, Finnish conductor; b. 14 April 1929, Helsinki; s. of Hjalmar and Siiri (Loiri) Berglund; m. Kirsti Kivekäs 1958; one s. two d.; ed. Sibelius Acad. Helsinki; Violinist, Finnish Radio Symphony Orchestra 1949–56, Conductor 1956–62, Prin. Conductor 1962–71; Prin. Conductor Bournemouth Symphony Orch. 1972–79, Helsinki Philharmonic Orch. 1975–79, Prin. Guest Conductor Scottish Nat. Orchestra 1982–84; State Award for Music 1972; Hon. O.B.E. *Recordings:* complete Sibelius symphonies incl. first recording of Kullervo Symphony 1971–77, Má Vlast (Smetana), Shostakovich symphonies 5, 6, 7, 10, 11, many other recordings. *Publication:* A Comparative Study of the Printed Score and

the Manuscript of the Seventh Symphony of Sibelius 1970. *Address:* Munkkiniemenranta 41, 00330 Helsinki 33, Finland.

BERGMAN, Ingmar; Swedish film director and theatre producer; b. 14 July 1918, Uppsala; m. Ingrid Karlebovon Rosen; eight c.; ed. Stockholm Univ.; producer Royal Theatre, Stockholm 1940–42; scriptwriter and producer Svensk Filmindustri 1940–44; theatre-dir. Helsingborg 1944–46, Gothenburg 1946–49, Malmo 1954–63; leading Dir. Royal Dramatic Theatre, Stockholm 1963–66; has written the scripts of most of his films; Erasmus Prize 1965, Award for Best Dir. Nat. Soc. of Film Critics 1970, Order of the Yugoslav Flag 1971, Luigi Pirandello Int. Theatre Prize 1971, Goethe Award (Frankfurt) 1976, Gold Medal of Swedish Acad. 1977, European Film Award 1988; Dr. h.c. (Univ. of Rome) 1988; Commdr. Legion d'honneur 1985; author of plays A Painting on Wood, The City, The Rite (TV play), The Lie (TV play), Scenes from a Marriage (TV play); Dir. To Damascus 1974, The Merry Widow, Twelfth Night 1975, 1980, Tartuffe 1980, King Lear 1985, John Gabriel Borkman 1985, Miss Julie 1986, Hamlet 1986. *Films include:* Crisis 1945, It Rains on our Love 1946, A Ship Bound for India 1947, Music in Darkness 1947, Port of Call 1948, Prison 1948, Thirst 1949, To Joy 1949, Summer Interlude 1950, This Can't Happen Here 1950, Waiting Women 1952, Summer with Monika 1952, Sawdust and Tinsel 1953, A Lesson in Love 1954, Journey into Autumn 1955, Smiles of a Summer Night 1955, The Seventh Seal 1956, Wild Strawberries 1957, So Close to Life 1957, The Face 1958, The Virgin Spring 1959, The Devil's Eye 1960, Through a Glass Darkly 1961, Winter Light 1962, The Silence 1962, Now About these Women 1963, episode in Stimulantia 1965, Persona 1966, The Hour of the Wolf 1967, Shame 1968, The Rite 1970, A Passion 1970, The Touch 1971, Cries and Whispers 1972, Scenes from a Marriage 1974 (film and TV), The Magic Flute (film and TV) 1975, Face to Face (film and TV) 1975, The Serpent's Egg 1977, Sonate d'automne 1978, Aus dem Leben der Marionetten 1980, Fårö Document 1980, Fanny and Alexander 1981, After the Rehearsal 1984. *Publications:* Four Stories 1977, The Magic Lantern (autobiog.).

BERGMAN, Stephenie Jane, DIP.A.D.; British artist; b. 18 April 1946, London; d. of Jack 'Kid' Berg and Morya Bergman; ed. St Paul's Girls' School and St. Martin's School of Art; one-woman exhbns. at Garage Art Ltd., London 1973, 1975, Nottingham 1976, Cambridge 1977, Chester 1978, Anthony Stokes, London, 1978, 1980, Riverside Studios, London 1980, Crafts Council Gallery 1984, Butler's House, Kilkenny 1984; has participated in group exhbns. in London, France, Belgium, Australia, Zimbabwe, including 25 Years of Painting, Royal Academy, London 1976; Gulbenkian Award 1975. *Leisure interest:* horse racing. *Address:* 9 Berwick Street, London, W.1, England (Home).

BERGMANN, Felix, PH.D.; Israeli pharmacologist and academic; b. 17 Aug. 1908, Frankfurt; s. of Yehuda Bergmann and Hedwig Bergmann; m. Sarah Sulski 1938; one s. one d.; ed. Univ. of Berlin; Research Assoc. Weizman Inst. of Science, Rehovot, Israel 1934–46; Head Dept. of Pharmacology, Medical School, Jerusalem 1947–78, Emer. Prof. 1978–; Visiting Prof. Harvard Medical School 1946–47, Columbia Univ. 1947–48, Univ. of Cape Town 1987; mem. Israeli Acad. of Science, Hon. mem. Physiological Soc. of South America. *Publications:* over 350 publs. on organic chemistry, physiology, pharmacology and toxicology. *Leisure interest:* archaeology. *Address:* Department of Pharmacology, Medical School, Jerusalem 91010; Disraeli Street 3, Jerusalem 92222, Israel (Home). *Telephone:* (02) 428741; (02) 631138.

BERGONZI, Carlo; Italian tenor opera singer; b. 13 July 1924, Busseto, Parma; m. Adele; two c.; ed. Parma Conservatory; début (baritone) as Figaro (Il Barbiere di Siviglia) at Lecce 1948; début as tenor in title role of Andrea Chénier, Teatro Petruzzelli, Bari 1951; subsequently appeared at various Italian opera houses including La Scala, Milan; U.S. début in Il Tabarro and Cavalleria Rusticana, Lyric Opera, Chicago 1955; appeared at Metropolitan Opera, New York in Aïda (as Radames) and Il Trovatore (as Manrico) 1955–56; now appears at all the major opera houses in Europe, and also in U.S.A. and South America; repertoire includes many Verdi roles. *Address:* c/o Signor A. Ziliani, A.L.C.I., Via Paolo da Cannobio 2, 120122 Milan, Italy.

BERGQUIST, Patricia Rose, PH.D., D.SC., F.R.S.N.Z.; New Zealand professor of zoology; b. 10 March 1933, Auckland; d. of William and Bertha E. Smyth; m. Peter L. Bergquist 1958; one d.; ed. Takapuna Grammar School and Univ. of Auckland; Lecturer in Zoology, Auckland Univ. 1958; Postdoctoral research, Yale Univ. 1961–64; subsequently career concentrated on sponge biology, chemistry, chemo-taxonomy; pioneered application of chem. and pharmacology of marine sponges to resolving maj. questions of sponge phylogeny and relationships; int. consultant in marine sponge taxonomy and marine ecology; Prof. of Zoology (Personal Chair.), Univ. of Auckland 1981–, Head of Dept. 1986–. *Publications:* more than 50 articles in professional journals. *Leisure interests:* fishing, stamp collecting, classical music. *Address:* Zoology Department, University of Auckland, Private Bag, Auckland, New Zealand. *Telephone:* 737 999.

BERGSAGEL, John Dagfinn, PH.D.; Danish (b. Canadian) musicologist; b. 19 April 1928, Outlook, Sask.; s. of Rev. Knut Bergsagel and Alma Josephine Bergsagel née Anderson; m. 1st Sondra Rubin 1953 (divorced), 2nd Ingrid Charlotte Sørensen 1965; three s. one d.; ed. Gordon Bell High

School, Winnipeg, Man., Univ. of Manitoba, St. Olaf Coll., Minn., U.S.A., Cornell Univ., U.S.A., Oxford Univ., U.K., Royal Acad. of Music, London, U.K.; Lecturer, Concordia Coll., Minn. 1954–55; Assoc. Prof., Ohio Univ. 1955–59, Exec. Ed. Early English Church Music, Oxford, U.K. 1961–76; Tutor in History of Music, Oxford Univ. 1962–67, Lecturer, New Coll. 1966–67; Sr. Lecturer in Musicology, Manchester Univ. 1967–70; Lecturer in History and Theory of Music, Univ. of Copenhagen 1970–81, Prof. of Musicology 1981–; mem. Council of Plainsong and Mediaeval Music Soc., Nat. Cttee. for Monumenta Musicae Byzantinae, Exec. Bd., Danish Musicological Soc; Sr. Arts Fellow of Canada Council 1959; Gulbenkian Foundation Grant 1961; Fellow Royal Danish Acad. of Sciences and Letters. *Publications:* The Collected Works of Nicholas Ludford 1963, Early Tudor Masses I-II 1963, 1976, Engelske Anthems fra det 16. århundrede 1973, Musikk i Norge i Middelalder og Renessanse 1982, Music in Danmark at the Time of Christian IV: vol. 2, Music for Instrumental Ensemble 1988, vol. 6, Anonymous Mass and Occasional Motets (with H. Glahn) 1988; numerous articles, contribs. to encyclopaedias, transls. of many scholarly works. *Address:* Strandvejen 63, 2100 Copenhagen Ø, Denmark. *Telephone:* 31 20 02 02.

BERGSON, Abram, PH.D.; American professor of economics; b. 21 April 1914, Baltimore, Md.; m. Rita Macht 1939; three d.; ed. Johns Hopkins and Harvard Univs.; Asst. Prof. of Econs. Univ. of Texas 1940–42; mem. staff, Office of Strategic Services, Washington, D.C., then Chief, Russian Econ. Subdiv. 1944–45; various posts, finally Prof. of Econs. Columbia Univ. 1946–56; consultant, The Rand Corpn. 1948–; Prof. of Econs. Harvard Univ. 1956–, George F. Baker Prof. of Econs. 1971–, Prof. Emer. 1984–; Dir. Regional Studies Program—Soviet Union 1961–64, Dir. Russian Research Center 1964–68, Acting Dir. 1969–70, Dir. 1977–80, Frank W. Taussig Research Prof. 1970–71; mem. American Reparations Del. Moscow 1945, Social Science Advisory Bd., U.S. Arms Control and Disarmament Agency 1966–73, Chair. 1971–73; consultant various Fed. agencies; Chair. Advisory Cttee. on Nat. Income Estimates, World Bank 1983; mem. Nat. Acad. of Sciences, American Philosophical Soc.; Fellow, American Acad. of Arts and Sciences, Econometric Soc.; mem. Council, Int. Econ. Asscn. 1974–77; Pres. Comparative Econ. Assen. 1981; Trustee Nat. Council for Soviet and East European Research 1987–; Award, Distinguished Contribution, American Assen. for the Advancement of Slavic Studies 1975; Distinguished Fellow, American Econ. Assen.; Hon. LL.D. (Windsor) 1979, Hon. D.H.L. (Brandeis) 1985. *Publications:* several books, including The Structure of Soviet Wages: A Study in Socialist Economics 1944, Real National Income of Soviet Russia 1961, The Economics of Soviet Planning 1964, Essays in Normative Economics 1966, Planning and Productivity under Soviet Socialism 1968, Productivity and the Social System—The U.S.S.R. and the West 1978, Welfare, Planning and Employment: Selected Essays in Economic Theory 1982, The Soviet Economy: Towards the Year 2000 (co-ed. with Herbert Levine, and contrib.) 1983; Planning and Performance In Socialist Economies 1988; numerous articles and papers. *Address:* Department of Economics, Harvard University, Cambridge, Mass. 02138 (Office); 334 Marsh Street, Belmont, Mass. 02178, U.S.A. (Home). *Telephone:* 617-484 9171 (Home).

BERIĆ, Berislav, DR. SC.(MED.), F.R.C.S.(C.), F.I.A.C.; Yugoslav professor of obstetrics and gynaecology; b. 11 Nov. 1927, Belgrade; s. of Dr. Milenko Berić and Olga (née Pušić) Berić; m. Prof. Vesna Djukić 1956; one d.; ed. Zagreb and Belgrade Univs.; Asst. Docent Univ. Dept. of Obstetrics and Gynaecology, Sarajevo 1958–60; Docent and Prof. and Head of Dept. Novi Sad 1960–67, Dir. 1967–74; Dir. Dept. of Obstetrics and Gynaecology, Sherbrooke Univ., Quebec 1974–75; Head Inst. of Human Reproduction, Medical Faculty, Novi Sad 1975–; Consultant for WHO, Egypt, Iraq, Algeria 1968–87; Pres. Fed. Council for MCHP, Yugoslav Fertility and Sterilization Soc.; mem. Acad. of Science and Arts Vojvodina, Medical Acad. of Serbia, Medical Acad. of Croatia, Int. Acad. of Citology, Int. Acad. of Reproductive Medicine; Hon. mem. Socs. of Crynaecology and Obstetrics of Hungary, Romania and Egypt; recipient of over 70 int. and nat. awards, prizes, medals, diplomas, including Great Order of Labour (with Gold Wreath) Yugoslavia. *Publications:* 10 books on medicine and over 360 scientific and professional papers; newspaper articles. *Leisure interests:* history, politics, literature. *Address:* Sv. Markovića Str. 15, YU 21000 Novi Sad, Yugoslavia. *Telephone:* (021) 52-323.

BERIO, Luciano; Italian composer; b. 24 Oct. 1925; s. of Ernesto Berio and Ada dal Fiume; m. 1st Cathy Berberian 1950 (dissolved 1964), one d.; m. 2nd Susan Oyama 1964 (dissolved 1971), one s. one d.; m. 3rd Talia Pecker 1977, two s.; ed. Liceo Classico and Conservatorio G. Verdi, Milan; founder of Studio de Fonologia Musicale, Italian Radio; Teacher of Composition and Lecturer at Mills Coll. (Calif.), Darmstadt, and Harvard Univ.; now Prof. of Composition, Juilliard School of Music, N.Y. *Compositions include:* 5 Variazioni 1951, Nones for Orchestra 1954, Alleluyah I and II 1955–57, Thema (Omaggio a Joyce) 1958, Circles 1960, Visage 1961, Epifanie 63, Passagio 1962, Laborintus II 1965, O King 1968, Sinfonia 1969, This Means That ... 1970, Opera 1970, Sequenzas for solo instruments, A-Ronne for eight voices 1974–75, Coro for Chorus and Orchestra 1975–76, La Ritirata Notturna di Madrid 1975, Ritorno degli Snovidenia 1977, La Vera Storia 1978, Corale 1981, Un Re in Ascolto 1982, Requies 1983, Voci 1984. *Address:* Il Colombaio, Radicondoli, Siena, Italy.

BERIOSOVA, Svetlana; British ballerina; b. 24 Sept. 1932, Lithuania; d. of Nicolas and Maria Beriozoff; m. Mohammed Masud Khan 1959 (dissolved 1974); with Metropolitan Ballet 1946–49, Sadler's Wells Theatre Ballet 1949–52, Sadler's Wells ballet (now Royal Ballet) 1952–; teacher at the Royal Ballet, London Festival Ballet, N.Y. City Ballet, Australian Ballet, Northern Ballet Theatre, London City Ballet, Asama Maki, Tokyo, La Scala, Milan, Rio dé Joneiro; leading roles in Swan Lake, The Sleeping Beauty, Giselle, Coppélia, Trumpet Concerto, The Shadow, Rinaldo and Armida, The Prince of the Pagodas, Antigone, Baiser de la Fée, Perséphone, Les Sylphides, The Lady and the Fool, Ondine, Sylvia, Apollo, Lilac Garden, Cinderella, Les Biches, Les Noces, Enigma Variations 1968, Jazz Calendar 1969, La Bayadère, Checkpoint 1970, etc. *Leisure interest:* the arts. *Address:* 10 Palliser Court, Palliser Road, London, W.14, England.

BERKELEY, Sir Lennox Randal, Kt., C.B.E., B.A.; British composer; b. 12 May 1903, Boars Hill, Oxford; s. of Hastings Fitzhardinge Berkeley and Aline Carla (née Harris); m. Elizabeth Freda Bernstein; three s.; ed. Gresham's School, Holt, and Merton Coll., Oxford; studied music in Paris with Mlle. Nadia Boulanger 1927–31; mem. B.B.C. Music Dept. staff 1942–45; awarded Collard Fellowship in Music 1946; Composition Prof. Royal Acad. of Music, London 1946–68; Pres. Performing Right Soc. 1975–83, Pres. Composers' Guild 1975–; Vice-Pres. Bach Choir 1978–, Western Orchestral Soc. 1978–; Hon. Prof. of Music, Keele Univ. 1976–; fmr. Pres. Cheltenham Music Festival, now Pres. Emer.; Hon. Fellow Merton Coll., Oxford Univ.; Hon. D.Mus. (Oxford Univ.), (City Univ.) 1983; Foreign Hon. mem. American Acad. and Inst. of Arts and Letters 1980; Hon. mem. Royal Philharmonic Soc.; Cobbett Medal 1962; ordre de Mérite Culturel, Monaco 1967; Kt. of St. Gregory the Great 1973; Composer of the Year, Composers' Guild 1973. *Principal works include:* Orchestra: four Symphonies, Divertimento, Nocturne, Concerto for piano and orchestra, Concerto for two pianos and orchestra, Concerto for violin and chamber orchestra, Five Pieces for violin and orchestra, The Winter's Tale (suite), Voices of the Night, Guitar Concerto, Sinfonia Concertante for Oboe and Orchestra; Chamber Music: Three string quartets, string trio, Sonata for viola and piano, Trio for violin, horn and piano, Sextet for clarinet, horn and string quartet, Duo for cello and piano, Quintet for wind and piano; Piano: Sonata, six Preludes, four Concert studies; Vocal: Four Poems of St. Teresa for contralto and strings, Stabat Mater for six soloists and twelve instruments, Five Poems of W. H. Auden, Autumn's Legacy, Song Cycle for voice and piano, Mass for five voices, Songs of the Half-Light for high voice and guitar, Magnificat (City Festival, London) 1968, Guitar Concertino 1974, Five Chinese Songs; Opera: Nelson, A Dinner Engagement, Ruth, Castaway. *Address:* 8 Warwick Avenue, London, W.2, England. *Telephone:* 01-262 3922.

BERKELEY, Michael Fitzhardinge, A.R.A.M.; British composer; b. 25 May 1948, London; s. of Sir Lennox Berkeley and Freda Elizabeth Berkeley; m. Deborah Jane Coltman-Rogers 1979; one d.; ed. Westminster Cathedral Choir School, The Oratory School, Royal Acad. of Music; writer on music and arts for the Observer, Vogue and The Listener 1970–75; presents music programmes (including Proms) for BBC TV 1975–; BBC Radio 3 announcer 1974–79; mem. Exec. Cttee. Assen. of Professional Composers 1982–84; Cen. Music Advisory Cttee., BBC 1986–; Music Panel Adviser to Arts Council 1986–; apart from concert works, has written music for film, TV and Radio; The Guinness Prize for composition 1977· Assoc. of R.A.M. 1984. *Major works:* Meditations for Strings, Oboe Concerto, Fantasia Concertante, Gregorian Variations (orchestra), For The Savage Messiah (piano quintet), Or Shall We Die? (oratorio to text by Ian McEwan), 2 String quartets, Piano trio, Songs of Awakening Love. *Leisure interests:* walking, farming, reading. *Address:* 49 Blenheim Crescent, London, W11 2EF, England. *Telephone:* 01-229 6945.

BERKELEY, Norborne, Jr., LL.B.; American banker (retd.); b. 5 June 1922, Bethlehem, Pa.; s. of Norborne and Dorothea (née Randolph) Berkeley; m. Rowena Bauer Berkeley 1972; one s. two d. (by previous marriage); ed. Yale Univ., Univ. of Virginia, Harvard Univ.; Advanced Man. Program; joined Chemical New York Corpn. 1950; Sr. Vice-Pres. Chemical Bank (subsidiary of Chem. New York Corpn.) 1966–68, Exec. Vice-Pres. 1968–73; Pres. and Chief Admin. Officer, Chemical New York Corpn. and Chemical Bank Fed. 1973–81; Chair. Bd., Wildcat Service Corpn. 1973–, Dir. Uniroyal Inc., Hartz Mountain Corpn., Freeport Minerals Co., Beekman Downtown Hosp., Nat. Bd. of Boys' Clubs of America, Vera Inst. of Justice; Trustee, Nat. Recreation Foundation, Whitney Museum of American Art; mem. Assen. of Reserve City Bankers, President's Advisory Cttee. for Trade Negotiations. *Leisure interests:* golf, skiing. *Address:* 20 Pine Street, New York, N.Y. 10005 (Office); 41 Westcott Road, Princeton, N.J. 08540, U.S.A. (Home).

BERKHOUWER, Cornelis, LL.D.; Netherlands barrister and politician; b. 19 March 1919, Alkmaar; s. of Cornelis Berkhouwer and Neeltje Vroegop; m. Michelle Martel 1966; two s.; ed. Univ. of Amsterdam; barrister 1942–; mem. Second Chamber, States-Gen. 1956–79; European Parl., mem. 1963, Pres. Liberal Group 1968–72, Pres. European Parl. 1973–75; Commdr. Order of the Netherlands Lion; Grand Officer, Order of Merit (Italy, Spain). *Publications:* various articles in the field of law. *Leisure interests:* tennis, swimming, cycling, athletics, literature, music. *Address:* 56 Stationsweg, Heiloo, Netherlands. *Telephone:* 33791.

BERKOFF, Steven; British actor, writer and director; b. 1937, Stepney, London; s. of Al Berkoff and Polly Berkoff; founder London Theatre Group; appeared in Hamlet at Roundhouse, London; tours of Israel, Europe and U.S.A.; one-man show at Donmar Warehouse 1986–87; produces and stars in own shows in London; numerous film and TV appearances. *Films include:* Coming Out of the Ice, Octopussy, First Blood 2, Beverly Hills Cop, Absolute Beginners, Buster 1988, War and Remembrance (TV) 1988. Dir. Metamorphosis (play) 1987–, Coriolanus. *Publications:* Steven Berkoff's America 1988, I am Hamlet 1989. *Address:* c/o International Creative Management, 388/396 Oxford Street, London, W.1., England.

BERLIET, Paul; French industrialist; b. 5 Oct. 1918, Lyon; s. of Marius and Louise (née Saunière) Berliet; m. Colette Vignon-Carret 1942; two s. two d.; ed. Lycée Ampère, Lyon; Deputy Dir.-Gen. Société Automobiles M. Berliet 1954–58, Admin. Dir.-Gen. 1958–62, Pres., Dir.-Gen. 1962–74, Vice-Pres. and Dir.-Gen. 1975–78; Admin. Citröen S.A. 1968–75; Pres. Bd. Saviem 1975–76; Vice-Pres. Renault Véhicules Industriels (RVI) 1978–; Pres. Fondation de l'Automobile Marius Berliet 1982, Comité Rhône-Alpes de la Chambre de Commerce Franco-Arabe 1980, Comm. du commerce extérieur de la Chambre de commerce de Lyon 1983–; Officier, Légion d'honneur, Officier des Arts et Lettres. *Address:* Fondation de l'Automobile Marius Berliet, 39 avenue Esquirol, 69003 Lyon; La Cerisaie, rue Carnot, 69450 Saint-Cyr-au-Mont-d'Or, France.

BERLIN, Irving, D.MUS.; American composer and song writer; b. 11 May 1888 in Russia; s. of Moses and Leah L. Baline; m. 1st Dorothy Goetz 1913 (died 1913); m. 2nd Ellin Mackay 1926; three d.; ed. public schools in New York City; went to U.S.A. 1893; Pres. Irving Berlin Music Corpn.; U.S. Medal of Freedom 1977. *Songs include:* Alexander's Ragtime Band, Oh, How I Hate to Get up in the Morning, Always, Reaching for the Moon, White Christmas, God Bless America, Blue Skies, What'll I Do, All Alone, Remember, Everybody's Doing It, There's No Business Like Show Business, How Deep is the Ocean, among hundreds of others; musicals: This is the Army (comedy), Easter Parade (film), Annie Get Your Gun, Miss Liberty, Mr. President and Call Me Madam (stage musicals), Top Hat, Follow the Fleet, Alexander's Ragtime Band, Holiday Inn (films); hon. degrees, Temple Univ., Bucknell Univ., Fordham Univ.; Medal of Merit for This is the Army, special gold medal for God Bless America, Légion d'honneur, Medal of Freedom 1977. *Address:* Irving Berlin Music Corporation, 1290 6th Avenue, New York, N.Y. 10104, U.S.A.

BERLIN, Sir Isaiah, O.M., Kt., C.B.E., M.A., F.B.A.; British university teacher; b. 6 June 1909; s. of Mendel and Marie Berlin; m. Aline de Gunzbourg 1956; ed. St. Paul's School and Corpus Christi Coll., Oxford; Lecturer in Philosophy, New Coll., Oxford 1932–; Fellow of All Souls Coll., Oxford 1932–38, 1975–; Fellow and Tutor New Coll. 1938–50; attached to British Information Service New York 1941; First Sec., British Embassy, Washington 1942–46, Moscow 1945; lecturer, Oxford Univ. 1957–; Sub-Warden New Coll. 1949–50; Research Fellow, All Souls Coll. 1950–57; Chichele Prof. of Social and Political Theory, Oxford Univ. 1957–67; Visiting lecturer, Harvard 1949, 1951, 1953, Ford Research Prof. 1962, Mellon Lecturer, Wash., D.C. 1965; Visiting Prof., Princeton Univ. 1966; Mary Flexner Lecturer, Bryn Mawr Coll. 1952–53; Auguste Comte Memorial Lecturer, L.S.E. 1953; Northcliffe Lecturer, Univ. Coll., London; Alexander White Prof., Chicago Univ. 1955; Romanes Lecturer, Oxford Univ. 1971; Gov. Univ. of Jerusalem; Trustee, Nat. Gallery 1975–86; Dir. Royal Opera House, Covent Garden 1954–66, 1974–87; Prof. of Humanities, City Univ. of New York 1966–72; Pres. Wolfson Coll., Oxford 1966–75; Pres. British Acad. 1974–78; Hon. mem. American Acad. of Arts and Sciences, Arts and Letters; Fellow, American Philosophical Soc.; Hon. Dr., Hull, Oxford, Cambridge, Glasgow, East Anglia, Harvard, Columbia, Brandeis, Johns Hopkins, Northwestern, London, Liverpool, Sussex, Jerusalem, Tel-Aviv, Ben-Gurion and New York Univs., City Univ. of New York, New School of Social Research, N.Y.; Hon. Fellow, Corpus Christi Coll., Oxford, St. Anthony's Coll., Oxford, Wolfson Coll., Cambridge; Jerusalem Prize 1980, Erasmus Prize 1983, Benjamin E. Lippincott Award 1984, Giovanni Agnelli Prize 1988. *Publications:* Karl Marx 1939, The Hedgehog and the Fox, Historical Inevitability 1954, The Age of Enlightenment 1956, Two Concepts of Liberty, 1958, The Life and Opinions of Moses Hess 1959, Mr. Churchill in 1940 1964, Four Essays on Liberty 1969, Fathers and Children 1972, Vico and Herder 1976, Russian Thinkers 1978, Concepts and Categories 1978, Against the Current 1979, Personal Impressions 1980; trans. First Love (1950) and A Month in the Country (1980) by I. S. Turgenev. *Address:* All Souls College, Oxford, England.

BERLINER, Robert W., B.S., M.D.; American physician; b. 10 March 1915, New York; s. of William M. Berliner and Anna Weiner; m. Lea Silver 1941; two s. two d.; ed. Yale Univ. and Columbia Univ.; Intern, Presbyterian Hosp., New York 1939–41; Resident Physician, Goldwater Hosp., New York 1942–43; Research Fellow, Goldwater Memorial Hosp., and Asst. in Medicine, New York Univ. Coll. of Medicine 1943–44; Research Asst., Goldwater Memorial Hosp., and Instructor in Medicine, New York Univ. Coll. of Medicine 1944–47; Asst. Prof. of Medicine, Columbia Univ. 1947–50; Research Assoc., Dept. of Hosps., City of New York 1947–50; Chief, Lab. of Kidney and Electrolyte Metabolism, Nat. Insts. of Health, Bethesda, Md. 1950–62; Special Lecturer, George Washington School of Medicine, Wash., D.C. 1951–; Dir. of Intramural Research, Nat. Heart Inst., Nat.

Insts. of Health 1954–68; Dir. of Labs. and Clinics, Nat. Insts. of Health 1968–69, Deputy Dir. for Science 1969–73; Prof. Lecturer, Georgetown Univ. Schools of Medicine and Dentistry 1964–73; Prof. of Physiology and Medicine, Dean, Yale Univ. School of Medicine 1973–85, Prof. Emer. 1985–; mem. N.A.S. (Council 1978–81), American Acad. of Arts and Sciences, American Heart Asscn.; Pres. American Soc. of Nephrology 1968, Soc. for Experimental Biology and Medicine 1978–81; mem. numerous other medical socs.; Distinguished Service Award, Dept. of Health, Educ. and Welfare 1962, Homer W. Smith Award in Renal Physiology 1965, Alumni Award for Distinguished Achievement, Coll. of Physicians and Surgeons, Columbia Univ. 1966, Bicentennial Medal, Coll. of Physicians and Surgeons, Columbia Univ. 1967, Distinguished Achievement Award by Modern Medicine 1969, American Heart Asscn. Research Achievement Award 1970, A. Ross McIntyre Award (Univ. of Neb.) 1974, Joseph Mather Smith Prize 1978, Ray G. Daggs Award, American Physiological Soc. 1982. *Publications:* approx. 100 publs. in medical literature. *Leisure interests:* hiking, bird-watching, music. *Address:* Yale University School of Medicine, C203 Sterling Hall of Medicine, 333 Cedar Street, New Haven, Conn. 06510 (Office); 36 Edgehill Terrace, New Haven, Conn. 06511, U.S.A. (Home). *Telephone:* (203) 785-4672 (Office); (203) 777-1379 (Home).

BERLUSCONI, Silvio; Italian business executive; b. 1936, Milan; ed. Univ. of Milan; owner of Fininvest group (with interests in TV stations, real estate, insurance and financial services, 305-outlet cinema chain and Milan AC football club); began work on Milano 2 housing project 1969; Canale 5 network began broadcasting 1980; bought Italia 1 TV network 1983, Rete 4 TV network 1984; took stake in La Cinq commercial TV network 1985; bought Estudios Roma 1986; bought Milan AC Football Club 1986; bought La Standa (Italy's largest dept. store chain) 1988. *Address:* Villa San Martino, Milan, Italy.

BERMAN, Lazar; Soviet pianist; b. 26 Feb. 1930; s. of Naum Berman and Anna (Makower) Berman; m. 1968; one s.; ed. Moscow Conservatory; concert début 1934, orchestral début, with Moscow Philharmonic Orchestra 1940; concert pianist 1957–; London début 1958; U.S. début Miami Univ., Ohio 1976, Carnegie Hall début with N.J. Symphony Orchestra 1976; specialist in 19th century music; First Prize Int. Youth Festival, E. Berlin 1951; Fourth Prize Queen Elisabeth of Belgium contest, Brussels 1951; mem. Philharmonic Soc., Moscow; Founder-mem. U.S.S.R.-Belgium Soc. *Address:* c/o Jacques Leiser Artists' Management, Dorchester Towers, 155 West 68th Street, New York, N.Y. 10023, U.S.A.; c/o Dido Senger, 103 Randolph Avenue, London, W9 1DL, England. *Telephone:* 01-289 3736.

BERMAN, Yitzhak; Israeli lawyer and politician; b. 1913, Russia; ed. Teacher Training Coll., Jerusalem, Univ. Coll., London and Inner Temple, London; settled in Palestine 1921; served in British Army 1942–45; mem. Command, Irgun Zevayi Leumi, later Major, Israeli Defence Force 1948–50; Gen. Man. Willis Overland & Kaizer Assembly Plant, Haifa 1950–54; private law practice, Tel-Aviv 1954–80; mem. Cen. Cttee. Liberal Party 1968–; mem. Knesset 1977, Speaker March 1980–81; Leader Liberal Party of Israel 1986–, Jt. Leader New Liberal Party 1987. *Address:* c/o New Liberal Party, Tel-Aviv, Israel.

BERMÚDEZ, Enrique; Nicaraguan guerrilla fighter; fmr. Col. in army; C.-in-C. of 'Contras' 1981–; mem. Directorate of 'Contras' July 1988–.

BERN, Howard Alan, PH.D.; American professor of zoology and research endocrinologist; b. 30 Jan. 1920, Montreal, Canada; m. Estelle Bruck 1946; one s. one d.; ed. Univ. of California, Los Angeles; mil. service 1942–46; Nat. Research Council Postdoctoral Fellow in Biology, U.C.L.A. 1946–48; Instructor in Zoology, Univ. of Calif., Berkeley, Asst. Prof. 1950–56, Assoc. Prof. 1956–60, Prof. of Zoology and Research Endocrinologist, Cancer Research Lab. 1960–; research interests: comparative endocrinology of prolactin, control of prolactin secretion, mammary gland biology, long-term effect of perinatal exposure to hormones; hormones and genital epithelial cell growth; neurosecretion; Fellow, A.A.A.S., American Acad. of Arts and Sciences; Foreign Fellow, Indian Nat. Science Acad.; Assoc. Nat. Museum of Natural History, Paris; mem. N.A.S., American Soc. of Zoologists (Pres. 1967), Int. Organizing Cttee. on Comparative Endocrinology Symposia, Neuroendocrinology Panel of Int. Brain Research Org., Int. Organizing Cttee. on Neurosecretion Symposia, American Asscn. for Cancer Research, American Physiological Soc., Endocrine Soc., Int. Soc. of Neuroendocrinology, Int. Centre of Insect Physiology and Ecology, Soc. for Experimental Biology and Medicine. *Publications:* A Textbook of Comparative Endocrinology (with A. Gorbman) 1962; co-ed. of numerous books and publs.; author or co-author of approx. 300 papers. *Address:* Cancer Research Laboratory, University of California, Berkeley, Calif. 94720, U.S.A.

BERNABEI, Ettore; Italian journalist and broadcasting executive; b. 1921; ed. Univ. of Florence; Director Il Giornale del Mattino (Florence) 1951–56, Il Popolo (Rome) 1956–60; Ed. La Nazione del Popolo (Florence); Dir.-Gen. Radiotelevisione Italiana 1961–74; Pres. Italstat 1974–. *Address:* Italstat S.p.A., 9 Avenue Arno, Rome, Italy. *Telephone:* 844-8141.

BERNABÓ-BREA, Luigi; Italian archaeologist; b. 27 Sept. 1910, Genoa; ed. Univs. of Genoa and Rome and Italian School of Archaeology, Athens; Insp., Archaeological Museum, Taranto 38; Supt. of Antiquities for Liguria 1939–41, for Eastern Sicily 1941–73; Dir. Archaeological Museum, Syracuse 1941; founder and Dir. Aeolian museum, Lipari; Dir. Italian archaeological mission to Poliochni, Lemnos; mem. Acad. Naz. dei Lincei. *Publications:* Gli scavi nella Caverna delle Arene Candide di Finale Ligure, Vol. I 1946, Vol. II 1956, La scultura funeraria tarantina 1952, Akrai 1956, Sicily before the Greeks 1958, Poliochni, Vol. I 1964, Vol. II 1976, Mylai 1960, Meligunis Lipara, Vol. I 1960, Vol. II 1965, Vol. III 1968, Vol. IV 1978, Menandro e il teatro greco nelle terracotte Liparesi 1981, La ceramica policroma Liparese di età ellenistica 1986 in collaboration with M. Cavalier. *Address:* c/o Museo Eoliano, I 98055 Lipari, Aeolian Islands, Italy.

BERNADOTTE, Graf (Gustaf) Lennart (Nicolaus Paul); Swedish administrator; b. 8 May 1909, Stockholm; s. of Prinz Wilhelm of Sweden and Princess Marie Pavlovna; m. 1st Karin Nissvandt 1932–72, 2nd Sonja Haunz 1972; four s. five d.; ed. studies in forestry and land economy; owner, Insel Mainau, Lake Constance 1932–74 (now belongs to Lennart Bernadotte Foundation); Hon. Pres. Deutsche Gartenbaugesellschaft, Nobelpreisträgertagungen, Lindau; Hon. Senator, Technische Hochschule, Hannover; Hon. mem. Royal Horticultural Soc.; Dr. sc.agr. h.c. (Univ. of Hohenheim) numerous decorations and awards including Grosses Bundesverdienstkreuz mit Stern und Schulterband, Albert Schweitzer Gold Medal. *Address:* Schloss Mainau, D-7750 Insel Mainau, Federal Republic of Germany. *Telephone:* 07531/303-0.

BERNADOTTE, Count Sigvard Oscar Fredrik, B.A.; Swedish industrial designer; b. 7 June 1907; s. of late King Gustav VI of Sweden; m. Marianne Lindberg 1961; ed. Uppsala Univ., Royal Acad. of Arts, Stockholm and Munich; designed silverware, textiles, bookbindings, glass, porcelain 1930–; Partner, Bernadotte & Bjørn (Industrial Design) 1949–63, own firm Bernadotte Design AB 1964–69; Pres. Int. Council of Socs. of Industrial Design (ICSID) 1961–63; awarded Gold Medal, Silver Medal and Diploma at the Milan Triennale. *Address:* Villagatan 10, Stockholm, Sweden. *Telephone:* 10-20-20.

BERNAL Y GARCÍA PIMENTEL, Ignacio, PH.D.; Mexican anthropologist; b. 13 Feb. 1910, Paris, France; s. of Rafael Bernal and Rafaela García Pimentel (de Bernal); m. Sofía Verea 1944; two s. two d.; ed. Loyola Coll., Montreal, Canada, Univ. Nacional Autónoma de México, Escuela Nacional de Antropología, Mexico; Director, Dept. of Anthropology, Mexico City Coll. 1948–59; Prof., Univ. Nacional Autónoma de México 1949–; Sec. Soc. Mexicana de Antropología 1954–62; Perm. Del. to UNESCO, Mexico 1955–56; Dir., Nat. Museum of Anthropology, Mexico 1962–68, Nat. Inst. of Anthropology and History, Mexico 1968–70, Teotihuacan Project 1962–64; Dir. Nat. Museum of Anthropology 1971–77; Regular mem. El Colegio Nacional de México, British Acad., Acad. Mexicana de la Historia, Academia de la Lengua; Foreign Fellow, American Acad. of Arts and Sciences; mem. other Mexican and foreign anthropological orgs.; decorations from Netherlands, France, Italy, Belgium, Denmark, Senegal, U.K., Yugoslavia and German Fed. Repub. *Publications include:* Introduction to Archaeology 1952, Mesoamérica 1953, Huitzilopochtli Vivo 1957, Pintura Precolombina 1958, Tenochtitlan en una Isla 1959, Correspondencia de Bandelier 1960, Toynbee y Mesoamérica 1960, Bibliografía de Arqueología y Etnografía 1962, Mexico before Cortez 1963, Teotihuacan 1963, Mexican Wall Paintings 1963, Mexican Art 1963; various sections Handbook of Middle American Indians 1965, El Museo de Antropología 1967, La Cerámica de Monte Albán 1967, El Mundo Olmeca 1968, Ancient Mexico in Colour 1968, The Mexican National Museum of Anthropology 1968, The Olmec World 1969, History of Archaeology in Mexico 1980. *Address:* Tres Picos 65, 11560 México, D.F., Mexico. *Telephone:* 5-45-96-99.

BERNAR CASTELLANOS, Ignacio; Spanish economist; b. 11 Nov. 1929; s. of Manuel Bernar and Rosario Castellanos; m. Virginia Elorza Losada 1955; one s. five d.; ed. Commercial Univ. of Deusto and Cen. Univ. of Madrid; Dir., Macmor, S.A. until 1960; Dir.-Gen., Foreign Trade, Ministry of Trade 1962–68; Councillor, Instituto Español de Moneda Extranjera (IEME), Empresa Nacional Bazán, Almadén, Crédito y Caución, S.A. 1962–68; Dir.-Gen. Supreme Council of the Chamber of Commerce, Industry and Navigation 1968–76; Gran Cruz del Mérito Civil, Cruz de San Carlos (Colombia). *Leisure interests:* hockey, golf, tennis, trout fishing, hunting. *Address:* c/o Consejo Superior de las Cámaras Oficiales de Comercio, Industria y Navegación de España, Calle Claudio Coello 19, 1°, Madrid, Spain.

BERNARD, Henry; French architect; b. 21 Feb. 1912, Albertsville, Savoie; s. of Henri and Louise (née Vallat) Bernard; m. Marie-Thérèse de Malherbe 1945; two c.; ed. Ecole Nationale des Beaux-Arts and in Rome; served during Second World War 1939–45; architect to Palace of Versailles 1945; Deputy Chief Architect to City of Caen 1945, Architect-in-Chief 1953, Insp.-Gen. of Civil Buildings and Nat. Palaces 1963; Pres. Acad. of Architecture 1966–69; work includes St. Julien Church, several lycées and buildings of Univ. of Caen, Paris Radio Centre, univ. hosp. centres at Caen, Grenoble, Tours, prefecture of Val-d'Oise, Palais de l'Europe, Strasbourg, etc.; mem. de l'Institut (Acad. des Beaux Arts) 1968–; Officier, Légion d'honneur, Chevalier de l'ordre nationale du Mérite, Commdr. des Arts et des Lettres. *Publications:* articles in literary and specialized journals. *Address:* 44 avenue d'Iéna, 75116 Paris (Office); 7 rue de l'Yvette, 75016 Paris, France (Home).

BERNARD, Lucien, M.D.; French public health official; b. 30 Nov. 1913, Paris; s. of Noel Bernard and Paule Delage; m. Marguerite Hamelin 1939; one s. two d.; ed. Faculté de Paris and Inst. Pasteur, Paris; Dir. of Health Services and Prof. of Microbiology, School of Medicine, Rheims 1941–44; Chief of Communicable Diseases branch and Int. Health at Ministry of Public Health 1946–56; Asst. to Dir.-Gen. of Public Health 1956–58; Dir. of Health Services, Regional Office for S.E. Asia, World Health Org. (WHO) 1958–63, Dir. in the office of the Dir.-Gen., Geneva, and Personal Rep. of the Dir.-Gen. at Regional Office for Africa 1963–64; Asst. Dir.-Gen. WHO Feb. 1964–77; Corresp. Nat. Acad. of Medicine, Paris; Officier, Légion d'honneur, Croix de guerre 1939–45, etc. *Publications:* on microbiology, epidemiology and public health administration. *Leisure interests:* music, oriental art. *Address:* 29 route de Malagnou, 1208 Geneva, Switzerland. *Telephone:* 735-33-71.

BERNARDIN, H.E. Cardinal Joseph L.; American ecclesiastic; b. 2 April 1928, Columbia, Charleston; ordained priest 1952; Titular Bishop Lugara 1966; Archbishop of Cinncinnati 1972–82, of Chicago 1982–; mem. Sacred Congregation for Divine Worship; mem. Bishops' Synod; cr. Cardinal 1983. *Address:* 1555 North State Parkway, Chicago, Ill. 60610, U.S.A. *Telephone:* (312) 751-8200.

BERNARDINI, Gilberto, DR. PHYS.; Italian physicist; b. 20 Aug. 1906, Florence; s. of Alfredo Bernardini and Elvira Nannucci; m. Nella Magherini 1928; one s. one d.; ed. Univs. of Pisa and Florence and Kaiser Wilhelm Inst., Berlin-Dahlem; Prof. of Physics, Univ. of Bologna 1939, Univ. of Rome 1945; Research Prof. of Physics, Univ. of Ill., U.S.A. 1950; Visiting Prof., Columbia Univ. 1948–49 and 1949–50; Dir. of Research in S.C. Div. European Org. for Nuclear Research (CERN), Geneva 1957; Dir. of S.C. Div. CERN, Geneva 1958–59; Dir. of Research CERN 1960–62, Univ. of Rome 1963–64; Dir. Scuola Normale Superiore, Pisa 1964–77; Pres. Italian Inst. for Nuclear Studies; Pres. Italian Physical Soc. 1960–67; Pres. European Physical Soc. 1968–70; Vice-Pres. European Physical Soc. 1970–72; Vice-Pres. Istituto della Enciclopedia italiana 1972–79; mem. Accad. Nazionale dei XL, Accad. Pugliese delle Scienze 1967; Nat. mem. Accad. Nazionale dei Lincei; mem. Accad. Bologna, Modena, Bari and La Colombaria; mem. Council Istituto Accademico di Roma; Fellow, American Physical Soc; Hon. Fellow, Inst. of Physics 1971; Hon. degrees, Univ. of Rochester, Univ. of Aachen; awarded Int. Medal Augusto Righi, Somaini Prize 1955, Presidential Gold Medal (Italy), Italian Physical Soc. Gold Medal 1969, J. T. Tate Gold Medal (U.S.A.) 1971, Presidential Gold Medal (Italy) 1978. *Leisure interests:* music, poetry. *Address:* Scuola Normale Superiore, Piazza dei Cavalieri 7, 56100 Pisa, Italy. *Telephone:* 43554.

BERNASKO, Col. Frank George, B.SC., LL.B., B.L.; Ghanaian army officer (retd.); b. 7 Dec. 1930, Cape Coast; s. of Frank George and Sophia Rosetta Bernasko; m. Esther Nyahan Aaku 1960; ed. Cape Coast Govt. Boys' School, Adisadel Coll., Univ. of Ghana, Legon, and Army School of Educ., Beaconsfield, England; Instructor Ghana Mil. Acad. 1960–62; Deputy Adjutant-Gen. Ghana Armed Forces 1962–65; Dir. of Studies Ghana Mil. Acad. 1965–66; Chair. Scholarship Review Bd. 1966–67; Dir. of Educ. Ghana Armed Forces 1966–72; Pres. Military Court-Martial, Port-of-Spain, Trinidad 1970–71; Regional Commr. Cen. Region 1972–73; Commr. for Agriculture 1973–75; Commr. for Cocoa Affairs Feb.-Sept. 1975; Leader, Action Congress Party 1979; all political parties proscribed Dec. 1981–; Vice-Pres. World Food Congress, Rome 1974; now in private legal practice. *Leisure interests:* music, athletics, voluntary work. *Address:* P.O. Box 9271, Airport Branch Post Office, Accra, Ghana.

BERNE, Robert Matthew, A.B., M.D.; American professor of physiology; b. 22 April 1918, Yonkers, New York; s. of Nelson Berne and Julia Stahl; m. Beth Goldberg; two s. two d.; ed. Univ. of North Carolina, Chapel Hill and Harvard Medical School; Intern, Asst. Resident, Mount Sinai Hosp. of New York 1943–44; U.S. Army Medical Corps 1944–46; Resident in Medicine, Mount Sinai Hosp. 1947–48; Research Fellow in Physiology, Western Reserve Univ. 1948–49, Instructor 1949–50, Sr. Instructor 1950–52, Asst. Prof. 1952–55, Assoc. Prof. 1955–61, Prof. 1961–66; Chair. and Charles Slaughter Prof. of Physiology, Univ. of Va. 1966–; mem. Bd. Science Counsel Nat. Heart, Lung and Blood Inst. 1986–; Carl J. Wiggers Award for significant contrib. towards understanding of circulation in health and diseases 1975; Gold Heart Award, American Heart Asscn. 1985. *Publications:* The Heart, in Handbook of Physiology 1979, Cardiovascular Physiology (with M. N. Levy) 1981, The Regulatory Function of Adenosine (with others) 1983, Physiology (Ed., with M. N. Levy) 1983; 191 scientific papers (1986). *Leisure interests:* tennis and fishing. *Address:* Department of Physiology, Box 449, School of Medicine, University of Virginia, Charlottesville, Va. 22908, U.S.A. *Telephone:* (804) 924-5109.

BERNEA, Horia Mihai; Romanian painter; b. 14 September 1938; s. of Ernest Bernea and Maria Bernea; m. Margareta Cucu 1963; ed. Coll. of Physics, Coll. of Architecture Bucharest and Coll. of Fine Arts Bucharest; one-man exhbns. in England, Scotland, France, Poland, Venice Biennial 1978, 1980, Holland, Romania, U.S.A., France, Young Artists' Biennalle 1979; mem. Fine Arts Union in Romania; leader Young Artists' Union, Romania 1976–81; numerous prizes. *Address:* Str. Şelari No. 13, Bucharest, Romania.

BERNER, Peter, DR.MED.; Austrian psychiatrist and neurologist; b. 15 Nov. 1924, Karlsbad; s. of Emil Berner and Grete Berner; m. Claire Leenhardt; one s. two d.; ed. Vienna Univ., Psychiatric Neurological

Clinic, Vienna Univ.; Mental Health Adviser to UNHCR, Geneva 1960–62; Visiting Prof., Lausanne 1966–67; Asst. Dir. Psychiatric Clinic, Vienna Univ. 1969–71, Head 1971–; Visiting Prof., Paris 1986–87; Sec.-Gen. World Psychiatric Assen. 1977–83; mem. Royal Coll. of Psychiatrists; Foreign Assoc. mem. Société médico-psychologique, Paris; Corresp. mem. German Assen. of Psychiatrists and Neurologists, American Psychiatrists Assen. *Publications:* 4 scientific books, 270 scientific papers. *Address:* Annagasse 8, A-1010 Vienna, Austria.

BERNHARD LEOPOLD FREDERIK EVERHARD JULIUS COERT KAREL GODFRIED PIETER, H.R.H. Prince (see under Netherlands).

BERNSTEIN, Baron (Life Peer), cr. 1969, of Leigh; **Sidney Lewis Bernstein,** LL.D.; British business executive; b. 30 Jan. 1899; a founder, Film Soc. 1924; mem. Middx. County Council 1925–31; Films Adviser, Ministry of Information 1940–45; Liaison, British Embassy, Washington 1942; Chief, Film Section, Allied Forces HQ, N. Africa 1942–43; Chief, Film Section, SHAEF 1943–45; Gov. Sevenoaks School 1964–74; Chair. Granada Group PLC 1934–79, Pres. 1979–; lectured on Film and Int. Affairs, New York and Yale Univs.; mem. Nuffield Foundation Resources for Learning Consultative Cttee. 1965–72, Jerusalem Cttee. 1969–; Fellowship British Film Inst. 1984, Directorate Int. Council of Nat. Acad. of TV Arts and Sciences of America 1984. *Address:* 36 Golden Square, London, W1R 4AH, England (Office).

BERNSTEIN, Leonard; American conductor, composer and pianist; b. 25 Aug. 1918, Lawrence, Mass.; s. of Samuel J. and Jennie (Resnick) Bernstein; m. Felicia M. Cohn 1951 (died 1978); one s. two d.; ed. Boston Latin School, Harvard Univ. and Curtis Inst. of Music; Asst. at Berkshire Music Center 1942, mem. of Faculty 1948–55, Head, Conducting Dept. 1951–55; Asst. Conductor New York Philharmonic Symphony 1943–44; Dir. New York City Symphony 1945–48; Musical Adviser Israel Philharmonic Orchestra 1948–49, frequent conductor 1947–; Prof. of Music, Brandeis Univ. 1951–56; conductor, maj. orchestras of U.S. tours of Europe 1946–; Co-conductor New York Philharmonic 1957–58, Musical Dir. 1958–69, Laureate Conductor for Life; conducted leading orchestras of America and in the capitals of Europe 1944–; music lectures on "Omnibus" television programme 1954–62; Dir. New York Phil. Young People's Concerts on nationwide television 1958–71; tours in S. America, Europe, Near East and U.S.S.R.; Journey for Peace (concerts for 40th anniversary Hiroshima bombing); Pres. English Bach Festival 1972–; Hon. Pres. Santa Cecilia Orchestra 1983–; Charles Eliot Norton Prof. of Poetry, Harvard Univ. 1972–73; TV Acad. Award (for Young People's Concerts) 1960, (for Outstanding Classical Music Programme) 1976, Kennedy Center Honors 1980, Lifetime Achievement Grammy Awards 1985, Nat. Fellowship Award 1985, Gold Medal, American Acad. and Inst. of Arts and Letters, Gold Medal Royal Philharmonic Soc. 1987, Edward MacDowell Medal 1987, Gold Medal British Philharmonic Soc. 1988, Johannes Brahms Prize 1988; Hon. citizen of Vienna 1988; Order of the Aztec Eagle 1982, Commdr. Légion d'honneur 1986. *Compositions:* Clarinet Sonata 1942, Seven Anniversaries for Piano 1942, I Hate Music (song cycle) 1943, Symphony No. 1— Jeremiah 1943, Fancy Free (ballet) 1943, On the Town 1945, Facsimile (ballet) 1946, Four Anniversaries for Piano 1948, Symphony No. 2—The Age of Anxiety 1949, Trouble in Tahiti (one-act opera) 1952, Wonderful Town 1953, On the Waterfront 1954 (film score), Serenade for Violin, Strings and Percussion 1954, Candide 1956, West Side Story 1957, Symphony No. 3—Kaddish 1963, Chichester Psalms (for chorus and orchestra) 1965, Mass: A Theatre Piece for Singers, Players and Dancers 1971, Dybbuk (ballet) 1974, Songfest, Slava!, Three Meditations from Mass 1977, A Quiet Place (full-length opera) 1983, Jubilee Games (for Orchestra with Baritone solo) 1986, Swan Song (for voice and strings) 1986, Opening Prayer (for Orchestra with Baritone solo) 1986, Trial Song (from the Race to Urga) 1987, Missa Brevis (for A Capella Chorus with incidental Percussion) 1988, My Twelve Tone Melody (song for voice and piano) 1988, Thirteen Anniversaries (for piano) 1988, Arias and Barcarolles (for piano four-hands and mixed voices) 1988, and other scores for stage and songs. *Publications:* The Joy of Music 1959, Leonard Bernstein's Young People's Concerts for Reading and Listening 1962, The Infinite Variety of Music 1968, The Unanswered Question 1976, Findings 1982. *Address:* Amberson Enterprises, 24 West 57th Street, New York, N.Y. 10019, U.S.A.

BERNSTEIN, Richard Barry, PH.D.; American professor of physical chemistry; b. 31 Oct. 1923, New York; s. of Simon and Stella Grossman Bernstein; m. Norma B. Olivier 1948; one s. three d.; ed. Columbia Coll., N.Y. and Columbia Univ., N.Y.; Asst. Prof. Ill. Inst. of Technology (Chicago) 1948; Asst. Prof., Assoc. Prof. Univ. of Mich. 1953–63; Prof. Univ. of Wis. 1963–66, W. W. Daniells Prof. 1966–73; W. T. Doherty Prof. of Chem. and Prof. of Physics, Univ. of Tex. 1973–77; Higgins Prof. of Natural Science, Columbia Univ. 1977–82, Chair. Chem. Dept. 1979–81; Sr. Vice-Pres. Occidental Research Corpn. 1982–83; Prof. of Chemistry, Univ. of California at Los Angeles 1983–; Chair. Office of Chem. and Chem. Tech., Nat. Research Council of N.A.S. 1974–79; mem. N.A.S.; Fellow, American Acad. of Arts and Sciences, American Acad. for the Advancement of Science, American Physical Soc.; A. P. Sloan Fellowship 1956; Nat. Science Foundation Sr. Post-doctoral Fellowship 1960; Peter Debye Award in Physical Chem., American Chem. Soc. 1981; Ed., Chemical Physics Letters 1978–81. *Publications:* numerous scientific articles (particu-

larly on molecular collisions) 1947–, Molecular Reaction Dynamics (with R. D. Levine) 1974, Atom-Molecule Collision Theory: A Guide for the Experimentalist (Editor) 1979, Chemical Dynamics via Molecular Beam and Laser Techniques 1982. *Leisure interest:* music. *Address:* UCLA, Department of Chemistry, 405 Hilgard Avenue, Los Angeles, Calif. 90024, U.S.A.

BERNSTEIN, Robert Louis; American publisher; b. 5 Jan. 1923, New York City; s. of Alfred and Sylvia Bernstein; m. Helen Walter 1950; three s.; ed. Harvard Univ.; U.S. Army Air Force 1943–46; with Simon & Schuster (book publrs.) 1946–57, Gen. Sales Man. 1950–57; Random House Inc. 1958–, Vice-Pres. (Sales) 1961–63, First Vice-Pres. 1963–65, Pres. and C.E.O. 1966, Chair. 1975; Vice-Chair. Assen. of American Publrs. 1970–72, Chair. 1972–73; Chair. Assen. of American Publrs. Cttee. on Soviet-American Publishing Relations 1973–74, on Int. Freedom to Publish 1975; Chair. U.S. Helsinki Watch Cttee., New York, 1979–; Vice-Pres. and Dir. Int. League for Human Rights 1977; Chair. Fund for Free Expression, New York; mem. Council on Foreign Relations, Nat. Advisory Cttee. Amnesty Int.; mem. Bd., Blythedale Children's Hospital, Writers and Scholars Int., The Chamber Music Soc. of Lincoln Center, New York; mem. The Century Assen., N.Y.; mem. Soc. of Fellows, New York Univ.; mem. Americas Watch. *Leisure interests:* skiing, tennis, swimming. *Address:* Random House, Inc., 201 East 50th Street, New York, N.Y. 10022 (Office); P.O. Box 607, Bedford, N.Y. 10506, U.S.A. (Home). *Telephone:* (212) 572-2276 (Office); (914) 234-3748 (Home).

BERRI, (Claude) (pseudonym of Langmann, Claude Beri); French film director; b. 1 July 1934, Paris; s. of Hirsh Langmann and Beila Bercu; m. Anne-Marie Rassam 1967; one s.; ed. Lycée Turgot, Paris; theatre and film actor 1951–63; writer and dir. of films 1963–; Grand Prix de l'Acad. du Cinéma 1986. *Films include:* Le Poulet 1963 (Acad. Award for best short film 1966), Le Vieil Homme et l'Enfant 1966, Mazel Tov ou le Mariage 1968, Le Pistonné 1970, Le Cinéma de Papa 1971, Sex-Shop 1972, Le Mâle du Siècle 1975, La Première Fois 1976, Un Moment d'égarement 1977, Je vous aime 1980, Le Maître d'Ecole 1981, Tchao Pantin 1983, Jean de Florette 1986, Manon des Sources 1986. *Address:* 10 rue Lincoln, 75008 Paris, France.

BERRI, Nabih; Lebanese politician and lawyer; b. 1939, Tibnin; s. of Mustapha Berri; m. 1st, six c.; m. 2nd; Leader Shi'ite Amal Movement 1978–; mem. Nat. Salvation Front –1984; Minister of Water and Electrical Resources and Justice, of State for the South and Reconstruction 1984–. *Address:* Ministry of Justice, Beirut, Lebanon.

BERRILL, Sir Kenneth, K.C.B., B.SC.(ECON.), M.A.; British economist; b. 28 Aug. 1920, London; s. of Stanley Berrill and Lilian Blakeley; m. 1st Brenda West 1941 (divorced), one s.; m. 2nd June Phillips 1950 (divorced 1976), one s. one d.; m. 3rd Jane Marris 1977; ed. London School of Econs. and Trinity Coll., Cambridge; H.M. Treasury (Cen. Econ. Planning Staff) 1947–49; lecturer in Econs., Cambridge Univ. 1949–69; Prof. M.I.T. 1962; Special Adviser, H.M. Treasury 1967–69; Brit. Nat. Comm. for UNESCO 1967–70; Gov. Admin. Staff Coll. Henley 1969–85; mem. Council for Scientific Policy 1969–72; Chair. Univ. Grants Cttee. of G.B. 1969–73; mem. Advisory Bd. for Research Councils 1972–73, 1976–78; mem. Advisory Council for Applied Research and Devt. 1977–80; apptd. Head of Govt. Econ. Service and Chief Econ. Adviser to H.M. Treasury 1973–74; Dir. Cen. Policy Review Staff, Cabinet Office 1974–80; Chair. Vickers Da Costa and Co. 1981–85, Securities and Investment Bd. 1986–88; Pro-Chancellor, Open Univ. May 1983–; Deputy Chair. Universities Superannuation Scheme 1980–85; mem. Advisory Bd., Royal Coll. of Defence Studies 1974–80; mem. Review Bd. for Govt. Contracts 1981–85; Deputy Chair. Gen. Funds Investment Trust 1981–85; Chair. Robert Horne Group 1987–; mem. Council Lloyds of London 1983–; Pro-Chancellor and Chair. of Council of Open Univ. 1983–; sometime Econ. Adviser to OECD, IBRD, Guyana, Cameroon, Turkey; City Councillor, Cambridge 1964–69; Hon. Fellow (L.S.E., King's Coll. and St. Catharine's Coll., Cambridge, King's Coll. London); Hon. LL.D. (Bath, Cambridge, East Anglia, Leicester), Hon. D.Univ. (Open Univ.), Hon. D.Tech. (Loughborough), Hon. Sc.D. (Aston). *Leisure interests:* sailing, skiing, music, theatre. *Address:* Salt Hill, Bridle Way, Grantchester, Cambs., CB3 9NY, England (Home).

BERRILL, Norman John, F.R.S., F.R.S.C., PH.D., D.SC.; Canadian zoologist; b. 28 April 1903; s. of Percy and Kate (née Stiles) Berrill; m. Jacquelyn Batsel 1939; one s. two d.; ed. Bristol Grammar School and London Univ.; Lecturer in Zoology, Univ. of London 1925–27; Lecturer in Physiology, Univ. of Leeds 1927–28; Asst. Prof. in Zoology, McGill Univ. Montreal 1928–31, Assoc. Prof. 1931–46, Chair. Dept. of Zoology 1937–47, Strathcona Prof. of Zoology 1947–65, Guggenheim Fellow 1964–65; Lecturer in Biology, Swarthmore Coll., Pa. 1969; Fellow, A.A.A.S. 1978. *Publications:* The Tunicata 1951, The Living Tide 1951, Journey into Wonder 1952, Sex and the Nature of Things 1953, Man's Emerging Mind 1955, The Origin of Vertebrates 1955, You and the Universe 1957, Growth, Development and Pattern 1961, Worlds Apart 1965, Biology in Action 1966, Inherit the Earth 1966, Life of the Ocean 1966, The Person in the Womb 1968, Life of the Sea Islands 1969, Developmental Biology 1971, Animals in Action 1972, Development 1976, Adam in Blunderland 1987. *Leisure interests:* naturalism, writing, painting. *Address:* 410 N. Swarthmore Avenue, Swarthmore, Pa. 19081, U.S.A. (Home). *Telephone:* (215) 544-1762.

BERRY, Brian Joe Lobley, M.A., PH.D.; American geographer, policy analyst and planner; b. 16 Feb. 1934, Sedgley, Staffs., U.K.; s. of Joe and Gwendoline (Lobley) Berry; m. Janet E. Shapley 1958; one s. two d.; ed. Univ. Coll., London and Univ. of Washington; Asst. Prof., then Prof. Univ. of Chicago 1958–76; Faculty mem. Brookings Inst. 1966–76; Prof. Harvard Univ. 1976–81; Prof. and Dean, School of Urban and Public Affairs, Carnegie Mellon Univ. 1981–86; Prof. Univ. of Tex. at Dallas 1986–; Fellow, Univ. Coll. London 1983; mem. N.A.S., American Acad. of Arts and Sciences, Asscn. of American Geographers, American Inst. of Certified Planners, Urban Land Inst., Inst. of British Geographers; numerous awards and prizes; Hon. A.M. (Harvard) 1976. *Publications:* numerous books and articles. *Leisure interests:* family history, genealogy, travel. *Address:* P.O. Box 83-2130, Richardson, Tex. 75083, U.S.A. (Home).

BERRY, Chuck (Charles Edward Anderson Berry); American singer and composer; b. 18 Oct. 1926, St. Louis; popular artiste in rock and roll, plays guitar, saxophone, piano; concert and TV appearances 1955–; Grammy Award for Life Achievement 1984. *Albums:* After School Sessions 1958, One Dozen Berry's 1958, New Juke Box Hits 1960, Chuck Berry 1960, More Chuck Berry 1960, On Stage 1960, You Can Never Tell 1964, Greatest Hits 1964, Two Great Guitars 1964, Chuck Berry in London 1965, Fresh Berrys 1965, St. Louis to Liverpool 1966, Golden Hits 1967, At the Fillmore 1967, Medley 1967, In Memphis 1967, Concerto in B Goods 1969, Home Again 1971, The London Sessions 1972, Golden Decade 1972, St. Louis to Frisco to Memphis 1972, Let the Good Times Roll 1973, Golden Decade (Vol. II) 1973, (Vol. V) 1974, Bio 1973, Back in the U.S.A. 1973, I'm a Rocker 1975, Chuck Berry 75 1975, Motorvatin' 1976, Rockit 1979. *Films:* Go, Johnny Go, Rock, Rock, Rock 1956, Jazz on a Summer's Day 1960, Let the Good Times Roll 1973, Hail! Hail! Rock 'n' Roll 1987. *Publication:* Chuck Berry: The Autobiography 1989. *Address:* Berry Park, 691 Buckner Road, Wentzville, Mo. 63385, U.S.A.

BERRY, Richard Stephen, PH.D., A.M.; American professor of chemistry; b. 9 April 1931, Denver, Colo.; s. of Morris Berry and Ethel (Alpert) Berry; m. Carla Lamport Friedman 1955; one s. two d.; ed. Harvard Univ.; Instructor, Univ. of Mich. 1957–60; Asst. Prof. Yale Univ. 1960–64; Assoc. Prof. Univ. of Chicago 1964–67, Prof. Dept. of Chem., James Franck Inst., Cttee. on Public Policy Studies 1967–; Gaeslv Prof. Univ. of Copenhagen 1967, 1979; Visiting Prof., Univ. de Paris-Sud 1979–80; Minstrelwood Lecturer, Oxford 1980; Chair., Numerical Data Advisory Bd., National Research Council 1978–84; Newton Abraham Prof., Oxford Univ., England 1986–87; mem. Visiting Comm. of Applied Physics, Harvard Univ. 1977–; mem. N.A.S.; Foreign mem. Royal Danish Acad. of Sciences; Fellow, A.A.A.S., American Acad. of Arts and Sciences; MacArthur Prize Fellow. *Publications:* (with L. Gaines and T. V. Long II) TOSCA: The Social Costs of Coal and Nuclear Power 1979, (with S. A. Rice and J. Ross) Physical Chemistry 1980; approximately 200 scientific papers in specialist journals. *Leisure interests:* music, skiing, hiking and climbing, photography, fly fishing. *Address:* Department of Chemistry, University of Chicago, 5735 S. Ellis Avenue, Chicago, Ill. 60637 (Office); 5317 S. University Ave., Chicago, Ill. 60615, U.S.A. (Home). *Telephone:* (312) 702-7021 (Office).

BERRY, Walter; Austrian baritone singer; b. 8 April 1929, Vienna; s. of Franz Berry and Hilde Jelinek; m. 1st Christa Ludwig (q.v.) 1957 (divorced 1970), one s.; m. 2nd Brigitte Hohenecker 1973; ed. Vienna School of Eng. and Vienna Music Acad.; student mem. Vienna State Opera 1950–53, ordinary mem. 1953–; awarded title Kammersaenger by Austrian Govt. 1963; Guest singer at openings of opera houses in Vienna, Munich, Berlin, Tokyo, New York (Metropolitan Opera), at festivals in Salzburg, Munich, Aix-en-Provence, Lucerne, Netherlands, Stockholm, Saratoga; appearances in New York, Chicago, Buenos Aires, Tokyo, London, Paris, Berlin, Munich, etc.; Prizes from Music Concourses in Vienna, Verviers and Geneva. Roles include: Wozzeck, Ochs von Lerchenau, Barak, Olivier, Escamillo, Pizarro, Telramund, Klingsor, Wotan, Amonasro, Scarpia, Figaro, Guglielmo, Leporello; Mozart Prize. *Leisure interests:* listening to and taping music, yachting, swimming, archaeology, photography. *Address:* Strassergasse 43-47, A-1150 Vienna, Austria.

BERRY, Wendell, M.A.; American author; b. 5 Aug. 1934, Henry County, Ky.; m. Tanya Amyx 1957; one s. one d.; ed. Univ. of Ky.; mem. Faculty, Univ. of Ky. 1964–77, 1987–, Distinguished Prof. of English 1971–72. *Publications:* novels: Nathan Coulter 1962, A Place on Earth 1967, The Memory of Old Jack 1974; short stories: The Wild Birds 1986; poetry: The Broken Ground 1964, Openings 1968, Findings 1969, Farming: A Handbook 1970, The Country of Marriage 1973, Clearing 1977, A Part 1980, The Wheel 1982, Collected Poems 1985, Sabbaths 1987; essays: The Long-Legged House 1969, The Hidden Wound 1970, The Unforseen Wilderness 1971, A Continuous Harmony 1972, The Unsettling of America 1977, Recollected Essays 1965–80 1981, The Gift of Good Land 1981, Standing by Words 1985; co-ed. Meeting the Expectations of the Land 1985, Home Economics 1987. *Address:* Port Royal, Ky. 40058, U.S.A.

BERS, Lipman, DR.RER.NAT.; American (naturalized 1949) mathematician; b. 22 May 1914, Riga, Latvia; s. of I. A. and Bertha (née Weinberg) Bers; m. Mary Kagan 1938; one s. one d.; ed. Univs. of Zurich, Latvia and Prague; research instructor, Brown Univ. 1942–45; Asst. Prof., later Assoc. Prof. Syracuse Univ. 1945–50; mem. Inst. for Advanced Study 1948–50; Prof. New York Univ. 1950–64, Chair. Grad. Dept. Math. 1959–64; Prof.

of Math., Columbia Univ., New York 1964–, Chair. Dept. Math. 1972–75, Davies Prof. of Math. 1975–82, Davies Prof. Emer. 1982–, Special Prof. 1982–84; Visiting Prof. CUNY Grad. Center (Chair. Math. Section 1967–70, Comm. on Human Rights 1979–84); Pres. American Math. Soc. 1974–76; mem. N.A.S.; American Acad. of Arts and Sciences; Fellow, American Philosophical Soc.; Hon. Life mem. New York Acad. of Sciences. *Publications:* Mathematical Aspects of Gas Dynamics 1958, co-author (with F. John and M. Schechter) Partial Differential Equations 1967, Calculus 1969 (2nd edn. with F. Karal 1976), numerous research papers. *Address:* Department of Mathematics, Columbia University, New York, N.Y. 10027; 111 Hunter Avenue, New Rochelle, N.Y. 10801, U.S.A. (Home).

BERSON, Jerome Abraham, M.A., PH.D.; American professor of chemistry; b. 10 May 1924, Sanford, Fla.; s. of Joseph and Rebecca Bernicker Berson; m. Bella Zevitovsky 1946; two s. one d.; ed. City Coll. of New York, Columbia and Harvard Univs.; Asst. Prof., Univ. of Southern Calif. 1950–53, Assoc. Prof. 1953–58, Prof. 1958–63; Prof., Univ. of Wis. 1963–69, Yale Univ. 1969–79; Irénée duPont Prof. 1979–; Chair. Dept. of Chem., Yale Univ. 1971–74; Dir. Div. of Physical Sciences and Eng. 1983–; Sherman Fairchild Distinguished Scholar, Calif. Inst. of Tech. 1974–75; mem. N.A.S.; Fellow, American Acad. of Arts and Sciences; Nat. Research Council Post-doctoral Fellow; American Chem. Soc. (Calif. Section) Award 1963, James Flack Norris Award in Physical Organic Chemistry 1978, Sr. U.S. Scientist Award, Alexander von Humboldt Foundation 1980; Townsend Harris Medal 1984; William H. Nichols Medal 1985, Roger Adams Award 1987. *Publications:* scientific papers on organic chem. published mostly in Journal of the American Chemical Society. *Leisure interests:* hiking, squash. *Address:* Department of Chemistry, Yale University, Box 6666, New Haven, Conn. 06511, U.S.A. *Telephone:* (203) 432-3970.

BERTHELOT, Yves M.; French statistician and economist; b. 15 Sept. 1937, Paris; m. Doris Yeatman 1961; three s. one d.; ed. Ecole Polytechnique and Ecole Nationale de la Statistique et de l'Administration Economique; Dir. of Studies in the Ministry of Planning, Ivory Coast 1965–68; Chief of the Study of Enterprises Div., then Chief of Service of Programmes of INSEE (Institut national de la Statistique et des Etudes Economiques) 1971–75; Chief, Service des Etudes et Questions Int., French Ministry of Co-operation 1976–78; Dir of Research, Devt. Centre of OECD, Paris 1978–81; Deputy Sec.-Gen. of UNCTAD 1985–. *Publications:* numerous articles on economics. *Leisure interests:* sailing, skiing, squash. *Address:* c/o UNCTAD, Palais des Nations, 1211 Geneva (Office); 25 rue de la Filature, 1227 Carouge GE, Switzerland (Home).

BERTHELSEN, Asger, D.PHIL.; Danish geologist; b. 30 April 1928, Aarhus; ed. Copenhagen and Neuchatel Univ.; State Geologist 1959; Prof. of Geology, Aarhus Univ. 1961, Copenhagen Univ. 1966–; Order of Dannebrog (1st Class). *Publications:* On the geology of the Rupshu District 1953, Geology of Tovqussap Nuna 1960, Precambrian of Greenland 1965, Geological Map of Ivigtut 1975, Geologi pa Rösnäs 1975, Den lille Tektoniker 1976, The EUGENO-S Project 1988. *Leisure interest:* oil painting. *Address:* Institute of General Geology, Geological Department, Østervoldgade 10, 1350 Copenhagen K (Univ.); Dammegade 8, 4792 Askeby, Møn, Denmark (Home). *Telephone:* (45-1) 11 22 32 (Univ.); (45-3) 81 74 56 (Home).

BERTHOIN, Georges Paul, L. EN D., L. ÈS SC.; French civil servant; b. 17 May 1925, Nérac; s. of Jean Berthoin and Germaine Mourgnot; m. 1st Anne W. Whittlesey, 2nd Pamela Jenkins; two s. four d.; ed. Univ. of Grenoble, Ecole des Sciences Politiques, Paris and Harvard and McGill Univs.; Private Sec. to Minister of Finance 1948–50; Head of Staff, Prefecture of Alsace-Lorraine-Champagne 1950–52; Prin. Pvt. Sec. M. Jean Monnet, Pres. of ECSC 1952–55; Counsellor for Information, ECSC 1955–56; Deputy Chief Rep. of ECSC in U.K. 1956; Acting Chief Rep. of Comm. of EEC 1967–68, Deputy Chief Rep. 1968–71, Chief Rep. 1971–73; Exec. mem. Trilateral Comm. 1973–75, European Chair. 1975–; Int. Chair of European Movement 1978–81; Bd. mem. Aspen-Berlin Inst.; mem. Int. Advisory Bd. Johns Hopkins Univ., Bologna, Nine Wise Men Group on Africa; Médaille militaire, Croix de guerre, Médaille de la Résistance. *Leisure interests:* art, theatre, walking, collecting objects. *Address:* 67 avenue Niel, Paris 17, France.

BERTHOUD, Sir Martin (Seymour), K.C.V.O., C.M.G.; British diplomatist; b. 20 Aug. 1931; s. of Sir Eric Berthoud; m. Marguerite J.R. Phayre 1960; three s. one d.; ed. Rugby School and Magdalen Coll. Oxford; served with British embassies in Teheran 1956–58, Manila 1961–64, Pretoria/Cape Town 1967–71, Teheran 1971–73; Counsellor, Helsinki 1974–77; Insp. H.M. Diplomatic Service 1977–79; Head, N. American Dept. FCO 1979–81; Consul-Gen. Sydney 1982–85; High Commr. in Trinidad & Tobago 1985–; Commdr. Order of Lion (Finland) 1976. *Leisure interests:* squash, tennis, food and wine, photography, bird-watching. *Address:* Foreign and Commonwealth Office, London, SW1A 2AH, England.

BERTI, Luciano; Italian art historian; b. 28 Jan. 1922, Florence; s. of Ferdinando and Ines Berti; m. Anna Maria Tinacci 1959; no c.; ed. Univ. of Florence; attached to Superintendency of Florence 1949; arranged new museums of Casa Vasari, Arezzo 1950, Palazzo Davanzati 1955, Il Museo di Arezzo 1958, Il Museo di S. Giovanni Valdarno 1959, Museum of Verna 1961, Museum of S. Croce, Florence 1962; Dir. Museums of Arezzo, San Marco and Acad., Florence; Dir. Museo Nazionale del Bargello; Dir. Uffizi

Gallery, Florence 1969-; Dir. Monuments, Pisa Gallery 1973-; Dir. of Galleries, Florence 1974-; mem. Consiglio Superiore 1976-80; Silver Medal, Ministry of Public Educ.; Dott. Laurea in Lettere; Libera docenza in Storia dell'Arte. . *Publications:* Filippino Lippi 1957, Masaccio 1964, Pontormo 1964, Pontormo disegni 1965, Il Principe dello Studiolo 1967, Il Museo tra Thanatos ed Eros 1979, Catalogue to the Uffizi Gallery 1979, various articles and catalogues. *Leisure interests:* history of art, museology. *Address:* Galleria degli Uffizi, Piazzale degli Uffizi, Florence (Office); Via Giusti 6, Florence, Italy (Home). *Telephone:* 244938 (Home).

BERTOLA, Giuseppe M., D.ENG.; Swiss electrical engineer and business executive; b. 7 May 1910, Vacallo; s. of Giovanni Bertola and Aida Agustoni; m. Maria Giussani 1935; four d.; ed. Milan School of Eng.; Eng. Dept., Brown Boveri Baden, Switzerland 1933, Sales Dept. 1944-45, Sales Man. 1958-62, Man. Dir. 1962-76; with various electro-mechanical firms in Germany, Italy and U.S.A. 1934-43; worked for Brown Boveri in Latin America 1945-58; mem. Man. Cttee. Brown Boveri Group 1970-76; Head of Brown Boveri Int. 1970-76; mem. Bd. BBC Brown Boveri e Cy. Ltd. 1962-82, Banca Svizzera Italiana 1974-83, Union Bank of Switzerland 1969-81, TIBB (Milan) 1959-88, Banca Commerciale Italiana (Suisse); Hon. Chair. Bd. Chambre de Commerce Latino-Américaine, Saras Petroleum; Chair. Soc. Suisse pour l'Industrie Horlogère (SSIH) 1975-81. *Leisure interests:* books, golf. *Address:* Zürichbergstrasse 130, CH 8044-Zürich, Switzerland. *Telephone:* 01 251 88 83.

BERTOLI, H.E. Cardinal Paolo; Vatican diplomatist; b. 1 Feb. 1908, Poggio Garf (Lucca); s. of Carlo and Aride Poli; ordained priest 1930; Sec. Apostolic Nunciature, Belgrade 1933-38, France 1938-42; Chargé d'affaires a.i., Antilles Apostolic Nunciature, Port-au-Prince, Haiti 1942-46; Counsellor, Apostolic Nunciature, Berne 1946-52; Head of Mission of Emigration to S. America; Titular Archbishop of Nicomedia 1952; Apostolic Del. in Turkey 1952-53, Apostolic Nuncio in Colombia 1953-59, in Lebanon 1959-60; France 1960-69; Prefect of Congregation for the Causes of Saints 1969-73; cr. Cardinal 1969; Suburbicarian Bishop of Frascati 1979-; Camerlengo of the Roman Catholic Church 1979-85. *Address:* Piazza della Città Leonina 1, 00193 Rome, Italy. *Telephone:* 6877312.

BERTOLUCCI, Bernardo; Italian film director; b. 16 March 1940, Parma; s. of Attilio Bertolucci; worked with Pier Paolo Pasolini on Accattone; directed: La Commare Secca 1962, Prima della Rivoluzione 1964, Il Fico Infruttuoso in Vangelo 70 1968, Partner 1970, La Strategia del Ragno 1970, Il Conformista 1970, Last Tango in Paris 1972, 1900 1975, La Luna 1979, Tragedy of a Ridiculous Man 1981, The Last Emperor 1986; European Film Award 1988. *Publications:* In cerca del mistero (poems) 1962 (Viareggio Prize 1962). *Address:* Via del Babuino 51, Rome, Italy.

BERTOUILLE, André; Belgian politician; b. 29 Jan. 1932, Renaix; m. Marie-Louise Lison; one d.; Sec. of State for Walloon Region 1980; Minister and mem. Walloon Regional Exec. 1981; Minister for Nat. Educ. 1983-85. Minister, mem. Exécutif de la Communauté française of Belgium Dec. 1985-. *Address:* Rue Belliard 7, 1040 Brussels (Office); Rue du Beequerelle 22, 7500 Tournai, Belgium. *Telephone:* (02) 513.65.90 (Office); (069) 23.10.74.

BERUTOWICZ, Włodzimierz; Polish lawyer and politician; b. 3 Oct. 1914, Przedmość, Wieluń district; m.; two c.; ed. Wrocław Univ.; fmr. Chief Justice, Voivodship Court of Justice, Poznań and Wrocław; Chair. Dept. of Law and Civil Procedure, Wrocław Univ., Rector, Wrocław Univ. 1968-71; Minister of Justice 1971-76; Chair. Legis. Council 1972-76; First Pres. of Supreme Court 1976-87; Chair. State Tribunal 1982-87; Prof., Acad. of Internal Affairs, Warsaw 1976-80, Polish Acad. of Sciences, Inst. of State and Law 1980-85; mem. Scientific Council 1985-; Deputy to Seym 1980-85; mem. Polish United Workers' Party (PUWP); mem. Polish Lawyers' Assen.; Order of Banner of Labour (1st and 2nd Class), Commdr. Cross of Order of Polonia Restituta (with Star) and other decorations. *Publications:* Principles of Party Presentation in Civil Procedure 1957, Juridical Importance of the Assertion of Claims in Civil Proceeding 1966, Outline of Civil Procedure 1974, 1978, 1984 and over 100 articles on civil procedure, policy of justice and legislative policy.

BESCH, Werner Walter, DR.PHIL.; German professor of German; b. 4 May 1928, Erdmannsweiler, Schwarzwald; s. of Matthias and Elisabeth (née Fuss) Besch; m. Katharina Müller 1957; one s. two d.; Prof. of German Language and Early German Literature, Ruhr Univ., Bochum 1965-70, Univ. of Bonn 1970-; Rector, Univ. of Bonn 1981-83, Pro-Rector 1983-85; mem. Wiss.-Rat., Inst. für deutsche Sprache, Mannheim 1976-; Corresp. mem. Heidelberg Akad. der Wissenschaften; mem. Rheinisch-Westfälische Akad. der Wissenschaften. *Publications:* Lautgeographie u. Lautgeschichte im obersten Neckar-u. Donaugebiet 1961, Sprachlandschaften u. Sprachausgleich im 15. Jahrhundert 1967, Dialekt/Hochsprache-Kontrastiv 1977, Handbuch Dialektologie 1983, Handbuch Sprachgeschichte 1985. *Leisure interests:* joinery, skiing, walking. *Address:* Germanistisches Seminar, Universität Bonn, Am Hof Id, 5300 Bonn, Federal Republic of Germany. *Telephone:* 0228-73/7712; 0228-73/7660.

BESSIAH, Boulaem; Algerian politician; b. 1930, El-Bayadh; m.; two c.; mem. Secr. gén. du Conseil nat. de la revolution algérienne 1959-62; Amb. to Benelux, EEC, Egypt; Sec.-Gen. Ministry of Foreign Affairs; Special Envoy of the Pres. of Algeria to numerous Heads of State; Dir. Algerian Del., many sessions of the Arab League, OAU, Islamic Conf. and non-

aligned States; Amb. to Kuwait; fmr. Minister of Information and Culture, Posts and Telecommunications, Culture and Tourism; Minister of Foreign Affairs 1988-; mem. Central Cttee. of FLN 1979-. *Address:* 6 rue 16h-Batran, el-Mouradia, Algiers, Algeria. *Telephone:* (2) 60-47.44.

BESSIE, Simon Michael, B.A.; American publisher; b. 23 Jan. 1916, New York; s. of Abraham Bessie and Ella (née Brainin) Bessie; m. 1st Constance Ernst 1945; one s. one d.; m. 2nd Cornelia Schaeffer 1968; ed. Harvard Univ.; reporter, Newark Star Eagle 1936; Research Dept. RKO-Radio Pictures 1936-38; Ed. Market Research Monthly 1938; War Corresp. Look Magazine 1940-42; Ed. Harper & Bros. 1946-52, Gen. Ed. 1952-59; Co-founder, Atheneum Publishers 1959, Pres. 1953-75; Sr. Vice-Pres. Harper & Row 1975-81, Dir 1975-; Pres. Joshuatown Publishing Assocs. 1981-; Co-Publisher Cornelia and Michael Bessie Books 1981-; lecturer English Columbia Univ. 1953-59; Dir. Novel Workshop New School 1959-63, Franklin Book Programs 1963-72; Chair. Visiting Cttee. Harvard Univ. Press 1972-78, Bd. of Dirs. 1980-; Dir. American Book Publishers' Council 1964-69; Chair. Trade Book Div. Assen. of American Publishers 1970-72, Dir. 1972-76, Chair. 1974-75; Chair. Literary Panel, Nat. Arts Council 1971-74, Special Projects Panel 1974-81; mem. Exec. Cttee. Center for the Book, Library of Congress 1979-, Chair. 1983-; mem. Bd. of Dirs. Center for Communication 1981-; Medal of Freedom. *Publications:* Jazz Journalism 1938; numerous articles. *Address:* 10 E. 53rd Street, New York, N.Y. 10022 (Office); Joshuatown Road, Lyme, Conn. 06371, U.S.A. (Home).

BESSIS, Marcel Claude, M.D.; French research haematologist and university professor; b. 15 Nov. 1917, Tunis; s. of Victor and Camilla (née Nahum) Bessis; m. Claude Perrot 1952; three d.; ed. Lycée Janson de Sailly and Univ. de Paris (School of Medicine); Dir. of Research Lab. of Nat. Centre for Blood Transfusion 1947-65; Prof. Faculty of Medicine, Paris 1963; Dir. Inst. Pathologie Cellulaire, Bicêtre Hosp. 1966-85; mem. Nat. Cttee. for Scientific Research 1964-66; Laureate Acad. des Sciences et de Médecine; Ed. Nouvelle Revue française d'Hématologie 1946-80, Ed.-in-Chief Blood Cells 1975-85; mem. French Acad. of Sciences; Hon. mem. Harvey Soc. 1963, Hon. Fellow, American Coll. of Physicians; Chevalier Légion d'honneur, Commdr. de l'ordre national du Mérite, Officier des Arts et des Lettres. *Publications:* Cytology of Blood and Blood-forming Organs 1956, Living Blood Cells and their Ultra-structure 1973, Corpuscles 1974, Blood Smears Reinterpreted 1977. *Address:* Hôpital Pitié-Salpétrière, département d'haematologie, 75651 Paris (Office); 32 avenue de l'Observatoire, 75014 Paris, France (Home).

BESSMERTNOVA, Natalya Igorevna; Soviet ballet dancer; b. 19 July 1941; m. Yuriy V. N. Grigorovich (q.v.); ed. Bolshoi Theatre Ballet School; artiste of Bolshoi Theatre Ballet 1961-; People's Artist, U.S.S.R., Anna Pavlova Prize, U.S.S.R. State Prize, Lenin Prize 1986. *Important roles include:* Mazurka and 7th Valse (Chopiniana), Pas de trois (Swan Lake), variations (Class-concert), Giselle (Giselle), The Muse (Paganini, music by Rachmaninov), Florin (Sleeping Beauty), Leila (Leila and Medjnun, by Balasanyan), Shirin (Legend of Love), Odette-Odile (Swan Lake), Girl (Le Spectre de la Rose), Maria (The Fountain of Bakhtchisaray), Phrygia (Spartacus), Juliet (Romeo and Juliet), Masha (The Nutcracker), Nikia (The Kingdom of Shades), Rita (Golden Age). *Address:* State Academic Bolshoi Theatre of U.S.S.R., 1 Ploshchad Sverdlova, Moscow, U.S.S.R.

BESTOR, Arthur Eugene, M.A., PH.D., LL.D., LITT.D.; American historian; b. 20 Sept. 1908, Chautauqua, N.Y.; s. of Arthur Eugene Bestor and Jeanette Louise (Lemon) Bestor; m. 1st Dorothea Nolte 1931 (divorced), 2nd Anne Carr 1939 (deceased), 3rd Dorothy Alden Koch 1949; three s.; ed. Yale Univ.; instructor, Yale 1930-31, 1934-36; Asst. Prof. Columbia Univ. 1937-42; Asst. Prof. Humanities, Stanford Univ. 1942-45, Assoc. Prof. History 1945-46; Assoc. Prof. of History, Univ. of Ill. 1947-51, Prof. 1951-62; Guggenheim Fellow 1953-54, 1961-62; Harmsworth Prof. of American History, Oxford Univ. 1956-57; Prof. of History, Univ. of Wash. 1962-77, Emer. Prof. 1976-; Visiting Lecturer, Univ. of Wis. 1947; Fulbright Visiting Prof., Univ. of Tokyo 1967; mem. American Historical Assen. (Pres. Pacific Coast Br. 1975-76), Org. of American Historians, Ill. State Historical Soc. (Pres. 1954-55), Council for Basic Educ. (Pres. 1956-57), Wash. State Historical Soc., Southern Historical Assen.; Beveridge Prize of American Historical Assen. 1946. *Publications:* Education and Reform at New Harmony 1948, Backwoods Utopias 1950 (revised edn. 1970), Problems of American History (jointly) 1952 (4th edn. 1972), Educational Wastelands 1953 (2 edn. 1985), The Restoration of Learning 1955, Three Presidents and Their Books 1955 (jointly), State Sovereignty and Slavery 1961, The American Civil War as a Constitutional Crisis 1964, The American Territorial System 1973 (jointly), Separation of Powers in the Domain of Foreign Affairs 1974, Respective Roles of Senate and President in the Making and Abrogation of Treaties 1979. *Leisure interests:* walking, photography. *Address:* Department of History, University of Washington, Seattle, Wash. 98195; 4553 55th Avenue, N.E., Seattle, Wash. 98105, U.S.A. *Telephone:* (206) 524-4202.

BETANCUR CUARTAS, Belisario; Colombian politician; b. 1923, Amaga, Antioquia; m.; one s. two d.; mem. House of Reps., later Senator; Conservative Party Presidential Cand. 1962, 1970, 1978, Pres. of Colombia 1982-86; Minister of Labour 1963; Amb. to Spain 1974. *Address:* c/o Oficina del Presidente, Bogotá, Colombia.

BETANCUR-MEJIA, Dr. Gabriel; Colombian international civil servant; b. 26 April 1918, Bogotá; m. Yolanda Pulecio 1959 (dissolved); two d.; ed. Univ. Javeriana, Bogotá, Syracuse Univ., U.S.A., and School of Advanced International Studies, Washington; fmr. Sec. of Tech. and Econ. Affairs to Pres. of Colombia; fmr. Founder and Dir. Colombia Inst. for Advanced Training Abroad (ICETEX); Prof. of Finance and Int. Trade; fmr. Dir.-Gen. Colombian Assen. of Univs.; Asst. Dir.-Gen. of UNESCO (in charge of educational activities) 1963-66; Minister of Educ., Colombia 1955-56, 1966-68; mem. Exec. Bd. UNESCO 1970-75, Vice-Chair. 1972-74; Pres. Int. Conf. Educ., Geneva 1970; Chair. Bd. Dirs. Univ. Pedagógica; Founder-Pres. Fundación José María Córdova 1986; Org. of American States Educ. Award 1982. *Publication:* Documentos para la Historia del Planeamento Integral de la Educación (3 vols.) 1985. *Address:* Transversal 17A, Número 98-45, Bogotá, D.E., Colombia. *Telephone:* 257-81-12.

BETHE, Hans Albrecht, PH.D.; Alsatian-born American physicist; b. 2 July 1906; m. Rose Ewald 1939; one s. one d.; ed. Goethe Gymnasium (Frankfurt/Main) and Frankfurt/Main and Munich Univs.; Lecturer German Univs. 1928-33, Manchester and Bristol Univs. (England) 1933-35; Asst. Prof. Cornell Univ. 1935-37, Prof. 1937-75, Prof. Emer. 1975-; Dir. Theoretical Physics Div. Los Alamos Scientific Lab. 1943-46; mem., Pres.'s Science Advisory Cttee. 1956-59; mem. American Philosophical Soc., N.A.S., American Physical Soc. (Pres. 1954), American Astronomical Soc.; foreign mem. Royal Soc. (London); Hon. D.Sc. (Birmingham) 1956, (Manchester) 1981; Presidential Medal of Merit 1946, Max Planck Medal 1955, Enrico Fermi Award 1961, Nobel Prize for Physics 1967, Vannevar Bush Award (N.A.S.) 1985. *Publications:* Elementary Nuclear Theory 1947, Mesons and Fields 1955, Intermediate Quantum Mechanics 1964, 1968; contributions to Handbuch der Physik 1933, 1957, Review of Modern Physics 1936-37, etc., and to scientific journals. *Address:* Laboratory of Nuclear Studies, Cornell University, Ithaca, N.Y. 14853, U.S.A.

BETTELHEIM, Bruno, PH.D.; American child-psychoanalyst; b. 25 Aug. 1903, Vienna, Austria; m. Trude Weinfeld 1941; one s. two d.; ed. Univ. of Vienna; took up residence in U.S. 1939; Asst. Prof. of Educ. Psychology and Psychiatry, Univ. of Chicago 1944-47, Assoc. Prof. 1947-52, Prof. 1952-73, Stella M. Rowley Distinguished Service Prof. of Educ. 1963-73, Prof. of Psychology and Psychiatry 1963-73, Dir. Univ. of Chicago Sonia Shankman Orthogenic School 1944-73, the univ.'s residential treatment centre for severely emotionally disturbed children; has written many books on severely disturbed children, social psychology and related issues; founder mem. Emer. Nat. Acad. of Educ.; Fellow, American Psychological Assen., Orthopsychiatric Assen.; mem. Chicago Psychoanalytic Soc., Chicago Council for Child Psychiatry. *Publications include:* Love is Not Enough 1950, Symbolic Wounds 1954, Truants from Life 1955, The Informed Heart 1960, Dialogues with Mothers 1962, The Empty Fortress 1967, The Children of The Dream 1969, Obsolete Youth 1970, A Home for the Heart 1974, The Uses of Enchantment 1976, Surviving and Other Essays (with Morris Janowitz) 1979, On Learning to Read: The Child's Fascination with Meaning (with Karen Zelan) 1982, Freud and Man's Soul 1983, A Good Enough Parent 1987 and numerous magazine articles. *Address:* 718 Adelaide Place, Santa Monica, Calif. 90402, U.S.A.

BETTELHEIM, Charles, D. EN D., L. ÈS L.; French economist; b. 20 Nov. 1913, Paris; s. of Henri Bettelheim and Lucienne Jacquemin; m. Lucette Beauvallet; five c.; ed. Paris Univ.; Dir. Centre for Social Studies and Int. Relations, Ministry of Labour, Paris 1944-48; French rep. Conf. on Trade and Employment 1947; Prof. of Political Economy at Ecole Pratique des Hautes Etudes 1948-; Head of UN Mission for Tech. Assistance to Indian Govt. 1955-56; Prof. at Ecole Nat. d'Administration; Prof. at Inst. d'Etudes du Développement Economique et Social 1958-; mem. French Sociological Inst.; Dir. of the review Problèmes de Planification and Centre d'Etudes des Modes d'Industrialisation (C.E.M.I.). *Publications:* La Planification soviétique 1939, Les problèmes théoriques et pratiques de la planification 1946, L'économie allemande sous le Nazisme 1946, Bilan de l'économie française de 1918 à 1946 1947, Esquisse d'un tableau économique de l'Europe 1948, Initiations aux recherches sur les idéologies économiques et les réalités sociales 1948, Emploi et chômage devant la théorie économique 1949, L'économie soviétique 1950, Auxerre en 1950 1950, Théories contemporaines de l'emploi 1951, Nouveaux aspects de la théorie de l'emploi 1952, Long-Term Planning Problems 1956, Foreign Trade and Planning for Economic Development 1956, Studies in the Theory of Planning 1959, Some Basic Planning Problems 1960, Teoria de la Planificación 1961, Problemas Teóricos y Prácticos de la Planificación 1962, L'Inde indépendante 1962, Planification et croissance accélérée 1964, La construction du socialisme en Chine 1965, Los Marcos Socioeconómicos y la organización de la planificación Social 1966, Problèmes théoriques et pratiques de la planification 1966, La transition vers l'économie socialiste 1968, India Independent 1968, Calcul économique et formes de propriété 1970, Révolution culturelle et organisation industrielle en Chine 1973, Les luttes de classes en U.R.S.S.—1917-1923 1974, Class Struggles in the U.S.S.R. 1917-1923 1975, Les luttes de classes en U.R.S.S.—1923-1930 1977, Class Struggles in the U.S.S.R. 1923-30 1978, China since Mao 1978, Les luttes de classe en U.R.S.S.—1930-41, Vol. 1, Les dominés 1982, Vol. 2 Les dominants 1983, Moscou, Place du Manège 1984, Orwell et il 1984 del Socialismo reale (jtly.) 1984, Parcours. *Address:* c/o Centre d'Etudes des Modes d'Industrialisation,1 rue du 11 Novembre, 92120 Montrouge, France. *Telephone:* 40.92.01.99.

BETTENCOURT SANTOS, Humberto; Cape Verde diplomatist; b. 17 Feb. 1940, Santo Antao Island; m.; two c.; ed. Catholic Univ. of Louvain, Belgium; mem. del. in negotiations on colonial dispute with Portugal 1975; elected Deputy to Nat. Ass. 1975, re-elected 1980; Dir.-Gen. Fisheries 1975-82; Amb. to EEC and to Nordic and Benelux countries 1982-87; Perm. Rep. of Cape Verde to UN 1987-; mem. Nat. Comm. on Law of the Sea 1979-82. *Address:* Permanent Mission of Cape Verde to United Nations, 27 East 69th Street, New York, N.Y. 10021, U.S.A. *Telephone:* (212) 472-0333.

BETTS, Donald Drysdale, M.SC., PH.D., F.R.S.C.; Canadian professor of physics; b. 16 May 1929, Montreal; s. of Wallace Havelock Betts and Mary Drysdale Betts; m. 1st Vilma Mapp 1954 (divorced 1981), 2nd Patricia Giles McWilliams 1986; three s. one d. two step-s.; Queen Elizabeth High School, Halifax, Dalhousie Univ., Halifax and McGill Univ.; Nat. Research Council Fellow Univ. of Alberta, Edmonton 1955-56, Asst. Prof. of Physics 1956-61, Assoc. Prof. 1961-66, Prof. 1966-80; Dean of Arts and Science Dalhousie Univ. 1980-, Prof. of Physics 1980-; Visiting Prof. of Physics King's Coll., London 1970-71, of Chemistry and Physics Cornell Univ., New York Jan.-June 1975; Dir. Theoretical Physics Inst. Univ. of Alberta 1972-78; Fellow Japan Soc. for Promotion of Science 1982; NATO Science Fellowship 1963-64; Nuffield Fellowship 1970. *Publications:* some 80 refereed articles in physics journals. *Leisure interests:* game of Go, hiking, sailing, badminton and swimming. *Address:* Faculty of Arts and Science, Dalhousie University, Halifax, B3H 4H6, Canada (Office); 8 Simcoe Place, Halifax, Nova Scotia, B3M 1H3, Canada (Home). *Telephone:* (902) 424-3540; (902) 443-3916.

BEUGEL, Ernst Hans van der: Netherlands professor of international relations (retd.) and business executive; b. 2 Feb. 1918; ed. Univ. of Amsterdam; Govt. service 1945-60; Sec., Econ. Cttee. of the Cabinet, Ministry of Econ. Affairs; Dir. Bureau of the Marshall Plan, Ministry for Foreign Affairs 1947, Dir. Gen. Econ. and Mil. Aid Programme 1952; Sec. of State (Ministry of Foreign Affairs) for Foreign Affairs 1957-58; Amb. and Special Consultant to the Minister for Foreign Affairs 1959; Deputy Pres. KLM Royal Dutch Airlines 1960-61, Pres. 1961-63; now Dir. of several companies in Belgium, Netherlands, U.K. and U.S.A.; Prof. of Int. Relations, Leiden Univ. 1966-84; mem. council Int. Inst. for Strategic Studies, London; Trustee, Carnegie Foundation; Grand Cross of the Oak Crown (Luxembourg), Grand Cross of the Order of Leopold II (Belgium), Knight Commdr. of the Order of St. Michael and St. George (U.K.), Grand Officer of Dannebrog (Denmark), Commdr. Légion d'honneur (France), Kt. Netherlands Lion, Commdr. Order of Orange-Nassau, Hon. Cross Order of House of Orange; NATO Award 1985. *Address:* Smidswater 1, 2514BV The Hague (Office); Jan Muschlaan 84, 2597TZ, The Hague, Netherlands (Home). *Telephone:* 653850 (Office); 280548 (Home).

BEUKES, Wiets Daniel, B.A.; South African journalist; b. 25 Aug. 1927, Brandfort, O.F.S.; ed. Univ. of O.F.S.; journalist with Die Volksblad, Bloemfontein 1949, political columnist 1953, Asst. Ed. 1956; Asst. Ed. Die Burger 1976, Ed. 1977-; Dir. Nasionale Koerante Bpk. 1983. *Publications:* contrib. to anthology of Afrikaans short stories 1971, Afrikaans novel 1975. *Leisure interest:* tennis. *Address:* P.O. Box 692, Cape Town, South Africa. *Telephone:* 254850.

BEUTLER, Ernest, M.D.; American research scientist and professor of medicine; b. 30 Sept. 1928, Berlin, Germany; s. of Alfred David and Kaethe (Italiener) Beutler; m. Brondelle Fleisher 1950; three s. one d.; ed. Univ. of Chicago; Resident in Medicine, Univ. of Chicago Clinics 1951-53, Asst. Prof., Univ. of Chicago 1956-59; Chair. Div. of Medicine, City of Hope Medical Centre, Duarte, Calif. 1959-78; Chair. Dept. of Clinical Research, Scripps Clinic and Research Foundation, La Jolla, Calif. 1978-82, Chair. Dept. Basic and Clinical Research 1982-, Head, Div. of Haematology-Oncology 1982-; Clinical Prof. of Medicine, Univ. of Southern Calif., Los Angeles 1964-79, Univ. of Calif., San Diego, La Jolla, Calif. 1979-; mem. N.A.S., American Acad. of Arts and Sciences, American Assen. of Physicians; Gairdner Award 1975; Blundell Prize 1985. *Leisure interests:* music and computer programming. *Address:* Scripps Clinic and Research Foundation, 10666 North Torrey Pines Road, La Jolla, Calif. 92073; 2707 Costebelle Drive, La Jolla, Calif. 92037, U.S.A. (Home). *Telephone:* (619) 455-8040 (Office); (619) 457-5790 (Home).

BEUVE-MÉRY, Hubert, L. ÈS L., D. EN D.; French journalist; b. 5 Jan. 1902, Paris; s. of Hubert and Josephine (née Tanguy) Beuve-Méry; m. Geneviève Deloye 1928; four s. (one deceased); ed. Paris Univ.; Dir., Legal and Econ. Section, Inst. Français de Prague 1928-39; diplomatic corresp. of Temps, Prague 1934-38; with Inst. Français, Lisbon 1940-42, Dir. Nat. School, Uriage; F. Le Monde 1944, Dir. 1944-69; Pres. Centre de formation et de perfectionnement des journalistes 1973-80; Assoc. Prof. Univ. of Paris I 1970-73; mem. Admin. Council Agence-France-Presse 1970-78; Inst. Pasteur 1970-72, Haut Comité de l'environnement 1971-75; Administrator Soc. of Publs. of La Vie Catholique 1972-; writes under pseudonym "Sirius"; Gold Medal, Inst. of Journalists 1970, Golden Pen of Freedom, Int. Fed. of Newspaper Eds. 1972. *Publications:* La théorie des pouvoirs publics d'après François de Vittoria et ses rapports avec le droit public contemporain 1928, Vers la plus grande Allemagne 1939, Réflexions politiques 1951, Suicide de la IVe République 1958, Onze ans de règne, 1958-1969, vus par Sirius 1974. *Address:* 107 boulevard Raspail, 75006 Paris, France. *Telephone:* 45.48.54.78.

BEVAN, Sir Timothy Hugh, Kt.; British banker; b. 24 May 1927, London; s. of Hugh Bevan and Pleasance Scrutton; m. Pamela Murray (née Smith) 1952; two s. two d.; ed. Eton; called to the Bar, Middle Temple 1950; Dir. Barclays Bank Ltd. (now Barclays Bank PLC) 1966, Vice-Chair. 1968, Deputy Chair. 1973, Chair. 1981-87; Dir. Barclays Int. Ltd. 1971-; Dir. BET Public Ltd. Co. 1987-, Chair. 1988-; Foreign and Colonial Investment 1987-; fmr. Dir. Soc. Financière Européenne 1967, fmr. Dir. Commercial Union Assurance Co. Ltd., Union Discount Co. of London Ltd. 1976-; Chair. Cttee. London Clearing Bankers 1983-85; Chair. City Communications Centre 1982-83. *Leisure interests:* sailing, gardening. *Address:* c/o BET Public Limited Company, Stratton House, Picadilly, London, W1X 6AS, England.

BEVAN, William, M.A., PH.D; American psychologist and foundation executive; b. 16 May 1922, Plains, Pa.; s. of William Bevan and Elizabeth Merrill Jones Bevan; m. Dorothy L. Chorpening 1945; three s.; ed. Staunton Mil. Acad., Franklin and Marshall Coll. and Duke Univ.; Instructor to Asst. Prof. Heidelberg Coll. 1946, 1948; Instructor, Duke Univ. 1947; Asst. Prof. to Prof. Emory Univ. 1948-59; Fulbright Scholar, Univ. of Oslo 1952-53; Prof. Kansas State Univ. 1959-66; Fellow, Center for Advanced Study in Behavioral Sciences 1965-66; Prof. Johns Hopkins Univ. 1966-74, Vice-Pres. and Provost 1966-70; Exec. Officer, A. A. A. S. 1970-74; Publr. Science Magazine 1970-74; William Preston Few Prof. Duke Univ. 1974-, Provost 1979-83; Vice-Pres. John D. and Catherine T. MacArthur Foundation 1983-. *Publications:* numerous articles on psychology and on science policy. *Address:* The John D. and Catherine T. MacArthur Foundation, Suite 700, 140 S. Dearborn Street, Chicago, Ill. 60603 (Office); Apartment 202, Lake Residence, 666 North Lakeshore Drive, Chicago, Ill. 60611, U.S.A. (Home). *Telephone:* (312) 736-8000 (Office); (312) 943-3351.

BEVERIDGE, Gordon Smith Grieve, PH.D., A.R.C.S.T., F.R.S.E., F.ENG., F.I.CHEM.E.; British academic; b. 28 Nov. 1933, St. Andrews, Scotland; m. Geertruida H.J. Bruyn; two s. one d.; ed. Inverness Royal Acad., Univ. of Glasgow, Royal Coll. of Science & Tech. Glasgow and Univ. of Edin.; Asst. Lecturer Univ. of Edin. 1956-60, Lecturer 1962-67; Post-doctoral Harkness Fellow of Commonwealth Fund, Univ. of Minn. 1960-62; Sr. Lecturer, Reader, Heriot-Watt Univ. 1967-71; Prof. of Chemical Eng. and Head, Dept. of Chemical and Process Eng. Univ. of Strathclyde 1971-86; Pres. and Vice-Chancellor, Queen's Univ. Belfast 1986-; industrial consultant; Chair. Cremer & Warner Group of cos. 1985-; other professional appts. *Publications:* Optimization: theory and practice (with R.S. Schechter) 1970; articles in learned journals. *Leisure interests:* walking, Marlburian war games. *Address:* Vice-Chancellor's Office, Queen's University, Belfast, Northern Ireland. *Telephone:* (0232) 245133.

BEVERLOO, Cornelis Van; Netherlands painter; b. 1922; ed. Amsterdam Acad. of Fine Arts; co-founder, with Appel and Constant, of the experimental "Reflex" group; co-founder of "Cobra" group 1948; rep. at numerous exhibitions, including Brussels Int. Exhibition 1958, Dunn Int. Exhibition, London 1963; works under the name of "Corneille".

BEVERTON, Raymond John Heaphy, C.B.E., M.A., F.R.S., F.I.BIOL.; British professor of fisheries science; b. 29 Aug. 1922; s. of Edgar John Beverton and Dorothy Sybil Mary Beverton; m. Kathleen Edith Marner 1947; three d.; ed. Forest School, Snaresbrook, Downing Coll., Cambridge; joined Fisheries Research Lab. (Ministry of Agric., Fisheries and Food MAFF) 1947, Deputy Dir., Fisheries Research 1959-65; Sec. NERC 1965-80; Sr. Research Fellow, Univ. of Bristol, engaged on study of change and adaptation in scientific research careers 1981-82; Programme Integrator, Int. Fed. of Insts. for Advanced Study 1982-84; Prof. of Fisheries Science, Dept. of Applied Biology, Univ. of Wales Inst. of Science and Tech. (UWIST) 1984-89; Head School of Pure and Applied Biology, Univ. of Wales Coll. of Cardiff Aug. 1988-; Hon. Professorial Fellow UWIST 1982-84, Hon. D.Sc. (Wales) 1988; Chair. Comparative Fishing Cttee. of Int. Council for Exploration of the Sea (ICES) 1957-62, Research and Statistics Cttee. of Int. Comm. for Northwest Atlantic Fisheries 1960-63; mem. Ministry of Agric., Fisheries and Food Fisheries Research and Devt. Bd. 1972-79; Head U.K. Del. to Intergovernmental Oceanographic Comm. 1981-84; Chair. Natural Sciences Advisory Cttee. for UNESCO 1984-85; Pres. Fisheries Soc. of British Isles; Vice-Pres. Freshwater Biological Asscn. 1980-; mem. Council, Scottish Marine Biology Asscn. 1984-86; Trustee, World Wildlife Fund, U.K. 1983-; Ed. ICES Journal 1983-. *Publications:* On the Dynamics of Exploited Fish Populations (with S.J. Holt) 1957; papers on math. basis of fish population dynamics, theory and practice of fisheries conservation and various fisheries research topics. *Leisure interests:* fishing, sailing, golf, music. *Address:* Montana, Old Roman Road, Langstone, Gwent, NP6 2JU, Wales. *Telephone:* (0673) 412392.

BEWLEY, Thomas Henry, M.A., M.D., F.R.C.P.I., F.R.C. PSYCH.; Irish consultant psychiatrist; b. 8 July 1926, Dublin; s. of Geoffrey Bewley and Victoria Jane Wilson; m. Beulah Knox 1955; one s. four d.; ed. St. Columba's Coll., Dublin, Trinity Coll., Dublin Univ.; trained at St. Patrick's Hosp., Dublin,

Maudsley Hosp., London and Univ. of Cincinnati, U.S.A.; Consultant Psychiatrist, Tooting Bec and St. Thomas' Hosps., London 1961-; mem. Standing Advisory Cttee. on Drug Dependence 1966-71, Advisory Council on Misuse of Drugs 1972-84; Consultant Adviser on Drug Dependence to Dept. of Health and Social Security 1972-81; Consultant WHO 1969-; Pres. Royal Coll. of Psychiatrists 1984-87 (Dean 1977-82); Jt. Co-Founder and mem. Council, Inst. for the Study of Drug Dependence 1967-; M.D. (Hons.). *Publications:* Handbook for Inceptors and Trainees in Psychiatry 1976; papers on drug dependence, medical manpower and side effects of drugs. *Leisure interest:* Irish Georgian Society (London Chapter).

BEXON, Roger, M.A., M.S.; British business executive; b. 11 April 1926, London; s. of the late Macalister Bexon, and the late Nora Hope (née Jenner) Bexon; ed. Denstone Coll., St. John's Coll., Oxford Univ., Tulsa Univ., U.S.A.; m. Lois Loughran Walling 1952; one s. one d.; Geologist, Trinidad Petroleum Devt. Co. Ltd. 1946-57; managerial positions with British Petroleum Co. Ltd. (B.P.), E. Africa 1958-59, Libya 1959-60, Trinidad 1961-64, London 1964-66, Man. North Sea Operations 1966-68, Gen. Man., Libya 1968-70, Regional Co-ordinator for Middle East, London 1971-73, Gen. Man. Exploration and Prodn., London 1973-76, Man. Dir. B.P. Exploration Co. Ltd., London 1976-77, Man. Dir. B.P. 1981-86, Deputy Chair. Dec. 1983-86, Chair. B.P. Gas Ltd. 1981-86, Chair B.P. Exploration Co. Ltd. 1981-86; Dir. and Sr. Vice-Pres. Standard Oil Co., Cleveland, Ohio 1977-80, Dir. 1982-86; Dir. B.P. Canada Inc. 1981-87; Dir. BICC 1985-; Dir. J. H. Fenner (Holdings) PLC 1986-; Dir. Lazard Bros. & Co. Ltd. 1986-, Dir. Cameron Iron Works, Inc. 1986-, Majestic Wine PLC 1987; Chair. Laporte Industries (Holdings) PLC 1986-. *Leisure interests:* reading, golf, Times crosswords. *Address:* Laporte Industries (Holdings) PLC, 3 Bedford Square, London, WC1B 3RA, England.

BEYER, Frank Michael; German composer and professor of composition; b. 8 March 1928, Berlin; s. of Oskar Beyer and Margarete (née Löwenfeld) Beyer; m. Sigrid Uhle 1950; one s. one d.; ed. Beliner Kirchen-musikschule, Staatliche Hochschule für Musik (HDK), piano training in Leipzig; began career in church music; Docent Berliner Kirchenmusikschule 1953-62; with Hochschule für Musik Berlin, Prof. of Composition 1968-; initiated range of 'musica nova sacra' 1970-85; Supervisory mem. of Gema 1973-83; Exec. mem. German Music Bds. 1978-82; mem. Akademie der Künste Berlin 1979-, Dir. of Music Div. 1986-; mem. Bayerischen Akademie der Schönen Künste 1981-; Kunstpreis Berlin for Young Generation 1957, Bernhard-Sprengel Prize 1962. *Publication:* Orchester- und Kammermusik, Orgelwerke und solistische Musik Klavierstücke. *Leisure interest:* philosophy. *Address:* Söhtstrasse 6, 1 Berlin 45, Federal Republic of Germany. *Telephone:* 030/8338051.

BEYNON, John Herbert, D.SC., C.CHEM., F.R.S., F.R.S.C., C.PHYS., F.INST.P.; British professor of chemistry; b. 29 Dec. 1923, Ystalyfera, Wales; s. of Leslie Ewart and Phyllis (née Gibbon) Beynon; m. Yvonne Lilian Fryer 1947; Scientific Officer, Tank Armament Research 1943-47; Man. and Sr. Research Assoc., Physical Chemistry Research, ICI Dyestuffs Div.; Prof. of Chemistry and Dir. Mass Spectrometry Center, Purdue Univ., U.S.A. 1969-74; Visiting Prof., Univs. of Warwick and Essex 1974-; Royal Soc. Research Prof., Univ. Coll. of Swansea, 1974-87; Assoc. Inst. Jožef Stefan, Yugoslavia, Hon. mem. mass spectrometry Socs. of Japan, China and Yugoslavia, Hon. Fellow Bosnian Chem. Soc. 1982; 3M-Boomer Award 1965, Hasler Award for Spectroscopy 1979, Jan. Marc Marci Medal 1984, Gold Medal of the Int. Mass Spectrometry Soc. 1985, Frank H. Field and Joe L. Franklin Award of the American Chemical Soc. 1987, Hon. Fellow Univ. Coll. Swansea 1988. *Publications:* 10 books and over 400 scientific papers. *Leisure interests:* photography, golf. *Address:* Chemistry Building, University College of Swansea, Swansea, SA2 8PP (Office); 17 Coltshill Drive, Mumbles, Swansea, SA3 4SN, Wales. *Telephone:* 0792-295298 (Office); 0792-368718 (Home).

BEYNON, Sir (William John) Granville, Kt., C.B.E., F.R.S., PH.D.; British professor of physics; b. 24 May 1914; s. of William Beynon and Mary Beynon; m. Megan Medi James 1942; two s. one d.; ed. Gowerton Grammar School, Univ. Coll., Swansea; Scientific Officer, later Sr. Scientific Officer, Nat. Physical Lab. 1938-46; Lecturer, later Sr. Lecturer in Physics, Univ. Coll. of Swansea 1946-58; Prof. and Head of Dept. of Physics, Univ. of Wales, Aberystwyth 1958-81, Prof. Emer. 1981-; mem. S.R.C. 1976-80; mem. Schools Council 1965-76; Pres. URSI 1972-75, Hon. Pres. 1981-; Hon. Professorial Fellow, Univ. Coll. Swansea 1981-; Hon. D.Sc. (Leicester) 1981. *Publications:* Solar Eclipses and the Ionosphere (Ed.) 1956, Proceedings Mixed Commission on the Ionosphere (Ed.) 1948-58; numerous publs. in scientific journals. *Leisure interests:* music, cricket, tennis, rugby. *Address:* Caebryn, Caergôg, Aberystwyth; Bryn Eithin, 103 Dunvant Road, Swansea, Wales. *Telephone:* Aberystwyth 3947; Swansea 23585.

BEZOMBES, Roger; French painter; b. 17 Jan. 1913; has exhibited in Paris since 1937 and taken part in most overseas exhibitions of French art; work shown in Musée d'Art Moderne and Musée des Beaux Arts (Paris) and in museums in Paris, Menton, Algiers, Oran, Rabat, Athens, Jerusalem, etc.; one-man exhbn., Centre Georges Pompidou, Paris 1982; Prix Nat. de Peinture. *Works include:* paintings, illustrations for Le grain de Sable 1955, Les Fleurs du Mal (Baudelaire) 1986, lithographs; mural decorations for the steamer Ile de France and the liner France, also for apartments at the official residence of the Pres. of the Republic, etc.;

tapestries executed at Aubusson, including the collection for the Maison d'Afrique, Univ. of Paris; Nouvelle Maison de la Radio de Paris; Brussels Exhibition 1958; scenery and costume for the Metropolitan Opera N.Y. 1958; Peintre Officiel de la Marine; mem. Acad. des Sciences d'Outre Mer; Chevalier de la Légion d'honneur; Prof. Académie Julian. *Publication:* L'Exotisme dans l'art et la pensée 1954. *Address:* 3 quai Saint-Michel, 75005 Paris, France.

BHABHA, J. J., B.A.; Indian industrialist; b. 21 Aug. 1914, Bombay; ed. Gonville and Caius Coll., Cambridge, Lincoln's Inn, London; Chair. Tata Services Ltd., Tata McGraw-Hill Publishing Co. Ltd., Tata Press Ltd., Stewarts & Lloyds of India Ltd., Marg Educ. and Art Foundation; Vice-Chair. Associated Bldg. Co. Ltd.; Dir. Tata Sons Ltd., Indian Hotels Co. Ltd., CBS Gramophone Records and Tapes (India) Ltd., Vantech Investments Ltd.; Vice-Chair. and Trustee-in-Charge Nat. Centre for the Performing Arts; Man. Trustee Sir Dorabji Tata Trust; Trustee Lady Tata Memorial Trust, J.H. Bhabha Memorial Trust, Prince of Wales Museum of Western India, etc.; Chair. Governing Bd. Tata Inst. of Social Sciences; mem. Governing Council Nat. Inst. of Design, Admin. Council of the Int. Fund for the Promotion of Culture, UNESCO 1977–83, and other.; Kt. Commdr. of the Order of Merit (Italy) 1976, Commdr.'s Cross of the Order of Merit (Fed. Repub. of Germany) 1978, Commdr.'s Cross of the Order of the Crown, Belgium 1979, Austria Award of Honour 1984. *Address:* Tata Sons Ltd., Bombay House, Homi Mody Street, Bombay 400001 (Office); 12 Little Gibbs Road, Malabar Hill, Bombay 400006, India (Home).

BHAGAT, Bali Ram; Indian politician; b. 1 Oct. 1922; ed. Patna Coll.; Secretary Bihar Provincial Congress Cttee. 1949; mem. Provisional Parl. 1950–52, Lok Sabha 1952–77, Speaker 1976–77; Parl. Sec. Ministry of Finance 1952–55; Deputy Minister for Finance 1955–63; Minister of State for Planning 1963–67, for Defence March-Nov. 1967, for External Affairs 1967–69, 1985–86; Minister in charge of Foreign Trade and Supply 1969–70; Minister for Steel and Heavy Industry 1970–71. *Address:* c/o Indian National Congress, 5 Dr. Rajendra Prasad Road, New Delhi, India.

BHAGAT, Dhanraj; Indian sculptor; b. 20 Dec. 1917, Lahore, Pakistan; s. of B. Hargobind and Lakshmi Done; m. Kamla Devi 1943; two s. two d.; ed. Khalsa High School and Mayo School of Arts, Lahore; Teacher, Mayo School of Arts 1939 and 1944; lecturer in Sculpture, Delhi Polytechnic Art Dept. 1946–60, Sr. lecturer 1960–62, Asst. Prof. 1962–68, Prof. 1968–73; numerous commissions throughout India; works in stone, wood, plaster, cement and metal-sheet; ten one-man sculpture shows in India 1950–72; exhbns. abroad in London and Paris 1948, E. European countries 1955 and 1958, U.S.A. 1954, Fed. Repub. of Germany 1958, São Paulo 1962, S. Africa 1965; mem. Lalit Kala Acad. Punjab; mem. Nat. Cttee. of Int. Asscn. of Plastic Arts, Paris; invited to participate in first and second triennial exhbn. of World Art, New Delhi; works in Govt. Museum, Punjab, National Gallery of Modern Art, New Delhi, Lalit Kala Acad., Baroda Museum and Punjab Univ. Museum; Nat. Award of Lalit Kala Acad. 1961, State Award 1969. *Leisure interests:* reading art and philosophy books. *Address:* College of Art, 22 Tilak Marg, New Delhi; and H 20, New Delhi South Extension Part 1, New Delhi, India.

BHAGAT, H. K. L., M.A.; Indian politician; m.; three c.; mem. Lok Sabha 1971–; Minister of State in Ministry of Works and Housing 1975–77, 1982–83, Minister of State for Information, Broadcasting and Parl. Affairs 1983–84, Minister for Parl. Affairs and Tourism 1985–86, Minister of Parl. Affairs, Food and Civil Supplies 1986–88, of Parl. Affairs and Information and Broadcasting Feb. 1988–; Pres. Delhi Pradesh Congress Cttee. 1972–83; Head, several Indian int. dels. *Address:* Ministry of Information and Broadcasting, Shastri Bhavan, New Delhi 110001, India.

BHAGAVANTAM, Suri, M.SC.; Indian scientist and university professor; b. 1909, Gudivada, A.P.; s. of S. V. S. Sastry and S. Sitamma; m. Sitamahalakshmi 1924; four s. one d.; ed. Nizam Coll., Hyderabad and Madras Univ.; Prof. of Physics and Prin. Andhra Univ. until 1948; Scientific Liaison Officer, B.C.S.O. and Scientific Adviser to Indian High Commr. in U.K., London 1948–49; Prof. of Physics, Osmania Univ. 1949–52. Vice-Chancellor and Dir. Physical Labs. 1952–57; Dir. Indian Inst. of Science, Bangalore 1957–62; Scientific Adviser to Minister of Defence 1961–69; Pres. Cttee. on Science and Tech. in Developing Countries (COSTED) 1972–80; Chair. Bharat Electronics Ltd., Cttee. on Org. of Scientific Research; Vice-Pres. Int. Union of Pure and Applied Physics; Dir. Hindustan Aeronautics Ltd.; Hon. D.Sc., F.N.I. and F.A.Sc. *Leisure interests:* light reading, writing. *Publications:* Scattering of Light and Raman Effect 1940, Theory of Groups and Its Application to Physical Problems 1952, Crystal Symmetry and Physical Properties 1966. *Address:* Indian Institute of Technology, Madras 600036, India. *Telephone:* 414046.

BHAJAN LAL, Chaudhri; Indian politician; b. 6 Oct. 1930; ed. Bahwal Nagar, W. Pakistan; mem. Haryana Legis. Ass. 1968–, Minister in Haryana Cabinet 1970–75, Minister for Co-operation, Dairy Devt., Animal Husbandry, Labour and Employment 1978–79; Chief Minister of Haryana 1979–86; mem. Rajya Sabha 1986–; Union Minister of Environment and Forests Oct. 1986–88, of Agric. and Rural Devt. Feb. 1988–. *Leisure interests:* nature, wildlife. *Address:* Ministry of Agriculture and Rural Development, Krishi Bhavan, Dr. Rajendra Prasad Road, New Delhi, India.

BHANDARI, Sunder Singh, M.A., LL.B.; Indian politician; b. 12 April 1921, Udaipur, Rajasthan; s. of Dr. Sujan Singh Bhandari and Phool Bai; unmarried; ed. Sirohi, Udaipur and Kanpur; Advocate, Mewar High Court, Udaipur 1942–43; Headmaster, Shiksha Bhawan, Udaipur 1943–46; Divisional Pracharak, Rashtriya Swayamsewak Sangh, Jodhpur 1946–51; Provincial Sec. Bharatiya Jana Sangh (People's Party), Rajasthan 1951–57; All India Sec. Bharatiya Jana Sangh 1961–65, All India Organizing Sec. 1965–66; mem. Rajya Sabha 1966–72, 1976–82; Leader, Janasangh Group in Rajya Sabha 1967–68; Gen. Sec. Bharatiya Jana Sangh 1967–77; mem. Janata Party Cen. Exec. 1977–80, Cen. Election Panel; Deputy Parl. Leader Janata Party 1977–80; fmr. Convenor, Foreign Collaboration Comm. Janata Parl. Party; Vice-Pres. Bharatiya Janata Party (BJP) 1980–, in charge of Rajasthan, U.P., Bihar and W. Bengal 1983–85, in charge All India BJP org. wing 1986–, Deputy Leader, Bharatiya Janata Parl. Party 1980–82; mem. Panel of Farmers, Agric. Prices Comm. 1978–79, Sub-cttee. on Interests of Scheduled Tribes and Castes, Comm. on Subordinate Legislation 1980–82; Del. to Inter-Parl. Council session (Lisbon, Portugal) 1978. *Leisure interest:* reading. *Address:* 10 Dr. Rajendra Prasad Road, New Delhi; Panchayati Nohara, Udaipur, Rajasthan, India. *Telephone:* 387830 (New Delhi).

BHATIA, Prem Narain; Indian journalist and diplomatist; b. 1911, Lahore; s. of late H. N. D. Bhatia and late Puran Devi Bhatia; m. Shakuntala Ram 1942; two s. one d.; ed. Government Coll., Lahore, and Punjab Univ.; Army Service, Second World War; Dir. of Public Information, Bengal Govt. 1945–46; Political corresp. The Statesman (Calcutta and New Delhi) 1946–58; Public Relations Adviser, Indian Embassy, Moscow 1948; Ed. The Tribune, Ambala 1959; Resident Ed. The Times of India, Delhi 1960–62; Delhi Ed. The Indian Express 1963–65; Indian corresp. The Guardian (Manchester and London); High Commr. in Kenya 1965–68, in Singapore 1969–72; Ed.-in-Chief, Dir. India News and Features Alliance 1973–76, Tribune Group of Publs. 1977–86; Consultant The Tribune Trust 1986–; mem. Press Council of India, Nat. Integration Council; Dir. Press Inst. of India. *Publications:* All My Yesterdays, Indian Ordeal in Africa. *Leisure interests:* reading, golf. *Address:* The Tribune, Chandigarh-160020, India. *Telephone:* 23176.

BHATT, Ravishanker, M.A.; Indian merchant banker; b. 13 Dec. 1909; s. of Santoshram Bhatt; m. Pushpa N. Pathak; two s. two d.; ed. Samaldas Coll., Bhavnagar, Bombay School of Econs. and Sociology and London School of Econs.; Sec. Industrial Investment Trust Ltd. 1936–40, Sec. Diwan's Office, Bhavnagar State, subsequently Nayab Diwan (finance and railway) 1940–47; Finance Officer, Oriental Govt. Security Life Assurance Co. Ltd. 1948–53; Man. Dir. Bombay State Finance Corpn. 1953–57; mem. Govt. of India Tariff Comm. 1957–60; Exec. Dir. Indian Investment Centre 1960–64, Chair. –1972; Chair. Unit Trust of India 1964–72, Ahmedabad Electricity Co. Ltd., Surat Electricity Co. Ltd., Micro-Precision Pumps and Gears Ltd.; Dir. Premier Automobiles Ltd., Atul Products Ltd., Industrial Investment Trust Ltd., Jardine Henderson Ltd., Unichem Labs. Ltd.; Kesoram Industries Ltd., Gujerat Tubes Ltd., Gaekwar Mills Ltd., Zaudu Pharmaceutical Works Ltd.; Chair. Kanthal Bimetals India Ltd; fmr. Chair. Nat. Research Devt. Corpn. of India; Adviser, Merchant Banking Div., State Bank of India; Leader, Indian Del. to UN Comm. on Transnat. Corps.; Hon. Fellow, L.S.E. *Publications:* Capital for Medium and Small-Scale Industries; various articles on economic and financial subjects. *Leisure interests:* reading plays and poetry, long walks. *Address:* Ewart House, Homi Mody Street, Bombay 400023, India. *Telephone:* 272543.

BHATT, Uddhav Deo, M.A.; Nepalese diplomatist; b. 1 March 1932, Baitadi; m.; five c.; section officer, Ministry of Foreign Affairs 1960; First Sec. then Counsellor, New Delhi 1961–67; Chief of Protocol 1967–68; Deputy Perm. Rep. to UN, New York 1969–72; Joint Sec. Int. Org. Div., Ministry of Foreign Affairs 1972–75, Foreign Sec. 1975–79; del. to confs. of Non-Aligned heads of state and ministerial meetings 1973–; Perm. Rep. to UN 1979–87. *Address:* Ministry of Foreign Affairs, Kathmandu, Nepal.

BHATTACHARYA, Basu; Indian film director, producer and writer; b. 31 Jan. 1936, Murshidabad, W. Bengal; m. Rinki Bhattacharya 1963; one s. two d.; Pres. Indian Film Dirs. Asscn. 1978–85; Dir. Nat. Film Devt. Corpn. 1980–87; mem. Nat. Film Policy Working Group; mem. Jury, Moscow Int. Film Festival 1981; recipient of numerous film awards. *Films include:* Teesri Kasam 1966, Anubhav 1972, Sparsh 1981, Griha Pravesh 1982, Panchvati 1986. *Leisure interests:* poetry, painting, gardening. *Address:* Gold Mist, 36 Carter Road: Bandra, Bombay 50, India. *Telephone:* 6424727.

BHATTACHARYYA, Birendra Kumar, B.SC., M.A., PH.D.; Indian journalist and writer; b. 16 March 1924, Suffry Sibsagar, Assam; s. of Sashidhar and Aideo Bhattacharyya; m. Binita Bhattacharyya 1958; two s. one d.; ed. Jorhat Government High School, Cotton Coll., Gauhati, Calcutta Univ. and Gauhati Univ.; fmr. Science Teacher, Ukrul High School, Manipur; Ed. Ramdhenu 1951–61, Sadiniya Navayung 1963–67; lecturer in Journalism, Gauhati Univ. 1974–; Exec. mem. Janata Party, Assam; Sec. Archaeological Soc. of Assam; Sahitya Akademi Award for Assamese Literature 1961, Jnanpitho Award 1979. *Publications:* novels: Iyaruingam (won Akademi Award), Rajpathe Ringiai (Call of the Main Street), Mother, Sataghai (Killer), Mrityunjay, Pratipad, Nastachandra, Ballart, Kabar Aru Phul,

Ranga Megh, Daint; collections of short stories: Kolongajioboi (Still Flows the Kolong), Satsari (Necklace); Aurobindo (biography), A Survey of Assamese Modern Culture (in Assamese). *Address:* Kharghuli Development Area, Gauhati 4 Assam, India. *Telephone:* 25019.

BHICHAI RATTAKUL, Nai; Thai politician; b. 16 Sept. 1926, Bangkok; m. Nang Charoye; two s. one d.; ed. St. Peter's School, Bangkok, St. Stephen's Coll., Hong Kong; fmr. Man. Dir. Jawarad Co. Ltd., Pres. Thai Pharmaceutical Mfrs. Asscn., Vice-Pres. Druggists Asscn. of Thailand, Dir. Thai Chamber of Commerce, Bd. of Trade, and of Asscn. of Thai Industries, rep. of Thai Employers to Gen. Confs. of ILO, Geneva, Deputy mem. Asian Advisory Cttee. of ILO; joined Democrat Party 1958; M.P. for Bangkok Metropolis 1969-71, 1975-; mem. Nat. Convention, Nat. Legis. Ass., Constitution Scrutiny Cttee. 1973; Minister of Foreign Affairs 1975-86; Deputy Prime Minister 1986-; Deputy Leader Democrat Party. *Address:* Government House, Nakhan Pathan Road, Bangkok 10300, Thailand.

BHOGILAL, Pratap, M.A.(ECON.); Indian business executive; b. 25 Oct. 1916, Bombay; s. of Bhogilal Leherchand; m. Bhagwati Bhogilal 1939; one s. three d.; ed. Bombay Univ.; former Chair. Millowners' Asscn., Bombay Textile Research Asscn., Shree Ram Mills Ltd.; Pres. Indian Merchants' Chamber 1968, 1985; fmr. mem. Cttee. Fed. of Indian Chambers of Commerce and Industry, Bombay Chamber of Commerce and Industry; fmr. mem. Textile Wage Bd.; fmr. Trustee, Bombay Port Trust; now Vice-Pres. Employers' Fed. of India; Chair. Gov. Council Bhogilal Leherchand Inst. of Indology, Delhi; mem. Apex Council of Assoc. Chambers of Commerce and Industry; mem. Cttee. Indo-French Chamber of Commerce and Industry, Indian Merchants Chamber, Millowners' Asscn.; Chair. Batliboi & Co., Ltd. *Leisure interests:* swimming, bridge, long walks. *Address:* Batliboi & Co. Ltd., Apeejay House, V.B. Gandhi Marg, Fort, Bombay 4000 23, India. *Telephone:* 243823; 244332.

BHUIYAN, Rabia, B.C.L.; Bangladesh politician; b. 1 March 1944, Dhaka; m. Mozammel Hoque Bhuiyan; one s. one d.; fmr. Exec. Cttee. mem. and Asst. Sec., Supreme Court Bar Asscn., Bangladesh; Vice-Pres. Asian and Pacific Region, Int. Fed. of Women Lawyers; Pres. Bangladesh Mahila Ainjibi Samiti; mem. World Asscn. Muslim Scholars; mem. Faculty of Law, Dhaka Univ.; mem. Ethical Cttee., Bangladesh Medical Research Council; Dir. and f. mem. Inst. of Democratic Rights; mem. English and American Bar Asscns.; fmr. practising Barrister, Bangladesh Supreme Court; Minister for Social Welfare and Women's Affairs 1985-87; mem. numerous cttees. and councils. *Publications:* numerous contribs. to law journals. *Address:* c/o Ministry of Social Welfare and Women's Affairs, Bangladesh Secretariat, Bhaban 6, New Bldg., Dhaka, Bangladesh.

BHUMIBOL ADULYADEJ; King of Thailand; b. 5 Dec. 1927, Cambridge, Mass., U.S.A.; ed. Bangkok and Lausanne, Switzerland; youngest son of Their Royal Highnesses Prince and Princess Mahidol of Songkhla; succeeded his brother, the late King Ananda Mahidol, June 1946; married Her Majesty the present Queen Sirikit, daughter of H.H. the late Prince Chandaburi Suranath, 28th April 1950; formal Coronation 5th May 1950; one son, H.R.H. Crown Prince Maha Vajiralongkorn, b. 1952; three daughters, H.R.H. Princess Ubol Ratana, b. 1951, H.R.H. Princess Maha Chakri Sirindhorn, b. 1955, H.R.H. Princess Chulabhorn, b. 1957. *Address:* Chitralada Villa, Bangkok, Thailand.

BHUSHAN, Shanti, B.SC., LL.B.; Indian lawyer and politician; b. 11 Nov. 1925, Bijnor, Uttar Pradesh; set up legal practice in Allahabad High Court 1948; Sr. Standing Counsel 1962; Advocate-Gen. of Uttar Pradesh 1969-70; Chair. Uttar Pradesh Bar Council 1970-71; Treas. Working Cttee. of Org. Congress 1972-77; counsel for Raj Narain (q.v.) in Rae Bareli Constituency case; Treas. Janata Party Jan-April. 1977; Minister of Law, Justice and Company Affairs 1977-79; All-India Treas. Bharatiya Party 1979-86; Leader of Indian Del. to UN Confs. on the Law of the Sea New York June 1977, Sept. 1978, Geneva April 1979, to Commonwealth Law Ministers' Conf. Winnipeg Aug. 1977. *Address:* B-16, Sector 14, NOIDA, District Ghaziabad, Uttar Pradesh, India 201301 (Home).

BHUTTO, Benazir; Pakistani politician; b. 21 June 1953; d. of the late Zulfikar Ali Bhutto (died 1979) and of Begum Nusrat Bhutto (q.v.); m. Asif Ali Zardari 1987; one s.; ed. Harvard Univ. and Lady Margaret Hall, Oxford; under house arrest 1977-84; leader in exile of Pakistan People's Party with her mother Nusrat and involved in the Movt. for the Restoration of Democracy in Pakistan 1984-; returned to Pakistan 1986; Prime Minister Dec. 1988-. *Publication:* Daughter of The East (autobiog.) 1988. *Address:* Pakistan Secretariat, No 11, Rawalpindi, Pakistan.

BHUTTO, Nusrat; Pakistani politician; b. 1934; widow of Zulfikar Ali Bhutto (died 1979); two s. two d. (Benazir Bhutto q.v.); fmr. first lady of Pakistan; Chair. Pakistan People's Party and involved in the Movt. for the Restoration of Democracy in Pakistan 1984-.

BI DEXIAN; Chinese scientist; b. 21 Dec. 1908; Vice-Chancellor, Nanjing Coll. of Telecommunications and Eng.; researcher of cybernetics; Deputy, 2nd NPC 1959-64; mem. Dept. of Tech. Sciences, Academia Sinica 1985-. *Address:* 2 Yudaojie Biaoying Street, Najing, People's Republic of China.

BIAGGI, Francantonio; Italian consulting engineer; b. 1899; ed. Politecnico, Milan, and Pavia Univ.; Operation engineer, Società Orobia, Milan

1924-46, Engineering Man. 1946, later Deputy Gen. Man.; Gen. Man., later Man. Dir. Società Elettrica Bresciana Brescia 1946-; Man. Dir. Società Energia Elettrica (SENEL), Rome, Società Elettrica Valle Camonica; Vice-Pres. Società Lago d'Idro, Brescia; Dir. Rezzato-Vobarno Railway, Brescia; Appointee for Foreign Relations, Società Edison, Milan; expert OEEC Cttee. for Tariffs; Councillor, Federazione Nazionale Imprese Elettriche (FENIEL), Associazione Imprese Elettriche Lombarde Trentine Emiliane (AIELTE); fmr. mem. Italo-Austrian Cttee. for East Tyrol Hydro-Electric Plants; Italian Govt. del. to European Tech. Comm. of ECA for study of interconnection problems in U.S.A. 1949; Councillor Associazione Nazionale Imprese Produttrici e Distributrici di Energia Elettrica (ANIDEL); Dir. Società Italiana Autotrasporti (SIA). *Publications:* L'elettricità in Diritto 1946, Ordnungsprobleme der elektrischen Energiewirtschaft im Rahmen der Erfahrungen in Italien 1951, Report on the Tecaid Mission in the United States (with Marin) 1949. Wechselwirkungen zwischen Tarifpolitik und Ausbauplanung der Energieerzeugung (with Boselli) 1952. *Address:* Piazza Vittoria 7, 1-25100 Brescia, Italy.

BIAGGI, Mario, LL.B.; American politician and lawyer; b. 26 Oct. 1917, New York; s. of Salvatore Biaggi and Mary Biaggi; m. Marie Wassil 1941; two s. two d.; ed. Haaren High School, New York Law School; letter carrier, U.S. Postal Service 1936-42; served New York City Police Dept. 1942-65; entered law school at age of 45; admitted to New York Bar 1966; f. law firm Biaggi and Ehrlich 1967; Community Relations Specialist, New York State Div. of Housing 1961-63; Asst. to Sec. of State, New York 1963-65; mem. of Congress (19th Dist. New York; Democrat) 1969-; Adjunct Prof. of Political Science, Herbert H. Lehman Coll., Bronx, New York 1980-81; Pres. Nat. Police Officers' Asscn. 1967, Nat. Council of Columbia Asscns. 1958-; mem. American Bar Asscn. and other bodies; Medal of Honor for Valor, New York Police Dept. 1960; Cavaliere, Order of Merit (Italy); Kt. Commdr., Order of Merit of the Italian Republic; many other hon. degrees and awards. *Address:* 2428 Rayburn House Office Building, Washington, D.C. 20515, U.S.A.

BIAGGINI, Benjamin Franklin; American business executive; b. 15 April 1916, New Orleans, La.; s. of Benjamin F. Biaggini, Sr. and Maggie (Switzer) Biaggini; m. Anne Payton 1937; two d.; ed. St. Mary's Univ. of Texas and Harvard Business School; fmr. Chair., Dir., C.E.O. Southern Pacific Co.; Chair., C.E.O., Dir. Southern Pacific Transportation Co.; Chair., Dir. St. Louis Southwestern Railway Co.; Dir. Tenneco. Inc., Ticor, SRI Int.; Pres. Calif. Chamber of Commerce 1973; founder, Vice-Chair. Calif. Roundtable; mem. Business Council, Conf. Bd., Business Roundtable, Nat. Transportation Policy Study Comm. 1976-; Trustee, Calif. Inst. of Tech., Nat. Safety Council, Transportation Council of Calif., Transportation Cttee. of Chamber of Commerce of the U.S.A., American Railway Eng. Asscn.; Hon. LL.D. (St. Mary's, Tex.) 1965. *Address:* Southern Pacific Building, 1 Market Plaza, San Francisco, Calif. 94105, U.S.A.

BIAŁOSTOCKI, Jan, PH.D.; Polish art historian; b. 14 Aug. 1921, Saratov, U.S.S.R.; s. of late Jan Białostocki and Walentyna Wereninow; m. Jolanta Maurin 1950; one d.; ed. Univ. of Warsaw; Asst. Univ. of Warsaw 1946-50, Asst. Prof. 1959-62, Assoc. Prof. 1962-72, Prof. 1972-; Asst. Nat. Museum, Warsaw 1945-55, Curator and Head of Dept. of Foreign Art 1956-; Visiting Fellow, Princeton Univ. 1958; Visiting Prof. Yale Univ. 1965-66; Visiting mem. Inst. for Advanced Study, Princeton 1973, 1983; Visiting Prof. Coll. de France 1978; Slade Prof. Univ. of Cambridge 1985; Hon. LL.D. (Groningen) 1969; Hon. Ph.D. (Brussels) 1987; Herder Prize 1970, Polish Nat. Prize 1978, Warburg Prize 1980; Reuchlin Prize 1983. *Publications include:* Stil und Ikonographie 1966, Dürer and His Critics 1986, L'arte de Quattrocento nell' Europa Settentrionale 1988, The Message of Images 1988, festscrift Ars Auro Prior 1981. *Leisure interests:* music, mountain tourism. *Address:* Muzeum Narodowe, al. Jerozolimskie 3, PL 00-495 Warsaw (Office), Długa 30/34-7, PL 00-238 Warsaw, Poland (Home). *Telephone:* 211031 (Office); 318094 (Home).

BIANCHERI, Boris, B.L.; Italian diplomatist; b. 3 Nov. 1930, Rome; m.; one s. one d.; ed. Univ. of Rome; entered diplomatic service 1956, Office of the Sec. of State, Ministry of Foreign Affairs 1956-58; Italian Embassy, Athens 1959; Econ. Affairs Dept., Ministry of Foreign Affairs 1964-67, Counsellor 1967-71; Sec.-Gen. of Govt. Comm. for 1970 Universal Osaka Exhbn. 1968; Political Counsellor, Italian Embassy, London 1972-75; Head of Office of Sec.-Gen. Ministry of Foreign Affairs 1975-78, Chef de Cabinet Sec. of State for Foreign Affairs 1978, Minister Plenipotentiary 1979; Amb. to Japan 1980-84; Dir.-Gen. Personnel and Admin., Ministry of Foreign Affairs 1984, Dir.-Gen. Political Affairs 1985; Amb. to U.K. 1987-. *Leisure interests:* gardening, boating, swimming, horse-riding. *Address:* Italian Embassy, 14 Three Kings' Yard, London, S.W.1., England.

BIANCINI, Angelo; Italian sculptor; b. 1911; ed. Accademia di Santa Luca; Prof. and Artistic Dir. Istituto d'Arte, Faenza; Regular Exhibitor Venice Biennali and Rome Quadriennali 1934-58; international exhibitor throughout the world; Prize, Milan Triennale 1940, Venice Biennale 1958. Major works: three statues. Galleria d'Arte Moderna, Rome, Canadian Temple, Rome, Mosaic Marist Fathers' International Coll. etc. *Address:* Istituto d'Arte di Ceramica, Faenza, Italy.

BIANCO, Jean-Louis; French civil servant; b. 12 Jan. 1943, Neuilly-sur-Seine; s. of Louis Bianco and Gabrielle (née Vandries) Bianco; m. Martine

148

Letoublon 1971; two s.; ed. Lycée Janson-de-Sailly and Inst. d'études politiques, Paris; Auditor Conseil d'Etat 1971; Official Rep. Group central des villes nouvelles 1973–74; attached to Ministry of Health 1976–79; Counsel Conseil d'Etat 1976; Official Rep. Syndicat intercommunal de devt. Durance-Bléone 1979–81; Official Rep. to the advisers of the Pres. 1981; Sec.-Gen. to the Pres. 1982–; Pres. Bd. of Dirs., Nat. Office of Forestry. *Address:* Palais de l'Elysée, 33 rue du Faubourg Saint-Honoré, 75008 Paris, France.

BIBIN, Leonid Alekseyevich, CAND. ECON. SC.; Soviet politician; b. 1930; ed. Dnepropetrovsk Inst. of Eng. and Transport; work for Amur railways 1952; mem. CPSU 1953–; party work 1952–54; Second, First Sec. of Blagoveshchensky City Cttee. of CPSU 1958–63; head of section of Amur Dist. Cttee., of CPSU 1963–67; work for CPSU Cen. Cttee. 1967–71; dir. of state Econ. Planning Cttee., collegiate mem. of U.S.S.R. Ministry of Construction 1971–73; Deputy Minister, then first Deputy Minister of U.S.S.R. Ministry of Construction 1973–84; First Deputy Pres. of U.S.S.R. Gosplan 1984–86; First Deputy Pres. of U.S.S.R. State Cttee. for Construction, U.S.S.R. Minister 1986–; cand. mem. of CPSU Cen. Cttee. 1986–. *Address:* The Kremlin, Moscow, U.S.S.R.

BICH, Baron Marcel; French business executive; b. 29 July 1914, Turin, Italy; s. of Aime-Mario Bich and Marie Muffat de Saint-Amour de Chanaz; m. 1st Louise Chamussy (deceased), three s. one d.; one d. from union with Jacqueline de Dufourcq; m. 2nd Laurence Courier de Méré, two s. four d.; ed. Coll. Saint-Elme, Arcachon, Faculté de droit de Paris; Production Man. Stephens; f. and Pres. Société Bic 1950–; participated in America's Cup in his yacht France 1970, 1974, 1977, 1980; Chevalier Légion d'honneur. *Address:* 8 impasse des Cailloux, 92110 Clichy (Office); 80 rue de Chézy, 92200 Neuilly-sur-Seine, France (Home).

BIDDLE, Eric H.; American administrator; b. 27 April 1898, Philadelphia, Pa.; s. of Fred Davis Biddle and Estelle Harbeson; m. 1st Katharine Rogers 1926, three s.; m. 2nd Janet Mayo 1957, one step-d.; ed. Univ. of Pennsylvania and Oxford Univ.; Industrial Man. and Finance 1922–32; Relief Admin. of Pa. 1932–35; Exec. Dir. Community Fund of Philadelphia 1935–40; Exec. Vice-Pres. U.S. Cttee. for Care of European Children from the war zones 1940–41; mission to U.K. 1941, Head Special Mission to U.K. and missions to European, Middle East and Occupied Territories 1942–46 for various U.S. Govt. Depts.; Adviser U.S. Del. UNRRA 1945, UNESCO 1946, UN 1945–46; Chair. Advisory Group of Experts on Admin., Personnel and Budgetary questions to UN Gen. Ass. 1945–47; Special Asst. to Sec.-Gen. UN 1946; Special Asst. to Dir. of OIC, Consultant to Asst. Sec. of State for Public Affairs and special missions to Europe 1947; Special Asst. for Overseas Admin. ECA, Acting Chief ECA Mission to Korea and Asst. to U.S. Ambassador to Korea 1948; Consultant, ECA Mission to Italy and Special Asst. to Dir. of German and Austrian Affairs, Dept. of State 1949; Consultant to Chair., Nat. Sec. Resources Bd., exec. office of the Pres. 1949–51, and to various ECA and MSA officials 1951–53; Special Consultant to Exec. Chair. Tech. Assistance Bd. (UN); Management Consultant 1953–57, Vice-Pres. and Dir. Porter Int. Co. 1957–65; Vice-Pres. United States Leasing Corpn. 1958–61; Pres. Biddle Associates 1961–81. *Address:* 1200 N. Nash Street, Arlington, Va. 22209, U.S.A. (Home). *Telephone:* (703) 243-4766.

BIDE, Sir Austin (Ernest), Kt., B.SC., F.R.S.C., C.B.I.M., C.CHEM.; British business executive; b. 11 Sept. 1915, London; s. of Ernest Arthur and Eliza (Young) Bide; m. Irene Ward 1940; three s.; ed. Univ. of London; mem. of staff, Dept. of Govt. Chemist until 1940; Research Dept. Glaxo Laboratories Ltd., Deputy Sec. 1954, Sec. 1959; Dir. Glaxo Group Ltd. 1963; Deputy Chair. Glaxo Holdings Ltd. 1971–73; Chief Exec. 1973–80, Chair. 1973–85, Hon. Pres. 1985–; mem. Council CBI 1974–85, Chair, Research and Tech. Cttee. 1977–86, mem. Pres.'s Cttee. 1983–85; mem. Council British Inst. of Management 1976–81, 1982–, Companions Cttee. 1976–84, Chair. Finance Cttee. 1976–79, Dir. and Chair. B.I.M. Foundation 1977–79; Dir. British Leyland (now BL Ltd.) 1977– (non-exec. Deputy Chair. May 1980–82, non-exec. Chair. 1982–86, J. Lyons and Co. 1977–78; mem. Working Party on Biotechnology, Council of the Imperial Soc. of Knights Bachelor 1980–, British Inst. of Man. 1982–; Chair Visiting Cttee. of the Open Univ. 1982–; mem. Advisory Cttee. on Industry to Vice-Chancellors and Prins. of Univs. of U.K. 1984–; mem. Review Body, Univ. Grants Cttee., mem. Council of Inst. of Manpower Studies 1985–, Adam Smith Inst. 1985 (Chair. 1986–); Chair. Q-Ca Ltd 1985–, Microtest Research Ltd. 1987–; Trustee, British Motor Industry Heritage Trust 1983–86; mem. Court of British Shippers' Council 1984–; Chair. Salisbury Cathedral Appeal Cttee. 1986–; mem. MRC 1986; Hon. Fellow, Vice-Pres. Inst. of Industrial Mans. 1983, Hon. Fellow Inst. of Chemical Engineers; Hon. Fellow, Inst. of Biotechnological Studies, mem. Advisory Council 1985–; Hon. D.Sc. (Queen's, Belfast); Fellow St. Catharine's Coll., Cambridge. *Leisure interests:* fishing, handicrafts. *Address:* c/o Glaxo Holdings PLC, Clarges House, 6-12 Clarges Street, London, W.1, England.

BIDEN, Joseph Robinette, Jr., J.D.; American politician; b. 20 Nov. 1942, Scranton, Pa.; s. of Joseph R. Biden and Jean F. Biden; m. 1st Neilia Hunter (deceased), two s. one d.; m. 2nd Jill Tracy Jacobs 1977; one d.; ed. Univ. of Delaware, Newark and Syracuse Univ. Coll. of Law, N.Y.; Trial Attorney in the Public Defender's Office, Del. 1968; Founder of Biden & Walsh Law Firm, Wilmington; mem. New Castle Co., del. and

American Bar Asscns., American Trial Lawyers' Asscn.; admitted to practise before the Del. Supreme Court; mem. New Castle Co. Council 1970–72; Senator from Delaware 1972–, serving as a mem. of the Cttee. on Foreign Relations, Judiciary Cttee. (Chair.); named to the Democratic Steering Cttee.; Democrat. *Leisure interests:* sports, history, public speaking, American architecture. *Address:* 489 Russell Building, Washington, D.C. 20510, U.S.A. (Office).

BIDWELL, Charles Edward, PH.D.; American professor of education and sociology; b. 24 Jan. 1932, Chicago; s. of Charles L. Bidwell and Eugenia Campbell Bidwell; m. Helen Claxton Lewis 1959; one s.; ed. Univ. of Chicago; Lecturer in Sociology, Harvard Univ. 1959–61; Assoc. Prof. 1965–70, Prof. of Educ. and Sociology 1970–85, Reavis Prof. Educ. and Sociology 1985–, Chair. Dept. of Educ. 1978–; Guggenheim Fellow 1971–72; Fellow A.A.A.S.; mem. Nat. Acad. of Educ. *Publications:* The School as a Formal Organization, in Handbook of Organizations (Ed. J. March) 1965, The Organization and its Ecosystem (with J.D. Kasarda) 1985. *Leisure interests:* skiing and reading. *Address:* 5835 Kimbark Avenue, Chicago, Ill. 60637, U.S.A. *Telephone:* (312) 962-9456.

BIDWELL, Roger Grafton Shelford, PH.D., F.R.S.C.; Canadian scientist; b. 8 June 1927, Halifax, N.S.; s. of Rear-Adm. Roger E.S. Bidwell, R.C.N. and Mary G. (Bothamly) Bidwell; m. Shirley Mae Rachel Mason 1950; one s. three d.; ed. Dalhousie Univ., Halifax, Queen's Univ., Kingston, Ont.; Scientist, Nat. Research Council of Canada, Halifax 1956–59; Assoc. Prof. of Botany, Univ. of Toronto 1959–65; Prof. and Chair., Biology, Western Reserve Univ., Cleveland, Ohio, U.S.A. 1965–69; Prof. of Biology Queen's Univ., Kingston, Ont. 1969–79; Killam Univ. Research Prof., Dalhousie Univ., Halifax 1981–85; Exec. Dir. Atlantic Inst. of Biotechnology, Halifax 1985–88; Sr. Partner, Atlantic Research Assocs., Wallace, N.S. 1980–; Fellow A.A.A.S.; Queen Elizabeth II Silver Jubilee Medal 1977, Gold Medal, Canadian Soc. of Plant Physiologists 1979. *Publications:* 120 papers, chapters and articles, five books on plant physiology. *Leisure interests:* walking, birding, cross-country skiing, bicycling, music. *Address:* Rivendell, RR No.1, Wallace, N.S. B0K 1Y0, Canada. *Telephone:* (902) 257-2035.

BIEBER, Owen F.; American labour official; b. 28 Dec. 1929, North Dorr, Mich.; s. of Albert F. Bieber and Minnie Schwartz Bieber; m. Shirley M. Van Woerkom 1950; three s. two d.; ed. High School; elected Regional Dir., United Auto Workers (UAW) Region 1D 1974–80, Vice-Pres. Int. Union 1980–83, Pres. 1983–; Hon. D.Hum. (Grand Valley Coll.), Hon. Dr. Sc. (Ferris State Coll.). *Address:* 8000 E. Jefferson, Detroit, Mich. 48214, U.S.A. (Office). *Telephone:* 313 926 5201 (Office).

BIEDENKOPF, Kurt Hans, DR.JUR.; German lawyer and politician; b. 28 Jan. 1930, Ludwigshafen; s. of Wilhelm and Agathe (Schmidt) Biedenkopf; m. 1st Sabina Wautig, four c.; m. 2nd Ingrid Ries 1979; Prof. of Law, Ruhr Univ., Bochum 1964–70, Rector 1967–69; Chair. Govt. Comm. on co-determination 1968–70; Vice-Pres. Henkel Corpn., Düsseldorf 1970–73; Gen. Sec. Christian Democratic Party (CDU) 1973–77, Vice-Pres. 1977–83; Pres. CDU Regional Asscn., North Rhine-Westphalia 1977–87; mem. Bundestag 1976–80, 1987–; Chair. Inst. for Econ. and Social Policy, Bonn 1977–; mem. Landtag of North Rhine-Westphalia; mem. Senate Max Planck Gesellschaft; mem. Kuratorium, Volkswagenstiftung; Dr.jur. h.c. (Davidson Coll.) 1974, (Georgetown) 1978. *Publications:* Vertragliche Wettbewerbsbeschränkungen und Wirtschaftsverfassungen 1958, Grenzen der Tarifautonomie 1963, Fortschritt in Freiheit 1974, die programmierte Krise-Alternativen zur Staatlichen Schuldenspolitik, Die Neue Sicht der Diuge 1985. *Leisure interests:* skiing, sailing. *Address:* Bundeshaus, 5300 Bonn 12, Federal Republic of Germany.

BIEDRZYCKA, Jadwiga, M.A.; Polish politician; b. 17 Nov. 1945, Włocławek; m.; one d.; ed. Warsaw Univ.; apprentice, subsequently Insp. of Pres. of Municipal Nat. Council. Włocławek 1968–75; Deputy Mayor of Włocławek 1975–78, Mayor 1978–81; active leader of Women's League 1975–, former Chair. Mun. Bd., subsequently Deputy Chair. Voivodship Bd. in Włocławek, Chair. Gen. Bd. Polish Women's League Dec. 1981–; mem. Nat. Council of Patriotic Movt. for Nat. Rebirth (PRON) 1983–; Deputy to Seym (Parl.) 1985–, Deputy Marshal 1985–88; mem. Polish Pathfinders' Union 1956–63; mem. Polish United Workers' Party (PZPR) 1969–, mem. Exec. Town Cttee., Włocławek; Silver Cross of Merit. *Address:* PRON, Al. Ujazdowskie 13, 00-902 Warszawa, Poland. *Telephone:* 287103.

BIELER, Manfred, M.A.; German writer; b. 3 July 1934, Zerbst; s. of Richard and Elsbeth (née Tietz) Bieler; m. Marcella Matejovská 1966; one s. two d.; ed. Humboldt Univ., Berlin; mem. German Writers' Union 1956–57, freelance writer 1957–; fisherman on G.D.R. trawler 1960; resident in Prague, Czechoslovakia 1964–68; emigrated to Fed. Repub. of Germany 1968; mem. Bavarian Acad. of Fine Arts, PEN Club. *Publications:* Bonifaz 1963, Maria Morzek 1969, Der Passagier 1971, Der Mädchenkrieg 1975, Der Kanal 1978, Ewig und drei Tage 1980, Der Bär 1983 (novels), also three vols. of short stories, numerous plays for radio and television. *Leisure interest:* playing cembalo. *Address:* Gustav-Meyrink Strasse 17, D-8000 München 60, Federal Republic of Germany. *Telephone:* 089 8342855.

BIERICH, Marcus, PH.D.; German business executive; b. 29 April 1926; ed. Univs. of Münster and Hamburg; Bankhaus Delbrück Schickler & Co. 1956–61; Dir. Mannesmann AG, Düsseldorf 1961–67, mem. Man. Bd. 1967–80; mem. Man. Bd. Allianz Versicherungs-AG, Munich 1980–84; Chair.

Man. Bd. Robert Bosch GmbH, Stuttgart 1984–; Hon. Dr. rer. oec. (Bochum). *Address:* Robert Bosch GmbH, Postfach 50, 7000 Stuttgart 1, Federal Republic of Germany.

BIERMANN, Adm. Hugo Hendrik, S.S.A., O.B.E.; South African naval officer (retd.); b. 6 Aug. 1916, Johannesburg; s. of Hugo Hendrik Biermann; m. Margaret Elaine Cruwys 1940; one s. one d.; ed. Braamfontein Afrikaans Medium School, Volkskool Heidelberg, Transvaal, Jan van Riebeeck High School, Cape Town and training ship General Botha; served in Merchant Navy 1934–39; transferred to S.A. Navy 1940, with rank of Sub-Lieut.; served in Mediterranean and S.A. waters; Chief of S.A. Navy 1952, with rank of Commodore; promoted to rank of Rear-Adm. 1957, Vice-Adm. 1967, Adm. 1972; Chief of S.A. Defence Forces 1972–76; Dir. of various cos. *Leisure interest:* sports. *Address:* Canty Bay House, 196 Main Road, Muizenberg, South Africa. *Telephone:* Cape Town 885666.

BIERRING, Ole, LL.M.; Danish diplomatist; b. 9 Nov. 1926, Copenhagen; s. of Knud and Ester M. (Lorck) Bierring; m. Bodil E. Kisbye 1960; one s. three d.; ed. Univ. of Copenhagen and Princeton Univ., U.S.A.; joined Ministry of Foreign Affairs 1951; served in Washington, D.C. 1956–58, Vienna 1960–63, Brussels (NATO) 1968–72; Under-Sec. for Political Affairs 1976–80, Deputy Perm. Under-Sec. 1980; Amb. to France 1980–84; Amb. and Perm. Rep. to UN 1984–88, Rep. on the Security Council 1985–86; Amb. to NATO 1988–; Commdr. Order of Dannebrog and other decorations. *Leisure interests:* music, sailing. *Address:* Delegation de Danemark, OTAN/NATO, Boulevard Leopold III, 1110 Brussels, Belgium. *Telephone:* (02) 728-6111.

BIERWITH, John Cocks, B.A., J.D.; American business executive; b. 1 Jan. 1924, Lawrence, New York; m. Marion Moise 1946; ed. Yale and Columbia Univs.; Assoc. Law, White & Case, New York 1950–58; Asst. Vice-Pres. New York Trust Co. (now Chemical Bank), New York 1953–57; Asst. Treasurer, National Distillers, New York 1957–58, Vice-Pres. 1958–63, Gen. Man., Int. Div. 1963–66, Dir. Nat. Distillers 1966–69, Exec. Vice-Pres. 1969–72; Vice-Pres. Finance, Grumman Corpn., Bethpage, New York July–Nov. 1972, Pres. Grumman Int. Inc. 1972–74, C.E.O. 1974–, Chair. 1976–. *Address:* Grumman International Inc., 1111 Stewart Avenue, Mail Stop A02-GHQ, Bethpage, N.Y. 11714, U.S.A. *Telephone:* 516-575-2659.

BIESHEUVEL, Barend William; Netherlands agriculturist and politician; b. 5 April 1920, Haarlemmerliede; m. Wilhelmina Meuring 1945; one s. two d.; ed. Free Univ. of Amsterdam; Ministry of Agriculture 1945–47; Sec. for Foreign Relations, Fed. of Agriculture 1947–52; Gen. Sec. Nat. Protestant Farmers' Union 1952–59, Pres. 1959–63; mem. States-Gen. (Parl.) 1957–63, 1963–; mem. European Parl.; Deputy Prime Minister, Minister of Agriculture and Fisheries 1963–67; leader of Anti-Revolutionary Party; Prime Minister 1971–73; Pres. Supervisory Bd. Nat. Investment Bank 1973–; mem. Supervisory Bd. Johnson Wax Europlant, Mijdrecht, Advisory Bd. Unilever N.V. 1973–, Supervisory Bd. Centrale Suiker Maatschappij (CSM) 1974–. *Address:* The National Investment Bank, 4 Carnegieplein, 2517 KJ The Hague; Enschedeweg 7, Aerdenhout, Netherlands (Home). *Telephone:* (070) 425.425.

BIESHU, Mariya Lukyanovna; Soviet singer (soprano); b. 1934, Moldavia; graduated Kishinev Conservatoire (Moldavian S.S.R.) 1961; soloist with Moldavian Folk Orchestra 1958–60; with Moldavian Opera and Ballet 1961–; mem. La Scala, Milan 1965–67; with Bolshoi 1967–; awards include: 1st Prize Int. Puccini Competition, Tokyo 1967, People's Artist of U.S.S.R. 1970, Lenin Prize 1982.

BIFFEN, Rt. Hon. John, P.C., B.A.; British politician; b. 3 Nov. 1930; s. of Victor W. Biffen; m. Sarah Wood (née Drew) 1979; ed. Dr. Morgan's Grammar School, Bridgwater, Jesus Coll., Cambridge; M.P. for Oswestry 1961–83, for Shropshire North 1983–; with Tube Investments Ltd. 1953–60; with Economist Intelligence Unit 1960–61; Chief Sec. to the Treasury 1979–81, Sec. of State for Trade 1981–82; Lord Privy Seal and Leader of the Commons 1983–87; Dir. Glynwed Int. 1987–; Conservative. *Address:* House of Commons, Westminster, London, S.W.1; Middle Farm, Kinton, Nesscliffe, Salop, England.

BIFFI, H.E. Cardinal Giacomo; Italian ecclesiastic; b. 13 June 1928, Milan; ordained 1950; consecrated Bishop (Titular Church of Fidene) 1975; Archbishop of Bologna 1984; elevated to Cardinal 1985. *Address:* Arivesco-vado, Via Altabella 6, 40126 Bologna, Italy. *Telephone:* (051) 238.202.

BIFFOT, Laurent Marie, B.A., PH.D.; Gabonese diplomatist; b. 20 Feb. 1925, Nkoviè; m.; four c.; fmr. Head Psycho-sociological Dept. of Office for Overseas Scientific and Tech. Research; fmr. Dean, Vice-Rector then Rector Faculty of Arts and Social Sciences Omar Bongo Univ.; fmr. Dir. Social Sciences Research Inst. of Gabon; fmr. Dir. in charge of higher educ.; fmr. Dir. Univ. Centre for Political Sciences and Devt.; numerous teaching posts including Prof. of Sociology Franceville Govt. Acad. 1980–84; Ministerial Rep. to Minister for Cultural Arts and Popular Educ. 1983–84; Perm. Rep. to UNESCO, Paris 1984–87, to UN, New York 1987–. *Address:* Permanent Mission of Gabon to the UN, 820 2nd Avenue, Room 902, New York, N.Y. 10017, U.S.A. *Telephone:* (212) 867-3100.

BIGELEISEN, Jacob, A.B., M.S., PH.D.; American chemist; b. 2 May 1919, Paterson, N. J.; s. of Harry and Ida (Slomowitz) Bigeleisen; m. Grace Alice Simon 1945; three s.; ed. New York Univ., Washington State Univ. and

Univ. of California (Berkeley); S.A.M. Labs., Columbia Univ. (Manhattan District) 1943–45; Ohio State Univ. 1945–46; Univ. of Chicago 1946–48; Assoc. to Senior Chemist, Brookhaven Nat. Laboratory 1948–68; Prof. of Chemistry, Univ. of Rochester 1968–78, Chair. Dept. of Chemistry 1970–75, Tracy H. Harris Prof., Coll. of Arts and Sciences 1973–78, Leading Prof. of Chemistry, State Univ. of New York (Stony Brook) 1978–; Vice-Pres. for Research 1978–80, Dean of Graduate Studies 1978–80; Visiting Prof. Cornell Univ. 1953; Hon. Visiting Prof., Eidgenössische Technische Hoch-schule, Zürich 1962–63; Senior Postdoctoral Fellow, Nat. Science Found-ation 1962–63; Gilbert N. Lewis Lecturer, Univ. of Calif. 1963; Visiting Distinguished Prof., State Univ. of New York (Buffalo) 1966; Guggenheim Fellow 1974–75; mem. N.A.S., Chair. Assembly of Math. and Physical Science 1976–80; Fellow, American Acad. of Arts and Sciences, American Physical Soc., A.A.A.S.; American Chem. Soc. Nuclear Applications to Chemistry Award 1958, E. O. Lawrence Memorial Award and Presidential Citation 1964, Distinguished Alumnus Award (Washington State Univ.) 1983. *Publications:* Calculation of Equilibrium Constants of Isotopic Exchange Reactions 1947, Relative Reaction Velocities of Isotopic Mol-ecules 1949, The Significance of the Product and Sum Rules to Isotope Fractionation Studies 1957, Statistical Mechanics of Isotope Effects in Condensed Systems 1961, Quantum Mechanical Foundations of Isotope Chemistry 1974, and numerous publs. on ionization of strong electrolytes, organic photochemistry, semiquinones, acids and bases and particularly theoretical and experimental studies on the chemistry of isotopes. *Address:* 461 Graduate Chemistry Building, State University of New York, Stony Brook, Stony Brook, N.Y. 11794, U.S.A. *Telephone:* (516) 632-7905.

BIGGAM, Robin Adair; British chartered accountant and business execu-tive; b. 8 July 1938, Carluke; s. of Thomas Biggam and Eileen Biggam; m. Elizabeth McArthur (née McDougall) Biggam 1962; one s. two d.; ed. Lanark Grammar School; C.A. Peat Marwick Mitchell 1960–63, ICI 1964–81; Finance Dir. 1981–84; Exec. Dir. Dunlop 1984–85; Chair. Cadcentre Ltd 1983–86; Non Exec. Dir. Chloride Group PLC 1985–87, Abbey Life Group PLC 1985–; C.E.O. BICC PLC 1986–. *Leisure interests:* golf, gardening, swimming. *Address:* BICC PLC, Devonshire House, Mayfair Place, London, W1X 5FH, England. *Telephone:* (01) 629-6622.

BIGGS, Sir Norman Parris, Kt.; British banker; b. 23 Dec. 1907, Newry, Co. Down; s. of John G. Biggs and Mary Sharpe Dickson; m. Peggy Helena Stammwitz 1936; two s. one d.; ed. John Watson's School, Edinburgh; Bank of England 1927–46; Dir. Kleinwort, Sons & Co. Ltd. 1946–52; Dir. Esso Petroleum Co. 1952–57, Man. Dir. 1957–64, Vice-Chair. 1964–66; Vice-Pres. (Finance) Esso Europe Inc. 1966–67; Chair. Esso Petroleum Co. Ltd. 1968–71; Chair. United Int. Bank Ltd. 1970–79, Deputy Chair. Privat-banken Ltd. 1980–83; Chair. Williams and Glyn's Bank Ltd. 1972–76; Deputy Chair. Nat. and Commercial Banking Group Ltd. 1974–76; Dir. Gillett Bros. Discount Co. Ltd. 1963–77, Royal Bank of Scotland 1974–76, Banco de Bilbao 1981–87; mem. Bullock Cttee. on Industrial Democracy 1975–76. *Address:* Northbrook, Danworth Lane, Hurstpierpoint, Sussex, England. *Telephone:* 0273 832022.

BIGGS, Peter Martin, C.B.E., D.SC., F.R.C.V.S., F.R.C.PATH., F.I.BIOL., F.R.S.; Brit-ish veterinary scientist; b. 13 Aug. 1926, Petersfield; s. of Ronald and Cecile (née Player) Biggs; m. Alison Janet Molteno 1950; two s. one d.; ed. Bedales School, Petersfield, Cambridge School, Mass.; with R.A.F. 1944–48; with Royal Veterinary Coll., London 1948–53; Research Asst., Dept. of Veterin-ary Anatomy, Univ. of Bristol 1953–55; Lecturer in Veterinary Clinical Pathology, Dept. of Veterinary Medicine 1955–59; Prin. Scientific Officer, Houghton Poultry Research Station 1959–66, Sr. Prin. Scientific Officer 1966–1971, Deputy Dir. 1971–74, Dir. 1974–86; Dir. Inst. for Animal Health 1986–88; Chief Scientific Officer 1981–88; Visiting Prof. of Veterinary Micro-biology, Royal Veterinary Coll. London 1982–; Andrew D. White Prof.-at-Large, Cornell Univ., U.S.A.; Fellow of Inst. of Biology 1973, Royal Coll. of Pathologists 1978, Royal Coll. of Veterinary Surgeons 1979, Royal Veterin-ary Coll. 1983; Hon. Fellow Royal Agricultural Soc. 1986; Dalrymple—Champneys Cup and Medal of the British Veterinary Assccn.; Hon. Doc. of Veterinary Medicine (Ludwig-Maximilians Univ., Munich) and numerous others. *Publications:* more than 100 scientific papers. *Leisure interests:* music making, boating. *Address:* 'Willows', London Road, St. Ives, Hunting-don, Cambridgeshire, PE17 4ES, England. *Telephone:* 0480 63471.

BIGNONE, Maj.-Gen. Reynaldo Benito; Argentine army officer and politician; b. 21 Jan. 1928, Morón; m. Nilda Raquel Belen; three c.; ed. Nat. Mil. Acad., Superior War Coll.; Capt. 1954; Commdr. Cadet Corps, Nat. Mil. Acad. 1970; Sec. to Army High Command 1973; Deputy Commdr., later Commdr. Nat. Mil. Insts. 1980–81; fmr. Dir. Nat. Mil. Acad. and Sec.-Gen. of Army; retd. from active service Dec. 1981; Pres. of Argentina 1982–83; arrested Jan. 1984, released June 1984.

BIHALJI-MERIN, Oto; Yugoslav critic, essayist and novelist; b. 3 Jan. 1904, Belgrade-emun; s. of David Bihalji and Klara (Schoemann) Bihalji; m. Lisa Bihalji 1938; one d.; ed. Belgrade and Berlin Acads. of Fine Art; began his career as a painter; now works as an author, editor and art critic; also writes under the pseudonyms Peter Merin and Peter Thoene; Ed.-in-Chief Jugoslavia 1949–58; mem. Selection Cttee., Art Exhibition, Brussels Int. Exhbn. 1958; organized exhbn. The World of the Naïves, Haus der Kunst, Munich 1975; exhbn. Profile of an Art Critic, Belgrade 1976. *Publications:* Conquest of the Skies 1937 (English, French, German,

Dutch and Swedish edns.), Spain Between Death and Birth 1938 (English and German edns.), Modern German Art (English edn. 1938, Serbo-Croat edn. 1955), Au Revoir in October (novel) 1947, Yugoslavia, a Small Country between the Worlds 1954 (German edn. 1955, Dutch edn. 1956), Yugoslav Sculpture of the XX Century 1955 (English, French and German edns.), Peter Lubarda and the Painting "The Battle of Kossovo", The Invisible Door (play) 1956, Rencontres in Our Days (essays) 1957, Icons and Frescoes in Serbia and Macedonia (French, English and German edns.) 1958, Primitive Arts of the XX Century in Europe and America 1959, The Adventure of Modern Art (English, German, Japanese edns.) 1962-68, Bogosav Zivkovic, World of a Primitive Sculptor 1962, 1963, Bogomil Sculpture 1962, 1964 (The Bogomils in English 1963), Primitive Artists of Yugoslavia 1965, Die Welt von oben 1966, Art Treasures in Yugoslavia (Ed. and preface) 1969, Masks of the World 1970 (German and English), The End of Art in the Age of Science? (French and German) 1969, The Douanier Rousseau (with Lisa Bihalji-Merin) (German, English and Hungarian edns.) 1970, Time-Light-Movement (essay) (German, French, Serbo-Croat, Spanish) 1970, Modern Primitives 1971, Masters of Naïve Art (English, German, French, Italian, Serbo-Croat, Dutch) 1971, 1972, Bridges of the World (Ed. and preface) 1972, Image and Imagination (German, Serbo-Croat, Macedonian) 1974, Unity of the World in the Vision of Art (Serbo-Croat) 1974, Francisco Goya (Vol. I English, German, Italian, Spanish, Vol. II English, German, Spanish, Vol. III German) 1980, 1985, World Encyclopaedia of Naïve Art (with N. Tomasevic, in English, French, Serbo-Croat) 1984, Vangel Naumovski (English, Macedonian) 1983, 1984, Goya y Gea (essay) (Spanish) 1987; Critical Notes: Morris Hirshfield 1976, Mouvement et Aggressivité de Vladimir Veličković 1976, Painting behind Glass (German) 1978; Monographs on painters: Krsto Hegedusic 1965, Gabrijel Stupica 1968, Marij Pregelj 1971; also TV films in Frankfurt and Belgrade, and films on Impressionists and Modern Art. *Leisure interests:* talking with young people, travelling by aeroplane, listening to very old and very new music. *Address:* Nemanjina ul. 3, 11000 Belgrade, Yugoslavia. *Telephone:* Belgrade 641-571.

BIL'AK, Vasil, RSDR.; Czechoslovak politician; b. 11 Aug. 1917, Krajná Bystrá; ed. School of Political Studies at Central Committee of Communist Party of Czechoslovakia, Prague; took part in Slovak Nat. Rising 1944; full-time party official, Regional Cttee., CP of Slovakia, Bratislava 1950-51; Dept. Head, Cen. Cttee., CP of Slovakia 1953; Sec. and Chief Sec. Regional Cttee., CP of Slovakia, Prešov 1954-58; Minister-Commr., Comm. for Educ. and Culture of Slovak Nat. Council 1959-62, Minister 1960-62; Deputy Chair. Slovak Nat. Council 1960-63; Sec. Cen. Cttee. CP of Slovakia 1962-68, First Sec. 1968; mem. Cen. Cttee. CP of Czechoslovakia 1954-88, mem. Secr. 1968-88; mem. Presidium Cen. Cttee. CP of Czechoslovakia 1968-88, Chair. Ideological Cttee. 1970-88; Deputy to Slovak Nat. Council 1954-64; mem. Cen. Cttee. of CP of Slovakia 1955-71; Deputy to Nat. Assembly 1960-69; mem. Presidium, Cen. Cttee. of CP of Slovakia 1962-68; mem. Presidium Nat. Assembly 1963-68; Deputy to House of The People, Fed. Assembly 1969; mem. Presidium of Fed. Assembly 1969-71; Order of Labour 1967, Georgi Dimitrov Order 1968, Soviet Order of the Red Banner 1970, Soviet Memorial Medal 1970, Order of Repub. 1972, Order of Victorious Feb. 1973, hon. Hero of Socialist Labour 1977, 1987, Klement Gottwald Order 1977, Order of Lenin (U.S.S.R.) 1977. *Address:* Central Committee of Communist Party of Czechoslovakia, nábř. Ludvika Svobody 12, Prague 1, Czechoslovakia.

BILBY, Bruce Alexander, PH.D., F.R.S.; British emeritus professor of theory of materials and consultant; b. 3 Sept. 1922, London; s. of George A. Bilby and Dorothy J. (née Telfer) Bilby; m. 1st Hazel J. Casken 1946 (dissolved 1964), two s. one d.; m. 2nd Lorette W. Thomas 1966, two s.; ed. Dover County Grammar School, Peterhouse, Cambridge, and Univ. of Birmingham; Royal Soc. Sorby Research Fellow, Univ. of Sheffield 1951-57, J. H. Andrew Research Fellow 1957-58, Reader in Theoretical Metallurgy 1958-62, Prof. of Theoretical Metallurgy 1962-66, Prof. of the Theory of Materials 1966-84, Prof. Emer. 1984-. *Publications:* scientific papers in learned journals. *Leisure interest:* sailing. *Address:* Department of Mechanical Engineering, University of Sheffield, Mappin Street, Sheffield, S1 3JD (Office); Bushey Mount, 32 Devonshire Road, Totley, Sheffield, S17 3NT, England (Home). *Telephone:* Sheffield 78555 (Office); Sheffield 361086 (Home).

BILDT, Carl; Swedish politician; b. 1949; ed. Univ. of Stockholm; Political Sec. Moderata Samlingspartiet (Conservative Party) 1973; mem. Stockholm City Council 1974; Under-Sec. of State for Co-ordination and Planning 1979-81; Leader, Moderata Samlingspartiet 1986-. *Address:* Moderata Samlingspartiet, P.O. Box 1243, 111 82 Stockholm, Sweden.

BILGE, Ali Suat, LL.T.; Turkish professor of international law and politician; b. 1921, Istanbul; s. of Sulhiye and Sezai Bilge; m. Olcay Bilge 1965; one s.; ed. Univs. of Ankara and Geneva; Assistant, Faculty of Political Science, Univ. of Ankara 1950, Assoc. Prof. 1952, Prof. 1960; Hon. Legal Adviser, Ministry of Foreign Affairs 1960, First Hon. Legal Adviser 1965; Judge, European Court of Human Rights 1966; mem. Perm. Court of Arbitration, The Hague 1966; mem. UN Cttee. of Human Rights 1970; mem. Int. Law Comm. 1971-; Minister of Justice 1971-72; Amb. to Switzerland 1972-76; Special Adviser to Turkish Pres. 1983-. *Publications:* Diplomatic Protection of Compatriots 1953, International Politics 1966. *Leisure*

interest: fishing. *Address:* Bahçelievler 58 nci Sokak No. 2, Ankara, Turkey (Home). *Telephone:* 12-25-17.

BILGRAV-NIELSEN, Jens; Danish politician; b. 14 May 1936, Ølstrup; fmr. teacher; mem. Folketing (Parl.) 1966-67, 1979-; Minister of Energy 1988-; mem. Gen. Council, Radical Liberal Party 1973-, Deputy Chair. Parl. Group 1973-73, Nat. Council 1977-79; mem. N. Schleswig Cttee., Liaison Cttee. of Prime Minister's Dept., Defence Comm. 1969-73, Radio Council 1982-87, Finance Cttee. 1968-71, 1979-88. *Address:* Ministry of Energy, Slotsholmsgade 1, 1216 Copenhagen K, Denmark. *Telephone:* (01) 92-75-00.

BILHEIMER, Rev. Robert Sperry, B.A., B.D.; American ecclesiastic; b. 28 Sept. 1917, Denver, Colo.; s. of George Steven and Katherine Elizabeth Bilheimer; m. Dorothy Dodge 1942; three s.; ed. Phillips Exeter Acad., Yale Univ., Yale Divinity School; Minister, Westminster Presbyterian Church 1946-48; Sec. The Inter-Seminary Movement 1945-48; Programme Sec., World Council of Churches, New York 1948-54, Assoc. Gen. Sec., Dir. of the Division of Studies, Geneva 1954-63; Senior Minister, Central Presbyterian Church, Rochester, N.Y. 1963-66; Dir. Int. Affairs Programs, The Nat. Council of Churches of Christ in the U.S.A. 1966-74; Exec. Dir. Inst. for Ecumenical and Cultural Research, St. John's Univ. 1974-84; Hon. D.D. (Chicago Theological Seminary 1954, Butler Univ. 1954, Hamilton Coll. 1980). *Publications:* What Must the Church Do? 1947, The Quest for Christian Unity 1952, Faith and Ferment (Ed.) 1983, A Spirituality for the Long Haul 1984, Breakthrough, the Emergence of the Ecumenical Tradition 1989. *Leisure interests:* trout fishing, photography. *Address:* 15256 Knightwood Road, Cold Spring, Minn. 56320, U.S.A.

BILIP, Jerzy, M.ENG.; Polish politician and telecommunications engineer; b. 1932, Radom; m.; two s.; ed. Warsaw Tech. Univ. 1954; for many years worked in Kasprzak Wireless Plants, Warsaw, including Dept. of Tech. Inspection, then Chief of Unit of Depts.; Kasprzak Plants Plenipotentiary in Cuba, supervising construction, next production of Wireless Assembling Plants, Havana 1963-67; Deputy Dir. for tech. matters, Kasprzak Wireless Plants, Warsaw 1968-70; Tech. Dir. Unitra-Dom Electronic Industry Union, Warsaw 1970-77; Gen. Dir. Unitra-Polkolor Kinescope Plants, Piaseczno nr. Warsaw 1981-87; Minister of Industry Oct. 1987-88; mem. Polish United Workers' Party (PZPR); Kt.'s Cross of Polonia Restituta, Order of Banner of Labour (2nd Class) and other decorations.

BILL, Max; Swiss architect, sculptor, painter, politician and writer; b. 22 Dec. 1908, Winterthur; s. of Erwin Bill and Marie Geiger; m. Binia Spoerri 1931; one s.; ed. Zürich School of Art and Craft and Dessau Bauhaus; Dir. Inst. for Design, Ulm, Germany 1951-56; Prof. of Environmental Design, Inst. for Fine Arts, Hamburg 1967-74; mem. Fed. of Swiss Architects; mem. Zürich City Council 1961-68, Swiss Fed. Council 1967-71; Pres. Verein Bauhaus Archiv, Berlin 1985-; Hon. Fellow, American Inst. of Architects 1964; mem. Acad. of Arts, Berlin; Hon. Dr. Ing. 1979; Grand Prix Triennale Milan 1936 and 1951, Biennale São Paulo 1951 (1st Int. Sculpture prize), Kandinsky Prize 1949, Art Prize, City of Zürich 1968, City of Goslar 1982. *Address:* Rebhusstrasse 50, 8126 Zumikon, Switzerland (Home). *Telephone:* 918-08-28.

BILLAUD, Bernard; French civil servant; b. 3 Sept. 1942, Béziers; m. Claude Devitry 1967; three c.; ed. Inst. d'études politiques de Paris and Ecole nat. d'admin.; Auditor 1968, Public Auditor Cour des Comptes 1976-; Adviser to French Embassy, Holy See 1974-76; Official Rep. to the Prime Minister 1976; Dir. of Staff, Mayor of Paris 1979-83; Dir.-Gen. Int. Relations, Paris 1983-84; Gen. Commr. of the French language 1987-. *Address:* 32 rue de Babylone, 75007 Paris (Office); 77 rue Claude Bernard, 75005 Paris, France (Home). *Telephone:* 42 75 89 04 (Office).

BILLESKOV-JANSEN, Frederik Julius, DR.PHIL.; Danish professor; b. 30 Sept. 1907, Hvidbjerg; s. of Hans Billeskov-Jansen and Bothilde Schack-Schou; m. Vibeke Collet Henrichsen 1938; one s. two d.; ed. Københavns Universitet; Asst. lecturer in Danish, Univ. of Copenhagen 1935-38, Prof. 1941-77; lecturer, Univ. de Paris à la Sorbonne 1938-41; Ed. Orbis Litterarum 1943-50; mem. Emer. Royal Danish Acad. of Sciences and Letters, mem. Int. Asscns. of Comparative Literature and of German Language and Literature, mem. Danish Acad.; Pres. Søren Kierkegaard Soc., Alliance Française, Copenhagen; Commdr. Order of Dannebrog, Officier, Légion d'honneur, Officier, Ordre des Palmes académiques. *Publications:* Danmarks Digtekunst I-III 1944-58, Holberg som Epigrammatiker og Essayist 1939, Editions of Holberg: Moralske Tanker 1943, Epistler 1954, Memoirer 1963, Vaerker i tolv Bind 1969-71, Ludvig Holberg 1974; Søren Kierkegaards Litter≃re Kunst 1951, Søren Kierkegaards: Vaerker i Udvalg 1950, Poetik (Vols. I and II) 1941-48, Den Danske Lyrik 1961-66, Esthétique de l'œuvre d'art littéraire 1948, L'Age d'or 1953, Anthology of Danish Literature (French edn. 1964, English edn. 1971, Italian edn. 1973, Dutch edn. 1973, Japanese edn. 1976, German edn. 1978, Portuguese edn. 1981, Spanish edn. 1984), Verdens Litteraturhistorie I-XII (Chief Ed.) 1971-74, Verdenslitteratur 1982; also articles in Scandinavian and international reviews. *Address:* Frydendalsvej 20, 1809 Copenhagen V., Denmark. *Telephone:* 01-316369.

BILLET, Georges; French international civil servant; b. 1 June 1920, Paris; m. Jeannine Chaffenet 1943; two s.; ed. Ecole Nat. d'Administration; Head of Dept. in Div. of Personnel and Budget, Ministry of Public Works and Transport 1953, Asst. Dir. of Gen. Affairs in Ministry 1962, Head of Gen. Affairs and Transport Co-ordination in Land Transport Div. 1963, Head of Road and Urban Transport 1967, Insp.-Gen. of Public Works and Transport 1970; Officer responsible for Int. relations of Ministries of Equipment and Transport 1972-75; Sec.-Gen. Higher Council of Transport 1975-76; fmr. Sec.-Gen. European Conf. of Ministers of Transport; Officer, Ordre Nationale du Mérite, Légion d'honneur. *Address:* Conférence Européenne des Ministres des Transports, 19 rue de Franqueville, 75775 Paris (Office); 8 ter, rue de la Marne, 95220 Herblay, France (Home). *Telephone:* 524-97-10 (Office); 997-23-05 (Home).

BILLETDOUX, François-Paul; French writer, actor, director and producer; b. 7 Sept. 1927, Paris; s. of Paul and Adrienne (Vidal) Billetdoux; m. Evelyne Colin 1947; two d.; ed. Ecole d'Art Dramatique Charles Dullin and Institut des Hautes Etudes Cinématographiques; Producer and Dir. Radiodiffusion Française 1946-, in Caribbean 1949-50, Gen. Overseas Service 1957-58; journalist 1951; cabaret actor and disc jockey 1951-53; work for theatre, radio, television and films 1959-; Head of Research Dept., Radio France, and Nat. Audio-visual Inst. 1975-; Pres. Comm. for Cultural Affairs 1979; Vice-Pres. Société des Gens de Lettres (S.G.D.L.) 1979, Pres. 1981-86; Vice-Pres. Conseil Permanent des Écrivains 1980-; Chevalier, Légion d'honneur 1975, Officier ordre nat. du mérite. *Publications include:* L'animal (novel) 1955, Une rose pour Charles Cros 1957, Royal Garden Blues 1957, Brouillon d'un bourgeois 1961; Plays: Treize pièces à louer 1951, A la nuit 1955, Tchin-Tchin 1959, Le comportement des époux Bredburry 1960, Va donc chez Törpe 1961, Pour Finalie 1962, Comment va le monde, Môssieu?, Il tourne, Môssieu! 1964, Il faut passer par les nuages 1964, Silence! l'arbre remue encore! 1967, Je n'étais pas chez moi 1968, Quelqu'un devrait faire quelque chose 1969, 7 + Quoi? 1969, Femmes parallèles 1970, Rintru pa trou tar hin! 1971, Ne m'attendez pas ce soir 1971, Les veuves 1972, La nostalgie, camarade 1974; Television: Pitchi Poï ou la parole donnée 1967, Musique pour une ville 1969, Famine chez les rats 1970, Cantique des créatures 1970, L'apocalypse des animaux 1973; Radio: Ai-je dit que je suis bossu? 1981. *Address:* 31 square de Montsouris, 75014 Paris, France.

BILLINGHAM, Rupert Everett, M.A., D.PHIL., D.SC., F.R.S.; British zoologist; b. 15 Oct. 1921, Warminster, Wilts.; s. of Albert Everett Billingham and Helen Louise Green; m. Jean Mary Morpeth 1951; two s. one d.; ed. Oxford Univ.; Lecturer, Dept. of Zoology, Birmingham Univ. 1947-51; Research Fellow of British Empire Cancer Campaign, and Hon. Research Assoc., Dept. of Zoology, Univ. Coll. London 1951-57; mem. Wistar Inst. of Anatomy and Biology, Philadelphia, U.S.A. 1957-65; Prof. of Zoology, Univ. of Pa. 1958-71; Prof. and Chair. Dept. of Medical Genetics, and Dir. Phipps Inst. of Medical Genetics, Univ. of Pa., School of Medicine 1965-71; Prof. and Chair. Dept. of Cell Biology and Anatomy, Univ. of Tex. Health Science Centre at Dallas, Tex. 1971-86; Pres. The Transplantation Soc. 1974-76, Int. Soc. for Immunology of Reproduction 1983-86; Fellow, New York Acad. of Sciences, American Acad. Arts and Sciences; Fellow Royal Soc. 1961-; Alvarenga Prize, Coll. of Physicians of Philadelphia; Hon. Award Medal, American Assn. of Plastic Surgeons; Hon. D.Sc., Trinity Coll. (Conn.), F. L. Adair Award, American Gynaecological Soc. 1971. *Publications:* Transplantation of Tissues and Cells (ed. with W. K. Silvers) 1961, Wound Healing (ed. with W. Montagna) 1964, Epithelial-Mesenchymal Interactions (ed. with R. Fleischmajer) 1968, Immunology and the Skin (ed. with W. Montagna) 1971, The Immunobiology of Transplantation (with W. K. Silvers) 1971, The Immunobiology of Mammalian Reproduction (with A. E. Beer) 1976, numerous scientific publications on tissue transplantation immunology, immunological tolerance, immunological aspects of mammalian reproduction and the biology of skin, in Royal Soc. and other journals. *Leisure interests:* gardening, travel. *Address:* Route 2, Box 102B, Vineyard Haven, Mass. 02568, U.S.A. *Telephone:* (508) 693-7939.

BILLINGTON, James Hadley, PH.D.; American historian and librarian; b. 1 June 1929, Bryn Mawr, Pa.; s. of Nelson Billington and Jane Coolbaugh; m. Marjorie A. Brennan 1957; two s. two d.; ed. Princeton Univ. and Univ. of Oxford; Instructor in History, Harvard Univ. 1957-58, Fellow, Russian Research Center 1958-59, Asst. Prof. of History 1958-61; Assoc. Prof. of History, Princeton Univ. 1962-64, Prof. 1964-73; Dir. Woodrow Wilson Int. Center for Scholars, Washington, D.C. 1973-87; Librarian of Congress, Library of Congress, Washington, D.C. 1987-; Visiting Research Prof. Inst. of History of U.S.S.R. Acad. of Sciences 1966-67, Univ. of Helsinki 1960-61, Ecole des Hautes Etudes en Sciences Sociales, Paris 1985, 1988; visiting lecturer to various univs. in Europe and Asia etc.; Guggenheim Fellow 1960-61; mem. American Acad. of Arts and Sciences, Council on Foreign Relations; Chevalier, Ordre des Arts et des Lettres; seven hon. degrees. *Publications:* Mikhailovsky and Russian Populism 1958, The Icon and the Axe: An Interpretive History of Russian Culture 1966, Fire in the Minds of Men: Origins of the Revolutionary Faith 1980; contribs. to books and journals. *Address:* Library of Congress, First and Independence Avenues, Washington, D.C. 20540, U.S.A.

BILLINGTON, Kevin, B.A.; British film, theatre and television director; b. 12 June 1934; s. of Richard and Margaret Billington; m. Lady Rachel Mary Pakenham 1967; two s., two d.; ed. Bryanston School and Queens' Coll. Cambridge; film dir. BBC programme Tonight 1960-63; documentary film dir., BBC 1963-67; *feature films:* Interlude 1967, The Rise and Rise

of Michael Rimmer 1969, The Light at the Edge of the World 1970, Voices 1974, Reflections 1984; *television films:* And No One Can Save Her 1973, Once Upon a Time is Now (documentary) 1978, The Music Will Never Stop (documentary) 1979, Henry VIII 1979, The Jail Diary of Albie Sachs 1980, The Good Soldier 1981, Outside Edge 1982, The Sonnets of William Shakespeare 1984, The Deliberate Death of a Polish Priest 1986; *plays directed:* Find Your Way Home 1970, Me 1973, The Birthday Party 1974, The Caretaker 1975, Bloody Neighbours 1974, Emigrés 1976, The Homecoming 1978, Quartermaine's Terms 1982, The Deliberate Death of a Polish Priest 1985, The Philanthropist 1986, The Lover, A Slight Ache 1987; Screenwriters' Guild Award 1966, 1967, Guild of TV Producers and Directors Award 1966, 1967. *Address:* 30 Addison Avenue, London, W11 4QT, England.

BILLOTTE, Gen. Pierre; French army officer and politician; b. 8 March 1906, Paris; s. of Gen. Gaston Billotte and Catherine Nathan; m. 1951: two d.; ed. Ecole Militaire de Saint-Cyr, Ecole Supérieure de Guerre; Military Rep. of Free French in Moscow 1941-42; Chief of Staff to Gen. de Gaulle in London 1942-44, Sec. of Cttee. for Nat. Defence; Commdr. Brigade under Gen. Leclerc 1944; Commdr. 10th Infantry Division 1944; Asst. Gen. Chief of Staff Nat. Defence 1945-46; French Mil. Rep. to UN 1946-50; retired from army 1950; mem. Chamber of Deputies 1951-56, 1962-66, 1968-71, 1971-78; Minister of Nat. Defence and of the Armed Forces 1955; Rep. of France on various UN Cttees. 1955-62; Vice-Pres. UNR Group in Nat. Assembly 1962-66; Minister of State Overseas Depts. and Territories 1966-68; Mayor of Créteil 1965-77; Consul-Gen. in Senegal 1981-; Pres. Mouvement pour le socialisme par la participation; Commdr. Légion d'honneur; Compagnon de la Libération. *Publications:* Fatalité de la défaite allemande 1941, Le temps du choix 1950, L'Europe est née 1955, Considérations sur la stratégie mondiale 1957, Du pain sur la planche 1965, Le temps des armes 1973, Trente ans d'humour avec de Gaulle, Le passé au futur 1979. *Address:* Consulat général de France, 1 rue E.H. Amadou Assane Ndoye, P.O. Box 330 Dakar, Sénégal (Office); 15 bis rue de la Maison Blanche, 44100 Nantes, France (Home).

BILY, Mikhail Ulyanovich, PH.D.; Soviet scientist; b. 1922, Moskali, Chernigov Dist.; ed. Kiev State Univ.; served in Soviet Army 1940-43; mem. CPSU 1951-; Prof., corresp. mem. Ukrainian Acad. of Sciences 1948-; Head of Chair. of Experimental Physics 1951; Dean of Faculty of Physics, Kiev State Univ. 1962-, Rector 1970-; Chair. Ukranian Br. of U.S.S.R.-Canada Soc. 1971-; cand. mem. Cen. Cttee. Ukrainian CP 1971-76, mem. 1976-; mem. Supreme Soviet of Ukrainian S.S.R. 1971-, Deputy Chair. 1971-72, Chair. 1972-80. *Address:* Kiev State University, Vladimirskaya ul. 64, 252017 Kiev, Ukraine, U.S.S.R.

BINAISA, Godfrey Lukwongwa, LL.B.; Ugandan lawyer and politician; b. 30 May 1920, Kampala; ed. King's Coll., Budo, Makerere Univ., King's Coll., London, Lincoln's Inn, London; in private legal practice 1956-62, 1967-79; mem. of Uganda Nat. Congress, later of Uganda People's Congress; Attorney-Gen. 1962-67; Pres. Uganda Law Soc., Chair Law Devt. Centre 1968; mem. Uganda Judicial Service Comm. 1970; Chair. Organizing Cttee. for Commonwealth Lawyers' Conf., 1972; went into exile; in legal practice in New York; returned to Uganda 1979 after fall of Govt. of Pres. Idi Amin Dada (q.v.); Pres. of Uganda 1979-80, also Minister of Foreign Affairs June-July 1979, Minister of Defence; Chancellor, Makerere Univ. 1979-80; under house arrest 1980-81; left Uganda Jan. 1981; went to Britain.

BINDER, Theodor, M.D.; Peruvian physician; b. 1919; ed. Hebel-Gymnasium Lörrach, Univs. of Freiburg, Strasbourg, and Basel, and Swiss Tropical Inst., Basel; Clinic Chief, Swiss Tropical Inst. 1947-48; Public Health Officer, Oxapampa, Peru 1948-50; Staff, Medical School, Nacional Mayor de San Marcos de Lima 1951-56; Founder of Clinic for the Poor, and constructor of Hospital, Pucallpa 1956-60, Inauguration Hospital Amazónico Albert Schweitzer, Yarinacocha, Pucallpa 1960, Dir. 1960-; Founder and Dir. Instituto Tropical Amazónico 1963-; Exec. Dir. Amazonian Indian Int. Devt., Toronto and New York 1971-. *Publications:* Philosophy: Friedrich Nietzsche 1950, Goethe's Iphigenia and the Ethics 1951, A. Schweitzer as a Philosopher 1954, Heroism as an Attitude towards Life 1956, Personal Ethics in a Depersonalizing Age 1963, Tristes Tropiques or Land of Hope 1968, The Right to an Independent Development in the Third World 1970, Sense and Nonsense of the Christian Mission among Jungle Indians 1970, Problems of Intercultural Relations 1971; Medicine: Congenital Malaria 1950, Treatment of Hypertension 1952, Latin-America: Nonanalytical Psychotherapy 1958, Histoplasmosis in Eastern Peru 1964, Dermatomycosis and Deep Mycosis in Eastern Peru 1965, etc. *Address:* Taos Canyon, Taos, N.M. 87571, U.S.A.

BINDING, Günther, DR.ING., DR.PHIL.; German university professor; b. 6 March 1936, Koblenz; s. of Kurt Binding and Margot (née Masur); m. Elisabeth Dietz 1969; one s. two d.; ed. gymnasium in Arnsberg and Cologne, Technische Hochschule, Aachen, and Univs. of Cologne and Bonn; Dir. Lower Rhine section, Rheinisches Landesmuseum, Bonn 1964-70; Prof., Univ. of Cologne 1970-, Rector 1981-83, Pro-rector 1983-85; Vice-Pres. W. German Rectors' Conf. 1982-84; Ruhrpreis für Kunst und Wissenschaft 1966, Josef-Humar-Preis 1986, Rheinland-Taler 1987. *Publications:* 15 books and 150 articles about European architecture and history of art.

Address: 5060 Berg.-Gladbach 3, Wingertsheide 65, Federal Republic of Germany. *Telephone:* 02204/64956.

BING, Sir Rudolf, K.B.E.; British impresario; b. 9 Jan. 1902, Vienna, Austria; s. of Ernst and Stefanie Hoenigsvald Bing; m. 1st Nina Schelemskaya-Schelesnaya 1929 (died 1983); m. 2nd Carroll Lee Douglas 1987; Hessian State Theatre, Darmstadt 1928-30; Civic Opera, Berlin-Charlottenburg 1930-33; Gen. Man. Glyndebourne Opera, England 1935-49; Artistic Dir. Edinburgh Int. Festival 1947-49; Gen. Man. Metropolitan Opera, New York 1950-72; Distinguished Visiting Prof. of Music, Brooklyn Coll. 1972-75; Consultant, Columbia Artists Management Inc. 1974-; Adjunct Prof. of Theatre Management, N.Y. Univ. 1972-; Hon. D.Mus. (Lafayette Coll., Pa.), Hon. D.Litt. (Dickinson Coll., Pa.), Hon. D. Hum. Litt. (N.Y., Temple Univs., and Wagner Coll.), Hon. LL.D. (Jacksonville Univ., Fla.); Chevalier Légion d'honneur, Grand Officer Order of Merit (Italy), Grand Silver Medal of Honour (Austria), Commander's Cross of Order of Merit (Fed. Repub. of Germany). *Publications:* 5000 Nights at the Opera 1972, A Knight at the Opera 1981.

BINGAMAN, Jeff, J.D.; American lawyer and politician; b. 3 Oct. 1943, Silver City, N.M.; s. of Jesse Bingaman and Beth Ball; m. Ann Kovacovich 1968; one s.; ed. Harvard and Stanford Univs.; admitted to N.M. Bar 1968; partner Campbell, Bingaman & Black, Santa Fe 1972-78; Attorney-Gen., N.M. 1979-82; Senator from New Mexico Jan. 1983-; Democrat. *Address:* 502 Hart Senate Building, Washington, D.C. 20510, U.S.A.

BINGER, James Henry, A.B., LL.B.; American lawyer and business executive; b. 16 May 1916, Minneapolis, Minn.; s. of Dr. Henry E. and Vida Binger (née DeBar); m. Virginia E. McKnight 1939; one s. two d.; ed. Yale Univ. and Univ. of Minnesota; Assoc., Fletcher, Dorsey, Barker, Colman and Barber 1941-43; Minneapolis-Honeywell Regulator Co. (Honeywell Inc. 64) 1943-, Asst. Sec. 1945-46, Asst. Vice-Pres. 1946-50, Vice-Pres. and Gen. Man. Valve Div., Philadelphia 1949, Vice-Pres. 1952-61, Dir. 1959-, Pres. 1961-65, Chief Exec. Officer 1964-74, Chair. 1965-74, Chair. Exec. Cttee. 1974-78; fmr. Dir. North-western Bell Telephone Co., Northwest Airlines, Northwest Bancorporation, 3M Co., Chase Manhattan Bank; fmr. Vice-Pres. Univ. of Minnesota Foundation; fmr. Vice-Chair., Business Council. *Address:* 4522 I.D.S. Center, 80 South 8th Street, Minneapolis, Minn. 55402, U.S.A. *Telephone:* (612) 341-3500.

BINGHAM, John, F.R.S.; British scientist; b. 19 June 1930; mem. staff, Plant Breeding Inst., Cambridge, Deputy Chief Scientific Officer 1981-; research in plant breeding has culminated in production of improved, highly successful winter wheat varieties for British agric.; Mullard Medal of Royal Soc. 1975. *Address:* Plant Breeding Institute, Maris Lane, Trumpington, Cambridge, CB2 2LQ (Office); 25 Stansgate Avenue, Cambridge, CB2 2QZ (Home). *Telephone:* Trumpington 2411 (Office); Cambridge 247737 (Home).

BINKOWSKI, Johannes Aloysius Joseph, D.PHIL.; German newspaper publisher; b. 27 Nov. 1908, Neisse; s. of Emil and Anna (née Wilde) Binkowski; m. Helene Scholz 1937; ed. Univs. of Breslau and Cologne; Co-Founder and head of adult educ. programme, Aalen 1951; Co-Founder Südwestdeutscher Zeitungsverband 1954; Chair. Cttee. for Political Journalism and Studies, Assen. of Newspaper Publrs. 1962, Pres. Assen. 1970-80, Hon. Pres. 1980-; mem. German Press Council 1966-70; Chair. Verein Südwestdeutscher Zeitungsverleger 1967, Vice-Chair. 1970-; mem. Television Council, Zweites Deutsches Fernsehen, Chair. Policy and Co-ordination Cttee. 1962-; mem. Bd. of Govs. Stiftervereinigung der Presse 1966-; Vice-Pres. Int. Fed. of Newspaper Publrs. 1973; Pres. Ritterorden vom Heiligen Grabe zu Jerusalem; Grosses Verdienstkreuz 1969. *Publications:* Wertlehre des Duns Scotus 1935, Religiöse Erwachsenenbildung 1936, Christlicher Alltag 1937, Der Mensch am Scheideweg 1947, Die sozialen Enzykliken 1963, Mit den Massenmedien leben 1970, Wege und Ziel. Lebenserinnerungen eines Verlegers und Publizisten 1981, Jugend als Wegbereiter. Der Quickbron 1909-45, 1981, Flugblatt und Zeitung 1985. *Address:* 7 Stuttgart 1, Villastrasse 11 (Office); 7 Stuttgart 75 (Sillenbuch), Oberwiesenstrasse 47, Federal Republic of Germany (Home). *Telephone:* 26861-21 (Office); 473804 (Home).

BINNIG, Gerd; German physicist; b. 20 July 1947, Frankfurt; m. Lore Wagler 1969; one s. one d.; mem. Physics group, IBM Zürich Research Lab. Rüschlikon 1978-, Group Leader 1984-; Assignment to IBM Almaden Research Centre, San Jose, collaboration with Stanford Univ., Calif. 1985-86; IBM Fellow 1986; Visiting Prof. Stanford Univ. 1986-; Hon. Prof. (Univ. of Munich) 1986-; Hon. Fellow (Royal Microscopical Soc.) 1988; Foreign Assoc. mem. Acad. of Sciences, Wash. 1987; shared Nobel prize for Physics (with E. Ruska and H. Rohrer) 1986; German Physics Prize, Otto Klung Prize, Hewlett Packard Prize, King Faisal Prize, Eliot Cresson Medal (Franklin Inst., Phila.) 1987; D.S.M., O.M. (Fed. Repub. Germany) 1987; Minnie Rosen award (Ross Univ., N.Y.) 1988. *Leisure interests:* music, sports. *Address:* IBM Zürich Research Laboratory, Rüschlikon, Switzerland.

BINNS, Malcolm; British concert pianist; b. 29 Jan. 1936, Nottingham; s. of Douglas Priestley Binns and May Walker; ed. Bradford Grammar School, Royal Coll. of Music; soloist with maj. British orchestras 1960-; has performed many times at the Promenade Concerts and broadcast regularly on the BBC; has recorded over 30 maj. pieces, including the piano concertos

of Sir William Sterndale Bennett with the Philharmonia and London Philharmonic Orchestras; concerts at Aldeburgh, Leeds, Three Choirs and Canterbury Festivals; Chappell Medal 1956, Medal of Worshipful Co. of Musicians 1956. *Leisure interest:* gardening. *Address:* 233 Court Road, Orpington, Kent, BR6 9BY, England. *Telephone:* Orpington 31056.

BIOBAKU, Saburi Oladeni, C.M.G. PH.D.; Nigerian historian and university official; b. 16 June 1918; m. Muhabat Folasade Agusto 1949; four s.; ed. Government Coll., Ibadan, Higher Coll., Yaba, Univ. Coll. Exeter, Trinity Coll. Cambridge and Inst. of Historical Research, London; Master, Govt. Coll., Ibadan 1941-44; Educ. Officer 1947-50; Asst. Liaison Officer for Nigerian Students in U.K., Colonial Office, London 1951-53; Registrar, Univ. Coll., Ibadan 1953-57; Sec. to Premier and Exec. Council, W. Nigeria 1957-61; Pro-Vice-Chancellor, Univ. of Ife and Dir. Institutes of African Studies and Public Admin. 1961-65; Vice-Chancellor, Univ. of Zambia Feb.-March 1965; Vice-Chancellor Univ. of Lagos 1965-72, Prof. and Dir. of African Studies 1965; Research Prof. and later Dir. Inst. of African Studies, Univ. of Ibadan 1976-83; Chair. Cttee. of Vice-Chancellors, Nigeria 1967-70, Standing Cttee., Encyclopaedia Africana 1968-; mem. Exec. Bd. Assen. of African Univs. 1967-72; Pres. Historical Soc. of Nigeria 1968-71; Chair. Management Consultants Services Ltd. 1972-; created Balogun of Iddo 1958, Agbaakin of Igbore, Abeokuta 1972; Chief Maye of Ife, Chief Baapitan of Egbaland; Fellow, Nigerian Inst. of Man. 1980; Historical Soc. of Nigeria 1980; Hon. Fellow, W. African Assen. of Surgeons 1968. *Publications:* The Origin of the Yoruba 1955, The Egba and their Neighbours 1957, African Studies in an African University 1963, Sources of Yoruba History 1972, Living Cultures of Nigeria (Ed.) 1977. *Address:* P.O. Box 7741, Lagos, Nigeria.

BIOKE MALABO, Capt. Cristino Seriche; Equatorial Guinea politician and army officer; Second Vice-Pres. and Minister of Health 1981-82; Prime Minister of Equatorial Guinea 1982-; Minister of Govt. Co-ordination, Planning, Economic Devt. and Finance 1982-86, of Health 1986-. *Address:* Oficina del Primer Ministro, Malabo, Equatorial Guinea.

BIRCH, Arthur John, F.R.S., F.A.A., PH.D.; Australian professor of chemistry and scientific administrator; b. 3 Aug. 1915, Sydney, N.S.W.; s. of Arthur Spencer and Lily Bailey; m. Jessie Williams 1948; three s. two d.; ed Sydney Tach. High School, Sydney Univ., Oxford Univ.; Research Fellow, Oxford Univ. 1941-48; Smithson Fellow Royal Soc., Cambridge 1949-52; Prof. of Organic Chemsitry, Sydney Univ. 1952-55, Manchester Univ. 1955-67, Australian Nat. Univ. 1967-80; Dir. Research School of Chemistry 1967-70, Dean 1974-77; Chair. Independent Enquiry into CSIRO 1979; Chair. Marine Services and Technologies Advisory Cttee. 1978-81; Pres. Australian Academy of Science 1982-86; Pres. Royal Chemical Inst. 1979; Newton Abraham Prof., Oxford Univ. 1980; Prof. Emer. and Univ. Fellow Australian Nat. Univ. 1982-; Fellow U.S.S.R. Acad. of Sciences; 15 Medals including Davey Medal (Royal Soc.). *Publications:* over 400 scientific papers, numerous govt. reports, How Chemistry Works 1947, The Other Arts: Science and Technology (with M. J. Kaye) 1975. *Leisure interests:* gardening, surfing, languages. *Address:* Chemistry Department, ANU, P.O. Box 783, Canberra 2601 A.C.T., Australian Academy of Science, P.O. Box 783, Canberra 2601 A.C.T. (Offices); 30 Nungara Place, Aranda A.C.T. 2614, Australia (Home). *Telephone:* 493419, 486011 (Offices); (062) 513574 (Home).

BIRCH, Bryan John, PH.D., F.R.S.; British mathematician; b. 25 Sept. 1931, Burton-on-Trent; s. of Arthur Birch and Mary Birch; m. Gina Margaret Christ 1961; two s. one d.; ed. Shrewsbury School and Trinity Coll., Cambridge; Research Fellow, Trinity Coll. 1956-60; Sr. Research Fellow, Churchill Coll., Cambridge Univ. 1960-62; Sr. Lecturer, later Reader, Univ. of Manchester 1962-65; Reader in Mathematics, Oxford Univ. 1966-85, Prof. of Arithmetic 1985-, Fellow of Brasenose Coll. 1965-. *Publications:* scholarly articles, particularly on number theory. *Leisure interests:* theoretical gardening, listening to music, watching marmots. *Address:* Green Cottage, Boars Hill, Oxford, OX1 5DQ, England. *Telephone:* (0865) 735367.

BIRCH, L. Charles, B.AGR.SC., D.SC.; Australian academic; b. 8 Feb. 1918, Melbourne; s. of Harry Milton Birch and Honoria Eleanor Hogan; ed. Scotch Coll., Melbourne, Univs. of Melbourne and Adelaide; Research Fellow, Waite Agricultural Research Inst., Adelaide 1939-46; Sr. Overseas Research Scholar, Zoology Dept., Univ. of Chicago, U.S.A. 1946, Oxford Univ., U.K. 1947; Sr. Lecturer in Zoology, Univ. of Sydney 1948-54; Fulbright Research Scholar, Zoology Dept., Columbia Univ., New York 1954; Reader in Zoology, Univ. of Sydney 1954-60, Challis Prof. of Biology 1960-83, Prof. Emer. 1984-; Fellow Australian Acad. of Science; mem. Club of Rome; David Syme Prize, Univ. of Melbourne 1954; Visiting Prof. Univ. of Minn. 1958; Visiting Prof. of Genetics, Univ. of Calif., Berkeley 1967. *Publications:* Nature and God 1965, Confronting the Future 1976; (Co-author) The Distribution and Abundance of Animals 1954, Genetics and the Quality of Life 1975, The Liberation of Life 1981, The Ecological Web 1984. *Leisure interests:* surfing, music (organ). *Address:* 5A/73 Yarranabbe Road, Darling Point, N.S.W. 2027, Australia. *Telephone:* (02) 32-3268.

BIRCH, William Francis; New Zealand politician; b. 1934, Hastings; m.; four c.; ed. Hamilton Tech. Coll.; consultant in surveying and eng., Pukekohe 1957; mem. Parl. 1972-, Sr. Govt. Whip 1975; Minister of Energy, of

Nat. Devt. and of Regional Devt. 1978-84; regular rep. of N.Z. at meetings of Int. Energy Agency, Paris; National Party. *Address:* c/o Parliament Buildings, Wellington, New Zealand.

BIRCHALL, James Derek, F.R.S.; British research scientist; b. 7 Oct. 1930, Leigh, Lancs.; s. of David Birchall and Dora M. Leather; m. Pauline M. Jones 1956; two s.; ed. Mining Coll., Wigan, and Manchester Coll. of Tech.; Research Assoc., Imperial Chemical Industries (ICI) 1957, Research Leader 1965, ICI Research Assoc. 1970, ICI Sr. Research Assoc. 1975-; Visiting Prof., Univ. of Surrey 1976-88; M.I.T. 1984-86; Univ. of Durham 1987-; Industrial Fellow, Wolfson Coll., Oxford 1977-79; Prof. Assoc., Brunel Univ. 1984-; Visiting Prof., M.I.T. 1984-85; Awards: Ambrose Congreve Energy Award 1982, Mellor Memorial Lecture (Inst. of Ceramics) 1984, Rose Memorial Lecture 1983, Hurter Memorial Lecture 1985; Founders Lecture, Soc. of Chemical Industry 1989. *Publications:* numerous contributions to learned journals and encyclopaedias. *Leisure interest:* old books. *Address:* Braeside, Stable Lane, Mouldsworth, Chester, CH3 8AN, England. *Telephone:* (09284) 320.

BIRD, Rose Elizabeth, B.A., J.D.; American judge; b. 2 Nov. 1936; ed. Long Island Univ. and Univ. of Calif., Berkeley; called to Calif. Bar 1966; Clerk to Chief Justice, Nevada Supreme Court 1965-66; successively Deputy Public Defender, Sr. Trial Deputy, Chief, Appellate Div. Santa Clara County (Calif.) Public Defenders Office 1966-74; teacher, Stanford Univ. Law School 1972-74; Sec. Calif. Agricultural and Services Agency, also mem. Gov.'s Cabinet 1975-77; Chief Justice, Calif. Supreme Court 1977-87; Democrat. *Address:* P.O. Box 51376 Palo Alto, Calif. 94306, U.S.A.

BIRD, Vere Cornwall, Sr.; Antiguan politician; b. 9 Dec. 1909, St. John's; ed. St. John's Boys' School; joined Salvation Army as teenager; trained at Salvation Army Training School, Trinidad, then posted to Grenada; mem. Exec. Antigua Trades and Labour Union (AT&LU) on its foundation, 16 Jan. 1939; Pres. AT&LU 1943-67; elected mem. Legis. Council of Antigua 1945, re-elected 1946 (also mem. Exec. Council), 1951 (also a Chair. of Cttees., Exec. Council -1956); Minister of Trade and Production 1956-60; first Chief Minister of Antigua 1960-67; Premier of Antigua 1967-71, 1976-81; lost seat in Gen. Election 1971; re-elected to Parl. 1976, 1980; first Prime Minister of independent Antigua and Barbuda Nov. 1981-; Minister of Planning, External Affairs, Defence and Energy 1981-82, of Finance 1982-84; attended Caribbean Union Confs., Trinidad 1945, St. Kitts 1946, Jamaica 1947; West Indian Govt. Confs., Lancaster House, London 1953, 1956; with Errol Barrow (Barbados) and Forbes Burnham (Guyana), formed Caribbean Free Trade Assen. 1965; Leader del. to U.K. which gained Assoc. Statehood for Antigua 1966; Leader del. to U.K. which gained full independence for Antigua from Britain Dec. 1980; Leader Antigua Labour Party. *Leisure interest:* reading. *Address:* Office of the Prime Minister, Factory Road, Antigua, West Indies.

BIRENDRA BIR BIKRAM SHAH DEV, King of Nepal; b. 28 Dec. 1945, Kathmandu; s. of late King Mahendra and Princess Indra; m. Queen Aishwarya Rajya Laxmi Devi Rana 1970; two s. one d.; ed. St. Joseph's Coll., Darjeeling, Eton Coll., England, Univ. of Tokyo and Harvard Univ.; has travelled extensively throughout Europe, North and South America, U.S.S.R., Iran, Japan, China and several African countries; Grand Master and Col.-in-Chief, Royal Nepalese Army 1964; Supreme Commdr.-in-Chief 1972; Chief Scout, Nepal Boy and Girl Scouts; Chair. Nepal Assen. of Fine Arts; Chancellor Tribhuvan Univ.; Hon. Field-Marshal (U.K.) 1980 and numerous other decorations; came to the throne 31 Jan. 1972, crowned 24 Feb. 1975. *Leisure interests:* painting, swimming, riding, playing games, parachuting. *Address:* Narayanhity Royal Palace, Kathmandu, Nepal.

BIRENDRA SINGH, Rao, B.A.; Indian politician; b. 20 Feb. 1921, Rewari, Haryana; s. of Balbir Singh and Nihal Kaur; m. Chandra Prabha; three s. one d.; ed. Univ. of Delhi; served in Army as commissioned officer 1942-47, Territorial Army 1950-52; mem. Punjab Legis. Council 1954-56; Minister, Govt. of Punjab 1956-61; mem. Haryana Assembly 1967-71, Speaker 1967; Chief Minister, SVD Govt. March-Nov. 1967; f. Vishal Haryana Party; Leader of Opposition, Haryana Assembly 1968-71; mem. Lok Sabha 1971-77, 1980-; Minister of Agric. and Rural Reconstruction, 1980-85 (also Minister of Irrigation 1980-82), of Food and Civil Supplies 1985; Pres. and Trustee of several charitable and educational trusts. *Leisure interests:* reading, gardening and travelling. *Address:* Parliament Buildings, New Delhi, India.

BIRIDO, Omer Yousif, M.A.; Sudanese diplomatist; b. 1939; m.; five c.; ed. Univ. of Khartoum and Delhi Univ., India; Third Sec., Sudan Embassy, New Delhi 1963-66, Second Sec., London 1966-69; Deputy Dir., Consular Dept., Ministry of Foreign Affairs 1969-71; Counsellor Sudan Embassy, Kampala 1971-73; Minister Plenipotentiary, Perm. Mission of Sudan to the UN, New York 1973-76; Amb. and Dir. Dept. of Int. Orgs., Ministry of Foreign Affairs 1976-77, Dir. Dept. of African Affairs 1977-78; Perm. Rep. to UN, Geneva and Vienna, also mem. Sudan Del. and Rep. to Second Cttee. at UN Gen. Ass. 1979-83; Perm. Rep. to UN 1984-86. *Address:* c/o Ministry of Foreign Affairs, Khartoum, Sudan.

BIRINCIOGLU, Ahmet Ihsan; Turkish politician; b. 5 May 1923, Akçaabar; s. of Osman Birincioglu; m. Eminehatun Birincioğlu 1982; three c.; ed. Faculty of Law, Istanbul Univ.; worked as a lawyer; Justice Party Deputy 1965-69; Senator for Trabzon 1975; Minister of Customs and

Monopoly 1969-71; Defence Minister 1979-80; mem. Exec. Cttee. of the Post and Telegraph Org., of Ziraat Bankasi (Agric. Bank) 1981-85, of T. Çimento ve Toprak Sanayii T.A.Ş. (Turkish Cement and Earthenware Industry Co.) 1985-. *Leisure interests:* reading, surveying. *Address:* Hava Sok., 19/4 Çankaya, Ankara, Turkey. *Telephone:* 39-51-04.

BIRK, Roger Emil; American business executive; b. 14 July 1930, St. Cloud, Minn.; s. of Emil Birk and Barbara E. (née Zimmer) Birk; m. Mary Louise Schrank 1955; one s. three d.; ed. St. John's Univ., Collegeville, Minn.; Div. Dir. of Operations, Merrill, Lynch, Pierce, Fenner & Smith 1970-74, mem. Bd. of Dirs. 1971, Pres. 1974-76; mem. Bd. of Dirs. Merrill, Lynch & Co. Inc. (parent co.) 1974, Pres. 1976-81, Chair. of Bd. 1980-85, Chair. Emer. 1985-, C.E.O. 1980-84, mem. Advisory Council; Vice-Chair. Bd., New York Stock Exchange 1983-85; Chair. Bd. Int. Securities Clearing Corpn. 1986-87; Pres. and C.O.O. Fed. Nat. Mortgage Assen., Wash. 1987-. *Leisure interest:* golf. *Address:* Federal National Mortgage Association, 3900 Wisconsin Avenue, NW, Washington, D.C. 20016, U.S.A. (Office).

BIRKELUND, Palle; Danish librarian; b. 29 Jan. 1912; s. of the late Hans Birkelund and Fanny Møller; m. Gerda Birkelund; ed. Københavns Universitet and Aarhus Universitet; Library Asst., State Library, Aarhus and Univ. Library, Copenhagen, Asst. Librarian 1944; UNESCO Fellowship, U.S.A. 1949; Nat. Librarian 1952-82; UNESCO consultant, Burma 1968; Chair. Danish Assen. of Research Libraries; mem. Nordic Council for Information and Documentation, etc. *Publications:* Co-editor: Nordisk leksikon for bogvaesen 1947-62, Danmarkshistoriens Blå Bog 1971, Nordisk tidskrift för bok och biblioteksväsen, Bogens Verden 1959-78, Libri, International Library Review, library and bibliographical reviews, etc. *Leisure interest:* gardening. *Address:* 39 Overgaden neden Vandet 1414, Copenhagen, Denmark (Home). *Telephone:* 101-540189.

BIRKHOFF, Garrett, SC.D; American professor of mathematics; b. 10 Jan. 1911, Princeton, N.J.; s. of George David Birkhoff and Margaret Grabius; m. Ruth Wills Collins 1938; one s. two d.; ed. Harvard Univ. and Cambridge Univ., England; joined Harvard Faculty 1936, George Putnam Prof. of Pure and Applied Maths. 1969-81, Prof. Emer. 1981-; Guggenheim Fellow 1948; mem. Bd. of Eds. Encyclopaedia Britannica 1985-; consultant to various industrial and govt. labs.; mem. N.A.S., American Philosophical Soc., American Acad. of Arts and Sciences, Math. Assen. of America, Soc. Industrial Applied Math., A.A.A.S, American Math. Soc.; George D. Birkoff Prize, American Math. Soc. 1978; Dr. h.c. from Universidad Nacional de Mexico, Univ. of Lille, France, and Case Inst. of Tech. *Publications:* Hydrodynamics 1960, Lattice Theory 1967; co-author of: Survey of Modern Algebra 1977, Jets Wakes and Cavities 1957, Ordinary Differential Equations 1988, Algebra 1979, Modern Applied Algebra 1970, Source Book in Classical Analysis 1973 and Numerical Solution of Elliptic Problems 1983; about 200 research papers. *Address:* 45 Fayerweather Street, Cambridge, Mass. 02138, U.S.A.

BIRKIN, John Derek, T.D., C.B.I.M., F.R.S.A.; British company executive; b. 30 Sept. 1929, S. Elmsall, Yorks.; s. of Noah and Rebecca (née Stranks) Birkin; m. Sadie Smith 1952; one s. one d.; ed. Hemsworth Grammar School; Man. Dir. Velmar Ltd. 1966-67, Nairn Williamson Ltd. 1967-70; Man. Dir. Tunnel Holdings Ltd. 1971-75, Chair. and Man. Dir. 1975-83; Dir. Rio Tinto-Zinc Corpn. 1982-, Deputy Chief Exec. 1983-85, Chief Exec. and Deputy Chair. April 1985-; Dir. Smiths Industries Ltd. 1977-84, British Gas Corpn. 1982-85, George Wimpey PLC 1984-; Dir. CRA Ltd. (Australia) 1985-; Dir. Rio Algom Ltd. (Canada) 1985-; Dir. The Merchants Trust PLC 1986-; mem. Council, Industrial Soc. 1986-, U.K. Top Salaries Review Body 1986-; Dir. British Steel Corpn. 1986-. *Leisure interests:* opera, rugby, cricket. *Address:* RTZ Corporation, P.O. Box 133, 6 St. James's Square, London, SW1Y 4LD, England.

BIRKS, Jack, C.B.E., PH.D., F.ENG.; British company director; b. 1 Jan. 1920, Chapeltown, Sheffield; s. of the late Herbert Horace Birks and of Ann Birks; m. Vere Elizabeth Burrell-Davis 1948; two s. two d.; ed. Ecclesfield Grammar School, Univ. of Leeds; served with REME in Europe and India (despatches, rank of Captain) 1941-46; Exploration Research Div., Anglo-Iranian Oil Co. 1948-57; Man. of Petroleum Eng. Research, BP Research Centre, Sunbury 1957-59; Vice-Pres. Exploration, BP North America 1959-62; various posts then Dir. and Gen. Man. Iranian Oil Exploration and Production Co. 1962-70; Gen. Man. Exploration and Production Dept., British Petroleum Co. 1970-72; Tech. Dir. BP Trading Ltd. and Deputy Chair. BP Trading Exec. Cttee. 1972-77; Man. Dir. British Petroleum Co. Ltd. 1978-82; Chair. BP Minerals Int. 1981-82 (Dir. 1982-85), BP Coal 1981-82, LAE Energy Inc. 1981-88, London American Energy NV 1981-88, Charterhouse Petroleum PLC 1982-86, NMI Ltd. (now British Maritime Tech. Ltd.) 1982-85; Dir. George Wimpey 1981-, Jebsens Drilling UK 1982-; Pres. Inst. of Petroleum 1984-86; Chair. British Maritime Tech. Ltd. 1985-; Dir. Petrofina (U.K.) Ltd. 1986-, Mountain Petroleum PLC 1986-. *Publications:* articles in journals, scientific papers about oilfields developments and North Sea oil. *Leisure interests:* tennis, golf. *Address:* 1A Alwyne Road, Canonbury, London, N1 2HH; and High Silver, High Street, Holt, Norfolk, England. *Telephone:* 01-226 4905 (London); Holt 712847 (Norfolk).

BIRLA, Basant Kumar; Indian industrialist; b. 16 Feb. 1921, Calcutta; s. of the late Ghanshyam Das Birla and the late Mahadevi Birla; m. Sarala

Biyani 1942; one s. two d.; Chair. Jayshree Tea & Industries Ltd., Kesoram Industries Ltd., Century Enka Ltd., Mangalam Cement Ltd., Century Spg. & Mfg. Co. Ltd., Bharat Commerce & Industries Ltd., Mangalam Timber Products Ltd.; also dir. of many cos.; Trustee Birla Educ. Trust, Birla Inst. of Tech. & Science, Birla Acad. of Art and Culture, Birla Vidya Vihar Trust, Birla Sanskriti Trust; Menalik the Second Medal (Ethiopia). *Leisure interests:* music, fine arts, photography, sport. *Address:* 9/1 R.N. Mukherjee Road, Calcutta 700 001 (Office); Basant Vihar, 18 Gurusaday Road, Calcutta 700 019, India (Home). *Telephone:* 20-9453, 28-0135 (Office); 44-5426 (Home).

BIRLA, Ganga Prasad, B.SC.; Indian industrialist; b. 2 Aug. 1922, Calcutta; s. of the late B.M. Birla and Rukmani Devi Birla; m. Nimala Devi Birla 1952; one s. one d.; ed. Calcutta Univ.; Chair. Orient Paper & Industries Ltd. 1957, Pan-African Paper Mills (EA) Ltd., Kenya 1970-, Nigeria Eng. Works Ltd., Nigeria 1974-; Man. Dir. Birla Brothers Pvt. Ltd. 1982-; Dir. Pan-African Consultancy Services (Nigeria) Ltd., Nigeria 1975-; Chair. Bd. of Govs. Birla Inst. of Tech., Ranchi, Birla Inst. of Scientific Research, Calcutta Medical Research Inst.; Pres Indian Paper Mills Asscn., Calcutta 1947-48, 1954-55, 1955-56, Employers' Asscn., Calcutta 1962-63, 1964-65. *Leisure interests:* music, art, literature, archaeology, sport, travel. *Address:* Birla Building, 9/1 R.N. Mukherjee Road, Calcutta 700 001 (Office); Birla House, 8/9 Alipore Road, Calcutta 700 027, India (Home). *Telephone:* 20 3495-28 0135 (Office); 45 1286-45 9424 (Home).

BIRNBAUM, Robert J., LL.B., B.SC.; American stock exchange president; b. 3 Sept. 1927, New York; m. Joy Mumford 1957; one s. one d.; ed. New York Univ., Univ. of Calif. Hastings Coll. of Law, Georgetown Univ. Law School; law clerk, U.S. Gen. Accounting Office 1959-61; Branch Chief, U.S. Securities and Exchange Comm. 1961-66; Sr. Vice-Pres. American Stock Exchange 1967-75, Exec. Vice-Pres. 1975-77, Pres. 1977-85; Pres. New York Stock Exchange 1985-88; Special Counsel, Dechert Price and Rhoads 1988-. *Address:* Dechert Price and Rhoads, 477 Madison Avenue, N.Y. 10022, U.S.A. *Telephone:* (212) 326-3561.

BIRNEY, Earle, PH.D., D.LITT., LL.D., O.C., F.R.S.C.; Canadian author; b. 13 May 1904, Calgary, Alta; s. of William G. Birney and Martha Robertson; m. Esther Bull 1940 (divorced 1977); one s.; ed. Univs. of British Columbia, Toronto, Calif. and London; Lecturer during summer sessions, Univ. British Columbia 1927-34, 1936-37; Instructor in English, Univ. of Utah 1930-34; Lecturer, Asst. Prof. of English, Univ. of Toronto 1936-42; Personnel Selection Officer, Canadian Army, retd. with rank of Maj. 1942-45; Supervisor of European Foreign Language Broadcasts, Radio Canada 1945-46; Prof. of English, Univ. of British Columbia 1946-62, Prof. of Creative Writing, Head of Dept. 1963-65; Writer in Residence, Univ. of Toronto 1965-67, Univ. of Waterloo 1967-68, Univ. of Western Ontario 1981-82; Regents Prof. of Creative Writing, Univ. of Calif. 1968; Royal Soc. of Canada Scholarship 1934-36, Gov.-Gen.'s Medal for Poetry 1942, 1945, Leacock Medal for Humour 1949, Canadian Govt. Overseas Fellowship 1953, L. Pierce Medal for Literature 1954, Nuffield Fellowship 1958, Canada Council Travelling Fellowships to Latin America 1962, Australia, N.Z. 1968, Africa, S. Asia 1972, 1974-75, U.K. 1971, 1973, Canada Council Medal 1968. *Publications:* poetry: David 1942, Now is Time 1945, Strait of Anian 1948, Trial of a City 1952, Twentieth Century Canadian Poetry (anthology) 1953, Ed., Selected Poetry of Malcolm Lowry 1962, Ice, Cod, Bell or Stone 1962, Near False Creek Mouth 1964, Selected Poems 1966, Pnomes, Jukollages and Other Stunzas 1967, Memory No Servant 1968, Poems of Earle Birney 1969, Rag and Bone Shop 1971, What's So Big About Green? 1973, The Bear on the Delhi Road 1973, Collected Poems 1975, The Rugging and The Moving Times 1976, Damnation of Vancouver 1977, Alphabeings/poem-drawings 1977, Ghost in the Wheels 1977, Fall by Fury 1978, The Mammoth Corridors 1980; Nexus and Earle Birney (3 albums of poetry and music) 1982, Copernican Fix 1985, One Muddy Hand 1987; novels: Turvey 1949, Down the Long Table 1955; short stories: Big Bird in the Bush 1979; criticism: The Creative Writer 1966, The Cow Jumped over the Moon 1972, Spreading Time 1980, Essays on Chaucerian Irony (with Beryl Rowland) 1985, Words on Waves (radio plays) 1985. *Leisure interests:* swimming, travelling. *Address:* RR3, Uxbridge, Ont. L0C 1K0, Canada.

BIRÓ, József; Hungarian politician; b. 13 Feb. 1921; ed. Economic and Technical Academies, Univ. of Law; fmr. instrument maker, fitter and ywelder; fmr. Head of Wages Dept., Technical Dept., Imports Dept., Ministry of Foreign Trade; Managing Dir. foreign trade enterprise 1955-57; Head Commercial Dept., Hungarian Legation, London 1957-60; Sec. Party Cttee. of Ministry of Foreign Trade 1960-62, Deputy Minister of Foreign Trade 1962-63, Minister of Foreign Trade 1963-79 (retd.); mem. Parl. 1980-; Red Banner Labour Order of Merit 1979. *Address:* c/o Ministry of Foreign Trade, 1054 Honvéd-utca 13-15, Budapest, Hungary.

BIRT, John, M.A.; British television executive; b. 10 Dec. 1944, Liverpool; s. of Leo Vincent and Ida Birt; m. Jane Frances Lake 1965; one s. one d.; ed. St. Mary's Coll., Liverpool, St. Catherine's Coll., Oxford; Television Producer of Nice Time 1968-69, Jt. Editor World in Action 1969-70, Producer of The Frost Programme 1971-72, Exec. Producer of Weekend World 1972-74, Head of Current Affairs, London Weekend Television (LWT) 1974-77, Co-Producer of The Nixon Interviews 1977, Controller of Features and Current Affairs, LWT 1977-81, Dir. of Programmes 1982-87,

Deputy Dir. Gen. BBC March 1987-; mem. Media Law Group 1983-; mem. Working Party on New Techs., Broadcasting Research Unit, Exec. Cttee. 1983-. *Leisure interest:* walking. *Address:* BBC, Broadcasting House, Portland Place, London, W.1, England.

BIRTALAN, Stefan; Romanian handball player; b. 25 Sept. 1948, Zalău, Sălaj County; s. of Emeric and Valeria Birtalan; m. Eva Gherman 1973; one s. one d.; ed. Coll. of Physical Educ. and Sports, Bucharest; mem. Romanian nat. team 1969; world champion Paris 1970, Berlin 1974 (highest scorer in that event, with 43 goals); Silver Medal Olympic Games, Montreal 1976 (highest scorer with 32 goals), Bronze Medal Olympic Games, Munich 1972, Moscow 1980. *Address:* Ap. 192, Sc. 5, Bl. 0037, 20 Str. Maşina de Piine, Bucharest, Romania.

BIRTWISTLE, Sir Harrison, Kt.; British composer; b. 1934, Accrington, Lancs.; m. Sheila Birtwistle; three s.; ed. Royal Manchester Coll. of Music and Royal Acad. of Music, London; Dir. of Music, Cranborne Chase School 1962-65; Visiting Fellow Princeton Univ. (Harkness Int. Fellowship) 1966; Cornell visiting Prof. of Music, Swarthmore Coll., Pa. 1973-74; Slee Visiting Prof., New York State Univ., Buffalo, N.Y. 1975; Assoc. Dir. Nat. Theatre 1975-; Grawemeyer Award (Univ. of Louisville, Ky.) 1987; works have been widely performed at the major festivals in Europe including the Venice Biennale, the Int. Soc. of Contemporary Music Festivals in Vienna and Copenhagen, the Warsaw Autumn Festival and at Aldeburgh, Cheltenham and Edinburgh; formed, with Peter Maxwell Davies (q.v.), The Pierrot Players. Works: operatic and dramatic: The Mark of the Goat (cantata) 1965-66, The Visions of Francesco Petrarca (sonnets for baritone and orchestra) 1966, Punch and Judy (one-act opera) 1966-67; orchestral works: Chorales for Orchestra 1962-63, Three Movements with Fanfares 1964, Nomos 1968, The Triumph of Time 1970; for instrumental ensemble: Refrains and Choruses 1957, Monody for Corpus Christi 1959, The World is Discovered 1960, Entr'actes and Sappho Fragments 1964, Ring a Dumb Carillon 1965, Tragoedia 1965, Three Lessons in a Frame 1967, Verses for Ensembles 1969, Grimethorpe Aria 1973; choral works: Narration: Description of the Passing of a Year 1964, Carmen Paschale 1965; *additional compositions:* The Mask of Orpheus (opera) 1974-81, Down By The Greenwood Side 1969, Nenia on the Death of Orpheus 1970, Melencolia I 1976, Silbury Air 1977, Meridian, For O For O the Hobby Horse is Forgot 1977, agm. 1979, On the Sheer Threshold of the Night 1980, Pulse Sampler 1980, Yan Tan Tethera 1983, Still Movement, Secret Theatre 1984, Earth Danses, Words Overhead 1985, Fanfare for Will 1987; also several pieces of instrumental music. *Address:* c/o Allied Artists Agency, 42 Montpelier Square, London, SW7 1JZ, England.

BIRYUKOVA, Aleksandra Pavlovna; Soviet politician; b. 25 Feb. 1929, Voronezh Region; ed. Moscow Textile Inst.; mem. CPSU 1956-; Dept. head of Textile and Knitwear Admin., Sovnarkhoz, Moscow 1959-63; Chief Engineer, Cotton Combine, Moscow 1963-68; Sec. Cen. Council of Trade Unions 1968-85, Deputy Chair. 1985-86; Cand. mem. Cen. Cttee. CPSU 1971-76, mem. 1976, Sec. (responsible for light industry and consumer goods) 1986-88; mem. Comm. on Industry 1971-75; mem., Chair. of Comm. on Working and Living Conditions of Women, Mother and Child Care 1976-; Vice-Chair. Council of Ministers 1988-; Deputy Supreme Soviet of U.S.S.R. 1986-; non-voting mem. of Politburo 1988; Certificate of Honour, R.S.F.S.R. Supreme Soviet 1979. *Address:* The Kremlin, Moscow, U.S.S.R.

BISAR, Muhammad Abdul Rahman, PH.D.; Egyptian religious leader; b. c. 1910; ed. Univ. of London, England; fmr. Sec.-Gen. of Acad. of Islamic Research, Cairo, and Dir. Islamic Cultural Centre, Washington, D.C.; Minister of Waqfs and Minister of State charged with Al-Azhar Affairs 1978-79; Grand Sheikh of Al-Azhar 1979-82. *Address:* c/o Office of the Grand Sheikh, Al-Azhar Administration, Cairo, Egypt.

BISCHOFF, Bernhard, DR. PHIL.; German philologist; b. 20 Dec. 1906, Altendorf, Thuringia; s. of Emil Bischoff and Charlotte (née v. Gersdorff); m. Hanne Oehlerking 1935; two s. two d.; ed. Humanistisches Gymnasium Züllichau (Mark) and Univ. of Munich; Asst. to Prof. E.A. Lowe, Munich 1933-39; Dozent, Munich Univ. 1947, Full Prof. of Medieval Latin Philology 1953-77, Prof. Emer. 1977-; mem. Bayerische Akad. der Wissenschaft, Bayerische Benediktiner-Akad., Royal Irish Acad., Medieval Acad. of America, British Acad., Royal Historical Soc., Österreichische Akad. der Wissenschaft, Koninklijke Vlaamse Acad., American Acad. of Arts and Sciences, Royal Danish Acad., Acad. des Inscriptions et Belles-Lettres; D.Litt. h.c. (Dublin, Oxford and Milan); Bayerischer Maximilians-Orden für Wissenschaft und Kunst 1984. *Publications:* Die südostdeutschen Schreibschulen und Bibliotheken in der Karolingerzeit I 1940, II 1980, Libri Sancti Kyliani 1952, Mittelalterliche Studien I-III 1966, 1967, 1981, Carmina Burana (facsimile edn.) 1968, Carmina Burana (critical edn.) I, III (with O. Schumann) 1970, Lorsch im Spiegel seiner Handschriften 1974, Paläographie des römischen Altertums und des abendländischen Mittelalters 1979. *Leisure interest:* music. *Address:* 8033 Planegg bei München, Ruffini-Allee 27, Federal Republic of Germany. *Telephone:* 8596631.

BISCHOFF, Winfried Franz Wilhelm, B.COM.; German merchant banker; b. 10 May 1941, Aachen; s. of Paul H. and Hildegard (née Kühne) Bischoff; m. Rosemary E. Leathers 1972; two s.; ed. Marist Bros., Johannesburg and Univ. of the Witwatersrand; Man. Dir. Schroders & Chartered Ltd., Hong Kong 1971-82; Dir. J. Henry Schroder Wagg & Co. Ltd., London

1978, Head of Int. Issues 1982, Head of Corp. Finance 1983, Chair. 1983–; Dir. Schroders PLC 1983, Group Chief Exec. 1984–. *Leisure interests:* opera, music, golf. *Address:* 28 Bloomfield Terrace, London, SW1W 8PQ, England. *Telephone:* 01-730 1318.

BISHARA, Abdulla Yacoub; Kuwaiti diplomatist; b. 1936; m. Maryam Bishara; one s. one d.; ed. Cairo Univ., Balliol Coll., Oxford, St. John's Univ.; Second Sec., Kuwait Embassy, Tunisia 1963–64; Dir. Office of Ministry of Foreign Affairs, Kuwait 1964–71; Perm. Rep. to UN 1971–81; Amb. (non-resident) to Brazil and Argentina 1974–80; Sec.-Gen. Gulf Co-operation Council May 1981–; del. to numerous int. confs. *Leisure interest:* reading. *Address:* Gulf Co-operation Council Secretariat, P.O. Box 7153, Riyadh 11451, Saudi Arabia. *Telephone:* 4767646.

BISHOP, Charles Johnson, A.M., PH.D.; Canadian agrologist; b. 6 Jan. 1920, Semans, Sask.; s. of Lewis L. Bishop and Nellie E. Illsley; m. Katherine A. Corey 1951; one s.; ed. Acadia Univ., Harvard Univ.; Weather Forecaster 1942–45; Research Scientist (Agric.) 1947–52; Supt., Agricultural Experimental Station, Kentville, N.S. 1952–58; Asst. Supt., Agricultural Experimental Station, Summerland, B.C. 1958–59; Assoc. Dir. of Programme, Agric. Canada, Ottawa 1959–64, Research Co-ordinator 1964–85; retd. 1985; Chair. Editorial Policy Bd. Agric. Inst. of Canada 1962–65; mem. Editorial Bd. Scientia Horticulturae 1972–; Hon. D.Sc. (Acadia) 1982; Queen's Jubilee Medal 1977; Merit Award Canadian Horticultural Council 1972; Varilar Centenary Medal 1987. *Publications:* 24 scientific papers of original research in agric. and plant genetics and cytology. *Leisure interests:* curling, gardening, Rotarians. *Address:* 1968 Bel Air Drive, Ottawa, Ont., K2C 0W9, Canada. *Telephone:* (613) 727-1820.

BISHOP, Sir George Sidney, Kt., C.B., O.B.E., B.SC.; British company executive; b. 15 Oct. 1913, Wigan, Lancs. (now Greater Manchester); s. of late J. and M. Bishop; m. 1st Marjorie Woodruff (divorced 1961), one d.; m. 2nd Una Padel 1961; ed. Ashton-in-Makerfield Grammar School, London School of Econs.; social service work in distressed areas 1935–38; South West Durham Survey 1939; Ministry of Food 1940; Private Sec. to Minister of Food 1945–49; Under-Sec. Ministry of Agric., Fisheries and Food 1949–59, Deputy Sec. 1959–61; Dir. Booker McConnell Ltd. 1961–82, Vice-Chair. 1970–71, Chair. 1972–79; Chair. Int. Sugar Council 1957; Vice-Chair. Int. Wheat Council 1959; Chair. Bookers Agricultural Holdings Ltd. 1964–70; Dir. Nigerian Sugar Co. Ltd. 1966–70; mem. Panel for Civil Service Manpower Review 1968–70, Royal Comm. on the Press 1974–77; Dir. Barclays Bank Int. 1972–83, Agricultural Mortgage Corpn. Ltd. 1973–79, Barclays Bank 1974–83, Rank Hovis McDougall 1976–84, Int. Basic Economy Corpn., U.S.A. 1981–83; Chair. Overseas Devt. Inst. 1977–84; Pres. West India Cttee. 1977–, Britain-Nepal Soc. 1979–, Gov. Nat. Inst. of Econ. and Social Research 1968–; Vice-Pres. Royal Geographical Soc. 1981–84, Pres. 1983–84; mem. Council of CBI 1973–79. *Leisure interests:* mountaineering, photography. *Address:* Brenva, Egham's Wood Road, Beaconsfield, Bucks., England. *Telephone:* Beaconsfield 3096.

BISHOP, James Drew, B.A.; British journalist; b. 18 June 1929, London; s. of late Sir Patrick Bishop and Vera Drew; m. Brenda Pearson 1959; two s.; ed. Haileybury Coll., Hertford and Corpus Christi Coll., Cambridge; reporter, Northampton Chronicle 1953; editorial staff of The Times (London) 1954–64, Foreign Corresp. 1957–64, Foreign News Ed. 1964–66, Features Ed. 1966–70; Ed. The Illustrated London News 1971–87, Newsweek Int. Diary 1977–88; Dir. Int. Thomson Publishing Co. 1980–85; Editorial Dir. Orient Express, Connections and Natural World Magazines 1981–; Ed.-in-Chief Illustrated London News Publs. 1987–; contrib. to The Annual Register 1960–, mem. Advisory Bd. 1970–; Chair. Asscn. of British Eds. 1987–. *Publications:* A Social History of Edwardian Britain 1977, Social History of the First World War 1982, The Story of The Times (with O. Woods) 1983, Illustrated Counties of England (ed.) 1985. *Address:* The Illustrated London News, 91–93 Southwark Street, London, SE1 0HX (Office); 11 Willow Road, London NW3 1TJ, England (Home). *Telephone:* (01) 928-2111 (Office); 01-435 4403 (Home).

BISHOP, James Keough; American diplomatist; b. 21 July 1938, New Rochelle; s. of James K. Bishop and Dorothy O'Keefe Bishop; m. 1st Ann Heileman 1960, 2nd Kathleen Kirby 1977; one s. three d., two step-d.; ed. Iona Preparatory, Coll. of the Holy Cross and Johns Hopkins Univ.; joined Foreign Service Dept. 1960, Press Officer, State Dept. 1961–63; Vice-Consul, Auckland 1963–66; Econ. Officer, Beirut 1966–68, Yaoundé 1968–70; Int. Relations Officer, African Affairs Bureau 1970–74; Deputy Dir. Office West African Affairs 1974–76, Dir. North African Affairs 1977–79; Amb. to Niger 1979–81; Deputy Asst. Sec. of State for African Affairs 1981–87; Amb. to Liberia 1987–; Nat. Order of Niger; Pres. Meritorious Awards 1985, 1987. *Publication:* Samoa Comes of Age 1976. *Leisure interests:* squash, jogging, swimming, sailing, carpentry. *Address:* American Embassy, Box 101, APO New York 09155, U.S.A. *Telephone:* 222-991.

BISHOP, Peter Orlebar, A.O., M.B., B.S., D.SC., F.A.A., F.R.S.; Australian academic; b. 14 June 1917, Tamworth, N.S.W.; s. of the late Ernest John Hunter Bishop and Mildred Alice Havelock Vidal; m. Hilare Louise Holmes 1942; one s. two d.; ed. Barker Coll., Hornsby, N.S.W., Sydney Univ. Medical School; Resident Medical Officer and Neurological Registrar, Royal Prince Alfred Hosp., Sydney 1941–42; Surgeon Lieut., R.A.N.R. 1942–46; Fellow, Postgraduate Cttee. in Medicine, Univ. of Sydney 1946–50; at Nat.

Hosp. for Nervous Diseases, London 1946–47 and Dept. of Anatomy, Univ. Coll., London 1947–50; Fellow, Dept. of Surgery, Univ. of Sydney 1950–51, Sr. lecturer 1951–54, Reader 1954–55, Prof. and Head 1955–67, Dept. of Physiology, Univ. of Sydney; Prof. and Head of Dept. of Physiology, Australian Nat. Univ., Canberra 1967–82, Prof. Emer. 1983–; Visiting Fellow, Dept. of Behavioural Biology, Australian Nat. Univ., 1983–84; Visiting Scholar Univ of Sydney 1987–; Visiting Prof. Osaka Univ. Medical School 1974, Keio Univ. Medical School Tokyo 1982, Katholieke Univ., Leuven 1984–85, Univ. of Zürich 1985; Visiting Fellow, St. John's Coll., Cambridge 1986; hon. mem. various socs.; Hon. M.D. (Univ. of Sydney) 1983. *Leisure interest:* bushwalking. *Address:* Department of Anatomy, University of Sydney, N.S.W. 2006, Australia.

BISHOP, Richard Evelyn Donohue, C.B.E., PH.D., D.SC.(ENG.), SC.D., F.ENG., F.R.S.; British university professor and vice-chancellor; b. 1 Jan. 1925, London; s. of N. R. Bishop and Dorothy Mary Bishop (née Wood); m. Jean Paterson 1949; one s. one d.; ed. The Roan School, Greenwich, Univ. Coll. London and Stanford Univ., Calif., U.S.A.; served R.N.V.R. 1943–46; Sr. Scientific Officer, Ministry of Supply 1951–52; lecturer and Fellow of Pembroke Coll., Cambridge Univ. 1952–57; Kennedy Prof., Univ. Coll. London 1957–81; Vice-Chancellor and Prin., Brunel Univ. 1981–; several professional prizes and medals. *Publications:* author, co-author or ed. of books and of numerous scientific and tech. articles. *Leisure interest:* sailing. *Address:* c/o Brunel University, Uxbridge, Middlesex, UB8 3PH, England. *Telephone:* (0895) 74000.

BISHOP-KOVACEVICH, Stephen; American pianist; b. 17 Oct. 1940, San Francisco; s. of Nicholas and Loreta (née Zuban) Kovacevich; ed. Berkeley High School, Calif.; studied under Lev Shorr and Dame Myra Hess; London début 1961; subsequently appeared at int. music festivals in Edinburgh, Bath, Harrogate, Berlin, San Sebastian and Salzburg; a soloist at Henry Wood Promenade Concerts for fourteen seasons; tours frequently in Europe and America; numerous recordings; winner of Kimber Award, Calif. 1959, Mozart Prize, London 1962, Edison Award (for recording of Bartok's 2nd. Piano Concerto). *Publication:* Schubert Anthology. *Leisure interests:* table tennis, tennis, chess, cinema, Indian food. *Address:* c/o Harrison/Parrott Ltd., 12 Penzance Place, London, W11 4PA, England. *Telephone:* 01-229 9166.

BISMARCK, Klaus von; German administrator; b. 6 March 1912, Jarchlin; s. of Gottfried and Gertrud von Bismarck (née Kahn); m. Ruth-Alice von Wedemeyer 1939; seven s. one d.; ed. High School, Doberan, agricultural education (training); army training 1934–38; continued agricultural studies 1938–39; Second World War service rising to Lieut.-Col. and commdr. of infantry regt. 1939–45, P.O.W. 1945; Dir. Juvenile Welfare Office, Herford 1945–46, Jugendhof (Youth Leader Training Centre) Vlotho a.d. Weser 1946–49; Dir.-Gen. Westdeutscher Rundfunk 1961–76; Pres. Goethe-Institut, Munich 1977–; mem. Bd. of Trustees Int. Broadcasting Inst.; Hon. D. Theol. (Münster); Freiherr v. Stein Prize for social work 1954; Grosses Verdienstkreuz 1982. *Publications:* Papers on sociology and theology. *Leisure interests:* music, books, tennis, skiing, horse riding and other sports. *Address:* Römerstrasse 4, 8000 Munich 40, Federal Republic of Germany. *Telephone:* 59991.

BISSAT, Bahaeddine; Lebanese engineer and politician; b. 1923, Saida; s. of Sobhi Bissat and Mariam Mekkawi; m. Itaff Bissat 1950; two s. one d.; Pres. Order of Engineers and Architects 1970–72, 1974, 1975–; Chair. al-Makassed Soc., Saida, Lebanese Standards Inst. (LIBNOR); Minister of Hydraulic and Electric Resources, Housing and Co-operatives 1982–84; Pres. Bahaeddine Bissat UNIBUILD Contracting Co.; mem. Higher Council and Urban Planning. *Leisure interests:* reading, travelling. *Address:* P.O.B. 11-6460, 804 Corniche Mazraa, Beirut, Lebanon. *Telephone:* 300736; 301568.

BISSELL, Claude T(homas), C.C., PH.D.; Canadian university administrator; b. 10 Feb. 1916, Meaford, Ont.; s. of George Thomas Bissell and Maggie Editha (Bowen) Bissell; m. Christina Flora Gray 1945; one d.; ed. Runnymede Collegiate Inst., Toronto, Cornell and Toronto Univs; Reuben Wells Leonard Fellowship 1936, Cornell Fellowship 1937; Instructor in English, Cornell Univ. 1938–41; lecturer in English, Toronto Univ. 1941–42; served in Canadian Army in Europe 1942–45; on staff of Khaki Coll. England 1945–46; Asst. Prof. of English, Dean in Residence, Univ. Coll. Toronto Univ. 1947; Asst. to Pres. Toronto Univ. 1948, Assoc. Prof. 1951, Vice-Pres. of Univ. 1952–56, Pres. 1958–71, Univ. Prof. 1971–85; Pres. Carleton Univ., Ottawa 1956–58; Chair. Canada Council 1960–62; Pres. Nat. Conf. Canadian Univs. and Colls., World Univ. Service of Canada 1962–63; Chair. Canadian Univs. Foundation 1962–63; Pres. World Univ. Service of Canada 1962–63; Visiting Prof. of Canadian Studies on William Lyon Mackenzie King Endowment, Harvard Univ. 1967–68; Chair. Carnegie Foundation for Advancement of Teaching 1966; Hon. mem. American Acad. of Arts and Sciences 1968; Hon. D.Litt. (Manitoba, Laval, Western Ont., Lethbridge, Leeds, Toronto), Hon. LL.D. (McGill, Queen's, New Brunswick, Carleton, Montreal, St. Lawrence, British Columbia, Michigan, York, Windsor, St. Andrew's and Columbia Univs.); Companion of the Order of Canada 1969. *Publications:* Great Canadian Writing 1966, The Strength of the University 1968, Halfway Up Parnassus, A Personal Account of the University of Toronto, 1932–1971, Ed. and Contrib. to University College: A Portrait 1853-1953, Canada's Crisis in Higher Education, Our Living Tradition, The Humanities in the University 1977; many articles. *Leisure interests:* swimming, photography. *Address:* Massey College, University of Toronto, Toronto 5 (Office); 229 Erskine Avenue, Toronto, Ont. M4P 1Z5, Canada (Home). *Telephone:* 928-6446 (Office); 483-9616 (Home).

BISSET, Jacqueline; British actress; b. 13 Sept. 1944, Weybridge; ed. French Lycée, London; film debut in The Knack 1965. *Other films include:* Two for the Road 1967, Casino Royale 1967, The Sweet Ride 1968, The Detective 1968, Bullitt 1968, The First Time 1969, Airport 1970, The Grasshopper 1970, The Mephisto Waltz 1971, Believe in Me 1971, The Life and Times of Judge Roy Bean 1972, Stand Up and Be Counted 1972, The Thief Who Came to Dinner 1973, Day for Night 1973, Murder on the Orient Express 1974, The Spiral Staircase 1974, End of the Game 1974, St. Ives 1975, The Deep 1976, Le Magnifique 1977, Sunday Woman 1977, The Greek Tycoon 1978, Secrets 1978, Too Many Chefs 1978, I Love You, I Love You Not 1979, When Time Ran Out 1980, Rich and Famous 1981, Inchon 1981, Class 1982, Under the Volcano 1983, Forbidden 1986, Choices 1986, High Season 1988. *Address:* c/o International Creative Management, 8899 Beverly Boulevard, Los Angeles, Calif. 90048, U.S.A.

BISSINGER, Frederick Lewis, M.E., M.S., J.D.; American chemical executive; b. 11 Jan. 1911, New York; s. of Jacob Frederick Bissinger and Rosel (Ensslin) Bissinger; m. Julia E. Stork 1935; one s. one d.; ed. Stevens Inst. of Technology and Fordham Univ.; Chemistry Instructor, Stevens Inst. of Technology 1933-36; lawyer, Pennie, Davis, Marvin & Edmonds 1936-42; various exec. positions, including Pres., Industrial Rayon Corpn. 1942-61; Group Vice-Pres. Midland-Ross Corpn. 1961-62; Vice-Pres. and Dir. Stauffer Chem. Corpn. 1962-65; Vice-Pres. Allied Chemical Corpn. 1965-66, Dir. 1966-76, Exec. Vic-Pres. 1966-69, Pres. 1969-74, Vice-Chair. 1974-76; Counsel to Pennie & Edmonds 1976-; Chair. Bd. Trustees, Stevens Inst. of Tech. 1971-83, Chair. Emer. 1983-; Trustee Fordham Univ. 1970-75, Emer. 1985-; Dir. Selas Corpn.; Former Dir. Midlantic Nat. Bank, Nat. Starch and Chemical Corpn., Neptune Int. Corpn., Otis Elevator Corpn., Rheingold Corpn.; mem. Bar N.Y., Dist. of Colo., Ohio, Supreme Court. *Address:* 11 West Way, Bronxville, N.Y. 10708, U.S.A. *Telephone:* 914-337-3332.

BISSONNETTE, Hon. André; Canadian food executive and politician; b. 25 June 1945, Saint-Jean-sur-Richelieu; m.; two c.; ed. Saint-Georges d'Iberville School, European Inst. of Business Admin., Fontainebleau, France; entered food wholesale business, specializing in distribution to hotels, restaurants, insts. and food chains, founder and Man. Dir. of own firm; participated in trade missions for Canadian Int. Devt. Agency to Nigeria, Egypt; Minister of State (Small Businesses) 1984-86, (Transport) 1986-87; mem. Officers' Mess, Saint-Jean Royal Mil. Coll. *Leisure interest:* golf. *Address:* House of Commons, Ottawa, Ont., K1A 0A2, Canada.

BISTA, Kirti Nidhi, M.A.; Nepalese politician; b. 1927; ed. Tri-Chandra Coll., Kathmandu and Lucknow Univ.; Assistant Minister for Education 1961-62, Minister for Educ. 1962-64, for Foreign Affairs 1964; Vice-Chair. Council of Ministers and Minister for Foreign Affairs and Educ. 1964-66; Vice-Chair. Council of Ministers and Minister for Foreign Affairs and Econ. Planning 1966-67; Deputy Prime Minister and Minister for Foreign Affairs and Educ. 1967-68; Perm. Rep. to UN 1968-69; Prime Minister 1969-70, 1971-73, 1977-79, Minister of Finance, Gen. Admin. and Palace Affairs 1969-73, of Finance, Palace Affairs and Defence 1978-79; mem. Royal Advisory Cttee. 1969-70; Leader Nepalese dels. to UN Gen. Assemblies 1964, 1965, 1966, and to UNESCO Gen. Confs. 1962, 1964, 1966, and to various other confs; accompanied H.M. the King on many State Visits; Order of the Right Hand of Gurkhas (First Class), Fed. German Order of Merit, Légion d'honneur. *Address:* Singhdurbar, Kathmandu (Office); Gyaneshwor, Kathmandu, Nepal (Home).

BISZKU, Béla; Hungarian politician; b. 13 Sept. 1921, Márok, Bereg; Communist Party official 1944; Staff mem., later Head of Dept. of Cadres, Budapest Party Cttee. 1946-51; Sec. Budapest Party Cttee. 1951-53; Minister of Home Affairs 1957-61; Deputy Prime Minister 1961-62; mem. Political Cttee., Hungarian Socialist Workers' Party 1957-80; Sec. Central Cttee. 1962-78; Pres. Auditing Cttee. Hungarian Trade Unions 1980-; Order of Merit. *Publications:* Topical Points of the Proletarian Dictatorship in Hungary 1957, The 21st Congress of the Soviet Communist Party and its Effects on the International Workers Movement 1959, What are the Party's Tasks in Carrying the Resolutions of the 8th Congress into Effect? 1963, The Party and the State in the Service of the People 1972. *Address:* Szakszervezetek Országos Tanácsa, Budapest VI, Dózsa György ut 84/b, Hungary. *Telephone:* 428-333.

BISZTYGA, Jan, M.SC.; Polish diplomatist; b. Jan. 1933, Cracow; m. Otylia Bisztyga 1956; one s.; ed. Jagiellonian Univ., Cracow; Asst. Prof. Jagiellonian Univ. 1954-57; active in political youth movt. 1956-59; Ministry of Foreign Affairs 1959-63; Attaché, New Delhi 1963-64; Ministry of Foreign Affairs 1964-71; Deputy Foreign Minister 1972-75; Amb. to Greece 1975-78; Amb. to U.K. 1978-81; Visiting Prof., City of London Polytechnic 1981-82; official, Ideology Dept. of PZPR Cen. Cttee.; decorations from Poland, Egypt, Bulgaria, Ethiopia and Vietnam. *Leisure interests:* game shooting, fishing, history. *Address:* Komitet Centralny PZPR, ul. Nowy Świat 6, 00-497 Warsaw, Poland.

BITAT, Rabah; Algerian politician; b. 19 Dec. 1925, Constantine Region; two s. one d.; joined Parti du Peuple Algérien 1940, Mouvement pour le Triomphe des Libertés démocratiques 1947; participated in formation of Organisation spéciale 1948; detained, sentenced to 10 years; participated in foundation of Comité révolutionnaire d'Unité et d'Action 1954, later of Front de Libération National; arrested March 1955, held in France till 1962; hunger strike, granted political status after being appointed Minister of State in Provisional Revolutionary Govt. of Algerian Repub. 1958; mem. Political Bureau, in charge of Party Org. 1962-63; Deputy Premier 1962-63, Third Deputy Premier 1963; in exile in France 1963-65; Minister of State 1965-66; Minister of State in charge of Transport 1966-77; Pres. Nat. People's Assembly March 1977-; acting Pres. of Algeria 1978-79; Pres. Arab Parl. Union 1981-, African Parl. Union 1984-; mem. Exec. Cttee. Int. Parl. Union 1984, Vice-Pres. 1986-. *Address:* National People's Assembly, 18 Boulevard Ziroulh Youcef, Algeria.

BITOV, Andrei Georgevich; Soviet writer; b. 27 May 1937, Leningrad; m. Inga Petkevich; one d.; evacuated 1939-44; ed. Leningrad Mining Inst. worked as stevedore and lathe-operator 1958-62; researcher, Leningrad Mining Inst. 1962; started publishing 1962; mem. of 'Young Prose' group in 1960's with Aksyonov (q.v.) and Gladilin (q.v.); *Publications include:* The Big Balloon 1963, Such a Long Childhood 1965, A Summer Place 1967, Apothecary Island 1968, Way of Life 1972, Seven Journeys 1976, Days of Man 1976, Pushkin House 1978. *Address:* Leningrad Mining Institute, Leningrad, U.S.S.R.

BITSCH, Hans-Ullrich; German architect and industrial designer; b. 13 June 1946, Essen; s. of Prof. Heinz W. and Lore L. (née Falldorf) Bitsch; m. Evelyn R. Koch 1981; two s.; ed. High School, Saarbrücken, State Coll. of Art, Saarbrücken, and Illinois Inst. of Tech.; architect, Univ. of Saarbrücken 1968; Instr. Int. Inst. of Design, Washington, D.C. 1969; Visiting Lecturer, Harrington Inst., Chicago, Ill. 1970-71; Prof. Dept. of Architecture, Düsseldorf Univ. 1972-; Pres. German Inst. of Interior Architects 1977-82; Visiting Prof., Univ. of Texas 1981; Pres. Professor Bitsch & Assocs. (design and architectural office), Düsseldorf; work represented in Smithsonian Inst., Design Collection, Stuttgart, and Stiftung Preussischer Kulturbesitz; several awards for architecture and design. *Publications:* Menschengerechte Gestaltung des Kassenarbeitsplatzes 1978, Farbe und Industrie-Design 1982, Design und Formentwicklung von Stühlen 1988. *Leisure interests:* skiing, sailing, photography. *Address:* Florastrasse 53, 4000 Düsseldorf 1, Federal Republic of Germany. *Telephone:* (0211) 346031.

BIYA, Paul, L. EN D.; Cameroon politician; b. 13 Feb. 1933, Mvomeka'a; m. Jeanne (née Atyam); one c.; ed. Ndem Mission School, Edea and Akono Seminaries, Lycée Leclerc, Yaoundé, Univ. of Paris, Inst. d'Etudes Politiques, Inst. des Hautes Etudes d'Outre-Mer, Paris; Head of Dept. of Foreign Devt. Aid 1962-63; Dir. of Cabinet in Ministry of Nat. Educ., Youth and Culture 1964-65; on goodwill mission to Ghana and Nigeria 1965; Sec.-Gen. in Ministry of Educ., Youth and Culture 1965-67; Dir. of Civil Cabinet of Head of State 1967-68; Minister of State, Sec.-Gen. to Pres. 1968-75; Prime Minister 1975-82; Pres. of Cameroon Nov. 1982-; Second Vice-Pres., Central Cttee., mem. Union Nationale Camerounaise (UNC), Pres. 1982-, mem. Politbureau; Commdr. de l'Ordre de la Valeur Camerounaise, Commdr. of Nat. Order of Fed. Repub. of Germany and of Tunisia, Grand Cross of Nat. Order of Merit of Senegal, Grand Officier, Légion d'honneur (France). *Address:* Office of the President, Yaoundé, Cameroon.

BJARNASON, Gudmundur; Icelandic politician; b. 9 Oct. 1944, Húsavík; m. Vigdís Gunnarsdottir; three d.; ed. Húsavík Secondary School and Co-operative Coll.; with Co-operative Soc., Húsavík 1963-67; Húsavík Br. Co-operative Bank of Iceland 1967-77, Br. Dir. 1977-80; elected mem. Húsavík Town Council 1970, Chair. 1974; mem. Althing 1979-; Minister of Health and Social Security 1987-; mem. Althing Appropriation Cttee. 1979-, Vice-Chair 1983-; Chair. Cttee. on Housing Affairs; mem. jt. cttee. on public projects; Bd. Research Council; vice-mem. Nordic Council. *Address:* c/o Ministry of Health and Social Security, Laugavegi 116, 150 Reykjávík, Iceland.

BJARNASON, Matthias; Icelandic businessman and politician; b. 15 Aug. 1921, Isafjordur; s. of Bjarni Bjarnason and Audur Johannesdóttir; m. Kristin Ingimundardóttir 1944; one d. one s.; ed. Commercial Coll. of Iceland; Man. ferry co., Isafjordur 1942-68, Isafjordur Fishing Vessels' Mutual Insurance Soc. 1960-74; Man. Kögur Fishing Co. 1959-66; mem. Bd. Isfirdingur Fishing Co. 1947-59, Chair. 1950-59; mem. Isafjordur Town Council 1946-70, Chair. 1950-52; Chair. Bd. Isafjordur Electric Power Works 1946-51; Ed. Vesturland 1953-59; mem. Bd. Union of Icelandic Fishing Vessel Owners 1962-74, also other owners' socs.; mem. Cttee. State Shipping Authority 1966-; Supplementary mem. Althing 1963-67, mem. for West Fjords 1967-; Chair. Icelandic Fishing Vessels Joint Insurance Inst. 1967-74; mem. Bd. Icelandic Fish Industries Fund 1969-74, Employment Equalization Fund 1970-71, Econ. Devt. Inst. 1972-; Chair. Exec. Cttee. Fish Industry Bd. 1968-74; mem. Independence Party, on Cen. Cttee. 1970-; Minister of Fisheries, Health and Social Security 1974-78, of Health, Social Security and Communications 1984-85, of Trade and Commerce 1985-87. *Leisure interests:* reading, travelling. *Address:* Tjaldanes 5, Gardabaer, Iceland. *Telephone:* (1) 25000.

BJELKE-PETERSEN, Hon. Sir Johannes, K.C.M.G.; Australian politician; b. 13 Jan. 1911, Dannevirke, New Zealand; s. of Carl G. and Maren (née Poulsen) Bjelke-Petersen; m. Florence Gilmour 1952; one s. three d.; ed. Taabinga Village Primary School, correspondence courses and private studies; Farmer; mem. Queensland Legislative Assembly 1947-; Minister for Works and Housing, Queensland 1963-68, later of Aboriginal and Island Affairs, and Police; Leader of Country (National) Party of Queensland 1968-87, (split 1987), Leader New Nat. Party of Australia (right wing of old party) 1987-; Premier of Queensland 1968-87. *Leisure interests:* flying, reading, bush-walking. *Address:* Office of the Premier, Executive Building, Brisbane, Queensland 4000, Australia.

BJERRUM, Jannik, M.SC., DR. PHIL.; Danish professor of chemistry (retd.); b. 5 April 1909, Copenhagen; s. of Niels J. Bjerrum and Ellen E. Dreyer; m. Grethe V. Ehlers 1937; five s. two d.; ed. Sortedan Gymnasium., Copenhagen and Univ. of Copenhagen; Rockefeller Fellow, Rockefeller Inst. New York 1935-36; Asst. Prof. Univ. of Copenhagen 1938-48, Prof. of Chem. 1948-79, Pro-Vice-Chancellor 1965-67; Provost, Coll. Regenson, Copenhagen 1967-79; mem. Royal Danish Acad., Royal Norwegian Acad., Royal Swedish Acad. and other learned socs.; Commdr. Order of Dannebrog; Dr.h.c. (Debrecen) 1979, (Lund) 1984; Otto Bruun Prize 1957; Augustinus Prize 1958. *Publications:* Metal Ammine Formation in Aqueous Solution 1957, Stability Constants I-II (co-author) 1957-58; about 150 papers mainly in Coordination Chemistry. *Address:* Chemistry Laboratory I, The H.C. Ørsted Institute, Universitetsparken 5, 2100 Copenhagen Ø (Office); Reersøgade 2, 2100 Copenhagen Ø, Denmark (Home). *Telephone:* 01 35 31 33 (Office).

BJERVE, Petter Jakob, CAND. OECON., D.PHIL.; Norwegian economist and fmr. politician; b. 27 Sept. 1913, Stjördal; s. of Petter Jakob Bjerve and Kristine Arnstad; m. Rannveig Bremer 1942; three s.; ed. Univ. of Oslo; Research Asst. Economics Inst., Oslo Univ. 1939-40; Research Fellow, Oslo Univ. 1945-49; Chief of Div. Ministry of Finance 1945-49; Dir.-Gen. Central Bureau of Statistics of Norway 1949-60, 1963-80; Visiting Prof., Stanford Univ. 1954-55; Minister of Finance 1960-63; mem. advisory missions to Zambia 1964, Sri Lanka 1971; Adviser to the Govt. of Pakistan 1968-69, Bangladesh 1973, Sri Lanka 1976, Bangladesh 1979, 1982; mem. tax inquiry comm. Zimbabwe 1983-85; UN Consultant on UN Handbook of Statistical Orgs. 1977; mem. Labour Party. *Publications:* Hva krigen kostet Norge (What the War Cost Norway) 1945, Government Economic Planning and Control 1950, Planning in Norway 1947-56, 1959, Trends in Norwegian Planning 1945-1975, 1976, 2 Addresses on Statistical Co-operation 1976, 3 Decades of the Conference of European Statisticians: Past Achievements and Perspectives for the Future 1982, International Trends in Official Statistics 1985, Economy, Population Issues and Statistics; Selected Works by Petter Jakob Bjerve; Ed. Cen. Bureau of Statistics 1985, Ragnar Frisch ag Ökosirksystemet, Oslo 1987. *Leisure interests:* fishing, gardening. *Address:* c/o Central Bureau of Statistics, Oslo (Office); Breidablikkvn. 10D, Oslo 11, Norway (Home). *Telephone:* 283759.

BJÖRK, Anita; Swedish actress; b. 25 April 1923, Tällberg Dalecarlia; m. Stig Dagerman (deceased); one s. two d.; ed. Royal Dramatic Theatre School, Stockholm; has toured around U.S.A., Canada, U.K. and France; numerous stage appearances at Royal Dramatic Theatre, Stockholm, including Miss Julie 1948, Agnes (Brand, Ibsen), Celia (The Cocktail Party, Eliot), Rosalind (As You Like It, Shakespeare), Juliet (Romeo and Juliet, Shakespeare), Eliza (Pygmalion, Shaw), Solange (Les Bonnes, Genet), The girl (Look Back in Anger, Osborne), Johanna (Les séquestrés d'Altona, Sartre), Siri von Essen (Night of The Tribades, P. O. Enquist), Madame Arkadina (The Seagull, Chekhov) 1982-83, Hanna Heiburg (Life of the Rainsnakes, Euquist), Christa Wolf (Kassandra, Wolf). *Films acted in include:* Himlaspelet 1942, Räkna de lyckliga stunderna blott (Count Your Blessings) 1944, Hundra dragspel och en flicka (One Hundred Concertinas and a Girl) 1946, Ingen väg tillbaka (No Return) 1947, Kvinna utan ansikte 1947, Det kom en gäst (There Came a Guest) 1947, På dessa skuldror (On these Shoulders) 1948, Människors rike (The Realm of Men and Women) 1949, Kvartetten som sprängdes (The Quartet that was Broken) 1950, Fröken Julie 1950-51, Han glömde henne aldrig 1952, Night People 1953, Die Hexe 1954, Giftas 1955, Der Cornet 1955, Moln över Hellesta (Dark Clouds over Hellesta) 1956, Sängen om den eldröda blommen 1956, Gäst i eget hus (Guest in One's Own House) 1957, Mannekäng i rött 1958, Tärningen är kastad 1960, Goda vänner trogna grannar 1960, Vita frun 1962, Älskande par 1964. *Address:* Baggensgatan 9, 1131 Stockholm, Sweden.

BJÖRKLUND, Ilkka-Christian; Finnish politician and administrative official; b. 20 Jan. 1947, Helsinki; s. of Stig G. and Anja Kaaja-Björklund; m. Helena Salli 1978; mem. Parl. 1972-82, 1987-; Sec.-Gen. Nordic Council 1982-87. *Address:* Parliament of Finland, SF-00102 Helsinki, Finland. *Telephone:* (90) 4321.

BJÖRKMAN, Olle Erik, PH.D., D.SC.; American professor of plant biology; b. 29 July 1933, Jönköping, Sweden; s. of Erik Gustaf Björkman and Dagmar Kristina Björkman (Svensson); m. Monika Birgit Waldinger 1955; two s.; ed. Univs. of Stockholm and Uppsala; Research Fellow, Swedish Natural Science Research Council, Univ. of Uppsala 1961-63; Postdoctoral Fellow, Carnegie Inst. Washington, Stanford, Calif. 1964-65; Faculty mem. 1966-, Prof. of Biology by courtesy, Stanford Univ. 1967-; mem. Cttee. on Carbon Dioxide Effects, U.S. Dept. of Energy 1977-82, Cttee. on Bioscience Research in Agric. 1984-85; Scientific Adviser, Desert Research Inst., Nevada 1980-81; mem. N.A.S.; Fellow, American Acad. of Arts and Sciences, A.A.A.S.; Corresp. (Foreign) mem. Australian Acad. of Sciences; Linnaeus Prize, Royal Swedish Physiographic Soc. 1977, The Stephen Hale's Award, American Soc. of Plant Physiologists 1986, The Selby Award, Australian Acad. of Sciences 1987. *Publications:* Experimental Studies on the Nature of Species V (co-author) 1971, Physiological Processes in Plant Ecology 1980, more than 100 articles in scientific journals. *Leisure interest:* opera. *Address:* Carnegie Institution of Washington, Department of Plant Biology, Stanford, Calif. 94305, U.S.A. (Office); 3040 Greer Road, Palo Alto, Calif. 94303, U.S.A. (Home). *Telephone:* (415) 325-1521 (Office); (415) 858-0880 (Home).

BJÖRKSTRAND, Hilding Gustav Mattias, PH.D.; Finnish politician; b. 25 Oct. 1941, Kaarlela; s. of Gunnar Björkstrand and Siri Björkstrand (née Lurden); m. Annlis Carita Karlsson 1965; one s. one d.; headmaster, Uusikaarlepyy People's Coll.; Lecturer, Åbo Akademi 1975-78, Acting Prof. of Church History 1978-83; Prof. of Practical Theology 1988-; mem. Uusikaarlepyy City Council 1975-83, Parl. 1987-; Chair. Legis. Cttee. 1987-, Nordic Council 1987-; Minister, Ministry of Educ. and Science 1983-87, of Nordic Co-operation 1983-87; Swedish People's Party. *Leisure interest:* literature. *Address:* Gustav Björkstrand, Seminariegatan 20, 66900 Nykarleby, Finland. *Telephone:* (967) 21302.

BJØRNHOLM, Sven, DR.PHIL.; Danish physicist; b. 8 Sept. 1927, Tønder; s. of Lieut.-Col. H. L. Bjørnholm and Inger Hillerup; m. Iran Park 1957; two s. one d.; ed. Tech. Univ. of Denmark, Sorbonne, Paris and Univ. of Copenhagen; Research Asst. Niels Bohr Inst. Copenhagen 1955-68; Assoc. Prof. Univ. of Copenhagen 1968-; visiting scientist at research insts. in France, U.S.S.R., U.S.A., Germany and Brazil 1951-86; mem. Bd. Int. Fed. of Insts. of Advanced Study 1972-77, Danish Natural Science Research Council 1973-79, Danish Energy Policy Council 1976-86, Int. Union of Pure and Applied Physics (IUPAP) Comm. on Nuclear Physics 1978-84, European Community Comm. on Research and Devt. 1980-82; Pres. Danish Physical Soc. 1978-80; mem. Royal Danish Acad., Danish Acad. of Tech. Sciences, Danish Acad. of Future Studies, Danish Pugwash Cttee.; Ole Rømer Award 1965, Ulrich Brinch Award 1973. *Publications:* Energy in Denmark 1990-2005 1976 and articles in professional journals. *Address:* The Niels Bohr Institute, Blegdamsvej 17, 2100 Copenhagen Ø (Office); Frederiksberg Alle 45, 1820 Frederiksberg C, Denmark (Home). *Telephone:* 45-1-421616 (Office); 45-1-224885 (Home).

BJØRNVIG, Thorkild Strange, DR. PHIL.; Danish poet and writer; b. 2 Feb. 1918; s. of Adda and Theodor Bjørnvig; m. 1st Grete Damgaard Pedersen 1946, 2nd Birgit Hornum 1970; two s. one d.; ed. Cathedral School, Aarhus, and Univ. of Aarhus; mem. Danish Acad. 1960; several prizes. *Publications:* poetry; Stjaernen bag gavlen 1947, Anubis 1955, Figur og Ild 1959, Vibrationer 1966, Ravnen 1968, Udvalgte digte 1970, Morgenmørke 1977; essays: Rilke og tysk Tradition 1959, Begyndelsen 1960, Kains Alter 1964, Ôprør mod neonguden 1970, Virkeligheden er til 1973, Pagten, mit venskab med Karen Blixen 1974, Delfinen 1975, Stoffets Krystalhav 1975, Det religiøse menneskes ansigter 1975, Også for naturens skyld 1978, Barnet og dyret i industrisamfundet 1979, Abeguder, Miljødigte 1975-80 1981. *Address:* Issehoved, 8795 Nordby, Denmark. *Telephone:* 06596259.

BJURSTRÖM, Per Gunnar, PH.D.; Swedish museum director; b. 28 March 1928, Stockholm; s. of Gunnar and Claire (née Hellgård) Bjurström; m. Eva Gunnars; two d.; m. 2nd Görel Cavalli-Björkman; Asst. curator, Nationalmuseum 1950-68, curator of prints and drawings 1968-79; Dir. Nat. Swedish Art Museums 1980-; guest prof., Yale Univ. 1968; mem. Bd. Gen. Art Asscn. of Sweden 1964-, Prince Eugen's Waldemarsudde 1980-; Vice-Chair. Soc. of Art History 1965-; Chair. Int. Cttee. of Museums of Fine Art 1983-; mem. Royal Acad. of Letters, History and Antiquities and Royal Acad. of Fine Art. *Publications:* Giacomo Torelli and Baroque Stage Design 1961, Stage Design in Sweden 1964, Feast and Theatre in Queen Christina's Rome 1966, German Drawings in Swedish Public Collections 1972, French Drawings in Swedish Public Collections 1976, 1982, 1986, Italian Drawings in Swedish Public Collections 1979, Johan Tobias Sergel 1975, Three Decades of Swedish Graphic Art 1946-1976, Roman Baroque Scenery 1977, Philip von Schantz 1979. *Address:* Blasieholmskajen, Box 16176, 103 24 Stockholm (Office); Albavägen 23, 181 33 Lidingö, Sweden. *Telephone:* 08-767 58 07.

BLACK, Conrad M., LITT.D., LL.D.; Canadian business executive and publisher; b. 25 Aug. 1944, Montreal, Quebec; s. of George Montegu and Jean Elizabeth (Riley) Black; m. Shirley Gail Hishon 1978; two s. one d.; ed. Carleton, Laval, McGill, St. Francis Xavier, McMaster and Windsor Univs.; Chair. of Bd., Chair. Exec. Cttee. and C.E.O. Argus Corpn. Ltd., Chair. and C.E.O. Ravelston Corpn. Ltd.; Chair. The Daily Telegraph PLC 1987-; Chair. Saturday Night Magazine Inc.; Chair. and C.E.O. Hollinger Argus Ltd.; Deputy Chair. American Publishing Co.; Vice-Chair. and mem. Exec. Cttee. Norcen Energy Resources Ltd.; mem. Exec. Cttee. and Dir. Canadian Imperial Bank of Commerce; acquired Daily Telegraph newspaper group 1985; Dir. CFRB Ltd., Carling O'Keefe Ltd., Confed. Life Insurance Co., Domgroup Ltd., Eaton's of Canada Ltd., T. Eaton Acceptance Co. Ltd., Financial Post Co. Ltd., M.A. Hanna Co., Hees Int. Corpn., Iron

Ore Co. of Canada, Labrador Mining and Exploration Co. Ltd.; Trustee Clarke Inst. of Psychiatry. *Publication:* Duplessis 1977. *Address:* 10 Toronto Street, Toronto, Ont. M5C 2B7, Canada (Office).

BLACK, Sir Douglas Andrew Kilgour, Kt., M.D., F.R.C.P.; British physician; b. 29 May 1913, Delting, Shetland; s. of Rev. Walter Kilgour Black and Mary Jane Crichton; m. Mollie Thorn 1948; one s. two d.; ed. St. Andrews Univ.; Lecturer, Reader and Prof., Dept. of Medicine, Manchester Univ. 1946-77, now Emer., Sir Arthur Sims Commonwealth Travelling Prof. 1971; on secondment as Chief Scientist, Dept. of Health and Social Security 1972-77; Pres. Royal Coll. of Physicians, London 1977-83; Pres. Inst. of Medical Ethics 1984-; Pres. British Medical Assen. 1985-86; Lectureships (Royal Coll. of Physicians, London): Goulstonian 1953, Bradshaw 1965, Lumleian 1970, Harveian 1977; Hon. D.Sc. (St. Andrew's) 1972, Hon. D.Sc. (Manchester) 1978. *Publications:* The Logic of Medicine 1968, Essentials of Fluid Balance (4th edn.) 1967, An Anthology of False Antithesis 1984, Invitation to Medicine 1987, Recollections and Reflections 1987. *Leisure interests:* reading and writing. *Address:* The Old Forge, Duchess Close, Whitchurch-on-Thames, Reading, RG8 7EN, England. *Telephone:* Pangbourne 4693.

BLACK, Sir James (Whyte), Kt., F.R.C.P., F.R.S., F.R.S.E. (HON.); British professor of analytical pharmacology; b. 14 June 1924; ed. Beath High School, Cowdenbeath and Univ. of St. Andrews; Asst. Lecturer in Physiology, Univ. of St. Andrews 1946; lecturer in Physiology, Univ. of Malaya 1947-50; Sr. Lecturer Univ. of Glasgow Veterinary School 1950-58; with ICI Pharmaceuticals Ltd. 1958-64, Head of Biological Research and Deputy Research Dir. Smith, Kline & French, Welwyn Garden City 1964-73; Prof. and Head of Dept. of Pharmacology, Univ. College, London 1973-77; Prof. of Analytical Pharmacology, King's Coll. Hosp. Medical School, Univ. of London 1984-; Dir. Therapeutic Research, Wellcome Research Labs. 1978-84; mem. British Pharmacological Soc. 1961-; Mullard Award, Royal Soc. 1978, Nobel Prize for Medicine 1988. *Address:* Analytical Pharmacology Unit, Rayne Institute, 123 Coldharbour Lane, London, SE5 9NU, England. *Telephone:* 01-274 7437.

BLACK, Matthew, D.D., D.LITT., LL.D., F.B.A., F.R.S.E.; British academic; b. 3 Sept. 1908, Kilmarnock, Ayrshire, Scotland; s. of James Black and Ellen Black; m. Ethel Mary Hall 1938; one s. one d.; ed. Kilmarnock Acad., Univ. of Glasgow, Univ. of Bonn, Germany; Asst. to Prof. of Hebrew, Univ. of Glasgow 1935-37; Asst. Lecturer in Semitic Languages and Literature, Univ. of Manchester 1937-39; Lecturer in Hebrew and Biblical Criticism, Univ. of Aberdeen 1939-42; Parish Minister of Dunbarney, Bridge of Earn, Perthshire 1942-47; lecturer in New Testament Language and Literature, Univ. of Leeds 1947-52; Prof. of Biblical Criticism and Biblical Antiquities, Univ. of Edin. 1952-54; Prof. of Divinity and Biblical Criticism and Prin. of St. Mary's Coll., Univ. of St. Andrews 1954-78, Prof. Emer. 1978-; mem. Royal Swedish Soc. of Sciences of Uppsala; Corresp. mem. Göttingen Akademie der Wissenschaften; Burkitt Medal (British Acad.). *Publications:* The Scrolls and Christian Origins 1961, A Christian Palestinian Syriac Horologion Cambridge 1964, An Aramaic Approach to the Gospels and Acts (3rd edn.) 1967, Apocalypsis Henochi Graece 1970, The Book of Enoch or I Enoch 1985, Ed. of New Testament Studies 1954-78. *Leisure interest:* golf. *Address:* 40 Buchanan Gardens, St. Andrews, Fife, KY16 9LX, Scotland. *Telephone:* (0334) 74686.

BLACK, Robert Denis Collison, M.A., PH.D., F.B.A., M.R.I.A.; British economist; b. 11 June 1922, Dublin; s. of William R. and Rose M. (née Reid) Black; m. Frances M. Weatherup 1953; one s. one d.; ed. Sandford Park School, Dublin and Trinity Coll., Dublin; Deputy for Prof. of Political Econ., Trinity Coll. Dublin 1943-45; Asst. Lecturer in Econ. Queen's Univ. Belfast 1945-46, Lecturer 1946-58, Sr. Lecturer 1958-61, Reader 1961-62, Prof. 1962-85, Prof. Emer. 1985-, Pro-Vice-Chancellor 1971-75; Rockefeller Post-doctoral Fellow, Princeton Univ. 1950-51; Visiting Prof. Yale Univ. 1964-65; Research Fellow, Japan Soc. for Promotion of Science 1980; Hon. D.Sc. (Queen's Univ.) 1988; Hon. Fellow, Trinity Coll., Dublin 1982, Distinguished Fellow, History of Econs. Soc., U.S.A. 1987. *Publications:* Economic Thought and the Irish Question 1817-1870 1960, Catalogue of Pamphlets on Economic Subjects 1750-1900 1969, Readings in the Development of Economic Analysis 1971, Papers and Correspondence of W. S. Jevons (Vols. I-VII) 1972-81, Ideas in Economics (Ed.) 1986. *Leisure interests:* travel, music, classic cars. *Address:* Queen's University, Belfast, BT7 1NN, Northern Ireland. *Telephone:* Belfast 245133.

BLACK, Robert Lincoln, M.D.; American pediatrician; b. 25 Aug. 1930, Los Angeles; s. of Harold Black and Kathryn Stone; m. Jean Wilmott McGuire 1953; two s. one d.; ed. Stanford Univ., Kings County Hosp., Brooklyn, Stanford Univ. Hosp., Palo Alto; Capt. U.S. Air Force Medical Corps 1956-58; Asst. Clinical Prof., Stanford Univ. 1962-68, Assoc. Prof. 1968-79, Prof. of Pediatrics 1980-; mem. Bd. of Educ. Monterey Peninsula Unified School Dist. 1965-73; mem. Bd. Mid Coast Health System Agency 1975-81; mem. variousa cttees. of American Acad., of Pediatrics 1962-, Alt. Chapter Chair. 1984-87; Consultant, State of Calif. Dept. of Health Service 1976-82, and of Office of Statewide Health Planning 1975-81; currently Pediatrician with pvt. practice; mem. Inst. of Medicine, N.A.S., Calif. State Maternal, Child, Adolescent Health Bd. *Publications:* California Health Plan for Children, California's Use of Health Statistics in Child Health Planning. *Leisure interests:* music, hiking, travel, photography.

Address: 920 Cass Street, Monterey, Calif. 93940 (Office); 976 Mesa Road, Monterey, Calif. 93940, U.S.A. (Home). *Telephone:* (408) 372-5841 (Office); (408) 372-2594 (Home).

BLACK, Shirley Temple; American actress and diplomatist; b. 23 April 1928, Santa Monica, Calif.; d. of George F. and Gertrude Temple; m. 1st John Agar, Jr. 1945 (dissolved 1949), one d.; m. 2nd Charles A. Black 1950, two c.; ed. privately and Westlake School for Girls; career as film actress commenced at 3½ years; first full-length film was Stand Up and Cheer; narrator/actress in TV series Shirley Temple Storybook 1958; hostess/actress Shirley Temple Show 1960; Del. to UN, New York 1969-70; Amb. to Ghana 1974-76, White House Chief of Protocol 1976-77; mem. U.S. Comm. for UNESCO 1973-; mem. U.S. Delegation on African Refugee Problems, Geneva 1981; Dir. Nat. Multiple Sclerosis Soc.; Dame, Order of Knights of Malta (Paris) 1968; American Exemplar Medal 1979, Gandhi Memorial Int. Foundation Award 1988; numerous state decorations. *Films include:* Little Miss Marker, Baby Take a Bow, Bright Eyes, Our Little Girl, The Little Colonel, Curly Top, The Littlest Rebel, Captain January, Poor Little Rich Girl, Dimples, Stowaway, Wee Willie Winkie, Heidi, Rebecca of Sunnybrook Farm, Little Miss Broadway, Just Around the Corner, The Little Princess, Susannah of the Mounties, The Blue Bird, Kathleen, Miss Annie Rooney, Since You Went Away, Kiss and Tell, That Hagen Girl, War Party, The Bachelor and the Bobby-Soxer, Honeymoon. *Publication:* Child Star 1988. *Address:* 115 Lakeside Drive, Woodside, Calif. 94062, U.S.A.

BLACK, Stanley, O.B.E.; British conductor, composer and pianist; b. 14 June 1913, London; m. Edna Kaye 1947; one s. one d.; ed. schools in London; BBC Staff conductor 1944-52; Musical Dir. Assoc. British Film Studios, Elstree 1952-61; freelance 1962-; has composed and musically directed scores of some 95 British and Anglo-American productions since 1944; as conductor has appeared with most of the major British orchestras and in Japan, Scandinavia, Belgium, Netherlands, New Zealand, Australia, Canada and U.S.A.; records for Decca; Life Fellow Inst. of Arts and Letters 1963-, and numerous others; Freedom of the City of London 1988; several gold awards. *Leisure interests:* theatre, literature, music, children, grandchildren. *Address:* 118 Wardour Street, London, W.1., England.

BLACKMAN, Donald George, PH.D.; Barbadian politician, diplomatist and fmr. professor of African studies; b. 22 May 1935; ed. Lincoln's Inn, London, York Univ., Toronto, New York Univ., New School for Social and Econ. Research, New York; served in Barbados, U.K. and Canadian Civil Services 1955-58; Tutor, New York Dept. of Foster Care 1968-69; lecturer in Afro-American History and Literature, Long Island Univ. 1969-70; Instructor in Philosophy and Social Science, State Univ. of New York at Stony Brook 1970-71; Chair. and Assoc. Prof., African Studies Dept., State Univ. of New York 1971-76; Perm. Rep. to UN 1976-78; mem. Senate; Minister of Labour and Community Services 1978-80, of Transport and Works 1981-83, of Health and Community Services 1983-84, of Transport and Works Oct. 1988-. *Address:* Ministry of Transport and Works, P.O. Box 25, Bridgetown, Barbados.

BLACKMAN, Harold Alphonso, B.SC. (ECON.); Barbadian politician; b. 5 Sept. 1940; m. Marcia L. Boucher; two s. one d.; ed. Combermere School and Univ. of West Indies, Cave Hill, Barbados; formerly with Cable & Wireless (W.I.) Ltd.; Barbados External Telecommunications 1958-86; mem. Parl. 1981-; Minister of Housing and Lands 1986-; Democratic Labour Party. *Leisure interest:* cricket. *Address:* Ministry of Housing and Lands, Marine House, Hastings, Christ Church, Barbados.

BLACKMAN, Honor; actress; film début in Fame is the Spur 1947. *Films include:* Green Grow the Rushes 1951, Come Die My Love 1952, The Rainbow Jacket 1953, The Glass Cage 1954, Dead Man's Evidence 1955, A Matter of Who 1961, Goldfinger 1964, Life at the Top 1965, Twist of Sand 1967, The Virgin and the Gipsy 1970, To the Devil a Daughter 1975, Summer Rain 1976, The Cat and the Canary 1977. *TV appearances include:* Four Just Men 1959, Man of Honour 1960, Ghost Squad 1961, Top Secret 1962, The Avengers 1962-64, The Explorer 1968, Visit from a Stranger 1970. Out Damned Spot 1972, Wind of Change 1977, Robin's Nest 1982, Never the Twain 1982, The Secret Adversary 1983, Lace 1985, The First Modern Olympics 1986, Minder on the Orient Express 1986, Dr Who 1986, William Tell 1986. *Address:* c/o London Management Ltd., 235-41 Regent Street, London, W1A 2JT, England. *Telephone:* 01-493 1610.

BLACKMUN, Harry A.; American judge; b. 12 Nov. 1908, Nashville, Ill.; s. of Corwin Manning and Theo Huegely (Reuter) Blackmun; m. Dorothy E. Clark 1941; three d.; ed. Harvard Univ. and Harvard Law School; admitted to Minnesota Bar 1932; private legal practice until 1950; Instructor, William Mitchell Coll. of Law 1935-41, Univ. of Minnesota Law School 1945-47; Judge, U.S. Court of Appeals Eighth Circuit 1959-70; Assoc. Justice U.S. Supreme Court 1970-; mem. Judicial Conf. Advisory Cttee. on Judicial Activities 1969-79; Rep. Judicial Branch, Nat. Historical Publs. and Records Comm. 1975-82, 1986-; participant, Franco-American Colloquium on Human Rights 1979; co-moderator seminar on justice and the individual, Rome 1987; mem. American Bar Assen., Minnesota State, Third Judicial District (Minn.) and Olmsted County (Minn.) Bar Assens., American Judicature Soc.; Hon. LL.D. (DePauw, Drake, Hamline and Ohio Wesleyan Univs., Vermont Law School, Dartmouth Coll.; Morningside Coll., Wilson

Coll., Dickinson School of Law, Southern Ill., Pepperdine, Emory Univs., Rensselaer Polytechnic Inst., McGeorge School of Law, Univ. of the Pacific, Univ. of Neb., New York Law School, Vermont Law School, Dartmouth Coll., Carleton Coll., Luther Coll., Drury Coll., Tufts Univ. IIT Chicago Kent Coll. of Law, N. Ill. Univ., Brooklyn Law School); D.H.L. (Oklahoma City Univ., Mass. School of Professional Psychology); D.Litt. (Dickinson School of Law); D.P.S. (Ohio Northern); Chair. Faculty, Salzburg Seminar in American Studies (Law) 1977; co-moderator, Seminar on Justice and Society, Aspen Inst. 1979-88; co-moderator Seminar on Justice and Soc., Aspen Inst. Italia, Rome 1986; Visiting instructor on Constitutional Law, Louisiana State Univ. Law School Summer Session, Aix-en-Provence, France 1986. *Address:* United States Supreme Court, Washington, D.C. 20543, U.S.A.

BLACKWELL, Julian Toby; British bookseller; b. 10 Jan. 1929; s. of the late Sir Basil H. Blackwell and Marion C. Soans; m. Jennifer J.D. Wykeham 1953; two s. one d.; ed. Winchester Coll. and Trinity Coll., Oxford; served 5th Royal Tank Regt. 1947-49; 21st SAS (TA) 1950-59; Dir. and Chair. various Blackwell cos. since 1956; Chair. The Blackwell Group Ltd. 1980-; Chair. Council, ASLIB 1966-68; Pres. Booksellers' Assen. 1980-82; D.L. (Oxfordshire) 1988. *Leisure interests:* sawing firewood, sailing. *Address:* c/o 50 Broad Street, Oxford, OX1 3BQ, England.

BLACKSTONE, Baroness (Life Peer) cr. 1987, of Stoke Newington in Greater London, **Tessa Ann Vosper Blackstone,** PH.D.; British college principal; b. 27 Sept. 1942, London; d. of Geoffrey Vaughan Blackstone and Joanna Blackstone; m. (marriage dissolved); one s. one d.; ed. Ware Grammar School, London School of Economics, Univ. of London; Assoc. Lecturer, Enfield Coll. 1965-66; Asst. Lecturer, then Lecturer, Dept. of Social Admin., L.S.E. 1966-75; Fellow, Centre for Studies in Social Policy 1972-74; Adviser, Cen. Policy Review Staff, Cabinet Office 1975-78; Prof. of Educational Admin., Univ. of London Inst. of Educ. 1978-83; Deputy Educ. Officer (Resources), then Clerk and Dir. of Educ., Inner London Educ. Authority 1983-87; Master, Birkbeck Coll., Univ. of London 1987-; Dir. Royal Opera House 1987-; Chair. General Advisory Council BBC 1988-; Chair. Bd. of Trustees, Inst. for Public Policy Research 1988-; *Publications:* A Fair Start 1971, Education and Day Care for Young People in Need 1973, Social Policy and Administration in Britain 1975; co-author: Students in Conflict 1970, The Academic Labour Market 1974, Disadvantage and Education 1982, Education Policy and Educational Inequality 1982, Response to Adversity 1983, Testing Children 1983, Inside the Think Tank: Advising the Cabinet 1971-83, 1988. *Leisure interests:* tennis, walking, ballet, opera. *Address:* Birkbeck College, Malet Street, London, WC1E 7HP (Office); 2 Gower Street, London, WC1E 6DP, England (Home). *Telephone:* 01-631 6274 (Office); 01-636 0067 (Home).

BLAGOY, Dmitriy Dmitriyevich; Soviet literary historian; b. 28 Jan. (9 Feb., new style) 1893, Moscow; ed. Moscow Univ.; mem. Acad. Pedagogical Soc. RSFSR 1947-; Prof. Moscow Univ. 1943-; Corresp. mem. USSR Acad. Sciences 1953-; mem. USSR Acad. Pedagogical Soc. 1967-; State Prize-winner 1951, 1975; several orders and medals. *Publications:* deal mainly with the work of A. S. Pushkin and include: Fonvizin - A Biocritical Account 1945, The Evolution of Pushkin's Art 1813-26 1950, The Evolution of Pushkin's Art 1826-30 1967, The World As Beauty: 'The Vesperal Lights' of A. A. Fet 1975 (State Prize), The Soul in the Lyre 1978, From Kantemir to the Present Day 1978, also numerous works on history of Russian literature of the 18th, 19th, 20th centuries.

BLAHNIK, Manolo; Spanish couturier; b. 28 Nov. 1943, Santa Cruz, The Canary Islands; ed. Univ. of Geneva; f. and Dir. Manolo Blahnik Int. Ltd.; opened shop in Chelsea, London 1973, U.S.A. 1981; Biannual collections in Madrid, Spain; Fashion Council of America Award 1988. *Publications:* various int. publs. on fashion. *Leisure interests:* painting, travel, reading. *Address:* Manolo Blahnik International Ltd., 49-51 Old Church Street, London, SW3, England.

BLAHNÍK, Col.-Gen. Miloslav; Czechoslovak army officer; b. 22 Dec. 1927; First Deputy Minister of Nat. Defence 1979-; Chief of Staff, Czechoslovak People's Army 1979-; mem. House of Nations, Fed. Ass. 1979-89; mem. Cen. Cttee., CP of Czechoslovakia 1981-; mem. State Defence Council 1979-; Order of Labour 1977, Order of the Red Star (U.S.S.R.) 1983. *Address:* Ministry of Defence, Prague, Czechoslovakia.

BLAIN, Francis René; Gambian diplomatist; b. 8 Nov. 1943, Banjul; m.; three c.; ed. Univ. of Sierra Leone; with Gambian Civil Service (local govt.) 1970-74, Sr. Asst. Minister for External Affairs 1974-76; Counsellor High Comm., London 1976-79; Deputy Perm. Rep. to UN and Consul-Gen., New York 1980-82, Perm. Rep. to UN 1982-85. *Address:* c/o Ministry of Foreign Affairs, Banjul, The Gambia.

BLAINEY, Geoffrey Norman, O.A.; Australian author and historian; b. 11 March 1930, Melbourne; s. of Rev. Samuel C. Blainey and Hilda Blainey; m. Ann Heriot 1957; one d.; ed. Ballarat High School, Wesley Coll., Univ. of Melbourne; freelance historian 1951-61; Reader in Econ. History, Univ. of Melbourne 1963-68, Prof. 1968-76, Ernest Scott Prof. 1977-, Dean of Faculty of Arts 1982-87; Prof. of Australian Studies, Harvard Univ. 1982-83; Chair. Australia Council 1977-81, Fed. Govt.'s Australia-China Council 1979-84, Commonwealth Literary Fund 1971-73; Pres. Council, Queen's Coll., Univ. of Melbourne 1971-; Chair. Australian Selection

Cttee. Commonwealth Fund (Harkness) Fellowships 1983-; Gold Medal, Australian Literature Soc. 1963, Capt. Cook Bicentenary Literary Award 1970, Britannica Award for dissemination of learning, N.Y. 1988. *Publications include:* The Peaks of Lyell 1954, Centenary History of the University of Melbourne 1957, Gold and Paper: a History of the National Bank 1958, Mines in the Spinifex 1960, The Rush That Never Ended 1963, The Tyranny of Distance 1966, Across a Red World 1968, The Rise of Broken Hill 1968, The Steel Master 1971, The Causes of War 1973, Triumph of the Nomads: A History of Ancient Australia 1975, A Land Half Won 1980, Our Side of the Country 1984, All for Australia 1984, The Great Seesaw 1988. *Leisure interests:* travel, wood-chopping, Australian football. *Address:* 43 Hotham Street, East Melbourne, Vic. 3002, Australia. *Telephone:* 03-417 77363.

BLAIR, Gordon Purves, PH.D., D.SC., F.ENG., F.I.MECH.E.; British professor of mechanical engineering; b. 29 April 1937, Larne, Northern Ireland; s. of Gordon Blair and Mary H.J. Blair; m. Norma Margaret Millar 1964; two d.; ed. Larne Grammar School and The Queen's Univ. of Belfast; Asst. Prof., Mechanical Eng., New Mexico State Univ. 1962-64; Lecturer in Mechanical Eng., Queen's Univ. Belfast 1964-71, Sr. Lecturer 1971-73, Reader 1973-76, Prof. 1976-82, Prof. and Head of Dept. of Mechanical and Industrial Eng. 1982-, Dean of Faculty 1985-; consultant to many industries world-wide on engine design; Fellow S.A.E.; Colwell Technical Merit Award (S.A.E.); Crompton Lanchester Medal (I.Mech.E.); Trident TV Award (IBA). *Publications:* 45 tech. papers in int. journals. *Leisure interests:* golf, fishing, photography. *Address:* Ashby Building, The Queen's University of Belfast, Belfast, BT9 5AH, Northern Ireland. *Telephone:* (0232) 661111.

BLAIR-CUNYNGHAME, Sir James Ogilvy, Kt., O.B.E.; British banker; b. 28 Feb. 1913, Edinburgh; s. of late Edwin Blair-Cunynghame and late Anne Tod; ed. Sedbergh School and King's Coll. Cambridge; with Unilever Ltd. 1935-38; Fellow, St. Catherine's Coll. Oxford 1939-; served World War II 1939-45, Lt.-Col. 1944; Foreign Office 1946-47; Chief Personnel Officer, BOAC 1947-55; Dir.-Gen. of Staff, Nat. Coal Bd. 1955-57, full-time mem. of Staff, 1957-59; joined Royal Bank of Scotland 1960, Deputy Chair. 1961, Chair. 1965-68, 1970-76; Chair. Nat. and Commercial Banking Group Ltd. 1968-78, Williams and Glyn's Bank Ltd. 1976-78; Deputy Chair. Provincial Insurance Co. Ltd. and Provincial Life Assurance Co. Ltd. 1979-85; Dir. Provincial Insurance Investment Cttee., Provincial Life Assurance Co. Ltd., The Scottish Mortgage and Trust Co. Ltd. 1965-74; mem. Court of Govs., LSE; various other positions; mem. Queen's Body Guard for Scotland; Companion, British Inst. of Man., Inst. of Personnel Man.; Hon. LL.D. (St. Andrews) 1965, Hon. D.Sc., Social Science (Edinburgh) 1969, Hon. F.R.C.S. (Edinburgh) 1978. *Publications:* various articles on financial and econ. matters and on personnel aspects of gen. management. *Leisure interest:* fishing. *Address:* Broomfield, Moniaive, Thornhill, Dumfriesshire, Scotland (Home). *Telephone:* Moniaive 217 (Home).

BLAIS, Marie-Claire, C.C.; Canadian writer; b. 5 Oct. 1939, Quebec City; ed. Quebec, Paris and United States; Guggenheim Foundation Fellowship, New York 1963; Hon. Prof. Calgary Univ. 1978; Dr. h.c. (York Univ., Toronto) 1975; Order of Canada; Prix de la langue française 1961, Prix France-Quebéc 1964, Prix Médicis 8471966, Prix de l'Acad. Française 1983, and others. *Publications:* La belle bête 1959, Tête blanche 1960, Le jour est noir 1962, Une saison dans la vie d'Emmanuel 1965, L'insoumise 1966, David Sterne 1967, Manuscrits de Pauline Archange 1968, Vivre, Vivre 1969, Les Voyageurs sacrés 1966, Les Apparences 1970, Le Loup 1972, Un Joualonais sa Joualonie 1973, Une liaison parisienne 1976, Les nuits de l'underground 1978, Le sourd dans la ville 1980, Visions d'Anna 1982, Pierre 1984 (novels); Pays voiles (poems) 1964; L'ocean 1967, L'exécution 1968, Fievre 1974, La nef des sorcieres 1976, Sommeil d'Hiver 1985, Fière 1985 (plays). *Leisure interests:* painting, handwriting analysis. *Address:* c/o John C. Goodwin et Associés, 4235 avenue de l'Esplanade, Montréal, Que. H2W 1T1, Canada. *Telephone:* 844-2139.

BLAIS-GRENIER, Suzanne, M.A., PH.D.; Canadian politician; m.; two c.; ed. Univ. of Paris, Laval Univ., McGill Univ.; fmrly. at Unemployment Insurance Comm., Corpn. des travailleurs sociaux du Quebec, Agence Metropolitain-sud, Laval Univ.; Dir. Social Services Div., Dept. Health and Welfare 1975-78; Dir. Canadian Human Rights Comm. 1978-81; Exec. Dir. Assen. paritaire pour la santé et la sécurité du travail du Québec 1981-; Minister of Environment 1984-85, of State (Transport) 1985-86; Progressive Conservative. *Address:* House of Commons, 485 Confederation Building, Ottawa, Ont. 21A 0A6, Canada.

BLAIZE, Herbert Augustus, M.P., J.P.; Grenada solicitor and politician; b. 26 Feb. 1918; m. Venetia Davidson; three s. three d.; ed. Grenada Boys' School; mem. Parl. 1957-; Minister for Trade and Production 1957-60; Chief Minister of Grenada 1960-61, 1962-67; Premier of Grenada March-Aug. 1967; mem. Parl. Opposition 1967-69; Leader, New Nat. Party (NNP) 1984-89; Prime Minister, and Minister of Finance with responsibility for Security, Energy, Information, Planning, Trade and Industrial Devt. 1984-, also for Carriacou and Petit Martinique Affairs. *Address:* Office of the Prime Minister, St. George's, Grenada.

BLAKE, Baron (Life Peer), cr. 1971, of Braydeston, Norfolk; **Robert Norman William Blake,** M.A., F.B.A., J.P.; British academic; b. 23 Dec. 1916,

Blofield, Norfolk; s. of William J. Blake and Norah L. Daynes; m. Patricia M. Waters 1953; three d.; ed. King Edward VI School, Norwich, and Magdalen Coll., Oxford; mil. service during World War II (R.A.), P.O.W. in Italy 1942–44; Lecturer in Politics, Christ Church, Oxford 1946–47, Student and Tutor in Politics 1947–68, Hon. Student 1977; Censor 1950–55; Sr. Proctor 1959–60; Ford's Lecturer in English History 1967–68; mem. Hebdomadal Council 1959–81; Provost, The Queen's Coll., Oxford 1968–87; Pro-Vice-Chancellor, Univ. of Oxford 1971–87; Ed. Dictionary of Nat. Biog. 1980–; Pres. Electoral Reform Soc. 1986–; mem. Royal Comm. on Historical Manuscripts (Chair. 1982–), Bd. of Trustees of British Museum; Rhodes Trustee 1971–87, Chair. 1983–86; mem. Bd. of Channel 4 TV 1983–87; Hon. D.Litt. (Glasgow) 1972, (East Anglia) 1983, (Buckingham) 1988. *Publications:* The Private Papers of Douglas Haig 1952, The Unknown Prime Minister (Life of Andrew Bonar Law) 1955, Disraeli 1966, The Conservative Party from Peel to Churchill 1970, The Office of Prime Minister 1975, A History of Rhodesia 1977, Disraeli's Grand Tour 1982, The English World (ed.) 1982, The Conservative Party from Peel to Thatcher 1985, The Decline of Power 1985, Salisbury: the man and his policies (co-ed.) 1987, World History: From 1800 to the Present Day 1988. *Address:* Riverview House, Brundall, Norfolk, England. *Telephone:* 0603-712133.

BLAKE, John Clemens, M.A., R.C.A.; American artist; b. 11 Jan. 1945 Providence, R.I.; s. of John Holland Blake and Elizabeth Clemens (now Romäno); ed. Carnegie Inst. of Tech. (now Carnegie-Mellon Univ.), Yale Univ., Royal Coll. of Art, London; freelance visual artist in various media including drawing, installations, photographic constructions, audio constructions, film, etc.; approx. 40 solo exhbns. in Europe and U.S.A. 1972–, including Victoria and Albert Museum, London, Museum of Modern Art, Oxford, Project Studios One (PS1), New York, ICA, London, Krzysztofory, Krakow, Poland, Corps de Garde, Groningen, de Vleeshal, Middelburg and Bonnefantenmuseum, Maastricht, Netherlands, Orchard Gallery, Londonderry, Northern Ireland; teaching has included Hull Polytechnic 1975–76; London Coll. of Printing 1978–82; S. Glamorgan Inst. of Higher Educ., S. Wales 1983–84; Fulbright Fellow 1967–69; Nat. Endowment (U.S.A.) 1977; Arts Council Award (U.K.) 1979; Hokkaido Foundation Award (Japan) 1984. *Publications:* John Blake 1980, de Vleeshal 1983, Their Eyes 1983, Drawings and Constructions 1986. *Address:* 103 Earls Court Road, London, W.8, England; Oz. Voorburgwal 131, 1012-ER Amsterdam, Netherlands. *Telephone:* 01-373 8281 (London); (020) 277-740 (Amsterdam).

BLAKE, Peter Thomas, C.B.E., R.A.; British artist; b. 25 June 1932; s. of Kenneth William Blake; m. Jann Haworth 1963 (dissolved 1982); two d.; ed. Gravesend Tech. Coll., Gravesend School of Art, Royal Coll. of Art; works exhibited in Inst. of Contemporary Art 1958, 1960, Guggenheim Competition 1958, Cambridge 1959, Royal Acad. 1960, Musée d'Art Moderne, Paris 1963; retrospective exhbn. City Art Gallery, Bristol 1969, Tate Gallery, London 1983; works in perm. collections, Trinity Coll., Cambridge, Carlisle City Gallery, Tate Gallery, Arts Council of G.B., Museum of Modern Art, New York, Victoria and Albert Museum, and other maj. galleries. *Publications:* illustrations for Oxford Illustrated Old Testament 1968, several Arden Shakespeares and in various periodicals and magazines. *Address:* c/o Waddington Galleries Ltd., 2 Cork Street, London, W1X 1PA, England.

BLAKEMORE, Colin Brian, SC.D.; British neuro-physiologist and professor of physiology; b. 1 June 1944, Stratford-on-Avon; s. of Cedric Norman and Beryl Ann Blakemore; m. Andrée Elizabeth Washbourne 1965; three d.; ed. King Henry VIII School, Coventry, Corpus Christi Coll., Cambridge, Univ. of Calif. Berkeley; Harkness Fellowship, Univ. of Calif. 1965–67; Univ. Demonstrator, Physiological Laboratory, Cambridge 1968–72; Lecturer in Physiology, Cambridge 1972–79; Fellow and Dir. of Medical Studies, Downing Coll. 1971–79; Visiting Prof. New York Univ. 1970, M.I.T. 1971; Locke Research Fellow, Royal Soc. 1976–79; Waynflete Prof. of Physiology, Oxford 1979–; Professorial Fellow of Magdalen Coll. Oxford 1979–; Visiting Scientist, The Salk Inst., San Diego 1982–83; mem. Editorial Bd. Perception 1971–, Behavioral and Brain Sciences 1977–, Journal of Developmental Physiology 1978–86, Experimental Brain Research 1979–, Language and Communication 1979–, Reviews in the Neurosciences 1984–, News in Physiological Sciences 1985–, Clinical Vision Sciences 1986–; Chinese Journal of Physiological Sciences 1988–; Hon. Assoc. Rationalist Press Assen. 1986–; mem. U.K. Advisory Panel IRL Press 1987; Ed.-in-Chief IBRO News 1986–; Leverhulme Fellowship 1974–75; BBC Reith Lecturer 1976; Lethaby Prof., R.C.A., London 1978; Storer Lecturer, Univ. of Calif. at Davis 1980; Macallum Lecturer, Univ. of Toronto 1984; Robert Bing Prize, Swiss Acad. of Medical Sciences 1975, Man of the Year (Royal Soc. for Disability and Rehabilitation) 1978, Common Sense, Christmas Lectures for Young People, Royal Inst. 1982; John Locke Medal, Worshipful Soc. of Apothecaries 1983, Prize of Acad. Nat. de Médecine, Paris 1984; Bertram Louis Abrahams Lecture, Royal Coll. of Physicians 1986; Cairns Memorial Lecture and Medal, Soc. of British Neurological Surgeons 1986; Norman McAllister Gregg Lecture and Medal, Royal Australian Coll. of Ophthalmologists 1988. *Publications:* Ed. Handbook of Psychobiology 1975, Mechanics of the Mind 1977, Ed. Mindwaves 1987, Ed. Images and Understanding 1989, The Mind Machine 1988; contributions to Constraints on Learning 1973, Illusion in Art and Nature 1973, The Neurosciences Third Study Program 1974 and to professional journals. *Leisure interests:* running and the arts. *Address:* University

Laboratory of Physiology, Parks Road, Oxford OX1 3PT, England (Office). *Telephone:* (0865) 272471.

BLAKENEY, Allan Emrys, Q.C., P.C., L.L.B., M.A.; Canadian politician; b. 7 Sept. 1925, Bridgewater, Nova Scotia; s. of John Cline Blakeney and Bertha May Davies; m. 1st Mary Elizabeth Schwartz 1950 (died 1957), one s. one d.; 2nd Anne Gorham, one s. one d.; ed. Dalhousie and Oxford Univs.; Sec. and legal adviser to Crown Corpn., Govt. of Saskatchewan 1950–55; Chair. Sask. Securities Comm. 1955–58; partner law firm of Davidson, Davidson & Blakeney 1958–60; mem. Legis. Ass. 1960–88 (retd.); Govt. of Sask. Minister of Educ. 1960–61, Provincial Treas. 1961–62, Minister of Health 1962–64, Leader of the Opposition 1970–71, Premier 1971–82, Leader of the Opposition 1982–87; mem. Senate, Univ. of Sask. 1960–62; Chair. of Wascana Centre Authority 1962–64; partner Griffin, Blakeney, Beke (law firm) 1964–70; Pres. New Democratic Party of Canada 1969–71; Dr. h.c. (Mount Allison Univ.) 1980, (Dalhousie). *Publications:* Articles on Sask. Crown Corpns. in Proc. of the Inst. of Public Admin. of Canada and The Public Corporation edited by W. Freedman, Press Coverage of Saskatchewan Medicare Dispute, Queens' Quarterly, autumn, 1963. *Address:* P.O. Box 4375, Regina, Saskatchewan, S4P 3W7, Canada.

BLAKENHAM, 2nd Viscount (cr. 1963), of Little Blakenham; **Michael John Hare**; British business executive; b. 25 Jan. 1938, London; s. of 1st Viscount Blakenham and Hon. Beryl N. Pearson; m. Marcia P. Hare 1965; one s. two d.; ed. Eton Coll. and Harvard Univ.; army service in Life Guards 1956–57; with English Electric Co. 1958; Lazard Bros. 1961–63; Standard Industrial Group 1963–71; Royal Doulton 1972–77; Pearson PLC 1977–, Chair. and C.E.O. 1983– (Man. Dir. 1978–83); Chair. Madame Tussaud's 1975–, Financial Times 1984–; Dir. Lazard Bros. 1975–, Sotheby's Holdings Inc. 1987–; Partner, Lazard Partners 1975–. *Address:* 17th Floor, Millbank Tower, London, SW1P 4QZ, England.

BLAKEY, Art (Abdullah Ibn Buhaina); American jazz drummer; b. 11 Oct. 1919, Pittsburgh, Pa.; worked in steel mills, playing piano in clubs at night; started playing drums with bands in Pittsburgh area, then moved to New York; worked with Mary Lou Wiliams 1942, with Fletcher Henderson 1943; led own band, Boston 1944; with Billy Eckstine's Big Band 1944–47; subsequently led own group, played with Lucky Millinder and Buddy De Franco, freelance recording artist; formed Jazz Messengers 1955; many int. tours including The Giants of Jazz tour with Dizzy Gillespie (q.v.) and Thelonious Monk 1971–72.

BLALOCK, Hubert Morse, Jr., PH.D.; American professor of sociology; b. 23 Aug. 1926, Baltimore, Md.; s. of Hubert Morse and Helen Dorothy Welsh Blalock; m. Margaret Ann Bonar 1951; one s. two d.; ed. Dartmouth Coll., Brown Univ. and Univ. of North Carolina, Chapel Hill; Instructor and Asst. Prof., Dept. of Sociology, Univ. of Mich. 1954–61; Assoc. Prof., Dept. of Sociology, Yale Univ. 1961–64; Prof. Dept. of Sociology, Univ. of North Carolina 1964–71; Prof. Dept. of Sociology, Univ. of Wash. 1971–, Prof. of Statistics 1980–83; mem. N.A.S.; Fellow, American Acad. of Arts and Sciences and American Statistical Assen.; Pres. American Sociological Assen. *Publications:* Social Statistics 1960, Causal Inferences in Nonexperimental Research 1964, Toward a Theory of Minority Group Relations 1967, Theory Construction 1969, Intergroup Processes 1979, Conceptualization and Measurement in the Social Sciences 1982, Basic Dilemmas in the Social Sciences 1984. *Leisure interests:* hiking, boating, New Orleans jazz. *Address:* 40536 Skunk Bay Road, N.E., Hansville, Wash. 98340, U.S.A. *Telephone:* (206) 638-2159.

BLAMEY, Norman Charles, R.A.; British painter; b. 16 Dec. 1914, London; s. of Charles H. Blamey and Ada Blamey (née Beacham); m. Margaret Kelly 1948; one s. ed. Holloway School and School of Art, The Polytechnic, Regent Street, London; Lecturer and Sr. Lecturer, School of Art, Regent St. Polytech. 1938–63; military service 1941–46; Sr. Lecturer, Chelsea School of Art, London 1963–79; Visitor at Ruskin School of Drawing and of Fine Art, Univ. of Oxford 1978–80; Visitor (since 1975) at Royal Acad. Schools, London. *Works include:* mural decoration, St. Luke's, Leagrave, Beds. 1956, Lutheran Church of St. Andrew, Ruislip Manor, Middx. 1964, official portraits since 1975 and works in perm. collections including Tate Gallery, Chantry Bequest, King George V Gallery, Port Elizabeth, S.A., Pa. State Univ. Museum of Art, U.S.A., La Salle Coll. Art Gallery, Philadelphia, U.S.A. and Victoria and Albert Museum, London; Roy Miles Award 1978, Rowney Bicentenary Award 1983 Charles Wollaston Award 1984. *Leisure interest:* walking. *Address:* 39 Lyncroft Gardens, London, NW6 1LB, England. *Telephone:* 01-435 9250.

BLAMONT, Jacques Emile, D.SC.; French physicist; b. 13 Oct. 1926, Paris; s. of Emile Blamont; five c.; ed. École Normale Supérieure; Prof. Univ. of Paris 1961–; Scientific and Tech. Dir. Centre Nat. d'Études Spatiales (first successful launches of satellites by Diamant rocket) 1962–72, Chief Scientist 1972–82, Adviser to Dir. Gen. 1982–; Dir. Service d'Aéronomie C.N.R.S. 1962–85; control of first launches of French Véronique rockets 1959; Prime Investigator on many U.S. and Soviet spacecraft 1960–69; mem. NASA/SSG Grand Tour and Pioneer-Venus missions, U.S.S.R. Vega mission to Venus and Halley's Comet 1970–; Co-investigator Voyager, Pioneer-Venus and Vega missions; Promoter and Prime Investigator first launch of balloons in Venus atmosphere 1985; involved in discovery of interaction of electromagnetic radiation with multilevel atomic systems, interstellar wind, turbopause of Earth's atmosphere, hydrogen envelope of comets; mem. Int. Acad. of Astronautics 1969-, French Acad. of Science 1979-; Foreign Fellow Indian Nat. Science Acad. 1978-; Foreign Assoc. N.A.S.; Guggenheim Int. Medal of Astronautics 1967, NASA Medal for Exceptional Scientific Achievement 1972, Order of People's Friendship, U.S.S.R. 1986. *Publications:* Vénus dévoilée, voyage autour d'une planète 1987, and over 200 publs. on atmospheric research 1951-. *Address:* Centre National d'Études Spatiales, 2 place Maurice Quentin, 75039 Paris cedex 01 (Office); 7 villa Scheffer, 75116 Paris cedex, France (Home). *Telephone:* 45 08 76 11 (Office); 45 04 56 32 (Home).

BLAMONT, Philippe Lucien, DIPL.SC.POL.; French international official; b. 17 Nov. 1927, Paris; s. of Emile Armand Blamont and Perle Odette Amélie Cohen; m. Evelyne Bernheim 1950; two d.; ed. Faculté de Droit de Paris; Sec. of conf. of Advocates at Council of State and Court of Cassation 1951; mem. office of Dir.-Gen. Int. Labour Office (ILO), Geneva 1952-53, Int. Organizations Div. 1953-57, Liaison Office with UN, New York 1957-59; Exec. Asst. to Dir.-Gen., Geneva 1960-64; Dir. Liaison Office with UN 1964-66, Int. Centre for Advanced Technical and Vocational Training, Turin 1966-74; Pres. Nat. Comm. on Future Training 1974-75; Pres., Dir.-Gen. Bossard Inst. 1975-79; Vice-Pres. Soc. de formation et d'assistance technique internationale 1979-85, Hon. Pres. 1986; Chevalier, Ordre national du Mérite. *Address:* 92 rue du Bac, 75007 Paris; L'Hermitage du Montaiguet, 13590 Meyreuil, France.

BLANC, Marcel, L. EN D.; French prefect; b. 23 April 1925, Lyon; s. of Emile Blanc and Eugenie (née Pochat) Blanc; m. Monique Giraud 1956; one s. two d.; ed. Lycées du Parc and Champollion, Inst. d'études politiques, Grenoble, Inst. de géographie alpine and Ecole Nationale d'Admin.; Deputy Prefect 1950, Prefect, La Corrèze 1965, Région Languedoc-Roussillon, l'Hérault 1974, Loiret 1978; Prin. Pvt. Sec. to the Sec.-Gen. for Algerian Affairs 1960; Econ. and Finance Adviser to the Minister of the Interior 1964; Prin. Pvt. Sec. to the Minister of Works and Housing 1968; Dir.-Gen. for the Protection of Nature and the Environment 1970, for Local Communities 1977, Office Nat. des Anciens Combattants et Victimes de Guerre 1986-; Official Rep. for Econ. and Financial Affairs, Ministry of the Interior 1973, responsible for Defence 1980-84; Commandeur Légion d'honneur, ordre national du Mérite, Mérite Agricole, ordre du Mérite espagnol, Officier ordre du Mérite de la République italienne; Croix du Combattant Volontaire de la Resistance. *Leisure interest:* mountains. *Address:* Office National des Anciens Combattants et Victimes de Guerre, Hôtel National des Invalides, 75700 Paris (Office); Résidence Champ Lagarde, 4 allée des Gardes Royales, 78000 Versailles, France (Home). *Telephone:* 47 05 33 95 (Office); 39 53 82 58 (Home).

BLANCARD, Jean Raymond Edouard; French engineering administrator; b. 18 Aug. 1914; s. of Pierre Blancard and Louise Regal; m. Jeannine Maraquin 1940; one s. one d.; ed. Ecole Polytechnique; Engineer, then Chief Engineer of Mines; Dir. of Fuels Central Admin. of Ministry of Industry and Commerce 1951-59; mem. Admin. Council Gaz de France 1959-69, Pres. 1975-79; Ministerial Del. for Air Force 1959-61; Pres. Bureau de recherches de pétrole (B.R.P.) 1959-65; Vice-Pres. Entreprise de recherches et d'activités (ERAP) 1965-68; Pres. Dir.-Gen. Soc. auxiliaire de l'Erap (AUXERAP) 1965, Soc. française de recherches et d'exploitation pétrolières (SOFREP) 1966-68; Pres. Industrial Equipment Cttee., Atomic Energy Comm. 1961; Vice-Pres. Régie nat. des Usines Renault 1961-65; Pres. Dir.-Gen. SNECMA 1964-68; Perm. Under-Sec. for Armaments 1968-73; Sec. for Energy 1973-75; Pres. Admin. Council Gaz de France 1975; Dir. Turboméca, Nord-Aviation, Sud-Aviation; Vice-Pres. Union Syndicale des industries aéronautiques et spatiales 1965; mem. Atomic Energy Cttee. 1968-74; Vice-Pres. Gen. Council of Mines 1969; Pres. Consultative Comm. for Production of Nuclear Electricity 1974-75; Dir. S.N.C.F. (French Railways) 1974, Soc. Nat. Elf-Aquitaine 1977, Compagnie française des pétroles 1977; Commdr. Légion d'honneur. *Address:* 19 boulevard Flandrin, 75116 Paris, France.

BLANCAS BUSTAMANTE, Carlos; Peruvian lawyer and politician; b. 4 Nov. 1946, Lima; ed. Pontífica Universidad Católica del Perú; Sec.-Gen. Juventud Demócrata Cristiana, mem. World Cttee. of Int. Union of Young Christian Democrats 1972; mem. Nat. Political Comm., Democracia Cristiana 1981-83, Nat. Chair., Democracia Cristiana 1983; Prof. of Constitutional Law and Labour Law, Universidad Católica 1975-85; Minister of Labour 1985-86, of Justice 1986-87; mem. Colegio de Abogados de Lima; lawyer acting for many trade unions and individual workers. *Address:* c/o Ministry of Justice, Palacio de Gobierno, Pescadéeria, Lima, Peru. *Telephone:* 278181.

BLANCH, Baron (Life Peer), cr. 1983, of Bishopthorpe in the County of North Yorkshire; **Rt. Rev. and Rt. Hon. Stuart Yarworth Blanch,** P.C., M.A. (OXON.); British ecclesiastic; b. 2 Feb. 1918, Blakeney, Glos.; s. of the late William Edwin and Elizabeth Blanch; m. Brenda Coyte 1943; one s. four d.; ed. Alleyn's School, Dulwich, St. Catherine's Coll. and Wycliffe Hall, Oxford; Law Fire Insurance Soc. Ltd. 1936-40; Navigator, R.A.F. 1940-46; Curate, Highfield, Oxford 1949-52; Vicar of Eynsham, Oxford 1952-57; Tutor and Vice-Principal, Wycliffe Hall 1957-60, Chair. 1967-; Oriel Canon of Rochester and Warden of Rochester Theological Coll. 1960-66; Bishop of Liverpool 1966-75; Archbishop of York 1975-83; Sub-Prelate, Order of St. John 1975; Hon. LL.D (Liverpool) 1975, Hon. D.D.

(Hull) 1977, Hon. doctorate (York) 1979, Hon. D.D. (Wycliffe Coll., Toronto) 1979, (Manchester) 1984. *Publications:* The World Our Orphanage 1972, For All Mankind 1976, The Christian Militant 1978, The Burning Bush 1978, The Trumpet in the Morning 1979, The Ten Commandments 1981, Living by Faith 1983, Way of Blessedness 1985, Encounters with Christ 1988. *Leisure interests:* music, walking, squash, meteorology. *Address:* Bryn Celyn, The Level, Shenington, Nr. Banbury, OX15 6NA, England.

BLANCHARD, Francis, L.L.B.; French international civil servant; b. 21 July 1916, Paris; s. of Antoine and Marie (née Séris) Blanchard; m. Marie Claire Boué 1940; two s.; ed. Univ. of Paris; French Ministry of the Interior 1942-47; Int. Org. for Refugees, Geneva 1947-51; Int. Labour Office, Geneva 1951-; Asst. Dir.-Gen. 1956-68, Deputy Dir.-Gen. 1968-74, Dir.-Gen. 1974-89; Préfet 1956. *Leisure interests:* skiing, tennis. *Address:* Prébailly, 01170 Gex (Ain), France (Home). *Telephone:* 50.41.51.70 Gex (Home).

BLANCHARD, James J., M.B.A., J.D.; American state governor; b. 8 Aug. 1942, Detroit, Mich.; m. Paula Parker (divorced); one s.; ed. Michigan State Univ. and Univ. of Minnesota; admitted to Mich. Bar 1968; Legal Aid, elections bureau, Office of the Sec. of State, Mich. 1968-69; Asst. Attorney-Gen., Mich. 1969-74, Admin. Asst. to Attorney-Gen. 1970-71, Asst. Deputy Attorney-Gen. 1971-72; mem. House of Reps. 1975-83; Gov. of Mich. Jan. 1983-; mem. Pres.'s Comm. on Holocaust; Democrat. *Address:* Office of the Governor, The Capitol, Lansing, Mich. 48933, U.S.A.

BLANC-LAPIERRE, André Joseph Lucien, D. ÉS SC.; French scientist; b. 7 July 1915, Lavaur; s. of Victor Blanc-Lapierre and Jeanne Garrigues; m. Jacqueline Masson 1940; two s. six d.; ed. Ecole Normale Supérieure de Paris; Staff mem., Ecole Normale Supérieure 1940-44; Head of electronic Dept., Centre National d'Etudes des Télécommunications 1945-48; Prof. Univ. of Algiers and Dir. Inst. d'Etudes Nucléaires 1948-61; Prof. Univ. of Paris XI 1961-83; Dir. Laboratoire de l'Accélérateur Linéaire, Paris 1961-69; Dir.-Gen. Ecole Supérieure d'Electricité 1969-78; Pres. Consultative Cttee. for Scientific and Tech. Research 1963-65; Pres. Comm. for Scientific Research of Plan 1964-66; mem. Acad. des Sciences 1970-, Vice-Pres. 1983-84, Pres. 1985-86; mem. Acad. Pontificale des Sciences; Commdr. Légion d'honneur, Ordre national du Mérite et des Palmes académiques; several prizes. *Publications:* numerous books and articles in professional journals. *Leisure interests:* bridge, travel. *Address:* Laboratoire des Signaux et Systèmes, Plateau du Moulon, 91190 Gif-sur-Yvette (Office); Résidence Voltaire, 92290 Châtenay-Malabry, France (Home). *Telephone:* 941-80-40 (Office).

BLANCO, David, B.A.; Bolivian banker; b. 6 Jan. 1946; s. of Humberto Blanco and Gabriela Zabala; m. María Eugenia Sejas 1973; three d.; ed. Univ. of Chile, American Univ., Washington, D.C.; Prof., School of Econs., Univ. of Chile 1970-71; Prof. of Econ. Policy, Catholic Univ. of Bolivia 1971-72; Econ. Adviser, Cen. Bank of Bolivia 1971-72; Financial Adviser to Pres. of Bolivia 1972-73; Under-Sec. of Finance 1973-77, Minister of Finance 1977-78; Dir. Cen. Bank of Bolivia 1975-77; Corporacion Minera de Bolivia 1976-77; Gov. Inter-American Devt. Bank 1977-78; Gov. World Bank 1977; Alt. Exec. Dir. (Argentina, Bolivia, Chile, Paraguay, Uruguay) World Bank 1978-80, Exec. Dir. (incl. Peru) 1980-82. *Leisure interests:* tennis, swimming, skiing. *Address:* 6 Soldiers Field Park, Apt. 206, Boston, Mass., 02163, U.S.A. *Telephone:* (202) 477-2235 (Office); 795343 (La Paz, Bolivia).

BLANCO, Dr. Salvador Jorge; Dominican politician; b. 1926; Attorney-Gen. 1965; mem. comm. negotiating withdrawal of U.S. troops from Dominican Repub. 1965; mem. Senate; presidential cand. Partido Revolucionario Dominicano (PRD) 1982; Pres. Dominican Repub. 1982-86. *Address:* c/o Oficina del Presidente, Santo Domingo, Dominican Republic.

BLANCO-CERVANTES, Dr. Raúl; Costa Rican chest specialist and politician; b. 1903, San José, s. of Macedonio Blanco Alvarez and Dolores Cervantes Castro; m. Dora Martín Chavarría 1939; one s. four d.; ed. Liceo de Costa Rica and Ludwig-Maximilians-Univ. München; Medical Dir., Sanatorio Carlos Durán 1933-67; Dir. of Anti-Tuberculosis Dept., Ministry of Public Health 1937-67; Minister of Public Health 1948-49; Pres. Coll. of Physicians and Surgeons of Costa Rica 1946, 1947; Dir.-Gen. of Assistance, Ministry of Public Health 1950, 1951; First Vice-Pres. of Costa Rica 1953-58, 1962-66; Acting Pres. of Costa Rica 1955; Dir. Hospital Nacional para Tuberculosis 1958-; Pres. Colegio de Médicos y Cirujanos de Costa Rica 1946-47; Hon. mem. Sociedad Mexicana de Tisiología; mem. of WHO Expert Advisory Panel on tuberculosis 1954-71; Gov. American Thoracic Soc., American Coll. of Chest Physicians until 1966; First Pres. and Founder Sociedad Centroamericana de Tisiologia; several decorations. *Leisure interests:* reading, gardening. *Address:* Apdo. 918, San José, Costa Rica. *Telephone:* 21-20-82.

BLANCO ESTRADE, Dr. Juan Carlos; Uruguayan politician; b. 9 June 1934, Montevideo; ed. Univ. de Montevideo; worked in Banco Hipotecario, Uruguay; Central Govt. office, later President's office, until 1965; Gen. offices of OAS, and simultaneously alternate Rep. of Latin-American Assen. of Free Trade (LAFTA) 1965-68; Dir. LAFTA 1968-71; Under-Sec. for Foreign Affairs 1971-72; Minister for Foreign Affairs 1972-76; Perm. Rep to UN 1982-85. *Address:* c/o Ministerio des Asuutos Exteriores, Montevideo, Uruguay.

BLANCPAIN, Marc; French writer; b. 29 Sept. 1909; three s.; ed. Collèges d'Hirson et de Laon, Univ. de Nancy, Univ. de Paris à la Sorbonne and Ecole Normale Supérieure, Saint-Cloud; teacher, Ecole Internationale de Genève 1931–35, Lycée Français, Cairo 1935–39; Sec.-Gen. of Alliance Française 1945–, Pres. 1978–; Pres. Carnegie Comm., France 1984–; mem. PEN Club, Soc. des Gens de Lettres, Acad. Stanislas, Acad. des Sciences d'Outre-Mer; Commdr. Légion d'honneur, Croix de guerre 1939–44, Commdr. Ordre des Palmes académiques, Grand Officier, Ordre national du Mérite, Commdr. Ordre des Arts et des Lettres, and orders from Peru, Chile, Senegal, Brazil and Belgium; Grand Prix du Roman, Acad. Française 1945, Prix Courteline 1946, Prix Scarron 1955, Prix Engelmann (Belgium) 1956, Grand Prix du Rayonnement Français (Acad. Française) 1961. *Publications include:* novels: Le solitaire 1945, Les contes de la lampe à graisse 1946, Le carrefour de la désolation 1951, Ulla des Antipodes 1967, La femme d'Arnaud vient de mourir 1958; essays: Voyages et verres d'eau 1952, Les lumières de la France 1967; for children: Contes de Vermeil 1958; short stories: Vincennes Neuilly 1963; also: Les peupliers de la Prétentaine 1961, Grandes heures d'un village de la frontière 1964, Les truffes du voyage 1965, Aujourd'hui, l'Amérique latine 1966, La saga des amants séparés, Vol. I 1969, Vol. II 1970, Vol. III 1972–, Le plus long amour 1971, En français malgré tout 1973, Nous l'appelions Bismarck 1974, Paul-Emile et Emily 1977, Quand Guillaume II gouvernait "de la Somme aux Vosges" 1980, Histoires du Périgord 1982, La vie quotidienne au temps des invasions 1814-1944 1983, Le sentier de la douane, La Bachelière de Landouzy 1984, Le Mardi de Rocroi 1985, Monsieur le Prince 1986, Anne de Montmorency 1988. *Address:* 101 boulevard Raspail, Paris 6e (Office); 12 boulevard Jean Mermoz, 92 Neuilly-sur-Seine, France (Home). *Telephone:* 47-47-92-10 (Home).

BLANDY, John Peter, M.A., D.M., M.CH., F.R.C.S., F.A.C.S.; British consultant surgeon and professor of urology; b. 11 Sept. 1927, Calcutta, India; s. of Sir E. Nicolas Blandy and Dorothy Kathleen née Marshall; m. Anne Mathias 1953; four d.; ed. Clifton Coll., Balliol Coll., Oxford, London Hosp. Medical Coll.; House Physician and House Surgeon, London Hosp. 1952; served R.A.M.C. 1953–55; Surgical Registrar and Lecturer in Surgery, London Hosp. 1956–60; Exchange Fellow, Presbyterian St. Luke's Hosp., Chicago, U.S.A. 1960–61; Sr. Lecturer, London Hosp. 1961; Resident Surgical Officer, St. Paul's Hosp. 1963–64; Consultant Surgeon, London Hosp. 1964–, St. Peter's Hosp. for the Stone 1969–; Prof. of Urology, Univ. of London 1969–; mem. B.M.A., Royal Soc. of Medicine, Council, Royal Coll. of Surgeons 1982–, Int. Soc. of Pediatric Urology Surgeons, Int. Soc. of Urological Surgeons, British Asscn. of Urological Surgeons (Pres. 1984), European Asscn. of Urology (Pres. 1986–88); Fellow Asscn. of Surgeons; Hon. Fellow Urological Soc. of Australasia, Mexican Coll. of Urology; St. Peter's Medal, Freyer Medal, Diaz Medal 1988. *Publications:* Tumours of the Testicle (with A.D. Dayan and H.F. Hope-Stone) 1970, Transurethral Resection 1971, Urology (Ed.) 1976, Lecture Notes on Urology 1976, Operative Urology 1978, The Prostate (Ed. with B. Lytton) 1986, Urology for Nurses (with J. Moore) 1989; papers in scientific journals. *Leisure interest:* painting and sculpture. *Address:* The London Hospital, Whitechapel, London, E.1, England. *Telephone:* 01-377 7000.

BLANTON, Leonard Ray, B.S.; American businessman and politician; b. 10 April 1930, Hardin Co., Tenn.; s. of Leonard Alonza Blanton and Ova A. Delaney Blanton; m. 1st Betty Littlefield 1949; two s. one d.; m. 2nd Karen Flint 1988; ed. Old Shiloh High School and Univ. of Tennessee; mem. House of Reps. 1964–66; mem. for Tenn., U.S. House of Reps. 1966–72; Gov. of Tenn. 1975–79; fmr. mem. Exec. Cttee. Nat. Governors' Conf.; fmr. Chair. Dem. Nat. Governors' Conf. Task Force on Int. Trade and Tourism; Chair. Tennessee-Tombigbee Waterway Devt. Authority; sentenced to three years imprisonment for extortion and conspiracy 1981, served two; Democrat. *Leisure interests:* hunting, fishing, golf. *Address:* c/o Exec. Chamber Tenn. State Capitol, Nashville, Tenn. 37219, U.S.A. *Telephone:* (615) 741-2001 (Office); (615) 383-5401 (Home).

BLASCHKO, Hermann, F.R.S.; British university reader emeritus; b. 4 Jan. 1900, Berlin; s. of Alfred Blaschko and Johanna, née Litthauer; m. Mary Douglas Black 1944; no c.; ed. Univs. of Berlin, Freiburg im Breisgau and Cambridge; scientific work with Otto Meyerhof, Berlin-Dahlem 1925–28; Univ. Asst. in Physiology, Jena 1928–29; scientific work with A. V. Hill, Univ. Coll. London 1929–30; Asst. Inst. of Physiology, Kaiser-Wilhelm-Inst. für Medizinische Forschung, Heidelberg 1930–32; Demonstrator, Physiological Lab. Cambridge 1934–44; Sr. Research Officer, later Univ. Reader, Dept. of Pharmacology, Oxford 1944–67; Reader Emer. and Emer. Fellow, Linacre Coll., Oxford 1967–; Dr.med. h.c. (Freie Univ., Berlin and Berne); hon. mem. of several scientific socs. *Publications:* numerous papers in scientific journals. *Address:* University Department of Pharmacology, South Parks Road, Oxford, OX1 3QT; 24 Park Town, Oxford, OX2 6SH, England (Home). *Telephone:* Oxford 275200.

BLASHFORD-SNELL, Col. John Nicholas, M.B.E., F.R.S.G.S.; British soldier and explorer; b. 22 Oct. 1936, Hereford; s. of Rev. Prebendary Leland John Blashford Snell and Gwendolen Ives Sadler; m. Judith Frances Sherman 1960; two d.; ed. Victoria Coll., Jersey, R.M.A., Sandhurst; Commissioned Royal Engineers 1957; Commdr. Operation Aphrodite (Expedition), Cyprus 1959–61; Instructor Jr. Leaders Regt. Royal Engineers 1962–63; Instructor, R.M.A., Sandhurst 1963–66; Adjt. 3rd Div. Engin-

eers 1966–67; Commdr. The Great Abbai Expedition (Blue Nile) 1968; attended Staff Coll., Camberley 1969; Chair. Scientific Exploration Soc. 1969–; Commdr. Dahlak Quest Expedition 1969–70, British Trans-Americas Expedition (Darien Gap) 1971–72; Officer Commdg. 48th Field Squadron Royal Engineers 1972–74; Commdr. Zaire River Expedition 1974–75; C.O. Jr. Leaders Regt. Royal Engineers 1976–78; Dir. of Operations Operation Drake 1978–81; Staff Officer Ministry of Defence 1978–82, 1983–; Commdr. Fort George Volunteers 1982; Operations Dir. Operation Raleigh 1982–88, Dir.-Gen. 1989–; Dir. SES Tibet Expedition 1987; Chair. Explorers' Club (British Chapter); The Livingstone Medal, The Darien Medal, The Segrave Trophy; Hon. D.Sc.; Freeman of the City of Hereford. *Publications:* Weapons and Tactics (with T. Wintringham) 1972, Where the Trails Run Out 1974, In the Steps of Stanley 1975, Expeditions the Experts' Way (with A. Ballantine) 1977, A Taste for Adventure 1978, Operation Drake (with M. Cable) 1981, Mysteries, Encounters with the Unexplained 1983, Operation Raleigh, The Start of an Adventure 1987, Operation Raleigh, Adventure Challenge (with Anne Tweedy) 1988. *Leisure interests:* shooting, photography, food and wine, scuba diving. *Address:* c/o Operation Raleigh, Alpha Place, Flood Street, London SW3, England.

BLAŠKOVIČ, Dionýz, MU.DR., DR.SC.; Czechoslovak virologist; b. 2 Aug. 1913, Jablonica; s. of Koloman Blaškovič and Gabriela Blaškovičova; m. 1st Milada Janatová 1941; m. 2nd Vlasta Černá 1972; two d.; ed. Charles Univ., Prague; research work, Inst. of Bacteriology and Immunology, Charles Univ.; bacteriological research 1934–46; Rockefeller Foundation Fellow, United States 1946–47; Head, Dept. of Epidemiology and Microbiology, State Health Inst., Bratislava 1945–52; Prof. Med. Faculty, Comenius Univ., Bratislava 1954–84, Prof. Nat. Science Faculty 1969–84; Dir. Inst. of Virology, Slovak Acad. of Sciences, Bratislava 1953–78; Sec.-Gen. Int. Council of Scientific Unions (ICSU) 1963–66; Pres. Slovak Acad. of Sciences 1961–65; mem. Presidium Czechoslovak Acad. of Sciences 1965–70; Hon. mem. All-Union Soc. of Hygienists, Epidemiologists, Microbiologists and Infectionists of U.S.S.R. 1956; WHO expert; Fellow, New York Acad. of Sciences 1959; Hon. mem. Austrian Microbiological Soc. 1959, Polish Microbiological Soc. 1964, Hungarian Microbiological Soc. 1976, Czechoslovak Microbiological and Epidemiological Soc. 1979, G.D.R. Soc. for Microbiology and Epidemiology 1980, Serbian Acad. of Sciences and Arts 1981; Foreign mem. U.S.S.R. Acad. of Sciences 1966, Polish Acad. of Sciences 1977; mem. Int. Org. for Cell Research, Brussels, Deutsche Akad. Naturforscher Halle/Saale 1967; Hon. mem. Bulgarian Soc. for Microbiology, Epidemiology and Virology 1986; State Prize for Science 1951, Klement Gottwald State Prize 1976; Purkyně Medal in Medical Sciences 1956, Max Planck Gold Medal 1965, J. E. Purkyne Gold Plaque 1968; Order of Labour 1963; Order of the Repub. 1982. *Address:* Virological Institute, Bratislava, Mlynská dolina 1; Novosvetská 18, Bratislava, Czechoslovakia. *Telephone:* 371-046 (Office), 313-610 (Home).

BLASSE, George, D.SC.; Netherlands professor of chemistry; b. 28 Aug. 1934, Amsterdam; m. S. Vel 1961; three s.; ed. Univ. of Amsterdam; employed at Nat. Defence Lab. 1958–60, Philips Research Labs. 1960–70; Prof. of Solid State Chem., Univ. of Utrecht 1970–; mem. Royal Dutch Acad. of Sciences; Gold Medal Chem. Soc. *Publications:* articles in journals. *Leisure interest:* bird watching. *Address:* J. F. Kennedylaan 36, Bunnik, Netherlands.

BLATTY, William Peter, M.A., D.HUM.LITT.; American author; b. 7 Jan. 1928, New York; s. of Peter and Mary (née Mouakad) Blatty; m. Julie Alicia Witbrodt 1983; two s. three d.; ed. Georgetown Univ., George Washington Univ. and Seattle Univ.; served in U.S.A.F. 1951–54; ed. with U.S. Information Agency 1955–57, Publicity Dir. Univ. Southern Calif. 1957–58, Public Relations Dir. Loyola Univ., Los Angeles 1959–60. *Publications:* Which Way to Mecca, Jack? 1959, John Goldfarb, Please Come Home 1963, I, Billy Shakespeare 1965, Twinkle, Twinkle, 'Killer' Kane 1966, The Exorcist 1970, I'll Tell Them I Remember You 1973, The Exorcist: From Novel to Film 1974, The Ninth Configuration 1978, Legion 1983. *author of screenplays:* The Man from the Diner's Club 1961, Promise Her Anything 1962, A Shot in the Dark 1964, The Great Bank Robbery 1967, What Did You Do in the War, Daddy? 1965, Gunn 1967, Darling Lili 1968, The Exorcist 1973; awards include: Golden Globe award for best movie screenplay (Twinkle, Twinkle, 'Killer' Kane, The Exorcist) 1981, Academy Award of Acad. Motion Picture, Arts and Sciences 1973. *Address:* c/o Simon and Schuster, 1230 Avenue of the Americas, New York, N.Y. 10020, U.S.A.

BLAU, Peter Michael, PH.D.; American professor of sociology; b. 7 Feb. 1918, Vienna, Austria; s. of Theodore Blau and Bertha Selka; m. 1st Zena Smith 1948; m. 2nd Judith Fritz 1968; two d.; ed. Elmhurst Coll., Ill., Columbia Univ.; Instructor, Wayne State Univ. 1949–51, Cornell Univ. 1951–53; Asst. Prof., Univ. of Chicago 1953–58, Assoc. Prof. 1958–63, Prof. 1963–70; Pitt Prof. of American History and Insts., Univ. of Cambridge 1966–67; Prof. Columbia Univ. 1970–, Quetelet Prof. 1977–, Chair Sociology Dept. 1982–85; Visiting Prof., State Univ. of New York at Albany 1978–79, Distinguished Prof. 1979–82; Hon. D. Litt. (Elmhurst Coll.) 1974; ASA Sorokin Award 1968, ASA Distinguished Scholarship Award 1980. *Publications:* The Dynamics of Bureaucracy 1955, Bureaucracy in Modern Society 1956, Formal Organizations: A Comparative Approach (with W. Richard Scott) 1962, Exchange and Power in Social Life 1964, The American Occupational Structure (with Otis Dudley Duncan) 1967, The Structure of Organizations (with Richard A. Schoenherr) 1971, The Organization of Academic Work 1973, On the Nature of Organizations 1974, Approaches to the Study of Social Structure (Ed.) 1975, Inequality and Heterogeneity 1977, Crosscutting Social Circles (with Joseph E. Schwartz) 1984, Continuities in Structural Inquiry (ed. with R. K. Merton) 1984. *Leisure interests:* theatre, reading, travel. *Address:* 25 Claremont Avenue, New York, N.Y. 10027, U.S.A. *Telephone:* (212) 316-0100.

BLAUDIN De Thé, Guy (see de Thé, Guy Blaudin).

BLAUSTEIN, Albert Paul, J.D.; American lawyer and professor; b. 12 Oct. 1921, New York, N.Y.; s. of Karl Allen and Rose (née Brickman) Blaustein; m. Phyllis Migden 1948; two s. one d.; ed. Michigan and Columbia Univs.; reporter and rewrite man, Chicago Tribune and City News Bureau, Chicago 1941–42; army service, major 1942–46; 1950–52; admitted to New York bar 1948, New Jersey bar 1962; mem. Blaustein and Blaustein law firm, New York, N.Y. 1948–50, 1952–55; Counsel with Nierenberg, Zeif and Weinstein, New York, N.Y. 1972–85; Pres. Blaustein Assoc. Ltd.; Asst. Prof. and Law Librarian, New York Law School 1953–55; Assoc. Prof. Rutgers Univ. School of Law 1955–59, Prof. of Law 1959–; mem. Civil Rights Reviewing Authority, U.S. Dept. of Educ. 1984–; Fellow, Center for Int. Studies, L.S.E. 1984–85; Chair. Constitutions Associates; Pres. Constitutions Research Centre; constitutional consultant to Bangladesh, Cambodia, Liberia, Peru, Zimbabwe, Niger and Uganda movements; Pres. and Chair. Human Rights Advocates Int. Inc.; Ed.-in-Chief The Influence of the U.S. Constitution Abroad; consultative work in the field of law school devt., civil rights and constitutional law in many countries; mem. Int. Bar Asscn., Int. Law Asscn., American Bar Asscn., World Bar Asscn. for Peace through Law, Asscn. of the Bar of the City of New York, American Soc. of Int. Law, Int. Soc. for Military Law and Law of War, Int. Asscn. Jewish Lawyers and Jurists, professional and specialist orgs. in various countries; Ford Fellow 1962. *Publications:* author and co-author: Public Relations for Bar Associations 1952, The American Lawyer 1954, Fiction goes to Court 1954, Desegregation and the Law 1957, Doctor's Choice 1957, Deals with the Devil 1958, Invisible Men 1960, Civil Affairs Legislation, Selected Cases and Materials 1960, Fundamental Legal Documents of Communist China 1962, Manual on Foreign Legal Periodicals and their Index 1962, Civil Rights U.S.A., Public Schools in Cities in the North and West 1962, Human and Other Beings 1963, Public Schools in Camden and Environs 1964, Civil Rights and the American Negro 1968, Civil Rights and the Black American 1970, Law and the Military Establishment 1970, Intellectual Property: Cases and Materials (1960–70) 1971, Constitutions of the Countries of the World (19 vols., continually updated) 1971, Housing Discrimination in New Jersey 1972, Human Rights and the Bangladesh Trials 1973, The Common Law in French: A Bibliography 1974, Constitutions of Dependencies and Special Sovereignties (7 vols.) 1975–; Independence Documents of the World 1977, The Arab Oil Weapon 1977, The First 100 Justices: Statistical Studies on the Supreme Court of the U.S. 1978, The Military and American Society 1978; Disinvestment 1985, Influence of the United States Constitution Abroad 1986, Resolving Language Conflict: A Study of the World's Constitutions 1986, Human Rights Source Book 1987, Constitutions That Made History 1988, The Bicentennial Concordance 1988, The Role of the Military in Modern Government: A Constitutional Analysis 1988; numerous articles, contributions, reviews. *Leisure interests:* amateur theatricals, philately, travel. *Address:* Rutgers University School of Law, Camden, N.J. 08102; 230 Park Avenue, New York, N.Y. 10017 (Office); 415 Barby Lane, Cherry Hill, N.J. 08003, U.S.A. (Home). *Telephone:* (212) 986-5555 (N.Y. Office); (609) 757-6373 (University); (609) 429-9184 (Home).

BLAUVELT, Howard W., C.P.A.; American petroleum executive (retd.); b. 11 Feb. 1917, New York; s. of the late Harry O. W. Blauvelt and Lillian M. Woelfert Blauvelt; m. 1st Margaret D. Hahn 1939 (died 1970), 2nd Mary E. Cassity 1970; one s. one d.; ed. Yale Univ. and Columbia Graduate School of Business Admin., N.Y.; Treas., Meyer and Medelsohn, Inc. 1949–51; Asst. Controller, Continental Oil Company (CONOCO), Oklahoma 1952–57, Controller, Texas 1962–65, Vice-Pres. Co-ordinating and Planning, New York 1965–66, Dir. 1966–, Exec. Vice-Pres. New York 1966–69, Pres. Conoco Chemicals Div. 1969–72, Exec. Vice-Pres., Stamford, Conn. 1972–74, Pres. March-May 1974, Chair. and Chief Exec. Officer May 1974–79; Senior Vice-Pres. Hudson's Bay Oil & Gas Co. Ltd., Canada 1957–62; Dir. American Petroleum Inst. 1974–79, Bankers Trust, New York 1975–, General Telephone & Electronics 1975–, Gen. Reinsurance Co. 1977–, Colgate-Palmolive Co. 1978–, Atibiti Paper Co. 1978–. *Leisure interest:* golf. *Address:* c/o Conoco, Continental Oil Company, Wilmington, Del., U.S.A.

BLAXTER, Sir Kenneth (Lyon), Kt., F.R.S., F.R.S.E.; British scientist; b. 19 June 1919; s. of Gaspard Culling Blaxter and Charlotte Ellen Blaxter; m. Mildred Lillington Hall 1957; two s. one d.; ed. City of Norwich School, Univ. of Reading, Univ. of Ill., U.S.A.; Scientific Officer, Nat. Inst. for Research in Dairying 1939–40, 1941–44; Research Officer, Ministry of Agric. Veterinary Lab. 1944–46; Commonwealth Fellow, Univ. of Ill. 1946–47; Head Dept. of Nutrition, Hannah Inst., Ayr, Scotland 1948–65; Dir. Rowett Research Inst., Bucksburn, Aberdeen, and Consultant Dir. Commonwealth Bureau of Nutrition (fmrly. Animal

Nutrition) 1965–82, Hon. Research Assoc., 1982–; Visiting Prof. in Agricultural Biochemistry, Univ. of Newcastle Upon Tyne 1982–; Chair. Individual Merit Promotion Panel, Cabinet Office 1984–; Pres. British Soc. of Animal Production 1970–71, Nutrition Soc. 1974, Royal Soc. of Edinburgh 1979–82; Pres. Inst. of Biology 1986–88; Foreign mem. Lenin Acad. of Agricultural Sciences 1970; Hon. M.R.C.V.S 1978; Thomas Baxter Prize and Gold Medal 1960; Gold Medal Royal Agricultural Soc. of England 1964, Wooldridge Gold Medal, British Veterinary Asscn. 1973; De Laval Medal, Royal Swedish Acad. of Engineering Sciences 1976; Messel Medal Soc. of Chemistry Industry 1976; Keith Medal and Prize, Royal Soc. of Edinburgh 1977; Massey Ferguson Award 1977; Wolf Foundation, Int. Prize 1979; Hon. D.Sc. (Queen's Univ. Belfast) 1974, (Leeds) 1977, (Newcastle upon Tyne) 1983; Hon. LL.D. (Aberdeen) 1981; Hon. D.Agric. (Agricultural Univ., Norway) 1975. *Publications:* Energy Metabolism of Ruminants 1962, Energy Metabolism 1965, People, Food and Resources 1986; scientific papers in various learned journals. *Leisure interest:* painting. *Address:* Stradbroke Hall, Stradbroke, Nr. Eye, Suffolk, IP21 5HH, England. *Telephone:* Stradbroke 8191.

BLAŽEK, Vladimír; Czechoslovak government official; b. 5 April 1929, Štepánov; ed. Railway Coll., Žilina. Various posts with Czechoslovak State Railways 1955–75, Head of Cen. Railway Admin., Olomouc 1975; Fed. Minister of Transport 1975–88; Head of Del. to CMEA Perm. Comm. for Transport and Civil Aviation Jan. 1976–; Distinction for Outstanding Work 1975, Order of Labour 1979. *Address:* Ministry of Transport, Na Příkopě 33, Prague 1, Czechoslovakia.

BLAZEVIC, Juraj Jakov; Croatian politician; b. 24 March 1912, Bužim near Gospić; m. 1st Sabina Blažić 1945 (divorced 1976); three d.; m. 2nd Vera Gerovac 1976; ed. Zagreb Univ; joined Communist Party of Yugoslavia 1928; imprisoned for six months for communist activities 1931; Sec. Dist. Cttee. of Croatia in Lika 1940; Del. First Nat. Conf. of CP of Croatia; mem. Cen. Cttee. CP of Croatia; at Fifth Party Conf. elected mem. Cen. Cttee. CP of Yugoslavia; organized Croatian uprising First Partisan Detachment Velebit in Lika district; sentenced to death by Italian Mil. Court 1943; mem. 1st, 2nd and 3rd Zavnoh Convention; Public Prosecutor of Croatia 1945–48; Minister of Commerce and Supply 1948–50, Vice-Pres. Govt. and Pres. Econ. Council of Croatia 1950–53; Pres. of Croatia 1953–62; Pres. Fed. Chamber of Commerce, mem. Fed. Exec. Council 1962–65; Vice-Pres. 1965–67; Pres. of Assembly of Croatia 1967–74, Pres. of Presidency of Croatia 1974–82; fmr. mem. Presidency of Yugoslavia; Medal of Nat. Hero; Partisan Memorial Medal 1941; numerous other decorations. *Address:* Tuskanac 82, Zagreb, Yugoslavia. *Telephone:* 426-355.

BLEANEY, Brebis, C.B.E., F.R.S., D.PHIL.; British physicist and university professor; b. 6 June 1915, London; s. of Frederick Bleaney and Eva Johanne Petersen; m. Betty Isabelle Plumpton 1949; one s. one d.; ed. St. John's Coll., Oxford; lecturer in Physics, Oxford 1945–57; Fellow of St. John's Coll., Oxford 1947–57, Hon. Fellow 1968–; Dr. Lee's Prof. of Experimental Philosophy, Oxford 1957–77; Fellow of Wadham Coll. 1957–; Royal Soc. Warren Research Fellow 1977–80, Leverhulme Emer. Fellow 1980–82; Corresp. mem. Acad. des Sciences de l'Institut de France 1974–78, Associé Etranger 1978–; Abigail and John Van Vleck lecturer, Minneapolis 1985; Foreign Hon. mem. American Acad. Arts and Sciences 1978–; D.Sc. h.c. (Porto) 1987; Hughes Medal, Royal Soc. 1962; C. V. Boys Prize, Physical Soc. of London 1952, ISMAR Prize 1983, Holweck Prize, British and French Physical Socs. 1984. *Publications:* Electricity and Magnetism (with B. I. Bleaney) 1957, Electron Paramagnetic Resonance (with A. Abragam) 1970. *Leisure interests:* music, tennis, travel. *Address:* Clarendon Laboratory, Oxford; Garford House, Garford Road, Oxford, England (Home). *Telephone:* 272324 (Laboratory); 59589 (Home).

BLECH, Harry, C.B.E., F.R.S.A.; British conductor; b. 2 March 1910, London; s. of Polish parents; m. 2nd Marion Manley 1957; one s. three d. (and one s. two d. by 1st marriage); ed. Central London Foundation, Trinity Coll. of Music and Manchester Coll. of Music; Violin soloist 1928–30; with B.B.C. Symphony Orchestra 1930–36; Founder mem. Blech Quartet 1933–50, London Wind Players 1942, London Mozart Players 1949, Haydn-Mozart Soc. 1949, London Mozart Choir 1952; Conductor Royal Acad. of Music Chamber Orchestra 1961–65; Hon. mem. Royal Acad. of Music; Fellow, Royal Manchester Coll. of Music, Trinity Coll. of Music. *Leisure interest:* reading. *Address:* The Owls, 70 Leopold Road, Wimbledon, London, SW19 7JQ, England. *Telephone:* 01-946 8135.

BLECHA, Karl; Austrian politician; b. 16 April 1933, Vienna; ed. Univ. of Vienna; became vocational adviser in Vienna Employment Exchange and later worked as reader in publishing firm; Dir. Inst. for Empiric Social Research 1963–75; mem. Lower Austrian SPÖ (Austrian Socialist Party) Exec. 1964–; mem. Nationalrat 1970–; Gen. Sec. SPÖ H.Q. 1976–81, Vice-Chair. SPÖ 1981–; Federal Minister of the Interior 1983–89. *Address:* c/o Federal Ministry of the Interior, Herrengasse 7, 1014, Vienna, Austria.

BLEEHEN, Norman Montague, M.A., F.R.C.P., F.R.C.R.; British professor of clinical oncology; b. 24 Feb. 1930, Manchester; s. of Solomon Bleehen and Lena Bleehen; m. Tirza Loeb 1959; no c.; ed. Haberdashers' Aske's Hampstead School and Univ. of Oxford; Registrar and Sr. Registrar, The Middx. Hosp. London and Mt. Vernon Hosp. Northwood 1961–67; Research Fellow, Dept. of Radiology, Stanford, Calif. 1966–67; Locum Consultant

Radiotherapist, The Middx. Hosp. 1967-69; Prof. of Radiotherapy and Head, Academic Dept. of Radiotherapy, Middx. Hosp. Medical School 1969-75, Hon. Consultant Radiotherapist 1975-; Cancer Campaign Prof. and Head of Dept. of Clinical Oncology and Radiotherapeutics, Univ. of Cambridge 1975-; Hon. Consultant, Dir. MRC Unit, Clinical Oncology and Radiotherapeutics 1975-; Dir. Radiotherapeutic Centre, Addenbrooke's Hosp. Cambridge 1984-. *Publications:* contributions to numerous books and scientific journals. *Leisure interests:* reading, music, television. *Address:* Department of Clinical Oncology and Radiotherapeutics, Addenbrooke's Hospital, Hills Road, Cambridge, CB2 2QQ (Office); 21 Bentley Road, Cambridge, CB2 2AW, England (Home). *Telephone:* 354320.

BLEGEN, Judith; American opera and concert singer; b. Lexington, Ky.; d. of Dr. Halward Martin and Dorothy Mae (Anderson) Blegen; m. 1st Peter Singher 1967 (divorced 1975), one s.; m. 2nd Raymond Gniewek 1977; ed. Curtis Inst. of Music, Philadelphia, Pa., Music Acad. of the West, Santa Barbara, Calif.; leading soprano, Nuremberg Opera, Fed. Republic of Germany 1965-68, Staatsoper, Vienna, Austria 1968-70, Metropolitan Opera, New York 1970-; Vienna roles include Zerbinetta (Ariadne auf Naxos), Rosina (The Barber of Seville), Aennchen (Der Freischütz), Norina (Don Pasquale); numerous performances at Metropolitan include Marzelline (Fidelio), Sophie (Werther), Mélisande (Pelléas et Mélisande), Sophie (Der Rosenkavalier), Adina (L'Elisir d'amore), Juliette (Roméo et Juliette), Susanna (The Marriage of Figaro); other appearances include Susanna (The Marriage of Figaro), San Francisco, title-role in Manon, Tulsa Opera, Gilda (Rigoletto), Chicago, Despina (Così fan tutte), Covent Garden, Blondchen (The Abduction from the Seraglio), Salzburg Festival, Mélisande (Pélleas et Mélisande), Spoleto Festival, Susanna (The Marriage of Figaro), Edinburgh Festival, Sophie, Paris Opera; Fulbright Scholarship, Grammy Awards. *Numerous recordings, including:* La Bohème (Puccini), Carmina Burana (Orff), Symphony No. 4 (Mahler), Harmonienmesse (Haydn), The Marriage of Figaro (Mozart), A Midsummer Night's Dream (Mendelssohn), Lord Nelson Mass (Haydn), Gloria (Poulenc), Peer Gynt Suite (Grieg), Lieder recital (Richard Strauss and Hugo Wolf), baroque music recital. *Address:* c/o Thea Dispeker, 59 East 54th Street, New York, N.Y. 10022, U.S.A.

BLEICKEN, Jochen, DR.PHIL.; German professor of history; b. 3 Sept. 1926, Westerland/Sylt; s. of Max Bleicken and Marie (née Jensen) Bleicken; ed. Univs. of Kiel and Frankfurt a. M.; Asst. Althistorische Seminar, Göttingen 1955-62, Teacher in Early History 1961; Prof. in Early History, Hamburg 1962-67, Frankfurt a. M. 1967-77, Göttingen 1977-; mem. Wissenschaftlich Geschichte, Johann Wolfgang Goethe Univ., Frankfurt 1967-, Deutschen Archäologischen Instituts (DAI) 1976-, Akad. der Wissenschaften in Göttingen 1978. *Publications:* Das Volkstribunat der klassische Republik 1955, Staatliche Ordnung und Freiheit in der Römische Republik 1972, Lex Publica: Studien zu Gesetz und Recht in der Römische Republik 1975, Verfassung und Sozialgeschichte der Römische Kaiserzeit 1981, Geschichte der Römische Republik 1982, Die Athenische Demokratie 1985, Die Verfassung der Römische Republik 1985. *Leisure interest:* numismatics. *Address:* Obernjesaer Strasse 8, 3403 Friedland 4, Federal Republic of Germany. *Telephone:* 05504-381.

BLENDON, Robert J., SC.D., M.P.H., M.B.A.; American foundation executive; b. 19 Dec. 1942, Philadelphia, Pa.; s. of Edward G. Blendon and Theresa M. Blendon; m. Marie C. McCormick 1977; no c.; ed. Marietta Coll., Univ. of Chicago and Johns Hopkins Univ.; Instructor Johns Hopkins Univ. School of Hygiene and Public Health, Baltimore 1969, Asst. to Assoc. Dean (Health Care Programs) 1969-70, Asst. Prof. 1970-71, Asst. Dir. for Planning and Devt., Office of Health Care Programs 1970-71; Special Asst. for Health Affairs to Deputy Under-Sec. for Policy Co-ordination, Dept. of Health Educ. and Welfare 1971-72, Special Asst. for Policy Devt. to Asst. Sec. for Health and Scientific Affairs 1971-72; Visiting Lecturer, Princeton Univ. 1972-80, Co-ordinator, Medicine in Modern America Course 1980-; Sr. Vice-Pres. The Robert Wood Johnson Foundation 1980-87; Prof. and Chair. Dept. of Health Policy and Management, Harvard Univ. School of Public Health 1987-; numerous other professional appts. *Publications:* articles in professional journals. *Address:* Harvard University School of Public Health, 677 Huntington Avenue, Boston, Mass. 02115 (Office); 466 Sayre Drive, Princeton, N.J., U.S.A. *Telephone:* (609) 987-0721.

BLESSED, Brian; British actor; b. 1937, Yorks.; has appeared in numerous TV series, plays and films including: Z-Cars, Three Musketeers, Cold Comfort Farm, I Claudius, The Black Adder, The Recruiting Officer, Churchill's People, The Sweeney, Space 1999, Hound of the Baskervilles, Master of Ballantrae, The Last Days of Pompeii, William the Conqueror, Treasure Island; appeared with RSC at Stratford-on-Avon 1985. *Films include:* The Trojan Women, Henry VIII, Man of La Mancha, Flash Gordon, High Road to China. *Address:* c/o Miller Management, 82 Broom Park, Teddington, Middx., TW11 9RR, England.

BLEUSTEIN-BLANCHET, Marcel; French advertising executive; b. 21 Aug. 1906; s. of Abraham Bleustein and Elise Gross; m. Sophie Vaillant 1939; 3 c.; founder Publicis 1927-; founded Radio Cité 1935; founder and Dir.-Gen. Régie Press 1938-; founder Les Drugstores Publicis 1958; founder and Pres. Fondation de la Vocation 1960-; Pres. Publicis S.A. 1970-; Founding Co-Pres. Confédération de la Publicité Française 1966-67; Grand Officier Légion d'honneur, Croix de guerre, Médaille de la Résistance,

Médaille de l'aéronautique, Médaille des Evadés; Commdr. Economie nat. et du Mérite commercial; Officier de la Santé publique; Chevalier des Palmes Académiques. *Publications:* Sur mon antenne 1948, La rage de convaincre 1970, La nostalgie du futur 1976, Les Ondes de la Liberté 1984, Memoires d'Un Lion 1988. *Leisure interests:* aviation, yachting. *Address:* 131 avenue des Champs-Elysées, 75008 Paris (Office).

BLEVIN, William Roderick, D.SC., F.T.S., F.A.A.; Australian research physicist; b. 31 Oct. 1929, Inverell, N.S.W.; s. of late W. R. Blevin; m. Doreen Graham 1952; one s. two d.; ed. Tamworth High School, N.S.W. and Univ. of Sydney; research scientist to Chief Research Scientist, Div. of Physics, CSIRO 1953-79; Chief Standards Physicist, Div. of Applied Physics, CSIRO 1980-88, Chief of Div. 1988-; Expert Consultant, U.S. Nat. Bureau of Standards 1973; mem. of Council, Univ. of New England 1976-84; mem. Nat. Standards Comm. 1980-, Chair. 1981-85; Pres. Consultative Cttee. for Photometry and Radiometry 1980-; mem. Int. Cttee. of Weights and Measures 1982-. *Leisure interests:* gardening, tennis. *Address:* CSIRO Division of Applied Physics, P.O. Box 218, Lindfield, N.S.W. 2070 (Office); 61 Boronia Avenue, Cheltenham, N.S.W. 2119, Australia (Home). *Telephone:* (02) 467 6211 (Office); (02) 86 5835 (Home).

BLEWETT, Neal, M.A., PH.D., F.R.HIST.S.; Australian politician; b. 1933, Sydney; m.; two c.; ed. Launceston High School, Tasmania, Univ. of Tasmania, Oxford Univ.; Lecturer, Oxford Univ. 1959-64; Prof., Dept. of Political Theory and Insts., Flinders Univ. 1974-; M.P. for Bonython, S. Australia 1977-; Minister for Health 1983-87, for Community Services and Health 1987-; fmr. mem. Jt. House Cttee. on Foreign Affairs and Defence; fmr. mem. parl. dels. visiting several overseas countries; Australian Labor Party. *Publications:* Playford to Dunstan: The Politics of Transition (with Dean Jaensch) 1971, The Peers, the Parties and the People 1972. *Leisure interests:* reading, walking, cinema. *Address:* Parliament House, Canberra, A.C.T. 2600, Australia.

BLIM, Richard Don, M.D.; American pediatrician; b. 8 Nov. 1927, Kansas City; s. of Miles Blim and Latha Daniels Blim; m. Myrle Tingstad 1952; two s. one d.; ed. Univ. of Kansas; Pres. Kansas City S.W. Pediatric Soc. 1963; Pres. Mo. Chapter American Acad. of Pediatrics 1964-67; Exec. Bd. American Acad. of Pediatrics 1973-79, Vice-Pres. 1979-80, Pres. 1980-81; Pres. Pediatrics Assocs. 1970-; Pres. Univ. of Kansas Medical Alumni 1973; mem. Inst. of Medicine 1983-; Pres. of Health Plan Mid America 1984-; Outstanding Medical Alumnus, Univ. of Kansas 1978; Grulee Award, American Acad. of Pediatrics 1984. *Publications:* several articles on pediatrics. *Leisure interests:* medicine, tennis, children, grandchildren. *Address:* 4400 Broadway, Kansas City, Miss. 64111, U.S.A. *Telephone:* 816 561 8100.

BLIN-STOYLE, Roger John, D.PHIL., F.R.S., F.R.S.A.; British academic; b. 24 Dec. 1924, Leicester; s. of C. B. and A. M. (née Nash) Blin-Stoyle; m. Audrey Elizabeth Balmford 1949; one s. one d.; ed. Alderman Newton's Boys' School, Leicester, Wadham Coll., Oxford; Lecturer in Mathematical Physics Birmingham Univ. 1953-54; Sr. Research Officer in Theoretical Physics Oxford 1952-62, Fellow and Lecturer in Physics Wadham Coll. 1956-62, Hon. Fellow 1987; Visiting Assoc. Prof. of Physics M.I.T. 1959-60; Dean, School of Mathematical and Physical Sciences Sussex Univ. 1962-68, Prof. of Theoretical Physics 1962-, Pro-Vice-Chancellor 1965-67, Deputy Vice-Chancellor 1970-72, Pro-Vice-Chancellor (Science) 1977-79; Chair. School Curriculum Devt. Cttee. 1983-88; Rutherford Medal and Prize, Inst. of Physics 1976. *Publications:* Theories of Nuclear Moments 1957, Fundamental Interactions and the Nucleus 1973; Ed. Students Physics Series and various articles in scientific and educational journals. *Leisure interest:* making music. *Address:* School of Mathematical and Physical Sciences, University of Sussex, Brighton, Sussex, BN1 9QH (Office); 14 Hill Road, Lewes, Sussex, BN7 1DB, England (Home). *Telephone:* 0273 606755 (Sussex), 0273 473640 (Home).

BLISS, Anthony Addison, B.A., LL.B.; American lawyer; b. 19 April 1913, New York; s. of Cornelius Newton Bliss and Zaidee Cobb Bliss; m. 1st Barbara Field 1937 (divorced 1941); 2nd Jo Ann Sayers 1942 (divorced 1967); 3rd Sally Brayley 1967; four s. two d.; ed. Groton, Harvard Univ. and Univ. of Virginia Law School. Assoc.; Milbank, Tweed, Hope & Hadley 1940-41, 1945-51, Partner 1952-61; Partner Milbank, Tweed, Hadley & McCloy 1961-74, Consulting Partner 1974-; Dir. Metropolitan Opera Assen. Inc. 1949-, Pres. 1956-67, Exec. Dir. 1974-81, Gen. Man. 1981-; Chair. Foundation for Joffrey Ballet 1970; Hon. Chair. Nat. Corporate Fund for Dance, Inc. 1972-; Trustee, U.S. Trust Co. of New York 1959-; Dir. Lincoln Center for the Performing Arts, Inc. 1961-67, Great Atlantic and Pacific Tea Co., Inc. 1963-70; mem. Nat. Council on the Arts 1965-68, Advisory Panel on Dance, Nat. Endowment for the Arts 1968-71, Music Panel 1968-69; Trustee, Nat. Opera Inst. 1969-74; Dir. New York Foundation for the Arts, Inc. 1971-; Trustee, Portledge School 1973-. Foundation Center 1974-75; mem. American Bar Assen., N.Y. State Bar Assen., Assen. of the Bar of the City of New York, Nassau County Bar Assen; Hon. D.F.A. (Long Island) 1979. *Leisure interests:* breeding Chesapeake Bay Retrievers, tennis, swimming. *Address:* Metropolitan Opera Association, Inc., Lincoln Center Plaza, New York, N.Y. 10023; Milbank, Tweed, Hadley & McCloy, Chase Manhattan Plaza, New York, N.Y. 10005 (Office); Centre Island, Oyster Bay, N.Y. 11771, U.S.A. (Home). *Telephone:* (212) 799-3100, (212) 422-2660 (Office).

BLISS, John William Michael, PH.D., F.R.S.C.; Canadian historian and writer; b. 18 Jan. 1941, Kingsville, Ont.; s. of Quartus Bliss and Anne L. Crow; m. Elizabeth J. Haslam 1963; one s. two d.; ed. Kingsville Dist. High School and Univ. of Toronto; Teaching Asst. Harvard Univ. 1967–68; lecturer, Dept. of History, Univ. of Toronto 1968–72, Asst. Prof., Assoc. Prof., Prof. 1972–; several awards including Tyrrell Medal, Royal Soc. of Canada 1988. *Publications:* A Living Profit 1974, A Canadian Millionaire: The Life of Sir Joseph Flavelle 1978, The Discovery of Insulin 1982, Banting: A Biography 1984, Northern Enterprise: Five Centuries of Canadian Business 1987. *Leisure interests:* skiing, jogging. *Address:* Department of History, University of Toronto, M5S 1A1 (Office); 314 Bessborough Drive, Toronto, M4G 3L1, Canada (Home). *Telephone:* 416-978-8480 (Office); 416-485-1979.

BLISSETT, William, PH.D. F.R.S.C.; Canadian professor of English; b. 11 Oct. 1921, Saskatchewan; s. of Ralph R. Blissett and Gladys Jones; ed. Univs. of British Columbia and Toronto; lecturer in English, Univ. of Toronto 1948–50; Assoc. Prof. Univ. of Sask. 1950–57, Prof. 1957–60; Prof. and Head, Dept. of English, Huron Coll. Univ. of W. Ont. 1960–65; Prof. of English, Univ. Coll. Univ. of Toronto 1965–87, Prof. Emer. 1987–; Hon. Fellow, Huron Coll. 1966. *Publications:* The Long Conversation, A Memoir of David Jones 1981; numerous articles on Spenser, Shakespeare, Jonson, literary Wagnerism, T. S. Eliot, David Jones. *Leisure interests:* travel, opera, book collecting. *Address:* University College, University of Toronto, M5S 1A1 (Office); 36 Castle Frank Road, Apt. 212, Toronto, M4W 2Z7, Canada (Home). *Telephone:* (416) 978-3326 (Office); (416) 924-1297 (Home).

BLITZ, Gérard; Belgian business executive; b. 28 Feb. 1912; ed. Collège d'Anvers; Diamond cutter 1932–50; Founder, Vice-Chair., Club Méditerranée (holiday org.) 1950–; Pres. S.P.V.Y. 1966–; Croix de guerre. *Address:* 8 rue de la Bourse, 75002 Paris (Office); 6 rue du Printemps, 75017 Paris, France (Home).

BLIX, Hans Martin, LL.D., PH.D.; Swedish lawyer and international official; b. 28 June 1928, Uppsala; s. of Gunnar and Hertha (née Wiberg) Blix; m. Eva Kettis 1962; two s.; ed. Uppsala Univ., Univ. of Cambridge, Columbia Univ., New York, Univ. of Stockholm; Asst. Prof. of Int. Law, Univ. of Stockholm 1960–63; Legal Consultant on Int. Law, Foreign Ministry 1963–76; Under-Sec. of State for Int. Devt. Co-operation, Foreign Ministry 1976–78, 1979–81; Minister for Foreign Affairs 1978–79; Dir.-Gen. Int. Atomic Energy Agency (IAEA), Vienna 1981–; mem. Swedish del. to UN Gen. Assembly 1961–81; mem. del. to Conf. on Disarmament, Geneva 1962–78. *Publications:* Treaty-Making Power (dissertation), Statsmyndigheternas Internationella Förbindelser (monograph) 1964, Sovereignty, Aggression and Neutrality 1970, The Treaty-Maker's Handbook 1973, and articles in scientific journals. *Leisure interests:* skiing, hiking, art. *Address:* International Atomic Energy Agency, Wagramerstrasse 5, P.O. Box 100, A-1400 Vienna, Austria. *Telephone:* Vienna 2360.

BLOCH, Konrad, PH.D.; American (b. German) biochemist; b. 21 Jan. 1912; ed. Technische Hochschule, Munich, and Columbia Univ.; emigrated to U.S.A. 1936, naturalized 1944; Instructor and Research Assoc., Columbia Univ. 1939–46; Asst. Prof. of Biochemistry, Univ. of Chicago 1946–50, Prof. 1950–54; Higgins Prof. of Biochemistry, Harvard Univ. 1954–; Fellow American Acad. of Sciences; mem. N.A.S.; Fritzsche Award, American Chemical Soc. 1964; Nobel Prize for Medicine with Prof. Theodor Lynen for discoveries concerning the mechanism and regulation of cholesterol and fatty acid metabolism 1964. *Publication:* Lipide Metabolism 1961. *Address:* Department of Biochemistry, Harvard University, 12 Oxford Street, Cambridge, Mass. 02138, U.S.A.

BLOCH, Raymond, D. ÈS L.; French archaeologist; b. 4 May 1914, Paris; s. of Oscar Bloch and Marguerite Katz; m. Denise Cornet 1946; three s.; ed. Lycée Buffin and Ecole Normale Supérieure; mem. Ecole Française de Rome 1938–39, 1945–47; mil. service and prisoner of war 1940–45; Dir. of Studies, Ecole Pratique des Hautes Etudes 1949–; mem. Conseil Supérieur de la Recherche Archéologique 1963–78; mem. C.N.R.S. 1971–75; mem. Inst. de France (Acad. des Inscriptions et Belles Lettres); Chevalier, Légion d'Honneur; Commdr. des Palmes Académiques. *Publications:* numerous books and articles on archaeology, history and the religion of ancient Italy. *Leisure interests:* swimming, tennis. *Address:* 12 rue Emile Faguet, 75014 Paris, France. *Telephone:* 4.540.63.82.

BLOCH-LAINÉ, François, D. EN D.; French banker; b. 25 March 1912, Paris; s. of Jean-Frédéric Bloch-Lainé and Suzanne Lainé; m. Anne-Marie d'Abbadie d'Arrast 1935 (deceased); four s.; ed. Univ. of Paris; entered Inspection des Finances 1936; directed finances of Resistance; Deputy Dir. of Treasury 1944; financial adviser in China and Chief, French Financial Mission to Far East 1945–46; Dir. of Schuman Cabinet 1946; Dir. of Treasury 1947–53; Dir.-Gen. Caisse des Dépôts 1953–67; Insp.-Gen. of Finances 1963–; Pres. Soc. centrale immobilière de la Caisse des dépôts 1955–67, Soc. centrale pour l'équipement du territoire, Centre d'Etudes et de recherches sur l'aménagement urbain; Pres. Crédit Lyonnais 1967–74, Hon. Pres. 1984–; mem. Gen. Council, Banque de France 1947–67; posts in Soc. Nat. des Pétroles d'Aquitaine, Banque de Bruxelles, la Cie. Bancaire, Crédit Nat., Crédit Foncier Franco-Canadien, Crédit Foncier de France, SNCF (French railways) ORTF, etc.; Vice-Pres. Asscn. profes-

sionelle des Banques 1973–74; Pres. Fondation pour la recherche médicale française; Pres. Comm. chargée d'établir le rapport sur l'état de la France 1981; Pres. du Conseil d'Admin. de l'Établissement public de l'Opéra de la Bastille 1983–85; Grand Officier Légion d'honneur, Croix de guerre, Médaille de la Résistance, Commdr. Ordre des Palmes académiques. *Publications:* L'emploi des loisirs ouvriers et l'éducation populaire 1935, La zone franc 1953, Le trésor public 1960, Pour une réforme de l'entreprise 1963, Profession: fonctionnaire 1976. *Address:* 93 rue de Rivoli, 75056 Paris R.P. (Office); 11 rue de l'Hôtel-Colbert, 75005 Paris, France (Home).

BLOCK, Herbert Lawrence (Herblock); American cartoonist; b. 13 Oct. 1909, Chicago; s. of David Julian Block and Tessie Lupe; ed. Lake Forest Coll., Ill., Art Inst., Chicago; editorial cartoonist Chicago Daily News 1929–33; Nat. Educ. Asscn. Service 1933–43; served World War II; editorial cartoonist The Washington Post 1946–; Pulitzer Prize 1942, 1954, 1979, American Newspaper Guild Award 1948, Heywood Broun Award 1950, Sidney Hillman Award 1953, Reuben Award, Nat. Cartoonists Soc. 1957, Lauterbach Award for Civil Liberties 1959, Florina Lasker Award, New York Civil Liberties Union 1960, Distinguished Service Journalism Award 1963, Bill of Rights Award 1966, Nat. Headliners Award 1976, Power of Printing Award 1977, Nat. Press Club 4th Estate Award 1977, Nat. Educ. Asscn. Human Relations Award 1979, etc.; Hon. LL.D. (Lake Forest Coll.) 1957; Hon. Litt.D. (Rutgers Univ.) 1963; Hon. L.H.D. (Williams Coll. 1969, Haverford Coll. 1977, Univ. of Md. 1977). *Publications:* The Herblock Book 1952, Herblock's Here and Now 1955, Herblock's Special for Today 1958, Straight Herblock 1964, The Herblock Gallery 1968, Herblock's State of the Union 1972, Herblock Special Report 1974, Herblock On All Fronts 1980, Herblock Through the Looking Glass 1984, Herblock At Large 1987; designed U.S. postage stamp commemorating 175th anniversary of Bill of Rights 1966. *Address:* The Washington Post, Washington, D.C. 20071, U.S.A.

BLOCK, John Rusling; American farmer and politician; b. 1935, Ill.; m.; three c.; ed. U.S. Mil. Acad., West Point; farmer, Galesburg, Ill.; fmr. mem. Bd. Ill. Farm Bureau; served on Cttee. and Agricultural Export Task Force, Nat. Govs. Asscn.; Dir. Ill. Dept. of Agric. until 1980; U.S. Sec. of Agric. 1981–85; Pres. Nat. American Wholesale Grocers Asscn.; Dir. Deeve and Co. 1986–; Republican. *Leisure interest:* running (competed in Boston marathon). *Address:* Galesburg, Ill., U.S.A. (Home).

BLOCK, John Rusling; Jewish Fed. of Chicago 1931–52, Pres. 1947–50; Vice-Pres. and Dir. Exec. Service Corps. of Chicago 1978–; Hon. Dir. Nat. Merit Scholarship Corpn., Chair. 1971–75; Hon. Dir. Cttee. for Econ. Devt.; Hon. Trustee, Ill. Inst. of Tech.; Trustee, First Non-Profit Risk Pooling Trust 1978–; Hon. Life Trustee, Museum of Science and Industry, Chicago; mem. Ill. Bd. of Higher Educ. 1967–79, Vice-Chair. 1973–79; mem. Welfare Service Cttee., Cook Co. Dept. of Public Aid 1968–80, Chair. 1968–71; Hon. LL.D. St. Joseph's Coll. (Collegeville), Ind., Bradley Univ., Roosevelt Univ., Ill. Inst. of Tech., Northwestern Univ., Univ. of Illinois at Chicago Circle, Hon. LH.D. DePaul Univ., Hon. D.Eng. Rose Polytechnic Inst. *Leisure interests:* golf, collecting Lincolnia. *Address:* 30 West Monroe Street, Chicago, Ill. (Office); 1325 Astor Street, Chicago, Ill., U.S.A. (Home).

BLOEMBERGEN, Nicolaas, DR.PHIL.; American (naturalized 1958) professor of applied physics; b. 11 March 1920, Dordrecht, Netherlands; s. of Auke Bloembergen and Sophia M. Quint; m. Huberta D. Brink 1950; one s. two d.; ed. Univs. of Utrecht and Leiden; Research Fellow, Leiden Univ. 1947–49; Soc. of Fellows, Harvard Univ. 1949–51, Gordon McKay Assoc. Prof. 1951–57, Prof. of Applied Physics 1957–, Rumford Prof. of Physics 1974–80, Gerhard Gade Univ. Prof. 1980–; Guggenheim Fellow 1957; Lorentz Guest Prof., Leiden 1973; Raman Visiting Prof., Bangalore Univ. 1979; Visiting Prof., Coll. de France 1980; mem. N.A.S. (U.S.A.); Corresp. mem. Royal Dutch Acad. of Sciences; Foreign Assoc. mem. Acad. des Sciences, Inst. de France 1981–; Commdr., Order of Orange 1988; foreign mem., Indian Acad. of Sciences, Akad. Leopoldina (G.D.R.); Hon. D.Sc. (Laval Univ., Quebec, Univ. of Conn.); Buckley Prize, American Physical Soc., Liebmann Prize, Inst. of Radio Engineers, Ballantine Medal, Franklin Inst., Royal Dutch Acad. of Arts and Sciences, Half Moon Trophy, Netherland Club of New York, Nat. Medal of Science 1974, Lorentz Medal, Royal Dutch Acad. of Sciences 1978, Frederick Ives Medal, Optical Soc. of America 1979, Alexander von Humboldt Senior U.S. Scientist Award, Munich 1980, shared Nobel Prize in Physics 1981 for contribution to development of laser spectroscopy, Medal of Honor, Inst. of Electrical and Electronics Engineers 1983. *Publications:* Nuclear Magnetic Relaxation 1961, Nonlinear Optics 1965, over 300 papers in professional journals. *Leisure interests:* travel, skiing, tennis. *Address:* Pierce Hall, Harvard University, Cambridge, Mass. 02138, U.S.A.

BLOKHIN, Nikolay Nikolayevich, M.D.; Soviet surgeon and cancer specialist; b. 4 May 1912, Lukoyanov, Gor'kiy Region; s. of Nikolay I. Blokhin and Yevdokiya I. Blokhina; m. Nadyezhda G. Blokhina 1956; one d.; ed. Gor'kiy State Medical Inst.; intern at Gor'kiy Medical Inst. 1934–37, Asst. Prof. in Surgical Clinic 1937–47, Prof. and Chief of Surgical Clinic 1947–52, Dir. of Inst. 1951–52; Dir. Inst. of Experimental and Clinical Oncology of U.S.S.R. Acad. Medical Sciences 1952, later Dir. Cancer Research Centre; Pres. U.S.S.R. Acad. Medical Sciences 1960–68, 1977–87, mem. 1960–; Deputy to U.S.S.R. Supreme Soviet 1966–; mem. CPSU 1948–; Pres. Comm. awarding Int. Lenin prizes 1974–; Pres. U.S.S.R.-U.S

Friendship Soc.; Pres. Int. Union against Cancer 1966–70; Foreign mem. Polish Acad. Sciences, Czech and G.D.R. Acads. of Sciences; Hon. mem. Purkyné Czech Medical Soc.; Life mem. New York Acad. of Sciences; Hon. Dr. (Semmeweis Medical Univ., Bulgarian Medical Acad., Poznan Medical Acad.) 1980; Hero of Socialist Labour, Order of Lenin (four times), Order of Labour Red Banner, Order of Red Star, Order of October Revolution, State Prize 1982. *Publications:* Skinplastic 1956, Problems of Chemiotherapy of Malignant Tumours (Ed.) 1960, Modern Diagnostic Methods in Malignant Tumours (Ed.) 1967, Manual on Clinical Oncology 1972, and numerous other publications on surgery and cancer research. *Address:* All-Union Cancer Research Center, U.S.S.R. Academy of Medical Sciences, Kashirskoye chaussée, 24, Moscow 115478, U.S.S.R. *Telephone:* (324) 11-34.

BLOM-COOPER, Louis Jacques, Q.C., F.R.S.A.; British lawyer and author; b. 27 March 1926; s. of Alfred Blom-Cooper and Ella Flesseman; m. 1st 1952 (dissolved 1970), two s. one d.; m. 2nd Jane E. Smither 1970; one s. two d.; ed. Seaford Coll., King's Coll., London, Municipal Univ. of Amsterdam and Fitzwilliam Coll., Cambridge; army service 1944–47; called to Bar, Middle Temple 1952, Bencher 1978; mem. Home Sec.'s Advisory Council on the Penal System 1966–78; Chair. Howard League for Penal Reform 1973–84, Vice-Pres. 1984–; Chair. Panel of Inquiry into death of Jasmine Beckford 1985; on several comms. of inquiry 1986–87; Judge Court of Appeal, Jersey and Guernsey 1988–; Chair. Mental Health Act Comm. 1988–, Press Council Jan. 1989–; Visiting Prof. Queen Mary Coll., London 1983–. *Publications:* Bankruptcy in Private International Law 1954, The Law as Literature 1962, The A6 Murder (A Semblance of Truth) 1963, A Calendar of Murder (with T. P. Morris) 1964, Language of the Law 1965, Separated Spouses (with O. R. McGregor and C. Gibson) 1970, Final Appeal: A Study of the House of Lords in its Judicial Capacity (with G. Drewry) 1972, ed. Progress in Penal Reform 1975, Law and Morality (with G. Drewry) 1976; articles in legal journals, etc. *Leisure interests:* watching and reporting on Association football, reading, music, writing, broadcasting. *Address:* 1 Dr. Johnson's Buildings, London, EC4Y 7AX; 25 Richmond Crescent, London, N1 0LY, England. *Telephone:* 01-353 9328; 01-607 8045.

BLOMQUIST, John E., A.B.; American business executive (retd.); b. 22 Aug. 1914, Kansas City; s. of Arthur and Mary (née Meeker) Blomquist; m. Harriet T. Rohner 1943; one d.; ed. Univ. of Missouri; joined Reynolds Metals Co. 1940, then Pres. and C.O.O., Vice-Chair. 1983–85; Dir. Reynolds Metals and subsidiaries, and Robertshaw Controls Co.; mem. Aluminum Asscn. (Pres. 1978–80), Soc. of Automotive Engineers. *Address:* Office of the President, Reynolds Metals Co., 6601 Broad Street Road, Richmond, Va. 23261, U.S.A.

BLOMSTEDT, Henrik Lennart, LL.B.; Finnish diplomatist; b. 26 June 1921, Helsinki; s. of Lennart Blomstedt and Mary Blomstedt; m. Ulla Westin 1960; one s.; ed. Univ. of Helsinki; joined Foreign Service 1947; Amb. to Ethiopia (accred. to Kenya, Tanzania, Uganda, Zambia) 1965–69; Head Legal Dept., Foreign Ministry 1970–73; Amb. to Netherlands and Ireland 1973–78, to Japan and Repub. of Korea 1978–84, the Philippines 1978–80, to Norway 1984–88; Commdr. First Class, Order of the White Rose of Finland, of the Lion of Finland, Order of Diplomatic Service Merit and several foreign decorations. *Leisure interests:* literature, chess. *Address:* Mellstensvägen 9F2, 02170 Esbo, Finland. *Telephone:* 4521779.

BLOMSTEDT, Herbert Thorson; Swedish music director and conductor; b. 7 Nov. 1927, Springfield, Mass., U.S.A.; s. of Adolphe Blomstedt and Alida Armintha Thorson; m. Waltraud Regina Peterson 1955; four d.; ed. Royal Acad. of Music, Stockholm and Uppsala Univ.; Music Dir., Norrkoping Symphony Orchestra 1954–61; Prof. of Conducting, Swedish Royal Acad. of Music 1961–70; Perm. Conductor, Oslo Philharmonic 1962–68; Music Dir. of Danish Radio Symphony Orchestra 1967–77, of Dresden Staatskapelle Orchestra 1975–85, of Swedish Radio Symphony Orchestra 1977–82; Music Dir. and Conductor, San Francisco Symphony Orchestra 1985–; Hon. Conductor NHK Symphony, Tokyo 1986; Hon. D.Mus. (Andrews); Jenny Lind Scholarship, Swedish Royal Acad. of Music; Kt. Royal Order of the North Star (Sweden); Kt. Royal Order of Dannebrog (Denmark); Litteris et Artibus, Gold Medal (Sweden). *Leisure interests:* hiking, reading, art. *Address:* San Francisco Symphony Orchestra, 201 Van Ness, San Francisco, Calif. 94102, U.S.A.; Interartists, Frans van Mierisstraat 43, 1071 RK, Amsterdam, Netherlands. *Telephone:* 415-552-8000.

BLONDIN, Antoine, L. ÉS L.; French writer; b. 11 April 1922, Paris; s. of Pierre Blondin and Germaine Ragoulleau; m. 1st Sylviane Dollfus, one s. one d.; m. 2nd Françoise Barrère 1969; ed. Lycée Louis-le-Grand and Univ. de Paris; contributor to Paris-Presse, Arts, La Parisienne, etc.; wrote scenarios for the films La route Napoléon, Obsession, La foire aux femmes, Cran d'arrêt, le Dernier Saut, Sur le tour de France, La vie entre les lignes, Le tour de France en quatre et vingt jours; Prix des Deux-Magots 1949, Prix Interallié for Un singe en hiver 1959, Grand Prix (Literature) Académie Française 1979 and other prizes; Officier Ordre Arts et des Lettres. *Publications include:* L'Europe buissonnière, Les enfants du bon Dieu, L'humeur vagabonde, Un singe en hiver, Un garçon d'honneur, Nous reviendrons à pied, Quat'saisons, Vivre à Paris, Certificats d'études. *Leisure interests:* sport, gastronomy. *Address:* 72 rue Mazarine, 75007 Paris, France.

BLOOM, Allan, A.M., PH.D.; American professor of political science; b. 14 Sept. 1930, Indianapolis; s. of Allan Bloom and Malvina D. Glasner; ed. Univs. of Chicago, Paris and Heidelberg; reader, Univ. of Paris 1954–55; lecturer, Liberal Arts, Univ. of Chicago 1955–60; Visiting Asst. Prof. of Political Science, Yale Univ. 1962–63; Asst. Prof., Assoc. Prof. of Govt. Cornell Univ. 1963–70; Prof. of Political Science, Univ. of Toronto 1970–79; Prof. Comm. on Social Thought and the Coll., Univ. of Chicago 1979–; Visiting Prof. Univ. of Tel Aviv 1969, Ecole des Hautes Etudes, Paris 1984–; Fellow, Rockefeller Foundation 1957–58, Cornell Soc. for Humanities 1968–69; Guggenheim Fellow 1975–76; Clark Distinguished Teaching Award 1967; Prix Jean Jacques Rousseau, Geneva 1987. *Publications:* Shakespeare's Politics 1964, The Closing of the American Mind 1987; translations of Plato and Rousseau. *Address:* 1126 E 59th Street, Chicago, Ill. 60637 (Office); 5811 Dorchester Avenue, Apt. 12G, Chicago, Ill. 60637, U.S.A.

BLOOM, Claire; British actress; b. 15 Feb. 1931, London; d. of Edward Bloom and Elizabeth Grew; m. 1st Rod Steiger (q.v.) 1959 (divorced); one d.; ed. London, Bristol and New York; Oxford Repertory Theatre 1946, Stratford-on-Avon 1948; first major stage appearances in The Lady's Not For Burning 1949, Ring Around the Moon 1950; at Old Vic 1951–53, Duel of Angels 1956. *Other stage performances include:* Andromache in The Trojan women 1964, Sascha in Ivanov, London 1966, Nora in A Doll's House, New York 1971, London 1973, Hedda Gabler in Hedda Gabler, New York 1971, Mary, Queen of Scots in Vivat, Vivat Regina!, New York 1972, A Streetcar Named Desire, London (Evening Standard Drama Award for Best Actress) 1974, The Innocents, U.S.A. 1976, Rosmersholm, London 1977, The Cherry Orchard, Chichester Festival 1981; Fellow, Guildhall School of Music and Drama 1975. *Films include:* Limelight, Man Between, Richard III, Alexander the Great, Brothers Karamazov, Buccaneer, Look Back in Anger, Three Steps to Freedom 1960, The Brothers Grimm, The Chapman Report 1962, The Haunting 1963, 80,000 Suspects 1963, Alta Infedeltà 1963, Il Maestro di Vigevano 1963, The Outrage 1964, Spy Who Came in from the Cold 1965, Charly 1966, Three into Two Won't Go 1967, Illustrated Man 1968, Red Sky at Morning 1970, A Doll's House 1973, Islands in the Stream 1975, The Clash of the Titans 1979, Always 1984, Sammy and Rosie Get Laid 1987, Brothers 1988. *Television appearances:* A Legacy 1975, The Orestea 1978, Henry VIII 1979, Brideshead Revisited 1979, Hamlet 1980, Cymbeline 1982, Separate Tables 1982, The Ghost Writer 1982, King John 1983, Time and the Conways 1984, Shadowlands 1985, Promises to keep us 1985, Oedipus the King 1985, Lightning Always Strikes Twice 1985; mini series in U.S.: Ellis Island 1984, Florence Nightingale 1984, Liberty 1985, Anastasia 1986, Queenie 1986, The Belle of Amherst 1986, Intimate Contact 1987, A Shadow on the Sun 1988 (U.S. mini series). Also performs her one woman show These are Women, A portrait of Shakespeare's Heroines, throughout the U.S.A. *Publication:* Limelight and After 1982. *Leisure interests:* walking, music. *Address:* c/o William Morris, 31/32 Soho Square, London W.1, England.

BLOOM, Harold, PH.D.; American professor of humanities; b. 11 July 1930, New York; s. of William Bloom and Paula Lev; m. Jeanne Gould 1958; two s.; ed. Cornell and Yale Univs.; mem. Faculty, Yale Univ. 1955–, Prof. of English 1965–77, DeVane Prof. of Humanities 1974–77, Prof. of Humanities 1977–, Sterling Prof. of Humanities 1983–; Visiting Prof. Hebrew Univ. Jerusalem 1959, Breadloaf Summer School 1965–66, Soc. for Humanities, Cornell Univ. 1968–69; Visiting Univ. Prof. New School of Social Research, New York 1982–84; Charles Eliot Horton Prof. of Poetry, Harvard Univ. 1987–88; mem. American Acad. of Arts and Sciences; Guggenheim Fellow 1962; Fulbright Fellow 1955; Newton Arvin Award 1967; Melville Cane Award, Poetry Soc. of America 1970; Zabel Prize, American Inst. of Arts and Letters 1982; MacArthur Prize Fellowship 1985. *Publications:* Shelley's Mythmaking 1959, The Visionary Company 1961, Blake's Apocalypse 1963, Commentary to Blake 1965, Yeats 1970, The Ringers in the Tower 1971, The Anxiety of Influence 1973, Wallace Stevens: The Poems of Our Climate 1977, A Map of Misreading 1975, Kabbalah and Criticism 1975, Poetry and Represseion 1976, Figures of Capable Imagination 1976, The Flight to Lucifer: A Gnostic Fantasy 1979, Agon: Towards a Theory of Revisionism 1981, The Breaking of the Vessels 1981, The Strong Light of the Canonical 1987, Freud: Transference and Authority 1988, Poetics of Influence: New and Selected Criticism 1988. *Address:* 179 Linden Street, New Haven, Conn. 06511, U.S.A.

BLOOM, Myer, PH.D., F.R.S.C., F.A.P.S.; Canadian professor of physics; b. 7 Dec. 1928, Montreal; s. of Israel Bloom and Leah Ram; m. Margaret P. Holmes 1954; one s. one d.; ed. Baron Byng High School, McGill Univ. and Univ. of Illinois at Urbana; NRC Travelling Postdoctoral Fellow, Univ. of Leiden, Netherlands 1954–56; Research Assoc. Univ. of B.C. 1956–57, Asst. Prof. 1957–60, Assoc. Prof. 1960–63, Prof. of Physics 1963–; Visiting Prof. Harvard 1964–65, Kyoto Univ. 1965, Univ. de Paris Sud 1971–72, 1978–79, Univ. of Rome 1986, Danish Tech. Univ. 1986; mem. Canadian Assocn. of Physicists; Alfred P. Sloan Fellow 1961–65; Steacie Prize 1967, Biely Prize 1969; Canadian Assocn. of Physicists Gold Medal 1973. *Publications:* numerous research and review articles. *Leisure interests:* hiking, skiing, squash, wine-making. *Address:* Department of Physics, University of British Columbia, 6224 Agriculture Road, Vancouver, B.C., V6T 2A6 (Office); 5669 Kings Road, Vancouver, B.C., V6T 1K9, Canada (Home). *Telephone:* 604-224-6432 (Home).

BLOOMFIELD, Sir Kenneth Percy, K.C.B., M.A.; British civil servant; b. 15 April 1931, Belfast; s. of Mr and Mrs Harry P. Bloomfield; m. Mary E. Ramsey 1960; one s. one d.; ed. Royal Belfast Academic Inst. and St. Peter's Coll., Oxford; joined N. Ireland Civil Service 1952; Private Sec. to Ministers of Finance 1956–60; Deputy Dir. British Industrial Devt. Office, New York 1960–63; Asst. later Deputy Sec. to Cabinet, N. Ireland 1963–72; Under-Sec. N. Ireland Office 1972–76; Perm. Sec. Office of Exec. N. Ireland 1976–78; Perm. Sec. Dept. of Environment, N. Ireland 1978–81, Dept. of Econ. Devt. 1981–84; Head, N. Ireland Civil Service and Second Perm. Under-Sec. of State, N. Ireland Office 1984–. *Leisure interests:* reading history and biographies, swimming. *Address:* Central Secretariat, Stormont Castle, Belfast, BT4 3ST, Northern Ireland. *Telephone:* Belfast 63011.

BLOUIN, Georges Henri, LL.B; Canadian diplomatist; b. 4 June 1921, Montreal; s. of Charles-Henri Blouin and Hermine Panneton; m. Denise Angers 1949; one s. one d.; ed. Coll. Ste.-Marie, Montreal and Univ. of Montreal; joined foreign service 1949; served New Delhi, San Francisco, Athens, Brussels 1951–65; Amb. to Cameroon (also accred. to Gabon, Chad, Cen. African Repub.) 1965–67; Minister, Washington, D.C. 1967–70; Dir.-Gen. of Personnel, Dept. of External Affairs 1970–73; Amb. to Spain (also accred. to Morocco) 1973–77; Asst. Deputy Minister for External Affairs 1977–79; Amb. to Netherlands 1979–83; Chief of Protocol of Canadian Govt. 1983–. *Leisure interests:* golf, walking. *Address:* Chief of Protocol, Department of External Affairs, 20 Driveway, Apt. 602, Ottawa, Ont., K2P 1C8, Canada. *Telephone:* (613) 235-3540.

BLOUNT, Winton Malcolm; American business executive; b. 1 Feb. 1921, Union Springs, Ala.; s. of Winton M. Blount and Clara Belle Chalker Blount; m. Carolyn Self; four s. one d.; ed. Public School, Union Springs, Staunton Military Acad., Univ. of Alabama; bomber pilot—World War II; founded Blount Brothers Corpn. 1946, Chair. of Bd. and C.E.O.; Pres. Chamber of Commerce of U.S. April-Dec. 1968; Postmaster-Gen. of U.S. 1969–71; Chair. Exec. Cttee. Blount Inc. 1973–, Chair. of Bd., Pres. 1974–; Dir. Union Camp Corpn., Munford Inc., Friends of American Art in Religion, Alabama Shakespeare Festival, Alabama Foundation for Educ. Excellence, Folger's Library, President's Cttee. on Arts and Humanities; mem. Business Council, Business Cttee. for the Arts, Conf. Bd., Chief Exec. Org., American Enterprise Inst.; Trustee Univ. of Alabama, Rhodes Coll., Alabama Trust Fund Bd.; Hon. doctorates at Judson Coll., Huntingdon Coll., Birmingham-Southern, Rhodes Coll., Seattle Pacific Coll., Univ. of Alabama, Samford, Troy State Univ., Washington, Jefferson Coll., St. John's Univ.; Citation for Distinguished Service to City of Montgomery, Alabama Acad. of Honor, Golden Plate, American Acad. of Achievement 1980, Annual Gold Medal Award from Pope John Paul II 1981 and other awards; Republican. *Leisure interests:* skiing, tennis, hunting. *Address:* 5801 Vaughn Road, Montgomery, Ala. 36116, U.S.A.

BLOUT, Elkan R(ogers), A.B., PH.D.; American biochemist; b. 2 July 1919, New York, N.Y.; s. of Eugene and Lillian Blout; m. 1st Joan Dreyfus Blout 1939, two s. one d.; m. 2nd Gail Ferris Blout 1985; ed. Phillips Exeter Acad. and Princeton and Columbia Univs.; Assoc. Dir. of Research, Polaroid Corpn. 1948–58, Vice-Pres. and Gen. Man. of Research 1958–62; Lecturer on Biophysics, Harvard Medical School 1960–62, Prof. of Biological Chem. 1962–, Edward S. Harkness Prof. of Biological Chem. 1964–, Chair. Dept. of Biological Chem. 1965–69, Dean Academic Affairs, Harvard School of Public Health 1978–, Chair. Dept. of Environmental Science and Physiology 1986–88, Dir. Div. of Biological Sciences 1987–; Dir. Center for Blood Research 1972–, CHON Corpn. 1974–83; Gov. Weizmann Inst. of Science, Rehovot, Israel 1977–; mem. Finance Cttee., N.A.S. 1976–, Inst. of Medicine 1979–, Advisory Cttee. on the U.S.S.R. and Eastern Europe 1979–; mem. Finance Cttee. American Soc. of Biological Chemists 1973–, Corpn. of the Museum of Science, Boston 1974–, Advisory Council of the Dept. of Biochemical Sciences, Princeton Univ. 1974–83, Finance Cttee. American Acad. Arts and Sciences 1976–, Conseil de Surveillance, Compagnie Financière du Scribe 1975–81, Editorial Bd. International Journal of Peptide and Protein Research 1978–, Editorial Bd. Journal of the American Chemical Society 1978–82, Assembly of Math. and Physical Sciences, Nat. Research Council 1979–82, Scientific Advisory Council, American Cttee. for the Weizmann Inst. of Science 1979–, Governing Bd., Nat. Research Council 1980–, Council, N.A.S. 1980–, Exec. Cttee. of Governing Bd., Nat. Research Council 1980–, Investments Advisory Cttee., Fed. of American Socs. for Experimental Biology 1981–, Council, Int. Org. for Chemical Sciences in Devt. 1981– (Vice-Pres. and Treas. 1985–), Comm. on Physical Sciences, Maths. and Resources, Nat. Research Council 1982–; Treas. Nat. Acad. of Sciences 1980–, Advisory Council of the Program in Molecular Biology, Princeton Univ. 1983–; mem. Bd. of Dirs., ESA Inc. 1985–, Auburn Investment Man. Corpn. (also Investment Manager) 1985–; mem. Bd. of Dirs., Nat. Health Research Foundation 1985–, Organization for Chemical Sciences in Devt. 1985–, and Sec.-Treas., Nat. Acads. Corpn. 1986–; Chair. Research Advisory Cttee., Children's Hosp. Medical Center 1986–; Gen. Partner, Gosnold Investment Fund Ltd. Partnership; foreign mem. U.S.S.R. Acad. of Sciences 1976; Nat. Research Fellow, Harvard Univ.; Fellow, American Acad. of Arts and Sciences, A.A.A.S., Optical Soc. of America, New York Acad. of Sciences; Trustee, Bay Biochemical Research 1973–82, Boston Biomedical Research Inst. 1972–; Hon. A.M. (Harvard Univ.) 1962, Hon. D.Sc. (Loyola Univ.) 1976; Class of 1939 Achievement Award, Princeton Univ. 1970. *Publications:* Various articles in specialized

journals, including Journal of American Chemical Society, etc. *Leisure interests:* boating, deep-sea fishing. *Address:* Harvard School of Public Health, 677 Huntington Avenue, Boston, Mass. 02115 (Office); 1010 Memorial Drive, Apt. 12A, Cambridge, Mass. 02138, U.S.A. (Home). *Telephone:* (617) 868-1010 (Home).

BLOW, David Mervyn, PH.D., F.R.S., F.INST.P.; British professor of biophysics; b. 27 June 1931; s. of Rev. Edward Mervyn Blow and Dorothy Laura Blow; m. Mavis Sears 1955; one s. one d.; ed. Kingswood School, Corpus Christi Coll., Cambridge; Fulbright Scholar, Nat. Inst. of Health, Bethesda, Md. and M.I.T., U.S.A. 1957–59; MRC Unit for Study of Molecular Biological Systems, Cambridge 1959–62; MRC Lab. of Molecular Biology, Cambridge 1962–77; Coll. Lecturer and Fellow, Trinity Coll., Cambridge 1968–77; Prof. of Biophysics, Imperial Coll., Univ. of London 1977–, Dean of Royal Coll. of Science 1981–84; Pres. British Crystallographic Asscn. 1984–87; Biochemistry Soc. CIBA Medal 1967, Charles Léopold Meyer Prize 1979, Wolf Prize for Chem. 1987. *Publications:* papers and reviews in scientific journals. *Leisure interests:* hill walking, sailing. *Address:* Blackett Laboratory, Imperial College of Science, Technology and Medicine, University of London, SW7 2BZ, England.

BLOW, Sandra, R.A.; British artist; b. 14 Sept. 1925; d. of Jack Blow and Lily Blow; ed. St. Martin's School of Art, Royal Acad. Schools, Accademia di Belle Arti, Rome; tutor, Painting School, R.C.A. 1960–75; one-person exhbns.: Gimpel Fils 1952, 1954, 1960, 1962, Saidenbury Gallery, New York 1957, New Art Centre, London 1966, 1968, 1971, 1973; group exhbns. in U.K., U.S.A., Italy, Denmark and France; works in collections of Peter Stuyvesant Foundation, Nuffield Foundation, Arts Council of G.B., Arts Council of Northern Ireland, Walker Art Gallery, Liverpool, Allbright Knox Art Gallery, Buffalo, New York, Museum of Modern Art, New York, Tate Gallery, Gulbenkian Foundation, Ministry of Public Bldg. and Works, Contemporary Art Soc.; silk screen prints in Victoria and Albert Museum, Fitzwilliam Museum, Cambridge, City of Leeds Art Gallery, Graves Art Gallery, Sheffield; painting purchased for liner Queen Elizabeth II; won British Section of Int. Guggenheim Award 1960; Second Prize, John Moore's Liverpool Exhbn. 1961; Arts Council Purchase Award 1965–66. *Address:* 12 Sydney Close, London, S.W.3, England. *Telephone:* 01-589 8610.

BLUCK, Duncan Robert Yorke, O.B.E.; British company director; b. 19 March 1927, Shanghai, China; s. of T. E. Bluck; m. Stella Wardlaw Murdoch 1952; one s. three d.; ed. Taunton School, Somerset; joined John Swire & Sons, Far East 1948, Chair. Swire Group, Hong Kong 1981–84, Exec. Dir. John Swire & Sons, London April 1984–; Chief Exec. Cathay Pacific Airways 1971–80, Chair. 1981–84; Chair. British Tourist Authority April 1984–; Chair. English Tourist Bd. Nov. 1984–; Chair. Kent Econ. Devt. Bd. 1986–; Gov. Marlborough House School 1986–. *Leisure interest:* sailing. *Address:* Elfords, Hawkhurst, Kent, TN18 4RP; 41 Markham Square, London SW3 4XA, England. *Telephone:* (0580) 752153 (Kent); 01-352 8948 (London).

BLÜM, Norbert, DR.PHIL.; German politician; b. 21 July 1935, Rüsselsheim; s. of Christian and Margarete (née Beck) Blüm; m. Marita Binger 1964; one s. two d.; ed. Volksschule, Univs. of Cologne and Bonn; apprentice, Opel AG, Rüsselsheim, 1949–53, toolmaker 1953–57; worked in building trade and as lorry driver while studying evenings 1957–61; univ. student 1961–67; Chief Man. Social Comm. of Christian Democrat employees' asscn. 1968–75, Regional Chair. Rhineland-Palatinate 1974–77, Fed. Chair. 1977–; mem. Fed. Exec. C.D.U. 1969–; mem. Bundestag 1972–; Senator for Fed. Affairs for Berlin 1981; Minister of Labour and Social Affairs 1982–; teaching assignments, Fachhochschule, Mainz 1976–. *Publications:* Reaktion oder Reform—Wohin geht die CDU 1972, Gewerkschaften zwischen Allmacht und Ohnmacht 1979, Werkstücke 1980. *Leisure interests:* reading, mountaineering. *Address:* Bundesminister für Arbeit und Sozialordnung, 5300 Bonn 1, Federal Republic of Germany.

BLUM, Yehuda Z., M.JUR., PH.D.; Israeli lawyer and diplomatist; b. 2 Oct. 1931, Bratislava; m. Moriah Rabinovitz-Teomim; two s. one d.; ed. Hebrew Univ., Jerusalem, Univ. of London; detained in Nazi concentration camp of Bergen-Belsen 1944; Asst. to Judge Advocate-Gen. of Israel Defence Forces 1956–59; Senior Asst. to Legal Adviser, Ministry for Foreign Affairs 1962–65; Prof. of Int. Law Hebrew Univ. 1968–; UNESCO Fellow, Univ. of Sydney July-Aug. 1968; Office of UN Legal Counsel Sept.-Dec. 1968; Senior Research Scholar, Univ. of Michigan Law School 1969; Visiting Prof., School of Law, Univ. of Texas, Austin 1971, New York Univ. 1975–76, Univ. of Mich. Law School 1985; mem. Israeli del., Third UN Conference on Law of the Sea 1973, 31st Session of UN Gen. Assembly 1976; Perm. Rep. to UN 1978–84; holder of Hersch Lauterpacht Chair in Int. Law, Hebrew Univ., Jerusalem; Law Ed. Encyclopedia Hebraica 1973–; Jabotinsky Prize 1984; Dr. Jur. h.c. (Yeshiva Univ.) 1981. *Publications:* Historic Titles in International Law 1965, Secure Boundaries and Middle East Peace 1971, For Zion's Sake 1987. *Address:* Faculty of Law, Hebrew University, Mount Scopus, Jerusalem, Israel. *Telephone:* 882-562.

BLUMBERG, Baruch Samuel, M.D., PH.D., F.R.C.P.; American research physician; b. 28 July 1925, New York; s. of late Meyer and of Ida (Simonoff) Blumberg; m. Jean Liebesman 1954; two s. two d.; ed. Union Coll., Schenectady, Columbia Univ. Coll. of Physicians and Surgeons, Balliol

Coll., Oxford; served U.S. Navy 1943–46; Intern and resident, First (Columbia) Div., Bellevue Hosp., New York 1951–57; Ship's Surgeon 1952; Fellow in medicine, Presbyterian Hosp., New York 1953–55; Dept. of Biochem., Oxford Univ., U.K. 1955–57; Chief of Geographic Medicine and Genetics Section, Nat. Insts. of Health, Bethesda, Md. 1957–64; Assoc. Dir. for Clinical Research, Inst. for Cancer Research, Philadelphia 1964–86, Vice-Pres. for Population Oncology, Fox Chase Cancer Centre 1986–; Univ. Prof. of Medicine and Anthropology, Univ. of Pennsylvania 1977–; George Eastman Visiting Prof., Univ. of Oxford 1983–84, Raman Visiting Prof., Indian Acad. of Sciences, Bangalore, India, Jan.–April 1986; Ashland Visiting Prof., Univ. of Ky. 1986–87; Master (elect) Balliol Coll., Oxford 1989–; attending physician, Pa. Hosp., Hosp. of Univ. of Pennsylvania; mem. Asscn. of American Physicians, various other medical socs.; Fellow, N.A.S.; Hon. Fellow, Balliol Coll., Oxford 1976; numerous hon. degrees; Bernstein Award, Medical Soc. of New York, 1969, Passano Award 1974, Modern Medicine Distinguished Achievement Award 1975, Karl Landsteiner Award 1975; shared Nobel Prize in Physiology or Medicine for discoveries concerning new mechanisms for origin and dissemination of infectious diseases 1976, and numerous other awards. *Publications:* Australia Antigen and the Biology of Hepatitis B 1977; numerous papers to scientific journals. *Leisure interests:* middle-distance running, squash racquets, canoeing, cattle raising. *Address:* Fox Chase Cancer Center, 7701 Burholme Avenue, Fox Chase, Philadelphia, Pa. 19111, U.S.A. (Office). *Telephone:* (215) 728-2203 (Office).

BLUME, Peter; American painter; b. 27 Oct. 1906, Smorgon, Russia; s. of Harry and Rose Blume; m. Grace Douglas Gibbs Craton 1931; ed. New York Educational Alliance Art School; exhibited Daniel Gallery New York 1926–31, Julien Levy Gallery 1937, Durlacher Bros. 1947, Kennedy Gallery 1968, Danenberg Gallery New York 1970, Coe Kerr Gallery 1974, Terry Dintenfass Gallery 1980; Retrospective Exhbn., Paintings and Drawings 1926–65, Manchester, N.H., and Hartford, Conn. 1964, Paintings, Drawings and Sculpture, Museum of Contemporary Art, Chicago 1976, Museum of American Art 1982, New Britain, Conn. and museums throughout U.S., Italian Drawings 1956–62, Mead Museum, Amhurst Coll. 1985; works in Museum of Modern Art, Whitney, Metropolitan, Newark, Boston, Columbus, Cleveland, Philadelphia and Fogg Museums, Wadsworth Atheneum, Williams, Randolf-Macon Colls., Art Inst. Chicago; mem. Nat. Inst. of Arts and Letters 1950, American Acad. of Arts and Letters 1960; prizeman Carnegie Int. Exhbn., Pittsburgh 1934, and Artists for Victory Exhbn. 1942; Guggenheim Fellowship 1932, renewal 1936; awarded grant of American Acad. of Arts and Letters and Inst. of Arts and Letters 1947; elected Assoc. Nat. Acad. of Design 1948. *Works:* South of Scranton, Parade, Light of the World, The Eternal City, The Rock, Passage to Etna, Tasso's Oak, Winter, Summer, Recollection of the Flood, etc. *Publication:* Peter Blume-Frank Anderson Trapp. *Leisure interest:* gardening. *Address:* Route 1, Box 185, Sherman, Conn. 06784, U.S.A.

BLUMENTHAL W(erner) Michael, PH.D.; American business executive; b. 3 Jan. 1926, Germany; s. of Ewald Blumenthal and Rose Valerie (Markt) Blumenthal; ed. Univ. of California at Berkeley and Princeton Univ; went to U.S. 1947, naturalized 1952; Research Assoc., Princeton Univ. 1954–57; Vice-Pres., Dir. Crown Cork Int. Corpn. 1957–61; Deputy Asst. Sec. of State for Econ. Affairs, Dept. of State 1961–63; also served as U.S.A. Rep. to UN Comm. on Int. Commodity Trade; President's Deputy Special Rep. for Trade Negotiations (with rank of Amb.) 1963–67; Chair. U.S. Del. to Kennedy Round tariff talks in Geneva; Pres. Bendix Int. 1967–70; Dir. Bendix Corpn. 1967–77, Vice-Chair. June-Dec. 1970, Pres. and Chief Operating Officer 1971–72, Chair. and Chief Exec. Officer 1972–77; Sec. of the Treasury 1977–79; Dir. Burroughs Corpn. (now Unisys) 1979–, Vice-Chair. 1980, C.E.O. Sept. 1980–, Chair. Jan. 1981–; The Pillsbury Co. 1979–, the Chemical New York Corpn. 1979–, the Chemical Bank 1979–, (mem. Advisory Bd. 1986–); mem. Bd. of Dirs. Detroit Renaissance Inc., New Detroit Inc., The Econ. Club of Detroit, United Foundation of Detroit, Tenneco Co.; Detroit Symphony Orchestra; mem. The Business Council, American Econ. Asscn.; Trustee, mem. U.S. Corporate Council on S. Africa 1985–, Steering Cttee. U.S.–Japan Business Council; Dir. America-China Soc.; Charter Trustee Emer., Princeton Univ. *Leisure interests:* tennis, skiing. *Address:* Unisys Corporation, P.O.Box 418, Burroughs Place, Detroit, Mich. 48232, U.S.A. (Office).

BLUMGART, Leslie Harold, B.D.S., M.D., F.R.C.S., F.R.C.S.E., F.R.C.P.S.; British professor of surgery; b. 7 Dec. 1931, South Africa; s. of Harold Herman Blumgart and Hilda Blumgart; m. 1st Pearl Navias 1955 (deceased), 2nd Sarah Raybould Bowen 1968; two s. two d.; ed. Jeppe High School, Johannesburg, Univ. of Witwatersrand, Johannesburg, Univ. of Sheffield, England; Sr. Lecturer and Deputy Dir., Dept. of Surgery, Welsh Nat. School of Medicine, Cardiff 1970–72; St. Mungo Prof. of Surgery, Univ. of Glasgow, Hon. Consultant Surgeon, Glasgow Royal Infirmary 1972–79; Prof. of Surgery and Dir. Dept. of Surgery, Royal Postgraduate Medical School, Univ. of London and Hon. Consultant, Hammersmith Hosp., London 1979–86; Prof. of Visceral and Transplantion Surgery, Univ. of Berne and Inselspital Bern, Switzerland 1986–; Moynihan Fellowship, Asscn. of Surgeons of G.B. and Ireland 1972; Hon. mem. Soc. for Surgery of the Alimentary Tract, U.S.A., Danish Surgical Soc. 1988; mem. Hong Kong Surgical Soc., Hellenic Surgical Soc., L.A. Surgical Soc.; Pres. Int. Biliary Asscn. 1986; Order of Prasidda Prabala Gorkha-Dakshin Bahu (Nepal)

1984. *Publications:* Essentials of Medicine and Surgery for Dental Students (with A. C. Kennedy), 4th edn. 1982, The Biliary Tract, in Clinical Surgery Int., vol. 5 1982, Liver Surgery, in Clinical Surgery Int., vol. 12 (with S. Bengmark) 1986, Surgery of the Liver and Biliary Tract, Vols. 1 and 2 1988; numerous publs. concerned with medical educ., gastrointestinal surgery and aspects of oncology with particular interest in surgery of the liver, pancreas and biliary tract. *Leisure interests:* watercolour painting, wood carving. *Address:* Klinik für Viszerale und Transplantations Chirurgie, Inselspital, 3010 Berne, Switzerland; 12 Glebe Road, Barnes, London, SW13 0EA, England. *Telephone:* (031) 64 24 12 (Berne); 01-878 3752 (London).

BLUNDELL, Sir Michael, K.B.E.; Kenyan farmer and politician; b. 7 April 1907, London; s. of Alfred Herbert Blundell and Amelia Woodward Richardson; m. Geraldine Lötte Robarts 1946; one d.; ed. Wellington Coll.; emigrated to Kenya 1925; served in Royal Engineers (Col.) 1939–45; Comm. for European Settlement 1946–47; Chair. Pyrethrum Bd. of Kenya 1949–54, Allsopps African Investments 1949–54; mem. Kenya Legislative Council for Rift Valley Constituency 1948–58, 1961–62; specially selected mem. under Lennox-Boyd Constitution for Kenya, April 1958–61; Acting Leader, European Elected mems. 1951, Leader 1952; Minister on Emergency War Council 1954; Minister of Agric. 1955–59, 1961–62; Hon. Col. 3rd King's African Rifles 1955–60; Leader New Kenya Party 1959–63; Chair. E. A. Breweries Ltd. 1964–77, Uganda Breweries Ltd. 1965–76; Dir. Barclays Bank of Kenya 1968–81; Chair. Egerton Agricultural College 1962–72, Kenya Soc. for the Blind 1978–82; Freeman Goldsmiths' and Silversmiths' Co. 1953–. *Publications:* So Rough a Wind 1964, The Wild Flowers of Kenya 1982, Collins Guide to the Wild Flowers of East Africa 1987. *Leisure interests:* gardening, music, porcelain, wild-life. *Address:* P.O. Box 30181, Nairobi, Kenya. *Telephone:* Nairobi 512278.

BLUNDELL, William Richard Charles, B.A.SC.; Canadian business executive; b. 13 April 1927, Montreal; s. of Richard C. Blundell and Did Aileen Payne; m. Monique Audet 1959; one s. three d.; ed. Univ. of Toronto; joined Canadian Gen. Electric (now Gen. Electric Canada Inc.) 1949, Treas. 1966, Vice-Pres. Finance 1968, Vice-Pres. and Div. Exec. Consumer Products 1970, Vice-Pres. and Div. Exec. Apparatus and Heavy Machinery 1972, Pres. and C.O.O. 1983–84, Chair. and C.E.O. Dec. 1984–; Pres. and C.E.O. Camco Inc. 1979–83. *Leisure interest:* sport. *Address:* 2300 Meadowood Boulevard, Mississauga, Ont. L5N 5F (Office); 45 Stratheden Road, Toronto, Ont. M4N 1E5, Canada (Home). *Telephone:* (416)-489-7386 (Home).

BLUNDEN, Sir George, Kt., M.A.; British central banker; b. 31 Dec. 1922, Sutton, Surrey; s. of George Blunden and Florence Holder; m. Anne Bulford 1949; two s. one d.; ed. City of London School, Univ. Coll., Oxford; war service, Royal Sussex Regt. 1941–45; Bank of England 1947–55; Economist, Balance of Payments Div., Int. Monetary Fund 1955–58; various posts, Bank of England 1958–65, Deputy Principal, Discount Office 1965–67, seconded to Monopolies Comm. 1968, Deputy Chief Cashier 1968–73, Chief of Man. Services 1973–74, responsible for banking supervision with rank of Head of Dept. 1974–76, Exec. Dir. 1976–84, Non-Exec. Dir. 1984–85, Deputy Gov. 1986–; Chair. Group of Ten Cttees. on banking supervision 1975–77 and on payments systems 1981–83. *Address:* Bank of England, Threadneedle Street, London, EC2R 8AH, England.

BLUYSSEN, Most Rev. Johannes Wilhelmus Maria; Netherlands ecclesiastic; b. 10 April 1926, Nijmegen; ed. St. Michielsgestel and Haaren Episcopal Seminaries; Curate, Veghel 1950–52; Vice-Prefect Seminary St. Michielsgestel 1952–54; studied in Rome 1954–57; Spiritual Dir. Seminary St. Michielsgestel 1957–61; Joint Bishop of 's-Hertogenbosch 1961–66, Bishop 1966–86. *Address:* Parade 11, 's-Hertogenbosch, Netherlands. *Telephone:* 073-125488.

BLY, Robert, M.A.; American writer and poet; b. 23 Dec. 1926, Madison, Minn.; s. of Jacob Thomas Bly and Alice (Aws) Bly; m. 1st Carolyn McLean 1955 (divorced 1979), 2nd Ruth Counsell 1980; five c.; ed. Harvard Univ. and Univ. of Iowa; served U.S. Navy 1944–46; first book, Silence in the Snowy Fields, publ. 1962; f. The Fifties 1958, later The Sixties and Seventies Press; f. American Writers Against the Vietnam War 1966; Fulbright Award 1956–57; Amy Lowell Fellow 1964–65; Guggenheim Fellow 1965–66; Rockefeller Foundation Fellow 1967; Nat. Book Award in Poetry 1968. *Publications:* (poems) Silence in the Snowy Fields 1962, The Light Around the Body 1967, This Tree Will Be Here for a Thousand Years 1979, Sleepers Joining Hands 1973, Jumping out of Bed 1973, Old Man Rubbing his Eyes 1975, The Man in the Black Coat 1982, Loving a Woman in Two Worlds 1985, Selected Poems 1986; (prose poems) The Morning Glory 1973, This Body is Made of Camphor and Gopherwood 1977; (criticism) Leaping Poetry 1975; Ed. Forty Poems Touching on Recent American History 1967, A Poetry Reading Against the Vietnam War 1966 and The Sea and the Honeycomb 1966; trans. of vols. of poetry from Swedish, Norwegian, German, Spanish and Hindi. *Address:* 308 First Street, Moose Lake, Minn. 55767, U.S.A.

BLYTH, Sir James, Kt., M.A.; British business executive; b. 8 May 1940; s. of Daniel Blyth and Jane Power Carlton; m. Pamela Anne Campbell Dixon 1967; one d. (one s. deceased); ed. Spiers School, Glasgow Univ.; Mobil Oil Co. 1963–69; Gen. Foods Ltd. 1969–71; Mars Ltd. 1971–74; Dir.

and Gen. Man. Lucas Batteries Ltd. 1974–77, Lucas Aerospace Ltd. 1977–81; Dir. Joseph Lucas Ltd. 1977–81; Head of Defence Sales, Ministry of Defence 1981–85; Man. Dir. Plessey Electronic Systems 1985–86; Man.-Dir. Plessey Co. PLC 1986–87; C.E.O. Boots Co. PLC Oct. 1987–; Non-Exec. Dir. Imperial Group PLC 1984–86, Cadbury-Schweppes PLC 1986–; mem. Council, Dir. of British Aerospace Cos. 1977–81, 1986–. *Leisure interests:* skiing, tennis, paintings, theatre. *Address:* Boots Co. PLC, Nottingham, NG2 3AA, England.

BO, Hideo; Japanese politician; b. 1905; began career as journalist; elected 10 times to House of Reps. for constituency in Wakayama Prefecture; assoc. of Takeo Fukuda (q.v.) since early 1960s; fmr. Parl. Vice-Minister of Health; fmr. Chair. Research Comm. on Tax System, Liberal-Democratic Party (LDP); various posts in admin. of late Eisaku Sato 1964–72, incl. Minister of Health, also Vice-Chair. Policy Research Council of LDP; Minister of Finance 1976–77; Gov. IMF March-Nov. 1977. *Leisure interest:* karate. *Address:* c/o Ministry of Finance, 1-1, Kasumigaseki 3-chome, Chiyoda-ku, Tokyo, Japan.

BO, Jørgen; Danish architect; b. 8 April 1919, Copenhagen; s. of Alf and Anne Marie Bo; m. Gerda Bennike 1941 (divorced 1966); two s. two d.; ed. Royal Danish Acad. of Fine Arts; own firm since 1943; tech. consultant for Soc. for Preservation of Natural Amenities of Denmark 1944–52; mem. Danish Nature Conservancy Bd. 1952–61; mem. Charlottenborg Adjudicating Bd. 1958–61; mem. Slotsholm Cttee. 1961–63; mem. San Cataldo Council, Italy 1966; Fellow, Royal Danish Acad. in Rome 1968–70; consultant planner for Danish Nat. Museum; mem. of various int. juries; Fellow, Royal Danish Acad. of Fine Arts, Prof. 1960–; Kt. of the Dannebrog. *Works include:* domestic housing 1945–58, the Louisiana Museum 1956–58, Educ. Centre, Monastir, Tunisia 1960, Museum of Music History 1965, IBM HQ in Denmark 1968–73, Danish Embassy in Brasília 1968–73, IBM Int. Educ. Centre, Belgium 1969–75, Ny Carlsberg Glyptotek 1971–78, restoration work for Carlsberg Foundation and Royal Danish Acad. 1973–76, Extension of Louisiana Museum, Art Museum, Bochum, and offices and housing in Baghdad 1978–83, Lübcke Museum, Hamm, Fed. Repub. of Germany 1984–, Weisbord Pavilion, Israel Museum, Jerusalem 1987–88, 20th Century Art Pavilion, Israel Museum 1988. *Address:* Løvstræde 8, DK-1152 Copenhagen K (Office); Lindevangs vej 22, DK-3460 Birteroed, Denmark (Home). *Telephone:* (01) 145070 (Office); (02) 821813 (Home).

BO YIBO; Chinese government official; b. 1908, Dinxian Co.; m. Hu Ming (died 1966); five s. two d.; ed. Taiyuan Normal School and Beijing Univ.; joined Chinese CP about 1927; arrested for subversive activities 1932; organized Sacrifice for Nat. Salvation League in Taiyuan 1937; during Sino-Japanese War was Chair. S.E. Admin. Office of Shanxi Govt., Commdr. Taiyuan Mil. Area and Special Commissar in 3rd Admin. Commissar's Office 1937–45; mem. Cen. Cttee. of CP 1945–67; Chair. Shanxi-Hebei-Shandong-Henan Border Region Govt. 1945–47, also reportedly Vice-Chair. Revolutionary Mil. and Political Acad. for Korean Cadres, Yenan; Deputy Political Commissar Cen. China PLA, Commdr. 8th Column 1947–48; Political Commissar N. China Mil. Area, First Vice-Pres. N. China People's Govt., Chair. N.E. Finance and Econ. Cttee. and mem. CPN China Bureau 1948; mem. Preparatory Cttee. for CPPCC 1949; mem. Govt. Admin. Council, Vice-Chair. Cttee. of Finance and Econs., and Minister of Finance 1949–53; Political Commissar Suiyuan Mil. Area 1949; mem. Bd. All-China Fed. of Co-operatives 1950; Chair. Govt. Econ. Investigation Cttee. (led anti-corruption drive) 1951; mem. State Planning Comm. 1952–67, Deputy Chair. 1962–67; mem. Constitution Drafting Cttee. 1953; mem. NPC 1954–67, May 1979–; Chair. State Construction Comm. 1954–56; Head of Third Office, State Council 1955–59; Vice-Chair. Planning Comm. for Scientific Devt. 1956–67; Chair. State Econ. Comm. 1958–67; Alt. Mem. Politburo of CP 1958–69; Vice-Premier 1958–67, June 1979–; Deputy Dir. State Office of Industry and Communications 1959–61, Dir. 1961–67; criticized during Cultural Revolution 1966; arrested 1967; rehabilitated 1979; Vice-Premier, State Council 1979–82; Minister in Charge of State Machine Building Comm. 1979–82; mem. 11th Cen. Cttee. CCP 1979–82; Vice-Chair. Cen. Advisory Comm., CCP 1982–; State Councillor, State Council 1982–83; Vice-Minister, State Comm. for Restructuring Econ. System 1982–83; mem. Party Cttee. of Special Orgs. 1983–; Vice-Chair. Cen. Party Consolidation Comm. 1983–; Hon. Pres., Finance Soc., Acad. of Social Sciences 1980–; Hon. Chair. China Council for Promotion of Int. Trade 1984–; Hon. Chair. Bd. of Dirs. China Nat. Tech. Import Corpn. 1984–; Hon. Pres. Beijing Garment Assen. 1984–; Hon. Chair. All-China Fed. of Handicraft Cooperatives 1986–. *Address:* c/o The State Council, Beijing, People's Republic of China.

BOARDMAN, Baron (Life Peer), cr. 1980, of Welford in the county of Northamptonshire; **Thomas Gray Boardman,** M.C., T.D., D.L.; British lawyer and company director; b. 12 Jan. 1919, Staverton Hall, Northants; s. of John Clayton and Janet Boardman; m. Norah Mary Deirdre Chaworth-Musters (née Gough) 1948; two s. one d.; ed. Bromsgrove School; served Northamptonshire Yeomanry 1939–45, later Commdr.; qualified solicitor 1947; Conservative M.P. for Leicester South West, later for Leicester South 1967–74; Minister for Industry 1972–74; Chief Sec. to the Treasury Jan.-March 1974; Pres. Assen. of British Chambers of Commerce 1977–80; Chair. Steetley PLC 1978–83; Dir. Nat. Westminster Bank (Chair. 1983–89); Dir. MEPC PLC 1980–, Pritchard Services Group 1982–83; High Sheriff

of Northants. 1979–80; Hon. Jt. Treas. Conservative Party 1980–82. *Leisure interests:* riding, fox hunting. *Address:* 41 Lothbury, London, EC2P 2BP (Office); 29 Tufton Court, Tufton Street, London, SW1P 3QH; The Manor House, Welford Northamptonshire, England (Home). *Telephone:* 01-726 1000 (Office); 01-222 6793 (London); Welford 235 (Home).

BOARDMAN, Norman Keith, PH.D., SC.D., F.A.A., F.R.S.; Australian biochemist; b. 16 Aug. 1926, Geelong, Vic.; s. of William R. and Margaret Boardman; m. Mary C. Sheperd 1952; two s. five d.; ed. Melbourne Univ. and St. John's Coll., Cambridge; Research Officer, Wool Research Section, CSIRO 1949–51; Sr. Research Scientist, Div. of Plant Industry, CSIRO 1956–61, Prin. Research Scientist 1961–64; Fulbright Scholar, Univ. of Calif., Los Angeles 1964–65; Sr. Prin. Research Scientist, Div. of Plant Industry, CSIRO 1966–68, Chief Research Scientist 1968–77, mem. of Exec., CSIRO 1977–85, Chair. and Chief Exec. 1985–86, C.E.O. 1986–; Lemberg Medal, Australian Biochem. Soc. 1969; David Syme Research Prize, Melbourne Univ. 1967; mem. Australian Nat. Univ. Council, Australian Research Grants Cttee., Australian Centre for Int. Agric. Research (ACIAR). *Publications:* scientific papers on plant biochemistry, particularly photosynthesis and structure, function and biogenesis of chloroplasts. *Leisure interests:* listening to music, fishing, reading, tennis. *Address:* Commonwealth Scientific and Industrial Research Organisation, P.O.B. 225, Dickson, A.C.T. 2602 (Office); 6 Somers Crescent, Forrest, A.C.T. 2603, Australia. *Telephone:* (062) 951746 (Home); 951746 (Office).

BOATEN, Frank Edmund; Ghanaian diplomatist; b. 17 Dec. 1923; s. of late Hanson Edmund Acheampong and of Madam Christiana Tumtuo; m. Christina Esther (Amoo-Gottfried) 1955; ed. Univ. Coll. of the Gold Coast and Univ. of London; First Sec., Ghana High Comm., New Delhi 1957–59; Counsellor, Ghanaian Embassy, Moscow 1960; Dir. Eastern European Div. and later Dir. of Admin., Accra 1960–62; Sec.-Gen. Accra Assembly 1962–66; Del. numerous confs. Australia, Finland, Sweden, Switzerland, U.S.S.R., U.K. and U.S.A.; Prin. Sec. Ministry of Foreign Affairs 1966–71; mem. Ghana Constitutional Assembly 1969; Visiting Fellow, Queen Elizabeth House and Senior Assoc. mem. St. Antony's Coll., Oxford 1971–72; Perm. Rep. to UN. 1972–78, concurrently Amb. to Cuba, Jamaica, Trinidad and Tobago and Suriname 1974–78; Amb. to Denmark 1979; Vice-Pres. UN Gen. Assembly 1974–79; Chair. UN Financial Emergency Cttee. 1976–79, First Cttee. for the 32nd Session of the UN Gen. Assembly 1977; fmrly. Assoc. mem. Royal Inst. of Int. Affairs, Inst. of Commonwealth Studies; Companion of the Order of the Volta. *Leisure interests:* coin collecting, tennis. *Address:* c/o Ministry of Foreign Affairs, Accra, Ghana.

BOATENG, Ernest Amano, M.A., M.LITT.; Ghanaian geographer, educationalist and environmentalist; b. 30 Nov. 1920, Aburi; s. of the late Rev. C. R. Boateng and Adelaide Boateng; m. Evelyn Kensema Danso 1955; four d.; ed. Achimota Coll. and St. Peter's Hall, Oxford; lecturer in Geography, Univ. Coll. of Ghana 1950–57, Sr. lecturer 1958–61, Prof. and Head of Dept. 1961–69, Dean, Faculty of Social Studies 1962–69; Principal, Univ. Coll. of Cape Coast 1969–71, Vice-Chancellor, Univ. of Cape Coast 1972–73; Exec. Chair. Environmental Protection Council of Ghana 1973–81; Environmental consultant 1981–; Chair. West African Examinations Council 1977–85; Smuts Visiting Fellow, Univ. of Cambridge 1965–66, Visiting Prof., Univ. of Pittsburgh 1966; Fellow, Ghana Acad. of Arts and Sciences (Pres. 1973–77); Pres. Governing Council of UNEP 1979; Chair. Land Use Planning Cttee. of Ghana 1979; mem. Constituent Ass. 1978–79; mem. Pres. Task Force on Investments 1980; rep. of Ghana at many Int. confs. inc. 31st session of UN Gen. Assembly 1976; Sr. Consultant to UN Environment Programme 1981–; Fellow Royal Soc. of Arts, Royal Geographical Soc., Hon. mem. Ghana Inst. of Planners; Hon. D.Litt. (Legon) 1979; Henry Oliver Beckit Memorial Prize, Oxford 1949, Grand Medal (Ghana) 1968, Ghana Nat. Book Award 1978. *Publications:* A Geography of Ghana 1959, Independence and Nation Building in Africa 1973, A Political Geography of Africa 1978, African Unity: the Dream and the Reality 1978; articles on Ghana in Encyclopaedia Britannica 1961–, and other reference works; numerous articles in geographical journals. *Leisure interests:* gardening, photography, classical music, architecture, carpentry. *Address:* Environmental Consultancy Services, P.O. Box 84, Trade Fair Site, Accra; 3 Aviation Road, Airport Residential Area, Accra, Ghana. *Telephone:* 777875.

BOBBIO, Norberto, DR. JUR. ET PHIL.; Italian professor; b. 18 Oct. 1909, Turin; s. of Luigi and Rosa Caviglia; m. Valeria Cova 1943; three c.; ed. Univ. of Turin; Prof. of Legal Philosophy, Univs. of Camerino 1935–38, Siena 1938–40, Padua 1940–48 and Turin 1948–; Ordinary Fellow, Accad. dei Lincei. *Publications:* L'analogia nella logica del diritto 1938, Politica e cultura 1955, Italia civile 1964, Da Hobbes a Marx 1965, Giusnaturalismo e positivismo giuridico 1965, Saggi sulla scienza politica in Italia 1969, Una filosofia militante 1971, Dalla struttura alla funzione 1977, Quale socialismo? 1977. *Address:* Via Sacchi 66, Turin, Italy. *Telephone:* 59-70-56.

BOBKOV, Gen.-Col. Filipp Demisovich; Soviet intelligence official; b. 1925; ed. CPSU Cen. Cttee. Higher Party School; komsomol work 1942–; mem. CPSU 1944–; served in Soviet Army 1942–45; K.G.B. service 1945–; head of section and collegiate mem. of U.S.S.R. K.G.B. 1978–; Deputy Pres. of K.G.B. 1982–85, First Deputy Pres. 1985–; rank of Gen.-Col. 1984. *Address:* The Kremlin, Moscow, U.S.S.R.

BO-BOLIKO LOKONGA MONSE MIHOMO; Zairian trade unionist and politician; b. (as André Bo-Boliko) 15 Aug. 1934, Lobamiti, Bandundu; ed. Saint Raphael School, Léopoldville (now Kinshasa), and Ecole Sociale d'Heverlée-Louvain, Belgium; Perm. Regional Sec. and Nat. Admin. Sec. Confed. of Christian Trade Unions of the Congo 1959; Sec.-Gen. Union of Congolese Workers (UTC) 1960; on secondment to govt., mem. Coll. of Commrs. Gen., Asst. Commr. for Labour and Social Services 1960-61; elected Nat. Pres. UTC 1961; Pres. Trade Union Fed. of the Congo 1962, Nat. Council of Congolese Trade Unions 1967; Sec.-Gen. Nat. Union of Congolese Workers 1967-80 (from 1971 Nat. Union of Zairian Workers); mem. Senate 1965; mem. Political Bureau, Mouvement Populaire de la Révolution (MPR) 1968-, mem. Perm. Cttee. 1975-, Exec. Sec. 1980; People's Commr. and Pres. Nat. Ass. (now Nat. Legislative Council) 1970-79; First State Commr. 1979-80; mem. Constitutional Comm., Luluabourg (now Kananga) 1964; Admin., Nat. Inst. of Political Studies; Vice-Pres. Parliamentary Conf. of Assen. of the EEC and the African, Caribbean and Pacific Nations 1973; Pres. Zaire Nat. Group of the Inter-Parl. Union; Hon. mem. African Consultative Comm. for Labour, ILO; Grand cordon, Ordre National du Léopard, Grand croix, Légion d'honneur (Togo), Nat. Orders of Chad, Congo, Ivory Coast, Liberia, Mauritania, Romania, Senegal and Tunisia. Address: c/o Cabinet du Secrétaire Exécutif, Mouvement populaire de la révolution, B.P. 5808, Kinshasa, Zaire.

BOBOVIKOV, Ratmir Stepanovich; CAND. TECH. SC.; Soviet politician; b. 1927; ed. Leningrad Electrotech. Inst.; operator at electric power station 1944-52; mem. CPSU 1947-; engineer at inst. for study of electrophysical apparatus 1952-62; party work 1962-69; First Sec. of regional cttee., Leningrad 1969-72, Sec. 1972-78; Second Sec. of Leningrad CPSU Dist. Cttee. 1978-80, Pres. 1980-83; First Sec. of Vladimir Dist. Cttee. Dec. 1983-; mem. of CPSU Cen. Auditing Comm. 1976-; mem. of CPSU Cen. Cttee. 1981-; Deputy to U.S.S.R. Supreme Soviet. Address: The Kremlin, Moscow, U.S.S.R.

BOBROWSKI, Czesław; Polish economist; b. 17 Feb. 1904, Sarny, m.; ed. Warsaw Univ. and Ecole des Sciences Politiques, Paris; Dir. Econ. Dept. of Ministry of Agric. and Agricultural Reform 1935-39; took part in September 1939 campaign in Poland and campaign 1940 in France, helped organize assistance to Poles in France 1940-45; Pres. Cen. Planning Office and Vice-Chair. Econ. Cttee. of Council of Ministers 1945-48; Polish envoy in Sweden 1948-49; acting Vice-Chair. Econ. Council of Council of Ministers 1957-63; Prof. Warsaw Univ., Head Dept. of Planning and Econ. Policy, Dean Faculty of Econs. 1958-68; researcher Inst. of Political Sciences, Paris 1953, Centre Nat. de la Recherche Scientifique, Paris 1954-56; Dir. of studies Ecole Pratique des Hautes Etudes, Paris 1963; Prof. Associé Paris I Univ. 1969-71; lectured in Turin and Algiers; UN planning adviser in Algeria 1965-75; Chair. Main Council of Polish Econ. Soc. 1981-86; Chair. of Council of Experts of Prime Minister 1981; Chair. Consultative Econ. Council 1982-87; Hon. Chair. Polish Econ. Assen. 1985; mem. Consultative Council, attached to Chair. Council of State 1986-; deputy to Seym 1947-52; Dr. h.c. (Paris I Univ.) 1977, (Econ. Acad., Cracow) 1986; Order of Builders of People's Poland, Commdr.'s Cross with Star of Order of Polonia Restituta, Gold Cross of Merit with Swords, Commdr.'s Cross with Star and White Lion Order (Czechoslovakia). Publications: U źródeł planowania socjalistycznego 1956, Jugosławia socjalistyczna 1957, Essays on Economic Dynamics (co-author) 1965, Planowanie gospodarcze 1981, numerous articles on theory and methodology of planning and on current affairs. Leisure interests: travel, gardening, grandchildren. Address: ul. Śmiała 36 m.1, 01-523 Warsaw, Poland. Telephone: 39-22-01 (Home).

BOBYKIN, Leonid Fedorovich; Soviet government official; b. 1930; First Sec. Ordzhonikidze Regional Cttee. CPSU 1966-71; First Sec. Sverdlovsk City Cttee. CPSU 1971-77; Deputy of R.S.F.S.R. Supreme Soviet 1975-85; Second Sec. Sverdlovsk Dist. Cttee. CPSU 1977-83; Deputy Head, Dept. of Light Industry and Consumer Goods of Cen. Cttee., CPSU 1983-84, First Deputy Head 1984-86, Head 1986-; Cand. mem. Cen. Cttee. CPSU 1986-; Badge of Honour 1973. Address: The Kremlin, Moscow, U.S.S.R.

BOBYSHEV, Dmitri Vasilevich; Russian poet, essayist, literary critic; b. 1936, Maryupol; s. of Vasily Meshcheryakoy (adopted by Vasily Bobyshev); ed. Leningrad Tech. Inst.; emigrated for religious and political reasons to U.S.A. 1979. Poetry published in Soviet and émigré periodicals, including Vremya i my, Kontinent, Ziyaniya: Collected Verse and Poems 1979. Address: c/o Kontinent, A. Niemans, Buchvertrieb, Bauerstrasse 28, 8000 Munich, Federal Republic of Germany.

BOCHENSKI, Joseph, O.P., D.D., PH.D.; Swiss (b. Polish) philosopher; b. 30 Aug. 1902, Czuszów, Poland; s. of Adolph and Maria Dunin-Borkowska; ed. Univs. of Lwów and Poznań; lecturer, Angelicum, Rome 1934-36; Prof. 1937-40; Dozent Univ. of Cracow 1938; served Polish Army Great Britain 1940-44, Italy 1944-45; Extr. Prof. Univ. of Fribourg 1945-48, Prof. 1948-72, Dean Faculty of Arts 1950-52, Rector 1964-66, Vice-Rector 1966-68; Visiting Prof. Univ. of Notre Dame. Ind. 1955-56, Univ. of Pittsburgh 1958, Univ. of Calif. 1958-59, Univ. of Kansas 1960, Univ. of Salzburg 1976; Dir. East-European Study Centre, Fribourg 1958, Ost-Kolleg, Cologne 1962; Hon. LL.D. (Notre Dame) 1966, Hon. Ph.D. (Buenos Aires) 1977, Hon. D. Mathematics (Milan) 1981. Publications: De cognitione Exist. Dei 1936, Elementa logicae Graecae 1937, Nove lezioni di logica simbolica 1938, S. Thomae Aq. De modalibus 1940, La logique de Théophra-ste 1947, Petri Hispani Summulae Logicales 1947, Europäische Philosophie der Gegenwart 1947, On Analogy 1948, Précis de logique mathématique 1949, Diamat 1950, Ancient Formal Logic 1951, Die zeitgenössischen Denkmethoden 1954, Formale Logik 1956, Handbuch des Weltkommunismus (ed.) 1958, Wege zum philosophischen Denken 1960, Die dogmatischen Grundlagen der sowjetischen Philosophie 1960, Logic of Religion 1965, Was ist Autorität? 1974, Über d. Sinn des Lebens 1987, Sto Zabobonow 1987; ed. Studies in Soviet Thought, Sovietica. Leisure interest: flying. Address: 2 Square des Places, CH-1700 Fribourg, Switzerland. Telephone: 037-22-28-02.

BOCHET, Bernard Adrien Jacques; French diplomatist; b. 21 March 1926, Paris; m. Suon Sarin 1962; ed. Ecole Nat. de la France d'Outre-mer; overseas service 1946-55; Head of Econ. and Tech. Assistance Mission, Laos 1955-59; central admin. (econ. affairs) 1959-82; Amb. to Mexico 1982-86, to Algeria 1986-; Chevalier, Légion d'honneur; Ordre Nat. du Mérite. Address: French Embassy, 6 rue Larbi Alik, Algiers, Algeria.

BOCK, Edward John, M.S.; American chemicals executive; b. 1 Sept. 1916, Fort Dodge, Ia.; s. of Edward J. and Maude (Juday) Bock; m. Ruth Kunerth 1941; two s. two d.; ed. Iowa State Univ.; joined Monsanto Co. as an engineer 1941; Plant Man. Columbia, Tenn. 1948; Assoc. Dir. of Marketing, Inorganic Chemicals Div. 1956, Dir. of Marketing 1957, Asst. Gen. Man. 1958, Vice-Pres. 1960, Gen. Man. 1960, Vice-Pres. (Admin.), mem. Bd. of Dirs. and mem. Exec. Cttee. 1965; mem. Corporate Devt. Cttee. 1967; Pres. of Monsanto Co., Chair. Corporate Devt. Cttee. and Exec. Cttee. 1968-72; Dir. Internorth, Inc. of Omaha, Midcoast Aviation Inc., Harbour Group Ltd. 1976-84; Pres. and C.E.O. Cupples Co., St. Louis 1976-84; mem. Bd. of Govs., Iowa State Univ. Foundation; Anson Marston Eng. Award. Leisure interests: amateur radio, golf, hunting, boating. Address: 7 Huntleigh Woods, St. Louis, Mo. 63131, U.S.A.

BOCK, Fritz, LL.D.; Austrian politician; b. 1911; ed. Univ. of Vienna; joined Austrian People's Party 1945, Head of its section of Social Policy 1947; Gen. Counsellor Austrian Nat. Bank 1947-51; M.P. 1949-62; Sec. of State, Fed. Ministry of Commerce and Reconstruction 1952-55, Fed. Ministry of Finance 1955-56, Fed. Minister of Commerce and Reconstruction 1956-66; Vice-Chancellor and Minister of Commerce, Trade and Industry 1966-68; Chair. Supervisory Bd. of Creditanstalt-Bankverein; numerous decorations. Address: c/o Creditanstalt-Bankverein, Schottengasse 6, A-1010 Vienna, Austria.

BOCK, Jerry (Jerrold Lewis); American composer; b. 23 Nov. 1928, New Haven; s. of George and Rebecca (Alpert) Bock; m. Patricia Faggen 1950; one s. one d.; ed. Univ. of Wisconsin; wrote scores for high school and coll. musicals; author of sketches for television 1951-54; composed songs for film Wonders of Manhattan 1956; composed music for show Mr. Wonderful 1956, and with Sheldon Harnick (q.v.) The Body Beautiful 1958, Fiorello 1959 (Pulitzer Prize, Antoinette Perry (Tony) Awards), Tenderloin 1960, She Loves Me 1963, Fiddler on the Roof 1964, The Apple Tree 1966, The Rothschilds 1970; mem. Wilderness Soc., Horticultural Soc., New York, Broadcast Music Inc., American Civil Liberties Union. Address: 145 Wellington Avenue, New Rochelle, N.Y. 10804, U.S.A. (Home).

BOD'A, Koloman, DR.SC.; Czechoslovak doctor of veterinary medicine and politician; b. 4 April 1927, Horná Strehová; s. of Koloman Bod'a and Jolana Jankovská; m. 1951; one s. one d.; ed. Coll. of Veterinary Medicine, Brno; Asst. Faculty of Veterinary Medicine, Agricultural Coll., Košice 1951-63; Postgraduate studies, Moscow Veterinary Acad. 1955-58; Asst. Prof. Agricultural Coll., Košice 1959-62, Prof. 1962, Vice-Dean 1958-60, Pro-Rector 1960-63; Commr. of Slovak Nat. Council for Agric. and Food 1963-68; Minister, Chair. of Fed. Cttee. for Agric. and Food 1969-70; Alt. mem. Cen. Cttee. CP of Slovakia 1958-62, 1966-69, mem. 1967-71; Alt. mem. Cent. Cttee. CP of Czechoslovakia 1962-66, mem. 1966-71; mem. Presidium Slovak Nat. Council 1963-68, Deputy 1966-71; Alt. mem. Presidium of Cen. Cttee. CP of Slovakia 1966-68, mem. 1968-69; Deputy to House of Nations, Fed. Assembly 1968-71; mem. Econ. Council of Fed. Govt. 1969-70; mem. Int. Austronautic Acad. 1987; Corresp. mem. Czechoslovak Acad. of Sciences 1965-, mem. 1988-, Slovak Acad. of Sciences 1966-80, mem. Slovak Acad. of Sciences 1980-; Chair. Czechoslovak Agricultural Acad. 1969-74; Dir. of Research Inst. of the Physiology of Farm Animals, Slovak Acad. of Sciences 1972-; Dr. h.c. (Humboldt Univ.) 1981; Distinction for Merit in Construction 1962, Klement Gottwald State Prize 1967, Silver Plaque of Czechoslovak Agric. Acad. 1977, Hon. Golden Medal, Slovak Acad. of Sciences 1977, J. G. Mendel Hon. Golden Plaque of the Czechoslovak Acad. of Sciences for Merits in Biological Sciences 1982, Order of Labour 1987, Silver Plaque for Devt. and Mankind 1987 (Czechoslovak Acad. of Sciences). Address: Institute of the Physiology of Farm Animals, Slovak Academy of Sciences, 040 00 Košce, Dukelskych Hrdinov 1/B, Czechoslovakia.

BODELUN, Rogelio, DR. ING.; Spanish business executive; b. 21 Sept. 1936, Ponferrada; ed. Escuela Tecnica Superior Ingenieros Industriales, Madrid; mem. Bd. of Dirs. Sefanitro 1973-77; Commercial Dir. HIDRONITRU 1977-83; Gen. Dir. ENSIDESA 1983-88; Asst. Dir. Instituto Nacional de Industria (INI) Aug. 1988-. Publications: numerous articles in newspapers. Leisure interests: golf, dominoes. Address: Paseo Habana 26-6-12, 28036 Madrid, Spain. Telephone: 261 45 86.

BODEN, Margaret Ann, M.A., PH.D., F.B.A.; British professor of philosophy and psychology; b. 26 Nov. 1936, London; d. of Leonard F. Boden and Violet D. (Dawson) Boden; m. John R. Spiers 1967 (divorced 1981); one s. one d.; ed. Newnham Coll., Cambridge and Harvard Grad. School (Harkness Fellow); lecturer in Philosophy, Univ. of Birmingham 1959-65; lecturer, then Reader in Philosophy and Psychology, Univ. of Sussex 1965-80, Prof. 1980-, Founding Dean School of Cognitive Sciences 1987; co-founder, Harvester Press Ltd. 1970, Dir. 1970-85. *Publications:* Purposive Explanation in Psychology 1972, Artificial Intelligence and Natural Man 1977, Piaget 1979, Minds and Mechanisms 1981, Computer Models of Mind 1988. *Leisure interests:* dressmaking, travelling. *Address:* c/o School of Cognitive Sciences, University of Sussex, Brighton, BN1 9QN, England.

BODIAN, David, PH.D., M.D.; American medical scientist and professor of anatomy; b. 15 May 1910, St. Louis, Mo.; s. of Harry Bodian and Tillie Franzel; m. Elinor Widmont 1944; two s. three d.; ed. Univs. of Chicago, Michigan and Johns Hopkins Univ.; Asst. in Anatomy, Univ. of Chicago 1935-38; Research Fellow, Univ. of Michigan 1938, Johns Hopkins Univ. 1939-40; Asst. Prof. of Anatomy, Western Reserve Univ. 1941-42; Asst. Prof of Epidemiology, Johns Hopkins Univ. 1942-46, Assoc. Prof. 1946-57, Prof. of Anatomy and Dir. Dept. of Anatomy 1957-75, Prof. Neurobiology, Dept. Otolaryngology 1975-85, Emer. Prof. 1985-; mem. Bd. Scientific advisers Nat. Inst. of Neurological Diseases 1968-73; mem. N.A.S., American Acad. of Arts and Sciences, American Asscn. of Anatomists (Pres. 1971-72), American Soc. of Cell Biology, American Philosophical Soc., Soc. for Neuroscience, A.A.A.S.; Hon. mem. Soc. Française de Neurologie, Paris, Anatomical Soc. of G.B. and Ireland; Lashley Prize, American Philosophical Soc. 1985; E. Mead Johnson Award 1941, Distinguished Service Award, Univ. of Chicago Alumni 1955, U.S. Public Health Service Award 1956, Poliomyelitis Hall of Fame, Georgia Warm Springs 1957. *Publications:* Neural Mechanisms in Poliomyelitis (with H. A. Howe) 1942; numerous articles on neurobiology, poliomyelitis and experimental neurology in scientific journals 1936-84. *Leisure interests:* gardening, reading, music, tennis, chess. *Address:* School of Medicine, Johns Hopkins University, 720 Rutland Avenue, Baltimore, Md. 21205 (Office); 4100 Charles Street, Baltimore, Md. 21218, U.S.A. (Home). *Telephone:* 301-955-3877.

BODMER, Sir Walter Fred, Kt., PH.D., F.R.C.PATH., F.R.S.; British research scientist; b. 10 Jan. 1936, Frankfurt-am-Main, Germany; s. of Ernest J. and Sylvia E. Bodmer; m. Julia G. Pilkington 1956; two s. one d.; ed. Manchester Grammar School and Univ. of Cambridge; Research Fellow, Clare Coll., Cambridge 1958-60, Fellow 1961-; Demonstrator, Dept. of Genetics, Univ. of Cambridge 1960-61; Fellow, Visiting Asst. Prof., Dept. of Genetics, Stanford Univ. 1961-62, Asst. Prof. 1962-66, Assoc. Prof. 1966-68, Prof. 1968-70; Prof. of Genetics, Univ. of Oxford 1970-79; Dir. of Research, Imperial Cancer Research Fund, London 1979-; Vice-Pres. Royal Inst. 1981-82; Pres. Royal Statistical Soc. 1984-85; Pres. British Asscn. for Advancement of Science 1987-88; mem. Advisory Bd. for the Research Councils 1983-88; Chair. BBC Science Consultative Group 1981-87; mem. BBC Gen. Advisory Council; Pres. Asscn. for Science Ed. 1989; Chair. Bd. of Trustees, British Museum (Natural History) 1989-; Foreign Hon. mem. American Acad. of Arts and Sciences, American Asscn. of Immunologists; Foreign Assoc. N.A.S.; Hon. Fellow, Keble Coll., Oxford; Foreign mem. Acad. of Sciences 1988-; Hon. F.R.C.P.; Hon. F.R.C.S., Hon. M.D. Bologna; Hon. D.Sc. (Bath), (Oxford); William Allan Memorial Award (American Soc. of Human Genetics) 1980, Conway Evans Prize (Royal Coll. of Physicians/Royal Soc.) 1982, Rabbi Shai Shacknai Memorial Prize Lectureship in Immunology and Cancer Research 1983, John Alexander Memorial Prize and Lectureship (Univ. of Pa. Medical School) 1984, Rose Payne Distinguished Scientist Lectureship 1985, Ellison Cliffe Lecture and Medal 1987. *Publications:* co-author, The Genetics of Human Populations 1971, Our Future Inheritance—Choice or Chance? 1974, Genetics, Evolution and Man 1976; papers in scientific and medical journals. *Leisure interests:* playing piano, riding, swimming. *Address:* Imperial Cancer Research Fund, P.O. Box 123, Lincoln's Inn Fields, London, WC2A 3PX, England. *Telephone:* 01-242 0200.

BODSON, Victor Hubert Joseph, LL.D.; Luxembourg barrister; b. 24 March 1902, Luxembourg; s. of Leon Bodson and Therese Kimmes; m. Aline Krancher 1952; two s. three d.; ed. Athénée de Luxembourg and Univs. of Strasbourg, Algiers and Montpellier; mem. Luxembourg Socialist Labour Party 1930; mem. Communal Council 1934-40; Minister of Justice, Transport and Public Works 1940-47, 1951-59; mem. Chamber of Deputies 1934-61, Vice-Pres. 1937-40, 1948-51, 1959-61, Pres. 1964-67, Hon. Pres. 1967-; Councillor of State 1961-64, Hon. Councillor of State 1964-; Pres. Int. Asscn. of French-language Parliamentarians 1967-72, Hon. Pres. 1979-; mem. Comm. of European Communities 1967-70; mem. for Luxembourg (Socialist) of Action Cttee. for United States of Europe 1959-67; numerous foreign decorations. *Leisure interests:* hunting, travel, archaeology, history. *Address:* 23 rue Aldringan (Office); Villa Malpaartes, Mondorf-les-Bains, Grand Duchy of Luxembourg (Home). *Telephone:* 42155 (Office); 68915 (Home).

BODSTRÖM, Lennart, PH.D.: Swedish politician; b. 1928, Gothenburg; ed. Gothenburg and Uppsala Univs.; lecturer Political Science Dept., Uppsala Univ. 1961-63; mem. Research staff Swedish Cen. Org. of Salaried Employees 1964, Deputy Gen. Man. 1966-70, Chair. 1970; mem. Econ. Planning Council 1970; Vice-Chair. Bd. Cen. Fed. of People and Defence 1970-82; mem. Consultative Cttee. EFTA 1970-82; mem. Bd. Council of Nordic Trade Unions 1973-82; mem. Trade Union Advisory Cttee. OECD 1970, Chair. 1980-82; mem. Bd. Int. Confed. of Free Trade Unions 1981-82; Minister of Foreign Affairs 1982-85, of Educ. and Cultural Affairs Oct. 1985-; Chair. Nat. Union of Students 1959; mem. Directorate Nat. Bd. of Univs. and Colls. 1969-74; mem. Swedish Labour Market Bd. 1970-82. *Address:* Ministry of Education and Cultural Affairs, S-103 33 Stockholm, Sweden.

BODYUL, Ivan Ivanovich, D.PHIL.SCI.; Soviet politician; b. 3 Jan. 1918; ed. Moscow Mil. Veterinary Acad. and Higher Party School, Central Cttee. of CPSU; Veterinary Surgeon, Soviet Army 1938-46; Asst. Chief. Agricultural Group, Moldavian Council of Ministers 1946-48; Govt. Controller of State Farms, Moldavian S.S.R. 1948-51; econ. work 1952-54; party work 1951-52, 1954-56; Apparatus of Cen. Cttee. of CPSU 1958-59; Second Sec. CP of Moldavian S.S.R. 1959-61, First Sec. 1961-80; Vice-Chair. Comm. on Foreign Affairs of Soviet 1980-; a Vice-Chair. U.S.S.R. Council of Ministers 1980-85; mem. Cen. Cttee. of CPSU 1981-; Deputy to Supreme Soviet of U.S.S.R. 1965-, and Moldavian S.S.R. 1965-; Order of Lenin (three times), and other decorations. *Address:* c/o Council of Ministers, The Kremlin, Moscow, U.S.S.R.

BOEHM, Gottfried Karl, DR.PHIL.; German art historian; b. 19 Sept. 1942, Braunau, Bohemia; s. of Karl and Olga Boehm; m. Margaret Hunold 1980; one d.; ed.; Univs. of Cologne, Vienna and Heidelberg; lecturer, History of Art, Ruhr Univ. Bochum 1975-79, Prof. 1977; Prof. of History of Art, Justus Liebig Univ., Giessen 1979-86, Univ. of Basel 1986-; Vice-Pres. Inst. für die Wissenschaften vom Menschen, Vienna 1981-. *Publications:* Studien zur Perspektivität, Philosophie und Kunst in der frühen Neuzeit 1969, Zur Dialektik der ästhetischen Grenze 1973, Philosophische Hermeneutik 1976, Die Hermeneutik und die Wissenschaften 1978, Bildnis und Individuum, Uber den Ursprung des Porträts in der italienischen Renaissance 1985 Cézanne, Montagne Sainte Victoire 1987, articles and contributions, etc. *Address:* Kunstgeschichtliches Seminar, St. Albangraben, CH-405A Basel (Office); Sevogelplatz 1, CH-4052 Basel, Switzerland (Home). *Telephone:* 061-233595 (Office); 061-416241 (Home).

BOEHMER, Gerhard Walter, D.JUR.; German diplomatist and civil servant; b. 24 Nov. 1935, Tilsit; s. of Walter Boehmer and Elsa Boehmer; m. Renate Walther 1961; three s.; ed. Univs. of Heidelberg and Munich; Research Fellow Max-Planck Inst. of Int. Law, Heidelberg 1961-65; Deputy Chief, Europe and Middle East Div., Fed. Ministry for Econ. Cooperation, Bonn 1965-67; Del. to Devt. Assistance Cttee., Perm. Mission to OECD 1967-68; Attaché, Embassy, Turkey 1969-73; Div. Chief to UN (Del. to UN Gen. Ass.) and Int. Devt. Bank, Fed. Ministry for Econ. Cooperation, Bonn 1974-85; Exec. Dir. IBRD 1985-. *Publication:* International Treaties in the German Legal System 1965. *Address:* 4431 Westover Place N.W., Washington, D.C. 20016, U.S.A.; Am Kottenforst 76, 5300 Bonn 1, Federal Republic of Germany. *Telephone:* (202) 244-1052 (Washington); (228) 25 26 86 (Bonn).

BOEKELHEIDE, Virgil Carl, PH.D.; American professor of chemistry; b. 28 July 1919, S. Dakota; s. of Charles F. Boekelheide and Eleanor Toennies; m. Caroline A. Barrett 1945; two s. one d.; ed. Univ. of Minnesota; Instructor, Univ of Illinois 1943-46; Asst. Prof. Univ. of Rochester 1946-60; Prof. of Chem., Univ. of Oregon 1960-; mem. N.A.S. 1962-; Guggenheim Fellow 1953-54; Swiss American Foundation Fellow 1960; Roche Anniversary Fellow 1963-64; Welch Lecturer 1968; Fulbright Distinguished Prof., Yugoslavia 1972; Distinguished Scholar Exchange Program, People's Repub. of China 1981; mem. Bd. of Eds. Organic Reactions 1956-, Organic Syntheses 1956-64, Journal of American Chemical Society 1964-74; mem. Council for Int. Exchange of Scholars (Sr. Fulbright-Hayes Awards); Centenary Lecturer, Royal Soc. of G.B. 1983-; Alexander v. Humboldt Prize (Fed. Repub. of Germany) 1974-75; Coover Award 1981. *Publications:* over 200 original research papers. *Leisure interests:* tennis and music. *Address:* 2017 Elk Drive, Eugene, Ore. 97403, U.S.A.

BOEKER, Paul Harold, M.A.; American diplomatist; b. 2 May 1938, St. Louis, Missouri; s. of Victor W. Boeker and Marie D. Bernthal; m. Margaret Macon Campbell 1961; one s. two d.; ed. Dartmouth Coll., Princeton Univ. and Univ. of Michigan; Dir. Office of Devt. Finance Dept. of State 1969-71, Policy Planning Staff 1974, mem. Sec. of State's Policy Planning Council 1983-84; First Sec. U.S. Embassy, Bonn 1971-73; Deputy Asst. Sec. of State for Int. Finance and Devt. 1974-76; Sr. Deputy Asst. Sec. of State for Econs. and Business Affairs 1976-77; Amb. to Bolivia 1977-80; Dir. U.S. Foreign Service Inst. 1980-81; Amb. to Jordan 1984-87; Adviser U.S. Del. to UN Gen. Ass. 1987-; Arthur S. Fleming Award 1975; Presidential Distinguished Service Award 1985, 1987. *Leisure interests:* music, tennis and squash. *Address:* 3701 Blackthorn Court, Chevy Chase, Md. 20815, U.S.A.

BOENISCH, Peter H.; German journalist; b. 4 May 1927, Berlin; s. of Konstantin Boenisch and Eva Boenisch (née Premysler); m. Victoria von Schack 1959 (divorced); ed. Dr. Hugo Eckner Coll., Berlin Univ.; Political Ed. Die Neue Zeitung 1945-49; Ed. Tagespost 1949-52; Special Asst. to Pres. Nordwest-Deutsche-Rundfunk 1952-55; Ed. Kindler Publishing Co.

1955–59, Springer Publishing Corpn. (Berliner Illustrierte, Bild-Zeitung, Bild am Sonntag) 1959–81; Chair. Ed. Bd. Die Welt 1978–81; fmr. Vice-Chair. Axel Springer Group, responsible for planning and development; Chief Govt. Spokesman and Leader, Fed. Press and Information Office 1983–85; Man. Dir of Burda Magazines 1986–; Order of Merit (Fed. Repub. of Germany), Bayerischer Verdienstorden 1976, Order of Leopold II (Belgium) 1985. *Leisure interests:* golf, antiques. *Address:* c/o Burda Verlag, Postfach, 7600 Offenburg/Baden, Federal Republic of Germany.

BOERMA, Addeke Hendrik; Netherlands agricultural engineer; b. 3 April 1912, Anloo; m. Dinah Johnston 1953; ed. Agricultural Univ., Wageningen; Netherlands Farmers' Org. 1934–38; Adviser to Food Office, Ministry of Agric. 1938–41; Dir. Crop Marketing Bd. and of Dutch Purchasing Office for Agric. Produce 1941–44; Govt. Commr. for Food and Agric., liberated parts of Netherlands 1944–45; Acting Dir.-Gen. of Food 1945–46; Govt. Commr. for Foreign Agricultural Relations 1946–48; Regional Rep. for Europe, Food and Agric. Org. of the United Nations (FAO) 1948–51, Dir. Econs. Div. FAO 1951–58, Head of Program and Budgetary Service, FAO 1958–62, Asst. Dir.-Gen. FAO 1960–67, Exec. Dir. World Food Program, FAO 1962–67, Dir.-Gen. FAO 1968–76; Dr. h.c. (Netherlands, Belgium, Hungary, Italy, Greece, U.S.A., Canada); Commdr. Order of Lion (Netherlands) 1975, Order of Leopold II (Belgium) 1948, Officer Ordre du Mérite agricole (France) 1948, Cavaliere di Gran Croce (Italy) 1976, Waterler Peace Prize, Carnegie Foundation, The Hague 1976. *Leisure interests:* history, music. *Address:* Vienna, Austria.

BOESAK, Rev. Allan; South African clergyman; b. 23 Feb. 1946, Kakamas; s. of Andreas Boesak and Sarah Helena Boesak; m. Dorothy Rose Martin 1969; one s. three d.; prominent anti-apartheid campaigner; elected Pres. World Alliance of Reformed Churches, Geneva 1982; Pres. Assen. of Christian Students in S.A. 1984–; Pres. S.A. Council of Churches 1984–87; Hon. D.D. (Victoria) 1983, (Yale) 1984, (Interdenominational Theological Centre Atlanta) 1985; numerous awards; co-f. United Democratic Front 1983. *Publication:* A Call for an End to Unjust Rule 1986, If This is Treason, I am Guilty (Speeches) 1988. *Address:* World Alliance of Reformed Churches, 150 route de Ferney, 1211 Geneva 20, Switzerland.

BOESCHENSTEIN, William Wade; American glass executive; b. 7 Sept. 1925, Chicago, Ill.; s. of Harold and Elizabeth (Wade) Boeschenstein; m. Josephine Moll 1953; four s.; ed. Phillips Acad. and Yale Univ.; Owens-Corning Fiberglas Corpn., Detroit 1950–, Branch Man. 1955–59, Vice-Pres. (Central Region) 1959–61, Vice-Pres. (Sales Branch Operations) 1961–63, Vice-Pres. (Marketing) 1963–67, Exec. Vice-Pres. 1967–71, Pres. Aug. 1971–88, C.E.O. 1973–, Chair. 1981–. *Leisure interests:* golf, skiing, tennis. *Address:* Owens-Corning Fiberglas Corporation, Fiberglas Tower, Toledo, Ohio 43659 (Office); 3 Locust Street, Perrysburg, Ohio 43551, U.S.A. (Home). *Telephone:* 419-248-7300 (Office).

BOEYNANTS, Paul Van Den; Belgian politician; b. 22 May 1919; ed. Collège Saint-Michel; fmr. butcher; mem. Chamber of Reps. 1949–; Minister of Middle Classes 1958; Dir. 1958 Exhbn., Brussels; Chair. Social Christian Party 1961–68, 1979–81; Minister of State 1969; Prime Minister 1966–68, (acting) 1978–79; Deputy Prime Minister 1979–81; Minister of Defence 1972–79, of Brussels Affairs 1974–77; received three year suspended prison sentence for tax fraud and forgery 1986; kidnapped Jan. 1989, released Feb. 1989. *Address:* 41 rue des Deux Eglises, 1040, Brussels, Belgium.

BOFILL, Ricardo; Spanish architect; b. 5 Dec. 1939, Barcelona; s. of Emilio Bofill and Maria Levi; ed. Ecole Française, Barcelona, architectural studies in Geneva; two s.; founder mem. and leader Taller de Arquitectura (design team), Paris, Barcelona; works incl. Les Espaces d'Abraxas, Marne-la-Vallée, Les Echelles du Baroque, Paris, Antigone, Montpellier, Le Lac and Le Viaduc, Versailles, airports (Barcelona), theatres (Metz and Barcelona), offices, wine cellars and other residential bldgs.; exhbns. incl. Architectural Assocn., London Jan. 1981; Museum of Modern Art, New York June–Sept. 1985. *Address:* c/o 14 Avenue Industria, 08960 Saint Just Desvern, Barcelona, Spain; 18 rue de l'Université, 75007 Paris, France; 394 West Broadway, New York 10012, U.S.A. *Telephone:* (3) 3715950 (Spain); (1) 42964209 (France); (212) 431-5820 (U.S.A.).

BOGAERS, Petrus Clemens Wilhelmus Maria, DRS.ECON.; Netherlands trade unionist and politician; b. 2 July 1924, Cuyk a/d Maas; s. of Petrus P. M. J. Bogaers and Henrica Maria Hermans; m. 1st Femmigje Visscher 1950 (divorced 1980), 2nd Yvonne M. H. L. Bogaers 1981 (divorced 1986); four s. three d.; ed. Episcopal Coll. Grammar School, Roermond, and Tilburg School of Economics; Asst. to Prof. v.d. Brink 1947; Econ. Adviser to Roman Catholic Worker's Union 1948, Head Scientific Advisory Section 1957–63; mem. Socio-Economic Council 1954; mem. Econ. and Social Cttee. European Economic Communities 1958; mem. Second Chamber, Netherlands Parl. 1959; Minister of Housing and Building 1963–65; Minister of Housing and Physical Planning 1965–66; Pres. Gooiland Region 1968–74, Netherlands Asthma Foundation 1976–; mem. Supervisory Bds. various Dutch cos. 1976–; Commdr. Order of Orange-Nassau. *Leisure interests:* reading, tennis, open-air life. *Address:* Lingenskamp 25, 1251 Laren, North Holland, Netherlands. *Telephone:* 83148 (02153).

BOGARDE, Dirk (Van den Bogaerde, Derek Niven); British actor; b. 28 March 1921; ed. Allan Glen's School, Glasgow, Univ. Coll. School, London, and Chelsea Polytechnic; Army Service 1940–46; Chevalier de l'Ordre des Arts et des Lettres 1982; Hon. D.Litt. (St. Andrews Univ.) 1985; BAFA Acad. Award 1988. *Roles in plays include:* Cliff in Power without Glory 1947, Orpheus in Point of Departure 1950, Nicky in The Vortex 1953, Alberto in Summertime 1955–56, Jezebel 1958. *Films include:* Hunted, Appointment in London, They Who Dare, The Sleeping Tiger, Doctor in the House, Doctor at Sea, Doctor at Large, The Spanish Gardener, Cast a Dark Shadow, Ill Met by Moonlight, A Tale of Two Cities, The Wind Cannot Read, The Doctor's Dilemma, Libel, Song Without End, The Angel Wore Red, The Singer Not the Song, Victim, H.M.S. Defiant, Password is Courage, The Mind Benders, I Could Go on Singing, The Servant, Doctor in Distress, Hot Enough for June, High Bright Sun, King and Country, Darling ..., Modesty Blaise, Accident, Our Mother's House, Sebastian, Justine, The Fixer, Upon This Rock, The Damned, Death in Venice, The Serpent, The Night Porter, Permission to Kill, Providence, A Bridge Too Far, Despair; adapted for TV and starred in May We Borrow Your Husband 1986. *Publications:* A Postillion Struck by Lightning (autobiog.) 1977, Snakes and Ladders (autobiog.) 1978; A Gentle Occupation (novel) 1980, Voices in the Garden (novel) 1981, An Orderly Man (autobiog.) 1983, West of Sunset 1984, Backcloth (autobiog.) 1986, The Complete Autobiography 1988. *Address:* c/o London Management, 235 Regent Street, London W1, England.

BOGDANOV, Michael, M.A.; British theatre director; b. 15 Dec. 1938, London; s. of Francis Bogdin and Rhoda Rees; m. Patricia Ann Warwick 1966; two s. one d.; ed. Trinity Coll., Dublin, Munich Univ., Sorbonne; Producer/Dir. Radio Telefis Eireann 1966–68; Asst. Dir. R.S.C. 1969–71; Assoc. Dir. Tyneside Theatre Co. 1971–73; Dir. Phoenix Theatre, Leicester 1973–77; Dir. Young Vic Theatre 1978–80; Assoc. Dir. Nat. Theatre 1980–88, also Co. Dir.; founded (with Michael Pennington) English Shakespeare Co. 1986, Jt. Artistic Dir. 1986–; Intendant Deutsches Schauspielhaus, Hamburg Sept. 1989–; Assoc. Peter Brook's (q.v.) production of A Midsummer Night's Dream, R.S.C. 1971; Two Gentlemen of Verona, Teatro Escobar, São Paolo, Brazil, Rabelais (Jean-Louis Barrault) 1971; Dir. Gawain and the Green Knight, Hunchback of Notre Dame, Nat. Theatre 1977, The Taming of the Shrew, R.S.C., Hamlet, Stuttgart, and Düsseldorf 1978–79, Shadow of a Gunman, Knight of the Burning Pestle, R.S.C., The Seagull, Tokyo 1980; Dir. The Romans in Britain, Mayor of Zalamea, The Hypochondriac, A Spanish Tragedy, Uncle Vanya, all for Nat. Theatre; Hiawatha (Nat. Theatre Christmas production) 1980, 1981, 1982; Lorenzaccio, You Can't Take it With You, National Theatre 1983; Hamlet, Dublin Abbey Theatre 1983, Romeo and Juliet, Tokyo Imperial Theatre 1983; The Story of a Horse, Ancient Mariner, both for Nat. Theatre 1984; The Mayor of Zalamea, Washington 1984, Measure for Measure, Stratford, Ont. 1985, Mutiny, London 1985, Donnerstag Aus Licht, Covent Garden 1985, Romeo and Juliet, Royal Shakespeare Co. 1986, Julius Caesar, Hamburg 1986, Henry IV (parts I and II), Henry V, U.K., Europe, Canada, U.S.A. 1986–87, Reineke Fuchs, Hamburg 1987, The Wars of the Roses (7 play history cycle) 1987–89 Montag aus Licht, (Stockhausen) La Scala 1988; Dir. of Year, Soc. of West End Theatres, for the Taming of the Shrew 1979. *Television includes:* Channel 4 series Shakespeare Lives, also for Channel 4, Hiawatha. *Publications:* Hiawatha 1981, The Magic Drum 1983, Ancient Mariner. *Leisure interests:* cricket, reading, music. *Address:* c/o The National Theatre, South Bank, Waterloo, London, S.E.1, England. *Telephone:* 01-928 2033 (Office).

BOGDANOVICH, Peter; American film director, writer, producer and actor; b. 30 July 1939, Kingston, N.Y.; s. of Borislav and Herma (Robinson) Bogdanovich; m. 1st Polly Platt 1962 (dissolved 1970), two d.; m. 2nd Cybill Shepherd 1971 (dissolved 1978), 3rd Louise Hoogstratten 1989; Actor, American Shakespeare Festival, Stratford Conn. 1956, N.Y. Shakespeare Festival 1958; Dir. Producer off-Broadway plays, The Big Knife 1959, Camino Real, Ten Little Indians, Rocket to the Moon 1961, Once in a Lifetime 1964; film feature-writer for Esquire, New York Times, Village Voice, Cahiers du Cinéma, Los Angeles Times, New York Magazine, Vogue, Variety etc.; Owner Crescent Moon Productions Inc., Los Angeles 1986–; mem. Dirs. Guild of America, Writers' Guild of America, Acad. of Motion Picture Arts and Sciences; N.Y. Film Critics' Award (1971) and B.A.F.T.A. Award for Best Screenplay (The Last Picture Show) 1971, Writers' Guild of America Award for Best Screenplay (What's Up, Doc?) 1972, and other awards and prizes. *Films include:* The Wild Angels (2nd Unit Dir., co-wrote, acted in) 1966, Targets (directed, co-wrote, produced, acted in) 1968, The Last Picture Show (dir., co-wrote) 1971, Directed by John Ford (dir., wrote) 1971, What's Up Doc? (dir., co-wrote, prod.) 1972, Paper Moon (dir., prod.) 1973, Daisy Miller (dir., prod.) 1974, At Long Last Love (dir., wrote, prod.) 1975, Nickelodeon (dir., co-wrote) 1976, Saint Jack (dir., co-wrote, acted in) 1979, They All Laughed (dir., wrote) 1981, Mask (dir.) 1985, Illegally Yours (dir., prod.) 1988. Regular commentator for C.B.S. This Morning 1987–89. *Publications:* The Cinema of Orson Welles 1961, The Cinema of Howard Hawks 1962, The Cinema of Alfred Hitchcock 1963, John Ford 1968, Fritz Lang in America 1969, Allan Dwan, the Last Pioneer 1971, Pieces of Time, Peter Bogdanovich on the Movies 1961–85, The Killing of the Unicorn: Dorothy Stratten (1960–80) 1984. *Address:* c/o Camp and Peiffer, 2040 Avenue of the Stars, Century City, Calif. 90067, U.S.A.

BOGERS, Willem Adrianus Johannes; Netherlands business executive (retd.); b. 18 June 1922, Venlo; s. of Petrus A. Bogers and Wilhelmina A.

C. van Rijt; m. Willy J.Th.M. Coehorst 1951; one s. two d.; ed. Univ. of Econ. Science, Tilburg; with Univ. of Econ. Science; joined DSM 50, Man. Dir. 1966–73, Chair. 1973–84, Pres. Man. Bd. 1975–84; Chair. Supervisory Bd. DSM 1985–88; Commdr., Order of Orange-Nassau, Leopold II, St. Gregory the Great. *Leisure interests:* reading, walking, swimming. *Address:* Zandweg 22, Heerlen, Netherlands (Home).

BOGIANCKINO, Massimo, PH.D.; Italian opera director; b. 10 Nov. 1922, Rome; s. of Edoardo T. Bogianckino and Fiorangela Liberi; m. Judith Matthias 1950; ed. Conservatory of Music and Acad. Santa Cecilia, Rome and Univ. of Rome; fmr. musicologist and concert pianist; Dir. Enciclopedia dello Spettacolo 1957–62; Dir. Accademia Filarmonica, Rome 1960–63; Dir. Teatro dell' Opera, Rome 1963–68; Artistic Dir. Festival of Two Worlds, Spoleto 1968–71; Dir. of Concert Programs, Accad. Santa Cecilia, Rome 1970–71; Artistic Dir. La Scala, Milan 1971–74; Gen. Man. Teatro Comunale, Florence 1974–82; Admin. Gen. Paris Opera 1982–; Grosses Bundesverdienstkreuz (Fed. Repub. of Germany). *Publications:* L'arte clavicembalistica di D. Scarlatti 1956 (English version 1968), Aspetti del teatro musicale in Italia e in Francia nell' età Barocca 1968, Le canzonette e i madrigali di V. Cossa 1981. *Address:* Théatre National Opéra, Paris, France. *Telephone:* 266 50 22.

BOGNÁR, József; Hungarian politician and scholar; b. 5 Feb. 1917, Szombathely; s. of Gyula Bognár and Erzsébet Kutrovits; m. Ida Kutzián 1946; ed. in Budapest; studied literature and philosophy; taught in a grammar school; joined the "March Front" Resistance Movement during 1939–45 war; joined Smallholders Party, organizer and Sec. 1945; mem. Parl. 1945–; Minister of Information 1946; Mayor of Budapest 1947–48; Minister of Internal Trade 1948–53, of Internal and Foreign Trade 1953–54, of External Trade 1954–56; Prof. of Econs., Karl Marx Univ. of Econ. Science, Budapest 1957–; Chair. Hungarian World Alliance 1959–; Pres. Inst. for Cultural Relations 1961–69; Econ. Adviser to Ghanaian Govt. 1962; Vice-Pres. Presidium Patriotic People's Front 1965–; Chair. Cttee for Planning and Budget Hungarian Parl. 1966–88; Corresp. mem. Hungarian Acad. of Sciences 1966–73; Dir. Inst. for World Econs., Hungarian Acad. of Sciences 1966–87; Dir.-Gen. Hungarian Acad. of Sciences Engaged in Econs. 1988–; Pres. Hungarian Scientific Council for World Economy 1969–; mem. Hungarian Acad. of Sciences 1973–; mem. Club of Rome 1980–, Int. Prospects Acad., Geneva 1983–, Panel of Special Advisers, Int. Fed. of Insts. of Advanced Studies 1983–; mem. Advisory Council, UNITAR 1983–; mem. Council UN Univ. 1983–86; Vice-Pres. Hungarian Econ. Soc.; Ed.-in-Chief Studies on Developing Countries, Trends in World Economy; mem. Ed. Bd. The New Hungarian Quarterly, Mondes en developpement, Paris, Asian Journal of Econs., India, Hon. Ed. Advisory Bd. World Dev., Oxford; Fellow World Acad. of Art and Sciences (WAAS) 1982–; Hungarian State Prize 1970. *Publications include:* Planned Economy in Hungary: Achievements and Problems 1959, Kereslet és Keresletkutatás a Szocializmusban (Demand and Demand Analysis in Socialism) 1961, Economic Growth in the Developing Countries 1966, Economic Policy and Planning in Developing Countries 1968, Les nouveaux mécanismes de l'économie socialiste en Hongrie 1969, Világgazdasági Korszakváltás (Beginning of a New Era in the World Economy) 1976, End of Century Crossroads of Development and Co-operation 1980, and numerous articles. *Leisure interests:* reading memoirs and historical novels. *Address:* Scientific Council for World Economy, Budapest XII, Kálló esperes u. 15; Budapest II, Érmelléki-utca 1, Hungary. *Telephone:* 664-572; 155-206.

BOGNER, Willy; German business executive, film director and producer; b. 23 Jan. 1942, Munich; s. of Willy and Maria Bogner; m. Sonia Ribeiro 1973; ed. Altes Realgymnasium, Munich, and business and technical studies in Munich and Hohenstein; Man. Willy Bogner GmbH & Co. KG (sportswear co.), Willy Bogner Film GmbH, Munich; mem. German Nat. Olympic Cttee.; dir. of documentary, advertising, sports (esp. skiing) films, etc. and special cameraman for James Bond films 1960–; several times German ski champion and participated in Winter Olympics, Squaw Valley 1960, Innsbruck 1964, and World Ski Championships, Chamonix 1962, Portillo (Chile) 1966. *Films include:* Skivision 1974, 1975, 1979, Skifaszination, Ski Fantasie 1981, Crystal Dreams 1982, Fever und Eis 1986. *Leisure interests:* sport (tennis, skiing, diving), filming and photography. *Address:* Firma Willy Bogner GmbH & Co. KG, Sankt-Veit-Strasse 4, D-8000 Munich 80, Federal Republic of Germany. *Telephone:* (089) 41491.

BOGOLYUBOV, Klavdiy Mikhailovich; Soviet politician; b. 1909; ed. Leningrad Pedagogical Inst. mem. CPSU 1938–; Higher Party School of Cen. Cttee. CPSU 1944; teacher; served in Soviet Army 1939–41; party work in Vologda Dist. 1930–39, 1941–42; party work in apparatus of Cen. Cttee. CPSU 1944–63, 1965–; Deputy Chair. of U.S.S.R. State Comm. on Press 1963–65; First Deputy Head of Dept. of Cen. Cttee. CPSU 1968–; mem. U.S.S.R. Cen. Auditing Comm. 1971–81; Deputy to U.S.S.R. Supreme Soviet. *Address:* Central Committee of the Communist Party of the Soviet Union, Staraya pl.4, Moscow, U.S.S.R.

BOGOLYUBOV, Mikhail Nikolayevich; Soviet philologist; b. 24 Jan. 1918, Kiev; ed. Leningrad Univ.; Service in the Army 1941–45; lecturer and Researcher Leningrad Univ. 1944–60, Prof. 1959–, Dean Oriental Dept. 1960–; Corresp. mem. U.S.S.R. Acad. of Sciences 1966–. *Address:* Leningrad State Univ., Oriental Faculty, II Universitetskaya Naberezhnaya, Leningrad, U.S.S.R.

BOGOLYUBOV, Nikolay Nikolayevich; Soviet mathematician; b. 21 Aug. 1909, Gorky; Prof. Kiev and Moscow Univs. 1936–; mem. Ukrainian S.S.R. Acad. of Sciences 1948–; U.S.S.R. Acad. of Sciences 1953–, Academician-Sec. Dept. of Math. 1963–, mem. Presidium; Dir. Joint Inst. for Nuclear Research, Dubna 1965–; Deputy to U.S.S.R. Supreme Soviet 1966–; Foreign mem. Polish 1962–, German Dem. Repub. 1966–, Heidelberg 1968–, Bulgarian 1970– Acads. of Sciences, American Acad. of Sciences and Arts, Boston 1969–; Foreign Assoc. N.A.S. of U.S.A. 1969–; Foreign mem. Mongolian Acad. of Sciences 1983–; State Prize 1947, 1953, Lenin Prize 1958, Heineman Prize 1966, Hero of Socialist Labour 1969; Helmholz Gold Medal 1969, Max Planck Gold Medal 1973, Franklin Gold Medal 1974, Order of Lenin (five), Hammer and Sickle Gold Medal (twice), Order of the October Revolution. *Publications:* Introduction to Non-linear Mechanics 1937, On some Statistical Methods in Mathematical Physics 1945, Problems of a Dynamical Theory in Statistical Physics 1946, Problems of Statistical Mechanics of Quantum Systems 1949, Asymptotic Methods in the Theory of Non-linear Oscillations 1958, Problems of the Theory of Dispersion Relations 1958, A new Method in the Theory of Superconductivity 1958, Introduction to Axiomatic Quantum Field Theory 1969, Introduction to the Theory of Quantized Fields 1976. *Address:* Joint Institute for Nuclear Research, Dubna, P.O. Box 79, Moscow, U.S.S.R.

BOGOMOLOV, Aleksey Fedorovich; Soviet physicist; b. 2 June 1913, Sitskoe Village, Smolensk Region; ed. Moscow Power Inst.; Postgraduate, Research Assoc. Moscow Power Inst. 1937–41; Army Service 1941–45; mem. CPSU 1944; Asst. Prof. Head of Chair, Moscow Power Inst. 1945–; Doctor of Tech. Sciences, Prof. 1958–; Merited Scientist of R.S.F.S.R.; Corresp. mem. U.S.S.R. Acad. of Sciences 1966–; Hero of Socialist Labour 1957; Order of Lenin (three times); Hammer and Sickle Gold Medal. *Publications:* Works on radiophysics and radio engineering. *Address:* Moscow Power Institute, 14 Krasnokazarmennaya ulitsa, Moscow, U.S.S.R.

BOGOMOLOV, Oleg; Soviet economist; b. 20 Aug. 1927, Moscow; s. of T. I. Bogomolov and K. P. Zhelyabaeva; m. 1st Larisa Sokolova, one s. (died 1962); m. 2nd Inna Yermakova 1966 (divorced 1977); m. 3rd Tatyana Yarikova 1978; ed. Moscow Inst. of Foreign Trade; Ministry of Foreign Trade 1949–50; with CMEA 1954–56; Scientific Inst. for Economical Researches of State Cttee. for Planning 1956–62; mem. Cen. Cttee. of CPSU, Official 1962–69; Section Chief, Econ. Research Inst., State Planning Cttee. 1958–; lecturer, then Prof. Moscow Univ. 1967–77; Dir. Inst. of Econs. of the World Socialist System of Acad. of Sciences 1969–; mem. Exec. Cttee. Int. Econ. Assen. 1974–; Corresp. mem. U.S.S.R. Acad. of Sciences 1981; Dr. h.c. (Karl Marx Univ. of Econ., Budapest); decorations include Order of October Revolution, Order of Red Banner (twice). *Publications:* Teoria i metodologia mezhdunarodnogo sotsialisticheskogo razdelenia truda 1967, Economischeskaja effectivnost mezhdunazodnogo razdelenia truda 1967, Strany sotsialisma v mezhdunatodnom razdelenii truda 1980, Integration by Market Forces and through Planning Proceedings of the Fourth Congress of the IEA 1976, World Socialist Economy: Problems of Political Economy 1982, Socialism and Reconstruction of International Economic Relations 1982, Structural Changes: Economic Interdependence in World Economy of the Seventh Congress of the IEA 1983, Soglasovanie ekonomicheskei politiki Stran SEV 1986. *Leisure interests:* photography, music, tennis. *Address:* 117418, Novo-Cheremushkinskaya, 46, Moscow, U.S.S.R. *Telephone:* 120-82-00.

BOGOMOLOV, Sergey Aleksandrovich; Soviet diplomatist; b. 1926; mem. of diplomatic service 1948–; posts at embassies in U.S.A., France; Sec.-Gen. of U.S.S.R. Del. at Geneva Disarmament Conf., Amb. to Spain 1977–78; Chief Admin. for General Int. Problems, Ministry of Foreign Affairs 1978–. *Address:* Ministry of Foreign Affairs, Moscow, U.S.S.R.

BOGORAD, Lawrence, PH.D.; American biologist; b. 29 Aug. 1921, Tashkent, U.S.S.R.; s. of Boris and Florence (Bernard) Bogorad; m. Rosalyn G. Sagen 1943; one s. one d.; ed. Univ. of Chicago; Instructor, Dept. of Botany, Univ. of Chicago 1948–51, Asst. Prof. 1953–57, Assoc. Prof. 1957–61, Prof. 1961–67; Visiting Investigator, Rockefeller Inst. 1951–53; Prof. Dept. of Biology, Harvard Univ. 1967–, Maria Moors Cabot Prof. of Biology 1980–, Chair. Dept. of Biology 1974–76; Dir. Maria Moors Cabot Foundation, Harvard Univ. 1976–; mem. N.A.S., Chair. Botany Section 1974–77; mem. American Philosophical Soc.; Foreign mem. Royal Danish Acad. of Sciences and Letters; Fellow, American Acad. of Arts and Sciences; Pres. American Soc. of Plant Physiologists 1968; Pres. Soc. of Developmental Biology 1983–84; mem. Bd. of Dirs. A.A.A.S. 1982–86, Pres. 1986–87, Chair. Bd. of Dirs. 1987–88; Fulbright Fellowship 1960, Stephen Hales Award 1982 and other academic awards. *Publications:* various papers in scientific journals. *Address:* Harvard University, The Biological Laboratories, 16 Divinity Avenue, Cambridge, Mass. 02138, U.S.A. *Telephone:* 617-495-4292.

BOHAN, Marc; French couturier; b. 22 Aug. 1926; s. of Alfred Bohan and Geneviève Baudox; m. Huguette Rinjonneau (deceased); one d.; ed. Lycée Lakanal, Sceaux; Asst. with Piguet 1945, later with Molyneux and Patou; Dior organization, London 1958, later Paris; Artistic Dir. Soc. Christian Dior 1960–; Chevalier, Légion d'honneur, and l'ordre de Saint-Charles (Monaco). *Address:* 30 avenue Montaigne, 75008, Paris, (Office); 71 rue des Saints-Pères, 75006 Paris, France (Home).

BOHIGAS GUARDIOLA, Oriol; Spanish architect; b. 10 Dec. 1925, Barcelona; s. of Pere Bohigas and María Guardiola; m. Isabel Arnau 1957; five c.; founder-mem. of Grupo R 1951; partnership with Josep Martorell 1952; Special Technician in town-planning, Instituto de Estudios de Administración Local 1961; partnership with David Mackay 1963; lecturer, Escuela Técnica Superior de Arquitectura, Barcelona 1964–66, Prof. 1971–, Dir. 1977–80; Head of town-planning, Barcelona City Council 1980–84, Adviser to Mayor 1984–; mem. Accad. Nazionale di San Luca de Roma; prizes from Foment de les Arts Decoratives for best building in Barcelona 1959, 1962, 1966, 1976, 1979, Delta de Plata (industrial design) 1966; First Prize, Internationale Bauhausstellung Berlin 1980. *Publications include:* Barcelona entre el pla cerda i el barraquisme 1963, Arquitectura modernista 1968–1969, Les escoles tecniques superiors i l'estructura professional 1968, 1970, Contra una arquitectura adjetivada 1969, La arquitectura española de la Segunda República 1970, 1978, Polemica d'arquitectura catalana 1970, Reseña y catálogo de la arquitectura modernista 1972, Proceso y erótica del diseño 1972, 1979, Once arquitectos 1976, Catalunya. Arquitectura i urbanisme durant la republica 1978, Reconstrucció de Barcelona 1984. *Address:* calle Calvet, 71 Barcelona 21; calle Camp, 61 Barcelona 22, Spain. *Telephone:* 200 10 61; 211 14 00.

BOHMAN, (Bo) Gösta, B.L.; Swedish politician; b. 15 Jan. 1911, Stockholm; s. of Conrad Bohman and Berta Gabrielson; m. Gunnel Mossberg 1939; one s. four d.; ed. Univ. of Stockholm 1936; Officer in Reserve 1932–; Asst. Dir. Stockholm Builder's Assen. 1939–42; Sec. Stockholm Chamber of Commerce 1942–48, Deputy Man. Dir. 1948–70; mem. Riksdag (Parl.) 1958–; Pres. Moderata Samlingspartiet (Conservative Party) 1970–81; Minister of Econ. 1976–78, 1979–81; Kt. Commdr.'s Cross, Royal Order of Vasa, Kt. Commdr.'s Cross, Royal Order of Northern Star, Stella della Solidarità (Italy), Great Cross of the Order of the Lion (Finland). *Publications:* Tankar om mitt Sverige (Reflections on my Sweden) 1974, Så var det (The Way it Was) 1983, Maktskifte (Change in Power) 1984. *Leisure interests:* skiing, skating, hunting, fishing. *Address:* Villagatan 13B, 114 32 Stockholm, Sweden (Home).

BÖHME, Hans-Joachim; German politician and history teacher; b. 25 April 1931, Leipzig; m. Helga Böhme; one s. two d.; First Deputy Sec. Sozialistische Einheitspartei Deutschlands (SED) 1955–59, First Sec. SED party org. Karl Marx Univ., Leipzig 1959–66, Cand. mem. Cen. Cttee. SED 1971–73, mem. 1973–; Head of Student Section, Moscow Embassy 1966–68; State Sec. and First Deputy Minister 1968–70; Minister of Higher and Tech. Educ. 1970; Prof. at Humboldt Univ. 1970–; Vaterländischer Verdienstorden in Silver and other awards. *Address:* Ministerrat, Berlin, German Democratic Republic.

BOHR, Aage Niels, DR.PHIL., D.SC.; Danish physicist; b. 19 June 1922, Copenhagen; s. of Prof. Niels Bohr and Margrethe Nørlund; m. 1st Marietta Bettina (née Soffer) (died 1978), two s. one d.; m. 2nd Bente Scharff (née Meyer) 1981; ed. Univ. of Copenhagen; Assoc. D.S.I.R., London 1943–45; Research Asst., Inst. of Theoretical Physics, Copenhagen 1946; Prof. of Physics, Univ. of Copenhagen 1956–; Dir. Niels Bohr Inst. 1963–70, Nordita 1975–81; mem. Danish, Norwegian, Pontifical, Swedish, Polish, Finnish, Yugoslav Acads. of Science, Nat. Acad. of Sciences, U.S.A., American Acad. of Arts and Sciences, American Philosophical Soc., Royal Physiograph Soc., Lund, Sweden, Acad. of Tech. Sciences, Copenhagen, Deutsche Acad. der Naturforscher Leopoldina; Hon. Ph.D. (Oslo, Heidelberg, Trondheim, Manchester, Uppsala); Dannie Heineman Prize 1960, Pius XI Medal 1963, Atoms for Peace Award 1969, Ørsted Medal 1970, Rutherford Medal 1972, John Price Wetherill Medal 1974, Nobel Prize for Physics 1975. *Publications:* Rotational States of Atomic Nuclei 1954, Nuclear Structure Vol. I 1969, Vol. II 1975 (with Ben R. Mottelson). *Address:* Strandgade 34, 1-sal, 1401 Copenhagen, Denmark.

BOIKO, Viktor Grigorevich; Soviet politician; b. 19 July 1931; ed. Mining Inst., Krivoi Rog, Dnepropetrovsk Dist.; served in Soviet Army 1951–54; mem. CPSU 1954–; Instructor, Head of Dept., Dnepropetrovsk Dist. Cttee., Ukrainian CP 1961–70; Chair. of Exec. Cttee., Dnepropetrovsk City Workers' Soviet 1970–74; Deputy, Ukrainian S.S.R. Supreme Soviet 1971–80; First Sec., Dnepropetrovsk City Cttee., Ukrainian CP 1974–76; mem. Cen. Cttee. Ukrainian CP 1976–; Chair., Exec. Cttee. Dnepropetrovsk Dist. Workers' Soviet 1978–83; Deputy to Council of Nationalities, U.S.S.R. Supreme Soviet 1979–; First Sec. Dnepropetrovsk Dist. Cttee. Ukrainian CP 1983–; mem. Cen. Cttee. CPSU 1986–; diplomatic work 1987–; Order of Red Banner 1981. *Address:* Dnepropetrovsk District Committee of the Ukrainian Communist Party, Kiev, Ukrainian S.S.R., U.S.S.R.

BOILEAU, Oliver Clark, Jr.; American business executive; b. 31 March 1927, N.J.; s. of Oliver Clark Boileau Sr. and Florence Mary Smith; m. Nan Eleze Hallen 1951; two s. two d.; ed. Univ. of Pennsylvania and M.I.T. (Sloan Fellow 1964); served U.S. Navy 1944–46; worked in aircraft electronics with RCA; joined Boeing Co. as research engineer 1953, then several tech. and man. positions, Vice-Pres. 1968, Pres. Boeing Aerospace Co. 1973; Pres. and mem. Bd. of Dirs. Gen. Dynamics Corpn. 1980–87, Vice-Chair. 1987–88; Fellow American Inst. of Aeronautics and Astronautics; mem. Air Force Assen., American Defense Preparedness Assen., Assen. of U.S. Army, Nat. Acad. of Eng., Nat. Aeronautics Assen.,

National Space Club, Navy League. *Address:* c/o General Dynamics Corporation, Pierre Laclede Center, St. Louis, Mo. 63105, U.S.A.

BOISDEFFRE (Néraud le Mouton de), Pierre Jules Marie Raoul; French writer, diplomatist and broadcasting official; b. 11 July 1926, Paris; s. of Gen. de Boisdeffre; m. Béatrice Wiedemann-Goiran 1957; three s.; ed. Lycée Condorcet, Collège Stanislas, Ecole Libre des Sciences Politiques, Ecole Nationale d'Administration and Harvard Univ.; Civil Servant, Ministry of Nat. Educ. 1950–55; Deputy Dir. of Press Affairs, Ministry of Foreign Affairs 1958–63; Dir. of Sound Broadcasting, Office de Radiodiffusion et Télévision Française (O.R.T.F.) 1963–68; Cultural Counsellor, French Embassy, London 1968–71, Brussels 1972–77, Ministry of Foreign Affairs 1977–78; Minister Plenipotentiary 1979; Amb. to Uruguay 1981–84, to Colombia 1984–88; Perm. Rep. to the Council of Europe 1988–; Officier de la Légion d'honneur, Officier de l'Ordre national du Mérite, Commdr. des Arts et des Lettres, Chevalier des Palmes académiques, Officier de l'Etoile Polaire, Commdr. de l'Ordre de la Couronne, Commdr. de l'Ordre national du Cèdre, Commdr. de l'Ordre du Christ; Grand Prix de la Critique (for Métamorphose de la littérature) 1950. *Publications:* Métamorphose de la littérature (Vol. I de Barrès à Malraux, Vol. II de Proust à Sartre) 1950, Où va le Roman? 1962, Les écrivains français d'aujourd'hui 1963, Une histoire vivante de la littérature d'aujourd'hui (1939–64) 1964, Une anthologie vivante de la littérature d'aujourd'hui I 1965, II 1966, La cafetière est sur la table 1967, Lettre ouverte aux hommes de gauche 1969, Les écrivains de la nuit, les poètes français d'aujourd hui 1973, La foi des anciens jours 1977, Le roman français depuis 1900 1979, Les nuits, l'Ile aux livres, Paroles de vie, la Belgique 1980; critical portraits: Barrès parmi nous 1952, André Malraux 1952, Kafka (with R. M. Albérès) 1960, Barrès 1962, Giono 1965, Vie d'André Gide (Vol. I: Gide avant la fondation de la N.R.F.) 1970, De Gaulle malgré Lui 1978; Theatre: Goethe m'a dit 1981. *Address:* 40 rue de Verdun, 67000 Strasbourg, France.

BOISI, James O., D.JUR.; American banker; b. 30 April 1919, New York; s. of the late Henry L. and Mary Magdalene (Davolio) Boisi; m. Edith M. Mullen 1945; three s. three d.; ed. Brooklyn Coll. and Fordham Univ. Law School; Sr. Assoc. Amend and Amend (Law Firm) 1942–56; Real Estate Attorney, N.Y. Cen. Railroad 1956–57, Dir. of Real Estate 1957–59, Vice-Pres. of Real Estate 1959–64; Vice-Pres. Morgan Guaranty Trust Co. of New York 1964–67, Sr. Vice-Pres. 1967–70, Exec. Vice-Pres. 1970–72; Exec. Vice-Pres. J. P. Morgan & Co. Inc. 1972–79, Vice-Chair. 1979–84; Exec. Vice-Pres. Helmsley Enterprises Inc. 1984–. *Leisure interests:* golf, gardening. *Address:* Helmsley Enterprises, 60 East 42nd Street, New York, N.Y. 10165, U.S.A.

BOISSIEU DEAN DE LUIGNÉ, Gen. Alain Henri Paul Marie-Joseph de; French army officer; b. 5 July 1914, Chartres; s. of Henri de Boissieu Dean de Luigné and Marguérite Froger de Mauny; m. Elizabeth de Gaulle, d. of Gen. Charles de Gaulle, 1946; one d.; ed. Saint-Cyr Mil. Acad.; Cavalry Second Lieut. 1938, First Lieut, 1940; prisoner of war, escaped, later detained in U.S.S.R.; joined Free French Forces 1941; Capt. 1942; Staff, High Commr. in Indian Ocean 1944–45; Maj. 1945, Lieut.-Col. 1953; Commdg. Officer 4th Regiment of Chasseurs, Algeria 1956–58; Col. 1958; Chief Mil. Staff, High Commr. in Algeria 1958; Chief of Staff Armoured Directorate 1959; Commdg. Officer 2nd Armoured Brigade 1962; Brig.-Gen. 1964; Commdg. Gen. Saint-Cyr Mil. Acad. and Ecole Mil. Inter-Armes de Coëtquidan 1964–67; Commdg. Gen. 7th Div. 1967; Maj.-Gen. 1968; Inspector of Armour 1969; Lieut.-Gen. 1970; mem. Army Council 1971; Gen., Chief of Staff of French Army 1971–75; fmr. Grand Chancellor, Légion d'honneur, fmr. Chancellor, Ordre national du Mérite 1975–81; Grand Croix Légion d'honneur, Compagnon de la libération, Grand Croix de l'Ordre national du Mérite, Croix de guerre, Croix de la Valeur militaire, Knight of Malta; Hon. K.B.E., and other decorations. *Leisure interests:* riding, hunting. *Address:* 233 rue de Vaugirard, 75015 Paris, France.

BOITEUX, Marcel; French business executive; b. 9 May 1922, Niort; s. of René Boiteux and Suzanne Vezes; m. Juliette Barraud 1946; one s. two d.; ed. Ecole Normale Supérieure and Inst. d'Etudes Politiques; Attaché C.N.R.S. 1946–49; Dir.-Gen. Electricité de France 1967–79, Pres. Bd. of Dirs. 1979–87; Prof. of Economy, Ecole Supérieure d'Electricité 1957–62, Ecole Nat. des Ponts et Chaussées 1963–67; Pres. Centre Européen de l'Entreprise Publique 1981–84, Inst. des Hautes Etudes Scientifiques 1985–, World Energy Conf. 1986–89, Pasteur Inst. 1988–, Fondation EDF pour le Mécénat 1987–, Comm. Perspectives 1993 1987–; Hon. Pres. EDF; Dr. h.c. (Yale) 1982. *Leisure interests:* skiing, golf. *Address:* 26, rue de la Baume, 75008 Paris, France (Office). *Telephone:* (33-1) 40 42 30 70 (Office).

BOITSOV, Vasiliy Vasiliyevich, DR.SC.; Soviet technologist and politician; b. 1 Jan. 1908, Alabino, Moscow Oblast; ed. Baumann Higher Technical School, Moscow; engineering posts 1937–46; Deputy Minister Aircraft Industry 1947–63; Dir. of Scientific Research of Tech. Inst. 1947–63; Chair. State Cttee. of Standards, Measures and Measuring Instruments 1963, U.S.S.R. Council of Ministers 1970–78, U.S.S.R. State Cttee. of Standards 1978–; Pres. Int. Org. for Standardization (ISO) 1977–79; mem. CPSU 1939–, Cand. mem. Cen. Cttee. 1981–; Deputy to U.S.S.R. Supreme Soviet 1966–, Deputy to Supreme Soviet of R.S.F.S.R.; Order of Lenin (three), Order of October Revolution, and other decorations. *Address:* State Committee of Standards, 9 Leninsky Prospekt, Moscow, U.S.S.R.

BOJART ORTEGA, Rafael; Argentine university professor; b. 12 April 1920, Buenos Aires; s. of Rafael Bojart Ceballos and Hemilce Ortega; m. Haydée Albistur Pando 1944; two s.; ed. Univs. de Buenos Aires, El Salvador, Barcelona and Columbia Univ., New York; Founder Academia de Estudios Históricos Bartolomé Mitre 1958, Univ. de Morón 1960, Instituto Enrique Larreta 1964, Academia Internacional de Historia 1965, Instituto Americano de Futurología 1975; Pres. Academia de Estudios Históricos Bartolomé Mitre, Academia Internacional de la Historia; fmr. Rector, Univ. de Morón; mem. Real Academia Hispano-americana de Cádiz, Academia Argentina de Diplomacia, Academia de Estudios Parlamentarios y Legislativos Internacionales, Instituto de Cultura Americana de Madrid, Instituto Argentino Hispánico, Asociación Internacional de Derecho, Academia de Letras (Uruguay), Club des intellectuels français, Univ. Int. Moctezuma, World Constituent Assembly, U.S.A.; Médaille Etoile Civique, Paris, Gran Cruz del Inst. de Estudios Franciscanos, Médaille Grand Prix Humanitaire de France. *Publications:* Introducción a la filosofía, Filosofía de la Historia, La Poesía Epica Medieval, La Estética Contemporánea, La Esencia de la Poesía, El Motivo de la Angustia en el Existencialismo, La Poesía de Carlos Obligado, La Inteligencia en el Gobierno de los Pueblos, Ricardo Rojas y el Futuro de América, El Hispanismo en Larreta, La Poesía de César Rosales, Como Hacer un Best Seller, Qué es la Futurología, Borges Escritor, La Fuerza del Occidente, Una Obra Inédita de Enrique Larreta, Que Piensa Arnold Toynbee del Futuro; novels: La Música de la Montaña, El Hombre Nuevo, Una Aventura en el Año 2000, Hombres Celebres del Siglo XX; plays: Polichinela, Los Hijos que no Nacieron. *Address:* Mitre 1491, 19th Floor, Department G, 7600 Mar del Plata, Argentina. *Telephone:* 023-42334.

BOK, Derek, M.A., J.D.; American university administrator; b. 22 March 1930, Bryn Mawr, Pa.; s. of late Curtis Bok and Margaret Plummer (now Mrs. W. S. Kiskadden); m. Sissela Ann Myrdal (d. of Karl Gunnar and Alva Myrdal *q.v.*) 1955; one s. two d.; ed. Univs. of Stanford, Harvard, George Washington and Inst. of Political Science, Paris Univ.; served U.S. Army 1956-58; Asst. Prof. of Law, Harvard Univ. 1958, Prof. 1961-; Dean, Harvard Law School 1968-71; Pres. Harvard Univ. 1971-. *Publications include:* The First Three Years of the Schuman Plan, Cases and Materials on Labor Law (with Archibald Cox), Labor and the American Community (with John Dunlop), The Federal Government and the University, Beyond the Ivory Tower: Social Responsibilities of the Modern University 1982, Higher Learning 1986. *Leisure interests:* gardening, tennis, swimming. *Address:* Office of President, Harvard University, Cambridge, Mass. 02138, U.S.A. *Telephone:* 617-495-1502.

BOKASSA, Marshal Jean Bédel; Central African Republic army officer and politician; b. 22 Feb. 1921, Bobangui, Lobay; s. of the late Mindogon Mgboundoulou and Marie Yokowo; m. Catherine Dengueade; ed. Ecole Sainte Jeanne-d'Arc, M'Baiki, Ecole Missionnaire, Bangui, and Ecole Missionnaire, Brazzaville; joined French Army 1939, Capt. 1961; organized Central African Empire (Central African Republic until 1976) Army, C.-in-C. 1963-79; took power in mil. coup Dec. 1965; Pres. 1966-79 (Pres. for Life 1972-79), Prime Minister 1966-75; Minister of Defence 1966-76, of Justice 1966-70, of Information 1970-74, of Agric. and Stockbreeding 1970-74, of Public Health and Population 1971-76, also Minister of Civil and Mil. Aviation and of Civil Service 1973-76, of Land, River and Air Transport 1973-76, of Trade and Industry 1973-74, April-Sept. 1976, of Mines 1973-76, of Posts and Telecommunications and Information April-Sept. 1976; proclaimed Emperor Dec. 1976, self-crowned Dec. 1977, overthrown in coup 1979, sentenced to death in absentia 1980; lived in France until Oct. 1986, then returned to C.A.R. where he was put on trial, convicted and sentenced to death for murder, cannibalism and embezzlement of public funds in July 1987, sentenced to forced labour for life 1988; Leader Mouvement d'évolution sociale de l'Afrique noire (MESAN); fmr. Pres. Union douanière et économique de l'Afrique central (UDEAC) 1979; Pres. Council of Cen. African Revolution 1976-79; Légion d'honneur, Croix de guerre; Marshal of CAR 1974. *Publication:* My Truth 1985.

BOKOV, Nikolai K.; Soviet writer; b. 1945, Moscow; ed. Moscow Univ.; associated with literary society SMOG in 1960s; emigrated 1975 after samizdat publication of "Contact with the KGB as a Psycho-Sociological Phenomenon" and "The Philosophy of an Accused Philosopher". *Publications include:* The City of the Sun 1971, The Door 1972, Laughter after Midnight 1972, The Cross 1972, Natasha and Pivovarov (play) 1976, Nobody, or the Disgospel According to Maria Dementnaya 1975, Everyday Opposition 1975, Swings of Fate 1978, Best-Seller and Other Prose 1978. *Address:* U.S.S.R. Union of Writers, 52, ul. Vorovskogo, Moscow, U.S.S.R.

BOKSENBERG, Alexander, PH.D., F.R.S.; British astronomer; b. 18 March 1936; s. of Julius Boksenberg and Ernestina Steinberg; m. Adella Coren 1960; one s. one d.; ed. Stationers' Co.'s School, Univ. of London; S.R.C. Research Asst., Dept. of Physics and Astronomy, Univ. Coll. London 1960-65, Lecturer in Physics 1965-75, Head of Optical and Ultraviolet Astronomy Research Group 1969-81, Reader in Physics 1975-78, SRC Sr. Fellow 1976-81, Prof. of Physics 1978-81; Dir. Royal Greenwich Observatory 1981-; Visiting Prof., Dept. of Physics and Astronomy, Univ. Coll. London 1981-, Astronomy Centre, Univ. of Sussex 1981-; Dr. h.c. (l'Observatoire de Paris) 1982. *Publications:* contribs. to learned journals. *Address:* Herstmonceux Castle, Hailsham, East Sussex, BN27 1RP, England (Office).

BOLDIN, Valeriy Ivanovich, CAND. ECON. SC.; Soviet politician; b. 1935; ed. Timiryazev Agric. Acad., Moscow; radio signalisation expert on Moscow-Ryazan Railway 1953-60; on literary staff of Pravda 1960-; mem. CPSU 1960-; work with CPSU Cen. Cttee. 1961-65, 1980-; Deputy Ed. Pravda, Ed. 1969-, mem. Bd. 1973-; asst. to Gen. Sec. of CPSU Cen. Cttee. 1985-; cand. mem. of CPSU Cen. Cttee. 1986-; Head of Section of CPSU Cen. Cttee. 1987-; Deputy mem. of U.S.S.R. Supreme Soviet. *Address:* Pravda, ul. Pravdy 24, Moscow, U.S.S.R.

BOLDYREV, Ivan Sergeyevich; Soviet politician; b. 1937; ed. Inst. of Finance and Econs. and Higher Party School, Rostov-on-Don; teacher 1954-55; Komsomol work 1955-; mem. CPSU 1956-; deputy head of section of Stavropol CPSU Dist. Cttee. 1964-74; First Sec. of Pyatigorsk City Cttee. 1974-83; Sec. of Stavropol CPSU Dist. Cttee. 1983-85; work for CPSU Stavropol Dist. Cttee. 1985-; mem. of CPSU Cen. Cttee. 1986-. *Address:* The Kremlin, Moscow, U.S.S.R.

BOLDYREV, Vil Konstantinovich; Soviet diplomatist; b. 1924; sr. posts in Ministry of Foreign Affairs at home and abroad 1956-69; Embassy Counsellor and Envoy to India 1969-75; Deputy Chief of South Asia Dept. of Ministry of Foreign Affairs 1975-78, Chief of Middle East Dept. 1978-82; Amb. to Iran 1982-. *Address:* U.S.S.R. Embassy, Neauphle-le-Château Avenue, Teheran, Iran.

BOLE, Filipe Nagera, C.B.E., M.A.; Fijian diplomatist; b. 23 Aug. 1936; ed. Victoria Univ. and Auckland Teachers' Coll., New Zealand; joined Civil Service as teacher then Educ. Officer (Secondary) and Chief Educ. Officer (Secondary); Deputy Sec. for Educ. 1972-73; Perm. Sec. for Urban Devt., Housing and Social Welfare 1973-74, for Educ., Youth and Sport 1974-80; Perm. Rep. to UN and Amb. to U.S.A. (also accred. to Canada) 1980-83; Project Admin. for Pacific Islands Devt. Programme, Honolulu 1983-86; Minister of Educ. 1986-87, Dec. 1987-; mem. Council, Univ. of South Pacific, Fiji 1974-80; served on several Govt. Cttees. on education and sport. *Address:* c/o Ministry of Education, Suva, Fiji.

BOLESŁAWSKI, Jerzy, M.ENG.; Polish politician; b. 25 Feb. 1940, Przemyśl; ed. Warsaw Tech. Univ.; mem. Socialist Youth Union 1961-70; Foreman, then Chief of Dept., Cast Steel Foundry of Warszawa Steelworks 1965-71; Sec. Factory Cttee. of Polish United Workers' Party (PZPR) 1971-72; Deputy Head, Propaganda Dept. of PZPR Warsaw Cttee. 1972-74, Head 1974-75; Chair., Warsaw Council of Fed. of Socialist Unions of Polish Youth and Chair. Voivodship Bd. of Polish Socialist Youth Union 1975-79; Councillor, Capital Nat. Council, Warsaw 1976-80, Chair. Dist. Nat. Council, Warsaw 1979-80; First Sec. PZPR Dist. Cttee., Warsaw (Centre) 1979-80, Sec. PZPR Warsaw Cttee. 1980-86; Mayor of Warsaw 1986-; Chair. Capital Bd. of Polish-Russian Friendship Soc. 1980-; mem. PZPR 1966-, mem. PZPR Cent. Control and Revisional Comm. 1986-; Officer's Cross of Order of Polonia Restituta and other decorations. *Address:* Urząd m. stoł. Warszawy, Pl. Dzierżyńskiego 13-5, 00-142 Warsaw, Poland. *Telephone:* 201395.

BOLGER, James Brendan; New Zealand farmer and politician; b. 1935, Taranaki; m.; nine c.; ed. in Taranaki; farms sheep and beef cattle and runs Hereford cattle stud at Te Kuiti; mem. Parl. 1972-; Minister of Fisheries and Assoc. Minister of Agric. 1977; Minister of Labour 1978-84; Minister of Immigration 1978-81; Deputy Leader Nat. Party 1984-85, Parl. Leader 1985-; del. to various ILO confs., Pres. 1983. *Leisure interests:* squash, fishing, reading. *Address:* Parliament Buildings, Wellington, New Zealand.

BOLGER, William F.; American postal and government official; b. 13 March 1923, Waterbury, Conn.; s. of George and Catherine (Leary) Bolger; m. Marjorie Tilton 1949; two d.; ed. George Washington and Columbus Univs., Washington, D.C.; joined U.S. Postal Service 1941, various managerial posts 1955-, Regional Postmaster Gen. for North-East 1973-78, mem. Bd. of Govs. 1975-, Deputy Postmaster Gen. 1975-78, U.S. Postmaster Gen. 1978-84; Pres. Air Transport Assocn. America 1986-; mem. Exec. Cttee. Nat. Bd. of Trustees, Leukaemia Soc. of America Inc. and numerous other cttees. and socs.; Nat. Advisory Bd., Univ. of America; Bd. of Dirs. Nat. Council on Alcoholism; Wolf Trap Foundation; Bausch and Lomb; Hon. D.Lit. (St. Bonaventure Coll., N.Y.). *Leisure interests:* golf, swimming. *Address:* 1709 New York Avenue, NW, Washington, D.C. 20006-5206, U.S.A. (Office).

BOLIN, (Axel) Bertil; Swedish lawyer and international official; b. 8 Nov. 1923, Törnevalla; s. of A. G. and Gotty Bolin; one s. one d.; ed. Univ. of Uppsala; Legal Adviser to Swedish Confed. of Trade Unions 1954-62, Dir. for Int. Affairs 1962; mem. Swedish Del. to UN Gen. Assembly 1962-68; Chair. Industrial Devt. Bd. 1966-67; mem. ILO Gov. Body 1965-68, Asst. Dir.-Gen. 1968-74, Deputy Dir.-Gen. 1974-89; mem. Int. Comm. of Jurists, Int. Assocn. for Industrial Relations, Swedish Labour Law Assocn., several Swedish Royal Comms. *Publications:* Swedish Labour Law, Holidays with Pay (in Swedish), Labour Market and Trade Unions in Developing Countries (in Swedish), Consumer Rights. *Leisure interests:* skiing, tennis, gardening. *Address:* c/o International Labour Office, 4 Chemin des Morillons, 1211 Geneva 22, Switzerland; Strandgatan 38, 27051 Skillinge, Sweden (Home).

BOLING, Edward J., M.S., ED.D.; American university president; b. 19 Feb. 1922, Sevier County, Tenn.; s. of Sam R. and Nerissa (Clark) Boling; m. Carolyn Pierce 1950; three s.; ed. Univ. of Tennessee and George Peabody Coll.; with Union Carbide Corpn. of Oak Ridge, Tenn. 1951–54; State Budget Dir. 1954–58; Commr. of Finance and Admin. 1958–61; Vice-Pres. for Devt. and Admin., Univ. of Tenn. 1961–70, Pres. Univ. of Tenn. 1970–; mem. Educ. Comm. of States 1970–, mem. Southern Regional Educ. Bd. 1957–61, 1970–81, 1983–. *Publications:* Forecasting University Enrolment (with D. A. Gardiner) 1952, Methods of Objectifying the Allocation of Tax Funds to Tennessee State Colleges 1961. *Leisure interests:* boating, tennis, skiing. *Address:* Suite 800, Andy Holt Tower, University of Tennessee, Knoxville, Tennessee 37996, U.S.A. *Telephone:* 615-974-2241 (Office); 615-525-4090 (Home).

BOLKIAH MU'IZUDDIN WADDAULAH, H.M. Sultan Sir Muda Hassanal, D.K., P.S.P.N.B., P.S.N.B., P.S.L.J., S.P.B.M. P.A.N.B.; Sultan of Brunei, b. 15 July 1946; s. of former Sultan Sir Muda Omar Ali Saifuddin, K.C.M.G. (q.v.); m. 1st Rajah Isteri Anak Saleha 1965, one s. five d.; m. 2nd Pengiran Isteri Hajjah Mariam 1981, one s.; ed. privately, and Victoria Inst., Kuala Lumpur, Malaysia, and Royal Mil. Acad., Sandhurst; Appointed Crown Prince and Heir Apparent 1961; Ruler of State of Brunei Oct. 1967–; Prime Minister of Brunei Jan. 1984–, Minister of Finance and Home Affairs 1984–86, of Defence Oct. 1986–; Hon. Capt. Coldstream Guards 1968; Sovereign and Chief of Royal Orders instituted by Sultans of Brunei. *Address:* Istana Darul Hana, Brunei; The Aviary, Osterley, England.

BÖLKOW, Ludwig, DIP.ENG.; German aviation executive (retd.); b. 30 June 1912, Schwerin; ed. Technische Hochschule, Berlin; engineer, Messerschmitt AG 1939–45; Founder Bölkow (IBB) engineering co., Stuttgart 1948; Founder Bölkow-Entwicklungen KG (later Bölkow G.m.b.H.) 1956; Shareholder and Pres. Messerschmitt-Bölkow-Blohm G.m.b.H., Ottobrunn 1977; Founder, Ludwig Bölkow-Stiftung 1979; mem. Bd. of Dirs., Deutsche Gesellschaft für Luft- und Raumfahrt e.V., Berlin, Chair. 1980–; Dr. Ing. h.c. Technische Universität, Stuttgart; Dr. Ing. e.h. Bundeswehrhochschule; Bavarian Order of Merit, Ring of Honour, Soc. of German Engineers, Gold Diesel medal, Ludwig-Prandtl ring, Deutsche Gesellschaft für Luft- und Raumfahrt, Pionierkette der Windrose, Distinguished Service Cross with Star, Gold Medal of Royal Aeronautical Soc., Grashof-Gedenkmünze, VDI, Fed. Repub. of Germany Order of Merit, Werner-von-Siemens Ring of Honour; Fellow, A.I.A.A.. *Address:* c/o Messerschmitt-Bölkow-Blohm G.m.b.H., 8012 Ottobrunn, Federal Republic of Germany.

BOLLARD, Edward George, C.B.E., PH.D.; New Zealand plant physiologist; b. 21 Jan. 1920, Athlone, Westmeath, Ireland; s. of Edward D. and Elizabeth (née Allen) Bollard; m. 1st Constance M. Esmond 1947 (died 1971); m. 2nd Joy E. Cook 1972; two s. one d.; ed. Mount Albert Grammar School, Auckland, and Univs. of Auckland and Cambridge; with N.Z. Dept. of Scientific and Industrial Research 1948–80, latterly Dir. Div. of Horticulture and Processing; Hon. Prof., Univ. of Auckland 1973; Fellow, Royal Soc. of N.Z., Pres. 1981–85; Harkness Fellow, Cornell Univ. 1956–57; Hector Medal, Royal Soc. of N.Z. 1972; Jubilee Medal 1977; Hon. D.Sc. (Auckland). *Publications:* Science and Technology in New Zealand: Opportunity for the Future 1986, research papers in the field of plant nutrition and on the development of the horticultural industry in N.Z. *Leisure interest:* keel boat sailing.

BOLLING, Claude; French pianist, composer and orchestral and band leader; b. 10 April 1930, Cannes; s. of Henri Bolling and Geneviève Brannens; m. Irène Dervize-Sadyker 1959; two s.; studied with private music teachers including Maurice Duruflé; maj. compositions for jazz piano trios including Sonate pour deux pianistes, suites for flute, for violin, for cello, for chamber orchestra, Guitar Concerto, Picnic Suite, Toot Suite; piano solos, trios and all kinds of compositions; hundreds of orchestral originals; has composed more than 100 film soundtrack scores including Le Jour et l'Heure, Borsalino, Lucky Luke, Le Magnifique, Willie and Phil, California Suite, La Mandarine, L'Homme en Colère, Jazz Memories and Les Brigades du Tigre; U.S. and Canada Gold Records, Médaille d'or Maurice Ravel, Officier Arts et Lettres-Chevalier Ordre Nat. du Mérite, Citoyen d'Honneur de L.A. *Leisure interest:* model railroading. *Address:* 20 avenue de Lorraine, 92380 Garches, France. *Telephone:* (47) 41 41 84 and (47) 41 84 84.

BOLLMANN, Niels; Danish politician; b. 11 July 1939, Brons, South Jutland; s. of Heinrich Bollmann; ed. Customs Admin. School; early career in Customs Admin., Sr. Examining Officer 1971–77; M.P. 1977–, Minister of Housing 1982–87; Centre Democrat. *Address:* c/o Ministry of Housing, Slotsholmsgade 12, 1216 Copenhagen K, Denmark.

BOLLNOW, Otto Friedrich, DR. PHIL.; German philosopher; b. 14 March 1903, Stettin; s. of Otto and Frida Bollnow; m. Dr. Ortrud Bürger 1938; one s. two d.; ed. Univs. von Berlin, Greifswald and Göttingen; teacher of Philosophy and Educ., Göttingen 1931–39; Prof. of Psychology and Educ., Giessen 1939–46; Prof. of Philosophy and Educ., Mainz 1946–53, Tübingen 1953–70, Prof. Emer. 1970–; Dr. h.c. *Publications:* Dilthey 1936, Das Wesen der Stimmungen 1941, Existenzphilosophie 1943, Einfache Sittlichkeit 1947, Rilke 1951, Die Pädogogik der deutschen Romantik 1952, Neue Geborgenheit: Das Problem einer Überwindung des Existenzialismus 1955, Die Lebensphilosophie 1958, Wesen und Wandel der Tugenden 1958, Existenz-

philo-sophie und Pädagogik 1959, Mensch und Raum 1963, Die pädagogische Atmosphäre 1964, Französischer Existentialismus 1965, Sprache und Erziehung 1966, Philosophie der Erkenntnis Vol. I 1970, Vol. II 1975, Das Verhältnis zur Zeit 1972, Vom Geist des Übens 1978, Studien zur Hermeneutik, I 1982, II 1983, O. F. Bollnow im Gespräch 1983, Zwischen Philosophie und Pädagogik 1988. *Address:* Waldeckstrasse 27, 74 Tübingen 1, Federal Republic of Germany. *Telephone:* 07071-24511.

BOLT, Robert Oxton, C.B.E.; British playwright; b. 15 Aug. 1924; s. of Ralph and Leah Bolt (née Binnion); m. 1st Celia Roberts 1950 (divorced), 2nd Sarah Miles 1967 (divorced); two s. two d.; m. 3rd Ann Zane 1980 (divorced 1985); ed. Manchester Grammar School and Manchester Univ.; office boy, Insurance Office, Manchester 1941–42; Manchester Univ. 1943; R.A.F. and W. African Frontier Force 1943–46; teacher, Bishopsteignton Village School 1950–51, Millfield School, Somerset 1951–58; freelance writer 1958–; Oscar for A Man for All Seasons (film) 1967. *Plays:* Flowering Cherry 1957, The Tiger and the Horse 1959, A Man for All Seasons 1961 (film 1967), Gentle Jack 1963, The Thwarting of Baron Bolligrew (for children) 1966, Brother and Sister 1967, Vivat! Vivat Regina! 1970, State of Revolution 1977; Filmscripts: Lawrence of Arabia 1962, Dr. Zhivago 1964, Ryan's Daughter 1970, Lady Caroline Lamb 1972 (also Dir.), The Bounty 1984, The Mission 1986. *Address:* c/o Margaret Ramsay Ltd., 14A Goodwin's Court, St. Martin's Lane, London, WC2N 4LL, England.

BOMANI, Paul Lazaro, M.A.; Tanzanian politician; b. 1 Jan. 1925, Musoma; s. of Rev. Lazaro Bomani; ed. Ikizu Secondary School; employee, Williamson Diamonds Ltd. 1945–47; Asst. Sec., later Sec. Mwanza African Traders' Co-operative Soc.; Organizer, Lake Province Growers' Asscn. 1952; studied Co-operative Devt. at Loughborough Coll. 1953–54; mem. Legislative Council 1955; Man. Victoria Fed. of Co-operative Unions Ltd. 1955; Minister of Agric., Tanganyika 1960–62, of Finance 1962–64, Minister of Finance of Tanzania 1964–65, for Econ. Affairs and Devt. Planning 1965–67, of Commerce 1967–72, and of Industries 1970–72, of Minerals –1984, of Natural Resources and Tourism 1984–86, of Agric. and Livestock Devt. 1986–87, Gov. of IBRD (World Bank) for Tanzania 1967–70; Amb. to U.S.A. 1972–83 (also accred. Mexico 1975–83); Vice-Pres. Int. Inst. of Cotton 1976–80, Pres. 1980–. *Leisure interests:* soccer, swimming, fishing, music, reading. *Address:* c/o Ministry of Natural Resources and Tourism, Dar es Salaam, Tanzania.

BOMBASSEI FRASCANI DE VETTOR, Giorgio; Italian diplomatist; b. 29 June 1910, Florence; s. of Alfredo Bombassei Frascani de Vettor and Margherita Tidone Peri; m. Eli Tramontani 1940; one s.; ed. Università degli Studi, Florence and Inst. of Political and Social Sciences "Cesare Alfieri", Florence; Italian Diplomatic Service 1933–, served Egypt, U.S.A., France, Ceylon, U.S.S.R., Switzerland, Brazil 1933–50; Deputy Dir. of Int. Co-operation, Ministry of Foreign Affairs 1952, Deputy Dir.-Gen. of Political Affairs 1956; Perm. Rep. of Italy to Council of Europe 1957–61; Amb. to Luxembourg 1961–67; Perm. mem. Italian Del. to Special Council of Ministers of ECSC 1961–65; Amb. to Netherlands 1965–67; Perm. Rep. of Italy to the European Communities 1967–76; Vice-Pres. EIB and Vice-Chair. Bd. Dirs. 1976–82, Hon. Vice-Pres. June 1982–; Grand Cross Officer Order of Merit (Italy), Medal of Freedom (U.S.A.), Knight S.M. Order of Malta; and other decorations. *Leisure interests;* golf, bridge. *Address:* 8 rue de Crayer, 1050 Brussels, Belgium.

BOMERS, Henricus J.A.; Netherlands ecclesiastic; b. 19 April 1936, Eibergen; Novitiate, Lazarist Fathers 1957; ordained 1964; Lecturer in Philosophy, Interdiocesan Seminary, Addis Ababa 1967–73; Regional Superior, Lazarist Brothers in Ethiopia 1973–78; Sec.-Gen. for Food Aid 1973–74; Apostolic Vicar of Gimma, Ethiopia 1977; Bishop of Haarlem 1983–. *Address:* Nieuwe Gracht 80, 2011 NJ Haarlem, Netherlands. *Telephone:* 023-319450.

BOND, Alan, A.O.; Australian business executive; b. 22 April 1938; s. of Frank Bond and Kathleen Bond; m. Eileen Teresa Hughes 1956; two s. two d.; ed. Perivale School, London and Fremantle Boy's School, W.A.; f. and Exec. Chair. Bond Corpn. Holdings Ltd. 1969; interests in brewing, property, oil and gas, electronic media, minerals, airships; Syndicate Head America's Cup Challenge 1983 Ltd.; Australia Winners of 1983 America's Cup Challenge; named Australian of the Year 1977. *Leisure interest:* yachting. *Address:* Dalkeith, Western Australia.

BOND, Christopher Samuel; American lawyer and politician; b. 6 March 1939, St. Louis; s. of Arthur Doerr and Elizabeth Green Bond; m. Carolyn Reid 1967; ed. Deerfield Acad., Mass., Woodrow Wilson School of Public and Int. Affairs, Princeton Univ., Univ. of Virginia; Clerk, Fifth Circuit, U.S. Court of Appeals 1963–64; with law firm, Covington and Burling, Washington, D.C. 1964–67; private practice 1968; Asst. Attorney-Gen., Chief Counsel of Consumer Protection Div. 1969–70; State Auditor, Missouri 1970–72; Gov. of Missouri 1973–77, 1981–84; Chair. Republican Govs.' Asscn. 1974–75, Midwestern Govs.' Conf. 1976; Exec. Cttee. Nat. Govs.' Conf. 1974–75; Chair. NGA Cttee. on Econ. Devt. 1981–82; Pres. Great Plains Legal Foundation, Kansas City, Mo. 1977–81; Partner, law firm Gage and Tucker, Kansas City and St. Louis 1981–; Senator from Missouri Jan. 1987–; Hon. LL.D. (Westminster and William Jewell Colls., Mo.) 1973, Hon. D.Litt. (Drury Coll., Springfield, Mo.) 1976; Republican. *Address:* 14 S. Jefferson Road, Mexico, Mo. 65265, U.S.A. (Home).

BOND, Edward; British playwright; b. 18 July 1934, London; m. Elizabeth Pablé 1971; Resident Theatre Writer, Univ. of Essex 1982–83; winner, George Devine Award, John Whiting Award 1968; Hon. D.Litt. (Yale). *Publications:* plays: Saved 1965, Narrow Road to the Deep North 1968, Early Morning 1968, The Pope's Wedding 1971, Passion 1971, Black Mass 1971, Lear 1972, The Sea 1973, Bingo 1974, The Fool 1976, A-A-merica! (Grandma Faust and The Swing) 1976, Stone 1976, The Bundle 1978, The Woman 1979, The Worlds 1980, Restoration 1981, Summer: A Play for Europe 1982, Human Cannon 1985, War Plays (Red Black and Ignorant, The Tin Can People, Great Peace) 1985, Jackets 1989, In the Company of Men 1989; librettos: We Come to the River 1977, The English Cat 1983; translations: Chekhov's The Three Sisters 1967, Wedekind's Spring Awakening 1974; others: Theatre Poems and Songs 1978, Collected Poems 1978–1985, 1987. *Address:* c/o Margaret Ramsay, 14A Goodwin's Court, St. Martin's Lane, London, WC2N 4LL, England. *Telephone:* 01-240 0691.

BOND, Julian; American civil rights leader; b. 14 Jan. 1940; s. of Horace Mann Bond and Julia Agnes (née Washington); m. Alice Louise Clopton 1961; three s. two d.; ed. Morehouse Coll.; co-founder, Cttee. on Appeal for Human Rights, Atlanta Univ. 1960, later Exec. Sec.; co-founder Student Non-violent Co-ordinating Cttee. 1960, Communications Dir. 1961–66; reporter, feature writer Atlanta Inquirer 1960–61, Man. Ed. 1963; mem. Ga. House of Reps. 1966–75, excluded 1966 by House for criticizing U.S. involvement in Viet-Nam, exclusion overruled in Supreme Court; mem. Ga. Senate 1975–87; Chair. Bd., Southern Elections Fund; Pres. Emer. Southern Poverty Law Center; Pres. Inst. of Southern Studies; mem. Bd. of Dirs. African-American Inst., Delta Ministry Project of Nat. Council of Churches, Robert F. Kennedy Memorial Fund, Martin Luther King Jr. Center for Social Change, Centre for Community Change, Southern Regional Council, New Democratic Coalition, Voter Educ. Project, Nat. Asscn. for Advancement of Coloured People, and other bodies; mem. Nat. Advisory Council of American Civil Liberties Union, Southern Correspondents Reporting Racial Equality Wars, hon. degrees from 17 Colls. and Univs. *Publications:* A Time to Speak, A Time to Act, poems and articles in books and periodicals, syndicated weekly newspaper column. *Address:* 361 Westview Drive, S.W., Atlanta, Ga. 30310, U.S.A. (Office). *Telephone:* 404-755 2051.

BOND, Sir Kenneth (Raymond Boyden), Kt., F.C.A.; British business executive; b. 1 Feb. 1920; s. of James E. Bond and Gertrude Deplidge Bond; m. Jennifer M. Crabbe 1958; three s. three d.; ed. Selhurst Grammar School; T.A. Service 1939–46; Partner Cooper & Cooper, Chartered Accountants 1954–57; Dir. Radio & Allied Industries Ltd. 1957–62; Financial Dir. Gen. Electric Co. PLC 1962–66, Deputy Man. Dir. 1966–85, Vice-Chair. 1985–. *Leisure interest:* golf. *Address:* Woodstock, Wayside Gardens, Gerrards Cross, Bucks., England. *Telephone:* Gerrards Cross 883513.

BONDARCHUK, Sergey Fedorovich; Soviet film actor and director; b. 25 Sept. 1920, Byelozerka, Odessa Region; one s. two d.; ed. All Union State Inst. of Cinematography. *Principal roles:* Othello, Shevchenko (Taras Shevchenko), Valko (The Young Guard), Dymov (The Grasshopper), Yershov (An Unfinished Tale), Ivan Franko (Ivan Franko), Matvei Krylov (The Soldiers Go On), Sokolov (Destiny of a Man), Korostylov (Seryozha), Pierre Bezukhov (War and Peace), Astrov (Uncle Vanya), Sergey Tutarinov (Gold Star Winner), Fyodor (It was Night in Rome), Martin Evens (The Silence of Doctor Evens), Ivan Nikolayevich (This High Mountain), Kurchatov (Choosing the Goal), Zvyagintsev (They Fought for the Motherland) Emelyan (Steppe). *Films directed include:* Destiny of a Man, War and Peace 1962–67, Waterloo 1970, Uncle Vanya 1974, They Fought for the Motherland 1975, Steppe 1979, Father Sergius 1979, Mexico in Flames 1982; Order of Lenin (twice), People's Artist of U.S.S.R., Order of Red Banner, Hero of Soviet Labour 1980, U.S.S.R. State Prize 1984 and other awards. *Publications:* Intimate Thoughts 1979. *Leisure interests:* drawing, sculpture, wood carving. *Address:* Gorky Street 9, 75, Moscow 9, U.S.S.R. *Telephone:* 229-27-95.

BONDAREV, Yuriy Vasiliyevich, Soviet author and state official; b. 1924, Orsk; ed. Gor'kiy Inst., Moscow 1951; writer 1949–; mem. CPSU 1944–; First Deputy Chair. of RSFSR Writers' Union; served Soviet Army 1941–45; Deputy to Supreme Soviet 1975–80 and Deputy Chair.; Hero of Socialist Labour 1984. *Publications include:* novels: On the Big River 1953, Young Comrades 1956, Fire for the Battalions 1957, Last Salute 1959, The Last Gulp 1968, Hot Snow 1970, The Shore 1979, A Choice 1980. *Address:* U.S.S.R. Union of Writers, Ulitsa Vorovskogo 52, Moscow, U.S.S.R.

BONDE, Peder, B.L.; Swedish business executive; b. 2 Sept. 1923, Stockholm; s. of Count Carl Bonde and Countess Ebba Bonde (née Wallenberg); m. Jacqueline Madeleine Fernande Rouchier 1957; two s. one d.; Asst. Vice-Pres. Stockholms Enskilda Bank 1957, Vice-Pres. 1961, Exec. Vice-Pres. 1969; Man. Dir. and Deputy Chief Exec. Skandinaviska Enskilda Banken 1972–73, Special Rep., Zürich 1977; Exec. Vice-Pres. Saléninvest AB 1973–76; Chief Exec. Banque Scandinave en Suisse, Geneva 1978–82; Exec. Vice-Chair., Investor AB, Providentia AB 1983–; Dir. several Swedish corpns. *Address:* Box 16174, S-103 24 Stockholm, Sweden. *Telephone:* (+46 8) 23-37-90.

BONDI, Sir Hermann, K.C.B., M.A. F.R.S.; British mathematician; b. 1 Nov. 1919, Vienna, Austria; s. of late Samuel and Helene Bondi; m. Christine M. Stockman 1947; two s. three d.; ed. Real Gymnasium, Vienna, and Trinity Coll., Cambridge; Fellow, Trinity Coll., Cambridge 1943–49, 1952–54; Lecturer in Math., Cambridge Univ. 1948–54; Research Assoc. Cornell Univ. 1951, Harvard Coll. Observatory 1953; Visiting Prof. Cornell Univ. 1960; Prof. of Math. King's Coll., Univ. of London 1954–71, Titular Prof. 1971–84, Prof. Emer. 1985–; Dir.-Gen. European Space Research Org. (ESRO), Paris 1967–71; Chief Scientific Adviser to Ministry of Defence 1971–77; Chief Scientist Dept. of Energy 1977–80; Chair. Offshore Energy Bd., Dept. of Energy 1977–80, Advisory Council on Research and Devt. for Fuel and Power 1977–80, Severn Barrage Cttee. 1978–81, Natural Environment Research Council 1980–84; Fellow, Royal Soc. 1959, Royal Astronomical Soc. (Sec. 1956–64), Cambridge Philosophical Soc.; Chair. Nat. Cttee. for Astronomy 1964–67; Pres. Inst. of Math. and its applications 1974–75, Asscn. of British Science Writers 1981–83, British Humanist Assen. 1982–, Pres. Hydrographical Soc. 1985–87; Master, Churchill Coll., Cambridge Sept. 1983–; Hon. Fellow Regent's Coll. 1988; Hon D.Sc. (Sussex, Bath, Surrey) 1974, (York) 1980, (Southampton) 1981, (Salford) 1982, (Birmingham) 1984, (St. Andrews) 1985, Gold Medal (Inst. of Mathematics and Its Application) 1988. *Publications:* Cosmology 1960, The Universe at Large 1961, Relativity and Common Sense 1964, Assumption and Myth in Physical Theory 1967, numerous papers. *Address:* Churchill College, Cambridge, England. *Telephone:* (0223) 336142.

BONDURANT, Stuart, B.S., M.D.; American professor and university administrator; b. 9 Sept. 1929, Winston-Salem, N.C.; m. Margaret Fortescue 1954; one s. two d.; ed. Univ. of North Carolina at Chapel Hill, Duke Univ. School of Medicine, Durham, N.D.; Assoc. Dir. Indiana Univ. Cardiovascular Research Centre, Indiana Univ. Medical Center, Indianapolis, Ind. 1961–67; Chief, Medical Br. Artificial Heart-Myocardial Infarction Program, Nat. Health Inst., Nat. Insts. of Health 1966–67; Prof. and Chair., Dept. of Medicine, Albany Medical Coll., Physician-in-Chief, Albany Medical Center Hosp., New York 1967–74, Pres. and Dean 1974–79; Prof. of Medicine and Dean, Univ. of N.C. School of Medicine 1979–; Hon. F.R.C.P. (E.); Hon. D.Sc. (Indiana). *Address:* Office of the Dean, University of North Carolina School of Medicine, 125 MacNider Building 202H, Chapel Hill, N.C. 27514; 623 Greenwood Road, Chapel Hill, N.C. 27514, U.S.A. (Home.) *Telephone:* (919) 966-4161 (Office).

BONELL, Carlos Antonio; British musician, teacher, guitarist and composer; b. 23 July 1949, London; m. Pinuccia Rossetti 1971; two s.; ed. William Ellis School, London and Royal Coll. of Music, under John Williams (q.v.); solo début as guitarist, Wigmore Hall, London 1971; concerto début with Royal Philharmonic Orchestra 1975; American début, Avery Fisher Hall, New York 1978; concert appearances with London Symphony, London Philharmonic, Philharmonia, English Chamber and London Sinfonietta orchestras, many prov. orchestras, concerts in all maj. European centres, appearances with John Williams, Teresa Berganza (q.v.), Pinchas Zukerman (q.v.) and own ensemble 1975–; Prof. Royal Coll. of Music 1972–, London Coll. of Music 1983–; Hon. A.R.C.M. *Recordings include:* Guitar Music of Spain 1975, Guitar Music of the Baroque 1976, Showpieces 1981, Rodrigo Concerto 1981, Paganini Trios and Quartets with Salvatore Accardo 1983, Twentieth Century Music for Guitar. *Publication:* Twenty First Pieces 1982. *Leisure interests:* reading, walking, snooker. *Address:* c/o Harold Holt Ltd., 31 Sinclair Road, London, W14 0NS, England. *Telephone:* 01-603 4600.

BONETTI, Mattia; Swiss designer, decorator and artist; b. 2 May 1952, Lugano; s. of Giorgio Bonetti and Stella Frossard; ed. Centro Scolastico Industrie Artistiche, Lugano; Exhbns.: Musée des Arts Décoratifs, Bordeaux 1985, Galerie Neotu, Paris 1985–87, Furniture of the 20th Century, New York 1985, 1987, 1988, Mairie de Villeurbanne 1986, Galerie David Gill, Vic. and Albert Museum, London 1988; decorated Bernard Picasso's Boisgeloop Castle 1987, Christian Lacroix Showroom and Graphics 1987–88; Hon. Citizen City of Villeurbanne. *Leisure interests:* swimming, photography. *Address:* 14 rue Vavin, 75006 Paris, France. *Telephone:* 43 26 21 45.

BONFIELD, Peter Leahy, B.TECH., C.B.I.M., C.B.E.; British business executive; b. 3 June 1944; ed. Loughborough Univ.; Div. Dir. Texas Instruments Inc. 1966–81; Group Exec. Dir. Worldwide Operations, Int. Computers Ltd. 1981–84; Man. Dir. Int. Computers Ltd. 1984; Chair. and Man. Dir. STC Int. Computers Ltd. 1986–. *Leisure interests:* music, sailing, jogging. *Address:* STC International Computers Ltd., Bridge House, Fulham, London, SW6 3JX, England. *Telephone:* 01-788 7272.

BONGO, Albert-Bernard (Omar); Gabonese politician; b. 30 Dec. 1935, Lewai, Franceville; m.; three c.; ed. primary school at Bacongo (Congo—Brazzaville) and technical coll., Brazzaville; Civil Servant; served Air Force 1958–60; entered Ministry of Foreign Affairs 1960; Dir. of Private Office of Pres. Léon Mba 1962, in charge of Information 1963–64, Nat. Defence 1964–65; Minister-Del. to Presidency in charge of Nat. Defence and Co-ordination, Information and Tourism 1965–66; Vice-Pres. of Govt., in charge of Co-ordination, Nat. Defence Planning, Information and Tourism 1966–67; Vice-Pres. of Gabon March-Nov. 1967, Pres. 1967–, Minister of Defence 1967–81, of Information 1967–80, of Planning 1967–77, Prime Minister 1967–75, Minister of the Interior 1967–70, of Devt. 1970–77, of Women's Affairs 1976–77, and numerous other portfolios; Pres. UDEAC 1981; Founder and Sec.-Gen. Parti Démocratique Gabonais 1968; High Chancellor, Ordre Nat. de l'Etoile Equatoriale; decorations from the Ivory Coast,

Niger, Chad, Cameroon, Central African Republic, Mauritius, Togo, Taiwan, Zaire, France, U.K. and Guinea. *Address:* Présidence de la République, Boîte Postale 546, Libreville, Gabon. *Telephone:* 26-90.

BONGO, Martin; Gabonese politician; b. 4 July 1940, Lekei; ed. Ecole Normale de Mitzic; fmrly. school dir. in Franceville, then Insp. for Primary Instruction for Upper-Ogooué Region; fmr. Dir. of Cabinet to the Vice-Pres.; Deputy Dir. of Cabinet to the Pres. 1968-69; Commr.-Gen. for Information April-Dec. 1969; Sec. of State to the Presidency, for Penitentiary Services 1969-70, for Nat. Educ. in charge of Special Missions 1970-72, Head of State's Personal Rep. 1972-73; Minister of Educ. and Scientific Research 1973-75, of Nat. Educ. 1975-76, of Foreign Affairs and Co-operation 1976-81, of State for Foreign Affairs and Co-operation 1981-; Commdr. Order of the Equatorial Star, Grand Officer, Nat. Order of Merit (Mauritania), Grand Officer, Order of Merit (Italy), Commdr. Ordre national du Mérite. *Address:* Ministère des Affaires Etrangères et de la Coopération, Libreville, Gabon.

BONIFACIO, Francesco Paolo; Italian jurist and government official; b. 3 May 1923, Castellammare di Stabia; s. of Vincenzo and Elvira Bonifacio; m. Flora Acanfora 1947; ed. Law Faculty, Univ. of Naples; elected to Higher Council of Magistrates 1959; Dean, Faculty of Law, Univ. of Bari 1961; later Prof. of Roman Law, Univ. of Naples, Prof. of Constitutional Justice, Univ. of Rome 1975-; mem. Communal Council of Castellammare di Stabia 1956-60, also mem. Provincial Council 1956-60; Judge, Constitutional Court (Supreme Court) 1963-73, Pres. 1973-75; Minister of Justice 1976-79; mem. Senate for Campania June 1979-; Pres. First Cttee. 1983-. *Address:* c/o The Senate, Piazza Madama, 00100 Rome, Italy.

BONIN, Bernard, D. EN SC. (ECON.), F.R.S.C.; Canadian economist; b. 29 Sept. 1936, Joliette; s. of Georges Bonin and Thérèse Racette; m. Andrée Gregoire 1960; one s. one d.; ed. Montreal and Paris; Prof. of Econs. Ecole des Hautes Etudes Commerciales, Montreal 1962-74; Asst. Deputy Minister for Immigration, Govt. of Quebec 1974-77, for Intergovernmental Affairs 1977-79; Prof. of Econs., Ecole Nat. d'Admin. Publique, Montreal 1979-, on leave to Conseil des Universités 1985-. *Publications:* L'investissement étranger à long terme au Canada 1967, A propos de l'association économique Canada-Québec 1980, L'entreprise multinationale et l'état 1984, Innovation industrielle et analyse économique 1988. *Leisure interests:* music, reading, sport. *Address:* Conseil des Universités, 2700 boulevard Laurier, Sainte-Foy, Quebec, G1V 2L8 (Office); 946 Dunlop Avenue, Outremont, Quebec, Canada (Home). *Telephone:* (418) 643-1954 (Office); (514) 737-5685 (Home).

BONNEFOUS, Edouard; French politician; b. 24 Aug. 1907; ed. Ecole des Sciences Politiques and Inst. des Hautes Etudes Internationales; Minister of Commerce, Faure Cabinet 1952, Minister of State, Mayer Cabinet Jan. 1953, Minister of Posts and Telegraphs until 1956, Minister of Transport and Public Works 1957-58; Deputy from Seine-et-Oise 1946-58, Senator from Yvelines 1959-86; Del. to UN 1948-52; fmr. Chancellor Inst. de France, Pres. French Cttee., Ligue Européenne de Coopération Economique, Pres. Comm. on Foreign Affairs, Nat. Assembly; Pres. Comm. on Finance, Senate 1972-86; Pres. Assen. Professionnelle de la Presse Républicaine, Asscn. and Féd. Française pour la Défense de l'Environnement contre les Pollutions et les Nuisances; later Pres. Conservatoire Nat. des Arts et Métiers, later Vice-Pres. Exhbn. Cttee.; Hon Pres. Soc. of Political Econ., Asscn. Nat. de Protection des Eaux; Vice-Pres. Inst. Océanographique; Prof. Inst. des Hautes Etudes Internationales; mem. Inst. de France, later mem. Central Admin. Comm.; mem. Conseil Régional de l'Ile-de-France, Pres. Conseil d'Admin. de l'Agence des Espaces Verts de la Région de l'Ile-de-France; fmr. mem. Acad. de Sciences morales et politiques; Pres. Fondation Singer-Polignac 1984; Vice-Pres. Fondation del Duca 1986; Grand Prix Gobert, Acad. Française 1968, Prix de Cercle Européen/Sévigné (Louise Weiss) 1976, Prix Berthault, Académie des Sciences 1972. *Publications:* Le corporatisme, Devant et derrière le rideau de fer, A travers l'Europe mutilée, L'Idée européenne et sa réalisation, L'Europe en face de son destin, Encyclopédie de l'Amérique Latine, La réforme administrative, Les grands travaux, Histoire politique de la IIIe République (7 vols.), La terre et la faim des hommes, L'Année politique (43 vols.), Les milliards qui s'envolent, Le monde est-il surpeuplé?, L'Homme ou la nature, Sauver l'humain, A la recherche des milliards perdus, Le monde en danger 1982, Avant l'oubli: La vie en France 1900-40 1984, 1940-70 1987. *Address:* 6 rue de l'Elysée, Paris, France.

BONNEFOUS, Marc, D. EN D.; French diplomatist; b. 5 Jan. 1924, Bordeaux; s. of Henri Bonnefous and Renée Teillac; m. Monique Lesbegueris 1946; one s. one d.; ed. Lycée de Bordeaux, Faculté de Droit, Bordeaux and Ecole Nat. d'Admin. Paris; Insp. of diplomatic postings 1973-77; Amb. to Congo, Brazzaville 1970-72, to Israel 1978-82; Dir. Dept. of North African and Middle East Dept. Ministry of Foreign Affairs 1982-86; Asst. Sec.-Gen. Ministry of Foreign Affairs 1986-87; Perm. Rep. of France at OECD 1987-. *Publication:* Europe et Tiers-Monde 1961. *Address:* 20 chaussée de la Muette, 75106 Paris, France. *Telephone:* 45202833.

BONNEFOY, Yves Jean, L. ÈS L.; French writer; b. 24 June 1923, Tours; s. of Elie Bonnefoy and Hélène Maury; m. Lucille Vine 1968; one d.; ed. Lycée Descartes, Tours, Faculté des Sciences, Poitiers, and Faculté des Lettres, Paris; lived in Paris 1943-; Prof. Collège de France 1981; contribu-

tor to Mercure de France, Critique, Encounter, L'Ephémère, La Nouvelle Revue Française etc.; has travelled in Europe, Asia and N. America; lectures or seminars at Brandeis, Johns Hopkins, Princeton, Geneva, Nice, Yale and other univs.; Prix Montaigne 1980, Grand Prix de poésie (Acad. Française) 1981, Prix Florence Gould 1987; Hon. D. Hum Litt. (American Coll., Paris) 1988. *Publications:* poems: Du mouvement et de l'immobilité de Douve 1953 (English 1968), Pierre écrite 1964 (English 1976), Selected Poems 1968, Dans le leurre du seuil 1975, Poèmes (1947-1975) 1978, Ce qui fut sans lumière 1987, essays: L'Improbable 1959, Arthur Rimbaud 1961 (English translation 1973), Un rêve fait à Mantoue 1967, Le nuage rouge 1977, Rue traversière 1977; on art: Peintures murales de la France Gothique 1954, Miró 1963, Rome 1630 1969, L'Arrière-Pays 1972, Entretiens sur la poésie 1981; La Présence et l'Image 1983, Récits en rêve 1987; other work: Hier régnant désert 1958, co-editor L'Ephémère, translations of Shakespeare. *Address:* 63 rue Lepic, 75018 Paris, France.

BONNER, James, PH.D.; American professor of biology; b. 1 Sept. 1910, Ansley, Neb.; s. of Walter D. and Grace Gaylord Bonner; m. Ingelore Silberbach 1967; one s. three d.; ed. Univ. of Utah, Calif. Inst. of Tech. and Oxford Univ.; Nat. Research Council Fellow, Utrecht, Zürich and Leiden 1934-35; Instructor, Calif. Inst. of Tech. 1936-38, Asst. Prof. 1938-43, Assoc. Prof. 1943-46, Prof. 1946-81, Prof. Emer. 1981-; Chair. Phytogen Inc. 1981-; mem. Nat. Acad. of Sciences. *Publications:* Plant Biochemistry 1950, Principles of Plant Physiology 1952, The Next 100 Years 1957, The Nucleohistones 1964, The Molecular Biology of Development 1965, The Next 90 Years 1967, The Next 80 Years 1977, The World's People, the World's Food 1980, and c. 500 scientific publs. *Leisure interests:* skiing, mountain climbing, travel. *Address:* California Institute of Technology, Pasadena, Calif. 91125 (Office); 1914 Edgewood Drive, South Pasadena, Calif. 91030, U.S.A. (Home). *Telephone:* 818-356-4928 (Office); 818-799-8224 (Home).

BONNER, John Tyler, PH.D., D.SC.; American biologist; b. 12 May 1920, New York; s. of Paul Hyde Bonner and Lilly Marguerite Stehli; m. Ruth Ann Graham 1942; three s. one d.; ed. Harvard Univ.; U.S. Air Corps 1942-46; Asst. Prof., then Prof., Princeton Univ., N.J. 1947-, George M. Moffett Prof. 1966-, Chair. Dept. of Biology 1965-77, 1983-84, 1987-88; Sheldon Travelling Fellow, Panama, Cuba 1941; Rockefeller Travelling Fellow, Paris 1953; Guggenheim Fellow, Edin. 1958, 1971-72; Nat. Science Foundation Sr. Postdoctoral Fellow, Cambridge, England 1963; Commonwealth Foundation Book Fund Fellow, Edin. 1971 and 1984-85; Josiah Macy Jr. Foundation Book Fund Fellow, Edin. 1978; Fellow American Acad. of Arts and Sciences, A.A.A.S.; mem. American Philosophical Soc., N.A.S.; mem. Editorial Bd. Growth 1955-, Differentiation 1976-, Oxford Surveys in Evolutionary Biology 1982-; fmr. mem. Editorial Bd. American Naturalist, American Scientist and other publs. *Publications:* Morphogenesis: An Essay on Development 1952, Cells and Societies 1955, The Evolution of Development 1958, The Cellular Slime Molds 1959, The Ideas of Biology 1962 (several edns. in transl.), Size and Cycle 1965, The Scale of Nature 1969, On Development: The Biology of Form 1974, The Evolution of Culture in Animals 1980 (several edns. in trans.), On Size and Life 1983; The Evolution of Complexity 1988; Ed. abridged edn. of Growth and Form (D'Arcy Thompson) 1961. *Leisure interests:* fishing, walking. *Address:* Department of Biology, Guyot Hall, Princeton University, Princeton, N.J. 08544 (Office); 148 Mercer Street, Princeton, N.J. 09540, U.S.A. (Home). *Telephone:* (609) 452-3841 (Office); (609) 924-1255 (Home).

BONNER, Paul Max; British television executive; b. 30 Nov. 1934, Banstead, Surrey; s. of Frank and Jill Bonner; m. Jenifer Bonner 1956; two s. one d.; ed. Felsted School; with Longmans Green & Co., Publrs. 1952; trainee reporter, Southend Standard 1953; Nat. Service 1953-55; Asst. Press Officer, E.K. Cole Ltd. 1955; freelance work for Evening Standard 1955; Trainee Studio Asst., BBC, Bristol 1955-56, Studio Man. 1956-58, Acting Asst. Producer, Talks Dept., West Region 1958-59, Production Asst., Talks Dept., TV 1961-65, Sr. Producer, Travel and Features Programmes 1965-74, Ed. BBC Community Programmes 1974-77, Special Asst. to Controller BBC2 1977, Chair. Small Integrated Multi-Role Production Unit Study Group 1977, Head of Science and Features Dept., TV 1978-81; Channel Controller, Channel Four TV Co. Ltd. 1981-83, Controller of Programmes and Exec. Dir. 1983-87; Dir. of Programme Planning Secr. ITV Asscn. 1987-; Chair. Edin. TV Festival 1979; a Man., Royal Inst. 1982-85; Gov. of Nat. Film and TV School 1981-88; Bd. mem., Broadcasting Support Services; Chair. Media Group, Cttee. on Public Understanding of Science; Fellow Royal TV Soc. *Publication:* The Third Age of Broadcasting 1983. *Leisure interests:* photography, sailing, walking. *Address:* ITV Association, Knighton House, 56 Mortimer Street, London, W1N 8AN. *Telephone:* (01) 636-6866.

BONNER, Robert William, LL.B., Q.C.; Canadian politician and business executive; b. 10 Sept. 1920, Vancouver; m. Barbara Newman 1942; one s. two d.; ed. Univ. of British Columbia; army service in U.K., N. Africa, Sicily, Italy 1942-45; mem. Legis. Ass., B.C. 1952-68; Attorney-Gen., B.C. 1952-68; at various times concurrently Minister of Educ., of Industrial Devt., of Trade and Commerce, of Commercial Transport; Senior Vice-Pres. Admin., MacMillan Bloedel Ltd. 1968-71, Dir. 1968-, mem. Exec. Cttee. 1969, Vice-Chair. 1971-72, Pres., Chief Exec. Officer 1972-73, Chair. 1973-74, retd. 1974; Chair, B. C. Hydro & Power Authority 1976-85;

Partner, Robertson Ward Suderman 1985–; Dir. Terramar Resource Corpn.; mem. Bd Grace Hosp., Energy Supplies Allocation, Canadian Bar Asscn., Vancouver Bar Asscn., Life Bencher Law Soc. of B.C., Bd. of Montreal Trust. *Leisure interests:* photography, boating. *Address:* Box 47, 1800 Four Hundred Burrard, Vancouver, B.C. V6C 3A6 (Office); 5679 Newton Wynd, Vancouver, B.C. V6T 1H6, Canada (Home).

BONNET, Christian, D. EN D.; French industrialist and politician; b. 14 June 1921, Paris; s. of Pierre Bonnet and Suzanne Delebecque; m. Christiane Mertian 1943; five c.; ed. Univ. of Paris and Ecole des sciences politiques; Pres. Les Grandes Marques de la conserve 1952–61, Del. Conseil supérieure de la conserve; MRP Deputy for Morbihan 1956–58, 1981–; Deputy for the second constituency of Morbihan 1963–; Gen. Councillor, Belle-Ile 1958–; Mayor of Carnac 1964–; fmr. Sec.-Gen. Républicains Indépendants; Chair. Cttee. on the Merchant Marine budget; Pres. Supervisory Council, Caisse des dépots et consignations; Sec. of State for Supply, Housing and Territorial Devt. 1972–74; Minister of Agric. 1974–77, of the Interior 1977–81; Senator for Morbihan 1983. *Address:* Palais du Luxembourg, 75291 Paris Cedex 06, France.

BONNEY, J. Dennis, B.S., LL.M.; American business executive; b. 22 Dec. 1930, Blackpool, England; s. of John P. Bonney and Isabel Evans; m. Elizabeth Shore-Wilson; three s. two d.; ed. Oxford Univ. and Univ. of California, Berkeley; lawyer (self-employed), Liverpool 1956–59; Exec. Iraq Petroleum Co., London and Baghdad 1959–60; Exec. Standard Oil Co. (now Chevron Corp), San Francisco 1960–, elected Vice-Pres. 1972, Dir. 1986, Vice-Chair. 1987–. *Leisure interests:* music, tennis, sailing. *Address:* Chevron Corporation, 225 Bush Street, San Francisco, Calif. 94104, U.S.A. *Telephone:* (415) 894-3232.

BONNICI, Emanuel, LL.D., M.P.; Maltese lawyer and politician; b. 17 May 1928, Valletta; ed. the Lyceum and Univ. of Malta; practising lawyer 1953–87; mem. Exec. Cttee. Nationalist Party 1963–; mem. Parl. 1966–; Minister for Devt. of Tertiary Sector May 1987–; fmr. Pres. Civic Council of Valletta. *Address:* Ministry for the Development of the Tertiary Sector, Valletta, Malta.

BONNICI, Karmenu Mifsud (see Mifsud Bonnici, Karmenu).

BONNICI, Ugo Mifsud (See Mifsud Bonnici, Ugo).

BONO VOX (b. Paul Hewson); Irish rock singer; b. 10 May 1960; formed rock group U2 with friends, Dublin 1978. *Recordings include:* Boy 1980, October 1981, War 1983.

BONYNGE, Richard, C.B.E.; Australian conductor; b. 20 Sept. 1930, Sydney; s. of C. A. Bonynge; m. Joan Sutherland (q.v.) 1954; one s.; trained as a pianist; début as conductor with Santa Cecilia Orchestra, Rome 1962; conducted first opera Faust, Vancouver 1963; has conducted in most of leading opera houses; Artistic Dir., Principal Conductor Sutherland/Williamson Int. Grand Opera Co., Australia 1965; Artistic Dir. Vancouver Opera Asscn. 1974–; Musical Dir. Australian Opera 1975–85. Has conducted La Sonnambula, La Traviata, Faust, Eugene Onegin, L'Elisir d'amore, Orfeo 1967, Semiramide, Florence 1968, Giulio Cesare, Lucia di Lammermoor, Hamburg, New York 1969–71, Norma and Orfeo, N.Y. 1970, The Tales of Hoffmann, N.Y. 1973, Sydney Opera House 1974. *Major recordings include:* Alcina, La Sonnambula, Norma, Beatrice di Tenda, I Puritani, Faust, Semiramide, Lakmé, La Fille du Régiment, Messiah, Don Giovanni, Les Huguenots, L'Elisir d'amore, Lucia di Lammermoor, Rigoletto, The Tales of Hoffmann, Thérèse (Massenet), numerous orchestral works, ballet including Giselle, Coppélia, Sylvia, The Nutcracker. *Publication:* The Joan Sutherland Album (with Dame Joan Sutherland) 1986. *Address:* c/o Ingpen and Williams, 14 Kensington Court, London W.8., England.

BÖÖHER, Edward E.; American publisher; b. 29 June 1911, Dayton, Ohio; s. of Wilfred Elsworth Booher and Cora Bell Middlestetter Booher; m. 1st Selena Read Knight 1939, 2nd Agnes Martin Whitaker 1961; two s. one d., two step-s. one step-d.; ed. Antioch Coll.; McGraw-Hill Book Co., Vice-Pres. 1944–54, Exec. Vice-Pres. 1954–60, Pres. 1960–68, Chair. 1968–70; Pres. Books and Educ. Services Group, McGraw-Hill Inc. 1970–76; mem. Bd. of Dirs. Henry Holt and Co., Inc., Scientific American, Inc.; Dir. Nat. Enquiry into Scholarly Publishing 1976–78, Scholastic Magazines Inc.; Woodrow Wilson Fellow; Trustee, Edward W. Hazen Foundation; L.H.D. (Rutgers). *Leisure interests:* education, tennis, swimming, travel. *Address:* 34 Wilson Road, Princeton, N.J. 08540, U.S.A. *Telephone:* 609-921-7822.

BOOKER, Henry George, PH.D.; American professor of applied physics; b. 14 Dec. 1910, Barking, Essex, U.K.; s. of Charles Henry Booker and Gertrude Mary Booker; m. Adelaide Mary McNish 1938; two s. two d.; ed. Cambridge Univ.; Research Fellow, Christ's Coll., Cambridge 1935–40; Scientific Officer in British Radar Research Establishment 1940–45; Univ. lecturer in Math., Cambridge Univ. 1945–48; Prof. of Electrical Eng., Cornell Univ. 1948–65, Prof. of Eng. Physics 1949–65, IBM Prof. of Eng. and Applied Math. 1962–65, Dir. School of Electrical Eng. 1959–63; Prof. of Eng., Univ. of Calif., San Diego 1965–; Research Assoc. Carnegie Inst. of Washington 1937–39; Guggenheim Fellow, Cambridge Univ. 1954–55; Staff Scientist, Stanford Research Inst. 1962–63, 1977; Hon. Prof. of Space Physics Wuhan Univ., China 1981–; Hon. Pres. Int. Union of Radio Science 1978–; mem. N.A.S. and numerous other socs.; numerous prizes. *Publications:* Over fifty scientific works. *Leisure interest:* swimming.

Address: Department of Electrical Engineering and Computer Sciences, University of California, San Diego, La Jolla, Calif. 92093, U.S.A. *Telephone:* 614-452-4496.

BOOKOUT, John Frank, Jr., M.A.; American petroleum executive; b. 31 Dec. 1922, Shreveport, La.; s. of the late John Frank and Lena (Hagen) Bookout; m. Mary Carolyn Cook 1946; one s. two d.; ed. Centenary Coll., Shreveport, La., Univ. of Texas, Austin, Tex.; joined Shell Oil Co., Geologist, Tulsa, Okla. 1950–59, Man. Exploration Div. 1959–61, Area Exploration Man., Denver, Colo. 1961–63, the Hague, Netherlands 1963–64, Exploration Man., New Orleans 1964, Man. Exploration and Production Econs. Dept., New York 1965, Vice-Pres. Denver Area 1966, Vice-Pres. Southeastern Exploration and Production Region 1967–70; Pres. and Chief Exec. Officer, Shell Canada Ltd. 1970–74; Exec. Vice-Pres. Shell Oil Co. 1974–76, Pres., Dir. and Chief Exec. Officer 1976–87; Dir. Irving Trust Co., Houston Chamber of Commerce, Methodist Hospital, Houston, Safeway Stores Inc.; mem. Bd. of Visitors Tulane Univ., Southern Regional Advisory Bd. of Inst. of Int. Educ., British-North America Cttee., Geology Foundation Advisory Council of Texas Univ., Man. Cttee. American Petrol Inst., Advisory Cttee. of Houston Reg. Minority Purchasing Council, American Assen. of Petrol Geologists, Business Roundtable, Nat. Petroleum Council, The Conf. Bd., Business Higher Educ. Forum of American Council on Educ.; Trustee U.S. Council of Int. Chambers of Commerce, Foundations for Business, Politics and Econs.; Hon. D.Sc. (Tulane). *Leisure interests:* hunting, fishing. *Address:* P.O. Box 13614, Houston, Tex. 77019, U.S.A. (Home).

BOOMS, Hans, DR.PHIL.; German historian and archivist; b. 22 June 1924, Haldern/Reis; s. of Theodor Booms and Agnes Kamps; m. 1st Renate Welter 1949, 2nd Brigitte Ludwig 1981; one s. two d.; ed. Gymnasium, Emmerich and Univ. of Cologne; Hon. Prof. Univ. of Cologne 1970; Pres. Fed. Archives of Fed. Republic of Germany 1972–; Pres. Int. Council on Archives 1984–; Bundesverdienstkreuz; Commdr. Ordre de la Couronne de Chêne. *Publications:* historical and archival books and articles. *Address:* Potsdamerstrasse 1, Am Berliner Ring, 5400 Koblenz (Office); Emser Landstrasse 9, 5420 Lahnstein, Federal Republic of Germany (Home). *Telephone:* 0261-505-200 (Office); 02621-7845 (Home).

BOOMSTRA, Sjoerd, D.JUR.; Netherlands financial executive; b. 12 Sept. 1913, Rotterdam; m. Henny Brons 1954; two c.; ed. secondary school, Bandung, Indonesia, Univ. of Leiden; Netherlands Clearing Inst. and Deviezen Inst. 1938; joined Ministry of Finance 1945, Deputy Dir., then Dir. External Finance 1953; Vice-Pres. EIB 1970–76, Hon. Vice-Pres. 1976–. *Address:* Ridderlaan 25, The Hague, Netherlands. *Telephone:* 24-41-67.

BOON, Henrik Nicolaas, LL.D.; Netherlands diplomatist (retd.); b. 23 Aug. 1911, Rotterdam; s. of Jan Boon and Elizabeth Johanna Mees; m. Charlotte Talitha Mees 1936; four d.; ed. Univs. of Leiden, London, Paris and Geneva School of Int. Studies; served Ministry of Foreign Affairs 1936–39; served in Madrid, Brussels, Washington, Tsjoengking, Jakarta and Nanking 1939–47; Deputy and later Chief of Diplomatic Affairs Div., Ministry of Foreign Affairs 1947–49; Sec.-Gen. Ministry of Foreign Affairs 1949–52, Minister later Amb. to Italy (also accred. to Malta) 1952–58 and 1970–77, Amb. to Venezuela 1958–61; Amb. on Special Mission; Perm. Rep. to NATO 1961–70; Chair. A. Pearson Museum Foundation, Netherlands Venice Cttee.; Hon. CG of Malta; Kt. Order of Netherlands Lion, Grand Officer, Order of Orange-Nassau, Grand Cross Order of Adolf van Nassau of Luxembourg, Grand Officer Order of the Crown of Belgium, Commdr. Légion d'honneur, Grand Cross Ordine al Merito, Italy. *Publications:* Rêve et réalité dans l'oeuvre économique et social de Napoléon III, Bagatellen, Afscheidsaudientie (Farewell Audience), Uitgevaren-thuisgevaren, Indonesian Diary 1946–49 (ed. Wiebes and Zeeman). *Leisure interests:* archaeology, classical music, horse-riding. *Address:* Parkflat Marlot 16, Offenberglaan 1, 2594 BM 's-Gravenhage, Netherlands. *Telephone:* (070) 852039.

BOON, John Trevor, C.B.E.; British publisher; b. 21 Dec. 1916; s. of Charles Boon and Mary Cowpe; m. Felicity A. Logan 1943; four s.; ed. Felsted School and Trinity Hall, Cambridge; war service 1939–45; Historical Section, War Cabinet 1945–46; joined Mills & Boon, Ltd. 1938, Man. Dir. 1963–, Chair. 1972–; Dir. Wood Bros. Glass Works Ltd. 1968, Chair. 1973–75, Deputy Chair. 1975–78; Vice-Chair. Harlequin Enterprises Ltd., Toronto 1972–83; Chair. Harlequin Overseas 1978–, Marshall Editions 1977–; Dir. Harmex 1978–82, Harlequin France 1980–82 (Chair. 1978–80), Torstar Corpn. Toronto 1981–85, Open Univ. Educational Enterprises 1977–79, etc.; Pres. Publishers Assen. 1961, Int. Publishers' Assen. 1972–76, Soc. of Bookmen 1981; Hon. M.A. (Open Univ.) 1983. *Leisure interests:* walking, swimming, wine, books, friends. *Address:* c/o Royal Bank of Scotland (Holt's Branch), Kirkland House, Whitehall, London, S.W.1., England.

BOON, William Robert, PH.D., F.R.S.; British chemist (retd.); b. 20 March 1911, London; s. of Walter and Ellen Boon; m. Marjorie Betty Oury 1938; one s. two d.; ed. St. Dunstan's Coll. Catford and King's Coll. London; Research in Chemotherapy and Agrochemicals, ICI 1936–67; Dir. Jealott's Hill Research Station 1960–67; Man. Dir. Plant Protection Ltd. (ICI) 1967–73; mem. Advisory Bd. Research Councils 1973–76, Natural Environment Research Council 1976–79; Mullard Medal, Royal Soc. 1972; Fellow,

King's Coll. 1976. *Publications:* papers in Biochemical Journal, Journal of the Chemical Soc., Journal of the Soc. of Chemical Industry. *Leisure interest:* reading. *Address:* The Gables, Sid Road, Sidmouth, Devon, EX10 9AQ, England. *Telephone:* (0395) 514069.

BOONYACHAI, Admiral Sonthi; Thai politician and fmr. naval officer; b. 20 June 1917; ed. Suan Kularb Coll., Bangkok, Royal Naval Acad.; naval positions afloat and ashore included C.O. HTMS Po Sam Ton 1953, Asst. Navy C.-in-C. 1973, Deputy Navy C.-in-C. 1976; Deputy Prime Minister 1983–88. *Address:* c/o Government House, Nakhon Pathom Road, Bangkok 10300, Thailand.

BOONZAIER, Hugh Murray; South African stockbroker; b. 31 July 1933, Cape Town; ed. Observatory Boys' High School and Univ. of Cape Town; qualified as chartered accountant 1956; Accountant, Cape Portland Cement, various jobs, London, England, on staff of Southern Paper Industries, Cape Town, Man. Trainee, Alcan Aluminium, Pietermaritzburg, then Johannesburg; became mem. Johannesburg Stock Exchange 1963, Pres. 1985–86; Dir. Allied Group Ltd. 1986, African Cables 1987; Hon. Life mem. J.S.E. 1986. *Address:* P.O. Box 61028, Marshalltown 2107, Johannesburg, South Africa.

BOORMAN, John; British film director, producer and screenwriter; b. 18 Jan. 1933; s. of George and Ivy (Chapman) Boorman; m. Christel Kruse 1956; one s. three d.; ed. Salesian Coll., Chertsey; Broadcaster and critic, BBC Radio, also contributor to Manchester Guardian and magazines 1950–54; army service 1951–53; Film Editor, ITN London 1955–58; Dir. and Producer Southern TV 1958–60; Head of Documentaries, Bristol, BBC TV; left BBC to work as film director; Chair. Nat. Film Studios of Ireland 1975–85; Gov. British Film Inst. 1983–; Best Director Prize, Cannes Festival 1970, many film awards; Chevalier de l'Ordre des Arts et Lettres 1985. *Television:* founded magazine Day by Day, Dir. The Citizen 1963, The Newcomers 1960–64. *Films:* Catch us if you can 1965, Point Blank 1967, Hell in the Pacific 1968, Leo the Last 1969, Deliverance 1970, Zardoz 1973, The Heretic 1976, Excalibur 1981, The Emerald Forest 1985, Hope and Glory 1987 (Golden Globe Award 1988). *Publication:* The Legend of Zardoz 1973 (novel), Money into Light 1985. *Leisure interests:* hacking the Wicklow Hills, losing gracefully at tennis, skiing in the wake of my kids. *Address:* The Glebe, Annamoe, Co. Wicklow, Ireland. *Telephone:* Wicklow (404) 5177.

BOORSTIN, Daniel J., M.A., LL.D.; American historian, author and administrator; b. 1 Oct. 1914, Atlanta, Ga.; s. of late Samuel Boorstin and Dora Olsan; m. Ruth Carolyn Frankel 1941; three s.; ed. Harvard Coll., Balliol Coll., Oxford, Cambridge and Yale Univs.; Harvard Coll. and Harvard Law School 1938–42; Office of Lend-Lease Admin., Washington 1942; Asst. Prof., Swarthmore Coll. 1942–44; Prof. of American History and Preston and Sterling Morton Distinguished Service Prof. of History, Univ. of Chicago 1944–69; Prof. American History, Univ. of Paris 1961–62; Pitt Prof. American History and Institutions and Fellow, Trinity Coll. Cambridge 1964–65; Dir. Nat. Museum of History and Tech. 1969–73; Shelby and Kathryn Cullom Davis Lecturer, Graduate Inst. of Int. Studies, Geneva 1973–74; Senior Historian Smithsonian Inst., Washington, D.C. 1973–75; The Librarian of Congress 1975–87, Librarian Emer. 1987–; mem. Bd. Trustees Colonial Williamsburg, Bd. Dirs. Thomas Gilcrease Museum, Comm. on Critical Choices for Americans, Bd. Editors Encyclopedia Britannica; numerous hon. degrees; Pulitzer Prize for History 1974, and several other prizes; Chevalier Legion d'Honneur 1984, Grand Officer of the Order of Prince Henry the Navigator (Portugal) 1985, Japanese Order of the Sacred Treasure, (First Class) 1986, Watson-Davis Prize of the History of Science (Soc. for Discoverers) 1986. *Publications:* The Mysterious Science of the Law 1941, Delaware Cases 1792–1830 (3 vols.) 1943, The Lost World of Thomas Jefferson 1948, The Genius of American Politics 1953, The Americans: The Colonial Experience 1958, America and the Image of Europe 1960, The Image or What Happened to the American Dream 1962, The Americans: The National Experience 1965, The Landmark History of the American People (2 vols.) 1968, 1970, The Decline of Radicalism 1969, The Sociology of the Absurd 1970, The Americans: The Democratic Experience 1973, Democracy and its Discontents 1974, The Exploring Spirit 1976, The Republic of Technology 1978, A History of the United States (with Brooks Kelley) 1980, The Discoverers 1983, Hidden History 1987; Ed.: An American Primer 1966, American Civilization 1972. *Leisure interests:* gardening, bird watching, hiking. *Address:* U.S. News and World Report, 2400 North Street, N.W., Washington D.C. 20037 (Office); 3541 Ordway Street, N.W., Washington, D.C. 20016, U.S.A. (Home). *Telephone:* (202) 955-2652 (Office); (202) 287-5205 (Home).

BOOTH, Rt. Hon. Albert Edward, P.C., C.I.MECH.E.; British politician; b. 28 May 1928; s. of Albert Henry Booth and Janet Mathieson; m. Joan Amis 1957; three s.; ed. South Shields Marine School, Rutherford Coll. of Technology; worked as a marine eng. draughtsman; elected to Tynemouth Borough Council 1962; Tynemouth Election Agent 1951, 1955; M.P. for Barrow-in-Furness 1966–83; Minister of State, Dept. of Employment 1974–76; Sec. of State for Employment 1976–79; Opposition Spokesman for Transport 1979–83; Dir. S. Yorkshire Passenger Transport 1983–87; Public Transport Officer, Hounslow Council 1988–; Treas., The Labour Party 1984–85. *Address:* 128 Brooklands Crescent, Sheffield, England.

BOOTH, Charles Leonard, C.M.G., L.V.O., M.A.; British diplomatist; b. 7 March 1925, Rochdale; s. of Charles and Marion Booth; m. Mary G. Emms 1958; two s. two d.; ed. Heywood Grammar School and Univ. of Oxford; served R.A. 1943–47; joined diplomatic service 1950; Second and Third Sec., Rangoon 1951–55, Head of Chancery 1963–64, Amb. 1978–82; Foreign Office 1955–60, 1967–69; First Sec. Rome 1960–63; Head of Chancery, Bangkok 1964–67; Deputy High Commr., Kampala 1969–71; Consul Gen., Washington, D.C. 1971–73; Counsellor, Belgrade 1973–77; High Commr. in Malta 1982–85; with FCO 1985–. *Leisure interests:* books, opera, gardening. *Address:* c/o Foreign and Commonwealth Office, King Charles Street, London, SW1A 2AH, England.

BOOTH, Eric Stuart, C.B.E., F.R.S.; British electrical engineer; b. 14 Oct. 1914; s. of Henry Booth and Annie Booth; m. 1st Mary Elizabeth Melton 1945 (died 1987); two d.; m. 2nd Pauline Margaret Ford 1988; ed. Batley Grammar School, Liverpool Univ.; apprentice, Metropolitan Vickers Electrical Co. Ltd. 1936–38; Tech. Eng., Yorks. Electric Power Co. 1938–46; Deputy, then City Electrical Eng. and Man., Salford Corpn. 1946–48; posts involving construction of power stations with Cen. Electricity Authority 1948–57, Deputy Chief Eng. (Generation Design and Construction) 1957, Chief Engineer (Design and Construction) 1958; mem. bd. for Eng. Cen. Electricity Generating Bd. 1958–72, Chief Design and Construction Eng., 1972–79; Chair. Yorks. Electricity Bd. 1972–79; part-time mem. UKAEA 1965–72; Pres. I.E.E. 1976–77; Consultant to Electricity Council 1979–84; Dir. British Electricity Int. 1979–84; Hon. D. Tech (Bradford) 1980. *Address:* Pinecroft, Upper Dunsforth, York, Y05 9RU, England. *Telephone:* 0423 32 2821.

BOOTH, I. MacAllister, B.S., M.B.A.; American business executive; b. 7 Dec. 1931, Atlanta, Ga.; m.; two s. two d.; ed. Cornell Univ.; joined Polaroid Corpn. 1958, Pres. and C.E.O. 1986–; Dir. Western Digital Corpn. *Address:* Polaroid Corporation, 549 Technology Square, Cambridge, Mass. 02139, U.S.A. *Telephone:* (617) 577-2000.

BOOTH-CLIBBORN, Rt. Rev. Stanley Eric Francis, M.A.; British ecclesiastic; b. 20 Oct. 1924, London; s. of Theodore Booth-Clibborn and Lucille Booth-Clibborn; m. Anne Forrester; two s. two d.; ed. Highgate School, London and Oriel Coll., Oxford; Curate, Attercliffe, Sheffield 1952–54; Training Officer Christian Council of Kenya 1956–63; Ed.-in-Chief East African Venture Christian Papers Target and Lengo 1963–67; Leader Lincoln City Centre Team Ministry 1967–70; Vicar of Great St. Mary's Cambridge 1970–79; Bishop of Manchester 1979–. *Leisure interests:* tennis, photography, reading and walking. *Address:* Bishopscourt, Bury New Road, Manchester, M7 0LE, England.

BORBÁNDI, János; Hungarian politician; b. 1923; ed. Univ. of Political Econ., Party Acad.; joined Communist Party 1945; machine fitter Csepel Iron Works until 1949; political posts in factory and party headquarters 1949–53; Sec. Factory Party Cttee., Lenin Foundry Works, Diósgyor 1953–55; First Sec. Party Cttee., Budapest District II 1958–61; Deputy Minister of Defence 1961–66; Leader Admin. Dept., Cen. Cttee., Hungarian Socialist Workers' Party 1966, mem. Cen. Supervisory Dept. 1962–66, Cen. Cttee. 1970–; mem. Parl. 1962–66; Deputy Prime Minister 1974–84. *Address:* Office of the Prime Minister, Kossuth Lajos tér 1, 1357 Budapest, Hungary. *Telephone:* 123-500.

BORBÉLY, Sándor; Hungarian politician; b. 1931, Nagybun.; began career as toolmaker; entered politics 1947; full-time communist youth leader 1949–55; mem. Hungarian Working People's Party 1950–56, Hungarian Socialist Workers' Party (HSWP) 1956–; mem. Youth Cttee. of HSWP and organizing Cttee. of Communist Youth League (CYL) 1956; Sec. of Cen. Cttee. of CYL, First Sec. of Budapest Cttee. of CYL 1957; alt. mem. Cen. Cttee. of HSWP 1957; Sec. of Party Cttee., Csepel Iron and Metal Works 1962, First Sec. 1970; First Sec. of HSWP Cttee., 21st District of Budapest 1966–70; Head of Industry, Agric. and Transport Dept. of HSWP Cen. Cttee. 1975, Sec. of Cen. Cttee. 1976–80; Nat. Commdr. of Workers Militia. *Address:* Central Committee of the Hungarian Socialist Workers' Party, Széchenyi rakpart 19, Budapest V, Hungary.

BORCH, Otto Rose; Danish diplomatist; b. 1 Sept. 1921, Randers; s. of A. Borch and Ninna Borch; m. Astrid Lundbye 1951; two d.; ed. Copenhagen and Columbia Univs; joined Foreign Service 1948; Embassy Sec., Bonn 1954–59; Head of Section Ministry of Foreign Affairs 1959–61, Head of Dept. 1961–64; Deputy Perm. Rep. North Atlantic Council 1964–67; Perm. Rep. to UN 1967–74; Under-Sec. of State for Political Affairs, Copenhagen 1974–76; Amb. to U.S.A. 1976–83, to Sweden 1988–; Perm. Rep. to North Atlantic Council 1983–88; Commdr. Order of the Danebrog, Royal Order of the Polar Star (First Class), Star of the Royal Norwegian Order of St. Olav (First Class). *Address:* Danish Embassy, Box 1638, S-111 86 Stockholm, Sweden.

BORCHERS, Elisabeth; German editor; b. 27 Feb. 1926, Homberg; d. of Rudolf Sarbin and Claire (née Beck) Sarbin; m. (divorced); two s.; ed. Luchterhand 1960–71, Suhrkamp Verlag and Insel Verlag 1971–; mem. PEN, Acad. of Sciences and Literature in Mainz; Erzahlerpreis Suddeutscher Rundfunk, German Industry Culture Prize, Roswitha-Gedenk-Medaille, Friedrich-Hölderlin-Preis. *Publications:* poetry, prose, translations, children's books. *Address:* Arndtstrasse 17, 6000 Frankfurt 1; Federal Republic of Germany. *Telephone:* (069) 74 63 91.

BORCHERT, Wilhelm: German actor; b. 13 March 1907, Berlin; s. of Wilhelm Borchert and Marie Klatt; m. Marga Klas 1949; ed. Reichersche Hochschule für dramatische Kunst; Ostpreussische Bühne, Königsberg 1927–28; Landestheater, Sonderhausen 1928–29; Städtische Bühnen, Erfurt 1929–34, Cologne 1934–38; Hebbeltheater, Volksbühne and Deutsches Theater, Berlin 1938–, Schillertheater 1950–; noted for interpretation of works of Goethe, Schiller, Büchner, Wedekind etc.; TV appearances; mem. Frankfurt and Berlin Acads.; Berliner Staatsschauspieler 1963, Berliner Kunstpreis 1976. *Films:* Die Mörder sind unter uns, Schicksal aus zweiter Hand, Herr über Leben und Tod, Hunde wollt ihr ewig leben. *Leisure interests:* literature, music. *Address:* 1000 Berlin 28, Zeltingerstrasse 14, Federal Republic of Germany.

BORD, André; French politician; b. 30 Nov. 1922, Strasbourg; s. of Alphonse Bord and Marie-Anne Sigrist; m. 1st Germaine Fend, two s.; m. 2nd Francine Heisserer; ed. Saint-Etienne Coll., Strasbourg; mem. of Nat. Assembly 1958–66, 1967, 1968, 1973, 1978; mem. Municipal Council, Strasbourg 1959–, Deputy Mayor 1959–71; mem. Conseil Général, Strasbourg-Est 1961–73, of Strasbourg 8 1973–79; Pres. Corbeil-Général du Ba's-Rhin 1967–79; Pres. Groupe de l'Union démocratique européenne, European Parl. 1961–66, mem. European Parl. 1982–84; Sec. of State for Interior 1966–72, for Ex-Servicemen and War Victims 1972–77, for Relations with Parl. 1977–78; Sec.-Gen. UDR 1975–76; Founder, Pres. Asscn. for Industrial Devt., Alsace 1967; Pres. Regional Council of Alsace 1973–77, Asscn. Départementale du Tourisme, Commission Interministérielle de Coopération France-République Fédérale d'Allemagne 1986–; Médaille militaire, Médaille de la France libre, Médaille de la Résistance, Croix de guerre avec palme; Grand Officer, Order of Orange-Nassau (Netherlands), Order of Polonia Restituta (Poland), Chevalier, Légion d'Honneur, and others. *Address:* 27 route de Wolfisheim, 67810 Holtzheim, France.

BORDABERRY AROCENA, Juan Maria; Uruguayan politician; b. 17 June 1928, Montevideo; s. of Domingo Bordaberry and Elisa Arocena de Bordaberry; m. Josefina Herrán Puig; seven s. one d.; ed. Univ. Montevideo; Chair., Nat. Meat Bd. 1959; mem. Hon. Comm. for Agric. Devt. Plan 1960; mem. Nat. Wool Bd. 1960–62; Chair. Comm. Against Foot and Mouth Disease 1962; mem. Senate 1962–64; Chair. Liga Federal de Acción Ruralista 1964; Minister of Agric. 1969–72; Pres. of Uruguay 1972–76 (deposed). *Address:* Joaquín Suárez 2868, Montevideo, Uruguay. *Telephone:* 20-14-12.

BORDAZ, Robert, D. EN D., L. ÉS L.; French lawyer; b. 6 July 1908, Argenton-le-Château, Deux Sèvres; s. of Louis Bordaz and Marguerite Michel; m. Mathilde Lacoste 1947; two s. one d.; Communications and Merchant Marine Office, Algiers 1943; Ministry of Public Works, Paris; Master of Petitions, Council of State 1944; Ministry of Nat. Economy 1945; Govt. Commr., Banque de Paris et des Pays Bas 1946–48; Head of Private Office of Minister of Construction 1948–51; Dir. Bank Inst. of Cambodia, Laos and Viet-Nam 1951–54; Deputy Commr. Indo-China 1954–56; Commercial Counsellor and Head of Dept. of Econ. Expansion, Moscow 1956–58; Counsellor of State 1958; Pres. Inst. d'Aménagement et d'Urbanisme de la Ville de Paris 1960–62; Dir.-Gen. Radiodiffusion-Télévision Française 1962–64; mem. Bd. of Agence France-Presse; Commr.-Gen. French section Expo 1967, Montreal 1964–67; Pres. Etablissement Public du Centre Georges Pompidou 1970–77, Union Centrale des Arts Décoratifs 1975–, Institut France/Canada 1977–; Avocat, Cour de Paris 1977–82; Pres. Ecole Speciale d'Architecture 1983–, Musée des Arts de la Mode 1986–; Grand Officier, Légion d'honneur, Médaille de la Résistance, Commdr. des Arts et des Lettres. *Publications:* La nouvelle économie soviétique 1935–1960 1960, monthly column in La Nouvelle Revue des Deux Mondes 1970–75, Le Centre Pompidou, une nouvelle culture 1977. *Leisure interest:* cinema. *Address:* Union centrale des arts décoratifs, 107 rue de Rivoli, 75001 Paris (Office); 15 rue Gay-Lussac, 75005 Paris, France (Home). *Telephone:* 359-3005 (Office); 033-10-31 (Home).

BORDIER, Primrose; French designer; b. 27 March 1929, Paris; d. of Marcel Bordier and Germaine de Fonds Lamothe; m. Charles Gombault (died 1983); ed. Couvent de l'Assomption, Paris; worked as textile designer 1949–54, with Cosserat (mfrs. of velvet) 1954–57, with Boussac 1958–60, with Printemps (Dept. Store) 1960–62; cr. own Co. (Couleurs, Dessins et Modèles) 1975, Man. 1975–82, Dir. 1982–; signed an exclusive contract with Descamps 1970, first Descamps shop opened 1975; Chevalier de la Légion d'honneur. *Address:* 57 avenue d'Iena, 75116 Paris, France.

BORDIER, Roger; French writer; b. 5 March 1923; s. of Robert Bordier and Valentine Jeufraux; m. Jacqueline Bouchaud; ed. secondary school; journalist in the provinces, later in Paris; contributor to Nouvelles Littéraires and Aujourd'hui; radio and television writer; Prix Renaudot 1961. *Publications:* poems: Les épicentres 1951; novels: La cinquième saison 1959, Les blés 1961, Le mime 1963, L'Entracte 1965, Un âge d'or 1967, Le tour de ville 1969, Les éventails 1971, L'océan 1974, Meeting 1976, Demain l'été 1977; plays: Les somnambules 1963, Les visiteurs 1972; essays: L'objet contre l'art 1972, Le progrès: Pour qui? 1973, L'art moderne et l'objet 1978; novels: La Grande Vie 1981, Les Temps heureux 1983, La longue file 1984, 36 La fête 1985, La belle de mai 1986, Les saltimbanques de la Révolution 1989. *Address:* 8 rue Geoffroy St. Hilaire, 75005 Paris, France. *Telephone:* 535-22-56.

BOREHAM, Sir Arthur John, K.C.B., B.A.; British civil servant (retd); b. 30 July 1925, Hindhead; s. of late Venerable Frederick and Caroline Mildred Boreham; m. Heather Horth 1948; three s. one d.; ed. Marlborough Coll., Trinity Coll., Oxford; Temporary Higher Executive Officer, Ministry of Food 1950–52; with Ministry of Agriculture and Fisheries 1952–55, Gen. Register Office 1955–58, 1963–67, Central Statistical Office 1958–63 and 1971–85, Ministry of Technology 1967–71; Asst. Dir. Cen. Statistical Office 1971–72, Deputy Dir. 1972–78, Dir. and Head of Govt. Statistical Service 1978–85; Visiting Fellow, Nuffield Coll., Oxford 1981–88; Pres. Inst. of Statisticians 1983–. *Leisure interests;* music, country life, golf. *Address:* Piperscroft, Brittains Lane, Sevenoaks, Kent, TN13 2NG, England. *Telephone:* Sevenoaks 454678.

BOREL, Jacques; French writer, teacher and critic; b. 17 Dec. 1925, Paris; s. of Pierre Borel and Lucie Dubée; m. Christiane Idrac 1948; one s. four d.; ed. Lycée Henri IV, Paris and Univ. de Paris; teacher, Lycée de Clermont-Ferrand 1952–56, Lycée Rodin, Paris 1956–67; Visiting Prof. Middlebury Coll. 1966, Portland State Coll. 1967, Univ. of Hawaii 1968, Univ. of Calif. (Irvine) 1969, Univ. of Calif. (Riverside) 1980, Univ. of N.Y. 1983; Literary Adviser Gallimard 1969–75, Balland 1978–82; Cultural Attaché, French Embassy in Belgium 1984–86; contributes poems and essays to Nouvelle Revue Française, Critique, Cahiers du Chemin, Mercure de France, Botteghe Oscure, Cahiers du Sud, Figaro, etc.; Prix Goncourt 1965, Chevalier Arts et Lettres 1971, Officier 1986. *Publications:* Ed.: Verlaine's Complete Works 1959–60, Poetical Works 1962, Complete Works in Prose 1972; novels: L'adoration 1965, Le retour 1970, Histoire de mes vieux habits 1979; play: Tata ou de l'education 1967; essays: Marcel Proust 1972, Commentaires 1974, Poésie et nostalgie 1979; diaries: La dépossession 1973, Un voyage ordinaire 1975; autobiography: Petite Histoire de mes Rêves 1981; Translated: James Joyce's The Cat and the Devil 1966, Collected Poems 1967, Prefaces to Romanciers au travail 1967, Du Bellay's Poetical Works 1967, Guillevic's Terraqué 1968, Fargue's Vulturne and épaisseurs 1971, Francis Jammes' De l'Angélus de l'aube à l'Angélus du soir 1971, Verlaine's Poèmes Saturniens, Fêtes galantes, Romances sans paroles 1973, Victor Hugo: Choix de poèmes 1983, Paroles Ecrites 1986, L'Enfant Voyeur 1987, Lettres d'Europe 1988. *Address:* 22 rue Charles de Gaulle, 91440 Bures-sur-Yvette, Essonne; 68 rue du Moulin, 91120 Palaiseau, Essonne, France. *Telephone:* 69 07 57 29; 60 10 33 57.

BOREL, Jacques Paul; French restaurant and hotel executive; b. 9 April 1927, Courbevoie; s. of William and Marie (née Le Monnier) Borel; m. Christiane Roubit 1949; two s. one d.; ed. Lycées Condorcet and Carnot, Paris, Ecole des Hautes Etudes Commerciales; mem. Sales Force IBM France 1950–57, Man. Saigon (Viet-Nam) Branch Office IBM; Founder Restaurant Chain Jacques Borel 1957, became Compagnie des Restaurants Jacques Borel (CRJB) 1960, then Jacques Borel Int. (J.B. Int.) 1970, Pres., Dir.-Gen. –1977; Pres. J.B. Enterprises Soc. 1977–; Dir. Sofitel Jacques Borel, Jacques Borel Belgie NV-Belgique SA, Jacques Borel Do Brasil, Jacques Borel Deutschland, Jacques Borel Italia, Jacques Borel Nederland, Jacques Borel Iran, Jacques Borel Misr (Egypt), Jacques Borel Venezuela, Hoteles Jacques Borel (Barcelona), Farah Maghreb (Casablanca); Founder Syndicat Nat. des Restaurants Economiques 1966, become Syndicat Nat. des Chaînes d'Hôtels et de Restaurants de Tourisme et d'Entreprise 1970, Pres. until 1972, then Founder-Pres.; Pres. Groupement HEC Tourisme-Hôtellerie. *Leisure interests:* music, painting, sailing.

BOREN, David L., M.A., J.D.; American lawyer and politician; b. 21 April 1941, Washington, D.C.; s. of Lyle H. and Christine (McKown) Boren; m. 1st, one s. one d.; m. 2nd Molly W. Shi 1977; ed. Yale, Oxford and Oklahoma Univs. Rhodes Scholar 1965; mem. Okla. House of Reps. 1966–74; Chair. Govt. Dept., Okla. Baptist Univ. 1969–74; Gov. of Okla 1975–79; Senator from Okla. 1979–. *Leisure interests:* family, reading, rowing, tennis. *Address:* 452 Russell Senate Office Building, Washington, D.C. 20510 (Office); 2369 South Queen Street, Arlington, Va. 22202, U.S.A. (Home). *Telephone:* (202) 224-4721 (Office).

BORG, Björn Rune; Swedish tennis player; b. 6 June 1956, Södertälje; s. of Rune Borg; m. Mariana Simionescu 1980 (divorced 1984); one s.; ed. Blombacka School; professional player since 1972; Italian Champion 1974, 1978; French Champion 1974, 1975, 1978, 1979, 1980, 1981; Wimbledon Champion 1976, 1977, 1978, 1979, 1980 (runner-up 1981); WCT Champion 1976; Grand Prix Masters Champion 1980, 1981; World Champion 1979, 1980; played Davis Cup for Sweden 1972, 1973, 1974, 1975, 1976, 1977, 1978, 1979, 1980; announced retirement from tennis Jan. 1983. *Publication:* Bjorn Borg—My Life and Game (with Eugene Scott) 1980. *Leisure interest:* fishing. *Address:* c/o International Management Group, The Pier House, Strand on the Green, Chiswick, London W4 3NN, England.

BORG, Kim, M.SC.; Finnish singer; b. 7 Aug. 1919, Helsinki; s. of Kaarlo Borg and Hilkka Stenius; m. Ebon Ringblom 1950; one s. one d.; ed. Helsinki Inst. of Technology and Sibelius-Acad., Helsinki. Début, Helsinki 1945; Royal Theatre, Copenhagen 1952–70; Finnish Nat. Opera 1952–70; Munich State Opera 1956–57; Glyndebourne Opera Co. 1956, 1959 and 1968; Metropolitan Opera Co., New York 1959–62; Royal Theatre, Stockholm 1963–75; Hamburg State Opera 1964–69; Prof. Royal Conservatory, Copenhagen 1972–; guest appearances at State Opera, Vienna and Bolshoi Theatre, Moscow; tours in Europe, N. and S. America, Asia, Australia and Africa; numerous recordings; composed chamber music and orchestral music; Chair. Det danske Sangselskab 1972-82; mem. Bd. Dirs. Danish-Finnish Soc.; Cross of Liberty (Finland); Kt. of White Rose (Finland); Kt. of Dannebrog (Denmark); Pro-Finlandia Medal; Hon. Cross for Arts and Sciences (Austria), Commdr. of North Star (Sweden). *Leisure interests:* Scandinavian co-operation, literature. *Publications:* Suomalainen laulajanaapinen (ABC for the Finnish singer) 1972. *Address:* Det Kgl. danske Musikkonservatorium, Copenhagen (Office); Österbrogade 158, DK 2100 Copenhagen, Denmark (Home). *Telephone:* 01-290731; 02-190027.

BORG, Lars Göran, LIC.SC., DR.SC.; Swedish mathematician; b. 19 Nov. 1913, Kumla; s. of Eric J. Borg and Elna Peterson; m. Gunborg Sjölinder, M.D., 1939; two s. one d.; ed. Univ. of Uppsala. Research Prof., Univ. of Uppsala 1945-52; Prof. of Math. Royal Inst. of Tech., Stockholm 1953-76, Rector 1968-74; Pres Bd. for Educ. Org. for Teachers in Tech. 1964-67; Pres. Bd. Microwave Inst. Stockholm 1968-78; Deputy, Bd. of L. M. Ericsson Telephone Co. 1972-80; Man. Dir C. Trygger Foundation 1980-; mem. Nat. Science Council 1961-67, Advisory Council of Bd. of Univ. Chancellor 1964-70, Swedish Bd. for Technical Development 1971-77, Royal Acad. of Eng. Sciences (Vice-Pres. 1972-74), Advisory Council to Wallenberg Foundation 1972-74, Swedish Math. Soc. (Pres. 1957-60), Swedish Operational Analysis Soc. (Pres. 1963), Swedish Soc. of Future Studies (Pres. 1971), New York Acad. of Science, American Math. Soc., American Assoc. for the Advancement of Science, Bd. of SEFI, Brussels 1973-74, Bd. of Inst. for Applied Math. 1975-84, Swedish UNESCO Comm. 1975-80, several govt. cttees. on educ., research, industry, radio and television, etc.; Hon. LL.D. (Dundee); Commdr. Order of Polar Star. *Publications:* Über die Stabilität gewisser Klassen von linearen Differentialgleichungen 1944, Eine Umkehrung der Sturm-Liouvilleschen Eigenwertaufgabe 1945, Inverse Problems in the Theory of Characteristic Values 1947, Bounded Solution of a System of Differential Equations 1948, On a Liapounoff Criterion 1949, On the Completeness of some Sets of Functions 1949, co-author several books on science policy, technology and economy 1978-80. *Leisure interests:* technical constructions, building. *Address:* C. Trygger Foundation, Artillerigatan 4, S-11451 Stockholm, Sweden (Office). 118 Alviksvagen, S-161 38 Stockholm-Bromma, Sweden (Home). *Telephone:* 08-663 86 00 (Office); 08-25-21-40 (Home).

BORGE, Victor; American entertainer; b. 3 Jan. 1909, Copenhagen; s. of Bernhard and Frederikke (née Lichtinger) Borge; m. Sarabel Sgaper; two s. three d. (including one s. and one d. by previous marriage); ed. Borgerdydskolen and Copenhagen Conservatoire, and in Berlin and Vienna under Frederic Lamond and Egon Petri; concert pianist 1922-34; revue, theatre and film career as composer, actor and musical comedian 1934-; settled in U.S.A. 1940, U.S. citizen 1948; Hon. D. Mus. (Butler Univ., Dana Coll., Neb.); Order of Dannebrog, Order of Vasa (Sweden) 1972, Order of St. Olav (Norway) 1973, Order of the White Rose (Finland) 1981. *Publication:* My Favourite Intervals 1974. *Leisure interest:* boating. *Address:* Field Point Park, Greenwich, Conn. 06830, U.S.A.

BORGE MARTÍNEZ, Tomás; Nicaraguan politician; b. 13 Aug. 1930, Matagalpa; ed. Nat. Univ., Léon; first took part in guerrilla activities 1958; f. Frente Sandinista de Liberación Nacional (F.S.L.N.) (Sandinist Nat. Liberation Front) 1961; arrested, nine months in prison, Tipitapa 1977-78; mem. Nat. Directorate F.S.L.N. Dec. 1978-; Minister of Interior July 1979-; Second in Command People's Army. *Address:* c/o Frente Sandinista de Liberación Nacional, Managua, Nicaragua.

BORGEAUD, Pierre, DIPL.ENG; Swiss business executive; b. 31 March 1934; m.; three c.; ed. Swiss Fed. Inst. of Tech.; Research Dept. of Sulzer Bros. Ltd 1959-73, Man. of Sulzer Eng. Works and of Swiss Locomotive and Machine Works, Winterthur 1973-75, Gen. Man., Sulzer Bros. Ltd. 1975-81, Pres. also C.E.O. of Corp. Exec. Man. 1981; Chair. Presidential Bd. of Swiss Fed. of Commerce and Industry; mem. Bd. of Dirs. Winterthur Insurance Co. and of Swiss Bank Corpn. *Address:* Sulzer Brothers Ltd., Zuercherstr. 9, CH-8401 Winterthur, Switzerland. *Telephone:* (052) 81 11 22.

BORGEN, Kjell; Norwegian politician; b. 21 Oct. 1939, Oslo; m.; Municipal Projects Leader and local Mayor 1968-77; mem. Storting 1977; Chair. Standing Cttee. on Communications 1981-85; Vice-Chair. Standing Cttee. on Local Govt. and the Environment, until 1986; Minister of Communications 1986-88, of Local Govt. and Labour June 1988-. *Address:* Ministry of Local Government and Labour, Møllergt. 43, P.O. Box 8112, Dep., 0030 Oslo 1, Norway. *Telephone:* (2) 11-90-90.

BORGES, Jacobo; Venezuelan painter; b. 28 Nov. 1931; ed. Escuela de Artes Plásticas Cristóbal Rojas, Caracas and Ecole des Beaux Arts, Paris; mem. of Young Painters' Group and Illustrator of magazines and record covers while in Paris 1951-56, also exhibited in French Nat. Exhbns.; Prof. of Scenography and Plastic Analysis, Escuela de Artes Plásticas Cristóbal Rojas, Caracas 1958-65; Prof. of Scenography, Theatre School of Valencia and Dir. Experimental Art Centre, Univ. Central de Venezuela 1966-; one-man exhbns. in Caracas at Galeria Lauro 1956, Museo de Bellas Artes 1956, Galeria G 1963 and Galeria Techo 1965; represented in numerous group exhbns. including São Paulo Bienal 1957, 1963, 1965, Venice Biennale 1958, Brussels World Fair 1958, and Int. Exhbns. at Guggenheim Museum, New York 1964, 1965; Nat. Painting Prize 1963, Armando Reverón Bienal Prize 1965. *Major works:* La Lámpara y la Silla

1951, La Pesca 1957, Sala de Espera 1960, Todos a la Fiesta 1962, Ha Comenzado el Espectáculo 1964, Altas Finanzas 1965; series of Las Jugadoras and Las Comedoras de Helados 1965-66. *Address:* c/o Museo de Bellas Artes, Avenida los Caobos, Caracas, Venezuela.

BORGES, José Joaquim Almeida, LL.D.; Portuguese judge; b. 25 Oct. 1910, Celorico da Beira; s. of José Joaquim Borges and Ana da Conceição de Almeida; m. Maria da Graça Pimenta 1947; three s. one d.; ed. S. Pedro Coll., Coimbra Coll. and Univ., Lisbon Univ.; Magistrate 1934-42; Judge, lower and appellate courts 1942-74, Judge for judicature in Flowers Island, Azores 1942-44; Counsellor Judge, Supreme Court of Justice June 1974-, Pres. 1975-81; Pres. of the Portuguese Maritime Law Comm. (Navy). *Publications:* co-author of specialist law publs. *Leisure interest:* nautical sports. *Address:* Rua Conde Sabugosa no. 25, 7°, Lisbon, Portugal. *Telephone:* 894863.

BORGMAN, Jan. PH.D.; Netherlands astronomer; b. 30 Nov. 1929, Groningen; m. Cobi Koops 1957; three s.; ed. Univ. of Groningen; faculty mem. Univ. of Groningen 1955-81, Dean Faculty of Natural Sciences 1975-78, Vice-Pres. for Academic Affairs 1971-81, Pres. of Univ. 1981-88; faculty mem. Univ. of Ariz. 1963; various consultancies to European Space Agency, European Southern Observatory, Max Planck Gesellschaft 1961-80; Dir. Kapteyn Observatory, Roden, Netherlands 1964-72; Pres. Netherlands Science Org. 1988-; mem. Royal Netherlands Acad. of Arts and Sciences. *Address:* Prof. v.d. Leeuwplantsoen 27, 9301 H S Roden, Netherlands. *Telephone:* 05908-19414.

BORGNINE, Ernest; American actor; b. 24 Jan. 1917, Hamden, Conn.; s. of Charles B. and Anna (née Baselli) Borgnine; m. Tove Newman 1972; ed. New Haven public schools; *Films include:* From Here to Eternity, Bad Day at Black Rock, Marty, Violent Saturday, Square Jungle, Three Brave Men, Hell Below, The Rabbit Trap, Man on String, Barabbas, Flight of the Phoenix 1966, The Oscar 1966, The Split, Ice Station Zebra, The Dirty Dozen 1968, Willard 1971, The Poseidon Adventure 1972, Emperor of the North 1972, Sunday in the Country 1974, Law and Disorder 1975, Convoy 1978, Goin' South 1979, The Black Hole 1980, All Quiet on the Western Front 1980, Last Days of Pompeii 1984, Dirty Dozen: The Next Mission 1985; Acad. Award for Best Performance in Marty 1956. *Address:* c/o Selected Artists Agency, 13111 Ventura Boulevard, Studio City, Calif. 91604, U.S.A.

BORGOMEO, Rev. Pasquale S.J., D.LIT.; Italian ecclesiastic; b. 20 March 1933, Naples; s. of Vincenzo Borgomeo and Letizia De Meo; ed. Pontano Coll.; entered Soc. of Jesus 1948; ordained Priest 1963; Ed.-in-Chief Vatican Radio 1970-78, Programme Dir. 1978-83, Asst. Dir. Gen. 1983-85, Dir. Gen. 1985-; mem. Bureau Univ. Radiophonique et Télévisuelle Int., Paris 1976-, Bd. of Dirs Centro Televisivo Vaticano 1984-; Pres. Int. Broadcasting Working Party of European Broadcasting Union 1983-. *Publication:* L'Eglise de ce temps dans la prédication de Saint Augustin 1972. *Address:* Vatican Radio, 00120 Vatican City (Office); Via dei Penitenzieri, 20, 00193 Rome, Italy (Home). *Telephone:* 698-3945 (Office); 68-69-357 (Home).

BORISEVICH, Nikolai Aleksandrovich; Soviet physicist; b. 21 Sept. 1923; ed. Byelorussian Univ., Minsk; mem. CPSU 1945-; served in Soviet Army 1941-45; Deputy Dir. and Head of Lab. of Inst. of Physics, Byelorussian Acad. of Sciences 1955-69, Prof. 1967-; mem. Acad. and Pres. of Byelorussian Acad. of Sciences 1969; corresp. mem. U.S.S.R. Acad. of Sciences 1972, mem. 1981-; U.S.S.R. State Prize 1973; mem. Acad. Cttee. of Byelorussian CP 1971-; mem. U.S.S.R. Supreme Soviet 1971-; Hero of Socialist Labour 1978; Lenin Prize 1980. *Address:* Academy of Sciences of the U.S.S.R., Leninsky Prospekt 14, Moscow V-71, U.S.S.R.

BORJA CEVALLOS, Rodrigo, LL.D. ; Ecuador academic and politician; b. 1937; m. Carmen Calisto de Borja; one s. three d.; ed. Cen. Univ. of Ecuador; Deputy in Nat. Congress 1962-82; Founder and Leader Partido Izquierda Democrática; Prof. of Political Sciences, Cen. Univ. of Ecuador 1963-88; Pres. of Ecuador 1988-; Pres. Law School Assocn., Cen. Univ. of Ecuador 1958; mem. Special Comm. of Lawyers on Ecuador's Political Constitution 1966. *Publications:* Political Constitutional Law (2 vols.) 1964, 1971, Democratic Socialism 1983; numerous essays. *Address:* Office of the President, Palacio Nacional, García Moreno 1043, Quito, Ecuador. *Telephone:* 216-300.

BORK, Robert Heron, J.D.; American judge, lawyer and educationalist; b. 1 March 1927, Pittsburgh; s. of Harry Philip Bork and Elizabeth Kunkle; m. 1st Claire Davidson 1952 (died 1980); two s. one d.; m. 2nd Mary Ellen Pohl 1982; ed. Univ. of Chicago; admitted to Illinois Bar 1953; Assoc., mem. Kirkland, Ellis, Hodson, Chaffetz & Masters 1955-62; Assoc. Prof. Yale Law School 1962-65, Prof. of Law 1965-73, Chancellor Kent Prof. of Law 1977-79, Alexander M. Bickel Prof. of Public Law 1979-81; Solicitor-Gen. 1973-77; Acting Attorney-Gen. 1973-74; mem. Kirkland & Ellis, Washington 1981-82; Circuit Judge, Dist. of Columbia Court of Appeals 1982-88; nominated as Justice of U.S. Supreme Court and rejected by Senate 1987; Appellate Court Judge until 1988; Resident Scholar, American Enterprise Inst., Washington, D.C. 1977, adjunct scholar 1977-82; Fellow, American Acad. of Arts and Sciences; Francis Boyer Award, American Enterprise Inst. 1982; Hon. LL.D. (Creighton Univ.) 1975, (Notre-Dame) 1982; Hon. D.Hum.Litt. (Wilkes-Barre Coll.) 1976, Juris Dr. h.c. (Brooklyn Law School) 1984. *Publication:* The Antitrust Paradox: A Policy at War with Itself 1978. *Address:* 5171 Palisade Lane, N.W., Washington, D.C. 20016, U.S.A. (Home).

BORKH, Inge; Swiss soprano opera singer; b. 26 May 1921; ed. Drama School, Vienna, and Vienna Acad.; theatre performances (dancing, piano) in Vienna and Milan, then in Switzerland in German version of Konsul (Menotti); Int. career 1951-, Bayreuth, Paris, Vienna, Edinburgh Festival; first visit to U.S.A. 1953; World Première of Irische Legende (Egk) 1955; appeared as Salome and Elektra, Carnegie Hall, New York 1958; Metropolitan Opera, N.Y. 1958; Bavarian Court Singer 1963; appeared at opening of Nationaltheater, Munich, in Die Frau ohne Schatten 1963; Grand Prix du Disque for Elektra, Antigone (Orff), and Schönberg's Gurrelieder; Reinhard Ring Award 1973. *Address:* D 7000 Stuttgart 75, Florentinerstrasse 20, Apartment 2018, Federal Republic of Germany. *Telephone:* 47022018.

BORLAUG, Norman Ernest, PH.D.; American agricultural scientist; b. 25 March 1914, Cresco, Ia.; s. of Henry O. and Clara (Vaala) Borlaug; m. Margaret G. Gibson 1937; one s. one d.; ed. Univ. of Minnesota; with U.S. Forest Service 1938-39; Instructor, Univ. of Minn. 1941; Microbiologist, E. I. DuPont de Nemours Foundation 1942-44; Research Scientist, Wheat Rockefeller Foundation, Mexico 1944-60, Centro Internacional de Mejoramiento de Maíz y Trigo (Int. Maize and Wheat Improvement Center), Mexico 1964-79; Leonard L. Klinck Lecturer, Agric. Inst. of Canada 1966; mem. Citizens' Comm. on Science, Law and Food Supply 1973-, Comm. on Critical Choices for America 1973-, Council of Agric. Science and Tech. 1973-; Assoc. Dir. Rockefeller Found. 1964-, Consultant 1983-; Distinguished Prof. of Int. Agriculture, Texas A+M Univ. Jan. 1984-; mem. N.A.S.; Foreign mem. Royal Swedish Acad. of Agric. and Forestry 1971, Indian Nat. Science Acad. 1973; Hon. Foreign mem. Acad. Nacional de Agronomia y Veterinaria de Argentina, N. I. Vavilovi Acad. (U.S.S.R.); Hon. Fellow Indian Soc. of Genetics and Plant Breeding 1968; Hon. D.Sc. (Punjab Agric. Univ.) 1969, (Royal Norwegian Agric. Coll.) 1970, (Mich. State Univ.) 1971, (Univ. of Florida) 1973, and others; Medal of Freedom 1977 and numerous Mexican awards. *Leisure interests:* hunting, fishing, baseball, wrestling, football, golf. *Address:* Texas A+M University System, College Station, Tex. 77843, U.S.A. (Office); Agustín Ahumada 310-F, Lomas de Chapultepec, Mexico 10, D.F., Mexico (Home).

BORMAN, Frank; American astronaut; b. 14 March 1928, Gary, Ind.; m. Susan Bugbee; two s.; ed. U.S. Military Acad., Calif. Inst. of Tech.; pilot training, Williams Air Force Base, Arizona; assigned to various fighter squadrons in U.S. and Philippines; Instructor in Thermodynamics and Fluid Mechanics, U.S. Mil. Acad. 1957; Master's degree from Calif. Inst. of Tech. 1957; graduated from U.S. Air Force Aerospace Research Pilots School 1960; Instructor 1960-62; selected by NASA as astronaut Sept. 1962; Command Pilot Gemini VII 1965; Commdr. Apollo VIII spacecraft which made flight round the moon Dec. 1968; Deputy Dir. for Flight Operations, NASA, until May 1969; Field Dir. of a NASA Space Station Task Group 1969-70; Vice-Pres. Eastern Airlines Inc. 1970-74, Vice-Pres. for Eastern Operations 1974-75, Pres. 1975, Chair. of Bd. 1976-86; Vice-Chair., mem. Bd. of Dirs. Texas Air 1986-; NASA Exceptional Service Medal, Harmon Int. Aviation Trophy 1966, Gold Space Medal, Int. Aeronautics. Feb 1969, Encyclopedia Britannica Achievement in Life Award 1980. *Address:* Texas Air Corporation, 4040 Capital Bank Plaza, Houston, Tex. 77002, U.S.A.

BORN, Gustav Victor Rudolf, D.PHIL., M.B., CH.B., F.R.S, F.R.C.P.; British professor of pharmacology; b. 29 July 1921; s. of the late Prof. Max Born; m. 1st Wilfrida Ann Plowden-Wardlaw 1950 (divorced 1961), two s. one d.; m. 2nd Dr Faith Elizabeth Maurice-Williams 1962, one s. one d.; ed. Oberrealschule, Göttingen, Germany, Perse School, Cambridge, Edin. Acad. and Univs. of Edin. and Oxford; Medical Officer, R.A.M.C. 1943-47; Medical Officer, Graham Research Lab., Univ. Coll. Hosp. Medical School, London 1947-49; Studentship, training in research methods of MRC 1949-52; mem. scientific staff, Toxicology Research Unit, MRC 1952-53; Sr. Research Officer Nuffield Inst. for Medical Research and Medical Lecturer St. Peter's Coll., Oxford 1953-60; Vandervell Prof. of Pharmacology, Royal Coll. of Surgeons and London Univ. 1960-73; Sheild Prof. of Pharmacology, Cambridge Univ. and Fellow, Gonville and Caius Coll. Cambridge 1973-78; Prof of Pharmacology, King's Coll., London Univ. 1978-86, Prof. Emer. 1986-; fmr. mem. Council of the Int. Soc. of Thrombosis and Haemostasis (Pres. 1977-79), Cttee. of British Pharmacological Soc., Working Party on Antihaemophilic Globulin of MRC, Official Cttee. of Enquiry into Relationship of Pharmaceutical Industry with Nat. Health Service, Medical Advisory Bd., British Council and numerous other cttees. and bds.; Hon. D.Sc. (Bordeaux, Paris, Brown Univ.), Hon. M.D. (Münster, Leuven, Edin.); Hon. Fellow St. Peter's Coll., Oxford; Chevalier de l'Ordre National du Mérite; mem. Akademie Leopoldina; Hon. Life mem. New York Acad. of Sciences; Royal Soc. Royal Medal, and other medals. *Leisure interests:* music, history. *Address:* King's College, Strand, London, WC2R 2LS; 10 Woodland Gardens, London, N10, England (Home). *Telephone:* 01-836 5454 (College); 01-444 7911 (Home).

BORN, Jorge; Argentine businessman; b. 24 July 1900; ed. Athenée, Royal Antwerp, Belgium, and Univ. de Bruxelles, Belgium; Dir. Bunge y Born S.A. 1926-, Pres. and Chair. 1956-; Vice-Pres. Molinos Río de la Plata S.A. 1951-, Bunge y Born Foundation 1964-; breeder of pedigree cattle

(Hereford) and controls ownership of ranches in several Argentine provinces; Kt. Order of Leopold, Officer Order of Crown (Belgium). *Address:* 25 de Mayo 501, Buenos Aires, Argentina.

BORNEWASSER, Hans (Johannes Antonius), D.HIST.; Netherlands professor of ecclesiastical history; b. 15 July 1924, Voorst; m. Maria van den Berg 1956; three c.; teacher of History and Politics, Canisius Coll. Nijmegen 1950-67; teacher of History, Katholieke Leergangen, Tilburg 1956-80; Prof. of Church History, Tilburg Univ. 1967-; Pres. Netherlands Historical Assen. 1969-73; mem. Royal Netherlands Acad. of Arts and Sciences. *Publications:* Kirche und Staat in Fulda unter Wilhelm Friedrich von Oranien 1802-1806 1956, Vÿftig jaar Katholieke Leergangen 1912-1962 1962, Katholieke Hogeschool Tilburg, deel I. 1927-54 1978, In de Geest van Thÿm 1985. *Address:* Jericholaan 1, 6564 BR Nijmegen, Netherlands. *Telephone:* 80-224 7 27.

BORODIN, Leonid Aleksandrovich; Soviet politician; b. 1923, Stalingrad (now Volgograd); ed. Volgograd Agricultural Inst.; mem. CPSU 1948-; Soviet Army 1941-46; Production Man. in Volgograd 1946-49; mem. Macheshansky Regional Dept. for Agric. and Regional Cttee. CPSU; Deputy Chief of Volgograd Dist. Cttee.; First Sec. Novoanninsky Regional Cttee. of Volgograd CPSU 1949-59; Sec. of Chuvash Dist. Cttee. CPSU 1959-62; Inspector of Agricultural Dept. for RSFSR at CPSU Cen. Cttee. 1962-63; Second Sec. Bashkir Dist. Cttee. CPSU 1963-67; Deputy to U.S.S.R. Supreme Soviet 1966-; First Sec. Astrakhan Dist. Cttee. CPSU 1967-; Cand. mem. Cen. Cttee. CPSU 1971-80, mem. 1980-; Order of Lenin. *Address:* Communist Party of the Soviet Union, Staraya pl. 4, Moscow, U.S.S.R.

BOROTRA, Jean (Robert), C.B.E.; French civil engineer, company director and fmr. tennis player; b. 13 Aug. 1898, Biarritz; s. of Henry Borotra and Marguerite Revet; m. Mabel de Forest 1938 (divorced 1947); one s.; ed. Lycées Saint Louis and Michelet, Paris, Univ. de Paris and Ecole Polytechnique; Civil Engineer 1922; Commercial Man Satam. 1924-30, Dir. 1930-75, Consultant 1975; Commissar-Gen., Gen. Educ., and Sport in Marshal Pétain's Govt. 1940-42, deported by Gestapo 1942-45; Vice-Pres. French Lawn Tennis Assen. 1930-68, Hon. Pres.; Pres. Comm. Doctrine of Sport, High Cttee. of Sport, Paris 1962-68; Pres. Int. Lawn Tennis Fed. 1960-61, Vice-Pres. 1961-69, Hon. Pres. 1969-; Vice-Pres. Int. Council for Sport and Physical Educ. (ICSPE) 1960-68, Deputy Pres. 1968-76; Hon. Vice-Pres. 1982, Pres. Int. Cttee. for Fair Play 1966, Vice-Pres. 1966-82, Hon. Vice-Pres. 1982-; Hon. Pres. Assen. pour défendre la mémoire du Maréchal Pétain 1980-; winner of numerous lawn tennis prizes, including six Wimbledon Championships (two for singles, three for doubles, and one for mixed doubles), and mem. French Davis Cup Team 1922-47; Commdr. Légion d'honneur, Croix de guerre (1914-18, 1939-45); Hon. C.B.E. and several other foreign decorations. *Address:* 35 avenue Foch, 75116 Paris, France. *Telephone:* 500.05.27; 500.28.80.

BOROV, Todor; Bulgarian bibliographer and librarian; b. 30 Jan. 1901, Lom; m. Haritina Ivanova Peeva 1930; two s.; ed Sofia and Berlin Univs. Prof. in Library Science, Univ. of Sofia; Ed. Bǎlgarska kniga (The Bulgarian Book) 1930, Yearbook of Bulgarian Bibliographical Inst. 1945-63. *Publications:* Knigi, biblioteki, bibliografija (Books, Libraries, Bibliography) 1941, Pǎtija kǎm knigite (The Road to Books) 1942, Cehov i Bǎlgarija 1955, Bulgarische Bibliographie 1960, Die Bibliographie als Universitätslehrfach 1963, Ausbildung von Bibliothekaren 1964, Zivot s knigi (Life with Books) 1973, Kniga i literatura 1981. *Address:* Khan Krǔm 15, 1000 Sofia, Bulgaria. *Telephone:* 87-52-40, 55-38-29.

BOROVIK-ROMANOV, Viktor-Andrey Stanislavovich; Soviet physicist; b. 18 March 1920, Leningrad; m. Tatyana Petrovna Belikova 1947; one s.; ed. Moscow Univ; Research Assoc. Inst. of Physical Problems U.S.S.R. Acad. of Sciences 1947-48, 1956-62, Assoc. and Deputy Dir. 1962-; Research Assoc. Moscow Inst. of Measures and Measuring Instruments 1948-55; Inst. of Physico-Technical and Radio Measurements 1955-56, Prof. Moscow Physico-Technical Inst. 1967-; Ed. JETP Letters 1968-; Corresp. mem. U.S.S.R. Acad. of Sciences 1966-72, Academician 1972-, Order of Lenin, Order Red Banner of Labour, Order of Labour (Silver Degree, Hungary). *Publications:* works on experimental and theoretical physics. *Address:* Institute of Physical Problems, 2 Ul. Kosygina, Moscow 117334, U.S.S.R. *Telephone:* 137-61-85.

BOROVKOV, Aleksandr Alekseyevich; Soviet mathematician; b. 6 March 1931, Moscow; ed. Moscow Univ.; Postgraduate, Research Assoc. Moscow Univ. 1954-60; Assoc. Head of Dept. Inst. of Math., Siberian Branch U.S.S.R. Acad. of Sciences 1960-; lecturer 1961-, Prof., Assoc. Head of Chair Novosibirsk Univ. 1965-; Corresp. mem. U.S.S.R. Acad. of Sciences 1966-; State Prize 1979. *Publications:* works on contiguous problems of theory probabilities and mathematical statistics. *Address:* Institute of Mathematics, Akademgorodok, Novosibirsk, U.S.S.R.

BORRELLI, Mario, M.SC.; Italian sociologist; b. 1922, Naples; s. of Gennaro Borrelli and Lucia Morvillo; m. Jilyan West 1971; one d.; ed. Posillipo Theological Univ., School of States Archives, Naples, London School of Econs.; Founder of "Casa dello Scugnizzo", Naples 1950; Founder-Dir. Lo Scugnizzo (monthly magazine) 1950-; Founder Materdei Community Centre, Naples 1970; Pres. IPRI (Italian Peace Research Inst.). *Publications:* La Concezione Copernico Galileiana e la Filosofia di Tomaso

D'Aquino 1961, La Relazione tra il Conservatorio dei Poveri di Gesù Cristo e l'Oratorio di Napoli 1961, Il Largo dei Girolamini 1962, A Streetlamp and the Stars 1963, Memorie Baroniane dell'Oratorio de Napoli 1963, Opere e Documenti sul Baronio Presso The British Museum Library 1964, I Documenti dell'Oratorio Napoletano 1964, Le Testimonianze Baroniane dell'Oratorio di Napoli, Documenti sul Baronio Presso The Bodleian Library, L'Epistolario del Giusto Calvino nei suoi Rapporti col Baronio 1965, L'Architetto Nencioni Dionisio Di Bartolomeo 1967, Le Costituzioni dell' Oratorio Napoletano 1968, Diario delle Baracche 1969, Unearthing the Roots of the Sub-Culture of the South Italian Sub-Proletariat 1969, Socio-political Analysis of the Sub-Proletarian Reality of Naples and Lines of Intervention for the Workers of the Centre 1973, Basic Concepts for Community Action in the Urban Sub-Proletariat 1974, Practical Directions for Intervention in a Community Action in Favour of the Urban Sub-Proletariat 1974, Hypothesis of the Existence of a "Peripheral" Europe with consequent different types of Social Policy Intervention 1975, Exclusion from the Productive Process, Social Deviance and Mental Illness 1975, Alimentation and Directions of Social Intervention among the Neapolitan Sub-Proletariat 1975, Communication and Consciousness-Raising 1975, Socio-political Analysis of the Neapolitan Reality and Programme of Intervention for the Social Operators of the Centre 1976, Integration between Peace Research, Peace Education and Peace Action 1977, New Trends in the International Division of Labour and their Effects on the Conditions of Workers in Industrialized and "Third World" Countries 1977, Tourism as an Expression of Economic Subordination: Relationships between Emigration and Tourism 1977, Italian Compulsory School and Mental Retardation 1978, Human Needs, Human Rights and Peace Education (An Analysis by Means of the Practical Experience of the Materdei Community Centre of Naples), Exploration of the Preliminary Conditions for a Defensive and Economic Strategy for Central Europe leading to its Balance Insertion in the Mediterranean and African Areas 1981, Human Rights and a Methodology for Peace 1983, The Development of the Concept of Peace Education in the IPRA Archipelago 1983, An Approach to the Political Dimension of Disarmament Education 1984. *Address:* Largo San Gennaro a Materdei 3A, Naples; Via Vecchia, S. Gennaro, Palazzo Nardi, Pozzuoli, Naples, Italy. *Telephone:* 34-22-59 (Office); (081) 8675701 (Home).

BORRIE, Sir Gordon, Kt., Q.C., F.R.S.A.; British lawyer; b. 13 March 1931; s. of Stanley Borrie; m. Dorene Toland 1960; ed. John Bright Grammar School, Llandudno and Univ. of Manchester; called to Bar, Middle Temple 1952; Bencher 1980; Barrister, London 1954-57; Lecturer, later Sr. Lecturer in Law, Coll of Law 1957-64, Univ. of Birmingham 1965-68, Prof. of English Law and Dir. Inst. of Judicial Admin. 1969-76, Dean Faculty of Law 1974-76; Dir.-Gen Office of Fair Trading 1976-; mem. Parole Bd. for England and Wales 1971-74, Consumer Protection Advisory Cttee. 1973-76, Equal Opportunities Comm. 1975-76; Vice-Pres. Inst. of Trading Standards Admin. 1985-; Labour candidate, Croydon 1955, Ilford 1959; Gov. Birmingham Coll. of Commerce 1966-70. *Publications:* Commercial Law 1962, The Consumer, Society and the Law (with Prof. A. L. Diamond) 1963, Law of Contempt (with N. V. Lowe) 1973, The Development of Consumer Law and Policy 1984. *Leisure Interests:* gastronomy, piano playing, travel. *Address:* Manor Farm, Abbots Morton, Worcestershire; 1 Plowden Buildings, Temple, London EC4, England. *Telephone:* Inkberrow 792330; 01-353 4434.

BORRIE, Wilfred David, C.B.E., M.A.; British demographer; b. 2 Sept. 1913, Waimate, New Zealand; s. of Peter and Isobella Borrie; m. Alice H. Miller 1941; one d.; ed. Waitaki Boys High School, Oamaru, New Zealand, Univ. of Otago, N.Z. and Cambridge Univ; Lecturer, Social History and Econs., Sydney Univ. 1944-46, Senior Lecturer 1946-48; Research Fellow, Research School of Social Sciences, Australian Nat. Univ. 1949-52, Reader 1952-57, Prof. and Head of Dept. of Demography 1957-68, Dir. Research School of Social Sciences 1968-73, Prof. of Demography 1973-78, Emer. 1979-; Visiting Prof., Office of Population, Research, Princeton Univ. 1959-60; Vice-Pres. Int. Union for Scientific Study of Population 1961-63; Pres. Social Science Research Council of Australia 1962-64, Australian Council of Social Services 1963-64, Australian and New Zealand Assen. for the Advancement of Science (ANZAAS) 1975, Population Comm., UN, Chair. 1965-69; Chair. and Dir. Nat. Population Inquiry 1970-78; Emeritus Prof. Australian Nat. Univ. Jan. 1979-; Dir. Acad. of Social Sciences in Australia 1979-85; mem. Immigration Planning Council of Australia 1965-74, Australian Population and Immigration Council 1972-81; Patron Australian Population Assen. 1980-; Hon.D.Litt (Tasmania) 1975, Hon. D.Sc. (Sydney) 1979; Hon. LL.D. (Australian Nat. Univ.) 1982. *Publications:* Immigration 1948, Population Trends and Policies 1949, Italians and Germans in Australia 1954, The Cultural Integration of Immigrants (Part I and General Ed.) 1959, Australia's Population Structure and Growth (with G. Spencer) 1965, The Growth and Control of World Population 1970, Population Environment and Society 1973, Population and Australia (First Report of the Nat. Population Inquiry, 2 vols.) 1975, Supplementary Report (Recent Trends and their Implications) 1978, Implications of Australian Population Trends (Ed.) 1981. *Leisure interests:* writing demographic history, gardening. *Address:* 29 Norman Street, Deakin, A.C.T., Australia 2600. *Telephone:* 814114.

BORSOS, Miklós; Hungarian sculptor and graphic artist; b. 13 Aug. 1906, Nagyszeben; s. of Lajos Miklós Borsos and Erzsébet Mosolygó; m. Ilona

Gabriella Kéri 1933; no c.; ed. Budapest Coll. of Fine Arts and self-taught in Italy and France; started as painter, switched to stone-modelling and copper engraving 1933; mem. Arts Council 1945; Prof. Budapest Coll. of Applied Arts 1946-60; Univ. Prof. of Fine Art, Univ. of Budapest 1981-; Exhbns. Budapest 1957, Tihany 1965, Venice Biennale 1966, Zürich and Rome 1967; f. museum of own work, Győr 1979; First Prize Carrara sculpture exhbn. 1959, Munkácsy Prize 1954, Kossuth Prize 1957, Merited Artist 1967; Labour Order of Merit, Golden Degree 1971, Eminent Artist 1972, "For Socialist Hungary" Award, Merited Citizen 1979 (Győr), Banner Order of Hungarian People's Repub. 1981. *Works include:* Smile 1933, Buffalo 1942, portraits of József Egry 1951, Lőrinc Szabó 1962, Mihály Babits 1962, Gyula Derkovits 1968, St. Steven, Janus Pannonius, Haydn, Mother Teresa, Apollo, Echo 1986, János Ferencsik tomb 1987; Béla Bartók tomb 1988, Luther Medal for Centenary of Budapest Opera House; illustrations for Dante's Commedia, King David Psalms. *Writings:* Visszanéztem félutamból 1971, 1975, A toronyból (studies) 1979. *Leisure interests:* playing violin, literature. *Address:* Romer Flóris-utca 53, Budapest II, Hungary. *Telephone:* 357-958.

BORTEN, Per; Norwegian agronomist and politician; b. 3 April 1913, Flå Gauldal; s. of Lars and Karen Borten; m. Magnhild Rathe 1948; three c.; ed. Norwegian Agricultural Univ; Asst. Head, Tech. Section, Provincial Agric. Admin., Sör-Tröndelag 1946-65; Chair. Flå Municipal Council 1945, Provincial Council, Sör-Tröndelag 1948; fmr. Head of Youth Movement of Agrarian Movement, Sör-Tröndelag; mem. Storting 1950-77, Pres. Odelsting 1961-65, 1973-77; Chair. Senterpartiet 1955-67, Chief Spokesman 1958-65; Prime Minister 1965-71; *Address:* c/o Storting, Oslo, Norway.

BORTOLUZZI, Paolo; Italian ballet dancer; b. 17 May 1938, Genoa; m. Jaleh Kerendi 1970; one s. one d.; studied ballet under Ugo Dell'Ara, Genoa 1954; joined Del Balletto Italiano, Milan 1957; Leone Massine's Festival de Nervi 1960; with Maurice Béjart's Ballet of the Twentieth Century 1960-72; Perm. Guest Artist, American Ballet Theater 1972, La Scala, Milan, Düsseldorf Opera, now Artistic Adviser and Choreographer La Scala, Milan; repertoire includes Romeo and Juliet, Les Sylphides, Giselle, The Sleeping Beauty, Orpheo, The Nutcracker, Cinderella, Swan Lake, Firebird, Nomos Alpha, Apollon Musagète, Albinoni Adagio, L'Après-midi d'un faune, Sheherazade, Spectre-de-la-Rose, as well as many avant-garde works, notably Béjart's Nijinsky: Clown of God, IXe Symphonie, Messe Baudelaire. *Address:* Nuovo Corso Torino 11, 1-10098, Rivoli, Turin, Italy.

BORZOV, Valeriy; Soviet athlete; b. 20 Oct. 1949, Sambor, Ukraine; m. Ludmila Tourischeva; competed Olympic Games Munich 1972, winning gold medals at 100 m. and 200 m; bronze medal at 100 m, Montreal 1976; European Junior Champion 100 m. and 200 m. 1968; European Champion 100 m. 1969; 100 m. and 200 m. 1971, 100 m. 1974; European Indoor Champion 60 m. 1970, 1971, 1972, 50 m. 1974, 1975, 1976; held European record at 100 m. and 200 m. and World record at 60 m; Master of Sport. *Address:* c/o Light Athletic Federation, Skatertnyi per 4, Moscow G. 69, U.S.S.R.

BOSCH, Juan; Dominican writer and politician; b. 1909; ed. La Vega and Santo Domingo; founded literary group Las Cuevas (The Caves); exile in Puerto Rico and Cuba, travelled extensively in Latin America 1937-61; founded Partido Revolucionario Dominicano 1939, Pres. until Oct. 1966; fmr. Prof. of Inst. of Political Science of Costa Rica; Pres. of Dominican Repub. Feb.-Sept. 1963 (deposed by mil. coup); unsuccessful candidate for Presidency 1966. *Publications:* Camino Real (Royal Path—short stories), Indios (Indians), La Mañosa (The Shrew—novel), Mujeres en la Vida de Hostos (Women in the life of Hostos), Hostos—El Sembrador (Hostos, the Sower), Dos Pesos de Agua (Two Pesos worth of Water), Ocho Cuentos (Eight Tales), La Muchacha de la Guaira (The Girl from La Guaira), Cuba, la Isla Fascinante (Cuba, the Fascinating Island), Cuentos de Navidad (Christmas Stories), Life of Bolívar, Cuentos escritos en el Exilio (Tales written in Exile), Trujillo: Causas de una tiranía sin Ejemplo (Trujillo: Causes of a Tyranny without Equal), The Unfinished Experiment: Democracy in the Dominican Republic 1965, David 1966, Pentagonism 1969.

BOSCHWITZ, Rudy, B.S., LL.B.; American politican; b. 1930, Berlin, Germany; m. Ellen Boschwitz; four s.; ed. Johns Hopkins Univ. and New York Univ.; admitted to New York State Bar 1954, Wis. Bar 1959; founder, owner, operator, Plywood Minn. 1963-; Senator from Minnesota 1979-; Republican. *Address:* 506 Hart Senate Bldg., Washington, D.C. 20510, U.S.A.

BOSCO, Giacinto; Italian lawyer and politician; b. 25 Jan. 1905, Santa Maria Capua Vetere (Caserta); m. Rosa Sagnelli 1929; two s. one d.; Prof. of Int. Law, Rome Univ.; fmr. Ed. Rivista di Studi Politici Internazionali, Florence; Ed. Rivista di Studi Europei, Rome; fmr. Legal Adviser, Ministry of Foreign Affairs; mem. Senate 1948-, Vice-Pres. 1958-60; Under-Sec. of State for Defence 1953-58, Minister for Educ. 1960-62 and Justice 1962-63, of Labour and Social Security 1963-64; Chief, Italian Del. at UN 1965, 1968-69, Minister of Labour and Social Security 1966-68, Finance 1968-69, Special Political Affairs 1969-70, without Portfolio March-July 1970, Posts and Telecommunications 1970-1972; Vice-Pres. Consiglio superiore della Magistratura 1972-76; Judge, Court of Justice of the European Communities 1976-88, Pres. First Chamber 1976-82, First and Fourth Chambers

1984–85; Christian Democrat. *Address:* Court of Justice, Centre Européen, Plateau de Kirchberg, P.O. Box 1406, L-2920, Luxembourg; Viale Tito Livio 53, 1-00136 Rome, Italy.

BOSERUP, Ester Talke, M.A.(ECON.); Danish author and consultant; b. 18 May 1910, Frederiksberg; d. of Holger and Talke (née Hansen) Børgesen; m. Mogens Boserup 1931 (died 1978); two s. one d.; ed. Univ. of Copenhagen; Direktorat for Vareforsyning, Danish Govt. Service 1936–47; Research Div., UN Econ. Comm. for Europe, Geneva 1947–57; freelance author and consultant on devt. problems 1957–, various assignments included stays in India 1957–59, Senegal 1964–65; mem. UN Expert Cttee. of Devt. Planning 1971–80; mem. Bd. Scandinavian Inst. of Asian Studies 1978–80, UN Int. Research and Training Inst. for Advancement of Women 1979–85. *Address:* Nevedone, 6614 Brissago, Switzerland.

BOSHER, John Francis, B.A., D.ÈS SC., PH.D., F.R.S.C.; Canadian professor of history; b. 28 May 1929, Sidney, B.C.; s. of John Ernest Bosher and Grace Simister; m. Kathryn Cecil Berry 1968; one s. three d.; ed. Univ. of British Columbia, Univ. of Paris and Univ. of London; Jr. Admin. Asst. and Personnel Selection Officer Civil Service Comm., Ottawa 1951–53; Asst. Lecturer King's Coll., London 1956–59; Asst. Prof. Univ. of British Columbia 1959–67; Prof. of History Cornell Univ. 1967–69; York Univ., Toronto 1969–. *Publications:* The Single Duty Project: A Study of the Movement for a French Customs Union in the 18th Century 1964, French Finances 1775–1795: From Business to Bureaucracy 1970, French Society and Government: Essays in Honour of Alfred Cobban (Ed.) 1973, The Canada Merchants 1713–1763, 1987, The French Revolution 1988, numerous articles on France. *Leisure interests:* gardening and music. *Address:* Department of History, York University, 4700 Keele Street, North York, Ont., M3J 1P3, Canada.

BOSHOFF, Carel Willem Hendrik, M.A., D.D.; South African theologian; b. 9 Nov. 1927, Nylstroom; s. of W. S. and A. M. Boshoff; m. Anna Verwoerd, d. of late Hendrik Verwoerd (Prime Minister of S.A. 1958–66) 1954; five s. two d.; ed. Nylstroom High School, Pretoria Univ.; Missionary Dutch Reformed Church 1953–63, Sec. of Missions 1963–66; Prof. and Head of Dept. of Theology, Missiology and Science of Religion, Univ. of Pretoria 1967–88, Dean, Theology Faculty 1978–80; Chair. S.A. Bureau of Racial Affairs (SABRA) 1972–; Chair. N. G. Kerkboekhandel 1976–; Chair. Council of Inst. for Missiological Research 1978–; Exec. Chair. Afrikaner Vryheidstigting 1988–; mem. numerous theological and scholarly cttees. *Publications:* Die Begin van die Evangelie van Jesus Christus 1963, Uit God Gebore 1968, Die Nuwe Sendingsituasie 1978, Swart Teologie van Amerika Tot in Suid-Afrika 1980. *Leisure interests:* small farming, breeding Nooitgedracht ponies. *Address:* 55 Kesselaar Avenue, Brummeria, 0184 Pretoria, South Africa. *Telephone:* (012) 436051 (Office); (012) 865225 (Home).

BOSKIN, Michael Jay, PH.D.; American economist, educator and politician; b. 23 Sept. 1945, N.Y.; s. of Irving Boskin and Jean (née Kimmel) Boskin; m. Chris Dornin 1981; ed. Univ. of California, Berkeley; Asst. Prof. Stanford Univ., Calif. 1970–75, Assoc. Prof. 1976–78, Prof. 1978–; Dir. Centre for Econ. Policy Research 1986–; Wohlford Prof. Econs. 1987–; Visiting Prof. Harvard Univ., Cambridge, Mass. 1977–78; nominated Chair. of the Council of Econ. Advisers Dec. 1988; mem. Bd. Dirs., Equitec-Siebel Mutual Fund Group, Oakland, Calif.; Faculty Research Fellow Mellon Foundation 1973; mem. American Council on Capital Formation Bd. Dirs. 1986–; mem. Nat. Chamber Foundation Bd. Dirs. 1987–. *Publications:* Too Many Promises: The Uncertain Future of Social Security 1986, Reagan and the Economy: Successes, Failures, Unfinished Agenda 1987 and articles in various professional journals. *Leisure interests:* tennis, skiing, reading, theatre. *Address:* Stanford University, Department of Economics, Stanford, California 94305; Office of the Chairman, Old Executive Office Building, Washington, D.C. 20500, U.S.A.

BOSKOVSKY, Willi; Austrian conductor; b. 16 June 1909; ed. Akademie für Musik, Vienna; Conductor of New Year Concerts of Vienna Philharmonic Orchestra 1954–; Founder of Vienna Octet; Leader of Philharmonic Orchestra of Vienna State Opera; soloist in chamber music; numerous decorations including Mozart Medal, Salzburg and Vienna, Österreichisches Ehrenkreuz, Kreisler Prize.

BOSQUET, Alain, M.A. (pseudonym of Anatole Bisk); French writer and critic; b. 28 March 1919, Odessa, Russia; s. of Alexander Bisk and Berthe Bisk (née Turiansky); m. Norma E. Caplan 1954; ed. Athénée d'Uccle, Univ. Libre de Bruxelles and Univ. de Paris (Sorbonne); served with Belgian, French and U.S. Armies 1940–45; served with Allied Control Council, Berlin, then with Dept. of State 1945–51; Prof. of French Literature, Brandeis Univ., U.S.A. 1958–59; Prof. of American Literature, Univ. of Lyons 1959–60; Columnist, Combat 1953–74; Literary Critic, Le Monde, Le Figaro, Quotidien de Paris and various literary reviews; Vice-Pres. Acad. Mallarmé; mem. juries for Theophraste-Renaudot and Max Jacob Prizes; Prix Guillaume Apollinaire for Langue morte 1952, Prix Sainte-Beuve for Premier Testament 1957, Prix Max Jacob for Deuxième Testament 1959, Prix Fémina-Vacaresco for Verbe et vertige 1962, Prix interallié for La confession mexicaine 1965, Grand Prix de Poésie de l'Académie Française for Quatre Testaments et autres poèmes 1967, Grand Prix du Roman de l'Académie Française for Une mère russe, Prix Marcel Proust for L'enfant que tu étais, Prix Chateaubriand 1987. *Publications:* poems:

A la mémoire de ma planète 1948, Langue morte 1951, Quel royaume oublié 1955, Premier Testament 1957, Deuxième Testament 1959, Maître objet 1962, 100 notes pour une solitude 1970, Notes pour un Amour 1972, Notes pour un pluriel 1974, Le livre du doute et de la grâce 1977, Poèmes, Un, (1945-1967) 1979, Deux (1970-74) 1981, Sonnets pour une Fin de Siècle 1981, Un Jour après la Vie 1984, Le tourment de Dieu 1987; essays: Saint-John Perse, Emily Dickinson, Walt Whitman, Anthologie de la poésie américaine 1956, 35 jeunes poètes américaines 1961, Verbe et vertige (on contemporary poetry) 1961, Entretiens avec Salvador Dali 1967; novels: La grande éclipse 1952, Le mécréant 1960, Un besoin de malheur 1963, Les petites éternités 1964, La confession mexicaine 1965, Les tigres de papier 1968, Chicago oignon sauvage 1971, Monsieur Vaudeville 1973, L'amour bourgeois 1974, Les bonnes intentions 1975, Une mère russe 1978, Jean-Louis Trabart, Médecin 1981, L'enfant que tu étais 1982, Ni Guerre ni Paix 1983, Les Fêtes cruelles 1984, Lettre à mon père qui aurait eu cent ans 1987; short stories: Un homme pour un autre 1985. *Address:* c/o Gallimard, 5 rue Sébastien Bottin, Paris 7e, France.

BOSSANO, Joe; Gibraltar politician; b. 1938; Gen. Sec. Gibraltar Socialist Labour Party; Chief Minister of Gibraltar March 1988–. *Address:* c/o Gibraltar Socialist Labour Party, 6 Covenant Place, Gibraltar.

BOSSARD, André, D.IUR.; French international police official (retd.); b. 18 June 1926, St. Ouen; s. of Charles and Aline (Sirugue) Bossard; m. Francine Agen 1956; two d.; ed. Lycée Louis le Grand, Paris Univ.; called to Bar 1949; joined police service with rank of Commissaire 1950, Commissaire Principal 1958, Commissaire Divisionnaire 1968; Tech. Adviser at Police Judiciaire HQ 1970; Head of a Div. Int. Criminal Police Org. (INTERPOL) 1971–77; Contrôleur Gén. de la Police Nat. 1977; Sec.-Gen. INTERPOL 1978–85; Chevalier Légion d'honneur. *Leisure interest:* painting. *Address:* International Criminal Police Organization (INTERPOL), 26 rue Armengaud, 92210 Saint-Cloud, France (Office). *Telephone:* 602-5550 (Office).

BOSSIDY, Lawrence Arthur, B.A.; American business executive; b. 5 March 1935, Pittsfield, Mass.; m. 1956; three s. six d.; ed. Colgate Univ.; joined Gen. Electric Co. 1957, now Vice-Chair. and Dir.; Chair. and Dir. Gen. Electric Credit Corpn. New York. *Address:* General Electric Credit Corporation, 570 Lexington Avenue, New York, N.Y. 10022, U.S.A.

BOSSON, Bernard; French politician; b. 25 Feb. 1948, Annecy; s. of Charles Bosson and Claire Bosson; m. Danielle Blaise 1976; one d.; ed. Coll. Saint-Michel and Faculté de droit de Lyon; barrister, Annecy 1976–; Mayor of Annecy March 1983–; Deputy to Nat. Ass. March 1986–; Sec. of State, Ministry of the Interior 1986, Del. Minister, Ministry of Foreign Affairs 1986; Vice-Pres. Del. for EEC Oct. 1988–, mem. Nat. Del. Union Democratique Française for European Affairs Oct. 1988–. *Address:* 8 rue Royale, 74000 Annecy, France.

BOSTERUD, Helen; Norwegian politician; b. 15 Feb. 1940, Oslo; mem. Akershus Co. Council 1975–79; mem. Storting 1977; State Sec. Ministry of Health and Social Affairs 1980–81; Chair. Storting's Standing Cttee. on Justice 1981–; Minister of Justice May 1986–. *Address:* Ministry of Justice, P.O. Box 8005, Dep., Oslo 1, Norway. *Telephone:* (2) 11-90-90.

BOSTRÖM, Curt; Swedish politician; b. 31 Dec. 1926, Öjebyn; active in Social Democratic Labour Party 1940s–; with Byske Municipality, Västerbotten; accountant Log Driving and Measurement Asscn., Norrbotten and Västerbotten 1946–; mem. Riksdag (Parl.) 1974–; mem. Riksdag Cttee. on Taxation; Minister of Transport and Communications 1982–86; mem. Exec. Parl. Social Democratic Labour Party, Second Vice-Chair. 1979–, Head Research Dept.; Chair. Norrbotten Dist. Social Democratic Labour Party 1981–82; mem. Bd. Swedish Union of Clerical and Tech. Employees in Industry, Norrbotten branch. *Address:* Ministry of Transport and Communications, 103-33 Stockholm, Sweden.

BOTELHO, Carlos; Portuguese painter; b. 18 Sept. 1899, Lisbon; s. of Carlos and Josefina Botelho; m. Beatriz Dos Santos 1922; one s. one d.; ed. Lisbon and Paris Acads. of Fine Arts; decorated Portuguese pavilion, Colonial Exhbn., Paris 1931, Universal Exhbn., Paris 1937; rep. XXV Venice Biennale 1950, São Paulo Biennale 1951–53, 1955, 1957, Brussels Int. Exhbn. 1958; exhibited at 50 Years of Modern Art Exhbn. Brussels and Art and Work Exhbn. Charleroi 1958; organized in conjunction with British Council Henry Moore Exhbn. in Lisbon 1959; retrospective exhbn. Lisbon 1959; "Promotion of Architecture" Exhbn., Barcelona 1960; Rep. XXX Biennale, Venice 1960; Exhbn., Madrid 1961; one-man Exhbn., New York 1963, Lisbon 1964, New York 1965; Exhbns. São Paulo, London, Rio de Janeiro 1965, Madrid 1966; Gulbenkian Exhbn., Brussels, Paris, Madrid 1967, Lisbon 1979; itinerant exhbn. in major cities of Brazil 1970; Bertrand Russell Centenary Exhbn., London 1972; Grand Prix, Paris Int. Exhbn.; Sousa Cardoso Prize 1939, Columbano Prize 1940, S. Paulo Biennale, Prix d'Acquisition 1951, Mention d'honneur 1953, Hallmark Award Prix, New York 1952; Silver Medal Brussels Exhbn 1958; Gulbenkian Prize, Lisbon 1961, Distinguished Gold Medal of City of Lisbon 1979. *Leisure interest:* playing the violin. *Address:* Avenue João XXI-3-3D-F, 1000 Lisbon, Portugal. *Telephone:* 896399.

BOTERO; Colombian artist; b. 19 April 1932, Medellín; s. of David and Flora Botero; m. Cecilia Botero 1964; four c.; first group exhbn., Medellín 1948; first one-man exhbn., Galería Leo Matiz, Bogotá 1951; studied at

Acad. San Fernando and El Prado Museum, Madrid 1952; visited Paris and Italy and studied art history with Roberto Longhi, Univ. of Florence 1953–54; lived in Mexico 1956; one-man exhbn. Pan American Union, Washington, D.C. 1957, Colombia 1958–59; lived in New York 1960–; first one-man exhbn. in Europe, Baden-Baden and Munich 1966; visited Italy and Germany 1967, studied work of Dürer; travelling retrospective exhbn. of 80 paintings in five German museums 1970; one-man exhbn. Hanover Gallery, London 1970; moved to Paris 1973; concentrated on Sculpture 1976–77, first one-man exhbn. of sculpture, Foire Int. d'Art Contemporain, Paris 1977; retrospective exhbn., Hirshorn Museum and Sculpture Garden, Washington, D.C. 1979; first one-man exhbn. in Japan, Tokyo, Osaka 1981; paintings in public collections in Belgium, Finland, Germany, Israel, Italy, S. America, Spain and U.S.A.; Guggenheim Nat. Prize for Colombia 1960.

BOTHA, Jan Christoffel Greyling (Stoffel), B.A., LL.B.; South African politician; b. 29 Sept. 1929, Standerton; s. of Pieter Fourie Botha and Helena Jacomina Greyling; m. Lucy Homer Nicholson 1955; two s. two d.; ed. Helpmekaar High School, Johannesburg and Witwatersrand Univ.; joined law firm, specializing in commercial law; farmed in Natal; Dir. Natal Agricultural Co-operative; M.P. for Eshowe 1974–79; Admin. of Natal 1979–84; Minister of Educ. and Culture 1984–85, of Home Affairs July 1985–Nov. 1986, of Home Affairs and Communications Nov. 1986–; Leader Nat. Party Natal; Nat. Party. *Address:* 1002 Civitas Building, cnr. of Andries and Struben Street, Private Bag X741, Pretoria 0001; 815 Hendrik Verwoerd Building, Plein Street, Private Bag 9102, Cape Town 8000, South Africa. *Telephone:* (012) 268 081 (Pretoria); (021) 465 818 (Cape Town).

BOTHA, Matthys Izak, B.A., LL.B.; South African diplomatist; b. 31 Oct. 1913, Bloemfontein; s. of Johannes H. J. Botha and Anna M. J. Botha (née Joubert); m. Hester le Roux (née Bosman) 1940; two s.; ed. Selborne Coll., East London and Univ. of Pretoria; Dept. of Finance 1931–44; Dept. of Foreign Affairs 1944–, Washington 1944–51, UN, New York 1951–54; Head of Political Div., Dept. of Foreign Affairs, Pretoria 1955–58; Minister to Switzerland 1959–60; Minister, London 1960–62; Perm. Rep. to UN 1962–70; Amb. to Canada 1970–73, to Italy and Panama 1973–76, also accred. to Costa Rica and El Salvador 1973–74, to U.K. 1977–78, to Ciskei 1983–85; mem. Transvaal Bar; mem. S.A. Foundation, Van der Stel Foundation, Huguenot Soc.; Kt. Grand Cross, Order of Merit (Italy). *Leisure interests:* boating, skiing, golfing. *Address:* 7 de Jongh Street, Strand 7140, South Africa.

BOTHA, Pieter Willem, D.M.S., M.P.; South African politician; b. 12 Jan. 1916, Paul Roux district, O.F.S.; m. Elize Rossouw 1943; five c.; ed. Univ. of Orange Free State; mem. Parl. for George 1948–84; Chief Sec. Cape Nat. Party 1948–58, Deputy Minister of the Interior 1958–61; Minister of Community Devt., Public Works and Coloured Affairs 1961–66, of Defence 1966–80, of Nat. Security 1978–84; Prime Minister 1978–84; State Pres. of South Africa Sept. 1984–; hospitalized Jan. 1989; C.-in-C. of the Armed Forces 1984–; Leader Nat. Party 1978–89; Leader Nat. Party in Cape Prov. 1966–86; Chancellor Univ. of Stellenbosch 1984–; Dr. h.c. (Univ. of O.F.S.); Decoration for Meritorious Service (S.A.) 1976, Order of the Star of S.A. and various foreign awards. *Leisure interests:* horse riding, hunting game, reading, walking. *Address:* Tuynhuys, Cape Town 8000, South Africa.

BOTHA, Roelof Frederik (Pik), B.A., LL.B.; South African diplomatist; b. 27 April 1932, Rustenburg; m. Helena Bosman 1953; two s. two d.; ed. Volkskool, Potchefstroom, Univ. of Pretoria; joined Dept. of Foreign Affairs 1953; served with diplomatic missions in Europe 1956–66; mem. S. African legal team in S.W. Africa case, Int. Court of Justice, The Hague 1963–66, 1970–71; Agent of S. African Govt., Int. Court of Justice 1965–66; Legal Adviser Dept. of Foreign Affairs 1966–68, Under-Sec. and Head S.W. Africa and UN sections 1968–70; mem. Parl. for Wonderboom 1970–74, for Westdene 1977–, served on various select Parl. cttees. 1970–74; Sec. Foreign Affairs Study Group of Nat. Party's mems. of Parl. 1974; Amb. and Perm. Rep. to UN 1974–77; Amb. to U.S.A. 1975–77; Minister of Foreign Affairs 1977–, for Information 1980–86; mem. S. African Del. to UN Gen. Assembly 1967–69, 1971, 1973–74; National Party; Grand Cross, Order of Good Hope, Decoration for Meritorious Service (S.A.), Grand Cordon, Order of the Brilliant Star (Taiwan). *Leisure interests:* hunting and fishing. *Address:* Ministry of Foreign Affairs, Union Buildings, Private Bag X152, Pretoria; House of Assembly, Cape Town, South Africa. *Telephone:* 455848.

BOTHAM, Ian Terence; British cricketer; b. 24 Nov. 1955, Heswall, Cheshire; m. Kathryn Waller 1976; one s. two d.; ed. Milford School; right-hand batsman, right-hand, fast-medium bowler; made debut for Somerset 1974, awarded county cap 1976; Test debut 1977; went on tours of Pakistan and N.Z. 1977–78, Australia 1978–79, Australia and India 1979–80, West Indies 1981, India and Sri Lanka 1981–82, Australia 1982–83, N.Z. and Pakistan 1983–84; Capt. of England 1980–81; Capt. of Somerset County Cricket Club 1983; player for Queensland, Australia and Worcestershire County Cricket Club 1987–; became first player to score a century and take 8 wickets in an innings in a Test Match, v. Pakistan (Lord's) 1978; took 100th wicket in Test cricket in record time of 2 years 9 days 1979; achieved double of 1,000 runs and 100 wickets in Tests to create world record of fewest Tests (21), and English records of shortest time (2 years

33 days) and at youngest age (23 years 279 days) 1979; became first player to have scored 3,000 runs and taken 250 wickets in Tests (55) Nov. 1982; first player to score a century and take 10 wickets in a Test Match, v. India; has scored over 1,000 runs and taken more than 100 wickets in Tests against Australia; has also played soccer for Scunthorpe United. *Publications:* It Sort of Clicks 1986, Cricket My Way 1989. *Leisure interests:* shooting, golf, flying, fishing.

BOTHWELL, Thomas Hamilton, D.SC., M.D., F.R.C.P., F.R.S.S.A., F.A.C.P.(HON.); South African physician and professor of medicine; b. 27 Feb. 1926; s. of Robert Cooper Bothwell and Jessie Isobel (née Hamilton) Bothwell; m. Alexandrine Moorman Butterworth 1957; one s. two d.; ed. St. John's Coll., Johannesburg, Univ. of Witwatersrand and Univs. of Oxford and Washington; physician, later Sr. Physician Dept. of Medicine, Univ. of the Witwatersrand 1956–67, Prof. of Medicine and Head Dept. of Medicine 1967–; Chief Physician Johannesburg Hosp. 1967–; Dir. MRC Iron and Red Cell Metabolism Research Unit, Univ. of the Witwatersrand 1969–; Gold Medal, S.A. Medical Research Council. *Publications:* 250 articles in the field of iron metabolism, 50 chapters and two books: Iron Metabolism 1962, Iron Metabolism in Man 1979. *Leisure interests:* reading, walking, dogs. *Address:* Department of Medicine, University of the Witwatersrand, Medical School, 7 York Road, Parktown 2193, Johannesburg, South Africa. *Telephone:* 488-3621.

BOTSTEIN, David, PH.D.; American professor of genetics; b. 8 Sept. 1942, Zürich, Switzerland; one d.; ed. Harvard Univ. and Univ. of Mich.; Instructor, M.I.T. 1967–69, Asst. Prof. of Genetics 1969–73, Assoc. Prof. 1973–78, Prof. 1978–; mem. N.A.S., American Acad. of Arts and Science; Woodrow Wilson Nat. Fellowship 1963; Nat. Insts. of Health Career Devt. Award 1972–77; Eli Lilly & Co. Award in Microbiology and Immunology 1978. *Address:* Massachusetts Institute of Technology, Cambridge, Mass. 02139, U.S.A.

BOTT, Martin Harold Phillips, PH.D., F.R.S.; British professor of geophysics; b. 12 July 1926, Stoke-on-Trent; s. of Harold Bott and Dorothy Bott (née Phillips); m. Joyce Cynthia Hughes 1961; two s. one d.; ed. Clayesmore School, Dorset, Keble Coll. Oxford (army short course) and Magdalene Coll. Cambridge; Nat. Service in army (Royal Signals) 1945–48, rank of Lieut.; Turner & Newall Research Fellow, Univ. of Durham 1954–56, Lecturer in Geophysics 1956–63, Reader 1963–66, Prof. 1966–88, Research Prof. in Geophysics 1988–; Head of Dept. of Geological Sciences 1970–73, 1976–82; Chair. British Nat. Cttee. for Geodesy and Geophysics 1985–; Murchison Medal, Geological Soc. of London 1977, Clough Medal, Geological Soc. of Edin. 1979, Sorby Medal, Yorks. Geological Soc. 1981. *Publications:* The Interior of the Earth 1971, Structure and Development of the Greenland-Scotland Ridge: new methods and concepts (Co-Ed.) 1983, Sedimentary Basins of Continental Margins and Craters (Ed.) 1976, and many scientific papers in journals. *Leisure interests:* Lay Reader (Anglican Church), mountain walking, skiing etc. *Address:* Department of Geological Sciences, University of Durham, South Road, Durham, DH1 3LE (Office); 11 St Mary's Close, Shincliffe, Durham, DH1 2ND, England (Home). *Telephone:* (091) 374 2511 (Office); (091) 386 4021 (Home).

BOTT, Raoul, D.SC.; American (naturalized) mathematician; b. 24 Sept. 1923, Budapest, Hungary; s. of Rudolph and Margit (Kovacs) Bott; m. Phyllis H. Aikman 1947; one s. three d.; ed. McGill Univ. and Carnegie Inst. of Tech.; mem. Inst. for Advanced Study, Princeton 1949–51, 1955–57; Instructor in Math., Univ. of Mich. 1951–52, Asst. Prof. 1952–55, Prof. 1957–59; Prof. of Math., Harvard Univ. 1959–67, Higgins Prof. of Math. 1967–79, Graustein Prof. of Math. 1978–; Ed. Topology, Annals of Mathematics 1958–59, American Journal of Mathematics 1969; mem. Nat. Acad. of Sciences, American Math. Soc., American Acad. of Arts and Sciences; Master Dunster House 1978–84; Hon. Fellow London Math. Soc. 1983, St. Catherine's Coll., Oxford 1984; Hon. D.Sc. (Notre Dame) 1981, (McGill Univ.) 1986; Veblen Prize, American Math. Soc. 1964 (Vice-Pres. 1973–75), Nat. Medal for Science 1987. *Leisure interests:* music, swimming, skiing. *Address:* Mathematics Department, Harvard University, Science Center, 1 Oxford Street, Cambridge, Mass. 02138 (Office); 1 Richdale Avenue No. 9, Cambridge, Mass. 02140, U.S.A. (Home). *Telephone:* (616) 864-2482 (Home).

BOTTAI, Bruno; Italian diplomatist; b. 10 July 1930, Rome; unmarried; ed. Univ. of Rome; entered Ministry of Foreign Affairs 1955; served Tunis, Brussels, London, Vatican and Ministry of Foreign Affairs 1955–76; Amb. to the Holy See and the Sovereign Mil. Order of Malta 1979; Dir.-Gen. of Political Affairs, Ministry of Foreign Affairs 1981; Amb. to U.K. 1985–87. *Leisure interest:* modern paintings. *Address:* c/o Ministry of Foreign Affairs, Piazzale della Farnesina 1, 00194 Rome, Italy.

BÖTTIGER, Lars Erik, PH.D.; Swedish professor of medicine; b. 23 Oct. 1924, Stockholm; s. of Erik Böttiger and Ebba Lisa Åkerhielm; m. Margareta Westerlund 1948; three d.; ed. Karolinska Inst., Stockholm; Resident, Dept. of Internal Medicine Karolinska Inst. 1951–60, Assoc. Prof., Dept. of Medicine 1960–72, Prof. and Head 1972–84; Prof. and Head, Pharmacotherapeutic Div., Dept. of Drugs, Nat. Bd. of Health and Welfare 1972–74; Vice-Pres. and Medical Dir., Kabi Ltd. 1985–. *Publications:* over 350 scientific papers. *Leisure interest:* literature. *Address:* Kabi Ltd., S-112 87 Stockholm, Sweden. *Telephone:* 46-8-13 80 00.

BOTTO DE BARROS, Adwaldo Cardoso; Brazilian international official; b. 19 Jan. 1925, Aracajú, Sergipe; m. Neida de Moura Botto de Barros 1951; one s. two d.; ed. Mil. Coll. of Resende, Mil. Eng. Inst., Catholic Univ. of São Paulo and Getulio Vargas Foundation; Chief Eng. railway construction 1952–54; Dir. of industries in São Paulo and Curitiba 1955–64; Dir. Handling Sector, São Paulo Pref., Financial Adviser to São Paulo Eng. Faculty and Adviser on industrialization of Suzano Prefecture, São Paulo 1965–71; Regional Dir. Brazilian Telegraph and Post Office Enterprise, São Paulo 1972–74; Pres. Brazilian Telegraph and Post Office Enterprise, Brasilia 1974–84; Chair. Exec. Council, Universal Postal Union (UPU) 1979–84, Dir.-Gen. Int. Bureau 1985–; numerous awards and honours. *Leisure interests:* philately, sport. *Address:* International Bureau of the UPU, Weltpoststrasse 4, 3000 Berne 15, Switzerland. *Telephone:* 031/43 22 11.

BOTTOMLEY, Sir James Reginald Alfred, K.C.M.G., M.A.; British diplomatist; b. 12 Jan. 1920, London; s. of Sir Cecil Bottomley and Alice T. Bottomley (née Robinson); m. Barbara E. Vardon 1941; two s. (and one deceased) two d.; ed. King's Coll. School, Wimbledon and Trinity Coll., Cambridge; served in British Army 1940–46; joined Dominions Office 1946 (now Foreign and Commonwealth Office); served in South Africa 1948–50, Pakistan 1953–55, U.S.A. 1955–59, Malaysia 1963–67; mem. British Nat. Export Council 1970–71, British Overseas Trade Bd. 1972, Cttee. on invisible exports 1970–72; Amb. to South Africa 1973–76; Perm. Rep. to UN Office and other orgs. in Geneva 1976–78 (retd.); Dir. Johnson, Matthey PLC 1979–85. *Leisure interests:* reading, golf. *Address:* 22 Beaufort Place, Thompsons Lane, Cambridge, CB5 8AG, England. *Telephone:* (0223) 328760.

BOTTRALL, Francis James Ronald, O.B.E., K.C.ST.J., M.A., F.R.S.L.; British poet and literary historian; b. 2 Sept. 1906, Camborne, Cornwall; s. of Francis John Bottrall and Clara Jane Rowe; m. 1st Margaret F. Saumarez-Smith 1934; one s.; m. 2nd Margot Pamela Samuel 1954; ed. Redruth County School and Pembroke Coll., Cambridge; Lecturer in English, Helsinki Univ. 1929–31; Commonwealth Fund Fellowship Princeton Univ. U.S.A. 1931–33; Johore Prof. of English Language and Literature Raffles Coll. Singapore 1933–37; Asst. Dir. and Prof. of English Literature British Inst. Florence 1937–38; Sec. London Univ. School of Oriental and African Studies 1939–45; seconded to Air Ministry, Priority Officer 1940; British Council Rep. Sweden 1941–44, Italy 1945–50; Controller Educ. Div. British Council 1950–54; Rep. Brazil 1954–56, Greece 1957–59. Japan 1959–61; Chief, Fellowships and Training Branch, FAO of UN 1963–65; Coronation Medal 1953; Syracuse Int. Poetry Prize 1954; Grand Officer of Order of Merit of Republic of Italy 1973, Kt. Commdr. of the Order of St. John of Jerusalem (Malta) 1977. *Publications:* The Loosening and Other Poems 1931, Festivals of Fire 1934, The Turning Path 1939, T. S. Eliot: Dikter i Urval 1942, Farewell and Welcome 1945, Zephyr Book of English Verse 1945, Selected Poems 1946, The Palisades of Fear 1949, Adam Unparadised 1954, Collected Poems 1961, Rome (Art Centres of the World) 1968, Day and Night 1974, Poems 1955–1973 1974, Reflections on the Nile 1980, Against A Setting Sun 1984. *Leisure interests:* music, travel, watching sport. *Address:* Flat 4, New Cavendish Court, 39 New Cavendish Street, London, W1M 7RJ, England. *Telephone:* 01-486 1144.

BOTVIN, Aleksandr Platonovich; Soviet politician and diplomatist; b. 1918, Ukraine; ed. Kharkov Inst. of Aviation; mem. CPSU 1943–; foreman and chief metallurgist and Cen. Cttee. organizer in a plant in Khabarovsk 1941–55; First Sec. Regional Cttee. Ukrainian CP (Kharkov), Second Sec. Kiev Dist. Cttee. Ukrainian CP 1955–62; First Sec. Kiev City Cttee. Ukrainian CP 1962–63; Second Sec. Kiev Dist. Cttee. Ukrainian CP, 1963–65; Deputy to Supreme Soviet of Ukrainian S.S.R. 1963–79; mem. Cen. Cttee. Ukrainian CP 1965–; First Sec. Kiev City Cttee. Ukrainian CP 1965–79; mem. Auditing Cttee. CPSU 1966–71; Deputy to Supreme Soviet of U.S.S.R. 1966–79; cand. mem. Cen. Cttee. of CPSU 1971–76, mem. 1976–79; mem. Politburo Cen. Cttee. of Ukrainian CP 1976–79; U.S.S.R. Amb. to Czechoslovakia 1980–84. *Address:* c/o Ministry of Foreign Affairs, 32-34 Smolenskaya-Sennaya, Ploshchad, Moscow, U.S.S.R.

BOTVINNIK, Mikhail Moiseyevich, D.SC.; Soviet chess player; b. 17 Aug. 1911, Repino (near Leningrad); s. of Moisey and Serafina Botvinnik; m. Gajane Ananova 1935; one d.; ed. Leningrad M. I. Kalinin Polytechnic Inst; Chess Champion of U.S.S.R. 1931, 1933, 1939, 1941, 1944, 1945, 1952; World Champion 1948–57, 1958–60, 1961–63; Chess Grandmaster of U.S.S.R. 1935; Senior Scientific Assoc. All-Union Scientific Research Inst. of Electrical Energy 1955–; mem. CPSU, 1940–; Int. Grand Master 1950; Honoured Master of Sport of U.S.S.R. 1945, Order of Lenin, Order of Red Banner of Labour, Order of Honour (twice) and other decorations. *Publications:* Selected Games (1926–46) 1951, Soviet School of Chess 1951, Algorithms of the Game of Chess 1968, Controlled AC Machines (with Y. Shakarian) 1969, Computers, Chess and Long-Range Planning 1971, Botvinnik's Best Games 1947–70 1972, Three Matches of Anatoly Karpov 1975, On Cybernetic Goal of Game 1975. *Address:* Flat 154, 3 ja Frunzenskaja W. 7, Moscow G-270, U.S.S.R. *Telephone:* 2421586.

BOUABID, Maati, L. EN D.; Moroccan lawyer and politician; b. 11 Nov. 1927, Casablanca; ed. Lycée Lyautey, Casablanca, Univ. of Bordeaux, France; in practice as Barrister, Casablanca 1953–56; Public Prosecutor, Tangier 1956–57; Attorney-Gen. Court of Appeal 1957–58; Minister of Labour and Social Affairs 1958–60, of Justice 1977–81; Prime Minister 1979–84; Head, Union Constitutionelle; fmr. Pres. of Municipal Council of Casablanca; fmr. mem. Union Nat. des Forces Populaires; Medal of the Green March. *Address:* c/o Présidence du Conseil de Gouvernement, Rabat, Morocco.

BOUCETTA, M'Hamed, L. EN D.; Moroccan politician; b. 1925, Marrakesh; ed. Ecole Sidi Mohamed, Lycée Moulay Idriss, Fez, Univ. of Paris, France, Inst. des Etudes Supérieures, Paris; worked as lawyer in Casablanca; joined Istiqlal Party, Dir. Al-Istiqlal (party newspaper) 1955, mem. Political Bureau 1956, Exec. Cttee. 1963–, Sec.-Gen. 1974–; Sec. of State for Foreign Affairs 1956; Minister of Justice 1961–63; Minister of State without Portfolio March-Oct. 1977, 1984–85, for Foreign Affairs 1977–84, and for Cooperation 1977–81, Minister of State without Portfolio in Interim Govt. 1985. *Address:* c/o Majlis al-Nuwab, Rabat, Morocco.

BOUCHARD, Benoit, B.A.; Canadian politician; b. 16 April 1940, Roberval, Quebec; m. Jeannine Lavoie, three c.; ed. Laval Univ.; teacher Coll. Classique, Coll. Notre-Dame, then Prin. Coll. Notre-Dame and Villa étudiante, Roberval; Dir. St. Felicien CEGEP 1979; alderman, Roberval 1973–80; Minister of State (Transport) Sept. 1984–85, Minister of Communications 1985–86, of Employment and Immigration 1986–88, of Transport 1988–; fmrly. active in numerous social and professional orgs. including Féd. des Cégeps, St. Félicien Zoo, Solidarité econ. régionale. *Address:* House of Commons, Ottawa, Ont. K1A 0AZ, Canada.

BOUCHARDEAU, Huguette; French politician; b. 1 June 1935, Saint-Etienne; d. of Marius Briaut and Rose (née Noel) Briaut; m. Marc Bouchardeau 1955; one s. two d.; teacher of philosophy, Lycée Honoré d'Urfé 1961–70; lecturer in educ. sciences, Univ. of Lyon 1970–; Sec.-Gen. Parti Socialiste unifié 1979–83; unsuccessful presidential cand. 1981; Sec. of State for Environment and Quality of Life 1983–84; Minister for the Environment 1984–86. *Publications:* Pas d'histoire, les femmes 1977, Hélène Brion: La voie feministe 1978, Un coin dans leur monde 1980, Le ministère du possible 1986, Choses dites de profil 1988. *Address:* Assemblée nationale, 126 rue de l'Université, 75355 Paris, France (Home).

BOUCHIER, Ian Arthur Dennis, M.B., CH.B., M.D., F.R.C.P., F.R.C.P.E., F.R.S.E.; British professor of medicine; b. 7 Sept. 1932, Cape Town, S. Africa; s. of E. A. Bouchier and May Bouchier; m. Patricia N. Henshilwood 1959; two s.; ed. Rondebosch Boys' High School and Univ. of Cape Town; junior staff positions, Groote Schuur Hosp. Cape Town 1955–60; Registrar, Lecturer, Royal Free Hosp. London 1961–63; Research Fellow, Instr. Boston Univ. 1963–65; Sr. Lecturer, Univ. of London 1965–70, Reader in Medicine 1970–73; Prof. of Medicine, Univ. of Dundee 1973–86, Univ. of Edin. 1986–; Sec.-Gen. World Org. of Gastroenterology 1982; Visiting Prof. Univ. of Michigan 1979; Madras Medical Coll. 1981; McGill Univ. 1983, Royal Postgrad. Medical School 1984, Univ. of Hong Kong 1988, China Medical Univ. 1988; Chair. Educ. Cttee. and mem. Council British Soc. of Gastroenterology; mem. Council, Royal Soc. of Edin. 1986–; Royal Coll. of Physicians; Chief Scientist Cttee.; Ed.-in-Chief Current Opinion in Gastroenterology; mem. numerous editorial bds. *Publications:* 16 textbooks and 350 articles mainly on gastroenterological topics. *Leisure interests:* music of Berlioz, history of whaling, cooking. *Address:* Department of Medicine, University of Edinburgh, Royal Infirmary, Edin., EH3 9YW, Scotland. *Telephone:* 031-229 2477 (Ext. 2055).

BOUDART, Michel, M.A., PH.D.; American professor of chemical engineering; b. 18 June 1924, Brussels, Belgium; s. of François Boudart and Marguerite Swolfs; m. Paula M. d'Haese 1948; three s. one d.; ed. Princeton Univ.; Asst. then Assoc. Prof. Princeton Univ. 1954–61; Prof. Univ. of Calif. (Berkeley) 1961–64; William Keck Sr. Prof. of Chemical Eng. Stanford Univ. 1964–; co-founder and Dir. Catalytica Asscn. Inc. 1973–; mem. N.A.S., Nat. Acad. of Eng. *Publications:* Kinetics of Chemical Processes 1968, Kinetics of Heterogenous Catalytic Reactions 1984 (with G. Djéga-Mariadasson). *Address:* Department of Chemical Engineering, Stanford University, Calif. 94305 (Office); 512 Gerona Road, Stanford, Calif. 94305, U.S.A. (Home). *Telephone:* (415) 723-4748 (Office); (415) 324-2480 (Home).

BOUDOURIS, Georges; Greek university professor and engineer; b. 11 Sept. 1919, Kyparissia; s. of Odysseas Boudouris and Eustathia Rombola; m. Irma Terzakis 1952; two s.; ed. Nat. Tech. Univ. of Athens, École Supérieure d'Électricité, Paris and Univ. of Paris; Scientific Research C.N.R.S., Paris 1955–56; Asst. Prof. École Supérieure d'Électricité 1964–65; Consultant Univ. of Patras, Greece 1965–66; Assoc. Prof. Agricultural High School of Athens 1966–68; returned to France in 1968, became naturalised citizen but retained Greek nationality; Prof. Polytechnic Inst. and Univ. of Grenoble 1968–76; returned to Greece 1976; Prof. of Physics Nat. Tech. Univ. of Athens 1976–87, Rector 1983–86, re-elected 1986, resgnd. 1987, Prof. Emer. 1987–; fmr. Visiting Prof. Univs. of Pisa and Paris; Gov. Hellenic Telecommunication Org. 1981–82; Pres. Nat. Foundation of Scientific Research 1982–83; Vice-Pres. Greek Cttee. for UNESCO 1982–85; mem. Perm. Cttee. Conf. of European Univ. Rectors 1983–87, Exec. Cttee. European Scientific Foundation 1982–84, Admin. Council Community of Mediterranean Univs. 1983–87, Council for Higher Educ., Greek Ministry of Nat. Educ. 1983–87, mem. numerous other scientific, cultural and social orgs. and insts. *Publications:* about 60 research papers on atomic and molecular physics, 15 textbooks, and numerous articles, reports and other publs. concerning univ. educ., energy problems and peace protection. *Leisure interests:* social and cultural activities. *Address:* Odos Xiroyanni, Zografou 157.71, Athens, Greece. *Telephone:* 7796 560.

BOUEY, Gerald Keith, O.C., B.A.; Canadian banker; b. 2 April 1920, Axford, Sask.; s. of J. A. Bouey; m. Anne Margaret Ferguson 1945; one s. one d.; ed. Queen's Univ., Kingston, Ont.; joined Research Dept., Bank of Canada 1948, Asst. Chief 1953–56, Deputy Chief 1956–62; Chief 1962–65, Adviser to the Govs. 1965–69, Deputy Gov. 1969–71, Senior Deputy Gov. 1972–73, Gov. and Dir. 1973–87; Dir. Fed. Business Devt. Bank, Export Devt. Corpn., Canada Deposit Insurance Corpn.; Hon. LL.D. (Queen's Univ.). *Leisure interests:* golf, skiing. *Address:* 79 Kamloops Avenue, Ottawa, Canada (Home). *Telephone:* (613) 733-5710 (Home).

BOULANGER, Paul, M.SC., M.D.; French professor of biochemistry; b. 21 Nov. 1905, Roubaix; m. Renée Brochen 1933; two s. one d.; ed. Univ. of Lille; Asst. in Biochem., Univ. of Lille (later Univ. of Lille II) 1931, Assoc. Prof. 1939, Prof. 1942–77, Hon. Prof. 1977–; Dir. Research Unit for Protein Chem., Inst. Nat. de la Santé et de la Recherche médicale 1961–78; engaged in research in amino acid metabolism, polypeptid and protein structure 1932–77; mem. Nat. Acad. of Medicine; Commdr. Légion d'honneur, Ordre national du Mérite, Ordre des Palmes académiques. *Publications:* Medical Biochemistry 1940, General Biochemistry 1959; many papers and reviews in biochemical journals. *Address:* les Jardins d'Arcadie, 6 place Saint-Louis, 67000 Strasbourg, France.

BOULDING, Kenneth Ewart, M.A.; American university professor; b. 18 Jan. 1910, Liverpool, England; s. of William C. Boulding and Elizabeth Ann Boulding (née Rowe); m. Elise Biorn-Hansen 1941; four s. one d.; ed. Liverpool Collegiate School, New Coll., Oxford, and Univ. of Chicago; Commonwealth Fellow 1932–34; Asst. Edinburgh Univ. 1934–37; Instructor, Colgate Univ., U.S.A. 1937–41; Economist, L.N. 1941–42; Prof. Fisk Univ. 1942–43; Assoc. Prof. Iowa State Coll. 1943–46; Angus Prof. of Political Economy and Chair. of Dept., McGill Univ. 1946–47; Prof. Iowa State Coll. 1947–49; Prof. of Econs., Univ. of Michigan 1949–68; Prof. of Econs. and a Programme Dir. Inst. of Behavioral Science, Univ. of Colorado 1968–81, Distinguished Prof. of Econs. 1977–80, Prof. Emer. 1980–, Research Assoc. and Project Dir. Inst. of Behavioral Science 1981–; Pres. American Econ. Assch. 1968, Distinguished Fellow 1969; Pres. American Assch. for the Advancement of Science 1979; Fellow, Center for Advanced Study of Behavioral Science, Stanford, Calif. 1954–55; Fellow, American Acad. Arts and Sciences, American Philosophical Soc.; Corresp. Fellow, British Acad. 1982–; mem. Nat. Acad. of Sciences 1975, Sr. mem. Inst. of Medicine 1983–; numerous hon. degrees; John Bates Clark Medal, American Econ. Assch. 1949, Prize for Distinguished Scholarship in the Humanities 1962, Frank E. Seidman Distinguished Award in Political Economy 1976, Lentz Int. Research Award 1976, Rufus Jones Award 1979, Leadership Award, Soc. for General Systems Research 1984. *Publications:* Economic Analysis 1941 (fourth edn. 1966), The Economics of Peace 1945, The Naylor Sonnets 1945, A Reconstruction of Economics 1950, The Organizational Revolution 1953, The Image 1956, Principles of Economic Policy 1958, The Skills of the Economist 1958, Conflict and Defense 1962, The Meaning of the Twentieth Century 1964, The Impact of the Social Sciences 1966, Beyond Economics 1968, Economics as a Science 1970, A Primer on Social Dynamics 1970, The Prospering of Truth (1970 Swarthmore Lecture) 1970, Peace and the War Industry (ed.) 1970, Readings in Price Theory (ed. with G. J. Stigler) 1972, Linear Programming and the Theory of the Firm (ed. with W. A. Spivey) 1960, Disarmament and the Economy (ed. with Emile Benoit) 1963, Economic Imperialism (ed. with T. Mukerjee) 1972, Redistribution to the Rich and the Poor (ed. with Martin Pfaff) 1972, Kenneth E. Boulding/Collected Papers Vols. I and II (ed. Fred Glahe) 1971, Vols. III–VI (ed. Larry Singell) 1973–85, The Appraisal of Change (in Japanese) 1972, Transfers in an Urbanized Economy (ed. with Martin and Anita Pfaff) 1973, The Economy of Love and Fear: a Preface to Grants Economics 1973, Sonnets from the Interior Life and Other Autobiographical Verse 1975, Stable Peace 1978, Ecodynamics: A New Theory of Societal Evolution 1978, The Social System of the Planet Earth (co-author) 1980, Redistribution through the Financial System: The Grants Economics of Money and Credit (ed. with Thomas F. Wilson) 1978, Beasts, Ballads and Bouldingisms (ed. R. P. Beilock) 1980, Evolutionary Economics 1981, A Preface to Grants Economics: The Economy of Love and Fear 1981, The Optimum Utilization of Knowledge: Making Knowledge Serve Human Betterment (ed. with L. Senesh) 1983, The Economics of Human Betterment (ed.) 1984, Human Betterment 1985, The World as a Total System 1985, Bibliography of Published Works by Kenneth E. Boulding (compiled by V. L. Wilson) 1985. *Leisure interests:* poetry, sketching, water-colours. *Address:* Institute of Behavioral Science, University of Colorado, Campus Box 484, Boulder, Colo. 80309-0484 (Office); 624 Pearl Street, 206, Boulder, Colo. 80302, U.S.A. (Home). *Telephone:* (303) 492-7526 (Office).

BOULET, Gilles, O.C., L.TH., L.PH., M.A., D.E.S.; Canadian university administrator; b. 5 June 1926, Quebec; s. of Georges Alidor and Yvonne (née Hamel) Boulet; m. Florence Lemire 1971; one s. one d.; ed. Coll. St. Gabriel, St. Tite, Séminaire St. Joseph, Trois-Rivières, Laval Univ., Univ. Catholique de Paris; Prof. of Literature and History, Séminaire Ste. Marie, Shawinigan 1953–61; Prof. of French, Faculty of Literature, Laval Univ.,

Quebec 1955–62, Aggregate Prof., Faculty of Arts 1959; Founder and Dir. Centre d'études universitaires, Trois-Rivières 1960–69, Prof. of Literature and History 1961–66; Rector Université du Quebec, Trois-Rivières 1969–78, Pres. 1978–; Dr. h.c (Rio Grande do Norte) 1983; Hon. Master of Admin. (Guerrero) 1984; Duvernay Award for Literature, La Société St. Jean Baptiste de Trois-Rivières 1978; nominated Rector-Founder Université du Québec à Trois-Rivières by Bd. of Dirs. of Univ. 1979; Commdr. of l'Association Belgo-Hispanique 1980, Mérite et Dévouement Français 1980; Gold Medal Univ. Fed. da Bahia, Brazil 1983, of Merit 'Sousandrade' Univ. Fed. do Maranhão, Brazil 1986. *Publications:* author and co-author several books on secondary school French, French literature, Canadian history and national affairs. *Leisure interests:* reading, skiing, skating, hunting and fishing. *Address:* Université du Québec, 2875 boulevard Laurier, Sainte Foy, Quebec G1V 2M3, Canada. *Telephone:* (418) 657-3551.

BOULEZ, Pierre, C.B.E.; French composer and conductor; b. 26 March 1925, Montbrison; s. of Léon Boulez and Marcelle Calabre; ed. Paris Conservatoire; studied with Messiaen, Vaurabourg-Honegger and Leibowitz; Dir. of Music to Jean-Louis Barrault theatre co. 1948; aided by Barrault and Madeleine Renaud Barrault he founded the Concert Marigny which later became the Domaine Musicale, Paris; Prin. Guest Conductor Cleveland Symphony Orchestra 1968; Prin. Conductor BBC Symphony Orchestra 1971–75; Musical Dir. New York Philharmonic 1971–77; Dir. Inst. de Recherches et de Coordination Acoustique/Musique 1975–; conducted the centenary production of Wagner's Ring, Bayreuth 1976–80; Consultant for Special Events, Orchestra Nat. de France 1987–; Hon. D.Mus. (Oxford) 1987. *Works:* First Piano Sonata 1946, Sonata for Two Pianos 1946, Sonatina for Flute and Piano 1946, Le Visage Nuptial (5 poems of René Char for 2 solo voices, female choir and orch.) 1946–50, Second Piano Sonata 1948, Le Soleil des Eaux (2 poems of René Char for voice and orch.) 1948, Livre pour Quattuor (string quartet) 1949, Symphonie Concertante (piano and orch.) 1950, Le Marteau sans Maître (cantata for voice and instruments to texts by René Char, also ballet 1965) 1955, Structures (2 pianos) 1964, Third Piano Sonata 1957–58, Improvisations sur Mallarmé (soprano and chamber ensemble) 1958, Doubles (orch.) 1958, Poésie pour Pouvoir (orch.) 1958, Tombeau (soprano and orch.) 1959, Pli selon Pli 1958–62, Figures—doubles-prismes 1964/74, Eclats and Eclats Multiples 1965, Domaines 1968–69, Cummings ist der Dichter 1970, Explosante Fixe 1973, Rituel 1974, Messagesquisse 1977, Notations 1979, Répons 1981–86, Dérive 1985; Hon. Dir. (Cambridge, Univ. of S. Calif.). *Publications:* Penser la musique aujourd'hui 1966, Relevés d'apprenti (essays) 1967, Par volonté et par hasard 1975, Points de repère 1981, Orientations: Collected Writings 1986, Dominique Jameau 1988. *Address:* 31 rue St. Merri, 75004 Paris, France; Postfach 22, 757 Baden-Baden, Federal Republic of Germany.

BOULTING, Roy; British film producer and director; b. 21 Nov. 1913; s. of Arthur Boulting and Rose Bennet; twin brother of John Boulting; m. Hayley Mills (q.v.) 1971 (divorced 1977); m. (5th) Sandra Payne 1978; ed. Reading School; formed independent film production co. with John Boulting 1937; war service, RAC, finishing as Capt.; Dir. British Lion Films Ltd. 1958–72; Jt. Man. Dir. Charter Film Productions Ltd. 1973–. *Films produced include:* Brighton Rock 1947, Seven Days to Noon 1950, Privates Progress 1955, Lucky Jim 1957, I'm All Right Jack 1959, Heaven's Above! 1962. *Films directed include:* Pastor Hall 1939, Thunder Rock 1942, Fame is the Spur 1947, The Guinea Pig 1948, High Treason 1951, Singlehanded 1952, Seagulls over Sorrento, Crest of the Wave 1953, Josephine and Men 1955, Run for the Sun 1955, Brothers in Law 1956, Happy is the Bride 1958, Carlton-Browne of the FO 1958–59, I'm All Right Jack 1959, The Risk 1960, The French Mistress 1960, Suspect 1960, The Family Way 1966, Twisted Nerve 1968, There's a Girl in My Soup 1970, Soft Beds, Hard Battles 1974, Danny Travis 1978, The Last Word 1979, The Moving Finger (for BBC TV) 1985. *Play:* Favourites 1976. *Address:* Charter Film Productions Ltd., Twickenham Film Studios, St. Margarets, Twickenham, Middlesex, England (Office).

BOULTON, David; British journalist, author and television producer; b. 3 Oct. 1935, Richmond, Surrey; s. of Charles and Lily Boulton; m. Anthea Ingham 1968; two d.; ed. Hampton Grammar School; Staff writer and Deputy Ed. Tribune 1959–63; Ed. Sanity 1963–65; Press Officer, Granada TV 1965–66, Producer, Regional Programmes 1966–68, What the Papers Say programme 1968–69, World in Action programme 1969–74, Ed. World in Action 1974–75, Ed. Drama-documentary Dept. 1976–79, Head, Current Affairs 1979–82, Producer, Writer and Dir. 1982–, Head, News, Current Affairs and Regional Programmes 1985–87, Head Arts 1987–; Chair. What the Papers Say Press Awards 1979–87; British Asscn. for Film and TV Arts Awards 1975; Int. Emmy Award 1978, 1979; Royal TV Soc. Award 1981. *Publications:* Objection Overruled 1968, The UVF: Protestant Paramilitaries in Ulster 1973, The Lockheed Papers 1978, The Grease Machine 1978, Adam Sedgwick's Dent 1984, Dales Historical Monographs (Ed.). *Leisure interest:* social history. *Address:* Granada TV Ltd., Quay Street, Manchester, M60 9EA, England; Hobsons Farm, Dent, Sedbergh, Cumbria; 46 High Street, Belmont, Bolton, Lancs., England. *Telephone:* (061) 832 7211 (Office); (05875) 321 (Dent); (020481) 273 (Belmont Village).

BOUMAH, Augustin; Gabonese politician; b. 7 Nov. 1927, Libreville; m.; ten c.; ed. French Inst. of Overseas Studies, College Moderne de Libreville, Ecolé des Cadres Supérieurs, Brazzaville; Dir. de Cabinet, Ministry of

Labour 1963; fmr. Dir. Gabonese School of Admin.; mem. Exec. Cttee., Parti Démocratique Gabonais (PDG); Minister of Youth, Sports and Cultural Affairs Jan.-April 1967, of Justice and Keeper of the Seals April-Sept. 1967, of the Interior and Justice 1967-68, of Finance and the Budget 1968-72; Minister of State at Presidency in charge of Planning and Devt. and Land Admin. 1972, 1972-75; Pres. Supreme Court 1975-80; Pres. Nat. Ass. of Gabon; numerous decorations. *Address:* c/o Supreme Court, B.P. 1043, Libreville, Gabon.

BOURASSA, Robert, M.A.; Canadian politician and economist; b. 14 July 1933, St. Pierre Claver, Mercier; s. of Aubert Bourassa and Adrienne Courville; m. Andrée Simard 1958; one s. one d.; ed. Jean-de-Brébeuf Coll., Montreal, Montreal Univ., Univ. of Oxford and Harvard; admitted to Quebec Bar 1957; Fiscal Adviser to Dept. of Nat. Revenue, lecturer in Econs. and Public Finance, Ottawa Univ. 1960-63; Sec., Dir. of Research, Bélanger Comm. on Public Finance 1963-65; Special Adviser to Fed. Dept. of Finance; mem. Nat. Assembly for Mercier 1966-76; Pres. Liberal Party Political Comm., mem. Party's Strategy Cttee.; Prof. of Public Finances, Montreal and Laval Univs.; Leader Liberal Party of Quebec 1970-77, 1983-, Financial Critic; Prime Minister of Quebec 1970-76, Dec. 1985-; Minister of Finance 1970, of Intergovt. Affairs 1971-72. *Address:* 190 Maplewood Street, Outremont, Quebec H2V 2M7, Canada.

BOURBON BUSSET, Comte Jacques Louis Robert Marie de; French diplomatist and writer; b. 27 April 1912, Paris; s. of François de Bourbon, Comte de Busset, and Guillemette de Colbert; m. Laurence Ballande 1944; three s. one d.; ed. Ecole Normale Supérieure, Paris; embassy attaché 1939; Pres. French Red Cross 1944-45; Dir. de Cabinet, Ministry of Foreign Affairs 1948-52, Dir. of Cultural Affairs 1952-56, Minister 1954; mem. Acad. Française 1981; Grand Prix Roman de l'Académie Française 1957, Prix Marcel Proust 1980. *Publications:* 32 works including Le Livre de Laurence (10 vols.) and Lettre à Laurence 1966-85. *Address:* 91610 Ballancourt, France. *Telephone:* (6) 4932902.

BOURDET, Claude; French journalist; b. 28 Oct. 1909, Paris; s. of Edouard Bourdet and Catherine Pozzi; m. Ida Adamoff 1935; two s. one d.; ed. Coll. de Normandie, Lycée Hoche (Versailles), Fed. Inst. of Tech. (Zürich); attached to Cabinet of Minister of Nat. Economy 1936-39; Man. La Manda (soap and oil firm) 1940-41; mem. Dir. Cttee. "Combat" Movement and Man. of secret paper 1942; mem. Conseil Nat. de la Résistance; arrested and imprisoned in Oranienburg and Buchenwald concentration camps 1944; Vice-Pres. Consultative Assembly 1945; Dir.-Gen. Radiodiffusion Française 1945; Man. Combat 1947-50; Founder and Ed. L'Observateur (now Le Nouvel Observateur) 1950-63; founder Centre d'Action des Gauches Indépendants 1952; mem. Municipal Council of Paris 1959-71, Nat. Cttee. Parti Socialiste Unifié 1960-63; Pres. Mouvement pour le Désarmement, la Paix, la Liberté; Vice-Pres. Int. Peace Bureau, Foreign Ed. Témoignage Chrétien 1967-; Compagnon de la Libération, Commdr. de l'Ordre des Arts et Lettres. *Publications:* Le schisme Yougoslave 1950, Les chemins de l'unité 1964, A qui appartient Paris 1972, L'aventure incertaine 1975, L'Europe truquée 1977. *Address:* 47 avenue d'Iéna, 75116 Paris, France. *Telephone:* 4720 8875.

BOURDIEU, Pierre; French professor of social sciences; b. 1 Aug. 1930, Denguin; s. of Albert Bourdieu and Noémie Duhau; m. Marie-Claire Brizard 1962; three s.; ed. Ecole Normale Supérieure; Prof., Lycée de Moulins 1954-55; Asst., Faculty of Arts, Algiers 1958-60, Faculty of Arts, Paris 1958-60; Dir. of Educ., Faculty of Arts, Lille 1961-64; Dir. of Studies, Ecole pratique des hautes études 1964-; Ecole normale supérieure 1964-84; Dir. Collection "Le Sens Commun" (Editions de Minuit) 1964-; Visiting mem. Inst. for Advanced Studies, Princeton 1972-73; mem. Scientific Council of Max Planck Inst. für Bildungsforschung 1974-76; Dir. Review Actes de la recherche en Sciences Sociales 1975-; Consulting Ed. American Journal of Sociology 1975; mem. Ed. Bd. The Sociological Review 1976, Media, Culture and Society 1980; Dir. Centre de sociologie européenne (CSE) of Collège de France, and Ecole des hautes études en Sciences Sociales 1985-; Prof., Coll. de France 1981-; mem. American Acad. of Arts and Sciences. *Publications* (in English): The Algerians 1958, The Inheritors 1964, Reproduction in Education, Society and Culture 1970, Outline of a Theory of Practice 1972, Algeria 1960 1977, Distinction 1979, Homo Academicus 1984, Language and Symbolic Power 1987. *Address:* Collège de France, 11 Place Marcelin Berthelot, 75005 Paris, France.

BOUREAU, Edouard; French academic; b. 31 Jan. 1913, Maine-et-Loire; s. of Edouard Boureau and Elise (née Decouard) Boureau; m. Jane Vallet 1943; two s.; Deputy Dir. Museum Nat. d'Histoire Naturelle 1946-59; Prof. of Paleobotany, Univ. Pierre-et-Marie-Curie, Paris 1959-81, Prof. Emer. 1981-; Sec.-Gen., Pres. Org. int. de la Paléobotanique 1954-80; mem. Acad des Sciences (Inst. de France) 1977-; Laureat Acad. des Sciences 1950-65, Officier des Palmes Academiques 1949. *Publications:* Anatomie végétale (3 vols) 1954-57, Traite de Paleobotanique (4 vols) 1964-75; World Report on Paleobotany (9 vols) 1954-73, La Terre, Mère de la vie 1986. *Leisure interest:* scientific history. *Address:* 64 rue de Paris, 94340 Joinville-Le-Pont, France. *Telephone:* (1) 48 83 83 61.

BOURGES, Hervé; French journalist and administrator; b. 2 May 1933, Rennes, Ile-et-Vilaine; s. of Joseph Bourges and Marie-Magdeleine Desjeux;

m. Marie-Thérèse Lapouille 1966; ed. Lycée de Biarritz, Coll. Saint-Joseph, Reims, École supérieure de journalisme; Ed. then Ed.-in-Chief Témoignage Chrétien 1956-62; attached to the Keeper of the Seals 1959-62, Dir. Algerian Ministry of Youth and Popular Education, attached to Ministry of Information; Asst. Lecturer Univ. de Paris II 1967-; f. and Dir. École supérieure de journalisme de Yaoundé, Cameroun 1970-76; Dir. then Pres. Admin. Council École nat. supérieure de journalisme de Lille 1976-80; Dir. Information Service and Dir.-Gen.'s Messenger UNESCO 1980-81; Dir. then Dir.-Gen. Radio France Int. 1981-83; Chair. Dir.-Gen. TV Française 1 (T.F.1) 1983-; Docteur d'état en sciences politiques; Chevalier, Légion d'honneur. *Publications:* L'Algérie à l'épreuve du pouvoir 1967, La Révolte étudiante 1968, Décoloniser l'information 1978, Les cinquante Afriques (jtly.) 1979, Le village planétaire (jtly.) 1986. *Address:* T.F.1, 15 rue Cognacq-Jay, 75340 Paris, France (Office).

BOURGES, Yvon, L. EN D.; French overseas administrator and politician; b. 29 June 1921, Pau; m. Odile Fontaine 1943; two s. three d.; ed. Univ. de Rennes; Chef de Cabinet to Prefect of the Somme 1944-45, of Bas-Rhin 1945-47; Sub-Prefect of Erstein 1947-48; with Ministry of Overseas Territories 1948, Dir. de Cabinet, High Comm. in French Equatorial Africa 1948-51, in French West Africa 1951-56; Gov. Upper Volta 1956-58; High Commr. (French) Equatorial Africa 1958-61; Chef de Cabinet, Ministry of Interior 1961-62; Deputy for Ille-et-Vilaine 1962-80; Mayor of Dinard 1962-67, 1971-83; Sec. of State for Scientific Research 1965-66, for Information 1966-67, for Co-operation 1967-72; Minister of Commerce 1972-73, of Defence 1975-80; Chair. Regional Council of Brittany 1986-; mem. Senate; Chevalier Légion d'honneur and numerous foreign decorations. *Address:* Palais du Luxembourg, 75291 Paris Cedex 06, (Office); 47 boulevard Féart, 35800 Dinard, France (Home).

BOURGÉS-MAUNOURY, Maurice; French politician; b. 19 Aug. 1914; s. of Georges Bourgès and Geneviève Maunoury; m. 2nd Jacqueline Lacoste; two s. one d.; ed. Collège Stanislas and Univ. of Paris; active with Resistance Movement 1941-44; mem. Constituent Assembly 1946; Radical Socialist Deputy for Haute Garonne 1956-58; Sec. of State (Budget) in Schuman Cabinet 1947-48; Sec. of State (Armed Forces) in Marie and Schuman Cabinets July-Sept. 1948; returned to Govt. as Minister of Public Works July 1950; Sec. of State, Présidence du Conseil 1950-51; Deputy Minister of Nat. Defence, Pleven Cabinet 1951-52; Minister of Armaments, Faure Cabinet Jan.-Feb. 1952; French Del. to 7th Session of the UN 1952; Minister of Finance, Mayer Cabinet Jan.-July 1953; Minister of the Interior until 1956, of Nat. Defence 1956-57; Prime Minister 1957; Minister of Interior 1957-58; Mayor of Bessières (Haute-Garonne) 1949-71; municipal councillor 1949-73; Dir. of paper la Dépêche du Midi 1960-; Pres. Société industrielle et financière de l'Artois 1960-; et des Mines de Kali 1963-; Chevalier Légion d'honneur, and other decorations. *Address:* 67 rue la Boétie, 75008 Paris, France.

BOURGUIBA, Habib Ben Ali; Tunisian politician; b. 3 Aug. 1903, Monastir; m. 1st Mathilde Lorrain 1927 (divorced 1961, deceased 1976), one s.; m. 2nd Mrs. Wassila Ben Ammar 1962 (divorced 1986); ed. Univ. of Paris, Ecole Libre des Sciences Politiques; active in politics and journalism since 1928; mem. Destour Party 1921, broke away and formed Neo-Destour Party (outlawed by the French) 1934; imprisoned by the French 1934-36 and 1938-43; escaped to Middle East 1945, travelled to promote Tunisian independence 1945-49, world tour during Tunisian negotiations with French Govt. 1951; arrested 1952, placed under surveillance at Tabarka (Jan.), imprisoned at Remada (March), in solitary confinement, Ile de la Galite (May) until 1954; released 1954, under surveillance in France 1954-55, during negotiations; returned to Tunisia following Franco-Tunisian Agreements 1955; Pres. Tunisian Nat. Assembly, Prime Minister, Pres. of the Council, Minister of Foreign Affairs, of Defence 1956-57, Head of Cabinet 1957-87; Pres. of Tunisia 1957-87, Pres. for Life 1975-87; Pres. Neo-Destour Party (Pres. for Life 1974); Ordre du Sang, Ordre de la confiance en diamants. *Publications:* Le Destour et la France 1937, La Tunisie et la France 1955; under house arrest, Mornag, S. Tunisia 1987-.

BOURGUIBA, Habib, Jr., L ÉS D.; Tunisian diplomatist; b. 9 April 1927, Paris, France; s. of Pres. Habib Bourguiba (q.v.); m. Neila Zouiten 1954; two s. one d.; ed. Collège Sadiki, Law School, France; collaborated in nat. liberation movement, especially 1951-54; lawyer in negotiating, Tunis 1954-56; Counsellor, Tunisian Embassy, Washington 1956-57; Amb. to Italy 1957-58, to France 1958-61, to U.S.A. 1961-63, to Canada 1961-62, to Mexico 1962-63; Perm. Rep. to UN 1961-62; Sec.-Gen. to Presidency of Repub. 1963-64; in charge of Dept. of Youth and Sports, Dept. of Tourism, Nat. office of Artisanship and Information Dept. 1963-64; elected mem. Nat. Assembly Nov. 1964; Sec. of State for Foreign Affairs 1964-70; Special Adviser to the Pres. 1977-86; Pres., Gen. Man. Banque de Développement de l'Economie de la Tunisie 1971-; many Tunisian and foreign decorations. *Leisure interests:* staying home with family, golf. *Address:* Banque de Développement Économique de Tunisie, 68 avenue Habib Bourguiba, BP 280, 1000 Tunis; Dar Essalam, 14 Rue Chédli Zouiten, La Marsa 2070, Tunisia. *Telephone:* (216-1) 27.15.05.

BOURJAILY, Vance, B.A.; American novelist; b. 17 Sept. 1922, Cleveland, Ohio; s. of Monte Ferris and Barbara Webb Bourjaily; m. Bettina Yensen 1946; one s. two d.; ed. Handley High School, Va. and Bowdoin Coll., Maine; American Field Service 1942-44; U.S. Army 1944-46; Publisher,

Record, New Castle, Va. 1947–48; Staff Writer, San Francisco Chronicle 1949–50; Ed. Discovery 1951–53; Instructor, Mexico City Coll. 1953; Dramatic Critic, The Village Voice 1955–56; freelance TV writer 1956–57; Visiting lecturer, Univ. of Iowa 1957–59, Prof. 1961; Specialist, U.S. State Dept. 1960. *Publications:* novels: The End of My Life 1947, The Hound of Earth 1953, The Violated 1957, Confessions of a Spent Youth 1960, The Man Who Knew Kennedy 1967, Brill Among the Ruins 1970, Now Playing at Canterbury 1976; non-fiction: The Unnatural Enemy 1963, Country Matters 1973, The Great Fake Book 1986; plays: Time is a Dancer 1950, The Quick Years 1956, Confessions 1971. *Leisure interests:* politics, mycology, conservation. *Address:* c/o Owen Laster, William Morris Agency, 1350 Avenue of the Americas, New York, N.Y. 10019 (Office); Redbird Farm, Route One, Iowa City, Iowa 52240, U.S.A. (Home).

BOURKE, William Oliver; American business executive; b. 12 April 1927, Chicago, Ill.; s. of Robert E. and Mabel E. D'Arcy Bourke; m. 1st Mary C. Cassell 1948; m. 2nd Elizabeth M. Philbey 1970; three s. one d.; ed. DePaul Univ.; Asst. Gen. Sales Man., Studebaker Corpn., South Bend, Ind. 1952–56; Exec. Vice-Pres. Ford Motor Co., Dearborn, Mich. 1956–80; Pres. Reynolds Metal Co. (now Reynolds Aluminium) 1981–88, C.E.O. 1986–, Chair. April 1988–; Dir. Dart & Kraft Inc., Abex Corpn., Robertshaw Controls Co. *Address:* Reynolds Aluminium Company, 6601 West Broad Street, Richmond, Va. 23261, U.S.A. *Telephone:* 804–281–2676.

BOURLIÉRE, François (Marie Gabriel), M.D., SC.D.; French biologist and university professor; b. 21 Dec. 1913, Roanne, Loire; s. of Gabriel Bourlière and Marie Deroche; m. Jacqueline Butez 1942; two s. one d.; ed. Univ. of Paris; Research Asst., School of Medicine, Paris Univ. 1942; Prof. of Physiology, School of Medicine, Rouen 1946–49; Prof. of Gerontology, Univ. of Paris 1959–83; Ed. of Revue d'Ecologie and Gerontology; Pres. Int. Union for Conservation of Nature and Natural Resources 1963–66; Convener Int. Biological Programme (Terrestrial Ecology) 1964–69; Dir. Nat. Foundation of Gerontology 1968–80; Pres. Société Nat. de Protection de la Nature 1972–82; Pres. Special Cttee. for the Int. Biological Programme (ICSU) 1969–74; Chair. Int. Co-ordination Cttee., Man and the Biosphere Program, UNESCO 1971–75; Chair. Interdisciplinary Research Programme on Environmental Problems, C.N.R.S. 1981–83; Pres. Int. Asscn. of Ecology (INTECOL) 1982–86; Chevalier Légion d'honneur 1970, Commdr. Order of Golden Ark (Netherlands) 1974, Officier Ordre national du Mérite 1978. *Publications:* Eléments d'un guide bibliographique du naturaliste (2 vols.) 1940–41, Formulaire technique de zoologiste 1941, Vie et moeurs des mammifères 1951, Le monde des mammifères 1954, The Natural History of Mammals 1954, Sénescence et sénilité 1958, Introduction à l'écologie des ongulés 1960, The Land and Wildlife of Eurasia 1964; Précis de gérontologie 1956, African Ecology and Human Evolution 1963, Ed.; Problèmes de production biologique 1967, Progrès en gérontologie 1969, Problèmes d'échantillonnage des peuplements animaux terrestres 1969, Problèmes d'échantillonnage des peuplements animaux aquatiques 1971, Zoologie, Vol. IV, Pléiade 1974, La démographie des populations sauvages de vertébrés 1975, Structure et fonctionnement des écosystèmes terrestres 1978, Gérontologie: Biologie et Clinique 1982, Tropical Savannas 1983, A Primate Radiation 1988, Vertebrates in Complex Tropical Systems 1989. *Leisure interest:* wildlife photography. *Address:* 15 avenue de Tourville, 75007 Paris, France. *Telephone:* 45.51.44.83.

BOURNE, Charles Beresford, B.A.(HONS.), LL.M., S.J.D., F.R.S.C.; Canadian barrister and professor of law; b. 19 Feb. 1921, Barbados, W.I.; s. of Rev. Beresford Bourne and Lilian M. Ward; m. Barbara J. Farmer; one s. two d.; ed. The Lodge School, Barbados, Univ. of Toronto, St. John's Coll. Cambridge and Harvard Law School; Asst. Prof. of Law, Univ. of Saskatchewan 1947–50; Assoc. Prof. of Law, Univ. of B.C. 1950–57, Prof. 1957–86, Prof. Emer. 1986–; Ed.-in-Chief, Canadian Yearbook of Int. Law 1962–; Read Medal (Canadian Council of Int. Law). *Publications:* articles in legal journals especially on the law of international water resources and constitutional law. *Leisure interests:* reading, walking, gardening, bridge. *Address:* 1576 Newton Crescent, Vancouver, B.C., V6T 1W7, Canada. *Telephone:* (604) 228-5624 (Office); (228) 0590 (Home).

BOURNE, Kenneth, PH.D., F.R.HIST.S., F.B.A.; British historian; b. 17 March 1930, Wickford, Essex; s. of Clarence Arthur Bourne and Doris Bourne (née English); m. Eleanor Anne Wells 1955; one s. one d.; ed. Southend High School, Univ. Coll. of South West and L.S.E.; Research Fellow, Inst. of Historical Research, Univ. of London 1955–56; Research Fellow, Reading Univ. 1956; asst. lecturer, then lecturer, L.S.E. 1957–69, Reader in Int. History 1969–76, Prof. 1976–; Albert B. Corey Prize (American and Canadian Historical Asscns.) 1968. *Publications:* Britain and the Balance of Power in North America 1967, Studies in International History (with D. C. Watt) 1967, The Foreign Policy of Victorian England 1970, The Blackmailing of the Chancellor 1975, Letters of Viscount Palmerston 1979, Palmerston: The Early Years 1983, British Documents on Foreign Affairs (with D. C. Watt) 1983–. *Leisure interest:* book collecting. *Address:* 15 Oakcroft Road, London, SE13 7ED, England. *Telephone:* 01-852 6116.

BOURNE, Larry Stuart, PH.D., F.R.S.C.; Canadian professor of geography and planning; b. 24 Dec. 1939, London, Ont.; s. of Stuart H. Bourne and Florence (Adams) Bourne; m. Paula T. O'Neill 1967; one s. one d.; ed. Univs. of Western Ontario, Alberta and Chicago; Asst. Prof. of Geography, Univ. of Toronto 1967–69, Assoc. Prof. and Assoc. Dir., Centre for Urban

and Community Studies (CUCS) 1969–72, Prof. and Dir. 1973–78, 1979–84, Prof. of Geography and Planning, Co-ordinator of Graduate Studies 1985–; Visiting Scholar, Univ. of Monash, Australia and L.S.E., U.K. 1972–73, Centre for Environmental Studies, London, U.K. 1978–79; Visiting Prof., Univ. of Alberta, Univ. of Tex., U.S.A. 1984, Marburg (W. Germany) 1985, Melbourne 1988; Chair. Comm. on Urban Systems in Transition, Int. Geographical Union 1988–; consultant to local, nat. and int. agencies; Award for Scholarly Distinction, Canadian Asscn. of Geographers, Honors Award 1985, Asscn. of American Geographers 1985. *Publications:* 14 books, including Internal Structure of the City 1971, Urban Systems: Strategies for Regulation 1975, The Geography of Housing 1981, Urbanization and Settlement Systems 1984, Urban Systems in Transition 1986; numerous articles in journals. *Address:* Department of Geography, University of Toronto, 100 St. George Street, Toronto, Ont., M5S 1A1 (Office); 26 Anderson Avenue, Toronto, Ont., M5P 1H4, Canada (Home).

BOURSEILLER, Antoine; French theatre director and producer; b. 8 July 1930, Paris; s. of Marcel Edouard Bourseiller and Denise Fisteberg; m. Chantal Darget 1966; one s. one d.; Dir. of Theatre, Studio des Champs-Elysées 1960–63, Poche 1964–66, Centre Dramatique National de Marseille 1966–75, Recamia 1975–78, Orléans 1980–82; Dir.-Gen. Opéra-Théâtre de Lorraine 1982–; Dir. (plays): Va donc chez Torpe 1961, Axel 1963, L'Amérique 1964, Metro Fantôme 1965, Striptease 1965, Silence, l'arbre. . . 1967, Les Brigands 1972, Jean Harlow 1972, Leuco 1974, Kennedy's Children 1975, La Tour 1976, S.T. 1979; (opera): La Clémence de Titus (Aix-en-Provence Festival) 1973, Le Barbier de Seville (Théâtre Lyrique du Sud) 1979, Mireille (Geneva) 1981, (London) 1983, Carmen (Nancy) 1981, Woyzeck (Angers) 1982; Boulevard Solitude 1984, Cantate d'Octobre, Erwartung 1986, Donna Abbandonata 1987, King Priam 1988 (all at Lorraine); Lulu (Nantes), Lady Macbeth de Mtsensk (Nancy) 1989; Chevalier, Légion d'honneur; Officer des Arts et Lettres. *Address:* 1 rue Sainte Catherine, Nancy; 20 Villa Seurat, 75014 Paris, France. *Telephone:* 83.37.28.63. (Nancy); 43.35.26.17. (Paris).

BOUSFIELD, Edward Lloyd, M.A., PH.D., F.R.S.C.; Canadian biologist; b. 19 June 1926, Penticton, B.C.; s. of late Reginald H. Bousfield and Marjory Frances (née Armstrong) Bousfield; m. 1st Barbara Joyce Schwartz 1953 (died 1983), 2nd Margaret I. Tuer 1984; one s. three d.; ed. Riverdale Collegiate Inst., Univ. of Toronto and Harvard Univ.; Invertebrate Zoologist Nat. Museum of Natural Sciences, Ottawa 1950–64, Chief Zoologist 1964–74, Sr. Scientist 1974–86, Curator Emer. 1986–; Research Assoc. Royal Ont. Museum, Toronto 1984–; Outstanding Achievement Award (Public Service of Canada) 1985. *Publications:* more than 100 scientific and other works on marine and aquatic invertebrate life, including Shallow-water Gammaridean Amphipoda of New England 1973 and A History of the Canadian Society of Zoologists–The First Decade (1961–71) 1971. *Leisure interests:* music (stringed instruments and horns), curling, lawn bowling and golf. *Address:* P.O. Box 3443, Station "D", K1P 6P4 (Office); 25 Hawthorn Avenue, Toronto, Ont., M4W 2Z1 Canada (Home). *Telephone:* (613) 956-7678 (Office).

BOUSSENA, Sadek; Algerian politician; b. 1948; m.; two c.; teacher Univ. of Algiers 1970–73; Head of Studies, Ministry of Industry and Energy 1973–75; Dir. to Ministry of Industry and Energy 1976–78; Dir.-Gen. Planning, MEIPC 1978–81; Dir.-Gen. SONATRACH 1988; Minister of Energy and Petrochemical Industries 1988–. *Address:* 80 rue Ahmad Ghermoul, Algiers, Algeria. *Telephone:* (2) 66-33-00.

BOUTALEB, Abdelhadi; Moroccan politician and educationist; b. 23 Dec, 1923; m. Touria Chraïbi 1946; two s. one d.; ed. Al Qarawiyin Univ.; Prof. of Arabic History and Literature, and Tutor to Prince Moulay Hassan and Prince Moulay Abdallah; Founder-mem. Democratic Party of Independence 1944–51; campaigned, through the Party, for Moroccan independence, and for this purpose attended UN Session, Paris 1951, and Negotiating Conf. at Aix-les-Bains 1955; Minister of Labour and Social Affairs in Bekkai Govt. 1956; Chief Ed. of journal Al-Rai-Alaam 1956–61; Amb. to Syria Feb 1962; Sec. of State, Ministry of Information Nov. 1962, Ministry of Information, Youth and Sports Jan. 1963; Interim Minister in Charge of Mauritania and Sahara Nov. 1963; Minister of Justice 1964–67, of Nat. Educ. and Fine Arts 1967; Minister of State 1968; Minister of Foreign Affairs 1969–70; Pres. Chamber of Reps. 1970–71; Prof. of Constitutional Law and Political Insts., Rabat Law Univ. 1974; Amb. to U.S.A., 1975–77; Adviser to H.M. Hassan II Oct. 1977–78, Tutor to Crown Prince Sidi Mohamed 1978–; Minister of State in Charge of Information 1978; Commdr. of the Throne of Morocco, Grand Cordon of the Repub. of U.A.R., and other decorations. *Publications:* many cultural and literary works. *Leisure interests:* sports, music, reading. *Address:* c/o Ministry of State in Charge of Information, Rabat, Morocco.

BOUTEFLIKA, Abdul Aziz; Algerian politician; b. 2 March 1937, Melilla; ed. Morocco; Major, Nat. Liberation Army and Sec. of Gen. Staff; mem. Parl. for Tlemcen 1962–; Minister of Sports 1962–63, of Foreign Affairs 1963–79; Counsellor to the Pres. March 1979–80; mem. F.L.N. Political Bureau 1964–81; mem. Revolutionary Council 1965–79; led negotiations with France 1963–66, for nationalization of hydrocarbons 1971; leader of dels. to many confs. of Arab League, OAU 1968, Group of 1977 1967, Non-aligned countries 1973, 7th Special Session of UN Gen. Assembly 1975,

Int. Conf. on Econ. Co-operation, Paris 1975–76; Pres. 29th UN Gen. Ass. 1974. *Address:* Front de Libération Nationale, place Emir Abdelkader, Algiers, Algeria.

BOUTIN, Bernard Louis, PH.B.; American management consultant; b. 2 July 1923, Belmont, N.H.; s. of Joseph L. Boutin and Annie E. (Laflam) Boutin; m. Alice M. Boucher 1945; six s. five d.; ed. St. Michael's Coll., Winooski, Vt., and Catholic Univ. of America, Washington, D.C.; Pres. and Treas. Boutin Insurance Agency Inc., Laconia, N.H. 1948–63; Proprietor, Boutin Real Estate Co., Laconia 1955–63; Mayor of Laconia 1955–59; Deputy Admin. Gen. Services Admin. (G.S.A.), Washington D.C. Feb.-Nov. 1961; Admin. G.S.A. 1961–64; Exec. Vice-Pres. Nat. Asscn. Home Builders 1964–65; Admin. of Small Business Admin. 1966–67; Deputy Dir. Office of Econ. Opportunity 1965–66; Exec. Sanders Assoc. Inc. 1967–69; Chair. N.H. State Bd. of Educ. 1968–69; mem. Nat. Highway Safety Comm. 1969–70; Democratic Candidate for Gov. of N.H. 1958, 1960; Pres. St. Michael's Coll. 1969–75; Exec. Vice-Pres. Burlington Savings Bank (Vt.) 1975–76, Pres., Trustee 1976–80; Treas. and Trustee Medical Center Hospital of Vermont 1978–80; Dir. New England College Fund 1979–80; numerous awards; Hon. LL.D. (St. Michael's Coll.); Hon. L.H.D. (Plymouth Coll. of the Univ. of New Hampshire), Hon. H.H.D. (Franklyn Pierce Coll.). *Leisure interests:* golf, fishing. *Address:* 26 Wildwood Village, Laconia, N.H. 03246, U.S.A. *Telephone:* (603) 528-1014.

BOUTOS, Ioannis; Greek politician; b. 1925, Athens; m. Maria V. Sourrapa 1957; three s.; ed. Univ. of Athens, London School of Econs.; mem. Parl. 1950, re-elected 1956, 1961, 1963, 1964; Under-Sec. of Co-ordination 1961–63, 1967; Under-Sec. to Prime Minister; Minister of Commerce 1974–75; Alt. Minister for Co-ordination 1975–76, Minister May–Oct. 1980; Minister of Agric. 1976–77, of Finance 1977–78, of Agric. 1978–80; mem. Interparl. European Comm. for Asscn. of Greece with EEC. *Address:* c/o Ministry of Co-ordination, Athens, Greece.

BOUTROS, Fouad; Lebanese lawyer and politician; b. 1920, Beirut; m. Tania Shehade 1953; one s. two d.; ed. Coll. des Frères, Beirut; Judge, Civil and Mixed Commercial Court, Beirut 1944–47; Judge Mil. Tribunal and Court Lawyer 1947–50; Govt. Lawyer 1951–57; Minister of Nat. Educ. and of the Plan 1959–60; mem. Chamber of Deputies 1960–; Deputy Speaker, Chamber of Deputies 1960–61; Minister of Justice 1961–64; Vice-Pres. of the Council, Minister of Educ. and Defence 1966–67; Vice-Pres., Council of Ministers, Minister of Foreign Affairs and of Tourism Feb.-Oct. 1968; Deputy Prime Minister and Minister of Foreign Affairs 1976–82, of Defence 1976–80; numerous decorations. *Address:* Sursock Street, Fouad Boutros Building, Beirut, Lebanon (Home). *Telephone:* 334110 (Home).

BOUTROS GHALI, Boutros, LL.B., PH.D.; Egyptian politician and international civil servant; b. 14 Nov. 1922, Cairo; ed. Cairo Univ. and Paris Univ.; fmr. Prof. of Int. Law and Head Dept. of Political Sciences, Cairo Univ.; fmr. mem. Cen. Cttee. Arab Socialist Union; Pres. Cen. of Political and Strategic Studies, Al Ahram; Minister of State for Foreign Affairs Oct. 1977–; Vice-Pres. Egyptian Soc. of Int. Law; mem. Cttee. on Application of Conventions and Recommendations of Int. Labour Org.; mem. Int. Comm. of Jurists, Geneva, and Council and Exec. Cttee. of Int. Inst. of Human Rights, Strasbourg. *Publications:* Contribution à l'étude des ententes régionales 1949, Cours de diplomatie et de droit diplomatique et consulaire 1951, Le principe d'égalité des états et les organisations internationales 1961, Foreign Policies in World Change 1963, L'Organisation de l'unité africaine 1969, La ligue des états arabes 1971, Les Conflits des frontières en Afrique 1973. *Address:* 2 avenue El Nil, Giza, Cairo, Egypt.

BOUYGUES, Francis Georges; French business executive; b. 5 Dec. 1922, Paris; s. of Georges Bouygues and Edmée Regnault.; m. Monique Tézé 1946; three s. one d.; ed. Coll. Stanislas, Paris, Ecole Centrale des Arts et Manufactures, Paris; founder and Pres.-Dir.-Gen. Société Bouygues 1951; Chair. Société Commerciale d'Affrètements et de Combustibles (SCAC) 1978–; Vice-Pres. Fondation pour entreprendre 1986–; Chair. TF-1 (TV) 1987–; Officier, Légion d'honneur; Officier, Ordre Nat. du Mérite. *Leisure interests:* yachting, hunting, fishing. *Address:* 381 avenue du Général-de-Gaulle, 92142 Clamart (Office); 14 rue des Sablous, 75116 Paris, France (Home).

BOUZEGHOUB, Mohamed Tahar; Algerian politician; b. 2 Feb. 1947, El-Main; m.; five c.; numerous positions of authority in the Nat. People's Ass.; Dir.-Gen. Air-Algeria 1980–81, S.N.T.A. 1981–88; Minister of Light Industry 1988–; mem. Central Cttee. Nat. Liberation Front 1979–. *Address:* 3 rue Ahmad Bey, Algiers, Algeria. *Telephone:* (2) 60-11-44.

BOUZIRI, Najib; Tunisian diplomatist; b. 3 Sept. 1925, La Maasa; s. of Manoubi Bouziri and Habiba Bouderbala; m. Ferida Hamza 1958; two s. one d.; ed. Paris Univ. and Inst. d'Etudes politiques; joined Néo-Destour Party (now Destour Socialist Party) 1941, mem. Cen. Cttee. 1964–; practised law in France; mem. Tunisian del., autonomy negotiations 1954–55; served with Home and Foreign Ministries 1955–56; Chargé d'affaires, Paris 1956; Chef de Cabinet, Foreign Ministry 1957–58; Amb. to Italy 1958–61 (concurrently to Austria 1959–61), to Fed. Repub. of Germany 1961–64; Sec. of State for P.T.T. Feb.-Nov. 1964; 2nd Vice-Pres. Nat. Assembly 1964–65; Amb. to U.S.S.R. 1965–70, concurrently to Poland 1967; Amb. to Belgium and Luxembourg 1970–72, to Morocco 1972–73, to Algeria 1973–75, to Spain 1975–78; Leader, Tunisian del. to confs. on Maritime

Law, Geneva 1960, Diplomatic Relations, Vienna 1961, Consular Relations, Vienna 1963; Chair. Admin. and Budgetary Cttee. of UN Gen. Assembly 1965, mem. Human Rights Cttee. 1979–82, 1982–86; Vice-Chair., Tunisian Rep. Cttee. to ECOSOC 1982–; Perm. Rep. of Tunisia to the UN, 1984–87. *Leisure interests:* tennis, painting, music. *Address:* c/o Ministry of Foreign Affairs, Tunis, Tunisia.

BOVET, Daniel, DR.SC.; Italian physiologist; b. 1907, Neuchâtel, Switzerland; s. of Pierre Bovet and Amy Babut; m. Filomena Nitti 1938; one s.; ed. Univ. of Geneva; Asst. in Physiology, Univ. of Geneva 1928–29; Asst. Inst. Pasteur, Paris 1929–39, Dir. of Laboratory 1939–47; Dir. of Laboratories of Therapeutical Chemistry, Istituto Superiore di Sanità, Rome 1947–64; Prof. of Pharmacology, Univ. of Sassari 1964–71; Prof. of Psychobiology, Univ. of Rome 1971–82, Hon. Prof. 1982–; Dir. Laboratory of Psychobiology and Psychopharmacology, Consiglio Naz. delle Ricerche 1969–75; mem. Accad. Naz dei Lincei; Foreign mem. Royal Soc. (U.K.); Nobel Prize for Physiology and Medicine 1957; Grand Officer of the Order of the Italian Repub.; Hon. Doctorates Palermo, Geneva, Rio de Janeiro, etc. *Publications:* Structure chimique et activité pharmacodynamique des médicaments du système nerveux végétatif (with F. Bovet-Nitti) 1948, Curare and Curare-like Agents (with F. Bovet-Nitti and G. B. Marini-Bettolò) 1959, Controlling Drugs (with R. H. Blum and J. Moore), 1974. *Address:* Piazza San Apollinare 33, 00186 Rome, Italy (Home). *Telephone:* (06) 6565297 (Home).

BOVIN, Aleksandr Yevgeniyevich; Soviet journalist; b. 9 Aug. 1930, Leningrad; s. of Yevgeni Bovin and Agnessa Bovin; m. Lena Bovin 1962; one d.; ed. Rostov Univ.; mem. CPSU 1952–; party work in Krasnodar Dist. 1954–56; served on editorial staff of Kommunist 1959–63; posts in Cen. Cttee. CPSU 1963–72; political observer for Izvestiya 1972–; mem. Cen. Auditing Comm., CPSU 1981–86. *Address:* Izvestiya, Pushkinskaya pl. 5, Moscow, U.S.S.R. *Telephone:* (095) 209–61–36.

BOWDEN, Baron (Life Peer), cr. 1963 of Chesterfield, **Bertram Vivian Bowden,** M.A., PH.D., M.SC.TECH., F.I.E.E., F.I.E.E.E.; British college principal, physicist and politician (retd.); b. 18 Jan. 1910, Chesterfield; s. of Bert C. Bowden; m. 1st Marjorie Browne 1939 (died 1957), 2nd Mary Maltby 1967 (died 1971), 3rd Phyllis James 1974 (dissolved); one s. two d.; ed. Chesterfield Grammar School, Emmanuel Coll., Cambridge, and Univ. of Amsterdam; schoolmaster, The Collegiate School, Liverpool 1935–37; Chief Physics Master, Oundle School 1937–40; Telecommunications Research Establishment, Swanage and Malvern 1940–43; Naval Research Laboratory, Washington 1943–45; M.I.T. 1945–46; Atomic Energy Research Establishment, Harwell 1946; Partner, Sir Robert Watson-Watt and Partners 1946–50; Ferranti Ltd. (in charge of application of digital computers) 1950–53; Prin., Manchester Municipal Coll. of Tech. (now Univ. of Manchester Inst. of Science and Tech.) 1953–64, 1966–76; Minister of State, Dept. of Educ. and Science 1964–65; Pres. Nat. TV Rental Asscn. 1976–82; Hon. D.S. (Rensselaer Polytechnic, U.S.A.) 1974, Hon. LL.D. (Manchester) 1976; Pioneer Award, I.E.E.E. Aerospace and Electronic Systems Group 1973. *Publications:* Faster than Thought—A Symposium on Digital Computers 1953, The Proposals for the Development of the Manchester College of Science and Technology 1956, numerous papers and articles on education. *Leisure interests:* garden, music, reading *Address:* Pine Croft, 5 Stanhope Road, Bowdon, Altrincham, Cheshire, WA14 3LB, England. *Telephone:* 061-928 4005.

BOWDLER, William Garton, M.A.; American diplomatist; b. 27 March 1924, Argentina; s. of George A. and Ruth N. Bowdler; m. Margaret Clark 1945; two s. one d.; ed. Univ. of Richmond, Va., Fletcher School of Law and Diplomacy; served in U.S. Army 1944–46; various positions in Dept. of State 1950–56; Embassy in Havana, Cuba 1956–61; Int. Relations Officer, Washington, D.C. 1961–64; Deputy Co-ordinator of Cuban Affairs 1964–65; senior mem. Nat. Security Council staff 1965–68; U.S. Amb. to El Salvador 1968–71, to Guatemala 1971–73; Deputy Asst. Sec.-Gen. for Inter-American Affairs 1973–75; Amb. to South Africa 1975–78; Envoy of Pres. Carter to Nicaragua 1978; Dir. Bureau of Intelligence and Research 1978–79; Asst. Sec. for Inter-American Affairs 1979–81. *Address:* c/o Department of State, 2201 C Street, Washington, D.C. 20520, U.S.A.

BOWEN, Edward George, C.B.E., M.SC., PH.D., F.A.A., F.R.S.; British scientist (retd.); b. 14 Jan. 1911, Swansea; s. of George Bowen; three s.; ed. Univs. of Wales, London and Sydney; mem. Radar Devt. Team, Orfordness 1935; Air Ministry Research Station, Bawdsey 1936–40; Tizard Mission to U.S.A. 1940; British Air. Comm., Washington, D.C. 1940–42; Radiation Lab., M.I.T. 1943; Chief, Div. of Radiophysics, CSIRO 1946–71; Chair. Anglo-Australian Telescope Bd. 1967–73; Counsellor (Scientific), Australian Embassy, Washington, D.C. 1973–76; Foreign mem. American Acad. of Arts and Sciences, American Acad. of Eng.; Thurlow Award, American Inst. of Navigation 1950; U.S. Medal for Freedom 1947. *Publication:* Radar Days 1987. *Leisure interest:* yachting. *Address:* 1/39 Clarke Street, Narrabeen, N.S.W. 2101, Australia. *Telephone:* (02) 98.8565.

BOWEN, Howard Rothmann, PH.D., D.LITT., LL.D.; American economist; b. 27 Oct. 1908, Spokane, Wash.; s. of Henry G. Bowen and Josephine Bowen; m. Lois Schilling 1935; two s.; ed. Washington State Univ., and Univ. of Iowa; postdoctoral study, Cambridge Univ. and L.S.E., England 1937–38; Assoc. Prof., Univ. of Ia. 1935–42; Chief Economist, Cttee. on Internal

Revenue Taxation, U.S. Congress 1943–45; Chief Economist, Irving Trust Co., New York 1945–47; Dean and Prof., Coll. of Business Admin., Univ. of Ill. 1947–52; Prof., Williams Coll. 1952–55; Pres. Grinnell Coll. 1955–64; Pres. Univ. of Ia. 1964–69; Chancellor Claremont Univ. Center 1969–74; Prof. of Econs., Claremont Graduate School 1974–85, Prof. Emer. 1985–; 22 hon. degrees and many awards. *Publications:* Toward Social Economy 1948, Social Responsibilities of the Businessman 1953, Graduate Education in Economics 1953, Efficiency in Liberal Education 1971, Investment in Learning 1977, The Costs of Higher Education 1980, The State of the Nation and the Agenda for Higher Education 1982, American Professors: A National Resource Imperiled 1986, Academic Recollections 1988. *Leisure interests:* reading, music, hiking. *Address:* 916 W. Harrison Avenue, Claremont, Calif. 91711, U.S.A. *Telephone:* (714) 624-8433.

BOWEN, Lionel Frost; Australian politician; b. 28 Dec. 1922, Sydney; m. Claire Bowen; eight c.; ed. Univ. of Sydney; fmrly. in practice as solicitor; mem. N.S.W. Parl. 1962–69; mem. House of Reps. (Fed. Parl.) 1969–; Postmaster-Gen., Special Minister of State and Minister for Mfg. Industry 1972–75; Deputy Leader of Opposition 1977–83; Deputy Prime Minister, Minister for Trade and Minister assisting Prime Minister in Commonwealth-State Affairs 1983–84, Deputy Prime Minister, Attorney-Gen. 1984–, Minister assisting the Prime Minister 1984–88, Vice-Pres. of Exec. Council 1984–87; Australian Labor Party. *Address:* House of Representatives, Canberra, A.C.T., Australia.

BOWEN, Most. Rev. Michael George, S.T.L., PH.L.; British ecclesiastic; b. 23 April 1930, Gibraltar; s. of late Maj. C. L. J. Bowen and of Mary J. Pedley; ed. Downside Abbey School, Trinity Coll., Cambridge, and Gregorian Univ., Rome; wine trade 1951–52; Venerable English Coll., Rome 1952–59; ordained R.C. priest 1958; curate, Earlsfield and Walworth, Diocese of Southwark 1959–63; teacher of Theology, Pontifical Beda Coll. Rome 1963–66; Chancellor, Diocese of Arundel and Brighton 1966–70; Coadjutor Bishop 1970–71, Bishop of Arundel and Brighton 1971–77; Archbishop and Metropolitan, Diocese of Southwark 1977–; Freeman of City of London 1984. *Leisure interests:* golf, tennis. *Address:* Archbishop's House, 150 St. George's Road, London, SE1 6HX, England. *Telephone:* 01-928 5592/2495.

BOWEN, Hon. Sir Nigel Hubert, A.C., K.B.E., B.A., LL.B., Q.C.; Australian judge; b. 26 May 1911, Summerland, British Columbia, Canada; s. of Otway Percival Bowen and Dorothy Joan Bowen; m. 1st Eileen Cecily Mullens 1947 (died 1983), three d.; m. 2nd Ermyn Krippner 1984; ed. King's School, Parramatta, N.S.W. and St. Paul's Coll., Univ. of Sydney; admitted to N.S.W. Bar 1936, Victoria Bar 1954; Q.C. 1953; Ed. Australian Law Journal 1946–58; Vice-Pres. Law Council of Australia 1957–60; lecturer in Company Law and Taxation, Univ. of Sydney 1957–58; Pres. N.S.W. Bar Council 1959–61; mem. of Parl. 1964–73; Attorney-Gen. 1966–69; Minister of Educ. and Science 1969–71, Attorney-Gen. 1971; Minister of Foreign Affairs 1971–72; Judge, N.S.W. Supreme Court and Court of Appeal 1973–76; Chief Judge in Equity 1974–76; Chief Justice, Fed. Court of Australia 1976–; leader of Australian del., Vice-Pres. UN Int. Conf. on Human Rights 1968; leader of del. UNESCO Int. Conf. on Cultural Policies 1970, UN Gen. Assembly 1971, 1972. *Leisure interests:* music, swimming. *Address:* 21st Level, Law Courts Building, Queens Square, Sydney, N.S.W. 2000, Australia.

BOWEN, Otis Ray, M.D.; American physician and politician; b. 26 Feb. 1918, Fulton Co., Ind.; s. of Vernie Bowen and Pearl Bowen (née Wright); m. 1st Elizabeth A. Steinmann 1939 (died 1981), three s. one d.; m. 2nd Rose Mary Hochstetler 1981; ed. Indiana Univ. and Indiana Univ. Medical School; physician 1942–; served U.S. Army Medical Corps, commissioned First Lieut. later Capt. 1942–45; Intern Memorial Hospital, South Bend, Ind.; private practice Bremen, Ind. 1946–72; fmr. mem. of staff Bremen Community, Parkview, St. Joseph's of South Bend, St. Joseph's of Mishawaka and Memorial Hospital; fmr. Marshall County Coroner; mem. House of Reps. 1957–72, House Minority Leader 1965–67, Speaker 1967–72, mem. Legislative Advisory Cttee. and Vice-Chair Legis. Council, Ind. Gen. Assembly 1967–68, Chair. 1970–72; Gov. of Indiana 1973–81; Del. Repub. Nat. Convention 1972 and 1976; Vice-Chair. Repub. Govt. Asscn. 1977–78, Chair. 1978–79; mem. Exec. Cttee. Nat. Govt. Asscn. 1978–79, Cttee. on Crime Reduction and Public Safety 1973, Chair. 1973–78; mem. Exec. Cttee. Midwest Govs. Great Lakes Caucus, 1973–81; Chair. Interstate Mining Compact 1978; mem. Council State Govts. 1973–81, Educ. Comm. States 1973–81, Chair. elect 1976–77, Chair. 1977–81; mem. Midwest Govs. Conf. 1973–81, Vice-Chair. 1977–81, Chair. 1978–81; mem. Republican Govs.', Conf. 1973–81, Nat. Govs.' Conf. 1973–81; Sec. Dept. of Health and Social Services 1985–89; Chair. Advisory Council on Social Security; fmr. mem. Intergovt. Relations Cttee. and Task Force on Urban Affairs, Nat. Legislative Conf.; Trustee, Ancilla Coll.; mem. District, State and American Medical Asscns., Ind. Mental Health Asscn., Bremen Chamber of Commerce; mem. President's Comm. on Fed. Paperwork 1975–, on Science and Tech. 1976–; Hon. LL.D. (Valparaiso Univ., Butler Univ., Anderson Coll., Indiana Univ., Vincennes Univ., Tri-State Univ., Calumet Univ., Univ. Evansville, Indiana State Univ., Rose-Hulman Inst., Notre Dame Univ., Ball State Univ., Purdue Univ., Calumet); Merit Award, Ind. Public Health Asscn. 1971, Dr. Benjamin Rush Bicentennial Award, American Medical Asscn. 1973, and other awards; Republican. *Leisure interests:* collecting

quotes, fishing, watching baseball, basketball, football and racing. *Address:* c/o Department of Family Medicine, Long Hospital, 1100 West Michigan Street, Indianapolis, Ind. 46223, U.S.A. (Office).

BOWEN, William Gordon, PH.D.; American university president; b. 6 Oct. 1933, Cincinnati, Ohio; s. of Albert A. Bowen and Bernice Pomert; m. Mary Ellen Maxwell 1956; one s. one d.; ed. Denison and Princeton Univs.; Asst. Prof. of Econs., Princeton Univ. 1958–61, Assoc. Prof. 1961–65, Prof. 1965–; Dir. of Graduate Studies, Woodrow Wilson School of Public and Int. Affairs, Princeton Univ. 1964–66; Provost, Princeton Univ. 1967–72, Pres. 1972–87; Head Andrew W. Mellon Foundation, New York 1987–; Dir. NCR Corpn. 1975–; Regent Smithsonian Inst. 1980–; Trustee, Denison Univ. 1966–75, Center for Advanced Study in the Behavioral Sciences 1973–84, 1986–. *Publications:* The Wage-Price Issue: A Theoretical Analysis 1960, Performing Arts: The Economic Dilemma (with W. J. Baumol) 1966, The Economics of Labor Force Participation (with T. A. Finegan) 1969. *Leisure interests:* swimming, tennis, reading. *Address:* Princeton University, 1 Nassau Hall, Princeton, N.J. 08544, U.S.A. (Office); Andrew W. Mellon Foundation, 140 East 62nd Street, New York, N.Y. 10021, U.S.A. (Office).

BOWER, Gordon, M.S., PH.D.; American professor of psychology; b. 30 Dec. 1932, Scio, Ohio; s. of Clyde W. Bower and Mabelle Bosart Bower; m. Sharon Anthony 1957; one s. two d.; ed. Western Reserve (now Case Western Reserve) and Yale Univs.; Asst. Prof. Stanford Univ. 1959, Assoc. Prof. 1963, Prof. 1965, A. R. Lang Chair Prof. 1975–, Chair. Dept. of Psychology 1978, Assoc. Dean, Stanford Univ. 1983–85; Ed. The Psychology of Learning and Motivation 1964–; mem. N.A.S., American Acad. of Arts and Sciences, Soc. of Experimental Psychologists. *Publications:* co-author of five books. *Leisure interests:* reading, sport. *Address:* Department of Psychology, Stanford University, Stanford, Calif. 94305, U.S.A.

BOWERS-BROADBENT, Christopher Joseph, F.R.A.M.; British organist and composer; b. 13 Jan. 1945, Hemel Hempstead; s. of Henry W. Bowers-Broadbent and Doris E. Mizen; m. Deirdre Cape 1970; one s. one d.; ed. Berkhamsted School and Royal Acad. of Music; chorister, King's Coll. Cambridge 1954–58; appointed organist and choirmaster of St. Pancras Parish Church 1965–88, West London Synagogue 1973 and Gray's Inn 1983–, holding all three posts together; debut organ recital, Camden Festival 1966; Prof. of Organ, Royal Acad. of Music 1976–. *Leisure interests:* sketching, wine-making. *Address:* 94 Colney Hatch Lane, Muswell Hill, London, N10 1EA, England.

BOWIE, David (David Robert Jones); British musician and actor; b. 8 Jan. 1947, Brixton, London; s. of Hayward Jones and Margaret Mary (née Burns) Jones; m. Angela Barnett 1970 (divorced 1980); one s.; singer/songwriter 1967–; first hit single Space Oddity 1969, numerous tours and TV appearances; *recordings include:* The Man Who Sold The World, Hunky Dory 1971, The Rise and Fall of Ziggy Stardust and the Spiders From Mars 1972, Aladdin Sane, Pin Ups 1973, David Live, Diamond Dogs 1974, Young Americans 1975, Station to Station 1976, Low, Heroes 1977, Lodger (with Brian Eno) 1979, Scary Monsters and Super Creeps 1980, Let's Dance 1983; *appeared in films:* The Man Who Fell to Earth 1976, Just a Gigolo 1981, The Hunger 1983, Merry Christmas Mr Lawrence 1983, Ziggy Stardust and the Spiders from Mars 1983, Absolute Beginners 1986, Labyrinth 1986, The Last Temptation of Christ 1988; appeared in play The Elephant Man, New York 1980; appeared in TV play Baal (Brecht) 1982. *Leisure interests:* boxing, martial arts instruction, listening to Polish and Chinese Communist music. *Address:* Suite 2411, 250 West 57th Street, New York, N.Y. 10107, U.S.A.

BOWIE, Stanley Hay Umphray, D.SC., F.R.S., F.ENG., F.R.S.E.; British economic geologist; b. 24 March 1917, Bixter; s. of James Cameron Bowie and Mary Nicolson; m. Helen Elizabeth Pocock 1948; two s.; ed. Aberdeen Grammar School, Univ. of Aberdeen; with Meteorological Office 1942; commissioned R.A.F. 1943–46; Geologist, Sr. Geologist, Prin. Geologist, Geological Survey of Great Britain (GSGB) 1946–55, Chief Geologist, Atomic Energy Div. 1955–68; Chief Geochemist, Asst. Dir. Inst. of Geological Sciences 1968–77; Chief Consultant Geologist to UKAEA 1955–77; Visiting Prof. of Applied Geology, Univ. of Strathclyde 1968–85; Geological Consultant 1977–; Visiting Prof., Royal School of Mines, Imperial Coll. 1985–; Chair. DOE Research Advisory Group, Radioactive Waste Man. 1984–85; Chair. Shetland Sheep Breeders' Group 1988–; Hon. Fellow Inst. Mining and Metallurgy; Silver Medal R.S.A., Sr. Kilgour Research Scholarship, Mitchell Prize for Geology (Univ. of Aberdeen). *Publications:* contrib. to Nuclear Geology 1954, Physical Methods in Determinative Mineralogy 1967, Applied Environmental Geochemistry 1963, The Bowie Simpson System for the Microscopic Determination of Ore Minerals (with P. R. Simpson) 1980 and others, Ed. (Jt.) Uranium Prospecting Handbook 1972, Mineral Deposits of Europe 1978, Environmental Geochemistry and Health 1985. *Leisure interests:* photography, gardening, survival of endangered breeds of domesticated animals. *Address:* Tanyard Farm, Clapton, Crewkerne, Somerset, TA18 8PS, England. *Telephone:* (0460) 72093.

BOWLES, Paul; American composer and writer; b. 30 Dec. 1910, New York; s. of Dr. Claude Dietz Bowles and Rena (Winnewisser) Bowles; m. Jane Auer 1938; ed. Univ. of Virginia and in Berlin and Paris; Music Critic for New York Herald Tribune 1942–45; recipient of Guggenheim Fellowship and Rockefeller Grant. *Compositions of music for films, for the theatre:* Doctor Faustus, Twelfth Night, The Glass Menagerie, Cyrano de Bergerac, Watch on the Rhine, Summer and Smoke, Sweet Bird of Youth, The Milk Train Doesn't Stop Here Any More, etc.; scores for ballets: Yankee Clipper, Pastorela (American Ballet Company), Colloque Sentimental (Marquis de Cuevas); operas: Denmark Vesey, The Wind Remains, Yerma; and a number of sonatas, concertos, etc.; also wrote novels, The Sheltering Sky, Let it come Down, The Spider's House, Up Above the World; short stories, collections, A Little Stone, The Hours after Noon, A Hundred Camels in the Courtyard, Pages from Cold Point, Things Gone and Things Still Here, Midnight Mass, Call at Corazón; non-fiction, Their Heads are Green, Yallah! Without Stopping, Points in Time; Poetry: Scenes, The Thicket of Spring, Next to Nothing; trans. No Exit (by Jean-Paul Sartre), A Life Full of Holes (by Driss ben Hamed Charhadi), Love with a Few Hairs, The Lemon (by Mohammed Mrabet), M'Hashish, the Boy Who Set the Fire (by Mohammed Mrabet), For Bread Alone (by Mohamed Choukri), Jean Genet in Tangier (by Mohamed Choukri), Tennessee Williams in Tangier (by Mohamed Choukri), The Oblivion Seekers (by Isabelle Eberhardt), Look and Move On (by Mohammed Mrabet), Harmless Poisons, Blameless Sins (by Mohammed Mrabet), The Big Mirror (by Mohammed Mrabet), The Beach Café (by Mohammed Mrabet), Five Eyes (by five Moroccans), The Chest (by Mohammed Mrabet), A Distant Episode 1989. *Address:* 2117 Tanger Socco, Tangier, Morocco; c/o William Morris Agency, Inc., 1350 Avenue of the Americas, New York, N.Y. 10019, U.S.A.

BOWMAN, John, M.A., D.PHIL., F.A.H.A.; Australian ecclesiastic and university professor; b. 13 May 1916, Ayr, Scotland; s. of Matthew Bowman and Sarah (née Andrew) Bowman; m. Margaret Fanny Stanton 1944; two s. five d.; ed. Ayr Acad., Glasgow Univ., Christ Church, Oxford Univ.; lecturer in Hebrew, Faculties of Arts and Divinity, Glasgow Univ. 1945–46; Sr. Lecturer, Head of Dept. of Semitic Languages and Literature, Leeds Univ. 1946–59; Prof., Univ. of Melbourne, Dept. of Middle Eastern Studies 1959–78, Prof. Emer. 1978–; Ordained Priest 1954; became Australian citizen 1961; UNESCO Fellow 1964. *Publications:* founder and Ed. Abr Nahrain 1961–80, Milla wa-Milla. *Leisure interests:* planting trees, walking. *Address:* 15 Haines Street, North Melbourne, Vic. 3051, Australia.

BOWNESS, Sir Alan, Kt., C.B.E.; British art historian; b. 11 Jan. 1928; s. of George and Kathleen (née Benton) Bowness; m. Sarah Hepworth-Nicholson; one s. one d.; ed. Univ. Coll. School, Downing Coll., Cambridge, Courtauld Inst. of Art, Univ. of London; with Friends' Ambulance Unit and Friends' Service Council 1946–50; Regional Art Officer, Arts Council of G.B. 1955–57; Courtauld Inst. 1957–79, Deputy Dir. 1978–79; Reader, Univ. of London 1967–78, Prof. of History of Art 1978–79; Visiting Prof. Humanities Seminar, Johns Hopkins Univ., Baltimore 1969; Dir. Tate Gallery 1980–88, Henry Moore Foundation 1988–; mem. Arts Council 1973–75, 1978–80, Art Panel 1960–80 (Vice-Chair. 1973–75, Chair. 1978–80), Arts Film Cttee. 1968–77 (Chair. 1972–75); mem. Fine Arts Cttee., British Council 1960–69, 1970– (Chair. 1981–); mem. Exec. Cttee., Contemporary Art Soc. 1961–69, 1970–86, Cultural Advisory Cttee., U.K. Nat. Comm. for UNESCO 1973–82; Gov. Chelsea School of Art 1965–; Hon. Sec. Asscn. of Art Historians 1973–76; Dir. Barbara Hepworth Museum, St. Ives, Cornwall 1976–; mem. Council Royal Coll. of Art 1978–; mem. int. juries for Premio Di Tella, Buenos Aires 1965, São Paulo Bienal 1967, Lehmbruck Prize, Duisburg 1970; Rembrandt Prize 1982; Venice Biennale 1986; Hon. Fellow, Downing Coll., Cambridge 1980, Bristol Polytechnic 1980, Royal Coll. of Art 1982; Hon. D.Lit. (Liverpool) 1988; Chevalier Ordre des Arts et des Lettres 1973. *Publications:* William Scott Paintings 1964, Impressionists and Post Impressionists 1965, Henry Moore: complete sculpture 1955–64 1965, Modern Sculpture 1965, Barbara Hepworth Drawings 1966, Alan Davie 1967, Recent British Painting 1968, Gauguin 1971, Barbara Hepworth: complete sculpture 1960–70 1971, Modern European Art 1972, Ivon Hitchens 1973, Picasso 1881–1973 (contrib.) 1973, The Genius of British Painting (contrib.) 1975, Henry Moore: complete sculpture 1964–73 1977, Henry Moore: Complete Sculpture 1974–80 1983. *Leisure interest:* listening to music, reading, especially poetry and fiction. *Address:* 91 Castelnau, London, SW13 9EL, England. *Telephone:* 01-748 9696.

BOWRING, Edgar Rennie Harvey, M.C., M.A., C.B.I.M.; British lawyer and company executive; b. 5 Nov. 1915, Calif., U.S.A.; s. of Arthur and Margaret Bowring; m. Margaret Grace Brook 1940; two s. one d.; ed. Eastbourne Coll., Clare Coll., Cambridge, and Yale Univ.; served Kent Yeomanry and Royal Artillery 1939–46; admitted solicitor 1949; Partner, Cripps Harries Hall and Co. 1950–55; Solicitor, Dir. C. T. Bowring and Co. (Insurance) Ltd. 1960–73; mem. Lloyd's 1962–; Dir. C. T. Bowring and Co. Ltd. 1963–81; Chair. English and American Insurance Co. Ltd. 1966–77, Deputy Chair. and Chief Exec. C. T. Bowring (Insurance) Holdings Ltd. 1970–73; Chair. Crusader Insurance Co. Ltd. 1973–77; Chair. Bowmaker Ltd. 1973–77; Chair. The Bowring Group of Companies 1973–77; Dir. Singer and Friedlander 1971–77; Deputy Pres. Insurance Inst. of London 1970–71, Pres. 1971–72; Dir. Marsh and McLennan Cos. Inc. 1980–88; Fellow, Corpn. of Insurance Brokers. *Leisure interests:* golf, gardening. *Address:* Leopards Mill, Horam, Sussex, England. *Telephone:* Horam Road 2687 (Sussex).

BOWRING, Peter, F.R.S.A.; British company director; b. 22 April 1923, Bromborough; s. of Frederick Clive and Agnes Walker (née Cairns) Bow-

ring; m. Barbara Ekaterina Brewis 1946 (divorced), one s. one d.; m. 2nd Carol Gillian Hutchings 1979 (divorced); m. 3rd Carole Mary Dear 1986; ed. Shrewsbury School; commissioned, Rifle Brigade 1942, served in Egypt, North Africa, Italy and Austria (mentioned in despatches); Dir. C. T. Bowring & Co. Ltd. 1956; Chair. C. T. Bowring Trading (Holdings) Ltd. 1967; Deputy Chair. C. T. Bowring and Co. Ltd. 1973; Chair. Bowmaker (Plant) Ltd. 1972–77, Bowmaker Ltd. 1978–82, C. T. Bowring & Co. Ltd. 1978–82; Dir. Marsh and McLennan Companies Inc. 1980–85, Vice-Chair. 1982–84; Dir. Aldeburgh Foundation 1975–, Chair. 1982–89; Chair. Help the Aged Ltd. 1977–87; Bd. of Govs. St. Dunstan's Educational Foundation; Deputy Chair. Bd. Govs. Shrewsbury School; Dir. Independent Primary and Secondary Educ. Trust; Centre for Policy Studies 1983–88; Int. Human Assistance Programs Inc. 1985–; Rhein Chemie Holding GmbH 1968; Fellow Inst. of Dirs. *Leisure interests:* sailing, motoring, music, walking, cooking. *Address:* 79 New Concordia Wharf, Mill Street, London, SE1 2BA, England. *Telephone:* 01-237 0818.

BOWYER, William, R.A., R.P., R.W.S.; British artist; b. 25 May 1926; m. Vera Mary Small 1951; two s. two d.; ed. Burslem School of Art, Royal Coll. of Art; Head of Fine Art, Maidstone Coll. of Art 1971–82; Hon. Sec. New English Art Club. *Leisure interests:* cricket, snooker. *Address:* 12 Cleveland Avenue, Chiswick, London, W4 1SN, England. *Telephone:* 01-994 0346.

BOX, Betty Evelyn, O.B.E.; British film producer; m. Peter Edward Rogers 1949; no c.; ed. privately; Dir. Welbeck Film Distributors Ltd. 1958–, Ulster TV 1955–85. *Films include:* Dear Murderer, When the Bough Breaks, Miranda, Blind Goddess, Huggett Family series, It's Not Cricket, Marry Me, Don't Ever Leave Me, So Long at the Fair, Appointment with Venus, Venetian Bird, A Day to Remember, The Clouded Yellow, Doctor in the House, Mad About Men, Doctor at Sea, The Iron Petticoat, Checkpoint, Doctor at Large, Campbell's Kingdom, A Tale of Two Cities, The Wind Cannot Read, The 39 Steps, Upstairs and Downstairs, Conspiracy of Hearts, Doctor in Love, No Love for Johnnie, No, My Darling Daughter, A Pair of Briefs, The Wild and the Willing, Doctor in Distress, Hot Enough for June, The High Bright Sun, Doctor in Clover, Deadlier than the Male, Nobody Runs Forever, Some Girls Do, Doctor in Trouble, Percy, The Love Ban, Percy's Progress. *Address:* Pinewood Studios, Iver, Bucks., England.

BOYCOTT, Prof. Brian Blundell, F.R.S.; British professor of biology; b. 10 Dec. 1924, Croydon, Surrey; s. of Percy Blundell Boycott and Doris Eyton Lewis; m. Marjorie Mabel Burchell 1950; two s. (one deceased); ed. Royal Masonic School, Birkbeck Coll., Univ. of London; Tech., Nat. Inst. Medical Research; at Univ. Coll., Univ. of London 1946–70, Asst. Lecturer in Zoology 1946–47, Hon. Research Asst. Anatomy 1947–52, Lecturer in Zoology 1952–62, Univ. Reader in Zoology 1962–68, Prof. of Zoology 1968–70; at M.R.C. 1971–, Prof. of Biology 1971–, Dir. Cell Biophysics Unit 1980–; mem. Advisory Council, British Library Bd. 1976–80, Council Open Univ. 1975–87, Council Royal Soc. 1976–78; Scientific Medal (Zoological Soc.), London 1965. *Publications:* articles on structure and function of nervous systems in scientific journals. *Address:* c/o Department of Cell Biophysics, King's College, 26-29 Drury Lane, London, WC2B 5RL, England. *Telephone:* 01-836 8851.

BOYCOTT, Geoffrey, O.B.E.; British cricketer; b. 21 Oct. 1940, Fitzwilliam, Yorks.; s. of late Thomas Wilfred Boycott and Jane Boycott; ed. Kinsley Modern School and Hemsworth Grammar School; fmrly. in civil service, debut as cricketer (right-hand batsman) for Yorkshire 1962, received County Cap 1963, Capt. of Yorkshire 1970–78; played for England 1964–74, 1977–82; appointed Vice-Captain, England team to Pakistan and N.Z. 1977–78, took over captaincy on injury of M. J. Brearley, Jan. 1978; only Englishman to achieve average of 100 in English County season 1971; repeated this achievement in 1979; scored 100th hundred, England v. Australia, Headingly, Leeds Aug. 1977; became 18th batsman in history of game to score 100 hundreds and the first to achieve this in a Test Match; became top run-scorer in Tests, India 1981; barred from representing England in Tests for three years for taking part in unofficial tour of South Africa 1982, dismissed from Yorkshire 1983, reinstated 1984, mem. Gen. Cttee.; 100 centuries for Yorkshire 1985, 7th batsman to do this for a county; 151 first-class centuries. *Publications:* Geoff Boycott's Book for Young Cricketers 1976, Put to the Test: Ashes Series in Australia 1978/79 1979, Geoff Boycott's Cricket Quiz 1979, Boycott on Batting 1980, Opening Up 1980, In the Fast Lane 1981, Master Class 1982, Boycott on Boycott (autobiog.) 1986. *Leisure interests:* golf, tennis. *Address:* c/o Yorkshire County Cricket Club, Headingley Cricket Ground, Leeds, LS6 3BV, England.

BOYD, Alan Stephenson, LL.B.; American transportation executive and politician; b. 20 July 1922, Jacksonville, Fla.; s. of Clarence and Elizabeth (Stephenson) Boyd; m. Flavil Townsend 1943; one s.; ed. Univ. of Virginia; Chair. U.S. Civil Aeronautics Bd. 1961–65; U.S. Under-Sec. of Commerce 1965–66; first U.S. Sec. of Transportation 1966–67; Pres. Ill. Cen. Gulf Railroad 1969–76; U.S.-U.K. Bilateral Air Traffic Negotiation Leader 1977; Pres. and Chair. Amtrak 1978–82; Chair. and Pres. Airbus Industrie North America 1982–86, Pres. and C.E.O. 1986–; Trustee, Anser Inc. 1969–; Dir. ERC Environmental Services Inc, 1989–. *Leisure interests:* golf, historic preservation. *Address:* 2301 Connecticut Avenue, N.W., Washington, D.C. 20008, U.S.A. (Home).

BOYD, Aquilino Edgardo; Panamanian lawyer and diplomatist; b. 1921; ed. La Salle, Panama City, Holy Cross Coll., U.S.A., Univs. de la Habana and Panamá; First Sec. Cuba 1946–47, Washington 1947–48; mem. Panama Nat. Assembly 1948–64; Pres. Nat. Assembly 1949; Minister Foreign Affairs 1956–58, 1976–77; Perm. Rep. to UN 1962–67, 1968–76, 1983–86; Amb. to U.S.A. 1983–86. *Address:* Ministry of Foreign Affairs, Panama 4, Panama.

BOYD, Arthur Merric Bloomfield, A.O., O.B.E.; Australian painter; b. 24 July 1920, Murrumbeena; s. of Merric Boyd and Doris Gough; m. Yvonne Lennie 1945; one s. two d.; taught painting and sculpture by parents and grandfather; painted and exhibited in Australia 1937–59, in England 1959–; first one-man exhbn. London 1960; retrospective, Whitechapel Gallery, London 1962; designed for Ballet at Edinburgh Festival and Sadler's Wells Theatre 1961, Covent Garden Opera House 1963, retrospective exhbn., Adelaide 1964; now works in England and Australia; Britannica Award for Distinguished Service to Art 1979. *Address:* c/o Westpac Banking Corpn., Walbrook House, Walbrook, London EC4, England.

BOYD, Howard Taney, J.D., LL.D.; American lawyer and retd. business executive; b. 5 June 1909, Woodside, Maryland; s. of Howard T. Boyd and Mary Violet (Stewart); m. Lucille Belhumeur 1935; one s. two d.; ed. Georgetown Prep School, Georgetown Univ.; admitted D.C. Bar 1934, Texas Bar 1953; fmr. Prof. Nat. Law School (now Nat. Law Center), Washington Coll. of Law (now American Univ.); Sec. to Attorney-Gen. of U.S. 1934; Special Attorney, Dept. of Justice 1935; Asst. U.S. Attorney, D.C. 1935–39; Partner, law firm Hogan and Hartson, Washington 1939–52; with El Paso Natural Gas Co. (renamed The El Paso Co. 1974) 1952–79, Chair. 1965–79; Partner law firm, Liddell, Sapp, Zivley, Hill and La Boon 1979–; fmr. Dir. Armour and Co., Texas Commerce Bank–Houston, Texas Commerce Bankshares, El Paso Co., Greyhound Corpn., Houston Symphony; fmr. mem. U.S.-U.S.S.R. Trade and Econ. Council, American Heart Asscn., World Energy Conf., and numerous other orgs.; mem. Int. Trade Asscn., Nat. Petroleum Council, A.B.A., etc.; Chevalier, Légion d'honneur; Sovereign Mil. Order of Malta; Golden Plate Award 1977. *Address:* 3300 Texas Commerce Tower, Houston, Texas 77002 (Office); 6042 Crab Orchard Street, Houston, Texas 77057, U.S.A. (Home).

BOYD, Joseph Aubrey, M.S., PH.D.; American business executive; b. 25 March 1921, Oscar, Ky.; s. of Joseph R. Boyd and Relda J. Myatt; m. Edith A. Atkins 1942; two s.; ed. Univs. of Ky. and Mich.; Instr., Asst. Prof. of Electrical Eng. Univ. of Ky. 1947–49; mem. Faculty, Univ. of Mich. 1949–62, Prof. of Electrical Eng. 1958–62, Dir. Willow Run Labs. 1958–62, Dir. Inst. of Science and Tech. 1960–62; Exec. Vice-Pres. Radiation Inc., Melbourne, Fla. 1962–63, Pres. 1963–72; Exec. Vice-Pres. Electronics, Harris Corpn. Cleveland (now in Melbourne, Fla.) 1967–71, Exec. Vice-Pres. Operations 1971–72, Dir. 1972–, Pres. 1972–85; consultant, Inst. for Defense Analyses 1956–, Nat. Security Agency 1957–62; special consultant to Army Combat Surveillance Agency 1958–62; Chair. Advisory Group, Electronic Warfare, Office of Dir. of Defense Research, Dept. of Defense 1959–61, consultant 1959–; Fellow, A.A.A.S., Inst. of Electrical and Electronic Engs. *Publications:* articles in professional journals. *Address:* Harris Corporation, 1025 W. Nasa Boulevard, Melbourne, Fla. 32919, U.S.A.

BOYD, Robert Hugh Steele (Robin), B.A., PH.D., D.D.; British ecclesiastic; b. 14 May 1924, Belfast; s. of Robert Boyd and Annie (née Higgison) Boyd; m. Frances Amy Paton 1954; two d.; ed. Royal Belfast Academical Inst., Trinity Coll., Dublin and Univs. of Edinburgh and Basel; ordained in Presbyterian Church, Ireland 1951; Sec. Theol. Colls. Dept. Student Christian Movt., London 1951–53; Missionary, Gujarat State, India 1954–74; lecturer Gujarat United School of Theol., Ahmedabad 1961–74; Presbyter Church of N. India 1970–74; Assoc. Minister Presbyterian Church, Toorak, Melbourne 1974–77, Uniting Church in Australia 1977–80; Dir. Irish School of Ecumenics, Dublin 1980–87; Minister Wesley Church, 1988–. *Publications:* Introduction to Indian Christian Theology 1969, India and the Latin Captivity of the Church 1975, Church History of Gujarat 1981. *Leisure interests:* railways, industrial archaeology, local history and music. *Address:* Wesley Church, 148 Lonsdale Street, Melbourne, Vic. 3000, (Church); 41 Kawarren Street, North Balwyn, Vic. 3104, Australia (Home). *Telephone:* 662 2355; 857 5378 (Home).

BOYD, Sir Robert Lewis Fullarton, Kt., C.B.E., PH.D., A.C.G.I., F.R.S.; British chartered engineer and emeritus professor of physics; b. 19 Oct. 1922, Saltcoats, Ayrshire; s. of late Dr. and Mrs. W. J. Boyd; m. Mary Higgins 1949; two s. one d.; ed. Whitgift School, Croydon, Imperial and Univ. Colls., London; experimental officer, Admiralty Mining Establishment 1943–46; Research Asst., Dept. of Math., Univ. Coll., London 1946–49; ICI Research Fellow 1949–50, ICI Research Fellow, Dept. of Physics 1950–52, Lecturer in Physics 1952–58, Reader 1959–62, Prof. 1962–83, Hon. Research Fellow 1983–; Dir. Mullard Space Science Lab., Univ. Coll., London 1965–83; Prof. of Astronomy (part-time), Royal Inst. 1961–67; Fellow, Inst. of Physics, Inst. of Elec. Engs., Royal Astron. Soc.; Hon. D.Sc. (Heriot Watt) 1979, Fellow, Univ. Coll. London 1988. *Publications:* over 100 scientific books and papers. *Leisure interest:* elderly Rolls-Royce motor cars.

Address: Roseneath, 41 Church Street, Littlehampton, West Sussex, BN17 5PU, England. *Telephone:* 0903-714438.

BOYD, William B., B.S.; American business executive; ed. Texas A & M Univ.; Gen Man. household refrigeration, Gen. Electric Co. until 1975; various positions, Carrier Air Conditioning Co. New York; C.O.D.. American Standard Inc., New York until 1985, Vice-Chair. 1985–86, C.E.O. 1985–, Chair. 1986–, Pres. 1987–, also Dir.; Dir. Stanley Interiors Corpn. *Address:* American Standard Inc., 40 W. 40th Street, New York, N.Y. 10018, U.S.A.

BOYD OF MERTON, 2nd Viscount (cr. 1960); **Simon Donald Rupert Lennox-Boyd,** M.A.; British business executive; b. 7 Dec. 1939, London; s. of the late Alan Lennox-Boyd (Viscount Boyd of Merton) and of Lady Patricia Guinness; m. Alice Clive 1962; two s. two d.; ed. Eton, Christ Church Coll., Oxford; Dir. Iveagh Trustees Ltd. 1967–; Chair. Overseas Cttee. Save the Children 1980–; Deputy Chair. Arthur Guinness & Sons 1981–86; Pres. Council of British Exec. Service Overseas 1985–; Trustee, Guinness Trust 1974–; Chair. Scottish Licensed Trade Asscn. 1983–84. *Leisure interests:* yachting, gardening. *Address:* Iveagh House, 41 Harrington Gardens, London, S.W.7; 9 Warwick Square, London, S.W.1; Wivelscombe, Saltash, Cornwall, England. *Telephone:* 01-373 7261 (Iveagh House); 01-821 1618 (Warwick Square); Saltash 2672.

BOYD-CARPENTER, Baron (Life Peer), cr. 1972, of Crux Easton in the County of Southampton; **Rt. Hon. John Archibald Boyd-Carpenter,** P.C.; British administrator; b. 2 June 1908, Harrogate; s. of late Sir Archibald, M.P., and Lady Boyd-Carpenter; m. Margaret Mary Hall 1937; one s. two d.; ed. Stowe School and Balliol Coll., Oxford; Pres. Oxford Union Soc. 1930; called to Bar 1934; practised S.E. Circuit; joined Scots Guards 1939, served until 1945; M.P. 1945–72; Financial Sec. to Treasury 1951–54; Privy Councillor 1954; Minister of Transport and Civil Aviation 1954–55, of Pensions and Nat. Insurance 1955–62, Chief Sec. to Treasury and Paymaster-Gen. 1962–64; Opposition Front Bench Spokesman on Housing and Land 1964–66; Chair. Public Accounts Cttee. House of Commons 1964–70, Local Govt. Advisory Cttee. of Conservative Greater London Area Org. 1968; Dir. Orion Insurance Co. 1967, 1972, Chair. 1969–72, C.L.R.P. Investment Trust 1967, Chair. 1970–72, Life Asscn. of Scotland 1970–72; mem. Council, Trusthouse-Forte Ltd. 1970–72, 1977–; Dir. Rugby Portland Cement Co. 1971–84, Chair. 1977–84; Dir. Bell Group Int. 1982–88; Heylesbury (U.K.) 1988–; Chair. U.K. Civil Aviation Authority 1972–77; High Steward of Kingston upon Thames and Deputy Lieut. for Greater London 1973–; elected Deputy Chair. Asscn. of Independent Unionist Peers Nov. 1979, Chair. 1980–; Chair. Carlton Club 1979–86; Dir. TR Australia Investment Trust; Gov. of Stowe School. *Publication:* Way of Life (memoirs) 1980. *Leisure interests:* swimming, tennis. *Address:* 12 Eaton Terrace, London S.W.1; Crux Easton House, Crux Easton near Highclere, Hants.,England. *Telephone:* 01-730 7765 (Home); (0635) 25037 (Country).

BOYE, Ibrahima; Senegalese judge; b. 29 March 1924, Saint Louis; s. of Amadou Abdoulaye Boye and Marème Sène; m. Marie Anne Cissé 2948; three s. four d.; ed. Univ. of Montpellier; Attorney-at-Law, Court of Appeals, Nîmes, France 1947–48; mem. Public Prosecutor's Office at Court of Appeals of Montpellier 1948–50; later French Judge, Guinea, Pres. of Colonial Court of Appeals, Dahomey; Examining Magistrate, Cotonou and Abidjan; Justice of the Peace, Agbonville, Ivory Coast; mem. Criminal Court, Dahomey and Ivory Coast 1956–57; Technical Adviser in Ministry of Justice, Mali Fed. 1960, later Dir. of Cabinet and Justice of Supreme Court, Senegal; fmr. Attorney-Gen., Senegal; mem. UN Comm. on Human Rights 1967–72, Chair. 1968, Chair. ad hoc working group of experts 1967–72; Amb. and Perm. Rep. of Senegal to UN 1968–71; Rep. of Senegal, UN Security Council 1968, 1969, Pres. 1969; Vice-Pres. UN Gen. Assembly 1970; Amb. to U.S.S.R., Poland, Hungary, Czechoslovakia 1971–77, to Bulgaria 1973–77, to Romania 1976–79, to Canada 1979–81; Grand Officer Nat. Order of Senegal, of Lebanon; Officier Palmes académiques. *Publications:* Works on human rights, study of racial discrimination throughout the world. *Leisure interest:* African-negro poetry. *Address:* c/o Ministère des Affaires étrangères, place de l'Independance, Dakar, Senegal.

BOYE, Mohamed Mahjoub Ould, M.A.; Mauritanian diplomatist; b. 1947; m.; four c.; ed. Sorbonne Univ.; teacher in higher educ., Nouakchott Advanced School; Chargé de Mission to President's Office 1978–80; Amb. to Iraq 1980; Chef de Cabinet to the Prime Minister 1980–81; Minister of Water and Housing 1981–84; Perm. Rep. to UN 1984–. *Address:* Permanent Mission of Mauritania to the United Nations, 37th Floor, 600 Third Avenue, New York, N.Y. 10016, U.S.A.

BOYE, Thore Albert, LL.B.; Norwegian diplomatist; b. 27 Oct. 1912, Oslo; s. of Thorvald and Mia (née Esmarch) Boye; m. Augusta Sophie Siem 1945; two s.; ed. Univ. of Oslo; Asst. Dist. Judge, Tromsö 1936; Sec. at Ministry of Foreign Affairs 1938, and Ministry of Finance (London) 1940; Head of Division, Norwegian Ministry of Defence (London) 1942; Commercial Counsellor Brussels Embassy and Delegate to Inter-Allied Reparation Agency, Brussels 1946; Head of Division, Ministry of Foreign Affairs 1948; Chief Sec., North European Regional Planning Group, NATO, London 1949; Deputy Dir. Gen., Dept. of Econ. Affairs, Ministry of Foreign Affairs 1951; Director Gen., Dept. of Political Affairs 1953; Sec. Gen., Ministry of

Foreign Affairs 1966; Amb. to Rome and Athens 1962, to Madrid 1973, to Stockholm 1978–81; Exec. Vice-Pres. Scandinavian Airlines System 1955–61. *Address:* c/o Norwegian Foreign Ministry, 7 juni plassen 1, P.O. Box 8114, Oslo, Norway.

BOYER, Paul Delos, PH.D.; American professor of biochemistry; b. 31 July 1918, Provo, Utah; s. of Dell Delos Boyer and Grace Guymon; m. Lyda Wicker 1939; one s. two d.; ed. Brigham Young Univ. and Univ. of Wisconsin; Research Asst., Univ. of Wis. 1939–43; Instructor, Stanford Univ. 1943–45; Assoc. Prof., Univ. of Minn. 1947–53, Prof. 1953–56, Hill Prof. of Biochem. 1956–63; Prof. of Biochemistry, Univ. of Calif. at Los Angeles 1963–, Dir. Molecular Biology Inst. 1965–83; mem. Nat. Acad. of Sciences; Fellow, American Acad. of Arts and Sciences, Vice-Pres. Biological Sciences 1985–87; Pres. American Soc. of Biol. Chemists 1969–70; Guggenheim Fellowship 1955; American Chem. Soc. Award 1955; Tolman Medal 1981; Rose Award (American Soc. of Biochemistry and Molecular Biology) 1989; Dr. h.c., Univ. of Stockholm 1974. *Publications:* Author or co-author of over 200 scientific papers in biochem. and molecular biology; Ed. Annual Biochemistry Review 1964–89, Ed. Biochemical and Biophysical Research Communications 1968–80, The Enzymes 1970–. *Leisure interest:* tennis. *Address:* University of California at Los Angeles, Molecular Biology Institute, 408 Hilgard Avenue, Los Angeles, Calif. 90024 (Office); 1033 Somera Road, Los Angeles, Calif. 90077, U.S.A. (Home). *Telephone:* (213) 825-1416 (Office).

BOYER SALVADOR, Miguel; Spanish politician; b. 5 Feb. 1939, San Juan de Luz, France; m. 1st Elena Arnedo (deceased); two s.; m. 2nd Isabel Preyslev 1988; graduated in physics and econ. sciences; joined Spanish Socialist Workers' Party 1960, imprisoned for 6 months for political activities; fmr. economist, Studies Group of Banco de España; Dir. Studies Group, Nat. Industrial Inst., Strategic Planning Group, Explosivos Rio Tinto S.A., Strategic Planning, Nat. Hydrocarbons Inst.; Minister of Economy, Finance and Commerce 1982–85; Chair. Banco Exterior de España 1985–; Gov. IBRD; Rep. to IDB 1983–85. *Address:* c/o Banco Exterior de España, Carrera de San Jerónimo 36, Madrid 14, Spain.

BOYESEN, Jens Mogens; Norwegian diplomatist; b. 9 Oct. 1920, Oslo; s. of Einar and Birghild Boyesen; m. Erle Bryn 1947; ed. Oslo Univ.; active in Resistance 1940–45; degree in law 1947; Asst. Judge 1948; entered Foreign Service 1949; Under-Sec. Ministry of Foreign Affairs 1951–54, Ministry of Defence 1954–55; Amb. to NATO 1955–63, to OEEC 1955–61, to OECD 1961–63; Under-Sec. of State for Foreign Affairs 1964–65; Assoc., Norwegian Defence Research Establishment Jan. 1967–; Amb. to Int. Orgs. in Geneva 1968–73; Amb. to European Communities, and to Belgium and Luxembourg 1973–76; Amb. to OECD 1977–86. *Address:* c/o Ministry of Foreign Affairs, P.O. Box 8114, 7-juni Plassen, Oslo, Norway.

BOYLAND, Eric, D.SC., PH.D.; British university professor; b. 24 Feb. 1905, Manchester; s. of Alfred E. and Helen Boyland; m. Margaret Esther Maurice, two s. one d. (died 1985); ed. Univs. of Manchester and London; Lister Inst. for Preventive Medicine 1928–30; Kaiser Wilhelm Inst. für Medizinische Forschung, Heidelberg 1930–31; Physiological Chemist to Royal Cancer Hospital, London 1931; Reader in Biochem., Univ. of London 1935–47, Prof. of Biochem. in Univ. of London, at the Chester Beatty Research Inst. of the Royal Cancer Hospital 1948–70, Emeritus Prof. 1970–; Visiting Prof. in Toxicology, London School of Hygiene and Tropical Medicine 1970–76; Hon. Ph.D. (Frankfurt) 1982, Hon. M.D. (Malta) 1985; Judd Award for Cancer Research, N.Y. 1948, Mem of Société de Chimie biologique 1956. *Leisure interests:* walking, painting. *Address:* London School of Hygiene and Tropical Medicine, Keppel Street, London, WC1E 7HT (Office); 42 Bramerton Street, London, S.W.3., England (Home). *Telephone:* 01-636 8636 (Office); 01-352 2601 (Home).

BOYLE, Marshal of the R.A.F. Sir Dermot Alexander, G.C.B., K.C.V.O., K.B.E., A.F.C.; British officer; b. 2 Oct. 1904, Durrow, Eire; s. of A. F. Boyle; m. Una Carey 1931; two s. one d.; ed. St. Columba's Coll., Ireland, and R.A.F. Coll., Cranwell; commissioned R.A.F. 1924; Staff Officer, H.Q., R.A.F. India 1933–35; Staff Coll., Andover 1936; Chief Flying Instructor, Cranwell 1937–39; 83 Squadron, Scampton 1940–41; Asst. Sec. War Cabinet Office 1941; Senior Air Staff Officer, H.Q. No. 83 Group 1943–45; A.D.C. to the King 1943; A.O.C. No. 11 Group 1945; Imperial Defence Coll. 1946; Dir-Gen. of Manning 1949–51; A.O.C. No. 1 Group, Bomber Command 1951–53; C.-in-C. Fighter Command 1953–55; Air Chief Marshal 1956; Chief of Air Staff 1956–59; Vice-Chair. British Aircraft Corpn. 1962–71; Chair. of Trustees, R.A.F. Museum 1965–74; Master of Guild of Air Pilots and Air Navigators 1965–66; Chair. Court of Govs. Mill Hill School 1969–76. *Address:* Fair Gallop, Brighton Road, Sway, Lymington, Hants., England.

BOYLE, J. Allan; Canadian banker; b. 10 May 1916, Orillia, Ont.; s. of Mr. and Mrs. W. J. Boyle; ed. Orillia Collegiate Inst., Univ. of Western Ontario; joined Toronto-Dominion Bank, Orillia 1934; worked Toronto, Ont. and New York; served Royal Canadian Air Force 1940–45; Special Rep. then Agent Toronto-Dominion Bank, New York 1956–66, Asst. Gen. Man., Int. Div. 1966–68, Gen. Man. Admin. 1968, Deputy Chief Gen. Man. 1968–72, Exec. Vice-Pres., Chief Gen. Man. 1972–78, Pres. 1978–81; Dir. Toronto-Dominion Bank, Costain Ltd., Excelsior Life Insurance Co., Aetna Casualty Co. of Canada, Jannock Ltd., Echo Bay Mines Ltd., Westinghouse

Canada Inc. *Address:* c/o Toronto-Dominion Bank, Head Office, P.O. Box 1, Toronto Dominion Centre, Toronto, Ont. M5K 1A2, Canada (Office).

BOYNTON, Robert Merrill, PH.D.; American professor of psychology; b. 28 Oct. 1924, Evanston, Ill.; s. of Merrill Holmes Boynton and Eleanor Matthews Boynton; m. Alice Neiley 1947; three s. one d.; ed. Amherst Coll. and Brown Univ.; Asst. Prof., Univ. of Rochester 1952–57, Assoc. Prof. 1957–61, Prof. 1961–74, Dir. and Founder, Center for Visual Science 1963–71, Chair. Dept. of Psychology 1971–74; Prof., Dept. of Psychology, Univ. of Calif. at San Diego 1974–; Assoc. Dean, Graduate Studies and Research 1987–; Chair. Visual Sciences B Study Section, Nat. Inst. of Health 1972–75; Chair. Bd. of Eds. Vision Research 1982–85; mem. N.A.S.; Godlove Award, Inter-society Color Council 1982, Tillyer Medal, Optical Soc. of America 1972. *Publications:* Human Color Vision 1979 and 150 scientific articles. *Address:* Department of Psychology C-009, University of California at San Diego, La Jolla, Calif. 92093; 376 Bellaire Street, Del Mar, Calif. 92014, U.S.A. (Home). *Telephone:* (619) 534-3976 (Univ.); (619) 481-0263 (Home).

BOYSE, Edward Arthur, M.D., F.R.S.; British/American research physician; b. 11 Aug. 1923, Worthing, Sussex; s. of Arthur Boyse and Dorothy V. (née Mellersh) Boyse; m. 1st Jeanette Grimwood 1951; two s. one d.; m. 2nd Judith Bard 1987; ed. St. Bartholomew's Hosp. Medical School, Univ. of London; various hospital appts. 1952–57; Research Fellow in Pathology, Guy's Hospital, London 1957–60; Assoc. mem. Sloan-Kettering Inst., New York 1964–67, mem. 1967–; Prof. of Biology, Cornell Univ. Grad. School of Medical Sciences 1969–; Adjunct Prof. of Pathology New York Univ. School of Medicine 1964–; Harvey Lecturer 1975; Fellow American Acad. of Arts and Sciences 1977, N.A.S. 1979; Cancer Research Inst. Award in Tumour Immunology 1975; Isaac Adler Award of Rockefeller and Harvard Univs. 1976. *Publications:* papers relating to genetics and immunology to devt. and cancer. *Address:* Memorial Sloan-Kettering Cancer Center, 1275 York Avenue, New York, N.Y. 10021, U.S.A.

BOZANGA, Simon-Narcisse; Central African Republic politician; b. 26 Dec. 1942, Bangassou; Dir. of Legal Studies, Ministry of Foreign Affairs 1972–74, Sec.-Gen. 1974–78; Amb. to Gabon 1978–79; Sec.-Gen. to Govt. 1979–80; Minister of Justice 1980–81; Prime Minister and Head of Govt. April–Sept. 1981 (deposed by mil. coup); Dir.-Gen. Société Centrafricaine des Hydrocarbures (CentraHydro) 1982–. *Address:* Société Centrafricaine des Hydrocarbures, B.P. 724, Bangui, Central African Republic.

BOZER, Prof. Dr. Ali Husrev; Turkish jurist; b. 28 July 1925, Ankara; s. of Mustafa Fevzi Bozer and Zehra Bozer; m.; three s.; ed. Ankara and Neuchâtel Univs. and Harvard Law School; Asst. judge, Ankara 1951; Asst., Faculty of Law, Ankara Univ. 1952–60, Agrégé 1955–60, Head of Dept. 1961–, Prof. of Commercial Law 1965–; lawyer at bar, Ankara 1952–; Dir. Inst. de Recherche sur le Droit commercial et bancaire 1960–; Judge, European Court of Human Rights 1974–76; mem. Admin. Council, Turkish Radio-TV Corpn. 1968–71, Vice-Pres. 1971–73; Minister of Customs and Monopolies 1981–83, of State for Relations with EEC Oct. 1986–. *Publications:* Les droits d'administration et de jouissance des père et mère sur les biens de l'enfant, Nantissement commercial, Aperçu général sur le droit des assurances sociales en droit turc, Droit commercial pour les employés de banques, Papiers valeurs pour les employés de banques; monographs and articles in several reviews in Turkish and French. *Leisure interest:* tennis. *Address:* Ahmet Rasim sok. 35/5, Gankaya, Ankara, Turkey. *Telephone:* 271845, 191322.

BOZO, Dominique; French museum administrator; b. 1935, Alençon; Curator Musée national d'art moderne 1969–72, redesign of the nat. collections and collections of contemporary art, in charge of museum graphics scheme; at Centre national d'art et de culture Georges-Pompidou (CNAC) 1972-, Acting Dir. 1973–74, Dir. 1981–86; designer of new Musée Picasso at l'hôtel Salé 1974–; co-Dir. Picasso Retrospective Exhbn., New York 1980; organizer numerous exhbns. of artists including Naum Gabo, Victor Brauner, Soutine, Rothko, Hajdn, Matisse, Henry Moore (drawing and sculpture); Chevalier Légion d'honneur. *Address:* c/o C.N.A.C. Georges Pompidou, 75191 Paris, Cedex 04, France.

BRAAMS, Cornelis Marius, PH.D.; Netherlands physicist; b. 5 July 1925, Den Bosch; s. of R. Braams and B. J. Straver; m. A. G. Planting 1952; two s. two d.; ed. Univ. of Utrecht; experimental nuclear physics at M.I.T., Cambridge, U.S.A. 1952–54; with Foundation for Fundamental Research on Matter (FOM) 1955–, Research Assoc. 1955–57, Scientific Head of Thermonuclear Group 1957–58, Dir. Inst. for Plasma Physics 1958–86; part-time Prof. of Plasma Physics, Univ. of Utrecht 1962–87; Visiting Scientist, Boeing Scientific Research Laboratories, Seattle 1963–65. *Leisure interests:* sailing, field-hockey, gardening. *Address:* Joh. Wagenaarkade 33, Utrecht, Netherlands (Home). *Telephone:* 30-931132.

BRABHAM, Sir Jack (John Arthur), Kt., O.B.E.; Australian professional racing driver (retd.); b. 2 April 1926, Sydney, Australia; m. Betty Evelyn, 1951; three s.; ed. Hurstville Tech. Coll., Sydney; served in R.A.A.F. 1944–46; started own engineering business 1946; Midget Speedway racing 1946–52; numerous wins driving a Cooper-Bristol, Australia 1953–54; went to Europe 1955; Australian Grand Prix 1955, 1963; World Champion, Formula II 1958; Formula II Champion of France 1964; World Champion Driver 1959–60, 1960–61, 1966; First in Monaco and U.K. Grandes Epreuves

1959; won Grand Prix of Netherlands, Belgium, France, U.K., Portugal, Denmark 1960, Belgium 1961, France 1966, 1967, U.K. 1966; began building own cars 1961; Man. Dir. Jack Brabham (Motors) Ltd., Jack Brabham (Worcester Park) Ltd., Engine Devts. Ltd.; Ferodo Trophy 1964, 1966; RAC Gold Medal 1966, BARC Gold Medal 1959, 1966, 1967; Formula I Mfrs. Championship 1966, 1967. *Publications:* Jack Brabham's Book of Motor Racing 1960, When the Flag Drops 1971. *Address:* P.O. Box 441, Bankstown, N.S.W., Australia.

BRACE, William Francis, PH.D.; American professor of geology; b. 26 Aug. 1926, Littleton, N.H.; s. of Frank Charles Brace and Frances Badger Dodge Brace; m. Margaret T. Grant 1955; two s. one d.; ed. M.I.T., Cambridge, Mass.; Asst. Prof. of Geology, M.I.T., 1954-61, Assoc. Prof. of Geology 1961-64, Prof. of Geology 1964-; mem. American Acad. of Arts and Sciences, N.A.S. *Publications:* numerous technical articles. *Leisure interests:* woodworking, music, rowing, running, climbing, skiing. *Address:* Room 54-722, Department of Earth, Atmospheric and Planetary Sciences, Massachusetts Institute of Technology, Cambridge, Mass. 02139 (Office); 49 Hillcrest Street, Concord, Mass. 01742, U.S.A. (Home). *Telephone:* (617) 253-3391 (Office).

BRACHER, Karl Dietrich, DR. PHIL.; German political scientist and historian; b. 13 March 1922, Stuttgart; s. of Theodor Bracher and Gertrud Zimmermann; m. Dorothee Schleicher 1951; one s. one d.; ed. Gymnasium, Stuttgart, Univ. of Tübingen and Harvard Univ.; Research Asst. and Head of Dept., Inst. of Political Science, Berlin 1950-58; lecturer, German Hochschule für Politik, Berlin; Privatdozent and Prof. Free Univ., Berlin 1955-58; Prof. of Political Science and Contemporary History, Univ. of Bonn 1959-; Pres. Comm. for History of Parl. and Political Parties, Bonn 1962-68; Fellow, Center for Advanced Study in the Behavioral Sciences, Stanford, U.S.A. 1963-64; Chair. German Assen. of Political Science 1965-67; mem. Inst. for Advanced Study, Princeton, U.S.A. 1967-68, 1974-75; mem. Wilson Center, Wash. 1980-81; Chair. Bd., Inst. für Zeitgeschichte, Munich 1980-88, German Assen. of Foreign Policy, German PEN Centre; Visiting Prof. Oxford Univ. 1971, Tel Aviv Univ. 1974, European Univ. Inst. (Florence) 1975-76; Hon. mem. American Acad. of Arts and Sciences; Hon. D. Hum. Litt., Dr. Jur., D. Rev. Pol.; Corresp. Fellow, British Acad., American Philosophical Soc., Austrian Akad. der Wissenschaften, mem. Deutsche Akad. für Sprache und Dichtung, Rhenish-Westfalian Acad. of Sciences; Ed. Vierteljahrshefte für Zeitgeschichte; mem. Editorial Bd., Politische Vierteljahresschrift until 1970, Neue Politische Literatur, Bonner Historische Forschungen, Journal of Contemporary History, Government and Opposition, Societas, Zeitschrift für Politik, Tempo Presente, Risorgimento, European Journal of Int. Affairs, History of the Twentieth Century, Bonner Schriften zur Politik und Zeitgeschichte, Quellen zur Geschichte des Parliamentarismus, Modern Constitutionalism and Democracy (joint editor) 2 vols. 1966, Nach 25 Jahren (editor) 1970, Bibliographie zur Politik (joint editor) 1970, 1976, 1982, Dokumente zur Deutschlandpolitik 1972-, Nationalsozialistische Diktatur 1983, Das Gewissen steht auf 1984, Geschichte der BR Deutschland 1981-87, Die Weimarer Republik 1987. *Publications:* Conscience in Revolt (with others) 1954, Die Auflösung der Weimarer Republik 1955, Staat und Politik (with E. Fraenkel) 1957, Die Nationalsozialistische Machtergreifung (with others) 1960, The Foreign Policy of the Federal Republic of Germany 1963, Problems of Parliamentary Democracy in Europe 1964, Adolf Hitler 1964, Deutschland zwischen Demokratie und Diktatur 1964, Theodor Heuss 1965, Internationale Beziehungen (with E. Fraenkel) 1969, The German Dictatorship (Italian, Spanish, French, Japanese, Hebrew trans.) 1970, Das deutsche Dilemma 1971 (English trans. 1974), Western Europe (in Times History of Our Times) 1971, Democracy (in Europe Tomorrow) 1972, Zeitgeschichtliche Kontroversen 1976, Die Krise Europas 1917-1975 1976 and 1979 (Italian trans.), Schlüsselwörter in der Geschichte 1978, Geschichte und Gewalt 1981, Zeit der Ideologien 1982 (English and Italian trans. 1985), Die totalitäre Erfahrung 1987. *Leisure interest:* piano music. *Address:* Stationsweg 17, Bonn, Federal Republic of Germany. *Telephone:* 284358.

BRACHES, Ernst; Netherlands professor; b. 8 Oct. 1930, Padang, Indonesia; m. Maartje van Hoorn 1961; three s. and one foster s.; ed. Univ. of Amsterdam; Asst. Univ. of Amsterdam 1957-65; Keeper, Western Printed Books, Univ. Library, Leiden 1965-73; Asst. Dir. Rijksmuseum Meermanno-Westreenianum, The Hague 1973-77; Librarian, Univ. of Amsterdam 1977-88; Prof. History of the Modern Book, Dr. P. A. Tiele Foundation, Univ. of Amsterdam; hon. mem. Soc. de la Reliure Originale, Paris. *Publications:* Het Boek als Nieuwe Kunst 1973, Engel en Afgrond 1983; publications on Goethe, Henry James, Thomas Mann, book conservation, history of modern printing etc. *Address:* University Library, Singel 425, 1012 WP Amsterdam (Office); Vrijburglaan 53, 2051 LB Overveen, Netherlands (Home). *Telephone:* (020) 5252310 (Office); (023) 253246 (Home).

BRACK, Robert William, A.O., B.A., F.A.I.M.; Australian business executive; b. 15 Nov. 1921, Melbourne, Victoria; s. of late James Brack and late Frances Lillian Brack (née Downey); m. Joan Mackey 1952; one s. one d.; ed. Telopea Park High School, Canberra and Melbourne Univ.; with Dept. of Trade and Customs 1938-41; served 8th Div. A.I.F. 1941-45, P.O.W. Singapore and Thailand; Australian High Comm., London 1949-51, 1956-57; Australian Embassy, Washington, D.C. 1952-53; Asst. Comptroller-Gen. of Customs, Canberra 1959-63; Collector of Customs for N.S.W. 1963-64;

joined Australian Consolidated Industries Ltd., Commercial Man. 1964-66, Asst. Gen. Man. 1966-67, Gen. Man. 1967-, Dir. 1974-, Man. Dir. 1978-81; Chair. Australian Telecommunications Comm. 1981-88; Commr. Australian Nat. Airlines Comm. 1978, Vice-Chair. 1979-83; Dir. Ramtron Australia Ltd., Former Dir. Standard Chartered Bank Australia Ltd., Sandhurst Trustees Ltd., Australian Reinsurance Co. Ltd.; fmr. Vice-Chair. Australian Admin. Staff Coll.; Fellow Inst. of Dirs. (Australia), Australian Inst. of Man., Chair. The Victoria Leasing Co. Ltd. *Address:* 9, Springfield Avenue, Toarak, 3142 Vic., Australia. *Telephone:* (03) 241-3800.

BRADBROOK, Muriel Clara, M.A., PH.D., LITT.D.; British university professor; b. 27 April 1909, Wallasey, Cheshire; d. of Samuel Bradbrook and Annie (née Harvey) Bradbrook; ed. Hutchesons' School, Glasgow, Oldershaw School, Wallasey, and Girton Coll., Cambridge; Fellow of Girton Coll., Cambridge 1932-35, 1936-; Mistress of Girton Coll. 1968-76; in residence Somerville Coll., Oxford 1935-36; Bd. of Trade, Industries and Manufactures Depts. 2 and 3 1941-45; Univ. lecturer, Cambridge 1945-62, Reader 1962-65, Prof. of English 1965-76; in residence Folger Library, Washington, and Huntington Library, Calif. 1958-59; tour of Far East for Shakespeare's Fourth Centenary 1964; Trustee, Shakespeare's Birthplace 1967; Visiting Prof. Santa Cruz, Calif. 1966, Kuwait 1969, Kenyon Coll., U.S.A. 1977; Hon. Prof. Warwick Univ. 1987; Foreign mem. Norwegian Acad. of Arts and Sciences 1966; Freedom of City of Hiroshima; F.R.S.L. 1947; Hon. Litt. D. (Liverpool Univ.) 1964, (Sussex Univ.) 1972, (London Univ.) 1973, Hon. LL.D. (Smith Coll., U.S.A.) 1965, Hon. Ph.D. (Gothenburg) 1975, Hon. D. Litt. (Kenyon Coll., U.S.A.) 1977; Fellow, Nat. Humanities Center, N.C. 1979; Visiting Lecturer, Rhodes Univ. S.A. 1979; Visiting Fellow, Japan Soc. for Promotion of Science 1985, Fudan Univ., Shanghai 1985. *Publications:* Elizabethan Stage Conditions 1932, Themes and Conventions of Elizabethan Tragedy 1934, The School of Night 1936, Andrew Marvell (with M. G. Lloyd Thomas) 1940, Joseph Conrad 1941, Ibsen the Norwegian 1947, T. S. Eliot 1950, Shakespeare and Elizabethan Poetry 1951, The Queen's Garland 1953, The Growth and Structure of Elizabethan Comedy 1955, Sir Thomas Malory 1957, The Rise of the Common Player 1962, English Dramatic Form 1965, That Infidel Place: A History of Girton College 1969, Shakespeare the Craftsman 1969, Literature in Action 1972, T. S. Eliot: the Making of "The Waste Land" 1972, Malcolm Lowry: His Art and Early Life 1974, The Living Monument 1976, Shakespeare, the Poet and his World 1978, John Webster, Citizen and Dramatist 1980, Collected Papers (Vols. 1-4) 1982-89, Muriel Bradbrook on Shakespeare 1984. *Leisure interests:* travel, theatre. *Address:* 91 Chesterton Road, Cambridge, CB4 3AP, England. *Telephone:* 352765.

BRADBURY, Malcolm Stanley, M.A., PH.D.; British author and professor of American studies; b. 7 Sept. 1932, Sheffield, Yorks.; s. of Arthur and Doris Ethel (Marshall) Bradbury; m. Elizabeth Salt 1959; two s.; ed. Univ. Coll., Leicester, Queen Mary Coll., Univ. of London, Univ. of Manchester, Indiana Univ.; Staff Tutor in Literature and Drama, Dept. of Advanced Educ., Univ. of Hull 1959-61; lecturer in English Language and Literature, Univ. of Birmingham 1961-65; lecturer, later Senior lecturer and Reader, School of English and American Studies, Univ. of East Anglia 1965-70, Prof. of American Studies 1970-; Visiting Fellow, All Souls, Oxford 1969; Visiting Prof., Univ. of Zürich 1972; Royal Soc. of Literature Prize for The History Man 1975; Hon. Fellow, Queen Mary Coll., London 1985; Hon. D.Litt. (Leicester) 1986. *Publications:* Eating People is Wrong (novel)1959, Evelyn Waugh 1962, E. M. Forster: a Collection of Critical Essays (editor) 1965, Stepping Westward (novel) 1965, What is a novel? 1969, A Passage to India: a Casebook 1970, A Penguin Companion to Literature: Vol. III, American Literature (with E. Mottram) 1971, The Social Context of Modern English Literature 1972; Possibilities: Essays on the State of the Novel 1973, The History Man (novel) 1975, Modernism (with J. W. MacFarlane) 1976, Who Do You Think You Are? (short stories) 1976, The Novel Today (editor) 1977, Saul Bellow 1982, The After Dinner Game (plays) 1982, All Dressed Up and Nowhere To Go 1982, The Modern American Novel 1983, Rates of Exchange (novel) 1983, Why Come to Slaka 1986, No Not Bloomsbury 1986, Cuts: A Very Short Novel 1987, Mensonge: Structuralism's Hidden Hero: My Strange Quest for Henri Mensonge 1987, The Penguin Book of Modern Short Stories (ed.) 1987, No, Not Bloomsbury (essays) 1987, The Modern World: Ten Great Writers 1988, Unsent Letters 1988. *Address:* School of English and American Studies, University of East Anglia, University Plain, Norwich, Norfolk, England. *Telephone:* 56161.

BRADBURY, Norris Edwin, B.A., PH.D.; American physicist; b. 30 May 1909; s. of Edwin Bradbury and Elvira Norris; m. Lois Platt 1933; three s.; ed. Pomona Coll., California, Univ. of California and M.I.T.; Asst. Prof. of Physics, Stanford Univ. 1934-37, Assoc. Prof. 1937-42, Prof. 1942-51; Prof. of Physics, Univ. of Calif. 1951-70; Dir. Los Alamos Scientific Laboratory, New Mexico 1945-70; Capt. U.S. Naval Reserve 1941-61; Fellow N.A.S., American Physical Soc.; Enrico Fermi Award 1970. *Address:* 1451 47th Street, Los Alamos, New Mexico 87544, U.S.A. (Home).

BRADBURY, Ray (Douglas); American author; b. 1920; s. of Leonard Bradbury and Esther Bradbury; m. Marguerite McClure 1947; four d.; Pres. Science-Fantasy Writers of America 1951-53; mem. Bd. of Dirs. Screen Workers Guild of America 1957-61. *Publications:* Dark Carnival 1947, The Meadow (play) 1948, The Martian Chronicles 1950, The Illustrated Man 1951, It Came from Outer Space (screenplay) 1952, Fahrenheit

451 1953, The Golden Apples of the Sun 1953, Moby Dick (screenplay) 1954, The October Country 1955, Switch on the Night 1955, Dandelion Wine 1957, A Medicine for Melancholy (play as The Day it Rained Forever) 1966, Icarus Montgolfier Wright (screenplay) 1961, R is for Rocket 1962, Something Wicked This Way Comes 1962, The Anthem Sprinters and Other Antics (play) 1963, The World of Ray Bradbury (play) 1964, The Machineries of Joy (short stories) 1964, The Vintage Bradbury 1965, The Wonderful Ice-Cream Suit (play) 1965, The Autumn People 1965, Tomorrow Midnight 1966, The Pedestrian (play) 1966, S is for Space 1966, The Picasso Summer (screenplay) 1968, I Sing the Body Electric! 1969, Christus Apollo (play) 1969, Old Ahab's Friend and Friend to Nosh, Speaks His Piece: A Celebration 1971, The Halloween Tree 1972, The Wonderful Ice Cream Suit and Other Plays: For Today, Tomorrow and Beyond Tomorrow 1972, When Elephants Last in the Dooryard Bloomed (poetry) 1972, The Small Assassin 1973, Zen and the Art of Writing 1973, Mars and the Mind of Man 1973, The Son of Richard III 1974, Long After Midnight (stories) 1976, Pillar of Fire and Other Plays 1976, Where Robot Mice and Robot Men Run Round in Robot Towns, New Poems Both Light and Dark 1977, Beyond 1984 1979, The Stories of Ray Bradbury 1980, The Ghosts of Forever 1981, The Haunted Computer and the Android Pope 1981, The Last Circus 1981, The Complete Poems of Ray Bradbury 1982, The Love Affair 1983, The Dinosaur Tales 1983, A Memory for Murder 1984, Forever and the Earth 1984, Death is a Lonely Business 1985. *Address:* 10265 Cheviot Drive, Los Angeles, Calif. 90064, U.S.A.

BRADFORD, Barbara Taylor; British journalist and author; b. 10 May 1933 Leeds, England; d. of Winston Taylor and Freda Walker; m. Robert Bradford 1963; ed. privately; reporter, Yorkshire Evening Post 1949-51, Women's Ed. 1951-53; Fashion Ed. Woman's Own 1953-54; columnist, London Evening News 1955-57; Exec. Ed. London American 1959-62; Ed. Nat. Design Center Magazine 1965-69; syndicated columnist, Newsday Specials, Long Island 1968-70; nat. syndicated columnist, Chicago Tribune-New York (News Syndicate), New York 1970-75, Los Angeles Times Syndicate 1975-. *Publications:* Complete Encyclopaedia of Homemaking Ideas 1968, A Garland of Children's Verse 1968, How to be the Perfect Wife 1969, Easy Steps to Successful Decorating 1971, Decorating Ideas for Casual Living 1977, How to Solve your Decorating Problems 1976, Making Space Grow 1979, A Woman of Substance (novel) 1979, Luxury Designs for Apartment Living 1981, Voice of the Heart 1982, Hold the Dream 1984, Act of Will (novel) 1986, To Be The Best 1988. *Address:* 450 Park Avenue, New York, N.Y. 10022, U.S.A.

BRADFORD, William E.; Canadian banker; b. 14 Oct. 1933, Montreal; s. of the late Elwood Joseph Bradford and Jessie (née Murray) Bradford; m. Dolores MacDonnell 1954; three s. four d.; ed. Concordia Univ., Montreal; with Northern Electric Co. Ltd. 1950-59, Canada Iron Foundries Ltd. 1959-62; Asst. Controller, Reynolds Extrusion Co. Ltd. 1962-66; Vice-Pres. and Controller, Churchill Falls (Labrador) Corpn. Ltd. 1967-70; Vice-Pres. and Sr. Financial Officer, Brinco 1970-74; Exec. Vice-Pres. for Finance, Bank of Montreal 1975, for Finance and Admin. 1976, Exec. Vice-Pres. and Deputy Gen. Man. Domestic Banking 1978, also Gen. Man. 1979, Exec. Vice-Pres., Chief Gen. Man. Bank of Montreal 1980, Pres. 1981-83, Deputy Chair. 1983-87; Pres. and C.E.O. N. American Life Assurance Co. Nov. 1987-; Fellow, Certified Gen. Accountants' Assen. of Ont., Financial Execs. Inst. *Leisure interests:* tennis, squash, golf, skiing, hunting, fishing. *Address:* North American Life Assurance Company, 5650 Yonge Street, North York, Ont., M2M 4G4, Canada; 1333 Watersedge Road, Mississauga, Ont., L5J 1AE, Canada (Home). *Telephone:* (416) 867-5717 (Office).

BRADLEY, Bill, M.A.; American politician; b. 28 July 1943, Crystal City, Mo.; s. of Warren W. Bradley and Susan Crowe; m. Ernestine Schlant 1974; one d.; ed. Princeton and Oxford Univs.; player, New York Knickerbockers Professional Basketball Team 1967-77; Senator from New Jersey 1979-; Democrat. *Publications:* Life on the Run 1976, The Fair Tax 1984. *Address:* 731 Hart Senate Office Building, Washington, D.C. 20510, U.S.A.

BRADLEY, Clive, M.A.; British publishing and communications executive; b. 25 July 1934, London; s. of late Alfred Bradley and Annie K. Bradley; ed. Felsted School, Essex, Clare Coll. Cambridge and Yale Univ.; B.B.C. 1961-63; Broadcasting Officer, Labour Party 1963-65; Political Ed., The Statist 1965-67; Group Labour Adviser, Int. Publishing Corpn. and Deputy Gen. Man. Mirror Group Newspapers 1967-73; Dir. The Observer 1973-75; Chief Exec. The Publishers Assen. 1976-; Dir. Confed. of Information Communication Industries 1984-. *Publications:* many articles and broadcasts on politics, econs. and current affairs. *Leisure interests:* politics, reading, walking. *Address:* 19 Bedford Square, London, WC1B 3HJ (Office); 8 Northumberland Place, Richmond upon Thames, Surrey, TW10 6TS, England (Home). *Telephone:* 01-580 6321 (Office); 01-940 7172 (Home).

BRADLEY, Daniel Joseph, PH.D., F.R.S.; Irish professor of optical electronics; b. 18 Jan. 1928; s. of John and Margaret Bradley; m. Winefriede M. T. O'Connor 1958; four s. one d.; ed. St. Columb's Coll., Derry, St. Mary's Training Coll., Belfast, Birkbeck and Royal Holloway Colls., London; primary school teacher, Londonderry 1947-53, secondary school teacher, London area 1953-57; Asst. Lecturer, Royal Holloway Coll. 1957-60; lecturer, Imperial Coll. of Science and Tech. 1960-64; Reader, Royal Holloway Coll. 1964-66; Prof. and Head of Dept. of Pure and Applied Physics, Queen's Univ., Belfast 1966-73; Prof. of Optics, Imperial Coll.

1973-80, Head, Dept. of Physics 1976-80, Emer. Prof. London Univ. 1980-; Prof. of Optical Electronics, Trinity Coll., Dublin 1980-; Visiting Scientist M.I.T. 1965; Consultant, Harvard Observatory 1966; Chair. Laser Facility Cttee. S.R.C. 1976-79, British Nat. Cttee. for Physics 1979-80, Quantum Electronics Comm. IUPAP 1982; mem. Rutherford Lab. Establishment Cttee. S.R.C. 1977-79, Science Bd., S.R.C. 1977-80; mem. Council, Royal Soc. 1979-80; Fellow, Optical Soc. of America; mem. Royal Irish Acad.; New Univ. of Ulster h.c. 1983; Belfast h.c. 1986; Thomas Young Medal, Inst. of Physics 1975; Royal Medal, Royal Soc. 1983. *Publications:* papers on optics, lasers, spectroscopy, chronoscopy and astronomy in learned journals. *Leisure interests:* television, walking. *Address:* Trinity College, Dublin 2, Ireland.

BRADLEY, Donald Charlton, PH.D., D.SC., F.R.S.C., F.R.S.A., F.R.S.; British inorganic chemist; b. 7 Nov. 1924; m. Constance Joy Hazeldean 1948 (died 1985); one s.; ed. Hove Co. School for Boys, Birkbeck Coll., Univ. of London; Research Asst., British Electrical and Allied Industries Research Assen. 1941-47; Asst. Lecturer in Chem., Birkbeck Coll. 1949-52, Lecturer 1952-59; Prof. of Chem., Univ. of Western Ont. 1959-64; Prof. of Inorganic Chem., Queen Mary Coll., Univ. of London 1965-87, Emer. Prof. 1988-, Head of Chem. Dept. 1978-82; Chair. Bd. of Studies in Chem. and Chemical Industries, Univ. of London 1977-79; mem. Senate, London Univ. 1981-87, Soc. of Chem. Industry; Exec. Ed. Polyhedron 1982. *Publications:* (jt. author) Metal Alkoxides 1978, numerous scientific papers. *Leisure interests:* travelling, gardening, music, archaeology. *Address:* Department of Chemistry, Queen Mary College, Mile End Road, London, E1 4NS, England. *Telephone:* 01-980 4811.

BRADLEY, Thomas (Tom), LL.D.; American police officer and politician; b. 29 Dec. 1917, Calvert Tex.; s. of Lee and Crenner (Hawkins) Bradley; m. Ethel Arnold 1941; two d.; ed. Polytechnic High School, Univ. of California at Los Angeles, Southwestern Univ. Law School; served Los Angeles Police Dept. 1940-61, attained rank of Lieut.; Attorney at Law 1961-63; Councilman, Los Angeles 10th Dist. 1963-73; Mayor, City of Los Angeles July 1973-; Democrat. *Leisure interests:* reading, jazz, home movies, sports. *Address:* Office of Mayor, City Hall, Los Angeles, Calif. 90012, U.S.A. *Telephone:* (213) 485-3311.

BRADMAN, Sir Donald George, Kt., A.C.; Australian cricketer and company director; b. 27 Aug. 1908, Cootamundra, N.S.W.; s. of George and Emily Bradman; m. Jessie Menzies 1932; two s. (one deceased) one d.; ed. Bowral Intermediate High School; played cricket for N.S.W. 1927-34, for S. Australia 1935-49; played for Australia 1928-48, Capt. 1936-48; in test cricket made 6,996 runs (average 99.9), in all first-class cricket 28,067 runs (average 95); scored 117 centuries in first-class matches; fmr. mem. Australian Bd. of Control for Int. Cricket, Chair. 1960-63, 1969-72; Vice-Pres. S. Australia Cricket Assen. 1951-65, Pres. 1965-73; fmr. Australian Test Selector; fmr. mem. Stock Exchange of Adelaide; Champion Mt. Osmond Country Club (Golf) 1936, 1949; fmr. S. Australia Amateur Squash Champion; Life Vice-Pres. of M.C.C. 1988-. *Publications:* Don Bradman's Book 1930, How to Play Cricket 1935, My Cricketing Life 1938, Farewell to Cricket 1950, The Art of Cricket 1958. *Leisure interests:* cricket, tennis, golf, squash. *Address:* 2 Holden Street, Kensington Park, South Australia.

BRADSHAW, Anthony David, M.A., PH.D., F.R.S.; British botanist; b. 17 Jan. 1926; m. Betty Margaret Bradshaw; three d.; ed. St. Paul's School, London, Jesus Coll., Cambridge; Lecturer Univ. Coll. N. Wales, Bangor 1952-63, Sr. Lecturer 1963-64, Reader in Agricultural Botany 1964-68; Holbrook Gaskell Prof. of Botany, Univ. of Liverpool 1968-88; mem. Nature Conservancy Council 1969-78, Natural Environment Research Council 1969-74; Bd. of Man. Sports Turf Research Inst. 1976-; Pres. British Ecological Soc. 1981-83. *Publications:* (jt. ed.) Teaching Genetics 1963, (with M. J. Chadwick) The Restoration of Land 1980, (with others) Quarry Reclamation 1982, (with others) Mine Wastes Reclamation 1982, (with R. A. Dutton) Land Reclamation in Cities 1982, (jt. ed.) Ecology and Design in Landscape 1985, numerous learned papers. *Leisure interests:* sailing, gardening, landscape appreciation. *Address:* Botany Department, The University, Liverpool, L69 3BX, England.

BRADSHAW, Peter, B.A., F.R.S.; British professor of aerodynamics; b. 26 Dec. 1935, Torquay; s. of J. W. N. Bradshaw and F. W. G. Bradshaw (née Finch); m. Sheila Dorothy Brown 1969; ed. Torquay Grammar School, St. John's Coll., Cambridge; Scientific Officer, Aerodynamics Div., Nat. Physical Lab., Teddington 1957-69; Sr. Lecturer, Dept. of Aeronautics, Imperial Coll., Univ. of London 1969-71, Reader 1971-78, Prof. of Experimental Aerodynamics 1978-88; Prof. Thermosciences Div., Dept. of Mechanical Eng., Stanford Univ. 1989-; Royal Aeronautical Soc. Bronze Medal 1971, Royal Aeronautical Soc. Busk Prize 1972. *Publications:* Experimental Fluid Mechanics 1964, An Introduction to Turbulence 1971, Momentum Transfer in Boundary Layers (with T. Cebeci) 1977, Engineering Calculation Methods for Turbulent Flow (with T. Cebeci and J. H. Whitelaw) 1981, Convective Heat Transfer (with T. Cebeci) 1984. *Leisure interests:* ancient history, walking. *Address:* Thermosciences Division, Department of Mechanical Engineering, Stanford Univ., Stanford, Calif. 94305-3030, U.S.A. *Telephone:* (415) 725 0704.

BRADY, Conor, M.A.; Irish journalist; b. 24 April 1949, Dublin; s. of Conor Brady and Amy MacCarthy; m. Ann Byron 1971; two s.; ed. Mount St.

Joseph Cistercian Abbey, Univ. Coll. Dublin; Asst. Ed. The Irish Times 1978-81; Ed. The Sunday Tribune 1981-82; Deputy Ed. The Irish Times 1984-86, Ed. 1986-, Dir. Irish Times Ltd. 1986-; Award for Outstanding Work in Irish Journalism 1979. *Publication:* Guardian of the Peace 1974. *Leisure interests:* travel, reading, swimming. *Address:* c/o The Irish Times, d'Olier Street, Dublin 2, Ireland. *Telephone:* 792022.

BRADY, James S., B.S., J.D.; American lawyer and government official; b. 17 Sept. 1944, Grand Rapids, Mich.; s. of George Joseph and Emily Mae (Sherman) Brady; m. Catherine Ann Yared 1966; two s., one d.; ed. Univs. of Western Michigan and Notre Dame; admitted to Mich. bar 1969; assoc. Roach, Twohey, Maggini and Brady law firm 1969-77, partner 1972-77; Adjunct Prof. Cooley Law School, Lansing, Mich. 1975-76; U.S. Attorney Western Dist., Mich. Grand Rapids 1977-81; mem. Miller, Johnson, Snell and Cummiskey 1981-; Press Sec. to Pres. Reagan 1981-89; mem. American, Fed., Mich. and Grand Rapids bar asscns., State Bar, Mich., American Trial Lawyers' Assn. *Address:* 1700 Fisk S.E., Grand Rapids, Mich. 49506, U.S.A. (Home).

BRADY, Nicholas F.; American financier and politician; b. 11 April, 1930, New York; s. of James C. Brady and Eliot Brady; m. Katherine Douglas 1952; two s. one d.; ed. Yale and Harvard Univs.; with Dillon, Read and Co. Ltd. 1954-82, Chair. C.E.O. 1982-; Chair., Exec. Comm. Purolator Courier Corpn. Inc. Basking Ridge, N.J. 1983-; U.S. Treasury Sec. 1988-; appointee to U.S. Senate from N.J. 1982; Dir. Bessemer Securities Corpn., Doubleday & Co., Wolverine World Wide Inc., ASA Ltd., Media Gen. Inc., NCR Corpn.; mem. MX Missile Options Panel, Cen. American Study Comm.; Chair. Jockey Club, New York. *Address:* c/o Dillon Read & Co., 535 Madison Avenue, N.Y. 10022, U.S.A.

BRADY, Roscoe Owen, M.D.; American medical research scientist; b. 11 Oct. 1923, Philadelphia, Pa.; s. of Roscoe O. and Martha Roberts Brady; m. Bennett Carden Manning 1972; two s.; ed. Pennsylvania State Univ., Harvard Medical School and Univ. of Pennsylvania; Thyroid Clinic Assoc., Univ. of Pa. School of Medicine 1950-52; Officer-in-Charge, Dept. of Chemistry, U.S. Naval Medical School 1952-54; Section Chief. Nat. Inst. of Neurological Diseases and Blindness (now Nat. Inst. of Neurological and Communicative Disorders and Strokes) 1954-67, Acting Chief, Laboratory of Neurochemistry 1967-68, Asst. Chief 1969-71, Chief, Developmental and Metabolic Neurology Branch 1972-; Professorial Lecturer, Dept. of Biochemistry, George Washington Univ. School of Medicine 1963-73; Adjunct Prof. of Biochemistry, Dept. of Biochemistry, Georgetown Univ. School of Medicine 1965-; mem. Inst. of Medicine, Nat. Acad. of Sciences; Gairdner Foundation Int. Award, Passano Foundation Award and Lasker Foundation Award. *Publications:* Neurochemistry of Nucleotides and Amino Acids (ed. with D. B. Tower) 1960, The Basic Neurosciences (ed.) 1975, The Molecular Basis of Lysosomal Storage Disorders (ed. with J. A. Barranger) 1984 and 400 scientific publs. *Leisure interests:* piano, tennis, bridge. *Address:* Building 10, Room 3D04, National Institutes of Health, Bethesda, Md. 20892 (Office); 9501 Kingsley Avenue, Bethesda, Md. 20814, U.S.A. (Home). *Telephone:* (301) 496-3285 (Office); (301) 530-8864 (Home).

BRAGG, Melvyn, M.A., F.R.S.L.; British author and television presenter; b. 6 Oct. 1939; s. of Stanley Bragg and Mary E. Park; m. 1st Marie-Elisabeth Roche 1961 (deceased); one d.; m. 2nd Catherine M. Haste 1973; one s. one d.; ed. Nelson-Thomlinson Grammar School, Wigton and Wadham Coll. Oxford; BBC Radio and TV Producer 1961-67; TV Presenter and Ed. The South Bank Show for ITV 1978-; Head of Arts, London Weekend TV 1982-; Deputy Chair. Border TV 1985-; writer and broadcaster 1967-; novelist 1964-; mem. Arts Council and Chair. Literature Panel 1986-; Pres. Cumbrians for Peace 1982-, Northern Arts 1983-, Nat. Campaign for the Arts 1986-; Hon. D.Litt. (Liverpool) 1986. *Plays:* Mardi Gras 1976, Orion 1977, The Hired Man 1984. *Screenplays:* Isadora, Jesus Christ Superstar, Clouds of Glory (with Ken Russell). *Publications:* Speak for England 1976, Land of the Lakes 1983, Laurence Olivier 1984, Rich, The Life of Richard Burton 1988; *novels:* For Want of a Nail 1965, The Second Inheritance 1966, Without a City Wall 1968, The Hired Man 1969, A Place in England 1970, The Nerve 1971, Josh Lawton 1972, The Silken Net 1974, A Christmas Child 1976, Autumn Manoeuvres 1978, Kingdom Come 1980, Love and Glory 1983; weekly column in Punch and contributions to journals. *Address:* 12 Hampstead Hill Gardens, London, N.W.3, England.

BRAHAM, Allan John Witney, PH.D.; British museum curator and author; b. 19 Aug. 1937, Croydon; s. of Dudley Braham and Florence Meaks; m. Helen Clare Butterworth 1963; two d.; ed. Dulwich Coll., London Univ. and the Courtauld Inst.; Asst. Keeper Nat. Gallery 1962, Deputy Keeper 1973, Keeper and Deputy Dir. 1978-; Hitchcock Medal, Bannister Fletcher Prize. *Publications:* François Mansart (with Peter Smith) 1973, Carlo Fontana: The Drawings at Windsor (with Hellmut Hager) 1977, The Architecture of the French Enlightenment 1980, El Greco to Goya 1981. *Leisure interest:* history of architecture. *Address:* The National Gallery, Trafalgar Square, London, WC2N 5DN (Office); 15A Acol Road, London, NW6 3AA, England (Home).

BRAHIMI, Abdelhamid, D.ECON.; Algerian politician; b. 2 April 1936, Constantine; m.; one c.; officer, Nat. Liberation Army 1956-62; Wali of Annaba (govt. rep. in province of Annaba) 1963-65; Dir. O.C.I. (Algerian-French Bd. for promotion of industrial co-operation) 1968-70; Prof. of

Econs., Univ. of Algiers 1970-75; Chair. SONATRACH Inc., U.S.A. 1976-78; Minister of Planning and Regional Devt. 1979-83; Prime Minister of Algeria 1984-88. *Address:* c/o Office du Premier Ministre, Palais du gouvernement, Algiers, Algeria. *Telephone:* 60-23-40.

BRAHIMI, Lakhdar; Algerian diplomatist; b. 1934; ed. Medersa Algiers, Faculté de Droit et Inst. des Sciences Politiques, Algiers, then Paris; Student Leader 1953-56; Algerian Front of Nat. Liberation (F.L.N.) to 1956; Perm. Rep. of F.L.N. and later of Provisional Govt. of Algeria in S.E. Asia 1956-61; Gen. Secr., Ministry of External Affairs 1961-63; Amb. to U.A.R. (Egypt) and Sudan 1963-69; Perm. Rep. to Arab League 1963-70, Deputy Sec. Gen. 1984-; Amb. to U.K. 1971-79; mem. Cen. Cttee., F.L.N. 1979-83. *Address:* Arab League, 31 Avenue Kheireddine Pacha, Tunis, Tunisia. *Telephone:* 890100.

BRAHMANANDA Palahally Ramaiya, PH.D.; Indian professor of economics; b. 27 Sept. 1926, Bangalore; s. of Ramaiya and Jayalaxshamma Ramaiya; ed. Mysore Univ. and Bombay Univ.; Research Asst., Bombay Univ. 1950-54, Lecturer in Econs. 1954-56, Reader in Monetary Econs. 1956-63, Prof. 1963-, Dir. Dept. of Econs. 1976-; Ed. Indian Economic Journal 1956-; Nat. Lecturer in Econs., Univ. Grants Comm.; Pres. Indian Econs. Assn. 1977; Nat. Fellow in Econs., Univ. Grants Comm. 1978-81; Best Teacher Award, Govt. of Maharashtra 1983; Visiting Prof. Delhi Univ. 1985. *Publications:* Planning for a Shortage Economy 1952, Economics of Electricity Planning 1952, Planning for an Expanding Economy 1956 (all with C. N. Vakil), Studies in Welfare Maximization 1959, The new Classical vs. the Neo-Classical Economics 1967, The Gold-Money Rift—A Classical Theory of International Liquidity 1969, Explorations in the New Classical Theory of Political Economy and a Connected Critique of Economic Theory 1974, Determinants of Real National Income and of Price Level 1976, The Falling Economy and How to Revive It 1977, Planning for a Futureless Economy—A Critique of the 6th Plan 1978, Growthless Inflation by Means of Stockless Money 1980, Essays in Honour of Professor V. L. D'Souza (ed. with D. M. Nanjundappa and B. K. Narayan) 1980, The I.M.F. Loan and India's Economic Future 1982, Productivity in the Indian Economy: Rising Inputs for Falling Outputs 1982, Employment Policy in a Developing Country: A Case Study of India, Vols. I-II (ed. with A. Robinson and L. K. Deshpande) 1983, New Models for the American Economy 1985; Keynes' 'General Theory': A New-Classical Critique 1986, Monetary Theory—A Real Angle 1986; over 300 articles on different aspects of economic theory and the Indian economy. *Address:* Department of Economics, University of Bombay, Vidyanagari P.O., Vidyanagari Marg, Bombay 400098, India. *Telephone:* 6127010.

BRAIDWOOD, Robert John, PH.D.; American archaeologist and anthropologist; b. 29 July 1907, Detroit; s. of Walter Braidwood and Rhea Nimmo; m. Linda Schreiber 1937; one s. one d.; ed. Michigan, Berlin and Chicago Univs.; field archaeology in Iraq, Illinois, Syria, New Mexico, Turkey and Iran; mem. Oriental Inst., Univ. of Chicago 1933-, Prof. Old World Prehistory 1954-76, Prof. Emer. 1976-; Prof. Anthropology, Univ. of Chicago 1954-76, Prof. Emer. 1976-; Co-Dir. Istanbul-Chicago Univs. Jt. Prehistoric Project in Southeastern Turkey 1963-; Fellow, American Acad. of Arts and Sciences, N.A.S., American Philosophical Soc.; Hon. Fellow, Soc. of Antiquaries, London; Corresp. mem. Deutsches Archäologisches Institut, Österreichische Akademie der Wissenschaft, Académie de France, etc.; Dr. h.c. (Indiana) 1972, (Sorbonne) 1975, (Rome) 1984. *Publications:* Excavations in the plain of Antioch I (with Linda Braidwood), Prehistoric investigations in Iraqi Kurdistan (with Bruce Howe, et al.). *Address:* Prehistory Laboratory, Oriental Institute, University of Chicago, Chicago, Ill. 60637, U.S.A.

BRAININ, Norbert, O.B.E.; British (b. Austrian) violinist; b. 12 March 1923, Vienna; s. of Adolph Brainin and Sophie Brainin; m. Kathe Kottow 1948; one d.; started studies Vienna; emigrated to U.K. 1938; studied with Carl Flesch and Max Rostal; won Carl Flesch prize for solo violinists, Guildhall School of Music, London 1946; Leader of Amadeus String Quartet, which he founded 1947; Prof. for Chamber Music R.A.M. 1986-; D. Univ. (York) 1968; Grand Cross of Merit, First Class (Fed. Repub. of Germany) 1972; Cross of Hon. for Arts and Science (Austria) 1972. *Address:* 19 Prowse Avenue, Bushey Heath, Herts., England. *Telephone:* 01-950 7379.

BRAITHWAITE, Eustace Adolphe, M.SC.; Guyanese author and diplomatist; b. 27 June 1922; ed. New York Univ. and Cambridge Univ.; R.A.F., Second World War; schoolteacher, London 1950-57; Welfare Officer, London County Council 1958-60; Human Rights Officer, World Veterans Foundation, Paris 1960-63; lecturer and Educ. Consultant, UNESCO, Paris 1963-66; Perm. Rep. of Guyana to UN 1967-68; Amb. to Venezuela 1968-69; Franklin Prize; Ainsfield Wolff Literary Award for To Sir, With Love. *Publications:* To Sir, With Love 1959 (film 1967), A Kind of Homecoming 1961, Paid Servant 1962, A Choice of Straws, 1965, Reluctant Neighbours 1972, Honorary White 1976. *Address:* Billingsley Trail, Golders Bridge, New York 10526, U.S.A.

BRAKKE, Myron Kendall, PH.D.; American research chemist (retd.); b. 23 Oct. 1921, Minn.; s. of John T. and Hulda C. Marburger Brakke; m. Betty-Jean Einbecker 1947; two s. two d.; ed. Rochester Jr. Coll., Minnesota and Univ. of Minnesota; Research Assoc., Brooklyn Botanic Garden, Brooklyn, New York 1947-52, Univ. of Illinois 1952-55; Research Chemist,

U.S. Dept. of Agric. Lincoln, Neb. 1955–86; Prof. of Plant Pathology, Univ. of Nebraska 1955–86, Prof. Emer. 1986–; mem. N.A.S., A.A.A.S., American Chem. Soc. and numerous professional socs. etc.; several achievement awards. *Publications:* more than 100 research articles. *Leisure interests:* reading, gardening, forestry. *Address:* Route 1, Box 57, Crete, Neb. 68333, U.S.A.

BRAKOV, Yergeniy Alekseyevich; Soviet engineer; b. 1937; ed. Higher Tech. School, Moscow Likhachev Automobile Works; served with Soviet Army 1956–57; technician at Inst. of Automobile Industry 1957–59; mem. CPSU 1963–; engineer, head of workshop 1959–73; dir. of mechanical ass. production, head of production of a factory co-operative 1973–80; Deputy Chief engineer, Deputy General Dir. of Production 1980–86; General Dir. of Moscow Likhachev Automobile Works 1986–; cand. mem. of CPSU Cen. Cttee. 1986–. *Address:* Likhachev Automobile Works, Moscow, U.S.S.R.

BRAKS, Gerrit J. M., M.AGR.; Netherlands politician; b. 23 May 1933, Odiliapeel; m. Frens Bardoel; two s. three d.; ed. Agricultural Univ., Wageningen; worked on parents' farm –1955; Asst. Govt. Agricultural Advisory Service, Eindhoven 1955–58; Directorate for Int. Econ. Co-operation, Ministry of Agric. and Fisheries 1965–66; Deputy Agricultural Attaché, Perm. Mission of Netherlands to EEC, Brussels 1966–67; Sec. North Brabant Christian Farmers' Union (NCB), Tilburg 1967–69; Agricultural Counsellor, Perm. Mission of Netherlands to EEC 1969–77; mem. Second Chamber of Parl. 1977–80, 1981–82; Chair. Standing Cttee. on Agric., Second Chamber 1979–80 parl. year; Minister of Agric. and Fisheries 1980–81, Nov. 1982–; Kt. Order of the Netherlands Lion 1981. *Leisure interest:* gardening. *Address:* Ministry of Agriculture and Fisheries, Bezuidenhoutseweg 73, P.O.B. 20401, 2500 EK The Hague, Netherlands. *Telephone:* (070) 792000.

BRAMALL, Life Peer (cr. 1987), of Bushfield in the County of Hampshire; **Field Marshal Sir Edwin (Noel Westby) Bramall,** G.C.B., O.B.E., M.C.; British army officer; b. 18 Dec. 1923, Tunbridge Wells, England; s. of Maj. Edmund Haselden Bramall and Katherine Bridget (Westby) Bramall; m. Dorothy Avril Wentworth Vernon 1949; one s. one d.; ed. Eton Coll.; commissioned in Kings Royal Rifle Corps 1943, served in North-west Europe 1944–45; occupation of Japan 1946–47; Instructor, School of Infantry 1949–51; served Middle East 1953–58; Instructor, Army Staff Coll. 1958–61; on staff of Lord Mountbatten with special responsibility for reorg. of Ministry of Defence 1963–64; CO 2nd Green Jackets (Kings Royal Rifle Corps) 1965–66; Commdr. 5th Airportable Brigade 1967–69; G.O.C 1st Div. BAOR 1972–73; rank of Lieut. Gen. 1973; Commdr. British Forces Hong Kong 1973–76; Col. Commdt. 3rd Royal Green Jackets 1973–84, SAS Regt. 1985–; Col. 2nd Goorkhas 1976–86; rank of Gen. 1976; C.-in-C. U.K. Land Forces 1976–78; Vice-Chief of Defence Staff (Personnel and Logistics) 1978–79; Chief of Gen. Staff and ADC Gen. to H.M. The Queen 1979–82; rank of Field Marshal 1982; Chief of Defence Staff 1982–85; Lord Lieut. of Greater London 1986–; Dir. Vickers 1986–; Pres. of M.C.C. Oct. 1988–; Trustee Imperial War Museum 1983–; J.P. London 1986; K.St.J. 1986. *Leisure interests:* cricket, painting, travel, tennis. *Address:* c/o Ministry of Defence, Whitehall, London, S.W.1, England. *Telephone:* 52-89-819.

BRANAGH, Kenneth; British actor and director; b. 10 Dec. 1960, Belfast; ed. Royal Acad. of Dramatic Art; Bancroft Gold Medal RADA 1982; f. Renaissance Theatre Co. April 1987. *Theatre:* Another Country 1982 (Soc. of W. End Theatres Award for Most Promising Newcomer), The Madness 1983, Francis, Henry V, Hamlet, Love's Labours Lost, Golden Girls, Tell Me Honestly (wrote and dir.) 1986, Romeo and Juliet (prod. and dir.) 1986, Much Ado About Nothing, As You Like It, Hamlet. *TV:* Easter 2016, The Boy in the Bush, Billy (Trilogy), To the Lighthouse, Maybury, Derek, Coming Through, Ghosts, Lorna, Fortunes of War, Strange Interlude, The Lady's Not for Burning. *Films:* High Season, A Month in the Country; Dir., Writer, actor (film) Henry V 1989. *Address:* c/o Marmont Management, Langham House, 308 Regent Street, London, W.1, England.

BRANCA, Vittore (Felice Giovanni), D.LITT.; Italian educationist; b. 9 July 1913, Savona; m. Olga Montagner 1938; one s. three d.; ed. Univ. of Pisa; Prof. Accad. della Crusca, Florence 1937–48; Prof. of Italian Literature, Maria Assunta Univ., Rome 1948–50; Prof. of Italian Literature, Univ. of Catania 1950–53, Univ. of Padua 1953–; Rector Univ. of Bergamo 1968–72; Head, Div. of Arts and Letters, UNESCO 1950–53; Vice-Pres. Nat. Italian Comm. of UNESCO; Pres. Int. Asscn. for Study of Italian Language and Literature; Vice-Pres. Fondazione Giorgio Cini; mem. Cttee. Int. Fed. of Modern Languages and Literatures; literary adviser to publishing houses; Ed. Lettere Italiane and Studi sul Boccaccio (magazines) and of numerous series of classical texts and essays; Pres. Istituto Veneto Scienze Lettere e Arti; mem. Accad. dei Lincei, Accad. Arcadia, Accad. Polacca della Scienze, Accad. du Monde Latin (Inst. de France), Medieval Acad. of America, Hon. mem. Modern Language Asscn. of America, American Acad. of Arts and Sciences, Union of Writers, Moscow; Dr. h.c. (Univs. of Budapest, New York, Bergamo, Paris Sorbonne, McGill Univ.); Gold Medal of Italian Ministry of Educ. and of Polish Ministry of Culture. *Publications:* editions and critical studies of San Francesco, Petrarch, Boccaccio, Poliziano, Alfieri, Manzoni, other classical authors and Romanticism; methodological works including Boccaccio Medievale 1958, Filologia e critica 1977, Poliziano e l'umanesimo della parola 1983, Dizionario critico della litteratura italiana 1986. *Address:* San Marco 2885, Venice, Italy.

BRANCH, Harllee, Jr., B.A., LL.B.; American business executive (retd.); b. 21 June 1906, Atlanta, Ga.; s. of Harllee Branch and Bernice Simpson Branch; m. Katherine Hunter 1932; three s. one d.; ed. Boys High School, Atlanta, Davidson Coll., N. Carolina, and Lamar School of Law, Emory Univ., Atlanta; Dir., Fed. Reserve Bank of Atlanta 1953–55; Pres. Southeastern Electric Exchange 1954–55, Edison Electric Inst. 1955–56; Pres. and Dir. The Southern Co. 1957–69, Chair. of Bd. 1969–71, Exec. Consultant 1986–; Chair. of Bd., Southern Services Inc. 1961–71; Vice-Pres. and Dir. Alabama, Georgia, Gulf and Mississippi Power Companies 1957–68; mem. U.S. Business Advisory Council 1962–, Nat. Comm. on Productivity 1970–71, Corporate Advisory Council, Gen. Motors Corpn. 1980–; Dir. Nat. Center for Voluntary Action 1970–71, Gen. Motors Corpn. 1965–78, U.S. Steel Corpn. 1961–79; Senior Fellow, Woodrow Wilson Nat. Fellowship Foundation 1973–; Guest Lecturer Execs. on Campus Programme 1978–86; Hon. LL.D., Hon. D.H.L. *Leisure interests:* golf, fishing. *Address:* 3106 Nancy Creek Road, N.W., Atlanta, Ga. 30327, U.S.A. *Telephone:* (404) 355-7906.

BRANCO, Joaquim Rafael; São Tomé and Príncipe diplomatist; b. 1953; m.; two c.; ed. Univ. of Havana, Cuba; began as teacher of History and Portuguese 1975; fmr. Gen. Co-ordinator with Nat. Radio; fmr. Chief of Dept. of Political Affairs of Ministry of Foreign Affairs, fmr. Sec.-Gen.; Sec. of State for Educ. and Culture 1982–84; Minister for Information 1982–84; Perm. Rep of São Tomé and Príncipe to UN 1984–. *Address:* Permanent Mission of São Tomé and Príncipe to United Nations, 801 Second Ave., Suite 1504, New York, N.Y. 10017, U.S.A. *Telephone:* (212) 697-4211.

BRANDAUER, Klaus Maria; Austrian actor; b. 1944; m. Karin Brandauer 1965; mem. Burgtheater, Vienna; extensive stage repertoire, Cannes Film Festival Prize for film Mephisto 1981; Acad. Award (Oscar) for title role in film Mephisto 1982; appeared as Jedermann at Salzburg Festival 1983. *Films include:* Mephisto 1980, Colonel Redl 1985, Out of Africa 1985, Burning Secret 1988, Hannussen 1988. *Address:* Bartensteingasse 8/9, A-1010 Vienna, Austria.

BRANDO, Marlon; American actor; b. 3 April 1924; s. of Marlon and Dorothy Penebaker (née Myers) Brando; m. 1st Anna Kashfi 1957 (divorced 1959); one s.; m. 2nd Movita Brando (divorced); one c.; ed. Shattuck Military Acad. *Stage appearances include:* I Remember Mama, Candida, A Flag is Born, The Eagle has Two Heads, A Streetcar Named Desire, etc. *Film appearances include:* The Men 1950, A Streetcar Named Desire 1951, Viva Zapata 1952, Julius Caesar 1953, The Wild Ones 1953, Desirée 1954, On the Waterfront 1954, Guys and Dolls 1955, Teahouse of the August Moon 1956, Sayonara 1957, The Young Lions 1958, The Fugitive Kind 1960, The One-Eyed Jacks (also Dir.) 1960, Mutiny on the Bounty 1962, The Ugly American 1963, Bedtime Story 1964, The Saboteur 1965, The Chase 1966, Appaloosa 1966, A Countess from Hong Kong 1967, Southwest to Sonora 1966, Reflections in a Golden Eye 1967, Candy 1968, The Night of the Following Day 1969, Queimada 1970, The Nightcomers 1971, The Godfather 1972, Last Tango in Paris 1972, The Missouri Breaks 1975, Apocalypse Now 1977, Superman 1978, The Formula 1980, Dry White Season 1989, Jericho (wrote and acted in). *TV appearance:* Roots: The Next Generations 1979; Acad. Award for the best actor of the year 1954, Golden Globe Award for the most popular actor 1972; refused Oscar for The Godfather 1973. *Address:* Hawley Road, Mundelein, Ill. 60060, U.S.A. (Home).

BRANDON, Henry, C.B.E.; British journalist; b. 9 March 1916, Liberec, Czechoslovakia; s. of Oscar and Ida Brandon; m. Mabel H. Brandon 1971; one d.; ed. Prague and Lausanne Univs.; with The Sunday Times, London 1939–83, War Corresp. in N. Africa and W. Europe 1943–45, Paris Corresp. 1945–46, Roving Diplomatic Corresp. 1947–49, Washington Corresp. and Chief American Corresp., then Assoc. Editor 1950–83; Syndicated Columnist, Washington Star 1979–81; Columnist N.Y. Times World Syndicate 1983–; Guest Scholar, The Brookings Inst., Washington, D.C. 1983–; D.Lit. (Williams Coll.); Foreign Corresp. Award, Univ. of Calif. 1957, Lincoln Univ. Award, Mo. 1962, Hannen Swaffer Award 1964. *Publications:* As We Are 1961, In the Red 1966, Conversations with Henry Brandon 1966, The Anatomy of Error 1970, The Retreat of American Power 1973. *Leisure interests:* skiiing, tennis, swimming, photography. *Address:* 3604 Winfield Lane, N.W., Washington, D.C. 20007, U.S.A. *Telephone:* (202) 338-8506.

BRANDON OF OAKBROOK, Baron (Life Peer), cr. 1981; **Henry Vivian Brandon,** Kt., P.C., M.C., B.A.; British lawyer; b. 3 June 1920, Worthing; s. of the late Capt. V.R. Brandon and Joan Elizabeth Maud Simpson; m. Jeanette Rosemary Janvrin 1955; three s. one d.; ed. Winchester Coll., King's Coll., Cambridge; Officer, R.A. 1939–45; served in U.K., Madagascar, India, Burma; Major 1944–45; called to Bar, Inner Temple 1946; mem. Bar Council 1951–53; Q.C. 1961; Judge, High Court (Probate, Divorce and Admiralty Div.) 1966–71, (Family Div.) 1971–78, Admiralty Court 1971–78, Commercial Court 1971–72, 1977–78; Lord Justice of Appeal 1978–81, Lord of Appeal in Ordinary 1981–; Hon. LL.D. (Southampton) 1984. *Leisure interests:* cricket, travel, bridge. *Address:* House of Lords, London, S.W.1; 6 Thackeray Close, Wimbledon, London, SW19 4JL, England. *Telephone:* 01-219 3110 (House of Lords); 01-947 6344 (Home).

BRANDT, Cornelis J.; Netherlands executive and journalist; b. 14 Feb. 1913, Amsterdam; m. W. J. van den Bosch 1937; two s.; ed. Netherlands Inst. of Chartered Accountants; began career as accountant and Sec. to agricultural and banking organizations; Acting Ed.-in-Chief Amsterdamsche Effectenblad and Het Financieele Dagblad 1943-49; Financial Ed. De Telegraaf 1949-52, Ed.-in-Chief 1952-79; Man. Dir. 1964-79; Chair. of the Bd. of Dirs. N.V. Holdingmaatschappij De Telegraaf 1979-. *Publication:* Preference Shares 1946. *Leisure interest:* bridge. *Address:* Hartelstein 3, 1082 A.J., Amsterdam, Netherlands (Office). *Telephone:* 020-421023.

BRANDT, Willy; German politician; b. (as Herbert Ernst Karl Frahm) 18 Dec. 1913, Lübeck; s. of Martha Frahm; m. 1st Carlota Thorkildsen 1941, one d.; m. 2nd Rut Hansen 1948 (divorced 1980), three s.; m. 3rd Brigitte Seebacher 1983; ed. Lübeck and Oslo Univ.; apprentice ship-broker 1932; emigrated to Norway 1933; journalist and Sec. of Norwegian charity 1933-40; German and Norwegian resistance movements 1940-45; journalist and Norwegian Press Attaché in Berlin 1945-48; Chief Ed. Berliner Stadtblatt 1950-51; Sec. Exec. Cttee. of SPD in Berlin 1948-49, mem. 1950-63, Deputy Chair. 1954-58, Chair. 1958-63; Deputy Chair. SPD 1962-64, Chair. 1964-87, Hon. Chair. 1987-; mem. Berlin Chamber of Deputies 1950-69, Pres. 1955-57; Gov. Mayor of Berlin 1957-66; mem. Fed. Parl. (Bundestag) 1949-57, 1969-87; Pres. Fed. Council (Bundesrat) 1957-58; Pres. Deutscher Städetag 1958-63; Minister of Foreign Affairs and Fed. Vice-Chancellor 1966-69; Fed. Chancellor 1969-74; Pres. Socialist Int. 1976; Chair. Independent Comm. on Devt. Issues 1977; mem. European Parl. 1979-83; Senator Max-Planck Asscn.; numerous Hon. degrees and foreign decorations; Nobel Peace Prize 1971, Reinhold Niebuhr Award 1972, Aspen Inst. for Humanistic Studies Prize 1973, B'nai Brith Gold Medal 1981, Einstein Int. Peace Prize 1985; Social Democrat (SPD). *Publications include:* Krigen i Norge 1945, Ernst Reuter (with R. Lowenthal) 1957, Von Bonn nach Berlin 1957, My Road to Berlin 1960, The Ordeal of Co-existence 1963, Begegnung mit Kennedy 1964, Draussen (with G. Struve) 1966, Schriften Während der Emigration 1966, A Peace Policy for Europe 1968, Der Wille zum Frieden 1971, Über den Tag Hinaus 1974, Briefe und Gespräche 1972 bis 1975, Zusammen mit Bruno Kreisky und Olof Palme 1975, Willy Brandt/Helmut Schmidt: Deutschland 1976—zwei Sozialdemokraten im Gespräch 1976, Begegnungen und Einsichten 1976, People and Politics 1960-1975 1978, Frauen heute 1978, Links und Frei 1982. *Leisure interests:* reading, fishing, swimming. *Address:* Sozialdemokratische Partei Deutschlands, Erich-Ollenhauer-Haus, 5300 Bonn, Federal Republic of Germany. *Telephone:* 5321.

BRANSCOMB, Lewis McAdory, M.S., PH.D.; American physicist; b. 17 Aug. 1926, Asheville, N.C.; s. of Bennett Harvie Branscomb and Margaret Vaughn Branscomb; m. Anne Wells 1951; one s. one d.; ed. Duke and Harvard Univs.; Instructor in Physics, Harvard Univ. 1950; Lecturer in Physics, Univ. of Maryland 1950-51; Chief, Atomic Physics Section, Nat. Bureau of Standards, Washington, D.C. 1954-60, Chief Atomic Physics Div. 1960-62; Chair. Jt. Inst. for Laboratory Astrophysics 1962-65, 1968-70; Chief, Lab. Astrophysics Div., Nat. Bureau of Standards, Boulder, Colo. 1962-69; Dir. Nat. Bureau of Standards 1969-72; Chief Scientist, Vice-Pres. IBM Corpn. 1972-86; Prof., Dir. Public Policy Program Kennedy School of Govt., Harvard Univ. 1986-; mem. Bd., General Foods Corpn., Mobil Corpn., IBM World Trade Europe/Middle East/Africa Corpn.; mem. Nat. Acad. of Sciences, Inst. of Medicine, Nat. Acad. of Eng.; Fellow, American Acad. of Arts and Sciences, American Philosophical Soc.; mem. Nat. Acad of Public Admin., Harvard Univ. Bd. of Overseers; Trustee, Carnegie Inst. of Washington, Vanderbilt Univ., Nat. Geographic Soc., Woods Hole Oceanographic Inst.; several awards and hon. degrees. *Publications:* numerous articles in professional journals. *Leisure interests:* skiing, sailing. *Address:* Kennedy School of Government, Harvard University, 79 J. F. Kennedy Street, Cambridge, Mass. 02138, U.S.A.

BRANSON, Richard; British business executive; b. 18 July 1950; s. of Edward James Branson; m. 1969 (diss.); one s. one d. by Joan Templeman; ed. Stave School; set up Student Advisory Centre (now Help) 1970; founded Virgin mail-order co. 1969, first Virgin record shop 1971, recording co. 1973, nightclub (The Venue) 1976, Virgin Atlantic Airlines 1984, took Virgin Group public 1986, bought back shares 1988; Group also includes publishing, broadcasting, construction, heating systems, holidays; Chair. UK 2000 July 1986-; Dir. Intourist Moscow Ltd. 1988-; captured Blue Riband Title for Fastest Atlantic Crossing 1986, Segrave Trophy 1987. *Leisure interest:* sailing. *Address:* c/o Virgin Group PLC, 120 Campden Hill Road, London, W8 7AR, England.

BRANSTAD, Terry Edward, B.A., J.D.; American state governor; b. 17 Nov. 1946, Leland, Iowa; s. of Edward Arnold Branstad and Rita Garland; m. Christine Ann Johnson 1972; two s. one d.; ed. Univ. of Iowa and Drake Univ.; admitted to Iowa Bar; sold interest in Branstad/Schwarm, Lake Mills, Iowa; farmer, Lake Mills; mem. Iowa House of Reps. 1972-78; Lieut.-Gov. of Iowa 1979-82, Gov. of Iowa Jan. 1983-; Republican. *Address:* State Capitol, Des Moines, Iowa 50319, U.S.A.

BRASSEUR, Claude; French actor; b. 15 June 1936, Paris (as Claude Espinasse; s. of late Pierre Espinasse (known as Pierre Brasseur) and of Odette Joyeux; m. 2nd Michèle Cambon 1970; one c.; ed. René Girard and René Simon drama schools, Paris. *Plays include:* Un ange passe, L'enfant du dimanche, Match 1964, La calèche 1966, Britannicus 1966, Du côté de chez l'autre 1971, Les jeux de la nuit 1974. *Films include:* Rue des prairies, Les yeux sans visage 1959, Le noeud de vipères, La verte moisson, Pierrot la tendresse 1960, Le caporal épinglé, La bride sur le cou 1961, Germinal 1962, Dragées au poivre, Peau de banane 1963, Bande à part, Lucky Joe 1964, L'enfer (unfinished), Le chien fou, Du rififi à Paname 1966, Un homme de trop, Caroline chérie 1967, La chasse royale, Catherine ou il suffit d'un amour 1968, Le viager, Le portrait de Marianne, Un cave 1971, Une belle fille comme moi 1972, Bel ordure 1973, Les seins de glace 1974, Il faut vivre dangereusement, L'agression 1975, Attention les yeux 1976, Barocco, Le grand Escogriffe, Un éléphant ça trompe énormément 1976, Monsieur papa, Nous irons au paradis, L'état sauvage 1977, L'argent des autres, Une histoire simple 1978, La guerre des polices 1979, La boume 1980, Une langouste au petit déjeuner, Une robe noire pour un tueur, L'ombre rouge, Une affaire d'hommes 1981, Josepha, Guy de Maupassant 1982, Légitime violence 1982, T'es heureuse? Moi toujours 1983, la Crime 1983, Signes extérieurs de richesse 1983, Souvenir, Le Léopard 1984, Palace 1985, Les loups entre eux 1985, La gitane 1986, Taxi Boy 1986, Descente aux enfers 1986. *Television appearances include:* Le paysan parvenu, La misère et la gloire, Don Juan, Le mystère de la chambre jaune (as Rouletabille), Les eaux mêlées, Vidocq, Les nouvelles aventures de Vidocq, L'équipe; Beatrix Dussane trophy 1974, Caesar awards for Best Supporting Actor in Un éléphant ça trompe énormément 1976, Best Actor in La guerre des polices 1980; Chevalier, Ordre Nat. du Mérite. *Leisure interests:* boxing, swimming, football, bobsleighing, skiing. *Address:* 1 rue Séguier, 75006 Paris, France.

BRATBY, John, R.A., A.R.C.A., F.I.A.L., F.R.S.A., R.B.A.; British painter; b. 19 July 1928; s. of George Alfred and Lily Beryl (née Randall) Bratby; m. 1st Jean Cooke (q.v.) 1953 (divorced 1977), three s. one d.; m. 2nd Patti Prime 1977; ed. Tiffin Boys School, Kingston Art School, Royal Coll. of Art, London; Works in Tate Gallery, London, Nat. Gallery of Canada, Nat. Gallery of New South Wales, New York Museum of Modern Art, Walker Art Gallery, Arts Council, Glasgow Museum of Art, etc.; numerous one-man exhbns.; rep. at Pittsburgh Int. Festival 1955, 1957, Venice Biennale 1956; executed painting for the film The Horse's Mouth 1958, Mistral's Daughter 1984 (TV Series 1985); Guggenheim Nat. Award 1956 and 1958. *Publications:* fiction: Breakdown 1960, Breakfast and Elevenses 1961, Brake-Pedal Down 1962, Break 50 Kill 1963, Ed.-in-Chief Art Quarterly, Stanley Spencer 1969. *Leisure interests:* sex, garden care, preservation of local buildings, eating out, drinking beer, philosophy. *Address:* The Cupola, Belmont Road, Hastings, Sussex, England. *Telephone:* Hastings 434037.

BRATCHENKO, Boris Fedorovich; Soviet mining engineer, economist and politician; b. 9 Oct. 1912; worked at coal mines in Rostov Region 1935-49, at big combine in Karaganda, Kazakhstan 1949-53; Govt. posts 1953-; Vice-Chair. Council of Ministers of Kazakhstan 1961-65; Deputy Chair. Council of Ministers 1961-; Chair. Kazakh State Planning Cttee. 1961-65; Minister of Coal Industry 1965-85; cand. mem. Cen. Cttee. of CPSU 1966-71, mem. 1971-; Deputy to U.S.S.R. Supreme Soviet 1962-; mem. CPSU 1940-; U.S.S.R. State Prize, Order of Lenin (twice), Hero of Socialist Labour 1982. *Address:* c/o Ministry of Coal Industry, 23 Building 2, Prospekt Kalinina, Moscow, U.S.S.R.

BRATZ, Jens-Harvard; Norwegian business executive and politician; b. 21 April 1920, Aker; ed. Oslo Commercial Gymnasium, in England and U.S.A.; joined A/S Grorud Jernvarefabrik 1950, Man. Dir. 1962-; mem. Bd. several industrial, banking and shipping concerns; Chair. Asscn. of Norwegian Mfrs. of Iron and Non-Ferrous Metal Products 1965-68; Pres. Norwegian Fed. of Industries 1971-73; Minister of Industry 1981-83; Conservative. *Address:* c/o Ministry of Industry, Akersgaten 42, Pb. 8014, Oslo, Norway.

BRAUER, Arik; Austrian artist; b. 4 Jan. 1929, Vienna; s. of Simon Moses Brauer and Hermine Brauer; m. Naomi Dahabani 1957; three d.; ed. Wiener Kunstakademie; underground, Vienna 1942-45; after studies in Vienna travelled in Africa, France, Spain, Austria, Greece and Israel 1950-58, U.S.A., E. Africa, Ethiopia, Japan 1965-74; one-man exhbns. 1956-, in Austria, Germany, Switzerland, France, Denmark, Liechtenstein, Italy, Canada, Sweden, Yugoslavia, Bulgaria, Norway, Japan, Israel and U.S.A.; world travelling exhbn. 1979-; group exhbns., incl. travelling exhbns. with Wiener Schule des Phantastischen Realismus 1962-, in W. Europe, U.S.A., S. America, England, Yugoslavia, Israel, Iran, Turkey, Japan; Scenery for The Seven Mortal Sins (Vienna 1972), Bomarzo (Zürich 1970); scenery and costumes for Medea (Vienna 1972), The Magic Flute (Paris 1977); book, design and costumes for Sieben auf einen Streich (Vienna 1978); mural design for Univ. of Haifa, Israel 1982-; Guest Lecturer, Int. Summer Acad. for Fine Arts, Salzburg 1982, 83; two gold records for Erich Brauer LP (poetry, music and songs) 1971. *Publications:* Zigeunerziege 1976, Runde Fliegt 1983. *Leisure interests:* alpinism, skiing, windsurfing. *Address:* c/o Joram Harel Management, P.O. Box 28, A-1182 Vienna, Austria. *Telephone:* 34-71-60.

BRAUER, Jerald Carl, A.B., B.D., PH.D.; American church historian and educator; b. 16 Sept. 1921, Fond du Lac, Wisconsin; s. of Carl L. and Anna M. Brauer; m. Muriel I. Nelson 1945; two s. one d.; ed. Carthage Coll., Northwestern Lutheran Theological Seminary and Univ. of Chicago; Instructor, Church History and History of Christian Thought, Union Theological Seminary, New York City 1948-50; Asst. Prof. of Church

History, Federated Theological Faculty, Univ. of Chicago 1950–54, Assoc. Prof. 1954–59, Prof. 1959–; Dean, Federated Theological Faculty 1955–60; Visiting Prof. Univ. of Frankfurt 1961; Naomi Shenstone Donnelley Prof. History of Christianity 1969–, Dean, Divinity School 1960–70; Visiting Lecturer Univ. of Tokyo and Kokugakin Univ. 1966; mem. Bd. of Augustana Coll.; mem. Bd. of Theological Educ., Lutheran Church in America 1961–70; Pres. 1961–68; mem. Bd. of Govs., International House 1970–, Pres. 1973–; Fellow, Center for Policy Studies, N.Y. Educ. Dept. 1969–, Nat. Endowment of the Humanities 1977–78; Visiting Fellow, Center for the Study of Democratic Insts. 1972, 1974; Trustee, Council on Religion and Int. Affairs, Chair. of Bd. 1979–83; Del. of Lutheran Church in America to Lutheran World Fed. Assembly, Helsinki 1963; Observer to Vatican Council Sessions 1964, 1965; mem. American Soc. of Church History, Pres. 1961; Hon. D.D. (Miami), Hon. L.L.D. (Carthage Coll.), Hon. S.T.D. (Ripon Coll.), Hon. L.H.D. (Gettysburg Coll.). *Publications:* Protestantism in America 1953, rev. edn. 1966, Luther and the Reformation (with Jaroslav Pelikan) 1953, Basic Questions for the Christian Scholar 1954; Ed.: The Future of Religions by Paul Tillich 1966, Essays in Divinity (8 vols.) 1967, My Travel Diary by Paul Tillich 1970, Westminster Dictionary of Church History 1971, Religion and the American Revolution 1976, The Lively Experiment Continued 1987. *Leisure interests:* painting, music, drama. *Address:* Swift Hall 207, Univ. of Chicago, Chicago, Ill. 60637 (Office); 5620 South Blackstone Avenue, Chicago, Ill. 60637, U.S.A. (Home). *Telephone:* (312) 753-4061 (Office); (312) 493-6886 (Home).

BRAUMAN, John I., PH.D.; American professor of chemistry; b. 7 Sept. 1937, Pittsburgh, Pa.; s. of Milton and Freda S. Brauman; m. Sharon Lea Kruse 1964; one d.; ed. M.I.T. and Univ. of California (Berkeley and Los Angeles); Asst. Prof., Stanford Univ. 1963–69, Assoc. Prof. 1969–72, Prof. 1972–80, J. G. Jackson-C. J. Wood Prof. 1980–, Chair. 1979–83; Deputy Ed. Science 1985–; mem. Editorial Bds. several journals including Nouveau Journal de Chimie 1977–85, Chemical Physics Letters 1982–85, Chemical and Engineering News 1982–84, Journal of Physical Chemistry 1985–87; mem. Nat. Research Council Bd. on Chemical Sciences and Tech., advisory panels of NASA, Nat. Science Found., Atomic Energy Comm.; mem. N.A.S. and A.A.A.S.; Award in Pure Chemistry and Harrison-Howe Award, American Chemical Soc., James Flack Norris Award in Physical Organic Chemistry, Arthur C. Cope Scholar Award. *Publications:* over 200 publs. in scientific journals. *Address:* Department of Chemistry, Stanford University, Stanford, Calif. 94305 (Office); 849 Tolman Drive, Stanford, Calif. 94305, U.S.A. (Home). *Telephone:* (415) 497-3023 (Office); (415) 493-1378 (Home).

BRAUN, Fernand; Luxembourg administrator; b. 14 March 1925, Esch-sur-Alzette; ed. Paris Univ.; Journalist 1950–58; joined EEC 1958, Chef de Cabinet to Head of Luxembourg del. to EEC Comm., then Chef de Div., Secr.; Dir. for Industry, Commerce and Crafts, Directorate-Gen. of Internal Market 1961; mem. del. to negotiations of Kennedy Round; Chef de Cabinet to Luxembourg mem. of Comm. responsible for transport 1967–68; Prin. Adviser Directorate-Gen. of Industrial Affairs 1968–69, Asst. Dir.-Gen. 1969–73; Dir.-Gen. of Internal Market 1973–77, of Internal Market and Industrial Affairs 1977–. *Address:* Directorate-General of Internal Market, Commission of the European Communities, 200 rue de la Loi, 1049 Brussels, Belgium. *Telephone:* 35 00 40; 35 80 40.

BRAUN, Pinkas; Swiss actor and director; b. 7 Jan. 1923, Zürich; s. of Chaja and Nathan Braun; m. (divorced); one s. one d.; ed. drama school, Zürich; mem. of co. of Schauspielhaus Zürich 1945–50, 1952–56; own co. 1950–51; freelance 1957–; has undertaken theatre work as actor and Dir. in Germany, Austria and Israel, and television and cinema work in Germany, Austria, France, Italy and U.K. *Roles include:* Woyzeck, Baron (in Nachtasyl), Pelegrin (in Santa Cruz), Salieri (in Amadeus), Shylock (in The Merchant of Venice), Iago (in Othello). *Publications:* translation into German of all of Edward Albee's plays. *Address:* Unterdorf, CH 8261 Hemishofen /SH, Switzerland. *Telephone:* 054/413370.

BRAUN, Baron Sigismund von; German diplomatist (retd.); b. 15 April 1911, Berlin; s. of the late Baron Magnus von Braun and Emmy von Braun (née von Quistorp); m. Hildegard Margis 1940; one s. four d.; ed. Univs. of Hamburg, Berlin, and Cincinnati, Ohio; Counsellor, German Embassy, London 1953–58; Chief of Protocol, Foreign Office, Bonn 1958–62; Observer (with rank of Amb.) of Fed. Repub. of Germany to the UN 1962–68; Amb. to France 1968–70, 1972–76; State Sec. Ministry of Foreign Affairs 1970–72; Dr. h.c. and numerous decorations. *Leisure interest:* shooting. *Address:* Graf Stauffenbergstrasse 21, D-5300 Bonn, Federal Republic of Germany. *Telephone:* 235621.

BRAUNFELS, Michael; German composer, pianist and teacher; b. 3 April 1917, Munich; s. of Walter and Bertele (von Hildebrand) Braunfels; m. Mechthild Russel 1954; two s. three d.; studied piano in Basle under Paul Baumgartner and composition with Frank Martin; concert pianist in all West European music centres, Near East, Asia and Africa 1949–; Prof. of Piano, Cologne Music Coll. 1954–. *Compositions include:* 2 piano concertos, Cembaloconcerto 1956, Oboe concerto 1960, Symphony for 12 celli 1975, Concerto for cello and piano with orchestra 1976, Concerto for string trio and string orch. 1978, Das Parlament (variations for orchestra) 1982, Sinfonietta serena seria 1984, The King's Messenger (musical for children), chamber music, lieder and piano music. *Leisure interest:* history. *Address:*

Dransdorferstrasse 40, D-5000 Cologne 51, Federal Republic of Germany. *Telephone:* (0221) 383660.

BRAUNITZER, Gerhard, DR.RER.NAT.; German biochemist; b. 24 Sept. 1921, Marburg; s. of Alfons Braunitzer and Fanny Werdisch; m. Heide Butenandt 1965; one s. two d.; ed. Univs. of Graz, Tübingen and Munich; Asst. Max-Planck-Inst. für Biochemie, Tübingen 1950, Munich 1964; Scientific mem. Max-Planck-Gesellschaft 1964; Dir. Dept. of Proteinchemistry, Max-Planck-Inst. für Biochemie, Martinsried 1972–; mem. Deutsche Akad. der Naturforscher Leopoldina, Bavarian Acad. of Sciences, Serbian Acad. of Arts and Sciences; Annual award of Bavarian Acad. of Sciences 1962; Feldberg Prize 1965; one prize one medal from Univ. of Brussels. *Leisure interest:* chamber music. *Address:* Max-Planck-Institut für Biochemie, 8033 Martinsried, Federal Republic of Germany.

BRÄUTIGAM, Hans Otto, D.JUR., LL.M.; German diplomatist; b. 6 Feb. 1931, Völklingen, Saar; s. of Maximilian Bräutigam and Margarethe Senewald; m. Dr. Hildegard Becker 1961; two s. one d.; ed. Bonn Univ. and Harvard Law School; research asst. in int. law, Heidelberg 1958–62; served in foreign service of Fed. Repub. of Germany 1962–74; Deputy Head, Perm. Representation of Fed. Repub. of Germany to German Democratic Repub. (G.D.R.) 1974–77, Head 1982–; Dir. Fed. Chancellor's Office, Bonn 1977–80; Foreign Office, Bonn 1980–82. *Leisure interests:* arts, mountain climbing. *Address:* Hannoversche Strasse 30, 1040 Berlin, German Democratic Republic.

BRAY, John Jefferson, A.C., LL.D.; Australian lawyer and poet; b. 16 Sept. 1912, Adelaide; s. of Harry Midwinter Bray and Gertrude Eleanore Midwinter (née Stow); ed. St. Peter's Coll., Adelaide, Univ. of Adelaide; admitted to South Australian Bar 1933; Q.C. 1957; Chief Justice of South Australia 1967–78; Chancellor Univ. of Adelaide 1968–83; mem. State Library Bd. 1944–87. *Publications:* Poems 1962, Poems 1961–1971 1972, Poems 1972–1979 1979, The Bay of Salamis and Other Poems 1986, Satura: Selected Poetry and Prose 1988, The Emperor's Doorkeeper: Occasional Addresses 1988. *Leisure interests:* reading, walking, swimming. *Address:* 39 Hurtle Square, Adelaide, South Australia 5000. *Telephone:* 223 4196; (08) 2234196.

BRAYBROOKE, David, PH.D.; Canadian philosopher, university professor and author; b. 18 Oct. 1924, Hackettstown, N.J.; s. of Walter Leonard Braybrooke and Netta Rose Foyle; m. 1st Alice Boyd Noble 1948 (divorced 1982), 2nd Margaret Eva Odell 1984; two s. one d.; ed. Hobart Coll., New School for Social Research, Downing Coll., Cambridge, U.K., Harvard and Cornell Univs., U.S.A., New College, Oxford, U.K.; Instructor, History and Literature, Hobart and William Smith Colls. 1948–50; Teaching Fellow, Econ., Cornell Univ. 1950–52; Instructor, Philosophy, Univ. of Mich., U.S.A. 1953–54, Bowdoin Coll. 1954–56; Asst. Prof. of Philosophy, Yale Univ., U.S.A. 1956–63; Assoc. Prof. of Philosophy and Politics, Dalhousie Univ., Halifax 1963–65, Prof. 1965–; Fellow American Council of Learned Socs. 1952–53; Rockefeller Foundation Grant 1959–60; Guggenheim Fellow 1962–63; Leave Fellowships, Canada Council etc.; Visiting Fellow, Wolfson Coll., Cambridge, U.K. 1985–86. *Publications:* A Strategy of Decision: Policy Evaluation as a Social Process (with C. E. Lindblom) 1963, Philosophical Problems of the Social Sciences 1965, Three Tests for Democracy 1968, Traffic Congestion Goes through the Issue-Machine 1974, Ethics in the World of Business 1983, Philosophy of Social Science 1987, Meeting Needs 1987. *Leisure interests:* reading (poetry, fiction, history), listening to music, walking, swimming. *Address:* Department of Philosophy, Dalhousie University, Halifax, N.S. B3H 3J5; Department of Political Science, Dalhousie University, Halifax, N.S. B3H 4H6; 6045 Fraser Street, Halifax, N.S. B3H 1R7, Canada (Home). *Telephone:* (902) 424-3810 (Dept. of Philosophy); (902) 424-2396 (Dept. of Political Science); (902) 422-5086 (Home).

BRAYER, Yves; French painter; b. 18 Nov. 1907, Versailles; s. of Gen. Victor Brayer and Lydie Passabosk; m. Hermione Falex 1945; one s.; ed. Ecole Nationale des Beaux-Arts, Paris; exhibited in Paris, New York, London, Nice 1959, 1967, Geneva 1961, Bordeaux 1963, Madrid 1963, Cologne, Berlin, Japan 1981; sets and costumes for ballet at the Paris Opéra, Royal Opera in Amsterdam and Festival of Cimiez; in addition to watercolours, etchings and lithographic works, has painted murals for public buildings and illustrated numerous books; work represented in Musée National de l'Art Moderne, Paris and in numerous museums and private collections throughout the world; Prof., Acad. de la Grande Chaumière; Hon. Pres. Salon d'automne; mem. Inst. de France; Ex.-Dir. Musée Marmottan, Paris; Premier Grand Prix, Rome 1930; Officier Légion d'honneur, des Palmes académiques, Commdr. des Arts et des Lettres, Commdr. dell'Ordine al Merito della Republica (Italy). *Address:* 22 rue Monsieur le Prince, 75006 Paris, France. *Telephone:* 43 54 00 01.

BREAM, Julian, C.B.E.; British guitarist and lutanist; b. 15 July 1933; m. 1st Margaret Williamson; one adopted s.; 2nd Isobel Sanchez 1980; ed. Royal Coll. of Music; began professional career Cheltenham 1947, London début, Wigmore Hall 1950; tours in Europe, America, Japan, Australia, India and the Far East; appeared at festivals at Aldeburgh, Bath, Edinburgh, Three Choirs, King's Lynn, Holland, Ansbach, Berlin, and Stratford (Canada); research into Elizabethan Lute music which led to revival of interest in that instrument; has encouraged contemporary English compositions for the guitar (incl. works by Britten, Walton and Tippett);

formed Julian Bream Consort 1960; inaugurated Semley Festival of Music and Poetry 1971; F.R.C.M. 1981; Hon. D.Univ. (Surrey) 1968, A.R.A.M. 1969, F.R.N.C.M. 1983, Hon. D.Mus. (Leeds) 1984. *Leisure interests:* playing the guitar, cricket, table tennis, gardening, backgammon. *Address:* c/o Harold Holt Ltd., 31 Sinclair Road, London, W.14, England. *Telephone:* 01-603 4600.

BREARLEY, John Michael (Mike), O.B.E.; British cricketer and psychoanalyst; b. 28 April 1942, Harrow, Middlesex; s. of Horace and Midge Brearley; ed. City of London School and St. John's Coll., Cambridge; right-hand batsman, occasional wicket-keeper; played for Cambridge Univ. 1961-64, captained Cambridge Univ. 1963, 1964; awarded county cap (Middlesex) 1964; Capt. of Middlesex (winning County Championships four times and Gillette Cup twice) 1971-82; Test debut 1976; Capt. of England 1977-80, 1981 (four Tests); went on tours of South Africa 1964-65, Pakistan 1967, India, Sri Lanka and Australia 1976-77, Pakistan 1977-78, Australia 1978-79, Australia and India 1979-80; holds record for most runs scored at Cambridge Univ. (4,310 at an average of 38.48) 1964; scored 312 not out for M.C.C. under-25 v. North Zone, Peshawar 1966-67; Lecturer in Philosophy, University of Newcastle upon Tyne 1968-71; Counsellor, Westminster School. *Publications:* (with Dudley Doust) The Return of the Ashes 1978, (with Dudley Doust), The Ashes Retained 1979, Phoenix: the Series that Rose from the Ashes 1982, The Art of Captaincy 1985. *Address:* c/o Middlesex County Cricket Club, Lord's Cricket Ground, St. John's Wood Road, London, NW8 8QN, England. *Telephone:* 01-289 1300.

BREAUX, John B., J.D.; American politician; b. 1 March 1944, Crowley, La.; s. of Ezra Breaux and Katie Breaux; m. Lois Gail Daigle 1964; two s. two d.; ed. Southwestern Univ. and State Univ. of Louisiana; called to La. Bar 1967; Partner Brown, McKernan, Ingram and Breaux 1967-68; Legislative Asst. to U.S. Congressman 1968-69; Dist. Asst. 1969-72; mem. 92nd-99th Congresses from 7th Dist., La. 1971-87; Senator from Louisiana Jan. 1987-; mem. House of Democrats Policy and Steering Cttee.; mem. Senate Cttee. on Commerce, Science and Transportation, on Environment and Public Works, Special Cttee. on Aging, Democratic Leadership Council; Chair. Nuclear Regulation Subcttee, Democratic Senatorial Campaign Cttee., Nat. Water Alliance 1987-88; fmr. Chair House Subcttee. on Fisheries and Wildlife and the Environment; American Legion Award; Neptune Award, American Oceanic Org. 1980; Democrat. *Address:* 516, Hart Senate Office Building, U.S. Senate, Washington, D.C. 20510, U.S.A. *Telephone:* (202) 224-4623.

BRECHER, Michael, PH.D., F.R.S.C.; Canadian professor of political science; b. 14 March 1925; s. of Nathan Brecher and Gisela Hopmeyer; m. Eva Danon 1950; three d.; ed. McGill and Yale Univs.; mem. Faculty, McGill Univ. 1952-, Prof. of Political Science 1963-; Visiting Prof. Univ. of Chicago 1963, Hebrew Univ. Jerusalem 1970-75, Univ. of Calif. Berkeley 1979, Stanford Univ. 1980; Nuffield Fellow 1955-56; Rockefeller Fellow 1964-65; Guggenheim Fellow 1965-66; many other awards and distinctions. *Publications:* The Struggle for Kashmir 1953, Nehru: A Political Biography 1959, The New States of Asia 1963, Succession in India 1966, India and World Politics 1968, Political Leadership in India 1969, The Foreign Policy System of Israel 1972, Decisions in Israel's Foreign Policy 1975, Studies in Crisis Behavior 1979, Decisions in Crisis 1980, Crisis and Change in World Politics 1986, Crises in the 20th Century: Handbook of International Crises, (Vol I, II) 1987, over 50 articles in journals. *Address:* McGill University, 855 Sherbrooke Street West, Montreal, P.Q., H3A 2T7, Canada (Office); 5 Dubnov Street, Jerusalem, Israel (Home). *Telephone:* 514-398-4816 (Office).

BRECKENRIDGE, Alasdair Muir, M.D., M.SC., F.R.C.P.; British professor of clinical pharmacology; b. 7 May 1937, Arbroath, Scotland; s. of Thomas Breckenridge and Jane Breckenridge; m. Jean M. Boyle 1967; two s.; ed. Bell-Baxter School, Cupar, Fife and Univ. of St. Andrews; House Physician and Surgeon, Dundee Royal Infirmary 1961-62; House Physician, Registrar, Lecturer, Sr. Lecturer, Hammersmith Hosp. and Royal Postgrad. Medical School 1963-74; Prof. of Clinical Pharmacology, Univ. of Liverpool 1974-; mem. Cttee. on Safety of Medicines 1981-; Councillor Int. Union of Pharmacology 1981-87; Foreign Sec. British Pharmacological Soc. 1983-; Vice-Chair. Advisory Cttee. on Drugs 1985-; Goulstonian Lecturer, Royal Coll. of Physicians 1975; Paul Martini Prize for Clinical Pharmacology 1974. *Publications:* articles in scientific and medical journals. *Leisure interests:* stock market, golf. *Address:* Department of Pharmacology and Therapeutics, University of Liverpool, Liverpool, L69 3BX (Office); Cree Cottage, Feather Lane, Wirral, L69 3BX, England (Home). *Telephone:* 051-709 6022 (Office); 051-342 1096 (Home).

BREDSDORFF, Elias, DR. PHIL.; Danish author and retd. university reader; b. 15 Jan. 1912, Roskilde; s. of Thomas Bredsdorff and Margrete Lunn; m. 1st Marlie Brande 1935, 2nd Anne Lise Neckelmann 1954; one s. one d.; ed. Roskilde Grammar School, Copenhagen Univ. and Univ. Coll. London; lecturer, Vordingborg Teachers' Training Coll. 1939-43; underground activities in Danish Resistance Movt. 1943-45; Ed. Frit Danmark 1945-46; Queen Alexandra Lecturer in Danish, Univ. Coll. London 1946-49; lecturer in Danish, Univ. of Cambridge 1949-60; Reader and Head of Dept. of Scandinavian Studies 1960-79; Fellow, Peterhouse, Cambridge 1963-79, Fellow Emer. 1979-; Ed. Scandinavica 1962-75; Fellow, Royal Danish Soc.; Hans Christian Andersen Award 1975. *Publi-*

cations: D. H. Lawrence 1937, Hans Christian Andersen and Charles Dickens 1956, Hans Christian Andersen og England 1954, Henrik Pontoppidan og Georg Brandes 1-2 1964, Den store nordiske krig om seksualmoralen 1973, Hans Christian Andersen: The Story of his Life and Work 1975. *Leisure interest:* travel. *Address:* Kronprinsesse Sofiesvej 28, 2000 Copenhagen F, Denmark. *Telephone:* 01 199117.

BRÉE, Germaine; French university professor; b. 2 Oct. 1907, Lasalle, Gard; d. of Walter Brée and Lois Andrault; ed. Jersey Ladies Coll., St. Helier, Jersey, Univ. de Paris, Bryn Mawr Coll., U.S.A.; teacher Lycée d'Oran 1932-36; Prof. of French Bryn Mawr Coll., U.S.A. 1936-53; Chair. French Dept. Washington Square Coll., Univ. of New York 1953-54; Head Romance Languages Graduate School, New York 1954-57, at Univ. of New York 1957-60; Prof. Inst. Research in Humanities Univ. of Wis. 1960-73; Visiting Prof. at Princeton, Williams, Wis. and Ohio State Univs.; Kenan Prof. of Humanities at Wake Forest Univ. 1973-85, Prof. Emer. 1985-; mem. Asscn. int. des études françaises, Modern Language Asscn., Pres. 1976; mem. PEN Club, American Acad. Arts and Sciences; Chevalier, Légion d'honneur, Bronze Star Medal. *Publications:* Du temps perdu au temps retrouvé, An Age of Fiction (with Margaret Guiton), Du Surréalisme à l'Empire de la Critique (with Ed Morot) 1981, Albert Camus, André Gide, l'insaisissable Protée, The World of Marcel Proust, Camus and Sartre: crisis and commitment, Women Writers in France, Littérature française (Vol. 16) XXᵉ siècle, 1920-1970. *Address:* 2135 Royall Drive, Winston-Salem, N.C. 27106, U.S.A.

BRÉGOU, Christian Robert; French publisher; b. 19 Nov. 1941, Neuilly-sur-Seine, Hauts-de-Seine; s. of Robert Brégou and Lucienne Poirier; m. Florence Bourgois 1966; two s.; ed. Inst. de Sainte-Croix, Neuilly, Lycée Carnot, Paris and École Supérieure des Sciences Économiques et Commerciales; apptd. Financial Dir. Havas Group 1971; Dir.-Gen. C.E.P. Communication 1975, Pres. 1979-; Pres. Dir.-Gen. de Groupe Larousse-Nathan 1984-; mem. Bd. Centre Français du Commerce Extérieur. *Leisure interests:* golf, tennis, horse-riding. *Address:* 13 rue Bonaparte, 75006 Paris, France (Home).

BREGVADZE, Nani Georgevna; Soviet-Georgian singer; b. 1938; ed. Tbilisi Conservatoire (pianoforte class under Machutadze); soloist with Georgian State Philharmonic Orchestra 1959-, with Georgian popular orchestra 'Rero' 1959-64, with 'Orera' 1964-; specialises in Georgian music and Russian romances; has toured abroad on numerous occasions; People's Artist of U.S.S.R. 1983. *Address:* Georgian State Philharmonic Orchestra, Tbilisi, Georgian S.S.R., U.S.S.R.

BREITKOPF, Jerzy, LL.M.; Polish journalist and politician; b. 13 Sept. 1930, Wilno (now Vilnius), Lithuania; ed. Law Faculty of Warsaw Univ.; fmr. journalist in press of Gen. Board of Polish Youth Union (ZMP), Drużyna and Sztandar Młodych; staff mem., man. sub-editor of journal Rada Narodowa, subsequently journals Gospodarka, Administracja; active in youth movement incl. Deputy Commdr.-in-Chief, Polish Pathfinders' Union (ZHP) 1957-59, mem. ZHP Cen. Revisional Comm. 1973-81; Head, Team for Co-operation with Nat. Councils and Inhabitants' Self-Govt., All-Poland Cttee. of Nat. Unity Front 1973-77; Dir. Chair.'s Office, Chancellery of State Council 1978-83, Acting Chief, Chancellery of State Council 1983-84, Chief April 1984-; mem. Polish United Workers' Party (PZPR). *Address:* Kancelaria Rady Państwa, ul. Wiejska 4/6, 00-902 Warsaw, Poland.

BREITSCHWERDT, Werner; German business executive; b. 23 Sept. 1927, Stuttgart; m. Nelly Breitschwerdt; two c.; joined Daimler-Benz AG 1953, mem. Admin. Bd. 1979, Chair. 1983-87; mem. Supervisory Bd. AEG, Dornier GmbH, MTU Gesellschaft; Hon. Prof. Univ. of Karlsruhe; Hon. Dir. Ing. (Bochum) 1982. *Address:* Daimler-Benz AG, Mercedesstrasse 136, 7000 Stuttgart 60, Federal Republic of Germany.

BREKHOV, Konstantin Ivanovich; Soviet engineer and politician; b. 6 March 1907; ed. Kharkov Machine Building Inst; Engineer, machine-building factories 1931-42; mem. CPSU 1931-; Dir. Irkutsk Heavy Machine-Building Works 1944-54; Deputy Minister of Building and Road Machine Building U.S.S.R. 1954-57; econ. work, Moscow Region 1957-59; Chair. Moscow Regional Econ. Cttee. 1959-64; Chair State Cttee. for Building of Machinery for Chemical and Oil Industries 1964-65; U.S.S.R. Minister for Chemical and Oil Eng. 1965-86; Cand. mem. Cen. Cttee. of CPSU 1961-71, mem. 1971-; Deputy to Supreme Soviet of U.S.S.R. 1962-; Order of Lenin (twice) and other decorations. *Address:* c/o Ministry for Chemical and Oil Engineering, 25 Bezbozhny Pereulok, Moscow, U.S.S.R.

BREKHOVSKIKH, Leonid Maksimovich, D.SC.; Soviet physicist; b. 6 May 1917, Strunkino Village, Arkhangelsk Region; ed. Perm. State Univ; jr. research worker, sr. research worker, Head of Dept., Inst. of Physics, U.S.S.R. Acad. of Sciences 1939-54; Dir. Inst. of Acoustics 1954-64, Head of Laboratory 1964-; Sec.-Academician, Dept. of Oceanography, Physics of Earth Atmosphere and Geography, U.S.S.R. Acad. of Sciences 1969-; mem. CPSU 1959-; Prof. Moscow Univ. 1953; Corresp. mem. U.S.S.R. Acad. of Sciences 1953-68, mem. 1968-; State Prize 1950, 1976. *Publications:* numerous scientific works in fields of ocean acoustics, radiophysics and theoretical physics. *Address:* U.S.S.R. Academy of Sciences, 14 Leninski Prospekt, Moscow, U.S.S.R.

BREMRIDGE, Sir John Henry, K.B.E., M.A.; British colonial administrator; b. 12 July 1925, White River, South Africa; s. of Godfrey and Monica (née Bennett) Bremridge; m. Jacqueline Everard 1956; two s. two d.; ed. Dragon School, Cheltenham, St. John's Coll., Oxford; served Rifle Brigade; Chair. John Swire and Sons (Hong Kong) Ltd. 1973–80; Financial Sec., Hong Kong 1981–86; Chair. John Swire and Sons Ltd., Hon. D.Soc. (Chinese Univ. of Hong Kong) 1980; Hon. D.C.L. (Hong Kong Univ.) 1982. *Leisure interests:* reading, golf, boating, swimming. *Address:* 40 Redburn Street, London, S.W.3; Church House, Bradford-on-Avon, Wilts., England. *Telephone:* 01-351 1657; (022) 16-6136.

BRENCHLEY, Thomas Frank, C.M.G., M.A.; British diplomatist (retd.) and international consultant; b. 9 April 1918, Stockton-on-Tees; s. of Robert B. and Alice (née Brough) Brenchley; m. Edith Helen Helfand 1946 (died 1980), three d.; ed. Merton Coll., Oxford and the Open Univ.; served in British Army 1939–46; entered Civil Service 1947, transferred to Foreign Office 1949; served in Singapore, Cairo, Foreign Office and Middle East Centre for Arabic Studies 1950–59; Khartoum, Jeddah and Foreign Office 1960–66; Asst. Under-Sec. for Middle East Affairs, Foreign and Commonwealth Office 1967–68; Amb. to Norway 1968–72, to Poland 1972–74; Deputy Sec., Cabinet Office 1975–76; Deputy Sec.-Gen., C.E.O. Arab-British Chamber of Commerce 1976–83; Chair. Inst. for the Study of Conflict 1983–. *Publications:* Britain and the Middle East: An Economic History 1945-1987, 1989. *Leisure interests:* collecting books, chess. *Address:* 19 Ennismore Gardens, London, S.W.7, England. *Telephone:* 01-584 7981.

BRENDEL, Alfred; Austrian pianist and writer; b. 5 Jan. 1931, Wiesenberg; s. of Ing. Albert and Ida (née Wieltschnig) Brendel; m. 1st Iris Heymann-Gonzala 1960 (divorced 1972); one d.; 2nd Irene Semler 1975; one s. two d.; studied piano under Sofija Deželić (Zagreb), Ludovika v. Kaan (Graz), Edwin Fischer (Lucerne), Paul Baumgartner (Basel), Edward Steuermann (Salzburg); studied composition under A. Michl (Graz) and harmony under Franjo Dugan (Zagreb); first piano recital 1948; concert tours through Europe, Latin America, North America 1963–; Australia 1963, 1966, 1969, 1976; has appeared at many music festivals, including Salzburg 1960–, Vienna, Edinburgh, Aldeburgh, Athens, Granada, Puerto Rico and has performed with most of the major orchestras of Europe and U.S.A., etc.; numerous recordings, including complete piano works of Beethoven, Schubert's piano works 1822-28; Hon. R.A.M.; Hon. D.Mus. (London) 1978, (Oxford) 1983; Hon. D.Litt. (Sussex) 1981; Premio Città de Bolzano, Concorso Busoni 1949, Grand Prix du Disque 1965, Edison Prize 1974, Grand Prix des Disquaires de France 1975, Deutscher Schallplattenpreis 1976 and 1977, Wiener Flötenruhm 1976, Gramophone Award 1978, Japanese Grand Prix 1978, Franz Liszt Prize 1980, Frankfurt Music Prize 1984, Commdr., Arts et Lettres 1985. *Publications:* essays on music and musicians in Phono, Fono Forum, Österreichische Musikzeitschrift, Music and Musicians, Hi-Fi Stereophonie, Musical Thoughts and Afterthoughts 1976, etc. *Leisure interests:* books, theatre, the visual arts, films, baroque and romanesque architecture, unintentional humour, kitsch. *Address:* c/o Ingpen and Williams, 14 Kensington Court, London, W.8, England. *Telephone:* 01-937 5158.

BRENNAN, Edward A.; American business executive; b. 16 Jan. 1934, Chicago; s. of Edward Brennan and Margaret Bourget; ed. Marquette Univ.; joined Sears, Roebuck and Co., Madison, Wis. as salesman 1956, held several positions in co.'s nat. HQ and elsewhere, Exec. Vice-Pres. South 1977, Pres. of Sears 1980, Chair. and C.E.O. Sears Merchandise Group 1981, Pres. and C.O.O. Sears, Roebuck and Co. 1984–86, Chair. and C.E.O. 1986–; mem. Bd. of Trustees Atlanta, DePaul and Marquette Univs. and Chicago Museum of Science and Industry; mem. Bd. of Govs. United Way of America. *Address:* Sears, Roebuck and Co., Sears Tower, Chicago, Ill. 60684, U.S.A.

BRENNAN, Joseph Edward, B.S., LL.B.; American state governor; b. 2 Nov. 1934, Portland, Me.; s. of John J. and Katherine (née Mulkerin) Brennan; one s. one d.; ed. Boston Coll., and Univ. of Maine; admitted to Maine Bar 1963; pvt. practice, Portland 1963–70; County Attorney, Cumberland County 1971–72; partner Brennan and Brennan, Portland 1972–74; Attorney-Gen. State of Maine 1975–79; Gov. of Maine 1979–87; mem. Maine House of Reps. 1965–70, Maine Senate 1973–74; mem. House of Reps. from 1st Maine Dist. 1987–; mem. Nat. Govs. Asscn.; Democrat. *Address:* Room 1535, Longworth House Office Building, Washington, D.C. 20515 (Office); 104 Frances Street, Portland, Me. 04102, U.S.A. (Home).

BRENNAN, William Joseph, Jr., B.S., LL.B.; American judge; b. 25 April 1906, Newark; s. of William Brennan and Agnes McDermott; m. 1st Marjorie Leonard 1928 (deceased), two s. one d.; m. 2nd Mary Fowler 1983; ed. Pennsylvania and Harvard Univs.; admitted to N.J. Bar 1931; practised in Newark, N.J. 1931–49; Superior Court Judge 1949–50, Appellate Div. Judge 1950–52; Justice, Supreme Court of N.J. 1952–56; Assoc. Justice, Supreme Court of the U.S. 1956–; served as Col., Gen. Staff Corps, U.S. Army in Second World War; Legion of Merit; Hon. D.C.L. (New York and Colgate Univs.), Hon. S.J.D. (Suffolk Univ.), Hon. LL.D. (Wesleyan, St. John's, Pa., Rutgers, George Washington, Harvard, Princeton, Columbia, Brandeis, Notre Dame and Yale Univs., Jewish Theological Seminary of America, New York and John Marshall Law Schools, Ohio State Coll. of Law 1987, Yale Univ. 1987). *Address:* Supreme Court of the United States,

Supreme Court Building, 1 First Street N.E., Washington, D.C. 20543, U.S.A. *Telephone:* (202) 252-3000.

BRENNER, Sydney, C.H., M.B., D.PHIL., F.R.S., F.R.C.P.; British scientist; b. 13 Jan. 1927, Germiston, South Africa; s. of Morris Brenner and Lena Blacher; m. May Woolf Balkind; one s. two d.; ed. Univ. of the Witwatersrand, Johannesburg, and Oxford Univ.; Lecturer in Physiology, Univ. of Witwatersrand 1955–57; mem. Scientific Staff of Medical Research Council at M.R.C. Laboratory of Molecular Biology, Cambridge 1957–, and Dir. 1979–86; Medical Research Council 1978–82, 1986–, Dir. MRC Molecular Genetics Unit 1986–; Fellow of King's Coll., Cambridge 1959–; Foreign Hon. mem. American Acad. of Arts and Sciences 1965, Hon. mem. Deutsche Akademie der Natursforscher Leopoldina 1975, Soc. for Biological Chemists 1975; Foreign Assoc. Nat. Acad. of Sciences 1977; Hon. Fellow of Royal Soc. of Edinburgh 1979; Foreign mem. of American Philosophical Soc. 1979; Fellow of the Royal Coll. of Physicians 1979, Foreign Assoc. Royal Soc. of S. Africa 1983, Hon. Fellow, Exeter Coll. 1985; Foreign mem. of Real Academia de Ciencias 1985; External Scientific mem. Max Planck Soc. 1988; mem. Acad Europaea 1989; Hon. Fellow Indian Acad. of Sciences 1989; Hon. D.Sc. (Dublin, Witwatersrand, Chicago, London, Leicester, Oxford); Hon. LL.D. (Glasgow); Warren Triennial Prize 1968, William Bate Hardy Prize, Cambridge Philosophical Soc. 1969, Gregor Mendel Medal of German Acad. of Science Leopoldina 1970, Albert Lasker Medical Research Award 1971, Gairdner Foundation Annual Award (Canada) 1978; Royal Medal of Royal Soc. 1974, Prix Charles Leopold Mayer, French Acad. 1975, Krebs Medal, Fed. of European Biochemical Socs. 1980, Ciba Medal, Biochemical Soc. 1981, Feldberg Foundation Prize 1983, Neil Hamilton Fairley Medal, Royal Coll. of Physicians 1985, Croonian Lecturer Royal Soc. of London 1986, Rosenstiel Award, Brandeis Univ. 1986, Prix Louis Jeantet de Médecine (Switzerland) 1987, Genetics Soc. of America Medal 1987, Harvey Prize, Israel Inst. of Tech. 1987, Hughlings Jackson Medal, Royal Soc. of Medicine 1987, Waterford Bio-Medical Science Award (The Research Inst. of Scripps Clinic) 1988. *Address:* Medical Research Council Molecular Genetics Unit, Hills Road, Cambridge CB2 2QH (Office); 17b St. Edward's Passage, Cambridge, CB2 3PJ, England. (Home).

BRENT, Richard Peirce, PH.D., F.A.A.; Australian professor of computer sciences; b. 20 April 1946, Melbourne; s. of Oscar Brent and Nancy Brent; m. Erin O'Connor 1969; two s.; ed. Melbourne Grammar School, Monash Univ., Stanford Univ., U.S.A.; Research Scientist, IBM T. J. Watson Research Center, Yorktown Heights, New York, U.S.A. 1971–72; Research Fellow etc., A.N.U., Canberra 1972–78, Prof. of Computer Studies 1978–; Australian Math. Soc. Medal 1984. *Publications:* Algorithms for Minimization without Derivatives 1973, Topics in Computational Complexity and the Analysis of Algorithms 1980. *Leisure interests:* music, chess, walking, astronomy. *Address:* Computer Sciences Laboratory, Research School of Physical Sciences, Australian National University, G.P.O. Box 4, Canberra, A.C.T. 2601, Australia. *Telephone:* (61) (62) 44332.

BRENTON, Howard, B.A.; British playwright; b. 13 Dec. 1942, Portsmouth; s. of Donald and Rosalind Brenton; m. Jane Fry 1970; two s.; ed. Chichester High School for Boys and St. Catharine's Coll., Cambridge; resident writer, Royal Court Theatre, London 1972–73; writer-in-residence, Warwick Univ. 1978–79; John Whiting Award 1970, Standard Best Play of the Year Award 1976, Standard Best Play of the Year (jtly. with David Hare) 1985. *Publications:* Revenge 1969, Christie in Love 1969, Hitler Dances 1972, Magnificence 1973, Brassneck (with David Hare) 1973, The Churchill Play 1974, Government Property 1975, The Saliva Milkshake 1975, Weapons of Happiness 1976, Sore throats 1979, Plays for the Poor Theatre 1980, The Romans in Britain 1980, Thirteenth Night 1981, The Genius 1983, Sleeping Policemen (with Tunde Ikoli) 1983, Bloody Poetry 1984, Pravda (with David Hare) 1985, Dead Head 1986, Greenland 1988, Diving for Pearls (novel) 1989. *Leisure interest:* painting. *Address:* c/o Margaret Ramsay Ltd., 14A Goodwins Court, St Martin's Lane, London, WC2 4NL, England. *Telephone:* 01-240 0691.

BRESLOW, Lester, M.D., M.P.H.; American professor of public health; b. 17 March 1915; s. of Joseph Breslow and Mayme Danziger; m. Devra Miller 1967; three s.; ed. Univ. of Minnesota; Dist. Health Officer, Minn. 1941–43; U.S. Army 1943–46; Chief, Bureau of Chronic Diseases, Calif. Dept. of Public Health 1946–60, Div. of Preventative Medicine 1960–65; Dir. Calif. Dept. of Public Health 1965–68; Prof. School of Public Health, Univ. of Calif. (Los Angeles) 1968–, Dean 1972–80, Dir. for Cancer Control Research, Jonsson Comprehensive Cancer Center 1982–86; Sedwick Medal, American Public Health Assnc.; Lasker Award. *Publication:* Health and Ways of Living: The Alameda County Study 1983. *Leisure interest:* gardening. *Address:* School of Public Health, University of California, Los Angeles, Calif. 90024 (Office); 10926 Verano Road, Los Angles, Calif. 90077, U.S.A. (Home).

BRESLOW, Ronald Charles, PH.D.; American professor of chemistry; b. 14 March 1931, Rahway, N.J.; s. of Alexander Breslow and Gladys Fellows; m. Esther Greenberg 1956; two d.; ed. Harvard Univ.; Instructor, Columbia Univ. 1956–59, Assoc. Prof. 1959–62, Prof. 1962–67, Mitchill Prof. of Chem. 1967–; Sloan Fellowship 1961–63; Fellow A.A.A.S. 1986; mem. Nat. Acad. of Sciences, American Acad. of Arts and Sciences, American Philosophical Soc., Exec. Cttee. of Organic Div. of American Chemical Soc.; mem. Ed. Bd. Organic Syntheses 1965–, Bd. of Eds. Journal of Organic Chem. 1968,

Tetrahedron, Tetrahedron Letters 1977, Chemical Eng. News 1980-83; Procurator, N.A.S. 1984; Trustee, American-Swiss Foundation for Scientific Exchange Inc. 1969-71; Chair. Div. of Organic Chem., American Chemical Soc. 1970-71; Chair. Div. of Chem., N.A.S. 1974; Chair. Dept. of Chem., Columbia Univ. 1976-; mem. Advisory Bd., Chemical and Engineering News 1980; Chair. Bd. of Scientific Advisers, Sloan Foundation 1981-; mem. Bd. of Scientific Advisers, Gen. Motors 1982-; Centenary Lecturer, London Chemical Soc. 1972; Trustee, Rockefeller Univ. 1981-; A. R. Todd Visiting Prof., Univ. of Cambridge 1982; Annual Ciba Foundation Lecturer, London 1982; American Chemical Soc. Award in Pure Chem. 1966; Eresinius Award 1966, Mark van Doren Award 1969, Baekeland Medal 1969, Harrison Howe Award 1974, Remsen Medal 1977, Roussel Prize 1978, American Chemical Soc. James Flack Norris Award in Physical Organic Chemistry 1980, Richards Medal in Chemistry 1984, Arthur Cope Award 1987, George Kenner Award 1988, Nichols Medal 1989, Nat. Acad. of Sciences Chemistry Medal 1989. *Publications:* Organic Reaction Mechanisms 1965; over 250 scientific papers. *Address:* 566 Chandler Laboratories, Department of Chemistry, Columbia University, New York, N.Y. 10027, U.S.A. *Telephone:* (212) 280-2170.

BRESSANI, Ricardo, PH.D.; Guatemalan biochemist; b. 28 Sept. 1926, Guatemala; s. of César Bressani and Primina Castignoli de Bressani; m. Alicia Herman 1949; five s. two d.; ed. Univ. of Dayton, Iowa State Univ. and Purdue Univ.; Visiting Prof. M.I.T., Rutgers Univ.; Ed.-in-Chief, Archivos Latino-americanos de Nutrición; Head and Research Dir., Div. of Agric. and Food Sciences, Inst. of Nutrition of Cen. America and Panama (INCAP); Foreign mem. N.A.S., Afralasian Acad. of Sciences; mem. American Inst. of Food Technologists; Babcock Hart Award 1970, McCollum Award 1976, World Science Award "Albert Einstein" 1984; Dr. h.c. (Purdue). *Publications:* over 450 scientific publications in related professional fields including books, monographs and articles in scientific journals. *Leisure interests:* swimming, horseback-riding. *Address:* Institute of Nutrition of Cental America and Panama, Carretera Roosevelt zona 11 Guatemala, 01911, Apartado Postal 1188, Guatemala 01001 (Office); 6a calle "A" 7-71 zona 9, Guatemala City, 01909 Guatemala (Home). *Telephone:* 72 37 62-8 Ext. 221 (Office); 62-1-25 (Home).

BRESSON, Robert; French film writer and director; b. 25 Sept. 1901, Bromont-Lamothe (Puy-de-Dôme); s. of Léon Bresson and Marie-Elisabeth Clausels; m. 1st Leidia Van der Zee 1926, 2nd Marie-Madeleine van der Mersch; ed. Lycée Lakanal, Sceaux; started as painter; made first film 1934; Hon. Pres. Soc. des Réalisateurs de films 1968; Officier Légion d'honneur, Grand Officier Ordre nat. du Mérite, Commdr. Arts et Lettres; Grand Prix du Cinéma français 1943, 1951, Prix Louis-Delluc 1950, Grand Prix du Film d'avant garde 1950, Grand Prix des Arts et des Lettres 1978, Akira Kurosowa Award 1988 and numerous foreign awards. *Films directed include:* Anges du péché 1943, Les dames du Bois de Boulogne 1945, Journal d'un curé de campagne 1951 (Venice Film Festival Grand Prize 1951), Un condamné à mort s'est échappé 1956 (Best Dir. Award, Cannes 1957), Pickpocket 1959 (prix du Meilleur Film de l'année 1960), Le procès de Jeanne d'Arc 1962 (prix spécial, Cannes Festival 1962), Au hasard, Balthasar 1966, Mouchette 1966 (prix du Cinéma français 1967, Hommage unanime du jury Cannes 1967, grand prix, Panama Festival 1968), Une femme douce 1969 (Coquille d'argent, Festival de Saint Sébastien), Quatre nuits d'un rêveur 1971, Lancelot du lac 1974, Le diable probablement 1977 (Ours d'argent, Berlin 1977), l'Argent (Grand Prix, Cannes festival 1983). *Publication:* Notes sur le cinématographe 1975. *Address:* 49 quai de Bourbon, 75004 Paris, France.

BREUER, Rolf-E., DR. JUR.; German Banker; deputy mem. of Bd. of Managing Dirs. Deutsche Bank AG, Frankfurt; Chair. Supervisory Bd. Deutsche Grundbesitz Anlagegesellschaft mbH, Cologne, Deutsche Vermögensbildungsgesellschaft mbH, Frankfurt, Lombardkasse AG, Frankfurt; Vice-Chair. Supervisory Bd. Deutscher Auslandskassenverein AG, Frankfurt, Frankfurter Kassenverein AG, Frankfurt; mem. of Bd. Asia Fund Management Co. S.A., Luxembourg; Chair. Deutsche Bank Capital Markets (Asia), Euro-Clear Clearance System Ltd., London; Vice-Chair. Deutsche Bank Capital Corp., Frankfurt, Deutsche Bank Capital Markets Ltd., London. *Address:* Deutsche Bank, Postfach 10 06 01, D-6000 Frankfurt 1 (Office); Taunusanlage 12, D-6000, Frankfurt am Main, Federal Republic of Germany.

BREWER, Leo, PH.D.; American professor of chemistry; b. 13 June 1919, St. Louis, Mo.; s. of Abraham and Hannah (Resnik) Brewer; m. Rose Strugo 1945; one s. two d.; ed. Calif. Inst. of Tech. and Univ. of California (Berkeley); Research Assoc. Manhattan Dist. Project, Univ. of Calif. (Berkeley); Research Assoc. Lawrence Berkeley Lab. (Univ. of Calif.) 1943-61, Head Inorganic Materials Div. 1961-75, Prin. Investigator 1961-; Assoc. Dir. Lawrence Berkeley Lab. 1967-75; Asst. Prof. Coll. of Chem., Univ. of Calif. 1946-50, Assoc. Prof. 1950-55, Prof. 1955-; mem. N.A.S. 1959-, American Acad. of Arts and Sciences 1979-; Great Western Dow Fellow 1942, Guggenheim Fellow 1950; Leo H. Baekland Award 1953, E. O. Lawrence Award 1961, Palladium Medal and Award of Electrochemical Soc. 1971; several hon. lectureships 1963-67, 1970-72, 1974, 1979, 1981, 1983, 1986; Distinguished Alumni Award, Calif. Inst. of Technology 1974; William Hume-Rothery Award, Metallurgical Soc. A.I.M.E. 1983. *Publi-*

cations: Thermodynamics (co-author) 1961 and numerous articles in professional journals. *Leisure interest:* gardening. *Address:* Department of Chemistry, University of California, Berkeley, Calif. 94720, U.S.A. *Telephone:* (415) 486-5946.

BREWER, Richard George, PH.D.; American atomic physicist; b. 8 Dec. 1928, Los Angeles; s. of Louis Ludwig and Elise Brewer; m. Lillian Magidow 1954; one s. two d.; ed. California Inst. of Technology and Univ. of California, Berkeley; Instructor, Harvard Univ. 1958-60; Asst. Prof., Univ. of Calif., Los Angeles 1960-63; IBM Research Staff mem., San José, Calif. 1963-73; Consulting Prof., Applied Physics, Stanford Univ. 1977-; IBM Fellow, San José, Calif. 1973-; mem. N.A.S.; Fellow American Physical Soc. and Optical Soc. of America; Albert A. Michelson Gold Medal, Franklin Inst. 1979. *Publications:* more than 120 papers in scientific journals. *Leisure interests:* growing magnolias, swimming, classical music, travel, Hawaii. *Address:* IBM Almaden Research Center, 650 Harry Road, San José, Calif. 95120-6099, U.S.A.

BREZHNEV, Vladimir Arkadevich; Soviet politician; b. 1931; ed. Odessa Hydro-technical Inst.; worker at metallurgical plant 1949-55; man. of a trust in the transport-construction industry 1955-75; mem. CPSU 1959-; deputy, first deputy minister 1975-85; Minister of Transport Construction for U.S.S.R. 1985-; cand. mem. of CPSU Cen. Cttee. 1986-; Deputy to U.S.S.R. Supreme Soviet. *Address:* The Kremlin, Moscow, U.S.S.R.

BREZHNEV, Yuriy Leonidovich; Soviet politician; b. 1933, Ukraine; s. of L. I. Brezhnev; ed. Dnepropetrovsk Metallurgical Inst. and U.S.S.R. Acad. of Foreign Trade 1955-60; Deputy Dir. of Bureau of Foreign Trade 1960-65; U.S.S.R. Trade Mission, Sweden 1965-66, Deputy Dir. 1966-68, Dir. 1968-70; Chair. of Foreign Trade Org. dealing in raw materials 1970-76; U.S.S.R. Deputy Minister of Foreign Trade 1976-82, First Deputy 1982-86 (rank of Lieut.-Gen.); cand. mem. of Cen. Cttee. of CPSU 1982-. *Address:* c/o Ministry of Foreign Trade, Moscow, U.S.S.R.

BRICKER, Neal S., M.D.; American physician; b. 18 April 1927, Denver, Colo.; s. of Eli D. Bricker and Rose (Quiat) Bricker; m. 1st Miriam Thalenberg (died 1974), 2nd Ruth Baker 1980; one s. three d.; ed. Univ. of Colorado, School of Medicine; intern and resident, Bellevue Hosp.; mem. staff, Peter Bent Brigham Hosp. and mem. Faculty, Harvard Medical School; Dir. Renal Div., Washington Univ. Medical School 1956-72; Chair. Dept. of Medicine, Albert Einstein Coll. of Medicine, New York 1972; Distinguished Prof. of Medicine, Univ. of Calif., Los Angeles School of Medicine 1978-86; Distinguished Prof. of Medicine, Loma Linda Univ., School of Medicine 1986-; a founder, American Soc. of Nephrology; Pres. American Soc. for Clinical Investigation 1972; mem. N.A.S. Inst. of Medicine 1975; Pres. Int. Congress on Nephrology 1981-84; has lectured extensively throughout the U.S.A., Canada, Western Europe, Asia, Central and S. America; has served on editorial bds. of several leading medical journals; mem. numerous advisory panels etc.; recipient of many int. awards in nephrology and other distinctions. *Publications:* some 150 scientific papers and 37 chapters in textbooks. *Address:* Loma Linda University, School of Medicine, Department of Medicine, Loma Linda, Calif. 92350, U.S.A.

BRIDGES, 2nd Baron; Thomas Edward Bridges, G.C.M.G., M.A.; British diplomatist (retd.); b. 27 Nov. 1927, London; s. of Edward, 1st Baron Bridges, K.G., and Hon. Katharine D. Farrer; m. Rachel M. Bunbury 1953; two s. one d.; ed. Eton and New Coll., Oxford; joined diplomatic service 1951; served Bonn, Berlin, Rio de Janeiro, Athens and Moscow; Asst. Private Sec. to Foreign Sec. 1963-66; Private Sec. (Overseas Affairs) to Prime Minister 1972-74; Commercial Minister, Washington, D.C. 1976-79; Deputy Sec. (for int. econ. affairs), FCO 1979-83; Amb. to Italy Feb. 1983-87; Dir. Consolidated Gold Fields PLC 1988-. *Address:* 73 Church Street, Orford, Woodbridge, Suffolk, IP12 2NT, England.

BRIDGES, Alan; British film director; dir. of numerous films and dramas for TV including The Intrigue, The Ballade of Peckham Rye, Alarm Call: Z Cars, The Brothers Karamazov, The Idiot, Days to Come, Great Expectations, Les Miserables, Dear Brutus etc. *Films include:* Act of Murder, Invasion, The Lie, The Wild Duck, Shelley, The Hireling (Golden Palm Award, Best Film, Cannes Festival 1973), Brief Encounter, Out of Season, Summer Rain, The Girl in Blue Velvet, Very Like a Whale, Rain on the Roof, The Return of the Soldier, The Shooting Party, Displaced Persons. *Address:* c/o John Redway, 16 Berners Street, London, W.1, England.

BRIDGES, Sir Phillip Rodney, Kt., C.M.G., Q.C.; British lawyer; b. 9 July 1922; s. of Capt. Sir Ernest and Lady Bridges; m. 1st Rosemary Ann Streeten 1951 (dissolved 1961), two s. one d.; m. 2nd Angela Mary (née Dearden) Huyton; ed. Bedford School, England; army service 1941-47, Capt. Royal Artillery with Royal West African Frontier Force, W. Africa, India, Burma; admitted as solicitor England 1951; barrister and solicitor, The Gambia 1954; Solicitor-Gen. of The Gambia 1961, Attorney-Gen. 1964, Chief Justice 1968-82. *Address:* Weavers, Coney Weston, Bury St. Edmunds, Suffolk, England.

BRIERLEY, Sir Ronald Alfred, Kt.; New Zealand business executive; b. 2 Aug. 1937, Wellington; ed. Wellington Coll.; Chair. Brierley Investments Ltd. 1961-, Bank of N.Z. 1987-; Chair. Industrial Equity Pacific Ltd., Tozer Kemsley & Millbourn Holdings PLC, The Citizens & Graziers

Life Assurance Co. Ltd., Acmex Holdings Ltd.; Dir. The Australian Gas Light Co., Australian Oil & Gas Corpn. Ltd., Brick & Pipe Industries Ltd., Southern Farmers Group Ltd., New South Wales Investment Corpn.; mem. N.Z. Cricket Council, N.Z. Cricket Foundation; Trustee Sydney Cricket & Sports Ground Trust. *Leisure interests:* cricket, ballet, stamp collecting, chess. *Address:* Level 44, Grosvenor Place, 225 George Street, Sydney, Australia (Office); Level 9, CML Building, 22–24 Victoria Street, Wellington (Office); 2 Bayview Terrace, Wellington, New Zealand (Home). *Telephone:* 235-3700 (Office, Australia); 738-199 (Office, New Zealand).

BRIGGS, Baron (Life Peer), cr. 1976, of Lewes in the County of Sussex; **Asa Briggs**, M.A., B.SC., F.B.A.; British historian; b. 7 May 1921, Keighley, Yorks.; s. of William Walker Briggs and Jane Briggs; m. Susan Anne Banwell 1955; two s. two d.; ed. Keighley Grammar School and Sidney Sussex Coll., Cambridge; Fellow, Worcester Coll., Oxford 1945–55, Reader in Recent Social and Econ. History, Univ. of Oxford 1950–55; Prof. of Modern History, Leeds Univ. 1955–61; Prof. of History, Univ. of Sussex 1961–76, Dean of Social Studies 1961–65, Pro-Vice-Chancellor 1961–67, Vice-Chancellor 1967–Sept. 1976; Provost Worcester Coll., Oxford 1976–; Chancellor, Open Univ. 1979–; Deputy Pres. Workers Educational Asscn. 1954–58, Pres. 1958–67; Chair. Appts. Comm. Press Council 1972–; mem. Univ. Grants Cttee. 1959–67; Trustee, Int. Broadcast Inst. 1968–86; Gov. British Film Inst. 1970–76; Chair. European Inst. of Educ. 1974–; mem. Council of UN Univ. 1974–80; Chair. Advisory Bd. for Redundant Churches 1983–; Chair. Cttee. on Nursing 1970–72, Heritage Educ. Group 1976–86; Pres. Social History Soc. 1976–; Pres. Ephemera Soc. 1982–; Vice-Pres. Historical Asscn. 1986–; Vice-Chair. of Council, UN Univ. 1978–80; mem. American Acad. of Arts and Sciences 1970–; Hon. LL.D., Hon. D.Litt., Hon. D.Sc.; Marconi Medal for Services to Study of Broadcasting 1975; Medal of French Acad. for Architecture 1982. *Publications:* Patterns of Peacemaking (with D. Thomson and E. Meyer) 1945, History of Birmingham, 1865-1938 1952, Victorian People 1954, Friends of the People 1956, The Age of Improvement 1959, Ed. Chartist Studies 1959, History of Broadcasting, Vol. I 1961, Vol. II 1965, Vol. III 1970, Vol. IV 1979, Victorian Cities 1963, The Nineteenth Century (editor) 1970, Cap and Bell (with Susan Briggs) 1972, Essays in the History of Publishing (editor) 1974, Essays in Labour History 1918-1939 1977, Governing the BBC 1979, From Coalbrookdale to the Crystal Palace 1980, The Power of Steam 1982, Marx in London 1982, A Social History of England 1983, The BBC—The First Fifty Years 1985, The Collected Essays of Asa Briggs, (vol. 1, 2), The Franchise Affair (with Joanna Spicer) 1986, Victorian Things 1988. *Leisure interest:* travel. *Address:* Worcester College, Oxford (Office); The Caprons, Keere Street, Lewes, Sussex, England (Home). *Telephone:* Oxford 247777; Lewes 4714704 (Home).

BRIGGS, Raymond Redvers, N.D.D., D.F.A., F.S.I.A.D.; British illustrator, writer and cartoonist; b. 18 Jan. 1934, Wimbledon; s. of Ernest R. Briggs and Ethel Bowyer; m. Jean T. Clark 1963 (died 1973); no c.; ed. Rutlish School, Merton, Wimbledon School of Art and Slade School of Fine Art, London; free-lance illustrator 1957–; children's author 1961–; awards include Kate Greenaway Medal 1966, 1973, and BAFTA Award (British Acad. of Film and Television Arts). *Publications:* The Strange House, 1961, Midnight Adventure 1961, Sledges to the Rescue 1963, Ring-a-Ring o'Roses 1962, The White Land 1963, Fee Fi Fo Fum 1964, The Mother Goose Treasury 1966, Jim and the Beanstalk 1970, The Fairy Tale Treasury 1972, Father Christmas 1973, Father Christmas Goes on Holiday 1975, Fungus the Bogeyman 1977, The Snowman 1978, Gentleman Jim 1980, When the Wind Blows 1982 (stage and radio version 1983, animated film version 1987), The Tinpot Foreign General and the Old Iron Woman 1984, The Snowman Pop-Up 1986, Unlucky Wally 1987, Unlucky Wally Twenty Years On 1989. *Leisure interests:* second-hand books, walking, gardening. *Address:* Weston, Underhill Lane, Westmeston, nr. Hassocks, Sussex, England.

BRIGGS, Winslow Russell, M.A., PH.D.; American biologist; b. 29 April 1928, St. Paul, Minn.; s. of John Briggs and Marjorie (Winslow) Briggs; m. Ann Morrill 1955; three d.; ed. Harvard Univ.; Instructor in Biological Sciences, Stanford Univ. 1955–57, Asst. Prof. 1957–62, Assoc. Prof. 1962–66, Prof. 1966–67; Prof. of Biology, Harvard Univ. 1967–73; Dir. Dept. of Plant Biology, Carnegie Inst. of Washington, Stanford 1973–; Prof. of Biology, Stanford Univ. 1973–; Guggenheim Fellow 1973–74; mem. Nat. Acad. of Sciences. *Publications:* Life on Earth (with others) 1973; articles in professional journals. *Leisure interests:* hiking, Chinese cooking. *Address:* Department of Plant Biology, Carnegie Institution of Washington, 290 Panama Street, Stanford, Calif. 94305 (Office); 480 Hale Street, Palo Alto, Calif. 94301, U.S.A.

BRIGHT, Sir Keith, Kt., PH.D., C.CHEM., F.R.S.C., F.C.I.T.; British industrialist; b. 30 Aug. 1931, Witham, Essex; s. of Ernest W. and Lillian M. Bright; m. 1st Patricia Anne Bright 1959 (divorced), 2nd Margot Joan Norman 1985; one s. two d.; ed. Univ. of London; Chief of Research, Passfield Research Labs.; Man. Dir. Formica Int. Ltd. 1967–73; Group C.E.O. Sime Darby (Holdings) Ltd. 1974–77, Assoc. Biscuit Mfrs. Ltd. 1977–82; Non-Exec. Dir. Extel group 1980–87; London and Continental Advertising Holdings 1979–87; Electrocomponents PLC 1987–; Chair. and C.E.O. London Transport (now London Regional Transport) 1982–88; Nationalised Industries Overseas Group 1987–; mem. Nationalised Industries Chair-

men's Group. *Publications:* 21 papers in technical and scientific journals. *Leisure interests:* music, golf. *Address:* c/o London Regional Transport, 55 Broadway, London, SW1H 0BD, England.

BRIGHTMAN, Baron (Life Peer), cr. 1982, of Ibthorpe in the County of Hampshire; **John Anson Brightman**, Kt., P.C.; British lawyer; b. 20 June 1911, St. Albans, Herts.; s. of William Henry Brightman and Minnie Boston (née Way) Brightman; m. Roxane Ambatielo 1945; one s.; ed. Marlborough Coll., St John's Coll., Cambridge; called to the bar, Lincoln's Inn 1932; Able Seaman 1939–40; Lieut.-Commdr. R.N.V.R. 1940–46; Asst. Naval Attaché Ankara 1944; Q.C. 1961; Bencher 1966; Attorney-Gen., Duchy of Lancaster, and Attorney and Serjeant within the County Palatine of Lancaster 1969–70; a Lord Justice of Appeal 1979–82; a Lord of Appeal in Ordinary 1982–86; Judge, Nat. Industrial Relations Court 1971–74; mem. Gen. Council of the Bar 1956–60, 1966–70; Hon. Fellow, St. John's Coll., Cambridge 1982. *Leisure interests:* sailing, skiing, mountain walking. *Address:* House of Lords, London, S.W.1, England.

BRILLINGER, David Ross, PH.D., F.R.S.C.; Canadian professor of statistics; b. 27 Oct. 1937, Toronto; s. of Austin C. Brillinger and Winnifred E. Simpson; m. Lorie Silber 1961; two s.; ed. Univ. of Toronto and Princeton Univ.; lecturer in Math. Princeton Univ., concurrently mem. tech. staff, Bell Telephone Labs. 1962–64; lecturer, then Reader, London School of Econs. 1964–69; Prof. of Statistics, Univ. of Calif. Berkeley 1969–; Guggenheim Fellow 1975–76, 1982–83. *Publication:* Time Series: Data Analysis and Theory 1975. *Address:* Department of Statistics, University of California, Berkeley, Calif. 94720, U.S.A. *Telephone:* 415-642-0611.

BRIM, Orville G., Jr., PH.D.; American foundation administrator and author; b. 7 April 1923, Elmira, New York; s. of Orville Gilbert and Helen Whittier Brim; m. Kathleen J. Vigneron 1944; two s. two d.; ed. Yale Univ.; Instructor in Sociology, Univ. of Wis. 1952–53, Asst. Prof., Sociologist 1953–55; Sociologist, Russell Sage Foundation, New York 1955–60, Asst. Sec. 1960–64, Pres. 1964–74; Pres. Foundation for Child Devt. 1974–85; Chair., Bd. of Dirs., Automation Eng. Lab. 1959–67, Special Comm. on the Social Sciences, Nat. Science Foundation 1968–69; mem. Drug Research Bd., N.A.S. 1964–65; Vice-Chair., Bd. of Trustees, American Insts. for Research 1971–88, Chair. 1988–; MacArthur Foundation Research Cttee. on Successful Aging 1985–; Kurt Lewin Memorial Award 1979; Social Research in Child Devt. Award for Distinguished Scientific Contribs. to Child Devt. Research 1985. *Publications:* Sociology and the Field of Education 1958, Education for Child Rearing 1959, Personality and Decision Processes 1962, Intelligence: Perspectives 1964, Socialization after Childhood: Two Essays 1966, American Beliefs and Attitudes Toward Intelligence 1969, The Dying Patient 1979; Ed.: Lifespan Development and Behavior, Vols. 2–5 1979–83, Constancy and Change in Human Development 1980. *Leisure interests:* sports and world ocean beaches. *Address:* 503, River Drive, Vero Beach, Fla. 32963, U.S.A.

BRIMELOW, Baron (Life Peer), cr. 1976, of Tyldesley in the County of Lancashire; **Thomas Brimelow**, G.C.M.G., O.B.E.; British diplomatist; b. 25 Oct. 1915, Tyldesley, Lancs.; s. of William Brimelow and Hannah Smith; m. Jean E. Cull 1945; two d.; ed. New Mills Grammar School and Oriel Coll. Oxford; Laming Travelling Fellow, Queen's Coll., Oxford 1937; Probationer Vice-Consul, Danzig 1938; Consulate, Riga 1939, Acting Consul 1940; served in Consulate-Gen., New York 1940; in charge of Consular Section of Embassy, Moscow 1942–45; Foreign Office 1945; First Sec., Havana 1948; in Moscow 1951–54; Counsellor (Commercial) Ankara 1954–56; Head of Northern Dept., Foreign Office 1956–60; Counsellor, Washington 1960–63; Minister, Moscow 1963–66; Amb. to Poland 1966–69; Deputy Under-Sec. Foreign and Commonwealth Office 1969–73; Rep. on Council of WEU 1969–73; Perm. Under-Sec., Head of Diplomatic Service 1973–75; mem. European Parl. (Socialist Group) 1977–78; Chair. Occupational Pensions Bd. 1978–82; Hon. Fellow, Oriel Coll., Oxford 1973, Queen's Coll., Oxford 1974. *Address:* 12 West Hill Court, Millfield Lane, London, N6 6JJ, England. *Telephone:* 01-340 8722.

BRIMMER, Andrew Felton, M.A., PH.D.; American economist and government official; b. 13 Sept. 1926, Newellton, La.; s. of Andrew Brimmer and Vellar Davis Brimmer; m. Doris Millicent Scott 1953; one d.; ed. Univ. of Washington, Univs. of Delhi and Bombay (India), and Harvard Univ.; Teaching Fellow, Harvard Univ. 1954–55; Economist, Fed. Reserve Bank of New York 1955–58; Asst. Prof. of Econs. Michigan State Univ. 1958–61, Asst. Prof. of Finance, Wharton School, Univ. of Pa. 1961–63; Deputy Asst. Sec. for Econ. Affairs, U.S. Dept. of Commerce 1963–65, Asst. Sec. 1965–66; mem. Bd. of Govs. Fed. Reserve System 1966–74; Thomas Henry Carroll Ford Foundation Visiting Prof., Graduate School of Business Admin., Harvard 1974–76; Pres. Brimmer & Co. Inc., Washington 1976–; Dir. Du Pont Co.; Dir. Bank of America, American Security Bank, Int. Harvester Co., United Air Lines, Gannett Co.; fmr. Overseer Harvard Coll.; Gov. Commodity Exchange Inc.; Trustee, Tuskegee Inst., Chair. of Bd. New York Univ.; Fellow, American Acad. of Arts and Sciences, American Philosophical Soc., Nat. Assoc. of Business Economists; mem. American Econ. Assoc., American Finance Assoc., Nat. Economists Club, Council on Foreign Relations, Assoc. for the Study of Afro-American Life and History; Govt. Man of Year, Nat. Business League 1963; Arthur S. Flemming Award 1966; Russworm Award 1966; Golden Plate Award, American Acad. of Achievement 1967; Public Affairs Award of Capital

Press Club; Hon. LL.D. (Marquette, Nebraska Wesleyan, Atlanta, Colgate, Tufts, Michigan, Washington and Southern California Univs., Univ. of Notre Dame and Middlebury, Uppsala and Bishop Colls.), other hon. degrees from Univ. of Miami, Boston and Oberlin Colls., Ohio and Long Island Univ. *Publications:* Life Insurance Companies in the Capital Market 1962, Survey of Mutual Fund Investors (with Arthur Freedman) 1963, Economic Development: International and African Perspectives 1976, The World Banking System: Outlook in a Context of Crisis 1985, International Banking and Domestic Economic Policies 1986; contribs. to many professional journals. *Address:* Brimmer & Co. Inc., 4400 MacArthur Boulevard, N.W., Washington, D.C. 20016, U.S.A. (Office). *Telephone:* 202-667-7176.

BRIND, (Arthur) Henry, C.M.G.; British diplomatist (retd.); b. 4 July 1927; s. of the late T. H. Brind and N. W. B. Brind; m. Barbara Harrison 1954; one s. one d.; ed. St. John's Coll., Cambridge; nat. service 1947-49; in Colonial Admin. Service, Gold Coast/Ghana 1950-60, Regional Sec., Trans-Volta Togoland 1959; joined H.M. Diplomatic Service 1960; Acting High Commr. Uganda 1972-73; High Commr. Mauritius 1974-77; Amb. to Somali Democratic Repub. 1977-80; Visiting Research Fellow, Royal Inst. of Int. Affairs 1981-82; High Commr. in Malawi 1983-87. *Leisure interests:* walking, swimming, books. *Address:* 20 Grove Terrace, London, NW5 1PH, England (Home).

BRINDLEY, Giles Skey, M.A., M.D., F.R.C.P., F.R.S.; British physiologist; b. 30 April 1926; s. of late Arthur James Benet and Dr. Margaret Beatrice Marion Skey; m. 1st Lucy Dunk Bennell 1959 (dissolved); m. 2nd Dr. Hilary Richards 1964; one s. one d.; ed. Leyton Co. High School, Downing Coll., Cambridge, London Hosp. Medical School; clinical and research posts 1950-54; Russian Language Abstractor, British Abstracts of Medical Sciences 1953-56; Demonstrator, then Lecturer and Reader in Physiology, Univ. of Cambridge 1954-68; Prof. of Physiology, Univ. of London Inst. of Psychiatry 1968-; Hon. Dir. MRC Neurological Prostheses Unit 1968-; Hon. Consultant Physician Maudsley Hosp. 1971-; Hon. F.R.C.S.; Fellow King's Coll., Cambridge 1959-62, Trinity Coll., Cambridge 1963-68; Chair. Editorial Bd. Journal of Physiology 1964-66; Visiting Prof. Univ. of Calif., Berkeley 1968; Liebrecht-Franceschetti Prize, German Ophthalmological Soc. 1971, Feldberg Prize, Feldberg Foundation 1974, St. Peter's Medal, British Asscn. of Urological Surgeons 1987. *Publications:* Physiology of the Retina and Visual Pathway 1960, numerous scientific papers. *Leisure interests:* skiing, orienteering, cross-country and track running, designing and playing musical instruments. *Address:* 102 Ferndene Road, London, S.E.24, England. *Telephone:* 01-274 2598.

BRÎNDUS, Nicolae, D.MUS.; Romanian composer; b. 16 April 1935, Bucharest; s. of Niculae Brânduş and Elena Brânduş (née Mahalla); m. Ioana Moroiu Ieronim 1982; two s. one d.; ed. Ciprian Porumbescu Conservatory, Bucharest, piano 1952-56, composition 1960-64; soloist pianist Philharmonic Orchestra, Ploieşti, Romania 1959-69, dir. 1968-69; Prof. at the C. Porumbescu Conservatory, Bucharest 1969-81; ed. Muzica review, Bucharest 1981-; mem. Romanian Composers' Union; mem. S.A.C.E.M. (Société des Auteurs, Compositeurs et Editeurs de Musique, Paris); The Order of Cultural Merit 1969, Prize of the Romanian Composers' Union 1974, Prize of the Romanian Radio and TV 1975, 1977, Prize of the Romanian Acad. 1977. *Works include:* The Ghosts (opera pantomime), Mamsell Hus (cantata), Phtora (cycle for orchestra, chamber ensembles, choir, tapes), Kitsch-N (clarinet/saxophone/flute, tapes), Infrarealism (instrumental theatre), DI$<^{\text{ALO}}_{\text{VA}}>G<^{\text{OS}}_{\text{UES}}$ (piano concert), Rhythmodia (percussion), La ţigănci (At the Gypsies, opera), Syn-Euphonia (electronic poem), Sonata for Two Pianos, Eight Madrigals, Interrelations, (vol. of musical studies). *Leisure interests:* theatre, literature. *Address:* Str. Dr. Felix 101, Bl. 19 sc. A, et. 9, apt. 42, 70672 Bucharest, Romania. *Telephone:* 507409.

BRINK, André Philippus; South African writer; b. 29 May 1935, Vrede; s. of Daniel and Aletta (née Wolmarans) Brink; three s. one d.; ed. Potchefstroom Univ., Sorbonne, Paris; began writing at an early age; first novel (Afrikaans) published 1958; on return from Paris became mem. and spokesman of young Afrikaans writers' group Sestigers; returned to Paris 1968; went back to South Africa with intention of resisting apartheid through writing; novel Kennis van die Aand banned 1973 (first Afrikaans novel to be banned); began to write in English as well; dir. several plays, but abandoned theatre due to censorship; founder-mem. Afrikaans Writers' Guild; Prof. of Afrikaans and Dutch Literature, Rhodes Univ. (previously lecturer) 1980-; C.N.A. Award for Literature, South Africa 1965, 1978 and 1982; Martin Luther King Memorial Prize 1979; Prix Médicis Etranger, France 1979; Légion d'honneur 1983; Officier Ordre des Arts et des Lettres 1987; Hon. D.Litt. (Wits Univ.) 1975. *Publications include:* novels: Looking on Darkness 1974, An Instant in the Wind 1976, Rumours of Rain 1978, A Dry White Season 1979, A Chain of Voices 1982, The Wall of the Plague 1984, The Ambassador 1985; Mapmakers (essays); States of Emergency 1988; several plays 1965-75. *Address:* Rhodes University, 6140 Grahamstown, South Africa.

BRINK, Andries Jacob, M.D., F.R.C.P., D.SC.; South African professor of medicine; b. 29 Aug. 1923, Potchefstroom; s. of Andries J. Brink and Petronella J. Havenga; m. Maria Ruskovich 1949; two s. two d.; ed. Jeppe High School, Univs. of Witwatersrand, Pretoria, and Stellenbosch; Post-Graduate Medical School, Hammersmith Hosp., London 1951; Fellow in Paediatrics, Johns Hopkins Hosp., U.S.A. 1952; Internist, Sr. Lecturer, Univ. of Pretoria 1953-56; Founder Prof. Dept. of Medicine, Univ. of Stellenbosch 1956, Chief Cardiologist and Founder, Dept. of Cardiology 1956-78, Dean, Faculty of Medicine 1971-83; Dir. Molecular and Cellular Cardiac Research Unit, MRC 1956-69, Pres. (part-time) S.A. Medical Research Council 1969-83, Full-time Pres. 1984-; mem. Bd. Scientific Advisory Council to Prime Minister 1972, S.A. Medical and Dental Council 1971; several awards and prizes, including Decoration for Meritorious Service; D.Sc. h.c. (Natal) 1976, (Potchefstroom). *Publications:* 115 scientific and general medical publications. *Leisure interests:* hiking, reading, chess, music. *Address:* South African Medical Research Council, P.O. Box 70, Tygerberg 7505 (Office); 13 Lindenberg Avenue, Durbanville 7550, Republic of South Africa. *Telephone:* (021) 932-0311 (Office); (021) 96-1786.

BRINK, David Maurice, D.PHIL., F.R.S.; British physicist; b. 20 July 1930, Tasmania, Australia; s. of Maurice Ossian Brink and Victoria May (née Finlayson) Brink; m. Verena Wehrli 1958; one s. two d.; ed. Friends' School, Hobart, Univ. of Tasmania, Univ. of Oxford; Rhodes Scholar 1951-54, Rutherford Scholar 1954-58; Lecturer, Balliol Coll., Oxford 1954-58, Fellow and Tutor 1958-; Instructor M.I.T. 1956-57; Rutherford Medal and Prize, Inst. of Physics 1982. *Publications:* Angular Momentum 1962, Nuclear Forces 1965, Semi-Classical Methods 1985. *Leisure interests:* bird-watching, mountaineering. *Address:* 21 Northmoor Road, Oxford, OX2 6UW, England. *Telephone:* (0865) 513613.

BRINK, Frank, Jr., B.S., M.S., PH.D.; American biophysicist; b. 4 Nov. 1910, Easton, Pa.; s. of Frank Brink, Sr., and Lydia (Wilhelm) Brink; m. Marjory Gaylord 1939; one s. one d.; ed. Easton High School, Pennsylvania State Univ., Calif. Inst. of Tech. and Univ. of Pennsylvania; Research Asst. Johnson Research Foundation, Univ. of Pennsylvania 1937-38; Fellow 1938-40; Instructor in Physiology, Cornell Medical Coll., New York City 1940-41; Johnson Foundation Fellow and Lecturer in Biophysics, Univ. of Pa. 1941-47, Asst. Prof. 1947-48; Assoc. Prof. Johns Hopkins Univ. 1948-53; Prof. and mem. Rockefeller Inst. (now Univ.) 1953-81, acting Dean of Graduate Studies 1954-58, Dean of Graduate Studies 1958-72, Detlev W. Bronk Prof. 1974-81, Prof. Emer. July 1981-; White Fellowship, Pa. State Coll. (now Univ.); Lalor Fellowship, Univ. of Pa.; mem. Nat. Acad. of Sciences, American Acad. of Arts and Sciences; Hon. D.Sc. (Rockefeller Univ.) 1983. *Publications:* articles in scientific journals. *Leisure interest:* reading. *Address:* Rockefeller University, New York, N.Y. 10021 (Office); Pine Run, Apt. E-1, Ferry and Iron Hill Roads, Doylestown, Pa. 18901, U.S.A. (Home). *Telephone:* (212) 570-8383 (Office); (215) 348-1792 (Home).

BRINKHOUS, Kenneth Merle, M.D., D.SC.; American pathologist; b. 29 May 1908, Clayton County, Iowa; m. Frances Benton 1936; two s.; ed. Univ. of Iowa; Assoc. in Pathology, Univ. of Iowa 1935-37, Asst. Prof. of Pathology 1937-45, Assoc. Prof. of Pathology 1945-46, Prof. 1946-61; Chair. of Pathology, Univ. of N. Carolina 1946-73, Alumni Distinguished Prof. of Pathology 1961-80, Prof. Emer. 1981-; mem. N.A.S.; Hon. D.Sc. (Univ. of Chicago); several awards including J. F. Mitchell Int. Award for Heart and Vascular Research, N. Carolina Award in Sciences 1969, Murray Thelin Award, Nat. Haemophilia Foundation 1972, Gold Headed Cane Award, American Asscn. of Pathologists 1981, Maude Abbott Award, Int. Acad. of Pathology 1985, Distinguished Service Award, American Medical Asscn. 1986. *Publications:* several publications on haemophilia, blood coagulation, thrombosis atherosclerosis, snake venoms and related topics. *Leisure interests:* travel, reading, hiking. *Address:* Department of Pathology, CB7525, University of North Carolina, School of Medicine, Chapel Hill, N.C. 27514 (Office); 524 Dogwood Drive, Chapel Hill, N.C. 27514, U.S.A. (Home). *Telephone:* (919) 966-1061 (Office); (919) 942-4956 (Home).

BRINKHUES, Josef; German ecclesiastic; b. 21 June 1913, Aachen; s. of Heinrich Brinkhues and Cläre (née Führen); m. Dr Ilse Volckmar 1946; one s. one d.; ed. Frankfurt and Bonn; ordained priest 1937; consecrated bishop 1966; mem. Int. Old Catholics Bishops' Conf. of Utrecht Union 1966-; Bishop Emer. of Old-Catholic Church in Germany. *Leisure interests:* music, walking. *Address:* Oberdorf 18, D-5305 Impekoven/Alfter, Federal Republic of Germany. *Telephone:* (0228) 64 33 01.

BRINKLEY, David; American broadcaster; b. 10 July 1920, Wilmington, N.C.; s. of William G. Brinkley and Mary West; m. 1st Ann Fischer 1946; three s.; m. 2nd Susan Adolph 1972; reporter, Wilmington, N.C. Star-News 1938-41; reporter, bureau man. various cities, United Press Asscn. 1941-43; news writer, broadcaster, radio and TV, NBC, Washington 1943-, Washington Corresp. 1951-81; Anchorman, This Week (ABC) 1981-; duPont Award, Peabody Award, and other awards for journalism. *Address:* ABC News, 1717 DeSales Street, N.W., Washington, D.C. 20036, U.S.A.

BRINKMAN, Leonard Cornelis (Eelco), DR. RER.POL.; Netherlands politician; b. 5 Feb. 1948, Dirksland; m. J. Salentijn; three c.; ed. Gymnasium, Dordrecht, Free Univ., Amsterdam; research post in the Public Admin. Dept., Free Univ. 1969-74; mem. Co-ordination Office for North of West Holland conurbation 1974-75; Head of Office of Sec.-Gen., Ministry of Home Affairs 1976-79, Dir.-Gen. Jan. 1980-82; Minister for Welfare, Health and Cultural Affairs Nov. 1982-; Christian Democratic Alliance. *Publications:* articles on public admin. in specialist journals. *Address:* c/o Ministry of Welfare, Public Health and Culture, Sir Winston Churchilllaan 362-

366, P.O.B. 5406, 2280 EH Rijswijk, Netherlands. *Telephone:* (070) 40-79-11.

BRINNIN, John Malcolm, B.A.; American teacher and author; b. 13 Sept. 1916, Halifax, Canada; s. of John Thomas Brinnin and Frances Malcolm; ed. Univ. of Michigan and Harvard Univ.; Dir., The Poetry Center, New York, N.Y. 1949–57; Instructor in English, Vassar Coll. 1942–47; Assoc. Prof. of English, Univ. of Conn. 1951–62; Emer. Prof. of English, Boston Univ.; mem. Nat. Inst. of Arts and Letters, Award 1968; Centennial Medal for Distinction in Literature (Michigan Univ.), Gold Medal of Poetry Soc. of America. *Publications:* Dylan Thomas in America 1955, The Third Rose, Gertrude Stein and Her World 1958, The Selected Poems of John Malcolm Brinnin 1964, The Sway of the Grand Saloon: A Social History of the North Atlantic 1971, Sextet: T. S. Eliot & Truman Capote & Others 1981. *Leisure interests:* Venice, archaeology. *Address:* King Caesar Road, Duxbury, Mass. 02332, U.S.A. (Home). *Telephone:* (617) 934-5386 (Home).

BRISCO, Milo Martin; American business executive; b. 1912, Maud, Okla.; m.; two s.; ed. Univ. of Oklahoma; with Tropical Oil Co., Colombia, and other affiliates of Standard Oil Co. (N.J.) 1935–51; Asst. Gen. Man. Int. Petroleum, Colombia 1951–53, Gen. Man., Peru 1953, Colombia 1954–56, Exec. Vice-Pres. 1957–61, Pres. 1961–66; mem. Bd. of Dirs. Jersey Standard 1966–69, Vice-Pres. 1967, Exec. Vice-Pres. and mem. Bd. Exec. Cttee. 1968; Pres. Standard Oil Co. (N.J.) 1969–72; Dir. Int. Exec. Service Corps, Econ. Devt. Council New York, American Petroleum Inst., First Nat. City Bank, First Nat. Corpn., Council for Financial Aid to Educ. Inc.; Trustee, Univ. of Miami; mem. Bd. of Govs., United Way of America; mem. American Inst. of Mining, Metallurgical and Petroleum Engineers, New York Urban Coalition Inc., Council on Foreign Relations Inc., Brookings Inst., Econ. Club of New York. *Address:* c/o Exxon Corpn., 1251 Avenue of the Americas, New York, N.Y. 10020, U.S.A.

BRISSENDEN, Robert Francis, A.O., M.A., PH.D.; Australian novelist, poet and former professor; b. 13 March 1928, Wentworthville, N.S.W.; s. of Arthur Piercy Brissenden and Nellie Annie Rogers; m. Rosemary Lorna Groves 1959; two s. one d.; ed. Cowra High School, Sydney Univ. and Univ. of Leeds; Sr. Tutor in English Univ. of Melbourne 1951–52; Asst. Lecturer Canberra Univ. Coll. 1953–54, lecturer and Sr. Lecturer 1957–66; lecturer and Sr. Lecturer in English Australian Nat. Univ. 1957–66, Sr. Research Fellow in History of Ideas 1966–69, Reader in English 1969–85; now full-time novelist and poet; Literary Ed. The Australian 1964–65; Sr. Research Fellow Univ. of California, L.A. 1971; Pres. Australasian and Pac Soc. for 18th Century Studies 1970–76, A.C.T., and Canberra and S.E. Region Environment Centres 1974–81; mem. then Chair. Literature Bd. Australia Council 1977–81; Fellow Australian Acad. of Humanities 1976–. *Publications:* poems: Winter Matins 1971, Elegies 1974, Building a Terrace 1974, The Whale in Darkness 1980, Gough and Johnny were Lovers (light verse) 1984; Virtue in Distress 1974, The Gift of the Forest (with Rosemary Brissenden) 1982, Poor Boy (novel) 1987. *Leisure interests:* gardening, fishing, wine. *Address:* 1 Solander Court, Yarralumla, A.C.T. 2600, Australia. *Telephone:* (062) 81 3386.

BRISTOL, Bishop of (see Tinsley, Rt. Rev. Ernest John).

BRITTAIN, Alfred, III, B.A.; American business executive; b. 22 July 1922, Evanston, Ill.; s. of Alfred, Jr. and Sibyl (née Collins) Brittain; m. Beatrice Memhard 1948; one s. one d.; ed. Phillips Exeter Acad. and Yale Univ.; served with Army Air Corps 1942–46; with Bankers Trust Co., New York 1947–, Nat. Banking Dept. 1951–64, Head of Dept. 1964, later Vice-Pres. Special Industries Div., Asst. Treas. 1951, Asst. Vice-Pres. 1954, Vice-Pres. 1957, First Vice-Pres. 1962, Senior Vice-Pres. 1964, Pres. 1966–74, Chair. 1975–87; Dir. Bankers Trust New York Corpn., Fed. Reserve Bank of New York Dec. 1982–, Philip Morris Inc., Collins & Aikman Corpn., Econ. Devt. Council, New York, New York Chamber of Commerce and Industry, Royal Group Inc., New York Partnership Inc. *Address:* 505 Indian Field Road, Greenwich, Conn. 06830, U.S.A. (Home).

BRITTAN, Rt. Hon. Sir Leon, Kt., P.C., M.A.; British politician and barrister; b. 25 Sept. 1939, London; s. of the late Dr. Joseph Brittan and of Rebecca Brittan; m. Diana Peterson 1980; ed. Haberdashers' Aske's School, Trinity Coll., Cambridge, Yale Univ.; Chair. Cambridge Univ. Conservative Assen. 1960; Pres. Cambridge Union 1960, debating tour of U.S.A. 1961; called to Bar, Inner Temple 1962; Chair. Bow Group 1964–65; contested N. Kensington seat 1966, 1970; Ed. Crossbow 1966–68; mem. Political Cttee. Carlton Club; Vice-Chair. of Govs. of Isaac Newton School 1968–71; M.P. for Cleveland and Whitby 1974–83, for Richmond (N. Yorks.) 1983–89; U.K. Commr. with responsibility for Competition Policy and Financial Insts., Comm. of the European Communities Jan. 1989–; Vice-Chair. Parl. Conservative Party Employment Cttee. 1974–76; Opposition Spokesman on Devolution 1976–78, on Employment 1978–79; Minister of State, Home Office 1979–81; Chief Sec. to the Treasury 1981–83, Home Sec. 1983–85; Sec. of State for Trade and Industry 1985–86; Dir. Phicom 1987–; Distinguished Visiting Fellow Inst. of Political Studies 1988–; Chair. Soc. of Conservative Lawyers 1986–88. *Leisure interests:* walking, cricket, opera. *Publications:* contributed to The Conservative Opportunity, jt. author Millstones for the Sixties, Rough Justice, Infancy and the Law, How to Save your Schools. *Address:* European Parliament, Centre Européen, Plateau de Kirchberg, BP 2929, Luxembourg.

BRITTEN, Roy John, PH.D.; American biophysicist and molecular biologist; b. 1 Oct. 1919, Washington, D.C.; s. of Rollo H. Britten and Marion (Hale) Britten; m. (divorced); two s.; ed. Univ. of Virginia, Johns Hopkins and Princeton Univs.; staff mem. Biophysics Group, Dept. of Terrestrial Magnetism, Carnegie Inst. of Washington 1951–71; inventor, quadrupole focusing of energetic beams; discoverer, repeated DNA sequences in genomes of higher organisms; Visiting Assoc. Calif. Inst. of Tech. and staff mem. Dept. of Terrestrial Magnetism, Carnegie Inst. of Washington 1971–73; Sr. Research Assoc. Calif. Inst. of Tech. and staff mem. Carnegie Inst. of Washington 1973–81; Distinguished Carnegie Sr. Research Assoc. in Biology, Calif. Inst. of Tech. and staff mem. Carnegie Inst. of Washington 1981–; mem. N.A.S., Acad. Arts and Sciences. *Publications:* articles in professional journals. *Leisure interest:* sailing. *Address:* Kerckhoff Marine Laboratory, California Institute of Technology, 101 Dahlia Avenue, Corona del Mar, Calif. 92625, U.S.A. *Telephone:* (714) 675-2159.

BROACKES, Sir Nigel, Kt.; British businessman; b. 21 July, 1934, Wakefield; s. of the late Donald and Nan Broackes; m. Joyce Horne 1956; two s. one d.; ed. Stowe School; with Stewart & Hughman Ltd. 1952–55; Man. Dir. Trafalgar House Investments Ltd. 1958, Deputy Chair. and Jt. Man. Dir. 1968, Chair. 1968–; Chair. London Docklands Urban Devt. Corpn. 1981–84, Ship and Marine Tech. Requirements Bd. 1972–77; Deputy Chair. Offshore Energy Tech. Bd. 1975–77; non-exec. Dir. The Distillers Co. PLC 1985–, Dir. 1986–; British Chair. Euroroute 1984–86; mem. Advisory Council, Victoria and Albert Museum 1980–83; Trustee, Royal Opera House Trust, Nat. Maritime Museum 1987–. *Publication:* A Growing Concern 1979. *Address:* 41 Chelsea Square, London, S.W.3; Checkendon Court, Checkendon, Nr. Reading, Oxon., England.

BROADBENT, Donald Eric, C.B.E., SC.D., F.R.S.; British psychologist; b. 6 May 1926, Birmingham; s. of Herbert Arthur Broadbent and Hannah Elizabeth Broadbent (née Williams); m. 1st Margaret Elizabeth Wright 1949, two d.; m. 2nd Margaret Hope Pattison Gregory 1972; ed. Pembroke Coll., Cambridge; Staff mem. Applied Psychology Unit, Medical Research Council 1949–58, Dir. 1958–74, External Staff 1974–; Pres. British Psychological Soc. 1965, Psychological Section, British Assen. for the Advancement of Science 1967, Experimental Psychology Soc. 1973; Fellow, British Psychological Soc., Acoustical Soc. of America, Human Factors Soc., Wolfson Coll., Oxford, Royal Coll. of Psychiatry, Faculty of Occupational Medicine; Foreign Assoc. N.A.S.; H.M. Vernon Prize, Kenneth Craik Award, Dist. Scientific Contribution Award of American Psychological Assen.; Lister Lecturer, British Assen. for the Advancement of Science; Gregynog Lecturer (Aberystwyth), Pillsbury Lecturer (Cornell), Fitts Lecturer (Michigan), William James Lecturer (Harvard); Fletcher-Stevens Lecturer (Utah), Bartlett Lecturer (Experimental Psychological Soc.); Hon. D.Sc. (Southampton, Loughborough, City, Brussels), Dr. h.c. (York). *Publications:* Perception and Communication 1958, Behaviour 1961, Decision and Stress 1971, In Defence of Empirical Psychology 1973. *Leisure interests:* reading, camping, photography. *Address:* Department of Psychology, 1 South Parks Road, Oxford, OX1 3UD, England. *Telephone:* 0865-271444.

BROADBENT, Edward Granville, M.A., SC.D., F.R.A.E.S., F.I.M.A., F.R.S., F.ENG., F.R.S.A.; British scientist; b. 27 June 1923, Huddersfield, Yorks.; s. of Joseph C. F. and Lucetta (née Riley) Broadbent; m. Elizabeth B. Puttick 1949; ed. Huddersfield Coll. and St. Catharine's Coll., Cambridge; Govt. Scientist, Royal Aircraft Establishment, Farnborough 1943–83, Deputy Chief Scientific Officer (Aerodynamics Dept.) 1969–83, Consultant 1983–85; Visiting Prof. Dept. of Math., Imperial Coll., London 1983–; Consultant, Royal Armament Research and Defence Establishment, Fort Halstead 1983–85; Simms and Wakefield Medals, Royal Aeronautical Soc. *Publications:* various scientific papers. *Leisure interests:* music, theatre, chess, duplicate bridge, garden. *Address:* Imperial College, Huxley Building, Queen's Gate, London, SW7 2BZ (Office); 11 Three Stiles Road, Farnham, Surrey, GU9 7DE, England (Home). *Telephone:* 01-589 5111, ext. 5733 (Office); 0252 714621.

BROADBENT, Hon. John Edward, PH.D.; Canadian professor and politician; b. 21 March 1936, Oshawa, Ont.; s. of Percy E. Broadbent and Mary A. Welsh; m. Lucille Munroe 1971; one s. one d.; ed. High School in Oshawa, Univ. of Toronto, London School of Econs. and Political Science; Prof. of Political Science, York Univ., Ont. 1965–68; mem. House of Commons 1968–; Co-Chair. Policy Review Cttee. for New Democratic Party Fed. Convention 1969; Chair. Fed. Caucus 1972–74; Parl. Leader of Fed. Caucus 1974–75; Nat. Leader of New Democratic Party 1975–89; Vice-Pres. Socialist Int. *Publications:* The Liberal Rip-Off 1970. *Leisure interests:* reading contemporary fiction, listening to music, skiing. *Address:* Room 629c, House of Commons, Ottawa (Office); c/o New Democratic Party, 200 Albert Street, Suite 600, Ottawa K2P 1R9, Ont., Canada (Office). *Telephone:* 995-7224; (613) 236-3613.

BROBECK, John R., M.D., PH.D.; American professor of medicine; b. 12 April 1914, Steamboat Springs, Col.; s. of James A. and Ella Johnson Brobeck; m. Dorothy W. Kellogg 1940; two s. two d.; ed. Wheaton Coll., Ill., Northwestern and Yale Univs.; mem. Faculty, Yale Univ. School of Medicine, Dept. of Physiology 1943–52; Chair. Dept. of Physiology, Univ. of Pennsylvania School of Medicine 1952–70, Herbert C. Rorer Prof. in Medical Sciences 1970–82, Prof. Emer. 1982–; mem. Nat. Acad. of Sciences; Fellow, American Acad. of Arts & Sciences. *Publications:* articles on control of food intake, body temperature, body weight, energy balance. *Address:* Department of Physiology, School of Medicine, University of Pennsylvania, Philadelphia, Pa. 19104-6085 (Office); 224 Vassar Avenue, Swarthmore, Pa. 19081, U.S.A. (Home). *Telephone:* (215) 898-8072 (Office); (215) 544-5898 (Home).

BROCCOLI, Albert Romolo; American film producer; b. 5 April 1909, New York City; s. of Giovanni and Christina Broccoli; m. Dana Natol Wilson 1959; two s. two d.; Asst. dir. 20th Century Fox 1941–42; theatrical agent Charles Feldman 1948–51; producer, Warwick Films 1951–60, Eon Productions 1960–; mem. Producers' Guild, American Film Inst. *Films include:* Red Beret 1952, Hell Below Zero 1953, Prize of Gold 1955, Safari 1956, Arrivederci Roma 1957, How to Murder a Rich Uncle 1957, Jazz Boat 1960, The Trials of Oscar Wilde 1960, Chitty Chitty Bang Bang 1967; *Co-produced:* Dr No 1962, From Russia with Love 1963, Goldfinger 1963, Thunderball 1964, You Only Live Twice 1966, On Her Majesty's Secret Service 1969, Diamonds are Forever 1971, Live and Let Die 1972, The Man with the Golden Gun 1974, The Spy Who Loved Me 1977, Moonraker 1979, For Your Eyes Only 1981, Octopussy 1983, A View to a Kill 1987, The Living Daylights 1987. *Address:* c/o Gang, Tyre and Brown, 6400 Sunset Building, Los Angeles, Calif. 90028, U.S.A.

BROCHES, Aron, LL.D., J.D.; Netherlands international lawyer and arbitrator; b. 22 March 1914, Amsterdam; s. of Abraham Broches and Chaja Broches (née Person); m. Catherina Johanna Pothast 1939 (died 1982); one s. one d.; ed. Univ. of Amsterdam and Fordham Univ. Law School; Legal adviser, Netherlands Econ. Mission and American Embassy, New York and Washington, D.C. 1942–46; Sec. Netherlands Del. to UN Monetary and Financial Conf., Bretton Woods 1944; Sec. and Legal Adviser, Netherlands Del. to Inaugural Meeting, IMF; Int. Bank for Reconstruction and Development (IBRD) 1946–79, Gen. Counsel 1959–, mem. President's Council 1965–, Vice-Pres 1972–; Sec.-Gen. Int. Centre for Settlement of Investment Disputes 1967–80; Chief IBRD Econ. Survey Mission to Nigeria 1953–54; Trustee, Int. Legal Center 1969–77; mem. N.Y. Bar; Exec. Council, American Soc. of Int. Law 1969–73; Int. Council for Commercial Arbitration 1972–; Advisory Council, World Peace Through Law; Int. Law Cttee. American Arbitration Asscn. 1984–; Commdr. Order of Orange-Nassau (Netherlands) 1979. *Publications:* numerous works on int. arbitration and legal aspects of economic development including International Legal Aspects of the Operations of the World Bank 1959, The Convention on the Settlement of Investment Disputes between States and Nationals of Other States 1972. *Leisure interest:* music. *Address:* Suite 300, 1919 Pennsylvania Avenue, N.W., Washington, D.C. 20006 (Office); 2600 Tilden Place, N.W., Washington, D.C. 20008, U.S.A. (Home). *Telephone:* (202) 659-8847 (Office); (202) 362-3335 (Home).

BRØCHNER-MORTENSEN, Knud, M.D.; Danish physician; b. 4 July 1906, Fredericia; s. of Vald Brøchner-Mortensen and Ingrid Schaffer; m. Else Stein 1932; two s. two d.; ed. Univ. of Copenhagen; Prof. of Medicine and Dir. of Medical Dept. A, Univ. Hospital of Copenhagen 1949–76; Dean of Medical Faculty, Univ. of Copenhagen 1956–57, mem. Konsistorium 1963–74, Chair. Medical Educ. Cttee. 1962–74; mem. Danish State Research Foundation 1963–68; Chair. Medical Council, Univ. Hospital of Copenhagen 1958–64; mem. Danish Forensic Council 1964–76; Hon. mem. American Rheumatism Asscn., Sociedad Argentina de Reumatologia, Japanese Rheumatism Asscn., Swedish Rheumatism Asscn., Norwegian and Finnish Soc. of Internal Medicine, European Rheumatism League; Copenhagen Univ. Medal 1979; Heberden Oration Medal 1957, Klein Prize 1977. *Publications:* Uric Acid in Blood and Urine 1937. *Leisure interest:* history of medicine. *Address:* Fridtjof Nansens Plads 3, 2100 Copenhagen Ø, Denmark. *Telephone:* 01-262210.

BROCK, William Emerson, B.S.; American politician; b. 23 Nov. 1930, Chattanooga; s. of William Emerson Jr. and Myra (Kruesi) Brock; m. Laura Handly 1957; three s. one d.; ed. McCallie School and Washington and Lee Univ.; with Brock Candy Co., Chattanooga 1956–63; mem. House of Reps. 1963–71; U.S. Senator from Tenn. 1971–77; Chair. Republican Nat. Cttee. 1977–80; U.S. Trade Rep. (Cabinet status) 1981–85; U.S. Sec. of Labor 1985–87; Chair. Dole for Pres. Cttee. 1987–88. *Address:* c/o 200 Constitution Ave., N.W., Washington, D.C. 20210, U.S.A.

BROCKHOUSE, Bertram Neville, O.C., PH.D., F.R.S.; Canadian professor of physics; b. 15 July 1918; s. of Israel Bertram Brockhouse and Mabel Emily (née Neville) Brockhouse; m. Doris Isobel Mary Miller 1948; four s. two d.; ed. Univ. of British Columbia, Univ. of Toronto; served with Royal Canadian Navy 1939–45; Lecturer Univ. of Toronto 1949–50; Research Officer, Atomic Energy of Canada Ltd. 1950–59, Br. Head, Neutron Physics Br. 1960–62; Prof. of Physics, McMaster Univ. 1962–84, Prof. Emer. 1984–; Hon. D.Sc. (Waterloo Univ.) 1969, (McMaster Univ.) 1984. *Publications:* about 75 papers in learned journals. *Address:* P.O. Box 7338, Ancaster, Ont. L9G 3N6, Canada.

BROCKINGTON, Ian Fraser, M.PHIL., M.D., F.R.C.P., F.R.C.PSYCH.; British professor of psychiatry; b. 12 Dec. 1935, Chillington, Devon; s. of Fraser Brockington and Joyce Brockington; m. Diana Hilary Pink 1969; two s. two d.; ed. Winchester Coll., Univ. of Cambridge, Univ. of Manchester Medical School; Wellcome Research Fellow, Royal Postgraduate Medical School and Univ. of Ibadan, Nigeria 1966–69; Visiting Prof. Univ. of

Chicago, U.S.A. 1980–81, Washington Univ., St. Louis, U.S.A. 1981; Prof. of Psychiatry, Univ. of Birmingham 1983–; Pres. The Marcé Society 1982–84; Cottman Fellow, Monash Univ. 1988. *Publications:* papers on African heart diseases 1966–80, on schizoeffective psychosis, puerperal psychosis 1978–82; Motherhood and Mental Illness (with R. Kumar) 1982; Puerpal Mental Disorders 1978–88. *Leisure interest:* choral singing. *Address:* Lower Brockington Farm, Bredenbury, Bromyard, Herefordshire, England (Home). *Telephone:* (021) 414 6863 (Office); (088548) 3245 (Home).

BRODAL, Alf, M.D.; Norwegian neuroanatomist; b. 25 Jan. 1910, Oslo; s. of Peter Brodal and Helene Obenauer; m. Inger Hannestad 1935; one s. two d.; ed. Univ. of Oslo; Assistant Dept. of Anatomy, Odontological High School of Norway, Oslo 1937–43; Prosector of Anatomy, Univ. of Oslo 1943–50, Prof. of Anatomy 1950–77, Dean Medical Faculty 1964–66, Pro-Rector 1967–69; Rockefeller Fellowship, Dept. of Human Anatomy, Oxford Univ. 1946–47; Fellow, Norwegian Acad. of Sciences 1944; mem. Royal Soc. of Medicine, London 1946; Assoc. mem. Nordic Neurosurgical Asscn. 1947; Hon. mem. American Neurological Asscn. 1967, Norwegian Neurological Asscn. 1973, American Asscn. Anatomists 1977, Anatomical Soc. of Great Britain and Ireland 1979, Belgian Acad. of Medicine 1983; mem. Deutsche Akad. Naturforscher Leopoldina 1964; Commdr. Order of St. Olav 1979; Fridtjof Nansen Prize 1952, Monrad-Krohn Prize 1941 and 1960; Barany Medal (Uppsala) 1963; Anders Jahre's Medical Prize 1966; Dr. h.c. (Univ. of Uppsala) 1966, (Univ. of Paris) 1975, (Univ. of Oxford) 1983. *Publications:* (Monographs) The Reticular Formation of the Brain Stem 1957 (Russian edn. 1960), (with Jan Jansen) Aspects of Cerebellar Anatomy 1954, (with Jan Jansen) Das Kleinhirn 1958, (with Pompeiano and Walberg) The Vestibular Nuclei and their Connections 1962; (Textbooks) Neurological Anatomy in Relation to Clinical Medicine 1948, 1969, 1981 (Italian trans. 1983, Portuguese trans. 1984), The Cranial Nerves 1959, 1965, The Biology of Myxine 1963 (jt. ed. with R. Fänge), Basic Aspects of Central Vestibular Mechanisms 1972 (joint ed. with O. Pompeiano). *Leisure interests:* literature (fiction), carpentry, painting, out-door recreation. *Address:* Anatomical Institute, University of Oslo, Karl Johans gt. 47, Oslo 1 (Office); Preståsen 14, Blommenholm, Baerum, Norway (Home). *Telephone:* 02-42-90-10 (Office); 54-83-50 (Home).

BRÖDER, Ernst-Günther, D.ECON.; German economist and banker; b. 6 Jan. 1927, Cologne; ed. Univs. of Cologne, Mainz, Freiburg and Paris; mem. corpn. staff, Bayer AG, Leverkusen 1956–61; Projects Dept. World Bank (IBRD) 1961–64; joined Kreditanstalt für Wiederaufbau 1964, Deputy Man. 1968–69, Man. 1969–75, mem. Man. Bd. 1975–84, Man. Bd. Spokesman 1980–84; Dir. European Investment Bank (EIB) 1980–84, Pres. and Chair. Bd. of Dirs. Aug. 1984–; mem. Supervisory Bd. DEG Deutsche Finanzierungsgesellschaft für Beteiligungen in Entwicklungsländern GmbH 1980–84; mem. Panel of Conciliators, Int. Centre for Settlement of Investment Disputes 1976–, Special Advisory Group, Asian Devt. Bank 1981–82. *Address:* European Investment Bank, 100 boulevard Konrad Adenauer, L-2950 Luxembourg. *Telephone:* 43 79-1.

BRODIE, Bernard Beryl, PH.D.; American pharmacologist; b. 7 Aug. 1907, Liverpool, England; s. of Samuel Brodie and Esther Ginsburg; m. Anne L. Smith 1950; no c.; ed. McGill Univ., Montreal and New York Univ; Research Asst. in Pharmacology, New York Univ. Medical School 1935–38, Instructor in Pharmacology 1938–41, Instructor, Dept. of Medicine (Biochem.) 1941–43, Asst. Prof. of Pharmacology 1943–47, Assoc. Prof. of Biochem. 1947–50; Chief, Laboratory of Chemical Pharmacology, Nat. Heart and Lung Inst., Bethesda, Md. 1950–70; Senior Consultant Hoffman-La Roche Inc. 1971–; Founder Life Sciences; U.S. Ed. and Co-Founder Pharmacology; Ed. Medicina et Pharmacologia Experimentalis; Co-Founder and mem. Ed. Advisory Bd. International Journal of Neuropharmacology; mem. of Ed. and Advisory Bds. of other medical journals; Claude Bernard Prof. Univ. of Montreal; Visiting Prof. Pa. State Univ. 1975, Visiting Prof. Univ. of Arizona 1972–75, 1982–; Scientist Emer., Nat. Inst. of Health; Fellow, New York Acad. of Science; Hon. Life mem. N.A.S., New York Acad. of Sciences; mem. Inst. of Medicine; Hon. mem. Soc. of Pharmaceutical Sciences, Italy; Paul Lamson Memorial Lecture 1971; Rosemary Cass Memorial Lecture, Univ. of Dundee 1971; T. Edward Hicks Memorial Lectureship in Pharmacy, Univ. of Iowa 1971; Hon. D.Sc. (Univs. of Louvain, Paris, Ariz. and Barcelona, Philadelphia Coll. and New York Medical Coll.); Hon. M.D. (Karolinska Inst., Univ. of Cagliari), (Ohio Medical Coll.); Distinguished Service Award of Dept. of Health, Educ. and Welfare 1958, Torald Sollmann Award in Pharmacology 1963, Distinguished Achievement, Modern Medicine 1964, Albert Lasker Award for Basic Medical Research 1967, Nat. Medal of Science 1968, Schmiedeberg-Plakette 1969, Oscar B. Hunter Memorial Award, Golden Plate Award 1970, Intra-Science Foundation Medallist 1972. *Publications:* Metabolic Factors Controlling Duration of Drug Action 1963, Drug Enzyme Interactions 1964, Handbuch der exp. Pharmakologie 1971, Bioavailability of Drugs 1973, Principles and Perspectives of Drug Availability 1979 and about 500 articles on biology. *Leisure interests:* bridge, swimming, reading. [*Died 6 March 1989.*]

BRODIE, Harlow Keith Hammond, M.D.; American academic; b. 24 Aug. 1939, Stamford; s. of Lawrence Sheldon and Elizabeth Hammond Brodie; m. Brenda Ann Barrowclough 1967; three s. one d.; ed. Princeton Univ.

and Columbia Univ. College of Physicians and Surgeons; Asst. Resident in Psychiatry, Columbia-Presbyterian Medical Center, New York 1966–68; Clinical Assn., Sec. on Psychiatry, Lab. of Clinical Science, Nat. Inst. of Medical Health 1968–70; Asst. Prof., Dept. of Psychiatry, Stanford Univ. School of Medicine 1970–74; Program Dir., Gen. Clinical Research Center, Stanford Univ. School of Medicine 1973–74; Prof. and Chair., Dept. of Psychiatry, Duke Univ. School of Medicine 1974–82; Chief, Psychiatry Service, Duke Univ. Hosp. 1974–82; Chancellor Duke Univ. 1982–85, Acting Provost 1982–83, Pres. 1985–, James B. Duke Prof. of Psychiatry and Law 1981–, Adjunct Prof. of Psychology 1980–; mem. Coll. of Physicians and Surgeons of Columbia Univ. Asscn. of Alumni Gold Medal 1985. *Publications:* co-author Modern Clinical Psychiatry 1982, co-ed. Critical Problems in Psychiatry, Signs and Symptons in Psychiatry, also numerous articles. *Leisure interests:* tennis, reading, hiking. *Address:* Office of the President, 207 Allen Building, Duke Univ., Durham, N.C. 27706 (Office); 63 Beverly Drive, Durham, N.C. 27706, U.S.A. *Telephone:* 919-684 2424 (Office); 919-493-2447 (Home).

BRODSKY, Iosif Aleksandrovich; Russian-Jewish poet; b. 24 May 1940, Leningrad; ed. secondary school; began writing poetry 1955; sentenced to five years' hard labour in Arkhangelsk region for "social parasitism" 1964; sentence commuted 1965; refused visa to attend Poetry Int., London, and Festival of Two Worlds, Spoleto 1969; involuntary exile in U.S. after brief stays in Vienna, London; appeared at Poetry Int. 1972; Poet in residence, Univ. of Mich. 1972–73; Queen's Coll., New York 1973–74; Poet in residence, Univ. of Mich. 1974–; Nobel Prize for Literature 1987. *Publications:* A Christmas Ballad 1962, Elegy for John Donne 1963, Isaac and Abraham 1963, New Stanzas to Augusta 1964, Einem alten Architekten in Rom 1964, Verses on the Death of T. S. Eliot 1965, Verse and Poems (New York) 1965, French trans. Collines et autres poèmes 1966, German trans. Gedichte (Cologne) 1966, English trans. Elegy to John Donne & Other Poems 1967, Song Without Music 1969, A Stop in the Desert: Verse and Poems 1970, Selected Poems (Penguin) 1973. *Address:* c/o University of Michigan, Ann Arbor, Mich. 48109, U.S.A.

BRODY, Jane Ellen, M.S.; American journalist; b. 19 May 1941, Brooklyn; d. of Sidney Brody and Lillian Kellner; m. Richard Engquist 1966; twin s.; ed. New York State Coll. of Agric., Cornell Univ. and Univ. of Wis.; reporter, Minn. Tribune 1963–65; science writer, personal health columnist, New York Times 1965–; mem. Advisory Council, New York State Coll. of Agric. 1971–77; numerous awards including Howard Blakeslee Award, American Heart Asscn. 1971; Science Writers' Award, ADA 1978; J.C. Penney-Univ. of Mo. Journalism Award 1978; Lifeline Award, American Health Foundation 1978. *Publications:* Secrets of Good Health (with R. Engquist) 1970, You Can Fight Cancer and Win (with A. Holleb) 1977, Jane Brody's Nutrition Book 1981, Jane Brody's New York Times Guide to Personal Health 1982, Jane Brody's Good Food Book 1985. *Address:* c/o New York Times, 229 W. 43rd Street, New York, N.Y. 10036, U.S.A.

BROERS, Alec Nigel, PH.D., F.I.E.E., F.ENG., F.R.S.; British professor of electrical engineering; b. 17 Sept. 1938, Calcutta; s. of Alec W. Broers and Constance A. (Cox) Broers; m. Mary T. Phelan 1964; two s.; ed. Geelong Grammar School, Melbourne Univ. and Gonville & Caius Coll. Cambridge; mem. research staff and man. of photon and electron optics groups, IBM Thomas Watson Research Center 1965–80; Man. Semiconductor Lithography and Process Devt. and Advanced Devt. IBM East Fishkill Lab. 1981–84; mem. Corp. Tech. Cttee. IBM Corp. H.Q. 1984; Prof. of Electrical Eng. and Head of Electrical Eng. Div. Univ. of Cambridge 1984–; Fellow, Trinity Coll. Cambridge 1984–; IBM Fellow 1977; Prize for Industrial Applications of Physics, American Inst. of Physics 1982; Cledo Brunetti Award, Inst. of Electrical and Electronic Engs. 1985. *Publications:* patents, papers and book chapters on electron microscopy, electron beam lithography and integrated circuit fabrication. *Leisure interests:* music, small-boat sailing, skiing, tennis. *Address:* The Oak House, Hinxton, Essex, CB10 1RF, England. *Telephone:* (0779) 30245.

BROMLEY, David Allan, PH.D., F.R.S.A.; American professor of physics; b. 4 May 1926, Westmeath, Ont., Canada; s. of Milton E. and Susan (Anderson) Bromley; m. Patricia J. Brassor 1949; one s. one d.; ed. Queen's Univ., Kingston, Ont., and Univ. of Rochester, N.Y.; operating engineer, Hydro Electric Power Comm., Ont. 1947–48; research officer, Nat. Research Council of Canada 1948; Instructor, then Asst. Prof. of Physics, Univ. of Rochester 1952–55; Sr. Resident Officer, Atomic Energy Canada Ltd. 1955–60; Assoc. Prof. of Physics, Yale Univ. 1960–61, Henry Ford II Prof. 1961–, Chair. Dept. of Physics 1970–77; mem. White House Science Council 1981–; discovered first nuclear molecules, created first completely integrated computer-based nuclear data acquisition system; Dir. and consultant of several cos. and mem. various scientific advisory bodies; Pres. American Asscn. for Advancement of Science (A.A.A.S.) 1981–85; Pres. Int. Union of Pure and Applied Physics 1984–; Assoc. Ed. of several learned journals; Fellow, A.A.A.S., American Physical Soc.; Benjamin Franklin Fellow, Royal Soc. of Arts. 1979; several hon. degrees and other distinctions. *Publications:* Large Electrostatic Accelerators 1976, Detectors in Nuclear Science 1978, Nuclear Science in China 1980, Heavy Ion Science, 8 vols. 1984, numerous scientific and tech. publs. *Address:* Wright Nuclear Structure Laboratory, Yale University, 260 Whitney, New Haven, Conn. 06520 (Office); 35 Tokeneke Drive, North Haven, Conn. 06473, U.S.A. (Home).

BROMLEY, Yulian Vladimirovich, D.HIST.; Soviet historian; b. 21 Feb. 1921, Moscow; ed. Moscow Univ; Junior Research Assoc. Inst. of Slav Studies 1950–51; Scientific Sec. Dept. of History, U.S.S.R. Acad of Sciences 1951–66; Dir. Inst. of Ethnography, U.S.S.R. Acad. of Sciences 1966–; Second Sec. to History Dept. of Acad. of Sciences 1968–; Corresp. mem. U.S.S.R. Acad. of Sciences 1966–; mem. Anthropological Inst. of G.B. and Ireland 1977–; mem. CPSU 1944–. *Publications:* Works on general history and ethnology include Middle Ages in Croatia, Ethnos and Ethnography 1973, Soviet Ethnology and Anthropology Today (ed.) (English trans.) 1974, Soviet Ethnography: Main Trends 1976, Contemporary Ethnic Processes in U.S.S.R. (editor) 1977. *Address:* N. N. Miklukho-Maklai Institute of Ethnography, 19 Ulitsa Dmitriya Ulyanova, Moscow 117036, U.S.S.R.

BRØNDSTED, Morgens; Danish professor of Nordic literature; b. 12 Nov. 1918, Copenhagen; s. of Prof. Johannes Brøndsted; m. Else Baadsgaard 1947; two s. one d.; lecturer Oslo Univ. 1946–50, Uppsala Univ. 1950–57; librarian Kongelige Bibliotek, Copenhagen 1957–61; lecturer Univ. of Copenhagen 1961–63, Asst. Prof. 1963–66; Prof. of Nordic Literature, Odense Univ. 1966–88, Rector 1966–71; Dr. Phil.h.c. (Uppsala). *Publications:* Henrik Hertzes teater 1946, Henrik Ibsen antologi 1951, Danske i Norge 1953, Digtning og skæbne 1958, Meir Goldschmidt 1965, Goldschmidts fortællekunst 1967, Danmarks litteratur (with S. M. Kristensen) 1963, Oehlenschlägers Fynsrejse 1970, H. C. Andersen og avisen 1972, Ed. Nordens litteratur I-II 1972. *Leisure interest:* music. *Address:* Åløkken 50, 5250 Odense SV, Denmark. *Telephone:* 09-961884.

BRONFENBRENNER, Urie, PH.D.; American (b. Russian) psychologist; b. 29 April 1917, Moscow; s. of Alexander Bronfenbrenner and Eugenia (Kamenetski) Bronfenbrenner; m. Liese Price 1942; six c.; ed. Cornell and Harvard Univs. and Univ. of Michigan; psychologist, Univ. Lab. School, Univ. of Mich. 1940–42; mil. service as psychologist, U.S.A.A.F. 1942–46; Asst. Chief Clinical Psychologist for Admin. and Research, Veterans' Admin. Cen. Office, Washington, D.C. 1946; Asst. Prof. of Psychology, Univ. of Mich. 1946–48; Jacob Gould Schurman Prof. of Human Devt. and Family Studies and of Psychology, Cornell Univ. 1948–; Hon. Ph.D. (Gothenburg) 1980, (Munster) 1981, (Tech. Univ. Berlin) 1986; Hon. Dr. Family Sciences (Brigham Young Univ.) 1982; several awards from American Psychological Asscn. *Publications:* Two Worlds of Childhood: U.S. and U.S.S.R. 1970, Is Early Intervention Effective? 1974, Influences on Human Development (with M. Mahoney, eds.) 1975, Childhood in China (with W. Kessen and others) 1975, The Ecology of Human Development: Experiments by Nature and Design 1979. *Leisure interests:* hiking, music, literature. *Address:* Department of Human Development and Family Studies, Cornell Univ., Ithaca, N.Y. 14853; 108 McIntyre Place, Ithaca, New York, N.Y. 14850 (Home). *Telephone:* (607) 255-0833 (Office).

BRONFMAN, Charles Rosner, O.C.; Canadian industrialist; b. 27 June 1931, Montreal, Quebec; s. of the late Samuel and of Saidye (Rosner) Bronfman; m. 2nd Andrea Morrison 1982; one s. one d. from previous m.; ed. Selwyn House School, Montreal, P.Q., Trinity Coll., Port Hope, Ont., McGill Univ., Montreal; joined The Seagram Co. Ltd. 1951, Dir. and Vice-Pres. 1958–71, Exec. Vice-Pres. 1971–75, Chair. Exec. Cttee. 1975–, Deputy Chair. 1979–86, Co.-Chair. 1986–; fmr. Chair. Cemp Investments Ltd.; Hon. Chair. Canada-Israel Securities Ltd.; Dir. E.I. du Pont de Nemours Co., Canadian Council of Christians and Jews, Power Corpn. of Canada; Hon. Chair. and Dir. Super-Sol Ltd., Israel; Chair. Montreal Expos Baseball Club. *Leisure interests:* tennis, golf. *Address:* The Seagram Company Ltd., 1430 Peel Street, Montreal, Quebec H3A 1S9, Canada. *Telephone:* (514) 849-5271.

BRONFMAN, Edgar M., B.A.; American business executive; b. 20 June 1929, Montreal, Quebec; s. of late Samuel Bronfman and of Saidye (Rosner) Bronfman; ed. Trinity Coll. School, Port Hope, Ont., Williams Coll., Williamstown, Mass., and McGill Univ., Montreal; exec. in charge of co.'s plants in Canada, Distillers Corpn.-Seagrams Ltd. 1953–55; Chair. Admin. Cttee., Joseph E. Seagram & Sons Inc., N.Y. 1955, Pres. and Dir. 1957–71; Pres. Distillers Corpn.-Seagrams (now The Seagrams Co. Ltd.), Montreal July 1971–75, Chair. and C.E.O., N.Y. May 1975– (Co.-Chair. Nov. 1986–); Dir. Int. Exec. Service Corps., American Technion Soc.; Chair. Clevepak Corpn., Pres. World Jewish Congress; Dir. E.I. duPont de Nemours & Co., United Negro Coll. Fund, Weizmann Inst. of Science, American Cttee.; Trustee Salk Inst. for Biological Studies, Mt. Sinai Hosp. and School of Medicine; mem. Bd. of Dirs. Inter-racial Council for Business Opportunity; mem. Foreign Policy Asscn., Center for Inter-American Relations Inc., Cttee. for Econ. Devt., Dir. U.S.-U.S.S.R. Trade and Econ. Council, Inc., etc. *Address:* The Seagram Company Ltd., 1430 Peel Street, Montreal, Quebec H3A 1S9, Canada. *Telephone:* (514) 849-5271.

BRONIAREK, Zygmunt; Polish journalist and broadcaster; b. 27 Aug. 1925, Warsaw; s. of Wacław Broniarek and Marianna Broniarek; m. Elżbieta Sarcewicz 1972; ed. Main School of Planning and Statistics, Warsaw; Radiotelegraphic operator and stenographer, Czytelnik publishers, Warsaw 1945–48; Corresp. Trybuna Ludu 1950–, Perm. Corresp. in U.S.A. 1985; in U.S.A. 1955, 1958, 1975, Latin America 1956, Paris 1959–60, 1969–73, Washington 1960–67, East Africa 1975, West Africa 1976, Nordic Countries 1977–82; mem. Polish United Workers' Party (PZPR) 1956–; Corresp., Polish Radio and TV, for Finland and Sweden; Chair. Polish Asscn. of Int. Journalists and Writers 1974–77; mem. Bd. of

Foreign Press Assen., Stockholm 1979-81; mem. Presidium of Journalists' Assen. Polish People's Repub. 1983-; Vice-Pres. Polish Club of Int. Journalism 1984-; Corresp. Trybuna Ludu, L.A. Olympic Games 1984; Special Corresp. in Australia 1984; Corresp. Polish Press Agency to U.S.A. 1986; Presenter The Guests of Mr. Broniarek (TV), The Inner History of the Great Policy (TV) 1983, Behind the Scenes of Int. Politics (TV) 1983-85; Int. Journalists Club of Polish Journalistic Assen. Prize 1978, Golden Screen Award of Weekly Ekran 1984; Bolesław Prus Award, First Class (SD PRL) 1984; Gold Cross of Merit, Commdr's. Cross Order of Polonia Restituta, Order of Banner of Labour (Second Class) 1984, Commdr.'s Cross with star of Infante Dom Henrique the Navigator (Portugal), Victor Prize (TV) 1985. *Publications:* Od Hustonu do Mississipi 1956, Gorące dni Manhattanu 1960, Szczeble do Białego Domu, Walka o Pałac Elizejski 1974 1974, Kto się boi rewolucji (co-author) 1975, Angola zrodzona w walce 1977, Jak się nauczyłem sześciu języków 1977, Od Kissingera do Brzezińskiego 1980, Szaleństwo zbrojeń (co-author) 1982, Żródła spirali zbrojeń (co-author) 1985, Tajemnice Nagrody Nobla 1987. *Leisure interests:* good company, good food. *Address:* Ul. Grójecka 81/87 m. 79, 02-094 Warsaw, Poland; 3450 Toledo, Terr. Apt. 715, Hyattsville, Md. 20782, U.S.A. *Telephone:* 28-34-01; 301-559 3339.

BRONSON, Charles (Charles Buchinsky) American actor; b. 3 Nov 1922, Ehrenfield, Pa.; m. 1st Harriet Fendler (divorced), two c.; m. 2nd Jill Ireland 1969, one d.; played small parts in Hollywood films in the 1950s before coming into prominence in The Magnificent Seven 1960; other films include: A Thunder of Drums, 1961, Lonely Are the Brave 1962, The Great Escape 1963, The Sandpiper 1965, Battle of the Bulge 1965, This Property is Condemned 1966, The Dirty Dozen 1967, Guns for San Sebastian 1969, Rider in the Rain 1969, Twinky 1969, You Can't Win Them All 1970, Cold Sweat 1971, The Family 1971, Chato's Land 1972, The Mechanic 1972, The Valachi Papers 1972, Wild Horses 1973, The Stone Killer 1973, Mr. Majestyck 1974, Death Wish 1974, Breakout 1975, Hard Times 1975, Breakheart Pass 1976, From Noon till Three 1976, St. Ives 1976, The White Buffalo 1976, Telefon 1977, Love and Bullets 1979, Cabo Blanco, Death Wish II 1981, Murphy's Law 1986, Assassination 1987; television includes Raid on Entebbe 1976; also appeared on many American series during 1950s and 1960s. *Address:* c/o Paul Kohner, 9169 Sunset Boulevard, Los Angeles, Calif. 90069, U.S.A.

BRONSTON, Samuel; American film producer; ed. Université de Paris (Sorbonne); fmr. film distributor, Paris; fmr. unit production exec. with Columbia Studios Hollywood; founder Samuel Bronston Pictures Inc., now Pres. *Productions include:* King of Kings, El Cid 1960, 55 Days to Peking 1962, Fall of the Roman Empire 1963, The Magnificent Showman (Circus World, U.K.) 1964.

BROOK, Adrian G., PH.D.; Canadian professor of chemistry; b. 21 May 1924, Toronto; s. of Frank A. Brook and Beatrice M. Wellington; m. Margaret E. Dunn 1954; two s. one d.; ed. Lawrence Park Collegiate and Univ. of Toronto; Lecturer in Chem. Univ. of Toronto 1953-56, Asst. Prof. 1956-60, Assoc. Prof. 1960-62, Prof. 1962-, Acting Chair. Dept. of Chem. 1969-71, Chair. 1971-74, Chair. Univ. of Toronto Research Bd. 1976-81, Univ. Prof. 1987; Nuffield Fellow 1950-51; Stanley Kipping Award (American Chem. Soc.) 1973; CIC Medal (Chem. Inst. of Canada) 1986. *Publications:* about 130 papers on aspects of organic chemistry. *Leisure interests:* windsurfing, computer hacking. *Address:* Department of Chemistry, University of Toronto, Toronto, M5S 1A1 (Office); 79 Glenview Avenue, Toronto, M4R 1P7, Canada (Home). *Telephone:* (416) 978-3573 (Office); (416) 483-9987 (Home).

BROOK, Peter Stephen Paul, C.B.E.; British theatre and film director; b. 21 March 1925; s. of Simon Brook; m. Natasha Parry 1951; one s. one d.; ed. Westminster and Gresham's Schools, and Magdalen Coll., Oxford; joined Royal Shakespeare Co. 1962; Producer, Co-Dir. Royal Shakespeare Theatre; founded Int. Theatre Research Centre, Paris 1970, has toured with group in Iran, W. Africa; Hon. D.Litt. (Birmingham); Officier, Ordre des Arts et des Lettres, Legion d'honneur 1987; Freiherr von Stein Foundation, Shakespeare Award 1973. *Productions include:* Dr. Faustus 1943, Pygmalion, King John, Lady from the Sea 1945, Romeo and Juliet (at Stratford) 1947, Dir. of Productions at Covent Garden Opera 1949-50, The Beggar's Opera (film) 1952, Faust (at Metropolitan Opera, N.Y.) 1953, The Dark is Light Enough (London) 1954, House of Flowers (N.Y.) 1954, Cat on a Hot Tin Roof (Paris) 1956, Eugene Onegin (N.Y.) 1958, View from the Bridge (Paris) 1958, The Fighting Cock (N.Y.) 1959, Moderato Cantabile (film) 1960, Irma la Douce 1960, Lord of the Flies (film) 1962, King Lear 1963, The Physicists (N.Y.) 1964, The Marat/Sade (N.Y.) 1965 (film) 1966, US 1966, Tell Me Lies (film) 1968, Oedipus (Seneca) 1968, A Midsummer Night's Dream 1970, King Lear (film) 1971, The Conference of the Birds 1973, Timon of Athens (Paris) 1974, The Ik (Paris) 1975, (London) 1976, (U.S.A.) 1976, Ubu (Paris) 1977, Meetings with Remarkable Men (film, also dir. screenplay) 1977, Antony and Cleopatra (Stratford and London) 1978, Measure for Measure (Paris) 1978, Conference of the Birds, L'os (Festival Avignon and Paris) 1979, (New York) 1980, The Cherry Orchard (Paris) 1981, (New York) 1988, (Moscow) 1989, La Tragédie de Carmen (opera) (Paris) 1981, Le Mahabharata (Avignon and Paris) 1985, (World tour) 1988. *Publications:* The Empty Space 1968, The Shifting Viewpoint: Forty years of theatrical exploration 1946-87, 1988. *Address:* c/o C.I.R.T., 9 rue du Cirque, 75008 Paris, France.

BROOK, Robert H., M.D., SC.D., F.A.C.P.; American professor of medicine; b. 3 July 1943, New York; s. of Benjamin N. Brook and Elizabeth Berg; m. 1st Susan Weiss 1966, 2nd Jacquiey Kosecoff 1981; one s. three d.; ed. Univ. of Arizona, Johns Hopkins Medicial School, Johns Hopkins School of Hygiene and Public Health; mil. service, U.S. Public Health Services 1972-74; currently Prof. of Medicine and Public Health, Deputy Dir. Health Sciences Program, Rand Corpn.; Chief of Div. of Geriatrics, Univ. of California Center for the Health Sciences; Dir. Robert Wood Johnson Clinical Scholar Program; mem. Inst. of Medicine, Nat. Acad. of Sciences, American Soc. of Clinical Investigation, American Assen. of Physicians; Commendation Medal; Richard and Hinda Rosenthal Foundation Award; Baxter Health Services Research Prize 1988; Sonneborn Distinguished Lecturer, Univ. of Pa.; Hollister Univ. Lecturer, Northwestern Univ. *Publications:* over 250 articles on medicine. *Leisure interests:* tennnis, swimming, golf. *Address:* Robert Wood Johnson Clinical Scholars Department of Medicine, University of California, B-973 Louis Factor Building, Los Angeles, Calif. 90024; The Rand Corporation, P.O. Box 2138, 1700 Main Street, Santa Monica, Calif. 90406-2138, U.S.A.

BROOK, Sir Robin (Ralph Ellis), Kt., C.M.G., O.B.E.; British business executive; b. 19 June 1908; s. of Francis Brook, F.R.C.S.; m. Helen Knewstub 1937; two d.; ed. Eton and Kings Coll., Cambridge; mil. service 1941-46, Brig. 1945; Dir. Bank of England 1946-49; Deputy Chair. British Tourist and Holidays Bd. 1946-50, Colonial Devt. Corpn. 1949-53; Chair. London Chamber of Commerce and Industry 1966-68, Pres. 1968-72; Pres. Assen. of British Chambers of Commerce 1972-74, Conf. of Chambers of Commerce of EEC; Dir. British Petroleum Co. 1970-73; Dir. C. E. Coates and Co. Ltd., United City Merchants; mem. Cttee. on Invisible Exports 1969-75, mem. Sports Council 1971-78, Chair. 1975-78; Council and Exec. Cttee. King Edward's Fund, City and East London AHA 1974-82, Vice-Chair. 1974-79; mem. City and Hackney Dist. Health Authority 1982-86; Treas. and Chair. St. Bartholomew's Hospital 1964-74, Gov. 1962-74, Chair. Trustees 1974-; Gov. Royal Free Hospital 1962-74; Past Master Haberdashers' Co.; Gov. Sports Aid Foundation; British Sabre Champion 1936; Olympic Games 1936, 1948; Commdr. Legion of Merit; Legion of Honour; Croix de guerre and Bar; Order of Leopold (Belgium); Belgian Croix de guerre. *Address:* 31 Acacia Road, London, NW8 6NS, England. *Telephone:* 01-722 5844.

BROOKE, Christopher Nugent Lawrence, M.A., LITT.D., F.B.A., F.R.HIST.S., F.S.A.; British historian; b. 23 June 1927; s. of Zachary Nugent Brooke and Rosa Grace (Stanton) Brooke; m. Rosalind Beckford Clark 1951; three s.; ed. Gonville and Caius Coll. Cambridge, Fellow 1949-56, 1977-; Asst. Lecturer, Univ. of Cambridge 1953-54, Lecturer 1954-56; Prof. of Medieval History, Univ. of Liverpool 1956-67; Prof. of History, Westfield Coll., Univ. of London 1967-77; Dixie Prof. of Ecclesiastical History, Univ. of Cambridge 1977-; Hon. D. Univ. (York) 1984; Pres. Soc. of Antiquaries 1981-84; Corresp. Fellow, Medieval Acad. of America; Corresp. mem. Monumenta Germaniae Historica; Fellow Società Internazionale di Studi Francescani; mem. Royal Comm. on Historic Monuments 1977-83, Reviewing Comm. on Export of Works of Art 1979-82. *Publications:* The Dullness of the Past 1957, From Alfred to Henry III 1961, The Saxon and Norman Kings 1963, Europe in the Central Middle Ages 1964, Time the Archsatirist 1968, The Twelfth Century Renaissance 1969, Structure of Medieval Society 1971, Medieval Church and Society (selected papers) 1971, Marriage in Christian History 1977, A History of Gonville and Caius College 1985, The Church and the Welsh Border in the Central Middle Ages 1986, The Medieval Idea of Marriage 1989; co-author of numerous works, including Gilbert Foliot and his Letters (with A. Morey) 1965, London 800-1216 (with G. Keir) 1975, Popular Religion in the Middle Ages, 1000-1300 (with Rosalind Brooke) 1984, Oxford and Cambridge (with Roger Highfield and Wim Swaan) 1988; ed. of numerous works, including Oxford (fmrly. Nelson's) Medieval Texts, Nelson's History of England (Gen. Ed.); articles and reviews in professional journals. *Address:* Faculty of History, West Road, Cambridge, CB3 9EF, England.

BROOKE, Edward William, LL.D.; American lawyer and politician; b. 26 Oct. 1919, Washington, D.C.; s. of Edward and Helen Brooke; m. 1st Remigia Ferrari Scacco 1947 (divorced 1979); two c.; m. 2nd Anne Flemming 1979; ed. Howard Univ. and Boston Univ; Admitted to Mass. Bar 1948; Chair. Finance Comm., Boston 1961-62; Attorney-Gen. of Mass. 1963-67; U.S. Senator from Mass. 1967-79; Chair. Boston Opera Co.; Gen. Partner, O'Connor and Hannan, Washington, D.C. 1979-; Chair. Nat. Low-Income Housing Coalition 1979-; Counsel Csaplar and Bok, Boston 1979-; Ltd. Partner, Bear and Stearns, N.Y. 1979-; Fellow, American Bar Assen., American Acad. of Arts and Sciences; numerous hon. degrees; Republican. *Address:* O'Connor and Hannan, 1919 Pennsylvania Avenue, N.W., Washington, D.C. 20006, U.S.A. *Telephone:* (202) 887-1400.

BROOKE, Rt. Hon. Peter, M.A., M.B.A., P.C.; British politician; b. 3 March 1934, London; s. of Lord Brooke of Cumnor, C.H. and Baroness Brooke of Ystradfellte, D.B.E.; m. Joan Smith 1964 (died 1985); four s. (one deceased); ed. Marlborough Coll., Balliol Coll., Oxford, Harvard Business School, U.S.A.; Research Assoc., IMEDE, Lausanne and Swiss Corresp. of Financial Times 1960-61; Spencer Stuart Man. Consultants 1961-79, Chair. of parent co. 1974-79; M.P. for City of London and Westminster S. 1977-; Govt. Whips' Office 1979-83; Dept. of Educ. and Science Parl. Under-Sec.

1983–85; Minister of State, H.M. Treasury 1985–87, Paymaster Gen. 1987–; Chair. Conservative Party 1987–. *Leisure interests:* churches, conservation, cricket, visual arts. *Address:* House of Commons, London, S.W.1., England. *Telephone:* 01-219 5041.

BROOKER, Robert Elton; American businessman; b. 18 July 1905, Cleveland, Ohio; s. of Robert and Isadora (Roberts) Brooker; m. Sally Burton Smith 1933; two s.; ed. Univ. of Southern California; with Southern California Edison Co. 1928–34, Firestone Tire and Rubber Co. 1934–44, Sears, Roebuck & Co. 1944–58; Pres. Whirlpool Corpn. 1958–61; Pres. Montgomery Ward & Co. 1961–66, Chair. 1966–70, Chair. Exec. Cttee. 1970–75; Chair. Marcor Inc. 1968–70, Chair. Exec. Cttee. 1970–75, Chair. and C.E.O. 1975–. *Address:* Executive Services Corps., 25 E. Washington Street, 8th Floor, Chicago, Ill. 60603 (Office); 1500 Sheridan Road, Wilmette, Ill. 60091, U.S.A. (Home). *Telephone:* (312) 467-3859 (Office).

BROOKES, Baron (Life Peer), cr. 1975, of West Bromwich, West Midlands; **Raymond Percival Brookes,** Kt.; British business executive; b. 10 April 1909, West Bromwich, Staffs.; s. of William Percival and Ursula Brookes; m. Florence E. Sharman 1937; one s.; ed. West Bromwich School, Kenrick Tech. Coll.; apprenticed as engineer 1923; joined GKN as joint Gen. Man. of Carringtons Ltd. 1941, subsequently Man. Dir. and Chair.; Chair. GKN Forgings and Castings Ltd. 1965–74, Life Pres. Jan. 1975–; fmr. Chair. Joseph Sankey and Sons Ltd. (now GKN Sankey Ltd.); Dir. Guest Keen and Nettlefolds Ltd. 1953, Deputy Group Man. Dir. 1962, Group Man. Dir. 1964, Group Chair. and Man. Dir. (subsequently relinquished Man. Directorship) 1964, Group Chair. and C.E.O. 1966–75, Life Pres. 1975–; part-time mem. British Steel Corpn. 1967–68; First Pres. British Mechanical Eng. Confederation 1968–70; Vice-Pres. Eng. Employers' Fed. 1967–75; mem. Council Soc. of Motor Mfrs. and Traders Ltd. 1969–, mem. Exec. Cttee. 1970–, Pres. 1974–75; mem. Council CBI 1968–75, BNEC 1969–71, Wilberforce Court of Inquiry into electricity supply industry dispute Jan. 1971, Industrial Development Advisory Bd. 1972–75, Man. Bd. UNI-Cardan Group Lohmar, Fed. Repub. of Germany 1975–78; former Chair. Rea Brothers (Isle of Man) Ltd.; Dir. AMF Inc. U.S.A. (retd. 1979), Mannin Industries Ltd., Mannin Trust Bank Ltd. (retd. 1980); non-Exec. Dir. Plessey Co.; Hon. Fellow, Inst. of Sales Engineers 1973; Pres. Motor Ind. Research Assen. 1973–75. *Leisure interests:* fly-fishing, golf. *Address:* Mallards, Santon, Isle of Man.

BROOKNER, Anita; British teacher and author; b. 16 July 1938; d. of Newson and Maude Brookner; ed. James Allen's Girls' School, King's Coll., London, Courtauld Inst. and Paris; Visiting Lecturer, Univ. of Reading 1959–64; Slade Prof., Univ. of Cambridge 1967–68; lecturer, Courtauld Inst. of Art 1964, Reader 1977–87; Fellow, New Hall, Cambridge; Booker Prize for Fiction for Hôtel du Lac 1984. *Publications:* Watteau 1968, The Genius of the Future 1971, Greuze: the rise and fall of an Eighteenth Century Phenomenon 1972, Jacques-Louis David 1980, The Stories of Edith Wharton (ed.) 1988; novels: A Start in Life 1981, Providence 1982, Look at Me 1983, Hôtel du Lac 1984, Family and Friends 1985, A Misalliance 1986, A Friend from England 1987, Latecomers 1988; articles in Burlington Magazine etc. *Address:* 68 Elm Park Gardens, London, S.W.10., England. *Telephone:* 01-352 6894.

BROOKS, Chandler McCuskey, PH.D.; American physiologist and administrator; b. 18 Dec. 1905, Waverly, W. Va.; s. of Earle Amos Brooks and Mary McCuskey Brooks; m. Nelle I. Graham 1932 (died 1982); ed. Everett High School, Mass., Oberlin Coll. and Princeton and Harvard Univs.; Teaching Asst. Oberlin Coll., then Princeton and Harvard Univs.; 1928–33; Instructor, Assoc. Prof. of Physiology, Johns Hopkins Medical School 1933–48; Guggenheim Fellow, Asst., Univ. of Otago, N.Z. 1946–48; Prof. and Chair. Physiology and Pharmacology Dept., Long Island Coll. of Medicine 1948–52, then State Univ. of New York Medical Center; Chair. and Prof. of Physiology, Downstate Medical Center, State Univ. of New York 1956–72, Dean Graduate School 1965–72, Dean of Medicine and Acting Pres. Downstate Medical Center 1968–72, Distinguished Prof. 1972–; Chair. of Grants Cttee., Int. Foundation, and Trustee 1974–; mem. N.A.S. 1975; Fellow Center of Theological Inquiry 1987–; Hon. mem. Japanese Physiological Soc. 1985; Hon. D.MSc. (Berea Coll., Ky.) 1979, (State Univ., New York) 1986; Order of the Rising Sun (3rd Rank), Japan 1979. *Publications:* Excitability of the Heart 1955, History of Physiological Thought 1960, Humors, Hormones and Neural Secretions 1962, Pacemaker of the Heart 1972, Japanese Physiology 1965, The Life and Contributions of Walter B. Cannon 1975, Integrative Function of the Autonomic Nervous System 1979, Neurovegetative Control Systems 1986; Ed.-in-Chief and Founding Ed. Journal of Autonomic Nervous System 1978–. *Leisure interest:* history and philosophy of science and religion. *Address:* Physiology 31, Downstate Medical Center, State University of New York, 450 Clarkson Avenue, Brooklyn, N.Y. 11203; c/o C.T.I., 50 Stockton Street, Princeton, N.J. 08540; 623 Second Street, Brooklyn, N.Y. 11215, U.S.A. (Home). *Telephone:* (718) 270-3106 (Office); (609) 683-0896. (718) 788-7047 (Home).

BROOKS, Cleanth, A.M., B.LITT.; American university professor; b. 16 Oct 1906, Murray, Ky.; s. of Cleanth Brooks and Bessie Lee Witherspoon; m. Edith Amy Blanchard 1934 (died 1986); ed. The McTyeire School, Vanderbilt Univ., Tulane Univ. and Oxford Univ; Prof. of English, Louisiana State Univ. 1932–47, Yale Univ. (now Gray Prof. Emer. of Rhetoric) 1947–; Man. Ed., later Ed. (with Robert Penn Warren) Southern Review, Baton

Rouge, Louisiana 1935–42; Hon. Consultant, Library of Congress 1952–62, mem. Council of Scholars 1984–; Cultural Attaché American Embassy, London 1964–66; mem. American Acad. of Arts and Sciences, Nat. Inst. of Arts and Letters, American Philosophical Soc., Royal Soc. of Literature; Hon. D.Litt., L.H.D. *Publications:* Modern Poetry and the Tradition 1939, The Well-Wrought Urn 1947; with Robert Penn Warren: Understanding Poetry 1938, Understanding Fiction 1943, Modern Rhetoric 1950; Literary Criticism: A Short History (with W. K. Wimsatt, Jr.) 1957, The Hidden God 1963, William Faulkner: the Yoknapatawpha Country 1963, A Shaping Joy 1971, American Literature: the Makers and the Making (with R. W. B. Lewis and R. P. Warren) 1973, William Faulkner: Toward Yoknapatawpha and Beyond 1978, The Rich Manifold 1983, William Faulkner: First Encounters 1983, The Language of the American South 1985, On the Prejudices, Predilections and Firm Beliefs of William Faulkner 1987; Gen. Ed. (with David N. Smith) The Percy Letters, 10 vols. 1942–; Ed.: The Correspondence of Thomas Percy and Richard Farmer 1946, The Correspondence of Thomas Percy and William Shenstone 1977. *Address:* 70 Ogden Street, New Haven, Conn. 06511, U.S.A. *Telephone:* (203) 776-9038.

BROOKS, Gwendolyn; American writer; b. 7 June 1917, Topeka, Kan.; d. of David Brooks and Keziah Wims; m. Henry Blakely 1939; one s. one d.; ed. Englewood High School and Wilson Junior Coll; Poet Laureate for State of Illinois 1968–; Teacher of poetry at Northeastern Illinois State Coll., Columbia Coll., Chicago and Elmhurst Coll.; mem. Nat. Inst., American Acad. of Arts and Letters, Poetry Soc. of America, Nat. Assen. for Advancement of Colored People, Third World Press; cited for creative writing by American Acad. of Arts and Letters 1946; Guggenheim Fellow 1946, 1947; Pulitzer Prize for Poetry for Annie Allen 1950; Anisfield-Wolf Award 1969, Shelley Memorial Award. *Publications:* A Street in Bronzeville 1945, Annie Allen 1949, Maud Martha 1953, Bronzeville Boys and Girls 1956, The Bean Eaters 1960, Selected Poems 1963, In the Mecca 1968, Riot 1969, Family Pictures 1970, Aloneness 1971, Report From Part One (autobiog.) 1972, Tiger who wore White Gloves 1974, Beckonings 1975, Primer for Blacks 1980, Young Poet's Primer 1980, To Disembark 1981, The Near-Johannesburg Boy 1986, Blacks 1987. *Address:* 7428 South Evans Avenue, Chicago, Ill. 60619, U.S.A.

BROOKS, Harvey, A.B., PH.D.; American physicist; b. 5 Aug. 1915, Cleveland, Ohio; s. of Chester Kingsley Brooks and Elizabeth Brown Brooks; m. Helen Gordon Lathrop 1945; one s. three d.; ed. Yale and Harvard Univs; Soc. of Fellows, Harvard Univ. 1940–41, Research Assoc. Harvard Underwater Sound Laboratory 1942–45; Gordon McKay Prof. of Applied Physics 1950–75, Benjamin Pierce Prof. of Tech. and Public Policy 1975–86, Prof. Emer. 1986–, Dean of Eng. and Applied Physics 1957–75; Asst. Dir. Ordnance Research Laboratory, Pa. State Univ. 1945–46; Assoc. Laboratory Head, Knolls Power Laboratory, Gen. Electric Schenectady 1946–50; Ed.-in-Chief Physics and Chemistry of Solids; Dir. Raytheon Co.; mem. Bd. of Trustees, German Marshall Fund, Case Western Reserve Univ., Tufts Univ., Woods Hole Oceanographic Inst., Environmental Law Inst.; fmr. Pres. American Acad. of Arts and Sciences; mem. Council on Library Resources, Nat. Acad. of Eng., Nat. Acad. of Sciences, American Philosophical Soc.; Hon. D.Sc.; Ernest Orlando Lawrence Award 1960. *Publications:* The Government of Science 1968; numerous articles in Physical Review, Nuclear Science and Engineering, and other scientific journals. *Address:* 226 Aiken Computation Laboratory, Harvard University, Cambridge, Mass. 02138 (Office); 46 Brewster Street, Cambridge, Mass. 02138, U.S.A. (Home). *Telephone:* (617) 495-2831 (Office); (617) 354-7170 (Home).

BROOKS, James; American painter; b. 18 Oct. 1906, St. Louis, Mo.; s. of William R. Brooks and Abigail Williamson; m. 1st Mary Macdonald 1933, 2nd Charlotte Park 1947; ed. Southern Methodist Univ., Art Students League, N.Y.C., and with Wallace Harrison; Federal Arts Mural Projects 1938–42; taught at Columbia and Yale Univs. and at Queens Coll. 1947–67; several one-man shows 1949–88; Visiting Artist, New Coll, Sarasota, Fla. 1965–67; represented in Museum of Modern Art, Metropolitan Museum, Guggenheim, Whitney, Brooklyn, New York, Tate Gallery, London, Nat. Museum of American Art, Washington, D.C., Hirshhorn Museum, Washington, D.C.; several shows abroad; retrospective exhbn. Whitney Museum of American Art 1963–64, Dallas Museum of Art 1972, Portland Museum of Art 1983; Artist in Residence, American Acad. in Rome 1963; Prof., Queen's Coll. 1968; Guggenheim Fellowship 1967–68; Visiting Critic, Univ. of Pennsylvania 1971–72, 1973; Carnegie Int. Prize 1952, Art Inst. of Chicago Prize 1957, 1961; Ford Foundation 1962; Gold Medal Nat. Arts Club, New York 1985; mem. American Inst. of Arts and Letters, Century Assen. *Address:* 128 Neck Path, Springs, East Hampton, N.Y. 11937, U.S.A.

BROOKS, Mel (Melvin Kaminsky); American actor, writer, producer and director; b. 1926, New York; m. 1st Florence Baum, two s. one d.; m. 2nd Anne Bancroft (q.v.) 1964, one s.; script writer for TV series Your Show of Shows 1950–54, Caesar's Hour 1954–57, Get Smart 1965–70; set up feature film production co. Brooksfilms; *films include:* The Critic (cartoon) 1963, The Producers 1968, The Twelve Chairs 1970, Blazing Saddles 1974, Young Frankenstein 1975, Silent Movie 1976, High Anxiety 1978, The Elephant Man (producer) 1979, History of the World Part I 1981, To Be or Not to Be 1983 (actor, producer), Spaceballs 1987 (actor, producer), 84 Charing Cross Road 1987; Academy awards for The Critic 1964, The

Producers (Best Screenplay) 1968. *Address:* Brooksfilms, c/o Twentieth Century-Fox Film Corporation, P.O. Box 900, Beverly Hills, Calif. 90213, U.S.A.

BROOKS, Richard; American film writer and director; b. 18 May 1912; m. Jean Simmons (q.v.); ed. Temple Univ.; fmrly. with NBC as writer and commentator; now directs and writes screenplays for films. Wrote and directed: Deadline, U.S.A., Battle Circus, Last Hunt, Something of Value, The Brothers Karamazov, Cat on a Hot Tin Roof, Elmer Gantry (Acad. Award for Screenplay 1961), Sweet Bird of Youth, Lord Jim (also producer), In Cold Blood, The Professionals, The Man with the Deadly Lens 1982; Directed and collaborated on screenplays of: Last Time I Saw Paris, Blackboard Jungle, Looking for Mr Goodbar; Directed: Take the High Ground, Flame and the Flesh, Catered Affair, The Happy Ending, Dollars (The Heist, U.K.), Bite The Bullet; Wrote screenplay for: Swell Guy, White Savage, Brute Force, To the Victor, Crossfire. *Publications:* (novels) Brick Fox Hole, Boiling Point, The Producer. *Address:* c/o Geald Lipsky, 190 North Canon Drive, Beverly Hills, Calif. 90210, U.S.A.

BROOME, David, O.B.E.; British farmer and professional show jumper; b. 1 March 1940, Cardiff; s. of Fred and Amelia Broome; m. Elizabeth Fletcher 1976; one s.; ed. Monmouth Grammar School for Boys; European Show Jumping Champion, riding Sunsalve, Aachen 1961, riding Mr. Softee, Rotterdam 1967 and Hickstead 1969; World Champion, riding Beethoven, La Baule (France) 1970; Professional Champion of World, riding Sportsman and Philco, Cardiff 1974; Master of Foxhounds. *Publications:* Jump-Off 1970, Horsemanship (with S. Hadley) 1983. *Leisure interests:* hunting, shooting, golf. *Address:* Mount Ballan Manor, Crick, Newport, Gwent, Wales. *Telephone:* Caldicot 42077.

BROPHY, Brigid, F.R.S.L.; British novelist and critic; b. 12 June 1929, London; d. of late author John Brophy and Charis (Grundy); m. Sir Michael Levey (q.v.) 1954; one d.; ed. St. Paul's Girls' School, London, and St. Hugh's Coll., Oxford; Founder mem. Writers' Action Group 1972–82; Exec. Councillor Writers' Guild of Great Britain 1975–78; mem. British Copyright Council 1976, Vice-Chair. 1977–80. *Publications:* Hackenfeller's Ape 1953, The King of a Rainy Country 1956, Black Ship to Hell (non-fiction) 1962, Flesh 1962, The Finishing Touch 1963, The Snow Ball 1964, Mozart the Dramatist (non-fiction) 1964, The Waste Disposal Unit (play) 1965, Don't Never Forget (non-fiction) 1966, The Burglar (play) 1967 (published with preface 1968), Black and White, A Portrait of Aubrey Beardsley (non-fiction) 1968, In Transit 1969, Prancing Novelist (non-fiction) 1973, The Adventures of God in His Search for the Black Girl 1973, Pussy Owl 1976, Beardsley and his World (non-fiction) 1976, Palace Without Chairs 1978, The Prince and the Wild Geese (non-fiction) 1983, A Guide to Public Lending Right (non-fiction) 1983, Baroque-'n'-Roll (non-fiction) 1987, Reads (non-fiction) 1989. *Address:* Flat 3, 185 Old Brompton Road, London, SW5 0AN, England.

BROPHY, Theodore F., B.A., LL.B.; American business executive; b. 4 April 1923, New York; s. of Frederick H. and Muriel W. (née Osborne) Brophy; m. Sallie M. Showalter; one s. one d.; ed. Yale Univ. and Harvard Univ. Law School; Assoc. law firm of Root, Ballantine, Harlan, Bushby & Palmer 1950–55; Gen. Counsel, The Lummus Co. 1955–58; GTE Corpn., Counsel 1958–59, Vice-Pres. and Gen. Counsel 1959–68, Exec. Vice-Pres. 1968–69, Dir. 1969–, Pres. 1972–76, Chair. and C.E.O. 1976–; mem. American Bar Assocn. and Past Chair. Public Utility Law Section; mem. Fed. Communications Bar Assocn.; Public mem. Admin. Conf. of the U.S. 1970–72. *Address:* One Stamford Forum, Stamford, Conn. 06904, U.S.A. (Office). *Telephone:* (203) 965-2104 (Office).

BROST, Erich Eduard; German publisher and journalist; b. 29 Oct. 1903, Elbing; s. of Gustav Brost and Maria Brost; m. Anneliese Brinkmann 1975; one s.; ed. St. Peter and St. Paul's High School, Danzig; Ed. Danziger Volksstimme 1924–36; journalist in Poland, Sweden, Finland and G.B. 1936–45, in Essen and Berlin 1945–48; Publr. Westdeutsche Allgemeine Zeitung, Essen 1948–. *Address:* Zeissbogen 28, D-4300 Essen, Federal Republic of Germany. *Telephone:* 711235.

BROUSSE, Pierre, French politician; b. 30 Nov. 1926, Limoges, Haute Vienne; s. of Louis Brousse and Marie Jeanne Borzeix; m. Edmée Nouchy 1954; ed. Lycée de Tulle, Corrèze, Institut d'Etudes Politiques, Paris and Univ. of Paris; Pres. Radical Students Group 1949; Ministry of Industry 1954–56; Pres., Young Radicals Group 1956–58; Jt. Sec.-Gen. Radical Party 1958–61, Sec.-Gen. 1961–69; mem. and Délégué général, Fédération de la gauche démocrate et socialiste 1966–69; Mayor of Béziers 1967–77; Gen. Counsellor of Hérault 1967–82, Hon. Gen. Counsellor 1982–; Senator for Hérault 1968–76; Minister of Commerce and Handicrafts and Small Businesses 1976–77; Vice-Pres. Radical Party 1969–71, 1977–80, Hon. Pres. 1980–; Hon. Freeman, Co. Borough of Stockport, England; Conseiller d'Etat 1977; Chevalier Légion d'honneur. *Address:* 14 rue Ernest Psichari, 75007 Paris, France.

BROUWENSTYN, Gerarda; Netherlands opera singer; studied in Amsterdam; joined the Amsterdam opera and subsequently became First Soprano; has appeared in London, Berlin, Stuttgart, Brussels, Copenhagen, Paris, Vienna, Bayreuth, Barcelona, Buenos Aires, etc.; repertoire includes Forza del Destino, Tosca, Aida, Otello, Un Ballo in Maschera, Tannhäuser, Die Walküre, Die Meistersinger, Le Nozze di Figaro, Jenufa, Troubadour, Cavalleria Rusticana, Don Carlos, etc.; Order of Orange-Nassau.

BROVIKOV, Vladimir Ignatyevich, CAND. PHIL. SC.; Soviet politician; b. 1931, Vetka, Gomel Dist.; ed. Byelorussian State Univ. and CPSU Cen. Cttee. Acad. of Social Sciences; posts in press 1955–63; party posts 1963–70; Sec. Vitebsk Dist. Cttee. of Byelorussian CP 1970–72; posts in Cen. Cttee. of CPSU, Deputy Chief of Organizational Party Work, Cen. Cttee. of CPSU 1972–78; mem. U.S.S.R. Supreme Soviet 1979–; mem. Cen. Cttee. of CPSU 1981–; Pres. Byelorussian Council of Ministers 1983–86; Amb. to Poland 1986–. *Address:* Kommunisticheskaya Partiya Sovietskogo Soyuza, Staraya pl. 4, Moscow, U.S.S.R. *Telephone:* (095) 206-25-11.

BROWALDH, Tore, B.A., LL.M., DR.ENG., DR.ECON.; Swedish banker; b. 23 Aug. 1917, Vaesteraas; s. of Ernfrid and Ingrid (née Gezelius) Browaldh; m. Gunnel Ericson 1946; three s. one d. Financial Attaché Swedish Legation, Washington, D.C. 1943; Asst. Sec. Swedish Royal Cttee. of Post-War Econ. Planning 1944–45; Admin. Sec. Swedish Industrial Inst. for Econ. and Social Research 1944–45; Sec. Bd. of Man., Svenska Handelsbanken 1946–49, Chief Gen. Man. 1955–66, Chair. 1966–78, Vice-Chair. 1978–88, Hon. Chair. 1988–; Dir. Econ., Social, Cultural and Refugee Dept., Sec.-Gen. Council of Europe 1949–51; Exec. Vice-Pres. Confed. of Swedish Employers 1951–54; mem. Bd. Swedish Bankers Assocn., Chair. 1959–61; Chair. AB Industrivärden 1966–88, Svenska Cellulosa AB 1960–88, Swedish IBM, Swedish Unilever AB; Deputy Chair. Nobel Foundation 1966–88, AB Volvo; mem. Bd. IBM World Trade Corpn. 1976–88; mem. Advisory Bd. Unilever, Rotterdam 1976–88; mem. Bd. Dag Hammarskjöld Foundation 1961–63, Swedish Govt. Research Advisory Bd. 1966–70, Swedish Govt. Industrial Policy Comm. 1968–70, Swedish Govt. Econ. Planning Comm. 1962–; Special Adviser to Int. Fed. of Insts. for Advanced Studies; mem. UN Group to Study Multinational Corpns.; mem. Swedish Royal Acad. of Sciences 1980, Swedish Acad. of Eng. Sciences, Royal Acad. of Arts and Sciences, Uppsala; St. Erik Medal, Commdr. Order of Vasa, Kt. Grand Cross Order of the Northern Star. *Publications:* Management and Society 1961, The Pilgrimage of a Journeyman 1976, The Road Ahead 1980, Ascent and Tailwind 1984. *Address:* Svenska Handelsbanken, Arsenalsgatan 11, S-103 28 Stockholm (Office); 14 Sturegatan, 114 36 Stockholm, Sweden (Home). *Telephone:* 08-661 96 43.

BROWDER, Felix Earl, M.A., PH.D.; American professor of mathematics; b. 31 July 1927, Moscow, U.S.S.R.; s. of Earl Browder and Raissa Berkmann; m. Eva Tislowitz 1949; two s.; ed. Yonkers High School and Princeton Univ.; C.L.E. Moore Instr. in Math. M.I.T. 1948–51; Instr. in Math. Boston Univ. 1951–53; U.S. Army 1953–55; Asst. Prof. of Math. Brandeis Univ. 1955–56; from Asst. Prof. to Prof. Yale Univ. 1956–63; Prof. of Math. Univ. of Chicago 1963–72, Louis Block Prof. of Math. 1972–82, Max Mason Distinguished Service Prof. 1982–87; Vice-Pres. for Research and Univ. Prof. Rutgers Univ. 1986–; mem. N.A.S.; Fellow, American Acad. of Arts and Sciences. *Publications:* Problèmes non-linéaires 1966. *Address:* Rutgers University, P.O. Box 201, New Brunswick, N.J. 08903, U.S.A. *Telephone:* (201) 932-8329 (Office); (201) 297-6040 (Home).

BROWN, Alexander Claude, PH.D., F.R.S.S.A.; South African professor of zoology and marine biology; b. 19 Aug. 1931, Cape Town; s. of Alexander John Brown and Doris Hilda (née Todd) Brown; m. Rosalind Jane Roberts 1957; three s.; ed. Rhodes Univ. and Univ. of Cape Town; lecturer in Zoology, Rhodes Univ. 1954; Research Officer Council for Scientific and Industrial Research 1954–57; lecturer and Sr. Lecturer Univ. of Cape Town 1957–74; Prof. and Head Dept. of Zoology 1975–; Deputy Dean, Faculty of Music 1970–80; worked at the Univs. of London, Manchester, Cambridge and Plymouth Marine Lab.; expeditions to Chile and Antarctica; mem. Ed. Bd. Journal of Experimental Marine Biology and Ecology; Past Pres. Royal Soc. of South Africa; Life Fellow Univ. of Cape Town; Gold Medal, Zoological Soc. of Southern Africa. *Publications:* Ed. A History of Scientific Endeavour in South Africa (Royal Soc. of South Africa), several textbooks; Ed. Transactions of the Royal Soc. of South Africa 1968–72; about 150 research papers on the ecophysiology of sandy beach animals and marine pollution. *Leisure interests:* music, musicological research. *Address:* Department of Zoology, University of Cape Town, Rondebosch 7700 (Office); 10 Monroe Road, Rondebosch 7700, South Africa (Home). *Telephone:* 6503603 (Office); 613504 (Home).

BROWN, Arthur Joseph, C.B.E., M.A., D.PHIL., F.B.A.; British professor of economics; b. 8 Aug. 1914, Great Warford, Cheshire; s. of Joseph and Adelene Brown; m. Joan Hannah Margaret Taylor 1938; three s. (one deceased); ed. Bradford Grammar School and Queen's Coll. Oxford; Fellow of All Souls Oxford 1937–46; Foreign Research and Press Service (Foreign Office) 1940–43; Foreign Office Research Dept. (Head of Econ. Section) 1943–45; Econ. Adviser, Econ. Section, Cabinet Office 1945–47; Prof. of Econs., Univ. of Leeds 1947–79, Pro-Vice-Chancellor 1975–77, Emer. Prof. 1979–; Pres. Royal Econ. Soc. 1976–78, Vice-Pres. 1978–; Hon.D.Litt. (Bradford, Sheffield, Kent); Hon. LL.D. (Aberdeen); Hon. Fellow Queen's Coll. *Publications:* Applied Economics: Aspects of the World Economy in War and Peace 1948, The Great Inflation 1939–51 1955, The Framework of Regional Economics in the United Kingdom 1972, World Inflation since 1950 1985. *Leisure interests:* gardening, walking. *Address:* 24 Moor Drive, Leeds, LS6 4BY, England. *Telephone:* (0532) 755799.

BROWN, Daniel McGillivray, PH.D., F.R.S.; British reader in organic chemistry; b. 3 Feb. 1923; s. of David C. Brown and Catherine S. (McGillivray) Brown; m. Margaret J. Herbert 1953; one s. three d.; ed. Glasgow Acad. and Glasgow, London and Cambridge Univs.; Research Chemist, Chester Beatty Research Inst. 1945–53; Fellow, King's Coll. Cambridge 1953–; Asst. Dir. of Research, Univ. of Cambridge 1953–58, Lecturer 1959–67, Reader in Organic Chem. 1967–83, Reader Emer. 1983–; Vice-Provost, King's Coll. Cambridge 1974–81; Attached Fellow, Lab. of Molecular Biology, Cambridge; Visiting Prof. U.C.L.A. 1959–60, Brandeis Univ. 1966–67. *Publications:* articles in professional journals. *Leisure interests:* modern art, gardening, spasmodic fly-fishing. *Address:* 60 Hartington Grove, Cambridge, CB1 4UE, England. *Telephone:* Cambridge 245304.

BROWN, Sir David, Kt., M.I.A.E., F.I.MECH.E.; British engineer and business executive; b. 1904; s. of Frank and Caroline Brown; m. 1st Daisie M. Firth 1926 (dissolved 1955), one s. one d.; m. 2nd Marjorie Deans 1955 (dissolved 1980); m. 3rd Paula Benton Stone 1980; ed. Rossall School, private tuition, and Huddersfield Tech. Coll; David Brown and Sons (Huddersfield) Ltd. 1921, Dir. 1929–32, Man. Dir. 1932; founder David Brown Tractors Ltd. 1935; Chair. David Brown Holdings 1951–78; Chair. Vosper Private Ltd., Singapore 1978–86; fmr. Chair. Vosper Thornycroft; Dir. David Brown Gear Industries (Pty.) Ltd., South Africa, David Brown Corpn. Pty. Ltd., Australia, David Brown Inc., U.S.A., David Brown Int. B.V. Netherlands; fmr. Dir. David Brown Gear Industries Ltd.; underwriting mem. Lloyd's; past mem. Bd. of Govs. Huddersfield Royal Infirmary, Council of Huddersfield Chamber of Commerce; Hon. Dato SPMJ (Johore) 1979. *Leisure interests:* hunting, yachting, tennis. *Address:* L'Estoril, 31 avenue Princesse Grace, Monte Carlo, Monaco.

BROWN, Donald David, M.S., M.D.; American biologist; b. 30 Dec. 1931, Cincinnati, Ohio; s. of Louise R. and Albert L. Brown; m. Linda Weil 1957; three c.; ed. Walnut Hills High School, Cinn. Dartmouth Coll and Univ. of Chicago; Intern, Charity Hosp., New Orleans 1956–57, Sr. Asst. Surgeon, U.S. Public Health Service, Bethesda 1957–59; Postdoctoral Fellow, Pasteur Inst. 1958–60, Dept. of Embryology, Carnegie Inst. of Washington, Baltimore 1960–62, staff mem. 1962–76, Dir. 1976–; Prof., Dept. of Biology, Johns Hopkins Univ. 1968–; Pres. Life Sciences Research Foundation 1981–; U.S. Steel Award in Molecular Biology 1973, V. D. Mattia Award 1976, Boris Pregel Award, New York Acad. of Science 1977, Rose Harrison-ISDB Award 1981, Ernst W. Bertner Award, Texas Univ. Cancer Center 1982, Louisa Gross Horwitz Award, Columbia Univ. 1985, Rosensteil Award 1985, Feodor Lynen Medal, Miami Winter Symposium 1987. *Address:* Department of Embryology, Carnegie Institution of Washington, 115 W University Parkway, Baltimore, Md 21210 (Office); 5721 Oakshire Road, Baltimore, Md. 21209, U.S.A. (Home). *Telephone:* 301-467-1414 (Office).

BROWN, Donald S., B.A.; American administrator; b. 2 April 1928; m.; three s.; ed. Antioch Coll., Ohio; Asst. Program Officer, U.S. Agency for Int. Devt. (AID), mission to Iran 1956–58, to Libya 1958–60, Program Officer, mission to Somalia 1960–63, then to the Sudan; Exec. Sec., Washington, D.C. 1963–65, Deputy Dir. then Dir., mission to Zaire 1967–70, to Morocco 1970–72, Deputy Asst. Admin. of Africa Bureau 1972–76; Dir., mission to Egypt 1976–82, Special Asst. to Admin. of AID 1982–; Woodrow Wilson Fellow, Univ. of Princeton 1965–66; Vice-Pres. Int. Fund for Agricultural Devt. (IFAD) 1983–. *Address:* International Fund for Agricultural Development, Via del Serafico 107, 00142 Rome, Italy.

BROWN, Edmund Gerald (Pat), LL.B.; American lawyer and politician; b. 21 April 1905; s. of Edmund Joseph and Ida (née Schuckman) Brown; m. Bernice Layne 1930; one s. three d.; ed. Lowell High School, San Francisco, Univ. of California Extension Div., San Francisco Coll. of Law; admitted to bar 1927; asst. and successor to Milton L. Schmitt; Dist. Attorney, San Francisco 1943; Attorney-Gen., Calif. 1950, re-elected on nomination of both Democratic and Republican parties 1954; Gov. of Calif. 1959–66; Chair. Nat. Comm. on Reform of Criminal Laws 1967–; Sr. Partner Ball, Hunt, Hart and Brown; Vice-Pres. N.Y. Bd. of Trade; Democrat. *Address:* Ball, Hunt, Hart and Brown, 4525 Wilshire Blvd., Third Floor, Los Angeles, Calif. 90010-3886, U.S.A.

BROWN, Edmund Gerald, Jr., A.B., J.D.; American lawyer and politician; b. 7 April 1938, San Francisco; s. of Edmund G. Brown (q.v.) and Bernice Layne; ed. Univ. of California at Berkeley, Yale Law School; Research Attorney, Calif. Supreme Court 1964–65, Attorney, Los Angeles 1966–69; Sec. of State, Calif. 1971–74; Gov. of Calif. 1975–83; Chair. Calif. State Democratic Party Feb. 1989–; partner Reavis and McGarth; Trustee, Los Angeles Community Colls. 1969. *Address:* Kakmakura, Japan; 8942 Wonderland Park Avenue, Los Angeles, Calif. 90046, U.S.A.

BROWN, Sir (Ernest) Henry Phelps, Kt., M.B.E., M.A., F.B.A.; British economist; b. 10 Feb. 1906, Calne, Wilts.; s. of Edgar W. Brown and Ada L. Bibbing; m. Dorothy E.M. Bowlby 1932; two s. one d.; ed. Taunton School, Wadham Coll., Oxford; Fellow of New Coll., Oxford 1930–47; Rockefeller Travelling Fellow in U.S.A. 1930–31; served with R.A. 1939–45; Prof. of Econs. of Labour, Univ. of London 1947–68; mem. Council on Prices, Productivity and Incomes 1959, Nat. Econ. Devt. Council 1962–66, Royal Comm. on the Distribution of Income and Wealth 1974–78. *Publications:* The Framework of the Pricing System 1936, A Course in Applied Econ-

omics 1951, The Balloon (novel) 1953, The Growth of British Industrial Relations 1959, The Economics of Labour 1962, A Century of Pay 1968, The Inequality of Pay 1977, The Origins of Trade Union Power 1983, Egalitarianism and the Generation of Inequality 1988. *Leisure interests:* walking, gardening. *Address:* 16 Bradmore Road, Oxford, OX2 6QP, England. *Telephone:* Oxford 56320.

BROWN, Fred, PH.D., F.R.S.; British chemist; b. 31 Jan. 1925, Clayton, Lancs.; s. of Fred Brown and Jane E. Fielding; m. Audrey Alice Doherty 1948; two s.; ed. Burnley Grammar School, Victoria Univ. of Manchester; Head, Biochem. Dept., Animal Virus Research Inst., Pirbright, Surrey 1955–83, Deputy Dir. 1980–83; Head, Virology Dept., Wellcome Biotechnology Ltd. 1983–. *Publications:* numerous papers on virology. *Leisure interests:* fell walking, reading scientific biographies. *Address:* Wellcome Biotechnology Ltd., Langley Court, Beckenham, Kent, BR3 3BS (Office); Syndal, Glaziers Lane, Normandy, Surrey, England (Home). *Telephone:* 01-658 2211 (Office); 0483-811107 (Home).

BROWN, Gavin, PH.D., F.A.A.; Australian academic; b. 27 Feb. 1942, Lundin Links, Scotland; s. of Frank B. D. Brown; m. Barbara Routh 1966; one s. one d.; ed. Madras Coll., St. Andrews Univ., Univ. of Newcastle upon Tyne and Univ. of Edinburgh; mem. Faculty Univ. of Liverpool 1966–75; Prof. School of Maths. Univ. of New South Wales 1976–; Visiting Prof. Univ. of Paris 1975, York Univ. 1979, Washington Univ. 1983, Cambridge Univ. 1968; Sir Edmund Whittaker Memorial Prize 1977; Australian Mathematical Soc. Medal 1982. *Address:* 19 Eastern Avenue, N.S.W. 2033, Australia.

BROWN, Sir (George) Malcolm, Kt., D.SC., M.A., D.PHIL., F.R.S., F.R.S.E.; British geologist; b. 5 Oct. 1925; s. of George A. Brown and Anne Brown; m. 1st Valerie J. Gale 1963 (dissolved 1977); m. 2nd Sally J. Marston 1985; two step-d.; ed. Coatham School, Redcar and Univs. of Durham and Oxford; service in R.A.F. 1944–47; Harkness Fellow, Princeton Univ. 1954–55; Lecturer in Petrology, Univ. of Oxford 1955–66; Fellow, St. Cross Coll. Oxford 1965–67; Carnegie Inst. Research Fellow, Geophysical Lab., Washington, D.C. 1966–67; Prof. of Geology, Univ. of Durham 1967–69, Prof. Emer. 1979–, Dean, Faculty of Science 1978–79, Pro-Vice-Chancellor 1979; UN Consultant 1986–; NASA Prin. Investigator, Apollo Moon Programme 1967–75; Dir. British Geological Survey 1979–, Geological Museum 1979–, Geological Survey of N. Ireland 1979–; Geological Adviser to Minister of Overseas Devt. 1979–; Hon. D.Sc. (Leicester) 1984; Murchison Medal 1981. *Publications:* Layered Igneous Rocks (with L. R. Wager) 1968; contribs. to books and scientific journals. *Address:* Dove House, Leafield, Oxford, OX8 5NP, England.

BROWN, Harold, PH.D.; American physicist and fmr. government official; b. 19 Sept. 1927, New York City; s. of A. H. Brown and Gertrude Cohen; m. Colene McDowell 1953; two d.; ed. New York City public schools and Columbia Univ.; Lecturer in Physics, Columbia Univ. 1947–48, Stevens Inst. of Tech. 1949–50; Univ. of Calif. Radiation Laboratory, Berkeley 1950–52; Livermore Radiation Laboratory, 1952–61, Dir. 1960–61; mem. Polaris Steering Cttee., Dept. of Defense 1956–58; Consultant to Air Force Scientific Advisory Bd. 1956–57; mem. Scientific Advisory Cttee. on Ballistic Missiles to Sec. of Defense 1958–61; mem. President's Science Advisory Cttee. 1961; Sec. of Air Force 1965–69; Pres. Calif. Inst. of Tech. 1969–77; U.S. Sec. of Defense 1977–81; Distinguished Visiting Prof. of Nat. Security Affairs, School of Advanced Int. Studies, Johns Hopkins Univ. 1981–84, Chair. Johns Hopkins Univ. Foreign Policy Inst. 1984–; business consultant 1981–; Dir. Amax, CBS Inc., IBM, Philip Morris, Cummins Engine Co. 1981–; mem. Del. to Strategic Arms Limitation Talks 1969; mem. N.A.S.; Hon. D.Eng. (Stevens Inst. of Tech.), Hon. LL.D. (Long Island Univ., Gettysburg Coll., Occidental Coll., Univ. of Calif., Univ. of S.C., Franklin and Marshall Coll., Brown Univ.), Hon. D.Sc. (Univ. of Rochester). *Publication:* Thinking About National Security 1983. *Address:* 1619 Massachusetts Avenue, N.W., Washington, D.C. 20036, U.S.A.

BROWN, Headley Adolphus, PH.D.; Jamaican central bank governor; b. St. Thomas; m.; two c.; ed. Kingston Tech. High School, Univ. of West Indies; Research Economist, Ministry of Industry and Trade 1964–66, Chief Economist 1966–72; Dir. Sectoral and Social Planning, Nat. Planning Agency 1972–75; mem. tech. group which designed framework for EEC/ACP Agreement, Jamaica's rep., tech. group which designed common external tariff for Caricom 1972–75; Dir. Econ. Stabilization Comm. 1976–77; Trade Admin. 1977–81; Chief Tech. Dir. Nat. Planning Agency 1981–84; Dir. Gen. Planning Inst. of Jamaica, Chair. Bd. of Dirs. 1984–; Gov. Bank of Jamaica, Chair. Bd. of Dirs. 1985–; Alt. Gov. IMF, World Bank, Caribbean Devt. Bank, Inter-American Devt. Bank 1985–; Chair. Nat. Export-Import Bank of Jamaica 1985; Dir. Bd. of Nat. Investment Bank of Jamaica 1985, Bd. of Pegasus Hotels of Jamaica 1985; Commdr. of Order of Distinction, Order of Jamaica. *Leisure interests:* lawn tennis, cricket, reading. *Address:* Bank of Jamaica, Nethersole Place, P.O. Box 621, Kingston (Office); 23 Dillsbury Avenue, Kingston 6, Jamaica (Home). *Telephone:* 92-20750 (Office).

BROWN, Helen Gurley (see Gurley Brown, Helen).

BROWN, Herbert Charles, PH.D., D.SC.; American (naturalized 1935) professor of chemistry; b. 22 May 1912, London, England; s. of Charles Brown and Pearl Gorinstein; m. Sarah Baylen 1937; one s.; ed. Wright Junior

Coll., Chicago and Univ. of Chicago; Eli Lilly Post-doctorate Fellow, Univ. of Chicago 1938–39, Instructor 1939–43; Asst. Prof. and Assoc. Prof. Wayne Univ. 1943–47; Prof. Purdue Univ. 1947–59, R. B. Wetherill Research Prof. 1959–78, Emer. 1978–; mem. Bd. of Govs., Hebrew Univ., Jerusalem; Harrison Howe Lecturer 1953; Esmark-Estech Visiting Prof., Univ. of Calif., San Diego 1979; Centenary Lecturer, Chem. Soc. London 1955, Baker Lecturer 1968, Ingold Memorial Lecturer, Chemical Soc., London 1978, IBM Lecturer for Brazil 1983, AID Lecturer for Thailand 1985; mem. Nat. Acad. of Sciences, American Acad. of Arts and Sciences; Corresp. mem. Acad. of Arts and Sciences, Puerto Rico; Hon. mem. Pharmaceutical Soc. of Japan, Chemical Soc. of Japan; Bd. of Visitors, Boston Univ. 1977; Foreign Fellow, Indian Nat. Science Acad. 1977; Hon. D.Sc. (Univ. of Chicago) 1968, Hon. Fellow, Chemical Soc. 1978; Nichols Medal 1959, A.C.S. Award 1960, S.O.C.M.A. Medal 1960, Linus Pauling Medal 1968, Nat. Medal of Science 1969, Roger Adams Medal 1971, Chandler Medal 1973; Madison Marshall Award 1975; CCNY Scientific Achievement Award Medal 1976, Elliot Cresson Medal, Franklin Inst., Philadelphia 1978, Allied Chemical Award 1978, Ingold Memorial Lecturer and Medal 1978, Nobel Prize in Chemistry 1979, Priestley Medal 1981, Perkin Medal 1982, Medal of Pharmaceutical Soc. of Japan 1982, Gold Medal of the American Inst. of Chemists 1985, N.A.S. Award in Chemical Sciences 1987. *Publications:* Hydroboration 1962, Boranes in Organic Chemistry 1972, Organic Syntheses via Boranes 1975, The Nonclassical Ion Problem 1977, Borane Reagents 1988 (with A. Pelter, K. Smith); many articles in professional journals. *Leisure interest:* travel. *Address:* Department of Chemistry, Purdue University, West Lafayette, Ind. 47907 (Office); 1840 Garden Street, West Lafayette, Ind. 47906, U.S.A. (Home). *Telephone:* (317) 494-5316 (Office); (317) 463-5651 (Home).

BROWN, James; American singer and broadcasting executive; b. 17 June 1928; leader, Famous Flames (musical group) 1956–; now solo performer and recording artist with King, Smash Records; Pres. J.B. Broadcasting, Ltd. 1968–, James Brown Network 1968–; arrested Dec. 1988 for attempted assault, received six-year sentence; *films include:* Come to the Table 1974, The Blues Brothers 1980; recordings include Original Disco Man, Please, Please, Hot on the One, Poppa's Got a Brand New Bag; Grammy award 1965; 44 Gold Record awards. *Address:* c/o Brothers Management Associates, 141 Dunbar Avenue, Fords, N.J., U.S.A.

BROWN, John Canvin, PH.D., F.R.S.C.; Canadian professor of physiology; b. 10 Oct. 1938, U.K.; s. of Thomas Brown and Eliza Canvin; m. Anne J. Robinson 1963; one s. two d.; ed. Univs. of Durham and Newcastle-upon-Tyne; Visiting Prof. Univ. of Washington 1964–65; Asst. Prof. Univ. of British Columbia 1965–69, Assoc. Prof. 1969–72, Prof. of Physiology 1972–; Dir. MRC Regulatory Peptide Group 1986–; Hon. Prof. Beijing Medical Univ.; Oppenheimer Award, Endocrinology Soc.; McLaughlin Medal, Royal Soc. of Canada; Gold Medal, B.C. Sciences Council. *Leisure interest:* fly fishing. *Address:* University of British Columbia, Department of Physiology, MRC Regulatory Peptide Group, 2146 Health Sciences Mall, Vancouver, B.C., V6T 1W5, Canada.

BROWN, Sir John Gilbert Newton, Kt., C.B.E.; British publisher; b. 7 July 1916, London; s. of John Brown and Molly Purchas; m. Virginia Braddell 1946; one s. two d.; ed. Lancing Coll., Hertford Coll., Oxford; Man. Oxford Univ. Press, Bombay 1937–40, London 1946–49, Sales Man. 1949–55, Deputy Publr. 1955, Publr. 1956–74, Publr. Gen. Div. and Deputy Sec. 1974–80; served R.A. 1940–41, Japanese P.O.W. 1942–45; Chair. B. H. Blackwell Ltd. 1980–83, Basil Blackwell Publishers Ltd., Univ. Bookshops (Oxford) Ltd.; Dir. Blackwell Group Ltd., Willshaws Ltd., Manchester, Book Tokens Ltd.; mem. Publrs. Asscn., Pres. 1963–65; mem. Bd. British Library 1974–80; mem. Bd. British Council; Prof. Fellow of Hertford Coll., Oxford; Jt. Treas. Royal Literary Fund. *Leisure interest:* gardening. *Address:* B. H. Blackwell Ltd., 50 Broad Street, Oxford, OX1 3BQ (Office); Milton Lodge, Great Milton, Oxon., England (Home). *Telephone:* 084-46217 (Home).

BROWN, John Joseph; Australian politician; b. 19 Dec. 1931, Sydney; m.; four s. one d.; ed. Sydney Univ.; worked as distributor and co. dir. in wholesale meat business; Alderman, Parramatta City Council 1977–70; M.P. for Parramatta, N.S.W. 1977–; Minister for Sport, Recreation and Tourism 1983–87 (also Minister assisting the Minister for Defence), for Admin. Services 1983–84; Chair. N.S.W. Wholesale Meat Traders' Assen. 1974–76; mem. Australasian Meat Industry Employees' Union; Labor Party. *Leisure interests:* golf, jogging, horse racing, theatre, opera, gardening. *Address:* Parliament House, Canberra, A.C.T. 2600, Australia.

BROWN, L. Dean; American diplomatist; b. 1920, New York, N.Y.; s. of Lewis P. Brown and Elizabeth Crossley; m. June Vereker Farquhar 1942; one s.; ed. Wesleyan Univ. and Imperial Defence Coll., London; served in U.S. Army 1942–46; joined U.S. Foreign Service 1946; postings to Congo, Canada, France, U.K., Morocco, Senegal; Amb. to Senegal and The Gambia 1967–70, to Jordan 1970–73; Deputy Under-Sec. of State for Man. 1973–75; Pres. Middle East Inst., Washington, D.C. 1975–; Dir. Pres. Task Force on Vietnam 1975; Special Pres. Envoy to Cyprus 1973, to Lebanon 1976. *Address:* 1761 N Street, N.W., Washington, D.C. 20036 (Office); 3030 Cambridge Place, Washington, D.C. 20007, U.S.A. (Home).

BROWN, Lawrence Michael, B.SC., M.A., PH.D., F.R.S.; Canadian physicist; b. 18 March 1936, Windsor, Ont.; s. of B. W. and Edith Brown; m. Susan

Drucker 1965; one s. two d.; ed. Univ. of Toronto, Univ. of Birmingham, England; work in Cambridge 1960–, Fellow, Gonville and Caius Coll. 1963–, Univ. Demonstrator in Physics 1966, Reader in Structure and Properties of Materials, Dept. of Physics 1982–; Fellow and Coll. Lecturer in Natural Science (Physical), Robinson Coll. 1977–; Rosenhain Medal, Metals Soc. 1980. *Publications:* many papers in Philosophical Magazine and Acta Metallurgica. *Leisure interests:* reading, gardening. *Address:* Cavendish Laboratory, Madingley Road, Cambridge, CB3 0HE; 74 Alpha Road, Cambridge, CB4 3DG, England (Home). *Telephone:* (0223) 337291 (Office); (0223) 62987 (Home).

BROWN, Sir Mervyn, K.C.M.G., O.B.E., M.A.; British diplomatist (retd.); b. 24 Sept. 1923, Durham; s. of William Brown and Edna Penman; m. Elizabeth Gittings 1949; ed. Ryhope Grammar School, Sunderland and St. John's Coll., Oxford; Third Sec., Foreign Office 1949–50; Buenos Aires 1950–53; Second Sec., New York 1953–56; First Sec., Foreign Office 1956–59; Singapore 1959–60; Vientiane 1960–63; Foreign Office 1963–67; Amb. to Madagascar 1967–70; Diplomatic Service Insp. 1970–72; Head of Communications Operations Dept., FCO 1973–74, Dir. of Communications 1974; High Commr. in Tanzania 1975–78, concurrently Amb. to Madagascar 1976–78; Deputy Perm. Rep. to UN 1978; High Commr. in Nigeria 1979–83; Chair. Anglo-Malagasy Soc. *Publication:* Madagascar Rediscovered. *Leisure interests:* music, history, tennis. *Address:* 195 Queen's Gate, London, S.W.7, England.

BROWN, Michael Stuart, B.A., M.D.; American professor of genetics; b. 13 April 1941, New York; s. of Harvey Brown and Evelyn Katz; m. Alice Lapin 1964; two d.; ed. Univ. of Pennsylvania; Intern, then Resident, Mass. Gen. Hosp. Boston 1966–68; served with U.S. Public Health Service 1968–70; Clinical Assoc. Nat. Inst. of Health 1968–71; Asst. Prof. Univ. of Texas Southwestern Medical School, Dallas 1971–74, Paul J. Thomas, Prof. of Genetics and Dir. Center of Genetic Diseases 1977–; mem. N.A.S. and other scientific socs.; Pfizer Award (American Chemical Soc.) 1976; Lounsbery Award (N.A.S.) 1979, Lita Annenberg Hazen Award 1982, Albert Lasker Medical Research Award 1985. *Address:* University of Texas Health Center, Department of Internal Medicine-Biophysics, 5323 Harry Hines Boulevard, Dallas, Tex. 75235, U.S.A.

BROWN, Robert, D.SC., F.R.S.; British professor of botany; b. 29 July 1908; s. of Thomas W. Brown and Ethel M. Brown; m. Morna D. Mactaggart 1940; ed. English School, Cairo and Univ. of London; Asst. Lecturer in Botany, Univ. of Manchester 1940–44; Lecturer in Botany, Bedford Coll. London 1944–46; Reader in Plant Physiology, Univ. of Leeds 1946–52; Prof. of Botany, Cornell Univ. 1952–53; Dir. Agricultural Research Council Unit of Plant Cell Physiology 1953–58; Regius Prof. of Botany, Univ. of Edin. 1958–77, Prof. Emer. 1977–. *Publications:* articles in professional journals. *Address:* 5 Treble House Terrace, Blewbury, Didcot, Oxon., OX11 9NZ, England. *Telephone:* Blewbury 850415.

BROWN, Robert Hanbury, A.C., D.SC., M.I.E.E., F.R.A.S., F.A.A., F.R.S.; British professor of astronomy and consulting engineer; b. 31 August 1916, Aruvankadu, India; s. of Col. B. H. Brown and Joyce Brown (née Blaker); m. Hilda Chesterman 1952; two s. one d.; ed. Tonbridge School, Kent, Brighton Tech. Coll., City and Guilds Coll., Univ. of London; Scientific Officer Air Ministry (radar) 1936–42; Hon. Comm. Flight Lieut. R.A.F. 1940–45; Asst. Head Combined Research Group, Naval Research Lab., Washington, D.C. 1942–45; Prin. Scientific Officer Telecommunications Research Establishment and Head Navigation Div., Ministry of Supply 1945–47; Partner Sir Robert Watson-Watt and Partners Ltd. 1947–49; Prof. Radio-Astronomy Univ. of Manchester 1949–64; Prof. Physics Univ. of Sydney, Australia 1964–, Prof. of Physics (Astronomy) 1964–81, Emer. Prof.; Dir. Narrabri Observatory, Foundation Research Fellow 1982–88; Pres. Int. Astronomical Union; Hon. D.Sc. (Sydney and Monash Univs.), numerous awards including Hughes Medal of The Royal Soc. 1971, Britannica Australia Medal 1971, Hon. F.A.Sc. 1975, Hon. F.N.A. 1975, Michelson Medal of Franklin Inst. 1982. *Publications:* The Exploration of Space by Radio (with A. C. B. Lovell) 1960, The Intensity Interferometer 1974, Man and the Stars 1978, Photons, Galaxies and Stars 1985, The Wisdom of Science 1986. *Address:* White Cottage, Penton Mewsey, Andover, Hants, SP11 0RQ, England. *Telephone:* (026477) 2344.

BROWN, Robert McAfee, M.DIV., PH.D.; American professor and clergyman; b. 28 May 1920, Illinois; s. of George William Brown and Ruth McAfee Brown; m. Sydney Elise Thomson 1944; three s. one d.; ed. Amherst Coll., Union Theological Seminary, Columbia Univ.; U.S. Navy Chaplain, Pacific 1945–46; Asst. Chaplain, Instructor in Religion, Amherst Coll. 1946–48; Instructor, Union Theological Seminary 1950–51; Prof. and Head of Dept. of Religion, Macalester Coll. 1951–53; Auburn Prof. of Systematic Theology, Union Theological Seminary 1953–62; Prof. of Religious Studies, Stanford Univ. 1962–76; Prof. of Ecumenics, Union Theological Seminary 1976–79; Prof. of Theology and Ethics, Pacific School of Religion 1979–86, Prof. Emer. 1986–; Fulbright Scholar 1949–50; Montgomery Fellow, Dartmouth Coll. 1966; various hon. doctorates. *Publications:* numerous books, including The Spirit of Protestantism 1961, the Ecumenical Revolution 1967, Religion and Violence 1973, Is Faith Obsolete? 1974, Making Peace in the Global Village 1981, Elie Wiesel: Messenger to All Humanity 1982, Unexpected News: Reading the Bible with Third World Eyes 1984, Saying Yes and Saying No: On Rendering to God and Caesar 1986, Spirituality and Liberation: Overcoming the Great Fallacy; several transls. *Leisure interests:* cello, carpentry, grandchildren. *Address:* 2090 Columbia Street, Palo Alto, Calif. 94306, U.S.A. *Telephone:* (415) 857 0870.

BROWN, Roger William, M.A., PH.D.; American professor of social psychology; b. 14 April 1925, Detroit; s. of Frank H. Brown and Muriel L. Brown; ed. Univ. of Michigan; Asst. Prof. Social Psychology, Harvard Univ. 1952–57; Assoc. Prof. of Social Psychology, Mass. Inst. of Tech., Prof. of Social Psychology 1960–62, Prof. of Social Psychology, Harvard Univ. 1962–, John Lindsley Prof. of Psychology in Memory of William James 1974–, Chair. Dept. of Social Relations 1967–70; mem. N.A.S.; Hon. Doctorate York Univ., England, (Bucknell Univ.) 1980, (Northwestern Univ.) 1983; Fyssen Int. Prize in Cognitive Sciences 1984. *Publications:* Words and Things 1958, The Acquisition of Language 1964, Social Psychology 1965, 1986, Psycholinguistics 1970, A First Language 1973, Psychology (with R. Herrnstein) 1975. *Leisure interests:* music and literature. *Address:* 1270 William James Hall, Harvard University, Cambridge, Mass. 02138 (Office); 100 Memorial Drive, Cambridge, Mass. 02142, U.S.A. (Home).

BROWN, Ronald Drayton, PH.D.; Australian professor of chemistry; b. 14 Oct. 1927, Melbourne; s. of William Harrison Brown and Linda Grace Drayton; m. Florence Catherine Mary Stringer 1950; two s. one d.; ed. Wesley Coll., Melbourne, Univs. of Melbourne and London; lecturer, Univ. Coll., London, U.K., Melbourne Univ.; Prof. of Chem., Monash Univ. 1959–, Chair. Chem. Dept.; current research interests cover theoretical chem., spectroscopy, galactochemistry and life in space; Vice-Pres. Comm. 51 (Search for Extraterrestrial Life) of Int. Astronomical Union; Discipline Specialist, Int. Halley Watch; mem. Spectroscopy Comm., Int. Union of Pure and Applied Chem.; Fellow Australian Acad. of Science (fmr. mem. Council and Vice-Pres. of Physical Sciences); Masson Medal, Royal Chemical Inst. 1948, Rennie Medal 1951, Smith Medal 1959; David Syme Prize for Research, Univ. of Melbourne 1959; Edgeworth-David Medal, Royal Soc. of N.S.W. 1961; Royal Soc. Medal of Victoria 1977. *Address:* Department of Chemistry, Monash University, Wellington Road, Clayton, Vic., 3618 (Office); 21 Brolga Street, Mount Waverley, 3149 Vic., Australia (Home). *Telephone:* (03) 565 4550 (Office); (03) 277 9109 (Home).

BROWN, Ronald H.; American attorney and politician; b. 1941; ed. Middlebury Coll., Vermont; joined Urban League; staff mem. to Senator Ted Kennedy 1980; Nat. Convention Man. Jesse Jackson Campaign for Pres. 1988; Chair. Nat. Democratic Cttee. Feb. 1989–. *Address:* Office of the Chairman, 430 South Capitol Street, S.E., Washington, D.C. 20003, U.S.A.

BROWN, William Lacy, PH.D.; American plant geneticist and business executive; b. 16 July 1913, Arbovale, W. Va.; s. of Tilden L. and Mamie Hudson (Orndoff) Brown; m. Alice Hevener Hannah 1941; one s. one d.; ed. Bridgewater Coll., Va. and Washington Univ., St. Louis; Cytogeneticist, Dept. of Agric., Washington 1941-42; Dir. Maize Breeding, Rogers Bros. Co., Olivia, Minn. 1942-45; with Pioneer Hi-Bred Int. Inc. 1945–, Vice-Pres., Dir. of Corpn. Research, Des Moines 1965-75, Pres. 1975-79, C.E.O. 1975-81, Chair., Dir. 1979-83; Dir. American Farmland Trust; Extra-Mural Prof. of Botany, Washington Univ. 1957-65; Chair. Bd. on Agric., Nat. Research Council, N.A.S. 1981–; Univ. Fellow, Drake Univ. 1981–; Fellow American Soc. of Agronomy; mem. A.A.A.S., N.A.S., American Genetics Assscn., American Inst. of Biological Sciences, Botanical Soc. of America; Fulbright Advanced Research Scholar, Imperial Coll. of Tropical Agric., Trinidad 1952-53; Distinguished Econ. Botanist Award, Soc. of Econ. Botany 1980. *Publications:* papers on maize cytogenetics, evolution and germplasm conservation. *Address:* 6800 Pioneer Parkway, Johnston, Ia. 50131 (Office); 5770 Linden Court, Johnston, Ia. 50131 U.S.A. (Home).

BROWNE-WILKINSON, Rt. Hon. Sir Nicolas Christopher Henry, Kt., P.C., Q.C., B.A.; British judge; b. 30 March 1930; s. of Canon A. R. Browne-Wilkinson and Molly Browne-Wilkinson; m. Ursula de Lacy Bacon 1955 (died 1986); three s. two d.; ed. Lancing Coll., Magdalen Coll. Oxford; called to Bar, Lincoln's Inn 1953, Bencher 1977; Q.C. 1972; Jr. Counsel to Registrar of Restrictive Trading Agreements 1964-66, to Attorney-Gen. in Charity Matters 1966-72, in bankruptcy, to Dept. of Trade and Industry 1966-72; a Judge of the Courts of Appeal of Jersey and Guernsey 1976-77; a Judge of the High Court, Chancery Div. 1977-83; a Lord Justice of Appeal 1983-85; Vice-Chancellor of the Supreme Court 1985–; Pres. Employment Appeal Tribunal 1981-83, Senate of the Inns of Court and the Bar 1984-86. *Leisure interests:* farming, gardening. *Address:* Royal Courts of Justice, Strand, London, WC2A 2LL, England.

BROWNELL, Herbert, A.B., LL.B.; American lawyer; b. 20 Feb. 1904, Peru, Neb.; s. of Herbert Brownell and May Miller Brownell; brother of Samuel Miller Brownell (q.v.); m. 2nd Marian R. Taylor 1987; two s. two d.; ed. Univ. of Nebraska and Yale Univ. School of Law; admitted to New York Bar 1928; law practice, Root, Clark, Buckner, Howland and Ballantine 1928-29; mem. N.Y. State Assembly 1932-37; practising attorney Lord, Day & Lord 1929-53, 1957-89; Attorney-Gen. of U.S. 1953-57; Pres. Assscn. of Bar of City of N.Y. 1962-64; Chubb Fellowship, Yale Univ. 1959–; Assoc. Fellow Silliman Coll., Yale Univ. 1955–; Chair. Comm. on Int. Rules of Judicial Procedure 1958-59, American Bar Asscn. Cttee. on Constitutional Amendment relating to Presidential Disability; Pres. Amer-

ican Judicature Soc. 1966-68; Vice-Chair. U.S. Bicentennial Comm. on Constitution. *Address:* 2 East 70 Street, New York, N.Y. 10021, U.S.A. *Telephone:* (212) 744-7187.

BROWNELL, Samuel Miller, M.A., PH.D.; American educationist; b. 3 April 1900, Peru, Neb.; s. of Herbert Brownell and May Miller Brownell; brother of Herbert Brownell (q.v.); m. Esther Delzell 1927; four c.; ed. Lincoln (Neb.) High School, Univ. of Nebraska and Yale Univ.; teacher, Demonstration High School, State Teachers Coll., Peru, Neb. 1921-23; Asst. Prof. of Educ., N.Y. State Coll. for Teachers 1926-27; Supt. of Schools, Grosse Pointe, Mich. 1927-38; Prof. of Educational Admin., Yale Univ. 1938-56; Pres. New Haven State Teachers, Coll. 1947-53; U.S. Commr. of Educ. 1953-56; Supt. of Schools, Detroit 1956-66; Prof. Urban Educational Admin., Yale Univ. and Univ. of Conn. 1966-70; Consultant Urban Educ. and Dir. Mid-Career Program, City School Admin. 1970-73; Prof. Emer. Yale Univ.; many hon. degrees. *Publications:* Progress in Educational Administration 1935, Urban Education 1962; Ed. Issues in Urban Education 1971. *Leisure interests:* spectator sports, travel. *Address:* Apartment 1L, 70 Livingston Street, New Haven, Conn. 06511, U.S.A. *Telephone:* (203) 562-8545.

BROWNING, Most Rev. Edmond L., B.D.; American ecclesiastic; b. 11 March 1929, Texas; s. of Edmond L. Browning and Cora M. Lee; m. Patricia Sparks 1953; four s. one d.; ed. Univ. of the South, Sewanee, Tenn., School of Theology, Sewanee and Japanese Language School, Okinawa; First missionary Bishop of Okinawa 1968-71; Bishop-in-Charge, Convocation of American Churches in Europe 1971-74; Exec. for Nat. and World Mission, Episcopal Church Center 1974-76; Bishop of Hawaii 1976-85; Presiding Bishop, Episcopal Church, U.S.A. 1985–. *Address:* 815 Second Avenue, New York, N.Y. 10017, U.S.A. *Telephone:* 212 867-8400.

BROWNING, Keith Anthony, D.I.C., PH.D., F.R.S., A.R.C.S.; British meteorologist; b. 31 July 1938, Sunderland; s. of late James Anthony Browning and of Amy Hilda Greenwood; m. Ann Baish 1962; one s. two d.; ed. Imperial Coll. of Science and Tech., Univ. of London; Research Atmospheric Physicist, Air Force Cambridge Research Labs., Mass., U.S.A. 1962-66; Chief Meteorological Officer, Meteorological Office Radar Research Lab., Royal Signals and Radar Establishment, Malvern, Worcs. 1966-74, 1975-85; Chief Scientist, Nat. Hail Research Experiment, Nat. Center for Atmospheric Research, Boulder, Colo., U.S.A. 1974-75; Deputy Dir. (Physical Research), Meteorological Office, Bracknell, Berks. 1985-89, Dir. of Research 1989–; Chair. Meteorology & Atmospheric Physics Sub-Cttee. of British Cttee. for Geodesy and Geophysics 1985–; mem. Natural Environment Research Council 1984-87; Visiting Prof., Dept. of Meteorology, Univ. of Reading 1988–; Pres. Royal Meteorological Soc. 1988-90; awards from Royal Meteorological Soc., American Meteorological Soc. and Inst. of Physics. *Publications:* numerous articles on meteorology. *Leisure interests:* home and garden. *Address:* Meteorological Office, London Road, Bracknell, Berks, RG12 2SZ, England.

BROWNING, Robert, M.A., D.LITT., F.B.A.; British historian; b. 15 Jan. 1914, Glasgow, Scotland; s. of Alexander M. Browning and Jean M. Browning (née Miller); m. 1st Galina Chichekova 1946, 2nd Ruth Gresh 1972; two d.; ed. Glasgow Univ., Balliol and Merton Colls. Oxford; served in army 1939-46; lecturer, Univ. Coll. London 1947-55, Reader 1955-65; Prof. of Classics and Ancient History, Birkbeck Coll., Univ. of London 1965-81, Emer. Prof. 1981–; Pres. Soc. for the Promotion of Hellenic Studies 1974-77; Fellow of Dumbarton Oaks, Washington D.C., U.S.A. 1973-74, 1982, 1983-(91); Chair. British Cttee. for the Restitution of the Parthenon Marbles 1982–, Nat. Trust for Greece 1985–; Vice-Pres. Assscn. Int. des Etudes Byzantines 1981–; Hon. D.Litt. (Birmingham) 1980, Hon. Dr. (Athens) 1988; Corresp. mem. Athens Acad; Commdr., Order of the Phoenix, Greece 1984. *Publications:* Medieval and Modern Greek 1969, 1983, Justinian and Theodora 1971, Byzantium and Bulgaria 1975, The Emperor Julian 1976, The Byzantine Empire 1980, The Greek World, Classical, Byzantine and Modern (ed.) 1985. *Address:* 17 Belsize Park Gardens, London, NW3 4JG, England. *Telephone:* (01) 586 2135.

BROWNLEE, George, D.SC., PH.D., F.K.C.; British professor of pharmacology; b. 8 Sept. 1911, Edinburgh; s. of late George R. Brownlee and Mary C. C. Gow; m. 1st Margaret P. M. Cochrane 1940 (died 1970); m. 2nd Betty J. Gaydon (divorced 1981); three s.; ed. Tynecastle School and Heriot-Watt Coll., Edinburgh and Univ. of Glasgow; mem. scientific staff, Wellcome Research Labs. 1939-49, MRC Toxicology Unit, Carshalton 1949; Reader in Pharmacology, King's Coll. London 1949-55, Prof. of Pharmacology 1955-78, Prof. Emer. 1978–. *Publications:* Experimental Pharmacology (with J. P. Quilliam) 1952; contribs. to scientific journals. *Leisure interests:* herbals, history of medicine, making things. *Address:* 602 Gilbert House, Barbican, London, EC2Y 8BD, England. *Telephone:* 01-638 9543.

BROWNLIE, Ian, Q.C., D.C.L., F.B.A.; British barrister and university teacher; b. 19 Sept. 1932, Liverpool; s. of Amy Isabella Atherton and John Nason Brownlie; m. 1st Jocelyn Gale 1958, one s. two d.; m. 2nd Christine Apperley 1978; ed. Alsop High School, Liverpool, Hertford Coll. Oxford and King's Coll. Cambridge; called to Bar (Gray's Inn) 1958; in practice 1967–; Q.C. 1979; Bencher of Gray's Inn 1988; teaching and research at Nottingham Univ. 1957-63; Fellow Wadham Coll. Oxford 1963-76; Prof. of Int. Law, London Univ. (attached to L.S.E.) 1976-80; Chichele Prof. of

Public Int. Law, Oxford and Fellow of All Souls 1980-. *Publications:* International Law and the Use of Force by States 1963, Principles of Public International Law 1966, Encyclopaedia of African Boundaries 1979, State Responsibility, Part I 1983; British Year Book of International Law (Jt. Ed.). *Leisure interests:* travel, book collecting, maps. Address: All Souls College, Oxford, OX1 4AL; 2 Hare Court, Temple, London, EC4Y 7BH (Chambers); 43 Fairfax Road, Chiswick, London, W4 1EN, England (Home). *Telephone:* (0865) 279342 (Coll.); 01-583 1770 (Chambers); 01-995 3647 (Home).

BROWNLOW, Kevin; British film historian and television director; b. 2 June 1938, Crowborough, Sussex; s. of Robert Thomas Brownlow and Niña Fortnum; m. Virginia Keane 1969; one d.; ed. University College School, Hampstead; joined World Wide Pictures 1955; became film Ed., then jt. Dir. 1964; with Thames TV 1975-. *Films* include: It Happened Here 1964, Winstanley 1975 (both with Andrew Mollo). *Publications:* Parade's Gone By... 1968, The War, the West and the Wilderness 1978, Napoleon (Abel Gance's Classic Film) 1983. *Television* includes 13-part series Hollywood 1980, three-part Unknown Chaplin 1983, three-part British Cinema 1986, three part Buster Keaton—A Hard Act to Follow 1987 (all with David Gill). *Address:* c/o Thames Television, 306 Euston Road, London, N.W.1, England (Office). *Telephone:* 01-387 9494.

BROYLES, William Dodson, Jr., M.A.; American journalist; b. 8 Oct. 1944, Houston; s. of William Dodson and Elizabeth (née Bills) Broyles; m. Sybil Ann Newman 1973; one s. one d.; ed. Rice Univ., Houston, Oxford Univ.; U.S. Marine Corps Reserve 1969-71; teacher Philosophy U.S. Naval Acad. 1970-71; Asst. Supt. Houston Public Schools 1971-72; Ed.-in-Chief Texas Monthly 1972-82; Ed.-in-Chief California Magazine 1980-82; Ed.-in-Chief Newsweek Magazine 1982-84; Columnist, U.S. News and World Report 1986; Bronze Star. *Address:* Diskant and Co., 1033 Gayley Avenue, 202 Los Angeles, Calif. 90024, U.S.A.

BRUBECK, David Warren, B.A.; American musician; b. 6 Dec. 1920, Concord, Calif.; s. of Howard P. Brubeck and Elizabeth Ivey; m. Iola Whitlock 1942; five s. one d.; ed. Pacific and Mills Colls.; formed his own trio 1950, Dave Brubeck Quartet 1951; numerous tours and recordings; many awards from trade magazines, Metronome, Downbeat, Billboard, Melodymaker; Hon. Ph.D. (Univ. of Pacific, Fairfield Univ., Univ. of Bridgeport, Mills Coll.); Jazz Pioneer Award, BMI 1985; Compostela Humanitarian Award 1986; Connecticut Arts Award 1987; American Eagle Award, Nat. Music Council 1988; Duke Ellington Fellow, Yale Univ.; composer of 250 jazz pieces and songs. *Extended works:* Points of Jazz (ballet), Elementals (orchestral), The Light in the Wilderness (oratorio), The Gates of Justice (cantata), Truth Is Fallen (cantata), La Fiesta de la Posada (cantata), They all sang Yankee Doodle (orchestral), Glances (ballet), Beloved Son (oratorio), Tritonis (piece for flute and guitar), Festival Mass: To Hope, Variations on Pange Lingua, The Voice of the Holy Spirit (oratorio) 1985. *Address:* Derry Music Company, 601 Montgomery Street, San Francisco, Calif. 94111; Box 216, Wilton, Conn. 06897, U.S.A.

BRUBECK, William H.; American government official; b. 19 Aug. 1920, Hannibal, Mo.; s. of Zorah Moab Brubeck and Marcia Little; m. 1st Margaret Bramwell Houser 1947 (deceased), one d.; m. 2nd Lois Sidenberg 1960; one s. two d.; ed. St. John's Coll., Maryland and Harvard Univ.; U.S. Army service 1942-46; Teaching Fellow, St. John's Coll. 1946-48, Harvard Univ. 1950-52; Asst. Prof. Williams Coll. 1952-56; Visiting Lecturer, Salzburg Seminary, Austria 1955, Columbia Univ. 1957; Legislative Asst. to mems. of Congress 1956; Consultant, pvt. firm 1957-60, to Devt. Loan Fund 1961; Special Asst. to Under-Sec. of State 1961, Deputy Exec. Sec., Exec. Secr. 1961-62, Special Asst. to Sec. of State, Exec. Sec. of Dept. of State 1962-63; mem. Nat. Security Council, White House 1963-65; Political Counsellor, London 1965-69; Deputy Head of Mission, Jordan 1970-73; at Dept of State 1976-; Exec. Dir. Middle East Working Group, State Dept., 1977-78; Man. Ed. Daedalus 1978-. *Address:* 7 Linden Street, Harvard, Cambridge, Mass. 02138, U.S.A.

BRUCE, Frederick Fyvie, M.A., D.D., F.B.A.; British university professor (retd.); b. 12 Oct. 1910, Elgin, Scotland; s. of Rev. Peter Fyvie Bruce and Mary Maclennan; m. Betty Davidson 1936; one s. one d.; ed. Elgin Acad., Univs. of Aberdeen, Cambridge and Vienna; Asst. Lecturer in Greek, Univ. of Edinburgh 1935-38; Lecturer in Greek, Univ. of Leeds 1938-47; Prof. of Biblical History and Literature, Univ. of Sheffield 1947-59; Rylands Prof. of Biblical Criticism and Exegesis, Univ. of Manchester 1959-78; Prof. Emer. 1978-; Burkitt Medal in Biblical Studies (British Acad.) 1979; Hon. D.Litt. (Sheffield) 1988. *Publications:* The Acts of the Apostles: Greek text with introduction and commentary 1951, Biblical Exegesis in the Qumran Texts 1960, Tradition Old and New 1970, Paul: Apostle of the Free Spirit 1977, History of the Bible in English 1978, In Retrospect 1980, New Testament History 1982, Galatians: Greek Text with introduction and commentary 1982, 1 and 2 Thessalonians 1982, The Hard Sayings of Jesus 1983, The Epistles to Colossians, Philemon, and Ephesians 1984, The Work of Jesus 1984, The Real Jesus 1985, The Pauline Circle 1985, Paul and His Converts 1985, The Canon of Scripture 1988. *Leisure interest:* foreign travel. *Address:* The Crossways, 2 Temple Road, Buxton, Derbyshire, SK17 9BA, England. *Telephone:* 0298-3250.

BRUCE-CHWATT, Leonard Jan, C.M.G., O.B.E., M.D., M.P.H., F.R.C.P.; British professor of tropical hygiene; b. 9 June 1907, Lodz, Poland; s. of Michael Chwatt and Anna Marquitante; m. Joan M. Bruce 1948; two s.; ed. Univs. of Warsaw, Paris and London and Harvard School of Public Health; wartime service in Polish Army 1939-41, thereafter in R.A.M.C.; Sr. Malariologist, Fed. Medical Service, Nigeria 1948-58; Chief, Research and Technical Intelligence, WHO, Geneva 1958-68; Prof. of Tropical Hygiene and Dir. Ross Inst. Univ. of London 1968-74 (retd.); Assoc. Wellcome Tropical Inst. 1985-; Darling Medal and Prize, Laveran Medal, Rudolf Leuckart Medal, German Soc. for Parasitology. *Publications:* Dynamics of Tropical Disease (with V. Glanville) 1973, Rise and Fall of Malaria in Europe (with J. de Zulueta) 1980, Essential Malariology (2nd edn.) 1985, Chemotherapy of Malaria 1985 (2nd edn.). *Leisure interests:* music, travel. *Address:* 21 Marchmont Road, Richmond, Surrey, England. *Telephone:* 01-387 4477 (Office); 01-940 5540 (Home).

BRUCE-MITFORD, Rupert Leo Scott, M.A., F.B.A.; British museum keeper (retd.); b. 14 June 1914, London; s. of C. E. Bruce-Mitford and Beatrice Allison; m. 1st Kathleen Dent 1941 (dissolved 1972), one s. two d.; m. 2nd Marilyn R. Luscombe 1975 (dissolved 1984); ed. Christ's Hospital and Hertford Coll. Oxford; Temporary Asst. Keeper, Ashmolean Museum 1937; Asst. Keeper, Dept. of British and Medieval Antiquities, British Museum 1938; Royal Signals 1939-45; Keeper of British and Medieval Antiquities, British Museum 1954-69, of Medieval and Later Antiquities 1969-75, Research Keeper 1975-77; F.S.A. Scotland; Slade Prof. of Fine Art, Univ. of Cambridge 1978-79; Visiting Fellow, All Souls Coll. Oxford 1978-79; Professorial Fellow, Emmanuel Coll. Cambridge 1978-79; Faculty Visitor, Australian Nat. Univ., Canberra 1981; mem. numerous archaeological insts. etc.; Hon. Litt.D. (Dublin) 1966, (Oxford) 1987. *Publications:* The Sutton Hoo Ship-burial, 3 vols. 1975-83, and other works on archaeology. *Leisure interests:* reading, playing chess, watching sport, travel. *Address:* 12 Cambray Place, Cheltenham, Glos., GL50 1JS, England.

BRUCHÉSI, Jean, B.A. LL.L., D.LITT. D.POL.SC.; Canadian university professor and civil servant; b. 1901; ed. Univs. of Montreal and Paris, Ecole Libre des Sciences Politiques, Paris, and Ecole des Chartes, Paris; admitted to the Bar 1924; Prof. of Gen. History, Univ. of Montreal 1927-37, Prof. of Political Science and External Politics 1929-58; Prof. of Canadian History, Marguerite-Bourgeoys Coll. Montreal 1932-59; Prof. of Econ. History of Canada, Ecole Supérieure de Commerce, Laval Univ. 1943-52; Under-Sec. of the Prov. of Quebec 1937-59; Amb. to Spain 1959-64, to Morocco 1962-69, to Argentina, Uruguay and Paraguay 1964-67; Ed. of Foreign Politics, Le Canada, Montreal 1928-31; Chief Ed. La Revue Moderne 1930-35, L'Action Universitaire 1934-37; mem. (and founder) Soc. des Ecrivains canadiens 1937-, mem. Royal Soc. of Canada 1940- (Pres. 1953-54); Pres. Inst. Canadien de Québec 1946-59; fmr. Pres. Canadian Catholic Historical Asscn., Canadian Historical Asscn., Canadian Arts Council; Chevalier Légion d'honneur, Kt. Grand Cross (Spain, Vatican), etc. *Publications:* Aux Marches de l'Europe 1931, L'Epopée Canadienne 1934, Histoire du Canada pour tous 1934-36, Rappels 1941, De Ville-Marie à Montréal 1942, Le Chemin des Ecoliers 1944, Evocations 1947, Canada, réalités d'hier et d'aujourd'hui 1948, Histoire du Canada 1951, Le Canada 1952, L'Université 1953, Voyages ... Mirages 1957, Témoignages d'hier 1961, Souvenirs à vaincre 1974, Souvenirs d'ambassade 1975. *Address:* Apt. 903, 2 Square Westmount, Boulevard de Maisonneuve, Montreal, Que. H3Z 2S4, Canada.

BRÜCK, Hermann Alexander, C.B.E., D.PHIL., PH.D., M.R.I.A., F.R.S.E.; British astronomer; b. 15 Aug. 1905, Berlin, Germany; s. of H. H. Brück and Margaret Brück; m. 1st Irma Waitzfelder 1936 (died 1950), 2nd Mary T. Conway 1951; two s. three d.; ed. Augusta Gymnasium, Berlin-Charlottenburg and Univs. of Bonn, Kiel, Munich and Cambridge; astronomer, Potsdam Astrophysical Observatory 1928; Lecturer, Berlin Univ. 1935; Research Assoc., Vatican Observatory 1936; Asst. Observer, Solar Physics Observatory, Cambridge 1937; John Couch Adams Astronomer, Cambridge Univ. 1943; Asst. Dir. Cambridge Observatory 1946; Dir. Dunsink Observatory and Prof. of Astronomy, Dublin for Inst. Advanced Studies 1947-57; Astronomer Royal for Scotland and Regius Prof. of Astronomy, Univ. of Edinburgh 1957-75, Dean Faculty of Science 1968-70; Vice-Pres. Royal Astronomical Soc. 1959-61; mem. Pontifical Acad. of Sciences; Corresp. mem. Akad. der Wissenschaften, Mainz; Hon. D.Sc. (Nat. Univ. of Ireland, St. Andrews Univ.). *Publications:* Astrophysical Cosmology (Jt. Ed.) 1982, The Story of Astronomy in Edinburgh 1983, The Peripatetic Astronomer. The Life of Charles Piazzi Smyth (with Mary T. Brück) 1988; Scientific papers in journals and observatory publications. *Leisure interest:* music. *Address:* Craigower, Penicuik, EH26 9LA, Midlothian, Scotland. *Telephone:* Penicuik 75918.

BRÜCK, Jean François Julien; Belgian trade union official; b. 4 July 1918, Verviers; m. Jeanne Cuypers 1947; two s. one d.; ed. state secondary school, Verviers; Permanent Sec. Young Christian Workers Regional Fed., Verviers 1937-39; Nat. Treas. Belgian Young Christian Workers 1939-47; Deputy Sec.-Gen. Office Employees' Nat. Union 1947-51, Sec.-Gen. 1951-57; Sec.-Gen. Confed. of Christian Trade Unions of the Congo 1957-62; Dir. Int. Solidarity Fund, Int. Fed. of Christian Trade Unions (IFCTU) 1962-68; Sec.-Gen. World Confed. of Labour 1968-76; Head Int. Relations, Confed. Christian Trade Unions, Belgium 1977; Special Adviser to EEC for Devt. Co-operation 1977-. *Leisure interests:* physical education, swimming, mountaineering. *Address:* 20 rue d'octobre, 1200 Brussels, Belgium. *Telephone:* 771-22-26.

BRUCKMANN, Gerhart, PH.D., M.P.; Austrian politician and statistician; b. 9 Jan. 1932, Vienna; s. of Friedrich Bruckmann and Anny (née Pötzl) Bruckmann; m. Hilde Bartl 1961; two s.; ed. Univ. of Graz, Vienna and Rome, Antioch Coll., U.S.A.; with Austrian Fed. Chamber of Commerce 1957–67; Prof. of Statistics, Univ. of Linz 1967–68, Univ. of Vienna 1968–; Dir. Inst. for Advanced Studies 1968–73; Consultant Int. Inst. for Applied Systems Analysis 1973–83, Council mem. 1983–86; M.P. 1986–; mem. Austrian Acad. of Sciences, Club of Rome. *Publications:* Auswege in die Zukunft 1974, Sonnenkraft statt Atomenergie 1978, Groping in the Dark (with D. Meadows and J. Richardson) 1982, Megatrends für Österreich 1988. *Leisure interest:* collecting anchor building blocks. *Address:* Institut für Statistik und Informatik, Universitätsstrasse 5/9, A-1010, Vienna (Office); Zehenthofgasse 11, 1190, Vienna, Austria (Home). *Telephone:* (222) 434159 (Office).

BRÜCKNER, Christine; German author; b. 10 Dec. 1921, Schmillinghausen, Waldeck; d. of Carl and Clotilde (née Schulze) Emde; m. Otto H. Kühner 1967; Asst., Kunstinstitut, Marburg 1947–51; Ed. Frauenwelt, Nürnberg 1951–52; freelance author 1954–; assisted production, State Theatre, Kassel 1960–61; Vice-Pres. German PEN 1980–84; f. (with O. H. Kühner) of Kasseler Literaturpreis für grotesken Humor 1984; novel prize, Bertelsmann Verlag 1954; Goetheplakette, State of Hessen 1982; Hon. Citizen, Kassel 1987. *Publications:* Ehe die Spuren verwehen 1954, Die Zeit danach 1961, Der Kokon 1966, Das glückliche Buch der a.p. 1970, Überlebensgeschichten 1971, Jauche und Levkojen 1975, Nirgendwo ist Poenichen 1977, Erfahren und erwandert 1979, Das eine sein, das andere lieben 1981, Mein schwarzes Sofa 1982, Wenn du geredet hättest, Desdemona 1983, Die Quints 1985, Deine Bilder/Meine Worte (with O. H. Kühner) 1987, Hat der Mensch Wurzeln? (autobiographical essays) 1988; novels, short stories, radio plays, dramas, etc. *Leisure interests:* modern art, travel, especially on foot. *Address:* Hans-Böckler-Strasse 5, 3500 Kassel, Federal Republic of Germany.

BRUECKNER, Keith Allan, M.A., PH.D.; American professor of physics; b. 19 March 1924, Minneapolis, Minn.; s. of Leo John and Agnes Holland Brueckner; two s. one d.; ed. Univs. of Minnesota and California (Berkeley), Inst. for Advanced Study, Princeton; Asst. Prof. Indiana Univ. 1951–54, Assoc. Prof. 1954–55; Physicist, Brookhaven Nat. Lab. (N.Y.) 1955–56; Prof. of Physics, Univ. of Pa. 1956–59; Prof. of Physics, Univ. of Calif. (San Diego) 1959–; Vice-Pres. and Dir. of Research, Inst. for Defense Analyses, Wash., D.C. 1961–62; Tech. Dir. KMS Tech. Center, San Diego 1968–71; Exec. Vice-Pres. and Tech. Dir. KMS Fusion Inc., Ann Arbor 1971–74; Consulting Ed., Pure and Applied Physics Series, Academic Press 1964–; mem. N.A.S.; Hon. D.Sc. (Indiana Univ.) 1976; Dannie Heinemann Prize for Mathematical Physics 1963. *Publications:* Numerous articles in scientific journals. *Leisure interests:* mountain climbing, skiing, sailing, surfing. *Address:* Department of Physics, University of California at San Diego, La Jolla, Calif. 92093 (Office); 4018 Nobel Drive, 201 San Diego, Calif. 92122, U.S.A. (Home). *Telephone:* (619) 452-2892 (Office).

BRUEL, Jean-Marc André; French business executive; b. 18 Feb. 1936, Akbou, Algeria; s. of René Bruel and Jeanine Poirson; m. Anne-Mary Barthod 1962; two s. two d.; ed. Ecole Centrale des arts et Manufactures; Head of tech. services, Rhodiaceta, Brazil 1964; Dir. nylon polyester factory, Rhône-Poulenc, Brazil 1968; Deputy Dir.-Gen. of textile production Rhône-Poulenc, Brazil 1971; Deputy Dir.-Gen. Div. of plant hygiene, groupe Rhône-Poulenc 1975, Dir.-Gen. 1976; Asst. to Pres. and mem. Exec. Cttee. Rhône-Poulenc 1979–80, Deputy Dir.-Gen. 1980, Dir.-Gen. 1982–84; mem. Exec. Cttee. Sandoz, Basle 1985–. *Leisure interests:* tennis, sailing. *Address:* Sandoz, Lichstrasse 35, CH 4002, Basle, Switzerland.

BRUGGER, Ernst; Swiss politician and banker; b. 10 March 1914, Bellinzona; s. of Alois Brugger and Ida Müller; m. Eleonora Ringer 1937; five s.; ed. Univs. of Zürich, London, Paris; Secondary school teacher, Gossau 1936; Deputy to Kantonsrat 1947–59; Mayor of Gossau 1949–59; mem. Zürich Canton Govt. 1959–69, Dir. of Interior and Justice Depts. 1959–67, Dir. of Public Economy Dept. 1967–69; mem. Fed. Council 1970–78, Vice-Pres. Jan.-Dec. 1973, Pres. Jan.-Dec. 1974; Head of Fed. Dept. of Public Economy 1970–78, retd. from Govt. Feb. 1978; Chair. Finland-EFTA Jt. Council at Ministerial level and of Consultative Cttee. 1974; Chair. of Bd. of Dirs. Swiss Volksbank –1986, Swiss charitable org. Pro-Infirmis; Radical Democrat. *Leisure interest:* mountaineering. *Address:* 8625 Gossau ZH, Switzerland. *Telephone:* (01) 935 16 73.

BRUGMANS, Hendrik, D. ÈS L.; Netherlands literary critic and historian; b. 13 Dec. 1906, Amsterdam; s. of Prof. Hajo Brugmans and Marie Keizer; m. Engelina Carolina Mary Kan 1934 (divorced); two s. (one deceased) one d., one step d.; ed. Lycée Fontanes, Paris, Amsterdam Univ. and the Sorbonne; teacher at Arnhem, Terneuzen and Amersfoort; Pres. Workers' Educational Inst.; Socialist mem. of Parl. 1939–40; teacher at Amersfoort and Amsterdam 1940–42; arrested and imprisoned as hostage in St. Michielsgestel camp 1942–44; released and joined "Je Maintiendrai" resistance movement 1944; sent to report to Netherlands Govt. in Exile in London 1945; Dir. of Information and Political Sec. of Prime Minister in first postwar Govt.; mission in Thailand and Indonesia 1946; has devoted himself to the European Federalist Movement since 1946; first Pres. Union Européenne des Fédéralistes 1946; Rector, Coll. of Europe, Bruges 1950–72; Gold Medal "Bene Meriti della Cultura" (Italy); Charlemagne Prize; Légion d'honneur; Officer Order of Orange-Nassau; Commdr. Order of Leopold

II; Grosses Verdienstkreuz des Verdienstordens der Bundesrepublik Deutschland; Dr. h.c. (Catholic Univ. of Louvain); Netherlands Labour Party (Partij van de Arbeid). *Publications:* Denis de Rougemont et le Personalisme français, La Littérature française contemporaine, Les Trésors littéraires de la France, Jean-Jacques Rousseau, Histoire de la Littérature française moderne, Crise et Vocation de l'Occident, Introduction à une Histoire européenne (Vol. I Les Origines de la Civilisation européenne 1958, Vol. II L'Europe prend le Large 1960), L'Europe des Nations Vol. III 1970; also the federalist programme La Cité Européenne, Panorama de la Pensée fédéraliste, Le Fédéralisme contemporain (with P. Duclos), L'Idée européenne, 1920–1970, Visages de l'Europe, La pensée politique du Fédéralisme, L'Europe vécue 1979; together with several works on Europe and Federalism (in Dutch) and numerous articles on European problems in periodicals. *Leisure interests:* reading, mountain climbing, listening to people. *Address:* Carmersstraat 85, 8000 Bruges, Belgium.

BRULLER, Jean Marcel (see Vercors).

BRUNDAGE, Howard Denton, B.A.; American publisher and advertising executive; b. 9 Nov. 1923, Newark, N.J.; s. of Edgar Rae and Salome (Denton) Brundage; m. Nancy Williams 1945; one s. three d.; ed. Dartmouth Coll. and Harvard Graduate School of Business Admin.; with Morgan, Stanley and Co., New York 1945–50; Asst. Sec. The Hanover Bank, New York 1950–52; with J.H. Whitney and Co., New York 1952–58, Partner 1958–61; Pres. New York Herald Tribune Inc. 1958; Exec. Vice-Pres. (Finance) and Dir. J. Walter Thompson Co. 1962–74, Dresdner and Brundage Asscns. 1974–77, Conn. Investment Man. Inc. 1978–87; Vice-Pres. Smith Barney Harris Upham 1987–; Dir. Smith, Barney Equity Fund, and various insurance cos.; Trustee, Mountainside Hospital, Montclair, N.J. *Leisure interests:* travel, tennis, bridge. *Address:* Ely's Ferry Road, Lyme, Conn. 06371, U.S.A. (Home).

BRUNDTLAND, Gro Harlem, M.D., M.P.H.; Norwegian physician and politician; b. 20 April 1939, Oslo; d. of Gudmund and Inga Harlem; m. Arne Olav Brundtland 1960; three s. one d.; ed. Oslo and Harvard Univs.; Consultant, Ministry of Health and Social Affairs 1965–67; Medical Officer, Oslo City Health Dept. 1968–69; Deputy Dir. School Health Services, Oslo 1969; Minister of Environment 1974–79; Deputy Leader Labour Party 1975–81, Leader Labour Parl. Group 1981–; Prime Minister of Norway Feb.-Oct. 1981, 1986–; mem. Parl. Standing Cttee. on Foreign Affairs, fmr. mem. Parl. Standing Cttee. on Finance; Chair. UN World Comm. on Environment and Devt.; fmr. Vice-Chair. Sr. Secondary Schools' Socialist Asscn., Students' Asscn. of Labour Party. *Publications:* Articles on preventive medicine, school health and growth studies. *Leisure interest:* cross-country skiing. *Address:* Office of the Prime Minister, P.O. Box 8001, Dep., N-0030 Oslo 3, Norway; Th. Løvstads vei 19, N-0286 Oslo 2, Norway (Home). *Telephone:* 47 2 11 90 60 (Office).

BRUNEI, Sultan of (see Bolkiah).

BRUNER, Jerome Seymour, PH.D.; American professor of psychology; b. 1 Oct. 1915, New York; s. of Herman Bruner and Rose Bruner; m. 1st Katherine Frost 1940 (divorced 1956); one s. one d.; m. 2nd Blanche Marshall McLane 1960 (divorced 1984), m. 3rd Carol Fleisher Feldman; ed. Duke and Harvard Univs.; U.S. Intelligence 1941–42; Assoc. Dir. Office of Public Opinion Research, Princeton 1942–44; Political Intelligence, France 1943; Research, Harvard Univ. 1945–72, Prof. of Psychology 1952–72, Dir. Center for Cognitive Studies 1961–72; Ed. Public Opinion Quarterly 1943–44; Lecturer, Salzburg Seminar 1952; Bacon Prof., Univ. of Aix-en-Provence 1965; Watts Prof. of Psychology, Oxford Univ. 1972–80; Univ. Prof., New School for Social Research, New York; Hon. D.H.L. (Lesley Coll.) 1964, Hon. D.Sc. (Northwestern) 1965, (Sheffield) 1970, (Bristol) 1965, (Columbia) 1988, Hon. M.A. (Oxford) 1972, Hon. LL.D. (Temple) 1965, (Cincinnati) 1966, (New Brunswick) 1969, Hon. D.Litt. (North Mich.) 1969, (Duke) 1969, Dr. h.c. (Sorbonne) 1974, (Leuven) 1976, (Ghent) 1977, (Madrid) 1986, Dr.·h.c. (Free Univ. Berlin) 1988; mem. American Acad. of Arts and Sciences; Fellow, New York Inst. for the Humanities; Int. Balzan Foundation Prize 1987. *Publications:* Mandate from the People 1944, The Process of Education 1960, On Knowing: Essays for the Left Hand 1962, Toward a Theory of Instruction 1966, Processes of Cognitive Growth: Infancy, (Vol. 111) 1968, The Relevance of Education 1971, Under Five in Britain 1980, Communication as a Language 1982, In Search of Mind 1983, Child's Talk 1983, Actual Minds, Possible Worlds 1986; also co-author of several books. *Leisure interest:* sailing. *Address:* 200 Mercer Street, New York, N.Y. 10012, U.S.A.

BRUNET, Jacques, L. en D.; French banker; b. 10 May 1901, Paris; s. of Gustave and Thérèse (née Blanche) Brunet; m. Antoinette Vigier 1930; four s. one d.; ed. Paris Univ.; Sec. to Raymond Poincaré 1928; Deputy Dir., later Dir. Ministry of Finance 1935–46; Gen. Man. Banque d'Algérie et de Tunisie 1946–48; Pres. and Gen. Man. Crédit Nat. 1949–60; Gov. Banque de France 1960–69, Hon. Gov. 1969–; Hon. Insp. Gen. of Finances 1969; Grand Croix Légion d'honneur, Grand Croix Ordre national du Mérite. *Address:* 5 avenue Kléber, 75116 Paris (Office); 14 boulevard Emile-Augier, 75016 Paris, France (Home).

BRUNET, Jean-Pierre; French diplomatist; b. 20 Jan. 1920; m. Geneviève Didry 1970; ed. Lycée Saint-Louis, Paris and Ecole Navale, Brest; Sub-Lieut., French Navy 1940; joined Free French Naval Forces 1940, served in submarines 1940–45; Diplomatic Service 1945–82; French Embassy, London 1946–47; Ministry of Foreign Affairs 1948–61; Deputy Rep. of France to EEC 1961–64; Head of Econ. Co-operation Section, Ministry of Foreign Affairs 1965–66, Dir. of Econ. and Financial Affairs 1966–75; Amb. to Japan 1975–77, to Fed. Repub. of Germany 1977–82; Chair. and C.E.O. Cie. Gen. d'Electricité 1982–84; Pres. Banque DB-Pargesa; Sr. Vice-Pres. (Int.) Drexel Burnham Lambert 1987; Dir. several large French cos.; mem. Gen. Council of Banque de France 1966–73; Commdr. Légion d'honneur. *Leisure interests:* skiing, sailing. *Address:* 4 rue Monsieur, 75007 Paris, France (Home). *Telephone:* 47.83.81.61 (Home).

BRUNHART, Hans; Liechtenstein politician; b. 28 March 1945, Balzers; s. of Andreas and Rosa Brunhart; m. Bernadette Biedermann 1972; two s. one d.; ed. Lyceum Gutenberg in Balzers, Univs. of Freiburg and Basel, Switzerland; Dir. Liechtenstein Nat. Library and Liechtenstein State Archives, Vaduz 1972–74; Deputy to Head of Govt. 1974–78; Head of Govt. April 1978–; Head Depts. Foreign and External Affairs, Educ., Finance and Bldg. 1982–; Grand Cross, Liechtenstein Princely Order of Merit. *Publications:* contributions to Der Schriftsteller und sein Verhältnis zur Sprache 1971, 2 essays in Liechtenstein Politische Schriften 1972, 1973. *Address:* Government Palace, 9490 Vaduz, Liechtenstein.

BRUNNER, Guido, D.JUR., LL.L.; German diplomatist and politician; b. 27 May 1930, Madrid, Spain; m. Dr. Christa Speidel 1958; ed. Bergzabern, Munich, German School, Madrid and Univs. of Munich, Heidelberg and Madrid; Diplomatic service 1955–74; Foreign Minister's Office 1956, Office of Sec. of State for Foreign Affairs 1958–60, German Observer to UN, New York 1960–68; Scientific and Technological Relations Div., Foreign Office 1968–70, Spokesman 1970–72, Head, Planning Staff 1972–74; Amb. and Head, del. to Conf. on Security and Co-operation in Europe, Helsinki/Geneva 1972–74; mem. Comm. European Communities 1974–80 (Commr. for Energy, Research, Science and Education); mem. of Bundestag 1980–; Mayor and Senator (Minister) for the Economy, W. Berlin 1981; Amb. to Spain 1982–; Freie Demokratische Partei (FDP); Hon. Doctorates, Univ. of Patras (Greece), Heriot-Watt Univ. (Edinburgh), City Univ. (London); Melchett Medal (Inst. of Energy) 1978. *Publications:* Bipolarität und Sicherheit 1965, Friedenssicherungsaktionen der Vereinten Nationen 1968, Stolz wie Don Rodrigo 1982, articles in periodicals. *Address:* Embassy of the Federal Republic of Germany, Calle Fortuny 8, Madrid, Spain. *Telephone:* 419 91 00.

BRUNO, Michael, PH.D.; Israeli university professor; b. 30 July 1932, Hamburg, Germany; s. of Hans and Lotte Bruno; m. Ofra Hirshenberg 1958; two s. one d.; ed. Reali School, Haifa, King's Coll., Cambridge, Stanford Univ., U.S.A.; Sr. Economist, Bank of Israel 1957–61, Deputy Dir. 1961–63, Jt. Dir. Research Dept. 1964–65; on staff of Hebrew Univ. of Jerusalem 1963–, Prof. of Econs. 1970–; Dir. of Research, Maurice Falk Inst. for Econ. Research in Israel 1972–75; Econ. Policy Adviser to Minister of Finance 1975–76; Pres. Israel Econ. Assn. 1977–79; Visiting Prof. of Econs., Harvard Univ. and M.I.T. 1965–67, 1970–71, 1976–77, 1981; Adviser to Ministry of Finance 1985–; Gov. Bank of Israel 1986–; mem. Israel Acad. of Sciences and Humanities; Hon. Foreign mem. American Acad. of Arts and Sciences; Fellow and Pres. of Econometric Soc.; Rothschild Prize in Social Science 1974; mem. team formulating econ. stabilization programme 1985–86; Gov. of Bank of Israel 1986–. *Publications:* articles in economic journals. *Leisure interests:* music, hiking. *Address:* Bank of Israel, P.O. Box 780, Jerusalem, Israel. *Telephone:* (02) 552-701.

BRUNSVIG, Per, DR. IUR.; Norwegian lawyer and business executive; b. 26 Sept. 1917, Skien; s. of Nils J. Brunsvig and Aagot Elisa (née Christoffersen) Brunsvig; m. Gerd Elin Juul Olsen 1946; one s. one d.; ed. Univ. of Oslo and Harvard Law School; Legal Sec. Royal Norwegian Ministry of Justice, London 1944–45; Assoc. Dist. Judge 1945–48; Assoc., later partner Thommessen, Karlsrud, Heyerdahl and Brunsvig 1949–; Chair. Norwegian Asscn. for the Protection of Industrial Property 1968–82, Norwegian Bar Asscn. 1976–79, mem. Bd. numerous Norwegian cos.; Kt. Royal Order of St. Olav (First Class). *Publications:* Liability for defective skip design 1973, 20 treatises in legal periodicals and books. *Address:* Tollbodgt. 27, 0157 Oslo 1 (Office); Risalléen 20A, 0374 Oslo 3, Norway (Home). *Telephone:* (02) 421810 (Office); (02) 140079 (Home).

BRUNT, Peter Astbury, M.A., F.B.A.; British professor of ancient history; b. 23 June 1917, Croydon; s. of Rev. Samuel Brunt and Gladys Eileen Brunt; ed. Ipswich School, Oriel Coll., Oxford; Temporary Civil Servant 1940–45; Craven Fellow, Oxford Univ. 1946–47; Lecturer in Ancient History, Univ. of St. Andrews 1947–51; Fellow and Tutor, Oriel Coll., Oxford 1951–67; Fellow and Sr. Bursar, Gonville and Caius Coll., Cambridge 1968–70; Camden Prof. of Ancient History, Oxford, and Fellow of Brasenose Coll. 1970–82, Prof. Emer. 1982–; Hon. Fellow of Oriel Coll., Oxford. *Publications:* Italian Manpower 225 B.C.–A.D. 14 1971, Social Conflicts of Roman Republic 1971, Arrian's Anabasis and Indica, 2 vols. (ed.) 1976, The Fall of the Roman Republic and related essays 1987, numerous articles and reviews in academic journals. *Address:* 34 Manor Road, Oxford, England (Home). *Telephone:* 73993 (Home).

BRUNTON, Sir Gordon Charles, Kt.; British business executive; b. 27 Dec. 1921, London; s. of Charles A. Brunton and Hylda Pritchard; m. 1st Nadine Sohr 1946 (divorced 1965), one s. (one s. deceased) two d.; m. 2nd

Gillian A. Kirk 1966, one s. one d.; ed. Cranleigh School and London School of Econs.; war service 1942–46; joined Tothill Press 1947, Exec. Dir. 1956; Man. Dir. Tower Press Group 1958; Exec. Dir. Odhams Press 1961; joined Thomson Org. 1961, Dir. 1963, Man. Dir. and C.E.O. 1968–; Man. Dir. Thomson Publications 1961; Chair. Thomson Travel 1965–68; Pres. Int. Thomson Org. Ltd. 1978–84; Man. Dir. and C.E.O. Int. Thomson Org. PLC 1978–84; Dir. Times Newspapers Ltd. 1967, Bemrose Corpn. 1974 (Chair. 1978–), Sotheby Parke Bernet Group PLC 1978–85, Cable and Wireless PLC, Yattendon Investment Trust Ltd.; non-exec. Dir. Cable and Wireless PLC, South Bank Bd. (Arts Council), Information Scientist Publs. Ltd.; Pres. Periodical Publishers' Asscn. 1972–74, 1981–82, Nat. Advertising Benevolent Soc. 1973–75; Chair. Econ. Devt. Council for Civil Eng. 1978–84, Appeals Cttee., Independent Adoption Soc., Communications and Gen. Consultants Ltd., Mercury Communications Ltd., Cavendish Shops PLC, Community Industry Ltd., Euram Consulting Ltd., Focus Investments Ltd., and other limited cos.; Gov. and Fellow L.S.E., Henley Man. Coll. 1983–86; Pres. The History of Advertising Trust 1981–84; mem. Council, Templeton Coll. (fmrly. Oxford Cen. for Man. Studies). *Leisure interests:* books, breeding horses. *Address:* Communications and Gen. Consultants Ltd., 90 Long Acre, London, WC2E 9NP (Office); North Munstead, North Munstead Lane, Godalming, Surrey, GU8 4AX, England (Home). *Telephone:* 01-528 2025 (Office); 048-68 6313 (Home).

BRUS, Włodzimierz, D.PHIL.; Polish professor of economics; b. 23 Aug. 1921, Płock; m. 1st Helena Wolińska 1940; m. 2nd Irena Stergien 1945, two d.; m. 3rd Helena Wolinska 1956, one s.; ed. Warsaw, Lvov, Saratov (U.S.S.R.), Univ. of Leningrad, School of Planning, Warsaw; Asst. Prof. of Political Econ., Cen. School of Planning, Warsaw 1949–52, Extraordinary Prof. 1952–54; Extraordinary Prof., Univ. of Warsaw 1954–65, Ordinary Prof. 1965–68, Dean Faculty of Econs. 1958–60; Dir. Research Bureau, Planning Comm. of Poland 1956–58; Vice-Chair. Econ. Council 1957–63; Research Worker, Inst. of Housing, Warsaw (after dismissal from univ.) 1968–72; Visiting Prof. Univ. of Rome 1971, Catholic Univ. of Louvain, Belgium 1973, Visiting Research Fellow, Univ. of Glasgow 1972–73, Sr. Research Fellow, St. Antony's Coll., Oxford 1973–76; Official Fellow Wolfson Coll., Oxford, and Univ. Lecturer in Modern Russian and East European Studies, Oxford Univ. 1976; Prof. 1985–88, Emer. Prof. 1988–; Ford Foundation Fellow 1961; Sr. Fellow, Harriman Inst. for Advanced Studies of U.S.S.R. Columbia Univ., New York, 1982; Distinguished Visiting Prof., Johns Hopkins Univ., Bologna Centre 1983; Isaac Deutscher Memorial Prize 1976. *Publications include:* The Economy of Pre-War Poland 1945, The Problems of Transition to Socialism (co-author) 1954, The Law of Value and Economic Incentives 1956, General Problems of Functioning of the Socialist Economy 1961, The Market in a Socialist Economy 1972, Political Economy of Socialism 1963, Economics and Politics of Socialism 1972, Socialist Ownership and Political Systems 1975, Economic History of Communist Eastern Europe 1983. *Leisure interests:* walking, swimming. *Address:* Wolfson College, Oxford; 21 Bardwell Court, Bardwell Road, Oxford, England. *Telephone:* (0865) 53790 (Home).

BRUSTAD, Tor; Norwegian biophysicist; b. 20 Dec. 1926; s. of Johan Ludwig and Aslaug Brustad; m. Berte-Marie Brustad 1953; one s. two d.; ed. Univs. of Oslo and California; Research Fellow, Univ. of Oslo 1953–54, Norwegian Cancer Soc. 1954–57, U.S. Nat. Acad. of Sciences 1957–59; Research Assoc. Univ. of California 1959–60; Chair. Dept. of Biophysics, Norsk Hydro's Inst. for Cancer Research (Chair. Exec. Council 1975–84), Oslo 1962–; Chair. Dept. of Medical Physics, The Norwegian Radium Hospital (Chair. Admin. Council 1978–81), Oslo 1968–; Prof. of Radiation Biophysics, Univ. of Trondheim 1970; mem. Norwegian Acad. of Science and Letters, Royal Norwegian Soc. of Science and Letters 1978. *Publications:* on radiation effects on various biological systems. *Address:* Norsk Hydro's Institute for Cancer Research, Montebello, Oslo (Office); Nordvegen 30, 1342 Jar, Norway (Home). *Telephone:* Oslo 24-97-50 (Home).

BRUSTEIN, Robert, M.A., PH.D.; American actor, producer and drama critic; b. 21 April 1927, New York, N.Y.; m. Norma Cates 1962 (deceased 1979); one s. one step-s; ed. Amherst Coll. Yale Univ. Drama School, Columbia Univ.; played about 70 roles in theatre groups and TV plays 1950–; Instructor, Cornell Univ. 1955–56, Vassar Coll. 1956–57; lecturer, Columbia Univ. 1957–58, Asst. Prof. 1958–63, Assoc. Prof. 1963–65, Prof. 1965–66; Prof. of English, Yale Univ., Dean of Yale Drama School, Artistic Dir. and Founder, Yale Repertory Theatre 1966–79; Artistic Dir. and Founder American Repertory Theatre Ensemble, Loeb Drama Center, Cambridge, Mass. 1979–; Prof. of English, Harvard Univ. 1979–; Drama Critic, The New Republic 1959–67, 1979–, Contributing Ed. 1959–; host and writer, The Opposition Theatre (Net TV) 1966–; regular contributor to New York Times 1967–; Founder and Publr. Yale/Theatre 1967–; Advisory Ed., Theatre Quarterly 1967–; Guest Critic, The Observer, U.K. 1972–73; Trustee, Sarah Lawrence Coll. 1973–77; Panel mem. Nat. Endowment for the Arts 1970–72, 1981–; Fulbright Fellow 1953–55, Guggenheim Fellow 1961–62, Ford Fellow 1964–65; George G. Nathan Prize in Criticism 1962, George Polk Memorial Award in Criticism 1964, Jersey City Journal Award in Theatre Criticism 1967; Eliot Norton Award for Theatre; New England Theatre Conf. Award for Excellence in Theme; Litt.D. (Lawrence Univ.) 1968, (Amherst Coll.) 1972, L.H.D. (Beloit Coll.) 1975; Hon. Dr. of Arts (Bard Coll.) 1981. *Publications:* Introduction to The Plays of Chekhov 1964; Ed. The Plays of Strindberg 1964; author: The

Theatre of Revolt 1964, Seasons of Discontent 1965, The Third Theatre 1969, Revolution as Theatre 1971, The Culture Watch 1975, The Plays and Prose of Strindberg (editor), Critical Moments 1980, Making Scenes 1981, Who Needs Theatre 1989; articles in well-known journals and newspapers. *Address:* Loeb Drama Centre, 64 Brattle Street, Cambridge, Mass. 02138, U.S.A.

BRUTON, John Gerard, B.A., B.L.; Irish politician and farmer; b. 18 May 1947, Dublin; s. of Matthew Joseph Bruton and Doris Mary Delany; m. Finola Gill 1981; one s. two d.; ed. Clongowes Wood Coll., Univ. Coll., Dublin, King's Inn, Dublin; mem. Dáil Éireann (House of Reps.) 1969–; Fine Gael Spokesman on Agric. 1972–73; Parl. Sec. to Minister for Educ. 1973–77, to Minister for Industry and Commerce 1975–77; Fine Gael Spokesman on Agric. 1977–81, on Finance Jan.–June 1981; Minister of Finance 1981–82, of Industry, Trade, Commerce and Tourism 1982–86, of Finance 1986–87; Deputy Leader of Fine Gael, Fine Gael Spokesman on Industry and Commerce 1987–; Barrister; Hon. Citizen, Sioux City, Iowa, U.S.A. *Leisure interests:* history, folk music, tennis. *Address:* Cornelstown, Dunboyne, County Meath, Ireland (Home). *Telephone:* Dublin 255573.

BRUTUS, Dennis, B.A.; South African educationist and poet; b. 28 Nov. 1924, Salisbury, S. Rhodesia (now Harare, Zimbabwe); s. of Francis Henry Brutus and Margaret Winifred (née Bloemetjie); m. May Jaggers 1950; four s. four d.; ed. Paterson High School, Port Elizabeth, Fort Hare and Witwatersrand Univs.; language teacher, Paterson High School, Cen. Indian High School; office boy and law student, Witwatersrand Univ.; imprisoned for opposition to apartheid 1964–65, exiled 1966, political asylum in U.S.A. 1983; Dir. World Campaign for Release of S. African Political Prisoners; worked for Int. Defence and Aid Fund, fmrly. UN Rep.; Visiting Prof. Denver Univ.; Prof. of English, Northwestern Univ., Evanston, Ill.; Visiting Prof., English Dept., African and Afro-American Studies and Research Center, Univ. Tex., Austin, 1974–75; Visiting Prof., Dept. of English, Amherst Coll., Mass. 1982–83, Dartmouth Coll., N.H. 1983; Adjunct Prof. Northeastern Univ., Boston, Mass. 1984; Pres. S. African Non-Racial Olympic Cttee. (SAN-ROC); Chair. Int. Campaign Against Racism in Sport (ICARIS), Africa Network 1984–; Founding Chair., Exec. mem. African Literature Assen., fmr. Chair. ARENA (Inst. for Study of Sport and Social Issues); mem. of Bd., Black Arts Celebration, Vice-Pres. Union of Writers of the African People; mem. Bd. of Dirs. UN Assen. of Chicago and Ill., Editorial Bd. Africa Today; Dir. Troubadour Press; Fellow, Int. Poetry Soc.; mem. Modern Language Assen. 1972, Int. Platform Assen. 1979–, Int. Jury Books Abroad Award 1976; Hon. H.L.D. (Worcester State Coll.) 1982; Mbari Prize for Poetry in Africa, Chancellor's Prize for Bilingualism (Univ. of S. Africa); Freedom Writers' Award, Kenneth David Kaunda Humanism Award, Academic Excellence Award, Nat. Council for Black Studies 1982, UN Human Rights Day Award 1983. *Publications:* Sirens, Knuckles, Boots 1963, Letters to Martha 1968, Poems from Algiers 1970, Thoughts Abroad (John Bruin) 1971, A Simple Lust 1973, China Poems 1975, Strains 1975, Stubborn Hope 1978, 1979, 1983, Salutes and Censures 1980. *Leisure interests:* sport, music, chess. *Address:* English Department, Northwestern University, Evanston, Ill. 60201; 624 Clark Street, Evanston, Ill. 60201, U.S.A.; 18 Hilton Avenue, London, N.12, England. *Telephone:* 312-328-9154 (Evanston); 01-445 6109 (London).

BRUUN, Egon, M.D.; Danish physician; b. 1 Feb. 1909, Copenhagen; m. Birte Dela 1936; two s. one d.; ed. Københavns Univ.; specialist in allergies; has trained at Univs. of Münster and Berlin 1938, Forlanini Inst., Rome 1940, Stockholm 1943, Hôpital Broussais and Inst. Pasteur, Paris 1950, London and Oxford 1952; Head Physician, Danish Red Cross Asthma Sanatorium in Norway 1946–52; Lecturer on Clinical Allergy, Univ. of Copenhagen 1950; Head Physician of Allergy Clinic, Univ. Hospital, Copenhagen 1955–; Pres. Danish Soc. of Allergology 1950–54, 1958–60; Treas. Int. Assen. of Allergology 1954–64; Fellow, American Acad. of Allergy 1952; Pres. (elect) European Acad. of Allergology 1958–62, Pres. 1962–65; Pres. Northern Soc. of Allergology 1962–65; official of other medical orgs.; Hon. mem. French, Argentine, Belgian, Finnish and Northern Allergy Soc., European Acad. of Allergology; Illum Prize of Honour and several awards. *Leisure interests:* editing Acta Allergologica, gardening, historical literature. *Address:* 8 Gersonsvej, Copenhagen-Hellerup, Denmark. *Telephone:* HE 178.

BRYAN, Sir Arthur, Kt.; British company director; b. 4 March 1923, Stoke-on-Trent; s. of William Woodall Bryan and Isobel Alan (née Tweedie); m. Betty Ratford 1947; one s. one d.; ed. Longton High School; served with R.A.F.V.R. 1941–45; joined Wedgwood Ltd. 1947, sales rep. 1949, Asst. London Man. 1950–53, London Man. and Gen. Man. of Wedgwood Rooms 1953–59, Gen. Sales Man. 1959–60; Dir. and Pres. Josiah Wedgwood & Sons Inc. of America 1960–62; Man. Dir. Wedgwood PLC 1963–85; Chair. 1968–86; Pres. Waterford Wedgwood Holdings PLC 1986–; Dir. Waterford Glass Group PLC 1986–; Dir. Friends' Provident Life Assen. 1985–; Pres. British Ceramic Mfrs. Fed. 1970–71; mem. Court, Univ. of Keele; Companion, British Inst. of Man. 1968; Fellow, Inst. of Marketing, Royal Soc. of Arts 1964; Companion, Inst. Ceramics; K. St. J. 1972; Lord Lieut. of Staffordshire 1968–. *Leisure interests:* walking, reading. *Address:* Waterford Wedgwood Holdings PLC, Barlaston, Stoke-on-Trent, Staffs (Office); Parkfields Cottage, Tittensor, Stoke-on-Trent, Staffs, England (Home).

BRYAN, John Henry, Jr., B.A.; American business executive; b. 5 Oct. 1936, West Point, Miss.; s. of John H. Bryan, Sr.; m. Neville Frierson Bryan 1958; two s. two d.; ed. Southwestern Univ. (now Rhodes Coll.), Memphis; joined Bryan Packing Co. 1960, Pres., C.E.O. 1968–74; Exec. Vice-Pres., Dir. Sara Lee Corpn. March–Oct. 1974, Pres. 1974–75, C.E.O. 1975–, Chair. 1976–; mem. Bd. of Dirs. Amoco Corpn., First Chicago Corpn., The First Nat. Bank of Chicago, Nat. Merit Corpn.; fmr. Chair. and mem. Bd. of Dirs. of Grocery Mfrs. of America, Inc.; mem. Business Roundtable, bds. Catalyst, Nat. Women's Econ. Alliance, Art Inst. of Chicago; fmr. Dir. Nat. Merit Scholarship Corpn.; Dir. Business Cttee. for Arts; Prin. of Chicago United; Trustee Rush-Presbyterian-St. Luke's Medical Center, Univ. of Chicago; Trustee Cttee. for Econ. Devt. *Address:* Sara Lee Corpn., 3 First National Plaza, Chicago, Ill. 60602-4260 (Office). *Telephone:* (312) 726-2600 (Office).

BRYAN, Richard H., LL.B.; American state governor; b. 16 July 1937, Washington; m.; three c.; ed. Univ. of Nev. and Hastings Coll. of Law, Univ. of Calif.; admitted to Nev. Bar 1963, U.S. Supreme Court Bar 1967; Deputy Dist. Attorney, Clark Co., Nev. 1964–66; Public Defender, Clark Co. 1966–68; Counsel Clark Co. Juvenile Court 1968–69; mem. Nev. Assembly 1969–71; Nev. Senate 1973–77; Attorney-Gen., Nev. 1979–82; Gov. of Nevada Jan. 1983–89; Senator from Nevada Jan. 1989–; Democrat. *Address:* c/o Office of the Governor, Capitol Complex, Carson City, Nev. 89710, U.S.A.

BRYANT, Douglas Wallace, A.B., A.M.L.S.; American librarian; b. 20 June 1913, Visalia, Calif.; s. of Albert George and Ethel (Wallace) Bryant; m. Rene Kuhn 1953; one d.; ed. Univs. of Munich, Stanford, Michigan; translator, Stanford Univ. 1934–35; Asst. Curator of Printed Books, Univ. of Michigan 1936–38; Detroit Public Library 1938–42; Lt.-Commdr., U.S. Naval Reserve 1942–46; Asst. Librarian, Univ. of Calif. 1946–49; Dir. of Libraries, American Embassy, London 1949–52; Admin. Asst. Librarian, Harvard Coll. Library 1952–56; Assoc. Dir. Harvard Univ. Library and Assoc. Librarian, Harvard Coll. 1956–64; Univ. Librarian, Harvard Univ. 1964–72, Dir. of Library and Prof. of Bibliography 1972–79, Emer. 1979–; Trustee and Exec. Dir. American Trust for the British Library. *Address:* P.O. Box 463, Cambridge, Mass. 02238, U.S.A.

BRYANT, Michael, C.B.E.; British actor; b. 5 April 1928; has acted on stage in London and Broadway and in TV drama series; appearances with Nat. Theatre, London 1977–. *Plays include:* Five Finger Exercise, Ross, The Double Dealer. *Films include:* A Life for Ruth, The Mindbenders, Goodbye Mr Chips, The Happy Family, Nicholas and Alexandra, The Ruling Class, A Fortunate Man, Caravan to Vaccares, Gandhi, Sakharov. *Address:* 38 Killyon Road, London, S.W.8, England.

BRYANT, Thomas Edward, M.D., J.D.; American physician and attorney; b. 17 Jan. 1936, Ala.; s. of Howard Edward Bryant and Alibel Nettles Bryant; m. Lucie Elizabeth Thrasher 1961; one s. one d.; ed. Emory Univ., Atlanta; Dir. of Health Affairs, U.S. Office of Econ. Opportunity 1969–70; Pres. Nat. Drug Abuse Council 1970–78; Chair. Pres. Comm. on Mental Health 1977–78; Dir. Children of Alcoholics Foundation 1983–; mem. Inst. of Medicine, N.A.S. 1972–; Chair. The Public Cttee. on Mental Health 1977–, Council for Understanding Mental Illnesses 1983–; Practising Attorney specializing in Health Law with Webster and Sheffield 1980–; Pres. The Friends of the Nat. Library of Medicine 1985–. *Address:* 3414 Volta Place, N.W., Washington D.C. Zone 7, U.S.A. *Telephone:* 202-965 7190.

BRYARS, (Richard) Gavin, B.A.; British composer and professor of music; b. 16 Jan. 1943, Goole, Yorks.; s. of Walter Joseph Bryars and Miriam Eleanor Bryars; m. Angela Margaret Bigley 1971; two d.; ed. Goole Grammar School, Sheffield Univ. and private composition study with George Linstead; freelance Double Bassist 1963–66; freelance Composer/Performer 1968–70; Lecturer in Dept. of Fine Art, Portsmouth Polytechnic 1969–70; Sr. Lecturer, School of Fine Art, Leicester Polytechnic 1970–78, Sr. Lecturer and Head of Music, School of Performing Arts 1978–85, Prof. of Music 1985–; mem. Collège de Pataphysique, France 1974–; Ed. Experimental Music Catalogue 1972–81; British Rep. Int. Soc. for Contemporary Music Festival 1977; Arts Council Comms. 1970, 1980, 1982, Bursary 1982. *Works:* The Sinking of the Titanic 1969, Jesus' Blood Never Failed Me Yet 1971, Out of Zaleski's Gazebo 1977, The Vespertine Park 1980, Medea (opera with Robert Wilson) 1982, My First Homage 1978–82, Effarene 1984, String Quartet No.1 1985, Pico's Flight 1986, By the Vaar 1987, The Invention of Tradition 1988, Glorious Hill 1988; recordings on Editions EG, Crépuscule and ECM (Munich). *Leisure interests:* cricket (mem. Yorks. Country Cricket Club) and detective fiction. *Address:* c/o Erica Bolton and Jane Quinn Ltd., 15 Prebend Gardens, London W4 1TN and School of Performing Arts, Leicester Polytechnic, Scraptoft, Leicester, LE7 9SU, England. *Telephone:* 01-995 5592/5245 (London) and (0533) 431011 (Leicester).

BRYMER, Jack, O.B.E., F.G.S.M.; British clarinettist; b. 27 Jan. 1915, South Shields, Co. Durham; s. of John Brymer and Mary Dixon; m. Joan Richardson 1939; one s.; ed. Goldsmith's Coll., London Univ.; Principal Clarinet, Royal Philharmonic Orchestra 1947–63, BBC Symphony Orchestra 1963–72, London Symphony Orchestra 1972–; Prof., Royal Acad. of Music 1950–56; Prof. of Clarinet, Royal Mil. School of Music, Kneller Hall 1970–73; Prof.

of Clarinet Guildhall School of Music and Drama 1982–; mem. Wigmore Ensemble, Prometheus Ensemble, London Baroque Ensemble, Delme Ensemble, Robles Ensemble and Dir./Founder London Wind Soloists; world-wide soloist recitals and numerous recordings; lecturer on musical topics on radio and television; two demonstration films on history, development and use of the clarinet as a solo and orchestral instrument; Hon. F.R.A.M.; Hon. M.A. (Univ. of Newcastle) 1973. *Publications:* The Clarinet 1976, From Where I Sit (autobiog.) 1978, In the Orchestra 1987. *Leisure interests:* golf, tennis, swimming, gardening, carpentry, photography. *Address:* Underwood, Ballards Farm Road, South Croydon, Surrey, England. *Telephone:* 01-657 1698.

BRYNIELSSON, Harry Anders Bertil; Swedish executive; b. 20 March 1914, Stockholm; s. of Georg and Gurli Brynielsson; m. Wera Wahrenby 1940; two s. one d.; ed. Royal Inst. of Tech., Stockholm; with Kema-Bolagen, Stockholm 1936–43; Man. Dir. LKB-Produkter Fabriks Aktiebolag, Stockholm 1943–51; Man. Dir. Aktiebolaget Atomenergi (Swedish Atomic Energy Co.) 1951–69; mem. Bd. Boliden AB 1955–84; Pres. European Atomic Energy Soc. 1958–61; Chair. Swedish Corrosion Inst. 1972–, Swedish Plant Inspection 1975–85; Svenska B.P. 1979–84; Delegation for Scientific and Tech. Information 1979–85; mem. Swedish Acad. of Eng. Sciences. *Address:* Ytterbyudd, S-185 00 Vaxholm, Sweden (Home). *Telephone:* 0764-373-65.

BRYSON, Adm. Sir Lindsay Sutherland, K.C.B., D.SC., (ENG), F.ENG., F.R.S.E., F.I.E.E., F.R.AE.S.; British naval officer (retd.) and engineer; b. 22 Jan. 1925, Glasgow; s. of James McAuslan Bryson and Margaret Whyte; m. Averil Curtis-Willson 1951; one s. two d.; ed. Allan Glen's School, Glasgow; entered Royal Navy as Electrical Mechanic 1945, rank of Lieut. 1948, Commdr. 1960, Capt. 1967; Commdg. Officer, R.N. Air Station, Lee-on-Solent 1970–71; Dir. Naval Guided Weapons 1973–75; Dir. Surface Weapon Projects as Commodore 1975–76; rank of Rear-Adm. 1977; Dir. Gen. Weapons (Navy) 1977–80; rank of Vice-Adm. 1979; Chief Naval Engineer Officer 1979–80; Controller of the Navy 1981–84; rank of Admiral 1983; retd. from Navy 1985; Pres. I.E.E. 1985–86; Dir. (non-exec.) ERA Tech. PLC 1985, Molins PLC 1988; Chair. Marine Technology Directorate PLC 1986–; Deputy Chair. GEC-Marconi Ltd.; Hon. D.Sc.(Eng.) (Bristol) 1988. *Leisure interests:* opera, sailing. *Address:* 74 Dyke Road Avenue, Brighton, Sussex, BN1 5LE, England. *Telephone:* 0273-553638.

BRZEZINSKI, Zbigniew K., PH.D.; American (naturalized 1958) professor of government and politician; b. 28 March 1928, Warsaw, Poland; m. Emilie Anna (Muska) Benes 1955; two s. one d.; ed. McGill and Harvard Univs.; settled in N. America 1938; Instructor in Govt. and Research Fellow, Russian Research Center, Harvard Univ. 1953–56; Asst. Prof. of Govt., Research Assoc. of Russian Research Center and of Center for Int. Affairs, Harvard Univ. 1956–60; Assoc. Prof. of Public Law and Govt., Columbia Univ. 1960–62, Prof. 1962– (on leave 1966–68, 1977–81) and Dir. Research Inst. on Communist Affairs 1961– (on leave 1966–68, 1977–81); mem. Policy Planning Council, Dept. of State 1966–68; mem. Hon. Steering Cttee., Young Citizens for Johnson 1964; Dir. Foreign Policy Task Force for Vice-Pres. Humphrey 1968; Asst. to the Pres. for Nat. Security Affairs 1977–81; Sr. Adviser, Center for Strategic and Int. Studies, Washington, D.C. Jan. 1981–; now Herbert Lehman Prof. of Govt., Columbia Univ.; Fellow, American Acad. of Arts and Sciences 1969–; mem. Nat. Security Council 1977–81, Council on Foreign Relations, New York, Inst. for Strategic Studies (London), Bd. of Trustees, Freedom House; Guggenheim Fellowship 1960, Ford Fellowship 1970; Presidential Medal of Freedom 1981; Hon. Dr. (Alliance Coll.) 1966, (Coll. of the Holy Cross) 1971, (Fordham Univ.) 1979, (Williams Coll.) 1986, (Georgetown Univ.) 1987. *Publications include:* Political Controls in the Soviet Army 1954, The Permanent Purge—Politics in Soviet Totalitarianism 1956, Totalitarian Dictatorship and Autocracy (co-author) 1957, The Soviet Bloc—Unity and Conflict 1960, Ideology and Power in Soviet Politics 1962, Africa and the Communist World (Ed. and contrib.) 1963, Political Power: U.S.A./U.S.S.R. (co-author) 1964, Alternative to Partition: For a Broader Conception of America's Role in Europe 1965, Dilemmas of Change in Soviet Politics (Ed. and contrib.) 1969, Between Two Ages: America's Role in the Technetronic Era 1970, The Fragile Blossom: Crisis and Change in Japan 1972, Power and Principle 1983, Game Plan 1986, The Grand Failure: The Birth and Death of Communism in the 20th Century, 1989. *Address:* Centre for Strategic and International Studies, Suite 400, 1800 K Street, N.W., Washington, D.C. 20006, U.S.A. (Office).

BU HE; Chinese party and government official; b. 1927, Inner Mongolia; s. of Ulanhu; Deputy for Nei Monggol, 1st NPC 1954; Deputy Dir. Cultural Office, Nei Monggol 1961; Dir. Propaganda Dept., CCP Cttee., Nei Monggol 1978–79; Vice-Minister of State, Nationalities Affairs Comm., Hohhot City 1981–; Deputy Sec., CCP Cttee., Nei Monggol Jan. 1982–; mem. 13th Cen. Cttee. CCP 1987–; Chair. Provincial Govt., Nei Monggol April 1983–. *Address:* Office of the Regional Governor, Hohhot, Nei Monggol, People's Republic of China.

BUBENNOV, Mikhail Semyonovich; Soviet writer; b. 1909, Vtoroe Polomoshnevo, Altai; teacher 1927–; first published work 1927; mem. CPSU 1951–; Order of Red Banner of Labour, Stalin Prize. *Publications:* The Thundering Year 1932, Collected Stories 1940, Immortality (novel) 1940,

The White Birch 1947 (vol. 2) 1952, and many others. *Address:* USSR Union of Writers, Ul. Vorovskogo 52, Moscow, USSR.

BUCALOSSI, Pietro; Italian cancer specialist and politician; b. 9 Aug. 1905, San Miniato; s. of Alfredo and Maria (née Casetti) Bucalossi; m. Eugenia Goisis 1938; ed. Università degli Studi, Pisa; Director-Gen. Nat. Cancer Inst., Milan; fmr. Pres. Fatebenefratelli Hospital, Milan; Mayor of Milan 1964–; mem. Exec. Cttee. of the Int. Union Against Cancer (UICC); Pres. Italian League Against Cancer, Italian Cancer Soc., fmr. Pres. Work and Social Care Comm.; Dir. Tumori; mem. numerous medical socs.; Hon. Deputy, Chamber of Deputies; fmr. Pres. Justice Comm.; Minister without Portfolio in charge of Scientific Research 1973–74; Minister of Public Works 1974–76; Vice-Pres. Chamber of Deputies 1976–; Republican. *Publications:* numerous articles on cancer and malignant tumours. *Address:* Via Bigli 15, 1-20121 Milan, Italy. *Telephone:* 700-510.

BUCCI, Maurizio, B.L.; Italian diplomatist; b. 29 Aug. 1923, Sant'Angelo del Pesco (Isernia); s. of Onorato Bucci and Tina Marracino; m. Anna Maria Costa 1956; one d.; ed. Terenzio Mamiani High School, Rome, and Univ. of Rome; entered diplomatic service 1949; Second Sec. Italian Mission to NATO 1952; Deputy Consul-Gen. Paris 1955; First Sec. Luxembourg 1958; Chief of Cabinet of Vice-Pres. of EEC Exec. Cttee. 1961; Counsellor, Italian Mission to European Communities, Brussels 1963; Head, Research and Planning Div., Econ. Dept., Ministry of Foreign Affairs 1968; Amb. to Syria 1973–76, to Brazil 1976–79; Dir. Gen. of Econ. Affairs, Ministry of Foreign Affairs 1979–84; Perm. Rep. to UN 1984–; Gran Croce, Merito Repubblica Italiana. *Address:* Permanent Mission of Italy to the United Nations, 2 United Nations Plaza, 24th Floor, New York, N.Y. 10017, U.S.A. *Telephone:* (212) 486-9191.

BUCCIARELLI DUCCI, Brunetto; Italian politician; b. 18 June 1914; ed. Collegio Nazionale, Arezzo and Univ. degli Studi, Florence; Judge, Tribunale di Arezzo; joined Christian Democrat Party immediately after the war; Deputy; Vice-Pres. Chamber of Deputies 1958–63, Pres. 1963–68; then Judge, Corte Costituzionale. *Publications:* Partiti Gruppi e Parlamento, Introduzione allo Studio del Diritto Parlamentare, Cento Anni di Vita del Parlamento Italiano, Alcide de Gasperi e il suo Magistere Politico, La crisi dei partiti e la responsabilità dei cattolici, Siena e Dante, La figura e l'opera di Pio XI, Legislazione e Sport, Il Voto alle Donne, Il poeta Giosuè Borsi a 50 anni dalla morte. *Address:* 172 via Nazionale, 00184 Rome, Italy.

BUCERIUS, (Karl Anton Martin) Gerhard, DR.JUR.; German publisher and lawyer; b. 19 May 1906, Hamm, Westphalia; s. of Karl Ludwig Walter and Maria (née Rump) Bucerius; m. Gertrud Müller 1947; ed. at schools in Essen, Hanover and Hamburg, law studies 1925–32; Judge in Kiel and Flensburg 1932; Lawyer in Hamburg 1933–; Publr. and Propr. of Die Zeit newspaper, Hamburg 1946–; mem. Bd. of Dirs. Bertelsmann AG & Gruner & Jahr AG; Grosses Bundesverdienstkreuz mit Stern 1956, Schulterband 1986. *Publications:* Der angeklagte Verleger 1974, Der Adenauer 1976, Zwischenrufe und Ordnungsrufe 1984. *Address:* Leinpfad 19, 2000 Hamburg 60, Federal Republic of Germany.

BUCHACHENKO, Anatoliy Leonidovich, DR. PHYS. SC.; Soviet chemophysicist; b. 1935; ed. Gorky Univ.; post-graduate, jr. then sr. scientific asst. 1958–68; mem. CPSU 1964–; head of lab. of U.S.S.R. Acad. of Sciences Inst. of Chemo-Physics 1970–; Prof. 1975–; State Prize 1977, Lenin Prize 1986. *Address:* U.S.S.R Institute of Chemo-Physics, Moscow, U.S.S.R.

BUCHANAN, Sir Colin Douglas, Kt., C.B.E.; British town planner; b. 22 Aug. 1907, Simla, India; s. of William Ernest and Laura Kate Buchanan; m. Elsie Alice Mitchell 1933 (died 1984); two s. one d.; ed. Berkhamsted School and Imperial Coll. of Science and Technology, London; with Public Works Dept., Sudan 1930–32; Regional Planning Studies with F. Longstreth-Thompson, London 1932–35; at Ministry of Transport 1935–39; served with Royal Engineers 1939–46; at Ministry of Town and Country Planning (later Ministry of Housing and Local Govt.) 1946–61; Urban Planning Adviser, Ministry of Transport 1961–63; Prof. of Transport, Imperial Coll., London 1963–72; Dir. School of Advanced Urban Studies, Univ. of Bristol 1973–75; Visiting Prof., Imperial Coll. 1975–78; Consultant with Colin Buchanan and Partners and to various public authorities; mem. Comm. on Third London Airport 1968–70, Royal Fine Art Comm. 1972–73; Pres. Council for the Protection of Rural England 1980–85, Friends of the Vale of Aylesbury 1985–; Gold Medal, Town Planning Inst. 1968; Int. Road Fed. "Man of the Year" 1971. *Publications:* Mixed Blessing, the Motor in Britain 1958, Traffic in Towns 1963, Bath: A Study in Conservation 1969, No Way To the Airport: The Stansted Controversy 1981, and numerous papers on town planning and related subjects. *Leisure interests:* woodworking, photography, caravanning. *Address:* Appletree House, Boars Hill, Oxford OX1 5DU, England. *Telephone:* Oxford 739458.

BUCHANAN, George Duncan, B.A., M.DIV.; South African ecclesiastic; b. 23 April 1935, South Africa; s. of Kelsey Buchanan and Dale Nichols; m. Diana Margaret Dacombe 1959; two d.; ed. Rhodes Univ., Grahamstown and Ripon Hall, Oxford; ordained Deacon, Canterbury Cathedral 1959; ordained priest, Cathedral of St. John the Divine 1960; Curate, St. Paul's Church, Durban 1961; Rector in Diocese of Natal 1962–65; Sub-Warden, St. Paul's Theological Coll., Grahamstown 1966–75, Warden 1976–86; Archdeacon of Albany 1975–86; Dean, Cathedral of St. Mary the Virgin,

Johannesburg 1986; Bishop of Johannesburg 1986–; Hon. D.D. *Publication:* The Counselling of Jesus 1985. *Leisure interest:* carpentry. *Address:* P.O. Box 1131, Johannesburg 2000; 4 Crescent Drive, Westcliff, Johannesburg 2193, South Africa (Home). *Telephone:* (011) 29-8724; (011) 486-1014 (Home).

BUCHANAN, Isobel; British opera singer; b. 15 March 1954, Glasgow; d. of Mr and Mrs S. Buchanan; m. Jonathan King (actor Jonathan Hyde) 1980; two d.; ed. Cumbernauld Comprehensive High School and Royal Scottish Acad. of Music and Drama; professional début in Sydney, Australia with Richard Bonynge and Joan Sutherland 1976–78; British début, Glyndebourne 1978; U.S. and German débuts 1979; Vienna Staatsoper début 1979; ENO début 1985; now freelance artist working with all major opera cos. and orchestras; has made several recordings. *Leisure interests:* cooking, reading, gardening, yoga, knitting. *Address:* c/o Sandor Gorlinsky, 36 Dover Street, London, W1, England. *Telephone:* 01-299 9166.

BUCHANAN, James McGill, M.A., PH.D.; American professor of economics; b. 2 Oct. 1919, Murfreesboro, Tenn.; s. of James Buchanan and Lila Scott; m. Anne Bakke 1945; ed. Middle Tenn. State Coll. and Univs. of Tenn. and Chicago; Prof. of Econs. Univ. of Tenn. 1950–51, Fla. State Univ. 1951–56, Univ. of Va. 1956–62; Paul. G. McIntyre Prof. of Econs. Univ. of Va. 1962–68; Prof. of Econs. Univ. of Calif. Los Angeles 1968–69; Univ. Distinguished Prof. of Econs. Va. Polytechnic Inst. 1969–83, Dir. Center for Public Choice 1969–; Univ. Distinguished Prof. of Econs. George Mason Univ. 1983–; Fulbright Research Scholar, Italy 1955–56; Ford Faculty Research Fellow 1959–60; Fulbright Visiting Prof. Univ. of Cambridge 1961–62; Nobel Prize for Econs. 1986; Seidman Award 1984; Fellow, American Acad. of Arts and Sciences; Distinguished Fellow, American Econ. Asscn.; Dr. h.c. (Giessen) 1982, (Zürich) 1984. *Publications:* author and co-author of numerous books on financial policy and other econ. matters; articles in professional journals. *Address:* P.O. Box G, Blacksburg, Va. 24060, U.S.A.

BUCHANAN, John Machlin, D.SC., PH.D.; American professor of biochemistry; b. 29 Sept. 1917, Winamac Ind.; s. of Harry J. and Eunice B. (Miller) Buchanan; m. Elsa Nilsby 1948; two s. two d.; ed. De Pauw Univ., Univ. of Michigan and Harvard Univ.; Instructor, Dept. of Physiological Chem., School of Medicine, Univ. of Pa. 1943–46, Asst. Prof. 1946–49, Assoc. Prof. 1949–50, Prof. 1950–53; Nat. Research Council Fellow in Medicine, Nobel Inst., Stockholm 1946–48; Prof., Head, Div. of Biochem., Dept.of Biology, Mass. Inst. of Technology 1953–67, Wilson Prof. of Biochem. 1967–88, prof. emer. 1988–; mem. Medical Fellowship Bd. 1954–; Fellow, Guggenheim Memorial Foundation; mem. Nat. Acad. of Sciences, American Soc. of Biological Chemists, American Chem. Soc., Int. Union of Biochemists, American Acad. of Arts and Sciences; Eli Lilly Award in Biological Chem., A.C.S. 1951. *Address:* Room 16-619, Department of Biology, Massachusetts Institute of Technology, Cambridge, Mass. 02139 (Office); 56 Meriam St., Lexington, Mass. 02173, U.S.A. (Home).

BUCHANAN, John MacLennan, B.SC., Q.C., D.E., D.C.L., LL.D., M.L.A.; Canadian politician, barrister and solicitor; b. 22 April 1931, Sydney, Nova Scotia; s. of Murdoch William and Flora Isabel (née Campbell) Buchanan; m. Mavis Olive Charlotte Forsyth 1954; two s. three d.; ed. Mount Allison and Dalhousie Univs.; elected to N.S. Legislature 1967, re-elected 1970, 1974, 1978, 1981, 1984 and 1988; Minister of Finance, Public Works and Fisheries 1969; Leader, Progressive Conservative Party, N.S. 1971–; Leader of the Opposition 1971–78; Premier of N.S. Oct. 1978–; Hon. D.Eng. (Technical Univ. of N.S.) 1979, Hon. D.C.L. (Mount Allison Univ.) 1980, LL.D. h.c. (St. Mary's Univ.) 1982; Centennial Medal. *Leisure interests:* skating, water skiing, swimming, reading, history, politics. *Address:* Province House, P.O. Box 726, Halifax, Nova Scotia B3J 2T3, Canada. *Telephone:* (902) 424-4119.

BUCHANAN, J. Robert, M.D.; American professor of medicine; b. 8 March 1928, Newark, N.J.; m. Susan Carver; one s. one d.; ed. Amherst Coll. and Cornell Univ. Medical School; Intern, then Asst. Resident Physician, New York Hosp. 1954–58, Research Fellow in Medicine 1956–57; Research Fellow in Endocrinology, Cornell Univ. Medical Coll., New York 1960–61; WHO Travelling Fellow 1963; Instructor in Medicine, Cornell Univ. Medical Coll. 1961–63, Asst. Prof. 1963–67, Asst. to Chair. Dept. of Medicine 1964–65, Assoc. Dean 1965–69, Clinical Assoc. Prof. 1967–69, Assoc. Prof. 1969–71, Prof. 1971–76, Acting Dean, then Dean 1969–76; Prof. of Medicine, Univ. of Chicago, Ill. 1977–82; Assoc. Dean, Pritzker School of Medicine, Chicago 1978–82; Prof. of Medicine, Harvard Medical School, Boston, Mass. 1982–; Gen. Dir., Mass. Gen. Hosp. 1982–; physician at hosps. in New York, Chicago and Boston 1956–; mem. Admin. Bd., Council of Teaching Hosps. 1984–, mem. Exec. Council 1985–; Dir. Mass. Div., American Cancer Soc. 1984–; Bd. of Dirs. Bank of New England 1986–, Exec. Cttee. Mass. Hosp. Asscn. 1987–, Charles River Labs.; Chair. Council of Teaching Hosps., Assn. of American Medical Colls. 1988; mem. N.A.S. Cttee. to review Inst. of Medicine, American Cancer Soc., Mass. Div., Soc. of Medical Admins.; Fellow American Coll. of Physicians. *Publications:* numerous papers and articles in journals. *Address:* Massachusetts General Hospital, Boston, Mass. 02114, U.S.A.

BUCHANAN, Patrick Joseph, M.S.; American government official; b. 2 Nov. 1938; s. of William Buchanan and Catherine Crum; m. Shelley A. Scarney 1971; ed. Georgetown and Columbia Univs.; editorial writer, St. Louis Globe Democrat 1962–64, asst. editorial writer 1964–66; Exec. Asst.

to Richard Nixon 1966–69; Special Asst. to Pres. Nixon 1969–73; consultant to Pres. Nixon and Ford (qq.v.) 1973–74; Asst. to Pres., Dir. of Communications, White House, Washington, D.C. 1985–87; syndicated columnist, political commentator, New York Times special features 1975–78, Chicago Tribune-New York News Syndicate 1978–85; commentator, NBC Radio Network 1978–82; appeared as host and panellist in TV shows 1978–85; Republican. *Publications:* The New Majority 1973, Conservative Votes, Liberal Victories 1975. *Address:* 1017 Savile Lane, McLean, Va. 22101, U.S.A.

BUCHHEIM, Lothar-Günther; German publisher and author; b. 6 Feb. 1918, Weimar, Thüringen; m. Diethild Wickboldt 1955; one s. one d.; ed. Dresden Acad., Art Acad., Munich; served in German navy; f. Kunstbuchverlag, Feldafing, and started collection, "the most important private collection", of the work of German Expressionists; owner and publr. Buchheim Verlag, Feldafing; Dr. h.c. (Duisburg) 1985; Bundesverdienstkreuz 1983; Grosses Verdienstkreuz des Verdienstordens 1986; Bayerischer Verdienstorden 1988. *Publications:* Tage und Nächte steigen aus dem Strom 1941, Die Künstlergemeinschaft "Brücke" 1956, Der Blaue Reiter und die Neue Künstlervereinigung München 1958, Graphik des deutschen Expressionismus 1959, Max Beckmann 1959, Otto Mueller 1963, Das Boot 1973, U-Boot-Krieg 1976, Staatsgala 1977, Mein Paris 1977, Die Tropen von Feldafing 1978, Staatszirkus 1978, Der Luxusliner 1980, U 96 1981, Der Film-Das Boot 1981, Das Segelschiff 1982, Die U-Boot-Fahrer 1985, Das Museum in den Wolken 1986, Zu Tode gesiegt-Der Untergang der U-Boote 1988, Malerbuch 1988. *Address:* Biersackstr. 23, D-8133 Feldafing, Federal Republic of Germany. *Telephone:* 08157 1221.

BÜCHI, George H., D.SC.; American professor of chemistry; b. 1 Aug. 1921, Baden, Switzerland; s. of George and Martha Büchi; m. Anne Westfall Barkman 1955; ed. Fed. Inst. of Technology, Zürich; Firestone Fellow, Univ. of Chicago 1948–49; Instructor, Univ. of Chicago 1949–51; Asst. Prof. of Chem., Mass. Inst. of Tech. 1951–56, Assoc. Prof. 1956–58, Prof. 1958–71, Dreyfus Prof. 1971–; mem. N.A.S. 1965–; Swiss Chemical Soc. (Ruzicka Award 1957), American Chemical Soc.; Fritzsche Award for outstanding contributions to field of structure determination of terpenes, American Chemical Soc. 1958; Award for creative work in synthetic organic chem. 1973; Dr. h.c. (Heidelberg) 1983; Order of the Rising Sun (Japan) 1986. *Publications:* Photochemical Reactions XIII: A Total Synthesis of Thujopsene 1964, Terpenes XIX: Synthesis of Patchouli Alcohol 1964, The Structures of Aflatoxins B_1 and G_1 1965, The Total Synthesis of Iboga Alkaloids 1966, A Structurally Selective Method for the Preparation of Certain Diels-Alder Adducts 1967, Biosynthesis of Aflatoxins 1968. *Leisure interests:* hunting, hiking and skiing. *Address:* Room 18-287, Massachusetts Institute of Technology, Cambridge, Mass. 02139, U.S.A. (Office).

BUCHSBAUM, Solomon J., PH.D.; American physicist and business executive; b. 4 Dec. 1929, Stryj, Poland; s. of Jacob Buchsbaum and Berta (Rutherfer) Buchsbaum; m. Phyllis N. Isenman 1955; two s. one d.; ed. McGill Univ., Quebec, Canada and M.I.T.; Dept. Head, Solid State and Plasma Physics Research, AT&T Bell Labs. 1961–65, Dir. Electronics Research Lab. 1965–68; Vice-Pres., Research, at Sandia Labs., Sandia Corpn. 1968–71; Exec. Dir., Research, Communications, Science Div., AT&T Bell Labs. 1971–75, Exec. Dir., Transmission Systems Div. 1975–76, Vice-Pres., Network Planning and Customer Services 1976–79, Exec. Vice-Pres., Customer Systems 1979–; Chair. White House Science Council 1982–; Trustee Rand Corpn. 1982–; mem. Bd. Dirs. Draper Lab. Corpn. 1983–; Anne Molson Gold Medal, McGill Univ., Sec. of Defense Medal for Outstanding Service 1977; Sec. of Energy Award for Exceptional Public Service 1981; Nat. Medal of Science 1986; I.E.E.E. (Frederik Philips) Award 1987. *Publications:* Waves in Anisotropics Plasma (with W. P. Allis and A. Bers) 1963; 50 articles in plasma and solid state physics. *Leisure interests:* tennis and skiing. *Address:* AT&T Bell Laboratories, Crawfords Corner Road, Holmdel, N.J. 07733, U.S.A. *Telephone:* (201) 949-5564.

BUCHTHAL, Fritz, M.D.; Danish neurophysiologist; b. 19 Aug. 1907, Witten, Germany; s. of Sally Buchthal and Hedvig Weyl; m. Margaret A. Lennox, M.D.; ed. Albert-Ludwig-Universität, Freiburg im Breisgau, Germany, Stanford Univ., California, U.S.A., and Humboldt-Universität zu Berlin; Asst. in Physiology, Univ. of Berlin 1930–32; Inst. for Theory of Gymnastics, Copenhagen Univ. 1933–43; Physiological Inst., Lund Univ. 1943–45; Dir. Inst. of Neurophysiology, Copenhagen Univ. 1946–77, Prof. of Neurophysiology 1955–77; Chief, Dept. of Neurophysiology, Univ. Hospital 1945–77; Consultant, Nat. Inst. of Health, U.S.A. 1959; Visiting Scientist, Nat. Inst. of Neurological and Communicative Disorders and Stroke, Nat. Inst. of Health, Bethesda 1982–84, Consultant 1984–; Visiting Prof. Univ. of California 1962, Academia Sinica 1964, N.Y. Univ. 1965; mem. Royal Danish Acad. Sciences 1946, Danish Acad. of Technical Sciences, Royal Swedish Acad. of Sciences 1968, Royal Soc. of Sciences (Sweden) 1972, Polish Acad. of Sciences 1988; Hon. mem. French Neurological Soc., British Asscn. of Neurologists, Polish Neurological Soc., Danish Neurological Soc., American Neurological Asscn., American Acad. of Neurophysiology, German EEG Soc., English EEG Soc., Italian EEG and Clinical Neurophysiological Soc. and American Soc. for Electrodiagnosis and Electromyography; Corresp. mem. German Physiological and Neurological Socs., Italian Neurological Soc., Acad. de Ciencias Médicas, Cordoba; Hon. M.D. (Münster, Zürich, Lund, Munich); Hon. D.Sc. (Medical Coll., Wisconsin); numerous awards. *Publications:* Mechanical Properties of Muscle Fibre 1942, Rheology of Muscle 1951, An Introduction to Electromyography 1957, Electrophysiological Aspects of Myopathy 1963, Evoked Action Potential and Conduction Velocity in Human Sensory Nerve 1966, Electrical and Mechanical Responses of Normal and Myasthenic Muscle 1968, Human Nerve Potentials Evoked by Tactile Stimuli 1982. *Leisure interest:* gardening. *Address:* 289 El Cielito Road, Santa Barbara, Calif. 93105, U.S.A. *Telephone:* (805) 966-5304.

BUCHTHAL, Hugo H., PH.D.; British professor of history of art; b. 11 Aug. 1909, Berlin, Germany; m. Amalia Serkin 1939; one d.; ed. Univs. of Heidelberg, Paris and Hamburg; Librarian, Warburg Inst., Univ. of London 1940, lecturer in History of Art 1949; Prof. of History of Byzantine Art, Univ. of London 1951; Prof. of Fine Arts, Inst. of Fine Arts, New York Univ. 1965–75; Hon. Fellow Warburg Inst. 1975–. *Publications:* Miniatures of the Paris Psalter 1938, Miniature Painting in the Latin Kingdom of Jerusalem 1958, Historia Trojana 1971, Patronage in 13th Century Constantinople (with H. Belting) 1978, The "Musterbuch of Wolfenbuettel" 1981, numerous articles and book reviews in learned journals. *Leisure interest:* music. *Address:* 22 Priory Gardens, London, N6 5QS, England. *Telephone:* 01-348 1664.

BUCHWALD, Art; American journalist, author and playwright; b. 20 Oct. 1925, New York; s. of Helen Kleinberger and Joseph Buchwald; m. Ann McGarry 1952; one s. two d.; ed. Univ. of Southern Calif., Los Angeles; columnist, Herald Tribune, Paris 1948–62; syndicated columnist to 550 newspapers throughout the world 1952–; Prix de la Bonne Humeur; Pulitzer Prize for Outstanding Commentary 1982; Horatio Alger Award 1989; mem. American Acad. and Inst. of Arts and Letters 1986. *Publications:* Paris After Dark, Art Buchwald's Paris, I Chose Caviar, More Caviar, A Gift from the Boys, Don't Forget to Write, How Much Is That in Dollars? 1961, Is It Safe to Drink the Water? 1962, I Chose Capitol Punishment 1963, And Then I Told the President 1965, Son of the Great Society 1967, Have I Ever Lied to You? 1968, Oh, to Be a Swinger 1970, Getting High in Government Circles 1971, I Never Danced at the White House 1973, I Am Not a Crook 1974, Washington Is Leaking 1976, Down the Seine and Up the Potomac 1977, The Buchwald Stops Here 1978, Laid Back in Washington with Art Buchwald 1981, While Reagan Slept 1983, You *Can* Fool All of the People All of the Time 1985, I Think I Don't Remember 1987. *Address:* 2000 Pennsylvania Avenue, N.W., Washington, D.C. 20006, U.S.A. *Telephone:* Washington 393-6680.

BUCK, Robert Follette, B.A., LL.B.; American lawyer and banker; b. 7 June 1917, Superior, Neb.; s. of Samuel R. Buck and Faye Follette; m. Barbara J. Carlson 1963; one s. one d. by previous m.; admitted Washington Bar 1946, D.C. Bar 1960; Pres. Orcas Power & Light Co., Eastsound, Wash. 1947–54; Regional Dir. Small Business Admin. Seattle 1954–59; Deputy Admin., Small Business Admin. Washington, D.C. 1959–61; Vice-Pres. Rainier Nat. Bank, Seattle 1961–66, Sr. Vice-Pres. 1966–74, Exec. Vice-Pres. 1974–82; Prosecuting Attorney, San Juan County, Wash. 1947–54; Pres. Pacific Northwest Trade Assen. 1969–70; Trustee, Assen. of Wash. Business 1968–, Chair. 1978–79; Trustee, Seattle Mun. League 1964–72, Econ. Devt. Council, Puget Sound 1970–, Wash. State Int. Trade Fair 1963–; mem. American Bankers Assen. (Dir. 1976–78). *Address:* 4100 Seafirst, Fifth Avenue Plaza, 800 Fifth Avenue, Seattle, Wash. 98104 (Office); 909 E. Newton, D9 Seattle, Wash. 98102, U.S.A. (Home).

BUCKINGHAM, Prof. Amyand David, F.R.S.; Australian professor of chemistry; b. 28 Jan. 1930, Sydney; s. of the late Reginald Joslin Buckingham and Florence Grace Buckingham; m. Jillian Bowles; one. s. two d.; ed. Barker Coll., Hornsby, N.S.W., Univ. of Sydney, Corpus Christi Coll., Cambridge; Lecturer, then Student and Tutor, Christ Church, Univ. of Oxford 1955–65, Univ. Lecturer in Inorganic Chem. 1958–65; Prof. of Theoretical Chem., Univ. of Bristol 1965–69; Prof. of Chem., Univ. of Cambridge, Aug. 1969–, Fellow, Pembroke Coll., Cambridge 1970–; Pres. Faraday Div. of Royal Soc. of Chem. 1987–89; *Publications:* over 200 papers in scientific journals, The Laws and Applications of Thermodynamics 1964, Organic Liquids: Structure, Dynamics and Chemical Properties 1978. *Leisure interests:* cricket, tennis, travel, walking. *Address:* University Chemical Labratory, Lensfield Road, Cambridge, CB2 1EW, England (Office). *Telephone:* 0223-336377.

BUCKLE, (Christopher) Richard (Sandford), C.B.E.; British writer, critic and exhibition designer; b. 6 Aug. 1916; ed. Marlborough Coll. and Balliol Coll., Oxford; founded Ballet 1939; army service 1940–46; Ballet Critic, The Observer 1948–55, Sunday Times 1959–75; Dir. Theatre Museum Assen. 1978–; organizer The Diaghilev Exhibition, Edinburgh Festival and London 1954, The Observer Film Exhibition, London 1956, Telford Bicentenary Exhibition 1957, Epstein Memorial Exhibition, Edinburgh 1961, The Shakespeare Exhibition (for Quatercentenary), Stratford-on-Avon and Edinburgh 1964; designer, Exhibition Rooms, Harewood House, Yorks. and area in "Man in the Community" Pavilion, Expo 1967 exhbn. Montreal, Gala of Ballet, London 1971, Happy and Glorious exhbn. London 1977; Plays: Gossip Column, Q Theatre 1953 and Family Tree, Worthing 1956. *Publications:* John Innocent at Oxford (novel) 1939, The Adventures of a Ballet Critic 1953, In Search of Diaghilev 1955, Modern Ballet Design 1955, The Prettiest Girl in England 1958, Harewood (a guide book) 1959, Dancing for Diaghilev (the Memoirs of Lydia Sokolova) 1960, introductions

to Epstein Drawings 1962, and Epstein: An Autobiography 1963, Jacob Epstein: Sculptor 1963, Monsters at Midnight (ltd. edn.) 1966, The Message, a Gothick Tale of the A1 (ltd. edn.) 1969, Nijinsky 1971, Diaghilev 1978, U and Non-U revisited (Ed.) 1978, Self Portrait with Friends: Selected Diaries of Cecil Beaton 1926–74 (Ed.) 1979, Buckle at the Ballet (selected criticism) 1980, Designing for the Dancer (with others) 1981, The Most Upsetting Woman (autobiog.) 1981, In the Wake of Diaghilev (autobiog.) 1982, The Englishman's Room (contrib.) 1986, Sir Iain Moncrieffe of that Ilk (contrib.) 1986, George Balanchine, Ballet Master (with John Taras) 1988. *Address:* Roman Road, Gutch Common, Semley, Shaftesbury, Dorset, England.

BUCKLEY, James Lane, LL.B.; American politician; b. 9 March 1923, New York, N.Y.; m. Ann F. Cooley 1953; six c.; ed. Yale Univ.; served U.S. Navy 1943–46; Senator from New York 1971–77; Under-Sec. of State for Coordinating Security Assistance Programs 1981–82; Pres. Radio Free Europe—Radio Liberty 1982–85; Circuit Judge, U.S. Court of Appeals, D.C. Circuit 1985–; Republican. *Publication:* If Men Were Angels 1975. *Address:* c/o U.S. Courthouse, Constitution at 3rd, N.W., Washington, D.C. 20001, U.S.A.

BUCKLEY, Stephen, M.F.A.; British artist; b. 5 April 1944, Leicester; s. of Nancy Throsby and Leslie Buckley; m. Stephanie James 1973; one s. one d.; ed. Univs. of Newcastle upon Tyne and Reading; taught at Canterbury Coll. of Art 1969–79, Leeds Coll. of Art 1970, Chelsea School of Art 1971–80; Artist in Residence, King's Coll., Cambridge 1972–74; one-man exhbns. throughout world including Museum of Modern Art, Oxford 1985, Yale Center for British Art, New Haven, Conn., U.S.A. 1986; worked with Rambert Dance Co., London 1987–88; works in public collections in U.K., Venezuela, U.S.A., N.Z., Australia; comms. include Neal St. Restaurant 1972, mural painting for Penguin Books 1972, Leith's Restaurant 1973; prizewinner, John Moores Exhbn. 1974, 1985, Chichester National Art Exhbn. 1975, Tolly-Cobbold Exhbn. 1977. *Address:* c/o Knoedler Gallery, 22 Cork Street, London, W1X 1HB, England. *Telephone:* (01) 439 1096.

BUCKLEY, William Frank, Jr.; American editor and author; b. 24 Nov. 1925, New York; s. of William Frank and Aloise (Steiner) Buckley; m. Patricia Taylor 1950; one s.; ed. Univ. of Mexico and Yale Univ.; formerly on staff American Mercury; Ed. National Review 1955–88, Ed.-in-Chief 1988–; syndicated columnist 1962–; host of weekly television series Firing Line 1966–; lecturer New School for Social Research 1967; mem. U.S.I.A. Advisory Comm. 1969–72; mem. U.S. del. to UN 1973; contributor to Harper's, Esquire, Foreign Affairs, Atlantic, etc.; numerous hon. degrees. *Publications:* God and Man at Yale 1951, Up from Liberalism 1959, Rumbles Left and Right 1963, The Unmaking of a Mayor 1966, The Jeweler's Eye 1968, The Governor Listeth 1970, Cruising Speed 1971, Inveighing We Will Go 1972, Four Reforms 1973, United Nations Journal 1974, Execution Eve 1975, Saving the Queen 1976, Airborne, Stained Glass 1978, A Hymnal 1978, Who's on First 1980, Marco Polo, If You Can 1982, Atlantic High 1982, Overdrive 1983, The Story of Henri Tod 1984, See You Later, Alligator 1985, Right Reason (articles and essays) 1985, The Temptation of Wilfred Malachey 1986, High Jinx 1986, Racing through Paradise 1987, Mongoose R.I.P. 1988; co-author McCarthy and His Enemies 1954; Ed. The Committee and Its Critics 1962, Odyssey of a Friend 1970, Did You Ever See a Dream Walking 1970. *Leisure interests:* skiing, sailing, music. *Address:* National Review, 150 East 35th Street, New York, N.Y. 10016, U.S.A. *Telephone:* (212) 679-7330.

BUCKSTEIN, Mark, J.D., B.S.; American lawyer; b. 1 July 1939, New York; s. of Henry Buckstein and Minnie Buckstein; m. Rochelle J. Buchman 1960; one s. one d.; ed. New York Univ. Law School and City Coll. of New York; Sr. Partner, Baer, Marks & Upham (law firm), New York 1968–86; Special Prof. of Law, Hofstra Univ. School of Law 1981–89; Sr. Vice-Pres. and Gen. Counsel, Trans World Airlines Inc. 1986–. *Leisure interests:* tennis, puzzles, reading, music. *Address:* Trans World Airlines Inc., 100 South Bedford Road, Mt. Kisco, N.Y. 10549 (Office); 306 Vista Drive, Jericho, N.Y. 11753, U.S.A. (Home). *Telephone:* (914) 242-400 (Office); (516) 433-7190 (Home).

BUDDEN, Kenneth George, M.A., PH.D., F.R.S.; British physicist; b. 23 June 1915; s. of late George E. Budden and Gertrude H. Rea; m. Nicolette A. L. de Longesdon Longsdon 1947; no c.; ed. Portsmouth Grammar School and St. John's Coll. Cambridge; Telecommunications Research Establishment 1939–41; British Air Comm. Washington, D.C. 1941–44; Air Command, S.E. Asia 1945; Fellow, St. John's Coll. Cambridge 1947–; Reader in Physics, Univ. of Cambridge 1965–82, Emer. 1982–. *Publications:* four books and numerous articles in professional journals. *Leisure interest:* gardening. *Address:* 15 Adams Road, Cambridge, England. *Telephone:* Cambridge 354752.

BUDDENBERG, Hellmuth, DR.RER.POL.; German economist and business executive; b. 5 May 1924, Bünde, Westphalia; s. of Friedrich and Anna (née Nehl) Buddenberg; m. Hildburg Röhr 1948; ed. Hamburg Univ.; joined OLEX (now Deutsche BP AG), Hamburg 1949, Head, Finance and Financial Accounts Dept. 1959; Man. 1960, Deputy mem. Bd. of Man. 1965–, mem. 1967–, Deputy Chair. with responsibility for technology, organization, planning, marketing, petrochemicals, finance, personnel 1972–76, Chair. 1976–; Chair. Bds. numerous cos. *Leisure interests:* sport, history. *Address:* Deutsche BP Aktiengesellschaft, Überseering 2, 2000 Hamburg 60, Federal Republic of Germany.

BUDGE, (John) Donald; American tennis player (retd.); b. 13 June 1915, Oakland, Calif.; s. of John Budge and Pearl Kincaid; m. 1st Deirdre Conselman 1941, 2nd Loriel McPherson 1967; two s. one step-s.; ed. Univ. of California at Berkeley; amateur player until 1938, when he turned professional; Triple Wimbledon Champion (singles, men's doubles and mixed doubles) 1937, 1938; U.S.A. Champion 1937, 1938; Australian Champion 1938; French Champion 1938; first player to win the Grand Slam of the world's four major titles in the same year; played Davis Cup for U.S.A. 1935, 1936, 1937, 1938; World professional champion 1939–46; Pres. Budge Enterprises Ltd. (includes Don Budge Tennis Campus, Baltimore, Md. 1964–); mem. Cttee. Int. Fed. of Tennis to name annual Men's World Champion 1977–, Bd. of Dirs. Nat. Tennis Hall of Fame. *Publications:* Budge and Tennis 1939, Don Budge: A Tennis Memoir 1969. *Leisure interests:* jazz, building stone walls, making furniture, reading, travel. *Address:* c/o The All England Club, Church Road, Wimbledon, London, S.W.19, England.

BUDOWSKI, Gerardo, PH.D.; Venezuelan agronomist and silviculturalist; b. 10 June 1925, Berlin, Germany; s. of Dr. Issar Budowski and Marguerite Wolffgang; m. Thelma T. Palma 1958; two d.; ed. Univ. Central de Venezuela, Inter-American Inst. of Agricultural Sciences, Turrialba, Costa Rica and Yale Univ. School of Forestry; Div. of Research, Ministry of Agriculture Forestry Service 1947–49, Head 1949–52; Forester, Inter-American Inst. of Agricultural Sciences, Havana 1953–55, Turrialba 1956–58, Head, Forestry Dept. 1958–67; Visiting Prof. of Geography and Forestry, Univ. of Calif., Berkeley 1967; Programme Specialist for Ecology and Conservation, UNESCO, Paris 1967–70; Dir.-Gen. Int. Union for Conservation of Nature and National Resources 1970–76; Head, Renewable Natural Resources Dept., Tropical Agricultural Research and Training Center, Costa Rica 1976–86; Dir. Natural Resources Univ. for Peace, Costa Rica; Int. Coordinator for Agroforestry, UN Univ. (Tokyo) 1978–; mem. Bd. Int. World Wildlife Fund, Switzerland; Int. Network of Resources Centre, Hungary; Order of the Golden Ark (Netherlands) 1976, Order Henry Pittier, 1st Class (Venezuela) 1979. *Publications:* La Conservación como instrumento para el desarro 1985, and more than 180 articles. *Leisure interest:* chess (several times champion of Venezuela and mem. of Olympic team). *Address:* University for Peace, P.O. Box 199, 1250 Escazú, Costa Rica (Office); P.O. Box 198, 2300 Curridabat, San José, Costa Rica (Home). *Telephone:* 49-10-72 (Office); 24-40-05 (Home).

BUDYKA, Aleksandr Dmitrievich, CAND. ECON. SC.; Soviet politician; b. 1927; ed. Inst. for Construction of Agric. Machinery, Rostov-on-Don; mem. CPSU 1949; sr. engineer, dir. of plant 1953–57; pres. of collective farm in Stavropol Dist. 1957–60; Dir. of N. Caucasus Research Station 1960–61; deputy head of section of Stavropol Dist. Cttee. 1961–62; chief in charge of regional production of collective farm man. 1962–64; head of section of Stavropol CPSU Dist. Cttee. 1964–71; deputy pres. of Stavropol Dist. Cttee. 1971–80; deputy head of section of CPSU Cen. Cttee. 1980–87; cand. mem. of CPSU Cen. Cttee. 1986–. *Address:* The Kremlin, Moscow, U.S.S.R.

BUECHE, Wendell F., B.S.; American business executive; b. 7 Nov. 1930, Flushing, Mich.; ed. Univ. of Notre Dame, Ind.; joined Allis-Chalmers Corpn. 1952, subsequently Sales Engineer, machine tools, then responsible for all co. electrical and mechanical equipment sales; and apptd. Utility Group Sales Man., Cleveland Dist. 1959, Dist. Man., Detroit, Mich. 1961, Sales Man., Gen. Products Div., 1964, Man. of Planning, Process Equipment and Systems Div. 1966, subsequently Marketing Man., then Div. Gen. Man. of Crushing and Screening Equipment Div. 1969, Corp. Vice-Pres. 1973, Exec. Vice-Pres. Electrical Groups 1976, Pres. Allis-Chalmers Power Systems, Dir. Allis-Chalmers Corpn. 1981, C.E.O. and Pres. 1984–, Chair. 1986–; Dir. M & I Corpn., M & I Marshall & Ilsley Bank, WICOR Inc., Wisconsin Gas Co., Svenska Fluidcarbon A.B., Siemens-Allis Inc., Farm and Industrial Equipment Inst.; mem. Exec. Cttee. Machinery and Allied Products Inst.; Dir. numerous cos. *Address:* Allis-Chalmers Corporation, P.O. Box 512, Milwaukee, Wis. 53201, U.S.A. *Telephone:* (414) 457-3360.

BUERO VALLEJO, Antonio; Spanish playwright; b. 29 Sept. 1916, Guadalajara; s. of Teniente Coronel Francisco Buero and Cruz Vallejo; m. Victoria Rodriguez 1959; two s.; ed. Instituto de Segunda Enseñanza de Guadalajara and Escuela de Bellas Artes de Madrid; visiting lecturer numerous Univs. in U.S.A. 1966; Hon. Fellow, Círculo de Bellas Artes, Ateneo de Madrid, American Asscn. of Teachers of Spanish and Portuguese, Soc. of Spanish and Spanish-American Studies, Modern Language Asscn., Deutscher Hispanistenverband; mem. Hispanic Soc. of America, Real Acad. Española, Int. Cttee. of the Theatre of the Nations; Premio Lope de Vega 1949; Premio Nacional de Teatro 1957, 1958, 1959, 1980; Premio Maria Rolland 1956, 1958, 1960; Premio March de Teatro 1959; Premio de la Crítica de Barcelona 1960; Premio Larra 1962; Medalla de Oro del Espectador y la Crítica 1967, 1970, 1974, 1976, 1977, 1981, 1984, 1986; Premio Leopoldo Cano 1968, 1972, 1974, 1975, 1977; Premio Mayte 1974; Premio Foro Teatral 1974; Medalla de Oro "Gaceta Ilustrada" 1976; Premio Pablo Iglesias 1986, Premio Cervantes 1986. *Plays:* Historia de una Escalera 1949, Las palabras en la arena 1949, En la Ardiente Oscuridad 1950, La Tejedora de Sueños 1952, La señal que se espera 1952, Casi un Cuento de Hadas 1953, Madrugada 1953, Irene, o el Tesoro 1954, Hoy es

Fiesta 1956, Las Cartas boca Abajo 1957, Un Soñador para un Pueblo 1958, Las Meninas 1960, El Concierto de San Ovidio 1962, Aventura en lo Gris 1963, El Tragaluz 1967, La doble historia del Dr. Valmy 1967, Mito 1968, El Sueño de la razón 1970, Llegada de los dioses 1971, La Fundación 1974, La Detonación 1977, Jueces en la noche 1979, Caimán 1981, Dialogo secreto 1984, Lázaro en el laberinto 1986; *essays:* Tres Maestros ante el público 1973. *Leisure interest:* painting. *Address:* Calle General Díaz Porlier 36, 28001 Madrid, Spain. *Telephone:* 402-56-14.

BUFFET, Bernard; French painter; b. 10 July 1928, Paris; s. of Charles Buffet and Blanche-Emma Colombe; m. 1st Agnès Nanquette 1948 (divorced); m. 2nd Anabelle Schwob 1958, one s. two d.; ed. Lycée Carnot, Ecole Nat. Supérieure des Beaux-Arts; annual exhbns. 1949–56 in Galerie Drouant-David, and in Galerie David & Garnier 1957–67, Galerie Maurice Garnier 1968–; exhbns. in many foreign countries, including retrospective exhbns. Paris 1958, Berlin 1958, Belgium 1959, Tokyo 1963; illustrator of books, engraver, lithographer and stage designer; mem. Acad. des Beaux-Arts 1974–; Chevalier, Légion d'honneur; Officier des Arts et des Lettres; Grand Prix de la Critique 1948. *Address:* Galerie Maurice Garnier, 6 avenue Matignon, 75008 Paris (Office); Domaine de la Beaume, Route d'Aups, Tourtour, 83690 Salernes, France (Home).

BUFFUM, William Burnside, M.LITT.; American diplomatist; b. 10 Sept. 1921, Binghamton, N.Y.; m. Alma Bauman; three d.; ed. Oneonta State Teachers' Coll., Univ. of Pittsburgh, Oxford and Harvard Univs.; served U.S. Army 1943–46; entered Foreign Service 1949; has served in Stuttgart 1949, Bonn 1953–58; Deputy Dir. UN Political Affairs, Dept. of State 1963–65, Dir. 1965–66; Deputy Asst. Sec. of State for Int. Org. Affairs 1965–67; Deputy Perm. Rep. to UN 1967–70; Amb. to Lebanon 1970–73; Asst. Sec. of State for Int. Org. Affairs 1973–; UN Under Sec.-Gen. in charge of Political and Gen. Assembly Affairs 1975–87; rep. to several sessions of UN Gen. Assembly. *Address:* c/o Department of State, Washington, D.C., U.S.A.

BUGAYEV, Air Chief Marshal Boris Pavlovich; Soviet pilot and politician; b. 29 July 1923, Markovka, Cherkassy Region, Ukraine; ed. School of Civil Aviation; entered Soviet Army 1943, served World War II; Deputy Minister, then First Deputy Minister, U.S.S.R. Ministry of Civil Aviation 1966–70; Minister of Civil Aviation May 1970–; Deputy to U.S.S.R. Supreme Soviet 1970–; mem. CPSU 1946–, Cen. Cttee. CPSU 1971–; Air Chief Marshal 1977–; Chair. U.S.S.R. Comm. for ICAO, CMEA Standing Comm. for Civil Aviation; Merited Pilot, Hero of Socialist Labour 1966, 1983, Hammer and Sickle Gold Medal (twice), Order of Lenin (five times), Red Banner (twice), Badge of Honour, U.S.S.R. State Prize 1972 and other decorations. *Address:* Ministry of Civil Aviation, 37 Leningradsky prospekt, Moscow, U.S.S.R.

BUHARI, Maj.-Gen. Muhammadu; Nigerian army officer and government official; b. 17 Dec. 1942, Daura, Katsina Province of Kaduna; m. Safinatu Yusuf 1971; two d.; ed. Katsina Provincial Secondary School, Nigerian Mil. Training Coll., Mons Officers' Cadet School, Aldershot, England; joined Army 1962; commissioned 1963; served 2nd Bn. in Congo (now Zaire) 1963–64; Army Service Corps 1964–66; staff and command appointments in 1st and 3rd Infantry Divs.; Defence Service Staff Coll., Wellington, India 1972–73; Acting Dir. of Supply and Transport, Nigerian Army 1974–75; Mil. Gov. of North Eastern State (divided into three States Feb. 1976) 1975–76, of Borno State Feb.-March 1976; Fed. Commr. for Petroleum 1976–78; Chair. Nigerian Nat. Petroleum Corpn. 1976–80; Mil. Sec. Nigerian Army 1978; mem. Supreme Mil. Council 1976–77; overthrew govt. of Shehu Shagari (q.v.); Head of State, Chair. Supreme Mil. Council and C. in C. of Armed Forces 1983–85; detained 1985–88, released 1988. *Leisure interests:* tennis, squash, golf.

BUHECHAOLU; Chinese engraver; b. 1928, Inner Mongolia; Art ed. Inner Mongolia Daily. *Address:* CCP Inner Mongolian Autonomous Region, Huhehotet, People's Republic of China.

BUHLER, Robert, R.A., F.R.C.A.; British painter; b. 23 Nov. 1916, London; s. of the late Robert Buhler and Lucy Kronig; m. 1st Eve Rowell 1935; m. 2nd Prudence Beaumont 1962; three s. one d; ed. Westbourne Park Grammar School, London, St. Martin's School of Art, Royal Coll. of Art, London, also in Switzerland; teacher, Chelsea School of Art 1945–47; Cen. School of Art and Design 1945–47; Royal Coll. of Art 1948–75; Trustee Royal Acad. 1975–; Wollaston Prize, Royal Acad. 1982, Huntingdon Prize 1983. *Publications:* various articles for Observer magazine; Monograph by Colin Hayes 1986. *Leisure interests:* literature, crosswords, language, homes. *Address:* 3 Avenue Studios, Sydney Close, London, S.W.3, England. *Telephone:* 01-589 4983.

BÜHLER, Winfried, DR. PHIL.; German professor of classics; b. 11 June 1929, Münster; s. of Ottmar Bühler and Maria Michels; m. Ria Fisser 1958; one s.; ed. Univs. of Bonn and Munich; Privatdozent, Univ. of Munich 1962–66; Assoc. Prof. of Classics, Univ. of Calif. Los Angeles 1966–67; Prof. of Classics and Dir. Thesaurus Linguae Graecae, Univ. of Hamburg 1967–; Fellow, Göttingen Acad.; corresp. Fellow, British Acad., Bavarian Acad. of Sciences. *Publications:* Die Europa des Moschos 1960, Beiträge zum Schrift vom Erhabenen 1964, Zenobii Athoi Proverbia, (Vol. 4) 1982, (Vol. 1) 1987. *Leisure interests:* music, tennis. *Address:* Oberstrasse 89,

2000 Hamburg 13, Federal Republic of Germany. *Telephone:* (040) 44 33 66.

BUIRA, Ariel, M.A.; Mexican economist; b. 20 Sept. 1940, Chihuahua; s. of Antonio Buira and Enriqueta Seira de Buira; m. Janet Clark 1965; two s.; ed. Univ. of Manchester, England; Lecturer, Centre for Econ. and Demographic Studies, El Colegio de México 1966-68; Prof. of Econs., Graduate School of Business, Instituto Tecnológico de Monterrey 1968-70; Economist, IMF 1970-74; Econ. Adviser to Gov., Man. for Int. Research, Banco de México, S.A. 1975-78; Deputy Dir. then Dir. for Int. Orgs. and Agreements Dec. 1982-; Del. to Conf. on Int. Econ. Co-operation (CIEC) (Financial Affairs Comm.) 1976-77; Alt. Exec. Dir., IMF 1978-80, Exec. Dir. for Mexico, Spain, Venezuela, Cen. America 1980-82; First Prize, Course on Econ. Integration, Coll. Européen des Sciences Sociales et Economiques 1963. *Publications:* 50 Años de Banca Central (jointly) 1976, LDC External Debt and the World Economy 1978, Directions for Reform— The Future of the International Monetary System (jointly) 1984, México: Crisis Financiera y Programa de Ajuste en América Latina: Deuda, Crisis y Perspectivas 1984; Is There a Need for Reform? 1984; contrib.: Politics and Economics of External Debt Crisis—The Latin American Experience 1985, Incomes Policy (ed. V. L. Urquidi) 1987, Money and Finance Vol. I (ed. R. Tandon) 1987, Adjustment with Growth and the Role of the IMF 1987, and numerous articles. *Leisure interests:* music, literature. *Address:* Sierra Tezonco No. 174, Lomas de Chapultepec, Delegación Miguel Hidalgo, 11000-Mexico, D.F. *Telephone:* 520.46.17; 540.02.37.

BUJONES, Fernando; American ballet dancer; b. 9 March 1955, Miami, Fla.; s. of Fernando and Maria (Calleiro) Bujones; m. Marcia Kibitschek 1980; ed. School of American Ballet; joined American Ballet Theater 1972, Soloist 1973, Prin. Dancer 1974-85, Guest Prin. 1976; Guest Artist, Boston Ballet 1987-; has danced with Nat. Ballet of Canada, Berlin Opera, Vienna State Opera, Scottish Ballet, Rome Opera and Stuttgart Ballet; appeared in film The Turning Point; has produced own dance corpn. Bujones Ltd.; choreographed Grand Pas Romantique 1985; Varna Gold Medal 1974, Dance Magazine Award 1982, Florida Prize 1986. *Ballets:* Coppelia 1974, Swan Lake 1975, Sleeping Beauty 1976, Giselle 1977. *Address:* c/o International Performing Artists Inc., 3848 North Circle Drive, Hollywood, Fla. 33021, U.S.A.

BUKOVAC, Martin, PH.D.; American professor of horticulture; b. 12 Nov. 1929, Johnston City, Ill.; s. of John Bukovac and Sadie Fak; m. Judith A. Kelley 1956; one d.; ed. Michigan State Univ.; Asst. Prof., Dept. of Horticulture, Mich. State Univ. 1957-61, Assoc. Prof. 1961-63, Prof. 1963-; Postdoctoral Fellow, Univs. of Oxford and Bristol, England 1965-66; Adviser, Eli Lilly Co. 1971-; Fellow A.A.A.S., American Soc. of Horticultural Science; mem. N.A.S.; numerous awards. *Publications:* over 250 research articles. *Leisure interests:* photography, sports. *Address:* Department of Horticulture, Michigan State University, East Lansing, Mich. 48824-1112; 4428 Seneca Drive, Okemos, Mich. 48864, U.S.A. (Home). *Telephone:* (517) 355-5207 (Office); (517) 349-1952 (Home).

BUKOVSKY, Vladimir, M.A.; Russian writer and scientist; b. 30 Dec. 1942, Belebey; s. of Konstantin and Nina Bukovsky; ed. Moscow State Univ., Cambridge Univ.; worked at Moscow Centre of Cybernetics; arrested for possessing banned literature 1963, confined to Leningrad Psychiatric Prison Hospital for 15 months; arrested for demonstration on behalf of Soviet writers 1965, confined for 8 months in psychiatric institutions; arrested for civil rights work 1967, on trial Sept. 1967 and sentenced to 3 years' corrective labour; arrested for delivering information on psychiatric abuse to the West 1971, on trial 1972 and sentenced to 2 years in prison, 5 in a labour camp and 5 in exile; after world-wide campaign for his release, was exchanged for Chilean Communist Party leader Luis Corvalán in Zürich Dec. 1976; research work, Stanford Univ., Calif. 1982-; Hon. mem. several human rights orgs., several PEN clubs; Konrad Adenauer Freedom and Literature Prize 1984. *Publications:* short stories in Russia's Other Writers 1970, and in Grani, Opposition—Eine neue Geisteskrankheit in der U.S.S.R. (German edition) 1972, A Manual on Psychiatry for Dissenters (with Semyon Gluzman) 1974, To Build a Castle: My Life as a Dissenter (in English; trans. in Swedish, Italian, Spanish, French and German) 1978, Cette lancinante douleur de la liberté 1981, The Peace Movement and the Soviet Union 1982. *Leisure interests:* the arts, architecture. *Address:* c/o Department of Psychology, Stanford University, Stanford, Calif. 94305, U.S.A.

BULATOVIĆ, Moidrag; Yugoslav writer; b. 20 Feb. 1930, Okladi, Bijelo Polje; s. of Milorad Bulatović and Milica Čuljković; m. Kansky Nuša 1964; two s. one d.; ed. Univ. of Belgrade; wrote his early works in hospitals and Red Cross centres while leading a wandering life; Nin Prize for Best Yugoslav Novel 1976, Cen. Library of Serbia Prize 1977. *Publications:* Djavoli dolaze (Devils Arrive) short stories 1956, Vuk i Zvono (The Wolf and the Bell) novel-poem 1958, Crveni Petao leti prema nebu (The Red Cockerel) novel 1960, Heroj na magarcu (Hero on a Donkey) novel 1965, Godot je došao (Godot Came) play 1966, Ljudi sa četiri prsta (The Thumbless) novel 1975, Rat je bio bolji (The War was Better) novel 1977. *Address:* Belgrade, Francuska 7, Yugoslavia.

BULATOVIĆ, Vukoje; Yugoslav journalist; b. 18 March 1927, Medevce, Medvedja; s. of Sava and Milosava Ćalović; m. Branka Gavrilović 1960;

one s.; ed. Univ. of Belgrade; scientific Assoc., Inst. for Int. Labour Movt., Belgrade 1957-60; Rome Corresp. for Komunist newspaper 1964-69, Foreign Desk Ed. 1970; Sec. of Information, Socialist Repub. of Serbia 1970-74; mem. Exec. Cttee. of the Presidency of the Cen. Cttee., League of Communists of Serbia 1974-75; Dir. of Politika Publrs., Ed.-in-Chief Politika daily 1975-82; Memorial Order 1941; Order for Courage (twice); Order of Merit for the People; Grand Officer of Italian Repub. *Leisure interest:* fishing. *Address:* c/o Politika, Makedonska ulica 29, Belgrade, Yugoslavia. *Telephone:* 329-367, 325-609.

BÜLBRING, Edith, M.A., M.D., F.R.S.; British pharmacologist; b. 27 Dec. 1903; d. of Karl D. Bülbring and Hortense L. Bülbring (née Kann); ed. Univs. of Bonn, Munich and Freiburg; Dept. of Pharmacology, Berlin Univ. 1929-31; Pediatrics, Univ. of Jena 1932; Virchow Krankenhaus, Berlin Univ. 1933; Pharmacological Lab. of Pharmaceutical Soc. of G.B., Univ. of London 1933-38; Pharmacology Dept., Univ. of Oxford 1938-71, Reader 1960-67, Prof. of Pharmacology 1967-71, now Emer.; Hon. Fellow, Lady Margaret Hall, Oxford; various honours and distinctions. *Leisure interest:* music. *Address:* 15 Northmoor Road, Oxford, England. *Telephone:* Oxford 57270.

BULDAKOV, Gennadiy Nikonorich; Soviet architect; b. 1924; army service; ed. Leningrad Inst. of Eng. and Construction 1951; mem. CPSU 1945-; worked for 'Lenproyekt' 1951-71; Chief Architect of Leningrad 1971-; Work includes (with others) gen. planning of Leningrad and suburbs 1960-64; gen. town-plan of Zelenogorsk 1966; Sestroretsk 1972, Shuvalov Lakes Region, Leningrad 1966, S.-W. Region, Leningrad 1976, Restoration of Palace Square 1974, Grazhdanskiy Prospekt Underground Station 1978; 'Chernaya rechka' 1982; corresp. mem. U.S.S.R. Acad. of Arts 1979; People's Architect 1984. *Address:* Office of the Chief Architect, Leningrad, U.S.S.R.

BULGER, Roger James, M.D.; American physician; b. 18 May 1933, Brooklyn; s. of William J. Bulger and Florence D. (Poggi) Bulger; m. Ruth E. Grouse 1960; two d.; ed. Harvard Univ., Emmanuel Coll., Cambridge, Univ. of Washington and Boston Univ.; intern, Resident, Univ. of Washington Hospitals 1960-62, 1964-65; Asst. Prof., Assoc. Prof. Univ. of Washington Medical School, Seattle 1966-70; Medical Dir. Univ. Hospital, Seattle 1967-70; Prof. of Community Health Sciences, Duke Univ. Medical Center 1970-72; Exec. Officer, Inst. of Medicine, N.A.S. 1972-76; Prof. of Internal Medicine, George Washington Univ. School of Medicine 1972-76; Prof. of Internal Medicine, Family and Community Medicine, Dean, Medical School, Chancellor, Worcester Campus, Univ. of Mass. 1976-78; Pres. Univ. of Tex. Health Sciences Center, Houston 1978-88; Pres. and C.E.O. Asscn. Acad. Health Centers, Washington, D.C. Feb. 1988-; mem. numerous professional socs. etc. *Publications:* Hippocrates Revisited 1973, In Search of the Modern Hippocrates 1987; articles and book chapters. *Address:* Office of the President, Association of Academic Health Centers, 11 Dupont Circle, Washington, D.C., 20036, U.S.A.

BULIN, René Henri; French aeronautical engineer; b. 8 Aug. 1920, Langres; s. of Louis and Louise (née Walter) Bulin; m. 1st Claudine Prostot 1955, 2nd Catherine Tambuscio 1982; ed. Ecole Polytechnique Paris, Ecole Nationale Supérieure de l'Aéronautique; engineer responsible for setting up Centre d'Essais des Propulseurs 1946-53; instructor, Ecole Nationale de l'Aviation Civile 1955-63; Deputy Dir., then Dir. Air Navigation Secrétariat Général de l'Aviation Civile, France 1956-61; first Dir.-Gen. European Org. for the Safety of Air Navigation (EUROCONTROL) 1961-78, responsible for having set up the Air Traffic Services Agency, Brussels and the EUROCONTROL Experimental Centre, Bretigny-sur-Orge and for establishing the Upper Area Control Centres, Maastricht, Netherlands, Karlsruhe, Germany, Shannon, Ireland, and the EUROCONTROL Inst. of Air Navigation Services, Luxembourg; Adviser Thomson-C.S.F. 1978-83; Special Adviser to European Community Aeronautical Comm.; Commdr., Légion d'honneur, Officier, Ordre de Léopold 1er, Chevalier des Palmes académiques, Commdr. Ordre de Luxembourg, Portugal, Order of the Lion of Judah (Ethiopia); Médaille de l'aéronautique. *Publication:* Technique du Transport Aérien 1958. *Address:* Altirama, avenue Frédéric Mistral, 06130, Grasse (Home).

BULL, Lt.-Gen. Odd; Norwegian air force officer and United Nations official; b. 28 June 1907, Oslo; s. of Gjert Bull and Sigrid Bull (née Oddvin); m. Inga-Lisa Furugård 1953; one s.; ed. Vestheim School, Oslo Univ. and Norwegian Army Acad; Norwegian Army 1928-31, Air Force 1931; Norwegian Air Force in Norway, U.K. and Canada 1940-45, Norway 1945-48; Deputy Chief of Air Staff Royal Norwegian Air Force 1948-51, Deputy Chief of Staff Operations, Allied Air Forces, N. Europe 1951-53; Air Commdr., N. Norway 1953-56; Commdr. Tactical Air Forces, Norway 1956-58; Exec. mem. UN Observation Group, Lebanon 1958; Special Rep. of UN Sec.-Gen. for British Air Evacuation and Flight Control from Jordan Oct. 1958; Commdr. Tactical Air Forces, Norway 1959-60, Chief of Air Staff, Royal Norwegian Air Force 1960-63; Chief of Staff, UN Truce Supervision Org. Palestine June 1963-70; co-operated with Israel and Jordanian authorities to secure Pope Paul's pilgrimage to the Holy Land, Jan. 1964; mem. Advisory Bd. Int. Peace Acad.; Grand Cross Order of St. Olav and other awards; UN Medal "In the Service of Peace" (twice); Hon. Citizen of Texas. *Publications:* Norwegian Air Force Participation in World War II: Outside Norway 1948, On Duty in the Middle East 1973,

War and Peace in the Middle East 1976. *Leisure interests:* skiing, swimming, reading (especially history). *Address:* Nedre Baastad Vei 48, 1370 Asker, Norway. *Telephone:* 02-782214.

BULLARD, Sir Giles Lionel, K.C.V.O., C.M.G.; British diplomatist (retd.); b. 24 Aug. 1926, Oxford; s. of the late Sir Reader Bullard and Miriam Bullard (née Smith); m. 1st Hilary Chadwick Brooks 1952 (died 1978); two s. two d.; m. 2nd Linda Rannells Lewis 1982; three step-c.; ed. Blundell's School, Balliol Coll., Oxford; served Army 1944–48; with H. Clarkson and Co., Bishopsgate 1952–55; with diplomatic service 1955–86, served in Bucharest 1957–58, Brussels 1958–60, Panama City 1960–64, London 1964–67, Bangkok 1967–69, Islamabad 1969–73, Inspectorate 1974–77, Consul Gen., Boston 1977–80, Amb. to Bulgaria 1980–83, High Comm. in Barbados (also accred. to St. Kitts/Nevis, Antigua/Barbuda, Dominica, St. Lucia, St. Vincent and the Grenadines, Grenada) 1983–86. *Leisure interests:* walking, cinema, country pursuits. *Address:* Manor House, West Hendred, Wantage, Oxon., England.

BULLARD, Sir Julian (Leonard), G.C.M.G.; British diplomatist (retd.); b. 8 March 1928, Athens; s. of the late Sir Reader Bullard and Miriam Smith; m. Margaret Stephens 1954; two s. two d.; ed. Rugby School, Magdalen Coll., Oxford; Fellow of All Souls Coll., Oxford 1950–57; nat. service Army 1950–52; joined H.M. Diplomatic Service 1953, served at Foreign Office 1953–54, Vienna 1954–56, Amman 1956–59, Foreign Office 1960–63, Bonn 1963–66, Moscow 1966–68, Dubai 1968–70, FCO (Head of E. European and Soviet Dept.) 1971–75; Minister, Bonn 1975–79; Deputy Under-Sec. of State 1979–84; Deputy to Perm. Under-Sec. of State and Political Dir. 1982–84; Amb. to Fed. Repub. of Germany 1984–88. *Address:* 18 Northmoor Road, Oxford, OX2 6UR, England. *Telephone:* 0865-512981.

BULLER, Prof. Arthur John, B.S., E.R.D., F.R.C.P., F.I.BIOL., F.R.S.A.; British physiologist; b. 16 Oct. 1923; s. of Thomas Alfred and Edith May (née Wager) Buller; m. Helena Joan Pearson 1946; one s. two d. (one deceased); ed. Duke of York's Royal Mil. School, Dover, St. Thomas's Hospital Medical School; Kitchener Scholar 1941–45; Lecturer in Physiology St. Thomas's Hospital 1946–49; Maj. R.A.M.C., Specialist in Physiology, Jr. Sec. Mil. Personnel Research Cttee. 1949–53; Lecturer in Medicine St. Thomas's Hospital 1953–57; Reader in Physiology King's Coll., London 1961–65; Gresham Prof. of Physics 1963–65; Prof. of Physiology Univ. of Bristol 1965–82 (now Prof. Emer.), Dean Faculty of Medicine 1976–78; Chief Scientist (on secondment) Dept. of Health and Social Security 1978–81; Visiting Prof. Monash Univ., Australia 1972; Long Fox Memorial Lecturer, Bristol 1978; Hon. Consultant in Clinical Physiology, Bristol Dist. Hospital 1970–85; Royal Soc. Commonwealth Fellow, Canberra, Australia 1958–59; mem. Bd. of Govs. Bristol Royal Infirmary 1968–74, Avon Health Authority 1974–78, MRC 1975–81; Chair. Neurosciences and Mental Health Bd., MRC 1975–77; External Scientific Adviser, Rayne Inst. St. Thomas's Hospital 1979–85; Research Devt. Dir., Muscular Dystrophy Gp. of G.B. and N.I. 1982–; mem. BBC, IBA Cen. Appeals Advice Cttee. 1983–; Milroy Lecturer, Royal Coll. of Physicians 1983. *Publications:* articles in books and journals on normal and abnormal physiology. *Leisure interests:* clarets and conversation. *Address:* Lockhall, Cow Lane, Steeple Aston, Oxon., OX5 3SG, England. *Telephone:* Steeple Aston 47502.

BULLOCK, Baron (Life Peer) cr. 1976, of Leafield in the County of Oxfordshire; **Alan Louis Charles Bullock,** Kt., F.B.A., M.A., D.LITT.; British historian and university administrator; b. 13 Dec. 1914, Trowbridge; s. of Rev. Frank A. Bullock; m. Hilda Yates Handy 1940; three s. two d. (one deceased); ed. Bradford Grammar School, Wadham and Merton Colls., Oxford; BBC European Service diplomatic and political corresp. 1940–45; Fellow, Dean and Tutor of New Coll., Oxford 1945–52; Master of St. Catherine's Coll., Oxford 1960–80, Fellow by Special Election 1980–87, Hon. Fellow and Founding Master 1987–; Trustee, The Observer 1957–69, Dir. 1977–81; mem. Arts Council 1961–64, British Library Organizing Cttee. 1972–73, Cttee. of Vice-Chancellors and Principals 1969–73; Vice-Chancellor, Univ. of Oxford 1969–73; Chair. Inquiry into Teaching of Reading and Other Uses of Language 1972–74; Chair. Trustees of Tate Gallery 1973–79; Chair. Cttee. on Industrial Democracy 1975–76; Trustee, Wolfson Foundation 1974–87; Aspen Inst., Berlin; Chair. Research Cttee. and mem. Council, Royal Inst. of Int. Affairs (Chatham House) 1954–78; fmr. Chair. Nat. Advisory Council on Training and Supply of Teachers; mem. Advisory Council on Public Records to 1976; fmr. Chair. The Schools Council, Bd. of Int. Assen. for Cultural Freedom; Joint Ed. Oxford History of Modern Europe, Int. Comm. of Historians for publication of documents on German Foreign Policy 1918–45; Hon. doctorates (Aix-Marseilles, Bradford, Newfoundland, Reading, Open Univ., Leicester, Sussex Univs.); Hon. Fellow, Merton, Wadham, Wolfson and Linacre Colls., Oxford; Chevalier Légion d'honneur 1970, Hon. F.R.I.B.A. *Publications:* Hitler, a Study in Tyranny 1952, 1962, The Liberal Tradition 1956, Schellenberg Memoirs 1956, The Life and Times of Ernest Bevin, Vol. I 1960, Vol. II 1967, Vol. III 1983, The Twentieth Century (ed.) 1971, The Fontana Dictionary of Modern Thought (co-ed. with Oliver Stallybrass) 1977, 2nd Ed. (with Stephen Trombley) 1988, Faces of Europe 1979, Fontana Dictionary of Modern Thinkers (co-ed. with R. B. Woodings) 1983, The Humanist Tradition in the West 1985. *Address:* St. Catherine's College, Oxford; 30 Godstow Road, Oxford, OX2 8AJ, England. *Telephone:* Oxford 271700; Oxford 513380 (Home).

BULLOCK, Theodore Holmes, PH.D.; American professor of neurosciences; b. 16 May 1915, Nanking, China; s. of A. Archibald and Ruth Beckwith Bullock; m. Martha Runquist 1937; one s. one d.; ed. Univ. of California, Berkeley; Sterling Fellow, Yale Univ. 1940–41; Rockefeller Fellow 1941–42; Instructor in Neuroanatomy, Yale Univ. 1942–44; Asst. Prof. of Anatomy, Univ. of Missouri 1944–46; Instructor and sometime Head, Invertebrate Zoology, Marine Biol. Lab., Woods Hole, Mass.; Asst. Prof., Assoc. Prof., Prof. of Zoology, Univ. of Calif., Los Angeles 1946–66; Prof. of Neurosciences, Univ. of Calif. San Diego School of Medicine 1966–82, Prof. Emer. 1982–; Head of Neurobiology Unit, Scripps Inst. of Oceanography; mem. Brain Research Inst., Univ. of Calif. at Los Angeles; mem. N.A.S., American Phil. Soc.; Pres. Int. Soc. for Neuroethology 1984–87; fmr. Pres. American Soc. of Zoology, Soc. for Neuroscience; Lashley Prize, American Philosophical Soc. 1968; Gerard Prize, Soc. for Neuroscience 1984. *Publications:* Structure and Function in the Nervous Systems of Invertebrates (with G. A. Horridge) 1965, Introduction to Nervous Systems (with R. Orkand and A. D. Grinnell) 1977, Electroreception (with W. Heiligenberg) 1986. *Address:* A-001 Department of Neurosciences, University of California, San Diego, La Jolla, Calif. 92093, U.S.A. *Telephone:* (619) 534-3636.

BULMER-THOMAS, Ivor (see Thomas, Ivor Bulmer-).

BUMBRY, Grace; American opera singer; b. 4 Jan. 1937, St. Louis, Mo.; d. of Benjamin and Melzia Bumbry; ed. Boston and Northwestern Univs., Music Acad. of the West; début, Paris Opera as Amneris, Aida March 1960; Basel Opera 1960–63; Carmen with Paris Opera, and toured Japan; Royal Opera, Brussels; Die Schwarze Venus, Tannhäuser, Bayreuth Festival 1961 and 1962; Vienna State Opera 1963; Covent Garden 1963, 1968, 1969, 1976, 1978; Salzburg Festival 1964; Metropolitan Opera 1965–79; La Scala 1964–79, Chicago Lyric 1962–78; Richard Wagner Medal 1963; Grammy Award 1979, Royal Opera House Medal 1988; Hon. D.H. (Univ. of St. Louis), (Rust Coll.); Hon. D.Mus. (Rockhurst Coll.); Hon. Citizen of Baltimore, Los Angeles, Philadelphia, St. Louis. *Leisure interests:* interior decorating, designing clothes. *Address:* c/o Bruce Zemsky, 165 West 57th Street, New York City, N.Y. 10019, U.S.A.

BUMPERS, Dale Leon, LL.D.; American politician; b. 12 Aug. 1925, Charleston, Ark.; s. of William Rufus and Lattie (née Jones) Bumpers; m. Betty Flanagan 1949; two s. one d.; ed. Univ. of Arkansas and Northwestern Law School; propr. Charleston Hardware and Furniture Co. 1951–66, Angus Breeding Farm 1966–70; Attorney, Charleston, Ark. 1951–70; Gov. of Arkansas 1971–74; U.S. Senator from Arkansas Jan. 1975–; Democrat. *Leisure interests:* reading, tennis, hunting. *Address:* Room SD-229 Dirksen Senate Office, Washington, D.C. 20510, U.S.A. *Telephone:* (202) 224-4843.

BUND, Karlheinz, DR.ING., DR.RER.POL.; German business executive; b. 18 March 1925, Saarlouis; m. Anni Kronenberger; Chair. Man. Bd. of Ruhrkohle AG 1973–85; Chair. EVG and Chair. Advisory Bd. INNOTEC 1985–; mem. Supervisory Bd. Brown, Boveri & Cie. AG, Deutsche Babcock Anlagen AG, Klöckner-Humboldt-Deutz AG, Mobil Oil AG, Strabag Bau AG; mem. Advisory Bd. Allianz AG, Klöckner & Co., Ruhrgas AG, Rheinisch-Westfälische Elektrizitätswerk AG; mem. cttee. Max-Grundig-Stiftung; Pres. Int. Coal Devt. Inst. (ICDI). *Address:* Huyssenallee 82-84, 4300 Essen 1, Federal Republic of Germany. *Telephone:* 0201-233 600.

BUNDY, McGeorge; American professor and foundation official; b. 30 March 1919, Boston, Mass.; s. of Harvey H. and Katharine L. (Putnam) Bundy; brother of William P. Bundy (q.v.); m. Mary B. Lothrop 1950; four s.; ed. Yale Univ.; political analyst, Council of Foreign Relations 1948–49; Visiting Lecturer, Harvard Univ. 1949–51, Assoc. Prof. of Govt. 1951–54, Dean, Faculty of Arts and Sciences 1953–61, Prof. 1954–61; Special Asst. for Nat. Security Affairs, The White House 1961–66; Pres. Ford Foundation 1966–79; Prof. of History, New York Univ. 1979–. *Publications:* On Active Service in Peace and War (with H. L. Stimson) 1948, Pattern of Responsibility (Ed.) 1952, The Strength of Government 1968. *Address:* 19 University Place, New York 10003, U.S.A. *Telephone:* 212 673-9270.

BUNDY, William Putnam; American editor and former government official; b. 24 Sept. 1917, Washington, D.C.; s. of Harvey H. and Katharine L. (Putnam) Bundy; brother of McGeorge Bundy (q.v.); m. Mary Acheson 1943; two s. one d.; ed. Groton School, Yale Coll., Harvard Graduate School and Harvard Law School; U.S. Army 1941–46; Lawyer with Covington and Burling, Washington D.C. 1947–51; CIA 1951–61; Deputy Asst. Sec. of Defense, International Security Affairs 1961–63, Asst. Sec. of Defense, Int. Security Affairs Nov. 1963–64; Asst. Sec. for East Asian and Pacific Affairs, Dept. of State 1964–69; Massachusetts Inst. of Technology 1969–71; Ed. Foreign Affairs (quarterly) 1972–84; Lecturer, Princeton Univ. 1985–87; Fellow, Yale Corpn. 1961–80; Trustee, American Assembly 1963–84; Bd. of Dirs., Council on Foreign Relations 1964–72; Hon. American Sec.-Gen. Bilderberg Meetings 1975–80; Legion of Merit, Hon. M.B.E. *Leisure interest:* farming. *Address:* 1087 Great Road, Princeton, N.J. 08540, U.S.A. *Telephone:* (609) 924-8826.

BUNN, Charles William, D.SC., F.INST.P., F.R.S.; British research scientist (retd.); b. 15 Jan. 1905; s. of Charles J. Bunn and Mary G. Bunn; m. Elizabeth M. Mold 1931; one s. one d.; ed. Wilson's Grammar School, London and Exeter Coll. Oxford; mem. Research Staff, Imperial Chemical Industries (ICI), Winnington, Northwich, Cheshire 1927–41; ICI Plastics

Div. 1946-63; Dewar Research Fellow, Royal Inst. of G.B. 1963-72. *Publications:* Chemical Crystallography 1945, Crystals: Their Role in Nature and Science 1964; papers in scientific journals. *Leisure interests:* music, horticulture. *Address:* 6 Pentley Park, Welwyn Garden City, Herts., England. *Telephone:* Welwyn Garden 323581.

BÜNNING, Erwin, DR.PHIL.; German botanist; b. 23 Jan. 1906, Hamburg; s. of Hinrich and Hermine Bünning; m. Eleonore Walter 1935; one s. two d.; ed. Univs. of Berlin and Göttingen; Lecturer, Univ. of Jena 1931-35, Univ. of Königsberg 1935-42, Prof. 1938; Prof., Univ. of Strasbourg 1942-44, Univ. of Cologne 1944-46; Prof. of Botany, Univ. of Tübingen 1946-72; mem. Leopoldina Acad., Halle, and Acads. of Berlin, Heidelberg, Göttingen, Munich, New York; Foreign Assoc., N.A.S., Washington; Hon. mem. Japanese Botanical Soc., American Soc. Plant Physiology, Deutsche Botanische Gesellschaft, Indian Acad. of Sciences, European Soc. of Chronobiology; Corresp. mem. American Botanical Soc.; Hon. LL.D. (Glasgow), Dr.rer.nat. (Freiburg, Göttingen and Erlangen). *Publications:* Entwicklungs-und Bewegungsphysiologie der Pflanze 1953, Theoretische Grundfragen der Physiologie 1948, In den Wäldern Nord-Sumatras 1948, Der tropische Regenwald 1956, Die physiologische Uhr 1963, (in Russian 1958), The Physiological Clock 1973, Wilhelm Pfeffer 1975; about 260 publications in several fields of biology, especially plant physiology, movements, differentiation, photobiology. *Address:* Institut für Biologie 1, Auf der Morgenstelle 1, 74 Tübingen, Federal Republic of Germany. *Telephone:* Tübingen 62608.

BUNSHAFT, Gordon, B.ARCH., M.ARCH.; American architect; b. 9 May 1909, Buffalo, N.Y.; s. of David and Yetta Bunshaft; m. Nina Elizabeth Wayler 1943; ed. Mass. Inst. of Technology; Chief Designer, Skidmore, Owings and Merrill 1937-42, Partner 1949-; mem. Pres. Comm. of Fine Arts 1963-72; mem. Int. Council of Museum of Modern Art, American Inst. of Architects, Nat. Acad. of Design, Nat. Inst. of Arts and Letters; Fellow American Inst. of Architects; Trustee, Museum of Modern Art, Carnegie Mellon Univ., Pittsburgh; Hon. mem. Buffalo Fine Arts Acad.; American Inst. of Arts and Letters Architectural Award 1955, Brunner Award, Inst. of Arts and Letters 1955; Hon. Dir. Fine Arts Univ. of Buffalo; Chancellor's Medal, Univ. of Buffalo 1969, Gold Medal American Acad. Arts and Letters 1984, Jt. Pritzker Prize Winner 1988. *Projects include:* Lever House (New York), Manufacturers Trust Co. (Fifth Avenue, New York), Conn. Gen. Life Insurance Co. building (Hartford, Conn.), Beinecke Rare Book and Manuscript Library (Yale Univ.), Banque Lambert (Brussels), Albright-Knox Art Gallery (Buffalo, N.Y.), Library-Museum of Performing Arts (Lincoln Center, N.Y.), H. J. Heinz Co. Ltd. (Middx., England), Hirshhorn Museum (Washington), Lyndon Baines Johnson Library and S. & W. Richardson Hall, Univ. of Texas (Austin, Tex.), American Can Co. Headquarters (Greenwich, Conn.), Marine Midland Bldg. (New York, N.Y.), Haj Terminal and Support Complex, Jeddah Int. Airport (Saudi Arabia). *Leisure interest:* collecting of art. *Address:* 200 East 66th Street, New York, N.Y., U.S.A. (Home).

BUNTING, Sir (Edward) John, A.C., K.B.E., B.A.; Australian civil servant (retd.); b. 13 Aug. 1918, Ballarat, Vic.; s. of late G. B. Bunting and Ellen Withers; m. Peggy MacGruer 1942; three s.; ed. Trinity Grammar, Trinity Coll., Melbourne Univ.; Asst. Sec., Prime Minister's Dept. 1949-53; Official Sec. Australian High Comm., London 1953-55; Deputy Sec., Prime Minister's Dept. 1955-58, Sec. 1959-68; Sec. to the Cabinet 1959-75; Sec. Dept. of Cabinet Office 1968-71, Dept. of Prime Minister and Cabinet 1971-75; High Commr. in U.K. 1975-77; Chair. Official Establishment Trust; Deputy Chair. Sir Robert Menzies Memorial Trust; Fellow, Trinity Coll., Melbourne Univ. *Publication:* R. G. Menzies: A Portrait 1988. *Leisure interests:* golf, music, reading. *Address:* 3 Wickham Crescent, Red Hill, A.C.T. 2603, Australia. *Telephone:* (062) 95-8803.

BUNTING, John R.; American banker; b. 29 June 1925, Philadelphia, Pa.; m.; two c.; ed. The Hill School, Pottstown, Pa. and Temple Univ.; Federal Reserve Bank of Philadelphia 1950-64, Vice-Pres. 1962-64; Vice-Pres. and Economist, The First Pennsylvania Banking and Trust Co. 1964 (now first Pennsylvania Bank N.A.), Exec. Vice-Pres. 1965, Pres. Sept. 1968-81, Chair. and C.E.O. 1972-81; Lecturer in Econs., Temple Univ. 1956-60; guest lecturer at many other univs. and colls.; Dir. City Stores Co., Fidelity Mutual Life Insurance Co., Greater Philadelphia Chamber of Commerce; Dir. or Trustee of many civic and educational orgs.; Hon. D.B.A. (St. Joseph's Coll., Philadelphia); Hon. LL.D. (Temple Univ.); Hon. Fellow, Hebrew Univ., Israel. *Publications:* The Hidden Face of Free Enterprise 1964, and numerous articles in business and financial publications. *Address:* Bunting-Rubinsohn Associates, Inc., Benson Manor, Suite 221, Jenkintown, Pa. 19046, U.S.A.

BURAKIEWICZ, Janusz; Polish politician (retd.); b. 20 Nov. 1916, Leningrad, U.S.S.R.; s. of Wincenty Burakiewicz and Janina Chełmińska; m. Wanda Slusarczyk 1945; three s.; ed. Main School of Commerce, Warsaw; bank employee, Warsaw until 1939; during Second World War took part in campaign of Sept. 1939; in Auschwitz and Sachsenhausen Concentration Camps 1941-45; at Cen. Bd. of Metallurgical Industry, Katowice 1945-47; at various important posts at Ministry of Industry and Trade, Ministry of Foreign Trade and Office of Council of Ministers 1945-56; Commercial Counsellor, Budapest 1950-53, Berlin 1956-58; Deputy Minister of Foreign Trade 1958-64; Minister of Shipping 1964-69; Minister of Foreign Trade

1969-71; mem. Polish Workers' Party 1945-48, Polish United Workers' Party 1948-; Vice-Pres. Union of Fighters for Freedom and Democracy 1969-72; Amb. to Yugoslavia 1971-78; Pres. Polish Chamber of Foreign Trade 1978-82; Order of Banner of Labour 1st and 2nd Class, Knight's and Commdr. Cross of Order Polonia Restituta, Great Ribbon of the Homayoun Order of Iran, Gold Cross of Merit, Medal of 10th Anniversary of People's Poland. *Leisure interests:* gardening, fishing.

BURBIDGE, (Eleanor) Margaret Peachey, PH.D., F.R.S.; American astronomer; d. of Stanley John and Marjorie (née Stott) Peachey; m. Geoffrey Burbidge (q.v.) 1948; one d.; ed. Frances Holland School, London and Univ. Coll., London; Second Asst., Asst. Dir. and acting Dir. Univ. of London Observatory 1946-51; Research Fellow, Yerkes Observatory, Harvard Coll. Observatory 1951-53, Calif. Inst. of Technology 1955-57; Research Fellow and Assoc., Prof. Univ. of Chicago 1957-62; Assoc. Research Physicist, Univ. of Calif., San Diego 1962-64, Prof. 1964-, Univ. Prof. 1984-; Dir. Royal Greenwich Observatory 1972-73; Dir. Center for Astrophysics and Space Sciences, Univ. of Calif., San Diego 1979-88; Ed. Observatory 1948-51; mem. Editorial Bd. Astronomy and Astrophysics 1969-85; Lindsay Memorial Lecture NASA 1985; mem. Royal Astronomical Soc., American Astronomical Soc. (Pres. 1978), American Acad. of Arts and Science, N.A.S., A.A.A.S. (Fellow 1981, Pres. 1982), American Philosophical Soc., Soc. Royale des Sciences de Liège, Astronomical Soc. of the Pacific, New York Acad. of Sciences; Fellow, Univ. Coll., London, Lucy Cavendish Coll., Cambridge, Girton Coll., Cambridge; numerous prizes and awards including Helen B. Warner Prize (jointly with Geoffrey Burbidge) 1959; Bruce Gold Medal, Astronomical Soc. of the Pacific 1982; Hon. D.Sc. (Smith Coll., Mass., Rensselaer Political Inst. and Univs. of Sussex, Leicester, Bristol, Mich., Mass., City Univ., Notre Dame, London and Williams Coll.). *Publications:* Quasi-Stellar Objects (with Geoffrey Burbidge) 1967; numerous articles in scientific journals. *Address:* Center for Astrophysics and Space Sciences, C-011, University of California at San Diego, La Jolla, Calif. 92093, U.S.A.

BURBIDGE, Frederick Stewart, B.A., LL.B.; Canadian transport executive; b. 30 Sept. 1918, Winnipeg; s. of Frederick M. and Susan M. (Stewart) Burbidge; m. Cynthia A. Bennest 1942; two s.; ed. Ravenscourt School, Winnipeg, Univ. of Manitoba, Manitoba Law School; called to the Bar, Manitoba 1946; joined Law Dept. of Canadian Pacific 1947, Asst. Solicitor Winnipeg 1947-50, Montreal 1950-57, Solicitor 1957-60, Asst. Gen. Counsel 1960, Asst. Vice-Pres. Traffic 1962, Vice-Pres. Rail Admin. 1966, Vice-Pres. and Exec. Asst. 1967, Vice-Pres. Admin. 1969, Vice-Pres. Marketing and Sales 1969, Sr. Exec. Officer Canadian Pacific Rail; Vice-Pres. Canadian Pacific 1971, Pres. 1972-81, Chair. and C.E.O. 1981-85, Chair. 1985-86; Dir. Canadian Pacific Ltd., Canadian Pacific Steamships Ltd., Canadian Pacific (Bermuda) Ltd., Canadian Pacific Enterprises, Cominco Ltd., Bank of Montreal, Soo Line Railroad Co., Marathon Realty Co. Ltd., C.I.L. Inc., Canadian Pacific Air; Dir. and mem. Exec. Cttee. Bank of Montreal; Dir. Royal Victoria Hosp. Foundation, AMCA Int. Ltd., CNCP Telecommunications, Pan Canadian Petroleum Ltd.; Dir. and Sr. mem. The Conf. Bd. of Canada; mem. Business Council on Nat. Issues, Bd. of Govs., McGill Univ., Citizens' Advisory Bd., Salvation Army. *Address:* Canadian Pacific, P.O. Box 6042, Station A, Montreal H3C 3E4, Que., Canada. *Telephone:* 514-395 6589.

BURBIDGE, Geoffrey, PH.D., F.R.S.; British physicist; b. 24 Sept. 1925; s. of Leslie and Eveline Burbidge; m. Margaret Peachey 1948 (q.v. Eleanor Margaret Peachey Burbidge); one d.; ed. Bristol Univ. and Univ. Coll., London; Asst. Lecturer, Univ. Coll. London 1950-51; Agassiz Fellow, Harvard Univ. 1951-52; Research Fellow, Cavendish Lab., Cambridge 1953-55; Carnegie Fellow, Mount Wilson and Palomar Observatories 1955-57; Asst. Prof. Dept of Astronomy, Univ. of Chicago 1957-58; Assoc. Prof. 1958-62; Assoc. Prof. Univ. of Calif. (San Diego) 1962-63, Prof. 1963-84, 1988-; Dir. Kitt Peak Nat. Observatory 1978-84; Emer. Prof., Univ. of Calif., San Diego 1984-87; Phillips Visiting Prof., Harvard Univ. 1968; Pres. Astronomical Soc. of the Pacific 1974-76; Dir. Associated Univs. for Research in Astronomy 1971-74; Fellow, Univ. Coll., London; Ed. Annual Review of Astronomy and Astrophysics 1974-; Trustee, Associated Univs. Inc. 1973-82. *Address:* Center for Astrophysics and Space Sciences, University of California, San Diego, La Jolla, Calif. 92093, U.S.A. *Telephone:* (619) 534-6626.

BURBRIDGE, Kenneth Joseph, M.A., B.C.L., PH.D.; Canadian diplomatist; b. 2 July 1911, Bathurst, N.B.; s. of Harry J. Burbridge and Elizabeth Foley; m. Marion C. Smith 1943; one s. one d.; ed. St. Thomas and St. Francis Xavier Univs., and Univs. of New Brunswick and Ottawa; private legal practice, St. John, New Brunswick 1939-41; various public appointments incl. Legal Counsel, Dept. of Munitions and Supply, Ottawa 1941-43; Chief Legal Adviser to Nat. Selective Service (Mobilization), Dept. of Labour, Ottawa 1943-44; Legal Adviser to Unemployment Insurance Comm., Ottawa 1945; Counsellor to Sec. of State and Dir. of War Claims, Dept. of Sec. of State, Ottawa 1945-47; Adviser and Del. to various int. bodies 1947-53; Canadian Deputy Perm. Rep. to North Atlantic Council (NATO) and OEEC 1954-57; Consul-Gen. of Canada, Seattle 1957-62; Canadian del. to Colombo Plan Conf., Seattle 1958; High Commr. to New Zealand 1963-67; Dir. U.S.A. Div., Dept. of External Affairs 1967-70; Canadian del. to IMCO and ECE Conf. on Int. Combined Transport,

London 1970, to UNCTAD Conf. on Int. Shipping Legislation, Geneva 1971, to Int. Conf. on Unlawful Interference with Civil Aviation 1971; Exec. Dir. Int. Transport Policy Cttee., Canadian Transport Comm. 1971–78; Canadian Del. to Gen. Assembly of Int. Civil Aviation Org. (ICAO) 1974, 1977; Canadian del. to UNCTAD Confs. on int. multi-modal transport, Geneva 1972–77; Dir. Canadian Branch Int. Law Asscn.; Admin. Maritime Pollution Claims Fund, Ottawa. *Leisure interests:* oil painting, golf, skiing. *Address:* Tower "A", Place de Ville, Ottawa, Ont. K1A 0N5 (Office); 930 Sadler Crescent, Ottawa Ont. K2B 5H7, Canada (Home).

BURCH, Dean, LL.B.; American attorney and government official; b. 20 Dec. 1927, Enid, Okla.; s. of Bert Alexander and Leola (Atkisson) Burch; m. Patricia Meeks 1961; one s. two d.; ed. Univ. of Arizona; Asst. Attorney-Gen., Ariz. 1953–54; Admin. Asst. to Senator Barry Goldwater 1955–59; mem. firm Dunseath, Stubbs & Burch, Tucson 1959–63; Deputy Dir. Goldwater for Pres. Cttee. 1963–64; Chair. Republican Nat. Cttee. 1964–65; Partner, Dunseath, Stubbs & Burch 1965–69; Chair. Fed. Communications Comm. 1969–74; Counsellor to Pres. Nixon March–Aug. 1974, to Pres. Ford 1974–75; Sr. Adviser to Reagan-Bush Cttee. July–Nov. 1980, Aug.–Dec. 1984; Chief of Staff to George Bush Nov. 1980–Jan. 1981; Head U.S. Del. to First Session of World Admin. Radio Conf. on Use of Geostationary–Satellite Orbit & Planning of Space Service, Geneva June 1984–; Dir.-Gen. Intelsat April 1987–; mem. Exec. Cttee., Reagan-Bush Transition Cttee.; Partner, Pierson, Ball & Dowd, Washington, D.C. 1975–. *Leisure interests:* golf, tennis. *Address:* 1000 Ring Building, Washington, D.C. 20036 (Office); 9311 Persimmon Tree Road, Potomac, Md. 20854, U.S.A. (Home). *Telephone:* (202) 947-7800 (Office); 301-983-1294 (Home).

BURCHAM, William Ernest, C.B.E., PH.D., F.R.S., F.INST.P.; British emeritus professor of physics; b. 1 Aug. 1913, Norfolk; s. of Ernest Barnard Burcham and Edith Pitcher; m. 1st Isabella Mary Todd 1942 (died 1981), two d.; m. 2nd Patricia Newton Marson 1985; ed. City of Norwich School and Trinity Hall, Cambridge; Scientific Officer, Ministry of Supply 1939–44; with U.K. Atomic Energy 1944–45; Lecturer, Fellow, Selwyn Coll., Univ. of Cambridge 1945–51; Demonstrator, Lecturer, Univ. of Cambridge 1945–51; Oliver Lodge Prof. of Physics, Univ. of Birmingham 1951–80, Emer. Prof. of Physics 1981–; Hon. Life Fellow, Coventry Polytechnic 1984. *Publications:* Nuclear Physics: An Introduction 1963, Elements of Nuclear Physics 1979. *Address:* 95 Witherford Way, Birmingham, B29 4AN, England. *Telephone:* (021) 4721226.

BURCHFIELD, Robert William, C.B.E., M.A.; New Zealand lecturer in English Language and author; b. 27 Jan. 1923, Wanganui; s. of Frederick Burchfield and Mary Blair; m. 1st Ethel May Yates 1949 (dissolved 1976), one s. two d.; m. 2nd Elizabeth Austen Knight 1976; ed. Wanganui Tech. Coll., Victoria Univ. Coll., Wellington and Magdalen Coll., Oxford; war service with Royal N.Z. Artillery 1941–46; Jr. Lecturer in English Language, Magdalen Coll., Oxford 1952–53; Lecturer in English Language, Christ Church, Oxford 1953–57; Lecturer, St. Peter's Coll., Oxford 1955–63, Tutorial Fellow 1963–79, Sr. Research Fellow 1979–; Ed., Notes and Queries 1956–62, A Supplement to the Oxford English Dictionary 1957–86; Chief Ed., The Oxford English Dictionaries 1971–84; Pres. English Asscn. 1978–79; Hon. Sec. Early English Text Soc. 1955–68, mem. Council 1968–80; Hon. Foreign mem. American Acad. of Arts and Sciences 1977–; Hon. D.Litt. (Liverpool) 1978, Hon. Lit.D. (Victoria Univ. of Wellington) 1983. *Publications:* The Oxford Dictionary of English Etymology (with C. T. Onions and G. W. S. Friedrichsen) 1966, A Supplement of Australian and New Zealand Words (in the Pocket Oxford Dictionary) 1969, A Supplement to the Oxford English Dictionary (Vol. I) 1972, (Vol. II) 1976, (Vol. III) 1982, (Vol IV) 1986. The Quality of Spoken English on BBC Radio (with D. Donoghue and A. Timothy) 1979, The Spoken Language as an Art Form 1981, The Spoken Word 1981, The English Language 1985, The New Zealand Pocket Oxford Dictionary 1986, Studies in Lexicography 1987, Unlocking the English Language 1988. *Leisure interests:* travelling, English grammar, country life. *Address:* The Barn, 14 The Green, Sutton Courtenay, Oxon., OX14 4AE, England. *Telephone:* (0235) 848645.

BURDICK, Quentin Northrop, B.A., LL.B.; American lawyer and politician; b. 19 June 1908, Munich, N.D.; s. of late Usher L. Burdick and Emma Robertson; m. 1st Marietta Janecky (died 1958), m. 2nd Mrs. Jocelyn Birch Peterson; seven c.; ed. Williston High School, Univ. of Minnesota; admitted to N. Dakota Bar 1932, practised Fargo 1932–58; Cand. for Gov. 1946, for U.S. Senator 1956; elected to House of Reps. 1958; Senator from N. Dakota 1961–; Democrat. *Address:* 511 Hart Senate Building, Washington, D.C. 20510 (Office); 1110 South 9th Street, Fargo, North Dakota, U.S.A. (Home).

BURELLI RIVAS, Miguel Angel, LL.B., DR.POL.SC.; Venezuelan lawyer and diplomatist; b. 8 July 1922; ed. Univ. de Los Andes, Bogotá, Univ. Central de Venezuela et de Ecuador, Univ. Nacional de Bogotá, Univ. de Madrid and Univ. di Firenze; pre-seminary Prof. of Political Sociology and Chief Prof. of Mining and Agrarian Legislation, Faculty of Law, Univ. de Los Andes, Bogotá, Chief Prof. of Humanities I and II, Faculty of Civil Eng., Dir. of Univ. Culture, Founder of School of Humanities, Founder-Dir. of Univ. reviews, Bibliotheca and Universitas Emeritensis; Political Dir. Ministry of the Interior; Dir.-Gen. Ministry of Foreign Affairs (nine times Acting Minister); Interim Minister of Foreign Affairs; returned to legal profession 1961; mem. Venezuelan Supreme Electoral Council 1961; Minister of Justice 1964–65; Amb. to Colombia 1965–67, U.K. 1967–69;

Presidential Candidate 1968, 1973; Amb. to U.S.A. 1974–76; numerous decorations. *Address:* c/o Ministerio de Asuntos Exteriores, Caracas, Venezuela.

BURESCH, Eugen F., LL.D.; Austrian diplomatist (retd.); b. 9 Oct. 1915, Vienna; s. of Karl Buresch, LL.D., Federal Chancellor; m. 1st Joan Dulles 1954, 2nd Edda Grieshoffer 1961; two s. three d.; 3rd Natascha Vinograd-skava 1982; ed. High School Theresianum, Vienna, Univ. of Vienna and Ecole des Sciences Politiques, Paris; Officer, Comité Int. du Bois, Brussels 1938–39; First Sec., Rome 1946–49; in Political Dept., Foreign Office, Vienna 1949; First Sec., London 1950–51; Dir. Austrian Information Service, N.Y. 1952–55; Chargé d'affaires, Austrian Embassy, Iran 1955, Minister 1958, Amb. 1960, concurrently to Afghanistan; Amb. to Canada 1960–64; Head of Austrian negotiating del. with EEC, Brussels and Luxembourg 1965–68; Amb. to UN at Geneva 1968; Amb. to Mexico 1973–77; Head of Economic Section, Fed. Ministry of Foreign Affairs, Vienna 1977–78; Vice-Dir. Danube Comm., Budapest 1978–83; mem. Alumni Theresianische Akad. *Publications:* Weder Heil Noch Opfer 1985, and articles in newspapers. *Address:* Grünbergstrasse 4, A-Vienna, Austria. *Telephone:* 836556.

BURG, Josef, DR. PHIL.; Israeli politician; b. 31 Jan. 1909, Dresden, Germany; m. Rivka Slonim 1943; one s. two d.; ed. Univs. of Berlin and Leipzig; Pedagogical Inst. Leipzig, Rabbinical Seminary Berlin and Hebrew Univ. of Jerusalem; Directorate, Palestine Office, Berlin 1936; Nat. Exec. Mizrachi; Zionist Gen. Council 1939–51; mem. Exec. Hapoel Hamizrachi 1944–; Deputy Speaker First Knesset (Israeli Parl.) 1949–51; Minister of Health, Govt. of Israel 1951–52, of Posts and Telegraphs Dec. 1952–58, of Social Welfare 1959–70, of the Interior 1970–76, of Welfare July–Nov. 1975, of Interior and Police 1977–84, of Religious Affairs 1981–84, 1985–86; Chair. Ministerial Cttees. on Jerusalem, Devt. of the Galilee, Crime Prevention and Cabinet procedures; Nat. Religious Party. *Address:* 6 Ben Maymon Street, Jerusalem, Israel. *Telephone:* 02-639092.

BURGAN, Salih Khalil, M.D.; Jordanian physician, politician and international civil servant; b. 19 July 1918, Kerak; s. of Khalil Burgan and Labeebah (née Halasa); m. Blanche (née Khoury) 1949; three s. one d.; ed. American Univ. of Beirut; Physician, Transjordan Frontier Forces (T.J.F.F.) 1943–46, Dir. of Arab Physicians (T.J.F.F.) 1946–48; private physician at Zerka, Jordan 1948–63; mem. Parl. 1961–62, Senate 1963–69; Minister of Health 1963–64, of Social Affairs and Labour 1966, of Public Health 1966–67, of Social Affairs and Labour and Minister of Interior for Municipal and Rural Affairs 1967–69; Dir. Int. Labour Office, Beirut 1969–75, Asst. Dir.-Gen., Geneva June 1975–; Al Kawkab Medal (1st Grade); Grand Kt. of the Holy Tomb. *Leisure interests:* reading, classical music. *Address:* International Labour Office, Case Postale 500, CH-1211 Geneva 22; Residence: 11 Parc de Budé, 1202 Geneva, Switzerland.

BURGARD, Horst; German banker and company executive; b. 28 Jan. 1929; member of Man. Bd., Deutsche Bank AG, Frankfurt am Main; Chair. Supervisory Bd., DLW AG, Bietigheim-Bissingen, Didier-Werke AG, Hutschenreuther AG; Chair. of Supervisory Bd., Frankfurter Hypothekenbank; Deputy Chair. Bertelsmann AG, Gütersloh; mem. Supervisory Bd., AEG AG, Berlin/Frankfurt, Rütgerswerke AG, Frankfurt, Allgäuer Alpenmilch AG, Munich, Heidelberger Zement AG, Deutsche Bank AG, Hamburg, Messer Griesheim GmbH, Frankfurt, Linde AG, Wiesbaden. *Address:* Taunusanlage 12, D-6000 Frankfurt am Main, Federal Republic of Germany.

BURGEN, Sir Arnold (Stanley Vincent), Kt., M.D., F.R.S.; British scientist; b. 20 March 1922, London; s. of the late Peter and Elizabeth (née Wolfers) Burgen; m. Judith Browne 1946; two s. one d.; ed. Christ's Coll., Finchley, London, Middlesex Hospital Medical School; Demonstrator, later Asst. Lecturer, Middlesex Hospital Medical School 1945–49; Prof. of Physiology, McGill Univ., Montreal 1949–62; Deputy Dir. McGill Univ. Clinic, Montreal Gen. Hospital 1957–62; Sheild Prof. of Pharmacology, Univ. of Cambridge 1962–71; Dir. Nat. Inst. of Medical Research, London 1971–82; Master Darwin Coll., Cambridge Oct. 1982–; mem. Medical Research Council (MRC) 1969–71, 1973–77, Hon. Dir. MRC Molecular Pharmacology Unit 1967–72; Pres. Int. Union of Pharmacology 1972–75; Foreign Sec. Royal Soc. 1981–86; Fellow, Downing Coll., Cambridge 1962–71, Hon. Fellow 1972; mem. Deutsche Akad. der Naturforscher Leopoldina 1984; Corresp. mem. Royal Acad. of Spain 1984; Foreign Assoc. Nat. Acad. of Sciences, U.S.A.; Pres. Academia Europaea 1988–; Hon. D.Sc. (McGill, Leeds); Hon. M.D. (Zürich) 1983, (Utrecht); Hon. D. Univ. (Surrey) 1983; Hon. F.R.C.P., Canada. *Publications:* Physiology of Salivary Glands 1961, papers in journals of pharmacology and physiology. *Leisure interests:* sculpture, music. *Address:* Darwin College, Cambridge, England. *Telephone:* (0223) 335670.

BURGER, Alewyn Petrus, F.R.S.S.A., M.SC., D.SC.(TECH); South African scientist; b. 31 Jan. 1927, Middelburg, Transvaal; s. of the late D. J. Burger and M. M. Burger; m. Erica L. van der Merwe 1952; one s. four d.; ed. Univ. of Pretoria and Tech. Univ., Delft; Research Meteorologist S.A. Weather Bureau, Pretoria 1950–57; Head Dept. of Applied Math., Nat. Physics Research Lab., Council for Scientific and Industrial Research (CSIR) 1957–61; Dir. Nat. Research Inst. for Math Sciences, CSIR 1961–73, Vice-Pres. CSIR 1973–76, Consultant in Atmospheric Sciences 1982–; Chair. Scientific Advisory Council to the Prime Minister, Special Adviser and Head of Science Planning 1977–81; Man. Impetus Magazine 1985–;

Chair. S.A. Math. Soc. 1961–63, 1973–75; Pres. Jt. Council of Scientific Socs. 1972–73; mem. Council for Natural Scientists 1988–; mem. S.A. Acad. of Arts and Sciences 1968–; Hon. Prof. of Applied Math., Univ. of Stellenbosch 1979–80; Havenga Prize for Math. Sciences 1973. *Publications:* numerous scientific articles in int. journals. *Leisure interests:* Christian work, piano, athletics, tennis. *Address:* P.O. Box 4485, Pretoria 0001, South Africa.

BURGER, Warren E(arl); American judge; b. 17 Sept. 1907, St. Paul; s. of Charles Joseph Burger and Katharine Schnittger; m. Elvera Stromberg 1933; one s. one d.; ed. Univ. of Minnesota, St. Paul Coll. of Law; admitted to Minn. Bar 1931; Partner, Faricy, Burger, Moore & Costello 1931–53; mem. Faculty, Mitchell Coll. of Law 1931–46; Asst. Attorney-Gen. of U.S. 1953–56; Judge, U.S. Court of Appeals, Washington, D.C. 1956–69; Chief Justice of U.S. 1969–86; Hon. Chair. Inst. of Judicial Admin.; Chair. Comm. on Bicentennial of U.S. Constitution; Faculty Appellate Judges' Seminar, New York Univ. 1958–; Guest Lecturer Fordham Univ., New York 1973, Frankfurt Univ., Stockholm Univ., Uppsala Univ., Salzburg Seminar for American Studies; Chair. Criminal Justice Project, American Bar Asscn.; Churchill Lecturer 1987; Pres. Bentham Club, Univ. Coll. London 1972–73; Chancellor, Bd. of Regents, Smithsonian Inst., Washington, D.C.; Chair. Bd. of Trustees, Nat. Gallery of Art, Washington, D.C.; Trustee Emer. William Mitchell Coll. of Law, St. Paul, Minn., Mayo Foundation, Rochester, Minn., and Macalester Coll., St. Paul, Minn.; Trustee, Nat. Geographic Soc.; Hon. Master of the Bench, Middle Temple, London 1969; Hon. LL.D. (Columbia Univ, New York Univ., Univ. of Penn., Georgetown Univ., American Univ., Univ of Minn., George Washington Univ.); Presidential Medal of Freedom 1988. *Address:* 1 First Street, N.E., Washington, D.C. 20543, U.S.A.

BURGESS, Anthony, B.A., F.R.S.L.; British writer; b. 25 Feb. 1917, Manchester; s. of Joseph Wilson and Elizabeth Burgess; m. 1st Llewela Isherwood Jones 1942 (deceased); m. 2nd Liliana Macellari, Countess Pasi 1968; one s.; ed. Xaverian Coll., Manchester and Manchester Univ.; British Army 1940–46; Chief Instructor, Western Command Coll. 1946–48; Lecturer in Speech and Drama, Ministry of Educ. 1948–50; Master Banbury Grammar School 1950–54; Educ. Officer Malaya and Borneo 1954–59; freelance writer 1959–; reviewer for many British newspapers and journals incl. Listener, Observer, Sunday Times, Spectator, Harpers and Queen; Visiting Prof. Univ. of N. Carolina 1969–70, Princeton Univ. 1970–71; Distinguished Prof., City Coll., N.Y. 1972–73; Prof. Columbia Univ. 1973–; Fellow, Royal Soc. of Literature; Literary Adviser, Guthrie Theater, Minn.; Hon. D.Litt. (Manchester) 1982; Commandeur de Mérite Culturel (Morocco) 1986, des Arts et des Lettres 1986; U.S. Nat. Arts Club Gold Medal; Knight of Mark Twain. *Publications:* fiction: Malayan Trilogy (The Long Day Wanes) 1956–59, The Doctor Is Sick 1960, The Worm and the Ring 1961, Devil of a State 1961, A Clockwork Orange 1962, The Wanting Seed 1962, Honey for the Bears 1963, Inside Mr. Enderby (as Joseph Kell) 1963, Nothing Like the Sun 1964, The Eve of St. Venus 1964, Tremor of Intent 1965, Enderby Outside 1968, MF 1970, Napoleon Symphony 1974, The Clockwork Testament 1974, A Long Trip to Teatime 1976, Beard's Roman Women 1977, Abba Abba 1977, L'Homme de Nazareth 1977, 1985 1978, Christ the Tiger 1978, Earthly Powers 1980, On Going to Bed 1982, The End of the World News 1982, Enderby's Dark Lady 1984, Flame into Being 1985, Kingdom of the Wicked 1985, The Piano Players 1986, Any Old Iron 1988; biography: Shakespeare 1971, Ernest Hemingway and his World 1978, Little Wilson and Big God (autobiog.) 1986; trans.: Cyrano de Bergerac 1971, Oedipus the King 1972; philology: Language Made Plain 1965; criticism: The Novel Today 1963, Here Comes Everybody—an introduction to James Joyce 1965, The Novel Now 1967, Joysprick 1973, Ninety-Nine Novels 1984, Homage to Qwert Yuiop: Selected Journalism 1978–85 1986; This Man and Music (autobiog.) 1982; poetry: Moses 1976; television: Lots of Fun at Finnegans Wake 1973, Moses 1973, Michelangelo 1975, Jesus of Nazareth 1976; radio: Blooms of Dublin 1982; musical compositions: Symphony in C 1975, The Brides of Enderby 1978, Mr. WS (a ballet) 1979. *Leisure interests:* travel, playing organ, piano, harpsichord, musical composition, philology, linguistics, cooking. *Address:* 44 rue Grimaldi, MC 98000, Monaco.

BURGESS, Ian Glencross, B.SC.; Australian business executive; b. 26 Nov. 1931, Sydney; s. of Athol V. Burgess and Malitza Boiadjieff; m. Barbara J. Hastie 1957; ed. The King's School, Parramatta and Univ. of N.S.W.; Gen. Man. Raw Sugar Marketing, CSR Ltd. 1978–81, Gen. Man. Personnel 1981, Gen Man. Bldg. Materials 1982–84, Gen. Man. Sugar 1984–86, Exec. Dir. 1986, Man. Dir. 1987–. *Leisure interests:* reading, golf. *Address:* CSR Limited, Level 35, Grosvenor Place, 225 George Street, Sydney 2000, N.S.W., Australia. *Telephone:* 235 8333.

BURGH, Sir John Charles, K.C.M.G., C.B., B.SC.(ECON.), M.A.; British administrator; b. 9 Dec. 1925, Vienna, Austria; m. Ann Sturge 1957; two d.; ed. Friends' School, Sibford, London School of Economics; Leverhulme postintermediate Scholarship, L.S.E., Pres. of Union 1949; Asst. Prin., Bd. of Trade 1950; Pvt. Sec. to successive Ministers of State, Bd. of Trade 1954–57; Colonial Office 1959–62; mem. U.K. Del. to UN Conf. on Trade Devt. 1964; Asst. Sec., Dept. of Econ. Affairs 1964; Prin. Pvt. Sec. to successive First Secs. of State and Secs. of State for Econ. Affairs 1965–68; Under-Sec., Dept. of Employment 1968–71; Deputy Chair. Community

Relations Comm. 1971–72; Deputy Sec. Cabinet Office (Cen. Policy Review Staff) 1972–74, Dept. of Prices and Consumer Protection 1974–79, Dept. of Trade 1979–80; Dir.-Gen. British Council 1980–87; Pres. Trinity Coll., Oxford Oct. 1987–; Sec. Nat. Opera Co-ordinating Cttee. 1972–; Sec. Opera Cttee. Royal Opera House, Covent Garden 1972–80; Gov. L.S.E. 1980–, Chair. 1985–87; Vice-Pres. Royal Inst. of Public Admin. 1985–88; mem. Exec., Political and Econ. Planning 1972–78, Council, Policy Studies Inst. 1978–85, Council Voluntary Service Overseas 1980–87, Wilton Park 1984–87; Chair. Assoc. Bd. Royal Coll. of Music 1987–; Vice-Chair. Int. Student House 1985–86, Chair. 1987–; Hon. Fellow L.S.E.; Hon. LL.D. (Bath); Hon. mem. Royal Northern Coll. of Music. *Leisure interests:* friends, music, the arts generally. *Address:* Trinity College, Oxford, OX1 3BH, England. *Telephone:* 0865-279900.

BURGHARDT, Walter J., M.A., PH.L., S.T.L., S.T.D.; American professor of theology; b. 10 July 1914, New York; ed. Woodstock Coll., The Catholic University of America; Prof. Patristic (Historical) Theology, Woodstock Coll. 1946–74; Lecturer Union Theological Seminary, New York City 1971–74; Prof. Patristic Theology, The Catholic Univ. of America 1974–78, Prof. Emer. 1978–; Visiting Lecturer in Theology, Princeton Theological Seminary 1972–73; Research Assoc. Woodstock Theological Center, Washington, D.C. 1974–; Ed. Theological Studies 1967–, Man. Ed. 1946–67; Co-ed. Ancient Christian Writers 1958–; mem. Bd. of Patrons, Ecumenical Inst. for Advanced Theological Studies in Jerusalem (Tantur) 1981–; Chair. Cttee. on Theology and Ethics, The Catholic Health Asscn. of the U.S. 1985–; mem. Corpn. Jesuit Int. Volunteers Inc. 1986–; mem. American Theological Soc., Assocn. Int. d'Etudes Patristiques, Catholic Comm. on Intellectual and Cultural Affairs, Catholic Theological Soc. of America, Mariological Soc. of America, North American Acad. of Ecumenists, North American Patristic Soc.; Mariological Award 1958, Cardinal Spellman Award 1962; several hon. degrees. *Publications include:* The Image of God in Man According to Cyril of Alexandria 1957, All Lost in Wonder: Sermons on Theology and Life 1960, Saints and Sanctity 1965, Seasons That Laugh or Weep: Musings on the Human Journey 1983, Preaching: The Art and Craft 1987, etc.; also author and ed. of many booklets, radio and TV programmes, lectures. *Address:* Office of Theologian in Residence, Georgetown University, Washington, D.C. 200057, U.S.A.

BURGIN, Victor, A.R.C.A., M.F.A.; British author, lecturer and artist; b. 24 July 1941, Sheffield; s. of Samuel Burgin and Gwendolyne A. Crowder; m. Hazel P. Rowbotham 1964 (divorced 1975); two s.; ed. Firth Park Grammar School, Sheffield, Sheffield Coll. of Art, Royal Coll. of Art, London, and Yale Univ, U.S.A.; Sr. Lecturer, Trent Polytechnic, Nottingham 1967–73; Prof. of History and Theory of Visual Arts, Faculty of Communication, Polytechnic of Cen. London 1973–; U.S./U.K. Bicentennial Arts Exchange Fellowship 1976–77; Deutscher Akademischer Austauschdienst Fellowship 1978–79; Picker Professorship, Colgate Univ., Hamilton, New York 1980; mem. Arts Advisory Panel, Arts Council of G.B. 1971–76, 1980–81; numerous mixed and one-man exhbns. at galleries around the world since 1965. *Publications:* Work and Commentary 1973, Thinking Photography 1982, The End of Art Theory 1986, Between 1986, and exhbn. catalogues. *Leisure interests:* listening to and playing music, especially baroque (lute) and modern jazz (saxophone). *Address:* Polytechnic of Central London, Faculty of Communication, 18–22 Riding House Street, London, W.1 (Office); 56a Albert Street, London, NW1 7NR, England (Home). *Telephone:* 01-486 5811 Ext. 6518 (Office); 01-387 2144 (Home).

BURGON, Geoffrey, G.G.S.M.; British composer and conductor; b. 15 July 1941, Hambledon; s. of Alan and Vera (née Isom) Burgon; m. Janice Garwood 1963 (divorced); one s. one d.; ed. Pewley School, Guildford, Guildhall School of Music; freelance trumpeter/composer 1964–71; conductor 1964–; full-time composer 1971–; compositions include (dramatic works): Epitaph for Sir Walter Raleigh 1968, Joan of Arc 1970, The Fall of Lucifer 1977, Orpheus 1982 (orchestral music): Concerto for String Orchestra 1963, Gending 1968, Alleluia Nativitas 1970 (with voices): Acquainted with Night 1965, Think on Dredful Domesday 1969, Canciones del Alma 1975, Requiem 1976, Magnificat and Nunc dimittis 1979, The World Again 1983, Revelations 1984, Title Divine 1986 (ballet music): The Golden Fish 1964, The Calm 1974, Running Figures/Goldberg's Dream 1975, Songs, Lamentations and Praises 1979, Mass 1984, Prometheus 1988 (chamber music): Four Guitars 1977, Six Studies 1980 (with voices): Hymn to Venus 1966, Five Sonnets of John Donne 1967, Worldës Blissë 1971, Two Love Songs, Lunar Beauty 1986 (choral music): Three Elegies 1964, Short Mass 1965, Golden Eternity 1970, The Fire of Heaven 1973, Dos Coros 1975 (music for children): Divertimento 1964, Five Studies 1965, Now Welcome Summer 1966, Beginnings 1969 (film music): Life of Brian 1979, Dogs of War 1980, Turtle Diary 1985 (TV Music): Dr Who 1975, Tinker Tailor Soldier Spy 1979, Brideshead Revisited 1981, Testament of Youth 1979, How Many Miles to Babylon 1981, Bewitched 1983, The Death of the Heart 1985, Happy Valley 1987, The Old Wives Tale 1988; recipient of Ivor Novello Awards 1980, 1981, Gold Disc 1986. *Leisure interests:* cricket, jazz, wasting money on old Bristols. *Address:* Chester Music, 8–9 Frith Street, London W1V 5T2, England.

BURHAN XAHIDI, PH.D.; Chinese politician; b. Wensu Co., Xinjiang; m. Lashida; ed. Berlin Univ.; Vice-Gov. Xinjiang 1946–48; Gov. Xinjiang 1948; joined CCP 1949; mem. CPPCC 1951; mem. Standing Cttee. CPPCC 1953;

Vice-Chair. CPPCC 1954–65; mem. Dept. of Philosophy and Social Sciences, Academia Sinica 1955–66; in disgrace during Cultural Revolution 1966–77; mem. Standing Cttee. 5th CPPCC 1978; Chair. Chinese Islamic Asscn. 1979–; Vice-Chair. 6th CPPCC 1983–88; Vice-Chair. 7th CPPCC 1988–. *Publications:* Half Century in Xinjiang. *Address:* Chinese People's Political Consultative Conference, Taiping Qiao Road, Beijing, People's Republic of China.

BURIN DES ROZIERS, Etienne; French diplomatist; b. 11 Aug. 1913, Paris; s. of André Burin des Roziers and Madeleine Heurteau; m. Jane d'Oilliamson 1950; two s. one d.; ed. Ecole Libre des Sciences Politiques, Faculties of Law and Letters, Univ. of Paris, and Univ. of Oxford; Head, French Del. to Int. Comm. of Enquiry on Former Italian Colonies 1947–48; Sub-Dir. of the Saar, Ministry of Foreign Affairs 1948–50; Atlantic Pact Del. 1950–52; Tech. Adviser to Prime Minister 1953; Chargé d'affaires, Yugoslavia 1954–55; Deputy to French Resident in Morocco 1955–56; Consul-Gen., Milan 1956–58; Amb. to Poland 1958–62; Sec.-Gen. of the Presidency of the Repub. 1962–67; Amb. to Italy 1967–72; Perm. Rep. to Comm. of European Communities 1972–75; Conseiller d'Etat 1975–84; Pres. Council Agence France-Presse 1976; Grand Officier de la Légion d'honneur, Croix de guerre, Médaille de la Résistance, other decorations. *Publications:* Retour aux Sources, 1962 l'année décisive 1986. *Address:* 40 Quai des Célestins, Paris 75004, France. *Telephone:* 4272-66 25.

BURKARD, Otto Michael, DR. PHIL.; Austrian academic; b. 24 Nov. 1908, Graz; s. of Otto A. Burkhard; m. Herta Waidbacher 1942; three s. one d.; ed. Univ. of Graz; Prof. of Math. and Physics, Eng. School 1938; Head, Inst. of Meteorology and Geophysics, Univ. of Graz 1949–79; now Prof. Emer.; Dir. Inst. for Space Research, Austrian Acad. of Sciences 1973–84; mem. Austrian Acad. *Publications:* approximately 90 publs. on physics of the ionosphere and space. *Leisure interests:* mountaineering, gardening. *Address:* Grillparzerstrasse 32, 8010 Graz, Austria. *Telephone:* 0316/33-92-92.

BURKE, Admiral Arleigh A., American naval officer (retd.); b. 19 Oct. 1901, Boulder, Colo.; s. of Oscar A. Burke and Claire Mokler Burke; m. Roberta Gorsuch 1923; ed. U.S. Naval Acad. and Univ. of Michigan; commissioned 1923, served all ranks to Rear-Admiral 1950; served 1939–45 war; Head of Research and Devt. Div., Bureau of Ordnance, Washington 1945; Chief of Staff to Commdr. Eighth Fleet in Atlantic 1946, to C.-in-C. Atlantic Fleet 1945–47; Deputy Chief of Staff to Commdr. Naval Forces, Far East; Commdr. Cruiser Div. Five; mem. Mil. Armistice Comm. under Commdr. Naval Forces, Far East 1951; Dir. Strategic Plans Div., Navy Dept. 1952; Commdr. Cruiser Div. Six 1954; Commdr. Destroyers Atlantic Fleet 1955; Chief of Naval Operations (with rank of Admiral) 1955–61, retd. 1961; Counsellor to Center for Strategic and Int. Studies, Georgetown Univ.; Dir. of numerous cos.; Hon. D.Sc., Hon. LL.D., Hon. D.Eng.; Navy Cross; Legion of Merit (two gold stars with oak leaf cluster); Purple Heart; and others. *Leisure interests:* gardening, hunting, sailing. *Address:* The Virginian, Apt. 323, 9229 Arlington Boulevard, Fairfax, Va. 22031, U.S.A. *Telephone:* (703) 385-0555.

BURKE, Bernard Flood, PH.D.; American physicist and astrophysicist; b. 7 June 1928, Boston, Mass.; s. of Vincent Paul Burke and Clare Aloyse Brine; m. Jane Chapin Pann 1953; three s. one d.; ed. Mass. Inst. of Technology; mem. of staff, Carnegie Inst. of Washington 1953–65; Chair. Radio Astronomy Section, Carnegie Inst. of Washington, Dept. of Terrestrial Magnetism 1962–65; Prof. of Physics, M.I.T. 1965–, William Burden Prof. of Astrophysics 1981–; Visiting Prof., Leiden Univ. 1971–72; Trustee Associated Univ. Inc. 1972–; Trustee and Vice-Chair. N.E. Radio Observatory Corpn. 1973–82, Chair. 1982–; mem. American Acad. of Arts and Sciences, N.A.S.; Fellow, A.A.A.S.; Helen B. Warner Prize, American Astron. Soc. 1963, Rumford Prize, American Acad. of Arts and Sciences 1971; Sherman Fairchild Scholar, Calif. Inst. of Tech. 1984–85; Smithsonian Regents Fellow 1976; Pres. American Astronomical Soc. 1986–88; Ed. Comments on Astrophysics 1984–87. *Publications:* Microwave Spectroscopy 1953–54, Radio Noise from Jupiter 1955–61, Galactic Structure 1959–, Very Long Baseline Interferometry 1968–, Interstellar Masers 1968–, Gravitational Lenses 1980–, miscellaneous publs. in radio astronomy 1955–. *Leisure interests:* skiing, sailing, hiking, chamber music. *Address:* Room 26-335, Department of Physics, Massachusetts Institute of Technology, Cambridge, Mass. 02139 (Office); 10 Bloomfield Street, Lexington, Mass., U.S.A. (Home). *Telephone:* 617-253-2572 (Office); 617-862-8939 (Home).

BURKE, Hon. Brian Thomas, A.C., J.P., M.L.A.; Australian politician; b. 25 Feb. 1947, Perth; s. of late Thomas Burke and of Madeleine Burke; m. Susanne May Nevill 1965; four s. two d.; ed. Marist Brothers Coll., Univ. of W. Australia; journalist W. Australian Newspapers, 6 PM and TVW Channel 7 1965–70; mem. Legis. Ass. for Balcatta (now Balga) 1973–83; Opposition Shadow Minister 1976–83, Leader 1981–83; Premier of W. Australia, State Treasurer, Minister for Women's Interests 1983–88; Minister of Tourism and Forests 1983–85; Minister Co-ordinating Econ. and Social Devt. 1983–87; Amb. to Ireland and the Holy See 1988–; Labor. *Leisure interests:* stamp-collecting, swimming, fishing, reading, writing poetry. *Address:* Australian Embassy, 6th Floor, Fitzwilton House, Wilton Terrace, Dublin 2, Ireland; 66 Balcombe Way, Balga, W. Australia 6061 (Office). *Telephone:* 349-6597 (Home).

BURKE, Kenneth; American writer; b. 5 May 1897, Pittsburgh, Pa.; s. of James Leslie Burke and Lillyan May Duva; m. 1st Lily Mary Batterham 1919, 2nd Elizabeth Batterham 1933; two s. three d.; ed. Ohio State and Columbia Univs.; research worker Laura Spelman Rockefeller Memorial 1926–27; music critic The Dial 1927–29; mem. staff Bureau of Social Hygiene 1928–29; Music Critic Nation 1934–36; Lecturer in Practice and Theory of Literary Criticism New School for Social Research 1937, Univ. of Chicago 1938, 1949–50, Kenyon Coll. 1950, Ind. Univ. 1952, 1958, Drew Univ. 1962, 1964, Bennington Coll. 1943–61, Pennsylvania State Univ. 1963; Regents Prof., Univ. of Calif. (Santa Barbara) 1964–65; Prof. Central Washington State Coll. 1966, Harvard 1967–68, Washington Univ. 1970–71, Wesleyan Univ. 1972; Andrew W. Mellon Visiting Prof. of English, Univ. of Pittsburgh 1974; Walker-Ames Visiting Prof. of English, Washington Univ. 1976; Guggenheim Fellowship 1935; mem. Nat. Inst. of Arts and Letters, American Acad. of Arts and Letters, American Acad. of Arts and Sciences; Fellow Center for Advanced Study in Behavioral Sciences 1957–58; Hon. D.Litt., Bennington Coll., Rutgers Univ., Dartmouth Coll., Hon. D.Hum. Litt. (Fairfield Univ., Northwestern Univ., Univ. of Rochester); Brandeis Univ. Creative Arts Awards Comm. Award for Notable Achievements in the Arts 1967, award from Nat. Council on the Arts 1969, Horace Gregory Award, New School for Social Research 1970, Ingram Merrill Foundation Award in literature 1970, Award for contribution to Humanities (American Acad. of Arts and Science) 1977; Nat. Medal for Literature 1981; mem. Century Asscn. *Publications:* The White Oxen 1924, Counter-Statement 1931, 1953, 1968, Towards a Better Life 1932, 1966, Permanence and Change—Anatomy of Purpose 1935, 1954, 1965, Attitudes Towards History—Vol. I Acceptance and Rejection, The Curve of History, Vol. II Analysis of Symbolic Structure 1937, 1959, 1961, The Philosophy of Literary Form-Studies in Symbolic Action 1941, 1957, revised edn. 1967, A Grammar of Motives 1945, 1962, 1969, A Rhetoric of Motives 1950, 1962, 1969, Book of Moments: Poems 15-54 1955, The Rhetoric of Religion 1961, 1970, Perspectives by Incongruity 1965, Terms for Order 1965, Language as Symbolic Action, Essays on Life, Literature and Method 1966, Collected Poems 15-67 1968, Complete White Oxen 1968, Dramatism and Development 1972; translator Thomas Mann's Death in Venice 1925, Emil Ludwig's Genius and Character 1927, and Emil Baumann's Saint Paul 1929. *Leisure interests:* trying to keep from becoming too unfit, punishing the piano, worrying about the military-industrial complex. *Address:* 154 Amity Road, Andover, N.J. 07821, U.S.A. *Telephone:* (201) 347-3249.

BURKE, Prof. Philip George, F.R.S., M.R.I.A.; British professor of mathematical physics; b. 18 Oct. 1932, London; s. of Henry Burke and Frances Mary Burke; m. Valerie Mona Martin 1959; four d.; ed. Univ. of Exeter, Univ. Coll., Univ. of London; Research Fellow Univ. Coll., Univ. of London 1956–57, Lecturer Computer Unit 1957–59; Research Physicist, Berkeley, Calif. 1959–62; Prin. Scientific Officer, then Sr. Prin. Scientific Officer, Atomic Energy Research Establishment, Harwell 1962–67; Prof. of Math. Physics Queen's Univ., Belfast 1967–; Head Div. Theory and Computational Science, Science and Eng. Research Council, Daresbury Lab., Cheshire 1977–82; Fellow Univ. Coll., London 1985–; Hon. D.Sc. (Exeter) 1981. *Publications:* over 200 articles in many specialist journals, author or co-author of four books. *Leisure interests:* reading, walking, swimming. *Address:* Department of Applied Mathematics, Queen's University, Belfast (Office); 33 Leverogue Road, Lisburn, BT27 5PP, Northern Ireland (Home). *Telephone:* 0232-245133 (Office); 0232-826416 (Home).

BURKE, Ray; Irish politician; b. 30 Sept. 1943, Dublin; m. Anne Fassbender; two d.; ed. O'Connell's Co. Boys' School, Dublin; mem. Dublin County Council 1967–78, Chair. 1985–87; mem. Dail 1973–; Minister of State, Dept. of Industry and Commerce and Energy 1978–80, Minister for Environment 1980–81, 1982, for Energy and Communications 1987–88, for Industry, Commerce and Communications 1988–; Fianna Fail. *Address:* Briargate, Malahide Road, Swords, Co. Dublin, Ireland (Home).

BURKE, Richard, M.A.; Irish politician and administrator; b. 29 March 1932, New York, N.Y., U.S.A.; s. of David Burke and Elizabeth Kelly; m. Mary Freeley 1961; two s. three d.; ed. Christian Brothers, Thurles, Univ. College and Kings Inns, Dublin; teacher in Blackrock until 1969; mem. of the Dail for Dublin South Co. 1969–77, for West Dublin 1981–82; fmr. Chief Whip of Fine Gael; Shadow Minister for Posts and Telegraphs 1969–73; Minister for Educ. 1973–76; mem. Comm. European Communities 1977–84, Vice-Pres. 1977–81, Commr. for Consumer Affairs, Transport and Taxation 1977–80, for Personnel and Admin., Joint Interpreting and Conf. Service, Statistical Office 1982–84; Assoc. Fellow, Center for Int. Affairs, Harvard Univ. 1980–81. *Leisure interests:* music, golf. *Address:* 67 Ailesbury Road, Dublin 4, Ireland; Avenue Louise 300, Bte 6, 1050 Brussels, Belgium.

BURKE, Samuel Martin, M.A., F.R.S.A.; Pakistani diplomatist; b. 3 July 1906, Martinpur; s. of K. D. Burke; m. Queenie Louise Burke; four d.; ed. Govt. Coll., Lahore, and School of Oriental Studies, London; Indian Civil Service 1931–47; Dist. Officer and Dist. and Sessions Judge; Pres. Election Tribunal, Punjab 1946; Pakistani Foreign Office 1948–49; served as Sec. to Pakistani Del. to Inter-Dominion Confs. with India 1948 and 1949; Counsellor to Pakistani High Comm. in London 1949–52; Minister in Washington 1952–53; led Special Missions to Dominican Republic and Mexico 1952; Chargé d'affaires, Rio de Janeiro 1953; mem. UN Cttee. on

Contributions 1953-55; Deputy High Commr. for Pakistan in U.K. 1953; Minister to Sweden (concurrently to Norway, Denmark and Finland) 1953-56; Amb. to Thailand and Minister to Cambodia and Laos 1956-59; mem. Pakistani Del. to SEATO Council Meetings 1957, 1958, 1959; High Commr. in Canada 1959-61; led Special Mission to Argentina 1960; Prof. and Consultant in South Asian Studies, Dept. of Int. Relations, Univ. of Minnesota 1961-75; Founder, Burke Library, South Asia Collection, Hamline University; mem. UNITAR Consultative Panel on Training 1983; Fellow, Royal Soc. of Arts; Sitara-i-Pakistan. *Publications:* Zafrulla Khan: The Man and His Career, Pakistan's Foreign Policy: An Historical Analysis, Mainsprings of Indian and Pakistani Foreign Policies, Akbar, the Greatest Mogul. *Leisure interests:* cricket, riding, tennis. *Address:* 3 Pine Walk, Great Bookham, Surrey, KT23 4AS, England. *Telephone:* Bookham 56384.

BURKE, Thomas Kerry, B.A., M.P.; New Zealand politician; b. 24 March 1942, Christchurch; m. 2nd Helen Paske 1984; one s. (two s. from 1st m.); ed. Univ. of Canterbury, Christchurch Teachers' Coll.; general labourer in Auckland 1965-66, Factory del., Auckland Labourers' Union; teacher, Rangiora High School 1967, Chair. Rangiora Post-Primary Teachers' Asscn. 1969-71; M.P. for Rangiora 1972-75, for West Coast 1978-; teacher Greymouth High School 1975-78; Minister of Regional Devt., and of Employment and Immigration 1984-87; Speaker, New Zealand Parl. 1987-; Labour. *Leisure interests:* skiing, swimming. *Address:* Parliament Buildings, Wellington, New Zealand.

BURKHARDT, François; Swiss architect; b. 16 April 1936, Ruschein; m. Linde Honold; ed. Haute Ecole Tech. Fed., Lausanne, Ecole Fed. d'architecture, Berne and Ecole des Beaux-Arts, Hamburg; Dir. Musée des Beaux-Arts, Hamburg 1969-71, Int. Design Centre, Berlin 1971-84; Prof. Ecole Supérieure de Design, Kiel 1970-71, Ecole des Beaux-Arts, Berlin 1980-83, Domus Acad. 1983, Ecole Polytechnique Univ. de Milan 1987, Ecole des Arts Appliqués, Vienna 1987; Dir. Nat. Council of Design, Darmstadt 1974-80, Exhbn. Council, Inst. of External Relations, Stuttgart 1977-84; mem. Deutsches Werkbund, Berlin 1972-84, Bauhaus-Archive Cttee., Berlin 1977-84. *Publications:* Produkt-Form-Geschichte 150 Jahre deutsches Design (with Ernest Fuchs) 1985, Wie ein Stil entsteht- am Beispiel von Ettore Sottsass 1986, Mésurer, adapter, mettre en forme: un processus culturel? 1986, numerous articles. *Address:* 3 rue de Venise, 75004 Paris, France.

BURKILL, John Charles, SC.D., F.R.S.; British mathematician; b. 1 Feb. 1900, Holt; s. of H. R. Burkill; m. Margareta Braun 1928; one s. two d. (two deceased); ed. St. Paul's School, and Trinity Coll., Cambridge; Prof. of Pure Maths., Univ. of Liverpool 1924-29; Hon. Fellow, Tutor of Peterhouse, Cambridge 1929-67, Master of Peterhouse 1968-73, Emer. Reader in Mathematical Analysis; mem. Inst. of Advanced Study, Princeton 1947, Visiting Prof. Rice Inst. 1956, Tata Inst., Bombay 1959; Adams Prize 1949. *Publications:* mathematical books and papers. *Address:* 2 Archway Court, Barton Road, Cambridge, CB3 9LW, England.

BURKITT, Denis Parsons, C.M.G., F.R.S., M.D., F.R.C.S.; British medical research scientist; b. 28 Feb. 1911, Enniskillen; s. of James P. and Gwendoline (née Hill) Burkitt; m. Olive M. Rogers 1943; three d.; ed. Dublin Univ.; surgeon, R.A.M.C. 1941-46; joined H.M. Colonial Service, Uganda 1946, Govt. Surgeon and Lecturer in Surgery, Makerere Univ. Coll. Medical School 1946-64; Sr. Consultant Surgeon, Ministry of Health, Uganda 1961-64; mem. Medical Research Council External Scientific Staff, Uganda 1964-66, London 1966-76; Hon. D.Sc. (Univ. of E. Africa) 1970, (Leeds), (London) 1984, (West Va.) 1985; Hon. M.D. (Bristol Univ.); Hon. F.R.C.S.I.; Hon. F.R.C.P.I.; Hon. Fellow, Trinity Coll., Dublin 1979-; Harrison Prize, Ear Nose and Throat Section, Royal Soc. of Medicine 1966, Stuart Prize, British Medical Asscn. 1966, Arnott Gold Medal, Irish Hospitals and Medical Schools Asscn. 1968, K. B. Judd Award, Sloan Kettering Inst., N.Y. 1969, Robert de Villiers Award, American Leukemia Soc. 1970, Walker Prize, Royal Coll. of Surgeons 1971, Paul Ehrlich-Ludwig Darmstaedter Prize (with Jan Waldenström, q.v.) 1972; shared Albert Lasker Medical Award in Clinical Cancer Chemotherapy 1972, Gairdner Foundation Award 1973, British Medical Asscn. Gold Medal, Bristol-Myers Award for Cancer Research (U.S.A.) 1982, Gen. Motors Mott Award for Cancer Research 1982, Beaumont Bonelli Award, Italy 1983, Prix Mondial Cino del Duca (France) 1987. *Publications:* Treatment of Burkitt's Lymphoma (co-ed.) 1967, Burkitt's Lymphoma (co-ed.) 1970, Refined Carbohydrate Food and Disease (co-ed.) 1975, Don't Forget the Fibre in your Diet 1979, Western Diseases, Their Emergence and Prevention 1981 (co-ed.), Dietary Fibre, Fibre-Depleted Foods and Disease 1985 (co-ed). *Leisure interests:* photography, carpentry. *Address:* Hartwell Cottage, Wells Road, Bisley, Glos., England (Home).

BURLINGAME, John Francis, B.SC.; American business executive; b. 18 June 1922, Somerville, Mass.; s. of John Francis Burlingame and Irene Walsh Burlingame; m. Genevieve Keohane 1947; four c.; ed. Somerville High School and Tufts Univ.; Lieut. U.S.N.R. 1943-46; joined Gen. Electric 1946-, Vice-Pres. Computer Systems Div. 1964-71, Corporate Employee Relations 1971-73, Group Exec. Int. 1973-79, Vice-Chair. 1979-85; Dir. American Arbitration Asscn. 1972-79; Dir. Foreign Policy Asscn. 1974-79; mem. Conf. Bd. 1979-85; mem. Trilateral Comm. 1979-84; Dir. U.S. Chamber of Commerce 1979-82; Dir. Alcan Aluminium Ltd. 1984-87,

Eastman Kodak Co. 1984-, Hershey Foods Corpn. 1984-, Merrill Lynch and Co. 1985-; mem. Advisory Council, Stanford Research Inst. 1980-85. *Address:* 45 Hancock Lane, Darien, Conn. 06820, U.S.A. (Home). *Telephone:* (203) 373 2520 (Office).

BURNET, Alastair (see Burnet, Sir J. W. A.).

BURNET, Sir James William Alexander (Alastair), Kt.; British journalist; b. 12 July 1928, Sheffield, Yorks.; s. of late Alexander and Schonaid Burnet; m. Maureen Sinclair 1958; ed. The Leys School, Cambridge, and Worcester Coll., Oxford; Sub-Ed. and Leader Writer, Glasgow Herald 1951-58, Leader Writer The Economist 1958-62; Political Ed., Independent Television News 1963-64, rejoined ITN 1976-, Dir. 1981-, Assoc. Ed. ITN 1981-; Ed. The Economist 1965-74; Ed. Daily Express 1974-76; Contributor to TV current affairs programmes, This Week, Panorama, News at Ten, etc.; Ind. Dir. Times Newspapers 1982-; mem. Council of the Banking Ombudsman 1985-; Dir. United Racecourses Ltd. 1985-. *Publication:* The Time of Our Lives (with Willie Landels) 1981. *Address:* 43 Hornton Court, Campden Hill Road, London, W.8, England; and 33 Westbourne Gardens, Glasgow, G12, Scotland. *Telephone:* 01-937 7563 (London); 041-339 8073 (Glasgow).

BURNETT, Most Rev. Bill Bendyshe, M.A., L.TH.; South African ecclesiastic; b. 31 May 1917, Koffiefontein; s. of Richard Evelyn Burnett and Louisa Martha Dobinson; m. Sheila Trollip 1945; two s. one d.; ed. Diocesan Coll., Rondebosch, Michaelhouse School, Rhodes Univ. Coll. and St. Paul's Coll., Grahamstown and Queen's Coll., Birmingham, U.K.; schoolmaster St. John's Coll., Umtata 1940; Army Service 1940-45; Deacon St. Thomas', Durban 1947; Chaplain Michaelhouse 1947-54; Vicar of Ladysmith 1954-57; Bishop of Bloemfontein 1956-67; Gen. Sec. S. A. Council of Churches 1967-69; Bishop of Grahamstown 1969-74; Archbishop of Cape Town 1974-81; Hon. D.D. (Rhodes Univ.) 1980. *Publications:* Anglicans in Natal 1953, Be My Spirit: Renewal in the Worldwide Anglican Church (ed.) 1988. *Address:* c/o St. Alban's Rectory, 5 Durham Road, Vincent, East London, 5247; 20 Milner Street, Grahamstown, 6140, South Africa.

BURNEY, Leroy Edgar, M.D., M.P.H.; American physician; b. 31 Dec. 1906, Burney, Ind.; s. of Robert E. Burney and Mabel C. Howell; m. Mildred Hewins 1932; one s. one d.; ed. Indiana and Johns Hopkins Univs.; joined U.S. Public Health Service 1932, established first mobile venereal disease clinic, in Brunswick, Ga. 1937-39; Asst. Chief, Div. of States Relations 1943-44; detailed to U.S. Navy 1944; Dir. U.S. Public Health Service, District IV, New Orleans 1945; Sec. and State Health Commr., Ind. State Bd. of Health 1945-54; Asst. Surgeon-Gen. and Deputy Chief, Bureau of State Service, U.S. Public Health Service 1954-56; Surgeon-Gen. U.S. Public Health Service 1956-61; Pres. World Health Assembly 1958; Vice-Pres. Health Sciences, Temple Univ. 1961-70; fmr. Pres. Milbank Memorial Fund, Sedgwick Memorial Award, American Public Health Asscn. 1975; Hon. D.Sc. (Jefferson, Woman's Medical Colls., Indiana Univ., De Pauw Univ.), Hon. LL.D. (Seton Hall Univ.). *Leisure interests:* golf and gardening. *Address:* Milbank Memorial Fund, 40 Wall Street, New York, N.Y. 10005, U.S.A.

BURNEY, Sayed Muzaffir Hussain, M.A.; Indian politician; b. 14 August 1923, Bulandshahr, Uttar Pradesh; entered Indian Admin. Service; various posts, including Jt. Sec., Ministry of Agric. 1965-72, Additional Sec. in Ministry of Petroleum and Chemicals 1973-75, Sec., Ministry of Information and Broadcasting 1975-77, Sec., Ministry of Home Affairs 1980-81; served Orissa Govt. as Divisional Commr. and Chief Sec. 1979-80; Gov. of Nagaland, Manipur and Tripura, then Haryana 1984-88. *Publications:* many articles in English and Urdu on literary subjects and public admin. *Address:* Raj Bhawan, Chandigarh, Haryana, India.

BURNHAM, James B., PH.D.; American banker; b. 22 Oct 1939, New York; s. of James Burnham and Marcia Lightner; m. Anne Mullin 1964; two s. two d.; ed. Milton Acad., Princeton Univ., Washington Univ., St. Louis; Economist and special asst., Federal Reserve Bd., Washington, D.C. 1969-71; Sr. Economist, Mellon Bank, Pittsburgh, Pa. 1971-74, Vice-Pres. 1974-81, Sr. Vice-Pres. 1985-, Office of Govt. Affairs 1979-81, Chair. Country Review Cttee. 1977-81; Staff Dir. and Special Asst. to Chair., Pres.'s Council of Economic Advisers, Washington, D.C. 1981-82; U.S. Exec. Dir. IBRD, Washington, D.C. 1982-85; Fulbright Scholar, Univ. of Sao Paulo, Brazil 1962. *Publications:* articles on contemporary economic subjects. *Leisure interests:* canoeing, bridge. *Address:* Mellon Bank, 1 Mellon Bank Centre, Suite 0400, Pittsburgh, Pa. 15258, U.S.A.

BURNLEY, James H., IV, J.D.; American government official; b. 30 July 1948, High Point, N.C.; s. of James H. Burnley and Dorothy M. Rockwell; m. Jane Nady; ed. Yale and Harvard Univs.; Assoc. Brooks, Pierce, McLendon, Humphrey & Leonard 1973-75; Partner, Turner, Enochs, Foster, Sparrow & Burnley 1975-81; Dir. VISTA 1981-82; Assoc. Deputy Attorney-Gen., Dept. of Justice, Washington, D.C. 1982-83; Gen. Counsel, Dept. of Transport 1983, Deputy Sec. 1983-87, Sec. of Transport Dec. 1987-89. *Address:* c/o Department of Transport, 400 7th Street, S.W., Washington, D.C. 20590, U.S.A.

BURNS, Benedict DeLisle, M.R.C.S., L.R.C.P., F.R.S.; British neurophysiologist; b. 22 Feb. 1915, London; s. of C. DeLisle Burns and Margaret Hannay; m. 1st Angela Ricardo 1938, 2nd Monika Kasputis 1954; four s.

one d.; ed. Univ. Coll. School, London, Tübingen and Cambridge Univs. and Univ. Coll. Hospital, London; operational research for Prof. S. Zuckerman (q.v.) 1939–45; research staff, MRC Nat. Inst of Medical Research 1945–50; Assoc. Prof. of Physiology, McGill Univ., Canada 1950–58, Prof. 1958–66, Chair. Dept. of Physiology 1965–66; Head, Div. of Physiology and Pharmacology, MRC Nat. Inst. of Medical Research 1966–76; External staff of MRC, Dept. of Anatomy, Univ. of Bristol 1976–80, Hon. Prof. of Neurobiology 1976–80; now Guest Research Worker, Dept. of Anatomy, Univ. of Newcastle-upon-Tyne. *Publications:* The Mammalian Cerebral Cortex 1958, The Uncertain Nervous System 1968. *Leisure interests:* painting, walking, house decoration. *Address:* Department of Anatomy, Medical School, University of Newcastle-upon-Tyne, NE2 4HH, England. *Telephone:* Newcastle 2328511, Ext. 2948.

BURNS, George (Nathan Birnbaum); American comedian; b. 20 Jan. 1896, New York; m. Gracie Allen 1926 (deceased); one s. one d.; appeared regularly in vaudeville with wife Gracie Allen; made radio début on the BBC; Dr. h.c. (Hartford) 1988. *Films include:* The Big Broadcast, 1932, International House 1932, Love in Bloom 1933, We're Not Dressing 1934, The Big Broadcast of 1938, 1938, Many Happy Returns, 1939, Honolulu, 1939, The Sunshine Boys, 1975, Oh God! 1977, Going in Style 1979, Just You and Me, Kid 1979, Oh God! II, Oh God! You Devil III 1984; TV Series: Burns and Allen Show 1950–58, George Burns Show, 1959–60, Wendy and Me 1964; produced TV series Mona McCluskey and is co-owner of the series, Mr. Ed.; has appeared in various concerts and nightclubs, including Carnegie Hall, February 29, 1976; Academy Award for Best Supporting Actor for The Sunshine Boys; Kennedy Award 1988. *Publications:* I Love Her, That's Why, 1955, Living It Up, or They Still Love Me in Altoona, 1976, How to Live to be One Hundred or More 1983, Dear George, Dr. Burns' Prescription for Happiness 1986, Gracie: A Love Story 1988. *Address:* c/o Putnam Publications Group, 200 Madison Avenue, New York, N.Y. 10016, U.S.A.

BURNS, John, PH.D.; American pharmacologist; b. 8 Oct. 1920, Flushing, N.Y.; ed. Queens Coll. and Columbia Univ.; Deputy Chief, Lab. of Chemical Pharmacology, Nat. Heart Inst. 1958–60; Dir. of Research, Pharmacodynamics Div. The Wellcome Research Labs. 1960–66; Vice-Pres. for Research and Devt. Hoffman-La Roche 1966–84; Adjunct Prof. Rockefeller Univ. 1985–; Adjunct mem. Roche Inst. of Molecular Biology 1985–; mem. N.A.S.; mem. N.A.S. Inst. of Medicine; Fellow American Inst. Chemists. *Leisure interests:* equestrian sports. *Address:* Roche Institute of Molecular Biology, Nutley, N.J. 07110 (Office); 480 Catamount Road, Fairfield, Conn. 06430, U.S.A. (Home). *Telephone:* (201) 235-2811.

BURNS, Kevin Francis Xavier, C.M.G.; British diplomatist; b. 18 Dec. 1930; m. Nan Pinto 1963 (died 1984); one s. two d.; ed. Finchley Grammar School and Trinity Coll. Cambridge; Commonwealth Relations Office 1956–58; Asst. Pvt. Sec. to Sec. of State 1958, Second Sec. 1959, First Sec. 1960–63; served Colombo 1960–63, Montevideo 1967–70; Counsellor, U.K. Mission, Geneva 1973–79, Royal Coll. of Defence Studies 1979–80; Head, S.E. Asian Dept, F.C.O. 1980–83; High Commr. to Ghana 1983–86, Barbados 1986–. *Address:* c/o Foreign and Commonwealth Office, London, S.W.1, England.

BURNS, Norman, M.A.; American economist and educationist; b. 14 Nov. 1905, Versailles, Ohio; s. of Marley and Mabel B. Burns; m. Constance Albrech 1935; ed. Wittenberg Univ., Ohio, Yale Univ. and Univ. of Montpellier, France; Asst. Prof. of Econs., American Univ. of Beirut 1929–32; U.S. Govt. Service as Foreign Trade Economist, U.S. Tariff Comm., Dir. Foreign Service Inst. of State Dept., Deputy Dir. for Near East and South Asia, Int. Co-operation Admin., Econ. Adviser, UN Relief and Works Agency, Beirut, Dir. United States Operations Missions, Amman 1934–61; Pres. American Univ. of Beirut 1961–65; mem. Bd. of Dirs. Musa Alami Foundation of Jericho, Washington, D.C. 1968; Hon. LL.D. (Wittenberg Univ.). *Publications:* Government Budgets of Middle East Countries 1956, Planning Economic Development in the Arab World 1959, Education in the Middle East 1965, The Challenge of Education in the Developing Countries 1973, The Energy Crisis and U.S. Middle East Policy 1973. *Leisure interests:* hiking and local history.

BURNS, Sir Terence, Kt. B.A.ECON.; British economist; b. 13 March 1944, Durham; s. of the late Patrick O. Burns and of Doris Burns; m. Anne Elizabeth Powell 1969; one s. two d.; ed. Houghton-le-Spring Grammar School and Victoria Univ. of Manchester; held various research positions at the London Business School 1965–70, Lecturer in Econs. 1970–74, Sr. Lecturer in Econs. 1974–79, Dir. Centre for Econ. Forecasting 1976–79, Prof. of Econs. 1979; Chief Econ. Adviser to the Treasury and Head Govt. Econ. Service 1980–; Vice-Pres. Soc. of Business Economists 1985–; Fellow, London Business School 1988–; mem. Council Royal Econ. Soc. 1986–. *Publications:* various articles on economic matters. *Leisure interests:* watching football, music and golf. *Address:* c/o H.M. Treasury, Parliament Street, London, S.W.1, England.

BURNS, Tom, B.A., F.R.A.; British professor of sociology; b. 16 Jan. 1913; s. of John Burns and Hannah Burns; m. Mary Elizabeth Nora Clark 1944; one s. four d.; ed. Parmiters Foundation School, and Univ. of Bristol; teacher, pvt. schools in Tunbridge Wells and Norwich 1935–39; Friends Ambulance Unit 1939–45; P.O.W., Germany 1941–43; Research Asst., W.

Midland Group on Post-war Reconstruction and Planning 1945–49; lecturer, Sr. lecturer and reader, Univ. of Edin. 1949–65, Prof. of Sociology 1965–81, Visiting Prof., Harvard Univ. 1973–74; mem. Social Science Research Council 1969–70; *Publications:* Local Government and Cen. Control 1954, The Management of Innovation (with G.M. Stalker) 1961, (ed.) Industrial Man 1969, (ed. with E. Burns) Sociology of Literature and Drama 1973, The BBC: Public Institution and Private World 1977, articles in a number of journals in Britain, U.S.A., France etc. *Leisure interests:* music, walking. *Address:* Inchgarvie Lodge, South Queensferry, West Lothian, EH30 9SJ, Scotland.

BURNSTOCK, Geoffrey, PH.D., D.SC., F.A.A., F.R.S.; Australian university professor; b. 10 May 1929, London, England; s. of James Burnstock and Nancy Green; m. Nomi Hirschfeld 1957; three d.; ed. London and Melbourne Univs.; Nat. Inst. for Medical Research, London 1956–57; Dept. of Pharmacology, Oxford Univ. 1957–59; Dept. of Physiology, Illinois Univ. 1959; Sr. Lecturer, Dept. of Zoology, Melbourne Univ. 1959–62, Reader 1962–64, Prof. and Chair. 1964–75, Assoc. Dean (Biological Sciences) 1969–72; Visiting Prof., Dept. of Pharmacology, Univ. of Calif. 1970; Vice-Dean, Faculty of Medical Sciences, Univ. Coll., London 1980–83, Prof. of Anatomy and Head of Dept. of Anatomy and Developmental Biology 1975–, Convenor, Centre for Neuroscience 1979–; Royal Soc. of Vic. Silver Medal 1970; Hon. M.R.C.P. 1987. *Publications:* Adrenergic Neurons: Their Organisation, Function and Development in the Peripheral Nervous System 1975, An Atlas of the Fine Structure of Muscle and its Innervation 1976; Ed. Purinergic Receptors 1981, Somatic and Nerve-Muscle Interactions 1983, Nonadrenergic Innervation of Blood Vessels 1988; Ed.-in-Chief, Journal of the Autonomic Nervous System. *Leisure interests:* wood sculpture, tennis. *Address:* Department of Anatomy and Developmental Biology and Centre for Neuroscience, University College London, Gower Street, London, WC1E 6BT, England. *Telephone:* 01-387 7050.

BURNYEAT, Myles Fredric, F.B.A.; British professor of philosophy; b. 1 Jan. 1939; s. of Peter James Anthony Burnyeat and Cynthia Cherry Warburg; m. 1st Jane Elizabeth Buckley 1971 (divorced 1982); one s. one d.; m. 2nd Ruth Sophia Padel 1984; one d.; ed. Bryanston School and King's Coll., Cambridge; Asst. Lecturer in Philosophy, Univ. Coll., London 1964, Lecturer 1965; Lecturer in Classics, Cambridge Univ. 1978, Fellow and Lecturer in Philosophy, Robinson Coll. 1978; Laurence Prof. of Ancient Philosophy, Cambridge 1984–. *Publications:* Co-Ed. Philosophy As It Is 1979, Doubt and Dogmatism 1980, Science and Speculation 1982; Ed. The Skeptical Tradition 1983. *Leisure interest:* travel. *Address:* Robinson College, Cambridge, England.

BURRELL, J. Earl, BS.CHEM.ENG.; American company executive; b. 7 Sept. 1919, Aurora, Ill.; s. of Fred W. Burrell and the late Rosa (Greenman) Burrell; m. Margaret Macatee 1942; three s. three d.; ed. Michigan and Harvard Univs.; joined PPG Industries, Inc. as Chemical Eng., Research in Chem. Div., Barberton, Ohio 1941; Asst. to Vice-Pres. Operations, Chem. Div., Pittsburgh, Pa. 1956; Vice-Pres. Operations, Chem. Div. 1961; Vice-Pres., Gen. Man. Chem. Div. 1966–75; Exec. Vice-Pres., Operations 1975; Pres. and C.O.O., PPG Industries, Inc. 1976–85. *Leisure interests:* golf, tennis. *Address:* 136 Devonwood Drive, Pittsburgh, Pa. 15241, U.S.A.

BURRENCHOBAY, Sir Dayendranath, K.B.E., C.M.G., C.V.O., B.SC.; Mauritian administrator; b. 24 March 1919, Plaine Magnien; s. of Mohabeer Burrenchobay and Anant Coomaree Ramnath; m. Oomawati Ramphul 1957; one s. two d.; ed. Royal Coll., Curepipe, and Imperial Coll., London Univ.; Graduate Apprentice with British Electricity Authority 1949–50; Chief Educ. Officer, Mauritius 1951; successively Senior Educ. Officer, Chief Educ. Officer 1951–64; Perm. Sec. Ministry of Educ. and Cultural Affairs 1964–68; Perm. Sec. Ministry of External Affairs, Tourism and Emigration, and Prime Minister's Office 1968–76; Sec. to the Cabinet and Head of the Civil Service 1976–78; Gov.-Gen. 1978–83; Chair. Cen. Electricity Bd. 1968–78; Chevalier de la Légion d'honneur. *Address:* S. Ramphul Street, Curepipe Road, Mauritius. *Telephone:* 86-5750.

BURRIS, Robert Harza, PH.D., D.SC.; American professor of biochemistry; b. 13 April 1914, Brookings, S. Dak.; s. of Edward Thomas Burris and Mable Harza Burris; m. Katherine Irene Brusse 1945; one s. two d.; ed. S. Dakota State Coll. and Univ. of Wisconsin; Research Asst., Univ. of Wis. 1936–40; Nat. Research Council Postdoctoral Fellow, Columbia Univ. 1940–41; Instructor in Bacteriology, Univ. of Wis. 1941–44, Asst. Prof. of Biochemistry 1944–46, Assoc. Prof. 1946–51, Prof. 1951–, Chair. Dept. of Biochemistry 1958–70; mem. N.A.S., American Acad. of Arts and Sciences, American Philosophical Soc., Foreign Fellow of the Indian Nat. Science Acad. 1985; Guggenheim Fellow 1954; Pres. American Soc. of Plant Physiologists 1960; Hon. D.Sc. (S. Dakota State Univ.) 1966; Merit Award of Botanical Soc. of America 1966; American Soc. of Plant Physiologists Stephen Hales Award 1968, Charles Reid Barnes Award 1977, Soc. for Industrial Microbiology Charles Thom Award 1977, American Soc. of Agronomy Edward W. Browning Award 1978, Nat. Medal of Science 1980, N.A.S. Carty Award 1984, Wolf Award 1985. *Publications:* Manometric Techniques 1945; 307 scientific papers 1936–88. *Leisure interests:* photography, canoeing. *Address:* Department of Biochemistry, University of Wisconsin, Madison, Wis. 53706, U.S.A. *Telephone:* (608) 262-3042.

BURROUGHS, William Seward, B.A.; American writer; b. 5 Feb. 1914, St. Louis; s. of Perry Mortimer and Laura (Lee) Burroughs; m. Joan

Vollmer 1945 (deceased); one s. (deceased); ed. Harvard Univ.; worked as bar-tender, private detective, factory hand, (pest) exterminator, newspaper reporter, advertising copy writer 1936–41; addicted to heroin 1944–58; moved to Mexico 1949; began writing 1949 (first work Junkie publ. 1953); travelled in Colombia, Peru, Ecuador and corresponded with Allen Ginsberg (q.v.) (publ. as The Yage Letters) 1951–53; in Morocco 1954–58, France 1959–64, Britain 1965–73, U.S.A. 1974–; adopted collage style of writing ("cutting up") 1960; mem. American Acad., Inst. of Arts and Letters 1983. *Publications include:* Junkie: Confessions of an Unredeemed Drug Addict 1953, The Naked Lunch 1959, The Exterminator (with Brion Gysin) 1960, The Soft Machine 1961, Minutes To Go 1961, The Ticket That Exploded 1962, The Yage Letters (with Allen Ginsberg) 1963, Dead Fingers Talk 1963, Nova Express 1964, The Job (with Daniel Odier) 1969, The Wild Boys 1971, Last Words of Dutch Schultz 1975, Electronic Revolution and Other Writings 1978, City of Red Night 1979, The Third Mind (with Brion Gysin) 1978, Ah Pook Is Here and other texts 1979, Roosevelt after Inauguration 1980, Cities of the Red Night 1981, The Place of Dead Roads 1984, Queer 1985, The Adding Machine (collected essays) 1986, The Western Lands 1988. *Address:* c/o Grove Press Inc., 920 Broadway, 16th Floor, New York, N.Y. 10010, U.S.A.

BURROW, John Wyon, M.A., PH.D., F.B.A.; British professor of history; b. 4 June 1935, Southsea; s. of Charles Burrow and Alice (Vosper) Burrow; m. Diane Dunnington 1958; one s. one d.; ed. Exeter School and Christ's Coll. Cambridge; Research Fellow, Christ's Coll. Cambridge 1959–62; Fellow and Dir. of Studies in History, Downing Coll. Cambridge 1962–65; Reader, School of European Studies, Univ. of E. Anglia 1965–69; Reader in History, Univ. of Sussex 1969–82, Prof. of Intellectual History 1982–; Visiting Prof. Univ. of Calif. Berkeley 1981; Visiting Fellow, History of Ideas Unit, Australian Nat. Univ. 1983; Carlyle Lecturer, Oxford Univ. 1985; delivered Gauss Seminars, Princeton Univ. 1988; Hon. Dr. Sci. Pol. (Bologna) 1988; Wolfson Prize for History 1981. *Publications:* Evolution and Society 1966, A Liberal Descent 1981, That Noble Science of Politics 1983, Gibbon 1985, Whigs and Liberals 1988. *Leisure interest:* cooking. *Address:* Arts Building, University of Sussex, Falmer, Brighton, East Sussex, BN1 9QN (Office); 7 Ranelagh Villas, Hove, East Sussex, BN3 6HE, England (Home). *Telephone:* (0273) 606755 (Office); (0273) 731296 (Home).

BURROWES, Norma Elizabeth, B.A.; British opera and concert singer; b. Bangor, Co. Down; d. of Henry and Caroline Burrowes; m. 1st Steuart Bedford (q.v.) 1969 (divorced 1980); m. 2nd Emile Belcourt 1987; one s. one d.; ed. Queen's Univ., Belfast, Royal Acad. of Music; début with Glyndebourne Touring Opera singing Zerlina in Don Giovanni 1969, début with Royal Opera House, Fiakermili in Arabella 1976; roles include Blöndchen in The Abduction from the Seraglio, Oscar (Ballo in Maschera), Despina (Cosi Fan Tutte), Woodbird (Siegfried), Sophie (Der Rosenkavalier), Cunning Little Vixen, Manon (Massenet), Titania (Midsummer Night's Dream), Nanetta (Falstaff), Gilda (Rigoletto), Marie (Daughter of the Regiment), Juliet (Romeo and Juliet), Adina (Elisir d'Amore), Susanna (Nozze di Figaro), Lauretta (Gianni Schicchi); sings regularly with Glyndebourne Opera, Scottish Opera, Aldeburgh Festival, English Nat. Opera, Welsh Nat. Opera and others; abroad: Salzburg, Paris, Munich, Aix-en-Provence, Avignon, Ottawa, Montreal, New York, Vienna, Chicago, Buenos Aires; has sung with all the prin. London orchestras and on BBC radio and television; numerous recordings; Hon. D.Mus. (Queen's Univ., Belfast) 1979; Order of Worshipful Co. of Musicians. *Leisure interests:* gardening, embroidery. *Address:* 56 Rochester Road, London, NW1 9JG, England. *Telephone:* 01-485 7322.

BURROWS, Sir Bernard Alexander Brocas, G.C.M.G.; British fmr. diplomatist; b. 3 July 1910; m. Ines Walter 1944; one s. one d.; ed. Eton and Oxford Univ.; entered Foreign Service 1934; served Cairo 1938–45; Foreign Office 1945–50; Counsellor, Washington 1950–53; Political Resident in the Persian Gulf 1953–58; Amb. to Turkey 1958–63; Deputy Under-Sec. at the Foreign Office 1963–66; U.K. Perm. Rep., North Atlantic Council 1966–70; Dir.-Gen., Fed. Trust for Educ. and Research 1973–76 now Consultant. *Publications:* The Security of Western Europe (with C. Irwin) 1972, The Defence of Western Europe (with G. Edwards); Contributor to: Devolution or Federalism 1980; A Nation Writ Large 1973, Federal Solutions to European Issues 1978, The Third World War 1985, 1978, The Third World War: the untold story 1982. *Address:* Rubens West, Droke, East Dean, Chichester, West Sussex, England.

BURROWS, Eva, A.O., B.A., M.ED.; British Salvation Army officer; b. 15 Sept. 1929, Newcastle, Australia; d. of Robert J. Burrows and Ella M. Watson; unmarried; ed. Brisbane State High School and Queensland, London and Sydney Univs.; Missionary educator, Howard Inst., Zimbabwe 1952–67; Prin. Usher Inst., Zimbabwe 1967–69; Vice-Pres. Int. Coll. for Officers, London 1970–73, Prin. 1974–75; Leader, Women's Social Services in G.B. and Ireland 1975–77; Territorial Commdr. Sri Lanka 1977–79, Scotland 1979–82, Australia 1982–86; Gen. of the Salvation Army July 1986–; Hon. Dr. Liberal Arts (Ewha Woman's Univ., Seoul) 1988, Hon. Dr. Laws (Asbury Coll., U.S.A.) 1988. *Leisure interests:* classical music, reading, travel. *Address:* Salvation Army International Headquarters, 101 Queen Victoria Street, London, EC4P 4EP, England. *Telephone:* 01-236 5222.

BURROWS, (James) Stuart; British opera singer; b. Cilfynydd, S. Wales; s. of Albert Burrows and Irene (Powell) Burrows; m. Enid Lewis 1957; one s. one d.; ed. Trinity Coll. Camarthen; school teacher until début Royal Opera House, Covent Garden 1967; a leading lyric tenor and has sung in world's major opera houses including San Francisco, Vienna, Paris, Buenos Aires (Théâtre Cologne) and Brussels (Théâtre de la Monaie) as well as Covent Garden and Metropolitan Opera, New York; toured Far East with Royal Opera 1979 and sang with co. at Olympic Festival, Los Angeles 1984; four U.S. tours with Metropolitan Opera; concert appearances throughout Europe and N. America, under Solti, Barenboim, Mehta, Ozawa, Bernstein and Ormandy, including two recitals in Brahmssaal, Vienna; BBC TV series Stuart Burrows Sings every year since 1978; many recordings, including Die Zauberflöte, Don Giovanni, Die Entführung aus dem Serail, La Clemenza di Tito, La Damnation de Faust, Les Contes d'Hoffmann, Maria Stuarda, Anna Bolena, Eugene Onegin, The Midsummer Marriage, Messiah, Grande Messe des Morts (Berlioz), Les Nuits d'Eté, Das Klagende Lied, Beethoven's 9th (Choral) Symphony and single discs of Mozart arias, Operetta Favourites, German and French songs, popular ballads and Welsh songs; Hon. D.Mus. (Wales) 1981. *Address:* c/o Harrison-Parrott Ltd., 12 Penzance Place, London, W11 4PA, England.

BURSON, Harold, B.A.; American business executive; b. 15 Feb. 1921, Memphis; s. of Maurice Burson and Esther Burson; m. Bette Foster 1947; two s.; ed. Univ. of Mississippi; Acting Dir. Ole Miss News Bureau 1938–40; Reporter Memphis Commercial Appeal 1940; Asst. to Pres. and Public Relations Dir., H. K. Ferguson Co. 1941–43; operated own Public Relations Firm for six years; formation of Burson-Marsteller, Chair. 1953–, C.E.O. 1953–88; Exec. Vice-Pres. of Young and Rubicam Inc., mem. Exec. Cttee. 1979–85; Garrett Lecturer on Social Responsibility, Columbia Univ., Graduate School of Business 1973; Vice-Pres. and Mem. Exec. Cttee. Nat. Safety Council 1964–77; Int. Trustee World Wildlife Fund 1977–81; trustee and mem. Exec. Cttee. Foundation for Public Relations Research and Educ. 1978–84; Founder and Sec. Corporate Fund, John F. Kennedy Centre for the Performing Arts 1977–; Dir. Kennedy Cen. Productions Inc. 1974–; presidential appointee to Fine Arts Comm. 1981–85; White House appointee to Exec. Cttee. Young Astronauts Co. 1984–88; Advisory Cttee., Medill School of Journalism, Northwestern Univ. 1985–; Graduate School of Business, Emory Univ., 1986–; trustee Ray Simon Inst. of Public Relations, Syracuse Univ. 1985–; mem. Public Relations Soc. of America, Int. Public Relations Asscn. of Business Communicators, Overseas Press Club, N.Y. Soc. of Security Analysts, Exec. Cttee., Catalyst Inc. 1977–88, Public Relations Advisory Cttee., U.S. Information Agency 1981–; assoc. mem. N.Y. Acad. of Medicine; Counsellor Nat. Press Foundation; trustee The Economic Club of N.Y.; Chair. Jt. Council on Econ. Educ., Public Relations Seminar 1983; Hon. D. Hum. Litt. (Boston Univ.) 1988; Public Relations Professional of the Year Award (Public Relations News) 1977, Gold Anvil Award (Public Relations Soc. of America) 1980, Univ. of Mississippi Alumni Hall of Fame 1980, Silver Em Award (Mississippi Press Asscn.) 1982; Arthur Page Award, Univ. of Texas 1986, Horatio Alger Award 1986, Nat. Public Relations Achievement Award, (Ball State Univ.). *Leisure interests:* stamp collection, West Highland white terriers. *Address:* 260, Beverly Road, Scarsdale, N.Y. 10583 (Home); 230, Park Avenue South, N.Y. 10003, U.S.A. *Telephone:* (212) 614-4444.

BURSTYN, Ellen; American actress; b. 7 Dec. 1932, Detroit, Mich.; d. of John Austin and Coriene Marie (née Hamel) Gilloly; m. 1st William C. Alexander, 2nd Paul Roberts, 3rd Neil Burstyn; one s.; ed. Cass Tech. High School, Detroit, Mich.; co-artistic dir. The Actor's Studio, New York 1982–; Pres. Actors' Equity Assen. 1982–; Best Supporting Actress, The Last Picture Show (New York Film Critics Award, Nat. Soc. of Film Critics Award); Best Actress, Alice Doesn't Live Here Anymore (Acad. Award, British Acad. Award); Best Actress, Same Time Next Year (Tony Award, Drama Desk Award, Outer Critics Circle Award); dir. Judgement (off Broadway) 1981, Into Thin Air 1985. *Stage Productions include:* Fair Game 1957, Same Time Next Year 1975, 84 Charing Cross Road. *Film appearances (leading parts) include:* Goodbye Charlie 1964, For Those who Think Young 1965, Tropic of Cancer 1969, Alex in Wonderland 1970, The Last Picture Show 1971, The King of Marvin Gardens 1972, Thursday's Game (TV), 1973, The Exorcist 1973, Harry and Tonto 1974, Alice Doesn't Live Here Anymore 1975, Providence 1976, Dream of Passion 1978, Same Time Next Year 1978, Resurrection, Silence of the North 1980, Alamo Bay 1985, Twice in a Lifetime 1985, Hannah's War 1987. *Address:* The Actor's Studio Inc., 432 West 44th Street, New York, N.Y. 10036, U.S.A.

BURT, Richard, M.A.; American diplomatist; b. 3 Feb. 1947, Sewell, Chile; s. of Wayne Burt and Dorothy Burt; m. Gahl Lee Hodges 1985; ed. Cornell and Tufts Univs., U.S.A.; fmr. research assoc. and Asst. Dir. of Int. Inst. for Strategic Studies, London and Advanced Research Fellow at U.S. Naval War Coll., Rhode Island; fmr. Nat. Security Affairs Corresp. for New York Times; Dir. Bureau of Politico-Mil. Affairs, State Dept. 1981–82; Asst. Sec. of State for European and Canadian Affairs 1982–85; Amb. to Fed. Rep. of Germany 1985–. *Publications:* numerous learned articles on strategic affairs. *Address:* Box 215, American Embassy, Bonn, APO, New York, N.Y. 09080, U.S.A. *Telephone:* 49-228-339-2330.

BURT, Robert Amsterdam, M.A., J.D.; American professor of law; b. 3 Feb. 1939, Philadelphia, Pa.; s. of Samuel Mathew Burt and Esther Amsterdam

Burt; m. Linda Gordon Rose 1964; two d.; ed. Princeton, Oxford and Yale Univs.; Law Clerk, U.S. Court of Appeals, Dist. of Columbia Circuit 1964–65; Asst. Gen. Counsel, Exec. Office of the Pres. of U.S.A. 1965–66; Legis. Asst., U.S. Senate 1966–68; Assoc. Prof. of Law, Chicago Univ. 1968–70; Assoc. Prof. of Law, Michigan Univ. 1970–72, Prof. of Law 1972–73, Prof. of Law and Prof. of Law in Psychiatry 1973–76; Prof. of Law, Yale Univ. 1976–, Southmayd Prof. of Law 1982–; Rockefeller Fellowship in Humanities 1976; mem. Bd. of Dirs., Benhaven School for Autistic Persons 1977–, Chair. 1983–; mem. Inst. of Medicine and N.A.S. 1976. *Publications:* Taking Care of Strangers: The Rule of Law in Doctor-Patient Relations 1979, Two Jewish Justices: Insider and Outsider in American Society 1987. *Leisure interest:* running. *Address:* Yale Law School, 127 Wall Street, New Haven, Conn. 06520 (Office); 66 Dogwood Circle, Woodbridge, Conn. 06525, U.S.A. (Home). *Telephone:* (203) 432-4960 (Office); (203) 393-3881 (Home).

BURTCHAELL, Rev. James Tunstead, S.T.L., S.S.L., PH.D., L.H.D.; American ecclesiastic and professor of theology; b. 31 March 1934, Portland, Ore.; s. of James T. Burtchaell Jr. and Marion M. Murphy; ed. Columbia Prep. School, Portland, Univ. of Notre Dame, Pontificia Università Gregoriana, Rome, Catholic Univ. of America, Ecole Biblique et Archéologique Française de Jérusalem and Univ. of Cambridge; mem. Faculty, Univ. of Notre Dame 1966–, Chair. Dept. of Theology 1968–70, Provost, Trustee 1970–77, Prof. of Theology 1975–; Pres. American Acad. of Religion 1970–71; Visiting Fellow, Princeton Univ. 1980–81; Sr. Fulbright Fellow, Univ. of Cambridge 1985–86; Hon. L.H.D. (St. Mary's Coll.). *Publications include:* Catholic Theories of Biblical Inspiration Since 1810 1969, Philemon's Problem 1973, Bread and Salt 1978, For Better for Worse 1985, There is No More Just War: The Teaching and Trial of Don Lorenzo Milani 1988, The Giving and Taking of Life: Essays Ethical 1989. *Leisure interests:* classical music, travel, contention. *Address:* Department of Theology, University of Notre Dame, Notre Dame, Ind. 46556, U.S.A. *Telephone:* 219-239-7662.

BURTON, Glenn Willard, PH.D.; American research geneticist and plant breeder; b. 5 May 1910, Clatonia, Neb.; s. of Joseph F. Burton and Nellie Rittenburg; m. Helen Jeffryes 1934; four s. one d.; ed. Univ. of Nebraska and Rutgers Univ.; part-time agronomist and graduate study 1932–36; Research Geneticist, U.S. Dept. of Agric.-A.R.S. 1936–; Chair. Agronomy Div., Univ. of Ga. 1950–64; mem. N.A.S.; Hon. D.Sc. (Neb., Rutgers and 45 others); U.S. Dept. of Agric. Distinguished Award 1980; Nat. Medal of Science 1983. *Publications:* 619 papers and book chapters. *Leisure interests:* music, photography, travel, reading. *Address:* P.O. Box 748, Coastal Plain Experimental Station, Tifton, Ga. 31794 (Office); 421 West 10th Street, Tifton, Ga. 31794, U.S.A. (Home). *Telephone:* (912) 382-2469 (Home).

BURTON, Ian, M.A., PH.D., F.R.S.C.; Canadian-British geographer, environmental scientist and consultant; b. 24 June 1935, Derby, England; s. of Frank Burton and Elsie Victoria Barnes; m. 1st Lydia Demodoff 1962 (divorced 1977); one s. one d.; m. 2nd Anne V. T. Whyte 1977; one adopted s. two d. (one adopted); ed. Derby School, Univ. of Birmingham and Oberlin Coll., Ohio; Lecturer Univ. of Ind. 1960–61; Queen's Univ., Kingston, Ont. 1961; Consultant Ford Foundation, India 1964–66; Prof. Univ. of Toronto 1968–, Dir. Inst. for Environmental Studies 1979–84; Prof. of Environmental Science Univ. of E. Anglia 1972–73; Sr. Adviser Int. Devt. Research Centre, Ottawa 1972–75; Sr. Connaught Fellow, École des Hautes Études en Sciences Sociales, Paris 1984–86; Dir. Int. Fed. of Insts. for Advanced Study 1986–, January Corpn.; numerous cttee. and consultant assignments with UNESCO, WHO, UN Environment Programme, Ford Foundation, projects in Sudan and Nigeria etc.; Order of Zvonkova (U.S.S.R.). *Publications:* co-wrote: The Human Ecology of Coastal Flood Hazard in Megalopolis 1968, The Hazardousness of a Place: A Regional Ecology of Damaging Events 1971, The Environment as Hazard 1978; co-ed.: Readings in Resource Management and Conservation 1986, Environmental Risk Assessment 1980, Living with Risk 1982, Geography, Resources and Environment 1986. *Leisure interests:* swimming, sailing, hiking, cricket. *Address:* 387 Sackville Street, Toronto, Ont., M5A 3G5; 560 Hillsdale Road, Rockcliffe Park Village, Ottawa, Ont., K1M 0S1, Canada. *Telephone:* 613-744 4786.

BURTON, Kenneth, M.A., PH.D., F.R.S.; British professor of biochemistry; b. 26 June 1926; s. of Arthur Burton and Gladys Burton; m. Hilda Marsden 1955; one s. one d.; ed. High Pavement School, Nottingham, Wath-upon-Dearne Grammar School and King's Coll. Cambridge; Asst. Lecturer in Biochemistry, Univ. of Sheffield 1949, Lecturer 1952; Research Assoc. Univ. of Chicago 1952–54; MRC Unit for Research in Cell Metabolism, Oxford 1954–66; Prof. of Biochem. Univ. of Newcastle-upon-Tyne 1966–88, Dean, Faculty of Science 1983–86, Emer. Prof. 1988–. *Publications:* articles in scientific journals. *Leisure interests:* music, hill-walking. *Address:* 42 Cade Hill Road, Stocksfield, Northumberland, NE43 7PU, England. *Telephone:* 0661-842289.

BURWELL, Robert L., Jr., M.S., PH.D.; American professor of chemistry; b. 6 May 1912, Baltimore, Md.; s. of Robert L. and Anne H. (Lewis) Burwell; m. Elise Frank 1939; two d.; ed. St. John's Coll., Annapolis, Md. and Princeton Univ.; Instr. Trinity Coll., Hartford, Conn. 1936–39; Instructor Northwestern Univ. 1939–45, Asst. Prof. 1946, Assoc. Prof. 1946–52, Prof. 1952–70, Ipatieff Prof. 1970–80, Ipatieff Prof. Emer. 1980–; Humboldt Sr. Scientist Award, Tech. Univ. Munich 1981; Prof. Associé, Univ. Pierre et Marie Curie Paris 1982; Pres. The Catalysis Soc. 1973–77,

Int. Congress on Catalysis 1980–84; mem. American Chem. Soc.; recipient of awards from American Chem. Soc. and Catalysis Soc. *Publications:* articles on heterogeneous catalysis and surface chemistry. *Leisure interests:* tennis and history. *Address:* Department of Chemistry, Northwestern University, Evanston, Ill. 60201 (Office); 2759 Girard Avenue, Evanston, Ill. 60201, U.S.A. (Home). *Telephone:* (312)491-3632 (Office); (312) 475-8315 (Home).

BURY, Józef, M.ECON.; Polish politician; b. 1928, Miechowice; ed. Main School of Planning and Statistics, Warsaw; Sr. counsellor at Ministry of Bldg. 1953–60; Dir. of Dept. in Labour and Wages Cttee. 1961–70; employee Dept. for Planning and Econ. Analyses of Polish United Workers' Party (PZPR) Cen. Cttee. 1971–79; econ. adviser to Chair. of Council of Ministers 1980–81; Under-Sec. of State, Ministry of Labour, Wages and Social Affairs 1981–86, Head of Ministry 1982–83; Diplomatic Service 1986–; mem. PZPR.

BUSBY, Sir Matt(hew), Kt., C.B.E.; British football manager (retd.); b. 26 May 1909, Bellshill, Scotland; s. of Alexander and Helen Busby; m. 1931; one s. one d.; ed. St. Brides, Bothwell and Park Street, Motherwell; played football with Denny Hibs (Scottish Junior Club); joined Manchester City 1926; transferred to Liverpool 1936; army physical training instructor 1939–45; Man. Manchester United Football Club 1945–71, Dir. 1971–82, Pres. 1980–; Kt. Commdr. Order of St. Gregory the Great; Freeman, City of Manchester. *Publication:* My story 1957. *Leisure interests:* football, golf. *Address:* 10 Cedar Court, Wilbraham Road, Manchester, England.

BUSCH, August A., Jr.; American brewing executive; b. 28 March 1899; m. 1st Gertrude Buholzer 1952, 2nd Margaret M. Snyder 1981; ed. Smith Acad.; Gen. Supt. Anheuser-Busch Inc. 1924–26, Sixth Vice-Pres. and Gen. Man. 1926–31, Second Vice-Pres. and Gen. Man. 1931–34, First Vice-Pres. and Gen. Man. 1934–41, Pres. 1946–72, Chair. 1956–77, C.E.O. 1971–75, Hon. Chair. 1977–; Pres. Chair., C.E.O. St. Louis Cardinals 1953–; official of numerous other cos. *Address:* Anheuser-Busch Inc., 1 Busch Place, St. Louis, Mo. 63118, U.S.A.

BUSCH, Rolf T.; Norwegian diplomatist; b. 15 Nov. 1920, Spydeberg; s. of Aksel Busch and Alette (née Tunby); m. Solveig Helle 1950; one s.; ed. Oslo Univ. and Nat. Defence Coll.; Deputy Judge 1946–47; entered Norwegian Foreign Service 1947; Ministry of Foreign Affairs 1947–50; Sec., Cairo 1950–52; Vice-Consul, New York 1952–54; Ministry of Foreign Affairs 1954–56; Nat. Defence Coll. 1956–57; First Sec., Norwegian Del. to NATO, Paris 1957–60; Ministry of Foreign Affairs 1960–65; Counsellor and Deputy Perm. Rep. Norwegian Del. to NATO, Paris and Brussels 1965–70; Dir.-Gen. Ministry of Foreign Affairs 1970; Perm. Rep. to North Atlantic Council 1971–77; Amb. to Fed. Repub. of Germany 1977–82, to U.K. 1982–; Commdr. Norwegian Order of St. Olav, Officer, Order of the Nile, Commdr. with Star, Icelandic Order of the Falcon; Grand Cross, Order of Merit (Fed. Repub. of Germany). *Address:* 25 Belgrave Square, London, S.W.1 (Office); 10 Palace Green, London, W.8, England (Home). *Telephone:* 01-235 7151 (Office); 01-937 6449 (Home).

BUSER, Walter Emil, DR.IUR.; Swiss government official; b. 14 April 1926, Lausen; s. of Emil and Martha Buser; m. Renée Vuille 1947; ed. Humanistic Gymnasium, Basel, Univs. of Basel and Berne; Ed. Sozialdemokratische Bundeshauskorrespondenz 1950–61; Legal Consultant 1962–64; Head, legal and information service, Fed. Dept. of Interior 1965–67; Vice-Chancellor of the Swiss Confed. 1968–81, Chancellor July 1981–; Hon. Dozent (Basel). *Publications:* Das Bundesgesetz über die Ordnung des Arbeitsverhältnisses vom 27.6.19, Die Rolle der Verwaltung und der Interessengruppen im Entscheidungsprozess der Schweiz, Betrachtungen zum schweizerischen Petitionsrecht, Die Organisation der Rechtsetzung, in Hundert Jahre Bundesverfassung 1874–1974, Das Institut der Volksinitiative in rechtlicher und rechtspolitischer Sicht. *Address:* Federal Chancellery, Swiss Confederation, 3003 Berne, Switzerland.

BUSH, Alan, D.MUS. (LOND.); British composer, conductor and pianist; b. 22 Dec. 1900, London; s. of Alfred Walter Bush and Alice Maud Bush (née Brinsley); m. Nancy Rachel Head 1931; three d. (one deceased); ed. Highgate School, Royal Acad. of Music and Humboldt Univ., Berlin; Prof. of Composition, Royal Acad. of Music 1925–78; Fellow 1938–, Lecturer on History of Music 1936–38; served army 1941–45; Chair. Composers' Guild of G.B. 1947–48; Pres. Workers' Music Assen. 1941–; has conducted leading orchestras in Europe and the U.S.S.R. and appeared frequently as pianist and lecturer; Corresp. mem. German Acad. of Arts 1958; Carnegie Award for String Quartet 1924, Arts Council Opera Prize 1951, Handel Prize 1962; D.Mus. h.c. (Dunelm) 1971. *Works include:* Choral: Winter Journey 1946, Ballad of Freedom's Soldier 1953, Alps and Andes of the Living World 1968, Africa Is My Name 1976, Mandela Speaking for Baritone (for Chorus and Orchestra) 1986; Orchestral: Dance Overture 1935, Piano Concerto 1937, First Symphony 1940, English Suite 1946, Violin Concerto 1948, Nottingham Symphony 1949, Concert Suite for 'Cello 1952, Dorian Passacaglia and Fugue 1959, Byron Symphony 1960, Variations, Nocturne and Finale for Piano and Orchestra 1962, Partita Concertante 1964, Scherzo (for Wind Orchestra, with Percussion) 1969, Africa is My Name (for Piano and Orchestra) 1971, Concert-Overture for an Occasion 1971, Liverpool Overture 1973, Song and Dance for Junior String Orchestra 1981, Lascaux Symphony 1983, Song Poem and Dance Poem (for String Orchestra and Pianoforte) 1986; Chamber music: Dialectic (for String Quartet) 1929,

Concert Piece (for Cello and Piano) 1936, Lyric Interlude (for Violin and Piano) 1944, Three Concert Studies (for Piano Trio) 1947, Prelude, Air and Dance (for Violin, String Quartet and Percussion) 1963, Suite (for Two Pianos) 1967, Time Remembered (for Chamber Orchestra) 1969, Serenade (for String Quartet) 1969, Suite of Six (for String Quartet), Sonata for Recorders and Piano 1975, Sonatina (for Viola and Piano) 1978, Rhapsody (for 'Cello and Piano) 1979, Meditation and Scherzo (for Double-Bass and Piano) 1980, Trio (for Clarinet, 'Cello and Piano) 1980, Concertino (for two Violins and Piano) 1981, Summer Fields and Hedgerow (for Clarinet and Piano) 1983, Piano Quintet 1984, Octet (for Flute, Clarinet, Horn, String Quartet and Piano) 1984, Canzona (for Flute, Clarinet, Violin and Piano) 1985, Two Preludes and Fugues (for Violin and Piano), Serenade and Duet (for Violin and Piano); Piano solo: Prelude and Fugue 1927, Relinquishment 1928, Le Quatorze Juillet 1943, Nocturne 1957, Sonata in A Flat 1970, Corentyne Kwe-Kwe 1972, Letter Galliard, 24 Preludes for Piano 1976, Scots Jigganspiel for Piano 1981, Six Short Pieces for Piano 1983, Sonata in G 1986, Two Pieces for Nancy 1986; Operatic: Wat Tyler 1950, Men of Blackmoor 1955, The Sugar Reapers 1963, Joe Hill: The Man Who Never Died 1967; Operas for Schools: The Press Gang 1946, The Spell Unbound 1953, The Ferryman's Daughter 1961; Vocal solo: Song-Cycle Voices of the Prophets (for Tenor and Piano) 1953, Song-Cycle The Freight of Harvest (for Tenor and Piano) 1969, Song Cycle Life's Span (for Mezzo-Soprano and Piano) 1974, Song Cycle Woman's Life 1977, Song Cycle De Plenos Poderes to Poems by Pablo Neruda 1977. *Publication:* Strict Counterpoint in Palestrina Style, In My Eighth Decade and Other Essays. *Leisure interests:* walking through countryside and viewing animal scenes on TV. *Address:* 25 Christchurch Crescent, Radlett, Herts., WD7 8AQ, England. *Telephone:* Radlett 6422.

BUSH, Dorothy Vredenburgh; American politician; b. 8 Dec. 1916, Baldwyn, Miss.; d. of Will Lee McElroy and Lany Holland McElroy; m. 1st Peter Vredenburgh, 1940 (deceased); one step s. (deceased); 2nd John W. Bush 1962; ed. George Washington Univ. and Mississippi State Coll. for Women; Sec. to Dir. of Tenn. Coal, Iron and Rail Road Co. 1937-40; Ala. Ctteewoman for Young Democrats of America 1941-50; Asst. Sec. Young Democrats of America 1941, Vice-Pres. 1943-48, Acting Pres. 1944; Sec. Democratic Nat. Cttee. 1944-; Sec. Democratic Nat. Conventions 1944, 1948, 1952, 1956, 1960, 1964, 1968, 1972, 1976, 1980, 1984; Chair. DNC Alumni Council 1981-; Co-Chair. Nat. Party Advisory Cttee. on Sr. Issues 1983-84; Dir. Coastal Caribbean Oils & Minerals Ltd., Pancoastal Inc.; mem. Nat. Fed. of Business and Professional Women. *Leisure interests:* tatting, fundraising for scholarship at Miss. State Coll. for Women. *Address:* Democratic National Committee, 430 South Capital Street, S.E., Washington, D.C. 20003 (Office); 106 Moorings Park Drive, Apartment 104, Naples, Fla. 33942, U.S.A. (Home).

BUSH, Geoffrey, M.A., D.MUS.; British composer and university teacher; b. 23 March 1920, London; s. of Christopher Bush and Winifred Bush; m. Julie Kathleen McKenna 1950; two s.; ed. Salisbury Cathedral School, Lancing Coll., Balliol Coll., Oxford; Lecturer in Music, Oxford Univ. Extra-Mural Dept. 1947-52; Staff Tutor in Music, London Univ. Extra-Mural Dept. 1952-64, Sr. Staff Tutor 1964-80; Visiting Prof. in Music, King's Coll., London 1969-; Music Adviser John Ireland Trust 1969-; Hon. Fellow Univ. Coll. of Wales, Aberystwyth 1986-; Chair. Composers Guild of G.B. 1957; Performing Right Soc. Mems. Fund 1987-; Royal Philharmonic Prize for Yorick (overture) 1949. *Publications:* Left, Right and Centre (Essays) 1983, Musica Britannica, Vols. 37 (1972), 43 (1979), 49 (1982), 52 (1986). *Compositions:* Christmas Cantata 1947, Yorick (overture) 1949, Summer Serenade 1948, In Praise of Mary 1955. *Operas:* If the Cap Fits 1956, The Equation 1967, Lord Arthur Saville's Crime 1972; also two symphonies, chamber music and choral music. *Leisure interests:* Detective fiction, theatre, tennis, bridge, walking, watching cricket, cooking. *Address:* 43 Corringham Road, London, NW11 7BS, England. *Telephone:* 01-458 3928.

BUSH, George Herbert Walker, B.A. (ECONS); American politician; b. 12 June 1924, Milton, Mass.; s. of the late Prescott Sheldon Bush and of Dorothy Walker; m. Barbara Pierce 1945; four s. one d.; ed. Phillips Acad., Andover, Mass., and Yale Univ.; naval carrier pilot 1942-45 (D.F.C., three Air Medals); co-founder, Dir. Zapata Petroleum Corpn. 1953-59; founder, Pres. Zapata Offshore Co. 1956-64, Chair. 1964-66; mem. House of Reps. for 7th Dist. of Texas 1967-71; Perm. Rep. to UN 1971-72; Chair. Republican Nat. Cttee. 1973-74; Head U.S. Liaison Office, Peking (now Beijing) 1974-75; Dir. C.I.A. 1976-77; Vice-Pres. of U.S.A. Jan. 1981-89, Pres. of U.S.A. Jan. 1989-; numerous hon. degrees. *Publication:* Looking Forward: An autobiography (with Victor Gold) 1988. *Leisure interests:* tennis, jogging, boating, fishing. *Address:* Office of the President, The White House, 1600 Pennsylvania Avenue, Washington, D.C. 20501, U.S.A.

BUSHELL, John Christopher Wyndowe, C.M.G.; British diplomatist (retd.); b. 27 Sept. 1919, Harrow; s. of late Col. and Mrs. C. W. Bushell; m. Theodora Senior; two s. one d.; ed. Winchester Coll. and Cambridge Univ.; R.A.F. 1939-45; entered U.K. Diplomatic Service 1945, served in Moscow, Rome, Baghdad, Ankara, Aden and with NATO, Paris, Brussels; seconded to Cabinet Office 1968; Minister and Deputy Commdt., British Mil. Govt., Berlin 1970; Amb. to Repub. of Viet-Nam 1974-75; sabbatical year, SOAS, London Univ. 1975-76; Amb. to Pakistan 1976-79. *Address:* 19 Bradbourne Street, London S.W.6, England. *Telephone:* 01-736 5716 (Home).

BUSHMIN, Aleksey Sergeyevich; Soviet literary historian; b. 1910, Levaya Roskosh, Voronezh; ed. Inst. for Veterinary Science, Voronezh, and Voronezh Pedagogical Inst.; research worker in literary history 1946-; Dir. Inst. of Russian Literature; mem. U.S.S.R. Acad. of Sciences 1955-. *Publications include:* About Early Russian Prose 1953, A. S. Serafimovich 1954, numerous works on Russian literature and culture. *Address:* Institute of Russian Literature, Academy of Sciences, Nab. Makarova 4, Leningrad, U.S.S.R.

BUSHUK, Walter, PH.D., F.R.S.C., F.C.I.C.; Canadian cereal chemist; b. 2 Jan. 1929, Poland; s. of Anton Bushuk and Helen Mucha; m. Jean Huston 1955; two s.; ed. Univ. of Manitoba and McGill Univ.; research scientist, Grain Research Lab., Canadian Grain Comm. 1953-66; Dir. of Research, Ogilvie Flour Mills Ltd., Montreal 1962-64; Prof. Univ. of Manitoba 1966-78; Head, Dept. of Plant Science, Univ. of Manitoba 1978-80; Assoc. Vice-Pres. (research), Univ. of Manitoba 1980-84; Prof. Dept. of Plant Science, Univ. of Manitoba 1984-86; NSERC Research Prof. Dept. of Food Science 1986-; Osborne Medal, American Asscn. of Cereal Chemists. *Publications:* more than 150 scientific and technical publications on aspects of breadmaking, quality of wheat and related cereals; cereal grain proteins—structure and function. *Address:* Food Science Department, University of Manitoba, Winnipeg, Man., R3T 2N2 (Office); 26 Millikin Road, Winnipeg, Man., R3T 2N2, Canada (Home). *Telephone:* (204) 474-6480 (Office); (204) 261-9842 (Home).

BUSQUIN, Philippe; Belgian politician; b. 6 Jan. 1941; m.; ed. Université Libre de Bruxelles; fmr. Prof. of Biology and Physics; Deputy for Hainaut 1977-78, for Charleroi 1978-; Minister of Nat. Educ. 1980-81, of the Interior and Nat. Educ. Feb.-Dec. 1981, for the Budget and Energy (French region) 1982-85, of the Economy and Employment (French region) Feb.-May 1988, of Social Affairs May 1988-. *Address:* Ministry of Social Affairs, 56 rue de la Loi, 1040 Brussels, Belgium. *Telephone:* (02) 230-01-70.

BUSSE, Felix; German lawyer; b. 30 April 1940, Wernigerode/Harz; s. of Max Busse and Magdalene Eicke; m. Regine Bohn; one s. one d.; ed. Oberschule, Wernigerode and Univs. of Bonn, Kiel and Berlin; legal practice in Bonn 1967-, specialist in admin. law 1988-; Sec. Deutscher Juristentag e.V. 1978-; mem. Bd. German Union of Lawyers 1978-, Vice-Pres. 1988-; Ehrenzeichen der Republik Österreich. *Publications:* Der Umfang des Entschädigungsanspruchs aus Enteignung, Die aussergerichtliche Tätigkeit des Anwalts in Verwaltungssachen. *Leisure interests:* music, climbing, sailing. *Address:* 5300 Bonn 1, Oxfordstrasse 10, Federal Republic of Germany. *Telephone:* (02 28) 65 80 35.

BUSTELO Y GARCÍA DEL REAL, Carlos, LL.B.; Spanish civil servant; b. 21 Oct. 1936, Ribadeo (Lugo); s. of Francisco and Carlota Bustelo y García del Real; m. Teresa Tortella 1961; three c.; ed. Univ. of Madrid and Econ. Devt. Inst.; Country Studies Div., Dept. of Econ. Affairs, OECD 1963; Dir. Balance of Payments Office, Gen. Technical Secr., Ministry of Commerce 1965-66; Alt. Exec. Dir. IMF 1968; Under-Sec. of Commerce 1977; Minister of Industry and Energy 1979-80; Chair. Instituto Nacional de Industria (I.N.I.) April 1981-; adviser, Interim Cttee. for Int. Monetary Reform; fmr. mem. Exec. Bd., Bank of Spain; mem. Bd. ASESA (oil), ENASA (trucks); adviser HISPANOIL; Financial Dir. ENAGAS. *Publications:* articles in specialized magazines and journals. *Address:* Instituto Nacional de Industria, Plaza del Marqués de Salamanca 8, Madrid 6, Spain. *Telephone:* (341) 2752265.

BUSYGIN, Mikhail Ivanovich, CAND. ECON. SC.; Soviet politician; b. 1930; ed. Urals Inst. of Foresty; mem. CPSU 1952-; engineer 1950-56; Sr. engineer Perm Dist. 1956-60; First Sec. Solikamsk City Cttee. 1960-62; Dir. Solikamsk Cellulose and Paper Combine 1962-68; Head of Man. and collegiate mem. U.S.S.R. Ministry of Cellulose and Paper Industry 1968-74; Deputy Minister of Pulp and Paper Industry 1974-80; First Deputy Minister of Timber, Cellulose and Paper, and Wood Processing Industries 1980-82, Minister 1982-; Cand. Mem. CPSU Cen. Cttee. 1986-; Deputy to USSR Supreme Soviet. *Address:* Ministry of Timber, Cellulose and Paper, and Wood Processing Industries, Telegrafny per. 1, Moscow, U.S.S.R. *Telephone:* (095) 208-00-56.

BUTCHER, David John, B.A. (HONS.); New Zealand politician; b. 1948, England; m.; ed. Victoria Univ. of Wellington; fmr. union field officer and research officer for Dept. of Labour, Wages Tribunal and Industrial Comm.; mem. Parl. 1978-; fmr. Parl. Under-Sec. to Ministers of Agric., Lands and Forests; Minister of Energy, Minister of Regional Devt. and Assoc. Minister of Finance 1987-88, of Commerce Sept. 1988-; Labour Party. *Address:* Parliament House, Wellington, New Zealand.

BUTCHER, Willard Carlisle; American banker; b. 25 Oct. 1926, Bronxville, N.Y.; s. of Willard F. and Helen (Calhoun) Butcher; m. 1st Sarah Catherine Payne 1949 (died 1955), two d.; m. 2nd Elizabeth Allen 1956 (died 1978), one s. one d.; m. 3rd Carole Elizabeth McMahon 1979, one s.; served U.S.N.R. 1944-45; with Chase Nat. Bank (now Chase Manhattan Bank) 1947-, Asst. Treas. Grand Cen. Branch 1953-56, Asst. Vice-Pres. 1956-58, Vice-Pres. 1958-61, Sr. Vice-Pres. 1960-69, Exec. Vice-Pres. 1969-72, Vice-Chair. 1972, Pres. 1972-80, C.E.O. Jan. 1980-, Chair. April 1981-; Dir. ASARCO Inc.; Trustee, Brown Univ. *Address:* 1 Chase Manhattan Plaza, New York, N.Y. 10081, U.S.A. (Office).

BUTEMENT, William Alan Stewart, C.B.E., B.SC., D.SC., F.I.E.E., F.INST.P., F.A.I.P., F.I.R.E.E., F.T.S.; Australian scientist; b. 18 Aug. 1904, Masterton, New Zealand; s. of Dr. William Butement; m. Ursula Florence Alberta Parish 1933; two d.; ed. Scots Coll., Sydney, Australia, Univ. Coll. School, Hampstead and Univ. Coll., London; Scientific Officer, War Office 1928–39; Asst. Dir. Scientific Research, Ministry of Supply 1939–47, planned and directed devt. of searchlight radar; First Chief Supt., Research Establishment and Rocket Range, Woomera, Australia 1947–49, developed anti-tank weapon Malkara and anti-submarine weapon Ikara; Chief Scientist, Australian Dept. of Supply in charge Australian Defence Science 1949–66; Dir. Plessey Pacific 1967–81. *Publication:* Precision Radar 1945–46. *Leisure interests:* amateur radio transmission, fishing. *Address:* 5A Barry Street, Kew, Victoria 3101, Australia. *Telephone:* 861-8375.

BUTENANDT, Adolf Friedrich Johann, D.PHIL.; German physiological chemist; b. 24 March 1903, Bremerhaven-Lehe; s. of Otto Butenandt and Wilhelmine Butenandt (née Thomfohrde); m. Erika von Ziegner 1931; two s. five d.; ed. Oberrealschule Bremerhaven, Univs. of Marburg and Göttingen; Scientific Asst. Chemical Inst., Göttingen Univ. 1927–30, Dozent in organic and biological chemistry 1931, leader organic and biological chemistry laboratories 1931–33; Prof. of Chemistry, Dir. Organic Chemistry Inst., Danzig Inst. of Technology 1933–36; Dir. Kaiser Wilhelm Inst. of Biochemistry, Berlin-Dahlem (later at Tübingen) (now Max Planck Inst. of Biochemistry, Munich) 1936–72; Prof. of Physiological Chemistry, Munich Univ. 1956–71; Prof. Emer. 1971–; Pres. Max-Planck Soc. 1960–72, Hon. Pres. 1972–; Foreign mem. Royal Soc. (U.K.) 1968; Nobel Prize for Chem. 1939, Ordre Pour le Mérite (Arts and Sciences) 1962, Österreichisches Ehrenzeichen für Wissenschaft und Kunst 1964, Commdr. Légion d'honneur 1969, Commdr. Ordre des palmes académiques 1972, Adolf-von-Harnack-Medaille, Max-Planck-Soc. 1973 (in gold 1983), Bayerischer Maximiliansorden für Wissenschaft und Kunst 1981, Grosskreuz des Verdienstordens 1985; Foreign mem. Acad. des Sciences, Paris 1974. *Publications:* Biochemie der Wirkstoffe (Sexualhormone, Genchemie, Insektenphysiologie); numerous articles in Hoppe-Seyler's Zeitschrift für Physiologische Chemie, Chemische Berichte, Zeitschrift für Naturforschung, etc. *Address:* Marsopstrasse 5, 8 Munich 60, Federal Republic of Germany (Home). *Telephone:* 089-885490 (Home).

BUTHELEZI, Chief Gatsha, B.A.; South African (Zulu) leader and politician; b. 27 Aug. 1928, Mahlabatini; s. of late Chief Mathole Buthelezi and Princess Magogo; m. Irene Audrey Thandekile Mzila 1952; three s. four d.; ed. Adams Coll., Fort-Hare Univ.; installed as Chief of Buthelezi Tribe 1953; assisted King Cyprian in admin. of Zulu people 1953–68; elected leader of Zululand territorial authority 1970; Chief Minister of KwaZulu 1976–; Leader of S.A. Black Alliance 1978–; Pres. Inkatha; Hon. LL.D. (Zululand and Cape Town); George Meany Human Rights Award 1982; Kt. Commdr. Star of Africa (Liberia), Commdr. Ordre Nat. du Mérite 1981, and numerous other awards. *Address:* Private Bag X01, Ulundi 3838, KwaZulu, South Africa. *Telephone:* Ulundi 1/2/3.

BUTHELEZI, Rt. Rev. Bishop Manas, S.T.M., PH.D.; South African ecclesiastic; b. 10 Feb. 1935, Mahlabathini; s. of Absalom Buthelezi and Keslinah Mkhabase; m. Grace Mhlungu 1963; two s. two d.; ed. St. Francis Coll. and Yale and Drew Univs., U.S.A.; high school teacher 1957; Visiting Prof., Heidelberg Univ., Fed. Repub. of Germany 1972, Wesley Seminary 1975; Bishop, Central Diocese, Evangelical Lutheran Church 1977–; Pres. S.A. Council of Churches; mem. Comm. on Studies, Lutheran World Fed. 1970–77, Comm. on World Mission and Evangelism, WCC 1975–83; mem. Standing Cttee. Faith and Order Comm., Pvt. Sector Council on Urbanization, Int. Comm. on Lutheran/Catholic Dialogue, Iliff School of Theology; several hon. degrees. *Leisure interests:* music and photography. *Address:* P.O. Box 32413, Braamfontein 2017, South Africa.

BUTLER, Basil Richard Ryland, O.B.E., M.A., F.ENG.; British business executive; b. 1 March 1930, Hexham; s. of Hugh Montagu Butler and Annie Isabelle Wiltshire; m. Lilian Joyce Haswell 1954; one s. two d.; ed. St. John's Coll., Cambridge; Operations Man. Sinclair and BP Colombian Inc. 1968–70, Operations Man. BP Alaska Inc. 1970–72, Gen. Man. BP Petroleum Devt. Ltd. 1978–81, Chief Exec. BP Exploration Co. Ltd. 1981–86, Man. Dir. BP Co. PLC 1986–; Gen. Man. of Kuwait Oil Co. Ltd. 1972–75, of Sullom Voe Devt. 1975–78. *Leisure interests:* sailing, music. *Address:* The British Petroleum Company PLC, Britannic House, Moor Lane, London, EC2Y 9BU, England.

BUTLER, Sir Clifford Charles, Kt., PH.D., F.R.S.; British physicist; b. 20 May 1922, Reading, Berks; s. of Charles and Olive Butler; m. Kathleen Betty Collins 1947; two d.; ed. Reading Univ.; Asst. Lecturer in Physics, Manchester Univ. 1945–47, Lecturer 1947–53; Reader in Physics, Imperial Coll., London 1953–57, Prof. 1957–70, Head, Dept. of Physics 1963–70; Dir. Nuffield Foundation 1970–75; Vice-Chancellor, Loughborough Univ. of Tech. 1975–85; Sec.-Gen. Int. Union of Pure and Applied Physics 1963–72, First Vice-Pres. 1972–75, Pres. 1975–78; Chair. Council for the Educ. and Training of Health Visitors 1977–83; Chair. Advisory Cttee. on Supply and Education of Teachers 1980–85; Chair. Educational Counselling and Credit Transfer Information Service (ECCTIS) Steering Cttee. 1982–; Chair. ABRC/NERC Working Group on Geological Surveying 1985–87; Chair. Working Party on Research Selectivity, N. Ireland 1986–87; Vice-Chair. Open Univ. Council 1986–; Hon. D.Sc. (Reading Univ.) 1976; Hon. D.Univ.

(Open Univ.) 1986; Hon. D.Tech. (Loughborough) 1987. *Publications:* scientific papers on cosmic rays and high energy physics. *Address:* Low Woods Farm House, Low Woods Lane, Belton, Loughborough, Leics., LE12 9TR, England. *Telephone:* (0530) 223125.

BUTLER, Colin Gasking, O.B.E., M.A., PH.D., F.I.BIOL., F.R.S.; British entomologist (retd.); b. 26 Oct. 1913; s. of Rev. Walter G. Butler and Phyllis Pearce; m. Jean M. Innes 1937; one s. one d.; ed. Monkton Combe School, Bath and Queens' Coll. Cambridge; Ministry of Agric. and Fisheries Research Scholar, Cambridge 1935–37; Supt. Cambridge Univ. Entomological Field Station 1937–39; Asst. Entomologist, Rothamsted Experimental Station 1939–43, Head of Bee Dept. 1943–72, Head of Entomology Dept. 1972–76; Pres. Royal Entomological Soc. 1971–72, Int. Union for Study of Social Insects 1969–73; Hon. Fellow, British Beekeepers' Asscn.; Royal Entomological Soc.; R.S.A. Silver Medal 1945. *Publications:* The Honeybee: an introduction to her sense, physiology and behaviour 1949, The World of the Honeybee 1954, Bumblebees (with J. B. Free) 1959; scientific papers. *Leisure interests:* nature photography, fishing, sailing. *Address:* Silver Birches, Porthpean, St. Austell, Cornwall, PL26 6AU, England. *Telephone:* St. Austell 72480.

BUTLER, Sir (Frederick Edward) Robin, K.C.B., C.V.O.; British public servant; b. 30 Jan. 1938, Poole, Dorset; s. of Bernard Butler and Nora Butler (née Jones); m. Gillian Lois Galley 1962; one s. two d.; ed. Harrow University Coll., Oxford; with H.M. Treasury 1961–69, Private Sec. to the Financial Sec. 1964–65, Sec. Budget Cttee. 1965–69; seconded to Cabinet Office as mem. Central Policy Review Staff 1971–72; Private Sec. to Prime Minister 1972–74, 1974–75, 1982–85; Head of General Expenditure Policy Group 1977–80; Principal Establishment Officer, H.M. Treasury 1980–82; Second Perm. Sec., Public Services 1985–87; Sec. to Cabinet and Head of Home Civil Service Jan. 1988–; Gov. Harrow School 1975–. *Leisure interests:* competitive games, opera. *Address:* Cabinet Office, 70 Whitehall, London, S.W.1, England.

BUTLER, Frederick Guy, M.A.; South African poet and university professor; b. 1918, Cradock, Cape Province; s. of E. C. Butler and Alice E. (née Stringer) Butler; m. Jean Murray Satchwell 1940; three s. one d.; ed. Rhodes Univ., Grahamstown, and Brasenose Coll., Oxford; war service Egypt, Lebanon, Italy, U.K. 1940–45; Oxford 1945–47; lecturer in English, Univ. of Witwatersrand 1948–50; Prof. of English, Rhodes Univ. 1952–; Hon. D.Litt. (Univ. of Natal) 1970, (Univ. of Witwatersrand) 1984 (South Africa). *Publications:* Stranger to Europe (poems) 1952, 1960, The Dam (play) 1953, The Dove Returns (play) 1956, A Book of South African Verse 1959, South of the Zambesi (poems) 1966, Cape Charade (play) 1968, When Boys were Men 1969, Take Root or Die (play) 1970, The 1820 Settlers (history) 1974, Selected Poems 1975, Karoo Morning (autobiog. 1918–1935) 1977, Songs and Ballads 1978, A New Book of South African Verse in English 1979 (ed. with Chris Mann), Richard Gush of Salem (play) 1982, Bursting World (autobiog. 1936–1945) 1983, The Re-interment on Buffels-Kop (Diary, ed. with N. W. Visser) 1983, A Pilgrimage to Dias Cross (poem) 1987, Out of the African Ark (ed. with David Butler) 1988, The Magic Tree (ed. with Jeff Opland) 1989, Tales of the Old Karoo 1989, Selected Poems 1989, A Rackety Colt (novel) 1989. *Address:* c/o Rhodes University, Grahamstown, South Africa. *Telephone:* 2-2023.

BUTLER, Graham Wesley, Q.S.O., M.SC., FIL. DR., F.R.S.N.Z.; New Zealand scientist and administrator; b. 27 Feb. 1928, Auckland; s. of Joseph H. W. Butler and Olive B. (née Clark) Butler; m. Beris Quiney Boyce 1958; two s. one d.; ed. Auckland Univ. Coll., Univ. of Lund, Sweden; Research Scientist, D.S.I.R., Palmerston North 1949–65, Dir. Plant Chem. Div. 1965–74, Asst. Dir.-Gen. D.S.I.R. responsible for agric. and biological research, Dir.-Gen. 1983–84; Research Officer N.Z. Futures Trust, 1987–; Fellow N.Z. Inst. of Agric., N.Z. Inst. Chem. *Publications:* Chemistry and Biochemistry of Herbabe, Vols. 1, 2 & 3 1974; over 80 articles in scientific journals. *Leisure interests:* golf, gardening, reading. *Address:* New Zealand Futures Trust, P.O. Box 12-008, Wellington N. (Office); 58 Churton Drive, Churton Park, Wellington 4, New Zealand (Home).

BUTLER, Michael; American financier; b. 26 Nov. 1926, Chicago; ed. Univ. of Colorado; Pres. Butler Communications Corpn.; Chair. Natoma Productions Inc., Talisman Co., Michael Butler Associates; fmr. Vice-Pres. Butler Co.; Exec. Vice-Pres. and Dir. Butler Engineering & Construction, Butler Overseas; Dir. Butler Paper Corpn., Int. Sports Core, J. W. Butler Paper Co. of Chicago, Butler Paper Co., Basic Investment Corpn., Intrafi, Overseas Bank Ltd., Drake Oak Brook Hotel, Oak Brook Landscaping Co., Oak Brook Utility, Ondine Inc.; fmrly. Chancellor, Lincoln Acad. of Ill.; Pres. Org. of Econ. Devt., Ill. Sports Council; Commr. Chicago Regional Port District; Special Adviser on India and Middle East Affairs to the late Senator John F. Kennedy; World Producer of Hair, Catonsville 9; Co-Producer of Lenny; mem. Chicago Historical Soc., Nat. Geographic Inst., Oceanographic Inst.; Order of the Sword and Cutlass, Order of Lincoln, Order of Colonial Wars. *Address:* 3500 Midwest Road, Oak Brook, Ill. 60522, U.S.A.

BUTLER, Sir Michael Dacres, G.C.M.G.; British diplomatist (retd.); b. 27 Feb. 1927, Nairobi, Kenya; s. of Thomas D. and Beryl M. (née Lambert) Butler; m. Ann Clyde 1951; two s. two d.; ed. Winchester Coll. and Trinity Coll., Oxford; joined Foreign Office 1950; served U.K. Mission to UN

1952–56, Baghdad 1956–58, Paris 1961–65, U.K. Mission to UN at Geneva 1968–70; sabbatical year at Harvard 1970–71; served at Washington, D.C. 1971–72; Head of European Integration Dept., FCO 1972–74, Under-Sec. for European Community Affairs 1974–76, Deputy Under-Sec, for Econ. Affairs 1976–79; Perm. Rep. to European Community 1979–85; Deputy Chair. Bd. of Trustees, Victoria and Albert Museum 1985–; Dir. The Wellcome Foundation, PLC 1985–; Dir. Hambros PLC 1986; Exec. Dir. Hambros Bank 1986; Chair. Oriental Art Magazine 1987; Chair. European Strategy Bd. I.C.L. 1986–; Adolphe-Bentinck Prize 1987. *Publications:* Chinese Porcelain at the End of the Ming (O.C.S. Transactions, Vol. 48), and at the Beginning of the Qing (O.C.S. Transactions, Vol. 49), Europe—More than a Continent 1987, etc. *Leisure interests:* collecting Chinese porcelain, skiing, tennis. *Address:* 36A Elm Park Road, London, S.W.3, England.

BUTLER, Richard Edmund, A.A.S.A.; Australian international official; b. 25 March 1926, Melbourne; m. Patricia Carmel Kelly 1951; three s. two d.; held various positions in Australian Post Office including Chief Industrial Officer 1955–60, Exec. Officer, Deputy Asst. Dir.-Gen. (Ministerial and External Relations) 1960–68; apptd. in absentia Sec. of Australian Telecommunications Comm. 1975, later Dir. Corporate Planning Directorate; Sec.-Gen. ITU Oct. 1982–; mem. Admin. Cttee. of Co-ordination for UN and Heads of Specialised Agencies; fmr. mem. Australian Del. Int. Telecommunication Satellite Consortium, Plenipotentiary Conf. 1965; mem. Admin. Council and Planning Cttees. 1962–68; Fellow Royal Inst. of Public Admin., Inst. of Electronic and Telecommunication Engineers; mem. CTA, Melbourne, Royal Commonwealth Soc., Royal Overseas League; Hon. mem. Greek Soc. of Air and Space Law 1984; Grand Insignia of Order of Merit for Telecommunications (Spain) 1983, Philipp Reis Medal 1987. *Leisure interests:* golf and reading. *Address:* 222B route d'Hermance, 1246 Corsier, Geneva (Home); International Telecommunications Union, Place des Nations, 1211 Geneva 20, Switzerland (Office).

BUTLER, William Joseph; American lawyer; b. 22 March 1934, Brighton, Mass.; s. of Patrick L. Butler and Delia Conley; m. Jane Hays 1945; one s. one d.; ed. Harvard Univ. and New York Univ. School of Law; mem. New York Bar 1950; Assoc. Hays, St. John, Abramson & Schulman, New York 1949–53; partner Butler, Jablow & Geller, New York 1953–; special counsel American Civil Liberties Union; Lecturer, Practising Law Inst. 1966; Sec., Dir., Cen. Counsel, Walco Nat. Corpn., FAO Schwarz, New York; mem. Comm. on Urban Affairs, American Jewish Congress 1965–70; mem. Bd. of Dirs. New York Civil Liberties Union, Int. League for Rights of Man; mem. Exec. Cttee. League to Abolish Capital Punishment; mem. Standing Cttee. on Human Rights, World Peace Through Law Center, Geneva; Chair. Advisory Cttee. Morgan Inst. for Human Rights; mem. Int. Comm. of Jurists, American Bar Assscn., Council on Foreign Relations, Int. Law Assscn., American Soc. of Int. Law, etc.; int. legal observer, Int. Human Rights Org. at trials in Greece, Burundi, Iran, Nicaragua, S. Korea, Philippines, Uruguay, Israel; Hon. D.Hum.Litt. (Cincinnati) 1988. *Publications:* Human Rights and the Legal System in Iran 1976, The Decline of Democracy in the Philippines 1977, Human Rights in United States and United Kingdom Foreign Policy 1977; contribs. to professional journals. *Address:* 400 Madison Avenue, New York, N.Y. 10017 (Office); 24 E 10th Street, New York, N.Y. 10003, U.S.A.

BUTLER, Robin (see Butler, (Frederick Edward) Robin).

BUTLER-SLOSS, Rt. Hon. Lord Justice, Dame (Ann) Elizabeth (Oldfield), D.B.E., P.C.; British judge; b. 10 Aug. 1933; d. of late Sir Cecil Havers, Q.C., and Enid Snelling, sister of Lord Havers (q.v.); m. Joseph W. A. Butler-Sloss 1958; two s. one d.; ed. Wycombe Abbey School; called to Bar, Inner Temple 1955, Bencher 1979; contested Lambeth, Vauxhall as Conservative Cand. 1959; practising barrister 1955–70; Registrar, Prin. Registry of Probate, later Family Div. 1970–79; Judge, High Court of Justice, Family Div. 1979–87; Lord Justice of Appeal Jan. 1988–; a Vice-Pres. Medico-Legal Soc.; Pres. Honiton Agricultural Show 1985–86. *Publications:* Jt. Ed. Phipson on Evidence (10th ed.), Corpe on Road Haulage (2nd ed.), fmr. ed. Supreme Court Practice 1976, 1976. *Address:* c/o Royal Courts of Justice, Strand, London, W.C.2, England.

BUTLIN, Martin Richard Fletcher, M.A., D.LIT., F.B.A.; British museum curator and art historian; b. 7 June 1929, Birmingham; s. of K.R. Butlin and Helen M. (née Fletcher) Butlin; m. Frances C. Chodzko 1969; ed. Trinity Coll., Cambridge and Courtauld Inst. of Art., Univ. of London; Asst. Keeper, Tate Gallery, London 1955–67, Keeper of the Historic British Collection 1967–89; Mitchell Prize (jointly) 1978. *Publications:* works on J. M. W. Turner, William Blake, Samuel Palmer, catalogues, articles, reviews etc. *Leisure interests:* music, travel.

BUTOR, Michel; French lecturer and writer; b. 14 Sept. 1926, Mons-en-Baroeul, Nord; s. of Emile Butor and Anne Brajeux; m. Marie-Josephe Mas 1958; four d.; ed. Univ. of Paris; teacher at Sens (France) 1950, Minieh (Egypt) 1950–51, Manchester (England) 1951–53, Salonica (Greece) 1954–55, Geneva (Switzerland) 1956–57; Visiting Prof. Bryn Mawr and Middlebury, U.S.A. 1960, Buffalo, U.S.A. 1962, Evanston, U.S.A. 1965, Albuquerque, U.S.A. 1969–70, 1973–74, Nice and Geneva 1974–75; Assoc. Prof. Vincennes 1969, Nice 1970–73; Prof. of Modern French, Geneva 1975–; Reader Éditions Gallimard 1958–; Chevalier de l'Ordre nationale du Mérite, Ordre

des Arts et des Lettres; Prix Felix Féneon 1957, Prix Renaudot 1957, Grand prix de la critique littéraire 1960. *Publications:* Novels: Passage de Milan 1954, L'emploi du temps 1956, La modification 1957, Degrés 1960, Intervalle 1973; Essays: Le Génie du lieu 1958, Répertoire 1960, Histoire extraordinaire 1961, Mobile 1962, Réseau aérien 1963, Description de San Marco 1963, Les oeuvres d'art imaginaires chez Proust 1964, Répertoire II 1964, Portrait de l'artiste en jeune singe 1967, Répertoire III 1968, Essais sur les essais 1968, Les mots dans la peinture 1969, La rose des vents 1970, Le génie du lieu II 1971, Dialogue avec 33 variations de L. Van Beethoven 1971, Répertoire IV 1974, Matière de rêves 1975, Second sous-sol 1976, Troisième dessous 1977, Boomerang 1978, Quadruple Fond 1981, Répertoire V 1982; Poetry: Illustrations 1964, 6,801.000 litres d'eau par second 1965, Illustrations II 1969, Travaux d'approche 1972, Illustrations III 1973, Illustrations IV 1976, Envois 1980, Brassée d'Avril 1982, Exprès 1983, Herbier Lunaire 1984, Mille et un plis 1985. *Leisure interest:* teaching. *Address:* Aux Antipodes, Chemin de Terra Amata, 23 boulevard Carnot, 06300 Nice, France. *Telephone:* (93) 897118.

BUTT, Michael Acton, M.A.; British business executive; b. 25 May 1942, Thruxton; s. of Leslie Acton Kingsford Butt and Mina Gascoigne Butt; m. 1st Diana Lorraine Brook 1964; two s.; m. 2nd Zoe Benson 1986; ed. Rugby, Magdalen Coll., Oxford and INSEAD, France; joined Bland Welch Group 1964; Dir. Bland Payne Holdings 1970; Chair. Sedgwick Ltd. 1983–87; Deputy Chair. Sedgwick Group PLC 1985–87; Chair. and C.E.O. Eagle Star Holdings PLC 1987–; Chair. and C.E.O. Eagle Star Insurance Co. 1987–; Dir. BAT Industries PLC 1987–. *Leisure interests:* travel, tennis, opera, reading, family, the European movt. *Address:* 4 Maida Avenue, Little Venice, London, W.2., England. *Telephone:* 01-723 9657.

BUTTERFIELD, Alexander P., D.F.C., M.S.; American air service and business executive and fmr. public official; b. 6 April 1926, Pensacola, Fla.; s. of Admiral Horace Butterfield and Susan Armistead Alexander Butterfield; m. Charlotte Mary Maguire 1949; one s. two d.; ed. Univ. of Calif. at Los Angeles, Univ. of Maryland, George Washington Univ. and Nat. War Coll.; served with U.S.A.F. 1948–69; pilot; promoted to rank of Col.; mem. Sky Blazers, U.S.A.F. Europe jet aerobatic team; Operations Officer McGhee-Tyson Base, Knoxville, Tenn.; Commdr. fighter squadron Kadena Base, Okinawa; Commdr. tactical air reconnaissance operations, S.E. Asia; F-111 Project Officer and Sr. U.S. Mil. Rep., Australia; staff positions include Academic Instructor, Air Force Acad., Sr. Aide to C.-in-C. Pacific Air Forces, Policy Planner, Pentagon, Mil. Asst. to Special Asst. to Sec. of Defence; Deputy Asst. to Pres. Nixon and Sec. to Cabinet 1969–73; Administrator Fed. Aviation Admin. 1973–75; lecturer, 1975–76; Exec. Vice-Pres. Int. Air Service Co. Ltd. 1977–79; Pres. Calif. Life Corpn. 1979–80; Chair. GMA Corpn. 1981–82; Pres. and Chair. and C.E.O. Armistead and Alexander, Inc. 1983–; mem. Bd. of Dirs. Aloha Airlines, Los Angeles Co. Museum of Natural History, Pres. Appointee, Bd. of Dirs. Smithsonian Inst.; Legion of Merit and other awards. *Address:* 2040 Avenue of the Stars, Suite 400, Los Angeles, Calif. 90067, U.S.A. (Office).

BUTTERFIELD, Baron (Life Peer) cr. 1988, of Stechford in the County of West Midlands; **(William) John (Hughes) Butterfield,** D.M., M.D., F.R.C.P., F.A.C.P.; British physician; b. 28 March 1920, Birmingham; s. of the late William Hughes Butterfield and of Doris Butterfield (née Pritchard); m. 1st Ann West Sanders 1946 (died 1948); m. 2nd Isabel-Ann Foster Kennedy 1950; three s. one d.; ed. Solihull School, Exeter Coll. Oxford, Johns Hopkins Medical School; Royal Army Medical Corps 1946–48; scientific staff of Medical Research Council 1950–58; Prof. Guy's Hosp. 1958–70; Vice-Chancellor Univ. of Nottingham 1970–75; Regius Prof. of Physic, Cambridge Univ. 1976–87; Master of Downing Coll., Cambridge 1978–87; Vice-Chancellor Cambridge Univ. 1983–85; Chair. East Midlands Econ. Planning Council 1974–75, Medicines Comm. 1976–81; Health Promotion Research Trust 1983–, Jardine Educ. Trust (H.K.) 1982–; mem. Health Educ. Council 1972–78, Inter-univ. Council for Higher Educ. Overseas 1973–, Trent Regional Health Authority 1974–76, Hong Kong Univ. and Polytechnic Grants Cttee. 1975–81, Medical Research Council 1976–80; East Anglian Regional Health Authority 1980–; Dir. Prudential Corpn. 1981–; Trustee, Croucher Foundation, Hong Kong 1980–; Specialist Adviser House of Lords Sub Cttee. Priorities in Medical Research; Hon. Fellow, New York Acad. of Science, Hon. LL.D. (Nottingham), Hon. D.Med.Sci. (Keio), Hon. D.Sc. (Florida Int. Univ.). *Publications:* On Burns 1952, Tolbutamide after Ten Years 1966, Priorities in Medicine 1968, Health Behaviour in an Urban Community 1970, about 100 articles on diabetes, vascular disease, health care delivery, etc. *Leisure interests:* tennis, cricket, conversation, visiting Wellfleet, Mass. *Address:* c/o Downing College, Cambridge, England. *Telephone:* 0223-334800.

BUTTERWORTH, Sir (George) Neville, Kt.; British business executive; b. 27 Dec. 1911, Hastings; s. of Richard Butterworth and Hannah Wright; m. Barbara M. Briggs 1947; two s.; ed. Malvern Coll. and St. John's Coll., Cambridge; joined English Sewing Cotton Co. Ltd. 1933, Joint Man. Dir. 1964, Man. Dir. 1966, Deputy Chair. 1967, Chair. Tootal Ltd. (fmrly. English Calico Ltd.) 1968–74; High Sheriff of County of Greater Manchester 1974, Deputy Lieut. 1974–; fmr. Chair. North West Regional Council, Confed. of British Industry (CBI); fmr. mem. North Regional Bd., Nat. Westminster Bank Ltd., Court of Govs. of Univ. of Manchester, Textile Council, Royal Comm. on the Distribution of Income and Wealth 1974–79;

fmr. mem. Grand Council of CBI; Fellow, B.I.M.; Companion of the Textile Inst. *Address:* Oak Farm, Ollerton, Knutsford, Cheshire, England. *Telephone:* Knutsford 3150 (Home).

BUTTERWORTH, Prof. Ian, C.B.E., F.R.S.; British professor of physics; b. 3 Dec. 1930, Tottington; s. of Harry and Beattie Butterworth; m. Mary Therese Gough, 1964; one d.; ed. Bolton County Grammar School, Univ. of Manchester; Scientific Officer, then Sr. Scientific Officer UKAEA, Harwell A.E.R.E. 1954–58; Lecturer in Physics Imperial Coll., Univ. of London 1958–64, Sr. Lecturer 1965–68, Head High Energy Nuclear Physics Gp., Univ. Prof. of Physics 1971–83, Head of Physics Dept. 1980–83; Visiting Physicist Lawrence Berkeley Lab., Univ. of Calif. 1964–65; Sr. Prin. Scientific Officer Rutherford Lab. 1968–71; Research Dir. C.E.R.N. (on leave of absence from Imperial Coll.) 1983–86; Principal Queen Mary Coll., Univ. of London Aug. 1986–. *Publications:* numerous papers on particle physics in scientific journals. *Leisure interest:* history of art. *Address:* Queen Mary Coll., Mile End Road, London, E1 4NS, England. *Telephone:* 01-980 4811.

BUTTON, John, B.A., LL.B.; Australian politician; b. 30 June 1933, Ballarat, Vic.; m. 1st Marjorie Bowen 1960; two s.; m. 2nd Dorothy O'Neill 1985; ed. Univ. of Melbourne; former sr. partner in Melbourne law firm specializing in industrial law; mem. Senate 1974–; Opposition Spokesman 1976–83; Deputy Leader of Opposition in Senate 1978–80, Leader 1980–83; Leader of Govt. in Senate, Minister for Industry and Commerce and Minister assisting Minister for Communications March 1983–, for Tech. Dec. 1984–; Chair. Cabinet sub-cttee. on industry restructuring, trade competitiveness; Australian Labor Party. *Leisure interests:* skiing, languages, films, literature, theatre and the arts. *Address:* Parliament House, Canberra, A.C.T., Australia.

BUTZ, Earl, PH.D.; American agriculturist; b. 3 July 1909, Noble County, Ind.; s. of Herman Lee Butz and Ada Tillie Lower; m. Mary Emma Powell 1937; two s.; ed. Purdue Univ.; farmer, Noble County 1932–33; Fellow in Agricultural Econs., Purdue Univ. 1933–35; Research Fellow, Fed. Land Bank of Louisville 1935–37; Instructor in Agricultural Econs., Purdue Univ. 1937–38, Asst. Prof. 1938–42, Assoc. Prof. 1942–46, Prof. and Head of Agricultural Econs. 1946–54; Asst. Sec. of Agric., Washington, D.C., and mem. Bd. of Dirs. Commodity Credit Corpn. 1954–57; Dean of Agriculture 1957–67, Dean of Continuing Educ. and Vice-Pres. Purdue Research Foundation, Purdue Univ. 1968–71; U.S. Sec. of Agric. 1971–76; Counsellor to the Pres. for Natural Resources Jan.–May 1973; Chair. U.S. Del. to FAO, Rome 1955–56, 1972–74, to World Food Conf. 1974; mem. American Farm Econs. Assen., Int. Conf. of Agricultural Economists, American Assen. of Univ. Profs., etc.; numerous directorships, awards and hon. degrees. *Publications:* The Production Credit System for Farmers 1944, Price Fixing for Foodstuffs 1952, various pamphlets, research bulletins and articles in journals and magazines. *Leisure interest:* travel. *Address:* 312 Jefferson Drive, West Lafayette, Ind. 47906, U.S.A. *Telephone:* (317) 494-4307 (Office); (317) 743-1097 (Home).

BUXTON, Andrew Robert Fowell; British banker; b. 5 April 1939; m. Jane M. Grant 1965; two d.; ed. Winchester Coll. and Pembroke Coll. Oxford; joined Barclays Bank Ltd. 1963; Dir. Barclays Bank UK Ltd. 1978; Gen. Man. Barclays Bank PLC 1980, Vice-Chair. 1984–; Chair. Barclays Merchant Bank 1986–, Man. Dir. 1988–. *Address:* Barclays Merchant Bank, Ebbgate House, Swan Lane, London, E.C.4, England. *Telephone:* 01-623 4321.

BUYOYA, Maj. Pierre; Burundi politician; b. 1949; ed. Royal Mil. Acad., Brussels; mem. Cen. Cttee. UPRONA party 1982–87; fmr. C.O.O. Ministry of Nat. Defence; led mil. coup against fmr. Pres. Bagaza Sept. 1987; Pres. of Third Repub. and Minister of Nat. Defence Sept. 1987–; Chair. Mil. Cttee. for Nat. Salvation Sept. 1987–. *Address:* Office of the President and Minister of National Defence, Bujumbura, Burundi. *Telephone:* 6063.

BWAKIRA, Melchior; Burundi diplomatist and politician; b. 1937, Kabuye, Bujumbura Prov.; five c.; ed. State Univ., Leningrad; Gen. Dir. Ministry of Foreign Affairs 1969–72; Minister of Communications and Aeronautics 1972–75; Minister of Foreign Affairs and Co-operation 1975–76; Prof. of Letters and Human Sciences, Univ. of Burundi 1976–78; Amb. to Ethiopia 1978–81; Perm. Rep. of Burundi to the UN 1981–87. *Address:* c/o Ministry of Foreign Affairs, Bujumbura, Burundi.

BYAM SHAW, Nicholas Glencairn; British publisher; b. 28 March 1934, London; s. of the late Lieut.-Commdr. David Byam Shaw and of Clarita Pamela Clarke; m. Joan Elliott 1956 (divorced 1973); two s. one d.; ed. Royal Naval Coll., Dartmouth; served R.N., retiring with rank of Lieut. 1951–56; on staff of Collins (printers and publrs.), Sales Man. 1956–64; joined Macmillan Publrs. Ltd. as Sales Man. 1964, Deputy Man. Dir. 1968, Man. Dir. 1970–, Man. Dir. Macmillan Ltd. 1983–; Dir. St. Martins Press, Pan Books Ltd., Book Devt. Council; mem. British Council Publishers' Advisory Cttee., Byam Shaw School Council. *Leisure interests:* travel, gardening, reading, music. *Address:* 9 Kensington Park Gardens, London, W11 3HB, England. *Telephone:* 01-221 4547.

BYATT, Antonia Susan, B.A. (HONS.), F.R.S.L.; British author; b. 24 Aug. 1936; d. of His Honour John F. Drabble, Q.C. and late Kathleen M. Bloor; m. 1st Ian C. R. Byatt 1959 (dissolved 1969), one s. (deceased), one d.; m.

2nd Peter J. Duffy 1969, two d.; ed. Sheffield High School, The Mount School, York, Newnham Coll., Cambridge, Bryn Mawr Coll., Pa., U.S.A. and Somerville Coll., Oxford; Extra-Mural Lecturer, Univ. of London 1962–71; Lecturer in Literature, Cen. School of Art and Design 1965–69; Lecturer in English, Univ. Coll., London 1972–81, Sr. Lecturer 1981–83; Assoc. Newnham Coll., Cambridge 1977–; mem. Bd. of Creative and Performing Arts 1985–; Kingman Cttee. on English Language; Man. Cttee. Soc. of Authors 1984– (Chair. 1986–88); broadcaster, reviewer and judge of literary prizes. *Publications:* Shadow of a Sun 1964, Degrees of Freedom 1965, The Game 1967, Wordsworth and Coleridge in their time 1970, Iris Murdoch 1976, The Virgin in the Garden 1978, Still Life 1985, Sugar and Other Stories 1987. *Address:* 37 Rusholme Road, London, S.W.15, England. *Telephone:* 01-387 7050 (Office); 01-789 3109 (Home).

BYATT, Sir Hugh Campbell, K.C.V.O., C.M.G., M.A.; British diplomatist (retd.); b. 27 Aug. 1927, Edinburgh; s. of late Sir Horace Byatt and Lady Byatt (née Olga Campbell); brother of R.A.C. Byatt (q.v.); m. Fiona M. C. Coats 1954; two s. one d.; ed. Gordonstoun and New Coll., Oxford; Royal Navy 1945–48; Nigerian political service 1952–57; Commonwealth Office 1957; subsequently served in Bombay, Lisbon; seconded Cabinet Office 1965–67; Consul-Gen. Mozambique 1972–73; Inspector H.M. Diplomatic Service 1973–75; Royal Coll. of Defence Studies 1976; Deputy High Commr. in Kenya 1977–78; Amb. to Angola 1978–81 (also accred. to São Tome and Príncipe 1980–81), to Portugal 1981–86; Chair. of Govs., Centre for Information on Language Training and Research; Dir. Dragon Trust PLC, Consultant; Kt. Grand Cross Mil. Order of Christ 1985. *Leisure interests:* sailing, fishing, gardening. *Address:* Leargnahension by Tarbert, Argyll, PA29 6YB, Scotland.

BYATT, Ronald (Robin) Archer Campbell, C.M.G.; British diplomatist; b. 14 Nov. 1930; s. of late Sir Horace Byatt and Lady Byatt (née Olga Campbell); brother of Sir H. C. Byatt (q.v.); m. Ann Brereton Sharpe 1954; one s. one d.; ed. Gordonstoun, New Coll., Oxford; joined Diplomatic Service 1959; Foreign Office 1959, 1963; served in Havana 1961, Kampala 1970; with U.K. Mission to UN, New York 1966, Counsellor and Head of Chancery 1977–79; Head of Rhodesia Dept., Foreign Office 1972–75; Asst. Under-Sec. of State for Africa 1979–80; High Commr. in Zimbabwe 1980–83; Amb. to Morocco 1985–87, in N.Z. (also accred. to Western Samoa) 1987–; Visiting Fellow, Glasgow Univ. 1975–76; Civilian Dir. Royal Coll. of Defence Studies, London 1983–84; Trustee Beit Trust 1987–. *Address:* c/o Foreign and Commonwealth Office, London, S.W.1, England (Office); Drimna-Vullin, Lochgilphead, Argyll, Scotland (Home).

BYCHKOV, Semyon; Soviet-born conductor; b. 1952, Leningrad; ed. Leningrad Conservatory (pupil of Musin); invited to conduct Leningrad Philharmonic Orchestra; left. U.S.S.R. 1975; debut with Concertgebouw, Berlin Philharmonic 1984–85; toured Germany with Berlin Philharmonic 1985; Music dir. of Buffalo Philharmonic Orch. 1986–87, of Orchestre de Paris 1989–90. *Operas include:* La Finta Giardiniera 1984, Ariadne auf Naxos 1985, Rosenkavalier 1987, Aida Lyon Opera 1987. *Address:* c/o Harold Holt Ltd., 31, Sinclair Rd., London, W14 0NS, England.

BYERS, Horace Robert, SC.D.; American meteorologist; b. 12 March 1906, Seattle, Wash.; s. of Charles H. Byers and Harriet E. Byers; m. Frances Clark 1927; one d.; ed. Univ. of California and M.I.T.; Research Meteorologist, U.S. Weather Bureau 1935–40; Assoc. Prof., Univ. of Chicago 1940–45, Prof. 1945–65, Chair. Dept. of Meteorology 1948–60; Distinguished Prof., Tex. A.&M. Univ. 1965–74, Dean, Coll. of Geosciences 1965–68, Vice-Pres. for Academic Affairs 1968–71; Professeur Associé, Univ. of Clermont-Ferrand, France 1975; Prof. Emer. 1975–; mem. N.A.S.; Robert M. Losey Award, Inst. of Aeronautics and Astronautics 1941; Charles F. Brooks Award, American Meteorological Soc. 1960, Cleveland Abbe Award 1972. *Publications:* General Meteorology (4th edn.) 1974, Elements of Cloud Physics 1965 and more than 75 scientific articles and monographs. *Address:* 300 Hot Springs Road, Apartment 178, Santa Barbara, Calif. 93108, U.S.A. *Telephone:* (805) 969-8295.

BYERS, Sir Maurice Hearne, C.B.E., Q.C.; Australian barrister; b. 10 Nov. 1917, Sydney; s. of Arthur Tolhurst and Mabel Florence (née Hearne) Byers; m. Patricia Therese Davis 1949; two s. one d.; ed. St. Aloysius Coll., Milson's Point, Sydney and Sydney Univ.; barrister-at-law 1944–, Q.C. 1960–; Solicitor-Gen. of Australia 1973–83; Vice-Pres. N.S.W. Bar Assen. 1964–65, Pres. 1965–67; Chair. N.S.W. Police Bd. 1984–88; mem. Exec. Council of the Law Council of Australia 1966–68, Australian Law Reform Comm. 1984–86; Leader, Australian del., UN Comm. on Int. Trade Law 1974, 1976–81, Australian del. to Diplomatic Conf. on Sea Carriage of Goods (Hamburg) 1979; Chair. Australian Constitutional Comm. 1986–88; mem. Council of Australian Nat. Univ. 1975–78. *Leisure interests:* reading, talking. *Address:* 6th Floor, Wentworth Chambers, 180 Phillip Street, Sydney, N.S.W. (Office); 14 Morella Road, Clifton Gardens, N.S.W., Australia (Home). *Telephone:* 232 4766 (Office); 969 8257 (Home).

BYKOV, Vasily Vladimirovich (Bykaŭ, Vasil'); Soviet (Byelorussian) writer; b. 1924, Chernovshchina, Vitebsk district; ed. Vitebsk School of Art; writer 1951–; Kolas Literature Prize 1964, Lenin Prize 1974, 1986, Order of the Red Star, Hero of Socialist Labour. *Publications include:* The Cry of the Cranes 1960, Frontline Pages 1960, The Third Rocket

1962, Alpine Ballad 1963, The Dead Feel No Pain 1966, Cursed Height 1968, Kruglyansky Bridge 1969, Sotnikov 1972, Obelisk. Stories 1973, When You Want to Live (play) 1974, The Wolf-Pack 1975. *Address:* U.S.S.R. Union of Writers, Ulitsa Vorovskogo 52, Moscow, U.S.S.R.

BYRD, Harry Flood, Jr.; American newspaperman and politician; b. 20 Dec. 1914; s. of late Harry Flood Byrd; m. Gretchen B. Thomson 1941; two s. one d.; ed. John Marshall High School, Richmond, Virginia Military Inst. and Univ. of Virginia; Ed. writer Winchester Evening Star 1935, Ed. and Publr. 1935–, Ed. and Publr. Harrisonburg Daily News-Record 1937–; also active in firm of H. F. Byrd, Inc., apple growers; mem. Virginia State Senate 1947–65; mem. Democratic State Cen. Cttee. 1940–70; served U.S. N.R. 1941–46; Dir. Associated Press 1950–66; U.S. Senator from Virginia (succeeding his father, Harry Flood Byrd) 1965–83; Independent. *Address:* Rockingham Publishing Co. Inc., 2 North Kent Street, Winchester, Va. 22601, U.S.A.

BYRD, Robert C., J.P.; American politician; b. 20 Nov. 1917, North Wilkesboro, N.C.; s. of Cornelius Sale and Ada Byrd; m. Erma O. James 1936; two d.; ed. George Washington Univ. Law School and Washington Coll. of Law (American Univ.); mem. West Virginia House of Delegates 1946–50, W.Va. Senate 1950–52; mem. U.S. House of Representatives rep. 6th Dist. of W.Va. 1952–58; Senator from West Virginia 1958–; Asst. Democratic Leader in Senate 1971–77, Majority Leader 1977–81, Minority Leader 1981–87, Majority Leader 1987–88; mem. Senate Appropriations, Judiciary and Rules and Admin. Cttees.; Democrat. *Address:* 311 Hart Senate Office Building, Washington, D.C. 20510, U.S.A.

BYSTEDT, (Petrus) Gösta, M.ENG.; Swedish business executive; b. 14 May 1929, Häggdånger; s. of Petrus and Anna Bystedt; m. Kerstin Elmer; one s. two d.; ed. Royal Inst. of Tech., Stockholm and Stockholm School of Econs.; Asst. Royal Inst. of Tech., Inst. for Industrial Org. and Econ. 1953–55, Asst. Lecturer 1955–58; Head of Org. and Methods Dept., AB Electrolux 1958–65, Head of Vacuum Cleaner Div. 1965–68, Deputy Man. Dir. 1968–74, Man. Dir. 1974–81, C.E.O. 1981–85, C.E.O. and Exec. Vice-Chair. 1985–86, Exec. Vice-Chair. 1986–; Pres. Gränges AB 1982–. *Leisure interest:* shooting, golf. *Address:* AB Electrolux, S-105 45, Stockholm, Sweden.

BYZANTINE, Julian Sarkis, A.R.C.M.; British classical guitarist; b. 11 June 1945, London; s. of Carl Byzantine and Mavis Harris; ed. Royal Coll. of Music, London and Accademia Chigiana, Siena, Italy; studied with John Williams at R.C.M., subsequently with Julian Bream and with Andrés Segovia and Alirio Diaz in Siena; taught at R.A.M. 1966–68; has performed in 67 countries and is regular touring artist for British Council; has performed concerts with leading British orchestras including Royal Philharmonic, City of Birmingham Symphony, Scottish Chamber, BBC Symphony; numerous radio and TV appearances; three records for Classics for Pleasure; awarded first A.R.C.M. for guitar 1966; Scholarships to study with Segovia from Vaughan Williams and Gilbert Foyle Trusts. *Publication:* Arrangements of Six Albeniz Piano Works for Guitar 1984. *Leisure interests:* collecting Chinese porcelain, archaeology, tennis. *Address:* Flat 1, 42 Ennismore Gardens, London, SW7 1AQ, England. *Telephone:* 01-584 7486.

C

CAAN, James; American actor and director; b. 26 March 1939, Bronx, New York; s. of Arthur and Sophie Caan; ed. Hofstra Coll.; m. 1st. DeeJay Mathis 1961 (divorced 1966); one d.; m. 2nd. Sheila Ryan 1976; one s.; made theatre début in the off-Broadway production of La Ronde 1960; Broadway début in Blood Sweat and Stanley Poole, 1961. *Films include:* Irma La Douce 1963, Lady in a Cage 1964, The Glory Guys 1965, Countdown 1967, Games 1967, Journey to Shiloh 1968, Submarine XI 1968, Man Without Mercy 1969, The Rain People 1969, Rabbit Run 1970, T. R. Baskin 1971, The Godfather 1972, Slither 1973, Cinderella Liberty 1975, Freebie and the Bean 1975, The Gambler 1975, Funny Lady 1975, Rollerball 1975, The Killer Elite 1975, Harry and Walter Go to New York 1976, Silent Movie 1976, A Bridge Too Far 1977, Another Man, Another Chance 1977, Comes a Horseman 1978, Chapter Two 1980, Thief 1982, Kiss Me Goodbye 1983, Bolero 1983, Gardens of Stone 1988; Dir. Hide in Plain Sight 1980, Violent Streets 1981; starred in television movie, Brian's Song, 1971; numerous TV appearances. *Address:* c/o Martin Licker, 9025 Wilshire Blvd., Suite 313, Beverly Hills, Calif. 90211, U.S.A.

CABALLÉ, Montserrat; Spanish (soprano) opera singer; b. Barcelona; m. Bernabe Marti (tenor) 1964; one s.; ed. Conservatorio del Liceo; studied under Eugenia Kemeny, Conchita Badia and Maestro Annovazi; début as Mimi (La Bohème), State Opera of Basel; N. American début in Manon, Mexico City 1964; U.S. début in Lucrezia Borgia, Carnegie Hall 1965; appeared at Glyndebourne Festival as the Marschallin in Der Rosenkavalier and as the Countess in The Marriage of Figaro 1965; début at Metropolitan Opera as Marguerite (Faust) Dec. 1965; now appears frequently at the Metropolitan Opera and numerous other opera houses throughout the U.S.A.; has performed in most of the leading opera houses of Europe including Gran Teatro del Liceo, Barcelona, La Scala, Milan, Vienna State Opera, Paris and Rome Operas, Bayerische Staatsoper (Munich), etc., and also at Teatro Colón, Buenos Aires; repertoire of over forty roles; recordings of Lucrezia Borgia, La Traviata, Salomé, Aida; Most Excellent and Illustrious Doña and Cross of Isabella the Catholic, numerous hon. degrees, awards and medals, including Commdr. des Arts et des Lettres 1986. *Address:* c/o Carlos Caballé, Via Augusta 59, 08006 Barcelona, Spain.

CABALLERO CALDERÓN, Eduardo; Colombian diplomatist and writer; b. 6 March 1910; ed. Gimnasio Moderna de Bogotá and Univ. Externado de Colombia; Sec, Embassy, Lima 1937–40; business official, Madrid 1946–48; Rep. in Congress, Bogotá 1958–61; Amb. to UNESCO, Paris 1962–66; Ed. El Tiempo 1966; mem. Colombian Acad. 1966–; Corresp. mem. Royal Spanish Acad.; Eugenio Nadal Prize for El Buen Salvaje 1965. *Publications:* Tipacoque (short stories) 1939, Suramérica, Tierra del Hombre (essays) 1941, Brevario del Quijote 1947, Ancha es Castilla 1947, Diario de Tipacoque 1949, Americanos y Europeos 1949, Historia Privada de Los Colombianos 1949, Cartas Colombianas 1951; novels: El Cristo Espaldas 1950, El Arte de Vivir sin soñar 1950, La Penúltima Hora 1953, Siervo sin Tierra 1954, Memorias Infantiles 1964, Manuel Pacho 1965, El Buen Salvaje 1965, Cain 1969. *Address:* Calle 37, No. 19-07, Bogotá, D.E., Colombia.

CABANILLAS DE LLANOS DE LA MATA, Mercedes, D. EN EDUC.; Peruvian politician; ed. Escuela de Admin. de Negocios para Graduados (ESAN); Escuela de Ciencias Políticas de San José de Costa Rica; Inst. Golde Meir, Israel; Lecturer Univ. Nacional Federico Villarreal; fmr. Head Dept. of Acad. grades and titles; Deputy for Dept. of Lima; Pres. Chamber of Deputies Comm. on Educ. and Univs.; Minister of State for Education 1987–; mem. Partido Aprista Peruano (PAP). *Address:* Ministerio de Educación, Lima, Peru.

CABANILLAS GALLAS, Pío; Spanish lawyer and politician; b. 13 Nov. 1923, Pontevedra; m. María Teresa Alonso García; one s.; ed. Univ. of Granada; Prof. of Commercial Law, Univ. of Madrid; founder Revista de Derecho Notarial; Under-Sec. Ministry of Information and Tourism 1962–73; Minister of Information and Tourism 1973–74, of Culture and Social Welfare 1977–79, in Prime Minister's Office 1980–81, of Justice 1981–82; Deputy for Orense; Co-founder Partido Popular 1976; Pres. Tabacalera, S.A.; mem. Real Acad. de Jurisprudencia y Legislación and other Acads.; Grand Cross of Civil Merit, Order of San Raimundo de Peñafort, Order of Carlos III, Order of Alfonso X el Sabio. *Publications:* La Ley de Venta a Plazos, Estatuo de la Publicidad, Modernas Orientaciones del Derecho Inmobilario, El Convenio de Exclusiva, Tópica y Dogmática Jurídica, El Poder en la Sociedad Anónima. *Address:* Alberto Alcocer, 13, Madrid, Spain (Home).

CABANIS, José, L.ÈS.L., D.EN.D.; French writer; b. 24 March 1922; s. of Gaston Cabanis and Françoise de Bellomayre; one s. one d.; ed. Univ. de Toulouse; Grand Prix de Littérature de l'Acad. Française 1976; Chevalier des Arts et des Lettres; Chevalier Légion d'honneur; *works include:* novels: L'age ingrat 1952, Juliette Bonviolle 1954, Les mariages de raison 1958, Le bonheur du jour (Prix des Critiques) 1961, Les cartes du temps (Prix des Libraires) 1962, Les jeux de la nuit 1964, La Bataille de Toulouse (Prix Théophraste Renaudot) 1966, Les jardins de la nuit 1973; Un essai

sur Marcel Jouandeau 1960, Plaisir et lectures 1964 (criticism), Plaisir et lectures II 1968, Des jardins en Espagne 1969, Le sacre de Napoléon 1970, Charles X roi ultra (Prix des Ambassadeurs) 1972, Saint-Simon l'Admirable (Grand Prix de la Critique) 1975, Les profondes années 1976, Michelet, le prêtre et la femme 1978, Petit entracte à la guerre 1981, Lacordaire et quelques autres 1983, Le Musée espagnol de Louis-Philippe Goya 1985. *Address:* 5 rue Darquié, 31000 Toulouse (Office); Nollet, 31130 Balma, France (Home).

CABANNES, Jean, L. EN D.; French lawyer; b. 2 March 1925, Mirande; s. of Serge Cabannes and Lucienne (née Casteran) Cabannes; m. Lucienne Pons 1951; two c.; ed. Lycée d'Auch and Faculté de Droit de Toulouse; trainee lawyer, Toulouse 1945; Deputy Public Prosecutor, Saint Flour 1951; Del. Ministry of Justice 1952; Sec.-Gen. Grande Chancellerie de la Légion d'honneur 1958-69; Sec.-Gen. Ordre nat. du Mérite 1964-69; Attorney-Gen., Paris 1969-76; Adviser to the Supreme Court of Appeal 1976, 1st Attorney-Gen. 1981-; Dir. of Staff for the Minister of Justice 1977-80; Commdr. Légion d'honneur, Ordre nat du Mérite, Croix de guerre 39-45. *Address:* Cour de Cassation, Palais de Justice, 5 quai de l'Horloge, 75001 Paris, France (Office). *Telephone:* (1) 43 29 99 88.

CABOT, Paul Codman, A.B., M.B.A.; American banker; b. 21 Oct. 1898, Brookline, Mass.; s. of Henry B. Cabot and Anne Codman; m. Virginia Converse 1924; five c.; ed. Harvard Univ.; with First Nat. Bank 1923-24; Treas. State Street Investment Corpn. 1924-34, Pres. 1934-58, Chair. of Bd. 1958-; Sr. Partner State Street Research and Management Co. 1924-; Treas. Harvard Univ. 1948-65. *Address:* 653 Chestnut Street, Needham, Mass., U.S.A. (Home).

CABOU, Daniel, L. EN. D.; Senegalese economist and politician; b. 16 June 1929, Mandina; s. of Benoît Cabou and Angélique N'Deye; m. Eleonore Mendy 1959; one s. five d.; ed. Lycée Van Vollenhoven, Dakar, Univ. of Dakar, Lycée Louis le Grand, Paris, Ecole Nat. de la France d'Outre-Mer, Univ. of Paris; responsible for liaisons with the Grand Council of the French African Community in the Cabinet of Xavier Torre, Sec.-Gen. of the French African Community 1954-58; Chef de Cabinet for Pierre Lami, Head of Senegalese Territory 1958; Tech. Councillor for Mamadou Dia; Pres. Council of Ministers 1959; Dir.-Gen. Entente coopérative Sénégalaise (ENCOOP) 1959; Gov. Fleuve region 1960-61; Dir. de Cabinet for André Peytavin, Minister of Finances 1961-62; Sec. of State for Public Works, responsible for Hydraulics, Housing and Urban Devt. Nov.-Dec. 1962; Sec. of State for Finance and Econ. Affairs 1962-63; Minister of Finance 1963-64, of Commerce, Industry and Labour 1964-68, for Secr. of the Presidency 1968-70, of Industrial Devt. 1970-72; Deputy Gov. Central Bank of West African States 1972-75, Sec.-Gen. 1975-85. *Address:* 49 avenue Raymond Poincaré, 75116 Paris, France (Home).

CABOUAT, Jean-Pierre Noël, L. ES L., L. EN D.; French diplomatist; b. 25 Dec. 1921, Paris; s. of Paul Cabouat and Isabelle Steege; m. 1st Claire Chicoteau (divorced), two s. two d.; m. 2nd Huguette Chatard (divorced), one s. one d.; m. 3rd Noëlle Rivero 1983, one s. one d.; ed. Facultés des Lettres et de Droit, Paris; served Genoa 1946-48, Prague 1949-52; First Sec. Perm. Mission of France at European Communities, Brussels 1959, Second Counsellor 1962-63; First Counsellor, Washington, D.C. 1966-70; Dept. Head 1970-75; Amb. to Libya 1975-79; Dir. of personnel and gen. admin., Ministry of Foreign Affairs 1981-83; Amb. to Canada 1984-; Officier, Légion d'honneur, Commdr. Ordre Nat. du Mérite, Croix de Guerre; Médaille de la Résistance. *Address:* French Embassy, 42 Promenade Sussex, Ottawa, Ont., K1M 2C9, Canada; 36 rue Pierre-Nicole, 75005 Paris, France (Home).

CABRAL, Alfredo Lopes, B.SC; Guinea-Bissau diplomatist; b. 1946, Dakar, Senegal; m.; joined Mouvement de Libération Nationale de la Guinée-Bissau 1964; regularly attended meetings of OAU and the Non-Aligned Movt. 1970-; Chef de Cabinet, Guinea-Bissau Foreign Ministry 1973-75, Dir. Afro-Asian Div. 1975-79; First Counsellor, Guinea-Bissau Perm. Mission, New York 1979-83; Amb. to Algeria and M.E. 1983-86; Perm. Rep. to UN 1986-. *Address:* Permanent Mission of Guinea-Bissau to the United Nations, 211 East 43rd Street, Room 604, New York, N.Y. 10017, U.S.A. *Telephone:* 661-3977, 3978, 3979.

CABRAL, Luis de Almeida; Guinea-Bissau politician; b. 1931, Bissau; brother of late Amílcar Cabral; founded Partido Africano da Independencia da Guiné e Cabo Verde (PAIGC) with Amílcar Cabral 1956; mem. Political Bureau and Cen. Cttee., PAIGC 1956-70; fled to Senegal; Sec.-Gen. Nat. Union of Workers of Guinea-Bissau 1961; mem. PAIGC Council of War 1965-80, Perm. Comm. of Exec. Cttee., in charge of Nat. Reconstruction of the liberated areas 1970-72, Asst. Sec.-Gen. 1972-80; Pres. State Council (Head of State) of the self-proclaimed independent state of Guinea-Bissau 1973-74, Pres. of State Council of Guinea-Bissau 1974-80 (deposed in coup); under arrest 1980; released 1 Jan. 1982; went to Cuba.

CACCIA, Baron (Life Peer), cr. 1965, of Abernant; **Harold Anthony Caccia,** G.C.M.G., G.C.V.O.; British diplomatist; b. 21 Dec. 1905, Pachmarhi,

India; s. of late Anthony Caccia, C.B., M.V.O. and Fanny Theodora Birch; m. Anne Catherine Barstow 1932; one s. two d.; ed. Eton, Trinity Coll., and Queen's Coll., Oxford; entered Foreign Service as Third Sec. Foreign Office 1929, Legation, Peking 1932; promoted to Second Sec. 1934; transferred to Foreign Office 1935; Asst. Private Sec. to Sec. of State 1936; Legation, Athens 1939; First Sec. 1940; Foreign Office 1941; seconded for service with Resident Minister North Africa 1943; Vice-Pres. Allied Control Comm., Italy 1943; Political Adviser G.O.C.-in-C. Land Forces, Greece 1944; Minster, local rank, British Embassy, Athens 1945; Asst. Under-Sec. of State, Foreign Office 1946, Deputy Under-Sec. of State 1949; Minister, Vienna 1949, Minister and High Commr. 1950-51, Amb. and High Commr. 1951-54; Deputy Under-Sec., Foreign Office 1954-56; Amb. to the U.S.A. 1956-61; Perm. Under-Sec. Foreign Office 1961-64; Head of Diplomatic Service 1964-65; Provost of Eton 1965-77; Chair. Standard Telephones and Cables Ltd. 1968-79, ITT (U.K.) Ltd. 1979-81; Dir. Nat. Westminster Bank 1965-75, Prudential Assurance Co. 1965-80, Foreign and Colonial Investment Trust 1965-76, Eurotrust 1977-84; Lord Prior, Order of St. John 1969-80; Hon. Fellow, Trinity Coll., Oxford 1963, Queen's Coll., Oxford 1974. *Address:* Abernant, Builth Wells, Powys, LD2 3YR, Wales. *Telephone:* Erwood 233 (Wales).

CÁCERES CONTRERAS, Carlos; Chilean politician; b. 7 Oct. 1940, Valparaíso; m. Inés Consuelo Salarzano; three c.; ed. Colegio de los Sagrados Corazones, Valparaíso, Univ. Católica de Chile, Valparaíso, and Cornell Univ., Ithaca, N.Y.; Lecturer, Dept. of Econs. and Finance, Universidad Católica de Valparaíso School of Business Studies 1964, Head, Firms and Finances Dept. 1973; Visiting Lecturer, Ohio State Univ. 1971; mem. Council of State 1976; mem. Mont Pelerin Soc. 1981; Pres. Banco Central de Chile 1982; mem. and founder, Inst. of Econ. Studies of Paris 1983; Minister of Finance 1983-84, of the Interior Oct. 1988-. *Address:* Palacio de la Moneda, Santiago, Chile.

CACOYANNIS, Michael, Greek film and stage director and actor; b. 11 June 1922, Limassol, Cyprus; s. of the late Sir Panayotis and Lady Cacoyannis; brother of Mrs. Stella Soulioti, q.v.; ed. Greek Gymnasium, and London at Gray's Inn, Central School of Dramatic Art and Old Vic School; called to the Bar 1943; Producer for Overseas Service of BBC 1941-50; screen and stage producer 1950-; Hon. Doctorate (Columbia Coll., Chicago) 1981; Order of the Phoenix (Greece) 1965; Commdr. des Arts et des Lettres 1987. *Stage appearances include:* Wilde's Salomé as Herod 1947, in Camus's Caligula 1949, in Two Dozen Red Roses 1949, etc. *Directed films:* Windfall in Athens 1953, Stella 1955, A Girl in Black 1957, A Matter of Dignity 1958, Our Last Spring 1959, The Wastrel 1960, Electra 1961, Zorba the Greek 1964, The Day the Fish Came Out 1967, The Trojan Women 1971, The Story of Jacob and Joseph 1974, Attila 74 1975, Iphigenia 1977, Sweet Country 1986; also a number of stage productions in Athens, New York, etc., including The Trojan Women, Paris 1965, The Devils, New York 1966, Mourning Becomes Electra, Metropolitan Opera, New York 1967, Romeo and Juliet, Paris 1968, Iphigenia in Aulis, New York 1968, La Bohème, New York 1972, King Oedipus, Dublin 1973, The Bacchae, Comédie Française, Paris 1977, Antony and Cleopatra, Athens 1979, The Bacchae, New York 1980, Zorba (musical), U.S.A. 1983, Sophocles' Electra, Epidaurus Festival 1983, Gluck's Iphigenia in Aulis and Iphigenia in Taulis, Frankfurt State Opera 1987. *Publications:* translations into Greek of Shakespeare: Antony and Cleopatra 1980, Hamlet 1985; into English: The Bacchae 1982. *Address:* 15 Mouson Street, Athens 117-41, Greece. *Telephone:* 922-2054.

CADBURY, Sir (George) Adrian (Hayhurst), Kt., M.A.; British food manufacturer; b. 15 April 1929, Birmingham; s. of the late Laurence J. Cadbury and Joyce Cadbury; m. G. M. Skepper 1956; two s. one d.; ed. Eton and King's Coll., Cambridge; Man. Dir. Cadbury Schweppes PLC 1969-73, Deputy Chair. 1974, Chair. 1975-89; Chair. West Midlands Econ. Planning Council 1967-70, CBI Econ. and Financial Policy Cttee. 1974-80, Food and Drink Industries Council 1981-83, Pro Ned 1984-; Dir. Bank of England 1970-, IBM U.K. Ltd. 1975-89; Pres. Birmingham Chamber of Industry and Commerce 1988-89; Chancellor Univ. of Aston, Birmingham 1979-; mem. Supervisory Bd. DAF B.V. 1988-, Covent Garden Market Authority 1974-; Freeman of the City of Birmingham 1982; Hon. D.Sc. (Aston) 1973, (Cranfield Inst. of Tech.) 1985; Hon. LL.D. (Bristol) 1986. *Address:* Cadbury Schweppes PLC, Bournville, Birmingham, B30 2LU, England. *Telephone:* 021-458 2000.

CADBURY-BROWN, Henry Thomas, O.B.E., T.D., R.A., F.R.I.B.A.; British architect; b. 20 May 1913; s. of Henry William Cadbury Brown and Marion Ethel Sewell; m. Elizabeth Romeyn 1953; ed. Westminster School, Architectural Asscn. School of Architecture; pvt. practice since winning competition for British Railway Branch Offices 1937; taught at Architectural Asscn. School 1946-49; Tutor, Royal Coll. of Art. 1952-61; architect in partnership with John Metcalfe 1962-; Visiting Critic, School of Architecture, Harvard Univ. 1956; Prof. of Architecture, Royal Acad. 1975-; mem. group partnership with Eric Lyons, Cunningham partnership for W. Chelsea redevt. for Royal Borough of Kensington and Chelsea; work includes: pavilions for "The Origins of the People", main concourse and fountain display, Festival of Britain; schools, housing, display and interiors; new civic centre, Gravesend; halls of residence, Birmingham Univ.; new premises for Royal Coll. of Art. (with Sir Hugh Casson (q.v.) and Prof.

Robert Gooden); lecture halls, Univ. of Essex; mem. R.I.B.A. Council 1951-53, British Cttee. of Int. Union of Architects 1951-54, Modern Architectural Research group (MARS); Pres. Architectural Asscn. 1959-60; Hon. Fellow, R.C.A. *Address:* Church Walk, Aldeburgh, Suffolk, England. *Telephone:* Aldeburgh 2591.

CADIEUX, Pierre H., B.A., LL.B., B.C.L.; Canadian lawyer and politician; b. 6 April 1948, Hudson, Quebec; s. of Antonio Cadieux and Thérèse Leduc; ed. Hudson, Collège de Valleyfield, McGill Univ.; Lawyer, mem. Quebec Bar Asscn., Canadian Bar Asscn., Montreal Estate Planning Council, Quebec Asscn. for Fiscal and Estate Planning; M.P. 1984-; Minister of Labour 1986-89, for Indian Affairs and Northern Devt. Jan. 1989-; Progressive Conservative. *Address:* Department of Indian and Northern Affairs., Terrasses de la Chaudière, 10 Wellington Street, Ottawa K1A 0G2, Canada.

CADOGAN, John Ivan George, C.B.E., PH.D., F.R.S., F.R.S.E., C.CHEM., F.R.S.C.; British chemist; b. 1930, Pembrey, Carmarthen; s. of Alfred and Dilys Cadogan; m. Margaret J. Evans 1955; one s. one d.; ed. Grammar School, Swansea, and King's Coll., London; research at King's Coll., London 1951-54; Civil Service Research Fellow 1954-56; Lecturer in Chem., King's Coll., London 1956-63; Purdie Prof. of Chem. and Head of Dept., St. Salvator's Coll., Univ. of St. Andrews 1963-69; Forbes Prof. of Organic Chem., Univ. of Edinburgh 1969-79; Chief Scientist, BP Research Centre 1979-81; Dir. of Research, British Petroleum 1981-, C.E.O. BP Ventures 1988-; Dir. BP Gas Int. Ltd., BP Chemicals Int. Ltd., BP Venezuela Ltd., BP Advisory Materials Int. 1987-; Visiting Prof., Imperial Coll., London 1979-; Professorial Fellow, Univ. Coll. of Swansea 1979-; mem. Council, Royal Inst. 1984-; Past Pres. Royal Soc. of Chemistry 1982-84; mem. numerous scientific cttees. etc.; recipient of several prizes and five hon. degrees. *Publications:* about 220 papers in professional journals. *Leisure interest:* supporting rugby football. *Address:* British Petroleum Company PLC, Britannic House, Moor Lane, London, EC2Y 9BU, England. *Telephone:* 01-920 6457.

CADWALLADER, Sir John, Kt.; Australian business executive (retd.); b. 25 Aug. 1902, Melbourne; s. of Daniel Cadwallader and Florinda Margaretta Cust; m. Helen S. Moxham 1935; two s. one d.; ed. Sydney Church of England Grammar School; Man. Dir. Mungo Scott Pty. Ltd. until incorporation of Allied Mills Ltd. 1919-49; Chair. and Man. Dir. Allied Mills Ltd. 1949-78; Dir. Bank of New South Wales 1945-78, Pres. 1959-78; fmr. Chair. Bushells Investments Ltd.; Dir. Queensland Insurance Co. Ltd. 1946-74. *Leisure interests:* golf, reading, rural interests. *Address:* 27 Marian Street, Killara, N.S.W. 2071, Australia. *Telephone:* 49-1974.

CAGATAY, Mustafa; Cypriot politican; b. 20 April 1937, Limassol; s. of Ali Hasan and Fehime Ali; m. Tuncay Çağatay 1965; two s. one d.; ed. Nicosia Turkish Lycée; started Law Practice in Limassol 1963; elected dep. for Limassol, Turkish Communal Chamber 1970; elected mem. for Kyrenia, Legis. Assembly, Turkish Federated State of Cyprus 1976; Minister of Finance 1976, of Labour, Social Security and Health May-Dec. 1978; Prime Minister 1978-83; mem. Turkish Cypriot Cttee., Turkish and Greek Cypriot Talks on Humanitarian Issues 1974; mem. Nat. Unity Party. *Leisure interests:* reading, swimming, walking. *Address:* 6 D Kolordu Street, Kyrenia (Office); 60 Cumhuriyet Caddesi, Kyrenia, Cyprus (Home).

CAGE, John; American composer, author and artist; b. 5 Sept. 1912, Los Angeles, Calif.; s. of John Milton Cage and Lucretia Harvey; m. Xenia Andreyevna Kashevaroff 1935 (divorced 1945); ed. Pomona Coll.; studied composition, harmony and counterpoint with Richard Buhlig, Adolph Weiss, Arnold Schoenberg and Henry Cowell; Teacher of Composition, New School for Social Research, New York 1955-60; Musical Dir. Merce Cunningham and Dance Co., New York 1944-68; Fellow, Center for Advanced Studies, Wesleyan Univ. 1960-61; Composer in Residence, Univ. of Cincinnati 1967; Visiting Research Prof., School of Music, Univ. of Ill. 1967-69, Artist in Residence, Univ. of Calif. (Davis) 1969; Charles Eliot Norton Prof. of Poetry, Harvard Univ. 1989-90; Dir. concert percussion music sponsored by Museum of Modern Art and League of Composers 1943; mem. Cunningham Dance Foundation; mem. of Bd., Foundation for Contemporary Performance Arts; mem. Nat. Inst. of Arts and Letters 1969-, American Acad. of Arts and Letters 1988-; Guggenheim Fellow 1949; Thorne Music Grant 1968-69; award for extending boundaries of Musical Art, Nat. Acad. of Arts and Letters, Carl Sczuka Prize for Roaratorio, An Irish Circus on Finnegans Wake 1979, Poses Creative Arts Award (Brandeis) 1983, and other awards; commissioned works include The Seasons (Ballet Soc.) 1949, 34'46. 766 for Two Pianists (Donaueschinger Musiktage) 1954, Atlas Eclipticalis (Montreal Festival) 1961, Cheap Imitation (Koussevitzky Music Foundation) 1972, Renga with Apartment House 1776 (National Endowment for the Arts and the Boston Symphony Orchestra) 1976, Thirty Pieces for Five Orchestras (Orchestre de Lorraine and Centre Européen pour la Recherche Musicale de Metz) 1981. *Publications include:* The Life and Works of Virgil Thomson (with Kathleen O'Donnell Hoover) 1958, Silence 1961, A Year from Monday 1967, Notations (with Alison Knowles) 1969, Mushroom Book (with Lois Long and Alexander H. Smith) 1972, Not Wanting to Say Anything about Marcel, M 1973, Empty Words 1978, Writing Through Finnegans Wake 1978, X 1983; *etchings include:* Signals, Changes and Disappearances, On the Surface 1977-81. *Leisure interest:* amateur mycology (founding mem. New York

Mycological Soc.). *Address:* 101 West 18th Street, New York, N.Y. 10011, U.S.A.

CAGIATI, Andrea, LL.B.; Italian diplomatist; b. 11 July 1922, Rome; m. Sigrid von Morgen 1968; one s. one d.; ed. Univ. of Siena; entered Foreign Service 1948; Sec., Paris 1950-51; Prin. Private Sec. to Minister of State for Foreign Affairs 1951-53; Vice-Consul-Gen., New York 1953-55; Prin. Private Sec. to Minister of State for Foreign Affairs, then with Dept. of Political Affairs 1955-57; Counsellor, Athens 1957-60, Mexico 1960-62; Del. Disarmament Cttee., Geneva March-Dec. 1962; mem. Italian del. to UN June 1962; Head NATO Dept. 1962-66; Minister-Counsellor, Madrid 1966-68; Amb. to Colombia 1968-71; Inst. for Diplomatic Studies 1971-72; Diplomatic Adviser to Prime Minister 1972-73; Amb. to Austria 1973-80, to U.K. 1980-86, to the Vatican 1986-; Hon. G.C.V.O. 1980. *Leisure interests:* sculpture, golf. *Address:* c/o Ministry of Foreign Affairs, Piazzale della Farnesina 1, 00100 Rome, Italy.

ÇAĞLAYANGIL, Ihsan Sabri; Turkish politician; b. 1908, Istanbul; s. of Saleri and Belkis Çağlayangil; m. Füruzende Çağlayangil 1933; one s. one d.; ed. School of Law, Istanbul; fmrly. with Ministry of Interior; Gov. of Antalya 1948-53; of Çannakale 1953-54, of Sivas 1954, of Bursa 1954-60; Senator for Bursa 1961; Minister of Labour Feb.-Oct. 1965, of Foreign Affairs 1965-71; Pres. Senate Foreign Affairs Cttee. 1972-79, of the Senate 1979; Minister of Foreign Affairs 1975-77, July-Dec. 1977; Acting Pres. of Turkey April-Sept. 1980; detained June-Sept. 1983, released 1983; Justice Party. *Address:* Şehit Ersan Caddesi 30/15, Çankaya, Ankara, Turkey. *Telephone:* 27-28 56.

CAGLIOTI, Vincenzo; Italian chemist and university professor; b. 26 May 1902; ed. Università di Napoli; Prof. Univ. of Florence 1936; Prof. Univ. of Rome 1938-77; Pres. Consiglio Nazionale delle Ricerche 1965; mem. Accad. Nazionale dei Lincei; Nat. Prize for Chemistry Accad. Nazionale dei Lincei 1957. *Address:* c/o Consiglio Nazionale delle Ricerche, Piazzale Aldo Moro 7, Rome, Italy.

CAHEN, Alfred; Belgian diplomatist; b. 28 Sept. 1929, Ixelles-Lès-Bruxelles; s. of Max Cahen and Rose Hazaert; m. Nicole Debeauvais 1961; one s. one d.; ed. Athénée Robert Catteau, Brussels and Université Libre de Bruxelles; Barrister at the Brussels Bar 1953-56; Attaché at Ministry of Foreign Affairs 1956; Attaché to Belgian Del. to OECD 1959-61; Sec. Embassy, Léopoldville, Congo (now Kinshasa, Zaire) 1962-64; Counsellor to Minister-Sec. of State for European Affairs in Brussels 1964-66; First Sec. to Belgian Del. to UN 1966-68; Asst. Chef de Cabinet to Minister for Foreign Trade 1968-70; Minister-Counsellor, Embassy, Kinshasa 1970-74; Minister-Counsellor, Embassy, Washington, D.C. 1974-77; Chef de Cabinet to Minister for Foreign Affairs 1977-79; Ambassador-Political Dir., Ministry for Foreign Affairs, Foreign Trade and Devt. Co-operation 1979-85; Sec.-Gen. WEU 1985-; Lecturer, Université Libre de Bruxelles 1980-; Chair. Study Centre on Int. Relations Univ. Libre de Bruxelles; Chair. Scientific Cttee. Royal Inst. of Int. Relations, Brussels 1985-; Hon. Prof., Nat. Inst. of Political Studies, Kinshasa; Medal for excellence in Int. Finance, School of Int. and Public Affairs, Columbia Univ., New York. *Publications:* numerous articles on int. relations. *Leisure interest:* reading. *Address:* Western European Union, 9 Grosvenor Place, London, SW1X 7HL, England. *Telephone:* 01-235 5351.

CAHILL, Teresa Mary, L.R.A.M.; British opera and concert singer; b. 30 July 1944, Maidenhead, Berks.; d. of Henry D. Cahill and Florence née Dallimore; m. John A. Kiernander 1971 (divorced 1978); ed. Notre Dame High School, Southwark, Guildhall School of Music and Drama and London Opera Centre; debut at Glyndebourne 1969, Covent Garden 1970, La Scala, Milan 1976, Philadelphia Opera 1981; specializes in works of Mozart and Strauss; has given concerts with all the London orchestras, Boston Symphony Orchestra, Chicago Symphony Orchestra, Berlin and Vienna Festivals, and throughout Europe, U.S.A. and the Far East; Master Classes, Dartington Festival 1984, 1986; recordings include works of Elgar, Strauss, Mahler; Worshipful Company of Musicians Silver Medal 1966, John Christie Award 1970. *Leisure interests:* cinema, theatre, travel, reading, collecting antique furniture, photography. *Address:* 65 Leyland Road, London, SE12 8DW, England.

CAI NINGLIN; Chinese government official; mem. Standing Cttee. CCP Prov. Cttee. Fujian, 1985-; Exec. Vice-Gov. Fujian Prov. People's Govt. 1983-. *Address:* Fujian Provincial People's Government, Fuzhou, People's Republic of China.

CAI QIJIAO; Chinese poet; b. 12 Dec. 1918, Jingjiang Cty., Fujian; s. of Cai Zhongsi and the late Chen Kuanzhi; m. Xu Jingci 1943; three s. one d.; ed. Shanghai Jinan Univ., Yarian Lu Xun Art Coll.; participated in Dec. 9th Movement; studied in Literature Dept., Lu Xun Acad. of Literature and Art, Yan'an; army corresp., Zhangjiakou, after World War II; taught in N. China Univ.; Vice-Chair. Fujian Writers Assen. 1959-. *Publications:* Prayer, Double Rainbows. *Address:* Fujian Writers Association, Fuzhou City, People's Republic of China.

CAI ZAIDU; Chinese government official; Dir. Taiwan Affairs Office, Foreign Ministry 1986-. *Address:* Office of the Director, Taiwan Affairs, Ministry of Foreign Affairs, Beijing, People's Republic of China.

CAIN, Sir (Henry) Edney (Conrad), Kt., O.B.E.; Belizean chartered accountant and diplomatist; b. 2 Dec. 1924, Belize; s. of late Henry E. C. Cain and of Rhoda Stamp; m. Leonie E. Locke 1951; ed. St. George's and St. Michael's Colls. Belize and Balham and Tooting Coll. of Commerce, London; auditor, Audit Dept. Belize 1959; Asst. Accountant-Gen. Belize 1961, Accountant-Gen. 1963; Man. Dir. Monetary Authority of Belize 1976; Gov. Central Bank of Belize 1982; Amb. to U.S.A. 1983; First Sec. Ministry of Finance 1985; High Commr. in U.K. 1987-. *Leisure interests:* music, travel. *Address:* 492 Finchley Road, London, NW11 8DE, England (Residence); 18 Albert Street West, Belize City, Belize (Home). *Telephone:* 01-458 2905 (London).

CAIN, John, LL.B.; Australian politician; b. 26 April 1931; s. of late John Cain; m. Nancye Williams 1955; two s. one d.; ed. Northcote High School, Scotch Coll. and Melbourne Univ.; mem. Council Law Inst. of Vic. 1967-76, Exec. Law Council of Australia 1973-76; Vice-Chair. Vic. Br. Australian Labor Party 1973-75; Pres. Law Inst., Vic. 1972-73, Chair. Council 1971-72; mem. Legis. Ass. for Bundoora, Vic. 1976-; Leader of Opposition 1981-82; Premier of Vic. April 1982-; Attorney-Gen. and Minister for Fed. Affairs 1982; Treas. Law Inst., Vic. 1969-70; part-time mem. Law Reform Comm. of Australia 1975-77; Trustee, Melbourne Cricket Club 1982-. *Leisure interests:* tennis, swimming, jogging. *Address:* 9 Magnolia Road, Ivanhoe, Vic. 3079, Australia.

CAIN, Stanley Adair, PH.D.; American ecologist and professor of botany (retd.); b. 19 June 1902, Jefferson Co., Ind.; s. of Oliver E. and Lillian F. Cain; m. Louise Gilbert Marston 1940; one s.; ed. Butler Univ. and Univ. of Chicago; engaged in research at Butler Univ. 1924-30, Indiana Univ. 1931-33, Cold Spring Harbor Biological Lab. 1935-39; Chief, Science Section, American Army Univ. 1945-46; worked at Cranbrook Inst. of Science 1946-50; Dir. Inst. for Environmental Quality, Prof. of Botany and Prof. of Conservation, Univ. of Mich. 1950-70; UNESCO Expert in Ecology, Tech. Mission to Brazil 1955-56; Asst. Sec. for Fish, Wildlife, Parks and Marine Resources, Dept. of the Interior 1965-68; Prof. of Environmental Studies, Univ. of Calif. 1971-81; mem. World Acad. of Art and Science, Nat. Acad. of Sciences 1970; fmr. mem. Task Force on Natural Resources 1968; Benjamin Franklin Fellow, R.S.A.; Pres. First Nat. Biological Congress, American Inst. of Biological Sciences 1970; Hon. D.Sc. (Montreal, Williams Coll., Butler Univ. and Drury Coll.); Conservation Award, U.S. Dept. of the Interior 1964, Eminent Ecologist, Ecological Soc. of America 1969, Distinguished Service Award, U.S. Dept. of the Interior 1970. *Leisure interests:* plant sketching, travel. *Address:* 109 Oak Knoll Drive, Santa Cruz, Calif. 95060, U.S.A. *Telephone:* 408-438-0677.

CAINE, Marco, M.B., B.S., F.R.C.S., M.S., F.A.C.S.; British-Israeli urological surgeon; b. 23 May 1923, London; s. of Theodore Caine and Bella S. Fedderman; m. Deborah B. Binstock 1945; three s.; ed. St. Paul's School, London and St. Bartholomew's Hosp. Medical School, Univ. of London; Sr. Surgical Registrar, St. Paul's Hosp. London 1950-51; Research Asst. Inst. of Urology, Univ. of London 1951-52; Sr. Surgical Registrar, North Middx. Hosp. London 1953-59; Head, Dept. of Urology, Hadassah Univ. Hosp. Jerusalem 1959-; Prof. of Urology, Hebrew Univ. Jerusalem 1972-. *Publications:* The Pharmacology of the Urinary Tract 1984; book chapters and approximately 100 papers in int. scientific journals. *Leisure interests:* music, electronics. *Address:* 2 Hovevei Zion Street, Talbia, Jerusalem 92226, Israel. *Telephone:* 02-632884.

CAINE, Michael; British actor; b. (as Maurice Joseph Micklewhite) 14 March 1933, London; s. of late Maurice Joseph Micklewhite and of Ellen Frances Marie Micklewhite; m. 1st Patricia Haines 1954 (divorced), one d.; m. 2nd Shakira Khatoon Baksh 1973, one d.; ed. Wilson's Grammar School, Peckham; army service, Berlin and Korea 1951-53; worked at repertory theatres, Horsham and Lowestoft 1953-55; Theatre Workshop, London 1955; mem. IBA 1984-. Acted in: over 100 TV plays 1957-63; play: Next Time I'll Sing to You 1963; films: A Hill in Korea 1956, How to Murder a Rich Uncle 1958, Zulu 1964, The Ipcress File 1965, Alfie 1966, The Wrong Box 1966, Gambit 1966, Funeral in Berlin 1966, Billion Dollar Brain 1967, Woman Times Seven 1967, Deadfall 1967, The Magus 1968, Battle of Britain 1968, Play Dirty 1968, The Italian Job 1969, Too Late the Hero 1970, The Last Valley 1970, Kidnapped 1971, Pulp 1971, Get Carter 1971, Zee and Co. 1972, Sleuth 1973, The Black Windmill, The Marseilles Contract, Peeper, The Wilby Conspiracy 1974, Fat Chance, The Romantic Englishwoman, Harry and Walter Go to New York, The Eagle has Landed, The Man Who Would be King 1975, A Bridge Too Far, The Silver Bears 1976, The Swarm, California Suite 1977, Ashanti 1978, Beyond the Poseidon Adventure 1979, The Island 1979, Dressed to Kill 1979, Escape to Victory 1979, Deathtrap 1981, The Hand 1981, Educating Rita 1982, Jigsaw Man 1982, The Honorary Consul 1982, Blame it on Rio 1983, Water 1984, The Holcroft Covenant 1984, Sweet Liberty 1985, Mona Lisa 1985, The Whistle Blower 1985, Half Moon Street 1986, The Fourth Protocol 1986, Hannah and Her Sisters (Acad. Award for Best Supporting Actor) 1986, Surrender 1987, The Impostor of Baker Street 1988 (now called Without a Clue), Jack the Ripper (TV mini-series) 1988 (Golden Globe Award), Dirty Rotten Scoundrels 1988. *Publications:* Michael Caine's File of Facts 1987, Not Many People Know This is 1988. *Leisure interests:* gardening, reading. *Address:* c/o Dennis Sellinger, International Creative Management, 388-396 Oxford Street, London W1, England.

CAINE, Sir Michael Harris, Kt., B.A.; British business executive; b. 17 June 1927, Welwyn, Herts.; s. of Sir Sydney Caine (q.v.) and Muriel Anne Harris; m. 1st Janice Denise Mercer 1952 (divorced 1987); one s. one d.; m. 2nd Emma Nicholson, M.P. 1987; ed. Bedales, Lincoln Coll., Oxford and George Washington Univ., Washington; joined Booker McConnell PLC 1952, Dir. 1964-, Chief Exec. 1975-85, Chair. May 1979-; Dir. Arbor Acres Farm, Inc. 1980-, Commonwealth Devt. Corpn. 1985-; Chair. Council for Tech. Education and Training for Overseas Countries 1973-75; Chair. Inst. of Race Relations 1971-72; mem. Council, Bedford Coll., London 1966-85, Governing Body, Inst. of Devt. Studies, Univ. of Sussex 1975-; Gov. Nat. Inst. for Econ. and Social Research 1979-; Chair. U.K. Council for Overseas Student Affairs 1980-; Commonwealth Scholarship Comm. in the U.K. 1987-; Chair. of Council Royal African Soc. 1984-; mem. IBA 1984-. *Leisure interests:* reading, walking, gardening. *Address:* c/o Booker PLC, Portland House, Stag Place, London, SW1E 5AY, England.

CAINE, Sir Sydney, K.C.M.G.; British civil servant and university administrator; b. 27 June 1902, London; s. of Harry Edward Caine; m. 1st Muriel Anne Harris (died 1962), 2nd Doris Winifred Folkard 1965 (died 1973), 3rd Elizabeth Crane Bowyer 1975; one s. (Michael Harris Caine, q.v.); ed. Harrow County School and London School of Economics; Asst. Inspector of Taxes 1923-26; Asst. Prin., Colonial Office 1926-35, Prin. 1935-37; Financial Sec., Hong Kong 1937-40; Asst. Sec., Colonial Office 1940-44; Asst. Under-Sec. of State, Colonial Office 1944-47, Deputy Under-Sec. of State 1947-48; Third Sec. H.M. Treasury 1948; Head of U.K. Treasury Del. and British Supply Office, Washington, D.C., 1949-51; Head of Int. Bank Mission to Ceylon 1951-52; Vice-Chancellor Univ. of Malaya 1952-56; Chair. Caribbean Fed. Fiscal Comm. June-Sept. 1955; Dir. L.S.E. 1957-67; Chair. Int. Inst. of Educational Planning (UNESCO) 1963-70; Gov. Reserve Bank of Rhodesia 1965-67; Head, Indonesian Sugar Study 1971-72; participation in other sugar industry studies in British West Indies 1969, Portugal 1973, Thailand 1974, Dominican Repub. 1975, Tanzania 1976, Ethiopia 1977; Chair. Univ. Coll. of Buckingham 1969, mem. of Council Univ. of Buckingham 1983-86; Hon. LL.D. (Univ. of Malaya) 1956; Hon. D.Sc. (Univ. of Buckingham) 1980; Grand Officer Order of Orange-Nassau (Netherlands), Order of Dannebrog (Denmark). *Publications:* The Foundation of the London School of Economics 1963, British Universities: Purpose and Prospects 1969, The Price of Stability . . . ? 1983. *Address:* Buckland House, Tarn Road, Hindhead, Surrey, England. *Telephone:* Hindhead 5557.

CAIRD, Most Rev. Donald Arthur Richard, M.A., B.D.; Irish ecclesiastic; b. 11 July 1925, Dublin; s. of George R. Caird and Emily F. Dreaper; m. Nancy B. Sharpe 1963; one s. two d.; ed. Wesley Coll., Dublin and Trinity Coll., Univ. of Dublin; Curate-Asst. St. Mark's, Dundela, Belfast 1950-53, Asst. Master and Chaplain The Royal School, Portora 1953-57; Lecturer in Philosophy, Univ. of Wales 1957-60; Rector Rathmichael Parish, Co. Dublin 1960-69; Dean of Ossary, Kilkenny 1969-1970; Bishop of Limerick, Ardfert and Aghadoe 1970-76; of Meath and Kildare 1976-1985; Archbishop of Dublin and Bishop of Glendalough 1985-; Hon. D.D. (Trinity Coll., Dublin) 1988; Sr. Exhibitioner, Foundation Scholar and Sr. Moderator, Univ. of Dublin. *Leisure interests:* tennis, walking and swimming. *Address:* The See House, 17 Temple Road, Dublin 6, Ireland. *Telephone:* 01-977849.

CAIRNCROSS, Sir Alexander Kirkland, K.C.M.G., M.A., PH.D., F.B.A.; British economist and civil servant; b. 11 Feb. 1911, Lesmahagow, Scotland; s. of Alexander Kirkland Cairncross and Elizabeth Andrew Wishart; m. Mary Frances Glynn 1943; three s. two d.; ed. Hamilton Acad., Univ. of Glasgow and Trinity Coll., Cambridge; Lecturer, Univ. of Glasgow 1935-39; held various Civil Service posts 1940-46; on staff of The Economist 1946; Econ. Adviser, Bd. of Trade 1946-49; Dir. Econ. Div. OEEC 1950; Prof. of Applied Econs., Univ. of Glasgow 1951-61; Dir. Econ. Devt. Inst., Washington, D.C. 1955-56; Econ. Adviser to British Govt. 1961-64; Head of British Govt. Econ. Service 1964-69; Master, St. Peter's Coll., Oxford 1969-78, Hon. Fellow 1978-; Supernumerary Fellow St. Antony's Coll., Oxford 1978-; Pres. Royal Econ. Soc. 1968-70, Scottish Econ. Soc. 1969-73; mem. Council of Man. Nat. Inst. of Social and Econ. Research, Court of Govs. L.S.E.; mem. of numerous cttees., including Working of the Monetary System 1957-59, Police Pay 1977-79; Adviser to Minister of Transport on Proposals for Channel Tunnel 1979-81; Pres. Section F, B.A.A.S. 1969, Pres. B.A.A.S. 1970-71; Foreign mem. American Acad. of Arts and Sciences; Chancellor Univ. of Glasgow 1972-; Pres. Girls' Public Day School Trust 1972-; Hon. Fellow, L.S.E. 1981; Hon. LL.D. (Mount Allison Univ., Glasgow, Reading, Exeter), Hon. D.Litt. (Heriot Watt), Hon. D.Sc. (Univ. of Wales, Queen's Univ., Belfast), Dr. h.c. (Stirling). *Publications:* Introduction to Economics 1944, Home and Foreign Investment 1870-1913 1953, Monetary Policy in a Mixed Economy 1960, Economic Development and the Atlantic Provinces 1961, Factors in Economic Development 1962, Essays in Economic Management 1971, Control of Longterm International Capital Movements 1973, Inflation Growth and International Finance 1975, Snatches 1980, Sterling in Decline 1983, Years of Recovery 1985, The Price of War 1986, Economics in Disarray (ed.) 1984, A Country to Play With 1986, The Diaries of Robert Hall (ed.) 1989, The Economic Section 1939-61 (with Nita Watts) 1989. *Address:* 14 Staverton Road, Oxford, England. *Telephone:* (0865) 52358.

CAIRNS, David Adam, M.A.; British journalist and musicologist; b. 8 June 1926, Loughton; s. of Sir Hugh and Barbara (née Smith) Cairns; m.

Rosemary Goodwin 1959; three s.; ed. Winchester Coll., Univ. of Oxford, Princeton Univ.; Library Clerk, House of Commons 1951-53; critic, Record News 1954-56; mem. Editorial Staff, Times Educational Supplement 1955-58; music Critic, Spectator 1958-63, Evening Standard 1958-63; Asst. Music Critic, Financial Times 1963-67; Music Critic, New Statesman 1967-70; mem. staff, Philips Records, London 1968-70, Classic Programme Co-ordinator 1970-73; Asst. Music Critic, Sunday Times 1975-84, Music Critic 1984-; Visiting Prof. of Music, Univ. of Calif., Davis 1985; Leverhulme Research Fellow 1972-74; Chevalier, Ordre des Arts et des Lettres 1975. *Publications:* The Memoirs of Hector Berlioz 1969 (editor and translator), Responses: Musical Essays and Reviews 1973, The Magic Flute, Falstaff (co-author, ENO Opera Guides) 1981, 1982. *Leisure interests:* conducting, reading, walking, cinema, theatre, cricket. *Address:* 21 Oakhill Court, Oakhill Road, London, S.W.15, England.

CAIRNS, H. Alan C., M.A., D.PHIL., F.R.S.C.; Canadian professor of political science; b. 2 March 1930, Galt, Ontario; s. of Hugh Cairns and Lily Cairns; m. Patricia Ruth Grady 1958; three d.; ed. Univ. of Toronto and Univ. of Oxford; Instructor Dept. of Political Science Univ. of British Columbia 1960-63, Asst. Prof. 1963-66, Assoc. Prof. 1966-70, Prof. 1971-, Chair. Dept. 1973-80; Visiting Prof. Memorial Univ., Newfoundland 1970-71, of Canadian Studies Univ. of Edinburgh 1977-78, William Lyon Mackenzie King Visiting Prof. Harvard Univ. 1982-83; Dir. of Research (Insts.) Royal Comm. on Econ. Union and Devt. Prospects for Canada 1983-85; Queen's Silver Jubilee Medal 1977; Canada Council 25th Anniversary Molson Prize 1982. *Publications:* Prelude to Imperialism 1965, Constitution, Citizenship and Society (ed. with Cynthia Williams) 1986, The Politics of Gender, Ethnicity and Language in Canada (ed. with Cynthia Williams) 1986 and many articles. *Leisure interests:* golf, theatre, swimming. *Address:* Department of Political Science, University of British Columbia, C472-1866 Main Mall, Vancouver, B.C., V6T 1W5, Canada (Office); 4424 West 2nd Avenue, Vancouver, B.C., V6R 1K5, Canada (Home). *Telephone:* (604) 228-3844 (Office); (604) 228-9319.

CAIRNS, Hugh John Forster, D.M., F.R.S.; British professor of microbiology; b. 21 Nov. 1922; ed. Univ. of Oxford; Registrar, Radcliffe Infirmary, Oxford 1945; Intern, Postgraduate Medical School, London 1946; Pediatric Intern, Royal Victoria Infirmary, Newcastle 1947; Chemical Pathologist, Radcliffe Infirmary 1947-49; Virologist, Hall Inst. Melbourne 1950-51; Virus Research Inst. Entebbe, Uganda 1952-54; Research Fellow, then Reader, Australian Nat. Univ. Canberra 1955-63; Dir. Cold Spring Harbor Lab. of Quantitative Biol. 1963-68, staff mem. 1968-; Hon. Prof. of Biology, State Univ. of N.Y. Stony Brook 1968-73; Head, Imperial Cancer Research Fund Mill Hill Labs. 1973-80; Prof. of Microbiology, Harvard School of Public Health 1980-. *Address:* Department of Microbiology, Harvard School of Public Health, 677 Huntington Avenue, Boston, Mass. 02115, U.S.A. *Telephone:* 617-732-1240.

CAIRNS, James Ford, PH.D.; Australian politician; b. 4 Oct. 1914, Carlton, Victoria; ed. state schools, Univ. of Melbourne; Jr. Clerk, Australian Estates Co. Ltd. 1932-35; with Victoria Police Detective Force 1935-44; Australian Infantry Forces 1944-46; Sr. Lecturer of Econ. History, Univ. of Melbourne 1946-55; mem. House of Reps. for Yarra 1955-69, for Lalor 1969-77; Minister for Overseas Trade 1972-74, of Secondary Industry 1972-73; Deputy Prime Minister 1974-75, Fed. Treas. 1974-75, Minister of Environment and Conservation June-July 1975; mem. Fed. Parl. Labor Party Exec. 1960-62, 1964-75. *Publications:* Australia 1952, Living with Asia 1965, The Eagle and the Lotus 1969, Silence Kills 1970, Tariffs and Planning 1971, The Quiet Revolution 1972, Oil in Troubled Waters 1976, Vietnam: Scorched Earth Reborn 1976, Theory of the Alternative 1976, Growth to Freedom 1979, Survival Now, the Human Transformation 1983. *Leisure interests:* sleeping, reading. *Address:* 21 Wattle Road, Hawthorn, Victoria 3122, Australia.

CAIRNS, Theodore Lesueur, PH.D.; American organic chemist; b. 20 July 1914, Edmonton, Alberta, Canada; s. of Albert W. Cairns and Theodora I. Cairns; m. Margarget Jean McDonald 1940; two s. two d.; ed. Univs. of Alberta and Illinois; Instructor in Organic Chem. Univ. of Rochester 1939-41; Research Chemist, Cen. Research and Devt. Dept., E.I. du Pont de Nemours & Co. 1941-45, Research Supervisor 1945-51, Lab. Dir. 1951-61, Dir. Basic Sciences 1962-66, Dir. of Research 1966-67, Asst. Dir. 1967-71, Dir. 1971-79; mem. N.A.S., American Chem. Soc., American Acad. Arts and Sciences; mem. Ed. Bd. Organic Reactions 1969-; mem. Soc. of Chem. Industry; mem. Gov.'s Council on Science and Tech. 1969; mem. President's Science Advisory Comm. 1970-73; mem. of Pres. Cttee. on Nat. Medal of Science 1974-75; Chair. Office of Chemistry and Chemical Tech., Nat. Research Council 1979-81; Regents Prof. Univ. of Calif., Los Angeles 1965-66; Fuson Lecture, Univ. of Nevada 1968; Marvel Lecture, Univ. of Arizona 1971; Perkin Medal, American Section of Soc. of Chemical Industry 1973, Cresson Medal, Franklin Inst. 1974; Hon. Dr.Iur. (Univ. of Alberta). *Publications:* numerous patents and articles on chemistry. *Leisure interest:* tennis. *Address:* c/o E. I. Du Pont de Nemours, Experimental Station, Wilmington, Del. 19898, U.S.A.

CAKOBAU, Ratu Sir George Kadavulevu, G.C.M.G., G.C.V.O., O.B.E., J.P.; Fijian administrator and politician; b. 6 Nov. 1911, Suva; s. of Ratu Popi Epeli Seniloli Cakobau; m. 1st Adi Veniana Gavoka, one s. two d.; 2nd Adi Seruwaia Lealea Belekiwai, three s. one d.; ed. Levuka Public School,

Queen Victoria School, Fiji, Newington Coll., N.S.W. and Wanganui Technical Coll., N.Z.; Fiji Civil Service 1936-39; Roko and Fijian Magistrate 1940-42, 1946-56; Sub-Insp. of Police 1944-46; mem. Legis. Council and Parl. 1951-72; Econ. Devt. Officer and Roko 1956-62; Native Lands Commr. 1962-67; Asst. Minister for Fijian Affairs and Local Govt. 1969, Minister 1970-72; Minister without Portfolio May-Dec. 1972; Gov.-Gen. of Fiji 1973-83; K.St.J., Royal Victorian Chain 1982; "Vuni Valu" of Fiji. *Leisure interests:* fishing, shooting, rugby, cricket, tennis and athletics. *Address:* Bau Island, Tailevu, Fiji.

CALAN (Comte de la Lande de), Pierre; French business executive; b. 18 July 1911, Paris; s. of Comte Jean de la Lande de Calan and Elisabeth Barbier de la Serre; m. Madeleine de Frondeville 1936; three s. three d.; ed. Ecole Libre des Sciences Politiques; Insp. of Finance 1936-50; Vice-Pres. Syndicat de L'Industrie Cotonnière 1950-64; Pres. Banque Cotonnière (Bancotex) 1960-68, Société Française des Constructions Babcock et Wilcox 1965-70, Babcock Atlantique 1968-73, Cie. Industrielle et Financière Babcock Fives 1970-73, Barclays Bank S.A. 1976-82; Vice-Pres. Conseil Nat. du Patronat Français 1972-75; Pres. European Business School 1976-, Univ. Libre des Sciences de l'Homme; Dir. of numerous cos. etc.; mem. Inst. de France (Acad. des Sciences Morales et Politiques); Prix Paul Flat (Acad. Française), Grand Prix André Arnoux, Prix Renaissance de l'Economie; Croix de Guerre; Officier, Légion d'honneur. *Publications:* Les cousins vraisemblables (stories) 1949, Les écrivains (play) 1959, Les jours qui viennent (essay) 1974, Côme ou le désir de Dieu (novel) 1977, Renaissance des libertés économiques et sociales 1963, Interdit aux économistes 1972, Chère inflation 1975, Le patronat piégé 1977, Inacceptable chômage 1985. *Leisure interests:* theatre, literature, gardening. *Address:* 25 rue du Faubourg Saint Honoré, 75008 Paris, France. *Telephone:* 42 65 00 09.

CALAZANS DE MAGALHÃES, Camillo, B.ECON.; Brazilian banker; b. 22 Jan. 1928, Aracaju; s. of Estevão Coelho de Magalhães and Heitorina Calazans de Magalhães; m. Evany Pereira Reis; four c.; ed. Faculdade de Economia do Rio de Janeiro, Ohio State Univ. and Inst. Interamericano Ciências Agrícolas, Mexico; Tech. Consultant, Banco do Brasil S.A. 1967-69, mem. Bd. of Dirs. 1969-74, Chair. and Pres. 1985-88; Pres. Brazilian Coffee Inst. 1974-79; Chair. and Pres. Banco do Nordeste do Brasil S.A. 1979-85; fmr. adviser to Ministries of Agric. and Finance; mem. numerous delegations and special missions representing Banco do Brasil or Govt.; Pres. or Dir. of several financial insts. etc.; Comendador, Ordem do Rio Branco and decorations from Italy and Colombia. *Leisure interests:* reading, soccer. *Address:* Banco do Brasil S.A., Edifício Sede III-19° andar, Setor Bancário Sul-Lote 32, 70073 Brasilia (DF), Brazil. *Telephone:* (061) 224-3496, 223-7466.

CALCUTT, David Charles, Q.C., M.A., LL.B., MUS.B.; British barrister; b. 2 Nov. 1930; s. of Henry Calcutt; m. Barbara Walker 1969; ed. Christ Church Oxford (chorister), Cranleigh School (music scholar), King's Coll. Cambridge (choral scholar, Stewart of Rannoch Scholar 1952); called to Bar, Middle Temple 1955 (Bencher 1981); Harmsworth Law Scholar 1956; on staff of The Times 1957-66; Deputy Chair. Somerset Quarter Sessions 1970-71; a Recorder 1972-; Fellow Commoner, Magdalene Coll. Cambridge 1980-85; Master 1986-; a Judge of the Courts of Appeal of Jersey and Guernsey 1978-; Chair. Civil Service Arbitration Tribunal 1979-; Deputy Pres., Lloyd's of London Appeal Tribunal 1983-; Chair. Inst. of Actuaries' Appeal Bd. 1985-, Falkland Islands Comm. of Inquiry 1984, Cyprus Servicemen Inquiry 1985-86; Chair. City Takeover's Panel, April 1989-; mem. Criminal Injuries Compensation Bd. 1977-, Council on Tribunals 1980-86, Colliery Independent Review Body 1985-; mem. Gen. Council of the Bar 1968-72, Crown Court Rules Cttee. 1971-77, Senate of the Inns of Court and the Bar 1979-85, Chair. of the Senate 1984-85, Chair. of the Bar 1984-85; mem. U.K. Del., Consultative Cttee., Bars and Law Socs., EEC 1979-83; Chancellor of Dioceses of Exeter and Bristol 1971-, and of Gibraltar in Europe 1983-; mem. Council, Royal School of Church Music 1967-, R.C.M. 1980-; Gov. Soc. for Propagation of Christian Knowledge 1980-, British Inst. of Human Rights 1983-; Fellow Int. Acad. of Trial Lawyers, New York; Hon. mem. American Bar Asscn., Canadian Bar Asscn. *Leisure interest:* living on Exmoor. *Address:* Magdalene College, Cambridge; Lamb Building, Temple, London, E.C.4, England.

CALDECOTE, 2nd Viscount, cr. 1939, of Bristol; **Robert Andrew Inskip,** K.B.E., D.S.C., M.A., F.ENG., F.I.E.E.; British chartered engineer and business executive; b. 8 Oct. 1917, London; s. of Thomas Walker Hobart Inskip, 1st Viscount Caldecote, and Lady Augusta, widow of Charles Orr Ewing; m. Jean Hamilla Hamilton 1942; one s. two d.; ed. Eton and King's Coll., Cambridge; R.N.V.R. 1939-45; Royal Naval Coll., Greenwich 1946-47; Asst. Man. Vickers-Armstrong Naval Yard, Walker-on-Tyne 1947-48; Fellow, King's Coll., Cambridge, and Lecturer, Engineering Dept., Cambridge Univ. 1948-55; Man. Dir. English Electric Aviation 1960-63; Deputy Man. Dir. British Aircraft Corpn. 1961-67; Dir. English Electric Co. 1953-69, D. Napier and Son Ltd. 1959-69, British Aircraft Corpn. (Holdings) 1960-69, Marconi Int. Marine Co. Ltd. 1960-71, Delta Group PLC 1969-82 (Chair. 1972-82); Dir. Consolidated Gold Fields Ltd. 1969-79, Cincinnati Milacron Ltd. 1969-75, Lloyds Bank Ltd. 1975-88, Lloyds Bank Int. Ltd. 1979-85; Chair. Legal and Gen. Group Ltd. 1977-80, Investors in Industry Group PLC 1980-87; Vice-Pres. Eng. Employers' Fed. 1980-83; Dir. Equity

Capital for Industry 1980-86; mem. U.K. del to UN 1952; Bd. British Rail 1979-85; Chair. The Design Council 1972-80; Pres. Soc. of British Aerospace Companies 1965-66, Parl. and Scientific Cttee. 1966-69, Assen. Int. des Constructeurs de Matériel Aérospatial (AICMA) 1966-68, Australian-British Trade Assen. 1973-78, Fellowship of Eng. 1981-86; Chair. Econ. Devt. Cttee. for the Movement of Exports 1965-72; mem. Review Bd. for Govt. Contracts 1969-76, Inflation Accounting Cttee. 1975-76, Eng. Industries Council 1975-82, British North American Cttee. 1980-88, Advisory Council for Applied Research and Devt. 1981-84, Eng. Council 1982-85; Chair. Export Council for Europe 1970-71; Chair. Gen. Advisory Council, BBC Nov. 1982-85, Mary Rose Trust 1983-; Pres. Dean Close School; Pro-Chancellor Cranfield Inst. of Tech. 1976-84; W. S. Atkins Ltd 1985-; Hon. F.I.Mech.E., Hon. F.I.C.E.; Hon. D.Sc. (Cranfield Inst. of Tech.), Hon. D.Sc. (Aston), Hon. D.Sc. (Bristol), Hon. D.Sc. (City), Hon. LL.D. (London), (Cambridge). *Leisure interests:* sailing, shooting, golf. *Address:* Orchard Cottage, South Harting, Petersfield, Hants., GU31 5NR, England (Home). *Telephone:* Harting 529 (Home).

CALDER, John Mackenzie; British publisher, critic and playwright; b. 25 Jan. 1927; m. 1st Mary A. Simmonds 1949, 2nd Bettina Jonic 1960 (dissolved 1975); two d.; ed. Gilling Castle, Yorks., Bishops Coll. School, Canada, McGill Univ., Montreal, Sir George Williams Coll. and Univ. of Zürich, Switzerland; f. and Man. Dir. John Calder (Publishers) Ltd. 1950-, Calder and Boyars Ltd. 1950-; expanded to Edinburgh 1971; organized literature confs., Edinburgh Festival 1962, 1963, Harrogate Festival 1969; f. Ledlanet Nights (music and opera festival) Kinross-shire 1963-74; Pres. Riverrun Press Inc., New York 1978-; acquired book-selling business of Better Books, London 1969; Chair. North American Book Clubs 1982-, Fed. of Scottish Theatres 1972-74; co-founder, Defense of Literature and the Arts Soc.; dir. of other cos. assoc. with opera, publishing etc.; Chevalier des Arts et des Lettres, Chevalier Ordre nat. du Mérite. *Publications:* A Samuel Beckett Reader, The Burroughs Reader 1981, New Beckett Reader 1983, Henry Miller Reader 1985, Nouveau Roman Reader 1986, The Defence of Literature 1989. *Leisure interests:* writing, reading, chess, conversation, travelling, promoting good causes, good food and wine. *Address:* John Calder (Publishers) Ltd., 18 Brewer Street, London, W1R 4AS, England; Riverrun Press Inc., 1170 Broadway, Room 807, New York 10001, U.S.A. *Telephone:* 01-734 3786 (England); (212) 889-6850 (U.S.A.).

CALDERA RODRÍGUEZ, Dr. Rafael; Venezuelan lawyer and politician; b. 24 Jan. 1916, San Felipe, Yaracuy; s. of Dr. Rafael and Rosa Sofia R. Caldera; m. Alicia P. Caldera 1941; three s. three d.; Sec., Cen. Council of Soc. of Venezuelan Catholic Youth 1932-34; founded U.N.E. (Nat. Union of Students) 1936; graduated as lawyer 1939; founded Acción Nacional 1942; mem. Chamber of Deputies 1942; unsuccessful Pres. Candidate for Partido Social-Cristiano (COPEI) 1947; Fellow of Acad. of Political and Social Sciences 1952, 1983; unsuccessful COPEI Pres. Candidate 1958; Pres. of Chamber of Deputies 1959-61; unsuccessful COPEI Pres. Candidate 1963, 1986; Pres. of Dem. Christian Org. of America (ODCA) 1964-69; Pres. of Venezuela 1969-74; Senator-for-life 1974; Pres. of Inter-Parliamentary Council 1980-83; Prof. Emer. of Sociology and Labour Jurisprudence, Univ. Cen. de Venezuela; Fellow of Venezuelan Acad. of Languages; mem. many Venezuelan and Latin American Insts. of Political Science, Spanish Language and Sociology; Dr. h.c. from more than 20 American and European univs. *Publications:* essays on legal matters, sociology and politics. *Address:* Avenida Urdaneta 33-2, Apdo. 2060, Caracas, Venezuela. *Telephone:* 561-3726.

CALDERÓN, Alberto Pedro, PH.D.; American mathematician; b. 14 Sept. 1920, Mendoza, Argentina; s. of Pedro J. Calderón and Haydée Cores; m. Mabel Molinelli Wells 1950; one s. one d.; ed. Montana Inst., Zug, Switzerland, Colegio Nacional, Mendoza, Argentina, Univs. of Buenos Aires and Chicago; Head of Practical Studies, Univ. of Buenos Aires 1947-48; Rockefeller Fellow, Univ. of Chicago 1949-50; Visiting Assoc. Prof., Ohio State Univ. 1950-53; mem. Inst. of Advanced Study, Princeton 1953-55; Assoc. Prof. of Mathematics, M.I.T. 1955-59; fmr. Visiting Prof., Univs. of Buenos Aires, Cornell, Sorbonne, Stanford, Madrid, Bogotá (Colombia) Rome and Collège de France; Prof. of Mathematics, Univ. of Chicago 1959-; Louis Block Prof. of Mathematics, Univ. of Chicago 1968-; Chair. Dept. of Mathematics, Univ. of Chicago 1970-72; Prof. of Mathematics, M.I.T. 1972-75; Univ. Prof., Univ. of Chicago 1975-; Hon. Prof., Univ. of Buenos Aires 1975-; fmr. Assoc. Ed., Transactions of the American Medical Soc., Duke Mathematical Journal, Illinois Journal of Mathematics; Assoc. Ed., Journal of Functional Analysis, Journal of Differential Equations, Annals of Mathematics; mem. American Acad. of Arts and Sciences, Nat. Acad. of Sciences of Buenos Aires, N.A.S., U.S.A., Royal Acad. of Sciences, Spain, Latin American Acad. of Sciences, Fellow Third World Acad. of Sciences, Foreign Assoc. French Acad. of Sciences; Hon. Ph.D. (Buenos Aires) 1969; Bôcher Memorial Prize 1978, Wolf Foundation Prize 1989. *Publications:* numerous papers on mathematical topics. *Address:* Department of Mathematics, University of Chicago, Chicago, Ill., U.S.A.; also Departamento de Matemáticas, Facultad de Ciencas Exactas, Ciudad Universitaria, Buenos Aires, Argentina.

CALDWELL, John Bernard, O.B.E., PH.D., D.SC., F.ENG., F.R.I.N.A.; British professor of naval architecture; b. 26 Sept. 1926, Northampton; s. of John R. Caldwell and Doris (Bolland) Caldwell; m. Jean M. F. Duddridge 1955;

two s.; ed. Bootham School, York and Univs. of Liverpool and Bristol; Prin. Scientific Officer, R.N. Scientific Service 1957–60; Asst. Prof. R.N. Coll., Greenwich 1960–66; Visiting Prof. M.I.T. 1962–63; Prof. of Naval Architecture, Univ. of Newcastle-upon-Tyne 1966–, Head, Dept. of Naval Architecture 1966–83, Head, School of Marine Tech. 1975–80, 1986–88, Dean, Faculty of Eng. 1983–86; Pres. Royal Inst. of Naval Architects 1984–87; Dir. Nat. Maritime Inst. Ltd. 1983–85, Marine Design Consultants Ltd. 1985–, Marine Tech. Directorate 1986–; mem. Eng. Council 1988–; Gold Medal of N.E.C.I.S. 1973; Froude Medal of R.I.N.A. 1984; David Taylor Medal of S.N.A.M.E. (U.S.A.) 1987. *Publications:* over 40 papers in various eng. and scientific publs. *Leisure interests:* music, walking, reading. *Address:* The White House, Cade Hill Road, Stocksfield, Northumberland, NE43 7PT, England. *Telephone:* 0661-843445.

CALDWELL, Philip, M.B.A.; American motor manufacturing executive; b. 27 Jan. 1920, Bourneville, Ohio; s. of Robert Clyde and Wilhelmina (née Hemphill) Caldwell; m. Betsey Chinn Clark 1945; one s. two d.; ed. Muskingum Coll. and Harvard Univ.; served U.S. Navy, later Lieut. 1942–46; Navy Dept. 1946–53, Deputy Dir. of Procurement Policy Div. 1948–53; joined Ford Motor Co. 1953, Vice-Pres. 1968–85, Dir. 1973; Gen. Man. Truck Operations 1968–70; Pres. and Dir. Philco-Ford Corpn. 1970–71; Vice-Pres. of Mfg. Group 1971–72; Chair., C.E.O. and Dir. Ford Europe Inc. 1972–73; Exec. Vice-Pres. with responsiblity for int. automotive operations 1973–77, Vice-Chair. and Deputy C.E.O. 1978–79, Pres. of Ford Motor Co. 1978–80, C.E.O. 1979–85, Chair. 1980–85; also Dir. of Ford Latin America, Ford Asia-Pacific Inc., Ford of Europe, Ford Motor Credit Co., Ford of Canada, Ford Mid-East and Africa Inc., Chase Manhattan Corpn., Chase Manhattan Bank N.A., Digital Equipment Corpn., Federated Dept. Stores Inc., Russell Reynold Assocs. Inc.; Sr. Man. Dir. Shearson Lehman Bros. 1985–; mem. Int. Advisory Cttee., Chase Manhattan Bank 1979–, Business-Higher Educ. Forum; Trustee, Cttee. for Econ. Devt., Muskingum Coll.; Sec. Motor Vehicle Mfrs.' Assocn.; Dir. Detroit Symphony Orchestra; Meritorious civilian service award, U.S. Navy 1953, 1st William A. Jump memorial award 1950, Golden Plate Award, American Acad. of Achievement 1984 and several other awards; Hon. D.H. (Muskingum Coll.) 1974; Hon. D.B.A. (Upper Iowa) 1978; Hon. LL.D. (Boston Univ. 1979, Eastern Mich. Univ. 1979, Miami Univ. 1980, Davidson Coll. 1982, Lawrence Inst. of Tech. 1984, Ohio Univ. 1984). *Address:* c/o Shearson Lehman Hutton Inc., American Express Tower, World Financial Center, New York, N.Y. 10285, U.S.A. (Office).

CALIFANO, Joseph Anthony, Jr., A.B., LL.B.; American lawyer and government official; b. 15 May 1931, Brooklyn, New York; s. of Joseph A. Califano and Katherine Gill Califano; m. 2nd Hilary Paley Byers 1983; two s. one d. from previous marriage; ed. Holy Cross Coll. and Harvard Univ.; admitted to New York Bar 1955; U.S.N.R. 1955–58; with firm Dewey Ballantine, Bushby, Palmer Wood, New York 1958–61; Special Asst. to Gen. Counsel, Dept. of Defense 1961–62; Special Asst. to Sec. of Army 1962–63; Gen. Counsel, Dept. of Army 1963–64; Special Asst. to Sec. and Deputy Sec. of Defense 1964–65; Special Asst. to Pres. 1965–69; Sec. of Health, Educ. and Welfare 1977–79; Special Counsel to House of Reps. Cttee. on Standards of Official Conduct 1982–83; admitted to U.S. District Court; U.S. Court of Appeals for 2nd Circuit; U.S. Supreme Court Bar 1966; mem. Fed. Bar Assocn., American Bar Assocn., American Judicature Soc.; mem. firm Arnold & Porter 1969–71, Williams, Connolly & Califano 1971–77, Califano, Ross & Heineman 1980–82, Dewey, Ballantine, Bushby, Palmer Wood 1983–; General Counsel, Democratic Nat. Cttee. 1971–72; mem. Democratic Party's Nat. Charter Comm. 1972–74; Chair. Inst. for Social Policy in the Middle East, Kennedy School of Govt., Harvard Univ.; mem. Bd. of Dirs. Chrysler Corpn., The American Can Co., Automatic Data Processing Inc.; Trustee, New York Univ., Kaiser Family Foundation, Urban Inst.; Distinguished Civilian Service Medal, Dept. of Army 1964, Dept. of Defense 1968; Man of Year Award, Justinian Soc. Lawyers 1966; hon. degrees from Coll. of Holy Cross, Coll. of New Rochelle, Univ. of Michigan, Davis and Elkins Coll., Howard Univ., Univ. of Notre Dame, City Coll., New York. *Publications:* The Student Revolution, A Global Confrontation 1969, A Presidential Nation 1975, The Media and the Law (with Howard Simons) 1976, The Media and Business (with Howard Simons) 1978, Governing America: An Insider's Report from the White House and the Cabinet 1981, Report on Drug Abuse and Alcoholism 1982, America's Health Care Revolution: Who Lives? Who Dies? Who Pays? 1984; numerous articles for various newspapers and other publications. *Leisure interest:* jogging. *Address:* 1775 Pennsylvania Avenue, N.W., Washington, D.C. 20006, U.S.A.

CALIFICE, Alfred; Belgian politician; b. 2 Oct. 1916, Melen; m. Marcelle David; four d.; Publicity section, Jeunesse Ouvrière Chrétienne 1937–40; local govt. employee 1940–42; Sec. Fédération des Syndicats Chrétiens, Charleroi district 1944–65; mem. Parl. 1965–, of European Parl. 1968–72; Sec. of State for Housing and Planning 1972–73; Minister of Public Works 1973–74, of Employment and Labour, Walloon Affairs, Planning and Housing 1974–77, for Social Security 1977–80, for Health and Environment 1980–81. *Address:* c/o Ministry of Social Security, Brussels, Belgium.

CĂLINOIU, Nicolae, Romanian musicologist and academic; b. 3 Aug. 1926, Dobriţa commune; s. of Constantin Călinoiu and of Maria Călinoiu (née Gugu); m. Veronica-Emilia Modoran; one s.; ed. Ciprian Porumbescu Conservatory Bucharest; Prof. C. Porumbescu Conservatory Bucharest 1963–, Rector 1981–; Dir. of the Dept. of Music, Council of Socialist Culture and Educ. 1968–78; Dir. Dept. of Arts and Shows and Concerts, Council of Socialist Culture and Educ. 1978–81; Chair. of the Romanian Composers' Union 1982–; Labour Award 1964, Order of Cultural Merit 1966, 1968, Prize of the Romanian Acad. 1966, Prize of the Romanian Composers' Union 1983. *Works include:* monographs on the music of socialist Romania 1964, 1965, 1973, The Methods of Vocal Music Teaching (a treatise). *Address:* Uniunea Compozitorilor, Str. C.Esarcu no. 2, Bucharest, Romania.

CALISHER, Hortense, A.B.; American author; b. 20 Dec. 1911, New York; d. of Joseph H. Calisher and Hedvig (Lichtstern) Calisher; m. 1st.; two s.; m. 2nd Curtis Harnack 1959; ed. Barnard Coll., New York; Adjunct Prof. of English, Barnard Coll. 1956–57; Visiting Lecturer, State Univ. of Iowa 1957, 1959–60, Stanford Univ. 1958, Sarah Lawrence Coll. Bronxville, New York 1962, 1967; Adjunct Prof. Columbia Univ., New York 1968–70, City Coll. of New York 1969; Visiting Prof. of Literature, Brandeis Univ. 1963–64, Univ. of Pa. 1965, Southern Univ. of New York, Purchase 1971–72; Regent's Prof. Univ. of Calif. 1976; Visiting Prof. Bennington Coll. 1978, Washington Univ., St. Louis 1979, Brown Univ. 1986; Guggenheim Fellow 1952, 1955; mem. American Acad. and Inst. Arts and Letters (Pres. 1987–); American PEN (Pres. 1986–); Acad. of Arts and Letters Award 1967; Nat. Council Arts Award 1967; Hon. Litt.D. (Skidmore Coll.) 1980. *Publications:* novels: Tale for the Mirror 1961, Extreme Magic 1963, The Railway Police and The Last Trolley Ride 1965, Queenie 1969, Standard Dreaming 1971, Herself (autobiog.) 1972, Eagle Eye, On Keeping Women 1977, Mysteries of Motion 1984, The Bobby Soxer 1986, Age 1987; several novellas and volumes of short stories, articles and reviews etc. *Address:* c/o Candida Donadio, 231 West 22nd Street, New York, N.Y. 10011, U.S.A.

CALKINS, Robert D., M.A., LL.D., PH.D.; American economist; b. 19 Jan. 1903, Lebanon, Conn.; s. of Robert D. Calkins and Ethel Mae (Chambers); m. 1929; one s. one d.; ed. Coll. of William and Mary, and Stanford Univ.; Research Assoc., Food Research Inst., Stanford 1925–27, 1930–32; Teaching Asst. and Instructor, Stanford 1929–31; Asst. Prof. of Econs., Univ. of Calif. 1932–36, Assoc. Prof. 1936–40, Prof. 1940–41, Chair. of Dept. of Econs. 1935–41, Dean, Coll. of Commerce 1937–41; Prof. and Dean, School of Business, Columbia Univ. 1941–46; Vice-Pres. and Dir.-Gen. Educ. Bd., New York 1947–52; Pres. The Brookings Inst., Washington, D.C. 1952–67, Dir. 1952–; Vice-Chancellor, Social Sciences and Prof. of Econs., Univ. of Calif., Santa Cruz 1967–70; Dir. New York Fed. Reserve Bank 1943–49; Mediator, War Labor Bd. 1942–45; Consultant to Nat. Resources Planning Bd. 1940–42, Office of Price Admin. 1942, War Dept. 1942, etc. *Address:* Brookings Institution, 1775 Massachusetts Avenue, Washington, D.C. 20036 (Office); 5415 Connecticut Avenue, Washington, D.C. 20015, U.S.A.

CALLAGHAN OF CARDIFF, Baron (Life Peer) cr. 1987, of the City of Cardiff in the County of South Glamorgan; **(Leonard) James Callaghan,** K.G., P.C.; British politician; b. 27 March 1912, Portsmouth; m. Audrey Elizabeth Moulton 1938; one s. two d.; ed. Portsmouth Northern Secondary School; Tax Officer 1929; Asst. Sec. Inland Revenue Staff Assoc. 1936–47; service in Royal Navy 1939–45; M.P. 1945–87; Parl. Sec. Ministry of Transport 1947–50; Parl. and Financial Sec., Admiralty 1950–51; Chancellor of the Exchequer 1964–67; Home Sec. 1967–70; Sec. of State for Foreign and Commonwealth Affairs 1974–76; Leader of Parl. Labour Party 1976–80; Prime Minister 1976–79; Leader of the Opposition 1979–80; mem. Consultative Assembly, Council of Europe 1948–50, 1954; Chair. Co-ordinating Advisory Cttee. on Oil Pollution of the Sea 1953–64; Consultant to Police Fed. 1955–64; mem. Nat. Exec. Cttee. Labour Party 1957–80; Treas. Labour Party 1967–76, Chair. 1973–74; Hon. Life Fellow, Nuffield Coll., Oxford 1967; Hon. Fellow (Univ. Coll., Cardiff) 1978, (Portsmouth Polytechnic) 1981; Pres. U.K. Pilots' Assocn. 1963–76, Swansea Univ. Coll., Univ. of Wales 1986–; Hon. Pres. Int. Maritime Pilots' Assocn. 1971–76; Freedom of City of Cardiff 1975; Hon. Master of the Bench of the Inner Temple 1976; Hubert Humphrey Int. Award 1978; Freeman of Sheffield 1978; Grand Cross (1st Class) of the Order of Merit (Fed. Repub. of Germany) 1979; Hon. LL.D. (Univ. of Wales) 1976, Hon. LL.D. (Sardar Patel Univ., India) 1978, Hon. LL.D. (Univ. of Birmingham) 1981, Hon. LL.D. (Univ. of Sussex) 1988. *Publication:* A House Divided 1973, Time and Chance (autobiog.) 1987. *Address:* House of Lords, Westminster, London, S.W.1, England.

CALLAGHAN, Morley (Edward), C.C.; Canadian novelist; b. 1903, Toronto; s. of Thomas and Mary (née Dewan) Callaghan; m. Lorrete Florence 1929; two s.; ed. St. Michael's Coll., Univ. of Toronto, and Osgoode Hall Law School; Hon. D.Litt. (Windsor) 1973; Canada Council Medal Winner 1966; Royal Bank of Canada Award 1970. *Publications:* Strange Fugitive 1928, Native Argosy 1929, It's Never Over 1930, No Man's Meat 1931, Broken Journey 1932, Such is My Beloved 1934, They Shall Inherit The Earth 1935, More Joy in Heaven 1936, Now that April's Here 1937, Jake Baldwin's Vow (for children) 1948, The Varsity Story 1948, The Loved and the Lost 1955, The Man with the Coat 1955, A Many Coloured Coat 1960, A Passion in Rome 1961, That Summer in Paris 1963, Morley Callaghan Vols. I and II 1964, A Fine and Private Place 1975, Close to the Sun Again 1975, No Man's Meat and the Enchanted Pimp 1978, A Time for Judas 1983, over 100 short stories. *Address:* 20 Dale Avenue, Toronto, Ontario, Canada.

CALLAHAN, Harry M.; American photographer and academic (retd.); b. 22 Oct. 1912, Detroit, Mich.; s. of Harry A. Callahan and Hazel Mills; m. Eleanor Knapp 1936; one d.; ed. Michigan State Coll.; photographer 1938–; Instructor of Photography at Chicago Inst. of Design 1946–49, appointed Head of Dept., established Graduate Program 1950; Prof. of Photography, Rhode Island School of Design 1961–76, fmr. Head of Dept. of Photography (established Undergraduate and Graduate Program); numerous photographic awards. *Publications:* numerous monographs. *Address:* 153 Benefit Street, Providence R.I. 02903; 145 Street, N.E., 421 Atlanta, Ga. 30361, U.S.A. *Telephone:* 351 0053; 881 8680.

CALLAN, Harold Garnet, M.A., D.SC., F.R.S.; British professor of zoology; b. 5 March 1917, Maidenhead, Berks.; s. of Garnet George Callan and Winifred Edith (née Brazier); m. Amarillis M. S. Dohrn 1944; one s. two d.; ed. King's Coll. School, Wimbledon, and St. John's Coll., Oxford; served Second World War, Telecommunications Research Establishment 1940–45; Hon. Comm. Squadron Leader R.A.F.V.R.; Senior Scientific Officer, Agricultural Research Council, Inst. of Animal Genetics, Edinburgh 1946–50; Prof. of Natural History, St. Salvator's Coll., St. Andrews 1950–82, Emer. Prof. 1982–; Master of United Coll. of St. Salvator's and St. Leonard's 1967–68; mem. Advisory Council on Scientific Policy 1963–64; Trustee, British Museum (Natural History) 1963–66; Visiting Prof., Univ. of Indiana 1964–65; mem. Science Research Council 1972–76; mem. Council Royal Soc. 1974–76. *Publications:* Scientific papers, mostly on cytology and cell physiology; monograph on lampbrush chromosomes 1986. *Leisure interests:* shooting, carpentry. *Address:* Gatty Marine Laboratory, University, St. Andrews; 2 St. Mary's Street, St. Andrews, Scotland (Home). *Telephone:* St. Andrews 76161 (Office); St. Andrews 72311 (Home).

CALLARD, Sir Jack (Eric John), Kt., M.A., F.ENG., F.R.S.A.; British business executive (retd.); b. 15 March 1913, Torquay, Devon; s. of late Frank and Ada Mary Callard; m. Pauline Mary Pengelly 1938; three d.; ed. Queen's Coll., Taunton, St. John's Coll., Cambridge; Dir. Imperial Chemical Industries Ltd. (ICI), Paints Div. 1951–55, Man. Dir. 1955–59, Chair. 1959–64; Dir. ICI Ltd. 1964–75, Deputy Chair. 1967–71, Chair. 1971–75; Dir. Pension Funds Securities Ltd. 1963–67, Imperial Metal Industries 1964–67, Imperial Chemical Insurance 1966–70; Chair. ICI (Europa) Ltd. 1965–67; mem. Council Univ. of Manchester, Manchester Business School 1964–71, Vice-Pres. 1971–; mem. Council, British Inst. of Man. 1964–69, Companion 1966–; mem. Council, Export Council for Europe 1966–71; Chair. Industrial Co-partnership Assc. 1967–71; Pres. Industrial Participation Assc. 1971–74; mem. Council of Industry for Man. Educ. 1967–73; Co-opted mem. Univ. of Cambridge Appointments Bd. 1968–71; Vice-Pres. Combustion Eng. Assc. 1968–75; Dir. Midland Bank Ltd. 1971–87, Equity Bank 1976–84, British Home Stores 1975–82 (Chair. 1976–82), Commercial Union Assurance Ltd. 1975–83, Ferguson Industrial Holdings Ltd. 1975–86; Gov. London Graduate School of Business Studies 1972–75; Fellow, British Inst. of Man.; Hon. Fellow, Inst. of Mechanical Engineers; Hon. D.Sc. (Cranfield Inst. of Tech.) 1974. *Leisure interests:* fly fishing, gardening. *Address:* Crookwath Cottage, Dockray, Nr. Penrith, Cumbria, CA11 0LG, England.

CALLAWAY, Howard H.; American public official; b. 2 April 1927, LaGrange, Ga.; s. of Cason J. Callaway and Virginia Hand Callaway; m. Elizabeth Walton 1949; three s. two d.; ed. U.S. Military Acad.; served in Infantry, participating in Korean War in Far Eastern Command, later becoming Instructor, Infantry School, Fort Benning, Ga. 1949–52; mem. 89th Congress, rep. third district of Georgia 1965–66; Republican candidate for Gov. of Georgia 1966; Civilian Aide for Third Army Area 1970–73; Sec. of the Army May 1973–75; fmr. Campaign Man. for President Ford, 1976 Pres. Election; fmr. Chair. Interfinancial Inc. of Atlanta; Chair. Crested Butte Mountain Resort Inc.; Chair. Colo. Republican Party; Dir. United Bank of Denver; fmr. mem. Bd. of Regents Univ. System of Nat. 4-H Service Cttee., Bd. of Trustees, Nat. Recreation Assc., Ida Cason Callaway Foundation. *Leisure interests:* skiing, sailing, tennis, trout fishing. *Address:* P.O. Box A, Mt. Crested Butte, Colo. 81225, U.S.A.

CALLIL, Carmen Therese, F.R.S.A., B.A.; Australian publisher; b. 15 July. 1938, Melbourne; d. of Lorraine Claire Allen and Frederick Alfred Louis Callil; ed. Star of the Sea Convent, Loreto Convent, Melbourne, and Melbourne Univ.; settled in England 1963; Buyer's Asst., Marks and Spencer 1963–65; Editorial Asst., Hutchinson Publishing Co. 1965–66, B. T. Batsford 1966–67, Publicity Man., Granada Publishing 1967–70, André Deutsch 1971–72; f. Carmen Callil Ltd., Book Publicity Co. and Virago Press 1972; Chairwoman and Man. Dir. Virago Press 1972–82, Chairwoman 1983–, Man. Dir. Chatto and Windus, The Hogarth Press 1982–; Dir. Channel 4 1985–; Distinguished Service Award (Int. Women's Writing Guild). *Leisure interests:* friends, reading, animals, films, gardening. *Address:* 30 Bedford Square, London, W.C.2; Flat 2, Loreto House, 17 Pembridge Villas, London, W11 3EW, England. *Telephone:* 01-631 4434.

CALLOW, Simon Philip Hugh; British actor, director and writer; b. 15 June 1949; s. of Neil Callow and Yvonne Mary Callow; ed. London Oratory Grammar School, Queen's Univ., Belfast, Drama Centre; debut Edin. Festival 1973; repertory seasons, Lincoln and Traverse Theatre, Edin.; work at the fringe theatre, the Bush, London; joined Joint Stock Theatre Group 1977. *Stage appearances include:* Schippel 1975, A Mad World My Masters 1977, Arturo Ui, Mary Barnes 1978, As You Like It, Amadeus 1979, The Beastly Beatitudes of Balthazar B, Total Eclipse, Restoration

1981, The Relapse 1983, On The Spot 1984, Kiss of the Spider Woman 1985, Faust I and II, Lyric, Hammersmith 1988, A Question of Attribution 1988, Single Spies 1988. *Films include:* Amadeus 1983, A Room With A View 1986, The Good Father 1986, Maurice 1987. *Television includes:* Chance In A Million 1983, 1985–86, David Copperfield 1986. *Directed:* Loving Reno, Bush 1984, The Passport 1985, Nicolson Fights, Croydon 1986, Offstage, Amadeus, Theatre Clwyd 1986, The Infernal Machine 1986, Cosi fan Tutte, Switzerland 1987, Jacques and His Masters, L.A. 1987, Shirley Valentine, Vaudeville 1988. *Publications:* Being An Actor 1984, A Difficult Actor: Charles Laughton 1987. *Leisure interest:* planning the future of the British theatre. *Address:* c/o Marina Martin, 7 Windmill Street, London, W.1, England. *Telephone:* 01-323 1216.

CALLWOOD, June, O.C.; Canadian journalist, b. 2 June 1924, Chatham; d. of Harold Callwood and Gladys LaVoie; m. Trent Frayne 1944; two s. (one deceased) two d.; founding mem. and Vice-Pres. Canadian Civil Liberties Assc. 1965–88; Pres and f. Nellie's Hostel for Women 1974–78, Dir. 1985–89; Pres. Jessie's Centre for Teenagers 1982–83, 1987–; Pres. and founding mem. Learnx Foundation 1977–79, Justice for Children 1979–80; f. and Pres. Casey House Hospice (for AIDS) 1988–89–; Chair. The Writers' Union of Canada 1979–80; mem. Council, Amnesty International (Canada) 1978–; Dir. Canadian Inst. for Admin. of Justice 1983–84; Columnist Toronto Globe and Mail 1983–; Guest Lecturer on Human Rights, Univ. of Ottawa 1984; Vice-Pres. PEN (Canada-English-Speaking) 1987–88, Dir. 1988–89; Judge, Gov.-Gen.'s Literary Awards 1983–86; involved in many other public and humanitarian activities; Hon. D.Univ. (Ottawa) 1987; Hon. Dr. of Sacred Letters (Trinity Coll.) 1988; Hon. LL.D. (Memorial Univ., Newfoundland) 1988, (Univ. of Toronto) 1988, (York Univ.) 1988; Hon. Litt.D. (Carleton Univ.) 1988, (Univ. of Alberta) 1988; Canadian Newspaper Hall of Fame 1984, Bencher Law Soc. of Upper Canada 1987–(91) and other awards. *Publications;* Love, Hate, Fear and Anger 1964, The Law is Not for Women 1973, Portrait of Canada 1981, Emma 1984, Emotions 1986, Twelve Weeks in Spring 1986, Jim: A Life with AIDS 1988, and 16 other books. *Leisure interests:* swimming, biking, books. *Address:* 21 Hillcroft Drive, Islington, Ontario, M9B 4X4, Canada. *Telephone:* (416) 231-1923.

CALMES, Christian, D. EN D.; Luxembourg lawyer and civil servant; b. 11 July 1913, Oberursel, Germany; s. of Albert Calmes; m. Anne Raus 1939; three s. two d.; ed. Echternach Gymnasium, Strasbourg and Paris Univs.; called to the Bar 1938; successively Attaché, Sec., Counsellor and Minister Plenipotentiary, Ministry of Foreign Affairs; Sec.-Gen. Special Council of Ministers of ECSC 1952–58, Council of Ministers of European Communities (ECSC, EEC, and EURATOM) 1958–73, Hon. Sec.-Gen. 1973–; Chamberlain of H.R.H. the Grand Duke 1973–; mem. historic section of Institut Grand-Ducal de Luxembourg, Hon. Minister Plenipotentiary; Marshal of the Court 1981–85, Prime Chamberlain 1986. *Publications:* L'Affaire du Luxembourg 1967, Geôles sanglantes 1947 1968, Le Luxembourg dans la guerre de 1870 1970, Au fil de l'histoire Tome 3 1970, 1914–1919: Le Luxembourg au centre de l'annexionnisme belge 1976, Fil de l'histoire 1977, Le referendum Luxembourgeois du 28 Septembre 1919 1979, Une Banque raconte son histoire 1981, Luxembourg in the U.S.A. 1985, Jean, Grand-Duke of Luxembourg 1986, The Making of a Nation; From 1815 to the Present 1988. *Leisure interest:* history. *Address:* Ehnen 5489, Luxembourg, Grand Duchy of Luxembourg. *Telephone:* 761 33.

CALMON DE SÁ, Angelo (see Sá, Angelo Calmon de).

CALNE, Sir Roy Yorke, Kt., M.A., M.S., F.R.C.S., F.R.S.; British professor of surgery; b. 30 Dec. 1930; s. of Joseph R. Calne and Eileen Calne; m. Patricia D. Whelan 1956; two s. four d.; ed. Lancing Coll. and Guy's Hospital Medical School, London; RAMC 1954–56; Departmental Anatomy Demonstrator, Univ. of Oxford 1957–58; Sr. House Officer, Nuffield Orthopaedic Centre, Oxford 1958; Surgical Registrar, Royal Free Hospital 1958–60; Harkness Fellow in Surgery, Peter Bent Brigham Hosp. Harvard Medical School 1960–61; Lecturer in Surgery, St. Mary's Hosp. London 1961–62; Sr. Lecturer and Consulting Surgeon, Westminster Hosp. 1962–65; Prof. of Surgery, Univ. of Cambridge 1965–; Fellow, Trinity Hall Cambridge 1965–; Hon. Consulting Surgeon, Addenbrooke's Hosp. Cambridge 1965–; Royal Coll. of Surgeons: Hallet Prize, Jacksonian Prize, Hunterian Prof. 1962, Cecil Joll Prize 1966; numerous other honours and awards including Lister Medal 1984. *Publications:* books and scientific papers on renal and liver transplantation and gen. surgery. *Leisure interests:* tennis, squash. *Address:* 22 Barrow Road, Cambridge, England. *Telephone:* Cambridge 59831.

CALOGERO, Guido; Italian philosopher and university professor; b. 4 Dec. 1904, Rome; s. of Giorgio Calogero; m. Maria Comandini; fmr. Prof., Florence and Pisa Univs.; one of the leaders of Liberal-Socialist Movement, arrested 1942 as anti-Fascist; Ed. for the section of philosophy of Italian Encyclopaedia; Visiting Prof. of Philosophy, McGill Univ., Montreal 1948–49; Dir. Italian Inst., London 1950–55; Visiting Prof. of Philosophy, Univ. of Calif., Berkeley 1956–57; mem. Inst. for Advanced Study, Princeton 1962–63; Pres. Inst. Int. de Philosophie 1963–66; fmr. Prof. of Philosophy, Rome Univ.; mem. Accad. Nazionale dei Lincei. *Publications:* I fondamenti della logica aristotelica 1927, Studi sull'Eleatismo 1932, La scuola dell'uomo 1939, Lezioni di Filosofia 1946–48, Logo e Dialogo 1950, Scuola sotto inchiesta 1957, Filosofia del Dialogo 1962. *Address:* Via S. Alberto Magno 5, 1-00153 Rome, Italy.

ČALOVSKI, Mitko; Yugoslav politician; b. 1930, Bitola, Macedonia; ed. High School of Journalism and Diplomacy, Belgrade; successively mem. Cttee. League of Communists, Fed. Secr. for Internal Affairs; mem. Municipal Cttee. Socialist Alliance of Working People, Borough of Vračar, Belgrade; mem. Comm. for Int. Relations and Co-operation, Fed. Conf. of Socialist Alliance of Working People of Yugoslavia (SAWPY), also its Electoral Comm.; Chef de Cabinet to Pres. and mem. Group for Current Political Issues, Fed. Conf. SAWPY; Consul-Gen. Toronto; Head Analysis Planning Group, Fed. Secr. for Foreign Affairs; Deputy Gen. Sec. Collective Presidency of Yugoslavia; fmr. Amb. to Canada; Minister of Information 1982–86. *Address:* Federal Secretariat for Information, Omladinskih brigada, 11000 Belgrade, Yugoslavia.

CALVET, Jacques; French banker and business executive; b. 19 Sept. 1931, Boulogne-sur-Seine; s. of Prof. Louis Calvet and Yvonne Olmières; m. Françoise Rondot 1956; two s. one d.; ed. Paris Univ. and Nat. School of Admin.; at Cour des Comptes 1957–63; Chargé de mission to office of Valéry Giscard d'Estaing (Sec. of State for Finance) 1959–62, Dir. 1962–66; Dir. Financial Affairs, Paris Dist. 1966–68; Prin. Pvt. Sec. to Minister of Finance 1968–74; Deputy Gen. Man., Banque Nat. de Paris (BNP) 1974–75, Gen. Man. 1975–79, Chair. 1979–82, Chair. BNP Intercontinentale 1979–; Vice-Chair. Peugeot 1982–84, Pres. Sept. 1984–; Chair. Automobiles Peugeot 1982–84, Pres. Peugeot Citroën 1983–, Chair. P.S.A. 1984–; Dir. Talbot Motor Co. 1982–; Officier, Légion d'honneur, Chevalier des Palmes académiques, Ordre nat. du Mérite, du Mérite agricole. *Leisure interest:* tennis. *Address:* 75 avenue de la Grande Armée, 75116 Paris (Office); 31 avenue Victor Hugo, 75116 Paris, France (Home).

CALVET, Pierre Louis, LL.L.; French civil servant; b. 27 June 1910, Troyes; s. of Louis and Marthe (née Bauer) Calvet; m. Luce Petitjean-Saglio 1933; one s. one d.; ed. Lycée Buffon, Law Faculty, Univ. of Paris, Ecole Libre des Sciences Politiques; Financial Insp. 1933; Financial Attaché, London 1945; Gen. Dir. Office des Changes 1947; Vice-Pres. European Payments Union 1950; Deputy Gov. Bank of France 1952–66; Vice-Pres. Banque Nationale de Paris 1966–70, Hon. Vice-Pres and Admin. 1971–; mem. Council Nat. Museums; Commdr. Légion d'honneur; Grand Officier Ordre nat. du mérite; Order of Orange-Nassau; Officier Ordre de Léopold; Grand Officer, Order of Merit (Italian Repub.). *Leisure interests:* reading, walking, music. *Address:* 33-35 rue de Valois, 75001 Paris, France (Home). *Telephone:* 244-72-83 (Office); 261-49-14 (Home).

CALVIN, Melvin, PH.D.; American chemist; b. 8 April 1911, St. Paul, Minn.; s. of Elias and Rose (Hervitz) Calvin; m. Marie Genevieve Jemtegaard 1942; one s. two d.; ed. Michigan Coll. of Mining and Tech. and Univ. of Minnesota; Instructor Dept. of Chemistry, Univ. of Calif., Berkeley 1937–40, Asst. Prof. 1941–45, Assoc. Prof. 1945–47, Prof. 1947–, Univ. Prof. of Chemistry 1971–; Dir. Chem. Biodynamics Group, Lawrence Radiation Lab. 1946–80; nat. defence work 1941–45; Dir. Lab. of Chem. Biodynamics, Univ. of Calif., Berkeley 1960–80; Assoc. Dir. Lawrence Radiation Lab., Berkeley 1967–80; selected to carry out research on lunar samples from Apollo XI, XII; non-Exec. Dir. Dow Chem.; mem. N.A.S.; Foreign mem. The Royal Soc.; recipient of several scientific awards; Nobel Prize for Chemistry 1961; Davy Medal, Royal Soc. 1964; Priestley Medal, A.C.S. 1978; Gold Medal A.I.C. 1979. *Publications:* The Theory of Organic Chemistry (with G.E.K. Branch) 1941, Isotopic Carbon (with Heidelberger, Reid, Tolbert and Yankwich) 1949, The Chemistry of the Metal Chelate Compounds (with Martell) 1952, The Path of Carbon in Photosynthesis (with Bassham) 1957, Chemical Evolution 1961, Photosynthesis of Carbon Compounds (with Bassham) 1962, Chemical Evolution: Molecular Evolution towards the Origins of Living Systems on Earth and Elsewhere 1969. *Address:* Department of Chemistry, University of California, Berkeley, Calif. 94720 (Office); 2683 Buena Vista Way, Berkeley, Calif., U.S.A. (Home).

CALVO-SOTELO, Jaoquin; Spanish writer; b. 5 March 1905, La Coruña; m. Giuliana Arioli 1949; two c.; author of 50 plays; Sec. Instituto de España; Hon. Pres. Confédération Internationale des Sociétés d'Auteurs et Compositeurs; mem. Royal Academy; fmr. Pres. Sociedad de Autores de España, Círculo de Bellas Artes de Madrid; Grandes Cruces de Isabel la Católica, Mérito Civil, Alfonso X, S. Raimundo; Caballero, Orden de Malta; Officier, Légion d'honneur; Commendatore (Italy); Infante D. Enrique de Portugal. *Address:* Calle Alvarez de Baema 7, 28006 Madrid, Spain. *Telephone:* 91.261.17.26.

CALVO-SOTELO BUSTELO, Leopoldo, D.C.ENG.; Spanish engineer and politician; b. 14 April 1926, Madrid; m. Pilar Ibáñez Martín Mellado; eight c.; ed. Escuela de Ingenieros de Caminos, Canales y Puertos, Madrid; Pres. Spanish Railways 1967–68; Dir.-Gen. (now Adviser), Unión Explosivos Rio Tinto 1963–67, 1968–75; Procurador 1971–; Minister of Commerce 1975–76, of Public Works 1976–77; Minister for Relations with European Communities 1978–80; Second Deputy Prime Minister, Econ. Affairs 1980–81, Prime Minister of Spain 1981–82; mem. of European Parl. 1986–; Pres. Union of the Democratic Centre (UCD) 1981–82. *Address:* Buho 1, Somosaguas, Madrid, Spain.

CALVOCORESSI, Peter; British writer and book publisher; b. 17 Nov. 1912, Karachi, India; s. of Pandia J. Calvocoressi and Irene (Ralli); m. Barbara Dorothy Eden 1938; two s.; ed. Eton Coll. and Balliol Coll., Oxford; called to Bar 1935; R.A.F. Intelligence 1940–45; assisted Trial of Major War Criminals, Nuremberg 1945–46; on staff, Royal Inst. of Int. Affairs 1949–54; partner Chatto & Windus, publishers 1955–65; Reader in Int. Relations, Sussex Univ. 1965–71; Ed. Dir. Penguin Books 1972, Publr. and Chief Exec. 1973–76; Chair. Open Univ. Enterprises Ltd. 1979–; mem. UN sub-comm. on the Prevention of Discrimination 1961–71; Chair. The London Library 1970–73. *Publications:* Nuremberg: The Facts, the Law and the Consequences 1947, Survey of International Affairs: Vols. for 1947–48, 1949–50, 1951, 1952 and 1953, Middle East Crisis (with Guy Wint) 1957, South Africa and World Opinion 1961, World Order and New States 1962, World Politics Since 1945 1968, Total War (with Guy Wint) 1972, The British Experience: 1945–75, Top Secret Ultra 1980, Oskar Kokoschka 1886–1890 1986, A Time for Peace 1987, Who's Who in the Bible 1987. *Leisure interests:* music, tennis. *Address:* 1 Queens Parade, Bath, England. *Telephone:* Bath 333903.

CAMARA, Assan Musa; Gambian politician; b. 1923, Mansajang; ed. St. Mary Anglican Mission School, Bathurst (now Banjul) and Anglican Mission School, Kristu Kunda; Teacher in govt. and mission schools 1948–60; mem. House of Assembly (Independent) 1960–; Minister without Portfolio 1960, of Health and Labour 1960–62, of Educ. and Social Welfare 1962–65, of Works and Communications 1965–66, of Educ., Labour and Social Welfare 1966–68, of External Affairs 1968–74, of Local Govt. and Lands 1974–77, of Educ., Youth and Sports 1977, 1981–82, of Finance and Trade 1977–79; Vice-Pres. of The Gambia 1973–77, 1978–82; Order of the Cedar of Lebanon, Commdr. Nat. Order of Senegal, Grand Band, Order of Star of Africa, Grand Cross, Brilliant Star of China. *Address:* c/o Office of the Vice-President, Banjul, The Gambia.

CÂMARA, Most Rev. Helder Pessôa; Brazilian (Roman Catholic) ecclesiastic; b. 7 Feb. 1909, Fortaleza; ordained priest 1931; consecrated Bishop 1952; Titular Bishop of Salde 1952; Titular Archbishop of Salde 1955–64; Archbishop of Olinda and Recife 1964–84, Archbishop Emer. 1985–; organized Brazilian Conf. of Bishops and co-operated in organization of CELAM (the Latin-American Conf. of Bishops); an active campaigner for social reform in Latin-America; René Sande Award 1962, Via Int. Peace Prize (Italy) 1970, Martin Luther King Jr. Award 1970, John XXII Memorial Award from Pax Christi, Spain 1970, Niwano Peace Prize 1983, Christopher Award 1987; Dr. h.c. (Univs. of St. Louis, Louvain, Münster, Fribourg and Sorbonne); People's Peace Prize 1974. *Address:* Rua Henrique Dias, 208—Derbi 50070, Recife, Brazil.

CAMARGO, Sérgio de; Brazilian sculptor; b. 1930; ed. Academia Altamira, Buenos Aires, and Univ. de Paris à la Sorbonne; in France 1948–50, 1951–54, 1961–; visited China 1954; specializes in wood reliefs; Int. Sculpture Prize, Paris Biennale 1963; works are in permanent collections of Nat. Museum of Art, Rio de Janeiro, Museum of Art, São Paulo, Musée d'Art Moderne de la Ville de Paris, Tate Gallery, London, Galleria d'Arte Moderna, Rome, and in numerous private collections; represented in exhbns. in Paris and Brussels 1963, Mannheim, Arras, London and Paris 1964, 1974, New York 1965, and Latin-American exhbns. 1954–.

CAMBIE, Richard Conrad, D.SC., PH.D., D.PHIL., F.R.S.N.Z.; New Zealand university professor; b. 11 Nov. 1931, Tauranga; s. of David Gilbert Carlton Cambie and Sybil Lorna Cambie; m. 1956; two s.; ed. Tauranga Coll., Auckland Univ., Oxford Univ., U.K.; jr. lecturer, Univ. of Auckland 1957, Lecturer in Chem. 1958–60, Sr. Lecturer 1961–63, Assoc. Prof. 1964–69, Prof. of Organic Chem. 1970–, Head of Chem. Dept. 1984–; Asst. to Vice-Chancellor (Student Accommodation and Welfare) 1978–; Fellow N.Z. Inst. of Chem.; I.C.I. Medal (N.Z. Inst. of Chem.) 1964, Royal Soc. of N.Z. Hector Medal 1967, N.Z. Asscn. of Scientists Research Medal 1969. *Publications:* Co-author: New Zealand Medicinal Plants 1981, 1987, Economic New Zealand Plants 1988; 280 scientific papers on organic natural products chem. 1958–. *Leisure interest:* lawn bowling. *Address:* Chemistry Department, University of Auckland, Private Bag, Auckland (Office); 109 Riddell Road, Glendowie, Auckland, New Zealand (Home). *Telephone:* 737-999 (Office); 556-503 (Home).

CAMBITOGLOU, Alexander, A.O., PH.D., D.PHIL., F.S.A.; Australian classical archaeologist; b. Thessaloniki, Greece; s. of Anthony Cambitoglou and Helen Cambitoglou (née Antoniadou); ed. Univ. of Thessaloniki, Univs. of Manchester, London and Oxford, U.K.; Asst. Prof. Univ. of Miss., U.S.A. 1954–56, Asst. Prof., Bryn Mawr Coll., Pa. 1956–60; Sr. Lecturer in Classical Archaeology, Univ. of Sydney, Australia 1961–63; Prof. of Archaeology 1963–78, Arthur and Renee George Prof. of Classical Archaeology 1978–; Curator, Nicholson Museum, Sydney 1963–; Dir. Australian Archaeological Inst. at Athens 1981–; Fellow Australian Acad. of the Humanities, Athens Archaeological Soc.; Corresp. mem. Athens Acad., German Archaeological Inst. *Publications:* The Brygos Painter 1958; Co-author: Apulian Red-Figured Vase-Painters of the Plain Style 1961, Zagora I. Excavations of a Geometric Settlement on the Island of Andros, Greece 1978, Zagora II 1989, Eine Gruppe Apulischer Grabvasen in Basel 1976, The Red-Figured Vases of Apulia Vol. I 1978, Vol. II 1982, A Guide to the Archaeological Museum in Andros 1981, Le Peintre de Darius et son Milieu 1986; Ed.: Studies in Honour of Arthur Dale Trendall 1979. *Leisure* *interests:* swimming, music. *Address:* Australian Archaeological Institute at Athens, c/o Department of Archaeology (A14), University of Sydney, Sydney, N.S.W. 2006, Australia. *Telephone:* 692-2759.

CAMDEN, John, B.SC.; British civil engineer; b. 18 Nov. 1925, Malvern, Worcs.; s. of late Joseph R. R. J. Camden and of Lilian Kate McCann; m. 3rd Diane Mae Friese 1972; two d., (one s. two d. from fmr. m.); ed. Worcester Royal Grammar School, Birmingham Univ.; Royal Tank Corps and Intelligence Corps 1943–47; joined Ready Mixed Concrete Group 1952, Dir. European Operations 1962, Group Man. Dir. 1966–85, Chair. 1974–; Grand Decoration of Honour in Silver (Austria). *Leisure interests:* golf, gardening. *Address:* RMC Group PLC, RMC House, 53-55 High Street, Feltham, Middx., England (Office). *Telephone:* 01-890 1313.

CAMDESSUS, Jean-Michel: French civil servant; b. 1 May 1933, Bayonne; s. of Alfred Camdessus and Madeleine Cassembon; m. Brigitte d'Arcy 1957; two s. four d.; ed. Notre Dame Coll., Betharram, Faculty of Law, Paris; civil servant, Treasury, Ministry of Finance 1960–66; Chief, Bureau of Industrial Affairs, Treasury, Ministry of Econ. and Finance 1969–70; Chair. "Investissements" Sub-Cttee. of Treasury 1971–; Deputy Dir. of Treasury 1974–82, Dir. 1982–84; Financial Attaché, Perm. Representation, EEC, Brussels 1966–69; mem. Monetary Cttee., EEC 1978–, Pres. 1982–; Sec. Conseil de Direction du Fonds de Développement Economique et Social 1971–; Asst. Dir. "Épargne et Crédit" Sub-Cttee. 1972–; Deputy Gov. IMF 1982–, Man. Dir. and Chair. Jan 1987–; Gov. Banque de France 1984–87, Hon. Gov. 1987–; Dir. Banque Européenne d'Investissements, Banque Cen. des Etats de l'Afrique de l'Ouest, Air France, Soc. Nat. des Chemins de fer Français, Crédit Lyonnais (all 1978–); Pres. Club de Paris 1978–; Chevalier Légion d'honneur, de l'ordre nat. du Mérite, Croix de la Valeur militaire. *Address:* International Monetary Fund, 700 19th Street, N.W., Washington, D.C. 21431, U.S.A. (Office); 18 rue de Bourgogne, 75007 Paris, France (Home).

CAMERON, Averil Millicent, F.B.A., F.S.A., M.A., PH.D.; British professor of ancient history; b. 8 Feb. 1940, Leek, Staffs.; d. of Tom Roy Sutton and Millicent Drew; m. Alan Douglas Edward Cameron 1962 (dissolved 1980); one s. one d.; ed. Somerville Coll., Oxford, Univ. of London; Asst. Lecturer Classics, King's Coll., London 1965, Lecturer 1968, Reader in Ancient History 1970, Prof. 1978–88, Prof. Late Antique and Byzantine Studies 1988–, Chair. Dept. 1989–; Visiting Prof., Columbia Univ., New York 1967–68; Visiting mem., Inst. for Advance Study, Princeton 1977–78; Summer Fellow, Dumbarton Oaks 1980; Sather Prof. of Classical Literature, Univ. of Calif. 1985–86; Visiting Prof. Coll. de France 1987; Ed. Journal of Roman Studies. *Publications:* Procopius 1967, Agathias 1970, Corippus, In laudem Iustini minoris 1976, Images of Women in Antiquity (ed.) 1983, Continuity and Change in Sixth-Century Byzantium 1981, Constantinople in the Eighth Century (ed.) 1984, Procopius and the Sixth Century 1985. *Address:* Department of Classics, King's College, London, Strand, London, WC2R 2LS, England. *Telephone:* 01-836 5454.

CAMERON, Clyde Robert, A.O.; Australian politician (retd.); b. 11 Feb. 1913, Murray Bridge; s. of Robert Cameron II and Adelaide Hilder; m. 1st Ruby Helen Krahe 1939; m. 2nd Doris Maud Bradbury 1967; two s. one d.; ed. Gawler High School, South Australia; worked in shearing sheds 1928–38; Organizer S. Australian Branch, Australian Workers' Union (AWU) 1938, Sec. 1941–49, Pres. 1956; Fed. Vice-Pres. 1942–50; Industrial Officer 1944–48; mem. House of Reps. for Hindmarsh 1949–80; mem. Fed. Parl. Labor Party Exec. 1953–80; Minister for Labour 1972–74, for Labor and Immigration 1974–75, of Science and Consumer Affairs June–Nov. 1975; parl. del. to UN Gen. Assembly 1976; mem. S.A. Broadcasting Advisory Cttee. 1945–49, 1964–75; mem. House of Reps. Privileges Cttee. 1959–75, 1977, Parl. Retiring Allowances Trust Fund 1978; Pres. S.A. Branch, Australian Labor Party 1946–49, 1958, 1963; Chair. S. Pacific Labour Ministers' Conf. 1973; Vice-Chair. Asian Labour Ministers' Conf. 1973, Chair. 1975; Dir. Care Australia; Labor Party. *Publications:* China, Communism and Coca Cola, The Cruel Dilemma—Labor and the Unions, Oral History (650 hours, 6 million words), Unions in Crisis, Grappling with the Giants. *Leisure interests:* research and recording oral history. *Address:* 19 Sunlake Place, Tennyson, 5022, S. Australia. *Telephone:* 08-3560019.

CAMERON, Kenneth, C.B.E., PH.D., F.R.HIST.S., F.S.A., F.B.A.; British professor of English language (retd.); b. 21 May 1922, Burnley, Lancs.; s. of late Angus W. Cameron and of E. Alice Cameron; m. Kathleen Heap 1947 (died 1977); one s. one d.; ed. Burnley Grammar School and Univ. of Leeds; pilot, R.A.F. 1941–45; Asst. Lecturer in English Language, Univ. of Sheffield 1947–50; Lecturer in English Language, Univ. of Nottingham 1950–59, Sr. Lecturer 1959–62, Reader 1962–63, Prof. 1963–87, Head, Dept. of English Studies 1984–87; Hon. Fil.Dr. (Uppsala) 1977. *Publications:* The Place-Names of Derbyshire 1959, English Place-Names 1961, Scandinavian Settlement in the Territory of the Five Boroughs 1965, The Meaning and Significance of Old English *walh* in English Place-Names 1980, The Place-Names of the City of Lincoln 1985; articles in professional journals. *Leisure interests:* sports, home. *Address:* 292 Queens Road, Beeston, Nottingham, England. *Telephone:* Nottingham 254503.

CAMERON, Peter Duncanson, LL.B., PH.D.; British lawyer and consultant; b. 21 June 1952, Glasgow; s. of Stewart Cameron and Margaret Cameron; ed. Bishop Vesey Grammar School, High School of Stirling and Univ. of Edinburgh; lecturer in Law, Univ. of Dundee 1977–86; Visiting Research Assoc., Oxford Univ. Centre for Socio-Legal Studies 1980, Visiting Scholar, Stanford Law School 1985; Adviser UN Centre on Transnat. Corpns. 1985–86; Vice-Chair. Utility Law Cttee., Int. Bar Asscn. Section on Business Law 1988–; Adviser UN ESCAP 1988–89; Dir. Int. Inst. of Energy Law, Univ. of Leiden. *Publications:* Property Rights and Sovereign Rights: the Case of North Sea Oil 1983, Petroleum Licensing 1984, The Oil Supplies Industry: a Comparative Study of Legislative Restrictions and their Impact 1986, Nuclear Energy Law after Chernobyl (with L. Hancher) 1988. *Leisure interest:* long-distance running. *Address:* Internationaal Instituut voor Energierecht, Univ. of Leiden, Hugo de Grootstraat 27, 2311 XK Leiden, Netherlands. *Telephone:* (071) 277736.

CAMERON, Roy James, C.B., M.ECON., PH.D.; Australian government official; b. 11 March 1923, S. Australia; s. of Kenneth and Amy Jean Cameron (née Davidson); m. Dorothy Olive Lober 1951; two s. one d.; ed. Univs. of Adelaide and Harvard, U.S.A. Lecturer in Econs., Canberra 1949–51; Economist Int. Bank for Reconstruction and Devt. 1955–56; with Australian Treasury 1956–73, First Asst. Sec., Transport and Industry Div. 1966–73; Amb., Del. to OECD 1973–77, Australian Statistician 1977–85. *Address:* 10 Rafferty Street, Chapman, A.C.T. 2611, Australia.

CAMILIÓN, Oscar Héctor, PH.D.; Argentine politician; b. 6 Jan. 1930, Buenos Aires; s. of Oscar Juan Camilión and Lucía Fernández; m. Susana María Lascano 1956; two s. two d.; ed. Colegio San Salvador, Univ. Nacional de Buenos Aires; Asst., then Head of Research, Inst. of Constitutional Law, Univ. Nacional de Buenos Aires, Sec.-Gen. 1955, Prof. of Constitutional Law, concurrently at Univ. Católica de La Plata 1957; Prof. of Int. Law, Argentine Inst. of Hispanic Culture; Prof. of Int. Politics, Argentine Nat. Coll. of Defence; entered Ministry of Foreign Affairs 1958, held posts of Minister, Chief of Cabinet, Dir. of Personnel, Minister-Counsellor, Argentine Embassy, Brazil 1959–61, Under-Sec. 1961–62; mem. dels. to UN Gen. Assembly, Confs. of OAS and other regional orgs., to Conf. of Guaranteeing Countries of Peru-Ecuador Peace Protocol 1960, 1981; Chief Ed. Clarin newspaper, Buenos Aires 1965–72; Amb. to Brazil 1976–81; Minister of Foreign Affairs and Worship March–Dec. 1981; f. Argentine Council of Int. Relations; mem. Interamerican Dialogue, Atlantic Confs.; decorations from Brazil, Peru, Bolivia, Venezuela, Colombia, Honduras, El Salvador. *Publications:* several papers on historical, political and diplomatic subjects. *Leisure interests:* golf, classical music, history. *Address:* Montevideo 1597-4°, Buenos Aires 42-9557, Argentina.

CAMILLERI, Charles, MUS.BAC.; British/Maltese composer; b. 7 Sept. 1931, Malta; s. of Carmel Camilleri and Josephine Quinton; m. Doris Vella 1957; one s. one d.; ed. Lyceum High School and Toronto Univ., Canada; composer, teacher, lecturer, conductor in Malta up to 1949, Australia 1949–53, U.K. 1954–57, Toronto, conductor with CBC, Toronto 1958–63, London 1964–; apptd. Dir. Inst. of Mediterranean Music Foundation of Int. Studies, UNESCO 1987; comm. by UNESCO Songs of Infant Species for soprano and piano 1987; commissioned by Aga Khan Foundation: Mimar for piano, vibraphone and gongs 1987; visits to many countries in Far East, Europe and N. America 1949–; many Arts Council Awards. *Publications:* over 80, including Missa Mundi 1968, 2nd Piano Concerto 1969, Piano Trio 1970, String Quartet 1973, Cosmic Vixions 1974, Five Books on Improvisation 1983, 3rd Piano Concerto 1985. *Leisure interest:* research in primitive and folk music. *Address:* 24 Orchard Avenue, Finchley, London, N3 3NL, England. *Telephone:* 01-349 1728.

CAMMANN, Helmuth Carl, DR. RER. POL.; German economist; b. 8 Feb. 1927, Düsseldorf; s. of Carl Cammann and Maria Döpp; m. Helga Herweg 1957; one s. one d.; ed. Technological Univ., Karlsruhe and Cologne Univ.; Foreign Trade and Balance of Payments Section, Econ. Research Inst., Essen 1950–53; Econ. Adviser, Perm. German Del. to OEEC 1953–56; Head of Div., Econ. Directorate, ECSC, Luxembourg 1956–57; Econ. Sec. Del. in U.K. of ECSC 1957–61; Head of Perm. Del. of EEC Comm. to OECD, Paris 1961–66; Sec.-Gen. Bundesverband deutscher Banken e.V., Cologne (Asscn. of German Banks) 1966–; mem. Econ. and Social Cttee., EURATOM 1970–. *Address:* Mohrenstrasse 35, 5000 Cologne, Federal Republic of Germany. *Telephone:* 1663215.

CAMOYS, 7th Baron, (cr. 1264) Ralph Thomas Campion George Sherman Stonor; British banker; b. 16 April 1940; s. of 6th Baron Camoys and Mary Jeanne Stourton; m. Elisabeth Mary Hyde Parker 1966; one s. three d.; ed. Eton Coll., Balliol Coll., Oxford; Gen. Man. and Dir., Nat. Provincial and Rothschild (London) Ltd. 1968; Man. Dir. Rothschild Intercontinental Bank Ltd. 1969; C.E.O. and Man. Dir. Amex Bank Ltd. 1975–77, Chair. 1977–78; Chair. Jacksons of Piccadilly Ltd. 1968–85; Man. Dir. Barclays Merchant Bank Ltd. 1978–84, Exec. Vice.-Chair. 1984–; Dir. Barclays Bank Int. Ltd. 1980–84, Barclays Bank PLC 1984–, Mercantile Credit Co. Ltd. 1980–84, Nat. Provident Inst. 1982–; C.E.O. Barclays de Zoete Wedd 1986–88, Deputy Chair. 1987–; Pres. Mail Users' Asscn. 1977–84; mem. House of Lords EEC Select Cttee. 1979–84, Court of Assistants, Fishmongers' Co. 1980–, Royal Comm. on Historical Manuscripts 1987–; Order of Gorkha Dakshina Bahu, 1st class (Nepal) 1981. *Leisure interests:* the arts, shooting. *Address:* Stonor Park, Henley-on-Thames, Oxon., RG9 6HF, England.

CAMP, Jeffery Bruce, R.A., A.R.A.; British artist; b. 1923, Oulton Broad, Suffolk; s. of George Camp and Caroline Denny; m. Laetitia Yhap 1963;

ed. Lowestoft and Ipswich Art Schools and Edinburgh Coll. of Art (under William Gillies); Andrew Grant Scholarship for travelling and study 1944, 1945, David Murray Bursary for landscape painting 1946; painted altarpiece for St. Alban's Church, Norwich 1955; Teacher Slade School of Fine Art, London 1961-; mem. London Group 1961; one-man exhbns.: Edinburgh Festival 1950, Galerie de Seine, London 1958, 1959, Beaux Arts Gallery, London 1961, 1963, New Art Centre, London 1968, Fermoy Art Gallery, King's Lynn 1970, S. London Art Gallery 1973, Royal Shakespeare Theatre, Stratford 1974, Serpentine Gallery, London (Arts Council) 1978, Bradford City Art Gallery 1979, Browse and Darby 1984, The 29th Aldeburgh Festival 1986, Nigel Greenwood Gallery, London 1986, Royal Acad. Retrospective 1988; in numerous mixed exhbns. 1958-; works in numerous public collections in U.K. *Publication:* Draw 1981. *Address:* c/o Nigel Greenwood Gallery, 4 New Burlington Street, London, W1X 1FE, England. *Telephone:* 01-223 5686.

CAMPAIGNE, Jameson Gilbert, B.A.; American editor and writer; b. 16 Jan. 1914, Brooklyn, New York; s. of Curtis Campaigne and Edna Amory Foote; m. Edith Louise Baker 1938; three s. one d.; ed. Montclair Acad., Williams Coll.; salesman, Yardley & Co. 1936-40; writer with Compton Advertising 1940-44; U.S. Marine Corps 1944-46; Chief Editorial Writer, Indianapolis Star 1946-51, Ed., Editorial Page 1951-60, Ed. 1960-69, editorial writer and columnist 1969-73; Editorial Writer, New York Daily News 1973-76; editorial consultant 1976-; mem. Mont Pelerin Soc.; Lincoln Nat. Life Foundation Award for best editorial on Lincoln; Freedoms Foundation Award for editorial writing 1951, 1952, 1957; Indiana Univ. World Affairs Award 1960. *Publications:* American Might and Soviet Myth 1960, Check-off 1961, International Background 1978; articles in Saturday Evening Post 1977. *Address:* 370 Orwell Lane, Encinitas, Calif. 92024, U.S.A.

CAMPBELL, Sir Alan Hugh, G.C.M.G.; British diplomatist (retd.); b. 1 July 1919, Worthing, Sussex; s. of Hugh Elphinstone and Ethel Marion (Warren) Campbell; m. Margaret Jean Taylor 1947; three d.; ed. Sherborne School and Cambridge Univ.; served in Devonshire Regt. 1940-46, Major 1945; Third Sec. in H.M. Foreign Service 1946; served in Singapore, Rome, Peking, New York, Paris and Foreign Office, London 1946-68; Amb. to Ethiopia 1969-72; Under-Sec. of State, Foreign Office (later Foreign and Commonwealth Office) 1972-76; Amb. to Italy 1976-79; Adviser to Rolls-Royce Ltd. 1979-81; Dir. Nat. Westminster Bank; Mercantile and Gen. Reinsurance Co., H. Clark Holdings PLC; Chair. Soc. of Pension Consultants 1982-87, British-Italian Soc. 1983-, British School at Rome 1987-. *Leisure interests:* painting in water colours, lawn tennis. *Address:* 45 Carlisle Mansions, Carlisle Place, London, S.W.1, England (Home). *Telephone:* 01-834 2827.

CAMPBELL, Hon. Alexander Bradshaw, P.C., Q.C., LL.B., LL.D.; Canadian lawyer and politician; b. 1 Dec. 1933, Summerside, P.E.I.; s. of late Thane A. Campbell and Cecilia Bradshaw; m. Marilyn Gilmour 1961; two s. one d.; practised law in Summerside 1959-66; mem. P.E.I. Legislature 1965-78, Leader of Liberal Party for P.E.I. Dec. 1965-78; Premier of P.E.I. 1966-78; Minister of Devt. 1969-72, of Agriculture and Forestry 1972-74, Pres. Exec. Council, Minister of Justice, Attorney and Advocate-Gen. 1974-78; Justice, Supreme Court of P.E.I. 1978-; mem. Privy Council for Canada Jan. 1967-; mem. and fmr. Sec. Summerside Bd. of Trade; Past Pres. of Y's Men's Club; fmr. Vice-Pres. and Exec. mem. P.E.I. Young Liberal Asscn.; Pres. Summerside Y.M.C.A. 1981-; Elder, United Church, Summerside; Founding Pres. Summerside Area Historical Soc. 1983-; Founding Chair. Duke of Edinburgh's Awards Cttee. (P.E.I.) 1984-; Hon. LL.D. (McGill, P.E.I.). *Leisure interests:* golf, swimming, gardening. *Address:* 330 Beaver Street, Summerside, Prince Edward Island, C1N 2A3 (Home); Sir Louis Davis Law Courts Building, Charlottetown, Prince Edward Island, Canada (Office).

CAMPBELL, Allan McCulloch, M.S., PH.D.; American professor of biology; b. 27 April 1929, Berkeley, Calif.; s. of Lindsay and Virginia Campbell; m. Alice Del Campillo 1958; one s. one d.; ed. Univ. of Calif. (Berkeley) and Univ. of Ill.; Instructor in Bacteriology, Univ. of Mich. Medical School, Ann Arbor 1953-57; Research Assoc., Carnegie Inst. of Washington, Dept. of Genetics 1957-58; Asst. Prof. to Prof. of Biology, Univ. of Rochester, 1958-68; Prof. of Biological Sciences, Stanford Univ. 1968-; Fellow, American Acad. of Arts and Sciences; mem. Nat. Acad. of Sciences; Hon. D.Sc. (Univ. of Chicago) 1978, (Univ. of Rochester) 1981. *Publications:* Episomes 1969, General Virology 1978. *Address:* Department of Biological Sciences, Stanford University, Stanford, Calif. 94305 (Office); 947 Mears Court, Stanford, Calif. 94305, U.S.A. (Home). *Telephone:* 723-1170 (Office); 493-6155 (Home).

CAMPBELL, Carroll Ashmore, D.HUM.LITT.; American politician; b. 24 July 1940, Greenville, S.C.; s. of Carroll Ashmore Campbell Sr. and Anne Williams; m. Iris Rhodes 1959; two s.; ed. American Univ. and Sherman Coll.; Pres. Handy Park Co. 1960-78; mem. S.C. House of Reps. 1970-74, S.C. Senate 1976; Exec. Asst. to Gov. of S.C. 1975; Asst. Regional Whip to various State dels. at Repub. Convention 1976, 1980, 1984; mem. 96th-99th Congresses from S.C. 4th Dist.; Gov. of South Carolina Jan. 1987-; mem. Advisory Council, White House Conf. on Handicapped Individuals; numerous awards including Guardian of Small Businesses Award, Watchdog of Treasury Award, Humanitarian Award, Rutledge Coll. and

Leadership Award, American Security Council; Republican. *Address:* Office of Governor, P.O. Box 11450, Columbia, S.C., U.S.A.

CAMPBELL, Sir Clifford Clarence, G.C.M.G., G.C.V.O.; Jamaican teacher and administrator; b. 28 June 1892, Petersfield, Westmoreland; s. of the late James Campbell and of Blanche (née Ruddock); m. Alice Estephene 1920; two s. two d.; ed. Petersfield Elementary School and Mico Training Coll.; Headmaster of various govt. schools 1916-44; mem. House of Reps. (Jamaica Labour Party) 1944-52; Chair. Cttee. for Educ. 1945-49; Speaker, House of Reps. 1950; Pres. of Senate 1962; Gov.-Gen. of Jamaica 1962-73; K.St.J. *Leisure interests:* music, painting, reading, agriculture, community and professional service. *Address:* 8 Cherry Gardens Avenue, Kingston 8, Jamaica.

CAMPBELL, Colin Kydd, F.R.S.C., F.R.S.A.; Canadian professor of electrical and computer engineering; b. 3 May 1927, St. Andrews, Scotland; s. of David Walker Campbell and Jean Bell Campbell; m. Vivian G. Norval 1954; two s. two d.; ed. Madras Coll. St. Andrews, Univ. of St. Andrews and Mass. Inst. of Technology; mil. service 1944-46; communications engineer, Diplomatic Wireless Service and Foreign Office, London, Washington and New York 1946-48; electronics engineer, Atomic Instrument Co., Cambridge, Mass. 1954-57; research scholar, Royal Naval Scientific Service, St. Andrews Univ. 1957-60; Asst. Prof. Electrical Eng. McMaster Univ. 1960-63, Assoc. Prof. 1963-67, Prof. of Electrical and Computer Eng. 1967-; Fellow, Eng. Inst. of Canada; Eadie Medal (Royal Soc. of Canada) 1983, Hon. B.Eng., Hon. M.S., Hon. PH.D., Hon. D.SC., Hon. F.I.E.E. *Publications:* Surface Acoustic Wave Devices and their Signal Processing Applications 1989, numerous scientific and eng. publs. in professional and tech. journals with specialization in surface acoustic wave devices. *Leisure interests:* fishing, travelling. *Address:* Department of Electrical and Computer Engineering, McMaster University, 1280 Main Street West, Hamilton, Ont., L8S 4L7 (Office); 160 Parkview Drive, Ancaster, Ont., L9G 1Z5, Canada (Home). *Telephone:* 416-525-9140 (Office); 416-648-3867 (Home).

CAMPBELL, Fergus William, M.A., M.D., PH.D., F.R.S.; British professor of neurosensory physiology; b. 30 Jan. 1924; s. of William Campbell and Anne Fleming; m. Helen M. Cunningham 1948; one s. two d. (and one d. deceased); ed. Univ. of Glasgow; Casualty and Eye Resident Surgeon, Western Infirmary, Glasgow 1946-47; Asst. Inst. of Physiology, Glasgow 1947-49, Lecturer 1949-52; Research Graduate, Nuffield Lab. of Ophthalmology 1952-53; Univ. Lecturer, Physiological Lab. Cambridge 1953-72, Reader in Neurosensory Physiology 1973-83, Prof. of Neurosensory Physiology 1983-; Hon. Prof. Dept. of Optometry, Univ. of Wales Inst. of Science and Tech. 1984-; Tillyer Medal, Optical Soc. of America 1980. *Publications:* papers in professional journals. *Leisure interests:* music, photography. *Address:* 96 Queen Edith's Way, Cambridge, CB1 4PP, England. *Telephone:* Cambridge 247578.

CAMPBELL, Finley Alexander, M.A., PH.D., F.R.S.; Canadian geologist; b. 5 Jan. 1927, Kenora, Ont.; s. of Finley McLeod Campbell and Vivian Delve; m. Barbara E. Cromarty 1953; two s. one d.; ed. Brandon Coll., Univ. of Man., Queen's Univ. Kingston, Ont. and Princeton Univ.; exploration and mine geologist 1950-58; Asst., Assoc. Prof. Univ. of Alberta 1958-65; Prof. and Head Dept. of Geology, Univ. of Calgary 1965-69; Vice-Pres. Capital Resources, Univ. of Calgary 1969-71, Vice-Pres. 1971-76, Prof. of Geology 1976-84, Vice-Pres. Priorities and Planning 1984-; Queen's Jubilee Medal and other awards and distinctions. *Publications:* over 40 publs. on geological topics. *Leisure interests:* sailing, golf, music, skiing, ballet. *Address:* The University of Calgary, 2500 University Drive N.W., Calgary, T2N 1N4 (Office); 3408 Bentor Drive N.W., Calgary Alta, T2L 1W8, Canada (Home).

CAMPBELL, John Garfield, C.A.; Canadian business executive; b. 13 March 1916; ed. public and high schools, Regina, Saskatchewan; Audit Clerk, Rooke Thomas & Co., Regina 1935-41; Gen. Auditor, Defence Industries Ltd., Montreal 1941-46; Comptroller, Victory Mills Ltd. 1946-51; Comptroller Canadian Breweries Ltd. 1951; Pres. Victory Mills Ltd. 1952; Vice-Pres. Canadian Breweries Ltd. 1954-59, Exec. Vice-Pres. 1959-65, Pres. 1965-.

CAMPBELL, Juliet Jeanne d'Auvergne, C.M.G., B.A.; British diplomatist; b. 23 May 1935, London; m. Alexander E. Campbell 1983; no c.; ed. Lady Margaret Hall, Oxford; Foreign Office 1957; U.K. Del. to Brussels Conf. 1961; Foreign Office 1963; Second, later First Sec. Bangkok 1964; First Sec. Paris (NATO) 1966; FCO 1967; The Hague 1970; FCO 1974; Counsellor, Paris 1977; Royal Coll. of Defence Studies 1981; Counsellor and Head of Chancery, Djakarta 1982; FCO 1984; Amb. to Luxembourg 1988-. *Address:* British Embassy, 14 boulevard Roosevelt, Luxembourg. *Telephone:* 29864.

CAMPBELL, Roderick Samuel Fisher, PH.D., M.R.C.V.S., F.R.S.E.; Australian professor of tropical veterinary science; b. 5 June 1924, Glasgow, Scotland; s. of Robert Campbell and Harriet Hodson; m. Barbara M. Morris 1956; three s.; ed. Allan Glens School, Glasgow, McLaren High School, Callander, and Glasgow Veterinary Coll.; Lecturer in Veterinary Pathology, Univ. of Glasgow 1948, Sr. Lecturer 1956-69; Prof. and Head, Grad. School of Tropical Veterinary Science, James Cook Univ. Townsville 1969-87, Emer. Prof. 1987-; Visiting Prof. Khartoum Univ. 1964-65, Purdue Univ. 1967-68; Project Man. Balitvet Inst. Project, Bogor, Indonesia 1981-; Consultant,

Food and Agric. Org., World Bank, Australian Centre for Int. Agric. Research; Hon. D.Sc. (James Cook); Kesteren Medal for Contrib. to Int. Veterinary Science. *Publications:* numerous scientific papers. *Leisure interests:* history, music, golf. *Address:* James Cook University, P.O. Box 4811, Townsville, Queensland (Office); 21 Potts Street, Townsville, Queensland, Australia (Home). *Telephone:* (077) 81 4288 (Office); (077) 72 6249 (Home).

CAMPBELL, Ronald Hugh, O.B.E., B.SC.; British business executive; b. 28 Nov. 1924, Renfrewshire; s. of Hugh Campbell and Agnes Blair Campbell; m. Hilda E. Probyn 1948; one s. one d.; ed. Greenock High School and Glasgow Univ.; engineer, Dowty Equipment 1944-50, Sperry Gyroscope 1950-56; Chief Engineer, Savage and Parsons 1956-59, UKAEA 1959-69; Gen. Man., The Nuclear Power Group 1969-73; Asst. Man. Dir. Nat. Nuclear Corpn. 1973-77; Dir. Babcock Int., Man. Dir., Babcock Power 1977-. *Leisure interests:* golf, gardening. *Address:* 165 Great Dover Street, London, SE1 4YB (Office); Larchwood, 34 Blueberry Road, Bowdon, Altrincham, Cheshire, WA14 3LU, England (Home). *Telephone:* 01-407 8383 (Office); 061 928 2920 (Home).

CAMPBELL, Ross, B.A., D.S.C.; Canadian fmr. government official and diplomatist; b. 4 Nov. 1918, Toronto, Ont.; s. of late William M. Campbell and Helen I. Campbell; m. Penelope Grantham-Hill 1945; two s.; ed. Univ. of Toronto Schools and Univ. of Toronto; Royal Canadian Navy 1940-45; joined Dept. of External Affairs, Canada 1945; Third Sec., Oslo 1946-47; Second Sec., Copenhagen 1947-50; European Div. Dept. of External Affairs, Ottawa 1950-52; First Sec., Ankara 1952-56; Head of Middle East Div., Ottawa 1957-59; Special Asst. to Sec. of State for External Affairs 1959-62; Asst. Under-Sec. of State for External Affairs 1962-64, Adviser to Canadian Dels. to UN Gen. Assemblies 1958-63, Adviser to Canadian Dels. to North Atlantic Council 1959-64; Amb. to Yugoslavia 1964-67, concurrently accred. to Algeria 1965-67; Perm. Rep. and Amb. to NATO, Paris May 1967, Brussels Oct. 1967-72; Amb. to Japan 1973-75 (concurrently accred. to Repub. of Korea 1973-74); Chair. Atomic Energy of Canada Ltd. 1976-79, Pres. Atomic Energy of Canada Int. 1979-80; Partner Canus Tech. Services Corpn. 1981-83, Inter Con Consultants 1983-; Dir. MBB Helicopter Canada Ltd. and UXB Int. Canada Ltd. *Leisure interest:* gardening. *Address:* Suite 705, 275 Slater Street, Ottawa, Ont. K1P 5H9 (Office); 890 Aylmer Road, Alymer, Quebec J9H 5T8, Canada (Home). *Telephone:* (613) 236-4451 (Office).

CAMPBELL, Steven MacMillan, B.A.; British artist; b. 19 March 1953, Glasgow; s. of George Campbell and Martha (née MacMillan) Dallas; m. Carol Ann Thompson 1975; one s. two d.; ed. Rutherglen Acad., Glasgow School of Art 1978-82, Pratt Inst., N.Y. 1982-83; Barbara Toll Fine Art Ltd; N.Y. 1983-86; Marlborough Fine Art Ltd., London 1986-. Major works for Hirshorn Museum, Tate Gallery, British Council, Wardsworth Atheneum, Metropolitan Museum. *Leisure interests:* angling, reading mathematics, detective novels, opera. Address: Inchwood Cottage, By Milton of Campsie, Glasgow G65 8AL, Scotland. *Telephone:* Kilsyth 822930.

CAMPBELL, Sir Walter Benjamin, A.C., Kt., K. St. J. 1986, M.A., LL.B.; Australian judge and state governor; b. 4 March 1921, Burringbar, N.S.W.; s. of late Archie Eric Gordon Campbell and Leila Mary Campbell (née Murphy); m. Georgina Margaret Pearce 1942; two s. (one deceased) one d.; ed. Downlands Coll., Univ. of Queensland; Pilot R.A.A.F. 1941-46; Barrister 1948-67; Q.C. 1960; Judge, Supreme Court of Queensland 1967-85; Chief Justice of Queensland 1982-85; mem. Senate Univ. of Queensland 1963-85, Chancellor 1977-85; Gov. of Queensland July 1985-; Pres. Bar Asscn., Queensland 1965-67; mem. Law Council Exec. 1965-67; Pres. Australian Bar Asscn. 1966-67; Chair. Law Reform Comm., Queensland 1969-73; sole mem. Academic Salaries Tribunal (Commonwealth) 1974-78, and Chair. Remuneration Tribunal (Commonwealth) 1974-82; Chair. Bd. of Govs. Utah Foundation 1977-85; Freeman, City of London 1987; Liveryman, Guild of Air Pilots and Air Navigators 1988; Hon. LL.D. (Univ. of Queensland) 1980, Hon. D.Litt. (James Cook Univ.) 1988. *Leisure interests:* golf, swimming, reading. *Address:* Government House, Brisbane, Queensland 4001, Australia.

CAMPBELL OF CROY, Baron (Life Peer), cr. 1974; **Gordon Thomas Calthrop Campbell,** M.C.; British politician; b. 8 June 1921, Quetta, Pakistan; s. of Maj.-Gen. and Mrs. J. A. Campbell; m. Nicola Madan 1949; two s. one d.; ed. Wellington Coll.; served in regular army 1939-46 (rank of Maj.), wounded and disabled; diplomatic service 1946-57, mem. U.K. mission to UN 1949-52, Cabinet Office 1954-56; M.P. for Moray and Nairn 1959-74; Lord Commr. of the Treasury 1962; Parl. Under-Sec. of State for Scotland 1963-64; Sec. of State for Scotland 1970-74; Opposition Spokesman in House of Lords 1975-79; Oil Industry Consultant 1975-; Partner in Holme Rose Farms and Estate 1969-; Dir. and Chair. Scottish Bd. of Alliance and Leicester Building Soc. 1985-; Chair. Advisory Cttee. on Pollution of the Sea 1987-89; Chair. Scottish Council of Independent Schools; Consultant in Oil Industry, Chair. Stoic Insurance Services 1979-; Chair. Scottish Cttee., Int. Year of Disabled 1981; Conservative. *Publication:* Disablement: Prospects and Problems in the U.K. 1981. *Leisure interests:* music, birds. *Address:* Holme Rose, Cawdor, Nairn, Scotland. *Telephone:* Croy 223.

CAMPBELL OF ESKAN, Baron (Life Peer) cr. 1966, of Camis Eskan; **John (Jock) Middleton Campbell,** Kt.; British business executive; b. 8

Aug. 1912, London; s. of the late Colin Algernon Campbell and Mary C. G. Barrington; m. 1st Barbara N. Roffey 1938, two s. two d.; m. 2nd Phyllis J. Gilmour Taylor 1949 (died 1983); ed. Eton and Exeter Coll., Oxford; Chair., Booker McConnell Ltd. 1952-67, Pres. 1967-79; Chair. Commonwealth Sugar Exporters 1950-84, Statesman and Nation Publishing Co. 1963-81, Milton Keynes Devt. Corpn. 1967-83; fmr. Pres. **W.** India Cttee.; Dir. Commonwealth Devt. Corpn. 1968-81; mem. Community Relations Comm. 1968-77; Pres. Town and Country Planning Asscn. 1980-; Trustee Runnymede Trust, Chequers Trust. *Leisure interests:* reading, hitting balls, painting. *Address:* Lawers, Crocker End, Nettlebed, Oxford, England (Home).

CAMPEN, Dr. Philippus Canisius Maria van; Netherlands business executive; b. 1 Jan. 1911, Nijmegen; Man. Co-operative Central Bank, Eindhoven 1946, Gen. Man. 1957-73; mem. Netherlands Senate and European Parl. until 1967; mem. Supervisory Bd., N.V. Philips Gloeilampenfabrieken 1963-, Chair. 1968, fmr. Vice-Chair. Supervisory Bd.; Pres. Assen. Co-operative Credit Banks, EEC 1971; mem. Supervisory Bd., Friesch-Groningsche Hypotheek Bank, Ballast Nedam (Chair.), D.S.M., Kas-Associatie. *Address:* Spechtlaan 9, Lieshout N. Br., Netherlands. *Telephone:* 04992-1517.

CAMPENHAUSEN, Hans Erich, Freiherr von, D.THEOL.; German university professor; b. 16 Dec. 1903, Rosenbeck, Livland; s. of Balthasar von Campenhausen and Lilli von Löwis of Menar; m. 1st Dorothee von Eichel 1931 (died 1964), three s. one d.; m. 2nd Dorothee Anders 1966 (died 1981); ed. Marburg, Heidelberg, Berlin and Rome; Lecturer in ecclesiastical history Marburg 1928-30, Göttingen 1930-35; Lecturer in Giessen, Kiel, Greifswald, Heidelberg and Vienna 1935-45; Prof. of Ecclesiastical History, Heidelberg 1945-68, now Emer.; Rector Univ. of Heidelberg 1946-47; mem. Heidelberg Akad. der Wissenschaften 1946, Göttingen Akad. der Wissenschaften, British Acad., A.A.A.S.; Hon. doctorates in Theology (St. Andrews, Göttingen, Oslo, Vienna and Uppsala). *Publications:* Ambrosius von Mailand als Kirchenpolitiker 1929, Die Passionssarkophage 1930, Die Idee des Martyriums in der alten Kirche 1936, Luther: Die Hauptschriften, Karl Müller: Kirchengeschichte I 1941, Kirchliches Amt und geistliche Vollmacht in den ersten drei Jahrhunderten 1953, 1963, Die griechischen Kirchenväter 1955, Lateinische Kirchenväter 1960, Tradition und Leben 1960, Die Jungfrauengeburt in der alten Kirche 1962, Aus der Frühzeit des Christentums 1963, Die Entstehung der christlichen Bibel 1968, Theologenspiess und-spass 1973, 1974, Urchristliches und Altkirchliches (Vorträge und Aufsätze) 1979. *Address:* Jaspers-Strasse 2, 6900 Heidelberg, Federal Republic of Germany.

CAMPO SAINZ DE ROSAS, Julián; Spanish politician; b. 1938, Las Arenas; m. Pilar Llopis; three c.; economist and industrial engineer; mem. Frente de Liberación Popular; mem. Partido Socialista Obrero Español 1974; tax and financial inspector; Asst. Dir. Instituto de Estudios Fiscales; Dir. Escuela Financiera y Tributaria; financial adviser, Spanish Embassy in Washington until 1981; Minister of Public Works and Town Planning 1982-86. *Leisure interests:* walking, and touring Spain. *Address:* Ministerio de Obras Públicas y Urbanismo, Avenida del Generalísimo, Madrid, Spain (Office).

CAMPOS, Roberto de Oliviera (see de Oliviera Campos, Roberto).

CAMU, Pierre, O.C., PH.D., L.LITT., F.R.S.C.; Canadian public official; b. 19 March 1923, Montreal; m. Marie-Marthe Trudeau; one s. two d.; ed. Univ. of Montreal and Johns Hopkins Univ., Baltimore; Prof. Econ. Geography and Dir. Research Center, Faculty of Commerce, Laval Univ. 1956-60; Consultant to shipping orgs. in Eastern Canada and U.S.A. 1956-60; Vice-Pres. St. Lawrence Seaway Authority 1960-65, Pres. 1965-73; Administrator Canadian Marine Transportation Admin. 1970-80; Pres. March Shipping Ltd. 1979-84; Chair. Canadian Road Transport Asscn. 1977-79; Pres. Royal Canadian Geographical Soc. 1967-77; Vice-Pres. Lavalin Inc. Consulting Engineers. *Leisure interests:* skiing, sailing, swimming. *Address:* Lavalin Inc., Royal Bank Centre, 90 Sparks Street, Ottawa, Ont., Canada.

CÂNDEA, Virgil; Romanian historian; b. 29 April 1927, Focşani; s. of Lucian Cândea and of Elena Cândea; m. Alexandrina M. Anastasiu 1957; two s. one d.; ed. Bucharest Univ.; head documentation dept. of the Romanian Acad. Library 1950-61; Dir. of Int. Assen. of South-East European Studies 1963-68; Prof. Institut Universitaire de Hautes Etudes Internationales, Geneva 1967-71; Sr. Fellow Inst. of South-East European Studies, Bucharest, 1968-; Gen. Sec. of Romania Assen. 1972-; Corresp. mem. Romanian Acad. of Social and Political Sciences 1970-; mem. Romanian Writers' Union 1971; Vice-Pres. Centro italo-rumeno di Studi Storici, Milan 1978-; Ordre du Cèdre Award (Lebanon); Prize of Romanian Acad. *Publications:* Pagini din istoria diplomaţiei româneşti (Pages from the History of Romanian Diplomacy) 1966, co-author; Stolnicul între contemporani (The High Steward Among Contemporaries) 1971; An Outline of Romanian History 1971; Raţiunea dominantă (The Prevailing Reason) 1979; co-author: Witnesses to the Romanian presence in Mount Athos 1979, Romanian Culture Abroad 1982, Présences culturelles roumaines 1985; critical editions of works by N. Bălcescu, A. Odobescu and D. Cantemir; Romanian translations from Nikitin, Bacon, Dante and others. *Leisure interests:* history, spirituality. *Address:* 5 Intr. Eminescu, 72111 Bucharest

(Office); 8 Intr. Cocora, 70262 Bucharest, Romania (Home). *Telephone:* 113557 (Office); 192063 (Home).

CANDELA (OUTERIÑO), Félix; Mexican builder, engineer and architect; b. 27 Jan. 1910, Madrid, Spain; s. of Félix Candela Magro and Julia Outeriño Echeverría; m. 1st Eladia Martin 1940 (died 1963); m. 2nd Dorothy Davies 1967; ed. Inst. de Cardenal Cisneros, Madrid, and Escuela Superior de Arquitectura, Madrid; service in Spanish Civil War on Republican side 1936–39; interned in France 1939; emigrated to Mexico 1939; supervision of architecture of La Colonia Santa Clara (Spanish Colony), Chihuahua 1939–40; draftsman Mexico City 1940; contractor Acapulco 1941; asst. architect, Mexico City 1942; partnership with his brother Antonio 1945–; first structure in thin-shell concrete 1949; established Cubiertas Alá, S.A. with his brother 1951; buildings include Cosmic Ray Pavilion, Ciudad Universitaria, Mexico 1950, Mexico City Stock Exchange, Church of San Antonio de las Huertas, Church of La Virgen Milagrosa, Lederle Laboratories, and warehouses, Sports Palace for 1968 Olympic Games, Mexico City; major exhbn. of his work, Univ. of South Calif. 1957; Prof., Escuela Nacional de Arquitectura, Mexico 1953–; Charles E. Norton Prof. of Poetry Harvard Univ. 1961–62; Jefferson Memorial Prof., Univ. of Virginia 1966; Andrew White Prof.-at-Large, Cornell Univ. 1969–74; Hon. Prof., Escuela Superior de Arquitectura de Madrid 1969; Prof. Dept. of Architecture, Univ. of Ill. at Chicago 1971–78; William Hoffman Wood Chair. of Architecture, Univ. of Leeds, England 1974–75; Hon. Prof., Univ. Nacional 'Federico Villareal', Lima 1977; mem. Sociedad y Colegio de Arquitectos Mexicanos, Colegio Oficial de Arquitectos de Madrid; Hon. mem. Sociedad de Arquitectos Colombianos, Sociedad Venezolana de Arquitectos and other societies; Hon. Fellow American Inst. of Architects 1963, Hon. Corresp. mem. R.I.B.A. 1963; Hon. D.F.A. (Univ. of New Mexico) 1964; Gold Medal Inst. of Structural Engineers 1961, Auguste Perret Prize of the Int. Union of Architects 1961, Gold Medal, Soc. of Mexican Architects 1963, and other awards. *Address:* P.O. Box 356, Bronxville, N.Y. 10708, U.S.A.; Avda America 14, Madrid 2, Spain.

CANDILIS, Georges; French architect; b. 11 April 1913, Baku, Russia; s. of Panayotis and Vera (née Skanavi) Candilis; m. Christiane Richard 1951; two s. one d.; ed. Athens Polytechnical School; architectural practice, Athens until 1940; fmr. Architect Greek Air Force, Asst. Prof. Athens Polytechnical School, Prof. Greek Nat. School of Building Technicians; Reserve Lieut. Greek Army 1940–45 (Cross of St. George); went to France 1945; Asst. to Le Corbusier, Paris and Architect of Le Corbusier's Housing Unit, Marseilles 1945–51; Dir. Atbat-Afrique Co., Casablanca 1951–54; Architectural practice, Paris 1956–, specializing in tropical architecture; Prof. Ecole Nat. Supérieure des Beaux-Arts 1963–; Pres. group of architects for the devt. of Languedoc-Roussillon seashore; Chief Architect Barcarès Leucate Tourist Station, Languedoc-Roussillon; Pres. Syndicat des Architectes de la Seine; mem. French Order of Architects and other professional orgs.; Hon. Fellow A.I.A.; Chevalier Légion d'honneur, Croix de guerre hellenique de l'ordre de Saint-Georges; many prizes. *Major works include:* new city of Bagnols sur Cèze; new city of Toulouse-Mirail; Free Univ. of Berlin; urban planning of Fort-Lamy (now N'Djamena) Chad, and numerous housing units, shopping centres, schools, hotels, etc. in France and abroad, including Algeria, Morocco, Iran, Tahiti and New Caledonia. *Address:* 18 rue Dauphine, 75006 Paris (Office); 17 rue Campagne-Première, 75014 Paris, France (Home). *Telephone:* 329.61.70 (Office).

CANEPA, Adolfo John; Gibraltar politician; b. 17 Dec. 1940, London; m.; three c.; ed. Gibraltar Grammar School, Univ. of Leicester and St. Mary's Coll. Twickenham; teacher 1964–69; Deputy Headmaster, Gibraltar Grammar School 1969–72; mem. House of Ass. 1972; Minister for Labour and Social Security 1972–81, also of Econ. Devt. and Trade 1980–81; Minister of Econ. Devt. and Trade 1981–87; Mayor of Gibraltar 1976–78; Chief Minister of Gibraltar 1987–88; Leader Gibraltar Labour Party Dec. 1987–. *Address:* 31 Governor's Parade, Gibraltar.

CANESTRI, H.E. Cardinal Giovanni; Italian ecclesiastic; b. 30 Sept. 1918, Alessandria; ordained 1941, elected to the titular Church of Tenedo 1961, consecrated Bishop 1961; transferred to Tortona 1971; prefect at the titular Church of Monterano 1975 with title of Archbishop; transferred to Cagliari 1984, Genoa 1987; cr. Cardinal 1987. *Address:* Arcivescovado, Piazza Matteotti 4, 16123 Genoa, Italy. *Telephone:* (010) 207 839.

CANETE, Alfredo; Paraguayan diplomatist; b. 14 March 1942, Asunción; m.; one s.; Sec. in Paraguayan Mission to UN 1961–62, Perm. Rep. to UN 1983–; Deputy Dir. Econ. Dept., Ministry of Foreign Affairs, then Dir. Dept. of Foreign Trade; Alt. Rep. to Latin-American Trade Asscn. 1973–78; Consul-Gen. and Chargé d'Affaires in U.K. 1978; Minister in Embassy, U.S.A. 1980–81; Amb. to Belgium, Netherlands and Luxembourg 1981–83; Head of Mission to EEC 1982–83; Cross of Kt., Order of Civil Merit, Spain. *Address:* Permanent Mission of Paraguay to the United Nations, Room 1206, 211 East 43rd Street, New York, N.Y. 10017, U.S.A.

CANETTI, Elias; British (b. Bulgarian of Spanish-Jewish descent) writer; b. 25 July 1905, Ruse (Ruschuk), Bulgaria; m.; ed. schools in England, Zürich, Frankfurt, Univ. of Vienna; family went to England 1911; settled in Vienna 1913; moved to France 1938, then London, England 1939–; writes in German; Nobel Prize for Literature 1981; Grosses Bundesverdienstkreuz

(Fed. Repub. of Germany) 1983. *Publications:* Hochzeit (Wedding) (play) 1932, Die Blendung (Auto da Fé) (novel) 1935, Komödie der Eitelkeit (The Comedy of Vanity) (play) 1950, Die Befristeten (The Deadlined) (play) 1956, Masse und Macht (Crowds and Power) (social psychology) 1960, Die Stimmen von Marrakesch (The Voices of Marrakesh) (travel book) 1967, Der andere Prozess (Kafka's Other Trial) (essay) 1969, Der Ohrenzeuge (Earwitness) 1974; Die gerettete Zunge (The Tongue Set Free) 1977 and Die Fackel im Ohr (The Torch in My Ear) 1980 (autobiog.), Das Augenspiel Lebensgeschichte (The Play of the Eyes) 1931–37 1985. *Address:* c/o C. & J. Worfers Ltd., 3 Regent Square, London, W.C.1 (Office); 8 Thurlow Road, Hampstead, London, N.W.3, England.

CANNON, Howard Walter, LL.B.; American lawyer and politician; b. 1912; s. of late Walter Cannon and Leah Sullivan; m. Dorothy Pace Cannon 1945; one s. one d.; ed. Arizona State Teachers' Coll. and Arizona Univ.; admitted to Arizona Bar 1937, to Utah Bar 1938, to Nevada Bar 1946; fmr. Reference Attorney, Utah State Senate and County Attorney, Washington County, Utah; City Attorney, Las Vegas 1949–59; Senator from Nevada 1959–83; Chair. Senate Cttee. on Rules and Admin. 1973–77, on Commerce, Science and Transportation 1978–80; Chair. Bd. of Dirs., Goldwater Scholarship and Excellence in Educ. Foundation; service with Air Force in Second World War, rising to rank of Maj.-Gen. U.S.A.F. Reserve; D.F.C., Air Medal with two Oak Leaf Clusters, American Defense Citation, Presidential Unit Citation, Croix de guerre with silver star, Purple Heart; Democrat. *Address:* Howard W. Cannon & Associates, 1919 Pennsylvania Avenue, N.W., Suite 400, Washington, D.C. 20006, U.S.A. (Office). *Telephone:* (202) 887-1417.

CANTACUZÈNE, Jean Michel, D.S.; French director of research; b. 15 Dec. 1933, Bucharest, Romania; s. of Dr Alexandre Cantacuzène and Marianne (née Labeyrie) Cantacuzène; m. 1st Anne-Marie Szekely 1956, 2nd Danièle Ricard 1971; two s. one d.; ed. Ecole Supérieure Chem. Industry, Lyon, Ecole Normale Superieure, Paris; Asst. Prof., Ecole Normale Supérieure, Paris 1960–62, Deputy Dir., Lab. Chimie 1964–67; Scientific attaché, French Embassy, Moscow 1962–64, Counsellor for Science and Tech., Washington, D.C. 1977–80; Prof. Organic Chem., Univ. of Paris 1967–73; Dir. Chem. Scientific Dept., CNRS Paris 1973–77, Counsellor for Industrial Affairs 1971–77; Scientific Dir. Total Co. Française des Petroles, Paris 1980–; Counsellor for Scientific Affairs, Ministry of Foreign Affairs, Paris 1971–77; Chair. Bd. SOLEMS 1983–86, AVRIST 1982–; mem. Advisory Comm. for Science and Tech. 1971–75, Industrial R and D Advisory Cttee., EEC, Brussels 1983–86, French Nuclear Safety Cttee., Paris 1982–, Industrial Innovation Cttee., Ministry of Industry, Paris 1989–; Le Bel Award 1968; Ordre Nat. Légion d'Honneur, Chevalier 1982, Ordre Nat. du Merite, Chevalier 1973, Officier 1988. *Publications:* Chimie Organique 3 Vols. (co-author) 1971–75, America, Science and Technology in the 80s, 2 Vols. 1981, over 60 papers in scientific journals. *Leisure interest:* book collecting. *Address:* Total CFP, 5 rue Michel Ange, 75781 Paris, Cedex 16 (Office); 9 avenue Constant Coquelin, 75007 Paris, France (Home).

CANTENOT, Jean; French engineer and business executive; b. 19 Sept. 1919, Paris; s. of Joseph and Marcelle (née Tournay) Cantenot; m. Nicole Berrier 1948; one d.; ed. Ecole Polytechnique and Ecole des Mines de Paris; dept. of iron-smelting, Ministry of Industry 1948–50; Chief Engineer, ARBED factory, Burbach-Saar 1950–57; Chief Engineer Schneider S.A. 1957–, Asst. Dir. 1963–68; Man. Dir., then Chair. Droitaumont-Bruville Mining Co. 1957–69; Chair. and Man. Dir. Aciéries de Pompey 1968–82; Chair. and Man. Dir. SACILOR (Steel Co.) 1980–83; Pres. Union des industries métallurgiques et minières 1973–85, Hon. Pres. 1985–, Lormines 1979–85; Chevalier, Légion d'honneur, Officier nationale du Mérite; Croix de guerre. *Address:* A.G.S., 8 rue de Lisbonne, 75008 Paris (Office); 1 rue Perronet, 92200 Neuilly-sur-Seine, Paris, France (Home).

CANTERBURY, Archbishop of (see Runcie, Most Rev. Robert Alexander Kennedy).

CANTO, Jorge del; Chilean economist; b. 1916; ed. Univ. de Chile and Univ. of Calif. (at Berkeley); officer, Chilean Foreign Office 1937–38; Adviser, Banco Central de Chile 1942–46; fmr. Prof. School of Econs. Univ. de Chile; Int. Monetary Fund 1946–; Dir. Western Hemisphere Dept. 1957–77. *Address:* 5412 Christy Drive, Washington, D.C. 20016, U.S.A.

CANTONI, Giulio L., M.D.; American laboratory chief; b. 29 Sept. 1915, Milan, Italy; s. of Umberto L. Cantoni and Nella Pesaro Cantoni; m. Gabriella S. Cantoni 1965; two d.; ed. Univ. of Milan, Italy; Instructor, New York Univ. 1943–45; Asst. Prof., Long Island Coll. of Medicine, New York 1945–48; Sr. Fellow, American Cancer Soc., New York 1948–50; Assoc. Prof., Western Reserve Univ., Cleveland, Ohio 1950–54; Chief, Lab. of Gen. and Comparative Biochemistry, Nat. Inst. of Mental Health 1954–; Distinguished Service Award, Dept. of Health and Human Services; mem. N.A.S. *Publications:* Onium compounds, in Handbook of Comparative Biochemistry (Eds. Florkin and Mason) 1960; papers in scientific journals. *Leisure interest:* chamber music. *Address:* National Institute of Mental Health, Building 36, Room 3D-06, Bethesda, Md. 20892, U.S.A. *Telephone:* (301) 496-3241.

CAO JIARUI; Chinese government official; Deputy Dir. Tech. Import and Export Dept., Ministry of Foreign Economic Relations and Trade 1984–.

Address: Ministry of Foreign Economic Relations and Trade, Beijing, People's Republic of China.

CAO KEQIANG; Chinese diplomatist; Counsellor, Embassy, Democratic People's Repub. of Korea 1957-60; Deputy Dir. Asia Dept., Ministry of Foreign Affairs 1961-72; Deputy Dir. W. Asia and N. Africa Dept., Ministry of Foreign Affairs 1972-74; Amb. to Syria 1974-78, to Sweden 1979-83, to France 1983-86; mem. Standing Cttee. CPPCC 1987-. *Address:* c/o Ministry of Foreign Affairs, Beijing, People's Republic of China.

CAO LUHE; Chinese government official; Dir. Exit-Entry Bureau, Ministry of Public Security 1986-. *Address:* Head Office, Gong An Ju, Beijing, People's Republic of China.

CAO YU; Chinese dramatist; b. 24 Sept. 1910, Hubei Prov.; m. 1st Zheng Xiu 1939 (divorced 1951), two d.; m. 2nd Deng Yisheng 1951 (died 1980), two d.; m. 3rd Li Yuni 1977; ed. Tsinghua Univ.; Chair. Chinese Dramatists' Asscn.; Vice-Pres. China Pen Centre 1982-; Pres. Beijing People's Art Theatre; *plays include:* Thunderstorm 1933, Bright Skies 1954, Wang Zhao Jun, Sunrise, Wildness. *Address:* Chinese Dramatists' Association, Beijing, People's Republic of China.

CAO YUANXIN; Chinese diplomatist; Amb. to Spain 1984-. *Address:* Embassy of the People's Republic of China, Arturo Soria 111-113, Madrid, Spain.

CAO ZHENFU; Chinese mathematician; b. 1962, Jiangsu Prov.; ed. Harbin Polytechnic Univ., Sichuan Univ. *Address:* Harbin Polytechnic University, Harbin, Heilongjiang Province, People's Republic of China.

CAO ZHENGWEN; Chinese writer; b. 14 Jan. 1950, Shanghai; m. Qimei Liu 1976; one d.; lecturer Fudan Univ. 1976-81; Ed. Xinmin Evening News 1981-; mem. Shanghai Writers Asscn.; Deputy Sec. Shanghai Essay Society. *Publications include:* Tang Bohu Failing in Imperial Examination, Puzzle of Men at the Age of 40, Golden Trap Purple Puzzle and numeraous other works. *Leisure interests:* reading, breeding birds, travelling. *Address:* Xinmin Evening News, Shanghai, People's Republic of China.

CAPLIN, Mortimer M., B.S., LLB., J.S.D.; American lawyer, educator and government official; b. 11 July 1916, New York; s. of Daniel Caplin and Lillian Epstein; m. Ruth Sacks 1942; three s. two d.; ed. Univ. of Virginia and New York Law School; law Clerk to U.S. Circuit Judge 1940-41; legal practice with Paul, Weiss, Rifkind, Wharton & Garrison, New York 1941-50; U.S.N.R., Beachmaster in Normandy landings 1942-45; Prof. of Law, Univ. of Virginia 1950-61, lecturer and Visiting Prof. 1964-87; Counsel to Perkins, Battle & Minor 1952-61; U.S. Commr. of Internal Revenue 1961-64; Partner, Caplin & Drysdale, Washington, D.C. 1964-; Chair. Nat. Civil Service League 1965-80, American Council on Int. Sports 1975-80, Nat. Citizens' Advisory Cttee. 1975-80, Asscn. of American Medical Colls.; Dir. Fairchild Industries Inc., Presidential Reality Corpn., Easco Hand Tools Inc.; mem. Public Review Bd., Arthur Andersen & Co.; mem. House of Dels., D.C. and Fed. Bar Asscns., Va and N.Y. State Bars, American Law Inst.; Ed.-in-Chief Virginia Law Review 1939-40; mem. Bd. of Trustees, George Washington Univ. and Coll. of the Virgin Islands, Univ. of Va. Law School Foundation, Arena Stage, Washington, D.C.; Hon. LL.D. (St. Michael Coll.) 1964; Order of the Coif, Raven Award, Alexander Hamilton Award, and other awards. *Publications:* Doing Business in Other States, Proxies, Annual Meetings and Corporate Democracy, and numerous articles on tax and corporate matters. *Leisure interests:* swimming, horseback riding, gardening. *Address:* 4536 29th Street, N.W., Washington, D.C. 20008, U.S.A. (Home); One Thomas Circle, N.W., Washington D.C. 20005, U.S.A. (Office). *Telephone:* (202) 244-3040 (Home); (202) 862-5050 (Office).

CAPO-CHICHI, Gratien Tonakpon; Benin diplomatist; b. 1938, Savalou; teacher, Lycée Michelet, Vanves 1963-64; teacher Lycée Technique Coulibaly, Cotonou 1964-75; Govt. Commr. Transit Operations, SOTRACOB 1975; Prefect of Oueme Prov. 1975-80; Minister for Literacy and Popular Culture 1980-84; lecturer Ecole Normale Supérieure, Nat. Univ. of Benin 1985-; Perm. Rep. to UN Feb. 1988-. *Address:* Permanent Mission of Benin, 4 East 73rd St, New York, N.Y. 10021, U.S.A. *Telephone:* (212) 249-6014.

CAPPELEN, Andreas Zeier; Norwegian lawyer and politician; b. 31 Jan. 1915, Vang, Hedmark; s. of Hans Blom Cappelen and Erna Margrethe Zeier; m. Olene Liberg; three s.; ed. Univ. of Oslo; Asst. District Court 1939-40, Barrister at Stavanger 1941-45, District Attorney, County of Rogaland 1945-47; Legal Lawyer and Asst. Chief of Wages to Municipal Authorities, Stavanger 1947-57, Deputy Mayor of Stavanger 1953, Sec. for Finance, Stavanger 1957-58; Minister for Municipal and Labour Affairs 1958-63, of Finance 1963-65; Sec. for Finance, Stavanger 1966-67, Judge, Stavanger 1967, Chair. of Bench 1969; Minister of Foreign Affairs 1971-72; Minister of Justice 1979-80. *Address:* c/o Ministry of Justice, Oslo, Norway.

CAPPELLO, Carmelo; Italian sculptor; b. 21 May 1912; m. Selene Varale Cappello; one s. one d.; ed. Istituto Superiore d'Arte di Monza; sculptor 1937-; regular exhibitor at Venice Biennali, Milan Triennali and Rome Quadriennali since 1947; represented in major collections and int. exhbns. throughout the world; mem. Nat. Cttee. of UNESCO Div. of Plastic Arts; mem. Accad. Nazionale di San Luca; numerous awards. *Major works:*

Freddoloso 1938, Uomo nello spazio 1955, Tempesta 1956, Cristo e i due ladroni 1955, Volo Stratosferico 1958, Il Folle 1948, Il Filosofo 1949, Tuffatori 1958, Gli Acrobati 1955, Eclisse 1959, Fughe ritmiche 1961, Involuzione del cerchio 1962, Fontana per curve d'acqua 1958, Ala 1960, Ritmi Chiusi 1963, Superficie-Spazio: Itinerario Circolare 1964, Traiet-toria Dal Piano Dello Spazio: 1965, Occhio di Cielo 1966, Cerchi in Movimento, Milan. *Address:* Via Melone 2, Milan, Italy. *Telephone:* 8058457 (Office); 8394658 (Home).

CAPPUCCILLI, Piero; Italian baritone opera singer; b. 9 Nov. 1929, Trieste; m. Graziella Bossi; ed. architectural studies in Rome; studied singing with Maestro Luciano Donaggio at Teatro Giuseppe Verdi, Trieste; debut as Tonio (I Pagliacci), Teatro Nuovo, Milan 1957; debut at La Scala Milan in Lucia di Lammermoor 1964; Covent Garden debut in La Traviata 1967; U.S. debut in I Due Foscari at Lyric Opera of Chicago 1969; appears at all leading Italian opera houses and major opera houses through the world; recordings include Lucia di Lammermoor (with Callas), La Gioconda, Aida, La Forza del Destino, Un Ballo in Maschera, Macbeth, Rigoletto. *Address:* c/o S. A. Gorlinsky Ltd., 33 Dover Street, London, W1X 4NJ, England.

CAPPUYNS, Baron Hendrik Frans Ferdinand, D. EN D.; Belgian business executive; b. 24 April 1913; s. of Hendrik and Maria Van Dingenen; m. Judith Smeets 1942; one s. one d.; ed. Univ. of Louvain; lawyer, Brussels bar 1936-37; Sec.-Gen. S.N.C.B., Brussels 1937-45; Sec.-Gen. Gevaert Photo-Producten N.V. 1945-52, Gen. Man. 1952-64, Man. Dir. 1957-81, Chair. 1975-85; Pres. Agfa-Gevaert N.V. (fmrly. Gevaert-Agfa N.V.), Mort-sel 1964-75, Vice-Pres. Agfa-Gevaert AG, Leverkusen 1964-71; Chair. Agfa-Gevaert Group 1971-75, Supervisory Bd. 1975-83; Chair. Ortelius 1957-, Uitgeversbedrijf Tijd 1969-84; Dir. Soc. Réunies d'Energie du Bassin de l'Escaut, EBES 1960-81; Dir. Royale Belge 1964-84, Vice-Pres. 1984-; Dir. Union Chimique Belge, UCB 1966-83; Dir. Vlaamse Uitgevers Maatschappij, VUM 1976-85; Censor Nat. Bank Belgium, Brussels 1962-67, Regent 1967-82, Hon. Regent 1982-; Dir. Foundation Industry-Univ. 1962-82; Dir. Nat. Investment Co. 1962-66; Dir. Nat. Co. for Credit to Industry 1964-66; Dir. Research Centre for Nuclear Energy 1975-81; Hon. Vice-Pres. Fed. of Belgian Industries; Hon. Pres. Vlaams Economisch Verbond VEV.; Dir. Group Bruxelles Lambert 1982-83, Cobepa N.V. 1982-88; mem. Supervisory Bd. Bayer 1982-87; Commdr. Ordre de la Couronne, Commdr. Ordre Léopold, Commdr. Ordre Léopold II, Officier Ordre Orange-Nassau. *Address:* Gevaert N.V., Septestraat 27, B-2510 Mortsel (Office).

CAPRA, Frank R.; American film director and producer; b. 18 May 1897, Palermo, Italy; s. of Salvatore Capra; m. Lucille Warner 1933; two s. one d.; ed. Calif. Inst. of Tech.; came to U.S.A. 1903; film dir. 1921-; served U.S. Army both World Wars; fmr. Pres. Acad. of Motion Picture Arts and Sciences, Screen Directors' Guild; Dir. Calif. Inst. Tech.; three Acad. Awards for best direction of year; Pres. Liberty Films Inc. (own co.); twice produced films which won Acad. Award as best picture of year; Life Achievement Award (American Film Inst.) 1982; Nat. Medal of Arts 1986. *Films produced, directed include:* Tramp, Tramp, Tramp 1926, The Strong Man 1926, Long Pants 1927, For the Love of Mike 1927, That Certain Thing 1928, Submarine 1928, Power of the Press 1928, The Donovan Affair 1929, Ladies of Leisure 1930, Platinum Blonde 1931, Forbidden 1932, American Madness 1932, Lady for a Day 1933, It Happened One Night (Acad. Awards for best picture and best dir.) 1934, Broadway Bill 1934, Mr. Deeds Goes to Town (Acad. Award for best dir.) 1936, Lost Horizon 1937, You Can't Take it With You (Acad. Awards for best picture and best dir.) 1938, Mr. Smith Goes to Washington 1939, Meet John Doe 1941, Why we Fight (propaganda series) 1941-45, Arsenic and Old Lace 1944, It's a Wonderful Life 1946, State of the Union 1948, Double Dynamite 1949, Riding High 1950, Here Comes the Groom 1951, A Hole in the Head 1959, Pocketful of Miracles 1961. *Publication:* The Name Above the Title 1971. *Address:* P.O. Box 980, La Quinta, Calif. 92253; and c/o Academy of Motion Picture Arts and Sciences, 8949 Wilshire Boulevard, Beverly Hills, Calif. 90211, U.S.A.

CAPRIA, Nicola; Italian politician and lawyer; b. 6 Nov. 1932, San Ferdinando di Rosarno, Reggio Calabria; joined Italian Socialist Party (PSI) 1953, mem. Cen. Cttee. 1968, subsequently mem. Nat. Exec.; Councillor, Messina 1964-70; Regional Deputy for Sicily 1967-76; Regional Sec. Italian Socialist Party 1974-; M.P. for Catania-Messina-Siracuse-Ragusa-Enna 1976-; Minister for Extraordinary Aid to Mezzogiorno (South) in second Cossiga Govt. and Forlani Govt.; Minister of Foreign Trade in first and second Spadolini Govts., fifth Fanfani Govt. and Craxi Govt.; Minister of Tourism 1986-87. *Address:* Camera dei Deputati, 00100 Rome, Italy.

CAPRIO, H.E. Cardinal Giuseppe, J.C.D., S.T.L.; Italian ecclesiastic; b. 15 Nov. 1914, Lapio, Avellino; ed. Diocesan and Regional Seminaries, Benevento, Pontifical Gregorian Univ., Rome, Pontifical Ecclesiastical Acad., Rome; ordained Roman Catholic Priest 1938; Attaché, Secretariat of State, Vatican City 1943-47; Sec., Apostolic Nunciature, Nanking, China 1947-51; Auditor, Apostolic Nunciature, Brussels, Belgium 1952-56; Apostolic Visitor to Repub. of Viet-Nam and later Regent of Apostolic Del. in Saigon 1956-59; Apostolic Nuncio to China, serving in Taiwan 1959-67; Titular Archbishop of Apollonia 1961; Apostolic Pro-Nuncio to India 1967-69; Sec. of Admin. of Patrimony of the Holy See 1969-77; Substitute of the

Secretariat of State 1977-79; Pres. of Admin. of the Patrimony of the Holy See 1979-81; Prefect of Vatican's Econ. Affairs Office 1981-; mem. Sacred Congregation for the Evangelization of Peoples, Pontifical Comm. for the Revision of Canon Law; created Cardinal 1979. *Address:* Office of Economic Affairs of the Holy See, 00120 Vatican City.

CAPRON, Alexander Morgan, LL.B; American professor of law; b. 16 Aug. 1944, Hartford, Conn.; s. of William M. and Margaret (Morgan) Capron; m. 1st Barbara A. Brown 1969 (divorced 1985); one s.; m. 2nd Kathleen M. West 1989; ed. Palo Alto High School, Swarthmore Coll. and Yale Law School; law clerk, U.S. Court of Appeals, D.C. Circuit 1969-70; Lecturer and Research Assoc. Yale Law School 1970-72; Asst. Prof. to Prof. of Law and Prof. of Human Genetics, Univ. of Pa. 1972-82; Exec. Dir. President's Comm. for Study of Ethical Problems in Medicine and Biomedical and Behavioural Research 1979-83; Prof. of Law, Ethics and Public Policy, Georgetown Univ. 1983-84; Topping Prof. of Law, Medicine and Public Policy, Univ. of Southern Calif. 1985-89, Univ. Prof. 1989-; Pres. American Soc. of Law and Medicine 1988-89; Chair. Bio-medical Ethics Advisory Cttee., U.S. Congress 1988-; several honours and awards. *Publications:* books including Catastrophic Diseases: Who Decides What? (with J. Katz) 1975, Law, Science and Medicine (with others) 1984, and 130 articles in journals and books. *Leisure interests:* swimming, films, travel. *Address:* The Law Center, University of Southern California, University Park, MC 71, Los Angeles, Calif. 90089-0071, U.S.A. *Telephone:* (213) 743-7734.

CAPUTO, Dante; Argentine professor and politician; b. 25 Nov. 1943, Buenos Aires; m. Anne Morel; three s.; ed. Salvador Univ. of Buenos Aires, Univ. of Paris, Univ. of Tuffs and Harvard, Boston; Adjunct Prof. of Political Sociology, Salvador Univ., Buenos Aires; Adjunct Prof. of Public Services and State Enterprises, Univ. of Buenos Aires; Dir. Center for Social Investigations on State and Admin. 1976; Adjunct investigator Nat. Center for Scientific Investigation, France; Minister of Foreign Affairs and of Worship Dec. 1983-. *Address:* Ministerio de Relaciones Exteriores y Culto, Reconquista 1088 C.P. 1003, Buenos Aires, Argentina.

CARADON, Baron (Life Peer), cr. 1964, of St. Cleer in the County of Cornwall; **Hugh Mackintosh Foot,** P.C., G.C.M.G., K.C.V.O., O.B.E. (brother of Lord Foot of Buckland Monachorum and Michael Foot, q.v.); British overseas administrator; b. 8 Oct. 1907, Plymouth; s. of Rt. Hon. Isaac Foot, P.C.; m. Sylvia Tod 1936 (died 1985); three s. one d.; ed. Leighton Park School, Reading and St. John's Coll., Cambridge; Pres. Cambridge Union 1929; Admin. Officer Palestine Govt. 1929-37; attached to Colonial Office 1938-39; Asst. British Resident, Transjordan 1939-43; British Mil. Admin., Cyrenaica 1943; Colonial Sec. Cyprus 1943-45; Colonial Sec. Jamaica 1945-47; Chief Sec. Nigeria 1947-50; Capt.-Gen. and Gov.-in-Chief of Jamaica 1951-57; Gov. and Commdr.-in-Chief of Cyprus 1957-60; U.K. Perm. Rep. UN Trusteeship Council 1961-62; Consultant to UN Special Fund 1963; Minister of State for Foreign Affairs and Perm. Rep. to UN Oct. 1964-70; Visiting Fellow at Princeton, Harvard and Georgetown Univs. 1977-79. *Publication:* A Start in Freedom 1964. *Address:* 203 Drake House, Dolphin Square, London, SW1V 3LX, England (Home). *Telephone:* 01-821 6550.

CARAZO ODIO, Rodrigo; Costa Rican politician; b. 27 Dec. 1926, Cartago; active mem. of Partido de Liberación Nacional (PLN) until resignation 1969, occupying posts as Dir. Nat. Inst. of Housing and Urbanization 1954-59, Adviser on Housing and Finance, Banco Obrero de Venezuela 1959-63, Dir. Banco Central de Costa Rica 1963-65; Deputy to Legislative Assembly of Costa Rica 1966, then Pres., Dir. Recope (state enterprise controlling distribution of petroleum products); founded Renovación Democrática, taking fourth place in presidential elections 1974; Leader of coalition party Unidad (Renovación Democrática, Republicano Calderonista, Unión Popular, Demócrata Cristiano) 1976-82; Pres. of Costa Rica May 1978-82; Prof. of Econs., Admin., Econ. Devt. and History, visiting lecturer to U.S.A. and South America; agricultural, commercial and industrial activities. *Address:* c/o Oficina del Presidente, San José, Costa Rica.

CARBERRY, H.E. Cardinal John J.; American ecclesiastic; b. 31 July 1904, Brooklyn; ordained 1929; Titular Bishop of Elis 1956; Bishop of Lafayette, Indiana 1957-65, of Columbus, Ohio 1965-68; Archbishop of St. Louis 1968-79; cr. Cardinal 1969; Pres. Cen. Applied Research in the Apostolate 1970-. *Address:* 4445 Lindell Boulevard, Saint Louis, Missouri 63108, U.S.A.

ÇARÇANI, Adil; Albanian politician; b. 5 May 1922, Fushë-Bardha; joined Albanian CP, now Albanian Party of Labour (APL) 1942; joined Nat. Liberation Army, became Deputy Commissar, Seventh Assault Brigade then Commissar of Fourth Div.; mem. People's Assembly 1950-; mem. APL Cen. Cttee. 1952-, mem. Politburo 1961-; Political Sec. APL Dist. Cttee. in Shkodër and Durrës 1945, then Gen. Sec. Prime Minister's Office, then Deputy Minister and Minister of Industry and Mining 1959-65; Deputy Chair. Council of Ministers 1965-82, Chair. Jan. 1982-. *Address:* c/o Council of Ministers, Tirana, Albania.

CARDEN, Joan Maralyn, A.O., O.B.E.; Australian opera singer; b. Melbourne; m. William Coyne 1962 (divorced 1980); two d.; ed. schools in Melbourne, language studies in London, Trinity Coll. of Music, London and London Opera Centre; voice studies with Thea Phillips and Henry Portnoj, Melbourne and Vida Harford, London; first opera engagement, world premiere of Williamson's Our Man in Havana, Sadler's Wells; joined The Australian Opera 1971; Covent Garden debut as Gilda (Rigoletto) 1974; Glyndebourne debut as Anna (Don Giovanni) 1977; U.S. debut at Houston as Amenaide (Tancredi) 1977; Metropolitan Opera Tour as Anna (Giovanni) 1978; perf. regularly in concert repertoire of Sydney Symphony Orchestra and Australian Broadcasting Comm.; Dame Joan Hammond Award for Outstanding Service to Opera in Australia 1987. *Leisure interests:* tennis, gardening, theatre, reading. *Address:* c/o Jenifer Eddy Artists' Management, Suite 11, 596 St. Kilda Road, Melbourne 3004, Vic., Australia.

CARDIFF, Jack; British film director and cameraman; b. 18 Sept. 1914; s. of John Joseph and Florence Cardiff; m. Julia Lily Mickleboro 1940; three s.; ed. various schools, including Medburn School, Herts.; began career as child actor 1918; switched to cameras 1928; asst. to many Hollywood cameramen 1936; world travelogues 1937-39; photographer for Ministry of Information Film Unit on War Dept. films, including Western Approaches 1942; films as cameraman include: Caesar and Cleopatra 1945, A Matter of Life and Death 1946, Black Narcissus 1946 (Academy Award, Golden Globe Award 1947), The Red Shoes 1948, Scott of the Antarctic, Under Capricorn, Black Rose, Pandora and the Flying Dutchman 1951, Magic Box, African Queen, War and Peace 1956, The Vikings 1958; began to direct films 1958; *films as director include:* Intent to Kill 1958, Beyond This Place 1959, Scent of Mystery 1960, Sons and Lovers 1960, My Geisha 1962, The Lion 1963, The Long Ships 1964, Young Cassidy 1965, The Liquidator 1967, The Mercenaries 1968, Girl on a Motor Cycle (also producer) 1969, The Mutation, Penny Gold 1974, Ride a Wild Pony 1976; Dir. of photography: The Prince and the Pauper, Beyond the Iron Mask, Death on the Nile, Avalanche Express, The Awakening, The Dogs of War, Ghost Story, Last Days of Pompeii, The Wicked Lady, Conan the Destroyer, Catseyes, First Blood II; TV includes: The Far Pavilions; Coup de Soir (France) 1951; Film Achievement Award, Look Magazine; B.S.C. Award for War and Peace; New York Critics Award for best film direction, Golden Globe Award for outstanding dir. for Sons and Lovers, Acad. Award for Black Narcissus; Hon. Dr. of Art, Rome 1953; Hon. mem. Assen. Française de Cameramen 1971. *Publication:* Autobiography 1975. *Address:* 32 Woodland Rise, London, N.10, England.

CARDIN, Pierre; French couturier; b. 2 July 1922, San Biagio di Callatla, Italy; fmrly. worked with Christian Dior; founded own fashion house 1949; founded Espace Pierre Cardin (theatre group); Dir. Ambassadeurs-Pierre Cardin Theatre (now Espace Pierre Cardin Theatre) 1970-; Chair. Maxims 1982-; Chevalier, Légion d'honneur 1974. *Publication:* Fernand Léger, Sa vie, Son oeurre, Son rêve 1971. *Address:* 59 rue du Faubourg-Saint-Honoré, 75008 Paris (Office); 11 quai Anatole-France, 75007 Paris, France (Home).

CARDINAL, Douglas Joseph, B.ARCH., F.R.A.I.C., R.C.A.; Canadian architect; b. 7 March 1934, Calgary, Alberta; s. of Joseph Treffle Cardinal and Frances Margarete Rach; m. Marilyn Zahar 1973; three s. two d.; ed. Univ. of Texas; design architect, Bissell & Halman, Red Deer 1963-64; Prin. Douglas Cardinal Architect, Red Deer 1964-67, Edmonton 1967-76, Douglas J. Cardinal Architect Ltd., Edmonton 1976-; major works include St. Mary's Church, Red Deer, Alberta, Grande Prairie Regional Coll., Grande Prairie, Alberta, Ponoka Provincial Bldg., Ponoka, Alberta, St. Albert Place, St. Albert, Alberta, Nat. Museum of Man, Hull, Quebec; awards include Honour Award, Alberta Assen. of Architects, for St. Mary's Church 1969 and Award of Excellence, Canadian Architect Magazine, for Grande Prairie Regional Coll. 1972. *Publications:* contribs. to Of the Spirit 1977 and Human Values: A Primary Motive in Planning 1981. *Address:* 6th Floor, 55 Murray Street, Ottawa, Ont. K1N 5M3, Canada.

CARDINALE, Claudia; Italian film actress; b. 15 April 1938, Tunis; d. of Franco and Yolanda Cardinale; m. Franco Cristaldi 1966; one s.; ed. Lycée Carnot and Collège Paul Cambon, Tunis; made first film 1958; awards include Nastro d'Argento, David di Donatello, Grolla d'Oro. *Films include:* 8½, The Pink Panther, The Leopard, The Professionals, Once Upon a Time in the West, Fury, The Magnificent Showman, La Scoumoune, Fitzcarraldo 1982, Le Ruffian 1982, History (TV), A Man in Love 1988. *Address:* via Flamina Km. 17,200, 1-0018 Rome, Italy.

CARDOSO E CUNHA, António José; Portuguese politician and agriculturist; worked in petrochem. industries, foreign trade and agric.; in Angola 1966-76; Sec. of State for Foreign Trade, Third Constitutional Govt., for Industries, Fourth Constitutional Govt.; mem. Assembly of the Repub., Social Democratic Party (PSD) Dec. 1979-; Minister of Agric. and Fisheries 1980-81; Commr. for Fisheries 1986-88, for Personnel and Admin., Energy, Small and medium-sized Business Jan. 1989-. *Address:* Commission of the European Communities, 200 rue de la Loi, 1049 Brussels, Belgium.

CARDWELL, John James, B.S., M.B.A.; American business executive; b. 3 Jan. 1931, New York; s. of John E. and Anne Boyle Cardwell; m. Mary Jean Carey 1956; two s. four d.; ed. U.S. Naval Acad., Harvard Business School; with McKinsey and Co. 1960-76, Prin. 1965-68, Dir. and Man. Dir. Chicago office 1968-76; Pres. and C.E.O. Consolidated Foods Corpn. 1976-. *Address:* 955 Hill Road, Winnetka, Ill. 60093, U.S.A. (Home). *Telephone:* (312) 726-6414 (Home).

CAREY, Hugh L., J.D.; American state governor; b. 11 April 1919, Park Slope, Brooklyn; s. of Margaret Collins and Dennis J. Carey; m. 1st Helen Owen Twohy 1945 (deceased); nine s. (two deceased) four d. one adopted d.; m. 2nd Evangeline Gouletas 1981; ed. St. Augustine's Acad., High School, Brooklyn, St. John's Univ.; served with U.S. Army in Europe 1939-46, rank of Lt.-Col.; joined family petrochemical business 1947; called to bar 1951; mem. U.S. House of Reps. rep. 12th Dist. of Brooklyn 1960-74, apptd. Deputy Whip, mem. House Educ. and Labour Cttee., House Cttee. on Interior and Insular Affairs, Senate-House Joint Econ. Cttee., Sub-cttee. on National Parks; Chair. Sub-cttee. on Territorial and Insular Affairs; mem. House Ways and Means Cttee. 1970; Gov., New York State 1974-83; Partner, Beer Sterns Feb. 1983-; Exec. Vice-Pres. W. R. Grace and Co, 1987; Bronze Star, Croix de guerre with Silver Star, Combat Infantryman's Badge; Democrat. *Address:* W. R. Grace and Co., 1114 Avenue of the Americas, New York, N.Y. 10036, U.S.A.

CAREY, John, M.A., D.PHIL., F.R.S.L.; British university professor and literary critic; b. 5 April 1934; s. of Charles William and Winifred Ethel (née Cook) Carey; m. Gillian Mary Florence Booth 1960; two s.; ed. Richmond and East Sheen County Grammar School, St. John's Coll., Oxford; served East Surrey Regt. 1953-54; Harmsworth Sr. Scholar, Merton Coll., Oxford 1957-58; lecturer, Christ Church, Oxford 1958-59; Andrew Bradley Jr. Research Fellow, Balliol Coll., Oxford 1959-60; Tutorial Fellow, Keble Coll., Oxford 1960-64, St. John's 1964-75; Merton Prof. of English Literature, Oxford Univ. 1976-. *Publications:* The Poems of John Milton (Ed. with Alastair Fowler) 1968, Milton 1969, The Violent Effigy: a Study of Dickens' Imagination 1973, Thackeray: Prodigal Genius 1977, John Donne: Life, Mind and Art 1981, The Private Memoirs and Confessions of a Justified Sinner, by James Hogg (Ed.), William Golding: The Man and His Books (Ed.) 1986, Original Copy: Selected Reviews and Journalism 1987, The Faber Book of Reportage (Ed.) 1987; articles in Review of English Studies, Modern Language Review, etc. *Address:* Brasenose Cottage, Lyneham, Oxon.; 57 Stapleton Road, Headington, Oxford, England. *Telephone:* Oxford 64304.

CAREY, Peter; Australian author; b. 1943; partner, McSpedden Carey Advertising Consultants, Sydney. *Publications:* The Fat Man in History (short stories) 1974 (in U.K. as Exotic Pleasures 1981), War Crimes (short stories) 1979, Bliss (novel) 1981, Illywhacker (novel) 1985, Oscar and Lucinda 1988 (Booker Prize for Fiction 1988). *Address:* c/o University of Queensland Press, P.O. Box 42, St. Lucia, Queensland 4067, Australia.

CAREY, Sir Peter Willoughby, G.C.B.; British business executive; b. 26 July 1923, London; s. of Jack Delves Carey and Sophie Searle; m. Thelma Young 1946; three d.; ed. Portsmouth Grammar School, Oriel Coll., Oxford and School of Slavonic Studies, London; Capt. Intelligence Corps 1943-45, Information Officer, Belgrade and Zagreb 1945-46; served in Foreign Office 1947-49, Bd. of Trade, Civil Service 1949-65, Royal Coll. of Defence Studies 1965; Asst. Sec. Bd. of Trade 1963-67, Under-Sec. 1967-69; Under-Sec. Ministry of Tech. 1969-71; Deputy Sec. Cabinet Office 1971-72; Perm. Sec. Dept. of Industry 1973-83; Dir. BPB Industries PLC 1983-, Cable and Wireless PLC 1984-; Chair. Dalgety PLC 1986-, Morgan Grenfell Group PLC 1987-; Hon. LL.D. (Birmingham). *Leisure interests:* music, theatre, travel, argument. *Address:* 23 Great Winchester Street, London E.C.2 (Office); 67 Church Road, London, S.W.19, England (Home). *Telephone:* 01-588 4545 (Office); 01-947 5222 (Home).

CARÍAS, Mario; Honduras diplomatist; b. 1 July 1941; m.; two c.; ed. San Miguel Salesian Inst., Tegucigalpa, Univs. of Barcelona and Paris, Acad. of Int. Law, The Hague; First Sec. in Embassy, Paris 1966-68, acting Chargé d'affaires 1968-71; Amb. to European Communities 1973-77; Perm. Rep. to UN, Geneva 1972-77, New York 1977-82; rep. to UNCTAD 1970 and 1976; Rep. to Gen. Assembly First Cttee. (Political and Security) and Second Cttee. (Econ. and Financial) 1971 and 1973; head of del. and Vice-Chair. of Drafting Cttee., Review Conf. of Parties to Treaty on Non-Proliferation of Nuclear Weapons 1975; Chair. of del. to 2nd, 3rd and 6th sessions, Third UN Conf. on the Law of the Sea 1974, 1975 and 1977; Vice-Pres., Trade and Devt. Bd. 1976; head of del. to UN Sugar Conf. April-May 1977; Chair. of "Group of 77" developing countries, Geneva, July-Sept. 1972, and Latin American Group May-June 1973. *Address:* c/o Ministry of Foreign Affairs, Tegucigalpa, Honduras.

CARL XVI GUSTAF; King of Sweden; b. 30 April 1946; s. of Prince Gustaf Adolf and Sibylla, Princess of Saxe-Coburg and Gotha; m. Silvia Sommerlath 1976; one s., Prince Carl Philip Edmund Bertil, b. 13 May 1979; two d., Crown Princess Victoria Ingrid Alice Désirée, b. 14 July 1977, and Princess Madeleine Thérèse Amelie Josephine, b. 10 June 1982; ed. in Sigtuna and Univ. of Uppsala; created Duke of Jämtland; became Crown Prince 1950; succeeded to the throne on death of his grandfather, King Gustaf VI Adolf 15 Sept. 1973. *Address:* Royal Palace, Stockholm, Sweden.

CARLI, Guido, D.IUR.; Italian economist and banker; b. 28 March 1914, Brescia; ed. Padua Univ.; Dir. Ufficio Italiano dei Cambi 1945; mem. Consulta Nazionale 1945; mem. Man. Bd. IMF 1947; Gen. Adviser Ufficio Italiano dei Cambi 1948; mem. European Payments Union Man. Bd. 1950-58, Pres. 1951-52; Pres. Mediocredito 1952, Consorzio Credito Opere Pubbliche 1959, Istituto Credito Imprese Pubblica Utilità 1959; Vice-Pres.

Istituto Mobiliare Italiano 1959, Ufficio Italiano dei Cambi 1959; Gen. Man. Banca d'Italia 1959-61, Gov. 1961; mem. Bd. Dirs. Bank of Int. Settlements 1960-70, Bd. European Monetary Agreement 1959-; mem. EEC Monetary Cttee. 1959-; Gov. for Italy Int. Bank for Reconstruction and Devt. 1962-75; Pres. Confindustria -1980; Pres. European Industrialists Fed., Brussels 1980-84; Adviser Robeco Group 1982-; M.P. 1983-; Minister of Foreign Trade 1957-58; Einaudi Prize 1964; Christian Democrat. *Publications:* Verso il multilateralismo degli scambi e la convertibilità delle monete, Evoluzione della legislazione italiana sul controllo degli scambi e dei cambi, Commercio Estero-Maggio 1957-Giugno 1958. *Address:* Viale Dell'Astronomia 30, 1-Rome, Italy.

CARLILE, Thomas, C.B.E., B.SC., F.C.G.I., F.ENG., F.I.MECH.E.; British engineer and company executive (retd.); b. 9 Feb. 1924, London; s. of James Love Carlile and Isobel Scott (Thompson) Carlile; m. Jessie Davidson Clarkson 1956; three d.; ed. Minchenden County School, City and Guilds Coll., London; joined Babcock and Wilcox Ltd. 1944, New York Rep. 1950-53, Asst. Gen. Works Man. 1953-60, Gen. Works Man. 1960-66, Man. Dir. 1968-83, Deputy Chair. 1978-84; Vice-Pres. Eng. Employers' Fed. 1979-84; Deputy Chair. Burnett and Hallamshire Holdings 1985-88 (Dir. 1984-); Dir. several cos. *Address:* 8 Aldenham Grove, Radlett, Herts., WD7 7BW, England (Home).

CARLIN, John William; American state governor; b. 3 Aug. 1940, Smolan, Kan.; s. of Jack W. and Hazel L. (Johnson) Carlin; m. 1st Ramona Hawkinson 1962, m. 2nd Karen Bigsby Hurley 1981; one s. one d., m. 3rd Diana Bartelli Prentice 1987; ed. Lindsborg High School, Kansas Univ.; farmer, dairyman, Smolan, Kan. 1962-; mem. Kan. House of Reps. for 93rd Dist. 1970-73, 73rd Dist. 1973-79, Minority Leader of House 1975-77, Speaker 1977-79; Gov. of Kansas 1979-87; Visiting Prof. of Public Admin. and Int. Trade Wichita State Univ. 1987-88; Visiting Fellow Kansas Univ. 1987-88; Pres. Econ. Devt. Assen. 1987-; fmr. Chair. Nat. Govs. Assen.; mem. Nat. Govs. Assen. (NGA) Exec. Cttee.; fmr. Chair. Midwestern Govs. Conf.; Hon. D.Iur. (Kansas); Democrat. *Leisure interests:* golf, swimming. *Address:* 700 Jackson, Suite 702, Topeka, Kan. 66603, U.S.A. (Office).

CARLISLE OF BUCKLOW, Baron (Life Peer) cr. 1987, of Mobberley in the County of Cheshire; **Mark Carlisle**, P.C., LL.B., Q.C., M.P.; British lawyer and politician; b. 7 July 1929; s. of Philip and Mary Carlisle; m. Sandra Des Voeux 1959, one d.; ed. Radley Coll., Manchester Univ.; called to the Bar, Gray's Inn 1953; M.P. for Runcorn 1964-83, for Warrington South 1983-87; mem. Home Office Advisory Council on the Penal System 1966-70; Joint Hon. Sec. Conservative Cttee. on Home Affairs 1965-69, Chair. 1983-87; Opposition Spokesman on Home Affairs 1969-70; Parl. Under-Sec. of State, Home Office 1970-72; Minister of State 1972-74; Sec. of State for Educ. and Science 1979-81; Recorder Crown Court 1976-79, 1981-; mem. Advisory Council, BBC 1975; Hon. Fellow, Coll. of Preceptors; Conservative. *Address:* House of Lords, Westminster, London, S.W.1, England (Office).

CARLSON, Edward Elmer; American airline executive (retd.); b. 4 June 1911, Tacoma, Wash.; s. of Elmer E. and Lula (Powers) Carlson; m. Nell Hinckley Cox 1936; one s. one d.; ed. Univ. of Washington; U.S. Navy 1942-46; Asst. to Pres. Western Int. Hotels 1946, Vice-Pres. 1947, Exec. Vice-Pres. 1953-61, Pres. 1961-69, Chair. and C.E.O. 1969-70, Chair. Exec. Cttee. 1971; mem. Bd. of Dirs. UAL Inc. Aug. 1970 (following merger of Western Int. Hotels and UAL, Inc.), Pres. and C.E.O. UAL Inc. and United Airlines 1970-75, C.E.O. 1975-83, Chair. 1979-83; Dir. Seattle First Nat. Bank, Dart Industries Inc., Deere and Co, Seafirst Corpn., First Chicago Corpn. (and its subsidiary First Nat. Bank of Chicago), etc.; Order of St. John of Jerusalem. *Leisure interests:* golf, sailing. *Address:* UAL Inc., P.O. Box 66919, Chicago, Ill. 60666 (Office); Boundary Lane, The Highlands, Seattle, Wash. 98177, U.S.A.

CARLSON, Robert J., B.A.; American executive; b. 12 Sept. 1929, Minneapolis, Minn.; s. of Carlyle R. Carlson, Jr., and Helen Wahl Carlson; m. Joann Ferguson 1952; three s. one d.; ed. Univ of Minnesota; served in various managerial positions in manufacturing, marketing and man. fields at Deere & Co. 1950-70, Sr. Vice-Pres. and Dir. 1970-79; Group Vice-Pres. United Technologies Corpn. and Pres. Pratt & Whitney Div. July-Nov. 1979; Exec. Vice-Pres. and Dir. United Technologies Corpn. 1979-83, Pres. May 1983-84; Pres., Chair. and C.E.O. BMC Industries Inc. 1985-. *Address:* BMC Industries Inc., Two Appletree Square, Bloomington, Minn. 55425, U.S.A.

CARLSSON, Ingvar Gösta, M.A.; Swedish politician; b. 9 Nov. 1934, Borås; m. Ingrid Melander 1957; two d.; ed. Lund Univ. and Northwestern Univ. U.S.A.; Sec. in Statsradsberedningen (Prime Minister's Office) 1958-60; Pres. Social Democratic Youth League 1961-67; Member of Parl. 1964-; Under Sec. of State, Statsradsberedningen 1967-69; Minister of Educ. 1969-73, of Housing and Physical Planning 1973-76, Deputy Prime Minister 1982-86, Minister of the Environment 1985-86, Prime Minister of Sweden March 1986-; mem. Exec. Cttee. Social Democratic Party, Chair. 1986-. *Address:* Statsrådsbereduingen, 10333 Stockholm, Sweden.

CARLSSON, Sten Carl Oscar, D.PHIL.; Swedish professor of history; b. 14 Dec. 1917, Uppsala; s. of Professor Gottfrid Carlsson and Lizzie Carlsson; m. Kerstin Wallstén 1945; one s. two d.; ed. Univ. of Lund; Docent in History, Lund Univ. 1945-56; Lecturer Gymnasium, Helsingborg 1953-56;

Prof. of History Uppsala Univ. 1956–83; Visiting Prof. Macalester Coll., St. Paul, Minn. 1969; Övralidspriset 1954, Zibets Pris, Swedish Acad. 1981, Commdr. White Rose of Finland 1986, Reltigska priset, Vi Herhetsakad 1988. *Publications:* Gustaf IV Adolf 1944, Ståndssamhälle och Ståndspersoner 1949, Lantmannapolitiken och Industrialismen 1953, Svensk Historia II 1961, Den Sociala Omgrupperingen i Sverige efter 1866 1966, Fröknar, Mamseller, Jungfrur och Pigor 1977, Anderstorp 1980, Swedes in North America 1638–1988, 1988. *Address:* Historiska Institutionen, St. Larsg. 2, S 75220, Uppsala (Office); St. Olofsgatan 12, S 75221, Uppsala, Sweden (Home). *Telephone:* 018 182500-1540 (Office); 018 146764 127760 (Home).

CARLUCCI, Frank Charles; American business executive and politician; b. 18 Oct. 1930, Scranton, Pa.; s. of Frank and Ruth Carlucci; m. 1st Jean Anthony 1954 (divorced 1974), one s. two d.; m. 2nd Marcia McMillan Myers 1974; ed. Princeton Univ. and Harvard Graduate School of Business Admin.; with Jantzen Co., Portland, Ore. 1955–56; Foreign Service Officer, Dept. of State 1956; Vice-Consul, Econ. Officer, Johannesburg 1957–59; Second Sec. Political Officer, Kinshasa 1960–62; Officer in charge of Congolese Political Affairs, Zanzibar 1962–64, Consul-Gen. 1964–65; Counsellor for Political Affairs, Rio de Janeiro 1965–69; Asst. Dir. for Operations, Office of Econ. Opportunity 1969–70, Dir. OEO 1970; Assoc. Dir. Office of Management and Budget 1971–72, Deputy Dir. 1972; Under-Sec. Dept. of Health, Educ. and Welfare 1972–74; Amb. to Portugal 1974–77; Deputy Dir. CIA 1977–81, Deputy Sec. of Defense 1981–82; Pres. C.O.O. Sears World Trade Inc. 1983–84, Chair. and C.E.O. 1984–86; Nat. Security Adviser to Pres. of U.S.A. 1986–87; Sec. of Defense 1987–89; Hon. D.Hum.-Litt.; Superior Service Award and Superior Honour Award, Dept. of State, Presidential Citizens Award, Distinguished Intelligence Medal and other awards. *Leisure interests:* tennis, swimming, jogging, squash.

CARLYLE, Joan Hildred; British soprano, b. 6 April 1931; d. of late Edgar J. Carlyle and Margaret M. Carlyle; m. Robert Duray Aiyar; two d.; ed. Howell's School, Denbigh, N. Wales; prin. Lyric Soprano, Covent Garden 1955–; *major roles sung in U.K. include:* Oscar, Ballo in Maschera 1957–58; Sophie, Der Rosenkavalier 1958–59; Nedda, Pagliacci (Zeffirelli production) 1959, Mimi, La Bohème 1960, Titania, Midsummer Night's Dream, Britten (Gielgud production) 1960, Pamina, Magic Flute 1962, 1966, Countess, Marriage of Figaro 1963, Zdenka, Arabella (Hartman Production) 1964, Suor Angelica 1965, Desdemona, Othello 1965, Arabella 1967, Marschallin, Der Rosenkavalier 1968, Jenifer, Midsummer Marriage 1969, Donna Anna 1970, Reiza, Oberon 1970, Adrianna Lecouvreur 1970, Russalka, Elizabetta, Don Carlos 1975; major roles sung abroad include Oscar, Nedda, Mimi, Pamina, Zdenka, Micaela, Donna Anna, Arabella, Elizabetta and Desdemona; debut at Salzburg, Metropolitan Opera, New York and Teatro Colón, Buenos Aires 1968; several recordings including Von Karajan's production of Pagliacci as Nedda and Midsummer Marriage as Jenifer. *Leisure interests:* gardening, travel, preservation of the countryside, interior design, cooking. *Address:* The Griffin, Ruthin, Clwyd, North Wales. *Telephone:* Ruthin 2792.

CARLZON, Jan, M.B.A.; Swedish airlines executive; b. 25 June 1941, Nyköping; ed. Stockholm School of Econs.; began career as Product Man. at Vingressor (tour operators and SAS subsidiary from 1971) 1967–74, Man. Dir. 1974–78; Pres. Linjeflyg (the domestic airline) 1978–80; C.O.O. SAS Airline 1980, C.E.O. and Pres. SAS Group 1981–; mem. of Bd. Linjeflyg, Enator, Pronator, Stockholms Fondkommission, Swedish Broadcasting Co.'s Friends of Music Radio, Swedish chapter of World Wildlife Fund; mem. Int. Air Transport Asscn.'s Exec. Cttee.; Pres. Swedish Br. Young Pres.'s Org.; co-owner Börsen nightclub; lectures overseas on man. and motivation issues. *Publication:* Moments of Truth. *Leisure interests:* golf, skiing, sailing. *Address:* Scandinavian Airlines System, Ulvsundavägen 193, 161 87 Stockholm-Bromma, Sweden.

CARMOY, Guy de, L. EN D., L. ÈS L.; French administrator and professor; b. 20 Feb. 1907, Paris; s. of Pierre de Carmoy and Marguerite Perquer; m. Marie de Gourcuff 1934; one s. three d. (one d. deceased); Insp. of Finances 1930–60; Gen. Information Commissariat 1939; Head of Film Dept., Ministry of Information 1940–41; Budgetary Controller 1941–43; deported to Germany 1943–45; Alt. Exec. Dir. Int. Bank for Reconstruction and Devt. 1946–48; mem. French del. for European Economic Co-operation 1948; Dir. of Admin. and Confs. Org. for European Economic Co-operation 1948–52; Prof. Inst. d'Etudes Politiques 1950–79; Prof. Inst. Européen d'Administration des Affaires (INSEAD, Fontainebleau, France) 1961–80, Prof. Emer. 1980–; Officier Légion d'honneur. *Publications:* Fortune de l'Europe 1953, Les politiques étrangères de la France (1944–66) 1967, Le dossier européen de l'energie 1971, Energy for Europe, Economic and Political Implications 1977, Western Europe in World Affairs (with Jonathan Story) 1986, 1987. *Leisure interest:* interior decoration. *Address:* 22 avenue de Suffren, 75015 Paris, France. *Telephone:* 45-67-12-73.

CARNÉ, Marcel; French film director; b. 18 Aug. 1906, Paris; s. of Paul Carné and Marie Racouët; took course for film technicians; work interrupted by military service; on discharge entered insurance business, later returned to film work; asst. operator for Les Nouveaux Messieurs 1928, asst. to Dir., Richard Oswald, for Cagliostro 1929; won competition for film criticism organized by Cinémagazine and joined editorial staff of this publication, directed Nogent, Eldorado du Dimanche 1929, assisted René

Clair in this direction of Sous les Toits de Paris 1930; wrote criticisms for various journals; Asst. Dir. to Jacques Feyder for Le Grand Jeu, Pension Mimosa, and La Kermesse Héroique; scored first great success as dir. with Jenny 1936; Commdr. Légion d'honneur; Commdr. Ordre des Arts et des Lettres; Grand Officier, Ordre national du Mérite; Membre de l'Institut, Prix Int., Venice Biennale 1938, 1953, Grand Prix de Cinéma 1958, Médaille de Vermeil 1972, Grand Prix Oecuménique, Cannes 1977, César des Césars 1979, Lion d'Or de Venise 1982; BFI Fellowship 1983. *Films include:* Drôle de drame 1937, Quai des brumes 1938, Le jour se lève 1939, Les visiteurs du soir 1941, Les enfants du Paradis 1943, Les portes de la nuit 1946, La Marie du port 1949, Juliette ou la clé des songes 1950, Thérèse Raquin 1953, L'air de Paris 1954, Le pays d'où je viens 1956, Les tricheurs 1958, Terrain vague 1960, Du mouron pour les petits oiseaux 1963, Trois chambres à Manhattan 1965, Les jeunes loups 1968, Les assassins de l'ordre 1970, La merveilleuse visite 1974, La Bible 1976. *Publication:* La vie à belles dents (autobiog.) 1975. *Address:* 16 rue de l'Abbaye, 75006 Paris, France. *Telephone:* 46 34 21 64.

CARNEGIE, Sir Roderick Howard, Kt., B.SC., M.A., M.B.A., F.T.S.; Australian mining executive; b. 27 Nov. 1932, Melbourne; s. of D. H. Carnegie; m. Carmen Clarke 1959; three s.; ed. Trinity Coll. Melbourne Univ., New Coll., Oxford, Harvard Business School; Assoc. McKinsey and Co., Melbourne and New York 1959–64, Prin. Assoc. 1964–68, Dir. 1968–70; Dir. Conzinc Riotinto of Aust. Ltd. (now CRA Ltd.) 1970–, Joint Man. Dir. 1971–72, Man. Dir. and Chief Exec. 1972–74, Chair. and Man. Dir. 1974–83, Chair. and Chief Exec. 1983–86; Dir. Comalco Ltd., CRA Ltd., Rio Tinto-Zinc Corpn. Ltd.; Chair. Consultative Cttee. on Relations with Japan 1984–; Pres. Business Council of Australia 1986–; Vice-Pres. Australian Mining Industry Council; mem. Int. Council Morgan Guaranty Trust, The Asia Soc., The Brookings Inst.; mem. IBM World Trade Asia/Pacific Group Bd.; Hon. D.Sc. *Address:* CRA Ltd., 55 Collins Street, Melbourne, Vic. 3000, Australia (Office). *Telephone:* 658 3311.

CARNEY, David PH.D., M.A., M.SC., DIP. PUB. ADMIN.; Sierra Leonean economist, administrator, teacher; b. 27 May 1925, Freetown; s. of David Edward and Esther Victoria Carney; m. 1st Helen Elizabeth Smith-Hall 1960 (deceased), one s. one d.; m. 2nd Ellen Ernst Gillespie; ed. Fourah Bay Coll., Sierra Leone, Univ. of Pennsylvania and School of Advanced Int. Studies, Johns Hopkins Univ., U.S.A.; lecturer, Fourah Bay Coll., Sierra Leone 1945–47; Statistician, Dept. of Statistics, Govt. of Nigeria, Lagos, and lecturer, Extra-Mural Dept., Univ. of Ibadan 1948–52; Headmaster, Ghana Nat. Coll., Cape Coast, Ghana 1952–53; lecturer, Lincoln Univ., Franklin and Marshall Coll., Pa., Fairleigh Dickinson Univ., N.J. 1953–58; Econ. Affairs Officer, Dept. of Econ. and Social Affairs, UN, New York 1958–60; Asst. Prof. of Econs., Antioch Coll., Yellow Springs, Ohio 1960–61; Econ. Adviser, Govt. of Sierra Leone 1961–63; UN African Inst. for Econ. Devt. and Planning, Dakar, Senegal 1963–70, Project Man. and Dir. 1967–70; Chair. Comm. on Higher Educ. Sierra Leone 1969, East African Community 1970–72; Deputy Chief Economist 1970–72; UN Econ. Devt. Planning Advisor, St. Lucia 1973–75; Head Econ. Devt. Unit, onchocerciasis control programme 1976–78; Sr. Devt. Adviser Lake Chad Basin Comm. 1978–; mem. Governing Bd. UNESCO Int. Inst. for Educational Planning 1970–73. *Publications:* Government and Economy in British West Africa 1961, A Ten-Year Plan of Economic and Social Development for Sierra Leone 1962/3–1971/2 1962, Patterns and Mechanics of Economic Growth 1967; numerous papers in nat. and int. journals. *Leisure interests:* writing poetry, stamp collecting. *Address:* 101 Regent Road, Freetown, Sierra Leone.

CARNEY, Patricia, M.A.; Canadian politician and economist; b. 26 May 1935, Shanghai, China; m.; two c.; ed. Univ. of British Columbia, British Columbia School of Community and Regional Planning; fmrly. econ. journalist and socio-econ. and communications consultant; first elected M.P. 1980, fmrly. Caucus Spokesperson for Energy, Mines and Resources, for Finance, fmr. Minister of State (Finance), Sec. of State, fmr. mem. Standing Cttee. on Finance, on Trade and Econ. Affairs, on Communications and Culture, on Justice and Legal Affairs; Minister of Energy, Mines and Resources 1984–86, of Int. Trade 1986–88; Pres. of Treasury Bd. 1988–; mem. Asscn. Professional Economists, B.C., Canadian Econs. Asscn., Inst. of Planners, Int. Inst. of Planners. *Address:* House of Commons, Ottawa, Ont., K1A 0A2, Canada.

CARNLEY, Most Rev. Peter Frederick, D.D., PH.D.; Australian archbishop and theologian; b. 17 Oct. 1937, New Lambton, N.S.W.; s. of F. Carnley; m. Carol Ann Dunstan, 1966; one s. one d.; ed. St. John's Theological Coll., N.S.W., Trinity Coll. Melbourne Univ., St. John's Coll., Univ. of Cambridge; Deacon 1962; Priest 1964; Chaplain Mitchell Coll. of Advanced Educ., N.S.W. 1970–72; Research Fellow St. John's Coll., Cambridge 1971–72; Warden St. John's Coll., Univ. of Queensland 1978–81; Anglican Archbishop of Perth and Metropolitan of the Province of Western Australia 1981–. mem. Archbishop of Canterbury's Comm. on Communion and Women in the Episcopate 1988. *Publications:* The Poverty of Historical Scepticism; in Christ, Faith and History 1972, The Structure of Resurrection Belief 1987. *Leisure interests:* gardening, music. *Address:* P.O. Box W2607, Perth, Western Australia 6001; 52 Mount Street, Perth, Western Australia 6000.

CARO, Sir Anthony, Kt., C.B.E., M.A.; British sculptor; b. 8 March 1924, London; s. of Alfred and Mary Caro; m. Sheila Girling 1949; two s.; ed. Charterhouse School, Christ's Coll., Cambridge, Regent St. Polytechnic and Royal Acad. Schools, London; Asst. to Henry Moore 1951–53; Part-time Lecturer St. Martin's School of Art, London 1953–79; taught at Bennington Coll. Vermont 1963–65; one-man exhbn. in Milan 1956, others subsequently in London, Washington, Toronto, New York, Houston, Hamburg, Zürich and in Netherlands, Japan, N.Z. and Australia; retrospective exhbn. Arts Council (Hayward Gallery, London) 1969; works in Tate Gallery, Arts Council, Museum of Modern Art (New York), Brandeis Univ. (Boston), Albright Knox Museum, Buffalo, N.Y., Cleveland Museum Ohio, Rijksmuseum Kroller-Muller (Otterloo, Netherlands); retrospective exhbn. (Sept. 1975–May 1976) Museum of Modern Art, New York, Walker Art Center, Minneapolis, Houston Museum of Fine Art, Boston Museum of Fine Art; Arts Council of G.B. touring collection 1982–83; initiated Triangle Summer Workshop, Pine Plains, New York 1982; presented keys of New York 1976; undertook commission for new East Building, Nat. Gallery of Art, Washington, D.C., 1977; Hon. Fellow, Christ's Coll. Cambridge 1981, R.C.A., London 1986; Trustee, Tate Gallery 1982, Fitzwilliam Museum, Cambridge 1984; Hon. D.Litt. (E. Anglia, York Univ., Toronto, Cambridge, Surrey); Sculpture Prize, Paris Biennale 1959, David E. Bright Award, Venice Biennale 1967; Prize for Sculpture, São Paulo Biennale 1969. *Leisure interest:* listening to music. *Address:* 111 Frognal, Hampstead, London, N.W.3, England (Home).

CARO, David Edmund, A.O., O.B.E., M.SC., PH.D., F.INST.P., F.A.I.P., F.A.C.E.; Australian university vice-chancellor (retd.); b. 29 June 1922, Melbourne; s. of George and Alice Caro; m. Fiona Macleod 1954; one s. one d.; ed. Geelong Grammar School, Univs. of Melbourne and Birmingham; war service, R.A.A.F. 1941–46; Demonstrator in Physics, Univ. of Melbourne 1947–49, Lecturer 1952, Sr. Lecturer 1954, Reader 1958, Prof. of Experimental Physics and Head of Dept. of Physics 1961–72, Deputy Vice-Chancellor 1972–77, Vice-Chancellor and Prin. 1982–87; Vice-Chancellor, Univ. of Tasmania 1978–82; Chair. Antarctic Research Policy Advisory Cttee. 1979–84, Australian Vice-Chancellors Cttee. 1982–83, Melbourne Theatre Co. 1982–87, S.S.A.U. Nominees Pty. Ltd. 1984–; Dir. Melbourne Business School Ltd.; mem. Council Asscn. Commonwealth Univs. 1982–84, Royal Melbourne Hosp. Cttee. of Man. 1982–86, Amalgamated Melbourne and Essendon Hosps. Cttee. of Man. 1986–; Interim Vice-Chancellor, N. Territory Univ. 1988–89; Pres. Victorian Coll. of the Arts 1989–; Exhbn. of 1851 Overseas Research Scholar 1949–51; Hon. LL.D. (Melbourne) 1978, (Tasmania) 1982; Hon. D.Sc. (Melbourne) 1987. *Publication:* Modern Physics (co-author) 1961. *Leisure interests:* skiing, gardening, theatre. *Address:* 17 Fairbairn Road, Toorak, Vic. 3142, Australia. *Telephone:* 241-2004.

CARON, Leslie Clair Margaret; French ballet dancer and actress; b. 1 July 1931, Boulogne-Billancourt; m. 1st George Hormel; m. 2nd Peter Reginald Frederick Hall (q.v.) 1956 (dissolved 1965), one s. one d.; m. 3rd Michael Laughlin 1969; ed. Convent of the Assumption, Paris, and Conservatoire de Danse; with Ballet des Champs Elysées 1947–50, Ballet de Paris 1954. *Films include:* An American in Paris, Man with a Cloak, Glory Alley, Story of Three Loves, Lili, Glass Slipper, Daddy Long Legs, Gaby, Gigi, The Doctor's Dilemma, The Man Who Understood Women, The Subterranean, Fanny, Guns of Darkness, The L-Shaped Room, Father Goose, A Very Special Favor, Promise Her Anything, Is Paris Burning?, Head of the Family, Madron, The Contract, The Unapproachable 1982, Deathly Moves 1983, Génie du Faux 1984, The Train 1987; stage appearances in Paris, London, U.S.A. and Australia. *Publication:* Vengeance 1983. *Address:* c/o Hugh J. Alexander International Artists Representation, 4th Floor, 235 Regent Street, London, W1R 8RU, England.

CARPENTER, Leslie Arthur; British business executive; b. 26 June 1927; s. of William Carpenter and Rose Carpenter; ed. Hackney Tech. Coll.; Dir. Country Life 1965, George Newnes 1966; Man. Dir. Odhams Press Ltd. 1968; Dir. Int. Publishing Corpn. 1972, Reed Int. 1974, IPC (America) Inc. 1975; Chair. Reed Holdings Inc. 1977, Reed Publishing Holdings Ltd. 1981; Chair. and Chief Exec. IPC Ltd. 1974; Chief Exec. Publishing and Printing, Reed Int. Ltd. 1979; Chief. Exec. Reed Int. PLC 1982–86, Chair. 1985–. *Leisure interests:* racing, gardening. *Address:* Reed International PLC, Reed House, Piccadilly, London, W1A 1EJ, England.

CARPINO, H.E. Cardinal Francesco; Italian ecclesiastic; b. 18 May 1905; Ordained Priest 1927; Titular Archbishop of Nicomedia 1951; Titular Archbishop of Sardica 1961; Archbishop of Palermo 1967–70; Titular Bishop of Albano; Assessor, Sacred Congregation of Bishops 1970–; created Cardinal by Pope Paul VI 1967. *Address:* Piazza St. Calisto 16, 1-00153 Rome, Italy.

CARPIO-CASTILLO, Ruben, PH.D.; Venezuelan diplomatist; b. 5 Aug. 1925; m.; three c.; ed. Instituto Pedagogico, Caracas, Univ. of Boston, Universidad Central de Venezuela; Prof. at Instituto Pedagogico de Caracas 1954–, Chief of Dept. of Social Sciences 1961–68; faculty mem., Universidad Central 1958, Dir., School of Geography 1974–; Deputy, Guarico State Legislative Council 1947; Deputy, Nat. Congress 1964–68, 1969–74; fmr. mem. Foreign Affairs Cttee., Chamber of Deputies; alt. Senator (until 1979); Amb. to Canada 1974–77, to Spain 1977–78; Perm. Rep. to UN 1978–79; mem. Congress of the Interparl. Union 1964–74, del. to Third UN Conference on the Law of the Sea 1974. *Publications:* (author or co-

author); Mexico, Cuba y Venezuela: Triangulo Geopolitico del Caribe 1962, Geografia de Venezuela, vol. II 1965, El Golfo de Venezuela: Mar Territorial y Plataforma Continental 1970, Accion Democratica, Bosquejo Historico de un Partido 1971, Humboldt, Caldes, Codazzi; Sintesis Geografica de America Latina 1973. *Address:* c/o Ministerio de Relaciones Exteriores, Caracas, Venezuela.

CARR, Sir (Albert) Raymond (Maillard), Kt., M.A., D.LITT., F.R.S.L., F.R.HIST.S., F.B.A.; British historian; b. 11 April 1919, Bath; s. of Reginald Henry Maillard Carr and Ethel Gertrude Marion Carr; m. Sara Ann Mary Strickland 1950; three s. one d.; ed. Brockenhurst School and Christ Church Oxford; Gladstone Research Exhibitioner, Christ Church 1941; Fellow All Souls Coll. Oxford 1946–53, New Coll. 1953–64; Dir. Latin American Centre 1964–68, Chair. Soc. for Latin American Studies 1966–68; Prof. of History of Latin America, Oxford Univ. 1967–68, Warden St. Antony's Coll. 1968–87; mem. Nat. Theatre Bd. 1980; Corresp. mem. Royal Acad. of History, Madrid 1968–77; Hon. Fellow Christ Church Coll., Oxford; Exeter Univ.; Grand Cross of the Order of Alfonso El Sabio (for services to Spanish history) 1983. *Publications:* Spain 1808–1939 1966, Latin American Affairs 1969, The Spanish Civil War 1971, English Fox Hunting 1976, The Spanish Tragedy: the Civil War in Perspective 1977, Spain: Dictatorship to Democracy 1979, Modern Spain 1980, Fox-Hunting 1982, Puerto Rico: A Colonial Experiment 1984. *Leisure interest:* foxhunting. *Address:* Burch, North Molton, South Molton, EX36 3JU, England. *Telephone:* (07697) 267.

CARR, Col. Gerald Paul, D.SC.; American astronaut and engineer; b. 22 Aug. 1932, Denver, Colo.; s. of the late Thomas E. Carr and Freda L. Carr (née Wright); m. JoAnn R. Petrie 1954 (dissolved); three s. three d.; m. 2nd Dr. Patricia L. Musick, 14 Sept. 1979; ed. Univ. of S. Calif., U.S. Naval Postgraduate School and Princeton Univ.; entered U.S. Navy 1949, commissioned U.S. Marine Corps 1954; selected as NASA astronaut April 1966; mem. astronaut support crew, Apollo VIII and XII flights; commdr. of Skylab III, launched Nov. 1973 on 84-day mission; retd. from U.S. Marine Corps 1975; retd. from NASA 1977; Sr. Vice-Pres. Bovay Engineers Inc. 1977–82; Sr. Consultant Applied Research Inc. 1982–84; Man. 7.6 m. Telescope Project, McDonald Observatory, Univ. of Tex. 1983–86; Vice-Pres. CAMUS Inc. 1984–; Dir. Houston POPS Orchestra, Space Foundation, Space Dermatology Foundation; Registered Professional Engineer (Tex.); Hon. D.Sc. (Parks Coll., St. Louis Univ.); U.S. Navy D.S.M., NASA D.S.M., F.A.I. Gold Medals, Komarov Diploma, Collier Trophy, Haley Astronautics Award, other mil. decorations and numerous awards. *Leisure interests:* woodworking, fishing, bird hunting. *Address:* CAMUS Inc., P.O. Box 919, Huntsville, Ark. 72740, U.S.A. *Telephone:* (713) 880-4592.

CARR, Jack, D.PHIL., F.R.S.E.; British mathematician; b. 29 Aug. 1948, Newcastle upon Tyne; s. of John George Carr and Elizabeth Eleanor Carr; m. Teresa Nancy Thorpe 1976; one s. two d.; ed. Walbottle Secondary School, Univ. of Bath, St. Catherine's Coll., Oxford; Lecturer, Heriot-Watt Univ., Edin. 1974–83, Reader in Math. 1983–; Visiting Prof., Brown Univ., U.S.A. 1978–79, Mich. State Univ., U.S.A. 1982, Ecole Polytechnique, Lausanne, Switzerland 1983. *Publication:* Applications of Centre Manifolds 1981. *Leisure interests:* spreading urban myths, playing cricket for the W.C.C. *Address:* 42 Balgreen Avenue, Edinburgh, EH12 5SU, Scotland.

CARR, Willard Zeller Jr., B.S., J.D.; American attorney; b. 18 Dec. 1927, Richmond, Ind.; s. of Willard Z. Carr and Susan E. Brownell Carr; m. Margaret Paterson Carr 1952; two s.; ed. Purdue Univ., Indiana Univ. School of Law; Capt. Judge Advocate Gen.'s Dept. U.S.A.F. 1951–52; partner Gibson, Dunn & Crutcher, Attorneys 1952–; admitted to U.S. Supreme Court 1963–; mem. Los Angeles County Bar Asscn., Calif. State Bar Asscn., American Bar Asscn., Int. Bar Asscn. (Chair. Labour Law Cttee. 1973–83); on Bd. of Visitors Southwestern Univ. Law School; on Advisory Council Int. and Comparative Law Center, Southwestern Legal Foundation; mem. Nat. Panel of Arbitrators, American Arbitration Asscn., World Affairs Council, Republican State Cen. Cttee. for Calif.; recipient of Jurisprudence Award from the Anti-Defamation League 1987. *Publications:* International Handbook on Contracts of Employment 1976, Symposium on Private Investments Abroad—Problems and Solutions in International Business 1982; numerous specialist articles. *Leisure interests:* tennis, travel. *Address:* 333 South Grand Avenue, 49th floor, Los Angeles, Calif. 90071, U.S.A. *Telephone:* (213) 229-7238.

CARR OF HADLEY, Baron (Life Peer), cr. 1975, of Monken Hadley in Greater London; **(Leonard) Robert Carr,** P.C., M.A.; British politician and business executive; b. 11 Nov. 1916, London; s. of Ralph Edward and Katie Elizabeth Carr; m. Joan Kathleen Twining 1943; one s. (deceased) two d.; ed. Westminster School and Gonville and Caius Coll., Cambridge; M.P. 1950–75, Parl. Pvt. Sec. to Sec. of State for Foreign Affairs 1951–55, to Prime Minister April-Dec. 1955, Parl. Sec. Ministry of Labour and Nat. Service 1955–58, Sec. for Tech. Co-operation May 1963–Oct. 1964; Sec. of State for Employment 1970–72; Lord Pres. of Council and Leader of House of Commons April-Nov. 1972; Sec. of State Home Dept. 1972–74; joined John Dale Ltd. 1938, Chief Metallurgist 1945–48, Dir. of Research and Development 1948–55, Chair. 1959–63 and 1965–70; Dir. Carr, Day & Martin Ltd. 1947–55, Isotope Developments Ltd. 1950–55; Deputy Chair. and Joint Man. Dir. Metal Closures Group Ltd. 1960–63, Dir. 1965–70; Dir. Scottish Union and Nat. Insurance Co. (London) 1958–63; Dir. S. Hoffnung and Co. 1963, 1965–70, 1974–80, Securicor Ltd. 1965–70, 1974–85; Norwich Union Insurance Group (London) 1965–70, 1974–76; Dir. S.G.B. Group Ltd. 1974–86; Dir. Prudential Assurance Co. 1976–85, Deputy Chair. 1979–80, Co-Chair. 1980–85; Dir. Prudential Corpn. Ltd. 1978–89, Deputy Chair. 1979–80, Chair. 1980–85; Dir. Cadbury Schweppes Ltd. 1979–87; mem. Political Honours Scrutiny Cttee. 1977–87; Fellow, Imperial Coll., London 1985; Conservative. *Publications:* Co-author One Nation 1950, Change is our Ally 1954, The Responsible Society 1958, One Europe 1965. *Leisure interests:* lawn tennis, gardening, music. *Address:* House of Lords, Westminster, London, S.W.1 (Office); 14 North Court, Great Peter Street, London, S.W.1, England (Home).

CARRANZA, Roque Guillermo, PH.D.; Argentine politician; b. 29 Sept. 1919, Buenos Aires; ed. Nat. Univ. of Buenos Aires; Adjunct Prof. in Math., Univ. of Buenos Aires; Tech. Sec. of Argentine Devt. Nat. Council 1963–66; consultant for the Econ. Dept. of UN 1967–68; consultant UN Devt. Program; consultant Org. of American States; consultant Cartagena Agreement Junta; Defense Minister 1983–86. *Address:* c/o Ministerio de Defensa, Avenida Paseo Colón 255 C.P. 1330, Buenos Aires, Argentina.

CARRELL, Robin Wayne, CH.B., M.SC., M.A., PH.D., F.R.A.C.P., F.R.S.N.Z.; New Zealand professor of haematology; b. 5 April 1936, Christchurch; s. of Ruane George Carrell and Constance Gwendoline (née Rowe) Carrell; m. Susan Wyatt Rogers 1962; two s. two d.; ed. Christchurch Boys' High School, Univ. of Otago, Univ.of Canterbury and Univ. of Cambridge; mem. MRC Haemoglobin Unit, Cambridge 1965–68; Dir. Clinical Biochemistry Christchurch Hosp., N.Z. 1968–75; lecturer Clinical Biochemistry Univ. of Cambridge 1976–86, Prof. of Haematology 1986–; Prof. of Clinical Biochemistry and Dir. Molecular Research Lab. Christchurch Clinical School of Medicine, Otago Univ. 1978–86; Commonwealth Fellow St. John's Coll., Cambridge and Visiting Scientist MRC Lab. of Molecular Biology 1985; Fellow Trinity Coll., Cambridge 1987–; Hector Medal (Royal Soc. of N.Z.) 1986. *Publications:* articles in scientific journals on genetic abnormalities of human proteins and new protein family, serpins. *Leisure interests:* gardening and walking. *Address:* 19 Madingley Road, Cambridge, CB3 OEG, England. *Telephone:* (0223) 312 970.

CARRERAS, José; Spanish tenor; b. 5 Dec. 1947, Barcelona; s. of José Carreras and Antonia Carreras; m. Ana Elisa Carreras; one s. one d.; opera début as Gennaro in Lucrezia Borgia, Liceo Opera House, Barcelona 1970–71 season; appeared in La Bohème, Un Ballo in Maschera, I Lombardi alla Prima Crociata at Teatro Regio, Parma, Italy 1972; U.S. début as Pinkerton in Madame Butterfly with New York City Opera 1972; début Metropolitan Opera as Cavaradossi 1974; début La Scala as Riccardo in Un Ballo in Maschera 1975; appeared in film Don Carlos 1980, West Side Story (TV) 1985; has appeared at maj. opera houses and festivals including Teatro Colón, Buenos Aires, Covent Garden, London, Vienna Staatsoper, Easter Festival and Summer Festival, Salzburg, Lyric Opera of Chicago; recordings include Un Ballo in Maschera, La Battaglia di Legnano, Il Corsaro, Un Giorno di Regno, I Due Foscari, Simone Boccanegra, Macbeth, Don Carlos, Tosca, Thais, Aida, Cavalleria Rusticana, Pagliacci, Lucia di Lammermoor, Turandot, Elisabetta di Inghilterra, Otello (Rossini). *Address:* c/o Columbia Artists Management, 165 West 57th Street, New York, N.Y. 10019, U.S.A.; c/o Opera Caballe, Via Augusta 59, Barcelona, Spain.

CARRICK, Hon. Sir John Leslie, K.C.M.G.; Australian politician (retd.); b. 4 Sept. 1918, Sydney; s. of Arthur James and Emily Ellen (Terry) Carrick; m. Diana Margaret Hunter 1951; three d.; ed. Sydney Technical High School, Univ. of Sydney; commissioned Univ. of Sydney Regt. 1939, served in Australian Imperial Force, sparrow Force; P.O.W. 1942–45; mem. Citizen Mil. Force 1948–51; Gen. Sec. N.S.W. Div. of Liberal Party of Australia 1948–71; mem. Senate 1971–88; mem. Library Cttee. 1971–73, Senate Standing Cttee. on Educ., Science and the Arts 1971–75, Senate Standing Cttee. on Foreign Affairs and Defence 1971–74, Joint Cttee. on Foreign Affairs 1971–72, on Foreign Affairs and Defence 1973–75, Senate Standing Cttee. on Standing Orders 1978–83, Senate Select Cttee. on Human Embryo Experimentation Bill 1985 Oct. 1985–, Standing Cttee. on Regulations and Ordinances 1983–86, Jt. Select Cttee. on Electoral Reform 1983–; Opposition Spokesman for Federalism and Intergovernment Relations 1975; Minister for Housing and Construction, for Urban and Regional Devt. Nov.-Dec. 1975; Minister for Educ. 1975–79, Minister assisting the Prime Minister in Fed. Affairs 1975–78; Leader of Govt. in the Senate 1978–83, Vice-Pres. of Exec. Council 1978–82; Minister for Nat. Devt. and Energy 1979–83. *Leisure interests:* swimming, running, reading. *Address:* 8 Montah Avenue, Killara, N.S.W. 2071, Australia (Home). *Telephone:* 02-498-6326 (Home).

CARRIER, George Francis, PH.D.; American professor of applied mathematics; b. 4 May 1918, Millinocket, Maine; s. of Charles Mosher Carrier and Mary Marcoux Carrier; m. Mary Casey Carrier 1946; three s.; ed. Cornell Univ.; Research Engineer, Harvard Univ. 1944–46; Asst. Prof. Brown Univ. 1946–47, Assoc. Prof. 1947–48, Prof. 1948–52; Gordon McKay Prof. of Mech. Eng., Harvard Univ. 1952–72, Coolidge Prof. of Applied Maths. 1972–; T. Jefferson Coolidge Prof. of Applied Math. 1972–88, Emeritus 1988–; mem. Nat. Acad. of Sciences; Fellow, American Acad. of Arts and Sciences, Nat. Acad. of Eng.; Assoc. Ed., Quarterly of Applied Math.; mem. American Philosophical Soc., Council for Engineering Coll., Cornell Univ.; Hon. mem. A.S.M.E.; Hon. Fellow, Inst. for Maths. and its Applications; Pi Tau Sigma Richards Memorial Award, A.S.M.E. 1963, Von Karman Prize, SIAM 1979, NAS Award in Applied Math and Numerical Analysis 1980; Von Karman Medal, American Soc. of Civil Engineers 1977, Timoshenko Medal, ASME 1978, ASME Silver Centennial Medal 1980, Fluid Dynamics Prize, American Physical Soc. 1984, Dryden Medal, A.I.A.A. 1989. *Publications:* Functions of a Complex Variable: Theory and Technique (with M. Krook and C. E. Pearson) 1966, Ordinary Differential Equations (with C. E. Pearson) 1968, Partial Differential Equations (with C. E. Pearson) 1976; numerous articles. *Address:* Pierce Hall, Harvard University, Cambridge, Mass. 02138, U.S.A.

CARRIER, Hervé; Canadian Jesuit, sociologist and Vatican official; b. 26 Aug. 1921, Gran-Mère, Quebec; s. of Fortunat Carrier and Cora Gelinas; ed. Univ. de Montréal, Jesuit Faculty, Montreal, Catholic Univ. of America, Washington and Sorbonne, Paris; Prof. of Sociology, Gregorian Univ. Rome 1959–, Rector 1966–78; Pres. Int. Fed. of Catholic Univs. 1970–80, Dir. Centre for Coordination of Research 1978–82; Sec. Pontifical Council for Culture, Vatican City 1982–; mem. Acad. des Lettres et des Sciences Humaines of Royal Soc. of Canada; Officier, Légion d'honneur; Dr. h.c. (Sogang Univ., Seoul and Fu Jen Univ., Taipei). *Publications:* Psycho-sociology of Religious Belonging 1965, Higher Education facing New Cultures 1982, Cultures: notre avenir 1985, Evangile et cultures 1987, Psico-sociologia dell'appartenenza religiosa 1988. *Address:* Pontifical Council for Culture, Vatican City; Piazza della Pilotta 4, 00187 Rome, Italy. *Telephone:* 06-6987321, 6987342; 06-67011.

CARRIÈRE, Jean P.; French international civil servant: b. 7 Nov. 1925, Chalon/Saône; s. of Julien Carrière and Alice Daubard; m. Françoise Emery 1953; two s. one d.; ed. Dijon Law School and Ecole Nat. d'Admin.; Administrateur Civil, Ministry of Finance 1957; Financial Attaché for Near and Middle East, Beirut 1962; Dir. Office of Int. Orgs., Ministry of Finance 1964, Deputy Dir. Information Dept. 1967; Financial Attaché, French Embassy, Washington and Alt. Exec. Dir. IBRD 1968–72; Dir. European Office of World Bank (IBRD) 1972–78; Gen. Man. S.E.I.T.A. 1978–81 and Pres. 1980–81; Pres. Soc. Lyonnaise de banque 1982–, Comm. de la communication de l'Asscn. Française de Banques 1986–; Order of the Cedar of Lebanon; Chevalier Légion d'honneur. *Publications:* La Relève de l'Or (under pseudonym Jean Dautun) 1966, L'Or Jaune et l'Or Noir 1976. *Address:* c/o Société Lyonnaise de Banque, 8 rue de la République, 69001 Lyon (Office); 24 rue de la Banque, 75002 Paris (Office); 15 quai Général Sarrail, 69006 Lyon, France (Home).

CARRIÈRE, Jean Paul Jacques; French author; b. 6 Aug. 1932, Nîmes; s. of Edmond Carrière and Andrée Paoli; m. 1st Michele Bollé, two s.; m. 2nd Françoise Battistini 1978, one s.; ed. Coll. Saint Stanislas, Coll. de l'Assomption and Lycée Alphonse Daudet, Nîmes; disc-jockey, Manosque 1958–63; producer, Radio Languedoc-Roussillon 1965–74; television producer, ORTF 1969–; mem. PEN Club; Prix de l'Acad. Française 1968; Prix Goncourt 1972. *Publications:* Les forêts du nouveau monde 1956, Lettre à une père sur une vocation incertaine 1956, Retour à Uzes 1968, L'Epervier de Maheux 1972, Jean Giono 1973, L'univers de Jean Carrière 1975, Noémie, Célestin, Joseph et autres paysans d'Ardèche 1976, La Caverne des Pestiférés (two vols.) 1978, 1979, Le nez dans l'herbe 1980, Jean Giono 1985, Les années sauvages (novel) 1986, Julien Gracq 1986, Le Prix du Goncourt (novel) 1986, Le Dernier Été d'Occident 1987, Voyage d'hiver en Provence 1987, Cévennes 1988, Jean Fusaro, ou La peinture réhabilitée 1988. *Leisure interests:* bicycling, walking, piano, cinema. *Address:* Les Broussanes, Domessargues 30350, Ledignan; Le Devois, Super Camprieu, 30750, Trèves, France. *Telephone:* (66) 83.30.76; (67) 82.61.12.

CARRILES GALLARAGA, Eduardo; Spanish government official; b. Nov. 1923, Santander; joined Nat. Lawyers' Asscn. 1944, later Asscn.'s adviser to Pres. of Council of Ministers; mem. Comm. for Admin. Reform; now Pres. Consumer Comm. of Devt. Planning Authority; Vice-Pres. of EDICA; Pres. Radio Popular; mem. Man. of CEU, Man. Bd. of UDE; many positions in pvt. business corpns.; mem. Consultative Cttee. of RENFE (Nat. Railways); Dir.-Gen. of Cía. de Seguros Reunidos La Unión y el Fénix Español (insurance co.) 1971–; Minister of Finance 1976–77. *Address:* Cia. de Seguros Reunidos La Unión y el Fénix Español, Paseo de la Castellana 37, Apdo. 67, F 1864, Madrid 1, Spain.

CARRILLO, Santiago; Spanish journalist and politician; b. 18 Jan. 1915, Gijón; s. of Wenceslao and Rosalía (Solares) Carrillo; m. Carmen Menéndez 1924; three s.; Sec.-Gen. de la Juventud Socialista Unificada 1936; Councillor of Public Order, Junta de Defensa de Madrid 1936; Sec.-Gen. Partido Comunista de España 1960–82, expelled from CP 1985; mem. Congress of Deputies July 1977–, Deputy for Madrid Oct. 1982–; Dir. Ahora June 1984–; Pres. de Unidad Comunista Oct. 1985–; Pres. Workers-Communist Unity Party Feb. 1987–. *Publications:* Después de Franco, Que?, Nuevos enfoques a problemas de hoy, Mañana España, Eurocomunismo y Estado, El año de la Constitución, Memoria de la transición 1983, Le communisme malgré tout 1983. *Address:* Calle Campomanes 6, 4°, Madrid 28013, Spain. *Telephone:* 4199002.

CARRINGTON, Alan, M.A., PH.D., F.R.S.; British professor of chemistry; b. 6 Jan. 1934; s. of Albert Carrington and Constance (Nelson) Carrington; m. Noreen H. Taylor 1959; one s. two d.; ed. Colfe's Grammar School and

Univs. of Southampton, Oxford and Cambridge; Asst. in Research, Univ. of Cambridge 1960, Asst. Dir. of Research 1963; Fellow, Downing Coll. Cambridge 1960; Prof. of Chem. Univ. of Southampton 1967, Royal Soc. Research Prof. 1979–84, 1987–; Royal Soc. Research Prof. and Fellow, Jesus Coll. Oxford 1984–87; numerous medals and awards. *Publications:* Introduction to Magnetic Resonance (with A. D. McLachlan) 1967, Microwave Spectroscopy of Free Radicals 1974; papers in learned journals. *Leisure interests:* family, music, fishing, golf, sailing. *Address:* 46 Lakewood Road, Chandler's Ford, Hants., England. *Telephone:* Chandler's Ford 65092.

CARRINGTON, 6th Baron; **Peter Alexander Rupert Carington**, K.G., P.C., C.H., G.C.M.G., M.C.; British politician and international administrator; b. 6 June 1919, London; s. of 5th Baron Carrington and the Hon. Sybil Marion Colville; m. Iona McClean; one s. two d.; ed. Eton Coll. and Royal Military Coll., Sandhurst; Grenadier Guards 1939, served N.W. Europe; Parl. Sec. Ministry of Agriculture 1951–54, Ministry of Defence 1954–56; High Commr. in Australia 1956–59; First Lord of the Admiralty 1959–63; Minister without Portfolio (at the Foreign Office), Leader of the House of Lords 1963–64; Leader of the Opposition in the House of Lords 1964–70, 1974–79; Sec. of State for Defence 1970–74, also Minister of Aviation Supply 1971–74; Sec. of State for Energy Jan.-March 1974, for Foreign and Commonwealth Affairs 1979–82, Minister of Overseas Devt. 1979–82; Sec.-Gen. NATO 1984–88; Chair. Christie's Int. PLC July 1988–; Leader of the Opposition, House of Lords 1974–79; Chair. Conservative Party 1972–74; Sec. for Foreign Correspondence and Hon. mem. R.A. of Arts 1982–; Chair. Bd. of Trustees, Victoria and Albert Museum 1983–; Pres. The Pilgrims 1983–; mem. Kissinger Assen. 1982–84; Pres. Chiltern Open Air Museum 1983–; Hon. Bencher of the Middle Temple 1983–; Hon. Fellow, St. Antony's Coll., Oxford 1982–; Hon. LL.D. (Cambridge) 1981, (Leeds) 1981, (Univ. of Philippines) 1982, (Univ. of Aberdeen) 1985; Hon. D.Univ. (Essex) 1983; Hon. Dr. Laws (Univ. of S.C.) 1983, (Harvard Univ.) 1986; Dr. h.c. (Essex) 1983; Hon. LL.D. (Harvard) 1986; Chancellor, Order of St. Michael and St. George 1984–, Grand Officier, Légion. d'honneur. *Publication:* Reflect on Things Past: The Memoirs of Lord Carrington 1988. *Address:* House of Lords, London, S.W.1; 32A Ovington Square, London, SW3 1LR; Manor House, Bledlow, nr. Aylesbury, Buckinghamshire, England. *Telephone:* 08444-3499.

CARROLL, Donal Shemus Allingham, F.C.A.; Irish industrialist and banker; b. 26 Dec. 1927, Ireland; s. of Col. J. D. Carroll and Sheila Maunsell (née Flynn); m. Monica D. M. Moran 1951; one s. one d.; ed. Glenstal Abbey School, Limerick and Trinity Coll., Dublin; joined P. J. Carroll & Co. Ltd. 1952, Dir. 1955, Chair. 1960–88 and Man. Dir. 1960–71; mem. court of Dirs., Bank of Ireland 1956–, Deputy Gov. 1962–64; Gov. 1964–70, 1982–85; Dir. Carreras Ltd. 1962, Vice-Chair. 1971–72; Dir. Rothmans Int. Ltd. 1972–, Deputy Chair. 1985–; Dir. Cen. Bank of Ireland 1970–81; Chair. Lloyds & BOLSA Int. Bank Ltd. 1971–73; mem. Public Services Advisory Council 1973–77; Dir. Dunlop Holdings Ltd. 1973–83; Dir. Irish Times Holdings, Irish Times Trust 1974–80; mem. Comm. on Taxation 1980–85; Hon. LL.D. (Dublin) 1969. *Leisure interests:* gardening, reading. *Address:* P. J. Carroll and Co. PLC, Grand Parade, Dublin 6, Ireland. *Telephone:* Dublin 604311.

CARROLL, John Bissell, PH.D.; American psychologist and educator; b. 5 June 1916, Hartford, Conn.; s. of William James Carroll and Helen M. (Bissell) Carroll; m. Mary Searle 1941; one d.; ed. Wesleyan Univ. and Univ. of Minnesota; Instructor in Psychology and Educ., Mount Holyoke Coll. 1940–42; Instructor in Psychology, Ind. Univ. 1942–43; lecturer in Psychology, Univ. of Chicago 1943–44; Aviation Psychologist, U.S.N.R. 1944–46; Research Psychologist, Dept. of the Army 1946–49; Asst. Prof., Graduate School of Educ., Harvard Univ. 1949–51, lecturer 1951–53, Assoc. Prof. 1953–56, Prof. of Educ. 1956–67; Sr. Research Psychologist, Educational Testing Service, Princeton, N.J. 1967–74; Prof. of Psychology, Univ. of N.C. at Chapel Hill 1974–82, Prof. Emer. 1982–; Dir. The L.L. Thurstone Psychometric Lab., Univ. of N.C. 1974–79; E.L. Thorndike Award, American Psychological Assen. 1970; Diamond Jubilee Medal, Inst. of Linguists, London 1971. *Publications:* The Study of Language 1953, Modern Language Aptitude Test 1959, Language and Thought 1964, Perspectives on School Learning: Selected Writings 1985. *Leisure interests:* music (piano and composition). *Address:* 409 Elliott Road North, Chapel Hill, North Carolina, U.S.A. *Telephone:* (919) 929-6587.

CARROLL, Julian Morton; American politician; b. 16 April 1931, Paducah, Ky.; s. of Elvie B. and Eva (née Heady) Carroll; m. Chariann Harting; two s. two d.; ed. Paducah Junior Coll., Univ. of Kentucky; served in U.S.A.F.; opened a law firm in Paducah; mem. from McCracken County, Ky. House of Reps. 1962–73; Speaker of Ky. House of Reps. 1968–71; Lieut.-Gov. of Ky. 1971–74, Gov. of Kentucky Dec. 1974–79; Pres. Paducah Optimist Club 1962; Chair. Nat. Govs.' Assen.; mem. McCracken County, Ky., American Bar Asscns.; Moderator, Ky. Synod of Cumberland Presbyterian Church; mem. Judiciary Bd. of Gen. Assembly of Cumberland Presbyterian Church; mem. Natural Resources and Environmental Man. Cttee. of Southern Govs.' Conf.; fmrly. States' Co-Chair. Appalachian Regional Comm.; Dr. h.c. from four Univs.; Minerva Award (Louisville Univ.). *Leisure interests:* hunting, fishing, golf. *Address:* 218 Raintree Road, Frankfort, Ky. 40601, U.S.A. (Home).

CARROLL, Kenneth Kitchener, M.A., PH.D., F.R.S.C.; Canadian professor of biochemistry; b. 9 March 1923, Carrolls, N.B.; s. of Lawrence Carroll and Sarah Della Estey; m. Margaret Aileen Ronson 1950; three s.; ed. Fredericton High School, Univs. of New Brunswick, Toronto, Western Ontario and Cambridge Univ., U.K.; Asst. Prof., Dept. of Medical Research, Univ. of Western Ont. 1954–57, Assoc. Prof. 1957–65, Prof. and Acting Head 1965–68, Prof., Dept. of Biochemistry 1968–; Career Investigator, Medical Research Council of Canada 1963–; Sec. Canadian Soc. of Nutritional Sciences 1965–67, Pres. 1978–79; Hon. Sec. Canadian Fed. of Biological Socs. 1967–71; Merck Fellowship 1952–53; Earle Willard McHenry Award, Canadian Soc. of Nutritional Sciences 1987. *Publications:* about 190 original research papers, review articles and book chapters on lipid metabolism, and nutrition in relation to heart disease and cancer. *Leisure interests:* sailing, curling. *Address:* Department of Biochemistry, University of Western Ontario, London, Ont., N6A 5C1 (Office); 561 St. George Street, London, Ont., N6A 3B9, Canada (Home). *Telephone:* (519) 661-3097 (Office); (519) 438-5502 (Home).

CARRUTHERS, Garrey Edward, M.S., PH.D.; American state governor; b. 29 Aug. 1939, Alamosa, Colo.; s. of William C. Carruthers and Frankie J. Shoults; m. Katherine Thomas 1961; one s. two d.; ed. New Mexico State Univ. and Iowa State Univ.; Asst. Prof., Assoc. Prof. Dept. of Agricultural Econs. and Agricultural Business, New Mexico State Univ. 1968–76, 1978–79, Prof. 1979–81, 1984–87; Special Asst. U.S. Sec. of Agric. 1974–75; Acting Dir. N.M. Water Resources Research Inst. 1976–78; Pres. Garrey Carruthers Assocs., Inc. 1979–; Asst. Sec. Interior for Land and Minerals Man. 1983–84; Gov. of New Mexico 1987–; mem. American Agricultural Econs. Assen., American Acad. of Political and Social Services etc.; Republican. *Publications:* articles in professional journals. *Leisure interests:* golf, flying, jogging, driving 1967 Mustang. *Address:* Office of the Governor, State Capitol, 4th Floor, Santa Fe, N.M. 87503, U.S.A.

CARRUTHERS, Robert, B.SC. (ENG.), C.ENG., A.C.G.I., F.I.E.E.; British electrical engineer; b. 29 Jan, 1921, Leeds; s. of Mr. and Mrs. J. Carruthers; m. Phyllis Kathleen Deal 1945; two d.; ed. Harrow County School and London Univ. City and Guilds Coll.; Research at Telecommunications Research Establishment, Swanage and Great Malvern 1941–46, Research engineer with Messrs. Standard Telecommunication Laboratories Ltd. devt. of R.F. equipment for microwave radio links 1946–47; research and devt. of synchrotrons, Atomic Energy Research Establishment 1947–51; research work on gas discharge phenomena and their application to the field of controlled thermonuclear reactors 1951–61; Sr. Prin. Scientist, Atomic Energy Research Establishment, Harwell; Head, Applied Physics and Tech. Division, Culham Laboratory 1961–79. *Address:* 11 Badgers Copse, Radley, Abingdon, Oxon., OX14 3BQ, England. *Telephone:* Abingdon 20386.

CARSBERG, Sir Bryan (Victor), Kt. M.SC.; British university professor and telecommunications executive; b. 3 Jan. 1939, London; s. of Alfred Victor and Maryllia Ciceley (née Collins) Carsberg; m. Margaret Linda Graham 1960; two d.; ed. L.S.E.; sole practice C.A. 1962–64; Lecturer in Accounting, L.S.E. 1964–68, Arthur Andersen Prof. of Accounting 1981–87, Visiting Prof. 1987–; Visiting lecturer, Graduate School of Business, Univ. of Chicago 1968–69; Prof. of Accounting, Univ. of Manchester 1969–78; Visiting Prof. of Business Admin. Univ. of Calif., Berkeley 1974; Asst. Dir. Research and Tech. Activities, U.S. Financial Accounting Standards Bd. 1978–81; Dir. of Research, Inst. of C.A. in England and Wales 1981–87; Dir.-Gen. of Telecommunications, Oftel 1984–; Inst. Medal, W. B. Peat Medal and Prize (Inst. of C.A., England); Chartered Accountants Founding Socs. Centenary Award 1988. *Publications:* An Introduction to Mathematical Programming for Accountants 1969, Analysis for Investment Decisions 1974, Economics of Business Decisions 1975 and others. *Leisure interests:* road running, theatre, music. *Address:* Oftel, Atlantic House, Holborn Viaduct, London, EC1N 2HQ (Office); 14 The Great Quarry, Guildford, Surrey, GU1 3XN, England (Home). *Telephone:* 01-822 1601 (Office); (0483) 572672 (Home).

CARSON, Edward Mansfield, B.S.; American banker; b. 6 Nov. 1929, Tucson, Ariz.; s. of Ernest L. Carson and Earline Mansfield; m. Nadine A. Severns 1952; one s. one d.; ed. Arizona State Univ. and Stonier School of Banking, Rutgers Univ.; with First Interstate Bank of Ariz., Phoenix 1951–85, Exec. Vice-Pres. 1969–72, Chief. Admin Officer 1972–75, Vice-Chair. of Bd. 1975–77, Pres. and C.E.O. 1977–85; Pres. First Interstate Bancorp, Los Angeles 1985–. *Address:* First Interstate Bancorp, 707 Wilshire Boulevard, Los Angeles, Calif. 90017, U.S.A.

CARSON, Hampton L(awrence), A.B., PH.D.; American professor of genetics; b. 5 Nov. 1914, Philadelphia, Pa.; s. of Joseph and Edith Bruen Carson; m. Meredith Shelton 1937; two s.; Instructor in Zoology, Pa. 1938–42, Washington (St. Louis) 1943–46, Asst. Prof. 1946–49; Assoc. Prof. Univ. of Hawaii 1949–55, Prof. 1956–70, Prof. of Genetics 1971–85, Prof. Emer. 1985–, Geneticist, Dept. of Entomology 1967–68; Visiting Prof. of Biology, Univ. of São Paulo 1951, 1977; Fulbright Research Scholar Dept. of Zoology, Univ. of Melbourne 1961; mem. American Acad. of Arts and Sciences, American Soc. of Naturalists (Pres. 1973), Genetics Soc. of America (Pres. 1982), Hawaiian Acad. of Sciences (Pres. 1975), N.A.S., Soc. for the Study of Evolution (Pres. 1971); Hon. Assoc. in Entomology and Trustee B. P. Bishop Museum; Medal for Excellence in Research, Univ.

of Hawaii 1979, Leidy Medal, Acad. of Natural Sciences, Philadelphia 1985. *Publications:* Heredity and Human Life and over 200 scientific articles. *Leisure interest:* bonsai training. *Address:* Department of Genetics, 1960 East-West Road, University of Hawaii, Honolulu, Hawaii 96822 (Office); 2001 Ualakaa Street, Honolulu, Hawaii 96822, U.S.A. (Home). *Telephone:* (808) 948-7662 (Office); (808) 941-6319 (Home).

CARSON, Johnny; American television personality; b. 23 Oct. 1925, Corning, Ia.; s. of Homer Carson and Ruth (née Hook) Carson; m. 1st Jody Wolcott 1948 (divorced 1963), three c.; m. 2nd Joanne Copeland 1963 (divorced); m. 3rd Joanna Holland 1972 (divorced 1983); m. 4th Alexis Maas 1987; ed. Univ. of Nebraska; announcer, radio station KFAB, Lincoln, Neb. 1948, then radio WOW and WOW-TV, Omaha, Neb., station KNXT, Los Angeles, Calif. 1950; TV show Carson's Cellar 1951; writer for comedian Red Skelton; introduced TV quiz show Earn Your Vacation 1954; the Johnny Carson Show, CBS 1955; introduced TV quiz show Who Do You Trust?, ABC-TV 1958–63; host Tonight programme, NBC-TV 1962–; numerous other TV appearances; performer Las Vegas 1954–; Entertainer of Year Award, American Guild of Variety Artists. *Publication:* Happiness is a Dry Martini 1965. *Address:* c/o NBC, 3000 West Almeda Avenue, Burbank, Calif. 91505, U.S.A.

CARSON, William Hunter, O.B.E.; British jockey; b. 16 Nov. 1942, Stirling, Scotland; s. of Thomas Whelan and Mary Hay (Hunter) Carson; m. 1st Carole Jane Sutton 1962 (divorced 1978), three s.; m. 2nd Elaine Williams 1982; ed. Riverside School; Apprentice with Capt. G. Armstrong 1957–62; rode first winner Pinker's Pond at Catterick 1962; rode for Sam Armstrong, Newmarket 1962–68; First Jockey to Lord Derby 1968, to Bernard van Cutsem 1971–75, to Maj. Dick Hern 1977, to H.M. The Queen 1977; Champion Jockey 1972, 1973, 1978, 1980, 1983; rode the winners of 11 English Classics, 7 Irish Classics, and 40 Group One races; best horse ridden Troy; bred and rode St. Leger winner Minster Son 1988. *Leisure interest:* fox hunting. *Address:* West Ilsley, nr. Newbury, Berks., England. *Telephone:* West Ilsley 348.

CARSTAIRS, George Morrison, M.A., M.D., F.R.C.P.E., F.R.C.PSYCH.; British psychiatrist; b. 18 June 1916, Mussoorie, India; s. of late Rev. George Carstairs, D.D., and of Elizabeth H. Carstairs; m. Vera Hunt 1950; two s. one d.; ed. George Watson's Coll., Edinburgh and Edinburgh Univ.; Medical Officer, Fighter Command, R.A.F. 1942–46; Commonwealth Fund Fellow, U.S.A. 1948–49, Rockefeller Research Fellow, India 1950–51, Henderson Research Scholar, India 1951–52; Registrar, Maudsley Hospital, London 1953; Scientific Staff, Medical Research Council Social Psychiatry Research Unit 1954–60, Hon. Consultant, Maudsley Hospital 1956–60; Dir. Medical Research Council Unit for Research on Epidemiology of Psychiatric Illness 1960–71; Prof. of Psychiatry, Univ. of Edinburgh 1961–73; Vice-Chancellor, Univ. of York 1974–78; Visiting Prof. of Psychiatry, Nat. Inst. of Mental Health and Neuro-Sciences, Bangalore, India 1978–81; B.B.C. Reith Lecturer 1962; Pres. World Fed. for Mental Health 1967–71; Fellow, Woodrow Wilson Center for Int. Scholars, Washington, D.C. 1981–82. *Publications:* The Twice Born 1957, This Island Now (the 1962 Reith Lectures) 1963, The Great Universe of Kota 1976, Death of a Witch 1983. *Leisure interests:* theatre, travel. *Address:* c/o 23 Lancaster Grove, London, N.W.3, England. *Telephone:* 01-435 8839.

CARSTENS, Karl, DR. IUR.; German lawyer and politician; b. 14 Dec. 1914, Bremen; m. Veronica Prior 1944; ed. Univs. of Frankfurt, Dijon, Munich, Königsberg, Hamburg and Yale; war service 1939–45; lawyer, Bremen 1945–49; Rep. of Free Hanseatic City of Bremen to Fed. Govt., Bonn 1949–54; Fed. German Del. to Council of Europe, Strasbourg 1954–55; Foreign Office, Bonn 1955–60; Sec. of State for Foreign Affairs 1961–66; Deputy of Fed. Minister of Defence 1966–67; Head of the Fed. Chancellor's Office 1968–69; Prof. of Law, Univ. of Cologne 1960–73; Dir. Research Inst., German Soc. for Foreign Affairs 1970–73; mem. Bundestag 1972–79, Pres. 1976–79; Pres. Fed. Repub. of Germany 1979–84; Parl. Leader Christian Democrats 1973–76; Chair. Cttee. for 750th Anniversary Celebration of Berlin 1985–87; Dr. h.c. (Tokyo Univ., Coimbra Univ., Speyer, Dijon, St. Louis Univs.); Charlemagne Prize 1984, Robert Schuman Prize 1985, Hans-Martin Schleyer Prize 1987. *Publications:* Grundgedanken der amerikanischen Verfassung und ihre Verwirklichung 1954, Das Recht des Europarats 1956, Politische Führung 1971, Bundestagsreden und Zeitdokumente 1978, Reden und Interviews, 5 vols. 1980–84, Anthologie Deutsche Gedichte 1983, Wanderungen in Deutschland 1985. *Leisure interests:* sailing, music. *Address:* Bundeshaus 5300 Bonn 1, Federal Republic of Germany.

CARTAN, Henri Paul, D. ÉS SC.; French mathematician; b. 8 July 1904, Nancy; s. of Elie Cartan; m. Nicole Weiss 1935; two s. three d.; ed. Lycée Buffon, Lycée Hoche, Versailles and Ecole Normale Supérieure; Teacher, Lycée, Caen 1928; Lecturer, Faculty of Science, Lille Univ. 1929–31; Prof. Faculty of Science, Strasbourg Univ. 1931–40, Univ. of Paris 1940–69, Univ. de Paris-Sud (Orsay) 1969–75; Pres. French Section, European Asscn. of Teachers 1957–75; Pres. Int. Mathematical Union 1967–70; Pres. Mouvement Fédéraliste Européen (France) 1974–85; mem. Royal Acad., Denmark 1962; Corresp. Acad. des Sciences 1965, mem. 1974–; Foreign mem. Royal Soc. 1971; Foreign Hon. mem. American Acad. 1950, Foreign Assoc. Nat. Acad. of Sciences, Washington 1972, Acad. Royale Belgique 1978; Corresp. Akad. der Wissenschaften Göttingen 1971, Royal Acad. of

Sciences, Madrid 1971, Bayerische Akad. der Wissenschaften 1974; hon. mem. Japan Acad. 1979; fmr. mem. Acad. Finland 1979; Foreign mem. Royal Swedish Acad. of Sciences 1981; (Polish Acad.) 1985, Hon. D.Sc. (ETH, Zurich) 1955, (Münster) 1952, (Oslo) 1961, (Sussex) 1969, (Cambridge) 1969, (Stockholm) 1978, (Oxford) 1980, (Zaragoza) 1985; Officier de la Légion d'honneur. *Address:* 95 boulevard Jourdan, 75014 Paris, France. *Telephone:* (1)-45-40-51-78.

CARTELLIERI, Ulrich; German banker; b. 21 Sept. 1937; mem. Bd. Deutsche Bank AG, Frankfurt; Chair. Deutsche Bank (Asia Credit) Ltd., Singapore, DB Finance (Hong Kong) Ltd., Hong Kong; Chair. Supervisory Bd. European Asian Bank AG, Hamburg; mem. Supervisory Bd. Deutsche Solvay-Werke GmbH, Solingen, Deutsche Telephonwerke und Kabelindustrie AG, Berlin, Euro-Pacific Finance Corpn. Ltd., Melbourne, Girmes-Werke AG, Grefrath-Oedt, Th. Goldschmidt AG, Essen, Wilhelm Karmann GmbH, Osnabrück, Thyssen Edelstahlwerke AG, Düsseldorf, G. M. Pfaff AG, Kaiserslautern.

CARTER, Angela; British writer; b. 1940; ed. Bristol Univ.; Fellow in Creative Writing, Sheffield Univ. 1976–78; Visiting Prof., Brown Univ., Providence, R.I. 1980–81; Writer-in-Residence, Univ. of Adelaide, S. Australia 1984; Visiting Prof., Univ. of Tex. at Austin 1985, Iowa Writers' Workshop 1986. *Publications:* Shadow Dance 1965, The Magic Toyshop (John Llewellyn Rhys Prize) 1967, Several Perceptions (Somerset Maugham Award) 1968, Heroes and Villains 1969, Love 1971, The Infernal Desire Machine of Dr. Hoffman 1972, The Passion of New Eve 1978, Fireworks, The Bloody Chamber (Cheltenham Festival of Literature Award) 1979, The Sadeian Woman: An Exercise in Cultural History 1979, Nothing Sacred: selected journalism 1983, Nights at the Circus 1984, Black Venus 1985, Wayward Girls and Wicked Women (Ed.) 1986; *film screenplay:* for film The Company of Wolves (based on her own short story) 1984. *Address:* c/o Virago Press Ltd., 41 William IV Street, London, WC2N 4DB, England.

CARTER, Brandon, D.SC., F.R.S.; British theoretical physicist; b. 26 May 1942, Sydney, Australia; s. of Harold B. Carter and Mary Brandon-Jones; m. Lucette Defrise 1969; three d.; ed. George Watson's Coll., Edinburgh, Univ. of St. Andrews, Univ. of Cambridge (Pembroke Coll.); Research Fellow, Pembroke Coll., Univ. of Cambridge 1967–72; staff mem., Inst. of Astronomy, Cambridge 1968–72; Asst. Lecturer, Dept. of Applied Math. and Theoretical Physics, Univ. of Cambridge 1973, lecturer 1974; Maître de Recherche, Centre Nat. de la Recherche Scientifique, Paris 1975–85, Directeur de Recherche 1986–; Directeur-Adjoint, Group d'Astrophysique Relativiste, Observatoire de Paris-Meudon 1975–82, Directeur 1983–86. *Publications:* Global Structure of the Kerr Family of Gravitational Fields 1968, Black Hole Equilibrium States 1973, Large Number Coincidences and the Anthropic Principle in Cosmology 1974, The General Theory of the Mechanical Electromagnetic and Thermodynamic Properties of Black Holes 1979, The Anthropic Principle and its Implications for Biological Evolution 1983. *Address:* Département d'Astrophysique Relativiste et Cosmologie, Observatoire de Paris, 92190 Meudon (Office); 19 rue de la Borne au Diable, 92310 Sèvres, France (Home). *Telephone:* 4534-7570.

CARTER, Sir Charles Frederick, Kt., M.A., F.B.A.; British economist; b. 15 Aug. 1919, Rugby, Warwicks.; s. of Frederick William and Edith Mildred Carter; m. Janet Shea 1944; one s. two d.; ed. Rugby School and St. John's Coll., Cambridge; Lecturer in Statistics, Univ. of Cambridge 1945–51; Prof. of Applied Econs., The Queen's Univ., Belfast 1952–59; Stanley Jevons Prof. of Political Economy and Cobden Lecturer, Victoria Univ. of Manchester 1959–63; Vice-Chancellor, Univ. of Lancaster 1963–79; Chair. Research Cttee., Policy Studies Inst. 1978–88, Pres. 1988–; Chair. Northern Ireland Econ. Council 1977–87, Goldsmiths Coll. (Univ. of London); Chair. numerous trusts; Fellow of Emmanuel Coll., Cambridge 1947–51, Hon. Fellow 1965–; numerous hon. degrees; Hon. Fellow Royal Irish Acad. *Publications:* The Measurement of Production Movements (with W. B. Reddaway and J. R. N. Stone, qq.v.) 1948, British Economic Statistics (with A. D. Roy) 1954, Industry and Technical Progress 1957, Investment in Innovation 1958, Science in Industry 1959 (all three with B. R. Williams, q.v.), The Science of Wealth 1960, The Northern Ireland Problem (with D. P. Barritt) 1962, Wealth 1968, Higher Education for the Future 1980, Policies for a Constrained Economy (with J. H. M. Pinder) 1982. *Leisure interest:* gardening. *Address:* 1 Gosforth Road, Seascale, Cumbria, CA20 1PU, England. *Telephone:* 09467-28359.

CARTER, Hon. Sir Douglas Julian, K.C.M.G., F.R.S.A.; New Zealand farmer, politician and diplomatist; b. 5 Aug. 1908, Foxton; s. of Walter Stephen Carter and Agnes Isobel Nimmo; m. Mavis R. Miles 1936; ed. Palmerston North High School, Waitaki Boys' High School; mem. Parl. (Nat.) Raglan 1957–75; Parl. Under-Sec. of Agriculture 1966–69; Minister of Agriculture 1969–72; High Commr. to U.K. 1976–79; Chair. Urban Transport Council (N.Z.) 1981–84; Vice-Pres. Royal Humane Soc., London 1979–; Exec. mem. Federated Farmers, N.Z. 1951–57; Chair. N.Z. Pig Producers' Council 1952–57, N.Z. Sharemilker Employers Asscn. 1954–69; mem. Ethics Cttee., Waikato Univ. 1980–. *Leisure interest:* travel.
[Died 7 Nov. 1988.]

CARTER, Edward W., M.B.A., LL.D.; American businessman; b. 29 June 1911; m. 2nd Hannah Locke Caldwell; one s. one d.; ed. Univ. of California, Harvard Univ.; Chair. Emer. and Dir. Carter Hawley Hale Stores, Inc.,

Los Angeles; fmr. Dir. American Telephone and Telegraph Co., Del Monte Corpn., Lockheed Corpn., Pacific Mutual Life Insurance Co., Southern Calif. Edison Co., First Interstate Bancorporation and its subsidiary First Interstate Bank, Novacar Medical Corpn.; mem. Bd. of Regents, Univ. of Calif.; Trustee of Los Angeles County Museum of Art, Occidental Coll., The Brookings Inst., Washington, D.C., Cttee. for Econ. Devt.; Dir. Los Angeles Philharmonic Asscn; Chair. San Francisco Opera Asscn., Stanford Research Inst., James Irvine Foundation, Santa Anita Foundation; mem. Business Council, Business Cttee. for the Arts, Harvard Business School Overseers Visiting Cttee., Harvard Visiting Cttees. for Art Museums, Dept. of Econs., Rockefeller Univ. Council, UCLA Business School Visiting Cttee., The Conf. Bd.; Council on Foreign Relations; Trustee, Nat. Humanities Center, mem. Council Woodrow Wilson Int. Center for Scholars, Sloan Comm. on Higher Education. *Address:* 550 South Flower Street, Los Angeles, Calif., U.S.A. *Telephone:* (213) 620-0150.

CARTER, Elliott Cook, Jr., A.B., A.M.; American composer; b. 11 Dec. 1908, New York; s. of Elliot and Florence (née Chambers) Carter; m. Helen Frost-Jones 1939; one s.; ed. Harvard Univ., Ecole Normale de Musique, Paris; Musical Dir. Ballet Caravan 1937–39; critic Modern Music 1937–42; tutor St. John's Coll., Annapolis 1939–41; teacher of composition Peabody Conservatory 1946–48, Columbia Univ. 1948–50, Queen's Coll. (N.Y.) 1955–56; Prof. of Music, Yale Univ. 1960–61; Prof. Dept. of Composition, Juilliard School, New York 1966–; Andrew White Prof.-at-Large, Cornell Univ. 1967–; mem. Bd. of Trustees, American Acad., Rome; mem. Int. Soc. for Contemporary Music, Dir. 1946–52, Pres. American Section 1952, Nat. Inst. of Arts and Letters; mem. American Acad. of Arts and Sciences; Hon. degrees Swarthmore Coll. and Princeton Univ. 1969, Univs. of Harvard, Yale and Boston 1970, Univ. of Cambridge 1983; American Composers' Alliance Prize (for Quartet for Four Saxophones) 1943, First Prize Liège Int. Music Competition 1953, Prix de Rome 1953, Pulitzer Prize (for Second String Quartet), Sibelius Medal (Harriet Cohen Foundation) 1960, New York Critics Circle Award (for Double Concerto) 1961, Pulitzer Prize (for Third String Quartet) 1973; Ernst Von Siemens Prize, Munich 1981; Gold Medal, Nat. Inst. of Arts and Letters 1971, Handel Medallion of New York 1978, awarded Nat. Medal of Art by Pres. Reagan 1985. *Works include: (Orchestral):* Symphony No. 1 1954, Variations for Orchestra 1955, Double Concerto 1961, Piano Concerto 1965, Concerto for Orchestra 1969, Symphony of Three Orchestras 1977, Triple Duo 1982, Penthode (for 20 players) 1985; *(Chamber):* Elegy 1943, Sonata for Cello and Piano, Woodwind Quintet 1948, Sonata for Flute, Oboe, Cello and Harpsichord 1952, Brass Quintet 1974, three String Quartets 1951–71; *(Vocal):* A Mirror on Which to Dwell 1975, In Sleep In Thunder 1983; *(Choral):* The Defense of Corinth 1949, *(Instrumental):* Piano Sonata 1946, Night fantasies (piano) 1980; *(Stage Works):* Pocahontas 1939, The Minotaur 1947. *Address:* Mead Street, Waccabuc, N.Y. 10597, U.S.A.

CARTER, H.E. Cardinal Gerald Emmett, C.C., M.A., PH.D., L.TH., D.H.L., C.C.; Canadian ecclesiastic; b. 1 March 1912, Montreal; s. of Thomas Joseph Carter and Mary (Kelty) Carter; ed. Grand Seminary, Montreal, Univ. of Montreal, Duquesne Univ.; ordained priest 1937; founder and prin. Prof. St. Joseph Teachers' Coll., Montreal 1939–61; Chaplain, Newman Club, McGill Univ. 1941–56; Charter mem. and first Pres. Thomas More Inst. of Adult Educ. 1945–61; mem. Montreal Catholic School Comm. 1948–61; Auxiliary Bishop of London, Ont. and titular Bishop of Altiburo 1961; Bishop of London, Ont. 1964–78; Archbishop of Toronto 1978–; Cardinal 1979; mem. Council for studying Econ. Affairs of Holy See. 1981–, Canon Law Comm., Holy See. 1981; Chair. Episcopal Comm. on Canadian Liturgy 1966–73; mem. Consilius of Liturgy, Rome 1965; Chair. Int. Cttee. for English in Liturgy 1971; Vice-Pres. Canadian Catholic Conf. 1973, Catholic Conf. of Ont. 1971–73; Pres. Canadian Conf. of Catholic Bishops 1975; mem. Council, Synod of Bishops 1977; Hon. Canon, Cathedral Basilica, Montreal; Hon. LL.D. (Western Ont.) 1966, (Concordia) 1976, (Windsor) 1977, (McGill) 1980, (Notre Dame, Ind.) 1981; Hon. D.Lit. (St. Mary's, Halifax, N.S.) 1980. *Publications:* The Catholic Public Schools of Quebec 1957, Psychology and the Cross 1959, The Modern Challenge to Religious Education 1961. *Leisure interests:* fishing and swimming. *Address:* 355 Church Street, Toronto, Ont. M5B 1Z8, Canada (Office). *Telephone:* (416) 377 1500.

CARTER, Herbert Edmund, A.B., M.S., PH.D.; American professor of biochemistry and college administrator; b. 25 Sept. 1910, Mooresville, Ind.; s. of George B. Carter and Edna Pidgeon Carter; m. Elizabeth DeWees 1933; two d.; ed. DePauw Univ. and Univ. of Illinois; Instructor in Biochemistry, Univ. of Ill., Urbana 1932–35, Assoc. 1935–37, Asst. Prof. of Biochem. 1937–43, Assoc. Prof. 1943–45, Prof. 1945, Head of Dept. of Chem. and Chem. Eng. 1954–67, Acting Dean, Graduate Coll. 1963–65, Vice-Chancellor for Academic Affairs 1967–71; Co-ordinator Interdisciplinary Programmes, Univ. of Ariz. 1971–77, Head Dept. of Biochemistry 1977–81; Research Fellow, Office, Arid Lands Studies 1981–; mem. Nat. Acad. of Sciences, American Acad. of Arts and Sciences, Nat. Science Bd. 1964, Chair. 1970, American Chemical Soc. (assoc. ed. Bio-Chemistry 1961–); Eli Lilly Award in Biochem. 1943; Nichols Medal 1965; American Oil Chemists Soc. Award in Lipid Chem. 1966; Kenneth A. Sencer Award 1968, Alton E. Bailey Award 1970. *Publications:* some 130 papers in various chemical and biochemical journals; Ed.-in-Chief Vol. I of Biochemical Preparations.

Leisure interests: squash, golf. *Address:* 2401 Cerrada de Promesa, Tucson, Ariz. 85718, U.S.A. (Home).

CARTER, Jimmy (James Earl, Jr.), B.S.; American farmer and politician; b. 1 Oct. 1924, Plains, Ga.; s. of the late James Earl Carter Sr. and Lillian Gordy; m. Rosalynn Smith 1946; three s. one d.; ed. Plains High School, Georgia Southwestern Coll., Georgia Inst. of Tech., U.S. Naval Acad., Annapolis, Md.; served U.S. Navy 1946–53, attained rank of Lieut.; peanut farmer, warehouseman 1953–77, businesses Carter Farms, Carter Warehouses, Ga.; State Senator, Ga. 1962–66; Gov. of Georgia 1971–74; Pres. of U.S.A. 1977–81; Distinguished Prof., Emory Univ. 1982–; mem. Sumter County, Ga., School Bd. 1955–62 (Chair. 1960–62), Americus and Sumter County Hospital Authority 1956–70, Sumter County Library Bd. 1961; Pres. Plains Devt. Corpn. 1963; Georgia Planning Assn. 1968; Dir. Ga. Crop Improvement Asscn. 1957–63 (Pres. 1961); Chair. West Cen. Ga. Area Planning and Devt. Comm. 1964; State Chair. March of Dimes 1968–70; District Gov. Lions Club 1968–69; Chair. Congressional Campaign Cttee., Democratic Nat. Cttee. 1974; several hon. degrees; World Methodist Peace Award 1984, Albert Schweitzer Prize for Humanitarianism 1987; Democrat. *Publications:* Why not the Best? 1975, A Government as good as its People 1977, Keeping Faith: Memoirs of a President 1982, The Blood of Abraham: Insights into the Middle East 1985, Everything to Gain: Making the Most of the Rest of Your Life 1987, An Outdoor Journal 1988. *Leisure interests:* reading, tennis. *Address:* The Carter Center, 1 Copenhill, Atlanta, Ga. 30307, U.S.A.

CARTER, Sir John, Kt., LL.B., Q.C.; Guyanese diplomatist (retd.); b. 27 Jan. 1919; s. of Kemp R. Carter; m. Sara Lou Harris 1959; two s.; ed. Queen's Coll., Georgetown, and London Univ.; called to Bar, Middle Temple, London 1942; Law practice British Guiana 1945–66; mem. British Guiana Legislature 1948–53, 1961–64; Pro-Chancellor Univ. of Guyana 1962–66; Perm. Rep. of Guyana to UN 1966; Amb. to U.S.A. 1966–69, to Yugoslavia 1969–70; High Commr. in U.K. 1970–76, concurrently Amb. to Fed. Repub. of Germany, France, Netherlands and U.S.S.R.; Amb. to People's Repub. of China (also accred. to Democratic People's Repub. of Korea) 1976–81, to Japan 1979–81; High Commr. in Jamaica 1981–83. *Address:* 3603 East West Highway, Chevy Chase, Maryland 20815, U.S.A.

CARTER, John Edwin, B.SC.; Canadian company executive; b. 3 April 1915, Jackson, Ga.; s. of Charles Luther and Marilu (née Holiman) Carter; m. Virginia Meredith Crickmer; one s. one d.; ed. Georgia Inst. of Tech.; Metallurgist, Huntington Alloys Inc. (a U.S. subsidiary of Inco Ltd.) 1937; rose to rank of Maj. in U.S. Army during World War II; various posts with Huntington Alloys, rising to Pres. 1945–71; transferred to Inco Ltd., Canada 1971, Vice-Pres. 1971–72, Exec. Vice-Pres. 1972–74, Dir. Feb. 1973–80; Pres. 1974–77, Chair. and C.E.O. 1977–80; Dir. Toronto-Dominion Bank, C. D. Howe Research Inst., Int. Copper Research Asscn. Inc.; mem. British-North American Cttee., Canadian Inst. of Mining and Metallurgy, American soc. for metals, american chem. soc.; pres. w.va. mfrs'. asscn. 1969–71; Gold Knight of Industry award, Nat. Man. Asscn. 1965. *Leisure interest:* golf. *Address:* 66 Collier Street, Toronto, Ont., M4W 1L9 Canada.

CARTER, Lieut.-Gen. Marshall Sylvester, M.S.; American army officer and government official; b. 16 Sept. 1909, Fortress Monroe, Va.; s. of the late Brig. Gen. Clifton Carroll Carter and Mai Coleman Carter; m. Préot Nichols 1934; one s. two d.; ed. U.S. Military Acad., Mass. Inst. of Tech., and Nat. War Coll.; 2nd Lieut., U.S. Army 1931; service with artillery, Honolulu, Panama; Staff Officer, Washington 1942–45; China Theatre 1945–46; Special Asst. to Sec. of State 1947–49; Minister, American Embassy, London 1949; Exec. to Sec. of Defense 1950–52; Deputy Commdg. Gen., U.S. Army Alaska 1952–55; Commdg. Gen. 5th Army Air Defense Region 1955–56; Chief of Staff, North American Air Defense Command, Colorado Springs 1957–59, Continental Air Defense Command 1956–59; Chief of Staff, 8th Army, Korea 1959–61; Commdg. Gen., Army Air Defense Center, Commdt. Army Air Defense School 1961–62; Deputy Dir. CIA 1962–65; Dir. Nat. Security Agency 1965–69; retd. from military service as Lieut.-Gen. 1969; Pres. George C. Marshall Research Foundation 1969–85, Emer. 1985–; Cheyenne Mountain Zoological Soc.; D.S.M. with two Oak Leaf Cluster, Legion of Merit with Oak Leaf Cluster, Bronze Star Medal, Distinguished Intelligence Medal, etc. *Leisure interests:* hunting, fishing, ecology. *Address;* 655 Bear Paw Lane, Colorado Springs, Colo. 80906, U.S.A. *Telephone:* (719) 634-0770.

CARTIER-BRESSON, Henri; French photographer; b. 22 Aug. 1908, Chanteloup; s. of André and Marthe (née Leverdier) Cartier-Bresson; m. Martine Franck 1970; ed. Ecole Fénelon and Lycée Condorcet, Paris; studied painting in André Lhote's studio; took up photography 1931; Asst. Dir. to Jean Renoir 1936, 1939; prisoner of war 1940–43, escaped; f. Magnum-Photos with Capa, Chim, and Rodger 1946; exhbns. Madrid, New York 1933, New York Museum of Modern Art 1946, 1968, The Louvre (Pavillon de Marsan), Paris 1954, Phillips Collection, Washington 1964, Tokyo 1965, Victoria and Albert Museum, London 1969, Grand Palais, Paris 1970, Palais de Tokyo, Paris 1985; drawing exhbns. New York, Zürich 1975, Musée d'art moderne, Paris, Museo de arte moderno, Mexico 1982; drawings, photographs and paintings exhbns. French Inst., Stockholm, Padiglione d'Arte Contemporanea, Milan, Univ. of Rome 1983, Museum of Modern Art, Oxford 1984, Palais Lichtenstein, Vienna, Salzburg 1986, Kunstverein Mannheim 1986; collection of 390 photographs at Menil

Foundation, Houston, U.S.A., Victoria and Albert Museum, London, Univ. of Fine Arts, Osaka, Japan, and Bibliothèque Nationale, Paris, exhibited Edinburgh Festival, Hayward Gallery, London 1978; made various documentary films; Grand Prix nationaux 1981; Hasselbladt Award 1983; Overseas Press Club awards; D.Lit. h.c., Oxford Univ. 1975, Prize Novocento Palermo 1986. *Publications:* Images à la sauvette (U.S. edition The Decisive Moment), The Europeans, From One China to the Other, The People of Moscow, Danses à Bali, The World of Henri Cartier-Bresson 1968, L'homme et la machine 1968, Vive la France 1970, Cartier-Bresson's France 1971, Faces of Asia 1972, About Russia 1974, Henri Cartier-Bresson, Photographer 1979, Photoportraits 1983. *Address:* c/o Magnum-Photos, 20 rue des Grands-Augustins, 75006 Paris, France; c/o Helen Wright, 135 East 74 Street, New York, N.Y., U.S.A.; c/o John Hillelson, Wheatsheaf House, 4 Carmelite Street, London, E.C.4, England.

CARTLAND, Barbara (Hamilton), F.R.S.A.; British authoress and playwright; b. 9 July 1901; d. of the late Maj. Bertram Cartland; m. 1st Alexander George McCorquodale 1927 (divorced 1933), one d.; m. 2nd Hugh McCorquodale 1936 (died 1963), two s.; author of sociology, philosophy, religion, poetry, biography, autobiography and romantic fiction; best-selling author in the world (Guinness Book of Records, sales number 370 million, 1984), Silver Medal of Paris 1988. *Publications include:* Jigsaw 1923, Cupid Rides Pillion (renamed Dangerous Love), A Virgin in Paris, The Irresistible Buck, The Outrageous Lady, Love and the Loathsome Leopard, The Twists and Turns of Love, Love Has His Way 1979, Kneel for Mercy, The Vibration of Love 1981, The Magic of Honey, The Incredible Honeymoon, The Romance of Food, Princess to the Rescue 1984; Co. Cadet Officer St. John Ambulance Brigade, Beds. 1943-47, County Vice-Pres. 1948-50, Deputy Pres. 1978-; County Vice-Pres. Nursing Cadets, Herts. 1951, Chair. St. John Council, Herts. 1972-; mem. many charitable bodies; numerous radio and TV appearances; mounted many pageants in aid of charity. *Address:* Camfield Place, Hatfield, Herts., England. *Telephone:* Potters Bar 42612.

CARTLEDGE, Sir Bryan George, K.C.M.G.; British diplomatist and college principal; b. 10 June 1931; s. of Eric Cartledge and Phyllis Shaw; m. Ruth Hylton Gass 1960; one. s. one d.; ed. Hurstpierpoint and St. John's Coll., Cambridge; served Queen's Royal Regt. 1950-51; Commonwealth Fund Fellow, Stanford Univ., Calif. 1956-57; Research Fellow, St. Antony's Coll., Oxford 1958-59; joined Foreign Service 1960, served Foreign Office 1960-61, British Embassy, Stockholm 1961-63, Moscow 1963-66, Diplomatic Service Admin. Office 1966-68, Teheran 1968-70, Harvard Univ. 1971-72, Counsellor, Moscow 1972-75, Head of E. European and Soviet Dept., FCO 1975-77, Pvt. Sec. (Overseas Affairs) to Prime Minister 1977-79, Amb. to Hungary 1980-83, Asst. Under Sec. of State, FCO 1983-84, Deputy Sec. of the Cabinet 1984-85, Amb. to U.S.S.R. 1985-88; Prin. Linacre Coll., Oxford Oct. 1988; Hon. Fellow, St. John's Coll., Cambridge 1985, St. Antony's Coll., Oxford 1987. *Address:* Linacre College, Oxford, OX1 3JA, England. *Telephone:* 0865-271650.

CARTLEDGE, Raymond Eugene, B.S.; American business executive; b. 6 June 1929, Pensacola, Fla.; s. of Raymond H. Cartledge and Meddie Brookins; m. Gale Perry 1962; one s. two d.; ed. Univ. of Alabama and Harvard Univ.; Sales Man. Kraft Paper & Bd., Union Camp 1967; Exec. Vice-Pres. Clevepak Corpn. 1971, Pres. 1975, C.E.O. 1977; Vice-Pres. and Gen. Man. Container Div. Union Camp 1980, Exec. Vice-Pres. 1982, mem. Bd. of Dirs. 1983-, Chair. and C.E.O. 1986-; mem. Bd. of Dirs. Mutual Benefit Life 1987-. *Leisure interests:* golf, tennis. *Address:* Union Camp Corporation, 1600 Valley Road, Wayne,.N.J. 07470, U.S.A.

CARTWRIGHT, Alton Stuart; American business executive (retd.); b. 7 Oct. 1922, Casper, Wyo.; s. of Alton Stuart Cartwright Sr. and Blanche (Harper) Cartwright; m. Adelaide Frances Igoe 1951; four s.; ed. Oregon State Univ.; joined General Electric Co. 1946; Vice-Pres. Canadian Gen. Electric Co., Toronto 1970-72, Exec. Vice-Pres. 1972, Pres. 1972-77, Chair. 1977-84, and C.E.O. 1977-84; Dir. Dominion Engineering Works Ltd., Montreal, Canadian Appliance Manufacturing Co. Ltd., Toronto. *Address:* 676 Ocean Road, Vero Beach, Fla. 32963, U.S.A. (Home).

CARTWRIGHT, Dame Mary Lucy, D.B.E., M.A., D.PHIL., SC.D., F.R.S.; British mathematician; b. 17 Dec. 1900, Aynhoe, Northants; d. of Rev. W. D. Cartwright and Lucy H. M. Cartwright; ed. Godolphin School, Salisbury, and St. Hugh's Coll., Oxford; Asst. Mistress, Alice Ottley School, Worcester 1923-24, Wycombe Abbey School, Bucks. 1924-27; Yarrow Research Fellow, Girton Coll. 1930-34; Faculty Asst. lecturer in Mathematics, Cambridge 1933-35; Fellow and lecturer, Girton Coll. 1934-49; Mistress of Girton Coll. 1949-68, Life Fellow 1968-, Univ. lecturer in Mathematics, Cambridge 1936-59, Reader in the Theory of Functions 1959-68, Emer. Reader 1968-; Consultant on U.S. Navy Mathematical Research Projects at Stanford and Princeton Univs. 1949; Fellow, Cambridge Philosophical Soc.; Vice-Pres. London Mathematical Soc. 1936-38; Pres. Mathematical Assocn. 1951-52; London Mathematical Soc. 1961-63; Visiting Prof. Brown Univ., Providence R.I. 1968-69, Claremont Graduate School 1969, Case Western Reserve Univ. 1970, Poland 1970, Univ. of Wales 1971, Case Western Reserve Univ. Cleveland 1971; Hon. F.R.S.E.; Hon. LL.D. (Edinburgh Univ.), Hon. D.Sc. (Leeds Univ., Hull Univ., Univs. of Wales, Oxford and Brown, R.I.); Commdr., Order of the Dannebrog (Denmark), Sylvester Medal of Royal Soc., De Morgan Medal of London Mathematical Soc.,

Medal of Univ. of Jyväskylä (Finland). *Publications:* Integral Functions 1956, papers in journals. *Address:* 38 Sherlock Close, Cambridge, CB3 0HP, England. *Telephone:* 352574.

CARVAJAL PRADO, Vice-Adm. Patricio; Chilean naval officer and politician; b. 13 Sept. 1916, Santiago; m. Teresa Carvallo 1948; two s. three d.; ed. Liceo Alemán de Santiago and naval coll.; Capt. Lautaro 1953, Esmeralda (training ship) 1960, Covadonga 1961, C. L. Prat 1966-67; Dir. of Gunnery School 1962-63; naval attaché U.K. 1964-66; Chief of Naval Gen. Staff 1969-70; Chief of Defence Staff 1973-; Minister of Defence 1973-74, Feb. 1983-, of Foreign Affairs 1974-78. *Leisure interest:* target shooting. *Address:* Ministerio de Defensa, Plaza Bulnes s/n, 4°, Santiago, Chile. *Telephone:* 6965271.

CARVALHO, José Candido de Melo, PH.D.; Brazilian zoologist and entomologist; b. 11 June 1914, Carmo do Rio Claro, Minas Gerais; s. of João Candido de Melo Carvalho and Ana da Silva Vilela Carvalho; m. Milza Freire Carvalho 1939; one d.; ed. Escola Superior de Agricultura e Veterinária, Viçosa, Univ. of Nebraska, and Iowa Univ. of Science and Tech.; Prof. of Biology and Zoology, Viçosa 1942-46; Zoologist, Museu Nacional, Rio de Janeiro 1946-84, Dir. of Museu Nacional 1955-61; Dir. Museu Goeldi, Belém 1954-55; Vice-Pres. Nat. Research Council, Brazil 1962-63; mem. Exec. Bd. Int. Union for Conservation of Nature 1963-70; Pres. Asscn. for Tropical Biology 1965-66; Prof. Nat. Coll. of Geology, Rio de Janeiro 1960-68; mem. Council, Univ. of Brazil 1955-61, Nat. Council for Protection of Indians 1955-58, Council for Nat. Culture 1959-60; Pres. Perm. Cttee. Int. Congress on Entomology 1952-84, Latin American Congresses on Zoology 1962-; mem. Brazilian Acad. of Sciences, Vice-Pres. 1955-56; John Simon Guggenheim Fellow 1954-55; British Council Fellow 1951; carried out twelve expeditions to Hyléa (Amazonas); Pres. Brazilian Foundation for Nature Conservation 1966-69, 1979-82; Hon. mem. Mexican Inst. Nat. Research 1967-; Fellow Agra Zoological Soc. 1964-72; mem. Directorate of Nat. Indian Foundation 1967-70; mem. Natural Resources Res. Comm. UNESCO 1969-71; Chief Assessor Pres. Brazilian Inst. Forestry Devt. 1971; Vice-Pres. Brazilian Soc. for Ecology 1971; Pres. Section Entomology, Int. Union of Biological Sciences 1972-80; mem. Council for Research and Post-Graduation, Fed. Univ. of Rio de Janeiro 1973; Consulting Ed. Biological Conservation 1968-; mem. Fed. Council of Culture 1974-84; Sr. Scientific Fellow, N.S.F. 1971; Co-ed. Amazoniana 1971-; mem. Brazilian Comm. on Man and the Biosphere 1975; Co-ordinator on Tech. Comm. of Brazilian Foundation for Nature Conservation 1975; Chair. Comm. on Zoology, Ecology, Botany, Brazilian Nat. Research Council 1975; Vice-Pres. Fed. Council of Culture 1977-84; Hon. Fellow Zoological Soc. London 1979; Prizes: Mello Leitão 1951, Costa Lima of Brazilian Acad. of Sciences 1966, Gold Medal World Wildlife Fund 1973. *Publications:* Notas de Viagem ao Rio negro 1952, Notas de Viagem ao Javari-Itacoai-Jurua 1955, Notas de Viagem ao Paru de Leste 1955, Key to the Genera of Miridae of the World 1955, Insects of Micronesia (Miridae) 1956, Catalogue of the Miridae of the World (5 vols.) 1957-60, The Miridae of Galapagos 1967, Notas de viagem de um zoólogo à região das catingas e áreas limítrofes 1969, and numerous papers on zoology, entomology, etc. *Address:* Museu Nacional, Quinta da Boa Vista, Rio de Janeiro, RJ; Rua Campos Sales 143, Apt. 601, Rio de Janeiro, RJ Brazil. *Telephone:* 2648262 (Office); 2486794 (Home).

CARVER, Baron (Life Peer), cr. 1977; **Field-Marshal Richard Michael Power Carver,** G.C.B., C.B.E., D.S.O., M.C.; British army officer; b. 24 April 1915, Bletchingley, Surrey; s. of Harold Power Carver and Winifred A. G. née Wellesley; m. Edith Lowry-Corry 1947; two s. two d.; ed. Winchester Coll. and Royal Military Acad., Sandhurst; with 7th Armoured Div. 1942, 1st Royal Tank Regt. 1943, 4th Armoured Brigade 1944; Ministry of Supply 1947; Allied Forces, Central Europe and SHAPE 1951-54; Deputy Chief of Staff, East Africa Command 1954-56; Dir. of Plans, War Office 1958-59; Commdr. 6th Infantry Brigade 1960-62; G.O.C. 3rd Div. (Maj.-Gen.) 1962-64; Dir. Army Staff Duties 1964-66; Commdr. Far East Land Forces (Lieut.-Gen.) 1966-67; C.-in-C. Far East (Gen.) 1967-69; G.O.C.-in-C. Southern Command 1969-71; Chief of Gen. Staff 1971-73; Chief of Defence Staff (Field-Marshal) 1973-76; Commr.-designate for Rhodesia 1977-78. *Publications:* Second to None 1950, El Alamein 1962, Tobruk 1964, War Lords (Ed.) 1976, Harding of Petherton 1978, The Apostles of Mobility 1979, War Since 1945 1980, A Policy For Peace 1982, The Seven Ages of the British Army 1984, Dilemmas of the Desert War 1986, Twentieth Century Warriors 1987. *Leisure interests:* writing, reading, gardening, tennis, sailing. *Address:* Wood End House, Wickham, near Fareham, Hants., PO17 6JZ, England (Home). *Telephone:* (0329) 832143.

CARVER, John Henry, A.M., PH.D., F.A.A.; Australian physicist; b. 5 Sept. 1926, Sydney; s. of J. F. Carver; m. Mary Fielding 1955; two s. two d.; ed. Fort St. Boys' High School, Sydney, Univs. of Sydney and Cambridge, U.K.; Cavendish Lab., Cambridge, U.K. 1949-53; Research School of Physical Sciences, Australian Nat. Univ. 1953-61; Atomic Energy Research Establishment, Harwell, U.K. 1958-59; Elder Prof. of Physics, Univ. of Adelaide 1962-78, Emer. Prof. 1979-; Naval Research Lab., Washington, D.C., U.S.A. 1968-69; Dir. and Prof. of Physics, Research School of Physical Sciences, Australian Nat. Univ. 1978-; mem. Radio Research Bd. of Australia 1964-82, Australian Science and Tech. Council 1979-86, Anglo-Australian Telescope Bd. 1978-, Australian Space Bd. 1986-; Chair. UN

Scientific and Tech. Sub-Cttee. on the Peaceful Uses of Outer Space 1970-; Fellow Australian Acad. of Technological Science and Eng.; mem. Int. Acad. of Astronauts. *Publications:* numerous articles on nuclear, atomic, molecular, atmospheric and space physics in scientific journals. *Address:* Research School of Physical Sciences, Australian National University, GPO Box 4, Canberra, A.C.T. 2601 (Office); 8 Holmes Crescent, Campbell, A.C.T. 2601, Australia (Home). *Telephone:* (062) 49 2476 (Office); (062) 49 8732 (Home).

CARY, Frank T., M.B.A.; American business executive; b. 14 Dec. 1920, Idaho; s. of Frank Taylor and Ida Cary; m. Anne Curtis 1943; three s. one d.; ed. Univ. of Calif. (Los Angeles) and Stanford Univ.; joined Int. Business Machines Corpn. 1948; IBM Vice-Pres. and Group Exec. and Gen. Man. Data Processing Group 1966; Sr. Vice-Pres. 1967; mem. Bd. of Dirs. IBM Corpn. 1968-; Pres. IBM Corpn. 1971-74, Chair. of the Bd. 1979-83, Chief Exec. 1973-81, Chair. Exec. Cttee. 1979-86; Dir. J. P. Morgan & Co., Morgan Guaranty Trust Co., American Broadcasting Co. Inc., Merck and Co. Inc.; mem. Business Council, Bd. of Trustees, American Museum of Natural History, Mass. Inst. of Technology, the Conf. Bd. *Address:* c/o International Business Machines Corpn., 2000 Purchase Street, Purchase, N.Y. 10577, U.S.A.

CASA-DEBELJEVIC, Lisa Della; Swiss singer; ed. Berne Conservatoire; Début at Zürich Opera House 1943; mem. Vienna State Opera Co. 1947-, New York Metropolitan Opera Co. 1953-; has appeared at Festivals at Salzburg 1947, 1948, 1950, 1953-58, Glyndebourne 1951, Bayreuth, Edinburgh 1952, Zürich, Lucerne, Munich 1951-58; has also appeared in London, Berlin, Paris, Milan, San Francisco and in South America, etc.; apptd. Austrian State Kammersängerin. *Address:* Schloss Gottlieben, Thurgau, Switzerland.

CASANOVA, Marc; French business executive; b. 14 Jan. 1926, Marrakech, Morocco; s. of Xavier Casanova and Berthe Cherfils; m. Daisy Pistorelli 1954; three d.; ed. Lycée Mangin, Marrakech; joined Mobil Oil Morocco 1946; Dir. Mobil Oil Tunisia 1953; Deputy Dir.-Gen. Mobil Oil N. Africa 1957, Mobil Oil W. Africa, Dakar 1961; Vice-Pres. and Deputy Dir.-Gen. Mobil Oil W. Africa, Paris 1963; Pres. Mobilrex and Mobil Sahara 1966-67, Mobil Oil AOEC 1967-68; Exec. Vice-Pres. Mobil Sekiyu-K K, Tokyo 1968-71; Vice-Pres. Mobil Far East, New York 1972-73; Pres. Mobil cos. Turkey 1973-78; Pres. Mobil Oil Italiana, Rome 1979-84; Pres. Dir.-Gen. Mobil Oil Française 1984-; Médaille Militaire, Croix de guerre. *Leisure interests:* golf, swimming. *Address:* Mobil Oil Française, Tour Septentrion, 92081 Paris-La-Défense cedex 9, France.

CASARDI, Alberico Aubrey; Italian diplomatist; b. 3 Feb. 1903, Siena; s. of Ruggero Casardi and Margaret Haskard; m. Virginia Harris 1935; Diplomatic Service 1927, New York, Lima, London, Berlin, Buenos Aires, UN, NATO, Brussels, Tokyo; joined Ministry of Foreign Affairs in Brindisi-Salerno 1943-44; Asst. to Sec.-Gen. 1944-48, and mem. Italian Del. to peace negotiations, Council of Foreign Ministers, London 1947, Peace Conf., Paris 1947, Council of Foreign Ministers, New York 1947, Buenos Aires 1948-51; Asst. to Sec.-Gen. of UN 1951-54, Observer and subsequently Amb. to UN 1955-56; Deputy Sec.-Gen. of NATO, Paris; Amb. to Belgium 1963-65; Amb. to Japan 1965-68; Italian Comm.-Gen. to Expo 70, 1968-70; special adviser to Banco Commerciale Italiana 1970-75. *Leisure interest:* painting. *Address:* Villa il Frosino, via delle Fontanelle 22, San Domenico di Fiesole, 1-50100 Florence, Italy. *Telephone:* (055) 59-111.

CASARÉS, Maria; French actress; b. 21 Nov. 1922, La Coruña, Spain; d. of Santiago Casarès Quiroga and Gloria Perez; ed. Conservatoire nationale d'art dramatique; Début, Théâtre des Mathurins, Paris 1942; mem. Comédie Française 1952, Théâtre national populaire 1955; appearances have included roles in Six personnages en quête d'auteur, Le triomphe de l'amour, Macbeth, La ville, Phèdre, La danse de mort, Antony and Cleopatra, Peer Gynt, Les possédés, Les paravents, Le borgne est roi, Les cuisines du château, La nuit de Madame Lucienne, Quai Ouest; film appearances include: Les enfants du paradis, Les dames du Bois de Boulogne, La chartreuse de Parme, Orphée, Ombre et lumière, Le testament d'Orphée, Blanche et Marie 1985; also appears on television; Commdr. des Arts et des Lettres. *Publication:* Résidente privilegiée (mémoires) 1980. *Address:* 8 rue Asseline, 75014 Paris, France (Home).

CASAROLI, H.E. Cardinal Agostino; Italian ecclesiasic; b. 24 Nov. 1914, Castel S. Giovanni, Piacenza; s. of Giovanni Emilio and Giuditta Casroli; ordained priest 1937; Titular Archbishop of Carthage 1967-; cr. Cardinal 1979; Sec. of State and Prefect of the Council for the Public Affairs of the Church July 1979-; mem. Sacred Congregation for the Doctrine of the Faith, Sacred Congregation for the Bishops, Pontifical Comm. for the Revision of Canon Law, Cardinals' Comm. for the supervision of the Istituto per le Opere di Religione, Secr. for Non-Believers; Pres. Pontifical Comm. for the Vatican City State; entitled Ss XII Apostoli; assigned to represent the Pontiff in the powers and responsibilities inherent in his sovereignty over the State of Vatican City 1984-. *Publication:* Der Heilige Stuhl und die Völkergemeinschaft 1981. *Address:* 00120 Città del Vaticano, Roma, Italy.

CASE, Everett Needham, M.A.; American educator and historian; b. 9 April 1901, Plainfield, N.J.; s. of James Herbert and Alice Needham Case; m. Josephine Young 1931; three s. one d.; ed. Princeton Univ., Corpus Christi Coll., Cambridge, and Harvard Univ.; Asst. in History, Harvard Univ. 1926-27; Asst. to Owen D. Young 1927-33; Exec. Sec. Central Banking and Industrial Cttee., Washington, D.C. 1932-33; Asst. Dean, Harvard Graduate School of Business Admin. 1939-42; Pres. Colgate Univ. 1942-62, Emer. 1962-; Consultant on Far Eastern Affairs to Sec. of State 1949; Chair. American Council on Educ. 1951-52; Pres. Alfred P. Sloan Foundation 1962-68; Dir. Fed. Reserve Bank of New York 1961-68, Chair. 1966-68; Dir. Nat. Educational Television 1954-61, 1962- (Chair. 1963-69); Trustee, Memorial Sloan-Kettering Cancer Center 1963-68, Sloan-Kettering Inst. for Cancer Research 1966-68, Millbrook School 1944-69 (Chair. 1960-68), Educational Broadcasting Corpn. 1965-68; mem. Council on Foreign Relations, UNA-U.S.A. China Panel 1966-68; Dir. Nat. Cttee. on U.S.-China Relations 1966-75; several hon. degrees. *Publication:* Owen D. Young and American Enterprise—A Biography (with Josephine Young Case) 1982. *Leisure interests:* music, swimming. *Address:* Van Hornesville, Herkimer County, N.Y. 13475, U.S.A. *Telephone:* (315) 858-0036.

CASEY, Albert V., M.B.A.; American airline executive; b. 28 Feb. 1920, Boston, Mass.; s. of John J. Casey and Norine Doyle; m. Eleanor Anne Welch 1945; one s. one d.; ed. Harvard Univ. and Graduate School of Business Admin.; Asst. Vice-Pres. and Asst. Treas. Southern Pacific Co. 1953-61; Vice-Pres. and Treas. REA Express 1961-63; Vice-Pres. Finance, Times Mirror Co. 1963-64, Exec. Vice-Pres. and Dir. 1964-66, Pres. and mem. Exec. Cttee. 1966-74; Pres. American Airlines Inc. 1974-85, Chair. 1974-85, Chief Exec. 1974-85; Postmaster-Gen. of U.S.A. Jan. 1986; Distinguished Prof. of Business Policy Edwin L. Cox School, Southern Methodist Univ., Dallas 1986-; Dir. Pacific American Income Shares Inc., Boys' Club of America, C.I.T. Financial Co., Times Mirror Co., LTV 1987-; mem. Bd. of Visitors of UCLA Graduate School of Man., Bd. of Councillors of Univ. of S. Calif. School of Business Admin., Visiting Cttee., Bd. of Overseers, Harvard Business School. *Leisure interests:* golf, tennis. *Address:* 2626 First Republic Bank Center, Tower II, Dallas, Tex. 75201, U.S.A.

CASEY, Most. Rev. Eamonn, L.PH., B.A.; Irish ecclesiastic; b. 23 April 1927, Firies, Co. Kerry; s. of John Casey and Helena Shanahan; ed. St. Munchin's Coll., Limerick and Univ. and Seminary at Maynooth; ordained, Diocese of Limerick 1951; curate and teacher 1951-55; attached to St. John's Cathedral, Limerick 1955-60; Chaplain to the Irish, Slough, Bucks. 1960-63; Nat. Dir. Catholic Housing Aid Soc., London 1963-69; Bishop of Kerry 1969-76; Bishop of Galway 1976-; mem. numerous comms. and socs. *Publication:* A Home of your Own (with Adam Ferguson). *Leisure interests:* music, theatre, concerts, films, conversation, motoring. *Address:* The Diocesan Office, The Cathedral, Galway (Office); Mount St. Mary's, Taylor's Hill, Galway, Ireland (Home). *Telephone:* (091) 63566 (Office).

CASEY, Michael Bernard, LL.B.; British fmr. civil servant and business executive; b. 1 Sept. 1928, Barnes, Surrey; s. of Joseph Bernard and Dorothy (née Love) Casey; m. Sally Louise Smith 1963; two s. two d.; ed. Colwyn Bay Grammar School, London School of Econs.; Hon. Soc. of Middle Temple, Manchester Business School; served in R.A.F. 1947-49; at Ministry of Agric., Fisheries and Food 1954-63, Office of the Minister for Science 1963-64, at Dept. of Econ. Affairs 1964-69, Asst. Sec. 1967; Asst. Sec., Ministry of Tech. 1969-70, Dept. of Trade and Industry 1971-72, Dept. of Prices and Consumer Protection 1973-75; Under-Sec. Head of Shipbuilding Policy Div., Dept. of Industry 1975-77; Chief Exec. and Deputy Chair., British Shipbuilders 1977-80; Chair. and Man. Dir. Mather and Platt 1980-81; Chair. Sallingbury Casey Ltd. (fmrly. Michael Casey & Assocs. Ltd.); Dir. Robin Marlar Ltd. 1982-, Marlar Int. Ltd. 1982-, Grosvenor Place Amalgamations Ltd. 1982-, IRPLAN Ltd. 1983-. *Leisure interest:* golf. *Address:* 10 Phillimore Terrace, London, W.8., England.

CASEY, Raymond, D.SC., PH.D., F.R.S.; British geologist (retd.); b. 10 Oct. 1917; s. of Samuel G. Casey and Gladys V. H. (Garrett) Casey; m. Norah K. Pakeman 1943 (died 1974); two s.; ed. St. Mary's, Folkestone and Univ. of Reading; Asst. Geological Survey and Geological Museum 1939, Asst. Experimental Officer 1946, Experimental Officer 1949, Sr. Geologist 1957, Prin. Geologist 1960; Sr. Prin. Scientific Officer, Inst. of Geological Sciences, London 1964-79. *Publications:* two books and numerous articles on Mesozoic palaeontology and stratigraphy in scientific journals. *Leisure interest:* research into early Russian postal and military history. *Address:* 38 Reed Avenue, Orpington, Kent, England.

CASEY, Robert P., J.D.; American state governor; b. 9 Jan. 1932; m. Ellen T. Harding; ed. Holy Cross Coll. and George Washington Univ.; Gov. of Pennsylvania 1987-; Democrat. *Address:* Office of the Governor, Main Capitol Building, Room 225, Harrisburg, Pa. 17120, U.S.A.

CASH, Sir Gerald Christopher, G.C.M.G., G.C.V.O., O.B.E., J.P.; Bahamas Governor-General; b. 28 May 1917, Nassau; s. of the late Wilfred Cash and the late Lillian Cash; m. Dorothy Cash; two s. one d.; ed. Govt. High School, Nassau, Middle Temple, London; called to Bar, Bahamas 1940, London 1948; private law practice 1940-45; J.P. 1941-; general law practice 1945-76; Acting Gov.-Gen. of the Commonwealth of the Bahamas 1976-78, Gov.-Gen. 1979-88; Chair. Bd. of Govs. of Govt. High School 1949-63; Chair. Labour Bd. (Bahamas) 1950-52; Chair. Nat. Cttee., United World Colls. 1977-81; Vice-Chancellor, Anglican Diocese of the Bahamas; mem. Bd. of Educ. 1950-62; mem. Immigration Cttee., Road Traffic Cttee., Air Transport Licensing Authority 1958-62; mem. Police Service Comm.

1964–69; mem. Bd. of Dirs., Cen. Bank of the Bahamas; Coronation Medal 1953, Silver Jubilee Medal 1977, Silver Medal of the Olympic Order 1983. *Address:* P.O. Box N-476, Nassau, Bahamas. *Telephone:* 322 2956 (Office); 393 4767 (Home).

CASH, Johnny D. H.; American singer, composer; b. 26 Feb. 1932, Kingsland, Ark.; s. of Ray and Carrie (née Rivers) Cash; m. 2nd June Carter 1968; one s., four d. by previous marriage; ed. Gardner-Webb Coll., Nat. Univ. San Diego; served with U.S.A.F. TV appearances include: The Johnny Cash Show 1969–71, Muscular Dystrophy Telethon 1972, Johnny Cash at San Quentin; documentary films: Trail of Tears, Johnny Cash, The Man, His World, His Music, United Way of America 1972; acted in films A Gunfight, North and South 1985, Stagecoach 1986; wrote, produced and narrated film The Gospel Road; compositions include: I Walk the Line, Folsom Prison Blues, At Folsom Prison, Man In Black, Don't Take Your Guns to Town; composer movie sound tracks: I Walk the Line, Little Fauss and Big Halsy; albums include: Folsom and San Quentin, John R. Cash, Last Gunfighter, The Baron, Believer Sings the Truth, The Holy Land, The True West; Pres. House of Cash Inc., Song of Cash Inc.; Vice-Pres. Family of Man Music Inc.; mem. Country Music Asscn., Country Music Hall of Fame 1980; Hon. D.Hum.Litt. (San Diego) 1976. *Publications:* Man in Black (autobiography) 1975, Man in White (religious novel) 1986. *Address:* c/o Agency for Performing Arts, 9000 Sunset Boulevard, 1200 Los Angeles, Calif. 90069, U.S.A.

CASH, Pat; Australian tennis player; b. 27 May 1965, Melbourne; coached by Ian Barclay; trainer Anne Quinn; winner U.S. Open 1982, Brisbane and in winning Australian Davis Cup team 1983, in quarter-finals Wimbledon 1985, finalist Australian Open 1987, Wimbledon Champion 1987. *Address:* Melbourne, Australia.

CASIMIR, Hendrik Brugt Gerhard, PH.D.; Netherlands physicist; b. 15 July 1909, The Hague; s. of Rommert Casimir and Teunsina Dina Borgman; m. Josina Maria Jonker 1933; one s. four d.; ed. Univs. of Leiden, Copenhagen, and at Zürich; various research positions, Leiden 1933–42; joined staff of Philips Research Labs., Eindhoven 1942, Dir. of Labs. 1946, mem. Bd. of Man. of Philips 1957–72, supervising Philips research activities in various countries; Pres. European Physical Soc. 1972–75; mem. Royal Acad. of Netherlands 1946– (Pres. 1973); Foreign Hon. mem. American Acad. of Arts and Sciences; mem. Royal Flemish Acad. of Science, Letters and Arts; Corresp. mem. Heidelberg Acad. of Science, Austrian Acad. of Sciences, Vienna; Foreign mem. Royal Soc., London 1970, Finnish Acad. of Technical Sciences, Helsinki, American Philosophical Soc., Philadelphia; Foreign Assoc. N.A.S., Acad. des Sciences, France, Nat. Acad. of Engineers, Washington, D.C.; Alfred Ewing Medal (London), Hon. D.Sc. Tech. Univ. Copenhagen, Louvain, Tech. Univ. Aachen, Edinburgh, Cranfield Inst. of Tech., Columbia Univ., Univ. of Paris VI, Univ. of Sussex. *Publications:* Haphazard Reality 1983, and many papers on theoretical physics, applied mathematics and low temperature physics. *Address:* De Zegge 7, 5591 TT Heeze, Netherlands. *Telephone:* 040-862233.

ČÁSLAVSKÁ, Věra; Czechoslovak gymnast; b. 3 May 1942, Prague; ed. Faculty of Physical Training and Sport, Charles Univ., Prague; coach, Sports Centre, Sparta Prague 1970–79; coach, Mexico 1979–; overall, vault and beam gold medals, Olympic Games, Tokyo 1964; overall, floor, asymmetric bars and vault gold medals, beam silver medal, Olympic Games, Mexico City 1968; overall and vault first place, beam and floor second place and mem. winning team World Championships, Dortmund 1966; five first places, European Championships, Sofia 1965 and Amsterdam 1967; Meritorious Master of Sports 1962, Order of the Republic 1968. *Address:* SVS Sparta Prague, Korunovační 29, Prague 7, Czechoslovakia.

CASORIA, H.E. Cardinal Giuseppe; Italian ecclesiastic; b. 1 Oct. 1908, Acerra; ordained priest 1930; made Bishop 1972; Titular Archbishop of Vescovia; Prefect of the Sacred Congregation of the Sacraments; Consultant to the Sacred Congregation of the Oriental Churches; mem. Pontifical Comm. for the Interpretation of the Decrees of the Vatican Council II; cr. Cardinal 1983; Dean of S. Giuseppe in Via Trionfale 1984–. *Address:* via Pancrazio Pfeiffer 10, 00193 Rome, Italy. *Telephone:* (06) 698-4245.

CASS, Geoffrey Arthur, M.A., C.B.I.M., F.I.I.M.; British publishing executive; b. 11 Aug. 1932; s. of late Arthur and Jessie Cass; m. Olwen M. Richards 1957; four d.; ed. Queen Elizabeth Grammar School, Darlington and Jesus Coll., Oxford; Nuffield Coll., Oxford 1957–58; R.A.F. 1958–60; Ed. Automation 1960–61; Consultant, PA Man. Consultants Ltd. 1960–65; Pvt. Man. Consultant, British Communications Corpn. and Controls and Communications Ltd. 1965; Dir. Controls and Communications Ltd. 1966–69; Dir. George Allen & Unwin 1965–67, Man. Dir. 1967–71; Man. Dir. Cambridge Univ. Press (Publishing Div.) 1971–72, Chief Exec. of the Press 1972–; Sec. Press Syndicate, Univ. of Cambridge 1974–; Univ. Printer 1982–83; Fellow, Clare Hall, Cambridge 1979–; Chair. Royal Shakespeare Co. 1985–, Royal Shakespeare Theatre Trust 1983–, British Int. Tennis and Nat. Training 1985–; mem. numerous other trusts, cttees. and advisory bodies particularly in connection with theatre and lawn tennis; Oxford tennis Blue, and badminton; played in Wimbledon Tennis Championships 1954, 1955, 1956, 1959; British Veterans Singles Champion, Wimbledon 1978; Chevalier, Ordre des Arts et des Lettres. *Publications:* articles in professional journals. *Leisure interests:* tennis, theatre. *Address:* Middlefield, Huntingdon Road, Cambridge, CB3 0LH, England.

CASSAB, Judy, A.O., C.B.E.; Australian painter; b. 15 Aug. 1920, Vienna, Austria; d. of Imre Kaszab and Ilona Kont; m. John Kampfner 1939; two s.; ed. Budapest and Prague; mem. Council for the Honours of Australia 1975–79; Trustee, Art Gallery of N.S.W. 1979–88; has held exhbns. in galleries throughout Australia, in London and Paris since 1963 and works are in many Australian galleries including Nat. Gallery, Canberra, galleries in U.K. including Nat. Portrait Gallery, London, in U.S.A. and at Nat. Gallery of Budapest; 4 individual exhbns. 1985; several prizes including Sir Charles Lloyd Jones Memorial Prize (four times). *Publication:* Ten Australian Portraits (lithographs) 1984, Judy Cassab, Places, Faces and Fantasies 1985, Artists and Friends 1988. *Address:* 16C Ocean Avenue Double Bay, Sydney, N.S.W., Australia 2028. *Telephone:* 326 1348.

CASSAR, Francis Felix; Maltese diplomatist; b. 10 May 1934, Malta; s. of Carmelo Cassar and Filomena Cassar; m. Doreen Marjorie 1969; two s.; ed. The Lyceum, Malta; emigrated to U.K. 1953; studied mechanical eng. 1953–58; Man. Dir. of own motor eng. co.; active in movement for independence; Sec. Maltese Labour Movement (U.K.); rep. Malta Labour Party in U.K. from 1971, and also at meetings of the Bureau of the Socialist Int.; Co. Sec. of Malta Drydocks (U.K.) Ltd. 1975; J.P. 1972–80; High Commr. in U.K. 1985–87. *Leisure interests:* music, football and Do-it-Yourself. *Address:* c/o Ministry of Foreign Affairs, Valletta, Malta.

CASSAR, Joseph, B.A., LL.D., M.P.; Maltese politician; b. 22 Jan. 1918, Qrendi; s. of late Giuseppe and Giovanna (née Magri) Cassar; m. Janie Pace 1948; ed. Bishop's Seminary, Gozo, the Lyceum, Malta, Univ. of Malta; with Home Guard Voluntary Force 1940–44; Barrister 1943–; mem. Council of Govt. 1945–46, Speaker, Legis. Assem. 1947–48; Minister of Justice 1949–50, 1951–53, 1955–58; Minister of Labour, Employment and Welfare 1971–74, Minister of Educ. and Culture 1974–76, Minister of Justice, Lands, Housing and Parl. Affairs 1976, Deputy Prime Minister 1976, and Deputy Leader for Govt. Affairs 1976, 1981–; Minister of Finance, Customs and People's Financial Investments 1979–81, Sr. Deputy Prime Minister and Minister of Justice and Parl. Affairs 1981–87; Labour. *Leisure interests:* reading, swimming, travel. *Address:* The Palace, Valletta, Malta.

CASSEL, Jean-Pierre; French actor; b. 27 Oct. 1932, Paris; m. Anne Célérier 1981; three s.; film debut in 1959; frequent TV appearances. *Films include:* Les Jeux de l'Amour, Le Caporal Epinglé, Paris brûle-t-il? Those Magnificent Men in Their Flying Machines, Oh What A Lovely War!, Baxter, The Discreet Charm of the Bourgeoisie, The Three Musketeers, Le Mouton Enragé, Murder on the Orient Express, That Lucky Touch, The Twist, Someone is Killing, The Great Chefs of Europe, Les Rendezvous d'Anna, From Hell to Victory, The Return of the Musketeers, Mangeclous; TV includes: Love in a Cold Climate, Shillingbury Tales, La Truite, Liberty, Casanova. *Address:* c/o I.C.M., 388/396 Oxford Street, London, W.I, England.

CASSELS, Field-Marshal Sir (Archibald) James (Halkett), G.C.B., K.B.E., D.S.O.; British army officer; b. 28 Feb. 1907, Quetta, then in India; s. of late Gen. Sir Robert A. Cassels and the late Lady Florence E. Cassels; m. 1st Joyce Kirk 1935 (died 1978), one s.; m. 2nd Joyce Dickson 1978; ed. Rugby School and Royal Military Coll., Sandhurst; commissioned 1926; served Second World War, G.O.C. 51st Highland Div. 1945, G.O.C. 6th Airborne 1946; G.O.C. 1st British Commonwealth Div., Korea 1951–52; Commdr. 1st British Corps 1953–54; Dir.-Gen. of Mil. Training, War Office 1954–57; Dir. of Operations, Malaya 1957–59; G.O.C.-in-C. Eastern Command 1959; C.-in-C. British Army of the Rhine and Commdr. NATO Northern Army Group 1960–63; Adjutant-Gen. to the Forces 1963–65; Chief of Gen. Staff 1965–68. *Leisure interests:* shooting and fishing. *Address:* Hamble End, Higham Road, Barrow, Bury St. Edmunds, Suffolk, England. *Telephone:* Bury St. Edmunds 810895.

CASSELS, James Macdonald, M.A., PH.D., F.R.S.; British physicist; b. 9 Sept. 1924, Penang, Malaysia; s. of Alastair Macdonald Cassels and Ada White Scott; m. 1st Jane Helen Thera Lawrence (died 1977); one s. one d.; m. 2nd Analesia Theresa Bestman (divorced 1989); ed. Rochester House School, Edinburgh, St. Lawrence Coll., Ramsgate, and Trinity Coll., Cambridge; Harwell Fellow and Prin. Scientific Officer, A.E.R.E., Harwell 1949–53; Lecturer 1953, Sr. Lecturer, Univ. of Liverpool, Prof. of Experimental Physics, Univ. of Liverpool 1956–59; Extraordinary Fellow, Churchill Coll., Cambridge 1959–60; Visiting Prof. Cornell Univ. 1959–60; Lyon Jones Prof. of Physics, Univ. of Liverpool 1960–82, Hon. Fellow 1982–83, now Prof. Emer.; mem. Council Royal Soc. 1968–69, Fellow; mem. Dept. of Energy Combined Heat and Power Cttee. 1973–77, Chair. Heat Load Density Working Party 1976–77; Rutherford Medal, Inst. of Physics 1973; Chair. Igitur Ltd. 1985–. *Publications:* Basic Quantum Mechanics 1970, and articles in scientific journals on atomic, nuclear and elementary particle physics, Energy Papers Nos. 20, 34, 35, H.M.S.O., Patents on sugar metabolism, AIDS, etc. *Leisure interests:* travelling, motoring and fishing. *Address:* 18 St. Michael at Plea, Norwich, NR3 1EP, England. *Telephone:* (0603) 660999.

CASSELS, John William Scott, M.A., PH.D., F.R.S., F.R.S.E.; British mathematician; b. 11 July 1922, Durham City; s. of John William Cassels and Muriel Speakman Cassels (née Lobjoit); m. Constance Mabel Senior 1949;

one s. one d.; ed. Neville's Cross Council School, Durham, George Heriot's School, Edinburgh, and Edinburgh and Cambridge Univs.; lecturer, Manchester Univ. 1949–50, Cambridge Univ. 1950–65; Reader in Arithmetic, Cambridge Univ. 1965–67; Sadleirian Prof. of Pure Mathematics, Cambridge Univ. 1967–84; Fellow of Trinity Coll., Cambridge 1949–. *Publications:* An Introduction to Diophantine Approximations 1957, An Introduction to the Geometry of Numbers 1959, Rational Quadratic Forms 1979, Economics for Mathematicians 1981, Local Fields 1986. *Leisure interests:* The Higher Arithmetic, gardening. *Address:* Department of Pure Mathematics and Mathematical Statistics, 16 Mill Lane, Cambridge, CB2 1SB, (Office); 3 Luard Close, Cambridge, CB2 2PL, England (Home). *Telephone:* (0223) 337975 (Office); (0223) 246108 (Home).

CASSIDY, Sheila Anne, B.M., B.CH., M.A.; British medical practitioner; b. 18 Aug. 1937, Lincs.; d. of late Air Vice-Marshal J. R. Cassidy and of Barbara Margaret Drew; ed. Our Lady of Mercy Coll., Parramatta, N.S.W., Univ. of Sydney and Oxford Univ.; resident posts, Radcliffe Infirmary, Oxford 1963–68, Leicester Royal Infirmary 1968–70; Medical Asst. 1970–71; Asst. Surgeon. Assistencia Pública, Santiago, Chile 1971–75; tortured and imprisoned for treating wounded guerilla Nov.–Dec. 1975; human rights lecturing 1976–77; studied monastic life, Ampleforth Abbey, York 1977–79; novice in Bernardine Cistercian Convent 1979–80; resident in radiotherapy, Plymouth Gen. Hosp. 1980–82, Research Registrar, Dept. Radiotherapy 1982–; Medical Dir., St. Luke's Hospice, Plymouth 1982–; Valiant for Truth media award. *Publications:* Audacity to Believe (autobiog.) 1977, Prayer for Pilgrims 1979, Sharing the Darkness 1988. *Leisure interests:* writing, broadcasting, drawing, walking, swimming. *Address:* St. Luke's Hospice, Stamford Road, Turnchapel, Plymouth, England.

CASSIERS, Juan, D. EN D.; Belgian diplomatist; b. 11 May 1931, Middelkerke; m. Daisy Lannoy 1956; two s. two d.; ed. St. Jean Berchmans Coll., Brussels and Catholic Univ., Louvain; entered Foreign Service 1956; Attaché Del. to NATO 1959–61; Embassy Sec., Washington 1962–67; Deputy Head Scientific Co-operation Office, Ministry of Foreign Affairs 1967–70; Deputy Perm. Rep. to OECD 1970–73, Perm. Rep. 1987–; Minister-Counsellor Embassy to China, Peking 1974–76, Embassy, Bonn 1976–79; Head Political and Mil. Affairs Office 1979–81; Prin. Pvt. Sec. to the Foreign Minister 1981; Amb. at Large 1981–82; Perm. Rep. to NATO 1983–87; Commdr. Order of the Crown, Order of Leopold, Order of Merit (Fed. Repub. of Germany). *Publication:* The Hazards of Peace 1975. *Address:* 4, Square du Ranelagh, 75016 Paris, France.

CASSILLY, Richard; American (tenor) opera singer; b. 14 Dec. 1927, Washington, D.C.; s. of Robert Rogers Cassily and Vera F. Swart; m. Helen Koliopulos 1951; four s. three d.; ed. Peabody Conservatory of Music, Baltimore, Md.; with New York City Opera 1955–66, Chicago Lyric 1959–, San Francisco Opera 1966–; Deutsche Oper Berlin 1965–, Hamburgische Staatsoper 1966–, Covent Garden 1968–, La Scala, Milan 1970, Wiener Staatsoper 1970, Staatsoper München 1970, Paris Opera 1972, Metropolitan Opera 1973–; Kammersänger 1973; television performances of Otello, Peter Grimes, St. of Bleeker Street, Fidelio, Wozzeck and Die Meistersinger; recordings for D.G., C.B.S., E.M.I. *Address:* c/o Robert Lombardo Associates, 61 West 62nd Street, 6F New York, N.Y. 10023, U.S.A.

CASSIRER, Henry R., PH.D.; American radio and television administrator; b. 2 Sept. 1911, Berlin; s. of Kurt and Eva (née Solmitz) Cassirer; divorced; one d.; m. 2nd Arlette Freund; ed. Odenwaldschule, Univs. of Frankfurt, Paris, Cologne, London School of Econs. and London Univ.; Announcer/translator, B.B.C. European Service 1938–40; Foreign News Ed., Columbia Broadcasting System (C.B.S.), New York 1940–44; Television News Ed., C.B.S. 1944–49; freelance producer of TV documentary programmes 1949–52; teacher of TV Production and Public Affairs Programming, New School for Social Research, New York Univ. School of Radio Techniques; with UNESCO 1952–71, Dir. Use of Mass Media in Out-of-School Educ.; Adviser on Educational Radio/TV to Govt. of India 1957, Pakistan 1960–, Israel 1961–, Senegal 1963–, Brazil 1967–, Mali 1968–, Algeria 1969–, Singapore, United States (Alaska) 1970, Morocco 1974–, Ghana 1975, Fed. Repub. of Germany and Ford Foundation for West Africa projects 1976, Portugal for World Bank 1976; Int. Consultant communication and educ. 1971–, parent education 1979 (Int. Year of the Child); Visiting Prof. Ontario Inst. for Studies in Educ. 1974; Hon. Devt. Consultant Univ. of London Dept. of Extra-Mural Studies 1979–; Communication and Education Consultant on Disability, UNESCO 1981–; Consultant to European Space Agency 1986–88; Vice-Pres. Groupement pour l'insertion des personnes handicapées physiques (G.I.H.P.), France 1981–; Vice-Pres. Collectif handicap de la région Annecienne. *Publications:* Television, a World Survey 1954, Television Teaching Today 1960, Bildung und Kommunikation 1974; films: Man of our Age—The Sculpture of Jo Davidson 19, Buma-African Sculpture Speaks 1952, Television Comes to the Land 1958, Adult Education and the Media 1984, Co-operation between the Media and Adult Education Bodies, UNESCO 1985. *Leisure interests:* stereo, photography, organic gardening. *Address:* Les Moulins, 74290 Menthon St. Bernard, France. *Telephone:* 50 60 18 53.

CASSON, Sir Hugh Maxwell, Kt., C.H., K.C.V.O., M.A., P.R.A., F.R.I.B.A., R.D.I., HON. DES. R.C.A.; British architect; b. 23 May 1910; s. of late Randal Casson; m. Margaret Macdonald Trap 1938; three d.; ed. Eastbourne Coll., St.

John's Coll., Cambridge, and Bartlett School of Architecture, Univ. Coll., London; private practice as architect 1935–; Camouflage Officer in Air Ministry 1940–44; Tech. Officer Ministry of Town and Country Planning 1944–46; Dir. of Architecture, Festival of Britain 1951; mem. MARS Group 1945–; Prof. of Environmental Design, R.C.A. 1953–75; mem. Royal Mint Advisory Cttee. 1972–; Pres. Royal Acad. of Arts 1976–84; Provost, R.C.A. 1980–86; Vice-Pres. Brighton Festival Soc. 1982–84; mem. Royal Danish Acad. 1954, Royal Fine Art Comm. 1960–84, British Council 1977–81; Hon. LL.D. (Birmingham) 1977, (Southampton) 1977; Hon. D.Litt. (Loughborough Univ.) 1979; Dr. h.c. (Royal Coll. of Art, London) 1985; Albert Medal, Royal Soc. of Arts 1984. *Publications:* Bombed Churches as War Memorials 1944, Houses: Permanence and Prefabrication (with Anthony Chitty) 1945, Homes by the Million 1945, An Introduction to Victorian Architecture 1948, Inscape: The Design of Interiors 1968, Nanny Says (with Joyce Grenfell) 1972, Diary 1981, Hugh Casson's London 1984, Hugh Casson's Oxford 1988. *Leisure interest:* drawing. *Address:* 6 Hereford Mansions, Hereford Road, London, W2 5BA, England. *Telephone:* 01-221 7774 (Office); 01-727 2999 (Home).

CASTAING, Raimond Bernard René; French professor of physics; b. 28 Dec. 1921, Monaco; s. of Fernand and Lucienne (née Mirot) Castaing; m. Jeanne Gadrat 1947; two s. one d.; ed. Lycée de Monaco, Collège de Condom, Gers, Lycée de Toulouse, Ecole Normale Supérieure, Paris; Research Eng., French Office for Aeronautical Research (ONERA) 1947–51, Dir.-Gen. 1968–73; Lecturer, Univ. of Toulouse 1952–56, Sorbonne 1956–59, Prof. Univ. of Paris Sud 1959–; mem. Deutsche Akademie der Naturforscher Leopoldina, Halle an der Saale, German Dem. Repub. 1968–, French Acad. des Sciences, Paris 1977–; Foreign mem. Royal Swedish Acad. of Sciences, Stockholm 1978–; First Pres. Soc. Française de Microscopie Electronique 1959–60, Pres. Soc. Française de Physique 1973; Hon. Dr. (Univ. of Tübingen, Fed. Repub. of Germany) 1963; Commdr. Ordre Nat. du Mérite 1976, Cmmdr., Légion d'Honneur 1986, Commdr. des Palmes académiques 1984; John Price Wetherill Medal (Franklin Inst., Pa.) 1960, Médaille Réaumur (Soc. Française de Métallurgie) 1963, Holweck Prize (Physical Soc. and Soc. Française de Physique) 1966, Grand Prix de la Technique de la Ville de Paris 1966, Albert Sauveur Achievement Award (American Soc. for Metals) 1967, Prix du Centenaire du Crédit Lyonnais (Acad. des Sciences, Paris) 1967 Maurice F. Hasler Award (Soc. for Applied Spectroscopy, U.S.A.) 1970, Gold Medal C.N.R.S. 1975, Brinell Medal (Swedish Acad. for Eng. Sciences, Stockholm) 1977, Roebling Medal (Mineralogical Soc. of America) 1977, Prix des Trois Physiciens 1984, Grande Médaille le Chatelier de la Société Française de Métallurgie 1985. *Publications:* about 100 publications since 1949, including Electron Probe Microanalysis 1960, Secondary Ion Microanalysis and Energy-Selecting Electron Microscopy 1971, Thermodynamique Statistique 1970. *Leisure interests:* mountaineering, family tree. *Address:* Laboratoire de Physique des Solides, Bat. 510, Université de Paris Sud, 91405 Orsay (Office); 64 bis, Avenue Paul Langevin, 92260 Fontenay-aux-Roses, France (Home). *Telephone:* 6941 5380 (Office); 4350 5234 (Home).

CASTAÑEDA, Jorge; Mexican diplomatist; b. 1 Oct. 1921, México, D.F.; s. of Jorge Castañeda and Carmen Alvarez de la Rosa; m. Alicia C. de Castañeda 1985; one s. one d.; ed. Univ. Nacional Autónoma de México; joined Mexican Foreign Service 1950; Legal Counsel, Ministry of Foreign Affairs 1955–58, Dir.-Gen. for Int. Orgs. 1959–60; Alt. Rep. to UN 1961–62; Amb. to Egypt 1962–65; Prin. Dir., Ministry of Foreign Affairs 1965–; Under-Sec. of State 1976; Perm. Rep. to Int. Orgs. in Geneva; Minister of Foreign Affairs 1979–82; Amb. Emer., Amb. to France 1983–; Prof. of Int. Public Law, Escuela Libre de Derecho 1958; Prof. of Int. Public Law, Univ. Nacional Autónoma de México 1959–; mem. UN Int. Law Comm. 1967– (Chair. 1973); del. to numerous int. confs. including many sessions of UN Gen. Assembly; mem. Inst. of Int. Law, Int. Law Asscn., Hispano-Luso-American Inst. of Int. Law; now Amb. at Large. *Publications:* México y el Orden Internacional 1956, Mexico and the United Nations 1958, Valor Jurídico de las Resoluciones de las Naciones Unidas 1967 (English version 1969), La No Proliferación de las Armas Nucleares en el Orden Universal 1969, and articles in various legal journals. *Address:* Embassy of Mexico, 9 rue de Longchamp, 75116 Paris, France; Anillo Periférico sur 3180, Depto 1120, Jardines del Pedregal, 01900 Mexico.

CASTAÑON DE MENA, Juan, D.ARCH.; Spanish army officer; ed. Escuela Técnica Superior de Arquitectura, Madrid, Acad. de Infantería and Escuela Superior de Guerra; Capt. Gen. Staff 1931; active service Corunna, 8th military div. and Gallegas Columns campaign 1936, later C.-in-C. Gen. Staff 82nd Div. at Teruel, Alfambra, Levante, Ebro, Cataluña and liberation of Madrid, promoted Lt. Col.; Prof., Gen. Staff School; Brig.-Gen. 1959; Tactics Prof. Senior Army School 1959; A.D.C. to Gen. Franco 1951–75; Mil. Gov., Madrid 1962; C.-in-C. 11th Mechanized Div. 1964; Lt.-Gen. 1965; Chief of Mil. House of Gen. Franco 1965; Minister of the Army 1969–73; several decorations, including Gran Cruz de Isabel la Católica, Gran Cruz de Carlos III, Commdr. Legion of Merit, U.S.A. *Address:* Lopez de Hoyez 15, Madrid 6 (Office); Lagasca 77-6°, Madrid 6, Spain (Home).

CASTELLI, Leo; American art gallery owner; b. 4 Sept. 1907, Trieste, Italy; s. of Ernest Krauss and Bianca Castelli; m. 1st Ileana Schapira 1933 (divorced 1960), 2nd Antoinette Fraissex du Bost 1963; one s. one d.; ed. Univ. of Milan and Columbia Univ., New York; early career in int. banking;

opened Galérie René Douin, Paris; worked in Knit-Goods Mfg. 1939–49; owner, Leo Castelli Gallery, New York 1957–; Hon. Pres. Modern Art Dept. Museo Revoltella, Trieste; Hon Ph.D. (School of Visual Arts, New York) Chevalier, Légion d'honneur; Butler Medal of Life Achievement in American Art 1987; and other awards. *Leisure interests:* tennis, reading. *Address:* Leo Castelli Gallery, 420 West Broadway, New York, N.Y. 10012, U.S.A.

CASTILLO, Michel Xavier Janicot del, L. ÉS L., L. EN P.; French writer; b. 2 Aug. 1933, Madrid, Spain; s. of Michel Janicot and Isabelle del Castillo; ed. Coll. des jésuites d'Ubeba, Spain, Lycée Janson-de-Sailly, Paris; mem. Soc. des gens de lettres, PEN; Prix des Neufs 1957, Prix des Magots 1973, Grand Prix des libraires 1973, Prix Chateaubriand 1975, Prix Renaudot 1981. *Publications:* Tanguy 1957, La Guitare 1958, Le Colleur d'affiches 1959, Le Manège espagnol 1960, Tara 1962, Gerardo Laïn 1969, Le Vent de la nuit 1973, Le Silence des pierres 1975, Le Sortilège espagnol 1977, Les Cyprés meurent en Italie 1979, Les Louves de l'Escurial 1980, La nuit du décret 1981, La Gloire de Dina 1984, Nos Andalousies 1985. *Address:* Le Mas des Bories, Saint-Victor-de-Malcap, 30500 Saint-Ambroise, France.

CASTILLO ARRIOLA, Eduardo; Guatemalan diplomatist; b. 5 Jan. 1914, Huehuetenango; m.; four s. four d.; ed. Institute Normal de Occidente, Quezaltenango and Universidad de San Carlos, Guatemala City; fmrly. Prof., Escuela Nacional de Comercio, Escuela Normal Central, Verones, School of Juridical and Social Sciences, Univ. de San Carlos; fmr. Prof. and Dir. Colegie Institute Cervantes; fmr. Vice-Pres. Colegio de Abogados; sometime Congressman and First Sec., Nat. Assembly; fmr. Chief, Legal Dept., Ministry of Foreign Affairs; has held various posts in public admin. and led Guatemalan dels. to UN Gen. Assembly 1951–54, 1967–69 and numerous int. confs.; Perm. Rep. to OAS 1971–78; Perm. Rep. of Guatemala to UN 1978–82; Minister of Foreign Affairs 1982–83. *Address:* c/o Ministry of Foreign Affairs, Guatemala City, Guatemala.

CASTILLO LARA, H.E. Cardinal Rosalio José, S.D.B.; Venezuelan ecclesiastic; b. 4 Sept. 1922, San Casimiro, Maracay; ordained 1949; consecrated Bishop (Titular See of Praecausa) 1973, Archbishop 1982; cr. Cardinal 1985; Pres. Pontifical Council for the Interpretation of the Legal Texts; Pres. Disciplinary Comm. of the Roman Curia. *Address:* Città del Vaticano, Rome, Italy.

CASTILLO MORALES, Carlos Manuel, PH.D., M.SC., D.ECON.; Costa Rican economist; b. 19 Dec. 1928; ed. Univ. de Costa Rica, and Univs. of Tennessee and Wisconsin; Head of Agricultural Section, UN Econ. Cttee. for Latin America (ECLA) 1956–59, in Mexican Office of ECLA as Sec. of Cen. Isthmus Econ. Co-operation Cttee. 1959–61, Asst. Dir. later Dir. of Office 1961–63, 1963–66; Sec.-Gen. Perm Secretariat of Gen. Treaty for Cen. American Econ. Integration 1966–70; Minister of Econs., Industry and Commerce 1971–72; Vice-Pres., Minister of the Presidency 1974–77; Pres. Banco Central de Costa Rica –1984. *Publications:* Análisis Exploratorio del Sistema de Tenencia de la Tierra en Costa Rica 1953, La Reforma Agraria y sus Efectos sobre la Tasa de Acumulación de Capital en la Economía 1953, El Régimen Agrario y el Funcionamiento de Mercado de los Factores 1955, La Economía Agrícola en la Región del Bajío 1956, Aspectos Políticos y Administrativos del Desarrollo Económico 1959, Growth and Integration in Central America 1966. *Address:* c/o Banco Central de Costa Rica, San José, Costa Rica.

CASTLE, Rt. Hon. Barbara Anne, P.C., B.A.; British politician; b. 6 Oct. 1910, Chesterfield; d. of F. Betts and Annie Rebecca Farrand; m. Edward Castle (later Lord Castle of Islington, died 1979) 1944; ed. Bradford Girls' Grammar School, St. Hugh's Coll., Oxford Univ.; Admin. Officer, Ministry of Food 1941–44; Corresp. for Daily Mirror 1944–45; M.P. 1945–79; mem. St. Pancras Borough Council, London 1937–45, Metropolitan Water Bd. 1940–45, Nat. Exec. Cttee. of Labour Party 1950–85; Chair. of Labour Party 1958–59; Minister of Overseas Devt. 1964–65; Transport 1965–68; First Sec. of State and Sec. of State for Employment and Productivity 1968–70, for Social Services 1974–76; mem. European Parl. for Greater Manchester North 1979–84, for Greater Manchester West 1984– (Vice-Pres. Socialist Group 1979–85, Leader British Labour Group 1979–85); Hon. Fellow St. Hugh's Coll., Oxford 1968; Hon. D. Tech. (Bradford 1968, Loughborough 1969). *Publications:* The Castle Diaries 1974–76 1980, The Castle Diaries 1964–70 1984, Christabel and Sylvia Pankhurst 1987. *Leisure interests:* walking, gardening, reading. *Address:* Headland House, 308 Grays Inn Road, London, WC1X 8DP, England. *Telephone:* 01-833 4898.

CASTLE, Michael N., J.D.; American lawyer and state governor; b. 2 July 1939, Wilmington, Del.; s. of J. Manderson and Louisa B. Castle; ed. Hamilton Coll. and Georgetown Univ.; admitted Del. Bar 1964, D.C. Bar 1964; Assoc. Connolly, Bove and Lodge, Wilmington 1964–73, partner, 1973–75; Deputy Attorney-Gen. State of Del. 1965–66; Partner, Schnee & Castle 1975–80; Lieut.-Gov. State of Del. 1981–85; Prin. Michael N. Castle 1981–; Gov. of Delaware 1985–; mem. Del. House of Reps. 1966–67, Del. Senate 1968–76; Republican. *Address:* Legislative Hall, Dover, Del. 19901, U.S.A.

CASTLE, William Bosworth, M.D., D.SC., M.S.; American physician and educator; b. 21 Oct. 1897, Cambridge, Mass.; s. of William Ernest and Clara (Sears) Bosworth Castle; m. Louise Müller 1933; one s. one d.; ed.

Harvard; Prof. of Medicine, Harvard Univ. 1937–57; George R. Minot Prof. of Medicine 1957–63; Dir. Thorndike Lab., Boston City Hosp. 1948–63, Hon. Dir. 1963–68; Francis W. Peabody Faculty Prof. of Medicine, Harvard Univ. 1963–68, Emeritus 1968–; Distinguished Physician, U.S. Veterans Admin. 1968–72; Senior Physician 1972–73, Consultant, Veterans Admin. Hospital, West Roxbury, Mass 1973–79; mem. N.A.S., American Philosophical Soc., Assen. of American Physicians; Hon. D.Sc. (Harvard, Pa., Marquette, Mount Sinai), Hon. LL.D. (Jefferson), Hon. S.M. (Yale), Hon. M.D. (Utrecht), Hon. S.D. (Chicago), Hon. L.H.D. (Boston Coll.); Hon. Curator, Harvard Medical School Archives 1969–84; John Phillips Memorial Prize 1932; Proctor Award, Philadelphia Coll. of Pharmacy and Science 1935, Walter Reed Medal, American Soc. of Tropical Medicine 1939, and Mead, Johnson and Co. Award 1950, for discovery of gastric intrinsic factor and its relation to vitamin B12 deficiency in pernicious anaemia, etc, Kober Medal of the Assen. of American Physicians 1962, John M. Russell Award of the Markle Scholars 1964, Oscar B. Hunter Memorial Award of the American Therapeutic Soc., Joseph Goldberger Award for Clinical Nutrition, Sheen Award of American Medical Assen. 1973, Distinguished Teacher Award of American Coll. of Physicans 1978, Distinguished Chair. Award of Assen.of Profs. of Medicine 1978. *Leisure interests:* small boat sailing, home repairs. *Address:* 22 Irving Street, Brookline, Mass. 02146, U.S.A.

CASTLEMAN, Christopher Norman Anthony, M.A.; British banker; b. 23 June 1941, Beaconsfield, Bucks.; s. of late S. Phillips and of Mrs. J. S. S-R-Pyper; m. 1st Sarah Victoria Stockdale 1965 (died 1979), one s. one d.; m. 2nd Caroline Clare Westcott 1980, two d.; ed. Harrow School and Clare Coll., Cambridge; joined M. Samuel and Co. Ltd. 1963; Gen. Man. Hill Samuel Australia 1970–72; Officer of Hill Samuel Inc., New York 1972–73; Dir. Hill Samuel and Co. Ltd., 1970–87; Man. Hill Samuel Int. Ltd. 1975–77, Hill Samuel Group (S.A.) Ltd. and Hill Samuel South Africa Ltd. 1978–80; Chief. Exec. Hill Samuel Group PLC 1980–87, Blue Arrow PLC 1987–88; Financial Adviser 1988–. *Leisure interests:* tennis, squash, sport in general, wildlife. *Address:* 190 Strand, London, WC2R 1DT, England. *Telephone:* 01-379 5040.

CASTON, Geoffrey, M.A., M.P.A.; British university administrator; b. 17 May 1926, Beckenham, Kent; s. of Reginald Caston and Lilian Caston; m. 1st Sonya Chassell 1956, two s. one d.; m. 2nd Judy Roizen 1983; ed. St. Dunstan's Coll., Peterhouse, Cambridge, Harvard Univ.; Sub-Lieut. R.N.V.R. 1945–47; Colonial Office 1951–58; First-Sec. U.K. Mission to UN 1958–61; Dept. of Tech. Co-operation 1961–64; Asst. Sec. Dept. of Educ. and Science 1964–66; Sec. Schools Council 1966–70; Under-Sec. Univ. Grants Cttee. 1970–72; Registrar of Univ. and Fellow of Merton Coll., Oxford 1972–79; Sec. Gen. Cttee. of Vice-Chancellors 1979–83; Vice-Chancellor, Univ. of South Pacific, Fiji 1983–; mem. numerous dels. and cttees., nat. and int., including UN Tech. Assistance Cttee. 1962–64, Visiting Mission to Trust Territory of Pacific Islands 1961; OECD Workshops on Educational Innovation 1969, 1970, 1971; Nat. Inst. for Careers Educ. and Counselling 1975–83; Exec. Cttee. Inter-Univ. Council for Higher Educ. Overseas 1977–83; George Long Prize for Jurisprudence 1950; Hon. LL.D. (Dundee) 1982. *Address:* University of the South Pacific, Suva, Fiji. *Telephone:* 313900.

CASTRO, Amado Alejandro, B.S., A.M., PH.D.; Philippine economist; b. 29 June 1924, Manila; ed. Univ. of the Philippines and Harvard Univ., U.S.A.; Instructor in Econs., Univ. of the Philippines 1948–53, Asst. Prof. 1954–56, Assoc. Prof. 1956–62, Head of Econs. Dept. 1956–58, Acting Dean, Coll. of Business Admin. Jan.-Sept. 1958, Prof. of Econs. 1962–, Dean, School of Econs. 1965–73, Prof. of Monetary Econs. 1972–; Gov. and Acting Chair. Devt. Bank of the Philippines 1962–66; Dir. Inst. of Econ. Devt. and Research 1958–66, Econ. Bureau ASEAN Secr. 1977–80. *Address:* School of Economics, University of the Philippines, Quezon City, Philippines 3041; 67 Valenzuela, San Juan, Metro Manila 3134, Philippines (Home).

CASTRO, Fidel (see Castro Ruz, Fidel).

CASTRO, Gen. Raúl (see Castro Ruz, Gen. Raúl).

CASTRO, Raul H., A.B., J.D.; American lawyer, politician and diplomatist; b. 12 June 1916, Cananea, Sonora, Mexico; s. of Francisco D. Castro and Rosario Acosta de Castro; m. Patricia M. Norris 1951; two d.; ed. Arizona State Coll., Flagstaff, and Univ. of Arizona, Tucson; fmr. owner and operator Castro Pony Farm, Tucson, Ariz.; in U.S. Foreign Service in Mexico 1941–46; Spanish Instructor, Univ. of Ariz. 1946–49; Sr. Partner law firm Castro and Wolfe 1949–52, Castro Zipf and Marable 1982–; Deputy District Attorney, Pima County, Ariz. 1952–54, District Attorney 1954–58; Judge of Superior Court, Ariz. 1959–61, Presiding Judge, Juvenile Court 1963–64; Amb. to El Salvador 1964–68, to Bolivia 1968–70, to Argentina 1977–80; int. law practice, Tucson 1969–75, Phoenix 1980–; Gov. of Arizona 1975–77; Hon. S.J.D., (N. Arizona Univ.), LL.D. (Arizona State Univ.); Dr. h.c. (Universidad Autonóma de Guadalajara, Mexico). *Leisure interests:* horseback-riding, hiking, reading. *Address:* Suite 250, 3030 E. Camelback Road, Phoenix, Ariz. 85016, U.S.A.

CASTRO JIJÓN, Rear-Adm. Ramón; Ecuadorean naval officer and politician; b. 1915; studied naval engineering in U.S.A.; fmr. Naval Attaché, London; C.-in-C. of Navy, Ecuador; Pres. Military Junta 1963–66; in exile 1966–. *Address:* Rio de Janeiro, RJ, Brazil.

CASTRO RUZ, Fidel, D.IUR.; Cuban politician; b. 13 Aug. 1927; m. Mirta Diaz-Bilart; one s.; ed. Jesuit schools in Santiago and Havana, Univ. de la Habana; law practice in Havana; began active opposition to Batista regime by attack on Moncada barracks at Santiago 26th July 1953; sentenced to 15 years' imprisonment 1953; amnestied 1956; went into exile in Mexico and began to organize armed rebellion; landed in Oriente Province with small force Dec. 1956; carried on armed struggle against Batista regime until flight of Batista Jan. 1959; Prime Minister of Cuba 1959-76; Head of State and Pres. of Council of State 1976-, Pres. of Council of Ministers 1976-; Chair. Agrarian Reform Inst. 1965-; First Sec. Partido Unido de la Revolución Socialista (PURS) 1963-65, Partido Comunista 1965- (mem. Political Bureau 1976-); Lenin Peace Prize 1961; Dimitrov Prize (Bulgaria) 1980; Hero of the Soviet Union 1963; Order of Lenin 1972, 1986, Order of the October Revolution 1976, Somali Order (1st Class) 1977, Order of Jamaica 1977, Gold Star (Vietnam) 1982. *Publications:* Ten Years of Revolution 1964, History Will Absolve Me 1968, Fidel (with Frei Betto) 1987. *Address:* Palacio del Gobierno, Havana, Cuba.

CASTRO RUZ, Gen. Raúl; Cuban politician; b. 3 June 1931; ed. Jesuit schools; younger brother of Fidel Castro Ruz (q.v.); sentenced to 15 years' imprisonment for insurrection 1953; amnestied 1954; assisted his brother's movement in Mexico, and in Cuba after Dec. 1956; Chief of the Armed Forces Feb. 1959; Deputy Prime Minister 1960-72; Minister of the Armed Forces 1960; First Deputy Prime Minister 1972-76; First Vice-Pres. Council of State 1976-, First Vice-Pres. Council of Ministers 1976-; Medal for Strengthening of Brotherhood in Arms 1977; Order of Lenin 1979, Order of the October Revolution 1981. *Address:* Oficina del Primer Vice-Presidente, Havana, Cuba.

CATALANO DI MELILLI, Felice; Italian diplomatist (retd.); b. 24 Jan. 1914; s. of Antonio and Verga Caterina; m. Rosana Muscatello; two s.; ed. Univ. degli Studi, Florence; joined Diplomatic Service 1938; Vice-Consul, Jerusalem 1939, Leipzig 1941-43; Sec., Washington 1945-52; at Ministry of Foreign Affairs 1952-55, 1958-59, 1961-65; Counsellor, Athens 1955-58; Minister, Bonn 1959-61; Acting Sec.-Gen. Ministry of Foreign Affairs 1965-66; Amb. to the U.A.R. 1966-69; Diplomatic Adviser to Prime Minister 1969-70; Perm. Rep. to N. Atlantic Council 1970-79; numerous honours including Gran Croce Ordine al Merito della Repubblica Italiana, Grosses Deutsches Verdienstkreuz, Grand Chancellor, Bailiff Grand Cross of Obedience, of Sovereign Military Order of Malta. *Address:* Via Monterone 2, 00186 Rome, Italy.

CATCHESIDE, David Guthrie, D.SC., M.A., F.R.S., F.A.A.; British professor of genetics; b. 31 May 1907, London; s. of the late David Guthrie and of Florence S. Catcheside; m. Kathleen M. Whiteman 1931; one s. one d.; ed. Strand School and King's Coll., Univ. of London; Asst. to Prof. of Botany, Glasgow Univ. 1928-30; Asst. Lecturer King's Coll., London 1931-33, Lecturer 1933-37; Rockefeller Int. Fellow, Calif. Inst. of Tech. 1936-37; Lecturer in Botany, Cambridge Univ. 1937-50, Reader in Cytogenetics 1950-51; Fellow and Lecturer, Trinity Coll., Cambridge 1944-51; Prof. of Genetics, Adelaide Univ. 1952-55; Prof. of Microbiology, Birmingham Univ. 1956-64; Research Assoc. Carnegie Inst. of Washington 1958; Visiting Prof. Calif. Inst. of Tech. 1961; Prof. of Genetics, John Curtin School of Medical Research, Australian Nat. Univ. 1964-67; Dir. and Prof. of Genetics, Research School of Biological Sciences, ANU 1967-72; Visiting Fellow 1973-75; Foreign Assoc. N.A.S. 1974; Hon. Research Assoc. Waite Agricultural Research Inst. 1976-. *Publications:* The Genetics of Micro-organisms 1951, Genetics of Recombination 1977, Mosses of South Australia 1980. *Leisure interests:* natural history, walking. *Address:* 16 Rodger Avenue, Leabrook, South Australia 5068, Australia. *Telephone:* (08) 332-3915.

CATER, Douglass; American educator, editor and government official; b. 24 Aug. 1923, Montgomery, Ala.; s. of Silas D. Cater, Sr. and Nancy Chesnutt Cater; m. Libby Anderson 1950; two s. two d.; ed. Philip Exeter Acad., Harvard Univ.; Washington Ed. The Reporter (magazine) 1950-63, Nat. Affairs Ed. 1963-64; Special Asst. to Pres. of U.S. 1964-68; writer and consultant 1968-; Vice-Chair. The Observer, London 1976-81; Pres. Observer Int. Inc. 1976-81; mem. Bd. of Eds., Encylopaedia Britannica 1978-; Pres. Washington Coll. 1982-; Special Asst. to Sec. of Army 1951; Consultant to Dir. of Mutual Security Agency 1952; Dir. Aspen Inst. Programme on Communications and Soc. 1970-76, Sr. Fellow Aspen Inst. for Humanistic Studies 1976-; Visiting Prof. Princeton Univ., Wesleyan Univ., Univ. of Calif., Stanford Univ.; Guggenheim Fellow 1955, Eisenhower Exchange Fellow 1957, George Polk Award 1961, New York Newspaper Guild, Page One Award 1961. *Publications:* Ethics in a Business Society (with Marquis Childs) 1953, The Fourth Branch of Government 1959, Power in Washington 1964, Dana: The Irrelevant Man 1970, TV Violence and the Child: The Evolution and Fate of the Surgeon General's Report (with Stephen P. Strickland) 1975. *Address:* Office of the President, Washington College, Chestertown, Md. 21620, U.S.A.

CATER, Sir Jack, K.B.E.; British colonial administrator; b. 21 Feb. 1922, London; s. of Alfred F. and Pamela E. (née Dukes) Cater; m. Peggy Gwenda Richards 1950; one s. two d.; ed. Sir George Monoux Grammar School, Walthamstow; war service 1939-45, Squadron Leader, R.A.F.V.R.; British Mil. Admin., Hong Kong 1945; joined Colonial Admin. Service, Hong Kong 1946; attended 2nd Devonshire Course, Queen's Coll., Oxford

1949-50; various posts incl. Registrar of Co-operative Socs. and Dir. of Marketing, Dir. of Agric. and Fisheries, Deputy Econ. Sec.; Imperial Defence Coll. (now Royal Coll. of Defence Studies) 1966; Defence Sec., Special Asst. to Gov. and Deputy Colonial Sec. (Special Duties) 1967; Exec. Dir. Hong Kong Trade Devt. Council 1968-70; Dir. Commerce and Industry, Hong Kong 1970-72; Sec. for Information 1972, for Home Affairs and Information 1973; Commr. Ind. Comm. Against Corruption 1974-78; Chief Sec., Hong Kong 1978-81 (Acting Gov. and Deputy Gov. on several occasions); Hong Kong Commr., London 1981-84; Man. Dir. Hong Kong Nuclear Investment Co. 1987-; Dir. Guangdong Nuclear Power Jt. Venture Co. Ltd. 1986- (First Deputy Gen. Man. 1985-86); Adviser to Consultative Cttee. for the Basic Law, Hong Kong 1986-; mem. Int. Bd. of Dirs., United World Colls., U.K. 1981-, Court, Univ. of Hong Kong 1982-, Hon. D.S.Sc. (Hong Kong Univ.) 1982. *Leisure interests:* walking, bridge, reading. *Address:* 97 Kadoorie Avenue, Kowloon, Hong Kong (Home).

CATER, Sir John Robert (Robin), Kt., M.A.; British businessman (retd.); b. 25 April 1919, Edinburgh; s. of the late Sir John Cater and of Lady Cater; m. Isobel Calder Ritchie 1945; one d.; ed. George Watson's Coll., Edinburgh, Cambridge Univ.; trainee, W. P. Lowrie & Co. Ltd. 1946; James Buchanan & Co. Ltd. 1949, Dir. 1950, Production Dir. 1959; Production Asst. The Distillers Co. Ltd. Edinburgh 1959, Dir. 1967; Man. Dir. and Vice-Chair. John Haig & Co. Ltd. 1965-70; Non-Exec. Dir. United Glass 1969, Chair. 1972; Chair. The Distillers Co. Ltd. 1976-83. *Leisure interests:* music, theatre, fishing. *Address:* "Avernish", Elie, Fife, KY9 1DA, Scotland. *Telephone:* Elie 667.

CATHALA, Thierry Gerard, D. EN D.; French judge; b. 23 Feb. 1925, Bordeaux; s. of Jean Cathala and Juliette Monsion; m. Marie F. Mérimée 1954; two s. one d.; ed. Saint-Genes Coll., Lycée Montaigne, Faculté de droit de Bordeaux and Paris; trainee barrister Bordeaux Bar 1946-48; Deputy Judge, Bordeaux 1948-51, Examining Magistrate 1951-65; Prin. Admin. EEC Comm., Brussels 1965-73; Judge Nanterre and Paris Courts 1974-81; Chief Justice French Polynesia Court of Appeal 1981-85; Judge Supreme Court of Appeal 1985-; French Rep. South Pacific Judicial Conf. 1982-84; mem. Supreme Judiciary Council 1987-; Chevalier Légion d'honneur, Ordre Nat. du Mérite. *Publications:* le Controle de la légalité administrative par les tribunaux judiciaires 1966, numerous articles on law. *Leisure interests:* geography, travelling, religious questions. *Address:* 5 quai de l'Horloge, 75001 Paris (Office); 8 rue Ploix, 78000 Versailles, France (Home). *Telephone:* 39 50 31 98 (Home).

CATHERWOOD, Sir (Henry) Frederick (Ross), Kt.; British industrialist and public official; b. 30 Jan. 1925, Co. Londonderry, N. Ireland; s. of the late of Stuart and of Jean Catherwood; m. Elizabeth Lloyd-Jones 1954; two s. one d.; ed. Shrewsbury and Clare Coll., Cambridge; Chartered Accountant 1951; Sec. Laws Stores Ltd., Gateshead 1952-54; Sec. and Controller, Richard Costain Ltd. 1954-55, Chief Exec. 1955-60; Asst. Man. Dir. British Aluminium Co. Ltd. 1960-62, Man. Dir. 1962-64; Chief Industrial Adviser, Dept. of Econ. Affairs 1964-66; mem. Nat. Econ. Devt. Council (N.E.D.C.) 1964-71, Dir. Gen. 1966-71; mem. British Nat. Export Council 1965-70; Vice-Chair. British Inst. of Man. 1972-74, Chair. 1974-76; Vice-Pres. 1976-; Chair. British Overseas Trade Bd. 1975-79; Chair. Mallinson-Denny Ltd. 1976-79 (Dir. 1974); Dir. John Laing Ltd. (Group Man. Dir. and Chief Exec. 1972-74) 1971-80, Goodyear Tyre and Rubber Co. (GB) Ltd. 1975-; Pres. Fellowship of Ind. Evangelical Churches 1977-78; mem. European Parl. for Cambridgeshire and Wellingborough, 1979-84, for Cambridgeshire and N. Bedfordshire 1984- (mem. Del. to U.S. Congress 1973-, Chair. Cttee. for External Econ. Relations 1979-84, Vice-Pres. European Democratic Group 1983-87, Chair. Land Use and Food Policy Inter-group 1987-); mem. Council Royal Inst. of Int. Affairs 1964-77; Treas. Int. Fellowship Evangelical Students 1979-; Hon. D.Sc. (Aston) 1972, Hon. D.Sc.Econ. (Queen's Univ., Belfast) 1973, Hon. D.Univ. (Surrey) 1979. *Publications:* The Christian in Industrial Society 1964, The Christian Citizen 1969, A Better Way 1975, First Things First 1979, God's Time God's Money 1987. *Address:* Sutton Hall, Balsham, Cambs., England. *Telephone:* (0223) 317672.

CATO, Rt. Hon. Robert Milton, P.C.; Saint Vincent politician and lawyer; b. 3 June 1915; m. Lucy-Ann Alexandra Cato; ed. St. Vincent Grammar School; called to Bar, Middle Temple 1948; served with First Canadian Army, Second World War; Chair. Kingstown Town Bd. 1952, mem. 1955-59; fmr. Chair. Labour Advisory Bd., Public Service Comm., Cen. Housing and Planning Authority; rep. to W. Indies Fed. Parl. 1958-62; fmr. Leader St. Vincent Labour Party; Chief Minister of Saint Vincent 1967-69; Premier 1969-72, 1974-79; Prime Minister of Saint Vincent and the Grenadines 1979-84, leader of the Opposition 1984-, also fmr. Minister of Finance, Information and Grenadines Affairs. *Address:* P.O. Box 138, Kingstown, St. Vincent and the Grenadines.

CATTANACH, Bruce MacIntosh, PH.D., F.R.S.; British geneticist; b. 5 Nov. 1932, Glasgow; s. of James Cattanach and Margareta May (née Fyfe) Cattanach; m. Margaret Bouchier Crewe 1966; two d.; ed. Heaton Grammar School, Newcastle-upon-Tyne, King's Coll., Univ. of Durham and Univ. of Edinburgh; Scientific Staff MRC Induced Mutagenesis Unit, Edin. 1959-62, 1964-66; N.I.H. Post-Doctoral Research Fellow Biology Div., Oak Ridge, Tenn., U.S.A. 1962-64; Sr. Scientist City of Hope Medical Centre, Duarte, Calif. 1966-69; Scientific Staff MRC Radiobiology Unit, Chilton, Oxon.

1969–, Head of Genetics Div. 1987–. *Publications:* numerous papers in scientific journals. *Leisure interests:* control of inherited disease in pedigree dogs; breeding, exhibiting and judging of dogs; and DIY house-building. *Address:* MRC Radiobiology Unit, Chilton, Didcot, Oxon., OX11 0RD (Office); Down's Edge, Reading Road, Harwell, Oxon., OX11 0JJ, England (Home). *Telephone:* (0235) 834393 (Office); (0235) 835410 (Home).

CATTO, Henry Edward; American business executive and diplomatist; b. 6 Dec. 1930, Dallas; s. of Henry Edward Catto and Maureen (née Halsell) Catto; m. Jessica Oveta Hobby 1958; two s. two d.; ed. Williams Coll.; Partner Catto & Catto, San Antonio 1955–; Dep. Rep. Org. of American States 1969–71; Amb. to El Salvador 1971–73; Chief of Protocol, The White House 1974–76; Amb. to the UN Office, Geneva 1976–77; Asst. Sec. of Defense, Pentagon, Washington 1981–83; mem. Bd. Dirs., Sovran/D.C. Nat. Bank; Columnist San Antonio Light 1985–; Amb. to the U.K. 1989–; mem. Council on Foreign Relations 1979; Trustee Inst. for Humanistic Studies. *Address:* American Embassy, Grosvenor Square, London W.1, England; 7718 Georgetown Pike McLean, Va. 22102, U.S.A. (Home).

CATTO, 2nd Baron, of Cairncatto; **Stephen Gordon Catto;** British banker and company director; b. 14 Jan. 1923, s. of 1st Baron Catto and Gladys Forbes Gordon; m. 1st Josephine Innes Packer 1948, 2nd Margaret Forrest 1966; three s. three d.; ed. Eton Coll. and Cambridge Univ.; Air Force service 1943–47; fmr. Chair. Morgan Grenfell & Co. Ltd., now Pres. Morgan Grenfell Group PLC, Chair. Australian Mutual Provident Soc. (U.K. Branch), Yule Catto & Co. PLC; Dir. Times Newspapers Holdings, The News Corpn., Gen. Electric Co. PLC and other cos.; mem. Advisory Council, Export Credits Guarantee Dept. 1959–65; Chair. R.A.F. Benevolent Fund; part-time mem. London Transport Bd. 1962–68. *Leisure interests:* gardening, music. *Address:* Morgan Grenfell Group PLC, 23 Great Winchester Street, London, EC2P 2AX, England. *Telephone:* 01-588 4545.

CAU, Jean, LIC. PHIL.; French writer and journalist; b. 8 July 1925, Bram (Aude); s. of Etienne and Rosalie (née Olivier) Cau; unmarried; ed. Lycée Carcassonne, Lycée Louis-le-Grand, and Univ. of Paris; Sec. to Jean-Paul Sartre 1947–56; Ed. Les Temps Modernes 1949–54; travelled extensively in U.S.A., Brazil, Greece, Italy, Spain, North Africa; journalist on L'Express, Le Figaro littéraire, Candide, France-Observateur, Paris-Match etc., Paris; writer for Figaro-Dimanche 1978–; Prix Goncourt 1961; Chevalier, Légion d'honneur. *Publications: novels:* Le coup de barre, Les paroissiens, La pitié de Dieu, Les enfants 1975; stories: Mon village; chronicle: Les oreilles et la queue, L'incendie de Rome 1964; plays: Les parachutistes, Le maître du monde, Dans un nuage de poussière 1967, Les yeux crevés 1968, Pauvre France 1972; translation of Who's Afraid of Virginia Woolf, Numance; Lettre ouverte aux têtes de chiens de l'Occident 1967, L'agonie de la vieille 1969, Tropicanas 1970, Le temps des esclaves, Les entrailles du taureau 1971, Traité de morale I: les écuries de l'occident 1973, II: la grande prostituée 1974, Toros 1973, Pourquoi la France 1975, Les otages 1976, Le chevalier, la mort et le diable, Une nuit à Saint-Germain des Prés, La conquête de Zanzibar et Nouvelles du Paradis 1980, Le grand soleil 1981, Une rose à la mer 1983, Proust, le chat et moi 1984, Croquis de mémoire 1985, Mon lieutenant 1985; scripts of films La curée 1966, Don Juan 1973 1973. *Address:* 13 rue de Seine, 75006 Paris, France.

CAUAS, Jorge; Chilean economist and banker; ed. Columbia Univ., New York; Vice-Pres. Banco Central de Chile 1967–70; Dir. Instituto de Economía, Catholic Univ. 1970–72; Dir. World Bank Devt. Research Centre 1972–74; Minister of Finance 1974–76; Amb. to U.S.A. 1977–78; Chair. Banco de Santiago 1978–83. *Address:* c/o Banco de Santiago, Ahumada 166, Santiago, Chile.

CAUSLEY, Charles Stanley, C.B.E., F.R.S.L.; British poet; b. 24 Aug. 1917, Launceston, Cornwall; s. of Laura and Charles Causley; ed. Horwell Grammar School, Launceston Coll., Peterborough Training Coll.; served in R.N. 1940–46; worked as a teacher for many years until 1976; Hon. D. Litt. (Exeter) 1977, Hon. M.A. (Open Univ.) 1982; Queen's Gold Medal for Poetry 1967, Cholmondeley Award 1971. *Publications:* Union Street 1957, Johnny Alleluia 1961, Underneath the Water 1968, Figgie Hobbin 1971, Puffin Book of Magic Verse (Ed.) 1974, Collected Poems 1951–75 1975, Puffin Book of Salt-Sea Verse (Ed.) 1978, The Ballad of Aucassin and Nicolette 1981, The Sun, Dancing (Ed.) 1982, Secret Destinations 1984, Kings' Children (trans. German ballads) 1986, 21 Poems 1986, Early in the Morning (poems) 1986, Jack the Treacle Eater 1987, A Field of Vision 1988. *Leisure interests:* theatre, cinema, foreign travel. *Address:* 2 Cyprus Well, Launceston, Cornwall, PL15 8BT, England. *Telephone:* (0566) 2731.

CAUSSE, Jean-Pierre; French scientist; b. 4 Oct. 1926, Montpellier; m. Françoise Villard; three d.; ed. Lycée de Montpellier and Ecole Normale Supérieure; Observatoire de Paris 1952–55; Physicist, Schlumberger Ltd. 1955–62; Dir. of Satellites Div., Centre Nat. d'Etudes Spatiales 1962–66; Dir. Brétigny Space Centre 1966–69; Deputy Sec.-Gen., European Launcher Devt. Org. 1969–73; Head Spacelab Programme, European Space Research Org. 1973–74; Vice-Pres. Cie. de Saint-Gobain 1974; Pres. European Industrial Man. Assen. 1985–; Officier, Légion d'honneur. *Address:* Les Miroirs, Cédex 27, 92096 Paris, la Défense, France. *Telephone:* 47-62-30-00.

CAUTE, (John) David, M.A., D.PHIL.; British writer; b. 16 Dec. 1936; m. 1st Catherine Shuckburgh (divorced 1970), two s.; m. 2nd Martha Bates 1973, two d.; ed. Edinburgh Acad., Wellington, Wadham Coll., Oxford; St. Anthony's Coll. 1959; army service Gold Coast 1955–56; Henry Fellow, Harvard Univ. 1960–61; Fellow, All Souls Coll., Oxford 1959–65; Visiting Prof. New York Univ. and Columbia Univ.; 1966–67; Reader in Social and Political Theory, Brunel Univ. 1967–70; Regents' Lecturer, Univ. of Calif. 1974, Visiting Prof. Univ. of Bristol 1985; Literary Ed., New Statesman 1979–80; Co-Chair. Writers' Guild 1982. *Plays:* Songs for an Autumn Rifle 1961, The Demonstration 1969, Fallout (for radio) 1972, The Fourth World 1973, Brecht and Company (BBC TV) 1979, The Zimbabwe Tapes (BBC Radio) 1983, Henry and the Dogs (BBC Radio) 1986. *Publications:* At Fever Pitch (novel, Authors' Club Award and John Llewelyn Rhys Prize 1960) 1959, Comrade Jacob (novel) 1961, Communism and the French Intellectuals 1914–1960 1964, The Left in Europe Since 1789 1966, The Decline of the West (novel) 1966, Essential Writings of Karl Marx (Ed.) 1967, Fanon 1970, The Confrontation: a trilogy (The Demonstration (play), The Occupation (novel), The Illusion) 1971, The Fellow-Travellers 1973, Collisions 1974, Cuba, Yes? 1974, The Great Fear 1978, Under the Skin: the Death of White Rhodesia 1983; The Baby-Sitters 1978, Moscow Gold 1980 (novels, both as John Salisbury), The K-Factor (novel) 1983, The Espionage of the Saints 1986, News from Nowhere (novel) 1986, Sixty Eight: the year of the barricades 1988, Veronica or the Two Nations. *Address:* 41 Westcroft Square, London, W6 0TA, England.

CAVACO SILVA, Anibal, PH.D.; Portuguese politician and university professor; b. 15 July 1939, Loulé; s. of Teodoro Silva and Maria do Nascimento Cavaco; m. Maria Cavaco Silva 1963; one s. one d.; ed. York Univ., U.K. and Inst. of Econ. and Financial Studies; taught Public Econs. and Political Economy, Inst. of Econ. and Financial Studies 1965–67, then at Catholic Univ. 1975–, and New Univ. of Lisbon 1977–; Research Fellow, Calouste Gulbenkian Foundation 1967–77; Dir. of Research and Statistical Dept., Bank of Portugal 1977–79, 1981; Minister of Finance and Planning 1980–81; Pres. Council for Nat. Planning 1981–; Leader, PSD 1985–; Prime Minister of Portugal 1985–; Dir. Economia (journal); Pres. Civic Inst. of Algarve; Social Democrat (PSD). *Publications:* Budgetary Policy and Economic Stabilization 1976, Economic Effects of Public Debt 1977, Public Finance and Macroeconomic Policy 1982, The Economic Policy of Sá Carneiro's Government 1982 and over 20 articles on financial markets, public economies and Portuguese economic policy. *Leisure interests:* tennis, gardening. *Address:* Office of the Prime Minister, Presidência do Conselho de Ministros, Rua du Imprensa 1, 1300 Lisboa, Portugal.

CAVAZOS, Lauro Fred, PH.D.; American professor of anatomy; b. 4 Jan. 1927, King Ranch, Tex.; s. of Lauro Fred and Tomasa (Quintanilla) Cavazos; m. Peggy Ann Murdock 1954; five s. five d.; ed. Texas Tech. Univ., Iowa State Univ.; Teaching Asst., Tex. Tech. Univ., Lubbock 1949–51; Instructor in Anatomy, Medical Coll. of Va., Asst. Prof. 1956–60, Assoc. Prof. 1960–64; Prof. of Anatomy, Tufts Univ. School of Medicine, Boston 1964–80, Chair. Dept. 1964–72, Assoc. Dean 1972–73, Acting Dean 1973–75, Dean 1975–80; Pres. Health Sciences Centre, Prof. of Biological Sciences, Prof. of Anatomy, Tex. Tech. Univ. 1980–88; mem. Bd. of Dirs. Shamrock R & M Inc. 1987–; Sec. of Educ. Sept. 1988–; mem. American Assen. of Anatomists, Endocrine Soc., Histochemical Soc., A.A.A.S., Assen. of American Medical Colls., Pan American Assen. of American Medical Colls., Pan American Assen. of Anatomy. *Address:* Department of Education, 400 Maryland Avenue, S.W., Washington, D.C. 20202, U.S.A.

CAWLEY, Evonne Fay, A.O., M.B.E.; Australian lawn tennis player; b. 31 July 1951, Barellan, N.S.W.; d. of the late Kenneth Goolagong; m. Roger Cawley 1975; one s. one d.; ed. Willoughby High School, Sydney; professional player since 1970; Wimbledon Champion 1971, 1980 (singles), 1974 (doubles); Australian Champion 1974, 1975, 1976, 1977; French Champion 1971; Italian Champion 1973; S.A. Champion 1972; Virginia Slims Circuit Champion 1975, 1976; played Federation Cup for Australia 1971, 1972, 1973, 1974, 1975, 1976. *Publication:* Evonne Goolagong (with Bud Collins) 1975. *Address:* Racquet Club, Hilton Mead, near Baufort, North Carolina, U.S.A.

CAYGILL, David Francis, LL.B., M.P.; New Zealand lawyer and politician; b. 15 Nov. 1948, Christchurch; m. Eileen E. Boyd 1974; one s. three d.; ed. Univ. of Canterbury; practised law in Christchurch legal firm 1975–78; mem. House of Reps. 1978–; Minister of Trade and Industry, Minister of Nat. Devt., Assoc. Minister of Finance 1984–87, of Health, Trade and Industry 1987–88, Deputy Minister of Finance 1988, Minister of Finance Dec. 1988–; mem. N.Z. Council Aug. 1987–; Labour Party. *Leisure interests:* collecting classical music records, following American politics. *Address:* Department of Finance, Private Bag, Wellington, New Zealand. *Telephone:* 720-030.

CAYROL, Roland; French producer, researcher and author; b. 11 Aug. 1941, Rabat, Morocco; two s. two d.; Prof. and Researcher Nat. Foundation of Political Sciences 1968; Resarch Dir. 1978–; Scientific Adviser Louis Harris France 1977–86; Assoc. Dir. CSA 1987–. *Television productions include:* Portrait d'un Président: François Mitterrand (with A. Gaillard) 1985. *Publications:* François Mitterrand 1945, Le Deputé Français (with J. L. Parodi and C. Ysmal) 1970, La Presse écrite et audiovisuelle 1973, La télévision fait-elle l'élection? (with G. Blumler and G. Thoueron) 1974, La nouvelle communication politique 1986. *Address:* Fondation National de Sciences Politiques, 10 rue de la Chaise, 75007 Paris (Office); CSA, 152 rue Montmartre, 75002 Paris, France (Office). *Telephone:* (33-1) 40 13 02 90 (Office).

CAYZER, Baron (Life Peer), cr. 1982; **(William) Nicholas Cayzer,** Bt.; British shipowner; b. 21 Jan. 1910, Scotland; s. of the late Sir Augustus Cayzer, 1st Bt. and the late Ina Frances Stancomb; m. Elizabeth Catherine Williams 1935; two d.; ed. Eton and Corpus Christi Coll., Cambridge; joined Clan Line Steamers Ltd. 1931; Chair. Liverpool Steamship Owners Asscn. 1944–45; Chair. Gen. Council of British Shipping 1959; Pres. Chamber of Shipping of the U.K. 1959, Chair. British Liner Cttee. 1960–63; Mem. Ministry of Transport Shipping Advisory Panel 1962–64; Pres. Inst. of Marine Engineers 1963; Prime Warden of the Worshipful Co. of Shipwrights 1969–70; Chair. British and Commonwealth Shipping Co. PLC (later British and Commonwealth Holdings) 1958–87, Life Pres. 1987–, Union-Castle Mail Steamship Co. Ltd., Clan Line Steamers Ltd., Cayzer Irvine and Co. Ltd., Caledonia Investments PLC, Scottish Lion Insurance Co. Ltd., Air Holdings Ltd., Air U.K. and various other cos. *Leisure interests:* gardening, golf. *Address:* The Grove, Walsham-le-Willows 263, Suffolk; 95J Eaton Square, London, S.W.1, England. *Telephone:* 01-235 5551.

CAZALET, Sir Peter (Grenville), Kt, M.A.; British business executive; b. 26 Feb. 1929, Weymouth; s. of Vice-Admiral Sir Peter Cazalet, K.B.E., C.B., D.S.O., D.S.C., and Lady Cazalet; ed. Uppingham School, and Univ. of Cambridge; m. Jane Jennifer Rew 1957; three s.; Gen. Man. BP Tanker Co. Ltd. 1968–70, Regional Co-ordinator, Australasia and Far East, BP Trading Ltd. 1970–72, Pres. BP North America Inc. 1972–75, Dir. BP Trading Ltd. 1975–81, Chair. BP Oil Int. Ltd. 1981–, Man. Dir. BP 1981–, Deputy Chair. 1986–89; Lloyds Register of Shipping Bd. 1981–86 and Gen. Cttee. 1981–, GKN PLC 1989–; Dir. Standard Oil Co., Cleveland, Ohio 1973–76, Peninsular & Oriental Steam Navigation Co. Ltd. 1980–, De La Rue Co. PLC 1983–, Trustee Uppingham School 1976–. *Leisure interests:* golf, theatre, fishing. *Address:* Britannic House, Moor Lane, London, EC2Y 9BU, England. *Telephone:* 01-920 7011.

CAZENEUVE, Jean, D. ÈS. L.; French academic; b. 1915, Ussel; s. of Charles Cazeneuve and Yvonne Renoul; m. Germaine Aladane de Paraize; one s. two d.; ed. Ecole normale supérieure and Harvard Univ.; Prof. of Sociology, Paris-Sorbonne 1966–84, Prof. Emer. 1984–; Pres. and Dir.-Gen. TF1 1974–78, Hon. Pres. 1978–; Amb. to the Council of Europe 1978–80; Vice-Pres. Haut Comité de la langue française 1980–81; mem. Acad. des Sciences morales et politiques 1973–; Commandeur Légion d'honneur; Dr. h.c. (Univ. of Brussels). *Publications:* Les Dieux dansent à Cibola 1957, Bonheur et civilisation 1966, Les pouvoirs de la télévision 1970, Sociologie du rite 1971, Dix grandes notions de la sociologie 1976, La raison d'être 1981, Le mot pour rire 1985. *Leisure interest:* tennis. *Address:* 25 bis boulevard Lannes, 75116 Paris, France. *Telephone:* 40 72 64 28.

CAZENOVE, Christopher de Lerisson; British actor; b. 17 Dec. 1945, Winchester; s. of Brig. Arnold and Elizabeth L. (née Gurney) Cazenove; m. Angharad M. Rees 1974; two s.; ed. Dragon School, Oxford, and Eton Coll.; trained as actor at Bristol Old Vic Theatre School; London stage appearances in The Lionel Touch, My Darling Daisy, The Winslow Boy, Joking Apart; New York appearance in play Goodbye Fidel; television appearances in The Regiment (two series), The Duchess of Duke Street (two series), The Riverman, Jennie's War, Dynasty, Hammer's House of Mystery, Lace, Windmills of the Gods. *Films:* Zulu Dawn, East of Elephant Rock, Eye of the Needle, Heat and Dust, Until September, Mata Hari, The Fantasist, Souvenir. *Address:* 32 Bolingbroke Grove, London, S.W.11, England.

CAZIMAJOU, Emile, L. ES L.; French diplomatist; b. 12 Dec. 1923, Pau; s. of Eugène-Jean Cazimajou and Berthe Haase; m. Martine Delomier 1967; two s.; ed. Lycée Berthollet, Annecy, Lycée Henri IV, Paris, and Faculty of Law, Grenoble and Paris; French High Commr.'s Office in Indochina 1948–56; French Embassy, Saigon 1956–59; Ministry of Foreign Affairs 1960–68; Deputy Perm. Rep. to EEC, Brussels 1968–77; Amb. to Turkey 1977–82; Perm. Rep. to OECD 1982–; Diplomatic Adviser to French Govt. 1987. *Address:* 37 quai d'Orsay, 75700 Paris (Office); 11 quai Paul Doumer, 92400 Courbevoie, France (Home).

CAZZANIGA, Vincenzo; Italian oil executive; b. 3 Nov. 1907; ed. Bocconi Univ., Milan; Exec. Soc. Italiana Lubrificanti Bedford (affiliate of Standard Oil Co.) 1932, Man. Dir. 1938; Head, N. Italy Mineral Oils Industrial Cttee. 1945, N. Italy Mineral Oils Dept. 1945–48, Head N. Italy Lubricants Dept., Italian Petroleum Cttee. 1945–48; Pres. Esso Standard Italiana 1951–74; mem. Exec. Cttee. Confindustria (Italian Mfrs. Asscn.) 1957; Dir. Int. Chamber of Commerce 1957; Pres. Unione Petrolifera 1958–73, Sarpom 1961, Esso Chimica 1966, Milan Experimental Fuel Station; Dir. Rasiom 1961, Stanic 1963, Esso Europe Inc. 1966–, Minn. Mining and Mfg. Co. 1970, Montedison 1972–, Istituto Bancario Italiano S.p.A. 1973, Fiduciaria Mobiliare & Immobiliare S.p.A. 1973; Vice-Pres. Bastogi Finanziaria 1972–; Chair. and Chief Exec. Bastogi Int. Ltd. 1973–; Pres. UCID (Christian Execs. Assn.) 1972–; Chair. Compagnia Tecnica Industrie Petroli, CTIP 1975–; Dr. h.c. 1971; Cavaliere del Lavoro, etc. *Address:* Via Porta Latina 8, 1-00179 Rome, Italy.

CEAUŞESCU, Elena, PH.D.(CHEM.); Romanian scientist and politician, wife of Nicolae Ceauşescu (q.v.), Pres. of Socialist Repub. of Romania; b. 7 Jan.

1919, Petreşti, Dîmboviţa; two s. one d.; ed. Coll. of Industrial Chemistry, Polytechnic Inst., Bucharest; involved in militant activities in Union of Communist Youth (UCY) and trade unions before and during World War II; mem. Romanian Communist Party (RCP) 1937–, mem. Cen. Cttee. RCP 1972–, mem. Exec. Cttee. 1973–, Political Exec. Cttee. 1974–, mem. Standing Bureau 1979–; Vice-Prime Minister, Council of Ministers 1980–; mem. Grand Nat. Assembly 1975–; mem. Nat. Council of Front of Democracy and Socialist Unity; Dir. Inst. of Chemical Research 1964–75; Gen. Dir. Cen. Inst. of Chemistry 1975–80; Chair., Nat. Council of Science and Tech. 1979–; Chair. Scientific Council of Cen. Inst. of Chemistry 1980–; mem. Nat. Council of Working People; Deputy Chair. Supreme Council on Socio-Economical Devt. 1982–; Chair. Nat. Council of Science and Educ. 1985–; mem. Romanian Acad. 1974–, New York Acad. of Sciences 1973–, European Acad. of Sciences, Arts and Humanities, Honour Cttee. (Paris) 1981–; Corresp. mem. Athens Acad. 1976–; Hon. mem. Int. Soc. of Industrial Chemistry, France 1970–, American Inst. of Chemists 1973–, Cen. Univ. Ecuador 1973–, Asscn. of Chemists and Chemical Engineers Costa Rica 1973–, Inst. of Natural Science, Quito 1975–, Chemical Soc. Mexico 1975–, Polymer Science Soc. Japan 1975–, Acad. of Arts and Sciences, Ghana 1977–, Acad. of Sciences, Illinois 1978–; Dr. h.c. (Univs. of Buenos Aires and Bahia Blanca) 1974, (Manila, Yucatán, Teheran) 1975, Tech. Univ. for the Middle East (Ankara) 1983, (Malta) 1983, (Islamabad) 1984; Hon. Prof. Nat. Univ. of Eng., Lima 1973, Polytechnic of Cen. London 1978; Prof. Extraordinary Autonomous Nat. Univ. of Mexico City 1975–; Chair. Nat. Romanian Comm. The Scientists and Peace 1981; Hero of Socialist Labour 1971; Order, Victory of Socialism; Star of Socialist Repub. of Romania 1979, Hero of Socialist Repub. of Romania 1981; Heroine of the Socialist Repub. 1989; numerous foreign awards and distinctions. *Publications:* Research Work on the Synthesis and Characterisation of Macromolecular Compounds 1974, Stereospecific polymerisation of Isoprene 1979, New Research Work on Macromolecular Compounds 1981, Studies on Chemistry and Technology of Polymers 1983, Encyclopedia of Chemistry (Vols. I, II, III) 1983, 1985, 1986, The Science and the Progress of Society 1985, Advances in Polymer Chemistry and Technology 1986; studies and articles in learned reviews, trans. in various languages. *Address:* Central Committee of the Romanian Communist Party, Bucharest, Romania.

CEAUŞESCU, Nicolae, D.ECON., DR.RER.POL.; Romanian politician; b. 26 Jan. 1918, Scorniceşti-Olt; s. of Andruţa and Alexandra Ceauşescu; m. Elena Petrescu (Ceauşescu, q.v.); two s. one d.; ed. Acad. of Econ. Studies, Bucharest; mem. Union of Communist Youth 1933– (Sec. Bucharest Org. 1935–36), Romanian Communist Party (RCP) 1933–; imprisoned for revolutionary and anti-fascist activities 1936–38, 1940–44; Sec. Cen. Cttee., Union of Communist Youth 1939–40, Sec.-Gen. 1944–46; mem. Cen. Cttee. RCP 1945–; mem. Grand Nat. Assembly 1946–; Deputy Minister of Agric. 1948–50; Deputy Minister of Armed Forces 1950–54; alt. mem. of Political Bureau 1954–55, mem. 1955–65; Sec. Cen. Cttee. of RCP 1954–65, First Sec. 1965, Sec.-Gen., Cen. Cttee 1965–69; Sec.-Gen. RCP 1969–; mem. Political Exec. Cttee. 1974–, mem. Exec. Cttee., Perm. Presidium 1965–74; Pres. State Council 1967–, Pres. Socialist Repub. of Romania 1974–; Pres. Nat. Council of Socialist Unity Front 1968–74; Socialist Unity Front 1974–80, Front of Democracy and Socialist Unity 1980–; Chair. Supreme Council on Socio-Econ. Devt. 1973–, Nat. Council of Working People 1977–; Chair. Defence Council, Supreme Commdr. of the Armed Forces 1969–; Hon. Pres. Acad. of Social and Political Sciences 1970–, Romanian Acad. 1985–; Dr. h.c. Univs. of Bucharest 1973, Cen. Univ. of Ecuador 1973, Univ. of San Marco, Peru 1973, Nat. Univ. of Eng., Peru 1973, Beirut Arab Univ., Lebanon 1974, Univ. of South Bahia Blanca, Argentina 1974, Univ. of Buenos Aires 1974, Nice Univ., France 1975, Univ. of the Philippines 1975, Yucatan Univ. 1975, Univ. of Teheran 1975; Hon. mem. Anversane Acad. (Italy) 1983; mem. Romanian Acad. 1985; Hero of Socialist Labour 1964; Hero of Socialist Repub. of Romania 1971, 1978, 1981, The Star of Socialist Repub. of Romania 1948, 1958, Victory of Socialism 1971, 1978, other Romanian distinctions; awarded the highest orders and distinctions from 64 states, awards, medals and distinctions from numerous public, cultural, scientific foreign organizations incl. Gold Medal of the World Peace Council, Gold Olympic Order 1985. *Publications:* Romania on the Way of Building Up the Multilaterally Developed Socialist Society (Vols. I–XXX) 1965–88, Selected Works (Vols. I–V) 1965–88, 159 other titles (biographies and selections from his works) in 22 foreign languages. *Leisure interests:* reading, cinema, music, sport. *Address:* Office of the President, Bucharest, Romania.

CEBRIÁN ECHARRI, Juan Luis; Spanish journalist; b. 30 Oct. 1944, Madrid; s. of Vicente Cebrián and Carmen Echarri; m. María Gema Torallas 1966 (divorced); two s. two d.; ed. Univ. of Madrid; founder-mem. of magazine Cuadernos para el Diálogo, Madrid 1963; Sr. Ed. newspapers Pueblo, Madrid 1962–67, Informaciones, Madrid 1967–69; Deputy Ed.-in-Chief, Informaciones 1969–74, 1974–76; Dir. News Programming, Spanish TV 1974; Ed.-in-Chief newspaper El País, Madrid 1976–; mem. Int. Press Inst. (Vice-Pres. 1982–86, Chair. 1986–88); Control Prize for Outstanding Newspaper Ed. 1976, 1977, 1978, 1979; Outstanding Ed. of the Year (World Press Review, New York) 1980, Spanish Nat. Journalism Prize 1983; Gold Medal, Spanish Inst. New York 1988. *Publications:* La prensa y la Calle 1980, La España que Bosteza 1980, ¿Qué pasa en el mundo? 1981, Red

Doll 1987. *Leisure interests:* music, literature. *Address:* Miguel Yuste 40, E-28017 Madrid, Spain.

CEBUC, Alexandru, PH.D.; Romanian art historian and critic; b. 5 April 1932, Păușești-Maglasi; s. of Ion and Ana Cebuc; m. Florica Turcu 1958; one d.; ed. Univ. of Bucharest; Head of Dept., Museum of History of City of Bucharest 1957–69; Vice-Pres. Culture Cttee. of City of Bucharest 1969–77; Dir. Art Museum of Romania 1977–; Order of Cultural Merit, Knight of Italian Repub. *Publications:* The History of the City of Bucharest 1966, The History of Passenger Transportation 1967, Historical and Art Monument of the City of Bucharest 1968, Ion Irimescu (monograph) 1983, Etienne Hadju (monograph) 1984. *Leisure interest:* art. *Address:* Str. 13 Decembrie nr. 31, et.1, ap.8, Bucharest, Romania. *Telephone:* 13.94.92.

CECCATO, Aldo; Italian conductor and director of music; b. 18 Feb. 1934, Milan; m. Eliana de Sabata; two s.; ed. Milan Conservatory, Hochschule für Musik Berlin; Musical Dir. Detroit Symphony 1973–77, Hamburg Philharmonic 1974–82, Norddeutsche Radio Orchestra 1985–, Bergen Symphony 1985–; guest conductor to all maj. symphony orchestras and opera houses in four continents; Hon. D. Mus. (Eastern Michigan Univ.). *Leisure interests:* tennis, stamps, books. *Address:* Chaunt da Crusch, 7524 Zuoz, Switzerland.

CEDAIN ZHOMA; Chinese singer; b. 1 Aug. 1937, Xigaze, Xizang; ed. Shanghai Music Coll.; performed in U.S.S.R. 1963; in political disgrace during Proletarian Cultural Revolutionary 1966–76; rehabilitated 1977; mem. Standing Cttee. 5th NPC 1978–83; Vice-Pres. Chinese Musicians Asscn.; mem. Standing Cttee. 6th NPC 1983–88. *Address:* Chinese Musician's Association, Beijing, People's Republic of China.

CEFIS, Eugenio; Italian business executive; b. 21 July 1921, Cividale; m. 1943; ed. Univ. of Milan; commissioned in Sardinian Grenadiers; Vice-Pres. Ente Nazionale Idrocarburi (ENI) until 1967, Pres. 1967–71; Pres. Montedison 1971–77, Chair. Montedison Ind. Holdings 1977–80; Dir. Snia Viscosa 1971–. *Address:* Snia Viscosa, Via Montebello 18, Milan, Italy.

CELA, Camilo José; Spanish writer; b. 11 May 1916; ed. Univ. de Madrid; fmr. Dir. and Publr. of journal Papeles de Son Armadans; mem. Real Acad. Española 1957; Premio de la crítica 1955. *Publications include:* La Familia de Pascual Duarte (novel) 1942, Pabellón de reposo 1943–57, Nuevas andanzas y desventuras de Lazarillo de Tormes 1944–55, Pisando la dudosa luz del día (poems) 1945, Mesa revuelta 1945 and 1957, Viaje a la Alcarria 1948, La colmena 1951, Del Miño al Bidasoa 1952, Mrs. Caldwell habla con su hijo 1953, La Catira 1955, Judíos, moros y cristianos 1956, El molino de viento (short stories) 1956, Nuevo retablo de don Cristobita 1957, Viaje al Pirineo de Lérida 1965, Diccionario Secreto I 1968, II 1971, San Camilo 1936 1969, María Sabina 1970, A vueltas con España (essays) 1973, Oficio de tinieblas 1973, Enciclopedia del Erotismo 1976–77, Vuelta de hoja 1981, Mazurca para dos muertos 1983, Cristo versus Arizona 1988. *Address:* La Bonanova, Palma de Mallorca, Spain.

CELEBREZZE, Anthony J., LL.B.; American politician and lawyer; b. 4 Sept. 1910, Anzi, Potenza, Italy; s. of Rocco and Dorothy (née Marcoguiseppe) Celebrezze; m. Anne Marco 1938; one s. two d.; ed. John Carroll and Ohio Northern Univs.; admitted Ohio Bar 1936; practised law in Cleveland; U.S. Navy Second World War; Senator, Ohio State 1950–53; Mayor of Cleveland 1953–62; U.S. Sec. of Health, Educ. and Welfare, July 1962–65; Judge, U.S. Court of Appeals 1965; Order of Merit (Italy); Doctor of Humanity (Wilberforce Univ.) and many other hon. degrees; Trustee of Catholic Charities, Nat. Conf. of Christians and Jews; Democrat. *Leisure interests:* reading, fishing, hunting. *Address:* 25043 Westwood Road, Westlake, Ohio 44145, U.S.A. (Home).

CELESTE, Richard F., PH.B.; American state governor; b. 11 Nov. 1937, Cleveland, Ohio; s. of Frank Celeste; m. Dagmar Braun 1962; three s. three d.; ed. Yale Univ. and Oxford Univ.; Staff Liaison Officer, Peace Corps 1963; Special Asst. to U.S. Amb. to India 1963–67; mem. Ohio House of Reps. 1970–74, Majority Whip 1972–74; Lieut.-Gov. of Ohio 1975–79, Gov. Jan. 1983–; Chair. Midwestern Govs.' Conf. 1987–88; Great Lakes Govs.' Asscn. 1987–89; Democrat. *Address:* State Capitol, Columbus, Ohio 43215, U.S.A.

CELIBIDACHE, Sergiu; German (b. Romanian) conductor, composer and musicologist; b. 28 June 1912; m. Joana Celibidache; ed. Jassy and Berlin; Conductor and Artistic Dir. Berlin Philharmonic Orchestra 1946–51; Dir. Swedish Radio Symphony Orchestra 1961–; Music Dir., Conductor Munich Philharmonic 1979–; now guest conductor to leading European orchestras; mem. Acad. of Fine Arts, Munich 1979; German Critics' Prize 1953, Berlin City Art Prize 1955; Grosses Verdienstkreuz (Fed. Repub. of Germany) 1954, Leonie-Sonnig Culture Award 1970. *Address:* Münchener Philharharmoniker, Rindermarkt 3-4, 8000 Munich 2, Federal Republic of Germany.

CÉLIER, Pierre, B.A., LL.B.; French company executive; b. 25 Feb. 1917, Paris; s. of Comte Alexandre Célier and Comtesse Elisabeth de Gastines; m. France-Victoire de Wendel 1942; one s. one d.; ed. Faculty of Arts and Faculty of Law (Paris); Inspecteur des Finances 1942–48; Asst. Dir.-Gen. De Wendel et Cie. 1952–70, Man. 1969–73; Dir.-Gen. Wendel-Sidélor 1968–73; Pres. of Directoire, Sacilor 1973–78; Joint Man. Petits-Fils de François de Wendel et Cie. 1961–70, Dir.-Gen. Cie. Lorraine Industrielle et Financière 1970–73; Dir. Solmer 1971–75; Pres. Admin. Bd. Marine-

Wendel July 1975–; Pres. Admin. Bd. Cie. Gen. d'Industrie et de Participation 1980–86, Hon. Pres. 1987–; Admin. numerous cos.; mem. Advisory Bd. S.A.E., Dilling; Officier, Légion d'honneur; Croix de guerre 1945. *Address:* 89 rue Taitbout, 75009 Paris, France (Office). *Telephone:* 42-85-30-00 (Office); 42-22-81-36 (Home).

CELIO, Nello, D.IUR.; Swiss lawyer and politician; b. 12 Feb. 1914; ed. Univs. of Basel and Berne; Sec. Cantonal Interior Dept. 1941–45; Public Procurator 1945–46; mem. Council of States 1946–49, Nat. Council 1963–; mem. Fed. Council 1967–73, Vice-Pres. Jan.-Dec. 1971, Pres. Jan.-Dec. 1972; Head of Fed. Mil. (Defence) Dept. 1967–68, of Finance and Customs Dept. 1968–73; fmr. Pres. Radical Democrat Party; Chair. Interfood, Banco Rasini, Milan 1984–. *Address:* Via Ronchi 13, Lugano, Switzerland.

ĆENAC, Winston Francis, LL.B., Q.C.; Saint Lucia lawyer and politician; b. 14 Sept. 1925, St. Lucia; s. of Frank and Leanese (née King) Cenac; m. Flora Marie Cenac 1952; ed. St. Mary's Coll. and Univ. of London; worked as Chief Clerk in District Court, then as Deputy Registrar, Supreme Court; called to the Bar Lincoln's Inn, London 1957; Registrar, Supreme Court, St. Lucia 1957; Acting Magistrate, Southern District, St. Lucia 1958; Chief Registrar of Supreme Court of Windward and Leeward Islands 1959; Attorney-Gen. of St. Lucia 1962, of St. Vincent 1964, of Grenada 1966; del. Constitutional Conf., Little Eight Constitution, London 1962; Dir. of Public Prosecutions, Grenada 1967; pvt. practice in St. Lucia 1969; Puisne Judge of St. Vincent 1971, of St. Kitts, Nevis and Virgin Islands 1972; returned to pvt. practice, St. Lucia 1973; mem. House of Ass. for Soufrière 1979–; Attorney-Gen. of Saint Lucia 1979–80, Prime Minister 1981–82; Pres. St. Lucia Bar Asscn. 1989; Life mem. Commonwealth Parl. Asscn. *Leisure interests:* reading, gardening, music. *Address:* 7 High Street, Box 629, Castries, Saint Lucia. *Telephone:* 23891 (Office); 28425 (Home).

CEREZO ARÉVALO, Mario Vinicio; Guatemalan politician; b. 26 Dec. 1942; s. of Marco Vinicio Cerezo; m. Raquel Blandón 1965; four c.; ed. Univ. of San Carlos; mem. Christian Democratic Party; Pres. of Guatemala Jan. 1986–. *Address:* Oficina del Presidente, Guatemala City, Guatemala.

ĆERNIK, Oldřich; Czechoslovak politician; b. 27 Oct. 1921, Ostrava; ed. Mining Coll., Ostrava; machine fitter at Vítkovice Iron Works 1937–49; Sec. District Cttee. of CP of Czechoslovakia, Opava 1949–54, Chair. Regional Nat. Cttee., Ostrava 1954–56; Sec. Cen. Cttee. of CP of Czechoslovakia 1956–60; mem. Econ. Comm. Cen. Cttee. 1963–70; Minister of Fuel and Power 1960–63, of Fuel 1963; Deputy Prime Minister and Chair. State Planning Comm. 1963–68; Prime Minister April-Dec. 1968, Prime Minister Fed. Govt. of Czechoslovak Socialist Repub. 1969–70; mem. Presidium Cen. Cttee. CP of Czechoslovakia 1966–70; mem. of Cen. Cttee. Bureau for directing party work in Czech lands 1969; Minister, Chair. of Cttee. for Technological and Investment Devt. 1970; Deputy to Nat. Assembly 1960–69; Deputy to House of the People, Fed. Assembly 1969–70; suspended from CP of Czechoslovakia 1970. *Address:* Committee for Technological and Investment Development, Prague 2, Slezská 7, Czechoslovakia.

ĆERNIK, Dr. Zdeněk; Czechoslovak diplomatist; b. 26 Feb. 1921, Ostrava; m.; two c.; ed. Inst. of Political and Social Sciences, Prague; joined Ministry of Foreign Affairs 1949; Deputy Head of Dept. of Int. Orgs. 1956–62, Head 1962–68; Deputy Perm. Rep. to UN 1959–62, Perm. Rep. 1968–73; Chief of Protocol 1973–77; Amb. to U.K. (also accred. to Ireland) 1977–83; Deputy Foreign Minister 1983–; Head Czechoslovak Del. to Eighteen-Nation Disarmament Conf., Geneva 1965–67; Order of the Repub. 1981. *Address:* c/o Ministry of Foreign Affairs, Loretánské nám. 5, Prague 1- Hradčany, Czechoslovakia.

CÉSAIRE, Aimé Fernand, L. ÈS L.; French (Martiniquais) poet, dramatist and politician; b. 25 June 1913, Basse-Pointe, Martinique; s. of Fernand and Marie (Hermine) Césaire; m. Suzanne Roussi 1937; four s. two d.; ed. Fort-de-France (Martinique) and Lycée Louis-le-Grand (Paris), Ecole Normale Supérieure and the Sorbonne; teaching career 1940–45; mem. Constituent Assemblies 1945 and 1946; Deputy for Martinique 1946–; Pres. Parti Progressiste Martiniquais; Mayor of Fort-de-France 1945–83, re-elected 1983 but result declared invalid by Tribunal; Pres. Conseil régional, Martinique 1983–86; Pres. Soc. of African Culture, Paris; Grand Prize for Verse 1982. *Publications:* Verse: Cahier d'un retour au pays natal, Les armes miraculeuses, Et les chiens se taisaient, Soleil cou coupé, Corps perdu, Cadastre, Ferrements, Moi, laminaire 1982; Essays: Discours sur le colonialisme; Theatre: La tragédie du roi Christophe, Une saison au Congo, Une tempête. *Address:* Assemblée Nationale, 75007 Paris, France; La Mairie, 97200 Fort-de-France, Martinique, West Indies.

CESAR, Jaroslav; Czechoslovak diplomatist; b. 1938; m.; two c.; ed. Charles Univ., Prague, State Inst. for Int. Relations, Moscow; lawyer with Ministry of Foreign Affairs 1963–65; with Czechoslovakian Embassy in Ethiopia 1965–69; Chargé d'Affaires in Somalia 1973–77; Head Dept., Ministry of Foreign Affairs 1977–81, mem. of Collegium and Chef de Cabinet of the Minister for Foreign Affairs 1981–84; Perm. Rep. to UN 1984–87. *Publications:* numerous articles on int. relations. *Address:* c/o Ministry of Foreign Affairs, Prague, Czechoslovakia.

CEYRAC, François, B.A., B.LL.; French trade union administrator; b. 12 Sept. 1912, Meyssac; s. of Paul and Suzanne (née Murat de Montaï) Ceyrac;

m. Renée Rihet (deceased); two s. three d.; ed. Lycée Louis-le-Grand and Univ. of Paris; Metal Workers' and Miners' Union branch chief 1936, Asst. Sec.-Gen. 1945, Deputy Sec.-Gen. 1952–68, Pres. 1969–73; Conseil Nat. du Patronat Français (French Nat. Business Council) 1946–, mem. of council 1967–, Vice-Pres. 1968–73, Pres. 1973–81, Hon. Pres. 1981; Pres. Econ. and Social Cttee. of the European Communities 1982–84; Pres. I.C.C. 1983–85; Pres. Supervisory Council Coparis 1986–; Admin. Soc. Arjomari-Prioux 1986–; founding mem. of Comité National pour le Développement des Grandes Ecoles; Vice-Pres. Mechanical and Metallurgical Asscn.; mem. Bd. Peugeot SA, Univ. of Paris IV; mem. Advisory Bd. Préservatrice Foncière Assurances; Officier, Légion d'honneur. *Leisure interest:* sailing. *Address:* 44 avenue d'Iéna, 75116 Paris; 16 avenue des Courlis, 78110 Le Vésinet, France (Home).

CEYSSON, Bernard; French museum director; b. 7 June 1939, Saint-Etienne; Dir. Musée d'art et d'industrie, Saint-Etienne 1967–86; Dir. Musée national d'art moderne 1986–. *Address:* Musée nationale d'art moderne, 75191 Paris Cedex 04, France.

CHA, Liang-Chien, S.J.D.; Chinese jurist, judge, government official and university professor; b. 17 June 1905, Hopeh, Chekiang; s. of Ho-Chi Cha; m. 1st Eunice Tsao 1931 (died 1951), two s.; m. 2nd Kay Chang 1955, two s.; ed. Nankai and Soochow Univs. and Michigan Univ., U.S.A.; Prof. of Law, Anhui Univ. and Nat. Cen. Univ. 1931–34; part-time Prof. Soochow Univ. 1934–49; Judge, Shanghai Special Dist. Court and Shanghai Br., Szechwan High Court; Counsellor, Ministry of Justice 1941–43; Tech. Expert, Far Eastern Comm. for Investigation and Trial War Criminals, UN 1942–45; Judge and Pres. Chungking Model Court and Shanghai Dist. Court 1943–49; Del. to UN Congress for Prevention of Crime and Treatment of Offenders 1960, to 18th and 19th Sessions of UN Gen. Ass. 1962 and 1963; Vice-Minister of Justice 1950–66; Pres. Supreme Court 1966–67; Minister of Justice 1967–70; Nat. Policy Adviser Repub. of China 1970–; Prof. and Dean, Graduate School of Law, Chinese Cultural Univ. 1970–; Bd. Chair. Tunghai Univ. 1970–; Pres. Sino-American Cultural Econ. Asscn., Repub. of China; Chin-shing 3rd Order of Honour and Distinction, 1955; N.R.B. Citation and Honour of Religious Leadership 1981. *Publications:* Criminology and Penology, Compulsory Execution of Civil Cases etc. *Leisure interests:* tennis, chess. *Address:* (Postal) 23-11F, Hang-chow N. Road, Sec. I, Taipei, Taiwan.

CHABAN-DELMAS, Jacques Michel Pierre; French politician; b. 7 March 1915; s. of Pierre Delmas; ed. Lycée Lakanal, Sceaux, Ecole Libre des Sciences Politiques, Paris; served army 1939–40, Brig.-Gen. 1944; nat. mil. del. responsible for co-ordination of mil. planning, Resistance 1944; Insp.-Gen. of Army Nov. 1944; Sec.-Gen. Ministry of Information 1945–46; Radical deputy for Gironde 1946–61; Mayor of Bordeaux 1947–; leader of Gaullist group (Républicains Sociaux) in Nat. Assembly 1954–58; Minister of Public Works 1954–55; Inspecteur des Finances 1956–57; Minister of Nat. Defence 1957–58; Pres. of Nat. Ass. 1958–69, 1978–81, 1986–88; Prime Minister 1969–72; Insp.-Gen. des Finances 1973; Pres. Regional Council, Aquitaine 1974–79, 1985–; Cand. for Pres. of France May 1974; Pres. of Comm. for Regional Econ. Devt. of Aquitaine 1964–69; Pres. European Assembly of Local Authorities 1975, United Towns Org. 1985; Commdr., Légion d'honneur; Croix de guerre; Compagnon de la Libération; Hon. LL.D. (Bristol) 1987. *Publications.* L'ardeur 1975, Charles de Gaulle 1980, La Libération 1984, Les Compagnons 1986. *Leisure interests:* tennis, rugby, golf. *Address:* Mairie de Bordeaux, 33077 Bordeaux (Office); Assemblée nationale, 75355 Paris (Office); La Mendicka, Urrugne, 64700 Hendaye, France (Home).

CHABAUD, André; French administrator; b. 26 Aug. 1921, Champs (Cantal); s. of late Annet Chabaud; m. Arlette F. Remy 1967; one s.; ed. Lycée de Maurice, Cantal, Faculté des Lettres et de Droit, Strasbourg and Paris; Asst. Prof. Lycée de Mentluçon 1941; Admin. Dir. Théâtres lyriques nationaux 1954; Admin. Reunion of Théâtres lyriques nationaux 1968; Sec.-Gen. Inventory of monuments and artistic treasures of France 1971; Dir. Musée du Louvre 1979–83; Chevalier, Légion d'honneur, Officier des Arts et des Lettres. *Address:* 50 bis, blvd. du Général Leclerc, 92200 Neuilly-sur-Seine, France.

CHABERT, Jos, DR. EN DROIT; Belgian lawyer and politician; b. 16 March 1933, Etterbeek; ed. Univs. of Brussels and Louvain; Advocate Court of Appeal; Alderman, Meise; mem. Bd. of Admin. Intercommunale Haviland; mem. Chamber of Reps. 1968–74, Senator 1974–; Pres. of Christian Social Party Group in Parl. 1972–73; mem. Finance and Steering Cttees., Cultural Council for the Dutch cultural community; Minister of Dutch Culture and Flemish Affairs 1973–74, of Communications 1974–80, of Public Works and Institutional Reforms (Dutch sector) 1980–81; Pres. Atelier protégé pour handicapés de Meise. *Address:* c/o Ministry of Public Works, rue de la Loi, 155, Brussels, Belgium.

CHABROL, Claude; French film director and producer; b. 24 June 1930, Paris; s. of Yves Chabrol and Madeleine Delarbre; m. 1st Agnès Goute, two s.; m. 2nd Colette Dacheville (Stéphane Audran, q.v.), one s.; ed. Paris Univ., Ecole Libre des Sciences Politiques; fmrly. film critic and Public Relations Officer in Paris for 20th-Century Fox; dir. and producer 1958–; Locarno Festival Grand Prix 1958, Berlin Festival Golden Bear 1959. *Films directed include:* Le beau Serge 1957, Les cousins 1958, A double

tour 1959, Les bonnes femmes 1959, Les godelureaux 1960, Ophélia 1962, L'oeil du malin 1961, Landru 1962, Les plus belles escroqueries du monde 1963, Le tigre aime la chair fraîche 1964, Le tigre se parfume à la dynamite 1965, Marie-Chantal contre le Docteur Kha 1965, Le scandale 1967, Les biches 1968, La femme infidèle 1968, Que la bête meure 1969, Le boucher 1970, La rupture 1970, Juste avant la nuit 1971, Doctor Popaul 1972, La décade prodigieuse 1972, Les noces rouges 1973, Nada 1973, Une partie de plaisir 1975, Les innocents aux mains sales 1976, Alice ou la dernière fugue 1977, Les liens de sang 1977, Violette Nozière 1978, The Twist, Blood Relations 1979, Le Cheval d'Orgueil 1980, Les fantômes du chapelier 1982, Cop au vin 1985, Inspecteur Lavardin 1986, Masques 1987, Une Affaire des Femmes 1988. *Publication:* Alfred Hitchcock (with E. Rohmer). *Address:* 15 Quai Conti, 75006 Paris, France.

CHADENET, Bernard; French international consultant; b. 16 Sept. 1915, Paris; s. of Julien and Geneviève (née Malézieux) Chadenet; m. Françoise Chêne-Carrère 1944; two d.; ed. Univ. de Paris à la Sorbonne and Ecole Supérieure d'Electricité, Paris, and Harvard Business School; Gen. Man. NEYRPIC, Grenoble 1958–64; Assoc. Dir. Projects Dept., World Bank 1964, Vice-Pres. for Admin., Org. and Personnel Man. 1972–, Vice-Pres. 1979; Int. Consultant 1980–; Officier Légion d'honneur. *Leisure interest:* skiing. *Address:* 6 rue Masseran, 75007, Paris, France (Home). *Telephone:* 45-67-28-62 (Home).

CHADHA, Indrajit Singh, M.SC.; Indian diplomatist; b. 9 July 1933, Rawalpindi; s. of Harnam Singh Chadha; m. Amrit Anand 1959; three d.; ed. Nagpur Univ.; lecturer in Physics, Coll. of Science, Nagpur 1954–56; joined Indian Foreign Service 1956; served Cairo 1958–59, Colombo 1959–62; Perm. Mission of India at UN, New York 1965–68; Chargé d'Affaires, Amman 1968–69; Officer on Special Duty, Ministry of External Affairs, New Delhi 1969–71; Deputy Chief of Mission, Brussels 1971–72; Resident Rep. of India to GATT and UNCTAD 1972–76; Dir. UNCTAD Secr. 1976–81; Joint Sec., later Additional Sec. Ministry of External Affairs 1982–85; High Commr. in Bangladesh 1985–. *Publications:* numerous articles in leading journals on int. econ. relations. *Leisure interests:* photography, bridge, badminton. *Address:* NE(K)-14, Gulshan Avenue, Dhaka, Bangladesh. *Telephone:* 603717.

CHADIRJI, Rifat Kamil, DIP.ARCH., F.R.I.B.A.; Iraqi architect; b. 6 Dec. 1926, Baghdad; s. of Kamil Chadirji; m. Balkis Sharara 1954; ed. Hammersmith School of Arts and Crafts, London; f. and Sr. Partner and Dir. Iraq Consult 1952–; Section Head, Baghdad Bldg. Dept. Waqaf Org. 1954–57; Dir.-Gen. Housing, Ministry of Planning, Baghdad 1958–59, Head Planning Cttee. Ministry of Housing 1959–63; returned to full-time private practice with Iraq Consult 1963–78; apptd. Counsellor to Mayoralty of Baghdad 1980–82; mem. Iraqi Tourist Bd. 1970–75; Loeb Fellow, Harvard Univ. 1983; *works include:* Council of Ministers Bldg., Baghdad 1975, Cabinet Ministers' Bldg., U.A.E. 1976, Nat. Theatre, Abu Dhabi, U.A.E. 1977, Al-Ain Public Library, U.A.E. 1978; exhbns. at Gulbenkian Hall, Baghdad 1966, Univ. of Khartoum, Sudan 1966, Ministry of Art and Culture, Accra, Ghana 1966, Kwame Nkrumah Univ. of Science and Tech., Ghana 1966, Middle East Tech. Univ., Ankara, Turkey 1966, Athens Tech. Insts., Greece 1966, American Univ. of Beirut, Lebanon 1966, Arab Engs. Conf., Jordan 1966, Amman, Jordan 1966, Hammersmith Coll. of Art 1966, Ain Shamis Univ., Cairo, Egypt 1967, Arab Engs. Conf., Kuwait 1975, Kuwait Engs. Union 1975, Iraqi Cultural Cen., London 1978, Middle East Construction Exhbn., Dubai, U.A.E. 1978, Vienna Tech. Univ., Austria 1978; many awards and prizes incl. First Prize for Council of Ministers Bldg., Baghdad 1975, First Prize New Theatre, Abu Dhabi, U.A.E. 1977, First Prize, Council of Ministers, Abu Dhabi, U.A.E. 1978. *Leisure interests:* photography and travel. *Address:* 28 Troy Court, Kensington High Street, London, W.8, England. *Telephone:* 01-937 3715.

CHADLI, Col. Bendjedid; Algerian army officer and politician; b. 14 April 1929, Sebaa; six c.; Joined Maquisards (guerrilla forces) in fight for independence against French 1955; mem. General Staff of Col. Boumedienne's army 1961; Commdr. Constantine Mil. Region, East Algeria 1962, of Second Mil. Region (Oran) 1963–79; mem. Revolutionary Council 1965; Acting Chief of Staff 1978–79; Sec.-Gen. National Liberation Front Feb. 1979–; President of Algeria, C.-in-C. of the Armed Forces and Minister of Defence Feb. 1979–; Medal of the Resistance 1984. *Address:* Présidence de la Republique, El Mouradia, Algiers, Algeria. *Telephone:* 60.03.60.

CHADWICK, Henry, D.D., MUS.B.; British professor emeritus of divinity; b. 23 June 1920, Bromley, Kent; s. of John Chadwick and Edith M. Chadwick; m. Margaret E. Brownrigg 1945; three d.; ed. Eton Coll. and Magdalene Coll. Cambridge; Fellow, Queens' Coll. Cambridge 1946–58, Hon. Fellow 1958–; Regius Prof. of Divinity, Univ. of Oxford 1959–69, Dean of Christ Church 1969–79; Regius Prof. of Divinity, Univ. of Cambridge 1979–83, Prof. Emer. 1983–, Fellow, Magdalene Coll. 1979–86; Del. Oxford Univ. Press 1960–79; hon. degrees from Glasgow, Leeds, Manchester, Uppsala, Yale and Chicago. *Publications:* Origen Contra Celsum 1953, Early Christian Thought and the Classical Tradition 1966, The Early Church 1967, Priscillian of Avila 1976, Boethius 1981, History and Thought of the Early Church 1982, Augustine 1986. *Leisure interest:* music. *Address:* Peterhouse, Cambridge, CB2 1RD, England. *Telephone:* (0223) 338211.

CHADWICK, John, M.A., LITT.D., F.B.A.; British classical scholar; b. 21 May 1920, East Sheen, Surrey; s. of Fred Chadwick and Margaret Bray; m. Joan Isobel Hill 1947; one s.; ed. St. Paul's School, London, Corpus Christi Coll., Cambridge Univ.; war service in Royal Navy 1940–45; Editorial Asst. Oxford Latin Dictionary 1946–52; Lecturer in Classics, Cambridge Univ. 1952–66, Reader in Greek Language 1966–69, Perceval Maitland Laurence Reader in Classics 1969–84; Collins Fellow, Downing Coll., Cambridge 1960–84, Hon. Fellow 1984–; Sec. Gen. Perm. Int. Cttee. for Mycenaean Studies 1975–; co-operated with Michael Ventris in the decipherment of the Minoan Linear B script; Corresp. mem. German archaeological Inst. 1957, Austrian Acad. of Sciences 1974; Foreign Assoc. Acad. des Inscriptions et Belles Lettres, Inst. de France 1985; Hon. Fellow Athens Archaeological Soc. 1974, Hon. Councillor 1987–; Hon. Doctorate, Athens Univ. Philosophical School 1958, Univ. Libre de Bruxelles 1969, Euskal Herriko Unibertsitatea, Vitoria 1985; Hon. Litt.D. (Trinity Coll., Dublin) 1971; Commdr., Order of the Phoenix (Greece) 1984. *Publications:* The Medical Works of Hippocrates (with W. N. Mann) 1950; Documents in Mycenaean Greek (with Michael Ventris) 1956; The Decipherment of Linear B 1958 trans. into 12 languages 1959–80; The Pre-History of the Greek Language (in Cambridge Ancient History, Vol. II) 1963; The Mycenaean World 1976 trans. into 5 languages 1977–81; Ed. The Mycenae Tablets III 1963; Jt. Ed. The Knossos Tablets IV 1971; Jt. Ed. Corpus of Mycenaean Inscriptions from Knossos, Vol. I Rome and Cambridge 1986, Linear B and Related Scripts 1987; Trans. The True Christian Religion by E. Swedenborg 1988; various articles in learned journals. *Leisure interest:* travel. *Address:* 75 Gough Way, Cambridge, CB3 9LN, England. *Telephone:* Cambridge 356864.

CHADWICK, Lynn Russell, C.B.E.; British sculptor; b. 24 Nov. 1914; s. of the late Verner Russell Chadwick and of Marjorie Brown (née Lynn) Chadwick; m. 1st Charlotte Ann Secord 1942, one s.; m. 2nd Frances Mary Jamieson (died 1964), two d.; m. 3rd Eva Reiner 1965, one s.; ed. Merchant Taylors School; works shown in London, New York, Paris, Brussels (Exposition 1958) and Venice, where he won the Int. Sculpture Prize at the Biennale 1956; 1st Prize Padua Int. Competition 1959; Hors Concours, Bienal São Paulo 1961; mem. Acad. di San Luca, Rome 1965, Premio Indebile El Circulo de Bellas Artes de Lerida, Spain 1970, Officier des Arts et Lettres 1986. *Address:* Lypiatt Park, Stroud, Glos., England. *Telephone:* (0452) 770 210.

CHADWICK, Owen, O.M., K.B.E., F.B.A.; British historian; b. 20 May 1916, Bromley, Kent; s. of John and Edith (née Horrocks) Chadwick; m. Ruth Hallward 1949; two s. two d.; ed. St. John's Coll., Cambridge; Fellow, Trinity Hall, Cambridge 1947–56; Master of Selwyn Coll., Cambridge 1956–83; Dixie Prof. of Ecclesiastical History, Cambridge Univ. 1958–68, Regius Prof. of Modern History 1968–83; Vice-Chancellor of Cambridge Univ. 1969–71; Pres. British Acad. 1981–85; Chancellor Univ. of E. Anglia 1985–; Wolfson Literary Award 1981; Hon. D.D. (St. Andrews) 1960, (Oxford) 1973, Hon. D.Litt. (Kent) 1970, (Columbia Univ.) 1977, (East Anglia) 1977, (Bristol) 1977, (London) 1983, (Leeds) 1986, (Cambridge) 1987, Hon. LL.D. (Aberdeen) 1986. *Publications:* From Bossuet to Newman 1957, The Victorian Church (2 vols.) 1966–70, The Mind of the Oxford Movement (2nd edn.) 1967, John Cassian (2nd edn.) 1968, The Reformation (20th edn.) 1986, The Secularization of the European Mind 1976, Catholicism and History 1978, The Popes and European Revolution 1981, Britain and the Vatican during the Second World War 1987; numerous articles and reviews in learned journals. *Leisure interests:* music and gardening. *Address:* Selwyn College, Cambridge, England.

CHADWICK, Peter, PH.D., SC.D., F.R.S.; British professor of mathematics; b. 23 March 1931; s. of Jack Chadwick and Marjorie (Castle) Chadwick; m. Sheila G. Salter 1956; two d.; ed. Huddersfield Coll., Univ. of Manchester and Pembroke Coll. Cambridge; Scientific Officer, then Sr. Scientific Officer, Atomic Weapons Research Establishment, Aldermaston 1955–59; Lecturer, then Sr. Lecturer in Applied Math. Univ. of Sheffield 1959–65; Prof. of Math. Univ. of E. Anglia 1965–, Dean, School of Math. and Physics 1979–82; Visiting Prof. Univ. of Queensland 1972. *Publications:* Continuum Mechanics 1976; articles in books and learned journals. *Address:* School of Mathematics, University of East Anglia, University Plain, Norwich, NR4 7TJ, England. *Telephone:* Norwich 56161.

CHAFEE, John H., B.A., LL.B.; American lawyer and politician; b. 22 Oct. 1922, Providence, R.I.; s. of John Sharpe and Janet Hunter Chafee; m. Virginia Coates, 1950; four s. one d.; ed. Deerfield Acad., Yale Univ., and Harvard Law School; U.S. Marine Corps 1942–46, 1951–52; admitted to Rhode Island Bar 1951; State Rep. R.I. House 1956–62; Gov. of Rhode Island 1963–69, Senator 1977–; Sec. of the Navy 1969–72; Hon. LL.D. (Brown Univ., Providence Coll., Univ. of R.I.); Visiting Chubb Fellow, Yale Univ. 1965; Chair. Compact for Educ. 1965, Republican Govs'. Assen. 1967–68, Republican Conf. 1985–; Trustee, Deerfield Acad. 1970–79, Yale Univ. 1972–78; Republican. *Leisure interests:* squash, tennis, sailing, skiing. *Address:* 3103 Dirksen Senate Office Bldg., Washington D.C. 20510, U.S.A. *Telephone:* 202-224-2921 (Office).

CHAGAS, Carlos, M.D., SC.D.; Brazilian biophysicist; b. 1910; ed. Colégio Rezende, Univ. do Brasil and Univ. de Paris; began career as Asst. at Inst. Oswaldo Cruz and Medical School, Univ. do Brasil; Prof. Univ. do Brasil Medical School 1937, Dir. Inst. of Biophysics 1946–64; mem. Brazilian Nat. Research Council 1950–55, UN Scientific Cttee. 1956–, WHO Scientific Advisory Cttee. 1959–61, Pan American Health Org. Scientific Advisory Cttee. 1962–; Chair. Exec. Cttee. Int. Brain Research Org.; Perm. Del. of Brazil to UNESCO; Adviser Puerto Rico Atomic Energy Comm.; mem. Brazilian Acads. of Science, Medicine and Pharmacy, Pontifical Acad. of Sciences, Assoc. Mem. Acad. de Médecine (Paris), Soc. de Biologie (Paris), London Physiological Soc.; fmr. Vice-Pres. ICSU; Dr. h.c. (Paris, Coimbra, Mexico, Recife Univs.); Premio Moinho Santista 1960; Commdr. Order of Christ (Portugal), of Merit (Italy); Officer, Légion d'honneur; Ordre de la Santé publique (France), Order of Polar Star (Sweden). *Publications include:* Homems e Cousas de Ciência (essays) and a large number of medical and scientific papers 1936–. *Address:* 38 Francisco Otaviano, Rio de Janeiro, RJ, Brazil.

CHAGULA, Dr. Wilbert K., M.B., CH.B., M.A.; Tanzanian public servant and administrator; b. 3 Feb. 1926, Shinyanga, Tanganyika; s. of Kiyenze Chagula; unmarried; ed. Tabora Govt. School, Makerere Univ. Coll., Uganda, King's Coll., Cambridge Univ., Univ. of W. Indies, Jamaica, Yale Univ., U.S.A.; Asst. Medical Officer, Tanganyika 1952; Asst. in Dept. of Anatomy, Asst. Lecturer, Lecturer in Anatomy, Makerere Univ. Coll. 1953–61; Rockefeller Foundation Fellow in Histochemistry, Jamaica and Yale Univs. 1961–63; Registrar and Vice-Prin., Univ. Coll., Dar es Salaam 1963–65, Prin. 1965–70; Minister for Water Devt. and Power 1970–72, for Econ. Affairs and Devt. Planning 1972–75, of Water Energy and Minerals 1975–77; Minister for Finance and Admin. (East African Community) 1977–78; Amb. to the UN, Geneva, 1978–86, to the UN, New York, 1986–; Chair. Tanzania Nat. Scientific Research Council 1972; mem. UN Advisory Cttee. for the Application of Science and Tech. to Devt. 1971– (Chair. sessions 1975–78), WHO Advisory Cttee. on Medical Research and WHO Expert Advisory Panel on Public Health Admin. 1976–77, UN Univ. Council 1977, Bd. of Trustees Int. Fed. of Science 1975, Editorial Bd. of Mazingira 1977–, E. African Acad. (Pres. 1963–, Fellow 1971), Medical Assen. of Tanzania, Econ. Soc. of Tanzania, The Third World Forum, Tanganyika African Nat. Union Nat. Exec. Cttee. 1969–75, Tanganyika Soc. of African Culture, Tanzania Soc.; Adviser Int. Fed. of Insts. of Advanced Studies. *Publications:* books and articles on education and health. *Leisure interests:* reading, writing. *Address:* Permanent Mission of Tanzania to the United Nations, 205 East 42nd Street, 13th Floor, New York, N.Y. 10017, U.S.A.

CHAI SHUFAN; Chinese politician; b. 1905, Hubei; joined CCP 1927; studied in Moscow 1927–30; on Long March; Vice-Chair. State Planning Comm. 1957–67, 1978; Minister of 6th Ministry of Machine Building 1978–81. *Address:* State Council, Beijing, People's Republic of China.

CHAI YANSHU; Chinese weightlifter; middleweight silver medalist in 1987 World Championships. *Address:* China Sports Federation, Beijing, People's Republic of China.

CHAI ZEMIN; Chinese diplomatist; b. 1915, Shanxi Prov.; m. Li Youfeng; Sec. CCP Cttee., Beijing Suburban Work Cttee. 1949; Deputy Sec.-Gen. Municipal People's Govt., Beijing 1950, mem. Financial and Econ. Cttee. 1950; Chair. Peasants' Assen., Beijing 1951; Pres. Suburban Branch, People's Court, Beijing 1952; Council mem. Municipal People's Govt., Beijing 1952, Inst. of Foreign Affairs 1955; Sec.-Gen. Municipal People's Council, Beijing 1955–57; Dir. Communications Dept., Municipal CCP Cttee., Beijing 1959; Amb. to Hungary 1961–64, to Guinea 1964–67, to Egypt 1970–74, to Thailand 1976–78; Head, Liaison Office, U.S.A. 1978; Amb. to U.S.A. 1979–82; Vice-Pres. Chinese People's Inst. for Foreign Affairs 1983–. *Address:* Beijing, People's Republic of China.

CHAILAKHYAN, Mikhail Khristoforovich, DR.SC.; Soviet plant physiologist; b. 21 March 1902, Nakhichevan-on-Don; ed. Yerevan State Univ.; Agronomist, Yerevan 1926–29; Lecturer, Faculty of Botany, Transcaucasian Zootechnical and Veterinary Inst. 1928–31; Aspirant (postgraduate), Lab. of Plant Physiology and Biochemistry, U.S.S.R. Acad. of Sciences, Leningrad 1931–34; Head of Lab., K. A. Timiriazev Inst. of Plant Physiology, U.S.S.R. Acad. of Sciences, Moscow 1935–; Faculty of Plant Anatomy and Physiology, Yerevan State Univ. 1941–48, Prof. 1943–, Chair. of Plant Physiology and Microbiology, Yerevan Agric. Inst., Prof. 1943–; Corresp. mem. Armenian S.S.R. Acad. of Sciences, Yerevan 1945–71, mem. 1971–; Hon. Scientist, Armenian S.S.R., Yerevan 1967–; mem. U.S.S.R. Acad. of Sciences, Moscow 1968–, German Acad. Leopoldina-Halle 1969–; Corresp. mem. American Soc. of Plant Physiologists 1963–, American Botanical Soc. 1969–; Foreign mem. Bulgarian Botanical Soc., Sofia 1974–; Dr. h.c. (Rostock Univ., G.D.R.) 1969–; Order of Lenin (twice) and other decorations. *Publications:* many scientific works in field of physiology of higher plant growth and development processes. *Address:* K. A. Timiriazev Institute of Plant Physiology, U.S.S.R. Academy of Sciences, Botanicheskaya 35, Moscow 127273, U.S.S.R. *Telephone:* 482-53-12.

CHAILLY, Riccardo; Italian conductor; b. 20 Feb. 1953, Milan; s. of Luciano Chailly and Anna Marie Motta; ed. Giuseppe Verdi and Perugia Conservatories and with Franco Caracciolo and Franco Ferrara; Asst. to Claudio Abbado, La Scala, Milan 1972–74; début as Conductor with Chicago Opera 1974; début, La Scala 1978, Covent Garden (operatic début) 1979; concert début with London Symphony Orchestra and Edin. Festival 1979; American concert début 1980; played with major orchestras 1980; début,

Metropolitan Opera 1982; Prin. guest Conductor, London Philharmonic Orchestra 1982-85; début, Vienna State Opera 1983; appearances Salzburg Festival 1984, 1985, 1986; Japan début, with Royal Philharmonic Orchestra 1984; début, New York Philharmonic Orchestra 1984; Chief Conductor of Radio Symphony Orchestra Berlin 1982-; Music Dir. Bologna Orchestra 1986-; Prin. Conductor Concertgebouw Orchestra 1988-. *Address:* c/o Harrison/Parrott, Penzance Place, London, W11 4PA, England.

CHAKAIPA, Patrick Fani; Zimbabwean ecclesiastic; b. 25 June 1932, Mhondoro; ed. St. Michael's Mission, Mhondoro, Kutama Training Coll.; ordained Roman Catholic priest 1965; Titular Bishop of Rucuma and Auxiliary Bishop of Salisbury (now Harare) 1972-76; Archbishop of Salisbury (now Harare) June 1976-. *Publications:* Karikoga Gumiremiseve 1958, Pfumo Reropa 1961, Rudo Ibofu 1961, Garandichauya 1963, Dzasukwa Mwana Asina Hembe 1967. *Leisure interest:* chess. *Address:* Archbishop's House, 66 Fifth Street, Harare (Home); P.O. Box 8060, Causeway, Harare, Zimbabwe (Office). *Telephone:* 792125 (Home); 727386 (Office).

CHAKOVSKY, Aleksandr Borisovich; Soviet writer; b. 26 Aug. 1913, St. Petersburg (Leningrad); s. of Boris and Nina Chakovsky; m. Raisa Chakovskya 1945; one s.; ed. Gorky Institute for Literature, Moscow; mem. CPSU 1941-; Ed.-in-Chief Literaturnaya Gazeta 1962-; Sec. of Bd., Union of Writers of U.S.S.R. 1963-; Deputy U.S.S.R. Supreme Soviet 1966-; Alt. mem. Cen. Cttee. CPSU 1971-86, mem. 1986-; U.S.S.R. State Prize 1950, 1983; State Prize in Literature 1983; Hero of Socialist Labour 1973; Order of Lenin (four times), Order of October Revolution, Red Banner of Labour, Red Star, War Medals. *Publications include:* It Was in Leningrad (trilogy) 1944, Lyda 1945, Peaceful Days 1947, It's Already Morning with Us 1950, Khvan Cher is on Guard 1952, A Year of One Life 1956, Roads We Take 1960, Light of Distant Star 1962 (made into film and play), Fiancée 1966 (made into film and play), Blockade (5 vols.) 1968-75 (made into film), Collected Works (six vols.) 1974-76, Victory (novel) (3 vols.) 1980-81, Unfinished Portrait 1984. *Leisure interest:* tennis. *Address:* Literaturnaya Gazeta, Kostiansky 13, Moscow, U.S.S.R. *Telephone:* 200-28-65.

CHAKRAVARTY, Sukhamoy, PH.D.; Indian professor of economics; b. 26 July 1934, Bengal; s. of Somnath Chakravarty and Bindubasini Devi; m. Lalita Chakravarty 1957; one d.; ed. Calcutta Univ., Netherlands School of Econ., Rotterdam; Visiting Fellow, Netherlands School of Econ., 1957-59; Asst. Prof., M.I.T., U.S.A. 1959-61; Prof., Presidency Coll., Calcutta 1961-63; Prof. of Econ., Delhi School of Econ. 1963-; Visiting Fellowships and Professorships, L.S.E., Johns Hopkins Univ., Univ. of Erasmus, Univ. of Cambridge 1963-; mem. Planning Comm,., Govt. of India 1971-77; Chair. Cttee. to Review Monetary System in India, Reserve Bank of India 1983-85, Econ. Advisory Council to the Prime Minister 1983-; Indian Council of Social Science Research 1987-; Chair. or mem. of numerous other nat. and int. cttees.; Pres. Indian Econometric Soc. 1983-, Indian Econ. Asscn. 1986-; Vice-Pres. Int. Econ. Asscn. 1983-86, Hon. Pres. 1987-; Fellow Econometric Soc.; Mahalanobis Memorial Gold Medal, Indian Econometric Soc. 1974, VKRV Rao Prize in Social Sciences 1978. *Publications:* Capital and Development Planning 1969, The Relationship between Food Aid and Non-Food Aid (with P. N. Rosenstein-Rodan) 1973, Reshaping the International Order (with Jan Tinbergen and others) 1977, Development Planning: The Indian Experience; book chapters, numerous articles in nat. and int. professional journals. *Leisure interest:* listening to music. *Address:* Delhi School of Economics, University of Delhi, University Road, Delhi-7, India.

CHALANDON, Albin Paul Henri, L. ES L.; French businessman and politician; b. 11 June 1920, Reyrieux, Ain; s. of Pierre Chalandon and Claire Cambon; m. Princess Salomé Murat 1951; two s. one d.; ed. Lycée Condorcet, Paris; Inspecteur des Finances; Dir. Banque Nationale pour le Commerce et l'Industrie (Afrique) 1950-51; Admin. and Dir.-Gen. Banque Commerciale de Paris 1952-64, Président-Directeur Général 1964-68; M.P. 1967-76; Minister of Industry May 1968, of Public Works, Housing and Urban Devt. 1968-72, of Justice 1986-88; Special Asst., Ministry of Foreign Affairs Feb.-Aug. 1974; Treas. Cen. Cttee. Union pour la Nouvelle République (now Union des Démocrates pour la République) 1958-59, Sec.-Gen. 1959, Deputy Sec.-Gen. UDR 1974-75; Pres. Entreprise de recherches et d'actions pétrolières (ERAP), now Soc. Nat. ELF Aquitaine (SNEA) 1977-80, Pres. SNEA 1977-83; mem. Social and Econ. Council 1963-67; Officier Légion d'honneur, Croix de guerre. *Publications:* Le système monétaire international 1966, Les joueurs de flûte, Le rêve économique de la Gauche 1977, Quitte ou Double 1986. *Address:* 12 rue de Lota, 75016, Paris, France (Home). *Telephone:* 4704-51-71.

CHALFONT, Baron (Life Peer), cr. 1964; (Arthur) Alun Gwynne Jones, P.C., O.B.E., M.C., F.R.S.A.; British politician; b. 5 Dec. 1919, Lantarnam, Wales; s. of Arthur Gwynne Jones and Eliza Alice Hardman; m. Mona Mitchell 1948; one d. (deceased); ed. West Monmouth School; commissioned into S. Wales Borderers (24th Foot) 1940; served in Burma 1941-44, Malaya 1955-57, Cyprus 1958-59; resgnd. comm. 1961; Defence Corresp. The Times, London 1961-64; Consultant on foreign affairs to BBC TV, London 1961-64; Minister of State for Foreign Affairs 1964-70, Minister for Disarmament 1964-67, 1969-70, in charge of day-to-day negotiations for Britain's entry into Common Market 1967-69; Perm. Rep. to Western European Union 1969-70; Foreign Ed. New Statesman 1970-71; Chair. All

Party Defence Group House of Lords 1980-; Industrial Cleaning Papers 1979-86; Peter Hamilton Security Consultants Ltd. 1984-86; U.K. Cttee. for Free World 1981-; European Atlantic Group 1983-; VSEL Consortium PLC 1987-; Deputy Chair. IBA Jan. 1989-; Pres. Hispanic and Luso Brazilian Council 1975-80; Royal Nat. Inst. for Deaf 1980-; Llangollen Int. Music Festival 1979-87; Abington Corpn. (Consultants) Ltd. 1981-; Nottingham Building Soc. 1983-; Dir. W. S. Atkins Int. 1979-83; IBM U.K. Ltd. 1973- (mem. IBM Europe Advisory Council 1973-); Lazard Brothers and Co. Ltd. 1983-; Pres. Freedom in Sport Int. 1988-; mem. Int. Inst. of Strategic Studies; Royal Inst.; Bd. of Govs. Sandle Manor School; mem. Inst. Dirs.; Hon. Fellow Univ. Coll. Wales, Aberystwyth 1974. *Publications:* The Sword and the Spirit 1963, The Great Commanders 1973, Montgomery of Alamein 1976; (Ed.) Waterloo: Battle of Three Armies 1979, Star Wars: Suicide or Survival 1985, Defence of the Realm 1987, By God's Will: A Portrait of the Sultan of Brunei; contribs. to Times and nat. and professional journals. *Leisure interests:* music and theatre. *Address:* House of Lords, London, SW1A 0PW, England.

CHALID, Idham (see Idham Chalid, Dr. Kjai Hadji).

CHALIDZE, Valeriy Nikolayevich; Soviet physicist; b. 1938, Moscow; m.; ed. Moscow Univ., then Faculty of Physics, Tbilisi Univ. 1965; head of research unit in Plastics Research Inst., Moscow 1965-70; removed from post 1970; mem. of U.S.S.R. Human Rights Cttee.; dissident activity 1969-, when started samizdat journal Obshchestvennyye problemy (Problems of Society), trip to U.S.A. to lecture on human rights in U.S.S.R., subsequently deprived of Soviet citizenship 1972; currently living in New York. *Publications* (apart from numerous samizdat articles and books) include: Ugolovnaya Rossiya (Capital Punishment in Russia) 1977, U.S.S.R.—The Workers' Movement 1978. A Foreigner in the Soviet Union. A Juridical Memoir 1980, Communism Vanquished (Stalin) 1981, The Responsibility of a Generation 1982.

CHALLIS, Anthony Arthur Leonard, C.B.E., PH.D.; British scientist; b. 24 Dec. 1921, Wolverhampton; s. of Leonard Hough and Dorothy (née Busby) Challis; m. Beryl Hedley 1947; two d.; ed. Newcastle Royal Grammar School, Univ. of Durham; joined Imperial Chemical Industries (ICI) 1946; Techn. Officer, Billingham Div. 1946-54, Research Section Man. Billingham Div. 1954-59, Research Group Head, Billingham Div. 1962-65; Research Dir. Mond Div. 1965-66; Head, Petrochemical and Polymer Lab. (now Corporate Lab.), ICI 1966-70; Gen. Man. Co. Planning, ICI 1970-74; Sr. Vice-Pres. ICI Americas Inc. 1974-77; Dir. Polymer Eng. Directorate, Science Research Council (SRC), now Science and Eng. Research Council 1977-80; Chief Scientist, Dept. of Energy 1980-83; mem. SRC 1973-83; Chair. Offshore Energy Tech. Bd. 1983-, Chair. Council Plastics and Rubber Inst. 1983-85, Pres. 1985-87; Assoc. Prof. Wolfson Unit for Materials Processing Brunel Univ. 1987; mem. Court, Univ. of Stirling 1968-74, Liveryman Worshipful Company of Horners. *Leisure interests:* music, walking, sailing. *Address:* Classeys, Low Ham, Langport, Somerset, England. *Telephone:* (0458) 250625.

CHALMERS, Floyd Sherman, C.C., LL.D., LITT.D., B.F.A.; Canadian publisher; b. 14 Sept. 1898, Chicago, Ill., U.S.A.; of Canadian-Scottish parentage; m. Jean A. Boxall 1921; one s. one d.; with Bank of Nova Scotia 1914; Reporter on Toronto News and Toronto World; joined Financial Post 1919, Montreal Ed. 1923, Ed. 1925-42; Exec. Vice-Pres. Maclean-Hunter Publishing Co. 1942-52, Pres. 1952-64, Chair. 1964-69, Hon. Chair. 1978-; Chancellor, York Univ. 1969-73; Warden, Hon. Co. of Freeman of City of London in North America; Civic Award of Merit, Toronto 1974, Diplôme d'hon., Canadian Conf. of the Arts 1974, Canadian News Hall of Fame 1975, Canadian Music Council, Special Award 1977, Queen's Jubilee Medal 1977, numerous other awards. *Leisure interest:* theatre. *Address:* Maclean Hunter Building, 777 Bay Street, Toronto, Ont. M5W 1A7 (Office); Apartment 4611, 44 Charles Street W., Toronto M4Y 1R8, Canada (Home). *Telephone:* (416) 596-5199 (Office); (416) 964-7667 (Home).

CHALMERS, (George) Everett N., O.C., D.SC., M.D.C.M., F.R.C.S.(C.), F.A.C.S.; Canadian surgeon and politician; b. 5 June 1905; m. 1st Eloise Roberts 1935, 2nd Winnifred W. Hickey 1956; three s. three d.; ed. Fredericton High School, Univ. of New Brunswick, McGill Univ., Montreal; began practice of medicine and surgery, Fredericton 1936; was for many years surgeon-in-chief of Victoria Public Hosp. (Dir. of Poliomyelitis Service Dept. 1941-51); Charter Mem. Fredericton Medical Clinic; has served on numerous hosp. building cttees. since 1937; Hon. Chair. Bd. of Dirs. Fredericton Regional Hosp.; Pres. N.B. Progressive Conservative Party 1959-61; mem. Legis. Ass. 1960-78; Chair. Alcoholism and Drug Dependency Comm. of N.B. 1978-; Hon. D.Sc. (Univ. of N.B.) 1974; Distinguished Citizen of Fredericton Award 1982; Officer, Order of Canada 1983; Dr. Paul Harris Award from Fredericton N. Rotary Club 1988. *Leisure interest:* sports. *Address:* P.O. Box 6000, 65 Brunswick Street, Fredericton, N.B., E3B 5H1, Canada. *Telephone:* 453-2136.

CHALONER, William Gilbert, PH.D., F.R.S.; British professor of botany; b. 22 Nov. 1928; s. of late Ernest J. Chaloner and L. Chaloner; m. Judith Carroll 1955; one s. two d.; ed. Kingston Grammar School and Univ. of Reading; Lecturer and Reader, Univ. Coll. London 1956-72; Visiting Prof. Pa. State Univ. 1961-62; Prof. Univ. of Nigeria 1965-66; Prof. of Botany, Birkbeck Coll. London 1972-79; Hildred Carlile Prof. of Botany and Head

School of Life Sciences, Royal Holloway and Bedford New Coll. 1985– (Bedford Coll. 1979–85); Visiting Prof. Univ. of Mass. 1981; mem. Bd. of Trustees, Royal Botanic Gdns. Kew; Pres. Linnean Soc. 1985–; mem. Senate London Univ.; corresp. mem. Botanical Soc. of America 1987–. *Publications:* papers in scientific journals. *Leisure interests:* swimming, tennis, visiting U.S.A. *Address:* 20 Parke Road, London, SW13 9NG, England. *Telephone:* 01-748 3863.

CHALUPA, Vlastimil, Ing., C.SC.; Czechoslovak politician; b. 17 Oct. 1919, Ratenice; ed. Transport Inst., Žilina; held various econ. and CP posts 1945–51; engaged in govt. admin. and postal services 1952–69; Deputy Chair., Fed. Cttee. for Posts and Telecommunications 1970; Minister of Posts and Telecommunications 1971–86; Head of Del. to CMEA Comm. for Posts and Telecommunications 1971–; Deputy Chair. Cttee. of Friendship between G.D.R. and Czechoslovakia 1973–80, Chair. 1980–, attached to the Czechoslovak Soc. for Int. Relations 1973–; Chair. Cttee. of Czech-Vietnamese Friendship, attached to the Czechoslovak Soc. for Int. Relations 1981–; Distinctions for "Merit in Construction" 1973, Order of Labour 1974, of the Republic 1979, Hon. Badge, Central Council of Trade Unions 1974, Gold Medal Czechoslovak Acad. of Sciences. *Address:* Federal Ministry of Posts and Telecommunications, Olšanská 5, CS-125 02 Prague 3, Czechoslovakia. *Telephone:* 714-11-11.

CHAMANT, Jean, L. EN D.; French lawyer and politician; b. 23 Nov. 1913, Chagny; s. of Eugène and Anne-Marie (née Retif) Chamant; m. Hélène Claret 1936; one s. three d.; Advocate, Court of Appeal, Paris; Deputy for l'Yonne 1946–77, Senator 1977–; Sec. of State, Ministry of Foreign Affairs 1955–56; Vice-Pres. Nat. Assembly 1959–67; Minister of Transport 1967–69, 1971–72; Pres. Conseil régional de l'Yonne 1970, de Bourgogne 1974–78. *Address:* Sénat, Palais du Luxembourg, 75291 Paris Cedex 06 (Office); 6 rue Masseran, 75007 Paris, France (Home). *Telephone:* 45-67-29-05 (Home).

CHAMBERLAIN, (George) Richard; American actor; b. 31 March 1935, Los Angeles; s. of Charles Chamberlain and Elsa Chamberlain; ed. Los Angeles Conservatory of Music and drama studies with Jeff Corey; stage appearances include King Lear, Hamlet, Richard II, The Lady's Not for Burning, Night of the Iguana, Cyrano de Bergerac; numerous TV appearances include Dr. Kildare 1961–65, Portrait of a Lady 1968, The Woman I Love 1973, The Count of Monte Cristo 1975, The Man in the Iron Mask 1978, Shogun 1980 (Golden Globe Award), The Thorn Birds 1983, Wallenberg: A Hero's Story 1985, Dream West 1986. *Films include:* Secret of Purple Reef 1960, Thunder of Drums 1961, Twilight of Honor 1963, Joy in the Morning 1965, Petulia 1968, The Madwoman of Chaillot 1969, The Music Lovers 1971, Julius Caesar 1971, Lady Caroline Lamb 1971, The Three Musketeers 1974, Towering Inferno 1974, The Four Musketeers 1975, The Slipper and the Rose 1977, The Swarm 1978, Murder by Phone 1982, King Solomon's Mines 1985, Alan Quartermain and The Lost City of Gold 1987. *Address:* c/o Creative Artists Agency, 1888 Century Park East, Suite 1400, Los Angeles, Calif. 90067, U.S.A.

CHAMBERLAIN, Joseph Wyan, A.M., M.S., PH.D.; American astronomer and geophysicist; b. 24 Aug. 1928, Boonville, Mo.; s. of Gilbert Lee Chamberlain and Jessie Wyan Chamberlain; m. Marilyn Roesler Chamberlain 1949; two s. one d.; ed. Univs. of Missouri and Michigan; Project Scientist in Aurora and Airglow, U.S.A.F., Cambridge Research Center 1951–53; Research Assoc., Yerkes Observatory, Univ. of Chicago 1953–55, Asst. Prof. of Astronomy 1955–59, Assoc. Prof. 1959–60, Assoc. Dir. Yerkes Observatory 1960–62, Prof. of Astronomy Jan.–June 1961, Prof. of Astronomy and Geophysical Sciences 1961–62; Assoc. Dir. for Planetary Sciences Div. (fmrly. Space Div.), Kitt Peak Nat. Observatory, Tucson, Ariz. 1962–70; Astronomer 1970–71; Dir. Lunar Science Inst., Houston, Texas 1971–73; Prof. Space Physics and Astronomy Dept., Rice Univ., Houston 1971–; Ed. Reviews of Geophysics and Space Physics 1974–80; mem. N.A.S.; mem. numerous int. comms. and recipient of numerous awards. *Publications:* Physics of the Aurora and Airglow 1961, Theory of Planetary Atmospheres 1978, revised edn. 1987, and over 125 technical publs. on aurora, airglow, planetary exospheres, and the atmospheres of the planets. *Leisure interests:* golf, music, reading. *Address:* Space Physics and Astronomy Department, Rice Univ., P.O. Box 1892, Houston, Texas 77251, U.S.A. *Telephone:* (713) 527-8101, Ext. 3641.

CHAMBERLAIN, Owen, PH.D.; American physicist; b. 10 July 1920, San Francisco; s. of Edward and Genevieve Lucinda (Owen) Chamberlain; m. 1st 1943 (divorced 1978); four c.; m. 2nd June Steingart Chamberlain 1980; ed. Germantown Friends School, Dartmouth Coll., and Univ. of Chicago; Research physicist Manhattan Project, Berkeley 1942–43, Los Alamos 1943–46; graduate student (under Enrico Fermi) Univ. of Chicago 1946–48; Instructor in Physics, Univ. of Calif., Berkeley 1948–50, Asst. Prof. 1950–54, Assoc. Prof. 1954–58, Prof. 1958–89, Prof. Emer. 1989–; on leave at Univ. of Rome as Guggenheim Fellow 1957–58; Loeb Lecturer, Harvard Univ. 1959; mem. N.A.S.; Fellow, American Acad. of Arts and Sciences; has specialized in research in spontaneous fission, proton scattering, discovery of antiproton, properties of antinucleons, etc.; shared Nobel Prize for Physics with Emilio Segre 1959. *Address:* Department of Physics, University of California, Berkeley, Calif. 74720, U.S.A.

CHAMBERS, George Michael; Trinidadian politician; b. 4 Oct. 1928; m. Juliana Jacobs; one d.; began as office boy in firm of solicitors; worked in

legal dept. of oil co.; People's Nat. Movement (PNM) Party Cand. 1966, elected MP for St. Ann's, N. Trinidad; re-elected until 1986; Minister of Finance 1971–75; also fmr. Minister of Public Utilities and Housing, of Nat. Security, of Educ. of Industry and Commerce, of Agric., Lands and Fisheries Jan.–March 1981; Prime Minister, also Minister of Finance of Trinidad and Tobago March 1981–86; Leader PNM 1981–88; Gov. Caribbean Devt. Bank 1981–. *Leisure interests:* opera, record playing, sea bathing, reading. *Address:* c/o Office of the Prime Minister, St. Ann's, Trinidad and Tobago.

CHAMBERS, Leigh Ross, M.A.; Australian professor of French; b. 19 Nov. 1932, Kempsey, N.S.W.; s. of Cecil Edward Chambers and Beryl Alma Fayle; ed. Univ. of Sydney and Univ. of Grenoble, France; McCaughey Prof. and Head Dept. of French Univ. of Sydney 1971–75; Prof. of French Univ. of Mich., Ann Arbor 1975–85, Marvin Felheim Distinguished Univ. Prof. of French and Comparative Literature 1985–; Fellow Australian Acad. of Humanities; Officier de l'Ordre des Palmes Académiques. *Publications:* Gérard de Nerval et la poétique du voyage 1969, La comédie au château 1971, L'Ange et l'automate 1971, Story and Situation 1984, Mélancholie et opposition 1987. *Address:* Department of Romance Languages, University of Michigan, Ann Arbor, Mich. 48109, U.S.A. (Office). *Telephone:* (313) 747 2339.

CHAMOUX, François, D.ÈS.L.; French academic; b. 4 April 1915, Mirecourt; s. of Emile Chamoux and Henriette Genvot; m. 1st Lucienne Cavaye 1938 (died 1971), 2nd Christiane Humeau 1973; one s. one d.; ed. Ecole Normale Supérieure, Ecole française d'Athènes, Sorbonne, Paris; lecturer in Greek, Univ. of Lille 1948–49; Lecturer in Archaeology, Sorbonne 1949–51; Prof. of Archaeology, Univ. of Nancy 1952–60; Prof. of Greek Literature and Civilization, Sorbonne 1960–83, Prof. Emer. 1983–; Dir. French Archaeological Mission in Libya 1976–81; mem. Institut de France (Académie des Inscriptions et Belles-Lettres) 1981–; Dr. h.c. (Neuchâtel); Officier, Légion d'honneur, Officier, Ordre du Mérite, Croix de guerre. *Publications:* Cyrène sous la monarchie des Battiades 1953, L'Aurige de Delphes 1955, La civilisation grecque archaïque et classique 1963, Art-grec 1966, La civilisation hellénistique 1981, Marc Antoine 1986; more than 120 learned articles on Greek literature, history and archaeology. *Leisure interest:* philological and historical research. *Address:* 6 avenue Paul-Appell, F-75014 Paris, France. *Telephone:* 45.40.51.30.

CHAMPAGNE, Andrée; Canadian politician and actress; ed. Institut Notre-Dame de Lorette, Saint-Hyacinthe; worked in radio, TV, theatre and film, as a writer, and in public relations; performed many roles with Montreal theatre cos. and with various summer theatre groups; Sec.-Gen. Union des artistes 1983–84; Pres. Chez-nous des artistes 1983–84; Minister of State for Youth 1984–86; Del. to Int. Fed. of Actors Conf. 1984; fmr. mem. Bd. of Dirs., Institut québécois du cinéma; Progressive Conservative Party. *Publications:* more than 200 poems and songs. *Address:* House of Commons, Parliament Buildings, Ottawa, Ont., K1A 0A6, Canada.

CHAMPIN, Pierre Marcel Henri; French businessman; b. 26 Aug. 1903; ed. Ecole des Sciences Politiques, Paris; fmr. Pres. and Gen. Man. Vallourec, fmr. Hon. Pres.; Officier Légion d'honneur. *Address:* 11 bis rue Jean Goujon, 75008 Paris, France (Home).

CHAN, Rt. Hon. Sir Julius, P.C., K.B.E.; Papua New Guinea politician; b. 29 Aug. 1939, Tanga, New Ireland; m. Stella Ahmat 1966; one d. three s.; ed. Maurist Brothers Coll., Ashgrove, Queensland and Univ. of Queensland, Australia; Co-operative Officer, Papua New Guinea Admin. 1960–62; Man. Dir. Coastal Shipping Co. Pty. Ltd.; mem. House of Assembly 1968–75, 1982–, Deputy Speaker, Vice-Chair. Public Accounts Cttee. 1968–72; Parl. Leader, People's Progress Party 1970–; Minister of Finance and Parl. Leader of Govt. Business 1972–77; Deputy Prime Minister and Minister for Primary Industry 1977–78, Prime Minister 1980–82, Deputy Prime Minister 1986–88, Minister of Trade and Industry 1986–88; Gov. for Papua New Guinea and Vice-Chair. Asian Devt. Bank 1975–77; Fellowship mem. Int. Bankers' Assn. Inc., U.S.A. 1976–; Hon. Dr. h.c. (Econ.), Dankook Univ., Seoul 1978; Hon. Dr. Tech., Univ. of Tech., Papua New Guinea 1983. *Address:* P.O. Box 717, Rabaul, Papua New Guinea.

CHAN SIANG SUN, Datuk; Malaysian politician; b. 2 Feb. 1933, Bentong Pahang; m. Chia Kwai Ying; six c.; ed. Massey Coll., Univ. of New Zealand; school teacher 1958; Deputy Minister of Educ. 1974–82, of Information 1982–85; Minister of Housing and Local Govt. Jan.–Aug. 1986, of Health Aug. 1986–; Vice-Pres. Malaysian Chinese Assen. (MCA) 1978–. *Address:* Ministry of Health, Jalan Cendera Sari, 50590 Kuala Lumpur, Malaysia.

CHANCE, Britton, M.S., PH.D., D.SC.; American biophysicist; b. 24 July 1913, Wilkes Barre, Pa.; s. of Edwin M. and Eleanor (Kent) Chance; m. 1st Jane Earle 1938 (divorced), 2nd Lilian Streeter Lucas 1955; four s. four d., two step s. two step d.; ed. Univ. of Pennsylvania and Cambridge Univ.; Acting Dir. Johnson Foundation 1940–41; Investigator Office of Scientific Research and Devt. 41; staff mem. Radiation Lab., M.I.T.; Asst. Prof. of Biophysics, Univ. of Pa. 1941–46, Prof., Chair. and Dir. Johnson Foundation 1949–83, E. R. Johnson Prof. of Biophysics 1949–, Prof. Emer. 1982–; Guggenheim Fellow, Nobel and Molteno Inst. 1946–48; scientific consultant, research attaché, U.S. Navy, London 1948; consultant, Nat. Science Foundation 1951–56; President's Scientific Advisory Cttee. 1959–60; NCI Working Group on Molecular Control 1973–; NIAAA Council 1971–75; Vice-Pres.

Int. Union Pure and Applied Biophysics 1972–75, Pres. 1975–; Dir. Inst. for Functional and Structural Studies, Philadelphia; mem. N.A.S., American Acad. of Arts and Sciences, American Philosophical Soc., Royal Acad. of Science, Uppsala, Biochemical Soc., Biophysical Soc., Int. Soc. for Cell Biology, Royal Soc. of Arts, Royal Swedish Acad., Acad. Leopoldina, etc.; Foreign mem. Max-Planck-Inst. für Systemphysiologie und Ernährungsphysiologie, Dortmund, Royal Soc. of London 1981; Fellow, Inst. of Radio Engineers; Philip Morris Lecturer 1978; Heineken Prize 1970, Presidential Certificate of Merit 1950, Paul Lewis Award in Enzyme Chemistry, American Chemical Soc. 1950, William J. Morlock Award in biochemical electronics, Inst. of Radio Engineers 1961, Netherlands Biochemical Soc. Award 1966, Keilin Medal 1966, Franklin Medal 1966, Gairdner Award 1972, Festschrift Symposium, Stockholm 1973, Semmelweis Medal 1974, Nat. Medal of Science 1974, DaCosta Oratusi 1976, etc. *Publications:* Waveforms (with Williams, Hughes, McNichol, Sayre) 1949, Electronic Time Measurements (with Hulsizer, McNichol, Williams) 1949, Enzyme-Substrate Compounds 1951, Enzymes in Action in Living Cells 1955, The Respiratory Chain and Oxidative Phosphorylation 1956, Techniques for Assay of Respiratory Enzymes 1957, Energy-Linked Functions of Mitochondria 1963, Rapid Mixing and Sampling Techniques in Biochemistry 1964, Control of Energy Metabolism 1965, Hemes and Hemoproteins 1966, Probes of Structure and Function of Macromolecules and Enzymes 1972, Alcohol and Aldehyde (3 vols.), Tunneling in Biological Systems 1979. *Leisure interests:* yacht sailing and cruising, amateur radio. *Address:* Department of Biochemistry and Biophysics, University of Pennsylvania, Philadelphia, Pa. 19104 (Office); 4014 Pine Street, Philadelphia, Pa. 19104, U.S.A. (Home). *Telephone:* 215-898-4342.

CHANCELLOR, Alexander Surtees, B.A.; British journalist; b. 4 Jan. 1940, Ware, Herts.; s. of Sir Christopher Chancellor, C.M.G. and Sylvia Mary Chancellor (née Paget); m. Susanna Elizabeth Debenham 1964; two d.; ed. Eton Coll., Trinity Hall, Cambridge; Reuters News Agency 1964–74, Chief Corresp., Italy 1968–73; ITV News 1974–75; Ed. The Spectator 1975–84; Asst. Ed. Sunday Telegraph 1986; Washington Ed. The Independent 1986–88; Ed. The Independent Magazine 1988–; Ed. Time and Tide 1984–86. *Address:* c/o The Independent, 40 City Road, London, EC1X 2DB (Office); 1 Souldern Road, London, W.14, England (Home).

CHANCELLOR, John; American newspaperman and TV compère; b. 14 July 1927; ed. Univ. of Illinois; Reporter, Chicago Sun-Times; NBC news staff 1950–65, corresp. Chicago, Vienna, London, Moscow, Brussels, Berlin; compère NBC TV Programme To-day 1961–62; Producer of Special Programmes 1962–63; Head of NBC Brussels Bureau to cover European Common Market July 1963–64; White House Corresp. of NBC 1964–65; Dir. Voice of America 1966–67; network nat. affairs corresp., NBC 1967–; Prin. Reporter NBC Nightly News 1970–82 (Commentator 1982–). *Address:* c/o NBC News, 30 Rockefeller Plaza, New York, N.Y. 10020, U.S.A.

CHANDAVIMOL, Abhai, M.A.; Thai educationist; b. 16 Feb. 1908, Chanthaburi; s. of Meng Chandavimol and Wann Punyasthiti; m. Tongkorn Punyasthiti 1942; three s. one d.; ed. Suan Kularb School, Bangkok, Imperial Service Coll., Windsor, Gonville and Caius Coll., Cambridge, Inner Temple, London; Teacher 1925–28, 1934–36; Sec. Dept. of Physical Educ. 1936–43; Chief Private School Div. 1943–47; Asst. Dir.-Gen. Dept. of Gen. Educ. 1947–51; Dir.-Gen. Dept. of Physical Educ. 1951–52, Dept. of Elementary and Adult Educ. 1952–61; Under-Sec. of State for Educ. 1961–68; Deputy Minister of Educ. 1970–71, Minister 1972–74; Senator 1975–76; mem. Exec. Cttee. Boy Scouts of Thailand 1952–; elected Boy Scouts World Cttee. 1965–71; elected Chair. Far East Scouts Advisory Cttee. 1966–68; Hon. Ed. D. (Chiengmai Univ.) 1978; Order of Crown of Thailand, Order of the White Elephant, Bronze Wolf Award of World Scout Cttee. *Publications:* translations of Lord Baden-Powell's books into Thai. *Leisure interests:* scouting, gardening, orchid cultivation, golf. *Address:* 85 Rajatapan Lane, Makkasan Bangkok 10400, Thailand. *Telephone:* 245-2512.

CHANDERNAGOR, André, L. EN D.; French politician; b. 19 Sept. 1921, Civray; s. of Clovis Chandernagor and Betzy Barbaud; m. Eliane Bernadet 1944; one s. two d.; ed. Collège de Civray, Lycée Henri-IV, Paris, Ecole nationale de la France d'outre-mer, Ecole nationale d'Admin.; Trainee Admin., Indochina civil service 1943; Asst. Admin., Overseas France 1945; Auditor, Council of State 1952, Maître des Requêtes 1957; Mayor of Mortroux 1953–83; Tech. Adviser, Ministry of Overseas France 1956–58; Deputy (Creuse) to Nat. Assembly 1958–81, Vice-Pres. 1967–68; Councillor, Bourganeuf 1961–83; mem. Steering Cttee., Section Française de l'Internationale Ouvrière (S.F.I.O.) 1963, Parti Socialiste 1969–79; Pres. Conseil de l'Union interparlementaire 1968–73; Pres. Departmental Assembly of Creuse 1973–83, and Limousin 1974–81; Pres. Int. Trade Inst. 1978; PS Rep., French Del. to UN 1978–79; Minister-Del. for European Affairs attached to Minister for External Relations 1981–83; Supreme Pres. Cour des comptes 1983–. *Publications:* Un parlement, pour quoi faire?, Réformer la démocratie? (with the late Alexandre Sanguinetti). *Address:* 13 rue Cambon, 75001 Paris (Office); 7 place des Vhernes, 91120 Palaiseau, France (Home).

CHANDLER, Colby H.; American photographic company executive; b. 1925; joined Kodak Park Div. of Eastman Kodak Co. as quality control eng. in colour print and processing org. 1950, Gen. Man. of Div. 1971; Dir.

of Photographic Programme Devt. for U.S. and Canadian Photographic Div. 1971–73, Dir. of Special Projects 1973, Gen. Man. of Div. 1974–75; mem. Bd. of Dirs. 1974; Exec. Vice-Pres. 1974–76, Pres. of Eastman Kodak Co. 1977–83, Chair. and C.E.O. July 1983–. *Address:* Eastman Kodak Company, 343 State Street, Rochester, N.Y. 14650, U.S.A.

CHANDLER, George, M.A., PH.D., F.L.A., F.R.HIST.S., F.R.S.A.; Australian (b. British) librarian; b. 2 July 1915, Birmingham; s. of late William Chandler and Florence Chandler; m. Dorothy Lowe 1937; one s.; ed. Central Grammar School, Birmingham, Birmingham and Midland Inst., Leeds Coll. of Commerce and Univ. of London; with Birmingham Public Libraries 1931–37, Leeds Public Libraries 1937–46; Borough Librarian and Curator, Dudley 1947–50; Deputy City Librarian, Liverpool 1950–52, City Librarian 1952–74; External Examiner, Sheffield Univ.; Pres. Soc. of Municipal and County Chief Librarians 1962–70; Chair. Exec. Cttee. of the Library Asscn. 1965–70; mem. Library Advisory Council for England and Wales 1965–72; Dir. Ladsirlac Tech. Information Centre; Pres. Int. Asscn. of Metropolitan City Libraries 1967–71; mem. Organizing Cttee., British Library 1971–73, British Library Bd. 1973–74; Dir.-Gen. Nat. Library of Australia 1974–80, Int. Research Fellow, Visiting Prof. and Consultant; Pres. Library Asscn. 1971. *Publications:* Dudley 1949, William Roscoe 1953, Liverpool 1957, Liverpool Shipping 1960, Liverpool under James I 1960, How to Find Out 1963, 1967, 1968, 1973, 1982, Liverpool under Charles I 1965, Libraries in the Modern World 1965, Four Centuries of Banking 1964, 1968, How to find out about Literature 1968, Libraries in the East 1971, International Librarianship 1972, Victorian and Edwardian Liverpool and the North West 1972, Libraries, Bibliography and Documentation in the Soviet Union 1972, Social History of Liverpool 1972, Merchant Venturers 1973, Victorian and Edwardian Manchester 1974, Liverpool and Literature 1974, Int. and Nat. Library and Information Services 1970–80, 1982. Ed. series: Library and Technical Information Division, Commonwealth and International Library (Gen. Ed.) 1962–, International Series on Library and Information Science 1963–, International Library Review 1969–, International Bibliographical and Library Surveys 1971–, Recent Advances in Library and Information Services 1980–; exhbn. of G. Chandler to mark Australian Bicentenary in U.K. 1988–. *Leisure interests:* travel, walking, dancing, foreign languages. *Address:* 43 Saxon Close, Stratford-on-Avon, England. *Telephone:* Stratford-on-Avon 294193.

CHANDLER, James Barton, M.A.; American international educational consultant; b. 27 May 1922, Conway Springs, Kan.; s. of James Perry Chandler and Bessie May (Stone) Chandler; m. Madeleine Racoux 1946; two s. one d.; ed. Univs. of Kansas and Michigan; Instructor, Mich. State Normal Coll. 1952–55; Language Educ. Adviser, Ethiopia 1955-57; Asst. Prof., Foreign Student Adviser, Eastern Michigan Univ. 1957–58; Teacher, Educ. Adviser, Laos 1958–60; Chief Educ. Adviser, Agency for Int. Devt. (AID), Laos 1960–63; Higher Educ. Adviser, AID, Tunisia 1963–65; Asst. Dir. Manpower, Industry and Public Admin., AID, Laos 1965–68; Deputy Mission Dir. 1968–73; Dir. Office of Educ., AID, Washington 1974–76; Assoc. Asst. Admin., Tech. Assistance 1976–77; retd. U.S. Dept. of State, AID 1977; Dir. Int. Bureau of Educ., UNESCO 1977–83; Bronze Star (World War II); Meritorious Honour Award, AID 1973, Presidential Certificate of Appreciation 1975, Distinguished Service Award 1977. *Leisure interests:* tennis, folk music, photography, hiking and camping. *Address:* 567 Hunt Place, Ypsilanti, Mich. 48198, U.S.A. (Home and Office). *Telephone:* (313) 481-1268.

CHANDLER, Otis; American newspaper executive; b. 23 Nov. 1927, Los Angeles; s. of Norman Chandler and Dorothy Buffum Chandler; m. 1st Marilyn Chandler 1951 (divorced 1981), m. 2nd Bettina Whitaker 1981; three s. two d.; ed. Andover Acad., Mass., and Stanford Univ.; Trainee, Times Mirror Co. 1953, Asst. to Pres. (assigned to Mirror-News) 1957, Marketing Man., Los Angeles Times 1958–60, Publr., Los Angeles Times 1960–80, Publr. and C.E.O. 1978–80; Vice-Pres. Times Mirror Co. 1961–, Dir. 1962, Sr. Vice-Pres. 1966–80; Vice-Chair. Bd. Times Mirror Co. 1968–80, Chair. and Ed.-in-Chief 1981–85, Chair. of Exec. Cttee. 1986–. *Leisure interests:* board surfing, hunting, fishing, photography, tennis, water skiing, track and field, sports cars. *Address:* Times Mirror Square, Los Angeles, Calif. 90053 (Office).

CHANDRA, Avinash; Indian artist; b. 28 Aug. 1931, Simla; s. of Kundan Lal and Ram Parai; m. Prem Lata; one c.; ed. Delhi Polytechnic, Delhi; on staff of Delhi Polytechnic, Delhi 1953–56; in London 1956, then New York 1966; executed glass mural for Pilkington Brothers' Head Office, St. Helens, Lancs and fibreglass mural for Indian Tea Centre, London 1964; Gold Medal, Prix Européen, Ostend 1962; John D. Rockefeller Third Fund Fellowship 1965. Works in following collections: Nat. Gallery of Modern Art, New Delhi, Tate Gallery, London, Victoria and Albert Museum, London, Arts Council of Great Britain, London, Ashmolean Museum, Oxford, Ulster Museum, Belfast, City Art Gallery, Birmingham, Gulbenkian Museum, Durham, Musée National d'Art Moderne, Paris, Whitworth Art Gallery, Manchester, Museum of Modern Art, Haifa, Punjab Museum, Chandigarh, etc.; one-man exhbns. in Srinagar, New Delhi, Belfast, London, Oxford, Paris, Bristol, Arnhem, Amsterdam, Zürich, Copenhagen, Stockholm, Chicago, Toronto, Geneva, etc. *Address:* 24 Willoughby Road, Hampstead, London, N.W.3, England.

CHANDRA, Ramesh, B.SC.; Indian newspaper executive; b. 15 Aug. 1925, Najibabad, Uttar Pradesh; s. of Raibahadur Sahu Jagmundar Das and Asharfi Devi; m. Chandrakanta Jain 1948; two s.; ed. Banaras Hindu Univ.; fmr. Sr. Vice-Chair. Municipal Bd. Najibabad; joined Times of India 1959; now Exec. Dir. Bennett, Coleman & Co. Ltd. (The Times of India Group of Publs.); Pres. Delhi Dahlia Soc.; fmr. Chair. Press Trust of India, Pres. Indian and Eastern Newspaper Soc.; mem. Cen. Advisory Bd. for Commercial Broadcasting; Trustee, Bharatiya Jnanpith; Hon. Sec.-Gen. All India Jain Parishad; Thomson Foundation Fellow, U.K. 1968. *Publications:* articles on newspaper management in various journals. *Leisure interests:* reading, gardening, cricket, music, theatre, social work, sports. *Address:* Times House, 7 Bahadurshah Zafar Marg, New Delhi 110002 (Office); 4 Tilak Marg, New Dehli 110001, India. *Telephone:* 3312277 (Office); 386560.

CHANDRA, Satish, M.A., B.SC.; Indian business executive and politician; b. 1917; ed. S.M. Coll., Chandausi, Govt. Agricultural Coll. Kanpur, and Bareilly Coll., Bareilly (Agra Univ.); Indian Nat. Congress 1936; mem. Indian Constituent Assembly 1948-50, Provisional Parl. 1950-52, Lok Sabha 1952-62; Parl. Sec. to Prime Minister 1951-52; Union Deputy Minister for Defence 1952-55, for Production 1955-57, for Commerce and Industry 1957-62; Chair. Indian Airlines Corpn. and Dir. Air-India 1963, 1964; Chair. British India Corpn. Ltd., The Elgin Mills Co. Ltd., Cawnpore Textiles Ltd., Cawnpore Sugar Works Ltd., Champarun Sugar Co. Ltd., Saran Eng. Co. Ltd. 1962-; Dir. other cos. *Address:* Chitrakut, Parbati Bagla Road, Kanpur, U.P., India.

CHANDRA SHEKHAR, N. L., M.A.; Indian politician; b. 1 July, 1927, Ibrahimpatti, Ballia Dist., Uttar Pradesh; m.; one s.; ed. Allahabad Univ.; Sec. Dist. Socialist Party, Ballia, Jt.-Sec. U.P. State Socialist Party, Gen.-Sec. 1955-56; mem. Rajya Sabha; joined Congress Party 1964, Gen.-Sec. Congress Parl. Party 1967; mem. Lok Sabha 1977-1984; Pres. Janata Party 1977-; mem. Working Cttee. during the emergency, imprisoned during the emergency; Ed. weekly newspaper Young Indian, Delhi. *Publications:* Meri Jail Diary, Dynamics of Social Change. *Address:* 7 Jantar Mantar Road, New Delhi 110001 (Office); 3 South Avenue Lane, New Delhi 110011, India (Home). *Telephone:* 383981 (Office); 376962 (Home).

CHANDRACHUD, Yeshwant Vishnu, B.A., LL.B.; Indian judge; b. 12 July 1920; s. of Vishnu Balkrishna and Indira Chandrachud; m. Prabha Chandrachud; one s. one d.; part-time Prof. of Law, Govt. Law Coll., Bombay 1949-52; practised at Bombay bar 1943-61; Govt. Pleader, Bombay High Court 1958-61, Judge 1961-72; Judge Supreme Court 1972-78, Chief Justice 1978-85; Pres. Int. Law Assen. (India Branch) 1978-, Indian Law Inst. 1978-. *Address:* 131 Budhwar Peth, Balkrishna Niwas, Poona 411002 India (Home). *Telephone:* 374053/372922 (Home).

CHANDRASEKHAR, Bhagwat Subrahmanya, B.SC.; Indian cricketer and bank executive; b. 17 May 1945, Mysore; m. Sandhya Rajarao 1975; one s.; ed. Nat. Educ. Soc., Bangalore; right-arm leg-spin, googly bowler; bowling arm withered by attack of polio at age of 6; debut in First Class Cricket 1963, Test Cricket 1964; had taken 242 Test wickets by early 1980; plays for Karnataka in Ranji Trophy competition (nat. championship of India); Arjuna Award; Padma Shri 1972; Hon. Life mem. MCC 1981-. *Leisure interests:* badminton, Indian classical music. *Address:* 571 31st Cross, 4th Block, Jayanagar, Bangalore 560011, India. *Telephone:* 41268.

CHANDRASEKHAR, Sivaramakrishna, PH.D., D.SC., SC.D., F.R.S.; Indian physicist; b. 6 Aug. 1930, Calcutta; s. of late S. and Sitalaxmi Sivaramakrishnan; m. Ila Pingle 1954; one s. one d.; ed. Univs. of Nagpur and Cambridge; Research Scholar, Raman Research Inst., Bangalore 1950-54; 1851 Exhbn. Scholar, The Cavendish Lab., Cambridge 1954-57; D.S.I.R. Fellow, Dept. of Crystallography, Univ. Coll., London 1957-59; Research Fellow, Royal Inst., London 1959-61; Prof. and Head, Dept. of Physics, Univ. of Mysore 1961-71; Prof. Raman Research Inst. 1971-; Nehru Visiting Prof. and Fellow of Pembroke Coll., Cambridge 1986-87; Fellow, Indian Nat. Science Acad. etc.; several Indian awards for outstanding contribs. to science. *Publications:* Liquid Crystals 1977; numerous scientific articles on crystal physics and liquid crystals. *Leisure interest:* painting. *Address:* Raman Research Institute, Bangalore 560080, India. *Telephone:* 345267 (Office); 342356 (Home).

CHANDRASEKHAR, Sripati, M.A., M.LITT., M.SC., PH.D.; Indian economist and demographer; b. 22 Nov. 1918, Rajahmundry; s. of Prof. Sripati Sarangapani and Rajamma Sarangapani; m. Dorothy Anne Downes 1947; three d.; ed. Presidency Coll., Madras, Univ. of Madras and Columbia, New York and Princeton Univ.; Visiting Lecturer, Univ. of Pa. and Asia Inst., New York 1944-46; Prof. of Econs., Annamalai Univ. 1947-50; Dir. Demographic Research, UNESCO, Paris 1947-49; Prof. of Econs. and Head of Dept., Baroda Univ. 1950-53; Nuffield Fellow, L.S.E. 1953-55; Dir. Indian Inst. for Population Studies 1956-67; mem. Rajya Sabha 1964-70; Minister of State for Health and Family Planning 1967-67; Minister of State in Ministry of Health, Family Planning and Urban Devt. 1967-70; Research Prof. of Demography, Univ. of Calif.; Visiting Fellow Battelle Research Centre ("Think Tank") Seattle 1971-72; Distinguished Visiting Prof. of Sociology, Calif. State Univ., San Diego 1972-74; Prof. of Demography and Public Health Univ. of Calif., Los Angeles, 1974-75; Regents Prof., Univ. of Calif., Santa Barbara 1975-; Vice-Chancellor Annamalai Univ., Chidambaram, South India 1975-78; Ed. Population Review;

Lucie Stern Trustee Prof. of Sociology, Mills Coll., Oakland, Calif. 1979-80; Visiting Prof. of Sociology, San Diego State Univ. 1981-; Visiting Prof., Univ. of Calif., Irvine 1982-; Distinguished Prof. of Demography, Univ. of Alaska, Fairbanks 1983-84, Visiting Prof. of Sociology, Univ. of Texas 1985-; Fellow, Indian Inst. of Advanced Study 1988-89; Dillingham Lecturer, East-West Centre, Honolulu 1977; Hon. D.Litt. (Redlands Univ., Kurukshetra Univ.); Hon. LL.D. (Punjabi Univ.); Hon. M.D. (Budapest); Hon. D.Sc. (Univ. of Pacific); numerous awards. *Publications:* India's Population 1946, Census and Statistics in India 1947, Indian Emigration 1948, Hungry People and Empty Lands 1952, Population and Planned Parenthood in India 1955, Infant Mortality in India 1959, China's Population 1959, Communist China Today 1961, Red China; An Asian View 1962, A Decade of Mao's China (ed.) 1963, American Aid and India's Economic Development 1965, Asia's Population Problems 1967, Problems of Economic Development 1967, India's Population: Fact, Problem and Policy 1968, Infant Mortality, Population Growth and Family Planning in India 1972, Abortion in a Crowded World: the Problem of Abortion with Special Reference to India 1974, Population and Law in India 1976, Ananda K. Coomaraswamy, A Critical Appreciation 1977, The Nagarathars of South India 1980, A Dirty Filthy Book 1981, From India to America 1983, From India to Canada 1986, From India to Mauritius 1987. *Leisure interests:* reading, European classical music. *Address:* 8976 Cliffridge Avenue, La Jolla, Calif. 92037, U.S.A. *Telephone:* (619) 455-6283.

CHANDRASEKHAR, Subrahmanyan, PH.D., SC.D., F.R.S.; American (b. Indian) university professor; b. 19 Oct. 1910, Lahore; m. Lalitha Doraiswamy 1936; ed. Presidency Coll., Madras, and Cambridge Univ.; Fellow of Trinity Coll., Cambridge 1933-37; Research Assoc. Univ. of Chicago 1937-38, Asst. Prof. 1938-41, Assoc. Prof. 1942-43, Prof. 1944-46; Distinguished Service Prof. of Theoretical Astrophysics 1947-52, Morton D. Hull Distinguished Service Prof. of Theoretical Astrophysics 1952-86, Prof. Emer. 1986-; Man. Ed. Astrophysical Journal 1952-71; mem. American Philosophical Society, American Academy of Arts and Sciences, N.A.S., Royal Soc. London; Bruce Gold Medal of Astronomical Soc. of the Pacific 1952; Gold Medal, Royal Astronomical Soc. 1953; Rumford Medal, American Acad. of Arts and Sciences 1957; Royal Medal, Royal Soc., London 1962; Nat. Medal of Science, U.S.A. 1967; Nehru Memorial Lecture 1968; Draper Medal, N.A.S. 1971; Heineman Prize, American Physical Soc. 1974; shared Nobel Prize for Physics 1983, R. D. Birla Award 1984, Copley Medal, Royal Soc. 1984. *Publications:* Introduction to the Study of Stellar Structure 1939, Principles of Stellar Dynamics 1942, Radiative Transfer 1950, Hydrodynamic and Hydromagnetic Stability 1961, Ellipsoidal Figures of Equilibrium 1969, The Mathematical Theory of Black Holes 1983, Eddington 1983. *Address:* Laboratory for Astrophysics and Space Research, 933 East 56th Street, Chicago, Ill. 60637, U.S.A. *Telephone:* (312) 702-7861.

CHANDRASEKHARAN, Komaravolu, M.A., PH.D.; Indian mathematician; b. 21 Nov. 1920, Masulipatam, India; m. A. Sarada 1944; two s.; ed. Presidency Coll., Madras, and Inst. for Advanced Study, Princeton; Prof. Eidgenössische Technische Hochschule (Swiss Fed. Inst. of Tech.), Zürich 1965-; Sec. Int. Mathematical Union 1961-66, Pres. 1971-74; Vice-Pres. Int. Council of Scientific Unions 1963-66, Sec.-Gen. 1966-70; mem. Scientific Advisory Cttee. to Cabinet, Govt. of India 1961-66; Fellow Nat. Inst. of Sciences of India, Indian Acad. of Sciences; Foreign mem. Finnish Acad. of Science and Letters 1975; lectured at more than 50 univs. in the U.S.A., U.S.S.R., Europe and Asia; Padma Shri 1959, Shanti Swarup Bhatnagar Memorial Award for Scientific Research 1963, Ramanujan Medal 1966. *Publications:* Fourier Transforms (with S. Bochner) 1949, Typical Means (with S. Minakshisundaram) 1952, Lectures on the Riemann Zeta-function 1953, Analytic Number Theory 1968, Arithmetical Functions 1970, Elliptic Functions 1985, Classical Fourier Transforms 1989; over 60 research papers. *Leisure interests:* painting, English literature, music. *Address:* Eidgenössische Technische Hochschule, 8092 Zürich, Rämistrasse 101 (Office); Hedwigstrasse 29, 8032 Zürich, Switzerland (Home). *Telephone:* 53-96-86.

CHANDY, Kanianthra Thomas, M.A., LL.M.; Indian business executive; b. 13 Jan. 1913; s. of K. I. Thomas and Mrs. A. Thomas; m. 1938; three s. two d.; ed. London Univ.; in legal practice; later joined Hindustan Lever Ltd., Dir. 1956-61; Dir. Indian Inst. of Man., Calcutta 1962-67; Chair. Food Corpn. of India 1966-68; Chair. Hindustan Steel Ltd. 1968-72; Chair. Kerala State Industrial Devt. Corpn. 1972-78, Nat. Productivity Council of India 1972-78, Asian Productivity Org. 1976-78, Carbon and Chemicals Ltd.; Vice-Chair. Kerala State Planning Bd. 1972-79; Dir. numerous govt. and joint sector cos.; fmr. Dir. Int. Iron and Steel Inst. Brussels; fmr. Chair. Indian Inst. of Tech.; fmr. mem. Univ. Grants Comm. *Address:* Kanianthra, Avittom Road, Medical College P.O., Trivandrum 695011, Kerala, India (Home). *Telephone:* 73855 (Home).

CHANEY, Frederick Michael, LL.B.; Australian lawyer and politician; b. 28 Oct. 1941, Perth; s. of Frederick Charles Chaney and Mavis Mary Bond; m. Angela Margaret Clifton 1964; three s.; ed. Univ. of Western Australia; solicitor, Perth 1964-74; Crown Prosecutor, Papua and New Guinea 1964-65; Senator from Western Australia 1974-; Senate Opposition Whip 1975, Govt. Whip 1976-78; Minister for Admin. Services 1978, Assisting the Minister for Educ. 1978-79, for Aboriginal Affairs 1978-80, Assisting the Minister for Nat. Devt. and Energy 1980, for Social Security 1980-83;

Leader of Opposition in Senate 1983–; Shadow Minister for Industrial Relations 1987–. *Leisure interest:* reading. *Address:* Parliament House, Canberra, A.C.T.; 5 Melville Street, Claremont, W.A. 6010, Australia. *Telephone:* 3254882 (Office).

CHANG BO; Chinese government official; Acting Dir. Mass Culture Bureau, Ministry of Culture 1986–. *Address:* Ministry of Culture, Beijing People's Republic of China.

CHANG CHI-CHENG, PH.D.; Chinese politician and banker; b. 7 Dec. 1918, Hwayang County, Szechwan; m.; two s.; ed. Nat. Tung-chi Univ. and Cornell Univ.; Chief, Gen. Affairs Div. Council for US Aid 1958–60, Chief 2nd Div. 1960–63; Sec.-Gen. Council for Int. Econ. Cooperation and Devt. 1963–65, 1969; Vice-Minister of Econ. Affairs 1965–69; Minister of Communications 1969–72; Vice-Chair. and Sec.-Gen. Council for Int. Econ. Cooperation and Devt. 1972–73; Chair. Econ. Planning Council 1973–76; Sec.-Gen. Exec. Yuan 1976–78; Minister of Finance 1978–81; Nat. Policy Adviser to Pres. and Chair. of Bd. Cen. Trust of China 1981–84; Gov. Cen. Bank of China 1984–. *Address:* Central Bank of China, 2 Roosevelt Road, Sec. 1, Taipei, Taiwan.

CHANG CHONGXUAN; Chinese government official; Vice-Minister for Family Planning 1985–. *Address:* State Family Planning Commission, Beijing, People's Republic of China.

CHANG DO YUNG, General; Korean army officer; b. 1923; ed. Tongyang Univ., Japan; fought in Japanese army in Second World War; further educ. in U.S.A. 1953; Deputy C.-in-C. of Gen. Staff, S. Korean Army 1956, later Commdr. Second Army; C.-in-C. of General Staff; Minister of Defence May-June 1961, Chair. Supreme Council of Nat. Reconstruction and Prime Minister May-June 1961; under house arrest July 1961; sentenced to death Jan. 1962, sentence commuted, later released 1962. *Address:* Seoul, Republic of Korea.

CHANG FENG-HSU, M.A.; Chinese politician; b. 5 Aug. 1928, Pingtung County; m.; one s.; ed. Nat. Taiwan Univ. and Univ. of New Mexico; specialist, Ministry of Foreign Affairs 1956–59; mem. Taiwan Provincial Ass. 1960–64; Magistrate, Pingtung County 1964–72; Mayor of Taipei 1972–76; Minister of Interior 1976–78; Minister of State 1978–; Pres. Chinese Taipei Olympic Cttee., Soc. for Taiwan Amateur Sports Fed., Soc. for Wildlife and Nature, Taiwan; Hon. D.Pol.Sc. (Kyung Hee Univ.) 1973. *Address:* The Executive Yuan, Taipei, Taiwan.

CHANG HONGSHENG; Chinese diplomatist; Amb. to Greece 1972–. *Address:* The Embassy of the People's Republic of China, Odos Krinon 2A, Palaio Psychico, Athens, Greece.

CHANG KING-YUH, LL.M., PH.D.; Chinese government official; b. 27 April 1937, Hsiangtan County, Hunan; m. Grace Yu 1964; two s.; ed. Nat. Taiwan Univ., Nat. Chengchi Univ. and Columbia Univ.; lecturer, Hofstra Univ., U.S.A. 1968–69; Asst. Prof. Western Ill. Univ. 1972; Assoc. Prof. Nat. Chengchi Univ. 1972–75, Chair. Dept. of Diplomacy 1974–77, Dir. Grad. School of Int. Law and Diplomacy 1975–77, Prof. 1975–, Deputy Dir. Inst. of Int. Relations 1977–81, Dir. 1981–84; Visiting Fellow, Johns Hopkins Univ. 1976–77; Distinguished Visiting Scholar, Inst. of E. Asian Studies, Univ. of Calif., Berkeley 1983; Dir.-Gen. Govt. Information Office 1984–87; Dir. Inst. of Int. Relations 1987–. *Leisure interests:* reading, mountain climbing and sports. *Address:* Office of the Director, Institute of International Relations, 64 Wan Shou Road, Mucha Taipei, Taiwan. *Telephone:* (02) 9394914.

CHANG, Kwang-chih, PH.D.; American professor of anthropology; b. 15 April 1931, Peiping (now Beijing), China; s. of Chang Wo-chün and Lo Hsin-hsiang; m. Hwei Li 1957; one s. one d.; ed. Nat. Taiwan Univ., Harvard Univ.; Lecturer on Anthropology, Harvard Univ. 1960–61, Prof. 1977–, Chair. Dept. of Anthropology 1981–84, now John E. Hudson Prof. of Archaeology, Curator of E. Asian Archaeology, Peabody Museum of Archaeology and Ethnology and Chair., Council on East Asian Studies; Instructor in Anthropology, Yale Univ. 1961–63, Asst. Prof. 1963–66, Prof. 1969–77, Chair. Dept. of Anthropology 1970–73; Hon. M.A.; mem. Acad. Sinica (Taipei) 1974–, N.A.S. (Washington, D.C.) 1979–. *Publications:* The Archaeology of Ancient China 1963, Rethinking Archaeology 1967, Prehistory of Taiwan 1969, Early Chinese Civilization 1972, Shang Civilization 1980, Art, Myth and Ritual: The Path to Political Authority in Ancient China 1983. *Address:* Department of Anthropology, Peabody Museum, Harvard University, Cambridge, Mass. 02138, U.S.A. *Telephone:* (617) 495-4389.

CHANG LIFU; Chinese party and government official; b. Shaanxi Prov.; Dir. Staff Office N.W. Mil. Admin. Council 1951, mem. Land Reform Cttee. 1951–54; Sec. Gen. Political and Legal Cttee. 1952; Sec. Gen. N.W. Admin. Cttee. 1953–54; Deputy Sec. Gen. and Dir. Office of Sec., State Council 1954–59; Chair. Shaanxi Prov. Br. Chinese People's Cttee. for World Peace 1960; Vice-Chair. Shaanxi Prov. CPPCC Cttee. 1960; Dir. United Front Work Dept. N.W. Bureau CCP Cen. Cttee. 1963–; Sec. Gen. Chinese People's Congress Shaanxi Prov. Cttee. 1979–; Vice-Chair. Shaanxi Prov. People's Congress 1979–; mem. Cen. Advisory Cttee. of CCP Cen. Cttee. 1982–. *Address:* Central Advisory Committee of the Central Committee of the Chinese Communist Party, Zhongnanhai, Beijing, People's Republic of China.

CHANG RENXIA, M.A.; Chinese artist, poet and art historian; b. 31 Jan. 1904, Anhui, N. China; m. 1st Lee Lan 1923 (deceased), one d.; m. 2nd Maeno Motoko 1936 (dissolved), one s.; m. 3rd Guo Sofen 1962, one s. one d.; ed. Nat. Cen. Univ., Nanjing, Imperial Univ., Tokyo; has lectured at Int. Univ. of Santiniketan, India, at Cen. Univ., Chongqing, and at Coll. of Oriental Studies, Kunming; Prof. of History of Art, Central Acad. of Fine Arts. *Publications:* Forget-Me-Not 1932, Harvest 1940, Mongolian Love Songs 1944, The Relationship in Art Between China and India 1955, The Classical Art of China 1956, A Study of Han Dynasty Paintings 1955, The Art of the Ajanta Caves 1956, Oriental Art 1956, An Art History of India and South East Asia 1964, The Relationship in Art Between China and Japan 1964, A Study of Silk Road 1979, The Silk Road and the Cultural Arts of Central Asia 1981, The History of Chinese Dance 1983, Talks on Chinese Arts 1983, Talks on Oriental Arts 1984, Aesthetics and History of the Chinese Arts 1984, On Archaeology of Ancient Arts 1984, The Silk Road by Sea and the Cultural Exchange 1985. *Leisure interests:* collecting old paintings, coins, and other treasures. *Address:* Central Academy of Fine Arts, Peking (Office); Dong Dan, Xi-Zong-Bu Hu Dong No. 51, Beijing, People's Republic of China. *Telephone:* 500.8343.

CHANG SHANA; Chinese artist; b. 1930, Lyon, France; d. of Chang Shuhong; ed. Boston Art Gallery and New York; returned to China 1950; Asst. to architect Liang Sicheng, Qinghua Univ. 1951–56; lecturer, Cen. Arts and Crafts Inst. 1956–66; del. 12th Conf. CCP 1982; Dir. Cen Arts and Crafts Inst. 1984–. *Address:* Central Arts and Crafts Institute, Beijing, People's Republic of China.

CHANG SHUHONG; Chinese artist; b. 1905; ed. Lyons and Paris; worked in Dunhuang, Gansu 1933–; Deputy, 3rd NPC 1964–66; Dir. Dunhuang Relics Research Inst. 1977–84; Deputy, 5th NPC 1978–83; Chair. Gansu Fed. of Literary and Arts Circles 1981; Hon. Dir. Dunhuang Relics Research Inst. 1984–. *Address:* Dunhuang Relics Research Institute, Gansu, People's Republic of China.

CHANGEUX, Jean-Pierre, DR. ÉS SC.; French research professor; b. 6 April 1936, Domont; s. of Marcel Changeux and Jeanne Benoit; m. Annie Dupont 1962; one s.; ed. Lycées Montaigne, Louis le Grand and St. Louis, Paris, and Ecole Normale Supérieure, Ulm; research asst. 1958–60; asst. lecturer, Science Faculty, Univ. of Paris 1960–66; post-doctoral Fellow, Univ. of Calif. 1966, Columbia Univ., New York 1967; Vice-Dir. Coll. de France (Chair. of Molecular Biology) 1967; Prof. Institut Pasteur 1974–; Prof. Coll. de France 1975–; corresp. mem. Turin Acad. of Medicine, Académie des Sciences, Akademia Leopoldina, Halle, N.A.S.; Chevalier, Légion d'honneur, Officier, Ordre nat. du mérite, Officier, Ordre des arts et des lettres, Alexandre Joannidès prize (Académie des Sciences), Gairdner Foundation Award 1978, Lounsbery Prize (N.A.S., U.S.A.) 1982, Co-recipient; Wolf Foundation Prize 1982, Céline Prize 1985, F.O. Schmitt Prize (Neurosciences Research Inst., New York) 1985. *Publications:* L'homme neuronal 1983, author and co-author of several research papers on allosteric proteins, on the acetylcholine receptor and on the devt. of the nervous system. *Leisure interests:* baroque paintings, organ music. *Address:* Laboratoire de Neurobiologie Moléculaire, Institut Pasteur, 25 rue du Docteur Roux, 75724 Paris Cedex 15 (Office); 47 rue du Four, 75006 Paris, France (Home). *Telephone:* 45-68-88-05 (Office); 45-48-44-64 (Home).

CHANG-HIM, Most Rev. French Kitchener, L.TH.; Seychelles ecclesiastic; b. 10 May 1938, Seychelles; s. of Francis Chang-Him and Amelia Zoé; m. Susan Talma 1975; twin d.; ed. Seychelles Coll., Lichfield Theological Coll., St. Augustine's Coll. Canterbury and Univ. of Trinity Coll. Toronto; primary school teacher 1958; man. of schools 1973–77; Chair. Teacher Training Coll. Bd. of Govs. 1976–77; Vicar-Gen. Diocese of Seychelles 1973–79; Archdeacon of Seychelles 1973–79; Bishop of Seychelles 1979–; Dean, Prov. of Indian Ocean 1983–84, Archbishop 1984–. *Publication:* The Seychellois: In Search of an Identity 1975. *Leisure interests:* reading, international affairs, cooking, gardening, fishing. *Address:* Bishop's House, P.O. Box 44, Victoria, Seychelles. *Telephone:* 24242.

CHANNING, Carol; American actress; b. 31 Jan. 1921; m. 3rd Charles Lowe 1956; one s.; Critics' Circle Award for Lend an Ear; Tony Award for Hello Dolly 1963, Golden Globe Award for Best Supporting Actress, Thoroughly Modern Millie 1967, Tony Award 1968. *Plays include:* No for an Answer, Let's Face It, So Proudly We Hail, Lend an Ear, Gentlemen Prefer Blondes, Wonderful Town, The Vamp, Hello Dolly, Lorelei. *Films include:* The First Traveling Saleslady 1956, Thoroughly Modern Millie 1967. *Address:* c/o William Morris Agency, 151 El Camino Boulevard, Beverly Hills, Calif. 90212, U.S.A.

CHANNON, Rt. Hon. (Henry) Paul Guinness, P.C., M.A.; British politician; b. 9 Oct. 1935; s. of late Sir Henry Channon and Lady Honor (née Guinness) Svejdar; m. Ingrid Olivia Georgia Wyndham 1963; one s. two d. (one d. deceased); ed. Eton Coll., Oxford Univ.; 2nd Lieut. Royal Horse Guards; M.P. for Southend West 1959–; Parl. Pvt. Sec. to Minister of Power 1960, to the Home Sec. and later to the Foreign Sec. 1961–64; Opposition Spokesman on the Arts 1967–70; Parl. Sec., Ministry of Housing 1970–72; Minister of State, Northern Ireland Office April-Nov. 1972; Minister for Housing and Construction 1972–74; Opposition Spokesman on Prices and Consumer Affairs June-Oct. 1974, on the Environment 1974–75; Minister of State, Civil Service Dept. 1979–81; Minister of State, Dept. of Education and Science (responsible for the Arts) 1981–83; Minister of State for Trade, Dept. of Trade and Industry 1983–86; Sec. of State for Trade and Industry 1986–87, for Transport June 1987–; Sponsor, Royal Comm. on Historical Monuments 1983–; Conservative. *Address:* 96 Cheyne Walk, London, S.W.10; Kelvedon Hall, Brentwood, Essex, England. *Telephone:* 01-351 0293; (0277) 362180.

CHAO MEI; Chinese woodcut artist; b. 2 April 1931, Heze Co., Shandong; s. of Chao Zhong Li and Zhuang Shu Zhi; m. Chen Yu Liang 1958; two s. one d.; Pres. Heilongjiang Artists' Asscn., Heilongjiang Woodcutters' Asscn.; Dir. Chinese Artists' Asscn. 1988–. *Address:* 133 Di Dun Street, Harbin, People's Republic of China. *Telephone:* 42446.

CHAO YAO-TUNG, M.SC.; Chinese politician; b. 29 Sept. 1915, Shanghai; m.; two s. one d.; ed. Nat. Wuhan Univ. and Mass. Inst. of Technology; Factory Man. Tientsin Machine Works 1946–48; Chief Eng. Jong-Been Textile Co. 1949–52, Acting Gen. Man. 1953–58; Project Man. Vietnam Textile Co. 1959–63, Sicovina Danang, Vietnam 1962–63, Singapore Textile Industries Ltd. 1964–66; Deputy Chair. Leader Textile and Fibre Industry 1967–68; Dir. Steel Mill Project, Ministry of Econ. Affairs 1968–70; Gen. Man. China Steel Corpn. 1971–78, Chair. Bd. of Dirs. 1978–81; Minister of Econ. Affairs 1981–84; Minister of State and Chair. Council for Econ. Planning and Devt., Exec. Yuan 1984–88. *Address:* c/o Council for Economic Planning and Development, Executive Yuan, Taipei, Taiwan.

CHAPEL, Alain Germain Gustave; French chef; b. 30 Dec. 1937, Lyon; s. of Roger Chapel and Eva (née Badin) Chapel; two s.; ed. Ecole de la Salle and Inst. des Lazaristes, Lyon; Chef and Restaurateur, Maison la Mère Charles, Mionnay 1969–; mem. Asscns. Tradition et Qualité, Grande Cuisine Française, Maîtres-Cuisiniers de France, Acad. Culinaire; Officier, Ordre Nat. du Mérite, Mérite Agricole, des Arts et Lettres; Meilleur Ouvrier de France 1972. *Leisure interests:* swimming, football, walking. *Address:* 01390 Mionnay, France.

CHAPELAIN-MIDY, Roger; French painter; b. 24 Aug. 1904, Paris; s. of Maurice and Hélène Chapelain-Midy; m. Ginette Chauvet 1935; two s.; ed. Lycée Louis le Grand, Paris; pictures hung in Musée d'Art Moderne and Musée des Beaux Arts, Paris, in museums in Boulogne, La Rochelle, Lyon, Saint-Etienne, Cambrai, Bordeaux, Dijon, Algiers, Tunis, etc.; also in Venice, Amsterdam, Brussels, Buenos Aires, Cairo, São Paulo and London; awards include Carnegie Prize 1938; Prix de l'Ile de France 1952; Prix de la Biennale de Menton 1953; Grand Prix de la Ville de Paris 1955; Prix du Costume de Théâtre at Int. Biennale São Paulo 1961; Officier, Légion d'honneur; Commdr. des Arts et des Lettres; mem. Acad. Royale de Belgique. *Works include (in addition to pictures):* murals in the theatre of the Palais de Chaillot, the Inst. Nat. Agronomique, and on the steamships Provence, Bretagne, Jean Laborde, France; theatrical costumes and decors, in particular for Les Indes Galantes 1952, Die Zauberflöte (Mozart) for the Théâtre National de l'Opéra 1954, and La Répétition (ballet) for Cologne Opera 1963, Les Femmes Savantes for the Comédie Française 1972, Comme le Sable entre les Doigts 1985. *Leisure interests:* everything related to gardens, plants, and nature in general. *Address:* 68 rue Lhomond, 75005 Paris, France. *Telephone:* 47-07-27-90.

CHAPIN, Schuyler Garrison; American musical impresario; b. 13 Feb. 1923, New York; s. of L. H. Paul Chapin and Leila H. Burden; m. Elizabeth Steinway 1947; four s.; ed. Longy School of Music; Spot Sales, NBC Television, New York 1947–53; Gen. Man. Tex and Jinx McCrary Enterprises, New York 1953; Booking Dir. Judson O'Neill and Judd Div., Columbia Artists Man. 1953–59; CBS Dir. Masterworks, Columbia Records Div. 1959–62, Vice-Pres. Creative Services 1962–63; Vice-Pres. Programming, Lincoln Center for the Performing Arts Inc. 1964–69; Exec. Producer, Amberson Productions 1969–72; Gen. Man. Metropolitan Opera Asscn. Inc. 1972–75; Dean of Faculty of Arts, Columbia Univ., New York 1976–87; Special Consultant, Carnegie Hall Corpn. 1979; Trustee, Naumburg Foundation 1962–; Bagby Music Lovers Foundation 1959–, mem. Bd. of Dirs., Amberson Enterprises Inc. 1972–; mem. The Century Asscn.; Trustee, Richard Tucker Music Foundation, Brooklyn Philharmonic, American Composers Orchestra; Franklin D. Roosevelt Four Freedoms Foundation 1983–, Vice-Pres. 1986; Chair. American Symphony Orchestra League 1982; Trustee, Curtis Inst. of Music 1986–; Hon. L.H.D. (New York Univ. and Hobart-William Smith Colls.); Hon. Litt.D. (Emerson Coll.) 1976; Air Medal 1945; N.Y. State Conspicuous Service Cross 1951; Christopher Award 1972, Emmy Awards 1972, 1976, 1980. *Publications:* Musical Chairs, A Life in the Arts 1977. *Leisure interests:* reading, tennis, bridge, swimming, gentle sailing. *Address:* 901 Lexington Avenue, New York, N.Y. 10021, U.S.A. *Telephone:* (212) 737-1761.

CHAPLIN, Arthur Hugh, C.B., B.A., F.L.A.; British librarian; b. 17 April 1905, Bexhill; s. of Rev. H. F. Chaplin and Florence B. Lusher; m. Irene Marcousé 1938; ed. Univ. Coll., London; Asst. Librarian, Reading Univ. 1927–28, Queen's Univ. Belfast 1928–29; Asst. Keeper, Dept. of Printed Books, British Museum 1930–55, Deputy Keeper 1955–59, Keeper 1959–66, Prin. Keeper 1966–70; Exec. Sec. I.F.L.A. Working Group on Cataloguing Principles 1954–59, Exec. Sec. Organizing Cttee. Int. Conf. on Cataloguing Principles (1961) 1959–66; mem. Council, Library Asscn. 1964–70; Chair. I.F.L.A. Cttee. on Cataloguing 1966–74; mem. Senate, London Univ. 1973–;

Pres. Microfilm Asscn. of Great Britain 1967–71. *Publication:* G.K.: 150 Years of the General Catalogue of Printed Books in the British Museum 1987. *Address:* 44 Russell Square, London, W.C.1, England. *Telephone:* 01-636 7217.

CHAPLIN, Boris Nikolaevich, CAND. TECH. SC.; Soviet diplomatist; b. 1931, Moscow; ed. Moscow Mining Inst.; mem. CPSU 1961–; miner 1955–57; party posts 1961–74; Asst. Prof. of Mining 1964–68; First Sec. of Cheremyshki Regional Cttee. of CPSU, Moscow Dist. 1968–74; Amb. to Vietnam 1974–86; U.S.S.R. Deputy Minister for Foreign Affairs 1986–; Cand. mem. of CPSU 1976–. *Address:* Ministry of Foreign Affairs, Moscow, U.S.S.R.

CHAPMAN, Dennis, PH.D., F.R.S.C., F.R.S.; British professor of biophysical chemistry; b. 6 May 1927, Co. Durham; s. of George Henry Chapman and Katherine Magnus; m. Elsie Margaret 1949; two s. one d.; ed. London, Liverpool and Cambridge Univs.; Comyns Berkeley Fellow, Gonville and Caius Coll., Cambridge Univ. 1960–63; Head of Gen. Research Div., Unilever Ltd., Welwyn 1963–69; Prof. Assoc., Biophysical Chem., Sheffield Univ. 1968–76; Sr. Wellcome Trust Research Fellow, Dept. of Chem., Chelsea Coll., Univ. of London 1976–77; Prof. of Biophysical Chem., Head Div. of Basic Medical Science Dept. of Protein and Molecular Biology, Royal Free Hosp. School of Medicine, Univ. of London 1977–; Hon. D.Sc. (Utrecht) 1978, (Memorial) 1980; Hon. M.R.C.P. *Publications:* Biomembranes (Vol. I–V) 1968–84; 400 scientific publs. in various int. journals. *Leisure interests:* reading, tennis and golf. *Address:* Department of Protein and Molecular Biology, Royal Free Hospital School of Medicine, Rowland Hill Street, London, NW3 2PF, England. *Telephone:* 01-794 0500 (Ext. 3246).

CHAPMAN, (F.) Ian; British publisher; b. 26 Oct. 1925, St. Fergus, Scotland; s. of late Rev. Peter Chapman and Frances Burdett; m. Marjory Stewart Swinton 1953; one s. one d.; ed. Shawlands Acad., Ommer School of Music, Glasgow, Scottish Royal Acad. of Music; served R.A.F. 1943–44; Miner (nat. service) 1945–47; with William Collins Ltd. (now William Collins PLC) 1947–, Sales Rep. 1950–51, Sales Man. 1955–60, Sales Dir. 1960–68, Jt. Man. Dir. 1967–76, Deputy Chair. 1976–81, Chair. 1981–87; Dir. William Collins overseas cos. 1968–89: Canada 1968–89, U.S.A. 1974–89, S. Africa 1978–89, N.Z. 1978–89, William Collins Int. Ltd. 1975–89; Chair. Radio Clyde 1972–, Harvill Press 1976–, Hatchards Ltd. 1976–, Granada Publishing Ltd. 1983–; Dir. Pan Books Ltd. 1962–, Publishing Dir. Dec. 1987–, Book Tokens Ltd. 1981–, Ind. Radio News 1983–; Trustee Book Trade Benevolent Soc. 1981–; mem. Gov. Council SCOTBIC; mem. Council Publishers Asscn. 1962–77, Vice-Pres. 1978, Pres. 1979–81. *Leisure interests:* music, golf, reading, skiing. *Address:* Kenmore, 46 The Avenue, Cheam, Surrey, England (Home). *Telephone:* 01-642 1820 (Home).

CHAPMAN, Orville Lamar, PH.D.; American professor of chemistry; b. 26 June 1932, New London, Conn.; m. Susan Parker Chapman 1981; two s.; ed. Virginia Polytechnic Inst. and Cornell Univ.; Prof. of Chem., Iowa State Univ. 1957–74, Univ. of Calif., Los Angeles 1974–; Arthur C. Cope Award (American Chem. Soc.), Texas Instrument Foundation Founders Prize, American Chem. Soc. Award in Pure Chem. *Publications:* over 130 research articles. *Address:* Department of Chemistry and Biochemistry, University of California, 405 Hilgard Avenue, Los Angeles, Calif. 90024, U.S.A. *Telephone:* (213) 825-4883.

CHAPMAN NYAHO, Daniel Ahmling, C.B.E., M.A.; Ghanaian teacher, public servant and business executive; b. 5 July 1909, Keta; s. of William and Jane (née Atriki) Chapman; m. Jane Abam Quashie 1941; two s. five d. (one deceased); ed. Bremen Mission School (Keta), Achimota Coll., Univ. of Oxford, Columbia Univ. and New York Univ.; Teacher Govt. Sr. Boys' School, Accra 1930, Achimota Coll. 1930–33, 1937–46; Gen. Sec. All-Ewe Conf. 1944–46; Area Specialist, UN Secr. Dept. of Trusteeship and Information from Non-Self-Governing Territories 1946–54; mem. Bd. of Man. of UN Int. School, New York 1950–54, 1958–59; Sec. to Prime Minister and Cabinet, Gold Coast 1954–57; Head of Ghana Civil Service 1957; Amb. to U.S.A. and Perm. Rep. to UN 1957–59; Chair. Mission of Ind. African States to Cuba, Dominican Repub., Haiti, Venezuela, Bolivia, Paraguay, Uruguay, Brazil, Argentina, Chile 1958; First Vice-Chair. Governing Council UN Special Fund 1959; Headmaster Achimota School 1959–63; Vice-Chair. Comm. on Higher Educ. in Ghana 1960–61, mem. Interim Nat. Council of Higher Educ. and Research, Ghana 1961–62; Fellow, Ghana Acad. of Arts and Sciences; mem. UN Middle East/North Africa Tech. Assistance Mission on Narcotics Control 1963; Dir. UN Div. of Narcotic Drugs 1963–66; mem. Political Cttee. of Nat. Liberation Council 1967; mem. Bd. of Trustees, Gen. Kotoka Trust Fund; Amb. Ministry of External Affairs 1967; Exec. Dir. Pioneer Tobacco Co. Ltd. (British-American Tobacco Group) 1967–70, Dir. 1970–; Dir. Standard Bank Ghana Ltd. 1970–75; Chair. Arts Council of Ghana 1968–69; Danforth Visiting Lecturer for Asscn. of American Colleges 1969, 1970; Chair. Council of Univ. of Science and Tech., Kumasi 1972–73; mem. Nat. Advisory Cttee. 1973; Dir. Ghana Film Industry Corpn. 1979–81, Ghana Nat. Honours and Awards Cttee. 1979–81; Deputy Chair. Ghana Constituent Assembly 1978–79. *Publications:* Our Homeland (Book I–A Regional Geography of South-East Gold Coast) 1945, The Human Geography of Eweland 1945. *Leisure interests:* music, walking, gardening, reading. *Address:* Tobacco House,

Liberty Avenue, P.O.B. 5211, Accra (Office); 7 Ninth Avenue, Tesano, Accra, Ghana (Home). *Telephone:* 21111 (Office); 27180 (Home).

CHAPPELL, Gregory (Greg) Stephen, M.B.E.; Australian cricketer and investment fund management executive; b. 7 Aug. 1948, Adelaide; s. of Arthur Martin and Jeanne Ellen (Richardson) Chappell; m. Judith Elizabeth Donaldson 1971; two s. one d.; ed. St. Leonards Primary School and Plympton High School, Adelaide, and Prince Alfred Coll., Adelaide; grandson of V. Y. Richardson (Australian Cricket Captain 1935-36); brother of I. M. Chappell (Australian Cricket Captain 1971-75); represented S. Australia 1966-73, Somerset (England) 1968-69, Queensland 1973-77; Captain of Queensland 1973-77, 1979-, of Australia 1975-77, 1979-81, 1981-83; retd. from cricket Jan. 1984; captained Australia in 47 test matches; signed contract for World Series Cricket and became their Australian Vice-Captain 1977; made century in test debut v. England, Perth 1970; only captain to have scored a century in each innings of 1st test as captain (v. West Indies, Brisbane 1975); holds record for most catches in a test match (7, v. England, Perth 1975), for most runs (aggregate) in a test match (247 not out and 133 v. New Zealand, Wellington 1974), for most test catches (122), for most test runs by an Australian, for the most test centuries (24); had test average of 73.6 in Australia v. India series 1980-81; Australian Sportsman of the Year 1976; Hon. Life mem. MCC 1985. *Leisure interests:* golf, tennis, reading, listening to music. *Address:* 40 Creek Street, Brisbane (Office); Watson Street, Wilston 4051, Australia (Home). *Telephone:* 229 1738 (Office).

CHAPPLE, Gen. Sir John (Lyon), G.C.B., C.B.E., ADC GENERAL, M.A., F.Z.S., F.L.S., F.R.G.S.; British army officer; b. 27 May 1931; s. of C. H. Chapple; m. Annabel Hill 1959; one s. three d.; ed. Haileybury and Trinity Coll., Cambridge; joined 2nd King Edward's Own Gurkhas 1954, served Malaya, Hong Kong, Borneo; Staff Coll. 1962, completed course at Jt. Services Staff Coll. 1969; Commdr. 1st Bn. 2nd Gurkhas 1970-72; Directing Staff, Staff Coll. 1972-73; Commdr. 48 Gurkha Infantry Brigade 1976; Gurkha Field Force 1977; Prin. Staff Officer to Chief of Defence Staff 1978-79; Commdr. British Forces, Hong Kong and Maj.-Gen. Brigade of Gurkhas 1980-82; Dir. of Mil. Operations 1982-84; Deputy Chief of Defence Staff (Programmes and Personnel) 1985-87; Col. 2nd Gurkhas 1986-; C.-in-C. U.K. Land Forces 1987-; Services Fellow Fitzwilliam Coll., Cambridge 1973; mem. Council Nat. Army Museum; Soc. for Army Historical Research; Trustee World Wildlife Fund (U.K.), King Mahendra Trust for Conservation, Nepal. *Address:* c/o Ministry of Defence, Whitehall, London, S.W.1, England.

CHARALAMBOPOULOS, Yannis; Greek politician; b. 1919, Psari, Messinia Pref.; ed. Mil. Acad., Woolwich Inst., London; co. commdr. fighting invading Italians in Albania 1939; served in Greek units attached to allied armies in Middle East during World War II; teacher at Mil. Acad. 1953; Tech. Adviser, Ministry of Finance 1954-58; resigned from army 1961 and joined Centre Union Party; Deputy to Parl. 1963, 1964-67; political prisoner 1967-72; leader, illegal Panhellenic Liberation Movt. 1972; arrested and imprisoned 1973-74; founding mem. Pasok, mem. of Cen. Cttee. and Exec. Office 1977; Pasok Parl. Rep. to European Parl. 1981; Minister of Foreign Affairs 1981-85, Deputy Prime Minister 1985-88, Minister of Defence April 1986-. *Address:* c/o Office of the Prime Minister, c/o Odos Zalokosta 3, Athens, Greece.

CHARBONNEAU, Hubert, M.A., PH.D., F.R.S.C.; Canadian demographer; b. 2 Sept. 1936, Montreal; s. of Léonel Charbonneau and Jeanne Durand; m. Marie-Christiane Hellot 1961; one d.; ed. Univs. of Montreal and Paris; Sr. Lecturer, Univ. of Montreal 1962-68, Asst. Prof. 1968-70, Assoc. Prof. 1970-76, Prof. 1976-; Visiting Prof. Univ. do Parana, Brazil 1978, 1980, 1983; Killam Sr. Research Scholarship 1974, 1975, 1976. *Publications:* author and co-author of several books on demographic topics. *Leisure interest:* genealogy. *Address:* Departement de démographie, Université de Montréal, C.P. 6128, succ. "A", Montreal, P.Q., H3C 3J7 (Office); 19 avenue Robert, Outremont, P.Q., H3S 2P1, Canada (Home). *Telephone:* (514) 343-7229 (Office); (514) 731-5503 (Home).

CHARBONNEL, Jean; French politician; b. 22 April 1927; m. Marielle Bal 1965; two s. two d.; ed. Lycées Henri IV and Louis-le-Grand, Paris, Univ. de Paris à la Sorbonne, Ecole Normale Supérieure and Ecole Nat. d'Administration; Research worker C.N.R.S.; with Cour des Comptes 1956; Prof. Inst. for Political Sciences, Sorbonne 1957-; Tech. Counsellor Ministry of Public Health and later Ministry of Justice 1959-62; Appeal Court Counsellor, Cour des Comptes 1962; mem. Chamber of Deputies 1962-73; Gen. Counsellor Brive-Nord area 1964-88; Mayor of Brive 1966-; Sec. of State for Foreign Affairs (Co-operation) 1966-67; mem. nat. secretariat Union des Démocrates pour la République 1967-68, Asst. Sec.-Gen. 1968-71; Pres. Comm. des Finances, Assemblée nationale 1971-72; Minister of Industrial and Scientific Devt. 1972-73; with Cour des Comptes 1974; Pres. Fédération des républicains de progrès 1976; Délégué Gén. du R.P.R. (1980-81); Député from Carrèze 1986-. *Publications:* L'aventure de la fidélité 1976, Comment peut-on être opposant? 1983, Le gaullisme aujourd'hui 1985, Politiques et Chrétiens, Edmond Michelet 1987. *Address:* 14 rue Dupont-des-Loges, 75007 Paris, France.

CHARGAFF, Erwin, DR.PHIL.; American professor of biochemistry and author; b. 11 Aug. 1905, Austria; s. of Hermann and Rosa Chargaff; m.

Vera Broido 1929; one s.; ed. Maximiliansgymnasium, Vienna, and Univ. of Vienna; Research Fellow, Yale Univ. 1928-30; Asst., Univ. of Berlin 1930-33; Research Assoc., Inst. Pasteur, Paris 1933-34; Columbia Univ., N.Y. 1935-, Asst. Prof. 1938-46, Assoc. Prof. 1946-52, Prof. of Biochemistry 1952-74, Chair. Biochemistry Dept. 1970-74, Prof. Emer. of Biochemistry 1974; Visiting Prof., Sweden 1949, Japan 1958, Brazil 1959; Einstein Chair., Collège de France, Paris 1965, Cornell Univ. 1967; mem. N.A.S., American Philosophical Soc.; Fellow American Acad. of Arts and Sciences, Boston; mem. Deutsche Akad. der Naturforscher Leopoldina; Foreign mem. Royal Swedish Physiographic Soc., Lund; Guggenheim Fellow 1949, 1958; Hon. Sc.D. (Columbia) 1976, Hon. Dr.Phil. (Basel) 1976; Pasteur Medal, Paris 1949; Neuberg Medal, N.Y. 1959; Charles Leopold Mayer Prize, Acad. des Sciences, Paris 1963; Dr. H.P. Heineken Prize, Royal Netherlands Acad. of Sciences, Amsterdam 1964; Bertner Foundation Award, Houston 1965; Gregor Mendel Medal, Halle 1973; Nat. Medal of Science, Washington 1975, New York Acad. of Medicine Medal 1980, Distinguished Service Award (Columbia Univ.) 1982, Johann Heinrich-Merck Prize, Deutsche Akad. für Sprache und Dichtung 1984. *Publications:* Essays on Nucleic Acids 1963, Voices of the Labyrinth 1977, Heraclitean Fire: Sketches from a Life before Nature 1978, Das Feuer des Heraklit 1979, Unbegreifliches Geheimnis 1980, Bemerkungen 1981; Warnungstafeln 1982, Kritik der Zunkunft 1983; Zeugenschaft 1985, Serious Questions 1986; Abscheu vor der Weltgeschichte-fragmente vom Menschen 1988; Editor: The Nucleic Acids (3 vols.) 1955, 1960; numerous scientific articles and other literary work. *Address:* 350 Central Park West, New York, N.Y. 10025, U.S.A. *Telephone:* 222-7994.

CHARLES, (Mary) Eugenia; Dominican politician; b. 15 May 1919, Pointe Michel; d. of John B. and Josephine (née Delauney) Charles; mem. Inner Temple, London 1947; legal practice, Barbados, Windward and Leeward Islands; political career began 1968; co-f. and first leader Dominica Freedom Party; M.P. 1975-; Leader of the Opposition 1975-79; Prime Minister, Minister of Foreign Affairs, Finance and Devt. July 1980-; fmr. Minister of Tourism and Devt.; fmr. Dir. Dominica Co-operative Bank; fmr. mem. Bd. Dominica Infirmary. *Leisure interests:* reading, travel. *Address:* Office of the Prime Minister, P.O. Box 121, Roseau, Dominica. *Telephone:* 809-448 2855.

CHARLES, Pearnel, M.P.; Jamaican politician; b. 31 Aug. 1936, Macedonia, Browns Town, St. Ann; s. of James and Mereta Charles; m. Gloria M. Hanson 1970; one s. four d.; ed. West Indies Coll., Mandeville and City Coll. of City Univ. of New York; held post with Bustamente Industrial Trade Union 1965, Area Supervisor 1967, Asst. Island Supervisor 1969; Senator 1972; Deputy Leader, Jamaica Labour Party 1974; mem. of Parl. for Eastern St. Thomas; Minister of Public Utilities and Transport 1982-89. *Publication:* Detained 1977. *Address:* c/o Ministry of Public Utilities and Transport, 2 St. Lucia Avenue, Kingston 5, Jamaica.

CHARLES, Ray (b. Ray Charles Robinson); American jazz musician; b. 23 Sept. 1930, Albany, Ga.; s. of late Bailey and Aretha Robinson; m. Della Charles; three s.; ed. St. Augustine's School, Orlando, Fla.; taught himself to play and write for every bass and wind instrument in the orchestra, specializing in piano, organ and saxophone; composes and arranges; played at Rockin' Chair Club, Seattle Elks Club, Seattle; joined Lowell Fulsom's Blues Band, toured for a year; played at Apollo, Harlem; formed group to accompany singer Ruth Brown; Leader of Maxim Trio; with Atlantic Records 1954-59, ABC Records 1959-62, formed own cos., Tangerine 1962-73, Crossover Records Co. 1973-, Columbia Records 1982-; tours with Ray Charles Revue; major albums include Ray Charles' Greatest Hits, Modern Sounds in Country and Western Music (Vols. 1 and 2), Message from the People, Volcanic Action of my Soul, Through the Eyes of Love; Songwriters Hall of Fame, Rock and Roll Hall of Fame 1986; Commdr. des Arts et des Lettres 1986; Kennedy Center Honor 1986. *Address:* c/o Triad Artists Inc., 90200 Sunset Blvd., Suite 823, Los Angeles, Calif. 90069, U.S.A.

CHARLES, Serge Elie, LL.D.; Haitian diplomatist; b. 19 Aug. 1941, Port-au-Prince; m.; two c.; ed. Mil. Acad. of Haiti, Univ. of Port-au-Prince and New York Univ.; Second Lieut. then mem. Coast Guard Haitian Army 1961-72; Legal Counsellor, Perm. Mission, New York 1972-75, Nat. Inst. Mineral Resources, Haiti 1975-77, Perm. Rep. to UN 1977-80, Amb. to U.S.A. and OAS 1980-81, to Fed. Repub. of Germany 1981-83; Perm. Rep. to UN 1983-87; Minister of Foreign Affairs Sept. 1988-; head of various dels. and confs. *Address:* c/o Ministry of External Affairs, Port-au-Prince, Haiti.

CHARLES-ROUX, Edmonde; French writer; b. 17 April 1920, Neuilly-sur-Seine; d. of François Charles-Roux and Sabine Gounelle; m. Gaston Defferre 1973 (deceased); ed. Italy; served as nurse, then in Resistance Movement, during Second World War, in which she was twice wounded; Reporter, magazine Elle 1947-49; Features Editor, French edn. of Vogue 1947-54, Editor-in-Chief 1954-66; mem. Acad. Goncourt 1983-; awarded Prix Goncourt 1966; Grand Prix Littéraire de Provence 1977. *Publications:* Oublier Palerme 1966, Elle Adrienne 1971, L'irrégulière 1974, Le temps Chanel 1979, Stèle pour un bâtard, Don Juan d'Autriche: 1545-1578 1980, Une enfance sicilienne 1981, Un désir d'Orient 1988. *Leisure interests:* music, sea and sailing. *Address:* Editions Grasset, 61 rue des Saints-Pères, Paris 75006 (Office).

CHARLOT, Gaston; French chemist; b. 11 June 1904, Paris; m. Dora Haimovici; one d.; ed. Ecole de Physique et de Chimie de Paris; Hon. Prof. Univs. of Paris, Ecole de Physique et de Chimie de Paris; mem. Acad. des Sciences (Inst. de France); Chevalier, Légion d'honneur; Grand Prix Scientifique de la Ville de Paris. *Publications:* numerous works on analytical chemistry. *Address:* 18 rue Berthollet, Paris 5e, France. *Telephone:* 45 87 00 36.

CHARLOT, Jean, D.LIT.; French professor of political science; b. 16 March 1932, Guingamp; m. Monica Huber 1956; three d.; ed. Inst. d'Etudes Politiques, Paris; Visiting Prof. Univs. of Lausanne and Liege 1971–75, lecturer, later Prof. of Political Science, Inst. d'Etudes Politiques, Paris 1978–; Sec.-Gen., later mem. Bd., French Political Science Asscn. 1975–79; former Jt. Ed. European Journal of Political Research; former political analyst for Le Point and Le Figaro; Hon. Dr. (Liège), Chevalier Ordre nat. du Merite. *Publications:* le Phenomène gaulliste 1970, les Partis politiques 1971, Quand la gauche peut gagner 1973, le Gaullisme d'opposition 1946–58 1983. *Address:* Institut d'Etudes Politiques, 27 rue Saint-Guillaume, 75007 Paris, France. *Telephone:* (1) 45 49 50 50.

CHARLTON, Robert (Bobby), C.B.E.; British football player; b. 11 Oct. 1937; s. of Robert and Elizabeth Charlton; m. Norma Charlton 1961; two d.; ed. Bedlington Grammar School, Northumberland; professional footballer with Manchester United 1954–73, played 751 games, scored 245 goals; F.A. Cup Winners' Medal 1963; First Div. Championship Medals 1956–57, 1964–65, 1966–67; World Cup Winners' Medal (with England) 1966; European Cup Winners' Medal 1968; 106 appearances for England 1957–73, scored 37 goals; Man. Preston North End 1973–75; Chair. N.W. Council for Sport and Recreation 1982–; Dir. Manchester United Football Club 1984–; Hon. Fellow Manchester Polytechnic 1979. *Publications:* My Soccer Life 1965, Forward for England 1967, This Game of Soccer 1967, Book of European Football, Books 1–4 1969–72. *Leisure interest:* golf. *Address:* Garthollerton, Chelford Road, Ollerton, nr. Knutsford, Cheshire, England.

CHARLTON, Robert William, M.B.B.CH., M.D., F.R.C.P.E.; South african university vice-chancellor; b. 27 Jan. 1929, Johannesburg; s. of Robert J.W. Charlton and Marjory Thomson; m. Margaret L. D. Ritchie 1960; one s. three d.; ed. St. John's Coll. Johannesburg and Univ. of the Witwatersrand; Sr. Physician, Johannesburg Hosp. 1961–87; Prof. of Experimental and Clinical Pharmacology, Univ. of the Witwatersrand 1967–83, Dean of Medicine 1978–79, Deputy Vice-Chancellor 1980–82, Vice-Prin. 1983–87, Vice-Chancellor and Prin. 1988–; Chair. Medicines Control Council of South Africa 1976–81. *Publications:* more than 100 articles in medical journals, mainly in the field of iron metabolism. *Leisure interests:* golf, fly fishing, music. *Address:* University of the Witwatersrand, 1 Jan Smuts Avenue, Johannesburg, 2001 South Africa. *Telephone:* (011) 7163200.

CHARMOT, Guy, M.D.; French physician; b. 1914, Toulon; s. of Ulysse Charmot and Claire Esmieu; m. Edith Dubuisson 1948; one d.; Medical Officer in reserve 1938; war service in Free French Forces 1940–45; served various hospitals in French-speaking Africa: Chad, Senegal, Congo, Madagascar 1945–66; now working at Hôpital Claude Bernard (infectious and tropical diseases), Paris; Pres. Société de Pathologie exotique; Commdr. Légion d'honneur, Companion de la Libération, Croix de guerre. *Publications:* numerous papers concerned chiefly with diseases of the liver and spleen, hereditary anaemia, malaria and amoeba-caused diseases. *Leisure interest:* mountaineering. *Address:* 72 boulevard de Reuilly, 75012 Paris, France. *Telephone:* 46.28.97.73.

CHARNOCK, Henry, M.SC., F.R.S.; British meteorologist and oceanographer; b. 25 Dec. 1920, Blackburn; s. of Henry Charnock and Mary Gray (McLeod); m. E. Mary Dickinson 1946; one s. two d.; ed. Queen Elizabeth's Grammar School, Municipal Tech. Coll., Blackburn and Imperial Coll., London; RAFVR 1943–46; Nat. Inst. of Oceanography 1949–58, 1960–66; Imperial Coll. 1958–59; Prof. of Physical Oceanography, Univ. of Southampton 1966–71, 1978–86, Visiting Prof. 1971–78, Prof. Emer. 1986–; Deputy Vice-Chancellor 1982–84; Dir. Nat. Inst. of Oceanography (now Inst. of Oceanographic Sciences) 1971–78; Pres. Int. Union of Geodesy and Geophysics 1971–75; Sec. Scientific Cttee. of Oceanic Research 1978–80, Vice Pres. 1980–82; Pres. Royal Meteorological Soc. 1982–84; mem. Royal Comm. Environmental Pollution 1985–. *Publications:* papers in scientific journals. *Address:* Department of Oceanography, The University, Southampton, SO9 5NH, England. *Telephone:* Southampton 559122.

CHARRETIER, Maurice Raymond Ferdinand, L. EN D.; French politician; b. 17 Sept. 1926, St.-Geniès-de-Colomas (Gard); s. of Elie Charretier and Raymonde Icard; m. Jacqueline Jouve 1949; ed. Coll. de Valence, Drôme, and Faculté de Droit, Aix-en-Provence; active in resistance 1943–44; served French Army 1944–45; lawyer, Carpentras 1947–78; Mayor of Carpentras 1965–; Conseiller-Gen., Vaucluse 1967–73; mem. Conseil Econ. et Social 1976–78; Deputy from Vaucluse (UDF) March 1978; mem. Nat. Bureau, Republican Party; Vice-Pres. Legal Comm., Nat. Assembly, and Titular Judge, High Court of Justice until 1979; mem. French del. to UN Gen. Assembly 1978; Minister of Commerce and Artisan Industries 1979–81; elected Deputy from Vaucluse March 1986 (gave up seat); elected Senator Sept. 1986; Croix du Combattant Volontaire de la Résistance. *Address:* Palais du Luxembourg, 75291 Paris cedex 06 (Office); 584 avenue Victor Hugo, 84200 Carpentras, France.

CHARTERIS, Leslie, F.R.S.A.; American author; b. 12 May 1907, Singapore; m. 1st Pauline Schishkin 1931, one d.; m. 2nd Barbara Meyer 1939, 3rd Elizabeth Borst 1943, 4th Audrey Long 1952; ed. Rossall School and King's Coll., Cambridge; Ed. The Saint Magazine 1953–67, Editorial consultant 1983–; producer of The Saint and other radio programmes; writer of the internationally syndicated Saint comic strip; originator of The Saint television programme; has written several film scripts; columnist, Gourmet Magazine 1966–68; mem. Mensa, Council of Int. Foundation for Gifted Children; Pres. Saint Club and Arbour Youth Centre; invented universal sign language Paleneo 1969. *Publications:* Meet the Tiger 1929, Enter the Saint 1931, The Last Hero 1931, The Avenging Saint 1931, Wanted for Murder 1931, Angels of Doom 1932, The Saint v. Scotland Yard 1932, Getaway 1933, The Saint and Mr. Teal 1933, The Brighter Buccaneer 1933, The Misfortunes of Mr. Teal 1934, The Saint Intervenes 1934, The Saint Goes On 1935, The Saint in New York 1935, Saint Overboard 1936, The Ace of Knaves 1937, Thieves' Picnic 1937, Juan Belmonte: Killer of Bulls (translated from Spanish) 1937, Follow the Saint 1938, Prelude for War 1938, The First Saint Omnibus 1939, The Saint in Miami 1940, The Saint Goes West 1942, The Saint Steps In 1943, The Saint at Large 1943, The Saint on Guard 1944, The Saint Sees It Through 1946, Call for the Saint 1948, Saint Errant 1948, The Second Saint Omnibus 1951, The Saint in Europe 1953, The Saint on the Spanish Main 1955, The Saint Around the World 1956, Thanks to the Saint 1957, Señor Saint 1958, The Saint to the Rescue 1959, Trust the Saint 1962, Saint in the Sun 1963, Vendetta for the Saint 1964, The Saint on TV 1968, The Saint Returns 1968, The Saint Abroad 1969, The Saint and the Fiction Makers 1969, The Saint in Pursuit 1970, The Saint and the People Importers 1971, Saints Alive 1974, Catch the Saint 1975, The Saint and the Hapsburg Necklace 1976, Send for the Saint 1977, The Saint in Trouble 1978, The Saint and the Templar Treasure 1978, Count on the Saint 1980, The Fantastic Saint 1982, Salvage for the Saint 1983. *Leisure interests:* reading, languages, horse racing, swimming, food and wine. *Address:* 3-4 Great Marlborough Street, London, W1V 2AR, England.

CHARUSATHIRA, General Prapas; Thai army officer and politician; b. 25 Nov. 1912, Udorn Prov.; m. Khunying Sawai; one s. four d.; ed. Chulachomklao Royal Mil. Acad. and Nat. Defence Coll; Army service 1933, rose through infantry to Gen. 1960; Minister of Interior 1957–71; Deputy Prime Minister 1963–71; Army Deputy Commdr. and Deputy Supreme Commdr. 1963–64, Supreme Commdr. 1964; mem. Nat. Exec. Council and Dir. of Security Council (Defence and Interior) 1971–72; Deputy Prime Minister, Minister of Interior 1972–73; Vice-Pres. and Rector, Chulalongkorn Univ. 1961–69; in exile 1973–77, returned to Thailand Jan. 1977; numerous decorations. *Publications:* The Role of the Ministry of Interior in the Development of National Security, The Role of the Ministry of Interior in Maintenance of National Peace and Order. *Leisure interests:* sport: boxing, soccer, golf, hunting, amateur ranching, arms collecting. *Address:* 132-5 Suan Puttan Residence, Bangkok, Thailand.

CHARYK, Joseph Vincent, PH.D., M.S., B.SC.; American scientist and administrator; b. 9 Sept. 1920, Canmore, Alberta, Canada; s. of John and Anna (Dorosh) Charyk; m. Edwina Rhodes Charyk; three s. one d.; ed. Univ. of Alberta, Calif. Inst. of Tech.; Instructor of Aeronautics, Calif. Inst. of Tech. 1945; Asst. (later Assoc.) Prof. of Aeronautics, Princeton Univ. 1946; Dir. of Aerophysics and Chemistry Lab., Lockheed Aircraft Corpn. 1955–56; Dir. of Missile Tech. Lab., Gen. Man. Space Tech. Div. Aeronutronic Systems Inc. (Subsidiary of Ford Motor Co.) 1956–59; Chief Scientist U.S.A.F. 1959, Asst. Sec. of Air Force for Research and Devt. 1959; Under-Sec. U.S.A.F. 1960–63; Pres. and Dir. Communications Satellite Corpn. 1963–79, C.E.O. 1979–85, Chair. and C.E.O. 1983–85; mem. Bd. of Dirs., Abbott Labs., American Security Corpn., Communications Satellite Corpn., Draper Labs.; mem. Int. Acad. of Astronautics; Fellow of American Inst. of Aeronautics and Astronautics; mem. Nat. Space Club, Armed Forces Communications and Electronics Asscn., Newcomen Soc., Nat. Inst. Social Sciences, and Conf. Bd., Nat. Acad. of Eng.; Hon. LL.D., Hon. Dr.Ing. *Leisure interests:* golf, tennis, photography. *Address:* 5126 Tilden Street, N.W., Washington, D.C. 20016, U.S.A. *Telephone:* (202) 244-3761.

CHASE, Robert Arthur, M.D.; American surgeon, anatomist and educator; b. 6 Jan. 1923, Keene, N.H.; s. of Albert Henry Chase and Georgia Beulah Bump; m. Ann Crosby Parker Chase 1946; one s. two d.; ed. Univ. of New Hampshire, Durham, N.H. and Yale Univ. School of Medicine, New Haven, Conn.; Teaching Fellow in Plastic Surgery, Univ. of Pittsburgh, Pa. 1957–59; Asst. Prof. then Assoc. Prof. of Surgery, Yale Univ. 1959–63; Prof. and Chair. Dept. of Surgery Stanford Univ. Medical School, Calif. 1963–74, Acting Chair. Dept. of Anatomy 1973–74, first Emile Holman Prof. of Surgery, Dept. of Surgery 1972–, Prof. of Anatomy and Chief, Div. of Human Anatomy 1977–; Pres. and Dir. Nat. Bd. of Medical Examiners, Philadelphia, Pa. 1974–77; Francis Gilman Blake Award, Yale Univ. 1962; Henry J. Kaiser Award for Innovation in Teaching 1978, 1979 and 1984; Fellow, Center for Advanced Study in the Behavioral Sciences, Stanford 1981–82. *Publications:* Atlas of Hand Surgery, ed. Videosurgery 1974–; contributions to numerous journals. *Leisure interest:* photography. *Address:* Department of Surgery, Stanford University Medical School,

Stanford, Calif. 94305; 797 N. Tolman Lane, Stanford, Calif. 94305, U.S.A. (Home). *Telephone:* (415) 723-8515 (Office); (415) 494-7821 (Home).

CHASTEL, André (Adrien), DR. ÉS LETTRES; French art historian; b. 15 Nov. 1912, Paris; s. of Adrien Chastel and Marie-Isabelle Morin; m. P.-M. Grand 1942; three s.(one deceased); ed. Sorbonne, Paris; Asst. in Art History, Sorbonne 1945-48; Focillon Fellowship, Yale 1949; Dir. of Studies for the History of the Renaissance, Ecole Pratique des Hautes Etudes 1951; Prof. History of Modern Art, Sorbonne 1957-70; Prof. Coll. de France 1970-85; Andrew Mellon Lecturer, Nat. Gallery, Washington, D.C. 1977; art critic, Le Monde 1950-; Sec. Comité Int. d'Histoire de l'Art 1961-69, Vice-Pres. 1969-; mem. Inst. de France 1975-, Accad. dei Lincei, Rome 1976-; Foreign Hon. mem. American Acad. of Arts and Sciences 1975-; Corresp. Fellow, British Acad. 1976, Corresp. mem. Bayerische Akademie der Wissenschaften 1986; Croix de guerre 1939-40; Commdr. Légion d'honneur 1986; Commdr., Ordre nat. du Mérite; Commdr. des Palmes académiques; Commdr. Ordine del Merito (Italy); Grand Prix National 1978. *Publications:* Vuillard 1946, L'art italien (2 vols.) 1957, 1982, Botticelli 1958, Art et humanisme à Florence au temps de Laurent le Magnifique 1959, 1982, L'âge de l'humanisme (with R. Klein) 1963, Italie 1460-1500 (2 vols.) 1965, Crise de la Renaissance 1968, Mythe de la Renaissance 1969, edition of Gauricus de Sculptura (1504) 1969, Fables, formes et figures (2 vols.) 1978, The Sack of Rome (1527) 1983, Chronique de la peinture italienne (1280-1580) 1984, Cardinal Louis d'Aragon 1986. *Leisure interests:* member of Racing-Club de France, farming. *Address:* 30 rue de Lübeck, 75116 Paris, France.

CHATAWAY, Rt. Hon. Christopher John, P.C.; British business executive, fmr. politician and fmr. athlete; b. 31 Jan. 1931; m. Carola Walker 1976; ed. Sherborne School and Magdalen Coll., Oxford.; rep. U.K. at Olympic Games 1952, 1956; holder of world 5,000 metres record 1954; Jr. Exec., Arthur Guinness, Son and Co. 1953-55; Staff Reporter, Ind. Television News 1955-56; Current Affairs Commentator, BBC Television 1956-59; mem. London County Council 1958-61; M.P. for Lewisham North 1959-66, for Chichester 1969-74; Parl. Private Sec. to Minister of Power 1961-62; Joint Parl. Under-Sec. of State, Dept. of Educ. and Science 1962-64; Alderman, Greater London Council 1967-70; Minister of Posts and Telecommunications 1970-72, for Industrial Devt. 1972-74; Man. Dir. Orion Royal Bank 1974-88; Chair. Kitcat and Aitken Ltd. 1986-88, Crown Communications 1987-, London Broadcasting Co. (L.B.C.) 1981-; Dir. British Electric Traction PLC, Petrofina (U.K.) Ltd.; Chair. ActionAid, Groundwork Foundation; Hon. D.Litt. (Loughborough) 1980; Conservative. *Address:* Crown Communications, 22 Newman Street, London W1P 4AJ (Office); 27 Randolph Crescent, London, W9 1DP, England (Home).

CHATENET, Pierre, LIC. EN DR.; French politician; b. 6 March 1917, Paris; s. of Henri Chatenet and Andrée Genès; m. Jacqueline Parodi 1947; one s.; ed. Lycée Buffon and Ecole des Sciences Politiques; Auditor Conseil d'Etat 1941; Chargé de Mission, Provisional Govt. 1944, Labour Office 1944-45; mem. French Del. UN Conf. San Francisco 1945; Maître des Requêtes, Conseil d'Etat 1946; Counsellor French Del. to UN 1946-47; Political Dir. Résidence Gen. Tunis 1947-50; Counsellor French Perm. Del. to NATO 1950-54; Dir. of Civil Service (Présidence du Conseil) 1954; mem. UN Rights of Man Comm., Consultative Cttee. Fonction Publique Int.; Sec. of State (Prime Minister's Office) Jan.-May 1959; Minister of the Interior May 1959-61; Pres. of EURATOM 1962-67; Conseiller d'Etat 1963-70; Pres. Comm. des Opérations de Bourse 1967-72; mem. Conseil Constitutionnel 1968-77; Pres. Creditel and Cofiroute 1973, de la Commission de la Privatisation 1986; mem. Bd. Soc. Lyonnaise des Eaux, SAFT, Soc. parisienne des eaux; Commdr. Légion d'honneur; Grand Croix de l'Ordre de la Couronne de Belgique. *Address:* 11 avenue Suffren 75007, Paris, France.

CHATT, Joseph, C.B.E., PH.D., SC.D.; British chemist; b. 6 Nov. 1914, Horden, s. of Joseph Chatt and Elsie Chatt (née Parker); m. Ethel Williams 1947; one s. one d.; ed. Nelson School, Wigton, Cumberland and Cambridge Univ.; Deputy Chief Chemist, later Chief Chemist, Peter Spence & Son Ltd. 1942-46; ICI Research Fellow, Imperial Coll., London 1946-47; Head of Inorganic Chemistry Dept., Butterwick, later Akers Research Labs., ICI Ltd. 1947-60; Akers Group Man. Research Dept. Heavy Organic Chemicals Div., ICI 1960-62, Group Head and Consultant, Petrochemical and Polymer Lab., ICI 1963; Dir. Unit of Nitrogen Fixation, Agricultural Research Council 1963-80; Prof. of Chemistry, Queen Mary Coll., London Univ. 1963-64, Univ. of Sussex 1965-80, Emer. Prof. 1980-; Fellow of Royal Soc., mem. Council 1975-77; Hon. Fellow Emmanuel Coll., Cambridge 1978; mem. Royal Soc. of Chem., of Council, Hon. Sec. 1956-62, Vice-Pres. 1962-65, 1972-74; Pres. Section B., British Asscn. for the Advancement of Science 1974-75; mem. American Chemical Soc.; mem. IUPAC Comm. on the Nomenclature of Inorganic Chemistry 1959-81, Chair. 1976-81; mem. A.R.C. Advisory Cttee. on Plants and Soils 1964-67; Hon. Life. mem. New York Acad. of Sciences 1978; corresp. mem. Acad. of Sciences, Lisbon 1978; Foreign Fellow, Indian Nat. Science Acad.; Hon. Fellow Indian Chemical Soc. 1983; Hon. mem. Royal Physiographical Soc. of Lund, Sweden 1984; Hon. Foreign mem. American Acad. of Arts and Sciences 1985; Distinguished Visiting Prof. of Chemistry, Pa. State Univ.; Visiting Prof. of Chemistry, Yale, Rajasthan and South Carolina Univs.; Debye Lecturer, Cornell Univ. 1975; Tilden Lecturer of Chemical Soc. 1962,

Liversidge Lecturer 1971-72, Nyholm Lecturer 1976-77, Arthur D. Little Lecturer, M.I.T. 1977; Univ. Lecturer in Chemistry, Western Ont. 1978; Stieglitz Lecturer Chicago Univ. 1978; Chandler Medallist and Lecturer, Columbia Univ., New York 1978; Stauffer Lecturer, Univ. of Southern Calif. 1979; Pres. Dalton Div. Chemical Soc. 1971-74; Sunner Memorial Lecturer (Lund Univ. Sweden) 1982; Hon. D.Sc. (East Anglia) 1974, (Sussex) 1982, Dr. h.c. (Univ. Pierre et Marie Curie, Paris) 1981, Dr. h.c. (Lund) 1986; Gordon Wigan Prize for Research in Chemistry Univ. of Cambridge 1939; American Chemical Soc. Award for Distinguished Service in the Advancement of Inorganic Chemistry 1971, Organometallic Award of Chemical Soc. 1971; Chugaev Commemorative Diploma and Medal, Kurnakov Inst. of Gen. and Inorganic Chemistry, Soviet Acad. of Sciences 1976; Davy Medal of the Royal Soc. 1979; Dwyer Memorial Medallist and lecturer, Univ. N.S.W. 1980, Wolf Laureate (Chemistry) 1981, G. W. Willand Award, Univ. of Chicago 1983. *Publications:* Scientific papers on complex chemistry, mainly in the journal of the Chemical Soc. *Leisure interests:* numismatics, history, art. *Address:* School of Chemistry and Molecular Sciences, University of Sussex, Brighton BN1 9QJ (Office); 16 Tongdean Road, Hove, East Sussex, BN3 6QE, England (Home). *Telephone:* 606755 (Office); 554377 (Home).

CHATTY, Habib; Tunisian diplomatist; b. 9 Aug. 1916, M'Saken; m. Souad Boulekbeche 1950; three c.; ed. Sadiki Coll., Tunis; Journalist 1937-52, Ed. Ez-Zohra 1943-50, Es-Sabah 1950-52; imprisoned 1952, 1953; Head, Press Cabinet of Pres. of Council 1954-55, Head, Information Service 1955; mem. Nat. Council, Neo-Destour Party 1955; Dir. Al Amal 1956; Vice-Pres. Constituent Nat. Assembly 1956; Amb. to Lebanon and Iraq 1957-59, to Turkey and Iran 1959-62, to U.K. 1962-64, to Morocco 1964-70, to Algeria 1970-72; Dir. of Presidential Cabinet 1972-74; Minister of Foreign Affairs 1974-77; mem. Political Bureau and Central Cttee. of Destour Socialist Party 1974-77; Deputy to Nat. Ass. 1974-; Sec. Gen. Org. of the Islamic Conf. 1979-85; several decorations. *Address:* Ministry of Foreign Affairs, place du Gouvernement, la Kasbah, Tunis, Tunisia.

CHATZIDAKIS, Manos; Greek composer; b. 1925.; composer of ballet music, incidental music for theatre and films, piano and orchestral music, and popular songs; numerous national and int. awards, including Oscar 1961; composed music for Lysistrata, Birds, Plutus (Aristophanes), and for films Stella 1956, Never on Sunday 1960, Topkapi 1964, etc.

CHAU, Dr. the Hon. Sir Sik-Nin, Kt., C.B.E., LL.D., M.B., B.S.; Hong Kong business executive; b. 1903, Hong Kong; s. of late Cheuk-Fan Chau; m. Ida Hing-Kwai Lau 1927 (died 1987); two s.; ed. St. Stephen's Coll., Hong Kong, Univs. of Hong Kong, London and Vienna; Hon. Chair. The Hong Kong Chinese Bank Ltd.; Chair. Hong Kong Trade Devt. Council 1966-70, Hong Kong Model Housing Soc., Kowloon Motor Bus Co., Pioneer Trade Devt. Co. Ltd., Repulse Bay Enterprises Ltd., Far East Insurance Co. Ltd., Nin Fung Hong Ltd., Oriental Express Ltd., Sik Yuen Co. Ltd., State Trading Corpn. Ltd.; Pres. Hong Kong Productivity Council 1970-73, Hong Kong Cttee. for Expo 1970, Osaka, Japan; Hon. Pres. Fed. of Hong Kong Industries; mem. Textiles Advisory Bd., Legis. Council 1946-60, Exec. Council 1947-62; Chair. Sub-Comm. on Trade, UN Econ. Comm. for Asia and Far East Conf. 1955, Indo-Pacific Comm., Int. Council for Scientific Man. 1964-67; Pres. Japan Soc. of Hong Kong; Pres. designate World Council of Man. 1977, Dir. official, educational and philanthropic orgs.; granted permanent title of Hon. by H.M. the Queen 1962; Hon. LL.D. (Hong Kong); Order of Sacred Treasure (Japan) 1969, Silver Jubilee Medal 1977. *Leisure interest:* racing. *Address:* IL 3547 Hatton Road, Hong Kong.

CHAUDHARY, Amarsingh Bhilabhai, B.ENG.; Indian engineer and politician; b. 31 July 1941, Dolvan Village, Vyara Taluka, Surat; ed. Maharaja Sayajirao Univ., Vadodara; Jr. Engineer, Surat Dist. Panchayat; joined Vyara Taluka Majdoor Sahakari Mandli as Sec. and Engineer 1969; Hon. Sec. Surat Dist. Majdoor Co-operative Socs. Union; joined Youth Congress 1971; mem. Legis. Ass., Deputy Minister, Public Works and Devt.; Minister for Social Welfare and Rural Housing 1972-74; Pres. Surat Dist. Congress Cttee. 1974; Gen. Sec. Pradesh Congress Cttee. 1974; mem. Legislative Ass. 1975-80, Minister for Agric. and Forestry 1976-77; mem. Legis. Ass. 1980-85, 1985-; Minister for Irrigation, Forest and Tribal Devt. 1980-85, for Home, Prohibition and Excise, Educ. and Youth and Cultural Activities 1985; elected Leader Congress (I) Legislative Party, Chief Minister of Gujarat 1985-; Pres. Gujarat Br., Friends of Soviet Union; Vice-Pres. All-India Tribal Council; Fellow All-India Inst. Engineers; Pres. Gujarat Branch, Indian Scouts and Guides. *Address:* Raj Bhavan, Gandhinagar, Gujarat, India.

CHAUDHURI, Naranarain (Sankho), B.A.; Indian sculptor; b. 25 Feb. 1916, Santhal Purganas, Bihar; s. of Narendra Narain and Kiron Moyee; m. Ira Chaudhuri; two s. one d.; ed. Armanitoba High School, Dacca and Bishwa Bharti Santiniketan, West Bengal.; freelance artist 1947-; Reader and Head Dept. of Sculpture, Univ. of Baroda 1949-50, Prof. of Sculpture 1957, Dean, Faculty of Fine Arts 1966-68; Prof. of Fine Arts, Univ. of Dar-es-Salaam 1980; mem. Lalit Kala Akademi 1956-(Sec. 1974, Chair. 1984-); Pres. Indian Sculptors' Assen. 1964-65; mem. Indian Cttee. Int. Assen. of Plastic Arts, All India Handicrafts Bd., Int. Jury 5th Triennale-India; exhibited São Paulo Bienal 1961, One-Man Exhbns. Bombay, New Delhi and Calcutta; numerous Indian awards; Padma Shri 1971. *Major* *works:* Sculptures, All India Radio, Delhi 1955, Statue of Mahatma Gandhi, Rio de Janeiro 1964, sculpture for Jyoti Ltd., Baroda 1968, brass sculpture for World Bank commissioned by Govt. of India 1976, Mahatma Gandhi, Copenhagen 1985, and works in collections in India, U.K. and U.S.A. *Address:* D-II/6 Cornwallis Road Flats, New Delhi 11003, India.

CHAUFOURNIER, Roger, D. EN D.; French international bank official; b. 23 Jan. 1924, Lignières; s. of Louis Chaufournier and Josephine Rome; m. Edna Hylton 1951; two s. one d.; ed. Univ. de Paris (Sorbonne) and Ecole des Hautes Etudes Commerciales, Paris; Post Doctoral Studies and Research, Univs. of Uppsala and Ill.; mem. Teaching and Research Staff, Dept. of Econs., Univ. of Ill. 1949-52; Int. Bank for Reconstruction and Devt. (World Bank) 1952-, economist 1952-56, Bank Rep. in Peru and Adviser to Peruvian Govt. 1956-60, Div. Chief, W. Hemisphere and European Depts. 1960-64, Deputy Dir. W. Hemisphere Dept. 1964-68, Dir. W. African Dept. 1968-72, Regional Vice-Pres. for Western Africa 1972-80, for Europe, Middle East and N. Africa 1980-84; mem. Bd. CIRAD; mem. Bd. N.-S. Devt.; Fellow, Swedish Inst. 1948; Fulbright Fellow 1949; Fellow, Inst. of Int. Educ.; Chevalier, Légion d'honneur. *Leisure interests:* reading, bridge, tennis, swimming, sailing. *Address:* 1 Pettit Court, Potomac, Md. 20854, U.S.A. (Home). *Telephone:* 869-3550 (Home).

CHAUNU, Pierre, D. ÉS L.; French professor of history; b. 17 Aug. 1923, Belleville, Meuse; m. 1947; four s. (one deceased) two d.; School of Advanced Hispanic Studies, Madrid 1948-51; C.N.R.S. 1956-59, now mem. Directorate; Univ. de Caen 1959; Prof. Univ. de Paris à la Sorbonne 1970-; Assoc. Prof., Faculté de Théologie Réformée, Aix-en-Provence 1974; mem. of Section, Conseil Econ. et Social 1976-77; Pres. Conseil Supérieur des Corps Universitaires 1977; mem. Scientific Cttee. (history section), C.N.R.S. 1980-; mem. Acad. des Sciences morales et politiques 1982-; Chevalier, Légion d'honneur. *Publications:* forty books including: Seville et l'Atlantique (1504-1650) (12 vols.), Le Pacifique des Ibériques, Civilisation de l'Europe classique, Civilisation de l'Europe des lumières, Temps des Réformes, L'Espagne de Charles Quint, La Mort à Paris, Histoire et Prospective, La Mémoire et le sacré, Le refus de la vie, La violence de Dieu, Un futur sans avenir, La mémoire de l'éternité, Le sursis 1979, Histoire et foi, Histoire et imagination 1980, Réforme et contre-réforme, Eglise, Culture et Société, Histoire et Décadence 1981, La France 1982, Ce que je crois 1982, Le chemin des mages 1983, Combats pour l'histoire 1983, L'historien dans tous ses états 1984, L'historien en cet instant 1985, Rétrohistoire, Au coeur religieux de l'histoire, L'aventure de la réforme 1986, Une autre voie (jtly.) 1986; 120 articles. *Address:* 12 rue des Cordeliers, 14300 Caen; 9 impasse Chartière, 75005 Paris 05, France. *Telephone:* (31) 81-61-51 (Caen); (1) 325-49-62 (Paris).

CHAUVIRÉ, Yvette; French ballerina; b. 22 April 1917, Paris; ed. Paris Opera Ballet School.; joined Paris Opera Ballet 1930, Danseuse Etoile 1942; with Monte Carlo Opera Ballet 1946-47; Artistic and Technical Adviser to Admin. of Paris Opera 1963-68; Dir. Acad. int. de danse, Paris 1970-; Officier Légion d'honneur; Commdr. des Arts et des Lettres; Commdr. Ordre nat. du Mérite; ballets in which she has performed leading roles include Istar, Les deux pigeons, David triomphant, Giselle, Les créatures de Prométhée, Roméo et Juliette, L'écuyère, Les suites romantiques, Lac des cygnes, L'oiseau de feu, Petrouchka, Sylvia, La belle Hélène, Casse-Noisette, Les mirages, Le cygne, La dame aux camélias. *Publication:* Je suis ballerine. *Leisure interests:* drawings, watercolours, collecting swans. *Address:* 21 Place du Commerce, 75015 Paris, France.

CHAVAN, Shankarrao Bhaorao, B.A., LL.B.; Indian politician; b. 14 July 1920, Paithan, Aurangabad Dist.; s. of Bhaorao and Laxmibi Chavan; m. Kusumati; one s.; ed. Univs. of Madras and Osmania; entered politics 1945; Pres. Nanded Town Municipality 1952-56; mem. Bombay Legis. Council 1956, Assembly 1957-; Deputy Minister for Revenue, Bombay Govt. 1956-60; Minister for Irrigation and Power, Maharashtra Govt. 1960-75; Deputy Leader Congress Legis. Party 1967-75, Leader 1975-; Chief Minister, Maharashtra Govt. 1975-77, 1986-88; mem. (Congress (I)) Lok Sabha 1980-; Minister of Educ. 1980-81, of Planning 1981-84, of Defence 1984-85, of Home Affairs 1985-86, of Finance July 1988-; Vice-Presidential cand. 1984; Vice-Pres. Nanded Co-operative Bank; Dir. Hyderabad State Co-operative Bank; mem. Exec. of Cen. Co-operative Union, Hyderabad; Exec. Cttee. of Maharashtra Pradesh Congress Cttee., A.I.C.C. *Address:* c/o Ministry of Finance, New Delhi, India.

CHAVES, Mañuel, LL.D.; Spanish politician; b. 1945, Ceuta; m.; two s.; Univ. Prof. of Labour Law; mem. Socialist Party (PSOE) 1968-; mem. Prov. Socialist Cttee. of Seville and Rep. of Nat. Cttee. 1968-75; M.P. for Cadiz 1977-; Exec. Sec., Nat. Exec. Comm. PSOE 1981; mem. Confederate Exec. Comm., Unión General de Trabajadores (UGT), Confederate Sec. for Information and Press Affairs; Minister for Labour and Social Security 1986-. *Address:* Ministerio de Trabajo y Seguridad Social, Neuvos Ministerios, Paseo de la Castellana s/n, Madrid 3, Spain. *Telephone:* Madrid 253 6000.

CHAVES DE MENDONÇA, Antônio Aureliano; Brazilian politician; b. 13 Jan. 1929, Três Pontas, Minas Gerais; s. of Jose Vieira and Luzia Chaves de Mendonça; m. Vivi Sanches de Mendonça; one s. two d.; ed. Itajuba Fed. School of Eng., Fluminense Faculty of Eng., War Coll.; teaching posts at Itajuba Fed. School of Eng. and Polytech. Inst. of

Catholic Univ. of Minas Gerais; Tech. Dir. ELETROBRAS 1961; Majority Leader in State Congress of Minas Gerais 1963-67; State Sec. for Educ. 1964, for Transport and Public Works 1965; Fed. Deputy 1967-75, Chair. Comm. for Mines and Energy 1971, later of Comm. for Science and Tech., also posts in various other comms.; Vice-Pres. of Brazil 1979-85, Acting Pres. Sept.-Nov. 1981; Minister of Mines and Energy 1988-; mem. Brazilian Geographical Soc., Brazilian Comm. for Large Dams, Brazilian Centre for Physical Research; various Brazilian medals; Arena party. *Publications:* several text books. *Address:* Esplanada dos Ministerios, Bloco 3, 70056, Brasília, Brazil.

CHÁVEZ, Ignacio, M.D.; Mexican physician; b. 31 Jan. 1897, Zirándaro, Michoacán; s. of Ignacio Chávez and Socorro Sánchez de Chávez; m. Celia Rivera de Chávez 1928 (died 1969); one s. one d.; ed. Univ. Nacional Autónoma de México; Clinical Prof. Univ. Nacional Autónoma de México 1923-50, Dir. Nat. School of Medicine 1933-34; Prof. of Cardiology, School of Graduates 1946-61, Rector of Univ. Nacional Autónoma de México 1961-66; Founder and Dir. Nat. Inst. of Cardiology of Mexico 1944-66, Hon. Dir. 1966-; Founder Mexican Cardiological Soc. 1935; founder-mem. Colegio Nacional 1943; Hon. Rector Univ. Michoacana de San Nicolás de Hidalgo; Hon. Prof. Univs. de Guadalajara, San Carlos de Guatemala, San Salvador, Rio de Janeiro, etc.; Hon. Pres. Interamerican Soc. of Cardiology; Pres. Int. Soc. of Cardiology 1958-62, Hon. Pres. 1962-; mem. Acads. of Medicine of Mexico, New York, Buenos Aires, etc.; hon. degrees Paris, Montpellier, Lyons, Mexico, São Paulo, Oxford, Bologna, Prague, Cracow, Jerusalem, Salamanca; Scientific Prize of Mexico; numerous Mexican and foreign decorations. *Publications:* La Digitalina a pequeñas dosis en el tratamiento de las Cardiopatias 1920, Lecciones de Clínica Cardiológica 1931, Exploración Funcional de los Riñones y Clasificación de la Nefropatias 1931, Enfermedades del Corazón, Cirugía y Embarazo 1945, Diego Rivera, Sus Frescos en el Instituto Nacional de Cardiología 1946, México en la Cultura Médica 1947, El Instituto Nacional de Cardiologia a los diez años de su fundación 1954, ... a los veinte años de su fundación 1964, El Nuevo Instituto Nacional de Cardiología 1978, Humanismo médico: Educación y Cultura 1978. *Leisure interests:* reading, history and literature, travelling, photography. *Address:* Paseo de la Reforma 1310, Lomas, México 10, D.F., Mexico. *Telephone:* 5-201176.

CHAVUNDUKA, Gordon Lloyd, M.A., PH.D.; Zimbabwean university professor and politician; b. 16 Aug. 1931, Umtali (now Mutare); s. of Solomon and Lillian Chavunduka; m. Rachel Chavunduka 1959; two s. four d.; ed. Univ. of California at Los Angeles, Univs. of Manchester and London; lecturer in Sociology, Univ. of Rhodesia, Salisbury 1966-79, Acting Head, Dept. of Sociology 1974-75; mem. Univ. Senate 1972; Dean, Faculty of Social Sciences 1978, Prof. 1979-, Dean, Faculty of Social Studies 1986-88; Sec.-Gen. African Nat. Council 1973; Pres. Asscn. of Univ. Teachers of Rhodesia 1974-, Zimbabwe Nat. Traditional Healers Asscn. 1980-. *Publications:* Traditional Healers and the Shona Patient; also papers in the field of sociology and contribs. to INCIDI, The Society of Malawi Journal, etc. *Leisure interests:* gardening, boxing (spectator), football. *Address:* University of Zimbabwe, P.O. Box M.P. 167, Mount Pleasant, Harare; 40 The Chase, Mount Pleasant, Harare, Zimbabwe (Home).

CHAYES, Abram, A.B., LL.B.; American professor of law; b. 18 July 1922, Chicago; m. Antonia Handler 1947; one s. four d.; ed. Harvard Univ.; U.S. Army service 1943-46; Legal Adviser to Gov. of Connecticut 1949-50; Assoc.-Gen. Counsel President's Materials Policy Comm. 1951; Law Clerk to Justice Felix Frankfurter 1951-52; private legal practice 1952-55; Asst. Prof. of Law, Harvard Univ. 1955-58, Prof. of Law 1958-61, 1965-76, Felix Frankfurter Prof. of Law 1976-; The Legal Adviser, Dept. of State 1961-64; Chair. Int. Nuclear Fuel Cycle Evaluation 1977-78; Guest Scholar, The Brookings Inst. 1977-78; represents Nicaragua at Int. Court of Justice; Fellow, American Acad. of Arts and Sciences; mem. Bars of Washington, D.C., Conn. and Mass., American Law Inst., American Soc. of Int. Law, Asscn. of the Bar of City of New York, Advisory Bd. Lawyers' Alliance for Nuclear Arms Control 1982-; Trustee, World Peace Foundation 1977-; Hon. LL.D. (Syracuse) 1987. *Publications:* The International Legal Process, (with T. Ehrlich and A. Lowenfeld) 1968, 1969, ABM, An Evaluation of the Decision to Deploy an Anti-Ballistic Missile System (with J. Wiesner) 1969, The Cuban Missile Crisis 1974, International Arrangements for Nuclear Fuel Reprocessing (Co-Ed. with W. Bennet Lewis) 1977. *Address:* 404 Griswold Hall, Harvard Law School, Cambridge, Mass. 02138 (Office); 3 Hubbard Park, Cambridge, Mass. 02138, U.S.A. (Home). *Telephone:* (617) 495-3122 (Office).

CHAZOV, Yevgeny, M.D., PH.D.; Soviet cardiologist and politician; b. 10 June 1929, Gorky; ed. Kiev Medical Inst.; Sr. Scientific Worker, Inst. of Therapy 1959; Deputy Dir. Inst. of Therapy, U.S.S.R. Acad. of Medical Science 1963-65, Dir. Inst. of Cardiology 1965-67; Deputy Minister of Public Health 1967-87, Minister Feb. 1987-; mem. Supreme Soviet 1974-(84); Dir. Cardiology Research Centre, Acad. of Medical Science 1975-82; mem. Cen. Cttee. CSPU 1982; mem. U.S.S.R. Acad. of Sciences 1979; Pres. U.S.S.R. Soc. of Cardiology 1975; Co-Pres. Int. Physicians for Prevention of Nuclear War (IPPNW) 1980-87, IPPNW awarded Nobel Prize for Peace 1985; Hero of Socialist Labour; State Prize 1969, 1976; Lenin Prize 1982, UNESCO Peace Prize 1984. *Publications:* Myocardial Infarction (with others) 1971, Cardiac Rhythm Disorders 1972, Anti-coagulants and Fibrinolytics 1977, and other monographs; over 300 articles on cardiology. *Leisure interests:* hunting, photography. *Address:* U.S.S.R. Ministry of Health, Rakhmanovsky per. 3, Moscow, U.S.S.R.

CHE PEIQIN; Chinese government official; alt. Gov. Asian Devt. Bank 1986–; mem. Council of People's Bank of China 1985–. *Address:* Head Office, Asian Development Bank, Beijing, People's Republic of China.

CHEBOTAREV, Dmitriy Fedorovich; Soviet gerontologist; b. 17 Sept. 1908, Kiev; ed. Kiev Medical Inst.; Intern Physiotherapeutical Inst., Chernigov 1933–36; Postgraduate 2nd Kiev Medical Inst. 1936–40; Army Surgeon 1941–44; Postgraduate, Senior Research Assoc. 1945–53; Deputy Dir. Inst. of Clinical Medicine, Kiev 1953–54, Prof. 1954; Chair. Learned Council of the U.S.S.R. Health Ministry 1955–64; Head of Chair, Inst. of Postgraduate Medical Training, Kiev 1953–61; Dir., Head of Dept., Inst. of Gerontology, U.S.S.R. Acad. of Medical Sciences 1961–87, Scientist Emer. 1987–; Corresp. mem. U.S.S.R. Acad. of Medical Sciences 1961, mem. 1966–; Pres. Int. Asscn. of Gerontology 1972–75; Chair. U.S.S.R. Soc. of Gerontologists and Geriatrists; mem. U.S.S.R. and Ukrainian Socs. of Internists, Presidium U.S.S.R. Soc. of Cardiologists; Chair. Gerontology and Geriatrics Comm., U.S.S.R. Ministry of Public Health; Order of Red Banner of Labour (three times), Order of October Revolution; Merited Scientist Ukrainian S.S.R. *Publications:* Over 180 works; monographs Hypertensive Syndrome of Pregnancy, Internal Pathology in Clinic of Obstetrics and Gynaecology, Cardio-vascular System of Ageing Organism, Care for Elderly and Old Patients, Geriatrics in the Clinic of Diseases of the Inner Organs. *Address:* Institute of Gerontology A.M.S. U.S.S.R., Vyshgorodskaya ul. 67, 252655 Kiev-114, U.S.S.R. *Telephone:* 430 40 68.

CHEBRIKOV, Viktor Mikhailovich; Soviet security officer; b. 1923, Ukraine; mem. CPSU 1944–; ed. Dnepropetrovsk Metallurgical Inst. 1950; served in Soviet Army 1941–46; rank of Col.-Gen.; party posts 1951–; mem. of Auditing Comm. of Ukrainian CP 1956–61; Second Sec. of Dnepropetrovsk City Cttee. of Ukrainian CP 1958–59, First Sec. 1961–63; cand. mem. of Cen. Cttee. of Ukrainian CP 1961–71, Sec. 1963–65; Second Sec. of Dnepropetrovsk Dist. Cttee. of Ukrainian CP 1965–67; Head of Personnel Dept. 1967–68; Deputy Chair. of U.S.S.R. State Security Cttee. (KGB) 1968–82, First Deputy Chair. 1982, Chair. 1982–88 (with rank of Gen.), State Comm. on Legal Reform 1988–; mem. Comm. to investigate crimes of Stalin 1988–; cand. mem. Cen. Cttee. of U.S.S.R. 1971–81, full mem. 1981–; cand. mem. Politburo 1983–85, mem. April 1985–; mem. Secr. 1988–; Order of Lenin 1983, Marshal Star 1984; mem. Foreign Affairs Comm., Soviet of Nationalities. *Address:* State Security Committee, The Kremlin, Moscow, U.S.S.R.

CHECKLAND, Michael, B.A.; British broadcasting executive; b. 13 March 1936, Birmingham; s. of Leslie and Ivy Florence Checkland; m. 1st. the late Shirley Checkland 1960; m. 2nd. Sue Zetter 1987; two s. one d.; ed. King Edward's Grammar School, Birmingham and Wadham Coll., Oxford; Accountant, Parkinson Cowan Ltd. 1959–62, Thorn Electronics Ltd. 1962–64; Sr. Cost Accountant, BBC 1964–67, Head, Cen. Finance Unit 1967, Chief Accountant, Cen. Finance Services 1969, Chief Accountant, BBC TV 1971, Controller, Finance 1976, Controller, Planning and Resource Man., BBC TV 1977, Dir. of Resources, BBC TV 1982, Deputy Dir.-Gen. BBC 1985–87, Dir.-Gen. Feb. 1987–; Dir. BBC Enterprises 1979 (Chair. 1986–87); Dir. Visnews 1980–85; Vice-Pres. RTS 1985–; Fellow 1987–; Pres. Commonwealth Broadcasting Assn. 1987–88. *Leisure interests:* sport, music, travel. *Address:* Orchard Cottage, Park Lane, Maplehurst, West Sussex, RH13 6LL (Home); British Broadcasting Corporation, Broadcasting House, London, W1A 1AA, England (Office).

CHEDID, Andrée, B.A.; French (b. Egyptian) writer; b. 20 March 1920, Cairo; d. of Selim Saab and Alice K. Haddad; m. Louis A. Chedid 1942; one s. one d.; ed. French schools, Cairo and Paris, American Univ. in Cairo; b. into family of Lebanese origin; has lived in Paris since 1946; Prix Louise Labé 1966, L'aigle d'or de la poésie 1972, Grand Prix des Lettres Françaises de l'Académie Royale de Belgique 1975, Prix de l'Afrique Méditerranéenne 1975, Prix de l'Académie Mallarmé 1976, Prix Goncourt for short story 1979; Chevalier, Légion d'honneur; Commandeur des Arts et des Lettres. *Publications:* poetry: Fraternité de la parole 1975, Epreuves du vivant 1983, Textes pour un pèome 1949–1970; novels: Le Sommeil délivré 1952, Le Sixième Jour 1960, L'Autre 1969, Nefertiti et le rêve d'Akhnaton 1974, La Maison sans racines 1985; plays: Bérénice d'Egypte, Les Nombres, Le Montreur 1981, Echec à la Reine 1984; essays, children's books, short stories. *Leisure interest:* collages. *Address:* c/o Flammarion, 26 rue Racine, 75006 Paris, France. *Telephone:* 40.51.31.00.

CHEEK, James Edward, PH.D.; American university president; b. 4 Dec. 1932, Roanoke Rapids, N.C.; s. of late King Virgil Cheek and Lee Ella (Williams) Cheek; m. Celestine J. Williams 1953; one s. one d.; ed. Shaw Univ., Raleigh, N.C., Colgate-Rochester Divinity School, Drew Univ., Madison, N.J.; Teaching Asst. in Historical Theology, Drew Theological School, Madison, N.J. 1959–60; Instructor in Western History, Union Junior Coll., Cranford, N.J. 1959–61; Asst. Prof. of New Testament and Historical Theology, Virginia Union Univ. 1961–63; Pres. Shaw Univ. 1963–69; Pres. Howard Univ., Washington, D.C. July 1969–; Dir. James S. Brady Presidential Foundation, First American Bank, N.A., Nat. Asscn. for Equal Opportunity in Higher Educ., Nat. Capital Area Council, Boy

Scouts of America, Nat. Permanent Federal Savings and Loan Asscn., UNA Bd. and Advisory Cttee.; Trustee, Washington Center for Metropolitan Studies, etc.; Bd. of Dirs., Public Broadcasting Service; Bd. of Trustees, Fisk Univ. and New York Inst. of Tech.; professional memberships include American Soc. of Church History, American Asscn. of Univ. Profs., American Acad. of Religion; mem. numerous advisory boards and cttees.; Pres. Medal of Freedom 1983; numerous honorary degrees. *Address:* Howard University, 2400 Sixth Street, Washington, D.C. 20059; 8035 16th Street, N.W., Washington, D.C. 20012, U.S.A. (Home).

CHÉHAB, Emir Maurice; Lebanese archaeologist and historian; b. 1904; s. of Emir Hafez; m. Olga Choribane 1945; two s. three d.; ed. Univ. St. Joseph, Beirut, Ecole du Louvre, and Ecole des Hautes Etudes Historiques, Paris; Conservator Lebanese Nat. Museum 1928; Chief of Antiquities Service 1937, Dir. 1944; Prof. Lebanese History, Ecole Normale and Gen. Diplomatic History, Ecole des Sciences Politiques 1945; Prof. of Oriental Archaeology, Inst. of Oriental Literature 1946; Prof., Ancient History, Univ. of Lebanon 1953–59; Dir. Tyre and Anjar Excavations 1950; Curator of Lebanese Antiquities, Nat. Museum of Lebanon 1953–59, Gen. Dir. 1959. *Address:* Direction des Antiquités, rue de Damas, Beirut, Lebanon.

CHEKARIN, Yevgeniv Mikhailovich; DR. PHIL. SC.; Soviet civil servant; b. 1924; ed. Moscow Law Inst.; asst. to regional procurator, Kozelsk 1949–52; mem. CPSU 1950–; Soviet Army 1941–43; sr lecturer, Deputy Dean, Moscow Law Inst. 1952–54; sr lecturer, Deputy Sec., Sec. of party cttee. of Moscow Univ. 1954–59; Sec., Second, then First Sec. of Leninsky Regional Cttee., Moscow 1959–62; Deputy, First Deputy, and head of section of CPSU Cen. Cttee. 1962–72; Rector of CPSU Cen. Cttee. Higher Party School 1972–78; U.S.S.R. Deputy Minister of Culture 1978–83; Deputy Pres. of RSFSR Council of Mins. 1983–; Pres. of Presidium of Cen. Cttee. of All-Union Society for Protection of Monuments of History and Culture 1984–; cand. mem. of CPSU Cen. Cttee. 1986–; Pres. of U.S.S.R. Acad. of Sciences Council on Problems of Russian Culture, July 1987–. *Address:* The Kremlin, Moscow, U.S.S.R.

CHEKANAUSKAS, Vitautas Algirdo; Soviet-Lithuanian architect; b. 1930, Šiauliai, Lithuania; ed. Lithuanian Art Inst., Vilnius; has designed exhibition pavilion in Vilnius 1967, and residential Dists. in Vilnius 1967–72, and other projects; Lenin Prize 1974, People's Architect of U.S.S.R. 1975. *Address:* Lithuanian S.S.R. State Arts Institute, Ul. Tiesos 6, Vilnius, Lithuanian S.S.R., U.S.S.R.

CHELI, Giovanni, M.THEOL., D.CN.L.; Italian ecclesiastic; b. 4 Oct. 1918, Turin; ed. Pontifical Lateran Univ., Pontifical Acad. for Diplomacy; ordained Roman Catholic priest 1942; Second Sec., Apostolic Nunciature in Guatemala 1952–55, First Sec., Madrid 1955–62; Counsellor, Nunciature in Rome 1962–67; served Council for Public Affairs of the Church, Vatican City 1967–73; Perm. Observer to UN 1973–86; Archbishop of Santa Giusta (Apostolic Nuncio), Sardinia 1978–; Pro-Pres. of the Pontifical Comm. for Migrations and Tourism, Vatican City 1986–; Kt. Commdr. Orden de Isabel la Católica (Spain), Ordine al Merito della Repubblica Italiana, Verdienstkreuz der Bundesrepublik Deutschland (Fed. Repub. of Germany). *Publications:* L'applicazione delle Riforme Tridentine nella diocesi di Asti 1952. *Leisure interests:* tennis, mountain climbing, reading, listening to classical music. *Address:* Pontifical Commission for Migrations and Tourism, Vatican City, Italy. *Telephone:* (06) 6987131.

CHELIDZE, Otar Silovanovich; Soviet author and poet; b. 8 Sept. 1929, Tbilisi, Georgia; ed. Univ. of Tbilisi; mem. CPSU 1958–; Gorky Inst. of Literature 1950–54; first works published 1943. *Publications include:* The Death of a Blacksmith, Ballad of a Tiger, The Second Hand, The Root, My Magnetic Field, Amirangora. *Address:* U.S.S.R. Union of Writers, ulitsa Vorovskogo 52, Moscow, U.S.S.R.

CHEN AILIAN; Chinese dancer and choreographer; b. 24 Dec. 1939, Shanghai; m. Weid Daoning; ed. China's Dance School; performed in northern Europe 1961; won four gold medals as a traditional dancer at 8th World Youth Festival in Helsinki 1962; in political disgrace during Cultural Revolution 1966–77; Choreographer, Guangdong Song and Dance Theater 1985–; mem. Nat. Cttee. 6th CPPCC 1986. *Address:* Guangdong Song and Dance Theater, Guangzhou, People's Republic of China.

CHEN BAICHEN; Chinese dramatist; b. 2 March 1908, Huaiyin Co., Jiangsu Prov.; ed. Shanghai Nanguo Art Coll.; joined CCP 1950; Sec. Chinese Writer's Asscn. 1956–60; Vice-Chair. Chinese Writers' Asscn. 1960–66; in political disgrace during Proletarian Cultural Revolutionary 1966–78; rehabilitated 1978; Vice-Chair. Chinese Dramatists' Asscn. 1982–; mem. China PEN Center 1983–. *Publications:* Plays: Taiping Heavenly Kingdom 1936–41, Hurricane Song 1980. *Address:* 141-2, Daqing Road, Nanjing City, People's Republic of China.

CHEN BANGZHU; Chinese party and government official; b. 1934, Jiujiang City, Jiangxi Prov.; Vice-Gov. Hunan Prov. 1984–86; Alt. mem. CCP Cen. Cttee. 1987–. *Address:* Central Committee of the Chinese Communist Party, Zhongnanhai, Beijing, People's Republic of China.

CHEN BIAO; Chinese astronomer; b. 26 Nov. 1923; researcher, Zijinshan (Purple Mountain) Observatory, Nanjing 1962–82; mem. Academic Degrees Cttee., Academia Sinica 1981–; Dir. Yunnan Observatory, Kunming 1983–;

mem. Dept. of Math. and Physics, Academia Sinica 1985–. *Address:* 71 Beijingdonglu, Nanjing, People's Republic of China.

CHEN BIN; Chinese politician; b. 1919, Sichuan; Minister, Comm. of Science, Tech. and Industry for Nat. Defence 1982–85; mem. 12th Cen. Cttee. CCP 1982–87; mem. Leading Group for Scientific Work under the State Council 1983–; mem. Cen. Advisory Comm. 1987–. *Address:* c/o State Council, Beijing, People's Republic of China.

CHEN BOJIAN; Chinese government official; b. 1922; Deputy Dir.-Gen. Xinhua News Agency, Beijing 1982–84; Deputy Dir. Hong Kong Br. of Xinhua 1984–. *Address:* New China News Agency, Kowloon, Hong Kong.

CHEN, Char-Nie, M.B., M.SC., D.P.M., F.R.S.M., F.R.C. PSYCH.; British university professor and college principal; b. 19 July 1938, Fukien Prov., China; s. of the late Kam-Heng Chen and of Mei-Ai Chen-Hsu; m. Chou-May Chien 1970; one s. two d.; ed. Nat. Taiwan Univ. and Univ. Coll., London; Rotating Intern, Nat. Taiwan Univ. Hosp. 1964–65, Resident, Dept. of Neurology and Psychiatry 1965–68; Sr. House Officer, Morgannwg Hosp., Wales 1968–69; Registrar, St. George's Hosp. Medical School, London 1969–71, Lecturer, Hon. Sr. Registrar 1971–72, 1973–78, Sr. Lecturer, Hon. Consultant Psychiatrist 1978–80; Prof. and Chair., Dept. of Psychiatry, Chinese Univ. of Hong Kong 1981–, mem. Univ. Senate 1981–, Head, Shaw Coll. 1987–; mem. Univ. Council 1987–; mem. Coll. Council, Hong Kong Baptist Coll. 1984–; Pres. Hong Kong Psychiatric Asscn. 1982–84, Hong Kong Soc. of Neurosciences 1983–84, 1988–89; Exec. Chair., Hong Kong Mental Health Asscn. 1983–; Pres., Pacific Rim Coll. of Psychiatrists 1988–90; Fellow of the Royal Australian and New Zealand Coll. of Psychiatrists; mem. British Medical Assen. 1979–; Visiting Prof., St. George's Hosp. Medical School, London 1984. *Publications:* over 30 scientific papers. *Leisure interests:* reading, travelling, good food. *Address:* Flat 8B, University Residence No. 9, The Chinese University of Hong Kong, Shatin, New Territories, Hong Kong. *Telephone:* (0) 604-5201.

CHEN CHI-LU, PH.D.; Chinese university professor and government official; b. 27 April 1923, Tainan City; s. of Chen Peng and Chen Cheng Shiu-Ming; m. Chen Chang-Jo; four s.; ed. St. John's Univ., Shanghai, Univs. of New Mexico, London and Tokyo; Research Asst. to Prof., then Head, Dept. of Archaeology and Anthropology, Nat. Taiwan Univ. 1949–69; Curator, Dept. of Anthropology, Taiwan Museum 1958–63; Visiting Prof. Michigan State Univ. 1969–70; Dir. Inst. of American Culture, Academia Sinica 1974–77; Dean, Coll. of Liberal Arts, Nat. Taiwan Univ. 1975–77; Deputy Sec.-Gen. Cen. Cttee., Kuomintang 1975–77; Minister of State 1977–81; Chair. Council for Cultural Planning and Devt., Exec. Yuan 1981; Prof. Coll. of Liberal Arts, Nat. Taiwan Univ. 1981–; mem. Academia Sinica. *Publications:* Woodcarving of the Paiwan Group of Taiwan 1961, Formosan Aboriginal Art, The Art of Paiwan Group of Southern Taiwan 1962, Material Culture of Formosan Aborigines 1968, The Aboriginal Art of Taiwan and Implication for the Cultural History of the Pacific 1972, Anthropological Studies in the Republic of China during the last three decades 1980, People and Culture 1981, over 170 books and articles. *Leisure interests:* calligraphy, painting. *Address:* 102 Ai-Kuo East Road, Taipei (Office); 7 Lane 52, Wenchow Street, Taipei, Taiwan (Home). *Telephone:* 3920059 (Office); 3512594 (Home).

CHEN DANQING; Chinese artist; b. 1953, Guangdong; self-taught; ed. Cen. Acad. of Fine Arts; lecturer, Cen. Acad. of Fine Arts. *Address:* Central Academy of Fine Arts, Beijing, People's Republic of China.

CHEN DUAN; Chinese diplomatist; Amb. to Mauritius 1985–. *Address:* Embassy of the People's Republic of China, Royal Road, Belle Rose, Quatre Bornes, Port Louis, Mauritius.

CHEN DUN; Chinese government official; Vice-Minister for Coal 1985–. *Address:* Ministry of Coal Industry, Beijing, People's Republic of China.

CHEN FANG; Chinese artist; b. 1957, Canton; lecturer Canton Univ. 1987–. *Address:* Canton University, Canton, Guangdong Province, People's Republic of China.

CHEN FUHAN; Chinese railway worker and trades union official; mem. 11th CCP Cen. Cttee. 1977; Deputy for Beijing Municipality to 5th NPC 1978; Vice-Chair. Railway Workers' Union 1978–; mem. Revolutionary Cttee. Beijing 1979; mem. 12th CCP Cen. Cttee. 1982–87. *Address:* Chinese Railway Workers' Union, Beijing, People's Republic of China.

CHEN GANG; Chinese composer; b. 1935; ed. Shanghai Music Conservatory. *Compositions include:* Liang Shanbo and Zhu Yingtai, Morning on the Miao Mountains. *Address:* Shanghai Music Conservatory, Shanghai, People's Republic of China.

CHEN GUANGYI; Chinese government official; b. 7 Aug. 1933, Putain City, Fujian; s. of Chen Zhao He and Li Mu Xin; m. Chen Xiu Yun 1961; two s. one d.; ed. China Northeast Industry Univ.; engineer, then section chief, div. chief, deputy Dir. Baiying Nonferrous Metal Industry Co., Gansu; mem. Gansu Metallurgy Industry Bureau, Gansu Prov. Planning Cttee.; Gov. of Gansu Prov. 1983–; elected mem. of Cen. Cttee. of CCP Sept. 1985; Sec. CCP Cttee., Fujian 1986–. *Address:* Office of the Provincial Governor, 1 Central Square, Lanzhou, Gansu Province, People's Republic of China. *Telephone:* 25941.

CHEN GUODONG; Chinese government official; b. 1911, Hunan; leading figure, Baoji (Shaanxi) Mil. Control Comm. 1949; Dir. Finance Dept., E. China Cttee. of Financial and Econ. Affairs 1949–50; mem. Cttee. of Financial and Econ. Affairs, E. China Mil. and Admin. Council and concurrently Dir. of its Finance Dept. 1950–52; mem. E. China Cttee. on Org. 1950; Dir. E. China Cttee. for Regulating and Distribution of Goods in Storage 1950; mem. E. China Cttee. for Govt. Offices Production Man. 1952; Vice-Minister of Finance, E. China Cttee. 1952–53; Vice-Minister of Food 1953; Sec. Leading Party Members' Group of CCP Cttee., Ministry of Food 1957; head, team of leading party members in rectification movement conducted in ministry 1957; mem. Cen. Famine Relief Cttee., for Nat. Conf. of Reps. of Outstanding Groups and Individuals in Culture and Educ. 1960, mem. Pres. of that Conf. 1960; mem. Presidium CCP 11th Nat. Congress 1977–; mem. CCP 11th Cen. Cttee. 1977–; Dir., All-China Fed. of Supply and Marketing Co-operatives 1978–79; Minister of Food 1979–80; First Sec. CCP Shanghai 1980–85, Chair. Advisory Comm. 1985–; mem. 12th Cen. Cttee. CCP 1982–85, Cen. Advisory Comm. 1982–; First Political Commr., Shanghai Garrison Dist. 1980–. *Address:* People's Republic of China.

CHEN HANSENG; Chinese economist; b. 5 Feb. 1897, Wuxi, Jiangsu Province; m. Gu Shuxing 1922; ed. Germany and U.S.A.; fmr. History Prof., Beijing Univ.; Head, World History Inst., Chinese Acad. of Social Sciences; after war became Prof. Washington State Univ. until return to China 1951; Vice-Pres. Chinese People's Inst. of Foreign Affairs 1951–66; Vice-Pres. Sino-Indian Friendship Assen. 1952–66; Del. for Hebei Province to the Nat. People's Congress 1954, 1958, and 1964; Deputy Dir. of Research, Inst. of Int. Relations 1956–66; Vice-Chair. of Editorial Bd. China Reconstructs 1952–66; Chair. Chinese Soc. for Central Asian Studies 1979–; Consultant, Chinese Acad. of Social Sciences 1977–83; Visiting Prof. Beijing Univ.; mem. Chinese People's Nat. Assembly for Political Consultation 1978–83; Hon. Pres. Research Inst. for World History 1983–. *Publications:* The Agrarian Regions of India and Pakistan 1959, Historical Data for the Study of Chinese Coolies Abroad 1980, Foreign Industrial Capital and the Chinese Tobacco Producers 1984, Collected Essays 1984; Foreign Industrial Capital and the Chinese Peasant 1984, Selected Essays 1985; articles on agrarian problems in various Chinese and foreign periodicals. *Leisure interest:* music. *Address:* Apt. 106, Bldg. 24, Fuxingmenwai Dajie, Beijing, People's Republic of China. *Telephone:* Beijing 36.1260.

CHEN HEQIAO, Maj.-Gen.; Chinese army officer; b. 1914, Huoqui Co., Anhui Prov.; joined Red Army 1932; made Maj.-Gen. PLA 1955; Commdr. 2nd Artillery Corps, PLA 1978; Political Commissar 2nd Artillery Corps, PLA 1981; mem. Standing Comm. 6th NPC 1983–, Overseas Chinese Comm. NPC 1986; Deputy Head China-Cape Verde Friendship Group 1986–. *Address:* People's Liberation Army Headquarters, Beijing, People's Republic of China.

CHEN HUANGMEI; Chinese literary critic; b. 23 Dec. 1913, Shanghai; s. of Bochao Chen and Youqing Zhang; m. Zhang Xin 1941; three d.; Cttee. mem. Fed. of Literature and Art since 1949; Deputy Dir., then Dir. of Film Bureau and Vice-Minister of Culture 1953–65; work suspended 1966–75; Deputy Dir. Research Inst. of Literature of Chinese Acad. of Social Sciences 1978–80; Vice-Chair. Chinese Writers' Assen. 1979–; Adviser to Ministry of Culture 1982–; Chair. Academic Cttee. of China Film Art Research Centre 1984–; Vice-Pres. of China P.E.N. Centre 1983–. *Publications include:* selections of short stories, prose, literary criticisms, film theses. *Leisure interest:* reading literary works. *Address:* Ministry of Culture, 2 N Shatan Street, Beijing, People's Republic of China. *Telephone:* 44-5668.

CHEN HUIGUANG; Chinese politician; b. 1939, Yulin City, Guangxi; fmr. engineer; ed. Guangxi Inst. of Coal Mining; Dongluo Mining Bureau, Guangxi, successively, Engineer, Mining Technician, Head of Production Section, Deputy Head and Head 1961–; Sec. CCP Municipal Cttee., Nanning 1983–85; Deputy Sec. CCP Cttee., Guangxi 1983–85, (Leading) Sec. 1985–; mem. 12th CCP Cen. Cttee. 1985–. *Address:* Guangxi Provincial Chinese Communist Party, Nanning, Guangxi, People's Republic of China.

CHEN JIDE; Chinese soldier; Political Commissar, Hubei PLA Mil. Dist. 1978–81; Dir. Political Dept., PLA Guangzhou Mil. Region 1981–. *Address:* Commissar's Office, Hubei Military District, People's Republic of China.

CHEN JING; Chinese bodybuilder and cycle acrobat; b. Sichuan Prov.; m.; Chengdu Acrobatic Troupe; women's nat. all-round individual body bldg. champion 1986. *Address:* China Sports Federation, Beijing, People's Republic of China.

CHEN JINGRUN; Chinese mathematician; b. 22 May 1933, Fujian Prov.; ed. Xiamen Univ.; researcher, Academia Sinica 1957–; Deputy for Tianjin Municipality to 5th NPC 1978; won First-Class Award for natural science in China 1982; Deputy for Fujian Prov. to 6th NPC 1983; Dept. of Math. and Physics, Academia Sinica 1985–. *Address:* Room 408, Bldg. 803, Huangzhuang, Haidian, Beijing 100080, People's Republic of China. *Telephone:* 283064 (Beijing).

CHEN JUNSHENG; Chinese government official; b. 1927; Sec. Gen. State Council 1985–88; Sec. CCP Cttee. of Cen. State Organs 1986–; Head Leading Group for Econ. Devt. in Poor Areas 1986–; mem. 13th CCP Cen.

Cttee. 1987–; State Councillor 1988–. *Address:* Office of the Secretary-General, State Council, Beijing, People's Republic of China.

CHEN KAIGE; Chinese film director; b. 1954, Beijing; ed. Beijing Cinema Coll.; worker, rubber plantation, Yunnan; soldier for four years. *Films include:* The Yellow Earth (Best Film, Berlin Film Festival). *Address:* Beijing Cinema College, Beijing, People's Republic of China.

CHEN LEI; Chinese politician; b. 1917; Council mem. People's Govt., Heilongjiang Prov. 1950; Sec.-Gen. CCP Cttee., Heilongjiang 1950; Vice-Gov. Heilongjiang 1958; Dir. Industry Dept., CCP Cttee., Heilongjiang 1959, Alt. Sec. CCP Cttee. 1964; Vice-Chair. Provincial Revolutionary Cttee., Heilongjiang 1977–79; Sec. CCP Cttee., Heilongjiang 1978–85; Vice-Gov. Heilongjiang 1979–80, Gov. 1980–85; mem. 12th CCP Cen. Cttee. 1982–87; mem. Cen. Advisory Comm. 1987–. *Address:* Office of the Provincial Governor, Harbin, Heilongjiang, People's Republic of China.

CHEN LI-AN, PH.D.; Chinese government official; b. 22 June 1937, Chingtien County, Chekiang; m. four s.; one d.; ed. Mass. Inst. of Tech. and New York Univ.; Eng. Honeywell Co., U.S.A. 1960–63; Prof. City Univ. of New York 1968–70; Pres Ming Chi Inst. of Tech. 1970–72; Dir. Dept. of Technological and Vocational Educ., Ministry of Educ. 1972–74; Pres, Nat. Taiwan Inst. of Tech. 1974–77; Vice-Minister, Ministry of Educ. 1977–78; Dir. Dept. of Org. Affairs, Cen. Cttee., Kuomintang 1979–80; Deputy Sec.-Gen. Cen. Cttee., Kuomintang 1980–84; Chair. Nat. Science Council, Exec. Yuan 1984–. *Address:* National Science Council, Executive Yuan, Taipei, Taiwan.

CHEN LUZHI; Chinese diplomatist; Amb. to Iceland 1984–87. *Address:* Ministry of Foreign Affairs, Beijing, People's Republic of China.

CHEN MINGYI, Maj.-Gen.; Chinese soldier and party official; b. 1917, Shancheng Co., Henan Prov.; joined Red Army 1931; joined CCP 1933; Gen. Staff Red 4th Front Army 1937; Commdr. Repair and Reconstruction HQ, Sikang-Tibet Highway 1954; Commdr. Rear Forces PLA Tibet Mil. Region 1955; Deputy Commdr. Tibet Mil. Region 1955–67; Deputy Commdr. Mil. Dist. Tibet 1955–71, Commdr. 1971–75; Maj. Gen. PLA 1957; mem. 3rd NPC Oct. 1964; Tibet Autonomous Region 1965–; Vice-Chair. Tibet Autonomous Region Revolutionary Cttee. 1968–75; Sec. Tibet Prov. CCP Cttee. 1971–75; Sichuan Prov. Revolutionary Cttee. 1977; Deputy Commdr. Chengdu Mil. Region 1978–85; alt. mem. CCP Cen. Cttee. 1987–. *Address:* Central Committee of the Chinese Communist Party, Zhongnanhai, Beijing, People's Republic of China.

CHEN MINGYUAN; Chinese linguist, computer scientist and poet; b. 5 Jan. 1941, Chongqing, Sichuan Prov.; s. of Chen Zaiwen and Shu Xiuhua; m. Guan Tinglu 1968; one s. one d.; ed. Shanghai High School, Shanghai Science and Tech. Univ.; Researcher, Electronics Inst. and Acoustics Inst., Academia Sinica, Beijing 1963–68; falsely charged with forging "Chairman Mao's Poems" and was branded a "counter-revolutionary" during the Cultural Revolution and in a labour-camp, 1968–77; rehabilitated, 1978; Researcher, Acoustics Inst., Academia Sinica 1978–81; Researcher, Committee for Reform Written Language of China, 1981–82; Lecturer, Beijing Languages Inst. 1982–; Special Correspondent of "RENWU" magazine, 1986–; Prof., Research Inst. of Buddhist Culture of China 1987–; Dir. Chinese Poetry Soc. 1987–; Vice-Pres. Beijing Poetry Assen. 1988–. *Publications:* On the Reform of Chinese Characters 1966, Poetry: Bloody Flowers 1976, Chinese Characters encoding 1978, Information Processing of Chinese Language 1981, Linguistics and Modern Science 1983, Rudiments of Chinese Phonetics 1984, Chinese Through Listening, Vol. 1-4 1984–86, Elementary Aural Comprehension 1986. *Poetry:* Underground grasses 1986, Chinese Onomastics 1987, Selected Poems of Chen Mingyuan 1988, and numerous articles on modern linguistics, teaching Chinese as a second language, reminiscences of Guo Moruo and Tian Han, cultural exchange between China and West, and has a patent on keyboard for Chinese information processing. *Leisure interests:* philately, music, photography. *Address:* Room 605, Building 919, Zhong Guan Cun, Beijing 100086, People's Republic of China.

CHEN MINZHANG; Chinese government official; Vice-Minister of Public Health 1984–87, Minister 1987–; alt. mem. 13th CCP Cen. Cttee. 1987–; Vice-Pres. Chinese Medical Assen. 1984–89, Pres. Feb. 1989–. *Address:* Ministry of Public Health, Beijing, People's Republic of China.

CHEN MUHUA; Chinese government and party official; b. 1920, Qinytian Co., Zhejiang Prov.; ed. Shanghai Jiatong Univ.; mem. 10th Cen. Cttee. of CCP 1973; Minister for Econ. Relations with Foreign Countries 1977–82, also in charge of the State Family Planning Comm. 1981–82, Minister of Foreign Trade 1982–85, a Vice-Premier 1978–82; Pres. People's Bank of China 1985–88; Dir. State Treasury Aug. 1985–; Chair. Council, People's Bank of China June 1985; alt. mem. Politburo, 11th Cen. Cttee. 1977–; Head Population Census Leading Group 1979–; mem. 12th CCP Cen. Cttee. 1982–87, 13th CCP Cen. Cttee. 1987–; State Councillor 1982–; Chair. Cen. Patriotic Sanitation Campaign Cttee. Cen. Cttee. 1981–; Chinese Gov. World Bank 1985–88, Asian Devt. Bank 1986–; Hon. Pres. Int. Econ. Cooperation Soc. 1983–, Florists' Assen. 1984–; Vice-Chair. NPC 7th Standing Cttee. 1988–; Pres. All-China Women's Fed. 1988–. *Address:* Standing Committee, National People's Congress, Tian Anmen Square, Beijing, People's Republic of China.

CHEN PEIQIU; Chinese artist; b. 1922, Nanyang, Henan; m. Xie Zhiliu; ed. S.W. Union Univ., Kunming, Nat. Coll. of Art. *Works include:* Lacebark Pine and Japanese Paradise Flycatcher, The Lotus Pond, Egret and Willow, Early Spring. *Address:* c/o National College of Art, Beijing, People's Republic of China.

CHEN PIXIAN; Chinese government official, b. 20 March 1916, Shanghang Co., Fujian Province; Secretary Children's Bureau CCP Cen. Cttee.; Sec. S. Jiangsu Provincial Cttee. Communist Youth League 1935; with Ts'ai Hui-wen Commdr. S. Jiangxi Mil. Dist.; Sec. and Deputy Sec. CCP Border Dist. Special Cttee. 1935; mem. CCP S. Jiangxi Dist. Special Cttee. 1936; Sec. CCP Cen. Jiangsu Dist. Cttee. 1937; Responsible Officer N. Jiangsu Army Corps. 1948; mem. Cen. Cttee. New Democratic Youth League 1949–53; Sec. CCP S. Jiangsu Dist. Cttee. 1949–52; Political Commissar, PLA, S. Jiangsu Mil. Dist. 1949–52; mem. E. China Mil. and Admin. Cttee. 1950–53; mem. S. Jiangsu Admin. Office 1950–52; Chair. Financial and Econ. Cttee. S. Jiangsu Admin. Office 1951–52; Fourth Sec. E. China Bureau CCP Cen. Cttee. 1952–54; Fourth Sec. CCP Shanghai Municipal Cttee. 1952–54; mem. E. China Admin. Cttee. 1953–54; Sec. Secr. CCP Shanghai Municipal Cttee. 1954–55; mem. Shanghai Municipal Fed. of Trades Unions 1955; mem. Shanghai Municipal People's Council 1955; Second Sec., Secr. CCP Shanghai Municipal Cttee. 1955–56; Sec. Secr. CCP Shanghai Municipal Cttee. 1956–65; mem. Exec. Cttee. China Welfare Inst. 1956; alt. mem. CCP 8th Cen. Cttee. 1956; Vice-Pres. Shanghai Branch Sino-Soviet Friendship Assen. 1957; Chair. Shanghai Municipal Cttee. CPPCC 1958; Political Commissar PLA, Shanghai Garrison HQ 1960; Sec. Secr., E. China Bureau CCP Cen. Cttee. 1964; mem. Pres. 4th Shanghai People's Political Consultative Conf. 1964; Chair. 4th Shanghai Municipal Cttee. CPPCC 1964; First Sec. CCP Shanghai Municipal Cttee. 1965–67; mem. Presidium 5th Shanghai People's Congress 1965; allegedly suppressed the Shanghai Worker Movement 1966; reportedly wrote a lengthy statement of confession 1967; tried by Shanghai workers at three televised struggles Dec. 1967, Mar. 1968, April 1968; mem. Presidium CCP 11th Nat. Congress 1977–; mem. CCP 11th Cen. Cttee. 1977; First Sec. Hubei CCP Prov. Cttee. 1978–83; Chair. People's Govt. (fmrly. Revolutionary Cttee.) 1978–79; First Political Commissar, Hubei Mil. Dist. 1978; Chair. Hubei People's Congress 1979; Political Commissar, Wuhan Mil. Region 1979–; Chair. Hubei People's Congress 1979–83; mem. and Sec. 12th Cen. Cttee. CCP 1982–87; Vice-Chair. Standing Cttee., 6th NPC 1983–, Sec.-Gen. Presidium 6th NPC 1986–; mem. Standing Cttee., Cen. Advisory Comm. 1987–. *Address:* Zongguo Gongchan Dang, Wuhan, Hubei Province, People's Republic of China.

CHEN PURU; Chinese politician; b. 1918, Boxin Co., Shandong Prov.; Chair. Zunyi Mil. Control Comm., Guizhou Prov. 1949; Dir. Industry and Commerce Dept., People's Govt., Guizhou 1950, Trade Dept. 1955; mem. Standing Cttee., CCP Cttee., Guizhou 1956; Vice-Gov. Guizhou 1957; Alt. mem. Secr., CCP Cttee., Guizhou 1960; Sec. CCP Cttee., Guizhou 1966–68; publicly denounced at least four times and disappeared 1968; Sec. CCP Cttee., Liaoning Prov. 1977–; Vice-Chair. Provincial Revolutionary Cttee., Liaoning 1977–80; mem. 11th Cen. Cttee. of CCP 1977–; Gov. Liaoning 1980–82; mem. 12th Cen. Cttee. CCP 1982–87; mem. Cen. Advisory Comm. 1987–; Minister of Railways 1982–85; Hon. Chair. China Regional Railways Assen. 1984–. *Address:* c/o Ministry of Railways, 10 Fuxing Road, Beijing, People's Republic of China.

CHEN RENHONG, Maj.-Gen.; Chinese army officer; b. 1917, Yanshan Co., Jiangxi Prov.; joined Red Army 1931, CCP 1932; Maj.-Gen. PLA forces in Tianjin 1962; cadre of the State Council 1970; cadre of Ministry of Public Health 1972; Deputy Political Commissar, Beijing Mil. Region 1974; Political Commissar, Jinan Mil. Region 1978–83; mem. 12th CCP Cen. Cttee. 1982–87; mem. Cen. Advisory Comm. 1987–. *Address:* Central Committee of the Chinese Communist Party, Beijing, People's Republic of China.

CHEN SHAOWU; Chinese academic; Pres. Acad. of Traditional Chinese Medicine 1985–. *Address:* Academy of Traditional Chinese Medicine, Beijing, People's Republic of China.

CHEN SHULIANG; Chinese diplomatist; b. 5 June 1911; s. of Chen Zen Hua and Jin Yang; m. Kang Dai Sha 1946; one s. one d.; Asst. Dir. Asia Dept., Ministry of Foreign Affairs 1950–51, Deputy Dir. 1955–57, Dir. 1957–62; Counsellor, Embassy, Indonesia 1952–55; Amb. to Cambodia 1962–67, to Romania 1979–82; Leader, Inst. of Int. Studies 1973–78; Vice-Pres. China-Romania Friendship Assen. 1984–. *Leisure interests:* literature, sports. *Address:* Ministry of Foreign Affairs, Beijing, People's Republic of China.

CHEN SONGLU; Chinese diplomatist; Amb. to the Philippines 1984–. *Address:* Embassy of the People's Republic of China, Manila, Philippines.

CHEN SUZHI; Chinese party and government official; b. 1931, Liaoning; ed. Liaoning Univ.; joined the CCP 1949; factory dir. 1978; Vice-Gov. Liaoning in charge of industrial work 1982; alt. mem. 12th CCP Cen. Cttee. 1982–87, 13th Cen. Cttee. 1987–; mem. Standing Cttee. CCP Prov. Cttee. Liaoning 1982–; Chair. Liaoning Prov. Trade Union Council 1983–. *Address:* Liaoning Trade Union Offices, Shenyang, People's Republic of China.

CHEN WEIDA; Chinese government official; native of Zhejiang; mem. Standing Cttee. CCP Zhejiang Prov. Cttee. 1957; Vice-Gov. Zhejiang 1958-64; mem. Pres. First Nat. Games 1959; Sec. CCP Zhejiang Provincial Cttee. 1960; mem. 11th Cen. Cttee. CCP 1977-; First Political Commissar, PLA Tianjin Garrison Dist. 1978-; Chair. Tianjin Municipal People's Govt. Cttee. (fmrly. Revolutionary Cttee.) 1978-79; First Sec. Tianjin CCP Cttee. 1978-84; mem. 12th Cen. Cttee. CCP 1982-85, Cen. Advisory Cttee. 1985-; Deputy Sec.-Gen. Comm. of Political Science and Law 1985-.

CHEN WEIQIANG; b. 1958, Shiling Co., Guangdong Prov.; Chinese weightlifter; equalled 52 kg. world junior record 1976; winner 60 kilogram div., Weightlifting, 1984 Olympics. *Address:* Chinese Sports Federation, Beijing, People's Republic of China.

CHEN XIEYANG; Chinese orchestral conductor; b. 4 May 1939, Shanghai; s. of Chen Dieyi and Liang Peiqiong; m. Wang Jianying 1973; ed. Music High School, Shanghai Conservatory; Conductor, Shanghai Ballet 1965-84; studied with Prof. Otto Mueller, Yale Univ., U.S.A. 1981-82; Conductor, Aspen Music Festival, Group for Contemporary Music, N.Y., Brooklyn Philharmonia, Honolulu Symphony, Philippines State Orchestra, Hong Kong Philharmonic, Shanghai Symphony Orchestra, Cen. Philharmonic, Beijing 1981-83, Symphony Orchestra of Vilnius, Kaunas, Novosibirsk, U.S.S.R. 1985, Tokyo Symphony Orchestra 1986; Music Dir. Shanghai Symphony Orchestra; has made recording for Kuklos CBE, France 1983; Dir., China Musicians' Assen.; Pres. Shanghai Symphonic Music Lovers' Soc.; Excellent Conducting Prize, Shanghai Music Festival 1986. *Leisure interest:* Beijing opera. *Address:* Shanghai Symphony Orchestra, 105 Hunan Road, Shanghai, People's Republic of China. *Telephone:* 373288; 521415.

CHEN XILIAN, Col.-Gen.; Chinese army officer; b. 1915, Hong'an Co., Hubei; ed. Red Army Acad.; joined Red Army 1929, CCP 1930; Battalion Commdr. 1931-33; on Long March 1934-35; Regimental Commdr. 1937; Commdr. 3rd Army Corps, 2nd Field Army 1949; Mayor of Chongqing 1949; Commdr. of Artillery Force, People's Liberation Army 1951; Gen. 1955; Alt. mem. 8th Cen. Cttee. of CCP 1956; Commdr. Shenyang Mil. Region, PLA 1959-73; Sec. of N.E. Bureau, CCP 1963-67; Chair. Liaoning Revolutionary Cttee. 1968; mem. Politburo, 9th Cen. Cttee. of CCP 1969, Politburo, 10th Cen. Cttee. 1973; First Sec. CCP Liaoning 1971-73; Commdr. Beijing Mil. Region, PLA 1974-80; a Vice-Premier State Council 1975-80; mem. Politburo, 11th Cen. Cttee. of CCP 1977-80, mem. Mil. Comm. CCP Cen. Cttee. 1978-80.; lost all posts Feb. 1980; mem. Standing Cttee., Mil. Comm., Cen. Cttee. CCP 1981, Standing Comm. Cen. Advisory Cttee. 1982-. *Address:* People's Republic of China.

CHEN XITONG; Chinese politician; b. 1930, Anyue Co., Sichuan; ed. Beijing Univ.; joined CCP 1930; Sec. Beijing CCP Cttee. 1981-; Dir. Beijing Planning and Construction Cttee. 1983-; Mayor Beijing 1983; mem. 13th CCP Cen. Cttee. 1987-; State Councillor 1988-. *Address:* Office of the Mayor, Beijing, People's Republic of China.

CHEN YI; Chinese musical composer and violinist; b. 4 April 1953; m. Zhou Long 1983; *Works:* Budding string concerto. *Address:* Central Conservatory of Music, Beijing, People's Republic of China.

CHEN YING; Chinese army officer; Deputy Political Commissar, PLA Gen. Logistics Dept. 1981-84; alt. mem. 12th CCP Cen. Cttee. 1982-87; Chair. 1990 Asian Games Organizing Cttee. 1985-. *Address:* General Logistics Department of the People's Liberation Army, Beijing, People's Republic of China.

CHEN YUN; Chinese politician; b. 1905, Qingbu Co., Jiangsu; m. Yu Ruomu; three s. two d.; joined CCP 1925; Trade Union activist 1925-27; mem. 6th Cen. Cttee. of CCP 1931; on Long March 1934-35; Deputy Dir. Org. Dept., CCP 1937, Dir. 1943; Dir. Peasants Dept., CCP 1939; mem. 7th Cen. Cttee. of CCP 1945; Vice-Premier, State Council 1949-75, 1978-80; Minister of Heavy Industry 1949-50; Sec., Secr. of Cen. Cttee., CCP 1954; Vice-Chair. CCP 1956-69; mem. Standing Cttee., Politburo of CCP 1956-69, 1978-87; Minister of Commerce 1956-58; Chair. State Capital Construction Comm. 1958-61; mem. 9th Cen. Cttee. of CCP 1969, 10th Cen. Cttee. 1973, 11th Cen. Cttee. 1977, 12th Cen. Cttee. 1982; First Sec. Cen. Cttee. for Inspecting Discipline 1979-87; Chair. Financial and Econ. Comm. State Council 1979-81; Vice-Chair. CCP 11th Cen. Cttee. 1979-81; mem. Standing Cttee. CCP 12th Cen. Cttee. 1982-87; Chair. Cen. Advisory Comm. 1987-. *Address:* People's Republic of China.

CHEN ZAIDAO, Col.-Gen.; Chinese army officer; b. 1909, Macheng Co., Hubei; guerrilla leader 1927; joined Red Army 1927, CCP 1928; Commdr. 4th Army 1934, 2nd Column, Cen. Plains Field Army 1944; Commdr. Henan Mil. District, People's Liberation Army 1949, Wuhan Mil. Region, PLA 1954-67; Gen. 1955; Leader of Wuhan Incident uprising (an anti-Maoist army revolt during Cultural Revolution, for which he was criticized and removed from office) 20 July 1967; Deputy Commdr. Fuzhou Mil. Region, PLA 1973; mem. Standing Cttee. 5th Nat. People's Congress 1978-83; Commdr. PLA Railway Corps. 1978-83; mem. Cen. Advisory Comm. 1982-87; Exec. Chair. 6th CPPCC Nat. Comm. 1983, Vice-Chair. 1983-. *Address:* People's Republic of China.

CHEN ZHAOBO; Chinese government official; Vice-Minister for Nuclear Industry 1984-. *Address:* Ministry of Nuclear Industry, Beijing, People's Republic of China.

CHEN ZHAOYUAN; Chinese diplomatist; b. 1918, Guangdong; Attaché Embassy, Sweden 1954; Deputy Dir. Int. Dept., Ministry of Foreign Affairs 1959-62; Chargé d'affaires, Embassy, India 1963-70; Amb. to Burma 1971-73, to Spain 1973-76, to India 1976-78, to U.K. 1983-85. *Address:* Ministry of Foreign Affairs, Beijing, People's Republic of China.

CHEN ZHI; Chinese musician; Head of Beijing Guitar Soc.; official at 1987 China Int. Guitar Festival, Guangdong. *Address:* Chinese Musicians' Association, Beijing, People's Republic of China.

CHEN ZHONGJING; Chinese academic; b. 1915; Dir. Inst. of Contemporary Int. Relations 1980-; Adviser, Ministry of State Security 1984-. *Address:* Chinese Academy of Social Sciences, Beijing, People's Republic of China.

CHEN ZHONGWEI; Chinese surgeon; b. 1 Oct. 1929, Hangzhou City, Zhejiang Prov.; ed. Shanghai Second Medical Coll.; succeeded in replanting the severed arm of a worker in Shanghai—the first operation of this kind in the world 1963; Chief of Orthopaedics Dept. of 6th People's Hosp. in Shanghai 1980-; Pres. of Int. Society of Reconstructive Microsurgery 1985-; Dir. Orthopaedics Dept. of Zhongshan Hospital, Shanghai 1985-. *Address:* 6th People's Hospital, Shanghai, People's Republic of China.

CHEN ZIZHUANG; Chinese artist; b. 1913, Yongchuan, Sichuan; studied under Qi Baishi and Huang Binhong.

CHEN ZUOHUANG, M.M., D.M.A.; Chinese orchestral conductor; b. 2 April 1947, Shanghai; s. of Chen Ru Hui and Li He Zhen; ed. Cen. Conservatory of Beijing, Univ. of Michigan; Musical Dir. China Film Philharmonic 1974-76; Assoc. Prof., Univ of Kansas, U.S.A. 1985-87; Prin. Conductor Cen. Philharmonic Orchestra of China 1987-. *Address:* The Central Philharmonic Orchestra, He Ping Li, Beijing, People's Republic of China. *Telephone:* 84-8770.

CHEN ZUOLIN; Chinese party and state official; Vice-Chair. Revolutionary Cttee., Zhejiang Prov. 1975-79; Deputy Sec. CCP Cttee., Zhejiang 1976, Sec. 1977-83; alt. mem. 11th CCP Cen. Cttee. 1977, 12th Cen. Cttee. 1982; Vice-Gov., Zhejiang 1979-83; Sec.-Gen. Comm. for Discipline Inspection 1985-87, Deputy Sec. 1987-. *Address:* Zhejiang Provincial People's Government, Hangzhou, Zhejiang, People's Republic of China.

CHENERY, Hollis Burnley, B.S., PH.D.; American economist; b. 6 Jan. 1918, Richmond, Virginia; s. of Christopher Chenery and Helen Bates; m. 1st Louise Seamster 1942 (dissolved); two d.; m. 2nd Mary Montgomery 1970; ed. Arizona, Oklahoma and Harvard Univs.; officer, U.S. Army Air Corps 1942-46; Economist, U.S. Econ. Co-operation Admin., Paris 1949-50; Head, Programme Div., U.S. Mutual Security Agency, Rome 1950-52; Econ. Consultant to Pakistan Govt. 1955, Japanese Govt. 1957-61, Bank of Israel 1959-61, Bank of Sicily 1961, Govt. of South Korea 1970; Prof. of Econs., Stanford Univ. 1952-61; Asst. Admin. for Program, Agency for Int. Devt., Dept. of State 1961-65; Prof. of Econs. and mem. Center for Int. Affairs, Harvard Univ. 1965-70, 1982-, Sr. lecturer 1975-80; Econ. Adviser to Pres., Int. Bank of Reconstruction and Devt. (World Bank) 1970-73, Vice-Pres. Devt. Policy 1973-82; Dir. Southern Natural Gas Co., Ala. 1952-74; Fellow, Econometric Soc.; mem. American Econ. Assen., American Acad. of Arts and Sciences, Royal Econ. Soc.; Guggenheim Fellowship. *Publications:* with others Arabian Oil 1949, Interindustry Economics 1959, Studies in Development Planning 1970, Redistribution with Growth 1974, Patterns of Development 1950-1970 1975, Structural Change and Development Policy 1979, Industrialization and Growth 1985. *Leisure interests:* tennis, hiking, skiing. *Address:* Harvard Institute for International Development (HIID), One Eliot Street, Cambridge, Mass. 02138 (Office); 5 Hemlock Road, Cambridge, Mass. 02138, U.S.A. (Home). *Telephone:* 495-2991 (Office); 491-1105 (Home).

CHENEY, Richard B.; American political administrator; b. 30 Jan. 1941, Lincoln, Neb.; m. Lynne Vincent; two d.; ed. Univ. of Wyoming, Univ. of Wisconsin; engaged on staff of Gov. of Wis. and as a Congressional Fellow on staff of a mem. of House of Reps.; also worked for an investment advisory firm; Exec. Asst. to Donald Rumsfeld 1969-71, Deputy 1971-73; Deputy Asst. to the Pres. 1974-75, Chief of White House Staff 1975-77; Congressman, At-large District, Wyoming, 1978-; Sec. of Defense March 1989-; Chair. House Republican Policy Cttee. 1980-; mem. American Political Science Assen.; Republican. *Address:* Department of Defense, The Pentagon, Washington, D.C., 20301, U.S.A.

CHENG JIANXIN; Chinese photographer; b. 1962, Yuexi Co., Anhui Prov. *Address:* Photography Society, Anqing Prefecture, Anhui Province, People's Republic of China.

CHENG LIANCHANG; Chinese government official; Vice-Minister of Astronautics 1976-, of Personnel 1988-. *Address:* Ministry of Personnel, Beijing, People's Republic of China.

CHENG MIAN; Chinese woodcut artist; b. 2 Nov. 1933, Shandong; s. of Cheng Qixiang and Zhang Qirong; m. Liu Qimei 1956; two s.; ed. Central Acad. of Fine Arts, Beijing; taught at the Acad. 1962; Art Ed. of Xinhua Daily 1963-78; full-time painter Jiangsu Art Gallery 1978-; one-man exhbn.

in Nanjing 1984, Qidong 1984; mem. China Artist Asscn.; mem. and Dir. China Woodcut Artist Asscn.; Vice-Pres. Jiangsu Woodcut Artist Asscn.; principal works include: book illustrations for Keep the Red Flag Flying, A Doctor on Night Shift 1977, Bank of Su River, Girl Carrying Water on Back, Moon in Water, Love, Morning Market, Perpetual Blood, Song for Bride, The People of Mount Taihang (series of woodcuts); many paintings shown in America, Britain, France and Denmark, woodcuts published in books and magazines. *Publications:* A Psychological Description of Artistic Creation; numerous articles on painting, block printing and engraving. *Leisure interests:* music and literature. *Address:* 266 Changjiang Road, Nanjing, Jiangsu, People's Republic of China. *Telephone:* Nanjing 41925.

CHENG QIKUN; Chinese agronomist; Dir. Tea Inst. 1983-. *Address:* Academy of Agricultural Sciences, Beijing, People's Republic of China.

CHENG SHIFA; Chinese artist; b. 1921, Songjiang Cty., Jiangsu; ed. Shanghai Coll. of Fine Arts; works at Shanghai Inst. of Painting. *Address:* Institute of Painting, Shanghai, People's Republic of China.

CHENG SHU-REN; Chinese sculptor; b. 2 April 1942, Nanjing; s. of Cheng Li-Jun and Qian Liang-Jie; m. Mai Zhu-Wei 1968; two d.; ed. Nat. Art Univ., Beijing 1965; Designer of Exhibition, Shanghai Arts and Crafts Import and Export Co. 1970-81; employed at Sculpture Studio, Shanghai Horticulture Bureau 1981-; *works include:* Composer of the National Anthem (granite, Kunming), Red Chamber Dream (white marble, outskirts of Shanghai, Qu Yuan (bronze) and Norman Bethune (woodcut) exhibited in Nat. Art Exhbn., large brick relief in Song Jiang Dist. and many others. *Address:* Room 303, No 665 Zhao Jia-bang Road, Shanghai, People's Republic of China.

CHENG YANAN; Chinese sculptor; b. 15 Jan 1936, Tianjin; d. of Cheng Goliang and Liuo Shijing; m. Zhang Zuoming 1962; one s. one d.; ed. Cen. Acad. of Fine Arts, Beijing; sculptor Beijing Architectural Artistic Sculpture Factory 1961-84, Sculpture Studio, Cen. Acad. of Fine Arts 1984-; mem. China Artists' Asscn.; exhbns. Jia Mei Shi Museum, Aomen 1986, and in Japan, France, Zaire, Congo, Hungary. *Address:* 452 New Building of Central Institute of Fine Arts, No 5 Shuaifuyan Lane, East District, Beijing, People's Republic of China.

CHENG ZIHUA; Chinese politician; b. 1904, Shanxi; educ. Whampoa Mil. Acad. 1926; alt. mem. 7th Cen. Cttee. CCP 1945; Gov. Shanxi 1950; Minister of Commerce 1958, of Civil Affairs 1978-82; Vice-Minister State Planning Comm. 1961; mem. 11th Cen. Cttee. CCP 1977; Deputy for Shanxi, 5th NPC 1978; mem. Presidium, NPC 1978; Vice-Chair. Nat. Cttee., 5th CPPCC 1980-83; mem. Standing Cttee. Cen. Advisory Cttee. 1982-, Party Cttee. of Special Orgs. 1983-, Cen. Comm. of Political Science and Law 1983-, Presidium CPCC 6th Nat. Comm. 1983-; Head of the Work Group for Foreign Affairs under CPPCC 1983-; Hon. Pres. Chinese Football Asscn. 1984-. *Address:* State Council, Beijing, People's Republic of China.

CHENOT, Bernard, L. EN DR., D.SC.POL.; French politician; b. 20 May 1909, Paris; s. of André Chenot and Marcelle Pellerin; m. Clélie Schmit 1934; one s. two d.; ed. Lycée Montaigne, Lycée Louis-le-Grand, Ecole libre des Sciences Politiques, Faculté de Droit, Paris; Chef de Cabinet in numerous Ministries 1932-39, including Public Health 1935, Public Works 1938 and 1939; Del.-Gen. of Tourism 1938-42; Sec.-Gen. Houillères nat. du Nord et du Pas de Calais 1944-46; Sec.-Gen. Conseil Economique 1951-58; Minister of Public Health and Population 1958-59 (de Gaulle Cabinet), 1959-61 (Debré Cabinet), Minister of Justice 1961-62 (Debré Cabinet); mem. Conseil Constitutionnel 1962; Président de la Cité internationale de l'Univ. de Paris; Pres. of Compagnies d'assurances générales 1964, Groupe des Assurances Générales de France 1968-70; Admin. Paribas Int. 1968-70; Pres. Comité de liaison d'étude et d'action républicaines 1968-71; Vice-Pres. Conseil d'Etat 1971-78, Hon. Vice-Pres. 1978-; Pres. Institut Français des Sciences Administratives 1974; fmr. Prof. Ecole Libre des Sciences Politiques, Inst. d'Etudes Politiques; Pres. French Section, Centre Européen de l'Entreprise Publique; mem. Admin. Council, Fondation des Sciences Politiques 1946, mem. Acad. des Sciences Morales et Politiques 1976, Sec. Perpetuel 1978, Acad. of Athens 1983; Hon. mem. Gray's Inn, London 1975; Grand Officier Légion d'honneur, Grand Cross, Sovereign Order of Malta, Ordre du Tresor Sacré, Gran Ufficiale, Ordine del Merito della Repubblica Italiana, Grand Croix Ordre de St.-Charles, Grand Croix Ordre du Cèdre (Lebanon), Grand Officier de l'Ordre de la Couronne (Belgium), Médaille d'Or, Education Physique et des Sports. *Publications:* Organisation économique de l'état 1951, Les entreprises nationalisées (Collection Que sais-je?) 1956; various published lectures, including Les institutions administratives de la France and Histoire des doctrines politiques, Etre Ministre 1967, Reflexions sur la Cité 1981, Morgane (Poèmes) 1985. *Leisure interests:* literature, sport. *Address:* 23 quai de Conti, 75006 Paris; 3 rue Mazarine, 75006 Paris, France (Home). *Telephone:* 326-31-35.

CHER (Cherilyn Lapierre Sarkisian); American actress and singer; d. of John Sarkisian and Georgina Holt; m. Sonny Bono (divorced 1975); one d.; m. 2nd Gregg Allman (divorced); one s.; half of singing duo Sonny and Cher; Sonny and Cher Comedy Hour (TV) 1971-75; own TV variety series and night club act; *Recordings include:* I Got You Babe, The Beat Goes On, Bang Bang, You Better Sit Down Kids; has won 11 gold and 3 platinum records; Best Actress Award, Cannes Film Festival, for Mask; Acad.

Award. for Moonstruck 1987; acted in play Come Back to the Five and Dime, Jimmy Dean, Jimmy Dean. *Films include:* Good Times, Chastity, Come Back to the Five and Dime, Jimmy Dean, Jimmy Dean, Silkwood, Mask, Witches of Eastwick, Moonstruck, Suspect.

CHÉREAU, Patrice; French theatre and opera director; b. 2 Nov. 1944; s. of Jean-Baptiste Chéreau and Marguerite Pélicier; ed. Lycée Louis-le-Grand and Faculté de Lettres, Paris; Co-Dir. Théâtre national populaire (T.N.P.) 1972-81; Dir. Théâtre des Amandiers, Nanterre 1982-; *theatre productions include:* L'Intervention 1964, L'Affaire de la rue de Lourcine 1966, Les Soldats 1967, La Révolte au Marché noir 1968, Don Juan, L'Italienne à Alger 1969, Richard II, Splendeur et Mort de Joaquin Murieta 1970, La Finta Serva 1971, Massacre á Paris 1972, La Dispute 1973, Lear 1975, Peer Gynt 1981, Les Paravents 1983, Combats de Nègre et de Chiens 1983, La Fausse suivante 1985, Quai Ouest 1986; *opera productions:* The Tales of Hoffmann 1974, Der Ring des Nibelungen (Bayreuth 1976-80), Lulu 1979; *films:* La Chair de l'Orchidée 1974, Judith Therpauve 1978, L'Homme blessé 1984; Officier des Arts et des Lettres. *Address:* Nanterre-Amandiers, 7 avenue Pablo Picasso, 92000 Nanterre, France (Office).

(three times), Order of Red Banner of Labour (twice), Badge of Honour, Hero of Socialist Labour and other decorations. *Address:* Lebedev Physics Institute of U.S.S.R. Academy of Sciences, Leninsky Prospekt 53, Moscow, U.S.S.R.

CHERIF, Safwat El-, B.SC.; Egyptian politician; b. 1933; m.; three c.; ed. studies in mil. science and at Int. Communications Inst., Fed. Repub. of Germany; held appts. in armed forces until 1957, in the Presidency until 1974; joined State Information Service 1975, Deputy Chair. 1977, Chair. 1978; mem. Standing Cttee. of Arab Information 1975-, Supreme Council of Family Planning and Population, Supreme Child Council; mem. People's Ass. for Kasr-el. Nil; Pres. Council of Radio and TV Fed. 1980; Minister of State for Information 1981-. *Address:* Ministry of Information, Radio and Television Building, Cairo (Maspiro), Egypt. *Telephone:* 749518.

CHERKASSKY, Shura; Russian-born American pianist; b. 7 Oct. 1911, Odessa; s. of Isaac Cherkassky and Lydia Schlemenson; m. Genia Ganz 1946 (divorced 1948); no c.; ed. Curtis Inst. of Music, Philadelphia; studied under his mother and then Josef Hofmann; emigrated to U.S.A. 1922; debut Baltimore 1923; first major European tour 1946; numerous world tours and frequent tours of Germany, U.S.A. and U.S.S.R. in particular; regular contributor to Salzburg Festival concerts; constant world-wide tours; has recorded for Deutsche Gramophon, Philips, Decca, Nimbus Records. *Leisure interest:* travel. *Address:* c/o Ibbs and Tillett, 18b Pindock Mews, Little Venice, London, W9 2PY, England.

CHERKEZIYA, Otari Yevtikhevich; Soviet politician; b. 1933; ed. Kirov Polytechnic, Georgia; mem. CPSU 1955-; head of section of Komsomol Cen. Cttee. of Georgia 1957-59; deputy head of section of Komsomol 1959-61; First Sec. of Komsomol Cen. Cttee. of Ga. 1961-67; First Sec. of Tbilisi Regional Cttee. 1967-70; head of section of Cen. Cttee. of Georgian CP 1970-73; deputy, First Deputy Pres. of Council of Ministers, Georgian S.S.R. 1973-86; Pres. of Georgian Council of Ministers, April 1986-; Deputy to U.S.S.R. Supreme Soviet. *Address:* Council of Ministers of Georgian S.S.R., Tbilisi, Georgia, U.S.S.R.

CHERMAYEFF, Serge, F.R.I.B.A., F.R.S.A.; American (b. Russian) architect, planning consultant and painter; b. 8 Oct. 1900, Russia; m. Barbara Maitland May 1928; two s.; practised in England and became a British citizen; went to U.S.A. 1940, became U.S. citizen 1946; essayist, lecturer, teacher, critic; fmr. Pres. Chicago Inst. of Design; fmr. Prof. Harvard Graduate School of Design; Emer. Prof. Yale Univ.; Hon. Dr. of Arts (Washington Univ.) 1967, (Murray Coll., Ill.), Hon. D.H. (Ohio State Univ.) 1980; Chicago Art Inst. Award 1947, 1949, Gold Medal, Royal Inst. of Canadian Architects 1974, Assoc. Collegiate Schools of Architecture Award 1980, Sir Misha Black Memorial Award (Royal Soc. of Industrial Artists and Designers) 1980, Dean's Gold Medal, Univ. of New York 1982. *Publications:* Community and Privacy (with Christopher Alexander) 1963, The Shape of Community 1971, Design and the Public Good (selected writings 1930-80) 1982. *Leisure interests:* painting, writing. *Address:* P.O. Box NN, Wellfleet, Mass. 02667, U.S.A.

CHERN, Shiing-Shen, B.S., M.S., D.SC.; American (naturalized 1961) professor of mathematics; b. 26 Oct. 1911, Kashing, China; s. of Lien Chin Chern and Mei Han; m. Shih Ning Cheng 1939; one s. one d.; ed. Nankai Univ., Tientsin, Tsing Hua Univ., Peking, and Univ. of Hamburg, Germany; Prof. of Mathematics, Tsing Hua Univ., Peking 1937-43; mem. Inst. for Advanced Study, Princeton, N.J., U.S.A. 1943-45; Acting Dir. Inst. of Mathematics, Academia Sinica, Nanking, China 1946-48; Prof. of Mathematics, Univ. of Chicago, U.S.A. 1949-60, Univ. of Calif. at Berkeley 1960-79, Prof. Emer. 1979-; Dir. Mathematical Sciences Research Inst., Berkeley 1982-84, Dir. Emer. 1984-; Dir. Nankai Inst. of Mathematics, Tianjin, China 1984-; mem. Academia Sinica, N.A.S., American Acad. of Arts and Sciences; Hon. mem. Indian Mathematical Soc.; Corresp. mem. Brazilian Acad. of Sciences; Foreign mem. Royal Soc. of London 1985-, Corresp. mem. Academia Peloritana, Messina, Sicily 1986; Hon. mem. London Math. Soc. 1986; Hon. LL.D. (Chinese Univ. of Hong Kong) 1969; Hon. D.Sc. (Univ. of Chicago) 1969, (Univ. of Hamburg, Germany) 1971, (State Univ. of New York at Stony Brook) 1985; Dr. h.c. (Eidgenossische Technische Hochschule,

Switzerland) 1982; Nat. Medal of Science (U.S.A.) 1975; Steele Prize, American Mathematical Soc. 1983; shared Wolf Foundation Prize, Israel 1983–84. *Publications:* S. S. Chern, Selected Papers 1978, Complex Manifolds without Potential Theory 1979. *Address:* 8336 Kent Court, El Cerrito, Calif. 94530, U.S.A. (Home).

CHERNAVIN, Admiral Vladimir Nikolayevich; Soviet naval officer; b. 1928; ed. Naval Acad., Mil. Acad. of Gen. Staff; command posts in Soviet Navy 1947–; mem. CPSU 1949–; Commdr. of Northern Fleet 1977–85, C.-in-C. Soviet Navy Dec. 1985–; Deputy Minister of Defence 1985–; Adm. 1978–; mem. U.S.S.R. Supreme Soviet 1979–; cand. mem. Cen. Cttee. CPSU 1981–; Hero of Soviet Union 1981. *Address:* c/o Ministry of Defence, Moscow, U.S.S.R.

CHERNOFF, Herman, PH.D.; American professor of statistics; b. 1 July 1923, New York; s. of Max Chernoff and Pauline Markowitz; m. Judith Ullman 1947; two d.; ed. Townsend Harris High School, City Coll. of New York, Brown and Columbia Univs.; Research Assoc., Cowles Comm. for Research in Econs., Univ. of Chicago 1947–49; Asst. Prof. of Mathematics, Illinois Univ. 1949–51, Assoc. Prof. 1951–52; Assoc. Prof. of Statistics, Stanford Univ. 1952–56, Prof. 1956–74; Prof. of Applied Math., M.I.T. 1974–85; Prof. of Statistics, Harvard Univ. 1985–; Dr. h.c. (Ohio State) 1983, (Technion) 1984; mem. N.A.S., American Acad. of Arts and Sciences; Townsend Harris Prize 1982, Wilks Medal 1987. *Publications:* numerous articles in scientific journals. *Address:* Department of Statistics SC713, Harvard University, Cambridge, Mass., 02138; 75 Crowninshield Road, Brookline, Mass. 02146, U.S.A. (Home). *Telephone:* (617) 495 5462 (Office); (617) 232 8256 (Home).

CHERNOMYRDIN, Viktor Stepanovich; CAND. TECH. SC; Soviet politician; b. 1938; ed. Kuybyshev Polytechnic; Soviet Army 1957–60; operator in oil refinery 1960–67; mem. CPSU 1961–; work with Orsk City Cttee. 1967–73; deputy chief engineer, dir. of Orenburg gas plant 1973–78; work with CPSU Cen. Cttee. 1978–82; U.S.S.R. Deputy Minister of Gas Industry, Chief of All-Union production unit for gas exploitation in Tyumen Dist. 1982–; U.S.S.R. Minister of Gas 1985–; mem. of CPSU Cen. Cttee. 1986–; Deputy to U.S.S.R. Supreme Soviet. *Address:* The Kremlin, Moscow, U.S.S.R.

CHERNY, Aleksey Klementevich; Soviet government official; b. 23 Feb. 1921; ed. Moscow Inst. of Chemical-Mechanical Eng.; technologist, then deputy dir. of plant in Komsomolsk-na-Amure 1942–49; mem. CPSU 1946–; Second Sec., Komsomolsk City Cttee. 1950–54; First Sec., Lazo Dist. Cttee. (Khabarovsk) CPSU 1954–56; Sec. Khabarovsk Dist. Cttee. CPSU 1956–59; First Sec. of Jewish Autonomous Dist. CPSU 1959–62; Deputy to R.S.F.S.R. Supreme Soviet 1959–63; Chair. of Exec. Cttee., Khabarovsk Dist. Soviet 1962–70; Deputy to Council of Nationalities, U.S.S.R. Supreme Soviet 1962–74; First Sec., Khabarovsk Dist. Cttee. CPSU, and mem. of Mil. Council, Far Eastern Mil. Dist. 1970–; mem. Cen. Cttee. CPSU 1971–; Deputy, Council of the Union, U.S.S.R. Supreme Soviet 1974–. Order of Lenin (four times), Order of the Red Banner of Labour and other medals. *Address:* The Kremlin, Moscow, U.S.S.R.

CHERNY, Gorimir Gorimirovich; Soviet scientist; b. 22 Jan. 1923, Kamenets-Podol'sky; ed. Moscow Univ.; served in Soviet Army 1941–45; worked for Cen. Inst. of Aircraft Engine Construction 1949–58; mem. CPSU 1954–; Prof. at Moscow Univ. 1958; Dir. Univ. Research Inst. of Mechanics 1960–; Corresp. mem. U.S.S.R. Acad. of Sciences 1962–; State Prize, five orders and various medals; author of numerous books and scientific articles on aerodynamics, theory of detonation and combustion, theory of gas-fired machines. *Address:* Institute of Mechanics, Moscow M.V. Lomonosov State University, Moscow, U.S.S.R.

CHERNYAKOV, Yuriy Nikolayevich; Soviet diplomatist; b. 1 Aug. 1918, Gorky; ed. Gorky Inst. of River Transport Engineers and Higher Diplomatic School; instructor, Gorky Inst. of River Transport Engineers 1943–46; entered diplomatic service 1948; Third Sec., Archives, Ministry of Foreign Affairs 1948–50; Third, Second then First Sec., Soviet Embassy, Budapest 1950–55; Counsellor, Ministry of Foreign Affairs 1955–57, Soviet Embassy, Budapest 1957–59; Deputy Head, Press Dept. 1959–65; Counsellor, Minister-Counsellor, Soviet Embassy, Washington, D.C. 1965–70; Head, Press Dept., Ministry of Foreign Affairs 1970–73; Sec.-Gen., Ministry of Foreign Affairs 1973–77; Amb. to Syria 1977–79; Head Press Dept., Ministry of Foreign Affairs 1979–; Badge of Honour, Order of the Great Fatherland War, Order of the Red Banner of Labour, Order of the Friendship of Peoples and other decorations. *Address:* Ministry of Foreign Affairs, 32-34 Smolenskaya-Sennaya Ploshchad, Moscow, U.S.S.R.

CHERNYAYEV, Anatoly Sergeyevich; Soviet party official; Deputy Head of Int. Dept. of Cen. Cttee. CPSU 1977–; mem. Cen. Auditing Comm. CPSU 1976–81; Cand. mem. Cen. Cttee. CPSU 1981–. *Address:* The Kremlin, Moscow, U.S.S.R.

CHERVONENKO, Stepan Vasiliyevich, M.SC.; Soviet diplomatist; b. 16 Sept. 1915, Okop, Poltava oblast; s. of Vassily Chervonenko and Agafia Kiritchenko; m. Loudmilla Chervonenko 1948; ed. Kiev State Univ.; headmaster, secondary school 1937–41; mem. CPSU 1940–; Soviet Army service 1941–44; Head, Marxism-Leninism Dept., Deputy Dir. Cherkass Pedagogical Inst. 1944–48; on staff of Cen. Cttee. CP Ukraine 1949–56; Sec. Cen.

Cttee. CP Ukraine 1956–59; Amb. to People's Repub. of China 1959–65, to Czechoslovakia 1965–73, to France (also accred. to Madagascar) 1973–82; Head of Section Cen. Cttee. CPSU 1982–; mem. Cen. Cttee. CPSU 1961–, parliamentary group of Supreme Soviet; Deputy to Supreme Soviet of U.S.S.R. 1958–62, 1984–, and to S.S.R. of Ukraine 1955–63; Order of Lenin (five times), Order of Red Banner of Labour, Order of White Lion, Order of October Revolution and other decorations. *Leisure interests:* hunting, sport. *Address:* Central Committee of the Communist Party of the Soviet Union, The Kremlin, Moscow, U.S.S.R.

CHESHIRE, Group Captain Geoffrey Leonard, V.C., O.M., D.S.O. (two bars), D.F.C., B.A.; British air force officer (retd.); b. 7 Sept. 1917, Chester; s. of the late Prof. G. C. Cheshire, F.B.A., D.C.L. and Primrose (Barstow) Cheshire; m. Margaret Susan Ryder, now Baroness Ryder of Warsaw, C.M.G. (q.v.); one s. one d.; ed. Stowe School, Merton Coll., Oxford; Perm. Comm. 1939; served 1939–45 in Bomber Command; Wing Commdr. commanding 617 Squadron (The Dambusters) 1943; official British observer at dropping of atomic bomb on Nagasaki 1945; Founder Leonard Cheshire Foundation Homes for the Disabled (operating 240 homes in 44 countries) and co-founder Ryder Cheshire Mission for the Relief of Suffering; Hon. Fellowship (Nottingham Univ., Manchester Polytechnic); Hon. D.C.L. (Oxford) 1984, (Kent) 1986, Hon. LL.D. (Liverpool) 1973, (Bristol Univ.) 1985, (Birmingham Univ.) 1986; Humanitarian Award, Variety Clubs Int. (with Sue Ryder-Cheshire) 1974. *Publications:* Bomber Pilot 1943, Pilgrimage to the Shroud 1956, Face of Victory 1961, The Hidden World 1981, The Light of Many Suns 1985. *Leisure interest:* tennis. *Address:* 26 Maunsel Street, London, SW1, England. *Telephone:* 01-828 1822.

CHESTERS, John Hugh, O.B.E., PH.D., F.ENG., F.R.S.; British engineer; b. 16 Oct. 1906; s. of Rev. George M. Chesters; m. Nell Knight 1936; three s. one d.; ed. High Pavement School, Nottingham, King Edward VII School, Sheffield and Univ. of Sheffield; Metropolitan-Vickers Research Scholar, Univ. of Sheffield 1928–31; Robert Blair Fellowship, Kaiser-Wilhelm Inst. für Silikatforschung, Berlin 1931–32; Commonwealth Fund Fellow, Univ. of Ill. 1932–34; joined United Steel 1934, Asst. Dir. of Research 1945–62, Deputy Dir. of Research 1962–67; Deputy Dir. of Research, Midland Group, British Steel Corpn. 1967–70; Dir. Corp. Labs. British Iron and Steel Research Assen. 1970–71; Consultant 1971–; Founder Chair., Watt Comm. on Energy 1976–86; Vice-Pres. Inst. Flame Research Foundation 1945–86; mem. several professional socs.; Foreign Assoc. Nat. Acad. of Eng. U.S.A.; numerous awards etc.; Hon. D.Sc. (Sheffield) 1975. *Publications:* four books and numerous articles in professional journals. *Leisure interests:* foreign travel, fishing. *Address:* 21 Slayleigh Lane, Sheffield, S10 3RF, England. *Telephone:* Sheffield 301257.

CHEVALIER, Louis; French university professor and political scientist; b. 29 May 1911, Vendeé; ed. Ecole Normale Supérieure; Prof. Coll. de France; Prof. Institut d'Etudes Politiques de Paris; fmr. mem. Conseil supérieur de la Recherche Scientifique; fmr. Pres. du Conseil Scientifique du Centre Int. d'Etude des Problèmes Humains de Monaco; fmr. mem. Conseil Economique et Social du District de Paris; Hon. degree (Columbia); Commdr. Légion d'honneur. *Publications:* Les paysans, Le problème démographique nord-africain, La formation de la population parisienne, Madagascar, Démographie générale; contributor to Population, Le choléra de 1832, Classes laborieuses et classes dangereuses, Les Parisiens, Histoire anachronique des Français, L'assassinat de Paris, Montmartre du plaisir et du crime, Histoires de la nuit parisienne, Les relais de mer, Les ruines de Suture-Montmartre de 1939 aux années 80. *Address:* 71 rue du Cardinal Lemoine, 75005 Paris, France.

CHEVALIER, Roger; French aeronautical engineer; b. 3 May 1922, Marseilles; s. of Louis Chevalier and Marie Louise Assaud; m. Monique Blin 1947; two s.; ed. Ecole Polytechnique and Ecole Nationale Supérieure de l'Aéronautique; Head of Dept., Aeronautical Arsenal 1948–53; Chief Engineer, Nord-Aviation 1954–60; Technical Dir. Soc. pour l'Etude et la Réalisation d'Engins Balistiques (SEREB) 1960, Dir.-Gen. 1967–70; Gen. Man. Société Nationale de l'Industrie Aérospatiale (SNIAS), Exec. Senior Vice-Pres. 1976–82, Vice-Chair. 1982–; Pres. Assen. Aéronautique et Astronautique de France; Pres. Int. Astronautical Fed. (IAF) 1980–82, Pres. Int. 1982–; Vice-Pres. Aero-Club de France 1981, French Acad. for Aeronautics and Astronautics; Pres. Soc. d'études de réalisation et d'applications techniques (SERAT) 1985–; Fellow, American Aeronautic and Astronautic Inst.; mem. Int. Acad. of Astronautics; Commdr. Légion d'honneur; Médaille de l'Aéronautique, Prix Galabert 1966, Commdr. Ordre national du mérite, Allan D. Emil Award 1982, Commdr. of Merit (Fed. Repub. of Germany) 1987. *Leisure interests:* tennis, hunting, reading. *Address:* 37 boulevard de Montmorency, 75016 Paris (Office); 4 rue Edouard Detaille, 75017 Paris, France. *Telephone:* 227-5928.

CHEVALLAZ, Georges-André, D.LITT.; Swiss politician; b. 7 Feb. 1915, Lausanne; m. Madeleine Roch 1945; two s.; ed. Univ. of Lausanne; Teacher, School of Commerce 1942–55; Dir. Canton Library, Reader in Diplomatic History, Univ. of Lausanne 1955–58; Syndic de Lausanne 1957–73; Nat. Councillor 1959–73; mem. Fed. Council 1973–, Head of Finance and Customs Dept. 1974–79; Vice-Pres. of Switzerland Jan.-Dec. 1979, Pres. Jan.-Dec. 1980, Head of Fed. Military (Defence) Dept. 1980–83; Radical Democrat. *Publications:* Aspects de l'agriculture vaudoise à la fin de l'ancien régime 1949, Histoire générale de 1789 à nos jours 1957, 1967, 1973, Les grandes conférences diplomatiques 1964, La Suisse ou le sommeil du juste 1967, La Suisse est-elle gouvernable? 1984, etc. *Address:* 1066 Epalinges, Switzerland (Home). *Telephone:* 021.784.19.19.

CHEVÈNEMENT, Jean-Pierre; French politician; b. 9 March 1939, Belfort; s. of Pierre Chevènement and Juliette Garessus; m. Nisa Grünberg 1970; two s.; ed. Lycée Victor-Hugo, Besançon, Univ. de Paris, Ecole Nationale d'Admin.; joined Parti Socialiste (PS) 1964; Commercial Attaché, Ministry of Econ. and Finance 1965-66; Sec.-Gen. Centre d'études, de recherches et d'éducation socialistes 1965-71; Commercial Adviser, Jakarta, Indonesia 1969; Political Sec. Fédération socialiste de Paris 1969-70; Dir. of Studies, Soc. Eres 1969-71; Nat. Sec. PS 1971-75, 1979-80, mem. Exec. Bureau 1971-81, 1986, Steering Cttee. 1971-; Deputy (Belfort) to Nat. Ass. 1973-81, 1986-; Vice-Pres. Departmental Ass. of Franche-Comté; mem. Bd. Dirs. Repères magazine; Minister of State, Minister of Research and Tech. 1981-82, of Industry 1982-83, of Nat. Educ. 1984-86, of Defence May 1988-; First Asst. to Mayor of Belfort 1977-83, Mayor 1983-; Pres. Conseil Régional de Franche-Comté 1981-82, mem. 1986-88, fmr. Vice-Pres.; Croix de la valeur militaire. *Publications:* (as Jacques Mandrin): L'enarchie ou les mandarins de la société bourgeoise 1967, Socialisme ou socialmédiocratie 1969, Clefs pour le socialisme 1973, Le vieux, la crise, le neuf 1975, Les socialistes, les communistes et les autres, Le service militaire 1977, Etre socialiste aujourd'hui 1979, Apprendre pour entreprendre 1985, Le pari sur l'intelligence 1985. *Leisure interest:* chess. *Address:* 14 rue Saint Dominique, 75700 Paris; Mairie de Belfort, 90020, Belfort cedex, France.

CHEVRILLON, Olivier; French museum administrator; b. 28 Jan. 1929, Paris; m. Marie France Renaud 1965; one d.; ed. Univ. of Paris-Sorbonne, Nat. Inst. of Political Studies and Nat. Admin. School; mem. Conseil d'Etat 1952-68; Vice-Pres. L'Express 1968-70, Chair. 1970-71; Chair. and columnist Le Point 1972-86; Dir. French Museums 1987-; Chevalier Légion d'Honneur, Commdr. Ordre Nat. des Arts et Lettres. *Address:* Palais du Louvre, 4 Quai des Tuileries, 75001 Paris, France.

CHEW, Geoffrey Foucar, PH.D.; American professor of physics; b. 5 June 1924, Washington, D.C.; s. of Arthur Percy Chew and Pauline Lisette Foucar; m. 1st Ruth Elva Wright 1945 (died 1971), one s. one d.; m. 2nd Denyse Mettel 1972, two s. one d.; ed. George Washington Univ. and Univ. of Chicago; Research Physicist, Los Alamos Scientific Lab. 1944-46; Research Physicist, Lawrence Radiation Lab. 1948-49, Head of Theoretical Group 1967-; Asst. Prof. of Physics, Univ. of California at Berkeley 1949-50, Prof. of Physics 1957-, Chair. Dept. of Physics 1974-78, Dean of Physical Sciences 1986-; Asst. Prof., then Assoc. Prof. of Physics, Univ. of Illinois 1950-55, Prof. 1955-56; Fellow, Inst. for Advanced Study 1956; Overseas Fellow, Churchill Coll., Cambridge 1962-63; Scientific Associate, CERN 1978-79; Prof. Miller Inst. 1981-82; Visiting Prof., Univ. of Paris 1983-84; mem. N.A.S., American Acad. of Arts and Sciences; Hughes Prize of American Physical Soc. 1962, Lawrence Award of U.S. Atomic Energy Comm. 1969. *Publications:* The S-Matrix Theory of Strong Interactions 1961, The Analytic S-Matrix 1966; over 100 scientific articles. *Leisure interests:* gardening, hiking. *Address:* Department of Physics, University of California, Berkeley, Calif. 94720 (Office); and Lawrence Radiation Laboratory, Berkeley, Calif. 94720; 10 Maybeck Twin Drive, Berkeley, Calif. 94708, U.S.A. (Home). *Telephone:* 642-4505 (Dept. of Physics); 486-5010, (Lawrence Radiation Lab.); 848-1830 (Home).

CHEYSSON, Claude; French public servant; b. 13 April 1920, Paris; s. of Pierre Cheysson and Sophie Funck-Brentano; m. 3rd Danielle Schwartz 1969; one s. two d. (and three c. from previous m.); ed. Ecole Polytechnique and Ecole d'Administration, Paris; escaped from occupied France to Spanish prison 1943; Officer in the Free French Forces 1943-45; entered French Diplomatic Service 1948; attached to UN Mission in Palestine 1948; Head of French liaison office with Fed. German Govt., Bonn 1949-52; adviser to Prime Minister of Vietnam, Saigon 1952-54; Chef de Cabinet to French Prime Minister (Mendès-France) 1954-55; technical adviser to Minister for Moroccan and Tunisian Affairs 1955-59; Sec.-Gen. Comm. for Technical Co-operation in Africa (C.C.T.A.), Lagos 1957-62; Dir-Gen. Sahara Authority (Organisme Saharien), Algiers 1962-65; Dir.-Gen. Organisme de coopération industrielle, Algiers 1966; Amb. to Indonesia 1966-69; Pres. Entreprise minière et chimique and Pres. Dir.-Gen. Cie. des potasses du Congo 1970-73; mem. Bd. Le Monde 1970-81; Commr. for Devt. Aid, Comm. of European Communities 1973-81; Minister of External Relations 1981-84; Commr. for Mediterranean Policy and North-South Relations, Comm. of European Communities Jan. 1985-; Bd. of Le Monde 1985-; Pres. Institut Mendès-France 1987-(89); Town Councillor, Bargemon, France; Dr. h.c. Univ. of Louvain; Commdr., Légion d'honneur, Croix de guerre, Grand Cross, from numerous countries, Grand Officier, Belgium, Benin, Chad, Cameroon, Gabon, Ivory Coast, Lebanon, Monaco, Nepal, Niger, Portugal, Rwanda, Senegal, Togo, Tunisia, Upper Volta, Commdr. Central African Republic, Gabon, Mali, Indonesia; Joseph Bech Prize 1978, Prix Luderitz (Namibia) 1983. *Leisure interest:* skiing. *Address:* Commission of the European Communities, 200 rue de la Loi, 1049 Brussels, Belgium (Office); Villa Samudra, 40150 Hossegor, France (Home).

CHHATWAL, H.E. Surbir Jit Singh, M.POL.SC.; Indian diplomatist; b. 1 Oct. 1931, Bannu; s. of Datar Singh Chhatwal and Rattan Kaur Chhatwal; m. Neelam Singh 1962; one s. one d.; ed. Agra Univ.; joined Foreign Service

1955; Ministry of External Affairs, including one year at Cambridge, U.K. 1955-58; Third Sec., Madrid 1958-60; Under-Sec., Ministry of External Affairs, New Delhi 1960-62; First Sec., Havana, Cuba 1962-64; Deputy Sec. (Co-ordinating), Ministry of External Affairs, New Delhi 1964-66; First Sec. and Acting High Commr., Ottawa, Canada 1966-68; First Indian Consul-Gen., Seoul, S. Korea 1968-71; Dir. Ministry of Foreign Trade, New Delhi 1971-73; Chief of Protocol, Ministry of External Affairs, New Delhi 1973-75; High Commr. in Malaysia 1975-79, in Sri Lanka 1982-85, in Canada 1985-; Amb. to Kuwait 1979-82. *Leisure interests:* reading, golf. *Address:* Indian High Commission, 10 Springfield Road, Ottawa, K1M 1C9 (Office); 585 Acacia Avenue, Rockcliffe, Ottawa, K1M 0M5, Canada (Home).

CHI BIQING; Chinese party official; b. 1920, Shanxi; joined CCP 1937; Cadre, Shanxi 1949; First Sec. CCP, Taiyuan City 1956; Sec. CCP, Shanxi 1957-67; Sec. N. China Bureau CCP 1963-67; criticized and removed from office during Cultural Revolution 1967; Second Sec. CCP, Inner Mongolia 1976-78; mem. 11th Cen. Cttee. CCP 1977; Second Sec. CCP, Guizhou Prov. 1978-79, First Sec. 1979-85; First Political Commissar, PLA Guizhon Mil. Dist. 1980-; mem. 12th Cen. Cttee. CCP 1982-87; mem. Cen. Advisory Comm. 1987-; Head Leading Group for Party Consolidation CCP, Guizhon Prov. 1984-. *Address:* Zhongguo Gongchan Dang, Guiyang, Guizhou Province, People's Republic of China.

CHI HAOTIAN, Gen.; Chinese army officer; Major, unit, Nanjing Mil. Region 1958; Deputy Political Commissar, Beijing Mil. Region 1975-77; Deputy Ed.-in-Chief, People's Daily 1977-82; Deputy Chief of Staff PLA 1977-82; Political Commissar, Jinan Mil. Region 1985-87; PLA Chief of Staff Dec. 1987-; mem. CCP Cen. Cttee. 1985-. *Address:* People's Liberation Army Headquarters, Jinan, People's Republic of China.

CHIANG KAI-SHEK, Madame (Soong, Mayling), LL.D., L.H.D.; Chinese sociologist; married (Pres.) Chiang Kai-shek 1927 (died 1975); ed. Wellesley Coll., U.S.A.; first Chinese woman appointed mem. of Child Labour Comm.; inaugurated Moral Endeavour Asscn.; established schools in Nanking for orphans of revolutionary soldiers; fmr. mem. Legislative Yuan; served as Sec.-Gen. of Chinese Comm. on Aeronautical Affairs; Dir.-Gen. New Life Movement; founded and directed Nat. Chinese Women's Asscn. for War Relief and Nat. Asscn. for Refugee Children; accompanied husband on mil. campaigns; Hon. Chair. American Bureau for Medical Aid to China and Cttee. for the promotion of the Welfare of the Blind; Patroness Int. Red Cross Cttee.; Hon. Chair. British United Aid to China Fund and United China Relief; First Hon. Mem. Bill of Rights Commemorative Soc.; first Chinese woman to be decorated by Nat. Govt. of China, awards include Gold Medal of Nat. Inst. of Social Sciences; L.H.D. (John B. Stetson Univ., Bryant Coll., Hobart and William Smith Colls., Nebraska Wesleyan Univ.), LL.D. (Rutgers Univ., Goucher Coll., Wellesley Coll., Loyola Univ., Russell Sage Coll., Hahnemann Medical Coll., Univs. of Michigan and Hawaii, and Wesleyan Coll., Macon); Hon. F.R.C.S. (Eng.); Hon. mem. numerous socs. *Publications:* Sian: A Coup d'Etat 1939, China in Peace and War 1939, China Shall Rise Again 1939, This is Our China 1940, We Chinese Women 1941, American Tour Speeches 1942-43, Little Sister Su 1943, The Sure Victory 1955, Madame Chiang Kai-shek: Selected Speeches 1958-59, Album of Reproductions of Paintings Vol. I 1952, Vol. II 1962, Religious Writings 1963, Madame Chiang Kai-shek: Selected Speeches 1965-66, Album of Chinese Orchid Paintings 1971, Album of Chinese Bamboo Paintings 1972, Album of Chinese Landscape Paintings 1973, Album of Chinese Floral Paintings 1974, Conversations with Mikhail Borodin 1977. *Address:* Lattingtown, Long Island, New York, U.S.A.

CHIARA, Maria; Italian opera singer; b. 24 Nov. 1939, Oderzo; m. Antonio Cassinelli; ed. Conservatorio Benedetto Marcello, Venice, with Maria Carbone; début as Desdemona in Otello, Doge's Palace, Venice, 1965, then Rome Opera début 1965; frequent performances (in Italy including Turandot with Placido Domingo, Verona 1969); débuts Germany and Austria 1970; début La Scala, Milan as Micaela, Carmen 1972; début Royal Opera House, Covent Garden, London, Turandot 1973; début Metropolitan Opera, New York in Traviata and at Lyric Opera, Chicago in Manon Lescaut 1977; sings in all major opera houses of Europe, U.S.A. and S. America; opened 1985/86 season at La Scala in Aida; has recorded Il Segreto di Susanna and a disc of operatic arias (Decca). *Address:* c/o S.A. Gorlinsky Ltd., 33 Dover Street, London, W1X 4NJ, England. *Telephone:* 01-493 9158.

CHIBESAKUNDA, Lombe Phyllis, BAR.-AT-LAW; Zambian lawyer and diplomatist; b. 5 May 1944; ed. Chipembi Girls' School, Nat. Inst. of Public Administration, Lusaka, Gray's Inn, England; State Advocate, Ministry of Legal Affairs 1969-72; private legal practice with Jacques and Partners 1972-73; M.P. for Matero Dec. 1973-; fmr. Solicitor-Gen. and Minister of State for Legal Affairs; Amb. to Japan 1975-77; High Commr. in the United Kingdom, concurrently Amb. to the Netherlands and the Holy See 1977-81; Judge of High Court; Chair. Industrial Court of Zambia; Chief Zambian del., UN Law of the Sea Conf. 1975, Rep. UN Comm. on the Status of Women; Chair. Equality Cttee. Sub-Cttee. UN Independence Party's Women's League; founded Social Action charity, Lusaka; Founder mem. Link Voluntary Org.; Life mem. Commonwealth Parl. Asscn.; Kt. Grand Cross of the Order of Pope Pius IX 1979. *Address:* High Court of Zambia, P.O. Box 50067, Lusaka, Zambia.

CHIBURDANIDZE, Mariya Grigorevna; Soviet chess player; b. 17 Jan. 1961, Kutaisi, Georgia; ed. Tbilisi Medical Inst. 1978–; Int. Grand Master 1977; Honoured Master of Sport 1978; U.S.S.R. Champion 1977; World Champion 1978–; winner of women's int. chess tournaments in Brasove, Romania 1974 and Tbilisi 1976; Capt. of winning Soviet team at 8th Women's Chess Olympics 1978.

CHIEN, Fredrick Foo, PH.D; Chinese politician; b. 17 Feb. 1935, Peiping; s. of Shih-liang and Wan-tu; m. Julie Tien 1963; one s. one d.; ed. Nat. Taiwan Univ., Yale Univ., Nat. War Coll.; Sec. Exec. Yuan, Taiwan 1962–63; Visiting Assoc. Prof. Nat. Chengchi Univ. 1962–64; Chief 1st Section, N. American Affairs Dept., Ministry of Foreign Affairs 1964–67, Deputy Dir. 1967–69, Dir. 1969–72; Visiting Prof. Nat. Taiwan Univ. 1970–72; Dir.-Gen. Govt. Information Office 1972–75; Deputy Minister of Foreign Affairs 1975–82; Rep. Coordination Council for N. American Affairs, Washington, D.C. 1983–; mem. Cen. Cttee 1976–; numerous awards and decorations. *Publications:* The Opening of Korea; A Study of Chinese Diplomacy 1876–85 1967, Speaking as a Friend 1975, More Views of a Friend 1976. *Address:* Coordination Council for North American Affairs, 4201 Wisconsin Avenue, N.W., Washington D.C. 20016-2137 (Office); 3828 Cathedral Avenue, N.W., Washington, D.C. 20016, U.S.A. (Home). *Telephone:* (202) 895-1800 (Office).

CHIEN, Robert Chun, M.A.; Chinese politician; b. 8 Feb. 1929, Peiping (Beijing); m. Ruth Cheng 1955; two d.; ed. Nat. Taiwan Univ. and Univ. of Minnesota; Dir. Econ. Research Dept., Bank of China 1963–68; Exec. Sec. Comm. on Taxation Reform, Exec. Yuan 1968–70; Dir. Secr. Cen. Bank of China 1970–73, Gen. Man. Banking Dept. 1973–77, Deputy Gov. 1972–85; Minister, Ministry of Finance 1985–88; Sec.-Gen. 1988–; Eisenhower Fellow 1970. *Address:* (0) 2, Ai-Kuo West Road, Taipei 10729, Taiwan.

CHIEPE, Gaositwe Keagakwa Tibe, M.B.E., P.M.S., B.SC., M.A., F.R.S.A.; Botswana diplomatist and politician; b. Serowe; d. of the late T. and S. T. Chiepe (née Sebina); unmarried; ed. secondary school in Tigerloof, S. Africa and Univs. of Fort Hare and Bristol; Educ. Officer, Botswana 1948, Senior Educ. Officer 1962, Deputy Dir. of Educ. 1965, Dir. of Educ. 1968; High Commr. in U.K. and Nigeria 1970–74, concurrently accredited to Sweden, Norway, Denmark, Fed. Repub. of Germany, France, Belgium and the EEC; Minister of Commerce and Industry 1974–77, of Mineral Resources and Water Affairs 1977–84, of External Affairs Sept. 1984–; Patron Botswana Forestry Soc.; Hon. Pres. Kalahari Conservation Soc.; Hon. LL.D. (Bristol). *Leisure interests:* music, gardening. *Address:* Ministry of External Affairs, Gaborone, Botswana.

CHIKANE, Rev. Frank, B.TH.; South African ecclesiastic; b. 3 Jan. 1951, Soweto; s. of James Mashi and Erenia Chikane; m.; two s.; ed. Turfloop Univ. and Univ. of S. Africa; worked with Christ for All Nations 1975–76; ordained Minister 1980; part-time research officer, Inst. of Contextual Theology 1981, Gen. Sec. 1983; Gen. Sec. S. African Council of Churches 1987–; Diakonia Peace Prize 1986; Star Crystal Award 1987. *Publications include:* Doing Theology in a Situation of Conflict 1983, The Incarnation in the Life of People in South Africa 1985, Children in Turmoil: Effect of the Unrest on Township Children 1986, Kairos Document—A Challenge to Churches. *Leisure interests:* reading, keeping fit (mentally, spiritually, physically). *Address:* South African Council of Churches, Khotso House, 42 De Villiers Street, Johannesburg 2000 (Office); 310 Zone 7, Pimville 1808, Soweto, South Africa (Home). *Telephone:* (011) 28-2251 (Office).

CHIKH, Slimane; Algerian politician; b. 13 July 1940, Beni Isguen; m.; four c.; ed. Coll. Sadiki de Kharznadar, Tunis and Univ. of Algiers; Dir. Inst., des Sciences politiques et de l'information, Univ. of Algiers 1975–78; Assoc. Prof., Univ. d'Aix-Marseille 1979–81; Rector Univ. of Algiers 1982–84; Prof. Univ. of Algiers 1984–88; Minister of Educ. and Training 1988–, *Address:* 8 ave de Pékin, El-Mouradia, Algiers, Algeria. *Telephone:* (2) 60-54-41.

CHIKIN, Valentin Vasilevich; Soviet journalist and official; b. 1932; ed. Moscow Univ.; literary corresp. for Moscow Konsomol newspaper 1951–58; mem. CPSU 1956–; literary corresp., Deputy Ed., Ed. of Komsomolskaya Pravda 1958–71; Deputy, First Deputy Ed.-in-Chief of Sovietskaya Rossiya 1971–84; First Deputy Pres. of State Cttee. on Publishng, Printing and the Book Trade 1984–86; Ed.-in-chief of Sovietskaya Rossiya; Sec. of U.S.S.R. Union of Journalists 1986–; cand. mem. of CPSU Cen. Cttee. 1986–. *Address:* Sovietskaya Rossiya, ul. Pravdy 24, Moscow, U.S.S.R.

CHILADZE, Tamaz Ivanovich; Soviet (Georgian) writer; b. 5 March 1931, Signakhi; s. of Ivane and Tamar Chiladze; ed. Univ. of Tbilisi; first published works in 1951; mem. CPSU 1967. *Publications include:* Sun Dial (poems) 1961, A Network of Stars 1961, Pony-trek 1963, The First Day 1965, Who Lives on the Stars 1970, White Smoke 1973, Memory (poems) 1978, Martyrdom of St. Shushanik (essay) 1978, Herald of Spring (essay) 1985; plays: Shelter on the Ninth Floor, Murder, Role for a Beginner Actress, Bird Fair. *Address:* 13 Machabeli Street, Tbilisi, 380007, Georgian S.S.R., U.S.S.R. *Telephone:* 99-59-19 (Office); 36-49-87 (Home).

CHILDS, Marquis William, A.B., A.M.; American writer; b. 17 March 1903; s. of William Henry and Lilan Malissa (née Marquis) Childs; m. 1st Lu Prentiss 1926 (deceased), one s. one d. (deceased); m. 2nd Jane Neylan McBaine; ed. Wisconsin and Iowa Univs.; with United Press 1923 and 1925–26; Corresp. St. Louis Post Dispatch 1926–44, Special Corresp. 1954–62, Washington Corresp. 1962–68; United Feature Syndicate Columnist 1944–54; Hon. LL.D. (Upsala Coll.); Pulitzer Prize for Commentary 1969, Order of North Star (Sweden), Order of Merit (Fed. Repub. of Germany). *Publications:* Sweden: The Middle Way, They Hate Roosevelt 1936, Washington Calling 1937, This is Democracy 1938, This is Your War, I Write from Washington 1942, The Cabin 1944, The Farmer Takes a Hand 1952, Ethics in Business Society (with D. Cater) 1954, The Ragged Edge 1955, Eisenhower: Captive Hero 1959, The Peacemakers 1961, A Taint of Innocence 1967, Witness to Power 1975, Sweden: The Middle Way on Trial 1980. *Address:* 1701 Pennsylvania Avenue, N.W., Washington, D.C. 20036 (Office); 2703 Dumbarton Avenue, N.W., Washington, D.C. 20007, U.S.A. (Home).

CHILES, Lawton Mainor; American politician; b. 3 April 1930, Lakeland, Fla.; s. of Lawton Chiles; m. Rhea May Grafton 1951; three s. one d.; ed. Univ. of Florida; served U.S. Army, Korea 1953–54; law practice, Lakeland 1955–70; mem. Fla. House of Reps. 1958–66, Fla. Senate 1966–70; Senator from Florida 1971–89; mem. Democratic Steering Cttee. 1971–; Chair. Budget Cttee. 1987–; Govt. Award for Conservation 1964; Wildlife Conservation Award of Nat. Wildlife Fed. 1965; Democrat. *Address:* 437 Russell Senate Office Building, Washington, D.C. 20510, U.S.A.

CHILLIDA JUANTEGUI, Eduardo; Spanish sculptor; b. 10 Jan. 1924, San Sebastian; ed. Colegio Marianistas, San Sebastian, and Univ. de Madrid; started sculpting 1947; first one-man exhbn., Madrid 1954; numerous one-man and group exhbns. in Europe, Japan and U.S.A.; has illustrated several books; Visiting Prof. Carpenter Centre, Harvard Univ.1971; Hon. mem. Hispanic Soc. of America, New York; Corresp. mem. Bayerische Akademie der Schönen Kunste, Munich; Gran Premio Int. de Escultura, Venice Biennale 1958, Prix Kandinsky 1960, Carnegie Prize, Pittsburgh Int. 1964, 1979, North Rhine Westphalian Prize for Sculpture 1965, Wilhelm Lehmbruck Prize, Duisburg 1966, Premio Rembrandt, Basel 1975 and numerous other prizes. *Address:* Villa Paz, Alto de Maracruz, San Sebastian, Spain.

CHILVER, Baron (Life Peer) cr. 1987, of Cranfield in the County of Bedfordshire; **Henry Chilver,** M.A., D.SC., F.ENG., C.B.I.M., F.R.S.; British university teacher and administrator; b. 30 Oct. 1926, Barking, Essex; s. of A. H. Chilver; m. Claudia Grigson 1959; three s. two d.; ed. Southend High School and Univ. of Bristol; Structural Eng., British Railways 1947–48; lecturer, Univ. of Bristol 1952–54, Univ. of Cambridge 1956–61, Fellow, Corpus Christi Coll., Cambridge 1958–61; Prof. of Civil Eng., London Univ. 1961–69; Dir. Centre for Environmental Studies 1967–69; Vice-Chancellor, Cranfield Inst. of Tech. 1970–89; Chair. Univs. Computer Bd. 1975–78, The Post Office 1980–81, Advisory Council for Applied Research and Devt. 1982–85, Milton Keynes Devt. Corpn. 1983–; Dir English China Clays, Powell Duffryn, Univs. Funding Council 1988– (Chair. 1988–), Base Int.; mem. or fmr. mem. various cttees. of inquiry, review bodies etc.; Pres. Inst. of Man. Services, of Materials Man. (fmrly. Materials Handling); Hon. Fellow, Corpus Christi Coll., Cambridge; hon. degrees (Leeds, Bristol, Salford, Strathclyde, Bath); Telford Gold Medal 1962 and Coopers Hill War Memorial Prize 1977, Inst. of Civil Engs. *Publications:* Problems in engineering structures (with R. J. Ashby) 1958, Strength of Materials and Structures (with J. Case) 1971; papers on structural eng. and stability. *Address:* English China Clays PLC, John Keay House, St. Austell, Cornwall, PL25 4DJ, England. *Telephone:* (0726) 74482.

CHIMUKA, Augustine Namakube, B.SC.(ECON.); Zambian international official; b. Dec. 1938, Monze; m. Masialeti Mwikisa 1966; three d.; ed. Canisius Coll., Chikuni, Munali Secondary School, Lusaka, Univ. Coll. of Rhodesia and Nyasaland, Salisbury, S. Rhodesia (now Zimbabwe), Univ. of London, Univ. of York, England, American Univ., Washington, D.C., Univ. of Clermont Ferrand, France; joined Zambian Civil Service as Asst. Principal, Ministry of Finance 1964; Principal, Ministry of Foreign Affairs 1966–68; First Sec., High Comm. of Zambia in the U.K. 1968–69; Senior Principal, Ministry of Foreign Affairs 1969–70, Asst. Sec. and Dir. of Africa and Middle East Dept. 1970–71, Under-Sec. 1971–72, Under-Sec. and Deputy Perm. Sec. with the Rank of Amb. 1972–73; Dir. Political Dept., Gen. Secretariat of the OAU 1973–78; Asst. Sec.-Gen. of OAU for Southern Africa Region July 1978, for Admin. Sept. 1978–. *Address:* General Secretariat of the Organization of African Unity, P.O. Box 3243, Addis Ababa, Ethiopia; c/o Ministry of Foreign Affairs, P.O. Box RW 69, Lusaka, Zambia.

CHIN A SEN, Dr. Hendrik Rudolf; Suriname politician and physician; b. 18 Jan. 1934, Albina, Marowijne Dist.; m. Shirley Ho A Fat; three s. one d.; ed. Medical School, Paramaribo, Univ. of Utrecht, Netherlands; mem. Nat. Republican Party; medical practice as specialist in internal diseases, Nieuw Nickerie Hosp. 1969–70, joined staff of St. Vincentius Hosp., Paramaribo 1970; continued medical studies at Nanjing Univ., China Aug.–Dec. 1979; Prime Minister of Suriname and Minister for Gen. and Foreign Affairs March–Nov. 1980; Pres. 1980–82; f. Movt. for the Liberation of Suriname, in exile in the Netherlands, returned 1987; fmr. Vice-Chair. Asscn. of Medical Doctors in Suriname; fmr. Chair. Robin Hood Football Club. *Leisure interests:* music, sport.

CHIN IEE CHONG; Korean lawyer and politician; b. 13 Dec. 1921, Kochang; ed. Seoul Imperial Univ.; joined Ministry of Commerce and Industry 1943, Dir. Bureau of Mines 1948–52; Admin. Vice-Minister 1960–64; New Democratic Party (NDP) mem. Nat. Ass. 1971, 1973, Minister of Health and Social Affairs 1979–81, Democratic Justice Party (DJP) mem. Nat. Ass. 1981, Chair. DJP 1983–84; Prime Minister 1983–85; practised law 1952–61; Vice-Pres. Korea Electric Co., Daihan Insurance Co. *Address:* c/o Office of the Prime Minister, Seoul, Republic of Korea.

CHINAUD, Roger Michel; French politician; b. 6 Sept. 1934, Paris; s. of Henri and Marcelle (née Zorninger) Chinaud; m. Christine Boisdon 1961; four s.; ed. Lycées Buffon, Montaigne and Louis-le-Grand and Law Faculty, Paris; Sec.-Gen. Féd. Région Nord 1956; Vice-Pres. Jeunesses Européennes Fédéralistes 1957; Asst., Gen. Secr. of Conseil des Communes d'Europe and Parl. Sec. 1958; Del.-Gen. Nat. Movt. for Local Candidates 1961–63; Asst. Dir.-Gen. Sable-Chaux Co. 1963–65; Asst. Sec.-Gen. Independent Republicans 1966, Nat. Political Sec. 1968; mem. finance section, Econ. and Social Council 1970–71; Deputy of Paris for Grandes-Carrières Independent Repub. group 1973–81, Asst. Sec.-Gen. for group 1973; Pres. parl. group of Independent Republicans 1974–75, later Vice-Pres.; Vice-Pres. Ile de France Regional Council 1976–81, 1986; Int. Vice-Pres. Paneuropean Union 1976–; Pres. UDF, Nat. Ass. 1978–81, Pres. Departmental UDF group, Paris 1978–86; Mayor of 18th arrondissement, Paris 1983–; Asst. to Mayor of Paris 1983–; Deputy to European Parl. 1984; elected to Senate for Paris Sept. 1986; Gold Medal of Gen. Council of Seine. *Leisure interests:* music, hunting. *Address:* Mairie du 18e, place Jules Joffrin, 75877 Paris Cedex 18 (Office); 2 square de Latour-Maubourg 75007 Paris, France (Home).

CHINNAPPA, Kuppanda Muthayya, B.E.; Indian business executive; b. 5 Feb. 1914, Bangalore; s. of Kuppanda Muthayya; ed. Coll. of Engineering, Guindy, Madras and Jamshedpur Tech. Inst.; Chair. Tata Projects Ltd., Tata Klockner Industrial Plants Ltd., Yashmun Engineers Ltd., Chemical Terminal Trombay Ltd.; Vice-Chair. Tata Hydroelectric Power Supply Co., Ltd., Andhra Valley Power Supply Co. Ltd., Tata Power Co. Ltd.; Vice-Chair. Tata Consulting Engineers; Dir. Tata Industries Ltd., Elpro Int. Ltd., Karnataka State Electronics Devt. Corpn. Ltd., DSMA-TATA Ltd., Toronto, Stewarts & Lloyds of India Ltd., Swede (India) Teltronics Ltd., Tata Consulting Engs. Int., AG, Zug; Fellow, Inst. of Engs. (India). *Leisure interest:* golf. *Address:* c/o Tata Services Ltd., Bombay House, Homi Mody Street, Fort, Bombay 400 023, India.

CHIPP, David Allan, M.A.; British journalist; b. 6 June 1927, Kew, London; s. of Thomas Ford Chipp and Isabel Mary Ballinger; unmarried; ed. Geelong Grammar School, Australia and King's Coll. Cambridge; sports reporter, Reuters 1950–52, Corresp. S.E. Asia 1952–55, first Western Resident Corresp. in Peking 1956–58, various managerial and editorial exec. positions in Asia, Africa and U.S.A. 1958–68, Ed. 1968–69; Ed.-in-Chief, Press Assen. 1969–1986; Dir. The Observer 1985–; TV-am News Co. 1986–; Reuter Foundation 1986–. *Leisure interests:* rowing (Steward of Henley Royal Regatta), theatre, reading, music. *Address:* 2 Wilton Court, 59/60 Eccleston Square, London, SW1V 1PH, England. *Telephone:* 01-834 5579.

CHIPP, Hon. Donald Leslie, B.COM., A.A.S.A.; Australian politician; b. 21 Aug. 1925, Melbourne, Victoria; s. of L. T. and J. S. Chipp; m. Idun G. Welz 1979; two s. four d.; ed. Northcote High School, Univ. of Melbourne; served in R.A.A.F. 1943–45; Registrar, Commonwealth Inst. of Accountants and Australian Soc. of Accountants 1950–55; Chief Exec. Officer Olympic Civic Cttee. 1955–56; Councillor, City of Kew 1955–61; mem. House of Reps. 1960–77; Senator 1977–; Minister for Navy and Minister in charge of Tourist Activities 1966–68, Minister for Customs and Excise 1969–72; Minister assisting Minister for Nat. Devt. 1971–72; Minister for Social Security, Health, Repatriation and Compensation Nov.-Dec. 1975; Liberal to March 1977, Leader Australian Democrats Party 1977–87. *Publications:* Don Chipp—The Third Man 1978 (with J. Larkin) and numerous articles. *Leisure interests:* cricket, football, tennis, rafting. *Address:* Parliament House, Canberra, A.C.T. 2600; 400 Flinders Street, Melbourne, Vic. 3000, Australia (Home). *Telephone:* 62-2521 (Office).

CHIRAC, Jacques René; French politician; b. 29 Nov. 1932, Paris; s. of François Chirac and Marie-Louise Valette; m. Bernadette Chodron de Courcel 1956; two d.; ed. Lycée Carnot, Lycée Louis-le-Grand and Ecole Nationale d'Administration; Military Service in Algeria; Auditor, Cour des Comptes 1959–62; Head of Dept., Sec.-Gen. of Govt. 1962; Head of Dept., Private Office of M. Pompidou 1962–65; Counsellor, Cour des Comptes 1965–67; Sec. of State for Employment Problems 1967–68; Sec. of State for Economy and Finance 1968–71; Minister for Parl. Relations 1971–72, for Agriculture and Rural Devt. 1972–74, of the Interior March-May 1974; Prime Minister of France 1974–1976, 1986–88; Sec.-Gen. Union des Démocrates pour la République (UDR) Jan.-June 1975, Hon. Sec.-Gen. 1975–76; Pres. Rassemblement pour la République (fmrly. UDR) 1976–; Hon. Sec.-Gen. 1977–80; elected to Nat. Assembly 1967, 1968, 1973, 1976, 1978, 1981, 1986; mem. European Parl. 1979; Counsellor-Gen., Meymac 1968, 1970; Pres. Gen. Council, La Corrèze 1970–79; Municipal Counsellor, Sainte-Féréole 1965–; Mayor of Paris March 1977–; mem. Comm. on Nat. Defence 1980–86; Grand Croix, Ordre nat. du Mérite, Chevalier du Mérite agricole, des Arts et des Lettres, etc. *Publications:* Discours pour la

France à l'heure du choix, La lueur de l'espérance: réflexion du soir pour le matin 1978. *Address:* Hôtel de ville, 75196, Paris RP, France.

CHIRAROCHANA, Gen. Sitthi; Thai army officer and politician; b. 25 April 1920, Thon Buri; ed. Wat Nuanorradit School, Chulachomklao Royal Mil. Acad., Bangkok, Army Staff Coll., Nat. Defence Coll., Command and Gen. Staff Coll., Leavenworth, U.S.A. and U.S. Naval Postgraduate School; began army career 1940; Chief of Staff, Royal Thai Army 1977; Deputy C.-in-C. Royal Thai Army 1978; Under-Sec. of State, Ministry of Defence 1979; Minister of Interior 1981–86. *Address:* Ministry of the Interior, Asdang Road, Bangkok 2, Thailand.

CHISHOLM, Donald Alexander, PH.D.; Canadian business executive; b. 7 May 1927, Toronto; s. of Douglas A. and Daisy (Smith) Chisholm; m. Marilyn Bayliss 1953; one s. one d.; ed. Univ. of Toronto; joined electron device Dept., Bell Telephone Labs. 1953, Dir. 1964; Man. Dir. Bellcomm Inc. 1968; Vice-Pres. for Research and Devt., Northern Electric Co. Ltd. 1969; Pres. Bell-Northern Research (GNR), Ltd. and Chair. of Bd., BNR Inc., Palo Alto 1971; Exec. Vice-Pres. Tech., Northern Telecom Ltd. (fmrly. Northern Electric Co., Ltd.); Chair. of Bd., Bell-Northern Research Ltd. 1976; Pres. Innovation & Devt., Northern Telecom Ltd. 1981–82 and Chair. of Bd. and Pres. Bell-Northern Research Ltd. 1981; Exec. Vice-Pres. Tech. and Innovation, Northern Telecom Ltd. 1982–; Chair. of Bd. Bell-Northern Research Ltd. 1977–; fmr. mem. Science Council of Canada; mem. and former mem. various govt. bds. and cttees.; Fellow, Inst. of Electrical and Electronics Engineers, New York, Ryerson Polytechnical Inst., Toronto; Dr.h.c. (Waterloo, Toronto, Quebec). *Address:* Northern Telecom Ltd., P.O. Box 458, Station A, Mississauga, Ont. L5A 3A2, Canada.

CHISHOLM, Geoffrey D., CH.M., F.R.C.S., F.R.C.S.(E.); British consultant surgeon and professor of surgery; b. 30 Sept. 1931, Hawera, N.Z.; s. of Sedman Arthur Chisholm and Ellen Marion Friston; m. Angela Jane Holden 1962; two s.; ed. Scot's Coll., Wellington, Malvern Coll., Worcs. and St. Andrew's Univ.; Research Fellow Johns Hopkins Hosp., Baltimore, Md. 1961–62; Consultant Urological Surgeon Hammersmith Hosp., London 1967–77; Hon. Sr. Lecturer Royal Postgraduate Medical School, London 1967–77; Inst. of Urology, London 1972–; Prof. of Surgery, Univ. of Edinburgh 1977–; Dir. Nuffield Transplant Unit 1977–; Chair. British Prostate Group 1975–80, European Soc. Urological Oncology and Endocrinology 1984–85; Pres. British Assen. Urological Surgeons 1986–88; Vice-Pres. British Assen. Surgical Oncologists 1984–85; Council mem. Royal Coll. of Surgeons of Edin. 1984–, Pres. 1988–; Ed. Urological Research 1977–81, British Journal of Urology 1977–; Memorial Lecture, Sydney 1983; Francisco Diaz Medal 1985, Pybus Medal 1986. *Publications:* Tutorials in Urology (Ed.) 1980, Scientific Foundations of Urology (Co-Ed.) 1982, Surgical Management (Co-Ed.) 1985. *Leisure interests:* medical journalism and wine tasting. *Address:* Department of Surgery/Urology, Western General Hospital, Edinburgh, EH4 2XU, Scotland (Office); 8 Ettrick Road, Edinburgh, EH10 5BJ, Scotland (Home). *Telephone:* 031-315 2522 (Office); 031-229 7173 (Home).

CHISSANO, Joaquim; Mozambique politician; b. 2 Oct. 1939, Chibuto; m. Marcelina Rafael Chissano; four c.; Asst. Sec. to Pres., Frente de Libertacão de Moçambique (FRELIMO) in charge of Educ. 1963–66, Sec. to Pres. FRELIMO 1966–69; Chief Rep. FRELIMO in Dar-es-Salaam 1969–74; Prime Minister, Transitional Govt. of Mozambique 1974–75, Minister of Foreign Affairs 1975–86, Pres. of Mozambique Oct. 1986–; Order, Augusto César Sandino (Nicaragua) 1988. *Address:* Office of the President, Avda Julius Nyerere, Maputo, Mozambique.

CHITTISTER, Joan D., M.A., PH.D.; American Benedictine prioress, social psychologist, author and lecturer; b. 26 April 1936, Dubois, Pa.; d. of Harold C. Chittister and Loretta Cuneo Chittister; ed. St. Benedict Acad. Erie, Mercyhurst Coll. Erie, Univ. of Notre Dame and Pennsylvania State Univ.; elementary teacher, 1955–59, secondary teacher 1959–74; taught Pa. State Univ. 1969–71; Pres. Fed. of St. Scholastica 1971–78; Prioress, Benedictine Sisters of Erie 1978–; Pres. Conf. of American Benedictine Prioresses 1974–; mem. Exec. Bd. Ecumenical and Cultural Inst. St. John's Univ. Collegeville 1976–; mem. Bd. of Dirs. Nat. Catholic Reporter; mem. Bd. of Corporators, St. Vincent Foundation; several awards and hon degrees. *Publications include:* Climb Along the Cutting Edge: An Analysis of Change in Religious Life 1977, Living the Rule Today 1982, Women, Church and Ministry 1983, Winds of Change: Women Challenge the Church 1986; numerous articles and lectures on religious life and peace-making. *Leisure interests:* fishing, music, reading. *Address:* Mount Saint Benedict Monastery, 6101 East Lake Road, Erie, Pa. 16511, U.S.A. *Telephone:* (814) 899-0614.

CHITTY, Sir Thomas Willes, Bt., F.R.S.L. (pen name **Thomas Hinde**); British author; b. 2 March 1926, Felixstowe; s. of Sir Thomas Henry Willes Chitty; m. Susan Elspeth Hopkinson 1951; one s. three d.; ed. Winchester Coll. and Univ. Coll., Oxford; served in Royal Navy 1944–47; with Shell group 1953–60; Granada Arts Fellow, Univ. of York 1964–65; Visiting lecturer, Univ. of Illinois 1965–67; Visiting Prof. Boston Univ. 1969–70; now freelance writer. *Publications include:* Mr. Nicholas 1952, For the Good of the Company 1961, The Day the Call Came 1964, High 1968, Our Father 1975, Daymare 1980; travel: The Great Donkey Walk 1977, The Cottage Book 1979, Stately Gardens of Britain 1983, A Field Guide to the

English Country Parson 1983, British Forests 1984, The Domesday Book: England's Heritage, then and now 1986, Courtiers: 900 years of Court Life 1986, Bath, an Informal History 1988; Sir Henry and Sons (autobiog.) 1980, A Field Guide to the English Country Parson 1983 (biography), Capability Brown 1986. *Leisure interests:* eating, drinking, talking, listening, gardening, reading, travelling. *Address:* Bow Cottage, West Hoathly, Sussex, RH19 4QF, England. *Telephone:* 0342 810 269.

CHIU CHUANG-HUAN; Chinese politician; b. 25 July 1925, Changhua County; ed. School of Political Science, Nat. Chengchi Univ.; Dir. 3rd Dept., Ministry of Personnel, Taiwan 1965-67; Dept. Dir. 5th Section, Cen. Cttee., Kuomintang 1967-68; Commr. Dept. of Social Affairs, Taiwan Prov. Govt. 1969-72; Dir. Dept. of Social Affairs, Cen. Cttee., Kuomintang 1972-78; Minister without Portfolio 1976-78; Deputy Sec.-Gen., Cen. Cttee., Kuomintang 1978; Minister of the Interior 1978-81; Vice-Premier Exec. Yuan, Repub. of China (Taiwan) 1981-84; Gov. of Taiwan 1984-; Hon. Ph.D. (Youngnam Univ., Repub. of Korea). *Publications:* Thought Regarding Social Welfare in the Three Principles of the People, A Summary of the Chinese Social Welfare System. *Address:* Taiwan Provincial Government, Foreign Affairs Department, 9th Floor, 15 Hangchow South Road, Section 1, Taipei 10044, Taiwan. *Telephone:* (049) 332201.

CHIZAKI, Usaburo; Japanese politician; b. 21 June 1919; ed. Ritsumeikan Univ.; mem. House of Reps 1963-; Chair. Standing Cttee. on Communications 1975-76, Standing Cttee. on Local Admin. 1976-78; Minister of Transport 1979-80; Pres. All Japan Construction Cos. Asscn. 1967-72, Hokkaido Amateur Sports Assn. 1965-. *Publication:* Watashi no Kyaku.

CHKHEIDZE, Revaz (Rezo); Soviet (Georgian) film director; b. 1924; studied acting at Tbilisi State Theatrical Inst. 1943-46, with Tengiz Abuladze (q.v.); studied under Sergei Yutkevich and Mikhail Romm. *Films include:* Magdana's Donkey 1956 (with T. Abuladze), Our Yard 1957, A Soldier's Father 1965, Our Youth 1970.

CHKHIKVADZE, Ramaz; Soviet (Georgian) actor; b. 1928, Georgia; grad. Rustaveli Georgian State Drama Inst.; since then with the Rustaveli Company, Georgia, for which he has played over 50 parts; *roles include:* Louis XIV (Bulgakov's Molière), Macheath (Brecht's Threepenny Opera), Adzhak (Caucasian Chalk Circle), Edward (King Lear), Richard (Richard III), has also acted in several films; awards include Best Leading Man at VIIIth Moscow Film Festival for film Saplings, Mardzhanishvili Prize for performance of title role in Kvarkvare, 1975; Prize Laureate for Caucasian Chalk Circle, 1979. *Address:* Rustaveli Company, Tbilisi, Georgia, U.S.S.R.

CHŇOUPEK, Bohuslav, Ing.; Czechoslovak politician; b. 10 Aug. 1925, Bratislava; ed. Coll. of Econ. Sciences, Bratislava; mem. editorial staff, Pravda 1958-60; Moscow corresp., Pravda 1960-65; Chief Editor, Predvoj 1965-67; Deputy Minister of Culture 1967-69; Gen. Dir. Czechoslovak Radio 1969-70; Amb. to U.S.S.R. 1970-71; Minister of Foreign Affairs 1971-88; alt. mem. Cen. Cttee. C.P. of Czechoslovakia 1967-69, mem. 1969-; Deputy to House of People 1972-; Klement Gottwald State Prize 1966; Order of Labour 1970, 1975, Order of Democracy (Colombia). *Publications:* Dunaj sa končí v Izmaile (The Danube Ends in Izmail) 1956, Dobyvatel vesmíru 1961, Generál s levom (The General with the Lion), Milníky (Milestones) 1975. *Address:* c/o Ministry of Foreign Affairs, Prague 1, Loretánské nám. 5, Czechoslovakia.

CHO, Kiyoko Takeda, D.LITT.; Japanese university professor; b. 20 June 1917, Hyogoken; d. of Takehira and Hiroko Takeda; m. Yukio Cho 1953; one s.; ed. Kobe Coll., Olivet Coll., U.S.A., Union Theological Seminary, Columbia Univ., U.S.A., and Tokyo Univ.; Instructor in History of Thought, Int. Christian Univ. 1953-55, Asst. Prof. 1955-61, Prof. 1961-83, Graduate School Prof. 1983-; lecturer, Tokyo Univ. 1962-72; Dir. Cttee. on Asian Cultural Studies 1958-71; Research Assoc. Princeton Univ. 1965-66, on Asian Studies, Harvard Univ. 1966-67; Dean Liberal Coll. of Arts, Int. Christian Univ. 1967-69, Dean Graduate School 1970-74; Dir. Inst. of Asian Cultural Studies 1971-83; mem. Pres. Cttee. World Council of Churches 1971-75; Senior Assoc. Fellow, St. Antony's Coll., Oxford 1975-76. *Publications:* Man, Society and History 1953, Conflict in Concept of Man in Modern Japan 1959, The Emperor System and Education 1964, Indigenization and Apostasy: Traditional Ethos and Protestants 1967, The Genealogy of Apostates: The Japanese and Christianity 1973, Between Orthodoxy and Heterodoxy 1976, The Dual Image of the Japanese Tenno Before and After 1945 1978, We and the World 1983, The Milestones for Women's Liberation in Modern Japan 1985; Ed. Method and Objectives of History of Thoughts—Japan and the West 1961, Educational Thoughts and Activities of Japanese Protestants 1963, Christianity in Modern Japan 1964, Theory of Comparative Modernization 1970, Human Rights in Modern Japan 1970, Collection of Religious Literature of the Meiji Period 1975, The Archetypes of Japanese Culture 1984; has translated works of Reinhold Niebuhr into Japanese. *Leisure interests:* folk art, floriculture. *Address:* 1-59-6 Nishigahara, Kita-ku, Tokyo, Japan. *Telephone:* 03-915-0886.

CHO, Ramaswamy, B.SC., B.L.; Indian journalist, playwright, actor, lawyer; b. 5 Oct. 1934, Madras; s. of R. Srinivasan and Rajammal Srinivasan; m. 1966; one s. one d.; ed. P.S. High School, Loyola Coll., Vivekananda Coll., Madras and Madras Law Coll., Madras Univ.; started practice as lawyer, Madras High Court 1957; Legal Adviser to T.T.K. Group of Cos. 1961-; film scriptwriter and actor 1966-; theatre dir., actor and playwright 1958-;

Ed. Tamil political fortnightly Thuglak 1970-; Pres. People's Union of Civil Liberties, Tamilnadu 1980-82; has acted in 170 films, written 14 film scripts, directed 4 films; Haldi Gati Award, Maharana of Mewar, for nat. service through journalism 1985; Veerakesari Award for investigative journalism 1986. *Publications:* 23 plays and 4 novels in Tamil; numerous articles on politics, in English and Tamil. *Leisure interest:* photography. *Address:* 5 Bishop Wallers Avenue, C.I.T. Colony, Madras, 600004, India. *Telephone:* 74222; 74142; 415643.

CHODOROW, Marvin, PH.D.; American physicist; b. 16 July 1913, Buffalo, N.Y.; s. of Isidor and Lena (Cohen) Chodorow; m. Leah Ruth Turitz 1937; two d.; ed. Univ. of Buffalo and M.I.T.; Research Assoc., Pennsylvania State Coll. 1940-41; Instructor in Physics, Coll. of City of New York 1941-43; Senior Project Engineer, Sperry Gyroscope Co. 1943-47; Asst. Prof. of Physics, Stanford Univ. 1947, Prof. of Physics and Electrical Engineering 1954, Barbara Kimball Browning Prof. of Applied Physics and Electrical Engineering 1975-78, Prof. Emer. 1978-; Dir. Microwave Lab. 1959-78, Chair. Dept. of Applied Physics 1962-69; lecturer, Ecole Normale Supérieure, Paris 1955-56; Visiting Research Assoc., Univ. Coll., London 1969-70; mem. N.A.S., Nat. Acad. of Engineering; Fellow, American Acad. of Arts and Sciences, American Physical Soc., Inst. of Electrical and Electronic Engineers; Fulbright Fellow, Cambridge Univ. (U.K.) 1962; W.R.G. Baker Award 1962; Hon. LL.D. (Glasgow) 1972. *Publications:* Fundamentals of Microwave Electronics (co-author), Progress and its Discontents (co-Ed.) 1982, Lamme Metal 1982. *Leisure interests:* travel, bridge, reading. *Address:* Edward L. Ginzton Laboratory, Stanford University, Stanford, Calif. 94305; 809 San Francisco Terrace, Stanford, Calif. 94305, U.S.A. (Home). *Telephone:* 415-497-0201 (Office); 415-858-1331 (Home).

CHOI, Man-Duen, PH.D., F.R.S.C.; Canadian professor of mathematics; b. 13 June 1945, Nanking, China; m. Pui-Wah Ip 1972; two s. one d.; ed. Chinese Univ. of Hong Kong and Univ. of Toronto; lecturer, Dept. of Math., Univ. of Calif. Berkeley 1973-76; Asst. Prof. Dept. of Math., Univ. of Toronto 1976-79, Assoc. Prof. 1979-82, Prof. of Math. 1982-; mem. American Math. Soc., Canadian Math Soc., Math. Assn. of America; Israel Halperin Prize 1980. *Publications:* numerous articles in mathematical journals. *Leisure interests:* swimming, yoga, stamps. *Address:* Department of Mathematics, University of Toronto, Toronto, Ont., M5S 1A1, Canada. *Telephone:* 416-978-3318.

CHOI, Sunu; Korean museum administrator; b. 27 April 1916, Kaesong; s. of Choi Chong-song and Yang Sun-som; m. Park Kum-som; one d.; ed. Songdo High School, Kaesong; Asst. Curator for Fine Art, Nat. Museum of Korea 1945, Chief Curator Nat. Museum of Korea 1973-74, Dir.-Gen. 1974-85. *Publications:* Korean Buddhist Painting 1957, Handicraft Art of the Choson Period 1977, 5,000 Years of Korean Art 1978, Korean Beauty, Korean Mind 1980, Paintings of Korea 1980. *Leisure interest:* rock collecting. *Address:* c/o Office of the Director-General, National Museum of Korea, Seoul, Republic of Korea. *Telephone:* 722-9428.

CHOI KYU-HAH; Korean politician; b. 16 July 1919, Wonju City, Kangwon-do; m. Kee Hong 1936; two s. one d.; ed. Kyung Gi High School, Seoul, Tokyo Coll. of Educ., Japan and Nat. Daedong Inst., Manchuria; Prof., Coll. of Educ., Seoul Nat. Univ. 1945-46; Dir. Econ. Affairs Bureau, Ministry of Foreign Affairs 1951-52; Consul-Gen. Korean Mission, Japan 1952-57, Minister 1959; Vice-Minister of Foreign Affairs 1959-60; Amb. to Malaysia 1964-67; Minister of Foreign Affairs 1967-71; Special Pres. Asst. for Foreign Affairs 1971-75; Acting Prime Minister 1975-76; Prime Minister 1976-79; Acting Pres. Oct.-Dec. 1979, Pres. 1979-80; Chief Korean del. to UN Gen. Assembly, 1967, 1968, 1969; del. to numerous int. confs. 1955-; Hon. Litt.D. (Hankook Univ. of Foreign Studies, Seoul); decorations from Ethiopia, Panama, El Salvador, Malaysia, Saudi Arabia, Tunisia and Belgium; Order of Diplomatic Service Merit. *Leisure interest:* angling. *Address:* c/o Chong Wa Dae, Seoul, Republic of Korea.

CHOJNOWSKA-LISKIEWICZ, Krystyna; Polish yachtswoman; b. 15 July 1936, Warsaw; d. of Juliusz and Kazimiera Chojnowski; m. Wacław Liskiewicz 1960; ed. Polytechnical Univ., Gdańsk; Shipbuilding engineer, Gdańsk 1960-; first woman to circumnavigate the world solo 28 March 1976-20 March 1978, in Yacht 'Mazurek'; Commdr. Cross of Order Polonia Restituta 1978; Hon. Medal Czechoslovakian Women's Union 1978; Prize of Minister of Foreign Affairs 1978, Slocum Award 1978, Médaille d'Argent de la Jeunesse et des Sports, France 1979, and other decorations. *Publication:* Pierwsza dookoła Świata (The First One Round the World) 1979. *Leisure interests:* sailing, skiing, music, books. *Address:* Ul. Norblina 29 m. 50, 80 304 Gdańsk-Oliwa, Poland. *Telephone:* 529371.

CHOMSKY, (Avram) Noam, M.A., PH.D.; American theoretical linguist; b. 7 Dec. 1928, Pennsylvania; s. of William Chomsky and Elsie Simonofsky; m. Carol Schatz 1949; one s. two d.; ed. Univ. of Pennsylvania; at M.I.T. 1955-, Prof. of Modern Languages 1961-66, Ferrari Ward Prof. of Modern Languages and Linguistics 1966-, Inst. Prof. 1976-; Nat. Science Foundation Fellow, Princeton Inst. for Advanced Study 1958-59; American Council of Learned Socs. Fellow, Center for Cognitive Studies, Harvard Univ. 1964-65; mem. American Acad. of Arts and Sciences, Linguistic Soc. of America, American Philosophical Assn., American Acad. of Political and Social Science, N.A.S., etc.; Hon. Fellow, British Psychological Soc. 1985; Hon. D.H.L. (Chicago) 1967, (Loyola Univ., Swarthmore Coll.) 1970,

(Bard Coll.) 1971, (Mass.) 1973; Hon. D.Lit. (London) 1967, (Delhi) 1972, Visva-Bharati (West Bengal) 1980, (Pa.) 1984; Kyoto Prize in Basic Sciences 1988. *Publications include:* Syntactic Structures 1957, Current Issues in Linguistic Theory 1964, Aspects of the Theory of Syntax 1965, Cartesian Linguistics 1966, Language and Mind 1968, The Sound Pattern of English (with Morris Halle) 1968, American Power and the New Mandarins 1969, At War with Asia 1970, Problems of Knowledge and Freedom 1971, Studies on Semantics in Generative Grammar 1972, For Reasons of State 1973, The Backroom Boys 1973, Bains de Sang (trans. of Counter-revolutionary Violence) (with Edward Herman) 1974, Peace in the Middle East? 1974, Reflections on Language 1975, The Logical Structure of Linguistic Theory 1975, Essays on Form and Interpretation 1977, Human Rights and American Foreign Policy 1978, The Political Economy of Human Rights (2 Vols., with Edward Herman) 1979, Rules and Representations 1980, Lectures on Government and Binding 1981, Radical Priorities 1981, Towards a New Cold War 1982, Concepts and Consequences of the Theory of Government and Binding 1982, Fateful Triangle 1983, Knowledge of Language: Its Nature, Origins and Use 1986, Turning the Tide 1986, Barriers 1986, Pirates and Emperors 1986, On Power and Ideology 1987, Language and Problems of Knowledge 1987, Language in a Psychological Setting 1987, The Culture of Terrorism 1988, Generative Grammar 1988, Manufacturing Consent (with Edward Herman) 1988, The Chomsky Reader 1988; numerous lectures. *Leisure interest:* gardening. *Address:* Department of Linguistics and Philosophy, Massachusetts Institute of Technology, 77 Massachusetts Avenue, Cambridge, Mass. 02139 (Office); 15 Suzanne Road, Lexington, Mass. 02173, U.S.A. (Home). *Telephone:* 617-253-7819 (Office); 617-862-6160 (Home).

CHONA, (Mathias) Mainza, BAR.-AT-LAW; Zambian politician; b. 21 Jan. 1930, Nampeyo, Monze; s. of Chief Chona; m. Yolanta Mainza 1953; two s. five d.; ed. Chona School, Chikuni Catholic Mission, Munali Govt. School, Lusaka and Gray's Inn, London; Interim Pres. UNIP (United National Independence Party) 1959–60, Vice-Pres. 1960–61, Gen. Sec. 1961–69, mem. Interim Exec. Cttee. 1969–71, mem. Cen. Cttee. 1969–81, Sec.-Gen. 1978–81; M.P. for Livingstone 1964, for Mankoya 1968; Minister of Justice 1964, of Home Affairs 1964–66, for Presidential Affairs 1967, without Portfolio 1968, for Central Province, without Portfolio, of Provincial and Local Govt. and Amb. to U.S.A. (also accred. to Chile) 1969–70; Vice-Pres. of Zambia 1970–73, Prime Minister 1973–75, 1977–78; Minister of Legal Affairs and Attorney Gen. 1975–77; Legal Practitioner 1981–84; Amb. to People's Repub. of China 1984–; Sec.-Gen. 3rd Non-Aligned Conf. (Lusaka) 1970; Pres. OAU Mediation Comm. 1971–; Chair. Comm. on Establishment of One Party Participatory Democracy 1971–72; mem. UN Inter-Action Council of Fmr. Heads of Govt. 1983–; Chair. Zambian Industrial and Mining Corpn. Ltd. (ZIMCO) 1977–78; del. to numerous int. congresses. *Publication:* Kabuca Uleta Tunji (novel, Margaret Wrong Medal 1956). *Leisure interests:* reading, writing. *Address:* Embassy of the Republic of Zambia, 5 Tung Sze Street, San Li Tun, Beijing, People's Republic of China. *Telephone:* 521554.

CHONG SOK-MO; Korean politician; b. 1929, Kongyu, S. Chungchong Prov.; ed. Seoul Nat. Univ.; fmr. mem. Home Affairs Ministry, Minister of Home Affairs 1985–86; elected to Nat. Ass. as mem. of Democratic Repub. Party 1979; mem. Democratic Justice Party 1981. *Address:* 77 Sejong-no, Chongno-ku, Seoul, South Korea. *Telephone:* 720-2466.

CHOONHAVAN, Maj.-Gen. Chatichai; Thai army officer, diplomatist, business executive and politician; b. 5 April 1922, Bangkok; ed. Chulachomklao Royal Mil. Acad. and Cavalry School, Royal Thai Army; served in Second World War and Korean War; fmr. Troop Commdr. First Royal Cavalry Guards, Asst. Mil. Attaché, Thai Embassy, Washington, D.C., U.S.A., Commandant Armour School, Bangkok, Amb. to Argentina, Austria, Turkey, Switzerland, Yugoslavia and UN; f. Erawan Trust Co. Ltd., Erawan International Co. Ltd.; Deputy Foreign Minister 1972, Foreign Minister 1975; Industry Minister 1976; Deputy Leader Chat Thai Party; Deputy Prime Minister 1986–88, Prime Minister of Thailand July 1988–. *Address:* Office of the Prime Minister, Government House, Nakhon Pathom Rd., Bangkok, Thailand.

CHOPPIN, Purnell Whittington, M.D.; American scientist; b. 4. July 1929, Baton Rouge, La.; s. of Arthur Richard Choppin and Eunice (Bolin) Choppin; m. Joan H. Macdonald 1959; one d.; ed. Louisiana State Univ.; Intern Barnes Hosp., St. Louis 1953–54, Asst. Resident 1956–57; Postdoctoral Fellow, Research Assoc., Rockefeller Univ., New York 1957–60, Asst. Prof. 1960–64, Assoc. Prof. 1964–70, Prof., Sr. Physician 1970–85, Leon Hess Prof. of Virology 1980–85, Vice-Pres. Acad. Programs 1983–85, Dean of Graduate Studies 1985; Vice-Pres., Chief Scientific Officer, Howard Hughes Medical Inst. 1985–87, Pres. 1987–; ed. Virology 1973–; Chair. Virology Study Section, Nat. Insts. of Health 1975–78; mem. Bd. of Dirs. Royal Soc. of Medicine Foundation Inc., New York 1978–, Advisory Cttee. on Fundamental Research, Nat. Multiple Sclerosis Soc. 1979–84, Advisory Council Nat. Inst. of Allergy and Infectious Diseases 1980–83, Sloan-Kettering Cancer Cttee., New York 1983–84, Comm. on Life Sciences, Nat. Research Council 1982–, Council for Research and Clinical Investigation, American Cancer Soc. 1983–; Chair. Advisory Cttee. on Fundamental Research 1983–84; Pres. American Soc. of Virology 1985–86; Fellow New York Acad. of Sciences, A.A.A.S.; mem. N.A.S., Asscn of American Physi-

cians, American Soc. of Microbiology, American Inst. of Biological Sciences, American Asscn. of Immunologists and other professional orgs.; Howard Taylor Ricketts Award, Univ. of Chicago 1978, Waksman Award for Excellence in Microbiology, N.A.S. 1984. *Publications:* numerous articles and chapters on virology, cell biology, infectious diseases. *Leisure interests:* fly fishing and stamp collecting. *Address:* 6701 Rockledge Drive, Bethesda, Md. 20814 (Office); 2700 Calvert Street, N.W., Washington, D.C. 20008; U.S.A. (Home).

CHOQUET, Gustave Alfred Arthur, D.ÈS.SC.; French professor of mathematics; b. 1 March 1915, Solesme; s. of Gustave Choquet and Marie Fosse; m. Yvonne Bruhat; one s. one d. (and two s. one d. from 1st marriage); ed. Lycée de Valenciennes, Lycée Saint-Louis, Paris, Ecole normale supérieure; taught at Institut français in Poland 1946–47; Lecturer, Faculty of Science, Univ. of Grenoble 1947–49; Lecturer, Faculty of Science, Univ. of Paris 1949–50, Prof. 1950–; Prof. of Math., Ecole polytechnique 1965–70; membre de l'Institut (Académie des sciences) 1976; Chevalier, Légion d'honneur. *Leisure interests:* mountain sports, walking, swimming. *Address:* 16 avenue d'Alembert, 92160 Antony, France (Home).

CHORZEMPA, Daniel Walter, PH.D.; American pianist, organist, musicologist and composer; b. 7 Dec. 1944, Minneapolis; s. of Martin Chorzempa Sr. and Henrietta Reiswig; ed. Univ. of Minnesota; former church organist; Organ Instructor, Univ. of Minn. 1962–65; Fulbright Scholar, Cologne 1965–66; extensive piano and organ recitals in Germany, Denmark, Italy and U.K. etc. since 1968; J. S. Bach Prize, Leipzig 1968; records for Philips. *Leisure interests:* mathematics, architecture, poetry, renaissance history and literature. *Address:* 5000 Cologne 1, Grosse Budengasse 11, Federal Republic of Germany. *Telephone:* 231271.

CHOTARD, Yvon, LIC. EN DROIT; French publisher; b. 25 May 1921, La Madeleine; s. of Joël Chotard; m. Adeline Levère 1943; three s. five d.; ed. Collège des Jésuites, Lille, Univs. of Paris and Lyon; Founder publisher Editions France-Empire 1945–; Founder, Pres. French Junior Chamber of Econs. 1952–55; Pres. Christian Centre for French Businessmen 1965–70; mem. Econ. and Social Council 1964–, Pres. Group of Private Enterprises; Vice-Pres., then Pres. Nat. Publishing Asscn. and Pres. Booksellers' Asscn. 1971–79; Cttee. mem., Dir. and Pres. Comm. for formation of Conseil national du patronat français 1971, then its Vice-Pres. 1973–81; First Vice-Pres. 1981–1986; Rep. of French Govt. at ILO, Geneva 1987; Commdr., Légion d'honneur and Commandeur des Arts et Lettres. *Leisure interest:* tennis. *Address:* 68 rue Jean-Jacques-Rousseau, 75001 Paris (Office).

CHOUDHURY, Abdul Barkat Ataul Ghani Khan, B.A.; Indian politician; b. 1 Nov. 1927, Malda Dist., W. Bengal; ed. Calcutta Univ., Inst. of Int. Affairs, Geneva; mem. W. Bengal Assembly 1952–; Minister for Irrigation, Govt. of W. Bengal 1971, for Irrigation and Power 1972–77; Pres. W. Bengal Congress (I) 1978; mem. Lok Sabha 1980–; Minister of Energy and Irrigation, Govt. of India 1980–81, of Energy 1981–82, of Railways 1982–85, of Programme Implementation 1985–87; mem. del. to UN 1972, 1976. *Address:* c/o Ministry of Programme Implementation, New Delhi, India.

CHOUDHURY, Humayan Rasheed, B.SC.; Bangladesh diplomatist and lawyer; b. 11 Nov. 1928; m.; one s. one d.; ed. Muslim Univ. of Aligarh, London Inst. of World Affairs, Fletcher School of Law and Diplomacy, Mass.; served at bar, London; joined Pakistani Foreign Service 1953, various assignments, Rome, Baghdad, Paris, Lisbon, Jakarta, New Delhi, then Chief Bangladesh Mission, New Delhi 1971–72, Amb. to Fed. Repub. of Germany (concurrently accred. to Switzerland, Austria, Holy See), also Perm. Rep. to IAEA, UNIDO 1972–76, to Saudi Arabia (concurrently accred. to Jordan, Oman), and Perm. Rep. to Org. of the Islamic Conf., then to U.S.A. 1982, del. to numerous int. confs. on Islamic Affairs 1977–81, to bilateral meetings including Indo-Bangladeshi talks on border delineation etc., to UN Gen. Ass. 1981, Vice-Pres. 39th Session; now Prin. Foreign Sec., Adviser for Foreign Affairs to Pres.; Minister of Foreign Affairs 1985–; Pres. 41st Session Gen. Ass. of UN 1986–87; mem. Exec. Cttee. and Chair. Finance Cttee. Islamic Centre of America, Washington; Mahatma Gandhi Peace Prize (William and Mary Univ., Va.) *Address:* c/o Ministry of Foreign Affairs, Topkhana Road, Dhaka, Bangladesh. *Telephone:* 236020.

CHOUFI, Hammoud el–; Syrian politician and diplomatist; b. 10 Aug. 1935; m.; three c.; ed. Univ. of Damascus; Sec.-Gen. Syrian Baath Party 1962–64; Amb. to Indonesia 1965–70, to India 1970–72; Dir. American Dept., Ministry of Foreign Affairs 1972–78; Perm. Rep. to UN 1978–79. *Publication:* History of the Sweida Region 1961. *Address:* c/o Ministry of Foreign Affairs, Damascus, Syria.

CHOW HONG-TAO, LL.B.; Chinese politician; b. 14 Dec. 1916, Fenghua County; m.; four d.; ed. Nat. Wuhan Univ. and Inst. of Nat. Defence; Sec. Nat. Govt. 1943–48, Office of Pres. 1948–57; Deputy Sec.-Gen. Cen. Cttee. Kuomintang 1950–59; Exec. Dir. Bank of China 1956–63; Vice-Minister, Ministry of Finance 1958–62; Commr. Dept. of Finance, Taiwan Provincial Govt. 1962–69; Exec. Dir. Bank of Taiwan 1963–69; Chair. Taiwan Provincial Land Devt. Co. 1964–69; Dir.-Gen., Directorate-Gen. of Budget, Accounting and Statistics, Exec. Yuan 1969–78; Minister of State, mem. Council for Econ. Planning and Devt. and Chair. Bd. of Dirs., Cttee. for Taipei World Trade Centre, Exec. Yuan 1978–. *Address:* The Executive Yuan, Taipei, Taiwan.

CHOW SHU-KAI; Chinese diplomatist; b. 21 Aug. 1913, Hupeh, China; ed. National Central Univ., Nanking and Univ. of London; Chinese Consul, Manchester, England 1944–45; Assoc. Prof. of Int. Relations, Univ. of Nanking 1946–47; Deputy Dir. Information Dept., Ministry of Foreign Affairs 1947–49; Minister, Chargé d'affaires, Manila 1953–55; Deputy Minister of Foreign Affairs 1956–60; Cabinet Minister and Chair. Overseas Chinese Affairs 1960–62; Amb. to Spain 1963–65, to U.S.A. 1965–71; Minister of Foreign Affairs 1971–72; Minister without Portfolio, Exec. Yuan (Cabinet) 1972–77; Ambassador to the Holy See 1978–. *Address:* Embassy of the Republic of China to the Holy See, Piazza delle Muse 7, 00197 Rome, Italy. *Telephone:* 803-166.

CHOWDHURY, Abul Fazal Mohammad Ahsanuddin, LL.B.; Bangladesh politician and judge; b. 1915, Mymensingh; m.; one s. two d.; ed. Univ. of Dacca; joined fmr. Bengal Civil Service (Judicial) 1942; served as Dist. Judge in several regions; elected to High Court of Bangladesh 1973; retd. from judiciary Nov. 1977; Pres. of Bangladesh March 1982–83; also in charge of Pres.'s Secr., Cabinet Div. and Ministries of Defence and Planning 1982–83. *Address:* Office of the President, Dhaka, Bangladesh.

CHOWDHURY, Major-Gen. Mahabbat Jan; Bangladesh army officer and government official; b. March 1934, Faridpur; ed. Armanitola High School, Chittagong Govt. Coll., Dacca Univ.; joined Pakistani Mil. Acad. 1953, Signals Corps Army 1955, served numerous posts including Instructor, Staff Officer, then Dir. Army Signals, then Deputy Dir.-Gen. Bangladesh Rifles, then Dir.-Gen. Forces' Intelligence; Minister of Food 1985–86. *Address:* c/o Ministry of Food, Bangladesh Secretariat, Bhaban 4, 2nd 9-Storey Building, 3rd Floor, Dhaka, Bangladesh.

CHOWDHURY, Mizanur Rahman; Bangladesh politician; b. 19 Oct. 1928, Chandpur; ed. Feni Coll.; m. 1955; Headmaster, Bamoni High School 1952, Teacher, Chandpur Nuria High School 1956; Vice-Chair. Chandpur Municipality 1959; elected mem. Nat. Ass. of Pakistan 1962, 1965, 1970; Organising Sec. East Pakistan Wing, Awami League 1966, Acting Gen. Sec. 1966, 1967, organized Awami League election campaign 1970, Jt. Convenor 1976; Minister of Information and Broadcasting 1972–73, Minister of Relief and Rehabilitation 1973; Minister of Posts and Telecommunications 1985–88; Prime Minister of Bangladesh 1986–88; Sr. Vice-Chair. Jatiya Dal Party 1984, Gen. Sec. 1985–86. *Leisure interest:* reading. *Address:* c/o Jatiya Dal, Dhaka, Bangladesh.

CHOWDHURY, Salahuddin Quader; Bangladesh politician; b. 13 March 1949, Chittagong; s. of the late Fazlul Quadar Chowdhury; two s. one d.; ed. Dhaka, Punjab and London Univs.; joined Bangladesh Muslim League 1978, Jt. Sec. 1980–; rep., Int. Seminar of World Youth Leaders, Washington 1983; Minister for Relief and Rehabilitation 1985–86, for Health and Family Planning 1986–88. *Address:* c/o Ministry of Health and Family Planning, Bangladesh Secretariat, Main Bldg., 3rd Floor, Dhaka, Bangladesh.

CHRAIBI, Driss; Moroccan and French novelist; b. 15 July 1926; s. of Haj Fatmi and Habiba Zwitten; m. 1st (dissolved); m. 2nd Sheena McCallion; two s.; ed. Lycée Lyautey, Casablanca, Paris; author of numerous novels including Le Passé Simple 1954, Les Boucs 1955, Une Enquête au Pays 1981, La Mère du Printemps 1983; various contributions to French radio. *Address:* c/o Editions du Seuil, 27 rue Jacob, 75261 Paris Cedex 06, France. *Telephone:* 3291215.

CHRÉTIEN, Hon. Joseph Jacques Jean, P.C., B.A., LL.L.; Canadian lawyer and politician; b. 11 Jan. 1934, Shawinigan; s. of Wellie Chrétien and Marie Boisvert; m. Aline Chaîné 1957; two s. one d.; ed. Laval Univ., Quebec; Dir., Shawinigan Senior Chamber of Commerce 1962; Liberal mem. House of Commons 1963–86; Parl. Sec. to Prime Minister, 1965, to Minister of Finance 1966; Minister without Portfolio 1967–68, of Nat. Revenue Jan.-July 1968, of Indian Affairs and Northern Devt. 1968–74; Pres. Treas. Bd. 1974–76; Minister of Industry, Trade and Commerce 1976–77, of Finance 1977–79, of Justice, Attorney-Gen. of Canada and Minister of State for Social Devt. 1980–82, of Energy, Mines and Resources 1982–84, Sec. of State for External Affairs, Deputy Prime Minister June–Sept. 1984; Legal Counsel, Lang, Michener, Cranston, Farquharson, Ottawa. *Leisure interests:* skiing, fishing. *Address:* 1 Bower Street, Ottawa, Ont., Canada (Home).

CHRISTENSEN, Jens, M.POL.SC.; Danish diplomatist; b. 30 July 1921, Copenhagen; s. of Christian and Sophie Dorothea Christensen; m. 1st Tove Jessen, one s. two d.; m. 2nd Vibeke Pagh; ed. Copenhagen Univ.; joined Danish Foreign Service 1945; Head of Section, Econ. Secretariat of Govt. 1947; Sec. to Del. to OECD 1949, to Del. to NATO 1952; Head of Section, Ministry of Foreign Affairs 1952; Acting Head of Div. 1954; Chargé d'affaires ad interim and Counsellor of Legation, Vienna, Austria 1957; Deputy Under-Sec., Ministry of Foreign Affairs 1960; Under-Sec. and Head of Econ./Political Dept. 1964–71; Head of Secretariat for European Integration 1966; Amb. Extraordinary and Plenipotentiary 1967; State Sec. for Foreign Econ. Affairs 1971; Amb. to U.K. 1977–81, to Austria 1984–89, to OECD, Paris 1989–; Danish Gov., Asian Devt. Bank 1967–73; Exec. Chair. Dansk Olie & Naturgas A/S 1980–83; Commdr., First Class, Order of Dannebrog; Kt. Grand Cross, Order of the Icelandic Falcon; Kt. Grand Cross, Order of the Northern Star (Sweden); Kt. Grand Cross,

Order of St. Olav (Norway), Hon. G.C.V.O. *Address:* 109 Avenue Henri Martin, Paris XVI, France.

CHRISTENSEN, Kai; Danish architect; b. 28 Dec. 1916, Copenhagen; s. of late J. C. Christensen and Jenny Christensen; m. Kirsten Vittrup Andersen 1941; two d.; ed. Royal Acad. of Fine Arts, Copenhagen; Dir., Technical Dept. of Fed. of Danish Architects 1947–52; Man. Dir. Danish Bldg. Centre 1952–61; Attached to Danish Ministry of Housing 1961–86; Graphic Adviser to Govt. Depts. 1986–; Chief, Scandinavian Design Cavalcade 1962–69; mem. Fed. of Danish Architects 1943, The Architectural Assocn., London 1955, Danish Cttee. for Bldg. Documentation 1950–79, Danish Soc. of History, Literature and Art 1969, Cttee. mem. 1979, Vice-Pres. 1981, Pres. 1985–; Fellow Royal Soc. of Arts, London 1977; Sec.-Gen. Nordisk Byggedag (Scandinavian Bldg. Conf.) VIII 1961, XIII 1977; Pres. Int. Conf. of Building Centres 1960, Danish Ministries Soc. of Art 1982–87; mem. Scandinavian Liaison Cttee. concerning Govt. Bldg. 1963–72; associated Ed. Building Research and Practice/Bâtiment International (C.I.B. magazine) 1968–85; awards and prizes in public competition. *Major works:* designs for arts and crafts, graphic design, exhbns., furniture for the Copenhagen Cabinet Makers' Exhbns., articles and treatises in technical magazines and daily press. *Leisure interests:* chamber music, chess, fencing. *Address:* 100 Vester Voldgade, DK-1552 Copenhagen V, Denmark. *Telephone:* (45) 33 12 13 37.

CHRISTESEN, Clement Byrne, O.B.E., D.LITT., F.A.H.A.; Australian editor and author; b. 28 Oct. 1911, Townsville, Queensland; s. of Patrick Christesen and Susan S. Byrne; m. Nina Maximoff 1942; ed. King's Coll. Univ. of Queensland; journalist, A.B.C. feature-writer and broadcaster, publicist for Queensland Govt. 1935–41; founder (1940) and ed./publisher, Meanjin Quarterly (literary journal) until 1974; Australian Man. Williams Heinemann Ltd. 1947–52; Lockie Fellow, Univ. of Melbourne 1966–74; Hon. bibliographer, Univ. of Melbourne; Emer. Fellow, Australia Council; Hon. Fellow, Australian Acad. of Humanities; Crouch Gold Medal 1965, Britannica Award for Humanities 1970, Priestley Gold Medal 1980. *Publications:* The Hand of Memory 1970, The Gallery on Eastern Hill 1970, Having Loved 1979. *Leisure interest:* painting. *Address:* Stanhope, Eltham, Australia.

CHRISTIAANSE, Jan Hendrikus, PH.D.; Netherlands professor of law; b. 8 Feb. 1932, Gouda; s. of J. Christiaanse and T. H. Christiaanse-Meerburg; m. Louise J. L. Dorrenboom 1956; one s. two d.; ed. Univ. of Leyden and Free Univ., Amsterdam; entered Fiscal Policy Dept., Ministry of Finance 1954–64; Prof. of Law Erasmus Univ., Rotterdam 1965–; Hon. Sec.-Gen. Int. Fiscal Assocn. 1969–88; Hon. Pres. Netherlands Youth Council 1964–72; mem. First Chamber of Parl. 1973–; Kt. of the Dutch Lion, La Medaille de la Ville de Paris, van Borssele Medal, Rotterdam. *Publications:* numerous papers and books on law. *Leisure interests:* tennis, history. *Address:* 50 Burg Oudlaan, 3000 Rotterdam (Office); 219 Molenlaan, 3055 Rotterdam, Netherlands (Home).

CHRISTIAN, John Wyrill, M.A., D.PHIL., F.R.S., F.INST.P., F.I.M., C.ENG., C.PHYS.; British professor of metallurgy; b. 9 April 1926, Scarborough, Yorks.; s. of late John W. and Louisa P. (née Crawford) Christian; m. Maureen L. Smith 1949; two s. one d.; ed. Scarborough Boys' High School and The Queen's Coll., Oxford; Pressed Steel Research Fellow, Oxford Univ. 1951–55, lecturer in Metallurgy 1955–58, George Kelley Reader in Metallurgy 1958–67, Prof. of Physical Metallurgy 1967–88, Prof. Ener. 1988–; Fellow, St. Edmund Hall, Oxford 1963–; has held visiting professorships at various U.S. univs.; recipient of several medals. *Publications:* Metallurgical Equilibrium Diagrams (co-author) 1952, The Theory of Transformations in Metals and Alloys 1965; papers in scientific journals. *Leisure interests:* theatre, gardening, walking. *Address:* Department of Metallurgy & Science of Materials, Parks Road, Oxford, OX1 3PH (Office); 11 Charlbury Road, Oxford, OX2 6UT, England (Home). *Telephone:* Oxford 73710 (Office); Oxford 58569 (Home).

CHRISTIANS, F. Wilhelm, DR.JUR.; German banker; b. 1 May 1922; mem. of Man. Bd., Deutsche Bank AG (jt. spokesman 1976–88); fmr. Pres. Bundesverband deutscher Banken e.V. (Fed. Assocn. of German Banks); Chair. Supervisory Bd. Deutsche Centralbodenkredit-AG, Deutsche Gesellschaft für Wertpapiersparen mbH Frankfurt, Mannesmann AG, Düsseldorf, Rheinisch-Westfälisches Elektrizitätswerk AG, VIAG 1983–; mem. Supervisory Bd. Otto Wolff AG, Cologne, Bayer AG, Leverkusen, Klöckner-Humboldt-Deutz AG, Volkswagenwerk AG, Wolfsburg, Karstadt AG, Essen, VEBA AG, Düsseldorf; Chair. Deutsche Bank Capital Corpn., New York; mem. ASIA Fund Management Co. S.A., Luxembourg, European Bank's Int. Co. S.A. (EBIC), Brussels. *Address:* Königsallee 51, 4000 Düsseldorf, Federal Republic of Germany.

CHRISTIANSEN, Ragnar Karl Viktor; Norwegian politician; b. 28 Dec. 1922, Drammen; ed. secondary school and Railway School; Norwegian State Railways, Drammen 1940, telegraphist 1942, Head Clerk 1961; mem. Nedre Eiker Municipal Council 1946–59, Chair. 1956–57; mem. Supervisory Bd. for Armaments Factories 1951–68; mem. Supervisory Bd. Konigsberg Arms Factory and Raufoss Munitions Factory 1969; mem. Consumers Council 1953–60; fmr. Chair. Nedre Eiker Labour Party; mem. Labour Party Cen. Council 1965–77; M.P. 1950–77; Minister of Finance 1971–72, of Transport and Communications 1976–78; Chief County Admin. Buskerud

1978–80; County Gov. Buskerud 1980–. *Address:* Fylkeshuset, 3000 Drammen, Norway.

CHRISTIANSEN, Wilbur Norman, D.SC.; Australian radio astronomer; b. 9 Aug. 1913, Melbourne; s. of Wilhelm Christiansen and Ilma C. Jones; m. Elsie M. Hill 1938; three s.; ed. Caufield Grammar School and Melbourne Univ.; Research engineer, Amalgamated Wireless 1937–48; research scientist, CSIRO 1948–60, Inst. d'Astrophysique, Paris 1954, ZWO, The Netherlands 1960–61, Peking Observatory 1966–67; Visiting Prof. Leiden Univ. 1970; Prof. of Electrical Engineering, Univ. of Sydney 1960–78; Visiting Fellow, Australian Nat. Univ. 1979–85; Vice-Pres. Int. Astronomical Union 1964–70; Pres. Int. Union for Radio Science 1978–81, Hon. Life Pres. 1984; Foreign Sec. Australian Acad. of Science 1981–85; Hon, D.Sc.Eng. (Sydney), Hon. D.Eng. (Melbourne); recipient of several awards and prizes. *Publications:* Radio-telescopes (with J. A. Hogbom) 1969, 1985 and many scientific papers. *Leisure interests:* farming activities, music, reading. *Address:* Bingera, RMB436 Mack's Reef Road, via Bungendore, N.S.W. 2621, Australia. *Telephone:* (062) 303287.

CHRISTIE, Sir George William Langham, Kt.; British music administrator; b. 31 Dec. 1934; s. of John Christie, C.H. and Audrey Mildmay Christie; m. Patricia Mary Nicholson 1958; three s. one d.; ed. Eton; Asst. to Sec. of Calouste Gulbenkian Foundation 1957–62; Chair. Glyndebourne Productions 1956–; mem. Arts Council of G.B. 1988–; Founder Chair. of London Sinfonietta; D.L.; Hon. F.R.C.M. 1986. *Address:* Glyndebourne, Lewes, East Sussex, BN8 5UU, England. *Telephone:* Ringmer 812250.

CHRISTIE, Ian Ralph, M.A., F.B.A., F.R.HIST.S.; British professor of history; b. 11 May 1919, Preston, Lancs.; s. of John R. Christie and Gladys L. née Whatley; ed. Royal Grammar School, Worcester and Magdalen Coll., Oxford; served in R.A.F. 1940–46; Asst. lecturer in History, Univ. Coll., London 1948, lecturer 1951, Reader 1960, Prof. of Modern British History 1966–79, Dean of Arts 1971–72, Chair. History Dept. 1975–79, Astor Prof. of British History 1979–84, Prof. Emer. 1984–; mem. Editorial Bd. History of Parliament Trust 1973–. *Publications:* several books and articles in historical journals and reviews. *Address:* 10 Green Lane, Croxley Green, Herts., England.

CHRISTIE, Julie Frances; British actress; b. 14 April 1940, Assam, India; d. of Frank St. John and Rosemary (née Ramsden) Christie; ed. Brighton Technical Coll., and Central School of Speech and Drama; Motion Picture Laurel Award, Best Dramatic Actress 1967, Motion Picture Herald Award 1967. *Films:* Crooks Anonymous 1962, The Fast Lady 1962, Billy Liar 1963, Young Cassidy 1964, Darling 1964 (Acad. Award 1966), Doctor Zhivago (Donatello Award) 1965, Fahrenheit 451 1966, Far From the Madding Crowd 1966, Petulia 1967, In Search of Gregory 1969, The Go-Between 1971, McCabe & Mrs. Miller 1972, Don't Look Now 1973, Shampoo 1974, Demon Seed, Heaven Can Wait 1978, Memoirs of a Survivor 1980, Gold 1980, The Return of the Soldier 1981, Les Quarantièmes rugissants 1981, Heat and Dust 1982, The Gold Diggers 1984, Miss Mary 1986, The Tattooed Memory 1986, Power 1987, Fathers and Sons 1988, Dadah is Death (TV) 1988. *Address:* c/o International Creative Management, 388–396 Oxford Street, London, W.1, England.

CHRISTMAN, Luther Parmalee, PH.D.; American professor of nursing and sociology; b. 26 Feb. 1915, Summit Hill, Pa.; s. of Elmer and Ellen (née Barnicott) Christman; m. Dorothy M. Black 1939; one s. two d.; ed. Pennyslvania Hosp. School, Philadelphia and Temple, Michigan State and Thomas Jefferson Univs.; Prof. of Sociology, Coll. of Arts and Sciences, Vanderbilt Univ., Nashville, Tenn. 1967–72, Dir., Nursing, Vanderbilt Univ. Hosp. 1967–72; Vice-Pres. Nursing Affairs, Rush-Presbyterian-St. Luke's Medical Center; Dean, Coll. of Nursing, Rush Univ. 1971–77; Prof. of Sociology, Rush School of Medicine 1972–78, Dean Emer. 1977–; Sr. Adviser, Center for Nursing, American Hosp. Assen. 1989–; Fellow, Nat. League for Nursing 1950–60; Visiting Fellow, N.Z. Nurses' Educ. and Research Foundation 1978; Dr. h.c. H.L.D. (Thomas Jefferson Univ.) 1980, Jesse M. Scott Award, American Nurses' Assen. 1988. *Publications:* Interpersonal Behavior and Health Care (with Michael Counte) 1981, Hospital Organization and Health Care Delivery (with Michael Counte) 1981. *Leisure interest:* horticulture. *Address:* Rush University, 1753 W. Congress Parkway, Chicago, Ill. 60612, U.S.A.

CHRISTO (Christo Javacheff); American (naturalized) artist; b. 13 June 1935, Gabrovo, Bulgaria; s. of Vladimir Ivan and Tzveta (née Dimitrova) Javacheff; m. Jeanne-Claude de Guillebon; one s.; ed. Fine Arts Acad., Sofia; went to Paris 1958. *Projects include:* Wrapped Objects 1958; project for Packaging of Public Building 1961; Iron Curtain Wall of Oil Barrels blocking rue Visconti, Paris, Wrapping a Girl, London 1962; Showcases 1963; Store Front 1964; Air Package and Wrapped Tree, Eindhoven, Netherlands 1966; 42,390 cu. ft. Package, Walker Art Center, Minneapolis School of Art 1966; Wrapped Kunsthalle Bern 1968; 5,600 cu. m. Package for Kassel Documenta 4 1968; Wrapped Museum of Contemporary Art, Chicago 1969; Wrapped Coast, Little Bay, Sydney, Australia, 1 m. sq. ft. 1969; Valley Curtain, Grand Hogback, Rifle, Colorado, suspended fabric curtain 1970–72; Running Fence, Calif. 1972–76; Wrapped Roman Wall, Rome 1974; Ocean Front, Newport 1974; Wrapped Walk-Ways, Kansas City 1977–78; Surrounded Islands, Biscayne Bay, Miami, Florida 1980–83;

The Pont Neuf Wrapped, Paris 1975–85. *Address:* 48 Howard Street, New York, N.Y. 10013, U.S.A. *Telephone:* (212) 966-4437 (after 10.30 a.m. only).

CHRISTODOULOU, Anastasios, C.B.E., M.A.; British educational administrator; b. 1 May 1932, Akanthou, Cyprus; s. of Christodoulos and Maria Haji Yianni; m. Joan P. Edmunds 1955; two s. two d.; ed. St. Marylebone Grammar School and The Queen's Coll., Oxford; Infantry Signaller, Royal Sussex Regt. 1950–52; Dist. Officer, Dist. Commr. and Magistrate, H.M. Overseas Civil Service, Tanganyika Govt. 1956–62; Asst. Registrar, Univ. of Leeds 1963–66, Deputy Sec. 1966–68; Sec. Open Univ. 1969–80; Sec.-Gen. Assen. of Commonwealth Univs. 1980–; Vice-Chair. Commonwealth Inst. 1982–; Jt. Sec. U.K. Commonwealth Scholarships Comm. 1980; mem. Bd. of Govs. The Commonwealth of Learning 1988–; Trustee Richmond Coll. 1988–; Hon. D.Univ. (Open Univ.) 1981, Hon. D.Univ. (Athabasca, Canada) 1981, Hon. Prof. (Mauritius Univ.) 1986. *Leisure interests:* rugby football, cricket, music, community service. *Address:* 22 Kensington Court Gardens, London, W8 5QP, England. *Telephone:* 01-937 4626.

CHRISTODOULOU, Efthymios, M.A.(ECONS.); Greek banker; b. 1932, Larissa; s. of Nicholas Christodoulou; ed. Athens Coll., Hamilton Univ., Utica, N.Y., and Columbia Univ., New York; scientific consultant Nat. Bank of Greece 1960, later Econ. Counsellor; Gen. Man. Nat. Investment Bank for Industrial Devt. 1971; Pres. Olympic Airways 1978–79; Gov. Nat. Bank of Greece 1980–82. *Address:* c/o National Bank of Greece, 86 Eolou Street (Plateia Cotzia), Athens 121, Greece.

CHRISTOFAS, Sir Kenneth (Cavendish), K.C.M.G., M.B.E.; British diplomatist (retd.); b. 1917; m. Jessica Laura Sparshott 1948; two d.; ed. Univ. Coll., London; served war 1939–45; rose to rank of Lieut.-Col.; Foreign Service 1948–76; Deputy Head of U.K. Del. to EEC 1959–61; Counsellor British High Comm., Lagos 1961–64; Head of Econs. Dept., Colonial Office 1964–66; Counsellor, Foreign and Commonwealth Office 1966–69; Minister and Deputy Head, U.K. del. to EEC 1969–72; Dir.-Gen. for Econ., Financial, Parl. and Institutional Affairs, Council of Ministers of European Communities 1973–82, Hon. Dir.-Gen. 1982–; Hon. Pres. U.K. Branch, Int. Assen. of "Anciens" of the European Communities 1985–. *Address:* 3 The Ridge, Bolsover Road, Eastbourne, Sussex, BN20 7JE, England. *Telephone:* 0323-22384.

CHRISTOFF, Boris, D.JUR.; Bulgarian singer; b. 18 May 1919, Plovdiv; s. of Kyryl Christoff and Rayna Teodorova; m. Franca de Rensis; ed. Sofia Univ. and Italy; began career as a lawyer; studied singing in Rome; interned in Austria in World War II; professional debut in Italy 1945; has appeared at principal European opera houses, including La Scala, Milan, Rome, Naples, Venice, Palermo, Paris, London and Vienna and in America; major roles include Boris Godunov, King Philip, Don Quixote, Ivan the Terrible, Mephistopheles, Pizarro, and others; Hon. mem. Paris Opera; Commendatore della Repubblica Italiana. *Complete recordings* of Boris Godunov, Gounod's Faust, Don Carlos and Mussorgsky's Songs. *Address:* Via Bertolini 1, Rome, Italy.

CHRISTOPHERSEN, Henning, M.ECON.; Danish politician; b. 8 Nov. 1939, Copenhagen; s. of Richard and Gretha Christophersen; m. Jytte Risbjerg Nielsen 1961; one s. two d.; ed. Univ. of Copenhagen; Head of the Economic Section of the Handicrafts Council 1965–70; mem. Folketing 1971–84, mem. of Parl. Finance Cttee. 1972–76, Vice-Chair. 1976–78, Minister of Foreign Affairs 1978–79; Deputy Leader, Danish Liberal Party 1972, Acting Party Leader 1977–78, Party Leader 1978–84; Deputy Prime Minister and Minister of Finance 1982–84; Vice-Pres. Comm. responsible for Budget, Financial Control, Personnel and Admin., Comm. of European Communities 1985–89, Econ. and Financial Affairs, Co-ordination of Structural Funds Jan 1989–; Nat. Order of Merit. *Publications:* En udfordring for de Liberale, and numerous articles on economics. *Address:* Commission of the European Communities, 200 rue de la Loi, 1049 Brussels, Belgium.

CHRISTOPHERSON, Sir Derman Guy, Kt., O.B.E., S.M., D.PHIL., F.R.S., F.I.MECH.E., M.I.C.E.; British academic; b. 6 Sept. 1915, Plumstead, Kent; s. of Derman and Edith F. Christopherson; m. Frances Edith Tearle 1940; three s. one d.; ed. Sherborne School, Univ. Coll., Oxford and Harvard Univ.; Scientific Officer, Research and Experiments Dept., Ministry of Home Security 1941–45; Lecturer in Eng., Cambridge Univ. and Fellow and Bursar of Magdalene Coll., Cambridge 1945–49; Prof. of Mechanical Eng., Univ. of Leeds 1949–55; Prof. of Applied Science, Imperial Coll. of Science and Technology, London 1955–60; Vice-Chancellor and Warden, Univ. of Durham 1960–78; mem. Royal Fine Art Comm. 1978–85, Chair. 1980–85; Fellow, Imperial Coll. of Science and Technology 1966–; Hon. Fellow, Magdalene Coll., Cambridge 1969–, Master 1979–85; Hon. Fellow, University Coll., Oxford 1977–; several hon. degrees; Clayton Prize, Inst. of Mechanical Engineers 1963. *Publications:* The Engineer in the University 1967, The University at Work 1973, and various articles in learned journals. *Address:* 43 Lensfield Road, Cambridge, CB2 1EN, England.

CHRISTOPHIDES, Andreas Nicolaou; Cypriot politician, broadcasting executive and author; b. 1937, Nicosia; two c.; ed. Pancyprian Gymnasium, School of Philosophy, Athens Univ., Greece, Columbia Univ., N.Y., U.S.A.; taught at Pancyprian Gymnasium 1958–63; Dir. of Greek Programmes, Cyprus Broadcasting Corpn. 1964–67, Dir.-Gen. 1967–; Govt. Spokesman 1983–; fmr. Minister of Educ.; Gov., Int. Foundation News Concern, London; mem. Int. Inst. of Communications; State Prize for Literature (three times), Order of the Phoenix, Greece, Chevalier, Ordre du Mérite, France. *Publications:* collections of essays: Points of View I, II, III, Black and White; poems: Strange Illustration, Analytical Propositions, Conversations of the Night; Anthology of Cyprus Poetry (ed. with Costas Montis), Anthology of Cypriot Short Stories (ed. with Panos Ioannides). *Address:* c/o Ministry of Education, Nicosia, Cyprus.

CHRISTOPHIDES, Ioannis; Cypriot barrister and politician; b. 21 Jan. 1924, Nicosia; s. of Cleanthis and Maris (née Ypsilantis) Christophides; m. Marvel Georgiadis 1953; two d.; ed. Pancyprian Gymnasium; called to the Bar, Gray's Inn, London 1947; joined Comptoir d'Escompte de Nicosie (family banking firm) and Cleanthis Christophides Ltd. (family insurance firm) 1948, Chief Exec. 1954–57; founder mem. and Chair. (until 1972), Merchant Credit Ltd., Universal Life Insurance Co. Ltd.; Minister of Foreign Affairs 1972–74, 1975–78; mem. Bd., Cyprus Telecommunications Authority, Chair. 1966–72; Vice-Chair. Commonwealth Telecommunications Council 1970–72; Chair. Commercial Union Assurance (Cyprus) Ltd., Universal Life Insurance Co. Ltd.; Pres. Cyprus Red Cross 1964–. *Leisure interest:* reading. *Address:* 25 El. Venizelou Street, Nicosia T.T. 109, Cyprus (Home). *Telephone:* 64653 (Home).

CHRISTOPHIDES, Takis; Cypriot politician and accountant; b. 1931; Famagusta; m. Erma Indianos; two d.; ed. Greek Gymnasium, Famagusta; qualified as certified accountant in U.K.; partner, Christophides Philippou Tsielepsis Accounting Firm (part of Price Waterhouse); Minister of Labour and Social Insurance 1988–; founding mem. Assen. of Chartered Accountants of Cyprus; fmr. mem. Bd., Cyprus Broadcasting Corpn. *Address:* Ministry of Labour and Social Insurance, Nicosia, Cyprus.

CHRISTY, Robert Frederick, B.A., M.A., PH.D.; American physicist; b. 14 May 1916, Vancouver; s. of Moise Jacques and Hattie Alberta (née McKay) Christy; m. 1st Dagmar Elizabeth Lieven 1941 (divorced 1971), two s.; m. 2nd I. Juliana Sackmann 1973, two d.; ed. Univs. of British Columbia, and California (Berkeley); on U.S. Atomic Energy Project, Chicago and Los Alamos (Calif.) 1942–46; Prof. of Physics, Calif. Inst. of Technology, Pasadena 1946–, Exec. Officer for Physics, Chair. of Faculty 1969–, Vice-Pres. and Provost 1970–80, Acting Pres. 1977; mem. American Astronomical Soc., Int. Astronomical Union, U.S. Nat. Acad. of Sciences 1965; Fellow, American Physical Soc., American Acad. of Arts and Sciences; Eddington Medal, Royal Astronomical Soc. (U.K.) 1967. *Publications:* Cosmic Ray Bursts 1941, The μ Meson Spin 1941, Determination of the Fine Structure Constant 1942, Angular Distribution of γ Rays 1949, The Coupling of Angular Momenta in Nuclear Reactions 1953, Low Excited States of F^{19} 1954, Analysis of Nuclear Scattering Data 1956, Corrections to Nuclear Q Values 1961, Direct Capture Nuclear γ Rays 1961, The Calculation of Stellar Pulsation 1964, A Study of Pulsation in RR Lyrae Models 1966, Review of Pulsation Theory 1966. *Leisure interests:* tennis, hiking, skiing, riding. *Address:* 1201 East California Boulevard, Pasadena, Calif. 91125; 1230 Arden Road, Pasadena, Calif. 91106, U.S.A. (Home). *Telephone:* 818-356 6918; 818-440 1801 (Home).

CHRYSSA; American artist; b. 1933, Athens; ed. Acad. Grand Shaumière, Paris, and San Francisco School of Fine Arts; one-woman shows, Solomon Guggenheim Museum, New York 1961, Museum of Modern Art, New York 1963, Walker Art Centre, Minneapolis 1968, Whitney Museum of Modern Art, New York 1972, Musée d'Art Contemporain, Montreal 1974, Musée d'Art Moderne de la Ville de Paris 1979, Nat. Pinacotheque Museum Alexander Soutsos, Athens 1980 and at galleries in New York, Boston, San Francisco, Paris, Cologne, Düsseldorf, Zurich, Turin and Athens since 1961; work has also appeared in many group exhbns. and belongs to numerous public collections in U.S.A. and Europe; Guggenheim Fellowship 1973; C.A.V.S., M.I.T. 1979. *Address:* 15 East 88th Street, New York, N.Y. 10028, U.S.A.

CHRYSSANTHOU, Christodoulos, LL.B.; Cypriot lawyer and politician; b. 24 May 1935, Pano Lefkara; m. Tereza Sika; one s. one d.; ed. Birmingham Univ., U.K.; admitted to Bar (Inner Temple); in pvt. practice, Nicosia 1963–; Minister of Justice 1988–. *Address:* Ministry of Justice, Nicosia, Cyprus.

CHU, Chi-Ming, M.B., PH.D., F.R.C.P.; Chinese medical scientist; b. 26 Aug. 1917, Yixing, Jiansu; m. Pauline Huang 1945; one s.; ed. Nat. Medical Coll. of Shanghai, Univ. of Cambridge, England; Asst. Tech. Expert, Nat. Epidemic Prevention Bureau, Kunming 1940–45; Research Fellow, Nat. Inst. for Medical Research, London 1948–50; Chief of Control Lab. and Second Research Lab., Nat. Vaccine and Serum Inst., Beijing 1951–55; Deputy Dir. Zhangchun Inst. of Biological Products, Zhangchun 1955–63; Prof. and Deputy Dir. Inst. of Virology, Chinese Acad. of Medical Sciences 1963–80, Dir. 1981–83; Prof. of Virology and Scientific Adviser, Chinese Acad. of Preventive Medicine 1984–; mem. NPC 1964–78, People's Political Consultative Cttee. 1986–; mem. Standing Cttee., Medical Scientific Council and Chair. Cttee. on Viral Diseases, Ministry of Health 1963–; Chair. Cttee. on Haemorrhagic Fever 1983–, Sub-Cttee. for Evaluation of Biologicals 1985–; Scientific Adviser, China Nat. Centre for Devt. of Biotechnology 1984–; Vice-Chair. for Evaluation of Medical Scientific Achievements 1986–; Chair. Advisory Cttee. on Infectious Diseases 1987–; Pres. Chinese Soc. for Microbiology 1983–; Chief Ed. Chinese Journal of Virology 1985–; Fellow of Chinese Acad. of Sciences 1980; at present working on expression

of viral genes in mammalian cells and in vaccinia vectors. *Publications:* over 150 papers on virology, microbiology and biotechnology, especially on influenza, adeno virus, vaccinia, measles and hepatitis B. *Leisure interests:* reading history and poetry. *Address:* Institute of Virology, 100 Ying Xin Jie, Xuan Wu Qu, Beijing, People's Republic of China. *Telephone:* Beijing 33-8621 (Ext. 63).

CHU, Peter, D. ÉS LETTRES; Chinese professor and businessman; b. 1902; ed. Univ. of Paris; Man. Dir. The Agricultural & Industrial Bank of China 1941–49; Publisher of Life Today; Prof. of Kwang Hsia Univ.; Dean of the Great China Univ.; Dir. South-Eastern Asia Development Corpn. Ltd. *Publications:* L'émigration japonaise depuis 1918, A Study of Scientific Management 1945.

CHU FU-SUNG, B.A.; Chinese diplomatist and politician; b. 15 Jan. 1915, Hsiangyang County, Hupeh; m.; ed. Univ. of Shanghai; Acting Dir. U.K. Office, Ministry of Information 1946–47; Dir. Int. Dept., Govt. Information Office, Exec. Yuan 1948–49; Counsellor, Taiwan Provincial Govt. 1949–50; Sr. Sec. and Counsellor, Exec. Yuan 1950–54; Adviser, Office of Govt. Spokesmen 1950–54; Dir. Information Dept. Ministry of Foreign Affairs 1952–56; Counsellor and Minister, Washington, D.C. 1956–60; Minister, Canada 1960–62; Vice-Minister, Ministry of Foreign Affairs 1962–65; Amb. to Spain 1965–71, to Brazil 1971–74, to Korea 1975–79; Nat. Policy Adviser to Pres. 1979–; Minister of Foreign Affairs 1979–87. *Address:* 262, Kuangfu S. Road, Taipei 100, Taiwan. *Telephone:* 3119292.

CHU JIANG; Chinese party and government official; b. 1917, Jiangsu; First Sec., Suzhou Region 1965; Sec., CCP Cttee., Nanjing 1976; Chair. Municipal Revolutionary Cttee., Nanjing 1977; mem. 11th Cen. Cttee. CCP 1977; Sec. CCP Cttee., Jiangsu 1977–; Sec., Comm. for Inspecting Discipline, CCP Cttee. Jiangsu 1977; First Sec. CCP Cttee., Nanjing 1978; Chair. Prov. People's Congress, Jiangsu 1983–88. *Address:* c/o Provincial People's Congress, Nanjing, Jiangsu, People's Republic of China.

CHUA SIAN CHIN, LL.B.; Singapore politician; b. 1934, Malacca, Malaya; m.; three c.; ed. Univs. of Malaya and London; barrister-at-law, Inner Temple, London 1959; returned to Singapore 1959 and began practice as advocate and solicitor; Chair. Univ. of Singapore Council 1967–68; mem. Parl. 1968–; Minister of Health 1968–75, of Home Affairs 1972–85, of Educ. 1975–79; Treas. People's Action Party 1970–. *Address:* c/o Ministry of Home Affairs, Singapore.

CHUAN LEEKPAI, LL.B.; Thai politician; b. 28 July 1938, Trang Prov.; ed. Painting and Sculpture School and Thammasat Univ.; studied for two years with Bar Assen. of Thailand; mem. Parl. from Trang Prov. 1969–; Minister of Justice 1975; Deputy Minister of Justice and Minister, Prime Minister's Office 1976; Minister of Justice, first Prem Govt.; Minister of Commerce 1981, of Agric. and Cooperatives 1981–83, of Educ. 1983–86, of Public Health Aug. 1988–. *Address:* c/o Ministry of Public Health, Devavesm Palace, Samsen Road, Bangkok 10200, Thailand.

CHUDAKOV, Aleksandr Yevgeniyevich; Soviet physicist; b. 16 June 1921, Moscow; s. of Yevgeny Chudakov; ed. Moscow Univ.; Research Assoc. Lebedev Inst. of Physics, U.S.S.R. Acad. of Sciences 1946–71, Inst. of Atomic Research 1971–; Corresp. mem. U.S.S.R. Acad. of Sciences 1966–; main works on nature and properties of cosmic rays; Lenin Prize 1960. *Publications:* works on nuclear physics. *Address:* U.S.S.R. Academy of Sciences, 14 Leninsky Prospekt, Moscow, U.S.S.R.

CHUDIN, Vitaliy Ivanovich; Soviet politician; b. 1929; ed. Altai Agric. Machine Bldg. Inst.; mem. CPSU 1954–; shop technologist, superintendent, Sec. CP Cttee.; Dir. of a machine-construction factory, Frunze 1963; Deputy to Supreme Soviet of Kirghiz S.S.R. 1963–; mem. Cen. Cttee. of Kirghiz CP 1963–; Deputy Chair. of Council of Ministers of Kirghiz S.S.R. 1967–80; U.S.S.R. Minister of Machine Building for Construction, Road Building and Municipal Services 1980–85; mem. Cen. Auditing Comm. CPSU 1981–. *Address:* c/o Council of Ministers, The Kremlin, Moscow, U.S.S.R.

CHU HUY MAN, Lieut.-Gen.; Vietnamese soldier and politician; b. 1920; mem. Cen. Cttee., Lao Dong Party; Maj.-Gen. in Viet-Nam People's Army; fmr. Political Commdr. in Western Highlands; mem. Politbureau of CP of Viet-Nam Dec. 1976; Vice-Pres. Council of State 1982; represents the ethnic minorities in Govt. *Address:* Central Committee of the Communist Party of Viet-Nam, No. 1-c, rue Hoang Van Thu, Hanoi, Viet-Nam.

CHUKHRAI, Grigoriy Naumovich; Soviet film director; b. 23 May 1921, Melitopol, Zaporozhye Region; s. of Naum Vladimirovich Roubanov and Klardia Petrovna Chukhrai; m. Irina Pavlovna Penkova 1944; one s. one d.; ed. All-Union State Inst. of Cinematography; Soviet Army 1939–45; mem. CPSU 1944–; Dir. Mosfilm 1955–64; Dir. Experimental Film Studio 1965–76; Honoured Art Worker of R.S.F.S.R., People's Artist of U.S.S.R., Lenin Prize 1961, Order of Red Star, Order of Patriotic War, Order of Red Banner of Labour (three times), Labour Order of Hungary, Partisan Star of Czechoslovakia. *Films:* The 41st 1956, Ballad of a Soldier 1959, The Clear Sky 1961, There Lived an Old Man and Old Woman 1964, Memory 1967, Quagmire 1978, Life is Beautiful 1980, I Will Teach You to Dream 1984. *Leisure interest:* the theory of economics. *Address:* Mosfilm Studio, 1 Mosfilmovskaya ulitsa, Moscow, U.S.S.R.

CHUKOVSKAYA, Lidia Korneyeva; Soviet author; b. 1907, Helsinki; d. of K. I. Chukovsky; widowed in 1930s; literary career 1928–; ed. of various publishing houses 1930-60. *Publications include:* The Deserted House 1965 (English and German trans. 1967), Confessions (poetry) 1960-72, Underwater Plunge 1972.

CHULASAPYA, Air Chief Marshal Dawee; Thai air force officer and politician; b. 8 Aug 1914, Thonburi; ed. Mil. Acad. (now Chulachomklao), Flying Training School and Command and Gen. Staff Coll., Fort Leavenworth, U.S.A.; fighter pilot, Royal Thai Air Force 1936, intelligence work and studies abroad during World War II; Dir. of Intelligence 1948-55; Acting Dir. Civil Aviation 1948-55; Air Marshal 1955; Chief of Air Staff 1955-61; Air Chief Marshal 1957; Chief of Staff, Supreme Command 1961-63; SEATO Mil. Adviser 1961-63; rank of Gen. and Admiral 1963; Special Officer, First Royal Guard Infantry 1963; Deputy Minister of Defence 1963-69; Minister of Communications 1969-71; Chair. Thai Maritime Navigation Co. 1969-74; Dir. of Nat. Devt. Agriculture and Communications in Nat. Exec. Council 1971; Minister of Agriculture and Co-operatives 1972-73, of Defence 1973-74; fmr. Chair. Joint Chiefs of Staff of Nat. Security Command; fmr. Deputy Dir. Communist Suppression Operations Command; concurrently Deputy C.-in-C. Armed Forces and Acting Supreme Commdr. 1973; retd. 1974; mem. House of Reps. for Mae Hong Son April-Oct. 1976; leader Social Justice Party 1976; Deputy Prime Minister 1976-80; Minister of Public Health April-Oct. 1976; Medal of Courage 1972, and numerous other awards. *Address:* Bangkok, Thailand.

CHUMAKOV, Mikhail Petrovich; Soviet virologist; b. 14 Nov. 1909, Ivanovka, Orlov oblast; ed. First Moscow Medical Inst.; Physician, Postgraduate, Senior Research Associate, Institute of Microbiology, U.S.S.R. Acad. of Sciences 1931-38; Sr. Research Assoc., Head of Lab., U.S.S.R. Inst. of Experimental Medicine 1938-44; Head of Dept. Inst. of Neurology, U.S.S.R. Acad. of Medical Sciences 1944-50, Corresp. mem. 1948, mem. 1960-; Dir., Head of Lab. Inst. of Virology 1950-55; Organizer, Dir. Inst. of Poliomyelitis and Virus Encephalitis 1955-72, Scientific Head 1972-76; mem. CPSU 1940; mem. Purkyně Medical Soc., Czechoslovakia; mem. Leopoldina Deutsche Akademie 1969; Order Badge of Honour, Red Banner of Labour, State Prize 1941, Ivanovsky Prize 1953, Lenin Prize 1963, Order of Lenin 1984, Hammer and Sickle Gold Medal, Hero of Socialist Labour 1984. *Publications:* Over 170 works on epidemiology of virus infections (tick encephalitis, trachoma, poliomyelitis, tick fever); monographs Poliomyelitis—Epidemic Infantile Paralysis, Antibioticotherapy of Trachoma. *Address:* c/o Academy of Medical Sciences, ul. Solyanka 14, Moscow 109801, U.S.S.R.

CHUN DOO-HWAN, Gen.; Korean army officer (retd.) and statesman; b. 18 Jan. 1931, Kyongsangnamdo Prov.; s. of Chun Sang-Woo and Kim Jum-Mun; m. Lee Soon-Ja; three s. one d.; ed. Heedoh Primary School, Taegu, Taegu Tech. High School, Mil. Acad., Army Coll.; commissioned Second Lieut. 1955; Adjutant-Gen. School 1959; U.S. Special Forces and Psychological Warfare School 1959; U.S. Army Infantry School 1960; Acting Planning Dir., Special Warfare Bureau Army HQ, 1960-61; Domestic Affairs Sec. to Chair. of Supreme Council for Nat. Reconstruction 1961-62; Dir. Personnel Admin. Bureau, Korean CIA 1963; Exec. Officer 1st Airborne Special Forces Group 1966-67; Commdr. 30th Bn., Capital Garrison Command 1967-69; Sr. Aide to Chief of Staff 1969-70; Commdr. 29th Regt., 9th Infantry Div. (Viet-Nam) 1970-71; Commdr. 1st Airborne Special Forces Group 1971; Asst. Dir. Presidential Security Office 1976; Commanding Gen. 1st Infantry Div. 1978; Commdr. Defence Security Command 1979-80; Acting Dir. Korean CIA April-June 1980; Chair. Standing Cttee. Special Cttee. for Nat. Security Measures June 1980; promoted to full Gen. Aug. 1980; retd. from army Aug. 1980; Pres. Repub. of Korea 1980-88; Pres. Democratic Justice Party 1981-87, Hon. Pres. 1987-88; in rural exile 1988; numerous decorations. *Leisure interest:* tennis. *Address:* c/o Democratic Justice Party, 155-2 Kwanhoon-dong, Chongno-ku, Seoul, Republic of Korea.

CHUNDER, Pratap Chandra, M.A., LL.B., PH.D.; Indian lawyer and politician; b. 1 Sept. 1919, Calcutta; s. of Nirmal and Suhasini Chunder; m. Leena Roy Chowdhury 1940; four s.; ed. Univ. of Calcutta; law practice in Calcutta since 1945; mem. Senate and Law Faculty of Calcutta Univ. 1961-68; mem. Exec. Council of Rabindra Bharati Univ. 1962-68; mem. West Bengal Legislative Ass. 1962-68; Pres. West Bengal Provincial Congress Cttee. 1967-69; Minister of Finance and Judiciary in State Govt. 1968; mem. Working Cttee. and Cen. Parl. Bd. of Org. Congress 1969-76; mem. Janata Party 1977-; mem. Lok Sabha from Calcutta North East March 1977-79; Union Minister of Education, Social Welfare and Culture 1977-79; mem. Inc. Law Soc. and Calcutta Bar Asscn.; Pres. Int. Educ. Conf. UNESCO 1977-79; Pres. Indo-American Soc. 1984-; Pres. Writers' Guild of India 1985-, Bengali Literary Conf. 1987-; fmr. editor several Bengali literary magazines; Hon. D.Litt., Hon. D.Sc.; Fellow, Asiatic Soc. of Calcutta 1975; Best Playwright award, Calcutta Univ. 1965. *Works:* four one-man exhbns. of paintings in Calcutta and New Delhi 1982, 1984, 1985, 1987, including one on China. *Publications:* Kautilya on Love and Morals, The Sons of Mystery, Job Charnock and his Lady Fair, Socialist Legality and Indian Law, Brother Vivekananda, and several novels and plays. *Leisure interests:* reading, writing, painting. *Address:* 23 Nirmal Chunder Street, Calcutta 700012, India. *Telephone:* 268248.

CHUNG, (Raymond) Arthur; Guyanese judge; b. 10 Jan. 1918, Windsor Forest, West Coast, Demerara; s. of Joseph and Lucy Chung; m. Doreen

Pamela Ng-See-Quan 1954; one s. one d.; ed. Modern High School, Georgetown and Middle Temple, London; land surveyor 1940; lived in England 1946-48; Asst. Legal Examiner, U.K. Inland Revenue Dept. 1947; returned to Guyana 1948; Magistrate 1954, Sr. Magistrate 1960; Registrar of Deeds of the Supreme Court 1961; Judge of the Supreme Court 1962-70; First Pres. of the Repub. of Guyana 1970-80. *Address:* Guijana House, 95 Carmichael Street, Georgetown, Guyana. *Telephone:* 62666-8.

CHUNG IL KWON, Gen.; Korean army officer (retd.), diplomatist and politician; b. 21 Nov. 1917; m. 1st Kye Won Yoon 1946, three d.; m. 2nd Hae Soo Park 1977; ed. Military Acad. of Japan, U.S.A. Command and General Staff Coll., Harvard and Oxford Univs.; fmr. Army Chief of Staff, Chair. Joint Chiefs of Staff; Amb. to Turkey, France, U.S.A., concurrently to Brazil, Chile, Colombia, Argentina, Paraguay and Ecuador; Minister of Foreign Affairs 1963; Prime Minister 1964-70, concurrently Minister of Foreign Affairs 1966-67; Chair. Korean-Japan Co-operation Council 1971-; Chair. Democratic Republican Party 1972-73; mem. Nat. Ass. 1971-, Speaker 1973-79; Standing Adviser to Pres. of Democratic Republican Party 1979-80. *Leisure interest:* horse-riding. *Address:* Hannam-dong, Yongsan-gu, Seoul, Republic of Korea.

CHUNG SHIH-YI; Chinese government official; b. 16 Oct. 1914, Taoyuan County, Hunan; m.; two s. two d.; ed. Hunan Univ., Finance and Quartermaster School, Nat. Defence Coll. and Nat. War Coll.; Chief, 2nd Div. Bureau of Budget, Ministry of Nat. Defence 1947-48; Chief, Nanking Disbursing Office, Combined Service Forces 1949; Dir. Disbursing Dept. Combined Service Forces 1949; Deputy Dir. Bureau of Budget, Ministry of Nat. Defence 1953-56; Supt. Finance School, Combined Service Forces 1957-58; Deputy Comptroller-Gen. Ministry of Nat. Defence 1958-63, Comptroller-Gen. 1963-70; Dir. Bureau of Finance, Taipei City Govt. 1970-72; Commr. Dept. of Finance, Taiwan Provincial Govt. 1972-78; Dir.-Gen. Directorate-Gen. of Budget, Accounting and Statistics, Exec. Yuan 1978-87; Auditor Gen., Ministry of Audit, Control Yuan 1987-. *Address:* 9, Lane 31, Juian Street, Taipei, Taiwan.

CHUNG, Kyung-Wha; Korean violinist; b. 26 Mar. 1948, Seoul; m. Geoffrey Leggett 1984; one s.; ed. Juilliard School of Music; studied under Ivan Galamian; started career in U.S.A.; winner of Leventritt Competition 1968; European debut 1970; has played under conductors such as Abbado, Barenboim, Davis, Dorati, Dutoit, Giulini, Haitink, Jochum, Kempe, Kondrashin, Leinsdorf, Levine, Maazel, Mehta, Muti, Previn, Rattle, Rozhdestvensky and Solti; has played with major orchestras including all London Orchestras, Chicago, Boston and Pittsburgh Symphony Orchestra, New York, Cleveland, Philadelphia, Berlin, Israel and Vienna Philharmonics, Orchestre de Paris; has toured world; recordings for Decca; played at Salzburg Festival with London Symphony Orchestra 1973, Vienna Festival 1981, 1984, Edinburgh Festival 1981, and at eightieth birthday concert of Sir William Walton March 1982. *Leisure interests:* arts, family. *Address:* c/o Jeanine Rose, 109 Avenue Victor Hugo, 75016 Paris, France; c/o 86 Hatton Garden, London, E.C.1, England.

CHUNG, Sir Sze-yuen, Kt., G.B.E., D.SC., PH.D., C.ENG., F.I.MECH.E., F.I.PROD.E., C.B.I.M., J.P.; Hong Kong business executive; b. 3 Nov. 1917; m. Nancy Cheung 1942 (died 1977); one s. two d.; ed Hong Kong and Sheffield Univs.; consulting eng. 1952-56; Gen. Man. Sonca Industries 1956-50, Man Dir. 1960-77, Chair. 1978-; mem. Hong Kong Legis. Council 1965-74, Sr. Unofficial Member 1974-78; mem. Hong Kong Exec. Council 1972-80, Sr. Unofficial Member 1980-; Chair. Hong Kong Polytechnic 1972-; holder of many other public appts.; Order of the Sacred Treasure (Japan); Silver Jubilee Medal 1977; Hon. D.Sc. (Hong Kong) 1976 and other awards and distinctions. *Publications:* articles in professional journals. *Leisure interests:* swimming, hiking, badminton. *Address:* House 25, Bella Vista, Silver Terrace Road, Clear Water Bay, Kowloon, Hong Kong. *Telephone:* 3-213506.

CHURBANOV, Yuriy Mikhailovich; Soviet politician; b. 1930, Moscow; m. Galina Brezhnev; ed. Moscow State Univ.; Head of Political Administration of Security Militia (MVD Troops) 1971-75; mem. Auditing Comm. of CPSU 1976-81; Cand. mem. Cen. Cttee. 1981; Deputy, U.S.S.R. Ministry of Internal Affairs 1977-80, First Deputy Minister 1980-84; convicted of corruption and imprisoned for 12 years 1988-.

CHURCH, Alonzo, A.B., PH.D.; American professor of mathematics and philosophy; b. 14 June 1903, Washington D.C.; s. of Samuel Robbins Church and Mildred H. L. Parker; m. Mary Julia Kuczinski 1925 (died 1976); one s. two d.; ed. Ridgefield School, Conn. and Princeton Univ.; Nat. Research Fellow in Mathematics, Harvard, Göttingen and Amsterdam Univs. 1927-29; Asst. Prof. of Maths., Princeton Univ. 1929-39, Assoc. Prof. 1939-47, Prof. 1947-61, Prof. of Maths. and Philosophy 1961-67; Ed. The Journal of Symbolic Logic 1936-79; Prof. of Philosophy and Maths., Univ. of Calif. at Los Angeles 1967-; mem. American Acad. of Arts and Sciences, Acad. Internationale de Philosophie des Sciences, Nat. Acad. of Sciences 1978-; Corresp. mem. British Acad. *Publications:* The Calculi of Lambda-Conversion 1941, Introduction to Mathematical Logic Vol. 1 1956; several research papers. *Address:* c/o Department of Philosophy, University of California at Los Angeles, Los Angeles, Calif. 90024, U.S.A. *Telephone:* 213-825-4641.

CHURCHILL, Odette Maria Céline (see Hallowes).

CHURIKOVA, Inna Mikhailovna; Soviet actress; b. 5 Oct. 1943; ed. Shchepkin Theatre School; with Moscow Youth Theatre 1965–68; with Lenin Komsomol Theatre, Moscow 1973–; début in films 1961; small parts in films in 1960s; Lenin Komsomol Prize 1976; R.S.F.S.R. People's Artist 1985. *Films include:* No Ford Through Fire (Panfilov) 1968, The Beginning 1970, May I Speak? 1976, Valentina 1981, Vassa 1983, War-Novel 1984 (Berlin Film Festival Prize). *Address:* Lenin Komsomol Theatre, Moscow, U.S.S.R.

CHUTE, Robert Maurice, SC.D.; American professor of biology and poet; b. 13 Feb. 1926, Bridgton, Me; s. of James Cleveland and Elizabeth Davis Chute; m. Virginia Hinds 1946; one s. one d.; ed. Univ. of Maine, The Johns Hopkins Univ.; Instructor and Asst. Prof. Middlebury Coll. 1953–59; Asst. Prof. Northridge State Coll. 1959–61; Assoc. Prof. and Chair. of Biology, Lincoln Univ. 1961; Prof. and Chair. of Biology, then Dana Prof. of Biology, Bates Coll. 1962–; Fellow A.A.A.S. *Publications:* Environmental Insight 1971; Introduction to Biology 1976. *Poetry:* Quiet Thunder 1975, Uncle George Poems 1977, Voices Great and Small 1977, Thirteen Moons/Treize Lunes 1982, Samuel Sewell Sails for Home 1986. *Leisure interests:* walking, reading, films. *Address:* RFD 1, Box 3868, Poland Spring, Maine 04274, U.S.A. *Telephone:* (207) 998-4338.

CHYNOWETH, Alan Gerald, B.SC., PH.D.; British physicist; b. 18 Nov. 1927, Harrow, Middx.; s. of James Charles Chynoweth and Marjorie Fairhurst; m. Betty Freda Edith Boyce 1950; two s.; ed. King's College, Univ. of London; Postdoctoral Fellow of Nat. Research Council of Canada, Chemistry Div., Ottawa 1950–52; mem. Tech. Staff, Bell Telephone Labs. 1953–60, Head, Crystal Electronics Dept. 1960–65, Asst. Dir. Metallurgical Research Lab. 1965–73, Dir. Materials Research Lab. 1973–76, Exec. Dir. Electronic and Photonic Devices Div. 1976–83, Vice-Pres., Applied Research, Bell Communications Research 1983–; Survey Dir. of Nat. Acad. of Sciences Cttee. on Survey of Materials Science and Eng. 1971–73, Comm. on Mineral Resources and the Environment 1973–75; mem. of Nat. Materials Advisory Bd., Wash. 1975–79, NATO Special Programme Panel on Materials 1977–82, Consultant to NATO Advanced Study Inst. Panel 1982–, Metallurgical Soc.; Fellow, Inst. of Electrical and Electronic Engineers, American Physical Soc., Inst. of Physics, London; W. R. G. Baker Prize Award 1967. *Publications:* over 60 papers in professional journals on solid state physics, 11 patents on solid state devices, Nat. Acad. of Sciences reports: Materials and Man's Needs, Materials Conservation through Technology, Resource Recovery from Municipal Solid Wastes. *Leisure interests:* travel, boating. *Address:* Bell Communications Research Inc., Morristown, N.J. 07960 (Office); 6 Londonderry Way Summit, New Jersey 07901, U.S.A. (Home). *Telephone:* 201-829-2100 (Office); 201-273-3956 (Home).

CIAMPI, Carlo Azeglio, LL.B.; Italian banker; b. 9 Dec. 1920, Livorno; s. of Pietro Ciampi and Marie Masino; m. Franca Pilla 1946; one s. one d.; ed. Scuola Normale Superiore di Pisa, Pisa Univ.; served in Italian Army 1941–44; with Banca d'Italia 1946, economist research dept. 1960–70, head research dept. 1970–73, Sec. Gen. 1973–76, Deputy Dir. Gen. 1976–78, Dir. Gen. 1978–79, Gov. 1979–; Chair. Ufficio Italiano dei Cambi, 1979–; mem. Bd. of Govs. for Italy IBRD, IDA, IFC; mem. Cttee. of Govs. EEC; mem. Bd. of Dirs. Consiglio Nazionale delle Ricerche, BIS; mem. Istituto Adriano Olivetti di Studi per la Gestione dell'Economia e delle Aziende; Military Cross, Grand Officer Order of Merit of the Italian Republic. *Address:* Banca d'Italia, Via Nazionale 91, 00184 Rome, Italy (Office). *Telephone:* (06) 47921.

CIAPPI, H.E. Cardinal Mario Luigi; Italian ecclesiastic; b. 6 Oct. 1909, Florence; ordained priest 1932; Titular Bishop of Miseno 1977; cr. Cardinal 1977; Deacon of Nostra Signora del S. Cuore; Theologian of the Papal Household; mem. Sacred Congregation for the Causes of Saints. *Address:* 00120 Città del Vaticano, Rome, Italy. *Telephone:* 698-3131.

CIHLARZ, Wolfgang, M.F.A.; German artist; b. 24 Aug. 1954, Karlsruhe; ed. Hochschule der Künste Berlin; works exhibited at Heftige Malerei, Haus am Waldsee, Berlin 1980, Medellin, Columbia, Westkunst, Cologne, Figures, Forms, Expression, Abright Knox Museum, Buffalo 1981, Sydney Biennale, Dokumenta Kassel, Zeitgeist, Berlin, Venice Biennale 1982, Frederik S. Wright Art Gallery, Univ. of Calif., Museum of Modern Art, Tel Aviv, Nat. Museum of Art., Osaka, Moderna Galerija, Ljublijana, Athens Pinacotecha 1983, Museum of Modern Art, New York 1984, Nationalgalerie, Berlin, Echnato Gallery, Cairo 1985, Akademie der Künste, Berlin, Bienal São Paulo, Hirshorn Museum, Washington, D.C. 1986; P.S.I. Grant Deutscher Akademischer Austauschdienst 1981, 1st Prize, German Shakespeare Soc. *Leisure interest:* art collecting. *Address:* Oranienstrasse 58, 1000 Berlin 61, Federal Republic of Germany; 1308 Factory Place 2-A, Los Angeles, Calif. 90013, U.S.A. *Telephone:* (030) 614 8850 (Berlin); (213) 627-3377 (Los Angeles).

CIKKER, Ján; Czechoslovak (Slovak) composer; b. 29 July 1911, Banská Bystrica; m. Kitty Fiedler 1950; ed. Banská Bystrica Conservatoire and Master School of Composition, Prague, and conducting under Felix Weingartner in Vienna; Prof. of Theory of Music Bratislava Conservatoire 1939–51; Dramaturge, Opera House 1945–48; Prof. of Composition, School of Musical Arts 1951–77; mem. Slovak Theatre Council 1970–75; Chair.

Czechoslovak Music Council 1975–77; Corresp. mem. Academy of Art, German Dem. Repub.; Czechoslovak Peace Prize 1951, State Prize 1955, 1963, 1975, Nat. Artist 1966, Herder Prize of Vienna Univ. 1966, Madach Prize, Hungary 1966, Order of Labour 1971, UNESCO Music Award 1979, Order of Victorious 1981. *Works include:* Sonatina for Piano 1933, Symphonic Prologue 1934, Two string quartets 1935, 1937, Capriccio 1936, Cantus Filiorum (cantata) 1940, About Life (trilogy of symphonic poems) 1941, 1943, 1946, Concertino for Piano and Orchestra 1942, Bucolic Poem (ballet music) 1944, scenic music for Hamlet 1947, and The Taming of the Shrew 1950, The Tatra Streams (three studies for piano) 1954, What the Children Told Me 1957, Meditation on the H. Schütz theme Glorified are the Dead 1964, orchestral studies 1965, Hommage à Beethoven 1970, Over the Old Trench (symphony) 1974, Symphonia 1945 1975, Ode to Joy (oratorio after Rufus) 1983; and operas: Juro Jánošík 1954, Beg Bajazid 1957, Resurrection (after Tolstoy) 1962, Mr. Scrooge (after Dickens) 1963, A play about Love and Death (after Romain Rolland) 1967, Coriolanus (after Shakespeare) 1974, Aquarelles 1977, Verdikt (after Kleist) 1978, The Storm of Bystrica (comic opera, after Mikszath) 1981, The Life of the Insect (after Čapek) 1985. *Address:* Fialkové údolie č. 2, Bratislava, Czechoslovakia. *Telephone:* 312555.

CILLIÉ, Petrus Johannes, B.SC.; South African journalist; b. 18 Jan. 1917, Stellenbosch; s. of late Prof. Gabriel Gideon Cillié and Maria Cillié (née Van Niekerk); m. Elizabeth Frederika Bester 1936; two d.; ed. Boys' High School, Stellenbosch, Stellenbosch Univ.; joined editorial staff Die Burger 1935, Chief Sub-Ed. 1938–44, Foreign Ed. 1944–45, Asst. Ed. 1945–54, Ed. 1954–77; Chair. Nasionale Pers Group (publishing house) 1977–; Prof. of Journalism, Stellenbosch Univ. 1977–83; mem. Stellenbosch Univ. Council 1984–; Hon. D.Litt. (Stellenbosch) 1975; Markus Viljoen Medal 1979; D.F. Malan Medal 1984; State Pres. Order for Meritorious Service (Gold) 1988. *Publications:* several books of essays and political articles. *Leisure interests:* music, books. *Address:* P.O. Box 692, Cape Town 8000 (Office); 27 Buxton Avenue, Cape Town 8001, South Africa. *Telephone:* 021-254850 (Office); 244408 (Home).

CIMINO, Michael; American film writer and director; b. 1943, New York; screenplay writer for Silent Running 1972, Magnum Force 1973; screenplay writer and dir. Thunderbolt and Lightfoot 1974; producer, writer and dir. The Deer Hunter (Academy Award for Best Dir. 1979) 1978; writer and Dir. Heaven's Gate 1980, Prod. and Dir. Year of the Dragon 1985, Dir. The Sicilian 1987.

CINADER, Bernhard, O.C., PH.D., D.SC., F.R.S.C.; Canadian university professor; b. 30 March 1919, Vienna, Austria; s. of Leon and Adele (Schwarz) Cinader; one d.; ed. Univ. of London; Research Asst. Lister Inst. of Preventive Medicine, London 1945–46, Jenner Memorial Student 1946–48; Fellow of Immunochemistry, Western Reserve Univ., Cleveland, Ohio 1948–49; Beit Memorial Fellow, Lister Inst. 1949–53, Grantee of Agric. Research Council 1953–56; research work, Inst. Pasteur, Paris 1955; Prin. Scientific Officer, Inst. of Animal Physiology, Cambridge, and Hon. Lecturer, Univ. Coll., London 1956–58; Head, Subdiv. of Immunochemistry, Ont. Cancer Inst., and Assoc. Prof. Univ. of Toronto 1958–69; Prof., Dept. of Medical Cell Biology, Univ. of Toronto 1969, Dept. of Medical Genetics 1969, Dept. of Clinical Biochem. 1970, Dir. Inst. of Immunology 1971–80; mem. Gov. Council, Univ. of Toronto 1980–; Chair. 6th Int. Congress of Immunology, Toronto 1986; mem. numerous nat. and int. scientific orgs. and research review cttees., etc.; several honours and awards, including Medal de la Société de Chimie Biologique, Paris 1954, Jubilee Medal 1977, Thomas W. Eadie Medal (Royal Soc. of Canada) 1982, Karl Landsteiner Congress Medal 1986; f. Hardi Cinader Prize (Univ. of Toronto) 1985; Bernhard Cinader Annual Lecture f. by Canadian Soc. of Immunology 1986. *Publications:* 6 books and 270 scientific papers and reviews; Ed. series Receptors and Ligands in Intercellular Communication (8 vols) 1983–, Intercellular and Intracellular Communication 1986–. *Leisure interest:* Canadian native art. *Address:* Department of Immunology, University of Toronto, Medical Sciences Building, Toronto, Ont. M5S 1A8, Canada. *Telephone:* (416) 978-6120; 463-3013.

CINTRA DO PRADO, Luiz, PH.D.; Brazilian engineer and university professor; b. 16 June 1904, Amparo; s. of Alfredo Patrício do Prado Paulista and Júlia Cintra do Prado; m. Maria Celina Ferreira 1939; two s. three d.; ed. Escola Politécnica, Univ. de São Paulo, Univ. de Paris (Sorbonne) and Collège de France; Asst. Lecturer Physics, Escola Politécnica, Univ. de São Paulo 1929–33, Prof. 1938–64, Dir. 1940–42, Prof. Emer. 1964–; lecturer Physics, Faculty of Medicine and Faculty of Science 1933–37, Prof. Applied Physics, Faculty of Architecture and Urbanism 1950–71, Dir. 1953–54; Vice-Rector, Univ. de São Paulo 1953–54, Chief Nuclear Eng. Dept., Inst. of Atomic Energy 1960–63, Dir. 1961–63; Prof. Pontifícia, Univ. Católica de São Paulo 1938–54; mem. Del. to Int. Atomic Energy Agency (IAEA) 1957–67; mem. Nat. Research Council 1951–64; mem. Brazilian Acad. of Sciences 1941–, Vice-Pres. 1959–64; mem. Scientific Advisory Cttee. (SAC) of UN and of IAEA 1960–72; mem. Int. Cttee. on Weights and Measures 1967–; Head Planning Dept. 1972–75; Consultant Adviser to Presidency, CESP Companhia Energética de São Paulo 1975–; Hon. Pres. Latin American Asscn. of Acoustics (GALA) 1980–; Prominent Engineer of the Year, Inst. of Engineers 1965. *Publications:* eight textbooks on pure and applied physics, over 160 scientific or technical papers. *Leisure interests:*

music, especially piano, walking, reading. *Address:* Alam. Itu 265, apt. 101, São Paulo, S.P. BR-01421, Brazil.

CIOARĂ, Gheorghe; Romanian politician; b. 23 Feb. 1924, Bucharest; ed. Polytechnic Inst., Bucharest, and Leningrad, U.S.S.R.; lecturer Polytechnic Inst., Bucharest 1950–56; Deputy Minister of Electric Power 1953–54, Minister 1954–57; Minister of Foreign Trade 1965–69; First Deputy Chair. State Planning Cttee. 1969–70; Vice-Prime Minister 1976–79; alt. mem. Cen. Cttee. Romanian CP 1960–65, mem. 1965–84, mem. Exec. Political Cttee. 1972–79; Vice-Chair. Supreme Council on Econ. and Social Devt. 1973–80; Deputy Rep. for Romania in Council for Mutual Econ. Assistance 1957–65; Chair. Municipal Cttee. and Gen. Mayor, Bucharest Municipality 1972–76; Minister of Industrial Construction 1978–79, of Electrical Power 1979–81; Minister and State Sec. for Nat. Council for Science and Tech. 1981–83; Amb. to Bulgaria 1983–84. *Address:* c/o Ministerul Afacerilor Externe, Bucharest, Romania.

CIOSEK, Stanisław, M.A.; Polish politician; b. 2 May 1939, Pawłowice, Radom Voivodship; s. of Józef and Janina Ciosek; m. Anna Ciosek 1969; two d.; ed. Higher School of Econs., Sopot; activist in youth orgs. 1957–75; Chair. Regional Council of Polish Students' Asscn. (ZSP), Gdańsk, Deputy Chair. and Chair. Chief Council, ZSP 1957–73; Chair. Chief Council of Fed. of Socialist Unions of Polish Youth (FSZMP) 1974–75; mem. PZPR, deputy mem. PZPR Cen. Cttee. 1971–80, First Sec. Voivodship Cttee. PZPR and Chair. Presidium of Voivodship Nat. Council, Jelenia Góra 1975–80, mem. PZPR Cen. Cttee. 1980–81, 1986–; Deputy to Seym 1972–85; Minister for Co-operation with Trade Unions Nov. 1980–85, for Labour, Wages and Social Affairs March 1983–84, Vice-Chair. Cttee. of Council of Ministers for Co-operation with Trade Unions 1983–85; Sec. Socio-Political Cttee. of Council of Ministers 1981–85; Head of Social and Legal Dept. of PZPR Cen. Cttee. 1985–86, Sec. PZPR Cen. Cttee. 1986–88; alt. mem. Political Bureau of PZPR Cen. Cttee. 1988–; Sec.-Gen. Nat. Council of Patriotic Movt. for Rebirth (PRON) 1988–; Kt.'s and Commdr.'s Cross, Order of Polonia Restituta. *Address:* PRON, Al. Ujazdowskie 13, Warsaw, Poland. *Telephone:* 287103.

CIPA, Walter Johannes, DR. RER. NAT.; German business executive; b. 29 Nov. 1928, Gleiwitz/Oberschl.; s. of Ernst and Marie (née Kus) Cipa; m. Eva Mayer 1958; no c.; ed. Technische Hochschule, Aachen and Universität Freiburg; Deutsche Erdöl AG, Hamburg 1955; Gelsenkirchener Bergwerks AG 1961– (name of firm changed to Gelsenberg AG 1969), mem. Man. Bd. 1965–75, Chair. of Man. Bd. 1969–75; Chair. Supervisory Bd. Aral AG until 1973; Deputy Chief Exec AEG-Telefunken 1975–76, Chair. Man. Bd. 1976–80. *Address:* Theodor-Stern-Kai, D-6000 Frankfurt 70, Federal Republic of Germany. *Telephone:* (0611) 600-5401.

CIRIANI, Henri; French architect and professor of architecture; b. 12 Dec. 1936, Lima, Peru; s. of Enrique Ciriani and Caridad Suito; m. Marcelle Espejo 1962; two d.; ed. Santa Maria School, Nat. Univ. of Eng. and Town Planning Inst., Lima; Asst. Architect Dept. of Architecture, Ministry of Devt. and Public Works, Lima 1956–60, Project Architect 1961–64; Pvt. Practice with Crousse and Paez 1961–64; Asst. Prof. of Design, Nat. Univ. of Eng., Lima 1961–64; emigrates to France 1964; f. Pvt. Practice, Bagnolet 1968, Paris 1976; Asst. Prof. of Architecture, Univ. de Paris VII 1969–71, Prof. 1971–; Prof. of Architecture, Ecole d'Architecture de Paris-Belleville 1971–; Visiting Prof. Tulane, New Orleans 1984, Univ. Coll., Dublin 1985, Univ. of Pennyslvania 1989; Sir Banister Fletcher Visiting Lecturer, Univ. Coll., London 1986–87; lectures worldwide; mem. Admin. Bd., Acad. de France, Rome 1987; Nat. Grand Prix of Architecture 1983, Equerre d'Argent 1983, Palme d'Or de l'Habitat 1988. *Public works include:* public bldgs., Ventanilla 1962–63, Matute 1963, Rimac San Felipe 1964, Marne-la-vallée Noisy I 1980, Noisy II 1981, Saint Denis 1982, Evry 1985, Lognes 1986; urban landscape at Grenoble 1968–74; Child-care Centre at St. Denis 1983; Cen. kitchen for St. Antoine Hosp., Paris 1985. *Leisure interests:* drawing, collecting postcards. *Address:* Ecole d'Architecture de Paris-Belleville, 78–80 rue Rébéval, 75019 Paris; 93 rue de Montreuil, 75011 Paris, France (Office). *Telephone:* (1) 42 41 33 60; (1) 43 56 72 09.

CIRKER, Hayward, B.S.; American book publisher; b. 1 June 1917, New York; s. of Sol Cirker and Sadie Goodman Cirker; m. Blanche Brodsky 1939; one s. one d.; ed. City Coll., New York; Founder, Owner and Pres. Dover Publs. Inc. 1942–. *Address:* 199 Woodside Drive, Hewlett, New York, N.Y. 11557, U.S.A.

CIROMA, Adamu, B.A.; Nigerian businessman and politician; b. 1934, Potiskum; s. of Muhammadu and Aishatu Ciroma; m. 1970; one d.; ed. Barewa Coll. and Univ. Coll. Ibadan; Admin. Officer, N. Nigeria Civil Service 1961–65; Sr. Asst. Sec., Fed. Civil Service 1965–66; Ed. New Nigerian 1966–69, Man. Dir. New Nigerian Newspapers 1969–74; business activities 1974–75; Gov. Cen. Bank of Nigeria 1975–77; mem. Constituent Assembly 1977–78; Minister of Industries 1979–82, of Agric. 1982–83, of Finance Nov.–Dec. 1983, arrested Dec. 1983, released Oct. 1984. *Leisure interest:* golf.

CIRY, Michel; French painter, etcher and graphic artist; b. 31 Aug. 1919, La Baule; s. of Georges and Simone (née Breune) Ciry; ed. Ecole des Arts Appliqués, Paris; studied music with Nadia Boulanger; religious and secular paintings and etchings; Prof. School of Fine Arts Fontainebleau 1957–58, Académie Julian 1960; fmr. mem. Conseil Supérieur de l'Enseignement

des Beaux-Arts; Vice-Pres. Comité National de la Gravure 1957–; numerous exhbns. in Europe and America including Paris, London, New York, Boston, Amsterdam, Rome and Berlin; works in Museums of Europe and America; has illustrated numerous books including books by Montherlant, Green, Claudel and Mauriac; Prix National des Arts 1945, Grande médaille de vermeil de la Ville de Paris 1962, Prix de l'Ile de France 1964, Prix Eugène Carrière 1964, Lauréate Acad. des Beaux-Arts 1968; mem. Acad. des Beaux-Arts, Florence 1964–; Prix Wildenstein 1968; Chevalier, Legion d'honneur, Chevalier des Arts et des Lettres. *Major Works:* Chemin de croix 1960–64, Stabat Mater 1960, 1961, 1963, 1965, Fièvres 1965, Christ's Passion 1955, 1957, 1960, 1964, Marie-Madeleine 1961, 1963, 1965, Saint François 1950, 1954, 1959, 1960, 1964, 1965. *Compositions include:* six sacred symphonies for choir and orchestra, several chamber works. *Publications:* nine vols. of autobiog. *Address:* La Bergerie, 76119 Varengeville-sur-Mer, Seine-Maritime, France.

CISSÉ, Jeanne Martin; Guinean fmr. diplomatist; b. 6 April 1926, Kankan; d. of Martin Cissé and Damaye Joséphine Soumah; m. Ansoumane Touré 1947; three s. three d.; teacher, Guinea 1945–54; Dir. of school 1954–58; mem. Teachers' Union 1958–64; Parti Démocratique de Guinée, Kindia Office of the Fed. Bureau 1959–68, Regional Women's Cttee. of Dalaba and Kindia and Nat. Women's Cttee.; Nat. Assembly, successively First Sec., Second Vice-Pres. and First Vice-Pres. until 1972; Sec.-Gen. Conf. of African Women 1962–72; Rep. UN Comm. on the Status of Women 1963–69; Perm. Rep. to UN 1972–76; attended sessions of Gen. Assembly 1961–63, 1966–68, OAU 1964, 1965, 1967–70, 1972 and Afro-Asian Conf. 1961; participated in UN Seminars on the Status of Women 1964 and 1971, and in world confs. of women, Moscow 1963 and Helsinki 1969; Minister of Social Affairs 1976–84; Lenin Peace Prize 1975.

CISSOKO, Col. Filifing; Mali army officer and politician; b. 8 Jan. 1936, Badeka; ed. Lycée Terrasson de Fourgère, Bamako and in Dakar, Senegal; joined French Army 1957, transferred to Mali Army 1960; Perm. Sec. of Mil. Cttee. for Nat. Liberation, Head of Cabinet of Pres. of the Repub. Oct. 1971; promoted Col. 1978; Pres. Nat. Comm. for preparation of Constitutional Congress of Union Démocratique du Peuple Malien (UDPM) Oct. 1978; mem. Cen. Exec. Bureau, Treas. UDPM March 1979–. *Address:* Union Démocratique du Peuple Malien, Bamako, Mali.

CISZEWSKI, Bohdan, D.TECH.SC.; Polish metallographist and metal physicist; b. 23 Dec. 1922, Grodno; m.; two c.; ed. Łódź Polytechnic; Asst. Metallography Dept., Łódź Tech. Univ. 1945–47; mem. staff, Warsaw Tech. Univ. 1947–68, Asst. Lecturer 1947–58, Asst. Prof. 1958–64, Extraordinary Prof. 1964–68; Lecturer, Military Tech. Acad., Warsaw 1951–, Prof. 1964–, Ordinary Prof. 1970–; Deputy Sec., Tech. Sciences Dept., Polish Acad. of Sciences 1975–80, Sec. 1981–86; mem. Scientific Secr. 1981–86; corresp. mem. Polish Acad. of Sciences 1973–86, mem. 1986–, mem. Presidium 1981–; hon. mem. Int. Inst. for Science of Sintering; mem. Metallurgy Cttee. of Polish Acad. of Sciences 1959–, Board of Polish Metallographic Soc. 1966–73; mem. Union of Fighters for Freedom and Democracy 1975–; numerous scientific awards include Award of Science and Technology Cttee. 1966, Minister of Nat. Defence Award 1968; Officer's and Kt's Cross, Order of Polonia Restituta, Order of Banner of Labour (2nd Class), Meritorious Teacher of Polish People's Rep. *Publications:* over 100 publications, including eight books and academic textbooks on metallography, material eng. and physics of metals. *Leisure interests:* ornithology, sightseeing. *Address:* ul. Świętojerska 24 m. 24, 00-202 Warsaw, Poland. *Telephone:* 20-33-03 (Office); 31-57-74 (Home).

CIUCU, George, PH.D.; Romanian mathematician; b. 12 July 1927, Cristian, Brasov county; ed. Science Coll., Bucharest Univ. 1950; instructor, Coll. of Mathematics, Bucharest Univ. 1950, lecturer 1956, Sr. lecturer 1958, Prof. 1966; Rector, Bucharest Univ. 1972–81; Deputy Minister of Educ. 1982–85; Pres. Romanian Comm. for UNESCO 1985–; corresp. mem. Romanian Acad. 1974–; Prize of Romanian Acad. 1960; Visiting Prof. Univ. of Rome 1961–62. *Publications:* Procese cu legături complete (Processes with Complete Links) (in collab.) 1960, Elemente de teoria probabilităţilor si statistica matematică (Elements of Probability Theory and Mathematical Statistics) 1963, Teoria jocurilor (Games Theory) (co-author) 1965, Probabilităţi şi procese stocastice (Probabilities and Stochastic Processes), with T. Constantin 1978. *Address:* c/o Universitatea Bucureşti, Bd. Gh. Gheorghiu-Dej 64, Bucharest, Romania.

CIUHA, Jože; Yugoslav artist and painter; b. 26 April 1924, Trbovlje; s. of Jože and Amalija Ciuha; m. Radmila Novak 1962; one s. one d.; ed. Acad. of Fine Arts, Ljubljana and Univ. of Rangoon, Burma (Buddhist art and philosophy); work includes painting on plexi-glass, print-making, murals, tapestry, scenography, illustrating and water colours; his extensive travels in Europe, Asia and S. America inspired deep interest in ancient cultures; over 100 one-man exhbns. in Europe and U.S.A.; more than 20 nat. and int. prizes. *Publications:* Petrified Smile, Conversations with Silence (based on sketchbooks from his S. American journey 1964–65), Travels to the Tenth Country (for children) *Leisure interest:* literature. *Address:* 61000 Ljubljana, Prešernova 12, Yugoslavia; and 4 Place de la Porte de Bagnolet, 75020 Paris, France. *Telephone:* 061/218 956 (Ljubljana) and 362 72 26 (Paris).

CIULEI, Liviu; Romanian actor, director, scenographer and architect; b. 7 July 1923, Bucharest; ed. Bucharest Univ. and Bucharest Acad. of

Dramatic Art; actor since 1945; stage dir. and scenographer since 1946; Dir. "Lucia Sturdza Bulandra" Theatre, Bucharest 1963–72, First Dir. 1972–; mem. Bd. of Dirs. Vivian Beaumont Theater, Lincoln Cen. 1978-; Art Dir. Minneapolis Theater 1980-; mem. Union of Plastic Artists, Assen. Artists of Theatrical and Musical Insts.; Pres. Romanian Centre of the O.I.S.T.T. (Int. Org. of Scenographers and Theatre Technicians); Artist Emer. 1957; acted at Bulandra, Odeon and C. Nottara theatres in Bucharest, as Puck in A Midsummer Night's Dream, Oliver in As You Like It, Krogstadt in Nora, Piotr in The Last Ones, Protasov in The Children Of The Sun, Treplev in The Seagull, Dunois in St. Joan, Danton in Danton's Death; directed Danton's Death, Bucharest 1966, and Schillertheater, West Berlin 1967, As You Like It, Bucharest 1961, Deutsches Theater Göttingen 1967, Macbeth, Bucharest 1968, The Seagull, Schillertheater 1968, Bucharest 1977, Richard II, Düsseldorfschauspielhaus 1969, Volpone, Freie Volksbühne, West Berlin 1970, Leonce and Lena, Bucharest 1970, Washington 1974, Vancouver 1976, Ionesco's Macbett, Munich 1973, The Threepenny Opera, Mannheim 1973, Paul Foster's Elizabeth the First, Bucharest 1974, Essen 1974, West German television 1975, Paris 1976, The Lower Depths, Bucharest 1975, Washington 1977, Sydney 1977, The Cherry Orchard, Essen 1975, Long Day's Journey into Night, Bucharest 1975, Spring Awakening, New York 1977, The Inspector General, New York 1978, Hamlet, Washington 1978, The Tempest, Bucharest 1978; numerous tours abroad with Romanian productions, including Budapest 1960, Leningrad and Moscow 1966, Florence 1969, 1970, Regensburg Frankfurt/Main, Essen 1970, Edinburgh Festival 1971, The Hague, Amsterdam 1972, etc.; State Prize 1962 for films; Grand Prize at the Int. Festival of Karlovy Vary 1960, for the film Valurile Dunării (The Waves of the Danube) as Dir. and interpreter; prize for the best direction at the Int. Festival at Cannes 1965, for the film Pădurea Spînzuraților (The Forest of the Hanged) as Dir. and interpreter. *Address:* Teatrul "Lucia Sturdza Bulandra", Bd. Schitu Măgureanu Nr. 1, Bucharest, Romania. *Telephone:* 149696, 129582.

CIUPE, Aurel; Romanian painter; b. 16 May 1900, Lugoj, Timiş County; ed. School of Fine Arts 1919, Coll. of Law, Bucharest; Julian Acad., Paris, and in Rome (with Pietro Coromaldi) 1919–24; Prof. School of Fine Arts 1925–49, then Ion Andreescu Coll. of Fine Arts, Cluj; Dir. of the Banat Museum, Timişoara 1940; exhbns. in Romania and abroad; Merited Master of Arts 1957, State Prize 1964. *Major works include:* landscapes (The Timis River at Lugoj, Winter), still life (Pink Table), interiors (Woman Indoors, A Room in the Evening). *Address:* 3400 Cluj-Napoca, Str. Rakoczi nr. 40, Romania.

CIVARDI, H.E. Cardinal Ernesto; Italian ecclesiastic; b. 21 Oct. 1906, Pavia; ordained priest 1930; Titular Archbishop of Sardica 1967-; cr. Cardinal 1979; Deacon of S. Teodoro; mem. Sacred Congregation for the Causes of Saints, for the Evangelization of the Peoples, Supreme Tribunal of the Apostolic Signatura. *Address:* 00193 Rome, Piazza del S. Uffizio 11, Italy. *Telephone:* 698.4171.

CIVIL, Alan, O.B.E.; British horn player and composer; b. 13 June 1929; m. Shirley Jean Hopkins; three s. three d.; ed. studied under Aubrey Brain, London, and Willy von Stemm, Hamburg; Prin. Horn, Royal Philharmonic Orchestra 1952–55; Co-Prin. Horn with late Dennis Brain, Philharmonia Orchestra 1955–57, Prin. 1957–66; Prof. of the Horn Royal Coll. of Music; Prin. Horn BBC Symphony Orchestra 1966–88; Guest Prin. Horn with Berlin Philharmonic Orchestra; mem. several Chamber Music Ensembles including London Wind Quintet, London Wind Soloists, Wigmore Ensemble, Prometheus Ensemble, Alan Civil Horn Trio, Music Group of London; has performed horn concertos as soloist in the U.S.A., South America, the Caribbean, Far East and Europe; Pres. British Horn Soc. 1979–; records for Columbia. *Compositions:* Symphony (for Brass and Percussion) 1950, Wind Octet 1951, Wind Quintet 1951, Horn Trio in E Flat 1952, Divertimento for Trombone Quartet, Suite for Two Horns; Songs, Music for Brass Ensemble, Horn Studies.
[*Died 19 March 1989.*]

CIVILETTI, Benjamin R., LL.B.; American lawyer; b. 17 July 1935, Peekskill, N.Y.; m. Gale Lundgren; three c.; ed. Johns Hopkins Univ., Baltimore, Md., Columbia Univ., New York, Univ. of Maryland; admitted Md. Bar 1961; law clerk to judge, U.S. District Court, Md. 1961–62; asst. U.S. attorney 1962–64; mem. firm, Venable, Baetjer & Howard 1964–77; Asst. Attorney-Gen., Criminal Div., U.S. Dept. of Justice 1977–79; Attorney-Gen. of U.S.A. 1979–81; law practice Baltimore 1981-; Chair., Dir. Healthcorp Inc. *Address:* 1800 Bank and Trust Building, 2 Hopkins Plaza, Baltimore, Md. 21201, U.S.A.

CIZIK, Robert, B.S., M.B.A.; American business executive; b. 4 April 1931, Scranton, Pa.; s. of John and Anna Paraska Cizik; m. Jane Morin 1953; three s. two d.; ed. Univ. of Connecticut and Harvard Grad. School of Business Admin.; Accountant with Price, Waterhouse & Co. 1953–54, 1956; financial analyst, Exxon Co. 1958–61; joined Cooper Industries 1961, Dir. 1971-, Pres. 1972-, C.E.O. 1975-, Chair. of Bd. 1983-; Dir. Temple-Inland Inc., Machinery and Allied Products Inst., The Texas Research League, Texas Eastern Corpn., Harris Corpn., Assocs. of Harvard Business School, Greater Houston Partnership, Cen. Houston, Inc., Business Cttee. for the Arts, Inc.; mem. Bd. of Trustees of The Conf. Bd., Cttee. for Econ. Devt.; mem. Texas Strategic Econ. Policy Comm., Rice Univ. Assocs., Bd. of Govs. Electrical Manufacturers Club, Business Roundtable, Houston Grand

Opera Bd. of Trustees; Co-Chair. Wortham Theatre Foundation; Hon. LL.D. (Kenyon Coll.) 1983 and other awards. *Address:* Cooper Industries, Inc., 1001 Fannin, Suite 4000, First City Tower Building, Houston, Tex. 77002, U.S.A. *Telephone:* 713-739-5400.

CLAES, Willy; Belgian politician; b. 24 Nov. 1938, Hasselt; m. Suzanne Meynen 1965; one s. one d.; ed. Univ. Libre de Bruxelles; mem. Exec. Cttee., Belgian Socialist Party, Joint Pres. 1975–77; mem. Limbourg Council 1964; mem. Chamber of Deputies 1968–; Minister of Educ. (Flemish) 1972–73, of Econ. Affairs 1973–74, 1977–81, Deputy Prime Minister 1979–81, May 1988-, Minister of Econ. Affairs, Planning and Educ. (Flemish Sector) May 1988-. *Address:* RAC-Arcades (6th Floor) 1010 Brussels; Berkenlaan 23, B3500 Hasselt, Belgium. *Telephone:* 011/21-25-68.

CLANCY, H.E. Cardinal, Edward Bede, A.O., D.D., L.S.S.; Australian ecclesiastic; b. 13 Dec. 1923, Lithgow, N.S.W.; s. of John Bede Clancy and Ellen Lucy Clancy; ed. St. Columba's Coll., Springwood, N.S.W., St. Patrick's Coll, Manly, N.S.W., Pontifical Biblical Inst. and Propaganda Fide Univ., Rome; Auxiliary Bishop, Archdiocese of Sydney 1974–78; Archbishop, Archdiocese of Canberra and Goulburn 1979–83; Archbishop of Sydney 1983-. cr. Cardinal 1988, with the titular Church of St. Maria in Vallicella. *Leisure interest:* golf. *Address:* St. Mary's Cathedral, Sydney, N.S.W. 2000, Australia. *Telephone:* 264-7211.

CLAPHAM, Sir Michael John Sinclair, K.B.E., M.A.; British printer and business executive; b. 17 Jan. 1912, Cambridge; s. of Sir John Clapham, C.B.E., and Lady Mary Margaret Clapham (née Green); m. Hon. Elisabeth Russell Rea (d. of 1st Baron Rea) 1935; three s. one d.; ed. King's Coll. Choir School, Cambridge, Marlborough Coll. and King's Coll., Cambridge; trained as printer 1933–38; joined Imperial Chemical Industries Ltd. (ICI) as Man. of Kynoch Press 1938; seconded to Tube Alloys Project (Atomic Energy) in Second World War; Dir. Metals Div., ICI (now IMI PLC) 1946–60, Chair. 1960–61, 1974–81; Dir. Main Bd. of ICI 1961–74, Deputy Chair. 1968–74; Dir. ICI of Australia and New Zealand Ltd. (renamed ICI Australia Ltd. 1971) 1961–74, Imperial Metal Industries Ltd. 1962–70, Chair. 1974–81; mem. Industrial Reorganization Corpn. April 1969–71; Chair. Council for Nat. Academic Awards 1971–77; Deputy Pres. CBI 1971–72, Pres. 1972–74, Vice-Pres. 1974–78; Dir. 1974–82 and Deputy Chair. Lloyds Bank 1974–80; Chair. BPM Holdings 1974–81; Dir. Grindlay's Bank 1975–84; Pres. Inst. of Printing 1980–82; Dir. Bell Group Int., fmrly. Associated Communications Corpn. PLC 1982–84; Dir. Stoll Moss Theatres Ltd. 1984-, Haytesbury (U.K.) Ltd. 1988-; mem. Court, Univ. of London 1969–86; Hon. D.Sc., LL.D. (London) 1984. *Publications:* Printing in History of Technology, Vol. III 1957, Multinational Enterprises and Nation States 1975. *Leisure interests:* sailing, swimming, cooking. *Address:* 26 Hill Street, London, W1X 7FU, England (Home). *Telephone:* 01-499 1240 (Home).

CLAPP, Norton, LL.D., J.D., D.C.L.; American businessman; b. 15 April 1906, Pasadena, Calif.; s. of Eben Pratt Clapp and Mary Bell Norton; m. 1st Mary Davis 1929 (deceased), 2nd Evelyn Booth Gardner 1941 (deceased), 3rd Jane Bumiller 1952 (divorced), 4th Jacqueline Hazen; six s. (three deceased); ed. Occidental Coll., and Univ. of Chicago; admitted to Calif. and Wash. Bars 1929, private practice 1929–42; U.S. Navy 1942–46; Chair. Metropolitan Building Corpn., Seattle 1954–78; Pres. Pelican (Alaska) Cold Storage Co. 1947–60, Chair. 1960–77; Pres. Boise (Ida.) Payette Lumber Co. 1949–55; Pres. Laird, Norton Co. 1950–60, Chair. 1960-; mem. Bd. of Dirs. 1946, Vice-Pres. Weyerhaeuser Co. 1956–57, Chair. 1957–60, 1966–76, Pres. 1960–66; dir. of numerous other cos.; Hon. Vice-Pres. Nat. Council Boy Scouts of America; Trustee Univ. of Puget Sound, Tacoma, The Menninger Foundation, Hon. Life Trustee, Univ. of Chicago; Officer Order of Leopold II (Belgium). *Leisure interests:* yachting, genealogy. *Address:* Norton Building, Seattle, Wash. 98104, (Office); P.O. Box 99, Medina, Wash. 98039, U.S.A. (Home). *Telephone:* (206) 464 5211.

CLAPPIER, Bernard; French economist; b. 9 Nov. 1913, Limoges; s. of Georges Clappier and Andrée Gérard; m. Tristane de Catheu 1941; one s. five d.; ed. École Polytechnique, Ecole Libre des Sciences Politiques; Deputy Sec.-Gen. Office of Industrial Production 1943; Dir. of the Cabinet of R. Schuman (Minister of Finance) 1947, (Minister of Foreign Affairs) 1948–50; Dir. External Econ. Relations, Ministry of Econ. Affairs 1951–64; Chair. Conf. between Member States of the European Communities and other states which applied for membership of the Communities 1962; Deputy Gov. Banque de France 1964–73, mem. Gen. Council 1973-, Gov. 1974–79; Hon. Gov. 1979; Insp.-Gen. of Finances 1964; Vice-Pres. of Monetary Cttee. EEC; Alt. Dir. Bank for Int. Settlements until 1973, Vice-Pres. 1983–86; Pres., Dir.-Gen. Crédit Nat. 1973–74. *Address:* 9 rue de Valois, 75001 Paris, France.

CLAPTON, Eric; British guitarist and songwriter; b. 30 March 1945, Bisley, Surrey; m. Patti Boyd 1988; guitarist with groups: Roosters, Yardbirds 1963–65, John Mayall's Bluesbreakers 1965–66, Cream 1966–68, Blind Faith 1969, Derek and the Dominoes 1970, Delaney and Bonnie 1970–72; solo performer 1972-; *recordings include:* Disraeli Gears, Wheels of Fire 1968, Goodbye Cream 1969, Layla 1970, Blind Faith 1971, Concert for Bangladesh 1971, Eric Clapton's Rainbow Concert 1973, Backless, Slowhand, 461 Ocean Boulevard 1974, E.C. Was Here, No Reason to Cry, Just One Night 1980, Money and Cigarettes 1983; compositions include

Presence of the Lord, Layla, Badge (with George Harrison); appeared in film Tommy 1974.

CLARE, David Ross, B.S.; American business executive; b. 21 July 1925, Perth Amboy, N.J.; s. of Robert Linn and Helen M. (née Walsh) Clare; m. Margaret Mary Corcoran 1947; two s. two d.; ed. M.I.T.; joined Johnson & Johnson 1946, Pres. Domestic Operating Co. 1970, Corporate Pres. 1976–, Dir. 1971–, mem. Exec. Cttee. 1971–, fmr. Chair.; mem. corpn. M.I.T. *Address:* 501 George Street, New Brunswick, N.J. 08903, U.S.A. (Office).

CLAREBROUGH, Leo Michael, F.A.A., PH.D.; Australian research scientist; b. 14 June 1924, Melbourne; s. of John A. Clarebrough and Josephine M. Carroll; m. Dorothy C. Rice 1951; two s. two d.; ed. Xavier Coll., Univs. of Melbourne and Birmingham, U.K.; research scientist Div. of Tribophysics, CSIRO 1947–78, Chief Research Scientist Chemical Physics 1978–87, Materials Science and Tech. 1987–88; Research Fellow CSIRO Div. of Materials Science and Tech. 1988–; mem. Council Australian Acad. of Science 1985–, Sec. (Physical Sciences) 1988–; David Syme Medal 1961. *Publications:* contribs. to Philosophical Magazine, Acta Metallurgica, Physica Status Solidi, Proc. Royal Soc., Australian Journal of Physics. *Leisure interest:* gardening. *Address:* 4 Logan St., Canterbury, Vic. 3126, Australia. *Telephone:* (03) 836-2058.

CLARK, Rt. Hon. (Charles) Joseph, P.C., M.A.; Canadian politician; b. 5 June 1939, High River, Alberta; s. of Charles A. Clark and Grace R. Welch; m. Maureen Anne (née McTeer) 1973; one d.; ed. Univ. of Alberta, Dalhousie Univ.; began career as a journalist; Nat. Pres. Progressive Conservative Party of Canada (PCP) Student Fed. 1963–65; First Vice-Pres. PCP Asscn. of Alberta 1966–67; Lecturer, Univ. of Alberta 1965–67; Special Asst. to Davie Fulton 1967; Exec. Asst. to PCP Leader Robert Stanfield (q.v.) 1967–70; mem. House of Commons 1972–; Leader of PCP 1976–83; Prime Minister of Canada 1979–80; Sec. of State for External Affairs Sept. 1984–; M.P. for Yellowhead 1984–; mem. Hillcrest Miners' Literary and Athletic Asscn.; Hon. LL.D. (New Brunswick) 1976, (Calgary) 1984; mem. Alberta Order of Excellence 1983. *Address:* Ministry of External Affairs, Lester B. Pearson Memorial Bldg., 125 Sussex Drive, Ottawa, K1A 0G2, Canada (Office). *Telephone:* (613) 995-1851.

CLARK, (Charles) Manning Hope, F.A.H.A., F.A.S.S.A., A.C., M.A.; Australian professor of history; b. 3 March 1915, Sydney; s. of late Rev. C. H. Clark and Catherine Clark; m. Hilma Dymphna Lodewyckx 1939; five s. one d.; ed. Melbourne Grammar School, Univ. of Melbourne, Balliol Coll., Oxford; schoolmaster 1939–44; lecturer in Political Science, Univ. of Melbourne 1944–46, in History 1946–48; Prof. Australian History, A.N.U. 1949–, now Prof. Emer.; Australian Literary Soc. Gold Medal 1970; Age Book Prize 1974; Prem's Literary Award 1979; Hon. D.Litt. (Melbourne, Newcastle and Sydney). *Publications:* numerous volumes and papers on Australian History, including A History of Australia 1962–87, A Short History of Australia 1963; fiction includes Disquiet and Other Stories 1969, In Search of Henry Lawson 1978. *Leisure interests:* fishing, music. *Address:* c/o Australian National University, Canberra A.C.T. 2600, Australia. *Telephone:* 495111.

CLARK, Colin Grant, M.A., D.LITT.; British economist; b. 2 Nov. 1905, Westminster, England; s. of James Clark and Marian Jolly; m. Marjorie Tattersall 1935; eight s. one d.; ed. Winchester Coll., and Brasenose Coll., Oxford Univ.; Asst. Social Surveys of London 1928–29, of Merseyside 1929–30; Econ. Advisory Council 1930–31; lecturer, Cambridge Univ. 1931–37; Visiting lecturer, Univs. of Sydney, Melbourne and Western Australia 1937–38; Under-Sec. of State for Labour and Industry, Dir. Bureau of Industry, Financial Adviser to Treasury, Queensland 1938–52; Dir. Inst. for Research in Agricultural Econs., Oxford 1953–69; now Consultant, Queensland Univ., Australia; Corresp. Fellow, British Acad.; Hon. Sc.D. (Milan); Hon. D.Econ. (Tilburg). *Publications:* The National Income, The Conditions of Economic Progress, The Economics of 1960, Welfare and Taxation, British Trade in the Common Market, Economics of Irrigation, Population Growth and Land Use, Starvation or Plenty?, The Value of Agricultural Land, Regional and Urban Location 1982, etc. *Leisure interest:* gardening. *Address:* Department of Economics, University of Queensland, St. Lucia, Queensland 4067 (Office); 102 Sunset Road, Kenmore 4069, Australia (Home). *Telephone:* 07-377-3720 (Office); 07-378-7775 (Home).

CLARK, Dick Clarence, M.A.; American politician; b. 14 Sept. 1928, Central City, Ia.; s. of Clarence and Bernice Clark; m. Jean Gross 1954 (divorced 1976), one s. one d.; m. 2nd Julie Kennett 1977; ed. Lamont High School, Upper Iowa Univ. and State Univ. of Iowa; U.S. Army, Germany, Private 1950, Corporal 1952; Teaching Asst., State Univ. of Ia. 1956–59; Asst. Prof. of History and Political Science, Upper Ia. Univ. 1959–64, Pres. of Faculty 1962; Chair. Office of Emergency Planning in Ia., and Ia. Civil Defense Admin. 1963–64; Admin. Asst. to Congressman John C. Culver 1965–71; Senator from Iowa 1973–79; Sr. Fellow on Foreign Affairs, Aspen Inst., Washington 1980–; fmr. Head of U.S. Refugee Programmes; mem. American Historical Asscn., Conf. on European History, American Assen. of Univ. Profs. and Conf. on Slavic and East European History, Members of Congress for Peace Through Law, fmr. mem. Senate Agriculture and Foreign Relations Cttees., Special Cttee. on Aging, Rules Cttee., Democratic Steering Cttee.; Nat. Oratorical and Debate Champion 1953, Sr.

Fellow of Aspen Inst. for Humanistic Studies; Hon. LL.D. (Upper Ia. Univ.) 1973; Hon. L.H.D. (Parsons Coll.) 1973, (Mount Mercy Coll., Drake Univ., Cornell Coll., Haverford Coll., St. Ambrose Coll.) 1977. *Leisure interests:* reading, tennis, painting, music, theatre. *Address:* Aspen Institute, 1333 New Hampshire Avenue, N.W., Washington, D.C. 20036 (Office); 4424 Edmunds Street, N.W., Washington, D.C. 20007, U.S.A. (Home). *Telephone:* 202-446-6410.

CLARK, George Whipple, PH.D.; American professor of physics; b. 31 Aug. 1928, Evanston; s. of Robert Keep Clark and Margaret Holmes Whipple; m. 1st. Elizabeth Kister 1954 (divorced 1972); m. 2nd Charlotte Reischer 1988; two d.; ed. Harvard Univ. and M.I.T.; Instructor, M.I.T. 1952–54, Asst. Prof. 1954–60, Assoc. Prof. 1960–65, Prof. 1965–, Breene M. Kerr Prof. of Physics 1984–; Prin. Investigator for X-ray astronomy projects on NASA satellites OSO-7, SAS-3 and HEAO-2; Guggenheim Fellow 1963; Fulbright Scholar 1963; NASA Distinguished Scientific Achievement 1982; mem. N.A.S., American Acad. of Arts and Sciences. *Publications:* numerous articles in scientific journals. *Leisure interests:* carpentry, tennis, sailing. *Address:* Massachusetts Institute of Technology, Room 37-611, Cambridge, Mass., U.S.A. *Telephone:* 617-253-5842.

CLARK, Helen, M.A.; New Zealand politician; b. 1950, Hamilton; m.; ed. Epsom Girls' Grammar School and Auckland Univ.; fmr. Lecturer, Dept. of Political Studies, Auckland Univ.; mem. Parl. 1981–; Minister of Housing and Minister of Conservation 1987–89, of Health 1989–; Labour Party. *Leisure interests:* badminton, tennis, films, theatre, concerts. *Address:* Parliament House, Wellington, New Zealand.

CLARK, Howard Longstreth; American business executive; b. 14 March 1916, South Pasadena, Calif.; s. of Warren and Florence Clark; m. Jean Beaven 1961; nine c.; ed. Stanford Univ., Harvard Law School and Columbia Univ. Graduate Business School; Price Waterhouse and Co. 1937–39; admitted to New York Bar 1942; War Service, Navy 1942–45; American Express Co. 1945–83, Vice-Pres. 1948, Senior Vice-Pres. 1952–56, Exec. Vice-Pres. 1956–60, Pres. and C.E.O. 1960–68, Chair. and C.E.O. 1968–74, 1975–77, Pres. 1974–75, Chair. Exec. Cttee. 1977–79; Dir. of numerous cos. *Address:* 660 Madison Avenue, Suite 1805, New York, N.Y. 10021 (Office); 10, Riverview Road, Hobe Sound, Fla. 33455, U.S.A. (Home).

CLARK, Ian Robertson, C.B.E., LL.D., F.C.C.A., I.P.F.A.; British administrator; b. 18 Jan. 1939, Motherwell, Scotland; s. of Alexander and Annie Dundas (née Watson) Clark; m. Jean Scott Waddell Lang 1961; one s. one d.; ed. Dalziel High School, Motherwell; trained as certified accountant; in local govt. 1962–76, reached post of Chief Exec. Shetland Islands Council 1976; mem. Bd. British Nat. Oil Corpn. 1976–82; Jt. Man. Dir. Britoil PLC 1982–85; Chair. Sigma Resources 1986–87; Chair. and Man. Dir. Clark and Assocs. 1986–; Chair. Ventures Div., Costain PLC 1987–; mem Scottish Econ. Council 1978–87; mem. Glasgow Univ. Court 1980–87; Hon. LL.D. (Glasgow) 1979. *Publication:* Reservoir of Power 1980. *Leisure interests:* walking and music. *Address:* 16 Pam's Gardens, Camberley, Surrey, GU15 1HY, England.

CLARK, Sir John A., Kt.; British business executive; b. 14 Feb. 1926; s. of Sir Allen and Lady Jocelyn Clark (née Culverhouse); brother of Michael William Clark (q.v.); m. 1st Deidre Waterhouse 1952 (dissolved 1962), one s. one d.; m. 2nd Olivia Pratt 1970, two s. one d.; ed. Harrow and Cambridge; Royal Naval Volunteer Reserve, Second World War; fmrly. with Metropolitan Vickers and Ford Motor Co.; studied American electronics industry in U.S.A.; Asst. to Gen. Man., Plessey Int. Ltd. 1949; Dir. and Gen. Man. Plessey (Ireland) Ltd. and Wireless Telephone Co. Ltd. 1950; mem. Bd. of Dirs. Plessey Co. Ltd. 1953, Gen. Man. Components Group 1957, Man. Dir. and Chief Exec. 1962–70, Deputy Chair. 1967–70, Chair. and Chief Exec. 1970–; Dir. ICL Ltd. 1968–79, Banque Nationale de Paris 1976–; Pres. Telecommunication Engineering and Mfg. Assen. 1964–66, 1972–74; Deputy Pres. Inst. of Works Mans.; Deputy Pres. Engineering Employers' Fed.; mem. Council and Pres.'s Cttee. of CBI Nat. Defence Industries Council; fmrly. mem. Review Body on Top Salaries; Fellow Inst. of Man.; Chair. of Wavertree Technology Park Co.; Companion I.E.E.; Order of Henry the Navigator (Portugal) 1973. *Leisure interests:* shooting, swimming, riding. *Address:* The Plessey Co. PLC, Millbank Tower, 21-24 Millbank, London, SW1P 4QP, England. *Telephone:* 01-834 3855.

CLARK, J(ohn) Desmond; C.B.E., F.B.A., F.S.A., SC.D., PH.D.; British anthropologist; b. 10 April 1916, London; s. of Thomas J. C. Clark and Catherine Wynne; m. Betty Cable Baume 1938; one s. one d.; ed. Monkton Combe School and Christ's Coll., Cambridge; Dir. Rhodes-Livingstone Museum, Livingstone, N. Rhodesia 1938–61; Prof. of Anthropology, Univ. of Calif. (Berkeley) 1961–86, Prof. Emer. 1986–, Faculty Research lecturer 1979; Mil. Service in E. Africa, Abyssinia, the Somalilands and Madagascar 1941–46; Founder mem. and Sec. N. Rhodesia Nat. Monuments Comm. 1948; Raymond Dart Lecturer, Univ. of the Witwatersrand, Johannesburg 1979; Fellow, American Acad. of Arts and Sciences 1965, Huxley Medallist, Royal Anthropological Inst., London 1972; Hon. Sc.D. (Univ. of Witwatersrand, Univ. of Cape Town) 1985; Sir Mortimer Wheeler Lecturer, British Acad. 1981; Foreign Assoc. N.A.S. 1986; Gold Plate Award of the American Men of Achievement 1982; Golden Mercury Int. Award 1982; Gold Medal, Soc. of Antiquaries 1985; Berkeley Citation, Univ. of Calif. 1986; Fellows'

Medal, Calif. Acad. of Science 1987; Hon. Fellow Royal Soc. of S. Africa 1988; Sr. Fellow Inst. for the Study of Earth and Man, Southern Methodist Univ., Dallas 1988; Medal, Archaeological Inst. of America 1989. *Publications:* The Stone Age Cultures of Northern Rhodesia 1950, The Prehistoric Cultures of the Horn of Africa 1954, The Prehistory of Southern Africa 1959, Prehistoric Cultures of Northeast Angola and their Significance in Tropical Africa 1963, Atlas of African Prehistory 1967, Kalambo Falls Prehistoric Site Vol. I 1969, Vol. II 1974, The Prehistory of Africa 1970, Ed. of and contrib. to Vol. I Cambridge History of Africa 1982, Ed. with G. R. Sharma of Palaeoenvironment and Prehistory in the Middle Son Valley, Madhya Pradesh, North Cen. India 1983, Ed. with S. A. Brandt and contrib. to From Hunters to Farmers: The Causes and Consequences of Food-Production in Africa 1984. *Leisure interests:* walking, photography, wood-cutting. *Address:* Dept. of Anthropology, University of California, Berkeley, Calif. 94720; 1941 Yosemite Road, Berkeley, Calif. 94707, U.S.A. (Home). *Telephone:* (415) 642-2533 (Office).

CLARK, John Grahame Douglas, C.B.E., M.A., PH.D., SC.D., F.B.A.; British archaeologist; b. 28 July 1907, Shortlands, Kent; s. of Lt.-Col. Charles Douglas Clark and Maud Shaw; m. Gwladys Maud White 1936; two s. one d.; ed. Marlborough Coll., and Peterhouse, Cambridge; research student Peterhouse, Cambridge 1930-32, Bye-Fellow 1932-35; Faculty Asst. lecturer in Archaeology, Cambridge 1935-46; Squadron Leader, R.A.F.V.R. 1941-45; Univ. lecturer in Archaeology, Cambridge 1946-52, Disney Prof. 1952-74; Head Dept. of Archaeology and Anthropology 1956-61, 1968, Master of Peterhouse 1973-80; Pres. Prehistoric Soc. 1959-62, also its Ed. 1935-70; Vice-Pres. Soc. of Antiquaries of London 1960-62; mem. Royal Comm. on Ancient Monuments 1957-69; mem. Ancient Monuments Bd. 1954-77; Trustee, British Museum 1976-80; Hon. mem. or Fellow of Danish, Dutch, Finnish, German, Irish, Italian, Swedish, Swiss and American Acads. and Socs.; Order of Dannebrog, Hodgkins Medal, Smithsonian Inst. 1967, Viking Medal, Wenner-Gren Foundation 1972, Drexel Medal, Pennsylvania 1974, Gold Medal of Soc. of Antiquaries, London 1978. *Publications:* The Mesolithic Settlement of Northern Europe 1936, Archaeology and Society 1939, 1958, Prehistoric England 1940, Prehistoric Europe: the Economic Basis 1952, Excavations at Star Carr 1954, World Prehistory—an Outline 1961, (with Stuart Piggott) Prehistoric Societies 1965, 1970, The Stone Age Hunters 1967, World Prehistory—a New Outline 1969, 1977, Aspects of Prehistory 1970, The Early Stone Age Settlement of Scandinavia 1975, World Prehistory in New Perspective 1977, Mortimer Wheeler Memorial Lectures 1978, Mesolithic Prelude 1980, The Identity of Man as seen by an Archaeologist 1982, Symbols of Excellence 1985, Prehistoric Archaeology at Cambridge and Beyond 1988, Economic Prehistory 1988. *Leisure interests:* gardening, sailing, contemporary art, oriental ceramics. *Address:* 36 Millington Road, Cambridge CB3 9HP, England. *Telephone:* Cambridge 353287.

CLARK, Rt. Hon. Joseph (see Clark, Rt. Hon. Charles Joseph).

CLARK, Kenneth Bancroft, PH.D.; American professor of psychology; b. 24 July 1914, Canal Zone, Panama; s. of Arthur Bancroft Clark and Miriam Hanson Clark; m. Mamie Phipps 1937; one s. one d.; ed. Howard Univ., Washington, D.C. and Columbia Univ., New York; Prof., Psychology Dept., City Coll., City Univ. of New York 1942-75; Founder and Dir. Harlem Youth Opportunity Unlimited, Inc. (HARYOU), New York 1964-66; Founder and Dir. Metropolitan Applied Research Center (MARC), New York 1967-75; Founder and Pres. Clark, Phipps, Clark & Harris, Inc., New York 1975-85; Pres. Kenneth B. Clark and Assocs., Inc., Hastings-on-Hudson, N.Y. 1986-; Springarn Medal 1961, Sidney Hillman Prize Book Award 1965, Kurt Lewin Award 1966, Coll. Bd. Medal of Distinguished Service to Educ. 1980. *Publications:* Prejudice and Your Child 1955, Dark Ghetto 1965, A Possible Reality 1972, Pathos of Power 1974, A Relevant War Against Poverty (with Jeannette Hopkins) 1968, The Negro American (Co-Ed. with Talcott Parsons) 1966. *Leisure interests:* writing and art. *Address:* Kenneth B. Clark and Assocs., Inc., 615 Broadway, Hastings-on-Hudson, N.Y. 10706, U.S.A. *Telephone:* (914) 478-1010.

CLARK, Ligia; Brazilian sculptress; b. 23 Oct. 1920, Belo Horizonte; d. of Jair and Ruth Pimentel Lins; m. Alnisio Clark Ribeiro 1938; one s. two d.; ed. Sacré Coeur de Marie, Belo Horizonte, Minas Gerais, and in Paris under Fernand Léger, Dobrinsky and Arpad Szénes; Co-founder Brazilian Neo-concrete Group 1959; first exhbn. of transformable sculptures Bichos 1960; took part in Biennale 1968, Sensorial Symposium of Art, Los Angeles 1970; lectured at Sorbonne, Paris 1970-75; Exhibitions in Paris, Rio de Janeiro, New York, São Paulo, Stuttgart and London; group exhbns. in France, Argentina, Germany, U.S.A., Italy, U.K., Israel, Czechoslovakia; numerous prizes and special exhbn., São Paulo Biennal 1963. *Address:* Avenida Prado Junior 16, Apdo. 801, Copacabana, Rio de Janeiro, RJ, Brazil.

CLARK, Michael William, C.B.E., D.L., C.I.E.R.E., C.I.E.E.; British business executive (retd.); b. 7 May 1927, London; s. of late Sir Allen and Lady Jocelyn Clark (née Culverhouse); brother of Sir John Clark (q.v.); m. Shirley MacPhadyen 1955 (died 1974); two s. two d.; ed. Harrow School; joined the Plessey Co. Ltd. 1950, Exec. Dir. 1951, Dir. 1953, Deputy Man. Dir 1962, Dir. of Corporate Planning 1965-67, Man. Dir. Telecommunications Group 1967-69, Man. Dir. The Plessey Co. Ltd. 1970-75, Deputy Chair. and Deputy Chief Exec. 1976-87; built up Plessey Defence business

1953-87; mem. of the Court, Univ. of Essex. *Leisure interests:* fishing, golf, forestry. *Address:* Braxted Park, Witham, Essex, England.

CLARK, Neil Rex, A.A.S.A., B.COM.; Australian banker; b. 9 July 1929; s. of R. H. Clark; m. Leona Buckley 1956; one s. one d.; ed. Homebush School, N.S.W. and Univ. of New South Wales; Personnel Man. Nat. Australia Bank 1973, Asst. State Man. 1974, Chief Admin. Officer E.D.P. and Systems 1976, State Man. 1979, Chief Man. Special Duties 1980, Gen. Man. Retail Banking and Finance 1981-84, Chief Gen. Man. 1984-, Chief Exec. 1985-. *Leisure interests:* golf, gardening. *Address:* c/o National Australia Bank, 500 Bourke Street, Melbourne, Vic. 3000, Australia.

CLARK, Petula; British singer and actress; b. (as Sally Olwen) 15 Nov. 1934, Epsom; d. of Leslie Norman and Doris Olwen; m. Claude Wolff 1961; one s. two d.; started career as child singer entertaining troops during Second World War; early appearances in films under contract to Rank Organization; made numerous recordings and television appearances in both England and France; success of single Downtown started career in the U.S.; *films:* Medal for the General 1944, Murder in Reverse 1945, London Town 1946, Strawberry Roan 1947, Here Come the Huggets, Vice Versa, Easy Money 1948, Don't Ever Leave Me 1949, Vote for Huggett 1949, The Huggetts Abroad, Dance Hall, The Romantic Age 1950, White Corridors, Madame Louise 1951, Made in Heaven 1952, The Card 1952, The Runaway Bus 1954, My Gay Dog 1954, The Happiness of Three Women 1955, Track the Man Down 1956, That Woman Opposite 1957, Daggers Drawn 1964, Finian's Rainbow 1968, Goodbye Mr. Chips 1969, Second Star to the Right 1980; *stage appearance:* Sound of Music 1981; has received two Grammy Awards and ten Gold Discs. *Address:* c/o J. Ashby, 235 Regent Street, London, W.1, England; c/o PROGENAR, 82 rue de Lausanne, Fribourg 1701, Switzerland.

CLARK, Ramsey, B.A., A.M., J.D.; American lawyer and government official; b. 18 Dec. 1927, Dallas, Tex.; s. of Thomas Campbell Clark; m. Georgia Welch 1949; one s. one d.; ed. Univs. of Texas and Chicago; Marine Corps 1945-46; admitted to Texas Bar 1951, U.S. Supreme Court 1956, New York Bar 1970; practised law, Texas 1951-61, New York 1970-; Asst. Attorney-Gen., Dept. of Justice 1961-65, Deputy Attorney-Gen. 1965-67, Attorney-Gen. 1967-69; Adjunct Prof., Howard Univ. 1969-72, Brooklyn Law School 1973-81. *Publication:* Crime in America 1970. *Address:* 36 East 12th Street, New York, N.Y. 10003 (Office); 37 West 12th Street, New York, N.Y. 10011, U.S.A. (Home). *Telephone:* (212) 475-3232 (Office); (212) 989-6613 (Home).

CLARK, Sir Robert Anthony, Kt., D.S.C.; British merchant banker; b. 6 Jan. 1924, London; s. of John Anthony Clark and Gladys Clark (née Dyer); m. Marjorie Lewis 1949; two s. one d.; ed. Highgate School, King's Coll., Cambridge; served in Royal Navy 1942-46; qualified as lawyer with Messrs. Slaughter and May, became partner 1953; Dir. Philip Hill, Higginson, Erlangers Ltd., now Hill Samuel & Co. Ltd. 1962-, Chair. 1974-87, Chief Exec. 1974-77, also Chief Exec. Hill Samuel Group 1976-80, Chair. 1980-; Chair. Review Bd. on Doctors' and Dentists' Remuneration 1979-86; Dir. Rover Group (fmrly. BL PLC) 1975-, Bank of England 1976-85; Chair. IMI PLC 1980-89; Chair. Marley 1984-; Dir. Shell Transport and Trading Co. 1982-, Alfred McAlpine PLC 1957-, Beecham Group PLC 1986- (Vice-Chair.); Chair. Charing Cross and Westminster Medical School 1982-. *Leisure interests:* music, reading. *Address:* 100 Wood Street, London, EC2P 2AJ (Office); Munstead Wood, Godalming, Surrey, England (Home). *Telephone:* 01-628 8011 (Office); Godalming 7867 (Home).

CLARK, Thomas H(enry), A.M., PH.D.; Canadian geologist; b. 3 Dec. 1893, London, England; s. of Thomas Clark and Elizabeth L. (née Anstiss) Clark; m. Olive M. Prichard 1927; one d.; ed. Harvard Univ.; Instructor in Geology Harvard Univ. 1919-23; Asst. Prof. Dept. of Geology, McGill Univ., Montreal 1924-28, Assoc. Prof. 1928-31, Logan Prof. of Palaeontology 1931-62, Chair. Dept. of Geology 1952-59, Prof. Emer. 1962-; Geologist, Geological Survey of Canada 1926-31; Curator Redpath Museum, McGill Univ. 1932-52; Geologist Quebec Dept. of Mines (later Natural Resources) 1938-63; Consultant Quebec Dept. of Natural Resources 1963-69; Advisor in Geology, Redpath Museum 1964-; Canada Centennial Medal 1967, Logan Gold Medal, Geological Asscn. of Canada 1971. *Publications:* Geological Evolution of North America (with C. W. Stearn) 1960 and over 100 scientific papers and reports. *Leisure interest:* English delftware. *Address:* Department of Geological Sciences, McGill University, Montreal, Quebec, H3A 2A7 (Office); 247 Chester Avenue, Town of Mount Royal, Quebec, H3R 1W4, Canada (Home).

CLARK, William P.; American lawyer and government official; b. 23 Oct. 1931, Oxnard, Calif.; s. of William Pettit and Bernice (née Gregory) Clark; m. Joan Brauner 1955; two s. three d.; ed. Stanford Univ., Law School, Loyola Univ., Los Angeles; admitted to Calif. Bar 1958; Sr. Partner Clark, Cole & Fairfield, Oxnard, Calif. 1958-66; Chief of Staff to Gov. Reagan, Sacramento 1966-69; Judge, Superior Court, San Luis Obispo County, Calif. 1969-71; Justice, Court of Appeals, Los Angeles 1971-73, Supreme Court of Calif., San Francisco 1973-81; Deputy Sec. of State, Washington, D.C. 1981; Asst. to the Pres. of the U.S.A. 1982-83; Sec. of Interior 1983-85; Chair. Task Group on Nuclear Weapons Program Man. 1985; mem. Comm. on Integrated Long-Term Strategy; Counsel, Rogers & Wells Law Firm 1985-; Bd. of Dirs. Lawter Int. 1985-, Pacific Telesis Group

1985–. *Address:* 1737 H Street, N.W., Washington, D.C. 20006; 201 N. Figueroa Street, Los Angeles, Calif. 90012, U.S.A.

CLARKE, Arthur Charles, B.SC.; British science writer and underwater explorer; b. 16 Dec. 1917, Minehead, Somerset; s. of Charles W. Clarke and Mary N. Willis; m. Marilyn Mayfield 1953 (dissolved 1964); ed. Huish's Grammar School, Taunton, and King's Coll., London; H.M. Exchequer and Audit Dept. 1936–41; R.A.F. 1941–46; Inst. of Electrical Engineers 1949–50; Technical Officer on first G.C.A. radar 1943; originated communications satellites 1945; Chair. British Interplanetary Soc. 1946–47, 1950–53; Asst. Ed. Science Abstracts 1949–50; engaged on underwater exploration on Great Barrier Reef of Australia and coast of Ceylon (Sri Lanka) 1954–; Chancellor, Univ. of Moratuwa, Sri Lanka, 1979–; Vikram Sarabhai Prof., Physical Research Lab., Ahmedabad 1980; extensive lecturing, radio and TV, U.K. and U.S.; UNESCO Kalinga Prize 1961; Fellow King's Coll., London; numerous prizes and awards, including Stuart Ballantine Medal, Franklin Inst. 1963; A.A.A.S.–Westinghouse Science Writing Award 1969; A.I.A.A. Aerospace Communications Award 1974; Nebula Award 1972, 1974, 1979, John Campbell Award 1974, Hugo Award 1974, Galaxy Award 1979, IEEE Centennial Medal 1984, Marconi Int. Fellowship 1984, Vidya Jyothi Medal 1986, Science Fiction Writers of America 'Grand Master' 1986, Charles A. Lindbergh Award 1987, Assoc. Fellow, Third World Acad. of Sciences 1987; Hon. D.Sc. (Beaver Coll.) 1971, (Moratuwa) 1979, Hon. D.Litt. (Bath) 1988. *Publications:* Non-fiction: Interplanetary Flight 1950, The Exploration of Space 1951, The Young Traveller in Space 1954 (publ. in U.S.A. as Going into Space), The Coast of Coral 1956, The Making of a Moon 1957, The Reefs of Taprobane 1957, Voice across the Sea 1958, The Challenge of the Spaceship 1960, The Challenge of the Sea 1960, Profiles of the Future 1962, Voices from the Sky 1965, The Promise of the Space 1968, The View from Serendip 1977, 1984, Spring 1984, Ascent to Orbit 1984, Astounding Days: A Science Fictional Autobiography 1989; with Mike Wilson: Boy Beneath the Sea 1958, The First Five Fathoms 1960, Indian Ocean Adventure 1961, The Treasure of the Great Reef 1964, Indian Ocean Treasure 1964; with R. A. Smith: The Exploration of the Moon 1954; with Editors of Life: Man and Space 1964; with the Apollo XI Astronauts: First on the Moon 1970; Report on Planet Three 1972; with Chesley Bonestell: Beyond Jupiter 1972; with Simon Welfare and John Fairley: Arthur C. Clarke's Mysterious World 1980 (also TV series), Arthur C. Clarke's World of Strange Powers 1984; with Peter Hyams: The Odyssey File 1984; Fiction: Prelude to Space 1951, The Sands of Mars 1951, Islands in the Sky 1952, Against the Fall of Night 1953, Childhood's End 1953, Expedition to Earth 1953, Earthlight 1955, Reach for Tomorrow 1956, The City and the Stars 1956, Tales from the White Hart 1957, The Deep Range 1957, The Other Side of the Sky 1958, Across the Sea of Stars 1959, A Fall of Moondust 1961, From the Ocean, From the Stars 1962, Tales of Ten Worlds 1962, Dolphin Island 1963, Glide Path 1963, Prelude to Mars 1965; with Stanley Kubrick: 2001: A Space Odyssey (novel and screenplay) 1968; The Lost Worlds of 2001 1971, 1972, Of Time and Stars 1972, The Wind from the Sun 1972, Rendezvous with Rama 1973, The Best of Arthur C. Clarke 1973, Imperial Earth 1975, The Fountains of Paradise 1979, 2010: Odyssey Two 1982, The Sentinel 1984, The Songs of Distant Earth 1986, Arthur C. Clarke's Chronicles of the Strange and Mysterious 1987, 2061: Odyssey Three 1988, Cradle (with Gentry Lee) 1988. *Leisure interests:* photography, table tennis, diving. *Address:* 25 Barnes Place, Colombo 7, Sri Lanka; c/o David Higham Associates, 5 Lower John Street, Golden Square, London, W1R 3PE, England. *Telephone:* Colombo 599757.

CLARKE, Brian; British artist; b. 2 July 1953, Oldham, Lancs.; s. of late Edward Ord Clarke and Lilian Clarke (née Whitehead); m. Elizabeth Cecilia Finch 1972; ed. Oldham School of Art and Crafts, Burnley School of Art, The North Devon Coll., Bideford School of Art; lived Düsseldorf 1981–82, Rome 1982–83, London 1983–84, New York 1984–; executed first of so-called "Punk Paintings" 1976; 45 paintings and stained glass for Queen's Medical Centre, Nottingham 1977; stained glass for mosque at King Khalid Airport, Saudi Arabia, in assoc. with Prof. Wayne Anderson of Boston 1981; designed Great Atrium stained glass for Buxton Thermal Baths, Derbyshire 1983–84; exhbns. Sheffield City Polytechnic 1978, Brian Clarke—New Paintings, Mappin Art Gallery, Sheffield 1980, Glass/Light Exhbn. (with John Piper), Festival of City of London 1979, Brian Clarke—New Paintings, Mappin Art Gallery, Sheffield 1980, Brian Clarke—New Paintings, Constructions and Prints, R.I.B.A., London 1981, Seriagraphen und Mosaik, Franz Mayerische Hofkunstanstalt, Munich 1982, Paintings from Rome and Düsseldorf, Robert Fraser Gallery, London 1983, Works on Paper, Robert Fraser Gallery, London 1984; paintings in numerous collections; council mem., Winston Churchill Memorial Trust; Churchill Fellowship in Religious Art, 1974, extension fellowship, art in architecture, 1975. *Publications:* Architectural Stained Glass 1979, The Two Cultures, A Tribute to C. P. Snow 1980, Brian Clarke Paintings 1983, Brian Clarke Drawings and Works on Paper 1985. *Leisure interests:* none. *Address:* c/o Simmons & Simmons, 14 Dominion Street, London E.C.2, England.

CLARKE, Bryan Campbell, M.A., D.PHIL., F.R.S.; British professor of genetics; b. 24 June 1932, Gatley, Cheshire; s. of Robert Campbell and Gladys (née Carter) Clarke; m. Ann G. Jewkes 1960; one s. one d.; ed. Fay School, Southborough, Mass., Magdalen Coll. School, Oxford and Magdalen Coll., Oxford; Nature Conservancy research student, Oxford Univ. 1956–59;

Asst. in Zoology, Univ. of Edinburgh 1959–63, lecturer 1963–69, Reader 1969–71; Prof. of Genetics, Univ. of Nottingham 1971–; Science Research Council Sr. Research Fellow 1976–81; Ed. Heredity 1978–85, Proceedings of the Royal Society, series B 1988–; Vice-Pres. Genetical Soc. 1981–83, Linnean Soc. 1984–86; Chair. Terrestrial Life Sciences Cttee. NERC 1984–87; mem. Biological Sub-Cttee., Univ. Grants Cttee. 1988–(90); *Publications:* Berber Village 1959, about 80 scientific publications. *Leisure interests:* painting, computing. *Address:* Department of Genetics, Queen's Medical Centre, Clifton Boulevard, Nottingham, NG7 2UH (Office); Linden Cottage, School Lane, Colston Bassett, Nottingham, NG12 3FD, England (Home). *Telephone:* (0602) 420639 (Office); (0949) 81243 (Home).

CLARKE, Sir Cyril Astley, K.B.E., M.D., SC.D., F.R.C.P., F.R.C.P.E., F.R.C.O.G., F.R.S., F.F.C.M., F.A.C.P., F.R.C.P.I., F.I.BIOL.; British professor of medicine; b. 22 Aug. 1907, Leicester; s. of Astley V. and Ethel Mary (née Gee) Clarke; m. Frieda M. M. (Féo) Hart 1935; three s.; ed. Oundle School, Caius Coll., Cambridge, and Guy's Hosp. Medical School; house physician, Guy's Hospital 1932–34, Demonstrator, Dept. of Pathology and Physiology 1934–35, Chief Clinical Asst., Dept. of Dermatology 1935–36; Life Insurance Work 1936–39; Medical Specialist, R.N. 1939–45; Medical Registrar, Queen Elizabeth Hospital, Birmingham 1946; Consultant Physician, United Liverpool Hospitals and Liverpool Regional Hospital Bd. 1946–58, Hon. Consultant Physician 1958–; Reader in Medicine, Univ. of Liverpool 1958, Dir. Nuffield Unit of Medical Genetics 1963–72, Prof. of Medicine 1965–72; Pres. Royal Coll. of Physicians 1972–77, Harveian Soc. of London 1977–78; Dir. Medical Service Study Group, Royal Coll. of Physicians 1977–83; Dir. Research Unit, Royal Coll. of Physicians 1983–; Nuffield Research Fellow, Dept. of Genetics, Univ. of Liverpool 1972–77; Hon. Research Fellow, Dept. of Genetic Medicine 1987–; Chair. British Heart Foundation 1982–87, British Soc. for Research on Ageing 1987–; Hon. Fellow, Caius Coll., Cambridge; Chair. of Council, Bedford Coll., London Univ. 1975–85; Hon. F.R.A.C.P.; Hon. D.Sc. (Edinburgh, Leicester, East Anglia, Birmingham, Liverpool, Sussex, Hull, Wales, London); Hon. F.R.C.P.Ed.; Hon. F.R.C.Path.; Fellow, Linnean Soc.; Hon. mem. Liverpool Medical Inst.; BMA Essay Prize 1932, Soc. of Apothecaries of London Gold Medal for Therapeutics 1970, James Spence Medal, 1973, Fothergillian Medal, Medical Soc. of London 1977, Gairdner Award 1977, Harveian Orator, Royal Coll. of Physicians 1979, Lasker Award New York 1980, Artois-Baillet Latour Health Prize 1981, Linnean Medal Zoology 1981, Nuffield Medal, Royal Soc. of Medicine 1984, First James Blundell Award, British Blood Transfusion Society 1984, Gold Medal, Royal Soc. of Medicine 1985–86. *Publications:* Genetics for the Clinician 1962 (2nd edn. 1964), Selected Topics in Medical Genetics 1969 (Editor), Human Genetics and Medicine 1970, 1977, 1987, Rhesus Haemolytic Disease, Selected papers and extracts (Editor) 1975, papers in professional journals. *Leisure interests:* small boat sailing, breeding butterflies. *Address:* Research Unit, Royal Coll. of Physicians, 11 St. Andrews Place, Regents Park, London, NW1 4LE (Office); 43 Caldy Road, West Kirby, Wirral, Merseyside, L48 2HF, England (Home). *Telephone:* 01-935 1174 (Office); 051-625 8811 (Home).

CLARKE, Edwin Sisterson, M.D., F.R.C.P.; British medical historian (retd.); b. 18 June 1919, Felling-on-Tyne; s. of Joseph C. Clarke and Nellie C. (née Sisterson) Clarke; m. 1st Margaret Morrison, two s.; m. 2nd Beryl Brock, one d.; m. 3rd Gaynor Crawford; ed. Cen. School, Jarrow-on-Tyne, Medical School, Univ. of Durham and Univ. of Chicago; Clinical Neurologist 1950–58; Asst. Sec. Wellcome Trust 1958–59; Asst. Prof. History of Medicine, Johns Hopkins Univ. 1960–61; Visiting Prof. History of Medicine, Yale Univ. 1961–63; Sr. Lecturer Univ. Coll. London 1966–72, Reader 1972–73; Dir. Wellcome Inst. for the History of Medicine 1973–79. *Publications:* The Brain and Spinal Cord (with C. D. O'Malley) 1968, Modern Methods in the History of Medicine (ed.) 1971, An Illustrated History of Brain Function (with K. E. Dewhurst) 1972, Die Historische Entwicklung by M. Neuburger (trans.), 19th Century Origins of Neuroscientific Concepts (with L. S. Jacyna) 1987. *Leisure interest:* history of Northumbria. *Address:* University Laboratory of Physiology, Parks Road, Oxford, OX1 3PT, England. *Telephone:* 0865-2-72543.

CLARKE, Sir Ellis Emmanuel Innocent, G.C.M.G., LL.B.; Trinidadian lawyer and diplomatist; b. 28 Dec. 1917, Port of Spain; s. of Cecil E. I. Clarke and Elma Pollard; m. Eyrmyntrude Hagley 1952; one s. one d.; ed. St. Mary's Coll., Port of Spain, Trinidad, London Univ. and Gray's Inn, London; private law practice, Trinidad 1941–54; Solicitor-Gen. Trinidad and Tobago 1954–56; Deputy Colonial Sec. 1956–57; Attorney-Gen. 1957–61; Constitutional Adviser to the Cabinet 1961–62; Amb. to the United States 1962–73, and to Mexico 1966–73; Perm. Rep. to UN 1962–66; Rep. on Council of OAS 1967–73; Chair. of Bd., British West Indian Airways 1968–73; Gov.-Gen. and C.-in-C. of Trinidad and Tobago 1973–76, Pres. 1976–87; Awarded first Trinity Cross (T.C.) 1969, K.St.J. 1973, Hon. Master of Bench, Gray's Inn 1980. *Leisure interests:* golf, racing, cricket. *Address:* c/o Office of the President, St. Ann's, Trinidad and Tobago. *Telephone:* 62-41261.

CLARKE, Graeme Wilber, M.A., LITT.D.; Australian professor of classics; b. 31 Oct. 1934, Nelson, New Zealand; s. of Wilber P. Clarke and Marjorie E. (née Le May) Clarke; m. Nancy J. Jordan 1963; three s. one d.; ed. Sacred Heart Coll., Auckland, N.Z., Univ. of Auckland, Balliol Coll., Oxford; lecturer, Dept. of Classics, Australian Nat. Univ. 1957, 1961–63,

Sr. Lecturer, Dept. of Classics and Ancient History, Univ. of Western Australia 1964–66, Assoc. Prof., Dept. of Classical Studies, Monash Univ. 1967–68, Prof. Dept. of Classical Studies, Univ. of Melbourne 1969–81; Deputy Dir. Humanities Research Centre, Australian Nat. Univ. 1982–, Prof. Emer. 1981–; Fellow Australian Acad. of the Humanities 1975–; with archaeological excavation in N. Syria at Jebel Khalid 1984–. *Publications:* The Octavius of Marcus Minucius Felix 1974, The Letters of St. Cyprian (4 vols.) 1984–88, Rediscovering Hellenism (ed.) 1988. *Leisure interest:* gardening. *Address:* Humanities Research Centre, Australian National University, G.P.O. Box 4, Canberra, A.C.T. 2601 (Office); 2 Hackett Gardens, Turner, A.C.T. 2601, Australia (Home). *Telephone:* 062-494357 (Office); 062-486549 (Home).

CLARKE, Sir (Henry) Ashley, G.C.M.G., G.C.V.O.; British diplomatist; b. 26 June 1903, Stourbridge, Worcs.; s. of H. H. R. Clarke, M.D. and Rachel Hill Duncan; m. Frances Pickett Molyneux 1962; ed. Repton and Pembroke Coll., Cambridge; served with diplomatic missions in Hungary 1925, Poland 1927, Turkey 1928–31; mem. British Del. to League of Nations and Disarmament Conf. 1932–34; mission to Japan 1934–38; at Foreign Office 1939–44, latterly as Head, Far-Eastern Dept.; Minister at Lisbon 1944–46; Minister in Paris 1946–49; Deputy Under-Sec. of State, Foreign Office 1950–53; Amb. to Italy 1953–62; Gov. of BBC 1962–67, of Nat. Theatre 1962–66, of British Inst. of Recorded Sound 1964–67; Chair. Royal Acad. of Dancing 1964–69; Chair. British-Italian Soc. 1962–67, Italian Art and Archives Rescue Fund 1966–70; mem. Cttee. of Man., Royal Acad. of Music 1967–73, Dir. 1973; mem. Advisory Council Victoria and Albert Museum 1969–73; Chair. Int. Torcello Cttee. 1976–83; Sec.-Gen. Europa Nostra 1969–71; London Adviser Banca Commerciale Italiana 1962–70, and mem. of Gen. Bd. Assicurazioni Generali, Trieste 1964–85; Vice-Chair. Venice in Peril Fund 1971–84, Pres. 1985–; Vice-Pres. Ancient Monuments Soc. 1982–; Fellow, Soc. of Antiquaries 1985–; Hon. Fellow, Pembroke Coll., Cambridge, Royal Acad. of Music; Hon. Dr. Pol.Sc. of Genoa Univ.; Torta Prize 1974, Grand Cross of the Order of Merit of the Italian Repub., Grand Cross of the Order of St. Gregory the Great, Kt. of St. Mark (Venice) 1979; Hon. Citizen of Venice 1985. *Publication:* Restoring Venice: the Church of the Madonna dell'Orto and the Porta della Carta (with Philip Rylands) 1977. *Leisure interests:* music and the arts. *Address:* Fondamenta Bonlini 1113, Dorsoduro, 30123 Venice, Italy; Bushy Cottage, The Green, Hampton Court, Surrey, KT8 9BS, England. *Telephone:* 5-206-530 (Italy); 01-943 2709 (England).

CLARKE, Mrs. Irene Fortune Irwin, O.C., C.M., M.A.; Canadian publisher; b. 21 March 1903; d. of John and Martha (Fortune) Irwin; m. William Henry Clarke 1927 (deceased); two s. one d.; ed. Parkdale Collegiate Inst., Victoria Univ., and Univ. of Toronto; Pres. (1955–81) and Chair. (1981–) Clarke, Irwin & Co. Ltd., since the death of her husband (the founder) in 1955; Chair. and f. of numerous women's groups. *Address:* 39 Old Mill Road, Apt. 2004, Toronto, Ont., M8X 1G6, Canada.

CLARKE, John, M.A., PH.D., F.R.S.; British professor of physics; b. 10 Feb. 1942, Cambridge; s. of Victor P. Clarke and Ethel M. Clarke; m. Grethe Fog Pedersen 1979; one c.; ed. Perse School, Cambridge and Univ. of Cambridge; Postdoctoral Scholar, Dept. of Physics, Univ. of Calif. Berkeley 1968–69, Asst. Prof. 1969–71, Assoc. Prof. 1971–73, Prof. 1973–; Prin. Investigator, Lawrence Berkeley Lab., Berkeley 1969–; Fellow, A.A.A.S., American Physical Soc.; Alfred P. Sloan Foundation Fellowship 1970–72; Adolph C. and Mary Sprague Miller Research Professorship 1975–76; Guggenheim Fellowship 1977–78, Calif. Scientist of the Year 1987, Fritz London Memorial Award 1987 and other honours and awards. *Publications:* approx. 150 publs. in learned journals. *Address:* Department of Physics, University of California, Berkeley, Calif. 94720, U.S.A. *Telephone:* (415) 642-3069.

CLARKE, Rt. Hon. Kenneth Harry, Q.C., M.P., B.A., LL.B.; British politician; b. 2 July 1940; s. of Kenneth Clarke; m. Gillian Mary Edwards 1964; one s. one d.; ed. Nottingham High School and Gonville and Caius Coll., Cambridge; called to the Bar, Gray's Inn 1963; practising mem. Midland circuit 1963–79; Research Sec. Birmingham Bow Group 1965–66; contested Mansfield, Notts. in General Elections 1964, 1966, M.P. for Rushcliffe Div. of Notts. 1970–; Parl. Pvt. Sec. to Solicitor Gen. 1971–72; an Asst. Govt. Whip 1972–74, Govt. Whip for Europe 1973–74; Lord Commr., H.M. Treasury 1974; Opposition Spokesman on Social Services 1974–76, on Industry 1976–79; Parl. Sec., Dept. of Transport, later Parl. Under Sec. of State for Transport 1979–82; Minister of State (Minister for Health), Dept. of Health and Social Security 1982–85; Paymaster-Gen. and Minister for Employment 1985–87; Chancellor of Duchy of Lancaster and Minister for Trade and Industry 1987–88, Minister for the Inner Cities 1987–88; Sec. of State for Health July 1988–; mem. Parl. Del. to Council of Europe and WEU 1973–74; Sec. Conservative Parl. Health and Social Security Cttee. 1974; Hon. Master of Bench, Gray's Inn. *Publication:* New Hope for the Regions 1979. *Leisure interests:* jazz, cricket, football. *Address:* c/o House of Commons, London, S.W.1, England.

CLARKE, Malcolm Roy, PH.D., D.SC., F.R.S.; British marine biologist; b. 24 Oct. 1930, Birmingham; m. Dorothy Knight 1958; three s. one d.; ed. Wallingford Co. Grammar School and Hull Univ.; Scientific Officer Nat. Inst. of Oceanography, Surrey 1958–71; Sr. Prin. Scientific Officer Marine Biological Asscn. of the U.K., Plymouth 1978–87; Visiting Prof., Liverpool

Univ. 1987–(90). *Publications:* A Review of the Systematics and Ecology of Oceanic Squids (in Advances in Marine Biology) 1966, Deep Oceans 1971, Cephalopoda in the Diet of Sperm Whales (in Discovery Report) 1980, Handbook for the Identification of Cephalopod Beaks 1986, The Mollusca (Vols. 10, 11, 12) 1986–87, Identification of Cephalopod "larvae" 1988. *Leisure interests:* boating, painting. *Address:* Ridge Court, Court Road, Newton Ferrers, Plymouth, PL8 1DD, England. *Telephone:* (0752) 872738.

CLARKE, Patricia Hannah, B.A., D.SC., F.R.S.; British professor of microbial biochemistry; b. 29 July 1919; d. of David S. Green and Daisy L. A. Willoughby; m. Michael Clarke 1940; two s.; ed. Howells School, Llandaff and Girton Coll. Cambridge; Armament Research Dept. 1940–44; Wellcome Research Labs. 1944–47; Nat. Collection of Type Cultures 1951–53; Lecturer, Dept. of Biochem. Univ. Coll. London 1953, Reader in Microbial Biochem. 1966, Prof. 1974–84, Prof. Emer. 1984–; Hon. Research Fellow, Chem. and Biochem. Eng. Dept. Univ. Coll. London 1984–; Leverhulme Emer. Fellow 1984–87; Hon. Professorial Fellow, Univ. of Wales Inst. of Science and Tech. 1984–. *Publications:* articles in professional journals. *Leisure interests:* walking, gardening, dress-making. *Address:* Glebe House, School Hill, Stratton, Cirencester, Glos., GL7 2LS, England.

CLARKE, Robert C., M.A.; British business executive; b. 28 March 1929, Eltham; s. of Robert H. Clarke and Rose (Bratton) Clarke; m. Evelyn M. Harper 1952; three s. one d.; ed. Dulwich Coll. and Pembroke Coll. Oxford; trainee, Cadbury Bros. Ltd. 1952; Gen. Man. John Forrest Ltd. 1954; Marketing Dir. Cadbury Confectionery 1957; Man. Dir. Cadbury Cakes Ltd. 1962; Chair. Cadbury Cakes Ltd. and Dir. Cadbury Schweppes Foods Ltd. 1969; Man. Dir. McVitie & Cadbury Cakes Ltd. 1971; mem. Bd. United Biscuits (UK) Ltd. 1974; Man. Dir. UB Biscuits 1977; Chair. and Man. Dir. United Biscuits (UK) Ltd. and Dir. United Biscuits (Holdings) PLC 1984; Group Chief Exec. United Biscuits (Holdings) PLC 1986–. *Leisure interests:* reading, walking, renovating old buildings and planting trees. *Address:* Easington Farmhouse, Chilton, Aylesbury, Bucks., HP8 9EX, England. *Telephone:* (0844) 208272.

CLARKSON, Thomas William, PH.D.; British professor; b. 1 Aug. 1932, Blackburn; s. of William Clarkson and Olive Jackson; m. Winifred Browne 1957; one s. two d.; ed. Univ. of Manchester; Instructor, Univ. of Rochester School of Medicine 1958–61, Asst. Prof. 1961–62, Assoc. Prof. 1965–71, Prof. 1971–, Head of Div. of Toxicology 1980–; Scientific Officer, Medical Research Council, U.K. 1962–64; Sr. Fellowship, Weizmann Inst. of Science 1964–65; Post-Doctoral Fellow, Nuffield Foundation 1956–57, and U.S. Atomic Energy Comm., Univ. of Rochester 1957–58; mem. Inst. of Medicine of N.A.S.; mem. La Academia Nacional de Medicina de Buenos Aires 1984; mem. Collegium Ramazzini 1983; Hon. Dr. Med. (Umea) 1986; J. Lowell Orbison Distinguished Service Alumni Prof. *Publications:* over 165 published papers; co-ed. of Reproductive and Developmental Toxicology, The Cytoskeleton as a Target for Toxic Agents. *Address:* University of Rochester School of Medicine, P.O. Box RBB, Rochester, New York, N.Y. 14642, U.S.A. *Telephone:* (716) 275-3911 (Office).

CLATWORTHY, Robert, R.A.; British sculptor; b. 31 Jan. 1928; s. of E. W. and G. Clatworthy; m. Pamela Gordon 1954 (divorced); two s. one d.; ed. Dr. Morgan's Grammar School, Bridgwater, West of England Coll. of Art, Chelsea School of Art, The Slade; teacher, West of England Coll. of Art 1967–71; Visiting Tutor, R.C.A. 1960–72; mem. Fine Art Panel of Nat. Council for Diplomas in Art and Design 1961–72; Governor, St. Martin's School of Art 1970–71; Head of Dept. of Fine Art, Central School of Art and Design 1971–75; exhbns. at Hanover Gallery, Waddington Galleries, Holland Park Open Air Sculpture, Battersea Park Open Air Sculpture, Tate Gallery (British Sculpture in the Sixties), Burlington House (British Sculptors 1972), Basil Jacobs Fine Art Ltd., Diploma Galleries, Burlington House, Photographers Gallery, Quinton Green Fine Art; work in collections of Arts Council, Contemporary Art Soc., Tate Gallery, Victoria and Albert Museum, GLC, Nat. Portrait Gallery (portrait of Dame Elisabeth Frink 1985); Monumental Horse and Rider, Finsbury Ave., London 1984. *Address:* Moelfre, Cynghordy, Llandovery, Dyfed, SA20 0UW, Wales. *Telephone:* Llandovery 20201.

CLAUDIUS-PETIT, Eugène Pierre; French politician and town planner; b. 22 May 1907, Angers; s. of Eugène Petit and Célestine Coué; m. Marie-Louise Moire (died 1975); one s. two d.; ed. Ecole Nationale Supérieure des Arts Décoratifs; fmr. cabinet maker and teacher; mem. Exec. Cttee. Franc-Tireur 1942; founder mem. Conseil Nat. de la Résistance; mem. Provisional Consultative Assembly of Algiers 1943–44; Pres. Mouvement de Libération Nationale 1945; founder mem. Union démocratique et socialiste de la Résistance (UDSR) 1945; Pres. Parl. Group of UDSR 1946–47, 1955; mem. two Constituent Assemblies 1945–46; mem. Nat. Assembly 1946–55, 1958–62, 1967–73, 1973–78; Minister of Reconstruction and Town Planning 1948–53; Minister of Labour 1954; Mayor of Firminy 1953–71; Vice-Pres. Nat. Assembly 1959–62, 1968–73, 1976–77; Pres. Entente Démocratique group, Nat. Assembly 1962, Progrès et Démocratie Moderne 1969–73; Vice-Pres. Centre Démocratie et Progrès 1969–73; Pres. Union Centrale des Arts Décoratifs 1961–72, Conseil supérieur de la création esthétique industrielle 1971–76; Chair. Gov. Body of Council of Europe Resettlement Fund for Nat. Refugees and Over-population 1979; Commandeur de la Légion d'honneur, Compagnon de la Libération, Rosette de la Résistance, Croix de guerre avec palme. *Address:* 15 rue des Barres, 75004 Paris, France.

CLAUSEN, Alden Winship (Tom); American banker; b. 17 Feb. 1923, Hamilton, Ill.; s. of Morton and Elsie (Kroll) Clausen; m. Mary Margaret Crassweller 1950; two s.; ed. Carthage Coll., and Univ. of Minnesota; joined Bank of America 1949; assigned to Nat. Div., Southern Calif. 1955; Asst. Vice-Pres. for financial relationships in electronics 1961–65; Head Nat. Div., San Francisco World H.Q. 1963; Senior Vice-Pres. 1965–68; Exec. Vice-Pres. and mem. Man. Cttee. 1968–69; Vice-Chair. Bd. of Dirs. 1969; Pres. and C.E.O., Bank of America 1970–81, 1986–; Dir. Wellcome 1986–; Pres. World Bank 1981–86; Dir. Int. Monetary Conf. of American Bankers Asscn., Pres. 1977; Dir. Assocs. of Harvard Business School; fmr. Pres. San Francisco Clearing House Asscn.; Dir. United Way of America; Dir. U.S.-U.S.S.R. Trade and Econ. Council, Nat. Council for U.S.-China Trade, S.R.I. International; Hon. mem. Asscn. of Reserve City Bankers; fmr. mem. Calif. Bar Asscn., Business Council; fmr. mem. U.S. Treasury's Advisory Cttee. on Reform of the Int. Monetary System, The Conference Bd., The Business Roundtable; Hon. LL.D. (Carthage Coll.) 1970; Grand Officer, Order of Merit of Italy, Grand Cross of the Order of Queen Isabel la Católica. *Address:* Bank of America, P.O. Box 3700, San Francisco, Calif. 94137, U.S.A.

CLAUSEN, Hans Peter; Danish politician; b. 31 Jan. 1928, Borg, Tønder; s. of Peter Clausen; ed. Copenhagen Univ.; apptd. Research Assoc., Univ. Inst. of Modern History, Århus Univ. 1955, Prof. of Political Science 1969, Head Librarian, State and Univ. Library 1984; Minister of Cultural Affairs 1986–88, of Transport and Communications 1988–. *Address:* Ministry of Transport, Frederiksholms Kanal 25–27, 1220 Copenhagen K, Denmark. *Telephone:* (01) 12-62-42.

CLAUSEN, John A., M.A., PH.D.; American sociologist; b. 20 Dec. 1914, New York; s. of Adam P. Clausen and Mary (Blum) Clausen; m. Suzanne Ravage 1939; four s.; ed. Cornell Univ. and Univ. of Chicago; Research Assoc., Virginia State Planning Bd. 1941–42; Study Dir. Troop att. Research Branch, War Dept. 1942–45; Chief, Surveys Design Section, Veterans Admin. 1945–46; Asst. Prof. Cornell Univ. 1946–48; Social Science Research Consultant, Nat. Inst. of Mental Health 1948–51, Chief, Lab. for Socioenvironmental Studies 1951–60; Prof. of Sociology, Univ. of Calif. 1960–82, Dir. Inst. of Human Devt. 1960–66, Chair. Dept. of Sociology 1976–79, Research Sociologist and Prof. Emer. 1982–; Commonwealth Award for Sociology 1986, Leo Reeder Award in Medical Sociology 1987. *Publications:* author and ed. of works on sociology and social psychology including The Life Course: A Sociological Perspective 1986. *Leisure interests:* music, nature study. *Address:* Institute of Human Development, 1203 Tolman Hall, University of California, Berkeley, Calif. 94720 (Office); 2851 Shasta Road, Berkeley, Calif. 94708, U.S.A. (Home). *Telephone:* 415-642-3635 (Office); 415-843-8898 (Home).

CLAUSSE, Gilbert-Roger; Belgian professor; b. 1 Dec. 1902, Saint-Mard, Luxembourg; m. Janine Huriau 1950; ed. Univ. de Liège; Prof. Athénée de St. Gilles 1928–37; Dir. French broadcasts, Institut Nat. Belge de Radiodiffusion 1937–46, Asst. Dir. of the Institut 1947–53, Dir.-Gen. 1953–57; Prof. Université Libre de Bruxelles 1945; Dir. Centre d'Etude des techniques de diffusion collective 1958. *Publications:* Critique matérialiste de l'éducation 1934, L'éducation de base pour un humanisme social 1935, Mesure des humanités anciennes 1937, La radio, huitième art 1945, La radio scolaire 1949, L'information à la recherche d'un statut 1951, L'information d'actualité: critique de la relation 1953, Synopsis de l'information d'actualité 1961, Les nouvelles: synthèse critique 1963, Turquie: développement du journalisme 1964, Le journal et l'actualité 1967, Belgique 1965—Presse, radio et télévision aux prises avec les élections 1968, L'enseignement universitaire du journalisme et de la communication sociale 1970.

CLAVÉ, Antoni; Spanish painter; b. 5 April 1913, Barcelona; ed. evening classes at Escuela Superior de Bellas Artes de San Jorge, Barcelona; magazine and book illustrator 1930–49; full-time painter since 1955; commenced carpet painting 1957 and metal work 1960; first one-man exhbn., Perpignan, France 1939, later in Paris, London, Oran, Gothenburg, Buenos Aires, Rome, Milan, Barcelona, Bilbao, Los Angeles, Geneva, Cologne, Luxembourg, Colmar, Toulouse, Venice and Tokyo; other exhbns.: "Thirty Years of Painting", Tokyo 1972, New York 1973, "En marge de la peinture", Centre Georges Pompidou, Paris 1978, Works 1958–78, Musée d'art moderne de la ville de Paris 1978, 1979; Musée d'Unterlinden, Colmar, peintures 1958–78, Septembre: A. H. Grafik, Stockholm, Dix Instruments étranges, gravures, Retrospective 1939–80, Museo de Arte Contemporaneo, Madrid 1980; Musée des Augustins, Toulouse, 1984, Biennale de Venise, Pavillon d'Espagne; 125 works 1958–84, paintings, sculptures, Museo de Arte contemporáneo, Madrid, 150 lithographs and carvings; exhbns in Paris and Perpignon 1985; and at Tokyo Metropolitan Teien Museum, Osaka Modern Art Museum, Yamanashi-ken Kiyoharu Museum 1986; Matarasso Prize, Biennal São Paulo 1957, UNESCO Prize, Kamakara Museum Prize. *Major works:* illustrations for La Dame de Pique, Pushkin 1946, black lithographs Candide, Voltaire 1948, Gargantua, Rabelais 1953, La Gloire des Rois, Saint-John Perse 1976. *Address:* 4 rue de Châtillon, 75014 Paris, France.

CLAVEL, Bernard; French writer; b. 29 May 1923, Lons-le-Saunier; s. of Henri Clavel and Héloïse Dubois; m. Josette Pratte 1982; three s. (of first marriage); ed. primary school; left school aged 14 and apprenticed as pâtissier 1937; subsequently held various jobs on the land and in offices; painter and writer since age 15; has written numerous plays for radio and television and contributed to reviews on the arts and pacifist journals; Prix Eugène Leroy, Prix populiste, Prix Jean Macé, Prix Goncourt (for Les fruits de l'hiver), Grand Prix littéraire de la Ville de Paris. *Publications:* Major works include: L'ouvrier de la nuit 1956, Qui m'emporte 1958, L'espagnol 1959, Malataverne 1960, Le voyage du père 1965, L'Hercule sur la place 1966, La maison des autres 1962, Celui qui voulait voir la mer 1963, Le coeur des vivants 1964, Les fruits de l'hiver 1968, Victoire au Mans 1968, L'espion aux yeux verts 1969, Le tambour du bief 1970, Le massacre des innocents 1970, Le seigneur du fleuve 1972, Le silence des armes 1974, Lettre à un képi blanc 1975, La boule de neige 1975, La saison des loups 1976, La lumière du lac 1977, Ecrit sur la neige 1977, La fleur de sel 1977, La femme de guerre 1978; Le Rhône ou la métamorphose d'un dieu 1979, Le chien des laurentides 1979, L'Iroquoise 1979, Marie Bon Pain 1980, La bourrelle 1980, Felicien le fantôme (with Josette Pratte) 1980, Terres de Mémoire 1980, Compagnons du Nouveau-monde 1981, Arbres 1981, Odile et le vent du large 1981, Le Hibou qui avait avalé la lune 1981, l'Homme du Labrador 1982, Harricana 1983, L'Or de la terre 1984, Le mouton noir et le loup blanc 1984, Le roi des poissons 1984, L'oie qui avait per du le nord 1985, Miserere 1985, Bernard Clavel qui êtes-vous? 1985, Amarok 1986, Au cochon qui danse 1986, l'Angelus du soir 1988, Le grand voyage de Quick Bearer 1988, and numerous essays, short stories and children's books. *Leisure interests:* sport, painting, handicraft. *Address:* Doon House, Maam, County Galway, Republic of Ireland. *Telephone:* 092-48049.

CLAVELL, James; British author, film director and producer; b. 10 Oct. 1924, Sydney, Australia; s. of late Commdr. R. C. Clavell and Eileen Ross Clavell; m. April Clavell 1953; two d.; ed. Portsmouth Grammar School; served as Capt. in R.A. during 2nd World War; Hon. Ph.D.(Maryland), Goldener Eiger (Austria) 1972. *Screenwriter:* The Fly 1958, Watussi 1958, The Great Escape 1960, Satan Bug 1962, 633 Squadron 1963. *Director:* Where's Jack? 1968. *Writer/Producer/Director:* Five Gates to Hell 1959, Walk like a Dragon 1960, To Sir with Love 1966, Last Valley 1969, Children's Story . . . But Not for Children 1982. *Publications:* King Rat 1962, Tai-Pan 1966, Countdown at Armageddon (play) 1986, , Shogun 1976, Noble House 1980, The Children's Story but not for Children 1982, Whirlwind 1986, Trump-O-Moto 1986. *Address:* c/o Creative Artists Agency, 1888 Century Park East, Suite 1400, Los Angeles, Calif. 90067, U.S.A.

CLAY, John Martin, B.A., F.B.I.M.; British banker; b. 20 Aug. 1927, Manchester; s. of the late Sir Henry Clay and of Gladys Priestman Clay; m. Susan Jennifer Miller 1952; four s.; ed. Eton Coll. and Magdalen Coll., Oxford; Director, Hambros Bank Ltd. 1961–84, Deputy Chair. 1972–84; Dir. Hambros 1970–, Vice-Chair. 1986–; Dir. Johnson and Firth Brown Ltd. 1973–, Chair. 1975–; Chair. Hambro Life Assurance Ltd. 1978–84; Dir. Bank of England 1973–83. *Leisure interest:* sailing. *Address:* 41 Tower Hill, London, E.C.3, England. *Telephone:* 01-480 5000.

CLAYBURGH, Jill; American actress; b. 30 April 1944, New York; d. of Albert H. and Julia (Door) Clayburgh; m. David Rabe 1979; ed. Sarah Lawrence Coll., Bronxville, N.Y.; Broadway debut in The Rothschilds 1979: *stage appearances include:* In the Boom Boom Room; *film appearances include:* Portnoy's Complaint 1972, The Thief Who Came to Dinner, The Terminal Man 1974, Gable and Lombard 1976, Silver Streak 1976, Semi-Tough 1977, An Unmarried Woman 1978, La Luna 1979, Starting Over 1979, It's My Turn 1980, I'm Dancing as Fast as I Can 1982, Hannah K 1983, Shy People 1987; has also appeared in television films; Best Actress Award, Cannes Film Festival, and Golden Apple Award for the best film actress for An Unmarried Woman. *Address:* Creative Artists Agency, 1888 Century Park East, Suite 1400, Los Angeles, Calif. 90067, U.S.A.

CLAYTON, Jack; British film director; b. 1921; m. 1st Christine Norden (dissolved); m. 2nd Katherine Kath (dissolved); entered film industry 1935; served in R.A.F. Film Unit 1939–45; Production Man. for An Ideal Husband; Assoc. Producer Queen of Spades, Flesh and Blood, Moulin Rouge, Beat the Devil, The Good Die Young, I am a Camera; Producer and Dir. The Bespoke Overcoat 1955; Dir. Room at the Top 1958; Producer and Dir. The Innocents 1961; Dir. The Pumpkin Eater 1964; Producer and Dir. Our Mother's House 1967; Dir. The Great Gatsby 1974, Something Wicked This Way Comes 1983, The Lonely Passion of Judith Hearn 1988. *Address:* c/o Batya Films, Herons Flight, Marlow, Bucks SL7 2LE, England.

CLAYTON, Sir Robert James, Kt., C.B.E., M.A., F.ENG.; British physicist; b. 30 Oct. 1915, London; m. Joy Kathleen King 1949; ed. Latymer Upper School, Christ's Coll., Cambridge; Man., Gen. Electric Co. (GEC) Applied Electronics Laboratories 1955; Deputy Dir. GEC Hirst Research Centre 1960; Man. Dir. GEC (Electronics) 1963, GEC (Research) 1966; Tech. Dir. The General Electric Co. Ltd. 1968–83; mem. GEC Main Bd. 1978–83; Chair. Ordnance Survey Advisory Bd.; 1982–84; mem. Monopolies Comm., Univ. Grants Cttee.; Pres. Inst. of Electrical Engs. 1975–76; Vice Pres. Fellowship of Engineering 1980–82; mem. British Library Bd. 1981–87, UGC 1982–; Trustee Science Museum 1980–; Hon. D.Sc. (Salford Univ., Univ. of Aston, City Univ., Univ. of Oxford); Hon. D.Eng. (Bradford)

Publications: GEC Research Labs. 1919–1984, papers in Proceedings of the Institution of Electrical Engineers. *Leisure interests:* theatre, music. *Address:* c/o GEC Hirst Research Centre, East Lane, Wembley, Middx., HA9 7PP, England. *Telephone:* 01-908 9007.

CLAYTON, Robert Norman, M.SC., PH.D., F.R.S.; British geochemist; b. 20 March 1930; s. of Norman Clayton and Gwenda Clayton; m. Cathleen Shelbourne Clayton 1971; one d.; ed. Queen's Univ. Canada and Calif. Inst. of Tech.; Research Fellow, Calif. Inst. of Tech. 1955–56; Asst. Prof. Pa. State Univ. 1956–58; Asst. Prof. Univ. of Chicago 1958–62, Assoc. Prof. 1962–66, Prof. Depts. of Chemistry and of the Geophysical Sciences 1966–. *Publications:* over 100 papers in geochemical journals. *Address:* 5201 South Cornell, Chicago, Ill. 60615, U.S.A.

CLEARY, Jon Stephen: Australian author; b. 22 Nov. 1917, Sydney, N.S.W.; s. of Mathew Cleary and Ida F. Brown; m. Constantina E. Lucas 1946; two d. (one deceased); ed. Marist Brothers School, N.S.W.; various jobs, including bush-working and commercial art 1932–40; served Australian Imperial Forces, Middle East, New Britain, New Guinea 1940–45; full-time writer since 1945, except for 3 years as journalist, Australian News and Information Bureau, London and New York 1948–51; winner, ABC Nat. Play Competition 1945; Crouch Literary Prize 1951; Edgar Award for Best Crime Novel 1974. *Publications:* 37 novels and two books of short stories (1983), including You Can't See Round Corners 1948, The Sundowners 1952, The High Commissioner 1966, High Road to China 1967, Mask of the Andes 1971, Spearfield's Daughter 1982, The Phoenix Tree 1984, The City of Fading Light 1985, Dragons at the Party 1987, Now and Then, Amen 1988, Babylon South 1989. *Leisure interests:* tennis, watching cricket, filmgoing, reading. *Address:* 71 Upper Pitt Street, Kirribilli, N.S.W. 2061, Australia.

CLEAVER, Alan Richard, M.A.; British couturier and business executive; b. 30 May. 1952, Northampton; s. of Terence Richard Cleaver and Miriam Elanor Tomlin; ed. Wellingborough Tech. Grammar School, Northampton School of Art, Kingston Coll. of Art and R.C.A.; worked with Michael Aukett Assoc. 1973–74; freelance stylist Maison de Marie Claire, Paris 1977–79; freelance design consultant, Paris 1976–79; Co. Designer Byblos, Italy 1980–; Man. Dir. S.R.L. Milan 1986–; External Examiner/Visiting Lecturer R.C.A. 1986–. *Leisure interests:* travel, opera, walking. *Address:* Via Vallone 11, Monte Conero, Sirolo; Bosco di San Francesco 6, Sirolo; Piazza Plebiscito 55, Ancona, Italy. *Telephone:* (071) 936 203; (071) 936 225; (071) 20-37-90.

CLEAVER, Anthony Brian, M.A.; British business executive; b. 10 April 1938, London; s. of William Brian Cleaver and Dorothea Early Cleaver (née Peeks); m. Mary Teresa Cotter 1962; one s.; ed. Berkhamsted School and Trinity Coll. Oxford; nat. service in Intelligence Corps 1956–58; joined IBM 1962, UK Sales Dir. 1976–77, DP Dir., mem. Bd., IBM UK (Holdings) 1977–80, Vice-Pres. of Marketing IBM Europe 1981–82, Asst. Gen. Man. IBM UK 1982–84, Gen. Man. 1984–85, Chief Exec. 1986–; Dir. Nat. Computing Centre 1977–80; mem. Council, Templeton Coll. Oxford 1982–, Assen. for Business Sponsorship of the Arts 1985; mem. Bd. CEED 1985–; Chair. Bd. of Govs., Birkbeck Coll. Sept. 1989–; Fellow of British Computer Soc. *Leisure interests:* sport, especially cricket, music, especially opera, and reading. *Address:* P.O. Box 41, North Harbour, Portsmouth, Hants., PO6 3AU, England.*Telephone:* (0705) 321212.

CLEDWYN OF PENRHOS, Baron (Life Peer), cr. 1979, of Holyhead in the County of Anglesey; **Cledwyn Hughes,** P.C., C.H., LL.B.; British politician; b. 14 Sept. 1916, Holyhead, Anglesey; s. of Rev. and Mrs. H. D. Hughes; m. Jean Beatrice Hughes 1949; one s. one d.; ed. Holyhead Grammar School and Univ. Coll. of Wales, Aberystwyth; Solicitor 1940; R.A.F.V.R. 1940–45; mem. Anglesey County Council 1946–52; M.P. Anglesey 1951, Chair. Welsh Parl. Party 1953–54, Welsh Labour Group 1955–56, mem. Cttee. of Public Accounts 1957–64; Minister of State for Commonwealth Relations 1964–66; Sec. of State for Wales 1966–68; Minister of Agric., Fisheries and Food 1968–70; Vice-Chair. Parl. Labour Party March–Oct. 1974, Chair 1974–79; Joint Chair. TUC–Labour Party Liaison Cttee. 1974–79; Prime Minister's Emissary to Southern Africa Nov.–Dec. 1978; Pres. Univ. Coll of Wales, Aberystwyth 1976–84; Pro-Chancellor, Univ. of Wales Jan. 1985–; mem. Cttee. of Privileges 1974–79; Commr. of House of Commons 1978–79; Deputy Leader of the Opposition, House of Lords 1981–82, Leader 1982–; Chair. House Select Cttee. on Agric. and Food, Welsh Cttee. on Econ. Affairs 1982–84; Dir. Shell UK 1980–84; Anglesey Aluminium Ltd. 1980–; Hon. LL.D. (Wales) 1970; Hon. Freedom, Beaumaris 1972, Freeman of Anglesey 1976; Hon. Fellow Univ. Coll. of Wales Aberystwyth 1987; Labour. *Publication:* Conditions on the Island of St. Helena. *Leisure interests:* walking, reading, writing. *Address:* Penmorfa, Trearddur, Holyhead, Gwynedd, Wales, *Telephone:* Trearddur 544.

CLEESE, John Marwood, M.A.; British writer and actor; b. 27 Oct. 1939; s. of Reginald and Muriel Cleese; m. 1st Connie Booth 1968 (dissolved 1978), one d.; m. 2nd Barbara Cleese 1981, one d.; ed. Clifton Sports Acad. and Downing Coll., Cambridge; started writing and making jokes professionally 1963; first appearance on British TV 1966; appeared in TV series: The Frost Report, At Last the 1948 Show, Monty Python's Flying Circus (co-writer), Fawlty Towers (co-writer with Connie Booth); f. and Dir. Video Arts Ltd. 1979–; appeared as Petruchio in The Taming of the Shrew, BBC TV Shakespeare cycle 1981; appeared in Cheers, for which he received an Emmy Award; Hon. LL.D. (St. Andrews). *Films include:* Interlude, The Magic Christian, And Now For Something Completely Different, Monty Python and the Holy Grail, Romance with a Double Bass, Life of Brian, Time Bandits, Privates on Parade, Yellowbeard 1982, The Meaning of Life 1983, Silverado 1985, Clockwise 1986, A Fish Called Wanda 1988, Erik the Viking 1988. *Publication:* Families and How to Survive Them (with Robin Skynner). *Leisure interests:* gluttony, sloth. *Address:* c/o David Wilkinson, 24 Denmark Street, London, WC2H 8NJ, England.

CLEGHORN, John E., B. COMM., C.A.; Canadian banker; b. 7 July 1941, Montreal, P.Q.; s. of H. W. Edward Cleghorn and Miriam Dunham; m. Pattie E. Hart 1963; two s. one d.; ed. McGill Univ.; Clarkson Gordon & Co. (chartered accountants) 1962–64; sugar buyer and futures trader, St. Lawrence Sugar Ltd., Montreal 1964–66; Mercantile Bank of Canada 1966–74; joined Royal Bank of Canada 1974, Sr. Vice-Pres. Planning and Marketing, Int. Div. 1979, Sr. Vice-Pres. and Gen. Man. British Columbia, Vancouver 1980, Exec. Vice-Pres. Int. Banking Div. Toronto 1983, Pres. June 1986–; numerous public appts. *Leisure interests:* skiing, jogging, tennis, fishing. *Address:* The Royal Bank of Canada, 1 Place Ville Marie, Montreal, Quebec, H3C 3A9, Canada.

CLEMEN, Wolfgang; German university professor; b. 29 March 1909, Bonn; s. of Prof. Paul Clemen; m. Ursula Gauhe 1943; two s. one d.; ed. Univs. of Heidelberg, Freiburg, Bonn, Berlin, Munich and Cambridge; lecturer, Cologne Univ. 1938, Kiel Univ. 1939; Prof. of English, Kiel Univ. 1940–46, Munich Univ. 1946–; mem. Bavarian Acad. of Sciences 1948; Vice-Pres. German Shakespeare Soc. 1949; Visiting Prof. Columbia Univ., New York 1953; Pres. Modern Humanities Research Assen. 1964; Corresp. mem. British Acad. 1964; Churchill Foundation Visiting Prof. Bristol 1964; Hon. mem. American Modern Language Assen. and Modern Humanities Research Assen. 1965; Life Trustee Shakespeare Birthplace Trust 1977; Hon. D.Litt. (Birmingham) 1964, Hon. D.Phil. (Rouen) 1967, Dr. h.c. (Uppsala) 1977; Grosses Bundesverdienstkreuz 1969; Hon. C.B.E. 1972; Orden pour le mérite für Wissenschaften und Künste 1981, Grosses Bundesverdienstkreuz mit Stern 1983, Bayer. Verdienstorden 1985, Bayer. Maximiliansorden 1988. *Publications:* Shakespeares Bilder 1936, Der junge Chaucer 1938, Shelleys Geisterwelt 1948, The Development of Shakespeare's Imagery 1951, 1977, English Tragedy before Shakespeare 1961, Chaucer's Early Poetry 1963, Kommentar zu Shakespeares Richard III 1957, Shakespeare's Soliloquies 1964, Spenser's Epithalamion 1964, Shakespeare's Midsummer Night's Dream (ed. 1963), Past and Future in Shakespeare's Drama 1966, A Commentary on Shakespeare's Richard III 1968, Das Problem des Stilwandels in der engl. Dichtung 1968, Was ist literarischer Einfluss? 1968, Das Drama Shakespeares 1969, Shakespeare's Dramatic Art 1972, Shakespeare and Marlowe 1972, G. M. Hopkins Gedichte (English and German edn.) 1973, The Pursuit of Influence 1974, Sympathielenkung bei Shakespeare, Einleitung 1977, Originalität und Tradition in der engl. Dichtungsgeschichte 1978, Some Aspects of Style in Shakespeare's Henry VI plays 1980, Der Leser und die Grenzen der Literaturwissenschaft 1983, Shakespeares Monologe: Ein Zugang zu seiner dramatischen Kunst 1985, Shakespeare's Soliloquies 1987. *Leisure interest:* chamber music. *Address:* 8207 Endorf, Hofhamer Weg 3, Upper Bavaria, Federal Republic of Germany. *Telephone:* 9326.

CLEMENS, Clive Carruthers, C.M.G., M.C.; British diplomatist (retd.); b. 22 Jan. 1924, Calcutta, India; s. of the late M. B. and Margaret Jane (née Carruthers) Clemens; m. Philippa Jane Bailey 1947; three s.; ed. Blundell's School, St. Catharine's Coll., Cambridge; H.M. Forces 1943–46; commissioned Duke of Cornwall's Light Infantry; served India and Burma entered Foreign Service, apptd. to Foreign Office (FO) 1947; Third Sec., Rangoon 1948–50, Third, later Second Sec., Lisbon 1950–53; FO 1953–54; First Sec., Budapest 1954–56, Brussels 1956–59, First Sec. and Consul, Seoul 1959–61; FO 1961–64; First Sec. (U.K. Del. to Council of Europe), Strasbourg 1964–67; Counsellor, Paris 1967–70; Prin. British Trade Commr., Vancouver 1970–74; Deputy Consul-Gen., Johannesburg 1974–78; Consul-Gen., Istanbul 1978–81; High Commr. in Lesotho 1981–84. *Leisure interests:* birdwatching, photography. *Address:* Orleton, 9 Saxonhurst, Downton, Salisbury, Wilts., England.

CLEMENT, John, C.B.I.M.; British business executive; b. 18 May 1932; s. of Frederick and Alice Eleanor Clement; m. Elisabeth Anne Emery 1956; two s. one d.; ed. Bishop's Stortford Coll.; Howards Dairies, Westcliff on Sea 1949–64; United Dairies London Ltd. 1964–69; Asst. Man. Dir. Rank Leisure Services Ltd. 1969–73; Chair. Unigate Foods Div. 1973; Chief Exec. Unigate Group 1976–, Chair. 1977–; Dir. Eagle Star Holdings 1981–86; Chair. (non-exec.) The Littlewoods Org. 1982–; mem. Securities and Investment Bd. 1986–; Trustee, Rank Prize Funds 1982–. *Leisure interests:* tennis, shooting, sailing, skiing, bridge, rugby. *Address:* Tuddenham Hall, Tuddenham, Ipswich, Suffolk, IP6 9DD, England. *Telephone:* Witnesham 217.

CLÉMENT, René; French film director; b. 18 March 1913, Bordeaux; s. of Jean Clément and Marguérite Bayle; m. Bella Gurwich 1940; ed. School of Architecture, Paris; founder mem. Inst. des hautes études cinématographiques; mem. Inst. (Acad. of Fine Arts) 1986; Chevalier, Légion d'honneur, Commdr. des Arts et des Lettres; Cannes Festival

Prize (1946, 1947, 1952, 1954), Grand Int. Prize Venice Biennale (1952), César d'honneur 1984, etc. *Films include:* Bataille du rail 1946, Les maudits 1947, Walls of Malapaga 1948, Château de verre 1950, Au delà des grilles (Oscar award for Best Foreign Film) 1951, Jeux interdits (Oscar award for Best Foreign Film) 1952, Lion d'or 1952, Monsieur Ripois 1954, Gervaise 1956, Sea Wall 1958, Demain est un autre jour 1962, Quelle joie de vivre, Purple Noon (Plein Soleil) 1960, The Love Cage (Les félins) 1964, Paris brûle-t-il? 1965, A la recherche du temps perdu 1966, Le passager de la pluie 1970, La maison sous les arbres 1971, La course du lièvre à travers les champs 1971, The Baby-Sitter 1975. *Publications:* Bataille du rail (with C. Audry) 1947. *Address:* 10 avenue Saint-Roman, Monte Carlo, Monaco; 91 avenue Henri Martin, 75016 Paris, France.

CLEMENTE, Carmine Domenic, A.B., M.A., PH.D.; American professor of anatomy; b. 29 April 1928, Penns Grove, N.J.; s. of Ermanno Clemente and Caroline (Friozzi) Clemente; m. Juliette G. Clemente 1968; no c.; ed. Univ. of Pennsylvania and Univ. Coll. London; U.S. Public Health Service Fellow and Asst. Instr. in Anatomy, Univ. of Pa. 1950-52; Instr. in Anatomy, Univ. of Calif. Los Angeles 1952-53, Asst. Prof. 1954-59, Assoc. Prof. 1959-63, Prof. and Chair. Dept. of Anatomy 1963-73, Prof. of Anatomy 1973-, Prof. of Surgery (Anatomy), Charles R. Drew Postgraduate Medical School 1974-, Dir. Brain Research Inst. 1996-; Consultant in Surgical Anatomy, Martin Luther King Hosp. Los Angeles 1971-; Consultant in Research Neurophysiology, Sepulvada Veterans Admin. Hosp.; mem. numerous advisory cttees. etc.; mem. Inst. of Medicine of N.A.S.; numerous awards and distinctions. *Publications:* books, films and some 190 scientific publs. *Leisure interest:* philately. *Address:* Brain Research Institute, UCLA School of Medicine, Los Angeles, Calif. 900024 (Office); 11737 Bellagio Road, Los Angeles, Calif. 90049, U.S.A. (Home). *Telephone:* (213) 825-5061 (Office); (213) 472-6207 (Home).

CLEMENTS, William Perry, Jr.; American state governor; b. 13 April 1917, Dallas, Tex.; s. of William P. Clements and Evelyn Cammack Clements; m. Rita Crocker Clements 1975; one s. one d. (by previous marriage); ed. Highland Park High School, Dallas, and Southern Methodist Univ., Dallas; founder, Chair., C.E.O. SEDCO Inc., Dallas 1947-73, 1977, 1983-; mem. Nat. Exec. Bd., Boy Scouts of America; mem. Bd. of Trustees and Bd. of Govs., Southern Methodist Univ.; Deputy Sec. for Defense 1974-77; Gov. of Texas 1979-83, Jan. 1987-; mem. Nat. Bipartisan Comm. of Cen. America 1983-84; Dept. of Defense Medal for Distinguished Service with Bronze Palm. *Address:* Office of the Governor, Box 12428, Capitol Station, Austin, Tex. 78711, U.S.A.

CLEMINSON, Sir James Arnold Stacey, Kt., M.C., D.L.; British company director; b. 31 Aug. 1921, Hull, Yorkshire; s. of Arnold Russell and Florence Stacey Cleminson; m. Helen Juliet Measor; one s. two d.; ed. Bramcote and Rugby schools; served British Army, Parachute Regt. 1940-46; joined Reckitt Colman Overseas 1946; Dir. and later Vice-Chair. J. J. Colman Norwich 1960-69; Dir. Reckitt and Colman 1969, Chair. Food Div. 1970, CEO 1973-80, Chair. 1977-86; Vice-Chair. Norwich Union 1981- (Dir. 1979-); Dir. United Biscuits Holdings 1982-89; Pres. CBI 1984-86; Pres. Endeavour Training 1984-86; Chair. British Overseas Trade Bd. July 1986-, Jeyes Hygiene PLC 1986-, Riggs A. P. Bank 1987- (Dir. 1985-); Dir. Eastern Counties Newspaper Group 1986-; Hon. LL.D. (Hull) 1985; Trustee, Army Benevolent Fund and Airborne Forces Security Fund. *Leisure interests:* riding, fishing, shooting, tennis, golf. *Address:* British Overseas Trade Board, 1-19 Victoria Street, London, S.W.1; Loddon Hall, Hales, Norfolk, England. *Telephone:* 01-215 4934 (Office).

CLEMMESEN, Johannes, D.M.SC.; Danish pathologist; b. 14 Nov. 1908, Copenhagen; s. of Capt. Johan Clemmesen and Marie Gran; ed. Metropolitan School and Univ. of Copenhagen; Pathologist, Old People's Town 1950-55; Assoc. Prof. of Pathology, Royal Dental Coll. 1951-56; Chief Pathologist, Finsen Inst., Copenhagen 1955-78; Dir. Danish Cancer Registry 1942-80; Exec. mem. WHO Sub-cttee. on Cancer Registration and other cttees. on statistics and endemiology of cancer 1950-82; mem. Exec. Cttee. Int. Union against Cancer 1954-62; mem. Secr., Cttee. on Geographical Pathology of Cancer 1950-62, Cttees. on Tumour Nomenclature 1950-65; Chair. Co-ordinating Cttee. for Human Tumour Investigations 1973-75; Pres. Int. Asscn. for Comparative Leukemia Research 1975-77; mem. Wissenschaftliches Beirat, Deutsches Krebsforschungszentrum, Heidelberg 1977-82; mem. Int. Comm. for Protection against Environmental Mutagens and Carcinogens 1978-85; Chair. Danish Assen. 1987; Dr. med. h.c. Aarhus 1978; Ramazzini Award 1988. *Publications:* X-radiation and Immunity to Heterotransplantation 1938, Statistical Studies in the Aetiology of Malignant Neoplasms 1965, 1969, 1974, 1977, Memoirs I 1986, Memoirs II 1988. *Address:* Stockholmsgade 43, Copenhagen 2100, Denmark. *Telephone:* 01-42-8600.

CLERCQ, Willy De, LL.D.; Belgian barrister and politician; b. 8 July 1927, Ghent; s. of Frans De Clercq and Yvonne Catry; m. Fernande Fazzi 1953; two s. one d.; Barrister, Court of Appeal, Ghent 1951; with Gen. Secretariat of UN, New York 1952; mem. Chamber of Reps. for Ghent-Ekloo 1958-; Deputy Prime Minister, in charge of Budget 1966-68; Deputy Prime Minister and Minister of Finance 1973-74, Minister of Finance 1973-77, Deputy Prime Minister and Minister of Finance and Foreign Trade Dec. 1981-85; Vice-Pres. Partij voor Vrijheid en Vooruitgang (PVV 1961); Pres. PVV 1971-73, 1977-81; mem. European Parl. 1979-81; Pres. European

Fed. of Liberal and Democratic Parties (ELD) 1980-85; part-time Prof. Univs. of Ghent and Brussels; Chair. of Interim Cttee. of the IMF 1976-77, 1983-85; Commr. for External Relations and Trade Policy, Comm. of European Communities 1985-89. *Leisure interests:* sport, travel. *Address:* Cyriel Bugssestraat 12, 9000 Ghent, Belgium (Home). *Telephone:* 091-225947.

CLERIDES, Glavkos John, B.A., LL.B.; Cypriot lawyer and politician; b. 24 April 1919, Nicosia; s. of John Clerides, Q.C., C.B.E.; m.; one c.; ed. Pancyprian Gymnasium, Nicosia, King's Coll., London Univ., Gray's Inn, London; served with R.A.F. 1939-45; shot down and taken prisoner 1942-45 (mentioned in despatches); practised law in Cyprus 1951-60; Head of Greek Cypriot Del., Constitutional Comm. 1959-60; Minister of Justice 1959-60; mem. House of Reps. 1960-, Pres. of House 1960-76; Acting Pres. of Cyprus July-Dec. 1974; rep. Greek Cypriots in UN sponsored intercommunal talks 1975-76; rep. to Consultative Assembly of the Council of Europe; Chair. Democratic Rally 1976, now Pres.; founder and leader of Unified Party; Gold Medal, Order of the Holy Sepulchre. *Address:* 56 Metochiou Street, Nicosia, Cyprus.

CLERMONT, Yves Wilfrid, PH.D., F.R.S.C.; Canadian professor of anatomy; b. 14 Aug. 1926, Montreal; s. of Rodolphe Clermont and Fernande Primeau; m. Madeleine Bonneau 1950; two s. one d.; ed. Univ. of Montreal, McGill Univ., Collège de France, Paris; Teaching Fellow, Dept. of Anatomy, Faculty of Medicine, McGill Univ., Montreal 1952-53, Lecturer 1953-56, Asst. Prof. 1956-60, Assoc. Prof. 1960-63, Prof. 1963-, Chair. of Dept. 1975-85; Vice-Pres. American Assen. of Anatomists 1979-83; mem. Review Group and Advisory Group of Expanded Programme of Research in Human Reproduction, WHO, Geneva 1971-76; Ortho Prize, Canadian Soc. of Fertility 1958, Prix Scientifique de la Province de Québec 1963, Siegler Award, American Fertility Soc. 1966, Van Campenhout Award, Canadian Fertility Soc. 1986, J.C.B. Grant Award, Canadian Assen. of Anatomists 1986, Distinguished Andrologist Award, American Assen. of Andrology 1988. *Publications:* more than 100 scientific articles in journals and books in the field of biology of reproduction and cell biology. *Leisure interests:* reading history and biography, gardening, listening to classical music. *Address:* Department of Anatomy, McGill University, 3640 University Street, Montreal, Quebec, H3A 2B2 (Office); 567 Townshend, St. Lambert, Quebec, J4R 1M4, Canada (Home). *Telephone:* (514) 398-6349 (Office); (514) 671-5606 (Home).

CLEVELAND, Harlan, A.B.; American administrator, educationist and government official; b. 19 Jan. 1918, New York; s. of Stanley Matthews and Marian Phelps (van Buren); m. Lois W. Burton 1941; one s. two d.; ed. Princeton and Oxford Univs.; served Allied Control Commission, Rome 1944-45; UNRRA, Rome and Shanghai 1946-48; Econ. Co-operation Admin., Washington 1948-51; Asst. Dir. for Europe, Mutual Security Agency 1952-53; Exec. Ed. The Reporter, New York 1953-55, Publr. 1955-56; Dean, Maxwell Graduate School of Citizenship and Public Affairs, Syracuse Univ. 1956-61; Asst. Sec. for Int. Organization Affairs, State Dept. 1961-65; Amb. to NATO 1965-69; Pres. Univ. of Hawaii 1969-74; Dir. Aspen Program in Int. Affairs Sept. 1974-80; Chair. Weather Modification Advisory Bd. 1977-78; Distinguished Visiting Tom Slick Prof. of World Peace, LBJ School of Public Affairs, Univ. of Texas 1979; Prof. of Public Affairs and Dean Hubert H. Humphrey Inst. of Public Affairs, Univ. of Minn. 1980-87, Prof. Emer. 1988-; 19 hon. degrees; U.S. Medal of Freedom, Woodrow Wilson Award (Princeton Univ.), Prix de Talloires; Democrat. *Publications:* The Promise of World Tensions (ed.) 1961, The Ethic of Power (co-ed.) 1962, Ethics and Bigness (co-ed.) 1962, The Obligations of Power 1966, NATO: The Transatlantic Bargain 1970, The Future Executive 1972, The Third Try at World Order 1977; Co-author: The Overseas Americans 1960, Human Growth: An Essay on Growth, Values and the Quality of Life 1978; Energy Futures of Developing Countries (ed.) 1980, Bioresources for Development (co-ed.) 1980, The Management of Sustainable Growth (ed.) 1981, The Knowledge Executive: Leadership in an Information Society 1985, The Global Commons (ed.) 1988. *Leisure interests:* sailing, golf, writing. *Address:* University of Minnesota, Hubert H. Humphrey Center, 301 19th Avenue South, Minneapolis, Minn. 55455, U.S.A. *Telephone:* (612) 625-6062.

CLEVELAND, Paul Matthews, M.A.; American diplomatist; b. 25 Aug. 1931, Boston, Mass.; s. of Paul Cleveland and Mary E. Chestnut; m. Carter Sellwood 1953; two s. two d.; ed. Yale Univ. and Fletcher School of Law and Diplomacy; Lieut. U.S.A.F. 1953-56, Dept. of the Navy 1956-57; Man. Analyst, Dept. of State 1957, Staff Asst. 1958; Econ. Officer, Canberra 1959-61, Political Officer 1961-63; Staff Aide, Bonn 1963-65; Econ. Officer, Jakarta 1965-68; Int. Economist, Washington 1968-70; Special Asst. to Asst. Sec. of State for East Asian and Pacific Affairs 1970-73; Political Officer, Seoul 1973-75; Counsellor for Political Affairs 1975-78; Deputy Dir. of Regional Affairs, Bureau of East Asian and Pacific Affairs 1978-79, Dir. 1979; Dir. Thai Affairs 1980-81, Korean Affairs 1981-82; Minister-Counsellor and Deputy Chief of Mission, Seoul 1982-85; Amb. to New Zealand 1985-, to Malaysia 1989-; Pres. Meritorious Service Award 1984. *Leisure interests:* golf, hiking, reading. *Address:* American Embassy, 376 Jalan Tun Razak, Kuala Lumpur, Malaysia (Office); 99 Ludlam Crescent, Lower Hutt, New Zealand (Home). *Telephone:* (03) 2489011 (Office).

CLEWLOW, Warren (Alexander Morton); South African business executive; b. 1936, Durban; m. Margaret Brokensha 1965; two s. three d.; ed.

Glenwood High School, Univ. of Natal; joined Barlow Rand Group as Co. Sec. Barlow's (OFS) Ltd. 1963; Financial Dir. Thos. Barlow & Sons (SWA) Ltd. 1967-68, Man. Dir. 1968-72; Man. Dir. Barlows Mfg. Co. Ltd. 1972-78, Alt. Dir. Barlow Rand Ltd. 1974, Dir. 1975; mem. Exec. Cttee. with various responsibilities Barlow Rand Group 1978-83; C.O.O. Barlow Rand Ltd. 1983-86, Deputy Chair. and Chief Exec. 1986-; Dir. Standard Bank Investment Corpn., Standard Bank SA Ltd.; Chair. SA Foreign Trade Org.; Pres. Keep South Africa Beautiful Asscn.; Council mem. Nat. Zoological Soc.; Hon. Treas. African Children's Feeding Scheme; Regional Gov. Univ. of Cape Town Foundation; Council mem. Univ. of South Africa; mem. State Pres. Econ. Advisory Council 1985-; Hon. Prof. Business Man. and Admin., Univ. of Stellenbosch 1986; Marketing Man of the Year, S.A. Inst. of Marketing 1984; Dr. G. Malherbe Award, Univ. of Natal 1986. *Leisure interest:* tennis. *Address:* P.O. Box 782248, Sandton, 2146 South Africa. *Telephone:* (011) 801-9111.

CLIBURN, Van (Harvey Lavan, Jr.); American pianist; b. 12 July 1934, Shreveport; s. of Harvey Lavan and Rildia Bee (née O'Bryan) Cliburn; studied with mother and at Juilliard School of Music; public appearances, Shreveport 1940; début, Houston Symphony Orchestra 1952, New York Philharmonic Orchestra 1954, 1958; concert pianist on tour U.S. 1955-56, U.S.S.R. 1958; appearances in Brussels, London, Amsterdam, Paris, etc.; Hon. H.H.D. (Baylor), winner first Int. Tchaikovsky Piano Competition, Moscow 1958; numerous prizes. *Address:* 455 Wilder Place, Shreveport, La. 71104, U.S.A. (Home).

CLIFFORD, Clark McAdams, LL.B.; American lawyer and government official; b. 25 Dec. 1906, Fort Scott, Kan.; s. of Frank Andrew and Georgia (née McAdams) Clifford; m. Margery Pepperell Kimball 1931; three d.; ed. Washington Univ.; Holland, Lashly and Donnell, St. Louis, Mo. 1928-33, Holland, Lashly and Lashly 1933-37, Partner, Lashly, Lashly, Miller and Clifford 1938-43, Senior Partner, Clifford & Miller, Washington 1950-68; Senior Partner, Clifford and Warnke 1969-; Special Counsel, President of U.S.A. 1946-50; Chair. Foreign Intelligence Advisory Bd. 1962-68; Sec. for Defense 1968-69; Chair. First American Bankshares 1982-; Dir. Knight-Ridder Newspapers. *Address:* 815 Connecticut Avenue, North West, Washington, D.C. 20006 (Office); 9421 Rockville Pike, Bethesda, Md. 20814, U.S.A. (Home). *Telephone:* (202) 828-4200 (Office); (301) 530-6193 (Home).

CLIFT, Richard Dennis, C.M.G., B.A.; British diplomatist; b. 18 May 1933, Weymouth, Dorset; s. of Dennis Victor Clift and Helen Wilmot Clift (née Evans); m. 1st Barbara Mary Travis 1957 (divorced 1982), 2nd Jane Rosamund Barker (née Homfray) 1982; three d. one step-d. three step-s.; ed. St. Edward's School, Oxford and Pembroke Coll. Cambridge; Foreign Office 1956-57; Office of Chargé d'Affaires, Peking 1958-61; Embassy, Berne 1961-62; U.K. Dels. to NATO, Paris 1962-64; Foreign Office 1964-68; High Comm. Kuala Lumpur 1969-71; FCO 1971-73; Counsellor (Commercial), Embassy, Peking 1974-76; Canadian Nat. Defence Coll. 1976-77; seconded to N.I. Office, Belfast 1977-79; Head, Hong Kong Dept., FCO 1979-84; High Commr. in Sierra Leone 1984-86; Political Adviser, Hong Kong Govt. 1986-. *Leisure interests:* sailing and walking. *Address:* c/o Foreign and Commonwealth Office, King Charles Street, London, SW1A 2AH, England.

CLIFTON, James Albert, B.A., M.D.; American physician, investigator, teacher and administrator; b. 18 Sept. 1923, Fayetteville, N.C.; s. of the late James A. Clifton, Sr. and Flora McNair Clifton; m. Katherine Rathe 1949; two d.; ed. Vanderbilt Univ.; Asst. Prof. of Medicine, Univ. of Iowa Coll. of Medicine 1954-58, Assoc. Prof. 1958-63, Prof. 1963-76, Roy J. Carver Prof. of Medicine 1976-; Chief, Div. of Gastroenterology, Univ. of Ia., Dept. of Medicine 1953-71; Chair. Dept. of Medicine, Univ. of Ia. Coll. of Medicine 1970-76; Pres. American Coll. of Physicians 1977-78, American Gastroenterological Asscn. 1970-71; Chair. Subspecialty Bd. in Gastroenterology, American Bd. of Internal Medicine 1972-75, American Bd. of Internal Medicine 1980-81; mem. Central Soc. for Clinical Research, American Physiological Soc., Assen. of American Physicians, Inst. of Medicine (N.A.S.), Royal Soc. of Medicine, London, Scientific Advisory Cttee., Ludwig Inst. for Cancer Research, Zürich, Switzerland, Health Task Force Cttee. (Nat. Insts. of Health), Nat. Advisory Council, Nat. Insts. of Arthritis, Metabolism, and Digestive Diseases (Nat. Insts. of Health); consultant to numerous U.S. medical schools; Visiting Scientist, Mount Desert Island Biological Research Lab., Bar Harbor, Maine 1964; Visiting Prof. of Medicine, St. Mark's Hosp. (Univ. of London), England 1984-85; Distinguished Medical Alumnus Award, Vanderbilt Univ., Alfred Stengel Award, American Coll. of Physicians. *Publications:* numerous scientific papers on intestinal absorption of nutrients, gastrointestinal motility and numerous publs. regarding philosophy and current affairs in internal medicine. *Leisure interests:* music, photography and travel. *Address:* Department of Medicine, University of Iowa Hospital and Clinics, Iowa City, Ia. 52242; RR2, Iowa City, Ia. 52240, U.S.A. (Home). *Telephone:* (319) 356-1771 (Office); (319) 351-1561 (Home).

CLINTON, Bill, J.D.; American politician; b. 19 Aug. 1946, Hope, Arkansas; s. of Roger Clinton and Virginia Dwire; m. Hillary Rodham 1975; one d.; ed. Hot Springs High School, Georgetown Univ., Univ. Coll., Oxford, Yale Law School; Professor, Univ. of Arkansas Law School 1974-76; Democratic Nominee, U.S. House Third District, Arkansas 1974; Attorney-General, Arkansas 1977-79, State Gov. 1979-81, Jan. 1983-; mem. counsel firm

Wright, Lindsey & Jennings 1981-83; Chair. Southern Growth Policies Bd. 1985-86; Chair. Nat. Govs.' Assen. 1987; Chair. Educ. Comm. of the States 1987; Chair. Democratic Party Affirmative Action 1975, Southern Growth Policies Bd. 1980, Democratic Governors' Assen. 1989-(90); mem. U.S. Supreme Court Bar, Bd. of Trustees, Southern Center for Int. Studies of Atlanta, Ga. *Leisure interests:* jogging, swimming, golf, reading. *Address:* State Capitol, Little Rock, Ark. 72201, U.S.A.

CLOSE, Glenn: American actress; b. 19 March 1947, Greenwich, Conn.; d. of William Close and Bettine Close; m. 1st Cabot Wade (divorced); m. 2nd James Marlas 1984 (divorced); one d. by John Starke; ed. William and Mary Coll.; joined New Phoenix Repertory Co. 1974. *Stage appearances include:* Love for Love, The Rules of the Game, The Singular Life of Albert Nobbs, Childhood, Real Thing (Tony Award), A Streetcar Named Desire, King Lear, The Rose Tattoo, Benefactors. *Films include:* The World According to Garp 1982, The Big Chill 1983, The Natural 1984, The Stone Boy 1984, Maxie 1985, Jagged Edge 1985, Fatal Attraction 1987, Dangerous Liaisons 1989. *Address:* c/o Creative Artists Agency Inc., 1888 Century Park East, Suite 1400, Los Angeles, Calif. 90067, U.S.A.

CLOUD, Preston, PH.D.; American research biogeologist; b. 26 Sept. 1912, Mass.; s. of Preston Cloud and Pauline Wiedemann; m. Janice Gibson 1972; one s. two d. (by previous marriage); ed. George Washington and Yale Univs; Geologist, U.S. Geological Survey 1942-61, 1974-79, Chief Paleontology and Stratigraphy Branch 1949-59, Rep. in Oceanography 1959-61; taught at Harvard Univ. 1946-48, Mo. School of Mines and Metallurgy 1940-41, Univ. of Minn. 1961-65, Univ. of Tex. 1962, 1978, U.C.L.A. 1965-68, Univ. of Calif. (Santa Barbara) 1968-74, Salzburg Seminar American Studies 1973, A. L. du Toit Memorial Lecturer 1975, H. R. Luce Prof. of Cosmology, Mount Holyoke Coll. 1979-80, Visiting Prof. Univ. Ottawa 1982, Guggenheim Fellow 1982-83; Queen's Sr. Fellow, Baas Becking Lab., Canberra, Australia 1981; has served on advisory panels to numerous orgs., including NASA, U.S. Dept. of Interior, Yale Univ. and Smithsonian Inst. and on Congressional panels; Assoc. Ed. American Journal of Science, Quarterly Review of Biology, Resources Policy and Precambrian Research; mem. and Chair. various cttees. of Nat. Research Council, N.A.S., American Acad. of Arts and Sciences and Geological Soc. of America; mem. N.A.S. (Council 1972-75, Exec. Cttee., 1973-75, Chair. Geology Section 1975-78), Nat. Research Council (Gov. Bd. 1972-75), American Philosophical Soc., American Acad. of Arts and Sciences; Foreign mem. Polish Acad. of Sciences; Fellow, Paleontological Soc. of America; Life Fellow, Geological Soc. of America (Council 1972-75), A.A.A.S.; Hon. mem. Paleontological Soc. of India; Corresp. mem. Soc. Géol. Belgium; Corresp. Fellow, Deutsches Paläontologische Gesellschaft; A. Cressy Morrison Prize, N.Y. Acad. of Sciences 1940, Rockefeller Public Service Award 1956, Distinguished Service Award and Gold Medal, U.S. Dept. of Interior 1959, Medal, Paleontological Soc. of America 1971, Lucius Wilbur Cross Medal, Yale Graduate School 1973, Penrose Medal of Geological Soc. of America 1976, C. D. Walcott Medal of N.A.S. 1977, R. C. Moore Medal of Soc. of Econ. Paleontologists and Mineralogists 1986. *Publications include:* Resources and Man 1969, Adventures in Earth History 1970, Cosmos, Earth and Man 1978, Oasis in Space 1988 and various technical books; contributions to professional journals on the biological and sedimentological aspects of geology, both land and marine, on the origin and early evolution of life and on the interactions between biospheric, atmospheric and lithospheric evolution. *Leisure interests:* gardening, travel, music. *Address:* Department of Geological Sciences, University of California, Santa Barbara, Calif. 93106; 400 Mountain Drive, Santa Barbara, Calif. 93103, U.S.A. (Home). *Telephone:* 805-965-7423 (Home); 805-961-3830 (Office).

CLOUDSLEY-THOMPSON, John Leonard, M.A., PH.D. (CANTAB.), D.SOC. (LOND.)/F.R.E.S., F.L.S., F.Z.S.; British professor of zoology; b. 23 May 1921, Murree, India; s. of A. G. G. Thompson and Muriel Elaine (née Griffiths) Thompson; m. J. Anne Cloudsley 1944; three s.; ed. Marlborough Coll., Pembroke Coll., Cambridge; war service 1941-44, commissioned 4th Queen's Own Hussars 1941; lecturer in zoology, King's Coll., Univ. of London 1950-60; Prof. of Zoology, Univ. of Khartoum and Keeper, Sudan Natural History Museum 1960-71; Prof. of Zoology, Birkbeck Coll., Univ. of London 1972-86, Prof. Emer. 1986-; Leverhulme Emer. Fellowship 1987-89; Visiting Prof. Univ. of Kuwait 1978, 1983, Univ. of Nigeria, Nsukka 1981, Univ. of Qatar 1986; Chair. British Naturalists' Assen. 1974-83, Vice-Pres. 1985; Pres. British Arachnological Soc. 1982-85, British Soc. for Chronobiology 1985-87, Linnaean Soc. 1975-76, 1977-78; mem. Royal African Soc. 1969 (Medal 1969), British Herpetological Soc. 1983; Liveryman Worshipful Co. of Skinners 1952; Silver Jubilee Gold Medal, 1981, Inst. of Biology Charter Award 1981; Hon. D.Sc (Khartoum Univ.); Ed. Journal of Arid Environments Vol. 1 1978-. *Publications:* Spiders, Scorpions, Centipedes and Mites 1958, Animal Behaviour 1960, Rythmic Activity in Animal Physiology and Behaviour 1961, Animal Conflict and Adaptation 1965, Animal Twilight 1967, Zoology of Tropical Africa 1969, The Temperature and Water Relations of Reptiles 1971, Desert Life 1974, Terrestrial Environments 1975, Insects and History 1976, Man and the Biology of Arid Zones 1977, The Desert 1977, Animal Migration 1978, Biological Clocks 1980, Tooth and Claw 1980, Evolution and Adaptation of Terrestrial Arthropods 1988. *Leisure interests:* music, photography, travel. *Address:* Department of Biology (Medawar Building), University College, Gower Street, London, WC1E 6BT (Office); Flat 9, 4 Craven Hill, London, W2 3DS, England (Home).

CLOUGH, Ray William, Jr., SC.D.; American professor of structural engineering; b. 23 July 1920, Seattle; s. of Ray W. Clough, Sr. and Mildred Eva Nelson; m. Shirley Claire Potter 1942; one s. two d.; ed. Univ. of Washington, Seattle, California Inst. of Tech., Pasadena, Calif. and Massachusetts Inst. of Tech., Cambridge, Mass.; served U.S.A.F. 1942–46; joined Civil Eng. Faculty, Univ. of Calif. as Asst. Prof. of Civil Eng. 1949, Assoc. Prof. 1954, Prof. 1959, Chair. Div. of Structural Eng. and Structural Mechanics 1967–70, Nishkian Prof. of Structural Eng. 1983–; Consultant in Structural Eng., specializing in structural dynamics, computer methods of structural analysis and earthquake eng. 1953–; mem. U.S. Civil Engineer Structural Design Advisory Bd. 1967–; mem. N.A.S., Nat. Acad. of Eng.; Research Prize, Howard Medal, Newmark Medal, Moisieff Medal (American Soc. of Civil Engineers). *Publication:* Dynamics of Structures (with J. Penzien) 1975. *Leisure interests:* skiing (cross-country) and hiking. *Address:* 775 Davis Hall, University of California, Berkeley, Calif. 94720; 576 Vistamont Avenue, Berkeley, Calif. 94708, U.S.A. (Home).

CLOUTIER, Gilles G., O.C., PH.D., F.R.S.C.; Canadian engineer and physicist; b. 27 June 1928, Quebec City; s. of late Philéas Cloutier and Valéda Nadeau; m. Colette Michaud 1954; two s. three d.; ed. Univ. Laval, Quebec and McGill Univ.; Prof. of Physics, Univ. de Montréal 1963–68; Man. of Basic Research Lab., Dir. of Research and Asst. Dir. of Inst., Research Inst. of Hydro-Quebec (IREQ) 1968–78; Pres. Alberta Research Council 1978–83; Exec. Vice-Pres. Tech. and Int. Affairs, Hydro-Quebec 1983–85; Rector, Univ. de Montréal 1985–; four hon. doctorates (Montreal, Alberta, McGill and Lyon II Univs.). *Address:* 2900 boulevard Edouard-Montpetit, Montreal, H3C 3J7 (Office); 3462 avenue Montclair, Montreal, H4B 2J2, Canada (Home).

CLOUTIER, Sylvain, O.C., C.A., M.COM., M.B.A.; Canadian government official; b. 4 Nov. 1929, Trois-Rivières, Quebec; s. of late Edmond and Hélène (Saint Denis) Cloutier; m. Denise Sauvé 1953; one s. one d.; ed. Univs. of Ottawa and Montreal and Harvard Univ.; Man. and/or Consultant in fields of financial admin., personnel management and industrial relations in various depts. and agencies of Govt. of Canada 1956–65; mem. Public Service Comm. 1965–67; Deputy Sec. Treasury Bd. 1967–70; Deputy Minister of Nat. Revenue for Taxation 1970–71, of Nat. Defence 1971–75, of Transport 1975–79; Chair. of Bd. and Pres. Export Devt. Corpn. 1979–86; Chair. of Bd. Canada Post Corpn. 1986–; Dir. Fed. Business Devt. Bank 1978–85; Vice-Chair. Univ. of Ottawa 1979–82; has held many other offices in various public bodies, hospital trusteeships and advisory posts etc.; awards include Canada Centennial Medal 1967, Silver Jubilee Medal 1977, Public Service Award 1978. *Leisure interest:* reading. *Address:* 1612–211 Wurtenburg, Ottawa, Ont. K1N 8R4, Canada (Home). *Telephone:* (613) 231-5309 (Home).

CLUFF, Algy; British business executive; b. 19 April 1940; s. of Harold Cluff and Freda Cluff; ed. Stowe School; army officer, served W. Africa, Cyprus, Malaysia 1959–64; Chief Exec. Cluff Oil (now called Cluff Resources) 1971–, Chair. 1979–; Proprietor, The Spectator 1981–85, Chair. 1985–; Chair. Apollo Magazine Ltd. 1985–. *Address:* 70 Arlington House, Arlington Street, London, S.W.1, England.

CLUFF, Leighton Eggertsen, M.D.; American physician and foundation executive; b. 10 June 1923; s. of Lehi E. Cluff and Lottie (Brain) Cluff; m. Beth Allen 1944; two d.; Intern, Johns Hopkins Hosp. 1949–50, Asst. Resident 1951–52; Asst. Resident Physician, Duke Hosp. 1950–51; Visiting Investigator, Asst. Physician, Rockefeller Inst. of Medical Research 1952–54; Fellow, Nat. Foundation of Infantile Paralysis 1952–54; mem. Faculty, Johns Hopkins School of Medicine; mem. staff, Johns Hopkins Hosp. 1954–66, Prof. of Medicine 1964–66; Prof. and Chair. Dept. of Medicine, Univ. of Florida 1966–76; Exec. Vice-Pres. Robert Wood Johnson Foundation 1976–86, Pres. 1986–; many other professional appts. etc. *Publications:* books and articles on internal medicine, infectious diseases, clinical pharmacology. *Address:* P.O. Box 2316, Princeton, N.J. 08540, U.S.A.

CLUTTON-BROCK, (Arthur) Guy; British agriculturist and social worker; b. 5 April 1906, Northwood, Middx.; s. of Henry and Rosa Clutton-Brock; m. Francys M. Allen 1934; one d.; ed. Rugby School and Magdalene Coll., Cambridge; Cambridge House Univ. Settlement 1927–29; Rugby House Settlement 1929–33; Borstal Service 1933–36; Principal Probation Officer, Metropolitan Area of London 1936–40; Head Oxford House Univ. Settlement 1940–45; Youth and Religious Affairs Officer, British Mil. Govt., Berlin 1945; with Christian Reconstruction in Europe 1946; farm labourer in U.K. 1947–48; Diocesan Agricultural Officer, Mashonaland (Southern Rhodesia) and Dir. of Farm Activities, St. Faith's Mission, Rusape (Southern Rhodesia) 1949–59; briefly detained by Rhodesian Govt. on declaration of emergency March 1959; Hon. Dir. Bamangwato Devt. Asscn., Bechuanaland Protectorate 1961–62; Field Officer of the African Devt. Trust 1962–65; Treas. non-racial Cold Comfort Farm Soc., S. Rhodesia; deported to Britain 1971; Pres. Britain-Zimbabwe Soc. 1981; Hon. Fellow Magdalene Coll., Univ. of Cambridge 1973. *Publications:* Dawn in Nyasaland 1959, Cold Comfort Confronted. *Leisure interest:* sitting under a tree with others talking and smoking. *Address:* Gelli Uchaf, Llandyrnog, Denbigh, L16 4HR, N. Wales. *Telephone:* Llandyrnog 482.

CLUZEL, Jean, L. EN D.; French politician; b. 18 Nov. 1923, Moulins; s. of Pierre Cluzel and Jeanne (née Dumont) Cluzel; m. Madeline Bonnaud 1947;

three s. one d.; ed. Lycée de Vichy and Univ. of Paris; Pres. and Dir.-Gen. Cluzel-Dumont 1947–71; Municipal Councillor St. Pourcain/Sioule 1959–65; Admin., later Pres. Soc. d'Equipement du Bourbonnais 1967; Conseiller Gen. Moulins-Ouest 1967, 1973, 1979, 1985; Pres. Regional Council, Allier 1970–76, 1985–; Senator, Allier 1971, 1980; mem. l'Union Centriste, Spokesman and Vice-Pres. Comm. des Finances du Senat; Pres. Cttee. for Econ. Expansion of Allier 1959–67; Pres. "Positions" and "L'Allier Demain", Fed. des Elus Bourbonnais 1972, Univ. Populaire de Bransat 1981; Chevalier Légion d'honneur. *Publications include:* Horizons Bourbonnais 1973, Les boutiques en colère 1975, Elu de peuple 1977, Télé Violence 1978, L'argent de la télévision 1979, Finances publics et pouvoir local 1980, Les pouvoirs publics et la transmission de la culture 1983, Les pouvoirs publics et les caisses d'épargne 1984, Les anti-monarque de la Vème 1985, Un projet pour la presse 1986, La loi de 1987 sur l'épargne 1987, La télévision après six réformes 1988. *Address:* Le Marais, Bransat, 03500 Saint-Pourcain, France (Home). *Telephone:* (16) 70 45 43 22 (Home).

CLYNE, Hon. John Valentine, C.C., B.A.; Canadian business executive; b. 14 Feb. 1902, Vancouver; s. of Henry Clyne and Martha Clyne; m. Betty Ventris Ann Somerset 1927; one s. one d.; ed. Florence Nightingale School and King Edward High School, Vancouver, Univ. of British Columbia, London School of Economics and King's Coll., London; various business firms 1923–29; Partner, Macrae, Duncan and Clyne, Vancouver 1929–46; Campney, Owen, Clyne and Murphy 1947–50; Judge of Supreme Court of British Columbia 1950–57; Chair. of Bd. MacMillian and Bloedel Ltd., Vancouver 1958–59; Chair. of Bd. and Chief Exec. Officer, MacMillan, Bloedel and Powell River Ltd. (name changed to MacMillan Bloedel Ltd. April 1966), Vancouver 1960–72, Chair. of the Bd. 1972–73, now Hon. Dir.; fmr. Chair. Canadian Maritime Comm.; Royal Commr. in Whatshan Power House Inquiry, Milk Industry Inquiry, Land Expropriation Inquiry; fmr. Chair. Prime Minister's Advisory Group on Executive Compensation in the Public Service; Dir. Emer. Canadian Imperial Bank of Commerce; Hon. Patron Canadian Inst. for Advanced Legal Studies; fmr. Chair. British Columbia Heritage Trust, Consultative Cttee. on Implications of Telecommunications for Canadian Sovereignty 1978–79; Chancellor, Univ. of British Columbia 1978–84; mem. Fed. Govt. Task Force on Deep Sea Shipping 1984–85; Hon. L.L.D. (McGill Univ.) 1981, (Univ. of British Columbia) 1984; Knight of Grace, Order of Knights of St. John 1959. *Publication:* Jack of All Trades: Memories of a Busy Life (autobiog.) 1985. *Leisure interests:* sport, especially rugby football, theatre. *Address:* MacMillan Bloedel Ltd., 1075 W. Georgia Street, Vancouver V6E 3R9 (Office); 3738 Angus Drive, Vancouver V6J 4H5, B.C., Canada (Home). *Telephone:* 661 8520 (Office); 733-6120 (Home).

CLYNE, Michael George, M.A., PH.D.; Australian professor of linguistics; b. 12 Oct. 1939, Melbourne; s. of Dr. John Clyne and Edith Clyne; m. Irene Donohoue 1977; one d.; ed. Caulfield Grammar School, Univs. of Melbourne, Bonn and Utrecht and Monash Univ.; Tutor then Sr. Tutor, Monash Univ. 1962–64, Lecturer then Sr. Lecturer 1965–71, Assoc. Prof. of German 1972–88, Prof. of Linguistics 1988–; Pres. Australian Linguistic Soc. 1986–88; Fellow, Acad. of Social Sciences in Australia, Australian Acad. of Humanities; other professional memberships, appts. etc. *Publications include:* Transference and Triggering 1967, Perspectives on Language Contact 1972, Deutsch als Muttersprache in Australien 1981, Multilingual Australia 1982, Language and Society in the German-Speaking Countries 1984, Australia: Meeting Place of Languages 1985, An Early Start: Second Language at the Primary School 1986. *Leisure interests:* music, philately, writing references. *Address:* Department of German, Monash University, 3168 (Office); 33 Quaintance Street, Mount Waverley, 3149 Australia (Home). *Telephone:* 03-5652291.

COALES, John Flavell, O.B.E., C.B.E., M.A., SC.D., F.I.E.E.E., F.ENG., F.R.S.; British emeritus professor of engineering; b. 14 Sept. 1907, Birmingham; s. of John Dennis and Marion Beatrice (Flavell) Coales; m. Mary Dorothea Violet Alison 1936; two s. two d.; ed. Berkhamsted School and Sidney Sussex Coll., Cambridge; Admiralty Dept. of Scientific Research 1929–46; Research Dir. Elliott Bros. (London) Ltd. 1946–52; Asst. Dir. of Research, Eng. Dept., Cambridge Univ. 1953, lecturer 1956, Reader 1958, Prof. 1965–74, now Emer.; Fellow, Clare Hall, Cambridge 1964–74, Emer. 1974–; Mackay Visiting Prof., Univ. of California, Berkeley 1963; mem. Research and Devt. Bd. of Tube Investments Ltd. 1957–61, Eastern Electricity Bd. 1967–73; Pres. Int. Fed. of Automatic Control (IFAC) 1963–66; Chair. U.K. Automation Council 1963–66; Pres. Inst. of Electrical Engs. 1971–72; Chair. Council of Eng. Insts. 1975, Chair. Educ., Training and Qualifications Cttee. of Council 1976–77, Chair. Commonwealth Engineering Education and Training Bd. 1975–79; Deputy Chair. BSA Group Research 1963–73; mem. Exec. Cttee. of Nat. Physical Laboratory 1958–63, Gov. Body of Nat. Inst. of Agricultural Eng. 1970–75, Training and Educ. Advisory Cttee. of R.A.F. 1976–79, Court of Cranfield Inst. of Tech. 1970–82, British Library Advisory Council 1975–81; Gov. Hatfield Coll. of Tech. and Hatfield Polytechnic 1952–71; Dir. Delta Materials Research Ltd. 1974–77, Exec. Cttee., Fellowship of Engineering 1976–80; Chair. Activities Cttee. of Fellowship of Eng. 1976–80; Hon. Fellow, Hatfield Polytechnic 1971–, Hon. Fellow, Inst. of Measurement and Control 1971, Inst. of Electrical Engineers 1985; Foreign mem. Serbian Acad. of Sciences 1981; Hon. Sc.D. (City) 1970; Hon. D.Tech. (Loughborough) 1977; Hon. D.Eng. (Sheffield) 1978; Harold Hartley Medal 1971; Giorgio Quazza Medal, Int. Fed. of

Automatic Control; Honda Prize 1982. *Publications:* many original papers on communications, radar, magnetic amplifiers, computers, control and systems eng., educ. and training in eng. *Leisure interests:* mountaineering, gardening, music, reading. *Address:* 4 Latham Road, Cambridge, CB2 2EQ, England. *Telephone:* 0223-63596.

COATES, Robert C., P.C., Q.C., B.A., LL.D.; Canadian politician; b. 10 March 1928, Amherst, Nova Scotia; m. Mary B. Wade; one s. one d.; ed. Mount Allison Univ., Sackville, N.B., Dalhousie Law School, Halifax, N.S.; called to Bar, N.S. 1955; practising lawyer, Amherst 1957–65; M.P. for Cumberland, Colchester 1957–; Nat. Pres. Progressive Conservative Assen. of Canada 1977–80; mem. numerous parl. assens. and groups; Minister of Nat. Defence 1984–85; Dr. h.c. (Chung Ang Cen. Univ., Seoul). *Address:* House of Commons, Ottawa, Ont., Canada.

COATS, David Jervis, C.B.E., D.SC., F.ENG., F.R.S.E.; British consulting civil engineer; b. 25 Jan. 1924, Edinburgh; s. of Rev. W. H. Coats; m. Hazel Bell Livingstone 1955; one s. two d.; ed. Glasgow Univ.; Maj. Royal Electrical and Mechanical Engs. 1943–47; Civil Engineer, Babtie, Shaw and Morton, Glasgow 1947–, Partner 1962–, Sr. Partner 1979–87, Consultant 1988–; Assen. of Consulting Engs. 1979–80; Vice-Pres. Int. Comm. on Large Dams 1983–86; Chair. The Univ. of Glasgow Trust 1986–; Chair, Scottish Construction Industry Group 1986–; Vice-Pres. Inst. of Civil Engineers 1987–; Lay mem. Inst. of Chartered Accountants of Scotland's Financial Services Authorization Cttee. 1988–; Hon. D.Sc. (Glasgow) 1984; ICE Telford Medal 1983; Fellow of the Fellowship of Engs. *Publications:* many tech. papers in professional journals and periodicals. *Leisure interests:* swimming, hill walking. *Address:* Babtie, Shaw and Morton, 95 Bothwell Street, Glasgow, G2 7HX (Office); 7 Kilmardinny Crescent, Bearsden, Glasgow, G61 3NP, Scotland (Home). *Telephone:* (041) 204 2511 (Office); (041) 942 2593 (Home).

COBB, Richard Charles, C.B.E., F.B.A.; British historian; b. 20 May 1917; s. of Francis Hills Cobb and Dora Swindale; m. Margaret Tennant 1963; four s. one d.; ed. Shrewsbury School and Merton Coll., Oxford; H.M. Forces 1942–46; research in Paris 1946–55; lecturer in History Univ. Coll. Wales, Aberystwyth 1955–61; Sr. Simon Research Fellow, Manchester 1960; lecturer Univ. of Leeds 1962; Fellow and Tutor in Modern History Balliol Coll., Oxford 1962–72, Hon. Fellow 1977; Reader in French Revolutionary History, Oxford 1969–72; Prof. of Modern History 1973–84; Sr. Research Fellow Worcester Coll., Oxford 1984–; Visiting Prof. in History of Paris Coll. de France 1971; several memorial lectures; Hon. Fellow Merton Coll. 1980; Hon. D. Univ. (Essex) 1981; Hon. D.Litt. (Leeds) 1988; Chevalier des Palmes Académiques, Officier, Ordre nat. du Mérite, Chevalier, Légion d'honneur. *Publications:* L'armée révolutionnaire à Lyon 1952, Les armées révolutionnaires du Midi 1955, Les armées révolutionnaires (vol. 1) 1961, (vol. 2) 1963, A Second Identity: essays on France and French History 1969, The Police and the People: French Popular Protest 1789–1820 1970, Reactions to the French Revolution 1972, Paris and its Provinces 1792–1802 1975, A Sense of Place 1975, Tour de France 1976, Death in Paris 1795–1801 1978 (Wolfson Prize 1979), Streets of Paris 1980, Promenades 1980, French and Germans, Germans and French 1983, Still Life; sketches from a Tunbridge Wells childhood 1983 (J. R. Ackerley Prize), A Classical Education 1985, People and Places 1985, Something to Hold onto (autobiog.) 1988, The French Revolution: Voices from a Momentous Epoch 1798–1895, 1989. *Address:* Worcester College, Oxford, England.

COBURN, James; American actor; b. 31 Aug. 1928, Laurel, Nebraska; ed. Los Angeles City Coll.; studied drama with Stella Adler; m. Beverly Kelly 1959; one s. one d.; made professional theatre debut with Vincent Price in Billy Budd at the La Jolla Community Playhouse, Calif. *Films include:* Ride Lonesome 1959, Faces of a Fugitive 1959, The Magnificent Seven 1960, Hell is for Heroes, 1962, The Great Escape 1963, Charade 1963, The Americanization of Emily 1964, Major Dundee 1965, High Wind in Jamaica 1965, The Loved One 1965, Our Man Flint 1966, What Did You Do in the War Daddy? 1966, In Like Flint 1966, The President's Analyst 1967, Duffy 1968, Candy 1968, Hard Contract 1968, A Fistful of Dynamite 1971, The Carey Treatment 1972, The Honkers 1972, Pat Garrett and Billy the Kid 1973, The Last of Sheila 1973, Harry in Your Pocket 1973, Hard Times 1976, Sky Riders 1976, Midway 1976, Cross of Iron 1977, The Internecine 1979, Golden Girl 1979, Firepower 1979, The Muppet Movie 1979, Loving Couples 1980, The Baltimore Bullet 1980, High Risk 1981, Locker 1981, Death of a Soldier 1986; producer, The President's Analyst 1967, Waterhole No. 3 1967; owner, Panpiper Productions, Hollywood; numerous TV appearances including The Dain Curse 1978. *Address:* c/o International Management, 8899 Beverly Boulevard, Los Angeles, Calif. 90048, U.S.A.

COBURN, John, A.M., A.S.T.C.; Australian artist; b. 23 Sept. 1925, Ingham, Queensland; s. of Edgar L. Cockburn and Alice Beatts; m. Barbara Woodward 1953 (deceased); two s. one d.; ed. All Souls' School, Charters Towers, and East Sydney Technical Coll.; has participated in major exhbns. of Australian art in Australia and abroad, including Australian Painting, Tate Gallery 1963; first one-man exhbn. Gallery of Contemporary Art, Melbourne 1957 and has since held many others in Australian cities, in Paris and Washington 1971 and New York 1977; art teacher, Nat. Art School, Sydney 1959–66; lived in France 1969–72 where designed many tapestries for the Aubusson workshops including two large tapestry curtains for

Sydney Opera House; Head, Nat. Art School, Sydney 1972–74; Trustee, Art Gallery of N.S.W., Sydney 1976–80; mem. Inst. Bd., City Art Inst., Sydney 1982–; work represented in Australian Nat. Gallery, Canberra, all Australian State galleries, Vatican Museum, Graphische Sammlung Albertina, Vienna and John F. Kennedy Center for the Performing Arts, Washington; Blake Prize for Religious Art 1970, 1977. *Address:* 50 Gurner Street, Paddington, N.S.W. 2021, Australia. *Telephone:* (02) 4496797.

COCHRAN, Thad; American politician; b. 7 Dec. 1937, Pontotoc, Miss.; s. of William Holmes and Emma Grace (née Berry) Cochran; m. Rose Clayton; two c.; ed. Mississippi Univ. and School of Law, Univ. of Dublin, Ireland; law practice in Jackson, Miss. 1965; Pres. Young Lawyers' section of Miss. State Bar, Chair. Miss. Law Inst.; mem. U.S. House of Reps. 1973–78, fmr. mem. Public Works and Transportation Cttee. Ethics Cttee., Select Cttee. on Aging; Southern States Rep. on House Republican Policy Cttee.; Senator from Mississippi Jan. 1979–; Sec. Republican Conf. in U.S. Senate 1985–, Chair. three Senate sub-cttees. *Address:* Senate Office Building, Washington, D.C. 20510, U.S.A.

COCHRAN, William, PH.D., F.R.S.; British professor of natural philosophy; b. 30 July 1922, Scotland; s. of James Cochran and Margaret W. Baird; m. Ingegerd Wall 1953; one s. two d.; ed. Boroughmuir School, Edinburgh and Univ. of Edinburgh; Asst. in Physics, Univ. of Edinburgh 1943–46; Research Asst., Univ. Demonstrator, Lecturer, Reader, Cavendish Lab., Cambridge 1946–64; Fellow, Trinity Hall, Cambridge 1953–64; Hon. Fellow 1982–; Prof. of Physics, later of Natural Philosophy, Univ. of Edinburgh 1964–87, Dean, Faculty of Science 1978–81, Vice-Principal 1983–87; Hughes Medal, Royal Soc. 1978. *Publications:* The Crystalline State, Vol. III (with H. S. Lipson) 1966, Dynamics of Atoms in Crystals 1973. *Leisure interests:* family history, Scots verse and light verse. *Address:* Department of Physics, The University, King's Buildings, Edinburgh, EH9 3JZ (Office); 71 Clermiston Road, Edinburgh, EH12 6UY, Scotland (Home).

COCKBURN, Sir Robert, K.B.E., C.B., PH.D., M.SC., M.A.(CANTAB.); British civil servant; b. 31 March 1909, Portsmouth, Hants; s. of Rev. R. T. Cockburn; m. Phyllis Hoyland 1935; two d.; ed. Municipal Coll., Portsmouth, and London Univ.; taught science at West Ham Municipal Coll. 1930–37; research in communications at Royal Aircraft Establishment, Farnborough 1937–39; radar research at Telecommunications Research Establishment, Malvern 1939–45; atomic energy research at A.E.R.E., Harwell 1945–48; scientific adviser to Air Ministry 1948–53; Principal Dir. of Scientific Research (Guided Weapons and Electronics), Ministry of Supply 1954–55, Deputy Controller of Electronics 1955–56, Controller of Guided Weapons and Electronics 1956–59; Chief Scientist, Ministry of Aviation 1959–64; Dir. Royal Aircraft Establishment, Farnborough 1964–69; Chair. Council, Nat. Computing Centre 1970–77; Fellow, Churchill Coll., Cambridge 1969–76; Chair. TV Advisory Cttee. 1971–; Chair. BBC Engineering Advisory Cttee. 1973–81; Hon. Fellow, Royal Aeronautical Soc.; U.S. Congressional Medal for Merit. *Address:* 1 Firethorn Close, Longmead, Fleet, Aldershot, Hants. GU13 9TR, England. *Telephone:* (0252) 615518.

COCKERELL, Sir Christopher (Sydney), Kt., C.B.E., M.A., F.R.S.; British engineer; b. 4 June 1910, Cambridge; s. of Sir Sydney Cockerell and Florence Kingsford; m. Margaret E. Belsham 1937; two d.; ed. Gresham's, Holt and Peterhouse, Cambridge; radio research Cambridge 1933–35; joined Marconi's 1935, in charge Airborne Devt. Section 1937, Airborne Div. and Navigational Research 1946–48, research 1948–50; started boat-building business later known as Ripplecraft Co. Ltd. 1948, Chair. 1950–79; inventor of Hovercraft 1954, formed Hovercraft Ltd. 1957; consultant to Ministry of Supply on Hovercraft Project 1957–58; consultant Hovercraft Devt. Ltd. 1958–70, Dir. 1959–66; Chair. Wavepower Ltd. 1974–82; mem. Ministry of Technology's Advisory Cttee. for Hovercraft 1968–70; f. and Pres. Int. Air Cushion Eng. Soc. 1969–71 (Vice-Pres. 1971–); Pres. U.K. Hovercraft Soc. 1972–; Fellow, Royal Soc. of Arts 1960–70, Hon. Fellow 1978–, Soc. of Engineers, Manchester Univ. of Science and Technology, Swedish Soc. of Aeronautics; Hon. Fellow, Downing Coll., Cambridge 1969, Fellow of the Royal Soc. 1967, Southampton Chamber of Commerce 1967; Hon. Fellow, Peterhouse, Cambridge 1974; Trustee, Nat. Portrait Gallery 1967–79; Hon. D.Sc. (Leicester and Heriot-Watt Univs.), Hon. D.Sc. (Royal Coll. of Art) 1968, (London Univ.) 1975; numerous medals. *Leisure interests:* fishing, gardening, visual arts. *Address:* 16 Prospect Place, Hythe, Southampton, Hants., SO4 6AU, England. *Telephone:* Southampton 842931.

COCKERHAM, C. Clark, PH.D.; American professor of statistics and genetics; b. 12 Dec. 1921, Mountain Park, N.C.; s. of Corbett C. Cockerham and Nellie B. McCann; m. Joyce E. Allen 1944; two s. one d.; ed. North Carolina State and Iowa State Colls.; Asst. Prof. Dept. of Biostatistics, School of Public Health, Univ. of N.C. 1952–53; Assoc. Prof. Dept. of Experimental Statistics, N.C. State Coll. 1953–59; Prof. Dept. of Statistics, N.C. State Univ., Raleigh 1959–72, William Neal Reynolds Prof. of Statistics and Genetics 1972–, Distinguished Univ. Prof. 1988–; mem. N.A.S. and other learned socs.; several awards. *Publications:* over 90 research papers on population and quantitative genetics and plant and animal breeding. *Address:* Department of Statistics, Box 8203, North Carolina State University, Raleigh, N.C. 27695-8203 (Office); 2110 Coley Forest Place, Raleigh, N.C. 27607, U.S.A. (Home). *Telephone:* (919) 737-2534 (Office); (919) 787-4844 (Home).

COCKFIELD, Baron (Life Peer), cr. 1978, of Dover in the County of Kent; **(Francis) Arthur Cockfield**, Kt., LL.B., B.SC.(ECON.).; British business executive; b. 28 Sept. 1916; m. Aileen Monica Mudie 1970; ed. Dover County School, London School of Economics; called to Bar, Inner Temple 1942; Inland Revenue Dept. of Civil Service 1938; Asst. Sec. Bd. of Inland Revenue 1945, Commr. 1951-52, also Dir. of Statistics and Intelligence to Bd. of Inland Revenue 1945-52; Finance Dir. Boots Pure Drug Co. Ltd. 1953-61, Man. Dir. and Chair. Exec. Man. Cttee. 1961-67; mem. Nat. Econ. Devt. Council (N.E.D.C.) 1962-64, 1982-; Special Adviser on Taxation to the Chancellor of the Exchequer 1970-73; Chair. Price Comm. 1973-77; Minister of State, Treasury 1979-82; Sec. of State for Trade 1982-83, Chancellor of the Duchy of Lancaster 1983-84; Commr. for Internal Market, Tax Law and Customs, Comm. of European Communities and a Vice-Pres. of the Comm. 1985-88; Adviser to Peat, Marwick McLintock 1989-; Hon. Fellow, L.S.E. 1972. *Address:* Connaught House, Mount Row, Berkeley Square, London, W.1, England.

COCKING, Edward Charles Daniel, PH.D., D.SC., F.I.BIOL., F.R.S.; British professor of botany; b. 26 Sept. 1931; s. of late Charles Cocking and of Mary (Murray) Cocking; m. Bernadette Keane 1960; one s. one d.; ed. Buckhurst Hill Co. High School, Essex and Univ. of Bristol; Civil Service Comm. Research Fellow, 1956-59; Lecturer in Plant Physiology, Univ. of Nottingham 1959-66, Reader 1966-69, Prof. of Botany and Head, Dept. of Botany 1969-; Trustee, Royal Botanic Gardens, Kew 1983-; Gov. Glasshouse Crops Research Inst. 1983-. *Publications:* Introduction to the Principles of Plant Physiology (with W. Stiles); articles in professional journals. *Leisure interests:* walking, travelling, chess. *Address:* Department of Botany, University of Nottingham, University Park, Nottingham, NG7 2RD; 30 Patterdale Road, Woodthorpe, Notts., NQ5 4LQ, England.

COCKS OF HARTCLIFFE, Baron (Life Peer) cr. 1987, of Chinnor in the County of Oxfordshire, **Michael Francis Lovell Cocks**, P.C., M.P.; British politician; b. 19 Aug. 1929; m. 1st Janet Macfarlane 1954, two s. two d.; m. 2nd Valerie Davis 1979; ed. Bristol Univ.; fmr. lecturer at Bristol Polytechnic; M.P. for Bristol South 1970-87; Asst. Govt. Whip 1974-76, Parl. Sec. to Treasury and Govt. Chief Whip 1976-79, Opposition Chief Whip 1979-85; Labour. *Address:* c/o House of Commons, Westminster, London, S.W.1, England.

COE, Sebastian Newbold, M.B.E., B.SC.; British athlete; b. 29 Sept. 1956, London; s. of Peter Coe and Angela Coe; ed. Loughborough Univ.; competed Olympic Games, Moscow 1980, winning Gold Medal at 1500 m. and Silver Medal at 800 m., and repeated this in Los Angeles 1984; European Junior Bronze Medallist at 1500 m. 1975; European Bronze Medallist at 800 m. 1978; European Silver Medallist at 800 m. 1982; European 800 m. Champion 1986; has held world records at 1500 m. and mile; world record holder at 800 m. and 1000 m.; est. new records at 800 m., 1000 m. and mile 1981; mem. 4 × 400 m. world record relay squad 1982; only athlete to hold world records at 800 m., 1000 m., 1500 m. and mile simultaneously; Pres. first athletes' del. to IOC, Baden-Baden 1981, and mem. first athletes' comm. set up after Congress by IOC 1981-; Vice-Chair. Sports Council 1986-, Sports Aid Trust 1987; Presenter BBC Breakfast Time 1989-; mem. Health Educ. Authority 1987, Health Educ. Council 1986-87; Vice-Patron Sharon Allen Leukemia Trust 1987-; BBC Sports Personality of 1979; Sir John Cohen Memorial Award 1981; Principe de Asturias Award (Spain) 1987; Hon. D. Tech. (Loughborough) 1985. *Publications:* Running Free (with David Miller) 1981, Running for Fitness 1983, The Olympians 1984. *Leisure interests:* reading, music (jazz), avoiding all strenuous activity away from the track. *Address:* Strand House, The Embankment, Twickenham, Middx., England.

COELHO, Tony, B.A.; American politician; b. 15 June 1942, Los Banos, Calif.; s. of Otto Coelho and Alice Branco; m. Phyllis Butler 1967; two d.; ed. Loyola Univ.; Agric. Asst. 1965-70, Admin. Asst. 1970-78; mem. and Majority Whip-at-Large, 96th-99th Congresses from 15th Calif. Dist.; Sec.-Treasurer United Democrats for Congress; Chair. Democrats' Congressional Campaign Cttee.; Majority Whip, House of Reps. Jan. 1987-; Democrat. *Address:* c/o House of Representatives, H148, Capitol Building, Washington, D.C. 20515, U.S.A.

COETSEE, Hendrik Jacobus, B.A., LL.B.; South African politician; b. 19 April 1931, Ladybrand, O.F.S.; m. Helena Elizabeth Malan 1956; two s. three d.; ed. Free State Univ.; lectured in law; qualified as attorney; practised, Bloemfontein -1972; called to the Bar 1972; M.P. for Bloemfontein West 1968-; mem. Exec. Cttee. Nat. Party, O.F.S. 1968-76, Chair. Congress 1979-85; Leader, Nat. Party, O.F.S. 1985-; Deputy Minister of Defence and Nat. Security 1978-80; Minister of Justice 1980-. *Leisure interests:* small scale mixed farming, fishing, clay pigeon shooting. *Address:* Ministry of Justice, Private Bag X276, Pretoria, South Africa.

COETZEE, John M., M.A., PH.D.; South African academic and writer; b. 9 Feb. 1940, South Africa; one s. one d.; ed. Univ. of Cape Town, Univ. of Texas; Asst. Prof. of English, State Univ. of New York 1968-71; Lecturer, Univ. of Cape Town 1972-76, Sr. lecturer 1977-80, Assoc. Prof. 1981-83, Prof. of General Literature 1984-; CNA Literary Award 1977, 1980, 1983, Geoffrey Faber Prize 1980, James Tait Black Memorial Prize 1980, Booker-McConnell Prize 1983, Prix Femina Etranger 1985 (for Life and Times of Michael K), Jerusalem Prize 1987; Hon. Dr. (Strathclyde) 1985. *Publications:* Dusklands 1974, In the Heart of the Country 1977, Waiting for

the Barbarians 1980, Life and Times of Michael K 1983, Foe 1986. *Address:* P.O. Box 92, Rondebosch, Cape Province 7700, South Africa.

COETZER, William Bedford, B.COMM., C.A.(S.A.), F.C.I.S.; South African business executive; b. 13 Sept. 1909, Rouxville; s. of Hendrik Coetzer and Sylvia Elza Coetzer (née Blake); m. Margaret de Waal-Davies 1935; two s. three d.; ed. Grey Univ., Bloemfontein and Stellenbosch Univ.; Articled Clerk, D. S. P. Ackerman, C.A., Aliwal North 1929-32; served in provincial admin., Cape Town 1934; Sec. and Man. Westelike Graanboere Cooperative Asscn., Malmesburg 1935-41; Commercial Consultant, Federale Volksbelegging Ltd., Cape Town 1941-, currently Dir.; Chair. Federale Mynbou Bpk. 1953, Siemens S.A. Ltd.; Dir. Hollardstraat-Ses Beleggings (Edms.) Bpk., Sentrust Ltd., Gen. Mining and Finance Corpn. (now Gen. Mining Union Corpn.) 1963-, Trust Bank of Africa Ltd., Lydenburg Platinum Ltd.; Hon. D.Phil. (Univ. of South Africa); Frans du Toit Medal for Industrial Leadership, S.A. Acad. for Science and Art 1973. *Address:* P.O. Box 65577, Benmore 2010, South Africa.

COFFEY, Shelby, III; American journalist; m. Mary Lee Coffey; ed. Univ. of Virginia; with Washington Post 1968-85, latterly Asst. Man. Ed. for nat. news and Deputy Man. Ed. for features; Ed. U.S. News and World Report 1985-86; Ed. Dallas Times Herald 1986-. *Address:* Dallas Times Herald, 1101 Pacific, Dallas, Tex. 75202, U.S.A.

COFFEY, Thomas (see Ó Cofaigh, Tomás).

COFFIN, Frank Morey; American lawyer and government official; b. 11 July 1919, Lewiston, Maine; s. of Herbert and Ruth Coffin; m. Ruth Ulrich 1942; one s. three d.; ed. Bates Coll., and Harvard Univ.; admitted to Maine Bar 1947, legal practice 1947-56; mem. U.S. House of Reps. 1957-61; Man. Dir. Devt. Loan Fund, Dept. of State 1961; Deputy Admin., Agency for Int. Devt. 1961-62; Deputy Admin. for Operations 1962-64; U.S. Rep. to Devt. Assistance Cttee., Org. for European Co-operation and Devt. (OECD), Paris 1964-65; U.S. Circuit Judge, Court of Appeals for First Circuit 1965-, Chief Judge 1972-83; Adj. Prof. Univ. of Maine School of Law 1986-; Dir. Overseas Devt. Council; mem. American Acad. of Arts and Sciences. *Publications:* Witness for Aid 1964, The Ways of a Judge 1980, A Lexicon of Oral Advocacy 1984. *Leisure interests:* sculpture, painting, boating. *Address:* 156 Federal Street, Portland, Maine 04112 (Office).

COGGAN, Baron (Life Peer), cr. 1980, of Canterbury and of Sissinghurst in the County of Kent; **Rt. Rev. and Rt. Hon. (Frederick) Donald Coggan**, D.D.; British ecclesiastic; b. 9 Oct. 1909, London; s. of Cornish and Fannie Coggan; m. Jean Strain 1935; two d.; ed. Merchant Taylors' School, St. John's Coll., Cambridge and Wycliffe Hall, Oxford; Asst. lecturer in Semitic Languages and Literature, Manchester Univ. 1931-34; Curate, St. Mary, Islington 1934-37; Prof. at Wycliffe Coll. Toronto 1937-44; Prin., London Coll. of Divinity 1944-56; Bishop of Bradford 1956-61; Archbishop of York 1961-74, of Canterbury 1974-80; Prelate Order of St. John of Jerusalem 1967-; Life Pres. Church Army 1981-; Chaplain of the Merchant Taylors' Co. 1980-81; Freedom of City of Canterbury 1976. *Publications:* A People's Heritage 1944, The Ministry of the Word 1945, The Glory of God 1950, Stewards of Grace 1958, Five Makers of the New Testament 1962, Christian Priorities 1963, The Prayers of the New Testament 1967, Sinews of Faith 1969, Word and World 1971, Convictions 1975, On Preaching 1978, The Heart of the Christian Faith 1978, Sure Foundation 1981, Mission to the World 1982, Paul: Portrait of a Revolutionary 1984, The Sacrament of the Word 1987, Cuthbert Bardsley: Bishop, Evangelist, Pastor 1989. *Leisure interests:* gardening, motoring, music. *Address:* 28 Lions Hall, St. Swithun Street, Winchester, SO23 911W, England. *Telephone:* 0962-64289.

COHAN, Robert Paul; British choreographer; b. 27 March 1925; s. of Walter and Billie Cohan; ed. Martha Graham School, New York; Partner, Martha Graham School 1950, Co-Dir. Martha Graham Co. 1966; Artistic Dir. Contemporary Dance Trust Ltd., London 1967-; Artistic Dir. and Prin. Choreographer, London Contemporary Dance Theatre 1969-87; Artistic Adviser, Batsheva Co., Israel 1980; Dir. York Univ., Toronto Choreographic Summer School 1977, Gulbenkian Choreographic Summer School, Univ. of Surrey 1978, 1979, 1982 and other int. courses; with London Contemporary Dance Theatre has toured Europe, S. America, N. Africa, U.S.A.; major works created: Cell 1969, Stages 1971, Waterless Method of Swimming Instruction 1974, Class 1975, Stabat Mater 1975, Masque of Separation 1975, Khamsin 1976, Nympheas 1976, Forest 1977, Eos 1978, Songs, Lamentations and Praises 1979, Dances of Love and Death 1981, Agora 1984, A Mass for Man 1985, Ceremony 1986, Interrogations 1986, Video Life 1986; Hon. Fellow York Univ., Toronto; Evening Standard Award for outstanding achivement in ballet 1975; Soc. of W. End Theatres Award for outstanding achivement in ballet 1978. *Publication:* The Dance Workshop 1986. *Leisure interest:* dancing. *Address:* The Place, 17 Dukes Road, London, W.C.1, England. *Telephone:* 01-387 0161.

COHEN, Alexander H.; American theatre and television producer; b. 24 July 1920, New York; s. of Alexander H. and Laura (Tarantous) Cohen; m. 1st Jocelyn Newmark 1942 (divorced), 2nd Hildy Parks 1956; two s. one d.; ed. New York Univ.; Producer, Broadway 1941-, London 1963-; New York productions include Anna Christie, Comedians, Ulysses in Nighttown, Good Evening, Home, Marlene Dietrich, John Gielgud's Ages

310

of Man, Black Comedy, Victor Borge, Hamlet, Beyond the Fringe, The Devils, The School for Scandal, The Unknown Soldier and his Wife, At the Drop of a Hat, Little Murders, Maurice Chevalier, The Homecoming, Mike Nichols and Elaine May, Baker Street, I Remember Mama, A Day in Hollywood/A Night in The Ukraine, 84 Charing Cross Road, Ben Kingsley as Edmund Kean, the Peter Brook production of Carmen, Memory; London productions include Applause, The Happy Apple, Who Killed Santa Claus, Halfway Up the Tree, 1776, Plaza Suite, Mixed Doubles, The Price, Ivanov, Man and Boy, The Rivals, Come As You Are, The Doctor's Dilemma, You Never Can Tell, The Merchant of Venice; productions for television: Annual Antoinette Perry (Tony) Awards 1967–, CBS: On The Air (A Celebration of Fifty Years) 1978, The Emmy Awards 1978, Applause, Night of 100 Stars 1982, Parade of Stars 1983, The Best of Everything 1983. *Address:* c/o Schubert Theatre, 225 West 44th Street, New York, N.Y. 10036. *Telephone:* New York 764-1900.

COHEN, Barry, B.A.; Australian politician; b. 3 April 1935, Griffith, N.S.W.; m. Rae Cohen; three s.; ed. Australian Nat. Univ.; served Citizens Mil. Forces (Army Reserve) 1953–57; mem. House of Reps. (parl.) for Robertson, N.S.W. 1969–; Minister for Home Affairs 1983–84, also for Arts, Heritage and Environment and Minister assisting the Prime Minister for the Bicentennial; Labor Party. *Leisure interests:* golf, squash, tennis. *Address:* Parliament House, Canberra, A.C.T. 2600, Australia.

COHEN, Bernard, D.F.A.; British artist; b. 28 July 1933, London; m. Jean Britton 1959; one s. one d.; ed. South West Essex School of Art, St. Martin's School of Art, London and Slade School of Fine Art, London; held teaching appts. at several art schools 1957–67; teacher of painting and drawing, Slade School of Fine Art 1967–73, 1977; Visiting Prof. Univ. of New Mexico 1969–70, faculty alumni 1974; guest lecturer, Royal Coll. of Art 1974–75; Visiting Artist, Minneapolis School of Art 1964, 1969, 1971, 1975, Ont. Coll. of Art 1971, San Fransisco Art Inst., Univ. of Vic., B.C. 1975; has lectured at several Canadian univs. since 1969; now Principal lecturer (Painting), Wimbledon School of Art; one-man exhbns. at various London galleries since 1958, Venice Biennale 1966, Betty Parsons Gallery, N.Y. 1967, Hayward Gallery, London (retrospective) 1972, Studio La Città, Verona 1972, 1975, Galleria Anunciata, Milan 1973, Tate Gallery, London (print retrospective) 1976, Gallery Omana, Osaka 1979; has participated in numerous group exhbns. in London, Europe, Japan and U.S.A. since 1953. *Publications:* articles and statements in journals and catalogues. *Leisure interests:* music, cinema, travel. *Address:* 17 Leybourne Park, Kew, Richmond, Surrey, England. *Telephone:* (01) 940 9999.

COHEN, Sir Edward, Kt., LL.B.; Australian lawyer and company director; b. 9 Nov. 1912, Malvern, Victoria; s. of Brig. H. E. Cohen; m. Meryl D. Fink 1939; one s.; ed. Scotch Coll., Melbourne and Ormond Coll., Univ. of Melbourne; served Australian Imperial Forces 1940–45; fmr. mem. Faculty of Law of Melbourne Univ., also of Bd. of Examiners and Council of Legal Educ.; mem. Council, Law Inst. of Victoria 1959–68, Pres. 1965–66; Chair. Pensions Cttee. of Melbourne Legacy 1961–84; fmr. Partner, now Consultant, Corrs, Pavey, Whiting and Byrne Solicitors, Melbourne; fmr. Chair. E.Z. Industries Ltd., Electrolytic Zinc Co. of Australasia Ltd., Nat. Commercial Union Ltd. (fmrly Commercial Union Ltd.), Emu Bay Railway Co. Ltd., CUB Fibre Containers Pty. Ltd., Carlton & United Breweries Ltd., Mfrs. Bottle Co. Vic., Derwent Metals; Dir. Herald and Weekly Times Ltd. 1974–77, Vice-Chair. 1976–77; Dir. Associated Pulp and Paper Mills Ltd. 1951–83, Deputy Chair. 1981–83, Standard Mutual Building Soc. 1951–64, Pelaco Ltd. 1959–68, Glazebrooks Paints and Chemicals Ltd. 1951–61, and other cos. *Address:* 350 William Street, Melbourne, Victoria 3000 (Office); Orrong Road, Toorak, Victoria 3142, Australia (Home).

COHEN, Gerald Allan, M.A., B.PHIL., F.B.A.; Canadian academic; b. 14 April 1941, Montreal; s. of Bella Lipkin and Morrie Cohen; m. Margaret Florence Pearce 1965; one s. two d.; ed. Morris Winchewsky Jewish School, Strathcona Acad. and McGill Univ., Montreal and New Coll. Oxford, England; lecturer in Philosophy, Univ. Coll. London 1963–78, Reader 1978–84; Chichele Prof. of Social and Political Theory and Fellow of All Souls, Oxford Jan. 1985–; Isaac Deutscher Memorial Prize. *Publications:* Karl Marx's Theory of History: A Defence 1978, History, Labour, and Freedom: Themes from Marx 1988. *Leisure interests:* Guardian crossword puzzles, Broadway and Hollywood musicals, architecture. *Address:* All Souls College, Oxford, England. *Telephone:* 0865-722251.

COHEN, Laurence Jonathan, M.A., D.LITT., F.B.A.; British university teacher; b. 7 May 1923, London; s. of Israel and Theresa Cohen; m. Gillian M. Slee 1953; three s. one d.; ed. St. Paul's School, London and Balliol Coll., Oxford; served Naval Intelligence to Lieut., R.N.V.R. 1942–45; Asst. Dept. of Logic and Metaphysics, Edinburgh Univ. 1947–50; lecturer in Philosophy, Univ. of St. Andrews at Dundee 1950–57; Fellow and Praelector, Queen's Coll., Oxford 1957–; Sr. Tutor 1985–; Commonwealth Fund Fellow, Princeton and Harvard Univs. 1952–53; Visiting Prof., Columbia Univ. 1967–68, Yale Univ. 1972–73; Visiting Fellow, Australian Nat. Univ. 1980, Northwestern Univ. Law School 1988; Pres. British Soc. for Philosophy of Science 1977–79; Co-Pres. Int. Union of History and Philosophy of Science 1987. *Publications:* The Principles of World Citizenship 1954, The Diversity of Meaning 1962, The Implications of Induction 1970, The Probable and the Provable 1977, The Dialogue of Reason 1986. An Introduction to the Philosophy of Induction and Probability 1988. *Leisure interest:*

gardening. *Address:* The Queens' College, Oxford, OX1 4AW, England. *Telephone:* 0865-279168.

COHEN, Marvin Lou, PH.D.; American (b. Canadian) professor of physics; b. 3 March 1935, Canada; s. of Elmo Cohen and Molly Zaritsky; m. Merrill Leigh Gardner 1958; one s. one d.; ed. Univs. of California (Berkeley) and Chicago; mem. Tech. Staff, Bell Labs., Murray Hill, N.J. 1963–64; Asst. Prof. of Physics, Univ. of Calif. (Berkeley) 1964–66, Assoc. Prof. 1966–68, Prof. 1969–; Prof. Miller Inst. Basic Research in Science, Univ. of Calif. 1969–70, 1976–77, 1983–, Chair. 1977–81; U.S. Rep., Semiconductor Comm., Int. Union of Pure and Applied Physics 1975–81; Visiting Prof., Univ. of Hawaii 1978–79; Alfred P. Sloan Fellow, Univ. of Cambridge 1965–67; Guggenheim Fellow 1978–79; Fellow, American Physics Soc. Exec. Council 1975–79, Chair. 1977–78; mem. N.A.S., Oliver E. Buckley Prize Comm. 1980–81, Chair. 1981; mem. Selection Cttee. for Presidential Young Investigator Awards 1983; mem. Cttee. on Nat. Synchotron Radiation Facilities 1983–84; Chair. 17th Int. Conf. on the Physics of Semiconductors 1984; mem. Govt.-Univ.-Industry Research Round Table 1984–, Vice-Chair. Working Group on Science and Eng. Talent 1984–; mem. Research Briefing Panels N.A.S. on Funding and on High Temperature Superconductivity 1987–, U.S.-Japan Workshop on Univ. Research 1988–89; Chair. Comstock Prize Cttee. N.A.S.; Oliver E. Buckley Prize for solid state physics 1979; Dept. of Energy Award 1981. *Publications:* over 400 articles on research topics. *Leisure interests:* music (clarinet), running. *Address:* Department of Physics, University of California, Berkeley, Calif. 94720 (Office); 10 Forest Lane, Berkeley, Calif. 94708, U.S.A. (Home). *Telephone:* 415-642-4753 (Office); 415-527-1750 (Home).

COHEN, Morris, D.SC.; American metallurgist and materials scientist; b. 27 Nov. 1911, Chelsea, Mass.; s. of late Julius H. and Alice Cohen; m. Ruth Krentzman 1937 (deceased); one s. one d.; ed. Massachusetts Inst. of Technology; Instructor of Metallurgy M.I.T. 1936, Asst. Prof. 1937, Assoc. Prof. 1941, Prof. of Physical Metallurgy 1946, Ford Prof. of Materials Science and Eng. 1962–74, Institute Prof. 1974–82, Inst. Prof. Emer. 1982–; fmr. consultant to U.S. Atomic Energy Comm. and mem. of several govt. panels and advisory cttees.; mem. N.A.S., Nat. Acad. of Eng.; Fellow, American Acad. of Arts and Sciences, New York Acad. of Sciences; Hon. mem. American Soc. for Metals (Pres. 1969), British Metals Soc., Japan Iron and Steel Inst., Japan Inst. of Metals, American Physical Soc., Indian Inst. of Metals, Korean Inst. of Metals, etc.; Fellow Metallurgical Soc. of AIME, A.A.A.S.; Foreign Assoc., Indian Nat. Science Acad.; has delivered numerous memorial lectures including several to American Soc. for Metals, and Coleman Lecture, Franklin Inst. 1960; Hon. D. Tekn. (Royal Inst. of Technology, Stockholm) 1977, Hon. D.Sc. (Israel Inst. of Tech., Haifa) 1979, Hon. D.Eng. (Colorado School of Mines) 1985; Kamani Medal, Indian Inst. of Metals 1952, Mathewson Gold Medal, AIME 1953, Clamer Medal, Franklin Inst. 1959, Gold Medal, American Soc. for Metals 1968, Gold Medal, Japan Inst. of Metals 1970, Médaille Pierre Chevenard, Soc. Française de Métallurgie 1971; Killian Faculty Achievement Award, M.I.T. 1974; Procter Prize, Research Soc. of N. America 1976; Nat. Medal of Science 1977, Albert Sauveur Achievement Award, American Soc. for Metals 1977, Joseph R. Vilella Award, American Soc. of Testing and Materials 1979, Hobart M. Kraner Award, American Ceramic Soc. 1981, ACTA Metallurgica Gold Medal 1981; Hon. Prof. Beijing Univ. of Science and Technology 1980, Hon. Prof. Beijing Univ. of Aeronautics and Astronautics 1980, Hon. mem. AIME 1981, New England Award, Eng. Socs. of New England 1987, Albert Easton White Distinguished Teacher Award, ASM Int. 1987, Kyoto Prize for Advanced Tech. 1987, Charles S. Barrett Award, ASM Int. 1988, Nat. Materials Advancement Award, Fed. of Materials Societies 1988. *Leisure interest:* art collecting. *Address:* Room 13-5046, Department of Materials Science and Engineering, Massachusetts Institute of Technology, Cambridge, Mass. 02139; 491 Puritan Road, Swampscott, Mass. 01907, U.S.A. (Home). *Telephone:* (617) 253-3325 (Office); (617) 595-1443 (Home).

COHEN, Philip Pacy, PH.D., M.D.; American professor of physiological chemistry; b. 26 Sept. 1908, Derry, N.H.; s. of David and Ada (Cottler) Cohen; m. Rubye H. Tepper 1935; three s. one d.; ed. Tufts Coll. and Univ. of Wisconsin; Prof. and Chair., Dept. of Physiological Chem., Univ. of Wisconsin 1948–75, H. C. Bradley Prof. of Physiological Chem. 1968–; Visiting Prof. Univ. of Calif. at Los Angeles 1976; Acting Dean, Univ. of Wisconsin Medical School 1961–63; Chair. Cttee. on Growth, Nat. Research Council 1954–56; mem. Bd. of Scientific Counsellors, Nat. Cancer Inst. 1957–59, Chair. 1959–61; mem. Nat. Advisory Cancer Council, Nat. Insts. of Health 1963–67; mem. Advisory Cttee. to Dir. Nat. Insts. of Health 1966–70; mem. Advisory Cttee. for Medical Research, Pan American Health Org. 1967–75; mem. Advisory Cttee. for Biology and Medicine, U.S. Atomic Energy Comm. 1963–71, Chair. 1969–70; mem. Nat. Advisory Arthritis and Metabolic Diseases Council, Nat. Insts. of Health 1970–74; mem. Nat. Comm. on Research 1978–; Visiting Prof., Univ. of Mexico 1981–; mem. N.A.S., American Chem. Soc., American Soc. of Biological Chemists, Biochemical Soc. (U.K.); hon. mem. Sociedad Argentina de Investigación Bioquímica, Nat. Acad. of Medicine, Mexico, Japanese Biochemical Soc., Harvey Soc.; Fellow, A.A.A.S.; Hon. Ph.D., Nat. Autonomous Univ. of Mexico 1979. *Publications:* over 200 papers in fields of intermediary nitrogen metabolism, enzymology, differentiation and development, comparative biochemistry. *Address:* Department of Physiological Chemistry,

587 Medical Sciences Bldg., University of Wisconsin. Madison, Wis. 53706; 1117 Oak Way, Madison, Wis. 53705, U.S.A. (Home).

COHEN, Robert; British cellist; b. 15 June 1959, London; s. of Raymond Cohen and Anthya Rael; m. Rachel Smith 1987; ed. Purcell School and Guildhall School of Music, cello studies with William Pleeth, André Navarra, Jacqueline du Pré and Mstislav Rostropovich; started playing cello at age of 5; Royal Festival Hall début (Boccherini Concerto), aged 12; London recital début, Wigmore Hall, aged 17; Tanglewood Festival, U.S.A. 1978; recording début (Elgar concerto) 1979; concerts U.S.A., Europe and Eastern Europe 1979; since 1980, concerts world-wide with maj. orchestras and with conductors who include Muti, Abbado, Dorati, Sinopoli, Mazur, Davis, Marriner and Rattle; regular int. radio broadcasts and many int. TV appearances; plays on the "Bonjour" Stradivarius cello dated 1692. *Recordings:* Elgar concerto, Dvořák concerto, Tchaikovsky Rococo Variations, Rodrigo Concierto en modo Galante, Beethoven Triple concerto, Grieg sonata, Franck sonata, Virtuoso Cello Music record, Dvořák Complete Piano trios with Cohen Trio, Schubert String Quintet with Amadeus Quartet. *Leisure interests:* photography, squash, cars, computers. *Address:* c/o Intermusica Artists' Management, 16 Duncan Terrace, London, N1 8BZ, England. *Telephone:* 01-278 5455.

COHEN, Ruth Louisa, C.B.E., M.A.; British university official; b. 10 Nov. 1906, Bushey Heath; d. of the late Walter and of Lucy (née Cobb) Cohen; ed. Newnham Coll., Cambridge; Commonwealth Fund Fellow, Stanford and Cornell Univs., U.S.A. 1930–32; Research Officer, Agricultural Research Inst., Oxford 1933–39; with Ministry of Food 1939–42, Bd. of Trade 1942–45; Fellow, Newnham Coll., Cambridge 1939–54, Principal 1954–72, Univ. lecturer in Econs. 1945–74; Gov. Hebrew Univ. of Jerusalem; lay mem. Gen. Medical Council 1961–76; City Councillor, Cambridge 1973–87. *Publications:* History of Milk Prices 1936, Economics of Agriculture 1939. *Address:* 2 Croft Lodge, Cambridge, England. *Telephone:* Cambridge 62699.

COHEN, Seymour Stanley, B.S., PH.D.; American biochemist; b. 30 April 1917, New York City; s. of Herman Cohen and Lena Tanz; m. Elaine Pear 1940; one s. one d.; ed. Coll. of City of New York and Columbia Univ.; NRC Fellow 1941–42 (to work with W. Stanley at Rockefeller Inst.), Research Assoc., Johnson Foundation, Univ. of Pa. 1943–45; Instructor in Dept. of Pediatrics, Univ. of Pa. 1945–50, Assoc. Prof. of Biochemistry and Pediatrics 1950–54, Prof. 1954–57, Charles Hayden American Cancer Soc. Prof. of Biochemistry 1957, Hartzell Prof. and Chair. Dept. of Therapeutic Research, School of Medicine, Univ. of Pa. 1963–71; American Cancer Soc. Prof. of Microbiology, Univ. of Colorado School of Medicine 1971–76; American Cancer Soc. Prof. of Pharmacological Sciences, New York State Univ. 1976–85, Prof. Emer. 1985–; Fellow, John Simon Guggenheim Foundation (to work with A. Lwoff and J. Monod at Pasteur Inst., Paris) 1947–48, 1982–83; Lalor Fellow, Marine Biology Lab., Woods Hole, Mass. 1951–52; Fellow Nat. Humanities Center 1982–83, 1985; Lady Davis Fellow 1983; Visiting Investigator, Virus Lab., Univ. of Calif. 1955, Inst. de Radium, Paris 1967; Instructor in Physiology, Marine Biology Lab. 1968–; mem. N.A.S., Serbian Acad. of Science and Arts; mem. American Acad. of Arts and Sciences; Visiting Prof. Hebrew Univ. (Jerusalem) 1974, Collège de France 1970; Consultant for Science, American Cancer Soc. 1973–76; mem. Inst. of Medicine 1973–; Fogarty Scholar, Nat. Insts. of Health 1973–74; Visiting Smithsonian Scholar 1973–74; Dr. h.c. (Univ. of Louvain, Belgium) 1972, (Univ. of Kuopio, Finland) 1982; Eli Lilly Award of American Soc. of Bacteriology 1951, Mead Johnson Award, American Acad. of Pediatrics 1952, Newcomb Cleveland Award (A.A.A.S.) 1955, Medal, Soc. Chimie Biologique 1964, Borden Award, Asscn. American Medical Colls., Passano Award 1974; Karl August Forster Prize of Mainz Acad. of Science and Letters 1978, Townsend Harris Medal of Coll. of City of New York Alumni Assn. 1978. *Publications:* Virus-Induced Enzymes (The Jesup Lectures) 1968, Introduction to the Polyamines 1971, about 280 papers. *Leisure interests:* tennis, history. *Address:* 10 Carrothill Road, Woods Hole, Mass. 02543, U.S.A. (Home). *Telephone:* (617) 548-7435 (Home).

COHEN, Stanley, B.A., PH.D.; American professor of biochemistry; b. 17 Nov. 1922, Brooklyn, New York; s. of Louis Cohen and Fruma Feitel; m. 1st Olivia Larson 1951, 2nd Jan Elizabeth Jordan 1981; three s.; ed. Brooklyn and Oberlin Colls., Univ. of Michigan; Teaching Fellow, Dept. of Biochemistry, Univ. of Mich. 1946–48; Instructor, Depts. of Biochemistry and Pediatrics, Univ. of Colo. School of Medicine, Denver 1948–52; Postdoctoral Fellow, American Cancer Soc., Dept. of Radiology, Washington Univ., St. Louis 1952–53; Asst. Prof. of Biochemistry, Vanderbilt Univ. School of Medicine, Nashville 1959–62, Assoc. Prof. 1962–67, Prof. 1967–86, Distinguished Prof. 1986–; mem. Editorial Bds. Excerpta Medica, Abstracts of Human Developmental Biology, Journal of Cellular Physiology; mem. N.A.S., American Soc. of Biological Chemists, Int. Inst. of Embryology, American Acad. of Arts and Sciences; Hon. D.Sc. (Chicago) 1985; Nobel Prize for Physiology and Medicine 1986 and many other prizes and awards. *Leisure interests:* camping, tennis. *Address:* Department of Biochemistry, Vanderbilt University School of Medicine, 507 Light Hall, Nashville, Tenn. 37232, U.S.A.

COHEN, Stanley, M.D.; American pathologist; b. 4 June 1937, New York; s. of Herman Joseph Cohen and Eva Lapidus; m. Marion Doris Cantor

1959; two s. one d.; ed. Stuyvesant High School, Columbia Coll. and Columbia Univ. Coll. of Physicians and Surgeons; Internship and Residency, Albert Einstein Medical Center and Harvard-Mass. Gen. 1962–64; Instructor, Dept. of Pathology, New York Univ. Medical Center 1965–66; Captain, M.C., U.S.A., Walter Reed Inst. of Research 1966–68; Assoc. Prof., State Univ. of New York at Buffalo 1968–72, Assoc. Dir., Center for Immunology 1972–74, Prof. of Pathology 1972–74; Assoc. Chair. Dept. of Pathology, Univ. of Conn. Health Center 1976–80, Prof. of Pathology 1974–; Chair. Dept. of Pathology, Hahnemann Medical Center 1986–; Kinne Award 1954; Borden Award 1961; Parke-Davis Award in Experimental Pathology 1977; Outstanding Investigator Award, Nat. Cancer Inst. 1986; Co-Chair. Int. Lymphokine Workshop 1979, 1982 and 1984. *Publications:* 175 scientific articles on cellular immunity, ed. 7 books including Mechanisms of Cell-Medicated Immunity 1977, Mechanisms of Immunopathology 1979, The Biology of the Lymphokines 1979, Interleukins, Lymphokines and Cytokines 1983, Molecular Basis of Lymphatic Action 1986, The Role of Lymphatics in the Immune Response 1989. *Leisure interests:* music, photography, karate. *Address:* Department of Pathology, Hahnemann Medical Center, Philadelphia, Pa. 19102, U.S.A. *Telephone:* (215) 448-8520.

COHEN, Stanley, B.A., M.D.; American educator and geneticist; b. 17 Feb. 1935, Perth Amboy, N.J.; s. of Bernard and Ida (Stolz) Cohen; m. Joanna Lucy Wolter 1961; one s. one d.; ed. Rutgers Univ., New Brunswick, N.J. and Univ. of Pennsylvania School of Medicine, Philadelphia, Pa.; intern, The Mount Sinai Hosp., New York 1960–61; Asst. Resident in Medicine, Univ. Hosp., Ann Arbor, Mich. 1961–62; Clinical Assoc., Arthritis and Rheumatism Branch, Nat. Inst. of Arthritis and Metabolic Diseases 1962–64; Sr. Resident in Medicine, Duke Univ. Hosp., Durham, N.C. 1964–65; American Cancer Soc. Postdoctoral Research Fellow, Dept. of Molecular Biology and Dept. of Developmental Biology and Cancer, Albert Einstein Coll. of Medicine, Bronx, New York 1965–67; Asst. Prof. of Medicine, Stanford Univ. School of Medicine 1968–71, Head, Div. of Clinical Pharmacology 1969–78, Assoc. Prof. of Medicine 1971–75, Prof. of Genetics 1977 and Prof. of Medicine 1975–, Chair. Dept. of Genetics 1978–86; Kinyoun Lecturer 1981, Wolf Prize in Medicine 1981, Marvin J. Johnson Award, American Chemical Soc. 1980, Albert Lasker Basic Medical Research Award 1980. *Address:* Department of Genetics S-337, Stanford University School of Medicine, Stanford, Calif. 94305, U.S.A. *Telephone:* (415) 497-5315.

COHEN, Prof. Sydney, C.B.E., M.D., PH.D., F.R.C.PATH., F.R.S.; British doctor of medicine and university professor; b. 18 Sept. 1921, Johannesburg, S. Africa; s. of Morris and Pauline Cohen; m. June Bernice Adler 1950; one s. one d.; ed. King Edward VII School, Witwatersrand Univ., Johannesburg, Univ. of London; Emergency Medical Service, U.K. 1944–46; lecturer, Dept. of Physiology, Univ. of Witwatersrand 1947–53; mem. Scientific Staff, Nat. Inst. for Medical Research, London 1954–60; Reader, Dept. of Immunology, St. Mary's Hosp., London 1960–65; Prof. of Chemical Pathology, Guy's Hosp. Medical School, London 1965–86; Consultant American Inst. of Biological Sciences 1987–; mem. MRC 1974–76, Chair. Tropical Medicine Research Bd. 1974–76, Assessor 1983–85; Chair. WHO Scientific group on Immunity to Malaria 1976–81; mem. Council, Royal Soc. 1981–83; Nuffield Dominion Fellow in Medicine 1954; Founding Fellow, Royal Coll. of Pathologists 1964; Hon. D.Sc. (Witwatersrand) 1987. *Publications:* papers and books on immunology and parasitic infections. *Leisure interests:* golf, gardening, hill-farming. *Address:* 4 Frognal Rise, London, NW3 6RD, England; Hafodfraith, Llangurig SY18 6GG, Wales (Homes). *Telephone:* (01) 435 6507 (London Home).

COHEN, William S., A.B., LL.B.; American politician; b. 28 Aug. 1940, Bangor, Maine; s. of Reuben and Clara (née Hartley) Cohen; ed. Bangor High School, Bowdoin Coll., Boston Univ. Law School; admitted to Maine Bar 1965; Asst. Ed.-in-Chief Journal of the American Trial Lawyers Assn. 1965–66; Asst. Attorney, Penobscot County, Maine 1968–70, instructor Husson Coll., Bangor 1968, Univ. of Maine at Orono 1968–72; City Councillor, Bangor 1969–72, Mayor 1971–72; elected to Congress 1972, re-elected 1974, 1976, Senator 1978–; Vice-Chair. Select Cttee. on Intelligence; mem. Armed Services Cttee., Projection Forces and Regional Defense Subcttee. (Ranking Republican), Sub-cttee. on Strategic Forces and Nuclear Deterrence, Sub-cttee. on Conventional Forces and Alliance Defense, Select Cttee. on Secret Mil. Assistance to Iran and the Nicaraguan Opposition, Governmental Affairs Cttee., Sub-cttee. on Oversight of Govt. Man. (Ranking Republican), Perm. Sub-cttee. on Investigations, Sub-cttee. on Governmental Efficiency, Federalism and the Dist. of Columbia; Founder and Co-Chair. Senate Footwear Caucus; Fellow of John F. Kennedy Inst. of Politics, Harvard 1972; award for Distinguished Public Service, Boston Univ. Alumni Assn. 1976, L. Mendel Rivers Award, Non-Commissioned Officers' Assn. 1983, President's Award, New England Assn. of School Superintendents 1984, Silver Anniversary Award, Nat. Collegiate Athletic Assn. 1987, numerous other awards. *Publications:* Of Sons and Seasons 1978, Roll Call 1981, Getting the Most out of Washington 1982 (with Prof. Kenneth Lasson), The Double Man 1985 (with Senator Gary Hart), A Baker's Nickel 1986, Men of Zeal (with Senator George Mitchell) 1988. *Leisure interests:* poetry, sport. *Address:* 322 Hart Senate Office Building, Washington, D.C. 20510, U.S.A. (Office). *Telephone:* 202-224-2523 (Office).

COHN, Haim; Israeli lawyer; b. 11 March 1911, Lübeck, Germany; s. of Zeev Cohn and Miriam Cohn (née Carlebach); m. 1st Else Benjamin 1933,

2nd Michal Smoira; one s. one d.; ed. Univs. of Munich, Hamburg and Frankfurt-on-Main, Germany, Hebrew Univ. of Jerusalem and Govt. Law School, Jerusalem; admitted to Bar of Palestine 1937; Sec. Legal Council Jewish Agency for Palestine, Jerusalem 1947; State Attorney, Ministry of Justice, Hakirya 1948, Dir.-Gen. 1949; Attorney-Gen., Govt. of Israel 1950; Minister of Justice and Acting Attorney-Gen. 1952; Attorney-Gen., later Justice, Supreme Court of Israel 1960–81; mem. Perm. Court of Arbitration, The Hague 1962–, UN Comm. on Human Rights 1957–59, 1965–67; Deputy Chair. Council of Higher Educ., Israel 1958–71; mem. Bd. of Govs., Int. Inst. of Human Rights, Strasbourg; fmr. Chair. Exec. Council Hebrew Univ. of Jerusalem; Visiting Prof. Emer. of Law, Univ. of Tel-Aviv; Visiting Prof. Emer. of Jurisprudence, Hebrew Univ. of Jerusalem; mem. Int. Comm. of Jurists, Pres. Int. Asscn. of Jewish Lawyers and Jurists, Israel Civil Rights Asscn. 1981–; Hon. Pres. Int. Center for Peace in the Middle East 1982–; Haim Cohn Chair of Human Rights, Hebrew Univ. of Jerusalem; LL.D. h.c. John Jay Coll. of Criminal Justice, City Univ. of N.Y. 1980, Georgetown Univ., Washington 1981, Univ. of Aberdeen 1981, Hon. D.Litt. (Hebrew Union Coll., Cincinnati) 1982, Hon. D.Sc. (Weizmann Inst. of Science, Rehovot) 1982. *Publications:* The Foreign Laws of Marriage and Divorce (English) 1937, Glaube und Glaubensfreiheit (German) 1967, The Trial and Death of Jesus (Hebrew) 1968, The Trial and Death of Jesus (English) 1971, Jewish Law in Ancient and Modern Israel (English) 1972, Human Rights in Jewish Law 1983. *Address:* 36 Tchernihovsky Street, Jerusalem, Israel. *Telephone:* (02) 63-9973.

COHN, Mildred, M.A., PH.D.; American professor of biochemistry and biophysics; b. 12 July 1913, New York City; d. of Isidore M. Cohn and Bertha Klein; m. Henry Primakoff 1938; one s. two d.; ed. Hunter Coll. and Columbia Univ.; Cornell Univ. Medical Coll., New York 1938–46; Washington Univ. Medical School, St. Louis, Mo. 1946–60; Prof. of Biophysics and Biophysical Chem., Univ. of Pa. School of Medicine 1961–75, Prof. of Biochemistry and Biophysics 1975–82; Benjamin Rush Prof. of Physiological Chem. 1975–82, Prof. Emer. 1982–; Career Investigator, American Heart Asscn. 1964–78; Sr. mem. Inst. for Cancer Research 1982–85; mem. American Acad. of Arts and Sciences, N.A.S., American Philosophical Soc.; Hon. Sc.D. (Women's Medical Coll. of Pennsylvania) 1966, (Radcliffe Coll.) 1978, (Washington Univ.) 1981, (Brandeis, Hunter Coll., Univ. of Pennsylvania) 1984, (N. Carolina) 1985, Hon. PH.D. (Weizmann Inst. of Science) 1988; Cresson Medal, Franklin Inst. 1975, Garvan Medal, American Chem. Soc, Nat. Medal for Science 1982, Chandler Medal, Columbia Univ. 1986, Distinguished Service Award, Coll. of Physicians, Phila 1987, Remsen Award, Maryland Section, American Chemical Soc. 1988. *Publications:* articles in professional journals, etc. *Leisure interest:* hiking. *Address:* Dept. of Biochemistry and Biophysics, Pa. Univ. School of Medicine, Philadelphia, Pa. 19104-6089 (Office); 747 Clarendon Road, Narberth, Pa. 19072, U.S.A. (Home). *Telephone:* (215) 898-8404 (Office); (215) 667-4674 (Home).

COHN, Norman, M.A., D.LITT., F.B.A.; British author and historian; b. 12 Jan. 1915, London; s. of August Cohn and Daisy Cohn (née Reimer); m. Vera Broido 1941; one s.; ed. Gresham's School, Holt and Christ Church Oxford; served in Queen's Royal Regt. and Intelligence Corps 1940–46; lecturer in French, Glasgow Univ. 1946–51; Prof. of French, Magee Univ. Coll. (then associated with Trinity Coll. Dublin), Ireland 1951–60; Prof. of French, King's Coll., Durham Univ. 1960–63; changed career to become Dir. Columbus Centre, Sussex Univ. and Gen. Ed. of Centre's Studies in Persecution and Extermination 1966–80; Professorial Fellow, Sussex Univ. 1966–73, Astor-Wolfson Prof. 1973–80, Prof. Emer. 1980–; Visiting Prof. King's Coll., London 1986–; Adviser, Montreal Inst. for Genocide Studies 1986–; Hon. LL.D. (Concordia, Canada); Anisfield-Wolf Award in Race Relations 1967. *Publications:* Gold Khan and other Siberian Legends 1946, The Pursuit of the Millennium: revolutionary millenarians and mystical anarchists of the middle ages 1957, Warrant for Genocide: the myth of the Jewish world-conspiracy and the Protocols of the Elders of Zion 1967, Europe's Inner Demons: an enquiry inspired by the great witch-hunt 1975. *Leisure interests:* travel, walking, looking at pictures, butterfly-watching. *Address:* Orchard Cottage, Wood End, Ardeley, Herts., SG2 7AZ, England. *Telephone:* (0438) 85-247.

COHN, Paul Moritz, PH.D., F.R.S.; British professor of mathematics; b. 8 Jan. 1924, Hamburg, Germany; s. of James and Julia (née Cohen) Cohn; m. Deirdre S. Sharon 1958; two d.; ed. Trinity Coll., Cambridge; Chargé de Recherches, Nancy, France 1951–52; lecturer, Univ of Manchester 1952–62; Visiting Prof., Yale Univ. 1961–62; Reader, Queen Mary Coll., London 1963–67; Visiting Prof, Univ. of Chicago 1964; Prof. and Head, Dept. of Math., Bedford Coll., London 1967–84; Prof., Univ. Coll. London 1984–, Astor Prof. of Mathematics 1986–; Pres. London Mathematical Soc. 1982–84; mem. Math. Cttee., S.R.C. 1977–80, Council, Royal Soc. 1985–87; L.R. Ford Award 1972, Berwick Prize 1974. *Publications:* Universal Algebra 1965, 1981, Free Rings and Their Relations 1971, 1985, Algebra 1, 2 1974, 1982 (books translated in Italian, Spanish, Russian, Chinese); research papers in algebra. *Leisure interest:* language in all its forms. *Address:* Department of Mathematics, University College, London: Gower Street, London, WC1E 6BT, England. *Telephone:* (01) 387 7050.

COING, Helmut, DR. JUR.; German jurist; b. 28 Feb. 1912; s. of Herman and Elisabeth (Krüger) Coing; m. Hilde Knetsch 1941; one d.; ed. Hanover,

Lille, Kiel, Munich and Göttingen; Prof. of Jurisprudence, Goethe Univ., Frankfurt (Main) 1940, Ord. Prof. 1948, Faculty Dean 1950–51, Univ. Rector 1955–57; Pres. West German Conf. of Rectors 1956–57, Wissenschaftsrat 1958–61; Chair. Wissenschaftlicher Beirat, F. Thyssen-Stiftung 1961–; Dir. Max Planck Inst. for History of European Law 1964–80; Vice-Pres. Max Planck Gesellschaft zur Förderung der Wissenschaften e.V., Munich 1978–84; Chancellor of Order Pour le Mérite für Wissenschaften und Künste 1984; mem. Bayerische Akad. der Wissenschaften, Accademia delle Scienze dell'Istituto di Bologna 1965; corresp. mem. Accademia Nazionale dei Lincei 1984; Commendatore Ordine al Merito (Italy); Stern zum Grossen Verdienstkreuz des Verdienstordens der Bundesrepublik Deutschland, Officier de la Légion d'honneur (France), Orden Pour le Mérite für Wissenschaft und Künste 1973, Premio Galileo Galilei (Italy) 1980, etc.; Dr. Iur. h.c. Lyon, Montpellier, Vienna, Aberdeen, Brussels and Uppsala. *Publications:* Die Rezeption des römischen Rechts in Frankfurt am Main 1939, Die obersten Grundsätze des Rechts 1947, Grundzüge der Rechtsphilosophie 1950, 1969, 1976, 1985, Lehrbuch des Erbrechts 1953, Staudinger-Kommentar zum Allgemeinen Teil des BGB 1957 and 1978–80, Römisches Recht in Deutschland (contribution to Ius Romanum Medii Aevi) 1964, Epochen d. Rechtsgeschichte in Deutschland 1967, 1971, Rechtsformen der privaten Vermögens-verwaltung insbesondere durch Banken in U.S.A. und Deutschland 1967, Die Treuhand, kraft privaten Rechtsgeschäfts 1973, Gesammelte Aufsätze zu Rechtsgeschichte, Rechtsphilosophie und Zivilrecht 1982; Ed. Handbuch der Quellen und Literatur der neueren europäischen Privatrechtsgeschichte Vol. I 1972, Vols. II/1 and II/2 1976/7, III/1 and III/2 1982, Aufgaben des Rechtshistorikers 1978, Europaisches Privatrecht 1500–1800 1985. *Leisure interests:* history, architecture. *Address:* Max-Planck-Institut für europäische Rechtsgeschichte, Freiherr-vom-Stein-Strasse 7, 6000 Frankfurt-am-Main (Office); Holzhecke 14, 6 Frankfurt-am-Main, Federal Republic of Germany. *Telephone:* 0611-7120 247 (Office).

COINTAT, Michel; French agronomist and politician; b. 13 April 1921, Paris; s. of Lucien Cointat and Marie-Louise Adam; m. Simone Dubois 1942; two s.; ed. Ecole Nat. des Eaux et Forêts; Insp. of water and forests, Uzès, Gard 1943–49; Insp. forests of Haute-Marne 1950–58; Dir. Gen. Soc. for Devt. of waste ground and scrub lands of the East 1948–61, Pres. 1961–71; Dir. du Cabinet, Ministry of Agriculture 1961–62, Dir. Gen. of Production and Supply 1962–67; Pres. Special Agricultural Cttee. to EEC 1965; Minister of Agriculture 1971–72, of External Trade 1980–81; Deputy Rassemblement pour la République (fmrly. Union Démocratique pour la République) for Ile-et-Vilaine 1967–71, 1981–; mem. European Parl. 1968–71, 1974–79; Mayor of Fougères 1971–83; Pres. Financial Comm. in Regional Council of Brittany; Pres. Special Comm. to examine proposed land law; Dir. Editions Ufap 1975–83; mem. various local socs.; Chevalier, Légion d'honneur; Officier de l'Ordre national du Mérite; Commandeur du Mérite agricole; Officier des Palmes académiques; Chevalier de l'Economie nationale; Grand Officier du Mérite (Fed. Repub. of Germany); Grand Officier de l'Ordre de Victoria; Commandeur du Mérite Italien; Grand Officier de l'Ordre de la Haute-Volta. *Publications:* about 500 articles on agriculture, forestry, fishing and related subjects; collections of poems: Souvenirs du temps perdu 1957, Poèmes à Clio 1965, Les heures orangées 1974, les Moments inutiles 1983. *Address:* Assemblée Nationale, 75355 Paris; 1 boulevard du Général Leclerc, 35300 Fougères, France.

COKE, Gerald Edward, C.B.E.; British merchant banker; b. 25 Oct. 1907, London; s. of Hon. Sir John Coke, K.C.V.O., and Hon. Mrs. Coke; m. Patricia Cadogan 1939; three s. (one s. deceased) one d.; ed. Eton and New Coll., Oxford; Lieut.-Col., Second World War; Chair. Rio Tinto Co. Ltd. 1956–62; Deputy Chair. Rio Tinto-Zinc Corpn. 1962–66, Dir. 1947–75; Deputy Chair. Mercury Securities Ltd. 1964–70; fmr. Dir. S. G. Warburg and Co. Ltd. 1945–75, U.K. Provident Inst. 1952–74 and other companies; Treas. Bridewell Royal Hospital (King Edward's School), Witley 1946–72; Chair. Glyndebourne Arts Trust 1955–75; Gov. Royal Acad. of Music 1957–73; Dir. Royal Opera House, Covent Garden 1959–64; Gov. of BBC 1961–66; Hon. F.R.A.M.; D.L. (Hants) 1974. *Publication:* In Search of James Giles 1983. *Address:* Jenkyn Place, Bentley, Hants., England. *Telephone:* Bentley 23118.

COKER, Peter Godfrey, R.A., A.R.C.A.; British artist; b. 27 July 1926; m. Vera J. Crook 1951; one s. (deceased); ed. St. Martin's School of Art, Royal Coll. of Art; one-man exhbns. include Zwemmer Gallery, 1956, 1957, 1959, 1964, 1967, Thackeray Gallery, London 1950, 1972, 1974, 1975, 1976, 1978, Gallery 10, London 1980, 1982, 1984–86; retrospective exhbn. Royal Acad. 1979; has participated in numerous group shows including Tate Gallery 1958, Royal Coll. of Art 1952–62, Royal Acad. Bicentenary Exhbn. 1968, British Painting 1952–77, Royal Acad. and at other galleries in U.K., Austria and Canada; works in numerous perm. collections in U.K. including Tate Gallery, Arts Council, Chantrey Bequest, Victoria & Albert Museum, Nat. Portrait Gallery, Nat. Maritime Museum etc.; Arts Council Award 1976. *Publication:* Etching Techniques 1976. *Address:* The Red House, Mistley, Manningtree, Essex, England. *Telephone:* Manningtree 2179.

ČOLAKOVIĆ, Božidar, D.SC.; Yugoslav physician; b. 10 Jan. 1931, Kosovska Mitrovica; m. Danica Čolaković 1955; one s. one d.; Dir. Medical Centre 1957–70; Sec. for Health and Social Politics of Serbia 1970–72; Gen. Dir. Inst. for Protection of Health, Repub. of Serbia 1972–74; Sec. for Health

COL INTERNATIONAL WHO'S WHO COL

and Social Politics of S.A.P. of Kosovo 1974–78; Chief of Dept. at Faculty of Medicine Univ. of Prishtina 1978–85; Dean, Faculty of Medicine 1983–85, Rector 1985–(89); recipient of several awards. *Publications:* more than 500 scientific and professional works. *Address:* University of Prishtina, 38000 Prishtina, M. Tita-53 (Office); Dardania SU6/2, 38000 Prishtina, Yugoslavia (Home).

COLBERT, Claudette (Lily Claudette Chauchoin); American actress; b. 13 Sept. 1903, Paris, France; d. of Georges and Jeanne (née Loew) Chauchoin; m. 1st Norman Foster 1928 (divorced 1934); 2nd Joel Pressman, 1935 (deceased 1968); made theatre début in The Wild Westcotts 1923; also appeared in We've Got to Have Money 1923, High Stakes 1924, Ginette in A Kiss in the Taxi, 1925; on Broadway in Fast Life 1928, Dynamo, See Naples and Die 1928; made London début as Lou in The Barker, 1928; also on Broadway in Janus 1956, Julio, Jake and Uncle Joe 1962, The Irregular Verb to Love 1963, The Kingfisher 1978, A Talent for Murder 1981, Aren't We All 1986. *Films include:* For the Love of Mike 1928, The Hole in the Wall 1929, The Lady Lies 1929, The Big Pond 1930, Young Man of Manhattan 1930, The Smiling Lieutenant 1931, Secrets of a Secretary 1931, His Woman 1931, Man From Yesterday 1932, The Sign of the Cross 1932, Cleopatra 1933, Tonight Is Ours 1933, I Cover the Waterfront 1933, Three Cornered Moon 1933, The Torch Singer 1933, Four Frightened People 1934, It Happened One Night 1934, Imitation of Life 1934, She Married Her Boss 1935, The Bride Comes Home 1935, I Met Him In Paris 1937, Tovarich 1937, Midnight 1939, It's a Wonderful World 1939, Drums Along the Mohawk 1939, Boom Town 1940, Arise my Love 1940, Skylark 1941, The Palm Beach Story 1942, So Proudly We Hail 1943, Since you Went Away 1944, Guest Wife 1945, The Egg and I 1947, Sleep My Love 1948, Bride For Sale 1949, Three Came Home 1950, Thunder on the Hill 1951, Love and the French Woman 1954, Texas Lady 1955, Parrish 1960; First appeared on television in the 1950's in such productions as Blithe Spirit, The Guardsman, One Coat of White; also hostess for the monthly documentary series Women 1959–60; Academy Award for Best Actress for It Happened One Night. *Address:* Bellerive, St Peter, Barbados, West Indies.

COLBERT, Edwin Harris, A.M., D.SC., PH.D.; American vertebrate palaeontologist; b. 28 Sept. 1905, Clarinda, Iowa; s. of George H. and Mary A. Colbert; m. Margaret Matthew 1933; five s.; ed. Univ. of Nebraska and Columbia Univ.; Student Asst. Univ. of Nebraska 1926–29; Univ. Fellow Columbia Univ. 1929–30; Research Asst. American Museum of Natural History 1930–32, Asst. Curator 1933–42, Curator and Chair. Dept. of Amphibians and Reptiles 1944–45, Chair. Dept. of Geology and Palaeontology 1958–60; Dept. of Vertebrate Palaeontology 1960–66, Curator 1966–70, Curator Emer. 1970–; Prof. Vertebrate Palaeontology, Columbia Univ. 1945–69, Prof. Emer. 1969–; Assoc. Curator, Acad. of Natural Sciences of Philadelphia 1937–48; Research Assoc., Museum of N. Ariz. 1954–68, Hon. Curator of Vertebrate Palaeontology 1970–; mem. N.A.S.; Pres. Soc. of Vertebrate Palaeontology 1946–47, Soc. for Study of Evolution 1958; Vice-Pres. Palaeontological Soc. 1963–; Daniel Giraud Elliot Medal (N.A.S.), American Museum of Nat. History Medal 1970. *Publications:* The Dinosaur Book 1951, Evolution of the Vertebrates 1955, 1969, 1980, Millions of Years Ago: Prehistoric Life in North America 1958, Dinosaurs 1961, Stratigraphy and Life History (with Marshall Kay) 1965, The Age of Reptiles 1965, Men and Dinosaurs 1968, Wandering Lands and Animals 1973, The Year of the Dinosaur 1977, A Fossil Hunter's Notebook 1980, Dinosaurs, An Illustrated History 1983, and over 300 papers, etc. *Leisure interests:* history, travel. *Address:* The Museum of Northern Arizona, Route 4, Box 720, Flagstaff, Arizona 86001, U.S.A. *Telephone:* 602-774-5211.

COLBERT, Lester Lum, B.B.A., LL.B.; American automobile manufacturer; b. 13 June 1905; s. of Lun and Sallie (née Driver) Colbert; m. Daisy Gorman 1928 (died 1970); two s. one d.; ed. Texas and Harvard Univs.; cotton buyer, Texas 1921–29; law practice with Larkin, Rathbone and Perry (New York) 1929–33; joined Chrysler Corpn. 1933; Resident Attorney 1933–36; Vice-Pres. Dodge Div. 1936–46; Gen. Man. Dodge Chicago plant (aircraft engines) 1943–46; Pres. Dodge Div. 1946–51; Vice-Pres. Chrysler Corpn. 1949–50, Dir. 1949–61, Pres. 1950–61, Chair. of Bd. 1960–61; Dir. Devt. Bd., Univ. of Tex. 1958–; Trustee Hanover Bank and Automotive Safety Foundation 1955–61; mem. Automobile Mfrs.' Assen. (Pres. 1958–61); mem. American Bar Assen.; mem. Nat. Industrial Conf. Bd.; Hon. LL.D. Bethany Coll.; Chevalier de la Légion d'honneur; Distinguished Alumnus, Univ. of Tex., Austin 1977. *Address:* 812 Colonial Court, Birmingham, Mich. 48009 (Office); 3401 Gulf Shore Boulevard N., Naples, Fla. 33940, U.S.A. (Home).

COLBY, William Egan, B.A., LL.B.; American lawyer, consultant and government official; b. 4 Jan. 1920, St. Paul, Minn.; s. of Elbridge and Margaret Colby (née Egan); m. 1st Barbara Heinzen 1945, three s. one d.; m. 2nd Sally Shelton 1984; ed. Princeton and Columbia Univs.; served to rank of Maj., U.S. Army 1941–45; admitted to N.Y. State Bar 1947, District of Colombia Bar 1976; Attorney Donovan, Leisure, Newton & Irvine 1947–49, Counsel 1987–; Attorney Nat. Labor Relations Bd. 1949–50; Attaché, American Embassy, Stockholm 1951–53, Rome 1953–58, First Sec., Saigon 1959–62; Head, Far East Div., Cen. Intelligence Agency 1963–67; Amb., Dir. Civil Operations and Rural Devt. Support, Saigon 1968–71; Exec. Dir. CIA 1972–73, Dir. Sept. 1973–76; law and consultancy practice, Washington, D.C. 1976–86; Silver Star Nat. Security Medal,

St. Olav Medal (Norway), Croix de guerre (France), CIA Distinguished Intelligence Medal, Dept. of State Distinguished Honor Award, Grand Officer, Nat. Order of Viet-Nam. *Publication:* Honorable Men—My Life in the CIA 1978. *Address:* 3028 Dent Place, N.W., Washington, D.C. 20007, U.S.A. *Telephone:* (202) 338-5231.

COLE, Sir (Alexander) Colin, K.C.V.O., O.ST.J., T.D., B.C.L., M.A., F.S.A., F.R.S.A., F.H.S.; British Garter King of Arms; b. 16 May 1922, London; s. of Capt. Edward Harold and Blanche Ruby Lavinia (Wallis) Cole; m. Valerie Card 1944; four s. three d.; ed. Dulwich Coll. and Brasenose Coll. Oxford; Barrister-at-Law, Inner Temple; Capt., Coldstream Guards 1939–45; rank of Major, Honourable Artillery Co. (TA); Lieut.-Col. Queen's Regt. (TA) RARO 1973; Hon. Col. 6/7th Bn. Queen's Regt. 1983–87; Fitzalan Pursuivant of Arms Extraordinary 1953; Portcullis Pursuivant of Arms 1957; Windsor Herald of Arms 1966–78, Garter Principal King of Arms 1978–; Kt. Prin., Imperial Soc. of Knights Bachelor 1983–; mem. Court of Common Council, City of London 1964–, Sheriff of City of London 1976–77; Master, Scriveners Co. of London 1978–79; Pres. Royal Soc. of St. George 1982–; mem. Int. Acad. of Heraldry; Cruz Distinguida (1st Class), Orden de San Raimundo de Penafort. *Publications:* numerous articles; illustrator: Visitation of London 1568, Visitation of Wiltshire 1623. *Leisure interests:* architecture, wine-tasting, archaeology. *Address:* The College of Arms, Queen Victoria Street, London E.C.4; Holly House, Burstow, Surrey, England. *Telephone:* 01-248 1188 (London).

COLE, Andrew Reginald Howard, D.PHIL., D.SC., F.R.A.C.I., F.A.A.; Australian professor of physical chemistry; b. 21 April 1924; s. of late J. H. Cole; m. Ursula Hagan 1955; one s. two d.; ed. Perth Modern School, Univ. of W. Australia and Oxford Univ.; Nuffield Research Fellow, Univ. of W. Australia 1952–55, Sr. Lecturer 1955–57, Reader in Physical Chem. 1958–68, Prof. of Physical Chem. 1969–, Dean, Faculty of Science 1975–77; Visiting Prof. Univ. of Tokyo, Tohoku Univ., Univ. of S. Carolina 1974; mem. Bureau, IUPAC 1973–81; Pres. Royal Australian Chemical Inst. 1981–82; other professional appts.; Leighton Memorial Medal 1984 and other awards. *Publications:* Chemical Properties and Reactions (jtly.) 1976, Tables of Wavenumbers for the Calibration of Infrared Spectrometers 1977. *Leisure interest:* golf. *Address:* 61 Haldane Street, Mt. Claremont, W.A. 6010, Australia. *Telephone:* (09) 384-2880.

COLE, Sir David Lee, K.C.M.G., M.C.; British diplomatist (retd.); b. 31 Aug. 1920, Newmarket, Suffolk; s. of Brig. and Mrs D. H. Cole; m. Dorothy Patton 1945; one s.; ed. Cheltenham Coll., and Sidney Sussex Coll., Cambridge; Royal Inniskilling Fusiliers, Second World War; Dominions Office 1947; U.K. Del. to UN, New York 1948–51; First Sec. British High Comm. New Delhi 1953–56, Private Sec. to Sec. of State for Commonwealth Relations 1956–60; Head, Personnel Dept., Commonwealth Relations Office 1961–63; Deputy High Commr. in Ghana 1963–64, Acting High Commr. 1963; High Commr. in Malawi 1964–67; Minister (Political), High Comm., New Delhi, 1967–70; Asst. Under-Sec. of State, Foreign and Commonwealth Office 1970–73; Amb. to Thailand 1973–78. *Publication:* Rough Road to Rome 1983. *Leisure interest:* watercolour painting. *Address:* 19 Burghley House, Somerset Road, London, SW19 5JB, England.

COLE, Keith David, D.SC., F.A.A.; Australian professor of physics; b. 2 March 1929, Cairns; s. of John C. Cole and Jessie O. Cole; m. A. A. Moore 1956 (dissolved 1981); two s. one d.; ed. Cairns High School and Univ. of Queensland; Australian Nat. Antarctic Research Expedition 1956; Theoretical Physicist, Antarctic Div. 1957–62; Research Assoc. Univs. of Chicago and Colorado 1963–66; Foundation Prof. of Physics, La Trobe Univ. Melbourne 1966–; Sr. Research Assoc. NASA, Goddard Space Flight Center 1969, 1974, 1982; Foreign Sec. and mem. of Council Australian Acad. of Science 1985–89; Pres. Int. Assen. of Geomagnetism and Aeronomy 1979–83, Scientific Cttee. on Solar Terrestrial Physics ICSU 1977–86; Appelton Prize, Royal Soc. *Publications:* over 120 scientific papers. *Leisure interest:* gardening. *Address:* Department of Physics, La Trobe University, Bondoora, Vic. 3083, Australia. *Telephone:* 4792735.

COLEMAN, Donald Cuthbert, B.SC., PH.D., LITT.D., F.R.HIST.S., F.B.A.; British emeritus professor of economic history; b. 21 Jan. 1920, London; s. of Hugh Augustus Coleman and Marian Stella Agnes Cuthbert; m. Jessie Ann Matilda Child (née Stevens) 1954; ed. Haberdashers' Aske's School and London School of Econs., Univ. of London; worked in insurance in London 1937–39; served in army 1940–46; Lecturer in Industrial History, L.S.E. 1951–58, Reader in Econ. History 1958–69, Prof. of Econ. History 1969–71, Hon. Fellow 1984; Prof. of Econ. History, Cambridge Univ. and Fellow of Pembroke Coll. 1971–81, Emer. Prof. 1981–; Visiting Assoc. Prof. of Econs., Yale Univ., U.S.A. 1957–58; English Ed. Scandinavian Economic History Review 1952–61; ed. Economic History Review 1967–72; Gov. Pasold Research Fund 1977–86, Chair. 1986–. *Publications:* The British Paper Industry, 1485–1860 1958, Sir John Banks 1963, Courtaulds: An Economic and Social History (3 vols.) 1969, 1980, The Economy of England, 1450–1750 1977, History and the Economic Past 1987. *Leisure interest:* gardening. *Address:* Over Hall, Cavendish, Sudbury, Suffolk, CO10 8BP, England. *Telephone:* (0787) 280325.

COLEMAN, James Samuel, PH.D.; American sociologist; b. 12 May 1926, Bedford, Ind.; s. of late James F. Coleman and Maurine L. Coleman; m. 1st Lucille Richey 1949 (divorced 1973), 2nd Zdzislawa Walaszek 1973; four

314

s.; ed. Purdue and Columbia Univs.; Research Assoc., Bureau of Applied Social Research, Columbia Univ. 1953–55; Fellow, Center for Advanced Study in the Behavioural Sciences 1955–56; Asst. Prof., Dept. of Sociology, Univ. of Chicago 1956–59; Assoc. Prof., Dept. of Social Relations, Johns Hopkins Univ. 1959, Prof. of Social Relations 1961–73; Prof. of Sociology, Univ. of Chicago 1973–; mem. President's Science Advisory Cttee. 1970–73, General Motors Science Advisory Cttee. 1973–83; mem. American Acad. of Arts and Sciences, N.A.S., Nat. Acad. of Educ., American Philosophical Soc., Royal Acad. of Sciences, Sweden; Guggenheim Fellow 1966; Fellow, Wissenschaftskolleg zu Berlin 1981–82; Hon. LL.D. (Purdue Univ.), (Univ. of Southern Calif.); Hon. D.Hum.Litt. (State Univ. of New York); Hon. Ph.D. (Hebrew Univ.); (Free Univ. of Brussels), (Univ. of Erlangen-Nuremberg); Hon. Prof. Univ. of Vienna. *Publications:* Union Democracy (co-author) 1956, The Adolescent Society 1961, Introduction to Mathematical Sociology 1964, Equality of Educational Opportunity (co-author) 1966, Resources for Social Change: Race in the United States 1971, The Mathematics of Collective Action 1973, Power and the Structure of Society 1974, Longitudinal Data Analysis 1981, The Asymmetric Society 1982, High School Achievement (co-author) 1982, Individual Interests and Collective Action 1986, Public and Private High Schools: The Impact of Communities (co-author) 1987. *Address:* Department of Sociology, University of Chicago, Chicago, Ill. 60637; 5625 Woodlawn Avenue, Chicago, Ill. 60637, U.S.A. (Home). *Telephone:* 312-702-8696 (Office); 312-241-7461 (Home).

COLEMAN, Sidney, PH.D.; American physicist and teacher; b. 7 March 1937, Chicago; s. of Harold Coleman and Sadie (Shanas) Coleman; m. Diana Teschmacher 1982; ed. Illinois Inst. of Tech. and California Inst. of Tech.; mem. Physics Dept., Harvard Univ. 1961–, Donner Prof. of Science 1980–; Fellow American Physical Soc., N.A.S., American Acad. of Arts and Sciences; Trustee, Aspen Center for Physics. *Publications:* numerous tech. papers on high-energy physics; Aspects of Symmetry 1985. *Address:* Physics Department, Harvard University, Cambridge, Mass. 02138; 1 Richdale Avenue, Unit 12, Cambridge, Mass. 02140, U.S.A. (Home). *Telephone:* (617) 495-3763 (Univ.); (617) 492 3491 (Home).

COLEMAN, Terry (Terence Francis Frank), LL.B.; British reporter and author; b. 13 Feb. 1931; s. of J. Coleman and D. I. B. Coleman; m. 1st Lesley Fox-Strangeways Vane 1954 (dissolved), two d.; 2nd Vivien Rosemary Lumsdaine Wallace 1981, one s. one d.; ed. 14 schools and Univ. of London; fmr. Reporter Poole Herald; fmr. Ed. Savoir Faire; fmr. Sub-Ed. Sunday Mercury, Birmingham Post; Reporter then Arts Corresp. The Guardian 1961–70, Chief Feature Writer 1970–74, 1976–79, New York Corresp. 1981, Special Corresp. 1982–89; Special Writer with Daily Mail 1974–76; Assoc. Ed. The Independent 1989–; Feature Writer of the Year, British Press Awards 1982, Journalist of the Year (What the Papers Say Award) 1988. *Publications:* The Railway Navvies 1965 (Yorkshire Post Prize for best first book of the year), A Girl for the Afternoons 1965, Providence and Mr Hardy (with Lois Deacon) 1966, The Only True History: collected journalism 1969, Passage to America 1972, An Indiscretion in the Life of an Heiress (Hardy's first novel) (Ed.) 1976, The Liners 1976, The Scented Brawl: collected journalism 1978, Southern Cross 1979, Thanksgiving 1981, Movers and Shakers: collected interviews 1987, Thatcher's Britain 1987. *Leisure interests:* cricket, opera and circumnavigation. *Address:* 18 North Side, London, S.W.4, England.

COLEMAN, William Thaddeus, Jr.; American lawyer and government official; b. 7 July 1920, Philadelphia; s. of William Thaddeus and Laura Beatrice (née Mason) Coleman; m. Lovinda Hardin 1945; two s. one d.; ed. Univ. of Pennsylvania, Harvard Law School; Law Sec. to Judge Herbert Goodrich, U.S. Court of Appeals, Third Circuit 1947; Law Clerk, U.S. Supreme Court 1948; Assoc. Paul, Weiss, Rifkind, Wharton & Garrison, law firm 1949–52; Assoc. Dilworth, Paxson, Kalish, Levy & Coleman 1952, Partner 1956–75; mem. President's Cttee. on Govt. Employment Policy 1959–61; Consultant to U.S. Arms Control and Disarmament Agency 1963–75; mem. Nat. Comm on Productivity 1971–72; U.S. Sec. for Transportation 1975–77; Sr. Partner O'Melveny & Myers, Washington 1977–; Dir. Pan-American Airways Inc., Penn Mutual Life Insurance Co., First Pa. Corpn.; mem. Bd. of Govs., American Stock Exchange; Trustee, Rand Corpn., Brookings Inst. *Address:* O'Melveny & Myers, 555 13th Street, N.W., Suite 500, Washington, D.C. 20036, U.S.A.

COLES, Anna L. Bailey, PH.D.; American professor of nursing; b. 16 Jan. 1925, Kansas City; d. of Lillie Mai Buchanan and Gordon A. Bailey; m. 1953 (divorced 1980); three d.; ed. Freedmen's Hosp. School of Nursing, Washington, D.C., Avila Coll., Kansas City, Mo. and Catholic Univ. of America; Instructor, Veterans Admin. Hosp., Topeka, Kan. 1950–52; Supervisor, Veterans Admin. Hosp., Kansas City 1952–58; Asst. Dir. In-Service Educ., Freedmen's Hosp. 1960–61, Admin. Asst. to Dir. 1961–66, Assoc. Dir. Nursing Service 1966–67, Dir. of Nursing 1967–69; Prof. and Dean, Howard Univ. Coll. of Nursing 1968–86, Dean Emer. 1986–, retd. 1986; mem. Inst. of Medicine; Meritorious Public Service Award, D.C. 1968. *Publications:* articles in professional journals; contrib. to Fundamentals of Stroke Care 1976; Nurses, in Encyclopedia of Black America 1981. *Leisure interests:* reading, outdoor cooking and travelling. *Address:* 6841 Garfield Drive, Kansas City, Kansas 66102, U.S.A. *Telephone:* (913) 299-3680.

COLES, John Morton, M.A., PH.D., SC.D., F.B.A., F.S.A., F.R.S.A.; Canadian archaeologist; b. 25 March 1930, Canada; s. of John L. Coles and Alice M.

Brown; m. 1st Mona Shiach 1958 (divorced 1985), two s. two d.; m. 2nd Bryony Orme 1985; ed. Univs. of Toronto, Edinburgh and Cambridge; Univ. Lecturer and Reader, Univ. of Cambridge 1960–80, Prof. of European Prehistory 1980–86; Fellow, Fitzwilliam Coll. Cambridge 1963–. *Publications:* The Archaeology of Early Man (with E. Higgs) 1969, Field Archaeology in Britain 1972, Archaeology by Experiment 1973, The Bronze Age in Europe (with A. Harding) 1979, Experimental Archaeology 1979, Prehistory of the Somerset Levels (with B. Orme) 1980, The Archaeology of Wetlands 1984, Sweet Track to Glastonbury (with B. Coles) 1986, Meare Village East: the excavations of A. Bulleid and H. St. George Gray 1932–1956 1987, People of the Welands (with B. Coles) 1989; numerous papers on European prehistory, field archaeology, experimental archaeology. *Leisure interests:* music, travel. *Address:* Fursdon Mill Cottage, Thorverton, Devon, EX5 5JS, England. *Telephone:* (0392) 860125.

COLES, Robert Martin, A.B., M.D.; American child psychiatrist; b. 12 Oct. 1929, Boston, Mass.; s. of Philip W. Coles and Sandra (Young) Coles; m. Jane Hallowell 1960; three s.; ed. Harvard Coll. and Columbia Univ.; Intern, Univ. of Chicago clinics 1954–55; Resident in Psychiatry, Mass. Gen. Hosp., Boston 1955–56, McLean Hosp., Belmont 1956–57; Resident in Child Psychiatry, Judge Baker Guidance Center, Children's Hosp., Roxbury, Mass. 1957–58, Fellow 1960–61; mem. psychiatric staff, Mass. Gen. Hosp. 1960–62; Clinical Asst. in Psychiatry, Harvard Univ. Medical School 1960–62; Research Psychiatrist in Health Services, Harvard Univ. 1963–, lecturer in Gen. Educ. 1966–, Prof. of Psychiatry and Medical Humanities, Harvard Univ. Medical School 1978–; numerous other professional appts.; mem. American Psychiatric Asscn.; Fellow, American Acad. of Arts and Sciences etc.; awards include Pulitzer Prize for Vols. II and III of Children of Crisis 1973, Sara Josepha Hale Award 1986. *Publications:* numerous books and articles in professional journals. *Leisure interests:* tennis, bicycle riding, skiing. *Address:* Harvard Health Services, Harvard University, 75 Mt. Auburn Street, Cambridge, Mass. 02138 (Office); Box 674, Concord, Mass. 01742, U.S.A. (Home). *Telephone:* 617-495-3736 (Office); 617-369-6498 (Home).

COLIN, Oswaldo Roberto, LL.B.; Brazilian banker; b. 24 March 1924, Joinville, Santa Catarina State; s. of Rodolpho and Maria Sophia Colin; m. 1st Roselys Carmen 1951 (deceased), three s. one d.; m. 2nd Maria Therezinha 1980; ed. School of Law, Rio de Janeiro State Univ.; joined Banco do Brasil 1942; successively Head., Accounting Dept., Rep. on Cttee. for Reformulation of Structure and Org. of Cen. Bank of Brazil, Admin. Dir. 1967–79; Chair. Bd. of Dirs. Banco do Brasil S.A. 1979–85; Pres. and mem. several int. financial insts. including: Euro-Latinamerican Bank Ltd. (EULABANK), (EUROBRAZ), Arab Latin American Bank S.A. (ARLABANK); mem. Brazilian Cttee. for Co-ordination of Implementation of Financial Techniques, Brazilian Council of Foreign Trade and Brazilian Monetary Council; Commendatore, Order of Rio Branco, Orden de Mayo Al Merito, Argentina. *Publication:* The New Image of the Banco do Brasil (monograph) 1966. *Address:* c/o Banco do Brasil S.A., Setor Bancário Sul-lote 23, Edifício Sede III—19 andar, P.O. Box 562, Brazil.

COLLADO, Emilio Gabriel, S.B., A.M., PH.D.; American company executive; b. 20 Dec. 1910, Cranford, N.J.; s. of Emilio Gabriel Collado and Carrie (Hansee) Collado; m. 1st Janet Gilbert 1932, one s. one d.; m. 2nd Maria Elvira Tanco 1972; ed. Phillips Acad., Andover, Massachusetts Inst. of Technology and Harvard, U.S.; U.S. Treasury Dept. 1934–36; Fed. Reserve Bank of New York 1936–38; U.S. State Dept. 1938–46; Assoc. Econ. Adviser, Special Asst. to Under-Sec., Dir. of Office of Financial and Devt. Policy, Deputy on Financial Affairs; Alt., Inter-American Financial and Econ. Advisory Cttee. 1939–45; Alt., Inter-American Econ. and Social Council 1945–46; mem. Inter-American Statistical Inst. 1943–46; Chair. Inter-American Coffee Bd. 1943–44; Trustee, Export-Import Bank of Washington 1944–45; U.S. Exec. Dir. Int. Bank for Reconstruction and Devt. 1946–47; Standard Oil Co. (New Jersey) (now Exxon Corpn.) 1947–75, Treas. 1954–60, Dir. 1960–75, Vice-Pres. 1962–66, Exec. Vice-Pres. 1966–75; Pres. Adela Investment Co., S.A. 1976–79; Chair. and Dir. Int. Planning Corpn. 1981–; mem. (fmr. Chair.) U.S.A./B.I.A.C. for OECD; Dir. J. P. Morgan and Co. and Morgan Guaranty Trust Co. (until 1981, then mem. of Dirs. Advisory Council), Americas Soc., Otto Wolff U.S. Holding Corpn., Work in America Inst.; Vice-Chair. Acad. of Political Science; Gov. Atlantic Inst.; mem. Council on Foreign Relations, Atlantic Council of U.S. (fmr. Vice-Chair.), Americas Soc.; Hon. Dir. Nat. Bureau of Econ. Research; mem. and fmr. Chair. Center for Inter-American Relations; Trustee and fmr. Chair. Cttee. for Econ. Devt.; Trustee Hispanic Soc. of America; mem. American Econ. Asscn., American Acad. of Arts and Sciences, Exec. Cttee. U.S. Council of Int. Chamber of Commerce (now U.S. Council for Int. Business). *Leisure interests:* swimming, tennis. *Address:* 1 Rockefeller Plaza, New York, N.Y. 10020; 130 Shu Swamp Road, Locust Valley, New York, N.Y. 11560, U.S.A. *Telephone:* 212-398 2345; 516-759-0680.

COLLARD, Jean Philippe; French solo pianist; b. 27 Jan. 1948, Mareuil S/AY (Marne); s. of Michel Collard and Monique (Philipponnat) Collard; m. Ariane de Brion; three s. one d.; ed. Conservatoire National de Musique de Paris; *numerous recordings:* music by Bach, Brahms, Debussy, Fauré, Franck, Rachmaninov, Ravel, Saint-Saens, Schubert Chopin, Mozart. *Leisure interests:* windsurfing, tennis. *Address:* Bureau de Concerts M. de Valmalete, 11 avenue Delcassé, 75008 Paris, France. *Telephone:* (1) 45.63.28.38 (Office).

COLLET, Bernt Johan; Danish politician; b. 23 Nov. 1941; s. of Harald Collett; m. Catharina Collet; two s. one d.; ran family estate, Lundbygaard; First Lieut. of the Reserve, Den Kongelige Livgarde 1964-; elected to Folketing 1981; Minister of Defence 1987-88; Conservative People's Party. *Address:* c/o Ministry of Defence, Slotsholmsgade 10, 1216 Copenhagen K, Denmark. *Telephone:* 01-92 33 20.

COLLIN, Fernand (Jozef Maria Fanny), LL.D.; Belgian company director and university professor; b. 18 Dec. 1897, Antwerp; s. of John F. Collin and Jeanne Verelst; m. Maria Bellekens 1968; two s. three d.; ed. Univ. of Louvain; Lawyer, Antwerp 1923-38; lecturer, Univ. of Louvain 1925, Prof. 1927-68, Dean Faculty of Law and mem. Rectorial Council 1945-48; Chair. Bd. of Dirs. Kredietbank 1938-73; Chair. Belgian Assoc. Investment Funds 1958-62, Imperial Products Co. 1959-65; Utrecht-Allerlei Risico's 1959-71, Banque Diamantaire Anversoise 1964-68, Continental Foods 1968-78; Dir. Gevaert Photo-Products 1952-73; mem. Man. Cttee. Inst. de Rescompte et de Garantie 1940-63; Chair. Benelux Cttee. 1959-66; Chair. Cen. Social Section, Belgian Banking Asscn. 1939-45; Chair. Supreme Family Council 1952-59; mem. Higher Council for Physical Educ. and Sports 1930-40; Royal Commissary to Middle Classes 1937; Chair. Cardiology Foundation Princess Liliane 1961-73; Pres. Int. Cardiology Fed. 1970-72; Commdr. Order of the Crown and Commdr. Order of Léopold, Grand Officer Order Léopold II (Belgium); Commdr. Order of Orange-Nassau (Neths.), Commdr. Italian Order of Merit, Commdr. Order St. Gregory the Great, Grand Officer Order of the Crown (Belgium), Grand Officer Order of Merit (Luxembourg), and other decorations. *Publications:* Enrico Ferri e l'avant-projet du code pénal italien de 1921 1925, Rapport sur les classes moyennes 1937, Strafrecht 1948, Code d'instruction criminelle et lois complémentaires (with M. H. Bekaert) 1949. *Leisure interests:* music, horse-riding. *Address:* Mechelsesteenweg 196, Antwerp, Belgium. *Telephone:* 03/237-86-39.

COLLIN, Jean, L.EN.D.; Senegalese politician; b. 19 Sept. 1924, Paris, France; s. of Louis Collin and Madeleine Meunier; m. Marianne Turpin 1973; one s. one d.; Chief Admin., French Overseas Territories; Chief Information Service and Dir. Radio-Dakar 1948; posted to Cameroon 1951-56; Dir. of Cabinet of Mamadou Dia, Vice-Pres. then Pres. of the Council 1957-58; Gov. of Cap-Vert March 1960-Dec. 1960; Sec.-Gen. of the Govt. 1960-62; Sec.-Gen. to the Presidency of the Repub. 1963-64, 1981-; Minister of Finance and Econ. Affairs 1964-71, of the Interior 1971-75, of State for the Interior 1975-81, of State, Sec.-Gen. of the Presidency 1981-; Acting Minister of the Interior 1987-88. *Address:* 25 Avenue Carde, Dakar, Senegal. *Telephone:* Dakar 215070.

COLLINS, Basil Eugene Sinclair, C.B.E., F.Z.S., F.I.D., F.B.I.M., F.R.S.A.; British business executive; b. 21 Dec. 1923, London; s. of Albert Collins and Pauline Alicia (née Wright); m. Doris Slott 1942; two d.; ed. Great Yarmouth Grammar School; joined L. Rose & Co. Ltd. 1945, Sales Man. at time of merger with Schweppes Ltd., Export Dir., Schweppes (Overseas) Ltd. 1958; Group Admin. Dir., Schweppes Ltd. 1964, Chair. Overseas Group 1968; Chair. Overseas Group of Cadbury Schweppes PLC 1969, Deputy Man. Dir. 1972, Man. Dir. 1974, Deputy Chair. and Group Chief Exec. 1980-83; Chair. Nabisco Group Ltd. 1984-; Vice-Pres. Royal Coll. of Nursing 1972-86, Chair. Finance and Gen. Purposes Cttee. 1970-86, Life Vice-Pres. 1986; Dir. Thomas Cook Group Ltd. 1980-85, British Airways 1982-; Dir. (non-exec.) Royal Mint Jan. 1984-; mem. Council, Inst. of Dirs. 1982-88; Fellow, American Chamber of Commerce 1979, Dir. 1984-; Man. Trustee Inst. of Econ. Affairs 1987-; Council mem. Univ. of East Anglia 1987-. *Leisure interests:* music, languages, travel, English countryside. *Address:* Nabisco Group Ltd., Bowater House, Knightsbridge, London, SW1 7LT (Office); Wyddial Parva, Buntingford, Herts., SG9 0EL, England (Home). *Telephone:* 01-225 1321 (Office).

COLLINS, Gerry; Irish politician; b. 16 Oct. 1938, Abbeyfeale, Co. Limerick; m. Hilary Tatten; ed. Univ. Coll. Dublin; fmr. vocational teacher; mem. Dail 1967-; Parl. Sec. to Minister for Industry and Commerce and to Minister for the Gaeltacht 1969-70; Minister for Posts and Telegraphs 1970-73; mem. Limerick County Council 1974-77; Minister for Justice 1977-81, 1987-; Minister for Foreign Affairs March-Dec. 1982; Fianna Fail. *Address:* The Hill, Abbeyfeale, Co. Limerick, Republic of Ireland. *Telephone:* 068 31126.

COLLINS, Jackie; British novelist. *Publications:* The World is Full of Married Men 1968, The Stud 1969, Sunday Simmons and Charlie Brick 1971, Lovehead 1974, The World is Full of Divorced Women 1975, The Hollywood Zoo 1975, Lovers and Gamblers 1977, The Bitch 1979, Chances 1981, Hollywood Wives 1983, Lucky 1985, Hollywood Husbands 1986, Rock Star 1988. *Address:* c/o Simon and Schuster, 1230 Avenue of the Americas, New York, N.Y. 10020, U.S.A.

COLLINS, Joan; British actress; b. 23 May 1933, London; d. of Joseph William and Elsa (née Bessant) Collins; m. 2nd Anthony Newley (divorced), one s. one d.; m. 3rd Ronald S. Kass 1972 (divorced), one d.; m. 4th Peter Holm 1985 (divorced 1987); *Films include:* I Believe in You 1952, Our Girl Friday 1953, The Good Die Young 1954, Land of the Pharaohs 1955, The Virgin Queen 1955, The Girl in the Red Velvet Swing 1955, The Opposite Sex 1956, Island in the Sun 1957, Sea Wife 1957, The Bravados 1958, Seven Thieves 1960, Road to Hong Kong 1962, Warning Shot 1966, The Executioner 1969, Quest for Love 1971, Revenge 1971, Alfie Darling 1974,

The Stud 1979, The Bitch 1980, The Big Sleep, Tales of the Unexpected, Neck 1983, Georgy Porgy 1983, The Nutcracker 1984; numerous TV appearances including Dynasty (serial) 1981, Cartier Affair 1985, Sins 1986, Monte Carlo 1986. *Publications:* Past Imperfect 1978, The Joan Collins Beauty Book 1980, Katy, A Fight for Life 1982, Prime Time 1988. *Address:* c/o Judy Bryer, 15363 Mulholland Drive, Los Angeles, Calif. 90077, U.S.A. *Telephone:* (818) 784-3003.

COLLINS, Martha Layne, B.S.; American politician; b. 7 Dec. 1936, Shelby County, Ky.; d. of Everett Larkin and Mary Lorena (Taylor) Hall; m. Bill Collins 1959; one s. one d.; ed. Lindenwood Coll. and Univ. of Kentucky; fmr. high school teacher; fmr. Lieut. Gov. State of Ky., Gov. 1983-87; mem. Woodford County (Ky.) Democratic Exec. Cttee.; mem. Democratic Nat. Cttee. 1972-76; Chair. Nat. Gov's. Task Force on Drug and Substance Abuse 1986; mem. Credentials Cttee. Democratic Nat. Cttee., Vice-Presidential Selection Process Comm.; mem. Ky. Democratic Cen. Exec. Cttee.; Sec. Ky. Democratic Party; elected Clerk of Court of Appeals 1975, then Clerk of Supreme Court, Ky. *Address:* P.O. Box 11890, Lexington, Ky. 40578-1890, U.S.A.

COLLINS, Michael; American fmr. astronaut and museum official; b. 31 Oct. 1930, Rome, Italy; m. Patricia M. Finnegan 1957; one s. two d.; ed. U.S. Military Acad. and Harvard Univ.; commissioned by U.S.A.F., served as experimental flight test officer, A.F. Flight Test Center, Edwards A.F. Base, Calif.; selected by NASA as astronaut Oct. 1963; backup pilot for Gemini VII mission 1965; pilot of Gemini X 1966; command pilot, Apollo XI mission for first moon landing July 1969; Asst. Sec. for Public Affairs, Dept. of State 1970-71; Dir. Nat. Air and Space Museum 1971-78, Under-Sec. Smithsonian Inst 1978-80; Maj.-Gen. U.S.A.F. Reserve; Vice-Pres. LTV Aerospace and Defense Co. 1980-85; Pres. Michael Collins Assocs. 1985-; Fellow, Royal Aeronautical Soc., American Inst. of Aeronautics and Astronautics; mem. Int. Acad. of Astronautics, Int. Astronautical Fed.; Exceptional Service Medal (NASA), D.S.M. (NASA), Presidential Medal of Freedom, D.C.M. (U.S.A.F.), D.F.C., F.A.I. Gold Space Medal. *Publications:* Carrying the Fire 1974, Flying to the Moon and Other Places 1976. *Address:* 4206 48th Place, N.W., Washington, D.C. 20016, U.S.A.

COLLINS, Phil; British pop singer, drummer and composer; b. 1951; former child actor appearing as the Artful Dodger in London production of Oliver; joined rock group Genesis as drummer 1970, lead singer 1975-; has also made own solo albums, including, Invisible Touch and No Jacket Required and sound-track singles including Throwing it Away, Land of Confusion, Tonight, Tonight, Tonight, In Too Deep, Against All Odds and Separate Lives (from White Nights); appeared in film Buster 1988.

COLLINSON, Patrick, PH.D., F.B.A.; British professor of history; b. 10 Aug. 1929, Ipswich; s. of William Cecil Collinson and Belle Hay Collinson (née Patrick); m. Elizabeth Albinia Susan Selwyn 1960; two s. two d.; ed. King's School, Ely, Pembroke Coll., Cambridge and Univ. of London; Research Asst., Univ. Coll. London 1955-56; Lecturer in History, Univ. of Khartoum, Sudan 1956-61; Lecturer in Ecclesiastical History, King's Coll. London 1961-69; Prof. of History, Univ. of Sydney, Australia 1969-75; Prof. of History, Univ. of Kent at Canterbury 1976-84; Prof. of Modern History, Univ. of Sheffield 1984-(88); Regius Prof. (elect) of Modern History, Univ. of Cambridge Oct. 1988-; Chair. Advisory Ed. Bd. Journal of Ecclesiastical History 1982-; Pres. Ecclesiastical History Soc. 1985-86; mem. Council British Acad. 1986-; Ford's Lecturer in English History, Oxford Univ. 1979. *Publications:* The Elizabethan Puritan Movement 1967, Archbishop Grindal 1519-1583: the Struggle for a Reformed Church 1979, The Religion of Protestants: the Church in English Society 1559-1625 (The Ford Lectures 1979) 1982, Godly People: Essays on English Protestantism and Puritanism 1984, English Puritanism 1984. *Leisure interests:* mountain walking and music. *Address:* 45 Parkers Road, Sheffield, S10 1BN, England. *Telephone:* (0742) 668394.

COLLMAN, James Paddock, PH.D.; American professor of chemistry; b. 31 Oct. 1932, Beatrice, Neb.; s. of Perry G. Collman and Frances Dorothy Palmer; m. Patricia Tincher 1955; four d.; ed. Univs. of Nebraska and Illinois; Instructor, Univ. of N.C. 1959-59, Asst. Prof. 1959-62, Assoc. Prof. 1962-66, Prof. of Organic and Inorganic Chem. 1966-67; Prof., Stanford Univ. 1967-, George A. and Hilda M. Daubert Prof. of Chem. 1980-; mem. N.A.S., American Acad. of Arts and Sciences; Alfred P. Sloan Foundation Fellow 1963-66; Nat. Science Foundation Sr. Postdoctoral Fellow 1965-66; Guggenheim Fellow 1977-78, 1985-86; Churchill Fellow (Cambridge) 1977-; Hon. Dr. (Univ. of Nebraska) 1988; Dr. h.c. (Univ. de Bourgogne) 1988; American Chemical Soc. Award in Inorganic Chem. 1975, Calif. Scientist of the Year Award 1983, Arthur C. Cope Award (from A.C.S.) 1986. *Publications:* Principles and Applications of Organo-transition Metal Chemistry (with Louis S. Hegedus) 1980, 1987 and 195 scientific papers. *Leisure interest:* fishing. *Address:* Department of Chemistry, Stanford University, Stanford, Calif. 94305, U.S.A. (University); 794 Tolman Drive, Stanford, Calif. 94305, U.S.A. (Home). *Telephone:* (415) 723-4648 (University); (415) 493-0934 (Home).

COLLYEAR, Sir John Gowen, Kt., B.SC., F.ENG., F.I.MECH.E., F.I.PROD.E, F.R.S.A., C.B.I.M.; British engineer; b. 19 Feb. 1927, Bushey; s. of John Robert and Amy Elizabeth (née Gowen) Collyear; m. Catherine Barbara Newman

1953; one s. two d.; ed. Watford Grammar School, Univs. of Manchester and Leeds; with Glacier Metal Co. Ltd. 1953, Jt. Man. Dir. 1969, Man. Dir. 1970-73; Man. Dir. Bearings Div., Assoc. Engineering Ltd. (now AE PLC) 1973-75, Group Man. Dir. 1975-81, Chair. 1981-86; Chair. M.K. Electrics Group 1987-88; Fulmer Research Inst. 1987-; United Machinery Group 1987-. *Publications:* Management Precepts 1975, The Practice of First Level Management 1976. *Leisure interests:* golf, bridge, music. *Address:* Walnut Tree House, Nether Westcote, Oxon., OX7 6SD, England. *Telephone:* Shipton under Wychwood 831247.

COLMAN, Rt. Hon. Fraser Macdonald, P.C.; New Zealand politician; b. 23 Feb. 1925, Wellington; s. of Kenneth Gordon Colman; m. Noeline Allen 1958; three d.; ed. Horowhenua Coll., Wellington Tech. Coll.; Boiler maker 1942-55, Asst. Sec. N.Z. Labour Party 1955-67; mem. Parl. for Petone 1967-, Minister of Mines and Immigration 1973-75, Postmaster General 1974-75, Minister of Works and Devt., Assoc. Minister of Energy 1984-87; Labour. *Address:* 103 Hine Road, Wainuiomata, New Zealand (Home).

COLMAN, 3rd Bt., cr. 1907; **Sir Michael Jeremiah Colman;** British business executive; b. 7 July 1928, London; s. of Sir Jeremiah Colman, 2nd Bt. and Edith Gwendolyn Tritton; m. Judith Jean Wallop (née William-Powlett) 1955; two s. three d.; ed. Eton; Capt. Yorks Yeomanry 1967; Dir. Reckitt and Colman PLC 1970-, Chair. 1986-; Dir. Foreign and Colonial Ventures Advisors Ltd. 1988-; Trade Affairs Bd. Chemical Industries Asscn. 1978-84, Council 1983-84; Council Mem. Royal Warrant Holders Assen. 1977-, Pres. 1984; Assoc. of Trinity House, mem. Lighthouse Bd. 1985-; mem. Bd. UK Centre for Econ. and Environmental Devt. 1985-; mem. of the Court of Skinners' Co. 1985-; mem. Council of Scouts Assen. 1985-; Special Trustee, St. Mary's Hosp., London 1988-(92). *Leisure interests:* farming, shooting, forestry, golf. *Address:* 40 Chester Square, London, SW1W 9HT, England (Home). *Telephone:* 01-730 3845 (Home).

COLMER, John Anthony, M.A., PH.D.; British/Australian academic, writer and critic; b. 2 Oct. 1921, Plymouth, England; s. of Vyvyan Colmer; m. Dorothy Mildred Penson 1951; two d.; ed. Keble Coll., Oxford; lecturer then Sr. Lecturer in English Univ. of Khartoum 1949-59; Research Fellow Univ. of Birmingham 1960-61; Sr. Lecturer in English Univ. of Adelaide 1961-64, Prof. 1964-78, Jury Prof. of English 1978-86, Emer. Prof. 1986-; Visiting Prof. Nat. Univ. of Singapore 1989-(90); Fellow Australian Acad. of Humanities 1971-. *Publications:* Coleridge: Critic of Society 1959, Coleridge: Selected Poems (Ed.) 1965, Approaches to the Novel 1966, E. M. Forster, A Passage to India 1967, New Choice 1967, Mainly Modern 1969, E. M. Forster: the Personal Voice 1975, Coleridge on the Constitution of the Church and State 1976, Coleridge to Catch-22 1978, Patrick White's Riders in the Chariot 1978, Patrick White 1984, Through Australian Eyes 1984, Penguin Book of Australian Autobiography 1987, The Changing Stage 1988, Australian Autobiography, The Personal Quest 1989. *Leisure interests:* painting, tennis, fishing. *Address:* 4 Everard Street, Glen Osmond, South Australia 5064. *Telephone:* 08 795707.

COLNBROOK, Baron (Life Peer) cr. 1987, of Waltham St. Lawrence in the Royal County of Berkshire; **Humphrey Edward Atkins,** K.C.M.G., M.P.; British politician; b. 12 Aug. 1922; s. of late Capt. E. D. Atkins; m. Margaret Spencer-Nairn 1944; one s. three d.; ed. Wellington Coll.; special entry cadetship, RN 1940, rank of Lieut. 1943, resgnd. 1948; M.P. for Merton and Morden 1955-70, for Spelthorne 1970-87; Parl. Private Sec. to Civil Lord of the Admiralty 1959-62; Hon. Sec. Conservative Party Cttee. on Defence 1965-67; Opposition Whip 1967-70; Treasurer of H.M. Household and Deputy Chief Whip 1970-73; Parl. Sec. to Treasury and Govt. Chief Whip 1973-74; Opposition Chief Whip 1974-79; Sec. of State for Northern Ireland 1979-81; Lord Privy Seal 1981-82; Chair. Commons Cttee. on Defence 1984-87; Chair. Campaign for Country Sports 1983-; Chair. Airey Neave Memorial Trust 1983-; fmr. Vice-Chair., Man. Cttee. Outward Bound. *Address:* House of Lords, Westminster, London, S.W.1, England.

COLOMBO, Emilio; Italian politician; b. 11 April 1920; ed. Rome Univ.; took active part in Catholic youth orgs.; fmr. Vice-Pres. Italian Catholic Youth Assen.; Deputy, Constituent Assembly 1946-48, Parl. 1948-; Under-Sec. of Agriculture 1948-51, of Public Works 1953-55; Minister of Agriculture 1955-58, of Foreign Trade 1958-59, of Industry and Commerce 1959-60, March-April 1960, July 1960-63, of the Treasury 1963-70, Feb.-May 1972; Prime Minister 1970-72; Minister without Portfolio in charge of Italian representation of UN 1972-73; Minister of Finance 1973-74, of the Treasury 1974-76, of Foreign Affairs 1980-83, of Budget and Econ. Planning 1987-88, of Finance April 1988-; mem. European Parl. 1976-80 (Pres. 1977-79); Pres. Nat. Cttee. for Nuclear Research 1961; mem. Cen. Cttee. Christian Democratic Party 1952, 1953. *Address:* Via Aurelia 239, Rome, Italy.

COLOMBO, H.E. Cardinal Giovanni; Italian ecclesiastic; b. 6 Dec. 1902, Milan; ordained priest 1926; consecrated Titular Bishop of Philippopolis in Arabia 1960; Archbishop of Milan 1963-79; mem. Cttee. of the Ecumenical Council on Catholic Seminaries and Educ.; created Cardinal 1965. *Address:* Corso Venezia 11, 20121 Milan, Italy.

COLOMBO, John Robert, B.A.; Canadian editor, author and consultant; b. 24 March 1936, Kitchener, Ont.; m. Ruth F. Brown 1959; two s. one d.; ed. Kitchener-Waterloo Collegiate Inst., Waterloo Coll. and Univ. of Toronto; editorial asst. Univ. of Toronto Press 1957-59; Asst. Ed. The Ryerson Press 1960-63; Consulting Ed. McClelland & Stewart 1963-70; Editor-at-Large 1970-; Centennial Medal 1967; Order of Cyril and Methodius 1979; Esteemed Kt. of Mark Twain 1979; Philips Information Systems Literary Prize 1985. *Publications:* more than 70 books of poetry, prose, reference, science fiction anthologies and translations from Bulgarian including Colombo's Canadian Quotations 1974, Colombo's Canadian References 1976, Colombo's Book of Canada 1978, Colombo's Book of Marvels 1979, Colombo's Canadiana Quiz Book 1983, Canadian Literary Landmarks 1984, We Stand on Guard 1985, 1,001 Questions about Canada 1986, Off Earth 1987, Colombo's New Canadian Quotations 1987, Mysterious Canada 1988, Extraordinary Experience 1989. *Leisure interest:* reading. *Address:* 42 Dell Park Avenue, Toronto, Ont. M6B 2T6, Canada.

COLOMBO, Vittorino; Italian politician; b. 3 April 1925, Albiate (Milan); ed. Università Cattolica, Milan; Deputy for Milan-Pavia to Chamber of Deputies 1958-76; Senator 1976-; mem. Nat. Council, Italian Workers' Catholic Action; mem. Federchimici. Fed. of Independent Trade Unions; mem. Nat. Council, Christian Democratic Party; fmr. Under-Sec. of State to Ministry of Finance; Minister of Foreign Trade 1968-69, of Health March-Oct. 1974, of Posts and Telecommunications 1976-78, of Transport and the Merchant Navy 1978-79, of Posts and Telecommunications 1979-80; fmr. Chair. of The Senate; Founder and Pres., Italo-Chinese Inst. for Econ. and Cultural Exchanges 1971-; Hon. Pres. Italo-Chinese Chamber of Commerce. *Address:* Via Carducci 18, 20123 Milan, Italy.

COLOTKA, Peter, J.U.DR., DR.SC.; Czechoslovak lawyer and politician; b. 10 Jan. 1925, Sedliacka Dubová; ed. Comenius Univ., Bratislava; Asst. lecturer, Faculty of Law, Comenius Univ., Bratislava 1950-56, Asst. Prof. 1956-64, then Prof., Vice-Dean 1956-57, Dean 1957-58, Pro-Rector of Univ. 1958-61; Commr. for Justice, Slovak Nat. Council 1963-68; Deputy to Slovak Nat. Council 1963-; mem. Presidium, Slovak Nat. Council 1963-68; Deputy Premier 1968-69; Deputy Premier, Fed. Govt. Sept. 1969-; mem. Cen. Cttee. CP of Czechoslovakia and Cen. Cttee. of CP of Slovakia 1966-; Deputy to House of Nations Fed. Assembly Dec. 1968-, Pres. of Fed. Assembly Jan.-April 1969; mem. Presidium of Fed. Assembly Jan.-April 1969; Premier of Slovak Socialist Repub. 1969-88; mem. Presidium of Cen. Cttee. CP of Slovakia 1969-88; mem. Presidium of Cen. Cttee. CP of Czechoslovakia April 1969-; Amb. to France Jan. 1989-; mem. Int. Court of Arbitration, The Hague 1962-70; Distinction for Merit in Construction 1965, Order of Labour 1966, Gold Medal of J. A. Comenius Univ. 1969, Order of Victorious February 1973, Order of the Repub. 1975. *Publications:* Personal Property 1956, Our Socialist Constitution 1961; scientific studies and articles in collaboration with Dr. Matoušek. *Address:* c/o Government of S.S.R., Bratislava, 1, Gottwaldovo nám. 45, Czechoslovakia.

COLSON, Elizabeth Florence, PH.D.; American anthropologist; b. 15 June 1917, Hewitt, Minn.; d. of Louis Henry Colson and Metta Damon Colson; unmarried; ed. Wadena Public High School, Univ. of Minnesota, Radcliffe Coll.; Sr. Research Officer Rhodes-Livingstone Inst. 1946-47, Dir. 1948-51; Sr. lecturer Manchester Univ., U.K. 1951-53; Assoc. Prof. Goucher Coll. 1954-55; Assoc. Prof. and Research Assoc., Boston Univ. 1955-59; Prof. Brandeis Univ. 1959-63; Prof. Univ. of Calif., Berkeley 1964-84, Prof. Emer. June 1984-, mem. N.A.S., American Acad. of Arts and Science; Fellow Center for Advanced Study in the Behavioral Sciences, Stanford Univ.; Fairchild Fellow Calif. Inst. of Technology; Hon. Fellow Royal Anthropological Soc., U.K.; Rivers Memorial Medal; Dr.h.c. (Brown, Rochester). *Publications:* The Makah 1953, Marriage and the Family among the Plateau Tonga 1958, Social Organization of the Gwembe Tonga 1962, Social Consequences of Resettlement 1971, Tradition and Contract 1974; (with Thayer Scudder) Secondary Education and the Formation of an Elite 1980, For Prayer and Profit 1988; (with Lemore Raiston and James Anderson) Voluntary Efforts in Decentralized Management 1983. *Address:* Department of Anthropology, University of California, Berkeley, Calif. 94720, U.S.A. *Telephone:* (415) 642-3391.

COMAN, Col.-Gen. Ion; Romanian army officer and politician; b. 25 March 1926, Bujoreni, Teleorman County; ed. Mil. Acad.; promoted to Maj. Gen. 1962, Sec. High Political Council of Armed Forces 1965-73, Chief of Gen. Staff 1974-76; mem. Grand Nat. Assembly 1965-, Chair. Defence Comm. 1980-; Deputy Minister of Nat. Defence 1965-73, First Deputy Minister 1974-76, Minister 1976-80; mem. Romanian CP 1945-, mem. Cen. Cttee. 1965-, Head of Section, Cen. Cttee. 1973-74, alt. mem. Exec. Political Cttee. 1976-79, mem. 1979-, Sec. Cen. Cttee. 1980-; mem. Nat. Council of Front of Socialist Democracy and Unity; Order of Star of Socialist Repub. of Romania and other Romanian and foreign decorations. *Publications:* works on military theory and history. *Address:* Comitetul Central al Partidul Comunist Român, Str. Academiei 34, Bucharest, Romania. *Telephone:* 15 02 00.

COMANECI, Nadia; Romanian gymnast; b. 12 Nov. 1961, Oneşti, Bacău County; now undergraduate student, Coll. of Physical Educ. and Sports, Bucharest; unmarried; overall European Champion Skien 1975, Prague 1977, Copenhagen 1979; overall Olympic Champion, Montreal 1976; overall World Univ. Games Champion, Bucharest 1981; Gold Medals European Championships, Skien 1975 (vault, asymmetric bars, beam), Prague 1977 (bars), Copenhagen 1979 (vault, floor exercises), World Championships,

Strasbourg 1978 (beam), Fort Worth 1979 (team title), Olympic Games, Montreal 1976 (bars, beam), Moscow (beam, floor), World Cup, Tokyo 1979 (vault, floor); World Univ. Games, Bucharest 1981 (vault, bars, floor and team title); Silver Medals European Championships, Skien 1975 (floor), Prague 1977 (vault), World Championships, Strasbourg 1978 (vault), Olympic Games, Montreal 1976 (team title), Moscow 1980 (individual all-round, team title), World Cup, Tokyo 1979 (beam); Bronze Medal Olympic Games, Montreal 1976 (floor); retd. May 1984, jr. team coach 1984–. *Address:* Clubul sportiv Cetatea, Deva, judeţul Hunedoara, Romania.

COMBS, Thomas Neal, J.D.; American lawyer; b. 30 Nov. 1942, Dallas, Tex.; s. of Thomas J. Combs and Edith Gibson; m. Dorothy E. Bell 1965; three s.; ed. Southern Methodist Univ.; admitted D.C. Bar 1968, U.S. Supreme Court Bar 1975, Mich. Bar 1976; Assoc. Alston, Miller & Gaines, Washington 1968–70, Marmet & Webster, Washington 1970–73; Assoc. then partner, Webster, Kilcullen & Chamberlain, Washington 1973–75; Vice-Pres., Gen. Counsel, Sec. Fruehauf Corpn., Detroit 1975–85, Exec. Vice-Pres. Finance and Legal, Chief Financial Officer, Sec. 1985–86, Pres., Chief Admin. and Financial Officer 1986–; mem. Bd. of Dirs Fruehauf Corpn., Fruehauf Int. Ltd., Fruehauf Canada. *Publications:* articles in professional journals. *Address:* Fruehauf Corporation, 10900 Harper Avenue, Detroit, Mich. 48213, U.S.A.

COMFORT, Alexander, M.A., M.B., D.SC., M.R.C.S., L.R.C.P., D.C.H.; British medical biologist and writer; b. 10 Feb. 1920; s. of Alexander Charles Comfort and Daisy Elizabeth Fenner; ed. Highgate School, Trinity Coll., Cambridge, and The London Hospital; medical and hospital practice 1944–48; lecturer in Physiology, The London Hospital 1948–51; Nuffield Research Asst. Univ. Coll., London 1951–54, Nuffield Research Fellow in Biology of Senescence 1954–63; Dir. Medical Research Council Research Group in Ageing, Univ. Coll., London 1963–70; Dir. of Research, Gerontology, Univ. Coll., London 1970–73; Clinical lecturer, Dept. Psychiatry, Stanford Univ. 1974–83; Prof. Dept. Pathology, Irvine Medical Coll., Univ. of Calif. 1976–78; Adjunct Prof., Dept. Psychiatry, Univ. of Southern Calif. 1977–81; Adjunct Prof. Dept. Psychiatry UCLA 1979–; Consultant, Geriatric Psychiatry, VA Hospital, Brentwood, Calif. 1977–. *Publications:* Novels: No Such Liberty 1941, The Almond Tree 1943, The Powerhouse 1945, On This Side Nothing 1948, A Giant's Strength 1952, Come out to Play 1961, Tetrarch (science fiction trilogy) 1981, Imperial Patient 1987, Walsingham's Drum 1989, The Philosphers 1989; Verse: A Wreath for the Living 1942, Elegies 1944, The Signal to Engage 1946, And All but he Departed 1952, Haste to the Wedding 1962, Poems for Jane 1979; Stories: Letters from an Outpost 1947; Essays: Art and Social Responsibility 1946, The Novel and Our Time 1948, The Pattern of the Future 1951, Darwin and the Naked Lady 1961; Other: Barbarism and Sexual Freedom 1948, Sexual Behaviour in Society 1949, First-Year Physiological Technique 1949, Authority and Delinquency in the Modern State 1950, The Biology of Senescence 1956, Sex in Society 1963, Ageing 1964, The Koka Shastra (trans.) 1964, The Process of Ageing 1964, Nature and Human Nature (essays) 1966, The Anxiety Makers 1967, The Joy of Sex 1972, More Joy 1964, A Good Age 1976, Sexual Consequences of Disability (ed.) 1978, I and That: the Biology of Religion 1979, The Facts of Love (with Jane Comfort) 1979, Practice of Geriatric Psychiatry 1980, What is a Doctor? (Essay) 1980, Reality and Empathy 1983, What About Alcohol 1983. *Address:* The Windmill House, The Hill, Cranbrook, Kent, England.

COMISKEY, Brendan, M.SC., D.D.; Irish ecclesiastic; b. 13 Aug. 1935, Tasson, Co. Monaghan; ed. Ireland and U.S.A., post-graduate educ. Catholic Univ. of America, Lateran Univ., Rome, Trinity Coll. Dublin; teacher and Dean Damien High School, La Verne, Calif; Chair. of Dept. Washington (D.C.) Theological Union; elected Prov., Anglo-Irish Prov. of the Congregation of the Sacred Hearts and Sec.-Gen. Conference of Maj. Religious Superiors 1974; named Auxiliary Bishop of Dublin 1979, ordained Bishop of St. Andrew's, Westland Row, Dublin 1980–84, then Bishop of Ferns 1984–; Chair. Bishops' Comm. for Communications; Pres. Catholic Communications Inst. of Ireland; mem. Nat. Episcopal Conf., Bishops' Comm. for Ecumenism, Jt. Comm. of Bishops and Religious Superiors, Comm. for Youth, Academic Council of Irish School of Ecumenics; Deputy Press Officer for the Catholic Hierarchy. *Address:* Bishop's House, Wexford, Republic of Ireland. *Telephone:* (053) 22657.

COMMAGER, Henry Steele, PH.B., M.A., PH.D., M.A.(Cantab.), M.A.(Oxon.); American historian; b. 25 Oct. 1902; ed. Chicago and Copenhagen Univ.; Prof. New York Univ. 1925–39, Columbia 1939–56, Cambridge 1942–43; Pitt Prof. Amercian History, Cambridge Univ. 1947–48; Harmsworth Prof. of American History, Oxford Univ. 1952–53; Gottesman Prof., Uppsala 1953; Prof. History, Amherst Coll. 1956–, Simpson Lecturer 1972–; Bullitt Prof. Univ. of Washington 1981–; Hon. Fellow, Peterhouse, Cambridge; Visiting Prof. Univ. of Copenhagen 1956; Commonwealth Lecturer, Univ. of London 1965; Visiting Prof. M.I.T. 1975, 1977; Patten Lecturer, Univ. of Ind. 1978; Vice-Pres. Nat. Conven. Effective Congress; consultant U.S. War Dept. Historical Branch, U.S. Office War Information, State Dept., U.S. Army I. & E. Div.; Trustee American Scandinavian Foundation, Friends of Cambridge Univ.; mem. U.S. War Dept. Comm. on History of War, UNESCO Nat. Comm., Exec. Cttee., U.S. Del. to UNESCO; mem. American Acad. of Arts and Letters; hon. degrees Columbia, Pa., Ohio State, Cambridge and numerous other univs. and colls.; Gold Medal for History, American Acad. of Arts and Letters 1972; Knight Order of Dannebrog, Sidney Hillman Award for Lifetime services to Civil Liberties. *Publications:* The American Republic (2 vols., with S. E. Morison) 1930, Documents of American History 1934, Theodore Parker 1936, America: Story of a Free People (with A. Nevins) 1942, Majority Rule and Minority Rights 1943, History of the Second World War 1945, The American Mind 1950, The Great Declaration 1959, The Great Proclamation 1960, The Great Constitution 1961, The Story of Human Rights 1961, Living Ideas in America 1951, America's Robert E. Lee 1951, The Blue and the Gray (2 vols.) 1951, Freedom, Loyalty and Dissent 1954, Joseph Story 1954, The Spirit of Seventy-Six (with R. B. Morris), Europe and America (with G. Bruun), Writings of Theodore Parker 1961, The Era of Reform 1961, Studies in Immigration 1961, Crusaders for Freedom 1961, History: Nature and Purpose 1965, Freedom and Order 1966, Search for a Usable Past 1967, Was America a Mistake? 1968, The Commonwealth of Learning 1968, The American Character 1970, The Use and Abuse of History 1972, Britain Through American Eyes 1974, The Defeat of America 1974, Essays on the Enlightenment 1974, Empire of Reason 1977; Ed. Tocqueville's Democracy in America 1947, America in Perspective 1948, St. Nicholas Anthology 1948, The Rise of the American Nation (50 vols. in progress), Documents of American History 1950, Chester Bowles: An American Purpose 1961, Lester Ward and the Welfare State, Defeat of the Confederacy, The Nature and Study of History 1965, The Struggle for Racial Equality 1967, Joseph Story, Selected Writings and Judicial Opinions, Winston Churchill, Marlborough 1968, Baedeker's United States, Britain Through American Eyes 1973, Jefferson, Nationalism and the Enlightenment 1975 (co-author), The Spirit of Seventy-Six 1975, This Day and Generation 1979. *Leisure interest:* music. *Address:* 405 S. Pleasant Street, Amherst, Mass., U.S.A. *Telephone:* (413) 253-3114.

COMMONER, Barry, A.B., M.A., PH.D.; American professor of plant physiology; b. 28 May 1917, New York; s. of Isidore Commoner and Goldie Yarmolinsky; m. 1st Gloria Gordon 1946, one s. one d.; m. 2nd Lisa Feiner 1980; ed. Columbia Coll. and Harvard Univ.; Asst. in Biology, Harvard Univ. 1938–40; Instructor, Queens Coll. 1940–42; U.S. Naval Reserve 1942–46; Assoc. Ed. Science Illustrated 1946–47; Assoc. Prof. of Plant Physiology, Washington Univ., St. Louis 1947–53, Prof. 1953–76, Univ. Prof. of Environmental Science 1976–81; Prof. of Earth and Environmental Sciences, Queens Coll., Flushing 1981–; Dir. Center for the Biology of Natural Systems 1981–; Visiting Prof. of Community Health, Albert Einstein Coll. of Medicine, New York 1981–; Chair. Dept. of Botany 1965–69, Dir. Center for the Biology of Natural Systems 1965–; Hon. Life Vice-Pres. Soil Asscn. 1968; Dir. A.A.A.S. 1967–74; Chair. A.A.A.S. Comm. on Environmental Alterations 1969–74; Pres. St. Louis Comm. for Nuclear Information 1965–66, mem. Bd. of Dirs. of St. Louis Comm. for Environmental Information 1958–, Pres. 1965–66; mem. Bd. of Dirs. Scientists' Inst. for Public Information 1963–, Co-Chair. 1967–69, Chair. 1969–78, Chair. Exec. Cttee. 1978–; Citizens Party Cand. for Presidency 1980. *Publications:* Science and Survival 1966, The Closing Circle 1971, La Tecnologia del Profitto 1973, The Poverty of Power 1976, Ecologia e Lotte Sociali 1976, Il Cerchio Da Chiudere 1986. *Leisure interest:* walking. *Address:* Center for the Biology of Natural Systems, Queens College, Flushing, N.Y. 11367, U.S.A.

COMPAGNON, Antoine Marcel Thomas; French university professor and writer; b. 20 July 1950, Brussels, Belgium; s. of Gen. Jean Compagnon and Jacqueline Terlinden; ed. Lycée Condorcet, The Maret School, Washington, D.C., U.S.A., Prytanée Militaire, La Flèche, Ecole Polytechnique, Paris, Ecole National des Ponts et Chaussées, Paris, Univ. of Paris VII; with Fondation Thiers and Research Attaché, Centre National de la Recherche Scientifique 1975–78; Asst. Lecturer, Univ. of Paris VII 1975–80; Asst. Lecturer, Ecole des Hautes Etudes en Sciences Sociales, Paris 1977–79; Lecturer, Ecole Polytechnique, Paris 1978–85; teacher at French Institute, London 1980–81; Lecturer, Univ. of Rouen 1981–85; Prof. of French, Columbia Univ., New York 1985–; Visiting Prof., Univ. of Pa. 1986; Guggenheim Fellow 1988; mem. Acad. of Literary Studies. *Publications:* La Seconde Main ou le travail de la citation 1979, Le Deuil antérieur 1979, Nous, Michel de Montaigne 1980, La Troisième République des lettres, de Flaubert à Proust 1983, Ferragosto 1985, critical edn. of Marcel Proust, Sodome et Gomorrhe 1988, Proust entre les siècles 1989; numerous articles on French literature and culture. *Address:* Columbia University, New York, N.Y. 10027 (Office); 29 Claremont Avenue, New York, N.Y. 10027, U.S.A.; 36 rue de Moscou, 75008 Paris, France (Home). *Telephone:* (212) 854-3208 (Office); (212) 222-2550 (Home, New York); 1-43-87-71-48 (Paris).

COMPAORÉ, Blaise; Burkina Faso army officer and politician; fmr. second in command to Capt. Thomas Sankara whom he overthrew in a coup in Oct. 1987; Chair. Popular Front of Burkina Faso and Head of Govt. Oct. 1987–. *Address:* Office of the President, Ougadougou, Burkina Faso.

COMPTON, Denis Charles Scott, C.B.E.; British cricketer (retd.), journalist and advertising executive; b. 23 May 1918, Hendon; s. of Harry Ernest Compton and Jessie Douthie; m. 3rd. Christine Franklin Tobias 1975; three s. from previous marriages; ed. Bell Lane School, Hendon; first played for Middx. County Cricket Club 1936, for England v. New Zealand 1937, v.

Australia 1938, v. West Indies 1939, v. India 1946, v. South Africa 1947; played in 78 Test Matches; made 122 centuries in first class cricket; retd. 1957; played Association Football, mem. Arsenal XI; England XI 1943; Cricket Corresp., Sunday Express 1951–; Commentator, BBC Television 1958–; Exec. in Advertising Co. 1958–; one of Wisden's Cricketers of the Year 1939; Sportsman of the Year 1947, 1948; Hon. mem. MCC 1957–; FA Cup Winners' Medal 1949–50. *Publications:* Testing Time for England 1948, Playing for England 1948, End of an Innings 1958, Denis Compton's Test Diary 1964, Cricket and All That (jointly) 1978. *Leisure interests:* golf, tennis, theatre. *Address:* c/o Sunday Express, Fleet Street, London, EC4P 4JT, England.

COMPTON, Rt. Hon. John George Melvin, P.C., LL.B.; St. Lucia politician; b. 1926, Canouan, St. Vincent and the Grenadines; m.; five c.; ed. London School of Econs.; called to the Bar (Gray's Inn); private practice in St. Lucia 1951–; independent mem. Legis. Council 1954; joined Labour Party 1954; Minister for Trade and Production 1957; Deputy Leader Labour Party 1957–61; resgnd. 1961; formed Nat. Labour Movt. 1961 (later became United Workers' Party); Leader, United Workers' Party 1964; Chief Minister of St. Lucia 1964; Premier 1967–79, Prime Minister Feb.-July 1979, May 1982–; also Minister of Foreign Affairs, Planning and Finance 1982–88, of Planning Finance, Statistics, Devt. and Home Affairs 1988–. *Address:* Office of the Prime Minister, Castries, St. Lucia.

CONABLE, Barber B., B.A., LL.B., Jr.; American former politician and administrator; s. of Barber B. Conable and Agnes Gouinlock; m. Charlotte Williams 1952; four c.; ed. Cornell Univ.; admitted to New York Bar 1948, practice in Buffalo 1948–50, Batavia 1952–64; served with U.S. Marine Corps. Reserve 1942–46, 1950–51; mem. New York State Senate 1963–64; mem. House of Reps. 1964–84; fmr. mem. House Cttee. on Ways and Means; Pres. Govt. Comm. on Defence Man. 1985–; Prof. Univ. of Rochester 1985–; Pres. and Chair. Exec. Dirs. The World Bank 1986–. *Address:* The World Bank, 1818 H Street, N.W., Washington D.C. 20433, U.S.A.

CONACHER, Desmond John, PH.D., F.R.S.C.; Canadian professor of classics; b. 27 Dec. 1918, Kingston; s. of William M. Conacher and Madeline M. (née Cashel) Conacher; m. Mary Smith 1952; one s. one d.; ed. Queen's Univ., Kingston, Univ. of Chicago; Master Upper Canada Coll., Toronto 1943–46; Lecturer in Classics Dalhousie Univ., Halifax 1946–47; Asst. Prof. Classics Univ. of Saskatchewan 1947–52, Assoc. Prof. 1952–58; Assoc. Prof. Trinity Coll., Univ. of Toronto 1958–65, Prof. 1965–84, Prof. Emer. 1984–, Head Dept. of Classics 1966–72, Chair. 1972–75; Bonsall Visiting Prof. Classics Dept. Stanford Univ. 1981, Visiting Prof. Princeton Univ. 1987, Univ. of Texas at Austin 1989; Nuffield Research Fellow, Oxford 1957–58; Dir. American Philological Asscn. 1974–77. *Publications:* Euripidean Drama 1967, Aeschylus' Prometheus Bound: A Literary Commentary 1980, Aeschylus' Oresteia: A Literary Commentary 1987, Euripides Alcestis (ed. with trans., introduction and commentary) 1988; articles on ancient Greek Tragedy in various classical journals. *Leisure interest:* tennis. *Address:* Trinity College, University of Toronto, Toronto, M5S 1H8 (Office); 126 Manor Road E., Toronto, Ont. M4S 1P8, Canada (Home). *Telephone:* (416) 978-3055 (Office); (416) 487-0777 (Home).

CONCHON, Georges; French author, screenwriter and journalist; b. 9 May 1925, Saint-Avit; s. of Gilbert Conchon and Marcelle Gancille; m. Yvonne Message 1946; one d.; ed. Lycée Henri IV, Paris, and Univ. de Paris à la Sorbonne; Sec. of Debates, Assemblée de l'Union française 1947–52, Divisional Head 1952–58; Sec.-Gen. Parl. Cen. African Repub. 1959; Sec. of Debates at the Senate 1960–80; artistic adviser at Antenne 2 (TV) 1982–; Oscar Black and White in Colour 1976, Prix des Libraires de France 1960, Prix Goncourt 1964. *Publications:* novels: Les grandes lessives 1953, Les honneurs de la guerre 1955, La corrida de la victoire 1959, L'état sauvage 1964, L'apprenti gaucher 1967, L'amour en face 1972, Le sucre 1977, Le bel avenir 1983, Colette Stern 1987; play: Pourquoi pas vamos 1965; films: 7 morts sur ordonnance 1975, Black and White in Colour 1976, L'état sauvage, Judith Therpauve, Le sucre 1978, La Banquière 1980, Une affaire d'hommes 1981, Mon beau-frère a tué ma soeur 1986. *Address:* 132 rue de Rennes, 75006 Paris, France. *Telephone:* 45-48-97-07.

CONDON, Richard Thomas; American author; b. 18 March 1915, New York; s. of Richard A. Condon and Martha I. Pickering; m. Evelyn R. Hunt 1938; two d. *Publications include:* novels: The Oldest Confession 1958, The Manchurian Candidate 1959, Some Angry Angel 1960, A Talent for Loving 1961, An Infinity of Mirrors 1964, Any God Will Do 1966, The Ecstasy Business 1967, Mile High 1969, Vertical Smile 1971, Arigato 1972, And then We Moved to Rossenarra 1973, The Mexican Stove 1973, Winter Kills 1974, The Star Spangled Crunch 1974, Money is Love 1975, The Whisper of the Axe 1976, The Abandoned Woman 1977, Bandicoot 1978, Death of a Politician 1978, The Entwining 1980, Prizzi's Honor 1982, A Trembling Upon Rome 1983, Prizzi's Family 1986; screenplays with Janet Roach: Prizzi's Honour 1984 (Best Screenplay Award, British Motion Picture Acad., Writers' Guild of America 1986), Arigato 1985. *Address:* c/o Abner Stein, 10 Roland Gardens, London, SW7 3PH, England.

CONG DEZI; Chinese army officer; mem. Standing Cttee., CCP Cttee., Fujian 1977; Commdr. Fujian Mil. Dist. 1977–; Deputy Commdr. Fuzhou Mil. Region 1981–. *Address:* Commanding Officers' Headquarters, Fuzhou Military Region, People's Republic of China.

CONG LIN; Chinese paper-cut artist; b. 1918, Penglai Co. *Address:* Beijing, People's Republic of China.

CONGAR, (Georges) Yves (Marie), M. EN THEOL.; French professor and author; b. 13 April 1904, Sedan; s. of George Congar, and Lucie (née Desoye) Congar; ed. Séminaire des Carmes (Inst. Catholique de Paris) Facultés Dominicaines du Saulchoir; entered the Ordre Frères Précheurs 1925, ordained 1930; Prof. 1931–54; Prisoner-of-War 1940–45; Ecole Biblique, Jerusalem 1954; Cambridge 1957; appt. by Pope John XXIII to the Theological Comm. for the Vatican Councils of 1962, 1965; Prof. l'Institut Supérieur d'Etudes Oecuméniques, l'Institut Catholique de Paris; 'Pensionnaire' l'Institution Nat. des Invalides 1984–; Croix de Guerre, Médaille des Evades, Légion d'honneur, Prix Bordin de l'Académie Française. *Publications:* Chrétiens désunis: Principes d'un oécuménisme catholique 1937, Esquisse du mystère de l'Eglise 1941, Vraie et fausse réforme dans l'Eglise 1950, Le Mystère du Temple 1958, La Tradition et les traditions (2 vols.) 1960, Chrétiens en dialogue 1964, Je crois en l'Esprit-Saint (3 vols.) 1979, Essais oécuméniques 1984, Le Concile Vatican II 1984, Entretiens d'automne 1987. *Address:* Institution Nationale des Invalides, 6 boulevard des Invalides, 75007 Paris, France.

CONLON, James, B.MUS.; American conductor; b. 18 March 1950, New York; s. of Angeline Conlon; ed. High School of Music and Art, New York and Juilliard School; fmr. faculty mem. Juilliard School of Music; since making début with New York Philharmonic has conducted every major U.S. orchestra and many leading European orchestras; début at Metropolitan Opera 1976, Covent Garden 1979, Paris Opéra 1982, Lyric Opera of Chicago 1988; Music Dir. Cincinnati May Festival 1979–, Rotterdam Philharmonic Orchestra 1983–; conducted opening of Maggio Musicale, Florence 1985; Chief Conductor, Cologne Opera (1989–); has conducted at major int. music festivals; Grand Prix du Disque for recording of Poulenc Piano Concertos (Erato); numerous recordings of works by Mozart, Liszt, Poulenc etc. *Address:* c/o Shuman Associates, 250 West 57 Street, New York, N.Y. 10107, U.S.A. *Telephone:* 212-315 1300.

CONN, Jerome W., M.D.; American professor of medicine; b. 24 Sept. 1907, New York; s. of Joseph H. Conn and Dora Kobrin; m. Elizabeth Stern 1932; one s. one d.; ed. Rutgers Univ. and Univ. of Michigan Medical School; Instructor of Internal Medicine, Univ. of Mich. Medical School 1935–38, Asst. Prof. 1938–44, Head of Div. of Endocrinology and Metabolism and Dir. of Metabolism Research Unit 1943–, Assoc. Prof. 1944–50, Prof. of Internal Medicine 1950–68, Louis Harry Newburgh Distinguished Univ. Prof. of Internal Medicine 1968–74; Prof. Emer. 1974–; Veterans' Admin. Distinguished Physician 1974–77; discoverer of Primary Aldosteronism, known as Conn's Syndrome; Hon. F.A.C.S.; mem. American Coll. of Physicians, N.A.S., Inst. of Medicine, U.S.A., Nat. Acad. of Medicine, Argentina; Hon. Sc.D. (Rutgers Univ.); Hon. M.D. (Univ. of Turin); numerous U.S. and foreign awards, including Modern Medicine Award and Citation 1957, Banting Medal of American Diabetes Asscn. 1958, Gordon Wilson Medal of American Clinical and Climatological Asscn. 1962, John Phillips Memorial Award of American Coll. of Physicians 1965, Gold Medal of Int. Soc. for Progress in Internal Medicine, Buenos Aires 1969, Gairdner Int. Award 1969, Stouffer Int. Award 1971. *Publications:* 428 articles and contribs. to 17 books, on metabolism, endocrinology and hypertension. *Leisure interests:* tennis, squash, fishing, writing. *Address:* Admiralty Point, 2369 Gulf Shore Boulevard North, Naples, Fla. 33940, U.S.A. *Telephone:* 813-262-1893.

CONNALLY, John Bowden, Jr., LL.B.; American lawyer and politician; b. 27 Feb. 1917, Floresville, Tex.; s. of John B. Connally and Lela Wright Connally; m. Idanell Brill 1940; two s. one d.; ed. Univ. of Texas; served in U.S. Navy 1941–46; fmr. exec. in oil, oilfield services, radio and television, carbon, ranches, insurance, New York Cen. Railroad; Sec. of the Navy Jan.-Nov. 1961; Gov. of Texas 1963–69; Sr. Partner, Vinson, Elkins, Houston (law firm) 1969–70, 1972–85; Sec. of the Treasury 1971–72; Dir. The Coastal Corpn., The Patten Corpn., Kaiser Tech., Methodist Hosp., Houston; Special Counsel: Bd. of Dirs. and Exec. Cttee., American General Cos., Houston; fmr. Dir. First City Bank Corpn. of Texas, Falconbridge Nickel Mines Ltd., First City Nat. Bank of Floresville, Justin Ind., Dr. Pepper Co., Santa Gertrudis Breeders Int., Continental Airlines Inc.; filed for Bankruptcy 1987; consultant, First City Bancorp 1989–; mem. and trustee Andrew W. Mellon Foundation 1973–; mem. Advisory Cttee. on Reform of Int. Monetary System 1973–; Vice-Chair. Houston Chamber of Commerce 1975–; Adviser to Pres. June-July 1973; mem. Saudi European Investment Corpn. May 1985–; Democrat until 1973, Republican 1973–. *Address:* 515 Post Oak Boulevard, Suite 600, Houston, Tex., 77024, U.S.A.

CONNELL, Elizabeth, B.MUS.; Irish opera singer; b. South Africa; ed. Univ. of the Witwatersrand and Johannesburg Coll. of Educ., S.A. and London Opera Centre; début at Wexford Festival, Ireland as Varvara in Katya Kabanova 1972; Australian Opera 1973–75; English Nat. Opera 1975–80; début Royal Opera House, Covent Garden, London as Viclinda in I Lombardi 1976; Ortrud in Lohengrin, Bayreuth Festival 1980; Electra in Idomeneo, Salzburg Festival 1984; début Metropolitan Opera, New York as Vitellia in La Clemenza di Tito 1985; début Vienna State Opera as Elisabeth in Tannhäuser 1985; début Glyndebourne, England as Electra in Idomeneo 1985; début La Scala, Milan as Ortrud in Lohengrin 1981; sang full range of dramatic mezzo repertoire until 1983 when moved into dramatic soprano field; sings worldwide, freelance in opera, oratorio, concert and recital work; Maggie Teyte Prize 1972. *Leisure interests:* reading, theatre, concerts, cooking, embroidery, writing and composing. *Address:* c/o S. A. Gorlinsky, 33 Dover Street, London, W1X 4NJ, England.

CONNELL, George Edward, O.C., B.A., PH.D., F.C.I.C., F.R.S.C.; Canadian professor of biochemistry and university administrator; b. 20 June 1930, Saskatoon, Sask.; s. of James Lorne Connell and Mabel Gertrude Killins; m. Sheila Harriet Horan 1955; two s. two d.; ed. Upper Canada Coll. and Univ. of Toronto; Prof. Dept. of Biochemistry Univ. of Toronto 1957-62, Chair. Dept. 1965-70. Assoc. Dean Faculty of Medicine 1972-74, Vice-Pres. Research and Planning 1974-77, Pres. Univ. 1984-; Pres. Univ. of Western Ont. 1977-84; Hon. LL.D. (Trent) 1984, (Western Ont.) 1985, (McGill) 1987. *Publications:* over 50 scientific articles in various journals. *Leisure interests:* tennis, skiing, wilderness canoe trips. *Address:* Simcoe Hall, Room 107, 27 King's College Circle, University of Toronto, Toronto, Ont., M5S 1A1 (Office); 93 Highland Avenue, Toronto, Ont. M4W 2A4, Canada (Home). *Telephone:* (416) 978-2121 (Office); (416) 929-3800 (Home).

CONNELL, John MacFarlane; British business executive; b. 29 Dec. 1924, Surrey; s. of late John M. Connell and of Mollie I. MacFarlane; m. Jean M. S. Mackay 1949; two s.; ed. Stowe School and Christ Church, Oxford; joined Tanqueray, Gordon & Co. Ltd. 1946, Man. Dir. 1962-70; mem. Bd. The Distillers Co. 1965, mem. Man. Cttee. 1971; Chair. United Glass Holdings PLC 1979-83; Chair. The Distillers Co. PLC 1983-86, Pres. 1986-; C.E.O. 1986; Past Pres. Royal Warrant Holders Asscn.; Chair. Gin Rectifiers and Distillers Assscn. 1967-70. *Leisure interests:* golf, shooting. *Address:* The Distillers Company PLC, 20 St. James's Square, London, SW1Y 4JF, England. *Telephone:* 01-930 1040.

CONNELL, Philip Henry, C.B.E., M.D., B.S., M.R.C.S., F.R.C.P., D.P.M.; British consultant psychiatrist; b. 6 July 1921, Leeds, Yorks.; s. of George Henry Connell and Evelyn Hilda Sykes; m. 1st Marjorie Helen Gilham 1948, two s.; m. 2nd Cecily Mary Harper 1973; ed. St. Paul's School, London, St. Bartholomew's Hosp., Univ. of London; St. Stephen's Hosp., London 1951-53; The Bethlem Royal Hosp. and The Maudsley Hosp. 1953-57; Consultant Psychiatrist, Newcastle Gen. Hosp. and Physician in charge of Child Psychiatry Unit in assscn. with King's Coll., Durham Univ., and Assoc. Physician, Royal Victoria Infirmary, Newcastle 1957-63; Physician, Bethlem Royal Hosp. and Maudsley Hosp. 1963-86, Consultant to Child and Adolescent Dept. 1963-86; Dir. Brixton Child Guidance Unit 1963-67, Drug Dependence Clinical Research and Treatment Unit 1968-86; Physician in charge of Boys' Adolescent Unit, Bethlem Royal Hosp. 1963-76; Emer. Physician, Bethlem Royal Hosp. and Maudsley Hosp. 1986-; mem. Bd. of Man., Inst. of Psychiatry 1968-74, Academic Bd. 1967-74; Consultant Adviser to Dept. of Health and Social Services on Drug Addiction 1966-71, 1981-86; Pres. Soc. for the Study of Addiction 1973-76; Vice-Pres. Int. Council on Alcohol and Addiction 1982-87, Chair. Scientific and Professional Advisory Bd. 1971-79, mem. Bd. of Man. 1982-87; Chair. Advisory Council on the Misuse of Drugs 1982-88; Fellow Royal Coll. of Psychiatrists (Vice-Pres. 1979-81), Chair. Child and Adolescent Psychiatry Specialist Section 1971-74; appt. mem. Gen. Medical Council by Royal Coll. of Psychiatrists 1979-, Preliminary Screener for Health 1982-84, Deputy Screener for Health 1984-; mem. WHO Panel of Experts on Alcohol and Drug Dependence 1968-86; mem. several editorial bds. int. journals. *Publications:* Amphetamine Psychosis (Maudsley Monograph No. 5) 1958, Cannabis and Man (Jt. Ed.) 1975; about 80 chapters and papers in scientific books and journals and proceedings of scientific confs. either solely or jtly. *Leisure interests:* theatre, bridge, family and friends. *Address:* 21 Wimpole Street, London, W1M 7AD (Consulting Rooms); 25 Oxford Road, Putney, London, SW15 2LG, England (Home). *Telephone:* 01-636 2220 (Consulting Rooms); 01-788 1416 (Home).

CONNELLY, John Francis; American business executive; b. 4 March 1905, Philadelphia; m. Josephine O'Neill 1938; two s. four d.; Dir. Crown Cork & Seal Co., Philadelphia 1956-, Pres. 1957-76, Chair. 1957-, C.E.O. 1979-; Chair. Connelly Containers Inc.; Hon. LL.D. (La Salle Coll., Villanova Univ.). *Address:* Crown Cork & Seal Co., 9300 Ashton Road, Philadelphia, Pa. 19136, U.S.A.

CONNERY, Sean; Scottish actor; b. 25 Aug. 1930; s. of Joseph and Euphamia Connery; m. 1st Diane Cilento 1962 (dissolved 1974), 2nd Micheline Boglio Roquebrun 1975; served in Royal Navy; Dir. Tantallon Films Ltd. 1972-; Hon.D.Litt. (Heriot-Watt) 1981; Acad. Award, Best Supporting Actor 1988; Fellow, Royal Scottish Acad. of Music and Drama 1984; Commdr. Ordre des Arts et des Lettres 1987. *Films include:* No Road Back 1955, Time Lock 1956, Action of the Tiger 1957, Another Time, Another Place, Hell Drivers, 1958, Darby O'Gill and the Little People 1959, Tarzan's Greatest Adventure 1959, On the Fiddle 1961, The Longest Day 1962, The Frightened City 1962, Woman of Straw 1964, Marnie 1964, The Hill 1965, A Fine Madness 1966, Shalako 1968, The Molly Maguires 1968, The Red Tent 1969, The Anderson Tapes 1970, The Offence 1973, Zardoz 1974, Murder on the Orient Express 1974, Ransom 1974, The Wind and the Lion 1975, The Man Who Would Be King 1975, Robin and Marian 1976, A Bridge Too Far 1977, The Great Train Robbery 1978, Meteor 1978, Cuba 1979, Outland 1981, The Man with the Deadly Lens 1982, The Untouchables 1986, The Name of the Rose 1987, The Presidio 1988, Family Business, Rosencrantz and Guildenstern are Dead; as James Bond in Dr.

No 1963, From Russia with Love 1964, Goldfinger 1965, Thunderball 1965, You Only Live Twice 1967, Diamonds are Forever 1971, Never Say Never Again 1982. *Address:* c/o C.A.A., 1888 Century Park East (Suite 1400), Los Angeles, Calif. 90067, U.S.A.; Málaga, Spain.

CONNICK, Robert Elwell, B.S., PH.D.; American professor emeritus of chemistry; b. 29 July 1917, Eureka, Calif., s. of Arthur E. Connick and Florence Robertson Connick; m. Frances Spieth 1951; two s. four d.; ed. Univ. of California; Prof. of Chem. Univ. of Calif., Berkeley 1952-88, Emer. 1988-, Chair. Dept. of Chem. 1958-60, Dean of Coll. of Chem. 1960-65, Vice-Chancellor for Academic Affairs 1965-67, 1969-71; mem. N.A.S. *Publications:* numerous articles in Journal of American Chem. Soc., Journal of Chem. Physics, Inorganic Chem., etc. *Leisure interest:* Indian petroglyphs. *Address:* Department of Chemistry, University of California, Berkeley, Calif. 94720 (Office); 50 Marguerita Road, Berkeley, Calif. 94707, U.S.A. (Home).

CONNOR, Frank J., B.A.; American business executive; b. 11 Sept. 1930, Yonkers, New York; s. of Nicholas J. Connor and Marie Fitz Simmons; m. A. Joan Taylor 1956; two s. two d.; ed. Maryknoll Coll., Newark Coll. of Eng., Wayne State Univ.; Mgt. Trainee, M & T Chemicals 1957-59, Sales Exec. 1959-67, Vice-Pres., Gen. Man. Corpn. Sales 1968-70, Vice-Pres. Group Operations 1970-71, Pres. 1972-75; Sr. Vice-Pres. and Group Exec. American Can Int. 1975-79, Sr. Vice-Pres., Sector Exec. Packaging, American Can Co. (now Primerica Corpn.) 1979-80, Exec. Vice-Pres., Sector Exec. Packaging and Metals Recovery 1980-81, Pres. 1981-87. *Leisure interests:* tennis, sailing, skiing. *Address:* c/o American Can Company, American Lane, Greenwich, Conn. 06830, U.S.A.

CONNOR, John Thomas, J.D., A.B.; American business executive and government official; b. 3 Nov. 1914, Syracuse, N.Y.; s. of Michael J. and Mary Sullivan Connor; m. Mary O'Boyle 1940; two s. one d.; ed. Holy Rosary High School, Syracuse, N.Y., Holy Rosary Grammar School, Harvard Law School and Syracuse Univ.; fmrly. assoc. with law firm Cravath, de Gersdorff, Swaine and Wood; General Counsel, Office of Scientific Research and Devt. 1942-44; U.S. Marine Corps 1944-45; Counsel, Office of Naval Research, later Special Asst. to U.S. Sec. of Navy 1945-47; Gen. Attorney, Merck & Co. (pharmaceuticals) 1947, Pres. 1955-65; U.S. Sec. of Commerce 1965-66; Pres. Allied Chemical Corpn. 1967-69, Chair. of Bd. 1969-79, Chief Exec. Officer 1969-79 and Dir. 1967-80; Dir., Gen. Motors Corpn., Merck & Co. Inc., American Broadcasting Cos., Inc., J. Henry Schroder Bank and Trust Co. 1980-, Schroders Ltd. (London) 1980, Schroders Inc. 1980, Chair. 1980; DNA Plant Technology Corpn. Chair. 1981-; numerous hon. degrees. *Leisure interests:* opera, golf. *Address:* Schroders Inc., 1 State Street, New York, N.Y. 10015 (Office); 1328 Lake Worth Lane, Lost Tree Village, N. Palm Beach, Fla., U.S.A. (Home). *Telephone:* 212-269-6500 (Office); 305-626-2147 (Home).

CONNOR, Joseph E., A.B., M.S.; American accountant; b. 23 Aug. 1931, New York; s. of Joseph E. Connor; m. Cornelia B. Camarata 1958; two s. one d.; ed. Univ. of Pittsburg and Columbia Univ.; joined Price Waterhouse & Co., New York 1956, Partner 1967-, Man. Partner, Western region, Los Angeles 1976-78, Chair. Policy Bd. 1978-88, Chair. Worldfirm 1988-; Consultant Foreign Direct Investment Programme, U.S. Dept. of Commerce; mem. Pres.'s Man. Advisory Council, Pres.'s Private Sector Survey on Cost Control. *Address:* Price Waterhouse & Co., 1251 Avenue of the Americas, New York, N.Y. 10020, U.S.A.

CONNOR, Ralph, B.S., PH.D.; American chemist; b. 12 July 1907, Newton, Ill.; s. of Stephen A. and Minnie (Ross) Connor; m. Margaret Raef 1931; one s.; ed. Univs. of Illinois and Wisconsin; Asst. Prof., Assoc. Prof. of Chem., Univ. of Pa. 1935-41; Technical Aide, Section Chief, and Chief of Div. 8, Nat. Defense Research Cttee. of Office of Scientific Research and Devt. 1941-45; Assoc. Dir. of Research, Rohm & Haas Co. 1945-48, Vice-Pres. and Dir. 1948-73 (in charge of Research 1948-70), Chair. of Bd. 1960-70, Chair. of Exec. Cttee. 1970-73; mem. Bd. of Dirs. American Chemical Soc. 1954-65, Chair. 1956-58; mem. Bd. of Dirs. Ursinus Coll. 1971-80, Life mem. 1980-; Hon. D.Sc. (Philadelphia Coll. of Pharmacy and Science, Univ. of Pa., Polytechnic Inst. of Brooklyn), Hon. LL.D. (Lehigh Univ.); several medals. *Address:* Royal Oaks, GH1007, 10035 Royal Oak Rd., Sun City, Ariz. 85351, U.S.A. *Telephone:* 602-9724742.

CONNORS, James Scott (Jimmy); American lawn tennis player; b. 2 Sept. 1952, East St Louis, Ill.; s. of James Scott Connors I and Gloria Thompson Connors; m. Patti McGuire 1978; one s.; ed. Univ. of California at Los Angeles; amateur player 1970-72, professional since 1972; Australian Champion 1974; Wimbledon Champion 1974, 1982; U.S.A. Champion 1974, 1976, 1978, 1982; S.A. Champion 1973, 1974; WCT Champion 1977, 1980; Grand Prix Champion 1978; played Davis Cup for U.S.A. 1976, 1981; BBC Overseas Sports Personality 1982. *Address:* c/o U.S. Tennis Association Membership, Department P.O. Box 1726, Hickville, New York, N.Y. 11802, U.S.A.

CONOMBO, Dr. Joseph Issoufou; Burkinabê fmr. politician; b. 9 Feb. 1917, Kombissiri, Upper Volta (now Burkina Faso); s. of Ousman Conombo and Tassombedo Timroko; m. 2nd Genevieve Nuninger di Illfurth 1975; two s. three d.; ed. Ecole Primaire et Supérieure, Bingerville, Ecole Normale "William Ponty", Dakar, Senegal; participated in World War II; Co-founder of Union Voltaïque 1946; medical practitioner 1946-48;

Consultant to Union Française 1948–51; Del. to Assemblée Nat. in Paris 1951–59; mem. Nat. Assembly of Togo 1952–80; Mayor of Ouagadougou 1960–65; Dir.-Gen. for Public Health 1966–68; Minister of Foreign Affairs 1971–73; Prime Minister 1978–80; mem. Rassemblement Démocratique Africain 1959–80; Pres. Upper Volta Red Cross Soc. 1961–80. *Address:* Avenue de la Liberté, B.P. 613, Dadoya, Ouagadougou, Burkina Faso.

CONRAD, Donald Glover, B.S., M.B.A.; American insurance company executive; b. 23 April 1930, St. Louis; s. of Harold Armin and Velma Glover (Morris) Conrad; m. M. Stephania Shimkus 1980; three c. by previous marriage; ed. Wesleyan and Northwestern Univs. and Univ. of Michigan; with Exxon Co. 1957–70; Financial Adviser, Esso Natural Gas, The Hague, Netherlands 1965–66, Treasurer Esso Europe, London 1966–70; Sr. Vice-Pres. Aetna Life & Casualty Co., Hartford, Conn. 1970–72, Exec. Vice-Pres. and Dir. 1972–; Dir. Terra Nova Insurance Co., Federated Investors Inc.; mem. Bd. and Exec. Cttee., American Council for the Arts. *Address:* Aetna Life and Casualty Co., 151 Farmington Avenue, Hartford, Conn. 06156, U.S.A.

CONRAD, Kent, M.B.A.; American politician; b. 12 March 1948, Bismarck, N.D.; m. Lucy Calantti 1987; one d.; ed. Univ. of Missouri, Stanford Univ. and George Washington Univ.; Asst. to tax commr. State of N.D. Tax Dept. Bismarck 1974–80, tax commr. 1981–86; Senator from North Dakota 1987–; Democrat. *Address:* 361 Dirksen Senate Building, Washington, D.C. 20510, U.S.A.

CONRAN, Shirley Ida; British designer and author; b. 21 Sept. 1932; d. of Ida and W. Thirlbey Pearce; m. 1st Sir Terence Conran (q.v.) (divorced 1962); 2nd John Stephenson; two s. one d.; ed. St. Paul's Girls' School and Portsmouth Art Coll.; Press Officer, Asprey Suchy (jewellers) 1953–54; Publicity Adviser to Conran Group Cos. 1955; org. and designed several kitchen and design exhbns.; ran Conran Fabrics Ltd. 1957; started Textile Design Studio 1958; Home Ed., Daily Mail 1962, Women's Ed. 1968; Women's Ed. The Observer Colour Magazine and contrib. to Woman's Own 1964; Fashion Ed. The Observer 1967, columnist and feature writer 1969–70; columnist Vanity Fair 1970–71; co-publr. Over 21 1972; has made numerous TV and radio appearances. *Publications:* Superwoman 1974, Superwoman Yearbook 1975, Superwoman in Action 1977, Futures 1979, Lace 1982, The Magic Garden 1983, Lace 2 1985, Savages (novel) 1987. *Leisure interests:* long distance swimming, yoga. *Address:* 19 Regent's Park Terrace, London, NW1 7ED, England.

CONRAN, Sir Terence Orby, Kt.; British designer and retailing executive; b. 4 Oct. 1931, Esher, Surrey; s. of Rupert Conran and Christina Halstead; m. Caroline Herbert 1963; four s. one d.; ed. Bryanston School and Cen. School of Art and Design, London; Chair. Conran Holdings Ltd. 1965–68; Jt. Chair. Ryman Conran Ltd. 1968–71; Chair. Habitat Group Ltd. 1971–, Habitat/Mothercare PLC 1982–; Chair. Habitat France SA 1973–, Conran Stores Inc. 1977–, J. Hepworth & Son Ltd. 1981–83 (Dir. 1979–83), Richard Shops 1983; Chair. Storehouse PLC 1986–, C.E.O. 1986–88; Dir. Conran Ink Ltd., The Neal Street Restaurant, Conran Roche Ltd., Electra Risk Capital 1981–84, Butler's Wharf Ltd. 1984–, Conran Octopus Ltd. 1983–, Heal & Son Ltd. 1983–87, FNAC 1985–, Michelin House Devt. 1985–, Savacentre 1986–, British Home Stores 1986–, Bibendum Restaurant Ltd. 1986–; mem. Royal Comm. on Environmental Pollution 1973–76; mem. Council, Royal Coll. of Art 1978–81, 1986–; mem. Advisory Council, Victoria & Albert Museum 1979–83, Trustee 1983–; R.S.A. Bicentenary Medal 1982 and other awards for design. *Publications:* The House Book 1974, The Kitchen Book 1977, The Bedroom & Bathroom Book 1978, The Cook Book (with Caroline Conran) 1980, The New House Book 1985, The Conran Directory of Design 1985, The Soft Furnishings Book 1986, Plants at Home 1986, Terence Conran's France 1987. *Leisure interests:* gardening, cooking. *Address:* Storehouse PLC, The Heal's Building, 196 Tottenham Court Road, London, W1P 9LD, England. *Telephone:* 01-631 0101 (Office).

CONSAGRA, Pietro; Italian sculptor; b. 4 Oct. 1920, Mazara; two s. two d.; ed. Acad. of Fine Arts, Palermo; one-man shows: Rome 1947, 1949, 1951, 1959, 1961; Milan 1958, 1961; Venice 1948; Brussels 1958; Paris 1959; Zürich 1961; São Paulo Bienal 1955, 1959; Venice Biennale 1956, 1960, New York 1962, Buenos Aires 1962, Boston 1962; Works in following museums: Tate Gallery, London; Nat. Museum and Middleheim Park, Antwerp; Museums of Modern Art, São Paulo, Paris, Rome, New York, Buenos Aires, Caracas, Zagreb, Helsinki; Guggenheim Museum, New York; Art Inst., Chicago; Carnegie Inst., Pittsburgh; Inst. of Fine Arts, Minneapolis and Houston; Grand Prize for Sculpture, Venice Biennale 1960. *Address:* Via Cassia 1162, Rome, Italy. *Telephone:* 6995119.

CONSALVI, Simón Alberto; Venezuelan diplomatist; b. 7 July 1929; m.; two c.; ed. Univ. Central de Venezuela; mem. Nat. Congress 1959–64, 1974–; Amb. to Yugoslavia 1961–64; Dir. Cen. Office of Information for the Presidency 1964–67; Pres. Nat. Inst. of Culture and Art 1967–69; Dir. Nat. Magazine of Culture; Int. Ed. El Nacional newspaper 1971–74; Minister of State for Information 1974; Perm. Rep. to UN 1974–77; Minister of Foreign Affairs 1977–79, 1985–88; fmr. Sec.-Gen. of Presidency; mem. Nat. Congress Foreign Relations Comm. *Address:* c/o Ministerio de Relaciones Exteriores, Casa Amoville, esq. Principal, Caracas, Venezuela.

CONSTÂNCIO, Vitor; Portuguese banker; b. 12 Oct. 1943, Lisbon; s. of António Francisco Constâncio and Ester Ribeiro Vieira Constâncio; m. Maria Jose Pardana Constâncio 1968; one s. one d.; ed. Instituto Superior de Ciências Económicas e Financeiras, Lisbon and Bristol Univ.; Asst. Prof. Faculty of Econs. 1965–73 and 1989–; Dir. of Global Planning Studies, Planning Research Centre 1973; Sec. of State for Planning and Budget 1974–75; Head of Econ. Research Dept., Banco de Portugal 1975; mem. Parl. 1976, 1980–82, 1987–; Chair. Parl. Comm. of Econ. and Finance 1976; Pres. of Comm. formed to negotiate with EEC 1977; Vice-Gov. Banco de Portugal 1977 and 1979–85, Gov. 1985; Minister of Finance and Planning 1978; Sec.-Gen. Socialist Party 1986–89. *Address:* rua do Caminho da Quinta, 7-A, 2780 Oeiras, Portugal. *Telephone:* 44 36 446.

CONSTANTINE XII; former King of the Hellenes; b. 2 June 1940; m. Princess Anne-Marie of Denmark 1964; three s. two d.; ed. Anavryta School and Law School, Athens Univ.; Military Training 1956–58; visited United States 1958, 1959; succeeded to throne March 1964; left Greece Dec. 1967; deposed June 1973; Monarchy abolished by Nat. Referendum Dec. 1974; Gold Medal, Yachting, Olympic Games, Rome 1960. *Address:* 4 Linnell Drive, Hampstead Way, London, N.W.11, England.

CONTAMINE, Claude Maurice; French television executive; b. 29 Aug. 1929, Metz, Moselle; s. of late Henry Contamine and Marie-Thérèse Dufays; m. Renée Jaugeon (deceased); one s.; ed. Lycée Malherbe, Caen, Facultés de Droit, Caen and Paris and Ecole Nat. d'Administration; public servant until 1964; Asst. Dir.-Gen. O.R.T.F. and Dir. of TV 1964–67; Pres. Dir.-Gen. Union générale cinématographique (U.G.C.) 1967–71; Consul-Gen. Milan 1971–72; Asst. Dir.-Gen. in charge of external affairs and co-operation, O.R.T.F. 1973–74; Minister plenipotentiary 1974; mem. Haut Conseil de l'Audiovisuel 1973–80; Pres. France-Régions (F.R.3) 1975–81; Conseiller Maître, Cour des Comptes 1981; Pres. Télédiffusion de France (T.D.F.) 1986; Pres. Dir.-Gen. société nat. de programme Antenne 2 1986–; mem. Supervisory Council, Agence-France-Presse (A.F.P.) 1987–; Chevalier, Légion d'honneur, Officier, Ordre Nat. du Mérite, Officier des Arts et des Lettres. *Address:* Antenne 2, 22 avenue Montaigne, 75387 Paris Cedex 08, France. *Telephone:* 42 99 53 35; 42 99 54 33.

CONTAMINE, Philippe, D. ÈS L.; French university professor; b. 7 May 1932, Metz; s. of Henry Contamine and Marie-Thérèse Dufays; m. Geneviève Bernard 1956; two s. one d.; ed. Lycée Malherbe, Caen, Lycée Louis-le-Grand, Paris, Sorbonne; History and Geography teacher, Lycée, Sens 1957–60, Lycée Carnot, Paris 1960–61; Asst. Prof. of Medieval History, Sorbonne 1962–65; Asst. lecturer, lecturer then Prof. of Medieval History, Univ. of Nancy 1965–73; Prof. of Medieval History, Univ. of Paris (Nanterre) 1973–, Dir. Dept. of History 1976–79; Sec. to Soc. de l'histoire de France 1984–; Scientific Dir. Centre Jeanne d'Arc Orléans 1985–; Premier Prix Gobert de l'Académie des Inscriptions et Belles-Lettres, Inst. de France 1972. *Publications:* La Guerre de cent ans 1968, Guerre, Etat et Société à la fin du Moyen Age 1972, La Vie quotidienne en France et en Angleterre pendant la guerre de cent ans 1976, La guerre au Moyen Age 1980, La France aux XIVe et XVe siècles 1981, La France de la fin du XVe siècle (co-ed.) 1985. *Address:* 11–15 rue de l'Amiral Roussin, 75015 Paris, France.

CONTE, Arthur; French journalist, politician and broadcasting executive; b. 31 March 1920, Salses, Pyrénées-Orientales; s. of Pierre Conte and Marie-Thérèse Parazols; m. Colette Lacassagne 1951; one s. one d.; ed. Montpellier Univ.; foreign leader writer, Indépendant de Perpignan 1945; later worked for Paris Match; subsequently leader-writer for Les Informations and contributor to Le Figaro, Historia, Les Nouvelles Littéraires; Sec. Socialist Party Fed. for Pyrénées-Orientales; Deputy to Nat. Assembly 1951–62, 1968–72; Sec. of State for Industry and Commerce 1957; Mayor of Salses 1947–72; Del. to Assembly of Council of Europe 1956–62; Pres. WEU Assembly 1961–62; Chair. and Dir.-Gen. ORTF 1972–73. *Publications:* La légende de Pablo Casals, Les étonnements de Mister Newborn, Les promenades de M. Tripoire, Les hommes ne sont pas des héros, La vigne sous le rempart, Yalta ou le partage du monde, Bandoung, tournant de l'histoire, Sans de Gaulle, Lénine et Staline, Les frères Burns, Hommes libres, L'épopée mondiale d'un siècle (5 vols.), Le premier janvier 1900, Le premier janvier 1920, Le premier janvier 1940, Le premier janvier 1960, Le premier janvier 1983, L'aventure européenne (2 vols.), L'homme Giscard, L'Après-Yalta, Karl Marx face à son temps, Les dictateurs du vingtième siècle, Les présidents de la cinquième république, Les premiers ministres de la Ve république, Verdun. *Leisure interest:* golf. *Address:* 94 avenue de Suffren, 75015 Paris, France. *Telephone:* 47 83 23 45.

CONTÉ, Gen. Lansana; Guinean army officer and politician; fmr. mil. commdr. of Boké Region, W. Guinea; Pres. Repub. of Guinea after mil. coup April 1984, also Prime Minister Dec. 1984–, also Minister of Defence, Security, Planning and Co-operation, and Information; Chair. Comité militaire de redressement nat. (CMRN) April 1984–. *Address:* Office du Président, Conakry, Guinea.

CONTEH, Abdulai Osman, LL.M., PH.D.; Sierra Leonean lawyer and politician; b. 5 Aug. 1945, Pepel; m.; two s. two d.; ed. Albert Acad., Freetown, London and Cambridge Univs., England; fmr. Barr.-at-Law, Lincoln's Inn; State Counsel 1974–75; private law practice 1974–77; lecturer in law, Fourah Bay Coll., Univ. of Sierra Leone 1975–77; Sec.-Gen. Sierra Leone Bar Asscn. 1975–76; Minister of Foreign Affairs 1977–84; Minister of Finance 1984–85; Attorney Gen. and Minister of Justice April 1987–;

Harold Porter Prize in Land Law, King's Coll., London Univ.; Gwang-Hwa Medal. *Leisure interests:* reading and gardening. *Address:* c/o Ministry of Justice, Freetown; P.O. Box 296, Freetown, Sierra Leone (Home). *Telephone:* 23498 (Office); 024/405 (Home).

CONTI, Rt. Rev. Mario Giuseppe, PH.L., S.T.L.; British ecclesiastic; b. 20 March 1934, Elgin; s. of Louis Joseph Conti and Josephine Quintilia Panicali; ed. Blairs Coll., Aberdeen, Pontifical Scots Coll. and Gregorian Univ., Rome; ordained Priest 1958; apptd. Curate St Mary's Cathedral, Aberdeen 1959, ordained Bishop 1977; apptd. Parish Priest St. Joschim's Wick 1962; Pres.-Treas. Scottish Catholic Int. Aid Fund 1978–84; Pres. Nat. Liturgy Comm. 1981–85, Nat. Comm. for Christian Doctrine and Unity 1985–; Vice-Pres. Comm. for Migrant Workers and Tourism 1978–84, Scottish Catholic Heritage Comm. 1980–; mem. Int. Comm. for English in the Liturgy 1978–87, (Roman Catholic) Secr. for Christian Unity 1985–; Order of Merit of the Italian Repub. 1982. *Publications:* occasional articles and letters in nat. and local press. *Leisure interests:* walking, travel, swimming, music and the arts. *Address:* Bishop's House, 156 King's Gate, Aberdeen, AB2 6BR, Scotland.

CONTI, Tom; British actor/director; s. of Alfonso Conti and Mary McGoldrick; m. Kara Wilson 1967; one d.; ed. Royal Scottish Acad. of Music; *London Theatre includes:* Savages (Christopher Hampton) 1973, The Devil's Disciple (Shaw) 1976, Whose Life is it Anyway? (Brian Clarke) 1978, They're Playing Our Song (Neil Simon/Marvin Hamlisch) 1980, Romantic Comedy (Bernard Salde); *Films include:* Flame, Full Circle, Blade on the Feather, Merry Christmas Mr. Lawrence, Reuben, American Dreamer, Saving Grace, Miracles, Heavenly Pursuits, Beyond Therapy, Roman Holiday, Two Brothers Running, White Roses, Shirley Valentine; *Television work includes:* Madame Bovary, Treats, The Glittering Prizes, The Norman Conquests. *Directed:* Last Licks, Broadway 1979, Before the Party 1980; West End Theatre Managers' Award; Royal Television Soc. Award, Variety Club of Great Britain Award 1978, Tony Award of New York 1979. *Leisure interest:* music. *Address:* APA, 9000 Sunset Boulevard, Los Angeles, Calif., U.S.A.; (Agent) Plant & Froggatt, 4 Windmill Street, London, W.1, England.

CONVERSE, Philip E., PH.D.; American author and professor of political science; b. 17 Nov. 1928, Concord, N.H.; s. of Rev. Ernest L. and Evelyn (Eaton) Converse; m. Jean G. McDonnell 1951; two s.; ed. Denison Univ. (Ohio), State Univ. of Iowa and Univ. of Michigan; Asst. Prof. of Sociology Univ. of Mich. 1960–63, Assoc. Prof. of Political Science 1963–65, Prof. of Sociology and Political Science 1965–, Program Dir. Survey Research Center 1965–, Robert C. Angell Distinguished Prof. of Political Science and Sociology 1975–, Dir. Center for Political Studies 1982–86; Dir. Inst. for Social Research 1986–; Fulbright Fellow 1959–60; Guggenheim Fellow 1975–76; Fellow American Acad. of Arts and Sciences, N.A.S., A.A.A.S.; Pres. Int. Soc. of Political Psychology 1980–81; Pres. American Political Science Asscn. 1983–84. *Publications:* The American Voter 1960, The Nature of Belief Systems in Mass Publics 1964, Elections and the Political Order 1966, The Human Meaning of Social Change 1972, The Quality of American Life 1976, Political Representation in France 1986, and many articles. *Leisure interests:* sports and music. *Address:* Institute for Social Research, The University of Michigan, Ann Arbor, Mich. 48104 (Office); 1312 Cambridge Road, Ann Arbor, Mich. 48104, U.S.A. (Home). *Telephone:* (313) 763-1347 (Office); (313) 663-3113 (Home).

CONWAY, Hugh Graham, C.B.E., M.A.; British mechanical engineer; b. 25 Jan. 1914, Vancouver, Canada; s. of George R. G. and A. E. Conway; m. Eva Gordon-Simpson 1937 (died 1980); two s.; ed. Merchiston Castle School, Edinburgh, and Univ. of Cambridge; aircraft industry 1936–; Chief Eng., then Man. Dir. Short Bros. and Harland Ltd., Belfast; Man. Dir. Bristol Siddeley Engines Ltd. 1964; Group Man. Dir. Rolls Royce Ltd. 1970; Dir. Rolls Royce (1971) Ltd. 1971; now engaged in consultancy; Deputy Chair. Design Council 1972–76; Pres. Inst. of Mech. Engs. 1967; mem. Decimal Currency Bd., generally credited with design of the 50p coin; Hon. D.Sc. *Publications:* several textbooks, books on Ettore Bugatti. *Leisure interest:* vintage motoring, especially Bugatti. *Address:* 33 Sussex Square, London, W.2, England. *Telephone,* 01-262 8136.

CONWAY, John Horton, M.A., PH.D., F.R.S.; British mathematician; ed. Gonville and Caius Coll., Cambridge; Lecturer in Pure Math., Cambridge Univ. 1973, Reader in Pure Math. and Math. Statistics 1973–83, Prof. of Math. 1983–; John von Neumann Prof. of Math., Princeton Univ.; Fellow Sidney Sussex Coll., Cambridge 1963–68, Gonville and Caius Coll., Cambridge 1968–; Polya Prize London Mathematical Soc. 1987. *Publications:* Regular Algebra and Finite Machines 1971, On Numbers and Games 1976, Atlas of Finite Groups 1985. *Address:* Department of Mathematics, Princeton University, Fine Hall, Washington Road, Princeton, N.J. 08544, U.S.A.

COOBAR, Abdulmegid; Libyan politician; b. 1909; ed. Arabic and Italian schools in Tripoli, and privately; with Birth Registration Section, Tripoli Municipal Council and later its Section Head, Adviser on Arab Affairs for the Council 1943–44; resigned from Govt. Service 1944; mem. Nat. Constitutional Assembly 1950, and mem. its Cttee. to draft the Libyan Constitution; mem. of Parl. for Eastern Gharian 1952–55, Pres. of Parl. Assembly 1952–55; Deputy Prime Minister and Minister of Communications

1955–56; again elected for Eastern Gharian to the new Chamber of Deputies 1955, Pres. 1956; mem. of Council of Viceroy 1956; Deputy Prime Minister and Minister of Foreign Affairs 1957; Prime Minister 1957–60; concurrently Minister for Foreign Affairs 1958–60; Independence Award (1st Class). *Address:* Sir Asadu el-Furat Street 29, Garden City, Tripoli, Libya.

COOK, Sir Alan Hugh, Kt. O.B.E., M.A., PH.D., SC.D., F.R.S., F.R.S.E., F.INST.P.; British professor of natural philosophy; b. 2 Dec. 1922, Felstead; s. of Reginald Thomas Cook and Ethel (née Saxon) Cook; m. Isabell Weir Adamson 1948; one s. one d.; ed. Westcliffe High School, Corpus Christi Coll., Cambridge; scientist Nat. Physical Lab., Teddington 1952–69; First Prof. of Geophysics, Univ. of Edin. 1969–72; Jacksonian Prof. of Natural Philosophy, Univ. of Cambridge 1972–; Master of Selwyn Coll., Cambridge 1983–; Visiting Fellow, Jt. Inst. for Lab. Astrophysics, Univ. of Colorado 1965–66; Visiting Prof. Univ. of Calif. at Los Angeles, Berkeley and San Diego 1981–82; Ed. Geophysical Journal 1958–85; Pres. Royal Astronomical Soc. 1977–79; Foreign Fellow Acad. Nazionale Lincei, Rome, C.V. Boys Prize. *Publications:* Gravity and the Earth 1969, Global Geophysics 1970, Interference/Electromagnetic Waves 1971, Physics of the Earth and Planets 1973, Celestial Masers 1977, Interiors of the Planets 1980, The Motion of the Moon 1988, and many contributions to learned journals. *Leisure interests:* travel, painting, listening to music. *Address:* The Master's Lodge, Selwyn College, Cambridge, CB3 9DQ; Cavendish Laboratory, Madingley Road, Cambridge, England. *Telephone:* (0223) 335889; (0223) 337324 (Laboratory).

COOK, Brian (Robert) Rayner, B.A., A.R.C.M.; British professional singer (baritone); b. 17 May 1945, London; s. of Robert Cook and Gladys Soulby; m. Angela M. Romney 1974; one s. one d.; ed. Univ. of Bristol, Royal Coll. of Music and privately with Alexander Young (vocal studies) and Helga Mott (repertoire); church organist and choirmaster at age 15; major conducting début (opera) 1966; professional singing début 1967; has appeared as soloist in oratorio, recitals, music-theatre and opera throughout the U.K. and Europe, in U.S.A., Canada, S. America, the Middle East, the Far East and N. Africa and broadcasts frequently in U.K. and Europe; has given first performances of various works written for him by distinguished composers; Dir. Singer's workshops and Jury men. int. singing competitions; Visiting Tutor in Vocal Studies, Birmingham School of Music 1980–; Welsh Coll. of Music and Drama, Cardiff 1988; Kathleen Ferrier Memorial Scholarship 1969 and many other major singing prizes; recordings include opera, oratorio and song ranging from Schütz and Charpentier to Fauré, Elgar, Delius and Vaughan Williams. *Leisure interests:* 78 r.p.m. records, Laurel and Hardy films, messing about in boats, relaxing, conjuring. *Address:* The Quavers, 53 Friars Avenue, Friern Barnet, London, N20 0XG, England. *Telephone:* 01-368 3010.

COOK, G(eorge) Bradford, J.D.; American lawyer and company executive; b. 10 May 1937, Lincoln, Neb.; s. of George B. Cook and Margaret Colman; m. Laura Shedd Armour 1966; one s. five d.; ed. Stanford Univ. and Univ. of Nebraska Law School; Partner, Winston & Strawn, Chicago, Ill. 1962–71; U.S. Securities and Exchange Comm. (SEC), Washington, D.C., Gen. Counsel 1971–72, Dir. Div. of Market Regulation 1972–73, Chair. March-May 1973 (resigned); Chair. of Bd. and Chief Exec. Officer Farragut Investments Inc. *Leisure interests:* skiing, hunting, fishing. *Address:* 4808 Rockwood Parkway, N.W., Washington, D.C. 20016; and Woman Lake, Longville, Minn. 56655, U.S.A. *Telephone:* 202-244-1240 and 218-363-2078 (Homes).

COOK, Gordon Charles, M.D., D.SC., M.R.C.S., F.R.C.P., F.R.A.C.P.; British physician; b. 17 Feb. 1932, London; s. of Charles F. Cook and Kate (Grainger) Cook; m. Elizabeth J. Agg-Large 1963; one s. three d.; ed. Wellingborough Grammar School, Kingston-upon-Thames, Raynes Park Grammar Schools and Royal Free Hospital School of Medicine, Univ. of London; junior appts. Royal Free Hosp., Brompton Hosp. and Royal Northern Hosp. 1958–60; medical specialist, R.A.M.C. and Royal Nigerian Army 1960–62; Lecturer in Medicine, Royal Free Hosp. School of Medicine 1963–65, 1967–69, Makerere Univ., Uganda 1965–67; Prof. of Medicine, Univ. of Zambia 1969–74, Univ. of Riyadh, Saudi Arabia 1974–75; Visiting Prof. of Medicine, Univs. of Basrah and Mosul, Iraq 1976; Sr. Lecturer in Clinical Tropical Medicine, London School of Hygiene and Tropical Medicine 1976–; Consultant Physician, Univ. Coll. Hosp. and Hosp. for Tropical Diseases, London 1976–; Hon. Consultant Physician, St. Luke's Hosp. for the Clergy 1988–; Prof. of Medicine and Chair. Clinical Sciences Dept., Univ. of Papua New Guinea 1978–81; Examiner, Royal Coll. of Physicians, Univs. of London and Makerere, Uganda; Ed. Quarterly Journal of Medicine and Journal of Infection; mem. Jt. Cttee. on Higher Medical Training; Medical Adviser, British Council and ICI; mem. numerous medical and scientific socs.; Frederick Murgatroyd Memorial Prize, Royal Coll. of Physicians, London 1973. *Publications:* Tropical Gastroenterology 1980, Communicable and Tropical Diseases 1988, 100 Clinical Problems in Tropical Medicine (jointly) 1987; more than 200 papers on physiology, gastroenterology, tropical medicine, nutrition and medical education. *Leisure interests:* cricket, cycling, walking, medical history, African and Pacific artefacts. *Address:* Department of Clinical Tropical Medicine, Hospital for Tropical Diseases, St. Pancras Way, London, NW1 0PE (Office); 11 Old London Road, St. Albans, Herts., AL1 1QE, England (Home). *Telephone:* 01-387 4411 (Office); (0727) 69000 (Home).

COOK, John Manuel, M.A., F.B.A., F.S.A.; British academic (retd.); b. 11 Dec. 1910, Sheffield; s. of Rev. Charles R. Cook and Mary M. Arnold; m. 1st Enid M. Robertson 1939, 2nd Nancy E. Law 1977; two s.; ed. Marlborough Coll. and King's Coll., Cambridge; Asst. and lecturer, Edinburgh Univ. 1936-46; war service in Royal Scots, Force 133 (Greece), H.Q. Land Forces, Greece, Lt.-Col. 1945; Dir. British School, Athens 1946-54, Visiting Fellow 1978; Lecturer, Reader and Prof. of Ancient History and Classical Archaeology, Univ. of Bristol 1954-76, Dean of Arts 1966-68, Pro-Vice-Chancellor 1972-75; C. E. Norton Lecturer, Archaeological Inst. of America 1961-62; Visiting Prof. Yale Univ. 1965; Gray Memorial Lecturer, Cambridge 1969; Geddes Harrower Prof., Univ. of Aberdeen 1977. *Publications:* The Greeks in Ionia and the East 1962, The Sanctuary of Hemithea at Kastabos (with W. H. Plommer) 1966, The Troad 1973, The Persian Empire 1983. *Address:* 8 Dalrymple Crescent, Edinburgh, EH9 2NU, Scotland. *Telephone:* 667-6563.

COOK, Lodwrick M., B.S., M.B.A.; American petroleum company executive; b. 1928, Grand Cane, La.; one s. three d.; ed. Louisiana State Univ. and Southern Methodist Univ.; Eng. Trainee, Atlantic Richfield Co. 1956-61, Man. positions in labour relations, refining, marketing, planning, supply and transportation 1961-70, Vice-Pres. 1979, Chair. of Owners' Cttee., Trans-Alaskan Pipeline System 1975-77, Sr. Vice-Pres., Transportation, Atlantic Richfield 1977-80, Exec. Vice-Pres. and mem. of Bd. 1980, C.O.O./Products 1982, Pres. and C.E.O. 1985, Chair. and C.E.O. Atlantic Richfield Co. 1986-. *Address:* Atlantic Richfield Company, 515 South Flower Street, Los Angeles, Calif. 90071, U.S.A. *Telephone:* (213) 486-2533.

COOK, Peter Edward, B.A.; British writer and entertainer; b. 17 Nov. 1937; s. of Alexander and Margaret Cook; m. 1st Wendy Snowden 1964, two d.; m. 2nd Judy Huxtable 1973; ed. Radley Coll., Pembroke Coll., Cambridge; appeared in and co-author of revues: Pieces of Eight 1958, One Over the Eight 1959, Beyond the Fringe, London and New York 1959-64; Behind the Fridge, Australia and London 1971-72; Good Evening, U.S.A. 1973-75; TV series Not Only but Also (with Dudley Moore, q.v.) 1965-71, Revolver 1978. *Films include:* The Wrong Box 1965, Bedazzled 1967, A Dandy in Aspic 1969, Monte Carlo or Bust 1969, The Bed-Sitting Room 1970, The Rise and Rise of Michael Rimmer 1971, The Hound of the Baskervilles 1978, Derek and Clive 1980, Yellowbeard 1983, Supergirl 1984, Whoops Apocalypse 1987, Mr Jolly Lives Next Door 1987. *Publications:* Dud and Pete: The Dagenham Dialogues 1971 and contributions to various humorous and satirical periodicals. *Leisure interests:* gambling, gossip, golf. *Address:* c/o Wright and Webb, 10 Soho Square, London, W.1, England. *Telephone:* 01-734 9641.

COOK, Robert Manuel, M.A., F.B.A.; British academic (retd.); b. 4 July 1909, Sheffield; s. of Charles Robert and Mary Manuel Cook; m. Kathleen Porter 1938 (died 1979); ed. Marlborough Coll. and Cambridge Univ.; Asst. Lecturer in Classics, Manchester Univ. 1934-38, Lecturer 1938-45; Laurence Reader in Classical Archaeology, Cambridge Univ. 1945-62, Laurence Prof. 1962-76; Chair. British School at Athens 1983-87; O.M. Deutsches Archäologishes Institut. *Publications:* Greek Painted Pottery 1960, Greek Art 1972, Clazomenian Sarcophagi 1981. *Address:* 15 Wilberforce Road, Cambridge, CB3 OEQ, England. *Telephone:* (0223) 352863.

COOK, Robert (Robin) Finlayson, M.A., M.P.; British politician; b. 28 Feb. 1946; s. of Peter Cook and Christina Cook (née Lynch); m. Margaret K. Whitmore 1969; two s.; ed. Aberdeen Grammar School and Univ. of Edinburgh; Tutor-Organiser with Workers' Educ. Asscn. 1970-74; Labour M.P. for Edinburgh Cen. 1974-83, for Livingston 1983-; Chair. Scottish Asscn. of Labour Student Orgns. 1966-67; Sec. Edin. City Labour Party 1970-72; mem. Edin. Corpn. 1971-74, Chair. Housing Cttee. 1973-74; an Opposition Treasury Spokesman 1980-83; Opposition Spokesman on Trade 1986-87; Labour's Campaign Co-ordinator 1984-86; Opposition Front Bench Spokesman on European and Community Affairs 1983-86, on Health and Social Security 1987-; mem. Tribune Group. *Leisure interests:* eating, reading and talking. *Address:* House of Commons, London, SW1A 0AA, England. *Telephone:* 01-219 5120.

COOK, Stanton R., B.S.; American newspaper publisher; b. 3 July 1925, Chicago, Ill.; s. of Rufus M. Cook and Thelma M. Borgerson; m. Barbara Wilson 1950; ed. Northwestern Univ.; Dist. sales rep. Shell Oil Co. 1949-51; Production Eng. Chicago Tribune Co. 1951-60, Asst. Production Man. 1960-65, Production Man. 1965-67, Production Dir. 1967-70, Dir. Operations 1970, Gen. Man. 1970-72, Publisher 1973-, Pres. 1972-74, Chief Officer 1974-76, Chair. 1974-81; Dir. Tribune Co. Chicago 1972-, Pres. and C.E.O. 1974-; Dir. A.P. 1975-84; Deputy Chair. and Dir. Fed. Reserve Bank of Chicago 1980-83, Chair. 1984-85. *Address:* Chicago Tribune, 435 North Michigan Avenue, Chicago, Ill. 60611, U.S.A.

COOK, Stephen Arthur, PH.D., F.R.S.C.; American university professor; b. 14 Dec. 1939, Buffalo, N.Y.; s. of Gerhard A. Cook and Lura Lincoln Cook; m. Linda Craddock 1968; two s.; ed. Univ. of Michigan and Harvard Univ.; Asst. Prof. of Math., Univ. of Calif. at Berkeley 1966-70; Assoc. Prof. of Computer Science, Univ. of Toronto, Canada 1970-75, Prof. 1975-85, Univ. Prof. 1985-; E.W.R. Staecie Memorial Fellowship 1977-78; Killam Research Fellow, Canada Council 1982-83; Turing Award, Assoc. Computing Machinery 1982; mem. N.A.S., American Acad. of Arts and Science. *Publi-*

cations: numerous articles in professional journals on theory of computation. *Leisure interests:* sailing, playing violin. *Address:* Department of Computer Science, University of Toronto, Toronto, M5S 1A4 (Office); 6 Indian Valley Crescent, Toronto, M6R 1Y6, Canada (Home).

COOKE, (Alfred) Alistair; American (b. British) writer and broadcaster; b. 20 Nov. 1908, Manchester, England; s. of Samuel Cooke and Mary Elizabeth Byrne; m. 1st Ruth Emerson 1934, 2nd Jane White Hawkes; one s. one d.; ed. Jesus Coll., Cambridge, Yale and Harvard Univs.; Film Critic, BBC 1934-37; London Corresp. Nat. Broadcasting Co. 1936-37; Special Corresp. on American Affairs, The Times 1938-41; Commentator on American Affairs BBC 1938-, wrote and narrated America: a Personal History of the United States, BBC TV 1972-73; American feature writer, Daily Herald 1941-44; UN Corresp. The Manchester Guardian (now The Guardian) 1945-48, Chief Corresp. in U.S.A. 1948-72; Peabody Award 1952, 1972, Writers' Guild Award for best documentary 1972, Dimbleby Award 1973, four Emmy Awards (Nat. Acad. of TV Arts and Sciences, U.S.A.) 1973, Benjamin Franklin Award 1973, Hon. K.B.E. 1973; Hon. LL.D. (Edinburgh, Manchester), Hon. Litt.D. (St. Andrews) 1975, Hon. D.Lit. (Cambridge) 1988, Medal for Spoken Language (American Acad. of Arts and Letters) 1983. *Publications:* Garbo and the Night Watchmen (edited) 1937, Douglas Fairbanks 1940, A Generation on Trial: U.S.A. v. Alger Hiss 1950, One Man's America (English title Letters from America) 1952, Christmas Eve 1952, A Commencement Address 1954, The Vintage Mencken (edited) 1955, Around the World in Fifty Years 1966, Talk about America 1968, Alistair Cooke's America 1973, Six Men 1977, The Americans: Fifty Letters from America on Our Life and Times 1979, Above London (with Robert Cameron), Masterpieces 1982, The Patient has the Floor 1986, America Observed: The Newspaper Years of Alistair Cooke 1989. *Leisure interests:* golf, music, travel, photography. *Address:* 1150 Fifth Avenue, New York, N.Y. 10028; Nassau Point, Cutchogue, Long Island, N.Y. 11935, U.S.A.

COOKE, George William, C.B.E., PH.D., C.CHEM., F.R.S.; British agricultural scientist; b. 6 Jan. 1916, Kingston-on-Soar; s. of William H. Cooke and Sarah J. (née Whittaker) Cooke; m. Elisabeth H. Hill 1944; one s. one d.; ed. Loughborough Grammar School, Univ. Coll., Nottingham; Ministry of Agric. research scholar, Rothamsted Experimental Station 1938-41, Scientific Officer, Chem. Dept. 1941-56, Head, Chem. Dept. 1956-75, Deputy Dir. 1962-75, Hon. Scientist attached to Soils Div. 1981-; Chief Scientific Officer, Agric. Research Council 1975-81; research medals of Royal Agric. Soc. of England and Soc. of Chem. Industry. *Publications:* Fertilizers and Profitable Farming 1959, Control of Soil Fertility 1967, Fertilizing for Maximum Yield 1972; some 200 papers in scientific journals. *Leisure interests:* advancing the use of agricultural science for the improvement of mankind's food supply; boats on inland waterways. *Address:* Rothamsted Experimental Station, Harpenden, Herts., AL5 2JQ (Office); 33 Topstreet Way, Harpenden, Herts., AL5 5TU, England (Home). *Telephone:* 058-27-63133 (Office); 058-27 2899 (Home).

COOKE, Herbert Basil Sutton, D.SC., F.R.S.S.A.; Canadian professor of geology; b. 17 Oct. 1915, Johannesburg, S.A.; s. of Herbert Sutton Cooke and Edith Mary Sutton; m. Dorothea Winifred Hughes 1943; two s.; ed. King Edward School, Johannesburg, Cambridge Univ. and Univ. of the Witwatersrand; geologist Cen. Mining and Investment Corpn., Johannesburg 1936-38; Jr. Lecturer, lecturer in Geology, Univ. of the Witwatersrand 1938-47, Sr. Lecturer 1953-61; Prin. Geologist Univ. of Calif. African Expedition 1947-48; Pvt. Geological Consultant, Johannesburg 1948-53; Prof. of Geology, Dalhousie Univ. N.S. 1961-81, Emer. Prof. 1981-, Dean Faculty of Arts and Science 1963-68; Geological Consultant B.C. 1981-85; Pres. S.A. Geographical Soc. 1949-50, S.A. Archaeological Soc. 1950-51, Nova Scotian Inst. of Science 1967-68, Royal Commonwealth Soc. 1985-89; Hon. LL.D. (Dalhousie) 1981; Canadian Centennial Medal 1967. *Publications:* Geology for South African Students (with G. N. Hamilton) 1939, Science in South Africa 1949, The Contribution of C. Van Riet Lowe to Prehistory in Southern Africa (ed. with B. D. Malan) 1962, Evolution of African Mammals (ed. with V. J. Maglio), over 80 scientific monographs and papers. *Leisure interests:* travel, photography. *Address:* 2133-154th Street, White Rock, B.C. V4A 4S5, Canada. *Telephone:* (604) 536 0363.

COOKE, Jean Esme Oregon, R.A.; British artist; b. 18 Feb. 1927; d. of Arthur Oregon Cooke and Dorothy E. Cranefield; m. John Bratby (q.v.) 1953 (divorced 1977); three s. one d.; ed. Blackheath High School, Cen. School of Arts and Crafts, Camberwell, City & Guilds School, Goldsmiths' Coll. School of Art and Royal Coll. of Art; pottery workshop 1950-53; lecturer in Painting, Royal Coll. of Art 1964-74; mem. Council, Royal Acad. 1983-85; numerous one-man shows in London and throughout Britain 1963-; works exhibited annually at Royal Acad. and in other group exhbns.; made TV film for B.B.C. Portrait of John Bratby 1978. *Publication:* Contemporary British Artists, The Artist 1980. *Leisure interests:* undergardening, talking, shouting, walking along the beach. *Address:* 7 Hardy Road, Blackheath, London, S.E.3, England. *Telephone:* 01-858 6288

COOKE, Rt. Hon. Sir Robin Brunskill, K.B.E., P.C., M.A., PH.D., Q.C.; New Zealand judge; b. 9 May 1926, Wellington; s. of Hon. Philip Brunskill Cooke, M.C. and Valmai Digby Gore; m. Phyllis Annette Miller 1952; three s.; ed. Victoria Univ. Coll., Wellington, Clare Coll., Cambridge, Gonville & Caius Coll., Cambridge; called to Bar, Inner Temple 1954; practised at

New Zealand Bar 1955–72; Judge of Supreme Court 1972–76, of Court of Appeal 1976–86, Pres. of Court of Appeal 1986–; Chair. Comm. of Inquiry into Housing 1970–71; Fellow Gonville & Caius Coll. 1952, Hon Fellow 1982; Hon. Bencher 1985; Yorke Prize 1954. *Publications:* Ed. Portrait of a Profession (Centennial Book of N.Z. Law Soc.); articles in law reviews. *Leisure interests:* The Times crossword, theatre, running. *Address:* 4 Homewood Crescent, Karori, Wellington 5, New Zealand. *Telephone:* 768-059.

COOKSON, Catherine, O.B.E.; British author, b. 20 June 1906, Jarrow, Northumberland; d. of Catherine Fawcett; m. Thomas Cookson 1940; worked as a laundress in a workhouse, Hastings until 1939. *Publications* include: Kate Hannigan 1950, Maggie Rowan 1954, A Grand Man 1954 (film: Jacqueline 1956), Rooney 1955 (filmed 1958), The Lord and Mary Ann 1956, The Menagerie 1958, The Devil and Mary Ann 1958, Love and Mary Ann 1961, The Garment 1962, Life and Mary Ann 1962, The Blind Miller 1963, Hannah Massey 1964, Marriage and Mary Ann 1964, Mary Ann's Angels 1965, Katie Mulholland 1967, Mary Ann and Bill 1967, The Round Tower 1968 (R.S.L. Winifred Holtby Award for the Best Regional Novel), Our Kate (autobiography) 1969, The Glass Virgin 1970, The Dwelling Place 1971, Pure as a Lily 1972, The Mallen Streak 1973, The Mallen Girl 1974, The Mallen Litter 1974, The Invisible Cord 1975, The Tide of Life 1976, The Girl 1977, The Cinder Path 1978, The Man who Cried 1979, Tilly Trotter 1980, Tilly Trotter Wed 1981, Tilly Trotter Widowed 1982, Hamilton 1983, The Whip 1983, The Black Velvet Gown 1984, Goodbye Hamilton 1985, A Dinner of Herbs 1985, Catherine Cookson Country (memoirs) 1986, Bill Bailey 1986, The Parson's Daughter 1986, Bill Bailey's Daughter 1989; also several novels as Catherine Marchant. *Address:* Bristol Lodge, Langley on Tyne, Northumberland, England.

COOKSON, Richard Clive, PH.D., F.R.S.C., F.R.S.; British chemist; b. 27 Aug. 1922, Hexham; s. of Clive and Marion (James) Cookson; m. Ellen Fawaz 1948; two s.; ed. Harrow School and Trinity Coll. Cambridge; Research Fellow, Harvard Univ. 1948; Research Chemist, Glaxo Labs. Ltd. 1949–51; Lecturer, Birkbeck Coll. London 1951–57; Prof. of Chem. Univ. of Southampton 1957–85, Prof. Emer. 1985–; Dir. Cookson Chemicals Ltd. 1986–. *Publications:* research papers. *Address:* Manor House, Stratford Tony, Salisbury, Wilts., SP5 4AT, England.

COOLEY, Denton Arthur, B.A., M.D.; American surgeon; b. 22 Aug. 1920, Houston, Tex.; s. of Ralph C. Cooley and Mary Fraley Cooley; m. Louise Goldsborough Thomas 1949; five d.; ed. Univ. of Texas and Johns Hopkins Univ. School of Medicine; Intern Johns Hopkins School of Medicine, Baltimore 1944–45, Instructor surgery 1945–50; Sr. Surgical Registrar Thoracic Surgery, Brompton Hospital for Chest Diseases, London 1950–51; Assoc. Prof. of Surgery Baylor Univ. Coll. of Medicine, Houston 1954–62, Prof. 1962–69; Surgeon-in-Chief (founder) Texas Heart Inst., Houston 1962–; Clinical Prof. of Surgery, Univ. of Texas Medical School, Houston 1975–; served Capt., Chief Surgical Service, Army Medical Corps, Linz, Austria 1946–48; has performed numerous heart transplants; implanted first artificial heart 1969; Hon. Fellow Royal Coll. of Physicians and Surgeons 1980, Royal Coll. of Surgeons 1984, Royal Australasian Coll. of Surgeons 1986; mem. numerous socs. and assocns.; Hon. Doctorem Medicinae (Turin) 1969; numerous awards and prizes include: Hoktoen Gold Medal 1954, Grande Médaille, Univ. of Ghent, Belgium 1963, René Leriche Prize, Int. Surgical Soc. 1965–67, Billings Gold Medal, American Medical Assen. 1967, Semmelweis Medal 1973, St. Francis Cabrini Gold Medal (first recipient) 1980, Theodore Roosevelt Award, Nat. Collegiate Athletic Assen. 1980, Presidential Medal of Freedom 1984; Knight Commdr., Order of Merit of Italian Repub., Order of the Sun, Peru and others. *Publications:* Surgical Treatment of Congenital Heart Disease 1966, Techniques in Cardiac Surgery 1975, Techniques in Vascular Surgery 1979, Techniques in Cardiac Surgery 1984, Essays of Denton A. Cooley—Reflections and Observations 1984; over 1,000 scientific articles. *Leisure interests:* golf, tennis, ranching. *Address:* Texas Heart Institute, P.O. Box 20345, 6621 Fannin Street, Houston, Tex. 77025 (Office); 3014 Del Monte, Houston, Tex. 77019, U.S.A. (Home). *Telephone:* 713/791-4900 (Office).

COOLS, André; Belgian politician; b. 1 Aug. 1927, Flémalle-Grande, Liège; s. of Marcel Cools; m. Thérèse Josis 1948; one s. one d.; fmr. Sec.-Receiver of Public Assistance Comm.; Socialist Deputy from Liège 1958–; Mayor of Flémalle-Haute; Minister of the Budget 1968–71, 1972–73, of Econ. Affairs 1971–72; Deputy Prime Minister 1969–73; Minister of State 1985; Co-Pres. Belgian Socialist Party 1973–81; Chevalier Ordre de Léopold, Grand Officer Order of Merit (Italy). *Address:* 75 Rue Village, 4110 Flémalle, Belgium. *Telephone:* (041) 336702.

COOMBS, Douglas Saxon, PH.D., F.R.S.N.Z.; New Zealand professor of geology; b. 23 Nov. 1924, Dunedin; m. Anne G. Tarrant 1956; two s. one d.; ed. King's High School, Dunedin, Univ. of Otago, Emmanuel Coll., Cambridge; Asst. Lecturer in Geology, Univ. of Otago 1947–48, lecturer 1949, 1952–55, Prof. 1956–; Exhbn. Scholar, Emmanuel Coll., Cambridge 1949–52; Visiting Prof. Pa. State Univ. 1960, Yale Univ. 1967–68, Geneva Univ. 1968, 1975, Univ. of Calif. 1982; Chair. Bd. of Govs., King's High School 1979–88; Fellow Mineralogical Soc. of America; Foreign Assoc. N.A.S. 1977; Hon. Fellow Geological Soc. of London 1968, Geological Soc. of America 1983; Hon. mem. Mineralogical Soc. of Great Britain and Ireland 1986; Mckay Hammer Award, Geological Soc. of N.Z. 1961, Hector

Medal, Royal Soc. of N.Z. 1969. *Publications:* numerous scientific papers. *Leisure interests:* cricket, fishing, walking. *Address:* Geology Department, University of Otago, P.O. Box 56, Dunedin (Univ.); 6 Tolcarne Avenue, Dunedin, New Zealand (Home). *Telephone:* (024) 797-520 (Univ.); (024) 775-699 (Home).

COOMBS, Herbert Cole, F.A.A., PH.D., F.A.S.S.A.; Australian fmr. banker; b. 24 Feb. 1906, Kalamunda, W. Australia; s. of the late F. R. H. Coombs and Rebecca M. Coombs; m. Mary A. Ross 1931; three s. one d.; ed. Univ. of Western Australia and London School of Economics and Political Science; Asst. Economist, Commonwealth Bank of Australia 1935; Economist to Commonwealth Treasury 1939; mem. Commonwealth Bank Bd. 1942; Dir. of Rationing 1942; Dir.-Gen. of Post-War Reconstruction 1943; Gov. Commonwealth Bank of Australia 1949–60; Chair. Commonwealth Bank Bd. 1951–60; Gov. Reserve Bank of Australia 1960–68, Chair. Reserve Bank Bd. 1960–68; Chair. Australian Council for Aboriginal Affairs 1968–75; Chair. Australian Council for the Arts 1968–74; Chancellor Australian Nat. Univ. 1968–76; Consultant to the Prime Minister 1972–75; Chair. Royal Comm. on Australian Govt. Admin. 1974–76; Hon. Fellow, L.S.E.; Visiting Fellow, Centre for Resource and Environmental Studies, Australian Nat. Univ. 1976–; Hon. LL.D. (Melbourne, Sydney and Australian Nat. Univs.), Hon. D.Litt. (Western Australia), Hon. D.Sc. (N.S.W.) 1985, Hon. F.A.A.H. *Publications:* Other People's Money 1971, The Fragile Pattern 1970: Institutions and Man, Kulinma: Listening to Aboriginal Australians 1978, Conservation (co-author), Trial Balance—Issues in a Working Life 1981, A Certain Heritage: Programs by and for Aboriginal Families (co-author) 1983, The Role of the National Aboriginal Conference 1984, Training and Employment for Aborigines (co-author) 1985, Land of Promises: Aborigines and Development in the East Kimberley (co-author) 1989, The Return of Scarcity: Essays Economic and Environmental. *Leisure interests:* music, cooking, walking, wine. *Address:* P.O. Box 4, Canberra, A.C.T. 2601 (Office); 119 Milson Road, Cremorne, N.S.W. 2090, Australia (Home). *Telephone:* 062-492011 (Office); 02-902866 (Home).

COOMBS, Philip H.; American economist and educator; b. 15 Aug. 1915, Holyoke, Mass.; s. of Chas and Nellie Coombs; m. Helena Brooks 1941; one s. one d.; ed. Holyoke Public Schools, Amherst Coll., Univ. of Chicago and Brookings Inst.; Instructor in Econs., Williams Coll., Mass. 1940–41; Economist, Office of Price Admin. 1941–42; Econ. Adviser, Office of Strategic Services 1942–45; Econ. Adviser to Dir. of Office of Econ. Stabilization 1945–46; Deputy Dir. Veterans Emergency Housing Program 1946–47; Prof. of Econs., Amherst Coll. 1947–49; Exec. Dir. President's Materials Policy Comm. (Paley Comm.) 1951–52; Sec. and Dir. of Research, Fund for Advancement of Educ. (Ford Foundation) 1952–61, Program Dir., Educ. Div., Ford Foundation 1957–61; Asst. Sec. of State for Educational and Cultural Affairs, Dept. of State 1961–62; Fellow Council on Foreign Relations 1962–63; Dir. Int. Inst. for Educational Planning (UNESCO), Paris 1963–68, Dir. of Research 1969–70; Co-founder Center for Educational Enquiry 1970; Vice-Chair. Int. Council for Educational Devt. 1970–; Faculty mem. Inst. of Social and Policy Studies, Yale Univ. 1970–72; Visiting Scholar, Univ. of London Inst. of Educ. 1983–86; official numerous educational orgs.; Hon. L.H.D. (Amherst Coll.), LL.D. (Brandeis Univ. and Monmouth Coll.). *Publications:* The Fourth Dimension of Foreign Policy 1964, Education and Foreign Aid 1965, The World Educational Crisis—A Systems Analysis 1968, Managing Educational Costs 1972, New Paths to Learning: for Rural Children and Youth 1973, Attacking Rural Poverty: How Nonformal Education Can Help 1974, Education for Rural Development: Cases Studies for Planners 1975, Meeting the Basic Needs of the Rural Poor: The Integrated, Community-Based Approach 1980, Future Critical World Issues in Education 1981, New Strategies for Improving Rural Family Life 1981, The World Crisis in Education: The View from the Eighties 1985, Cost Analysis: A Tool for Educational Policy and Planning 1987. *Leisure interests:* sailing, fishing, swimming, reading, touring, house repairs, community service. *Address:* International Council for Educational Development, Box 217, Essex, Conn. 06426 (Office); River Road, Essex, Conn. 06426 U.S.A. (Home). *Telephone:* (203) 767-8789.

COOMBS, Robert Royston Amos, SC.D., F.R.S., F.R.C.PATH.; British professor of immunology; b. 9 Jan. 1921; s. of Charles R. and Edris (née Coombs) Amos; m. Anne M. Blomfield 1952; one s. one d.; ed. Diocesan Coll., Cape Town, South Africa, Univs. of Edinburgh and Cambridge; Stringer Fellow, King's Coll., Cambridge 1947; Asst. Dir. of Research, Dept. of Pathology, Univ. of Cambridge 1948, Reader in Immunology 1963–66, Quick Prof. of Biology and Head, Immunology Div. Dept. of Pathology 1966–; Fellow, Corpus Christi Coll. Cambridge 1962–; foreign corresp. Royal Acad. of Medicine of Belgium, Hon. Fellow, American Coll. of Allergists; four hon. degrees and other awards and prizes. *Publications:* Serology of Conglutination and its relation to disease (co-author) 1960, Clinical Aspects of Immunology 1963; numerous papers on immunology. *Leisure interests:* retreat to the country. *Address:* 6 Selwyn Gardens, Cambridge, England. *Telephone:* Cambridge 352681.

COON, Minor Jesser, PH.D.; American professor of biological chemistry; b. 29 July 1921, Englewood, Colo.; s. of Minor Dillon Coon and Mary (née Jesser) Coon; m. Mary Louise Newburn 1948; one s. one d.; ed. Univ. of Colorado, Univ. of Illinois at Urbana; Postdoctoral Fellow, Univ. of Ill. 1946–47; Asst. Prof. of Physiological Chem., Univ. of Pa. 1949–53, Assoc.

Prof. 1953–55; Research Fellow Dept. of Pharmacology, Univ. of New York 1952–53; Prof. Dept. of Biological Chem., Univ. of Mich 1955–, Chair. Dept. 1970–, Victor Vaughan Distinguished Prof. of Biological Chem. 1983–; Special Research Fellow, Nat. Cancer Inst., U.S. Public Health Service 1952–53, Nat. Inst. of Gen. Medical Science 1961–62; Plenary Lecturer Int. Symposium on Microsomes, Drug Oxidations and Drug Toxicity, Tokyo 1981; Pres. Asscn. of Medical School Depts. of Biochemistry 1974–75; elected Fellow New York Acad. of Sciences 1977; mem. N.A.S. 1983, American Acad. of Arts and Sciences 1984; Sr. mem. Inst. of Medicine 1987; awards include American Chemical Soc. Award in Enzyme Chemistry 1959; William C. Rose Award in Biochemistry 1978; Bernard B. Brodie Award in Drug Metabolism 1980; Hon. D.Sc. (Northwestern) 1983, (Northeastern Ohio Univ. Coll. of Medicine) 1987. *Publications:* over 250 scientific papers and reviews; ed. of numerous books. *Leisure interest:* art. *Address:* Department of Biological Chemistry, Medical School, The University of Michigan, Ann Arbor, Mich. 48109 (Office); 1901 Austin Avenue, Ann Arbor, Mich. 48104, U.S.A. (Home). *Telephone:* (313) 764-8192 (Office); (313) 769-0783 (Home).

COONEY, Patrick, LL.B.; Irish solicitor and politician; b. 2 March 1931, Dublin; s. of Mark Aloysius Cooney and Margaret Blake; m. Brigid McMenamin; three s. one d.; ed. Castleknock Coll., Univ. Coll., Dublin; Fine Gael T.D. for Longford and Westmeath 1970–77; Minister of Justice 1973–77, of Transport, Posts and Telegraphs 1981–82, of Defence 1982–86, of Educ. 1986–87; Senator 1977–81; Deputy 1987–. *Address:* Leinster House, Kildare Street, Dublin 2 (Office); Garnafailagh, Athlone, Co. Westmeath, Ireland (Home). *Telephone:* (01) 789911 (Office); (0902) 75531 (Home).

COOPER, Imogen; British concert pianist; b. 28 Aug. 1949, London; d. of the late Martin Du Pré Cooper and of Mary Stewart; m. John Batten 1982; ed. Paris Conservatoire and pvtly. under Alfred Brendel, Vienna; TV début at Promenade Concerts, London 1975, has appeared regularly since then; first British woman pianist in South Bank Piano series, Queen Elizabeth Hall, London; broadcasts regularly for BBC; performances in Austria, France, Fed. Repub. of Germany, Iceland, Japan, the Netherlands, Portugal, S. America, Spain, Scandinavia, U.S.A., N.Z.; Premier Prix, Paris Conservatoire 1967, Mozart Memorial Prize 1969; recordings: Schubert four-hand piano music (with Anne Queffélec), Mozart two- and three-piano concertos (with Alfred Brendel and Acad. of St. Martin in the Fields and Neville Marriner) 1985, Schubert cycle: "The Last Six Years" 1986–. *Leisure interests:* visual arts, reading, hill-walking. *Address:* c/o Herzberger/Mebus, P.O. Box 251, NIJ KERK 3860 AG, The Netherlands. *Telephone:* (0) 3494-59744.

COOPER, John Allen Dicks, M.D., PH.D.; American physician and medical educator; b. 22 Dec. 1918, El Paso, Tex.; s. of John Allen Dicks Cooper and Cora (Walker); m. Mary Jane Stratton 1944; two s. two d.; ed. New Mexico State and Northwestern Univs.; Instructor in Biochemistry, Northwestern Univ., Evanston, Ill. 1943–47, Asst. Prof. 1947–51, Assoc. Prof. 1951–57, Prof. 1957, 1969, Assoc. Dean of the Medical School 1959–63, Dir. Integrated Program in Medical Educ. 1960–68, Dean of Sciences 1963–69, Assoc. Dean of Faculties 1963–69; mem. Faculty Georgetown Univ. 1970–; Pres. Asscn. of American Medical Colls., Washington D.C. 1969–; mem. Inst. of Medicine 1972–; Fellow A.A.A.S.; Hon. mem. American Hosp. Asscn.; selected by Eds. of U.S. News and World Report as one of the five most influential leaders in field of health 1977–81; Bd. of Trustees' Award, American Medical Asscn. 1985; numerous hon. degrees. *Publications:* over 250 articles in professional journals. *Address:* Association of American Medical Colleges, 1 Dupont Circle, N.W., Suite 200, Washington, D.C. 20036, U.S.A. *Telephone:* (202) 828 0460.

COOPER, John Philip, C.B.E., PH.D., F.R.S.; British professor of genetics; b. 16 Dec. 1923, Buxton, Derbys.; s. of Frank Edward Cooper and Nora Goodwin Stubbs; m. Christine Mary Palmer 1951; one s. three d.; ed. Univs. of Reading and Cambridge; Research Asst., Welsh Plant Breeding Station, Aberystwyth 1946–50; lecturer, Dept. of Agricultural Botany, Univ. of Reading 1950–54; Plant Geneticist, Welsh Plant Breeding Station 1954–59, Head Dept. of Developmental Genetics 1959–75, Dir. Welsh Plant Breeding Station and Prof. of Agricultural Botany, Univ. Coll. of Wales, Aberystwyth 1975–83, Emer. Prof., Univ. of Wales 1984–; Visiting Prof., Dept. of Agric., Univ. of Reading 1983–; mem. Int. Bd. for Plant Genetic Resources 1981–86. *Publications:* Potential Crop Production (with P. F. Wareing) 1971, Photosynthesis and Productivity in Different Environments 1975; over 100 papers on the genetics and physiology of crop plants. *Address:* Department of Agriculture, University of Reading, Earley Gate, Reading (Office); 31 West End, Minchinhampton, Stroud, Glos., England (Home). *Telephone:* (0734) 875123 (Office); (0453) 882533 (Home).

COOPER, Joseph, O.B.E., M.A., A.R.C.M.; British pianist and lecturer; b. 7 Oct. 1912; s. of Wilfrid Needham and Elsie (Goodacre) Cooper; m. 1st Jean Greig 1947 (died 1973); m. 2nd Carol Borg 1975; ed. Clifton Coll. (music scholarship), Keble Coll., Oxford (organ scholarship), studied piano under Egon Petri 1937–39; served in Royal Artillery 1939–46; solo pianist début, Wigmore Hall 1947; concerto début, Philharmonia Orchestra 1950; BBC début, Promenade Concerts, Royal Albert Hall 1953; tours specializing in lecture recitals in British Isles, Europe, Africa, India, Canada; Chair. BBC TV programme Face the Music 1971–84; Liveryman, Worshipful Co. of Musicians 1963–; mem. Music Panel of Arts Council and Chair. piano sub-

cttee. 1966–71; Trustee Countess of Munster Musical Trust 1975–80; Gov. Clifton Coll.; Ambrose Fleming Award, Royal TV Soc. 1971. *Publications:* Hidden Melodies 1975, Arrangement of Vaughan Williams Piano Concerto for 2 pianos (in collaboration with composer), Facing the Music (autobiog.) 1979; numerous recordings. *Leisure interests:* walking, church architecture. *Address:* Octagon Lodge, Ranmore, Nr. Dorking, Surrey, England. *Telephone:* 04865 2658.

COOPER, Leon N., D.SC., PH.D.; American professor of physics; b. 28 Feb. 1930, New York; s. of Irving Cooper and Anna Zola; m. Kay Anne Allard 1969; two d.; ed. Columbia Univ.; mem. Inst. for Advanced Study 1954–55; Research Assoc., Univ. of Ill. 1955–57; Asst. Prof., Ohio State Univ. 1957–58; Assoc. Prof. Brown Univ. 1958–62, Prof. 1974, Thomas J. Watson, Sr. Prof. of Science 1974–; Co-Dir. Center for Neural Science; Visiting Lecturer, Varenna, Italy 1955; Visiting Prof., Brandeis Summer Inst. 1959, Bergen Int. School of Physics, Norway 1961, Scuola Internazionale Di Fisica, Erice, Italy 1965, L'Ecole Normale Supérieure, Centre Universitaire Int., Paris 1966, Cargèse Summer School 1966, Radiation Lab., Univ. of Calif., Berkeley 1969, Faculty of Sciences, Quai St. Bernard, Paris 1970, 1971, Brookhaven Nat. Lab. 1972; Consultant for various industrial and educational orgs.; Chair. of Math. Models of Nervous System Fondation de France 1977–83; mem. Conseil supérieur de la Recherche Univ. René Descartes, Paris 1981–; Nat. Science Foundation Post-doctoral Fellow 1954–55; Alfred P. Sloan Foundation Research Fellow 1959–66; John Simon Guggenheim Memorial Foundation Fellow 1965–66; Fellow, American Physical Soc., American Acad. of Arts and Sciences; Sponsor, American Fed. of Scientists; mem. N.A.S., American Philosophical Soc.; Hon. D.Sc. (Columbia, Sussex), 1973, (Illinois, Brown) 1974, (Gustavus Adolphus Coll.) 1975, (Ohio State Univ.) 1976, (Univ. Pierre et Marie Curie, Paris) 1977; Comstock Prize, N.A.S. 1968; Nobel Prize 1972; Award in Excellence (Columbia Univ.) 1974; Descartes Medal, Acad. de Paris, Univ. René Descartes 1977; John Jay Award (Columbia Coll.) 1985. *Publications:* An Introduction to the Meaning and Structure of Physics 1968; numerous scientific papers. *Leisure interests:* skiing, music, theatre. *Address:* Physics Department, Brown University, Providence, R.I. 02912 (Office); 49 Intervale Road, Providence, R.I. 02906, U.S.A. *Telephone:* (401) 863-2172 (Office); (401) 421-1181 (Home).

COOPER, Warren Ernest; New Zealand politician; b. 21 Feb. 1933, Dunedin; s. of William Cooper; m. Lorraine Margaret Rees 1959; three s. two d.; ed. King's High School, Dunedin; fmrly. worked in family retail business, later as contract woolpresser, signwriter, in hotel and bldg. industries and then established motel in Queenstown; three times mayor of Queenstown; mem. House of Reps. 1975–; Minister of Tourism, of Regional Devt., Minister in charge of Publicity and Govt. Printing Office 1978–80; Postmaster-Gen. 1980–81, also of Broadcasting and Assoc. Minister of Finance 1981; Minister of Foreign Affairs and Minister of Overseas Trade 1981–84; Opposition Spokesman on Econ./Resource Allocation 1985–86, on Overseas Trade 1986–; mem. several select cttees; National Party. *Address:* c/o Parliament Buildings, Wellington; 12 Cluny Avenue, Kelburn, Wellington, New Zealand. *Telephone:* 749199.

COORE, David Hilton, B.A., B.C.L., Q.C., M.P.; Jamaican politician; b. 22 Aug. 1925, St. Andrew; s. of Clarence Reuben Coore and Ethlyn Maud Hilton; m. Rita Innis 1949; three s.; ed. Jamaica Coll., McGill Univ., Exeter Coll., Oxford; practised as barrister-at-law in Jamaica 1950–72; mem. Legis. Council 1960–62; Opposition Spokesman on Finance 1967–72; Chair. People's Nat. Party 1969–78; mem. Parl. 1972–; Deputy Prime Minister 1972–78, also Minister of Finance 1972–78, of Planning Jan. 1977–78; Chair. Bd. of Govs. Caribbean Devt. Bank 1972–73, Inter-American Devt. Bank 1973–74; Queen's Counsel 1961. *Leisure interests:* reading, swimming, golf. *Address:* c/o House of Assembly, Kingston, Jamaica.

COOREY, Chandana Aelian, B.SC.; Sri Lankan banker and administrator; b. 18 March 1921, Ceylon; s. of Dr. Henry Coorey and P. (née Jayawickrema) Coorey; m. Lakshmi de Silva 1951; two s. two d.; ed. Royal Coll., Colombo, Ceylon Univ. Coll.; Asst. Lecturer in Chem. Univ. Coll., Colombo 1942–44; Officer in Ceylon Civil Service 1945–65, sr. positions in Treasury 1959–63, Econ. Devt. Inst. World Bank, Washington, D.C. 1963–64, Sr. Asst. Sec. Ministry of Finance 1964–65; Deputy Sec. Treasury 1965–69, also Perm. Sec. Ministry of Finance 1969–72; Alt. Gov. for Ceylon, Bd. of Govs. World Bank, Washington and Asian Devt. Bank, Manila 1972–75; Alt. Exec. Dir. and Exec. Dir. Bd. of Dirs. Asian Devt. Bank 1975–79; Chair. Nat. Devt. Bank of Sri Lanka 1979–, Capital Devt. and Investment Co. Ltd. 1979–; Univ. Gold Medallist (Chem.). *Leisure interest:* reading. *Address:* National Development Bank of Sri Lanka, 6th Floor, Ceylinco House, Janadhipathi Mawatha, Colombo 1 (Office); No. 128 Park Road, Colombo 5, Sri Lanka (Home). *Telephone:* 547474 (Office); 581840 (Home).

COPITHORNE, Maurice Danby, B.A., LL.B., Q.C.; Canadian diplomatist; b. 3 July 1931, Vancouver, B.C.; m. Tamako Y. Agai 1963; two s.; ed. Univ. of British Columbia; called to Bar of B.C. 1956; joined Dept. of External Affairs 1956; served Indochina 1957–59; Teheran 1959–61, Kuala Lumpur 1964–67, Peking 1972–74; Fellow, Center for Int. Affairs, Harvard Univ. 1974–75; Dir.-Gen. Legal Affairs, then Legal Adviser, Dept. of External Affairs 1975–79; Amb. to Austria, concurrently Gov. IAEA and Perm. Rep. to UNIDO 1979–82; Asst. Under-Sec. of State for External Affairs 1982-83; Commr. for Canada, Hong Kong 1983–. *Publications:* articles in legal and other journals. *Address:* Office of the Commission for Canada, P.O. Box 20264, Hennessy Road Post Office, Hong Kong; 6 Goldsmith Road, Jardin's Lookout, Hong Kong. *Telephone:* 5-282222 (Office); 5-7906621 (Residence).

COPLAND, Aaron; American composer; b. 14 Nov. 1900, Brooklyn, New York; s. of Harris and Sarah (Mittenthal) Copland; enrolled Fontainebleau School of Music 1921; studied with Nadia Boulanger in Paris 1921–24; returned to U.S. 1924; Guggenheim Fellowship 1925–27; with Roger Sessions organised Copland-Sessions Concerts 1928–31; Dir. American Festival of Contemporary Music, Yaddo; toured South America 1941 and 1947; lecturer on Music, New School for Social Research New York 1927–37; has taught composition at Harvard and Berkshire Music Center; Charles Eliot Norton Prof. of Poetry, Harvard Univ. 1951–52; Dir. League of Composers, Edward MacDowell Asscn., Koussevitsky Music Foundation, Walter W. Naumberg Music Foundation and American Music Center; numerous awards, including Nat. Medal of Arts 1986, Congressional Gold Medal 1986, and three hon. degrees. *Works include:* First Symphony 1925, Concerto for Piano and Orchestra 1926, Two Pieces for String Quartet 1928, Lincoln Portrait 1942, Billy the Kid 1938, Violin Sonata 1943, Appalachian Spring 1944, Clarinet Concerto 1948, Twelve Poems of Emily Dickinson 1950, John Henry (revised 1957), The Tender Land 1954, Symphonic Ode 1955, Piano Fantasy 1957, Orchestral Variations 1958, Nonet 1960, Connotations for Orchestra 1962, Music for a Great City 1963, Emblems for Band 1964, Inscape for Orchestra 1967, Duo for Flute and Piano 1971, Three Latin American Sketches 1971, Night Thoughts for Piano 1971. *Publications:* What to Listen for in Music 1939, Our New Music 1941, Music and Imagination 1952, Copland on Music 1960, The New Music 1900–1960 1968, Copland: 1900 Through 1942 1984. *Address:* c/o Boosey & Hawkes Inc., 24 West 57th Street, New York, N.Y. 10019, U.S.A.

COPLESTON, Rev. Frederick Charles, S.J., PH.D., F.B.A.; British priest and academic (retd.); b. 10 April 1907, Taunton, Somerset; s. of Frederick Selwyn Copleston and Norah Margaret Copleston (née Little); ed. Marlborough Coll. and St. John's Coll. Oxford; Prof. of History of Philosophy, Heythrop Coll., Oxon 1939–70; Prof. of Metaphysics, Gregorian Univ., Rome, one semester each year 1952–69; Prin. Heythrop Coll., Univ. of London 1970–74, Dean, Faculty of Theology, Univ. of London 1972–74, Prof. of History of Philosophy (personal chair), Univ. of London 1972–74; Visiting Prof., Univ. of Santa Clara, Calif., U.S.A. 1975–82; Hon. Fellow of St. John's Coll. Oxford 1975–. *Publications:* A History of Philosophy, 9 vols. 1946–75, Nietzsche 1942, Schopenhauer 1946, Philosophies and Cultures 1980, Religion and the One 1982, Philosophy in Russia 1986, Religious Philosophy in Russia: Selected Aspects 1988. *Leisure interests:* Russian history and literature. *Address:* 114 Mount Street, London, W1Y 6AH, England. *Telephone:* 01-493 7811.

COPP, (Douglas) Harold, C.C., M.D., PH.D., F.R.S., F.R.S.C., F.R.C.P.(C); Canadian physiologist; b. 16 Jan. 1915; s. of Charles J. Copp and Edith (née O'Hara) Copp; m. Winnifred A. Thompson 1939; three d.; ed. Univ. of Toronto, Univ. of Calif., Berkeley, British Columbia Coll. of Physicians and Surgeons; Asst. Prof. of Physiology, Univ. of Calif. 1945–50; Co-ordinator Health Sciences, Univ. of British Columbia 1976–77, Prof. 1950, Head of Dept. of Physiology 1950–80; discovered calcitonin (ultimobranchial hormone) and teleocalcin (corpuscles of Stannius); Vice-Pres. and Pres. Acad. of Science 1978–81; Hon. LL.D. (Queen's Univ., Kingston, Ont.) 1970, (Univ. of Toronto) 1970, Hon. D.Sc. (Univ. of Ottawa) 1973, (Acadia Univ.) 1975, (Univ. of British Columbia) 1980. *Leisure interest:* gardening. *Address:* 4755 Belmont Avenue, Vancouver, B.C., V6T 1A8, Canada. *Telephone:* 604-224-3793.

COPPÉ, Albert; Belgian politician; b. 26 Nov. 1911, Bruges; s. of Albert Coppé and Helene Mahieu; m. Maria-H. Vandriessche 1940; four s. four d.; ed. Catholic Univ. of Louvain; mem. (Christian-Social Party) Chamber of Reps. 1946–52; Minister of Public Works 1950, of Economic Affairs and the Middle Classes 1950–52, of Reconstruction 1952; Vice-Pres. High Authority of the European Coal and Steel Community 1952–67, Acting Pres. 1967; mem. Combined Comm. of EEC, ECSC, and EURATOM 1967–73; Chair. Bd. Soc. Générale de Banque/Generale Bankmaatschappij 1977–81, Hon. Chair. 1982; mem. Bd. Philips Gloeilampenfabrieken-Eindhoven; Prof., Catholic Univ. of Louvain, 1940–82, Prof. Emer. 1982–; Dr. h.c. (Montreal and San Antonio, Texas); Commdr. Ordre de Léopold, Grand Cordon, Ordre du Chêne (Luxembourg), Great Cross Leopold II, Great Cross Verdienstorden (Fed. Repub. of Germany); *Publications:* De Europes e Uitdaging 1970, De Multinationale Onderneming 1972, Inflatie 1974. *Leisure interests:* walking, history, paleontology. *Address:* Liskensstraat 2, Tervuren 1980, Belgium. *Telephone:* 02-767.39.91.

COPPEL, Ronald Lewis, F.C.A.; Australian accountant and stock exchange official; b. 19 Dec. 1933, Belfast; s. of Marcus Coppel and Mabel Coppel; m. Valerie K. Bentley 1960; two s. one d.; ed. Royal Belfast Academical Inst. and Belfast Coll. of Tech.; partner, Coppel & Coppel (chartered accountants), Belfast 1957–63; Sr. Accountant, C.P. Bird & Assocs. Perth, W. Australia 1963–67; partner, Crowther, Bird & Spillsbury (public accountants), Perth 1967–70; Gen. Man. The Stock Exchange of Perth Ltd. 1970–74; Exec. Dir. Australian Associated Stock Exchanges 1974–87; Exec. Dir. Australian Stock Exchange Ltd. 1987–; mem. Accounting Standards Review Bd. *Leisure interests:* current affairs, walking, music, theatre.

Address: 137 Koola Avenue, Killara, N.S.W. 2071, Australia. *Telephone:* (02) 498.6185.

COPPEN, Alec James, M.D., D.SC., F.R.C.P., F.R.C.PSYCH.; British psychiatrist; b. 29 Jan. 1923; s. of Herbert J. W. Coppen and Marguerite M. A. Coppen; m. Gunhild M. Coppen 1952; one s.; ed. Dulwich Coll. and Univ. of Bristol; Registrar, then Sr. Registrar, Maudsley Hosp., London 1954–59; MRC Neuropsychiatry Research Unit 1959–74; MRC External Staff 1974–; now Dir. MRC Neuropsychiatry Lab. and Consultant Psychiatrist, West Park Hosp. Epsom; Consultant Psychiatrist, St. Ebba's Hosp. 1959–64; Hon. Consultant Psychiatrist, St. George's Hosp. 1965–70; Consultant, WHO 1977–79; Head, WHO-designated Centre for Biological Psychiatry in UK 1974–; Pres.-elect, Collegium Internationale Neuro-Psychopharmacologicum (CINP); mem. numerous nat. and int. professional socs. etc.; Anna Monika Prize 1969. *Publications:* more than 350 papers, contributions to textbooks etc. *Leisure interests:* golf, music, photography. *Address:* 5 Walnut Close, Epsom, Surrey, KT18 5JL, England. *Telephone:* Epsom 20800.

COPPENS, Yves; French professor of palaeoanthropology/and prehistory; b. 9 Aug. 1934, Vannes; s. of René Coppens and Andrée Coppens; m. Françoise Le Guennec 1959; ed. Univ. of Rennes, Univ. of Paris (Sorbonne); Research Asst. C.N.R.S., Paris 1956–69; Assoc. Prof., then Prof. Nat. Museum of Natural History 1969–83; Prof. of Palaeoanthropology and Prehistory, Collège de France 1983–; prizes include Silver Medal C.N.R.S., Kalinga Prize for Popularization of Science (UNESCO) 1984, Glaxo Prize; Chevalier, Légion d'honneur, Ordre National du Mérite, Officier Ordre National des Palmes Académiques, Ordre National Tchadien. *Publications:* c. 300 scientific papers and 20 books on palaeontology, anthropology and prehistory, also ed. and jt. author. *Address:* Collège de France, 11 place Marcelin Berthelot, 75005 Paris, France. *Telephone:* 43-29-12-11.

COPPIETERS, Emmanuel (Coppieters de ter Zaele, chevalier Emmanuel), DR. ECON., DR. IUR., M.SC. (ECON.); Belgian economist and jurist; b. 1925; m. Dr. Agnès de Munter 1982; ed. Louvain and London Univs.; Prof. Int. Econ. Orgs., Nat. Faculty of Econs., Univ. of Antwerp 1954–, Royal Mil. Coll. 1963–66; Dir.-Gen. Institut Royal des Relations Internationales, Brussels 1954–; Ed. Studia Diplomatica (fmrly. Chronique de Politique Etrangère); Co-Ed. Internationale Spectator, Tijdschrift voor Internationale Politiek; Consul-Gen. of Honduras 1961–; Minister chargé d'affaires a.i. of Honduras to the European Communities 1973–77; Public Auditor of Banks 1962–; Adviser for Foreign Trade to Govt. 1964–; mem. Belgian Nat. Council of Statistics 1959–70; mem. Royal Acad. of Overseas Sciences; Assoc. mem., Acad. Mexicana de Derecho Int.; mem. Int. Inst. for Strategic Studies 1960–; mem. Belgian Nat. Comm. UNESCO; Gov. Asscn. pour l'Etude des Problèmes de l'Europe, Paris 1959–82; Gov. European Cultural Foundation 1973–; Barrister; mem. American Political Science Asscn.; Hon. Lieut.-Col.; Hon. Fellow L.S.E.; Hon. Citizen, New Orleans; Grand Officier, Order of the Belgian Crown, Order of Morazan (Honduras), Tudor Vladimirescu (Romania), Commdr. Ordre de Léopold, Order of the Holy Sepulchre, Order of St. Gregory the Great, Order of Merit (Senegal), Orange-Nassau (Netherlands), Merit of Luxembourg, Merito Civil Español, Officier Order of Merit of Rwanda, Order of Polonia Restituta, Knight of the Order of Malta, mem. Order of the Leopard (Zaire), resistance and war volunteer medals. *Publications:* English Bank Note Circulation 1694-1954, L'accord monétaire européen et le progrès de la convertibilité des monnaies, Internationale organisaties en Belgische economie, La integración monetaria y fiscal europea, Culminación de la integración política, Les conséquences économiques d'un éventuel désarmement, Messages royaux et intégration européenne, Protocole, National et International, etc. *Address:* 88 avenue de la Couronne, Brussels; and Vijverskasteel, Loppem bij Brugge, Belgium. *Telephone:* 648-20-00; and (050)-822-888.

COPPOCK, John Terence, PH.D., F.B.A., F.R.S.E., F.R.S.A.; British professor of geography; b. 2 June 1921, Cardiff; s. of the late Arthur Leslie Coppock and Margaret Valerie Coppock (née Phillips); m. Sheila Mary Burnett 1953; one s. one d.; ed. Penarth County School, Queens' Coll., Cambridge; civil servant, Lord Chancellor's Office, Ministry of Works and Bd. of Customs and Excise 1938–47; war service in Army 1939–46; Departmental Demonstrator, Dept. of Geography, Univ. of Cambridge 1949–50; Asst. Lecturer in Geography, Univ. Coll. London 1950–52, Lecturer 1952–54, Reader 1954–65; Ogilvie Prof. of Geography, Univ. of Edin. 1965–86, Prof. Emer. 1986–; Visiting Sr. Lecturer, Dept. of Geography, Univ. of Ibadan, Nigeria 1963–64; Visiting Prof., Univ. of Tech., Loughborough 1986, Birkbeck Coll., London 1986–; Sec. and Treasurer Carnegie Trust for the Univs. of Scotland 1986–; mem. England Cttee., Nature Conservancy 1965–71; Specialist Adviser, Select Cttee. on Scottish Affairs 1971–72; Pres. Inst. of British Geographers 1973–74; mem. Ordnance Survey Review Cttee. 1978–79; Chair. British Nat. Cttee. for Geography 1979–84; mem. Scottish Sports Council 1976–; Ed. Int. Journal of Geographical Information Systems 1986–; Murchison Grant, Royal Geographical Soc. 1971, Victoria Medal 1985. *Publications:* The Changing Use of Land in Britain (with R. H. Best) 1962, An Agricultural Atlas of England and Wales 1964, An Agricultural Geography of Great Britain 1971, An Agricultural Atlas of Scotland 1976, Recreation in the Countryside (with B. S. Duffield) 1975, Agriculture in Developed Countries 1984, Institutional Innovation in Water Management: The Scottish Experience (with W. R. D. Sewell and A.

Pitkethly) 1985, Geography, Planning and Policy Making (Ed. with P. T. Kivell) 1986, and 15 other books; 130 articles. *Leisure interests:* walking, natural history, badminton, listening to music. *Address:* Carnegie Trust for the Universities of Scotland, Merchant Hall, 22 Hanover Street, Edinburgh, EH2 2EN; 57 Braid Avenue, Edinburgh, EH10 6EB, Scotland (Home); *Telephone:* (031) 225 5817 (Office); (031) 447 3443 (Home).

COPPOLA, Francis Ford; American film writer and director; b. 7 April 1939, Detroit, Michigan; s. of Carmine and Italia Coppola; m. Eleanor Neil; two s. one d.; ed. Hofstra Univ., Univ. of California. *Films include:* Dementia 13 1963, This Property is Condemned 1965, Is Paris Burning? 1966, You're A Big Boy Now 1967, Finian's Rainbow 1968, The Rain People 1969, Patton 1971, The Godfather 1972, American Grafitti 1973, The Conversation 1974, The Godfather Part II 1975, The Great Gatsby 1974, The Black Stallion (produced) 1977, Apocalypse Now 1979, One from the Heart 1982, Hammett (produced) 1982, The Escape Artist 1982, The Return of the Black Stallion 1982, Rumble Fish 1983, The Outsiders 1983, The Cotton Club 1984, Peggy Sue Got Married 1986, Gardens of Stone 1986, Life without Zoe 1988, Tucker: The Man and His Dream 1988; theatre direction includes Enrico IV at the American Conservatory Theatre, San Francisco 1971, Private Lives, The Visit of the Old Lady, San Francisco Opera Co. 1972; Artistic Dir. Zoetrope Studios 1969-; Cannes Film Award for The Conversation 1974; Director's Guild Award for The Godfather; Acad. Award for Best Screenplay for Patton, Golden Palm (Cannes) 1979 for Apocalypse Now, also awarded Best Screenplay, Best Dir. and Best Picture Oscars for The Godfather Part II; Commandeur, Ordre des Arts et des Lettres. *Address:* Zoetrope Studios, 916 Kearny Street, San Francisco, Calif. 94133, U.S.A.

CORBALLIS, Michael Charles, M.A., PH.D.; New Zealand-Canadian professor of psychology; b. 10 Sept. 1936, Marton, N.Z.; s. of Philip P. J. Corballis and late Alice E. (née Harris) Corballis; m. Barbara Elizabeth Wheeler 1962; two s.; ed. Univ. of N.Z., Univ. of Auckland and McGill Univ., Montreal, Canada; Lecturer in Psychology Univ. of Auckland 1966-68, Prof. 1978-; Asst. Prof., Assoc. Prof. and Prof. McGill Univ. 1968-77; Fellow N.Z. Psychological Soc., American Psychological Soc., Royal Soc. of N.Z., Asscn. for Advancement of Science. *Publications:* Psychology of Left and Right 1976, The Ambivalent Mind 1983, Human Laterality 1983. *Leisure interests:* ceramics, squash and cricket. *Address:* 86 Gladstone Road, Parnell, Auckland, New Zealand. *Telephone:* 775-404.

CORBALLY, John Edward, PH.D.; American university administrator; b. 14 Oct. 1924, South Bend, Washington; s. of John E. and Grace Williams Corbally; m. Marguerite Walker 1946; one s. one d.; ed. Univs of Washington and California (Berkeley); High School Teacher and principal, State of Wash. 1947-53; College of Educ. Faculty, Ohio State Univ. 1955-61, Dir. Personnel Budget 1959-61, Exec. Asst. to Pres. 1961-64, Vice-Pres. for Admin. 1964-66, Vice-Pres. for Academic Affairs and Provost 1966-69; Chancellor and Pres. Syracuse Univ. 1969-71; Pres. Univ. of Illinois 1971-79, Pres. Emer. and Distinguished Prof. of Higher Educ. 1979-; Pres. and Dir. John D. and Catherine T. MacArthur Foundation 1980-; Chair. Nat. Council on Educational Research 1973-79; Hon. LL.D. (Univ. of Md. 1971, Blackburn Coll. 1972, Ill. State Univ. 1977, Univ. of Akron 1978, Ohio State Univ. 1980). *Publications:* co-author: Educational Administration: The Secondary School 1961, School Finance 1962, An Introduction to Educational Administration 1984. *Leisure interests:* golf, model railroading, travel. *Address:* Suite 700, 140 S. Dearborn, Chicago, Ill. 60603 (Office); 1100 N. Lake Shore Drive, Chicago, Ill. 60611, U.S.A. (Home). *Telephone:* 312-726-8000 (Office); 312-951-8292 (Home).

CORBIN, Raymond Pierre Louis; French sculptor and professor; b. 23 April 1907, Rochefort-sur-Mer; s. of Georges Corbin and Hélène (née Boyau) Corbin; m. Charlotte Canale 1934; one s. three d.; ed. Ecole des Arts Appliqués de Paris and Ecole nat. supérieure des Beaux Arts de Paris; Prof. of Medal Engraving Ecole nat. supérieure des Beaux Arts de Paris 1955-77, Hon. Prof. 1977-; mem. Acad. des Beaux Arts 1970, Comité du Salon des Tuileries, Exhbns. Monnaie de Paris 1986, Cabinet des Médailles de Munich 1987. *Sculptures and medals include:* portraits of Charles Nodier, L. P. Fargue, Marcel Pagnol, Roland Dorgelès, Gérard de Nerval, Marie Curie, Colette, Guillaume Budé, Louis Pergaud; stone statue Ville de Borges; High Relief, Monument of Mount Valérien; Chevalier Légion d'honneur, Officier des Arts et Lettres; Prix Blumenthal 1936, Prix Germain Pilon 1969. *Address:* 32 rue Alphonse Bertillon, 75015 Paris (Office); 3 rue des Arts, 92100 Boulogne-Billancourt, France (Home).

CORBY, (Frederick) Brian, M.A., F.I.A.; British actuary and company executive; b. 10 May 1929, Raunds, Northants.; s. of Charles Walter and Millicent Corby; m. Elizabeth Mairi McInnes 1952; one s. two d.; ed. Kimbolton School and St. John's Coll., Cambridge; joined Prudential Assurance Co. Ltd. 1952, Asst. Gen. Man. (Overseas) 1968-73, Deputy Gen. Man. 1974-75, Gen. Man. 1976-79, Chief Actuary 1980-81, Group Gen. Man., Prudential Corpn. PLC 1979-82, Chief Exec. 1982-, Chief Gen. Man. Prudential Assurance Co. Ltd. 1982-85, Chair. 1985-; Vice-Pres. Inst. of Actuaries 1979-83; Deputy Chair. British Insurance Asscn. 1984-85; Chair. Assen. of British Insurers 1985-87; Dir. Bank of England 1985-. *Publications:* articles in Journal of Inst. of Actuaries. *Leisure interests:* reading, golf, gardening. *Address:* 142 Holborn Bars, London, EC1N 2NH, England (Office).

CORDEIRO, H.E. Cardinal Joseph; Pakistani ecclesiastic; b. 19 Jan. 1918, Bombay; Ordained 1946; Archbishop of Karachi 1958-; created Cardinal 1973. *Address:* St. Patrick's Cathedral, Karachi 3, Pakistan.

CORDEN, Warner Max, M.COMM., M.A., PH.D.; Australian professor of international economics; b. 13 August 1927, Breslau, Germany (now Wrocław, Poland); s. of late Ralph S. Corden; m. Dorothy Martin 1957; one d.; ed. Melbourne Boys High School, Univ. of Melbourne and L.S.E.; lecturer, Univ. of Melbourne 1958-61; Professorial Fellow, Australian Nat. Univ. 1962-67, Prof. of Econs. 1976-88; Prof. of Int. Econ., School of Advanced Int. Studies, Johns Hopkins Univ. 1989-; Nuffield Reader in Int. Econs. and Fellow of Nuffield Coll., Oxford 1967-76; Visiting Prof., Univ. of California (Berkeley) 1965, Univ. of Minn. 1971, Princeton Univ. 1973, Harvard Univ. 1986; Sr. Adviser, IMF 1986-88; Pres. Econ. Soc. of Australia and New Zealand 1977-80; mem. Group of Thirty; Bernard Harms Prize 1986. *Publications:* The Theory of Protection 1971, Trade Policy and Economic Welfare 1974, Inflation, Exchange Rates and the World Economy 1977, Protection, Growth and Trade 1985. *Address:* 1740 Massachusetts Avenue N.W., Washington D.C. 20036, U.S.A. *Telephone:* (202) 663 5679 (Office).

CORDOVEZ, Diego; Ecuador lawyer and diplomatist; b. 3 Nov. 1935, Quito; s. of Luis Cordovez-Borja and Isidora Zegers de Cordovez; m. Maria Teresa Somavia 1960; one s.; ed. Univ. of Chile; admitted to bar 1962; foreign service of Ecuador until 1963; joined UN as Econ. Affairs Officer 1963; political officer on special missions to Dominican Repub. 1965, Pakistan 1971; Dir. UN Econ. and Social Council Secr. 1973-78, Asst. Sec.-Gen. for Econ. and Social Matters, UN 1978-81; Special Rep. of UN Sec.-Gen. on Libya-Malta dispute 1980-82; Sec.-Gen.'s rep. on UN Comm. of Inquiry on hostage crisis in Teheran 1980; sr. officer responsible for efforts to resolve Iran/Iraq war 1980-88; Under-Sec.-Gen. for Special Political Affairs 1981-1988; UN Mediator, Afghanistan 1982-88, Rep. for implementation of Geneva Accords April 1988-; Minister for Foreign Affairs Aug. 1988-; UN Special Envoy to Grenada 1983; mem. American Soc. of Int. Law; Order of Merit (Ecuador). *Publication:* UNCTAD and Development Diplomacy 1971. *Leisure interests:* reading, carpentry. *Address:* Ministry of Foreign Affairs, Avda 10 de Agosta y Carrión, Quito, Eduador.

COREA, Gamani, D.PHIL.; Sri Lankan economist, diplomatist and UN official; b. 4 Nov. 1925, Colombo; s. of Dr. C. V. S. and Freda (née Kotelawala) Corea; ed. Univ. of Ceylon, Colombo, Corpus Christi Coll., Cambridge, and Nuffield Coll., Oxford; Dir. Planning Secr. and Sec. Nat. Planning Council 1956-60; Dir. of Econ. Research and Asst. to Gov. of Central Bank of Ceylon 1960-64; Perm. Sec. to Ministry of Planning and Econ. Affairs and Econ. Sec. to Cabinet 1965-70; Deputy Gov. Central Bank of Ceylon 1970-73; Amb. to EEC and Benelux countries 1973-74; Consultant to Sec.-Gen., UN Conf. on Trade and Devt.; fmr. Chief, UN Econ. Mission to British Honduras; Chair. UN Cttee. on Devt. Planning 1972-74, Cocoa Conf. 1972, Expert Groups on Int. Monetary Reform and Developing Countries, UNCTAD 1965, 1969; Sr. Advisor to Sec.-Gen., UN Conf. on Human Environment (Stockholm) 1971-72; Sec.-Gen. UNCTAD 1974-85; Sec.-Gen. UN Conf. on Least Developed Countries 1981; Chair. Expert Group on Regional Performance Evaluation, ECAFE 1972, Group on Review and Appraisal of 2nd Devt. Decade 1971, 1972; fmr. Pres. Section F, Ceylon Assen. for Advancement of Science, Pres. Assen. 1971; mem. Consultative Cttee. Asian Agricultural Survey, Asian Devt. Bank; Chair. Expert Panel on Devt. and Environment (Founex) 1971; mem. Bd. Govs. of Third World Forum, Int. Foundation for Development Alternatives, Dag Hammarskjöld Foundation (Sweden), Int. Inst. of Quantitative Econs., Concordia Univ., Canada, Int. Econ. Assen., Marga Inst. Devt. Studies (Chair), Sri Lanka; Research Fellow, Int. Devt. Research Centre, Canada 1973; Visiting Fellow, Inst. of Devt. Studies, Univ. of Sussex 1973, mem. Bd. of Govs. 1974-; Chancellor, Open Univ., Sri Lanka; Visiting Fellow, Nuffield College, Oxford 1974-79; Dr. h.c. (Nice) 1977, Hon. D.Litt. (Colombo Univ.); Fellow Commoner, Corpus Christi Coll., Cambridge 1985-86. *Publications:* The Instability of an Export Economy, Need for Change: Towards the New International Economic Order 1980 and numerous articles on economic and financial matters, Sri Lanka and the Third World. *Leisure interests:* photography, golf. *Address:* 9B Plateau de Frontenex, 1208 Geneva, Switzerland (Office); Horton Lodge, 21 Horton Place, Colombo 7, Sri Lanka (Home). *Telephone:* (022) 36 92 07 (Office).

CORELLI, Franco; Italian tenor; b. Ancona; ed. Pesaro Conservatory, Maggio Musicale, Florence; first appearance as Don José in Carmen, Spoleto; appeared in Spontini's La Vestale, La Scala, Milan 1954, Teatro San Carlo, Naples 1955, Cavaradossi, Covent Garden, London 1956, Rome 1957, 1958, Naples 1958, La Scala (with Maria Callas) 1960; Metropolitan Opera début as Manrico in Il Trovatore 1961; has sung major parts in Andrea Chénier, La Bohème, Turandot, Tosca, Ernani, Aïda, Don Carlos, Forza del Destino, Cavalleria Rusticana, I Pagliacci, etc.; performs regularly on American TV; recital tour with Renata Tebaldi; 1st Prize Spoleto Nat. Competition. *Address:* c/o S. A. Gorlinsky, 33 Dover Street, London, W1X 4NJ, England.

COREN, Alan, B.A.; British editor, author and broadcaster; b. 27 June 1938, London; s. of Samuel Coren and Martha (née Coren) Coren; m. Anne Kasriel 1963; one s. one d.; ed. East Barnet Grammar School, Wadham

Coll., Oxford, Univ. of California, Berkeley and Yale Univ.; Asst. Ed. Punch 1963–66, Literary Ed. 1966–69, Deputy Ed. 1969–77, Ed. 1977–87; Ed. The Listener 1988–89; Columnist The Times 1971–78, Daily Mail 1972–76, Mail on Sunday 1983–, Era 1983–; contrib. to Observer, Listener, Sunday Times, Atlantic Monthly, TV Guide, Tatler, Times Literary Supplement, London Review of Books, Daily Telegraph, Playboy, Guardian; Rector St. Andrew's Univ. 1974–77; British Soc. of Magazine Eds. Ed. of the Year 1986. *Publications:* The Dog it was that Died 1965, All Except the Bastard 1969, The Sanity Inspector 1974, The Collected Bulletins of Idi Amin 1974, Golfing for Cats 1975, The Further Bulletins of Idi Amin 1975, The Arthur Books (12 novellas) 1976–80, The Lady from Stalingrad Mansions 1977, The Peanut Papers 1977, The Rhinestone as Big as the Ritz 1979, Tissues for Men 1980, The Cricklewood Diet 1982, Bumf 1984, Something for the Weekend 1986, Bin Ends 1987. *Leisure interests:* bridge, tennis, riding. *Address:* 23 Tudor Street, London E.C.4, England. *Telephone:* 01-583 9199; 01-580 5577.

COREY, Elias James, PH.D.; American professor of chemistry; b. 12 July 1928, Methuen, Mass.; s. of Elias J. Corey and Tina Hasham; m. Claire Higham 1961; two s. one d.; ed. Massachusetts Inst. of Tech.; Instructor in Chem., Univ. of Ill. 1951–53, Asst. Prof. of Chem. 1953–55, Prof. 1956–59; Sheldon Emery Prof. of Chem., Harvard Univ. 1959–, Chair. Dept. of Chem. 1965–68; Alfred P. Sloan Foundation Fellow 1955–57, Guggenheim Fellow 1957, 1968–69; mem. American Acad. of Arts and Sciences 1960–68, N.A.S. 1966–; Hon. A.M., Hon. D.Sc.; Pure Chem. Award of American Chemical Soc. 1960, Fritzsche Award of American Chemical Soc. 1967, Intra-Science Foundation Award 1967, Harrison Howe Award, American Chemical Soc. 1970, Award for Synthetic Organic Chem. 1971, CIBA Foundation Award 1972, Evans Award, Ohio State Univ. 1972, Linus Pauling Award 1973, Dickson Prize in Science, Carnegie Mellon Univ. 1973, George Ledlie Prize, (Harvard) 1973, Remsen Award, Arthur C. Cope Award 1976, Nichols Medal 1977, Buchman Memorial Award (Calif. Inst. of Tech.) 1978, Franklin Medal 1978, Scientific Achievement Award Medal 1979, J. G. Kirkwood Award (Yale) 1980, C. S. Hamilton Award (Univ. of Nebraska) 1980, Chemical Pioneer Award (American Inst. of Chemists) 1981, Rosenstiel Award (Brandeis Univ.) 1982, Paul Karrer Award (Zurich Univ.) 1982, Medal of Excellence (Helsinki Univ.) 1982, Tetrahedron Prize 1983, Gibbs Award (American Chem. Soc.) 1984, Paracelsus Award (Swiss Chem. Soc.) 1984, V. D. Mattia Award (Roche Inst. of Molecular Biology) 1985, Wolf Prize in Chemistry (Wolf Foundation) 1986, Silliman Award (Yale Univ.) 1986, Japan Prize 1989, and numerous others. *Publications:* approx. 650 chemical papers. *Leisure interests:* outdoor activities and music. *Address:* Department of Chemistry, Harvard University, 12 Oxford Street, Cambridge, Mass. 02138 (Office); 20 Avon Hill Street, Cambridge, Mass. 02140, U.S.A. (Home). *Telephone:* 617-495-4033 (Office); 617-864-0627 (Home).

CORFIELD, Rt. Hon. Sir Frederick Vernon, Kt., P.C., Q.C.; British barrister-at-law and politician; b. 1 June 1915, London; s. of Brig. Frederick A. Corfield, D.S.O. and Mary Vernon; m. Ruth Taylor 1945; ed. Cheltenham Coll. and Royal Military Acad., Woolwich; regular army 1935–45, prisoner-of-war 1940–45; called to Bar, Middle Temple 1945; Judge Advocate Gen.'s Branch, War Office 1945–46; farming 1946–56; Conservative mem. Parl. for S. Glos. 1955–74; Joint Parl. Sec. Ministry of Housing and Local Govt. 1962–64; Minister of State, Bd. of Trade June-Oct. 1970; Minister of Aviation Supply 1970–71, Minister for Aerospace, Dept. of Trade and Industry 1971–72; mem. British Waterways Bd. 1974–83, Vice-Chair. 1980–83; mem. Mid-Kent Water Co.; Chair. London and Provincial Antique Dealers Asscn. Ltd.; Bencher, Middle Temple 1980–; Pres. Cheltenham Coll. Council 1985–. *Publications:* Corfield on Compensation 1959, A Guide to the Community Land Act 1975, Compulsory Acquisition and Compensation (joint author) 1978. *Leisure interest:* gardening. *Address:* 9 Randolph Mews, London, W.9; Wording's Orchard, Sheepscombe, Stroud, Glos., GL6 7RE, England.

CORFIELD, Sir Kenneth George, Kt., C.E., C.I.E.E., F.I.MECH.E.; British engineer and company executive; b. 27 Jan. 1924, Rushall; s. of Stanley Corfield and Dorothy Elisabeth (née Mason); m. Patricia Jean Williams 1960; one d.; ed. Elmore Green High School, South Staffs. Coll. of Advanced Tech.; Tech. Officer, ICI Ltd. 1947–50; Chief Exec., K.G. Corfield Ltd., camera mfrs. 1950–61; Exec. Dir. Parkinson Cowan Ltd. 1962–67; Vice-Pres., Dir. ITT Europe Inc. 1967–70; Man. Dir. Standard Telephones and Cables Ltd. 1970–85, Deputy Chair. 1974–79, Chair. and Chief Exec. 1979–85; Chair. Standard Telephones and Cables (N. Ireland) 1974–85; Vice-Pres. Int. Standard Electric Corpn., ITT Sr. Officer in U.K. 1974–84; Chair. Nat. Econ. Devt. Cttee. for Ferrous Foundries Industry 1975–78; Vice-Chair. British Inst. of Man. 1978–84; Vice-Pres. Inst. of Marketing 1980–; Chair. Eng. Council 1981–85; Dir. Midland Bank Group 1979–, Britoil 1982–, Octagon Group Ltd. 1987–, Distributed Information Processing Ltd. 1987–; Vice-Pres. Eng. Employers Fed. –1985; mem. Pres.'s Cttee. and Council, CBI –1985; mem. Council, Inst. of Dirs. 1981–85 (Pres. 1984–85); mem. Advisory Council, Science Museum 1975–83, Trustee 1984–; mem. Advisory Council for Applied Research and Devt. 1981, Nat. Econ. Devt. Cttee. for Electronics 1981; Hon. Fellow, Sheffield City Polytechnic 1983, Wolverhampton Polytechnic 1986; Dr. h.c. (Surrey), (Open Univ.) 1985, Hon. D.Sc. (City Univ.) 1981, (Bath) 1982, (Belfast, Queen's) 1982, (Loughborough) 1982, (Aston) 1985, Hon. LL.D. (Strathclyde) 1982, Hon. D.Sc.

(Eng.) Univ. of London 1982, Hon. D.Eng. (Bradford) 1983; Hon. F.I.E.E. *Publications:* Report on Product Design for NEDC 1979, Patterns of Change: Collected Essays 1983. *Leisure interests:* shooting, Hi Fi, photography, cinema. *Address:* 14 Elm Walk, Hampstead, London, NW3 7UP, England (Home).

CORFU, Haim; Israeli politician and lawyer; b. 1921, Jerusalem; m.; two c.; ed. Hebron, Tel Aviv yeshivas, Hebrew Univ.; mil. service Etzel and Israeli Defence Force; lawyer; served Jerusalem City Council; mem. Finance Cttee. Seventh Knesset, mem. sub-cttee. on Budget and Security, Eighth Knesset; mem. Foreign Affairs and Security Cttee., Knesset Cttee., Chair. Coalition Ninth Knesset; Minister of Transport 1981–88. *Address:* c/o Ministry of Transport, 97 Jaffa Street, Clal Center, Jerusalem, Israel.

CORI, Osvaldo, M.D.; Chilean professor of biochemistry; b. 11 Aug. 1921, Antofagasta; s. of Alejandro Cori and Aby Moully de Cori; m. Aída Traverso 1947; two s.; ed. Deutsche Schule and Liceo Eduardo de la Barra, Univ. of Chile Medical School, Harvard and New York Univs., U.S.A.; Asst. Prof. of Physiology, Medical School, Univ. of Chile 1947–61, Prof. of Biochemistry, Faculty of Pharmaceutical Sciences 1956–; research interest: mechanism of enzyme action in biochemical processes related to the biosynthesis of monoterpenes in plant tissues, physico-chemical and mechanistic aspects of biosynthetic reactions; Vice-Rector, Univ. of Chile 1975, Dir. Research Office 1976–78; Pres. Comisión Nacional de Investigaciones Científicas y Tecnológicas (CONICYT) 1985–87; mem. Academia Chilena de Ciencias, Academia de Ciencias de Latinoamérica, Academia de Ciencias Exactas, Físicas y Naturales, Argentina 1986; Hon. D.Sc. (Pontificia Univ. Católica de Chile) 1986. *Publications:* papers in scientific journals. *Leisure interests:* mountaineering, photography and music. *Address:* Flandes 1108, Santiago 10, Chile. *Telephone:* 2289485.

CORISH, Brendan; Irish politician (retd.); b. 1918; m. 1949; three s.; mem. of Parl. 1945–82; Vice-Chair. Labour Party 1949, Parl. Leader 1960–77, mem. Council of State 1964–77; Parl. Party Whip 1945–54; Parl. Sec. to Minister of Local Govt. and Minister of Defence 1948; Minister of Social Welfare 1954–57; Deputy Prime Minister and Minister for Health and Social Welfare 1973–77; Del. to Council of Europe 1955–59; Del. to Int. Affairs Asscn. Conf. 1949; Del. to Inter-Parl. Union Conf., Istanbul 1951; assoc. mem. Del. to Commonwealth Relations Conf., Ottawa 1952; mem. Wexford County Council 1979–. *Address:* Belvedere Road, Wexford, Ireland.

CORISH, Patrick Joseph, M.A., D.D.; Irish historian; b. 20 March 1921, Co. Wexford; s. of Peter William Corish and Brigid Mary O'Shaughnessy; ed. St. Peter's Coll., Wexford and Nat. Univ. of Ireland (St. Patrick's Coll., Maynooth and Univ. Coll., Dublin); ordained as Priest 1945; Prof. of Ecclesiastical History Pontifical Univ., Maynooth 1947–75; Prof. of Modern History, Maynooth, N.U.I. 1975–; mem. Royal Irish Acad. 1956; Sec. Catholic Record Soc. of Ireland 1948, ed. Soc.'s journal Archivium Hibernicum 1948–77; mem. Irish Manuscripts Comm. 1949; Domestic Prelate 1967. *Publications:* (ed. and contrib.) A History of Irish Catholicism 1967–71, The Catholic Community in the Seventeenth and Eighteenth Centuries 1981, The Irish Catholic Experience 1985. *Leisure interests:* travel, gardening. *Address:* St. Patrick's College, Maynooth, Co. Kildare, Ireland. *Telephone:* 01-285222.

CORK, Sir Kenneth (Russell), G.B.E., F.R.S.A., F.I.C.M., C.B.I.M., F.C.I.S., F.C.A.; British chartered accountant; b. 21 Aug. 1913; s. of William H. Cork and Maud A. Nunn; m. Nina Lippold 1937; one s. one d.; ed. Berkhamsted School; served World War II (rank of Lieut.-Col.); Sr. Partner, W. H. Cork, Gully & Co. 1946–80, Cork Gully (Chartered Accountants) 1980–83; Lord Mayor of London 1978–79; Pres. British Inst. of Man. (City Branch) 1986–; Visiting Prof. City of London Polytechnic 1988; Dir. (non-exec.) Brent Walker Group PLC 1986–; Chair. Advent Eurofund, Advent Capital, Advent Man. Ltd., Richmount Enterprize Zone Mans. Ltd., Dir. Ladbroke Group 1986–, Vice-Chair. 1986–; Pres. City Branch, Inst. of Dirs.; Gov. Royal Shakespeare Theatre 1967–, Chair. 1975–85, Pres. 1985–; Dir. Aitken Hume Int. PLC, Testaferrata Moroni Viani (Holdings) Ltd., decorations from France, Brazil, Portugal and Repub. of Korea; Hon. D.Litt. (City Univ.) 1978; Hon. G.S.M., K.St.J. *Publication:* Cork on Cork 1988. *Leisure interests:* sailing, photography, painting. *Address:* Cherry Trees, Grimms Lane, Great Missenden, Bucks., England. *Telephone:* Great Missenden 2628.

CORMACK, Allan MacLeod, M.SC.; American (formerly South African) physicist; b. 23 Feb. 1924, Johannesburg, S. Africa; s. of George Cormack and Amelia MacLeod; m. Barbara J. Seavey 1950; one s. two d.; ed. Rondebosch Boys' High School, Univs. of Cape Town and Cambridge; Junior Lecturer, Univ. of Cape Town 1946–47, lecturer 1950–56; Research Fellow, Harvard Univ. 1956–57; Asst. Prof. Tufts Univ., Medford, Mass. 1957–60, Assoc. Prof. 1960–64, Prof. 1964–80, Univ. Prof. 1980–, Chair. Dept. of Physics 1968–76; Hon. mem. Swedish Radiological Soc. 1979; Fellow, American Physical Soc., American Acad. of Arts and Sciences 1980, mem. N.A.S. 1983, Foreign Assoc., Royal Soc. of S.A. 1983; Hon. D.Sc. (Tufts Univ.) 1980; Ballou Medallist, Tufts Univ.; shared Nobel Prize for Physiology and Medicine 1979 with Dr. G. N. Hounsfield (q.v.) for work on computer-assisted tomography; Medal of Merit, Univ. of Cape Town 1980, Hogg Medallist, Univ. of Texas Cancer System 1981. *Leisure inter-*

ests: reading, sailing. *Address:* Department of Physics, Tufts University, Medford, Mass. 02155 (Office); 18 Harrison Street, Winchester, Mass. 01890, U.S.A. (Home). *Telephone:* 617-381-3655 (Office); 617-729-0735 (Home).

CORMAN, Roger William, A.B.; American film director and producer; b. 5 April 1926, Detroit, Mich.; ed. Stanford Univ. Calif., Oxford Univ., England; dir. Five Guns West 1955; *produced films:* Monster from the Ocean Floor 1953, Grand Theft Auto, I Never Promised You a Rose Garden, Thunder and Lightning, Avalanche, Deathsport, Piranha; *films as producer and director include:* The Day the World Ended 1956, The Fall of the House of Usher 1960, The Little Shop of Horrors 1960, The Pit and the Pendulum 1961, The Intruder 1962, The Raven 1963, Masque of the Red Death 1964, The Secret Invasion 1964, The Wild Angels 1966, The Saint Valentine's Day Massacre 1967, The Trip 1967, Bloody Mama 1970, Gas-s-s 1970; dir. Von Richthofen and Brown 1971; play: Little Shop of Horrors 1982; Pres. New World Pictures; distributed films including: Cries and Whispers, Amarcord, Fantastic Planet, The Story of Adele H, Small Change; mem. Producers' Guild of America, Directors' Guild of America. *Address:* c/o New Horizons Production Co., 11600 San Vincente Blvd., Los Angeles, Calif. 90049, U.S.A.

CORNEILLE (see Beverloo, Cornelis Van).

CORNER, Edred John Henry, C.B.E., F.R.S., F.L.S.; British fmr. botanist; b. 12 Jan. 1906, London; s. of Edred Moss Corner and Henrietta (née Henderson) Corner; ed. Rugby School; Asst. Dir. Gardens Dept., Straits Settlements 1929-45; Principal Field Scientific Officer, Latin America, UNESCO 1947-48; lecturer in Botany, Cambridge Univ. 1949-59, Reader in Plant Taxonomy 1959-65, Prof. of Tropical Botany 1966-73, Prof. Emer. 1973-; Fellow, American Asscn. for Advancement of Science and mem. or Corresp. mem. of many other foreign botanical and mycological socs.; Darwin Medal, Royal Soc. 1960, Patron's Medal, Royal Geographical Soc. 1966, Gold Medal, Linnean Soc. 1970, Victoria Medal of Honour, Royal Horticultural Soc. 1974, Allerton Award, Pacific Tropical and Botanical Garden, Hawaii 1981, Int. Prize for Biology 1985, Golden Key of the City of Yokohama, Japan 1985. *Publications:* Wayside Trees of Malaya 1940, Monograph of Clavaria 1950, Life of Plants 1964, Monograph of Cantharel- loid Fungi 1966, Natural History of Palms 1966, Illustrated Guide to Tropical Plants (with K. Watanabe) 1969, Boletus in Malaysia 1972, Seeds of Dicotyledons 1976, The Marquis 1981. *Leisure interest:* kindness. *Address:* 91 Hinton Way, Great Shelford, Cambridge, CB2 5AH, England. *Telephone:* (0223) 842167.

CORNESS, Sir Colin Ross, Kt., M.A.; British business executive; b. 9 Oct. 1931, Chorlton; s. of Thomas Corness and Mary Evlyne Corness; ed. Uppingham School, Magdalene Coll., Cambridge, Grad. School of Business Admin., Harvard; Dir. Taylor Woodrow Construction Ltd. 1961-1964; Man. Dir. Redland Tiles Ltd. 1965-70, Group Man. Dir. Redland PLC 1967-82, Deputy Chair. and Man. Dir. 1974-77, Chair. and C.E.O. 1977-; Dir. Chubb and Son PLC 1974-84, W.H. Smith and Son Holdings PLC 1980-87, S.E. Region, Nat. Westminster Bank PLC 1982-86, Courtaulds PLC 1986-, Gordon Russell PLC 1985-, Bank of England 1987-, S. G. Warburg Group PLC 1987-, Unitech PLC 1987-; Chair. Bldg. Centre 1974-77; mem. Econ. Devt. Cttee. for Bldg. 1980-84, Ind. Devt. Advisory Bd. 1982-84, U.K. Advisory Bd. of the British-American Chamber of Commerce 1987-. *Leis- ure interests:* squash, travel, music. *Address:* Redland PLC, Redland House, Reigate, Surrey, RH2 OSJ, England. *Telephone:* 0737 242488.

CORNFORTH, Sir John Warcup, Kt., C.B.E., D.PHIL., F.R.S.; Australian research scientist; b. 7 Sept. 1917, Sydney; s. of J. W. Cornforth and Hilda Eipper; m. Rita H. Harradence 1941; one s. two d.; ed. Univs. of Sydney and Oxford; Scientific Staff, Medical Research Council 1946-62; Dir. Milstead Lab. of Chemical Enzymology, Shell Research Ltd. 1962-75; Assoc. Prof. Univ. of Warwick 1965-71; Visiting Prof. Univ. of Sussex 1971-75; Royal Soc. Prof. Univ. of Sussex 1975-82; Foreign Hon. mem. American Acad. 1973-; Corresp. mem. Australian Acad. of Science 1977-; Foreign Assoc. U.S. Nat. Acad. of Sciences 1978-; Foreign mem. Royal Netherlands Acad. of Sciences 1978-; Hon. Fellow St. Catherine's Coll., Oxford 1976-; Hon. Prof. Beijing Medical Univ. 1986-; Hon. D.Sc. (ETH Zurich) 1975, (Oxford, Dublin, Liverpool, Warwick Univs.) 1976, (Aberdeen, Hull, Sussex, Sydney Univs.) 1977; Corday-Morgan Medal, Chem. Soc. 1953, Flintoff Medal, Chem. Soc. 1966, Ciba Medal, Biochem. Soc. 1966, Stouffer Prize 1967, Davy Medal, Royal Soc. 1968, Ernest Guenther Award, American Chemical Soc. 1969, Prix Roussel 1972, Nobel Prize for Chemistry 1975, Royal Medal, Royal Soc. 1976, Copley Medal, Royal Soc. 1982. *Publications:* The Chemistry of Penicillin (part author) 1949, and numerous papers on chemical and biochemical topics. *Leisure interests:* tennis, gardening, chess. *Address:* Saxon Down, Cuilfail, Lewes, East Sussex, BN7 2BE, England.

CORNILLON, Pierre, PH.D.; French IPU official; b. 5 March 1935, Lyon; m., separated; two c.; ed. Univ. of Geneva; previously worked as ed. and translator; Press Officer, Deputy Head, Information/Advertising Dept. Union Carbide S.A. Geneva 1962-64; teacher, Interpreters' School, Univ. of Geneva 1966-71; Research Officer, Cttee. Sec. IPU 1964-68, Asst. Sec. of Union 1968-72, Deputy Sec.-Gen. and Legal Adviser 1972-86, Sec.-Gen. 1987-. *Address:* Inter-Parliamentary Union, Place du Petit-Saconnex, Case

Postale 99, 1211 Geneva 19, Switzerland (Office); 1 Empasse des Bouchets, 74100 Vétraz-Monthoux, France (Home). *Telephone:* (022) 34 41 50 (Office); (50) 87 03 75 (Home).

CORNISH, William Rodolph, LL.B., B.C.L., F.B.A.; Barrister; b. 9 Aug. 1937, S. Australia; s. of Jack R. Cornish and Elizabeth E. Cornish; m. Lovedy E. Moule 1964; one s. two d.; ed. St. Peter's Coll., Adelaide, Adelaide Univ. and Oxford Univ., England; Lecturer in Law, L.S.E. 1962-68; Reader in Law, Queen Mary Coll., London Univ. 1969-70; Prof. of English Law, L.S.E. 1970-. *Publications:* The Jury 1968, Intellectual Property 1981, Encyclopaedia of U.K. and European Patent Law (with others) 1978. *Address:* 74 Palace Road, London, S.W.2, England. *Telephone:* 01-671 1564.

CORNWELL, David John Moore (pseudonym John le Carré); British writer; b. 19 Oct. 1931; s. of Ronald Thomas Archibald Cornwell and Olive Glassy; m. 1st Alison Ann Veronica Sharp 1954 (divorced 1971), three s.; m. 2nd Valerie Jane Eustace 1972, one s.; ed. St. Andrew's Preparatory School, Pangbourne, Sherborne School, Berne Univ., and Lincoln Coll., Oxford; Teacher, Eton Coll. 1956-58; in Foreign Service 1959-64; Somerset Maugham Award 1963, James Tait Black Award 1977. *Publications:* Call for the Dead 1961 (filmed as The Deadly Affair 1967), Murder of Quality 1962, The Spy Who Came in From the Cold 1963, The Looking Glass War 1965, A Small Town in Germany 1968, The Naive and Sentimental Lover 1971, Tinker, Tailor, Soldier, Spy 1974, The Honourable Schoolboy 1977, Smiley's People 1979, The Quest for Carla (collected edn. of previous three titles) 1982, The Little Drummer Girl 1983, A Perfect Spy 1986, The Russia House 1989. *Address:* 5-8 Lower John Street, Golden Square, London, W1R 4HA, England.

CORONEL DE PALMA, Luis, LL.B.; Spanish banker; b. 4 May 1925, Madrid; s. of Luís Coronel de Palma and Asunción Coronel de Palma; m. María del Rosario Martínez-Agulló Sanchis 1953; five c.; ed. Cen. Univ. of Madrid; Called to the Bar 1954; with Barcelona Treasury Office; Deputy Magistrate, High Court of Barcelona 1956; Dir.-Gen. Savings and Invest- ment, Gen. Banking and Exchange Office, Secr. of Bd. of Investments, Ministry of Finance 1957, Dir.-Gen. Confed. of Savings Banks 1959, 1976, Gen. Man.; Savings Banks Credit Inst. 1962; Nat. Econ. Adviser 1965; Gov. IBRD, IMF 1970; Gov. Banco de España 1970; mem. Royal Acad. of Jurisprudence 1955; Grand Cross, Civil Merit, Military Merit, Agricultural Merit, Mexican Order of Eagle-Azteca, Knight Commdr., Legion of Honour, and other decorations. *Leisure interests:* music, reading. *Address:* Avda del Campo, 21 Somosaguas, Madrid (11) (Home).

CORR, Edwin Gharst, M.A.; American diplomatist; b. 6 Aug. 1934, Edmond; s. of E. L. Corr and Rowena Gharst; m. Susanne Springer 1958; three d.; ed. Univ. of Okla.; officer Dept. of State, Foreign Office 1961-62; sent to Mexico 1962-66; Dir. Peace Corps, Cali, Colombia 1966-68; Panama Desk Officer, Dept. of State 1969-71; Program Officer InterAmerican Foundation 1971; Exec. Asst. to Amb., Embassy, Bangkok 1972-75; Coun- sellor Political Affairs, Embassy, Ecuador 1976; Deputy Chief of Mission 1977-78; Deputy Asst. Sec. Int. Narcotics Matters, State Dept. 1978-80; Amb. to Peru 1980-81, Bolivia 1981-85, El Salvador 1985-88; State Dept. Diplomat-in-Residence, Univ. of Oklahoma 1988-89; Nat. Order of Merit (Eduador), Condor of the Andes (Bolivia), Pres.'s Performance Award (USA), Award for Superior Performance (USA), Distinguished Service Award (USA), Distinguished Service Award (USA), Jose Matias Delgado Decoration (El Salvador). *Publications:* The Political Process in Colombia 1971, numerous articles in English and Spanish. *Address:* University of Oklahoma, 304 Dale Hall Tower, Norman, Okla. 73019 (Office); 544 Shawnee, Norman, Okla. 73071, U.S.A. (Home). *Telephone:* (405) 325-6621 (Office); (405) 321-7036 (Home).

CORREA, Charles M., M.ARCH.; Indian architect and planner; b. 1 Sept. 1930, Hyderabad; m. Monika Sequeira 1961; one s. one d.; ed. Univ. of Michigan and M.I.T.; Partner G. M. Bhuta & Associates, Bombay 1956-58; Pvt. Practice 1958-; Chief Architect New Bombay 1971-74; Consulting Architect to Govt. of Karnataka 1975-78; Governing Council Nat. Inst. of Design, Ahmedabad 1974-77; Dir. CIDCO, New Bombay 1976-; Chair. Housing Urban Renewal and Ecology Bd. (BMRDA) 1975-; Steering Cttee. Aga Khan Award for Architecture 1977-, Padma Shri, Pres. of India 1972; R.I.B.A. Gold Medal 1984, Gold Medal, Indian Inst. of Architects 1987; Hon. Fellow, American Inst. of Architecture 1977; Dr. h.c. (Univ. of Mich.) 1979. *Major works include:* Mahatma Gandhi Memorial Museum, Sabarmati Ashram, Ahmedabad, Jeevan Bima townships, Bombay and Bangalore, Kovalam beach Devt., Kerala, Kanchanjunga apartments, Bombay, Tara group housing, Delhi, plutonium plant, Bhabha Atomic Research Centre, Trombay, Cidade de Goa, Dona Paula, New India Centre, Delhi, performing arts centre, Kala Acad., Goa, Previ low-income housing, Peru, UNEP mission to Dodoma, Tanzania, consultant to HABITAT, etc. *Publication:* The New Landscape 1985. *Leisure interests:* model railways, old films, swimming. *Address:* 9 Mathew Road, Bombay 400004 (Office); Sonmarg, Napean Sea Road, Bombay 400006, India (Home). *Telephone:* 8111858/8111976 (Office); 8129091 (Home).

CORRÊA DA COSTA, Sérgio; Brazilian diplomatist; b. 19 Feb. 1919, Rio de Janeiro; s. of Dr. I. Affonso da Costa and Lavinia Corrêa da Costa; m. Zazi Aranha 1943; one s. two d.; ed. Univ. do Brasil and Univ. of California (Los Angeles); Sec., Brazilian Embassy, Buenos Aires 1944-46, Washington

D.C. 1946; Acting Rep. to Council of OAS and Inter-American ECOSOC 1946–48; Deputy Head, Econ. Dept., Ministry of Foreign Relations 1952; Head Div. of Int. Affairs, Brazilian War Coll. 1952; Acting Pres. Brazilian Nat. Tech. Assistance Comm. 1955–58; Minister Counsellor, Rome 1959–62; Amb. to Canada 1962–65; Sec.-Gen. Ministry of Foreign Relations 1967–68, Acting Minister 1968; Amb. to U.K. 1968–75; Perm. Rep. to UN 1975–83, Pres. UN Econ. and Social Council 1983; Amb. to U.S.A. 1983–86; Brazilian Rep., 18th and 21st Sessions, UN Gen. Assembly 1963 and 1966; mem. Brazilian Acad. of Letters; numerous orders. *Publications:* As Quatro Corôas de D. Pedro I 1941, Pedro I e Metternich—Tracos de uma guerra diplomática 1942, A Diplomacia Brasileira na questão de Letícia 1942, A Diplomacia do Marechal-Intervenção Estrangeira na Revolta da Armada 1945, Every Inch a King—A Biography of Dom Pedro I, First Emperor of Brazil 1950. *Leisure interests:* swimming, yachting, reading. *Address:* 3006 Massachusetts Avenue, N.W. Washington, D.C. 20008, U.S.A.

CORRÊA DO LAGO, Antonio, M.A., LL.B.; Brazilian diplomatist; b. 28 Aug. 1918, Pau, France; s. of Gen. Manoel Corrêa do Lago and Maria Helena Guerra do Lago; m. Delminda Aranha Corrêa do Lago 1948; five s.; ed. Colégio Santo Ignácio, Rio de Janeiro, Univ. do Brasil, Rio de Janeiro, and Univ. of S. California, Los Angeles; Foreign Service 1939–, Buenos Aires 1944, Montevideo 1945–47; Consul, Los Angeles 1951–53; Head, Econ. Div., Ministry of External Relations 1954–58; Consul-Gen. Paris 1959–61; Head of Brazilian Del. to Conf. of Latin American Free Trade Asscn. 1961; Amb. to Venezuela 1961–64; Perm. Rep. to European Office of UN, Geneva, and Del. to Disarmament Cttee. 1964–66; Dir. Instituto Rio Branco (Foreign Service Inst.) 1966–69; Del. to XXII Session UN Gen. Assembly 1967; Amb., Head Mission to European Communities, Brussels 1970–74; Amb. to Uruguay 1974–81, to Holy See 1981–84, to France 1985–86. *Address:* Laderia de Nossa Senhora 325, 22211 Rio de Janeiro, Brazil.

CORRIGAN, E. Gerald, PH.D.; American banker and economist; b. 1941, Waterbury, Conn.; ed. Fairfield and Fordham Univs.; Group Vice-Pres. (Man. and Planning) Fed. Reserve Bank of New York 1976–80, Pres. Jan. 1985–; Special Asst. to Chair., Bd. of Govs. Fed. Reserve System 1979–80; Pres. Fed. Reserve Bank of Minneapolis 1981–; Trustee, Macalester Coll., St. Paul, Minn. 1981–, Fairfield Univ., Fairfield, Conn. 1985–; mem. Council on Foreign Relations 1986–, Trilateral Comm. 1986–. *Address:* Federal Reserve Bank, P.O. Station, New York, N.Y. 10045, U.S.A.

CORRIGAN-MAGUIRE, Mairead; Northern Irish human rights activist; b. 27 Jan. 1944, Belfast; d. of Andrew Corrigan; m. 2nd Jackie Maguire 1981; one s.; ed. St. Vincent's Primary School, Belfast, Miss Gordon's Commercial Coll.; works as shorthand typist; Jt. winner of Nobel Peace Prize for launching the Northern Ireland Peace Movement (later renamed Community of the Peace People) 1976, Chair. 1980–81; Carl von Ossietzky Medal for Courage (Berlin Section, Int. League of Human Rights); Hon. LL.D. (Yale Univ.) 1976. *Address:* Community of the Peace People, 224 Lisburn Road, Belfast, BT9 6GE, Northern Ireland. *Telephone:* 663465.

CORRIPIO AHUMADA, H.E. Cardinal Ernesto; Mexican ecclesiastic; b. 29 June 1919, Tampico; ordained priest 1942; Titular Bishop of Zapara 1953–56; Bishop of Tampico 1956–67; Archbishop of Antequera 1967–76, of Puebla de los Angeles 1976–77; Archbishop of Mexico City and Primate of Mexico July 1977–; cr. Cardinal 1979; mem. Sacred Congregation for the Sacraments and Divine Worship, Pontifical Comm. for Latin America; entitled L'Immacolata al Tiburtino. *Address:* Apartado 22-796, 14000 México, México. *Telephone:* 5732222.

CORSARO, Frank Andrew; American theatre and opera director; b. 22 Dec. 1924, New York; s. of Joseph and Marie (née Quarino) Corsaro; m. Bonnie Leaders 1971; one s.; ed. Yale Univ.; began career as actor 1948, appearing since in productions including Mrs. McThing, Broadway 1951; first film appearance in Rachel, Rachel 1967; dir. of numerous plays including A Hatful of Rain, Broadway 1955–56, The Night of the Iguana 1961–62, Tremonisha 1975, 1600 Pennsylvania Avenue 1976, Cold Storage, Lyceum 1977–, Whoopee! 1979, Knockout 1979; directed and acted in numerous TV productions; one-man art show 1976; dir. numerous operas with New York City Opera 1958–, Washington Opera Soc. 1970–74, St. Paul Opera 1971, Houston Grand Opera 1973–77, Assoc. Artistic Dir. 1977–; productions include La Traviata, Madame Butterfly, Faust, Manon Lescaut, A Village Romeo and Juliet, L'Incoronazione di Poppea, The Angel of Fire, Rinaldo, Love for Three Oranges (Glyndebourne 1983), La Fanciulla del West (Deutsches Oper Berlin 1983), Rinaldo (Metropolitan Opera 1983), Fennimore and Gerda (Edinburgh Festival 1983), Where the Wild Things Are, Higgeldy, Piggeldy, Pop (Glyndebourne 1985), Alcina (Spitalfields 1985), (L.A. Opera Centre 1986). *Publications:* L'histoire du soldat (adaptation), La Bohème (adaptation), A Piece of Blue Sky (play), Maverik 1978, Libretto: Before Breakfast (music by Thomas Pasatieri). *Leisure interests:* painting, piano playing, writing. *Address:* c/o New York City Opera, State Theater, Lincoln Center Plaza, New York, N.Y. 10023 (Office); 33 Riverside Drive, New York, N.Y. 10023, U.S.A. (Home). *Telephone:* 212-874-1048 (Home).

CORSON, Dale R., PH.D.; American physicist and university administrator; b. 5 April 1914, Pittsburg, Kansas; s. of the late Harry R. Corson and of Alta Hill Corson; m. Nellie E. Griswold 1938; three s. one d.; ed. Coll. of Emporia, Univs. of Kansas and California; with Los Alamos Scientific Lab. 1945–46; Asst. Prof. of Physics, Cornell Univ. 1946–47, Assoc. Prof. 1947–52, Prof. 1952–56, Chair., Dept. of Physics 1956–59, Dean, Coll. of Eng. 1959–63, Univ. Provost 1963–69; Pres. Cornell Univ. 1969–77, Chancellor 1977–79, Pres. Emer. and Prof. Emer. 1979–; Fellow American Acad. of Arts and Sciences; mem. Nat. Acad. of Eng.; Public Welfare Medal, N.A.S. *Publications:* Introduction to Electromagnetic Fields and Waves (with Lorrain). *Leisure interests:* hiking, mountain climbing, canoeing, photography, sailing. *Address:* 615 Clark Hall, Cornell University, Ithaca, N.Y. 14853 (Office); 144 Northview Road, Ithaca, N.Y. 14850, U.S.A. (Home). *Telephone:* (607) 255-4320 (Office); (607) 272-1815 (Home).

CORSTEN, Severin, DR.PHIL.; German librarian; b. 8 Dec. 1920, Heinsberg/Rheinland; s. of Leo and Gertrud (née Heusch) Corsten; m. Dr. Margret Loenartz 1952; one s. two d.; ed. Univ. of Bonn; Librarian, Library of Ministry of Foreign Affairs, Bonn 1954–63; Deputy Dir. Universitäts- und Stadtbibliothek, Cologne 1963–71, Dir. 1971–85; Hon. Prof. Univ. of Cologne 1975–; Kt. of the Papal Order of St. Gregory; Verdienstkreuz am Bande des Verdienstordens. *Publications:* Das Domanialgut im Amt Heinsberg 1953, Die Anfänge des Kölner Buchdrucks 1955, Das Heinsberger Land im frühen Mittelalter 1959, Die Bibliothek des Auswärtigen Amtes 1961, Die Kölnische Chronik von 1499 1982, Studien zum Kölner Frühdruck 1985, Der Buchdruck im. 15. Jahrhundert, Vol. 1 1988, Untersuchungen zum Buch-und Bibliothekswesen 1988. *Leisure interest:* music. *Address:* Breslauer Strasse 14, D-5300 Bonn 2, Federal Republic of Germany. *Telephone:* 0228-375320.

CORTAZZI, Sir (Henry Arthur) Hugh, G.C.M.G.; British diplomatist (retd.); b. 2 May 1924, Sedbergh, Yorks. (now Cumbria); s. of F. E. M. Cortazzi and M. Cortazzi; m. Elizabeth Esther Montagu 1956; one s. two d.; ed. Sedbergh School, Univ. of St. Andrews and Univ. of London; served R.A.F. 1943–48; joined Foreign Office 1949; Third Sec., Singapore 1950–51; Second Sec., Tokyo 1951–54; Foreign Office, London 1954–58; First Sec., Bonn 1958–60, Tokyo 1961–65 (Head of Chancery 1963); Foreign Office 1965–66; Counsellor (Commercial), Tokyo 1966–70; Royal Coll. of Defence Studies 1971; Minister (Commercial), Washington 1972–75; Deputy Under-Sec. of State FCO 1975–80; Amb. to Japan 1980–84 (retd.); apptd. Dir. Hill Samuel and Co. Ltd., Foreign and Colonial Pacific Investment Trust, G. T. Japan Investment Trust 1984, Thornton Pacific Investment Trust S.A. 1986; apptd. Adviser (with Lady Cortazzi) to Mitsukoshi Dept. Store, Tokyo, Japan 1984; mem. Econ. and Social Research Council 1984–. *Publications:* trans. of Japanese short stories by Keita Genji 1972, A Diplomat's Wife in Japan: Sketches at the Turn of the Century (Ed.) 1982, Isles of Gold: Antique Maps of Japan 1983, Higashi No Shimaguni, Nishi No Shimaguni 1984, Dr. Willis in Japan (1862–1877) 1985, Mitford's Japan (Ed.) 1985, Zoku Higashi No Shimaguni, Nishi No Shimaguni (Ed.) 1987, Victorians in Japan: in and around the Treaty Ports 1987; Textbooks for Japanese students of English: Thoughts from a Sussex Garden 1985, Second Thoughts 1986, Japanese Encounter 1987. *Leisure interests:* the arts, especially literature and Japanese studies. *Address:* c/o Hill Samuel and Co. Ltd., 100 Wood Street, London, EC2P 2AJ, England.

CORTESI, Gaetano, D.ECON.; Italian industrial executive; b. 8 May 1912, Mesenzana, Varese; s. of late Giuseppe Cortesi and late Angela Ferrini; m. Fiorella Lello 1946; three s.; ed. Bocconi Univ., Milan; with Inst. for Industrial Reconstruction (IRI) group 1935–; first in textile industry, then with Banca Commerciale Italiana in New York and in Italy; Man. Control Dept. of IRI 1945, responsible for mechanical industries sector incl. Alfa Romeo 1957–60, Head of Man. Control Dept. 1960–66; assigned to superintend merger of Italian shipyards into Italcantieri, Trieste 1966; Pres. Italcantieri until 1971; Man. Dir. Fincantieri corpn. controlling 14 major ship-building and repair yards in Italy 1971–74; Chair., Man. Dir. Alfa Romeo S.p.A. 1974–78; also Chair. Alfa Romeo Alfasud S.p.A.; Pres. Cassa per il Mezzogiorno 1980–; Cavaliere del Lavoro. *Publication:* Pianificazione, Programmazione e Controlli Industriali 1955. *Leisure interest:* mountaineering. *Address:* Piazzale Kennedy 20, Eur, Rome, Italy.

CORTINA MAURI, Pedro; Spanish lawyer; diplomatist and politician; b. 1908; ed. Univ. of Madrid, Acad. of International Law, The Hague; Legal Adviser on Int. Affairs, Ministry of Foreign Affairs 1937–52; Consul-Gen. Tangiers 1945–52; Dir. Int. Orgs., Ministry of Foreign Affairs 1952–55; Consul-Gen. Paris, del. to Int. Orgs., Paris 1955–58; mem. del. to UN Gen. Ass. 1956; Under-Sec. Ministry of Foreign Affairs 1958–66; Amb. to France 1966–74; Minister of Foreign Affairs 1974–75; mem. Inst. of Int. Law; Grand Cross Order of Isabel la Católica, Order of Civil Merit, Order of San Raimundo de Penafort, Légion d'honneur. *Address:* c/o Ministerio de Asuntos Exteriores, Madrid, Spain.

CORWIN, Norman; American writer-producer-director of radio, television, stage and cinema; b. 3 May 1910, Boston, Mass.; s. of Samuel H. Corwin and Rose Ober; m. Katherine Locke 1947; one s. one d.; Newspaperman 1929–38; writer, director, producer for Columbia Broadcasting System 1938–48; Chief, Special Projects, UN Radio 1949–53; mem. Faculty of Theatre Arts Univ. of Calif., L.A.; Regents Lecturer Univ. of Calif., Santa Barbara; Visiting Prof. School of Journalism, Univ. of Southern Calif. 1980–; mem. Telecommunications faculty, Univ. of Southern Calif.; writer in residence, Univ. of N. Carolina; Patten Memorial Lecturer, Indiana

Univ. 1981; Co-Chair. Scholarship Cttee. of Acad. of Motion Picture Arts and Sciences; Chair. Documentary Awards Cttee. of Acad. of Motion Picture Arts and Sciences 1964–81; Distinguished Visiting Lecturer, San Diego State Univ. 1978; Chair. Writers Exec. Cttee. of Acad. of Motion Picture Arts and Sciences and mem. Bd. of Govs. 1979–, Chair. Documentary Awards Comm. 1967–82, 1985–, Sec. Acad. Foundation 1983–88; mem. Bd. of Dirs. Writers Guild of America; Trustee Filmex; writer, Dir. and host TV series, Norman Corwin Presents, Westinghouse Broadcasting Co.; Sec. Acad. of Arts and Sciences Foundation 1983; First Vice-Pres. Acad. of Motion Picture Arts and Sciences 1988; Stasheff Lecturer, Univ. of Mich. 1984; recipient of Peabody Medal, Edward Bok Medal; Award of American Acad. of Arts and Sciences 1942; American Newspaper Guide Page One Award 1944, 1945; Wendell Wilkie One-World Award 1946, entered in Radio Hall of Fame 1962; Hon. D.Litt. (Columbia Coll. of Communications); other awards. *Publications:* They Fly through the Air 1939, Thirteen by Corwin 1942, More by Corwin 1944, On a Note of Triumph (both as a book and album of recordings) 1945, Untitled, and Other Dramas 1947, Dog in the Sky 1952, Overkill and Megalove 1962, Prayer for the 70's 1969, Holes in a Stained Glass Window 1978, Greater than the Bomb 1981, A Date with Sandburg 1981, Trivializing America 1984, Jerusalem Printout 1984, Network at Fifty 1987; *Films:* The Blue Veil, The Grand Design, Lust for Life, The Story of Ruth, Yamashita, The Tiger of Malaya; *Cantatas:* The Golden Door, Yes Speak Out Yes (commissioned by UN 1968); Stage plays: The Rivalry, The World of Carl Sandburg, The Hyphen, Cervantes, Together Tonight 1975. *Leisure interests:* mineralogy, music, painting, chess. *Address:* 1840 Fairburn Avenue, Los Angeles, Calif. 90025, U.S.A.

COSGRAVE, Liam; Irish politician; b. 13 April 1920, Templeogue, Co. Dublin; s. of the late William T. Cosgrave (Pres. of the Exec. Council of the Irish Free State, 1922–32) and Louise Flanagan; m. Vera Osborne 1952; two s. one d.; ed. Christian Brothers' Schools, Dublin, St. Vincent's Coll., Castleknock, Co. Dublin and Kings Inns; called to the Bar 1943; Sr. Counsel 1958; served in Army, pvt.; T.D., Dublin Co. 1943–48, Dún Laoghaire and Rathdown 1948–81; Leader, Fine Gael Party 1965–77; Parl. Sec. to the Prime Minister and to Minister for Industry and Commerce 1948–51; Minister for External Affairs 1954–57; Prime Minister 1973–77; Minister for Defence 1976; Chair. and Leader of first Irish Del. to UN Gen. Ass. 1956; Hon. LL.D. (Duquesne Univ., St. John's Univ.) 1956, (De Paul Univ.) 1958, (Nat. Univ. of Ireland and Dublin Univ.) 1974; Kt. Grand Cross of Pius IX (Ordine Piaro). *Address:* Beechpark, Templeogue, Co. Dublin, Ireland.

COSMOS, Jean; French playwright; b. Jean Louis Gaudrat, 14 June 1923, Paris; s. of Albert Gaudrat and Maria Maillebuau; m. Alice Jarrousse 1943; one s. two d.; ed. Inst. St. Nicholas, Igny, Coll. Jean-Baptiste Say, Paris; songwriter 1945–50, writer for radio 1952–60, for TV 1964–; Comm. Soc. des auteurs dramatiques 1971–. *Plays:* author or adapter of numerous plays for the theatre including la Fille du roi 1952, Au jour le jour 1952, les Grenadiers de la reine 1957, Macbeth 1959, 1965, le Manteau 1963, la Vie et la Mort du roi Jean 1964, Arden de Faversham 1964, Monsieur Alexandre 1965, la Bataille de Lobositz 1969, Major Barbara 1970, le Marchand de Venise 1971, Sainte Jeanne des Abattoirs 1972; author of numerous TV plays including les Oranges (Albert Ollivier prize) 1964, le Pacte 1966, Un homme, un cheval 1968, le Petit vieux des Batignolles, la Pomme oubliée (after Jean Anglade), l'Ingénu (after Voltaire), Bonsoir Léon, la Tête à l'envers, le Trêve, le Coup Monté, Aide-toi, Julien Fontanes, magistrat; with Jean Chatenêt: 16 à Kerbriant, Ardéchois coeur fidèle (Critics' choice) 1975, Les Yeux Bleus, la Lumière des Justes (after Henri Troyat); with Gilles Perrault: le Secret des dieux, la Filière, seven-part serial of Julien Fontanes, Magistrat, regular contrib. to les Cinq dernières minutes; *film:* La dictée 1984; TV, Soc. des auteurs et compositeurs prizes 1970. *Address:* 7 avenue Porte-de-la-Plaine, 75015 Paris (Office); 2 avenue de la Porte-Briançon, 75015 Paris, France (Home).

COSSIGA, Francesco, LL.D.; Italian politician; b. 26 July 1928, Sassari; joined Democrazia Cristiana (DC) 1945, Provincial Sec. 1956–58, mem. Nat. Council 1958–; M.P. for Cagliari 1963–; Under-Sec. of State for Defence 1966–70; Minister for Public Admin. 1974–76, of the Interior 1976–78; Prime Minister 1979–80; Pres. of Senate July 1983–85; Pres. of Italy July 1985–; Chair. Parl. Group of DC; Dr. h.c. (Oxford) 1987. *Address:* Palazzo del Quirinale, 00187 Rome, Italy.

COSSINS, Edwin Albert, PH.D., D.SC., F.R.S.C.; Canadian professor of botany; b. 28 Feb. 1937, Havering, U.K.; s. of A.J. Cossins; m. Lucille J. Salt 1962; two d.; ed. Clark's Coll. Romford, S.E. Essex Tech. Coll., Chelsea Coll., Univ. of London and Purdue Univ.; Research Assoc. Purdue Univ. 1961–62; Asst. Prof. Univ. of Alberta 1962–65, Assoc. Prof. 1965–69, Prof. of Botany (Plant Biochemistry) 1969–, Assoc. Dean of Science 1983–88; Visiting Prof. Univ. of Geneva 1972–73, Univ. of California, Berkeley 1988; Pres. Canadian Soc. of Plant Physiologists 1976–77; other professional appts.; Centennial Medal, Govt. of Canada 1967. *Publications:* co-author of three books and author of over 95 publs. in scientific journals. *Leisure interests:* golf, gardening, cross-country skiing. *Address:* Department of Botany, University of Alberta, Edmonton, Alb., T6G 2E9 (Office); 99 Fairway Drive, Edmonton, Alb., T6J 2C2, Canada (Home). *Telephone:* (403) 432-4758 (Office); (403) 434-7613 (Home).

COSSLETT, Vernon Ellis, PH.D., SC.D., F.R.S.; British physicist; b. 16 June 1908, Cirencester; s. of Edgar William Cosslett and Annie Williams; m. 1st Rosemary Wilson 1936 (divorced 1940); m. 2nd Anna Joanna Wischin 1940 (died 1969); one s. one d.; ed. Cirencester Grammar School, Bristol and London Univs., Kaiser Wilhelm Institut, Berlin-Dahlem; lecturer, Faraday House Electrical Eng. Coll., London, 1935–39; Keddey-Fletcher Warr Research Student, London Univ. 1939–41; lecturer, Electrical Lab., Oxford 1941–46; ICI Research Fellow, Cavendish Lab., Cambridge Univ. 1946–49; lecturer in Physics 1949–65, Reader in Electron Physics 1965–75, Emer. 1975–; Fellow, Corpus Christi Coll., Cambridge 1963–; Pres. Royal Microscopical Soc., London 1961–64, Int. Fed. of Socs. for Electron Microscopy 1972–75; Hon. D.Sc. (Tübingen), Hon. D.Med.-Sci. (Gothenburg), Duddell Medal of Inst. of Physics, Royal Medal of Royal Soc. 1979. *Publications:* Introduction to Electron Optics 1946, The Electron Microscope 1947, Bibliography of Electron Microscopy 1950, Practical Electron Microscopy 1951, X-Ray Microscopy (with W. C. Nixon) 1960, Modern Microscopy 1966, Advances in Optical and Electron Microscopy (with R. Barer) 1966–87. *Leisure interests:* gardening, listening to music, skiing, mountain walking. *Address:* Corpus Christi College, Cambridge University; 31 Comberton Road, Barton, Cambridge, England (Home). *Telephone:* Cambridge 262423; Cambridge 338000; Cambridge 334563.

COSSONS, Neil, O.B.E., M.A., F.S.A.; British museum director; b. 15 Jan. 1939, Nottingham; s. of Arthur Cossons and Evelyn Cossons (née Bettle); m. Veronica Edwards 1965; two s. one d.; ed. Univ. of Liverpool; Curator of Tech., Bristol City Museum 1964; Deputy Dir., City of Liverpool Museums 1969; Dir. Ironbridge Gorge Museum 1971; Dir. Nat. Maritime Museum, Greenwich 1983; Dir. Science Museum, London 1986; Fellow of the Museums Assen.; Hon. Fellow R.C.A.; Hon. D.Soc.Sc. (Birmingham) 1979; Hon. D.Univ. (Open Univ.) 1984. *Publications:* Industrial Archaeology of the Bristol Region (with R.A. Buchanan) 1968, Transactions of the First International Congress on the Conservation of Industrial Monuments (Ed.) 1975, Rees's Manufacturing Industry (Ed.) 1975, Ironbridge—Landscape of Industry (with H. Sowden) 1977, The Iron Bridge—Symbol of the Industrial Revolution (with B.S. Trinder) 1979, The Management of Change in Museums (Ed.) 1985. *Leisure interests:* travel and design. *Address:* The Science Museum, London, SW7 2DD (Office); Church Hill, Ironbridge, Shropshire, TF8 7PW, England (Home). *Telephone:* 01-938 8003 (Office); (095245) 2701 (Home).

COSTA, Antonio Maria, PH.D.; Italian economist; b. 16 June 1941, Mondovi; s. of Francesco Costa and Maria Costa; m. Patricia Agnes Wallace 1971; two s. one d.; ed. Univ. of Calif. at Berkeley, Acad. of Sciences of the U.S.S.R. and Univ. of Turin; Visiting Prof. of Econs., Moscow Univ. and Acad. of Sciences of the U.S.S.R. 1965–67; Instructor of Econs., Univ. of Calif. at Berkeley 1968–70; Prof. of Econs., New York Univ., 1976–83; Sr. Econ. Adviser to the UN 1970–83; Special Counsellor in Econs. to the Sec.-Gen. of OECD 1983–87; Dir. Gen. Econ. and Financial Affairs, EEC 1987–. *Publications:* articles on econs. and politics. *Leisure interest:* work. *Address:* Drève de Lansrode, 7, 1640 Rhode St Genèse, Belgium. *Telephone:* (02) 358 45 40.

COSTA, Giovanni Mario, DR.ING.; Italian business executive; b. 17 June 1922, Genoa; s. of Alfredo Costa and Marie J. Bonfiglio; m. Maria Grossi 1948; two s.; maintenance and foundry foreman 1947–50; maintenance supt. 1951–54; gen. supt. mechanical plant 1954–57; Vice-Gen. Supt. steel-making plant 1957–61; Exec. Vice-Pres. eng. co. 1962–66, Pres. 1967–70; Exec. Vice-Pres. steel co. 1970–76; Pres. Financial Holding for Steel 1977–82, Vice-Chair. and Chair. Research Center 1983–86; Grand'Ufficiale della Repubblica Italiana. *Publications:* articles in professional journals. *Leisure interests:* sailing, tourism. *Address:* 00197 Rome, Via Bertoloni 30; 16122 Genoa, Via Mameli 3/5, Italy. *Telephone:* 873762 (Rome); 811763 (Genoa).

COSTA, Lucio; Brazilian architect; b. 1902; ed. England, France and Escola Nacional de Belas-Artes, Rio de Janeiro; with Le Corbusier and others designed Brazilian Govt. buildings 1936, with Niemeyer designed Brazilian Pavilion at New York World Fair 1939, won int. competition for design of city of Brasília 1957. *Address:* Brasília, D.F., Brazil.

COSTA, Manuel Pinto da; São Tomé politician; b. 5 Aug. 1937, Água Grande; Founded Movement for the Liberation of São Tomé and Príncipe (MLSTP) 1972; Sec.-Gen., MLSTP, based in Gabon 1972–75, Pres. 1978; Pres. of São Tomé and Príncipe July 1975–; Minister of Agric., Land Reform and Defence 1975–78, of Labour and Social Security 1977–78, of Territorial Admin. 1978–82, of Defence and Nat. Security 1982–86, fmr. Minister of Planning and Econs.; Prime Minister 1978–88; visited China and N. Korea Dec. 1975; Dr. h.c. (Berlin); José Marti Medal, Cuba. *Address:* Office of the President, C.P. 38, São Tomé, São Tomé and Príncipe.

COSTA-GAVRAS, (Henri) Kostantinos; film director; b. 1933, Athens; m. Michele Ray 1968; one s. one d.; ed. Sorbonne, Paris; fmr. ballet dancer in Greece; worked as Asst. to film Dirs. Yves Allegret, Jacques Demy (q.v.), René Clair, René Clément (q.v.); named Best Dir., Cannes Film Festival 1975. *Films directed include:* The Sleeping Car Murders (also writer), Z (also co-writer) 1969 (Acad. Award for Best Foreign Language Film), Un Homme de Trop (Moscow Film Festival Prize) 1966, L'Aveu (The Confession) 1970, State of Siege 1973, Madame Rosa 1978, Clair de

Femme 1979, Hanna K 1983, Missing 1984, Family Business 1988, Betrayed 1988, Music Box 1989.

COSTA MÉNDEZ, Dr. Nicanor; Argentine politician; b. 30 Oct. 1922; m.; two d.; ed. Univ. of Buenos Aires, Columbia Univ., New York; Adviser to Sec. of State for External Trade 1962; Adviser, Ministry of External Relations and Religion 1962; Amb. to Chile 1962–64; Minister of External Relations and Religion 1966–69, 1981–82; Pres. various Argentine dels. to UN; Del. to various int. confs.; Hon. Prof., Catholic Univ. of Argentina; contrib. to newspaper La Nación; Vice-Pres. Argentine Council for Int. Relations; mem. Interamerican Bar Asscn., Int. Law Asscn, Int. Inst. for Strategic Studies, Hon. mem. Spanish Cultural Inst. *Address:* c/o Ministerio de Relaciones Exteriores y Culto, Arenales No. 761, Buenos Aires, Argentina.

COSTANZO, Henry J., M.A.; American international finance official; b. 20 June 1925, Alabama; s. of Joseph and Mary Costanzo; m. Maxine Kruse 1955; two d.; ed. St. Mary's Univ. and Columbia Univ.; Economist, Econ. Co-operation Admin., Italy 1949–52; Asst. U.S. Treasury Rep., Rome 1952–53, Seoul 1954–55; Financial Adviser and Chief of Programme Planning, Int. Co-operation Admin. 1955; Adviser to IMF 1957–61; Economist, Office of Asst. Sec. of Treasury for Int. Affairs 1961; Dir. office of Latin America, Treasury Dept. 1962–67; Dir. Agency for Int. Devt., Seoul, 1967–69; Exec. Dir. for U.S.A. Inter-American Devt. Bank (IDB) 1969–71, Exec. Vice-Pres. 1972–74, Financial Man. 1976–; Exec. Sec. Jt. Ministerial Devt. Cttee. IBRD/IMF 1974–76. *Address:* Inter-American Development Bank, 1300 New York Avenue, N.W. Washington, D.C. 20577, U.S.A. *Telephone:* (202) 623-2201.

COSTIN, Alec Baillie, A.M., F.A.A., D.SC. AGR.; Australian consultant ecologist, farmer and grazier; b. 30 Sept. 1925, Sydney; two s. four d.; ed. North Sydney Boys' High School and Univ. of Sydney; soil conservationist, N.S.W. Soil Conservation Service 1942–50; Pawlett Scholar and Australian Services Canteens Scholar 1950–53; Prin. Research Officer, Soil Conservation Authority of Victoria 1953–55; Sr. Research Scientist, later Chief Research Scientist, CSIRO 1955–74; Visiting Fellow, Australian Nat. Univ. 1974–84; mem. or fmr. mem. of many Australian and int. socs. and cttees. on hydrology, conservation, environment and nat. parks. *Publications:* A Study of the Ecosystems of the Monaro Region of N.S.W., Studies in Catchment Hydrology in the Australian Alps, Trends in Vegetation at Kosciusko, Kosciusko Alpine Flora, Conservation, Phosphorus in Australia, Harvesting Water from Land. *Leisure interests:* surfing, windsurfing, bushwalking, tennis. *Address:* Widgett Farm, Bodalla, N.S.W., 2545, Australia. *Telephone:* 044-735203.

COT, Jean-Pierre; French academic and politician; b. 23 Oct. 1937, Geneva, Switzerland; s. of Pierre Cot and Luisa Phelps; m.; three c.; Prof., then Dean, Faculty of Law, Amiens 1968; Prof. of Int. Law and Political Sociology, Univ. of Paris I (Panthéon-Sorbonne) 1969, Dir. Disarmament Research and Study Centre (CEREDE); mem. Steering Cttee., Parti Socialiste (PS) 1970, 1973, mem. Exec. Bureau 1976; Mayor of Coise-Saint-Jean-Pied-Gauthier 1971–; Deputy (Savoie) to Nat. Ass. 1973–81; Gen. Councillor, Savoie 1973–81; PS Nat. Del. for matters relating to the European Communities 1976–79; mem. European Parl. 1978–79, 1984–, Pres. Budget Cttee. 1984–; Minister-Del. for Co-operation, attached to Minister for External Relations 1981–82; mem. Exec. Council UNESCO 1983–84. *Publication:* A l'épreuve du pouvoir: le tiers-mondisme, pour quoi faire? 1984, and numerous works on int. law and political science. *Address:* Coise-Saint-Jean-Pied-Gauthier, 73800 Montmélian, France (Home); Centre Européen, Kirchberg, Luxembourg.

CÔTÉ, Michel; Canadian politician; b. Quebec; ed. Laval Univ., École de dessin industriel, Quebec; fmr. Vice-Pres. of Finance, Giffen Recreation Ltée; f. accounting co. Richard, Côté and Cie 1972; fmr. Auditor, Samson, Belair et Associés, later with Besner, Tremblay, Richard et Associés –1982; Dir. of Promotion, Thorne Riddell, Poissant Richard 1982–; Minister of Consumer and Corporate Affairs 1984–86, of State for Regional, Industrial Expansion, Canada Post 1986–87, of Supply and Services 1987–88; mem. Ordre des comptables agrées du Québec 1969–; mem. Quebec City Chamber of Commerce and Industry, Red Cross Soc., Assen. québecoise de planification fiscale et successurale, Amicale des sommeliers du Québec, Conf. du Houblon d'Or; Progressive Conservative Party. *Address:* House of Commons, Parliament Buildings, Ottawa, Ont., K1A 0A6, Canada.

COTEANU, Ion, PH.D.; Romanian linguist; b. 6 Oct. 1920, Bucharest; ed. Univ. of Bucharest, Ecole Pratique des Hautes Etudes; Prof. 1962–, Dean of the Coll. of Romanian Language and Literature 1957–59, 1976–84; Deputy Dir. 1959–69, Dir. of the Inst. of Linguistics, Bucharest 1969–; ed. of Studii şi cercetări de lingvistică (Linguistic Studies and Researches) 1970–; founding mem. of the Romanian Soc. of Philological Sciences 1949 and Vice-Chair. 1968–; mem. of the Soc. of Romance Linguistics, Strasbourg 1968–; Corresp. mem. 1965, full mem. Romanian Acad. *Publications:* Prima listă a numelor românești de plante (The First List of the Romanian Names of Plants) 1942, Româna literară și problemele ei principale (Standard Romanian and its Main Problems) 1961, Morfologia numelui în protoromână (româna comună) (Noun Morphology in Proto-Romanian) 1969, Stilistica funcţională a limbii romăne (The Functional Stylistics of Romanian) 1973, 1985, Stil, stilistică, limbaj (Style, Stylistics, Language) 1973,

Limbajul Poeziei culte (The Language of Cultivated Poetry) 1985, Structura şi evoluţia limbii române (The Structure and Evolution of Romanian) 1981, Originile limbii române (The Origins of the Romanian Language) 1981, Gramatica de bază a limbii române (Basic Grammar of the Romanian Language) 1982; edited and collaborated in Sistemele limbii (Systems of the Language) 1970, Istoria limbii române (History of the Romanian Language) two vols. 1969, Limba română contemporană (Contemporary Romanian) 1974–75, Elemente de lingvistică structurală (Elements of Structural Linguistics) 1967, Semantică şi semiotică (Semantics and Semiotics) 1981, Etimologia si limba română (Romanian Etymology and Language) 1987, Dicţionarul limbii române (The Dictionary of the Romanian Language) 1965–83 (in collaboration), Dicţionar explicativ al limbii române (Explanatory Dictionary of the Romanian Language) 1975; numerous articles on linguistics in learned journals. *Address:* Institutul de lingvistică, Str. Spiru Haret 12, 79515 Bucharest, Romania.

COTRUBAŞ, Ileana; Romanian opera and concert singer; b. Galaţi; d. of Maria and Vasile Cotrubaş; m. Manfred Ramin 1972; ed. Conservatorul Ciprian Porumbescu, Bucharest; Lyric soprano range; début as Yniold in Pelléas et Mélisande at Bucharest Opera 1964; Frankfurt Opera 1968–70; Glyndebourne Festival 1968; Salzburg Festival 1969; Royal Opera House, Covent Garden 1971; Lyric Opera of Chicago 1973; Paris Opera 1974; La Scala, Milan 1975; Metropolitan Opera, New York 1977; operatic roles include Susanna, Pamina, Norina, Gilda, Traviata, Manon, Antonia, Tatyana, Mimi, Mélisande; concerts with all major European orchestras; Lieder recitals at Musikverein Vienna, Royal Opera House, Covent Garden, Carnegie Hall, New York, La Scala; First Prize, Int. Singing Competition, Hertogenbosch, Netherlands 1965, First Prize, Munich Radio Competition 1966; Austrian Kammersängerin 1981. *Recordings:* Bach Cantatas, Mozart Masses, Brahms Requiem, Mahler Symphonies 2, 8; complete operas including Le Nozze di Figaro, Die Zauberflöte, Hänsel und Gretel, Calisto, Louise, L'Elisir d'amore, Les Pêcheurs de perles, La Traviata, Rigoletto, Alzira Manon. *Address:* c/o The Royal Opera House, Covent Garden, London, W.C.2, England.

COTTA, Michèle; L. ES L., DR. ÉS. SC.POL.; French journalist; b. 15 June 1937, Nice; d. of Jacques Cotta and Hélène Scoffier; m. Claude Tchou (divorced); one s. one d.; ed. Lycée de Nice, Faculté de Lettres de Nice and Inst. d'études politiques de Paris; Journalist with L'Express 1963–69, 1971–76; Europ I 1970–71, 1986–; political diarist, France-Inter 1976–80; Head of political service, Le Point 1977–80, Reporter 1986–; Chief Political Ed. R.T.L. 1980–81; Pres. Dir.-Gen. Radio France 1981–82; Pres. Haute Autorité de la Communication Audiovisuelle 1982–86; Producer Faits de Société on TF 1 1987–. *Publications:* La collaboration 1940–1944, 1964, Les elections présidentielles 1966, Prague, l'été des Tanks 1968, Le VIème République 1974, Les miroirs de Jupiter 1986. *Address:* Le Point, 140 rue de Rennes, 75006 Paris; Europe 1, 26 bis rue François 1er, 75008, Paris, France.

COTTAFAVI, Luigi; Italian diplomatist (retd.); b. 7 March 1917, Turin; s. of Francesco Cottafavi and Gina Savio; m. Gabrielle de Rohan 1953; two s. one d.; ed. Liceo Tasso, Rome, Univs. of Rome, Florence and Neuchâtel; officer in Italian army 1939–45; joined diplomatic service 1948; served in Vienna 1950–52, Tel-Aviv 1953–57, London 1957–59, Oslo 1960–63; Deputy Diplomatic Adviser to Italian Prime Minister 1963–69; Chef de Cabinet to Minister of Foreign Affairs 1969–72; Amb. to Iran 1972–78; Under-Sec.-Gen., then Dir.-Gen., UN, Geneva 1978–83. *Leisure interests:* reading, mountaineering, skiing, rowing, tennis. *Address:* Via Salaria 400, Rome, Italy.

COTTEN, Joseph; American actor; b. Petersburg, Va.; s. of Joseph Cotton and Sally Wilson; m. 1st Lenore Kip (deceased), 2nd Patricia Medina 1960; ed. Robert Nugent Hickman Dramatic School, Washington; appeared in popular stage plays 1932–40; radio actor, America Ceiling Unlimited (Lockheed Aircraft weekly radio programme) 1943–44; Pres. Mercury Theatre 1944; film debut in Citizen Kane 1940; other films include The Third Man, September Affair, Half-Angel, Special Delivery, Caravans; stage appearances in New York in Sabrina Fair 1953–54, Once More with Feeling 1958–59, Hush, Hush, Sweet Charlotte 1964; has also appeared in TV shows and as TV host and narrator. *Address:* 6363 Wilshire Boulevard, Los Angeles, Calif. 90048, U.S.A.

COTTERILL, Rodney Michael John, PH.D.; Danish academic; b. 27 Sept. 1933, Bodmin, U.K.; s. of Herbert Cotterill and Aline Le Cerf; m. Vibeke Nielsen 1959; two d.; ed. Cowes and Newport High Schools, Isle of Wight, Univ. Coll. London, Yale Univ. and Emmanuel Coll. Cambridge; R.A.F. 1952–54; Assoc. Scientist, Argonne Nat. Lab. 1962–67; Prof. Tech. Univ. of Denmark 1967–; Guest Prof. Tokyo Univ. 1978, 1985; Fellow, Royal Danish Acad. of Sciences and Letters, Danish Acad. of Tech. Sciences, Danish Soc. of Natural Sciences, Inst. of Physics (U.K.); Kt., Order of the Dannebrog; Ellen and Hans Hermer Memorial Prize 1978. *Publications:* Lattice Defects in Quenched Metals (co-ed.) 1965, The Cambridge Guide to the Material World 1985, Computer Simulation in Brain Science (ed.) 1988; numerous articles on topics in physics, biology and materials science. *Leisure interests:* sailing, choral singing, writing. *Address:* Department of Structural Properties of Materials, Technical University of Denmark, Building 307, 2800 Lyngby (Office); Vibevangen 9, 3520 Farum, Denmark (Home). *Telephone:* 02-882488 (Office); 02-952698 (Home).

COTTESLOE, 4th Baron, cr. 1874, Baron of the Austrian Empire cr. 1816 (Baron Fremantle); **Sir John Walgrave Halford Fremantle**, Bt., G.B.E., T.D., M.A.; British businessman; b. 2 March 1900; s. of 3rd Baron and Florence Cottesloe; m. 1st Lady Elizabeth Harris 1926 (divorced 1945); one s. one d.; m. 2nd Gloria Dunn 1959; one s. two d.; ed. Eton and Trinity Coll., Cambridge; Chair. Thomas Tapling & Co., Heritage in Danger, Tate Gallery 1959-60, Arts Council of G.B. 1960-65, Reviewing Cttee. on Export of Works of Art 1954-72, South Bank Theatre Bd. 1962-77, N.W. Metropolitan Regional Hosp. Bd. 1953-60, Nat. Rifle Asscn. 1960-72, Hammersmith Hosp. 1967-73, British Postgraduate Medical Fed. 1959-73; Gov. King Edward VII's Hosp. Fund; Fellow Royal Postgraduate Medical School; Hon. Fellow Westfield Coll., Univ. of London; Pres. Hosp. Saving Asscn.; fmr. Vice-Chair. Port of London Authority; fmr. Pres. of Leander Club. *Leisure interests:* rowing, shooting (capt. the English Eight 1954-79). *Address:* 33 Edna Street, London, SW11 3DP, England. *Telephone:* 01-585 0208.

COTTING, James Charles, B.A.; American business executive; b. 15 Oct. 1933, Winchester, Mass.; s. of Edward L. Cotting and Mary E. Worrell; m. Marjorie A. Kirsch 1963; two s. one d.; ed. Ohio State Univ.; U.S. Steel Corpn. Pittsburgh 1959-61; Ford Motor Co. Dearborn, Mich. 1961-63; A.O. Smith Corpn., Milwaukee 1963-66; Gen. Foods Corpn. White Plains, New York 1966-71; Int. Paper Co. New York 1971-79; Sr. Vice-Pres. Finance and Planning, Chief Financial Officer, Navistar Int. Corpn. (formerly Int. Harvester Co.), Chicago 1979-82, Exec. Vice-Pres. Finance 1982-83, Vice-Chair., Chief Financial Officer 1983-87, Chair., C.E.O. 1987-; mem. Bd. of Dirs. Cera-Mite Corpn., ASARCO Inc., USG Corpn., Navistar Finance Corpn., Harbour Assurance (U.K.) Ltd., Harbour Assurance Co. of Bermuda. *Address:* Navistar International Corporation, 401 N. Michigan Avenue, Chicago, Ill. 60611, U.S.A.

COTTINGHAM, Robert; American artist; b. 26 Sept. 1935, Brooklyn, New York; s. of James and Aurelia Cottingham; m. Jane Weismann 1967; two d.; ed. Brooklyn Tech. High School, Pratt Inst.; army service 1955-58; Art Dir. with Young and Rubicam Advertising Inc., New York 1959-64, Los Angeles 1964-68; left advertising to paint 1968-; taught at Art Centre Coll. of Design, Los Angeles 1969-70; moved to London 1972-76; returned to U.S.A. 1976-; Nat. Endowment for the Arts 1974-76; numerous one-man exhbns. 1968-; works in many public galleries in U.S.A. and also in Hamburg Museum, Tate Gallery, London and Utrecht Museum. *Publications:* numerous print publs. (lithographs, etchings). *Leisure interests:* travel, music, history. *Address:* P.O. Box 604, Blackman Road, Newtown, Conn. 06470, U.S.A. *Telephone:* 203-426-4072.

COTTON, Fran(cis) Edward; British fmr. rugby player; b. 3 Jan. 1948, Wigan; s. of David and Alice (née Halsall) Cotton; m. Patricia Taylor-Walker 1977; one d.; ed. Newton-le-Willows Grammar School, Wigan Mining Coll., Loughborough Coll. of Education; played for England Under 25's 1970; joined Sr. England team 1971, touring in Far East 1971, S.A. 1972, N.Z. and Fiji 1973, Australia 1975; Toured with British Lions, S.A. 1974, 1980, N.Z. 1977; England Capt. 1975; mem. England Grand Slam winning side, Five Nations Championship 1980; 30 Full England Caps; mem. Coaching Advisory Panel, Rugby Football Union. *Publications:* Autobiog. and numerous articles for Rugby World, Rugby News and coaching publications for the Rugby Football Union. *Leisure interests:* all sports. *Address:* 102 Radnormere Drive, Cheadle Hulme, Cheshire, England. *Telephone:* 061-485 8249.

COTTON, Frank Albert, PH.D.; American chemist; b. 9 April 1930, Philadelphia, Pa.; s. of Albert Cotton and Helen M. Taylor; m. Diane Dornacher 1959; two d.; ed. Drexel Inst. of Tech., Temple and Harvard Univs.; Asst. Prof. Mass. Inst. of Tech. (M.I.T.) 1955-60, Assoc. Prof. 1960-61, Prof. 1961-71; Robert A. Welch Distinguished Prof., Texas A & M Univ. 1972-; mem. Nat. Science Bd. 1986-(92); mem. N.A.S. (Chair. Physical Sciences 1985-88), American Acad. of Arts and Sciences, Göttingen Acad. of Sciences, Royal Danish Acad. of Sciences and Letters, Indian Acad. of Sciences, Indian Nat. Science Acad., Royal Soc. of Edin.; American Chem. Soc. Awards in Inorganic Chem. 1962, 1974, Baekeland Award (N.J. section) 1963, Dwyer Medal (Univ. of N.S.W.) 1966, Centenary Medal (Chemical Soc. London) 1974, Nichols Medal (New York section) 1975, Harrison Howe Award (Rochester section) 1975, Edgar Fahs Smith Award (Philadelphia section) 1976, Pauling Medal (Oregon and Puget Sound Sections) 1976, Kirkwood Medal (Yale Univ.) 1978, Willard Gibbs Medal (Chicago Section, ACS) 1980, Nyholm Medal (Royal Soc. Chem.) 1982, Nat. Medal of Science 1982, Award in Physical and Mathematical Sciences (New York, Acad. Sciences), T. W. Richards Medal (New England Section, American Chem. Soc.); numerous hon. degrees. *Publications:* Advanced Inorganic Chemistry (with G. Wilkinson, F.R.S.) 5th edn. 1988, Chemical Applications of Group Theory 2nd edn. 1971, Chemistry, An Investigative Approach 2nd edn. 1973, Basic Inorganic Chemistry (with G. Wilkinson) 2nd edn. 1987, Multiple Bonds between Metal Atoms (with R. A. Walton) 1982, approx. 1050 research papers. *Leisure interests:* equitation, conservation. *Address:* Department of Chemistry, Tex. A & M University, College Station, Tex. 77843 (Office); Twaycliffe Ranch, Route 2, Box 285, Bryan, Tex. 77803, U.S.A. (Home). *Telephone:* (409) 845-4432 (Office); (409) 589-2501 (Home).

COTTON, Hon. Sir Robert Carrington, K.C.M.G., F.A.S.A.; Australian politician; b. 29 Nov. 1915, Broken Hill, N.S.W.; s. of H. L. Carrington and Muriel Cotton; m. Eve MacDougall 1937; one s. two d.; ed. St. Peter's Coll., Adelaide; fmr. Federal Vice-Pres. Liberal Party of Australia, State Pres. Liberal Party, N.S.W. 1957-60, Acting Pres. 1965; Senator for N.S.W. 1965-78; leader Del. of Fed. Parl. to meetings of Inter-Parl. Union in Majorca and Geneva 1967; Chair. Cottons' Pty. Ltd., Broken Hill; Minister of State for Civil Aviation 1969-72, Minister of Mfg. Industry, Science and Consumer Affairs Nov.-Dec. 1975, of Industry and Commerce 1975-78; fmr. Consul-Gen., New York; Amb. to U.S.A. 1982-85; Dir. Reserve Bank of Australia 1981-82. *Leisure interests:* golf, photography, writing, swimming. *Address:* 75 Pacific Road, Palm Beach, N.S.W. 2108, Australia (Home). *Telephone:* 919-5456.

COTTON, William (Bill) Frederick, O.B.E., J.P.; British television administrator; b. 23 April 1928; s. of William (Billy) Edward Cotton and Mabel Hope; m. 1st Bernadine Maud Sinclair 1950, three d.; m. 2nd Ann Corfield (née Bucknall) 1965, one step-d.; ed. Ardingly Coll.; Jt. Man. Dir. Michael Reine Music Co. 1952-56; BBC-TV producer, Light Entertainment Dept. 1956-62, Asst. Head of Light Entertainment 1962-67, Head of Variety 1967-70, Head of Light Entertainment Group 1970-77; Controller BBC 1 1977-81; Deputy Man. Dir. TV, BBC 1981-82, Dir. of Programmes, TV and Dir. of Devt., BBC 1982; Man. Dir., TV, BBC 1984-87; Chair. BBC Enterprises 1982-87. *Leisure interest:* golf. *Address:* 19 Model Cottages, East Sheen, London, SW14 7PH, England. *Telephone:* 01-878 2430.

COTTRELL, Sir Alan (Howard), Kt., PH.D., SC.D., F.ENG., F.R.S.; British scientist and professor of physical metallurgy; b. 17 July 1919, Birmingham; s. of Albert and Elizabeth Cottrell; m. Jean Elizabeth Harber 1944; one s.; ed. Moseley Grammar School, Univ. of Birmingham, Univ. of Cambridge; lecturer in Metallurgy, Univ. of Birmingham 1943-49, Prof. of Physical Metallurgy 1949-55; Deputy Head, Metallurgy Div., A.E.R.E., Harwell, Berks. 1955-58; Goldsmiths' Prof. of Metallurgy, Cambridge Univ. 1958-65; Deputy Chief Scientific Adviser (Studies), Ministry of Defence 1965-67, Chief Adviser 1967; Deputy Chief Scientific Adviser to H.M. Govt. 1968-71, Chief Scientific Adviser 1971-74; Master, Jesus Coll., Cambridge 1974-86, Vice-Chancellor, Cambridge Univ. 1977-79; Part-time mem. UKAEA 1962-65, 1983-87; Dir. Fisons PLC 1979-; mem. Advisory Council on Scientific Policy 1963-64, Cen. Advisory Council for Science and Technology 1967-, Exec. Cttee. British Council 1974-87, Advisory Council, Science Policy Foundation 1976-, U.K. Perm. Security Comm. 1981-; Hon. mem. American Soc. for Metals 1972, Fellow 1974; Hon. mem. The Metals Soc. 1977, Japan Inst. of Metals 1981; Foreign Assoc. N.A.S., U.S.A. 1972, Nat. Acad. of Eng., U.S.A. 1976; Foreign Hon. mem. American Acad. of Arts and Sciences 1960; Fellow Royal Soc., (Vice-Pres. 1964, 1976, 1977), Royal Swedish Acad. of Sciences 1970; Hon. Fellow Christ's Coll., Cambridge 1970 (Fellow 1958-70), Hon. Fellow Jesus Coll., Cambridge 1986; Hon. D.Sc. (Columbia) 1965, (Newcastle) 1967, (Liverpool) 1969, (Manchester) 1970, (Warwick) 1971, (Sussex) 1972, (Bath) 1973, (Strathclyde and Aston in Birmingham) 1975, (Cranfield Inst. of Tech.) 1975, (Oxford) 1979, (Essex) 1982, (Birmingham) 1983; Hon. D.Eng. (Tech. Univ. of Nova Scotia) 1984; Sc.D. (Cambridge) 1976; Rosenhain Medal, Inst. of Metals, Hughes Medal, Royal Soc. 1961, Réaumur Medal, Soc. Française de Métallurgie 1964; Inst. of Metals (Platinum) Medal 1965, James Alfred Ewing Medal, ICE 1967, Holweck Medal, Soc. Française de Physique 1969, Albert Sauveur Achievement Award, American Soc. for Metals 1969, James Douglas Gold Medal, American Inst. of Mining, Metallurgy and Petroleum Engineers 1974, Rumford Medal, Royal Soc. 1974, Harvey Prize (Technion, Israel) 1974, Acta Metallurgica Gold Medal 1976, Guthrie Medal and Prize, Inst. of Physics 1977, Gold Medal, American Soc. for Metals 1980, Brinell Medal, Royal Swedish Acad. of Eng. Sciences 1980, Kelvin Medal, ICE 1986. *Publications:* Theoretical Structural Metallurgy 1948, Dislocations and Plastic Flow in Crystals 1953, The Mechanical Properties of Matter 1964, Theory of Crystal Dislocations 1964, An Introduction to Metallurgy 1967, Portrait of Nature 1975, Environmental Economics 1978, How Safe is Nuclear Energy? 1981, Introduction to the Modern Theory of Metals 1988, and scientific papers in various learned journals. *Leisure interest:* music. *Address:* 40 Maids Causeway, Cambridge, CB5 8DD, England. *Telephone:* Cambridge 63806.

COTTRELL, Donald Peery, PH.D.; American university teacher and administrator; b. 17 Feb. 1902, Columbus, Ohio; s. of Dr. Harvey V. Cottrell and Della Stone Miller; m. Eleanor H. Westberg 1928; one s. (died 1984) one d.; ed. The Ohio State Univ. and Columbia Univ.; Public School Teaching and Admin. in Ohio 1923-26; Tutor, Hunter Coll. of the City of New York 1927-29; Asst. and Assoc. in Coll. Admin., Teachers' Coll., Columbia Univ. 1927-29; Asst. Prof. 1929-31, Assoc. Prof. 1931-41, Prof. 1941-46 (Educ.); Asst. Dir., Div. of Instruction 1941-44, Exec. Dir. Horace Mann-Lincoln School 1943-46, Exec. Officer, Div. of Instruction 1946 (all at Teachers' Coll., Columbia Univ.); Dean, Coll. of Educ., The Ohio State Univ. 1946-67, Prof. of Educ. 1967-72, Prof. Emer. 1972-; Expert Consultant, U.S. War Dept. to advise Mil. Govt. (U.S.) in the field of University Educ. in Germany 1947; Chair. of Comm. to survey the educational insts. of the Foreign Missions Conf. of N. America in the Philippines 1948; Chief UN Educational Planning Mission to Korea 1952-53; Pres. The American Asscn. of Colleges for Teacher Educ. 1957; Chair. The Nat. Comm. on Teacher Educ. and Professional Standards of the Nat.

Educ. Assen. 1962; Exec. Consultant in Secondary and Teacher Educ. to Ministry of Educ., Govt. of India, and U.S. A.I.D. Mission, India, 1958, 1961, 1964; Chair. Comm. on Educ. for the Teaching Profession 1966; Emer. mem. Bd. of Trustees, Talladega Coll., Alabama; L.H.D. h.c. (Talladega Coll.) 1977; Distinguished Service Award (Ohio State Univ.) 1982. *Leisure interest:* painting (oils and acrylics). *Address:* 6671 Olentangy River Road, Worthington, Ohio 43085, U.S.A. (Home).

COULOMB, Jean; French physicist; b. 7 Nov. 1904, Blida, Algeria; s. of Charles Coulomb and Blanche d'Izalguier; m. Alice Gaydier 1928; two s. two d.; ed. Ecole Normale Supérieure; Dir. Institut de Physique du Globe Algiers 1937–41; Dir. Institut de Physique du Globe Paris 1941–56; Prof. at the Sorbonne 1941–72; Visiting Prof. Istanbul Univ. 1954–55; Pres. Int. Assen. of Terrestrial Magnetism and Electricity 1951–54; Dir.-Gen. Centre Nat. de la Recherche Scientifique 1956–62; mem. of Cttee. for Int. Geophysical Year 1957–59; Pres. of Centre Nat. d'Etudes Spatiales 1962–67; Pres. Int. Union of Geodesy and Geophysics 1967–71; Pres. Bureau des Longitudes 1966–69; Vice-Pres. Int. Council of Scientific Unions 1968–72, Pres. 1972–74; mem. French Acad. of Sciences 1960– (Pres. 1977–78), Royal Danish Acad. 1969, Acad. Royale de Belgique 1971; Grand Officier, Légion d'honneur, Grand-Croix de l'ordre nat. du Mérite, Officier du Mérite Saharien. *Publications:* La physique des nuages (in collaboration) 1940, La constitution physique de la terre 1952, Physical Constitution of the Earth (in collaboration) 1963, Expansion des fonds océaniques 1969, Sea Floor Spreading and Continental Drift 1972, Traité de géophysique interne, Vol. I 1973, Vol. II 1975 (in collaboration). *Address:* 4 rue Emile Dubois, 75014 Paris, France. *Telephone:* (1) 45.88.43.01.

COULSON, Sir John Eltringham, K.C.M.G.; British diplomatist; b. 13 Sept. 1909, Gosforth, Northumberland; s. of Henry Coulson and Florence Eltringham; m. Mavis Beazley 1944; two s.; ed. Cambridge Univ.; entered Foreign Service 1932; served Romania 1934–37, Foreign Office, Ministry of Econ. Warfare and War Cabinet 1937–46; Counsellor, Paris 1946–48; Deputy U.K. Rep. OEEC, Paris 1948–50; Deputy Perm. Rep. to UN 1950–52; Asst. Under-Sec. of State, Foreign Office 1952–55; Minister in Washington 1955–57; Adviser to the Paymaster-Gen. 1957–59; Amb. to Sweden 1960–63; Deputy Under-Sec. of State, Foreign Office 1963–64; Chief of Admin., Diplomatic Service 1965; Sec.-Gen. European Free Trade Assen. (EFTA) 1965–72. *Address:* The Old Mill, Selborne, Hants., England.

COURANT, Ernest D., PH.D.; American (naturalized) physicist; b. 26 March 1920, Göttingen, Germany; s. of Richard Courant and Nina Runge; m. Sara Paul 1944; two s.; ed. Swarthmore Coll. and Univ. of Rochester, U.S.A.; Scientist Nat. Research Council (Canada), Montreal 1943–46; Research Assoc. in Physics, Cornell Univ. 1946–48; Physicist Brookhaven Nat. Lab., Upton, N.Y. 1948–60, Sr. Physicist 1960–; Prof. (part-time) Yale Univ. 1961–67, State Univ. of N.Y., Stony Brook 1967–85; co-discoverer of Strong-focusing principle, particle accelerators; mem. N.A.S. 1976; Fellow A.A.A.S. 1981; Hon. D.Sc. (Swarthmore Coll.) 1988; Pregel Prize, New York Acad. of Sciences 1979, Fermi Prize 1986, R. R. Wilson Prize 1987. *Publications:* various articles; contrib. to Handbuch der Physik 1959, Annual Review of Nuclear Science 1968. *Address:* Brookhaven National Laboratory, Upton, N.Y. 11973 (Office); 109 Bay Avenue, Bayport, N.Y. 11705, U.S.A. (Home). *Telephone:* (516) 282-4609 (Office); (516) 472-0510 (Home).

COURCEL, Geoffroy Chodron de, D. EN DR., L. ÈS L., DIP. ECOLE DES SC. POL.; French diplomatist; b. 11 Sept. 1912, Tours; s. of Louis de Courcel and Alice Lambert-Champy; m. Martine Hallade 1954; two s.; ed. Coll. Stanislas and Paris Univ.; Attaché Warsaw 1937; Sec. Athens 1938–39; joined Free French forces June 1940; Chef de Cabinet, Gen. de Gaulle 1940–41; mil. service in Egypt, Libya and Tunisia 1941–43; Deputy Dir. of Cabinet, Gen. de Gaulle 1943–44; Regional Commr. for Liberated Territories 1944; Deputy Dir. Cen. and Northern European Sections, Ministry of Foreign Affairs 1945–47; First Counsellor Rome 1947–50; Dir. Bilateral Trade Agreements Section, Ministry of Foreign Affairs 1950–53; Dir. African and Middle East Section, Ministry of Foreign Affairs 1953–54; Dir.-Gen. Political and Econ. Affairs, Ministry of Moroccan and Tunisian Affairs 1954–55; Perm. Rep. to Nat. Defence 1955–58; Perm. Rep. to NATO 1958–59; Sec. Gen. Présidence de la République 1959–62; Amb. to U.K. 1962–72; Ambassadeur de France 1965; Sec.-Gen. French Ministry of Foreign Affairs 1973–76 (retd.); Chair. France-Grande Bretagne 1978–87; Chair. French section Franco-British Council 1978–81; Pres. Institut Charles de Gaulle 1984; Grand Croix, Légion d'honneur, Compagnon de la Libération, Croix de guerre, Mil. Cross, Hon. G.C.V.O., etc.; Hon. D.C.L. (Oxford); Hon. LL.D. (Birmingham). *Publication:* L'influence de la Conférence de Berlin de 1885 sur le droit colonial international 1936. *Leisure interests:* shooting, swimming. *Address:* 7 rue de Medicis, 75006 Paris, France.

COURCHENE, Thomas Joseph, PH.D., F.R.S.C.; Canadian professor of economics; b. 16 Sept. 1940, Wakaw, Sask.; m. Margareta Strohhofer 1962; two s. one d.; ed. Univ. of Sask., Princeton Univ. and Univ. of Chicago; Prof. of Econs. Univ. of Western Ontario 1965–; Sr. Fellow, Howe Research Inst. 1981–; Chair. Ont. Econ. Council 1982–85; Robarts Prof. of Canadian Studies (North York) 1987–88; Visiting Prof. Univ. of Toronto 1970–71, Grad. Inst. of Int. Studies Geneva 1975–76, Queen's Univ. (Canada) 1982–83. *Publications include:* Money, Inflation and the Bank of Canada (Vol.

I) 1976, (Vol. II) 1981, Equalization Payments: Present and Future 1984, Economic Management and the Division of Powers 1986, Social Policy in the 1990s 1987, Les offrandes des rois-mages 1987. *Address:* Department of Economics, University of Western Ontario, London, Ont., N6A 3K7, Canada.

COURRÈGES, André; French couturier; b. 9 March 1923, Pau (Pyrénées); s. of Lucien Courrèges and Céline Coupe; m. Jacqueline Barrière 1966; one d.; ed. Ecole Supérieure Technique; studied eng.; moved to Paris and spent year as fashion designer 1945; went to Balenciaga's workrooms 1948 and served 11 years apprenticeship; f. Société André Courrèges 1961, Dir., then Chair. and Man. Dir. 1966–; Dir. and Admin, Sport et Couture Amy Linker 1969–; Dir. Société Courrèges design 1981–; launched his "Couture-Future" 1967; "Couture-Future" distributed by stores all over the world and by 45 exclusive boutiques in 10 countries including U.S.A., Canada, Japan, Australia. *Leisure interests:* pelote basque, physical fitness. *Address:* 40 rue François 1er, 75008 Paris (Office); 27 rue Delabordère, 92200 Neuilly-sur-Seine, France (Home).

COURT, Hon. Sir Charles Walter Michael, K.C.M.G., O.B.E. (MIL.), F.C.A., F.C.I.S.; Australian politician (retd.); b. 29 Sept. 1911, Crawley, Sussex, England; s. of late W. J. Court and Rose R. Court; m. Rita Steffanoni 1936; five s.; ed. Perth; Founder Partner, Hendry, Rae & Court, chartered accountants 1938; served Australian Imperial Forces 1940–46, rising to rank of Lieut.-Col.; mem. Legis. Ass. for Nedlands 1953–82; Deputy Leader of Opposition W. Australia 1957–59; Minister for Railways 1959–67, for Industrial Devt. and the N.W. 1959–71, for Transport 1965–66; Deputy Leader of Opposition 1971–72, Leader 1972–73; Premier, State Treas., Minister Co-ordinating Econ. and Regional Devt., W. Australia 1974–82; State Registrar (W. Australia) Inst. of Chartered Accountants in Australia 1946–52; Senator Jr. Chamber Int. 1971; Hon. Col. W. Australia Univ. Regt. 1969–74; Fellow of the Australian Soc. of Accountants; Life mem. Inst. of Chartered Accountants 1982; Hon. F.A.I.M. 1980; Hon. LL.D. (W. Australia) 1969, Hon. D.Tech. (W.A. Inst. of Tech.); Knight of the Order of Australia; Australian Mfrs. Export Council Award 1970, Inst. of Production Engs. Award 1971; Hon. Col. S.A.S. Regt. 1976–80; First Class Order of the Sacred Treasure, Japan; Liberal. *Publications:* many papers on industrial, economic and resource development matters. *Leisure interests:* music, occasional appearance as guest conductor. *Address:* 46 Waratah Avenue, Dalkeith, W. Australia 6009, Australia (Home). *Telephone:* 386-1257 (Home).

COURT, Margaret, M.B.E.; Australian fmr. lawn tennis player; b. (as Margaret Smith) 16 July 1942, Albury, N.S.W.; m. Barry Court 1967; one s. two d.; ed. Albury High School; amateur player 1960–67; professional 1968–77; Australian Champion 1960, 1961, 1962, 1963, 1964, 1965, 1966, 1969, 1970, 1971, 1973; French Champion 1962, 1964, 1969, 1970, 1973; Wimbledon Champion 1963, 1965, 1970; U.S.A. Champion 1962, 1965, 1969, 1970, 1973; holds more major titles in singles, doubles and mixed doubles than any other player in history; won two Grand Slams, in mixed doubles 1963, and singles, 1970; played Federation Cup for Australia 1963, 1964, 1965, 1966, 1968, 1969, 1971. *Publications:* The Margaret Smith Story 1964, Court on Court 1974. *Address:* 46 Waratah Avenue, Nedlands, W.A. 6009, Australia.

COURTENAY, Tom; British actor; b. 25 Feb. 1937; s. of Henry Courtenay and late Anne Eliza Quest; m. Cheryl Kennedy 1973 (dissolved 1982); ed. Kingston High School, Hull, Univ. Coll., London, Royal Acad. of Dramatic Art; started acting professionally 1960; stage performances in Billy Liar 1961–62, The Cherry Orchard 1966, Macbeth 1966, Hamlet 1968, She Stoops to Conquer 1969, Charley's Aunt 1971, Time and Time Again (Variety Club of G.B. Stage Actor Award) 1972, Table Manners 1974, The Norman Conquests 1974–75, The Fool 1975, The Rivals 1976, Clouds 1978, Crime and Punishment 1978, The Dresser (Drama Critics Award and New Standard Award for Best Actor) 1980, 1983, The Misanthrope 1981, Andy Capp 1982, Jumpers 1984, Rookery Nook 1986, The Hypochondriac 1987. *Films include:* The Loneliness of the Long Distance Runner 1962, Private Potter 1962, Billy Liar 1963, King and Country 1964, Operation Crossbow 1965, King Rat 1965, Doctor Zhivago 1965, The Night of the Generals 1966, The Day the Fish Came Out 1967, A Dandy in Aspic 1968, Otley 1969, One Day in the Life of Ivan Denisovitch 1972, Catch Me a Spy, The Dresser.

COURTHION, Pierre-Barthélemy; French art historian; b. 14 Jan. 1902, Geneva, Switzerland; s. of Louis Courthion and Elisa Bocquet; m. Pierrette Karcher 1927; one d.; ed. Univ. de Genève, Ecole des Beaux-Arts, Paris and Ecole du Louvre; fmr. Asst. Dir. Arts section at Int. Inst. of Intellectual Co-operation of Soc. des Nations and Dir. Archaeological Museum, Valère; fmr. Dir. fondation Suisse dans la Cité universitaire de Paris; fmr. Vice-Pres. Union of French Artistic Press; Vice-Pres. Int. Assen. of Art Critics; mem. Jury of Int. Guggenheim Prize 1960–; Cultural Mission to Brazil and Venezuela 1963, to American Univs. 1965, 1967, 1974, to Canadian Univs. 1969, to Japan and Republic of Korea 1973; Silver Medal Reconnaissance française, Prix Fondation Delmas 1979. *Publications:* Gabriele d'Annunzio 1925, Panorama de la peinture contemporaine 1927, Vie d'Eugène Delacroix 1927, Nicolas Poussin 1929, Claude Lorrain 1932, Courbet (2 vols.), Henri Matisse 1934, Genève ou le portrait des Töpffer 1936, Delacroix 1940, Henri Rousseau de Douanier 1944, Le Visage de Matisse 1945, Bonnard, Peintre du merveilleux 1945, Géricault 1947, Utrillo 1948, Peintres d'aujourd'hui, Raoul Dufy 1951, La Montagne, L'Art indépendant, Montmartre 1955, Paris d'autrefois 1957, Paris des temps nouveaux 1957, Le Romantisme 1961, Manet 1962, Georges Rouault 1962, Autour de l'impressionnisme 1965, Paris de sa naissance à nos jours 1966, Utrillo et Montmartre 1967, L'Ecole de Paris de Picasso à nos jours 1968, Seurat 1968, Soutine, peintre du déchirant 1972, Impressionism 1972, Pablo Gargallo 1973, Llorens Artigas et la céramique 1977, Les Impressionistes 1982, Tout l'Oeuvre peint de Courbet 1983, La peinture flamande et hollandaise 1983, Naissance et évolution de la peinture européene 1984; Dir. of art films: Ingres peintre du nu 1968, Georges Rouault 1971. *Leisure interests:* mountaineering, mushroom picking and music. *Address:* 11 rue des Marronniers, Paris 75016, France. *Telephone:* 647-58-03.

COUSINS, Norman, LITT.D., L.D.H., LL.D., D.E.; American editor and author; b. 24 June 1915, Union Hill; s. of Samuel and Sara (née Miller) Cousins; m. Ellen Kopf 1939; four d.; ed. Columbia Univ.; educ. writer with New York Evening Post 1935-36; Man. Ed. Current History 1936-40; Exec. Ed. Saturday Review 1940-42, Ed. 1942-71, 1973-77, Chair. Bd. of Eds. 1978-80, Ed. Emer. 1980-; Ed. World Magazine 1972-73; mem. Bd. Dirs. McCall Corpn. and Chair. Editorial Cttee. 1961-70; Ed. U.S.A. during Second World War; Adjunct Prof. Univ. of California, Los Angeles 1978-; Chair. Conn. Fact-Finding Comm. on Educ. 1951-54; Pres. United World Federalists 1954-56, Hon. Pres. 1956-; U.S. Presidential Rep. at Inauguration of Pres. of Philippines 1966; Hon. Pres. World Assen. of World Federalists 1965-; mem. Bd. of Dirs. UN Assen. of U.S.A., Nat. Educational Television, The Charles F. Kettering Foundation, Samuel H. Kress Foundation; officer of many orgs.; Encyclopædia Britannica Achievement in Life Award 1980; numerous Hon. degrees. *Publications:* The Good Inheritance, A Treasury of Democracy 1941, The Poetry of Freedom (with William Rose Benét) 1943, Modern Man is Obsolete 1945, Talks with Nehru 1951, Who Speaks for Man 1953, In God We Trust 1958, Ed. March's Dictionary Thesaurus 1958, Dr. Schweitzer of Lambaréné 1960, In Place of Folly 1961, Present Tense 1966, The Improbable Triumvirate 1972, The Celebration of Life 1974, Anatomy of an Illness 1979, Human Options 1981, The Physician in Literature 1981, The Healing Heart 1983, (Ed.) Words of Albert Schweitzer 1984, Albert Schweitzer's Mission 1985. *Address:* c/o Saturday Review, 214 Massachusetts Avenue, N.E. Suite 460, Washington, D.C. 20002; 2644 Eden Place, Beverly Hills, Calif. 90210, U.S.A. (Home).

COUSTEAU, Jacques-Yves; French marine explorer, writer, and film producer; b. 11 June 1910, St. André de Cubzac; s. of Daniel P. and Elizabeth (Duranthon) Cousteau; m. Simone Melchior 1937; two s. (one deceased); ed. Stanislas Acad., Paris, Brest Naval Acad.; Lieut. French Navy, World War II; partly responsible for invention of the Aqualung 1943; founder, Groupe d'études et de recherches sous-marines, Toulon 1946; Founder and Pres. Campagnes Océanographiques Françaises, Marseilles 1950; Founder and Pres. Office Français de Recherches Sousmarines, later became Centre d'Etudes Marines Avancées, Marseilles 1952; Leader Calypso Oceanographic Expeditions; Dir. Oceanographic Museum, Monaco 1957-; promoted Conshelf dive programme 1962; Gen. Sec. ICSEM 1966; went on scientific world cruise from Red Sea through Indian Ocean to Pacific, as far as North Alaska, filming TV series The Undersea World of Jacques-Yves Cousteau 1967; led expedition in Antarctic and along Chile coast, filming further TV series 1972; archaeological expedition in Greek waters 1975; mem. Soc. des Gens de Lettres de France 1976, Acad. Française 1988-; Foreign Assoc. mem. U.S. N.A.S. 1968; Corresp. mem. Hellenic Inst. of Marine Archaeology 1975; Fellow, Soc. of Film and TV Arts 1974; Hon. D.Sc. (Berkeley and Brandeis) 1970, (Rensselaer Polytechnic Inst.) 1979, (Ghent) 1983; Commdr., Légion d'honneur; Croix de guerre avec palmes; Mérite agricole, Mérite maritime; Officer Arts et Lettres; Potts Medal, Franklin Inst. 1970; Gold Medal, Grand Prix d'océanographie Albert Ier 1971; Gold Medal, Nat. Geographic Soc. 1971; Grande Médaille d'Or, Soc. d'encouragement au progrès 1973; Award of New England Aquarium 1973; Prix de la Couronne d'or 1973; Gold Medal "Sciences" (Arts, Sciences, Lettres) 1974; Pollena della Bravura 1974; Prix Manley Bendall, Acad. de Marine 1976; Special Prize of Cervia (Italy) for conservation of marine environment 1976; Int. Pahlavi Environment Prize 1977; Jean Sainteny Prize 1980, Kiwanis Int. Europe Prize 1980, Lindbergh Award 1982, Neptune Award 1982, Bruno H. Schubert Foundation Prize 1983, Medal of Freedom 1985; numerous awards, including ten Emmy Awards for documentary films at Festivals in Paris, Cannes, Venice. *Documentary films include:* The Silent World (Motion Picture Acad. Arts and Sciences Award (Oscar) for best documentary feature, and Grand Prix, Palme d'or, Cannes) 1956, The World without Sun (Oscar for best documentary feature) 1956, The Golden Fish (Oscar for the best short film) 1960, TV series: The World of Jacques-Yves Cousteau 1966-68, The Undersea World of Jacques-Yves Cousteau 1968-76, The Desert Whales, The Tragedy of the Red Salmon, Lagoon of Lost Ships, The Dragons of Galapagos, Secrets of the Southern Caves, The Unsinkable Sea Otter, A Sound of Dolphins, South to Fire and Ice, The Flight of Penguins, Beneath the Frozen World, Blizzard at Hope Bay, Life at the End of the World; Oasis in Space Series 1977; The Cousteau Odyssey Series 1977-81; The Cousteau/Amazon Series 1984-; Cousteau/Mississippi 1985, Cousteau/Rediscovery of the World 1986-. *Publications:* Par 18 mètres de fond 1946, La plongée en scaphandre 1950, The Silent World (Ed. with James Duggan)

1952, Captain Cousteau's Underwater Treasury (with James Duggan) 1962, The Living Sea 1962, World Without Sun (with P. Cousteau) 1965, The Shark: Splendid Savage of the Sea (with Ph. Diolé) 1971, Life and Death in a Coral Sea 1971, Diving for a Sunken Treasure 1971, The Whale: Mighty Monarch of the Sea 1972, Octopus and Squid 1973, Galapagos, Titicaca, the Blue Holes: Three Adventures 1973, Diving Companions 1974, Dolphins 1975, The Ocean World of Jacques Cousteau (Encyclopedia, 20 vols.), The Cousteau Almanac 1981, Jacques Cousteau's Calypso 1983, Jacques Cousteau's Amazon Journey (with Mose Richards) 1984; numerous articles for National Geographic Magazine 1952-66. *Address:* Musée Océanographique, Avenue Saint-Martin, Monaco-Ville, Monaco.

COUTINHO, Vice-Admiral António Alba Rosa; Portuguese naval officer (retd.); b. 14 Feb. 1926, Lisbon; s. of António Rodrigues Coutinho and Ilda dos Prazeres Alva Rosa Coutinho; m. Maria Candida Maldonado 1950; three s. one d.; ed. Portuguese Naval Acad., Libson Univ., Scripps Inst. of Oceanography, U.S.A.; commissioned in Portuguese Navy 1947; served on board naval vessels and attended naval courses 1948-54; Hydrographic Engineer, Chief of Hydrographic Mission, Angola 1959-61; in prison in Zaire 1961; several commissions and naval courses 1962-64; Dir. of Dredging Services, Mozambique 1964-72; Commdg. Officer of Frigate Admiral P. Silva 1973-74; mem. Portuguese Armed Forces Movt. 1974, mem. Mil. Junta 1974-75, mem. Supreme Revolutionary Council March-Nov. 1975; Pres. Angola Gov. Junta 1974, High Commr. in Angola 1974-75; accused of violating human rights Jan. 1977, acquitted by supreme discipline council July 1977, forced to retire by navy chief of staff Aug. 1977, reintegrated on active duty by decision of supreme mil. court Feb. 1978, retd. (on his own request) Dec. 1982; Distinguished Services Medal, Mil. Merit; Knight Aviz Order; Commdr. Order of Henry the Navigator; Vasco da Gama Naval Medal; Kt. of Spanish Naval Merit. *Leisure interests:* big game hunting, angling, sailing. *Address:* Rua Carlos Malheiro Dias 18, 3° esq., 1700 Lisbon, Portugal. *Telephone:* 883638.

COUTSOHERAS, John; Greek poet, lawyer and politician; b. 31 Dec. 1904, Ziria, Patras; s. of Panayotis and Katina Coutsoheras; m. Lena Strefi 1948; ed. Univs. of Athens and Paris; called to the Bar 1927; mem. Social Democratic Party 1932; Founder, Gen. Sec. Movt. for Democracy in Greece 1935; Pres. Soc. for the Study of Greek Problems 1956-; mem. Centre Union Party 1961; M.P. for Athens 1964-67, 1974-; under house arrest during dictatorship 1968-70; co-founder mem. Socialist Party 1974; mem. Council of Europe 1975-, Vice-Pres. Socialist group of Council of Europe 1979-81; mem. European Parl. 1981-82; Amb. to UNESCO 1985-; Pres. Greek PEN 1959-; Vice-Pres. Maison Int. de la poésie, Brussels 1987-; Founder Universal Centre of the World Citizen—Cosmopolitis, Brussels 1970; mem. many literary socs.; Medaglia d'oro di Poesia (Italy) 1969, Grand Prix de la Poésie libre, Syndicat des Journalistes et Ecrivains (France) 1970, Grand Prix de la Poésie, Cercle Int. de la Pensée et des Arts Français 1970, Grand Prix Int. du Disque d'Or, CIPAF 1971, Paris-Critique 1975, Coupe Int. Acad. of Lutece 1977, Grand Prix d'Europe, Paris 1985, and many others. *Publications:* poetry: Thoughts and Echoes 1942, Blue Breaths 1949, Greek Nights 1954, The Supper of Bethany 1959, The March of the Lilies 1959, Jordan, the Ever Running 1960, Smoke Spiralling Up 1960, Golgotha 1961, Markos Evgenikos 1964, The Man and the Sea 1965, Aphaia 1965, The Charioteer 1966, Men for Human Rights, Arise! 1969, The Golden Fleece 1970, With the Gull's Wing and Poseidon's Trident 1971, Au delà 1974, Silence and Scream of the Sea 1977, Eladica 1980 (poetry translated into many languages), Kalavitra '43, 1984, Saronicos 1984, Hiroshima Zero Hour 1984, The Symphony of the World Citizen 1984; essays: Poetry and Language 1954, Mon credo à l'homme libre 1970, and publications on law, economics and politics. *Leisure interests:* reading, music, swimming, people's company. *Address:* 60a Skoufa Street, Athens 106 80, Greece; 1 rue Miollis, 75015 Paris, France. *Telephone:* 361-35-16 (Athens); 47-34-49-75 or 45-67-35-96 (Paris).

COUTTS, Ronald Thomson, PH.D., F.R.S.C.; Canadian professor of medicinal chemistry; b. 19 June 1931, Glasgow, Scotland; s. of Ronald Miller Coutts and Helen Alexanderina Crombie; m. Sheenah Kirk Black 1957; two s. one d.; ed. Woodside Secondary School, Glasgow, Univ. of Strathclyde, Glasgow Univ. and Chelsea Coll., London; lecturer in Medicinal Chem. Sunderland Tech. Coll., England 1959-63; Asst. then Assoc. Prof. Univ. of Saskatchewan, Canada 1963-66; Prof. Univ. of Alberta 1966-, Distinguished Univ. Prof. 1984-, Pres. Faculty Assen. 1978-79, mem. Bd. of Govs. 1982-85, Hon. Prof. of Psychiatry 1979-; Pres. Xenotox Services Ltd. 1978-; Scientific Ed. Canadian Journal of Pharmaceutical Sciences 1967-72; mem. Ed. Bd. Asian Journal of Pharmaceutical Sciences 1978-85; Ed. Journal of Pharmacological Methods 1984-; Fellow, Pharmaceutical Soc. of G.B.; McNeil Research Award 1982; McCalla Prof. Univ. of Alberta 1985-86. *Publications:* 230 research manuscripts and reviews; several textbooks and chapters in textbooks. *Leisure interests:* golf, cross-country skiing, squash and music (playing and listening). *Address:* University of Alberta, Faculty of Pharmacy and Pharmaceutical Sciences, Edmonton, Alberta (Office); 4724-139 Street, Edmonton, Alberta, Canada (Home). *Telephone:* (403) 432-3362 (Office); (403) 436-4313 (Home).

COUTURE, Jean Désiré; French mining and energy executive; b. 23 June 1913, Paris; s. of Julien Couture and Mathilde Bouneau; brother of Pierre Julien Couture (q.v.); ed. Lycées Montaigne, Saint-Louis and Louis-le-

Grand, Ecole Polytechnique and Ecole Nationale Supérieure des Mines de Paris; Engineer 1937–45, Chief Engineer 1945–64 and Engineer-Gen. of Mines 1964–74; Dir. Cabinet of the Minister for Industrial Production 1946; Dir. of Industrial Production and Mines of Morocco 1947–48; Deputy Dir.-Gen. Charbonnages de France 1948–49, 1953–63; Deputy Dir.-Gen. Houillères de Bassin du Nord et du Pas-de-Calais 1949–53; Pres. Admin. Council 1957–63, Hon. Pres. 1963; Vice-Pres. Comité consultatif de l'utilisation de l'énergie 1948–63; Pres. Inst. français de l'énergie 1956–; Sec.-Gen. for Energy, Ministère de l'Industrie 1963–73; Admin., Société Nationale des Chemins de fer Français 1964–74; Pres. Comm. consultative pour la production d'électricité d'origine nucleaire 1967–73; Pres. Comm. de l'énergie au Commissariat général du Plan 1978–79; Pres. French Nat. Cttee. of World Energy Conf. 1975–80, Vice-Pres. 1980–; Sr. Adviser to Chair. of Société Générale 1974–84; Vice-Pres. Soc. Française d'Energie Nucléaire 1983–; Pres. Trans Energ 1984–; Commdr. Légion d'honneur; Croix de guerre 1939–45. *Address:* 3 rue Henri Heine, 75016 Paris (Office); 13 rue Monsieur, 75007 Paris, France (Home). *Telephone:* (1) 45-24-46-14 (Office).

COUTURE, Pierre Julien; French mining executive; b. 25 Feb. 1909, Paris; s. of Julien Couture and Mathilde Bouneau; brother of Jean Desiré Couture (q.v.); m. Yvonne Galot 1957; two s. (one died 1982) three d. (one died 1982); ed. Lycée St. Louis, Ecole Polytechnique and Ecole Nationale Supérieure des Mines de Paris; Engineer, Chief Engineer and Engineer-Gen. of Mines 1933–72; Asst. Dir.-Gen., Houillères de Lorraine 1946–50; Dir.-Gen. Mines de la Sarre 1950–57; Govt. Admin.-Gen., Commissariat of Atomic Energy 1958–63; Adviser, Charbonnages de France 1959–63; mem. Bd. of Dirs., Electricité de France 1959–63; mem. Council, Ecole Nat. des Mines de Paris 1959–69; Pres. Council Ecole Nat. des Mines de St-Etienne 1960–73; mem. Devt. Cttee., Ecole Polytechnique 1958–63; Pres. Bd. of Dirs., Les Mines Domaniales de Potasse d'Alsace 1964–67; Pres. Supervisory Bd. Soc. Commerciale des Potasses d'Alsace 1964–68; Pres. Soc. Potasses et Engrais Chimiques 1964–67; Pres. S.A. Pec-Rhin 1967–73, S.A. Tessenderloo-Chemie (Belgium) 1967–76; Pres. Bd. of Dirs. Entreprise minière et chimique 1967–72, Mines de Potasses d'Alsace S.A. 1968–72, SOFDI 1972–76, ENERCO 1974–78, GENERCO 1974–80; Pres. Soc. Industrie Minérale 1978–; Commdr., Légion d'honneur, Officier du Mérite Saharien, Officier des Palmes académiques, Commdr. Ordre Couronne (Belgium). *Leisure interests:* Rotary Club of Paris, shooting, skiing. *Address:* 22 rue Beaujon, 75008 Paris, France. *Telephone:* 763-37-95.

COUVE DE MURVILLE, (Jacques) Maurice; French politician; b. 24 Jan. 1907, Rheims; m. Jacqueline Schweisguth 1932; three d.; ed. Paris Univ.; Gen. Sec. to Gen. Giraud, Algiers March–June 1943; mem. French Cttee. for Nat. Liberation June-Nov. 1943; Italian Advisory Council 1944; Amb. to Italy 1945; Dir.-Gen. Political Affairs, Foreign Office 1945–50; Amb. to Egypt 1950–54, to U.S.A. 1955–56, to Fed. Repub. of Germany 1956–58; Minister of Foreign Affairs 1958–68, of Finance May-July 1968; Prime Minister July 1968–June 1969; Pres. N. Atlantic Council 1967–68; Inspector-Gen. of Finance 1969–; elected to Nat. Ass. 1968, 1973, 1978, 1981; Pres. Foreign Affairs Cttee. of Nat. Ass. 1973–81; Senator 1986–; mediator in Lebanon civil war 1975; Commdr. Légion d'honneur. *Publication:* Une politique étrangère 1958–69 1973. *Address:* 44 rue du Bac, 75007 Paris, France. *Telephone:* 42-22-98-10.

COUVE DE MURVILLE, Maurice Noel Leon, M.A., M.PHIL., S.T.L.; British ecclesiastic; b. 27 June 1929, St. Germain-en-Laye, France; s. of Noel Couve de Murville and Marie Souchon; ed. Downside School, Trinity Coll., Cambridge, Inst. Catholique, Paris and School of Oriental and African Studies; ordained priest for diocese of Southwark 1957; Curate, Dartford, Kent 1957–60; Priest-in-Charge St. Francis, Moulscoomb 1961–64; Catholic Chaplain Univ. of Sussex 1961–77; Sr. Catholic Chaplain Univ. of Cambridge 1977–82; Archbishop of Birmingham March 1982–. *Publications:* Catholic Cambridge (with Philip Jenkins) 1983, John Milner 1752–1826 1986. *Leisure interests:* walking, gardening, local history. *Address:* Archbishop's House, St. Chad's Queensway, Birmingham, B4 6EX; 57 Mearse Lane, Barnt Green, Birmingham, B45 8HJ, England (Home). *Telephone:* (021) 236-5535; (021) 445-1467 (Home).

COUZENS, Sir Kenneth (Edward), K.C.B.; British public official; b. 29 May 1925; s. of Albert and May (née Biddlecombe) Couzens; m. Muriel Eileen Fey 1947; one s. one d.; ed. Portsmouth Grammar School, Univ. of London and Caius Coll., Cambridge; served in R.A.F. 1943–47; Inland Revenue 1949–51; Private Sec. to Financial Sec., H.M. Treasury 1952–55, to Chief Sec. 1962–63; Asst. Sec. Treasury 1963–69; Under-Sec. Civil Service Dept. 1969–70, Treasury 1970–73; Deputy Sec. Incomes Policy and Public Finance 1973–77; Second Perm. Sec. (Overseas Finance), Treasury 1977–82; Vice-Chair. and Chair. Monetary Cttee. of the EEC 1981–82; Perm. Under-Sec. of State, Dept. of Energy 1982–85; Deputy Chair. British Coal 1985–88; Chair. Coal Products Ltd 1988–. *Address:* Coverts Edge, Woodsway, Oxshott, Surrey, England. *Telephone:* Oxshott 3207.

COVALIU, Brădut; Romanian painter; b. 1 April 1924, Sinaia, Prahova County; s. of Valeria Covaliu; m. Alexandrina Mihai; ed. Acad. of Fine Arts, Bucharest; exhbns. in Romania, Sofia, Prague, Berlin, Helsinki, Cairo, Paris, Athens, Ankara, Washington, Chicago, Ulan Bator, Venice since 1943; Sec. of the Romanian Fine Arts Union 1963–68, Chair. 1968–78; Prize of the Romanian Acad. 1962; Grand Prize of the Romanian Fine Arts Union 1979; Austrian Cross for Arts and Science 1976; Trionfo prize

of Rome 1981. *Works include:* cycles of paintings: Enthusiasm, Flyers, The Village, Don Quixote. *Address:* Uniunea Artistilor Plastici, Str. Nicolae Iorga 42, Bucharest, Romania. *Telephone:* 50.73.80.

COVENEY, James, D.D'UNIV., B.A., F.R.S.A.; British university professor of French; b. 4 April 1920, London; s. of James and Mary Coveney; m. Patricia Yvonne Townsend 1955; two s.; ed. St. Ignatius Coll., Stamford Hill, London, and Univs. of Reading and Strasbourg; Clerical Officer, London County Council 1936–40; served in Queen's Own Royal W. Kent Regt. (Second Lieut.) and as Pilot, R.A.F. (Flight-Lieut.) 1940–46; French Govt. Research Scholar, Univ. of Strasbourg 1950–51, Lecteur d'Anglais 1951–53; Lecturer in French, Univ. of Hull 1953–58; Asst. Dir of Examinations (Modern Languages), Civil Service Comm. 1958–59; UN Secretariat 1959–61; NATO Secretariat 1961–64; Sr. Lecturer and Head of Modern Languages, Univ. of Bath 1964–68, Prof. of French 1969–85, now Prof. Emer.; Joint Dir. Centre for European Industrial Studies 1969–75; Visiting Prof. Univ. of Buckingham 1974–85, Ecole Nat. d'Admin., Paris 1974–85, Bethlehem Univ. 1985; Nat. Inst. for Higher Educ., Limerick 1987–; Consultant Prof. Univ. of East Asia; Gov. Bell Educational Trust 1972–88; Corresp. mem. Acad. des Sciences, Agric., Arts et Belles-lettres, Aix-en-Provence 1975; Chevalier, Ordre des Palmes Académiques 1978; Officier, Ordre Nat. du Mérite 1986. *Publications:* La Légende de l'Empereur Constant 1955; Co-author: Glossary of French and English Management Terms 1972, Le français pour l'ingénieur 1974, Glossary of German and English Management Terms 1977, Glossary of Spanish and English Management Terms 1978, Guide to French Institutions 1978, Portuguese-English Business Dictionary 1982. *Leisure interests:* French politics, Arab studies. *Address:* 40 Westfield Close, Bath, BA2 2EB, England. *Telephone:* Bath 316670.

COVENTRY, Mgr. John Seton, S.J., M.A., S.T.L.; British ecclesiastic; b. 21 Jan. 1915, Deal, Kent; s. of Bernard S. Coventry and Annie Cunningham; ed. Stonyhurst Coll., Heythrop Coll. and Campion Hall, Oxford; joined Soc. of Jesus 1932; ordained priest 1947; Headmaster, Beaumont Coll. 1950–58; Provincial Superior English Prov. SJ 1958–64; lecturer in Theology Heythrop Coll. Oxon 1965–70, Heythrop Coll. Univ. of London 1970–76; Master, St. Edmund's Coll. (then House) Cambridge 1976–85; lecturer Emer. and Fellow, Heythrop Coll. 1985–87; now Tutor in Theology Manresa House; Hon. Fellow, St. Edmund's Coll. Cambridge. *Publications:* Morals and Independence 1949, The Breaking of Bread 1950, The Life Story of the Mass 1960, The Theology of Faith 1968, Christian Truth 1975, Faith in Jesus Christ 1980, Reconciling 1985. *Leisure interests:* music, pot plants. *Address:* Manresa House, 10 Albert Road, Birmingham, B17 0AN, England. *Telephone:* 021-427 2628.

COWAN, William Maxwell, M.A., D.PHIL., B.M., B.CH., F.R.S.; British biologist; b. 27 Sept. 1931, Johannesburg, South Africa; s. of Adam and Jessie (née Sloan) Cowan; m. Margaret Sherlock 1956; two s. one d.; ed. High School, S. Africa, Witwatersrand Univ., Oxford Univ.; Departmental Demonstrator in Anatomy, Oxford Univ. 1953–58, Univ. lecturer in Anatomy 1958–66; Fellow, Pembroke Coll., Oxford Univ. 1958–66; Assoc. Prof. of Anatomy, Univ. of Wis., U.S.A. 1966–68; Prof. and Head, Dept. of Anatomy and Neurobiology, Wash. Univ. School of Medicine 1968–80; Dir. Div. of Biology and Biomedical Sciences, Wash. Univ. 1975–80; Provost and Exec. Vice-Chancellor 1986–; Non-Resident Fellow, Salk Inst. for Biological Studies 1977–80; Prof. and Dir. Weingart Lab. for Developmental Neurobiology, Salk Inst. for Biological Studies 1980–86; Vice-Pres. Salk Inst. 1981–86; Fellow American Acad. of Arts and Sciences; Foreign Assoc. U.S. N.A.S. *Publications:* Studies in Developmental Neurobiology 1981; numerous articles in scientific journals; Ed.: Annual Reviews of Neuroscience 1975–, Journal of Comparative Neurology 1969–80, Journal of Neuroscience 1981–. *Leisure interests:* photography, reading, travel. *Address:* Office of the Provost, Washington University, 1 Brookings Drive, St. Louis, Mo. 63130; 6372 Forsyth Avenue, Clayton, Mo. 63105, U.S.A. (Home). *Telephone:* (314) 889-5151 (Office); (314) 726-3222 (Home).

COWDRAY, 3rd Viscount (cr. 1917), Weetman John Churchill, M.A.; British landowner and business executive; b. 27 Feb. 1910, London; s. of 2nd Viscount Cowdray and Agnes Beryl Spencer-Churchill; m. 1st Lady Anne Pamela Bridgeman 1939 (divorced), one s. two d.; m. 2nd Elizabeth Georgiana Mather Jackson, one s. two d.; ed. Eton Coll. and Christ Church Oxford; Capt., Surrey and Sussex Yeomanry 1939; Parl. Private Sec. to Under-Sec. of State for Air 1941–42; Dir. S. Pearson & Son Ltd. 1934–83, Chair. 1954–77, Pres. Pearson PLC 1983–. *Leisure interests:* polo, shooting and fishing. *Address:* 17th Floor, Millbank Tower, Millbank, London, SW1P 4QZ (Office); Cowdray Park, Midhurst, West Sussex, GU29 0AX; Dunecht House, Dunecht, Skene, Aberdeenshire, AB3 7DD, Scotland; 22 Kingston House South, Ennismore Gardens, London, SW7 1NF, England.

COWDREY, (Michael) Colin, C.B.E.; British cricketer and businessman; b. 24 Dec. 1932, Bangalore, India; s. of Ernest Arthur Cowdrey and Kathleen Mary Cowdrey (née Taylor); m. 1st Penelope Susan Chiesman 1956; three s. one d.; m. 2nd Baroness Herries of Terregles 1985; ed. Homefield, Sutton, Tonbridge and Brasenose Coll., Oxford; Capt. of Cricket Team, Oxford 1954, Kent 1957–70, England 25 times, MCC to West Indies 1968, to Pakistan and Ceylon 1969; mem. MCC Cttee. 1970–; 117 England caps; third highest run-maker in Tests; 107 centuries (22 in Tests); Dir. Whitbread Fremlins 1974–85; Exec. Barclays Int. 1975–, local Dir. Barclays,

Maidstone, then Brighton; Dir. Master Skinners Co.; mem. Council, Winston Churchill Memorial Trust 1971-, Britain Australia Soc. 1975-; Chair. Cook Soc. 1986. *Publications:* Cricket Today 1957, Tackle Cricket This Way 1960, Time for Reflection 1963, Incomparable Game 1969, MCC: Life of a Cricketer 1975. *Leisure interests:* golf, reading. *Address:* 54 Lombard Street, London, EC3P 3AH, England. *Telephone:* 01-626 1567.

COWEN, Rt. Hon. Sir Zelman, P.C., A.K., G.C.M.G., G.C.V.O., Q.C.; Australian academic; b. 7 Oct. 1919, Melbourne; s. of late Bernard Cowen and of Sara Granat; m. Anna Wittner 1945; three s. one d.; ed. Scotch Coll., Melbourne, Univ. of Melbourne, Univ. of Oxford; served in Royal Australian Naval Volunteer Reserve 1940-45; consultant to Mil. Govt. in Germany 1947; Australian Dominion Liaison Officer to Colonial Office 1951-66; Dean of Faculty of Law, Prof. of Public Law, Univ. of Melbourne 1951-66; Vice-Chancellor, Univ. of New England, N.S.W. 1967-70, Univ. of Queensland 1970-77; Gov.-Gen. of Australia 1977-82; Provost of Oriel Coll., Oxford Oct. 1982-; Visiting Prof., Univ. of Chicago 1949, Harvard Law School and Fletcher School of Law and Diplomacy 1953-54, 1963-64, Univ. of Utah 1954, Ill. 1957-58, Wash. 1959, Univ. of Calcutta, India 1975; Menzies Scholar in Residence, Univ. of Va., 1983; Pres. Adult Educ. Asscn. of Australia 1968-70; mem. and (at various times) Chair. Victorian State Advisory Cttee. to Australian Broadcasting Comm.; mem. Devt. Corpn. of N.S.W. 1969-70, Bd. of Int. Asscn. for Cultural Freedom 1970-75; Academic Gov. of Bd. of Govs., Hebrew Univ. of Jerusalem 1969-77, 1982-; mem. Bd. of Govs. Univ. of Tel Aviv 1984-; mem. of Council, Univ. of Lesotho 1976-77; a Dir. Australian Opera 1969-77; mem. Club of Rome 1974-77; Pres. Australian Inst. of Urban Studies 1973-77; Chair. Bd. of Govs., Utah Foundation 1975-77; Law Reform Commr., Commonwealth of Australia 1976-77; Chair. Australian Vice-Chancellor's Cttee. 1977, Australian Studies Centre Cttee. (London) 1982-, Press Council (U.K.) 1983-88, Nat. Council of Australian Opera 1983-, Victoria League for Commonwealth Friendship 1986-, of Trustees, Visnews Ltd. 1986-; Dir. Australian Mutual Provident Soc. Dec. 1982-; Trustee Sydney Opera House 1969-70, Queensland Overseas Foundation 1976-77, Sir Robert Menzies Memorial Trust (U.K.), Winston Churchill Memorial Trust (U.K.), Van Leer Inst. of Jerusalem (Chair. 1988-); Foreign Hon. Mem. American Acad. of Arts and Sciences; Fellow, Royal Soc. of Arts, Acad. of Social Sciences in Australia, Australian Coll. of Educ., Australian and N.Z. Asscn. for the Advancement of Science (now Hon. Fellow); Hon. Fellow New Coll., Oxford, Univ. House, Australian Inst. of Architects, Australian Acad. of Social Sciences, Australian Coll. of Educ., Univ. House of Australia, Nat. Univ., Australian Acad. of Technological Sciences, Royal Australasian Coll. of Physicians, Royal Australian Coll. of Medical Administrators, Royal Australian Coll. of Obstetricians and Gynaecologists, Australian Acad. of the Humanities, Australian Soc. of Accountants, Australian Inst. of Chartered Accountants, Australian Coll. of Rehabilitation Medicine; Hon. Master, Gray's Inn Bench 1976, Q.C. of the Queensland Bar, mem. Victorian Bar and Hon. Life mem. N.S.W. Bar Asscn.; Hon. Fellow, Trinity Coll., Dublin; Hon. LL.D. (Univs. of Hong Kong, Queensland, Melbourne, W.A., Turin, Australian Nat. Univ.), Hon. D.Litt. (Univs. of New England, Sydney, Oxford, James Cook Univ. of N.Queensland), Hon. D.H.L. (Hebrew Union Coll., Cincinnati), (Univ. of Redlands, Calif.), Hon. D.Univ. (Newcastle, Griffith), Hon. D.Phil. (Hebrew Univ. of Jerusalem, Univ. of Tel Aviv); Kt., Order of Australia, Kt. Grand Cross, Order of St. Michael and St. George, Royal Victorian Order, K.St.J. *Publications:* Specialist Editor, Dicey: Conflict of Laws 1949, Australia and the United States: Some Legal Comparisons 1954, (with P. B. Carter) Essays on the Law of Evidence 1956, American-Australian Private International Law 1957, Federal Jurisdiction in Australia 1959, (with D. Mendes da Costa) Matrimonial Causes Jurisdiction 1961, The British Commonwealth of Nations in a Changing World 1964, Sir John Latham and Other Papers 1965, Sir Isaac Isaacs 1967, The Private Man (A.B.C. Boyer Lectures 1969), Individual Liberty and the Law (Tagore Law Lectures 1975), The Virginia Lectures 1984, Reflections on Medicine, Biotechnology and the Law (Pound Lectures, Neb. Univ.) 1986, A Touch of Healing 1986. *Leisure interests:* music, performing and visual arts. *Address:* Provost's Lodgings, Oriel College, Oxford, OX1 4EW, England. *Telephone:* Oxford 722630, 276533.

COWLES, John, Jr., A.B.; American publisher; b. 27 May 1929, Des Moines, Iowa; s. of the late John Cowles and of Elizabeth Bates; m. Jane Sage Fuller 1952; two s. two d.; ed. Phillips Exeter Acad. and Harvard Coll.; joined Minneapolis Star and Tribune Co. (now Cowles Media Co.) 1953, Vice-Pres. 1957-68, Pres. 1968-73, 1979-83, Ed. 1961-69, Editorial Chair. 1969-73, Chair. 1973-79; Pres. Harper's Magazine Inc. 1965-68, Chair. 1968-72; Dir. Harper and Row, Publishers Inc. 1965-81, Chair. 1968-79; Dir. Des Moines Register and Tribune Co. 1960-, Associated Press, Guthrie Theatre Foundation 1960-71, Minneapolis Foundation 1975-77, American Newspaper Pubrs. Asscn. 1975-77, etc.; fmr. Dir. Equitable Life Insurance Co. of Iowa, Phillips Exeter Acad., First Bank System, Inc. (Minneapolis), etc.; Campaign Chair. Minneapolis United Fund 1967; Hon. Litt.D. (Simpson Coll.) 1965. *Address:* 1225 La Salle Avenue, Minneapolis, Minn. 55403, U.S.A. (Home).

COWLEY, John Maxwell, PH.D., F.A.A., F.R.S.; Australian professor of physics; b. 18 Feb. 1923, Australia; s. of Alfred E. Cowley and Doris R. Cowley; m. Roberta Beckett 1951; two d.; ed. Univ. of Adelaide and M.I.T., U.S.A.; Research Officer, Commonwealth Scientific and Industrial

Research Org., Australia 1945-62; Chamber of Mfrs. Prof. of Physics, Univ. of Melbourne 1962-70; Galvin Prof. of Physics, Arizona State Univ., U.S.A. 1970-, Dir. Facility for High Resolution Electron Microscopy 1983-; B.E. Warren Award, American Crystallographic Asscn. 1976, Distinguished Award, Electron Microscopy Soc. of America 1979, Ewald Award, Int. Union of Crystallography 1987; Fellow American Physical Soc. *Publications:* Diffraction Physics 1975, Modulated Structures—1979 (Ed.) 1979; approximately 300 scientific articles in journals. *Leisure interests:* painting and hiking. *Address:* Department of Physics, Arizona State University, Tempe, Ariz. 85287, U.S.A. *Telephone:* (602) 965-6459.

COWLEY, Malcolm, A.B.; American writer; b. 24 Aug. 1898, Belsano, Pa.; s. of William and Josephine (Hutmacher) Cowley; m. 2nd Muriel Maurer 1932; one s.; ed. Harvard and Montpellier Univs.; Copy writer Sweet's Architectural Catalogue 1920 and 1923-25; free-lance writer 1925-29; Literary Ed. The New Republic 1929-40; staff critic 1940-53; literary adviser to the Viking Press 1949-; mem. American Acad. of Arts and Letters (Chancellor 1967-77), Nat. Inst. of Arts and Letters (Pres. 1956-59, 1962-65); Hon. D. Litt. *Publications:* Exile's Return 1934, The Literary Situation 1954, Black Cargoes 1962 (with Daniel P. Mannix), The Faulkner-Cowley File 1966, Think Back on Us 1967, Blue Juniata: Collected Poems 1968, A Many-Windowed House 1970, A Second Flowering 1973, And I Worked at the Writer's Trade 1978, The Dream of the Golden Mountains 1980, The View from 80 1980, The Flower and the Leaf 1985; trans. Valéry's Variety 1926, Princess Bibesco's Catherine-Paris 1927, Gide's Imaginary Interviews 1944, etc.; Editor: Adventures of an African Slaver 1927, After the Genteel Tradition 1937, Books that Changed our Minds 1939, The Portable Hemingway 1944, The Portable Faulkner 1946, The Portable Hawthorne 1948, The Complete Whitman 1948, The Stories of F. Scott Fitzgerald 1951, Writers at Work 1958, etc. *Leisure interest:* gardening.
[Died 28 March 1989]

COWLEY, Roger A., F.R.S., F.R.S.E.; British professor of physics; b. 24 Feb. 1939, Essex; s. of C. A. Cowley; m. Sheila Joyce Wells 1964; one s. one d.; ed. Brentwood School and Univ. of Cambridge; Fellow of Trinity Hall, Cambridge 1962-64; Research Officer. Atomic Energy of Canada Ltd. 1964-70; Prof. of Physics, Univ. of Edinburgh 1970-88; Dr. Lee's Prof. of Experimental Philosophy, Univ. of Oxford 1988-; Max Born Medal and Prize. *Publications:* approx. 200 scientific publs. *Address:* Clarendon Laboratory, Parks Road, Oxford OX1 3P4 (Office); Tredinnock, Harcourt Hill, Oxford OX2 9AS, England (Home). *Telephone:* 0865-272224 (Office); 0865-247570 (Home).

COWLING, Thomas, F.R.S.; British professor emeritus of mathematics; b. 17 June 1906, London; s. of George and Edith Cowling; m. Doris Marjorie Moffatt 1935; one s. two d.; ed. Sir George Monoux Grammar School, Walthamstow and Brasenose Coll., Oxford; Demonstrator in Math. Imperial Coll., London 1933; Asst. lecturer in Math., Univ. Coll., Swansea; later lecturer in Math. Univ. Coll., Dundee and Manchester Univ.; Prof. of Math. Univ. Coll., Bangor 1945, Univ. of Leeds 1948-70, now Prof. Emer.; fmr. Pres. Royal Astronomical Soc.; Hon. mem. American Astronomical Soc.; Hon. Fellow, Brasenose Coll., Oxford; Royal Astronomical Soc. Gold Medal 1956, Bruce Medal, Astronomical Soc. of the Pacific 1985 and other distinctions. *Publications:* The Mathematical Theory of Non-Uniform Gases (with S. Chapman) 1939, Molecules in Motion 1949, Magnetohydrodynamics 1956. *Leisure interests:* gardening, crosswords. *Address:* 19 Hollin Gardens, Leeds, LS16 5NL, England. *Telephone:* (0532) 785342.

COWPER, Steve Cambreleng, J.D.; American lawyer and politician; b. 21 Aug. 1938, Petersburg, Va.; s. of Stephanie Smith; m. Michael Margaret Stewart; one s. two d.; ed. Univ. of N. Carolina; law practice, Norfolk, Va.; Asst. Dist. Attorney, State of Alaska, Fairbanks 1968-70; partner, Cowper & Madson, Fairbanks 1971-84; mem. Alaska House of Reps. 1974-78; newspaper columnist, Alaska 1979-80, 1985; Gov. of Alaska 1986-; Democrat. *Publication:* A Trail to Break—A History of Alaska Lands (documentary). *Leisure interests:* banjo, rugby, scuba diving, reading. *Address:* Office of the Governor, State Capitol, P.O. Box A, Juneau, Alaska 99811, U.S.A.

COX, Archibald, A.B., LL.B.; American lawyer; b. 17 May 1912, Plainfield, N.J.; s. of Archibald Cox and Frances Bruen; m. Phyllis Ames 1937; one s. two d.; ed. St. Paul's School, Concord, and Harvard Univ.; admitted to Mass. Bar 1937; in practice with Ropes, Gray, Best, Coolidge and Rugg, Boston 1938-41; Attorney, Office of Solicitor-Gen., U.S. Dept. of Justice 1941-43; Assoc. Solicitor, Dept. of Labor 1943-45; lecturer on Law, Harvard Univ. 1945-46, Williston Prof. of Law 1946-76; Carl M. Loeb Univ. Prof. 1976-85; Visiting Prof. of Law, Boston Univ. 1984-; Chair. Wage Stabilization Bd. 1952, Advisory Panel to Senate Cttee. on Educ. and Labour 1958-59; Solicitor-Gen. of U.S. 1961-65; Prosecutor, Watergate Investigation 1973; Pitt Prof. of American History and Insts., Cambridge Univ. 1974-75; Chair. Common Cause 1980-; mem. American Bar Asscn., American Acad. of Arts and Sciences, Bd. of Overseers, Harvard Univ. 1962-65. *Publications:* Cases on Labor law 1948, Law and the National Labor Policy 1960, Civil Rights, the Constitution and the Courts 1967, The Warren Court 1968, The Role of the Supreme Court in American Government 1976, Freedom of Expression 1981, The Court and the Constitution 1987, and articles in legal periodicals. *Address:* 34 Old Connecticut Path, PO Box 393, Wayland, Mass. 01778, U.S.A.

COX, Sir David (Roxbee), Kt, PH.D., F.R.S.; British professor of statistics; b. 15 July 1924, Birmingham; s. of Sam R. Cox and Lilian (née Braines) Cox; m. Joyce Drummond 1947; three s. one d.; ed. Handsworth Grammar School, Birmingham, and St. John's Coll. Cambridge; at Royal Aircraft Establishment 1944–46; Wool Industries Research Assen. 1946–50; Statistical Lab., Univ. of Cambridge 1950–55; with Dept. of Biostatistics, Univ. of N. Carolina 1955–56, Birkbeck Coll., London 1956–66; Bell Telephone Labs. 1965; Prof. of Statistics, Imperial Coll. of Science and Tech., London 1966–88; Warden Nuffield Coll., Oxford Aug. 1988–; Science and Eng. Research Council Sr. Research Fellow 1983–88; Ed. Biometrika 1966–; Hon. D.Sc. (Reading, Bradford, Helsinki, Limburg); Hon. Foreign mem.: U.S. Acad. of Arts and Sciences, Royal Danish Acad., N.A.S.; Guy Medals in silver and gold, Royal Statistical Soc., Weldon Medal, Univ. of Oxford. *Publications:* several books on statistics, articles in Journal of the Royal Statistical Soc., Biometrika etc. *Address:* Nuffield Coll., Oxford, OX1 1NF, England.

COX, Sir (Ernest) Gordon, K.B.E., T.D., F.R.I.C., F.INST.P., LL.D., D.SC., F.R.S.; British scientist; b. 24 April 1906, Bath, Avon; s. of Ernest and Rosina (née Ring) Cox; m. 1st Lucie Baker 1929 (died 1962), 2nd Mary Truter (née Jackman) 1968; one s. one d.; ed. City of Bath Boys' School and Univ. of Bristol; Research Asst. Davy-Faraday Laboratory, Royal Inst. 1927; Asst. Lecturer in Chemistry, Univ. of Birmingham 1929, Lecturer 1932, Sr. Lecturer 1939, Reader in Chemical Crystallography 1940; Prof. of Inorganic and Structural Chem., Univ. of Leeds 1945–60; mem. Agricultural Research Council 1957–60, Sec. 1960–71; Vice-Pres. Inst. of Physics 1950–53; Treas. Royal Inst. of Great Britain 1971–76; Hon. Sec. British Assen. 1971–75; Hon. Assoc. Royal Coll. of Veterinary Surgeons. *Publications:* papers, chiefly on the crystal structures of chemical compounds. *Leisure interests:* gardening, natural history, music, books. *Address:* 117 Hampstead Way, London, NW11 7JN, England. *Telephone:* 01-455 2618.

COX, Glenn A., B.B.A.; American business executive; b. 6 Aug. 1929, Sedalia, Mo.; s. of Glenn A. Cox and Ruth L. Atkinson; m. Veronica M. Martin 1953; two s. one d.; ed. Southern Methodist Univ., Dallas, Tex. and Central Methodist Coll., Fayette, Mo.; served as pilot, U.S.A.F. 1951–55; began career with Phillips Petroleum Co., in Treasury Dept. 1956, Asst. to Chair. of Operating Cttee. 1973, elected Vice-Pres. Man. Information and Control 1974, elected Exec. Vice-Pres. with responsibility for all corpn. financial matters 1980, elected mem. Bd. of Dirs. and Exec. Cttee. 1982, Pres. and C.O.O. 1985–; Order of the Ivory Coast. *Publication:* "Financing an Oil Company" in Energy Finance. *Leisure interests:* reading and jogging. *Address:* Phillips Petroleum Company, 18 Phillips Building, Bartlesville, Okla. 74004, U.S.A. *Telephone:* 918-661-7035.

COX, Graham Campbell, B.COM., LL.B.; South African attorney; b. 31 May 1932, Bloemfontein; s. of D. T. Cox and A. B. Cox; m. Jillian Jane Aston Key 1959; one s. two d.; ed. Diocesan Coll., Univ. of Cape Town; f. Cox, Yeats and Partners 1964; Chair. Standing Cttee. Assen. of Law Soc. on co. and tax matters 1979–84; Pres. Natal Law Soc. 1981–83; Chair. Legal Provident Fund 1981–87; Pres. Assen. of Law Soc. of S.A. 1985; Chair. Council of Univ. of Natal 1986–; mem. Standing Cttee. on Tax 1984–; Cttee. of Business Law Section of the Int. Bar Assen. 1985–88; Fellow of the Assen. of Arbitrators 1984–. *Publications:* numerous articles in legal journals. *Leisure interest:* fly fishing. *Address:* P.O. Box 3032, Durban 4000 (Office); 2 Woodlands Avenue, Westville 3630, South Africa (Home). *Telephone:* 3042851 (Office); 861874 (Home).

COX, Stephen Joseph; British artist; b. 16 Sept. 1946, Bristol; s. of Leonard John Cox and Ethel Minnie May McGill; m. Judith Atkins; two d.; ed. St. Mary Redcliffe, Bristol, West of England Coll. of Art, Bristol and Cen. School of Art and Design, London; part-time lecturer at several colls. of art, and Assoc. Lecturer, Brighton Polytechnic 1968–81; lives and works in London, Italy and India; many one-man exhbns. in London (Lisson Gallery, Nigel Greenwood Gallery, Tate Gallery), Bristol (Arnolfini Gallery) Nottingham (Midland Group Gallery), Oxford (Museum of Modern Art), Amsterdam, Bari, Milan, Rome, Spoleto (1982 Festival), Florence, Geneva, Basle, Paris and New Delhi; numerous group exhbns. in several countries, including Paris Biennale 1977, British Sculpture in 20th Century, Whitechapel Art Gallery, London 1981, Venice Biennale 1982, New Art, Tate Gallery, London 1983, Int. Garden Festival, Liverpool 1984 and Int. Survey of Painting and Sculpture 1984, M.O.M.A., New York, Forty Years of Modern Art 1945–85, Tate Gallery, Origins, Originally and Beyond, Sydney Biennale, Prospekt '86, Frankfurt, 19th Sculpture Biennale, Middlehiem, Belgium, British Art in the 1980s, Museum of Modern Art, Brussels; works in collections of Tate Gallery, Arts Council of G.B., British Council, Walker Art Gallery, Liverpool, Henry Moore Centre for Sculpture, Leeds City Gallery, Fogg Museum, U.S.A., Groningen Museum, Netherlands, Peter Ludwig Collection, Fed. Repub. of Germany and pvt. collections in U.S.A. and Europe; Arts Council Major Awards 1978, 1980, British Council Bursaries 1978, 1979, Hakone Open Air Museum Prize, Japan 1985. *Address:* 154 Barnsbury Road, Islington, London, N1 0ER, England. *Telephone:* 01-278 4184.

COX, Sir Trenchard, Kt., C.B.E., M.A., F.R.S.A., F.S.A., F.M.A.; British museum official; b. 31 July 1905; s. of the late William Pallett Cox and Marion Beverley; m. Mary Désirée Anderson 1935 (died 1973); ed. Eton Coll., and King's Coll., Cambridge; Asst. to Keeper, Wallace Collection 1932–39;

served 1939–45 war in Home Office; Dir. City Museum and Art Gallery, Birmingham 1944–55; Dir. and Sec. Victoria and Albert Museum 1956–66; Hon. Fellow Royal Acad. 1981; Hon. D.Litt. (Birmingham) 1956; Chevalier, Légion d'honneur 1967. *Publications include:* Jehan Foucquet 1931, David Cox 1947, Peter Bruegel 1951, Pictures: A Handbook for Collectors 1956. *Address:* 33 Queen's Gate Gardens, London, S.W.7, England. *Telephone:* 01-584 0231.

COXETER, Harold Scott MacDonald, PH.D., LL.D., D.MATH., D.SC., F.R.S., F.R.S.C.; British mathematician; b. 9 Feb. 1907, London; s. of Harold Samuel Coxeter and Lucy (née Gee) Coxeter; m. Hendrina Johanna Brouwer 1936; one s. one d.; ed. King Alfred School, London, St. George's School, Harpenden, and Trinity Coll., Cambridge; Rockefeller Foundation Fellow, Princeton 1932–33; Procter Fellow, Princeton 1934–35; Asst. Prof., Toronto 1936–43, Assoc. Prof. 1943–48, Prof. of Math. 1948–80, Prof. Emer. 1980–; Visiting Prof., Notre Dame 1947, Columbia Univ. 1949, Dartmouth Coll. 1964, Univ. of Amsterdam 1966, Univ. of Edin. 1967, Univ. of E. Anglia 1968, Australian Nat. Univ. 1970, Univ. of Sussex 1972, Univ. of Warwick 1976, Calif. Inst. of Tech. 1977, Univ. of Bologna 1978; foreign mem. Koninklijke Nederlandse Akademie van Wetenschappen; Hon. mem. Mathematische Gesellschaft in Hamburg, London Mathematical Soc., etc. *Publications:* Non-Euclidean Geometry 1942, 1965, Regular Polytopes 1948, 1973, The Real Projective Plane 1949, 1955, Introduction to Geometry 1961, 1969, Projective Geometry 1946, 1987, Twelve Geometric Essays 1968, Regular Complex Polytopes 1974. *Leisure interests:* music, travel. *Address:* 67 Roxborough Drive, Toronto M4W 1X2, Ont., Canada. *Telephone:* (416) 9625665.

COZAD, James William, B.S.; American oil executive; b. 10 Feb. 1927, Huntington, Ind.; s. of Emmett and Helen Motz Cozad; m. Virginia E. Alley 1948; three s. two d.; ed. Indiana Univ.; with Peat, Marwick, Mitchell & Co. (accountants) 1950–57; Treas., later Vice-Pres. Hygrade Food Products Corpn., Detroit 1957–67; Treas. Philip Morris Inc., New York 1967–69; Financial Vice-Pres. Amoco Oil Co., Chicago 1969–71; Vice-Pres. Financial Operations, Standard Oil Co. (Indiana) 1971–76, Vice-Pres. Finance and Chief Financial Officer 1976–78, Exec. Vice-Pres. 1978–83, Chief Financial Officer 1978–, Vice-Chair. 1983–. *Leisure interests:* golf, hunting, fishing. *Address:* Amoco Corporation, 200 E. Randolph Drive, Chicago, Ill. 60601 (Office); 1205 Central Road, Glenview, Ill. 60025, U.S.A. (Home). *Telephone:* (312) 856-6352 (Office).

CRABBE, Hon. Samuel Azu, B.A., LL.B.; Ghanaian judge; b. 18 Nov. 1918, Accra; s. of Q. L. Crabbe and Naa Adoley Addo; m. Dorice Martinson 1970; three s. two d.; ed. Achimota Coll. and Univ. Coll. London; Called to the Bar, Middle Temple 1948; Barrister and Solicitor, Gold Coast Bar 1948–52; mem. Accra Town Council 1950–51; Dist. Magistrate 1953–57, Acting Sr. Magistrate 1957; Acting Chief Registrar, Supreme Court and Acting Registrar, Ghana Court of Appeal 1957–58; Sr. Crown Counsel, Attorney-Gen.'s Office 1958; Acting Solicitor-Gen. 1959; Judge, High Court of Justice 1959–61, Supreme Court 1961; mem. Gen. Legal Council of Ghana 1961, Deputy Chair. 1965–66; Chair. Concessions Tribunal 1962; Justice of Appeal, Court of Appeal for Eastern Africa 1963–65; Judge, Court of Appeal 1966; Chair. Govt. Finance Bd. 1967, Chair. Business Cttee., Constituent Ass. 1968–69; Acting Chief Justice of Ghana 1970, Justice 1972; Justice Supreme Court 1971–77; Chief Justice of Ghana 1973–77; Pro-Chancellor Univ. of Cape Coast, Chair. Univ. Council 1972–76; Justice of the First Demonstration Int. Court of Justice, Belgrade; Chair. Advisory Cttee. Int. Assoc. of Trial Lawyers 1976, Salary Review Comm. 1979; Pres. Olympic and Commonwealth Games Assen. of Ghana 1968–70, 1979; Head, Ghanaian Sports Del. to Spartakiad Games, Moscow 1979; Chair. Comm. of Enquiry into specified Banks in Ghana 1979–81; Chair. Special Investigating Bd. (into Kidnapping and Killing) 1982; Mohammed Ali Jinnah Centenary Medal 1976, Int. Assoc. of Trial Lawyers Gold Medal 1977; Companion Order of the Volta (Ghana) 1977. *Publication:* John Mensah Sarbah (1874–1910), His Life and Works. *Leisure interests:* football, cricket, reading, swimming, classical music, golf. *Address:* Hillcrest, nr. Peduase, P.O. Box 01687, Osu, Accra, Ghana. *Telephone:* 76223.

CRADOCK, Sir Percy, G.C.M.G.; British diplomatist; b. 26 Oct. 1923; m. Birthe Marie Dyrlund 1953; joined FCO 1954; First Sec. Kuala Lumpur, Malaya 1957–61, Hong Kong 1961–62, Beijing (fmrly. Peking) 1962–63; Foreign Office 1963–66; Counsellor and Head of Chancery, Beijing 1966–68, Chargé d'affaires 1968–69; Head of FCO Planning Staff 1969–71; Asst. Under-Sec. of State and Head of Cabinet Office Assessments Staff 1971–76; Amb. to German Democratic Repub. 1976–78, concurrently Leader U.K. Mission to Comprehensive Test Ban Negotiations, Geneva 1977–78; Amb. to People's Repub. of China 1978–83; Deputy Under-Sec. with special responsibility for negotiations with China over Hong Kong 1983–85; Foreign policy adviser to Prime Minister, 1984–; Hon. Fellow St. John's, Cambridge 1982. *Address:* c/o 10 Downing Street, London, S.W.1, England.

CRAGG, Anthony Douglas, M.A.; British sculptor; b. 9 April 1949, Liverpool; s. of Douglas R. Cragg and Audrey M. Rutter; m. Ute Oberste-Lehn 1977; two s.; ed. Cheltenham and Wimbledon Schools of Art and Royal Coll. of Art; teacher, Düsseldorf Kunstakademie 1979–; one-man exhbns. include Whitechapel Gallery, London 1981, Kunsthalle, Bern 1983, Palais de Beaux-Arts, Brussels 1985, Staatsgalerie Moderner Kunst, Munich 1985, Musée d'Art Contemporain, Paris 1985, Brooklyn Museum 1986, Hayward

Gallery, London 1986; important group exhbns. include Venice Biennale 1980–86, São Paulo Bienale 1983, Sydney Bienale 1984 and Documental Kassel 1982; Turner Prize 1988. *Leisure interests:* walking, geology. *Address:* Jaegerstrasse 16, 5600 Wüppertal 1, Federal Republic of Germany. *Telephone:* (0202) 742607, (0202) 733118.

CRAIG, Marshal of the R.A.F. Sir David Brownrigg, G.C.B., O.B.E., M.A.; British air force officer; b. 17 Sept. 1929, Dublin; s. of Maj. Francis Brownrigg Craig and Olive Craig; m. Elizabeth June Derenburg 1955; one s. one d.; ed. Radley Coll. and Lincoln Coll., Oxford; commissioned in R.A.F. 1951, Commanding Officer R.A.F. Cranwell 1968–70; ADC to The Queen 1969–71; Dir. Plans and Operations, HQ Far East Command 1970–71, Commanding Officer R.A.F. Akrotiri 1972–75, ACAS (Ops) Ministry of Defence 1975–78, Asst. Officer Commanding No. 1 Group R.A.F. Strike Command 1978–80, Vice-Chief of the Air Staff 1980–82, Asst. Officer, C.-in-C., R.A.F. Strike Command and C.-in-C. U.K. Forces 1982–85, Chief of Air Staff 1985–88, Chief of Defence Staff Dec. 1988–; Air ADC to The Queen 1985–. *Leisure interests:* fishing, shooting, golf. *Address:* c/o The Royal Bank of Scotland, 9 Pall Mall, London, SW1Y 5LX, England.

CRAIG, David Parker, A.O., D.SC., F.R.S., F.R.S.A., F.A.A.; Australian professor of chemistry; b. 23 Nov. 1919, Sydney; s. of Andrew Hunter Craig and Mary Jane Parker; m. Veronica Bryden-Brown 1948; three s. one d.; ed. Univ. of Sydney and Univ. Coll. London; Capt., Australian Imperial Force 1941–44; lecturer in Chem., Univ. of Sydney 1944–46, Prof. of Physical Chem. 1952–56; Turner and Newall Research Fellow 1946–49; lecturer in Chem., Univ. Coll. London 1949–52, Prof. 1956–67, Visiting Prof. 1967–; Prof. of Chem., Australian Nat. Univ. 1967–85, Prof. Emer. 1985–, Dean, Research School of Chem. 1970–73, 1977–81; Firth Visiting Prof., Univ. of Sheffield 1973; Visiting Prof., Univ. Coll. Cardiff 1975–; Visiting Foreign Prof., Univ. of Bologna 1984; part-time mem. Exec. CSIRO 1980–85; Hon. D.Sc. (Sydney), (Bologna); Hon. F.R.S.C.; Fellow, Univ. Coll. London; H. G. Smith Memorial Medal. *Publications:* Excitons in Molecular Crystals—Theory and Applications (co-author) 1968, Molecular Quantum Electrodynamics: An Introduction to Radiation-Molecule Interactions (co-author) 1984; original papers on chemistry in scientific journals. *Leisure interest:* tennis. *Address:* Research School of Chemistry, Australian National University, G.P.O. Box 4, Canberra, A.C.T. 2601, Australia. *Telephone:* (062) 492839.

CRAIG, George Brownlee, Jr., PH.D.; American entomologist; b. 8 July 1930, Chicago; s. of George Brownlee Craig and Alice Madelaine McManus; m. Elizabeth Ann Pflum 1954; one s. three d. (one deceased); ed. Univ. of Chicago, Laboratory School, Univ. of Chicago Coll., Indiana Univ., Bloomington, Univ. of Ill., Urbana; Research Asst. in Entomology, Ill. Univ. 1951–53; Entomologist DesPlaines River Mosquito Abatement Dist., Ill., summers 1951–53; First Lieut. and Entomologist, U.S. Army Preventive Medicine Dept., Fort Meade, Md. 1954; Research Entomologist Insect Physiology Div., U.S. Army Chemical Centre, Md. 1955–57; Dir. Vector Biology Lab., Univ. of Notre Dame 1957–, Asst. Prof. of Biology 1957–61, Assoc. Prof. 1961–64, Prof. 1964–74, Clark Prof. of Biology 1974–; Dir. WHO Int. Reference Centre for Aedes Mosquito 1969–; Dir. Mosquito Biology Unit Int. Centre for Insect Physiology and Ecology, Nairobi, Kenya 1970–77; numerous consultantships on U.S. Public Health Service, WHO, N.A.S., Dept. Agric., Nat. Science Foundation, etc.; Fellow N.A.S., American Acad. of Arts and Sciences, Entomological Soc. of America; mem. Entomological Soc. of America (Governing Bd. 1969–75), American Soc. of Tropical Medicine and Hygiene (Governing Council 1978–83), Genetics Soc. of America, American Mosquito Control Assn. (Pres. 1988), numerous other acads. and scientific socs. including A.A.A.S., Indiana Acad. Science; Distinguished Research Award, American Mosquito Control Assn., Memorial Lecturer 1984; Charles Franklin Craig Memorial Lecturer, American Soc. of Tropical Medicine and Hygiene 1979. *Publications:* some 350 technical papers on Aedes mosquito. *Address:* Vector Biology Laboratory, University of Notre Dame, Notre Dame, Ind. 46556 (Office); 19645 Glendale Avenue, South Bend, Ind. 46637, U.S.A. (Home). *Telephone:* 219-239 7366 (Office); 219-272 2564 (Home).

CRAIG, Mary, M.A.; British author and broadcaster; b. 2 July 1928, St. Helens, Lancs.; d. of William Joseph Clarkson and Anne Mary Clarkson; m. Francis John Craig 1952; four s. (one deceased); ed. Notre Dame Convent, St. Helens, Liverpool Univ., St. Anne's Coll., Oxford Univ.; Market Researcher, Unilever 1949–50; taught at various schools 1950–64; N.-W. Organizer, Sue Ryder Trust 1962–68; TV Critic, Catholic Herald 1971–76; presenter and features writer (freelance) with BBC Radio 1969–77; interviewer, Thames TV, Southern TV (freelance); freelance journalist and book reviewer; The Christopher Book Award (for Blessings), U.S.A. 1979; Officer's Cross of Order of Polonia Restituta 1987. *Publications:* Longford 1978, Woodruff at Random 1978, Blessings 1979, Man from a Far Country 1979, Candles in the Dark 1983, The Crystal Spirit 1986, Spark from Heaven 1988; for children: Pope John Paul II 1982, Mother Teresa 1984, Lech Wałęsa 1989. *Leisure interests:* reading, cookery, knitting, embroidery. *Address:* Orton House, Tile Barn, Woolton Hill, Nr. Newbury, Berks., RG15 9UY, England. *Telephone:* (0635) 253524.

CRAIG, Michael; British actor; b. 1928 India; appeared in The Home-coming, New York 1967–68; frequent appearances on stage in Australia; actor and scriptwriter for TV plays and films in Australia; TV appearances

in U.K. *Films include:* The Love Lottery, Passage Home, The Black Tents, To the Night, Eyewitness, House of Secrets, High Tide at Noon, Campbell's Kingdom, The Silent Enemy, Nor the Moon by Night, The Angry Silence, Doctor in Love, The Mysterious Island, Payroll, No My Darling Daughter, A Life for Ruth, The Iron Maiden, Captive City, Summer Flight, Of a Thousand Delights, Life at the Top, Modesty Blaise, Funny Girl, Royal Hunt of the Sun, Twinky, Country Dance, Royal Hunt of the Sun, The Second Mrs Anderson, Inn of the Damned, A Sporting Proposition, The Irishman, Turkey Shoot, Stanley etc. *Address:* c/o Chatto & Linnit Ltd., Coventry Street, London W.1., England.

CRAIG, Very Rev. Robert, C.B.E., M.A., S.T.M., PH.D., D.D., D.LITT., LL.D.; British ecclesiastic, university professor and administrator; b. 22 March 1917, Markinch, Fife, Scotland; s. of late John Craig and Anne Peggie Craig; m. Olga Wanda Strzelec 1950; one s. one d.; ed. St Andrews Unv. and Union Theological Seminary, N.Y.; Asst. Minister, St. John's Kirk, Perth 1941–42; British Army Infantry Chaplain 1942–47; Despatches, Normandy 1944; Prof. of Divinity, Natal Univ., S. Africa 1950–57, Dean of Coll. 1953–54; Prof. of Religion, Smith Coll., Northampton, Mass., U.S.A. 1958–63; Prof. of Theology, Univ. Coll. of Rhodesia 1963–69, Vice-Prin. 1966, Acting Prin. 1967 and 1969; Prin. and Vice-Chancellor, Univ. of Rhodesia (now Zimbabwe) 1969–80, Emer. 1980; Minister, St. Andrew's Scots Memorial Church, Jerusalem 1980–85, Emer. 1985; Council Interfaith Cttee. 1981–85; Bd of Dirs. Int. YMCA 1982–85, Chair. 1984–85; Exec. Cttee, Spafford Community Centre 1982–85; Chair. Church of Scotland Israel Council 1981–85; Moderator, Presbytery of Jerusalem 1982–84; Chair. Ecumenical Theological Research Fraternity 1983–85; Moderator, Gen. Ass., Church of Scotland 1986–87; British Council Commonwealth Interchange Fellow, Cambridge Univ. 1966; Hon. Fellow, Zimbabwe Inst. of Engineers 1976; Hon. D.D. (St. Andrews) 1967, Hon. LL.D. (Witwatersrand) 1979, (Birmingham) 1980, (Natal) 1981, Hon. D.Litt. (Zimbabwe) 1981; Hon. Chaplain to the Forces 1947; City of Jerusalem Medal 1985. *Publications:* The Reasonableness of True Religion 1954, Social Concern in the Thought of William Temple 1963, Religion: Its Reality and its Relevance 1965, The Church: Unity in Integrity 1966, Politics and Religion: A Christian View 1972, On Belonging to a University 1974. *Leisure interests:* cinema, theatre, recent and contemporary history, light classical music, listening and talking to people. *Address:* West Port, Falkland, Fife, KY7 7BL, Scotland. *Telephone:* (0337) 57238.

CRAIG, Rt. Hon. William; British politician; b. 2 Dec. 1924; s. of the late John and Mary Kathleen (née Lamont) Craig; m. Doris Hilgendorff 1960; two s.; ed. Queen's Univ. Belfast; mem. (Ulster Unionist) Parl. of N. Ireland (Stormont) 1960–72; mem. N. Ireland Ass. 1973–74; Chief Whip 1962–63; Minister of Home Affairs 1963–64, 1966–68; Minister of Health and Local Govt. 1964; Minister of Devt. 1965–66; Leader, Ulster Vanguard 1972–74, Vanguard Unionist Party 1973–77; M.P. East Belfast (United Ulster Unionist Coalition) 1974–79; mem. Northern Ireland Convention, East Belfast 1975–76; mem. British Parl. Del. to Council of Europe and to WEU 1977–79. *Address:* 23 Annadale Avenue, Belfast, Northern Ireland, BT7 3JJ. *Telephone:* Belfast 644096.

CRAIK, Fergus Ian Muirden, PH.D., F.R.S.C.; British/Canadian professor of psychology; b. 17 April 1935, Edinburgh; s. of George Craik and Frances Crabbe; m. Anne Catherall 1961; two s.; ed. George Watson's Boys' Coll. Edinburgh and Univs. of Edinburgh and Liverpool; mem. scientific staff, MRC Unit for Research on Occupational Aspects of Ageing, Univ. of Liverpool 1960–65; lecturer in Psychology, Birkbeck Coll. London 1965–71; Assoc. Prof. then Prof. of Psychology, Univ. of Toronto 1971–, Chair. Dept. of Psychology 1985–; Fellow, Center for Advanced Study in Behavioral Sciences, Stanford Univ. 1982–83; Killam Research Fellowship 1982–84; Guggenheim Fellowship 1982–83; Fellow, Soc. of Experimental Psychologists, Canadian Psychological Assn., American Psychological Assn.; D. O. Hebb Award. *Publications:* Levels of Processing in Human Memory (ed. with L. S. Cormak) 1979, Ageing and Cognitive Processes (ed. with S. Trehub). *Leisure interests:* reading, walking, tennis, music. *Address:* Department of Psychology, University of Toronto, Toronto, Ont., M5S 1A1, Canada.

CRAINZ, Franco, M.D., F.R.C.O.G.; Italian university professor; b. 18 May 1913, Rome; s. of the late Silvio Crainz and Ada Fanelli Crainz; ed. Rome Univ.; Prof. and Head of Dept., School for Midwives, Novara 1956–64; Prof. and Head, Dept. of Obstetrics and Gynaecology, Univ. of Cagliari 1964–66, of Messina 1966–67, of Bari 1967–72; Prof. of Obstetrics and Gynaecology, Rome Univ. 1972–; Vice-Pres. Italian Soc. of the History of Medicine; Hon. mem. the Italian Soc. of Obstetrics and Gynaecology (Pres. 1977–80) and of the Portuguese, Romanian, Spanish and Swiss socs. *Publications:* An Obstetric Tragedy-The Case of H.R.H. the Princess Charlotte Augusta 1977; over 100 medical papers. *Leisure interests:* history of medicine, music, archaeology, history, gardening. *Address:* Via P. Mascagni 124, I-00199, Rome, Italy. *Telephone:* (06) 834318.

CRAM, Donald James, M.S., PH.D.; American professor of chemistry; b. 22 April 1919, Chester, Vt.; s. of Joanna Shelley and William Moffet Cram; m. Jane Maxwell 1969; no c.; ed. Rollins College Fla., Univ. of Nebraska and Harvard Univ.; Researcher, Merck & Co., Rahway, N.J. 1942–45; Instructor, American Chem. Soc. Fellowship, Univ. of Calif., L.A. 1947–48, Asst. Prof. 1948–51, Assoc. Prof. 1951–56, Prof. 1956–, S. Winstein Prof.

1985-; Fellow N.A.S., American Acad. of Arts and Sciences; Dr. h.c. (Uppsala Univ., Sweden) 1977, (Univ. of S. Calif.) 1983, (Rollins Coll.) 1988; A.C.S. Cope Award in Organic Chem. 1974, McCoy Award for Contribs. to Chem. 1965, 1975; Calif. Scientist of the Year 1974; several American Chemical Soc. Awards, including Roger Adams Award 1985, Gibbs Medal (Chicago Section) 1985, Tolman Medal (Southern Calif. Section) 1985, shared Nobel Prize in Chemistry 1987. *Publications:* Organic Chemistry (with Prof. George Hammond, Prof. James Hendrickson and Prof. Stanley Pine), Elements of Organic Chemistry (with Prof. John Richards and Prof. George Hammond), Essence of Organic Chemistry (textbook with Jane M. Cram) 1977, monograph Carbanions, 368 papers in Journal of American Chemical Society and other chemical journals from 1943. *Leisure interests:* tennis, surfing, skiing, guitar. *Address:* Department of Chemistry, University of California, 405 Hilgard Avenue, Los Angeles, Calif. 90024 (Office); 1250 Roscomare Road, Los Angeles, Calif. 90077, U.S.A. (Home). *Telephone:* (213)-825-1562 (Office); (213)-472-8477 (Home).

CRAMER, Friedrich D., DR.RER.NAT.; German director of Max-Planck-Institut für experimentelle Medizin; b. 20 Sept. 1923, Breslau; s. of Dr. Johannes Cramer and Ilse Cramer-Kribitzsch; m. Marie-Luise Erdel 1947; seven c.; ed. Breslau High School, Univ. of Breslau and Univ. of Heidelberg; Research Assoc. Chemistry Dept. Univ. of Heidelberg 1950-53, lecturer 1954-58; Visiting Lecturer Cambridge Univ. 1953-54; Prof. Tech. Univ. of Darmstadt 1959-62; Dir. Max-Planck-Inst. für experimentelle Medizin, Göttingen 1962-; mem. Acads. of Science of Poland, Göttingen and Heidelberg; Hon. mem. American Soc. of Biological Chemists 1980; Kopernikus Medal 1987. *Publications:* Einschlussverbindungen 1953, Paperchromatography 1955, Fortschritt durch Verzicht 1975, Chaos und Ordnung-über die Struktur des Lebendigen 1988, and about 300 papers in maj. journals on biochemistry of nucleic acids, protein-biosynthesis and cellular interaction. *Leisure interests:* painting and literature. *Address:* Max-Planck-Institut für experimentelle Medizin, Abteilung Chemie, Hermann-Rein-Strasse 3, D-3400 Göttingen, Federal Republic of Germany.

CRAMER, Jan ar Mars; Netherlands economist and statistician; b. 26 April 1928, The Hague; s. of P. J. S. Cramer and A. P. van Deventer; m. Mathilde van Gogh 1953; four c.; ed. Univ. of Amsterdam; Cen. Planning Bureau 1953-56, Dept. of Applied Econs., Cambridge 1956-59; CREDOC, Paris 1959-62; Prof. of Econometrics, Univ. of Amsterdam 1962-; Dir. Inst. of Econ. Research 1985-. *Publications:* Empirical Econometrics 1968, Econometric Applications of Maximum Likelihood Methods 1986. *Leisure interests:* reading, gardening. *Address:* Baambrugse Zuwe 194, 3645 AM Vinkeveen, The Netherlands. *Telephone:* (02949) 3060.

CRAMOND, William Alexander, O.B.E., M.D., F.R.C.PSYCH., F.R.A.N.Z.C.P.; British/Australian professor of clinical psychiatry; b. 2 Oct. 1920, Aberdeen; s. of W. J. Cramond and May Battisby; m. Bertine J. C. Mackintosh 1949; one s. one d.; ed. Robert Gordon's Coll. Aberdeen and Univ. of Aberdeen; Physician Superintendent, Woodilee Hosp. Glasgow 1955-61; Dir. of Mental Health, S. Australia 1961-65; Foundation Prof. of Mental Health, Univ. of Adelaide 1963-71; Prin. Medical Officer in Mental Health, Scottish Home and Health Dept. 1971-72; Foundation Dean, Faculty of Medicine, Univ. of Leicester 1972-75; Prin. and Vice-Chancellor, Univ. of Stirling 1975-80; Dir. of Mental Health, Health Comm. N.S.W. 1980-83; Prof. of Clinical Psychiatry, Univ. of Sydney 1980-83, The Flinders Univ. of S. Australia 1983-. *Leisure interests:* reading, theatre. *Address:* 28 Tynte Street, North Adelaide, South Australia 5006. *Telephone:* (08) 2671600.

CRANDALL, Robert Lloyd, B.A.; American business executive; b. 6 Dec. 1935, Westerly, R.I.; s. of Lloyd Evans Crandall and Virginia (née Beard) Crandall; m. Margaret Jan Schmults 1957; two s. one d.; ed. William and Mary Coll., Univ. of Rhode Island, Wharton School, Univ. of Pennsylvania; Dir. of Credit and Collections, then Vice-Pres. Data Services TWA 1967-73; C.O.O. 1973-85 and Sr. Vice-Pres. (Finance), American Airlines 1973-74, Sr. Vice-Pres. Marketing 1974-80, Dir. 1976-, Pres. 1980-85, Chair., CEO Jan. 1985-; Chair., CEO AMR Corpn. Jan. 1985-; Dir. of several cos. *Leisure interests:* skiing, tennis, running, reading. *Address:* c/o American Airlines Inc., P.O. Box 619616, Dallas/Fort Worth Airport, Tex. 75261, U.S.A.

CRANE, Horace Richard, PH.D.; American professor of physics; b. 4 Nov. 1907, Turlock, Calif.; s. of Horace Stephen Crane and Mary Alice Roselle; m. Florence Rhomer LeBaron 1934; one s. one d. (one d. deceased); ed. California Inst. of Tech.; Research Fellow Calif. Inst. of Technology 1934-35; on Faculty of Univ. of Mich. 1935-, Chair. of Dept. of Physics 1965-72, Distinguished Prof. 1972-78, Prof. Emer. 1978-; M.I.T. Radiation Lab. 1940; at Carnegie Inst. of Washington 1941; Henry Russel Lecturer Univ. of Mich.; mem. Standing Cttee. on Controlled Thermonuclear Research, U.S. Atomic Energy Comm. 1969-72; Chair. Bd. of Govs. American Inst. of Physics 1971-75; mem. Comm. on Human Resources 1977-80; mem. Council for Int. Exchange of Scholars 1977-80; Fellow, American Acad. of Arts and Sciences; mem. N.A.S.; Distinguished Service Award of Univ. of Mich. 1957, and of Calif. Inst. of Tech. 1968; Davisson-Germer Prize of American Physical Soc. 1968; Oersted Medal of American Asscn. of Physics Teachers 1976; Nat. Medal of Science 1986. *Publications:* over 150 scientific papers on nuclear physics, accelerators, electronics, biophysics and physics education, including Principles and Problems of Biological Growth (Scientific Monthly Vol. 70), Precision Measurement of

the g-factor of the Free Electron (with D. Wilkinson, The Physical Review Vol. 121) 1961. *Leisure interests:* ham radio, photography, horticulture. *Address:* 830 Avon Road, Ann Arbor, Mich. 48104, U.S.A.

CRANFIELD, Rev. Charles Ernest Burland, M.A., F.B.A.; British professor of theology; b. 13 Sept. 1915, London; s. of Charles Ernest Cranfield and Beatrice Mary Cranfield (née Tubbs); m. Ruth Elizabeth Gertrude Bole 1953; two d.; ed. Mill Hill School, Jesus Coll. Cambridge and Wesley House, Cambridge; research in Basle until outbreak of Second World War; Probationer in Methodist Church 1939; ordained 1941; Minister in Shoeburyness 1940-42; Chaplain to the Forces (from end of hostilities worked with German Prisoners of War, was first staff chaplain to P.O.W. Directorate in War Office) 1942-46; Minister in Cleethorpes 1946-50; admitted to Presbyterian Church of England (now part of United Reformed Church) 1954; Lecturer in Theology, Univ. of Durham 1950-62, Sr. Lecturer 1962-66, Reader 1966-78, Prof. of Theology (personal) 1978-80, Emer. Prof. 1980-; Jt. Gen. Ed., new series of International Critical Commentary 1966-; Hon. D.D. (Aberdeen) 1980. *Publications:* The First Epistle of Peter 1950, The Gospel according to Saint Mark 1959, I and II Peter and Jude 1960, A Critical and Exegetical Commentary on the Epistle to the Romans, Vol. 1 1975, Vol. 2 1979, Romans: a Shorter Commentary 1985, The Bible and Christian Life: a Collection of Essays 1985, If God Be For Us: a Collection of Sermons 1985. *Address:* 30 Western Hill, Durham City, Durham, DH1 4RL, England. *Telephone:* Durham 3843096.

CRANSTON, Alan; American politician; b. 19 June 1914, Palo Alto, Calif.; s. of William McGregor and Carol (née Dixon) Cranston; m. Geneva McMath 1940 (divorced 1977); two s.; m. 2nd Norma Weintraub 1978; ed. Mount View High School, Los Altos, Pomona Coll., Univ. of Mexico, and Stanford Univ.; Int. News Service, England, Germany, Italy, Ethiopia 1937-38; Chief, Foreign Language Div., Office of War Information 1940-44; U.S. Army 1944-45; Nat. Pres. United World Federalists 1949-52; Pres. Calif. Democratic Council 1953-58; Controller of Calif. 1958; re-elected 1962; business career in land investment and home construction; U.S. Senator from Calif. 1969-; Democratic Whip in the Senate 1977-. *Publications:* co-author The Big Story (play) 1940, The Killing of the Peace 1945, and numerous articles in newspapers and periodicals. *Leisure interests:* painting in oils, running. *Address:* 112 Hart Senate Building, Washington, D.C. 20510, U.S.A. (Office).

CRANSTON, Maurice (William), M.A.; British university professor; b. 8 May 1920; s. of William Cranston and Catherine Harris; m. Baroness Maximiliana von und zu Fraunberg 1958; two s.; ed. Univ. of London, St. Catherine's Coll., Oxford; London Civil Defence 1939-45; lecturer (part-time) in Social Philosophy, Univ. of London 1950-59; lecturer and Reader in Political Science, L.S.E. 1959-69, Prof. 1969-85; Visiting Professorships at Harvard Univ. 1965-66, Dartmouth Coll., U.S.A. 1970-71, Univ. of B.C., Canada 1973-74, Univ. of Calif. 1976, 1986-89, Ecole des Hautes Etudes, Paris 1977, Fondation Thiers 1983; Prof. of Political Science, European Univ. Inst. 1978-81; Carlyle Lecturer, Oxford Univ. 1984; Literary Adviser, Methuen Ltd. 1959-69; Vice-Pres. de l'Alliance Française en Angleterre 1964-; Foreign Hon. mem. American Acad. of Arts and Sciences 1970-; Pres. Institut Int. de Philosophie Politique 1976-79; James Tait Black Memorial Prize 1957, Commandeur Ordre des Palmes Académiques, Paris 1987. *Publications:* Freedom 1953, Human Rights Today 1954, John Locke: a Biography 1957, Jean-Paul Sartre 1962, What Are Human Rights? 1963, Western Political Philosophers (Ed.) 1964, A Glossary of Political Terms 1966, Rousseau's Social Contract 1967, Political Dialogues 1968, La quintessence de Sartre 1969, Language and Philosophy 1969, The New Left (Ed.) 1970, Hobbes and Rousseau (Editor with R. S. Peters) 1972, The Mask of Politics 1973, Idéologie et politique (Ed. with P. Mair) 1980, Jean-Jacques: The Early Life and Work of Rousseau 1983, Rousseau's Discourse on Inequality 1984, Philosophers and Pamphleteers 1986. *Leisure interest:* walking. *Address:* 1A Kent Terrace, Regent's Park, London, NW1 4RP, England. *Telephone:* 01-262 2698.

CRAVEN, Dr. Daniël Hartman, M.A., D.PHIL.; South African sports administrator; b. 11 Oct. 1910, Lindley, O.F.S.; s. of James Roos Craven and Maria Susanna Myra Hartman; m. 2nd Martha Jacoba Maria Vermeulen 1975; three s. one d. (by first m.); ed. Univ. of Stellenbosch; teacher St. Andrew's Coll., Grahamstown 1936-38; Dir. Physical Educ. for Defence Force 1938-41; Head Physical Training Branch, S. Africa Mil. Coll. 1941-46; Dir. Physical Training Bn. 1946-47; Prof. and Head, Dept. of Physical Educ., Univ. of Stellenbosch 1947-75, Dir. Sport and Recreation 1976-80, Dir. Sport Inst. 1981-84; played rugby union football for S. Africa, Capt. of Springboks in Tests *v.* British Lions; Selector 1949-56, Asst. Man. Springboks tour 1951, Man. 1956; Pres. S. Africa Rugby Bd.; Decoration for Meritorious Service, S. Africa; Hon. D.Phil. (Stellenbosch) 1979. *Publications:* about 25 books. *Leisure interests:* studying, rugby coaching and administration. *Address:* University of Stellenbosch, Stellenbosch, 7600; 10 Murray Street, Stellenbosch, 7600 Republic of South Africa (Home). *Telephone:* 02231-4163 (Office); 02231-3433 (Home).

CRAWFORD, Bryce, Jr., PH.D.; American professor of chemistry; b. 27 Nov. 1914, New Orleans, La.; s. of Bryce Low Crawford and Clara Hall Crawford; m. Ruth Raney 1940; two s. one d.; ed. Stanford Univ.; Nat. Research Council Fellow, Harvard Univ. 1937-39; Instructor, Yale Univ. 1939-40; Asst. Prof., Univ. of Minn. 1940-43, Assoc. Prof. 1943-46, Prof.

1946–82, Regents' Prof. 1982–85, Prof. Emer. 1985–, Chair. Dept. of Chem. 1955–60, Dean, Graduate School 1960–72; Fulbright Prof., Oxford Univ. 1951, Tokyo Univ. 1966; Ed. Journal of Physical Chem. 1970–80; Chair. Council of Graduate Schools 1962–63; Pres. Assen. of Graduate Schools 1970, Graduate Record Examinations Bd. 1968–72; mem. N.A.S. (Council 1975–78), Home Sec. 1979–; mem. American Acad. of Arts and Sciences 1977; American Chem. Soc. (Bd. of Dirs. 1969–77), Coblentz Soc., American Philosophical Soc.; Fellow, American Physical Soc.; Presidential Certificate of Merit 1946; Guggenheim Fellowships 1950, 1972; Fulbright Professorship 1951, 1966; Minn. Award, American Chem. Soc. 1969, Pittsburgh Spectroscopy Award 1977, Ellis Lippincott Award 1978, Priestley Medal 1982. *Publications:* Articles in scientific journals. *Address:* Dept. of Chemistry, University of Minnesota, 207 Pleasant Street SE, Minneapolis, Minn. 55455 (Office); 1545 Branston, St. Paul, Minn. 55108, U.S.A. (Home). *Telephone:* (612) 625-5394.

CRAWFORD, Michael, O.B.E.; British actor and singer; b. (as Michael Dumble-Smith) 19 Jan. 1942; ed. St. Michael's Coll., Bexley, Oakfield School, Dulwich; actor 1955–; films for Children's Film Foundation; hundreds of radio broadcasts; appeared in original productions of Noyes Fludde and Let's Make an Opera by Benjamin Britten. *Stage Roles include:* Travelling Light 1965, the Anniversary 1966, No Sex Please, We're British 1971, Billy 1974, Same Time, Next Year 1976, Flowers for Algernon 1979, Barnum 1981–83, 1984–86, Phantom of the Opera, London 1986–87, Broadway 1988, Los Angeles 1989. *Films include:* Soap Box Derby 1950, Blow Your Own Trumpet 1954, Two Living One Dead 1962, The War Lover 1963, Two Left Feet 1963, The Knack 1965, A Funny Thing Happened on the Way to the Forum 1966, The Jokers 1966, How I Won the War 1967, Hello Dolly 1969, The Games 1969, Hello Goodbye 1970, Alice's Adventures in Wonderland 1972, Condor Man 1980. *TV appearances include:* Sir Francis Drake (series) 1962, Some Mothers Do 'Ave 'Em (several series), Chalk and Cheese (series), Sorry (play) 1979; Tony Award 1988. *Address:* c/o Duncan Heath Associates Ltd, Paramount House, 162–170 Wardour Street, London, W.1, England. *Telephone:* 01-439 1471.

CRAWFORD, Michael Hewson, M.A., F.B.A.; British university teacher; b. 7 Dec. 1939, Twickenham, Middx.; s. of Brian Hewson Crawford and Margarethe Bettina née Nagel; ed. St. Paul's School, London and Oriel Coll. Oxford; Research Fellow, Christ's Coll. Cambridge 1964–69; Univ. Lecturer, Cambridge 1969–86; Jt. Dir. Excavations of Fregellae 1980–85, Valpolcevera Project 1987–; Visiting Prof. Pavia Univ. 1983, Ecole Normale Supérieure, Paris 1984, Padua Univ. 1986, Sorbonne, Paris 1989; Prof. of Ancient History, Univ. Coll. London 1986–. *Publications:* Roman Republican Coinage 1974, The Roman Republic 1978, La Moneta in Grecia e a Roma 1981, Sources for Ancient History 1983, Coinage and Money under the Roman Republic 1985, L'Impero Romano e la Struttura economica e sociale delle province 1986. *Address:* Department of History, University College London, Gower Street, London, WC1E 6BT, England. *Telephone:* 01-380 7396.

CRAWFORD, William Avery; American diplomatist; b. 14 Jan. 1915, New York; s. of John Raymond and Pauline Avery Crawford; m. 1st Barbara Gardner 1940, two s. three d.; m. 2nd Gudrun Hadell 1980; ed. Haverford Coll., Haverford, Pa., Centro de Estudios Históricos, Madrid, Ecole Libre des Sciences Politiques, Paris, Harvard Coll., Columbia Univ. and Nat. War Coll. Washington, D.C.; Foreign Service 1941–, Havana 1941–44, Dept. of State 1944–45, Moscow 1945–47, Dept. of State 1947–50, Paris 1950–54, Dept. of State 1954–57, Prague 1957–59; Dir. Office of Research and Analysis for Sino-Soviet Bloc, Dept. of State 1959–61; Minister to Romania 1961–64, Amb. 1964–65; Special Asst. for Int. Affairs to Supreme Allied Commdr., Europe, NATO 1965–67; Sr. Foreign Service Insp. 1967–70; Editorial Dir. Scholarly Resources Inc. 1970–73; Dir. WJS, Inc. 1974–83; Dir. Foreign Bondholders Protective Council, Inc. 1975–. *Address:* 4982 Sentinel Drive, Apartment 406, Bethesda, Md. 20816, U.S.A. *Telephone:* (301) 229-3880.

CRAWLEY, Frederick William, F.C.I.B., C.B.I.M.; British banker; b. 10 June 1926, London; m. Ruth E. Jungman 1951; two d.; entered Lloyds Bank 1942, Chief Accountant 1969, Asst. Gen. Man. 1973, Exec. Dir. Lloyds Bank Int. 1975, Asst. Chief Gen. Man. 1977, Deputy Chief Gen. Man. 1978–82, 1983–84, Vice-Chair. and C.E.O. Lloyds Bank Calif. 1982–83, Chief Gen. Man. Lloyds Bank PLC 1984–85, Deputy Group Chief Exec. 1985–87; Chair. Black Horse Agencies Ltd. 1985–88; Dir. Lloyds Bank 1984–88, Lloyds Devt. Capital Ltd. 1987–, FS Assurance Ltd. 1988–, FS Investment Mans. Ltd. 1988–, FS Investment Services Ltd. 1988–, Barratt Devts. Ltd. 1988–, Alliance & Leicester Bldg. Soc. 1988–, Alliance & Leicester Estate Agents Ltd. 1988–; Hon. Treas. R.A.F. Benevolent Fund Ltd. 1988–; Consultant Anglo-Airlines Ltd. 1988–; mem. U.K. Advisory Bd., The MAC Group (U.K.) Ltd. 1988–. *Leisure interests:* aviation, shooting, photography. *Address:* 4 The Hexagon, Fitzroy Park, London, N6 6HR, England. *Telephone:* 01-341 2279.

CRAWSHAW, Ralph, M.D.; American professor of psychiatry; b. 3 July 1921, New York; s. of Ralph and Grace Crawshaw; m. Carol Ann Strang 1948; one s. one d.; ed. Great Neck High School, Sea Cliff High School, Alfred Univ., Middlebury Coll., New York Univ. Coll. of Medicine; Staff Psychiatrist, C.F. Menninger Memorial Hosp., Topeka, Kan. 1954–57; Asst. Chief, V.A. Mental Hygiene Clinic, Topeka, Kan. 1957–60; Lecturer, Dept.

of Child Psychiatry, Univ. of Oregon Medical School 1961–63, Clinical Prof., Dept. of Psychiatry 1976–; Staff Psychiatrist, Community Child Guidance Clinic, Portland, Ore. 1960–63; Clinic Dir., Tualatin Valley Guidance Clinic, Beaverton, Ore. 1961–67; Private Practice, Portland, Ore. 1960–; Lecturer, Portland State Univ. 1964–67; mem. Inst. of Medicine, N.A.S. 1978, American Medical Assen., Nat. Medical Assen., Royal Soc. of Medicine, American Psychiatric Assen., American Psychological Assen., American Medical Writers' Assen., A.A.A.S. *Publications:* Contributing Ed. Western Journal of Medicine and The Pharos; over 80 articles on psychiatry. *Address:* Dept. of Psychiatry, Oregon Health Services Univ., Portland, Ore. 97201; 2525 NW Lovejoy, Portland, Ore. 97210, U.S.A.

CRAXI, Bettino; Italian journalist, writer and politician; b. 24 Feb. 1934, Milan; m. Anna Maria Moncini 1959; one s. one d.; active in Socialist Youth Movement and working on socialist daily and scientific review during 1950s; promoted "autonomist tendency" within Socialist Youth Movement, worked on *Energie nuove* (publ. of autonomist tendency) 1956–; Pres. Nat. Union of Students 1957; mem. Cen. Cttee. of Italian Socialist Party (PSI) 1957; mem. Community Council of Milan 1960–70; Pres. Inst. for Science of Public Admin. 1964; Provincial Sec. Milan Fed. of PSI and mem. PSI Nat. Exec. 1965; mem. Chamber of Deputies 1968–; Deputy Sec. PSI 1970–76; Gen. Sec. Socialist Party of Italy (PSI) 1976–; Vice-Pres. Socialist Int. 1977–; Prime Minister of Italy 1983–87. *Publications:* Socialismo e realtà 1973, Nove lettere da Praga 1973, Socialismo da Santiago a Praga 1976, Costruire il futuro 1977; co-author Inequality in the World 1977 (contributions by Willy Brandt, q.v., Felipe González, q.v., Carlos Andrés Pérez, q.v., Léopold Sédar Senghor, q.v.). *Leisure interests:* Italian history, especially Garibaldi. *Address:* Via del Corso 476, 00186 Rome, Italy.

CREAN, Hon. Frank, B.A., B.COM., A.A.S.A.; Australian accountant and politician; b. 28 Feb. 1916, Hamilton, Victoria; s. of John and Alison Crean; m. Mary Isabella Findlay 1946; three s.; ed. state schools, Melbourne Univ.; Income Tax Assessor for ten years; mem. Victoria Legis. Ass. for Albert Park 1945–47, for Prahan 1949–51; M.P. for Melbourne Ports 1951–77; mem. Fed. Parl. Labor Party Exec. 1956–72; Deputy Leader 1975–76; mem. Privileges Cttee. 1967–77, Joint Cttee. on Defence Forces Retirement Benefits Legislation 1970–72; Treas. 1972–74; Minister for Overseas Trade 1974–75; Deputy Prime Minister July-Nov. 1975; mem. several Parl. dels. abroad; Pres. Victoria Br., Australian Inst. for Int. Affairs 1983–86; Labor Party. *Publication:* Government and Politics (with W. Byrt) 1973. *Leisure interests:* walking, reading. *Address:* 31/27 Queens Road, Melbourne, 3004 Vic., Australia. *Telephone:* 690-1105.

CREAN, Simon, LL.B.; Australian trade union official; b. 26 Feb. 1949, Melbourne; s. of Frank Crean and Mary Crean; m. Carole Lamb 1973; two d.; ed. Middle Park Cen. School, Melbourne High School and Monash Univ.; Research Officer, Federated Storemen and Packers' Union of Australia 1970–74, Asst. Gen. Sec. 1974–79, Gen. Sec. 1979–85; Pres. Australian Council of Trades Unions 1985–; mem. Econ. Planning Advisory Council, Nat. Labor Consultative Council, ILO Gov. Body, Qantas Bd., Transport Industry Advisory Council, Business Educ. Council. *Leisure interest:* tennis. *Address:* Australian Council of Trades Unions House, 6th Floor, 393 Swanston Street, Melbourne, Vic. 3000, Australia. *Telephone:* 663 5266.

CREEDON, John J., LL.M.; American insurance executive; b. 1 Aug. 1924, New York; s. of Bartholomew and Emma Glynn Creedon; ed. New York Univ.; m. 1st Vivian Elser (deceased) 1947, two s. two d.; m. 2nd Diane Ardouin 1983, one s. one d.; with Metropolitan Life Insurance Co. 1942–, Asst. Gen. Counsel 1962–73, Sr. Vice-Pres. and Gen. Counsel 1973–76, Exec. Vice-Pres. 1976–80, Pres. 1980–83, Pres. and C.E.O. 1983–; Dir. numerous other cos.; mem. American Bar Assen., American Law Inst.; fmr. Pres. American Bar Foundation, Assen. Life Insurance Council; numerous other civic activities; Vanderbilt Gold Medal, New York Univ. *Leisure interests:* boating, swimming. *Address:* Metropolitan Life Insurance Company, 1 Madison Avenue, New York, N.Y. 10010, U.S.A.

CREEK, Malcolm Lars, L.V.O., O.B.E.; British diplomatist; b. 2 April 1931, Bradford; s. of Edgar Creek and Lily (Robertshaw) Creek; m. 1st Moira Pattison 1953, one s. one d.; m. 2nd Gillian Bell 1970, one s. two d.; ed. Belle Vue School, Bradford, London Univ.; in army (nat. service) 1950–52; FCO 1953–56; Vice-Consul, Mogadishu and Harar 1956–58; Second Sec., Mexico City 1959–62, Abidjan 1962–64, Santiago 1965–68; First Sec., San José 1968–71, Havana 1971–74, FCO 1974–77, Lima 1981–85; Head of Chancery, Tunis 1978–81; High Commr. in Vanuatu 1985–88; Consul-Gen., Auckland 1988–. *Leisure interests:* cricket, reading. *Address:* British Consulate General, Auckland, New Zealand. *Telephone:* 32-973.

CREELEY, Robert White, M.A.; American writer and professor of English; b. 21 May 1926, Arlington, Mass.; s. of Oscar Slade and Genevieve (Jules) Creeley; m. 1st Ann McKinnon 1946 (divorced 1955), two s. one d.; m. 2nd Bobbie Louise Hall 1957 (divorced 1976), three d.; m. 3rd Penelope Highton 1977, one s. one d.; ed. Univ. of New Mexico and Harvard Univ.; Instructor Black Mountain Coll. 1954–55; Visiting Lecturer Univ. of New Mexico, Albuquerque 1961–62, lecturer in English 1963–66, Visiting Prof. 1968–69, 1978, 1979, 1980; lecturer Univ. of B.C., Vancouver 1962–63; Prof. of English, State Univ. of N.Y., Buffalo 1967–, Gray Prof. of Poetry and Letters 1978–; Visiting Prof., San Francisco State Coll. 1970–71; Bicentennial Chair. of American Studies, Helsinki Univ. 1988–89; Ed. Black Mountain Review 1954–57; American Field Service 1944–45; mem. American Acad., Nat. Inst of Arts and Letters; D. H. Lawrence Fellow 1960, Guggenheim Fellow 1964, 1971; Rockefeller Grantee 1965; Levinson Prize of Poetry Magazine 1960, Blumenthal-Leviton Award of Poetry Magazine 1965, Union League Civic and Arts Foundation Prize, Poetry Magazine 1967, Shelley Memorial Award of Poetry Soc. of America 1981, Nat. Endowment for the Arts Grant in Writing 1982, DAAD Grant 1983, 1987, Leone D'Oro Premio Speciale 1985, Frost Medal, Poetry Soc. of America 1987. *Publications:* Le Fou 1952, The Immoral Proposition 1953, The Kind of Act of 1953, The Gold Diggers 1954, revised edn. 1965, All That is Lovely in Men 1955, If You 1956, The Whip 1957, A Form of Women 1959, For Love, Poems 1950–60 1962, The Island 1963, Words 1967, Numbers 1968, Pieces 1969, The Charm 1969, A Quick Graph 1970, The Finger 1970, St. Martins 1971, A Day Book 1972, Listen 1972, A Sense of Measure 1973, His Idea 1973, Contexts of Poetry 1973, Thirty Things 1974, Backwards 1975, Presences (with Marisol) 1976, Selected Poems 1976, Mabel: A Story 1976, Myself 1977, Hello 1978, Was That a Real Poem and Other Essays 1979, Corn Close 1979, Later 1979, Robert Creeley and Charles Olson: The Complete Correspondence, vols. 1 & 2, 1980, vol. 3 1981, vol. 4 1982, vol. 5 1983, vol. 6 1985, vols. 7 and 8 1987, Mother's Voice 1981, Echoes 1982, Collected Poems 1945–75, 1983, Mirrors 1983, The Collected Prose 1984, Memory Gardens 1986, The Company 1988, Collected Essays 1989; Edited: New American Story (with Donald M. Allen) 1965, The New Writing in the U.S.A. (with Donald M. Allen) 1967, Selected Writings of Charles Olson 1967, Whitman: Selected Poems 1972. *Address:* Clemens 306, State University of New York, Buffalo, N.Y. 14260 (Office). *Telephone:* 716-636-2575 (Office).

CREMER, Fritz; German sculptor; b. 22 Oct. 1906, Arnsberg; ed. Hochschule für bildende Künste, Berlin-Charlottenburg; studied in France, England and Italy 1934–39; master's studio, Prussian Acad. of Arts, Berlin 1938; Mil. service (prisoner-of-war) 1940–46; Prof. of Sculpture, Akad. für angewandte Kunst, Vienna 1946; return to Germany 1950; mem. Deutsche Akad. der Künste, Berlin 1950– (Vice-Pres. 1975); Corresp. mem. Accademia Nazionale di San Luca, Rome 1973; Hon. mem. Acad. of Arts, U.S.S.R. 1967; Art Prize of Freies Deutsches Gewerkschaftsbund 1961; Vaterländischer Verdienstorden in Gold 1965; Johannes R. Becher Medal (Gold) 1968; Nat. Prize (1st Class) 1972; Karl Marx Order (Gold) 1974; Held der Arbeit 1976; Fahnenorden (Hungary). *Address:* Akademie der Künste der Deutschen Demokratischen Republik, 1040 Berlin, Hermann-Matern-Strasse 58/60; 111 Berlin, Woldstrasse 76, German Democratic Republic.

CREMIN, Lawrence Arthur, PH.D.; American professor of education and foundation executive; b. 31 Oct. 1925, New York; s. of Arthur T. Cremin and Theresa B. Cremin; m. Charlotte Raup 1956; one s. one d.; ed. Coll. of the City of New York and Columbia Univ.; Instructor Teachers' Coll., Columbia Univ. 1949–51, Asst. Prof. of Educ. 1951–54, Assoc. Prof. 1954–57, Prof. 1957–, Frederick A.P. Barnard Prof. of Educ. 1961–, Pres. 1974–84; Pres. The Spencer Foundation 1985–; Bancroft Prize in American History 1962; Pulitzer Prize for History 1981. *Publications:* The Transformation of the School: Progressivism in American Education 1876–1957 1961, American Education: The Colonial Experience 1607–1783 1970, American Education: The National Experience 1783–1876 1980, American Education: The Metropolitan Experience, 1876–1980 1988. *Address:* Teachers' College Columbia University, 525 West 120th Street, New York N.Y. 10027; The Spencer Foundation, 875 North Michigan Avenue, Chicago, Ill. 60611; 35 East 85th Street, Box 106, New York, N.Y. 10028, U.S.A. (Home).

CREMONA, The Hon. John Joseph, K.M., LL.D., D.LITT., PH.D., DR.JUR.; Maltese jurist, historian and writer; b. 6 Jan. 1918, Gozo; s. of Dr. Antonio Cremona and Anne Camilleri; m. Beatrice Barbaro Marchioness of St. George 1949; one s. two d.; ed. Malta, Rome, London, Cambridge and Trieste Univs.; Crown Counsel 1947; Lecturer in Constitutional Law, Royal Univ. of Malta 1947–65; Attorney Gen. 1957–64; Prof. of Criminal Law, Univ. of Malta 1959–65; Prof. Emer. 1965–; Pres. of Council 1972–75; Crown Advocate-Gen. 1964–65; Vice Pres. Constitutional Court and Court of Appeal 1965–71; Judge, European Court of Human Rights 1965–, Vice-Pres. 1986–; Pro-Chancellor, Univ. of Malta 1971; Chief Justice of Malta, Pres. the Constitutional Court, the Court of Appeal and the Court of Criminal Appeal 1971–81; mem. UN Cttee. on Elimination of Racial Discrimination 1984–, Chair. 1986–; Judge, European Tribunal in Matters of State Immunity 1986–, Vice-Pres. 1987–; fmr. Acting Gov.-Gen., Acting Pres. of Malta; Chair. Human Rights Section, World Asscn. of Lawyers; Vice-Pres. Int. Inst. of Studies Documentation and Information for the Protection of the Environment 1980–; mem. Editorial Bd. several human rights journals in Europe and America; Fellow, Royal Historical Soc.; Hon. Fellow, L.S.E.; Hon. mem. Real Academia de Jurisprudencia y Legislación (Madrid); Kt. of Magisterial Grace, Sovereign Mil. Order of Malta; Commdr. Order of Merit (Italy); Kt. Grand Cross, Constantine St. George; Kt. Order of St. Gregory the Great; Kt. Most Venerable Order of St. John of Jerusalem. *Publications include:* The Treatment of Young Offenders in Malta 1956, The Malta Constitution of 1835 1959, The Legal Consequences of a Conviction in the Criminal Law of Malta 1962, The Constitutional Development of Malta 1963, From the Declaration of Rights to Independence 1965, Human Rights Documentation in Malta 1966; two volumes of poetry; articles in French, Italian, German and American law reviews.

Address: Villa Barbaro, Main Street, Attard, Malta, G.C. *Telephone:* 440818.

CRÉPEAU, Michel Edouard Jean; French lawyer and politician; b. 30 Oct. 1930, Fontenay-le-Comte; s. of Edouard Crépeau and Marcelle Pastureau; m. 1st Pierrette Perès 1955 (divorced), two s. and d.; m. 2nd Annie Meunier 1986; ed. Lycée Pierre-Loti, Rochefort-sur-Mer, Univ. of Bordeaux; Lawyer, La Rochelle 1955–; Gen. Councillor of Charente-Maritime 1967, re-elected 1973; Town Councillor and Mayor of La Rochelle 1971–; Pres. Poitou-Charente section, Mouvement des radicaux de gauche (MRG) 1971–, Nat. Vice-Pres. MRG 1976–78, Pres. 1978–81; Deputy (Charente-Maritime) to Nat. Ass. 1973–81, 1986–; MRG cand. in first round of presidential election April 1981; Minister of the Environment May 1981–83, of Commerce 1983–84, of Commerce, Crafts and Tourism 1984–86, of Justice 1986. *Leisure interest:* sailing. *Address:* Assemblée nationale, 75355 Paris, France (Home).

CREPEAU, Paul-André, O.C., Q.C., L.PH., LL.L., B.C.L.; Canadian professor of law; b. 20 May 1926, Gravelbourg, Sask,; s. of J. B Crepeau and Blanche Provencher; m. Nicole Thomas 1959; two s. one d.; ed. Univs. of Montreal, Ottawa, Oxford and Paris; Pres. Civil Code Revision Office 1965–77; Wainwright Prof. of Civil Law 1976–; Dir. Inst. of Comparative Law, McGill Univ. 1975–84; Dir. Quebec Research Centre of Private and Company Law 1975–; Chevalier de L'Ordre du Mérite (France); D.en D. h.c. (Ottawa) 1971, (York) 1984 and other awards and prizes. *Publications:* La responsabilité civile du médécin et de l'établissement hospitalier 1956, Rapport sur le Code civil 1978, Code civil, Edition historique et critique 1966–1980 1981. *Leisure interests:* reading, gardening. *Address:* Quebec Research Centre of Private and Comparitive Law, 3647 Peel Street, Montreal, Que. H3A 1X1 (Office); 5 Place du Vesinet, Montreal, Que. H2V 2L6, Canada, (Home). *Telephone:* 392-8024, 392-8004 (Office); 272-5941 (Home).

CRÉPIN, Général d'Armée Jean-Albert-Emile; French army officer; b. 1 Sept. 1908, Bernaville; s. of Albert and Jeanne (née Petit) Crépin; m. Simone Granday 1948 (deceased); two d.; ed. Ecole Polytechnique; served China, Cameroun 1933–39; with Free French Army 1940–44, served Chad, Fezzan, Tunisia, France, Germany; served Indo-China 1945; attached to 8th Infantry Div., Paris 1951; Insp.-Gen. of Works and Planning for the Armed Forces 1954–60; Général de Corps d'Armée, Algeria 1959; Commdr. Forces in Algeria 1960–61; Général d'Armée, C-in-C. French Forces in Germany 1961–63; C.-in-C. Allied Forces, Cen. Europe 1963–66; Pres. Nord-Aviation 1967–69; Pres. Euromissile 1972–75; Vice-Pres. Société Nationale Industrielle Aérospatiale (SNIAS) 1970–73, Counsellor for Mil. Affairs 1974–75; Grand Croix, Légion d'honneur, Compagnon de la Libération, Croix de guerre (1939–45), Croix de la Valeur militaire, Officer Legion of Merit, Grand Cross Order of Merit (Fed. Repub. of Germany), Hon. D.S.O. *Address:* 85 rue Dutot, 75015 Paris, France.

CRESPIN, Régine; French soprano; b. 23 Feb. 1927, Marseilles; d. of Henri and Marguerite (née Meirone) Crespin; m. Lou Bruder 1962; ed. Conservatoire Nat. d'Art Dramatique; Singer, Opéra, Paris 1951–; has sung in prin. concert houses, Europe and America; singing teacher, Higher Nat. Conservatory of Music 1976–; Chevalier, Légion d'honneur, Chevalier, Ordre national du Mérite, Commdr. Arts et Lettres. *Address:* c/o Michel Glotz, 141 boulevard Saint-Michel, 75005 Paris, France.

CRESSON, Edith; French politician; b. 27 Jan. 1934, Boulogne-sur-Seine; d. of Gabriel and Jacqueline Campion; m. Jacques Cresson 1959; two d.; Nat. Sec. Parti Socialiste; Youth Organizer, Parti Socialiste 1975; Mayor, Thuré 1977, Chatellerault 1983–; mem. European Parl. 1979; Minister of Agric. 1981–83, of Foreign Trade and Tourism 1983–84, of Industrial Redeployment and Foreign Trade 1984–86, of European Affairs May 1988–; Pres. L'Association démocratique des français de l'étranger 1986; mem. Nat. Ass. for Vienne 1986–88. *Publication:* Avec le soleil 1976. *Address:* Assemblée nationale, 75355 Paris, France.

CRESSWELL, Christopher Frederick, PH.D., F.R.S.S.A.; South African academic; b. 27 March 1933, Johannesburg; s. of Edward Coates Cresswell and Margaret Elizabeth (née Heard) Cresswell; m. Evelyn May Miller 1965; two s. one d.; ed. Rhodes Univ. and Bristol Univ.; jr. lecturer, Rhodes Univ. 1956–57; tutor, Wills Hall, Univ. of Bristol 1958–60; jr. lecturer, Dept. of Botany, Kings Coll., London 1961–63, lecturer 1963; Sr. Lecturer, Dept. of Botany, Univ. of Witwatersrand, Johannesburg 1963–65, Prof. and Head. of Dept. 1965–88, Dean of Science 1982–88; Deputy Vice-Chancellor and Vice-Prin. Univ. of Natal 1988–; Sir Percy Fitzpatrick Scholarship, Boots Research Scholarship; Recipient Claude Harris Leon Foundation Award. *Publications:* 124 scientific publs. on Inorganic Nitrogen Metabolism and Photosynthesis. *Leisure interests:* music, sailing, reading biographies. *Address:* University of Natal, King George V Avenue, Durban 4001 (Office); 222 South Ridge Road, Glenwood, Durban 4001, South Africa (Home).

CRETNEY, Stephen Michael, M.A., D.C.L., F.B.A.; British professor of law; b. 25 Feb. 1936, Witney, Oxon.; s. of Fred Cretney and Winifred Cretney; m. Antonia L. Vanrenen 1973; two s.; ed. Manchester Warehousemen and Clerks' Orphan Schools, Cheadle Hulme and Magdalen Coll., Oxford; Partner, Macfarlanes (Solicitors), London 1964–65; Lecturer, Kenya School of Law, Nairobi 1966–67, Southampton Univ. 1968–69; Fellow and Tutor in Law, Exeter Coll., Oxford 1969–78; mem. Law Comm. for England and

Wales 1978-83; Prof. of Law (Dean of Faculty 1984-88), Univ. of Bristol 1984-. *Publications:* Principles of Family Law (4th edition) 1984, Elements of Family Law 1987. *Address:* University of Bristol, Faculty of Law, Wills Memorial Building, Queen's Road, Bristol, BS8 1RJ (Office); 15 Canynge Square, Bristol, BS8 3LA, England (Home). *Telephone:* 0272-303030, 0272-303371 (Office); 0272-732983 (Home).

CREUTZ, Edward Chester, PH.D.; American physicist and consultant; b. 23 Jan. 1913, Beaver Dam, Wis.; s. of Lester Raymond Creutz and Grace Smith; m. 1st Lela Marie Rollefson 1937; m. 2nd Elisabeth Butler Cordle 1974; two s. one d.; ed. Univ. of Wisconsin; Instructor in Physics, Princeton Univ. 1939-42; Group Leader Manhattan Project 1942-46; Assoc. Prof. Carnegie Inst. of Tech. 1946-48, Prof. Physics and Head Dept. 1948-55; Vice-Pres. Research and Devt. Gen. Atomic Corpn. 1955-70; Asst. Dir. Research Nat. Science Foundation 1970-77; Dir. Bishop Museum, Honolulu 1977-84, Hon. Consultant 1984-; mem. N.A.S. *Publications:* Resonance Absorption of Neutrons in Uranium, Proton Scattering, Artificial Radioactivity, Flow of Gases through Porous Media, Fabrication of Uranium and Beryllium. *Leisure interests:* orchid growing, computer programming, radio-controlled model boats. *Address:* P.O. Box 2757, Rancho Santa Fe, Calif. 92067 U.S.A. *Telephone:* (619) 756-4980.

CREWE, Albert Victor, PH.D.; American physicist and professor; b. 18 Feb. 1927, Bradford, England; s. of Wilfred and Edith Fish (née Lawrence) Crewe; m. Doreen Crewe; one s. three d.; ed. Liverpool Univ.; Asst. Lecturer, Liverpool Univ. 1950-52, lecturer 1952-55; Research Assoc. Chicago Univ. 1955-56, Asst. Prof. of Physics 1956-59, Assoc. Prof. 1959-63; Dir. Particle Accelerator Div., Argonne Nat. Lab. 1958-61, Dir. 1961-67; Prof. Dept. of Physics and Biophysics Enrico Fermi Inst. 1963-, Univ. of Chicago 1963-71, Dean, Physical Sciences Div. 1971-81, William E. Wrather Distinguished Service Prof. 1977; Pres. Orchid One Corp. 1987-; constructed England's first diffusion cloud chamber with Dr. W. H. Evans at Liverpool Univ.; directed construction of large magnetic spectrometer for Chicago Univ.'s synchrocyclotron; consultant Sweden, Argentina; directed much of design and construction of Argonne's Zero Gradient Synchrotron; as Dir. Argonne Nat. Lab., developed relationships with U.S. Atomic Energy Comm., Argonne Univ. and Chicago Univ., expressed in Tripartite Agreement; invented the scanning transmission electron microscope; obtained first atom images 1971; Fellow, American Physical Soc., American Nuclear Soc.; mem. N.A.S., American Acad. of Arts and Sciences, Scientific Research Soc. for America, Electron Microscopy Soc. of America, Chicago Area Research and Devt. Council (Chair. 1964), Gov.'s Science Advisory Cttee. for State of Ill.; Hon. Fellow, Royal Microscopical Soc. 1984; Immigrant's Service League's Annual Award for Outstanding Achievement in the Field of Science 1962; "Industrial Research Man of the Year 1970"; Michelson Medal (Franklin Inst.) 1978; Ernst Abbe Award New York Microscope Soc. 1979; Duddell Medal, Inst. of Physics, U.K. 1980. *Leisure interests:* sculpture, photography. *Address:* Enrico Fermi Institute, 5640 Ellis Avenue, Chicago, Ill. 60637 (Office); 63 Old Creek Road, Palos Park, Ill. 60464, U.S.A. (Home).

CRICHTON, Sir Andrew James Maitland-Makgill-, Kt., F.R.S.A., F.C.I.T.; British shipping executive; b. 28 Dec. 1910, Bryn Garth, Hereford; s. of Lieut.-Col. D. M.-M.-Crichton and Phyllis née Cuthbert; m. Isabel McGill 1948; ed. Wellington Coll.; Man. Dir. P. & O. S. N. Co. 1957-69, Dir. 1970-81; Dir. Gen. Steam Navigation Co. Ltd. 1958-68; Chair. Port Employers and Registered Dock Workers Pension Fund Trustees Ltd. 1961-69, Nat. Asscn. of Port Employers and Jt. Chair. Nat. Council for Port Transport Industry 1958-65, E. Higgs (Air Agency) Ltd. 1963, investigation on the Post Office on behalf of N.E.D.C. 1965; Vice-Chair. British Transport Docks Bd. 1963-67, Port of London Authority (P.L.A.) 1967-76; Dir. British United Airways Ltd. 1962-68, British India Steam Navigation Co. Ltd. 1961-68; mem. Civil Service Arbitration Tribunal 1963-69, Nat. Freight Corpn. 1968-73, Council, Chamber of Shipping in U.K. 1958-, Industrial Court 1964; Chair. Overseas Containers Ltd. 1965-73; Vice-Pres. Inst. of Transport; mem. Police Council for G.B. 1966-75, Arbitrator 1975-79; mem. Court of the Chartered Bank 1970. *Leisure interests:* golf, collecting paintings, music. *Address:* 55 Hans Place, Knightsbridge, London, S.W.1; The Old Bakery, Yoxford, Suffolk, England. *Telephone:* 01-584 1209 (London); Yoxford 426.

CRICHTON-BROWN, Sir Robert, K.C.M.G., C.B.E., T.D.; Australian business executive; b. 23 Aug. 1919, Melbourne; s. of L. Crichton-Brown; m. Norah I. Turnbull 1941; one s. one d.; ed. Sydney Grammar School; Man. Dir. Security and Gen. Insurance Co., Ltd. 1952-; Chair. Security Life Assurances Ltd. 1961-85, NEI Pacific Ltd. 1961-85, Edward Lumley Ltd. (Group), Australia 1974- (Man. Dir. 1952-82), The Commercial Banking Co. of Sydney Ltd. 1976-82, Commercial and General Acceptance Ltd. 1977-82, Westham Dredging Co. Pty. Ltd. 1975-85, Rothmans of Pall Mall (Australia) Ltd. 1981-85; Vice-Chair. Nat. Australia Bank Ltd. 1982-85, Custom Credit Corpn. Ltd. 1982-85; Dir. Daily Mail & General Trust Ltd. (U.K.) 1979-; Exec. Chair. Rothmans Int. PLC 1985-88; Underwriting mem. Lloyd's 1946-; Dir. Royal Prince Alfred Hosp. 1970-84; Fed. Pres. Inst. of Dirs. in Australia 1967-80; Fed. Hon. Treas. Liberal Party of Australia 1973-85; Nat. Co-ordinator, Duke of Edinburgh's Award Scheme in Australia 1980-85; mem. or official of numerous professional and charitable orgs. in Australia; mem. Australia's winning Admiral's Cup Team

(Balandra) 1967; winner, Sydney-Hobart Yacht Race (Pacha) 1970. *Leisure interest:* sailing. *Address:* 15 Hill Street, London, W1X 7FB, England.

CRICK, Francis Harry Compton, PH.D., F.R.S.; British biologist; b. 8 June 1916; ed. Univ. Coll., London, and Cambridge Univ.; Scientist, Admiralty, Second World War; Medical Research Council (M.R.C.) Student, Strangeways Lab. Cambridge 1947-49: M.R.C. Lab. of Molecular Biology, Cambridge 1949-76; Kieckhefer Distinguished Research Prof., The Salk Inst., La Jolla, Calif. 1977-; Adjunct Prof. of Psychology and Chem., Univ. of Calif.; Fellow, Churchill Coll., Cambridge 1960-61, Hon. Fellow 1965; Fellow Univ. Coll., London 1962, A.A.A.S.; Hon. Fellow, Caius Coll., Cambridge 1976; Fellow, Indian Nat. Science Acad. 1982; Foreign Assoc. N.A.S. 1969; Assoc. Académie Française 1978; mem. German Acad. of Science 1969; Foreign mem. American Phil. Soc., Philadelphia 1972; Foreign Hon. mem. American Acad. of Arts and Sciences 1962, American Soc. Biological Chem. 1963, Hellenic Biochem. and Biophysics Soc. 1974; Hon. MRIA 1964; Hon. F.R.S.E. 1966; Nobel Prize for Medicine (with J. D. Watson and M. H. F. Wilkins) 1962; Royal Medal, Royal Soc. 1972; Copley Medal, Royal Soc. 1975, Michelson-Morley Award, Cleveland, U.S.A. 1981; numerous national lectures and other awards. *Publications:* numerous papers and articles on molecular and cell biology and on neurobiology; Of Molecules and Men 1967, Life Itself 1981, What Mad Pursuit 1988. *Address:* The Salk Institute for Biological Studies, P.O. Box 85800, San Diego, Calif. 92138 (Office); 1792 Colgate Circle, La Jolla, Calif. 92037, U.S.A. (Home).

CRICK, Ronald Pitts, F.R.C.S., F.R.S.M.; British ophthalmic surgeon; b. 5 Feb. 1917, Toronto, Canada; s. of Owen John Pitts Crick and Margaret Daw; m. Jocelyn Mary Grenfell Robins 1941; four s. one d.; ed. Latymer Upper School, London, King's Coll. Hosp. Medical School, London; surgeon, Merchant Navy 1939-40; Surgeon-Lieut., R.N.V.R. 1940-46; Ophthalmic Registrar, King's Coll. Hosp., London 1946-48; Surgical First Asst., Royal Eye Hosp., London 1947-50, Surgeon 1950-69; Ophthalmic Surgeon, Belgrave Hosp. for Children 1950-66; Consultant Ophthalmic Surgeon, King's Coll. Hosp 1950-82, Hon Consultant 1982; Recognized Teacher in Ophthalmology, Univ. of London 1960-82; Lecturer Emer., School of Medicine and Dentistry, King's Coll. 1982-; Chair. Ophthalmic Training Cttee., S.E. Thames Regional Health Authority 1973-82; Vice-Pres. Ophthalmology Section, Royal Soc. of Medicine 1964; Charter mem. Int. Glaucoma Congress of American Soc. of Contemporary Ophthalmology 1977-; Chair. Int. Glaucoma Asscn. 1974; Visiting Research Fellow Sussex Univ. 1976; Open Science Scholarship, King's Coll. Hosp. Medical School 1934; Sir Stewart Duke-Elder Glaucoma Award 1985. *Publications:* All About Glaucoma (with W. Leydhecker) 1981, A Text Book of Clinical Ophthalmology (with R. Trimble) 1987, Computerised Monitoring of Glaucoma, in Glaucoma: Contemporary International Concepts (Ed. Bellont) 1979; numerous articles in ophthalmic journals. *Leisure interests:* natural history, motoring, sailing, designing ophthalmic instruments. *Address:* King's College Hospital, Denmark Hill, London, SE5 9RS (Office); 6 Dartford Road, Sevenoaks, Kent, TN13; Sandbanks House, 2 Panorama Road, Sandbanks, Poole, Dorset BH13 7RD, England. *Telephone:* 01-274 6222 (Office); (0732) 452233 (Sevenoaks); (0202) 707560 (Sandbanks).

CRICKHOWELL, Baron (Life Peer) cr. 1987, of Port Esgob in the Black Mountains and County of Powys, **(Roger) Nicholas Edwards,** P.C., M.A., M.P.; British politician; b. 25 Feb. 1934; s. of late Ralph Edwards and of Marjorie Edwards (née Brooke); m. Ankaret Healing 1963; one s. two d.; ed. Westminster School, Trinity Coll., Cambridge; mem. Lloyd's 1965-; fmr. Dir. P.A. Int. and Sturge Underwriting Agency Ltd.; M.P. for Pembroke 1970-87; Opposition Spokesman on Welsh Affairs 1975-79; Sec. of State for Wales May 1979-87; Dir. HTV 1987-; Chair. Nat. River Authority Advisory Cttee. 1988-; Conservative. *Leisure interests:* gardening, fishing. *Address:* House of Lords, Westminster, London, S.W.1, England.

CRISTIANI, Alfredo; Salvadorean businessman and politician; b. c 1948; m. Margarita Cristiani; ed. Georgetown Univ., Washington, D.C., U.S.A.; fmr. exec. in family pharmaceutical, coffee and cotton businesses; Leader, Republican Nationalist Alliance (ARENA) 1985-; mem. Nat. Assembly 1988-; Pres. designate of El Salvador 1989 (takes office June 1989). *Address:* Alianza Republicana Nacionalista, San Salvador, El Salvador.

CRISTOFINI, Charles; French civil servant; b. 16 July 1913, Garlin; s. of Louis and Marie (Costeig) Cristofini; m. Solange Demerliac 1939; two d.; with Ministry of Finance 1938-48, Air Ministry 1948; Staff Dir. to M. Bourgès-Maunory 1950-52; Dir. Financial Dept. and Programmes, Ministry of Nat. Defence and Armed Forces 1952-55; Asst. Sec.-Gen. Western European Union 1955-59; founded Soc. pour l'étude et la réalisation d'engins balistiques (SEREB) 1959, Pres., Man. Dir. until 1969; Pres., Dir.-Gen. Soc. européenne d'études et d'intégration de systèmes spatiaux 1967-72; Man. Dir. Symphonie satellite consortium 1970-73; Pres., Dir.-Gen. Soc. girondine d'entretien et de réparation de matériels aéronautiques 1971-73; Dir.-Gen. Soc. nat. industrielle aérospatiale (SNIAS) 1973, Pres. 1974-75; Pres., Dir.-Gen. Groupement des industries de la mer et des activités sous-marines (Gimer) 1973-83; Commdr., Légion d'honneur. *Address:* 15 rue Tournefort, 75005 Paris, France. *Telephone:* 40.49.06.27.

CRISTOL, Stanley Jerome, PH.D.; American professor of chemistry; b. 14 June 1916, Chicago, Ill.; s. of Myer J. and Lillian (Young) Cristol; m. Barbara Wright Swingle 1957; one s. one d.; ed. Northwestern Univ. and Univ. of California, Los Angeles; Asst. in Chem., Univ. of Calif. at Los Angeles (UCLA) 1937-38, 1941-42; Research Chemist, Standard Oil Co. of Calif. 1938-41; Instructor, UCLA 1942-43; Post-doctoral Fellow, Univ. of Ill. 1943-44; Research Chemist, Bureau of Entomology and Plant Quarantine U.S. Dept. of Agric. 1944-46; Univ. of Colo., Asst. Prof. 1946-49, Assoc. Prof. 1949-55, Prof. 1955-, Chair. Dept. of Chem. 1960-62, Joseph Sewall Distinguished Prof. of Chem. 1979-, Dean, Graduate School 1980-81; mem. N.A.S., American Chem. Soc.; Guggenheim Fellow 1955-56, 1981-82; Fellow, A.A.A.S. (Councillor 1986-92), Chem. Soc., London; Robert L. Stearns Award 1971; James Flack Norris Award of the American Chemical Soc. 1972; Colo. Univ. Medal 1984. *Publications:* Organic Chemistry 1966 (with L. O. Smith, Jr.), numerous articles in scientific journals. *Leisure interests:* skiing, fishing. *Address:* Department of Chemistry, University of Colorado, Boulder, Colo. 80309 (Office); 2918 Third Street, Boulder, Colo. 80302, U.S.A. (Home). *Telephone:* (303) 492-6661 (Office); (303) 443-1781 (Home).

CRITCHLEY, Thomas Kingston, A.O., C.B.E., B.EC.; Australian diplomatist; b. 1916, Melbourne; s. of the late G. L. Critchley; m. Susan Cappel 1962; four d.; ed. North Sydney Boys' High School and Sydney Univ.; Asst. Econ. Adviser, Dept. of War Org. of Industry 1943-44; Head, Research Section, Far Eastern Bureau, New Delhi, British Ministry of Information 1944-46; Head, Econ. Relations Section, Dept. of External Affairs, Canberra 1946-47; Australian Rep. UN Cttee. of Good Offices on Indonesian Question 1948-49; Rep. UN Comm. for Indonesia 1949-50; Acting Australian Commr. Malaya 1951-52; Rep. UN Comm. for Unification and Rehabilitation of Korea (UNCURK) 1952-54; Head, Pacific and Americas Branch, Dept. of External Affairs, Canberra 1954-55; Commr. Fed. of Malaya 1955-57, High Commr. 1957-63, High Commr. in Malaysia 1963-65; Senior External Affairs Rep., Australian High Comm., London 1966-69; Amb. to Thailand 1969-74; High Commr. of Papua New Guinea 1974-75; Australian High Commr. in Papua New Guinea 1975-78; Amb. to Indonesia 1978-81; Consultant on S.E. Asia and Papua New Guinea 1981-; mem. Council of Australian Nat. Gallery 1982-86. *Publication:* Australia Foots the Bill (jointly) 1941. *Leisure interests:* golf, tennis. *Address:* 11 Walker Street, North Sydney, N.S.W. 2060, Australia. *Telephone:* (02) 922 1137.

CROCKER, Chester Arthur, PH.D.; American government official; b. 29 Oct. 1941; s. of Arthur and Clare Crocker; m. Saone Baron 1965; three d.; ed. Ohio State Univ., Johns Hopkins Univ.; editorial asst. Africa Report 1965-66, News Ed. 1968-69; lecturer American Univ. 1969-70; staff officer Nat. Security Council 1970-72; with Foreign Service Programme, Georgetown Univ. 1972-78; Dir. African Studies 1976-81; Asst. Sec. of State for African Affairs 1981-89; Chair. African working group, Reagan Campaign 1980. *Publications:* South Africa Defense Posture 1981, numerous articles. *Address:* c/o Bureau of African Affairs, Department of State, Washington, D.C. 20520, U.S.A.

CROCKER, Sir Walter Russell, K.B.E.; Australian diplomatist; b. 25 March 1902, Broken Hill; s. of Robert Crocker and Alma Bray; m. Claire Ward 1951 (dissolved 1968); two s.; ed. Balliol Coll., Oxford, Univ. of Adelaide, Australia, and Stanford Univ., California; with British Colonial Service 1930-34, L.N. and I.L.O. 1934-40; served army 1940-46; with U.N. 1946-50; Prof. of Int. Relations, Australian Nat. Univ. 1950-52, Acting Vice-Chancellor 1951; High Commr. for Australia in India 1952-55; Amb. to Indonesia 1955-57; High Commr. in Canada 1957-59; High Commr. in India 1959-62 and Amb. to Nepal 1960-62, to the Netherlands and Belgium 1962-65, to Ethiopia and High Commr. to Kenya and to Uganda 1965-67, to Italy 1967-70; Lieut.-Gov. of S. Australia 1973-82; Croix de guerre, Officer of the Lion (Belgium), Kt. Grand Cross of Italy, Grande Uff. Merito Melitense, Order of Malta. *Publications:* The Japanese Population Problem 1931, Nigeria: Critique of Colonial Administration 1936, On Governing Colonies 1946, Self-Government for Colonies 1949, Can the U.N. Succeed? 1951, The Racial Factor in International Relations 1955, Nehru 1966, Australian Ambassador 1971, Memoirs 1981, Sir Thomas Playford 1983. *Leisure interests:* gardening, music. *Address:* 256 East Terrace, Adelaide, South Australia 5000, Australia.

CROHAM, Baron (Life Peer), cr. 1978, of the London Borough of Croydon; **Douglas Albert Vivian Allen,** G.C.B.; British civil servant; b. 15 Dec. 1917, Surrey; s. of Albert Allen and Elsie Maria (née Davies); m. Sybil Eileen Allegro 1941; two s. one d.; ed. Wallington County Grammar School and London School of Econs.; Asst. Principal, Bd. of Trade 1939; served Royal Artillery 1940-45; Principal, Bd. of Trade 1945, Cabinet Office 1947, Treasury 1948; Asst. Sec., Treasury 1949-58; Under-Sec., Ministry of Health 1958-60, Treasury 1960-62; Third Sec., Treasury 1962-64; Deputy Under-Sec. of State, Dept. of Econ. Affairs 1964-66, Second Perm. Under-Sec. of State 1966; Perm. Under-Sec. of State, Dept of Econ. Affairs 1966-68; Perm. Sec., Treasury 1968-74; Head Home Civil Service, Perm. Sec. Civil Service Dept. 1974-77; Chair. Econ. Policy Cttee., OECD 1972-77, Deputy Chair. BNOC 1978-82, Chair. 1982-86; Adviser to Gov., Bank of England 1978-83; Dir. (non-exec.) Pilkington PLC 1978-; Trustee,

Anglo-German Foundation 1977-, Chair. 1982-; Pres. Inst. of Fiscal Studies 1978-; Chair. Inst. of Man. Econ. and Social Affairs Cttee. 1982-85, Trinity Insurance 1988-; Dir. (non-exec.) Guinness Peat Group 1983-87, Chair. Oct. 1983-86. *Leisure interests:* tennis, woodwork. *Address:* 9 Manor Way, South Croydon, Surrey, England (Home). *Telephone:* 01-688 0496 (Home).

CROISSIER, Luis Carlos; Spanish politician; b. 1950, Arucas, Las Palmas; m.; two s.; ed. Complutense Univ. of Madrid, Sorbonne, Paris; mem. Socialist Party (PSOE) 1974-; Sec.-Gen. Socialist Group of Majadahonda; Deputy Dir.-Gen. Office for Budgeting in Industry, Rep. of Ministry of Industry in Cttee. for Elaboration of Plan for Public Investments and in Inter-Ministerial Comm. for Rationalisation and Decentralisation of Public Expenditure 1980; Deputy Sec., Ministry of Industry 1982-84; then Pres. of Instituto Nacional de Industria (INI); Minister for Industry and Energy 1986-88. *Address:* c/o Ministerio de Industria y Energía, Paseo de la Castellana 160, Madrid 16, Spain.

CROMBIE, Hon. David Edward, B.A.(ECON.); Canadian politician and teacher; b. 24 April 1936, Toronto; s. of Norman M. Crombie and Vera Beamish; m. Shirley Bowden 1960; one s. two d.; ed. Earlhaig Collegiate, Willowdale, Ont., Univs. of Western Ontario and Toronto; lecturer, Ryerson Polytechnic Inst. 1962-71, Dir. of Student Services 1966-71; City Alderman, Toronto 1969; Mayor of Toronto 1972-78; mem. House of Commons 1978-; Spokesperson for Pres. Treasury Bd., then Minister of National Health and Welfare 1979-80, of Indian Affairs and Northern Devt. 1984-86, of Multiculturalism 1986-87, Sec. of State of Canada 1987-88; Head Royal Comm. on Devt. of Fed. Lands 1988-; cand. leader Fed. Progressive Conservative Party 1983; Commr. Toronto Hydro 1973-78. *Leisure interests;* handball, jogging, cross country skiing, swimming, golf, reading. *Address:* 81 Glencairn Avenue, Toronto, Ont., Canada.

CROMBIE, Leslie, C.CHEM., PH.D., D.SC., F.R.S.C., F.R.S.; British organic chemist; b. 10 June 1923, York; s. of Walter Leslie Crombie and Gladys May (née Clarkson) Crombie; m. Winifred Mary Lovell Wood 1953; two s. two d.; ed. Portsmouth Municipal Coll., King's Coll., London; Scientist Admiralty Chem. Lab., Portsmouth Naval Dockyard 1941-46; Lecturer Imperial Coll., London 1950-58; Reader in Organic Chem., King's Coll., London 1958-63; Prof. of Organic Chem., Univ. Coll., Cardiff 1963-69; Sir Jesse Boot Prof. of Organic Chem., Univ. of Nottingham 1969-88, Emer. Prof. 1988-, Dean of Science 1980-83; Fellow King's Coll., London 1978; Pres. Chemical Soc. Perkin Div. 1976-79, British Asscn., Section B; Vice-Chair. Phytochemical Soc. of Europe 1984-86, 1988-, Chair. 1986-88; mem. Jt. Chem. Educ. Cttee. 1981-82 (Chair. 1983-87), SERC Chem. Cttee. 1970-75, Enzyme Cttee. 1973-75, Univ. Grants Physical Science Sub-Cttee. 1978-85, Royal Soc. Educ. Cttee. 1983- (Chair. 1984-); Tilden Lecturer 1970, Simonsen Lecturer 1975, Hugo Muller Lecturer 1977, Pedler Lecturer 1982; Council mem. Chem. Soc. 1962-64, 1972-81; mem. Royal Inst. of Chem. 1975-78, Royal Soc. 1984-86; Royal Soc. of Chem. Natural Products Chem. Award 1980; Flintoff Medal 1984; Hon. Fellow Portsmouth Polytechnic 1983. *Publications:* numerous scientific papers. *Leisure interest:* gardening. *Address:* 153 Hillside Road, Bramcote, Beeston, Nottingham, England. *Telephone:* (0602) 259412.

CROMER, 3rd Earl of; George Rowland Stanley Baring, K.G., G.C.M.G., M.B.E., P.C.; British merchant banker and financial administrator; b. 28 July 1918; ed. Eton Coll., and Trinity Coll., Cambridge; served with Grenadier Guards, rising to rank of Lt. Col. 1939-46; Man. Dir. Baring Brothers and Co. Ltd. 1947-58, 1967-70, Adviser 1974-; Econ. Minister and Head of U.K. Treasury Del., Washington, U.K. Exec. Dir. IMF, IBRD, Int. Finance Corpn. 1959-61; Gov. Bank of England 1961-66; U.K. Gov., IBRD, Int. Finance Corpn., Int. Devt. Asscn. 1963-66; Partner Baring Brothers and Co. Ltd.; Dir. Union Carbide Corpn. 1967-71; Chair. IBM (U.K.) Ltd. 1967-71, 1974-79, Dir. IBM World Trade Corpn. 1977-83, mem. IBM European Advisory Council 1974-; Chair. Int. Advisory Council, Morgan Guaranty Trust Co. 1978-88; Int. Consultant Marsh and McLennan Cos. Inc.; Amb. to U.S.A. 1971-74; mem. Bd. Cie. Financière de Suez, Paris 1974-82; Dir. Shell Transport and Trading Co. 1974-, Barfield Trust Co., Guernsey 1979-; mem. Bd. P. & O. Steam Navigation Co. 1974-80, Daily Mail and General Trust Ltd., Supervisory Bd. ROBECO Group; Hon. LL.D. (New York) 1966. *Address:* Beaufield House, St. Saviour, Jersey. *Telephone:* (0534) 61671.

CRONE, Christian, M.D., SC.D.; Danish professor of physiology; b. 1 Feb. 1926, Copenhagen; s. of F. L. Crone and Betty Bredsdorff; m. Monna Nyeborg 1949; one s. three d.; ed. Univ. of Copenhagen, Univ. of Cambridge, England; Lieut. Royal Danish Navy 1952; Internship, Copenhagen City Hospitals 1953-56; Research Assoc., Dept. of Physiology, Univ. of Copenhagen 1957-66, Prof. of Physiology 1967-; Chair. Int. Comm. for Micro-circulation 1977-86, Nat. Comm. for Physiology 1977-88; Vice-Pres. Int. Union of Physiological Sciences (IUPS) 1983-; mem. Royal Danish Acad. of Sciences 1968-, Hon. Sec. 1980-85; mem. Bd. of Dirs. Carlsberg Foundation 1971-80; Visiting Prof., Faculty of Medicine, Paris 1984-85; Christian Bohr Award, Copenhagen 1963, Zweifach Int. Award, U.S.A. 1979, Novo Prize, Denmark 1983, Lucian Prof., McGill Univ., Montreal 1982; Malpighi Award 1986; Fernstrom Research Award (Lund Univ.) 1986. *Publications:* Diffusion of Organic Nonelectrolytes from Blood to Brain 1961, Capillary Permeability 1970, History of Capillary Physiology

1974, American Handbook of Physiology (Contrib.) 1984; numerous articles on capillary physiology and the blood-brain barrier. *Leisure interest:* music (active flautist). *Address:* Toldbodgade 79, 1253 Copenhagen K, Denmark. *Telephone:* (01) 143020.

CRONIN, Prof. James Watson, PH.D.; American professor of physics; b. 29 Sept. 1931, Chicago, Ill.; s. of James Farley Cronin and Dorothy Watson Cronin; m. Annette Martin 1954; one s. two d.; ed. Southern Methodist Univ., Dallas, Univ. of Chicago; Nat. Science Foundation Fellow 1952–55; Assoc. Brookhaven Nat. Lab. 1955–58; Asst. Prof. of Physics, Princeton Univ. 1958–62, Assoc. Prof. 1962–64, Prof. 1964–71; Prof. of Physics, Univ. of Chicago 1971–; Loeb Lecturer in Physics, Harvard Univ. 1976; mem. N.A.S., American Acad. of Arts and Sciences, American Physical Soc.; Research Corpn. Award 1968; Ernest O. Lawrence Award 1977; John Price Wetherill Medal, Franklin Inst. 1975; shared Nobel Prize for Physics 1980 with Prof. Val Fitch (q.v.) for work on elementary particles. *Publications:* numerous articles on physics. *Address:* Enrico Fermi Institute, University of Chicago, 5630 South Ellis Avenue, Chicago, Ill. 60637 (Office); 5825 South Dorchester Street, Chicago, Ill. 60637, U.S.A. *Telephone:* (312) 962 7102 (Office).

CRONKHITE, Leonard Wolsey, Jr., M.D.; American physician and research foundation executive; b. 4 May 1919, Newton, Mass.; s. of Leonard W. Cronkhite and Orpah G. (Brewster) Cronkhite; m. 1st Joan Dunn 1955 (divorced), 2nd Linda M. Marchky 1976; four d.; ed. Bowdoin Coll. and Harvard Univ.; army service 1940–45; Gen. Dir. Children's Hospital Medical Center, Boston 1962–71, Exec. Vice-Pres. 1971–73, Pres. 1973–77; Pres. Medical Coll. of Wisconsin, Milwaukee 1977–84; Pres. Medical Coll. of Wis. Research Foundation 1984–88; Bowdoin Prize 1973; Hon. LL.D. (Northeastern) 1970, (Bowdoin) 1979; Hon. L.H.D. (Curry Coll.) 1977. *Publications:* articles on medicine and medical educ. in professional journals. *Address:* 1935 River Park Court, Wauwatosa, Wis. 53226, U.S.A. (Home). *Telephone:* (414) 774-1590 (Home).

CRONKITE, Eugene Pitcher, M.D.; American physician; b. 11 Dec. 1914, Los Angeles; s. of Anita P. Cronkite and Clarence E. Cronkite; m. Elizabeth E. Kaitschuk 1940; one d.; ed. Univ. of California at Los Angeles and Stanford Univ. Medical School; Medical Officer U.S.N. 1942–54; Head of Haematology, Naval Medical Research Inst., Bethesda, Md. 1946–54; Head of Experimental Haematology, Medical Dept., Brookhaven Nat. Lab., Upton, New York 1954–67, Chair. Medical Dept. 1967–79, Chair. Emer. and Sr. Scientist 1979–; Prof. of Medicine, State Univ. of New York, Stony Brook 1969–; Medical Corps, U.S.N.R. (retd. as Rear Adm.) 1954–74; Ed. Experimental Hematology 1985–; mem. N.A.S.; Dr. Med. h.c. (Ulm) 1987; Sir Henry Wellcome Prize, Alfred Benzon Award (Denmark), L. Heilmeyer Gold Medal (Fed. Repub. of Germany), Semmelweis Medal (Hungary), Alexander von Humboldt Award (Fed. Repub. of W. Germany), DeVilliers Award (Leukemia Soc. of U.S.A.) 1989. *Publications:* over 400 publs. on radiation biology, leukaemia, cell proliferation, effects of radiation on humans. *Leisure interests:* tennis, photography and fishing. *Address:* Medical Department, Brookhaven National Laboratory, Upton, N.Y. 11973, U.S.A.

CRONKITE, Walter Leland, Jr.; American television correspondent; b. 4 Nov. 1916, St. Joseph, Missouri; s. of the late W. L. Cronkite and of Helene Fritsche; m. Mary Elizabeth Maxwell 1940; one s. two d.; ed. Univ. of Texas; News writer and Editor, Scripps-Howard & United Press, Houston, Kansas City, Dallas, Austin, El Paso and New York; United Press War Corresp. 1942–45, later Foreign Corresp., Chief Corresp. Nuremberg War Crimes Trials, Bureau Man., Moscow 1946–48; lecturer 1948–49; CBS, news corresp. 1950–81; Anchorman and Man. Ed., CBS Evening News with Walter Cronkite 1962–81, CBS News Special Corresp. 1981–, mem. Bd. of Dirs. CBS Inc.; several hon. degrees; Emmy Award (several times), Acad. TV Arts and Sciences 1970, George Polk Journalism Award 1971, Jefferson Award 1981, Presidential Medal of Freedom 1981, and other awards. *Publications:* Challenges of Change 1971; co-author South by Southeast 1983. *Leisure interest:* yachting. *Address:* c/o CBS News, 524 West 57th Street, New York, New York 10019, U.S.A.

CRONYN, Hume; Canadian actor and director; b. 18 July 1911, London, Ont.; s. of Hume Blake and Frances A. (née Labatt) Cronyn; m. Jessica Tandy 1942; one s. two d.; ed. Ridley Coll., St. Catharines, Ont., McGill Univ., New York School of Theatre, Mozarteum, Salzburg, and American Acad. of Dramatic Art, New York; after amateur experience with an acting group in Montreal, joined Cochran's Stock Co., Wash., D.C.; professional début in Up Pops the Devil 1931; made first film, Shadow of a Doubt 1943; dir. several Actor's Lab. productions 1946–57; staged (with Norman Lloyd) and co-starred in Phoenix Theatre's production Madam Will You Walk 1953; staged successful production of The Fourposter 1952, on tour 1951–53; inaugurated NBC radio series The Marriage 1953; has appeared in several films including Cleopatra 1963, Cocoon 1985, Batteries Not Included 1987, and numerous plays and has toured extensively with his productions; has appeared in all major U.S. TV drama series; mem. Bd. Dirs. Stratford Festival (first actor) 1978; nominated for Acad. Award for performance in The Seventh Cross 1944; Comoedia Matinee Club's Award for The Fourposter 1952, American Theatre Wings' Antoinette Perry Play Award (The Fourposter) 1952, Barter Theatre Award 1961, Delia Austria Medal, New York Drama League (Big Fish Little Fish)

1961, Antoinette Perry (Tony) Award and won Variety New York Drama Critics Poll for Polonius (Hamlet) 1964, Herald Theater Award for Tobias (A Delicate Balance), L.A. Drama Critics Circle Award for best actor (Caine Mutiny Court Martial) 1972, 1972–73 Obie Award (Krapp's Last Tape), Brandeis Univ. Creative Arts Awards for distinguished achievement 1978, L.A. Critics' Award (Gin Game) 1979, elected to American Hall of Fame 1979, Kennedy Center Honor 1986; Hon. LL.D. (Univ. of Western Ont.) 1974.

CROSBIE, John Carnell, B.A., B.L., M.P.; Canadian politician; b. 30 Jan. 1931, St. John's, Newfoundland; m. Jane Furneaux; three c.; ed. St. Andrew's Coll., Aurora, Ont., Queen's Univ., Ont., Dalhousie Law School, Univ. of London, L.S.E.; called to Newfoundland Bar 1957; Prov. Minister of Municipal Affairs and Housing 1966, mem. Newfoundland House of Ass. 1966, 1971–76; Minister of Finance, Econ. Devt., Fisheries, Inter-Govt. Affairs, Mines and Energy and Pres. of the Treasury Bd., Leader of House of Ass. 1975; mem. House of Commons 1976–; Minister of Finance 1979; Minister of Justice and Attorney Gen. of Canada 1984–86, of Transport 1986–89 , of Int. Trade Jan. 1989–; fmr. Chair. of Caucus Cttee. on Energy, Caucus spokesperson for Finance, External Affairs, Industry, Trade and Commerce; f. Newfoundland and Labrador Housing Corpn.; Progressive Conservative Party. *Address:* P.O. Box 9192, Station B, St. John's, Newfoundland, A1A 2X9; Place Bell Canada, 160 Elgin Street, Ottawa, Ont. K1A 0G5, Canada.

CROSBY, John Campbell; American writer; b. 18 May 1912, Milwaukee, Wis.; s. of Frederick and Edna (née Campbell) Crosby; m. 1st Mary B. Wolferth 1946 (divorced), one s. one d.; m. 2nd Katherine Blachford Wood 1964, one s. one d.; ed. Exeter, Yale Univ.; Reporter Milwaukee Sentinel 1933, New York Herald Tribune 1935–41, syndicated columnist 1946–65; U.S. Army 1941–46; columnist Observer, London 1965–75; John Crosby TV Programme (New York); Peabody Award, Newspaper Guild Award, George Polk Award. *Publications:* Out of the Blue 1952, With Love and Loathing 1963, Sappho in Absence 1970, The Literary Obsession 1973, The White Telephone 1974, An Affair of Strangers 1975, Nightfall 1976, The Company of Friends 1977, Dear Judgment 1978, The Party of the Year 1979, Penelope Now 1981, Men in Arms 1983, Take No Prisoners 1985, The Family Worth 1987, Wingwalker 1989. *Leisure interests:* reading, movies, farming. *Address:* Esmont, Va. 22937, U.S.A.

CROSS, Barry Albert, C.B.E., M.A., PH.D., F.R.C.V., F.INST.BIOL., F.R.S.; British anatomist and physiologist; b. 17 March 1925; s. of Hubert Charles Cross and Elsie May Cross; m. Audrey Lilian Crow 1949; one s. two d.; ed. Reigate Grammar School, Royal Veterinary Coll., London, St. John's Coll., Cambridge; ICI Research Fellow, Physiological Lab., Cambridge 1949–51; Demonstrator, Zoological Lab., Cambridge 1951–55, Lecturer 1955–58; Lecturer, Dept. of Anatomy, Cambridge 1958–67; Supervisor in Physiology, St. John's Coll. 1955–67; Prof. and Head of Dept. of Anatomy, Univ. of Bristol 1967–74, Chair. School of Preclinical Studies 1969–73; Dir. Inst. of Animal Physiology, Cambridge 1974–86, Inst. of Animal Physiology and Genetics, Cambridge and Edin. 1986–89; Fellow, Corpus Christi Coll., Cambridge 1962–67, 1974–, Pres. 1987–; Warden of Leckhampton 1975–80 (Pres. 1985–86, 1986–); mem. of Council Bristol Univ. Anatomical Soc. 1968–73 (Vice-Pres. 1973–74), Asscn. for the Study of Animal Behaviour 1959–62, 1973–75, Zoological Soc. of London 1985–; mem. of Cttee. Soc. for the Study of Fertility 1961–65, Physiological Soc. 1971–75 (Chair. 1974–75), Int. Soc. for Neuroendocrinology 1972–75, Pres. 1976–80), Inst. of Zoology 1982–, Council of Zoological Soc. of London 1986–; Chevalier Order of Dannebrog (Denmark) 1968, Commdr. d'honneur de l'Ordre du Bontemps de Médoc et des Graves 1973. *Publications:* numerous scientific papers. *Address:* 6 Babraham Road, Cambridge, England.

CROSS, G(eorge) L(ynn), M.S., PH.D.; American university president and professor; b. 12 May 1905, Woonsocket, S. Dakota; s. of George Washington Cross and Jemima Jane Dawson; m. Cleo Sikkink 1926; two s. one d.; ed. South Dakota Coll., and Univ. of Chicago.; Instructor Bacteriology, S. Dakota State Coll. 1927–28; Head Botany Dept., Univ. of S. Dakota 1930–34; Prof. of Botany, Univ. of Okla. 1934–38, Head of Botany Dept. 1938–42, Act. Dean Graduate Coll. 1942–44, Act. Dir. Research Inst. 1942–44, Pres. of the Univ. 1944–68; Chair. Bd. American Exchange Bank, Norman, Okla. 1964–86; Pres. Okla. Health Sciences Foundation 1968–78; mem. of many learned socs. *Publications:* The World of Ideas, Blacks in White Colleges: Oklahoma's Landmark Cases, The University of Oklahoma and World War II, Professors, Presidents and Politicians: Civil Rights at the University of Oklahoma 1890–1968, Presidents Can't Punt, Letters to Bill, The Seeds of Excellence The University of Oklahoma Research Inst. 1941–73; 50 papers in tech. journals. *Leisure interests:* golf, art, music, writing. *Address:* 812 Mockingbird Lane, Norman, Okla. 73071, U.S.A. *Telephone:* 405-321-4527.

CROSS, K. Patricia, A.M., PH.D.; American academic; b. 17 March 1926, Normal, Ill.; d. of Clarence L. and Katherine Dague Cross; ed. Illinois State Univ. and Univ. of Illinois; Asst. Dean of Women, Univ. of Ill. 1953–59; Dean of Students, Cornell Univ. 1959–63; research scientist, Educational Testing Service and Research Educator, Univ. of Calif. 1963–80; Sr. Lecturer on Higher Educ., Harvard Graduate School of Educ. 1980–, Chair. Dept. of Admin., Planning and Social Policy 1985–; Regents Medal of Excellence, New York; Distinguished Alumni Award, Ill. State

Univ. *Publications:* Beyond the Open Door: New Students to Higher Education 1971, Accents on Learning: Improving Instruction and Reshaping the Curriculum 1976, Adults as Learners 1981, and other works on education. *Address:* 406 Gutman Library, Harvard Graduate School of Education, Appian Way, Cambridge, Mass. 02138 (Office); 12 Hawthorne Park, Cambridge, Mass. 02138, U.S.A. (Home). *Telephone:* 617-495-3575 (Office); 617-491-3118 (Home).

CROSS OF CHELSEA, Baron (Life Peer), cr. 1971; **Geoffrey Cross**, P.C.; British judge (retd.); b. 1 Dec. 1904, Chelsea, London; s. of Arthur G. Cross and Mary E. Dalton; m. Joan Eardley Wilmot 1952; one d.; ed. Westminster School and Trinity Coll., Cambridge; Fellow, Trinity Coll., Cambridge 1927; called to the Bar 1930; K.C. 1949; Judge, Chancery Div., The High Court 1960–69; Lord Justice of Appeal 1969–71; Lord of Appeal in Ordinary 1971–75; Chair. Appeal Cttee. of City Take-over Panel 1976–81. *Publications:* Epirus 1932, The English Legal System (with G. R. Y. Radcliffe). *Address:* The Bridge House, Leintwardine, Craven Arms, Shropshire, England.

CROSSLAND, Bernard, C.B.E., D.SC., M.R.I.A., F.ENG., F.R.S.; British professor of mechanical engineering; b. 20 Oct. 1923, Sydenham; s. of Reginald F. and Kathleen M. (née Rudduck) Crossland; m. Audrey E. Birks 1946; two d.; ed. Simon Langton Grammar School, Derby Tech. Coll. and Nottingham Univ. Coll.; eng. apprentice, Rolls-Royce, Derby 1940–41, Tech. Asst. 1943–45; Asst. lecturer, lecturer, Sr. lecturer in Mech. Eng., Univ. of Bristol 1946–59; Prof. and Head, Dept. of Mechanical and Industrial Eng., Queen's Univ., Belfast 1959–82, Dean, Faculty of Eng. 1964–67, Pro-Vice-Chancellor 1978–82, Special Research Prof. 1982–84, Emer. Prof. 1984–; Consulting Eng. 1984–; Chair, N. Ireland Manpower Council 1981–86; Pres. Inst. of Mechanical Engineers 1986–87, Past Pres. 1987–; mem. Industrial Devt. Bd. for N. Ireland 1982–87, N. Ireland Econ. Council 1981–85; mem. Agricultural and Food Research Council 1981–87, Engineering Council; Assessor to King's Cross Underground Fire Investigation; George Stephenson Research Prize and Thomas Hawksley Gold Medal of Inst. of Mech. Eng.; Hon. mem. A.S.M.E.; Hon. D.Sc. (Aston) 1988. *Publications:* An Introduction to Mechanics of Machines 1964, Explosive Welding of Metals 1982; numerous papers on high-pressure eng. and explosive welding in int. journals. *Leisure interests:* walking, reading, travel. *Address:* The Queen's University, Belfast BT7 1NN; (Office); 16 Malone Court, Belfast, BT9 6PA, Northern Ireland. *Telephone:* (0232) 247303 (Office); (0232) 667495 (Home).

CROSSLAND, Sir Leonard, Kt.; British motor executive and farmer; b. 2 March 1914; s. of Joseph and Frances Crossland; m. 1st Rhona Griffin 1941; m. 2nd Joan Brewer 1963; two d.; ed. Penistone Grammar School; Purchase Dept. Ford Motor Co. Ltd. 1937–39; Royal Army Service Corps 1939–45; Purchase Dept., Ford Motor Co. Ltd. 1945–54, Chief Buyer, Tractor and Implement Dept. 1954–57, Chief Buyer, Car and Truck Dept. 1957–59, Asst. Purchase Man. 1959–60, Purchase Man. 1960–62, Exec. Dir. 1962–68, Supply and Services 1962–66, Dir. Mfg. Staff and Services 1966, Asst. Man. Dir. 1966–67, Man. Dir. June-Dec. 1967, Deputy Chair. Jan.-May 1968, Chair. May 1968–72; farmer 1974–; mem. Bd. Eaton Corpn., U.S.A. 1974–81; Chair. Eaton Ltd. U.K., Energy Research and Devt. Ltd. *Leisure interests:* fishing, shooting, golf. *Address:* Abbotts Hall, Great Wigborough, Colchester, Essex, England. *Telephone:* Peldon 456.

CROUZET, François Marie-Joseph, DR. ÉS L.; French professor of history; b. 20 Oct. 1922, Monts-sur-Guesnes; s. of Maurice Crouzet; m. Françoise J. T. Dabert-Hauser 1947; two s. one d.; ed. Lycée Hoche, Versailles, Ecole Normale Supérieure, Sorbonne, London School of Economics; Research Fellow, Centre Nat. de la Recherche Scientifique 1946–49; Asst. Lecturer, Sorbonne 1949–56; Reader in History, Univ. of Bordeaux 1956–58; Prof. of History, Univ. of Lille 1958–64, Univ. of Paris-Nanterre 1964–69, Univ. of Paris-Sorbonne 1969–; Corresp. Fellow British Acad., Royal Historical Soc.; mem. Franco-British Council, French Section; Hon. D.Lit. (Birmingham); Hon. C.B.E. *Publications:* l'Economie du Commonwealth 1950, l'Economie britannique et le Blocus continental 1958, 1988, Capital Formation in the Industrial Revolution 1972, Le Conflit de Chypre 1973, l'Economie de la Grande-Bretagne victorienne 1978, Britain and France: Ten Centuries (Ed. with F. Bedarida and D. Johnson) 1980, The First Industrialists 1985, De la supériorité de l'Angleterre sur la France 1985 and numerous articles on the history and economic history of Britain. *Leisure interests:* gardening, junk hunting. *Address:* Université de Paris-Sorbonne, 1 rue Victor-Cousin, 75230 Paris Cedex 05 (Office); 6 rue Benjamin Godard, 75116 Paris, France (Home). *Telephone:* 40.46.25.13 (Office); 4553-7803 (Home).

CROW, James F(ranklin), PH.D.; American geneticist; b. 18 Jan. 1916, Phoenixville, Pa.; s. of H. E. Crow and Lena Whitaker Crow; m. Ann Crockett 1941; one s. two d.; ed. Friends Univ. (Wichita, Kan.) and Univ. of Texas; Instructor and Asst. Prof. Dartmouth Coll. 1941–48; Asst. Prof., Assoc. Prof., Prof., Dept. of Genetics, Univ. of Wis., 1948–, Chair. of Dept. 1959–63, 1965–72, 1975–77; Acting Dean, Medical School, Univ. of Wis. 1963–65; mem. N.A.S.; Pres. Genetics Soc. of America 1959, American Soc. of Human Genetics 1967. *Publications:* Genetics Notes (8th edn.) 1982; various tech. articles on genetics; Introduction to Population Genetics Theory 1970, Basic Concepts in Population, Quantitative and Evolutionary Genetics 1986. *Leisure interest:* orchestral and chamber music. *Address:*

Department of Medical Genetics, University of Wisconsin, Madison, Wis. 53706; 24 Glenway, Madison, Wis. 53706, U.S.A. (Home). *Telephone:* 608-263-4438 (Office); 608-233-6709 (Home).

CROW, John W., B.A.; Canadian banker; b. 1937, London, England; s. of John Cornell Crow and Mary Winifred Weetch; m. Ruth Kent 1963; one s. one d.; ed. Oxford Univ.; Econ. IMF 1961–70; Chief N. American IMF 1970–73; Deputy Chief Research Dept. Bank of Canada 1973, Chief Dept. 1974, Adviser 1979–81, Deputy Gov. 1981–84, Sr. Deputy Gov. 1984–87, Gov. 1987–. *Leisure interests:* reading and gardening. *Address:* Bank of Canada, 234 Wellington Street, Ottawa, Ont., K1A 0G9, Canada. *Telephone:* (613) 782-8111.

CROWE, Sir Colin Tradescant, G.C.M.G.; British diplomatist (retd.); b. 7 Sept. 1913, Yokohama, Japan; s. of Sir Edward Crowe, K.C.M.G.; m. Bettina Lum 1938; ed. Stowe School and Oriel Coll., Oxford; served Embassy Peking 1936–38, 1950–53, Shanghai 1939–40, Washington 1940–45; mem. U.K. Del. to OEEC Paris 1948; served Tel-Aviv Legation 1949–50, Imperial Defence Coll. 1957; Chargé d'Affaires Cairo 1959–61; Deputy Perm. Rep. to UN 1961–63; Amb. to Saudi Arabia 1963–64; Chief of Admin., Diplomatic Service 1965–68; High Commr. in Canada 1968–70; Perm. Rep. to UN 1970–73; Supernumerary Fellow, St. Antony's Coll., Oxford 1964–65; Chair. Marshall Aid Commemoration Comm. 1973–85, Council Cheltenham Ladies Coll. 1974–86; Vice-Chair. Council, Univ. Coll. London 1974–85; Dir. Grindlays Bank Ltd. 1976–84. *Leisure interests:* bird watching, gardening. *Address:* Pigeon House, Bibury, Glos., England.

CROWE, Adm. William James, Jr., PH.D.; American naval officer; b. 2 Jan. 1925, La Grange, Ky.; s. of William J. Crowe and Eula Russell; m. Shirley M. Grennell 1954; two s. one d.; ed. U.S. Naval Acad., and Stanford and Princeton Univs.; commissioned ensign, U.S. Navy 1946; Commanding Officer U.S.S. Trout 1960–62; Commdr. Submarine Div. 31, San Diego 1966–67; Sr. Adviser, Vietnamese Navy Riverine Force 1970–71; Deputy to Pres.'s Special Rep. for Micronesian Status Negotiations 1971–73; Dir. E. Asia and Pacific Region, Office of Sec. of Defense, Washington until 1976; Commdr. Middle East Force, Bahrain 1976–77; Deputy Chief of Naval Operations, Dept. of Navy, Washington 1977–80; C.-in-C. Allied Forces, Southern Europe 1980–83; C.-in-C. Pacific 1983–85; Chair. Joint Chiefs of Staff 1985–; D.S.M., D.D.S.M., Legion of Merit, Bronze Star, Air medal with six oak leaf clusters. *Address:* The Pentagon, Washington, D.C. 20301, U.S.A.

CROWSON, Richard Borman, C.M.G., M.A., F.C.I.S.; British diplomatist; b. 23 July 1929, Gainsborough; s. of late Clarence B. Crowson and Cecilia M. (Ramsden) Crowson; m. 1st Sylvia Cavalier 1960 (dissolved 1974), 2nd Judith E. Turner 1983; one s. one d.; ed. Downing Coll. Cambridge; Overseas Civil Service Uganda 1955–62; FCO 1962–63; First Sec. Tokyo 1963–68; Deputy High Commr. Bridgetown, Barbados 1968–70; FCO 1970–74; Counsellor, Djakarta 1975–77, Washington, D.C. 1977–82, Berne 1983–85; High Commr. in Mauritius 1985–, also Amb. to the Comoros 1986–. *Leisure interests:* music, drama, travel. *Address:* c/o Foreign and Commonwealth Office, London, S.W.1; Westminster House, Floreal, Mauritius. *Telephone:* 865795 (Office); 865872 (Home).

CROZIER, Brian Rossiter; British writer and journalist; b. 4 Aug. 1918; s. of R. H. and Elsa (McGillivray) Crozier; m. Mary Lillian Samuel 1940; one s. three d.; ed. Lycée, Montpellier, Peterborough Coll., Harrow, Trinity Coll. of Music, London; music and art critic, London 1936–39; reporter and sub-ed., Stoke-on-Trent, Stockport, London 1940–41; aeronautical inspection 1941–43; sub-ed., Reuters 1943–44, News Chronicle 1944–48, sub-ed. and writer Sydney Morning Herald, Australia 1948–51; corresp., Reuters-AAP 1951–52; features ed., Straits Times, Singapore 1952–53; leader writer and corresp., The Economist 1954–64; BBC commentator, English, French and Spanish overseas services 1954–66; Chair. Forum World Features 1965–74; Ed., Conflict Studies 1970–75; Co-founder and Dir. Inst. for the Study of Conflict 1970–79, Consultant 1979–; Columnist, Now!, London 1980–81, Nat. Review, New York 1978–, The Times 1982–84. *Publications:* The Rebels 1960, The Morning After 1963, Neo-Colonialism 1964, South-East Asia in Turmoil 1965, The Struggle for the Third World 1966, Franco 1967, The Masters of Power 1969, The Future of Communist Power (in U.S.A.: Since Stalin) 1970, De Gaulle (vol. I) 1973, (vol. II) 1974, A Theory of Conflict 1974, The Man Who Lost China (Chiang Kai-shek) 1977, Strategy of Survival 1978, The Minimum State 1979, Franco: Crepúsculo de un hombre 1980, The Price of Peace 1980, Socialism Explained (co-author) 1984, This War Called Peace (co-author) 1984, The Andropov Deception (novel) (under pseudonym John Rossiter) 1984, The Grenada Documents, 1987, Socialism: Dream and Reality 1987, and contributions to journals in numerous countries. *Leisure interests:* taping stereo, piano, SX-70 photography. *Address:* Kulm House, Dollis Avenue, Finchley, London, N3 1DA, England (Home).

CRUICKSHANK, Durward William John, M.A., C.CHEM., SC.D., F.R.S.C., F.R.S.; British professor of chemistry; b. 7 March 1924; s. of William Durward Cruickshank and Margaret Ombler (née Meek) Cruickshank; m. Marjorie Alice Travis 1953 (died 1983); one s. one d.; ed.St. Lawrence Coll., Ramsgate, Loughborough Coll., Univ. of Cambridge, Univ. of Leeds; Eng. Asst. War Office and Admiralty 1944–46; Research Asst. Chemistry Dept., Leeds Univ. 1946–47, Lecturer 1950–57, Reader in Math. Chemistry 1957–62;

Joseph Black Prof. of Chem., Glasgow Univ. 1962–67; Prof. of Chem. UMIST 1967–83, Deputy Prin. 1971–72; Treas. Int. Union of Crystallography 1966–72, Gen. Sec. 1970–72; Chem. Soc. Award for Structural Chem. 1978; Fellow St. John's Coll., Cambridge 1953–56, Hon. Professorial Research Fellow UMIST 1983–. *Publications:* numerous scientific papers. *Leisure interests:* golf, genealogy. *Address:* Chemistry Department, University of Manchester Institute of Science and Technology, Manchester, M60 1QD (Office); 105 Moss Lane, Alderley Edge, Cheshire, SK9 7HW, England (Home). *Telephone:* 061-236 3311 (Office); (0625) 582656 (Home).

CRUMB, George, B.M., M.M., D.M.A.; American composer; b. 24 Oct. 1929, Charleston, W. Va.; s. of George Henry and Vivian Reed; m. Elizabeth Brown 1949; two s. one d.; ed. Mason Coll. of Music, Univ. of Illinois, Univ. of Michigan, Hochschule für Musik (Berlin); Prof., Univ. of Colorado 1959–63; Creative Assoc., State Univ. of New York at Buffalo 1963–64; Prof., Univ. of Pa., Annenberg Prof. 1983; Koussevitsky Int. Recording Award 1971; Pulitzer Prize for Music 1968. *Publications:* Ancient Voices of Children, Black Angels, Eleven Echoes of Autumn, 1965, Songs, Drones and Refrains of Death, Makrokosmos Vols. I-III, Music for a Summer Evening, Five Pieces for Piano, Night of the Four Moons, Night Music I, Echoes of Time and the River, Four Nocturnes, Star-child, Dream Sequence, Celestial Mechanics, Apparition, A Little Suite for Christmas 1979, Gnomic Variations, Pastoral Drone, Processional, A Haunted Landscape, The Sleeper, An Idyll for the Misbegotten, Federico's Little Songs for Children. *Leisure interest:* reading. *Address:* 240 Kirk Lane, Media, Pa. 19063, U.S.A. *Telephone:* (215) 565-2438.

CRUMPTON, Michael Joseph, PH.D., F.R.S.; British biochemist and immunologist; b. 7 June 1929; s. of Charles E. Crumpton and Edith Crumpton; m. Janet Elizabeth Dean 1960; one s. two d.; ed. Poole Grammar School, Univ. Coll., Southampton and Lister Inst. of Preventive Medicine, London; joined scientific staff Microbiological Research Establishment, Porton, Wilts. 1955–58; Visiting Scientist Fellowship, Nat. Insts. of Health, Bethesda, Md., U.S.A. 1959–60; Research Fellow, Dept. of Immunology, St. Mary's Hosp. Medical School, London 1960–66; mem. scientific staff Nat. Inst. for Medical Research, Mill Hill 1966–79, Head of Biochemistry Div. 1977–79; Deputy Dir. of Research, Imperial Cancer Research Fund Labs., London 1979–; Visiting Fellow, John Curtin School for Medical Research, Australian Nat. Univ., Canberra 1973–74; mem. Cell Bd. MRC 1979–83, Science Council, Celltech Ltd. 1980–, Council Royal Inst. 1986– (Chair. Davy Faraday Comm. 1987–), MRC 1986–; Biochemistry Soc. Visiting Lecturer, Australia 1983. *Publications:* numerous scientific papers. *Leisure interests:* gardening, reading. *Address:* 33 Homefield Road, Radlett, Herts., WD7 8PX, England. *Telephone:* (092 76) 4675.

CRUZ, Ivo; Portuguese composer and conductor; b. 1901, Corumba, Brazil; s. of Manuel Pereira da Cruz and Palmira Machado da Cruz; m. Maria Adelaide Soares Cardoso 1931; three s. one d.; ed. Univs. of Lisbon and Munich; has conducted in Austria, France, Germany, Switzerland, Spain, Holland, Belgium, Eire, Romania, Brazil and Portugal; his compositions have been played in Europe, N. America, Brazil, New Zealand, N. Africa and the Repub. of S. Africa; founder and Pres. Nat. Union of Musicians; Dir. Conservatoire Nat. de Lisbonne 1938–71; Head of the Lisbon Philharmonic Orchestra, of the Duarte Lobo Choral Soc., Pres. Pro Arte; Commdr. Order of St. Jacques; Knight Order of Alfonso el Sabio (Spain), Silver Medal (City of Lisbon) 1981, Nat. Order, Cruzeiro do Sul (Brazil) 1982. *Compositions include:* Sinfonia de Amadis, Sinfonia de Queluz, Homenagens a Falla and Pastoral (ballet), Aguarelas, Homenagens, Suite and Caleidoscopio, for piano; songs include Les amours du poète, Ballades lunatiques, Chansons perdues, Chansons profanes, Chansons sentimentales. *Leisure interest:* antiques. *Address:* Rua do Salitre, 166, 2° E, Lisbon, Portugal. *Telephone:* 680646.

CRUZ-DIEZ, Carlos; Venezuelan painter; b. 17 Aug. 1923; ed. School of Plastic and Applied Arts, Caracas; Dir. of Art. Venezuelan subsidiary of McCann-Erickson Advertising Agency 1946–51; Teacher, History of Applied Arts, School of Arts, Caracas 1953–55; in Barcelona and Paris working on physical qualities of colour now named *Physichromies* 1955–56; opened studio of visual arts and industrial design, Caracas 1957; Prof. and Asst. Dir. School of Arts, Caracas 1959–60; moved to Paris 1960; First one-man exhbn., Caracas 1947, later in Madrid, Genoa, Turin, London, Paris, Cologne, Munich, Oslo, Brussels, Ostwald Museum, Dortmund, Bottrop (Fed. Repub. of Germany), New York, Bogotá, Rome, Venice and Essen; Retrospective exhbns. at Signals, London and Galerie Kerchache, Paris 1965; represented at numerous Group exhbns.; works in Museo de Bellas Artes, Caracas, Victoria and Albert Museum, Tate Gallery, London, Casa de las Américas, Havana, Städtisches Museum, Leverkusen, Germany, Museum of Modern Art, N.Y., Museum of Contemporary Art, Montreal, Museum des 20. Jahrhunderts, Vienna, Univ. of Dublin, Museo Civico di Torino, Wallraf-Richartz Museum, Cologne, Museum of Contemporary Art, Chicago, Musée de Grenoble, Centre Georges Pompidou, Musée d'Art Moderne, Paris, Neue Pinakothek, Munich; Grand Prix at 3rd Biennale, Córdoba, Argentina; Prix Int. de Peinture à la IX Biennale de São Paulo. *Address:* 23 rue Pierre Semard, Paris 75009, France.

CRUZEIRO, Maria-Manuela da Silva Nunes Ribeiro, L. ES L.; Portuguese librarian and university teacher; b. 10 March 1934, Lisbon; d. of Armando Manuel Calabaça da Vila Nunes Ribeiro and Celsa Pereira da Silva Nunes Ribeiro; m. João Manuel Antunes da Silva Cruzeiro 1955; two s. one d.; ed. D. João de Castro Lyceum and Lisbon and Coimbra Univs.; Chief Librarian, Ministry of Econs. 1967–73, Nat. Inst. of Statistics 1974–78, New Univ. of Lisbon (Documentation Services) 1978–, Univ. Teacher of Documentation Sciences 1983–; Dir. Nat. Library 1978–80; Pres. Asscn. of Portuguese Librarians; Pres. Municipality Dept. *Publications:* poetry, novels and articles in magazines; Espelho de Cristina (medieval linguistics and literature); 2 vols., Book Industry and Commerce 1986, José Fontana-Work and Life, Woman Action in Portuguese Society; conf. papers on documentation science. *Leisure interests:* music, dance, reading, travelling and writing. *Address:* Praça do Principe Real 26, 1200 Lisbon (Office); Largo dos Lóios 3-3°, 1100 Lisbon, Portugal. *Telephone:* 370012/3/4 (Office); 861820 (Home).

CRVENKOVSKI, Krste; Yugoslav politician; b. 16 July 1921, Prilep, Macedonia; s. of Trajko and Balga Crvenkovski; m. Margarette Crvenkovski 1947; one s. one d.; ed. Higher Party School, Belgrade; mem. C.P. of Yugoslavia 1939–; active in People's Liberation Movt.; imprisoned 1943–44; mem. Political Bureau, Cen. Cttee. League of Communists of Macedonia 1948–51; Minister for Science and Culture, Govt. of Macedonia 1949–51; Organizational Sec., Cen. Cttee., League of Communists of Macedonia 1951–58, Political Sec. 1963–66, Pres. Cen. Cttee. 1966–69; mem. Fed. Exec. Council, Macedonia 1954–63, Sec. for Educ. and Culture 1958–63; mem. Exec. Bureau, Presidium of League of Communists of Yugoslavia (LCY) 1969–71; mem. Council of Fed. 1969; First Vice-Pres. Presidency of Repub. of Yugoslavia June 1971–72; Deputy to Ass., Socialist Repub. of Macedonia; Deputy to Fed. Ass.; del. to IPU 1965; leader or mem. del. to numerous congresses of Communist parties in other countries; numerous national decorations including Order of Nat. Hero, Order of Brotherhood and Unity, Order of Partisan Star, etc. *Publications:* The Problems of Education, The Leading Role of the League of Communists of Yugoslavia, The League of Communists and the National Question, The League of Communists and Society. *Leisure interests:* hunting, philately. *Address:* Vodnjanska 78, Skopje, Yugoslavia.

CSEHÁK, Dr. Judit; Hungarian physician and politician; b. 1940 Szekszárd; ed. Budapest Univ. of Medicine; joined Hungarian Socialist Workers' Party (HSWP) 1967; Asst. medical officer, Council Hospital of County Tolna; asst. dist. panel dr. in borough of Fadd; head of medical dept., Municipal Council of Szekszárd; Sec. cen. bd, Nat. Health Workers' Union 1975–78; Sec. Nat. Council of Trade Unions 1978–84; a Deputy to Chair. Council of Ministers 1984–87; Minister of Social Affairs and Health 1987–; mem. HSWP Political Cttee. 1987–; Pres. Nat. Youth Cttee. 1985–86; Labour Order of Merit 1984. *Address:* 1361 Budapest, Arany János utca 6–8, Hungary. *Telephone:* 323-100.

CSIKÓS-NAGY, Béla; Hungarian economist; b. 9 Sept. 1915, Szeged; s. of Dr. József Csikós-Nagy and Jolán Jedlicska; m. Dr. Livia Kneppó 1944; two d.; ed. Szeged Univ. and Univ. of Pécs; joined Hungarian CP 1945; Chair. Hungarian Bd. of Prices and Materials 1957–84; Exec. Co-Chair. Council of Industrial Policy 1984–; lecturer on Price Theory at Karl Marx Univ. of Econ. Sciences, Budapest 1959–, title of Univ. Prof. 1964, Dr. of Econ. Sc. 1967; Under-Sec. of State 1968–84; Pres. Hungarian Econ. Asscn. 1970–; Chair. Hungarian Soc. of Economists 1975–; mem. Exec. Cttee. Int. Econ. Asscn. 1971–77, 1983–86; Hon. Prof. Univ. of Vienna, mem. Oxford Energy Club 1977, Corresp. mem. Austrian Acad. of Sciences; mem. Hungarian Acad. of Sciences 1982–; Hon. Chair. Int. Soc. of Econs.; Pres. Hungarian Bridge Fed. 1983–; Hungarian State Prize 1970, Banner Order of Hungarian People's Repub. *Publications:* Pricing in Hungary 1968, General and Socialist Price Theory 1968, Hungarian Economic Policy 1971, Socialist Economic Policy 1973, Socialist Price Theory and Price Policy 1975, Towards a New Price Revolution 1978, On Hungarian Price Policy 1980, Economic Policy 1982, The Price Law in Socialist Planned Economy 1983, Topical Issues of Hungarian Price Policy 1985, Socialist Market Economy 1987; other studies on pricing theory and political economy. *Leisure interest:* card patience. *Address:* Iparpolitikai Tanács, Budapest V, Arany János u. 10, Hungary (Office). *Telephone:* 114-066.

CSIKSZENTMIHA'LYI, Miha'ly, PH.D.; American professor of psychology; b. 29 Sept. 1934, Fiume, Italy; s. of Alfred Csikszentmiha'lyi and Edith (Jankovich de Jessenice) Csikszentmiha'lyi; m. Isabella Selega 1961; two s.; ed. Univs. of Illinois and Chicago; went to U.S.A. in 1956; Assoc. Prof. and Chair., Dept. of Sociology and Anthropology, Lake Forest Coll. 1965–71; Prof. of Human Devt., Univ. of Chicago 1971–87, Chair. Dept. of Behavioral Sciences 1985–87; mem. Bd. of Advisers, Encyclopaedia Britannica 1985–; Consultant, The J.P. Getty Museum 1985–; Sr. Fulbright Scholar, Brazil 1984; Fellow Nat. Acad. of Educ., Nat. Acad. of Leisure Sciences. *Publications:* Beyond Boredom and Anxiety 1975, The Creative Vision 1976, The Meaning of Things 1981, Being Adolescent 1984, Optimal Experience 1988. *Leisure interests:* mountain climbing, chess and history. *Address:* 5333 South Hyde Park Boulevard, Chicago, Ill. 60615, U.S.A. (Home). *Telephone:* (312) 493-4681 (Home).

CUADRA MEDINA, Lieut.-Gen. Ramón; Spanish army officer; b. 29 Dec. 1910, Madrid; ed. Gen. Mil. Acad., Cavalry Acad.; Second Lieut. 1931, Cavalry Lieut. 1932, Capt. 1937, Major 1945, Lieut.-Col. 1957, Col. 1966, Brig.-Gen. 1969, Div. Gen. 1972, Lieut.-Gen. 1974–; Prof., Cavalry Acad. 1939–42, 1947–56, 1956–58, also Prof., Infantry Cavalry and Service Corps

Acad.; main commands held: 5th, then 2nd Cavalry Regt.; Security Corps at Valladolid; 2nd Regt. of Cavalry Brigade of Cen. Mil. Region; Flechas (arrows) Mixed Div.; 1st Regt. of Flechas Negras (black arrows); Guerrilla Sqn. of FET y de las JONS (the Falange) in Cáceres; Gen. Staff of 7th Army Corps, then of Cavalry Div., then of Castilla Army Corps; 2nd Chief of Gen. Staff, 7th Mil. Region; 12th Armoured Regt.; Deputy Insp. of Cavalry of 2nd, 3rd, 4th Mil. Regions; Mil. Gov. of La Plaza and Province of Santander; Deputy Insp. of Cavalry, 1st, 7th, 8th Mil. Regions; Dir. of Maintenance Services, Gen. Staff; now Chief of Gen. Staff in Canary Islands and Head of Jt. Command, Canary Islands Zone; Chief of Gen. Army Staff 1976; Cross of Mil. Merit (twice), Cross of War (twice), Bronze Medal for Mil. Valour, Cross, Plaque and Grand Cross, Royal Mil. Order of St. Hermenegildo, Cross and Grand Cross, Order of Mil. Merit, Grand Cross, Order of Naval Merit, Cross of Mil. Merit (Italy). *Address:* Ministerio del Ejército, Alcalá 51, Madrid 14, Spain.

CUATRECASAS, Pedro Martin, M.D.; American corporate executive and research scientist; b. 27 Sept. 1936, Madrid, Spain; s. of José and Martha Nowack Cuatrecasas; m. Carol Zies 1959; one s. three d.; ed. Washington Univ. and Washington Univ. School of Medicine; Internship and Residency, Johns Hopkins Hosp., Baltimore, Md. 1962–64; Clinical Assoc., Nat. Insts. of Health, Nat. Inst. of Arthritis and Metabolic Diseases 1964–66, Postdoctoral Fellow 1966–67, Medical Officer, Lab. of Chemical Biology 1967–70; Professorial Lecturer in Biochemistry (Enzymology), George Washington Univ. School of Medicine, Washington, D.C. 1967–70; Assoc. Prof. of Pharmacology and Experimental Therapeutics, Assoc. Prof. of Medicine, Dir. Div. of Clinical Pharmacology, Burroughs Wellcome Prof. of Clinical Pharmacology, Johns Hopkins Univ. School of Medicine, Baltimore, Md. 1970–72, Prof. of Pharmacology and Experimental Therapeutics, Assoc. Prof. of Medicine 1972–75; Asst. Physician, Johns Hopkins Hosp. 1972–75; Vice-Pres. of Research, Devt. and Medical, and Dept. Head, Molecular Biology, Wellcome Research Labs., Burroughs Wellcome Co., N.C. 1975–86; Vice-Pres. Research and Devt., Glaxo Research Labs., Glaxo Inc. 1986–, Dir. 1986–; Dir. Burroughs Wellcome Co. 1975–; Adjunct Prof., Dept. of Medicine and Dept. of Pharmacology and Physiology, Duke Univ., Durham, N.C. 1975–; Adjunct Prof., Dept. of Medicine and Dept. of Pharmacology, Univ. of N.C., Chapel Hill 1975–; Dir. Burroughs Wellcome Fund 1975–86; mem. N.A.S. and many medical socs.; mem. Council, Int. Soc. of Immunopharmacology; mem. editorial bd. of numerous scientific journals; several awards, including Laude Prize for int. medical-pharmaceutical research, Pharmaceutical World 1975, Wolf Prize 1987; Hon. Dr. (Barcelona Univ.) 1984. *Address:* Glaxo Research Laboratories, Glaxo Inc., Five Moore Drive, Research Triangle Park, N.C. 27709, U.S.A.

CUBILLOS SALLATO, Hernán; Chilean company director and government official; b. 25 Feb. 1936, Viña del Mar; s. of Hernán Cubillos Leiva and María Graciela Sallato; m. Marcela Sigall; three s. one d.; ed. Colegio de los Sagrados Corazones in Viña del Mar and Santiago, Oratory School, Bournemouth, England, Arturo Prat Naval Coll., Valparaíso; Officer, Chilean Navy 1953–61; Empresas Industriales El Melón S.A. 1961–62; Empresa Periodística El Mercurio, S.A.P. 1963–74; Pres. Revista Qué Pasa 1974–78, Santillana del Pacífico S.A. de Ediciones 1974–78, Compañía de Inversiones La Transandina, S.A. 1974–78, Transamerica S.A. de Comercio Exterior; Chair. Bd. Empresas CCT S.A., Ecom S.A.; Vice-Chair. Banco de Crédito e Inversiones 1981–; Minister of Foreign Affairs 1978–80; Dir. Inter-American Press Asscn. 1974–77; mem. Int. Press Inst.; Presidential Medal, Medal of City of Santiago 1953, Abdón Calderón Medal (Ecuador), Antonio Nariño Medal (Colombia), Grand Cross of Order of the Sun (Peru), Bicentenario del General Bernardo O'Higgins Award (Chile), Decoration for Services to the Nation (Chile). *Leisure interests:* yachting, photography. *Address:* Merced 22, P.O. Box 830, Santiago (Office); Candelaria Goyenechea 4241, Santiago, Chile.

CUCINO, Gen. Andrea; Italian army officer (retd.); b. 23 July 1914, Montecorvino Rovella; s. of Matteo and Giuseppina Lenza; m. Iolanda Saviani 1953; one s.; ed. Artillery and Eng. Acad., Scuola di Guerra, NATO Defence Coll.; promoted to the rank of Second Lieut., Artillery 1935, Lieut. 1937, Capt. 1942, Maj. 1946, Lieut.-Col. 1951, Col. 1957, Brig.-Gen. 1962, Div. Gen. 1967, Lieut.-Gen. 1970, Gen. 1972; Commdg. Officer 132nd Armoured Artillery Regt. 1959–60, 3rd Brigade of Ariete Armoured Div. 1963–64; mem. NATO Standing Group Int. Planning Team for 'Flexible Response' Strategy, Washington, D.C. 1960–63; Div. Commdr. Ariete Armoured Div. 1967–68; Insp. of Artillery 1968–72; Sec.-Gen. Ministry of Defence 1972–75; Chief of Gen. Staff 1975–77, retd. 1977; invited to People's Repub. of China as adviser on modernization of PLA 1978; Cavaliere di Gran Croce, Ordine al Merito della Repubblica Italiana, Grand Officer, Order of Merit (Fed. Repub. of Germany), Order of Tudor Vladimirescu 2nd Class (Romania), Commdr. Legion of Merit (U.S.A.), Silver and Bronze Medals for Mil. Valour, Italian Army. *Publications:* The Political and Military Ruling Classes in the Present Struggle for World Supremacy: Studies on Nuclear Strategy; numerous articles in Italian Military Review 1945–57. *Leisure interests:* sports, particularly tennis. *Address:* Via Ospedaletto Giustiniani, 1-4 00189 Rome, Italy. *Telephone:* (06) 3765675.

CUCKNEY, Sir John Graham, Kt., M.A.; British banker; b. 12 July 1925, India; s. of late Air Vice-Marshal E. J. Cuckney; m. 2nd Muriel Boyd 1960; ed. Shrewsbury, Univ. of St. Andrews; Civil Asst., Gen. Staff, War Office

1949–57; Dir. of various industrial and financial cos. 1957–72 incl. Lazard Bros. & Co. 1964–70, J. Bibby & Sons 1970–72; Chair. Standard Industrial Trust 1966–70, Mersey Docks and Harbour Bd. 1970–72, Bldg. Econ. Devt. Cttee. 1976–79; Ind. mem. Railway Policy Review Cttee. 1966–67; Special mem. Hops Marketing Bd. 1971–72; Chief Exec. (Second Perm. Sec.), Property Services Agency 1972–74; Sr. Crown Agent and Chair. of Crown Agents for Oversea Govts. and Administrations 1974–78; Chair. (part-time) Int. Mil. Services Ltd. 1974–85; Chair. (part-time) Port of London Authority 1977–79; Chair. (part-time) The Thomas Cook Group Ltd. 1978–87; Dir. Midland Bank PLC 1978–88, Royal Insurance PLC 1979–, Deputy Chair. 1982–85, Chair. May 1985–; Dir. Brooke Bond Liebig Ltd. (now Brooke Bond Group PLC) 1978–84, Vice-Chair. 1980–81, Chair. 1981–84; Dir. John Brown PLC 1981–86, Deputy Chair. 1982–83, Chair. 1983–86; Dir. and Deputy Chair. TI Group PLC 1985–; Dir. Brixton Estate PLC 1985–, Lazard Brothers & Co. Ltd. 1988–; Investors in Industry Group PLC (now 3i Group PLC) 1986– (Chair. 1987–); Chair. Int. Maritime Bureau 1981–85, Westland Group PLC 1985–89; Elder Brother of Trinity House 1980–. *Address:* 91 Waterloo Road, London, SE1 8XP, England. *Telephone:* 01-928 7822.

CUCU, Vasile, Romanian geographer; b. 7 April 1927, Igiroasa, Mehedinti county; s. of Sălică Cucu and Maria Cucu; m. Ana Popova 1954; two d.; ed. Coll. of Geography, Sverdlovsk Univ., U.S.S.R. 1954; Univ. lecturer Coll. of Geography, Bucharest Univ. 1965–69, Prof. 1969–; Pro-Rector, Bucharest Univ. 1968–72, of the Cen. Inst. of the Specialization of Teaching Staff 1972–74; Chair. Geography Dept., Bucharest Univ. 1975–85; ed.-in-chief of Geographical periodicals: Terra 1956–, Buletinul Societății de Stiințe Geografice 1972–, Analele Universității din București 1977–; mem. Int. Union of Geography Cttees. on Population 1966–, Town Planning 1968–, Nat. Demography Dept. 1974–; mem. Bd. of Geographical Sciences of the S.R. Romania 1956–, Vice-Pres. 1970–. *Publications:* Romania's Geography (in collaboration) 1966, 1977, 1987; Romania's Cities and Towns 1970, The Geography of Population and Human Settlements 1974, 1980, Geography and Urbanization 1976, The Systematization of Romania's Territory and Localities 1977, Millionaire Cities (in collaboration) 1983, Romania—A Geographical Synthesis 1984. *Address:* Facultatea de geologie-geografie, Bd. Nicolae Bălcescu No. 1, Bucharest 70111; Aleea Alexandru N9. 71273, sector 1, Bucharest, Romania. *Telephone:* 330217.

CUDLIPP, Baron (Life Peer), cr. 1974, of Aldingbourne in the County of West Sussex; **Hugh Cudlipp,** Kt., O.B.E.; British journalist; b. 28 Aug. 1913; s. of William Cudlipp; m. 2nd Eileen Ascroft (died 1962); m. 3rd Jodi Hyland; ed. Howard Gardens School, Cardiff; with various provincial newspapers in Cardiff and Manchester 1927–32; Features Ed. Sunday Chronicle 1932–35; Daily Mirror 1935–37; Ed. Sunday Pictorial 1937–40; served army 1940–46, C.O. British Army Newspaper Unit, C.M.F. 1943–46; Ed., Sunday Pictorial 1946–49; Man. Ed. Sunday Express 1950–52, Editorial Dir. Daily Mirror and Sunday Pictorial (now Sunday Mirror) 1952–63; Jt. Man. Dir. Daily Mirror Newspapers Ltd., Sunday Pictorial Newspapers Ltd. 1960–63; Chair. Daily Mirror Newspapers Ltd. 1963–68; Personal Consultant to Robert Maxwell, Mirror Group Newspapers 1984–; Chair. Odhams Press Ltd. 1961–63; Daily Herald (1929) Ltd. 1961–64; Dir. Associated TV Ltd. 1956–73, Reuters Ltd.; Editorial Dir. Int. Publishing Corpn. 1963–68, Deputy Chair. 1964–68, Chair. 1968–73; Deputy Chair. Reed Int. Ltd. 1970–73; mem. Royal Comm. on Standards of Conduct in Public Life 1974–76; Labour until 1981, joined SDP, now mem. S.L.D. *Publications:* Publish and be Damned! 1953, At Your Peril 1962, Walking on The Water (autobiog.) 1976, The Prerogative of the Harlot 1980. *Address:* House of Lords, London, SW1A 0PW; 14 Tollhouse Close, Avenue de Chartres, Chichester, West Sussex, PO19 1SF, England.

CUEVAS, José Luis; Mexican painter; b. 26 Feb. 1934, México, D.F.; s. of Alberto Cuevas and María Regla; m. Bertha Riestra 1961; three d.; ed. Univ. de México, School of Painting and Sculpture "La Esmeralda", Mexico; over forty one-man exhbns. in New York, Paris, Milan, Mexico, Buenos Aires, Toronto, Los Angeles, Washington, etc.; Group Exhbns. all over N. and S. America, Europe, India and Japan; works are in Museum of Modern Art, Solomon R. Guggenheim Museum, Brooklyn Museum (New York), Art Inst. Chicago, Phillips Collection, Washington, D.C., Museums of Albi and Lyons, France, etc.; First Int. Award for Drawing, São Paulo Bienal 1959, First Int. Award, Mostra Internazionale di Bianco e Nero de Lugano, Zürich 1962, First Prize, Bienal de Grabado, Santiago, Chile 1964, First Int. Prize for engraving, first Biennial of New Delhi, India 1968; has illustrated following books: The Worlds of Kafka and Cuevas 1959, The Ends of Legends String, Recollections of Childhood 1962, Cuevas por Cuevas (autobiog.) 1964, Cuevas Charenton 1965, Crime by Cuevas 1968, Homage to Quevedo 1969, El Mundo de José Luis Cuevas 1970, Cuaderno de Paris 1977. *Publications:* Cuevas by Cuevas 1964, Cuevario 1973, Confesiones de José Luis Cuevas 1975, Cuevas por Daisy Ascher 1979. *Address:* Galeana 109, San Angel Inn, México 20, D.F., Mexico; c/o Grace Borgenicht Gallery, 1018 Madison Avenue, New York, N.Y., U.S.A. *Telephone:* 548-78-20; 548-90-54 (both México, D.F.)

CUEVAS CANCINO, Francisco; Mexican diplomatist; b. 7 May 1921, Mexico City; m. Ana Hilditch 1946; two s. one d.; ed. Free School of Law, Mexico City, McGill Univ., Montreal, Ottawa, London and Columbia Univs.; Third Sec., London 1946–49; served UN Secr. 1950–53; Adviser to Minister of Foreign Affairs 1954; Asst. Dir. of Int. Orgs., Ministry of Foreign Affairs and Head, Tech. Assistance Programme in Mexico 1956-57; Legal Counsellor, Perm. Mission of Mexico at UN 1959-60; Dir. Centre for Int. Studies, Mexico City 1961; Alt. Rep. of Mexico at UN 1962, Perm. Rep. 1965-70, 1978; Perm. Del. of Mexico to UNESCO, Paris 1970-76, mem. Exec. Bd. UNESCO 1971-74; Consul Gen., Paris 1977; mem. Mexican del. to UN Gen. Ass. 1955-70; Amb. to EEC 1981-83, to U.K. Feb. 1983-86, to Austria 1986-; Perm. Rep. to UNIDO and IAEA 1986-. *Publications:* books on law, international affairs and history. *Address:* Mexican Embassy, Mattiellistrasse 2-4, 1040 Vienna, Austria.

CUI JUNZHI; Chinese musician; ed. Cen. Conservatory of Music; first modern exponent of the Konghou, (Chinese string instrument); participant in 3rd Int. Harp Conf., Vienna 1987; *Address:* Chinese Musician's Association, Beijing, People's Republic of China.

CUI NAIFU; Chinese politician; b. 1929, Shahe, Beijing; Dir. Propaganda Dept. and Dean of Studies, Lanzhou Univ.; Vice-Chair. Lanzhou Univ. Revolutionary Cttee.; Vice-Minister of Civil Affairs 1981, Minister 1982-; mem. 12th Cen. Cttee. CCP 1982-87, 13th Cen. Cttee. CCP 1987-; Deputy Head, Group for Resettlement of Demobilised Soldiers and Officers under the State Council 1983-; Chair. China Org. Comm. of UN Decade of Disabled Persons 1986-, Research Soc. for Theory of Civil Admin. and Social Welfare 1985-; Hon. Dir. China Welfare Fund for the Handicapped 1985-; Hon. Pres. China Assen. for the Blind and Deaf Mutes 1984-. *Address:* State Council, Beijing, People's Republic of China.

CUI YUELI, Gen.; Chinese politician; b. 1920, Shenxian Co., Hebei; engaged in underground activities 1940s; worked under Liu Ren 1948; Deputy Dir. United Front Work Dept., Municipal CCP Cttee., Beijing 1956, Dir. 1957, Dir. Dept. of Public Health and Physical Culture 1959; Deputy Mayor Beijing 1964; mem. Standing Cttee., Municipal CCP Cttee., Beijing 1965, Vice-Chair. 1965; disappeared during Cultural Revolution; Chair. Municipal CPPCC Cttee. Beijing 1977; Vice-Minister of Public Health 1978-82, Minister 1982-87; mem. 12th Cen. Cttee. CCP 1982-87, Cen. Advisory Comm. 1987-; Pres. All China Assen. for Traditional Chinese Medicine 1979-, Red Cross Soc. of China 1985-; Vice-Chair. Cen. Patriotic Public Health Campaign Comm. 1983-; Chair. Pharmacopeia Comm. Ministry of Public Health 1986-; Hon. Dir. Chinese Traditional Medicine Devt. Assen. 1985-. *Address:* State Council, Beijing, People's Republic of China.

CULLBERG, Brigit Ragnhild; Swedish choreographer; b. 3 Aug. 1908, Nyköping; d. of Carl Cullberg and Elna Westerström; m. Anders Ek 1942 (divorced); two s. one d.; ed. Univ. of Stockholm, Jooss School of Dance, Lilian Karina Ballet School; Choreographer, Swedish Opera Ballet 1951-57; Guest Choreographer, Royal Danish Ballet 1957-61, 1975, American Ballet Theatre 1958-64, New York City Ballet 1958, Nat. Ballet of Santiago de Chile, City Ballets of Cologne, Munich, Düsseldorf, Zürich, Dortmund, Oslo, Helsinki, Antwerp, Geneva, Warsaw, Teheran and West Berlin; Dir. Cullberg Ballet, The Swedish Nat. Theatre Centre 1967-; choreography includes: Miss Julie, Medea, Moon-reindeer, The Evil Queen (Prix d'Italia 1961), Lady from the Sea, Adam and Eve, Eurydice is Dead, Romeo and Juliet, Red Wine in Green Glasses (Prix d'Italia 1971), Revolt, Rapport (The 7th Symphony of Allan Pettersson), War Dances (9th Symphony), Dreams of Love and Death, Medea's Children, Pulcinella (in collaboration with Giuseppe Carbone). *Publication:* Ballet and Us 1954. *Leisure interests:* theatre, art, political and social problems, peace. *Address:* c/o Press Department, The Swedish National Theatre Centre, Rasunderagen 150, Solna, Sweden. *Telephone:* 8-652387.

CULLEN, Alexander Lamb, O.B.E., PH.D., F.R.S.; British professor of electrical engineering; b. 30 April 1920, London; s. of R.H. Cullen and J. Cullen; m. Margaret Lamb 1940; two s. one d.; ed. Lincoln School and Imperial Coll., London; Lecturer, Univ. Coll., London 1946-55, Pender Prof. of Electrical Eng. 1967-80, Sr. Research Fellow 1980-83, Hon. Research Fellow 1983-; Prof. of Electrical Eng. and Head, Dept. of Electrical Eng., Sheffield Univ. 1955-67; Prof. Emer., Univ. of London; Hon D.Eng. (Sheffield) 1985; Hon. D.Sc. (Chinese Univ. of Hong Kong) 1981, (Kent) 1986. *Publications:* Microwave Measurements 1950; numerous articles in scientific journals. *Leisure interest:* music. *Address:* Department of Electronic and Electrical Engineering, University College London, Torrington Place, London, WC1E 7JE; 3 Felden Drive, Hemel Hempstead, Herts., HP3 0BD, England. *Telephone:* 0442 58277.

CULLEN, Hon. Jack Sydney George Bud, P.C.; Canadian politician; b. 20 April 1927, Creighton Mine, Ont.; s. of Chaffey Roi Cullen and Margaret Evelyn Leck; m.; two s. two d.; ed. Sudbury High School, Univ. of Toronto and Osgoode Hall; Barrister-at-Law; M.P. for Sarnia-Lambton 1968-; Parl. Sec. to Minister of Nat. Defence, Minister of Energy, Mines and Resources and Minister of Finance; Minister of Nat. Revenue 1975-76; of Employment and Immigration 1976-79; Trial Div. Judge 1984-; first Pres. Sarnia Educ. Authority; mem. Sarnia School Bd., Sarnia and District Assen. for the Mentally Retarded; Liberal. *Address:* 125 Springfield Road, Unit 8, Ottawa, Ont. K1M 1CJ, Canada.

CULLEN, Michael John, M.A., PH.D.; New Zealand politician; b. 1945, London; two d.; ed. Christ's Coll. Christchurch, Canterbury Univ. and Univ. of Edinburgh; Asst. Lecturer, Canterbury Univ., Tutor Univ. of

Stirling, Sr. Lecturer in History, Univ. of Otago (Dunedin) and Visiting Fellow, Australian Nat. Univ. 1968-81; mem. Parl. 1981-; Minister of Social Welfare and Assoc. Minister of Finance 1987-88, Assoc. Minister of Health 1988-, Labour Party. *Leisure interests:* music, reading, house renovation. *Address:* Parliament House, Wellington, New Zealand.

CULLIGAN, John William; American business executive; b. 22 Nov. 1916, Newark, N.J.; m. Rita McBride 1944; two s. four d.; ed. Seton Hall, Utah, Chicago and Philippine Univs.; Pres. Whitehall Lab. (div. of American Home Products Corpn.) 1964-67; Vice-Pres. and mem. Operations and Finance Cttees., American Home Products Corpn. 1967-72, Exec. Vice-Pres. 1972-73, Dir. 1970, Pres. and Chair. Operations Cttee. 1973-81, Chair. of Bd. 1981-86, Chair. Exec. Cttee. Dec. 1986-; Vice-Pres. and Dir. The Proprietary Assen.; Dir. Valley Hosp. Foundation, N.J., Harvard Industries; Chair. and Dir. Calif. Biotechnology Inc.; Treas., Council of Family Health; Co-Chair. Archbishop's Cttee. of the Laity, Newark, N.J.; Papal Kt. of St. Gregory, Knight of Malta. *Leisure interest:* golf. *Address:* American Home Products Corporation, 685 Third Avenue, New York, N.Y. 10017, U.S.A. *Telephone:* (212) 878-5006.

CULLINAN, Brendan Peter; Irish judge; b. 24 July 1927, Dublin; s. of Patrick J. Cullinan and Elizabeth Kitchen; one s. (one deceased) two d.; ed. Christian Bros. School, Dublin, Univ. Coll. Dublin, Nat. Univ. of Ireland, King's Inns, Dublin and Irish Mil. Coll.; mil. service 1946-65; mem. Irish contingent, Equestrian Games of XVIth Olympiad, Stockholm 1956; called to Irish Bar 1963; legal officer, army Legal Service, Dublin 1963-65; seconded to Inst. of Public Admin. Dublin for service in Zambia and designated under Overseas Service Aid Scheme (OSAS) of Ministry of Overseas Devt. (now Overseas Devt. Admin.), London 1965-68; lecturer, Sr. Lecturer and Acting Head of Law School, Lusaka, Zambia 1965-68; legal officer, Army Legal Service, Dublin 1968-69; Resident Magistrate and Deputy Registrar, High Court, Lusaka 1969-70, Sr. Resident Magistrate and Registrar 1970-73; admitted to practice as legal practitioner in Zambia 1971; Puisne Judge Dec. 1973; called to Bar, Lincoln's Inn, London 1977; frequently Acting Judge of Supreme Court, Lusaka 1976-80, Judge of Supreme Court 1980; Dir. of Legal Services Corpn. Lusaka 1982-83; Puisne Judge of Supreme Court of Fiji, Lautoka and Suva 1984-87; Chief Justice of Lesotho May 1987-, Judge of Court of Appeal (ex officio) and Chair. Judicial Services Comm. *Leisure interests:* golf, swimming, gardening. *Address:* c/o High Court, P.O. Box 90, Maseru 100 (Office); Lerotholi Road, Maseru Central, Lesotho (Home); 16 Oak Park Gardens, London, S.W.19, England. *Telephone:* 324206/322183 (Office); 314714 (Maseru); 01-785 2260 (London).

CULLMAN, Joseph Frederick, III, B.A.; American business executive; b. 9 April 1912, New York; s. of Joseph F. Cullman, Jr. and Frances Nathan (Wolff) Cullman; one d.; ed. Hotchkiss School, Yale Univ.; Sales Man. Eastern Area, Webster Tobacco Co. 1936-41; served in U.S. Navy as Air Defence Officer and Commdr. 1941-45; Vice-Pres. Benson & Hedges 1946-53, Exec. Vice-Pres. 1953-55, Pres. 1955-61; Vice-Pres. Philip Morris Inc. 1954, Exec. Vice-Pres. 1955, Pres. and C.E.O. 1957-66, Chair. and C.E.O. Officer 1966-78, Chair. Exec. Cttee. of Bd. 1978-84; Dir. Philip Morris (Australia) Ltd., Benson and Hedges (Canada) Ltd., Mission Viejo Co. (operating co. of Philip Morris), IBM World Trade Europe/Middle East/Africa Corpn., Bankers Trust Co., Ford Motor Co., Braniff Int. and Levi Strauss and Co.; mem. Exec. Cttee. of Tobacco Inst., Wash., D.C.; mem. Finance Cttee. of Cttee. for Econ. Devt.; mem. Nat. Bd. of Smithsonian Assocs.; Trustee, New York State Nature and Historical Preserve Trust, American Museum of Natural History, Colonial Williamsburg Foundation; mem. Yale Devt. Bd., Advisory Council of Graduate School of Business, Stanford Univ., Conf. Bd.; Pres. Int. Atlantic Salmon Foundation; Dir. World Wildlife Fund—U.S. Appeal; Pres., Dir. Whitney M. Young, Jr. Memorial Foundation; New York City Chair. of United Negro Coll. Fund 1972 Campaign; Chair. U.S. Open Tennis Championships at Forest Hills 1969-70, Hon. Chair. 1971; Chair. Exec. Cttee. Nat. Tennis Found. and Hall of Fame; Ordre du Mérite commercial et industriel (France) 1963, Commdr. Order of Merit (Italy) 1966; Hon. D.Iur. (Bellarmine Coll., Louisville, Ky.) 1973, Hon. Dr. Commercial Science (Univ. of Richmond, Va.). *Leisure interests:* tennis, golf, fishing, hunting. *Address:* 100 Park Avenue, New York, N.Y. 10017, U.S.A. (Office). *Telephone:* 212-880-3500.

CULLMANN, Oscar, DR. THEOL., DR. PHIL., D.D.; French professor of theology; b. 25 Feb. 1902, Strasbourg; s. of Georges Cullmann and Frederique (née Mandel) Cullmann; ed. Univ. of Strasbourg, Sorbonne, Paris, Ecole des Hautes Etudes, Paris; Dir. of Protestant Seminary, Strasbourg 1925-30; Prof. New Testament and Ancient History of Christianity, Univ. of Strasbourg 1930-38, Univ. of Basle 1938-72; Rector Univ. of Basle 1968-69; Prof. Ecole des Hautes Etudes, Paris and Sorbonne 1948-72; Guest Lecturer U.S.A., U.K., Finland, Greece, etc. 1948-85; Prof. Emer. Sorbonne and Basle Univs. 1972; mem. Institut de France; Dr. h.c. Lausanne, Edinburgh, Lund, Manchester, Basle, Debrecen; Commdr. Légion d'Honneur; Corresp. mem. British Acad., Akademie Mainz, Royal Netherlands Acad. *Publications:* over 100 titles, including Christus und die Zeit (trans. English, French, Swedish, Greek, Italian) 1946, Petrus, Jünger, Apostel, Martyrer 1972, Der Staat in Neuen Testament 1956, Die Christologie des Neuen Testaments 1957, Der Johanneische Kreis 1975, Einheit Durch Vielheit 1986. *Leisure interest:* gardening. *Address:* Birmannsgasse 10A,

CH-4055, Basle, Switzerland; Rue Ravignan 20, 75018 Paris, France. *Telephone:* (61) 25.15.66 (Basle); 42-54-99-12 (Paris).

CULMANN, Herbert Ernst, DR.IUR.; German airline executive; b. 15 Feb. 1921, Neustadt; s. of Wilhelm Culmann and Cornelia Fuchs; m. Angelika Küstner 1949; two s. one d.; ed. Gymnasium Neustadt and Ruprecht-Karl Universität, Heidelberg; German Air Force 1939-45; legal studies and legal practice 1945-53; Deutsche Lufthansa A.G. 1953, Dir. of Cen. Admin. Div. (Int. relations, Org. Legal, Planning, Financial divs.) 1957-64, mem. Man. Bd. 1964-72, Chair. Exec. Bd. 1972-82; official of other companies; Vice-Pres. Féd. Aéronautique Int. (FAI) 1983-; Pres. Deutscher Aeroclub 1983-; mem. Aviation Advisory Cttee., Fed. Transport Ministry. *Leisure interests:* flying, music, sailing, skiing. *Address:* Neuer Trassweg 30, 5060 Bergisch-Gladbach 1, Federal Republic of Germany.

CULVER, David M., O.C., B.SC., M.B.A.; Canadian business executive; b. 5 Dec. 1924, Winnipeg, Man.; s. of Albert Ferguson and Fern Elizabeth (Smith) Culver; m. Mary Cecil Powell 1949; three s. one d.; ed. McGill Univ., Montreal, Harvard Graduate School of Business Admin.; joined Alcan Group 1949-, on staff of Centre d'Etudes Industrielles, Geneva, transferred to Co. sales office, New York, later Man.; Vice-Pres. and Dir. Alcan Int. Ltd. (Montreal) 1956-62, Pres. 1962-; Exec. Vice-Pres. and Dir. Alcan Aluminium Ltd. 1968-75, regional Exec. Vice-Pres. N. America and Caribbean 1975, Pres. 1977-, C.E.O. 1979-, Chair. Jan. 1987-, Pres. and C.E.O. Aluminium Co. of Canada Ltd. 1975, Chair. 1978-79, 1983-; Chair. Alcan Pacific Ltd. Oct. 1984-; Chair. Canada Japan Business Co-operation Cttee.; Dir. Int. Primary Aluminium Inst., Canadair, The Seagram Co. Ltd., American Express Co., American Cyanamid Co.; mem. Int. Man. Foundation Bd., Centre d'Etudes Industrielles Foundation Bd., Morgan Guaranty Trust Co. Int. Council. *Address:* Alcan Aluminium Limited, 1 Place Ville Marie, Montreal, Que. H3C 3H2, Canada (Office).

CULVER, John C., A.B., LL.B.; American politician; b. 8 Aug. 1932, Rochester, Minn.; s. of William Culver; m. 1st Ann Cooper 1958; one s. three d.; m. 2nd Mary Jane Checchi 1984; ed. Franklin High School, Cedar Rapids, Harvard Coll., Emmanuel Coll., Cambridge, Harvard Univ.; Dean of Men, Harvard Univ. Summer School 1960; Legis. Asst. to U.S. Senator Edward M. Kennedy 1962-63; mem. Congress (Iowa) 1965-75; U.S. Senator for Iowa 1975-80; partner, Arent, Fox, Kintner, Plotkin and Kahn 1981-; Democrat. *Leisure interests:* reading, sports, historical restoration. *Address:* 1050 Connecticut Avenue, N.W., Washington, D.C. 20036 (Office); 3434 Oakwood Terrace, N.W., Washington, D.C. 20010, U.S.A. (Home). *Telephone:* (202) 857-6152 (Office).

CUMBERLAND, Kenneth Brailey, C.B.E., M.A., D.SC., F.R.S.N.Z.; New Zealand farmer and professor emeritus of geography; b. 1 Oct. 1913, Bradford, England; s. of Ernest Cumberland, and Lucy Cumberland; m. 1st Marjorie Denham 1941 (deceased); one s. two d.; m. 2nd Gladys M. Johnston 1981; ed. Grange High School, Bradford, Univ. Coll. Nottingham; Asst. Lecturer Univ. Coll. London 1937-38; Lecturer Canterbury Univ. Coll., Christchurch, N.Z. 1938-48; Prof. of Geography, Univ. of Auckland 1949-78, Prof. Emer. 1978-; Vice-Pres. Int. Geographical Union 1960-68; f. N.Z. Geographical Soc. 1945; Ed. N.Z. Geographer; Hon Fellow Royal Geographical Soc., American Geographical Soc. *Publications:* Soil Erosion in New Zealand 1944, Southwest Pacific 1958, New Zealand: A Regional View 1968, Western Samoa: Land, Life and Agriculture 1962, The World's Landscapes: New Zealand 1970, Neuseeland: Antipode des Abendlandes 1972, Landmarks (Commentary of TV film) 1981. *Leisure interests:* farming, forestry, swimming, water polo. *Address:* Brookby, Rural Delivery, Manurewa, New Zealand. *Telephone:* (64-09) 530 8426.

CUMING, Frederick George Rees, R.A.; British painter, b. 16 Feb. 1930; s. of Harold and Grace Cuming; m. Audrey Cuming 1962; one s. one d.; ed. Univ. School, Bexley Heath, Sidcup Art School, Royal Coll. of Art; travelling scholarship to Italy; Exhbns. Redfern, Walker, New Grafton, Thackeray, Fieldborne Galleries; group shows at R.A., John Moore's London Group; one man exhbns. at Thackeray Gallery, and in Chichester, Lewes, Eastbourne, Guildford, Durham, Chester, Folkestone, Canterbury, New York; works in collections including Dept. of the Environment, Treasury, Chantrey Bequest, R.A., Kendal Museum, Scunthorpe Museum, Bradford, Carlisle, Nat. Museum of Wales, Brighton and Hove Museum, Maidstone Museum, Towner Gallery, Eastbourne, Monte Carlo Museum, etc.; works in galleries in Canada, France, Germany, Greece, Holland. *Leisure interests:* tennis, golf, snooker. *Address:* The Gables, Iden, nr. Rye, E. Sussex TN31 7UY, England.

CUMMINGS, Constance, C.B.E.; British actress; b. (as Constance Halverstadt) 15 May 1910, Seattle, U.S.A.; m. Benn W. Levy 1933 (died 1973); one s. one d.; ed. St. Nicholas School, Seattle; first appeared on the stage in Sour Grapes, since then in many stage, film and television roles; has performed Peter and the Wolf and played Joan in the Claudel-Honegger oratorio St. Joan at the Stake with the orchestra at the Albert Hall and Festival Hall; mem. Arts Council 1965-70; Chair. of Arts Council Young People's Theatre Panel 1965-74; mem. Royal Soc. of Arts 1975; mem. Council, English Stage Co. 1978-; Antoinette Perry Award for Best Actress in Wings. *Plays include:* Emma Bovary, The Taming of the Shrew, Romeo and Juliet, St. Joan, Lysistrata, Coriolanus, Long Day's Journey into Night, The Cherry Orchard, The Bacchae, Mrs. Warren's Profession,

Wings (U.S.A.) 1978-79, Hay Fever 1980, Chalk Garden (New York) 1982, The Old Ladies (BBC TV) 1983, Eve 1984, The Glass Menagerie 1985, Fanny Kemble at Home 1986, Crown Matrimonial 1987. *Films include:* Busman's Honeymoon 1940, Blithe Spirit 1945, John and Julie 1955, The Intimate Stranger 1956, The Battle of the Sexes 1959, Sammy Going South 1962, In the Cool of the Day 1963. *Leisure interests:* needlework, gardening. *Address:* 68 Old Church Street, London, S.W.3, England. *Telephone:* 01-352 0437.

CUMMINGS, Ralph W., PH.D.; American agriculturist; b. 13 Dec. 1911, Reidsville, N.C.; s. of William and Sarah Elizabeth (née Huffines) Cummings; m. Mary Parrish Cummings; three s. one d.; ed. N. Carolina State Univ., Ohio State Univ.; Asst. and Assoc. Prof. Cornell Univ. 1937-42; Prof. Head of Agronomy, N. Carolina State Univ. 1942-47, Asst. Dir. of Agricultural Research 1945-47, Dir. 1948-54; Chief N. Carolina Agricultural Research, Mission in Peru 1955-56; Field Dir., Chief Rep. in India, Rockefeller Foundation 1957-66, Assoc. Dir. for Agricultural Sciences 1963-68; Admin. Dean for Research N. Carolina State Univ. 1968-71, Emer. Prof. of Soil Science 1977-; Agric. Programme Adviser in Asia and the Pacific, Ford Foundation 1971-72; Dir. Int. Rice Research Inst., Philippines June-Nov. 1972, Int. Crops Research Inst. for the Semi-Arid Tropics, Hyderabad 1972-77; Chair. Tech. Advisory Cttee. Consultative Group on Int. Agric. Research 1977-82; Chair. Govt. of India Cttee. on Agricultural Univs. 1960-64; Consultant Agricultural Research Org., Indonesia 1970; Vice-Chair. Cttee. on Study of African Agricultural Research Capabilities, N.A.S., U.S.A. 1970-73; Acting Dir.-Gen. Int. Irrigation Man. Inst. 1983-84; Fellow, American Acad. of Arts and Sciences, American Soc. for Agronomy; mem. American Chem. Soc., Soil Science Soc. of America; Trustee Int. Council for Research in Agroforestry 1985-(91), Int. Livestock Center for Africa 1986- (Chair. 1987-); Sr. Consultant World Bank, West African Agric. Research 1985-87; Presidential End Hunger Award 1988; many hon. degrees; Int. Agronomy Award, Soc. of Agronomy 1970. *Address:* 812 Rosemont Avenue, Raleigh, N.C. 27607, U.S.A. (Home).

CUMMINGS, Tilden, B.S., M.B.A.; American banker; b. 18 Sept. 1907, Chicago; s. of William Charles and Frances May (née Stevens) Cummings; m. Hester Harton Browne 1933; three s. one d.; ed. Princeton Univ. and Harvard Graduate School of Business Admin.; Dir. Continental Ill. Nat. Bank and Trust Co. of Chicago, Pres. 1960-73; Dir. Northern Natural Gas Co., Omaha, American Brake Shoe Co., N.Y., Consolidated Foods Corpn., Chicago; Vice-Pres. Bd. of Trustees, Northwestern Univ.; Dir. Chicago, Milwaukee, St. Paul and Pacific Railroad Co. 1970-, Canteen Corpn., Chicago, Northern Natural Gas Co., Omaha; official of many civic and philanthropic orgs. *Address:* Continental Illinois National Bank and Trust Co. of Chicago, 231 South La Salle Street, Chicago, Ill. 60690 (Office); 1025 Hill Road, Winnetka, Ill., U.S.A. (Home).

CUNHAL, Alvaro; Portuguese politician; b. 10 Nov. 1913, Coïmbra; ed. Lisbon Univ.; mem. of Portuguese Communist Party 1931-; Sec.-Gen. Fed. of Communist Youth Movts. 1935; mem. PCP Cen. Cttee. 1936, Cen. Cttee. Secr. 1942-49, 1960-, active in party reorganization and devt. of links with Int. communist movt. 1942-49; imprisoned for political activities 1937-38, 1940, 1949-60; Sec.-Gen. PCP 1961-; Minister without Portfolio 1974-75; elected M.P. 1975, 1976, 1979, 1980, 1983, 1985; mem. Council of State 1983-; mem. many PCP Dels. abroad. *Publications:* numerous vols. concerning Portuguese social and econ. history and political tracts. *Leisure interests:* drawing and painting. *Address:* Partido Comunista Português, Rua Soeiro Pereira Gomes, 1, 1699 Lisbon, Portugal.

CUNNINGHAM, Alexander A.; American business executive; b. 7 Jan. 1926, Sofia, Bulgaria; Navigator-electronics radar specialist, R.A.F., World War II; joined Gen. Motors 1948, Gen. Motors Overseas Operations Div. 1953, Adam Opel A.G., Fed. Repub. of Germany 1953, Gen. Motors Ltd., London 1956; Works Man. Gen. Motors do Brasil 1958-62, Man. Dir. 1963; Works Man. Gen. Motors Argentina S.A. 1962-63; Man. Adam Opel, Bochum 1964; Asst. Gen. Mfg. Man. Adam Opel A.G. 1966-69, Gen. Mfg. Man. 1969-70, Man. Dir. 1970-74; Dir. European Operations, Gen. Motors Overseas Corpn. 1974-76; Vice-Pres. Group Exec. Overseas 1978; Group Exec., Body Ass. 1980; Exec. Vice-Pres., General Motors 1984-86; Trustee Detroit Symphony Orchestra 1983-. *Address:* c/o General Motors Overseas Corporation, Stag Lane, Kingsbury, London, N.W.9, England.

CUNNINGHAM, Harry Blair; American retail executive; b. 23 July 1907, Home Camp, Pa.; s. of Ezra James and Jane (née Farley) Cunningham; m. Margaret Diefendorf 1935; three d.; ed. Miami Univ., Oxford, Ohio; Newspaper Reporter Harrisburg Patriot 1927-28; S. S. Kresge Co., Lynchburg, Va. 1928-29, Washington 1930, Brooklyn 1931-32, Detroit 1933-35, Wheeling 1936, Lafayette (Ind.) 1936-38; Muncie (Ind.) 1939-40, Grosse Pointe (Mich.) 1940-41, Highland Park (Mich.) 1942-46, Superintendent, Stores 1947-50, Asst. Sales Dir. 1951-52, Sales Dir. 1953-57, Gen. Vice-Pres. 1957-59, Pres. 1959-70, Chair. of Bd. 1967-72, Hon. Chair. 1973-77; Hon. Chair. K-Mart Corpn. 1977-; official of other companies. *Address:* 1887 Pine Ridge Lane, Bloomfield Hills, Mich. 48013, U.S.A. (Office).

CUNNINGHAM, John A. (Jack), PH.D., M.P.; British politician; b. 4 Aug. 1939; s. of Andrew Cunningham; m. Maureen Cunningham 1964; one s. two d.; ed. Jarrow Grammar School and Univ. of Durham; former Research

Fellow in Chem. Univ. of Durham; school teacher; trades union officer; mem. Parl. for Whitehaven, Cumbria 1970-83, for Copeland 1983-; Parl. Pvt. Sec. to Rt. Hon. James Callaghan 1972-76; Parl. Under-Sec. of State, Dept. of Energy 1976-79; Opposition Spokesman on Industry 1979-83, on Environment 1983-; Labour. *Leisure interests:* fell walking, squash, gardening, classical and folk music, reading, listening to other people's opinions. *Address:* House of Commons, London, S.W.1, England.

CUNNINGHAM, Merce; American dancer and choreographer; b. 16 April 1919, Centralia, Wash.; s. of Mr. and Mrs. C. D. Cunningham; ed. Cornish School, Seattle and Bennington Coll. School of Dance; soloist with Martha Graham Dance Co. 1939-45; began solo concerts 1942; on faculty of School of American Ballet, New York 1949-50; formed own company 1953; opened his own dance school in New York 1959; Guggenheim Fellowships 1954, 1959; Dance Magazine Award 1960, Soc. for Advancement of The Dance in Sweden Gold Medal 1964, Gold Star for Choreographic Invention Paris 1966, Hon. D.Litt. (Univ. of Ill.) 1972, New York State Award 1975, Capezio Award 1977, Wash. State Award 1977, Samuel H. Scripps American Dance Festival Award 1982, Ordre des Arts et des Lettres 1982; Mayor of New York's Award of Honor for Arts and Culture 1983; Hon. mem. American Acad. and Inst. of Arts and Letters 1984; Kennedy Center Honors 1985, Laurence Olivier Award 1985; McArthur Fellowship 1985. *Works include:* The Seasons 1947, 16 Dances for Soloist and Company of Three 1951, Septet 1953, Minutiae 1954, Springweather and People 1955, Suite for Five 1956, Nocturnes 1956, Antic Meet 1958, Summerspace 1958, Rune 1959, Crises 1960, Aeon 1961, Story 1963, Winterbranch 1964, Variations V 1965, How to Pass, Kick, Fall and Run 1965, Place 1966, Scramble 1967, Rainforest 1968, Walkaround Time 1968, Canfield 1969, Second Hand 1970, Tread 1970, Signals 1970, Un Jour ou Deux 1973, Sounddance 1975, Rebus 1975, Torse 1976, Squaregame 1976, Travelogue 1977, Inlets 1977, Fractions 1978, Exchange 1978, Locale 1979, Duets 1980, Channels/Inserts, Gallopade 1981, Trails 1982, Quartet 1982, Coast Zone 1983, Roaratorio 1983, Pictures 1984, Doubles 1984, Phrases 1984, Native Green 1985, Arcade 1985, Grange Eve 1986, Points in Space 1986, Carousal 1987, Eleven 1988. *Publications:* Changes: Notes on Choreography 1969, The Dancer and the Dance, Conversations with Jacqueline Lesschaeve 1985. *Address:* 463 West Street, New York, N.Y. 10014, U.S.A. (Office).

CUOMO, Mario Matthew, LL.B.; American state governor; b. 15 June 1932, Queen's County N.Y.; s. of Andrea and Immaculata Cuomo; m. Matilda Raffa; two s. three d.; ed. St. John's Coll., and St. John's Univ.; admitted to N.Y. Bar 1956, Supreme Court Bar 1960; Confidential Legal Asst. to Hon. Adrian P. Burke, N.Y. State Court of Appeals 1956-58; Assoc., Corner, Weisbrod, Froeb and Charles, Brooklyn 1958-63, partner 1963-75; Sec. of State, N.Y. 1975-79; Lieut.-Gov. of New York State 1979-82, Gov. Jan. 1983-; mem. Faculty St. John's Univ. Law School 1963-75; Counsel to community groups 1966-72; N.Y. Rapallo Award, Columbia Lawyers' Asscn. 1976, Dante Medal, Italian Govt./American Asscn. of Italian Teachers 1976, Silver Medallion, Columbia Coalition 1976, Public Admin. Award, C. W. Post Coll. 1977; Democrat. *Publications include:* Forest Hills Diary: The Crisis of Low-Income Housing 1974, Maya 1984; articles in legal journals. *Address:* Governor's Residence, State Capitol, Albany, N.Y. 12224, U.S.A.

CURIEN, Gilles; French diplomatist; b. 26 Feb. 1922, Cornimont; s. of Robert Curien and Berthe Girot; m. Sophie Perier 1950 (deceased); two s. two d.; served embassies in Rome, Bonn and Washington, D.C. 1948-62; Counsellor, Ministry of Foreign Affairs 1962-68; Amb. to Congo (Brazzaville) 1968-70; Chief, Service des Affaires Scientifiques, Paris 1970-74; Dir. of Personnel, Ministry of Foreign Affairs 1974-79; Amb. to Switzerland 1979-82; Counsellor to the Government 1983-85; Amb., French Rep. to NATO 1985-87; Ambassadeur de France 1987; Head del. CSCE Vienna 1987-; Officier, Légion d'honneur; Commandeur, Ordre national de Mérite; Chevalier, Mérite agricole. *Publication:* La morale en politique 1962. *Address:* NATO, 1110 Brussels, Belgium (Office); 66 avenue de Breteuil, 75007 Paris, France (Home).

CURIEN, Hubert, D. ÉS SC.; French scientist and politician; b. 30 Oct. 1924, Cornimont, Vosges; s. of Robert Curien; m. Anne-Perrine Dumézil 1949; three s.; ed. Lycée d'Epinal, Coll. de Remiremont, Lycée Saint-Louis, Ecole Normale Supérieure and Faculté des Sciences, Paris; Prof., Faculté des Sciences, Paris 1956-; Scientific Dir. Centre Nat. de la Recherche Scientifique (CNRS) 1966-69, Dir.-Gen. 1969-73, Gen. Del. of Scientific and Tech. Research 1973-76, Pres. Admin. Council, Institut de biologie physico-chimique 1975-; Pres. Centre Nat. Etudes Spatiales 1976-84; Minister of Research and Technology 1984-86, May 1988-; Pres. Scientific Council of Defence 1986-; Pres. European Science Foundation 1979-84; Vice-Pres. Soc. of French Engineers and Sciences 1987-; Chair. Council, European Space Agency 1981-84; fmr. Pres. Soc. Française de Minéralogie et Cristallographie; Commandeur, Légion d'honneur, Commdr., Ordre nat. du Mérite, Commdr., Palmes académiques; Military Medal; Prize, Acad. des Sciences. *Publications:* scientific articles on solid state physics and mineralogy. *Address:* 24 rue des Fossés Saint-Jacques, 75005 Paris, France (Home). *Telephone:* 633-2636 (Home).

CURLEY, Walter Joseph Patrick, Jr., M.B.A.; American banker and diplomatist; b. 17 Sept. 1922, Pittsburgh; s. of Walter Joseph Curley and Marguerite Inez (née Cowan) Curley; m. Mary Walton 1948; three s. one

d.; ed. Phillips Acad., Yale Univ., Univ. of Oslo and Harvard Univ.; Man. Caltex Oil Co., India 1948-52, Italy 1952-55, New York City 1955-57; Vice-Pres. San Jacinto Petroleum 1957-60; Partner J. W. Whitney Co. 1961-75, Dir. various subsidiaries; Pres. Curley Land Co.; Dir. New York Life Insurance Co., Crane Co., Guinness Peat Aviation Inc., Bank of Ireland Man. Co. and numerous other cos.; Amb. to Ireland 1975-77, Amb. (desig.) to France 1989-; Hon. LL.D. (Trinity Coll., Dublin) 1976. *Publication:* Monarchs in Waiting 1974. *Address:* 2 avenue Gabriel, 75008 Paris, France; 1 Rockefeller Plaza, Suite 1401, New York, N.Y. 10020, U.S.A.

CURMAN, Johan; Swedish landowner and agronomist; b. 10 Oct. 1919, Ed, Sweden; s. of Carl G. Curman and Birgitta Palme; m. Britt Ekelund 1945; two s. two d.; ed. Royal Swedish Agricultural Coll.; Vice-Pres. Upplands Vaesby Property Admin. Co. 1956-79; Sec. C. F. Lundstrom Foundation 1957-; Pres. Bd. of Swedish Plant Protection Inst. 1968-76; Pres. Swedish Employer's Asscn. for Forestry and Agric. 1970-85, Swedish Soc. of Agricultural Eng. 1973-80, Royal Swedish Acad. of Agric. and Forestry 1980-83; mem. Bd. Swedish Employers' Asscn. 1979-85; Patron of Royal Uppsala Univ., Chorus of Sweden. *Address:* Edsby, S-194 90 Upplands Vaesby, Sweden. *Telephone:* 0760-30365.

CURRAN, Charles E., S.T.D.; American ecclesiastic and professor of moral theology; b. 30 March 1934, Rochester, N.Y.; s. of John F. Curran and Gertrude L. Beisner; ed. St. Bernard's Coll. Rochester, Gregorian Univ. Rome and Accademia Alfonsiana, Rome; ordained Roman Catholic priest 1958; Prof. of Moral Theology, St. Bernard's Seminary, Rochester, N.Y. 1961-65; Asst. Prof., Assoc. Prof., Prof. of Moral Theology, Catholic Univ. of America, Washington, D.C. 1965-; Sr. Research Scholar, Kennedy Center for Bio-Ethics, Georgetown Univ. 1972; Visiting Prof. of Catholic Studies Cornell Univ. 1987-88; External Examiner in Christian Ethics, Univ. of W.I. 1982-; Pres. Catholic Theological Soc. of America 1969-70, Soc. of Christian Ethics 1971-72; Treasurer American Theological Soc. 1983-; J. C. Murray Award (Catholic Theol. Soc.) 1972. *Publications:* numerous books, articles, lectures and addresses. *Leisure interests:* reading, golf. *Address:* Department of Theology, Catholic University of America, Washington, D.C. 20064, U.S.A. *Telephone:* 202-635-5481.

CURRAN, Sir Samuel Crowe, D.L., M.A., PH.D., D.SC., LL.D., SC.D., F.R.S.; British university principal and vice-chancellor; b. 23 May 1912, Ballymena, Ulster; s. of John Curran and Sarah Owen Crowe; m. Joan Elizabeth Strothers 1940; three s. one d.; ed. Glasgow Univ. and St. John's Coll., Cambridge; Royal Aircraft Establishment 1939-40; Ministry of Aircraft Production and Ministry of Supply 1940-44; Manhattan Project (Minstry of Supply), Univ. of Calif. 1944-45 (invention of scintillation counter 1944); Natural Philosophy Dept., Glasgow Univ. 1945-55; U.K. Atomic Energy Authority, Chief Scientist, Atomic Weapons Research Establishment, Aldermaston 1955-59; Prin., Royal Coll. of Science and Tech., Glasgow 1959-64; Principal and Vice-Chancellor, Univ. of Strathclyde, Glasgow 1964-80; mem. Council for Scientific and Industrial Research 1962-65; Science Research Council 1965-68, Advisory Council on Tech. 1964-70; Chair. Advisory Cttee. on Medical Research 1962-75, Advisory Bd. on Relations with Univs. 1966-70; Chief Scientific Adviser to Sec. of State for Scotland 1967-77; Deputy Chair. Electricity Council 1977-79, Electricity Supply Research Council 1980-82, Chair. 1978-79, Deputy Chair. 1980-82; Dir. Scottish Television Ltd. 1964-82, Int. Research and Devt. Co. Ltd. 1970-78, Cetec. Systems Ltd. 1965-77, Hall-Thermotank Ltd. 1969-76; mem. Advisory Cttee. on Safety of Nuclear Installations 1977-80; mem. Radioactive Waste Man. Advisory Cttee. 1978-81; Visiting Prof. of Energy Studies, Univ. of Glasgow 1980-86; Dir. Nuclear Structures (Protection) Ltd. 1980-; Fellow, Royal Soc. of London, Royal Soc. of Edin., Inst. of Energy, Fellowship of Eng.; Hon. FRCPS (Glasgow); Hon. Fellow, St. John's Coll., Cambridge; Hon. LL.D. (Glasgow, Aberdeen), Hon. Sc.D. (Łódź, Strathclyde), Hon. D.Eng. (Tech. Univ. N.S.); Commdr. of Order of St. Olav (Norway), Freeman of Burgh of Motherwell and Wishaw; Officer's Cross, Order of Polonia Restituta, Commdr. Order, Polish People's Repub.; St. Mungo Prize of The City of Glasgow; Freeman of City of Glasgow 1981. *Publications:* Counting Tubes 1949, Luminescence and the Scintillation Counter 1953, Alpha, Beta and Gamma Ray Spectroscopy 1964, Energy Resources and the Environment (with others) 1975, Energy and Human Needs 1979, Issues in Science and Education 1988; papers on education, nuclear research and energy. *Leisure interest:* horology. *Address:* 93 Kelvin Court, Glasgow, G12 0AH, Scotland. *Telephone:* 041-334 8329.

CURREA CUBIDES, Maj.-Gen. Hernando; Colombian army officer and politician; b. 7 Dec. 1919, Bogotá; s. of Miguel Angel Currea and María Cubides de Currea; m. Stella Pombo de Currea Cubides 1944; one s. three d.; ed. Colegio Americano, Bogotá and Escuela Militar de Cadetes; Dir. and Prof., Escuela Militar de Cadetes 1965; Chief of Staff and Commdr. of the Army 1968; C.-in-C. of Armed Forces 1969; Minister of Nat. Defence 1970-74; Amb. to Portugal 1975-79; Pres. Mil. Univ. of Nueva Granada; several decorations and medals. *Leisure interests:* golf, photography. *Address:* Escuela Militar de Cadetes, Calle 81 Carrera 36, Bogotá, Colombia.

CURTEIS, Ian Bayley; British playwright; b. 1 May 1935, London; m. 1st Dorothy Joan Armstrong 1964 (dissolved); two s.; m. 2nd Joanna Trollope 1985; two step-d.; ed. London Univ.; dir. and actor in theatres throughout U.K., and BBC TV script reader 1956–63; BBC and ATV staff dir. (drama) 1963–67; Chair. Cttee. on Censorship, Writers' Guild of Great Britain 1981–85. *Plays for TV:* Beethoven, Sir Alexander Fleming (BBC entry, Prague Festival 1973), Mr. Rolls and Mr. Royce, Long Voyage out of War (trilogy), The Folly, The Haunting, Second Time Round, A Distinct Chill, The Portland Millions, Philby, Burgess and Maclean (British entry, Monte Carlo Festival 1978, BAFTA nomination Best Play of the Year), Hess, The Atom Spies, Churchill and the Generals (Grand Prize for Best Programme of 1981, New York Int. Film and TV Festival and BAFTA nomination Best Play of the Year), Suez 1956 (BAFTA nomination Best Play of the Year), Miss Morison's Ghosts (British entry Monte Carlo Festival), BB and Lord D.; writer of numerous television series; screenplays: La condition humaine (André Malraux), Lost Empires (adapted from J. B. Priestley), Eureka, Graham Green's The Man Within (TV) 1983, The Nightmare Years (TV) 1989. *Publications:* Long Voyage out of War (trilogy) 1971, Churchill and the Generals 1980, Suez 1956, 1980, The Falklands Play 1987. *Leisure interest:* avoiding television. *Address:* The Mill House, Coln St. Aldwyns, Cirencester, Glos., England.

CURTI, Merle, A.B., PH.D.; American historian; b. 15 Sept. 1897, Papillion, Neb.; s. of John Eugene Curti and Alice Hunt Curti; m. 1st Margaret Wooster 1925 (deceased), 2nd Frances Becker 1968 (deceased); two d.; ed. Harvard; Dwight Morrow Prof. of History, Smith Coll. 1936–37; visiting Prof. Chicago and Calif. Univs. and Inst. of Tech. Calif.; Prof. Columbia Univ. 1937–42, Univ. of Wis. 1942–68; Frederick Jackson Turner Prof. of History, Univ. of Wis. 1947–68, Emer. Prof. 1968–; Visiting Prof. Univ. of Tokyo 1959–60; Hon. Consultant, Library of Congress 1969–72; Hon. Fellow Truman Inst. 1975–; mem. Bd. of Advisers American Council Learned Socs., mem. Social Science Research Princeton Univ. Advisory Council 1937–39; Pres. Miss. Valley Historical Assen. 1951–52; and American Historical Assen. 1953–54; Fellow, Center for Behavioral Sciences 1955–56; Fellow, Wis. Acad. of Sciences, Art and Literature 1982; Pulitzer Prize 1944, A.C.L.S. Prize for "extraordinary scholarly achievement" 1960; Kt. Order of Northern Star (Sweden); Hon. L.H.D., Hon. Lit.D. *Publications:* Austria and the United States 1848-1852 1926, Bryan and World Peace 1927, American Peace Crusade 1815-1861 1929, War or Peace: The American Struggle 1636-1936 1936, The Social Ideas of American Educators 1935, American Issues 1941, Growth of American Thought 1943, The Roots of American Loyalty 1946, American Scholarship in the Twentieth Century (jointly), Prelude to Point Four (jointly) 1954, Probing Our Past 1955, An American Paradox 1956, The Making of an American Community 1959, Rise of the American Nation (with Paul Todd) 1960, American Philanthropy Overseas: a History 1963, Philanthropy in the Shaping of American Higher Education (with Roderick Nash) 1965, Human Nature in American Historical Thought 1969, Human Nature in American Thought, A History 1980, etc. *Address:* 110 S. Henry Street, Madison, Wis. 53703, U.S.A. (Home).

CURTIN, David Yarrow, PH.D.; American chemist; b. 22 Aug. 1920, Philadelphia, Pa.; s. of Ellsworth F. Curtin and Margaretta (née Cope) Curtin; m. Constance O'Hara 1950; one s. three d.; ed. Swarthmore Coll. and Univ. of Illinois; Pvt. Asst. (with L. F. Fieser), Harvard Univ. 1945–46; Instructor in Chem., Columbia Univ. 1946–49, Asst. Prof. 1949–51; Asst. Prof. Univ. of Ill. 1951–52, Assoc. Prof. 1952–54, Prof. 1954–, Head, Div. of Organic Chem. 1963–65, Head, Div. of Chem. 1968–; mem. N.A.S. *Publications:* many scientific papers. *Leisure interests:* music, photography. *Address:* Department of Chemistry and Chemical Engineering, University of Illinois, Urbana, Ill. 61801 (Office); 3 Montclair Road, Urbana, Ill. 61801, U.S.A. (Home). *Telephone:* 217-344-5149.

CURTIN, Michael Edward, M.B.A.; American financial executive; b. 13 Aug. 1939, Tulsa, Oklahoma; s. of John Dorian Curtin and Marie Meyercord; m. Anne Elinor O'Grady 1963; one s. three d.; ed. Univs. of Notre Dame and Chicago; U.S. Peace Corps volunteer, Chile 1961–63; Exec. W. R. Grace & Co. in Chile and New York 1965–70; Vice-Pres. and Sec. Marine Int. Corpn. 1970–73; Chief Financial Officer and Treas. Satra Corpn. 1974–79; Int. Asst. Treas. Revlon Inc. 1979–81; Exec. Vice-Pres. Inter-American Devt. Bank 1981–. *Leisure interests:* golf, skiing. *Address:* 1300 New York Avenue, N.W., Washington, D.C. 20577 (Office); 3503 Springland Lane, N.W., Washington, D.C. 20008, U.S.A. (Home). *Telephone:* (202) 623-1200 (Office); (202) 364-8859 (Home).

CURTIS, David Roderick, M.B., PH.D., F.R.A.C.P., F.A.A., F.R.S.; Australian professor of pharmacology; b. 3 June 1927, Melbourne; s. of E. D. and E. V. Curtis; m. Lauris Sewell 1951; one s. one d.; ed. Melbourne High School, Univ. of Melbourne, and Australian Nat. Univ., Canberra; resident medical positions 1950–53; Research Scholar, Australian Nat. Univ. 1954–56, Research Fellow 1956–57, Fellow 1957–59, Sr. Fellow 1959–62, Professorial Fellow 1962–65, Prof. of Pharmacology 1966–68, Prof. of Neuropharmacology 1968–73; Prof. and Head, Dept. of Pharmacology, John Curtin School of Medical Research, Australian Nat. Univ. 1973–; Burnet Lecturer 1983; Pres. Australian Acad. of Science May 1986–. *Publications:* scientific papers on various topics concerned with neurophysiology and neuropharmacology. *Leisure interests:* tennis, gardening, carpentry. *Address:* Divison of Neuroscience, John Curtin School of Medical Research, GPO Box 334, Canberra, A.C.T. 2601, Australia. *Telephone:* (062) 49 2757, (062) 48 5664.

CURTIS, Jean-Louis; French author; b. 22 May 1917, Orthez; s. of Paul and Marie (née Sarlangue) Laffitte; ed. Collège Moncade, Orthez and the Sorbonne; High School teacher, Laon, Orleans, Paris 1943–54; Prof., Univ. of Philadelphia 1957–58; lecturing tours for Alliance Française in England, Scandinavia, Africa, Madagascar and Mauritius 1949–57; Visiting Prof. Haverford Coll., Pa. 1957–58; mem. Centre National du Cinéma Français 1962–70, Acad. Française 1986; Prix Goncourt 1947; Grand Prix de Littérature, Acad. Française 1972; Prix Pierre de Monaco 1981; Chevalier, Légion d'honneur, Chevalier des Arts et des Lettres. *Publications include:* Les jeunes hommes 1946, Les forêts de la nuit 1947, Haute école 1949, Chers corbeaux 1951, Les justes causes 1954, Un jeune couple 1967, Le roseau pensant 1971, L'horizon dérobé 1979, La moitié du chemin 1980, Le battement de mon coeur 1981, La France m'épuise 1982, Le mauvais choix 1984, Une Education d'écrivain 1985, Un rien m'agite 1985; translations of five Shakespeare plays. *Address:* c/o Flammarion, 26 rue Racine, 75006 Paris (Office); 40 rue Vaneau, 75007 Paris, France (Home).

CURTIS, Tony (Bernard Schwarz); American film actor; b. 3 June 1925, New York; s. of Manuel and Helen (née Klein) Schwarz; m. 1st Janet Leigh 1951 (divorced 1962); m. 2nd Christine Kaufmann 1963 (divorced); m. 3rd Leslie Allen 1968; ed. New School of Social Research; served in U.S. Navy. *Films include:* Houdini 1953, Black Shield of Falworth 1954, So This is Paris? 1954, Six Bridges to Cross 1955, Trapeze 1956, Mister Cory 1957, Sweet Smell of Success 1957, Midnight Story 1957, The Vikings 1958, Defiant Ones 1958, Perfect Furlough 1958, Some Like It Hot 1959, Spartacus 1960, The Great Imposter 1960, Pepe 1960, The Outsider 1961, Taras Bulba 1962, Forty Pounds of Trouble 1962, The List of Adrian Messenger 1963, Captain Newman 1963, Paris When It Sizzles 1964, Wild and Wonderful 1964, Sex and the Single Girl 1964, Goodbye Charlie 1964, The Great Race 1965, Boeing, Boeing 1965, Arriverderci, Baby 1966, Not with My Wife You Don't 1966, Don't Make Waves 1967, Boston Strangler 1968, Lepke 1975, Casanova 1976, The Last Tycoon 1976, The Manitou 1978, Sextette 1978, The Mirror Crack'd 1980, Venom 1982, Insignificance 1985. *Television includes:* Third Girl from the Left 1973, The Persuaders 1971–72, The Count of Monte Cristo 1976, Vegas 1978, Mafia Princess 1986. *Publication:* Kid Andrew Cody and Julie Sparrow 1977. *Address:* c/o Eli Blumenfeld, 1900 Avenue of the Stars, Suite 2440, Los Angeles, Calif. 90607, U.S.A.

CUSACK, Cyril James; Irish actor and writer; b. 26 Nov. 1910, Durban; s. of Alice Violet Cole and James Walter Cusack; m. Mary Margaret Kiely 1945; two s. four d.; ed. Univ. Coll., Dublin and Nat. Univ.; joined Abbey Theatre, Dublin 1932; Leading Actor, Nat. Theatre, Dublin 1932, 1945, 1946, Assoc. and Shareholder 1966–; Producer, Gaelic Players 1935–36; Man. Dir. Cyril Cusack Productions 1946–61; first London appearance in Ah Wilderness 1936; Produced Tareis An Aifrinn, Gate Theatre, Dublin 1942; Man. Gaiety Theatre, Dublin 1945; Hon. Litt.D. (Ulster) 1982; has played leading roles in many stage plays in Ireland, U.K., and Broadway including The Playboy of the Western World, The Moon for the Misbegotten, Julius Caesar (Cassius), The Physicists, Andorra, The Cherry Orchard, Mr. O, Arms and the Man (Int. Critics' Award 1961), Krapp's Last Tape (Int. Critics' Award 1961) The Plough and the Stars 1977, A Life 1980; since first film appearance in Knocknagow 1937, other films have included: The Small Back Room, Odd Man Out, The Elusive Pimpernel, The Man Who Never Was, Ill Met by Moonlight, A Terrible Beauty, The Blue Veil (Oscar nomination 1952), Johnny Nobody, The Waltz of the Toreadors, I Thank a Fool, 80,000 Suspects, One Spy Too Many, The Spy Who Came in from the Cold, The Taming of the Shrew, Oedipus Rex, Galileo Galilei, King Lear, David Copperfield, Country Dance, Day of the Jackal, Juggernaut, The Temptation of Mr. O, True Confessions 1981, Little Dorritt 1987; also appears in television plays and series including The Good and Faithful Servant (Canadian TV) 1974, Catholics (U.S.A. TV) 1974, Crystal and Fox (Irish TV) 1975, Jesus of Nazareth 1976, No Country for Old Men 1981, One of Ourselves 1983; extensive radio work and recordings. *Publication:* Timepieces (poetry) 1970. *Address:* Mont Alto, Deilginis, Dublin, Ireland; 2 Vincent Terrace, London, N.1, England. *Telephone:* Dublin 809707; 01-278 2681.

CUSHING, David Henry, M.A., D.PHIL., F.R.S.; British fisheries scientist; b. 14 March 1920; s. of W. E. W. Cushing and Isobel (née Batchelder) Cushing; m. Diana Antona-Traversi 1943; one d.; ed. Royal Grammar School, Newcastle upon Tyne, Balliol Coll., Oxford; with R. A. 1940–45, 1st Bn. Royal Fusiliers 1945–46; Fisheries Lab. 1946–80, Deputy Dir. Fisheries Research, England and Wales 1974–80; Rosenstiel Gold Medal for Oceanographic Science 1980, Albert Medal for Oceanography 1984, American Fisheries Soc. Award for Excellence 1987. *Publications:* The Arctic Cod 1966, Fisheries Biology 1968, Detection of Fish 1973, Fisheries Resources and their Management 1974, Marine Ecology and Fisheries 1975, Science and the Fisheries 1977, Climate and Fisheries 1982. *Address:* 198 Yarmouth Road, Lowestoft, Suffolk, England. *Telephone:* (0502) 65569.

CUSHING, Peter, O.B.E.; British actor; b. 26 May 1913, Kenley, Surrey; s. of George Edward and Nellie Maria (née King) Cushing; m. Helen Beck 1943 (deceased); ed. Purley, Surrey, and Guildhall School of Music and Drama; clerk in surveyor's office; stage début in The Middle Watch, Connaught Theatre, Worthing 1935; Hollywood film début in Vigil in the Night 1939; New York stage début in The Seventh Trumpet, Mansfield

Theatre 1941; London stage début in War and Peace, Phoenix Theatre 1943; English film début in Hamlet 1948; toured Australia and N.Z. with Old Vic Co. 1948; appeared as Bel Affris and Britannus in Caesar and Cleopatra, and as Alexas in Antony and Cleopatra at St. James's Theatre in Laurence Olivier (q.v.) season 1951; in Robert Helpmann's production of The Wedding Ring 1952, etc; Patron Vegetarian Soc. 1987-. *Films include:* The Curse of Frankenstein 1957, Dracula 1958, The Revenge of Frankenstein 1958, The Hound of the Baskervilles 1959, The Mummy 1959, Brides of Dracula 1960, Cash on Demand 1963, She 1965, Dr. Who and the Daleks 1966, Frankenstein Created Woman 1966, The Night of the Big Heat 1967, The House That Dripped Blood 1969, The Creeping Flesh 1973, The Satanic Rites of Dracula 1973, The Beast Must Die 1974, The Ghoul 1975, Legend of the Werewolf 1975, The Devil's People 1975, At The Earth's Core 1976, Star Wars 1976, The Silent Scream 1980, Black Jack 1981, House of the Long Shadows 1982, Sword of the Valiant 1982, Top Secret! 1983, Biggles 1985. *TV appearances include:* Sherlock Holmes, The Zoo Gang, Orson Welles Mystery Series, The New Avengers, The Eagle's Nest, The Great Houdini (U.S.A.), A Tale of Two Cities, Helen and Teacher, The Vorpal Blade (Tales of the Unexpected) 1982, The Masks of Death 1984; numerous plays 1951-. *Publications:* Peter Cushing: An Autobiography 1986, Past Forgetting (Memoirs of the Hammer Years) 1988. *Leisure interests:* country walks, collecting books. *Address:* c/o John Redway, 16 Berners Street, London, W1P 3DD, England.

CUTHBERT, Alan William, PH.D, F.R.S.; British professor of pharmacology; b. 1932, Peterborough; s. of Thomas William and Florence Mary (née Griffin) Cuthbert; m. Harriet Jane Webster 1957; two s.; ed. Deacons Grammar School, Peterborough, Leicester Coll. of Tech., Univs. of St. Andrews and London; Reader in Pharmacology, Univ. of Cambridge 1973-79, Shield Prof. of Pharmacology 1979-; Chair. Editorial Bd. British Journal of Pharmacology 1974-82; Fellow, Jesus Coll. Cambridge 1968-. *Publications:* numerous articles on physiology, pharmacology and biology. *Leisure interests:* painting, sculpture, photography, gardening, travel. *Address:* Department of Pharmacology, University of Cambridge, Hills Road, Cambridge, CB2 2QD (Office); 7 Longstanton Road, Oakington, Cambridge, England (Home). *Telephone:* Cambridge 336926 (Office); Histon 3676 (Home).

CUTLER, Sir (Arthur) Roden, V.C., A.K., K.C.M.G., K.C.V.O., C.B.E., K.ST.J., B.EC.; Australian public servant and diplomatist; b. 24 May 1916, Sydney; s. of Arthur and Ruby (née Pope) Cutler; m. Helen Morris 1946; four s.; ed. Sydney High School and Univ. of Sydney; Justice Dept. N.S.W. (Public Trust Office) 1935-42; State Sec. Retd. Servicemen's League N.S.W. 1942-43, State Pres. Retd. Servicemen's League Australian Capital Territory 1957-58; mem. of Aliens' Classification and Advisory Cttee. to advise Commonwealth Govt. 1942-43; Asst. Deputy Dir. of Security Service N.S.W. 1943; Commonwealth Asst. Commr. of Repatriation 1943-46; High Commr. in N.Z. 1946-52, in Ceylon 1952-55; Minister to Egypt 1955-56; Sec.-Gen. SEATO 1957; Chief of Protocol, Dept. of External Affairs, Canberra 1957; Australian High Commr. in Pakistan 1959-61; Australian Rep. to the Independence of the Somali Repub. 1960; Australian Consul-Gen., New York 1961-65; Del. to UN Gen. Ass. 1963-64; Australian Amb. to the Netherlands 1965-66; Gov. N.S.W. 1966-81; Chair. State Bank of N.S.W. 1982-86, Air N.S.W. 1982-, 1st Australian Prime Fund, and Investment Co. Ltd., Occidental Life Insurance Co. of Australia 1987-; Dir. Rothmans Holdings Ltd., Permanent Trustee Co. 1981-; Pres. Scout Assen. of N.S.W.; 2/5th Field Regt., A.I.F., Middle East 1940-42; Hon. Air Commodore R.A.A.F. 1981-; Hon. F.C.A.; Hon. LL.D. (Sydney), Hon. D.Litt. (New England Univ., Univ. of Wollongong), Hon. D.Sc. (Univ. of N.S.W., Univ. of Newcastle); Hon. Col. Royal N.S.W. Regt. and Sydney Univ. Regt. 1966-85. *Leisure interests:* sailing, swimming, photography. *Address:* 22 Ginahgulla Road, Bellevue Hill, N.S.W. 2023, Australia.

CUTLER, Sir Horace Walter, Kt., O.B.E., F.R.S.A.; British politician, builder and financier; b. 28 July 1912, London; s. of Albert B. and Mary A. Cutler; m. Christiane Muthesius 1957; two s. three d.; ed. Harrow Grammar School and Hereford; served R.N.V.R. 1941-46; mem. Harrow Borough Council 1952-65, Leader 1961-65; mem. Greater London Council (GLC) for Harrow West 1964-86, Deputy Leader of Opposition 1964-67, 1973-74, Leader of Opposition 1974-77, 1981-82; Deputy Leader of GLC 1967-73, Leader 1977-81; Chair. GLC Housing Cttee. 1967-70, Chair. Policy and Resources Cttee. 1970-73; mem. Milton Keynes New City Devt. Corpn. 1967-86; Chair. Cen. Milton Keynes Shopping Man. Co. Ltd. 1976-, Cen. Housing Advisory Cttee., Ministry of Housing and Local Govt. 1967-74, Nat. Housing and Town Planning Exec. Cttee. 1967-74; Dir. S. Bank Theatre Bd., Nat. Theatre Bd. 1975; Chair. Branch Retirement Homes 1985-; Hon. Freeman of Harrow 1977; Chair. Harrow West Conservative Assen. 1961-64, Pres. 1964-; Conservative. *Publication:* Rents—Chaos or Common Sense 1970, The Cutler Files 1982. *Leisure interests:* golf, skiing, classical music, travel. *Address:* Hawkswood, Hawkswood Lane, Gerrards Cross, Bucks., England. *Telephone:* Fulmer 3182.

CUTLER, Sir Roden (see Cutler, Sir Arthur Roden).

CUTLER, Walter Leon, M.A.; American diplomatist; b. 25 Nov. 1931, Boston, Mass.; s. of Walter Leon Cutler and Esther Dewey; m. 1st Sarah Gerard Beeson 1957 (divorced 1981), two s; m. 2nd Isabel Kugel Brookfield 1981; ed. Wesleyan Univ. and Fletcher School of Int. Law and Diplomacy;

Vice-Consul, Yaoundé, Cameroon 1957-59; Staff Asst. to Sec. of State 1960-62; Political-Econ. Officer, Algiers 1962-65; Consul, Tabriz, Iran 1965-67; Political-Mil. Officer, Seoul, Repub. of Korea 1967-69; Political Officer, Saigon, Repub. of Viet-Nam 1969-71; Special Asst., Bureau of Far Eastern Affairs, Dept. of State 1971-73, mem. Sr. Seminar on Foreign Policy 1973-74, Dir. Office of Cen. Africa 1974-75; Amb. to Zaire 1975-79, appointed Amb. to Iran 1979; Deputy Asst. Sec. of State for Congressional Relations 1979-81; Amb. to Tunisia 1981-83, Amb. to Saudi Arabia 1983-87; Amb. to Saudi Arabia April 1988-; mem. Council on Foreign Relations, New York; Order of the Leopard (Repub. of Zaire) 1979; King Abdulaziz Decoration (Saudi Arabia) 1985. *Leisure interests:* sports, ornithology. *Address:* Department of State, 2210 C Street, N.W. Washington, D.C. 20520, U.S.A.

CUTTS, Simon; British artist, poet and publisher; b. 30 Dec. 1944, Derby; s. of George Tom Cutts and Elizabeth Purdy; m. 1st Annira Uusi-Illikainen (divorced 1973); one s.; m. 2nd Margot Hapgood (died 1985); ed. Herbert Strutt Grammar School, Belper, Derbyshire, Nottingham Coll. of Art, Trent Polytechnic; travel and miscellaneous employment including The Trent Bookshop, Nottingham 1962-69; Jt. Ed. Tarasque Press 1964-72; publishing, lecturing and writing 1972-74; Dir. and Co-Partner Coracle Press Books (now Coracle Production and Distribution) 1975-87; Dir., Coracle Press Gallery 1983-86; Dir. Victoria Miro Gallery 1985-; org. of exhbns. in Europe and New York. *Publications:* numerous publs. including Quelque Pianos 1976, Pianostool Footnotes 1983, Petits-Airs for Margot 1986, Seepages 1988. *Leisure interests:* walking, running, cooking, eating, drinking and the nostalgia of innocence. *Address:* Victoria Miro, 21 Cork Street, London, W.1 (Office); 4/16 Courtfield Gardens, London, S.W.5, England (Home). *Telephone:* 01-734 5082 (Office); 01-370 4301 (Home).

CYBULKO, Mirosław; Polish physician and politician; b. 6 August 1932, Augustów, Suwałki Voivodship; s. of Władysław Cybulko and Jadwiga Cybulko; m. Danuta Starzycka 1959; one s.; ed. Medical Acad., Białystok; physician in District Hosp., Mońki, subsequently in The Jędrzej Śniadecki Voivodship Hosp. and in Specialist Outpatients' Dispensary Białystok 1964-77; Deputy Dir. Health and Social Welfare Dept. of Voivodship Office, Białystok 1977-81, then Voivodship Physician, Białystok; Dir., Jędrzej Śniadecki Voivodship Jt. Hosp., Białystok 1981-85; Minister of Health and Social Welfare 1985-87; mem. United Peasant Party (ZSL), mem. Presidium ZSL Voivodship Cttee., Białystok, Pres. ZSL Collective Circle of Health Service, Białystok; decorations including Kt.'s Cross of Order of Polonia Restituta. *Leisure interest:* tourism. *Address:* c/o Ministerstwo Zdrowia i Opieki Społecznej, ul. Miodowa 15, 00-923 Warsaw, Poland (Office). *Telephone:* 31-23-24 (Office).

CYBULSKI, Radosław, DR. ECON.; Polish librarian and researcher; b. 2 March 1924, Vilna; m. Halina Zabrzeska 1949; one s. one d.; ed. Mickiewicz Univ., Poznań, Acad. of Econs., Poznań; Publisher and Deputy Dir. of several publishing houses 1949-71; Deputy Librarian, Nat. Library of Poland 1972-81; Asst. Prof. Inst. of Librarianship and Information Science, Warsaw Univ. 1973-, Dir. of Inst. 1987-; Chief Librarian, Warsaw Univ. Library 1982-87. *Publications:* various publications on books and publishing. *Leisure interest:* tourism. *Address:* Białowieska 17, m. 19, 04-063 Warsaw (Home); Instytut Bibliotekoznawstwa i Informacji Naukowej UW, ul. Nowy Świat 69, 00-314, Warsaw, Poland (Office).

CYPRYNIAK, Kazimierz; Polish politician; b. 16 Dec. 1934, Wólka, Chełm Voivodship; ed. Higher Agric. School, Szczecin; official, Presidium of Dist. Nat. Council, Chełm Lubelski 1951; Head, Purchases Dept. of Commune Co-operative, Dorohusk 1951-53; mem. Polish Youth Union 1950-54, Polish United Workers' Party (PZPR) 1954-; Instructor, then Sec. of PZPR Dist. Cttee., Stargard 1960-63; First Sec. PZPR Dist. Cttee., Goleniów 1963-69, Stargard 1969-71; Sec. PZPR Voivodship Cttee., Szczecin 1971-80, First Sec. 1980-81; alt. mem. PZPR Cen. Cttee. 1980-81, 1985-86, mem. and Sec. PZPR Cen. Cttee. April-July 1981, Head, Organizational Dept. of PZPR Cen. Cttee. 1981-85, Head, Political-Organizational Dept. of PZPR Cen. Cttee. 1985-86, mem. and Sec. PZPR Cen. Cttee. 1986-; Chair. Comm. for Youth, Physical Culture and Tourism of PZPR Cen. Cttee. 1986-; Order of Banner of Labour (1st Class); Commdr.'s Cross of Order of Polonia Restituta and other decorations. *Address:* Komitet Centralny PZPR, ul. Nowy Świat 6, 00-497 Warsaw, Poland.

CZECHOWICZ, Tadeusz, D.SC.TECH.; Polish politician; b. 29 July 1935, Małecz; s. of Adam and Jozefa Czechowicz; m. Zofia Czechowicz 1960; two s.; ed. Łódź Tech. Univ.; master in Wool Industry Works, Łódź 1958-61; scientific worker in Textile Inst., Łódź 1961-69; Vice-Chair. Gen. Bd. of Textile Workers' Trade Union 1969-76; Dir. Centre for Advancement of Light Industry Cadre, Łódź 1976-77; Sec. Łódź Cttee. of Polish United Workers' Party (PZPR) 1977-80, First Sec. PZPR Voivodship Cttee., Łódź 1980-86, mem. PZPR Cen. Cttee. 1981-86, mem. Political Bureau of Cen. Cttee. 1981-86, Chair. Youth Comm. of PZPR Cen. Cttee. 1981-86; mem. PZPR 1959-, fmr. activist of Socialist Youth Union; Deputy to Seym (Parl.) 1985-; Amb. to Hungary 1986-; Kt.'s Cross of Order of Polonia Restituta and other decorations. *Address:* Embassy of the Polish People's Republic, Gorkij Fasor 16, 1068 Budapest, Hungary. *Telephone:* 425 566.

CZESZEJKO-SOCHACKI, Zdzisław, D.IUR.; Polish lawyer and diplomatist; b. 10 April 1927, Rokitno Wołyńskie; s. of Wiktor and Helena

Czeszejko-Sochacki; m. 1950 Amalia Czeszejko-Sochacka; two c.; ed. Jagiellonian Univ., Cracow; mem. Bar Co-operative No. 1, Opole 1953-67; mem. Bar Council, Opole 1953-67, Sec. 1953-56, Vice-Dean 1956-59, Dean 1959-67; mem. Bar Co-operative No. 6, Warsaw 1967-; Sec. Chief Bar Council 1967-70, Dean, Warsaw Bar Council 1970-72, Pres. Chief Bar Council 1972-81; mem. Cttee. of Legal Sciences, Polish Acad. of Sciences 1976-80; mem. Polish Lawyers' Asscn., mem. Presidium 1976-86, Pres. 1981-86; Vice-Pres. Int. Asscn. of Lawyers-Democrats 1984-; mem. PZPR 1953-; mem. Seym 1980-85; Amb. to Switzerland 1986-; numerous Polish decorations, including Officer's and Kt.'s Cross of Order of Polonia Restituta. *Publications:* over 100 publications on state and law, legal profession, penal substantive law and rules of penal court, including Odpowiedzialność dyscyplinarna adwokatów. Komentarz (co-author) 1971, Adwokatura PRL (co-author) 1974, Adwokat z urzędu w postępowaniu sądowym (co-author) 1975, Przestępstwo rozpijania małoletniego 1976, Prawo w Polsce. Wybrane zagadnienia (co-author) 1978, Minimum prawa, maksimum skuteczności 1985, Trybunał Konstytucyjny PRL 1986. *Leisure interests;* travelling, tennis, reading. *Address:* Botschaft der Volksrepublik Polen, Postfach 30, Elfenstrasse 20, 3006 Bern, Switzerland. *Telephone:* (031) 43-53-15.

CZIBERE, Tibor; Hungarian engineer and politician; b. 16 Oct. 1930, Tapolca; ed. Tech. Univ. of Heavy Industry, Miskolc; engineer with Ganz-MÁVAG Electricity Works 1956; rejoined Miskolc Univ. and active as lecturer 1963, Prof. and Dean of Mechanical Eng. Faculty 1968, Rector 1978-86, Prof. 1986-88; Minister of Culture 1988-; Corresp. mem. Hungarian Acad. of Sciences 1976, mem. 1985-, mem. of Parl. 1983-85, 1988-; Vice-Pres. Nat. Council of Patriotic People's Front; Kossuth Prize 1962, Labour Order of Merit 1971, Star Order of the People's Repub. *Address:* Ministry of Culture, 1055 Budapest, Szalay utca 10/14, Hungary. *Telephone:* 530-600.

CZIFFRA, Georges; French concert pianist; b. 5 Nov. 1921, Budapest, Hungary; s. of Julius Cziffra and Helen Nagy; m. Soleyka Abdin 1941; one s. (deceased); ed. Conservatoire of Music, Budapest; Cabaret pianist in Hungary 1938-50; went to Paris 1956; recitals and concerts in U.S.A., U.K., Canada, France, Israel, Belgium, Netherlands, Italy, Switzerland, Japan and South America; plays Liszt, Grieg, Tchaikovsky, Beethoven, Schumann, Chopin, etc.; f. Festival de la Chaise Dieu 1966, Biennial Concours Int. de Piano, Versailles, for young pianists 1968, and Cziffra Foundation 1975; works include Paraphrase—Transcriptions and Improvisations; Chevalier, Légion d'honneur 1973, Commdr., Ordre des Arts et des Lettres, Médaille d'or de l'Académie française. *Publications:* le Piano 1976, Des canons et des fleurs (autobiog.) 1977. *Address:* 4 rue Saint-Pierre, 60300 Senlis, France.

CZINEGE, Lajos; Hungarian politician; b. 24 March 1924, Karczag; s. of József Czinege and Mária Andrási; m. Maria Völgyi 1949; two s. one d.; agricultural labourer; official CP 1947-51; Lieut.-Col. 1951-54; Lieut.-Gen. 1960; Col.-Gen. 1962-78; Army Gen. 1978-; mem. Cen. Cttee., Hungarian Socialist Workers' Party 1959-, Substitute mem. Political Cttee. 1961-70; Minister of Defence 1960-84; a Deputy to Chair. Council of Ministers 1984-87; Order of the October Revolution (Soviet) 1980; Order of Lenin (twice). *Leisure interests:* mountaineering, wild game shooting. *Address:* Council of Ministers, 1055 Budapest, Parliament Building, Kossuth Lajos tér 1, Hungary. *Telephone:* 123-500.

CZUBIŃSKI, Lucjan, D.JUR.; Polish lawyer and politician; b. 21 July 1930, Dobrzelin, near Kutno; ed. A. Mickiewicz Univ., Poznań; Army 1949-; Officer of Public Prosecutor 1951-; Chief Mil. Prosecutor 1968-72; Brig.-Gen. 1970, Div.-Gen. 1984; mem. Cen. Revisional Comm. of Polish United Workers' Party, then mem. Presidium of Cen. Revisional Comm. 1971-75; Procurator Gen. 1972-81; Under-Sec. of State, Ministry of Internal Affairs 1983-; Deputy mem. Cen. Cttee. Polish United Workers' Party 1975-80, mem. 1980-81; lecturer, Dept. of Law and Admin., Univ. of Łódź 1976-; D.habil. Polit.-Law Dept., Internal Affairs Acad., Warsaw; Order of Banner of Labour (1st Class), Officer's Cross, Order of Polonia Restituta, Gold Cross of Merit, J. Krasicki Gold Award, Medal of 30th Anniversary of People's Poland. *Publications:* Niektóre problemy odpowiedzialności karnej żołnierzy 1968, Istota rozkazu wojskowego 1969, Kodeks karny, Część wojskowa 1969, Wychowawcze treści prawa wojskowego i regulaminów 1970, Problematyka egzekwowania posłuszeństwa w Ludowym Wojsku Polskim 1975. *Address:* Ministerstwo Spraw Wewnętrznych, ul. Rakowiecka 26, 00-904 Warsaw, Poland.

CZYREK, Józef, M.A.; Polish politician; b. 20 July 1928, Białobrzegi, Rzeszów Voivodship; ed. Jagiellonian Univ., Cracow; fmr. activist in youth orgs. Rural Youth Union (Wici) and Univ.; Polish Youth Union (ZAMP); Asst. Jagiellonian Univ., Cracow, and Higher School of Econs., Cracow 1949-52; numerous posts in Ministry of Foreign Affairs 1952-82, Under-Sec. of State 1971-80, Minister of Foreign Affairs 1980-82; mem. PZPR, Deputy mem. PZPR Cen. Cttee. 1971-80, mem. Cen. Cttee. Feb. 1980-, mem. Political Bureau of PZPR Cen. Cttee., Sec. Cen. Cttee. 1981-, Chair. Int. Comm. of PZPR Cen. Cttee. 1981-83, 1986-, Ideological Comm. of Cen. Cttee. 1983-86; Chair. Editorial Council Nowe Drogi 1986-; Vice-Chair. Provisional Nat. Council of Patriotic Movement for Nat. Rebirth (PRON) 1982-83, Vice-Chair. Exec. Cttee. of Nat. Council PRON 1983-87, mem. Exec. Cttee. of Nat. Council (PRON) 1987-; Deputy to Seym (Parl.) 1985-; Chair. Seym Comm. of Foreign Affairs 1985-; Chair. Polish Club of Int. Relations 1988-, Commdr.'s Cross, Order of Polonia Restituta, Commdr. de la Légion d'honneur, and other decorations. *Address:* Komitet Centralny PZPR, ul. Nowy Swiat 6, 00-497 Warsaw, Poland.

D

da NÓBREGA, Mailson Ferreira; Brazilian politician; Minister of Finance Jan. 1988–. *Address:* Ministry of Finance, Esplanada dos Ministérios, Bloco P, 5°, 70.048 Brasília, DF, Brazil.

DA SHICHANG; Chinese actor; Best Actor, Hundred Flowers Award for role in Return of the Swallows 1981. *Address:* People's Republic of China.

DAANE, James Dewey; American banker and educator; b. 6 July 1918, Grand Rapids, Mich.; s. of Gilbert L. and Mamie (née Blocksma) Daane; m. 1st Blanche M. Tichenor 1941 (dissolved); m. 2nd Onnie B. Selby 1953 (deceased); m. 3rd Barbara W. McMann 1963; three d.; ed. Duke Univ. and Harvard Univ.; Fed. Reserve Bank of Richmond 1939–60, Monetary Economist 1947, Asst. Vice-Pres. 1953, Vice-Pres., Dir., Research Dept., 1957; Chief, IMF Mission to Paraguay 1950–51; Vice-Pres., Econ. Adviser, Fed. Reserve Bank of Minneapolis May-July 1960; Asst. to Sec. of U.S. Treasury, Prin. Adviser to Under-Sec. for Monetary Affairs 1960–61; Deputy Under-Sec. of Treasury for Monetary Affairs and Gen. Deputy to Under-Sec. for Monetary Affairs 1961–63; mem. Bd. of Govs., Fed. Reserve System 1963–74; Vice-Chair. Commerce Union Bank 1974–; Vice-Chair. Tennessee Valley Bancorp 1975–78; Chair. Int. Policy Cttee., Sovran Financial Corpn./Cen. South 1978–; Dir. Nat. Futures Asscn., Ill. 1983–; Frank K. Houston Prof. of Banking and Finance, Graduate School of Man., Vanderbilt Univ. 1974–85, Valere Blair Potter Prof. of Banking and Finance 1985–; Dir. Whittaker Corpn. 1974–, Chicago Bd. of Trade 1979–82; mem. American Finance Asscn., American Econ. Asscn. *Address:* Sovran Bank/Central South, 1 Commerce Place, Nashville, Tenn. 37219 (Office); 102 Westhampton Place, Nashville, Tenn. 37205, U.S.A. (Home).

DABBAGH, Abdallah Tahir Al-, M.A.; Saudi Arabian civil servant; b. 1939, Makkah; s. of Mohammad Tahir Al-Dabbagh; m.; ed. Univ. of Colorado and Johns Hopkins Univ.; Dir. Int. Fairs and Expositions, Ministry of Commerce 1967–69, of Foreign Trade 1971–73; Deputy Commr. Gen., Osaka 1969–71; Commercial Counsellor Embassy, London 1973–77, Washington D.C. 1977–81; Gen. Man. Health Water Bottling Co., Riyadh 1976–77; Man. Dir. Arab Marketing Services Group 1981–83; Sec.-Gen. Council of Saudi Chambers of Commerce and Industry 1983–. *Address:* P.O. Box 16683, Riyadh 11474, Saudi Arabia. *Telephone:* (01) 4053200.

DACHEVILLE, Colette (pseudonym Stephane Audran); French actress; b. 8 Nov. 1932, Versailles; d. of Corneille Dacheville and Jeanne Rossi; m. 1st Jean-Louis Trintignant; m. 2nd Claude Chabrol 1964; one s.; ed. Lycée Lamartine, Paris, Cours Charles Dullin; studied drama under Tania Balachova and Michel Vitold. *Films include:* Les bonnes femmes 1959, Les godelureaux 1960, L'oeil du malin 1961, Landru 1962, Line of Demarcation 1966, Champagne Murders 1966, Les biches 1968, La femme infidèle 1968, La peau de torpedo 1969, La dame dans l'auto avec les lunettes et un fusil 1969, Le boucher 1970, La rupture 1970, Aussi loin que l'amour 1970, Juste avant la nuit 1971, Without Apparent Motive 1971, Un meurtre est un meurtre 1972, Dead Pigeon on Beethoven Street 1972, Discreet Charm of the Bourgeoisie 1972, Les noces rouges 1973, Comment réussir dans la vie quand on est con et pleurnichard 1973, Le cri du coeur 1974, Les dix petits nègres 1974, B Must Die 1974, The Black Bird 1975, Vincent, Francois, Paul and Others 1975, Folies bourgeoises 1976, Violette Nozière 1978, Le Gagnant, Le Soleil en face 1979, The Big Red One 1980, Coup de Torchon 1981, Boulevard des assassins 1982, On iras tous au paradis, Le sang des autres 1983, Poulet au vinaigre 1984, Babette's Feast 1988; TV appearance in Brideshead Revisited 1981. *Address:* 95 bis rue de Chezy, 92200 Neuilly-sur-Seine, France. *Telephone:* 6370069.

DACIE, Sir John (Vivian), Kt., M.D., F.R.C.P., F.R.C.PATH., F.R.S.; British professor of haematology; b. 20 July 1912; s. of John C. Dacie and Lilian M. Dacie; m. Margaret K. V. Thynne 1938; three s. two d.; ed. King's Coll. School, Wimbledon, King's Coll., London and King's Coll. Hosp.; various appts. King's Coll. Hosp. Postgrad. Medical School and Manchester Royal Infirmary 1936–39; Pathologist, Emergency Medical Service 1939–42; RAMC 1943–46, rank of Lieut.-Col.; Sr. Lecturer in Clinical Pathology, then Reader in Haematology, Postgrad. Medical School 1946–56; Prof. of Haematology, Royal Postgrad. Medical School of London, Univ. of London 1957–77, Prof. Emer. 1977–. *Publications:* Practical Haematology 1950, 6e. 1984, Haemolytic Anaemias 1954, 3e. 1985–88; papers on anaemia in medical journals. *Leisure interests:* music, entomology, gardening. *Address:* 10 Alan Road, Wimbledon, London, S.W.19, England. *Telephone:* 01-946 6086.

DACKO, David; Central African Republic politician; b. 24 March 1930, M'Baiki; ed. Ecole Normale, Brazzaville; Minister of Agriculture, Stockbreeding, Water and Forests, Cen. African Govt. Council 1957–58; Minister of Interior, Economy and Trade, Cen. African Provisional Govt. 1958–59; Premier, Cen. African Repub. 1959–66, Minister of Nat. Defence, Guardian of the Seals 1960–66; Pres. of Cen. African Repub. 1960–66 (deposed by mil. coup); mem. Mouvement pour l'Evolution Sociale de l'Afrique Noire (MESAN); under house arrest for several years; appointed Personal Adviser to Pres. (later Emperor) 1976; Pres. of restored Repub. 1979–81; ousted in coup Sept. 1981; Pres. UDEAC 1979.

DACRE OF GLANTON, Baron (Life Peer), cr. 1979, of Glanton, in the County of Northumberland; **Hugh Redwald Trevor-Roper,** F.B.A.; British historian; b. 15 Jan. 1914, Glanton, Northumberland; s. of the late Dr. B. W. E. Trevor-Roper and of Mrs. Trevor-Roper; m. The Lady Alexandra Haig 1954; ed. Charterhouse and Christ Church, Oxford; Research Fellow, Merton Coll., Oxford 1937–39; Student of Christ Church, Oxford 1945–57; Regius Prof. of Modern History of Oxford 1957–80; Master of Peterhouse, Cambridge 1980–87; Dir. Times Newspapers Ltd. 1974–88; Chevalier, Légion d'honneur 1976. *Publications:* Archbishop Laud 1940, The Last Days of Hitler 1947, Hitler's Table Talk (Ed.) 1953, The Gentry 1540-1640 1954, The Poems of Richard Corbett (Ed. with J. A. W. Bennett) 1955, Historical Essays 1957 (American title, Men and Events 1958), Hitler's War Directives (Ed.) 1964, The Rise of Christian Europe 1963, Religion, the Reformation and Social Change 1967 (American title The Crisis of the 17th Century 1968), The Philby Affair 1968, The European Witch-Craze in the 16th and 17th Centuries 1970, Queen Elizabeth's First Historian 1971, Princes and Artists: Patronage and Ideology at Four Habsburg Courts 1976, A Hidden Life: The Enigma of Sir Edmund Backhouse 1976, Goebbels Diaries, The Last Days (Ed.) 1978, Renaissance Essays 1985; Catholics, Anglicans and Puritans 1987; ed. The Golden Age of Europe: From Elizabeth to the Sun King 1987. *Address:* The Old Rectory, Didcot, Oxon., England. *Telephone:* Didcot 818568.

DADDAH, Moktar Ould, L. EN. D.; Mauritanian politician; b. 20 Dec. 1924, Boutilmit; ed. secondary school, Senegal and Paris; Interpreter; studied law; with firm Boissier Palun, Dakar; territorial councillor 1957; Premier, Islamic Repub. of Mauritania 1958–78; Pres. of the Repub. 1961–78; under house arrest 1978–79; left Mauritania, sentenced in absentia to hard labour for life Nov. 1980; Pres. Org. Commune Africaine et Malgache 1965; Chair. OAU 1971–72; Sec.-Gen. Parti du Peuple Mauritanien (suspended since the coup in July 1978).

DADZIE, Kenneth, B.A.; Ghanaian diplomatist and international official; b. 1930; ed. Univ. of Cambridge; entered govt. service 1952, Ghana Foreign Service 1955; First-Sec. Paris 1957–58, Dir. Admin. Div., Ministry of Foreign Affairs 1958–60, Counsellor, Perm. Mission of Ghana at UN 1960–62, Deputy Perm. Rep. 1962–63; mem. UN Secr. 1963–75, in Office of Inter-Agency Affairs 1970–75, Deputy Asst. Sec.-Gen. 1972–75; transferred to Geneva Office of UN 1975 as Dir. of External Relations and Inter-Agency Affairs; returned to Govt. Service 1975 as Perm. Rep. to UN in Geneva, concurrently Amb. to Austria and Switzerland 1975–78; Pres. UN Trade and Devt. Bd. 1975–76; Chair. Cttee. on Restructuring of the Econ. and Social Sectors of UN System 1976–77; Dir.-Gen. of Devt. and Int. Econ. Co-operation, UN Secr. 1978–82; High Commr. in U.K. with rank of Sec. of State 1982–86; Sec.-Gen. of UNCTAD Feb. 1986–. *Address:* c/o UNCTAD, Palais des Nations, 1211 Geneva 10, Switzerland. *Telephone:* 4122-34 60 11.

DAFALLAH, Gizouli; Sudanese physician and politician; b. Dec. 1935, Blue Nile Prov.; two d.; ed. Khartoum Medical Coll.; Chair. Alliance of the Nat. Forces April 1985 (after overthrow of Pres. Gaafar al-Nemery q.v. in coup); Chair. Doctors' Union; Prime Minister of Sudan 1985–86. *Address:* c/o Office of the Prime Minister, Khartoum, Sudan.

DAGENAIS, Camille A., O.C., LL.D., D.SC., D.A.SC., F.E.I.C.; Canadian engineer and business executive; b. 12 Nov. 1920, Montreal; s. of Gilbert and Charlotte (Mitchell) Dagenais; m. Pauline Falardeau 1947; three s.; ed. Ecole Polytechnique, Montreal, Alexander Hamilton Inst. and Ecole des Hautes Etudes Commerciales, Montreal; junior engineer (design), Canadian Industries Ltd. 1946–47, construction engineer 1947–50; project engineer H. J. Doran 1950–53; joined Surveyer, Nenniger & Chênevert Inc. 1953, Partner 1959, Chair. of Bd. and Gen. Man. 1965, Pres. 1966, Pres. SNC Enterprises Ltd. 1967, Chair. of Bd. and C.E.O., The SNC Group 1975–; Dir. Canadian Liquid Air Ltd. 1975–, Soc. d'investissement Desjardins 1977–, Royal Bank of Canada 1978–; Warden, Corpn. of Seven Wardens 1972–; Gov. Univ. of Québec, Conseil du Patronat du Québec; mem. Council, Conf. Bd. in Canada; mem. Nat. Research Council of Canada 1972–74; mem. Advisory Cttee., Centre of Int. Business Studies, Ecole des Hautes Etudes Commerciales; mem. Canadian Soc. for Civil Eng. (Pres. 1973), Asscn. of Consulting Engineers of Canada (Pres. 1967–68) and other professional asscns.; Hon. LL.D. (Toronto) 1973; Hon. D.A.Sc. (Sherbrooke) 1975; Hon. D.Sc. (Royal Mil. Coll. of Canada) 1975, (Laval) 1977. *Leisure interests:* hunting, fishing. *Address:* The SNC Group, 1, Complexe Desjardins, P.O. Box 10, Desjardins Postal Station, Montreal, Quebec H5B 1C8 (Office); 3495 Avenue de Musée, Montreal, Canada. *Telephone:* (514) 282-9551 (Office); (514) 613-6497 (Home).

DAGENAIS, Marcel Gilles, M.A., PH.D., F.R.S.C.; Canadian economist; b. 22 Feb. 1935, Montréal; s. of Emilien Dagenais and Antoinette Girard; m. Denyse Laberge 1958; two s. one d.; ed. Coll. Jean-de-Brébeuf, Univ. de Montréal and Yale Univ.; Asst. Prof. Univ. de Montréal 1961–66, Visiting Prof. 1972–73, Prof. of Econs. 1973–, Assoc. Fellow Centre de recherche et dévt. en écon. 1987–; Visiting Prof. Ecole des Hautes Etudes Commerciales de Montréal 1966–67, Assoc. Prof. 1967–70, Prof. 1970–72; Special Prof. Sir George Williams Univ. 1969–73; Woodrow Wilson Hon. Fellowship; Award of Soc. Canadienne de sciences écon.; Killam Research Fellow. *Publications:* numerous papers in economic journals. *Address:* C.R.D.E., Université de Montréal, P.O. Box 6128, Station A, Montréal, Québec, H3C 3J7 (Office); 60 Berlioz, Apt. 1002, Verdun, Québec, H3C 3J7, Canada. *Telephone:* (514) 343-6760 (Office); (514) 766-0473 (Home).

DAGWORTHY PREW, Wendy Ann, DIP.A.D.; British fashion designer; b. 4 March 1950, Gravesend; d. of Arthur S. Dagworthy and Jean A. Stubbs; m. Jonathan W. Prew 1973; one s.; ed. Medway Coll. of Design and Middx. Polytechnic; started own design co., designer and Dir. Wendy Dagworthy Ltd. 1972–; Dir. London Designer Collections 1982–; consultant to C.N.N.A. Fashion/Textiles Bd. 1982; Judge, Royal Soc. of Arts Bd.; judge of art and design projects for various manufacturers; participating designer in Fashion Aid and many charity shows; exhibits seasonally in London, Milan, New York and Paris; Lecturer and External Assessor at numerous polytechnics and colls. of art and design; frequent TV appearances; Fil d'Or Int. Linen Award 1986. *Leisure interests:* dining out, cooking, reading, painting, horse racing. *Address:* 15 Poland Street, London, W.1 (Office); 18 Melrose Terrace, London, W.6, England (Home). *Telephone:* 01-437 6105 (Office); 01-602 6676 (Home).

DAH, Michel Monvel; Burkina Faso diplomatist; b. 2 Dec. 1938, Yako; m.; ed. Acad. de Droit de la Haye, Coll. of Law, Ouagadougou, Faculty of Law and Econ. Science, Paris, Univ. of Abidjan, Int. Inst. of Admin. and Inst. of Int. Relations; regional journalist 1961–63; Attaché and First Sec. Embassy, Abidjan 1963–69; Examining Magistrate Court of First Instance, Ouagadougou 1969–71; Tech. Adviser Ministry of Justice 1971–72, 1973–75; Counsellor to Minister of Foreign Affairs 1975–77; Under-Sec.-Gen. Foreign Affairs, Burkina Faso 1978–81; Amb. to People's Republic of China, (also accred. to Democratic People's Repub. of Korea, India, Japan, Pakistan, Bangladesh, Viet Nam and Thailand) 1981–87; Perm. Rep. to UN Aug. 1987–. *Address:* Permanent Mission of Burkina Faso to the United Nations, 115 East 73rd Street, New York, N.Y. 10021, U.S.A. *Telephone:* (212) 288-7515.

DAHAB, Field Marshal Abdul-Rahman Swar al-; Sudanese army officer and politician; b. 1934, Omdurman; m.; two s. three d.; joined Sudanese Mil. Acad. 1954; trained at mil. acads. in Jordan, Britain and Egypt; Minister of Defence, C.-in-C. Sudanese Army March 1985–86; led. mil. coup April 1985; Chair. Transitional Mil. Council 1985–86; rank of Field Marshal 1987. *Address:* c/o Ministry of Defence, Khartoum, Sudan.

DAHANAYAKE, Wijeyananda; Ceylonese politician; b. 22 Oct. 1902, Galle; s. of Dionysius Sepala Panditha Dahanayake and Caroline Gunasekera; ed. Richmond Coll. Galle and St. Thomas' Coll. Mount Lavinia; trained teacher; elected mem. Galle Municipal Council 1935–59, Mayor of Galle 1939, 1940 and 1941; elected to the State Council for Bibile 1944; M.P. 1948; Minister of Educ. 1956–59; Prime Minister, 1959–60; Minister of Home Affairs 1965–70; mem. Nat. State Ass. 1972–77; M.P. 1979–; Minister of Co-operatives 1986–88; f. Ceylon Dem. Party 1959; Hon. LL.D. (Vidyalankara), Hon. D.Litt. (Vidyodaya). *Address:* "Sravasthi", 32 Sir Marcus Fernando Mawatha, Colombo 7 (Home); 225 Richmond Hill Road, Galle, Sri Lanka (Home). *Telephone:* 598279 (Home); 09-2403 (Home).

DAHL, Roald; British writer; b. 13 Sept. 1916; s. of Harald Dahl and Sofie Magdalene Hesselberg; m. Patricia Neal (q.v.) 1953 (divorced 1983); one s. three d. (and one d. deceased); 2nd Mrs Felicity Ann Crosland d'Abreu 1983; ed. Repton; Public Schools Exploring Soc. expedition to Newfoundland 1934; Eastern Staff, Shell Co. 1934–39 (served in Dar es Salaam); R.A.F. flying training, Nairobi and Habbanyah 1939–40; No. 80 Fighter Squadron, Western Desert 1940; Greece 1941; Syria 1941; Asst. Air Attaché, Wash. 1942–43; Wing Commdr. 1943; British Security Co-ordination, N. America 1943–45; TV series based on his Tales of the Unexpected 1979; Edgar Allan Poe Award (Mystery Writers of America) 1954 and 1959, Whitbread Children's Fiction Prize 1983; Dr h.c (Keele). *Publications:* Over to You 1945, Someone Like You 1953, Kiss Kiss 1960, Switch Bitch 1974, Tales of the Unexpected 1979, More Tales of the Unexpected (short stories) 1980, Roald Dahl's Completely Unexpected Tales (short stories) 1986; Sometime Never (A Fable for Supermen) 1948, My Uncle Oswald 1979 (novels); The Gremlins (with Walt Disney) 1943, James and the Giant Peach 1962, Charlie and the Chocolate Factory 1964, The Magic Finger 1966, Fantastic Mr. Fox 1970, Charlie and the Great Glass Elevator 1972, Danny, the Champion of the World 1975, The Wonderful Story of Henry Sugar and Six More 1977, The Enormous Crocodile 1978, The Twits 1980, Roald Dahl's Revolting Rhymes 1982, The BFG 1982, Dirty Beasts 1983, The Witches 1983, Book of Ghost Stories 1983 (children's books), Boy: Tales from Childhood (autobiog.) 1984, Going Solo (autobiog.) 1986; The Honeys (play) 1955; You Only Live Twice 1967, Chitty Chitty Bang Bang 1968, Willy Wonka and the Chocolate Factory 1971 (screenplays); articles in New Yorker, Harper's Magazine, Atlantic Monthly, Saturday Evening Post, Colliers, etc. *Leisure interest:* picking mushrooms. *Address:* Gipsy House, Great Missenden, Buckinghamshire, HP16 0PB, England. *Telephone:* Great Missenden 2757.

DAHL, Robert Alan, PH.D.; American professor of political science; b. 17 Dec. 1915; s. of Peter I. Dahl and Vera Lewis Dahl; m. 1st Mary Louise Barlett 1940 (died 1970), three s. one d.; m. 2nd Ann Goodrich Sale 1973; ed. Univ. of Washington, Div. of Econ. Research, Nat. Labor Relations Bd. and Yale Univ.; Man. Analyst, U.S. Dept. of Agric. 1940; Economist, Office of Production Man., O.P.A.C.S. and War Production Bd. 1940–42; U.S. Army 1943–45; Yale Univ., successively Instructor, Asst. Prof., Assoc. Prof. and now Sterling Prof. of Political Science 1964–86; Chair. Dept. of Political Science 1957–62; Ford Research Prof. 1957; Lecturer in Political Science, Flacso, Santiago, Chile 1967; Guggenheim Fellow 1950 and 1978; Fellow, Center for Advanced Study in the Behavioral Sciences 1955–56 and 1967; Pres. American Political Science Asscn. 1967; Fellow, American Acad. of Arts and Sciences, American Philosophical Soc., N.A.S.; Trustee, Center for Advanced Study in the Behavioral Sciences; fmr. mem. Educ. Advisory Bd., Guggenheim Foundation; Woodrow Wilson Prize 1963, Talcott Parsons Prize 1977; Bronze Star Medal with Cluster. *Publications:* Congress and Foreign Policy 1950, Domestic Control of Atomic Energy (with R. Brown) 1951, Politics, Economics and Welfare (with C. E. Lindblom) 1953, A Preface to Democratic Theory 1956, Social Science Research on Business (with Haire and Lazarsfeld) 1959, Who Governs? 1961, Modern Political Analysis 1963, Political Oppositions in Western Democracies 1966, Pluralist Democracy in the United States 1967, After the Revolution 1970, Polyarchy: Participation and Opposition 1971, Regimes and Opposition 1972, Democracy in the United States 1972, Size and Democracy (with E. R. Tufte) 1973, Dilemmas of Pluralist Democracy 1982, A Preface to Economic Democracy 1985, The Control of Nuclear Weapons: Democracy v Guardianship 1985. *Address:* Department of Political Science, 3532 Yale Station, Yale University, New Haven, Conn. 06520 (Office); 17 Cooper Road, North Haven, Conn. 06473, U.S.A. (Home).

DAHLBECK, Eva; Swedish actress and author; b. 8 March 1920, Nacka; d. of Edvard Dahlbeck and Greta Österberg; m. Col. Sven Lampell 1944; two s.; ed. Royal Dramatic Theatre School, Stockholm. *Films acted in include:* The Counterfeit Traitor 1961, Biljett till Paradiset 1961, För att inte tala om alla dessa Kvinnor 1964, Alskande par 1964, Kattorna 1965, Les créatures 1965, Den Röda Kappan 1966. *Plays acted in include:* Candida 1961, Ändå älskar vi varavdra 1963, Tchin-Tchin 1963, The Balcony 1964, Doctors of Philosophy 1964. *Publications:* Dessa mina minsta (play) 1955, Hem till Kaos (novel) 1964, S'is'ta Spegeln (novel) 1965, Den S'junde Natten (novel) 1966, Domen (novel) 1967, Med Seende Ögon (novel) 1972, Hjrätslagen (novel) 1974, Saknadens Dal (novel) 1976, Maktspråket 1978, I Våra Tomma Rum 1980. *Leisure interests:* reading, music.

DAHLERUP, Troels, D.THEOL.; Danish professor of modern history; b. 3 Dec. 1925, Frederiksberg; s. of Nicolai Frederik Bjerre Dahlerup and Inger Dahlerup; m. Merete (née Valt) Dahlerup 1958; three s.; ed. St. Jørgen Grammar School and Univ. of Copenhagen; grammar school teacher 1953; archivist Rigsarkivet 1956; Prof. of Modern History, Univ. of Aarhus 1968–; mem. Kongelige Danske Selskab for Faedrelandets Historie, Kongelige Danske Videnskabernes Selskab; Kt. Order of Danebrog. *Publications:* Studier i Senmiddelalderlig dansk Kirkeorganisation 1963, Det dabske Sysselprovsti i Middelalderen 1968; with A. E. Christensen, Aasum herreds Tingbog 1640–48 1956–62, Det Kongelige Rettertings Domme og Rigens Forfølgninger I-II 1959–69. *Address:* Bøgebjergvej 10, 8270 Højbjerg, Denmark.

DAHLFORS, John Ragnar, M.C.E.; Swedish engineer; b. 31 Dec. 1934, Stockholm; m. Anita Roger 1962; one s. two d.; ed. Royal Inst. of Tech., Stockholm; engineer with Gränges AB Liberia project 1962–66, Sales Man. Gränges Hedlund AB 1967–68, Pres. 1970–74, Tech. Man. Gränges Construction AB 1969, Pres. Gränges Aluminium AB 1974–78; Pres. Boliden AB 1979–86; Working Chair. Artus AB 1986–; mem. Bd., Sydkraft AB, Amdahl, Componenta AB, Latour Sila (Swedish Intercontinental Air Traffic, Swedish Chamber of Commerce, Gen. Export Asscn. of Sweden; mem. Industrial Advisory Bd. to the Swedish Acad. of Eng. Sciences. *Leisure interests:* sailing, golf, tennis. *Address:* Artus AB, Nybrogatan 9, S-114 34 Stockholm (Office); Sävstigen I, S-133 00 Saltsjöbaden, Sweden (Home). *Telephone:* 08-6653455 (Office); 08-717-2800 (Home).

DAHLSTEN, Gunnar, ECON.SC.; Swedish company executive; b. 25 July 1927, New York, N.Y., U.S.A.; s. of Gunnar and Kate (Wiberg) Dahlsten; m. Monica Louise Häller 1951; two s. two d.; ed. Gothenburg School of Econs.; Econ. Dept., Mölnlycke AB, Gothenburg 1951, Deputy Man. Dir. 1964, Man. Dir. and mem. Bd. of Dirs. 1965; Man. Dir. Swedish Match 1977–85; Kt. of Royal Order of Vasa (1st Class). *Leisure interest:* sailing. *Address:* Torild Wulffgatan 20, S-413 19 Gothenburg, Sweden.

DAHRENDORF, Sir Ralf (Gustav), K.B.E., F.B.A., DR.PHIL., PH.D.; British university administrator, sociologist and politician; b. 1 May 1929, Hamburg; s. of Gustav Dahrendorf and Lina Witt; m. Ellen Joan Krug 1980; ed. Hamburg Univ. and London School of Econs.; Asst., Univ. of Saar, Saarbrücken 1954; Privatdozent in sociology 1957; Fellow, Center for Advanced Study in the Behavioral Sciences, Palo Alto, U.S.A. 1957–58; Prof. of Sociology, Hamburg 1958, Tübingen 1960, Constance 1966 (on leave since 1969); Visiting Prof. at several European and U.S. Univs.; Vice-Chair. Founding Cttee. Univ. Constance 1964–66, First Dean Faculty of Social Science 1966–67; Adviser on educational questions to the Land Govt. of Baden-Württemberg 1964–68; mem. German Council of Educ. 1966–68; Chair. Comm. on Comprehensive Univ. Planning 1967–68; mem. Free Dem. Party (FDP) 1967, Fed. Exec. 1968–74; mem. Land Diet of

Baden-Württemberg and Vice-Chair. FDP Parl. Party 1968-69; mem. Fed. Parl. (Bundestag) and Parl. Sec. of State in Foreign Office 1969-70; mem. Comm. of the European Communities 1970-74; Chair. Royal Univ. of Malta Comm. 1972-74; mem. Hansard Soc. Comm. for Electoral Reform 1975-76, Royal Comm. on Legal Services 1976-78, Cttee. to Review the Functioning of Financial Insts. 1977-80; Dir. European Centre for Research and Documentation in Social Sciences 1966-82, L.S.E. 1974-84; Visiting Scholar, Russell Sage Foundation, New York 1986-87; Warden, St. Antony's Coll. Oxford 1987-; Pres. German Sociological Soc. 1967-70; Hon. Presidium Anglo-German Soc. 1973-; Chair. Social Science Council of the European Science Foundation 1976-77; Chair. Bd. Friedrich-Naumann-Stiftung 1982-87; mem. Council, British Acad. 1980-81, Vice-Pres. 1982-84; mem. German PEN Centre 1971-; Foreign Assoc., N.A.S. 1977; Foreign mem. American Philosophical Soc., Phila. 1977; Hon. mem. Royal Irish Acad. 1974; Foreign Hon. mem. American Acad. of Arts and Sciences 1975; Hon. mem. Royal Coll. of Surgeons 1982; Fellow Imperial Coll., London 1974, Royal Soc. of Arts 1977, British Acad. 1977; Hon. Fellow L.S.E. 1973; Trustee Ford Foundation 1976-88; Hon. D.Litt (Reading) 1973, LL.D. (Manchester) 1973, D.Sc. (Ulster) 1973, (Bath) 1977, D. Univ. (Open Univ.) 1974, D.H.L. (Kalamazoo Coll.) 1974, Litt.D. (Trinity Coll., Dublin) 1975, Hon. Dr. (Univ. Catholique de Louvain) 1977, Hon. LL.D. (Wagner Coll., Staten Is., New York) Hon. D.H.L. (Maryland) 1978, Hon. D. Univ. (Surrey) 1978, Hon. LL.D. (York, Ontario Univs.) 1979, Hon. D.H.L. (Johns Hopkins Univ., Baltimore) 1982; Dr. Social Sc. (Queen's Belfast); Hon. K.B.E.; Journal Fund Award for Learned Publications 1966; BBC Reith Lecturer 1974; Grand Croix de l'Ordre du Mérite du Sénégal 1971, Grand Croix de l'Ordre du Mérite du Luxembourg 1974, Grosses Bundesverdienstkreuz mit Stern und Schulterband (Feb. Repub. of Germany) 1974, Grosses goldenes Ehrenzeichen am Bande (Austria) 1975, Grand Croix de l'Ordre de Léopold II (Belgium) 1975. *Publications include:* Marx in Perspective 1953, Industrie- und Betriebssoziologie 1956, Homo Sociologicus 1958, Soziale Klassen und Klassenkonflikt 1957 and 1959, Die angewandte Aufklärung 1963, Gesellschaft und Demokratie in Deutschland 1965, Pfade aus Utopia 1967, Essays in the Theory of Society 1968, Konflikt und Freiheit 1972, Plädoyer für die Europäische Union 1973, The New Liberty: Survival and Justice in a Changing World (Reith Lectures) 1975, A New World Order? (Ghana Lectures 1978) 1979, Life Chances (also in German) 1979, On Britain (BBC TV Lectures) 1982/83, Reisen nach innen und aussen 1984, Law and Order 1985, The Modern Social Conflict 1988. *Address:* St. Antony's College, Oxford, OX2 6JF, England. *Telephone:* (0865) 59651.

DAI AILIAN; Chinese dancer and choreographer; b. 1916, Trinidad, W. Indies; studied in London 1931; worked with Modern Dance Co. of Ernst and Lotte Berk; studied at Jooss-Leeder Dance School, and with Anton Dolin, Margaret Craske, Marie Rambert; went to China 1941; teacher Nat. Opera School, Nat. Inst. of Social Educ. and Yucai School; since 1949 has been leader dance team attached to N. China Univ., Cen. Theatrical Inst., leader Cen. Song and Dance Ensemble, Artistic Dir. dance drama troupe, Cen. Experimental Opera Theatre; Pres. Beijing Dancing Acad., China Ballet Soc., China Labanotation Soc.; Vice-Chair. Chinese Dancers' Assen.; Adviser Cen. Ballet; mem. Int. Jury, Int. Youth Festival, Bucharest 1953, Moscow 1955, Choreography Competition, Turin 1983, 3rd U.S.A. Int. Ballet Competition, Jackson 1986, 2nd Int. Ballet Competition 1987, 3rd Tokyo Ballet Competition for Asia and Pacific 1987; Chair. China Nat. Ballet Competition 1984, New York 1987; Sr. Consultant, China Assen. for the Advancement of Int. Friendship; Cttee. mem. Int. Dance Council UNESCO, Vice-Chair. 1982-86, 1986-; mem. Cttee. China Int. Cultural Exchange Centre; mem. Int. Labanotation Council; mem. Standing Cttee. CPPCC; mem. Presidium 6th CPPCC Nat. Comm. 1983-. *Works include:* Lotus Dance, The Old Carries the Young, Flying Apsaras, The Women Oil-drillers' Dance. *Address:* Apartment 2-16, Overseas Chinese Mansions, Garden Village, Beijing, People's Republic of China.

DAI CHANG; Chinese traditional artist; b. 1943, Lantian Co. Shaanxi; ed. Middle School, Xian Coll. of Fine Arts 1964; mem. Shaanxi branch, Chinese Artists' Assen.

DAI QIANDING, M.A.; Chinese government official; b. 21 March 1925, Sichuan; m. Ye Zhiqing 1953; one s. two d.; ed. Central Univ., Nanking, China and Michigan Univ.; Deputy Man., People's Bank of China 1950-71, Deputy Gen. Man., Research Dept. 1972-80, Dir. Research Inst. of Int. Finance 1983-84, Dir. 1985-86, Gen. Man., Bank of China, London 1985-86; Alt. Exec. Dir. Int. Monetary Fund for China 1980-82, Exec. Dir. 1986-. *Publications:* The IMF and the World Bank 1978; numerous articles on int. finance. *Leisure interests:* travel, music, arts. *Address:* Room 13-400, International Monetary Fund, 700 19th Street, Washington, D.C. 20431, U.S.A.

DAI SULI; Chinese politician; b. Henan; Sec.-Gen. Secr., CCP Cttee., Henan 1960, mem. Standing Cttee. 1960; Alt. Sec. Secr., CCP Cttee., Henan 1965; Head Cultural Revolution Group, CCP Cttee., Henan 1966; Leading mem. Prov. Revolutionary Cttee., Henan 1968; purged 1968; mem. Standing Cttee., CCP Cttee., Henan 1972, Deputy Sec. CCP Cttee. 1973; Vice-Chair. Prov. Revolutionary Cttee. Henan 1973; Alt. mem. 11th Cen. Cttee. 1977; Sec. CCP Cttee., Henan 1977, Second Sec. 1981-; Vice-Gov. Henan 1979, Acting Gov. 1981, Gov. 1981-83; mem. 12th Cen. Cttee. CCP 1982-87; mem. Cen. Advisory Comm. 1987-; Sec. CCP Prov. Cttee.,

Liaoning 1983-86, Chair. Advisory Cttee. 1985-. *Address:* Governor's Office, Henan Province, People's Republic of China.

DAIBER, Hans Joachim, D.PHIL.; German professor of Arabic; b. 1 April 1942, Stuttgart; s. of Otto Daiber and Martha Daiber; m. Helga Brosamler 1971; one s. one d.; ed. Theological Seminaries of Maulbronn and Blaubeuren, Univs. of Tübingen and Saarbrucken; lecturer in Arabic, Univ. of Heidelberg 1975-77; Prof. of Arabic, Free Univ. Amsterdam 1977-; mem. German Oriental Inst., Beirut 1973-75, Royal Dutch Acad. of Arts and Sciences 1981-, German Oriental Soc., American Oriental Soc., Oosters Genootschap, Soc. Int. pour l'étude de la philosophie médiévale, Union Européenne d'Arabisants et d'Islamisants. *Publications:* Die arabische Übersetzung der Placita philosophorum 1968, Ein Kompendium der aristotelischen Meteorologie in der Fassung des Hunain Ibn Ishaq 1975, Das theologisch-philosophische System des Muammar Ibn Abbad as-Sulami 1975, Gott, Natur und menschlicher Wille im fruehen islamische Denken 1978, Aetius Arabus 1980, The Ruler as Philosopher: a new interpretation of al-Farabi's view 1986, Wasil Ibn Ata' als Prediger und Theologe 1988, Catalogue of Arabic Manuscripts in the Daiber Collection 1988, numerous articles in journals on Islamic philosophy, theology, history of sciences, Greek Heritage in Islam. *Address:* Free University, Letters, 10007 MC Amsterdam, The Netherlands (Univ.); Am Huettenhof 10, 4000 Düsseldorf 31, Federal Republic of Germany (Home). *Telephone:* (0211) 403714 (Home).

DAICHES, David, M.A. (EDIN.), D.PHIL (OXON.), PH.D. (CANTAB.), F.R.S.L., F.R.S.E.; British university professor and writer; b. 2 Sept. 1912, Sunderland; s. of Dr. Salis and Flora (née Levin) Daiches; m. 1st Isobel J. Mackay 1937 (died 1977) one s. two d.; m. 2nd Hazel Neville 1978 (died 1986); ed. George Watson's Coll., Edinburgh, Edinburgh Univ. and Balliol Coll., Oxford; Bradley Fellow, Balliol Coll., Oxford 1936-37; Asst. Prof. of English, Univ. of Chicago 1940-43; Second Sec. British Embassy, Washington 1944-46; Prof. of English, Cornell Univ. 1946-51; Univ. Lecturer in English, Cambridge Univ. 1951-61, Fellow of Jesus Coll., Cambridge 1957-62; Dean, School of English Studies, Univ. of Sussex 1961-67, Prof. of English 1961-77, Prof. Emer. 1977-; Dir. Inst. for Advanced Studies in the Humanities, Edinburgh Univ. 1980-86, Gifford Lecturer 1983; Sr. Fellow, Nat. Humanities Center, U.S.A. 1987-88; Hon. Litt.D. (Brown, Edinburgh, Sussex and Glasgow Univs.); Dr. h.c. (Sorbonne), Hon. D.Univ. (Stirling); many awards and prizes. *Publications:* 45 books including: The Novel and the Modern World 1939, A Study of Literature 1948, Robert Burns 1950, Two Worlds 1956, Critical Approaches to Literature 1956, Literary Essays 1956, Milton 1957, A Critical History of English Literature 1960, More Literary Essays 1968, Scotch Whisky 1969, Sir Walter Scott and his World 1971, A Third World (autobiography) 1971, Robert Burns and his World 1971, Prince Charles Edward Stuart 1973, Robert Louis Stevenson and his World 1973, Was 1975, Moses 1975, James Boswell and His World 1976, Scotland and the Union 1977, Glasgow 1977, Edinburgh 1978, Fletcher of Saltoun: Selected Political Writings and Speeches (Ed.) 1979, Literature and Gentility in Scotland 1982, God and the Poets 1984, Edinburgh: A Traveller's Companion 1986. *Leisure interests:* music, talking. *Address:* 12 Rothesay Place, Edinburgh, EH3 7SQ, Scotland.

DAILEY, Peter Heath, B.S.; American diplomatist; b. 1 May 1930, New Orleans; s. of John William and Abigail (née Heath) Dailey; m. Jacqueline Ann Biggerstaff 1953; one s. four d.; ed. Univ. of Calif., Los Angeles; progressed to Vice-Pres. Erwin Wasey Inc., Los Angeles 1956-63; Vice-Pres. Foote, Cone & Belding 1963-64; Sr. Vice-Pres. and Dir. Western and Far Eastern regions Campbell-Ewald Co., L.A. 1964-67; Chair. C.E.O. Dailey & Assocs., Los Angeles 1968-82; Vice-Chair. Interpublic, N.Y.; Amb. to Ireland 1982-84; Personal Envoy of Pres. for European Arms Control and Security Issues 1983; Pres. November Group (special advisory agency for Pres. Nixon) 1972; Dir. Shamrock Broadcasting. *Address:* 1999 Oak Knoll Avenue, San Marino, Calif. 91108, U.S.A.

DAINTITH, Terence Charles, M.A.; British professor of law; b. 8 May 1942, Coulsdon; s. of Edward Daintith and Irene M. Parsons; m. Christine Bulport 1965; one s. one d.; ed. Wimbledon Coll. and St. Edmund Hall, Oxford; called to Bar, Lincoln's Inn 1966; Assoc. in Law, Univ. of Calif. Berkeley 1963-64; lecturer in Constitutional and Admin. Law, Univ. of Edinburgh 1964-72; Prof. of Public Law, Univ. of Dundee 1972-83, Dir. Centre for Petroleum and Mineral Law Studies 1977-83; Prof. of Law, European Univ. Inst., Florence 1981-87; Dir. Inst. of Advanced Legal Studies and Prof. of Law, Univ. of London 1988-; mem. Conseil d'Admin. Assen. Int. de Droit Econ. 1985-; Trustee, Petroleum and Mineral Law Educ. Trust 1988-; Ed. Journal of Energy and Natural Resources Law 1983-. *Publications:* The Economic Law of the United Kingdom 1974, United Kingdom Oil and Gas Law (with G. D. M. Willoughby) 1977, Energy Strategy in Europe (with L. Hancher) 1986, The Legal Integration of Energy Markets (with S. Williams) 1987, Law as an Instrument of Economic Policy 1988. *Address:* 12 Viscount Court, 1 Pembridge Villas, London, W2 4XA, England; Pouzols, Josat, 43230 Paulhaguet, France. *Telephone:* 01-727 8069 (London).

DAINTON, Baron (Life Peer), cr. 1986, of Hallam Moors in South Yorkshire; **Frederick Sydney Dainton,** Kt., F.R.S., PH.D., SC.D.; British scientist and university administrator; b. 11 Nov. 1914, Sheffield; s. of George Whalley and Mary Jane Dainton; m. Barbara Hazlitt, PH.D., 1942; one s. two d.; ed. Central Secondary School, Sheffield, St. John's Coll., Oxford and

Sidney Sussex Coll., Cambridge; Univ. Demonstrator in Chem., Cambridge Univ. 1944, H. O. Jones Lecturer in Physical Chem. 1946; Prof. of Physical Chem. Leeds Univ. 1950–65; Vice-Chancellor, Univ. of Nottingham 1965–70; Prof. Dept. of Physical Chem., Univ. of Oxford 1970–73; Chancellor, Univ. of Sheffield 1978–; Chair. Council, Royal Postgraduate Medical School 1979–; Visiting Prof. Univ. of Toronto 1949; M.I.T. 1959; Tilden Lecturer Chemical Soc. 1950; lecturer, Univ. of Notre Dame, Indiana 1952; Cornell Univ. 1961, Univ. of Alberta 1962; Fellow, St. Catharine's Coll., Cambridge 1945, Praelector 1946; Chair., Assen. for Radiation Research 1964–66, Advisory Cttee. for Scientific and Tech. Information 1966–70, Nat. Radiological Protection Bd. 1978–85; mem. Council for Scientific Policy 1965–79, Chair. 1970–73, Cen. Advisory Council for Science and Tech. 1967–70; Chair. Advisory Bd. for Research Councils 1972–73; Chair. Univ. Grants Cttee. 1973–78, British Library Bd. 1978–85; Pres. Faraday Soc. 1965–67, Chemical Soc. 1972–73, Assen. for Science Educ. 1967; Centenary Pres. Library Assen. 1977; Pres. B.A.A.S. 1980, Arthritis and Rheumatism Council 1988–; mem. Genetic Manipulation Advisory Group 1979–82; Hon. mem. Royal Soc. of Science, Uppsala, American Acad. of Arts and Sciences, Göttingen Acad. of Sciences; Hon. Fellow, St. Catharine's Coll., Cambridge 1961, St. John's Coll., Oxford 1968, Goldsmiths' Coll., London, Queen Mary Coll., London, Birkbeck Coll., London, L.S.E.; Trustee British Museum (Nat. Hist.), Int. Council Educ. Devt.; Prime Warden, Goldsmith's Coll. 1982–83; Commr. on Museums and Galleries 1985–; Pres. Soc. of Designer-Craftsmen 1985–; Hon. F.R.C.P., Hon. F.R.S.C. 1983, Hon. Fellow Royal Coll. of Radiologists 1984; Hon. mem. British Inst. of Radiology 1987; many Hon. degrees from British and foreign Univs.; Sylvanus Thompson Medal, British Inst. of Radiology 1958, Davy Medal, Royal Soc. 1969, Faraday Medal, Chemical Soc. 1973, Crookshank Medal, Royal Coll. of Radiologists 1981; Rede Lecturer, Univ. of Cambridge 1981; Curie Medal, Poland 1985, John Snow Medal, Assen. of Anaesthetists 1987; Order of Merit, Poland 1985. *Publications:* Chain Reactions 1956, Photochemistry and Reaction Kinetics 1968, Choosing a British University 1981, Universities and the National Health Service 1983; numerous papers in scientific journals on reaction kinetics, especially photo and radiation chemistry, polymer chemistry and on scientific policy and education. *Leisure interests:* walking, colour photography. *Address:* Fieldside, Water Eaton Lane, Kidlington, Oxford, OX5 2PR, England (Home).

DAKOV, Mako; Bulgarian politician; b. 5 Dec. 1920, Pleven; m. Milka Stefanova 1951 (deceased), two d.; m. 2nd Nadka Lazarova 1979, one s.; ed. studies in forestry engineering; Dir. of Scientific Research, Inst. of Forestry 1950–51; Prof. Higher Forestry and Tech. Inst. 1951–57; Deputy Minister of Agric. and Forestry 1957, subsequently Chair. Cttee. for Forestry; Minister for Forestry and Forest Industry 1966–71; Deputy Chair. Council of Ministers 1971–78; mem. Bulgarian Acad. of Sciences, Vice-Pres. 1978–. *Publications:* more than 200 publications on politics, economics and forestry. *Leisure interest:* sport (especially tennis). *Address:* c/o Bulgarian Academy of Sciences, 7th November Street 1, 1040 Sofia, Bulgaria. *Telephone:* 8-41-41.

DAL, Erik, D.PHIL; Danish administrator; b. 20 Dec. 1922, Grenaa; s. of Johannes Dal and Karen (née Andersen) Dal; m. Estrid Bruun Jørgensen 1949; one s. one d.; ed. Univ. of Copenhagen; joined Danish Dept., Royal Library, Copenhagen 1953, Head 1953–67; Prof. of the History of the Printed Book 1967–74; ed. Royal Acad. of Sciences and Letters 1975–88, Pres. 1988; Admin. Danish Soc. of Language and Literature 1988–; numerous awards in the typographic field; Kt. of the Dannebrog Order 1st Class. *Publications:* works on folk ballads, Danish literature of the 16th and 17th centuries, Hans Christian Andersen, history of the book. *Address:* Frederiksholms Kanal 18A, DSL, 1220 Copenhagen (Office); Forchhammersvej 1, 1920 Copenhagen/Frederiksberg, Denmark (Home). *Telephone:* (0047) 1-130660 (Office); (0045) 1-241135 (Home).

DALAI LAMA, The (Tenzin Gyatso); temporal and religious head of Tibet; Fourteenth Incarnation; b. 6 July 1935, Taktser, Amdo Prov., N.E. Tibet; s. of Chujon Tsering and Tsering Dekyi; born of Tibetan peasant family in Amdo Province; enthroned at Lhasa 1940; rights exercised by regency 1934–50; assumed political power 1950; fled to Chumbi in S. Tibet after abortive resistance to Chinese 1950; negotiated agreement with China 1951; Vice-Chair. Standing Cttee., mem. Nat. Cttee. CPPCC 1951–59; Hon. Chair. Chinese Buddhist Assen. 1953–59; Del. to Nat. People's Congress 1954–59; Chair. Preparatory Cttee. for the "Autonomous Region of Tibet" 1955–59; fled Tibet to India after suppression of Tibetan national uprising 1959; Dr. of Buddhist Philosophy (Monasteries of Sera, Drepung and Gaden, Lhasa) 1959; Supreme Head of all Buddhist sects in Tibet (Xizang). *Publications:* My Land and People 1962, The Opening of the Wisdom Eye 1963, The Buddhism of Tibet and the Key to the Middle Way 1975, Kindness, Clarity, and Insight 1984, A Human Approach to World Peace 1984. *Leisure interests:* gardening, mechanics. *Address:* Thekchen Choeling, McLeod Ganj 176219, Dharamsala, Himachal Pradesh, India.

DALBERTO, Michel; French pianist; b. 2 June 1955, Paris; s. of Jean Dalberto and Paulette Girard-Dalberto; ed. Lycée Claude Bernard, Lycée Racine, Conservatoire National Supérieur de Musique, Paris; started piano aged 3½, first public appearance 5½; prin. teachers at Conservatoire: Vlado Perlemuter, piano and Jean Hubeau, chamber music; won first prizes

for piano, chamber music, harmony and counterpoint; started professional career 1975; concerts in major musical centres conducted by Colin Davis, Sawallisch, Rowicki, Bertini, Frühbeck de Burgos, Leinsdorf and others; played at festivals at Lucerne, Edin., Aldeburgh, Salzburg, Vienna, Berlin, Montreux; chamber music and recitals with Henryk Szeryng, Jessye Norman, Nikita Magaloff, Dumay and others; teaches at Musical Acad. des Arcs, Savoie; Clara Haskil Prize 1975; First Prize Leeds Int. Pianoforte Competition 1978; Acad. Charles Gros Award 1980 and Acad. Disque Français Award 1984, for recordings; has recorded Schubert and Beethoven sonatas, Schumann and Brahms pieces, Mozart Concertos and Chausson Mélodies (with Jessye Norman) 1980–. *Leisure interests:* skiing, tennis, golf. *Address:* Boulevard Henri Plumhof 13, 1800 Vevey, Switzerland. *Telephone:* (021) 922.64.21.

DALE, William B.; American financial official (retd.); b. 24 March 1924; ed. Wayne High School, Michigan, Univ. of Michigan and Fletcher School of Law and Diplomacy; Asst. U.S. Treasury Rep., Brussels 1948–50, Acting U.S. Rep. 1951–52; Deputy Chief, British Commonwealth and Middle East Div., U.S. Treasury Dept. 1952–53; U.S. Treasury Rep. in Middle East 1953–55; Program Man., Int. Research, Stanford Research Inst., Washington 1956–61; Dir. Bureau of Int. Programs, U.S. Dept. of Commerce 1961–62; Deputy Asst. Sec. for Int. Affairs, U.S. Dept. of Commerce 1962; U.S. Exec. Dir. IMF 1962–74, Deputy Man. Dir. 1973–84. *Address:* 6008 Landon Lane, Bethesda 14, Md., U.S.A. (Home).

DALGARNO, Alexander, PH.D., F.R.S.; British professor of astronomy; b. 5 Jan. 1928, London; s. of William Dalgarno and Margaret Dalgarno; m. Barbara Kane 1957 (divorced 1972); two s. two d.; ed. Univ. Coll. London; mem. Faculty, Applied Math., Queen's Univ. of Belfast 1951–67; Prof. of Astronomy, Harvard Univ. 1967–77, Chair. Dept. of Astronomy 1971–76, Dir. Harvard Coll. Observatory 1971–72, Phillips Prof. of Astronomy 1977–; Physicist, Smithsonian Astrophysical Observatory 1967–; Ed. Astrophysical Journal Letters 1973–; Hon. D.Sc. (Queen's, Belfast) 1972; Medal of Int. Acad. of Quantum Molecular Science 1969; Hodgkins Medal, Smithsonian Inst. 1977; Davisson-Germer Prize, American Physical Soc. 1980; Meggers Award, Optical Soc. of America 1986, Gold Medal, Royal Astronomical Soc. 1986. *Publications:* numerous scientific papers in journals. *Address:* Harvard-Smithsonian Center for Astrophysics, 60 Garden Street, Cambridge, Mass. 02138, U.S.A. *Telephone:* (617) 495-4403.

DALHOUSIE, 16th Earl of; Simon Ramsay, K.T., G.C.V.O., G.B.E., M.C., LL.D.; British politician and fmr. Governor-General; b. 17 Oct. 1914; s. of the late 14th Earl of Dalhousie and Lady Mary Adelaide Heathcote Drummond Willoughby; m. Margaret Elizabeth Stirling 1940; three s. two d.; ed. Eton Coll., and Oxford Univ.; served in Black Watch 1936–45; M.P., 1945–50; Conservative Whip 1946–48; Gov.-Gen. Fed. of Rhodesia and Nyasaland 1957–63; Lord Lieut. District of Angus 1965; Lord Chamberlain to H.M. Queen Elizabeth, the Queen Mother 1965; Chancellor of Dundee Univ. 1977–; Hon. LL.D. (Dundee Univ.) 1967. *Address:* Brechin Castle, Brechin, Scotland; 5 Margaretta Terrace, London, S.W.3, England. *Telephone:* Brechin 2176; 01-352 6477 (London).

DALITZ, Richard Henry, PH.D., F.R.S.; British research physicist; b. 28 Feb. 1925, Dimboola, Australia; s. of Frederick W. and Hazel Blanche (née Drummond) Dalitz; m. Valda Suiter 1946; one s. three d.; ed. Tooronga Rd. Cen. School and Scotch Coll., Melbourne, Univ. of Melbourne and Trinity Coll., Cambridge; Research Asst. in Physics, Univ. of Bristol 1948–49; lecturer in Math. Physics, Univ. of Birmingham 1949–55; Reader 1955–56; Prof. of Physics, Enrico Fermi Inst. for Nuclear Studies, Univ. of Chicago 1956–66; Royal Soc. Research Prof., Univ. of Oxford 1963–; Fellow, All Souls Coll., Oxford 1964–; Maxwell Medal, Inst. of Physics 1966; Jaffe Prize, Royal Soc. 1969; Hughes Medal, Royal Soc. 1975; J. Robert Oppenheimer Memorial Prize, Univ. of Miami 1980; Royal Medal, Royal Soc. 1982. *Publications:* Strange Particles and Strong Interactions 1962, Nuclear Interactions of the Hyperons 1965, Nuclear Energy Today and Tomorrow (co-author) 1971; numerous papers on theoretical physics, in scientific journals. *Leisure interests:* study of the history of the Wends and their emigration to the New World, walking, travelling hopefully and finding out why. *Address:* Department of Theoretical Physics, University of Oxford, 1 Keble Road, Oxford, OX1 3NP, England. *Telephone:* Oxford 273967.

dalla CHIESA, Romeo; Italian banker; b. 15 Oct. 1924, Livorno; s. of Romano dalla Chiesa and Maria L. Bergonzi; m. Ebba Tamm; five s.; ed. Torquato Tasso School, Florence, Orazio Flacco School, Bari, Univ. of Rome and American Univ., Washington, D.C.; at Gen. H.Q., Bank of Italy, Rome 1943–49; Economist and Econ. Consultant to Panamanian and Thai Govts. and Loan Officer, Far East Dept. IBRD (World Bank) 1949–58; Gen. Man. for Loans to European Community, EIB 1958–81; Gen. Financial Consultant, Banca Nazionale del Lavoro Rome 1981–82; Chair. of Bd. Banco di Roma Jan. 1983–; Commendatore della Repubblica Italiana. *Publications:* papers on economic, financial and banking subjects. *Leisure interests:* fine arts, literature, chess. *Address:* Banco di Roma, Vialell. Tupini 180, Rome, Italy. *Telephone:* (06) 54451.

DALLARA, Charles H., M.A., M.A.L.D.; American international finance official; b. 1948; ed. Univ. of S. Carolina and Fletcher School of Law and Diplomacy; int. economist, U.S. Treasury Dept. 1976–79; Special Asst. to

Under-Sec. for Monetary Affairs 1979–81; Special Asst. to Asst. Sec. for Int. Affairs 1981–82; Alt. Exec. Dir. IMF 1982–83; Deputy Asst. Sec. for Int. Monetary Affairs, U.S. Treasury Dept. 1983–84; Exec. Dir. IMF 1984–. *Address:* c/o International Monetary Fund, 700 19th Street, N.W., Washington, D.C. 20431, U.S.A.

DALLE, François Léon Marie-Joseph, L. EN D.; French business executive; b. 18 March 1918, Hesdin; s. of Joseph and Jeanne (Dumont) Dalle; m. 4th Genevieve Clément; three s. two d. (fmr. marriages); ed. Saint-Joseph de Lille, Faculty of Law, Paris; fmr. advocate, Court of Appeal, Paris 1941–42; Plant Man., then Asst. Gen. Man., Monsavon Co. 1945–48, Marketing Man., l'Oréal 1948–50, Asst. Gen. Man. 1950–57, Pres., Dir.-Gen. L'Oréal 1957–84; Pres. Union of perfumery and beauty salon suppliers 1957–; Pres. Saipo; Dir. Philips (France), Banque de Paris 1973–82, Editions Masson, Union des Annonceurs, Dir. and mem. bd. Nestlé S.A. 1975– (Vice-Pres. 1986–), fmr. Dir. Lancôme; Vice-Pres. Institut Pasteur 1970–78; Hon. Dir. 1978–; Pres. Exec. Cttee. Humanisme et Entreprise 1968–; mem. staff, Conseil Nat. du Patronat Français 1968, Exec. Council 1972–75; Founder and Pres. Asscn. Entreprise et Progrès 1969, mem. Exec. Cttee. 1971–; mem. Grandes Entreprises Françaises Asscn. (AGREF) 1977–82; mem. Futuribles Int. Asscn., INSEAD, council Centre d'Etudes Littéraires et Scientifiques Appliquées (CELSA), Founder and Vice-Pres. Institut de l'Entreprise 1975–; fmr. Pres. Mennen-France, Dir. Centre Européen d'Educ. Permanente; Pres. Comm. Nat. de l'Industrie 1984–; Commdre. Légion d'honneur, Ordre nat. du Mérite, Médaille de la Résistance, Commdr. des Palmes académiques, Commendatore della Repubblica Italiana. *Publications:* L'entreprise du futur (with Jean Bounine Cabalé) 1971, Quand l'entreprise s'éveille à la conscience sociale (with Jean Bounine Cabalé) 1975, Dynamique de l'auto-reforme de l'entreprise (with Nicolas Thiéry) 1976. *Leisure interests:* writing, hunting. *Address:* Centre Eugene Schueller, 41 rue Martre, 92117 Clichy (Office); 6 rue Frédéric-Le-Play, 75007 Paris, France (Home).

DALLEY, Christopher Mervyn, C.M.G., M.A., M.I.MECH.E., F.INST.PET.; British oil executive; b. 26 Dec. 1913, U.K.; s. of late Christopher Dalley; m. Elizabeth A. Gammell 1947; one s. three d.; ed. Epsom Coll., Surrey and Queens' Coll., Cambridge; served in Royal Navy 1939–45; joined British Petroleum Co. 1946; Iranian Oil Producing Co. 1954–62; Iraq Petroleum Co. and assoc. cos., Man. Dir. 1963–70, Chair. 1970–78; Dir. Viking Resources Trust 1973–84, London and Scottish Marine Oil Co. Ltd. 1979–84; Order of Homayoun (Iran). *Address:* Mead House, Woodham Walter, near Maldon, Essex, England (Home). *Telephone:* Danbury 2404.

DALMIA, Mriduhari; Indian business executive; b. 8 July 1941, Dalmianagar; s. of J. Dalmia and Krishna Devi Dalmia; m. Abha Dalmia 1962; one s. one d.; mem. Man. Cttee. Indian Refractory Makers Asscn. 1966–67, Chair. 1973–74; mem. Council Cement Research Inst. of India, Pres. 1976–77, Chair. Research Advisory Cttee. 1979; Vice-Pres. Cement Mfrs. Asscn. 1986–87; Vice-Chair. Bd. of Govs., Nat. Council for Cement and Bldg. Materials 1987; Pres. Orissa Cement Ltd.; Chair. Dalmia Inst. of Scientific and Industrial Research, Rockweld Electrodes India Ltd., Cement Distributors Ltd.; Dir. Dalton Int. Ltd., U.K.; mem. Refractory Panel of Directorate Gen. of Tech. Devt. *Leisure interests:* travelling, reading, music. *Address:* Orissa Cement Ltd., B-45 Connaught Place, New Delhi 110001, India. *Telephone:* 322481, 351351 (Office); 3019998, 3017575 (Home).

DALMIA, Vishnu Hari; Indian industrialist; b. May 1924; s. of J. Dalmia; Chair. Dalmia Dairy Industries Ltd., GTC Industries Ltd., The Shree Meenakshi Mills Ltd.; Advisor Dalmia Cement (Bharat) Ltd.; Dir. Devshree Cement Ltd., The Dalton Property Co. Ltd., Manchester, England; Chair. Advisory Cttee. of Asian Regional Office, World Fed. UN Asscns., Geneva; Dir. Export-Import Bank of India 1983–85; Pres. Cement Mfrs. Asscn. 1968–70, Indian Sugar Mills Asscn. 1969–70, All India Distillers' Asscn. 1963–64, Indian Nat. Cttee. of Int. Chambers of Commerce 1976–77; mem. Tourism Advisory Bd. 1984–86; Man. Trustee Dalmia Charitable Trust. *Address:* 11th Floor, Hansalaya, 15 Barakhamba Road, New Delhi-11 0001 (Office); 9 Tees January Marg, New Delhi-11 0011, India (Home). *Telephone:* 3315476, 3310121 (Office); 3013372, 3014498 (Home).

DALRYMPLE, Ian Murray, B.A., F.R.S.A.; British writer, film producer and director; b. 26 Aug. 1903, Johannesburg, S. Africa; s. of late Sir William Dalrymple and Lady Dalrymple; m. 2nd Joan Margaret Craig 1939; three s. one d.; ed. Rugby School and Trinity Coll., Cambridge; Film Ed. 1927–35; writer of screen plays 1935–40; Exec. Producer, Crown Film Unit, Ministry of Information 1940–43; Assoc. Exec. Producer, M.G.M.-London Films 1943–46; Producer and Man. Dir. Wessex Film Productions Ltd. 1946–; Advisory Producer, British Lion Film Corpn. Ltd. 1952–54; Chair. British Film Acad. 1957–58. *Principal productions:* A Cry from the Streets, The Admirable Crichton, A Hill in Korea, Raising a Riot, The Heart of the Matter, Bank of England, The Changing Face of Europe (a series of six short films in colour on European recovery), The Wooden Horse, All over the Town, Once a Jolly Swagman, Dear Mr. Prohack, Esther Waters, The Woman in the Hall, Western Approaches, Target for To-night, London Can Take It, Chaucer's Tale; as writer of screen plays: South Riding, The Citadel, Storm in a Teacup, Pygmalion, etc. *Leisure interests:* reading, weeding. *Address:* 3 Beaulieu Close, Cambridge Park, Twickenham, TW1 2JR, England.

DALSAGER, Poul Christian; Danish politician; b. 5 March 1929, Hirtshals; s. of the late Verner and Carla (née Svendsen) Dalsager; m. Betty Jørgensen 1951; two s.; mem. Folketing (Parl.) 1964–81; del. to UN Gen. Ass. 1969, 1971; Chair. Common Market Cttee., Parl. 1971–73; Minister of Agric. and Fisheries 1975–77, 1979–81; Minister of Agric. 1977–78; Vice-Pres. EEC Parl. 1973–74; EEC Commr. for Agric. 1981–84; Deputy Mayor, Hjørring 1986; Chair. Social Democratic Group in Parl. 1978; Pres. East of England Agric. Soc. 1983. *Address:* Gram Mikkelsensvej 12, 9800 Hjørring, Denmark. *Telephone:* 08-929390.

DALTON, Jack; American librarian; b. 21 March 1908, Holland, Va., s. of John Preston and Selma (Butler) Dalton; m. Mary Armistead Gochnauer 1933; one s.; ed. Virginia and Michigan Univs.; Instructor in English, Va. Polytechnic Inst. 1930–34; Reference Librarian, Univ. of Va. 1934–42, Assoc. Librarian 1942–50, Librarian 1950–56; Dir. Int. Relations Office, American Library Asscn. 1956–59; Dean, School of Library Service, Columbia Univ. 1959–70, Prof. 1970–76, Dean Emer. 1976–; Dir. Library Devt. Center, Columbia Univ. 1970–79; Library consultant 1979–. *Address:* 445 Riverside Drive, New York, N.Y. 10027, U.S.A. (Office). *Telephone:* MO3-3359.

DALTON, Timothy; British actor; b. 1946; TV appearances include: Flash Gordon, Centennial (U.S. TV series) 1981–82, Charlie's Angels, Jane Eyre, The Master of Ballantrae, Mistral's Daughter, Florence Nightingale, Sins. *Film appearances include:* A Lion in Winter, Le Voyeur (France), Cromwell, Wuthering Heights, Mary, Queen of Scots, Permission to Kill, The Man Who Knew Love (Spain), Sextette, Chanel Solitaire, The Doctor and the Devils, role of Ian Fleming's James Bond in Living Daylights 1987, Brenda Starr, Hawks, License Revoked 1989. *Stage appearances include:* Anthony and Cleopatra, The Taming of the Shrew, A Touch of the Poet 1988. *Address:* James Sharkey Associates, 15 Golden Square, London, W.1, England. *Telephone:* 01-434 3801.

DALY, Brendan; Irish politician; b. 2 Feb. 1940, Cooraclare; m. Patricia Carmody; two s. one d.; ed. Kilrush Co. Boys' School; mem. Dail 1973–; Minister of State, Dept. of Labour 1980–81; Minister for Fisheries and Forestry March–Dec. 1982, for the Marine 1987–; Fianna Fail. *Address:* Cooraclare, Kilrush, Co. Clare, Republic of Ireland (Home). *Telephone:* 065 59040.

DALY, Rt. Rev. Cahal Brendan, M.A., D.D.; Irish ecclesiastic; b. 1 Oct. 1917, Loughguile, Co. Antrim; s. of Charles Daly and Susan Connolly; ed. St. Malachy's Coll., Queen's Univ., Belfast, St. Patrick's Coll., Maynooth, Institut Catholique, Paris; Classics Master St. Malachy's Coll. 1945–46; Lecturer in Scholastic Philosophy, Queen's Univ., Belfast 1946–63, Reader 1963–67; Bishop of Ardagh and Clonmacnois 1967–82; Bishop of Down and Connor 1982–; *Publications:* Morals, Law and Life 1962, Natural Law Morality Today 1965, Violence in Ireland and Christian Conscience 1973, Theologians and the Magisterium 1977, Peace and the Work of Justice 1979, Communities Without Consensus: The Northern Irish Tragedy 1984, Renewed Heart for Peace 1984, Cry of the Poor 1986, contrib. to various philosophical works. *Address:* Lisbreen, 73 Somerton Road, Belfast, BT15 4DE, N. Ireland.

DALY, Rt. Rev. Edward Kevin, B.PHIL., S.T.L., D.D.; Irish ecclesiastic; b. 5 Dec. 1933, Co. Donegal; s. of Thomas Daly and Susan Flood; ordained as Priest 1957; Curate, Castlederg, Co. Tyrone 1957–62; St. Eugene's Cathedral, Derry 1962–74, Bishop of Derry 1974–; Religious Adviser to Radio Telefis Éireann (RTE) 1973–. *Leisure interests:* theatre, angling. *Address:* Bishop's House, St. Eugene's Cathedral, Derry, BT48 9AP, Ireland. *Telephone:* (0504) 262302.

DALY, Gabriel Conor, PH.D.; Irish priest and university lecturer; b. 18 Nov. 1927, Dublin; s. of John Anthony Daly and Maureen Mulhern; ed. St. Gerard's School, Bray, Gregorian Univ., Rome, Oxford Univ.; entered Order of St. Augustine 1944; ordained priest 1951; Sr. History Master and Housemaster, Austin Friars School, Carlisle, U.K. 1957–66; Tutor in History, Univ. Coll., Dublin 1967–69; Lecturer in Theology, Milltown Inst., Dublin 1969–85; part-time Lecturer in Theology, Irish School of Ecumenics 1970–; Lecturer in Theology, Trinity College, Dublin 1985–; Chair. Irish Theological Asscn. 1979–85. *Publications:* Transcendence and Immanence: A Study in Catholic Modernism and Integralism 1980, Asking the Father: A Study of the Prayer of Petition 1982, Creation and Redemption 1988; articles and reviews in various theological journals. *Leisure interests:* walking, music. *Address:* St. Augustine's, Taylor's Lane, Ballyboden, Dublin 16, Ireland. *Telephone:* 944966.

DALY, John (Charles), Jr.; American (b. South African) broadcaster; b. 20 Feb. 1914, Johannesburg; s. of John Charles and Helen Grant (Tennant) Daly; m. 1st Margaret Criswell Neal 1937 (deceased), 2nd Virginia Warren 1960; four s. two d.; ed. Boston Coll.; Schedule Engineer, Capital Transit Co., Washington 1935–37; Corresp. and News Analyst, Columbia Broadcasting System 1937–49; Special Events Reporter and White House Corresp. 1937–41, service in U.S.A., Europe and South America for C.B.S. 1945–49; Corresp.-Analyst, American Broadcasting Co., also Moderator, television programmes on all networks; Vice-Pres. American Broadcasting Co., in charge of News, Special Events and Public Affairs 1953–60; mem. Water Pollution Control Advisory Bd. 1960–62; Dir. Voice of America 1967–68, Consultant, Citibank, New York 1971–; Forum Moderator American Enterprise Inst., Washington, 1976–. *Address:* 1070 Park Avenue, New York, N.Y. 10028, U.S.A.

DALZIEL, Keith, PH.D., F.R.S.; British biochemist (retd.); b. 24 Aug. 1921, Salford, Lancs.; s. of Gilbert and Edith Dalziel; m. Sallie Farnworth 1945; two d.; ed. Royal Tech. Coll., Salford; Lab. Asst., Jewish Hosp., Manchester 1935–45; Asst. Biochemist, Radcliffe Infirmary, Oxford 1945–58; Rockefeller Travelling Fellowship in medicine, Stockholm 1956–58; Sorby Research Fellow, Royal Soc. 1958–63; lecturer in Biochem., Univ. of Oxford 1963–78, Reader 1978–83; Visiting Prof. of Biochem., Univ. of Mich. 1967; Fellow, Wolfson Coll., Univ. of Oxford 1970–83, now Emer.; mem. Council, Royal Soc. 1979–80. *Publications:* about 100 papers and articles in scientific journals, mostly on enzymology. *Leisure interests:* music, golf, literature. *Address:* Wolfson College, Oxford; 25 Hampden Drive, Kidlington, Oxford, England (Home). *Telephone:* (0865) 56711; (08675) 2623 (Home).

DAM, Kenneth W., J.D.; American lawyer and corporate executive; b. 10 Aug. 1932, Marysville, Kan.; s. of Oliver W. and Ida L. Dam; m. Marcia Wachs 1962; one s. one d.; ed. Univs. of Kansas and Chicago; law clerk, Mr. Justice Whittaker, U.S. Supreme Court 1957–58; Assoc., Cravath, Swaine & Moore, New York 1958–60; Asst. Prof., Univ. of Chicago Law School 1960–61, Assoc. Prof. 1961–64, Prof. 1964–71, 1974–76, Harold J. & Marion F. Green Prof. of Int. Legal Studies 1976–85; Provost, Univ. of Chicago 1980–82; Consultant, Kirkland & Ellis, Chicago 1961–71, 1974–80; Exec. Dir. Council on Econ. Policy 1973; Asst. Dir. for Nat. Security and Int. Affairs, Office of Man. and Budget 1971–73; Deputy Sec. of State 1982–85; Vice-Pres., Law and External Relations, IBM Corp. 1985–; Dir. Alcoa 1987–; Dir. American Council on Germany, Atlantic Council of the U.S., America-China Soc.; Gov. Atlantic Inst. for Int. Affairs, Foreign Policy Assoc.; Trustee The Asia Soc., U.S. States Council for Int. Business, Jt. Council on Econ. Educ.; mem. Council on Foreign Relations, U.S. Nat. Cttee. for Pacific Econ. Co-operation, Nat. Cttee. on U.S.-China Relations, American Acad. of Arts and Sciences, American Bar Assocn., American Law Inst., American Soc. of Int. Law. *Publications:* Federal Tax Treatment of Foreign Income (with L. Krause) 1964, The GATT: Law and International Economic Organization 1970, Oil Resources: Who Gets What How? 1976, Economic Policy Beyond the Headlines (with George P. Shultz) 1978, The Rules of the Game: Reform and Evolution in the International Monetary System 1982; numerous articles on legal and economic issues. *Address:* IBM Corporation, Old Orchard Road, Armonk, N.Y. 10504, U.S.A.

DAMAS, Aléka Georges; Gabonese politician; b. 18 Nov. 1902, Libreville; m.; eight c.; ed. Mission Catholique de Libreville, Ecole Universelle (correspondence course) Paris, diplomatic training course, Quai d'Orsay, Paris; worked in bank 1924–39; Chief Accountant, Cie. Maritime des Chargeurs Réunis, Libreville 1939–59; del. Conseil d'Admin., Gouvernement Gén. de l'Afrique Equatoriale Française 1943–46; deputy mem. Privy Council to Gov. of Gabon 1948–54; Town Councillor, Libreville 1956–63; Amb. to EEC, Belgium, Netherlands and Luxembourg 1961–64, to Fed. Repub. of Germany 1963–64; mem. Gabonese Nat. Ass. 1964–, Pres. 1964–75; High Councillor of State 1975–76; Admin., Shell-Gabon Co., Port Gentil 1960–; Composer of La Concorde (Gabon Nat. Anthem); Chevalier, Légion d'honneur, Etoile Noire du Bénin, Ordre des Arts et Lettres, Grand Officier, Etoile Equatoriale, Ordre nat. Gabonais, Ordre du Mérite Centraficaine, etc. *Publications:* L'homme noir, Recueil des allocutions prononcées par M. Georges Damas-Aléka. *Address:* Assemblée Nationale, Libreville, Gabon.

D'AMATO, Alfonse M., B.A., LL.B.; American lawyer and politician; b. 1 Aug. 1937, Brooklyn, New York; m.; four c.; ed. Syracuse Univ.; Receiver of Taxes, Town of Hempstead 1971–72, Supervisor, Hempstead 1972–78, Presiding Supervisor 1978–81; Senator from N.Y. State 1981–, on Banking, Housing and Urban Affairs Cttee. and Appropriations Cttee; Republican. *Address:* Senate Office Building, Washington, D.C. 20510 (Office); Island Park, N.Y. 11558, U.S.A. (Home).

DAMDIN, Paavangiyn; Mongolian politician; b. 1931; ed. Financial and Econ. Tech. School, Ulan Bator and a higher school of econs. in U.S.S.R.; Accountant, Finance Section of Mongolian People's Revolutionary Party (MPRP) Cen. Cttee 1950–52; Specialist, Head of Dept. State Planning Comm. 1958–60; Minister of Industry 1960–68; Minister of Light and Food Industry 1968–79; mem. MPRP Cen. Cttee. 1961–, Sec. 1979–87; alt. mem. Political Bureau 1987–; Deputy to People's Great Hural (Assembly) 1960–; awarded orders and medals of MPR. *Address:* Central Committee of the Mongolian People's Revolutionary Party, Ulan Bator, Mongolia.

DAN DICKO, Dankoulodo; Niger scientist and international official; b. 1934, Maradi; s. of Dankoulodo Madjara; m. Léontine Zafimahova 1960; two c.; ed. Acad. de Dakar-Bordeaux and Acad. de Montpellier; Asst. Lecturer in Chem., Univ. of Montpellier, France 1958–61; lecturer, Faculty of Science, Univ. of Abidjan, Ivory Coast 1966–67, Maître des Conférences, Abidjan 1967–72; Vice-Pres. Econ. and Social Council, Niger 1969–71; Minister of Nat. Educ., Youth, Sport and Culture, Niger 1971–74; Prof., Niamey 1971–74; Sec.-Gen. Agency for Cultural and Tech. Co-operation, Paris 1974–82; Dir. Dept. of Chem., Faculty of Sciences, Univ. of Niamey; mem. Exec. Council, Int. African Inst., London 1976–; Chevalier, Ordre de Mérite de la République de Côte d'Ivoire, Commdr., Ordre de Mérite de la République du Gabon, de la Pléiade (Francophonie), du Bren public. *Publications:* numerous scientific articles on medicinal plants and the

African pharmacopea. *Leisure interests:* agriculture, gardening. *Address:* B.P. 405, Niamey, Niger. *Telephone:* 73330; 733519.

DANCE, Charles; British actor; b. 10 Oct. 1946, Rednal, Worcs.; formerly worked in industry; with RSC 1975–80, 1980–85; *Television appearances include:* The Fatal Spring, Nancy Astor, Frost in May, Saigon–The Last Day, Thunder Rock (drama), Rainy Day Women, The Jewel in the Crown (nominated for Best Actor BAFTA Award), The Secret Servant, The McGuffin. *Films include:* For Your Eyes Only, Plenty, The Golden Child, White Mischief, Good Morning Babylon, Hidden City, Pascali's Island 1988. *Address:* c/o Caroline Dawson Associates, 47 Courtfield Road, London, S.W.7., England. *Telephone:* 01-370 0708.

DANDAVATE, Madhu; Indian politician and fmr. professor of physics; b. 21 Jan. 1924, Ahmed Nagar, Maharashtra; ed. Royal Inst. of Science, Bombay; participated in Independence Movement, later in Quit India Movement 1942; leader of passive resistance in Goa Campaign 1955; took part in Samyukta Maharashtra Movt. for formation of Maharashtra state; joined Praja Socialist Party (PSP) 1948, Chair. Maharashtra State Unit of PSP, later Jt. Sec. of All-India PSP; participated in Land Liberation Movt. 1969; associated with Maharashtra Citizens' Defence Cttee. during conflicts with People's Repub. of China and Pakistan; mem. Maharashtra Legis. Council 1970–71; mem. Lok Sabha from Rajapur 1971–79, 1980–; Vice-Prin. and Head of Physics Dept., Siddhartha Coll. of Arts and Science, Bombay until 1971; mem. Janata Party 1977–; Minister of Railways 1977–80. *Publications:* Gandhiji's Impact on Socialist Thinking, Three Decades of Indian Communism, Evolution of Socialist Policies, Kashmir—a Test for Secularism, Myth and Mystery of Congress Socialism, Bharatiya Swarajwad (in Marathi). *Address:* 10 Ashoka Road, New Delhi 110001, India.

DANELIUS, Hans Carl Yngve; Swedish lawyer and diplomatist; b. 2 April 1934, Stockholm; s. of Sven and Inga (née Svensson) Danelius; m. Hanneke Schadee 1961; three s. one d.; ed. Dept. of Legal Studies, Stockholm Univ.; Law Practice in Swedish Courts 1957–64; mem. Secr., European Comm. of Human Rights, Strasbourg 1964–67, mem. European Comm. of Human Rights 1983–; Asst. Judge, Svea Court of Appeal 1967–68; Adviser, Ministry of Justice 1968–71; Deputy Head, Legal Dept., Ministry for Foreign Affairs 1971–75, Head 1975–84, rank of Amb. 1977–84; Amb. to Netherlands 1984–88; Judge, Supreme Court of Sweden 1988–; mem. Perm. Court of Arbitration at the Hague 1982–; Chief Ed. Svensk Juristtidning (Swedish Law Journal) 1973–84; Dr. h.c. (Stockholm) 1988; Swedish and foreign decorations. *Publications:* Mänskliga Rättigheter (Human Rights) 1975, numerous articles in Swedish and foreign journals. *Address:* Supreme Court, Box 2066, S-10312 Stockholm (Office); Roslinvägen 33, S-16154 Bromma, Sweden (Home). *Telephone:* 8-236720 (Office); 8-373491 (Home).

DANFORTH, Douglas Dewitt, B.M.E.; American business executive; b. 25 Sept. 1922, Syracuse, New York; s. of Dewitt Ward Danforth and Ruth C. Ward; m. Janet M. Piron 1943; one s. three d.; ed. Fenn Coll. Cleveland and Syracuse Univ.; Supt. Planning, Easy Washer Machine Co., Syracuse 1942–46; Vice-Pres. Int. Gen Electric Co. 1947–53; Plant Man. Gen Electric Co., Baltimore 1953–55; Exec. Vice-Pres., Gen. Man. Industria Electrica De Mexico 1956–61; Vice-Pres. Westinghouse Electric Corpn., Pittsburgh 1962–65, Group Vice-Pres. 1965–69, Exec. Vice-Pres. 1969–74; Pres. Industry Products Co., Westinghouse 1974–78, Vice-Chair. and C.O.O. 1978–83, Chair. and C.E.O. 1983–; Dir. Pittsburgh Nat. Corpn., PPG Industries Inc., Whirlpool Corpn., Standard Oil, Nat. InterGroup. *Address:* Westinghouse Electric Corporation, Gateway Center, Westinghouse Building, Pittsburgh, Pa. 15222, U.S.A.

DANFORTH, John Claggett, L.H.D., LL.D., D.D.; American lawyer and politician; b. 5 Sept. 1936, St. Louis; s. of Donald and Dorothy Danforth; m. Sally B. Dobson 1957; four d. one s.; ed. Princeton and Yale Univs., Drury Coll., Lindenwood Coll., Lewis and Clark Coll.; Admitted to N.Y. bar 1964, Mo. bar 1966; David, Polk, Wardwell, Sunderland and Kiendl, law firm 1964–66, Bryan, Cave, McPheeters and McRoberts 1966–68; Attorney-Gen. of Mo. 1968–76; ordained Deacon of Episcopal Church 1963; Asst. Rector, N.Y. 1963–66; Assoc. Rector, Clayton, Mo. 1966–68, Grace Church, Jefferson City 1969–, Hon. Assoc. St. Albans Church, Washington 1977–; Senator from Missouri Jan. 1977–; Chair. Mo. Law Enforcement Assistance Council 1973; Republican. *Address:* 479 Russell Senate Building, Washington, D.C. 20510 (Office); Route 1, Box 91, Newburg, Mo. 65550, U.S.A. (Home).

DANGE, Shripad Amrit, M.P.; Indian trade union leader; b. 10 Oct. 1899; m. 1928; two d.; took a prominent part in organizing Textile Workers' Unions in Bombay; one of the founders of Indian Communist Party 1924; arrested on many occasions for TU and political activity; sentenced to twelve years' transportation in the Meerut conspiracy trial; released 1936; imprisoned 1939–43; Pres. Girni Kamgar Union; Pres. All-India TUC 1943–45; Del. to W.F.T.U. Paris 1945, Moscow 1946; Vice-Pres. W.F.T.U. 1948; Ed. and Founder of Socialist 1922, first Marxist paper in India; Ed. and Founder of Kranti, first working-class paper in Marathi language; mem. Legis. Ass., Bombay 1946–51; imprisoned 1948–50; Pres. All-India Trade Union Congress 1956–84; mem. Legis. Ass., New Delhi 1957–62, 1967–72; Chair. Nat. Council, Indian CP 1962–77; expelled from Communist Party 1981; Order of Lenin 1974. *Publications:* Gandhi versus Lenin 1921,

Hell Found 1927, Literature and the People 1945, India from Primitive Communism to Slavery 1949, One Hundred Years of our Trade Unions 1952, Mahatma Gandhi and History 1968, When Communists Differ 1970, etc. *Leisure interests:* history, philosophy, literature. *Address:* c/o All-India Trade Union Congress, 24 K. M. Munshi Lane, New Delhi 110001; 9, Kohinoor Road, Dadar, Bombay 400014, India.

DANIEL, Jean, L. ÈS L.; French journalist and author; b. 21 July 1920, Blida, Algeria; m. Michèle Bancilhon 1966; one d.; Cabinet of Felix Gouin, Pres. Council of Ministers 1946; founder and Dir. Caliban (cultural review) 1947–51; Prof. of Philosophy, Oran 1953; Asst. Ed.-in-Chief, subsequently Ed.-in-Chief, L'Express 1955–64; corresp., New Repub., Washington 1956–65; Associate, Le Monde 1964; founder and Dir. Le Nouvel Observateur 1964–; fmr. mem. Supervisory Council, Agence-France-Presse. *Publications:* L'Erreur 1953, Journal d'un journaliste, Le Temps qui reste 1973, Le Refuge et la source 1977, L'Ere des ruptures 1979, De Gaulle et l'Algérie 1985. *Leisure interest:* tennis. *Address:* Le Nouvel Observateur, 14 rue Dussoubs, 75002 Paris, France. *Telephone:* 42 33 37 48.

DANIEL-LESUR, J. Y.; French composer; b. 19 Nov. 1908, Paris; s. of Robert and Alice (née Thiboust) Lesur; m. Simone Lauer 1943; one s. one d.; ed. Paris Conservatoire; Musical Adviser to Radiodiffusion-Télévision Française; Prin. Insp. of Music at Ministry of Cultural Affairs; Admin. de la Réunion des Théâtres Lyriques Nationaux; Insp.-Gen. of Music, Ministry of Cultural Affairs; Pres. Acad. Charles Cros 1978–84, Hon. Pres. 1984–; contrib. to Arts, La Gazette des Lettres, Polyphonie, La Revue Musicale and other publs.; teaches and writes film music; Dir. hon. Schola Cantorum; French Comm. UNESCO; membre de l'Institut (Acad. des Beaux-Arts) 1982; Assoc. Mem. Acad. Royale des Sciences, des Lettres et des Beaux-Arts, Belgium 1984; Commdr. Légion d'honneur, Commdr. Ordre nat. du Mérite, Commdr. Ordre des Arts et des Lettres; Grand Prix du Conseil Général de la Seine, Grand Prix de Paris, Lauréat Acad. des Beaux Arts, Grand Prix Musical de la Soc. des Auteurs et Compositeurs de Musique. *Works include:* Suite française pour orchestre 1935, Passacaille 1937, Pastorale pour petit orchestre 1938, Ricercare pour orchestre 1939, Quatre lieder pour chant et orchestre 1933–39, Trio d'Anches 1939, Trois poèmes de Cécile Sauvage 1939, Quatuor à cordes 1941, L'enfance de l'art 1942, Variations pour piano et orchestre à cordes 1943, Clair comme le jour 1945, Suite pour trio à cordes et piano 1943, Suite médiévale pour flûte, harpe et trio à cordes 1944, Chansons cambodgiennes 1946, Berceuses à tenir éveillé (chant) 1947, Pastorale variée pour piano 1947, Ballade pour piano 1948, Andrea del Sarto (symphonic poem) 1949, Dix chansons populaires à trois voix égales 1950, Ouverture pour un festival 1951, Chansons françaises à quatre voix mixtes 1951, L'annonciation (cantata) 1952, Cantique des cantiques, pour 12 voix mixtes 1953, Concerto da camera pour piano et orchestre de chambre 1953, Cantique des colonnes pour ensemble vocal féminin et orchestre 1954, Sérénade pour orchestre à cordes 1954, Le bal du destin (ballet), Elégie pour deux guitares 1956, Symphonie de danses 1958, Messe du jubilé pour choeur mixte, orchestre et orgue 1960, Fantaisie pour deux pianos, Trois études pour piano 1962, Chanson de mariage pour choeur de voix de femmes 1964, Deux chansons de marins pour choeur d'hommes 1964, Deux chansons de bord pour choeur mixte 1964, Andrea del Sarto (2-act opera) 1968, Contre-fugue pour deux pianos 1970, Symphonie 1974, Nocturne pour hautbois et orchestre à cordes 1974, Berceuse pour piano 1975, Intermezzo pour violon et piano, Novelette pour flûte et piano 1977, Marine pour harpe 1978, Air à danser pour piano 1980, Ondine, opera in three acts 1981, La reine morte, opera in three acts 1987, Fantaisie: Dialogues Dans La Nuit 1988. *Leisure interest:* Racing Club de France. *Address:* 101 rue Sadi Carnot, 92800 Puteaux, France. *Telephone:* (1) 47-67-01-17.

DANIELL, Robert F.; American business executive; ed. Boston Univ. Coll. of Industrial Tech.; joined Sikorsky as design eng. 1956, program man. for S-61, S-62 and S-58 commercial helicopter programs 1968, Commercial Marketing Man. 1971, Vice-Pres. (Commercial Marketing) 1974, Vice-Pres. (Marketing) 1976, Exec. Vice-Pres. 1977, later Pres. and C.E.O. until 1982; Vice-Pres. United Technologies Corpn. 1982, Sr. Vice-Pres. (Defense Systems) 1983, Pres., C.O.O. and Dir. 1984–, C.E.O. 1986–, Chair. 1987–; Dir. Travelers Corpn., Hartford, Shell Oil Co., Houston; Fellow, Univ. of Bridgeport; Hon. D.Sc. (Bridgeport); Hon. LL.D. (Trinity Coll. and Boston Univ.). *Address:* United Technologies Corporation, United Technologies Building, Hartford, Conn. 06101, U.S.A.

DANIELS, Henry Ellis, M.A., PH.D., SC.D., F.R.S.; British professor of mathematical statistics; b. 2 Oct. 1912; s. of Morris Daniels and Hannah Daniels; m. Barbara E. Pickering 1950; one s. one d.; ed. Sciennes School, Edinburgh, George Heriot's School, Edinburgh, Edinburgh Univ. and Clare Coll., Cambridge; statistician, Wool Industries Research Asscn. 1935–47; Ministry of Aircraft Production 1942–45; Lecturer in Math. Univ. of Cambridge 1947–57; Prof. of Mathematical Statistics Univ. of Birmingham 1957–78, Prof. Emer. 1978–; Fellow, King's Coll., Cambridge 1975–76; Pres. Royal Statistical Soc. 1974–75; Fellow, Inst. of Mathematical Statistics; mem. Int. Statistical Inst.; Guy Medal (Silver) 1957, (Gold) 1984, Royal Statistical Soc.; Sc.D. (Cantab.) 1983. *Publications:* papers in learned journals. *Leisure interests:* playing the English concertina, repairing watches. *Address:* 12 Kimberley Road, Cambridge, CB4 1HH, England. *Telephone:* 0223 313402.

DANIELS, William B., PH.D., M.S.; American professor of physics; b. 21 Dec. 1930, Buffalo, N.Y.; s. of William C. Daniels and Sophia P. Daniels; m. Adriana A. Braakman 1958; two s. one d.; ed. Univ. of Buffalo and Case Inst. (now Case-Western Reserve Univ.); Asst. Prof. of Physics, Case Tech. 1957–59; Research Scientist, Union Carbide Corpn. 1959–61; Asst. Prof. Princeton Univ. 1961–63, Assoc. Prof. 1963–66, Prof. of Mechanical Eng. 1966–72; Unidel Prof. of Physics, Univ. of Del. 1972–, Chair. Physics Dept. 1977–80; Fellow, American Physical Soc.; John Simon Guggenheim Memorial Fellow 1976–77; Humboldt Sr. Award 1982. *Publications:* more than 100 articles on the physics of solids at high pressures. *Leisure interests:* sailing, mountaineering. *Address:* Physics Department, University of Delaware, Newark, Del. 19716 (Office); 100 Tanglewood Lane, Newark, Del. 19711, U.S.A. (Home). *Telephone:* (302) 451-2667 (Office).

DANIELSSON, Bengt Emmerik, PH.D.; Swedish anthropologist and writer; b. 6 July 1921, Krokek; m. Marie-Thérèse Sailley 1948; one s.; ed. Univ. of Uppsala, Sweden and Univ. of Washington, Seattle; field research among Jibaro Indians, Upper Amazonas 1946–47, in Tuamotu Archipelago, French Polynesia 1949–51, Australia 1955–56; mem. Kon-Tiki Expedition 1947; Assoc. Anthropologist Bernice P. Bishop Museum Honolulu, 1952–; mem. Pacific Science Bd. expedition to Tuamotu Archipelago 1952; Leader George Vanderbilt expedition to Soc. Islands 1957, Swedish TV expedition to S. Seas 1962; tech. adviser for film Mutiny on the Bounty 1961; Producer TV series Captain Cook's Voyages, Terry's South Sea Adventures; Swedish Consul, French Polynesia 1960–67, 1971–78; Dir. Nat. Museum of Ethnography, Stockholm 1967–71; Corresp. for Pacific Islands Magazine 1978–. *Publications:* The Happy Island 1951, The Forgotten Islands of the South Seas 1952, Love in the South Seas 1954, Work and Life on Raroia 1955, From Raft to Raft 1959, What Happened on the Bounty 1962, Gauguin in the South Seas 1965, La découverte de la Polynésie 1972, Moruroa, mon amour 1974, Mémorial Polynésien (6 vols.) 1976–80, Tahiti autrefois 1981, New Horizons in the Pacific 1986, Poisoned Reign 1986; Children's Books: Terry in the South Seas 1957, Terry in Australia 1958, Terry's Kon-Tiki Adventure 1963. *Address:* Papehue, Paea, Tahiti; Box 558, Papeete. *Telephone:* 582474, 582320.

DANINOS, Pierre; French writer; b. 26 May 1913, Paris; m. 1st Jane Marrain 1942, 2nd Marie-Pierre Dourneau 1968; one s. two d.; ed. Lycée Janson de Sailly; began as journalist 1931; liaison agent to the British Army, Flanders 1940; Columnist for Le Figaro. *Publications:* Les carnets du bon Dieu (Prix Interallié) 1947, Sonia, les autres et moi (Prix Courteline) 1952, Les carnets du Major Thompson 1954, Vacances à tous prix 1958, Un certain Monsieur Blot 1960, Le jacassin 1962, Snobissimo 1964, Le 36e dessous 1966, Les touristocrates 1974, Made in France 1977, La composition d'histoire 1979, Le Veuf Joyeux 1981, La Galerie des Glaces 1983, La France dans tous ses états 1985, Profession: Écrivain 1987. *Leisure interests:* loafing, tennis, collecting British hobbies. *Address:* 81 rue de Grenelle, 75007 Paris, France.

DANKWORTH, John Philip William, C.B.E., F.R.A.M.; British musician; b. 20 Sept 1927, London; m. Cleo Laine (q.v.) 1958; one s. one d.; ed. Monoux Grammar School, Royal Acad. of Music; founded large jazz orchestra 1958; *compositions include:* Improvisations (with Matyas Seiber) 1959, Escapade (commissioned by Northern Sinfonia Orchastra) 1967, Tom Sawyer's Saturday, for narrator and orchestra (commissioned by Farnham Festival) 1967, String Quartet 1971, Piano Concerto (commissioned by Westminster Festival) 1972, Grace Abounding (for Royal Philharmonic Orchestra) 1980, The Diamond and the Goose (for City of Birmingham Choir and Orchestra) 1981; *film scores include:* Saturday Night, Sunday Morning, Darling, The Servant, Morgan, Accident; Hon. M.A. (Open Univ.) 1975; Hon. D.Mus. (Berklee School of Music) 1982; Variety Club of G.B. Show Business Personality Award (with Cleo Laine) 1977. *Leisure interests:* driving, household maintenance. *Address:* c/o Laurie Mansfield, International Artistes' Representation, 235 Regent Street, London, W.1, England.

DANNEELS, H.E. Cardinal Godfried; Belgian ecclesiastic; b. 4 June 1933, Kanegem, Bruges; ordained priest 1957; Bishop of Antwerp 1977; apptd. Archbishop of Malines-Brussels 1979–; Castrene Bishop of Belgium 1980–; Pres. Episcopal Conf. of Belgium; mem. Synod of Bishops; mem. Sacred Congregation for the Doctrine of the Faith, Congregation for the Bishops, for the Evangelization, Council for the Public Affairs of the Church, Congregation of Catholic Educ., Congregation of Divine Worship, Secr. for Non-believers; cr. Cardinal 1983. *Address:* Aartsbisdom, Wollemarkt 15, B-2800, Mechelen, Belgium. *Telephone:* (015) 216501.

DANØ, Sven, M.SC., DR.POLIT.; Danish economist; b. 22 Feb. 1922, Copenhagen; s. of Hans Holger and Ingeborg D. (née Petersen) Danø; m. Ida Marianne Hauberg 1947; one s. one d.; ed. Univ. of Copenhagen; civil servant, Ministry of Housing 1947–61; lecturer in Econs., Univ. of Copenhagen 1960–66, Prof. of Managerial Econs. 1966–; Visiting Assoc. Prof. Univ. of Ill. 1958–59; Visiting Prof. Univ. of Kiel 1974–75. *Publications:* Linear Programming in Industry 1960, Industrial Production Models 1966, Nonlinear and Dynamic Programming 1975, Investeringsplanlægning 1988. *Address:* Institute of Economics, University of Copenhagen, Studiestræde 6, DK-1455 Copenhagen K (Office); Helsingevej 41, DK-2830 Virum, Denmark (Home). *Telephone:* 01-91 21 66, Ext. 317 (Office); 02-85 81 88 (Home).

DANSEREAU, Pierre, C.C., D.SC., F.R.S.C.; Canadian professor of ecology; b. 5 Oct. 1911, Montreal; s. of J.-Lucien Dansereau and Marie Archambault; m. Françoise Masson 1935; ed. Collège Sainte-Marie, Montreal, Institut Agricole d'Oka, Univ. of Geneva, Switzerland; Asst. Dir. of Tech. Services, Montreal Botanical Garden 1939–42; Dir. Service de Biogéographie, Montreal 1943–50; Assoc. Prof. of Botany, Univ. of Mich., Ann Arbor, U.S.A. 1950–55; Dean of Faculty of Science and Dir. of Botanical Inst., Univ. of Montreal 1955–61; Asst. Dir. and Head, Dept. of Ecology, The New York Botanical Garden, Bronx, 1961–68; Prof., Inst. of Urban Studies, Univ. of Montreal 1968–71; Prof. and Scientific Dir., Centre de Recherches Ecologiques de Montréal, Univ. of Quebec 1971–72, Prof. of Ecology attached to Centre de Recherches en Sciences de l'Environnement 1972–76, Emer. Prof. and Prof. of Ecology in Master's Programme in Environmental Sciences 1976–; many visiting professorships; Commonwealth Prestige Fellowship, Univ. of N.Z. 1961; numerous hon. degrees; 1st Prize (Prix David) Quebec, science section 1959, Massey Medal, Royal Canadian Geographical Soc. 1973, Molson Prize 1974, Canada Council 1975, Isaak Walton Killam Prize, Canada Council 1985, Lawson Medal, Canadian Botanical Asscn. 1986 and numerous other prizes and awards; Kt. of Ordre nat. du Québec. *Publications include:* Biogeography: an ecological perspective 1957, Contradictions et Biculture 1964, Dimensions of Environmental Quality 1971, Inscape and Landscape 1973, La Terre des Hommes et le Paysage Intérieur 1973, Harmony and Disorder in the Canadian Environment 1975, EZAIM: Écologie de la Zone de l'Aéroport International de Montréal-Le cadre d'une recherche écologique interdisciplinaire 1976, Essai de Classification et de Cartographie Ecologique des Espaces 1985, Les dimensions écologiques de l'espace urbain 1987. *Leisure interests:* swimming, cross-country skiing. *Address:* Université du Québec à Montréal, B.P. 8888, Succ.A., Montreal, Quebec, H3C 3P8, Canada. *Telephone:* (514) 282-3045.

DANSON, Hon. Barnett (Barney) Jerome, P.C.; Canadian politician; b. 8 Feb. 1921, Toronto; s. of Joseph B. and Saidie Eleanor Wolfe Danson; m. Isobel Bull 1943; four s.; ed. Public and High Schools, Toronto; served Queen's Own Rifles of Canada 1939–45; joined Joseph B. Danson & Sons Ltd., insurance brokers 1945; Sales Man. Maple Leaf Plastics Ltd. 1950–53; Chair. Danson Corpn. Ltd. 1953; M.P. for York North 1968–79; fmr. mem. Standing Cttee. on Finance, Trade and Econ. Affairs, fmr. Vice-Chair. Standing Cttee. on External Affairs and Nat. Defence; Parl. Sec. to Prime Minister Trudeau 1970–72; Minister of State for Urban Affairs 1974–76; Minister of Nat. Defence Nov. 1976–79; mem. Commonwealth team of observers scrutinizing Uganda elections Dec. 1980; Consul Gen. for Canada, Boston 1984–86; fmr. Pres. UN Conf. on Human Settlements (Habitat) 1976; Chair. de Havilland Aircraft of Canada Ltd., CSPG Consultants, Back Asscn. of Canada; Dir. Victoria and Grey Trust Co., Scintrex Ltd., Atlantic Council of Canada, Canadian Inst. of Strategic Studies, Canadian Council of Christians and Jews; mem. Canadian NATO Parl. Asscn., Canadian Group Inter-Parl. Union; Co-Chair. Canada/U.S. Interparl. Group; Del. to Interparl. Conf. on European Co-operation and Security 1973; fmr. Chair. Soc. of Plastics Industry in Canada; Pres. Dash-Air Inc., Toronto; mem. Bd. Soc. of Plastics Industry in New York, Canadian Mfrs. Asscn., Canadian Chamber of Commerce, Algoma Cen. Railway, Gen. Steelwares Ltd., Urban Transportation Devt. Corpn., Ballet Opera House Corpn., Toronto; Dir. Emer. Canadian Council of Native Business; Hon. Lt. Col. Queen's Own Rifles of Canada; Liberal. *Leisure interests:* fishing, wine, music. *Address:* 1106-561 Avenue Road, Toronto, Ont. M4V 2JB, Canada. *Telephone:* (414) 323 3274.

DANTON, J. Periam, M.A., PH.D.; American professor and librarian; b. 5 July 1908, Palo Alto, California; s. of George Henry and Annina Periam; m. Lois King 1948 (divorced 1973); one s. one d.; ed. Leipzig, Columbia and Chicago Univs., and Oberlin and Williams Colls.; served in N.Y. Public Library 1928–29; Williams Coll. Library 1929–30, American Library Asscn. 1930–33; Librarian and Assoc. Prof. Colby Coll. Library 1935–36, Temple Univ. 1936–46; Del. Int. Fed. of Library Asscns. meetings 1939, 1964, 1966–72; Visiting Prof., Univs. of Chicago 1942 and Columbia 1946; Lt., Lt.-Commdr., U.S.N.R. 1942–45; Prof. Librarianship, Calif. Univ. 1946–76, Dean, School of Librarianship 1946–61, Prof. Emer. 1976–; Pres. Asscn. American Library Schools 1949–50; Fulbright Research Scholar (Univ. Göttingen) 1960–61, (Vienna) 1964–65; Guggenheim Fellow 1971–72; U.S. Dept. of State, American Specialist, Ethiopia 1961; Ford Foundation Consultant on Univ. Libraries in Southeast Asia 1963; UNESCO Library Consultant, Jamaica 1968; Surveyor and Consultant, numerous libraries; Dir. U.S. Dept. of State-American Library Asscn. Multi-Area Group Librarian Program 1963–64; Guest lecturer, The Hague 1961, Univ. Toronto 1963, Hebrew Univ. Jerusalem 1965, 1985, Univs. Belgrade, Ljubljana and Zagreb 1965, Univ. of British Columbia 1968, McGill Univ. 1969, Univ. Puerto Rico 1970, Univ. of N. Carolina 1977, Univ. of Tex. 1978, Southern Ill. Univ. 1979; Hon. mem. Vereinigung Österreichischer Bibliothekare, Verein Deutscher Bibliothekare; Hon. Research Fellow, Univ. London 1974–75; Berkeley Citation 1976; mem. American Library Asscn., Asscn. of American Library Schools, Calif. Library Asscn. *Publications:* Library Literature, 1921–32 1934, Education for Librarianship 1949, United States Influence on Norwegian Librarianship 1890-1940 1957, The Climate of Book Selection: Social Influences on School and Public Libraries 1959, Book Selection and Collections: A Comparison of German and American University Libraries 1963, Jamaica: Library Development

1968, Index to Festschriften in Librarianship 1970, Between M.L.S. and Ph.D.: A Study of Sixth-Year Specialist Programs in Accredited Library Schools 1970, The Dimensions of Comparative Librarianship 1973, Index to Festschriften in Librarianship 1967-75, 1978; mem. Bd. of Editors Asscn. of Coll. and Research Libraries Monographs 1966-70, Library Quarterly 1968–, International Library Review 1968–. *Leisure interests:* classical music, tennis, swimming, travel. *Address:* School of Library and Information Studies, University of California, Berkeley, Calif. 94720, U.S.A. *Telephone:* (415) 642-1464.

DANTZIG, George Bernard, PH.D.; American professor of operations research and computer science; b. 8 Nov. 1914, Portland, Ore.; s. of Tobias and Anna G. Dantzig; m. Anne Shmuner 1936; two s. one d.; ed. Univs. of Maryland, Michigan and California (Berkeley); Statistician, U.S. Bureau of Labor Statistics 1937–39; Chief, Combat Analysis Branch, U.S.A.F. Jr. Statistical Control 1941–46; Math. Adviser, U.S.A.F. HQ 1946–52; Research Mathematician, Rand Corpn., Santa Monica, Calif. 1952–60; Chair. Operations Research Center and Prof., Univ. of Calif. (Berkeley) 1960–66; Prof. of Operations Research and Computer Science, Stanford Univ. 1966, C. A. Criley Chair. of Transportation Sciences 1966–; Int. Inst. for Applied Systems Analysis, Head of Methodology Project 1973–74; mem. N.A.S., Nat. Acad. of Eng.; Fellow, American Acad. of Arts and Sciences; Hon. mem. Inst. Electrical and Electronics Engineers; numerous Hon. degrees; Nat. Medal of Science, U.S.A. 1975, Harvey Prize 1985, Silver Medal Operational Research Soc., G.B. 1986. *Publications:* Linear Programming and Extensions 1963, Compact City (with Thomas L. Saaty) 1973; over 150 published technical papers. *Address:* 821 Tolman Drive, Stanford, Calif. 94305, U.S.A. (Home).

DANTZIG, Rudi Van; Netherlands choreographer; b. 4 Aug. 1933, Amsterdam; s. of Murk van Dantzig and Berendina Hermina Homburg; ed. High School and Art Coll.; took ballet lessons with Sonia Gaskell; joined Sonia Gaskell's co. Ballet Recital (later Netherlands Ballet), soloist 1959; won Prix de la Critique (Paris) for choreography in Night Island 1955; with Netherlands Dance Theatre 1959–60, artistic dir. and prin. choreographer Netherlands Nat. Ballet 1968–; has also worked for London Dance Theatre, Ballet Rambert, The Royal Ballet, Harkness Ballet (New York), Bat-Dor (Tel-Aviv), Ballet d'Anvers (Antwerp), Nat. Ballet of Washington, Royal Danish Ballet, American Ballet Theater, Nat. Ballet of Canada, Ballets of Munich and Cologne, Viennese Opera Ballet, Royal Winnipeg Ballet, Houston Ballet, Hungarian State Ballet, Finnish Opera Ballet, Pacific South-West Ballet (Seattle), Paris Opera Ballet; Ridder Oranje-Nassau 1969. *Choreography for:* Night Island 1955, Jungle 1961, Monument for a Dead Boy 1965, Romeo and Juliet 1967, Moments 1968, Epitaaf 1969, Astraal 1969, The Ropes of Time 1970, On Their Way 1970, Painted Birds 1971, Are Friends Delight or Pain 1972, The Unfinished 1973, Orpheus 1974, Ramifications 1974, Blown in a Gentle Wind (with Wade Walthall, for Rudolf Nureyev) 1975, Ginastera 1976, Gesang der Jünglinge 1977, Vier letzte Lieder 1978, Ulysses (for Nureyev) 1979, Life (with Toer van Schayk) 1979, Voorbÿ Gegaan 1979, About a Dark House 1978, Dialogues 1980, Underneath My Feet 1981, Room at the Top 1982, No-Mans Land 1982, I Just Simply Hold my Breath 1983, In Praise of Folly 1983, For We Know Not What We Are Doing 1986, To Bend or to Break 1987, Sans armes, Citoyens! 1987 (for the Paris Opera), Swan Lake (with Toer van Schayk) 1988. *Publications:* Nureyev, Aspects of the Dancer, Spectrum jaarboek 1979, Voorbÿ Gegaan—the making of a Pas-de-deux, Olga de Haas: A Memory, For a Lost Soldier (novel) 1986, articles in Ballet and Modern Dance; film appearances in Van Dantzig—Portrait of a Choreographer (by Jan Vrÿman), The Making of a Ballet (by Wilbert Bank). *Leisure interests:* literature, peace movement. *Address:* Het Nationale Ballet, Het Muziek theater, Waterlooplein 22, 1011 PG Amsterdam (Office); Emma-Straat 27, Amsterdam, Netherlands (Home). *Telephone:* 79-83-31 (Office).

DARBO, Bakary Bunja, B.A.; Gambian politician; b. 10 Aug. 1946, Dumbutto, The Gambia; s. of Bunja Darbo and Fatoumatta Saidykhan; m. Awa Kainde Darbo 1972; three d.; ed. Methodist Boys' High School and Gambia High School, Banjul, Univs. of Ibadan, Nigeria and Abidjan, Ivory Coast; Asst. Commr., Basse 1967–68; Asst. Sec. Prime Minister's Office, Ministry of External Affairs 1968–70, Commr., Kerewan 1970–71; Dir. Econ. and Tech. Affairs, Senegambian Perm. Secr. 1971–74; Man. Commercial Banking Operations, Gambia Commercial and Devt. Bank 1974–79; High Commr. in Repub. of Senegal, also accred. to Mali, Guinea-Bissau, Cape Verde, Mauritania and Morocco 1979–81; nominated mem. of Parl. and apptd. Minister of Information and Tourism 1981–82; Vice-Pres. and Leader of Govt. Business in Parl., Hon. Treas., mem. Cen. Cttee. of People's Progressive Party 1982–; Vice-Pres. and Minister of Educ., Youth, Sports and Culture 1987–. *Leisure interests:* reading, theatre. *Address:* c/o State House, Banjul, The Gambia. *Telephone:* 548.

DARBOVEN, Hanne; German artist; b. 29 April 1941, Munich; ed. Hochschule für Bildende Künste, Hamburg; one-man exhbns. in Düsseldorf 1967, 1968, 1970, 1971, 1975, Munich 1969, Cologne 1970, 1980, Amsterdam 1970, 1972, 1974, 1975, 1976, Leo Castelli Gallery, New York 1973, 1974, 1976, 1977, 1978, 1980, 1982; and in Paris, Brussels, Oxford, Turin, Milan, Bologna, Zürich, Basle, Houston, etc.; has participated in numerous group exhbns. of contemporary art in galleries in Europe, U.S.A., Canada, São

Paulo Biennale 1973, Venice Biennale 1982. *Publications:* books including: El Lissitzky, Hosmann, Hamburg und Yves Gevaert 1974, Atta Troll Kunstmuseum 1975, Baudelaire, Heine, Disecpolo, Maizi, Flores, Kraus: Pour écrire la liberté 1975, New York Diary 1976, Ein Jahrhundert, Vol. 1 1971–77. *Address:* Am Burgberg 26, D-21 Hamburg 90, Federal Republic of Germany. *Telephone:* 040/763-3033.

DARBY, Sir (Henry) Clifford, Kt., M.A., PH.D., LITT.D., C.B.E., F.B.A.; British professor of geography (retd.); b. 7 Feb. 1909, Resolven, Wales; s. of Evan Darby; m. Eva Constance Thomson 1941; two d.; ed. Neath County School, Wales, St. Catharine's Coll., Cambridge; lecturer in Geography, Cambridge Univ. 1931–45; Fellow, King's Coll., Cambridge 1932–45 and 1966–81; Intelligence Div., Admiralty 1941–45; Prof. of Geography, Univ. of Liverpool 1945–49, Univ. Coll., London 1949–66, Cambridge Univ., 1966–76; Emer. Prof. Univ. of Cambridge 1976–; Visiting Professorships at Chicago 1952, Harvard 1956, 1964–65, Washington 1963; mem. Royal Comm. on Historical Monuments 1953–77, Nat. Parks Comm. 1958–63, Water Resources Bd. 1964–68; holder of numerous awards and hon. degrees. *Publications:* The Medieval Fenland 1940, The Draining of the Fens 1940, The Changing Fenland 1983; Ed. and contrib. to: An Historical Geography of England 1936, The Domesday Geography of England (7 vols) 1952–76, A New Historical Geography of England 1973. *Address:* 60 Storey's Way, Cambridge, CB3 0DX, England. *Telephone:* (0223) 354745.

DARBY, William Jefferson, M.D., PH.D.; American professor of nutrition; b. 6 Nov. 1913, Galloway, Ark.; s. of William J. and Ruth (Douglass) Darby; m. Elva Louise Mayo 1935; three s.; ed. Univs. of Arkansas and Michigan; Asst. Prof., Biochemistry, Vanderbilt Univ. School of Medicine 1944–46, Assoc. Prof. Medicine 1944–46, Assoc. Prof. Biochemistry and Medicine 1946–48, Prof. Biochemistry, Chair. Dept., Dir. Div. of Nutrition 1949–71, Prof. Medicine in Nutrition 1965–79, Prof. Emer. of Biochemistry (Nutrition) 1979–; Archivist, American Inst. of Nutrition 1982–; mem. Council on Foods and Nutrition, American Medical Asscn. 1948–62, Chair. 1960–62; WHO expert panel on nutrition, consultant Yugoslavia, Austria, Indonesia, Egypt, Southern Rhodesia, Basutoland, Guatemala and other Cen. American countries 1950–; mem. Cttee. of Consultants Interdepartmental Cttee. on Nutrition for Nat. Defense and Dir. of Surveys in the Philippines, Ethiopia, Ecuador, Lebanon, Jordan and Nigeria 1955–63; Chair. Advisory Cttee. on Nutrition to the Office of the Surgeon Gen., U.S. Army 1959–72; mem. Panel on Nutrition, Space Science Bd., N.A.S. 1962–72; Nat. Consultant to the Surgeon Gen., U.S. Air Force 1967–72; mem. Scientific Advisory Cttee. the Nutrition Foundation Inc. 1967–71, Pres. 1972–81; Public Trustee, Food and Drug Law Inst. 1962–; Co-Chair. Hazardous Materials Advisory Cttee., Environmental Protection Agency 1971–75; mem. Bd. and Trustee, Swanson Center for Nutrition 1973–; mem. U.S. Nat. Cttee. for The Int. Union of Nutrition Sciences 1982–, Chair. 1986–; Trustee Helen Keller Int. 1975–, Int. Life Sciences Inst. 1978–82; Ed. Annual Review of Nutrition 1980–84; mem. N.A.S., and mem. or fmr. mem. of numerous other professional and public bodies; Hon. mem. El Colegio de Guatemala 1950, Austrian Public Health Assc. 1951, Nat. Medical Society of Panama 1951, Philippine Dietetic Assc. 1957, Serbian Acad. of Science 1959; Hon. D.Sc. (Univ. of Mich.) 1966, (Utah State Univ.) 1973; Conrad. A. Elvehjem Award for Public Service in Nutrition, American Inst. of Nutrition 1972, Thomas Jefferson Award, Vanderbilt Univ. 1969; Order of the Cedars of Lebanon 1972, Star of Jordan 1963, Order of Rodolfo Robles, Guatemala 1959, W. O. Atwater Memorial Lecturer 1975, Underwood-Prescott Memorial Award 1979; numerous other awards. *Publications:* (with J. S. McLester) Nutrition and Diet in Health and Disease 1952, (with V. N. Patwardhan) The State of Nutrition in the Arab Middle East, Food: The Gift of Osiris (with P. Ghalioungui and L. Grivetti) 1976, Fermented Food Beverages in Nutrition (with C. F. Gastineau and T. B. Turner) 1979, numerous other contributions to medical books, numerous articles. *Leisure interests:* bibliophily, history of nutrition. *Address:* Vanderbilt Univ. Medical Center Library, Nashville, Tenn. 37232 (Office); Route 1, Box 215, Thompson Station, Tenn. 37179, U.S.A. (Home). *Telephone:* 615-794-6888 (Home).

D'ARCY, Margaretta; Irish author and playwright; m. John Arden (q.v.) 1957; five c. (one deceased); Artistic Dir. Corrandulla Arts and Entertainment Club 1973–. *Publications:* Tell Them Everything (prison memoirs) 1981, The Happy Haven (with John Arden) 1961, Business of Good Government 1962, Ars Longa Vita Brevis 1964, The Royal Pardon 1966, Friday's Hiding 1967, The Hero Rises Up 1969, The Island of the Mighty 1974, The Non-Stop Connolly Show 1975, Vandaleur's Folly 1978, The Little Gray Home in the West (with John Arden) 1978, The Making of Muswell Hill (with John Arden) 1979, The Manchester Enthusiasts (with John Arden) 1984, Whose Is the Kingdom? (with John Arden) 1986. TV documentary (with John Arden) Profile of Sean O'Casey 1973. *Address:* c/o Margaret Ramsay, 14a Goodwins Court, London, WC2N 4LL, England.

DARGIE, Sir William Alexander, Kt., C.B.E., F.R.S.A., F.R.A.S.; Australian artist; b. 4 June 1912, Melbourne; s. of late A. Dargie; m. Kathleen Howitt; one s. one d.; official war artist with Australian Imperial Forces, Royal Australian Air Force, Royal Australian Navy; Head. Nat. Gallery, Vic. Art School 1946–53; Chair. Commonwealth Art Advisory Bd. 1969–73; mem. Interim Council, Nat. Gallery, Canberra 1968–73, Nat. Capital Planning Advisory Cttee. 1970–73, Aboriginal Arts Advisory Cttee. 1969–

71, Council, Nat. Museum of Vic. 1978–83; Trustee, Native Cultural Reserve, Port Moresby, Papua New Guinea 1969–75, Museum and Art Gallery, Papua New Guinea 1970–73; Chair. Bd. of Trustees, McLelland Gallery 1981–87; has painted portraits of H.M. Queen Elizabeth II, H.R.H. Duke of Gloucester, H.R.H. the late Princess Royal, H.R.H. the late Princess Marina, H.R.H. Princess Alexandra and many individuals distinguished in arts, sciences and politics in Australia, N.Z. and U.K.; exhibitor, Royal Acad. and Royal Soc. of Portrait Painters; M.A. (h.c.); Woodward and McPhillimy Awards 1940, Archibald Prize (eight times) N.S.W., MacKay Prize 1942. *Leisure interests:* tennis, folklore, material culture St Melanasia. *Address:* 19 Irilbarra Road, Canterbury, Vic. 3126, Australia. *Telephone:* 03/836 3396.

DARIDA, Clelio; Italian politician; b. 3 May 1927, Rome; joined Christian Democrat party (D.C.) 1946, elected mem. Rome Cttee. 1947, Dir. Propaganda Office 1954–55; M.P. for Rome 1963–69; Mayor of Rome 1969–76; M.P. for Rome 1976–; fmr. Under-Sec. of State, Ministry of Interior then fmr. Minister of Post and Telecommunications, of Public Admin. of Justice; Minister of State-owned Industries 1985–87. *Address:* Ministry of State Industry, Via Sallustiana 53, 00187 Rome, Italy.

DARIDAN, Jean-Henri; French diplomatist; b. 15 Aug. 1906; ed. Collège de Juilly, Ecole des Chartes and Univ. de Paris; entered French Ministry of Foreign Affairs 1932; Third Sec. Rome, Prague 1933–38; war and resistance services 1942–44; Counsellor Chungking 1945–46; Chargé d'affaires Bangkok 1947; Minister-Counsellor Washington 1948–54; Deputy High Commr. French Indochina 1954; Deputy Dir.-Gen. Political and Econ. Affairs, Paris 1955, Dir.-Gen. 1956; Amb. to Japan 1959–62; Diplomatic Adviser to French Govt. 1963–65; Amb. to India 1965–70, concurrently to Nepal 1965–67; Hon. Chair., France-Amérique; Chair. France Union-Indienne 1974; mem. Advisory Cttee. to French Nat. Museums; two prizes from Académie Française; Commdr., Légion d'honneur, Croix de guerre, Hon. K.B.E. (U.K.). *Publications:* John Law, père de l'inflation 1938, Abraham Lincoln 1962, Noirs et blancs, de Lincoln à Johnson 1965, De la Gaule à de Gaulle, une histoire de France 1977, Le chemin de la défaite 1980. *Address:* 32 avenue Marceau, 75008 Paris, France. *Telephone:* 47-20-55-43.

DARLING, Sir James Ralph, Kt., C.M.G., O.B.E., M.A.; Australian (b. British) teacher and administrator; b. 18 June 1899, Tonbridge, Kent; s. of the late Augustine M. Darling and Jane Baird (née Nimmo); m. Margaret Dunlop Campbell 1935; one s. three d.; ed. Repton School and Oriel Coll., Oxford; served in First World War; Schoolmaster, Liverpool 1921–24, Charterhouse, Godalming 1924–29; Headmaster, Geelong Church of England Grammar School, Australia 1930–61; mem. Commonwealth Univs. Comm. 1942–51, Australian Broadcasting Control Bd. 1955–61; Chair. Australian Broadcasting Comm. 1961–67; Hon. Fellow and Past Pres. Australian Coll. of Educ.; Chair. Australian Road Safety Council 1961–71; Chair. Australian Frontier Comm. 1962–71, Pres. 1971–73, Immigration Publicity Council 1962–71; mem. Melbourne Univ. Council 1933–71; Vice-Pres. Australian Elizabethan Theatre Trust 1964, Pres. 1964–81; Hon. D.C.L. (Oxford); Hon. LL.D. (Melbourne). *Publications:* The Education of a Civilised Man, Timbertop, Richly Rewarding 1978. *Address:* 3 Myamyn Street, Armadale, Victoria 3143, Australia. *Telephone:* Melbourne 20-6262.

DARMAN, Richard Gordon, M.B.A.; American banker and government official; b. 10 May 1943, Charlotte; m. Kathleen Emmet 1967; two. s.; ed. Harvard Univ.; Deputy Asst. Sec. Dept. of Health, Educ. and Welfare, Wash., D.C. 1971–72, Asst. to Sec., Dept. of Defense 1973, Special Asst. to Attorney-Gen. 1973; Asst. Sec. Dept. of Commerce 1976–77; Asst. to Pres. 1981–85; Deputy Sec. Treasury Dept. 1985–87; Dir. (desig.) Office of Man. and Budget Dec. 1988–; Prin. Dir. ICF Inc., Wash., D.C. 1975, 1977–80; lecturer in Public Policy and Man., Harvard Univ. 1977–80; Man. Dir. Shearson Lehman Brothers Inc., New York 1987–; Vice-Chair. Del. to UN Conf. on Law of Sea 1977; mem. Ocean Policy Cttee., N.A.S. 1978–80, Bd. of Dirs. American Capital and Research Corpn. 1988–, Council of Foreign Relations; Ed. Harvard Educ. Review 1970, Contributing Ed. U.S. News and World Report 1987–; trustee Brookings Inst. 1987–. *Address:* Office of Management and Budget, Old Executive Building, Washington, D.C. 20503, U.S.A.

DARMOJUWONO, H.E. Cardinal Justine; Indonesian ecclesiastic; b. 2 Nov. 1914, Godean; s. of Josef Surodikoro and Maria Ngatinah; ordained Priest 1947; Archbishop of Semarang 1963–81; Asst. parish priest, St. Maria Fatima, Semarang 1981–; cr. Cardinal by Pope Paul VI 1967; Chair. Conf. of Indonesian Bishops 1964–79; Bishop of the Indonesian Armed Forces 1964–83; mem. of Congregation for Sacraments; mem. Cen. Cttee., Fed. of Asian Bishops' Confs. 1970–79. *Address:* Jalan Kamfer Raya 49, Kelurahan Pedalangan, Semarang 50237, Indonesia. *Telephone:* Semarang 312504.

DARMON, Marco; French lawyer; b. 26 July 1930, Tunis; m. Elsa Lévy 1958; magistrate in Brittany 1957–59; joined Ministry of Justice 1959; Tech. Counsellor, Office of the Keeper of the Seals 1973–74; subsequently Vice-Pres. Tribunal de Grande Instance, Paris; Asst. Dir. Office of Keeper of the Seals 1981–82; Dir. of Civil Affairs and of the Seal of Ministry of Justice 1982; Advocate-Gen., European Court of Justice, Luxembourg

1984-. *Address:* Court of Justice of the European Communities, 2925 Luxembourg.

DARRIEUX, Danielle; French actress; b. 1 May 1917, Bordeaux; d. of Jean and Marie-Louise (née Witkowski) Darrieux; m. 3rd Georges Mitsinkides 1948; one s.; ed. Paris Univ.; First appeared in films 1931; in theatre 1937; Chevalier, Légion d'honneur, Commdr., Ordre des Arts et des Lettres, César d'honneur 1985. *Film appearances include:* Le bal, Mayerling, Un mauvais garçon, Battement de coeur, Premier rendez-vous, Ruy Blas, Le plaisir, Madame de ..., Le rouge et le noir, Bonnes à tuer, Le salaire du péché, L'amant de Lady Chatterley, Typhon sur Nagasaki, La ronde, Alexander the Great, Marie Octobre, L'homme à femmes, Les lions sont lâchés, Le crime ne paie pas, Le diable et les dix commandements, Le coup de grâce, Patate, Greengage Summer, Les demoiselles de Rochefort, 24 heures de la vie d'une femme, Divine, L'année sainte, En haut des marches, Le lieu du crime, Corps et biens; *Plays:* La robe mauve de Valentine 1963, Gillian 1965, Comme un oiseau 1965, Secretissimo 1965, Laurette 1966, CoCo 1970, Ambassador (musical) 1971, Folie douce 1972, les Amants terribles 1973, Boulevard Feydau 1978, L'intoxe 1981, Gigi 1985. *Address:* 6 rue Porte Blanche, 92430 Marnes-La-Coquette, France.

DĂSCĂLESCU, Constantin; Romanian politician; b. 1923, Breaza; ed. Bucharest Acad. of Econ. Studies; joined Romanian Communist Party (RCP) 1945; worker with Astra Romana until 1947; active in oil-workers' trade union 1947-49; attended Party school, Ploiesti, subsequently Dir.; held various offices in Admin. of Cen. Cttee. of RCP; Deputy to Grand Nat. Ass. 1965-; mem. State Council 1973-; Head, Org. Section, Cen. Cttee. of RCP 1974; mem. Cen. Cttee. of RCP 1965-, mem. Exec. Political Cttee. 1976-, Sec. of Cen. Cttee. 1976-82, mem. Perm. Bureau 1982-; Chair. Council of Ministers May 1982-; fmr. Chair. Nat. Union of Co-operative Producer Farms, Council of Econ. and Social Org.; fmr. Chair. Exec. Bureau, Nat. Council of Working People; Hero of Socialist Labour and other orders and medals. *Address:* Office of the Chair. of the Council of Ministers, Bucharest, Romania.

DASCHLE, Thomas Andrew, B.A.; American politician; b. 9 Dec. 1947, Aberdeen, S. Dak.; m. Linda Hall Daschle; one s. two d.; ed. S. Dak. State Univ.; served to 1st Lieut., U.S.A.F. 1969-72; Chief Legis. Aide and then Field Co-ordinator to U.S. Senator 1973-77; mem. 96th-97th Congresses from 1st S. Dak. Dist., 98th Congress 1977-87; Senator from S. Dak. Jan. 1987-; Democrat. *Address:* U.S. Senate, 2455 Rayburn House Office Building, Washington, D.C. 20510, U.S.A.

d'ASCOLI, Bernard Jacques-Henri Marc; French concert pianist; b. 18 Nov. 1958, Aubagne; ed. Marseille Conservatoire; became blind 1962; took up music 1970; youngest Baccalauréat matriculate of France 1974; first public appearances on both piano and organ 1974; elected as most talented French artist of the year (Megève) 1976; first prize Int. Maria Canals competition, Barcelona 1979; prizewinner, Leipzig Bach competition and Warsaw Chopin competition 1980; 3rd prize, Leeds Int. piano competition 1981; began int. professional career 1982, following débuts major London concert halls with Royal Philharmonic Orchestra and first recording; toured Australia with Chamber Orchestra of Europe 1983; début Amsterdam Concertgebouw 1984, U.S.A., with Houston Symphony Orchestra 1985, Musikverein, Vienna 1986, Henry Wood Promenade Concerts, London 1986, Tokyo Casals Hall and Bunka Kaikan Hall 1988. *Recordings:* Schumann CD, Nimbus 1989, Carnaval, Papillons, Fantaisie-stücke opus III. *Address:* c/o Van Walsum Management, 40 St. Peters Road, London, W6 9BH, England. *Telephone:* 01-741 5881.

DAS GUPTA, Bimal; Indian artist; b. 27 Dec. 1917; ed. Krishnalth Collegiate School, Berhampore, W. Bengal, and Govt. Coll. of Arts and Crafts, Calcutta; originally painted landscapes in water colours; is now avant-garde painter in oils; Sr. Lecturer in Painting, Coll. of Art, Delhi 1963-; paintings in Nat. Gallery of Modern Art, New Delhi, Nat. Gallery of Poland, Warsaw, Berlin Museum, Pilnitz Gallery, Dresden, Hermitage Gallery, Leningrad; one-man exhbns. in Delhi, Calcutta, Bombay, Madras, Amritsar, Mysore, Berlin, Poland, London, New York, Cairo, Moscow, Belgrade and Paris; exhibited at São Paulo Bienal, and int. exhbns. in Japan, New York and U.S.S.R. *Address:* 22 Tilak Marg, New Delhi 110001, India.

DAS GUPTA, Prodosh Kusum, B.A.; Indian sculptor and writer; b. 10 Jan. 1912, Dacca; s. of late Nalini Nath Das Gupta and Charubala Das Gupta; m. T. C. Kamala 1940; two s.; ed. Univ. of Calcutta Govt. Schools of Arts and Crafts, Lucknow and Madras, Royal Acad. of Arts, London and Ecole de Grand Chaumère, Paris; Founder, Calcutta Group (pioneer org. of modern art in India) 1943, Sec. 1943-51; Reader and Head, Dept. of Sculpture, Baroda Univ. 1950; Prof. of Sculpture, Govt. Coll. of Arts and Crafts, Calcutta 1951-57; Dir. Nat. Gallery of Modern Art, New Delhi 1957-70; Pres. Third Congress, Int. Asscn. of Arts, Vienna 1960; mem. Indian Artists' Dels. to U.S.A. and U.S.S.R.; represented India in int. sculpture competition The Unknown Political Prisoner, Tate Gallery, London; works in Nat. Gallery of Modern Art, New Delhi, Madras Museum, Acad. of Fine Arts Gallery, Calcutta and in private collections in India and abroad. *Publications:* My Sculpture, Temple Terracottas of Bengal, Fallen Leaves and other poems, and numerous articles on art. *Leisure*

interests: music, photography, poetry, writing on art. *Address:* K-5, Jangpura Ext., New Delhi 110014, India.

DA SILVA, Luis Inácio (Lula); Brazilian trades unionist; b. 1946; m.; two s.; metal-worker, São Bernardo do Campo 1968-, organized strike 1977 and became union leader; imprisoned 1977 and freed later that year; f. and Pres. Central Unica dos Trabalhadores (PT) 1980-; arrested 1981.

DASH, Mangaljavyn; Mongolian politician; b. 1925; ed. Mongolian State Univ.; teacher, Head of dept. Mongolian State Univ., then Vice-Rector, Inst. of Agric. 1947-59; Head of Dept. of the MPRP Cen. Cttee. 1959-68; Minister for Agric. and Chair. Supreme Council of Agricultural Co-operatives Union 1968-76; Amb. to Poland 1976-78, to Afghanistan 1978-80; Minister for Agric. 1980-81; Sec. MPRP Cen. Cttee. 1981-86; Deputy to People's Great Hural. *Address:* c/o Central Committee of the MPRP, Ulan Bator, Mongolia.

DASKALAKIS, Apostolos; Greek university professor; b. 1903, Sparta; s. of Vassilios and Maria Daskalakis; m. Hellen Vranicus 1935; two d.; ed. Athens Univ. and Univ. de Paris à la Sorbonne; began career as journalist 1921; Foreign Corresp. of various Athens newspapers 1927-32; Prof. of Medieval and Modern History, Athens Univ. 1939, of Ancient Greek History 1950-54, and of Modern Greek History 1955; Rector, Athens Univ. 1953-55; Cultural Counsellor, Ministry of Foreign Affairs 1950; Perm. Rep. of Greece to Council of Cultural Co-operation, Council of Europe, 1952-73, Pres. 1965; Hon. Prof. of many European univs. *Publications:* The Causes of the Greek War of Independence 1927, Chypre hellénique à travers quarante siècles d'histoire 1932, History of Modern Greece 1952, The Hellenism of the Ancient Macedonians 1960, La Bataille des Thermopyles 1962, Alexander the Great 1963, Rhigas Velestinlis 1964, Texts and Sources of the History of Greek War of Independence (6 vols.) 1968, The Greek People under the Turkish Empire 1970 and many other books and articles. *Address:* Apostolos Evrou 3, Athens 611, Greece. *Telephone:* 7770151.

DASSAULT, Serge; French engineer; b. 4 April 1925, Paris; s. of Marcel Dassault and of Madeleine Minckès; m. Nicole Raffel 1950; ed. Lycée Janson-de-Sailly, Ecole Polytechnique, Ecole Nat. Supérieure de l'Aéronautique, Centre de Perfectionnement dans l'Administration des Affaires, Inst. des Hautes Etudes de la Défense Nationale; Dir. of Flight Testing, Avions Marcel Dassault 1955-61, Export Dir. 1961-63; Dir.-Gen. Société Electronique Marcel Dassault 1963-67, Pres. Dir.-Gen. 1967-86; Admin. Avions Marcel Dassault-Breguet Aviation 1967-, Pres. Dir.-Gen. 1986-; Admin. Dassault Belgique Aviation 1968-; Town Councillor, Corbeil-Essonnes 1968-; mem. Comité de direction de la Fédération nationale des industries électroniques 1968-, Groupement des Industries Françaises Aéronautiques et Spatiales 1968-; Hon. Pres. Fondation des Oeuvres Sociales de l'Air 1968-; Commissaire Général des Salons Internationaux de l'Aéronautique et de l'Espace 1974-; Chief Engineer Armaments 1974-; Pres. Asscn. Française pour la Participation dans les Entreprises 1972; Pres. working group, Participation active dans l'entreprise, Nat. Council, Patronat Français 1985-; Chevalier, Légion d'honneur; Médaille de l'Aéronautique, Officier de l'Ordre national du Mérite ivoirien. *Publications:* la Gestion participative, J'ai choisi la vérité 1983. *Leisure interests:* golf, hunting, fishing. *Address:* les Mirages, 27 rue du Prof. Pauchet, 92420 Vaucresson, France. *Telephone:* (1) 47.41.79.21.

DASSIN, Jules; American film director; b. 18 Dec. 1911, Middletown, Conn.; s. of Samuel and Berthe (née Vogel) Dassin; m. 1st Béatrice Launer (divorced), one s. (deceased) two d.; m. 2nd Melina Mercouri (q.v.) 1966; ed. Morris High School; attended drama school in Europe 1936; Asst. Dir. to Alfred Hitchcock 1940; films directed in U.S. include Brute Force 1947, Naked City 1948, Thieves' Highway 1949; settled in France 1954 and directed Rififi (also acted) 1954, Celui qui doit mourir 1956, Never on Sunday (also acted) 1960, Phaedra 1961, Topkapi 1963, 10.30 p.m. Summer 1966, Up Tight 1968, Promise at Dawn 1970, The Rehearsal 1974, A Dream of Passion 1978, Circle of Two 1980, etc.; Director's Prize, Cannes Film Festival 1955 for Rififi. *Address:* Anagnostopoulou 25, Athens, Greece.

DATARS, William Ross, PH.D., F.R.S.C.; Canadian professor of physics; b. 14 June 1932, Desboro; s. of Albert J. Datars and Leona A. Fries; m. Eleanor R. Wismer 1959; three s.; ed. McMaster Univ. and Univ. of Wisconsin; Scientific Officer, Defence Research Board 1959-62; Asst. Prof. McMaster Univ. 1962-65, Assoc. Prof. 1965-69, Prof. of Physics 1969-; E.W.R. Steacie Research Fellow 1968-70; Fellow, American Physical Soc. *Publications:* 136 scientific papers. *Leisure interests:* farming, skiing, jogging. *Address:* R.R. 2, Lynden Ontario, L0R 1T0, Canada. *Telephone:* (519) 647-2327.

DATCU, Ion; Romanian diplomatist; b. 20 Feb. 1930, Braşov; s. of Ion and Maria Datcu; m. Viorica Datcu 1956; ed. history and philosophy; Cultural Attaché, Romanian Embassy, Moscow 1957-59; Press Attaché, Rome 1959-61; Dir., Div. of Int. Orgs. and mem. of the Bd., Min. of Foreign Affairs 1961-66; Del. to UN Gen. Ass. 1961-65; Rep. at confs. of the ILO, Econ. Comm. for Europe and UNESCO; Amb. to Japan 1966-69, also Australia 1967-69; Rep. at sessions of Econ. Comm. for Asia and the Far East, Tokyo 1967, Canberra 1968 and Singapore 1969; Rep. to UN Office and specialized agencies in Geneva, Del. to Cttee. on Disarmament Conf. and Rep. to ILO Governing Body 1969-71; Perm. Rep. to UN 1972-78, in Ministry of Foreign Affairs 1979-; Head Del. to Madrid Conf.

of Security and Co-operation in Europe 1980–82; Amb. to Switzerland 1982–86, Perm. Rep. to UN Office in Geneva 1983–86. *Publications:* articles and studies on Int. politics. *Leisure interests:* theatre, classical music. *Address:* Piaţa Victoriei No. 1, Bucharest, Romania.

DAUBE, David, D.IUR., PH.D., D.C.L., F.B.A.; university professor; b. 8 Feb. 1909, Freiburg-im-Breisgau, Germany; s. of Jakob Daube and Selma Daube (née Ascher); m. 1st 1936 (divorced 1964), three s.; m. 2nd Helen Smelser (née Margolis) 1986; ed. Berthold-Gymnasium, Freiburg, and Univs. of Freiburg, Göttingen and Cambridge; Fellow of Caius Coll., Cambridge 1938–46; lecturer in Law, Cambridge 1946–51; Prof. of Jurisprudence, Aberdeen 1951–55; Regius Prof. of Civil Law, Oxford, and Fellow of All Souls Coll. 1955–74, Emer. Regius Prof. 1970, Emer. Fellow 1980–; Dir. Robbins Hebraic and Roman Law Collections and Prof.-in-Residence, School of Law, Univ. of Calif., Berkeley 1970–80, Emer. 1980–; Sr. Fellow, Yale Univ. 1962; Gifford Lecturer, Edin. 1962, 1963; Olaos Petrie lecturer at Uppsala Univ. 1963; Ford Prof. of Political Science, Univ. of Calif., Berkeley 1964; Riddell Lecturer, Newcastle 1965; Gray Lecturer, Cambridge 1966; Pope John XXIII lecturer, Catholic Univ. of America, Wash. 1966, Lionel Cohen lecturer, Jerusalem 1970; Messenger Lecturer, Cornell Univ. 1971; Visiting Prof., Univ. of Constance 1966–78, Hon. Prof. 1980–; Charles Inglis Romson Prof. of Law, Univ. Colorado 1974; Fellow, British Acad., American and World Acad. of Arts and Sciences, American Acad. of Jewish Research; Pres. Soc. Int. des Droits de l'Antiquité 1957; Pres. Classical Assen. of G.B. 1976–77, Jewish Law Assen. 1983–85; Hon. Fellow, Oxford Univ. Centre for Postgraduate Hebrew Studies 1973–, Gonville and Caius Coll., Cambridge 1974–, American Soc. for Legal History; Founder-Pres. Oxford B'nai B'rith 1961; Corresp. mem. Göttingen and Bavarian Acads. of Sciences, Royal Irish Acad.; Hon. LL.D. (Edinburgh, Leicester and Cambridge); Dr. h.c. (Paris, Sorbonne, Munich); Hon. D.H.L. (Hebrew Union Coll.); Dr. Phil. h.c. (Göttingen); Grad. Theological Union, Berkely. *Publications:* Studies in Biblical Law 1947, The New Testament and Rabbinic Judaism 1956, Forms of Roman Legislation 1956, The Exodus Pattern in the Bible 1963, The Sudden in the Scriptures 1964, Collaboration with Tyranny in Rabbinic Law 1965, Roman Law 1969, Civil Disobedience in Antiquity 1972, Duty of Procreation 1977, Typologie im Werk des Flavius Josephus 1977, Ancient Jewish Law 1981, Ursprung der Detektivgeschichte 1983, Sons and Strangers 1984, Das Alte Testament im Neuen 1984, Witnesses in Bible and Talmud (with C. Carmichael) 1986, Appeasement or Resistance and other essays on New Testament Judaism 1987; Festschriften: Daube Noster (Ed. A. Watson) 1974, Studies in Jewish Legal History (Ed. B. S. Jackson) 1974, Donum Gentilicium (Ed. E. Bammel, C. K. Barrett and W. D. Davies) 1978. *Address:* School of Law, University of California, Berkeley, Calif. 94720, U.S.A.

DAUBEN, William Garfield, PH.D.; American professor of chemistry; b. 6 Nov. 1919, Columbus, Ohio; s. of H. J. Dauben and Leilah Stump; m. Carol Billings Hyatt 1947; two d.; ed. Ohio State, Harvard and Oxford Univs., and Eidgenössische Technische Hochschule, Zürich; Postdoctoral Fellow, Harvard Univ. 1944; at. Univ. of Calif., Berkeley 1945–, Prof. of Chem. 1958–; mem. Bd. of Dirs. Organic Syntheses, Organic Reactions; Consultant to U.S. Public Health Service, Nat. Science Foundation, American Chem. Soc. Petroleum Research Fund 1973–77; Ed.-in-Chief Organic Reactions 1967–83, Bd. Dirs. 1967–; mem. N.A.S. 1972–, Chair., Chem. Section 1977–80; American Chem. Soc., American Acad. of Arts and Sciences, Royal Soc. of Chem., Swiss Chem. Soc., Nat. Research Council, Ass. of Math. and Physical Sciences 1977–80; Hon. mem. Pharmaceutical Soc. of Japan; Dr. h.c., Univ. of Bordeaux 1980; E. Gunther Award American Chemical Soc. 1972, Sr. U.S. Scientist Award, Alexander von Humboldt Foundation 1980, 1984. *Publications:* scientific research articles in Journal of the American Chemical Society and Journal of Organic Chemistry. *Leisure interests:* golf, skiing. *Address:* 20 Eagle Hill, Berkeley, Calif. 94707, U.S.A. (Home). *Telephone:* 415-524-2142.

d'AUBUISSON ARRIETA, Maj. Roberto; Salvadorean politician and fmr. army officer; b. 23 Aug. 1943, San Salvador; s. of Roberto d'Aubuisson Andrade and Joaquina Arrieta Alvarado; m. Martaluz Angulo de d'Aubuisson; two s. two d.; 20 years in armed forces; fmr. mil. intelligence officer; Pres. Constituent Ass. 1982–83; fmr. Leader Alianza Republicana Nacionalista; Cand. 1984, Pres. Elections; Deputy, Legis. Ass. 1985–. *Address:* Alianza Republicana Nacionalista, San Salvador, El Salvador. *Telephone:* 24-27-79; 24-41-18; 24-40-30.

DAUD, Datuk Dr. Sulaiman bin Haj, B.D.S.; Malaysian politician; b. 4 March 1933, Kuching, Sarawak; m.; four c.; ed. Otago Univ., New Zealand and Univ. of Toronto; teacher 1954–56; Dental Officer, State Govt. of Sarawak 1963–68; State Dental Officer, Brunei 1971; Political Sec. Ministry of Primary Industries 1972; Minister for Land and Mineral Resources, Sarawak 1973–74; mem. Parl. 1974–; Deputy Minister of Land Devt. 1974–75, of Land and Mines 1975–76, of Land and Regional Devt. 1976–77, of Health 1978–81; Minister of Fed. Territory March 1981; Minister of Educ. July 1981, of Sport, Youth and Culture 1984–86, of Land and Regional Devt. 1986–; Vice-Pres. Party Pesaka Bumiputra Bersatu, Sarawak; other public appts. and leader of Malaysian dels. to int. confs.; Johan Bintang Sarawak; Panglima Negara Nintang Sarawak. *Address:* Ministry of Land and Regional Development, 13th Floor, Wisma Keramat, Jalan Gurney, 50514 Kuala Lumpur, Malaysia.

DAUGNY, Bertrand, L.ÉS SC.; French engineer and business executive; b. 5 Jan. 1925, Paris; s. of Pierre-Marie Daugny and Suzanne Hauser; m. 1st Nicole Wolff (deceased), one s. one d.; m. 2nd Elisabeth Joussellin 1958, two d.; ed. Faculté des Sciences, Paris, and Ecole Supérieure d'Electricité; engineer, later Head of Dept. Cie. Française Thomson-Houston 1948–54; founder, Electronic Dept., Avions Marcel Dassault 1954; Admin. and Asst. Dir.-Gen. Soc. Electronique Marcel Dassault 1963, Admin. and Dir.-Gen. 1967–, Vice-Pres. Soc. Electronique Serge Dassault 1983–86, Pres. Dir.-Gen. 1986–; Officier, Légion d'honneur, Ordre nat. du Mérite; Médaille Militaire, Croix de Guerre, Médaille Aéronautique. *Address:* 55 quai Marcel Dassault, 92214 Saint-Cloud, France. *Telephone:* (1) 49.11.80.00.

DAUSSET, Jean Baptiste Gabriel, M.D.; French doctor; b. 19 Oct. 1916, Toulouse; s. of Henri Pierre Jules Dausset and Elisabeth Brullard; m. Rose Mayoral Lopez 1962; one s. one d.; ed. Lycée Michelet, Faculty of Medicine, Paris; internship, Paris hosps. 1941; Asst. Faculty of Medicine, Univ. of Paris 1946; Dir. Lab., Nat. Blood Transfusion Cen. 1950–63; Chief, Immuno-haematology Lab., Inst. de Recherches sur les Leucémies et les Maladies du Sang, Paris 1961; Chief Biologist Service d'Hématologie-Serologie-Immunologie, Hôpital Saint-Louis, Paris 1963; Dir. of Research Unit on Immunogenetics of Human Transplantation, of Inst. Nat. de la Santé et la Recherche Médicale 1968–84; Prof. of Immunohaematology, Head Dept., Faculty of Medicine, Univ. of Paris 1968–77; Prof. of Experimental Medicine, Collège de France 1978–; mem. French Acads. of Science and Medicine 1977–87; Dir. Human Polymorphism Study Center 1984–; mem. N.A.S., Washington 1980; shared Nobel Prize for Physiology and Medicine 1980 with Dr. Baruj Benacerraf and Dr. George Snell (qq.v.) for work on histocompatibility antigens; Honda Prize 1987; Commdr., Légion d'honneur, des Palmes Academiques Grand Croix Ordre Nat. du Mérite; numerous other awards. *Publications:* Immuno-hématologie biologique et clinique 1956, numerous articles. *Leisure interest:* modern art. *Address:* CEPH, 27/29 rue Juliette Dodu, 75010 Paris (Office); 9 rue de Villersexel, 75007 Paris, France (Home). *Telephone:* 42-49-98-50 (Office); 42-22-18-82 (Home).

DAUX, Georges; French hellenist; b. 21 Sept. 1899, Bastia, Corsica; s. of Louis Daux and Célestine Digoy; m. Vida Pirjevec 1926; ed. Univ. of Paris; mem. French Archaeological School, Athens 1920–24; Cultural Counsellor, French Embassy, Istanbul 1924–26; Prof., Dean of the Faculty of Letters and Pres. of Dijon Univ. 1927–45; Prof. of Greek History, Sorbonne and Dir. of French Archaeological School at Athens 1945–69; mem. of Security Council's Comm. of Inquiry in the Balkans 1947; mem. Inst. for Advanced Studies, Princeton 1947–48; visiting Prof. Harvard 1949–50; Sather Prof. Berkeley 1956–57; Geddes-Harrower Prof., Aberdeen 1970; mem. Deutsches Archäologisches Inst., Berlin, Accademia Pontificale, Rome, Yugoslav Acad., Zagreb, Deutsche Akademie der Wissenschaften, Berlin, American Philosophical Soc., Philadelphia, Accademia dei Lincei, Rome, Acad. des Inscriptions, Paris, British Acad.; hon. life mem. Soc. for Promotion of Hellenic Studies, London, Archaeological Inst. of America, New York, Société Archéologique, Athens and others; Dr. h.c. (Brussels and Liège); Commdr. Légion d'honneur, Commdr. des Palmes académiques. *Leisure interests:* skiing, tennis, zoology. *Address:* 6 avenue Paul Appell, 75014 Paris, France. *Telephone:* Paris 45-40-49-28.

DAUZIER, Pierre Marie, B.A., LL.B.; French advertising executive; b. 31 Jan. 1939, Periquex; s. of late Maurice Dauzier and of Marie Faucher; m. Erle Fleischmann 1968; one s. one d.; ed. Ecole Bossuet, Lycée Henri IV, Univs. of Clermont-Ferrand and Paris and Inst. of Higher Advertising Studies; Account Exec. Havas Conseil (Advertising Agency) 1963–65, Sr. Account Exec. 1965–66, Head, Commercial Dept. 1966–68, Man. 1968–70, Man. Rep. at Needham Harper & Steers, New York 1970–72, Gen. Man. 1972–75, Pres. and C.E.O. UNIVAS 1975–80, Chair. and C.E.O. 1980–82; Gen. Man. Agence Havas 1982–86, Pres. and C.E.O. 1986–; Pres. and C.E.O. Information & Publicité 1986–; Chair. and C.E.O. Eurocom 1986–; Chevalier, Ordre Nat. du Mérite, Légion d'Honneur. *Address:* Agence Havas, 136 avenue Charles de Gaulle, 92200 Neuilly, France. *Telephone:* 1 47 47 30 00.

DAVAR, Dharmendar Nath, M.A., B. COM., S.A.S., C.A.I.I.B.; Indian financial official; b. 8 Aug. 1934; s. of Shri Daryai Lal and Smt. Bhagwanti; m. Santash Dawar 1960; one s. one d.; Man., Sr. Man. at various branches and head office of Punjab Nat. Bank 1960–68; Man. Industrial Finance Corpn. of India 1968–74, Gen. Man. 1980–82, Exec. Dir. 1982–84; Chair. April 1984–; Fellow, Econ. Devt. Inst. of IBRD; mem. Bd. of Govs., Man. Devt. Inst.; mem. Advisory Council, Devt. Banking Centre; Trustee Risk Capital Foundation, mem. Bd., Industrial Devt. Bank of India, Industrial Reconstruction Corpn. of India, Int. Devt. Inst. of India. *Address:* Industrial Finance Corporation of India, Bank of Baroda Building, 16 Sansad Marg, Post Box No. 363, New Delhi 110001, India. *Telephone:* (11) 2027012 (Office); 606757 (Home).

DAVENPORT, (Arthur) Nigel, M.A.; British actor; b. 23 May 1928; s. of Arthur H. Davenport and Katherine L. Meiklejohn; m. 1st Helena White 1951 (deceased); one s. one d.; m. 2nd Maria Aitken 1972 (divorced); one s.; ed Cheltenham Coll. and Trinity Coll. Oxford; entered theatrical profession and worked mainly in theatre 1951–61; since 1961 has starred in more than 30 films notably High Wind in Jamaica 1964, Man for All

Seasons 1966; frequent TV appearances; Pres. British Actors Equity Asscn. 1986-. *Leisure interests:* gardening, travel.

DAVEY, Kenneth George, PH.D., F.R.S.C.; Canadian professor, scientist and educator; b. 20 April 1923, Chatham, Ont.; s. of William Davey and Marguerite (Clark) Davey; m. Jeannette Isabel Evans 1959; one s. two d.; ed. McKeough Public School, Chatham, Chatham Collegiate Inst., Univ. of Western Ontario, Cambridge Univ.; N.R.C. Fellow (Zoology), Univ. of Toronto 1958-59; Drosier Fellow, Gonville and Caius Coll., Cambridge 1959-63; Assoc. Prof. of Parasitology, McGill Univ., Montreal 1963-66, Dir. Inst. of Parasitology 1964-74, Prof. of Parasitology and Biology 1966-74; Prof. of Biology, York Univ., Toronto 1974-, Chair. of Biology 1974-81, Dean of Science 1982-85, Distinguished Research Prof. of Biology 1984-, Vice-Pres. (Academic Affairs) 1986-; Ed. Int. Journal of Invertebrate Reproduction and Devt. 1979-85; mem. Bd. of Dirs. Huntsman Marine Lab. 1978-80, 1982-85, Pres. and Chair. of Bd. 1977-80; Pres. Biological Council of Canada 1979-82, Canadian Soc. of Zoologists 1981-82; Sec. Acad. of Science, Royal Soc. of Canada 1979-85; Fellow Entomological Soc. of Canada, Gold Medal 1981, Fry Medal (Canadian Soc. of Zoologists) 1987, Gold Medal (Biological Council of Canada) 1987. *Publications:* Reproduction in Insects 1964; 150 articles in the scholarly literature on insect endocrinology. *Leisure interests:* handweaving, food and wine. *Address:* Office of the Vice-President (Academic Affairs), York University, North York, Ont., M3J 1P3 (Office); 194 Banbury Road, Don Mills, Ont., M3B 3C5, Canada (Home). *Telephone:* (416) 736-5280 (Office); (416) 449-3160 (Home).

DAVICO, Oskar; Yugoslav poet and novelist; b. 1909; ed. Belgrade Univ.; imprisoned for working with Resistance 1941; escaped and joined partisans 1943; mem. Fed. Cttee. on Film Censorship 1958; recipient of several literary awards. *Publications:* With the Partisans of Markos, Poetry and Resistance, The Poem (novel), A Man's Man (poetic drama), Gedichte 1965. *Address:* c/o Serbian Writers' Association, Belgrade, Yugoslavia.

DAVID, Edward Emil, Jr., SC.D.; American scientist; b. 25 Jan. 1925, Wilmington, N.C.; s. of the late Edward Emil and Beatrice Liebman David; m. Ann Hirshberg 1950; one d.; ed. Georgia Inst. of Tech. and Mass. Inst. of Tech. (M.I.T.); joined Bell Telephone Labs. 1950; specialized in field of underwater sound and communication acoustics 1950-63, in research in computing science 1963-70; Science Adviser to Pres. Nixon and Dir. Office of Science and Tech. (Exec. Office of the Pres.) 1970-73; Exec. Vice-Pres. Gould Inc. 1973-77; Pres. Gould Labs. 1973-77, Edward E. David, Inc., Chicago, Ill. 1977-, Exxon Research and Eng. Co. 1977-86; Vice-Pres. Science and Tech., Exxon Corpn. 1978-80; U.S. Rep. to NATO Science Cttee.; mem. Bd. of Dirs., Materials Research Corpn.; Life-mem. Corpn., Exec. Cttee. and Energy Advisory Bd. M.I.T.; mem. Advisory Council, Stanford Research Inst.; Chair. Bd. of Trustees, Aerospace Corpn. 1975-81; mem. Bd. of Trustees, John Simon Guggenheim Memorial Foundation, Rensselaer Polytechnic Inst., Carnegie Inst., Washington; mem. N.A.S., American Asscn. för the Advancement of Science, Nat. Acad. of Eng.; Fellow, American Acad. of Arts and Sciences, Acoustical Soc. of America, Audio Eng. Soc., Inst. of Electrical and Electronics Engineers; hon. degrees, (Stevens Inst. of Tech., Polytechnic Inst. of Brooklyn, Carnegie-Mellon Univ., Univ. of Mich. etc.). *Publications:* Co-author of Man's World of Sound 1958, Waves and the Ear 1960, The Man-made World 1969; over 100 technical articles. *Leisure interests:* tennis, minerals, photography. *Address:* Edward E. David Inc., Box 435, Bedminster, N.J. 07921, U.S.A. (Office). *Telephone:* 201-765-1257.

DAVID, Jacques Henri; French business executive; b. 17 Oct. 1943, Ygrande (Allier); s. of André David and Suzanne Dupeyrat; m. Isabelle Lamy 1967; one d.; ed. Lycée Louis-le-Grand, Paris, Ecole Polytechnique, Inst. d'Etudes Politiques, Paris and Ecole Nat. Supérieure de la Statistique et des Études Économiques (Insee), Paris; Admin. Insee 1967-68; Head, econometric studies service, Banque de France 1969-75; Deputy Sec.-Gen. Conseil Nat. du Crédit 1973-75; Prof. Inst. d'Etudes Politiques 1975-; Insp. of Finance, Ministry of Econ. and Finance 1975-79; Adviser, Office of Minister of Econ. 1979, Deputy Dir. 1980, Dir. 1980-81; Sec.-Gen. Conseil Nat. du Crédit 1981; Finance Dir. Cie. Saint-Gobain 1984-86, Dir.-Gen. 1986-; Chevalier, Ordre Nat. du Mérite. *Publications:* La Politique monétaire 1974, Réévaluation et verité des bilans 1977, La Monnaie et la politique monétaire 1983, Crise financière et relations monétaires internationales 1985. *Leisure interests:* piano, skiing, tennis. *Address:* Cie. Saint-Gobain, 18 avenue d'Alsace, les Miroirs, 924000 Courbevoie, France.

DAVID, René, D.JUR., PH.D.; French jurist; b. 12 Jan. 1906, Paris; m. Hélène Labbé 1937, two s. two d.; ed. Univs. of Paris and Cambridge; Prof., Law Faculty, Grenoble Univ. 1929-42, Paris Univ. 1945-70, Aix-en-Provence Univ. 1970-76, European Univ. Inst. Florence 1976-78; Deputy Sec.-Gen. Int. Inst. for the Unification of Private Law (UNIDROIT), Rome 1929-33; Capt. Bataillon de Choc 1943-45; Legal Adviser to Imperial Govt. of Ethiopia 1954-58; Dr. h.c. (Edin., Brussels, Ottawa, Basel, Leicester, Helsinki, Florence); Hon. Bencher Middle Temple; Alciat Prize (Italy), Erasmus Prize (Netherlands); Commdr., Légion d'honneur. *Publication:* Major Legal Systems in the World Today 1985, Arbitration in International Trade 1985. *Address:* Le Tholonet, 13100 Aix-en-Provence, France. *Telephone:* 42-66-90-10.

DAVID, Václav; Czechoslovak politician and diplomatist; b. 23 Sept. 1910, Studený; ed. Commercial Coll., Prague; worked for ČKD Libeň 1929-32;

mem. of the illegal Cen. Cttee. of the CP of Czechoslovakia 1944-45; mem. of the Nat. Ass. 1945-69; Minister of Foreign Affairs 1953-68; Amb. to Bulgaria 1969-71; mem. of Cen. Cttee. of the CP of Czechoslovakia 1945-; Deputy to House of the People, Fed. Ass. 1969-, Chair. 1971; mem. Presidium, House of the People, Fed. Ass. 1971-86, Deputy Chair. Fed. Ass. 1971-; Deputy Chair. of Cen. Cttee. Czechoslovak-Soviet Friendship Union 1953-72, Chair. 1972; several decorations for part in Resistance Movement during World War II; Order of the Republic 1955, Klement Gottwald Order 1960, 1980, Order of Victorious February 1973. *Address:* Presidium, Sněmovna Lidu, Federální Shromáždění, Prague 1, Vinohradská 1, Czechoslovakia.

DAVIDOVICH, Bella; American (U.S.S.R. born) pianist; b. 16 July 1928, Baku, Azerbaijan; m. Julian Sitkovetsky 1950 (died 1958); one s.; ed. Moscow Conservatory; studied with Konstantin Igumnov and Jakob Flier; First Prize, Chopin Competition, Warsaw 1949; soloist with Leningrad Philharmonic for 28 consecutive seasons; toured Europe; went to U.S.A. 1978; became U.S. citizen 1984; has performed with world's leading conductors in U.S.A., Europe and Japan; recordings for Philips and Orfeo; Deserving Artist of the Soviet Union. *Address:* c/o Columbia Artists Management, 165 West 57th Street, New York, N.Y. 10019, U.S.A. *Telephone:* (212) 315-2430.

DAVIDSON, Alfred E.; American international lawyer; b. 11 Nov. 1911, New York; s. of Maurice P. Davidson and Blanche Reinheimer; m. Claire H. Dreyfuss 1934; two s.; ed. Horace Mann School, Harvard Univ. and Columbia Law School; Legis. Counsel, Exec. Office of Pres. of U.S.A. 1941-43; Asst. Gen. Counsel, Foreign Econ. Admin. 1944-45, Gen. Counsel 1945-; Gen. Counsel UNRRA 1945-46; Counsel Int. Refugee Org. (Preparatory Comm.), Geneva 1947; Dir. for Europe, Middle East and Africa, UNICEF 1947-51; Econ. Adviser to UN Sec.-Gen. 1951-52; Gen. Counsel Korean Reconstruction Agency, UN, New York 1952-54; Exec. Asst. to Chair. of Bd., Rio Tinto of Canada, New York 1955-58; int. law practice, including Dir. Channel Tunnel Study Group 1959-69, Technical Studies Inc. 1973-; Int. Econ. Adviser, Co. for Establishment of the Great Belt Bridge (Denmark) 1959-69; Special Rep. of IFC in Europe, Paris 1970-72; Counsel, Wilmer, Cutler & Pickering (law firm) 1972-75; mem. Bars of New York and D.C.; Co-Chair. Bipartisan Cttee. on Absentee Voting, Bipartisan Cttee. for MEDICARE Overseas; Hon. Chair. Democratic Party Cttee., France; co-founder, Asscn. for the Promotion of Humor in Int. Affairs; Hon. Chair. Common Cause (Overseas). *Publications:* articles in journals. *Leisure interests:* politics, reading, tennis, bridge. *Address:* 5 rue de la Manutention, 75116 Paris, France. *Telephone:* 47-23-51-68.

DAVIDSON, Basil; British historian; b. 9 Nov. 1914, Bristol; m. Marion Ruth Young 1943; three s.; served British Army 1940-45, Lieut.-Col. 1945; journalist with The Economist, The Star, The Times, New Statesman, Daily Herald, Daily Mirror, 1938-62; Visiting Prof. in African History, Univ. of Ghana 1964, Univ. of Calif., L.A. (UCLA) 1965; Regent's Lecturer in African History, UCLA 1971; Montague Burton Visiting Prof. of Int. Relations, Univ. of Edin. 1972; Hon. Research Fellow, Univ. of Birmingham 1974; Simon Sr. Research Fellow, Univ. of Manchester 1975-76; Hon. D.Litt. (Univ. of Ibadan) 1975, Hon. D.Univ. (Open Univ.) 1980, (Edin.) 1981; Hon. D.Litt. (Dar es Salaam) 1985; Mil. Cross; Bronze Star, U.S. Army; Zasluge za Narod, Yugoslav Army; Freeman City of Genoa 1945; Haile Selassie Award for African Research 1970; Medalha Amílcar Cabral 1976. *Publications:* principal works: Old Africa Rediscovered 1959, Black Mother—The African Slave Trade 1961 (revised 1980), The African Past 1964, History of West Africa to 1800 1965, History of East and Central Africa to the Late Nineteenth Century 1967, Africa in History: Themes and Outlines 1967, The Africans: A Cultural History 1969, The Liberation of Guiné 1969 (revised 1981), In the Eye of the Storm: Angola's People 1972, Black Star 1973, Can Africa Survive? 1975, Africa in Modern History, The Search for a New Society 1978, Special Operations Europe—Scenes from the anti-Nazi War 1980, The People's Cause: A History of Guerrillas in Africa 1981, Modern Africa 1982, Africa (TV series) 1984, The Story of Africa 1984, The Fortunate Isles 1988. *Address:* Old Cider Mill, North Wootton, Somerset, BA4 4HA, England.

DAVIDSON, George F., C.C., PH.D., LL.D., L.H.D., D.C.L.; Canadian public official; b. 18 April 1909, Bass River, Nova Scotia; s. of late Oliver Wendell Davidson and Emma Jane Sullivan; m. 1st Elizabeth Ruth Henderson 1935, two s. one d.; m. 2nd Anneke Irene Kuiper 1975; ed. Univs. of British Columbia and Harvard; Supt. of Welfare and Neglected Children for B.C. 1934; Exec. Dir. Vancouver Welfare Fed. and Council of Social Agencies 1935; Dir. of Social Welfare, B.C. 1939; Exec. Dir. of Canadian Welfare Council 1942; Deputy Minister of Nat. Welfare 1944-60, of Citizenship and Immigration 1960-63; Dir. Bureau of Govt. Org. 1963, Sec. of Treasury Bd. 1964-67; Pres. CBC 1968-72; Under-Sec.-Gen. of UN for Admin. and Man. 1972-79; Special Adviser to Exec. Dir. UN Fund for Population Activities 1980-86; has served since 1946 as Canadian Rep. or mem. Canadian dels. to various sessions of UN Gen. Ass., Econ. and Social Council and Social Comm. and Chair. of the Social, Humanitarian and Cultural Cttee. 1953; Pres. Inst. of Public Admin. of Canada 1951; Pres. of the UN Econ. and Social Council 1958; Pres. Int. Conf. of Social Work 1956-60; Chair. Nat. Jt. Council of Public Service 1954-60; numerous hon. degrees. *Leisure interests:* music, travel, swimming, people. *Address:* 1120

Beach Drive, Apt. 603, Victoria, B.C., Canada V85 2NI (Home). *Telephone:* 592-7020 (Home).

DAVIDSON, Janet Marjorie, M.A., F.R.S.N.Z.; New Zealand archaeologist and ethnologist; b. 23 Aug. 1941, Lower Hutt; m. Brian Foss Leach 1979; one d.; ed. Hutt Valley High School and Univ. of Auckland; Field Assoc. Bernice P. Bishop Museum, Honolulu 1964–66; E. Earle Vaile Archaeologist Auckland Inst. and Museum 1966–79; Hon. lecturer in Anthropology, Univ. of Otago 1980–86; ethnologist Nat. Museum of New Zealand 1987–; extensive archaeological field work in New Zealand and the Pacific; Rhodes Visiting Fellow, Lady Margaret Hall, Oxford 1974–76. *Publications:* Archaeology on Nukuaro Atoll 1971, The Prehistory of New Zealand 1984, numerous articles on the archaeology and prehistory of New Zealand and various Pacific Islands. *Leisure interests:* music, theatre, opera, ballet, cooking. *Address:* National Museum of New Zealand, Box 467, Wellington 1 (Office); 5 Hillview Crescent, Paparangi, Wellington 4, New Zealand (Home).

DAVIDSON, John Frank, SC.D., F.ENG., F.R.S.; British professor of chemical engineering; b. 7 Feb. 1926, Newcastle upon Tyne; s. of John and Katie (née Jarrat) Davidson; m. Susanne H. Ostberg 1948; one s. one d.; ed. Heaton Grammar School, Newcastle upon Tyne, and Trinity Coll., Cambridge; Reader in Chem. Eng., Univ. of Cambridge 1964–75, Prof. 1975–78, Shell Prof. of Chemical Eng., Univ. of Cambridge 1978–; Fellow, Trinity Coll., Cambridge; Visiting Prof., Univ. of Delaware, U.S.A. 1960, Sydney, Australia 1967; mem. Court of Inquiry into Flixborough disaster 1974–75; Foreign Assoc., Nat. Acad. of Eng. of U.S.A.; Dr.h.c. (Inst. Nat. Polytechnique de Toulouse); Leverhulme Medal, Royal Soc. 1984, Messel Medal Soc. of Chem. Industry 1986. *Publications:* with D. Harrison: Fluidized Particles 1963, Fluidization 1971; with D. Keairns: Fluidization 1978. *Leisure interests:* hill and mountain walking. *Address:* Department of Chemical Engineering, University of Cambridge, Pembroke Street, Cambridge (Office); 5 Luard Close, Cambridge, CB2 2PL, England. *Telephone:* 0223 358231 (Office); 0223 246104 (Home).

DAVIDSON, John Macdonald, A.M., B.ARCH., L.F.R.A.I.A., R.I.B.A.; Australian architect; b. 21 Oct. 1926, Sydney; s. of the late John H. Davidson and of Daisy Macdonald; m. Helen M. King 1954; two s. one d.; ed. Geelong Coll. and Univ of Melbourne; Assoc. Godfrey and Spowers (architects) 1954–61, Partner, later Dir. 1961, Chair. Godfrey and Spowers Australia Pty. Ltd. 1979–; Pres. Royal Australian Inst. of Architects 1978–79; mem. Expert Panel in Arch. (COPQ) 1978–; mem. Int. Council, Int. Union of Architects (UIA) 1981–85, Vice-Pres. UIA 1985–; Chair. Metropolitan Strategy Consultative Cttee. 1984–, South Yarra Collaborative Pty. Ltd. 1983–; Hon. Fellow American Inst. of Architects. *Publication:* The Awarding and Administration of Architectural Contracts 1961. *Leisure Interests:* music, art, farming. *Address:* 577 Little Collins Street, Melbourne 3000, Australia (Office). *Telephone:* (03) 614 6144.

DAVIDSON, Norman Ralph, PH.D.; American professor of molecular biology; b. 5 April 1916, Chicago, Ill.; s. of Bernard R. Davidson and Rose Lefstein; m. Annemarie Behrendt 1942; three s. one d.; ed. Univ. of Chicago and Oxford Univ.; Prof. of Chem., Calif. Inst. of Tech. 1957–82, Chandler Prof. of Chemical Biology 1982–84, Prof. Emer. 1984–; mem. N.A.S. *Publications:* Statistical Mechanics 1962, and numerous scientific articles. *Address:* Division of Chemistry and Chemical Engineering, California Institute of Technology, Pasadena, Calif. 91125 (Office); 318 East Laurel Avenue, Sierra Madre, Calif. 91024, U.S.A. (Home). *Telephone:* 213-356-6055 (Office); 213-355-1969 (Home).

DAVIDSON, Ralph P.; American magazine publisher; b. 17 Aug. 1927, Santa Fe, N.M.; s. of William Clarence and Doris Parsons Davidson; m. Jeanne Skidmore 1951 (divorced); two s.; ed. Stanford Univ.; with CIA 1952–54; Advertising Salesman Life Magazine 1954–56; European Advertising Dir. Time Magazine, London 1956–62; European Advertising Dir. Time-Life Int., London 1964, Man. Dir. Time-Life Int., New York 1967–; Asst. Publr. Time 1968, Assoc. Publr. 1969, Publr. 1972–78; Chair. Bd. Time Inc. 1972–. *Leisure interests:* reading, tennis, skiing. *Address:* Time Inc., Time & Life Building, Rockefeller Center, New York, N.Y. 10020 (Office); 494 Harbor Road, Southport, Conn., U.S.A. (Home). *Telephone:* 212-556-3456 (Office); 203-259-3861 (Home).

DAVIE, Alan, C.B.E.; British painter; b. 1920, Grangemouth, Stirlingshire; s. of James W. Davie and Elizabeth Turnbull; m. Janet Gaul 1947; one d.; ed. Edinburgh Coll. of Art; jazz musician and maker of jewellery; Gregory Fellowship, Leeds Univ. 1956–59; first one-man exhbn. Edinburgh 1946; one-man exhbns. in Europe and U.S.A. 1949–; rep. at Dunn Int. Exhbn., London 1963; Prize for the best foreign painter at his one-man exhbn. at the 7th Bienal de São Paulo, Brazil 1963; Gulbenkian Painting and Sculpture of a Decade Exhbn., Tate Gallery, London 1964; several exhbns. at the Salon de Mai; one-man exhbns. at Gimpel Galleries in London, New York and Zürich 1949–; exhbns. at Rome, Munich, Montreal, Texas, California 1970, Switzerland, Los Angeles, Norway, Poland, Geneva, Cologne 1971, New York 1972, Los Angeles, Chicago, Brussels 1976, London, Athens, Paris 1977, Australia 1979, Frankfurt 1981, Toronto, Hong Kong, Paris, Breda 1982, Amsterdam 1983, Bath, Windsor, Frankfurt, Jarrow 1984, London (Art Fair Olympia), Edinburgh and Bonn 1985, London, Ariz. and New York 1986; retrospective exhbn. Edinburgh Festival, R.S.A. Galleries

1972; exhbn. Tapestries, Paris 1977; first public music recital, Tate Gallery and Gimpel Fils, London 1971; four recordings 1972–86; music concerts 1972, concerts and broadcasts 1974; Hon. mem. Royal Scottish Acad. 1977; Saltire Award, Mosaic Scotland 1976. *Leisure interests:* gliding, music, photography, underwater swimming. *Address:* Gamels Studio, Rush Green, Hertford, England.

DAVIE, Donald Alfred, F.B.A.; British academic and literary critic; b. 17 July 1922, Barnsley, Yorks.; s. of George Clarke and Alice (née Sugden) Davie; m. Doreen John 1945; two s. one d.; ed. Barnsley Holgate Grammar School, St. Catharine's Coll., Cambridge; served with Royal Navy 1941–46; Lecturer, Dublin Univ. 1950–57, Fellow, Trinity Coll., Dublin 1954–57; Visiting Prof., Univ. of Calif. 1957–58; Lecturer, Univ. of Cambridge 1958–64, Fellow of Gonville and Caius Coll., Cambridge 1959–64; Prof. of Literature, Univ. of Essex 1964–68, Pro-Vice-Chancellor 1965–68; Prof. of English, Stanford Univ. 1968–74, Olive H. Palmer Prof. in the Humanities 1974–78; Clark Lecturer, Trinity Coll., Cambridge 1976; Andrew W. Mellon Prof. of Humanities, Vanderbilt Univ. 1978–88; Fellow, American Acad. of Arts and Sciences; Hon. Fellow Trinity Coll., Dublin 1978; Hon. D.Lit. (Southern Calif.) 1978, (Univ. of the South) 1982. *Publications:* poetry: Brides of Reason 1955, A Winter Talent 1957, The Forests of Lithuania 1959, A Sequence for Francis Parkman 1961, Events and Wisdoms 1964, Essex Poems 1969, Six Epistles to Eva Hese 1970, Collected Poems 1972, The Shires 1975, In the Stopping Train 1977, Collected Poems 1972–83 1983; literary criticism: Purity of Diction in English Verse 1952, Articulate Energy 1957, The Heyday of Sir Walter Scott 1961, Ezra Pound: Poet as Sculptor 1965, Thomas Hardy and British Poetry 1972, Pound 1976, The Poet in the Imaginary Museum (essays) 1978, A Gathered Church: the Literature of the English Dissenting Interest 1700–1930 1978, Dissentient Voice: Enlightenment and Christian Dissent 1982, Czeslaw Milosz and the Insufficiency of Lyric 1986; anthologies: The Late Augustans 1958 (with Angela Livingstone), Modern Judgement: Pasternak 1969, Augustan Lyric 1974, The New Oxford Book of Christian Verse 1981. *Leisure interests:* verse-translation, literary politics, travel. *Address:* 4 High Street, Silverton, Exeter, England. *Telephone:* 860-285.

DAVIES, Sir David Arthur, K.B.E., D.SC., F.INST.P.; British meteorologist; b. 11 Nov. 1913, Barry, Wales; m. Mary Shapland 1938; one s. two d.; ed. Univ. of Wales; Meteorological Office, Air Ministry 1936–39, R.A.F. 1939–47; Principal Scientific Officer, Meteorological Office, Air Ministry 1947–49; Dir. E. African Meteorological Dept., Nairobi 1949–55; Pres. WMO Regional Asscn. for Africa, mem. WMO Exec. Cttee.1951–55; Sec.-Gen. WMO 1955–79, Emer. 1980–; Vice-Pres. and Hon. Consultant, Welsh Centre for Int. Affairs 1983–; Vice-Pres. The Honourable Soc. of Cymmrodorion, London 1986–; Fellow, Inst. of Physics 1944; mem. Royal Inst. of Public Admin. 1950–; Hon. mem. American Meteorological Soc. 1970, Hungarian Meteorological Soc. 1975; Fellow, Univ. Coll. Cardiff 1985; Dr. h.c. (Univ. of Bucharest) 1970, (Eötvos Loránd Univ., Budapest) 1976, D. ès Sc. (Swiss Fed. Inst. of Tech., Lausanne) 1978, D.Sc. (Univ. of Wales) 1981; Fellow, Explorers Club, U.S.A. 1978; Gold Medal of Merit, Czechoslovak Acad. of Sciences 1978; UN Peace Medal 1979; Silver Medal, Royal Swedish Acad. of Science 1979; Cleveland Abbe Award, American Meteorological Soc. 1985; Int. Meteorological Org. Prize 1985. *Publications include:* meteorological papers and articles on international co-operative efforts through meteorology. *Leisure interests:* music, reading. *Address:* 2 Ashley Close, Patcham, Brighton, Sussex, BN1 8YT, England. *Telephone:* 509437.

DAVIES, David E. N., C.B.E., PH.D., F.I.E.E., F.I.E.R.E., F.ENG., F.R.S.; British electronic engineer; b. 28 Oct. 1935, Cardiff; s. of D. E. Davies and Sarah Samuel; m. Enid Patilla 1962; two s.; ed. Univ. of Birmingham; Lecturer, then Sr. Lecturer in Electrical Eng., Univ. of Birmingham 1961–67; Asst. Dir. Research Dept., British Railways Bd. 1967–71; Visiting Industrial Prof. of Electrical Eng. Loughborough Univ. 1969–71; Prof. of Electrical Eng. Univ. Coll. London 1971–88, Pender Prof. of Electrical Eng. 1985–88, Vice-Provost Univ. Coll. 1986–88; Dir. Strategy Ltd. 1974–79, Gaydon Tech. 1987–; Vice-Chancellor Loughborough Univ. of Tech. 1988–; I.E.E.E. Centennial Medal 1984 and other awards. *Publications:* about 120 publications on antennas, radar and fibre optics. *Address:* Loughborough University of Technology, Loughborough, Leics., LE11 3TU; Felden Thatch, Sheethanger Lane, Felden, Hemel Hempstead, Herts., HP3 OBG, England (Home).

DAVIES, David Reginald, D.PHIL.; American X-ray crystallographer and researcher; b. 22 Feb. 1927, Camarthen, Wales; s. of Theophilus Howel Davies and Gwladys Evelyn Evans (Hodges) Davies; m. 1st Cynthia Margaret Seaman 1951 (divorced 1981), two d.; m. 2nd Monica Walters 1985; ed. Magdalen Coll., Oxford, England, California Inst. of Tech., Pasadena, U.S.A.; Research Assoc., Albright & Wilson Ltd., Birmingham, England 1954–55; Visiting Scientist Nat. Insts. of Health, Bethesda, Md., U.S.A. 1955–61, Chief, Section on Molecular Structure 1961–; Visiting Scientist, MRC Lab. Molecular Biology 1963–64; mem. Study Section on Molecular Biology, Nat. Science Foundation 1969–77; mem. American Acad. of Arts and Sciences, N.A.S., American Soc. of Biological Chemists, American Crystallographic Asscn., Biophysical Soc. (Council 1960–65, 1973–78); Presidential Meritorious Exec. Award 1982, Presidential Rank Award 1988. *Publications:* articles in scientific journals. *Leisure interests:* tennis, sailing. *Address:* National Institutes of Health, NIDDK, Laboratory of Molecular Biology, 9000 Rockville Pike, Bethesda, Md. 20892; 4224 Franklin Street, Kensington, Md. 20895, U.S.A. (Home). *Telephone:* (301) 496-4295 (Office).

DAVIES, Rev. Jacob Arthur Christian, B.SC.; Sierra Leonean diplomatist; b. 24 May 1925; s. of Jacob S. and Christiana Davies; m. Sylvia Onikeh Cole; two s. two d.; ed. Univ. of Reading, Selwyn Coll., Cambridge Univ., Imperial Coll. of Tropical Agric.; served in various capacities at Ministry of Agric. and Natural Resources and later became Perm. Sec.; Co-Man. of a project of the UN Devt. Programme, FAO 1967-69, and later apptd. Chair. of the Public Service Comm.; fmr. Amb. to U.S.A.; High Commr. in the U.K. and non-resident Amb. to Denmark, Sweden and Norway 1972-74; Deputy Dir. Agric. Operations Div. UN FAO, Rome 1975-76, Dir. Personnel Div. 1976-82, Asst. Dir.-Gen., Regional Rep. for Africa 1982-. *Leisure interests:* philately, sports. *Address:* FAO Regional Office for Africa, P.O. Box 1628, Accra, Ghana.

DAVIES, John Arthur, M.A., PH.D., F.R.S.C.; Canadian research scientist; b. 28 March 1927, Prestatyn, Wales; s. of James Davies and Doris A. Edkins; m . Florence Smithson 1950; three s. three d.; ed. St. Michael's Coll. High School and Univ. of Toronto; Asst., later Assoc. Research Officer, Atomic Energy of Canada 1950-65, Sr. Research Officer 1965-70, Prin. Research Officer 1970-85; Part-time Prof. of Eng. Physics, McMaster Univ. 1970-; Adjunct Prof., Dept. of Electrical Eng, Univ. of Salford (U.K.) 1972-; Visiting Prof., Nobel Inst. of Physics, Stockholm, Sweden 1962, Univ. of Aarhus, Denmark 1964-65, 1969-70, Univ. of Osaka, Japan 1972; mem. Royal Danish Acad. of Arts and Sciences; D.Sc. h.c. (Royal Roads Mil. Coll.) 1984; Noranda Award (Chem. Inst. of Canada)1965; First T. D. Callinan Award (Electrochem. Soc.) 1968. *Publications:* co-author of over 150 research articles and five books in the fields of ion implantation, ion chanelling and ion beam analysis. *Leisure interests:* canoeing, cross-country skiing. *Address:* Department of Engineering Physics, Senior Sciences Building, McMaster University, Hamilton, Ont. L8S 4L8, Canada. *Telephone:* (416) 525-9140, Ext. 4690.

DAVIES, Sir Peter Maxwell, Kt., C.B.E., B.MUS.; British composer; b. 8 Sept. 1934, Manchester; s. of Thomas Davies and Hilda Howard; ed. Leigh Grammar School, Royal Manchester Coll. of Music, Manchester Univ.; studied with Goffredo Petrassi, Rome 1957 and with Roger Sessions, Milton Babbit, Earl Kim, Princeton Univ., N.J., U.S.A. (Harkness Fellow) 1962-64; Dir. of Music, Cirencester Grammar School 1959-62; lecture tours in Europe, Australia, U.S.A., Canada, Brazil; Visiting Composer, Univ. of Adelaide 1966; Prof. of Composition, Royal Northern Coll. of Music, Manchester 1965-80 (Fellow 1978); Pres. Schools Music Asscn. 1983-, Composers' Guild of G.B. 1986-; Co-Dir. (with Harrison Birtwistle, q.v.), Pierrot Players 1967-70, Fires of London 1971-87; Artistic Dir. Fires of London Productions 1987-; f. and Dir. St. Magnus Festival, Orkney Islands 1977-86, Pres. 1986-; Artistic Dir. Dartington Summer School of Music 1979-84; Assoc. Conductor and Composer Scottish Chamber Orchestra 1985-; Hon. mem. Royal Acad. of Music 1978; several hon. degrees including Hon. D.Mus. (Edin.) 1979, (Manchester) 1983, (Bristol) 1984, (Open Univ.) 1986; Olivetti Prize 1959; Koussevitsky Award 1964, Koussevitsky Recording Award 1966. *Compositions include:* St. Michael sonata for 13 wind instruments 1957, Prolation for orchestra 1958, O Magnum Mysterium for chorus, instruments and organ 1960, String Quartet 1961, Leopardi Fragments for soprano, contralto and chamber ensemble 1961, First Fantasia on John Taverner's In Nomine 1962, Veni Sancte Spiritus for chorus and orchestra 1963, Seven In Nomine 1963-65, Second Fantasia on John Taverner's In Nomine 1964, Shepherd's Calendar for young singers and instrumentalists 1965, Revelation and Fall for soprano and instrumental ensemble 1965, Ecce Manus Tradentis for mixed chorus and instruments 1965, Antechrist for chamber ensemble 1967, L'homme armé 1968, revised 1971, Stedman Caters for instruments 1968, St. Thomas Wake-Foxtrot for orchestra 1969, Worldes Blis 1969, Vesalii Icones 1969, Eram quasi Agnus (instrumental motet) 1969, Eight Songs for a Mad King 1969, Points and Dances from Taverner 1970, From Stone to Thorn for mezzo-soprano and instrumental ensemble 1971, Taverner (opera) 1972, Blind Man's Buff (masque) 1972, Hymn to Saint Magnus for chamber ensemble and soprano 1972, Stone Litany for mezzo-soprano and orchestra 1973, Miss Donni-thorne's Maggot for mezzo-soprano and chamber ensemble 1974; Ave Maris Stella for chamber ensemble 1975; Three Studies for Percussion 1975, Five Klee Pictures for percussion, piano and strings, revised 1976, Stevie's Ferry to Hoy (beginner's piano solo) 1976, Three Preludes for Organ 1976, Kinloche His Fantassie (Kinloch/Davies) 1976, Anakreontika (Greek songs for mezzo-soprano) 1976, The Blind Fiddler for soprano and chamberensemble 1976, Orchestral Symphony 1976, The Martyrdom of St. Magnus (chamber opera) 1976, Westerlings (unaccompanied part songs) 1977, A Mirror of Whitening Light for chamber orchestra 1977, Le Jongleur de Notre Dame (Masque) 1978, The Two Fiddlers 1978, Black Pentecost (for voices and orchestra) 1979, Symphony No. 2 1979, Solstice of Light (for Tenor, Chorus and Organ) 1979, A Welcome to Orkney (chamber ensemble) 1980, Little Quartet (string quartet) 1980, The Yellow Cake Revue (for voices and piano) 1980, Piano Sonata 1981, Little Quartet No. 2 (for string quartet) 1981, Lullabye for Lucy 1981, Salome 1984, Brass Quintet 1981, Songs of Hoy (Masque for children's voices and instruments) 1981, Sea Eagle (for horn solo) 1982, Image, Reflection, Shadow (for chamber ensemble) 1982, Sinfonia Concertante (for chamber orchestra) 1982, Into the

Labyrinth (tenor and chamber orchestra) 1983, Sinfonietta Academica (chamber orchestra) 1983, Guitar Sonata 1984, One Star, At Last (carol) 1984, Symphony No. 3 (for orchestra) 1984, Violin Concerto 1985, Oboe Concerto 1986, Resurrection (opera in one act with prologue) 1987, Cello Concerto 1987, Mishkenot (chamber ensemble) 1988, Trumpet Concerto 1988; has written music for films: The Devils, The Boyfriend, for the ballet Salome 1978, Cinderella (pantomime opera for young people) 1980, The Lighthouse (chamber opera) 1980 and many piano pieces, works for choir, instrumental works and realisations of fifteenth and sixteenth century composers. *Address:* c/o Judy Arnold, 50 Hogarth Road, London, SW5 0PU, England. *Telephone:* 01-370 1477.

DAVIES, Robert Ernest, PH.D., M.A., F.R.S.; British professor of molecular biology; b. 17 Aug. 1919; s. of William O. Davies and Stella Davies; m. Helen née Rogoff 1961; two step s.; ed. Manchester Grammar School, Univs. of Manchester, Sheffield, Pennsylvania and Oxford; Temporary Asst. Lecturer in Chem. Univ. of Sheffield; Ministry of Supply, Chemical Defence Research Dept. 1942; Medical Research Unit for Research in Cell Metabolism 1945; established staff, Medical Research Council 1947; Hon. Lecturer in Biochem. Univ. of Sheffield 1948-54; Prof. of Biochem. School of Medicine, Univ. of Pa. 1955-62, Graduate School of Medicine 1962-70, Prof. of Molecular Biology 1970-77, Benjamin Franklin Prof. of Molecular Biology and Univ. Prof. 1977-, Chair. Research Advisory Bd., Inst. for Environmental Medicine, School of Medicine 1970-. *Publications:* numerous articles in scientific journals. *Address:* Department of Animal Biology, School of Veterinary Medicine, University of Pennsylvania, Philadelphia, Pa. 19104 (Office); 7053 McCallum Street, Philadelphia, Pa. 19119, U.S.A. (Home).

DAVIES, Robertson, C.C., B.LITT., F.R.S.C., F.R.S.L.; Canadian writer and professor of English; b. 28 Aug. 1913, Thamesville, Ont.; s. of William Rupert Davies and Florence Sheppard Davies (née Mackay); m. Brenda Mathews 1940; three d.; ed. Renfrew and Kingston Schools, Upper Canada Coll., Toronto, Queen's Univ., Kingston, Ont., Balliol Coll., Oxford; teacher and actor, Old Vic Co., London 1938-40; Literary Ed. Saturday Night, Toronto 1940-42; Ed. and Publisher Examiner, Peterborough, Ont. 1942-63; Prof. of English, Univ. of Toronto 1960-81, and Master of Massey Coll. Univ. of Toronto 1963-81; Hon. mem. American Acad. and Inst. of Arts and Letters 1980; Hon. Fellow Balliol Coll., Oxford; Hon. LL.D. (Alberta) 1957, (Queen's Univ.) 1962, (Manitoba) 1972, (Toronto) 1981; Hon. D. Litt. (McMaster) 1959, (Windsor) 1971, (York Univ., Toronto, Mount Allison) 1973, (Memorial Univ. of Newfoundland, Univ. of W. Ontario, McGill, Trent) 1974, (Calgary) 1975, (Lethbridge, Waterloo) 1981, (Univ. of British Columbia) 1983, (Santa Clara, Calif.) 1985; Hon. D.C.L. (Bishop's Univ., Quebec) 1967; D.Hum. Litt. (Rochester Univ., U.S.A.) 1983; Louis Jouvet Prize 1949, Stephen Leacock Medal for Humour 1955, Lorne Pierce Medal of Royal Soc. of Canada 1961, Gov.-Gen.'s Award for Fiction 1973, City of Toronto Book Award 1986, Canadian Authors' Asscn. Literary Award for Fiction 1986, Medal of Honour for Literature, Nat. Arts Club, N.Y. 1986, Scottish Arts Council Neil Gunn Int. Fellowship 1988, and other awards. *Publications:* studies: Shakespeare's Boy Actors 1939, Stephen Leacock 1970, Feast of Stephen 1970; literary criticism: A Voice from the Attic 1960; history: (co-author) The Revels History of Drama in English Vol. VI 1975; text book: Shakespeare for Young Players 1942; essays: The Diary of Samuel Marchbanks 1947, The Table Talk of Samuel Marchbanks 1949, Samuel Marchbanks' Almanack 1967, One Half of Robertson Davies 1977, The Enthusiasms of Robertson Davies 1979, Robertson Davies: The Well-tempered Critic 1981, The Mirror of Nature 1983, The Papers of Samuel Marchbanks 1985; co-author (with Sir Tyrone Guthrie): Renown at Strat-ford 1953, Twice Have the Trumpets Sounded 1954, Thrice the Brinded Cat Hath Mew'd 1955; plays: Eros at Breakfast and Other Plays 1949, Fortune My Foe 1949, At My Heart's Core 1950, A Masque of Aesop 1952, A Jig for the Gypsy 1954, A Masque of Mr. Punch 1963, Hunting Stuart and Other Plays 1972, Question Time 1975; novels: Tempest Tost 1951, Leaven of Malice 1954, A Mixture of Frailties 1958, Fifth Business 1970, The Manticore 1972, World of Wonders 1975, The Rebel Angels 1981, What's Bred in the Bone 1985, The Lyre of Orpheus 1988; short stories: High Spirits 1981. *Leisure interests:* music, theatre. *Address:* Massey College, University of Toronto, 4 Devonshire Place, Toronto, Ont. M5S 2EI, Canada. *Telephone:* (416) 978-2890 (Office); (416) 964-6488 (Home).

DAVIES, Ryland; British (Welsh) opera and concert singer (tenor); b. 9 Feb. 1943, Cwm Ebbw Vale, Monmouthshire (now Gwent); s. of Joan and Gethin Davies; m. 1st Anne Howells (q.v.) 1966 (divorced 1981), 2nd Deborah Rees 1983, one d.; ed. Royal Manchester Coll. of Music (Fellow 1971); début as Almaviva in The Barber of Seville, Welsh Nat. Opera 1964, subsequent appearances including Tamino in The Magic Flute 1974; Glyndebourne Festival Chorus 1964-66, taking parts including Tamino, Belmonte in The Abduction from the Seraglio, Ferrando in Così fan tutte, Flamand in Capriccio, Lysander in A Midsummer Night's Dream, The Prince in Love of Three Oranges, Lensky in Eugene Onegin; appearances with Scottish Opera as Ferrando and as Fenton in Falstaff and as Nemorino in L'Elisir d'Amore, with Sadler's Wells Opera as Almaviva, Essex in Britten's Gloriana, with Royal Opera as Hylas in The Trojans, Don Ottavio in Don Giovanni, Ferrando, Cassio in Otello, Nemorino in L'Elisir d'Amore, Ernesto in Don Pasquale, Lysander in A Midsummer Night's Dream, and Almaviva, with English Nat. Opera as Eisenstein in Die Fledermaus;

overseas appearances include Salzburg Festival, at San Francisco, Chicago, Paris, at Metropolitan Opera, New York, Hollywood Bowl, Paris Opera, Geneva, Brussels, Lyons, Amsterdam, Mannheim, Israel, Buenos Aires, Stuttgart, Nice, Nancy, Philadelphia, Berlin, Hamburg; makes regular concert appearances in Europe and U.S.A. with all major orchestras. *Recordings include:* The Abduction from the Seraglio, L'Amore dei Tre Re (Montemezzi), La Navarraise (Massenet), The Trojans, Saul, Così fan tutte, Thérèse, Monteverdi Madrigals, Idomeneo, The Seasons (Haydn), Messiah, L'Oracolo (Leone), Judas Maccabaeus, Pulcinella, Il Matrimonio Segreto. *Video Films include:* Don Pasquale, A Midsummer Night's Dream, Die Entführung aus dem Serail, Love of Three Oranges, Trial by Jury. *Leisure interests:* antiques, art, cinema, sport. *Address:* 71 Fairmile Lane, Cobham, Surrey, KT11 2DG, England. *Telephone:* (0932) 63762.

DAVIGNON, Viscount Etienne, LL.D.; Belgian diplomatist; b. 4 Oct. 1932, Budapest, Hungary; m. Françoise de Cumont 1959; one s. two d.; Head of Office of Minister of Foreign Affairs 1963, Political Dir. 1969–76; Chair. Gov. Bd., Int. Energy Agency 1974–76; Commr. for Industry and Int. Markets, Comm. of European Communities 1977–81, Vice-Pres. for Industry, Energy and Research Policies 1981–84; C.E.O. SIBEKA 1986–; Man. Dir. Société Générale de Belgique 1985–; Chair. Spaak Foundation; Hon D. Hum. Litt. (American Coll. in Paris) 1988. *Leisure interests:* golf, skiing, tennis. *Address:* 12 avenue des Fleurs, Brussels, Belgium.

DAVIS, Andrew; British conductor; b. 1944; ed. Royal Coll. of Music, King's Coll., Cambridge; studied conducting with Franco Ferrara, Rome; continuo player with Acad. of St. Martin-in-the-Fields and English Chamber Orchestra; Festival Hall début conducting BBC Symphony Orchestra Nov. 1970; Asst. Conductor Philharmonia Orchestra and Prin. Guest Conductor Royal Liverpool Philharmonic Orchestra 1970; Music Dir. Toronto Symphony 1975–88, Conductor Laureate 1988–; Musical Dir. Glyndebourne Festival Opera 1989–; Chief Conductor BBC Symphony Orchestra 1989–; has conducted London Philharmonic, London Symphony, Royal Philharmonic, Boston, Chicago, Cleveland, Los Angeles Philharmonic, New York Philharmonic, Pittsburgh Symphony, BBC Symphony, Orchestre Nat. de France, Frankfurt Radio Orchestra, Tonhalle Orchestra, Stockholm Orchestra, Israel Philharmonic, Bavarian Radio Symphony and Berlin Philharmonic orchestras and London Sinfonietta; has conducted at Glyndebourne Festival Opera, Covent Garden Opera, Metropolitan Opera, Washington, D.C., Chicago Lyric Opera, Paris Opéra, La Scala, Milan, Sir Henry Wood Promenade Concerts, major British and European music festivals; tours of People's Republic of China 1978, Europe 1983 with Toronto Symphony Orchestra; recordings for CBS include Duruflé's Requiem (Grand Prix du Disque 1978), cycle of Dvořák symphonies and, for EMI, Tippett's The Mask of Time (won a Gramophone Record of the Year Award 1987), Grand Prix du Disque 1988. *Address:* c/o Harold Holt Ltd., 31 Sinclair Road, London, W14 0NS, England. *Telephone:* 01-603 4600.

DAVIS, Artemus Darius; American business executive; b. 22 Nov. 1905, Henderson, Ark.; s. of William M. and Ethel Chase Davis; m. Pauline K. McCormick 1970; two s. (by previous marriage); ed. Univ. of Idaho; Man. Table Supply Store, Little River, Fla. 1925–29, Vice-Pres. Table Supply Stores Inc. 1929–34, Pres. 1934–39; Pres. and Dir. Winn-Dixie Stores Inc., Jacksonville, Fla. 1939–65, Chair. Exec. Cttee. 1954–70, Vice-Chair. of Bd. 1965–. *Leisure interests:* hunting, ranching. *Address:* 5050 Edgewood Court, Jacksonville, Fla., U.S.A. *Telephone:* 904-384-5511.

DAVIS, Arthur H.; American diplomatist; b. 6 Oct. 1917, Brochton, Mass.; s. of Arthur H. Davis and Hazel E. (née Cornell) Davis; m. 1945; four c.; ed. Brochton High School and Univ. of Colo.; Warrant Officer U.S.A.A.F. 1942–45; Meteorologist Pan American Grace Airways, Chile 1945–56, United Airlines 1956–62; Vice-Pres. Von Frellick Assoc. 1962–64; Pres. New Engewood Corpn. 1964–68, Villa Enterprises Inc. 1968–77, Arthur Davis and Assoc. 1976–82; Amb. to Paraguay 1982–85, to Panama 1986–; Dept. of State Superior Honour Award 1985. *Leisure interests:* research, birds, animals, children. *Address:* U.S. Embassy, Box E Apo Miami, 34002-5000, U.S.A. *Telephone:* 271777 (Office); 649966 (Home).

DAVIS, Arthur John; British banker; b. 28 July 1924, Farnham; m. Jean Elizabeth Edna Hobbs; one s. one d.; ed. grammar schools; Dir. and Chief Gen. Man. Lloyds Bank PLC 1978–84, Vice-Chair. 1984–; Deputy Chair. Yorkshire Bank, Privatbanken Ltd. *Leisure interests:* beagling, gardening, music. *Address:* Lloyds Bank PLC, 71 Lombard Street, London, E.C.3 (Office); Little Barley End, Aldbury, Tring, Herts., England (Home).

DAVIS, Bernard D(avid), A.B., M.D.; American professor of microbiology; b. 7 Jan. 1916, Franklin, Mass.; s. of Harry and Tillie Davis; m. Elizabeth Menzel 1955; two s. one d.; ed. Harvard Univ. and Harvard Medical School; at Johns Hopkins Hosp. 1940–41; with U.S. Public Health Service 1942–54; Prof. of Pharmacology, New York Univ. Medical School 1954–57; Prof. of Bacteriology and Immunology, Harvard Medical School 1957–68; Adele Lehman Prof. of Bacterial Physiology, Harvard Medical School 1968–84, Prof. Emer. 1984–; mem. N.A.S., American Acad. of Arts and Sciences, World Acad. of Art and Science, American Soc. Biological Chem., American Soc. Microbiology, Inst. of Medicine. *Publications:* Microbiology (co-author) 1967 and subsequent edns., Storm over Biology 1986; numerous articles on science, and on science and society. *Leisure interest:* piano. *Address:* Harvard Medical School, Boston, Mass. 02115 (Office); 23 Clairemont Road,

Belmont, Mass. 02178, U.S.A. (Home). *Telephone:* 617-732-2022 (Office); 617-IV4-0460 (Home).

DAVIS, Bette (Ruth Elizabeth); American actress; b. 5 April 1908, Lowell, Mass.; d. of Harlow M. and Ruth F. Davis; m. 1st Harmon O. Nelson 1932 (dissolved); m. 2nd Arthur Farnsworth 1940 (died 1943); m. 3rd William G. Sherry 1945 (dissolved), one d.; m. 4th Gary Merrill 1950 (dissolved), one s. one d.; ed. Cushing Acad., Ashburnham, Mass.; Motion Picture Acad. Award as best actress of year, in Dangerous 1935, Jezebel 1938; received American Film Insts. Life Achievement in Motion Pictures Award 1977; Rudolf Valentino Life Achievement Award 1982, American Acad. of Arts 1983, Dept. of Defense Medal for Distinguished Public Service 1983, Women in Films Crystal Award 1983, César Award French Film Inst. 1986, Ordre des Arts et Belles Lettres (France) 1986, Kennedy Center Honors 1987; Légion d'honneur 1987. *Stage appearances include:* The World of Carl Sandburg, Night of the Iguana, Miss Moffat (musical). *Films acted in include:* Of Human Bondage, Bordertown, Dangerous, The Petrified Forest, Jezebel, Dark Victory, Juarez, The Old Maid, The Private Lives of Elizabeth and Essex, The Great Lie, The Bride Came C.O.D., All About Eve, Payment on Demand, Phone Call from a Stranger, The Star, The Virgin Queen, Storm Center, The Catered Affair, John Paul Jones, The Scapegoat, What Ever Happened to Baby Jane, Hush Hush, Sweet Charlotte, The Nanny, The Anniversary, Connecting Rooms, Bunny O'Hare, Madam Sin, The Game, Death on the Nile 1978, Watcher in the Woods 1979, Whales of August 1986; TV films: Strangers, the Story of a Mother and Daughter 1979, White Mama 1980, Skyward 1980, Family Reunion 1981, A Piano for Mrs. Cimino 1982; Little Gloria—Happy at Last 1982, Right of Way 1983, Hotel 1983, Murder with Mirrors 1984, As Summers Die 1985. *Publications:* The Lonely Life (autobiog.) 1962, This 'n That 1987. *Address:* c/o Gottlieb Schiff and Sendroff, P.C., 555 Fifth Avenue, New York, N.Y. 10017, U.S.A. *Telephone:* 212-922-1880.

DAVIS, Most Rev. Brian Newton, M.A., L.TH.; New Zealand ecclesiastic; b. 28 Oct. 1934, Stratford, N.Z.; s. of Leonard L. Davis and Ethel M. Davis; m. Marie L. Waters; four d.; ed. Ardmore Teachers Training Coll., Auckland Univ., Victoria Univ. of Wellington, Christchurch Theological Coll.; ordained Deacon 1960, Priest 1961, Asst. Curate St. Mark's, Wellington 1960–62, Parish of Karori and Makara 1962–64; Vicar of Makara and Karori West 1964–67, of Dannevirke 1967–73, of Cathedral Parish of St. John the Evangelist and Dean of Waiapu 1973–80; Vicar Gen. of Waiapu 1979–80; Bishop of Waikato 1980–86; Primate and Archbishop of N.Z. 1986–, Bishop of Wellington Sept. 1986. *Leisure interests:* tennis, water colour painting, reading, wood turning. *Address:* P.O. Box 12-046, Wellington (Office); Bishopscourt, 28 Eccleston Hill, Thorndon, Wellington, New Zealand (Home). *Telephone:* (04) 721-057 (Office); (04) 723-183 (Home).

DAVIS, Carl, B.A.; American composer; b. 28 Oct. 1936, New York; s. of Isadore and Sarah Davis; m. Jean Boht 1970; two d.; ed. Elizabeth Irwin High School, New York, Queen's Coll., New York, New England Conservatory, Boston, Tanglewood Music Festival, Bard Coll., New York; ed. privately in music 1955; toured with Robert Shaw Chorale as pianist 1955–56; répétiteur, Santa Fé Opera 1958, New York City Opera 1958–59; settled in London 1960; formed Sundergrade Music with Terry Oates 1979; Prin. Conductor, Bournemouth Pops 1984–; Assoc. Conductor (desig.) London Philharmonic Orchestra Sept. 1987–; Dir. Melbourne Music Festival 1989; B.A.F.T.A. Award for Original TV Music 1980, British Acad. Award 1982; Chevalier de l'ordre des Arts et des Lettres 1983. *TV scores include:* The Snow Goose 1971, World at War 1972, The Naked Civil Servant 1975, Our Mutual Friend 1976, Marie Curie 1977, Mayor of Casterbridge 1978, Hollywood 1980, Oppenheimer 1980, The Commanding Sea 1981, Aerodrome 1983, Unknown Chaplin 1983, Weather in the Streets 1983, The Tale of Beatrix Potter 1983, The Far Pavilions 1983, The Pickwick Papers 1985, Oscar 1985, The Day the Universe Changed 1985, Late Starter 1985, Silas Marner 1985, Sakharov 1985, Hotel du Lac 1986, Pride of Place 1986, See it Now 1986. *Film scores:* The French Lieutenant's Woman 1981, Champions 1984, King David 1985, The Big Parade 1985, Greed 1985, Intolerance 1988, Scandal 1988, The Rainbow 1988. *Silent film scores:* Napoléon (Abel Gance) (first performance Nov. 1980), The Crowd (King Vidor) (first performance Nov. 1981), Flesh and the Devil, Show People (first performances Nov. 1982) Broken Blossoms, The Wind (first performances Dec. 1983), The General 1987, Ben Hur 1987; Lines on London (symphony) (première July 1980). *Ballet scores:* Dances of Love and Death (ballet score for London Contemporary Dance Co.) (première, Edinburgh Festival 1981), Fire and Ice (ice ballet for Torvill and Dean) 1986, The Portrait of Dorian Gray 1987, A Simple Man (based on L. S. Lowry), for N. Ballet Theatre 1987; Last Night of the Poms—An Educational Sonorama with Music (lyrics by Barry Humphries), Royal Albert Hall Sept. 1981, The Thief of Bagdad 1984, The Big Parade (première London Film Festival 1985). *Address:* c/o Paul Wing, 35 Priory Road, London, N.8, England. *Telephone:* 01-348 6604.

DAVIS, Sir Colin Rex, Kt., C.B.E.; British musician; b. 25 Sept. 1927, Weybridge, Surrey; m. 1st April Cantelo 1949 (dissolved 1964), one s. one d.; m. 2nd Ashraf Naini 1964, three s. two d.; ed. Christ's Hospital and Royal Coll. of Music; Asst. Conductor, BBC Scottish Orchestra 1957–59; Conductor, Sadler's Wells Opera House 1960, Musical Dir. 1961–65; Chief Conductor, BBC Symphony Orchestra 1967–71, Chief Guest Conductor

1971–75; Artistic Dir. Bath Festival 1969; Musical Dir. Covent Garden Sept. 1971–86; Prin. Guest Conductor, Boston Symphony Orchestra 1972–86, London Symphony Orchestra 1974–; Chief Conductor Bavarian Radio Symphony Orchestra Sept. 1983–; Commendatore of the Repub. of Italy 1976, Légion d'Honneur 1982, Commdr.'s Cross of the Order of Merit, Fed. Repub. of Germany; Grosser Deutscher Schallplattenpreis 1978; Grammy Award 'Opera Recording of the Year' 1980; Grand Prix du Disque 1980; Gramophon Award for Best Recording 1983; Hamburg's Shakespeare Prize 1984. *Leisure interests:* poetry, tree-planting. *Address:* c/o 7A Fitzroy Park, London, N6 6HS, England.

DAVIS, Deane Chandler; American lawyer and politician; b. 7 Nov. 1900, E. Barre, Vt.; s. of Earle R. Davis and Lois S. Hillery; m. 1st Corrine Eastman 1924; m. 2nd Marjorie S. Conzelman 1952; one s. one d.; ed. Boston Univ.; practised law, Barre, Vt. 1922–31, 1936–40; City Attorney, Barre 1924–26, 1928–30; State Attorney, Washington County, Vt. 1926–28; Superior Judge, State of Vt. 1931–36; mem. law firm, Wilson, Carver Davis and Keyser Barre, Vt., and Chelsea, Vt. 1936–40; Gen. Counsel, Nat. Life Insurance Co. 1940–50, Vice-Pres. 1943–50, Pres. 1950–66, Chair. Bd. 1967–68; Gov. of Vermont 1969–73; Pres., Man. Dir. Co-operative Health and Information Center, Vermont 1973–76; Dir. Union Mutual Fire Insurance Co. 1941–85 (mem. Dirs.' Advisory Cttee. 1985–), Vermont Electric Co. 1976–85, Jonnergin Inc. 1983–; Republican. *Publications: Justice in the Mountains* 1981, *Nuthin' but the Truth* 1982. *Leisure interest:* breeding Morgan horses. *Address:* 5 Dyer Street, RD 1 Box 2220, Montpelier, Vt. 05602 U.S.A. (summer). *Telephone:* (802)-223-5000 (Montpelier).

DAVIS, Edgar Glenn, M.B.A.; American business executive; b. 12 May 1931, Indianapolis, Ind.; s. of Thomas C. Davis and Florence I. (Watson) Davis; m. Margaret L. Alandt 1953; one s. two d.; ed. Kenyon Coll., Gambier, O. and Grad. School of Business Admin., Harvard Univ.; joined Eli Lilly & Co. 1958, Dir. Pharmaceutical Market Research and Sales Manpower Planning Div. 1968, Dir. Pharmaceutical Marketing Plans Div. 1969, Exec. Dir. Worldwide Pharmaceutical Marketing Planning 1974, Exec. Dir. Corporate Affairs 1975, Vice-Pres. Corporate Affairs 1976–; mem. N.A.S. Inst. of Medicine; numerous other professional appts. etc. *Publications:* articles in journals. *Leisure interests:* sailing, golf, naval history. *Address:* Eli Lilly and Co., Lilly Corporate Center, Indianapolis, Ind. 46285 (Office); 502 Forest Boulevard, Williams Creek, Indianapolis, Ind. 46240, U.S.A. (Home). *Telephone:* 317-276-2780 (Office); 317-255-2793 (Home).

DAVIS, George Kelso, PH.D.; American nutrition biochemist; b. 2 July 1910, Pittsburgh, Pa.; s. of Ross I. Davis and Jennie (Kelso) Davis; m. Ruthanna Wood 1936; two s. four d.; ed. Pennsylvania State Univ. and Cornell Univ.; Research Asst. Cornell Univ. 1932–37; Research Asst. Prof. of Chem. Mich. State Univ. 1937–42; Prof. of Nutrition, Animal Nutritionist, Univ. of Fla., Gainesville 1942–79, Distinguished Prof. Emer. 1979–, Dir. Nuclear Sciences 1960–65, Dir. Biological Sciences 1965–70, Dir. Research 1970–75; Prof. of Nutrition, Univ. of Hawaii 1985; numerous other professional appts.; mem. N.A.S. and other professional socs.; Borden Award 1964, Elvehjem Award 1985 and other honours and distinctions. *Publications:* articles in professional journals and book chapters. *Address:* 2903 S.W. 2nd Court, Gainesville, Fla., U.S.A.

DAVIS, James Othello, M.D., PH.D.; American physician; b. 12 July 1916, Tahlequah, Okla.; s. of Zemry and Villa (Hunter) Davis; m. Florrilla L. Sides 1941; one s. one d.; ed. Univ. of Missouri and Washington Univ. School of Medicine, St. Louis, Mo.; Intern and Fellow, Barnes Hospital, St. Louis 1946; Investigator, Gerontology Unit, Nat. Heart Inst., Bethesda, Md. and Baltimore City Hospital 1947–49; Investigator, Lab. of Kidney and Electrolyte Metabolism 1949–57; Chief, Section on Experimental Cardiovascular Disease, Nat. Heart Inst., Bethesda, Md. 1949–66; Prof. and Chair. Dept. of Physiology, Univ. of Missouri School of Medicine 1966–82, Prof. Emer. 1982–; mem. N.A.S. and numerous other professional socs. and orgs.; several awards and honours. *Publications:* more than 260 scientific publications. *Leisure interests:* trout fishing, travel. *Address:* Department of Physiology, School of Medicine, University of Missouri, Columbia, Mo. 65212 (Office); 612 Maplewood Drive, Columbia, Mo. 65203, U.S.A.

DAVIS, Sir John Henry, Kt., C.V.O., F.C.I.S.; British industrialist; b. 10 Nov. 1906, London; s. of Sydney Myering Davis and Emily Harris; m. Felicity Rutland 1976; one s. three d. by earlier marriages; ed. City of London School; Chair. Rank Org. Ltd. 1962–77, Pres. 1977–83; Chief Exec. 1962–74; Joint Pres. Rank Xerox Ltd. 1972–83; Dir., Rank Foundation 1953–; Chair. and Trustee, Rank Prize Funds 1972–; Dir. Eagle Star Insurance Co. Ltd. 1949–82; Pres. E. Surrey Conservative Asscn. 1982–87; fmr. Gov. British Film Inst.; fmr. Pres. Advertising Asscn.; Hon. D.Tech. (Loughborough) 1975; Commdr., Ordre de la Couronne 1974, K.St.J. 1971. *Leisure interests:* farming, gardening, reading, travel, music. *Address:* 25 Victoria Street, London, SW1H 0EX (Office); 4 Selwood Terrace, London, SW7 3QN, England (Home). *Telephone:* 01-222 4808 (Office).

DAVIS, Miles Dewey; American jazz trumpet player and composer; b. 25 May 1926, Alton, Ill.; m. Cicely Tyson 1981; ed. Juilliard School; first played in High School band; performed with Eddie Randall, St. Louis

1941–43, with Charlie Parker, Coleman Hawkins, and on tour with Eckstine's Band 1945–48; leader bands Royal Roost; appeared Paris Jazz Festival 1949, New York 1950, 1951; on tour with Jazz Inc. 1952; appeared Café Bohemia, New York 1957; background music for *Elevator to the Gallows* (French film) 1958; retired from performing due to illness 1975–81; European tour 1982; JAY award poll (No. 4 jazz album *Miles Smiles*) 1967; named No. 1 Trumpeter, No. 2 Jazz Man of Year, No. 1 Small Group, No. 2 Jazz album (*Miles Smiles*) (3rd annual readers' poll) 1968; named No. 1 Combo, No. 1 Trumpet, No. 2 Record of Year (*Sorcerer*), 16th Int. Jazz Critics Poll 1968. *Recordings include:* Modern Idiom, Trumpet Stylists, Cool and Quintet, Miles Ahead, Miles Davis Plus 19, Relaxin', Walkin', Cookin', Bags' Groove, Collector's Items, Birth of the Cool, Round About Midnight, Sorcerer, Bitches' Brew, At Fillmore, Man with the Horn 1981. *Address:* c/o Elaine Geller, Warner Bros Records, 3300 Warner Boulevard, Burbank, Calif. 91510, U.S.A.

DAVIS, Nathanael Vining; Canadian businessman (retd.); b. 26 June 1915, Pittsburgh, Pennsylvania; s. of late Edward Kirk and Rhea (Reineman) Davis; m. Lois Howard Thompson 1941; one s. one d.; ed. Middlesex School, Harvard Univ., London School of Econs.; joined Alcan Group 1939; Man. Dir. Alcan Aluminium Ltd. (London Office) 1946–47, Pres. and Dir. 1947–72, Chair. and C.E.O. 1972–79, Chair. 1979–86. *Address:* 50 Fox Island Road, Box 309, Osterville, Mass. 02655, U.S.A.

DAVIS, Nathaniel, PH.D.; American diplomatist; b. 12 April 1925, Boston, Mass.; s. of Harvey Nathaniel Davis and Alice Marion Rohde; m. Elizabeth Kirkbride Creese 1956; two s. two d.; ed. Phillips Exeter Acad., Brown Univ., Fletcher School of Law and Diplomacy, Cornell Univ., Middlebury Coll., Columbia Univ., Univ. Central de Venezuela; Asst. in History, Tufts Univ. 1947; Lecturer in History, Howard Univ. 1962–65, 1966–68; Third Sec., U.S. Embassy, Prague 1947–49; Vice-Consul, Florence 1949–52; Second Sec., Rome 1952–53, Moscow 1954–56; Deputy Officer-in-Charge, Soviet Affairs, Dept. of State 1956–60; First Sec., Caracas 1960–62; Special Asst. to Dir. of Peace Corps 1962–63, Deputy Assoc. Dir. 1963–65; Minister to Bulgaria 1965–66; Senior Staff, Nat. Security Council, White House 1966–68; Amb. to Guatemala 1968–71, to Chile 1971–73; Dir.-Gen. U.S. Foreign Service 1973–75; Asst. Sec. of State for African Affairs April-Dec. 1975; Amb. to Switzerland 1975–77; State Dept. Adviser, Naval War Coll. 1977–83; Alexander and Adelaide Hixon Prof. of Humanities, Harvey Mudd Coll., Claremont, Calif; Hon. LL.D. (Brown Univ.) 1970; Hartshorn Premium 1942, Caesar Misch Premium 1942; Cinco Aguilas Blancas Alpinism Award 1962, U.S. Navy's Distinguished Public Service Award 1983. *Publication: The Last Two Years of Salvador Allende* 1985, *Equality and Equal Security in Soviet Foreign Policy* 1986. *Leisure interests:* skiing, mountain climbing, white water canoeing, water-colour painting. *Address:* 1783 Longwood Ave., Claremont, Calif. 91711, U.S.A. *Telephone:* 714-621-8000 (Office); 714-624-5293 (Home).

DAVIS, Peter J.; British business executive; b. 23 Dec. 1941, Heswall, Cheshire; s. of John S. Davis and Adri (de Baat) Davis; m. Susan J. Hillman 1968; two s. one d.; ed. Shrewsbury School; man. trainee, The Ditchburn Org., Lytham, Lancs. 1959–65; Gen. Foods Ltd., Banbury, Oxon 1965–72; Marketing Dir. Key Markets 1973; Man. Dir. David Grieg and Group Man. Dir. Key Markets, David Grieg 1975–76; Departmental Dir. (non-foods) J. Sainsbury PLC 1976, mem. Bd. responsible for marketing 1977, Asst. Man. Dir. Buying and Marketing and Dir. Sava Centre 1979–86; Dir. then Deputy Chair. Homebase Ltd. 1983–86; Dir. Shaws Supermarkets, U.S.A. 1984–86; Deputy Chief Exec. Reed Int. PLC 1986, Chief Exec. 1986–; Dir. (non-exec.) Granada Group 1987–; Dir. British Satellite Broadcasting (BSB) April 1988–. *Leisure interests:* sailing, swimming, ballet, opera. *Address:* Reed International PLC, 6 Chesterfield Gardens, London W1A 1EJ, England. *Telephone:* 01-491 8279.

DAVIS, Ralph Henry Carless, M.A., F.B.A.; British historian; b. 7 Oct. 1918, Oxford; s. of Prof. H. W. C. Davis and Mrs. R. J. Davis; m. Eleanor Maud Megaw 1949; two s.; ed. Leighton Park School, Reading and Balliol Coll., Oxford; Friends' Ambulance Unit 1939–45; Asst. Master Christ's Hosp., Horsham 1947–48; Asst. Lecturer and Lecturer, University Coll., London 1948–56; Fellow and Tutor, Merton Coll., Oxford 1956–70; Prof. and Head, Dept. of Medieval History, Univ. of Birmingham 1970–84; Ed. History 1968–78, Pres. The Historical Asscn. 1978–81. *Publications: A History of Medieval Europe* 1957, *King Stephen* 1967, *Regesta Regum Anglo-Normannorum,* vols iii and iv (with H.A. Cronne) 1968–69, *The Normans and their Myth* 1976, *The Medieval Warhorse* 1989. *Leisure interests:* archaeology, travel. *Address:* 349 Banbury Road, Oxford, OX2 7PL, England.

DAVIS, Raymond, Jr., PH.D.; American nuclear chemist; b. 14 Oct. 1914, Washington, D.C.; s. of Raymond Davis and Ida Rogers Davis; m. Anna Marsh Torrey 1948; three s. two d.; ed. Univ. of Maryland and Yale Univ.; Dow Chemical Co. 1937–38; served U.S.A.F. 1942–46; Monsanto Chemical Co. (Mound Lab.) 1946–48; Brookhaven Nat. Lab. 1948–84; Research Prof., Astronomy Dept., Univ. of Pa. 1985–; Boris Pregel Prize (with O. A. Schaeffer), New York Acad. of Sciences 1957; Comstock Award, N.A.S. 1978; American Chem. Soc. Award for Nuclear Chem. 1979. *Publications:* Several articles on neutrinos and lunar rock study. *Leisure interests:* sailing and tennis. *Address:* Astronomy Department, University of Pennsylvania,

Philadelphia, Pa. 19104; 28 Bergen Lane, Blue Point, N.Y. 11715, U.S.A. (Home). *Telephone:* (215) 898-8176 (Office); (516) 363-6521 (Home).

DAVIS, Sammy, Jr.; American singer and entertainer; b. 8 Dec. 1925, New York; s. of Sammy and Elvina (née Sanchez) Davis; m. 1st Loray White 1958 (divorced 1959); m. 2nd May Britt 1961 (divorced 1967), two s. one d.; m. 3rd Altovise Gore 1970; made stage début at age one in parents' vaudeville act; performed with father and uncle as Will Marstin Trio; Theatre includes On Broadway, Charlie Welch in Mr. Wonderful 1956; Joe Wellington in Golden Boy 1964; appeared at the Palladium in London 1968; one-man show at the Uris Theater, New York 1974, Stop the World, I Want to Get Off, New York 1978; *Films include:* The Benny Goodman Story 1956, Anna Lucasta 1958, Porgy and Bess 1959, Ocean's 11 1960, Pepe 1960, Johnny Cool 1963, Robin and the Seven Hoods 1964, Threepenny Opera 1965, Salt and Pepper 1968, Sweet Charity 1968, One More Time 1970, Save the Children 1973; *television includes:* Poor Devil (series) 1973, NBC Follies 1973; Sammy and Company 1975, GE Presents Sammy Davis Jr. 1977; also various guest appearances on many US series; Dr. h.c. (Atlanta Univ.) 1981. *Publications:* Yes I Can (autobiography) 1965, Hollywood in a Suitcase (autobiography) 1980. *Address:* c/o William Morris Agency, 1350 Avenue of Americas, New York, N.Y., U.S.A.

DAVIS, Stanley Clinton, LL.B.; British solicitor, politician and international official; b. 6 Dec. 1928, London; s. of late Sidney Davis and of Lily Davis; m. Frances J. Lucas 1954; one s. three d.; ed. Hackney Downs School, Bournemouth School, Mercers' School and King's Coll., London; fmr. Councillor and Mayor, London Borough of Hackney; mem. Parl. for Hackney Cen. 1970-83; Parl. Under-Sec. of State for Trade 1974-79; Opposition Spokesman for Trade 1979-81; Deputy Opposition Spokesman for Foreign Affairs 1981-83; Commr. of the European Communities for the Environment, Consumer Protection, Nuclear Safety, Forests and Transport Jan. 1985-86, for Environment, Transport and Nuclear Safety 1986-88; Labour. *Publication:* Good Neighbours? Nicaragua, Central America and the United States (co-author) 1982. *Leisure interests:* reading political biography, golf. *Address:* Essex Lodge, 354 Finchley Road, Hampstead, London, NW3, England.

DAVIS, Steve, M.B.E.; British snooker player; b. 22 Aug. 1957; s. of Harry George Davis and Jean Catherine Davis; ed. Alexander McLeod Primary School, Abbey Wood School, London; became professional snooker player 1978; has won numerous championships in U.K. and abroad; major titles include: U.K. Professional Champion 1980, 1981, 1984, 1985, 1986, 1987; Masters Champion 1981, 1982, 1988; Int. Champion 1981, 1983, 1984; World Professional Champion 1981, 1983, 1984, 1987, 1988. *Publications:* Steve Davis, World Champion 1981, Frame and Fortune 1982, Successful Snooker 1982. *Leisure interests:* chess, keep fit, listening to records (jazz/soul), Tom Sharpe books. *Address:* Ground Floor, 1 Arcade Place, South Street, Romford, Essex, RM1 1RS, England. *Telephone:* Romford 24023.

DAVIS, Sir Thomas Robert Alexander Harries, K.B.E., M.D.; Cook Islands politician; b. 11 June 1917, Ruatonga, Rarotonga; s. of Sydney Thomas Davis and Maryanne Harries; m. 1st Myra Lydia Henderson 1940, three s.; m. 2nd Pa Tepaeru Ariki 1978; three s.; ed. Otago Univ. and Medical School, Univ. of Sydney, Harvard School of Public Health; Medical Officer and Surgeon Specialist, Cook Islands Medical Service 1945-48; Research mem. Dept. of Nutrition, Harvard School of Public Health 1952; Head of Dept. of Environmental Medicine, Arctic Aero-medical Laboratory, Fairbanks, Alaska 1955-56; U.S. Army Medical Research Laboratory, Fort Knox, Ky. 1956-61; Dir. of Research, U.S. Army Research Inst. of Environmental Medicine 1961-63; employed by Arthur D. Littlem Inc. 1963-71; returned to Cook Islands 1971, formed Democratic Party; also runs medical practice in Rarotonga; Prime Minister of Cook Islands July 1978-87 (numerous other portfolios); Fellow, Royal Soc. of Tropical Medicine and Hygiene, Royal Soc. of Medicine; mem. Alaska Medical Assen., Cook Islands Medical and Dental Assen. Visitors' Bd. of Dirs., Bishop Museum, Hawaii; Silver Jubilee Medal 1977; Order of Merit, Fed. Repub. of Germany 1978. *Publications:* two books and over eighty other publications. *Leisure interests:* big game fishing, watching rugby football, ham radio, music, planting vegetables, yachting. *Address:* Private Bag, Rarotonga, Cook Islands. *Telephone:* 29-300; 29-301.

DAVIS, Sir (William) Allan, G.B.E., D.S.C., C.A., A.T.I.I., F.R.S.A.; British chartered accountant; b. 19 June 1921; s. of Wilfred E. Davis and Annie H. Davis; m. Audrey P. Louch 1944; two s. one d.; ed. Cardinal Vaughan School, Kensington; joined Barclays Bank 1939; Pilot, R.N.V.R., Fleet Air Arm 1940-44; apprentice, Dunn Wylie & Co. 1944, Partner 1952, Sr. Partner 1972-76; Partner, Armitage & Norton, London 1976-86, Sr. Partner 1979-86; Dir. Catholic Herald Ltd., Crowning Tea Co. Ltd., Dunkelman & Son Ltd., Fiat Auto (U.K.) Ltd., Internatio-Muller U.K. Ltd. and U.K. subsidiaries, NRG (U.K.) Holdings Ltd; Common Councilman 1971-76, Alderman 1976-, Sheriff, City of London 1982-83, Lord Mayor of London 1985-86; Gov. Hon. Irish Soc. 1986; mem. Council, City Univ. 1986; numerous civic and charitable appointments. *Leisure interests:* bridge, travel. *Address:* 168 Defoe House, Barbican, London, EC2Y 8DN, England. *Telephone:* 01-638 5354.

DAVIS, Hon. William Grenville, P.C., C.C., Q.C., M.P.; Canadian lawyer and politician; b. 30 July 1929, Brampton, Ont.; s. of late Albert Grenville and

Vera (Hewetson) Davis; m. 1st Helen MacPhee 1953 (died 1962); m. 2nd Kathleen Mackay 1963; two s. three d.; ed. Univ. of Toronto; called to the Bar 1955; mem. Ontario House of Ass. 1959-85; Minister of Educ., Provincial Govt. of Ont. 1962-71, also of Univ. Affairs 1964-71; Premier of Ont. and Pres. of Council 1971-85, Special Envoy on Acid Rain 1985-86; Counsel to Tory, Tory, DesLauriers and Billington, Toronto 1986-; Leader Progressive Conservative Party 1971-85; *Leisure interests;* boating, tennis, football. *Address:* Suite 3200, IBM Tower, P.O. Box 270, Toronto-Dominion Center, Toronto, Ont., M5K 1N2, Canada.

DAVISON, Edward Joseph, M.A., PH.D., F.I.E.E.E., F.R.S.C.; Canadian professor of engineering; b. 12 Sept. 1938, Toronto; s. of Maurice J. Davison and Agnes E. Quinlan; m. Zofia M. Perz 1966; four c.; ed. Royal Conservatory of Music, Toronto and Univs. of Toronto and Cambridge; Asst. Prof. Dept. of Electrical Eng., Univ. of Toronto 1964-66, Univ. of Calif. Berkeley 1966-67, Univ. of Toronto 1967-68; Assoc. Prof. Univ. of Toronto 1968-74, Prof. Dept. of Electrical Eng. 1974-; Pres. I.E.E.E. Control Systems Soc. 1983; Chair. Int. Fed. of Automatic Control 1987-; Dir. Electrical Eng. Assocs. Ltd., Toronto 1977-; Consulting Eng. Assen. of Professional Engs. of Prov. of Ontario 1979-; Killam Research Fellowship, E.W.R. Steacie Research Fellowship, Athlone Fellowship; I.E.E.E. Centennial Medal 1984; Hon. Prof. Beijing Inst. of Aeronautics and Astronautics 1986. *Publications:* more than 275 research papers in numerous journals. *Leisure interests:* backpacking, skiing. *Address:* Department of Electrical Engineering, University of Toronto, Toronto, Ont. M5S 1A4, Canada. *Telephone:* (416) 978-6342.

DAVISON, Ian Frederic Hay, B.SC., F.C.A.; British accountant; b. 30 June 1931; s. of Eric Hay Davison and the late Inez Davison; m. Maureen Patricia Blacker 1955; one s. two d.; ed. Dulwich Coll., L.S.E. and Univ. of Mich., U.S.A.; mem. Inst. of Chartered Accountants (mem. Council 1975-); Man. Partner Arthur Andersen & Co., Chartered Accountants 1966-82, Adviser 1986-; Ind. mem. NEDC for Bldg. Industry 1971-77; mem. Price Comm. 1977-79; Chair. Review Bd. for Govt. Contracts 1981; Chief Exec. and Deputy Chair. Lloyd's 1983-86; Dept. of Trade Insp., London Capital Securities 1975-77; Insp. Grays Bldg. Soc. 1978-79; Chair. Accounting Standards Cttee. 1982-84; Gov. L.S.E. 1982-; Chair. Monteverdi Trust 1979-84; Chair. CL-Alexanders Laing and Cruickshank Holdings 1986-; Dir. Morgan Grenfell Asset Man. 1986-, Newspaper Publishing PLC 1986-, Midland Bank PLC 1986-, The Independent 1986-, Storehouse PLC 1988-; Trustee, Victoria and Albert Museum 1984-; Dir. and Trustee, Royal Opera House, Covent Garden 1984-; Dir. (non-exec.) Newspaper Publishing Oct. 1986-. *Publication:* Lloyds: A View of the Room 1987. *Leisure interests:* music, theatre, squash, skiing. *Address:* 40 Earlham Street, London, W.C.2, England.

DAVISON, Rt. Hon. Sir Ronald Keith, G.B.E., C.M.G., P.C., LL.B.; New Zealand lawyer and judge; b. 16 Nov. 1920, Kaponga; s. of late Joseph James and late Florence Minnie Davison; m. Jacqueline May Carr 1948; two s. (one deceased) one d.; ed. Te Kuiti Dist. High School, Auckland Univ.; served in Army, reaching rank of lieut., 1940-46; Flying Officer, R.N.Z.A.F., Europe; called to bar 1948; partner, Milne, Meek and Davison 1948-53; private practice 1953-; Q.C. 1963-; Chief Justice of N.Z. 1978-; Chair. Legal Aid Bd. 1969-78; Chair. Environmental Council 1969-74; Chair. Aircrew Industrial Tribunal 1971-78; Chair. Montana Wines Ltd. 1972-78; mem. Auckland Dist. Law Soc. Council 1959-65, Pres. 1965-66; Dir., N.Z. Insurance Co. Ltd. 1975-78; mem., Auckland Electric Power Bd. 1958-71; mem., N.Z. Law Soc. Council 1964-66; fmr. mem. Torts and Gen. Law Reform Cttee.; Church Advocate, Auckland Diocese 1973-78; Vicar's Warden, St. Mark's Church, Remuera 1974-78. *Leisure interests:* golf, fishing. *Address:* Chief Justice's Chambers, High Court, Wellington (Office); 68 Rama Crescent, Khandallah, Wellington, New Zealand (Home). *Telephone:* 727 307 (Office).

DAVOS, Gen. Ioannis; Greek army officer (retd.); b. 23 Nov. 1918, Aghios Georgios, Dorion, Trifila; s. of Ioannis and Athanasia Davos; m. Anastasia Demetropoulou 1947; three s.; ed. Army Cadets Coll., War Coll., Nat. Defence Coll.; served Albania 1940-41, Resistance in Peloponnese 1941-42, Company Commdr. in anti-communist campaign in Greece 1946-49; Instructor at War Coll. 1959; Staff Officer, G3/HAGS 1960-62; Battalion Commdr., Mil. Cadets School 1962-64; Commdr. 30th Infantry Regt. 1967-68; 1st Field Army/AC of S G3 1968-69; Chief of Staff B Corps 1970-72; Commdr. XI Infantry Div. 1972-73; Commdr. C Corps 1973-74; Chief of Army Staff 1974-76; Commdr.-in-Chief, Supreme Greek Armed Forces Command 1976-80 (resigned); Deputy Minister for Nat. Defence 1980-; Gold Order of Merit for Bravery; Grand Commdr. Order of Honour; War Cross C Class (twice); Order of Cavalier de Madara with Epées, First Class (Bulgaria), Order Tudor Vladimirescu, First Class (Romania), Gran Croce dell'Ordine al Merito (Italy), Grosses Verdienstkreuz mit Stern (Fed. Repub. of Germany), Commdr., Ordre nat. du Mérite and numerous other Greek and foreign decorations. *Address:* c/o Ministry of National Defence, Holargos, Athens, Greece.

DAVTIAN, Vagan Armenakovich; Soviet (Armenian) author and poet; b. 1922, Arabkir, Turkey (family moved to Soviet Armenia 1925); ed. secondary school, Yerevan; served in Soviet Army 1941-45; Faculty of Philology, Yerevan State Univ. 1943-48; worked on various literary journals, first published works 1947; *Publications include:* First Love 1947, A Morning of Peace 1950, A Way Through the Heart 1952, Dawn in the Mountains 1957, and many others.

DAVYDOV, N.G.; Soviet party official; Second Sec. of Chemkent Dist. Cttee. of Kazakh CP 1978-82; cand. mem. of Cen. Cttee. of Kazakh CP 1981-83, mem. 1983-; First Sec. of Dzhezgazgan Dist. Cttee. of Kazakh CP 1982-86; cand. mem. of Cen. Cttee. of CPSU 1986-. *Address:* Central Committee of Kazakh Communist Party, Alma-Ata, Kazakh S.S.R., U.S.S.R.

DAVYDOV, Yuri Vladimirovich; Soviet author; b. 20 Nov. 1924, Moscow; m. Marotschina Branislava; two s.; served in Soviet Navy 1942-49; first works published 1945; mem. CPSU 1947-; political prisoner 1949-54; U.S.S.R. State Prize 1987. *Publications include:* On Seas and Journeys 1949, The Southern Cross 1957, The Captains Are Looking for the Way 1959, About Your Friends, Africa 1962, The Straw Guard 1987, Volunteer for Freedom 1988, An Evening at Kholmov 1989. *Address:* U.S.S.R. Union of Writers, ul. Vorovskogo 52, Moscow; 103107 Moscow, Malaia Bronnaia 12, Kb. 46, U.S.S.R. *Telephone:* 290 1027.

DAWES, Geoffrey Sharman, C.B.E., B.CH., D.M., F.R.C.O.G., F.R.C.P., F.R.S.; British medical research scientist; b. 21 Jan. 1918; s. of Rev. W. Dawes; m. Margaret Monk 1941; two s. two d.; ed. Repton School and New Coll., Oxford; Rockefeller Travelling Scholarship 1946; Fellow, Worcester Coll. Oxford 1946-85, Emer. Fellow 1985; Univ. Demonstrator in Pharmacology, Oxford 1947; Foulerton Research Fellow, Royal Soc. 1948; Dir. Nuffield Inst. for Medical Research, Oxford 1948-85; Dir. Charing Cross Medical Research Centre 1984-; other professional appts.; various awards and distinctions including Gairdner Foundation Award 1966; Hon. F.A.C.O.G. *Publications:* Foetal and Neonatal Physiology 1968; articles in professional journals. *Leisure interest:* fishing. *Address:* 8 Belbroughton Road, Oxford, OX2 6UZ, England. *Telephone:* Oxford 58131.

DAWKINS, John Sydney, DIP.AGR.; Australian politician; b. 2 March 1947, Perth; m.; two c.; ed. Scotch Coll., Roseworthy Agricultural Coll.; fmr. mem. Senate, Univ. of W. Australia; worked for Bureau of Agricultural Econs. and Dept. of Trade and Industry 1971-72; M.P., House of Reps., Seat of Tangney, W.A. 1974-75, Seat of Fremantle, W.A. 1977-; Minister for Finance and Minister Assisting the Prime Minister for Public Service Matters 1983-84, Minister for Trade and Minister Assisting the Prime Minister for Youth Affairs 1984-87, for Employment, Educ. and Training Nov. 1987-; fmr. mem. Nat. Exec., Australian Labor Party, Party Vice-Pres. 1982-; Press Officer, W.A. Trades and Labor Council 1976-77. *Address:* Parliament House, Canberra, A.C.T. 2600; Department of Employment, Education and Training, P.O.B. 826, Woden, A.C.T. 2606, Australia.

DAWSON, Rex Malcolm Chaplin, PH.D., F.R.S.; British biochemist; b. 3 June 1924; s. of James Dawson and Ethel M. (Chaplin) Dawson; m. Emily E. Hodder 1946; one s. one d.; ed. Hinckley Grammar School, Univ. Coll. London and Univ. of Wales; M.R.C. Fellowship, later Beit Memorial Fellowship, Neuropsychiatric Research Centre, Whitchurch Hosp., Cardiff 1947-52; Betty Brookes Fellow, Dept. of Biochem. Univ. of Oxford 1952-55; Prin. Scientific Officer, Inst. of Animal Physiology, Babraham, Cambridge 1955-59, Deputy Dir. and Head, Dept. of Biochem. 1969-84. *Publications:* three books and numerous papers in scientific journals. *Address:* Kirn House, Holt Road, Langham, Norfolk, NR25 7BX, England. *Telephone:* Binham 396.

DAY, Sir Derek (Malcolm), K.C.M.G.; British diplomatist; b. 29 Nov. 1927; s. of late Alan W. Day; m. Sheila Nott 1955; three s. one d.; ed. Hurstpierpoint Coll. and St. Catharine's Coll. Cambridge; R.A. 1946-48; entered diplomatic service 1951; served Tel Aviv 1953-56, Rome 1956-59, Washington, D.C. 1962-66, Nicosia 1972-75; Amb. to Ethiopia 1975-78; Asst. Under-Sec. of State FCO 1979, Deputy Under-Sec. of State 1980, Chief Clerk 1982-84; High Commr. in Canada 1984-. *Address:* c/o Foreign and Commonwealth Office, London, S.W.1, England.

DAY, Doris (Doris von Kappelhoff); American actress and singer; b. 3 April 1924, Cincinnati, Ohio; d. of Frederick Wilhelm and Alma Sophia von Kappelhoff; m. 1st Al Jorden 1941 (divorced 1943), one s.; m. 2nd George Weilder 1946 (divorced 1949); m. 3rd Marty Melcher 1951 (died 1968); professional dancing appearances, Doherty and Kappelhoff, Glendale, Calif.; singer Karlin's Karnival, radio station WCPO; singer with bands, Barney Rapp, Bob Crosby, Fred Waring, Les Brown; singer and leading lady, Bob Hope radio show (NBC) 1948-50, Doris Day Show (CBS) 1952-53; singer for Columbia Records 1950-; with Warner Bros. film studio. *Films include:* Romance on the High Seas 1948, My Dream is Yours 1949, Young Man With a Horn 1950, Tea for Two 1950, West Point Story 1950, Lullaby of Broadway 1951, On Moonlight Bay 1951, I'll See You in My Dreams 1951, April in Paris 1952, By the Light of the Silvery Moon 1953, Calamity Jane 1953, Lucky Me 1954, Yankee Doodle Girl 1954, Love Me or Leave Me 1955, The Pajama Game 1957, Teacher's Pet 1958, The Tunnel of Love 1958, It Happened to Jane 1959, Pillow Talk 1959, Please Don't Eat the Daisies 1960, Midnight Lace 1960, Lover Come Back 1962, That Touch of Mink 1962, Jumbo 1962, The Thrill of It All 1963, Send Me No Flowers 1964, Do Not Disturb 1965, The Glass Bottom Boat 1966, Caprice 1967, The Ballad of Josie 1968, Where Were You When the Lights Went Out? 1968, With Six You Get Egg Roll 1968; TV series The Doris Day Show

1968-72; appearance on TV in The Pet Set 1972. *Address:* c/o Terry Melcher Arwin Productions, P.O. Box 8166, Universal City, Calif. 91608, U.S.A.

DAY, John W.; American motor manufacturing executive; b. 25 Feb. 1933, Chicago, Ill.; s. of John W. Day and Gay Potters Day; m. Barbara Cline 1955; two d.; ed. Northwestern Univ.; Captain, U.S. Marine Corps 1955-57; Man. of Accounting, Missile Div. of U.S.A.F.T.A. 1957-61, Man. of Finance of U.S.A.F.T.A. 1961-63; Man. of Accounting and Audit, Chrysler Int. 1963-64; Finance Dir. Chrysler Peru 1964-67, Chrysler do Brasil 1967-69; Man. Dir. Chrysler Colmotores (Colombia) 1969-71, Chrysler Fevre Argentina 1971-73, Chrysler España 1973-75; Group Dir. of Chrysler cos. in France and Spain 1975; Vice-Pres. Chrysler Corpn. (Europe) 1976-77, Pres. Chrysler France 1976-78; Vice-Pres., Controller 1979-81; Int. Exec. Vice-Pres. Chrysler, Detroit 1981-84; Pres. Bendix Group of Allied-Signal Corpn. 1984-. *Address:* 20650 Civic Center Drive, P.O.B. 5029, Southfield, Mich. 48086, U.S.A.

DAY, Sir (Judson) Graham, Kt., LL.B.; Canadian business executive; b. 3 May 1933; s. of Frank C. Day and Edythe G. née Baker; m. Leda A. Creighton 1958; one s. two d.; ed. Queen Elizabeth High School, Halifax, N.S. and Dalhousie Univ., Halifax; pvt. law practice, Windsor, N.S. 1956-64; Canadian Pacific Ltd., Montreal and Toronto 1964-71; Deputy Chair. Org. Cttee. for British Shipbuilders and Deputy Chair. and Chief Exec. desig., British Shipbuilders 1975-76; Prof. of Business Studies and Dir. Canadian Marine Transportation Centre, Dalhousie Univ. 1977-81; Vice-Pres. Shipyards and Marine Devt., Dome Petroleum Ltd. 1981-83; Chair. and C.E.O. British Shipbuilders 1983-86; Chair. and C.E.O. The Rover Group (fmrly. BL) PLC 1986-; Chair. Cadbury Schweppes April 1989-. *Leisure interests:* reading, lakeside chalet in Canada. *Address:* The Rover Group PLC, 7-10 Hobart Place, London, SW1W 0HH, England. *Telephone:* (01) 235 4311.

DAY, Peter Rodney, PH.D.; American (b. British) agricultural scientist; b. 27 Dec. 1928, Chingford, Essex; s. of Roland Percy Day and Florence Kate (née Dixon); m. Lois Elizabeth Rhodes 1950; two s. one d.; ed. Chingford County High School and Birkbeck Coll., Univ. of London; John Innes Inst. 1946-63; Assoc. Prof., Ohio State Univ., Columbus, U.S.A. 1963-64; Chief, Genetics Dept., Conn. Agricultural Experiment Station, New Haven 1964-79; Dir. Plant Breeding Inst., Cambridge, England 1979-87; Dir. Center for Agricultural Molecular Biology, Rutgers Univ., N.B. 1987-, Rutgers Univ. Prof. of Genetics 1987-; Special Professorship, Univ. of Nottingham 1981-; Sec. Int. Genetics Fed. 1984-; Pres. British Soc. for Plant Pathology 1985; Chair. Cttee. on Managing Global Genetic Resources, N.A.S., U.S.A. 1986-; mem. Exec. Cttee., Norfolk Agricultural Station 1980-1987, Cttee. on Genetic Experimentation, Int. Council of Scientific Unions 1984-, Bd. of Trustees, Int. Centre for Maize and Wheat Improvement, 1986-; Fellow American Phytopathological Soc.: Frank Newton Prize, Birkbeck Coll., Univ. of London 1950; Commonwealth Fund Fellow, Univ. of Wis. 1954-56; John Simon Guggenheim Memorial Fellow, Univ. of Queensland 1972. *Publications:* Fungal Genetics (with J. R. S. Fincham) 1963, Genetics of Host-Parasite Interactions 1974; more than 100 scientific papers. *Leisure interests:* music, Scottish country dancing. *Address:* Center for Agricultural Molecular Biology, P.O. Box 231, Martin Hall, Cook College, Rutgers University, New Brunswick, N.J. 08903 (Office); 394 Franklin Road, North Brunswick, N.J. 08902, U.S.A. (Home). *Telephone:* (201) 932-8165 (Office); (201) 821-0746 (Home).

DAY, Sir Robin, Kt.; British television and radio journalist; b. 24 Oct. 1923, London; s. of William and Florence Day; m. Katherine Mary (née Ainslie) 1965 (divorced 1985); two s.; ed. Bembridge School, Oxford Univ.; Army Service 1943-47; Pres. Oxford Union 1950; called to the Bar 1952; BBC radio journalist 1954-55; Independent Television News newscaster and political corresp. 1955-59; BBC TV political interviewer and reporter specializing in current affairs 1959-; BBC radio World at One presenter 1979-87; introducer of Panorama 1967-72; Chair. Question Time, BBC 1979-; mem. Phillimore Cttee. on Law of Contempt 1971-74; Chair. Hansard Soc. for Parl. Govt. 1981-83, mem. Council 1977-; Richard Dimbleby Award, Soc. of Film and TV Arts 1974; Broadcasting Press Guild Award (for Question Time) 1980; RTS Judges Award for 30 years TV journalism 1985; Hon. LL.D. (Exeter) 1986, (Keele) 1988. *Publications:* Television—A Personal Report 1961, The Case for Televising Parliament 1963 (pamphlet), Troubled Reflections of a TV Journalist (article in "Encounter") May 1970, Day by Day 1975. *Leisure interests:* talking, skiing, reading. *Address:* c/o BBC Studios, Lime Grove, London, W.12, England.

DAY-LEWIS, Daniel; Irish actor; b. 20 April, London; s. of the late Cecil Day-Lewis and of Jill Balcon; ed. Sherington, S.E. London, Bedales and Bristol Old Vic Theatre School; plays: Class Enemy, Funny Peculiar, Bristol Old Vic; Look Back in Anger, Dracula, Little Theatre, Bristol and Half Moon Theatre, London; Another Country, Queen's Theatre; Futurists, Nat. Theatre; Romeo, Thisbe, R.S.C., Hamlet 1989; television: Insurance Man; films: My Beautiful Laundrette, A Room with a View, Stars and Bars, The Unbearable Lightness of Being. *Address:* c/o Julian Belfrage, 60 St. James's Street, London, S.W.1, England.

DAYAL, Rajeshwar, M.A.; Indian diplomatist; b. 12 Aug. 1909, Naini Tal. U.P.; s. of the late Mr. and Mrs. D. Dayal; m. Susheela Srivastava 1938;

ed. P.S. Coll., Naini Tal, U.P. Allahabad Univ., and New Coll., Oxford; entered Indian Civil Service 1932; Deputy Sec. Civil Supplies Dept., U.P. Govt. 1943-46, Home Sec. 1946-48; Minister-Counsellor and Chargé d'Affaires Moscow 1948-50; Special Commr. to Indian Govt. and Joint Sec. to Govt. External Affairs Dept. 1950; Alternate Rep. Security Council 1950-51, Perm. Rep. to U.N. 1952-54, mem. U.N. Peace Observation Comm., U.N. Comm. of Twelve on Disarmament, U.N. Comm. for Relief and Rehabilitation of Korea, U.N. Trusteeship Council, U.N. Human Rights Comm.; Amb. to Yugoslavia 1955-58, also accred. to Greece and Romania; High Commr. to Pakistan 1958-62, 1961-63; Personal Rep. of Sec.-Gen. of UN in the Congo Sept. 1960-May 1961; Special Sec. Ministry of External Affairs 1962-65; Commonwealth Sec. Ministry of External Affairs 1965; Amb. to France 1965-67; Sec.-Gen. Ministry of Foreign Affairs 1967-Nov.1968; Chair. UN Cttee. for Eradication of Racial Discrimination 1969-, Commonwealth Group for Monitoring Independence Elections in Rhodesia (Zimbabwe) 1980; Visiting Prof. Princeton Univ. 1969-70; Scholar in Residence, Aspen Inst. for Humanistic Studies 1972; Woodrow Wilson Fellow, Smithsonian Inst. 1971, 1973; Fellow, St. Antony's Coll., Oxford 1976; Visiting Fellow, Australian Nat. Univ., Canberra 1981; Chair. Rhodes Scholarship Cttee. 1972-81, Aga Khan Foundation, India 1980-; Padma Vibhushana 1969. *Publications:* Mission for Hammarskjöld (The Congo Crisis) 1976, A Martyred Country (Lebanon). *Leisure interests:* shooting, riding, music, gardening, reading. *Address:* 17 Palam Marg, New Delhi 57, India.

DAZA, Pedro; Chilean diplomatist; b. 1925; m.; five c.; ed. Nat. Inst., Santiago, Univ. of Chile and Univ. of Uruguay; joined Foreign Service 1945; posts at embassies in London and Buenos Aires 1951-57; Under-Sec. for External Affairs Ministry of Foreign Affairs 1962-64, Econ. Dir. 1972-74, Dir.-Gen. 1974-75; Prof. of Int. Politics and Int. Relations Univ. of Chile 1962-64; Amb. to Latin American Free Trade Asscn. 1964-73; Chair. Perm. Cttee. Inter-American Econ. and Soc. Council of OAS 1979-; Perm. Rep. of Chile to UN 1984-; Légion d'honneur; various hons. from govts. of Argentina, Brazil, Guatemala, Mexico, Venezuela, Fed. Repub. of Germany, Jordan and Yugoslavia. *Address:* Permanent Mission of Chile to United Nations, 809 United Nations Plaza, 4th Floor, New York, N.Y. 10017, U.S.A. *Telephone:* (212) 687-7547

DEAKIN, Sir William, Kt., D.S.O., M.A.; British university official (retd.); b. 3 July 1913, London; s. of Albert Whitney and Bertha Mildred Deakin; m. 1st Margaret Beatson Bell 1935 (dissolved); m. 2nd Livia Stela Nasta 1943; two s.; ed. Westminster School and Christ Church, Oxford; Fellow and Tutor, Wadham Coll., Oxford 1936-49, Research Fellow 1949, Hon. Fellow 1952; with Queen's Own Oxfordshire Hussars 1939-41; seconded to Special Operations, War Office 1941; led first British Mil. Mission to Marshal Tito 1943; First Sec. Embassy, Belgrade 1945-46; Warden of St. Antony's Coll., Oxford 1950-69, Hon. Fellow 1969; Hon. Fellow, British Acad. 1980, 1981; Hon. Student, Christ Church Coll., Oxford 1979; D.S.O. 1943; Russian Order of Valour 1944, Chevalier Légion d'honneur 1953, Bundesehrenkreuz (Fed. Repub. of Germany) 1958, and two Yugoslav mil. orders. *Publications:* The Brutal Friendship: Mussolini, Hitler and the Fall of Italian Fascism 1962, The Case of Richard Sorge 1964. The Embattled Mountain 1971. *Leisure interests:* travel, writing. *Address:* Le Castellet Village, 83 Var, France. *Telephone:* 94-32-63-21.

DEAN, Antony Musgrave, O.B.E.; British broadcaster; b. 7 Jan. 1921, Loose, Kent; s. of Arthur Edis Dean, C.B.E., M.A., M.LITT. and Elsie Georgina Dean (née Musgrave-Wood); m. 1st Anne Virginia Batcup 1943; m. 2nd Sheila Francis Whittingham 1956; three s. three d.; ed. The King's School, Canterbury; Commissioned Queen's Bays (2nd Dragoon Guards) 1941, wounded Western Desert 1942; forces Broadcasting Service Kenya 1945-46; Recording, feature film work and BBC news stringer 1947-52; Broadcasting Officer, Kenya Govt. 1952-59; Controller of Programmes, Kenya Broadcasting Service 1959-61, Operations Exec. 1962-64; Dir. of Radio Programme Dept., Sec. Radio Programme Cttee., European Broadcasting Union 1964-86; Media Consultant, Council of Europe 1986-; Hon. Citizen of Catalunya. *Leisure interests:* music, skiing. *Address:* 24 rue de la Printanière, 1293 Bellevue, Geneva, Switzerland; 6 The Carriage House, Lees Court, Sheldwich Lees, Faversham, Kent, ME13 0NQ, England. *Telephone:* (022) 742612 (Switzerland); (0795) 535581 (England).

DEAN, John Gunther, PH.D.; American diplomatist; b. 24 Feb. 1926, Germany; s. of Dr. Joseph and Lucy Dean; m. Martine Duphénieux 1952; two s. one d.; ed. Harvard Coll., Harvard and Paris Univs.; entered Govt. Service 1950; diplomatic posts in France, Belgium, Viet-Nam, Laos, Togo, Mali and in U.S. Dept. of State; Dir. Pacification Program in Mil. Region 1, Viet-Nam 1970-72; Deputy Chief Mission, American Embassy, Laos 1972-74; Amb. to Khmer Repub. 1974-75, to Denmark 1975-78, to Lebanon 1978-81, to Thailand 1981-85, to India 1985-; various U.S. and foreign decorations. *Leisure interest:* tennis. *Address:* Department of State, Washington, D.C. 20520, U.S.A.

DEAN, Sir Patrick Henry, G.C.M.G.; British diplomatist; b. 16 March 1909, Berlin, Germany; s. of Prof. Henry Roy and Irene Dean (née Wilson); m. Patricia Wallace Jackson 1947; two s.; ed. Rugby School and Gonville and Caius Coll., Cambridge; called to Bar at Lincoln's Inn 1934; legal practice 1934-39; Asst. Legal Adviser, Foreign Office 1939-45, Head German Political Dept. 1945-50, Minister in Rome 1950-51; Civilian Instructor

Imperial Defence Coll. 1952; Asst. Under-Sec. Foreign Office 1953-56, Deputy Under-Sec. 1956-60; Perm. Rep. to UN 1960-64; Amb. to U.S.A. 1965-69; Chair. ESU Dec. 1972-83, Cambridge Petroleum Royalties 1975-82; Governing Body Rugby School 1972-84; Dir. Taylor Woodrow Ltd., 1969-86, Int. Adviser 1986-; Int. Adviser to American Express 1969-; Hon. LL.D. (Columbia, Lincoln, Wesleyan Chattanooga, Hofstra Univs., William and Mary Coll.); Hon. Bencher Lincoln's Inn; Hon. Fellow Clare Coll. and Gonville and Caius Coll., Cambridge. *Leisure interest:* walking. *Address:* 5 Bentinck Mansions, Bentinck Street, London, W.1, England. *Telephone:* 01-935 0881.

DEAN, Winton Basil, M.A., F.B.A.; British author and musicologist; b. 18 March 1916, Birkenhead; s. of Basil Dean and Esther (née Van Gruisen); m. Hon. Thalia Mary Shaw 1939; one s. (two d. deceased) one adopted d.; ed. Harrow, King's Coll., Cambridge; mem. Music Panel, Arts Council of G.B. 1957-60; Ernest Bloch Prof. of Music, Univ. of Calif., Berkeley, U.S.A. 1965-66, Regent's Lecturer 1977; mem. Council, Royal Musical Asscn. 1965- (Vice-Pres. 1970-); mem. Vorstand, G.F. Händel-Gesellschaft, Halle 1980-, Kuratorium, Göttinger Händel-Gesellschaft 1982-; Hon. mem. R.A.M. *Publications:* Bizet 1948, Carmen 1949, Handel's Dramatic Oratorios and Masques 1959, Shakespeare and Opera 1964, Handel and the Opera Seria 1969, The New Grove Handel 1982, Handel's Operas 1704-1726 (with J. M. Knapp) 1987; maj. contribs. to new Oxford History of Music, vol. VIII 1982 and Grove's Dictionary of Music and Musicians, 5th and 6th edns. 1954, 1980. *Leisure interests:* shooting, naval history. *Address:* Hambledon Hurst, Godalming, Surrey, GU8 4HF, England. *Telephone:* Wormley 2644.

DEANE, Phyllis Mary, M.A., F.B.A., F.R.HIST.S.; British professor emeritus of economic history; economic historian; b. 13 Oct. 1918; d. of John Edward Deane and Elizabeth Jane Brooks; ed. Chatham County School, Hutcheson's Girls' Grammar School, Glasgow and Univ. of Glasgow; Carnegie Research Scholar 1940-41; Research Officer, Nat. Inst. of Econ. and Social Research 1941-45; Colonial Research Officer 1946-48; Research Officer, Colonial Office 1948-49; Dept. of Applied Econs., Cambridge Univ. 1950-61. Lecturer, Faculty of Econs. and Politics 1961-71, Reader in Econ. History 1971-81, Prof. 1981-82, now Prof. Emer.; Fellow of Newnham Coll. 1961-83, Hon. Fellow 1983; Ed. Economic Journal 1968-75; Pres. Royal Econ. Soc. 1980-82. *Publications:* The Future of the Colonies (with Julian Huxley) 1945, The Measurement of Colonial National Incomes 1948, Colonial Social Accounting 1953, British Economic Growth 1688-1959 (with W. A. Cole) 1962, The First Industrial Revolution 1965, The Evolution of Economic Ideas 1978, The State and the Economic System 1989, papers and reviews in econ. journals. *Leisure interests:* walking and gardening. *Address:* 4 Stukeley Close, Cambridge, CB3 9LT, England.

de ARÉCHAGA, Eduardo Jiménez (see Jiménez de Aréchaga, Eduardo).

DEARING, Sir Ronald Ernest, Kt., C.B., B.SC.ECON., C.B.I.M., F.INST.M.; British civil servant and business executive; b. 27 April 1930, Hull; s. of E. H. A. and M. T. (née Hoyle) Dearing; m. Margaret Patricia Riley 1954; two d.; ed. Malet Lambert High School, Doncaster Grammar School, Hull Univ.; Ministry of Labour and Nat. Service 1946-49; Ministry of Power 1949-62; Treasury 1962-64; Ministries of Power and Tech. and Dept. of Trade and Industry 1965-72; Regional Dir. Dept. of Trade and Industry 1972-74; Under Sec. Dept. of Industry 1974-76, Deputy Sec. for Nationalized Industry Matters 1976-80, Chair. of Nationalized Industries' Chairmen's Group 1983-84; Deputy Chair. Post Office 1980-81, Chair. 1981-87; Chair. CNAA 1987-88, Polytechnics and Colleges Funding Council 1987-, Review Cttee. on Accounting Standards 1987-88, Co. Durham Devt. Co.; Dir. (non-exec.) Whitbread 1987-, Prudential Corpn. PLC, I.M.I. PLC, British Coal, English Estates, Thorn Ericsson Ltd., Fellow of London Business School; Hon. D.Sc.(Econ.) (Hull) 1986. *Leisure interests:* music, genealogy. *Address:* 28 Westhawe, Bretton, Peterborough, PE3 8BA, England.

DEARNLEY, Christopher Hugh, M.A., D.MUS., F.R.C.O.; British organist; b. 11 Feb. 1930, Wolverhampton; s. of Rev. Charles Dearnley; m. Bridget Wateridge 1957; three s. one d.; ed. Cranleigh School and Worcester Coll., Oxford; Asst. Organist, Salisbury Cathedral 1954-57, Organist and Master of the Choristers 1957-67; Organist and Dir. of Music, St. Paul's Cathedral, London 1968-; Pres. Inc. Asscn. of Organists 1968-70; Chair. Friends of Cathedral Music 1971-, Percy Whitlock Trust 1982-; mem. Council, Royal Coll. of Organists 1980-; Dir. English Hymnal Co. 1970-, Harwich Festival 1981-. *Publications:* The Treasury of English Church Music Vol. III 1965, English Church Music 1650-1750 1970. *Leisure interests:* sketching, gardening. *Address:* 8b Amen Court, London, EC4M 7BU, England.

DEASY, Austin, T.D.; Irish politician; b. 26 Aug. 1936, Dungarvan, Co. Waterford; s. of Michael Deasy and Geraldine Deasy; m. Catherine Keating 1961; two s. two d.; ed. Dungarvan Christian Brothers' School, and Univ. Coll., Cork; former secondary school teacher; mem. Waterford County Council and Dungarvan Urban Council 1967-; mem. Seanad Eireann 1973-77; mem. Dail Eireann 1977-; Minister for Agric. 1982-87; Fine Gael. *Leisure interests:* golf, gardening, horse-racing. *Address:* Dáil Éireann, Leinster House, Dublin 2, Ireland. *Telephone:* 789911.

De BACKER-VAN OCKEN, Rika; Belgian politician; b. 1 Feb. 1923, Antwerp; seven c.; ed. St. Lutgardisschool, Antwerp and Catholic Univ.

of Leuven; worked on Winkler Prins voor de Vrouw encyclopaedia; Ed. KAV (Women's Christian Asscn.); Vice-Pres. Christian Social Party, Antwerp; mem. Provincial Senate for Antwerp 1971–74; mem. Senate 1974–; mem. Comms. for Nat. Educ., Culture, Justice; Minister of Dutch Culture and Flemish Affairs 1974–79, of the Flemish Community and Pres. Flemish Local Govt. 1979–80. *Address:* c/o Ministry of the Flemish Community, Jozef II straat 30, B 1040, Brussels, Belgium.

DeBAKEY, Michael Ellis, B.S., M.D., M.S.; American surgeon; b. 7 Sept. 1908, Lake Charles, Louisiana; s. of Shaker M. DeBakey and Raheeja Zorba; m. 1st Diana Cooper 1936 (died 1972); four s.; m. 2nd Katrin Fehlhaber 1975; one d.; ed. Tulane Univ., New Orleans; Instructor Tulane Univ. 1937–40, Asst. Prof. of Surgery 1940–46; War Service, Colonel, ultimately Dir. Surgical Consultant Div., Office of the Surgeon Gen. 1942–46; U.S. Army Surgical Consultant to Surgeon-Gen. 1946–; Assoc. Prof. Tulane Univ. 1946–48; Prof. Dept. of Surgery, Baylor Coll. of Medicine, Houston, Texas 1948–, Pres. 1969–79, Chancellor 1979–, Chair. 1948–, Dir. Nat. Heart and Blood Vessel Research and Demonstration Center, Baylor Coll. of Medicine 1974–84; Dir. DeBakey Heart Center 1985–; Surgeon-in-Chief, Ben Taub Gen. Hosp.; Senior Attending Surgeon, Methodist Hosp. and Consultant in Surgery, Veterans Administration Hospital, Houston; consultant surgeon to many hospitals in Texas; mem. Nat. Advisory Heart Council 1957–61, Program, Planning Cttee. and Cttee. on Training 1961–, Nat. Advisory Council on Regional Medical Programs 1965–, Advisory Council, Inst. for Advanced Research in Asian Science and Medicine, Brooklyn, New York 1978–, Advisory Council, Nat. Heart, Lung and Blood Inst. 1957–61, 1974–77, 1982–86, Tex. Science and Tech. Council 1984–86; Chair. Pres. Comm. on Heart Disease, Cancer and Stroke 1964–66; implanted first artificial heart in man April 1966; editorial boards of numerous medical journals and editor of General Surgery: Vol. II, History of World War II, co-editor American Lectures in Surgery, ed. Journal of Vascular Surgery 1983–88; mem. numerous American and foreign medical socs. and asscns. and holder of numerous advisory appointments; Encyclopaedia Britannica Achievement in Life Award 1980 and many other American and foreign awards including Harris County Hospital District 30-year Service Award, Clemson Award 1983, Presidential Medal of Freedom with Distinction 1969, Distinguished Service Award (American Surgical Asscn.) 1981, Theodore E. Cummings Memorial Prize for Outstanding Contribs. in Cardiovascular Disease 1987, Nat. Medal of Science 1987, and hon. degrees. *Publications:* The Living Heart 1977, The Living Heart Diet 1984; over 1,160 articles. *Address:* Baylor College of Medicine, Texas Medical Center, 1 Baylor Plaza, Houston, Texas 77030, USA. (Office). *Telephone:* (713) 797-9353.

DEBBASCH, Charles, D. EN D.; French professor of public law; b. 22 Oct. 1937, Tunis; s. of Max Debbasch; m. Odile Peyridier 1959; three s. one d.; tutorial asst. 1957; junior lecturer, law faculty, Aix-en-Provence Univ. 1959–62, Prof. of Law, Grenoble Univ. 1962–63, Aix-en-Provence 1963–67, Chair of Public Law, Faculty of Law and Econ. Sciences, Aix-en-Provence 1967, Dir. Centre of Research into Legal Admin. 1966–, Centre of Research and Study on Mediterranean Societies 1969–71; Head of Research Comm., Ministry of Educ. 1968–69; Dir. Teaching and Research Unit attached to faculty of Law and Pol. Sciences, Aix-Marseille Univ. 1970, Dean, Faculty of Law and Pol. Sciences 1971–73; Pres. Nat. Assen. of Pres. of Univs. specializing in law and politics and Deans of law faculties 1971–78; Prof. Coll. of Europe, Bruges 1975–81; Pres. Consultative Cttee. public law univs. 1978; tech. adviser Gen. Secr. French presidency 1978–81; Pres. Fondation Vasarely 1971; Dir. and Dir.-Gen. of Press Group, Dauphiné Libéré 1984–; Pres. Agence générale d'information 1985–; Officier, Ordre nat. du Mérite, Chevalier des Palmes Académiques, Grand Officer of the Aztec Eagle (Mexico), Commdr. Order of Tunisian Repub., Officer of Merit, Senegal. *Publications:* Procédure administrative contentieuse et procédure civile 1962, la République tunisienne 1962, Institutions administratives 1975, Traité du droit de la radio-diffusion 1967, le Droit de la radio et de la télévision 1970, l'Administration au pouvoir 1970, l'Université désorientée 1971, Droit administratif 1973, Science administrative 1980, la France de Pompidou 1974, Introduction à la politique 1982, Contentieux administratif 1985, les Chats de l'émirat 1976, Institutions et droit administratifs (4 vols., 1980–86), l'Etat civilisé 1979, L'Elysée dévoilé 1982, Lexique de politique 1984, Les constitutions de la France 1983, Droit constitutionnel 1986, Le Droit de l'audiovisuel 1984, Les Associations 1985, la Vᵉ République 1985, La Disgrace du socialisme 1985, Les recettes de la cuisine politique 1986. *Address:* Le Dauphiné Libéré, 38113 Veurey Voroize (Office); Université de Droit, d'Economie et des Sciences, 3 avenue Robert Schuman, 13628 Aix-en-Provence (Office); La Bergerole, 2 chemin de Bibemus, 13100 Aix-en-Provence, France (Home). *Telephone:* 42-59-24-12 (Office).

De BEER, Zacharias Johannes, M.B., CH.B.; South African physician, business executive and politician; b. 11 Oct. 1928, Woodstock, Cape; s. of the late Dr. Z. J. De Beer and Jean De Beer; m. 1st Maureen Strauss 1952, 2nd Mona Schwartz 1965; one s. two d.; ed. Diocesan Coll., Rondebosch and Univ. of Cape Town; House Surgeon, Groote Schuur Hosp. 1952; Medical Practitioner 1953–59; mem. Parl. 1953–61, 1977–80 (Progressive Fed. Party, Leader 1988–); Dir. P. N. Barrett Co. (S. African Advertising Contractors) 1962–67; joined Anglo American Corpn. of S. Africa 1968, Man. 1970–72, mem. Bd. 1974–; Chair. Anglo American Corpn. of Cen. Africa Ltd.

1972–80, Anglo-American Properties 1980–; Chair. LTA Ltd.; Deputy Chair. Southern Life Asscn. Ltd. 1984–85, Chair. 1985–; Exec. Dir. Anglo American Corpn. (South Africa) Ltd. *Publication:* Multi-Racial South Africa: the Reconciliation of Forces 1960. *Leisure interests:* bridge, politics, tennis. *Address:* P.O. Box 6946, Johannesburg (Office); 39 Cotswold Drive, Saxonwold, Johannesburg, South Africa (Home). *Telephone:* 638-3459 (Office); 42-9778 (Home).

De BENEDETTI, Carlo; Italian company executive; b. 14 Nov. 1934, Turin; m. Margherita Crosetti 1960; three s.; ed. Turin Polytechnic; Chairman and Chief Exec. Officer, Gilardini 1972–76; Dir. Euromobiliare Finance Co. 1973–, Vice-Chair. 1977–; Vice-Chair. and C.E.O. Compagnia Industriali Riunite (CIR) 1976–; with FIAT 1976; C.E.O. and Vice-Chair. Ing. C. Olivetti & Co. S.p.A. April 1978–; Chair. Sept. 1983–; Dir. SMI S.p.A. 1983–; Vice-Chair. and C.E.O. Compagnia Finanziaria De Benedetti (Cofide) 1985–; Chair. Cerus (Paris) 1986–; Vice-Pres. Confindustria 1984–; mem. Int. Council, Morgan Guaranty Trust 1980–; Co-Chair. Council for U.S.A. and Italy; mem. Centre for Strategic and Int. Studies; Hon. LL.D. (Wesleyan Univ., Conn., U.S.A.) 1986; Cavaliere del Lavoro 1983, Officier, Légion d'honneur 1987. *Publications:* lectures and articles in business journals. *Address:* Ing. C. Olivetti & Co. S.p.A., via Jervis 77, 10015 Ivrea, Turin, Italy. *Telephone:* 0125-522011.

DEBEYRE, Guy Edouard Pierre Albert; French university professor; b. 6 Nov. 1911; ed. Lille Univ.; Prof. Faculty of Law and Economic Sciences, Univ. of Lille 1945–55, Dean 1950–55, Rector 1955–72; Conseiller d'Etat 1972–76; Prof. Univ. Paris 1972–81; Pres.-Hon. Cttee. for Econ. Expansion of the North and Pas de Calais 1956–; Deputy Mayor of Lille 1977–; Hon. Pres. Lille Tourist Office 1975–; Grand Officier, Légion d'honneur, Croix de guerre (1939–45), Hon. C.B.E. *Publications:* La responsabilité de la puissance publique en France et en Belgique 1936, Le Conseil d'Etat belge 1947, Traité de droit administratif 1954, Le droit public des français 1956. *Address:* Mairie de Lille, 59033 Lille (Office); 112 rue Meurein, 59800 Lille, France (Home). *Telephone:* 20.57.21.56 (Home).

de BOER, Thymen Jan, PH.D., R.A.; Netherlands professor of chemistry; b. 24 Feb. 1924, Grootegast; s. of Bouwe de Boer and Antje van der Weg; m. Eva M. M. Rink 1954; two d.; ed. Univ. of Groningen, Univ. Coll. and Kings Coll., London; scientific officer Univ. of Amsterdam 1954; Sr. lecturer in Organic Chemistry 1957, Prof. of Organic Chemistry 1960–86; Vice-Pres. Netherlands Royal Acad., Chair. Science Div. 1988–; Hon. mem. Royal Dutch Chemical Soc.; Shell Prize, Holleman Prize, Kt., Orde van de Nederlandse Leeuw. *Publications:* numerous articles in nat. and int. journals. *Leisure interests:* chess, bridge, piano music, tennis. *Address:* Gunterstein 36, 1081 CJ, Amsterdam, The Netherlands. *Telephone:* (020) 424142.

de BONO, Edward Francis Charles Publius, D.PHIL., PH.D.; British academic and author; b. 19 May 1933; s. of the late Prof. Joseph de Bono and of Josephine de Bono; m. Josephine Hall-White 1971; two s.; ed. St. Edward's Coll., Malta, Royal Univ. of Malta and Christ Church, Oxford; Research Asst., Univ. of Oxford 1958–60, Jr. Lecturer in Medicine 1960–61; Asst. Dir. of Research, Dept. of Investigative Medicine, Cambridge Univ. 1963–76, Lecturer in Medicine 1976–83; Dir. Cognitive Research Trust, Cambridge 1971–; Sec.-Gen. Supranational Independent Thinking Org. 1983–; f. Edward de Bono Nonprofit Foundation; Hon. Registrar St. Thomas' Hosp. Medical School, Harvard Medical School; Hon. Consultant Boston City Hosp. 1965–66; creator of two TV series: The Greatest Thinkers 1981, de Bono's Thinking Course 1982. *Publications include:* The Use of Lateral Thinking 1967, The Five-Day Course in Thinking 1968, The Mechanism of Mind 1969, Lateral Thinking: a textbook of creativity 1970, The Dog Exercising Machine 1970, Technology Today 1971, Practical Thinking 1971, Lateral Thinking for Management 1971, The Greatest Thinkers 1976, Wordpower 1977, Future Positive 1979, Atlas of Management Thinking 1981, de Bono's Thinking Course 1982, Conflicts: a better way to resolve them 1985, Six Thinking Hats 1985, Letter to Thinkers 1987, and numerous publs. in Nature, Lancet, etc. *Leisure interests:* travel, toys, thinking. *Address:* The Edward de Bono Nonprofit Foundation, P.O. Box 3297, Dublin 8, Ireland. *Telephone:* Dublin 251342.

DEBRAH, Ebenezer Moses, M.V.; Ghanaian diplomatist; b. 9 July 1928; ed. Mfantsipim School, Achimota School, Univ. Coll. of Gold Coast (now Ghana), London School of Econs.; apptd. Admin. Officer 1954, Foreign Service Officer 1955; posted to Ghana Embassy in Liberia 1955, Egypt 1959, U.S.A. 1960; at Ministry of Foreign Affairs 1962–63; Amb. to Ethiopia 1963–67, to U.S.A. 1967–72; Principal Sec. Ministry of Foreign Affairs 1972–73; Sec. to Nat. Redemption Council 1973–75, to Supreme Mil. Council 1975–77; High Commr. in Australia 1977–78, in the U.K. 1978–80; Leader Commonwealth Team to monitor Ugandan elections 1980; Consultant to Govt. of Zimbabwe on Foreign Service Training 1981–82; Hon. LL.D. (Wilberforce Univ., Cedar Crest Coll., Benedict Coll.); mem. Order of the Volta Civil Division. *Address:* c/o Ministry of Foreign Affairs, P.O. Box M53, Accra, Ghana.

DEBRÉ, Michel, D. en D.; French politician; b. 15 Jan. 1912, Paris; m. Anne Marie Lemaresquier 1936; four s.; ed. Lycée Louis-le-Grand and Faculty of Law, Univ. of Paris; Auditeur, Conseil d'Etat 1934; Commr. de la République, Angers region 1944; mem. Comm. for Reform of the Civil

Service 1945; attached to Saar Econ. Mission 1947; Sec.-Gen. German and Austrian Affairs, Ministry of Foreign Affairs 1948; elected Senator from Indre et Loire 1948, re-elected 1955, Deputy from St. Denis, Réunion 1963–, re-elected 1967, 1968, 1973, 1978, 1981, 1986; Mayor, Amboise 1966–; Keeper of the Seals 1958–59; Prime Minister Jan. 1959–April 1962; Minister of Economic Affairs and Finance 1966–68, of Foreign Affairs 1968–69, of Defence 1969–73; elected to European Parl. 1979; Officier Légion d'honneur, Croix de guerre, Rosette de la Résistance; Rassemblement pour la République (RPR). *Publications:* Refaire la France 1944, Demain la paix 1945, La République et son pouvoir 1950, La République et ses problèmes 1953, La mort de l'état républicain, Ces princes qui nous gouvernent 1957, Refaire une démocratie, un Etat, un pouvoir 1958, Au service de la nation 1963, France, quelle jeunesse te faut-il? 1965, Sur le gaullisme 1967, A la jeunesse 1969, Lettres à des militants sur la continuité, l'ouverture et la fidélité 1970, Une certaine idée de la France 1972, Combat pour les élections de 1973 1973, Une politique pour la Réunion 1974, Ami ou ennemi du peuple? 1975, Français, choisissons l'espoir 1979, Lettre ouverte aux Français sur la reconquête de la France, Peut-on lutter contre le chômage? 1982, Trois républiques pour une France (mémoires) 1984. *Address:* 20 rue Jacob, 75006 Paris; L'Epine Fleurie, 37270 Montlouis-sur-Loire, France.

DEBREU, Gerard, D.SC; American professor of economics and mathematics; b. 4 July 1921, Calais, France; s. of Camille and Fernande (née Decharne) Debreu; m. Françoise Bled 1945; two d.; ed. Ecole Normale Supérieure, Paris, and Univ. of Paris; Research Assoc. C.N.R.S. 1946–48, Cowles Comm. for Research in Econs., Univ. of Chicago 1950–55; Assoc. Prof. of Econs. Cowles Foundation for Research in Econs. Yale Univ. 1955–61; Prof. of Econs., Univ. of Calif., Berkeley 1962–, also of Mathematics 1975–, Faculty Research Lecturer 1984–85, Univ. Prof. 1985–, Class of 1958 Chair. 1986–; Fellow, American Acad. of Arts and Sciences; mem. N.A.S., American Philosophical Soc.; Pres. Econometric Soc. 1971; Distinguished Fellow, American Econ. Asscn. 1982; (Pres. elect 1989); Foreign Assoc. French Acad. of Sciences; Nobel Prize for Econ. Sciences 1983; Dr.h.c. (Bonn, Lausanne, Northwestern Univ., Toulouse, Yale, Bordeaux); Chevalier, Légion d'honneur 1976, Commdr. de l'Ordre Nat. du Mérite 1984. *Publications:* Theory of Value: An Axiomatic Analysis of Economic Equilibrium 1959, Mathematical Economics. Twenty Papers of Gerard Debreu 1983. *Address:* Department of Economics, University of California, 250 Barrows Hall, Berkeley, Calif. 94720, U.S.A. *Telephone:* (415) 642-7284; (415) 642-1955.

de BROGLIE, Prince Gabriel Marie Joseph Anselme; French administrator; b. 21 April 1931, Versailles; s. of Prince Edouard de Broglie and Princess Hélène Le Bas de Courmont; m. Diane de Bryas 1953; one s. one d.; ed. Ecole Saint-Martin de France, Faculté de droit de Paris and Inst. d'études politiques; Auditor Conseil d'Etat 1960, Counsel 1967–; Legal Adviser to Sec.-Gen., Interdepartmental Cttee. on matters of European econ. co-operation 1964; Tech. Adviser, Ministry of Social Affairs 1966–68, to Prime Minister 1968–69, Minister of State for Cultural Affairs 1970; Sec.-Gen. Office de Radiodiffusion-Télévision Française 1971, Asst. Dir.-Gen. 1973; Dir. Radio-France 1975–77, Dir.-Gen. 1978–; Pres. Inst. nat. de l'audiovisuel 1979–1981; mem. Haut Conseil de l'Audiovisuel 1972; Pres. Univ. Radiophonique et Télévisuelle Int. 1976–87; Vice-Pres., later Pres. TV Historical Cttee. 1980–; mem. Comm. Nat. de la Communication et des Libertés Oct. 1986–, Pres. Nov. 1986; Chevalier Légion d'honneur, Ordre nat. du Mérite, Cmmdr. des Arts et Lettres; Prix Rocheron (Acad. Française). *Publications include:* Le Général de Valence ou l'insouciance et la gloire 1972, Ségur sans cérémonie, ou la gaieté libertine 1977, L'histoire politique de la Revue des Deux Mondes 1979, L'Orléanisme, la ressource libérale de la France 1981, Une image vaut dix mille morts 1982, Madame de Genlis (Gobert Prize) 1985, Le français, pour qu'il vive 1986. *Address:* 96 rue de Grenelle, 75007 Paris, France (Home).

de BRUYNE, Dirk; Netherlands petroleum executive; b. 1 Sept. 1920, Rotterdam; m.; one s. one d.; ed. Erasmus Univ., Rotterdam; joined Shell Group 1945, worked in Finance Div. 1945–55; worked with group in Indonesia 1955–58, Treas. Indonesia 1957–58; Deputy Treas., London 1958–60; Finance Man., The Hague 1960–62; Finance Man. Shell Italiana 1962–64, Exec. Vice-Pres. 1964–65; Regional Co-ordinator (Oil) for Africa 1965–68; Gen. Man. Deutsche Shell 1968–70; Dir. of Finance, London 1970; Dir. Shell Petroleum Co. Ltd. 1970, Man. Dir. 1971; Dir. Shell Petroleum N.V. 1970, mem. Presidium of Bd. of Dirs. 1971–, Vice-Chair. 1976–; Dir. Shell Int. Petroleum Co, Ltd. 1970, Man. Dir. and Chair.; Dir. Shell Transport and Trading Co. Ltd. 1971–74; Man. Dir. N.V. Koninklijke Nederlandsche Petroleum Maatschappij (Royal Dutch Petroleum Co. Ltd.) 1974–77, Pres. 1977–82, Chair. Cttee. of Man. Dirs. 1979–82, Dir. (non-exec.) 1982–, Chair. Supervisory Bd. 1987–; Chair. Shell Oil Co., U.S.A. 1977–82; Dir. National Nederlanden NV 1982–; Dir. (non-exec.) Ocean Transport and Trading 1982–, Deputy Chair. 1983–; Chair. Supervisory Bd. Algemene Bank Nederland 1983–; Kt., Order of the Netherlands Lion, Commdr., Order of Orange Nassau, Hon. C.B.E. *Address:* 30 Carel van Bylandtlaan, 2596 HR The Hague, The Netherlands.

de BRUYNE, Norman Adrian, PH.D., F.R.S., F.ENG.; American physicist; b. 8 Nov. 1904, Punta Arenas, Chile; s. of Pieter Adriaan and Maud de Bruyne (née Mattock); m. Elma Lilian Marsh 1940; one s. one d.; ed. Lancing Coll., Sussex, England and Trinity Coll., Cambridge; Fellow,

Trinity Coll. 1928–40; Man. Dir. Aero Research Ltd. 1934–48; Man. Dir. Ciba (ARL) Ltd. 1948–60; Dir., Eastern Electricity Bd. 1962–67; Man. Dir. Techne (Cambridge) Ltd. 1964–67; Pres. Techne Inc. 1967–73, Chair. 1973–; Founder-Chair. Techne Corpn. 1986–; Fellow, Inst. of Physics, Royal Aeronautical Soc. *Publication:* Adhesion and Adhesives (with R. Houwink) 1951. *Leisure interest:* inventing. *Address:* 3700 Brunswick Pike, Princeton, N.J. 08540, U.S.A. *Telephone:* (609) 452-9275.

DEBU-BRIDEL, Jacques, L. EN D.; French writer and politician; b. 22 Aug. 1902, Mézières en Drouais; s. of Gabriel Debu and Ernestine Bridel; m. Marie-Adélaïde Pluzanski 1927 (deceased); two d.; ed. Colls. of Lausanne and Dreux, Faculty of Law, Sorbonne, Paris, and Ecole Libre des Sciences Politiques; Journalist with l'Eclair 1922; then with various publs., notably l'Avenir and Comédia; co-founder of Federalist review Latinité; wrote for l'Ordre for six years; mem. of Ligue des Patriotes and Union pour la Nation; Chief Sec. to Minister for Merchant Marine 1939; French Army 1940; Leader of Resistance in Occupied Zone; mem. of Organisation Civile et Militaire and of Front National; rep. of Nat. Republicans to Council of Resistance 1943–45; Provisional Sec.-Gen. for Navy 1945; mem. of Provisional Consultative Ass. and of Comms. for National Defence, Propaganda and Information; Dir. of journal Front National, resgnd. because of Communist domination 1945; mem. of R.P.F. (Gaulliste); Vice-Pres. Organizing Cttee. R.P.F. for the Seine; Paris Municipal Councillor 1947–48; Senator for the Seine 1948, re-elected 1952–58; mem. Paris Municipal Council 1953; founder Union Démocratique du Travail 1958; Chair. of Budget Cttee. for Fine Arts, Council of the Republic; Dir. of Paris Services, Radio Monte Carlo 1960–66, Dir. of Information 1966–69; Dir. of weekly Notre République 1966; Hon. Pres. France Terre d'Asile, A.N.A.C.R.; Médaille de la Résistance, Officier, Légion d'honneur, Croix de guerre. *Publications:* Novels: Jeunes ménages 1935 (Prix Interallié), Exil au grand palais 1948, Déroute 1945, Sous la cendre 1951, Frère esclave (new edn. 1957); Essays: Alphonse Daudet et la famille 1929, Alger 1930, La grande tragédie du monde animal 1955; Biographies: La Fayette 1945, Emily Brontë 1950, Fourier; general: Journées révolutionnaires de Paris, Vol. I 1960, Vol. II 1961, Vol. III, Conjuration d'Amboise 1963, 20,000 siècles de chasse à la pierre ou l'épopée du silex, La résistance intellectuelle De Gaulle contestataire, De Gaulle et le C.N.R, L'actualité de Charles Fourier, Un vieil homme et sa caniche 1980. *Leisure interests:* horses, dogs, knitting. *Address:* 15 rue des Barres, 75004 Paris, France (Home). *Telephone:* TUR 21-61.

de BUNSEN, Sir Bernard, Kt, C.M.G., M.A.; British educator and administrator; b. 1907, Cambridge; s. of the late L. H. G. de Bunsen and Victoria (née Buxton) de Bunsen; m. Joan Harmston, M.B.E. 1975; ed. Leighton Park School and Balliol Coll., Oxford; Schoolmaster, Liverpool Public Elementary Schools 1931–34; Asst. Dir. of Education, Wiltshire County Council 1934–38; H.M. Inspector of Schools, Ministry of Educ. 1938–46; Dir. of Educ., Palestine 1946–48; Prof. of Educ., Makerere Univ. Coll. 1948, Acting Prin. Aug. 1949, Prin. 1950–63; Vice-Chancellor, Univ. of East Africa 1963–65; Prin., Chester Coll., England 1966–71; Chair. Africa Educ. Trust 1966–87, Africa Bureau 1971–77, Council for Aid to African Students 1976, Noel Buxton Trust 1978–83; Vice-Pres., Anti-Slavery Soc. 1975–, Royal African Soc. 1977, Britain-Tanzania Soc. 1986–; Hon. LL.D. (Univ. of St. Andrews). *Address:* 3 Prince Arthur Road, London, N.W.3, England. *Telephone:* 01-435 3521.

DECARIS, Albert Marius Hippolyte; French artist; b. 6 May 1901, Sotteville-les-Rouen; m. Micheline Bousquet (deceased); one d.; ed. Ecole Estienne, Ecole Nationale Supérieure des Beaux-Arts; Frescoes, Int. Exhibition, Paris 1937, New York 1938, Town Hall, Vesoul; engravings and book illustrations; design of French and French Overseas postage stamps; Premier Grand Prix de Rome 1919; mem. Acad. des Beaux Arts 1943–, Pres. 1960, 1966, 1978, 1984; Pres. Inst. de France 1960; Officier, Légion d'honneur, Arts et Lettres; Croix de guerre (1939–45). *Address:* 3 quai Malaquais, 75006 Paris, France. *Telephone:* 354 8261.

DECAUX, Alain; French historian and TV producer; b. 23 July 1925, Lille; s. of Francis Decaux and Louise Tiprez; m. 1st Madeleine Parisy 1957; one d.; m. 2nd Micheline Pelletier 1983; one s. one d.; ed. Lycée Faidherbe, Lille, Lycée Janson-de-Sailly, Paris, and Univ. of Paris; journalist 1944–; historian 1947–; Minister Del. attached to the Minister for Foreign Affairs: Francophone Countries July 1988–; cr. radio programme La tribune de l'histoire with André Castelot, Colin-Simard, and later Jean-François Chiappe 1951; created T.V. programmes: La caméra explore le temps with Stellio Lorenzi and André Castelot 1956, Alain Decaux raconte 1969, L'histoire en question 1981, Le dossier d'Alain Decaux 1985; f. magazine L'histoire pour tous 1960; Pres. Groupement syndical des auteurs de télévision 1964–66, 1971–72; Vice-Chair. Société des auteurs et compositeurs dramatiques 1965–67, 1969–71, Chair. 1973–75; Dir. Société Técipress 1967–; Vice-Chair. Syndicat nat. des auteurs et compositeurs 1968–73; Dir. Librairie Plon 1969–72; Dir. Historia Magazine 1969–71; worked on various periodicals, including Les nouvelles littéraires, Le Figaro littéraire, Historia, Histoire pour tous, Miroir de l'histoire, Lecture pour tous; Chair. Centre d'animation culturelle des Halles et du Marais (Carré Thorigny) 1971–73; mem. Conseil supérieur des lettres 1971–; mem. Man. Cttee. Centre nat. des lettres 1974–75; elected to Académie Française 1979; Chair. Centre d'action culturelle de Paris 1981–; Chair. Société des amis d'Alexandre Dumas; prix d'histoire, Académie Française 1950, grande médaille d'or, Ville de Versailles 1954, grand prix du disque for Révolution française 1963, prix Plaisir de lire 1968, Oscar de la télévision et de la radio 1968, 1973, prix de la Critique de Télévision 1972, médaille de vermeil de la Ville de Paris 1973, prix littéraire de la Paulée de Meursault 1973; Officier, Légion d'honneur, Commdr. Ordre National du Mérite, Ordre des Arts et des Lettres. *Publications:* Louis XVII 1947, Letizia, mère de l'empereur 1949, La conspiration du général Malet 1952, La Castiglione, dame de coeur de l'Europe 1953, La belle histoire de Versailles 1954, De l'Atlantide à Mayerling 1954, Le prince impérial 1957, Offenbach, roi de Second Empire 1958, Amours Second Empire 1958, L'énigme Anastasia 1960, Les heures brillantes de la Côte d'Azur, Les grands mystères du passé 1964, Les dossiers secrets de l'histoire 1966, Grands secrets, grandes énigmes 1966, Nouveaux dossiers secrets 1967, Les Rosenberg ne doivent pas mourir (play) 1968, Grandes aventures de l'histoire 1968, Histoire des Françaises (2 vols.) 1972, Histoire de la France et des Français (with André Castelot, 13 vols.) 1970–74, Le cuirassé Potemkine (co-writer, play) 1975, Blanqui 1976, Les face à face de l'histoire 1977, Alain Decaux raconte (4 vols.) 1978, 1979, 1980, 1981, L'Histoire en question (2 vols.) 1982–83, Notre-Dame de Paris (co-writer, play) 1978, Danton et Robespierre (co-writer, play) 1979, Un homme nommé Jésus (co-writer, play) 1983, Victor Hugo (biog.) 1984, Les Assassins 1986, Le Pape pélerin 1986, Destins fabuleux 1987, Alain Decaux raconte l'Histoire de France aux enfants 1987, l'Affaire du Courrier de Lyon 1987, Alain Decaux raconte la Révolution Française aux enfants 1988, La Liberté ou la mort (co-writer) 1988. *Address:* 37 quai d'Orsay, 75700 Paris (Office); 86 boulevard Flandrin, 75116 Paris, France.

de CASTELLA, (François) Robert, M.B.E., B.SC.; Australian athlete and biophysicist; b. 27 Feb. 1957, Melbourne; s. of Rolet François de Castella and Ann M. Hall; m. Gayelene J. Clews 1980; one d.; ed. Xavier Coll., Kew, Monash Univ. and Swinburne Inst. of Tech.; winner, Fukuoka Marathon (world's fastest for out-and-back course) 1981; Marathon Champion, Commonwealth Games, Brisbane 1982; winner Rotterdam Marathon 1983; World Marathon Champion, Helsinki 1983; winner Boston Marathon 1986; winner Commonwealth Games 1986. *Publication:* de Castella on Running 1984. *Leisure interests:* music, relaxation, sports cars, tennis. *Address:* c/o Australian Institute of Sport, P.O. Box 176, Belconnen, A.C.T. 2616, Australia. *Telephone:* 062-521253.

De CONCINI, Dennis, LL.B.; American lawyer and politician; b. 8 May 1937, Tucson, Ariz.; s. of Evo and Ora DeConcini; m. Susan Margaret Hurley 1959; one s. two d.; ed. Univ. of Arizona and Univ. of Arizona Coll. of Law; Committeeman, Pima County 1958–76; worked with family law practice 1963–65; special counsel to Gov. of Ariz. 1965, Admin. Asst. to Gov. 1965–67; Partner, DeConcini & McDonald, law firm 1968–73; Pima County Attorney 1973–76; Admin., Ariz. Drug Control District 1975–76; fmr. mem. Ariz. Democratic Exec. Cttee., Vice-Chair. 1964, 1970; Senator from Arizona Jan. 1977–; mem. judiciary cttee., appropriations cttee., Rules cttee., Special Select Cttee. on Indian Affairs, Veterans' Affairs Cttee.; served U.S. Army 1959–60, Judge Advocate Gen. Corps. 1964–67; mem. Pima County Bar Asscn., Ariz. Bar Asscn., American Bar Asscn., American Judicature Soc., American Arbitration Asscn., Nat. District Attorneys' Asscn.; mem. Ariz. County Attorneys' and Sheriffs' Asscn., Sec.-Treas. 1975, Pres. 1976. *Leisure interests:* tennis, golf, boating. *Address:* 328 Hart Senate Building, Washington, D.C. 20510, U.S.A. (Office). *Telephone:* (202) 224-4521.

de COTRET, Hon. Robert René, P.C., M.B.A.; Canadian politician; b. 20 Feb. 1944, Ottawa; m. Diane Chénier 1966; two s. one d.; ed. Univs. of Ottawa and Michigan and McGill Univ., Montreal; teaching Fellow in banking, finance and corporate finance, Univ. of Michigan, Ann Arbor 1969–70; sr. staff economist, Council of Econ. Advisers, Washington, D.C. 1970–71; Adviser on monetary affairs, Dept. of Finance, Ottawa 1971–72; Dir. of business econs., The Conference Bd. in Canada 1972–74, Vice-Pres. and Dir. of Applied Econ. Research and Information Centre 1974–75, Vice-Pres. and Dir. of Research 1975–76, Pres. Conf. Bd. 1976–78; mem. House of Commons 1978–79, mem. Senate 1979–; Minister of Industry, Trade and Commerce and Minister of State for Econ. Devt. 1979–80; Pres. Treasury Bd. 1984–87, Jan. 1989–, Minister of Regional Industrial Expansion and Minister of State for Science and Tech. 1987–89; Exec. Vice-Pres. Int., Nat. Bank of Canada 1982–84; Progressive Conservative. *Leisure interests:* skiing, summer cottage, billiards. *Address:* Place Bell Canada, 160 Elgin Street, Ottawa, Ont. K1A 0G5 (Office); 39 First Avenue, Ottawa, Ont., Canada (Home).

DECOURTRAY, H.E. Cardinal Albert; French ecclesiastic; b. 9 April 1923, Wattignies, Lille; ordained 1947; consecrated Bishop (Titular Church of Ippona Zárito) 1971, of Dijon 1974; Archbishop of Lyons 1981; cr. Cardinal 1985; Prelate of Mission de France; Chair. French Episcopal Conf. 1987. *Address:* Archevêché, 1 Place de Fourvière, 69321 Lyon Cédex 1, France. *Telephone:* 78-25-12-27.

DeCRANE, Alfred C., Jr.; American business executive; b. 11 June 1931, Cleveland, Ohio; m. Joan Elizabeth Hoffman 1954; one s. five d.; ed. Notre Dame and Georgetown Univs.; attorney, Texaco Inc., Houston and New York 1959, Asst. to Vice-Chair. 1965, to Chair. 1967, Gen. Man. Producing Dept., Eastern Hemisphere 1968, Vice-Pres. 1970, Sr. Vice-Pres. and Gen.

Counsel 1976, mem. Bd. of Dirs. 1977–, Exec. Vice-Pres. 1978–83, Pres. 1983–86, Chair. Jan. 1987–; mem. Bd. of Dirs., Arabian American Oil Co., CIGNA Corpn.; mem. Council of Arts and Letters, Notre Dame Univ.; Trustee, American Univ. of Beirut. *Address:* Texaco Inc., 2000 Westchester Avenue, White Plains, N.Y. 10650, U.S.A. *Telephone:* (914) 253-4000.

DEDEURWAERDER, Jose Joseph, B.S.(ENG.); Belgian business executive; b. 31 Dec. 1932, Halle; s. of Louis and Philippine (Paternot) Dedeurwaerder; m. Nelly Clemens 1955; one d.; ed. Ecole Technique Supérieure de Schaerbeek; Man. Dir. Renault Belgium 1958–67; Industrial Dir. Renault Argentina 1967–73; C.E.O. Renault Mexico 1973–76; Dir. Douai (France) ass. plant 1976–81; Exec. Vice-Pres., Dir. American Motors Corpn., Southfield, Mich. 1981–82, Pres. and C.O.O. 1982–84, Pres. and C.E.O. 1984–. *Address:* American Motors Corporation, 27777 Franklin Road, Southfield, Mich. 48034, U.S.A.

DÉDÉYAN, Charles, D. ÈS L; French university professor; b. 4 April 1910, Smyrna, Turkey; s. of Prince and Princess Dédéyan (née Emma Elisabeth Ekisler); m. Phyllis Sivrisarian 1938; four s. one d.; ed. Coll. Notre Dame de Ste. Croix, Neuilly and Sorbonne; Reader in French Literature, Univ. of Rennes 1942; Prof. of French and Comparative Literature, Univ. of Lyons 1945; Prof. of Comparative Literature at the Sorbonne 1949–; Sec.-Gen. Int. Fed. of Modern Languages and Literatures 1946–54; Dir. Inst. of Comparative Modern Literature, Sorbonne 1955–68, 1971; ed. of Encyclopédie permanente Clartés 1961–, and Revue des Etudes Gaulliennes. *Publications:* La "Sophonisbe" de Mairet 1945, Montaigne chez ses amis anglo-saxons 1946, Essai sur le journal de voyage de Montaigne 1946, Le journal de voyage de Montaigne 1947, Argile 1947, Studies in Marivaux, Stendhal, Du Fail, Balzac, V. Hugo 1950–53, Le thème de Faust dans la littérature européenne 1954–67, Madame de Lafayette, La nouvelle Héloïse, Stendhal et les Chroniques italiennes 1955, Voltaire et la pensée anglaise 1956, Le "Gil Blas" de Le Sage 1956, 1965, Gérard de Nerval et l'Allemagne 1957–59, L'Angleterre dans la pensée de Diderot 1959, Dante en Angleterre 1958–66, "Le Roman Comique" de Scarron 1959, Rilke et la France 1961, L'influence de Rousseau sur la sensibilité européenne à la fin du XVIIIe. siècle 1961, Stendhal chroniqueur 1962, Victor Hugo et l'Allemagne 1963, 1965, 1967, L'Italie dans l'oeuvre romanesque de Stendhal 1963, Le cosmopolitisme littéraire de Charles Du Bos 1968–70, Racine et sa "Phèdre" 1968, Le nouveau mal du siècle de Baudelaire à nos jours 1968–72, Une guerre dans le mal des hommes 1971, Chateaubriand et Rousseau 1972, Le cosmopolitisme européen sous la Révolution et l'Empire 1976, L'Arioste en France 1975–76, Lamartine et la Toscane 1978, Giorgione dans les lettres françaises 1979, Le Drame Romantique en Europe 1982, Dante dans le romantisme anglais 1983, Le Roman comique de Scarron 1983, Le critique en voyage 1985, Diderot et la Pensée anglaise 1986, Montesquieu ou l'Alibi persan 1987, Le Retour de Salente ou Voltaire et l'Angleterre 1988. *Leisure interest:* fine arts. *Address:* 27 rue de la Ferme, Neuilly-sur-Seine; Manoir de La Motte, 35780 La Richardais, France. *Telephone:* 4747-83-84 and 99-88-52-50.

DEDIJER, Vladimir, DR.IURIS, M.A.; Yugoslav writer; b. 4 Feb. 1914, Belgrade; m. 1st Olga Popović 1943, 2nd Vera Križman 1944; one s. two d.; ed. Belgrade Univ.; Lieut.-Col. in Tito's army, Second World War; Yugoslav Del. to U.N. Gen Assemblies 1945, 1946, 1948, 1949, 1951, 1952; mem. Yugoslav Del. to Peace Conf., Paris 1946; mem. Cen. Cttee. League of Communists of Yugoslavia 1952–54; Prof. of Modern History, Belgrade Univ. 1954–55; defended right of M. Djilas to free speech 1954; expelled from Cen. Cttee. of League of Communists 1954; sentenced to 6 months on probation 1955; Simon Sr. Fellow, Manchester Univ. 1960–62, now Hon. Fellow; Fellow of St. Antony's Coll., Oxford 1962–63; Research Assoc., Harvard Univ. 1963–64; Visiting Prof. Cornell Univ. 1964–65, Mass. Inst. of Technology 1969, Brandeis Univ. 1970–71; Pres. Bertrand Russell's Int. War Crimes Tribunal 1966; mem. Serbian Acad. of Sciences and Arts 1968–; Order of Liberation of Yugoslavia. *Publications:* Partisan Diary 1945, Notes from the United States 1945, Paris Peace Conference 1948, Yugoslav-Albanian Relations 1949, Tito 1952, The Beloved Land 1962, Sarajevo 1963, The Battle Stalin Lost 1969, History of Yugoslavia 1973, New Documents for Tito's Biography 1982; contrib. to Acta Scandinavica. *Leisure interests:* ping-pong, fortune-telling. *Address:* 52395 Savudrija, Yugoslavia. *Telephone:* 053-59504.

de DUVE, Christian René, M.D., M.SC.; Belgian scientist; b. 2 Oct. 1917, Thames Ditton, England; s. of Alphonse de Duve and Madeleine Pungs; m. Janine Herman 1943; two s. two d.; ed. Univ. of Louvain; Prof. of Physiol. Chemistry, Univ. of Louvain Medical School 1947–85; Prof. of Biochemical Cytology, Rockefeller Univ., New York City 1962–88; Pres. Int. Inst. of Cellular and Molecular Pathology, Brussels; mem. Royal Acad. of Medicine (Belgium), Royal Acad. of Belgium, American Chem. Soc., Biochem. Soc., American Soc. of Biol. Chem., Pontifical Acad. of Sciences, American Soc. of Cell Biology, Deutsche Akademie der Naturforschung, Leopoldina, Koninklijke Akademie voor Geneeskunde van België, etc.; Foreign mem. American Acad. of Arts and Sciences, Royal Soc., London; Foreign assoc. N.A.S., U.S.A.; Hon. D.Sc. (Keele Univ.) 1981; Hon. D.C.L. (Kent) 1988; Prix des Alumni 1949; Prix Pfizer 1957; Prix Franqui 1960; Prix Quinquennal Belge des Sciences Médicales 1967; Gairdner Foundation Int. Award of Merit (Canada) 1967; Dr. H. P. Heineken Prijs (Netherlands) 1973; Nobel Prize for Medicine 1974. *Leisure interests:* tennis, skiing, bridge. *Address:* 80 Central Park West, New York, N.Y. 10023, U.S.A.; Le Pré St. Jean, 5988 Nethen, Belgium. *Telephone:* (212)-724-8048 (U.S.A.); (010)-866628 (Belgium).

DEEDES, Baron (Life Peer), cr. 1986, of Aldington in the County of Kent; **William Francis Deedes,** P.C., M.C.; British fmr. politician and newspaper editor; b. 1 June 1913, Aldington, Kent; m. Evelyn Hilary Branfoot 1942; two s. (one deceased) three d.; ed. Harrow School; M.P. for Ashford (Kent) 1950-74; Parl. Sec., Ministry of Housing and Local Govt. 1954-55; Parl. Under-Sec. Home Dept. 1955-57; Deputy Lieut., Kent 1962; Minister without Portfolio (Information) July 1962-64; mem. Advisory Cttee. on Drug Dependence 1967-74; Chair. Select Cttee. on Immigration and Race Relations 1970-74; Ed. Daily Telegraph 1974-86; Hon. D.C.L. (Kent) 1988. *Address:* New Hayters, Aldington, Kent, England. *Telephone:* Aldington 269.

DEER, William Alexander, M.SC., PH.D., F.R.S.; British mineralogist and petrologist; b. 26 Oct. 1910, Manchester; s. of William Deer and the late Davina Cunningham; m. 1st Margaret Marjorie Kidd 1939 (died 1971), 2nd Rita Tagg 1973; two s. one d.; ed. elementary and Central High School, Manchester, and Univs. of Manchester and Cambridge; lecturer, Univ. of Manchester 1937-39; Senior 1851 Research Fellow 1939-40; Research Fellow, St. John's Coll., Cambridge 1939-47; served War of 1939-45, Royal Engs. (Lieut.-Col.); Demonstrator, Mineralogy Dept., Cambridge Univ. 1946-50; Tutor, St. John's Coll. 1948-50; Prof. of Geology, Manchester Univ. 1950-61; Prof. of Mineralogy and Petrology, Cambridge Univ. 1961-78, Prof. Emer. 1978-; Master of Trinity Hall, Cambridge 1966-75; Vice-Chancellor, Cambridge Univ. 1971-73; mem. Natural Environment Research Council 1968-71; Pres. Mineralogical Soc. 1968-70; Pres. Geological Soc. 1969-71; Greenland expeditions 1935, 1936, 1953, 1966; Hon. Fellow, St. John's Coll., Cambridge, Trinity Hall, Cambridge; Trustee, British Museum 1966-75; Hon. D.Sc. (Aberdeen) 1983; Daniel Pigeon Prize and Murchison Medal of Geological Soc., London; Bruce Medal of Royal Soc. of Edinburgh. *Publications:* Carsphairn Igneous Complex 1935, Petrology of the Skaergaard Intrusion, East Greenland (with L. R. Wager) 1939, Rock Forming Minerals 5 vols. (with R. A. Howie and J. Zussman) 1962-63, Petrology and Mineralogy of the Kangerdlugssuaq Alkaline Intrusion (with Dr. C. Kempe) 1970. *Leisure interests:* bassoon, music. *Address:* 82 New Road, Haslingfield, Cambridge, England. *Telephone:* 871602.

DEES, Bowen Causey, PH.D.; American science administrator; b. 20 July 1917, Batesville, Miss.; s. of John S. and Ida Lea (Causey) Dees; m. Sarah E. Sanders 1937; one d.; ed. Mississippi High Schools, Mississippi Coll., New York Univ.; Graduate Asst., New York Univ. 1937-42, Instructor in Physics 1942-43; Prof. of Physics, Mississippi Coll. 1943-44; Instructor in Electrical Communications, Radar School, M.I.T. 1944-45; Asst. Prof. of Physics, Rensselaer Polytechnic Inst. 1945-47; Physicist to Div. Dir., Scientific and Technical Div., Gen. H.Q., Supreme Commdr. for the Allied Powers, Tokyo 1947-51; Program Dir. for Fellowships, Nat. Science Foundation 1951-56; Deputy Asst. Dir. for Scientific Personnel and Educ. 1956-59, Asst. Dir. 1959-63; Assoc. Dir. for Educ. 1963-64, for Planning 1963-66; Vice-Pres. Univ. of Arizona 1966-68, Provost for Academic Affairs 1968-70; mem. Science Manpower Comm., Washington 1976-79; Pres. The Franklin Inst. 1970-82; U.S. Co-Chair. U.S.-Japan Comm. on Scientific Co-operation 1981-88; Hon. LL.D (Lehigh Univ.) 1976, Hon. D.Sc. (Temple Univ.) 1981. *Publications:* Fundamentals of Physics 1945; articles in educational and scientific journals. *Leisure interests:* photography, handicrafts. *Address:* 140 N. Camino Miramonte, Tucson, Ariz. 85716, U.S.A. (Home); *Telephone:* (602) 325-6064.

DEETMAN, Willem Joost, DR.POL.SC.; Netherlands politician; b. 3 April 1945, The Hague; s. of Egbert J. Deetman and G. Deetman-Scholten; m. Grietje T. Dijkstra 1970; one s. one d.; ed. Free Univ., Amsterdam; Dir. Pre-Univ. and Gen. Educ. Dept., Christian-Protestant Educ. Council 1968-78; mem. Second Chamber, States-Gen. (Parl.) 1978-81; State Sec. of Educ. and Science 1981-82; Minister of Educ. and Sciences 1982-. *Address:* Ministry of Education and Sciences, Europaweg 4, P.O. Box 25000, 2700 LZ Zoetemeer (Office); Blommesteisingel 54, 2804 EH Gouda, The Netherlands (Home). *Telephone:* 079-532884 (Office).

de FERRANTI, Sebastian Ziani; British electrical engineer; b. 5 Oct. 1927, Alderley Edge, Cheshire; s. of late Sir Vincent and of Lady de Ferranti (née Wilson); brother of Basil Reginald Vincent Ziani de Ferranti (q.v.); m. 1st Mona Helen Cunningham 1953; one s. two d.; m. 2nd Naomi Angela Rae 1983; ed. Ampleforth Coll.; served 4th/7th Dragoon Guards 1947-49; Brown Boveri, Switzerland and Alsthom, France 1948-50; Transformer Dept., Ferranti Ltd. 1950, Dir. 1954-82, Man. Dir. 1958-75, Chair. 1963-82; Dir. GEC PLC 1982-; Pres. BEAMA 1969-70, Manchester and Region Centre for Educ. in Science, Educ. and Tech. 1972-78; Chair. Inst. Electrical Assen. 1970-73; Vice-Pres. R.S.A. 1980-84; Commr. Royal Comm. for Exhbn. of 1851 1984-; Dir. Nat. Nuclear Corpn. 1984-; mem. Nat. Defence Industries Council 1969-77; Trustee, Tate Gallery 1971-78; Chair. North-West Civic Trust 1978-83; Hon. D.Sc. (Salford Univ.); Hon. Fellow, Manchester Univ. Inst. of Science and Tech.; Granada Guildhall Lecture 1966; Royal Inst. Discourse 1969; Louis Blériot Lecture, Paris 1970; Faraday Lecture 1970, 1971; Hon. D.Sc., Cranfield Inst. of Tech. 1973. *Address:* Henbury Hall, Macclesfield, Cheshire, England (Home). *Telephone:* 0625-22101.

DEFLASSIEUX, Jean Sébastien; French banker; b. 11 July 1925, Cap-d'Ail; s. of Alexis and Thérèse (née Dalmasso) Deflassieux; m. Christiane Orabona 1950; one s.; ed. Lycée de Monaco, Lycée Janson-de-Sailly, Law Faculty, Paris, London School of Econs., and Ecole d'organisation scientifique du travail; mem. Bd. of Dirs. for financial studies, Crédit lyonnais 1948-54, Man. of branch office 1954-56; attached to Cabinet of Jean Filippi (Sec. of State for the Budget) 1956-57 and of Arthur Conte (Sec. of State for Industry) 1957; Insp. of Paris branch offices, Crédit lyonnais 1958; Man. and Sub-Dir. Haute-Banque 1959-69, Dir of External Commerce 1969-72, of Int. Affairs 1972-, in charge of the Cen. Man. of Int. Affairs 1978-82; mem. man. cttee. Crédit Lyonnais 1972, Gen. Administrator 1982, Chair. 1982-86, Hon. Chair. 1986-; Chair. Int. Exchange Bank 1980-, Euralille 1988; Vice-Pres. Union de Banques Arabes et Françaises, Crédit Franco-Portugais 1973, Gulf Riyad Bank 1978-; Admin. East Asiatic Holding Co. 1972- and of numerous banks and other cos.; Pres. European League for Econ. Co-operation 1983; Councillor for External Trade for France 1959; Officier, Légion d'honneur, Officier, Ordre Nat. du Mérite, Croix de Guerre 1939-45, Chevalier des Palmes Academiques. *Leisure interest:* swimming. *Address:* 55 avenue Kléber, 75116 Paris (Office); 41 rue Vineuse, 75016 Paris, France (Home).

DEGA, Wiktor, M.D.; Polish surgeon, orthopaedist and educator; b. 7 Dec. 1896, Poznań; s. of Wiktor and Zofia D.; m. Maria Zelewska 1928; one s. two d.; ed. Berlin, Warsaw and Poznań Univs.; Asst.-Resident, Orthopaedic Clinic of Poznań Univ. 1924-30; Chief Asst., Orthopaedic Inst., Poznań 1930-37; Head Orthopaedic Dept. Municipal Hosp., Bydgoszcz 1938-39; Head Children's Surgery Dept., Karol and Maria Hosp., Warsaw 1940-45; Dir. Orthopaedic Clinic, Univ. and Medical Acad., Poznań 1945-67, Prof. Emer. 1967-; mem. Presidium All-Poland Cttee. of Nat. Unity Front June 1971-80; Chair. Polish Soc. for Rehabilitation, until 1960, Hon. Chair 1977-; mem. Polish Acad. of Sciences, Vice-Chair. Cttee. for Rehabilitation and Adaptation of Man 1971-82; mem. Int. Soc. of Orthopaedics and Traumatology, Int. Soc. of Surgeons, Int. Soc. of Brain Palsy, Polish Soc. of Surgeons; Hon. mem. Austrian, Czechoslovak, F.R.G., Finnish, French, G.D.R., Hungarian, Soviet, Polish, Yugoslav, Bulgarian Soc. of Orthopaedics and Traumatology, Polish Soc. of Rheumatology, Polish Medical Soc., Polish Medical Alliance U.S.A.; Polish Soc. of Friends of Sciences; Fed. German Orthopaedic Assen.; corresp. mem. American Acad. of Orthopaedic Surgery, Italian Soc. Orthopaedics and Traumatology; foreign mem. French Acad. Surgeons; fmr. Expert on Rehabilitation Affairs WHO; Dr. h.c. Medical Acad., Poznań 1969, Cracow 1974, Wrocław 1973, Łódź 1977, and Halle-Wittenberg 1977; Dr. h.c. Acad. of Physical Education, Poznań 1979; State Prizes 1951, 1968, (Special) 1979; Albert Lasker Prize 1966; Alfred Jurzvkowski Award, U.S.A. 1973; Order of Builders of People's Poland, Officer's and Commdr.'s Cross with Star of Order Polonia Restituta, Order of Banner of Labour (1st Class), Medal of Chief Cttee. for Physical Culture and Tourism 1977, Hon. Meritorious Physician of People's Poland 1979 and other awards. *Publications:* books, monographs and numerous articles in professional journals. *Leisure interests:* travelling, music. *Address:* ul. 28 Czerwca 1956 nr 135/147, 61-544 Poznań, Poland (Home). *Telephone:* 333-366.

de GAAY FORTMAN, Wilhelm Friedrich; Netherlands politician; b. 8 May 1911, Amsterdam; s. of Bastiaan and Elisabeth (Nolte) de Gaay Fortman; m. Margaretha Titia Hillegonda Woltjar 1936; two s. three d.; ed. Gymnasium Dordrecht, Reformed Gymnasium, Amsterdam, and Free Univ. Amsterdam; Special agricultural Office, Ministry of Econ. Affairs 1934-38; with Ministry of Social Affairs, later Head Industrial Relations Div. 1938-47; Principal, Nat. Protestant Trade Union Cadre Training Centre 1948-72; Prof. of Civil Law and Labour Law, Free Univ. of Amsterdam 1947, Rector 1962-63, 1965-72; Chamberlain (Extraordinary) to the Queen 1955; mem. Parl. (First Chamber) 1960-73, 1977-, Second Vice-Chair. First Chamber 1969; Party Leader in Chamber 1971; Minister for Home Affairs 1973-77; mem. Royal Comm. on Civil Law 1947, European Comm. of Human Rights 1965, Vice-Chair. 1972; mem. Bd. Netherlands Org. for the Advancement of Fundamental Research (ZWO) 1960-73; numerous church activities; Kt., Order of Netherlands Lion 1959, Commdr. Order of Orange-Nassau 1972; Medal for Energy and Ingenuity, Order of the House of Orange 1974. *Publications:* De onderneming in het arbeidsrecht 1936, De arbeider in de nieuwe samenleving 1952, De vakbeweging 1954, Recht doen 1972. *Address:* Zuidwerfplein 7, 2594 CV The Hague, Netherlands. *Telephone:* 070-850750.

DEGAZON, Frederick; Dominican politician; Speaker, House of Ass. until 1978; Pres. of Dominica 1978-79. *Address:* c/o Office of the President, Roseau, Dominica.

De GEER, Carl; Swedish diplomatist; b. 4 Jan 1923, Lund; m. Berit Jacoboson 1946; two s.; entered Swedish Foreign Service 1946, posted in Berlin, Paris and Washington 1948-67; Head of Econ. and Commercial Dept., Foreign Office 1970, Deputy Sec.-Gen. 1972; Amb. to the Int. Orgs., Geneva 1975-79; Amb. to U.S.S.R. 1979-82, to Denmark 1984-88. *Address:* c/o Ministry of Foreign Affairs, Gustav Adolfs torg 1, P.O. Box 16121, 103 23 Stockholm, Sweden.

DEGENHARDT, Johannes Joachim, DR.THEOL.; German ecclesiastic; b. 31 Jan. 1926, Schwelm; s. of Julius and Elfriede Degenhardt; ed. Albrecht Dürer Gymnasium, Hagen, and theological studies in Paderborn, Munich,

Münster and Würzburg; ordained in Paderborn 1951; subsequently student chaplain, Pädagogische Hochschule, Paderborn, and Bezirksdekan, Hochstift Paderborn; Bishop of Paderborn 1968, Archbishop 1974–; Chair. of Educ. Comm., Conf. of German Bishops. *Publication:* Lukas, Evangelist der Armen 1966. *Address:* Kamp 38, 4790 Paderborn, Federal Republic of Germany. *Telephone:* 20 73 27.

DEGENHART, Bernhard, DR. PHIL.; German art historian; b. 4 May 1907, Munich; s. of Max Degenhart and Matilde (née Raila) Degenhart; ed. Univs. of Munich, Vienna, Berlin; with Munich State Museums 1931–32; Asst. Bibliotheca Hertziana, Rome 1933–39; with Kustos Museum Albertina, Vienna 1940–46; Keeper Staatliche Graphische Sammlung (Print Room Munich) 1949–71; prizes include Medaglia ai Benemeriti della Cultura, Rome 1957, Premio Internazionale Galileo Galilei, University Pisa 1976; Dr. h.c. (Munich) 1972; mem. Accademia Nazionale di San Luca, Rome 1973, Akademie der Schönen Künste, Munich 1973, Accademia Marchigiana di scienze ed arti, Ancona 1979, Accademia degli Intronati, Siena 1980, Bayerische Maximiliansorden für Kunst und Wissenschaft 1984, Bayerische Akademie der Wissenschaften 1985, Accademia Ateneo Veneto, Venice 1986. *Publications:* Corpus der ital. Zeichnungen 1300–1450 (with Annegrit Schmitt), Parts 1-8 1968–82, Graphologie der ital. Handzeichnung 1937, Pisanello 1941, Europäische Handzeichnungen 1943, Jacopo Bellini 1984. *Leisure interest:* Italian drawings. *Address:* Meiserstrasse 10, D-8 Munich 2, Federal Republic of Germany.

DE GREY, Roger, P.R.A.; British artist and teacher; b. 18 April 1918; s. of Nigel de Grey and Florence Emily Frances (née Gore); m. Flavia Hatt (née Irwin) 1942; two s. one d.; ed. Eton Coll. and Chelsea School of Art, London; served in army 1939–45; Lecturer, Dept. of Fine Art, King's Coll., Newcastle upon Tyne 1947–51, Master of Painting 1951–53; Sr. Tutor, later Reader in Painting, R.C.A. 1953–73; Prin. City and Guilds of London Art School 1973–; Treasurer, R.A. 1976, Pres. 1985–; pictures in public collections including Arts Council of G.B., Contemporary Arts Soc., Chantrey Bequest, Queensland Gallery, Brisbane, Australia; Hon. A.R.C.A. 1959. *Address:* City and Guilds of London Art School, 124 Kennington Park Road, London, SW11 4DJ; 5 Camer Street, Meopham, Kent, England (Home). *Telephone:* 01-735 2306 (Office); Meopham 2327 (Home).

de GROOTE, Jacques, M.A. (ECON.); Belgian international finance official; b. 25 May 1927, Klerken; m. Jacqueline Wigny 1955; three d.; ed. Cambridge and Louvain Univs.; Adviser Nat. Bank of Belgium 1957–65; Prof. of Econs, Univ. of Namur 1963–; Adviser to Gov. of Nat. Bank of Zaire 1966–69; Financial Adviser to Belgian Del. to OECD 1965–71; Chief Adviser, Research Dept., Nat. Bank of Belgium 1971–73; Exec. Dir. Int. Bank for Reconstruction and Devt. (World Bank) and Int. Monetary Fund 1973–; Grand Officier Order of Leopold II (Belgium), and numerous others. *Leisure interests:* gardening, bird-watching. *Address:* 700 19th Street, N.W., Washington, D.C. 20431, U.S.A. (Office); 11 avenue de Mercure, 1180 Brussels, Belgium (Home). *Telephone:* (202) 623 4590 (Office).

DEGTYAR, Dmitriy Danilovich; Soviet diplomatist and politician; b. 1904; ed. Moscow Planning Inst. Trade Union activity 1935–38; State Exec. 1938–39; Chair. State Planning Cttee. of the R.S.F.S.R. 1939–47; Vice-Chair. U.S.S.R. State Planning Comm. 1949–53; Vice-Chair. Council of Ministers of the R.S.F.S.R. 1939–47; mem. later Deputy Chair. State Cttee. for Foreign Econ. Affairs 1957–62; Amb. to Guinea 1962–64; Deputy Chair. State Cttee. for Foreign Econ. Affairs 1965–. *Address:* State Cttee. for Foreign Economic Affairs, Ovchinnikovskaya nab. 18/1, Moscow, U.S.S.R. (Office).

DEHAENE, Jean-Luc; Belgian politician; b. 7 Aug. 1940, Montpellier; m.; four c.; ed. Univ. of Namur; adviser to various govt. ministries 1972–81; Minister of Social Affairs and Institutional Reforms 1981–88; Prime Minister and Minister of Communications and Institutional Reforms 1988–; Co-opted Senator 1982–. *Address:* Ministry of Communications, 65 rue de la Loi, 1040 Brussels, Belgium. *Telephone:* (02) 237-67-11.

de HAVILLAND, Olivia Mary; American (b. British) actress; b. 1 July 1916, Tokyo, Japan; d. of Walter Augustus de Havilland and Lilian Augusta (née Ruse); m. 1st Marcus Aurelius Goodrich 1946 (divorced 1953), one s.; m. 2nd Pierre Paul Galante 1955 (divorced 1979), one d.; ed. Saratoga Grammar School, Notre Dame Convent, Los Gatos Union High School; stage debut in A Midsummer Night's Dream 1934, film debut in screen version 1935; Pres. Cannes Film Festival 1965; on lecture tours in U.S.A. 1971–80; mem. Bd. of Trustees of American Coll. in Paris 1970–71, of American Library in Paris 1974–81; mem. Altar Guild, Lay Reader, American Cathedral in Paris 1971–81; numerous awards include: Acad. Award 1946, 1949; New York Critics Award 1948, 1949; Look Magazine Award 1941, 1946, 1949; Venice Film Festival Award 1948; Filmex Tribute 1978; American Acad. of Achievement Award 1978; American Exemplar Medal 1980, Golden Globe 1988. *Films include:* Captain Blood 1935, Anthony Adverse 1936, The Adventures of Robin Hood 1938, Gone with the Wind 1939, Hold Back the Dawn 1941, Princess O'Rourke 1942, To Each His Own (Acad. Award) 1946, The Dark Mirror 1946, The Snake Pit 1947, The Heiress (Acad. Award) 1949, My Cousin Rachel 1952, Not as a Stranger 1954, The Proud Rebel 1957, The Light in the Piazza 1961, Lady in a Cage 1963, Hush Hush Sweet Charlotte 1964, The Adventurers 1968, Airport '77 1976, The Swarm 1978; *Plays:* Romeo and Juliet 1951, Candida 1951–52,

A Gift of Time 1962; *TV:* Noon Wine 1966, Screaming Woman 1972, Roots, The Next Generations 1979, Murder is Easy 1981, Charles and Diana: A Royal Romance, 1982, North and South II 1986, Anastasia 1986 (Golden Globe Award), The Woman He Loved 1987. *Publication:* Every Frenchman Has One 1962. *Leisure interests:* crossword puzzles, reading tales of mystery and imagination, painting on Sunday. *Address:* B.P. 156, 75764 Paris Cedex 16, France.

DEHAYE, Pierre, L. EN D.; French administrator (retd.); b. 24 May 1921, St. Pol-sur-Mer; s. of Charles Dehaye and Thérèse (née Bonjour) Dehaye; m. Jacqueline Petit 1965 (deceased); two d.; ed. Collège municipal Pontoise, Faculté de Droit, Paris; Asst. Dir. Ministry of Finance 1954–60, Head of Service 1960–66; Dir. for Money and Medals at French Mint 1962–84; Pres. Société d'aide technique et de coopération (SATEC) 1964–82, Société d'encouragement aux métiers d'art 1976, 1981; mem. Council of Admin. ORTF 1970–72; mem. de l'Inst. de France (Acad. des Beaux Arts) 1975–, Royal Belgian Acad. of Science, Letters and Arts 1972–, Hon. mem. Worshipful Co. of Goldsmiths, London 1975–; Officier Légion d'Honneur, Commdr. Ordre des Arts et Lettres, Commdr. Ordre d'Isabelle la Catholique, Officier Ordre de Léopold de Belgique. *Publications:* Naître est une longue patience 1979, Parabole (poems) 1980, Un même mystère 1985, André Jacquemin, graveur 1986. *Address:* 45 rue Saint-Ferdinand, 75017 Paris, France.

DEHEM, Roger Jules, PH.D., F.R.S.C.; Belgian professor of economics; b. 24 July 1921, Wemmel; s. of Charles Dehem and Elise (née Masschelein) Dehem; m. Gertrude Montbleau 1950; two s. four d.; ed. Univ. of Louvain; Lecturer McGill Univ. 1947–49, Prof. Univ. of Montreal 1948–58; Prin. Admin. OEEC 1958–59; Economist Adv. Fabrimétal, Brussels 1959–60; Prof. Economics Laval Univ., Quebec 1961–; Fellow Rockefeller Foundation 1946–48; Pres. Canadian Econ. Assen. 1973–74. *Publications:* L'efficacité sociale du système économique 1952, Traité d'analyse économique 1957, L'utopie de l'économiste 1969, L'équilibre économique international 1970, De l'étalon sterling à l'étalon dollar 1972, Précis d'économique internationale 1982, Histoire de la pensée économique 1984, Les Economies capitalistes et socialistes. *Address:* Department of Economics, Université Laval, Quebec, G1K 7P4 (Office); 2000 rue Chapdelaine, Sainte-Foy, Quebec, G1V 1M3, Canada (Home). *Telephone:* (418) 681-9593.

DEHMELT, Hans Georg, DR.RER.NAT.; American physicist; b. 9 Sept. 1922, Görlitz, Germany; ed. Gymnasium Zum Grauen Kloster, Berlin, Breslau Tech. Univ., Göttingen Univ. and Inst. of Hans Kopfermann; served as private in German army 1940–46, P.O.W. 1945–46; Deutsche Forschungs-Gemeinschafts Fellow, Inst. of Hans Kopfermann 1950–52; co-discovered nuclear quadruple resonance 1949; postdoctoral work in microwave spectroscopy lab., Duke Univ., U.S.A. 1952–55; Visiting Asst. Prof., Univ. of Washington, Seattle, U.S.A. 1955–56, Asst. Prof. 1956–58, Assoc. Prof. 1958–61, Prof. 1961–; with others, achieved the most precise electron magnetic moment determination to date, through work on geonium 1976; became U.S. citizen 1961; Fellow American Physical Soc.; mem. N.A.S., American Acad. of Arts and Sciences; Dr. Rer. Nat. h.c. (Ruprecht Karl Univ., Heidelberg) 1986, Hon. D.Sc. (Chicago) 1987; Davisson-Germer Prize, American Physical Soc. 1970, Alexander von Humboldt Prize 1974, Award in Basic Research, Int. Soc. of Magnetic Resonance 1980, Count Rumford Prize, American Acad. of Arts and Sciences 1985. *Publication:* Radiofrequency Spectroscopy of Stored Ions 1967 and 1969. *Address:* University of Washington, Seattle, Washington 98195, U.S.A.

De HOFFMANN, Frederic, M.A., PH.D.; American scientist and industrialist; b. 8 July 1924, Vienna, Austria; s. of Otto and Marianne de Hoffmann; m. Patricia Lynn Stewart 1953; no c.; ed. Harvard Univ.; Scientific mem. Los Alamos Lab., U.S. Atomic Energy effort 1944–45, Alt. Asst. Dir. 1950–51; f. Gen. Atomic Div. of Gen. Dynamics Corpn. 1955; f. Gen. Atomic Europe 1960; Vice-Pres. and Senior Vice-Pres. Gen. Dynamics 1955–67, also Pres. Gen. Atomic and Gen. Atomic Europe; Pres. Gulf Gen. Atomic and Gulf Gen. Atomic Europe 1967–79; Vice-Pres. Gulf Oil Corpn. 1967–69; Chancellor, Salk Inst. for Biological Studies 1970–72, Pres. 1972–, mem. Bd. of Trustees 1970–; Chair. and Pres. Salk Inst. Biotech./Industrial Assocs. (SIBIA) 1981–; mem. Bd. Gulf Mineral Resources Co. 1968–73, S. Calif. First Nat. Bank 1971–75; Pres. Conf. on future of Science and Tech., Govt. of Austria 1972; Chair. Industrie 2000, Austrian Industry-wide conf., Vienna 1985, Int. Biology Panel, Singapore Govt. 1985; trustee various academic institutions, etc.; Grand Silver Cross of Merit and Cross of Science and Arts (Austria), Grand Silver Decoration of Merit, Grand Gold Decoration of Merit. *Leisure interests:* skiing, photography. *Address:* The Salk Institute, P.O. Box 85800, San Diego, Calif, 92138 (Office); 9736 La Jolla Farms Road, La Jolla, Calif. 92037, U.S.A. *Telephone:* 619-453-4100 (Office); 619-453-0454 (Home).

DEIGHTON, Len; British author; b. 1929, London. *Publications:* The Ipcress File, Horse under Water 1963, Funeral in Berlin 1964, Billion Dollar Brain 1966, An Expensive Place to Die 1967, Action Cook Book, Où est le Garlic, Len Deighton's London Dossier (guide book), Only When I Larf 1968, Bomber 1970, Declarations of War (short stories) 1971, Close-Up 1972, Spy Story 1974 (film 1976), Yesterday's Spy 1975, Twinkle, Twinkle, Little Spy 1976, Catch a Falling Spy 1976, Fighter: the True Story of the Battle of Britain 1977, SS 1978, Blitzkrieg 1979, XPD 1981, Goodbye Mickey Mouse 1982, Berlin Game 1983, Mexico Set 1984, London

Match 1985, Winter: a Berlin Family 1899-1945 1987, Spy Hook 1988, ABC of French Food 1989. *Address:* c/o Jonathan Cape Ltd., 30 Bedford Square, London, W.C.1, England.

De JAGER, Cornelis; Netherlands astronomer; b. 29 April 1921, Den Burg, Texel; s. of Jan de Jager and Cornelia Kuyper; m. Duotsje Rienks 1947; two s. two d.; ed. Univ. of Utrecht; Asst. in theoretical physics, Univ. of Utrecht 1946; Asst. in Astronomy, Univ. of Leiden; Asst. Astron. Inst., Utrecht; Assoc. Prof. of Stellar Astrophysics, Univ. of Utrecht 1957, Ordinary Prof. in Gen. Astrophysics 1960–; Extraordinary Prof., Univ. of Brussels and founder, Space Research Lab., Utrecht and Astron. Inst., Brussels 1961; Man. Dir. Utrecht Astron. Inst. 1963-78, Chair. Inst. Council 1978-83; Asst. Gen. Sec. Int. Astron. Union 1967-70, Gen. Sec. 1970-73; Pres. Netherlands Astron. Comm. 1975-83; mem. Exec. Council Cttee. on Space Research (COSPAR) 1970-72, Pres. 1972-78, 1982-86; mem. Exec. Council, ICSU 1970-82, Vice-Pres. 1976-78, Pres. 1978-80; Aggregate Prof., Univ. of Brussels 1970–; mem. Royal Netherlands Acad. of Art and Sciences, Foreign Sec. 1985–; mem. Royal Belgium Acad. of Art and Sciences; Assoc. mem. Royal Astron. Soc. (London); Corresp. mem. Soc. Royale de Science, Liège; mem. Int. Acad. Astronautics, Chair. Basic Sciences Section 1984; mem. Int. Scientific Acad. "Comenius", Uppsala; Foreign mem. Deutsche Akademie Leopoldina, Halle; Foreign Fellow Indian Nat. Scientific Acad.; Dr. h.c. Univ. of Wrocław, Poland 1975, Observatoire de Paris 1976; Yuri Gagarin Medal (U.S.S.R.) 1984, J. Janssen Medal (France) 1984, Ziolkowski Medal, U.S.S.R. Acad. of Sciences; Kt., Order of the Dutch Lion 1983; Gold Medal Royal Astronomical Soc., London 1988; Hale Medal, American Astronomical Soc. 1988; COSPAR Medal for Int. Co-operation in Space Science 1988. *Publications:* About 450 publications including: The Hydrogen Spectrum of the Sun 1952, Structure and Dynamics of the Solar Atmosphere 1959, The Solar Spectrum 1965, Solar Flares and Space Research (with Z. Svestka) 1969, Sterren-kunde 1969, Reports on Astronomy 1970, 1973, Highlights in Astronomy 1970, Ontstaan en Levensloop van Sterren (with E. van den Heuvel), 2nd edn. 1973, Image Processing Techniques in Astronomy (with H. Nieuwenhuyzen) 1975, The Brightest Stars 1980. *Leisure interests:* bird-watching and cinematography, jogging, ballroom dancing. *Address:* Observatory, Princetonplein 5, Utrecht; Space Research Laboratory Beneluxlaan 21, Utrecht (Offices); Zonnenburg 1, 3512 NL Utrecht, Netherlands (Home). *Telephone:* 030-937145 (Office); 030-314253 (Home).

DE JAGER, Gen. Cornelis; Netherlands army officer; b. 17 Aug. 1925, Oostburg; m. R. Hidding 1950; ed. Netherlands Mil. School; served with underground "Forces of Interior" 1944; joined Royal Netherlands Army (RNLA) 1947, Second Lieut., Artillery 1947-49, regular soldier 1949-53, Battery Commdr. 1953-54, Capt. attached to Royal Artillery School 1954-58, Major, Army HQ and Jt. Chiefs-of-Staff Cttee. 1961-67, Lieut.-Col. and Strategy Instructor, Head of Tactics Dept., Army Staff Coll. 1967-70, Commdr. 41 Field Artillery Battalion, Fed. Repub. of Germany 1970-71, Chief-of-Staff G2/3, Army HQ, Col. 1971, Chief of Personnel Div. 1972, Deputy Chief-of-Staff, HQ 1973, Vice-Chief of Gen. Staff and Deputy Commdr.-in-Chief RNLA, concurrently Maj.-Gen. Artillery 1974-77, Chief of Army Staff and Commdr.-in-Chief RNLA, concurrently Lieut.-Gen., Chief of Defence Staff, Gen. 1980; Aide-de-Camp in extraordinary service Dec. 1982–; Chair. NATO Mil. Cttee., Brussels 1983-86; Kt., Order of Netherlands Lion 1978; Officer, Order of Orange-Nassau, with Swords 1973; Officers' Long Service Medal; Grand Officer, Italian Order of Merit 1979; Commdr. Legion of Merit (U.S.A.) 1980, Commdr. Légion d'honneur (France) 1979; Kt., Order of Sword of Sweden 1955. *Leisure interests:* music, reading, painting. *Address:* c/o NATO Headquarters, boulevard Léopold III, 1110 Brussels, Belgium (Office).

DEJEAN DE LA BATIE, Bernard, L. EN D.; French diplomatist; b. 9 May 1927, Boulogne sur Mer; m. Claudine Perazio 1966; one s. one d.; ed. Coll. Saint-Joseph Poitiers, Univ. of Paris, Inst. d'études politiques de Paris and Ecole nat.d'admin.; Asst., later Second Sec., Embassy, London 1953-59; Dir. Econ. and Financial Affairs, Ministry of Foreign Affairs 1960-67; Embassy Adviser, Bucharest 1968-70, Cairo 1970-74; Rome 1974-78, Amb. Plenipotentiary 1975; Consul Gen., Geneva 1978-82; Asst. Dir. for Political Affairs, Ministry of Foreign Affairs 1982-85; Asst. Sec.-Gen. for Nat. Defence 1985–; Officier Légion d'honneur, ordre nat. du Mérite. *Address:* 51 boulevard de Latour-Maubourg, 75007 Paris, France (Office).

DEJID, Bugyn; Mongolian politician; b. 1927; ed. Mongolian State Univ. 1952-57; Chief Veterinary, Deputy Chair. of Exec. Cttee. of Gobi-Altai Prov. People's Deputies' Hural 1957-60; Deputy Chair. of Exec. Cttee. of Cen. Prov. People's Deputies' Hural 1960-63; First Sec. Party Cttee. of Cen. Prov. 1963-66; First Sec. Party Cttee., Bayan-Ulgii Prov. 1966-70; First Deputy Minister, Ministry of Public Security 1970-71, Minister 1971-81; Chair. Party Control Cttee. of MPRP Cen. Cttee. 1981-86; Alt. mem. Political Bureau of MPRP Cen. Cttee. 1981-83, mem. Dec. 1983–, Sec. of Cen. Cttee. 1986–; Deputy to People's Great Hural. *Address:* c/o Central Committee of the MPRP, Ulan Bator, Mongolia.

DEJMEK, Kazimierz; Polish actor and theatre director; b. 17 May 1924, Kowel; s. of Henryk and Włodzimiera Dejmek; m. 1st Irena Dejmek 1945, 2nd Danuta Dejmek 1954; one s. one d; ed. State Theatrical Acad., Łódź; Actor, Rzeszów, Jelenia Góra Companies 1945; Actor, Teatr Wojska Polskiego Łódź 1946-49; Founder and Gen. Dir. Teatr Nowy, Łódź 1949-61;

Head, State Theatrical Acad., Łódź 1952-55; Gen. Man. and Artistic Dir., Teatr Narodowy, Warsaw 1961-68; Assoc. Man. Teatr Dramatyczny, Warsaw 1972-74; Gen. Man. and Artistic Dir., Teatr Nowy, Łódź 1975-81; Teatr Polski, Warsaw 1981–; mem. Consultative Council attached to Chair. of Council of State 1986–; numerous decorations incl. Commdr. Cross of Order Polonia Restituta, Order of Banner of Labour (2nd class); State Prizes (2nd & 3rd class), Prize of Minister of Culture and Art (1st class), Alfred Jurzykowski Foundation Award 1975, Gottfried von Herder Prize 1979. *Principal productions:* Winkelried's Day (Andrzejewski and Zagórski) 1956, Measure for Measure, Julius Caesar (Shakespeare) 1956, 1960, Darkness Covers the Earth (Andrzejewski) 1957, Agamemnon (Aeschylus), Electra (Euripides), The Frogs (Aristophanes) 1961, 1963, The Story of the Glorious Resurrection of Our Lord (Nicolai of Wilkowiecko) 1961, 1962, 1975, Word about Jacob Szela (Bruno Jasieński) 1962, The Life of Joseph (Nicolai Rej) 1965, Kordian (Słowacki) 1965, Der Stellvertreter (Hochhuth), Dziady (A. Mickiewicz) 1967, Uncle Vanya (Chekhov) 1968, Jeux de Massacre (Ionesco) 1971, Baths and Bed-Bug (Mayakovsky) 1971, Trial Against Nine from Catonsville (Berrigan) 1971, Controller (Gogol) 1971, La Passione 1972, Acting About Resurrection 1972, opera Henry VI at the Chase (Karol Kurpiński) 1972, Philemon (Biedermann) 1973, opera Magic Flute (Mozart) 1973, Electra (Giraudoux) 1973, opera Devils of Loudun (Penderecki) 1974, Operetka (Gombrowicz) 1975, Dialogus de Passione 1975, Garbus (Mrożek) 1976, Patna (J. Conrad) 1976, Wielki Fryderyk (A. Nowaczyński) 1977, Cień (E. Szwarc, W. Młynarski) 1977, Die Frist (Dürrenmatt) 1977, Obecność (Słonimski) 1977, opera Franc-tireur (Carl Maria von Weber) 1978, Revange (Fredro) 1978, Vatzlav (Mrożek) 1978, Krakowiacy i górale (Bogusławski) 1978, Joseph's Life (Rey) 1985. *Leisure interests:* literature, music. *Address:* Ul. Rajców 8, 00-220 Warsaw, Poland.

DE JONG, Jan Willem, PH.D.; Dutch academic; b. 15 Feb. 1921, Leiden; s. of late Dirk Cornelis de Jong and Johanna Elisabeth van Biemen; m. Gisèle Fernande Bacquès 1949; one s. two d.; Gymnasium, Leiden, Univ. of Leiden, Harvard Univ. and Univ. of Paris; Prof. of Tibetan and Buddhist Studies Univ. of Leiden 1956-65, of S. Asian and Buddhist Studies Australian Nat. Univ., Canberra 1965-86; Visiting Fellow Dept. of Far Eastern History, A.N.U. 1987–; Co-Founder and Co-Ed. Indo-Iranian Journal 1956–; Corresp. mem. Royal Netherlands Acad. of Arts and Sciences 1978; Fellow Australian Acad. of the Humanities 1970; Hon. D.Litt. (Nava Nalanda Mahavihara, India) 1983. *Publications:* Cinq chapitres de la Prasannapadā 1949, Mi la ras pa'i rnam thar, Texte tibétain de la vie de Milarepa 1959, A Brief History of Buddhist Studies in Europe and America 1976, Textcritical Remarks on the Bodhisattvāvadānakalpalatā 1979, Buddhist Studies 1981. *Leisure interests:* tennis, walking. *Address:* 4 Jansz Crescent, Griffith, A.C.T. 2603, Australia. *Telephone:* (062) 953750.

de JONGH, Theunis Willem, M.SC., M.A., D.COM.; South African banker; b. 15 Dec. 1913, Gouda; s. of Petrus Johannes de Jongh and Rachel E. Wium; m. Anna F. Visser 1914; three s. two d.; ed. Stellenbosch, Pretoria and Columbia Univs.; Chief Statistician, Industrial Devt. Corpn. of S. Africa 1942-45; Head Econ. Research, S. African Reserve Bank 1946-62, Exec. Asst. 1962-67, Gov. and Chair. 1967-80; Chair. Nat. Finance Corpn. of S. Africa 1967–; Alt. Gov. IBRD, IFC and IDA 1967-72, Gov. 1972-80; mem. of Prime Minister's Econ. Advisory Council 1967–; Decoration for Meritorious Service, S. Africa 1975. *Publication:* An Analysis of Banking Statistics in South Africa 1947. *Leisure interests:* golf, tennis; keen follower of rugby and cricket. *Address:* 134 Eastwood Street, Arcadia, Pretoria 0002, South Africa (Home). *Telephone:* 74-2231 (Home).

DE JOSSELIN DE JONG, Patrick Edward, PH.D.; Netherlands professor of cultural anthropology; b. 8 July 1922, Peking, China; s. of Th. H. J. de Josselin de Jong and E. C. (née Persse-Sealy) de Josselin de Jong; m. Emilie A. M. Olivier; three s.; ed. Leids Stedelyk Gymnasium, Leiden Univ.; Curator of Islamic Dept., Nat. Museum of Ethnology, Leiden 1951-53; lecturer in Malay Studies, Univ. of Malaya, Singapore 1953-57; Prof. of Cultural Anthropology (special reference to S.-E. Asia), Leiden Univ. 1957-87, Prof. Emer. 1987–; Kt., Orde van de Nederlandse Leeuw; Hon. Fellow Royal Anthropological Inst. of G.B. and Northern Ireland. *Publications:* Minangkabau and Negri Sembilan 1980, Structural Anthropology in the Netherlands 1983, Unity in Diversity: Indonesia as a Field of Anthropological Study 1984. *Leisure interests:* golf, stamp collecting. *Address:* Willem de Zwygerlaan 33, 2341 EH Oegstgeest, The Netherlands. *Telephone:* 071-174484.

DEKEYSER, Willy Clément, D.SC.; Belgian university professor; b. 16 Feb. 1910, Ostend; s. of Georges and Eugenie Vanderputte; m. Marie Madeleine Vandenberge 1943; one d.; ed. Albert School and Athénée Royal, Ostend, Ghent Univ.; Teacher, Athénée Royal, Ghent 1931; Asst., Ghent Univ. 1938, Lecturer 1944; Prof. of Crystallography 1948-80, Prof. Emer. 1980–; mem. Scientific and Tech. Cttee. Euratom, Advisory Panel NATO, Flemish Acad. of Sciences; mem. Bd. Soc. Belge d'Optique et Instruments de Précision (OIP); Croix de guerre, Commdr. Ordre de Léopold. *Publications:* Les dislocations et la croissance des cristaux (with S. Amelinckx) 1955, The Structure and Properties of Grain Boundaries (with S. Amelinckx) in Solid State Physics Vol. 8, Reactivity of Solids (with W. P. Gomes) in Solid State Chemistry Vol. 4, 1974. *Leisure interest:* French literature. *Address:* Laboratorium voor Kristallografie en Studie van de Vaste Stof, Krijgslaan 281, B-9000 Ghent (Office); Green Park, Pacificatielaan 63, B-9000 Ghent, Belgium (Home). *Telephone:* 091-22-57-15.

de KLERK, Albert; Netherlands organist and composer; b. 4 Oct. 1917; ed. Amsterdamsch Conservatorium under Dr. Anthon van der Horst; Organist St. Joseph's Church, Haarlem 1934–; City Organist Haarlem 1956–82; Dir. of Catholic Choir, Haarlem 1946–; Prof. of Organ and Improvization, Sweelinck Conservatorium, Amsterdam 1964–85; numerous gramophone records for Telefunken, C.B.S., E.M.I.-Bovema, etc.; Prix d'Excellence, Amsterdam 1941, Prix du Disque, Prix Edison (for Die Kleinorgel) 1962. *Compositions:* several works for organ including three concertos for organ and orchestra, chamber-music, and liturgical music (seven masses). *Address:* Crayenesterlaan 22, Haarlem, Netherlands. *Telephone:* 023-280654.

de KLERK, Frederik Willem, LL.B.; South African politician; b. 18 March 1936, Johannesburg; s. of J. de Klerk; m. Marike Willemse 1959; two s. one d.; ed. Monument High School, Krugersdorp, Potchefstroom Univ.; in law practice 1961–72; mem. House of Assembly 1972; Information Officer Nat. Party, Transvaal 1975; Minister of Posts and Telecommunications and Social Welfare and Pensions 1978, subsequently Minister of Posts and Telecommunications and of Sport and Recreation 1978–79, of Mines, Energy and Environmental Planning 1979–80, of Mineral and Energy Affairs 1980–82, of Internal Affairs 1982–85, of Nat. Educ. and Planning Sept. 1984–; mem. Nat. Party, Transvaal Leader 1982–, Leader Feb. 1989–; Chair. Council of Ministers May 1985–. *Publications:* various articles and brochures for the Nat. Party Information Service. *Leisure interests:* golf, tennis. *Address:* House of Assembly, Cape Town, South Africa.

DE KOCK, Gerhardus Petrus Christian, M.A., PH.D.; South African banker; b. 14 Feb. 1926, Cape Town; s. of Machiel H. De Kock and Christina Magdalena De Jongh; m. Jocéne Hitchcock Visser 1949; two s. one d.; ed. Afrikaans Hoër Seunskool, Pretoria, Univ. of Pretoria and Harvard Univ.; Sr. lecturer in Econs., Univ. of Pretoria 1951–55; Economist, South African Reserve Bank 1956–61, Head, Econ. Dept. 1962–68; Special Econ. Adviser to Treasury 1966–67; Alt. Exec. Dir. IMF, Washington 1968–71; Deputy Gov. South African Reserve Bank 1971–76, Sr. Deputy Gov. 1976–80, Gov. 1980–; Special Econ. Adviser to Minister of Finance 1977–80; Gov. Devt. Bank of S. Africa; Hon. D.Econ. (Natal), Hon. D.Com. (Pretoria); Order for Meritorious Service, (1st Class), South Africa 1987; Euromoney Award as Central Banker of the Year (jtly with Gov. of Cen. Bank of Kuwait) 1988. *Publications:* History of the South African Reserve Bank 1920–52, Ekonomie - 'n Inleidende Studie (co-author). *Leisure interest:* golf. *Address:* South African Reserve Bank, P.O. Box 427, Pretoria 0001 (Office); 134 Eastwood Street, Arcadia, Pretoria 0083, South Africa (Home). *Telephone:* (012) 313-3751 (Office); (012) 43-2231 (Home).

De KOONING, Willem; American (b. Netherlands) artist; b. 24 April 1904, Rotterdam; m. Elaine Fried 1943 (died 1989); ed. Rotterdam Acad. of Fine Arts; display work, dept. stores in the Netherlands 1920–24; worked in Belgium 1924–25, America 1926, housepainter, muralist, New York 1926, Mural, Hall of Pharmacy, New York World's Fair 1939; Teacher, Black Mountain Coll. 1948, Yale 1950–51; One-man shows Egan Gallery 1948, 1950, Sidney Janis Gallery 1953, 1956, 1959, 1962; Knoedler & Co., Manhattan 1967, 1969; retrospective exhbns. at Tate Gallery, London 1968, Whitney Museum of American Art, New York 1983; pictures in Museum of Modern Art, New York, St. Louis Museum, Chicago Art Inst. and in private collections; Logan Purchase Prize, Chicago Art Inst. 1951; Nat. Medal of Arts 1986; Officer Order of Orange-Nassau (Netherlands). *Address:* Woodbine Drive, P.O. Box 1437, The Springs, East Hampton, N.Y. 11973, U.S.A.

DE KORTE, Rudolf Willem, DR.RER.NAT.; Netherlands politician; b. 8 July 1936, The Hague; m.; two c.; ed. Maerlant Gymnasium, The Hague, Leiden Univ., Harvard Business School; employed in industry, Hong Kong 1964–66, Ethiopia 1967–68; Gen. Sales Man. Unilever-Emery NV 1969–71, Dir. 1972–77; Sec. People's Party for Freedom and Democracy (VVD) 1971–78; M.P. 1977, Minister for Home Affairs March–July 1986, Deputy Prime Minister and Minister for Econ. Affairs July 1986–; mem. Wassenaar Municipal Council 1978–82; People's Party for Freedom and Democracy (VVD). *Address:* Ministry for Economic Affairs, Bezuidenhoutseweg 30, P.O. Box 20101, 2500 EC The Hague, Netherlands. *Telephone:* (070) 79-89-11.

de la BARRE de NANTEUIL, Luc, L. ÈS L.; French diplomatist; b. 21 Sept. 1925, Lhommaize; s. of Jean de la Barre de Nanteuil and Marguerite de Beauchamp; m. Hedwige Frerejean de Chavagneux 1973; two s. (by previous m.); ed. Faculty of Arts and Letters, Paris and Ecole Nat. d'Administration; Ministry of Foreign Affairs 1950–59; First Sec. Embassy London 1959–64; Asst. Dir. African and Middle East Affairs Dept., Paris 1964–70; promoted to rank of Minister Plenipotentiary 1969; Head, Econ. Co-operation Service, Directorate of Econ. Affairs 1970–76; Amb. to Netherlands 1976–77; Perm. Rep. to EEC, Brussels 1977–81, 1984–86; Perm. Rep. to UN Security Council and Head., Perm. Mission to UN, N.Y. 1981–84; Diplomatic Adviser 1986; Amb. to U.K. Sept. 1986–; Officier, Légion d'honneur, Commdr., Ordre Nat. du Mérite. *Publication:* a book on the painter Jacques-Louis David. *Leisure interests:* economics and arts. *Address:* French Embassy, 58 Knightsbridge, London, SW1X 7JT, England. *Telephone:* 01-235 8080.

DELACOMBE, Sir Rohan, K.C.M.G., K.C.V.O., K.B.E., C.B., D.S.O., K.ST.J., F.R.A.I.A.; British administrator and fmr. army officer; b. 25 Oct. 1906, Malta; s. of the late Lieut.-Col. and Mrs. A. Delacombe; m. Eleanor J. Foster, C.ST.J. 1941; one s. one d.; ed. Harrow, Royal Mil. Acad., Sandhurst, and Staff Coll., Camberley; served in Egypt, North China, India, active service Palestine 1937–39, France, Norway, Normandy, Italy, South-East Asia 1939–45; Deputy Mil. Sec., War Office 1953–55; Maj.-Gen. 1956; G.O.C., 52nd (Lowland) Div. 1955–58, Berlin 1959–62; retd. 1962; Gov. Victoria, Australia 1963–74; Administrator of Australia on four occasions; Pres. Royal British Legion, Wiltshire 1974–85; mem. Victoria Econ. and Devt. Corpn. (Europe); Freeman of Melbourne; Hon. LL.D. Univs. of Melbourne and Monash. *Leisure interests:* normal. *Address:* Shrewton Manor, Salisbury, Wilts., England. *Telephone:* (0980) 620253.

DE LA CONCHA Y LÓPEZ-ISLA, Manuel; Spanish stockbroker; b. 5 Oct. 1934, Madrid; s. of Manuel de la Concha and Amparo López-Isla; m. Paloma Giménez; five c.; ed. Instituto Ramiro de Maeztu and Univ. Complutense de Madrid and further stock exchange training in U.K. and U.S.A.; stockbroker 1957–; mem. Bd. of Govs., Madrid Stock Exchange 1973–76, Vice-Pres. 1976–80, Pres. 1981–. *Leisure interests:* reading, tennis, yachting. *Address:* Bolsa Oficial de Comercio de Madrid, Plaza de la Lealtad 1, Madrid 14; Velázquez 150, Madrid (Office); Darro 22, Madrid, Spain (Home). *Telephone:* 221-47-90 (Stock Exchange); 262-87-04 (Office); 457-71-49 (Home).

DELACÔTE, Jacques; French conductor; b. 16 Aug. 1942; s. of Pierre Delacôte and Renée Wagner Delacôte; m. Maria Lucia Alvares-Machado 1975; ed. Music Conservatoire, Paris, Acad. of Music, Vienna; among the orchestras conducted: Orchestre de Paris, Orchestre Nat. de France, New York Philharmonic, Vienna Philharmonic, Israel Philharmonic, Orchestre Nat. de Belgique, London Symphony Orchestra, San Francisco, Cleveland and Montreal Orchestras, Scottish Chamber, Scottish Nat., RIAS Berlin, WDR Cologne, SF Stuttgart, SWF Baden-Baden, Bavarian Radio, Munich, Royal Opera House Covent Garden (including Far East tour, Korea and Japan), English Nat. Opera, Scottish Opera, Opernhaus Zürich, Teatro Real Madrid, Vienna State Opera, Opera Düsseldorf, Welsh Nat. Opera, Teatro Liceo Barcelona, Opéra de Paris, Teatro Colón Buenos Aires, Canadian Opera Co., Royal State Opera Copenhagen, State Opera Hamburg, State Opera Munich; also recordings with EMI London; 1st Prize Conservatoire Paris, 1st Prize and Gold Medal Mitropoulos Competition, New York 1971. *Leisure interest:* chess. *Address:* Türkenschanzstrasse 20/10, 1180 Vienna, Austria.

DE LA CUADRA-SALCEDO FERNÁNDEZ DEL CASTILLO, Tomás; Spanish politician; b. 1946; m.; two c.; lecturer in admin. law, Univ. of Madrid; legal adviser, Cuadernos para el diálogo magazine 1968; lawyer, specializing in admin. law; worked in legal practice of Gregorio Peces-Barbo until 1982; sent to Latin America by Int. Fed. of the Rights of Man and Int. Movement of Catholic Jurists to investigate human rights situation 1976; fmr. mem. Federación Democrática Cristiana and then of Junta Democrática; joined Partido Socialista Obrero Español 1976; mem. comm. which drew up the García de Enterría report (preliminary to law of decentralization) 1981; Minister of Territorial Admin. 1982–86; Pres. Council of State 1986–. *Address:* El Consejo de Estado, Madrid, Spain.

DE LA MADRID HURTADO, Miguel; Mexican lawyer and politician; b. 1935; m. Paloma de la Madrid; five c.; ed. Harvard Univ., U.S.A.; successively with Bank of Mexico, Petróleos Mexicanos (PEMEX) (Asst. Dir. of Finances 1970–72); Dir. Public Sector Credit, later Under-Sec., Ministry of Finance; Sec. for Planning and Fed. Budget, Govt. of Mexico 1979–80; Institutional Revolutionary Party (PRI) cand. to succeed López Portillo as Pres. of Mexico Sept. 1981; Pres. of Mexico 1982–88. *Address:* c/o Palacio de Gobierno, México, D.F., Mexico.

de la MARE, Sir Arthur, K.C.M.G., K.C.V.O.; British diplomatist; b. 15 Feb. 1914, Jersey; s. of Walter de la Mare and Laura (née Syvret); m. Katherine Elisabeth Sherwood 1940; three d.; ed. Victoria Coll., Jersey, and Pembroke Coll., Cambridge; Diplomatic Service, served Tokyo and Seoul 1936–42, Washington 1942–43; Foreign Office 1943–47; Consul, San Francisco 1947–50; First Sec., Tokyo 1950–53; Counsellor, Foreign Office 1953–56, Washington 1956–60; Head of Far Eastern Dept., Foreign Office 1960–63; Amb. to Afghanistan 1963–65; Asst. Under-Sec. of State, Foreign Office 1965–68; High Commr. in Singapore 1968–70; Amb. to Thailand 1970–73; Chair. Anglo-Thai Soc. 1976–82; Chair. Royal Soc. for Asian Affairs 1978–84; Chair. Jersey Soc., London 1980–86. *Leisure interests:* gardening, walking, promoting the Norman-French language. *Address:* Havre de Grace, Rue de Fontaine, Trinity, Jersey, Channel Islands. *Telephone:* (0534) 63906.

de la MARE, Peter Bernard David, PH.D., D.SC., F.R.S.N.Z.; New Zealand professor of chemistry; b. 3 Sept. 1920, Hamilton; s. of the late F. A. de la Mare and S. R. Child; m. Gwynneth C. Jolly 1945; two d.; ed. Hamilton High School, Victoria Univ. Coll., Univ. of N.Z. and Univ. Coll. London; Asst. Chemist, N.Z. Dept. of Govt. 1942–44, Chemist 1945; Asst. Lecturer, Univ. Coll. London 1948–49, Lecturer 1949–56, Reader 1956–60; Prof. of Chem. and Head, Dept. of Chem. Bedford Coll. London 1960–67; Prof. of Chem. Univ. of Auckland 1967–82, Head, Dept. of Chem. 1967–81, Prof. Emer. 1982–; Fellow, Chem. Soc. (London), Royal Inst. of Chem., N.Z. Inst. of Chem., Royal Soc. of Chem.; Hon. D.Sc. (Victoria Univ. of Wellington) 1983; Hector Medal (Royal Soc. of N.Z.) 1985. *Publications:* Electrophilic Halogenation 1976; author and co-author of other books and some 190 scientific papers and reviews. *Leisure interests:* formerly cricket, cross-country running; now mountain-walking, table tennis, chess, stamp collecting. *Address:* 65 Grant's Road, Opotiki, New Zealand. *Telephone:* Opotiki 58-336.

DELAMURAZ, Jean-Pascal; Swiss politician; b. 1 April 1936, Paudex, Lausanne; m. Catherine Reymond 1962; one s. one d.; ed. Univ. of Lausanne; Mayor of Lausanne 1974; mem. Nat. Council, Fed. Assembly 1975; elected to Fed. Council (Cabinet) Dec. 1983; Head, Fed. Mil. Dept. (Ministry of Defence) 1984–86; Head, Fed. Dept. of Public Econ. (Industry, Trade, Labour and Agric.) 1987–; mem. cantonal govt., Canton of Vaud 1981; Silver Medal, Nat. Olympic Order. *Leisure interests:* sailing, travel, music. *Address:* Département de l'économie publique, Bundeshaus-Ost, 3003 Berne, Switzerland. *Telephone:* (031) 612001.

DELANO ORTUZAR, Juan Carlos; Chilean diplomatist; b. 14 June 1941, Santiago; m. María Paz Valenzuela; three s. one d.; ed. St. George's Coll., Catholic Univ. of Chile and Corporation Office for Development, Belgium; fmr. Partner, Distribuidora AUDICOL S.A. and Comercial Magara Ltda.; Pres. Trading Asscn. of Chile; Dir. Chamber of Commerce of Santiago 1979–83; Pres. Chilean Nat. Chamber of Commerce and Adviser to Confed. of Trade and Industry 1983–85; Minister of Economy, Promotion and Reconstruction 1985–87; Amb. to U.K. Nov. 1987–. *Address:* Embassy of Chile, 12 Devonshire Street, London, W1N 2DS, England. *Telephone:* 01-580 6392.

DE LA PEÑA, Javier, M.S.; Spanish petrochemical industry executive; b. 13 May 1940, Cortes, Navarra; s. of Juan-Jesus de la Peña and Julia de la Peña; m. Katherine Zegarra 1969; one s. three d.; ed. Univ. of Valencia and Univ. of Kansas, U.S.A.; joined Phillips Petroleum group 1965, Dept. of Eng. (Okla.) and Int. Dept. (New York), U.S.A. 1965–67, Marketing, Phillips Calatrava Ventas, Madrid 1967–68, Man. in charge of Projects for Latin America (New York) 1968–70, Marketing Man. Phillips Calatrava Ventas, Madrid 1970–72, Gen. Man. 1972–74, Devt. Man. Phillips Petroleum Chemicals, Brussels 1975–77, Vice-Pres., Devt. and Licensing 1978–82, Vice-Pres. and Man. Dir. for Petrochemicals (Olefins and Aromatics) of Phillips Petroleum Chemicals 1982–85; Vice-Pres. REPSOL PETROLEO, S.A., in charge of Petrochemical Group; REPSOL Rep. in Asscn. of European Petrochemical Producers 1985; Pres. REPSOL QUIMICA, S.A. 1986; Fulbright Scholar 1963–64. *Leisure interests:* sports, piano and music. *Address:* REPSOL PETROLEO, S.A., José Abascal 4, 28003 Madrid; REPSOL QUIMICA, S.A., Juan Bravo 3-b, 28006 Madrid, Spain. *Telephone:* 446 26 10 (REPSOL PETROLEO); 276 89 46 (REPSOL QUIMICA).

de la TOUR, Frances; British actress; b. 30 July 1944, Bovingdon, Herts.; d. of Charles de la Tour and Moyra (née Fessas); m. Tom Kempinski 1972 (divorced 1982); one s. one d.; ed. Lycée français de Londres, Drama Centre, London; with the R.S.C. 1965–71. *Stage appearances include:* As You Like It 1967, The Relapse 1969, A Midsummer Night's Dream 1971, The Man of Mode 1971, Small Craft Warnings (Best Supporting Actress, Plays and Players Award) 1973, The Banana Box 1973, The White Devil 1976, Hamlet (title role) 1979, Duet for One (Best Actress, New Standard Award, Best Actress, Critics Award, Best Actress, Soc. of W. End Theatres—SWET Award) 1980, Skirmishes 1981, Uncle Vanya 1982, Moon for the Misbegotten (Best Actress, SWET Award) 1983, St. Joan 1984, Dance of Death 1985, Brighton Beach Memoirs 1986, Lillian 1986, Façades 1988. *Films include:* Our Miss Fred 1972, To the Devil a Daughter 1976, Rising Damp (Best Actress, Standard Film Award) 1980, Murder with Mirrors 1984. *Television appearances include:* Crimes of Passion 1973, Rising Damp 1974, 1976, Cottage to Let 1976, Flickers 1980, Skirmishes 1982, Duet for One 1985, Partners 1986, Clem 1986, A Kind of Living (series) 1987/88. *Address:* c/o Saraband Associates, 265 Liverpool Road, London, N.1, England. *Telephone:* 01-609-5313.

DELAUNEY, Maurice Charles Jules, B. EN D.; French diplomatist; b. 31 July 1919, La Haye-du-Puits, Manche; s. of Charles Delauney and Hélène Lucas; m. Hélène Courcy 1947; one s.; ed. Collège de Saint-Lô, Collège Chaptal, Paris; Chef de subdivision et de région, Cameroon 1945–54; Chef de Cabinet civil of the High Comm., Madagascar 1954–55; Chargé de Mission, Ministry of French Overseas Depts. and Territories 1955–56; Chef de région, Bamileke, Cameroon 1956–58; Chargé de Mission to the Minister of State for Aid and Co-operation 1959; First Counsellor, High Comm. to Dahomey (now Benin) 1959–60; Resident Commr. of France in the New Hebrides 1960–65; Amb. to Gabon 1965–72, Minister Plenipotentiary 1969; Amb. to Madagascar 1972–75, to Gabon and São Tomé and Príncipe 1975–79; Pres. Cie. des Mines d'Uranium de Franceville (COMUF), Gabon 1979–; Special Minister Plenipotentiary (on leave) 1979–; Breveté de l'Ecole Nationale de France d'Outre-mer et du Centre des Hautes Etudes d'Administration musulmane; Officier, Légion d'honneur, Croix de guerre, Officier du Mérite agricole, Chevalier de l'Etoile noire, Grand Croix de l'Etoile équatoriale, Grand Officer of Merit (Spain), Commdr. dell'Ordine al Merito (Italy), Commdr. of Merit of the Sovereign Order of Malta. *Publication:* De la casquette à la jaquette, ou de l'administration coloniale à la diplomatie africaine. *Leisure interests:* tennis, golf, hunting. *Address:* B.P. 260, Libreville, Gabon; Tour Maine Montparnasse, 33 avenue du Maine, 75755 Paris; 150 rue de Rennes, 75006 Paris, France. *Telephone:* 42 22 30 63 (rue de Rennes).

De LAURENTIIS, Dino; Italian film producer; b. 8 Aug. 1919, Torre Annunziata, Naples; s. of Aurelio and Giuseppina (née Salvatore) De Laurentiis; m. Silvana Mangano 1949; one s. (deceased) three d.; founded Real Ciné, Turin 1941; Exec. Producer Lux Film 1942; acquired Safir Studios and f. Teatri della Farnesina 1948; co-founder Ponti-De Laurentiis S.p.A. 1950; Prin. De Laurentis Entertainment Group Inc. 1986–, now Chair. Bd.; numerous awards and prizes include Oscars for La Strada 1957, Le Notti di Cabiria 1958, Golden David Awards for Le Notti di Cabiria 1958, The Tempest 1959, Silver Ribbon (Italian Film Critics) for La Strada 1954, Venice Silver Lion for Europa 51 1952. *Films produced include:* La Figlia del Capitano, Il Bandito, Molti Sogni per la Strada, Anna, Bitter Rice, La Strada, Le Notti di Cabiria, Ulysses, War and Peace, The Tempest, This Angry Age, Europa 51, The Gold of Naples, The Great War, Five Branded Women, I Love, You Love, The Best of Enemies, Barabbas, To Bed or not to Bed, The Bible, The Three Faces of a Woman, Barbarella, A Man Called Sledge, Waterloo, The Valachi Papers, Serpico, Mandingo, Lipstick 1976, Buffalo Bill and the Indians 1976, Drum 1976, King Kong 1976, Hurricane 1979, Flash Gordon 1980, Ragtime 1981, Conan the Barbarian 1982, Firestarter 1984, The Bounty 1984, Dune 1984, Year of the Dragon 1985, Blue Velvet 1986, Trick or Treat 1986, King Kong Lives 1986, Crimes of the Heart 1986, Weeds 1987, Dracula's Widow 1987, Adult Education 1987. *Address:* De Laurentiis Entertainment Group, 8670 Wiltshire Boulevard, Beverly Hills, Calif, 90211, U.S.A.

DELBARRE, Florian François, D. EN MED.; French professor of medicine; b. 7 Sept. 1918, Paris; s. of Florian and Marguerite Delbarre; m. 2nd Jeanne Dacheux; two c. (of 1st m.); ed. Lycée Michelet, and Faculties of Science and Medicine, Paris; served as intern in Paris Hospitals 1943–49; Head of Clinic of Faculty of Medicine, Paris 1949–55; Fellow of the Faculty of Medicine, physician, Paris Hospitals 1955–60, Prof. of Rheumatology at the Faculty of Medicine 1960–, Prof. Clinic of Rheumatology 1967–; Dir. Research Inst. of Rheumatology at l'Hôpital Cochin; Hon. Dean of the Faculty of Medicine, Paris-Cochin; mem. of Bd. of the Nat. Centre of Scientific Research; Consultant to the WHO; Pres. Paris-René Descartes Univ. 1976–81; fmr. Pres. French League against Rheumatism; Officier, Légion d'honneur, Commdr. du Mérite, Chevalier, Ordre de la Santé Publique, Commdr., l'Ordre des Palmes académiques, Officier du Mérite de la République Italienne, Médaille d'Or des Hôpitaux de Paris, Lauréat de l'Académie Nat. de Médicine; several honorary degrees. *Publications:* L'insuffisance alimentaire (with Prof. C. Richet) 1950, Les stimulines hypophysaires (with Profs. Lemaire and Michard) 1950, Cortisone et cortico-stimuline en rhumatologie (with Profs. F. Coste and J. Cayla). *Address:* 62 boulevard Arago, Paris 75013, France. *Telephone:* 633-01 95.

De LEEUW, Ton; Netherlands composer; b. 16 Nov. 1926, Rotterdam; m. Arlette Reboul 1952; one s. three d.; ed. musical colls. in Netherlands and France and under Jaap Kunst, Amsterdam; with Radio Hilversum 1954–, responsible for annual radio programmes of Contemporary and non-Western Music 1956–; Prof. Composition Conservatoires of Amsterdam and Utrecht 1959–, lecturer, Univ. of Amsterdam 1962–; Dir. Conservatoire of Amsterdam 1972–; Study of Indian classical music and dance 1961; numerous prizes including Prix Italia 1956 and Prix des Jeunesses Musicales 1961. *Compositions:* Hiob (Radiophonic Oratorio) 1956, Mouvements Rétrogrades 1957, First String Quartet 1958, Antiphonie (chamber music with 4 electronic sound-tracks) 1960, Symphonies for Wind Instruments 1963, The Dream (Opera) 1963, Men go their ways (piano) 1964, Second String Quartet 1965, Syntaxis I (Electronic) 1966, Spatial music I-IV 1966–68, Haiku II (Sopr. and orch.) 1968, Lamento Pacis (vocal and instr.) 1969, Litany of our Time (Television play) 1970, Music for Strings 1970 and works for electronic instruments, Mountains (bass clarinet and tape) 1977, The Birth of Music 1978, Chronos (Electronic) 1980, Car nos Vignes sont en Fleur (Mixed Voices) 1980, And They Shall Reign Forever (vocal and instr.) 1981, Clair-Obscur (Electronic) 1982. *Publication:* The Music of the 20th Century 1964 and numerous articles on cultural interaction. *Address:* Costeruslaan 4, Hilversum, Netherlands. *Telephone:* 02150-15783.

DELELIS, André; French politician; b. 23 May 1924, Cauchy-à-la-Tour; s. of Eusèbe and Lucienne (née Flahaut) Delelis; m. Suzanne Soupart 1944; two d.; City Councillor and Deputy Mayor, Lens 1959; Gen. Councillor 1962–81; Mayor of Lens 1966–; Deputy (Pas-de-Calais) to Nat. Ass. 1967–81, Senator 1983–; mem. Steering Cttee., Parti Socialiste 1975–77; Minister of Trade and Handicrafts 1981–83. *Leisure interests:* football (Hon. Pres. Racing Club de Lens, 1st dir. team). *Address:* 36 rue Romuald Pruvost, 62300 Lens, France (Home). *Telephone:* 21-28-41-34.

DELEURAN, Aage; Danish journalist; b. 11 Oct. 1925, Korsør; s. of Holger Johannes and Agnete (née Lorentsen) Deleuran; m. Birthe Braae 1955. Staff reporter Korsør Avis 1942, Berlingske Aftenavis 1945, Paris Corresp. Berlingske Tidende 1952–56, Asst. Ed.-in-Chief 1961, Exec. Ed. 1967, Ed.-in-Chief 1970–; Dir. Berlingske House 1975–; Chair. Soc. of Danish Press History 1966–, Ritzau's News Agency 1971–76, 1980–, Asscn. of Danish Newspapers 1972–79, Vice-Chair. 1985–; Com- mdr. of the Order of Dannebrog; Officier, Légion d'honneur. *Publication:* April 40 1965. *Address:* 34 Pilestraede, 1147 Copenhagen K (Office); 1 Carl Johans Gade 2100 Copenhagen 1, Denmark (Home). *Telephone:* 01-157575 (Office).

DELFIM NETTO, Antônio, D.ECON.; Brazilian economist; b. 5 May 1928, São Paulo; s. of José Delfim and Maria Delfim; ed. School of Econs. and Management, Univ. de São Paulo; Univ. de São Paulo, Asst. Prof. 1952–54, Assoc. Prof. 1954–59, Prof. 1963; fmr. Dir. Insts. of Man. and Econ. Research, School of Econs. and Man.; mem. São Paulo State Planning Comm. for Devt. 1965; Sec. of Finance, São Paulo State Govt. 1966–67; Minister of Finance 1967–74, of Planning 1979–85; Consultant and Technical Adviser to several orgs. in São Paulo; Order of Merit of the Brazilian Armed Forces; Order of Boyaca (Colombia); Order of Christ (Portugal); Ordine del Merito (Italy); Légion d'honneur (France). *Publications:* O Mercado de Açucar no Brasil 1958, O Problema do Café no Brasil 1959, O Trigo no Brasil 1960, Alguns Aspectos da Inflação Brasileira 1963, Agricultura e Desenvolvimento 1966, Planejamento para o Desenvolvimento 1966. *Leisure interest:* reading. *Address:* 503 Avenida Aclimação, 01531 São Paulo, Brazil.

DELFINI, Delfo; Italian international civil servant; b. 6 July 1913, Rome; ed. Univ. of Rome; Captain in Army Reserve 1939–45; with Shell, Rome 1945–49; expert for econ. questions, Ministry of Foreign Affairs, mem. Italian Del. to OECD 1950–59; Head of Div., Econ. and Social Cttee., European Communities 1960, Dir. 1969, Acting Sec.-Gen. 1971, Sec.-Gen. March 1973–78. *Address:* c/o Ministry of Foreign Affairs, Farnesina, 00194 Rome, Italy.

DELFONT, Baron (Life Peer), cr. 1976, of Stepney in Greater London; **Bernard Delfont,** Kt.; British impresario and leisure executive; b. 5 Sept. 1909, Tokmak, Russia; s. of Isaac and Olga Winogradsky; brother of Lord Grade and uncle of Michael Grade (qq.v.); m. Carole Lynne 1946; one s. two d.; entered theatrical management in Britain 1941; first London production 1942, has since presented many shows in London; re-introduced variety to the West End at the London Casino 1947–48, presenting Laurel and Hardy, Sophie Tucker, Lena Horne, Olsen and Johnson, Mistinguette, etc.; presents summer shows in many seaside resorts; presented the annual Royal Variety Performance until 1978; assumed management of London theatres: Wimbledon 1942, Whitehall 1943, St. Martin's 1943, Winter Garden (with Mala de la Marr) 1944, Saville 1946, New Royalty 1960, Comedy and Shaftesbury theatres 1964; took over lease of Prince of Wales Theatre 1958, New London Theatre 1973; converted London Hippodrome into Talk of the Town theatre restaurant 1958; Chair. and C.E.O. Trusthouse Forte Leisure Ltd. 1981–82; C.E.O. EMI Ltd. March–Dec. 1979, Chair. EMI Film and Theatre Corpn. 1971–79; Dir. Bernard Delfont Org., Central Beach Amusements Ltd., Lewenstein-Delfont Productions Ltd., Bernard Delfont Ltd., Theatre Restaurants Ltd., and many other companies; Pres. Variety Artistes' Fed., Entertainment Artistes Benevolent Fund 1978–; Chair. & C.E.O. First Leisure Corpn. 1982–86, Exec. Chair. 1986–88, Group Pres. March–Nov. 1988, Chair. Nov. 1988–; Trustee, Theatres Trust 1977–; Past Chief Barker, Variety Club of Great Britain; fmr. Pres. Printers' Charitable Corpn. *Recent productions, alone or with others, include:* The Roar of the Greasepaint—The Smell of the Crowd, Pickwick, both in New York (with David Merrick), Barefoot in the Park, The Killing of Sister George, The Matchgirls, Funny Girl, The Odd Couple, Martha Graham Dance Co., Sweet Charity, The Four Musketeers, Golden Boy, Hotel in Amsterdam, Time Present, Mame, Your Own Thing, What the Butler Saw, Cat Among the Pigeons, Carol Channing with her 10 Stout-Hearted Men, The Great Waltz, Kean, Rabelais, Applause, The Threepenny Opera, The Good Old Bad Old Days, The Unknown Soldier and His Wife, A Doll's House, The Wolf, Brief Lives, Henry IV, A Streetcar Named Desire, Cinderella, The Good Companions, The Danny La Rue Show, Harvey, A Little Night Music, Dad's Army, The Plumber's Progress, The Exciting Adventures of Queen Daniella, Great Expectations, Mardi Gras, An Evening with Tommy Steele, It's Magic, Underneath the Arches, Little Me 1984. *Address:* 7 Soho Street, London, W1V 5FA, England. *Telephone:* 01-437 9727.

DELGADO, Alvaro; Spanish artist; b. 9 June 1922, Madrid; m. Mercedes Gal Orendain; one s.; ed. pupil of Vazquez Diaz 1936–39, Benjamin Palencia 1939–42; mem. Real Acad. de Bellas Artes, Real Acad. de San Fernando; Acad. Delegado de la Calcografia; Commdr. Order of Ethiopia; First Prize, Concurso Nacional de Carteles Para Teatro 1939; First Prize, Proyecto Para Figurines y Decorados 1940; Cuba Prize for Painting, IIa Bienal Arte Hispano Americano 1952; Grand Prize for Painting, Bienal de Arte Mediterraneo, Alejandria 1955; Grande Prize for Painting, Exposición Int., Alicante 1960; Primera Medalla de Dibujo, Exposición Nacional Bellas Artes 1960; Gold Medal, Salon Nacional del Grabado 1962; Vocal del Patronato del Museo del Prado, Madrid 1970. *Leisure interest:* constant travel. *Address:* Biarritz 5, Parque de las Avenidas, Madrid 28028, Spain.

DELHAYE, Jean, D. ÉS SC.; French astronomer (retd.); b. 25 Feb. 1921, Lourches; s. of Parfait Delhaye and Rosa Duc; m. Jeanne Guézel 1944; four c.; ed. Facultés des Sciences, Rennes and Paris and Univs. of Leiden and Stockholm; Astronomer, Observatoire de Paris 1943–57; Prof. and Dir. of Observatory, Univ. of Besançon 1957–64; Deputy Dir. Observatoire de Paris 1964–67, Dir. 1968–71; Dir. Inst. Nat. d'Astronomie et de Géophysique 1971–79; Astronomer, Paris Observatory 1979–87; corresp. mem. Acad. des Sciences, Soc. Royale des Sciences de Liège, Acad. Brasileira de Ciencias; mem. Bureau des Longitudes; Officier, Légion d'honneur; Officier, Ordre national du Mérite, Commdr., Ordre des Palmes Acad.

Publications: various articles on astronomy. *Address:* 2 rue de la Pléiade, 94240 L'Hay les Roses, France (Home). *Telephone:* (1) 46 64 57 71 (Home).

DELIBES, Miguel, D.IUR.; Spanish university teacher and writer; b. 17 Oct. 1920, Valladolid; s. of Adolfo and Mària Delibes; m. Angeles de Castro 1946 (died 1974); seven c.; ed. School of Higher Studies, Bilbao, Univ. of Valladolid, School of Journalism, Bilbao; Prof. Univ. of Valladolid 1945–85; Dir. El Norte de Castilla (newspaper) 1956–62; mem. Real Acad. de la Lengua 1973; recipient Premio Nadal, Premio Nacional de Literatura, Premio Príncipe de Asturias. *Publications:* La sombra del ciprés es alargada 1948, El camino 1950, Las ratas 1962, El libro de la caza menor 1964, Cinco horas con Mario 1966, Parábola del náufrago 1969, El disputado voto del señor Cayo 1978, Los santos inocentes 1981, El tesoro 1985, 377-A, madera de héroe 1988. *Leisure interests:* hunting, fishing, tennis. *Address:* c. Dos de Mayo No. 10, 47004 Valladolid, Spain. *Telephone:* 983/300250.

De L'ISLE, 1st Viscount, cr. 1956, 6th Baron De L'Isle and Dudley; **William Philip Sidney**, V.C., K.G., P.C., G.C.M.G., G.C.V.O., K.ST.J., M.A., D.L.; British Peer of the Realm; b. 23 May 1909, London; s. of late 5th Baron De L'Isle and Dudley and Winifred Bevan; m. 1st Hon. Jacqueline Corinne Yvonne Vereker 1940 (died 1962), one s. four d.; m. 2nd Margaret Lady Glanusk 1966; ed. Eton and Magdalene Coll., Cambridge; Fellow of Inst. of Chartered Accountants 1934; with Barclays Bank 1936–39; commissioned Grenadier Guards (Reserve) 1929; served France and Belgium 1939–40, Italy 1943–44; Conservative M.P. for Chelsea 1944–45; Parl. Sec. to Ministry of Pensions 1945; Jt. Treas. Conservative Party 1948; Sec. of State for Air 1951–55; Exec. with Schweppes (Home) Ltd. 1958–61; Gov.-Gen. of Australia 1961–65; Dir. Penshurst Man. Consultants Ltd., City Acre Property Investments Trust Ltd., Palmerston Property Devts., Morton D. Weiner and Co. (Miami); fmr. Dir. and Chair., Phoenix Assurance Co. Ltd. and other public cos.; Pres. British Heart Foundation 1976–84; Chair. and Trustee of the Winston Churchill Memorial Trust, Royal Armouries Museum 1983–86; Chancellor, Order of St. Michael and St. George 1968–84; Hon. Fellow Magdalene Coll., Cambridge 1955; Hon. Bencher Grays Inn; Hon. F.R.I.B.A.; Hon. LL.D. (Sydney) 1963, (Hampden Sidney Coll.) 1982. *Leisure interests:* fishing, shooting, oil painting, gardening, reading biographies. *Address:* Penshurst Place, near Tonbridge, Kent, England (Home). *Telephone:* (0892) 870223.

DELIVANIS, Dr. Dimitrios J.; Greek university teacher; b. 3 April 1909, Vienna; s. of John D. Delivanis and Helen J. Triantaphyllidis; m. Maria Negreponti 1959; one d.; ed. Univs. of Athens, Paris, Berlin and London School of Economics; Asst. Prof. Econs., Univ. of Athens 1938–44; Sec.-Gen. Ministry of Welfare 1939–41; Greek Co-ordinator, Joint Relief Cttee. for Greece 1943–45; Assoc. Prof. of Econs. Salonika Univ. 1944–47, Prof. 1948–74, now Emer.; mem. Exec. Cttee. Centre of Econ. Research 1961–64, Centre of Social Sciences, Athens 1960–67; Vice-Pres. Greek Econ. Asscn. 1961–70, Pres. 1971–75, Hon. Pres. 1975–; mem. Exec. Cttee. Int. Econ. Assscn. 1959–65, Treas. 1965–68; mem. Bd. of Mediterranean Social Sciences Research Centre 1961, Pres. 1965–69; mem. Bd. Inst. of Balkan Studies 1960–73, 1980–82, Exec. Dir. 1971–72, Pres. 1974–79; Vice-Rector, Univ. of Salonika 1964–65, Rector 1965–66, Pro-Rector 1966–67; Pres. Centre of Planning and Econ. Research 1968–73; mem. Bd. of Asscn. Française de Science Economique 1973–76; Corresp. Mem. Econs. Acad. of Barcelona 1967–, Acad. of Athens 1984, Acad. des Sciences Morales et Politiques, Paris 1987–; Guest Prof. at foreign univs. 1949–; Orders of Phoenix (First Class) and George I (Second Class), Greece; Officier, Légion d'honneur, France. *Publications:* La politique des banques allemandes en matière de crédit à court terme 1934, Greek Monetary Developments 1939–48 1949, L'économie sous-développée 1963, Die internationale Liquidität 1965, Economics (in Greek), six edns. 1952–71, L'influence de l'inflation sévissant depuis 1939 1970, Economic and Monetary Policy (in Greek) 5th edn. 1974, numerous articles in Greek, French, German and English. *Leisure interests:* mountaineering, travel. *Address:* Voukourestiou 50, Athens 10673; Morgenthaou 1, Thessaloniki 54622, Greece. *Telephone:* Athens 3613209.

DELL, Rt. Hon. Edmund, P.C., M.A.; British businessman and fmr. politician; b. 15 Aug. 1921, London; s. of Reuben and Frances Dell; m. Susanne Gottschalk 1963; ed. Owen's School, London, The Queens' Coll., Oxford; Lecturer, The Queens' Coll., Oxford 1947–49; Exec. Imperial Chemical Industries Ltd., 1949–63; mem. Manchester City Council 1953–60, Pres. Manchester and Salford Trades Council 1958–61; M.P. for Birkenhead 1964–79; Parl. Sec. Ministry of Tech. 1966–67, Parl. Under-Sec. of State, Dept. of Econ. Affairs 1967–68, Minister of State, Bd. of Trade 1968–69, Minister of State, Dept. of Employment 1969–70, Chair. Public Accounts Cttee. of House of Commons 1972–74, Paymaster-Gen. 1974–76; Sec. of State for Trade 1976–78; apptd. by the European Council as mem. of Cttee. of Three to report on mechanisms and procedures of the Institutions of the EEC 1978–79; Dir., Chair. Guinness Peat Group 1979–82; Founder-Chair. Channel Four TV Co. 1980–87; Chair. Public Finance Foundation 1984–, Prison Reform Trust 1988–; Deputy Chair. of Council, London Chamber of Commerce and Industry 1988–; Deputy Chair. Bd. of Govs., Imperial Coll., Univ. of London; Dir. (non-exec.) Shell Transport and Trading 1979–; Hon. Fellow Fitzwilliam Coll., Cambridge; mem. SDLP. *Publications:* Political Responsibility and Industry 1973; Report on European Institutions (with B. Biesheuvel and R. Marjolin) 1979, The Politics of Economic Interdependence 1987. *Leisure interest:* listening to music.

Address: 4 Reynolds Close, London, NW11 7EA, England. *Telephone:* 01-455 7197.

DELLA CASA-DEBELJEVIC, Lisa (see Casa-Debeljevic).

Del MAR, Norman Rene, C.B.E., F.R.C.M., F.G.S.M.; British conductor; b. 31 July 1919, London; m. Pauline Mann 1947; two s.; ed. Marlborough and Royal Coll. of Music; Asst. to Sir Thomas Beecham, Royal Philharmonic Orchestra 1947; Prin. Conductor English Opera Group 1949–55; Prof. of Conducting Guildhall School of Music 1953–60; Conductor BBC Scottish Orchestra 1960–65; Prin. Guest Conductor Gothenburg Symphony Orchestra 1969–73; Conductor Royal Acad. of Music 1973–77; Conductor and Prof. of Conducting, Royal Coll. of Music; Prin. Conductor Acad. of the BBC 1974–77; Artistic Dir., Norfolk and Norwich Triennial Festival 1979, 1982; Prin. Guest Conductor, Bournemouth Sinfonietta 1982–85; Artistic Dir. and Prin. Conductor Aarhus Symphony Orchestra 1985–88; freelance conductor in U.K. and abroad; Hon. D.Mus. (Glasgow, Bristol, Edinburgh), Hon. D.Litt. (Sussex), Hon. R.A.M. *Publications:* Richard Strauss (3 vols.) 1962–72, Mahler's Sixth Symphony—A Study 1980, Orchestral Variations 1981, Anatomy of the Orchestra 1981, Companion to the Orchestra 1987. *Address:* Witchings, Hadley Common, Herts., England (Home). *Telephone:* 01-449 4836.

DELON, Alain; French actor; b. 8 Nov. 1935; Sceaux; m. Nathalie Delon (dissolved); one s.; with French Marine Corps 1952–55; independent actor-producer under Delbeau (Delon-Beaume) Productions 1964– and Adel Productions 1968–; Commdr. des Arts et des Lettres. *Films include:* Christine 1958, Faibles femmes 1959, Le chemin des écoliers 1959, Purple Noon 1959, Rocco and His Brothers 1960, Eclipse 1961, The Leopard 1962, Any Number Can Win 1962, The Black Tulip 1963, The Love Cage 1963, L'insoumis 1964, The Yellow Rolls Royce 1964, Once a Thief 1964, Les centurions 1965, Paris brûle-t-il? 1965, Texas Across the River 1966, Les adventuriers 1966, Le samourai 1967, Histoires extraordinaires 1967, Diaboliquement votre 1967, Adieu l'ami 1968, Girl on a motorcycle 1968, La piscine 1968, Jeff 1968, Die Boss, Die Quietly 1969, Borsalino 1970, Madly 1970, Doucement les basses 1970, Le cercle rouge 1971, L'assassinat de Trotsky 1971, La veuve Couderc 1971, Un flic 1972, Le professeur 1972, Scorpio 1972, Traitement de choc 1972, Les granges brûlées 1973, Deux hommes dans la ville 1973, Borsalino & Co. 1973, Les seins de glace 1974, Creezy 1975, Zorro 1975, Le gitan 1975, Mr. Klein 1975, Le gang 1977, Mort d'un pourri 1977, Armaguedon 1977, L'homme pressé 1977, Attention, les enfants regardent 1978, Le toubib 1979, Trois hommes à abattre 1980, Pour la peau d'un flic 1981, Le choc 1982, Le battant 1982, Un Amour de Swann 1984, Notre Histoire 1984, Parole de flic 1985, Le passage 1986. *Stage performances:* 'Tis Pity She's a Whore 1961, 1962, Les yeux crevés 1967; also television appearances. *Address:* 4 rue Chambiges, 75008 Paris, France.

DE LORENZO, Francesco; Italian politician, surgeon and university teacher; b. 5 June 1938, Naples; Prof. of Biological Chem., Univ. of Naples; mem. Nat. Exec. of Italian Liberal Party; M.P. for Naples 1983–; Under-Sec. of State, Ministry of Health, Minister of the Environment 1986–87. *Address:* Camera del Deputati, Rome, Italy.

DELORME, Jacques Emile; French international civil servant; b. 2 Dec. 1926, Isques; s. of Albert Delorme and Louise Delorme-Vasseur; m. Armelle Sourrieu 1954; five d.; ed. Ecole Polytechnique, Ecole Supérieure du Génie Maritime; Gen. Chief armaments eng. 1966; Head of Tech. Services, Ministry of Industry 1970–75; Vice-Pres. European Patent Office 1976–; Officier, Ordre du Mérite, Officier, Légion d'honneur. *Leisure interests:* reading, sport. *Address:* European Patent Office, 2 Patentlaan, Rijswijk, Z.H. (Office); Belgischeplein 29A, The Hague, Netherlands (Residence); 5 rue du Parc, Meudon, France (Home). *Telephone:* 90-67-89 (Office).

DELORME, Jean; French mining engineer and company administrator; b. 25 Oct. 1902, Paris; s. of Paul Delorme and Marthe Frommel; m. Sabine Kablé 1937; two s. one d.; ed. Lycée Janson-de-Sailly, Ecole Nat. Supérieure des Mines, Paris; pit engineer, Béthune mines 1925, engineer 1927, Dir. Chemical Dept. 1933, Dir.-Gen. 1935; Pres. and C.E.O. Air Liquide 1945–85 (Hon. Chair. 1985–), Soc. d'oxygène et d'acétylène d'Extrême-Orient 1946–; Vice-Pres. Bd. of Dirs. La Soudure Co. 1956, Pres. 1971; Administrator Soc. Chimique de la Grande Paroisse, Lyonnaise industrielle et pharmaceutique; f. and Pres. Eurospace 1961–; Vice-Pres. Assen. Int. des Constructeurs de Matériel Aérospatial 1961; Pres. Bd. of Dirs. Monaco Oceanographie Inst. 1961; mem. Bd. Ecole Nat. d'Admin. 1971; Grand Officier, Légion d'honneur, Croix de guerre, Médaille de la Résistance. *Publications:* la Mer et l'espace, Nouvelles conquêtes dans l'espace et la mer. *Address:* 75 quai d'Orsay, 75007 Paris (Office); 1 avenue du Maréchal Maunoury, 75016 Paris, France (Home).

DELORME, Jean-Claude, O.C., Q.C., LL.L.; Canadian lawyer and business executive; b. 22 May 1934, Montréal; s. of Adrien Delorme and Marie-Anne Rodrigue; m. Paule Tardif 1961; two d.; ed. Coll. Sainte-Marie, Montréal, and Univ. of Montréal; admitted to Québec Bar 1960; with law firm Martineau, Allison, Beaulieu, Tetley and Phelan, Montréal 1960–63; Sec. and Gen. Counsel, Canadian Corpn. for Expo '67 1963–68; Gen. Counsel and Asst. to Chair. and C.E.O., Standard Brands Ltd. 1968–69; Vice-Pres. (Admin.), Sec. and Gen. Counsel, Telesat Canada 1969–71; Pres. and C.E.O. Teleglobe Canada 1971–; Chair. Capital Campaign, Montréal

Museum of Fine Arts 1985–; mem. numerous Bds., cos. etc. *Leisure interests:* reading, swimming, sailing, skiing, cycling. *Address:* Teleglobe Canada, 680 Sherbrooke Street West, Montréal, Qué. H3A 2S4 (Office); 3 Glendale Avenue, Beaconsfield, Qué. H9W 5P6, Canada (Home). *Telephone:* (514) 289-7777 (Office); (514) 697-5840 (Home).

DELORS, Jacques Lucien Jean; French politician and economist; b. 20 July 1925, Paris; s. of Louis Delors and Jeanne Rigal; m. Marie Lephaille 1948; one s. one d.; ed. Lycée Voltaire, Paris, Lycée Blaise-Pascal, Clermont-Ferrand, Univ. of Paris; Head of Dept., Banque de France 1945–62, attached to staff of Dir.-Gen. of Securities and Financial Market 1950–62, mem. Gen. Council 1973–79; mem. Planning and Investments Section, Econ. and Social Council 1959–61; Head of Social Affairs Section, Commissariat général du Plan 1962–69; Sec.-Gen. Interministerial Cttee. for Vocational Training and Social Promotion 1969–73; Adviser to Jacques Chaban-Delmas (q.v.) 1969, Chargé de mission 1971–72; mem. Bd. of Dirs. Banque de France 1973–79; Assoc. Prof. of Co. Man., Univ. of Paris IX 1973–79; f. Club Echange et Projets 1974; Dir. Labour and Soc. Research Centre 1975–79; Parti Socialiste Nat. Del. for int. econ. relations 1976–81; elected mem. Ass. of the European Communities 1979, Chair. Econ. and Monetary Cttee. 1979–81; Minister for the Economy and Finance 1981–83, for the Economy, Finance and Budget 1983–84; Mayor of Clichy 1983–84; Pres. Comm. of the European Communities Jan. 1985–, Commr. for Monetary Affairs 1985–, Gen. Admin. and Co-ordination of Structural Funds 1985–89; Hon. LL.D. (Univ. of Glasgow); Chevalier, Légion d'honneur. *Publications:* Les indicateurs sociaux 1971, Changer 1971, En sortir ou pas (jtly.) 1985; numerous articles; reports for UN on French planning (1966) and long-term planning (1969). *Address:* Commission of the European Communities, 200 rue de la Loi, 1049 Brussels, Belgium (Office); 19 boulevard de Bercy, 75012 Paris, France (Home). *Telephone:* 260 33 00 (Office).

de los ANGELES, Victoria; Spanish soprano singer; b. (as Victoria Gómez Cima) 1 Nov. 1923, Barcelona; m. Enrique Magriñá 1948 (deceased); two s.; ed. Univ. and Conservatoire of Barcelona; Barcelona début 1945, Paris Opera and La Scala, Milan 1949, Royal Opera House, Covent Garden, London 1950, Metropolitan Opera House, New York 1951, Vienna State Opera 1957; numerous appearances at other opera houses, concert tours and recordings; 1st Prize, Geneva Int. Competition 1947; Cross of Lazo de Dama of the Order of Isabel the Catholic, Condecoración Banda de la Orden Civil de Alfonso X (El Sabio), Spain and numerous other orders and decorations. *Address:* Avenida de Pedralbes 57, 08034 Barcelona, Spain.

DE LOSADA GONZALO, Sanchez; Bolivian politician; fmr. Minister of Planning; Pres. Cand. of Movimiento Nacionalista Revolucionario (MNR). *Address:* Movimiento Nacionalista Revolucionario, Genaro Saujines 541, Pasaje Kuljis, La Paz, Bolivia.

DELOUVRIER, Paul; French civil servant; b. 25 June 1914, Remiremont; s. of Roger and Suzanne (née François) Delouvrier; m. Louise van Lith 1946; four s. one d.; ed. Coll. Saint-Etienne, Strasbourg, Faculté de Droit and Inst. d'Etudes Politiques, Paris; Inspector, Ministry of Finance 1941; Dir. Finance Div., Monnet Plan Commissariat Gen. 1946–47; Dir. du Cabinet, Ministry of Finance 1947–48; Dir.-Gen. of Taxes 1948–53; Sec.-Gen. Interministerial Cttee. on European Econ. Co-operation; Dir. of Finance, European Iron and Steel Community 1955–58; Del.-Gen. in Algeria Dec. 1958–60; Prof. Inst. of Political Studies, Paris 1948–, mem. Bd. of Dirs. 1969–; Pres. Foyer d'accueil internat. de Paris 1968–; Del.-Gen. Paris Region 1961–69; Prefect of Paris Region 1966–69; Pres. Inst. of Housing and Town Planning, Paris Region 1962–69; Pres. Conseil d'Admin., Electricité de France 1969–79; Pres. West Atlantic Asscn. for Industrial Devt. 1970–80; Pres. Plan-Construction 1970–80, Founder-Pres. 1980–; Pres. Parc de la Villette 1979–84; mem. Conseil économique and social 1979–; Grand Prix d'Urbanisme de l'Acad. d'architecture, Prix Erasme 1985; Croix de guerre, Grand Croix, Légion d'honneur, Grand-Croix, Ordre nat. du Mérite, Commdr. de l'Etoile noire, Officier du Mérite civil. *Address:* 7 avenue de Ségur, 75007 Paris, France. *Telephone:* 705-14-64.

del PORTILLO, Monsignor Alvaro, D.C.ENG., D.PHIL.LITT., D.C.L.; Spanish priest; b. 11 March 1914, Madrid; s. of Ramón del Portillo and Clementina Diez de Sollano (deceased); ed. Higher Technical School of Civil Eng., Madrid, Univ. of Madrid, Angelicum Univ., Rome; trained as engineer; ordained Roman Catholic priest 1944; Procurator Gen. Opus Dei 1947–56, Sec.-Gen. 1940–47, 1956–75, Pres.-Gen. 1975–82; Prelate of Opus Dei 1982–; Consultor to the Sacred Congregation of the Religious, Vatican Curia 1954–66, to the Sacred Congregation of the Council 1959–66; Pres. Antepreparatory Comm. of Vatican Council II for the Laity 1960–61, Examiner of the Sacred Congregation of the Holy Office 1960, Judge 1960; Sec. Comm. for the Clergy, Vatican Council II 1962–65; Consultor to Conciliar Comm. for Bishops for Religious, for the Discipline of the Faith; Consultor to the Pontifical Comm. for Reform of the Code of Canon Law 1963–83, to the Congregation for the Doctrine of the Faith 1966–83, to the Sacred Congregation for the Clergy 1966–, to the Sacred Congregation for the Causes of the Saints 1982–, to the Pontifical Comm. for Social Communications 1984–; mem. Secr. Synod of Bishops 1983, mem. Synod of Bishops 1987; Grand Chancellor, Univs. of Navarra (Spain), Piura (Peru) 1975 and La Sabana (Colombia) 1980; Kt. of Honour and Devotion of the Supreme

Order of Malta 1958; Grand Cross of St. Raymond of Pennafort 1967, Hon. Academician, Pontificia Academia Theologica Romana 1982. *Publications:* Discovery and Explorations of the Coasts of California 1947, Faithful and Laity in the Church 1969, On Priesthood 1970, Ethics and Law 1971, Associations for Priests 1975, In Memory of Mgr. Escrivá de Balaguer 1976. *Address:* Viale Bruno Buozzi 73, 00197 Rome, Italy. *Telephone:* 879042.

De LUCCHI, Michele; Italian architect; b. 8 Nov. 1951, Ferrara; s. of Alberto De Lucchi and Giuliana Zannini; ed. Liceo Scientifico Enrico Fermi, Padua, Faculty of Architecture, Univ. of Florence; founder mem., Cavart (avant-garde design and architecture group) 1973-76; Asst. Prof., Univ. of Florence 1976-77; worked with Gaetano Pesce, Superstudio, Andrea Branzi, Ettore Sottsass 1977-80; Consultant, Centrokappa Noviglio, Milan 1978; Consultant, Olivetti Synthesis, Massa 1979-, Olivetti SpA, Ivrea 1984-; freelance designer, several furniture mfrs. 1979-; founder mem., Int. Designer Group Memphis 1981-. *Publication:* Architetture Verticali 1978. *Leisure interest:* travel photography. *Address:* Via Vittoria Colonna 8, 20149 Milan (Office); Via Cenisio 40, 20154 Milan, Italy (Home). *Telephone:* (02) 468556 (Office); (02) 314636 (Home).

DELVALLE, Eric Arturo; Panamanian politician; b. 2 Feb. 1937, Panama; m. Mariela Díaz de Delvalle; one s. two d.; ed. Colegio Javier, Panama City, Louisiana State Univ. and Soulé Coll. of Accountancy; fmr. Chair. and Dir. of several pvt. commercial enterprises; mem. Bd. of Dirs. Inst. for Econ. Promotion 1963; mem. Games Control Bd. 1960-64; Del. to Nat. Ass. 1968; Vice-Pres. Nat. Ass. 1968; Leader, Repub. Party; Vice-Pres. of Panama 1984, Pres. 1985-88 (removed from office for alleged drug-trafficking).

DEL VALLE ALLIENDE, Jaime; Chilean lawyer and politician; b. 2 July 1931, Santiago; m. Paulina Swinburn Pereira; four c.; ed. Escuela de Derecho de la Universidad Católica de Chile; taught at Catholic Univ. Law School from 1955, appt. Dir. 1969, Dean 1970; various posts in Supreme Court 1958-64; Public Prosecutor 1964-74; Pro-Rector, Pontificia Univ. Católica de Chile 1974; Dir.-Gen. nat. TV channel 1975-78; mem. Bd. Colegio de Abogados 1981-, Pres. 1982-83; Minister of Justice Feb.-Dec. 1983; Minister of Foreign Affairs 1983-87. *Address:* c/o Ministerio de Asuntos Exteriores, Palacio de la Moneda, Santiago, Chile. *Telephone:* 6982501.

DELVAUX, Paul; Belgian artist; b. 1897; ed. Brussels Acad. of Fine Arts; began as a painter of portraits, land- and sea-scapes; after travel in France and Italy adopted the surrealistic style; has executed murals in the Kursaal, Ostend, Inst. de Zoologie, Liège, and in private houses in Brussels; Prof. Inst. Nat. Supérieur d'Architecture et des Arts Décoratifs, Brussels; mem. Acad. Royale des Sciences, des Lettres et des Beaux Arts de Belgique; exhbn. at Piccadilly Gallery, London 1966. *Address:* c/o Académie Royale des Sciences, des Lettres et des Beaux Arts de Belgique, Palais des Académies, 1 rue Ducale, 1000 Brussels, Belgium.

de MAIZIÉRE, General Ulrich; German army officer; b. 24 Feb. 1912, Stade; s. of Walther de Maizière and Elisabeth Dückers; m. Eva Werner 1944; two s. two d.; ed. Humanistisches Gymnasium, Hanover; army service 1930, commissioned 1933; Battalion and Regimental Adjutant, 50th Infantry Reg.; Gen. Staff Coll., Dresden 1940; during Second World War Gen. Staff Duties with 18th Motorized Infantry Div., G3 and Chief of Staff of 10th Mechanized Div., wounded 1944, at end of war Deputy Chief of Operations Div. Army Gen. Staff; Prisoner-of-war 1945-47; dealer in books and sheet music 1947-51; Office of Fed. Commr. for Nat. Security Affairs 1951; Col. and Chief of Ops. Branch, Fed. Armed Forces Staff 1955; Commdr. of Combat Team A1 and Commdr. 2nd Brigade 1958; Deputy Commdr. 1st Armoured Infantry Div. 1959; Commdt. Fed. Armed Forces School for Leadership and Character Guidance 1960-62, Fed. Armed Forces Command and Staff Coll. 1962-64; Chief of Army Staff 1964-66; Chief of Fed. Armed Forces Staff 1966-72; Hon. Pres. Claüsewitz Gesellschaft; Commdr., Légion d'honneur 1962, Freiherr-von-Stein-Preis 1964, Commdr. Legion of Merit 1965, 1969, Grand Officier, Légion d'honneur 1969, Grosses Bundesverdienstkreuz mit Stern und Schulterband 1970, Hermann-Ehlers-Preis 1986; retd. *Publications:* Die Landesverteidigung im Rahmen der Gesamtverteidigung 1964, Soldatische Führung heute 1966, Bekenntnis zum Soldaten 1971, Führen im Frieden 1974, Verteidigung in Europa—Mitte 1975, In Der Pflicht (autobiog.) 1989. *Leisure interests:* classical music, literature, temporary history. *Address:* 5300 Bonn 2, Bad Godesberg, Eschenweg 37, Federal Republic of Germany. *Telephone:* 0228/321972.

DE MARCO, Guido, LL.D., M.P.; Maltese politician; b. 22 July 1931, Valletta; s. of Emmanuel de Marco and Giovanna Raniolo; m. Violet Saliba; three c.; ed. St. Aloysius Coll. and Royal Univ. of Malta; Crown Counsel 1964-66; mem. Parl. 1966-; Deputy Prime Minister and Minister for Internal Affairs and Justice 1987-; Nationalist Party. *Address:* Ministry of Justice, The Palace, Valletta, Malta.

De MARTINO, Ciro; Italian banker; b. 12 Dec. 1903; m. Renata Cametti; two d.; ed. Università degli Studi, Rome; joined Banca d'Italia, Cosenza br. 1927, Sec. to Vice Gen. Man. 1931, Asst. Insp. 1940; Rep. to Banca d'Italia at Interdepartmental Comm. on change of currency; Chair. Interbanks Cttee., negotiating re-establishment of Italian bank brs., in East

Africa 1948; Adviser to Somali authorities on Italian banking in the territory 1950; Senior Insp. in charge of Gen. Inspectorate, Banca d'Italia 1951, Head of Org. Dept. 1953, Gen. Insp. and Head of Banking Supervision Dept. 1960; resgnd. 1965; Chair. Bd. of Dirs., Banco di Sicilia, Palermo, 1965-78, Hon. Pres. 1978-; Kt. of Grand Cross, Ordine al Merito della Repubblica Italiana. *Address:* Via Dei Colli Della Farnesina 118, 00194 Rome, Italy (Home).

De MARTINO, Francesco; Italian university professor and politician; b. 31 May 1907, Naples; ed. Liceo Gianbattista Vico, Naples, and Univ. degli Studi, Naples; Prof. of History of Roman Law, Univ. of Naples 1934-38, Univ. of Messina 1938-40, Univ. of Bari 1940-50, Univ. of Naples 1950-, now Emer.; mem. Chamber of Deputies 1948-82; Sec. Partito Socialista Italiano 1964-66; Joint Sec. Unified Italian Socialist Party 1966-70; Sec.-Gen. Partito Socialista Italiano (PSI) 1972-76; Deputy Prime Minister 1968-69, 1970-72; Senator 1983-87; Fellow Accad. dei Lincei. *Publications:* Storia della Costituzione Romana, Vol. 5, Storia economica di Roma antica, Vol. 2, and numerous legal, historical and political articles. *Address:* Via Aniello Falcone 258, 1-80127 Naples, Italy.

DEMAS, William Gilbert, M.A.; Trinidadian economist and civil servant; b. 14 Nov. 1929, Port-of-Spain; s. of late Herman and Audrey (née Walters) Demas; m. Norma Taylor 1958; one d.; ed. Queen's Royal Coll., Trinidad and Emmanuel Coll., Cambridge; Adviser to W. Indies Trade Comm. U.K. 1957-58; Head, Econ. Planning Div., Govt. of Trinidad and Tobago 1959-66; Perm. Sec. Ministry of Planning and Devt. 1966-68; Econ. Adviser to the Prime Minister 1968-69; Sec.-Gen. Commonwealth Caribbean Regional Secr. 1970-74; Pres. Caribbean Devt. Bank 1974-; Dir. Cen. Bank; Chair. Multi-Sectoral Planning Task Force (Trinidad and Tobago) 1985-; Humming Bird Gold Medal (for public service). *Publications:* Economics of Development in Small Countries 1965, Planning and the Price Mechanism in the Context of Caribbean Economic Integration 1966. *Leisure interests:* films, listening to all kinds of music. *Address:* c/o Caribbean Development Bank, P.O.B. 408, Wildey, St. Michael, Barbados (Office); Harbour View, Collymore Rock, St. Michael, Barbados, West Indies (Home).

DE MATOS PROENCA, Joao Uva, D.JUR.; Portuguese diplomatist; m.; two c.; ed. Lisbon Univ.; entered Ministry of Foreign Affairs 1961, Consul in Porto Alegre, Brazil 1965, served in Portuguese Embassy Malawi 1970-72, Head of African and Asian Dept. 1974; Amb. to Nigeria 1976-79, to Czechoslovakia 1979-81; Dir. Gen. for Political Affairs in Foreign Ministry 1981-86; Perm. Rep. of Portugal to UN 1986-. *Address:* Permanent Mission of Portugal to the United Nations, 777 Third Avenue, 27th Floor, New York, N.Y. 10017, U.S.A. *Telephone:* 759-9444.

de MAYO, Paul, PH.D., D. ÉS SC., F.R.S.C., F.R.S.; Canadian chemist; b. 8 Aug. 1924, London; s. of Nissim de Mayo and Anna B. Juda; m. Mary Turnbull 1949; one s. one d.; ed. Univ. of Exeter and Birkbeck Coll., Univ. of London; Asst. Lecturer, Birkbeck Coll. 1954-55; Lecturer, Univ. of Glasgow 1955-57, Imperial Coll., Univ. of London 1957-59; Prof. Univ. of W. Ont. 1959-, Dir. Photochem. Unit 1969-72; Merck, Sharp & Dohme Lecture Award 1966; Centennial Medal (Canada) 1967, CIC Palladium Medal Award 1982, E. W. R. Steacie Award in Photochem. 1985. *Publications:* Ed. Molecular Rearrangements, Vol. I 1963, Vol. II 1964, Rearrangements in Ground and Excited States (3 vols.) 1980; Monographs: Mono and Sesquiterpenoids 1959, The Higher Terpenoids 1959; over 200 publications in scientific journals. *Leisure interests:* drinking wine, making furniture. *Address:* Department of Chemistry, University of Western Ontario, London, Ont. N6A 5B7 (Office); 436 St. George Street, London, Ont. N6A 3B4, Canada (Home). *Telephone:* 519-661-2171 (Office).

DEMCHENKO, Vladimir Akimovich; Soviet official; b. 1920; ed. Bauman Tech. School and CPSU Cen. Cttee. Party Higher School; design engineer 1944-45; mem. CPSU 1946-; Deputy Head of a Dept., Moscow City Cttee., League of Communist Youth (Komsomol) 1945-52; Sec. Moscow Dist. Cttee. CPSU 1952-63, First Sec. in charge of Industry 1963-64; Second Sec. Moscow Dist. Cttee. CPSU 1964-67; mem. (and mem. Presidium) R.S.F.S.R. Supreme Soviet 1963-67; cand. mem. Cen. Cttee. CPSU 1966-; mem. Auditing Comm. of U.S.S.R. Supreme Soviet 1966-70; Deputy Chair. R.S.F.S.R. Council of Ministers 1967-. *Address:* Council of Ministers of the R.S.F.S.R., Moscow, U.S.S.R.

DE MEL, Ronnie (Ronald Joseph Godfrey), B.A., D.LITT.; Sri Lankan politician; b. 11 April 1925, Moratuwa; m. Mallika Lakshmi Fernando 1952; three d.; ed. St. Thomas Coll., Mount Lavinia, Univs. of Sri Lanka and Cambridge; Asst. Govt. Agent, Ceylon Civil Service 1948; Asst. Sec. Ministry of Industries 1949, Ministry of Agric. and Lands 1950; Sen. Asst. Sec. Ministry of Irrigation, Lands and Land Devt. 1952; Controller of Immigration and Emigration 1955; Commr. of Co-operative Devt. and Registrar of Co-operative Socs. 1957; Dir.-Gen. of Broadcasting 1960; M.P. for Devinuwara 1967-; Minister of Finance 1977, of Finance and Planning 1978-88; Gov. World Bank and IMF; Vice-Pres. Asian Devt. Bank 1980-85, Pres. 1985-86, Chair. Bd. of Govs. 1985-86; Chair. Parl. Cttees. on Company Law Reform and Land Reform. *Publication:* Agricultural Plan of Sri Lanka 1958. *Leisure interests:* agriculture, landscape gardening, tennis, swimming, reading, collecting china, paintings and antique furniture. *Address:* Ministry of Finance and Planning, The Secretariat, Colombo 1; 5 Charles Drive, Colombo 3, Sri Lanka (Home). *Telephone:* 31028 (Office).

DE MELO, Eurico; Portuguese politician and chemical engineer; b. Sept. 1925; worked in the Textile industry; taught Textile Chem. at Faculty of Engineering, Oporto; mem. Popular Democratic Party (PPD, now PSD) May 1974–; Chair. District Political Cttee. of Braga; Civil Gov. of Braga 1975–76; Minister of the Interior 1980–81, of State and of Internal Admin. 1986–87; Deputy Prime Minister and Minister of Defence 1987–; mem. Social Democratic Party (PSD) Nat. Political Cttee. *Address:* c/o Ministerio da Defesa Nacional, Rua Gomes Teixeira, 1300 Lisbon, Portugal.

DEMERITTE, Richard C., F.A.I.A., F.C.A.A., G.G.A., F.B.I.M.; Bahamian diplomatist; b. 27 Feb. 1939, Nassau; s. of Richard and Miriam (née Whitfield) Demeritte; m. Ruth Smith 1966; one s. two d.; ed. Eastern Secondary School, Bahamas School of Commerce, Metropolitan Coll., London, and Century Univ., U.S.A.; Deputy Treas. Treasury Dept. 1956–79; Auditor-Gen. Commonwealth of the Bahamas 1980–84; High Commr. in U.K. 1984–87; Pres. Asscn. of Int. Accountants. *Leisure interests:* golf, chess, pool, electronic and mechanical gadgets. *Address:* P.O. Box N-4242, Nassau, Bahamas.

de MERODE, Prince Werner; Belgian diplomatist; b. 25 March 1914, St Gilles; m. Mathilde Rolin 1947; two s. four d.; ed. in Belgium; served Embassy in London 1944, in Paris 1944–46; Ministry of Foreign Affairs 1946–48; Second Sec., London 1948–51; Ministry 1951–53; First Sec., later Counsellor, Athens 1953–55; Counsellor, Ottawa 1955–58; Counsellor, Perm. Mission to EEC 1958–59; Minister Counsellor, Paris 1959–63, Minister Plenipotentiary 1963–65; Dir. of European Affairs, Ministry of Foreign Affairs, also Insp. of Personnel 1965–72; Amb. to Vatican City 1972–76, to France 1976–79; Chair. Banco di Roma (Belgio) S.A. 1980–; Grand Officier de l'Ordre de la Couronne (Belgium), Croix de guerre (Belgium), Croix des Evadés (Belgium), Grand Cross, Order of Pius IX (Vatican City), Commdr., Légion d'honneur, Croix de guerre, Hon. K.C.V.O. *Address:* Banco di Roma (Belgio) S.A., rue Joseph II 24, 1040 Brussels (Office); Rue Van Eyck 28, 1050 Brussels, Belgium (Home). *Telephone:* (02) 64844 21.

DE MICHELIS, Gianni; Italian politician and professor of chemistry; b. 26 Nov. 1940, Venice; Prof. of Chem., Univ. of Padua; Lecturer in Chem., Univ. of Venice; Nat. Chair. Unione Goliardica Italiana 1962–64; Councillor, Venice 1964–76; mem. Cen. Cttee. Italian Socialist Party (PSI) 1969–76, mem. Nat. Exec. 1976–; M.P. for Venice 1976–; fmr. Minister for State-owned Industries; Minister of Labour and Social Security 1986–87; Deputy Prime Minister April 1988–. *Address:* Camera del Deputati, Rome, Italy.

DEMICHEV, Pyotr Nilovich; Soviet politician; b. 3 Jan 1918; ed. Moscow Mendeleyev Chemical and Technological Inst.; Soviet Army 1937–44; Instructor, Moscow Mendeleyev Chemical and Technological Inst. 1944–45; Party Work 1945–56; Sec. Moscow Regional Cttee. CPSU 1956–58; Business-Man. U.S.S.R. Council of Ministers 1958–59; First Sec. Moscow Regional Cttee., CPSU 1959–60; mem. Bureau of CPSU Cen. Cttee. for R.S.F.S.R. 1959–61; First Sec. Moscow City Cttee., CPSU 1960–62; mem. Cen. Cttee. CPSU 1961–88, Sec. CPSU Cen. Cttee. 1961–74, Cand. mem. Politburo CPSU Cen. Cttee. 1964; Minister of Culture 1974–86; First Vice-Chair. Presidium U.S.S.R. Supreme Soviet 1986–88; Deputy to U.S.S.R. Supreme Soviet 1962–66; Sixty Years of Armed Forces of U.S.S.R. Medal; Order of Lenin (three times), Order of Red Banner and other decorations. *Address:* Supreme Soviet, Moscow, U.S.S.R.

DEMIDOVA, Alla Sergeyevna; Soviet film actress; b. 29 Sept. 1936; ed. Moscow Univ. and Shchukin Theatre School; acted with Taganka Theatre, Moscow 1964–; in films since 1957–; People's Artist of R.S.F.S.R. 1984. *Roles include:* Olga (Day Stars) 1968, Maria Spiridonova (The Sixth of July) 1968, Zhenya (A Degree of Risk) 1969, Julia von Meck (Tchaikovsky) 1970, Lesya Ukrainka (I Come to You) 1972, Jana (The Choice of a Goal), 1973, Liza (The Mirror) A. Tarkovsky, 1975, the Soothsayer (The Little Scarlet Flower) 1978, Pashenka (Father Sergius) 1978, Duchess of Marlborough (A Glass of Water) TV 1979, mother of Lida (Starfall) 1982. *Address:* Taganka Theatre, Moscow, U.S.S.R.

DEMIRCHIAN, Kamo Seropovich, D.TECH.SCI; Soviet scientist and academic; b. 25 October 1928, Rostov-on-Don; one d.; ed. Yerevan Electromechanical Inst. 1946; technician in Armenergo lab. 1946–47; ed. Leningrad Polytechnic Inst.; post-graduate Leningrad Polytechnic Inst. 1953–56, asst. dean, sr. researcher, Prof. 1956–76, Head of Dept. 1975–78; mem. CPSU 1963–; Prof. 1970, Head of lab. U.S.S.R. Acad. of Sciences Inst. of High Temperatures 1978–; Head of Dept. at Moscow Energetics Inst. 1981–; mem. U.S.S.R. Acad. of Sciences 1984; main work on theory of electromagnetic fields, complex electric chains etc. *Address:* U.S.S.R. Academy of Sciences, Moscow V-71, Leninksky Pr. 14, U.S.S.R.

DEMIRCHIAN, Karen Serpovich; Soviet politician; b. 1932, Yerevan, Armenia; mem. CPSU 1962; ed. Polytechnic Inst. and Party High School of Cen. Cttee. CPSU; Chief Engineer of a scientific research inst., Leningrad; Deputy Chief and Sec. of Party Cttee. of Electrotechnical Works, Yerevan 1954–58; Chief Engineer and Dir. Electrotechnical Works, Yerevan 1961–66; Second Sec. Yerevan City Dist. of Armenian CP 1966–72; mem. Cen. Cttee. Armenian CP 1966–; mem., later Sec., Politburo of Armenian CP 1972–74; First Sec. Cen. Cttee. of Armenian CP 1974–88; mem. Presidium of Armenian S.S.R. 1976–; mem. Cen. Cttee. CPSU 1986–; Chair. Mandate Comm. of U.S.S.R. 1979–; Head of Power Efficiency Dept., U.S.S.R. Acad.

of Sciences 1986–. *Address:* Office of the First Secretary, Communist Party, Yerevan, Armenia, U.S.S.R.

DEMIREL, Süleyman; Turkish engineer and politician b. 1924; ed. Istanbul Technical Univ.; qualified engineer; worked in U.S.A. 1949–51; 1954–55; with Dir.-Gen. of Electrical Studies, Ankara 1950–52; in charge of building various hydro-electric schemes 1952–54; Head of Dept. of Dams; Dir.-Gen. of Water Control 1954–55; first Eisenhower Fellow for Study in U.S.A. 1955; Dir. State Hydraulics Admin. 1955–60; teacher of Eng., Middle East Tech. Univ. 1960–64; in private practice 1961–65 (consultant to Morrison-Knudsen); Pres. Justice Party 1964–81, Correct Way Party 1987–; Deputy Prime Minister Feb.-Oct. 1965; Prime Minister 1965–71, 1975–June 1977, July-Dec. 1977, 1979–80; detained after coup Sept. 1980; released Oct. 1980, detained June-Sept. 1983, released Sept. 1983. *Address:* Ankara, Turkey.

De MITA, Luigi Ciriaco; Italian politician; b. 2 Feb. 1928, Fusco, Avellino; fmr. mem. Catholic Action; mem. Chamber of Deputies for Benevento-Avellino-Salerno 1963, 1972–; Nat. Counsellor Partito Democrazia Cristiana (Christian Democrats) (DC) 1964, later Political Vice-Sec.; Under-Sec. for the Interior; Minister of Industry and Commerce 1973–74, of Foreign Trade 1974–76; Minister without Portfolio with responsibility for the Mezzogiorno July 1976–79; Sec.-Gen. DC 1982–88; Prime Minister of Italy April 1988–. *Address:* c/o Partito Democrazia Cristiana, Piazza del Gesù 46, 00186 Rome, Italy.

DEMUS, Jörg; Austrian concert pianist; b. 2 Dec. 1928, St. Pölten, Lower Austria; s. of Dr. Otto and Erika (Budik) Demus; ed. Vienna State Acad. of Music and studies with various musicians; début at age 14; Gesellschaft der Musikfreunde, Vienna; débuts in London and Switzerland 1950, tour of Latin America 1951, Paris 1953, New York 1955, Japan 1961; has performed in almost all important musical centres; has made over 350 LP records; Dr. h.c. (Amherst Univ.); Premier Busoni at Int. Piano Competition, Bolzano 1956; Harriet Cohen Bach-Medal 1958; Hon. Prof. of Austria 1977; Beethoven Ring, Vienna Beethoven Soc. 1977; Mozart Medal, Mozartgemeinde, Vienna 1979; several Edison Awards and Grand Prix du Disque. *Publications:* Abenteuer der Interpretation (essays); co-author of a book on Beethoven's piano sonatas. *Leisure interests:* antiques, nature, collecting and restoring historic keyboard instruments. *Address:* Döblinger Hauptstrasse 77A, A-1190 Vienna, Austria. *Telephone:* (0222) 366238.

DEMUS, Otto, DR. PHIL., M.A.; Austrian art historian; b. 4 Nov. 1902, Harland; s. of Dr. Karl and Paula Demus; m. Dr. Margarete Demus 1953; ed. Univ. of Vienna; Asst. Inst. for History of Art, Univ. of Vienna 1928–29; keeper of monuments in Carinthia 1929–36; monuments officer in Fed. Monuments Office 1936–39; voluntary emigration to England 1939; returned to Austria 1946; Pres. Fed. Monuments Office 1946–; lecturer on History of Art, Univ. of Vienna 1937–39, 1946–51, Prof. 1951–; Slade Prof. Art, Cambridge 1968–69; mem. Vienna Acad. of Science and Inst. of Archaeology, Mainz Acad. of Sciences, Acad. des Inscriptions et Belles-Lettres, Acad. Palermo, British Acad., Acad. of Athens, Acad. of Serbia; Fellow, Soc. of Antiquaries 1960; mem. Ateneo Veneto; Dr.h.c. (Munich), (Padua); Austrian Cross of Honour for Science and Art (1st Class) 1959, Grosses Ehrenzeichen der Republik Österreich 1965, Commdr. Ordine al Merito della Repubblica Italiana 1965, Grosses österreichisches Verdienstzeichen für Kunst und Wissenschaft 1975, Mitchell Prize 1985. *Publications:* Byzantine Mosaics in Greece (with E. Diez) 1931, Die Mosaiken von San Marco in Venedig 1100-1300 1935, Byzantine Mosaic Decoration 1947, Sicilian Mosaics of the Norman Period 1949, The Church of San Marco in Venice 1960, Romanische Wandmalerei 1968, Byzantine Art and the West 1970, The Mosaics of San Marco 1984. *Leisure interests:* reading, music, walking, travel. *Address:* Prinz Eugenstrasse 27, 1030 Vienna III, Austria. *Telephone:* 78-42-094.

DEMUTH, Richard H., A.B., LL.B.; American lawyer and financier; b. 11 Sept. 1910, New York; s. of Leopold and Dora Holzman Demuth; m. Eunice Burdick 1947; one d.; ed. Princeton Univ. and Harvard Law School; Law Clerk to Fed. Circuit Judge 1934–35; practised law in New York with firm of Simpson, Thacher and Bartlett 1935–39; Special Asst. to U.S. Attorney-Gen., Office of Solicitor-Gen. 1939–42; Asst. to Chief of Procurement Div., Air Technical Service Command 1942–45; Legal Adviser, Industry Division, U.S. Mil. Govt. in Germany, mem. Cen. German Admin. Depts. (Economic) Cttee. Allied Control Council 1945–46; Asst. to Pres., IBRD 1946–47, Asst. to Vice-Pres. 1947–51, Dir. Tech. Assistance and Liaison 1951–61, Dir. Devt. Services Dept. 1961–73; Asst. to Pres. Int. Finance Corpn. 1956–57; Partner law firm of Surrey & Morse, Washington 1973–81, Counsel 1982–; led IBRD missions to Brazil 1949, Suriname 1951, Burma 1953, Spain 1958, Turkey 1965; mem. of President's Council; Chair. Int. Bd. for Plant Genetic Resources 1974–81, Chair. Emer. 1982–; fmr. Chair. Consultative Group on Int. Agricultural Research; fmr. mem. Governing Bd., Int. Inst. for Educational Planning. *Leisure interests:* tennis, golf. *Address:* 5404 Bradley Boulevard, Bethesda, Maryland 20814, U.S.A. (Home).

DEMY, Jacques; French film director; b. 5 June 1931, Pont Chateau; s. of Raymond Demy and Marie Louise Leduc; m. Agnès Varda (q.v.) 1962; one s. one d.; ed. Collège de Nantes and Ecole Nationale de Photographie et Cinématographie, Paris; Prix Louis Delluc 1964, Palme d'Or, Festival de Cannes 1964, Officier des Arts et des Lettres, Officier, Ordre nationale du Mérite, Grand Prix National 1982. *Short films:* Le sabotier du Val de Loire 1957, Le bel indifférent 1958, Ars 1959. *Full-length films:* Lola 1960, La baie des anges 1962, Les parapluies de Cherbourg 1963, Les demoiselles de Rochefort 1966, Model Shop 1968, Peau d'âne 1970, Pied Piper of Hamelin 1971, L'évènement le plus important depuis que l'homme a marché sur la lune 1973, Lady Oscar 1978, La Naissance du Jour 1980, Une chambre en ville 1982, Parking 1985, 3 Places pour le 26 1988. *Leisure interests:* painting, flying. *Address:* 77 rue Daguerre, 75014 Paris, France.

DENBIGH, Kenneth George, M.A., D.SC., F.R.S.; British university professor; b. 30 May 1911; s. of G. J. Denbigh; m. Kathleen Enoch 1935; two s.; ed. Queen Elizabeth Grammar School, Wakefield and Univ. of Leeds; Imperial Chemical Industries 1934-38, 1945-48; Lecturer, Southampton Univ. 1938-41; Ministry of Supply (Explosives) 1941-45; Lecturer, Chemical Eng. Dept. Univ. of Cambridge 1948-55; Prof. of Chemical Tech., Univ. of Edin. 1955-60; Prof. of Chemical Eng. Science, Univ. of London 1960-61; Prof. Emer. 1977-; Courtauld Prof. Imperial Coll. London 1961-66; Prin. Queen Elizabeth Coll. London 1966-77; Fellow, Imperial Coll. London 1976; Visiting Research Fellow, King's Coll. 1985-; Hon. D.ès Sc. (Toulouse) 1960; Hon. D. Univ. (Essex) 1967. *Publications:* several books and various scientific papers. *Address:* 19 Sheridan Road, Merton Park, London, SW19 3HW, England.

DENCH, Dame Judith (Judi) Olivia, D.B.E.; British actress; b. 9 Dec. 1934, York; d. of Reginald Arthur and Eleanora Olave (née Jones) Dench; m. Michael Williams 1971; one d.; ed. The Mount School, York, Central School of Speech Training and Dramatic Art; played in Old Vic seasons 1957-61, appearing in parts including Ophelia (Hamlet), Katherine (Henry V), Cecily (The Importance of Being Earnest), Juliet (Romeo and Juliet), appeared with Old Vic Co. at two Edinburgh Festivals, Venice, on tour to Paris, Belgium and Yugoslavia, and on tour to U.S.A. and Canada; appearances with R.S.C. 1961-62, including parts as Anya (The Cherry Orchard), Titania (A Midsummer Night's Dream), Dorcas Bellboys (A Penny for a Song), Isabella (Measure for Measure); on tour to W. Africa with Nottingham Playhouse 1963; subsequent roles include Irina (The Three Sisters), and Doll Common (Alchemist), Oxford Playhouse 1964-65, title-role in Saint Joan, and Barbara (The Astrakhan Coat), Nottingham Playhouse 1965, Amanda (Private Lives), Lika (The Promise) 1967, Sally Bowles (Cabaret) 1968, Grace Harkaway (London Assurance) 1970, 1972, Barbara Undershaft (Major Barbara) 1970; Assoc. Mem. R.S.C. 1969-, appearing as Bianca (Women Beware Women), Viola (Twelfth Night), Hermione and Perdita (Winter's Tale), Portia (Merchant of Venice), Duchess (Duchess of Malfi), Beatrice (Much Ado About Nothing), Lady Macbeth (Macbeth), Adriana (Comedy of Errors), also on tour with R.S.C. to Japan and Australia 1970, Japan 1972; other performances include Vilma (The Wolf), Oxford and London 1973, Miss Trant (The Good Companions), 1974, Sophie Fullgarney (The Gay Lord Quex) 1975, Nurse (Too True to be Good) 1975, 1976, Millament (Way of the World) 1978, Cymbeline 1979, Juno and the Paycock 1980-81, Lady Bracknell (The Importance of Being Earnest) 1982, Deborah (A Kind of Alaska) 1982, Pack of Lies 1983, Mother Courage 1984, Waste 1985, Mr. and Mrs. Nobody 1986, Antony and Cleopatra 1987, Entertaining Strangers 1987, Semi Monde 1987; Dir. Much Ado About Nothing 1988. *Films include:* A Study in Terror 1965, He Who Rides a Tiger 1966, Four in the Morning 1966, A Midsummer Night's Dream (R.S.C. Production) 1968, The Third Secret 1978, Dead Cert, Wetherby 1985, Room with a View 1986, 84 Charing Cross Road 1987, A Handful of Dust 1988, Henry V 1989. *TV Appearances in:* Major Barbara, Pink String and Sealing Wax, Talking to a Stranger, The Funambulists, Age of Kings, Jackanory, Hilda Lessways, Luther, Neighbours, Parade's End, Marching Song, On Approval, Days to Come, Emilie, Comedy of Errors, Macbeth, Langrishe Go Down, On Giants Shoulders, Love in a Cold Climate, A Fine Romance, The Cherry Orchard, Going Gently, Saigon—Year of the Cat 1982, Ghosts 1986, Behaving Badly 1989; mem. Bd., Nat. Theatre 1988-; numerous awards including Paladino d'Argentino (Venice Festival Award for Juliet) 1961, Best Actress of Year (Variety London Critics for Lika in The Promise) 1967, Most Promising Newcomer (British Film Acad. for Four in the Morning) 1965, Best Actress of the Year (Guild of Dirs. for Talking to a Stranger) 1967, Soc. West End Theatre Award (for Lady Macbeth) 1977, Best Actress New Standard Drama Awards (for Juno and the Paycock) 1980, (for Lady Bracknell in The Importance of Being Earnest and Deborah in A Kind of Alaska) 1983, (for Cleopatra in Antony and Cleopatra) 1987, Olivier Award for Best Actress in Antony and Cleopatra 1987; BAFTA Award for Best Television Actress 1981, for Best Supporting Actress (for A Room with a View) 1987; Hon. D.Litt. (Warwick) 1978, (York) 1983. *Publication:* Judi Dench: A Great Deal of Laughter (autobiog.). *Leisure interests:* painting, drawing, swimming, sewing, catching up with letters. *Address:* c/o 60 St. James' Street, London, S.W.1, England.

DENENBERG, Herbert Sidney, PH.D., J.D., LL.M.; American consumer reporter, lawyer and educator; b. 20 Nov. 1929, Omaha, Neb.; s. of David Aaron Denenberg and Fannie Molly (Rothenberg) Denenberg; m. Naomi Glushakow 1958; ed. Omaha Cen. High School, Johns Hopkins and Creighton Univs., Harvard Law School and Univ. of Pennsylvania; lawyer, Denenberg & Denenberg, Attorneys-at-Law 1954-55; lawyer, U.S. Army Judge Advocate Gen. Corps. 1955-58; Prof., Wharton School, Univ. of Pa. 1962-71; Insurance Commr., State of Pa. 1971-74; Special Adviser to Gov.

of Pa. on Consumer Affairs 1974; Commr., Pa. Public Utilities Comm. 1974-75; Consumer Reporter, WCAU-TV (CBS), Philadelphia 1975-, Consumer Columnist Philadelphia Daily News 1979-81, Philadelphia Journal 1981-82, Delaware Co. Daily Times 1987-, Bucks Co. Daily Times 1987-, and other newspapers; mem. Inst. of Medicine (N.A.S.), Advisory Bd. The People's Doctor 1988-; awards from Nat. Press Club and Nat. Acad. of TV Arts and Sciences. *Publications:* Risk and Insurance (textbook) 1964, Insurance, Government and Social Policy (textbook) 1969, Herb Denenberg's Smart Shopper's Guide 1980, The Shopper's Guidebook 1974, Life Insurance And/Or Mutual Funds 1967, Mass Marketing of Property and Liability Insurance 1970, The Insurance Trap 1972, Getting Your Money's Worth 1974, Cover Yourself 1974; hundreds of articles, govt. reports and statutes. *Address:* WCAU-TV, Philadelphia, Pa., 19131 (Office); P.O. Box 146, Wynnewood, Pa. 19096, U.S.A. (Home).

DENEUVE, Catherine (Catherine Dorléac); French actress; b. 22 Oct. 1943, Paris; d. of Maurice Dorléac and Renée Deneuve; m. David Bailey (q.v.) (divorced); one s. one d.; ed. Lycée La Fontaine, Paris; Film début in Les petits chats 1959; Pres., Dir.-Gen. Films de la Citrouille 1971-79; f. Société Cardeva 1983. *Films include:* Les portes claquent 1960, L'homme à femmes 1960, Le vice et la vertu 1962, Et Satan conduit le bal 1962, Vacances portugaises 1963, Les parapluies de Cherbourg 1963 (Palme d'Or, Festival de Cannes 1964), Les plus belles escroqueries du monde 1963, La chasse à l'homme 1964, Un monsieur de compagnie 1964, La Costanza della Ragione 1964, Repulsion 1964, Le chant du monde 1965, La vie de château 1965, Liebes Karusell 1965, Les créatures 1965, Les demoiselles de Rochefort 1966, Belle de jour 1967 (Golden Lion at Venice Festival 1967), Benjamin 1967, Manon 70 1967, Mayerling 1968, La chamade 1966, Folies d'avril 1969, Belles d'un soir 1969, La sirène du Mississippi 1969, Tristana 1970, Peau d'âne 1971, Ça n'arrive qu'aux autres 1971, Liza 1971, Un flic 1972, L'évènement le plus important depuis que l'homme a marché sur la lune 1973, Touche pas la femme blanche 1974, La femme aux bottes rouges 1975, La grande bourgeoisie 1975, Hustle 1976, March or Die 1977, Coup de foudre 1977, Ecoute, voir . . . 1978, L'argent des autres 1978, A nous deux 1979, Ils sont grands ces petits 1979, Le dernier métro 1980, Je vous aime 1980, Le choix des armes 1981, Hôtel des Amériques 1981, Le choc 1982, L'africain 1983, The Hunger 1983, Le bon plaisir 1984, Paroles et musiques 1984, Le lieu du crime 1986, Pourvu que ce soit une fille 1986. *Address:* c/o Artmedia, 10 avenue George V, 75008 Paris (Office).

DENG HENGGAO; Chinese state official; b. 1931; Minister, Comm. of Science, Tech. and Industry for Nat. Defence 1985-. *Address:* Commission of Science, Technology and Industry for National Defence, Beijing, People's Republic of China.

DENG LIQUN; Chinese party official; b. 1914, Guidong Co., Hunan Prov.; council mem. People's Govt. of Xinjiang 1949; Chair. Cultural and Educational Cttee., Xinjiang People's Govt. 1950; Assoc. Ed. Red Flag 1963; Deputy for Xinjiang 3rd NPC 1964; Deputy Chief Ed. HQ 1964; disappeared during Cultural Revolution; Deputy for Shanghai 5th NPC 1978; Adviser, State Econ. Comm., State Council 1979; Dir. Policy Research Office, Cen. Cttee. 1982, Propaganda Dept. 1982-85; mem. 12th Cen. Cttee. 1982-87; mem. Secr. Cen. Cttee. 1982-; mem. Cen. Party Consolidation Guidance Comm. 1983-; mem. Cen. Advisory Comm. 1987-; Head Leading Group for Educ. of Cadres 1985-; Ed. Contemporary China magazine 1982-; Deputy for Shanghai Municipality 5th NPC; Vice-Pres. Acad. of Social Sciences; Vice-Chair. Nat. Cttee. for Promoting Socialist Ethics 1983-. *Address:* Academy of Social Sciences, Beijing, People's Republic of China.

DENG XIAOPING; Chinese politician; b. 24 Aug. 1904, Guangan, Sichuan; m. Cho Lin; two s. three d.; ed. French School, Chongqing, in France and Far Eastern Univ., Moscow; Dean of Educ., Zhongshan Mil. Acad., Shaanxi 1926; Chief of Staff Red Army 1930; Dir. Propaganda Dept., Gen. Political Dept., Red Army 1932; on Long March 1934-36; Political Commissar during Sino-Japanese War; mem. 7th Cen. Cttee. of CCP 1945; Political Commissar 2nd Field Army, People's Liberation Army 1948-54; First Sec. E. China Bureau, CCP 1949; Sec.-Gen. Cen. Cttee. of CCP 1953-56; Minister of Finance 1953; Vice-Chair. Nat. Defence Council 1954-67; Vice-Premier, State Council 1954; mem. Politburo, CCP 1955-67; Secr. of Cen. Cttee., CCP 1956-67; Gen.-Sec. 8th Cen. Cttee. of CCP 1956; criticized and removed from office during Cultural Revolution 1967; mem. 10th Cen. Cttee. of CCP 1973; mem. Politburo, CCP 1974-76; Vice-Chair. Mil. Affairs Cttee. of CCP Cen. Cttee. 1975-76; Chief of Gen. Staff, PLA 1975-76; Vice-Premier, State Council 1975-76, 1977-80; attacked as "unrepentant capitalist roader" and removed from office April 1976; mem. Politburo 11th Cen. Cttee. CCP 1977-; Chair. Nat. Cttee., 5th CCP 1978-; mem. Standing Cttee., Politburo 12th Cen. Cttee. CCP 1982-87; Vice-Chair. CCP 1977-; Chief of Gen. Staff, PLA 1977-80; Chair. CCP Mil. Comm. July 1981-; Chair. Cen. Advisory Comm. CCP 1982-87; First Order of Socialist Repub. of Romania. *Publication:* Selected Works 1975-82. *Address:* Chinese Military Commission, Beijing, People's Republic of China.

DENG YINGCHAO; Chinese party official; b. 1903, Xinyang Henan Province; m. late Zhou Enlai (Premier of State Council 1949-76, died 1976) 1925; ed. Tianjin No. 1 Girls' Nat. School; arrested for part in May 4th Movement 1919; went to France as student with Zhou Enlai and others 1920; founded Paris Branch of CCP 1921; took part in Long March 1934-36;

Dir. Women's Work Dept., CCP 1937; Alt. mem. 7th Cen. Cttee., CCP 1945; Vice-Chair. All-China Democratic Women's Fed. 1953–; mem. 8th Cen. Cttee. CCP 1956, re-elected 9th Cen. Cttee. 1969, 10th Cen. Cttee. 1973; a Vice-Chair. Standing Cttee. Nat. People's Congress Nov. 1976-83, 5th Nat. People's Congress; mem. 11th Cen. Cttee. CCP 1977, 12th Cen. Cttee. CCP 1982-85; mem. Politburo, Cen. Cttee. CCP 1978-85; Sec. Cen. Comm. for Inspecting Discipline 1978; Head Taiwan Affairs Group 1980–; mem. Presidium CPPCC 6th Nat. Cttee. 1983–, Chair. 1983–; Hon. Chair. Chinese Nurses' Asscn. 1981–; Hon. Pres. Chinese People's Asscn. for Friendship with Foreign Countries 1982–; Adviser to Chinese Cttee. of Council of Chinese and Japanese Non-Governmental Personages 1984–. *Address:* Central Committee of the Chinese Communist Party, Beijing, People's Republic of China.

DENG YOUMEI; Chinese writer; b. 1931, Tianjin; messenger in CCP-led New 4th Army 1945; entered Cen. Research Inst. of Literature 1949; in political disgrace 1957-77; Sec. Secr. Chinese Writers' Asscn. Jan. 1985–. *Publications:* On the Precipice, Our Army Commander, Han the Forger, Tales of Taoranting Park.

DENG ZHUNJING; Chinese party official; mem. Standing Cttee. Nei Monggol Regional CCP Cttee. 1978–; Pol. Commissar Nei Monggol PLA Mil. Dist. 1978-81. *Address:* Nei Monggol, People's Republic of China.

DENHARDT, David Tilton, PH.D., F.R.S.C.; American professor of biological sciences; b. 25 Feb. 1939, Sacramento, Calif.; s. of David B. Denhardt and Edith E. Tilton; m. Georgetta Louise Harrar 1961; one s. two d.; ed. Swarthmore Coll., Pa. and Calif. Inst. of Tech. Pasadena; Instructor Biology Dept. Harvard Univ. 1964-66, Asst. Prof. 1966-70; Assoc. Prof. Biochemistry Dept. McGill Univ., Montreal 1970-76, Prof. 1976-80; Dir. Cancer Research Lab. and Prof. of Biochem., Microbiology and Immunology, Univ. of W. Ont. 1980-88; Prof. and Chair. Biological Sciences, Rutgers Univ. 1988–. *Leisure interests:* scuba diving, travel, reading, canoeing, skiing, camping. *Address:* Nelson Biological Laboratories, Rutgers University, P.O. Box 1059, Piscata Way, N.J., U.S.A.

DEN HARTOG, Jacob Pieter, E.E., PH.D.; American engineer; b. 23 July 1901, Java, Indonesia; s. of Maarten Den Hartog and Elisabeth Schol; m. Elisabeth Stolker 1926; two s.; ed. Delft Univ. of Technology, Netherlands and Univ. of Pittsburgh, Pa.; moved to Netherlands 1916; came to U.S. 1924; Engineer, Westinghouse Research Laboratory, Pittsburg 1924-32; Asst. Prof. and Assoc. Prof. Harvard Univ. 1932-41; Lieut.-Commdr. to Capt., U.S.N.R.; U.S.N. 1941-45; Prof. of Mechanical Eng., M.I.T. 1945-67, Head, Dept. of Mechanical Eng. 1954-58, Prof. Emer. 1967–; also Consulting Engineer; Fellow, A.I.A.A., I.Mech.E., London; mem., N.A.S., American Inst. of Consulting Engineers, Royal Inst. of Engineers, Netherlands; Hon. mem. A.S.M.E., Japan Soc. of Mechanical Engineers; Hon. A.M. Harvard Univ., Hon. Dr. Eng. Carnegie Inst. of Technology, Pittsburgh, Hon. Dr. Eng. Carnegie Inst. of Technology, Pittsburgh, Hon. Dr. Applied Sc. (Ghent), Hon. Dr. Tech. Sc. (Delft Univ. of Tech.), Hon. Sc.D. (Salford), Hon. Sc.D. (Newcastle-upon-Tyne); James Watt Int. Medal 1981. *Publications:* Mechanical Vibrations (trans. in 10 languages) 1st U.S. edn. 1934; also three other books and 35 papers. *Address:* Massachusetts Institute of Technology, Cambridge, Mass. 02139 (Office); 150 Barnes Hill Road, Concord, Mass. 01742, U.S.A. (Home). *Telephone:* 617-253-3298 (Office); 617-369-2907 (Home).

DENHOLM, John Ferguson, C.B.E., J.P.; British shipowner; b. 8 May 1927, Glasgow; s. of Sir William and Lady Denholm (née Ferguson); m. Elizabeth Murray Stephen 1952; two s. two d.; ed. Loretto School, Midlothian; Chair. Denholm Group of Companies 1974–; Deputy Chair. P & O Steam Navigation Co. 1980-83; Pres. Chamber of Shipping of U.K. 1973-74; Chair. North of England Protecting & Indemnity Asscn. 1976-78; Chair. Murray Group Investment Trusts 1985–; Chair. Murray Man. Ltd. 1985–; Chair. Finance and Econ. Policy Cttee., Gen. Council of British Shipping; mem. Nat. Ports Council 1974-77; mem. Scottish Transport Group 1975-82; mem. London Bd. of Bank of Scotland; Gov. Loretto School; D. L. Renfrewshire 1980; Hon. Norwegian Consul in Glasgow 1975–. *Leisure interests:* sailing, fishing. *Address:* Newton of Belltrees, Lochwinnoch, Renfrewshire, PA12 4JL, Scotland. *Telephone:* (0505) 842406.

DENIAU, Jean François, D. EN D., L. ÉS L.; French economist and diplomatist; b. 31 Oct. 1928, Paris; s. of Marc Deniau and Marie-Berthe Loth-Simmonds; brother of Xavier Deniau (q.v.); m. 1st Dominique de Mirbeck 1958, one s. one d.; m. 2nd Frédérique Dupuy 1971; ed. Inst. d'Etudes Politiques de Paris, Ecole Nat. d'Admin.; Ecole Nat. d'Admin. 1950-52; Finance Insp. 1952-55; Sec.-Gen. Inter-Ministerial Cttee. on European Econ. Co-operation 1955-56; Del. to OEEC 1955-56; Del. to Inter-Govt. Conf. on the Common Market and Euratom 1956; Head of Mission, Cabinet of Pres. of Counsel 1957-58; Tech. Adviser, Ministry of Industry and Commerce 1958-59; Dir. Comm. on countries seeking asscn. with EEC 1959-61; Head of Del., Conf. with States seeking membership of EEC 1961-63; Dir. External Econ. Relations, Ministry of Finance and Econ. Affairs (France) 1963; Amb. to Mauritania 1963-66; Pres. Comm. Franco-Soviétique pour la télévision en couleur; mem. Combined Comm. of EEC, ECSC, and Euratom 1967-73; Commr. for Devt. Aid, European Communities 1969-73; Sec. of State for Foreign Affairs 1973-74, for Agricultural and Rural Devt. 1974, for Agric. 1975-76; Amb. to Spain 1976-77; Sec. of State for Foreign Affairs 1977-78; Minister of Foreign Trade 1978-80, Minister Del. to the Prime Minister in Charge of Admin. Reforms 1980-81; lost seat in Nat. Ass. 1981, re-elected Deputy for Cher 1986, 1988; mem. European Parl. 1979-86, Vice-Pres. Political Comm., Vice-Pres. Sub-Comm. on Human Rights; Pres. Conseil Général, Cher 1981-85, re-elected 1985; Pres. Féd. Nat. des Clubs Perspective et Réalité 1982-84; Vice-Pres. Nat. Ass. Comm. on Foreign Affairs, 1988–; Chevalier, Légion d'honneur, Croix de guerre. *Publications:* Le marché commun 1958, 1960, La mer est ronde (Prix de la Mer) 1976, L'Europe interdite 1977, Deux heures après minuit 1985, La Désirade 1988. *Leisure interest:* sailing. *Address:* Assemblée nationale, 75355 Paris, France. *Telephone:* 40-63-60-00.

DENIAU, Xavier; French politician; b. 24 Sept. 1923, Paris; s. of Marc Deniau and Marie-Berthe Loth-Simmonds; brother of Jean François Deniau (q.v.); m. Irène Ghica-Cantacuzène 1953; five c.; ed. Univ. of Paris and Ecole Nat. de la France d'Outre-mer; successively Dir. of External Affairs, Cameroon, and Political Adviser to the Gen. High Commr. in Dakar 1944-55; mem. French del. to UN 1955-58, to NATO 1960-62; Tech. Adviser, Cabinet of the Minister for Armed Forces 1960-62; Maître des Requêtes, Council of State 1962–; Deputy for the fourth constituency of the Loiret 1962-72, 1973-80, 1981–; Chair. for Cultural Relations and Technical Co-operation, Foreign Affairs Comm., Nat. Ass. 1962-68, Vice-Pres. Foreign Affairs Comm., 1968-72, 1973–; Mayor of Escrignelles 1965–; Sec. of State in charge of Overseas Depts. and Territories 1972-73; Vice-Pres. of Council of Centre region 1974–; mem. Comm. nationale pour l'éducation, la science et la culture 1968; Sec.-Gen. Asscn. internationale des parlementaires de langue française 1967–; Vice-Pres. Asscn. nationale France-Canada 1966-69; Pres. Asscn. France-Québec 1969-72; Pres. friendship groups France-Cameroun 1963-72, France-Québec and France-Canada 1967-72, 1973–; Pres. Comité de la francophonie 1973–, Société d'ethnographie de Paris, Association pour la diffusion de la pensée française; mem. Société française d'onomastique; mem. Overseas Acad. of Sciences 1974–; Officier, Légion d'honneur, Croix de guerre 1939-45 and Croix de guerre des Théâtres d'Opérations Extérieurs, Commdr. Ordre du Christ; lauréat de l'Académie française pour 'la francophonie' paperback series (prix de la langue française); allied to Rassemblement pour la République (RPR). *Address:* Assemblée nationale, 75355 Paris (Office); La Tardivière, Escrignelles, 45250 Briare, France (Home).

DE NIRO, Robert; American actor; b. 1943, New York; s. of Robert De Niro and Virginia Admiral; m. Diahnne Abbott 1976; one s. one d. *Films include:* The Wedding Party 1969, Jennifer On My Mind 1971, Bloody Mama, Born to Win 1971, The Gang That Couldn't Shoot Straight 1971, Bang the Drum Slowly 1973, Mean Streets 1973, The Godfather, Part II 1974 (Acad. Award for Best Supporting Actor), The Last Tycoon, Taxi Driver 1976, New York, New York, 1900 1977, The Deer Hunter 1978, Raging Bull (Acad. Award Best Actor) 1980, True Confessions 1981, The King of Comedy 1982, Once Upon a Time in America 1984, Falling in Love 1984, Brazil 1984, The Mission 1985, Angel Heart 1986, The Untouchables 1987, Letters Home from Vietnam, Midnight Run 1988, We're No Angels. *Address:* c/o Jay Julien, 1501 Broadway, New York, N.Y. 10036, U.S.A. *Telephone:* (212) 221-7575.

DENISON, Edward Fulton, PH.D.; American economist; b. 18 Dec. 1915, Omaha, Neb.; s. of Edward Fulton Denison and Edith Barbara (Brown) Denison; m. Elsie Lightbown 1941; one s. one d.; ed. Cen. YMCA Coll., Chicago, Loyola Univ., Chicago, Oberlin Coll., Ohio, Brown Univ., Providence, R.I.; Instructor Brown Univ. 1940-41; Economist, Nat. Income Div., Office of Business Econs., Dept. of Commerce 1941-47, Acting Chief 1948; Asst. Dir. Office of Business Econs. 1949-56; Economist and Assoc. Dir. Research, Cttee. for Econ. Devt. 1956-62; Research Prof. Univ. of Calif. at Berkeley 1966-67; Assoc. Dir. for Nat. Econ. Accounts, Bureau of Econ. Analysis, Dept. of Commerce 1979-82; Sr. Fellow, Brookings Inst. 1962-78, Emer. 1979–; Fellow, American Acad. of Arts and Sciences and American Statistical Asscn.; mem. N.A.S.; Distinguished Fellow, American Econ. Asscn.; Distinguished Alumnus, Graduate School of Brown Univ.; W. S. Woytinsky Lectureship Award, Univ. of Mich., Shiskin Award, Washington Statistical Soc. *Publications:* The Sources of Economic Growth in the United States and the Alternatives Before Us 1962, Why Growth Rates Differ: Post-War Experience in Nine Western Countries 1967, Accounting for United States Economic Growth 1929-69 1974, How Japan's Economy Grew so Fast: the Sources of Post-War Expansion (with W. K. Chung) 1976, Accounting for Slower Economic Growth: the United States in the 1970s 1979, Trends in American Economic Growth 1929-82 1985, Estimates of Productivity Change by Industry: An Evaluation and an Alternative 1989. *Address:* The Brookings Institution, 1775 Massachusetts Avenue, N.W., Washington, D.C. 20036 (Office); 560 N Street, S.W., Apartment N-902, Washington, D.C. 20024 (Home); Cottage 846, Sherwood Forest, Md. 21405, U.S.A. *Telephone:* (202) 797-6135 (Office); (202) 554-1368 (Washington); (301) 849-2173 (Maryland).

DENISOV, Edison; Soviet composer; b. 6 April 1929, Tomsk; s. of Vasily Denisov and Antonina Titova; m. Ekaterina Kupzovskaia; one s. two d.; ed. Moscow Conservatory; teacher at Moscow Conservatory. *Compositions include:* The Sun of the Incas 1964, Les Pleurs 1966, Peinture pour Orchestre 1970, La Vie en Rouge 1973, Concerto for violin and orchestra 1977, Requiem 1980, L'Ecume des Jours (opera) 1981, Confession (ballet)

1984, Quatre Filles (opera) 1986, Clarinet quintet 1987, instrumental pieces, choral music, articles on music. *Address:* Studentscheskaia 44/28, kv. 35, 121165 Moscow, U.S.S.R. *Telephone:* 249 54 74.

DENISOV, Sergey Petrovich, DR. PHYS. SC.; Soviet physicist; b. 1937; ed. Moscow Univ.; sr. scientific asst., chief of lab. 1964–77; Sr. Section Head Inst. of High Energy Physics 1977; mem. CPSU 1978–; Prof. 1980–; Lenin Prize 1986 for work on Inclusive processes in the forceful interactions of elementary high energy particles and the discovery of scale invariants within these processes. *Address:* Institute of High Energy Physics, Moscow, U.S.S.R.

DENISSE, Jean-François; French astronomer, b. 16 May 1915, Saint-Quentin, Aisne; s. of Jean Julien Denisse and Marie Nicolas; m. Myriam Girondot 1948, two d., ed. Ecole Normale Supérieure; Teacher at Lycée, Dakar 1942–45; at Centre Nat. de la Recherche Scientifique (C.N.R.S.) 1946–47; Guest Worker, Nat. Bureau of Standards, U.S.A. 1948–49; Head of Research of C.N.R.S. at Ecole Normale Supérieure 1950–51, Dir. of Studies, Inst. des Hautes Etudes, Dakar 1952–53; Asst. Astronomer, Paris Observatory 1954–56, Astronomer 1956–63, Dir. 1963–68; Chair. of Bd. of Nat. Space Research Centre 1968–73; Dir. Institut Nationale d'Astronomie et de Géophysique 1968–71; Pres. Bureau des Longitudes 1974–75; mem. Atomic Energy Comm. 1970–75, Head of Research at the Ministry of Universities 1976–81; Pres. Council of the European Southern Observatory 1977–81; Pres. Cttee. for Space Research (COSPAR) 1978–82; mem. Acad. des Sciences 1967, Int. Acad. of Astronautics 1968–; Commdr., Légion d'honneur, Commdr., Ordre national du Mérite. *Leisure interest:* golf. *Address:* 48 rue Monsieur Le Prince, 75006 Paris, France (Home).

DENKTAŞ, Rauf R.; Cypriot politician; b. 27 Jan. 1924, Ktima, Paphos; s. of Judge M. Raif bey; m. Aydin Munir 1949; two s. (one deceased) two d.; ed. The English School, Nicosia, and Lincoln's Inn, London; law practice in Nicosia 1947–49; Jr. Crown Counsel 1949, Crown Counsel 1952; Acting Solicitor-Gen. 1956–58; Pres. Fed. of Turkish Cypriot Asscns. 1958–60; Pres. Turkish Communal Chamber 1960, re-elected 1970; Vice-Pres. of Cyprus 1973–; Pres. "Turkish Federated State of Cyprus" 1975–83; Pres. "Turkish Repub. of Northern Cyprus" Nov. 1983–. *Publications:* Secrets of Happiness 1943, Hell Without Fire 1944, A Handbook of Criminal Cases 1955, Five Minutes to Twelve 1966, The AKRITAS Plan 1972, A Short Discourse on Cyprus 1972, The Cyprus Problem 1973, A Discourse with Youth 1981, The Cyprus Triangle 1982. *Leisure interests:* reading, writing, sea sports, shooting, photography. *Address:* The Office of the President, "Turkish Republic of Northern Cyprus", Lefkoşa via Mersin 10, Turkey. *Telephone:* 9052071444.

DENMAN, Sir Roy, K.C.B., C.M.G., M.A.; British civil servant and administrator; b. 12 June 1924, Liverpool; s. of Albert Edward and Gertrude Ann Denman; m. Moya Lade 1966; one s. one d.; ed. Harrow Grammar School and St. John's Coll., Cambridge; Asst. Prin., Bd. of Trade 1948, Asst. Pvt. Sec. to successive Pres. 1950–52; First Sec., Embassy, Bonn, Fed. Repub. of Germany 1957–60; mem. del., Geneva 1960–61; Counsellor, Geneva 1965–67; mem. negotiating del. with European Communities 1970–72; Deputy Sec. Dept. of Trade and Industry 1970–75; Second Perm. Sec., Cabinet Office 1975–77; Dir.-Gen. of External Relations Comm. of EEC 1977–82; Head of EEC Del. to Washington 1982–. *Address:* Commission of the European Communities in Washington, 2100 M Street, Washington, D.C. 20037, U.S.A. *Telephone:* (202) 862-9500.

DENNING, Baron (Life Peer), cr. 1957, of Whitchurch; **Alfred Thompson Denning,** P.C., M.A.; British lawyer; b. 23 Jan. 1899; ed. Magdalen Coll., Oxford; called to the bar, Lincoln's Inn 1923; K.C. 1938; High Court Judge 1944; Lord Justice of Appeal 1948–57; Nominated Judge for War Pensions Appeals 1945–48; Chair. Cttee. on Procedure in Matrimonial Causes 1946–47; Lord of Appeal in Ordinary 1957–62; Master of the Rolls 1962–82; Chair. Cttee. on Legal Educ. for Students from Africa 1962; Treas. Lincoln's Inn 1964; Head of Security Enquiry 1963; Dimbleby Lecture 1980; Hon. D.C.L. (Oxford) 1965, Hon. LL.D. (Columbia) 1976, and 17 other hon. degrees; Hon. Fellow, British Acad. *Publications:* Freedom under the Law 1949, The Changing Law 1953, The Road to Justice 1955, The Discipline of Law 1979, The Due Process of Law 1980, The Family Story 1981, What Next in the Law 1982, The Closing Chapter 1983, Landmarks in the Law 1984, Leaves from my Library 1986. *Address:* The Lawn, Whitchurch, Hants., RG28 7AS, England.

DENNIS, Bengt, M.A.; Swedish banker; b. 1 Jan. 1930, Grengesberg; m. Turid Stroem 1962; one s. one d.; ed. Columbia Univ., N.Y.; econ. journalist 1959–67; Head of Dept., Ministry of Finance 1967–70; Under-Sec. of State, Ministry of Commerce 1970–76; Amb., Ministry of Foreign Affairs 1977–80; Ed.-in-Chief, Dagens Nyheter 1981–82; Gov. Cen. Bank of Sweden 1982–. *Leisure interests:* sailing, skiing, skating. *Address:* Diakongrend 32, 12353 Farsta, Sweden. *Telephone:* 08-640910.

DENNIS, Donna Frances; American sculptor and teacher; b. 16 Oct. 1942, Springfield, Ohio; d. of Donald P. and Helen Hogue Dennis; ed. Carleton Coll., Northfield, Minn., Paris and New York; teaching positions at Skowhegan School 1982, Boston Museum School (Visiting artist) 1983, State Univ. of N.Y., Purchase Coll. 1984–86, 1988–89, School of Visual Arts, New York 1983–, Princeton Univ. (Visiting Artist) 1984; one-woman exhbns. include West Broadway Gallery, New York 1973, Holly Solomon

Gallery, New York 1976, 1980, 1983, Contemporary Arts Center, Cincinnati 1979, Locus Solus Gallery, Genoa 1981, Neuberger Museum, State Univ. of N.Y., Purchase Coll. 1985, Univ. Gallery, Univ. of Mass. at Amherst 1985, Brooklyn Museum, New York 1987, Richard Green Gallery, New York 1987, 112 Greene St., New York 1987, Del. Art Museum, Wilmington 1988, Muhlenberg Coll. Center for the Arts, Allentown, Pa. 1988, Madison Art Center, Madison, Wis. 1989; group exhbns. include Walker Art Gallery, Minneapolis 1977, Biennial Exhbn. Whitney Museum 1979, Hirshhorn Museum, Washington, D.C. 1979, 1984, Developments in Recent Sculpture, Whitney Museum 1981, Venice Biennale 1982, 1984, New Art at the Tate, Tate Gallery, London 1983; recipient of several awards. *Publication:* 26 Bars (with Kenward Elmslie) 1987. *Leisure interests:* exotic cooking, reading fiction. *Address:* 131 Duane Street, New York, N.Y. 10013, U.S.A. *Telephone:* (212) 233-0605.

DENNIS, Sandy; American actress; b. 27 April 1937, Hastings, Neb.; d. of Jack Dennis; ed. Wesleyan Univ., Univ. of Nebraska; m. Gerry Mulligan 1965; studied acting, Herbert Berghof Studio, New York; stage début in Bus Stop, Palm Beach, Fla.; New York debut 1957. *Plays include:* Burning Bright 1960, Face of a Hero 1960, The Complaisant Lover 1961, A Thousand Clowns (Tony Award) 1962, Any Wednesday (Tony Award) 1964 (all Broadway), And Miss Reardon Drinks a Little (on tour 1971–72), Let Me Hear You Smile 1973, A Streetcar Named Desire 1974, Born Yesterday 1974, Absurd Person Singular 1975, Cat on a Hot Tin Roof 1975, Nasty Habits 1977. *Films include:* Splendour in the Grass 1961, Who's Afraid of Virginia Woolf? (Acad. Award as Best Supporting Actress) 1965, Up the Down Staircase (New York Film Critics Poll Award, Moscow Film Festival Best Actress Award) 1967, The Fox 1967, Sweet November 1968, Daphne in Cottage D, The Millstone, Same Time Next Year, A Hatful of Rain, That Cold Day in the Park, 1969, The Out-of-Towners 1969. *Address:* c/o Budgley, McQweeney and Connor, 9229 Sunset Blvd., 607 Los Angeles, Calif. 90069, U.S.A.

DENNISTON, Rev. Robin Alastair, B.LIT.HUM.; British publisher and ecclesiastic; b. 25 Dec. 1926; s. of late Alexander Guthrie Denniston and Dorothy Mary Gilliat; m. 1st Anne Alice Kyffin Evans 1950 (died 1985); one s. two d.; 2nd Rosa Susan Penelope Beddington 1987; ed. Westminster School and Christ Church, Oxford; Ed. Collins 1950–59; Man. Dir. Faith Press 1959–60; Ed. Prism 1959–61; Promotion Man. Hodder & Stoughton Ltd. 1960–64, Editorial Dir. 1966, Man. Dir. 1968–72, also Dir. Mathew Hodder Ltd. and subsidiary cos.; Deputy Chair. George Weidenfeld & Nicolson (and subsidiary cos.) 1973; Chair. (non-exec.) A. R. Mowbray & Co. 1974–; Chair. Sphere Books 1975–76, Thomas Nelson & Sons (and subsidiary cos.) 1975, Michael Joseph Ltd. 1975, George Rainbird Ltd. 1975; Dir. Thomson Publs. Ltd. 1975, Hamish Hamilton Ltd. 1975; Academic Publr. Oxford Univ. Press 1978, Deputy Sec. to the Dels. 1980–, Oxford Publr. 1984–; Student of Christ Church 1978–; ordained Deacon 1978, Priest 1979; Hon. Curate Parish of Clifton-on-Teme 1978. *Publications:* The Young Musicians 1956, Partly Living 1967, Part Time Priests? (Ed.) 1960. *Leisure interests:* music, farming, squash. *Address:* The Vicarage, Great Tew, Oxford, England.

DENNY, Floyd Wolfe, Jr., M.D.; American professor of paediatrics; b. 22 Oct. 1923, South Carolina; s. of Floyd W. Denny and Marion P. Denny; m. Barbara Horsefield 1946; two s. one d.; ed. Wofford Coll. and Vanderbilt Univ. School of Medicine; Asst. Prof. of Pediatrics, Univ. of Minn. 1951–53, Vanderbilt Univ. 1953–55; Asst. Prof. of Pediatrics and Preventive Medicine, Case Western Reserve Univ. 1955–60, Assoc. Prof. of Preventive Medicine 1960; Prof. of Pediatrics, Univ. of N.C. 1960–, Alumni Distinguished Prof. of Pediatrics 1973–, Chair. Dept. of Pediatrics 1960–81, Dir. Program on Health Promotion and Disease Prevention 1985–; Lasker Award; Hon. D.Sc. (Wofford Coll.) 1985. *Publications:* over 100 articles in medical journals on rheumatic fever, streptococcal infections, acute respiratory infections and sarcoidosis. *Leisure interests:* gardening, reading. *Address:* Program on HP/DP, Box 3 Wing DCB No. 7240, University of North Carolina, Chapel Hill, N.C. 27599 (Office); SR1102, Route 10 Box 56, Chapel Hill, N.C. 27516, U.S.A. (Home). *Telephone:* (919) 962 1136 (Office); (919) 929 2359 (Home).

DENNY, Robyn (Edward M. F.), A.R.C.A.; British artist; b. 3 Oct. 1930, Abinger, Surrey; s. of Sir Henry Denny, Bt. and Joan, Lady Denny; m. (divorced); two s. one d.; ed. Claysmore School, Dorset, St. Martin's School of Art and Royal Coll. of Art, London; first one-man exhbns. in London at Gallery One and Gimpel Fils 1958; has since given one-man exhbns. throughout Britain, Europe and U.S.A.; retrospective exhbn. Tate Gallery, London 1973; has represented Britain at Biennales in Paris, Tokyo, Milan, Brussels, U.S.A. and Australia and at 33rd Venice Biennale; works in numerous public collections; has received many public commissions for murals; teaching assignments have included Slade School, Univ. of London and Minn. Inst. of Fine Art; fmr. adviser, Arts Council of G.B., Inst. of Contemporary Arts, London; recipient of several awards and prizes. *Publications:* articles and criticism in int. publs. *Address:* 66 Royal Mint Street, London, E1 8LG, England.

DENSON, John Boyd, C.M.G., O.B.E.; British diplomatist (retd.); b. 13 Aug. 1926, Sunderland, Co. Durham; only s. of late George Denson and Alice Denson; m. Joyce Myra Symondson 1957; ed. Perse School and St. John's Coll., Cambridge; army service, Royal Artillery and Intelligence Corps

1944-48; St. John's Coll., Cambridge 1948-51; joined British Foreign Service 1951, served Hong Kong 1951-52, Tokyo 1952-53, Peking 1953-55, London 1955-57, Helsinki 1957-59, Washington 1960-63, Laos 1963-65; Asst. Head of Far Eastern Dept., Foreign Office, London 1965-68; Chargé d'affaires, Beijing 1969-71, Chargé d'affaires en titre 1971; Royal Coll. of Defence Studies, London 1972; Counsellor and Consul-Gen., Athens 1973-77; Amb. to Nepal 1977-82; mem. Univs. China Cttee. 1987-; Gorkha Dakshina Bahu 1980. *Leisure interests:* looking at pictures, the theatre and wine. *Address:* Pensile Road, Nailsworth, Stroud, Glos., England. *Telephone:* (045 383) 3829.

DENT, Sir John, Kt., C.B.E., F.ENG., F.R.AE.S., F.I.MECH.E., F.I.E.E.; British engineer and business executive; b. 5 Oct. 1923, Burton-on-Trent, Staffs.; s. of Harry F. Dent; m. Pamela A. Bailey 1954; one s.; ed. Burton-on-Trent Grammar School, King's Coll., London; with Admiralty Gunnery Establishments, Teddington and Portland 1944-55; Chief Eng., Guided Weapons Dept., Short Bros. and Harland Ltd., Belfast 1955-60; Chief Eng., Armaments Div., Armstrong Whitworth Aircraft Ltd., Coventry 1961-63; Dir. and Chief Eng., Hawker Siddeley Dynamics Ltd. 1963-67, Dir. and Div. Man., Guided Weapons Equipment and Systems 1967; Dir. Eng. Group, Dunlop Ltd. 1968-75; Dir. Dunlop Holdings Ltd. 1970-82; Man. Dir. Dunlop Ltd. 1978-82; Dir. Industrie Pirelli SpA 1978-80, Pirelli Gen. PLC 1980-, Pirelli Ltd. 1985-; Chair. Civil Aviation Authority 1982-86; Pres. Eng. Employers' Fed. 1974-76, Inst. of Travel Mans. 1986-, Int. Fed. of Airworthiness 1987-. *Leisure interests:* cabinet making, fishing, gardening, *Address:* Helidon Grange, Helidon, Daventry, Northants., NN11 6LG, England. *Telephone:* (0327) 60589.

DENTON, Derek Ashworth, M.M., B.S., F.A.A., F.R.A.C.P., F.R.C.P.; Australian research physiologist; b. 27 May 1924, Launceston, Tasmania; s. of A. A. Denton; m. Catherine M. Scott 1953; two s.; ed. Launceston Grammar School and Univ. of Melbourne; Haley Research Fellow, Walter & Eliza Hall Inst. of Medical Research 1943; Overseas Nat. Health and Medical Research Council (NH & MRC) Fellow, Cambridge 1952-53; Medical Research Fellow, later Sr. Medical Research Fellow, Nat. Health and Medical Research Council 1949-63, Prin. Research Fellow, Admin. Head and Chief Scientist 1964-70; Dir. and originating Bd. mem. Howard Florey Inst. of Experimental Physiology and Medicine 1971-; Dir. The David Syme Co. Ltd. 1984-, Australian Ballet Foundation 1983-; First Vice-Pres. Int. Union of Physiological Sciences 1983; Foreign Medical mem. Royal Swedish Acad. of Sciences; Hon. Foreign Fellow, American Acad. of Arts and Sciences; Hon. Foreign mem. American Physiology Soc. *Publications:* The Hunger for Salt 1982; 300 articles and reviews. *Leisure interests:* tennis, fishing, ballet, music, wine. *Address:* Howard Florey Institute of Experimental Physiology and Medicine, University of Melbourne, Parkville, Vic. 3052 (Office); 816 Orrong Road, Toorak, Vic. 3142, Australia (Home). *Telephone:* (03) 344-5639 (Office); (03) 2412640 (Home).

DENTON, Prof. Sir Eric James, Kt., C.B.E., F.R.S.; British physiologist; b. 30 Sept. 1923, Doncaster; s. of George Denton and Mary Anne Ogden; m. Nancy Emily Wright 1946; two s. one d.; ed. Doncaster Grammar School, St. John's Coll., Cambridge, University Coll., London; Lecturer, Dept. of Physiology, Univ. of Aberdeen 1948-56; Physiologist, Marine Biological Asscn. Lab., Plymouth 1956-64, Sec. of Asscn. and Dir. of Lab. 1974-87; Royal Soc. Research Prof., Univ. of Bristol 1964-74. *Publications:* numerous papers since 1948 in Journal of Marine Biological Asscn., Journal of Physiology and other scientific journals. *Leisure interest:* gardening. *Address:* The Laboratory, Citadel Hill, Plymouth, PL1 2PB (Office); Fairfield House, St. Germans, Saltash, Cornwall, PL12 5LS, England (Home). *Telephone:* 0752-221761 (Office); 0503-30204 (Home).

DENTON, Frank Trevor, M.A., F.R.S.C.; Canadian professor of economics; b. 27 Oct. 1930, Toronto; s. of Frank W. Denton and Kathleen M. Davies; m. Marilyn J. Shipp 1953; three s. one d.; ed. Univ. of Toronto; economist, Govt. of Ont. 1953-54, Govt. of Canada 1954-59, Philips Electronics Industries Ltd. 1959-60, Senate of Canada cttee. staff 1960-61, Govt. of Canada 1961-64; Dir. of Econometrics, Dominion Bureau of Statistics 1964-68; Consultant, Econ. Council of Canada 1964-68; Prof. of Econs. McMaster Univ. 1968-; Dir. McMaster Program for Quantitative Studies in Econs. and Population 1981-; various other consulting appts.; Fellow, American Statistical Asscn.; mem. Int. Statistical Inst., Int. Union for Scientific Study of Population. *Publications:* Growth of Manpower in Canada 1970; Co-author: Population and the Economy 1975, Working-Life Tables for Canadian Males 1969, Historical Estimates of the Canadian Labour Force 1967, The Short-Run Dynamics of the Canadian Labour Market 1976, Unemployment and Labour Force Behaviour of Young People: Evidence from Canada and Ontario 1980, Pensions and the Economic Security of the Elderly 1981; monographs, articles, technical papers. *Address:* Department of Economics, McMaster University, Hamilton, Ont., L8S 4M4 (Office); 382 Blythewood Road, Burlington, Ont., L7L 2G8, Canada (Home). *Telephone:* (416) 525-9140 Ext. 4595 (Office); (416) 639-9361 (Home).

DENVER, John (b. John Henry Deutschendorf); American singer and songwriter; b. 31 Dec. 1943, Rosell, N.M.; moved to L.A. 1964; sang in folk clubs, then joined Chad Mitchell trio 1965-69; TV appearances include own series, BBC-TV, U.K.; made film début in Oh God! 1977; started own record co., Windsong Records 1976. *Recordings include:* Rhymes and

Reasons 1969, Take Me Home, Country Roads 1971, Rocky Mountain High 1973, Sunshine on My Shoulders, Annie's Song 1974, Autograph 1980.

de OLIVEIRA CAMPOS, Roberto; Brazilian diplomatist; b. 17 April 1917, Cuiabá, Mato Grosso; s. of Waldomiro de Oliveira Campos and Honorina de Oliveira Campos; m. Maria Stella Tambellini de Oliveira Campos; two s. one d.; ed. Catholic Seminaries of Guaxupé and Belo Horizonte; George Washington Univ., Columbia Univ., N.Y., and New York Univ.; entered Brazilian Foreign Service 1939; Econ. Counsellor to Brazil, U.S.A. Econ. Devt. Comm. 1951-53; Dir., Gen. Man. and Pres. of Nat. Econ. Devt. Bank 1952-59; Sec.-Gen. Nat. Devt. Council 1956-59; Prof. of Money and Banking and Business Cycles, School of Econs., Univ. of Brazil 1956-61; Roving Amb. for Financial Negotiations in W. Europe 1961; Amb. to U.S.A. 1961-63; Minister of State for Planning and Co-ordination 1964-67; Amb. to U.K. 1975-82; mem. Inter-American Cttee. for the Alliance for Progress 1964-67; Pres. Inter-American Council of Commerce and Production 1968-70; mem. Bd. of Govs. Int. Devt. Research Centre, Bd. of Dirs. Resources for the Future, Inc.; numerous Brazilian and foreign orders and decorations. *Publications:* Ensaios de História Econômica e Sociologia Economia, Planejamento e Nacionalismo, A Moeda, O Govêrno e o Tempo, A Técnica e o Riso, Reflections on Latin American Development, Do outro lado da cerca, Temas e Sistemas, Ensaios contra a maré, Política Econômica e Mitos Políticos; co-author: Trends in International Trade (GATT report), Partners in Progress (report of Pearson Cttee., IBRD), A Nova Economia Brasileira, Formas Criativas No Desenvolvimento Brasileiro; technical articles and reports in journals. *Address:* c/o Ministry of Foreign Affairs, Brasilia, D.F., Brazil.

DÉON, Michel; French writer; b. 4 Aug. 1919, Paris; s. of Paul Déon and Alice de Fossey; m. Chantal d'Arc 1963; one s. one d.; ed. Lycée Janson-de-Sailly and Faculty of Law, Paris; journalist with l'Action française, Marie-Claire 1942-56; publisher 1954; devoted himself to writing 1956-; mem. Acad. Française 1978-; Chevalier, Légion d'honneur; Officier des Arts et des Lettres; Prix Interallié 1970, Grand Prix du Roman 1973. *Publications:* novels: Je ne veux jamais l'oublier 1950, La Corrida 1952, Le Dieu pâle 1954, Les trompeuses espérances 1956, Les gens de la nuit 1957, Tout l'amour du monde 1959, Le rendez-vous de Patmos (essays) 1963, Les poneys sauvages 1970, Un taxi mauve 1973, Le jeune homme vert 1976, Mes arches de Noé 1978, Un déjeuner de soleil 1981, Louis XIV par lui même 1983, Je vous écris d'Italie 1984, Bagages pour Vancouver 1985, La Montée du Soir, Ma Vie n'est plus un Roman (drama). *Leisure interests:* shooting, sailing. *Address:* The Old Rectory, Tynagh, Co. Galway, Ireland; 17 rue de l'Université, 75007 Paris, France. *Telephone:* Tynagh 743.

de ORIOL Y URQUIJO, Antonio María; Spanish lawyer and politician; b. 15 Sept. 1913; ed. Stonyhurst Coll., England, and Universidad Central de Madrid; Captain in civil war; later in private business; Dir.-Gen. of Charities and Social Works 1957-65; fmr. Pres. Supreme Ass. of Spanish Red Cross; Minister of Justice 1965-74; Pres. of the Council of State 1974-82; Gran Cruz del Mérito Civil and other decorations. *Address:* Finca Valgrande, El Plantio (Madrid), Spain.

DEPARDIEU, Gérard; French actor; b. 27 Dec. 1948, Chateauroux; s. of René Depardieu and Alice Depardieu (née Marillier); m. Elisabeth Guignot 1970; one s. one d.; ed. Ecole communale, Cours d'art dramatique de Charles Dullin and Ecole d'art dramatique de Jean Laurent Cochet; Best Actor, Venice Film Festival 1985; *appeared in short films:* le Beatnick et le minet 1966, Nathalie Grander 1971; *feature films:* Les gaspards 1974, Les valseuses 1974, 1900 1975, La dernière femme 1975, Pas si méchant que ça 1975, Sept morts sur ordonnance 1975, Maîtresse, Barocco 1976, René la Canne 1976, Les plages de l'Atlantique 1976, Baxter verra Baxter 1976, Dites-lui que je l'aime 1977, Le camion 1977, Préparez vos mouchoirs, Violanta 1978, Rêve de singe 1978, Le sucre 1978, Buffet froid 1979, Loulou 1980, Le dernier métro 1980 (César award Best Actor, France), Le choix des armes 1981, La femme d'à côté 1981, La chèvre 1981, Le retour de Martin Guerre 1982, Le grand frère 1982, Danton 1982, La lune dans le caniveau 1983, Les compères 1983, Tartuffe (also Dir.) 1984, Fort Saganne 1984, Rive Droite, Rive Gauche 1984, Les Compères 1984, Police 1985, One Woman or Two 1985, Jean de Florette 1986, Tenue de soirée 1986, Rue du départ 1986, Les fugatifs 1986, Sous le Soleil de Satan 1987, Camille Claudel 1988; *plays:* Boudu sauvé des eaux 1968, les Garçons de la bande 1969, Une fille dans ma soupe 1970, Sauvés 1971, Galapagos 1971, Clair obscure 1971, Home 1972, la Chevauchée sur le lac de Constance 1974, les Insensés sont en voie d'extinction 1978, Tartuffe (also Dir.) 1984, Lily Passion 1986; *TV series:* l'Inconnu 1974; Prix Gérard Philipe 1973; shared Best Actor Award, Montreal World Film Festival 1983. *Address:* Art Média, 10 avenue George V, 75008 Paris, France.

DE PEYER, Gervase, A.R.C.M.; British clarinettist and conductor; b. 11 April 1926, London; s. of Esme Everard Vivian de Peyer and Edith Mary Bartlett; m. 1st Sylvia Southcombe 1950 (divorced 1971), one s. two d.; m. 2nd Susan Rosalind Daniel 1971 (divorced 1979); m. 3rd Katia Perret Aubry 1980; ed. King Alfred's School, London, Bedales School, and Royal Coll. of Music, London; studied in Paris 1949; Int. soloist 1949-; Founder-mem. and Dir. Melos Ensemble; Prin. Clarinet, London Symphony Orchestra 1955-72; Founder and Conductor Melos Sinfonia; Dir. London Symphony Wind Ensemble; Assoc. Conductor Haydn Orchestra of London; solo clarinettist, Chamber Music Soc. of Lincoln Center, N.Y. 1969–; mem. Faculty, Mannes Coll. of Music, N.Y.; recording artist with all major companies; gives recitals and master classes throughout the world; Gold Medallist Worshipful Co. of Musicians 1948, Charles Gros Grand Prix du Disque 1961, 1962, Plaque of Honor for Acad. of Arts and Sciences of America for recording of Mozart concerto 1962. *Leisure interests:* theatre, good food, anything dangerous. *Address:* Porto Vecchio, 1020 South Washington Street, Alexandria, Va. 22314, U.S.A. *Telephone:* (703) 739-0824.

de PINIÉS, Jaime; Spanish diplomatist; b. 1918; m. Julia Ghirardi 1985; sec. to Spanish del. to UN Ass. 1956; interpreter to Gen. Franco for meeting with Pres. Eisenhower 1959; fmr. Perm. Rep. to UN, New York; Amb. to U.K. 1960-85; apptd. Special Amb. 1985; Pres. 40th Session of UN Gen. Ass. 1985-86. *Address:* Ministerio des Asuntos Exteriores, Plaza de la Provincial 1, Madrid 12, Spain.

De POUS, Jan Willem; Netherlands politician; b. 23 Jan. 1920, Aalsmeer; s. of Theunis de Pous and Aagje Maarse; m. Greta van Itterzon 1951; one s. two d.; ed. Amsterdam Univ. and Northwestern Univ., Chicago (Doctorate 1948); mem. staff of Trouw 1943-46; mem. Bd., Christian Nat. Press Org. for Neths. 1945–; Sec. and Econ. Adviser, Protestant Employers' Org. in the Netherlands 1949-59; lecturer Econ. Theory, Free Univ. of Amsterdam 1953-59; mem. Council of State 1958-59; Minister of Econ. Affairs May 1959-63; Pres. Social-Econ. Council 1964-85, Cen. Cttee. on Hospital Tariffs 1964-85; Pres. Mining Council 1967-85; Adviser Govts. of Suriname and Netherlands Antilles 1966-74; Pres. Del. Dutch-Belgian Jt. Venture Baalhoek canal 1969-75; Christian-Historical Union (now Christian Democratic Appeal); Pres. of Supervisory Bds., K.L.M. Royal Dutch Airlines 1964-85; fmr. mem. Supervisory Bds., Philips, R.S.V. Engineering Works and Shipyards, B.A.M. Batavian Contracting Co., Wolters Samsom Group; Hon. D. Econ. Sciences (Tilburg) 1977; Kt. Order of the Netherlands Lion; Commdr. Order Orange-Nassau; numerous other decorations. *Address:* Van Zaeckstraat 65, 2596 The Hague, Netherlands (Home). *Telephone:* 070-814341 (Office); 070-241575 (Home).

DEQUAE, André, L. ÉS SC.ECON.; Belgian politician; b. 3 Nov. 1915, Kortrijk; s. of F. Paul and M. Elodie Soen; m. Agnes Vandemoortele 1940; three s. three d.; ed. Louvain Univ.; mem. Chamber of Reps. 1946-77, Vice-Pres. 1958-60, First Vice-Pres. 1965-74, Pres. 1974-77; Minister of Reconstruction 1950, of Colonies 1950-54, of External Trade 1958, of Econ. Co-ordination 1960-61, of Finance 1961-65; Pres. of Belgian Farmers' Union 1977-81; Chair. and Pres. Bd. of Banque Bruxelles Lambert 1981-86; Pres. Confédération Internationale du Lin et du Chanvre; mem. Council of Europe 1965-77, and WEU 1965-77; Christian Social Party; Grand Cordon de l'Ordre de Léopold, Médaille de la Résistance, Médaille du Souvenir. *Leisure interests:* books, swimming. *Address:* Sint Eldoisdreef 32, Kortrijk, Belgium. *Telephone:* 056-351999.

de RACHEWILTZ, Igor, PH.D., F.A.H.A.; Italian historian and philologist; b. 11 April 1929, Rome; s. of Bruno Guido and Antonia Perosio; m. Ines Adelaide Brasch 1956; one d.; ed. St. Gabriel's Coll., Rome Univ. and A.N.U.; Research scholar A.N.U. 1956-60, Sr. lecturer Faculty of Asian Studies 1963-65, Fellow Inst. of Advanced Studies 1965-67, Sr. Fellow 1967–; lecturer in Asian Civilization, Canberra Univ. Coll. 1960-62; Visiting Prof. Bonn Univ. 1979, mem. Sonderforschungsbereich 12, 1979–. *Publications:* The Hsi-yu lu by Yeh-lü Ch'u-ts'ai 1962, Papal Envoys to the Great Khans 1971, Index to the Secret History of the Mongols 1972, The Preclassical Mongolian Version of the Hsiao-ching 1982, Repertory of Proper Names in Yüan Literary Sources 1988, numerous articles on Sino-Mongolian topics, medieval history and Altaic philology. *Leisure interest:* botany. *Address:* Department of Far Eastern History, Australian National University, P.O. Box 4, Canberra A.C.T. 2601 (Univ.); Ridley Street, Turner, A.C.T. 2601, Australia (Home). *Telephone:* 49-3171 (Univ.); 48-0557 (Home).

DERBYSHIRE, Sir Andrew George, Kt., M.A., A.A.DIP., F.R.I.B.A., F.S.I.A.; British architect; b. 7 Oct. 1923; s. of late Samuel Reginald and Helen Louise Puleston (née Clarke) Derbyshire; m. Lily Rhodes (née Binns); three s. one d.; ed. Chesterfield Grammar School, Queens' Coll., Cambridge, Architectural Assen., London; Admiralty Signals Establishment and Bldg. Research Station 1943-46; Farmer and Dark (Marchwood and Belvedere power stations) 1951-53; W. Riding Co. Architect's Dept. 1953-55; Asst. City Architect, Sheffield 1955-61; mem. Research Team, R.I.B.A. Survey of Architects' Offices 1960-62; mem. Robert Matthew, Johnson-Marshall and Partners 1961-, Chair. 1986–, involved with devt. of Univ. of York, Cen. Lancs. New Town, N.E. Lancs. Impact Study, Univ. of Cambridge, W. Cambridge Devt. and New Cavendish Lab., Preston Market and Guildhall, London Docklands Study, Hillingdon Civic Centre, Cabtrack and Minitram feasibility studies, Suez Master Plan Study, Castle Peak Power Station, Hong Kong, Harbour reclamation and urban devt., Hong Kong; mem. R.I.B.A. Council 1950-72, 1975-81, Vice-Pres. 1976; mem. Bldg. Industry Communications Research Cttee. 1964-66; mem. Ministry of Transport Urban Research and Devt. Group 1967; mem. Inland Transport Research and Devt. Council 1968; mem. Dept. of the Environment Planning and Transport Research Advisory Council 1971-76; mem. Standing Comm. on Energy and the Environment 1978–; mem. (part-time) Cen. Electricity Generating Bd. 1973-84, Environmental Consultant 1985–; mem. of Bd., Property Services Agency 1975-79; mem. Bd. London Docklands Devt.

Corpn. and Chair. of Planning Cttee.; Hoffman Wood Prof. of Architecture, Univ. of Leeds 1978-80; External Prof., Dept. of Civil Eng., Univ. of Leeds 1981; Hon. D.Univ. (York) 1972. *Publication:* The Architect and His Office 1962. *Leisure interest:* family. *Address:* 4 Sunnyfield, Hatfield, Herts., AL9 5DX (Home); 42 Weymouth Street, London, W1A 2BG, England (Office). *Telephone:* (07072) 65903 (Home); 01-486 4222 (Office).

DERINGER, Arved; German lawyer; b. 4 June 1913, Neustuttgart; s. of Nicolai Deringer and Gertrud von Toerne; m. Erika Stapff 1950; two s. three d.; ed. Univs. of Tübingen, Kiel, Berlin and Geneva; mem. Bundestag 1957-69; mem. European Parl. 1958-70; mem. Bar of Cologne 1962–; mem. Int. Bar Assen., British Inst. for Int. and Comparative Law, and various other legal assens.; Bundesverdienstkreuz; Ordine al Merito della Republica Italiana. *Publications:* Commentary on European Competition Law 1962-68; over 200 articles on German and European law, especially anti-trust law and European Community law. *Leisure interests:* swimming, walking, sailing, gardening. *Address:* Heumarkt 14, 5000 Cologne 1 (Office); Freibadstrasse 93, 7000 Stuttgart 80, Federal Republic of Germany (Home). *Telephone:* 221-205070 (Office); 711-733344 (Home).

de RIVOYRE, Christine Berthe Claude Denis, L. ÉS L.; French journalist and author; b. 29 Nov. 1921, Tarbes, Hautes-Pyrénées; d. of François de Rivoyre and Madeleine Ballande; ed. Insts. du Sacré-Coeur de Bordeaux and Poitiers, Faculté des lettres de Paris and School of Journalism, Syracuse Univ., N.Y.; journalist with Le Monde 1950-55; Literary Ed. of Marie-Claire 1955-65; mem. Haut comité de la langue française 1969–, Jury of Prix Médicis 1970–; Chevalier, Légion d'honneur, Chevalier des Arts et des Lettres: Prix Interallié (for Le petit matin) 1968; Prix des Trois Couronnes (for Boy) 1973; Grand Prix de la ville de Bordeaux 1973; Grand Prix littéraire Prince Rainier de Monaco 1982; Prix Paul Morand 1984. *Publications:* L'alouette au miroir 1956, La mandarine 1957, La tête en fleurs 1960, La glace à l'ananas 1962, Les sultans 1964, Le petit matin 1968, Le seigneur des chevaux (with Alexander Kalda) 1969, Fleur d'agonie 1970, Boy 1973, Le voyage à l'envers 1977, Belle alliance 1982, Reine-mère 1985. *Address:* Dichats Ha, Onesse-Laharie, 40110 Morcenx, France.

DERNESCH, Helga; Austrian opera singer; b. 3 Feb. 1939, Vienna; two c.; sang many operatic roles in Berne 1961-63, Wiesbaden 1963-66, Cologne 1966-69; freelance guest appearances at all maj. opera houses in Europe 1969–; regular appearances at Bayreuth Festival 1965-69, at Salzburg Easter Festival 1969-73; since 1979 has sung as mezzo-soprano; regular appearances at San Francisco Opera 1981–; début Metropolitan Opera, New York 1985; has sung in operas and concerts throughout Europe, N. and S. America, Japan; many recordings. *Leisure interests:* films, people, literature. *Address:* Neutorgasse 2/22, A-1013 Vienna, Austria.

De ROBERTIS, Eduardo Diego Patricio, M.D.; Argentine histologist, cytologist and embryologist; b. 11 Dec. 1913, Buenos Aires; s. of Francisco and Emilia De Robertis; m. Nelly Armand Ugon; one s.; one d.; ed. Univ. de Buenos Aires; Rockefeller Fellow, Chicago and Johns Hopkins Univs. 1940, 1944; at Biophysical Laboratory, Rio de Janeiro 1943; Dir. Dept. of Cellular Ultrastructure, Inst. de Investigaciones de Ciencias Biológicas 1946; Lecturer in Physiology, Texas Univ. 1952; Walker-Ames Prof. Univ. of Washington (Seattle) 1953; Prof. Histology, Univ. de Buenos Aires 1957, now Prof. Emer. and Dir. of Research; Pres. Int. Union of Biological Sciences 1979-82; mem. Argentine Acad. of Sciences, Argentine Acad. of Medicine, Argentine Research Council, American Acad. of Neurology, American Soc. for Neurochemistry; Fellow, New York Acad. of Sciences; Mitre Inst. Award, Van Meeter Award, Argentine Nat. Prize, Buenos Aires Gold Medal, Shell Foundation Prize 1969, Prize of Cuenca Villoro Foundation 1976, of Eugenio Rodríguez Pascuel Foundation 1977, Bunge and Born Prize 1984, Houssay Prize of the OAS 1985; Dr. h.c. (Loyola Univ.); Hon. mem. American Coll. of Physicians, Pan American Medical Assen. *Publications:* Citología General 1946, 1952, 1955 (English trans. 1948, 1954, Japanese trans. 1955, Russian trans. 1962; since 1965 appears as Cell Biology); Histophysiology of Synapses and Neurosecretion 1946 (French trans.), Cell and Molecular Biology 7th edn. (translated into Spanish, Italian, Russian, Hungarian, Polish), Synaptic Receptors: Isolation and Molecular Biology, Modern Pharmacology-Toxicology, Vol. 4 1975, Essentials of Cell and Molecular Biology 1981; more than 300 papers on cytology, thyroid gland, electromicroscopy, neurology and neuro-chemistry. *Address:* Galileo 2442 8B, 1425 Buenos Aires, Argentina. *Telephone:* 801-9643.

DeROBURT, Hammer, G.C.M.G., O.B.E.; Nauru politician and administrator; b. 25 Sept. 1923, Nauru; ed. Nauru Secondary School, Geelong Technical Coll., Victoria, Australia; Teacher 1940-42, 1951-57; deported by Japanese 1942-46; Educ. Liaison Officer, Dept. of Nauruan Affairs 1947-51; mem. Nauru Local Govt. Council 1955-68, Chair. and Head Chief of Nauru 1965-68; Chair. Transitional Council of State Jan.-May 1968; Pres. of Nauru 1968-76, May 1978– (also Minister for Internal Affairs, External Affairs, Island Devt., Industry and the Public Service); Leader of the Opposition 1976-78; Hon. LL.D. (Univ. of S. Pacific). *Address:* Office of the President, Nauru, Central Pacific.

DE ROMILLY, Jacqueline, D. ÉS L.; French academic; b. 26 March 1913, Chartres; d. of Maxime David and Jeanne Malvoisin; m. Michael Worms de Romilly 1940 (divorced 1973); ed. Ecole Nat. Supérieure, Univ. of Paris and Paris-Sorbonne; Prof. of Ancient Greek, Univ. of Lille 1949-57, Univ. of Paris-Sorbonne 1957-73; Prof. Coll. de France 1973-84, Hon. Prof. 1984-; mem. Acad. des Inscriptions et Belles Lettres, Inst. de France 1975-, Acad. Française 1988-; Corresp. mem. 7 Acads.; several French Acad. Prizes. *Publications:* L'enseignement en détresse 1984, Sur les chemins de Ste. Victoire 1987, numerous books on classical Greek literature. *Address:* 12 rue Chernoviz, 75016 Paris, France. *Telephone:* 42 24 59 07.

DERR, Kenneth T., M.B.A.; American business executive; m. Donna Mettler 1959; three c.; ed. Cornell Univ.; with Chevron Corpn. (formerly Standard Oil Co. of Calif.) 1960-, Vice-Pres. 1972-85; Pres. Chevron U.S.A. Inc. 1978-84; Head, merger program, Chevron Corpn. and Gulf Oil Corpn. 1984-85; Vice-Chair. Chevron Corpn. 1985-; mem. Bd. of Dirs. Citicorp; Dir. American Petroleum Inst. *Address:* Chevron Corporation, 225 Bush Street, San Francisco, Calif. 94104, U.S.A.

DERRIDA, Jacques; French philosopher; b. 15 July 1930, El Biar, Algiers; ed. Ecole Normale Supérieure, Paris; taught at Sorbonne 1960-64, at Ecole Normale Supérieure 1965-84. *Publications include:* La voix et le phénomène 1967, De la grammatologie 1967, L'écriture et la différence 1967, Marges 1972, La dissémination 1972, GLAS 1974, La vérité en peinture 1979, La carte postale 1980, Psyché 1987, De l'esprit 1987. *Address:* Ecole des Hautes Etudes en Sciences Sociales, 54 boulevard Raspail, 75006 Paris, France.

DERSHOWITZ, Alan Morton, LL.B.; American professor of law; b. 1 Sept. 1938, Brooklyn; s. of Harry Dershowitz and Claire Ringel; m.; two s.; ed. Brooklyn Coll. and Yale Univ.; admitted to D.C. Bar 1963, Mass. Bar 1968, U.S. Supreme Court Bar 1968; Law Clerk to Chief Judge David Bazelon, U.S. Court of Appeals 1962-63, to Justice Arthur J. Goldberg, U.S. Supreme Court 1963-64; mem. Faculty, Harvard Univ. 1964-, Prof. of Law 1967-; Fellow, Center for Advanced Study of Behavioral Sciences 1971-72; Consultant to Dir. Nat. Inst. of Mental Health 1967-69, to various Presidential Comms. etc.; mem. Comm. on Law and Social Action, American Jewish Congress 1978-; mem. Bd. of Dirs. American Civil Liberties Union 1968-71, 1972-75, Ass. of Behavioral and Social Sciences at N.A.S. 1973-76; Guggenheim Fellow 1978-79; Hon. M.A. (Harvard) 1967. *Publications:* Psychoanalysis, Psychiatry and the Law (with others) 1967, Criminal Law: Theory and Process 1974, The Best Defense 1982, Reversal of Fortune: Inside the von Bülow Case 1986; articles in professional journals. *Address:* Harvard Law School, Cambridge, Mass. 02138, U.S.A.

DERTHICK, Lawrence Gridley, Snr., B.A., M.A., LL.D.; American administrator and educationist; b. 23 Dec. 1906, Hazel Green, Kentucky; s. of Henry J. and Pearl S. Derthick; m. Helda L. Hannah 927; two s. one d.; ed. Univs. of Tennessee, Columbia and Chattanooga; has held many educational appointments since 1927; U.S. Commr. of Educ., Dept. of Health, Educ. and Welfare 1956-61; Asst. Exec. Sec. for Professional Devt. and Instructional Services, Nat. Educ. Assen. of U.S. 1961-71; Educ. Consultant 1972-. *Publications:* Be Safe and Live (co-author); numerous educ. and other works. *Leisure interests:* travel, volunteer service in civic and international activities. *Address:* c/o Alexian Village S-411, 100 James Boulevard, Signal MTN, Tenn. 37377, U.S.A. *Telephone:* (615) 870-0345.

de RUITER, Hendrikus; Netherlands business executive; b. 3 March 1934, The Hague; m. Theodora O. van der Jagt 1957; one s. two d.; ed. Technological Univ. of Delft; Research Chemist, Koninklijke/Shell Laboratorium Amsterdam (KSLA) 1956; Chief Technologist, Berre Refinery, Compagnie de Raffinage Shell-Berre 1965-67; returned to KSLA 1967; joined Shell Int. Petroleum Co. Ltd. (SIPC), London 1969; Man. Dir. Shell Co. of Thailand and Pres. Société Shell du Laos 1972; Coal Production and Trading Co-ordinator, SIPC 1975; Pres. Shell Int. Trading Co. 1979; Dir. Shell Internationale Petroleum Maatschappij B.V. 1981; Man. Dir. N.V. Koninklijke Nederlandsche Petroleum Maatschappij, mem. Presidium, Bd. of Dirs., Shell Petroleum N.V. and Man. Dir. The Shell Petroleum Co. Ltd. 1983-. *Address:* c/o Royal Dutch Petroleum Company, Carel van Bylandtlaan 30, P.O. Box 162, 2501 AN The Hague, Netherlands. *Telephone:* 070-774504.

de RUITER, Jacob (Job); Netherlands lawyer and politician; b. 1930; ed. Univ. of Utrecht; Judge, later Dist. Judge, Court of Zutphen; Prof. of Civil Law, Vrije Universiteit, Amsterdam, Rector 1976; Minister of Justice 1977-82, of Defence 1982-84; mem. Christian Democratic Appeal. *Address:* c/o Ministry of Defence, The Hague, Netherlands.

DERWINSKI, Edward Joseph, B.SC.; American government official and politician; b. 15 Sept. 1926, Chicago; s. of Casimir Ignatius Derwinski and Sophia (née Zmijewski) Derwinski; m. Bonita L. Derwinski; one s. one d.; ed. Loyola Univ.; mem. 86th-97th Congresses from 4th Dist., Ill. 1959-83; Counselor, U.S. Dept. of State, Washington 1983-87, Under-Sec. 1987-88; nominated Sec. of Veteran Affairs Dec. 1988; Vice Pres. Exec. Cttee., Treasury American Group Interparl. Union; served with infantry, U.S. Army 1945-46; mem. Veterans of Foreign Wars (VFW), Polish Highlanders (Nat. Dir.), Catholic War Veterans, American Legion, Polish Legion of American Veterans, Polish Roman Catholic Union, Polish Nat. Alliance; named one of ten Outstanding Young Men of Chicago 1959, 1961. *Address:* c/o Department of State, Washington DC 20520, U.S.A.

DERZSI, András; Hungarian engineer and politician, b. 1945, Kolozsvár (now Cluj, Romania); m.; one c.; ed. Budapest Tech. Univ.; designing engineer with General Edifice Designing Bureau; employed by Communication Directorate of Budapest Metropolitan Council 1972; mem. Metropolitan Council 1988; Minister of Bldg, Information and Communication 1988-. *Address:* 1077 Budapest, Dob utca 75/81, Hungary. *Telephone:* 220-220, 414-300.

De SAEGER, Jozef; Belgian accountant and politician; b. 1911, Boom, Province of Antwerp; Christian Democrat Deputy 1949-74; Minister of Public Works 1965-1973, of Public Health and Environment Jan.-Sept. 1973, of Public Health, Environment and Family 1973-74, of Public Health and Family Affairs 1974-77; Pres. Confed. of Caritas Insts. for Health and Social Welfare 1977-82; fmr. Pres. Christian Democrat Parl. Group; Minister of State 1978-. *Address:* 14 Willem Geetsstraat, 2800 Mechelen, Belgium.

DESAI, Hitendra Kanaiyalal, B.A., LL.B.; Indian politician; b. 9 Aug. 1915, Surat; s. of Kanaiyalal Desai and Mrs. Malvikaben; m. Mrs. Sagunaben 1954; ed. Bombay Univ. Faculties of Economics and Law; took part in anti-British political activities; imprisoned 1930, 1941, 1942-43; set up private legal practice in Surat 1939; elected mem. Surat Municipal Council 1939-57; mem. Bombay Legis. Assen. 1957-60; Minister of Educ., Bombay 1957-60; Minister of Revenue, Gujarat State 1960, later Home Minister; Leader of the House, Gujarat Ass. 1963; Chief Minister of Gujarat 1965-72; mem. Congress Party, elected to Supreme Exec. 1968; Pres. Gujarat Pradesh Congress Cttee. 1975-76; Minister of Works and Housing 1976-77, of Commerce and Civil Supplies 1979-80; elected to Lok Sabha from Godhra constituency (Gujarat) 1977; Treas. All India Congress Cttee. 1978; Freedom Fighters 'Sanman' Pension awarded by Govt. of India 1987. *Leisure interests:* reading, walking, social work. *Address:* Shahibag, Dafnala, Ahmedabad 380004, Gujarat, India. *Telephone:* 66552.

DESAI, Morarji Ranchhodji; Indian politician; b. 29 Feb. 1896, Bhadeli, Gujarat; s. of Ranchhodji Desai and Smt. Vajiyaben; m. Smt. Gajraben Desai 1911; one s. one d.; ed. Wilson Coll., Bombay Univ.; served in the Provincial Civil Service, Govt. of Bombay 1918-30; joined Civil Disobedience Movement led by Mahatma Gandhi 1930, convicted twice 1930-34; mem. All-India Congress Cttee. 1931-69, Treas. 1950-58, Sec. Gujarat Pradesh Congress Cttee. 1931-37, 1939-46; Minister for Revenue, Co-operation, Agric. and Forests 1937-39; imprisoned in the Quit India Movement 1940-41, detained 1942-45; Home and Revenue Minister, Bombay 1946-52; Chief Minister of Bombay 1952-56; Minister for Commerce and Industry 1956-58, for Finance 1958-63; resgnd. from Govt. to work for Congress Org. 1963; Chair. Admin. Reforms Comm., Govt. of India 1966-67; Deputy Prime Minister and Minister of Finance 1967-69; Chair. Parl. Group Congress Party (Opposition) 1969-77; arrested 1975-77; Chair. and Leader Janata Party (electoral alliance of 4 non-communist opposition parties) 1977-79; Prime Minister of India 1977-79, also fmr. Minister for Atomic Energy, Space, Electronics, Science and Tech.; mem. Lok Sabha 1957-79; Chancellor, Gujarat Vidyapeeth, Ahmedabad and Jawaharlal Nehru Univ.; Pres. Lok Bharati Univ.; mem. and Chair. numerous trusts; Hon. Fellow, Coll. of Physicians and Surgeons, Bombay; Hon. LL.D. (Karnatak Univ. 1957, Utkal Univ., Cuttack 1962). *Publications:* A View of the Gita, In My View, A Minister and His Responsibilities, The Story of My Life, Indian Unity: From Dream to Reality (Patel Memorial lectures). *Leisure interests:* spinning, sports, music. *Address:* 1 Safdarjung Road, New Delhi 110001, India.

DESAILLY, Jean; French actor; b. 24 Aug. 1920, Paris; m. Ginette Nicolas (divorced); two d.; ed. Paris Ecole des Beaux Arts; Pensionnaire, Comédie Française 1942-46; mem. Renaud-Barrault Company 1947-68; Dir. Théâtre Jacques Hébertot 1972-; mem. Council for Cultural Devt. 1971-73; Co-Dir., Théâtre de la Madeleine 1980-; mem. du Haut Comité de la langue française 1969-; Chevalier, Légion d'honneur, Officier, Ordre nat. du Mérite. *Plays include:* La nuit du diable, Le bossu, Malatesta, Le procès, On ne badine pas avec l'amour, Le château, Madame Sans-Gène, Tête d'or, La cerisaie, Le marchand de Venise, Comme il vous plaira, Hamlet, Andromaque, Le soulier de satin, Il faut passer par les nuages, Le mariage de Figaro, Brève rencontre, Un ami imprévu, Double jeu, Le légume, Dis-moi Blaise, Amphitryon 38 1976, Un ennemi du peuple 1977, Le Cauchemar de Bella 1978, Siegfried 1980, Arsenic et vieilles dentelles 1981, La dixième de Beethoven 1982, Sodome et Gomorrhe 1982, L'amour fou 1983, Les oeufs de l'autruche 1984, Un otage 1984, Comme de mal entendu 1985, Le silence éclaté 1986; Co-Dir. Tout dans le jardin. *Films include:* Le père Goriot, La symphonie pastorale, Le point du jour, Occupe-toi d'Amélie, Si Versailles m'était conté, Les grandes manoeuvres, Maigret tend un piège, Les grandes familles, Le baron de l'ecluse, Plein soleil, La mort de belle, Un soir sur la plage, Les sept péchés capitaux, Les amours célèbres, L'année du bac, La peau douce, Le doulos, Les deux orphelines, Le franciscain de Bourges, L'Ardoise, Comptes à rebours, L'assassinat de Trotsky, Un flic, L'ironie du sort, Le professionnel 1981, Le fou du roi 1984. *Address:* 53 quai des Grands Augustins, 75006 Paris, France.

DE ST JORRE, Danielle Marie-Madeleine, M.A.; Seychelles government official; b. 30 Sept. 1941; d. of Henri Jorre de St Jorre and Alice Corgat; m. 1965, divorced 1983; one s. one d.; ed. Univs. of York, London and Edinburgh; Principal, Teacher Training Coll., Seychelles 1974-76; Principal

Sec. Ministry of Foreign Affairs, Tourism and Aviation 1977-79, Ministry of Planning and External Relations 1983-86; Sec. of State, Dept. of Planning and External Relations 1986-; High Commr. in U.K. (also accred. to France, U.S.S.R., Canada and Cuba) 1983-85. *Publications:* Apprenons la nouvelle orthographe 1978, Dictionnaire Creole Seychellois-français 1982. *Leisure interests:* reading, lexicography, folklore, arts and crafts. *Address:* Department of Planning and External Relations, National House, P.O. Box 56, Victoria, Seychelles. *Telephone:* 24041.

DE SANCTIS, Roman William, M.D.; American physician and cardiologist; b. 30 Oct. 1930, Cambridge Springs, Pa.; s. of Vincent De Sanctis and Marguerita De Sanctis; m. Ruth A. Foley 1955; four d.; ed. Univ. of Arizona, Harvard Medical School; Resident in Medicine Mass. Gen. Hosp. 1958-60, Fellow in Cardiology 1960-62, Dir. Coronary Care Unit 1967-80, Dir. Clinical Cardiology 1980-, Physician 1970-; mem. Faculty of Medicine, Harvard Medical School 1962-, Prof. 1973-; U.S. Navy Consultant and to U.S. Congress 1956-58; Fellow American Coll. of Physicians, American Coll. of Cardiology, Inst. of Medicine; Distinguished Clinical Teaching Award, Harvard Medical School 1980; Hon. D.Sc. (Wittes Coll.). *Publications:* author and co-ed. of over 130 scientific papers. *Leisure interests:* travel, music. *Address:* 15 Parkman Street, Suite 367, Boston, Mass. 02114 (Office); 5 Thoreau Circle, Winchester, Mass. 01890, U.S.A. (Home). *Telephone:* (617) 7262889 (Office); (617) 729-1453 (Home).

de SAVARY, Peter John; British entrepreneur; b. 11 July 1944; m. Lucille Lana Paton; three d.; ed. Charterhouse; commercial holdings in the fields of energy, property, finance and leisure; Chair. Victory Syndicate, 1983, British Challenge for America's Cup, Blue Arrow Challenge for America's Cup 1987. *Leisure interests:* sailing, riding, carriage driving. *Address:* Littlecote House, Hungerford, Berks., England.

DESAZARS DE MONTGAILHARD, Baron (Jacques); French company executive; b. 21 May 1923, Epernay; s. of Jean Baron Desazars de Montgailhard and Francoise de Dumast; m. Geneviève de Nicolay 1950; three s.; ed. St. Louis de Gonzague, Paris, Univs. of Paris and Toulouse, Ecole nat. d'admin.; served in resistance in World War II, Sub-Lieut., wounded; Prof. Inst. des Etudes Politiques de Paris 1947-68; Finance Ministry 1947-53; Gen. Sec. and Dir. Banque Union Européenne 1953-60; Financial Dir., Deputy Man. Dir. Schneider S.A. 1960-69; Man. Dir. Ugine Kuhlmann 1969-71; Deputy Man. Dir. and then Man. Dir. Péchiney Ugine Kuhlmann 1972-75, Admin. Dir. Gen. 1975-83; Chair. Péchiney Ugine Kuhlmann Corpn., New York, N.Y. 1975-83, Société Générale de Brasserie 1985; mem. Econ. and Social Council 1970-71; Consultant and Dir. of several cos.; Commdr., Légion d'honneur, Croix de guerre, médaille de la Résistance française. *Address:* 33 avenue de Wigram, 75017 Paris, France. *Telephone:* 45 20 77 88.

DESBORDES, Joseph-Noël; French steel executive; b. 23 Dec. 1898, Bons; s. of François and Joséphine (née Vallentien) Desbordes; m. Jeanne Dautry 1927; ed. Ecole Polytechnique; Pres.-Dir.-Gen. Havre Drawing and Rolling Mills until 1962; Vice-Pres. Dir.-Gen. Tréfimétaux (merger of Havre Drawing and Rolling Mills and French Metal Co.) 1962-67, Pres. 1967, Hon. Pres. 1970-; Croix de guerre, Commdr., Légion d'honneur.

DESCHÊNES, Hon. Jules, B.A., LL.D., F.R.S.C.; Canadian judge; b. 7 June 1923, Montréal; s. of Wilfrid Deschênes and Berthe (Bérard) Deschênes; m. Jacqueline Lachapelle 1948; three s. two d.; ed. Ecole St.-Jean Baptiste Montréal, Coll. André-Grasset, Coll. de Montréal and Seminaire de Philosophie, Univ. of Montréal and Concordia Univ.; called to Bar of Québec 1946; Q.C. 1961; practised as barrister and solicitor 1946-72; Sr. Partner Deschênes, de Grandpré, Colas, Godin & Lapointe 1966-72; Justice, Court of Appeal Québec 1972-73; Chief Justice, Superior Court of Québec 1973-83; Lecturer in Private Int. Law, Univ. of Montréal 1962-69; mem. Exec. Cttee. Canadian Judicial Council 1977-83, Comm. of Inquiry on War Criminals 1985-86; Consultant, U.N. Centre for Social Devt. and Humanitarian Affairs, Vienna 1983-; Pres. World Asscn. of Judges' Cttee. on Expanding Jurisdiction of Int. Court of Justice 1977-82, Québec Bar Admission School 1988-; mem. Council, World Peace Through Law Center 1980-82; mem. Int. Law Asscn., Int. Comm. of Jurists, Canadian Council on Int. Law; Order of Malta 1978. *Publications:* The Sword and the Scales 1979, Les plateaux de la balance 1979, L'école publique confessionnelle au Québec 1980, Ainsi parlèrent les Tribunaux ... Conflits linguistiques au Canada 1968-80 1981, Justice et Pouvoir 1984, Ainsi parlèrent les Tribunaux II 1985, Co-author L'Université; son rôle, le rôle de ses composantes, les relations entre ses composantes 1969, Maîtres chez eux 1981, Judicial Independence: The Contemporary Debate 1985, and numerous articles. *Address:* 4854 Côte des Neiques, Montréal, Québec, H3V 1G7, Canada (Home).

D'ESCOTO BROCKMANN, Miguel; Nicaraguan politician; b. 5 Feb. 1933, Hollywood, U.S.A.; s. of Miguel D'Escoto Muñoz and Rita Brockmann Meléndez; ed. Instituto Pedagógico La Salle, Managua, Nicaragua, St. Mary's Coll., Moraga, Calif., Manhattan Coll., New York, State Univs. of New York and Columbia Univs. Sur le ligne de Feu 1988, New York, (studied philosophy, theology, educ. and political economy); Sub-Dir. Dept. of Social Communications, Maryknoll, New York, U.S.A. 1962-63; worked for Brazilian and Mexican church in slums of Belo Horizonte, Rio de Janeiro, Brazil and Mexico D.F. 1963-69, Dir. 1970-79; founder and Pres.

Fundación Nicaragüense Pro-Desarrollo Comunitario Integral, León, Nicaragua 1973; became involved with Frente Sandinista de Liberación Nacional from 1975; f. Grupo de los 12, a group of professionals and intellectuals supporting the Sandinista Front 1977; Minister of Foreign Affairs 1979-; elected mem. of Sandinista Ass. 1980. *Address:* Ministerio del Exterior, Detrás de Los Ranchos, Managua, JR, Nicaragua.

DESHMUKH, Shantaram Dwarkanath, M.A., B.SC.; Indian economist; b. 3 Oct. 1919, Roha, Maharashtra; s. of Dwarkanath Ganesh Deshmukh; m. Kamalini Jayavant 1943; one s.; ed. Univs. of Bombay and Cambridge; Research Officer, Reserve Bank of India 1948-51, Private Sec. to Gov. 1951-53, Deputy Dir. Research Dept. 1953-58, Dir. Int. Finance Div. 1958-60, Man. London Branch 1961-63, Sec. to Cen. Bd. 1963-66, Exec. Dir. Jan.-June 1977; Exec. Trustee, Unit Trust of India 1966-74; Adviser to Bank of Sierra Leone 1974-76; Exec. Dir. IMF for India, Bangladesh, Sri Lanka 1977-80. *Publications:* trans. of The Village Had No Walls 1956, short stories, tech. articles, book reviews, etc. *Address:* c/o Ministry of Foreign Affairs, New Delhi, India.

DESIO, Ardito, DR.RER.NAT., F.D.S., F.R.G.S., F.M.G.S.; Italian geologist, geographer and explorer; b. 18 April 1897, Palmanova, Udine; s. of Antonio Desio and Caterina Zorzella; m. Aurelia Bevilacqua 1932; one s. one d.; ed. Dept. of Natural Science, Univ. of Florence; Lecturer of Geology, Univ. of Milan 1926-31; Prof. of Geology, Univ. of Milan 1931; Dir. Inst. of Geology, Univ. of Milan, now Prof. Emer.; led 17 overseas exploratory expeditions and scientific missions in Libya, Sahara, Ethiopia, Jordan, Iran, Afghanistan, Pakistan (Karakoram), India, Philippines, Burma, Antarctica; discovered the first petroleum accumulations in subsurface of Libya 1938, and Mg and K deposits; leader of the first successful ascent of K2 (28,250 feet), second highest peak in the world 1954; organized expedition to Everest 1987; mem. Acad. Nazionale dei Lincei; Hon. mem. Italian Geog. Soc., Geol. Soc., London, Gesellschaft für Erdkunde, Bonn, Soc. Belge de Géologie, Indian Palaeontological Soc., Faculty of Sciences, Univ. of Chile; Patron's Medal Royal Geographical Soc. (U.K.), Antarctic Service Medal (U.S.A.), Gold Medal of Pakistan, Knight Grand Cross (Italy); numerous other awards. *Publications:* 426 publs. including a number of vols. about the geology and geography of Libya, Aegean Islands, Eastern Alps, Karakoram Range (Pakistan), Hindu Kush Range (Afghanistan), a monograph on the glaciers of Ortles-Cevedale massif, a treatise of geology applied to engineering, a vol. on the geology of Italy, eight vols. of scientific reports on expeditions to Karakoram and Hindu Kush, seven to Libyan Sahara, one on Antarctica, etc. *Leisure interests:* mountaineering, photography. *Address:* Dipartimento di Scienze della Terra, Università di Milano, Via Mangiagalli 34, 20133 Milan; Viale Maino 14, 20129 Milan, Italy (Home). *Telephone:* 236981-221 (Office); 76003845 (Home).

DESKUR, H.E. Cardinal Andrzej Maria; Polish ecclesiastic; b. 29 Feb. 1924, Sancygniów, Kielce; ordained 1950; consecrated Bishop (Titular See of Thenae) 1974, Archbishop 1980; cr. Cardinal 1985; Pres.-Emer. of the Pontifical Comm. for Social Communications; Pres. Pontifical Acad. of the Immaculate Conception. *Address:* 00120 Città del Vaticano, Rome, Italy. *Telephone:* (06) 698-3597.

DESLONGCHAMPS, Pierre, PH.D., F.R.S.C., F.R.S.; French-Canadian professor of chemistry; b. 8 May 1938, St.-Lin, Québec; s. of Rodolphe Deslongchamps and Madeleine Magnan; m. 1st Micheline Renaud 1960 (divorced 1975), two s.; m. 2nd Shirley E. Thomas 1976 (divorced 1983); m. 3rd Marie-Marthe Leroux 1987; ed. Montréal Univ., Univ. of New Brunswick; Post-doctoral Fellow Harvard Univ. 1965-66; Asst. Prof. Montréal Univ. 1966-67, Asst. Prof. Sherbrooke Univ. 1967-68, Assoc. Prof. 1968-72, Prof. 1972-; fellow numerous academic socs., including Chemical Inst. of Canada; Fellow Guggenheim Foundation, 1979; five hon. degrees. *Publications:* over 100 publs. in the area of organic synthesis and the development of the concept of stereo-electronic effects in organic chemistry, Stereo-electronic Effects in Organic Chemistry 1983. *Leisure interests:* reading, fishing, hunting, hockey, canoeing. *Address:* Département de chimie, Faculté des Sciences, Université de Sherbrooke, Sherbrooke, Québec, J1K 2R1 (Office); 1 North Hatley, Québec J0B 2C0, Canada (Home). *Telephone:* (819) 821-7002 (Office); (819) 842-4238 (Home).

DESMEDT, John E., M.D., PH.D.; Belgian neurologist; b. 19 Feb. 1926, Wavre; Prof. and Dir. Univ. of Brussels Brain Research Unit 1962-; also Chair. Dept. of Physiology and Pathophysiology, Univ. of Brussels Medical Faculty; Pres. Int. Fed. for Clinical Neurophysiology 1985-; mem. Acad. Royale de Médecine de Belgique, Acad. Royale de Belgique; foreign mem. Accademia Nazionale dei Lincei (Italy), Acad. Nat. de Médecine (France); Fellow, New York Acad. of Sciences, Royal Soc. of Medicine and mem. or hon. mem. of numerous other professional socs., int. scientific orgs. etc.; Francqui Prize 1972, Dautrebande Prize for Pathophysiology 1979, Maisin Prize (Fonds National de la Recherche Scientifique) 1985; Dr. h.c. (Palermo) 1975, (Strasbourg) 1981; Commdr. Ordre de Léopold. *Address:* Brain Research Unit, University of Brussels, 115 boulevard de Waterloo, Brussels 1000, Belgium.

DESMOND, Barry, M.COMM., T.D.; Irish politician; b. May 1935, Cork; s. of late Senator Con Desmond; m. Stella Murphy; four s.; ed. Presentation Brothers, Coláiste Chriost Rí, Cork, School of Commerce, Cork and Univ. Coll., Cork; mem. Dail Eireann for Dun Laoghaire 1969-; Labour Party spokesman on Social Welfare 1972–73; Labour Party Chief Whip 1973–81; Minister of State, Dept. of Finance 1981–82; Minister for Health and Social Welfare 1982–86, for Health 1986–87; mem. Inst. of Industrial Engs. *Address:* c/o Dáil Éireann, Leinster House, Dublin 2, Ireland.

DE SOMER, Pierre, M.D.; Belgian university rector; b. 22 Dec. 1917, Niel; s. of Polydoor de Somer and Maria Helena de Ridder; m. Paule Legein; four s. one d.; lecturer, Katholieke Universiteit Leuven, 1952, Prof. 1955, Dir. School for Clinical Assts. and Dieticians 1958, Rector, Dutch Section 1967, Rector of Univ. 1971–85; Dir. Rega-Inst. for Medical Research, Katholieke Univ. Leuven; Founder-Pres. Council of Dutch Speaking Univs. in Belgium; Vice-Pres. Int. Asscn. of Univ. Presidents; Pres. Comm. for Univ. Educ. and Fundamental Research, Nat. Council for Science Policy; WHO antibiotics expert. *Publications:* numerous papers on medicine in various journals. *Leisure interests:* the arts. *Address:* c/o Katholieke Universiteit Leuven, Naamse straat 22, 3000 Leuven, Belgium.

DE SOUZA, Robert; French diplomatist; b. 5 July 1921; ed. Ecole Nat. d'Administration; Tech. Consellor, Cabinet of Prime Minister Georges Pompidou 1962–65; Dir. Office of Sec. of State for Foreign Affairs 1968; served in Luxembourg, Damascus, Beirut, Athens; Amb. to Iran 1972, to the Netherlands 1977–80; Perm. Rep. to UN in Geneva 1981–86; Diplomatic Adviser to Govt. 1986–88. *Address:* 82 rue Lauriston, 75116 Paris, France.

DESPOTOPOULOS, Johannes (Jan); Greek architect; b. 7 Jan. 1909, Chios; s. of Georg Despotopoulos and Kleanthi Despotopoulos; m. Anastasia Travlos 1953; one s. two d.; ed. Bauhaus, Weimar-Dessau and Tech. Hochschule, Hannover; Hon. Prof. Technische Univ. Aachen; commissions have included housing, hosps. and cultural and community centres in Greece and Sweden; mem. Akad. der Künste, Berlin; numerous awards including five first prizes in architectural competitions. *Publications:* articles in professional publs. and book chapters. *Leisure interests:* sculpture, graphics, Greek history and philosophy. *Address:* Anapiron Polemou 7, 115 21, Athens, Greece. *Telephone:* 72 32 557; 72 32 564.

DESPRÉS, Robert, O.C., M.COM.; Canadian administrator; b. 24 Sept. 1927, Québec; m. Marguerite Cantin 1949; two s. two d.; ed. Laval Univ.; Comptroller, Québec Power Co. 1959–63; Man. Québec Regional Branch, Admin. and Trust Co. 1963–65; Deputy Minister of Revenue, Québec 1965–69; Pres. and Gen. Man., Québec Health Insurance Bd. 1969–73; Pres. Univ. of Québec 1973–78; Pres. and C.E.O. Netcom Inc. 1978–; Pres. and C.E.O. Nat. Cablevision and Comgen Inc. 1978–80; Chair. Atomic Energy of Canada Nov. 1980–; Dir. several cos.; fmr. mem. Québec Comm. of Inquiry on Financial Insts. and Royal Comm. of Inquiry on Financial Man. and Accountability; Fellow, Soc. of Man. Accountants of Canada, Canadian Certified Gen. Accountants' Asscn.; mem. Asscn. of Certified Gen. Accountants, Soc. of Man. Accountants. *Leisure interests;* golf, tennis, reading. *Address:* 890 Dessane Avenue, Québec, Qué. G1S 3J8, Canada.

DESTA, Fisseha; Ethiopian politician; Deputy Gen. Sec. Provisional Admin. Mil. Council; Vice-Pres. of Ethiopia Sept. 1987–. *Address:* Office of the Vice-President, Addis Ababa, Ethiopia.

de STRYCKER, Cecil A. J. F. J. M., D.S.C.; Belgian banker; b. 2 Feb. 1915, Derby, England; s. of Joseph de Strycker and Jeanne André Dumont; m. Elisabeth Braffort 1948; Hon. Gov. Banque Nationale de Belgique; Dir. Bank for Int. Settlements 1975–; Grand Officier de l'Ordre de Léopold, Grand Officier de l'Ordre de la Couronne. *Leisure interest:* gardening. *Address:* 14 avenue Bois du Dimanche, B-1150 Brussels, Belgium. *Telephone:* 770-3572 (Home).

de THÉ, Guy Blaudin, M.D., PH.D.; French cancer research specialist; b. 5 May 1930, Marseilles; s. of François Blaudin de Thé and Madeleine du Verne; m. Colette Pierrard de Maujouy 1958; one s. two d.; ed. Faculty of Medicine, Marseilles, Univ. of Paris, Sorbonne; Research Asst. Duke Univ. Medical Center, U.S.A. 1961–63; Visiting Scientist, Laboratory of Viral Oncology, Nat. Cancer Inst., U.S.A. 1963–65; Head of Unit of Electron Microscopy, Centre Nat. de Recherche Scientifique 1965–67; Chief, Unit of Biological Carcinogenesis, WHO Int. Agency for Research on Cancer, Lyons 1967–78; Dir. of Research CNRS, Faculty Med. A. Carrel, Lyon and Cancer Research Inst., Villejuif, Paris 1979–; mem. Scientific Council, ligue nat. française contre le cancer 1972–74; mem. Soc. française de Microbiologie, American Soc. for Cell Biology, American Asscn. for Cancer Research, A.A.A.S., European Asscn. for Cancer Research, Chevalier, Ordre nat. du Mérite; Scientific Prize, Acad. of Sciences 1971, Medical Research Foundation 1979, Collège de France 1981, Silver Medal, C.N.R.S 1981. *Publications:* many publs. on the cell virus relationship on avian and murine leukaemia viruses, and role of viruses in human tumours (Burkitt's lymphoma in Africa, Nasopharyngeal carcinoma in South-East Asia); Sur la piste du Cancer (popular scientific book) 1984, Modes de Vie et Cancers 1988. *Leisure interest:* arts. *Address:* Faculté de Médecine A. Carrel, rue Paradin, 69372 Lyon and Institut Santé et Développement, 15 rue de l'Ecole de Médecine, 75006 Paris (Offices); 36 Place Bellecour, 69002 Lyon, France (Home). *Telephone:* 43-26-12-08 (Paris Office); 78-74-47-52 (Lyon Office); 78-37-91-08 (Home).

DETHIER, Vincent Gaston, A.B., A.M., PH.D.; American professor of biology; b. 20 Feb. 1915, Boston, Mass.; s. of Jean Vincent Dethier and Marguerite Frances (Lally); m. Lois Evelyn Check 1960; two s.; ed. Harvard Coll. and Harvard Univ.; Instructor, Biology and Asst. Prof., John Carroll Univ. 1939–41; Lieut. to Major SNC, Army Air Corps 1942–46; Active Reserve, Lieut.-Col., Office of the Surgeon-Gen. 1946–62; Prof. of Zoology and Entomology, Ohio State Univ. 1946–47; Assoc. Prof. and Prof. of Biology, Johns Hopkins Univ. 1947–58; Prof. of Zoology and Psychology, and Assoc. of Neurological Inst. of School of Medicine, Univ. of Pa. 1958–67; Prof. of Biology, Princeton Univ. 1967–75; Prof. of Zoology, Univ. of Mass. 1975–; Pres. American Soc. of Zoologists 1967; Fellow, American Acad. of Arts and Sciences, Nat. Acad. of Sciences, Explorers Club; mem. Entomological Soc. of America, American Philosophical Soc.; Hon. Sc.D. (Ohio State Univ., Providence Coll., Univ. of Mass.), Hon. D.Univ. (Pau, France); Hon. Fellow, Royal Entomological Soc., London; Fellow, R.S.A. *Publications:* Chemical Insect Attractants and Repellents, Animal Behaviour (with E. Stellar), To Know a Fly, The Physiology of Insect Senses, Fairweather Duck, Biological Principles and Processes (with C. Villee) 1971, Man's Plague, The Hungry Fly, The Ant Heap, The World of the Tentmakers, The Ecology of a Summerhouse, A University in Search of Civility; and numerous scientific papers. *Leisure interests:* skiing, boating. *Address:* Department of Zoology, University of Massachusetts, Amherst, Mass. 01003, U.S.A. *Telephone:* 413-545-2046.

DETTMERING, Wilhelm Heinrich, DR. ING.; German engineer (retd.); b. 19 Jan. 1912, Bremen; s. of Wilhelm Dettmering and Anna Oentrich; m. Erika Dettmering 1944 (died 1973); one s.; ed. Tech. Univ. Berlin, Brunswick and Aachen; Research Engineer Luftwaffe Testing Stations, Travemünde and Peenemünde 1935–41; Sr. Engineer Tech. Hochschule, Aachen 1948–61; Prof. and Dir. Inst. für Strahlantriebe und Turbarbeitsmaschinen 1962–69; mem. Bd. (Research and Devt.), Fried. Krupp G.m.b.H. 1970–77; Pres. VDI 1975–77; mem. Rheinisch-Westfälische Akad. der Wissenschaften; Hon. mem. German Soc. for Air and Space Travel; Bundesverdienstkreuz. *Publications:* Nachverkehr, Probleme und Lösungsansätze; book chapters and some 80 professional publs. *Leisure interests:* sailing, history of science and technology. *Address:* 5100 Aachen, Luxemburger Ring 26, Federal Republic of Germany. *Telephone:* 0241-61468.

DETWEILER, David Kenneth, V.M.D., M.S.; American professor of physiology; b. 23 Oct. 1909, Philadelphia, Pa.; s. of David Rieser Detweiler and Pearl I. (Overholt) Detweiler; m. Inge Kludt 1965; two s. four d.; ed. Univ. of Pennsylvania; Asst. Instructor Veterinary School, Univ. of Pa. 1942–43, Instructor 1943–45, Assoc. Instructor 1945–47, Asst. Prof. 1947–51, Assoc. Prof. 1951–62, Prof. of Physiology and Head of Physiology Lab. 1962, Dir. Comparative Cardiovascular Studies Unit 1960–; Guggenheim Fellow 1955–56; mem. Inst. of Medicine, N.A.S.; Gaines Award and Medal, American Veterinary Asscn. 1960; D. K. Detweiler Prize for Cardiology established by German-speaking group of World Veterinary Medicine Asscn. 1982; Hon. D.Sc. (Ohio State Univ.) 1966; Hon. M.V.D. (Vienna) 1968; Hon. D.M.V. (Turin) 1969. *Publications:* some 150 publications on cardiology and cardiovascular physiology. *Leisure interests:* art, music, languages. *Address:* School of Veterinary Medicine, University of Pennsylvania, 3800 Spruce Street, Philadelphia, Pa. 19104 (Office); 4636 Larchwood Avenue, Philadelphia, Pa. 19143, U.S.A. (Home). *Telephone:* 215-898 8585.

DEUKMEJIAN, George, J.D.; American state governor; b. 6 June 1928, Albany, N.Y.; s. of C. George and Alice (née Gairdan) Deukmejian; m. Gloria M. Saatjian 1957; one s. two d.; ed. Siena Coll. and St John's Univ.; admitted to N.Y. State Bar 1952, Calif. Bar 1956, Supreme Court Bar 1970; partner Riedman, Dalessi, Deukmejian & Woods, Long Beach, Calif. –1979; mem. Calif. Ass. 1963–67, Calif. Senate (Minority Leader); Attorney-Gen., Calif. 1979–82; Gov. of California 1983–90; Republican. *Address:* Governor's Office, State Capitol, Sacramento, Calif. 95814, U.S.A.

DEUTEKOM, Cristina; opera singer; b. 28 Aug. 1938, Amsterdam; one d.; first major appearance at Munich State Opera 1966, then at Vienna Festwochen; sang at Metropolitan Opera, New York 1967; has sung in all the major opera houses in Europe, especially Italy, and U.S.A.; specializes in bel canto operas by Rossini, Bellini and Donizetti and the great Verdi operas; recordings for EMI, Decca and Philips; Grand Prix du Disque 1969, 1972. *Leisure interests:* driving round the world, singing, shopping (especially for shoes). *Address:* c/o S.A. Gorlinsky Ltd., 33 Dover Street, London, W1X 4NJ England; c/o H. R. Rothenberg, Johannisthaler Chaussee 421, 1 Berlin 47, Federal Republic of Germany.

DEUTSCH, André; British publisher; b. 15 Nov. 1917; s. of late Bruno Deutsch and Maria (Havas) Deutsch; unmarried; ed. Budapest, Vienna and Zürich; first publishing job with Nicholson & Watson 1942; independent publisher under imprint Allan Wingate (Publrs.) Ltd. 1945; formed André Deutsch Ltd. 1951, Chair. and Man. Dir. 1951–84, Co.-Chair. and Co-Man. Dir. 1984–87, Co-Chair. 1988–; f. African Univs. Press, Lagos 1962, E. Africa Publishing House, Nairobi 1964. *Leisure interests:* travel (preferably by train), skiing, publishing, talking. *Address:* 105–106 Great Russell Street, London, WC1B 3LJ, England.

DEUTSCH, Erwin, M.D.; Austrian professor of internal medicine; b. 12 April 1917, Klagenfurt; s. of Julius Deutsch and Maria Kempny; m. Alma Sitte 1958; one d.; ed. Gymnasium, Klagenfurt and Univ. of Vienna; First Dept. of Medicine, Univ. of Vienna 1940–41, 1942–43, 1945–87, Asst. Lecturer for Internal Medicine 1952, Extraordinary Prof. 1958, Prof. and Head of Dept. 1964–87; St. Josefs Hospital, Neunkirchen, Saar 1941–42,

1943–45; Knappschafts-krankenhaus, Frankenholz/Saar 1945; Hospital Neustadt 1945; Head, Dept. of Internal Medicine, Paracelsus Inst. Bad Hall 1964–; Theodor Körner Förderungspreis 1957; Vienna Science Prize 1958; Ehrenkreuz für Wissenschaft und Kunst 1987. *Publications:* Die Hemmkörperhamophilie 1948, Blutgerinnungsfaktoren 1955, Blutgerinnung und Operation 1973, Laboratoriums-diagnostik 1975; 400 scientific papers in journals. *Leisure interest:* music. *Address:* Medizinische Universitätsklinik, 1090 Vienna, Lazarettgasse 14 (Office); Siebensterngasse 2, 1070 Vienna, Austria (Home). *Telephone:* 0222-4800-2048 (Office); 0222-932663 (Home).

de VALOIS, Dame Ninette, C.H., D.B.E.; British choreographer; b. 6 June 1898, Baltiboys, Blessington, Co. Wicklow, Ireland; d. of Lieut.-Col. T. R. A. Stannus, D.S.O.; m. Dr. A. B. Connell 1935; Prima Ballerina, Royal Opera Season, Covent Garden 1919 and 1928; British Nat. Opera Co. 1918; mem. The Diaghileff Russian Ballet 1923–26; Choreographic Dir. to the Old Vic. Festival Theatre, Cambridge, and the Abbey Theatre, Dublin 1926–30; Founder and Dir. The Royal Ballet and the Royal Ballet School 1931–63, now Gov. Royal Ballet; fmr. Pres. London Ballet Circle; Hon. Mus. Doc. (London) 1947; Hon. D.Mus. (London, Sheffield, Trinity Coll. Dublin, Durham); Hon. D.Litt. (Reading, Oxford, New Univ., Ulster); Hon. D.F.A. (Smith Coll. Mass.) 1957; Hon. LL.D. (Aberdeen, Sussex) 1958; Chevalier, Légion d'honneur 1950; Erasmus Prize 1974; Irish Community Award 1980. *Choreographic works include:* Job, The Rake's Progress, Checkmate, The Prospect Before Us, Don Quixote. *Publications:* Invitation to the Ballet 1937, Come Dance with Me 1957, Step by Step 1977. *Address:* c/o Royal Ballet School, 153 Talgarth Road, London, W.14, England.

DEVAN NAIR, Chengara Veetil; Singapore trade unionist and politician; b. 5 Aug. 1923, Malacca, Malaysia; m. Avadai Dhanam 1953; three s. one d.; ed. Victoria Secondary School, Singapore; teacher, St. Andrew's School, Singapore 1949–51; Gen. Sec. Singapore Teachers' Union 1949–51; detained 1951–53; Convenor and mem. Cen. Exec. Cttee, People's Action Party (PAP) 1954–56; Sec. Singapore Factory and Shopworkers Union 1954–56; detained 1956–59; Political Sec. Ministry of Educ. 1959–60; Chair. Prisons Inquiry Comm. 1960; Chair. Adult Educ. Bd. 1960–64; Sec. Nat. Trades Union Congress (NTUC) and Dir. of its Research Unit, Singapore 1964–65; mem. House of Reps., Malaysia 1964–69; Founder and First Sec.-Gen. Democratic Action Party, Malaysia 1964–69; Dir. NTUC Research Unit 1969–81; Sec.-Gen. NTUC 1969–79, Pres. 1979–81; Pres. ICFTU Asian Regional Org. 1975–81; M.P. for Anson, Singapore 1979, re-elected 1980; resgnd. as M.P. and Pres. NTUC Oct. 1981; Pres. of Repub. of Singapore 1981–85; Consultant to AFL-CIO 1985–; Fellow Inst. of Advanced Study, Ind. Univ. U.S.A. 1985–87; Hon. D.Litt. (Univ. of Singapore) 1976; Public Service Star, Singapore 1963. *Publications:* Singapore Socialism that Works, Who Lives if Malaysia Dies?, Tomorrow—The Peril and the Promise, Asian Labour and the Dynamics of Change, Not By Wages Alone. *Leisure interests:* swimming, reading, music. *Address:* 39 Bin Tong Park, Singapore 1026. *Telephone:* 468-4008.

De VAUCOULEURS, Gerard Henri, DR. de L'UNIV. (Paris), D.SC. (Canberra); American (b. French) astronomer; b. 25 April 1918; ed Univ. of Paris; Asst. astronomer, Peridier Observatory 1939, 1941–42; C.N.R.S. research student, Physics Research Laboratory, Sorbonne 1943–45; Research Fellow, Astrophysics Inst. C.N.R.S., Paris 1945–49; Science programme, BBC London 1950–51; Research Fellow, Australian Nat. Univ. at Commonwealth Observatory, Mt. Stromlo 1951–54; Observer-in-Charge, Yale-Columbia Southern Station, Mt. Stromlo 1954–57; Astronomer, Lowell Observatory, Flagstaff, Ariz. 1957–58; Research Assoc. Harvard Coll. Observatory, Cambridge, Mass. 1958–60; Assoc. Prof. Astronomy, Univ. of Texas 1960–64; Prof. Univ. of Texas 1965–81; Ashbel Smith Prof. of Astronomy, Univ. of Texas 1981–82; Blumberg Centennial Prof. of Astronomy, Univ. of Texas 1983–88; Visiting Prof. Collège de France 1976; Visiting Fellow, Australian Nat. Univ. 1981–82; mem. N.A.S., Int. Astronomical Union, American Astronomical Soc., Royal Astronomical Soc. Astronomical Soc. of France; Herschel Medal, Royal Astronomical Soc. 1980. *Publications include:* Astronomie (with L. Rudaux) 1948, English, Spanish and Italian trans. 1959–67, Physique de la planète Mars 1951, English trans. 1954, Russian trans. 1956, Discovery of the Universe 1956, Manuel de photographie scientifique 1956, L'exploration des galaxies voisines 1958, Astronomical Photography 1961 (Russian trans. 1975), Reference Catalogue of Bright Galaxies (with A. de Vaucouleurs) 1964, Survey of the Universe (with D. Menzel and F. Whipple) 1976, Second Reference Catalogue of Bright Galaxies (with A. de Vaucouleurs and H. G. Corwin, Jr.) 1976, Topics in Extragalactic Astronomy 1977, Le monde des galaxies 1977, The Cosmic Distance Scale and the Hubble Constant 1982, S Andromedae 1987, and about 450 papers. *Address:* c/o Department of Astronomy, University of Texas, Austin, Texas 78712, U.S.A. (Office). *Telephone:* (512) 471-3465.

DEVAUX, Louis Armand; French business executive; b. 5 April 1907, Tananarive, Madagascar; s. of Louis-Séraphin Devaux and Estelle Charpentier; m. Suzanne Perche 1927; one s.; ed. Lycée St. Louis, Univ. de Paris à la Sorbonne and Ecole des Hautes Etudes Commerciales; with Banque de Paris et des Pays-Bas 1927–29; Cartier S.A. 1929–46, Pres. 1944–46, Chair. Bd. Cartier Inc., New York 1946–49; Pres. Pétroles Toneline S.A. 1949–51; Asst. Dir.-Gen. Compagnie des Produits Chimiques et Raffineries

de Berre 1949–51; Asst. Dir.-Gen. Shell Française 1952–60, Pres. Dir.-Gen. 1960–67; Pres. Soc. des Pétroles Shell Berre 1960–67; Pres. Dir.-Gen. Soc. Le Nickel 1967–71; Chair. Centre Français du Commerce Extérieur 1972–75; Chair. Laffitte-Tokyo 1973–77; Dir. Deutz et Geldermann S.A., Les Ateliers de Construction du Nord de la France, Soc. Générale de Fonderie 1975–82; Chair. Export Assistance Int.; Admin. Rio Tinto-Zinc. Corpn. 1967–75, Shell Française 1957–80, SICAV Laffitte-Tokyo 1978–80; Commdr., Légion d'honneur, Grand Officier Ordre national du Mérite, Croix de guerre. *Address:* 1 rue de la Paroisse, 78000 Versailles, France.

de VENOT DE NOISY, Jack; French international lawyer; b. 29 July 1916, Orléans; m. Lilian Marie Harel de la Coutancière; one s. one d.; ed. Ecole Saint-Grégoire, Pithiviers; Pres. Int. Fed. of Judicial and Fiscal Counsellors; Sec.-Gen. Int. Council of Space Law; Pres. Fed. of Latin Nations; Hon. Pres. order of Int. Lawyers of France; Vice-Pres. Int. Confed. of Assocns. of Experts and Advisers (UN); Officier, Légion d'honneur, Croix de guerre. *Leisure interests:* riding, hunting. *Address:* 2 avenue Foch, 75016 Paris, France. *Telephone:* 45 00 4826.

DEVER, Edmonde, LL.D.; Belgian diplomatist; b. 1921, Brussels; ed. Univ. of Liège and Free Univ. of Brussels; served in Cen. Admin., Brussels 1946–49, 1961–66, Belgian Embassy, London 1949–59; Consul-Gen., Johannesburg, South Africa 1959, Luanda, Angola 1959–61; Deputy Perm. Rep. of Belgium to the UN 1966–69, Perm. Rep. 1981–88; Amb. to Sweden 1973–78, to Austria 1978–81; Commdr. of the Order of Leopold, Commdr. of the Order of the Crown, Medal of Civic Merit (1st Class), Commdr. of the Order of the Oak of Luxembourg, Grand Ribbon of the Order of the Pole Star of Sweden, Grand Ribbon of the Order of Merit of Austria. *Address:* c/o Ministry of Foreign Affairs, 2 rue des Quatre Bras, 1000 Brussels, Belgium.

DEVESI, Sir Baddeley, G.C.M.G., G.C.V.O.; Solomon Islands politician and administrator; b. 16 Oct. 1941, East Tathiboko, Guadalcanal; s. of Mostyn Tagabasoe Norua and Laisa Otu; m. June Marie Barley 1969; four s. three d.; ed. St. Mary's School, Maravovo, King George VI School, Solomon Islands, Ardmore Teachers' Training Coll., Auckland, New Zealand; Teacher, Melanesian Mission schools, Solomon Islands 1965–69; elected mem. British Solomon Islands Legis. and Exec. Councils 1967–68; lecturer, Solomon Islands Teachers' Coll. 1970–72, Asst. Sec. for Social Services 1972, Internal Affairs 1972; Dist. Officer, S. Malaita 1973–75; Perm. Sec. Ministry of Works and Public Utilities 1976, Ministry of Transport and Communications 1977; Gov.-Gen. of Solomon Islands 1978–88; Chancellor, Univ. of S. Pacific 1980–83; Hon. D. Univ.; K.St.J. *Leisure interests:* swimming, lawn tennis, cricket, reading, snooker. *Address:* c/o Government House, Honiara, Solomon Islands.

De VILLIERS, David Pieter, B.A., LL.B.; South African business executive; b. 8 March 1918, George; m. Mavis de Villiers 1945; one s. four d.; ed. Stellenbosch Univ.; Registrar of Judge Pres. of Cape 1941; practising attorney, Cape Town 1942–47; Legal Adviser, Fed. Group of Cos. 1947–50; Dir. Sasol Ltd. (Sec. 1950–66, Man. Dir. 1966–77, Chair. 1977–87), Saambou Nat. Bldg. Soc., Nasionale Pers Beperk, Swiss-South African Reinsurance Co. Ltd., Small Business Devt. Corpn. Ltd., Volkskas Group Ltd.; Hon. LL.D (Rand Afrikaans Univ.); Hon. D.Comm. (Stellenbosch) 1985; Decoration for Meritorious Service 1984. *Leisure interest:* farming. *Address:* Sasol Ltd., P.O. Box 5486, Johannesburg 2000 (Office); P.O. Box 1617, Cape Town 8000, South Africa (Home).

de VILLIERS, Dawid Jacobus, M.A., D.PHIL.; South African diplomatist and politician; b. 10 July 1940, Burgersdorp; s. of C. V. de Villiers and E. Opperman; m. Suzaan Mangold 1964; one s. three d.; part-time lecturer in philosophy, Univ. of Western Cape 1963–64; Minister, Dutch Reformed Church, Wellington, Cape 1967–69; Lecturer in Philosophy, Rand Afrikaans Univ., Johannesburg 1969–72; mem. Parl. for Johannesburg West 1972–79, for Piketberg 1980–; Chair. Nat. Party's Foreign Affairs Cttee. in Parl. 1978–79; Pres. Convocation, Rand Afrikaans Univ. 1977–; Amb. to U.K. 1979–80; Minister of Trade and Industry 1980–86; Head Budget and Welfare, Ministers Council, House of Ass. 1986–88; Minister in Office of State Pres. in Charge of Comm. for Admin. and Privatization 1988–; rep. of S. Africa in int. rugby tours 1962–70, Capt. 1965–70; Abe Bailey Scholarship 1963–64, Markotter Scholarship 1964; State Pres.'s award for Sport 1968, 1970, S. African Sportsman of Year 1968, Jaycee's Outstanding Young Man of Year Award 1971, State Pres.'s Gold Decoration for Meritorious Service 1988. *Leisure interest:* squash. *Address:* c/o House of Assembly, Cape Town; Private Bag 9032, Cape Town 8000, South Africa.

DE VILLIERS, Jacobus Wynand Louw, D.SC., PR.ENG.; South African nuclear physicist; b. 27 Oct. 1929, Smithfield; s. of Adriaan Jacobus van Wyk de Villiers; m. Juanita S. Deetlefs 1953; two s. two d.; ed. Smithfield High School; Asst. Research Officer, C.S.I.R. 1952–54; Head, Mass Spectometry Div. NPRL, C.S.I.R. 1955–58; Fellow, Atomic Energy Bd. (AEB) 1958–59, Head, Reactor Physics Sub-div. 1959–67; spent two years at Argonne Nat. Lab. U.S.A.; Fellow, Research Assoc. Int. Inst. of Nuclear Science and Eng. 1959–61; Dir. Reactor Devt. Div. AEB 1967–70; Man. Dir. Fisika Praktika (Pty), Ltd. 1970–73; Deputy Pres. Atomic Energy Corpn. of South Africa Ltd., (AEC) 1976–79, Chair. AEC 1982–; Pres. AEB 1979–82; Chair. Science Advisory Council of Prime Minister 1982–; mem. South African Inst. for Physics, South African Inst. of Mechanical

Engs.; mem. Council, South African Acad. for Arts and Science. *Leisure interest:* tennis. *Address:* Atomic Energy Corporation of South Africa Ltd., P.O. Box 582, Pretoria 0001, South Africa.

De VILLIERS, Willem Johannes, PH.D.; South African engineer; b. 4 April 1921, Jacobsdal, Orange Free State; m. Francina Maria Meyer 1949; two s. one d.; ed. Grey Coll., Bloemfontein and Univ. of Cape Town; Engineer, Pretoria Power Station 1945-49; joined Anglo American Corpn. 1950, successively Engineer, Power Station Supt., Tech. Research and Devt. Engineer, Eng. Supt., Asst. Man. and Man., Rhokana Corpn., Kitwe, Zambia 1950-60; Consulting Mechanical Engineer responsible for method and work studies at the gold mines, Anglo American Corpn., Johannesburg and at Welkom 1961-65; played an important part in the planning of the Cabora-Bassa project; Man. Dir. L.T.A. Engineering 1965-68; Industrial Adviser to Sanlam 1968-70; Deputy Man. Dir., Gen. Mining Union Corpn. 1970-71, Man. Dir. 1971-76, Exec. Chair. 1976-82. *Leisure interests:* tennis, water-skiing. *Address:* c/o General Mining Union Corporation Ltd., 6 Holland Street, Johannesburg, South Africa (Office).

DEVINE, Grant, M.SC., PH.D., M.B.A.; Canadian politician, farmer and agricultural economist; b. 1944, Regina, Sask.; m. Chantal Guillaume 1966; two s. three d.; ed. Univs. of Saskatchewan, Alberta and Ohio State; marketing specialist, Agric. Commodity Legislation, Fed. Govt., Ottawa 1970-72; Adviser to Food Prices Review Bd. and Prov. Govts.; Graduate Asst., Ohio State Univ. 1972-76; Assoc. Prof. Agriculture, Econ. Univ. of Sask. 1975-79; Hon. Faculty Pres., Coll. of Agric. 1978; Leader, Progressive Conservative Party of Sask. 1979-; M.L.A. for Estevan 1982-; Premier of Sask. 1982-86, 1986-, also Min. of Agric. 1985-; mem. American Econ. Asscn., American Marketing Asscn., American Consumer Research, Canadian Agric. Econ. Soc., Consumers' Asscn., Canada; Vanier Award 1983. *Publications:* numerous papers in professional journals. *Leisure interests:* golf, skiing, baseball. *Address:* Office of the Premier of Saskatchewan, Legislative Building, 2405 Legislature Drive, Regina, Sask. S4S 0B3, Canada. *Telephone:* (306) 787-6271.

DE VITO, Salverino; Italian politician; b. 24 Jan. 1926, Brescia; Christian Democrat (D.C.) Senator 1968-; Sec., then Vice-Chair. D.C. Parl. Group; Minster for Extraordinary Aid to Mezzogiorno (South) Aug. 1986-87. *Address:* Camera del Deputati, Rome, Italy.

DEVITT, Edward James; American judge; b. 5 May 1911, St. Paul, Minnesota; s. of Thomas Philip and Catherine Ethel (née McGuire) Devitt; m. Marcelle LaRose MacRae 1939; one s. one d.; ed. Univ. of North Dakota; private legal practice, East Grand Forks, Minn. 1935-39, Municipal Judge 1935-39, Asst. Attorney-Gen., Minnesota 1939-42, Instructor in Law, Univ. of North Dakota 1935-39; St. Paul Coll. 1945-; mem. U.S. House of Reps. 1947-48; Probate Judge, Ramsey County, St. Paul 1950-54, Judge, U.S. District Courts, Minnesota 1954-, Chief Judge 1958. *Address:* 734 Federal Courts Building, 316 North Robert Street, St. Paul, Minn. 55101 (Office); 111 Kellogg Boulevard, St. Paul, Minn. 55101, U.S.A. (Home). *Telephone:* 612-228-7178 (Office).

DEVLETOGLOU, Evangelos A., PH.D.; Greek economist and politician; ed. Univ. of Athens, Columbia Univ., N.Y.; Reserve Officer Greek Navy; with Bank of Greece 1960-67; Sr. Economist, Int. Monetary Fund 1969; with IMF, Geneva 1972; Under-Sec. of Co-ordination and Planning July-Nov. 1974; M.P. Nov. 1974-; Minister of Finance 1974-77; Deputy Gov. Bank of Greece 1977-78; New Democracy Party. *Address:* 489 Bd. Messogion, Agia Paraskev, Athens, Greece. *Telephone:* 65939.

DEVLIN, Baron (Life Peer, cr. 1961), of West Wick in the County of Wiltshire, **Patrick Arthur Devlin,** Kt., P.C., F.B.A.; British lawyer; b. 25 Nov. 1905; s. of W. J. Devlin; m. Madeleine Oppenheimer 1932; four s. two d.; ed. Stonyhurst Coll., and Christ's Coll., Cambridge; called to the Bar 1929, K.C. 1945; Attorney-Gen. to the Duchy of Cornwall 1947-48; Justice of the High Court 1948-60; Master of the Bench of Gray's Inn 1947; Pres. of Restrictive Practices Court 1957-60; Lord Justice of Appeal 1960-61; Lord of Appeal in Ordinary 1961-63; Chair. Cttee. Inquiry into Dock Labour Scheme 1956, into decasualization of Dock Labour 1964, Nyasaland Inquiry Comm. 1959, Inquiry into the Port Transport Industry 1964-65, into Industrial Representation 1971-72, on Identification in Criminal Cases 1974; Chair. the Press Council 1964-69; Pres. British Maritime Law Asscn. 1962-76; a Judge of the Admin. Tribunal of ILO 1964-86; High Steward of Cambridge Univ. 1966-; Hon. LL.D. (Glasgow) 1962, (Toronto) 1962, (Cambridge, Leicester, Sussex) 1966, (Durham) 1968, (Liverpool) 1970, (St. Louis) 1980, Hon. D.C.L. (Oxford) 1965. *Publications:* (lectures) Trial by Jury 1956, Criminal Prosecution in England 1958, Samples of Lawmaking 1962, The Enforcement of Morals 1965, Too Proud to Fight: Woodrow Wilson's Neutrality 1974, The Judge 1979, Easing the Passing: The Trial of Dr. Adams 1985, The Jury in Two Constitutions 1988. *Address:* West Wick House, Pewsey, Wilts., England.

DEVLIN, Stuart Leslie, A.O., C.M.G.; Australian goldsmith, silversmith and designer; b. 9 Oct. 1931, Geelong; s. of Richard and Jesse Devlin; m. 1st Kim Hose 1962, 2nd Carole Hedley-Saunders 1986; ed. Gordon Inst. of Tech., Geelong, Royal Melbourne Inst. of Tech. and Royal Coll. of Art; art teacher, Victoria Educ. Dept. 1950-58; Royal Coll. of Art 1958-60; Harkness Fellow, New York 1960-62; lecturer, Prahan Tech. Coll., Melbourne 1962; Inspector of Art in Tech. Schools, Victoria Educ. Dept.

1964-65; working as goldsmith, silversmith and designer in London 1965-; exhbns. of gold and silver in numerous cities in U.K., U.S.A., Australia, Middle East, etc.; has executed many commissions for commemorative coins in gold and silver for various countries; designed and made cutlery for State Visit to Paris 1972, Duke of Edinburgh Trophy for World Driving Championship 1973, silver to commemorate opening of Sydney Opera House 1973, Grand National Trophy 1975 and Regalia for Order of Australia 1975-76; Centrepiece for Royal Engs. to commemorate their work in Northern Ireland 1984; Bas-relief portrait H.R.H. Princess of Wales for Wedgwood 1986; devised and executed Champagne Diamond Exhbn. 1987; granted Royal Warrant (goldsmith and jeweller to H.M. Queen Elizabeth II) 1982. *Leisure interests:* work, wind-surfing, squash. *Address:* Southbourne Court, Southwater, West Sussex RH13 7DJ, England. *Telephone:* (0403) 732706.

DEVONS, Samuel, PH.D., F.R.S.; British professor of physics; b. 30 Sept. 1914, Bangor, N. Wales; s. of David I. Devons and Edith Edlestein; m. Celia Ruth Toubkin 1938; four d.; ed. Trinity Coll., Cambridge; Scientific Officer, Air Ministry 1939-45; Fellow, Dir. of Studies, Lecturer in Physics, Trinity Coll., Cambridge 1946-49; Prof. of Physics, Imperial Coll. of Science 1950-55, Acting Dir. of Laboratory 1953-54; Langworthy Prof. of Physics and Dir. of Physical Laboratories, Manchester Univ. 1955-60; Visiting Prof. of Physics , Columbia Univ. New York 1959-60, Prof. 1960-85, Prof. Emer. 1985-, Chair. Dept. of Physics 1963-67; Visiting Prof., Barnard Coll., Colombia Univ., History of Physics 1969, Dir. History of Physics Lab.; mem. UNESCO Technical Aid, Argentina 1957; Royal Soc./Leverhulme Visiting Prof., India 1968-69; Racah Visiting Prof., Hebrew Univ., Jerusalem 1973-74; Balfour Visiting Prof., Weizmann Inst., Rehovot 1973; Memorial Lecturer, Royal Soc. Rutherford (Australia) 1989; Bd. of Govs. Weizmann Inst. 1971-; Rutherford Prize and Medal, Physical Soc. 1970. *Publications:* Excited States of Nuclei 1949, Biology and the Physical Sciences (Ed.) 1969, High Energy Physics and Nuclear Structure (Ed.) 1970. *Leisure interests:* writing, theatre. *Address:* Nevis Laboratory, Columbia University, P.O. Box 137, Irvington, N.Y. 10533 (Office); Lewis Road, Irvington, New York, N.Y. 10533, U.S.A. (Home). *Telephone:* 212-280-4124/914-591-8100 (Office); 914-591-7681 (Home).

DE VRIES, Michiel Josias, M.SC., DR.RER.NAT.; South African university professor; b. 5 May 1933, Riversdale; m. Renée Weber; three d.; ed. Univ. of Stellenbosch, Albert Ludwig Univ., Freiburg; frmly. Prof. in Physical Chemistry, Univ. of Stellenbosch, Dean Faculty of Natural Science 1974-76, Vice-Rector 1976-79, Rector July 1979, Prin. and Vice-Chancellor 1981-; Dir. Nasionale Pers Bpk., Boland Bank; Council mem. Mintek; mem. S.A. Acad. for Science and Art (mem. Council 1979-), Cttee. of Univ. Principals; Life-mem. Fed. of Afrikaans Cultural Socs.; Oppenheimer Memorial Trust Fellowship 1968; Carnegie Travel Bursary 1968; Gold Medal of S.A. Chemical Inst. for most eminent chemical publ. 1970. *Publications:* many scientific articles in nat. and int. magazines, co-author of 6 textbooks for schools on senior physics and chemistry. *Address:* Office of the Rector, Central Administration Building, University of Stellenbosch, Stellenbosch 7600; 51 Van der Stel Street, Stellenbosch 7600, South Africa. (Home).

DE VRIES, Peter, A.B.; American writer; b. 27 Feb. 1910; m. Katinka Loeser; three c.; ed. Calvin Coll., Michigan, and Northwestern Univ.; freelance writer 1931-; Assoc. Ed. Poetry 1938, co-Ed. 1942; joined editorial staff of New Yorker 1944; mem. American Acad. and Inst. of Arts and Letters. *Publications:* No But I Saw the Movie 1952, The Tunnel of Love 1954, Comfort Me with Apples 1956, The Mackerel Plaza 1958; dramatization of The Tunnel of Love (with Joseph Fields) 1957, The Tents of Wickedness 1959, Through the Fields of Clover 1961, The Blood of the Lamb 1962, Reuben, Reuben 1964 (dramatized as Spofford by Herman Shumlin 1967), Let Me Count the Ways 1965, The Vale of Laughter 1967, The Cat's Pyjamas and Witch's Milk 1968, Mrs. Wallop 1970, Into Your Tent I'll Creep 1971, Without A Stitch in Time 1972, Forever Panting 1973, The Glory of the Hummingbird 1974, I Hear America Swinging 1976, Madder Music 1977, Consenting Adults or The Duchess Will Be Furious 1980, Sauce for the Goose 1981, Slouching Towards Kalamazoo 1983, The Prick of Noon 1985, Peckham's Marbles 1986. *Address:* 170 Cross Highway, Westport, Conn. 06880, U.S.A.

DEVRIES, William Castle, M.D.; American surgeon; b. 19 Dec. 1943, Brooklyn; s. of Hendrik Devries and Cathryn L. Castle; m. Ane K. Olsen 1965; seven c.; ed. Univ. of Utah; intern Duke Univ. Medical Center 1970-71; Resident in cardiovascular and thoracic surgery 1971-79; Asst. Prof. of Surgery, Univ. of Utah until 1984; Chief of Thoracic Surgery, Salt Lake Hosp., Va. until 1984; Dir. Artificial Heart Project, Humana Hosp. Audubon, Louisville. *Address:* Humana Heart Institute, 1 Audubon Drive, Louisville, Ky. 40217, U.S.A.

DE WAAL, Marius Theodorus, B.SC., B.ING.; South African business executive; b. 12 March 1925, Paarl Dist.; s. of Pieter de Waal; m. Kitty du Plessis 1949; three s. one d.; ed. Univs. of Stellenbosch and Delft and Harvard Advanced Man. Programme, Swansea; town engineer, Bellville 1947-60; now Chair. Industrial Devt. Corp. of S.A. Ltd., Atlantis Diesel Engines (Pty) Ltd.; Dir. Sasol Ltd., Trustbank, Sage Holdings, Siemens Ltd., Iscor, Trust Bank of Africa Ltd. *Leisure interest:* tennis. *Address:* P.O. Box 7849055, Sandton 2146, South Africa.

de WAART, Edo; Netherlands conductor; b. 1 June 1941, Amsterdam; s. of M. de Waart and J. Rose; m. Katherine Hilst 1984; one s. one d. from 1st marriage; ed. Amsterdam Music Lyceum; Asst. Conductor, Concertgebouw Orchestra, Amsterdam 1966; Perm. Conductor, Rotterdam Philharmonic 1967, Musical Dir. and Prin. Conductor 1973-79; Prin. Guest Conductor, San Francisco Symphony Orchestra 1975-77, Music Dir. 1977-85; Music Dir. Minn. Orchestra 1986-; First Prize Dimitri Mitropoulos Competition, New York 1964. *Address:* Minnesota Orchestra, 1111 Nicollet Mall, Minneapolis, Minn. 55403, U.S.A.

DEWAR, Michael James Steuart, B.A., D.PHIL., M.A., F.R.S.; American (b. British) professor of chemistry; b. 24 Sept. 1918, Ahmednagar, India; s. of Francis Dewar and Nan Balfour Dewar; m. Mary Williamson 1944; two s.; ed. Winchester Coll. and Balliol Coll., Oxford; ICI Fellow, Oxford Univ. 1945; Physical Chemist, Courtaulds Ltd. 1945-51; Prof. of Chem. and Head of Dept., Univ. of London, Queen Mary Coll. 1951-59; Prof. of Chem., Chicago Univ. 1959-63; Robert A. Welch Prof. of Chem., Univ. of Texas in Austin 1963-; Fellow, Royal Soc. and American Acad. of Arts and Sciences; mem. N.A.S.; Reilly Lecturer, Notre Dame Univ. 1951; Tilden Lecturer, Chemical Soc. 1954; Visiting Prof., Yale Univ. 1957; Hon.-Sec. Chemical Soc. 1957-59; Harrison Howe Award, American Chem. Soc. 1961; Falk-Plaut Lecturer, Columbia Univ. 1963; Daines Lecturer, Univ. of Kansas 1963; Glidden Co. Lecturer, Western Reserve Univ. 1964; William Pyle Philips Visitor, Haverford Coll. 1964; Arthur D. Little Visiting Prof., M.I.T. 1966; Marchon Visiting Lecturer, Newcastle upon Tyne, England 1966; Glidden Company Lecturer, Kent State Univ. 1967; Grehn Lecturer, Eid Tech. Hochschule, Zurich, 1968; Barton Lecturer, Univ. of Okla. 1969; Benjamin Rush Lecturer, Univ. of Pa. 1971; Kahlbaum Lecturer, Univ. of Basel 1970; William Pyle Philips Visitor, Haverford Coll. 1970; Distinguished Visiting Lecturer, Yeshiva Univ. 1970; Kharasch Visiting Prof., Chicago 1971; Venable Lecturer, Univ. of N.C. 1971; Phi Lambda Upsilon Speaker, Johns Hopkins Univ. 1972; Firth Visiting Prof., Sheffield Univ., England, 1972; Foster Lecturer, State Univ. of N.Y. at Buffalo, 1973; Five College Chemistry Lecturer, Mt. Holyoke, Hampshire, Amherst, Smith Colls., Univ. of Mass., 1973; Robert Robinson Lecturer of the Chem. Soc. 1974; Special Lecturer, Univ. London 1974; Sprague Lecturer Univ. Wis. 1974; Distinguished Bicentennial Prof., Univ. of Utah 1976; Bircher Lecturer, Vanderbilt Univ., 1976; Pahlavi Lecturer, Iran 1976; Michael Faraday Lecturer, Northern Ill. Univ. 1977; Priestley Lecturer, Penn. State Univ. 1981; Research Scholar Lecturer, Drew Univ. 1984; J. Clarence Karcher Lecturer, Univ. of Okla. 1984; Charles A. Cowson Lecturer, Univ. of Georgia 1988; Hon. Fellow Balliol Coll., Oxford 1974; G. W. Wheland Memorial Medal, Univ. of Chicago 1976, Evans Award, Ohio State Univ. 1977, S.W. Regional Award A.C.S. 1978, Davy Medal, Royal Society 1982, James Flack Norris Award, A.C.S. 1984, Nichols Medal, A.C.S. 1986, Auburn—G. M. Kosolapoff Award A.C.S. 1988. *Publications:* The Electronic Theory of Organic Chemistry 1949, Hyperconjugation 1962, Introduction to Modern Chemistry 1965, The Molecular Orbital Theory of Organic Chemistry 1969, Computer Compilation of Molecular Weights and Percentage Compositions of Organic Compounds 1970, The PMO Theory of Organic Chemistry 1975; frequent contributions to scientific journals. *Leisure interests:* numerous and varied. *Address:* Department of Chemistry, University of Texas, Austin, Texas 78712 (Office); 6808 Mesa Drive, Austin, Tex. 78731, U.S.A. (Home). *Telephone:* (512) 471-5053 (Office); 512-345-0147 (Home).

DEWDNEY, Duncan Alexander Cox, C.B.E., B.SC.; British company director (retd.); b. 22 Oct. 1911, Hampton-on-Thames, England; s. of late Claude Felix Dewdney and Annie Ross; m. Edith Marion Riley 1935; two d.; ed. Bromsgrove School, Worcs., and Birmingham Univ.; Chemist, British Petroleum Co. 1932-36; Technical Asst., Standard Oil Devt. Co. 1936-40; R.A.F. 1940-45; Research and Devt. Adviser, Anglo-American Oil Co. Ltd. 1946-47; Man. Devt. Dept., Esso Devt. Co. 1947-49; Man. Esso European Laboratories 1949-51; with Refining Dept. Esso Petroleum Co. 1951-57, Dir. 1957-63, Man. Dir. 1963-68, Vice-Chair. 1968; Chair. Bd. Irish Refining Co. Ltd. 1957-65; Chair. Mechanical Eng. Econ. Devt. Comm. 1964-68, of Anglesey Aluminium Ltd. 1968-71, of RTZ Metals Ltd. 1968, of RTZ (Britain) 1969, of RTZ Devt. Enterprises Ltd. 1970-72; Exec. Dir. Rio Tinto-Zinc Corpn. Ltd. 1968-72; mem. Nat. Prices and Incomes Bd. 1965-69; Chair. Welsh Industrial Devt. Bd. 1972-75; Dir. The Coverdale Org. 1973-; Deputy Chair. Manpower Services Comm. 1974-77; Legion of Merit. *Address:* Salters, Harestock, Winchester, Hants., England. *Telephone:* 0962-52034.

de WECK, Philippe; Swiss banker; b. 2 Jan. 1919, Fribourg; s. of Pierre and Lucie (Glasson) de Weck; m. Alix de Saussure 1944; two s. five d.; ed. Fribourg Grammar School, Univ. of Fribourg; joined law firm of Mr. Bourgknecht (later Fed. Councillor) 1948-51; partner in Bank Weck, Aeby and Cie, Fribourg 1951-54; Man. Fribourg Branch Office, Union Bank of Switzerland 1954-56, Man. Geneva Branch Office 1956-62, Gen. Man. Head Office, Zürich 1964, Chair. Bd. 1976-80; Chair. Soc. Gén. de Surveillance Holding S.A., Geneva; mem. Bd. of Inquiry into affairs of Istituto per le Opere di Religione (Vatican Bank) 1982; mem. Bd. Nestlé S.A. (Vice-Chair.), Vevey. *Leisure interests:* skiing, sailing, mountain climbing. *Address:* c/o Union Bank of Switzerland, rue St.-Pierre 1, 1701 Fribourg, Switzerland. *Telephone:* 037-204 111.

DE WEERDT, Hon. Mark Murray, Q.C., M.A., LL.B.; Canadian lawyer and judge; b. 6 May 1928, Cologne, Germany; s. of Hendrik Eugen de Weerdt and Ina Dunbar Murray; m. Linda Anne Hadwen 1956; four s.; ed. Glasgow Univ., Univ. of B.C., Vancouver; Constable, Royal Canadian Mounted Police 1950-52; barrister and solicitor, B.C. 1956-70, 1973-81, N.W.T. 1958-81; Crown Attorney, N.W.T. 1958-63; City Solicitor, Yellowknife, N.W.T. 1969-71; Magistrate and Juvenile Court Judge, N.W.T. 1971-73; Gen. Solicitor, Insurance Corpn. of B.C. 1974-76; Sr. Counsel, Dept. of Justice of Canada, Vancouver 1976-79, Gen. Counsel and Dir. 1979-81; Judge of the Supreme Court of the N.W.T. 1981-; Justice of Appeal, Court of Appeal of the N.W.T. 1981-, Court of Appeal of the Yukon Territory 1981-; Chair. Judicial Council of the N.W.T. 1981-; Dir. Canadian Judges' Conf.; Dir. Canadian Inst. for the Admin. of Justice; mem. Canadian Bar Asscn.; Q.C. (Canada) 1968; mem. Int. Comm. of Jurists (Canadian Sec.), Advisory Council, Canadian Human Rights Inst., The Osgoode Soc., The Selden Soc. *Leisure interest:* general reading. *Address:* P.O. Box 1439, Yellowknife, North West Territories, X1A 2P1, Canada. *Telephone:* (403) 873 7105.

De WET, Dr. Carel, B.SC., M.B., B.CH.; South African physician, politician and diplomatist; b. 25 May 1924, Memel, Orange Free State; s. of Gen. Christian de Wet; m. Rina Maas 1949; one s. three d.; ed. Vrede High School, Orange Free State, Pretoria Univ., and Univ. of Witwatersrand; medical practice, Boksburg, Transvaal, Winburg, Orange Free State, and Vanderbijlpark, Transvaal; Mayor of Vanderbijlpark 1950-52; mem. House of Assembly for Vanderbijlpark 1954-64, for Johannesburg-West 1967-72; Amb. to U.K. 1964-67, 1972-77; Minister of Planning and Mines 1967-69, of Mines and Health 1969-72. *Leisure interests:* farming, shooting, deep-sea fishing, golf, rugby, cricket, trees. *Address:* P.O. Box 6424, Johannesburg 2000, South Africa *Telephone:* 726-2903 (Office); 706-6202 (Home).

DE WIED, David, M.D., PH.D.; Netherlands professor of pharmacology; b. 12 Jan. 1925, Deventer; s. of Izaak de Wied and Carolien Visser; m. Alijda Prins 1952; one s. three d.; ed. Univ. of Groningen; Asst. Prof. Dept. of Pharmacology, Univ. of Groningen 1950-58, Assoc. Prof. 1958-61, Prof. of Experimental Endocrinology 1961-63; Prof. of Pharmacology and Chair. of Inst. Univ. of Utrecht 1963-; Pres. Royal Netherlands Acad. of Sciences 1984-; Fellow, New York Acad. of Sciences; Foreign Corresp. mem. Royal Acad. of Medicine of Belgium; Foreign Fellow, Indian Nat. Science Acad.; corresp. mem. Portuguese Pharmacological Soc.; Kt., Order of Lion (Netherlands), Grosses Verdienstkreuz (Fed. Repub. of Germany), numerous awards, honours and prizes. *Publications:* papers in professional journals. *Leisure interests:* music, art. *Address:* Rudolf Magnus Institute, Vondellaan 6, 3521 GD Utrecht (Office); Lassuslaan 41, 3723 LH Bilthoven, Netherlands (Home). *Telephone:* 030-880521 (Office); 030-783328 (Home).

DE WIT, Cornelis T., PH.D.; Netherlands agronomist and crop ecologist; b. 27 Jan. 1924, Brummen; m. P. J. R. Blaauw 1950; two c.; ed. Agricultural Univ. Wageningen; Jr. Faculty mem. Agric. Univ. Wageningen 1947-53; Adviser, Soil Research, Dept. of Nat. Planning 1953-55; Sr. Scientist, Centre for Agro-Biological Research, Wageningen 1955-79; Adviser, Soil Research, Agric. Research Service, Wash., D.C. 1960-61; Prof. of Agronomy, Univ. of Calif. Davis 1968; Prof. of Theoretical Production Ecology, Agric. Univ. Wageningen 1968-; A. D. White Prof. at Large, Cornell Univ. 1977-83; mem. Advisory Council for Science Policy, The Hague 1976-86; mem. Scientific Council Govt. Policy 1978-87; Senator, Prov. of Gelderland 1968-74; mem. Royal Netherlands Acad., Lenin Acad. U.S.S.R., Ecology Soc., U.K.; Wolf Prize; Dr. h.c. (Ghent, Jerusalem). *Publications:* Placement of Fertilizers 1953, Transpiration and Crop Yields 1958, On Competition 1960, Theory and Model 1960, Ionic balance 1963, Photosynthesis of crops 1965, Simulation Transport Processes 1972, Simulation Ecological Processes 1974, Simulation Crops 1978, Future Studies 1978-84, Interactive Multiple Goal Planning of Agricultural Research and Development. *Leisure interest:* boating. *Address:* Department of Theoretical Production Ecology, P.O. Box 430, 6700 AK Wageningen (Office); Abersonlaan 31, 6703 GE Wageningen, Netherlands (Home).

DEWS, Peter Booth, M.B., CH.B., PH.D.; American professor of psychiatry and psychobiology; b. 11 Sept. 1922, Ossett, U.K.; s. of Ashley Dews and Ella Dews; m. Grace Miller 1949; three s. one d.; ed. Univ. of Leeds, U.K. and Univ. of Minnesota; Demonstrator in Pharmacology, Univ. of Leeds 1945-46, Lecturer 1946-47; Research Assoc. Mayo Clinic, Rochester 1952; Instr. in Pharmacology, Harvard Medical School 1953-54, Assoc. in Pharmacology 1954-56, Asst. Prof. 1956-58, Assoc. Prof. 1959-62, Stanley Cobb Prof. of Psychiatry and Psychobiology 1962. *Publication:* Caffeine 1984. *Address:* Harvard Medical School, Laboratory of Psychobiology, 220 Lockwood Avenue, Boston, Mass. 02115 (Office); 181 Upland Road, Newtonville, Mass. 02160, U.S.A. (Home). *Telephone:* 617-732-1680 (Office); 617-244-0663 (Home).

DEXTER, John; British film, theatre and opera director; b. 2 Aug. 1925, Derby, England; s. of Harry James Dexter and Rose Dexter; actor in repertory, television and radio until 1957; apptd. Assoc. Dir. English Stage Co. 1957; directed 15 plays at Royal Court Theatre 1957-72; Assoc. Dir. Nat. Theatre 1963-73, directed 14 plays; directed 13 plays elsewhere 1959-74; Dir. of Production, Metropolitan Opera, New York 1974-81, Adviser 1981-84; Dir. Buxton Festival, England. *Plays directed in 1963-66 include:* Chips With Things, Do I Hear a Waltz?, Royal Hunt of the

Sun, Black Comedy and White Lies, The Unknown Soldier and his Wife (all in New York); *in 1971-73 include:* Woman Killed With Kindness, Tyger, The Good Natur'd Man, The Misanthrope, Equus, The Party (all Nat. Theatre); The Old Ones 1972 (Royal Court), Pygmalion 1974, Phèdre Britannica 1975 (Nat. Theatre), The Merchant 1979 (Broadway), As You Like It (Nat. Theatre), Gallileo (Nat. Theatre) 1980, Shoemaker's Holiday (Nat. Theatre) 1981, The Portage to San Cristobal of A.H. (Mermaid Theatre) 1982, Gigi 1985, The Cocktail Party 1986, Portraits 1987. *Films directed:* The Virgin Soldiers 1968, The Sidelong Glances of a Pidgeon Kicker, Twelfth Night (on Granada TV). *Operas directed:* Benvenuto Cellini (Covent Garden) 1966, House of the Dead, Boris Godunov, Billy Budd, Ballo in Maschera, I Vespri Siciliani (Hamburg), The Devils (Sadler's Wells), I Vespri Siciliani (new production) (Metropolitan, New York and Paris), La Forza del Destino (Paris) 1975, La Gioconda 1975, Aïda (new production) 1976, Le Prophète (new production) 1977 (all Metropolitan Opera), Dialogues of the Carmelites, Lulu, Rigoletto (new productions) 1977 (Metropolitan Opera), Billy Budd, The Bartered Bride, Don Pasquale (new productions) 1978 (Metropolitan Opera), Don Carlos, Die Entführung aus dem Serail (Metropolitan Opera), The Rise and Fall of the City of Mahagonny (new productions) 1979 (Metropolitan Opera), Rossignol, Le Sacre du Printemps, Oedipus Rex (triple bill) (Metropolitan Opera) 1981, Parade 1981, The Nightingale (Covent Garden) 1983, The Devil and the Good Lord 1984, La Buone Figliola, Il Filosofo di Campagna (Buxton Festival) 1985, Nabucco (Zurich) 1986, Portraits (Malvern Festival) 1987, Madam Butterfly (New York) 1988; Tony Award for Equus 1975, Shakespeare Prize (Hamburg) 1978; Tony Award for Madame Butterfly 1988. *Leisure interest:* work. *Address:* c/o Eric Glass Limited, 28 Berkeley Square, London, W1X 6HD, England. *Telephone:* 01-629 7162.

DEXTRAZE, Gen. Jacques Alfred, C.C., C.B.E., C.M.M., D.S.O., C.D.; Canadian army officer (retd.); b. 15 Aug. 1919, Montréal; s. of Alfred and Amanda Dextraze; m. Francis Helena Pare; four s. (one deceased); ed. St. Joseph de Bethier, Montréal, MacDonald Business Coll.; with Dominion Rubber Co. 1938-40; Fusiliers Mount Royal 1939-45, Lt.-Col. and Commdg. Officer 1944-45; Commdg. Officer Hastings and Prince Edward Regt. 1945; with Singer Mfg. Co. 1945-50; Man. Forest Operations 1947-50; Commdg. Officer 2nd Bn., Royal 22e Regt. 1950-52; Officer in charge of Admin., E. Québec Area 1952-54; Gen. Staff Officer, Québec 1954-55, Col. and Chief of Staff, Québec 1956-57; Commdt. Royal Canadian School of Infantry 1957-60, Camp Valcartier 1960-62; Brig., Commdr. E. Québec Area 1962; Chief of Staff, H.Q., UN Operations in Congo 1963-64; Commdr. 2 Canadian Infantry Brigade Group 1964-66; Chief of Staff for Operations and Training, H.Q. Mobile Command 1966-67, Maj.-Gen., Deputy Commdr. Operations 1967; Deputy Chief of Personnel, Canadian Forces H.Q. 1969, Lt.-Gen., Chief of Personnel 1970-72, Gen., Chief of Defence Staff 1972-77; mem. Canadian Comm. to Tripartite Mil. Confs. 1957; mem. Inst. Cttee. for Standardization of Arms and Nat. Mil. Resources 1957-60; Hon. Aide-de-Camp to H.E. the Gov.-Gen. 1958; Chair. Bd. Canadian Nat. Railways 1977-82; Council for Canadian Unity, Canada Safety Council; Pres. J. A. Dextraze and Assocs., Ottawa; Hon.LL.D. (Wilfrid Laurier Univ.); Hon. Ph.D. (Sherbrooke Univ.); Commdr. Canadian Order of Mil. Merit, Canadian Forces Decoration, Cross of Grand Officer of the Order of the Crown (Belgium) 1977. *Leisure interests:* reading, bridge, golf, editing military papers. *Address:* 467 Crestview Road, Ottawa, Ont. K1H 5G7, Canada (Home).

DEY-DEVA, Mukul Chandra, A.R.C.A., I.E.S.; Indian artist and writer; b. 23 July 1895, Sridharkhola village, District Dacca; s. of Kula Chandra Dey and Purnasasi Basu; m. Srimati Bina Dey 1932; one d.; ed. Santiniketan School (West Bengal); studied art with Dr. Abanindra Nath Tagore (Calcutta), and in Japan, Chicago and London; exhibited Indian Soc. of Oriental Art, Calcutta 1913, Tokyo 1916, Art Int., Chicago 1916; studied Slade School of Art, London 1920; scholarship Royal Coll. of Art, London 1920-22; Art Teacher, King Alfred School, Hampstead 1920-21; Lecturer Indian Art, L.C.C. London 1925-27; Royal Acad. 1922-23; paintings and drypoint-etchings in perm. collection, British Museum, London 1924-28, 1st one-man show, London 1927; works exhibited to Their Majesties The King and Queen at Buckingham Palace 1927; executed murals Wembley Exhbn., London 1925; exhibited Philharmonic Hall, Berlin 1926; Prin. Govt. Coll. of Art, Calcutta; Officer-in-Charge Art Section and Keeper Govt. Art Gallery, Indian Museum, Calcutta; Trustee Indian Museum 1938-43; Co-founder (with Mahatma Gandhi) Kalika Art Gallery 1945; Fulbright Visiting Prof. of Art in U.S.A. 1953-54; Curator Nat. Gallery of Modern Art, Govt. of India, New Delhi 1955-57; received Fellowship Grant from Cultural Dept., Govt. of India 1984-85; Agani Gagan Purashkar Award (Visva-Bharati Univ.) 1988; exhbn., Commonwealth Inst., London 1960, Drypoint prints (etchings) at Visva-Bharati Univ. Santiniketan 1979; Award, Rabindra Bharati Univ., Calcutta 1972; D.Litt. (Rabindra Bharati) 1987; Fellow Lalit Kala Acad., Govt. of India 1987; has started collection of the works of Shri Gagonendranath Tagore and Abanindranath Tagore and paintings of Mukul Dey. *Works include:* paintings, portraits, drypoint-etchings, copies of frescoes in Ajanta and Bagh Caves, Pollonaruwa temples, Ceylon, Sittanavasal caves, S. India, British Museum, London, U.S.A., Germany, 150 engraved plates on Indian life and legends for seventy years (since 1915). *Publications:* 12 Portraits 1917, My Pilgrimages to Ajanta and Bagh 1925 and 1951, My Reminiscences 1938, 15 Drypoints 1939, Birbhum

Terracottas 1960, Indian Life and Legends (10 vols.) 1974-, Souvenir Illustrated Album 1987. *Leisure interests:* painting, drawing, writing, gardening. *Address:* Chitralekha, P.O. Santiniketan, West Bengal, India.

DEZZA, Paolo, B.A., D.PHIL., D.THEOL.; Italian ecclesiastic; b. 13 Dec. 1901, Parma; s. of Giovanni and Carla Riccadonna Dezza; ed. Milan, Barcelona, Innsbruck, Naples; Prof. of Philosophy, Pontifical Gregorian Univ., Rome 1929-33, 1941-62, Rector 1941-51; Pres. Faculty of Aloisian Philosophy 1934-41; Asst. Gen., Soc. of Jesus 1965-75; Consultant, Sacred Pontifical Congregation 1949-81; Pres. Pontifical Inst. Regina Mundi 1954-66; Papal Del. of the Co. of Jesus 1981-83; Dr. h.c. (Univ. of Santiago, Chile), Commdr. Order of Alfonso the Wise, Spain. *Publications:* Alle origini del Neotomismo 1940, I Neotomisti italiani del secolo XIX 1942-44, Metaphysica Generalis 1962, Filosofia 1988, Esercizi Ignaziani 1987. *Address:* Borgo Santo Spirito 5, Rome, Italy. *Telephone:* 686.9841.

DHANABALAN, Suppiah, B.A. (HONS.); Singaporean politician; b. 8 Aug. 1937; m. Tan Khoon Hiap 1963; one s. one d.; ed. Victoria School and Univ. of Malaya, Singapore; Asst. Sec. Ministry of Finance 1960-61; Sr. Industrial Economist, Deputy Dir. (Operations and Finance) Econ. Devt. Bd. 1961-68; Vice-Pres., Exec. Vice-Pres. Devt. Bank of Singapore 1968-78; M.P. for Kallang Dec. 1976-, Sr. Minister of State, Ministry of Nat. Devt. 1978-79, Ministry of Foreign Affairs 1979-80, Minister of Foreign Affairs June 1980-, for Culture 1981-84, for Community Devt. 1984-86, also Minister for Nat. Devt. 1987-. *Leisure interests:* reading, squash. *Address:* Ministry of Foreign Affairs, City Hall, St. Andrew's Road, Singapore 0617. *Telephone:* 3307401.

DHAR, Bansi, F.I.M.A., A.M.P.; Indian business executive; b. 7 March 1930, Delhi; s. of late Murli Dhar and Swaroop Devi; m. 1st Urmila Bansidhar 1953 (deceased), 2nd Suman Bansidhar 1976; three s.; ed. Harvard Univ.; trainee, eng. dept. DCM Ltd. 1952, various man. appts. 1957-71, Sr. Exec. Dir. 1971, Deputy Man. Dir. 1977, Jt. Man. Dir. also in charge of Shriram Fertilizers & Chemicals, Kota 1982, Chair. of Bd. and Sr. Man. Dir. 1985-. *Leisure interests:* badminton, gardening, philately, photography, Indian classical music, theatre, bridge. *Address:* DCM Ltd., 4th Floor, Kanchenjunga Building, Barakhamba Road, New Delhi 110001 (Office); 27 Sardar Patel Marg., New Delhi 110021, India (Home). *Telephone:* 3316801 (Office); 3015715 (Home).

DHARIA, Mohan; Indian politician; b. 14 Feb. 1925, Nate village, Kolaba; s. of Manikchand and Sitabai Dharia; ed. Mahad, Poona, Poona Law Coll.; took active part in Independence Movement, organized youth march to Mahad Tehsil 1942; associated with several trade unions; imprisoned five times after independence; joined Congress Party 1961; Gen. Sec. Maharashtra Pradesh Congress Cttee. 1962-67; mem. Rajya Sabha 1964-71; mem. Lok Sabha from Pune (Poona) 1971-79; Minister of State for Planning 1971-75; left Congress Party 1975; detained during emergency 1975-77; mem. Janata Party 1977-79; Minister of Commerce, Civil Supplies and Co-operation 1977-79; Chair. Blood Donors Foundation, Shri Amriteshwar Trust; Pres. Vanarai (People's Movt. for Green India); mem. Deccan Educ. Soc., Shikshan Prasarak Mandali, also several co-operative orgs. *Publications:* Fumes and the Fire 1975, Safar, Direction with Commitment, New Approach to National Reconstruction, For Effective Family Planning, 33 Years of Indian Republic, I Believe 1983, Afforestation in India: a great challenge, Yahi Jindagi. *Leisure interests:* reading, writing, gardening, bridge, chess. *Address:* Anant Smruti, 2064 Vijayanagar, Poona 411030, India. *Telephone:* 440464; 446118.

DHARMASAKTI, Sanya; Thai lawyer and judge; b. 5 April 1907, Bangkok; s. of Phaya Dharmsaravedya and Lady Dharmasaravedya; m. Panga Benjati 1935; two s.; ed. Bangkok and London; fmr. Chief Justice of Thailand; fmr. Rector, Thammasat Univ.; Prime Minister 1973-75; Pres. Privy Council 1976; Pres. World Fellowship of Buddhists 1984-(88). *Leisure interests:* gardening, reading. *Address:* 15 Sukhumvit Road, Soi 41, Bangkok, Thailand. *Telephone:* 251-1151 (Office); 258-8891 (Home).

d'HAUTERIVES, Arnaud Louis Alain; French artist; b. 26 Feb. 1933, Braine (Aisne); s. of Louis and Germaine (née Hincelin) d'Hauterives; m. Renée Delhaye 1959; two s. one d.; ed. Ecole des Beaux Arts, Reims, Ecole Supérieure des Beaux Arts, Paris; started painting as a career 1957; illustrator of some art books; Vice-Pres. Fondation Taylor 1982-, Pres. Société des Artistes Français 1982-, Jt. Pres. Soc. Int. des Beaux Arts 1983-, Contributor La Critique Parisienne 1984-, Pres. Acad. des Beaux Arts 1987, Vice-Pres. Institut de France 1987; Chevalier Légion d'Honneur, Premier Grand Prix de Rome 1957, Prix de la Critique 1967. *Leisure interest:* lithography, vol à voil. *Address:* 144 rue Salvador Allende, Nanterre 92000, France.

DHAVAN, Shanti Swarup; Indian judge and diplomatist; b. 2 July 1905; s. of Beli Ram Dhavan and Saraswati Dhavan (née Chopra); m. Shakuntala Kapur 1935; two s. one d.; ed. Government Coll., Lahore, Forman Christian Coll., Lahore, Emmanuel Coll., Cambridge, Middle Temple, London, and Univs. of Bonn and Heidelberg; fmr. Pres. Cambridge Union; Advocate, Allahabad High Court; Lecturer in Law, Univ. of Allahabad 1940-54; Senior Standing Counsel, Govt. of Uttar Pradesh 1956-58; Puisne Judge, Allahabad High Court 1958-67; High Commr. of India in U.K. 1968-69; Governor of W. Bengal 1969-71; Pres. Uttar Pradesh Section, Indo-Soviet Cultural Soc. 1965-67; mem. Law Comm. of India 1972-77; Sastri Memorial

Lecturer, Kerala Univ., Trivandrum 1973. *Publications:* several articles on Indian jurisprudence and the legal and judicial systems of Ancient India. *Address:* 28 Tashkent Marg, Allahabad 20001, Uttar Pradesh, India (Home).

DHILLON, Gurdial Singh; Indian politician; b. 6 Aug. 1915, Amritsar; s. of Hardit Singh; ed. Govt. Coll., Lahore, and Univ. Law Coll., Lahore; law practice 1937–40; active in Congress and Akali Dal movements; imprisoned twice before independence in 1947; journalist; Ed. Punjab daily Vartman 1948–52; Chief Ed. Urdu daily Sheri-e-Bharat 1948–50; Man. Dir. Sikh Newspapers Ltd.; founder mem. Fed. of Working Journalists of India; mem. Punjab Legis. Ass. 1952–67, Deputy Speaker 1952–54; Speaker of Punjab Vidhan Sabha 1954–62; Gen. Sec. and Chief Whip Congress Legis. Party 1964–67; Punjab State Minister of Transport 1965–66; mem. Lok Sabha (Parl. of India) 1967–77, Chair. Parl. Cttee. on Public Undertakings 1968–69, Speaker 1969–75; Minister of Shipping and Transport 1975–77; High Commr. in Canada 1980–82; India's Rep. Human Rights Comm., Geneva 1985, 1986; mem. A.I.C.C. 1975–; Pres. Commonwealth Speakers' Conf. 1970, Chair. Standing Cttee. of Commonwealth Speakers 1971–74; Pres. Commonwealth Parl. Assen. 1974; Pres. IPU Conf. 1969, acting Pres., Geneva 1973, Pres., Tokyo 1974; mem. Senate and Syndicate Punjab Univ. 1956–, Fellow 1968–69, Dean Faculty of Law 1974–80, 1982–85; mem. Lok Sabha 1985–, Minister of Agric. 1986–88, mem. Planning Comm. 1986–; Pres. Indian Confed. of Agric. 1986–; mem. Governing Body Indian Council of Cultural Relations; awarded Tamra Patra and Hon. degrees from several Indian and foreign univs. *Publications:* several brochures on current affairs. *Address:* M-4 Green Avenue, Amritsar, Punjab, India (Home).

DHOM, Robert; German banker; b. 16 Dec. 1919, Rosenheim; m. Irmentraut Bluhm 1944; Chair. Bd. of Man. Dirs., Commerzbank AG –Dec. 1980; mem. Bd. of Dirs., Int. Commercial Bank Ltd., London; Chair. Supervisory Bd. Rheinische Hypothekenbank; fmr. Chair. Supervisory Bd. Karstadt AG; mem. Supervisory Bd., Bayer AG, Daimler-Benz AG, Fichtel & Sachs AG, Heidelberger Druckmaschinen AG, Hutschenreuther AG, Linde AG, Standard Elektrik Lorenz AG, Thyssen Handelsunion AG, Sachs AG; Pres. Advisory Bd., Commerzbank Int. S.A., Luxembourg; mem. Advisory Bd., Allgemeine Kreditversicherung AG; mem. Bd. of Dirs., Bundesverband deutscher Banken e.V. (Fed. Assen. of German Banks), Cologne. *Address:* Commerzbank AG, Neue Mainzer Strasse 32-36, D-6000 Frankfurt am Main (Office); Reichenbachweg 24, 6240 Königstein 2, Federal Republic of Germany. *Telephone:* (0611) 13-62-1 (Office).

DIA, Mamadou; Senegalese politician; b. 18 July 1910, Kombole; ed. William Ponty School, Dakar; Councillor, Senegal 1946–52; Grand Councillor, French West Africa 1952–57; Founder mem. Bloc Démocratique Sénégalais (BDS), later Sec.-Gen.; Senator for Senegal 1949–55; Deputy to Nat. Ass., Paris 1956–59; Deputy to Legis. Ass., Senegal 1959; Vice-Pres., Council of Ministers, Senegal 1957–58, Pres. 1958–59; Vice-Pres., Mali Fed. 1959–60; Pres. Council of Ministers, Senegal 1960–62, concurrently Minister of Defence and Security 1962; Govt. overthrown Dec. 1962, sentenced to life detention May 1963, sentence reduced to 20 years imprisonment 1972, released 1974; political rights restored 1976; co-founder and Ed. of Ande Soppi (perodical) July 1977; Chevalier, Palmes académiques. *Publications:* Réflexions sur l'économie de l'Afrique noire 1953, Contributions à l'étude du mouvement coopératif en Afrique noire 1957, L'économie africaine 1957, Nations africaines et solidarité mondiale 1960. *Address:* Dakar, Senegal, West Africa.

DIAH, Burhanudin Mohamad; Indonesian journalist and diplomatist; b. 7 April 1917; s. of Mohamad Diah and Siti Saidah; m. Herawati Diah (q.v.) 1942; one s. two d.; ed. Taman Siswa High School, Medan, Sumatra and Ksatrian School for Journalism, Bandung, Java; Asst. Ed. daily Sinar Deli, Medan 1937–38; freelance journalist 1938–39; Chief of Indonesian Information Desk, British Consulate-Gen. 1939–41; Editor-in-chief Indonesian monthly Pertjaturan Dunia dan Film 1939–41; radio commentator and editorial writer daily Asia Raya 1942–45; Ed.-in-chief daily Merdeka 1945–49, (and Dir.) 1968–87; Pres. Merdeka Press Ltd., Masa Merdeka Printing Presses; active in political movement, especially during Japanese occupation; Chair. New Youth (underground) movement and jailed by Japanese in 1942 and again in 1945; active in forcing proclamation of Indonesian Independence Aug. 1945; mem. Provisional Nat. Cttee., Repub. of Indonesia 1945–49; mem. Provisional Indonesian Parl. 1954–56; mem. Nat. Council 1957–59; Amb. to Czechoslovakia 1959–62, to U.K. 1962–64, to Thailand 1964–66; Minister of Information 1966–68; Vice-Chair., Press Council of Indonesia 1970–; fmr. Amb. to Czechoslovakia, Hungary; Gov. for Indonesia to Int. Atomic Energy Agency (IAEA) in Vienna, Austria. *Leisure interests:* golf, swimming, gardening. *Address:* Jalan M. Sangaji 11, Jakarta (Office); Jalan Diponegoro 61, Jakarta, Indonesia (Home). *Telephone:* 364858 (Office); 341565 (Home).

DIAH, Herawati, B.A.; Indonesian journalist; b. 1917; m. Burhanudin Mohamad Diah (q.v.) 1942; ed. Barnard Coll. (Columbia Univ.); Announcer and feature writer, Indonesian Radio 1942; Sec. to Minister of Foreign Affairs, Republic of Indonesia Sept.-Dec. 1945; reporter daily Merdeka 1946; Ed. Indonesian Sunday paper Minggu Merdeka Jan.-July 1947 (when it was banned by Dutch authorities); reporter Merdeka 1947–48; Ed. illustrated weekly Madjalah Merdeka 1948–51, of Minggu Merdeka May 1951; Ed. of women's monthly magazines, Keluarga (Family) 1953–59,

of daily, Indonesian Observer 1955–59; Founder, Dir. Foundation for Preservation of Indonesian Art and Culture 1967–; mem. Int. Fund for Cultural Devt. (UNESCO body) 1977; mem. Exec. Bd. of Inst. for Man. and Educ. Devt. *Address:* Jalan Diponegoro 61, Jakarta, Indonesia.

DIAKITÉ, El Hadj Moussa; Guinean government official; b. 1927; ed. Ecole Primaire Supérieure, Ecole Technique Supérieure; Treasury 1954; Deputy Mayor of Kankan 1956; Vice-Pres. Grand Council of West Africa 1958; Sec. of State, Grand Council of West Africa 1958; Gov. Cen. Bank of Guinea and Minister of Finance 1960–63; Minister of Foreign Trade and Banking 1963–68; Sec. of State for Industry, Mines and Power 1968–71; Minister of the Interior and Security Domain 1972–79, Minister of the Environment and Town Planning 1979–84; Compagnon de l'Indépendance. *Address:* c/o Ministry of the Environment and Town Planning, Conakry, Republic of Guinea.

DIAKITÉ, Noumou; Mali diplomatist; b. 1943, Boulouli, Mali; m.; five c.; ed. Univ. of Algiers, Carnegie Foundation and Inst. des hautes études int., Geneva; Foreign Adviser 1970; Deputy Chief Political Div., Foreign Ministry 1970–71, 1972–74, Chief Africa-Middle East Section 1972–74; Counsellor Mission to UN 1974–76; Amb. accred. to Ghana, Nigeria, Benin and Togo 1979–80; accred. to Côte d'Ivoire, Niger, Upper Volta (now Burkina Faso) 1980–82, accred. to France, Spain, Portugal and Italy 1983–84; Acting Dir. Political Affairs, Ministry of Foreign Affairs and Int. Co-operation 1985–86, Dir.-Gen. 1987–88; Perm. Rep. to UN 1988–; Kt. Malian Nat. Order, Grand Officier Côte d'Ivoire Nat. Order, Officier Upper Volta Nat. Order. *Address:* Permanent Mission of Mali to the United Nations, 111 East 69th Street, New York, N.Y. 10021, U.S.A. *Telephone:* (212) 737-4150.

DIAMAND, Peter, C.B.E.; Netherlands (b. Austrian) arts administrator; b. 8 June 1913; m. 1st Maria Curcio (divorced 1971), 2nd Sylvia Rosenberg (divorced 1979); one s.; ed. Schiller-Realgymnasium, Berlin, and Friedrich Wilhelm Univ., Berlin; emigrated to Holland 1933, Private Sec. to Artur Schnabel 1934–39; Asst. Dir. Netherlands Opera 1946–48; Gen. Man. Holland Festival 1948–65, Artistic Adviser 1965–73; co-founder Netherlands Chamber Orchestra and mem. of Bd. 1955–77; Dir. Edinburgh Festival 1965–78; Consultant Orchestre de Paris 1976–; Dir. and Gen. Man. Royal Philharmonic Orchestra 1978–81; Dir. Paris Mozart Festival 1981–; Kt. Order of Oranje-Nassau, Netherlands, Grand Cross of Merit, Austria, Commdr. Order of Merit, Italy, Officier des Arts et des Lettres, France; Hon. LL.D. (Edinburgh). *Address:* 28 Eton Court, Eton Avenue, London, N.W.3, England. *Telephone:* (01) 586-1203.

DIAMOND, Baron (Life Peer), cr. 1970, of the City of Gloucester; **John Diamond,** F.C.A.; British politician; b. 30 April 1907, Leeds; s. of Solomon Diamond and Henrietta Beckerman; m.; two s. two d.; ed. Leeds Grammar School; Chartered Accountant; Labour M.P. for Blackley, Manchester 1945–51, Gloucester 1957–70; mem. Gen. Nursing Council and Chair. of its Finance and Gen. Purposes Cttee. 1947–53; Hon. Treas. Fabian Soc. 1950–64; Dir. Sadler's Wells Trust 1957–64; Hon. Treas. Labour Cttee. for Europe 1961–64; Chief. Sec. to the Treasury 1964–70; mem. Cabinet 1968–70; Hon. Treas. The European Movt.; Deputy Chair. of Cttees., House of Lords 1974; Chair. Royal Comm. on Distribution of Income and Wealth 1974–79, Prime Minister's Advisory Cttee. on Business Appts. of Crown Servants 1975–; Privy Councillor; Chair. Industry and Parl. Trust 1977–82; Trustee, S.D.P. 1981–82, Leader S.D.P. in House of Lords 1982–88; LL.D. h.c. 1978. *Publications:* Public Expenditure in Practice 1975, co-author: Socialism the British Way 1948. *Leisure interests:* music, golf and skiing. *Address:* House of Lords, London, S.W.1; Aynhoe, Doggetts Wood Lane, Chalfont St. Giles, Bucks., England. *Telephone:* (02404) 3229.

DIAMOND, Abel J., M.A. (OXON.), F.R.A.I.C., M.ARCH.; Canadian architect; b. 8 Nov. 1932, S. Africa; s. of Jacob Diamond and Rachel Zipporah Diamond (née Werner); m. Gillian Mary Huggins 1959; one s. one d.; ed. Univs. of Cape Town, Oxford and Pennsylvania; Asst. Prof. of Architecture and Architectural Asst. to Louis Kahn, Philadelphia 1963–64; Assoc. Prof., Univ. of Toronto 1964–69; Prof., Univ. of York 1969–72; Adjunct Prof., Univ. of Texas at Arlington 1980–81; Prin., A. J. Diamond and Partners, Architects and Planners 1975–; Chair. Nat. Capital Comm., Design Advisory Comm., Ottawa; 29 design prizes; mem. Royal Acad. of Arts (Canada), R.I.B.A., Canadian Inst. of Planners, American Inst. of Planners. *Works include:* Ontario Medical Assen. HQ 1970, Univ. of Alberta Long Range Plan 1970, Alcan HQ Office, Toronto 1972, Montreal 1976, Cleveland 1982, Queen's Univ. Housing, Kingston, Ont. 1976, Citadel Theatre, Edmonton, Alberta 1976 (with B. Myers and R. L. Wilkin), Nat. Ballet School Stage Training Facility, Toronto 1983, Burns Bldg. Renovation, Calgary 1983, Berkeley Castle Renovation, Toronto 1983, Metro Toronto Central YMCA 1984, Ont. Arts Council HQ Offices, Toronto 1985, Four Seasons HQ Offices, Toronto 1985, Imperial Theatre, Saint John, N.B. 1988, Earth and Sciences Center, Univ. of Toronto 1988, Curtiss Hall, Toronto 1988, Sunny Brook Hosp. 1988; mem. Bd. of Govs. Mt. Sinai Hosp., Toronto. *Leisure interests:* music, painting, squash. *Address:* 2 Berkeley Street, No. 600, Toronto, Ont. M5A 2W3, Canada (Office). *Telephone:* (416) 862-8800.

DIAMOND, Jared Mason, PH.D.; American biologist; b. 10 Sept. 1937, Boston; s. of Louis K. Diamond and Flora K. Diamond; m. Marie M. Cohen 1982; no c.; ed. Harvard Coll., Univ. of Cambridge, U.K.; Fellow Trinity

Coll., Univ. of Cambridge 1961–65, Jr. Fellow Soc. of Fellows, Harvard Coll. 1962–65; Assoc. in Biophysics, Harvard Medical School 1965–66; Assoc. Prof. of Physiology, Univ. of Calif. Medical School, Los Angeles 1966–68, Prof. 1968–; Research Assoc. Dept. of Ornithology American Museum of Natural History; mem. N.A.S., Fellow American Acad. of Arts and Sciences; Burr Award of Nat. Geographical Soc. *Publications:* contrib. Discover magazine; The Avifauna of the Eastern Highlands of New Guinea 1972, Ecology and Evolution of Communities 1975, Community Ecology 1985, several hundred research papers on physiology, ecology and ornithology. *Address:* Department of Physiology, University of California at Los Angeles Medical School, Los Angeles, Calif. 90024, U.S.A. *Telephone:* (213) 825-6177.

DIAMOND, William, PH.D.; American international finance official; b. 20 Dec. 1917, Baltimore, Md.; s. of Isidor and Yetta (née Mirtenbaum) Diamond; m. Lois Wilhelm 1946; ed. Johns Hopkins Univ.; with U.S. Bd. of Econ. Warfare and U.S. Foreign Econ. Admin. 1942–44; Economist on U.S. missions to Turkey and Czechoslovakia 1944–46; Econ. Adviser to UNRRA mission to Czechoslovakia, later in London; joined Loan Dept. of World Bank 1947; Deputy Dir. of Foreign Trade Admin. of Greece 1947–48; various posts, World Bank 1948–55; Econ. Devt. Inst. 1955–58; Adviser to Industrial Credit and Investment Corpn. of India 1959–60; Asst. Dir. Operations, Western Hemisphere, World Bank 1960–62; Dir. Devt. Finance Companies Dept., Int. Finance Corpn. 1962–68; Dir. Devt. Finance Companies Dept., World Bank 1968–72, Dir. S. Asia Dept. 1972–75; Special Asst. to Vice-Pres., Finance 1975–77; Sr. Fellow, Econ. Devt. Inst. 1977–78, Consultant 1978–. *Publications:* The Economic Thought of Woodrow Wilson 1943, Czechoslovakia between East and West 1947, Development Banks 1957, Development Finance Companies: Aspects of Policy and Operations (ed.) 1968. *Address:* Economic Development Institute, International Bank for Reconstruction and Development, 1818 H Street, N.W., Washington, D.C. 20433 (Office); 3315 Garfield Street, N.W., Washington, D.C. 20008, U.S.A. (Home). *Telephone:* 333-1863 (Home).

DIARRA, Col. Amadou Baba; Mali army officer and politician; b. 30 Dec. 1929, Bamako; ed. Ecole Normale Supérieure, Bamako, and Univ. de Montpellier, France; fmrly. at the Overseas Scientific and Tech. Research Bureau, Paris, then Minister of Public Works; Sec. of State for Labour and Social Affairs 1959–61, for the Civil Service and Labour 1961–65; Minister of Labour 1965–67; Asst. to Sec.-Gen. Nat. Council for Scientific and Technological Research 1967–68; Adviser to Minister of Foreign Affairs 1969–72; Minister of Finance and Commerce 1970–73, 1978–79, of Planning 1975–78; Minister of State for Equipment 1982–84, for Planning 1984–86; Vice-Pres. Mil. Cttee. of Nat. Liberation 1968–, Union Démocratique du Peuple Malien (UDPM) 1979–, mem. Cen. Exec. Bureau (UDPM) 1979–; fmr. Prof. of Political Econs. and Public Law, Nat. School of Admin.; Pres. UN Econ. Comm. for Africa 1962, Comm. on Apartheid 1964; Vice-Pres. African Regional Conf., ILO 1964; Pres. Council of Admin., ILO 1965–66; fmr. Adviser on African Affairs, Int. Centre for Advanced Tech. and Vocational Training. *Address:* Cabinet du Vice-Président, Comité Militaire de la Libération Nationale, Bamako, Mali.

DIAS, Anthony Lancelot, B.A., B.SC.(ECON.); Indian civil servant; b. 13 March 1910, Poona; s. of late Dr. and Mrs. E. X. Dias; m. Joan J. Vas 1939; 1our d.; ed. Deccan Coll., Poona, London School of Econs. and Magdalene Coll., Cambridge; entered Indian Civil Service 1933; Sec. Educ. Dept. 1952–55, Agricultural Dept. 1955–57, Home Dept. 1957–60; Chair. Bombay Port Trust 1960–64; Sec. Dept. of Food, Ministry of Food and Agric. 1964–70; Lieut.-Gov. of Tripura 1970–71; Gov. of West Bengal 1971–77; Chair. Indian Inst. of Man. 1976–84, Nat. Book Trust 1978–81; mem. Bd. of Govs., Int. Dept. Research Centre, Ottawa 1970–74; Padma Vibhushan 1970; Hon. Fellow L.S.E. 1978. *Publication:* Feeding India's Millions. *Leisure interests:* golf, photography. *Address:* 2 Darbhanga Mansions, Carmichael Road, Bombay 40026, India. *Telephone:* 492 4464.

DIAS, Felix (Bandaranaike); Ceylonese politician; b. 1931; Minister of Finance and Parl. Sec. to Minister of Defence and of External Affairs 1960–62; Minister without Portfolio Nov. 1962–63, of Agriculture, Food and Co-operatives 1963–65; Minister of Public Admin., Local Govt. and Home Affairs 1970–75, of Justice 1972–77, of Finance 1975–77. *Address:* Mahanuga Gardens, Colombo 3, Sri Lanka. *Telephone:* 27343.

DIATTA, Joseph, LL.B.; Niger diplomatist; b. 15 May 1948; m.; three c.; ed. Abidjan Univ. and Int. Inst. of Public Admin., Paris; Tech. Adviser for Legal Affairs, Office of the Minister for Foreign Affairs 1972–74, Dir. of Int. Orgs. in Ministry 1974–75, Sec. Gen. of Ministry 1975–79; Amb. to Ethiopia 1979–82, to the U.S.A. 1982–85; Perm. Rep. of Niger to the UN 1985–87. *Address:* c/o Ministry of Foreign Affairs and Co-operation, BP 396, Niamey, Niger.

DÍAZ, Jose Luís; Spanish mining engineer and executive; b. 30 Nov. 1929, León; m. Da. Raymonde Cassou Barès; two s. one d.; fmr. Chair. Bd. and C.E.O. Empresa Nacional del Petróleo, S.A. (ENPETROL). *Address:* José Abascal 4, Madrid 3, Spain. *Telephone:* 446-52-00.

DIAZ-DURAN, Fernando Andrade, LL.B.; Guatemalan diplomatist; b. 23 Sept. 1937; m.; six c.; ed. San Carlos Univ.; fmr. teacher of Political Science and Int. Law, Landivar, San Carlos and Francisco Marroquin Univs., Guatemala; Visiting Fellow, Political Science Dept. of Boston Univ., Mass.;

Minister of Foreign Affairs 1983–86; Perm. Rep. of Guatemala to OAS and Pres. of Perm. Council 1986; Perm. Rep. of Guatemala to UN 1986–; also rep. at a number of int. confs. *Address:* Permanent Mission of Guatemala to the United Nations, 57 Park Avenue, New York, N.Y. 10016, U.S.A. *Telephone:* 679-4760.

DIBA, Farah (see Pahlavi, Farah Diba).

DIBELA, Sir Kingsford, G.C.M.G., K.ST.J.; Papua New Guinea teacher and Governor-General; b. 16 March 1932; s. of Norman Dibela and Edna Dalauna; m. Winifred Tomalarina 1952; two s. four d.; ed. St. Paul's Primary School, Dogura; qualified as primary school teacher, teacher 1949–63; Pres. Weraura Local Govt. Council 1963–77; M.P. 1975–82, Speaker of Nat. Parl. 1977–80; Gov.-Gen. 1983–89. *Leisure interests:* golf, sailing and cricket. *Address:* c/o Government House, P.O. Box 79, Port Moresby, Papua New Guinea.

DI BELGIOJOSO, Lodovico Barbiano; Italian architect; b. 1 Dec. 1909, Milan; s. of Alberico Barbiano and Margherita (née Confalonieri) di Belgiojosa; m. Carolina Cicogna Mozzoni; ed. School of Architecture, Milan; Architect 1932; Prof. of Architecture 1949; Prof. Venice Univ. Inst. of Architecture 1956–63; Prof. of Architectural Composition, School of Architecture, Milan Polytechnic 1963–; private practice with Peressutti and Rogers in town planning, architecture, interior decoration and industrial design; mem. Nat. Council of Italian Town Planning Inst.; mem. Acad. di S. Luca, Rome; *works include* houses, factories, pavilions; Italian Merchant Navy Pavilion, Paris Int. Exhbn. 1937; health resort for children, Legnano 1939; Post Office, Rome 1939; monument to the dead in German concentration camps, Milan cemetery 1946; U.S. Pavilion at Triennale 1951; Olivetti Showroom, Fifth Avenue, New York, and Labyrinth at the Tenth Triennale 1954; restoration and re-arrangement of Castello Sforzesco Museums 1956; skyscraper Torre Velasca, Milan 1957; Canadian Pavilion, Venice Biennale; collaborator Italian Pavilion, Brussels Exhbn. 1958; Hispano Olivetti Building, Barcelona 1965. *Publications:* (in collaboration with Banfi, Peressutti and Rogers): Piano regolatore della Val d'Aosta 1937, Piano A.R. 1946, Stile 1936, etc. *Address:* Studio Architetti B.B.P.R., 2 via dei Chiostri, 1-20121 Milan, Italy.

diCENZO, Colin Domenic, C.M., C.D., M.Sc., D.I.C., F.E.I.C., F.I.E.E.E., F.C.A.E.; Canadian professor emeritus of electrical engineering; b. 26 July 1923, Hamilton, Ont.; s. of Fernando and Kathleen (Quickenden) diCenzo; m. Patricia E. Wright 1950; four s. two d.; ed. Hamilton Tech. Inst., Univ. of New Brunswick and Imperial Coll., London; Lecturer in Electrical Eng. Royal Mil. Coll., Kingston 1954–57; Project Eng. and Deputy Head, Sonar Eng. Naval HQ, Ottawa 1957–60; Head, Underwater Fire Control Systems Design Group 1960–62; Squadron Staff Officer, Second Canadian Destroyer Squadron, Pacific 1962–64; Systems Eng. Canadian Forces HQ, Ottawa 1964–65; Assoc. Prof. of Electrical Eng. McMaster Univ. 1965–72, Prof. 1972–79, also Prof. of Electrical and Computer Eng. 1979–80, Prof. Emer. 1980–; Dean of Eng. and Applied Science, Memorial Univ. of Newfoundland 1980–83; Dir (Canada) Continuing Eng. Educ., George Washington Univ. 1984–87, Canadian Inst. for Advanced Eng. Studies 1985–; Chair. Colpat Enterprises Inc. 1983–; Sr. Advisor Hickling Man. Consultants Ltd. 1983–85; Pres. Eng. Inst. of Canada 1979–80, Canadian Soc. of Electrical Eng. 1976–78; Adviser, Jadavpur Univ. 1981–83, Petroleum Directorate, Govt. of Newfoundland and Labrador 1981–83, Newfoundland Inst. Cold Ocean Science and mem. numerous other research and advisory cttees.; 54 publications and patents; several awards and honours including Canadian Decoration 1954, Centennial Medal 1967, Queen's Silver Jubilee Medal 1977, Eng. Medal (APEO) 1976, Julian C. Smith Medal (EIC) 1977. *Address:* 28 Millen Avenue, Hamilton, Ont. L9A 2T4, Canada (Home). *Telephone:* (416) 388-5614.

DICHTER, Ernest, PH.D.; American psychologist; b. 14 Aug. 1907, Vienna; s. of William Dichter and Matilde Schneider; m. Hedy Langfelder 1934; one s. one d.; ed. Univs. of Paris and Vienna; Consultant Psychologist on Programs, Columbia Broadcasting System 1942–46; developed application of social science to advertising, public service, politics (motivational research); Pres. Ernest Dichter Motivations Inc. *Publications:* Successful Living 1947, Strategy of Desire 1960, Handbook of Consumer Motivations 1964, Motivating Human Behavior 1971, The New World of Packaging 1973, Why Not: Management Problems of the 70s 1973, Die zweite Karriere 1976, Total Self Knowledge 1976, Motivforschung Mein Leben 1977, Getting Motivated by Ernest Dichter 1979, Comment vivrons-nous en l'an 2000? 1979, Die Jagd nach den Motiven 1980, So Führen Manager Ihr Unternehmen zu Spitzenleistungen 1984, How to be a Top Manager 1985, Dichter on Consumer Motivations 1985, How Hot a Manager Are You? 1987. *Leisure interests:* gardening, painting. *Address:* 24 Furnace Brook Drive, Peekskill, N.Y. 10566, U.S.A. *Telephone:* (914) 739-7405.

DICHTER, Misha, B.S.; American concert pianist; b. 27 Sept. 1945, Shanghai, China; s. of Leon Dichter and Lucy Dichter; m. Cipa Dichter 1968; two s.; ed. Juilliard School of Music under Rosina Lhevinne; winner, Silver Medal, Tchaikovsky Int. Competition, Moscow 1966; since then has performed with leading orchestras and at festivals and given recitals worldwide; also performs with wife as piano duo. *Publications:* articles in New York Times, Ovation and Keyboard magazines. *Leisure interests:*

tennis, jogging, drawing, sketching. *Address:* c/o Shuman Associates, 250 West 57th Street, Suite 1332, New York, N.Y. 10107, U.S.A.

DICK, John Kenneth, C.B.E., F.C.A., F.R.S.A.; British chartered accountant and executive; b. 5 April 1913; s. of late John Dick and Beatrice May Dick (née Chitty); m. Pamela Madge Salmon 1942; three s. (one deceased); ed. Sedbergh School; qualified with Mann Judd & Co., Chartered Accountants 1936, Partner 1947; Joint Man. Dir. Mitchell Cotts Group Ltd. 1957, sole Man. Dir. 1959, Deputy Chair. 1964, Chair. 1966–78; mem. Commonwealth Devt. Corpn. 1967–80; mem. British Nat. Export Cttee. 1968–71; Chair. Cttee. for Middle East Trade 1968–71; a Vice-Pres. Middle East Asscn. 1970, Pres. 1977–81; Chair. Hume Holdings Ltd. 1975–80, N.M. Rothschild (Leasing) Ltd. 1978–; Dir. N.M. Rothschild and Sons Ltd. 1978–, Esperanza Ltd. 1978–80, Sinclair Research Ltd. 1983–86, Biotechnology Investments Ltd. 1986–, Tiphook PLC 1986–; mem. Covent Garden Market Authority 1976–82. *Leisure interest:* golf. *Address:* "Overbye", 18 Church Street, Cobham, Surrey, England. *Telephone:* 01-280-5000 (Office).

DICK, Paul Wyatt, Q.C., B.A., B.C.; Canadian barrister and politician; b. 27 Oct. 1940, Kapuskasing, Ont.; s. of William Wyatt Dick and Constance Grace Harrison; m. Judith Ann Parish 1971; two s.; ed. Trinity Coll. School, Univ. of Western Ont., Univ. of New Brunswick; early career as a barrister and solicitor; Asst. Crown Attorney, Carleton Co. 1969–72; Chair. Ont. Fed. Progressive Conservative Caucus 1974–78; Q.C. 1981; Sr. Partner Dick and Nichols, Ottawa; Ont. Opposition Deputy House Leader 1983–84, Parl. Sec. to Govt. House Leader 1984, Parl. Sec. to Pres. of Queen's P.C. 1985; M.P. 1972–, Parl. Sec. to Pres. of Treasury Bd. 1985; Assoc. Minister of Nat. Defence 1986–89, Minister of State for Supply and Services Jan. 1989–; Progressive Conservative. *Address:* Department of Supply and Services, Canadian Government Publishing Centre, Ottawa K1A 0S9, Canada.

DICKE, Robert H(enry), A.B., PH.D.; American physicist; b. 6 May 1916, St. Louis, Mo.; s. of Oscar H. and Flora P. Dicke; m. Annie Currie 1942; two s. one d.; ed. Princeton Univ. and Univ. of Rochester; Microwave Radar Devt., M.I.T. 1941–46; Physics Faculty, Princeton Univ. 1946–, Cyrus Fogg Brackett Prof. of Physics 1957–75, Albert Einstein Prof. of Science 1975–84, Albert Einstein Emer. Prof. of Science 1984–, Chair. Physics Dept., Princeton Univ. 1967–70; mem. Advisory Panel for Physics, Nat. Science Foundation 1959–61; Chair. Advisory Cttee. on Atomic Physics, Nat. Bureau of Standards 1961–63; mem. NASA Cttee. on Physics 1963–70, Chair. 1963–66; Chair. Physics Panel, Advisory to Cttee. on Int. Exchange of Persons (Fulbright-Hays Act) 1964–66; mem. Visiting Cttee. Nat. Bureau of Standards 1974–79; Fellow American Physical Soc., American Geophysical Union, A.A.A.S.; mem. American Astronomical Soc., Nat. Acad. of Sciences, American Philosophical Soc.; Nat. Science Bd. 1970–76; Assoc. Royal Astronomical Soc.; Trustee Associated Univs., Inc. 1979–; Hon. D.Sc. (Edinburgh) 1972, (Rochester, Ohio Northern Univ.) 1981; Rumford Medal, American Acad. of Arts and Sciences 1967, Nat. Medal of Science 1970, Comstock Prize, Nat. Acad. of Sciences 1973, Medal for Exceptional Scientific Achievement, NASA, 1973, Cresson Medal, Franklin Inst. 1974, Michelson-Morley Award, Case Western Reserve Univ. 1987. *Publications:* (with Montgomery and Purcell) Principles of Microwave Circuits 1948, (with J. P. Wittke) An Introduction to Quantum Mechanics 1960, The Theoretical Significance of Experimental Relativity 1964, Gravitation and the Universe 1970. *Address:* 321 Prospect Avenue, Princeton, N.J. 08540, U.S.A. (Home).

DICKEL, Gen. Friedrich; German army officer and politician; b. 9 Dec. 1913, Wuppertal-Vohwinkel; ed. elementary school; fmr. moulder and high-frequency engineer; mem. Communist Youth League 1928–31; mem. Kommunistische Partei Deutschlands 1931–46, Sozialistische Einheitspartei (S.E.D.) 1946–, mem. Cen. Cttee. 1967–; lived abroad 1933–45; fought in Spanish Civil War 1936–37; First Deputy Minister of Nat. Defence 1956–57; studied at General Staff Academy of U.S.S.R. 1957–59; Deputy Minister of Nat. Defence 1959–63; Minister of Interior and Chief of People's Police (Volkspolizei) 1963–; Col.-Gen. 1965–84, rank of Gen. 1984; Deputy to Volkskammer 1967–; Karl Marx Orden, Hero of G.D.R., Vaterländischer Verdienstorden in Gold and other decorations. *Address:* Innenministerium, Berlin Mauerstrasse 29/31, 108 Berlin, German Democratic Republic.

DICKENS, Arthur Geoffrey, C.M.G., M.A., D.LIT., D.LITT., LITT.D., F.B.A., F.S.A.; British professor of history and university administrator (retd.); b. 6 July 1910, Hull, Yorks.; s. of Arthur J. Dickens and Gertrude H. (Grasby) Dickens; m. Molly Bygott 1936 (died 1978); two s.; ed. Hymers Coll., Hull and Magdalen Coll. Oxford; Fellow, Keble Coll. Oxford 1933–49; served R.A. 1940–45, rank of Capt.; Prof. of History and Head of Dept., Univ. of Hull 1949–62, Pro-Vice-Chancellor 1959–62; Prof. of History and Head of Dept., King's Coll. London 1962–67; Dir. Inst. of Historical Research, Univ. of London 1967–77; Foreign Sec. British Acad. 1967–77; mem. numerous cttees. and holder of various nat. and int. offices; Norton Medlicott Medal (Historical Asscn.) 1985; five hon. degrees; Commdr.'s Cross, Order of Merit (Fed. Repub. of Germany) 1980. *Publications:* Lübeck Diary 1947, Lollards and Protestants 1959, The English Reformation 1964, Reformation and Society in Europe 1966, The Age of Humanism and Reformation 1972, The German Nation and Martin Luther 1974, The Reformation in Historical Thought (with J. M. Tonkin) 1986; numerous articles in learned journals. *Leisure interests:* art history, especially English

painting 1890-1950. *Address:* c/o Institute of Historical Research, Senate House, London, WC1E 7HU, England.

DICKENS, Monica Enid, M.B.E.; British author and journalist; b. 10 May 1915, London; d. of late Henry Charles and Fanny Runge Dickens; m. Commdr. Roy Stratton, U.S.N. 1951; two d.; ed. Norland Place School, London and St. Paul's Girls' School, London; first book published 1937; nursing, aircraft factory work during war 1939–45; resident in U.S.A. 1951–86; joined The Samaritans (suicide prevention) 1968, founder The Samaritans, U.S.A. 1974. *Publications:* One Pair of Hands 1939, Mariana 1940, One Pair of Feet 1942, The Fancy 1942, Thursday Afternoons 1945, The Happy Prisoner 1946, Joy and Josephine 1948, My Turn to Make the Tea (autobiography) 1951, The Winds of Heaven 1955, The Angel in the Corner 1956, Man Overboard 1958, The Heart of London 1961, Cobbler's Dream 1963, Kate and Emma 1964, The Room Upstairs 1966, The Landlord's Daughter 1968, The Listeners 1970, Last Year When I Was Young 1974, The Horse of Follyfoot 1975, An Open Book 1978, Miracles of Courage 1984, View from the Seesaw 1984, Dear Doctor Lily 1988, Enchantment 1989, and 17 children's books. *Leisure interest:* riding. *Address:* Lavender Cottage, Brightwalton, Berks. RG16 0BY, England. *Telephone:* (04882) 302.

DICKEY, James, B.A., M.A.; American poet; b. 2 Feb. 1923, Atlanta, Georgia; s. of Eugene and Maibelle Swift Dickey; m. 1st Maxine Syerson 1948 (died 1976), two s.; m. 2nd Deborah Dodson 1976, one d.; ed. Clemson Coll. and Vanderbilt Univ.; served Second World War with U.S.A.A.F. and U.S.A.F. in Korea; Consultant in Poetry, Library of Congress, Washington 1966–68; Sewanee Review Fellow 1954–55, Guggenheim Fellow 1962–63; writer in residence and Prof. of English, Univ. of S. Carolina 1968–; mem. A.A.A.S.; Vachel Lindsay Award and Longview Award 1959; Prix Médicis 1971, Levinson Prize 1981. *Publications:* poetry: Into the Stone 1960, Drowning with Others 1962, Helmets 1964, Two Poems of the Air 1964, Buckdancer's Choice 1965 (Nat. Book Award), Poems 1959–1967 1967, The Eye-Beaters 1970, Exchanges 1971, The Zodiac 1976, The Owl King 1977, Veteran Birth 1978, Tucky the Hunter 1978, Head-Deep in Strange Sounds 1979, The Strength of Fields 1979, Scion 1980, Puella 1982, The Early Motion 1982, Falling, May Day Sermon and Other Poems 1982, The Central Motion 1983, Bronwen, The Traw and the Shape-Shifter 1986, Wayfarer 1988; Criticism: The Suspect in Poetry 1964, Babel to Byzantium 1968, Sorties 1971; Belles-lettres; Self-Interviews 1970, Night Hurdling 1983; Prose: Jericho: The South Beheld 1974, God's Images 1977; novels: Deliverance 1970, Alnilam 1987; *Films:* Call of the Wild (screenplay) 1975, Deliverance 1970. *Address:* 4620 Lelia's Court, Lake Katherine, Columbia, South Carolina 29206, U.S.A. *Telephone:* (803) 787-9962.

DICKIE, Lloyd M., PH.D., F.R.S.C.; Canadian ecologist; b. 6 March 1926, Kingsport, N.S.; s. of Ebenezer Cox Dickie and Pearl (née Sellars) Dickie; m. Marjorie C. Bowman 1952; one s. two d.; ed. Acadia Univ., Yale Univ., Univ. of Toronto; research scientist, Fisheries Research Bd., N.B. 1951–62, Great Lakes Inst., Toronto 1962–65; Dir. Marine Ecology Lab., Bedford Inst. Oceanography, Dartmouth, N.S. 1965–74; Chair. and Prof. of Oceanography, Dalhousie Univ., Halifax 1974–77, Dir. Inst. of Environmental Studies, Dalhousie Univ. 1974–76; Research Scientist, Marine Ecology Lab. and Marine Fish Div., Bedford Inst. of Oceanography, Dartmouth, N.S. 1976–, Sr. Research Scientist Biological Sciences Br., Dept. of Fisheries and Oceans 1987–. *Publications:* Ad Mare: Canada Looks to the Sea (with R. W. Stewart) 1971; some 75 scientific papers. *Address:* Bedford Institute of Oceanography, P.O. Box 1006, Dartmouth, N.S., B2Y 4A2 (Office); 7 Lakewood Court, Dartmouth, N.S., B2X 2R6, Canada (Home). *Telephone:* (902) 426-3248 (Office); (902) 435-1545 (Home).

DICKINSON, Christopher John, B.SC., M.A., D.M., F.R.C.P., A.R.C.O.; British physician and professor of medicine; b. 1 Feb. 1927, Sydney, Australia; s. of Reginald Ernest Dickinson and Margaret Dickinson; m. Elizabeth Patricia Farrell 1953; two s. two d.; ed. Berkhamsted School, Oxford Univ., Univ. Coll. Hosp. Medical School, London; jr. medical posts, Univ. Coll. Hosp., London 1953–54; R.A.M.C., jr. medical specialist 1955–56; Registrar and Research Fellow, Middx. Hosp., London 1957–60; Rockefeller Travelling Fellow, Cleveland Clinic, U.S.A. 1960–61; Lecturer, Sr. Lecturer and Consultant, Univ. Coll. Hosp. and Medical School, London 1962–75; Prof. of Medicine and Chair. Dept. of Medicine, St. Bartholomew's Hosp. Medical Coll., London 1975–; Sr. Censor and Sr. Vice-Pres., Royal Coll. of Physicians of London 1982–83; mem. MRC. *Publications:* Electrophysiological Technique 1950, Clinical Pathology Data 1951, Clinical Physiology 1959, Neurogenic Hypertension 1965, Computer Model of Human Respiration 1977, Software for Educational Computing 1980. *Leisure interests:* theatre, opera, playing the organ. *Address:* Griffin Cottage, 57 Belsize Lane, London, NW3 5AU, England (Home). *Telephone:* 01-601 7531 (Office); 01-431 1845 (Home).

DICKSON, Jennifer, R.A.; Canadian artist and photographer; b. 17 Sept. 1936, S. Africa; d. of John L. Dickson and Margaret J. (Turner) Dickson; m. Ronald A. Sweetman 1962; one s.; ed. Goldsmiths' Coll. School of Art, Univ. of London; Assoc. Atelier 17 (graphic workshop), Paris 1960–65; teacher, Brighton Coll. of Art 1961–68, Univ. of W. Indies, Jamaica 1968, Univ. of Wis. 1972, Saidye Bronfman Centre, Montreal 1970–71, 1982–83, Ohio State Univ., Athens 1973, 1979, Univ. of S. Ill. 1973, Calif. State Univ., Sacramento 1974, Denison Univ. 1976, Univ. of Ottawa 1980–83 (Sessional

Instructor 1980-85); visiting artist at many univs., colls. etc.; has held more than 55 one-woman exhbns. in six countries and participated in more than 150 group exhbns; works in numerous public collections in Canada, U.S.A., U.K., Europe, New Zealand, Australia and S. Africa including Nat. Gallery of Canada, Metropolitan Museum, New York, British Museum, London and Hermitage Museum, Leningrad; Fellow, Royal Soc. of Painter-Etchers and Engravers; fmr. mem. Royal Canadian Acad. of Arts (resgnd. 1987); Hon. LL.D. (Univ. of Alberta) 1988; awards include Prix de Jeunes Artistes pour Gravure, Biennale de Paris 1963, Special Purchase Award, World Print Competition, San Francisco Museum of Art 1974, Biennale Prize, 5th Norwegian Int. Print Biennale 1980. *Publications:* The Hospital for Wounded Angels 1975, and suites of original prints and photographs. *Leisure interests:* historic gardens, opera, films. *Address:* 20 Osborne Street, Ottawa, Ont., K1S 5Z9, Canada. *Telephone:* (613) 233-2315 (Studio); (613) 236-5602 (Home).

DICKSON, Robert George Brian, P.C., LL.B., D.CN.L.; Canadian lawyer; b. 25 May 1916, Yorkton, Sask.; s. of Thomas Dickson and Sarah Elizabeth Gibson; m. Barbara Melville 1943; three s. one d.; ed. Regina Collegiate Inst., Univ. of Manitoba and Manitoba Law School; served with Royal Canadian Artillery 1940-45; called to Man. Bar 1940; Lawyer, Aikins, MacAuley & Co. 1945-63; Lecturer, Man. Law School 1948-54; apptd. to Court of Queen's Bench, Man. 1963, Court of Appeal 1967, Justice, Supreme Court of Canada 1973-84, Chief Justice of Canada 1984-, Deputy Gov.-Gen.; Chair. Advisory Coucil of Order of Canada; Chair. Canadian Judicial Council; Life Bencher, Law Soc., Man.; Hon. Bencher, Lincoln's Inn 1984; Hon. Fellow, American Coll. of Trial Lawyers; Hon. Prof., Univ. of Man. 1985; Chancellor, Diocese of Rupert's Land, Anglican Church of Canada 1960-71; mem. Bd. of Trustees, the Sellers Foundation; Hon. LL.D. (Man.) 1973, (Sask.) 1978, (Ottawa) 1979, (Queen's) 1980, (Dalhousie) 1983, (York) 1985, (B.C.) 1986, (Toronto) 1986, (Laurentian) 1986, (Yeshiva) 1987, (McGill) 1987; K.St.J. 1985. *Leisure interest:* riding. *Address:* Supreme Court Building, Wellington Street, Ottawa, Ont. K1A 0J1 (Office); "Marchmont", Dunrobin, Ont., K0A 1T0, Canada. *Telephone:* (613) 995-4330 (Office).

DICKSON, Robert R. B.; Canadian banker (retd.); b. 21 Feb. 1927; joined Toronto-Dominion Bank 1948; Accountant, Bd. of Trade, Montreal 1957; Credit Officer, Montreal 1961; Asst. Man. Int. Operations, Montreal 1963, Man. 1966; Asst. Gen. Man. Far East, Cen. and S. America, Int. Div. 1969, Mexico, Cen. and S. America and the Caribbean 1970; Gen. Man. Europe, Middle East and Africa 1971; Vice-Pres. and Gen. Man. Regional Office, Europe and Africa 1973; Exec. Vice-Pres. Int. Banking Group 1976, Vice-Chair. 1981-87; Deputy Chair. Toronto-Dominion Bank Investments (U.K.) Ltd., Hong Kong Ltd.; Vice-Chair. Commercial Union Insurance; Dir. Toronto-Dominion Bank de Panamá, S.A., Toronto-Dominion Bank Pension Fund Soc.; Alt. Dir. Midland and Int. Banks Ltd., England; Hon. Assoc.'s Certificate, Fellows' Course, Inst. of Canadian Bankers, Int. Banking Summer School, Copenhagen 1969. *Address:* c/o Toronto-Dominion Bank, P.O. Box 1, Toronto-Dominion Centre, Toronto, Ont. M5K 1A2, Canada.

DIDION, Joan, B.A.; American writer; b. 5 Dec. 1934, Sacramento; d. of Frank Reese Didion and Eduene (née Jerrett) Didion; m. John G. Dunne 1964; one d.; ed. Univ. of California, Berkeley; Assoc. Features Ed. Vogue magazine 1956-63; fmr. columnist Saturday Evening Post, fmr. contributing ed. Nat. Review; now freelance writer; awarded 1st Prize Vogue's Prix de Paris 1956, Morton Dauwen Zabel prize (American Assen. of Arts and Letters) 1978. *Publications: novels* Run River 1963, Play It as It Lays 1971, A Book of Common Prayer 1977, The White Album 1979, Democracy 1984; *essays:* Slouching Towards Bethlehem 1969; *non-fiction* Salvador 1983; *Screenplays for films:* The Panic in Needle Park 1971, A Star is Born 1976. *Address:* c/o Wallace and Sheil, 118 East 61st Street, New York, N.Y., U.S.A.

DIDRIKSEN, Jan, LL.M.; Norwegian lawyer and business executive; b. 15 May 1917; m. Dagmar Mellgren 1946; ed. Oslo Univ. and Harvard Business School; District Commdr. Underground Mil. Forces 1941-42; Judge 1946-54; Chief, Law Dept., Norwegian Employers' Fed. 1954-62, Del. to Int. Labour Org. (ILO) 1956-62; Dir. Fed. of Norwegian Industries 1963-65, Dir.-Gen. 1965-85. *Address:* Sörkedalsveien 94, Oslo 3, Norway (Home). *Telephone:* Oslo 14-48-52 (Home).

DIEBENKORN, Richard Clifford, M.A.; American artist; b. 22 April 1922, Portland, Ore.; s. of Richard Diebenkorn and Dorothy Stephens; m. Phyllis Gilman 1943; one s. one d.; ed. Stanford Univ., Univ. of California and New Mexico and California School of Fine Arts; Teacher, Calif. School of Fine Arts 1947-50, Univ. of Ill. 1952-53, Calif. Coll. of Arts and Crafts 1955-60, San Francisco Art Inst. 1961-66; Prof. of Art, Univ. of Calif. at Los Angeles 1966-73; Artist-in-residence, Stanford Univ. 1963-64; Tamarind Fellowship 1962; mem. Nat. Council on the Arts 1966-69; mem. Nat. Inst. Arts and Letters, Nat. Foundation on Arts and the Humanities, American Acad. of Design, American Acad. of Arts and Letters; first one-man exhbn. San Francisco 1948; numerous one-man exhbns. in cities throughout U.S.A. 1948-, has exhibited in many group shows at Guggenheim Museum, Carnegie Internationals, Museum of Modern Art, San Francisco Museum of Art, Art. Inst. of Chicago, Museum of Fine Arts, Boston, Whitney Museum of American Art, New York, etc.; Venice Biennale 1968, retrospective exhbn. Albright Knox Art Gallery, Buffalo, New York 1977, Venice Biennale 1978, McDowell Medal 1978, Skowhegan Medal for Painting 1979. *Publication:* Drawing 1965, Etchings and Drypoints 1949-80, 1981, Small Paintings from Ocean Park 1985, Works on Paper 1987, Richard Diebenkorn 1987. *Address:* c/o Knoedler Gallery, 19 East 70th Street, New York, N.Y. 10021, U.S.A.

DIEBOLD, John, M.B.A., LL.D., SC.D., D.ENG.; American management consultant; b. 8 June 1926, Weehawken, N.J.; s. of William and Rose (Theurer) Diebold; m. 1st Doris Hackett 1951 (divorced 1975); one d.; m. 2nd Vanessa von der Porten 1982; one s.; ed. Swarthmore Coll. and Harvard Business School; with Griffenhagen & Assocs., management consultants, New York City, also Chicago 1951-57, owner 1957-, merged with Louis J. Kroeger and Assocs. to become Griffenhagen-Kroeger Inc., Chair. Bd. 1960-; established Diebold Group Inc., New York City 1954, Pres., Chair. Board, Los Angeles, Chicago 1954-; est. Urwick Diebold Ltd., England 1958, Co-Chair. 1958-; est. Raadgevend Bur. Berenschot-Diebold, N.V. 1958, Diebold Europe, S.A., Pres. 1960-; Chair. Diebold Computer Leasing Inc. 1967-, Gemini Computer Systems Inc. 1968-, Intermodel Transport Systems Inc. 1969-; Dir. Genesco 1969-; U.S. Council Trusteeship, Int. Chamber of Commerce 1972-; Dir. Acad. for Educ. Devt. 1972-; Dir. Prentice-Hall Inc. 1981-85; Trustee Nat. Planning Assen. 1973-, Carnegie Inst., Washington 1975-, Overseas Devt. Council 1974-82 (mem. Advisory Bd. 1982-), Lehigh Univ. June 1987-; Fellow, Int. Acad. of Man. 1983-; mem. Advisory Bd., Inst. of French Studies, N.Y. Univ. 1984, Advisory Comm. Deutsches Museum, Munich 1984-; Pres. World Man. Council (CIOS) 1986-; Order of Merit, Italy; Grand Cross 1971; Chevalier, Légion d'honneur; several hon. degrees; coiner of word automation. *Publications:* Automation—The Advent of the Automatic Factory 1952, Beyond Automation 1964, Man and the Computer Technology as an Agent of Social Change 1969, Business Decisions and Technological Change 1970, The Role of Business in Society 1983; Ed. World of the Computer 1973, Making the Future Work 1984, Business in the Age of Information 1985, Managing Information: The Challenge and the Opportunity 1985. *Address:* The Diebold Group Inc., 475 Park Avenue S., New York, N.Y. 10016, U.S.A. (Office).

DIEHL, Günter; German diplomatist; b. 8 Feb. 1916, Cologne; m. Helga von Rautenstrauch 1939; three s. one d.; ed. Univ. of Cologne, and Université de Bordeaux; entered Diplomatic Service 1939; Foreign Office 1945; Foreign Ed. Hamburger Abendblatt 1948; Foreign Dept. Press Office 1950; Foreign Office Spokesman 1952; Counsellor German Embassy, Santiago 1956; Head of Foreign Dept. Press and Information Service 1960; Head Planning Div. Foreign Office 1966; Chief, Press and Information Office, Fed. Repub. of Germany 1967-69; Amb. to India 1970-77, to Japan 1977-81; Pres. German Assen. for Asian Studies, German Soc. for Foreign Affairs 1981-87. *Publications:* Ferne Gefährten. Erinnerungen an Eine Botschaft in Japan 1987. *Leisure interests:* writing, painting, shooting. *Address:* Ölbergweg 2, Oberwinter, D-5480 Remagen 2, Federal Republic of Germany.

DIEMINGER, Walter E., DR. RER. TECH.; German aeronomist; b. 7 July 1907, Würzburg; s. of Ludwig and Anna (née Kraus) Dieminger; m. Dr. Ilse Günther 1935; two s. one d.; ed. Humanistisches Gymnasium, Würzburg and Technische Hochschule, Munich; Research Scientist and pilot, German Air Force Test Centre 1934-43; Head, Advisory Org. for Radio Propagation 1943-45; Head, Inst. for Ionospheric Research 1945-56; Man. Dir. Max-Planck-Inst. für Aeronomie 1956-65, Dir. 1965-75; Hon. Pres. German Nat. Cttee. URSI; mem. Finnish Acad. of Sciences, Acad. Leopoldina, Int. Acad. of Astronautics, Austrian Acad. of Sciences; Vice-Pres. URSI 1966-69, Pres. 1969-72, Hon. Pres. 1978; F. C. Gauss-Medal 1972, Cross of Merit, Hon. Citizen Community Katlenburg-Lindau. *Publications:* about 120 articles on radio propagation, aeronomy and space research; contribs. to encyclopaedias (including Brockhaus). *Leisure interests:* amateur radio, model railway, photography. *Address:* D 3412 Noerten-Hardenberg 1, O. T. Elvese, Berlinerstrasse 14, Federal Republic of Germany. *Telephone:* 05503-2689.

DIENER, Theodor Otto, D.SC.; American plant virologist; b. 28 Feb. 1921, Zürich, Switzerland; s. of Theodor E. Diener and Hedwig R. Baumann; m. Sybil Mary Fox 1968; three s.; ed. Swiss Fed. Inst. of Tech., Zürich; Plant Pathologist, Swiss Fed. Agricultural Research Station, Waedenswil 1948-49; Asst. Prof. of Plant Pathology Rhode Island State Univ., Kingston, U.S.A. 1950; Asst.-Assoc. Plant Pathologist, Wash. State Univ., Prosser 1950-59; Research Plant Pathologist, Plant Virology Lab., Agricultural Research Service, U.S. Dept. of Agric., Beltsville, Md. 1959-; Collaborator, Agricultural Reserve Service, U.S. Dept. of Agric., Beltsville, Md. 1988-; Prof., Center for Agric., Biotech. and Dept. of Botany, Univ. of Md. 1988-; discovered and named viroids, smallest known agents of infectious disease; mem. N.A.S., American Acad. of Arts and Sciences, Leopoldina (German Acad. of Nat. Scientists); Fellow N.Y. Acad. of Sciences, American Phytopathological Soc.; Campbell Award, American Inst. of Biological Sciences 1968; Superior Service Award, U.S. Dept. of Agric. 1969, Distinguished Service Award 1977; Alexander von Humboldt Award (Fed. Repub. of Germany) 1975; Wolf Prize 1987, E. C. Stakman Award, Univ. of Minn. 1988; Nat. Medal of Science (U.S.A.) 1987. *Publications:* Viroids and Viroid Diseases, Ed. The Viroids 1987, numerous chapters in scientific books and more than 190 scientific papers. *Address:* Plant Virology Laboratory, Agricultural Research Service, U.S. Department of Agriculture, Beltsville, Md. 20705 (Office); 4530 Powder Mill Road, Beltsville, Md. 20705 U.S.A. (Home). *Telephone:* (301) 344-3202 (Office).

DIENESCH, Marie-Madeleine; French politician; b. 3 April 1914, Cairo, Egypt; d. of Alfred Dienesch and Joséphine Grimaud; ed. Coll. Sainte Marie, Neuilly, Coll. Sévigné and Sorbonne, Paris; Prof. agregée Lycée de Saint-Brieuc 1939-43, 1944-45; Founder and Sec. Syndicat Général de l'Education Nationale des Côtes-du-Nord (S.G.E.N.) 1944; Founder and Pres. Union Féminine Civique et Sociale des Côtes-du-Nord 1944; Deputy for Côtes-du-Nord 1946-84; Rep. to Nat. Constituent Ass. 1945-46; Sec. Bureau of Nat. Ass. 1945; Vice-Pres. Nat. Ass. 1958-59; Int. Vice-Pres. Union of European Women 1962-69; Pres. French Section of Union of European Women 1969-74, Comm. of Cultural, Family and Social Affairs 1967-68; Gen. Counsellor March 1976, Regional Counsellor March 1978; French Rep. to Ass. of European Community 1979; Sec. of State for Educ. June-July 1968, for Social Affairs 1968-69, for Social Welfare 1969, for Social Action and Rehabilitation 1969-72, at Ministry of Health, responsible for Social Welfare 1972-74; Amb. to Luxembourg 1975-78; mem. European Parl. 1979-84; Pres. Democrates V movt. 1967-; Rassemblement pour la République; Chevalier, Légion d'honneur. *Address:* 79 avenue de Breteuil, 75015 Paris, France (Home).

DIEPGEN, Eberhard; German lawyer and politician; b. 13 Nov. 1941, Berlin; ed. Free Univ. of Berlin; joined CDU 1962, later Chair., W. Berlin CDU; mem. Berlin Chamber of Deputies 1971-81; mem. Bundestag (Parl.) as W. Berlin Rep. 1980-81; Mayor of Berlin 1984-88. *Leisure interest:* football. *Address:* Rathaus Schöneberg, 1000 Berlin 62, Federal Republic of Germany. *Telephone:* 783 33 00.

DIESEL, John Phillip, B.S.; American business executive; b. 10 June 1926, St. Louis, Mo.; s. of John Henry and Elsa A. (Poetting) Diesel; m. Rita Jan Meyer 1949; one s. three d.; ed Washington Univ., St. Louis, Mo.; Exec. Asst. Div. Man., McQuay-Norris Mfg. Co., St. Louis 1951-57; Partner Booz, Allen and Hamilton Inc., Chicago 1957-61; Vice-Pres. Operations, Operations Research Inc., Santa Monica, Calif. 1961-62; Vice-Pres., Treas. and Dir. Management Technology Inc., Los Angeles 1962-63; Dir. Marketing and Planning, A. O. Smith Corpn., Milwaukee, Wis. 1963-65, Dir. Mfg. and Engineering 1965-67, Vice-Pres. Mfg. and Planning 1967-70, Group Vice-Pres. 1970-72; Chair. Armor Elevator Can. Ltd. 1970-72; Chair. and Pres. Armor Elevator Co. Inc. 1970-72; Pres., C.E.O., Newport News (Va.) Shipbuilding and Dry Dock Co. 1972-78, Chair. 1976-78; Exec. Vice-Pres. Tenneco Inc. 1976-79, Pres. 1979-; Chair. Bd. of Albright and Wilson Ltd. (London, England) 1981-; Dir. Tenneco Inc., Aluminum Co. of America, Cooper Industries Inc., First City Bancorp. of Texas Inc., Poclain S.A., Allied Stores Corpn. *Address:* Tenneco Inc., P.O. Box 2511, Houston, Tex. 77002 (Office); 327 Longwoods Lane, Houston, Tex. 77024, U.S.A. (Home). *Telephone:* (713) 757-2374 (Office).

DIESEL, Jürgen, DR.JUR.; German diplomatist; b. 4 Jan. 1926, Berlin; m. Elenore von Dungern 1954; one s. two d.; ed. Univs. of Erlangen and Munich; Diplomatic Acad., Spreyer 1952-54; Attaché, German Embassy, Santiago 1954-56, First Sec., Caracas 1956-60; Disarmament Section, Ministry of Foreign Affairs 1960-64; Disarmament Negotiations, Geneva 1964-68; head, E. European Div., Ministry of Foreign Affairs 1968-73; Amb. to Switzerland 1973-77, to Czechoslovakia 1977-82; Deputy Sec.-Gen. WEU 1982-86; decorations from Germany, Chile, Romania, Sweden, Venezuela, Italy. *Leisure interests:* filming, mountains, travelling. *Address:* c/o Embassy of the Federal Republic of Germany, P.O. Box 30180, Nairobi, Kenya.

DIETRICH, Marlene; German-born American actress and singer; b. (as Maria Magdalena von Losch) 27 Dec. 1901; d. of Edward and Josephine (née Felsing) von Losch; m. Rudolf Sieber 1924; one d.; ed. Augusta Victoria School, Berlin; début in Berlin: worked with Max Reinhardt 1922-29; emigrated to U.S. 1930; naturalized U.S. citizen 1937; numerous stage and cabaret appearances; Officier, Légion d'honneur 1972, U.S. Medal of Freedom. *Films include:* The Blue Angel 1930, Morocco 1930, Dishonoured 1931, Shanghai Express 1932, Blonde Venus 1932, Song of Songs 1933, The Scarlet Empress 1934, The Devil is a Woman 1935, Desire 1936, The Garden of Allah 1936, Knight without Armour 1937, Angel 1937, Destry Rides Again 1939, Seven Sinners 1940, The Flame of New Orleans 1941, Manpower 1941, The Spoilers 1942, Kismet 1944, A Foreign Affair 1948, Stage Fright 1950, Rancho Notorious 1952, Around the World in Eighty Days 1956, Witness for the Prosecution 1957, Touch of Evil 1958, Judgement of Nuremburg 1961, Just a Gigolo 1978. *Publication:* My Life (autobiog.) 1988. *Address:* c/o Regency Artists Ltd., 9200 Sunset Boulevard, Suite 823, Los Angeles, Calif. 90069, U.S.A.

DIETZ, (Arno Kurt) Wolfgang; German librarian; b. 30 Aug. 1921, Leipzig; s. of Rudolf and Martha (Reichelt) Dietz; m. Gisela Selige 1963; one s. two d.; ed. Univ. of Leipzig and Deutsche Staatsbibliothek, Berlin; Librarian, Univ. Library, Leipzig 1956; Dir. Dept. for Univ. Publs., Deutsche Bücherei, Leipzig 1957-58; Parl. Librarian, Bibliothek des deutschen Bundestages, Bonn 1958-86; Consultant to Div. Insts. 1987. mem. various professional cttees. and advisory bodies; Bundesverdienstkreuz 1st Klasse; Silver Medal of the German Diet. *Publications:* articles in professional reviews. *Leisure interest:* classical music. *Address:* Am Wolfsbach 50, 5300 Bonn 3, Federal Republic of Germany. *Telephone:* 0228/481452.

DIEUDONNÉ, Jean Alexandre, D. ES SC.; French university professor; b. 1 July 1906, Lille (Nord); s. of Ernest Dieudonné and Léontine Lebrun;

m. Marie Odette Clavel 1935; one s. one d.; ed. Ecole Normale Supérieure and Inst. of Advanced Study, Princeton; Asst. Prof., Univ. of Rennes 1933-37, Univ. of Nancy 1937-48; Prof., Univ. of Nancy 1948-52, Univ. of Michigan 1952-53, Northwestern Univ. 1953-59, Inst. des Hautes Etudes Scientifiques, Paris 1959-64, Univ. of Nice 1964-70; retd. 1970; mem. French Acad. of Sciences; Pres. Soc. Mathématique de France 1964-65; Officier, Légion d'honneur. *Publications* La géométrie des groupes classiques 1955, Foundations of Modern Analysis 1960, Eléments d'analyse II 1968, III 1970, IV 1971, V-VI 1975, VII, VIII 1978, IX 1982, Calcul infinitésimal 1968, Introduction to the Theory of Formal Groups 1973, Cours de géométrie algébrique (2 vols.) 1974, Panorama des mathématiques pures 1977, History of Functional Analysis 1981, Pour l'honneur de l'esprit humain 1987, History of Algebraic and Differential Topology from 1900 to 1960 1988; 130 papers in mathematical journals. *Leisure interests:* music, cooking. *Address:* 120 avenue de Suffren, 75015 Paris, France. *Telephone:* 43-06-10-44.

DIEZ de VELASCO, Manuel, D. EN D.; Spanish professor of international law and magistrate; b. 22 May 1926, Santander; s. of Francisco Manuel Diez de Velasco and Mercedes Vallejo; m. Josefina-Tomasa Abellan y Vota 1959; ed. Valladolid, Madrid and Rome Univs., Int. Law Acad., The Hague; Prof. of Int. Law, Univ. of Granada 1959-61, Univ. of Barcelona 1961-71, Univ. of Madrid, Complutense Univ. 1974-; Judge Constitutional Court 1980-86, Court of Justice, EEC 1988-; mem. Inst. de Droit Int.; Dir. Revista de Inst. Europeas; Pres. Spanish Asscn. of Profs. of Int. Law and Int. Relations. *Publications include:* Curso de Derecho Internacional Publico, Vol. 1 1963, La Protection diplomatique des sociétés et des actionnaires 1974, and numerous papers on aspects of int. law. *Address:* Court of Justice of the European Communities, Kirchberg, 2925 Luxembourg. *Telephone:* 4303 2235 (Office).

DIFORIO, Robert G., B.A.; American publishing executive; b. 19 March 1940, Mamaroneck, N.Y.; s. of Richard John Diforio Sr. and Mildred Kuntz; m. Birgit Rasmussen 1983; one s. one d.; ed. Williams Coll., Mass. and Harvard Business School; Vice-Pres. Kable News Co. 1970; Vice-Pres. and Sales Man. New American Library (NAL) 1972, Sr. Vice-Pres. and Marketing Dir. 1976, Pres. and Publisher 1980, C.E.O. and Chair. Bd. NAL/E. P. Dutton 1985, C.E.O. NAL Penguin Inc. 1987-. *Leisure interests:* reading, children, golf. *Address:* NAL Penguin Inc., 1633 Broadway, New York, N.Y. 10019 (Office); Arrowhead Lane, Larchmont, N.Y. 10538, U.S.A. (Home). *Telephone:* (212) 397-8008 (Office); (914) 834-3461 (Home).

DIJKSTRA, Minne, M.SOC.PSYCH.; Netherlands broadcasting official; b. 11 Feb. 1937, Cornjum; ed. Univ. of Amsterdam; M.P. 1967-72, Chair. Standing Cttee. for Univ. Educ. and Science Policy 1971-72; mem. Bd. of Dirs. NOS (Dutch Broadcasting Corpn.) 1973-85, Vice-Pres. 1981-85; Chair. Bd. of Dirs. Radio Nederland Wereldomroep 1986-; mem. Bd. of Fryske Acad. 1974-85, Pres. 1978-85; mem. Bd. of Govs. Friese Pers Beheer BV 1979-; mem. Bd. SCO (Communication Assistance Foundation) 1986-, Foundation Public Information about Science and Tech. 1986-. *Address:* Postbus 222, 1200 JG Hilversum (Office); Leidsegracht 62, Amsterdam, The Netherlands (Home). *Telephone:* 035-16151 (Office); 020-225153 (Home).

DIJOUD, Paul Charles Louis; French politician; b. 25 July 1938, Neuilly-sur-Seine; s. of Jules-Raoul Dijoud and Andrée Claquin; m. Catherine Cochaux 1968 (divorced 1983); one s. one d.; ed. Lycée Condorcet, Faculté de Droit de Paris, Inst. d'Etudes politiques de Paris; Student at Ecole Nat. d'Admin. 1964-66; Commercial attaché, dept. of external econ. relations in Ministry of Econ. and Finance; elected to Nat. Ass. 1967, 1968, 1973, 1978, defeated 1981; Asst. Sec.-Gen. Ind. Republican Party 1967-69; Conseiller Général for canton of Embrun 1968-; Pres. Ind. Republican Exec. Cttee. for Provence-Côte d'Azur 1968-; Mayor of Briançon 1971-; Sec. of State attached to Prime Minister's Office 1973-74, later to Minister of Cultural Affairs and the Environment, to Minister of Employment with Responsibility for Immigrant Workers 1974, Secretary of State for Sport 1977, for Overseas Depts. and Territories 1978; Commercial Adviser to cen. admin. Ministry of Economy and Finance 1981; Man. Dir. Cie. Commerciale Sucres et Denrées 1982-84; Pres. Comidex 1984-; Pres. Conseil d'administration du parc national des Ecrins 1973-. *Address:* Compagnie Commerciale Sucres et Denrées, 133 avenue des Champs Elysées, 75008 Paris (Office); 37 rue de Chézy, 92200 Neuilly-sur-Seine, France (Home). *Telephone:* 723-55-77 (Office).

DIKSHIT, Uma Shankar; Indian politician and journalist; b. 12 Jan. 1901, Ugoo Dist., Uttar Pradesh; s. of late Ram Swarup and Jwala Devi Dikshit; m. Shiva Pyari Dikshit 1915; two s.; ed. Govt. School and Christchurch Coll., Kanpur; Sec. Kanpur City Congress Cttee. and mem. Uttar Pradesh Congress Cttee. 1920-25; imprisoned for participation in Non-Co-operation Movt. 1921-23; Pres. Uttar Bharatiya Sabha and Hindi Bhashi Sammendan 1925-30; active in underground movt. 1932, imprisoned 1931-33, 1931-33; Hon. Sec. Hindustani Prachar Sabha, Bombay 1934-41; joined Quit India Movt. 1942, detained until 1944; Custodian Evacuee Property, New Delhi 1948-52; Hon. Adviser, Nat. Small Industries Corpn. 1956; Man. Dir. Associated Journals Ltd., Lucknow 1957-71; mem. Rajya Sabha 1961-76; mem. All India Congress Cttee., mem. and Hon. Treas. Indian Nat. Congress 1969-76, Gen. Sec. 1971-72; Minister of Works and Housing, later also of Health and Family Planning 1971-73, of Home Affairs 1973-74, without Portfolio 1974-75, of Shipping and Transport Feb.-Nov. 1975; Gov.

of Karnataka 1976–77, resgnd. and rejoined working Cttee., All India Congress Cttee. Aug. 1977; Gov. West Bengal 1984–86; re-appointed mem. Congress Working Cttee. 1987; Chair. two Congress Organizational Cttees. 1987. *Leisure interests:* reading, swimming, badminton. *Address:* 1 Circular Road, New Delhi, India. *Telephone:* 3018990.

DILKS, David Neville, M.A., F.R.S.L.; British professor of international history; b. 17 March 1938, Coventry; s. of Neville Ernest and Phyllis Dilks; m. Jill Medlicott 1963; one s.; ed. Royal Grammar School, Worcester, Hertford Coll. and St. Antony's Coll., Oxford; Asst. lecturer, lecturer LSE 1962–70, Prof. of Int. History, Univ. of Leeds 1970–; Chair. and Founder Commonwealth Youth Exchange Council 1968–73, Chair. School of History, Univ. of Leeds 1974–79, Dean Faculty of Arts, Univ. of Leeds 1975–77; mem. Univs. Funding Council 1988–; Trustee Edward Boyle Memorial Trust 1982, Imperial War Museum 1983–, Lennox-Boyd Trust 1984–, Royal Commonwealth Soc. Library Trust 1987–; Curzon Prize, Univ. of Oxford 1960, Liveryman, Goldsmiths Co. 1984. *Publications:* Curzon in India (Vol. 1 & 2) 1969, 1970, The Diaries of Sir Alexander Cadogan 1971, Neville Chamberlain: Pioneering & Reform, 1869–1929 1984, and numerous articles in learned journals. *Leisure interests:* ornithology, steam railways, organ music, Bentley cars. *Address:* School of History, The University, Leeds, W. Yorks., LS2 9JT (Office); Wits End, Long Causeway, Leeds, LS16 8EX, England (Home). *Telephone:* (0532) 333585 (Office); (0532) 673466 (Home).

DILLARD, Annie, M.A.; American author; b. 30 April 1945, Pittsburgh, Pa.; d. of Frank Doak and Gloria Lambert; m. 1st R. H. W. Dillard 1965; 2nd Gary Clevidence 1979; one d., two step. d.; ed. Hollins College; contributing editor, Harper's Magazine 1974–85; Distinguished Visiting Prof. Wesleyan Univ. 1979–83, Adjunct Prof. 1983–, writer in residence 1987–; mem. Nat. Cttee. on U.S.-China Relations; Pulitzer Prize for Pilgrim at Tinker Creek 1974, Nat. Endowment for the Arts (Literature) Grant 1981, John Simon Guggenheim Memorial Grant 1985. *Publications:* Tickets for a Prayer Wheel (poetry), Pilgrim at Tinker Creek (prose) 1974, Holy the Firm 1978, Living by Fiction 1982, Teaching a Stone to Talk 1982, Encounters with Chinese Writers 1984, An American Childhood 1987. *Address:* c/o Blanche Gregory, 2 Tudor City Place, New York, N.Y. 10017, U.S.A.

DILLER, Barry; American entertainment executive; b. 2 Feb. 1942, San Franscisco; s. of Michael Diller and Reva (née Addison) Diller; Vice-Pres. feature films and movies of week ABC network 1971–74; Chair. Bd. Paramount Pictures Corpn. 1974–84; Pres. Gulf and Leisure Time Group 1983–84; Chair. and C.E.O. Twentieth Century Fox Film Corpn., Los Angeles 1984–, Fox Inc. 1985–; jr. partner TCF Holdings Inc. 1984–; mem. American Film Inst., Variety Clubs Int., Hollywood Radio and TV Soc., Acad. of Motion Picture Arts and Sciences. *Address:* Twentieth Century Fox Film Corporation, 10201 W. Pico Boulevard, Los Angeles, Calif. 90035, U.S.A.

DILLON, Brendan, M.A.; Irish diplomatist; b. 30 Nov. 1924, Dublin; s. of William Dillon and Pauline Kerrigan; m. Alice O'Keeffe 1949; four s. one d.; ed. Blackrock Coll. and Univ. Coll., Dublin; Chief of Protocol, Ministry of Foreign Affairs 1968; Amb. to Denmark, concurrently to Norway and Iceland 1970; Asst. Sec.-Gen., Ministry of Foreign Affairs 1972; Amb., Perm. Rep. to European Communities 1973–81, to France, concurrently to OECD 1981–86, to Holy See 1986–; Grand Cross, Order of Leopold II (Belgium), Grand Cross, Order of Merit (Luxembourg). *Address:* Embassy of Ireland to the Holy See, 1 via Giacomo Medici, 00153 Rome, Italy. *Telephone:* 581.01.34.

DILLON, C. Douglas, A.B.; American investment banker and diplomatist (retd.); b. 21 Aug. 1909, Geneva; s. of the late Clarence and of Anne (Douglass) Dillon; m. 1st Phyllis Elsworth 1931 (died 1982), two d.; m. 2nd Susan S. Sage 1983; ed. Groton School and Harvard Coll.; mem. New York Stock Exchange 1931–36; with U.S. and Foreign Securities Corpn. and U.S. and Int. Securities Corpn. 1937–53, Pres. 1946–53, Pres. U.S. and Foreign Securities Corpn. 1967–71, Chair. of Bd. 1971–84, Dir. 1938–53, 1967–71; Dir. Dillon, Read & Co. Inc. 1938–53, Chair. of Bd. 1946–53, Dir. 1971–81; served as Ensign, advancing to Lieut.-Commdr. U.S.N.R. 1941–45; awarded Air Medal, Legion of Merit with Combat Device; Amb. to France 1953–57; Under-Sec. of State for Econ. Affairs 1957–59; Under-Sec. of State 1959–61; Sec. of the Treasury 1961–65; Chair. Rockefeller Foundation, Brookings Inst.; Pres. Bd. of Overseers Harvard Univ. 1968–72, Metropolitan Museum of Art 1970–78; Chair. 1978–83; mem. Cttee. to Fight Inflation 1980–; Hon. LL.D. (Harvard, Columbia, New York, Hartford, Rutgers, Pennsylvania and Princeton Univs., Lafayette, Williams and Middlebury Colls.); Republican. *Address:* Suite 2300, 1270 Avenue of the Americas, New York, N.Y. 10022, U.S.A. *Telephone:* (212) 315-8353.

DIMBLEBY, David, M.A.; British broadcaster and newspaper proprietor; b. 28 Oct. 1938, London; s. of the late Richard Dimbleby and of Dilys Thomas; m. Josceline Gaskell 1967; one s. two d.; ed. Charterhouse, Christ Church, Oxford, Univs. of Paris and Perugia; News Reporter, BBC, Bristol 1960–61; presenter and interviewer, various scientific, religious and political programmes, BBC TV 1961–63, Foreign Affairs Film Reporter and Dir. 1964–65; Special Corresp. CBS News 1966; Reporter, Panorama, BBC TV 1967–69, Presenter 1974–77, 1980–81; Presenter, 24 Hours, BBC TV 1969–

72; Dimbleby Talk-In 1972–74; People and Power 1982; Gen. Election Results Programmes, BBC 1979, 1983, 1987; Presenter, This Week, Next Week, BBC TV 1984–86; Man. Dir. Dimbleby Newspaper Group 1966–86, Chair. 1986–; Man. Dir. Wandsworth Borough News Ltd. 1979–86, Chair. 1986–; Reporter The White Tribe of Africa, BBC TV 1979 (Royal TV Soc. Supreme Documentary Award). *Publication:* An Ocean Apart (with David Reynolds) 1988. *Leisure interests:* sailing, reading, music, not watching television. *Address:* 14 King Street, Richmond, Surrey, TW9 1NF, England.

DIMECHKIÉ, Nadim, B.A., M.A.; Lebanese diplomatist; b. 5 Dec. 1919, Lebanon; m. Margaret Alma Sherlock 1946; two s.; ed. American Univ. of Beirut; entered Ministry of Supply 1943, Dir. Econ. Affairs 1944; entered Foreign Service 1944; served London 1944–49, Ottawa 1949–51; Dir. Econ. and Social Dept., Ministry of Foreign Affairs 1951–52; Chargé d'affaires, Cairo 1952, Minister and Chargé d'affaires 1953–55; Minister to Switzerland 1955–57; Amb. to U.S.A. 1958–62; Dir. Econ. Affairs, Ministry of Foreign Affairs 1962–66; Amb to U.K. 1966–78; Amb. at large, Special Adviser on Foreign Affairs to Minister of Foreign Affairs and Prime Minister 1979; Hon. Consultant, Arab Fed. of Chambers of Commerce and Industry 1980–; mem. Bd. and Consultant, Bank de Credit Populaire Union Nat. 1985–, Union Foncier et Financing 1985–, Sterling Drugs Int. 1985–; Hon. G.C.V.O. 1978; Doyen of the Diplomatic Corps 1977–78; awards include Ordre du Cèdre, Egyptian Order of Ismail, Greek Order of Phoenix. *Leisure interest:* swimming. *Address:* c/o Ministry of Foreign Affairs, Beirut, Lebanon.

DIMÉNY, Dr. Imre, DR.AGR.SC.; Hungarian agronomist and politician; b. 3 Aug. 1922, Komolló; s. of János Dimény and Anna Illyés; m. Erzsébet M. Buzgó 1947; one d.; agronomic engineer; rural, county and ministry official 1945–55; Dept. Head, later Vice-Pres. Nat. Planning Bureau 1955–62; Alt. mem. Cen. Cttee. and Leader Agricultural Dept. Hungarian Socialist Workers' Party 1962–66; Minister of Agriculture and Food 1967–75; Prof., Univ. of Horticulture, Budapest 1975–, Rector 1975–86; Corresp. mem. Hungarian Acad. of Sciences 1982–. *Publications:* Determinants of the Power Machine Requirement in Domestic Agriculture 1961, Economy of Mechanization in Agriculture 1972, Agriculture and Technological Development 1973, Economy of Mechanization in Animal Husbandry 1974, Economy of Development of Mechanization in Agriculture 1975, Mechanization of Horticultural Branches 1980, Characteristics of Horticultural Production Systems 1980, Enterprise Fundamentals of Horticulture 1983, Agric. and Technical Development 1985. *Leisure interest:* reading. *Address:* University of Horticulture, Budapest XI, Villányi út 35–41, 1118 (Office); Budapest II, Szilágyi Erzsébet fasor 79, Hungary 1026 (Home).

DIMITRIOS I, (Dimitrios Papadopoulos); Archbishop of Constantinople and Ecumenical Patriarch; b. 8 Sept. 1914, Istanbul; ed. Theological School of Halki, Heybeliada-Istanbul; ordained Deacon 1937; ordained Priest 1942; Preacher in Edessa, Greece 1937–38; Preacher, Parish of Feriköy-Istanbul 1939–45; Priest of the Orthodox Community, Teheran 1945–50; Head Priest, Feriköy 1950–64; Bishop of Elaia, Auxiliary Bishop of the Patriarch Athenagoras in Istanbul 1964–72; Metropolitan of Imvros and Tenedos 1972; Archbishop of Constantinople and Ecumenical Patriarch July 1972–. *Address:* Rum Patrikhanesi, Fener, Istanbul, Turkey. *Telephone:* 23-98-50.

DIMITROVA, Ghena; Bulgarian opera singer; b. 6 May 1941, Beglej; ed. Bulgarian State Conservatoire (with Christo Bumbarov); début as Abigaille in Nabucco, Sofia Opera; Singer Laureate, Int. Competition, Treviso, Italy for interpretation of Amelia, Un Ballo in Maschera 1972; appearances France, Italy and Spain, early 1970s; appeared in Cen. and S. America and at Bolshoi, Moscow 1975–78; début Vienna Opera 1978; début Verona in La Gioconda 1980, several subsequent appearances there 1980–; début London, concert performance of La Gioconda at Barbican 1983; in Turandot, La Scala 1983; Macbeth, Salzburg Festival 1984; début Royal Opera House, Covent Garden in Turandot 1984; appears in opera houses of Vienna, Munich, Paris, Hamburg, Berlin, Madrid, Barcelona, Naples, Zürich, Rome, N.Y., San Francisco, Chicago; opened La Scala 1985/86 season in Aida; Gold Medal and First Prize, Fourth Int. Competition for Young Singers, Sofia 1970; People's Artist 1979; Golden Archer and Giovanni Zenatello Prizes (Rome and Verona) 1981; has recorded Nabucco and Oberto, Conte di San Bonifacio and discs of opera arias and Puccini arias. *Address:* c/o S. A. Gorlinsky Ltd., 33 Dover Street, London, W1X 4NJ, England.

DINCERLER, M. Vehbi; Turkish politician; b. 2 Aug. 1940, Gaziantep; s. of Esat and Şefika Dincerler; m.; three s. one d.; ed. Depts of Eng., Istanbul Tech. Univ., Business Inst., Istanbul Univ., Graduate School, Univ. of Syracuse, N.Y.; worked for State Planning Org.; joined Project Studies for Turkey at World Bank, studied economy of Ireland; academic at Middle East Tech. Univ., Gaziantep Campus; mem. Nat. Assembly 1983–(92), Minister of Educ., Youth and Sports 1983–85, Minister of State 1985–87; Chair. Nat. Ass. Foreign Relations Cttee. 1988–(90); Motherland Party. *Leisure interests:* music, social activities. *Address:* TBMM, Ankara, Turkey. *Telephone:* (4) 118 92 33, (4) 118 99 43.

DINE, James; American artist; b. 16 June 1935, Cincinnati, Ohio; m. Nancy Minto 1957; three s.; ed. Cincinnati Art Acad.; first one-man exhbn. Reuben Gallery, New York 1960; has subsequently held numerous one-man exhbns. in U.S.A. and throughout Europe including Palais des Beaux

Arts, Brussels 1963, 1970, Sidney Jannis Gallery, New York 1963, 1964, 1967, Robert Fraser Gallery, London 1965, 1966, 1969, Stedelijk Museum, Amsterdam (drawings) 1967, Museum of Modern Art, Munich 1969, Berlin Festival, Sonnabend Gallery, New York, and Whitney Museum of American Art, New York 1970; exhbn. of Designs for A Midsummer Night's Dream, Museum of Modern Art, New York 1967; has participated in numerous group exhbns. including Painting and Sculpture of a Decade, Tate Gallery, London 1964, Venice Biennale 1964, A Decade of American Drawings 1965, Young America 1965, and Art of the United States 1670-1966 1966 (all three at Whitney Museum of American Art), U.S. Pavilion, Expo 1967, Montreal, and Hayward Gallery, London 1969; work appears in many public collections including Guggenheim Museum, Moderna Museet, Stockholm, Museum of Modern Art, New York, Dallas Museum of Fine Arts, Tate Gallery, and Whitney Museum of Modern American Art. *Publications:* Welcome Home, Lovebirds 1969 (also illustrator); co-author and illustrator The Adventures of Mr. and Mrs. Jim & Ron 1970; illustrator The Poet Assassinated 1968. *Address:* c/o The Pace Gallery, 32 East 57th Street, New York, N.Y. 10022, U.S.A.

DING CONG; Chinese cartoonist; b. 1916, Shanghai City; s. of Ding Song; ed. Shanghai Fine Arts Inst.; worked on cartoon magazine Good Friends during 1930s; mem. editorial staff, Nat. Salvation Cartoons and Resisting the Japanese pictorial; Ed. Great Earth, Hong Kong 1938; worked on political and satirical magazine Qing Ming, Shanghai 1945, on journal The Age of Cartoons, Hong Kong 1947; Ed. (with Hu Kao) China Pictorial 1950s; in disfavour and prevented from working until late 1970s. *Address:* People's Republic of China.

DING FENGYING; Chinese party official; Chair. Hubei Branch, Chinese Women's Fed. 1973; Vice-Chair. Revolutionary Cttee., Hubei Prov. 1978-79; alt. mem. 12th CCP Cen. Cttee. 1982-87; First Sec. CCP Cttee., Huangguang Pref. 1983-; Deputy Sec. CCP Cttee., Hubei Prov. 1986-. *Address:* Huangguang Prefectural Chinese Communist Party, Huangguang, Hubei, People's Republic of China.

DING GU; Chinese government official; Dir. Bureau of External Cultural Relations 1983. *Address:* c/o Ministry of Culture, Beijing, People's Republic of China.

DING GUANGENG; Chinese state official; b. 1930; Minister of Railways 1985-88; Vice-Minister State Planning Comm. Aug. 1988-; Dir. Taiwan Affairs Office 1988-; mem. 12th CCP Cen. Cttee. 1985-; alt. mem. Political Bureau 1987-. *Address:* c/o Ministry of Railways, 10 Fuxing Road, Beijing, People's Republic of China. *Telephone:* 863 855 (Office).

DING GUANGXUN (Bishop K. H.); Chinese theologian and church leader; b. 1915; ed. Cen. Theological Seminary of the Chinese Anglican Church, and New York Union Theological Seminary, ordained 1942, Sec. Student Christian Movt. of Canada, World Christian Fed., Geneva; returned to China 1951; Pres. Nanking Theological Seminary 1952, consecrated Bishop 1955; Vice-Chair. Three-Self Patriotic Cttee. Movt. of the Protestant Churches of China 1961, later Chair. 4th Cttee.; Pres. Second Christian Council of China; a Deputy Chair. Chinese People's Political Conf. 1989-. *Address:* Christian Council of China, Beijing, China.

DING GUOYU; Chinese diplomatist; b. 1931; mem. Armistice Cttee. in Korea 1953; Amb. to Afghanistan 1955-58, to Pakistan 1958-66, to Egypt 1982-; Sec. Beijing CCP Cttee. 1966-67, 1971-78; Vice-Chair. Beijing Revolutionary Cttee. 1974-77. *Address:* Embassy of the Peoples Republic of China, 14 Sh. Bahgat Aly, Cairo, Egypt. *Telephone:* 651219.

DING HAO; Chinese diplomatist; Deputy Dir. Western Europe Dept., Ministry of Foreign Affairs 1965; Counsellor, Embassy, Denmark 1965; Chargé d'affaires Chile 1971; Amb. to Kuwait 1977-81, to Ecuador 1981.

DING JIEYIN; Chinese sculptor; b. 4 Feb. 1926, Yinxian, Zhejiang; d. of Ding Yong-sen and Gao Yu-ding; m. Hong Bo 1952; one d.; ed. Cen. Acad. of Fine Arts, Beijing; Asst. Researcher, Sculpture Studio, Cen. Acad. of Fine Arts; Ed. China Sculpture; Chief Ed. supplement Chinese Art, New Evening newspaper, Hong Kong; mem. China Artists' Asscn.; about 60 pieces of sculpture; works in jt. exhbn. of Women Sculptors, China Art Gallery and commissioned by various cities. *Publications:* Clay Figures in the Temples of Da Tong 1982, The Art of Colour Clay Sculpture in Jin Ancestral Temple 1988; articles in Meishu, Art Research, People's Daily and Chinese Art supplement, New Evening (Hong Kong). *Leisure interests:* literature, basketball. *Address:* Central Institute of Fine Arts, East Beijing, People's Republic of China. *Telephone:* 55.4731 (Ext. 275, 391).

DING SHENG; Chinese army officer; b. 1912, Jiangxi; ed. Red Army School and Mil. Coll.; participated in Long March 1934-35; Battalion Commdr 1937; Div. Commdr. 4th Field Army 1949; Commdr. 54th Army, People's Liberation Army, Xizang 1954-55; Deputy Commdr. Xinjiang Uygur Mil. Region, PLA 1963-68; Guangzhou Mil. Region, PLA 1968; mem. 9th Cen. Cttee. of CCP 1969; Sec. CCP Guangdong 1971; Commdr. Guangzhou Mil. Region, PLA 1972-73; Chair. Guangdong Revolutionary Cttee. 1972-79; First Sec. CCP Guangzhou 1972-73; mem. 10th Cen. Cttee. of CCP 1973; Commdr. Nanjing Mil. Region, PLA 1974-78. *Address:* People's Liberation Army, Nanjing Military Region, People's Republic of China.

DING SHISUN; Chinese mathematician and university administrator; b. 5 Sept. 1927, Shanghai; s. of Ding Rounong and Liu Huixian; m. Gui Linlin 1956; two s.; ed. Math. Dept., Tsing-hua Univ.; Asst. Tsing-hua Univ. 1950-52; joined staff Beijing Univ. 1952, promoted to Prof. of Math. 1979, Vice-Chair. Math. Dept. 1978-80, Chair. 1981-82, Pres. Peking Univ. 1984-; Math. Soc. of Beijing 1986-; visited Math. Dept., Harvard Univ., U.S.A. 1983; specializes in fields of algebra and number theory; Hon. Dr. (Soka, Japan) 1985. *Publications:* several books and papers. *Leisure interests:* classical music, reading novels. *Address:* Office of President, Beijing University, Haidian, Beijing, People's Republic of China. *Telephone:* 282471.

DING TINGMO; Chinese party official; Deputy Sec. Prov. CCP Cttee. Guizhou 1985-86; alt. mem. Cen. Cttee. 1985-. *Address:* Central Committee of the Chinese Communist Party, Zhongnanhai, Beijing, People's Republic of China.

DING XIMAN; Chinese dramatist; led the Shanghai Kunqu Troupe in Macbeth Edinburgh Festival 1987. *Address:* Shanghai Federation of Literary and Art Circles, Shanghai, People's Republic of China.

DING XUESONG; Chinese diplomatist; Vice-Chair. Inst. of Foreign Affairs 1964-Cultural Revolution; Cadre, S. China 1976; Amb. to Netherlands 1979-81, to Denmark 1982-84; first woman amb. in history of People's Repub.; Vice-Pres. China-Latin America Friendship Asscn. 1984-. *Address:* c/o Ministry of Foreign Affairs, Beijing, People's Republic of China.

DING YUANHONG; Chinese government official; Dir. Dept. of Policy Research, Foreign Ministry 1986; Deputy Rep. to the UN Nov. 1986-. *Address:* Ministry of Foreign Affairs, Beijing, People's Republic of China.

DINGELL, John David, Jr., B.S., J.D.; American congressman; b. 8 July 1926, Colorado Springs, Colo.; s. of John D. and Grace (Bigler) Dingell; ed. Georgetown Univ.; called to D.C. Bar 1952, to Mich. Bar 1953; Park Ranger U.S. Dept. of Interior 1948-52; Asst. Prosecuting Attorney, Wayne County, Mich. 1953-55; mem. 84th-101st Congresses; Chair. Cttee. on Energy and Commerce; mem. Migratory Bird Conservation Comm., Office Tech. Assessment. *Address:* Room 2221, Rayburn House Building, Washington D.C. 20515 (Office); Trenton, Mich. 48121, U.S.A. (Home).

DINI AHMED, Ahmed; Djibouti politician; b. 1932, Obock; Vice-Pres., Territorial Assembly, French Somaliland (now Repub. of Djibouti) 1959-60; Minister of Production 1963-64, of the Interior 1967-72; joined Ligue Populaire Africaine pour l'Indépendance 1972; Pres. Nat. Ass. of French Territory of the Afars and the Issas May-June 1977, of Repub. of Djibouti June-July 1977; Prime Minister July-Dec. 1977. *Address:* B.P. 300, Djibouti, Republic of Djibouti.

DINITZ, Simcha, M.SC.; Israeli diplomatist; b. 23 June 1929, Tel Aviv; s. of Josef and Bruria Dinitz; m. Vivian Dinitz 1954; two d. one s.; ed. Herzeliah High School, Tel Aviv, Univ. of Cincinnati and Georgetown Univ. School of Foreign Service; Israel Defence Forces 1948-50; Asst. to Dir. of Information Embassy of Israel, Washington 1954-58; Dept. of Information, Ministry for Foreign Affairs, Jerusalem 1958-61; Dir. of Bureau of Dir.-Gen. of Ministry for Foreign Affairs 1961-63; Dir. of Bureau and Political Sec. to Foreign Minister 1963; mem. Israel Del. to UN 1963-66; Minister to Rome 1966-68; Minister in charge of Information, Washington 1968-69; Political Adviser to Prime Minister 1969-73, also Dir.-Gen. of Prime Minister's Office 1972-73; Amb. to U.S.A. 1973-78; Vice-Pres Hebrew Univ. of Jerusalem 1979-84; mem. Knesset 1984-88; Chair. of Exec. of Jewish Agency and World Zionist Org. 1988-. *Leisure interests:* music, sports, reading. *Address:* 40 Nayot, Jerusalem, Israel. *Telephone:* 632314.

DINKOV, Vasily Alexandrovich; Soviet politician; b. 1924; ed. Azerbaijan Azizbekov Industrial Inst.; eng. tech. work in gas industry; mem. of CPSU 1946; head of main dept. for gas production, U.S.S.R. Ministry of the Gas Industry 1966-70, Deputy Minister 1970-79; First Deputy Minister 1979-81, Minister of the Gas Industry 1981-85, of the Oil Industry 1985-; mem. U.S.S.R. Supreme Soviet (10th convocation); Cen. Cttee. CPSU 1986-; State Prize, Order of Lenin, Hero of Socialist Labour 1984. *Address:* Ministry of the Oil Industry, Moscow, U.S.S.R.

DI NOLA, Raffaello; Italian business executive; b. 10 Aug. 1912, Naples; s. of Enrico di Nola and Maria Luisa de Rosa; m. Liliana Carisch 1942 (divorced); three c.; ed. Milan Univ.; commenced career with Rumianca (chemicals firm); joined the Pirelli Group 1939, subsequently became Gen. Man. and Man. Dir. and Dir. of other cos. in the group; Man. Dir. Alfa Romeo S.p.A. 1962-74, Vice-Pres., and Man. Dir. Alfa Romeo Alfasud S.p.A.; Pres. Alfa Romeo Int. S.A.; Pres. Spica S.p.A.; Pres. Breda Termomeccanica S.p.A.; Pres. Termosud S.p.A.; mem. Bd. Banca Popolare di Milano; Cavaliere di Gran Croce della Repubblica Italiana. *Leisure interests:* riding, skiing. *Address:* Via Fratelli Gabba 5, 1-20121 Milan, Italy. *Telephone:* 8858.

DION, Rev. Gérard, O.C., L.TH., L.PH., M.SOC.; Canadian social science educator; b. 5 Dec. 1912, Ste. Cécile, Qué.; s. of Albert Dion and Georgianna (née LeBlanc) Dion; ed. Coll. de Lévis, Laval Univ.; ordained priest R.C. Church 1939; Asst. Prof. Social Sciences Laval Univ. 1944-49, Prof. 1949-80, Prof. Emer. 1980-; Asst. Dir. Dept. Industrial Relations Laval Univ. 1946-56, Dir. 1956-63; Ed. Relations industrieles/Industrial Relations

1945–; Moderator Canadian Textile Labour-Man. Cttee. 1967–; Assoc. Hon. Ed. Royal Soc. of Canada 1975–; mem. Econ. Council Canada 1976–80, Canadian Social Sciences and Humanities Research Council 1978–81; Hon. LL.D. (McGill) 1975, (British Columbia) 1976, (Toronto) 1978, (Concordia) 1980; Hon. D.Litt. (St. Francis Xavier) 1977. *Publications:* Vocabulaire français-anglais des relations professionnelles/Glossary of Terms Used in Industrial Relations 1972, Dictionnaire canadien des relations du travail, 2e. 1986. *Address:* 909 Mgr. Grandin, P.Q., Canada, G1V 3X9A.

DIOP, Majhemout; Senegalese pharmacist and politician; b. 30 Sept. 1922, St. Louis; ed. Ecole Africaine de Médecine et de Pharmacie (Dakar), Paris Univ. and African Inst., Univ. of Moscow; Hospital pharmacist, Senegal and Gabon 1947–50; Pres. Senegalese students' asscn. in France 1951; studied Marxism at Bucharest 1953–56; Sec.-Gen. Parti Africain de l'Indépendance (PAI) 1957–76, Pres 1976–; exiled from Senegal 1961–76; engaged in research in political sociology at Inst. of Human Sciences, Mali 1968–76; dispensary pharmacist, Dakar 1977–. *Publications:* Contribution à l'Etude des problèmes politiques en Afrique Noire 1959, Classes et idéologies de class au Sénégal 1963, Notes sur la classe ouvrière sénégalaise 1965, Histoire des classes sociales dans l'Afrique de l'Ouest (Vol. I) 1971, (Vol. II) 1972, Etude sur le Salariat 1975, Essai sur l'esclavage en Afrique de l'Ouest (to be published); and many articles in review and journals. *Address:* 153 Avenue du Président Lamine Gueye, Dakar (Office); 210 HCM, Guediawaye, Dakar, Senegal (Home).

DIORI, Hamani; Niger politician; b. 16 June 1916; ed. Victor Ballot School, Dahomey, and Ecole William Ponty, Senegal; Deputy, Niger Territory, French Nat. Assembly 1946–51, 1956–58; Vice-Pres. Nat. Ass. 1957; Prime Minister, Republic of Niger 1958–60; Pres. of Republic of Niger 1960–74, Council of Ministers 1960–74, also Minister of Foreign Affairs until 1974; ousted by coup April 1974, imprisoned 1974–84, released April 1984; mem. Rassemblement Démocratique Africain (RDA); Chair. OCAM 1967–70; Pres. Conseil d'Entente 1967–74; Founder mem. Parti Progressiste Nigérien and fmr. Sec.-Gen.

D'IORIO, Antoine, PH.D.; Canadian university rector and vice-chancellor; b. 22 April 1925, Montréal; s. of Giuseppe D'Iorio and Assunta (Torino) D'Iorio; m. Ghislaine Chatel 1950 (deceased); three s. four d.; ed. Univs. of Montréal, Wisconsin and Oxford; Asst. Prof. of Physiology, Univ. of Montréal 1949–55, Assoc. Prof. 1956–61; Prof. of Biochem. and Chair. of Dept., Univ. of Ottawa 1961–69, Dean, Faculty of Science and Eng. 1969–76, Vice-Rector, Academic 1976–84, Rector and Vice-Chancellor 1984–; mem. Société médicale de Montréal; Ciba Award 1974, Parizeau Meal ACFAS 1974, Ottawa Biological Biochemical Soc. 1976, Queen Elizabeth II Silver Jubilee Medal 1978, Ordre du Mérite national (France) 1988. *Publications:* about 90 research papers in field of biological sciences. *Leisure interests:* photography, reading. *Address:* University of Ottawa, 550 Cumberland Street, Suite 212, Ottawa, Ont., K1N 6N5, Canada.

DIOUF, Abdou, L. EN D., L. ES SC.; Senegalese politician; b. 7 Sept. 1935, Louga; m. 1963; ed. Lycée Faidherbe, St. Louis, Dakar and Paris Univs.; Dir. of Technical Co-operation and Minister of Planning Sept.-Nov. 1960; Asst. Sec.-Gen. to Govt. 1960–61; Sec.-Gen. Ministry of Defence June-Dec. 1961; Gov. Sine-Saloum Region 1961–62; Dir. de Cabinet of Minister of Foreign Affairs 1962–63, of Pres. of Repub. 1963–65; Sec.-Gen. to Pres.'s Office 1964–68; Minister of Planning and Industry 1968–70; Prime Minister 1970–80; Pres. of Senegal Jan. 1981–, of Confed. of Senegambia Feb. 1982–; Chair. OAU 1985–86; mem. Nat. Assembly for Longa Département 1973–; mem. Sengalese Progressive Union (U.P.S.) 1961–, later Asst. Sec.-Gen.; fmr. Asst. Sec.-Gen. Parti Socialiste Sénégalais (P.S.), now Sec.-Gen; jt. winner Africa Prize for Leadership 1987. *Address:* Office of the President, avenue Roume, BP 168, Dakar, Senegal.

DIOUF, Jacques; Senegalese agronomist and international civil servant; b. 1 Aug. 1938, Saint-Louis; s. of Fara Diouf and Aissatou Diop Hameth; m. Aissatou Seye 1963; one s. four d.; ed. Lycée Faidherbe, Saint-Louis, Ecole Nat. Supérieure Agronomique, Paris/Grignon, France and Sorbonne, Paris; Exec. Sec. African Groundnut Council, Lagos 1965–71; Exec. Sec. West African Rice Devt. Assocn., Monrovia 1971–77; Sec. of State for Scientific and Tech. Research, Govt. of Senegal, Dakar 1978–83; mem. Nat. Ass., Chair. Foreign Affairs Comm. and elected Sec., Dakar 1983–84; Sec. Gen. Banque centrale des états de l'Afrique de l'ouest, Dakar 1985–; led Senegalese dels. to UN Confs. on Science and Tech., Vienna 1979 (Chair. of 1st Comm.), Industrial Devt., New Delhi 1980, New and Renewable Energy Sources, Nairobi (Vice-Chair.) 1981, Peaceful Use of Space, Vienna 1982; African Rep., Consultative Group on Int. Agricultural Research, Washington; mem. Bd. of Dirs. I.S.N.A.R., The Hague, I.C.R.A.F., Nairobi, Compagnie Air Afrique, Abidjan, Int. Foundation for Science, Stockholm; Chair. S.I.N.A.E.S., Dakar; mem. Consultative Cttee. on Medical Research, WHO, Geneva; Officier Légion d'honneur, des Palmes Académiques (France); Grand Commdr., Order of the Star of Africa (Liberia). *Publications:* La détérioration du pouvoir d'achat de l'Arachide 1972, Les fondements du dialogue scientifique entre les civilisations Euro-occidentale et Négro-Africaine 1979. *Leisure interests:* reading, music, sports. *Address:* Banque Centrale des Etats de l'Afrique de l'Ouest, Avenue du Barachois, Boîte Postale 3108, Dakar, Senegal. *Telephone:* 23.10.42; 23.16.15.

DIPRETE, Edward D.; American politician; b. 8 July 1934, Cranston, R. I.; s.of Frank A. Diprete and Maria Grossi; m. Patricia Hines 1956; three s. four d.; ed. Holy Cross, Worcester, Mass.; Councilman, City of Cranston 1975–79, Mayor 1979–85; Gov. of Rhode Island 1985–; Republican. *Address:* 222 State House, Providence, R.I. 02903, U.S.A.

DIRKSEN, Gebhard, DR.JUR.; German lawyer; b. 29 June 1929, Göttingen; s. of Wilhelm and Magdalene (née Güthenke) Dirksen; m. Renate Pöhl 1971; one s. two d.; ed. at schools in Gutersloh/Westfalen and Univs. of Mainz, Freibourg and Göttingen; articled in Göttingen, Hanover and Celle; Deputy Chair. Bd. of Dirs Norddeutschen Landesbank Girozentrale 1959–. *Address:* 3000 Hannover 51, Westpreussenufer 4, Federal Republic of Germany. *Telephone:* 64 787 46.

DISBROW, Richard Edwin, M.S.; American business executive; b. 20 Sept. 1930, Newark; s. of Milton A. Disbrow and Madeline C. Segal; m. 1st Patricia F. Warner 1953 (divorced 1972), one s. one d.; m. 2nd Teresa M. Moser 1973; ed. Lehigh Univ., Newark Coll. of Eng. and M.I.T.; with American Electric Power Service Corpn. New York 1954–80, Columbus, Ohio 1980–, Exec. Vice-Pres. 1974–75, Vice-Chair. Bd. 1975–79, Pres. and Chief Admin. Officer 1979–84, Pres. and C.O.O. 1985–, also Dir.; Pres., Dir. American Electric Power Co.; Dir. Ohio Nat. Bank, Edison Electric Inst.; Instr. Newark Coll. of Eng. 1959–64; Industrial Commr. Piscataway, N.J. 1960–64; mem. Visiting Cttee. Dept. of Mechanical Eng. and Mechanics, Lehigh Univ. 1960–64; Sloan Fellow M.I.T. *Address:* AEP Service Corporation, One Riverside Plaza, Columbus, Ohio 43215, U.S.A.

DISTEL, Sacha; French singer and songwriter; b. 29 Jan. 1933, Paris; s. of Léon and Andrée (née Ventura) Distel; m. Francine Breaud 1963; two s.; ed. Lycée Claude-Bernard, Paris; voted best guitarist by Jazz Hot magazine, and in critics poll 1957, 58, 59; acted in films, Les Mordus 1960, Nous irons à Deauville 1962, La Bonne Soupe 1964, Le Voyou 1970, Sans mobile apparent 1971; has sung more than 200 songs in French, English, Italian, German; TV presenter in France, England and Germany; producer of TV shows Sacha Show, Top à Sacha Distel 1973, Sacha's in Town (U.K.) 1972; producer and performer La Belle Vie TV programme 1984–; Chevalier des Arts et des Lettres 1987, numerous awards. *Publication:* Les Pendules à l'heure 1985. *Leisure interests:* swimming, skiing and tennis. *Address:* c/o Marovani Organization, 35 rue Marbeuf, 75008 Paris, France.

DITFURTH, Jutta; German politician and social scientist; b. 1951, Frankfurt; Nat. Spokesperson for the Green Party. *Address:* c/o Green Party, 36 Colmanstr., 5300 Bonn 1, Federal Republic of Germany.

DITYATIN, Aleksandr; Soviet gymnast; b. 7 Aug. 1957, Leningrad; ed. Leningrad Lesgaft Inst. of Physical Culture; many times Soviet champion and cup winner; overall champion Soviet Summer Games 1975, 1979, World Cup 1978, 1979; team and rings silver medals, Montreal Olympic Games 1976; overall bronze medallist world championships 1978; overall world champion 1979; overall gold medallist, team gold medal, rings gold medal, vault, parallel bars, pommel horse and horizontal bar silver medals, Moscow Olympic Games 1980.

DIXEY, Paul Arthur Groser; British underwriter; b. 13 April 1915, Herts.; s. of the late Neville Dixey and Marguerite Groser; m. Mary Margaret Baring Garrod 1939; one d. four s.; ed. Stowe School and Trinity Coll., Cambridge Univ.; served Royal Artillery,1939–45; mem. London Insurance Market Del. to Indonesia 1958; mem. Dunmow R.D.C. 1958–64; Cttee. of Lloyd's Underwriters' Asscn. 1962–74, Cttee. of Salvage Asscn. 1962–74 (Chair. 1964–65), Cttee. of Lloyd's 1964–70, 1972–75, Gen. Cttee. Lloyd's Register of Shipping 1964–; Deputy Chair. of Lloyd's 1967, 1969, 1972, Chair. 1973, 1974; mem. Council, Morley Coll. 1952–62; Chair. Govs., Vinehall School 1966–73. *Leisure interests:* riding, fly-fishing. *Address:* Little Easton Spring, Dunmow, Essex, England. *Telephone:* Great Dunmow 2840.

DIXIT, Jyotindranath, M.A.; Indian diplomatist; b. 8 Jan. 1936, Madras; m. Vijaya Sundaram 1958; three s. two d.; ed. Univ. of Delhi; served in different capacities in Indian embassies in Mexico, Chile, Bhutan, Japan, Austria 1958–69; at Ministry of External Affairs dealing with China, Pakistan and UN Affairs 1961–63, 1969–72; first Amb. (acting) to Bangladesh 1972–75; Minister Indian Embassy, Washington, U.S.A. 1975–78; Chief Spokesman on Foreign Policy, Govt. of India 1978–82; Amb. to Afghanistan 1982–85, to Pakistan 1989–; High Commr. to Sri Lanka 1985–89. *Publication:* Self in Autumn (poems) 1982. *Leisure interests:* reading, swimming, rowing, hiking. *Address:* Embassy of India, G-5, Diplomatic Enclave, Islamabad, Pakistan; 32A, Pocket B. Alakhnanda, Gangotri Enclave, New Delhi 19, India (Home). *Telephone:* 820116 (Office); 6434832 (Home).

DIXON, Alan John, B.S., LL.B.; American lawyer and politician; b. 7 July 1927, Belleville, Ill.; s. of William G. and Elsa (née Tebbenhoff) Dixon; m. Joan Louise Fox 1954; one s. two d.; ed. Univ. of Illinois, Washington Univ., St. Louis, Mo.; admitted to Ill. bar 1950; practised law, Belleville 1950–76; police magistrate, Belleville 1949; Asst. Attorney St. Clair County, Ill. 1950; mem. Ill. House of Reps. 1950–62; mem. Ill. Senate 1962–70 (minority whip); Treasurer State of Ill. 1970–76, Sec. of State 1977–81; Senator from Illinois 1981–; mem. Belleville Chamber of Commerce; Democrat. *Address:* U.S. Senate, Washington, D.C. 20510; 7606 Foley Drive, Belleville, Ill. 62223, U.S.A. (Home).

DIXON, Frank James, M.D.; American medical scientist; b. 9 March 1920, St. Paul, Minnesota; s. of Frank James and Rose Augusta (née Kuhfeld) Dixon; m. Marion Edwards 1946; two s. one d.; ed. Univ. of Minnesota, U.S. Naval Hospital, Great Lakes, Illinois; Research Asst., Dept. of Pathology, Harvard Medical School 1946–48; Instructor, Dept. of Pathology, Washington Univ. Medical School 1948–50; Asst. Prof. Dept. of Pathology 1950–51; Prof. and Chair. Dept. of Pathology, Univ. of Pittsburgh School of Medicine 1951–61, Chair. Biomedical Research Depts. 1970–74; Chair. Dept. of Experimental Pathology, Scripps Clinic and Research Foundation 1961–74, Dir. 1974–; Prof. in Residence, Dept. of Biology, Univ. of Calif. at San Diego 1965–68, Adjunct Prof. Dept. Pathology 1968–; mem. N.A.S., Asscn. American Physicians, A.A.A.S. and numerous other professional orgs.; Hon. Dr. Sc. (Medical Coll. of Ohio); Harvey Society Lecturer 1962; mem. numerous editorial bds. and advisory cttees.; Theobald Smith Award in Medical Sciences from A.A.A.S. 1952, Parke-Davis Award from the American Soc. for Experimental Pathology 1957, Award for Distinguished Achievement from Modern Medicine 1961, Martin E. Rehfuss Award in Internal Medicine 1966, Von Pirquet Medal from Annual Forum on Allergy 1967, Bunim Gold Medal from the American Rheumatism Assn. 1968, Mayo Soley Award from the Western Soc. for Clinical Research 1969, Gairdner Foundation Award 1969, Dickson Prize in Medicine, Univ. of Pittsburgh 1975, Albert Lasker Basic Medical Research Award 1975, Pahlavi Lecturer, Ministry of Science and Higher Educ., Iran 1976, Homer Smith Award in Renal Physiology, New York Heart Assn. 1976, Rous-Whipple Award of the American Assn. of Pathologists 1979, First award in Immunology from Kaiser Permanente Medical Group, Los Angeles, Calif. 1979. *Publications:* Ed. Advances in Immunology, and over 450 papers. *Leisure interests:* running, tennis, art collecting. *Address:* c/o National Academy of Sciences, 2101 Constitution Avenue, Washington, D.C. 20418; Research Institute, Scripps Clinic and Research Foundation, 10666 North Torrey Pines Road, La Jolla, Calif. 92037 (Office); 2355 Avenida de la Playa La Jolla, Calif. 92037, U.S.A. (Home). *Telephone:* (619) 455-8100.

DIXON, Gordon Henry, PH.D., F.R.S.C., F.R.S.; Canadian university professor; b. 25 March 1930, Durban, S.A.; s. of Walter James Dixon and Ruth Nightingale; m. Sylvia Weir Gillen 1954; three s. one d.; ed. Cambridgeshire High School for Boys, Trinity Coll., Cambridge, Univ. of Toronto, Canada; Asst. Prof., Dept. of Biochemistry, Univ. of Washington, Seattle, U.S.A. 1954–58; mem. staff MRC Unit for research in cell metabolism, Univ. of Oxford 1958–59; Research Assoc., Connaught Medical Research Lab., Univ. of Toronto 1959–60, Asst. Prof., Dept. of Biochemistry 1961–62, Assoc. Prof. 1962–63; Assoc. Prof., Dept. of Biochemistry, Univ. of B.C., Vancouver, Canada 1963–66, Prof. 1966–72; Prof. and Head, Biochemistry Group, Univ. of Sussex, England 1972–74; Prof. of Medical Biochemistry, Faculty of Medicine, Univ. of Calgary 1974–, Head of Dept. 1983–88; Visiting Fellow Commoner, Trinity Coll., Cambridge 1979–80; Pres. Canadian Biochemical Soc. 1982–83; Pres. Pan-American Assn. of Biochemical Socs. 1987–(90), Vice-Pres. 1984–87; Chair. Canadian Nat. Cttee. for Int. Union of Biochem. 1984–86, Exec. Cttee. Int. Union of Biochem. 1988–(94); Assoc. Ed. Journal of Molecular Evolution; Ayerst Award, Canadian Biochem. Soc. 1966, Steacie Prize 1968, Flavelle Medal, Royal Soc. of Canada 1980 and other awards. *Publications:* more than 200 articles in scientific journals. *Leisure interests:* hiking, gardening, skiing. *Address.* Faculty of Medicine, Department of Medical Biochemistry, Health Sciences Centre, 3330 Hospital Drive N.W., Calgary, Alberta, T2N 4N1; 3424 Underwood Place N.W., Calgary, Alberta, T2N 4G7, Canada (Home). *Telephone:* (403) 282-4394 (Home) or (403) 220-6022.

DIXON, Kenneth Herbert Morley, B.A.(ECON.); British business executive; b. 19 Aug. 1929, Stockport; s. of Arnold Morley Dixon and Mary Jolly; m. Patricia Oldbury Whalley 1955; two s.; ed. Cranbrook School, Sydney, Manchester Univ.; joined Rowntree & Co. Ltd. 1956, Dir. 1970, Chair. U.K. Confectionery Div. 1973–78; Deputy Chair. Rowntree Mackintosh Ltd. 1978–81; Chair. Rowntree Mackintosh PLC (now Rowntree PLC) 1981–; mem. Council Inc. Soc. of British Advertisers 1971–79, Council Cocoa, Chocolate and Confectionery Alliance 1972–79, Council Advertising Assn. 1976–79, CBI Cos. Cttee. 1979–84, Council CBI 1981–, B.I.M. Econ. and Soc. Affairs Cttee. 1980–, Food and Drink Fed. 1986–87, Exec. Cttee. 1986–; mem. Council York Univ. 1983–. *Leisure interests:* reading, music, fell walking. *Address:* Rowntree PLC, York, Y01 1XY, England (Office). *Telephone:* (0904) 653071 (Office).

DIXON, Richard Newland, SC.D., F.R.S.; British professor of chemistry; b. 25 Dec. 1930, Borough Green; s. of Robert T. Dixon and Lilian Dixon; m. Alison M. Birks 1954; one s. two d.; ed. Judd School, Tonbridge, King's Coll. London and St. Catharine's Coll. Cambridge; Scientific Officer, U.K.A.E.A. Aldermaston 1954–56; Postdoctoral Fellow, Univ. of Western Ont. 1956–57, Nat. Research Council, Ottawa 1957–59; ICI Fellow, Univ. of Sheffield 1959–60, Lecturer in Chemistry 1960–69; Prof. of Chemistry, Univ. of Bristol 1969–, Dean, Faculty of Science 1979–82; Sorby Research Fellow, Royal Soc. 1964–69; mem. Council, Faraday Div. Royal Soc. of Chem. 1985–, Cttees. of S.E.R.C., 1980–83, 1987–; Corday Morgan Medal and Spectroscopy Awards, Royal Soc. of Chem. *Publications:* Spectroscopy

and Structure 1965, Theoretical Chemistry, Vol. I 1972, Vol. II 1974, Vol. III 1977; numerous research articles in scientific journals. *Leisure interests.* mountain walking, photography, gardening, theatre-going. *Address:* School of Chemistry, University of Bristol, Cantock's Close, Bristol, BS8 1TS (Office); 22 Westbury Lane, Coombe Dingle, Bristol, BS9 2PE, England (Home). *Telephone:* (0272) 303030 (Office); (0272) 681691 (Home).

DIXON, Thomas F., B.S.ENG., B.S. AND M.S. CHEM.ENG., M.S.AERO.ENG.; American executive and aerospace engineer; b. 15 March 1916; m. Margaret Ann Donovan 1943; two s. two d.; ed. Vanderbilt and Michigan Univs., and California Inst. of Technology; Research Engineer, N. American Aviation 1946–54, Dir. Propulsion Center, Rocketdyne Div. N. American Aviation 1954–55, Chief Engineer 1955–60, Vice-Pres. Research and Eng. 1960–63, Vice-Pres. 1963–68; Deputy Assoc. Administrator Nat. Aeronautics and Space Admin. 1961–63; Chair. of the Bd., Airtronics Inc. 1967–69, 1973–; Pres. 1969–73; Exec. Vice-Pres. Teledyne McCormick Selph 1975–76, Pres. 1976–; Pres. Calif. Capital Tech. Resources, Inc. 1984–; Fellow, American Rocket Soc., A.I.A.A.; Robert M. Goddard Memorial Award 1957; shared Louis W. Hill Space Transportation Award 1961. *Address:* Teledyne McCormick Selph, 3601 Union Road, Hollister, Calif. 9502 (Office); 7 Via Las Encinas, Carmel Valley, Calif. 93924, U.S.A. (Home). *Telephone:* (408) 637-3731 (Office).

DIZ, Adolfo César, C.P.A., D.ECON., M.A., D.PHIL.; Argentine economist; b. 12 May 1931, Buenos Aires; s. of Agustín Diz and Elisa Aristizábal; m. Martha Solari 1959; five s.; ed. Univ. de Buenos Aires and Univ. of Chicago; Instructor of Statistics, Univ. de Buenos Aires 1951–55, 1958–59; Prof. of Statistics, Univ. Nacional de Tucumán 1959–60, Dir. Inst. of Econ. Research 1959–65, Prof. of Statistics and Econometrics 1960–61, 1964, Dir. of Monetary Theory 1962, 1965–66; Exec. Dir. Int. Monetary Fund (IMF) 1966–68; Envoy extraordinary and Minister plenipotentiary, Argentine Financial Rep. in Europe 1969–73; Dir. Center for Latin American Monetary Studies 1973–76; Pres. Banco Central de la República Argentina 1976–81; Dir. Per Jacobsson Foundation 1976–; Econ. Consultant 1981–; mem. of Argentine socs., American Econ. Assn. and Econometric Soc. *Publications:* Money and Prices in Argentina 1935–62, in Varieties of Monetary Experience (Ed. D. Meiselman), Money Supply Models (in Spanish), and numerous economic articles. *Address:* Callao Avenida 2049-P6 (1024), Buenos Aires, Argentina.

DIZDAREVIĆ, Raif; Yugoslav politician; b. 1926, Fojnica; with Nat. Liberation struggle 1943; mem. League of Communists 1945–, mem. Presidency Cen. Cttee. of Bosnia and Herzegovina 1974–; with state security organ 1945–51; Ministry of Foreign Affairs 1951–; Sec. and Chargé d'affaires Embassy, Bulgaria 1951–54, First Sec. Embassy, Moscow 1956–59, Counsellor Embassy, Prague 1963–67; Sec. Council of Confed. of Trade Unions of Yugoslavia 1967–72, mem. of the Presidency of the Council and Pres. of Council, Confed. of Trade Unions of Bosnia and Herzegovina 1974–78; Asst. Fed. Sec. for Foreign Affairs 1972–74, Fed. Sec. 1985–; mem. of Presidency of Repub. Conf. of Socialist and Workers Party of Bosnia and Herzegovina 1975–78; Pres. of Presidency of Socialist Repub. of Bosnia and Herzegovina and Pres. Council for Overall Nat. Defence 1978–82; Pres. Presidency of Socialist Fed. Repub. of Yugoslavia May 1988–; mem. Council for Nat. Defence of Yugoslavia 1978–83; mem. Cen. Cttee. League of Communists of Yugoslavia; mem. Fed. Ass. of Yugoslavia 1982–, Pres. 1982–83; Fed. Sec. Foreign Affairs SFR of Yugoslavia 1984; various medals and decorations. *Address:* Presidency of the Socialist Federal Republic of Yugoslavia, Bul. Lenjina 2, 11075 Novi Beograd, Yugoslavia.

DJEGHABA, Mohamed; Algerian politician; b. 1935, El Kentara; m.; four c.; ed. Univ. of Algiers; joined Nat. Liberation Army 1955, Officer; mem. Org. Cttee., Front Libération Nat. (FLN) 63, Central Cttee. 1979–; Vice-Pres. Conseil supérieur de la Jeunesse; Minister of War Veterans 1988–. *Address:* 2 rue Lt Benafa, Château-Neuf, Algiers, Algeria. *Telephone:* (2) 78-23-55.

DJERASSI, Carl, A.B., PH.D.; American chemist, educator, author; b. 29 Oct. 1923, Vienna; s. of Dr. Samuel Djerassi and Dr. Alice Friedmann; m. 1st Norma Lundholm (divorced 1976), one s. one d. (deceased); m. 2nd Diane W. Middlebrook 1985; ed. Kenyon Coll. and Univ. of Wisconsin; Research Chemist, Ciba Pharmaceutical Co., Summit, N.J. 1942–43, 1945–49; Assoc. Dir. of Research, Syntex, S.A., Mexico City 1949–51, Research Vice-Pres. 1957–60, Pres. Syntex Research 1968–72; Assoc. Prof. of Chem., Wayne State Univ., Detroit 1952–54, Prof. 1954–59, Stanford Univ. 1959–; Pres. of the Bd. Zoecon Corpn. (renamed Sandoz Crop Protection Corpn.) 1968–83, Chair. 1968–; Dir. Ridge Vineyards 1968–86, Cetus Corpn. 1972–, Teknowledge Inc. 1981–, Vitaphore Corpn. 1987–; Pres. Djerassi Foundation Resident Artists Program; Royal Chemical Soc. Centenary Lecturer 1964; Royal Swedish Acad. of Eng. Sciences thirteenth Chemical Lecturer 1969; Swedish Pharmaceutical Soc. Scheele Lecturer 1972; mem. Editorial Bd. Journal of the American Chemical Society 1968–76, Journal of Organic Chemistry 1955–58, Tetrahedron 1963–, Steroids 1963–, Proceedings of Nat. Acad. of Sciences 1964–70; mem. Nat. Acad. of Sciences Bd. on Science and Tech. for Int. Devt. 1967–76, Chair. 1972–76; mem. American Pugwash Cttee. 1967–1981; mem. Nat. Acad. of Sciences, N.A.S. Inst. of Medicine, Brazilian Acad. of Sciences, American Acad. of Arts and Sciences; Foreign mem. German Acad. of Natural Scientists (Leopoldina), Royal

Swedish Acad. of Sciences 1973, Bulgarian Acad. of Sciences 1979, Royal Swedish Acad. of Eng. Sciences 1984; Hon. Fellow Royal Chemical Soc. 1968, American Acad. of Pharmaceutical Science; Hon. D.Sc., Univ. Nacional de México, Kenyon Coll., Ohio, Fed. Univ. of Rio de Janeiro, Worcester Polytechnic Inst., Wayne State Univ., Columbia Univ., Univ. of Uppsala, Univ. of Geneva, Coe College, Iowa, Univ. of Ghent, Univ. of Manitoba; Award in Pure Chemistry 1958, Baekeland Medal 1959, Fritsche Medal 1960, Creative Invention Award 1973, American Chemical Soc.; Intra-Science Research Award 1969, Freedman Foundation Patent Award 1971, Chemical Pioneer Award 1973, Perkin Medal 1975, American Inst. of Chemists; Nat. Medal of Science 1973 (for synthesis of first oral contraceptive), Wolf Prize in Chemistry 1978, Award in the Chemistry of Contemporary Technological Problems 1983, Bard Award in Medicine and Science 1983. *Publications:* (author or co-author) Optical Rotatory Dispersion 1960, Steroid Reactions 1963, Interpretation of Mass Spectra of Organic Compounds 1964, Structure Elucidation of Natural Products by Mass Spectrometry (2 vols.) 1964, Mass Spectrometry of Organic Compounds 1967, The Politics of Contraception 1979, 1981, The Futurist and Other Stories 1988; of numerous scientific articles, also poems and short stories. *Leisure interests:* skiing, modern art, opera, poetry. *Address:* Department of Chemistry, Stanford University, Stanford, Calif. 94305, U.S.A. *Telephone:* 415-723-2783.

DJILAS, Milovan; Yugoslav writer and politician; b. 12 June 1911, Podbišće, Montenegro; s. of Nikola Djilas and Vasilija Radenović; m. 1st Mitra Mitrović 1937 (divorced 1948), one d.; 2nd Barić Štefanija 1952, one s.; ed. Belgrade Univ.; mem. Communist Party 1932, imprisoned 1932-35; mem. Cen. Cttee. Communist Party 1938, Politburo 1938 until expelled 1954; successively Minister, Head of Parl., Vice-Pres. of Yugoslavia until 1954; resgnd. from Communist Party 1954; imprisoned Nov. 1956-Jan. 1961, April 1962-Dec. 1966; 1969 Freedom Award (U.S.) 1968. *Publications:* Essays 1941-46 1947, Struggle of the Communist Party of Yugoslavia 1948, On National History as an Educational Subject 1949, Lerin and the Relations between Socialist States 1950, On New Roads to Socialism 1950, Reflections on Various Questions 1951, On the Aggressive Pressure of the Soviet Bloc against Yugoslavia 1951, The Legend of Njegoš 1952, The New Class 1957, Land without Justice (autobiography vol. 1) 1958, Conversations with Stalin 1962, Montenegro 1964, The Leper 1965, Njegoš 1966, The Unperfect Society: Beyond the New Class 1969, Under the Colors 1971, The Stone and the Violets 1971-72, Memoir of a Revolutionary (autobiography vol. 2) 1973, Parts of a Lifetime 1975, Tito 1980. *Address:* Ul. Palmotićeva 8/11, 11000 Beograd, Yugoslavia. *Telephone:* 340-957.

DJINDJIKHADZE, Vaya Gerontiyevich; Soviet banker; b. 1931; with Council of Ministers, Georgian S.S.R. -1965, First Deputy to Minister of Trade 1965-69; Man. Georgian S.S.R. Bd. of State Bank of U.S.S.R. 1969-76; mem. Bd. Foreign Trade Bank of U.S.S.R., then Deputy Chair. 1976-83; Chair. Bd. Int. Bank for Econ. Co-operation 1983-88; Govt. Official Georgian S.S.R. 1989-. *Address:* 380062 Tbilisi, pr. I, Chavchavadze, Georgian S.S.R., U.S.S.R.

DJOJOHADIKUSUMO, Sumitro; Indonesian politician; b. 29 May 1917, Kebumen, Central Java; s. of Margono Djojohadikusumo and Raden Ayu Siti Katumi; m. Dora Sumitro Djojohadikusumo 1947; two s. two d.; ed. Netherlands School of Economics, Rotterdam and the Sorbonne, Paris; Asst. to Prime Minister of Indonesia 1946; Pres. Indonesian Banking Corpn. 1947; Chargé d'affaires, Washington, D.C. 1949-50; Minister of Econ. Affairs 1950-51; Minister of Finance 1952-53, 1955-56; Prof. and Dean, Faculty of Econs., Univ. of Indonesia, Jakarta 1951-57; left the country after the PRRI/Permesta armed rebellion 1958; Minister of Trade 68-73; Minister of State for Research 1973-78. *Publications:* Strategic Variables in Indonesia's Long Term Growth 1977, Sciences, Resources and Development 1977, Technology and Global Economic Development, Structure, Performance and Prospects of the Indonesian Economy 1980; trans. Milton's Paradise Lost 1969, and over 80 articles about politics, literature, etc. *Leisure interests:* literature, philosophy, tennis. *Address:* Jalan Kartanegara 4, Jakarta, Indonesia (Home).

DJONDO, Koffi Gervais; Togolese financial administrator and politician; b. 4 July 1937, Ouidah; ed. Univ. of Paris, Inst. des Hautes Etudes D'Outre Mer; Pres. Econ. and Social Council 1968-, of Chamber of Commerce, Agric. and Industry 1977; Dir.-Gen. Caisse Nat. de Sécurité Sociale, Togo branch of Soc. Commerciale Occidentale Africaine; mem. Cen. Cttee., Rassemblement du Peuple Togolais; Minister of State Enterprises and Industry March 1985-. *Address:* Ministry of State Enterprises, Lomé, Togo. *Telephone:* 21-56-54.

DJOUDI, Hocine, LL.B.; Algerian diplomatist; b. 4 May 1930; m.; five c.; ed. Montpellier Univ.; Counsellor for Foreign Affairs and Deputy Chief of the Algerian Dept. of Int. Orgs. 1963, Counsellor, Algerian Embassy to the U.K. 1963-64, at the Perm. Mission to the UN 1964-68, Perm. Rep. 1984-; Counsellor, Office of the Minister for Foreign Affairs 1968-78; Amb. to Spain 1978-79, to Portugal 1979-82, to Mozambique and Lesotho 1982-84. *Address:* Permanent Mission of Algeria to the United Nations, 15 East 47th Street, New York, N.Y. 10017, U.S.A. *Telephone:* 750-1960.

DJURANOVIĆ, Veselin; Yugoslav politician; b. 17 May 1925, Martinići, near Danilovgrad, Montenegro; m. Vjera Djuranović; two s. one d.; joined

the Nat. Liberation War 1941, League of Yugoslav Communist Youth 1941; mem. CP (later renamed League of Communists) of Yugoslavia 1944-; various posts in party during post-war period; Pres. Cen. Cttee. Nat. Liberation Cttee. of Montenegro 1946-53; Dir. Radio Titograd 1953-54, Dir. and Editor-in-Chief Pobjeda newspaper 1954-58; mem. Exec. Cttee. of Cen. Cttee. of League of Communists of Montenegro 1959-66; Pres. Cen. Council of Socialist Alliance of Working People of Montenegro 1962-63; Pres. Exec. Council of Socialist Repub. of Montenegro 1963-66; Sec. of Exec. Cttee. Cen. Cttee. of League of Communists of Montenegro 1967-69; Pres. Cen. Cttee. League of Communists of Montenegro 1969-77; Pres. Fed. Exec. Council 1977-82; mem. and Pres. of the Presidency of the Socialist Repub. of Montenegro 1982-84; Pres. of Presidency of Social Fed. Repub. of Yugoslavia, 1984-85, mem. 1985-; awarded a number of distinguished Yugoslav and foreign decorations. *Address:* c/o Presidency of the Socialist Federal Republic of Yugoslavia, Bul. Lenjina 2, 11075 Novi Beograd, Yugoslavia.

DLAMINI, Prince Bhekimpi Alpheus; Swazi soldier, administrator and politician; served with Eighth Army 1937-45; mem. Swazi Nat. Council, participated in constitutional talks 1963; Asst. Minister of Admin. 1966, then Deputy Minister, Deputy Prime Minister's Dept.; Prime Minister of Swaziland 1983-86; imprisoned 1988.

DLAMINI, Sotsha; Swazi politician; fmr. Asst. Police Commr.-1984; Prime Minister of Swaziland Oct. 1986-. *Address:* Office of the Prime Minister, Mbabane, Swaziland.

DLAMINI, Timothy Lutfo Lucky, M.T.S., PH.D.; Swazi diplomatist; b. 1952, Swaziland; m.; one d.; ed. Botswana, Lesotho and Swaziland Univ., McCormick Theological Seminary, and Pittsburg Univ.; Teacher, Swazi Nat. High School 1973-75; Lecturing Asst., Dept. of Theology and Religious Studies, Univ. of Botswana, Lesotho and Swaziland (later renamed Univ. of Swaziland) 1975-76, Lecturer 1976-82 and part-time Lecturer, Faculty of Educ. 1976-83, Head of Dept., Theology and Religious Studies 1982-83; Private Sec. to Minister of Foreign Affairs 1983-85; Perm. Rep. of Swaziland to the UN 1985-. *Address:* Permanent Mission of Swaziland to the United Nations, 866 United Nations Plaza, Suite 420, New York, N.Y. 10017, U.S.A. *Telephone:* 371-8910.

DMITRIEV, Valentin Ivanovich; Soviet politician; b. 1927; ed. Odessa Hydro-Electrical Inst.; CPSU Cen. Cttee. Higher party School; served in Soviet Navy 1943-50; mem. CPSU 1947-; active service in World War II; engineer in various orgs. in Magnitogorsk 1955-59; Sec. of CPSU regional cttee., and party cttee. of Magnitostroy trust 1959-62; First Sec. of Magnitogorsk, of Chelyabinsk City Cttee., of CPSU 1962-79; work on CPSU Cen. Cttee. 1979-80; Second Sec. of Cen. Cttee. of Latvian CP 1980-86; cand. mem. of CPSU Cen. Cttee. 1981-; mem. to Ethiopia 1986-. *Address:* U.S.S.R. Embassy, Addis Ababa, Ethiopia.

DO AMARAL, Prof. Diogo Freitas, PH.D.; Portuguese politician and university professor; b. 21 July 1941, Povoa de Varzim; s. of Duarte P. C. Freitas do Amaral and Maria Filomena Campos Trocado; m. Maria José Salgado Sarmento de Matos 1965; two s. two d.; Prof. of Administrative Law, Lisbon Univ. 1968-, Portuguese Catholic Univ. 1978-; mem. Council of State 1974-75, Parl. 1975-82; Pres. Centre Democrat Party (CDS) 1974-82, 1988-; Pres. European Union of Christian Democrats 1981-82; Deputy Prime Minister and Minister for Foreign Affairs 1980-81, Deputy Prime Minister and Minister of Defence 1981-83; Presidential cand. 1986; Pres. Fundação Portugal Século XXI; Calouste Gulbenkian Prize (twice); Henry the Navigator Prize. *Publications:* A Utilização do Domínio Público Pelos Particulares 1965, A Execução das Sentenças dos Tribunais Administrativos 1967, Conceito e natureza do recurso hierárquico 1981, Uma Solução para Portugal 1985, Curso de Direito Administrativo I, 1986. *Leisure interests:* music, horses. *Address:* Casa 50, Quinta da Marinha, 2750 Cascais, Portugal.

DO MUOI; Vietnamese politician; b. 1917, Hanoi; joined movement against French colonial rule 1936; imprisoned by French; escaped in 1945 and took part in anti-Japanese uprising in Ha Dong Prov.; political and mil. leader in provs. of Red River delta during struggle against French 1951-54; Alt. mem. Cen. Cttee. Communist Party of Viet-Nam (CPV) March 1955-60, mem. 1960-; Alt. mem. Political Bureau CPV 1976-82, mem. 1982-87; Sec. CPV 1987-; Deputy to Nat. Ass. 2nd, 4th, 5th, 6th, 7th and 8th Legislatures; Minister of Commerce 1969; Deputy Prime Minister and Minister of Bldg. 1976-87; Vice-Chair. Council of Ministers in charge of Economy 1987-; Prime Minister June 1988-; Order of the October Revolution (U.S.S.R.) 1987 and several Vietnamese decorations. *Address:* Council of Ministers, Hanoi, Viet-Nam.

DOAN, Herbert D., B.CH.E.; American chemical executive; b. 5 Sept. 1922, Midland, Mich.; s. of Leland and Ruth Doan; two s. three d.; ed. Cornell Univ.; Man., Chemicals Dept., Dow Chemical Co. 1956-60, Exec. Vice-Pres. Dow Chemical Co. 1960-62, Pres. 1962-71, now Dir.; Partner Doan Assocs.; Chair. Doan Resources Corpn.; Pres. Mich. High Tech. Task Force, Inc., Ann Arbor, Mich.; Dir. Chemical Bank and Trust Co., Midland, Mich., Dow Corning Corpn., Michigan Bell Telephone Co., Detroit, Mich.; Chair. Bd. of Trustees, Michigan Molecular Inst.; Incorporator, Neurosciences Research Foundation, Brookline, Mass.; Trustee, Dow Foundation; fmr. Vice-Chair. Nat. Science Bd., Nat. Science Foundation, Washington,

D.C., mem. Gov's Comm. on Jobs and Econ. Devt., Lansing, Mich.; mem. A.I.Ch.E., Cornell Univ. Eng. Coll. Council; mem. emer. American Chem. Soc., Bd. of Fellows, Saginaw Valley Coll. *Leisure interests:* fine arts, tennis, golf, reading. *Address:* P.O.B. 1431, Midland, Mich. 48640 (Office); 3801 Valley Drive, Midland, Mich. 48640, U.S.A. (Home). *Telephone:* (517) 631-2471 (Office).

DOBBS, Mattiwilda; American singer; ed. Spelman Coll., Atlanta, and Columbia Univ.; m. 1st Luis Rodríguez García 1953 (died 1954); m. 2nd Bengt Janzon 1957; studied with Lotte Leonard 1946–50; Marian Anderson scholarship, soloist at Mexico Univ. Festival 1947; studied at Mannes Music School and Berkshire Music Center 1948, with Pierre Bernac, Paris 1950–52; 1st Voice Prize, Geneva Int. Competition 1951; concert tour Netherlands, France and Sweden 1952; debut La Scala (Milan) in L'Italiana in Algeri 1953; sang at Glyndebourne 1953, 1954, 1956, 1961, Royal Opera House, Covent Garden (London) 1954, 1955, 1956, 1959, San Francisco Opera 1955, Metropolitan Opera (New York) 1956–; Stockholm Royal Opera 1957–; Hamburg State Opera 1961–63; concert appearances in Europe, U.S.A., Mexico, Israel, Australia, New Zealand and U.S.S.R.; Order of the North Star (Sweden). *Address:* 1101 South Arlington Ridge Road., Arlington, Va. 22202, U.S.A. *Telephone:* (703) 892-5234.

DOBESCH, Gerhard, DR.PHIL.; Austrian professor of Roman history and archaeology; b. 15 Sept. 1939, Vienna; s. of Dr. Carl Dobesch and Gustave Dobesch; ed. Univ. of Vienna; lecturer in Ancient History 1967–73; Prof. of Greek and Roman History, Univ. of Graz 1973–76; Prof. of Roman History, Archaeology and Epigraphy, Univ. of Vienna 1976–; Corresp. mem. Austrian Acad. of Sciences 1976, mem. 1984–. *Publications:* Caesars Apotheose zu Lebzeiten und sein Ringen um der Königstitel 1966, Untersuchung zum Korinth, vol. 1 Der panhellen 1968, Wurde Caesar zu Lebzeiten in Rom als Staatsgott anerkannt?, vol. 2 1971, Nochmals zur Datierung des grossen Senatskonsultes 1971, Nikolaos von Damaskus und die Selbstbiographie des Augustus 1978, Die Kelten in Österreich nach den ältest 1980, Die Kimbern in dem Ostalpen und die Schlacht bei Noreia 1982; numerous specialist articles. *Leisure interests:* literature, art history. *Address:* Universität Wien, Institut für Alte Geschichte, Dr. Karl Lueger-Ring 1, A-1010 Vienna (Office); Spitalgasse 29/12, A-1090 Vienna, Austria (Home). *Telephone:* 4300-2207 (Office); 43 17 254 (Home).

DOBRACZYŃSKI, Jan; Polish writer; b. 20 April 1910, Warsaw; s. of Anthony and Valerie Dobraczyński; m. Danuta Kotowicz 1935 (died 1966); three d.; ed. Higher School of Commerce, Warsaw; writer and journalist since 1929, book début 1937; mem. Polish Writers' Asscn. 1945–83, PEN, ZAIKS Asscn. of Authors, Polish Writers' Asscn. 1983–; mem. European Soc. of Culture (SEC), Vice-Pres. Polish Section 1981–, mem. Exec. Council 1982–; Vice-Chair. Main Council, Union of Fighters for Freedom and Democracy; Pres. Nat. Council of Patriotic Movt. for Nat. Rebirth (PRON), Chair. Nat. Council 1983–; mem. of Parl. 1952–56, 1985–; Włodzimierz Pietrzak Literary Awards 1949, 1954, 1970, 1980, State Prize (2nd Class) 1970, (1st Class) 1986, Reinhold Schneider Prize (Fed. Repub. of Germany) 1972, Prize of Minister of Culture and Art (1st Class) 1977, City of Warsaw Prize 1980, City of Prato Prize (Italy) 1980, City of San Remo Prize 1985, Otto Nuschke Prize (German Democratic Repub.) 1985, Award of the Heroes of Warsaw, 1985, Bolesław Piasecki Prize 1986, Virtuti Militari 1983, Builder of People's Republic of Poland 1984; Commdr.'s Cross of Order of Polonia Restituta 1969, Order of Banner of Labour (1st Class) 1982, Warsaw Insurgent Cross and other decorations. *Publications:* Najeźdźcy 1946, W rozwalonym domu 1946, Klucz mądrości 1951, Listy Nikodema 1952, Przyszedłem rozłączyć 1959, Wyczerpać morze 1961, Błękitne hełmy na tamie 1965, Doścignięty 1967, Tylko w jednym życiu 1970, Truciciele 1974, Bramy Lipska 1976, Cień Ojca 1977, Samson i Dalila 1979, Małżeństwo Anny 1981, Ziemia Ewangelii 1982, Dzieci Anny 1983, Kto Was Zabije 1985, Świat Popiołów 1986, To Jest Zwycięzca 1986, Ptaki Spiewają 1987, W Panstwie Srodka 1987, Magdalena 1988. *Leisure interests:* walking, gardening, theatre. *Address:* ul. Hetmańska 42, 04-305 Warsaw, Poland. *Telephone:* 21-20-06 (Office).

DOBRESCU, Miu; Romanian politician; b. 30 Jan. 1927, Bucharest; ed. Bucharest Univ.; mem. of Romanian Communist Party (RCP) 1945–; Sec. Bucharest Cttee. Union of Communist Youth (UCY) 1953; mem. Cen. Cttee. UCY 1954; party worker Cen. Cttee. RCP 1954–66; alt. mem. Cen. Cttee. RCP 1965–69, mem. 1969–; First Sec. Iaşi Regional Cttee. RCP 1966–68; First Sec. R.C.P. Cttee. and Chair. Exec. Cttee. People's Council, Iaşi Co. 1968–71; Head of Section Cen. Cttee. 1971–72; First Sec. RCP Cttee. and Chair. Exec. Cttee. People's Council, Suceava Co. 1972–76; Chair. Council of Socialist Culture and Educ. 1976–79; First Sec. RCP Cttee. and Chair. Exec. Cttee. People's Council, Dolj Co. 1979–82; Chair. Grand Nat. Assembly Comm. for People's Councils and Local Admin. 1980–; alt. mem. Exec. Political Cttee. 1969–84, mem. 1984–; mem. Grand Nat. Assembly 1969–; mem. Nat. Council Front of Socialist Democracy and Unity 1969–; Sec. Cen. Cttee. RCP 1982–84, Chair. Cen. Party Collegium 1984–; Chair. Gen. Trades Union Confed. 1987–. *Address:* 14 Stefan Gheorgiu Street, Bucharest 71724, Romania.

DOBRYNIN, Anatoliy Fedorovich, M.SC.; Soviet diplomatist; b. 16 Nov. 1919, Krasnaya Gorka, Moscow Region; ed. technical coll.; engineer at aircraft plant, Second World War; joined diplomatic service 1946; Counsellor, later Minister-Counsellor, Soviet Embassy, Washington 1952–55; Asst.

Minister of Foreign Affairs 1955–57; Under-Sec.-Gen. for Political and Security Council Affairs UN 1957–59, Head American Dept., U.S.S.R. Ministry of Foreign Affairs 1959–61; Amb. to U.S.A. 1962–86; mem. CPSU 1945–, Cand. mem., CPSU Cen. Cttee. 1966–71, mem. 1971–, Sec. Cen. Cttee. for Foreign Affairs 1986–; Head Int. Dept. 1986–; Deputy of U.S.S.R. Supreme Soviet 1986–88; Adviser to Pres. Gorbachev (q.v.) 1988–; Hero of Socialist Labour 1982, Order of Lenin (five times), Order of Red Banner and other decorations. *Address:* The Kremlin, Moscow, U.S.S.R.

DOBSON, Frank Gordon, B.SC.ECON., M.P.; British politician; b. 15 March 1940; s. of James W. Dobson and Irene S. Dobson; m. Janet M. Alker 1967; three c.; ed. Archbishop Holgate's Grammar School, York and London School of Econs.; admin. appts. with Cen. Electricity Generating Bd. 1962–70, Electricity Council 1970–75; mem. Camden Borough Council 1971–76, Leader 1973–75; Asst. Sec. Comm. for Local Admin. 1975–79; M.P. for Holborn and St. Pancras South 1979–83, for Holborn and St. Pancras 1983–; Opposition Spokesman on Educ. 1981–83, on Health 1983–87; Shadow Leader of the House of Commons 1987–; Labour. *Address:* 22 Great Russell Mansions, Great Russell Street, London, W.C.1, England.

DOCTOROW, Edgar Lawrence, A.B.; American novelist; b. 6 Jan. 1931, New York; s. of David Richard and Rose (Levine) Doctorow; m. Helen Esther Setzer 1954; one s. two d.; ed. Kenyon Coll., Gambier, Ohio and Hobart Coll.; served with U.S. army 1953–55; Ed. New American Library, New York 1960–64; Ed.-in-Chief Dial Press., New York 1964–69, Publr. 1969; writer-in-residence Univ. of Calif., Irvine 1969–70; mem. faculty Sarah Lawrence Coll., Bronxville, N.Y., Authors Guild (Dir.), American P.E.N. (Dir.), Writers Guild of America East, Century Asscn.; Creative Writing Fellow Yale School of Drama 1974–75; Creative Artists Program Service Fellow 1973–74; Visiting Sr. Fellow Council on Humanities, Princeton Univ. 1980; Visiting Prof. New York Univ. 1982–; Arts and Letters Award (American Acad. and Nat. Inst. Art) 1976; Guggenheim Fellow 1973, American Book Award 1986; Hon. L.H.D. (Kenyon Coll.) 1976, (Hobart Coll.) 1979. *Publications:* Welcome to Hard Times 1960, Big as Life 1966, The Book of Daniel 1971, Ragtime 1975, Drinks before Dinner (play) 1975, Loon Lake 1980, Lives of the Poets: Six Stories and a Novella 1984, World's Fair 1986, Billy Bathgate 1988. *Address:* c/o Random House Publishers, 210 E 50th Street, New York, N.Y. 10022, U.S.A. (Office).

DODD, Christopher J., B.A., J.D.; American politician; b. 27 May 1944, Willimantic, Conn.; s. of Thomas J. and Grace (Murphy) Dodd; ed. Providence Coll., R.I., and Univ. of Louisville, Ky.; Volunteer with Peace Corps, Dominican Repub. 1966–68; admitted to Conn. Bar 1973; mem. House of Reps. 1975–81 from 2nd Dist. Conn.; Senator from Connecticut 1981–(93); Democrat. *Address:* U.S. Senate, Washington, D.C. 20510, U.S.A.

DODD, Edwin Dillon; American business executive; b. 26 Jan. 1919, Point Pleasant, W. Va.; s. of David Rollin and Mary G. (Dillon) Dodd; m. Marie Marshall 1942 (deceased 1984); one d.; ed. Upper Arlington High School, Columbus, Ohio, Ohio State Univ. and Harvard Graduate School of Business Admin.; joined Owens-Illinois Inc. 1946, Dir. of Public Relations 1949, Production Man. Libbey Glass Div. 1954, Factories Man. 1956; joined Forest Products Group 1958, Gen. Man. 1961; Vice-Pres. Owens-Illinois Inc. 1959, Exec. Vice-Pres. 1964, Dir. 1966, Pres. 1968–72, C.O.O. 1968–72, C.E.O. 1972–84, Chair. 1976–84, Chair. Emer. 1984–; Goodyear Tire and Rubber Co., Toledo Trust Co., U.S.A. Chamber of Commerce, Toledo Edison, Centerior Energy Corpn., American Life Insurance Co. of New York, Trustcorp Inc.; fmr. Dir. Great Atlantic and Pacific Tea Co., Ohio Bell Telephone Co., Nat. Petro-Chemicals Corpn., Distinguished Citizens Award; Legion of Merit; Military Medal (Philippines Govt.). *Leisure interests:* fishing, hunting, golf. *Address:* Owens-Illinois Inc., One Sea Gate, Toledo, Ohio 43666, U.S.A.

DODGE, John Vilas, B.S.; American editor; b. 25 Sept. 1909, Chicago; s. of George Dodge and Helen Porter; m. Jean Plate 1935; two s. two d.; ed. Northwestern Univ., Illinois and Univ. de Bordeaux; freelance writer 1931–32; Ed. Northwestern Univ. Alumni News, and Official Publications of Northwestern Univ. 1932–35, Exec. Sec. Northwestern Univ. Alumni Asscn. 1937–38; Asst. Ed. Encyclopaedia Britannica, and Assoc. Ed. Britannica Book of the Year 1938–43, Assoc. Ed. Ten Eventful Years (4 vol. History 1937–46) 1947; Asst. Ed. Encyclopaedia Britannica 1946–50, Man. Ed. 1950–60, Exec. Ed. 1960–64, Sr. Vice-Pres. Editorial 1964–65, Sr. Editorial Consultant 1965–70, 1972–; Ed. Britannica World Language Dictionary 1954; Editorial Adviser Encyclopaedia Universalis (Paris) 1968–, Britannica Int. Encylopaedia (Tokyo) 1969–, Enciclopedias Barsa (Rio de Janeiro and Mexico City) 1974–; Chair. Bd. of Eds. Encyclopaedia Britannica Publrs. 1977–. *Address:* 3851 N. Mission Hills Road, Northbrook, Ill. 60062, U.S.A. (Home). *Telephone:* 312-272-0254 (Home).

DODSON, Sir Derek Sherborne Lindsell, K.C.M.G., M.C., D.L.; British diplomatist (retd.); b. 20 Jan. 1920, Cambridge; s. of Charles Sherborne Dodson and Irene Frances Lindsell; m. Julie Maynard Barnes 1952; one s. one d.; ed. Stowe School, Royal Mil. Coll., Sandhurst; commissioned in Royal Scots Fusiliers 1939; Mil. Asst. to British Commr., Allied Control Comm. for Bulgaria 1945–46; Second Sec., Foreign Office 1947–48; Vice-Consul, Salonika, Greece 1948–50; in British Embassy to Spain 1950–53; at Foreign Office 1953–58; Head of Chancery, Embassy to Czechoslovakia 1958–62; Consul, Elisabethville (now Lubumbashi), Zaire 1962–63; Head of Central

Dept., FCO 1963-66; Counsellor, Embassy to Greece 1966-69; Amb. to Hungary 1970-73, to Brazil 1973-77, to Turkey 1977-80; Special Rep. of Foreign and Commonwealth Sec. 1981-; Gov. United World Coll. of the Atlantic 1982-; Chair. Anglo-Turkish Soc. 1982-, Beaver Guarantee Ltd. 1984-86; Dir. Benguela Railway Co. 1984-; Deputy Lieut. for Lincolnshire 1988-; Grand Cross of Cruzeiro do Sul (Brazil). *Leisure interests:* shooting, fishing, walking. *Address:* 47 Ovington Street, London, S.W.3; Gable House, Leadenham, Lincoln, England.

DODWELL, Charles Reginald, PH.D., LITT.D., F.B.A., F.R.HIST.S., F.S.A.; British professor of history of art; b. 3 Feb. 1922, Cheltenham; s. of William H. W. Dodwell and Blanche Dodwell; m. Sheila J. Fletcher 1942; one s. one d.; ed. Gonville and Caius Coll., Cambridge; served R.N. 1941-45; Research Fellow, Gonville and Caius Coll. 1950-51; Sr. Research Fellow, Warburg Inst. 1950-53; Lambeth Librarian 1953-58; Fellow, Lecturer, Librarian, Trinity Coll., Cambridge 1958-66; Visiting Scholar, Inst. of Advanced Studies, Princeton 1965-66; Pilkington Prof. of History of Art and Dir. Whitworth Art Gallery, Univ. of Manchester 1966-. *Publications:* Canterbury School of Illumination, Theophilus de Diversis Artibus, Reichenau Reconsidered, Painting in Europe 800-1200, Anglo-Saxon Art; articles in the Burlington Magazine, Gazette des Beaux Arts etc. *Leisure interests:* badminton, table-tennis, opera. *Address:* The Old House, 12 Park Road, Cheadle Hulme, Cheshire, SK8 7DA, England. *Telephone:* 061-485 3923.

DOE, Gen. Samuel Kanyon; Liberian army officer and politician; b. 6 May 1950, Tuzon, Grand Gedeh Co.; s. of Matthew and Anna Doe; m. Nancy B. Doe; four c.; ed. R.E.B. Richardson Baptist Jr. High School and Ministry of Nat. Defence Radio and Communication School, Monrovia; joined army as Pvt. 1969, Acting First Sergeant 1973-75, First Sergeant 1975-79, Master Sergeant and Adjutant 1979-81; overthrew Pres. William Tolbert in coup April 1980; Head of State April 1980-; Chair. People's Redemption Council 1980-85; Pres. Interim Nat. Ass. 1985-; rank of Gen. 1981-; C.-in-C. of Armed Forces 1981-; f. and Head, Nat. Democratic Party of Liberia 1984-; Hon. Ph.D. (Nat. Univ. of Seoul) 1982. *Leisure interest:* football. *Address:* Interim National Assembly, Monrovia, Liberia.

DOERING, William von Eggers, PH.D.; American professor of chemistry; b. 22 June 1917, Fort Worth, Tex.; s. of Carl Rupp Doering and Antoinette Mathilde von Eggers; m. 1st Ruth Haines 1947 (divorced 1954); two s. one d.; m. 2nd Sarah Cowles 1969 (divorced 1981); ed. Shady Hill School, Mass., Belmont Hill School, Mass. and Harvard Univ.; with Office of Scientific Research and Devt. 1941, Nat. Defense Research Cttee. 1942, Polaroid Corpn. 1943 (all in Cambridge, Mass.); Instructor, Columbia Univ. 1943-45, Asst. Prof. 1945-48, Assoc. Prof. 1948-52; Prof. Yale Univ. 1952-56, Whitehead Prof. of Chem. 1956-67; Prof. Harvard Univ. 1967-68, Mallinckrodt Prof. of Chem. 1968-86, Prof. Emer. 1986-; Chair. Council for a Livable World, Washington, D.C. 1964-73, Pres. 1973-78; U.S. Dir. People's Repub. of China-U.S.A. Chem. Graduate Program 1982-86; mem. N.A.S., American Acad. of Arts and Sciences; Hon. Prof. Fudan Univ., Shanghai 1980; John Scott Award 1945, American Chem. Soc. Award in Pure Chem. 1953, A. W. von Hoffman Medal (Gesellschaft Deutscher Chemiker) 1962, William C. DeVane Medal 1967, Theodore William Richards Medal 1970, and other awards from American Chem. Soc.; Hon. D.Sc. (Texas Christian Univ.); Hon. D. Nat. Sci. (Karlsruhe) 1987. *Publications:* Quinine 1944, Tropolone 1950, Tropylium Ion 1954, Carbenes 1954, Bullvalene 1962, Thermal Rearrangements 1966. *Leisure interests:* music, theatre, tennis, hiking. *Address:* Harvard University Dept. of Chemistry, 12 Oxford Street, Cambridge, Mass. 02138 (Office); 53 Francis Avenue, Cambridge, Mass. 02138, U.S.A. (Home). *Telephone:* 617-495-4263 (Office).

DOĞAN, Hüsnü; Turkish politician; b. 1944, Malatya; m.; one c.; ed. Dept. of Construction, Middle East Tech. Univ.; Project Eng. with State Electricity Bd.; Researcher, later Dir. Foreign Capital Dept., State Planning Org.; Special Adviser to Ministry of Agric., Research Planning Coordinator and Dir-Gen.; worked for State Procurement Office; Co-ordinator in Turkish automobile industry; Minister of Agric., Forestry and Rural Affairs 1983-89. *Address:* Tarim, Orman ve Koyisleri Bakanliği, Bakanliklar, Ankara, Turkey.

DOGRAMACI, Ihsan, M.D., LL.D., F.R.C.P., F.A.A.P.; Turkish pediatrician and educator; b. 3 April 1915, Erbil; s. of Ali Dogramaci and Ismet Kirdar; m. Ayser Hikmet Suleyman 1941; two s. one d.; ed. Istanbul, Harvard and Washington Univs.; Asst. Prof. of Pediatrics, Ankara Univ. 1947-49, Assoc. Prof. 1949-54, Prof. and Head of Dept. 1954-63; Dir. Research Inst. of Child Health, Ankara 1958-81; Prof. of Pediatrics and Head of Dept., Hacettepe Faculty of Medicine 1963-81, Dean of Faculty June-Nov. 1963; Pres. Ankara Univ. 1963-65; Chair. Bd. of Trustees Middle East Tech. Univ. 1965-67; Pres. Hacettepe Children's Medical Centre, Ankara 1965-81; Rector, Hacettepe Univ. 1967-75; Pres. UNICEF Exec. Bd. 1967-70; Pres. Int. Pediatric Asscn. 1968-77, Dir.-Gen. 1977-; Pres. Union of Middle-Eastern and Mediterranean Pediatric Socs. 1971-73, Turkish and Int. Children's Center, Ankara 1980-, Higher Educ. Council of Turkey 1981-; mem. of Standing Conf. of Rectors and Vice-Chancellors of the European Univs. 1969-81; Hon. Fellow, American Acad. Pediatrics 1959; Hon. mem. American Pediatric Soc., Deutsche Gesellschaft für Kinderheilkunde 1973, Soc. de Pédiatrie de Paris 1958, British Ped. Asscn. 1964, Finnish Pediatric Asscn. 1971, etc.; Corresp. mem. Acad. Nat. de Médecine, France 1973; Léon Bernard Foundation Prize 1981; Hon. LL.D. (Nebraska) 1965; Dr.

h.c. (Nice) 1973; hon. degrees also from Univs. of Glasgow, Anatolia, Bosporus, Baghdad, Marmara and Ain Shams; Fellow, Royal Coll. of Physicians (London) 1971; Grand Officier, Duarte, Sanchez y Mella 1976, Officier, Légion d'honneur 1978, Commdr., Order of the Lion of Finland (First Class). *Publications:* Annenin Kitabi—Mother's Handbook on Child Care 1952-84, Premature Baby Care 1954, ed. Turkish Journal of Pediatrics. *Address:* Turkish and International Children's Center, P.K. 2, 06572 Maltepe, Ankara, Turkey. *Telephone:* (90) 4-2234822.

DOHA, Aminur Rahman S., B.A., B.SC.; Bangladesh diplomatist; b. 24 Jan. 1929, Murshidabad; s. of A. H. M. Shams-ud Doha and Begum Hamida Shams-ud Doha; m.; two s.; Asst. Man. Imperial Tobacco Co., Ltd., 1948-50; commissioned 1952, Regimental Officer, Artillery Regts. 1952-61; School of Artillery and Guided Missiles, Oklahoma 1957-58; Command and Gen. Staff Coll., Quetta 1962; Gen. Staff Infantry Brigade HQ 1963; Royal Mil. Coll. of Science and Tech., Shrivenham 1964-65; Sr. Instructor, Gunnery 1965; Gen. Staff GHQ 1965-66; retd. from Army 1967; Ed. and Publr. Interwing, Rawalpindi 1968-71; Gen. Sec. Awami League, Rawalpindi 1969-71; Amb. to Yugoslavia and Romania 1972-74, to Iran and Turkey 1974-77; High Commr. in U.K. 1977-82; Minister of Information 1982-83, of Foreign Affairs 1982-84; fmr. Head, Ministry of Irrigation and Flood Control; del. to Non-Aligned Summits 1973, 1976, 1979; C.-in-C.'s commendation 1964; several mil. awards and decorations; Order of the Lance and Flag (Yugoslavia). *Publications:* Arab-Israeli War 1967, Aryans on the Indus. *Address:* Farm View, Indra Road, Tejgaon, Dhaka 15, Bangladesh (Home).

DOHERTY, Peter Charles, PH.D., F.A.A., F.R.S.; Australian research immunologist; b. 15 Oct. 1940, Brisbane; s. of Eric C. Doherty and Linda Doherty; m. Penelope Stephens 1965; two s.; ed. Indooroopilly High School and Univs. of Queensland and Edinburgh; veterinary officer, Queensland Dept. of Primary Industries 1963-66; Scientific Officer, Sr. Scientific Officer, Moredun Research Inst. Edinburgh 1967-71; Research Fellow, John Curtin School of Medical Research, Canberra 1972-75; Assoc. mem., mem. Wistar Inst. Philadelphia 1975-82; Prof. Dept. of Experimental Pathology, John Curtin School of Medical Research 1982-88; Chair. Dept. of Immunololgy, St. Jude Children's Research Hosp. Memphis 1988-; Paul Ehrlich Prize for Immunology 1983; Gairdner Int. Award for Medical Research 1986. *Publications:* 180 scientific papers and review articles. *Leisure interests:* reading, walking, skiing. *Address:* c/o St. Jude Children's Research Hospital, P.O. Box 318, Memphis, Tenn. 38101, U.S.A. *Telephone:* 901-522-0300.

DOHNÁNYI, Christoph von (see von Dohnányi, Christoph).

DOHNANYI, Klaus von (see von Dohnanyi, Klaus).

DOI, Takako; Japanese politician; b. 1929; fmr. univ. lecturer on Japanese constitution; mem. Lower House (Diet) 1969-; Leader, Japanese Socialist Party (JSP) Sept. 1986-. *Leisure interests:* singing, pachinko. *Address:* c/o Japanese Socialist Party, 1-8-1 Nagata-cho, Chiyoda-ku, Tokyo, Japan.

DOINAS, Stefan Augustin; Romanian writer; b. 26 April 1922, Caporal Alexa, Arad County; s. of Stefan Augustin Popa and Florita Popa; m. Silvia Lia Voicu 1958; ed. Coll. of Philology and Philosophy, Cluj Univ.; teacher 1948-55; Ed. of periodicals: Teatrul 1956-57, Lumea 1963-66, Secolul 20 1969-; deputy Ed.-in-chief of Secolul 20; Sec. of the Romanian Writers' Union; awards for poetry of the Romanian Writers' Union; the Prize of the Romanian Acad.; the Goethe medal for translations. *Works include:* vols of poetry Man with Compass 1966, Laokoon's Descendants 1967; Hypostases 1968, Hesperia 1980, Falcon Hunting 1985; essays; translations from Goethe, Dante, Hölderlin, Mallarmé and others. *Address:* 35 Bulevar 1848, Bucharest 70051, Romania. *Telephone:* 14.61.19.

DOJE CEDAIN; Chinese government official; b. 1924; m. Gesang Zhuoga; ed. Beijing Normal Univ.; Gov. of Xizang (Tibet) Autonomous Region 1983-85; Researcher, Inst. of Research on World Religions, Chinese Acad. of Social Sciences 1985-; Adviser United Front Work Dept. under CCP Cen. Cttee. 1986-; mem. Standing Cttee 6th NPC 1986-; Vice-Chair. Educ., Science, Culture and Public Health Cttee. under the NPC 1986-; Deputy Head China-Spain Friendship Group 1986-. *Address:* Chinese Academy of Social Sciences, 5 Jianguomen Nei Da Jie, Beijing, People's Republic of China.

DOJE CERING; Chinese (Tibetan) government official; b. 1938, Xiahe Co., Gansu Prov.; worked in Tibet 1959; country magistrate in Tibet 1962; mem. Tibet Autonomous Region CCP 1974-; mem., Standing Cttee. Tibet CCP 1977-; First Sec., Xigaze Municipality CCP 1979-82; Vice-Chair. Tibet Autonomous Region 1983-85, Acting Admin. Head 1986-88, Chair. 1988-. *Address:* Government of Xizang Autonomous Region, Lhasa City, People's Republic of China.

DOLAN, Beverly Franklin; American business executive; b. 1927, Augusta, Ga.; m.; ed. Univ. Georgia and Harvard Univ.; served with U.S. army 1952-54; Pres. and co-founder E-Z Go Car Corpn. 1954-60; joined Textron Inc. 1980, Pres. Homelit Div. 1976-79, Corpn. Exec. Vice-Pres. (Operations) 1979-80, Pres. and C.O.O. 1980-85, Pres., C.E.O. 1985-, Chair. 1986-, also Dir.; Dir. First Union Corpn., Alledale Mutual Insurance Co. *Address:* Textron Inc., 40 Westminister Street, Providence, R.I. 02903, U.S.A. (Office).

DOLANC, Stane; Yugoslav politician; b. 1925, Hrastnik, Slovenia; ed. Faculty of Law, Univ. of Ljubljana; active in Liberation Front of Slovenia 1941; mem. Nat. Liberation Army 1944; various mil. and political positions in Yugoslav People's Army –1960; mem. League of Communists of Yugoslavia (LCY) 1944–89; mem. Ass. of Socialist Repub. of Slovenia; Dir. Higher School of Political Science, Ljubljana 1963–67; mem. Cen. Cttee. LCY of Slovenia 1964–89, mem. Presidency of Cen. Cttee., Exec. Cttee. of Cen. Cttee.; Sec. Univ. Cttee. of League of Communists of Ljubljana 1967–; mem. Presidency of Cen. Cttee. and of Exec. Bureau of the Presidium, LCY 1968–89, Sec. Exec. Bureau 1972–78, Sec. 1978–79; Fed. Sec. for Internal Affairs 1982–84; mem. Fed. Exec. Council 1984–85; Vice-Pres. Collective State Presidency 1988–; numerous Yugoslav and foreign decorations. *Address:* Federal Executive Council, Bulevar Lenjina 2, 11075 Novi Beograd, Yugoslavia.

DOLCI, Danilo; Italian writer and social worker; b. 28 June 1924, Sesana (Trieste); ed. Faculty of Architecture, Milan Polytechnic; collaborated with Saltini, founder of Christian community Nomadelfia; social work in Sicily 1952; opened centres for study on problem of providing organic development for a traditionally under-employed population 1958; Head Centro Studi Partinico; Premio della Bontà, Milan 1954, Lenin Peace Prize 1958, Laurea philosophiae h.c. (Berne) 1968, Sonning Prize 1971, Premio Internazionale di Poesia Taormina 1975, Premio Gallileo, Pisa, 1988. *Publications:* Banditi a Partinico 1955, To Feed the Hungry 1959, Spreco 1960, Conversazioni 1962, Verso un mondo nuovo 1964, Chi gioca solo 1966, Chissà se i pesci piangono 1972, Esperienze e riflessioni 1974, Creatura di creature 1979, Da bocca a bocca 1981, The World is a Creature 1984, Palpitare di nessi 1985, Occhi Ancora Rimangono Sepolti 1987, Dal Transmettere al Communicare 1988, Bozzi di Manifesto 1989. *Address:* Centro Studi e Iniziative, Largo Scalia 5, Partinico (Palermo), Sicily, Italy. *Telephone:* (091) 8781905.

DOLE, Elizabeth Hanford, M.A., J.D.; American government official; b. 29 July 1936, Salisbury, N.C.; d. of John Van Hanford and Mary E. Cathey; m. Robert J. Dole (q.v.) 1975; ed. Duke and Harvard Univs. and Univ. of Oxford; called to Bar, Dist. of Columbia 1966; Staff Asst. to Asst. Sec. for Educ., Dept. of Health, Educ. and Welfare 1966–67; practising lawyer, Washington, D.C. 1967–68; Assoc. Dir. Legis. Affairs, then Exec. Dir. Pres.'s Comm. for Consumer Interests 1968–71; Deputy Dir. Office of Consumer Affairs, The White House, Washington, D.C. 1971–73; Commr. Fed. Trade. Comm. 1973–79; Asst. to Pres. for Public Liaison 1981–83; Sec. of Transport 1983–87; nominated Sec. of Labor Jan. 1989. *Address:* c/o Department of Labor, 200 Constitution Avenue, N.W., Washington, D.C. 20210, U.S.A.

DOLE, Robert; American politician: b. 22 July 1923, Russell, Kan.; s. of Mr. and Mrs. Doran R. Dole; m. Elizabeth Hanford Dole (q.v.) 1975; one d.; ed. Russell public schools, Univ. of Kansas and Washburn Municipal Univ.; mem. Kansas Legislature 1951–53; Russell County Attorney 1953–61; mem. House of Reps. 1960–68; U.S. Senator from Kansas 1968–; House Majority Leader 1985–87, Minority leader Jan. 1987–; Chair. Republican Nat. Cttee. 1971–72; Vice-Presidential Cand. 1976; Chair. Senate Finance Cttee. 1981–84; Dir. Mainstream Inc.; Adviser, U.S. Del. to FAO Conf., Rome 1965, 1974, 1977; mem. Congressional del. to India 1966, Middle East 1967; mem. U.S. Helsinki Comm., del. to Belgrade Conf. 1977; Trustee, William Allen White Foundation, Univ. of Kan.; mem. Nat. Advisory Cttee., The John Wesley Colls.; mem. American Bar Assocn.; mem. Nat. Advisory Cttee. on Scouting for the Handicapped, Kan. Assocn. for Retarded Children, Advisory Bd. of United Cerebral Palsy, Kan.; Hon. mem. Advisory Bd. of Kidney Patients Inc.; Republican. *Address:* 141 Hart Senate Office Building, Washington, D.C. 20510, U.S.A. *Telephone:* 202-224 6521.

DOLGIKH, Vladimir Ivanovich, M.SC.; Soviet politician; b. 5 Dec. 1924, Ilawskoi, Krasnoyarsk Krai; ed. Irkutsk Mining Institute; mem. CPSU 1942–; Army service 1941–43; Chief engineer at various plants in Krasnoyarsk 1949–58, Chief engineer 1958–62; Dir. of Zavenyagin Metallurgical Combine, Norilsk 1962–69; First Sec. Krasnoyarsk Krai Cttee., CPSU 1969–72; mem. of Cen. Cttee. CPSU 1971–, Sec. 1972–; Deputy Head of CC Dept. 1976–; Deputy to U.S.S.R. Supreme Soviet 1966–; cand. mem. Politburo of Cen. Cttee. 1986–88; Order of Lenin (six times), Hero of Socialist Labour 1965 and other decorations. *Address:* Central Committee of the CPSU, Moscow, U.S.S.R.

DOLGOPLOSK, Boris Aleksandrovich; Soviet organic chemist; b. 12 Nov. 1905, Lukoml, Byelorussia; ed. Moscow Univ.; at synthetic rubber plants 1932–46; on staff of Prof. Yaroslavl Tech. Inst. 1944–46; Assoc. All-Union Research Inst. of Synthetic Rubber 1946–61; Assoc., Inst. of High Molecular Compounds, U.S.S.R. Acad. of Sciences 1948–61; Inst. of Petrochemical Synthesis, U.S.S.R. Acad. of Sciences 1963–; mem. CPSU 1945–; Corresp. mem. U.S.S.R. Acad. of Sciences 1958–64, mem. 1964–; State Prize 1941, 1949, Lebedev Prize of U.S.S.R. Acad. of Sciences 1949, 1963; Lenin Prize 1984; Hero of Socialist Labour, Order of Lenin (twice), other awards. *Address:* Institute of Petrochemical Synthesis of the U.S.S.R. Academy of Sciences, Leninsky Prospekt 29, Moscow V-71, U.S.S.R. *Telephone:* 232-04-86.

DOLL, Sir (William) Richard (Shaboe), Kt., O.B.E., F.R.S., M.D., D.SC., F.R.C.P.; British epidemiologist and medical researcher; b. 28 Oct. 1912, Hampton;

s. of William and Kathleen Doll; m. Joan Faulkner (née Blatchford) 1946; one s. one d.; ed. Westminster School and St. Thomas's Hospital Medicial School, Univ. of London; Military Service 1939–45; with Medical Research Council's Statistical Research Unit 1948–69, Dir. 1961–69; mem. Advisory Cttee. on Medical Research WHO 1963, Council of Int. Epidemiological Asscn. 1961, Scientific Cttee. Int. Agency for Cancer Research 1965–70, 1975–78, Hebdomadal Council, Oxford Univ. 1975–81; Regius Prof. of Medicine, Oxford 1969–79, Warden Green Coll. 1979–83; Hon. Consultant, Imperial Cancer Research Fund, Cancer Epidemiology Unit, Radcliffe Infirmary, Oxford 1983–; mem. Royal Comm. on Environmental Pollution 1973–79; Comm. on Energy and the Environment 1978–81; Foreign Hon. mem. Norwegian Acad. of Sciences 1976, New York Acad. of Arts and Sciences 1977; Hon. Assoc. Physician Central Middx. Hospital 1949–69; David Anderson Berry Prize, Royal Soc. of Edin. (jointly) 1958, Bisset Hawkins Medal, Royal Coll. of Physicians, London 1962, UN Award for Cancer Research 1962, Rock Carling Fellow, Nuffield Provincial Hospitals Trust, London 1967, Gairdner Award 1970, Buchanan Medal, Royal Soc. 1972, Presidential Award, New York Acad. of Sciences 1975, Prix Griffuel, Paris 1975, John Snow Award, Epidemiology Section, American Public Health Asscn. 1976, Gold Medal, Royal Inst. of Public Health 1977, Charles S. Mott Prize for Prevention of Cancer 1979, Nat. Award, American Cancer Soc. 1981, Gold Medal, B.M.A. 1983, Wilhelm Conrad Röntgen Prize, Accademia dei Lincei 1984, Johann-Georg-Zimmermann Preis, Hanover 1985, Founders' Award, Chemical Inst. of Toxicology 1986, Royal Medal, Royal Soc. 1986, Alton Ochsner Award (jtly) 1988; Hon. D.Sc. Med. (Univ. of London) 1988. *Publications:* Articles on causes of cancer, aetiology of lung cancer, leukaemia, epidemiology, effects of ionizing radiations, oral contraceptives, treatment of gastric ulcers, etc. *Leisure interests:* conversation, good food. *Address:* 12 Rawlinson Road, Oxford, England. *Telephone:* Oxford 58887.

DOLLEZHAL, Nikolay Antonovich; Soviet academician and power engineering scientist; b. 27 Oct. 1899, Omelnik, Ukraine; ed. Moscow Higher Tech. School; Lecturer, Inst. of Nat. Economy, and Moscow Higher Tech. School 1923–32; Tech. Dir. Leningrad Inst. of Nitrogen Production Equipment 1932–34; Chief Eng. Kiev "Bolshevik" plant 1935–38; Dir. Moscow Research Inst. of Chemical Machinery 1942–53; Dir. Power Eng. Inst. of the U.S.S.R. State Atomic Energy Cttee. 1953–; mem. Bureau of Dept. of Physico—Tech. Problems of Energy of U.S.S.R. Acad. of Sciences 1953–62; corresp. mem. U.S.S.R. Acad. of Sciences 1953–62, mem. (Dept. Tech. Science), U.S.S.R. Acad. of Sciences 1962–; State Prize (four), Lenin Prize 1957, Hero of Socialist Labour 1949, Order of Lenin (four), Hammer and Sickle Gold Medal, etc. *Publications:* The Principles of Designing Steam Operated Power Units 1933, Theory of Compressor Valves 1941, Reactor of Atomic Power Station of U.S.S.R. Academy of Sciences 1956; Uranium-graphite reactors in power stations with steam heating 1957. *Address:* U.S.S.R. Academy of Sciences, 14 Leninsky Prospekt, Moscow, U.S.S.R.

DOLLFUS, Audouin, D. ÈS SC.; French astronomer; b. 12 Nov. 1924, Paris; s. of Charles Dollfus and Suzanne Soubeyran; m. Catherine Browne 1959; four c.; ed. Univ. de Paris; joined Observatoire de Meudon (astrophysical div. of Observatoire de Paris) 1946, now Head of Lab. for Physics of the Solar System; Astronomer, Observatoire de Paris 1965–; mem. Int. Acad. of Astronautics, Société Astronomique de France (Pres. 1979–81); Hon. mem. Royal Astronomical Soc. of Canada, Astronomy and Geophysics Soc. of U.S.S.R.; Assoc. Royal Astronomical Soc., London, Soc. Philomatique de Paris; Prize of Acad. des Sciences, Int. Award Galabert for Astronautics. *Publications:* 290 scientific publications on astrophysics. *Leisure interest:* ballooning (holds three official world records with gas balloons: duration, distance, altitude). *Address:* 77 rue Albert Perdreaux, 92370 Chaville, France. *Telephone:* 47-50-97-43.

DOLLING, Francis Robert; British banker; b. 21 Jan. 1923, London; s. of Frederick George Dolling and Edith Lilian Auriel Dolling; m. Maisie Alice Noquet 1949; two d.; ed. Tottenham County School; served with R.A.F. 1940–47; with Barclays Bank 1947–, Man. Dir. Barclays Nat. Bank Ltd., S. Africa 1974–76; Dir. and Sr. Gen. Man. Barclays Bank Int. Ltd. (now Barclays Int. Ltd.) 1976–80, Chair. 1983–85, 1985–; Dir. Barclays Bank Ltd. (now Barclays Bank PLC) 1976–80, Vice-Chair. 1980–82, Deputy Chair. 1983–85; Chair. Barclays Merchant Bank Ltd. 1980–85. *Leisure interests:* gardening, golf. *Address:* Barclays International Ltd., 54 Lombard Street, London, EC3P 3AH (Office); Rowan Cottage, The Ridgway, Pyrford, Surrey, England (Home). *Telephone:* 01-283 8989 (Office), Byfleet 43362 (Home).

DOLLINGER, Werner, DR. RER. POL.; German politician and industrialist; b. 10 Oct. 1918, Neustadt/Aisch; s. of Richard and Lisette (née Hösch) Dollinger; m. Herta Dehn 1945; one s. two d.; ed. School of Commerce, Nuremberg and Frankfurt Univ.; mil. service 1943–45; Chair. Neustadt Chamber of Commerce and Industry 1948; founder mem. of CSU and Neustadt Town Councillor 1946–; Dist. Chair. CSU 1951; Dist. Councillor 1952–; mem. Bundestag and CDU/CSU Parl. group 1953–; mem. ECSC Common Assembly 1956–58; Deputy Chair. CSU Land chapter in Bundestag 1957–62; Chair. CDU/CSU working cttee. on budget, finance and taxes 1957–62; Deputy Chair. CSU and Minister of Fed. Property 1962–66; Minister of Posts and Telecommunications 1966–69, of Transport 1982–87; Deputy Chair. CSU Land Chapter in Bundestag; Chair. CSU working group foreign affairs and defence, Chair. CDU/CSU working cttee. on Agric., Traffic and Housing. *Leisure interests:* tennis, skiing, swimming, walking. *Address:* Bundeshaus, 53 Bonn (Office); 30 Hampfergrundweg, 8530 Neustadt/Aisch, Federal Republic of Germany (Home).

DOLMAN, Claude Ernest, M.B., B.S., D.P.H., PH.D., F.R.C.P. (London), F.R.C.P. (Canada), F.R.S.C.; Canadian medical bacteriologist and writer; b. 23 May 1906, Porthleven, Cornwall, England; s. of John E. Dolman and Peternal E. Holloway; m. 1st Ursula Coray 1931, 2nd Clarisse Askanazy 1955; four s. two d.; ed. Wallingford Grammar School, Christ's Hospital, St. Mary's Hospital Medical School and several other London hospitals; Research and Clinical Assoc., Connaught Labs., Univ. of Toronto 1931-35, Research mem. 1935-72, Consultant 1972-73; Dir. Div. of Labs., Provincial Dept. of Health of British Columbia 1935-56, Acting Head Dept. of Nursing and Health, Univ. of British Columbia 1935-43, Prof. and Head 1943-51; Prof. and Head of Dept. of Bacteriology and Preventive Medicine, Univ. of B.C. 1936-51, Dept. of Bacteriology and Immunology 1951-65, Research Prof. Dept. of Microbiology 1965-71; Prof. Emer. of Microbiology 1971-; Hon. Lecturer Dept. of History of Medicine and Science 1964-; Assoc. Ed. Journal of Immunology 1946-57; Pres. Canadian Asscn. of Medical Bacteriologists 1964-66; Pres. Royal Soc. of Canada 1969-70; Hon. life mem. Canadian Asscn. of Medical Microbiologists 1971-, Canadian Public Health Asscn. 1973-, American Soc. for Microbiology 1977-, Int. Northwest Conf. on Diseases in Nature Communicable to Man 1978-; Cheadle Gold Medal for Medicine (St. Mary's Hospital) 1929, Coronation Medal 1953, Silver Jubilee Medal 1978. *Publications:* Bacterial Food Poisoning 1943, Report on a Survey of Medical Education in Canada and the United States 1946, Science and the Humanities 1950, The Epidemiology of Meat-Borne Diseases 1957, Type E Botulism: its Epidemiology, Prevention and Specific Treatment 1963, Water Resources of Canada (Editor) 1967, Bacteriophages of Clostridium botulinum 1972, Science as a Way of Life 1974; also numerous articles in scientific and medical journals on staphylococcus toxins, botulinus toxins and botulism, salmonella infections, brucellosis, etc., general public health and the history of microbiology; contributor to the Dictionary of Scientific Biography. *Leisure interests:* antiquarian, gardening. *Address:* 1611 Cedar Crescent, Vancouver B.C. V6J 2P8, Canada. *Telephone:* 604-738-8374 (Home).

DOLMATOVSKY, Yevgeniy Aronovich; Soviet poet; b. 5 May 1915, Moscow; s. of Aron and Adel Dolmatovsky; ed. Moscow Literature Inst.; Prof., Moscow Literature Inst.; mem. CP 1941-; State Prizewinner 1949; Orders of Great Patriotic War (1st Class), of Red Star, Badge of Honour, Red Banner of Labour (twice), of October Revolution, Order of Lenin and other decorations. *Publications:* Anthologies: Lyrics 1934, Song of the Dnieper 1942, Notes on the Steppes 1945, A Word About the Future 1959, African Poems 1961; Novel in verse Volunteers 1956, 1969, 1976; Selected Works 1959, Years and Songs 1963, Poems about Us 1964, Life of Lyrics 1965, Selected Works 1965, The Last Kiss 1967, The Girl in White 1968, Happiness, Ballads, Songs 1970, Selected Works (2 vols.) 1971, Victory Autographs 1972, Stories of your Songs 1973, I Ask the Floor 1974, It Was . . . (A Poet's Notes) Vol. 1 1975, Vol. 2 1979, Both Song and Poem 1975, Worries of Hope 1977, Collected Works 1978-79 (3 vols.), Spanish Themes 1980, Interpoems 1982, Green Brama 1983, 1985, 1989, I am to Say 1984, Poems 1985, Songs on Words of Yevgeniy Dolmatovsky 1986, Poetry from my Diary 1986, Comrade, My . . . 1987, It was . . . (A Poet's Notes) Vol. 3 1988. *Leisure interests:* driving, cooking. *Address:* Writers' Union, Ul. Vorovskogo 52, Moscow, U.S.S.R.

DOLMETSCH, Carl Frederick, C.B.E.; British musician; b. 23 Aug. 1911, Fontenay-sous-Bois, France; s. of Arnold Dolmetsch and Mabel Johnston; m. (dissolved); two s. (one deceased) two d.; ed. privately; first public concert performance at age of 7, and first concert tour aged 8; toured Alaska, Australia, Austria, Belgium, Canada, Colombia, Denmark, France, Germany, Netherlands, Italy, Japan, New Zealand, Sweden, Switzerland and the U.S.A.; Dir. Soc. of Recorder Players 1937-; Dir. Haslemere Festival of Early Music and Instruments 1940-, Dolmetsch Int. Summer School 1971-; Man. Dir. Arnold Dolmetsch Ltd. 1940-76, Chair. 1963-78; Chair. Dolmetsch Musical Instruments 1982-; mem. Art Workers' Guild, I.S.M.; Hon. Fellow, Trinity Coll. of Music (London), London Coll. of Music; Hon. D.Litt. (Exeter). *Publications:* many editions of recorder music; books on recorder playing 1957, 1962, 1970 and 1977. *Leisure interests:* ornithology, natural history. *Address:* Jesses, Haslemere, Surrey, England. *Telephone:* Haslemere 3818.

DOMB, Cyril, M.A., PH.D., F.R.S.; British professor of physics; b. London; s. of Joel and Sarah (nee Wulkan) Domb; m. Shirley Galinsky 1957; three s. three d.; ed. Hackney Downs School, London, Pembroke Coll., Cambridge; Fellow, Clarendon Lab., Oxford 1949-52; Univ. Lecturer in Mathematics, Cambridge 1952-54; Prof. of Theoretical Physics, London Univ. 1954-81; Prof. of Physics, Bar Ilan Univ., Israel 1981-; Academic Pres. Jerusalem Coll. of Technology 1985-; Rayleigh Prize 1947, Max Born Prize 1981. *Publications:* Co-operative Phenomena in Crystals, in Advances in Physics 1960, Phase Transitions and Critical Phenomena, Vols. 1-6 (ed. with M. S. Green), vols. 7-11 (ed. with J. L. Lebowitz), Challenge—Torah views on science and its problems (ed. with A. Carmell) 1976. *Leisure interests:* walking, swimming. *Address:* c/o Bar Ilan University, Ramat Gan, Israel; 28 St. Peter's Court, Queen's Road, London, N.W.4, England.

DOMENICI, Pete V., B.S., LL.B.; American senator; b. 7 May 1932; s. of Choppo and Alda Domenici; m. Nancy Burk 1958; two s. six d.; ed. Univs of Albuquerque, New Mexico, Denver; elected to Albuquerque City Comm. 1966, Chair. 1967; mem. Nat. League of Cities Revenue and Finance Steering Cttee. and the Resolutions Cttee. of the 1969 Annual Conf. of Mayors; served on Governor's Policy Bd. for Law Enforcement and on Middle Rio Grande Conf. of Govts.; U.S. Senator from New Mexico 1973-; Chair. Senate Budget Cttee. 1981-; Republican. *Leisure interests:* hunting, fishing. *Address:* Suite 434, Dirksen Senate Office Building, Washington, D.C. 20510 (Office); 11110 Stephalee Lane, Rockville, Md. 20852, U.S.A. (Home).

DOMERACKI, Lech, D.IUR.; Polish lawyer and politician; b. 17 Sept. 1929, Poznań; s. of Leon Domeracki and Apolonia Etter; m. 1955; one s.; ed. Faculty of Law, Poznań Univ.; successively apprentice, Dept. of Justice, assessor, judge, Dist. Court, Vice-Pres. Dist. Court, judge Voivodship Court, Poznań, Vice-Pres. Voivodship Court, Poznań, Dir. of Dept., Ministry of Justice, Pres. Voivodship Court, Poznań; Minister of Justice 1983-88; mem. PZPR 1955-; Golden Cross of Merit, Kt.'s and Officer's Cross of Order of Polonia Restituta, and other distinctions. *Leisure interests:* tourism, belles-lettres, history. *Address:* c/o Ministerstwo Sprawiedliwości, Al. Ujazdowskie 11, 00-567 Warsaw, Poland. *Telephone:* (28) 44-31.

DOMIN, Hilde, PH.D.; German author; b. 27 July 1912, Cologne; m. 1st Erwin W. Palm 1936, 2nd 1988; ed. Univs. of Heidelberg, Cologne, Berlin, Rome, Florence; language teacher, U.K., Prof., Univ. of Santo Domingo 1948-53; has given readings and lectures throughout Germany since 1961, also in U.S.A., Canada, U.K., throughout Europe and overseas; mem. Deutsche Akad. für Sprache und Dichtung, PEN; several medals and prizes including Rilke Prize 1976 and Nelly-Sachs Prize 1983. *Publications include:* poetry: Nur eine Rose als Stütze 1959, Rückkehr der Schiffe 1962, Hier 1964, Ich Will Dich 1970; Das zweite Paradies (novel) 1968 (original text 1986), Wozu Lyrik heute (essays) 1968, Von der Natur nicht Vorgesehen (autobiog.) 1974, Aber die Hoffnung: Autob. aus und über Deutschland 1982, Gesammelte Gedichte 1951-86 1987, Das Gedicht als Augenblick von Freiheit Frankfurter Poetik-vor-lasungen 1988. *Leisure interests:* literature, music, nature. *Address:* Graimbergweg 5, 69 Heidelberg, Federal Republic of Germany. *Telephone:* 06221/12545.

DOMINGO, Placido; Spanish opera singer; b. 21 Jan. 1941, Madrid; s. of the late Placido and Pepita (Embil) Domingo; m. Marta Ornelas; three s.; ed. Nat. Conservatory of Music, Mexico City; operatic début at Monterrey, Mexico 1961; début at Metropolitan Opera, New York, 1968; British début in Verdi's Requiem at Festival Hall 1969; Covent Garden début in Tosca 1971, returned to sing in Aïda, Carmen 1973, La Bohème 1974, Un ballo in maschera 1975, La Fanciulla del West; has taken leading roles in about 50 operas; with New York City Opera 1965-; Dr. h.c. (Royal Coll. of Music) 1982; Commdr. Légion d'honneur; recent engagements include Tosca (conducting), Romeo and Juliet at Metropolitan Opera, New York, N.Y., Aïda, Il Trovatore in Hamburg, Don Carlos in Salzburg, I vespri siciliani and La forza del destino in Paris, Turandot in Barcelona, Otello in Paris, London and Hamburg, Carmen in Edinburgh, Turandot at the Metropolitan, New York; film: Madame Butterfly with Von Karajan, La Traviata 1982; stage debut in My Fair Lady 1988; recent recordings include: Aïda, Un ballo in maschera, Tosca. *Publication:* My First Forty Years (autobiog.) 1984. *Address:* c/o Metropolitan Opera Company, Lincoln Center Plaza, New York, N.Y. 10023; c/o E. Semon Associates Inc., 111 West 57th Street, New York, N.Y. 10019, U.S.A.

DOMINIAN, Jacobus, D.SC., F.R.C.P.(E.), F.R.C.PSY.; British psychiatrist; b. 25 Aug. 1929, Athens, Greece; s. of Charles Dominian and Mary Scarlato; m. Edith Mary Smith 1955; four d.; ed. St. Mary's School, Bombay, Stamford Grammar School, England, Fitzwilliam Coll., Cambridge, Exeter Coll., Oxford and Inst. of Psychiatry, London; Sr. House Officer United Oxford Hosps. 1955-58; Registrar Maudsley Hosp., London 1958-61, Sr. Registrar 1961-64; Consultant Psychiatrist Cen. Middx. Hosp., London 1965-; Dir. Marriage Research Centre 1971-. *Publications:* Christian Marriage 1967, Marital Breakdown 1968, Depression 1976, Proposals for a New Sexual Ethic 1976, Authority 1976, Marital Pathology 1980, Marriage, Faith and Love 1981, The Capacity to Love 1985, Sexual Integrity: the answer to AIDS 1987. *Leisure interests:* swimming, theatre, music and reading. *Address:* Pefka, The Green, Croxley Green, Rickmansworth, Herts., WD3 3JA, England. *Telephone:* 0923-720972.

DOMITIEN, Elisabeth; Central African Republic politician; fmr. mem. Mouvement d'évolution sociale de l'Afrique noire (MESAN), Vice-Pres. 1975-79; imprisoned Nov. 1979, on trial Feb. 1980; Prime Minister of Central African Repub. 1975-76.

DOMOTO, Hisao; Japanese painter; b. 1928; ed. Kyoto Acad. of Fine Arts; First Prize, Acad. of Japan 1951 and 1953; studied in France, Italy and Spain 1952; settled in Paris 1955; abandoned traditional Japanese style and exhibited abstract paintings Salon des Indépendants, Salon de Mai, Paris 1956, 1957; rep. at Rome/New York Art Foundation first exhbn. Rome, "Otro Arte" Exhbn. Madrid, Facchetti and Stadler Galleries, Paris 1957; First Prize of Musée d'Art Moderne for foreign painters in Paris 1958; one-man exhbn. Martha Jackson Gallery, New York 1959.

DONABEDIAN, Avedis, B.A., M.D.; American physician and professor of public health; b. 7 Jan. 1919, Beirut, Lebanon; s. of Samuel Donabedian and Maritza (née Der Hagopian) Donabedian; m. Dorothy Salibian 1945; three s.; ed. Friends' Boys' School, Ramallah (Palestine), American Univ. of Beirut and Harvard Univ. School of Public Health, U.S.A.; Teaching Fellow in Pharmacology, American Univ. of Beirut 1938-40; Physician, then Acting Supt., English Mission Hosp., Jerusalem 1945-47; Instructor in Physiology, Clinical Asst. in Venereology, American Univ. of Beirut 1948-50, Physician, then Dir. Univ. Health Service 1951-54; Medical Assoc., Medical Care Evaluation Studies, United Community Services of Metropolitan Boston, Mass., U.S.A. 1955-57; Research Assoc., then Visiting Lecturer, Harvard School of Public Health 1955-57; Asst. Prof., then Assoc. Prof. of Preventive Medicine, New York Medical Coll. 1957-61; Assoc. Prof. of Public Health Econs., then Prof. of Public Health Econs., then Prof. of Medical Org., Univ. of Mich. School of Public Health 1961-79; Nathan Sinai Distinguished Prof. of Public Health, Univ. of Mich. 1979-; mem. Inst. of Medicine; several awards including Award in Recognition of a Distinguished Career in Health Services Research, Asscn. for Health Services Research 1985 and Baxter American Foundation Prize 1986. *Publications:* A Guide to Medical Care Administration: Vol. II, Medical Care Appraisal 1969, Aspects of Medical Care Administration 1973, Benefits in Medical Care Programs 1976, The Definition of Quality and Approaches to its Assessment 1980, The Criteria and Standards of Quality 1982, The Methods and Findings of Quality Assessment and Monitoring 1985. *Leisure interests:* gardening, photography, languages, literature and music. *Address:* Department of Health Services Management and Policy, School of Public Health, The University of Michigan, 109 South Observatory Street, Ann Arbor, Mich. 48109; 1739 Ivywood Drive, Ann Arbor, Mich. 48103, U.S.A. (Home). *Telephone:* (313) 764-5434 (Office); (313) 665-4565 (Home).

DONAHUE, Thomas Michael, PH.D.; American professor and atmospheric scientist; b. 23 May 1921, Healdton, Okla.; s. of Robert E. Donahue and Mary J. Lyndon; m. Esther McPherson 1950; three s.; ed. Rockhurst Coll. and Johns Hopkins Univ.; Asst. Prof., Prof. of Physics, Univ. of Pittsburgh 1951-74, Dir. Space Research Lab. 1966-74; Prof. of Atmospheric and Oceanic Science Univ. of Mich. 1974-87, Edward H. White II Distinguished Univ. Prof. of Planetary Science 1987-; mem. N.A.S., Univ. Space Science Bd. 1982-; mem. NASA Advisory Council 1982-; Chair. Science Steering Group, Pioneer Venus Mission 1974-; Chair. Cttee. on Solar Terrestial Research 1972-75; Chair. Atmospheric Sciences Advisory Panel 1968-72; mem. Cttee. on Atmospheric Science 1960-72, Rocket Research Cttee. 1966-69, Geophysics Research Forum (fmrly Bd.) 1972-75, 1982-, Climate Bd. 1979-82, Physical Science Cttee. 1972-76, Solar System Exploration Cttee. 1980-82; Henry Russel Lectureship, Univ. of Mich. 1986-; participated in Voyager Missions to Outer Planets 1977-, Galileo Mission to Jupiter 1976-; mem. NASA Science Center Assessment Study 1987-88; Fellow, American Physical Soc., A.A.A.S., American Geophysical Union (Pres. Solar Planetary Relations Section 1974-76); mem. American Astronomical Soc., Bd. of Trustees, Upper Atmosphere Research Corpn. 1968-80 (Chair. 1972), Univ. Space Research Corpn. for Atmospheric Research 1976-83 (Sec. 1978-[89], Vice-Chair. 1980-83), Int. Acad. of Astronautics 1987-; NASA Public Service Award 1977, Distinguished Public Service Medal 1980; Henry Arctowski Medal (N.A.S.) 1981; Fleming Medal, American Geophysical Union 1981; winner Space Science Award, American Inst. of Aeronautics and Astronautics 1987; Guggenheim Fellow (at Observatoire de Meudon, France) 1960; Hon. D.Sc. (Rockhurst Coll.) 1981. *Publications:* numerous scientific papers. *Leisure interests:* tennis, gardening, music (classical and traditional), Irish history. *Address:* Department of Atmospheric and Oceanic Science, University of Michigan, 2455 Hayward Avenue, Ann Arbor, Mich. 48109-2143, U.S.A. *Telephone:* (313) 763-2390.

DONALDSON, Charles Ian Edward, M.A., F.A.H.A.; British professor of English; b. 6 May 1935, Melbourne, Australia; s. of Dr. William Edward Donaldson and Elizabeth (née Weigall) Donaldson; m. Tamsin Jane Proctor 1962; one s. one d.; ed. Melbourne Grammar School, Melbourne Univ., Magdalen Coll., Oxford, Merton Coll., Oxford; Sr. Tutor in English, Melbourne Univ. 1958; Fellow and lecturer in English, Wadham Coll., Oxford 1962-69; CUF Lecturer in English, Oxford Univ. 1963-69; Chair. Oxford English Faculty 1968-69; Prof. of English, A.N.U. 1969-, Dir., Humanities Research Centre 1974-; visiting appointments at Univ. of Calif., Santa Barbara 1967-68, Gonville and Caius Coll., Cambridge 1985, Cornell Univ. 1988, Folger Shakespeare Library 1988; Corresp. Fellow of the British Acad. *Publications:* The World Upside Down: Comedy From Jonson to Fielding 1970, Ben Jonson: Poems (ed.) 1975, The Rapes of Lucretia: A Myth and its Transformations 1982, Jonson and Shakespeare (ed.) 1982, Transformations in Modern European Drama 1983, Seeing the First Australians (ed., with Tamsin Donaldson) 1985. *Address:* Humanities Research Centre, Australian National University, GPO Box 4, Canberra, A.C.T. 2601, Australia. *Telephone:* (062) 49-2700.

DONALDSON, Dame (Dorothy) Mary, G.B.E.; British local government official; b. 29 Aug. 1921, Wickham, Hants.; d. of late Reginald George Gale Warwick and Dorothy Alice Warwick; m. John Francis Donaldson (q.v.) 1945; one s. two d.; ed. Portsmouth High School of Girls, Wingfield Morris Orthopaedic Hosp., Middlesex Hosp., London; Chair. Women's Nat. Cancer Control Campaign 1967-69; Vice-Pres. British Cancer Council 1970; served

on numerous other medical and community bds. and Cttees.; Alderman, City of London (Ward of Coleman Street) 1975-, Sheriff 1981-82, first woman Lord Mayor of London 1983-84; Chair. Council responsible for Ombudsman in Banking 1985-; Hon. Fellow, Girton Coll.; Order of Oman 1982; Order of Bahrain 1984; Grand Officier, Ordre national du mérite (France) 1984; Pres.'s Medal of Inst. of Public Relations 1984; Hon. D.Sc. (City Univ.) 1983. *Leisure interests:* sailing, gardening, skiing. *Address:* c/o The Guildhall, London, E.C.2, England.

DONALDSON, Samuel Andrew, B.A.; American journalist; b. 11 March 1934, El Paso, Texas; s. of Samuel A. Donaldson and Chloe Hampson; m. 1st Billie K. Butler 1963; three s. one d.; m. 2nd Janice C. Smith 1983; ed. Univ. of Texas, El Paso and Univ. of S. Calif.; radio/TV news reporter/anchorman, WTOP, Washington 1961-67; Capitol Hill/corresp., ABC News, Washington 1967-77, White House Corresp. 1977-. *Address:* 1717 DeSales Street, N.W., Washington, D.C. 20036, U.S.A.

DONALDSON, Simon Kirwan, D.PHIL; British professor of mathematics; b. 20 Aug. 1957, Cambridge; s. of Peter Donaldson and Jane Stirland; m. Ana Nora Hurtado 1986; ed. Sevenoaks School, Kent, Pembroke Coll., Cambridge; Jr. Research Fellow, All Souls Coll., Oxford 1983-85; Wallis Prof. of Math., Oxford Univ. 1985-; Fields Medal 1986. *Leisure interest:* sailing. *Address:* 24-29 St. Giles, Oxford, OX1 3LB, England. *Telephone:* (0865) 54295.

DONALDSON OF KINGSBRIDGE, Baron (Life Peer), cr. 1967, of Kingsbridge; **John George Stuart Donaldson,** O.B.E.; British politician; b. 9 Oct. 1907; s. of Rev. S. A. Donaldson and Lady Albinia Donaldson (née Hobart-Hampden); m. Frances Annesley Lonsdale 1935; one s. two d.; ed. Eton and Trinity Coll., Cambridge; Pioneer Health Centre, Peckham 1935-38; Road Transport 1938-39; Royal Engineers 1939-45; farming in Glos., later Bucks. 1945-74; Parl. Under-Sec. of State, Northern Ireland Office 1974-76; Minister for the Arts 1976-79; Hon. Sec. Nat. Asscn. Discharged Prisoners Aid. Socs. 1961; Chair. Bd. of Visitors, H.M. Prison, Grendon 1963-69, Nat. Asscn. for Care and Resettlement of Offenders 1966-74, Consumer Council 1968-71, Nat. Cttee. for Family Service Units 1968-74, Cttee. of Inquiry into Conditions of Service for Young Servicemen 1969, Econ. Devt. Council for Hotel and Catering Industry 1972-74, British Fed. of Zoos; Pres. Royal Soc. for the Protection of Birds 1975-80; Chair. Apex Trust 1979-81; Dir. British Sugar Corpn. 1966-74; Dir. Royal Opera House, Covent Garden 1958-74, Sadler's Wells 1963-74; joined SDP April 1981, with SLD 1987. Spokesman in House of Lords on Northern Ireland, Arts and Penal Affairs. *Leisure interests:* music in general, opera in particular, golf. *Address:* 17 Edna Street, London, SW11 3DP; North Mays, Solmiston, East Sussex, England.

DONALDSON OF LYMINGTON, Baron (Life Peer), cr. 1988, of Lymington in the County of Hampshire; **John Francis Donaldson,** Kt.; British judge; b. 6 Oct. 1920, London; s. of Dr. M. Donaldson and Mrs. E. M. H. Maunsell; m. Dorothy M. Warwick (q.v.) 1945; one s. two d.; ed. Charterhouse School and Trinity Coll., Cambridge; called to the Bar, Middle Temple 1946; Judge of the High Court of Justice, Queen's Bench Div. 1966-79; Pres. Nat. Industrial Relations Court (NIRC) 1971-74; Pres. British Maritime Law Asscn. 1979-; Lord Justice of Appeal 1979-82; Chair. Advisory Council on Public Records 1982-; Master of the Rolls 1982-; Dr. h.c. (Essex) 1983, Hon. LL.D. (Sheffield) 1984. *Leisure interest:* sailing. *Address:* Royal Courts of Justice, Strand, London, W.C.2, England.

DO NASCIMENTO, H.E. Cardinal Alexandre; Angolan ecclesiastic; b. 1 March 1925, Malanje; s. of Antonio André do Nascimento and Maria Ana Alves da Rocha; ordained priest 1952; Bishop of Malanje 1975; Archbishop of Lubango 1977-86, of Luanda 1986-; Apostolic Admin. of Onjiva; mem. Sacred Congregation for the Propagation of the Faith and the Evangelization of the People; cr. Cardinal 1983; Pres. Caritas Internationalis; Preacher, Retreat of the Holy Father and the Roman Curia 1984; mem. Sacred Congregation Pro Culto Divino 1985. *Leisure interests:* reading, music. *Address:* Arcebispado, C.P. 87, Luanda, Angola. *Telephone:* 34640.

DONAT-CATTIN, Carlo; Italian journalist and politician; b. 26 June 1919, Finale Ligure; s. of Attilio Donat-Cattin and Maria Luisa Buraggi; m. Amelia Bramieri 1942; three s. one d.; trained as journalist; wrote for L'Italia until 1940, for Popolo Nuovo, Turin 1949-59; rep. Christian Democrat Party on Nat. Cttee. of Liberation, Ivrea and Canavese Dist.; joined Christian Democrat Regional Cttee. of Piedmont, Turin Prov. Cttee. and Nat. Council; mem. Cen. Cttee. Christian Democrat Party 1959-; helped organize Fed. of Ind. Labour Unions; fmr. mem. Gen. Council L.C.G.I.L., C.I.S.L. (Sec. of C.I.S.L., Turin 1948-56), Italian Catholic Action; elected to Chamber of Deputies 1958, 1963, 1968, 1972, 1976 for Turin constituency, to the Senate 1979, 1984; Under-Sec. for State Participations in 1st, 2nd and 3rd Moro govts. 1963-68; fmr. mem., Parl. Comm. to investigate Mafia; Minister of Labour and Social Security 1969-73; Minister without Portfolio in charge of Southern Devt. 1973-74; Minister of Trade and Industry 1974-78, of Health Aug. 1986-; Deputy Sec. Christian Democrat Party 1978-80. *Address:* Via Romagnano 27, 1-10145 Turin, Italy.

DONATH, Helen; American opera and concert singer; b. 10 July 1940, Corpus Christi, Tex.; d. of Jimmy Erwin and Helen Hamauei; m. Klaus Donath 1965; one s.; ed. Roy Miller High School, Del Mar Coll., Texas; studied with Paola Novikova, later with husband Klaus Donath (by whom all song-recitals are accompanied); début at Cologne Opera House 1962, at Hanover Opera House 1963-68, Bayerische Staatsoper, Munich 1968-72; guest appearances in London (Covent Garden), Vienna, Milan, San Francisco, Lisbon, etc.; has given concerts in all major European and American cities; major roles include, Pamina in Die Zauberflöte, Zerlina in Don Giovanni, Eva in Die Meistersinger, Sophie in Der Rosenkavalier, Susanna in Le Nozze di Figaro, Anne Trulove in the Rake's Progress, Ilia in Idomeneo, Micaela in Carmen; over 90 recordings 1962-; Pope Paul Medal, Salzburg 50 Year Anniversary Medal, Bratislava Festival Award, Deutscher Schallplattenpreis and Grosses Lob for her first song recital recording. *Leisure interests:* family, gardening, cooking, swimming, filming. *Address:* 3002 Wedemark 1, Bergstrasse 5, Federal Republic of Germany.

DONATI, Antigono; Italian banker; b. 20 Jan. 1910, Rome; s. of Giacomo and Olga Fano Donati; m. Margherita Flora; one s. one d.; ed. Liceo Tasso, Rome and Univs. of Rome and Padua; mem. Nat. Consultant. Assembly, Constituent Assembly, First Republican Parl. 1948-53; Pres. Italian Nat. Cttee. for Int. Econ. and Tech. Co-operation, Ministry of Foreign Affairs 1960-67; Pres. Cttee. of Tech. Co-operation, OECD 1963-66; Pres. Nat. Inst. for Foreign Trade 1965-69; Pres. Banca Nazionale del Lavoro 1967-78; Pres. Ente Finanziario Interbancario Efibanca 1968-85, Hon. Chair. 1985-; Pres. Int. de iure Assen. of Insurance Law, Luxembourg 1960-; Pres. Istituto Italiano di Studi Legislativi (ISLE) 1960-75, Istituto per lo Sviluppo Economico (ISVE) 1960-75; mem. bd. Istituto Nazionale delle Assicurazioni (INA) 1960-77, Le Assicurazioni d'Italia (Assitalia) 1960-77; mem. Consiglio Nazionale dell'Economia e del Lavoro (CNEL) 1961-; Prof. Univ. of Rome, Dean of Statistics Faculty 1954-72; Dr. jur. h.c. (Hamburg) and hon. Prof. Univs. of S. Calif. (Los Angeles), Mexico, Phoenix, Ariz.; Gold Medal for Culture and Arts 1960, INA Prize, Accad. Nazionale dei Lincei 1962, Cavaliere del Lavoro, Cavaliere di Gran Croce dell'Ordine al merito della Repubblica Italiana; honours of highest degree from Argentina, Brazil, Chile, Egypt, Finland, France, Fed. Repub. of Germany, Greece, Luxembourg, Mexico, Peru, Portugal and Spain. *Publications:* Il Contratto di assicurazione in abbonamento 1935, L'assicurazione per conto di chi spetta 1937, L'invalidità delle deliberazioni di assemblea di società anonime 1937, L'assicurazione nel Codice Civile, nel Commentario D'Amelio 1943, Trattato di diritto delle assicurazioni private (3 vols.) 1952-56, Manuale del Diritto delle assicurazioni 1956, Codice delle assicurazioni 1960, L'assicurazione nei Paesi del MEC 1963. *Address:* Via Cassia 1951, Rome, Italy.

DONATONI, Franco; Italian professor of musical composition; b. 9 June 1927, Verona; s. of Silvio Donatoni and Dolores Stefannuci; m. Susan Park 1958; one s. one d.; ed. Bologna and Rome; Prof. of Composition, Bologna 1953-55, Milan 1955-67, Turin 1967-69, Milan 1969; Docente, Advanced Course in Composition, Accad. Chigiana di Siena 1970; Marzotto Prize 1966, Koussevitsky Prize 1968 and other prizes for composition. *Works include:* Puppenspiel 1951, Sezioni 1960, Per Orchestra 1962, Quartetto IV 1963, Asar 1964, Puppenspiel (2) 1965, Souvenir 1967, Etwa ruhiger im Ausdruck 1967, Doubles II 1969-70, Questo 1970. *Address:* Via Bassini 39, 20133 Milan, Italy. *Telephone:* (02) 293408.

DONDELINGER, Albert Marie Joseph, D.JUR.; Luxembourg banker; b. 22 March 1934, Redange, Attert; s. of Jean Dondelinger and Simone Lamborelle; m. Francine Dandelinger-Gillen; one d.; ed. Coll. St. Michel, Brussels, Catholic Univ. of Louvain, Belgium; Alt. Gov. for Luxembourg, IBRD 1967-76; mem. European Monetary Cttee. 1971-76, Bd. of Belgium-Luxembourg Exchange Inst. 1972-76; Adviser to Group of Twenty and Assoc. mem. IMF Interim Cttee. 1972-76; mem. Bd. European Monetary Co-operation Fund and mem. Govs. Cttee., EEC Cen. Banks 1973-76; Govt. Commr. to State Savings Bank 1974-76; Co-Chair. Comm. for Financial Affairs of Conf. for Int. Econ. Co-operation (North-South Dialogue, Paris) 1975-76; Chair. Luxembourg Bankers' Assen. 1977-78; Man. Dir. and Chair. Exec. Bd., Banque Internationale à Luxembourg Jan. 1977-; Pres. European League for Econ. Co-operation (Luxembourg Bureau); Pres. BIL (Asia) Ltd., Singapore; mem. Bd., Treas. Foundation Prince Henri-Princesse Maria Teresa; mem. Bd. of Dirs. Luxair S.A., Soc. de la Bourse de Luxembourg S.A.; Dir. Henry Ansbacher Holdings PLC 1986-; mem. Monetary Comm., I.C.C. 1978-, Inst. Int. d'Etudes Bancaires 1978-; Officer, Order of Couronne de chêne (Luxembourg); Commdr. Order of the Crown (Belgium), in the Nat. Order (Ivory Coast); Officier, Ordre nat. du mérite, Order of Merit (Luxembourg). *Publication:* Le secret bancaire au Grand-Duché de Luxembourg 1972. *Leisure interests:* photography, bibliophily, golf, skiing, swimming. *Address:* Banque Internationale à Luxembourg S.A., 2 boulevard Royal, L-2953 Luxembourg-Ville (Office); 67 rue Cents, L-1319 Luxembourg (Home). *Telephone:* 4791-229 (Office).

DONEN, Stanley; American film producer and director; b. 13 April 1924, Columbia, S.C.; s. of Mortie and Helen Donen; ed. Univ. of South Carolina; Dir. of films including Fearless Fagan, Give the Girl a Break, Royal Wedding, Love is Better Than Ever, Deep in My Heart, Seven Brides for Seven Brothers, Funny Face, Kiss Them for Me; co-dir. Singin' in the Rain, It's Always Fair Weather, On the Town; producer-dir. Pajama Game, Indiscreet, Damn Yankees, Once More with Feeling, Surprise Package, The Grass is Greener, Charade, Arabesque, Two for the Road, Bedazzled, Staircase, The Little Prince, Lucky Lady, Movie, Movie, Saturn 3, Blame it on Rio 1984. *Address:* c/o Directors' Guild of America, 7950 West Sunset Boulevard, Hollywood, Calif. 90046, U.S.A.

DONG CHUNCAI; Chinese educationalist; Vice-Minister of Educ. 1952-65, 1979-82; Pres. Writers' Assen. for Dissemination of Scientific and Tech. Knowledge 1979-; mem. Standing Cttee., China Assen. for Promoting Democracy 1979; Chair. Cttee. for Reforming Chinese Written Language 1980-; Vice-Chair. Motions Cttee., CPPCC Nat. Cttee. 1983-; Head Work Group for Educ., CPPCC Nat. Cttee. 1983-; Hon. Chair. Abacus Assen. of China 1980-. *Address:* c/o State Council, Beijing, People's Republic of China.

DONG FURENG; Chinese economist; b. 26 July 1927, Ningbo, Zhejiang Prov.; s. of Dong Junmin and Zhao Jueying; m. Liu Ainian 1957; one s. one d.; ed. Wuhan Univ. and Moscow Nat. Inst. of Econs. of the Soviet Union; Teacher Dept. of Econs., Wuhan Univ. 1950-52, Lecturer 1957-58; Asst. Researcher Econs. Inst., Chinese Acad., and Deputy Head Group on Balance of Nat. Economy 1959-77; Deputy Dir. Econs. Inst., Chinese Acad. of Social Sciences 1978-85, Dir. Aug. 1985-; Sr. Researcher and Vice-Chair. Academic Cttee. Inst. of Econs. 1979-85; Prof., Beijing Univ. 1979-, Wuhan Teachers' Coll. 1980-, Wuhan Univ. 1986-, Chinese People's Univ.; mem. Academic Cttee. Inst. of Marxism and Mao Zedong Thought, Chinese Acad. of Social Sciences 1980-; Gen. Sec. Union of Chinese Socs. for Econ. Research 1981-87; Vice-Pres. Graduate School of Chinese Acad. of Social Sciences 1982-85; mem. Academic Senate of Chinese Acad. of Social Science 1982-85; Chair. Acad. Cttee. Inst. of Econs. 1985-; Short-term Consultant, The World Bank 1985; Visiting Prof. St. Antony's Coll. and Wolfson Coll., Univ. of Oxford 1985; Chief Ed. Journal of Econ. Research 1985-. *Publications:* Dynamic Analysis of the Soviet National Income 1959, Problems of the Socialist Reproduction and the National Income 1980, Socialist Economic Institution and its Superiority (ed.) 1981, Theoretical Problems of the Chinese Economy in the Great Transformation 1981, On Sun Yefang's Socialist Economic Theory 1983, Selected Works of Dong Fureng 1985 and over 80 essays on the Chinese economy. *Leisure interests:* arts, reading. *Address:* Institute of Economics (CASS), 2 Beixiaojie, Yuetan, Beijing, People's Republic of China (Office). *Telephone:* 895496 (Office).

DONG JICHANG; Chinese party official; alt. mem. 12th CCP Cen. Cttee. 1982-87, mem. 13th Cen. Cttee. 1987-; Deputy Sec. CCP Cttee., Shaanxi Prov. 1983-; Sec. CCP Cttee., Xian 1984-. *Address:* Shaanxi Provincial Chinese Communist Party, Xian, Shaanxi, People's Republic of China.

DONG KEJUN; Chinese woodcut artist; b. 18 Feb. 1939, Chongqing, Sichuan; s. of Dong Xueyuan and Gue Ximing; m. Lü Hengfen 1969; one s.; self-taught; Dir. of Chinese Artistic Assen.; Standing Dir. Chinese Woodcut Assen.; Vice-Chair. Guizhow Artistic Assen.; Chair. Guiyang Artistic Assen.; Vice-Pres. Acad. of Painting and Calligraphy; works on view at nat. exhbns. 1965-, also in Japan, U.S.A., France, Sweden and Africa; works include: Spring Returns to the Miao Mountain 1979, A Close Ball 1979, An Illustration of the Continuation of Feng Xuefeng's Fables (a hundred pieces) 1980, Company 1981, Go Back Drunkenly 1982, Lively Spring 1983, The Miao Nat. Sisters in Their Splendid Costume 1985, Contemporary Totem-1 1986, Mountain Breath 1986; Prizewinner, 9th Nat. Woodcut Exhbn. 1986. *Publication:* Dong Kejun Woodcut Works. *Leisure interests:* literature, music, film and dance. *Address:* Guiyang Artistic Assen., 4 Xing Shi Street, Guiyang, Guizhow Prov., People's Republic of China.

DONG QIZHONG; Chinese woodcut artist; b. 1935, Taihe Co. Jiangxi. *Address:* Shaanxi Artists' Assen, Xian, People's Republic of China.

DONG WENZHENG; Chinese artist; b. 1938, Suzhou, Jiangsu Prov.; ed. Nanjing Acad. of Art; created "Wu Mo" style of silkwork art. *Address:* China Federation of Literary and Art Circles, Beijing, People's Republic of China.

DONG ZHANLIN; Chinese army officer; Col. and Commdr. of a PLA Div. in N. Korea 1958; Deputy Commdr., Lanzhou Mil. Region 1981-; alt. mem. 12th CCP Cen. Cttee. 1982, 13th Cen. Cttee. 1987. *Address:* Lanzhou Military Region Headquarters, Lanzhou, Gansu, People's Republic of China.

DONG ZHENG; Chinese traditional physician; b. 3 Nov. 1926; specialises in treatment of bronchial disorders. *Address:* Guanganmen Hospital, Beijing, People's Republic of China.

DÖNHOFF, Gräfin (Countess) **Marion,** DR. RER. POL.; German journalist; b. 2 Dec. 1909, Friedrichstein, East Prussia; d. of August Graf Dönhoff and Ria (née von Lepel); unmarried; ed. in Potsdam, Königsberg, Frankfurt/Main and Basel Univ.; engaged in admin. of various agricultural estates in East Prussia 1936-45; joined Die Zeit 1946, Political Ed. 1955, Chief Ed. of Die Zeit 1968-72, Publr. 1973-; Hon. Dr. Smith Coll., U.S.A., Hon. Dr. (Columbia Univ., New York); Joseph E. Drexel Prize; Theodor Heuss Prize, Peace Prize of German Book Trade 1971. *Publications:* Namen, die keiner mehr nennt 1962, Die Bundesrepublik in der Ära Adenauers 1963, Reise in ein fernes Land (co-author) 1964, Welt in Bewegung 1965, Deutsche Aussenpolitik von Adenauer bis Brandt 1970, Menschen, die wissen, worum es geht 1976, Hart am Wind, The Political Career of Helmut Schmidt 1978 (Editor), Von Gestern nach Übermorgen-zur Geschichte der Bundesrepublik Deutschland 1981, Amerikanische Wechselbäder 1983, Weit ist der Weg nach Osten 1985. *Leisure interest:*

art (painting and graphic art). *Address:* c/o Die Zeit, Pressehaus, Postfach 10 68 20, 2000 Hamburg 1, Federal Republic of Germany.

DONINI, Ambrogio, PH.D.; Italian historian, politician and diplomatist; b. 8 Aug. 1903, Lanzo Torinese; s. of the late Pier Luigi and of Giaccone Irene; m. Olga Jahr 1930; one s.; ed. Univ. of Rome and Harvard Univ.; Reader in History of Christianity, Univ. of Rome 1926; mem. Communist Party of Italy since 1927; obliged to emigrate to U.S.A. in 1928 because of opposition to Fascist régime; research for Th.D. at Harvard Univ. Theological School 1928-30; Lecturer in Italian Literature, Brown Univ., Providence 1929; Asst. Prof. of Italian, Smith Coll., Northampton, Mass. 1930; antifascist political activity in Europe 1932-39; Ed. of anti-fascist daily La Voce degli Italiani, Paris; in U.S.A. as Ed. of Italian anti-fascist weekly L'Unità del Popolo 1939-45; Lecturer of History of Religion, Jefferson School, New York 1943-45; returned to liberated Italy after 17 years' exile 1945; Free Prof. of History of Christianity, Univ. of Rome; Dir. of Gramsci Cultural Inst., Rome 1949; joint ed. of Rome review Ricerche Religiose; elected to Rome City Council Nov. 1946; Amb. to Poland 1947-48; mem. World Peace Council 1950; elected to the Senate 1953, 1958; elected to Cen. Cttee. Communist Party of Italy 1948, to Central Control Cttee. 1956; Prof. History of Christianity, Univ. of Bari 1960; Dir. Interstampa (political monthly); retd. 1972. *Publications:* Ippolito di Roma, Polemiche teologiche e controversie disciplinari nella Chiesa di Roma agli inizi del III secolo 1925, Manuale introduttivo alla Storia del Cristianesimo (joint author) 1926, Per una storia del pensiero di Dante in rapporto al movimento gioachimita (Dante Prize, Harvard Univ.) 1930, Le basi sociali del Cristianesimo primitivo 1946, L'Italia al bivio 1955, I Manoscritti ebraici del Mar Morto e le origini del Cristianesimo 1957, Chiesa e Stato nell'Italia d'oggi 1958, Lineamenti di Storia delle Religioni 1959, Lezioni di Storia del Cristianesimo, Vol. I, Le Origini 1964, Storia del Cristianesimo dalle Origini a Giustiniano 1975, Enciclopedia delle Religioni 1977, Ernesto Buonaiuti: La Vita allo Sbaraglio 1980. *Leisure interests:* chess and classical music. *Address:* Contrada S. Sisinio, 00068 Rignano Flaminio, Rome, Italy. *Telephone:* 0761-50027.

DONLEAVY, James Patrick; American author; b. 23 April 1926, New York City; s. of Patrick and Margaret Donleavy; m. 1st Valerie Heron (divorced 1969); one s. one d.; m. 2nd Mary Wilson Price (divorced 1989); one s. one d.; ed. Preparatory School, New York, and Trinity Coll., Dublin; served in the U.S.N. during the Second World War; Brandeis Univ. Creative Arts Award, Evening Standard Drama Award, American Acad. and Nat. Inst. of Arts and Letters Award. *Publications: novels:* The Ginger Man 1955, A Singular Man 1963, The Beastly Beatitudes of Balthazar B 1968, The Onion Eaters 1971, A Fairy Tale of New York 1973, The Destinies of Darcy Dancer, Gentleman 1977, Schultz 1979, Leila 1983, Are You Listening Rabbi Low 1987; *plays:* The Ginger Man 1959, Fairy Tales of New York 1960, A Singular Man 1964, The Saddest Summer of Samuel S 1968, The Plays of J. P. Donleavy 1972, The Beastly Beatitudes of Balthazar B 1981; short stories and sketches: Meet My Maker the Mad Molecule 1964; novella: The Saddest Summer of Samuel S 1966; also: The Unexpurgated Code: A Complete Manual of Survival and Manners 1975, De Alfonce Tennis, The Superlative Game of Eccentric Champions. Its History, Accoutrements, Rules, Conduct and Regimen. A Legend 1984, J. P. Donleavy's Ireland: In All Her Sins and in Some of Her Graces 1986. *Leisure interest:* De Alfonce Tennis. *Address:* Levington Park, Mullingar, Co. Westmeath, Ireland.

DONNAY, J(oseph) D(ésiré) H(ubert), E.M., PH.D.; Canadian university professor; b. 6 June 1902, Grandville, Belgium; s. of Joseph Donnay and Marie Doyen; m. 1st Marie Hennin 1931, 2nd Gabrielle Hamburger 1949; three s. one d.; ed. Liège and Stanford Univs.; engineer and geologist, Société financière franco-belge de colonisation, French Morocco 1929-30; Research Assoc. and Teaching Fellow, Stanford Univ. 1930-31; Assoc. in Mineralogy and Petrography, Johns Hopkins Univ. 1931-39; Prof. Laval Univ. Quebec 1939-45; Research Chemist, Hercules Powder Co. 1942-45; Visiting Prof. Johns Hopkins Univ. 1945; Prof. Univ. of Liège 1946-47, Hon. Prof. 1948-; Prof. of Crystallography and Mineralogy, Johns Hopkins Univ. 1946-71, Emer. Prof. 1971-; Visiting Prof. Univ. of Marburg 1966, 1968; Chargé de cours, Univ. de Montréal 1970-72, Guest Prof. 1972-76; Research Assoc. in Crystallography, McGill Univ. 1978-; Sec.-Treas. American Soc. for X-ray and Electron Diffraction 1944-46; Vice-Pres. Soc. Géologique Belgique 1946-47; Vice-Pres. Mineralogical Soc. of America 1949 and 1952, Pres. 1953; Vice-Pres. Crystallographic Soc. of America 1946 and 1948, Pres. 1949; Corresp. mem. Société Royale des Sciences de Liège; Vice-Pres. Soc. française de Minéralogie 1949, Hon. mem. 1978; Vice-Pres. Geological Soc. of America 1954; Pres. American Crystallographic Assen. 1956; Fulbright Lecturer, Sorbonne 1958-59; Vice-Pres. Assen. française de Cristallographie 1959-60; Corresp. mem. Soc. Géologique Belgique 1966, Hon. mem. 1972; mem. Emer. Phila. Mineralogical Soc. 1974; Hon. mem. Japan Mineralogical Soc. 1982; Foreign Assoc. Académie Royale de Belgique 1976; Roebling Medal 1971, Médaille Trasenster 1977. *Publications:* Spherical Trigonometry 1945, Crystal Data 1954, 1963, 1972-73, Space Groups and Lattice Complexes 1973. *Leisure interest:* philology. *Address:* 3450 University Street, Montreal, Que. H3A 2A7 (Office); 516 rue d'Iberville, Mont-Saint-Hilaire, Que. J3H 2V7, Canada (Home). *Telephone:* (514) 392-5840 (Office); (574) 464-5652 (Home).

DONNELLY, James; Canadian atomic power administrator; b. 22 March 1931, Wishaw, Lanarkshire, Scotland; s. of Peter and Mary (née Morris) Donnelly; m. Brenda Marks 1956; three s. one d.; ed. Royal Tech. Coll., Glasgow; exec. posts, Gen. Electric Co. (GEC), England, and English Electric Co. 1954-74; Project Man. Hinkley Point and Sizewell nuclear power stations, U.K.; fmr. Man. Power Station Projects, GEC, and Commercial Dir. Turbine Generators; joined Int. Systems and Controls Corpn., Montreal 1974, Vice-Pres. Forestry Products -1978; Pres. Atomic Energy of Canada Ltd. Feb. 1978-; Dir. Canadian Nuclear Assen., Canadian Major Projects Assen., Canadian Nat. Cttee.-World Energy Conf., Nuclear Project Managers Canada Inc.; Chair. Advisory Bd. for the Center for Nuclear Eng., Univ. of Toronto; Assoc. Royal Tech. Coll., Glasgow; mem. Inst. of Electrical Engineers, U.K. *Leisure interests:* tennis, skiing, theatre. *Address:* Atomic Energy of Canada Ltd., 344 Slater Street, Ottawa, Ont. K1A 0S4 (Office); 111 Echo Drive, T.H. 3, Ottawa, Ont. K1S 5K8, Canada (Home).

DONNER, Andreas Matthias, D.IUR.; Netherlands jurist; b. 15 Jan. 1918; s. of Jan Donner and Golida van den Burg; m. Dina A. Mulder 1946; three s. six d.; ed. Amsterdam Free Univ.; Legal Adviser Assoc. of Christian Schools in the Netherlands 1941-45; Prof. of Constitutional Law, Free Univ. of Amsterdam 1945-58; Pres. Court of Justice of the European Communities 1958-64, Judge 1964-79, alt. Pres. of First Chamber; Prof. Constitutional Law Univ. of Groningen 1979-85, Prof. Emer. 1985-; mem. European Court of Human Rights 1986-88; Hon. Dr. Iur. (Louvain, Edinburgh, Freiburg); Pres., Royal Netherlands Acad. of Sciences and Art. *Publications:* Nederlands Bestuursrecht (Netherlands Administrative Law) 5th edn. 1986, Handboek van het Nederlandse Staatsrecht 11th edn. 1983. *Address:* Emmaplein 4, 9711 AP Groningen, Netherlands. *Telephone:* 050 122216.

DONNER, Clive; British film and theatre director; b. 21 Jan. 1926, London; s. of Alex and Deborah (née Taffel) Donner; m. Jocelyn Rickards 1971; Asst. film editor, Denham Studios 1942; free-lance film director 1956-; work has included documentary films for British television and direction of theatrical productions in London and New York; recipient of various awards at int. film festivals, incl. Silver Bear (Berlin Film Festival) for The Caretaker. *Films include:* Some People 1962, The Caretaker 1963, Nothing but the Best 1963, What's New Pussycat? 1965, Luv 1967, Here We Go Round the Mulberry Bush 1967, Alfred the Great 1969, The Scarlet Pimpernel, Arthur the King, To Catch a King, A Christmas Carol, Dead Man's Folly 1986, Babes in Toyland 1986, Stealing Heaven 1988. *Leisure interests:* classical music (particularly opera), popular music, reading, walking anywhere from the streets of London to the Australian sea shore. *Address:* 6 Melina Place, London, NW8 9SA, England.

DONNER, Jörn Johan, B.A.; Finnish film director and writer; b. 5 Feb. 1933, Helsinki; s. of Dr. Kai Donner and Greta von Bonsdorff; m. 1st Inga-Britt Wik 1954 (divorced); three s. one d.; m. 2nd Jeanette Bonnier 1974 (divorced 1988); ed. Helsinki Univ.; worked as writer and film dir. in Finland and Sweden, writing own film scripts; contributor and critic to various Scandinavian and int. journals; Dir. Swedish Film Inst., Stockholm 1972-75, Exec. Producer 1975-78, Man. Dir. 1978-82; Chair. Bd. Finnish Film Foundation, Helsinki 1981-; Man. Dir. Jörn Donner Productions; mem. Bd. Marimekko Textiles and other cos.; mem., Helsinki City Council 1969-1972, 1984; M.P. 1987-; Opera Prima Award Venice Film Festival 1963, Vittorio Sica Prize, Sorrento 1978. *Films:* A Sunday in September 1963, To Love 1964, Adventure Starts Here 1965, Rooftree 1967, Black on White 1968, Sixtynine 1969, Portraits of Women 1970, Anna 1970, Images of Finland 1971, Tenderness 1972, Baksmalla 1974, Three Scenes (with Ingmar Bergman), The Bergman File 1975-77, Men Can't Be Raped 1978, Dirty Story 1984, Letters from Sweden 1987. *Publications:* novels, short stories and non-fiction including: Report from Berlin 1958, The Personal Vision of Ingmar Bergman 1962. *Leisure interest:* fishing. *Address:* Pohjoisranta 12, 00170 Helsinki, Finland. *Telephone:* 652675 661212.

DONNER, Kai Otto, M.SC., PH.D.; Finnish professor of zoology; b. 19 Aug. 1922, Helsinki; s. of Karl R. Donner and Margareta von Bonsdorff; m. 1st Ulla Susanna Eklund 1948 (died 1983); two s. three d.; m. 2nd Marjatta Rouhiainen 1984; ed. Univ. of Helsinki; Lecturer in Zoology, Univ. of Helsinki 1953-72, Prof. 1973-85; junior and senior researcher, Acad. of Finland 1962-69, Research Prof. 1972-75, Chair. of Cen. Bd. 1980-85; hon. mem. Societas pro Fauna et Flora Fennica; Hon. mem. Soc. Scientiarum Fennica; foreign mem. Royal Swedish Acad. of Science. *Publications:* about 60 scientific articles. *Address:* Pohjoisranta 12 A 3, 00170 Helsinki, Finland (Home). *Telephone:* 6121646 (Home).

DONOGHUE, Denis, PH.D.; Irish literary critic; b. 1928; ed. Univ. Coll., Dublin; Admin. Office, Irish Dept. of Finance 1951-54; Asst. Lecturer, Univ. Coll., Dublin 1954-57, Coll. lecturer 1957-62, 1963-64, Prof. of Modern English and American Literature 1965-79; Visiting Scholar, Univ. of Pa. 1962-63; Univ. lecturer, Cambridge Univ., and Fellow, King's Coll. 1964-65; Henry James Prof. of Letters, New York Univ. 1979-; mem. Int. Cttee. of Assen. of Univ. Profs. of English; BBC Reith Lecturer 1982. *Publications:* The Third Voice 1959, Connoisseurs of Chaos 1965, The Ordinary Universe 1968, Emily Dickinson 1968, Jonathan Swift 1969, Yeats 1971, Thieves of Fire 1974, Sovereign Ghost: studies in Imagination 1978,

Ferocious Alphabets 1981, We Irish: Essays on Irish Literature and Society 1987; contribs. to reviews and journals and ed. of three vols. *Address:* New York University, 19 University Place, New York, N.Y. 10003, U.S.A.; Gaybrook, North Avenue, Mount Merrion, Dublin, Ireland.

DONOHOE, Peter; British pianist; b. 18 June 1953, Manchester; s. of Harold Donohoe and Marjorie Donohoe; m. Elaine Margaret-Burns 1980; one d.; ed. Royal Manchester Coll. of Music, studied with Yvonne Loriod, Paris; professional solo pianist 1974-; appears several times each season with major symphony orchestras in London and rest of U.K. and performs annually at the Promenade Concerts 1979-; signed exclusive contract with EMI 1989-; performances with the L.A. Philharmonic, Chicago Symphony, San Diego Symphony, Vancouver Symphony, and the Minn. Orchestra (with Sir Neville Marriner, q.v.), Rotterdam Philharmonic, Helsinki Philharmonic, Stockholm Philharmonic, a series of eight concerts with the NHK Symphony in Japan 1985, appeared with the Los Angeles Philharmonic at the Hollywood Bowl 1986 and at La Roque d' Antheron piano festival 1985; recordings include Messiaen's Turangalila Symphony (EMI) 1986, Dominic Muldowney Piano Concerto 1986, and Tchaikovsky's Piano Concerto No. 2 1986 (Gramophone magazine's Concerto of the Year) 1988; shared top prize at the Moscow Int. Tchaikovsky Competition 1982. *Leisure interests:* home-building, travelling. *Address:* 82 Hampton Lane, Solihull, West Midlands, B91 2RS, England. *Telephone:* (021) 704 4450.

DONOSO, Alvaro, M.A.; Chilean politician and financial official; b. 1951; ed. Catholic Univ., Univ. of Chicago; Chief Planning Dept., Office of Nat. Econ. Planning, subsequently Office Deputy Dir. 1978; Deputy Minister of Health 1980; Minister-Dir. Office of Nat. Econ. Planning 1981; Exec. Dir. IMF 1982-84, 1986-88. *Address:* c/o Ministerio de Relaciones Exteriores, Carrera 5, No. 15-80, Ps. 16-20, Bogotá, Colombia.

DONOSO, José, A.B.; Chilean writer; b. 5 Oct. 1924; s. of José and Alicia Donoso; m. María P. Serrano 1961; one d.; ed. The Grange School, Santiago, Instituto Pedagógico (Univ. de Chile), and Princeton Univ., U.S.A.; worked as shepherd in Patagonia before going to univ.; later lived in Buenos Aires; Doherty Foundation Scholarship to Princeton Univ.; Prof. of English Conversation, Univ. Católica de Chile 1952, later teacher of Techniques of Expression, School of Journalism, Univ. de Chile; journalist on Revista Ercilla, Santiago 1959-64; Visiting lecturer, Writers' Workshop, English Dept., Univ. of Iowa 1966-67; Premio Municipal de Santiago 1955; Chile-Italia Prize for Journalism 1960; William Faulkner Foundation Prize (for *Coronación*) 1962, Critics Award (for *Casa de Campo*) 1979, Guggenheim Fellow. *Publications: Veraneo y otros Cuentos* 1955, *Coronación* 1958, *El Charleston* (short stories) 1960, *Este Domingo* (novel) 1966, *El Lugar sin Limites* (novel) 1966, *El obsceno pájaro de la noche* (novel) 1971, *Cuentos* (short stories) 1971, *Historia Personal del "Boom"* (essay) 1972, *Casa de Campo* (novel) 1979, *La desesperanza* 1986. *Leisure interest:* film-making. *Address:* Calaceite, Province of Teruel, Spain.

DONOVAN, Hedley Williams; American journalist; b. 24 May 1914, Brainerd, Minn.; s. of Percy Williams Donovan and Alice (née Dougan) Donovan; m. Dorothy Hannon 1941 (died 1978); two s. one d.; ed. Univs. of Minn. and Oxford; Reporter at Washington Post 1937-42; war service in U.S. Navy; writer and Ed. Fortune magazine, New York 1945-51, Assoc. Man. Ed. 1951-53, Man. Ed. 1953-59; Ed. Dir. Time Inc. 1959-64, Dir. 1962-79, Ed.-in-Chief 1964-79; mem. Council Foreign Relations; Sr. Adviser to Pres. Carter 1979-80; Fellow, Faculty of Govt., Harvard Univ. 1980-87; Visiting Research Fellow, Nuffield Coll., Oxford, England 1986; Fellow, American Acad. of Arts and Sciences; Hon. Fellow, Hertford Coll., Oxford; Trustee, Nat. Humanities Centre; Rhodes Scholar 1934-37; several hon. degrees. *Publication:* Roosevelt to Reagan: A Reporter's Encounters with Nine Presidents. *Address:* 190 E. 72nd Street, New York, N.Y. 10021; Harbor Road, Sands Point, N.Y. 10020, U.S.A.

DONOVAN, Raymond J., B.A.; American businessman and politician; b. 31 Aug. 1930, Bayonne, N.J.; m. Catherine Sblendorio 1957; two s. one d.; ed. St. Andrew's School and Notre Dame Seminary, New Orleans, La.; with American Insurance Co., Parsippany, N.J. 1953-58; joined Schiavone Construction Co., N.J., as Vice-Pres. 1959, Exec. Vice-Pres. 1971-80; U.S. Sec. of Labor 1981-85. *Address:* c/o Department of Labor, 3rd Street and Constitution Avenue, N.W., Washington, D.C. 20210, U.S.A.

DONTSOP, Paul; Cameroonian civil administrator and politician; b. *c.* 1937, Bafou; ed. Inst. d'Hautes Etudes d'Outre-mer; Prefect 1965-75; Minister of Labour and Social Security 1975-80; Minister of State for Foreign Affairs 1980-83; Pres. Consultative Council, African Centre for Work Admin. (CRADAT). *Address:* c/o Ministère des Affaires Etrangères, Yaoundé, Cameroon.

DOOB, Joseph Leo, M.A., PH.D.; American professor of mathematics; b. 27 Feb. 1910, Cincinnati, Ohio; s. of Leo and Mollie Doerfler Doob; m. Elsie Haviland Field 1931; two s. one d.; ed. Harvard Univ.; Univ. of Illinois 1935-78, Prof. of Maths 1945-78, Prof. Emer. 1979-; mem. N.A.S., American Acad. of Arts and Sciences, French Acad. des Sciences; Nat. Medal of Science. *Publications:* Stochastic Processes, Classical Potential Theory and its Probabilistic Counterpart. *Leisure interest:* recorder. *Address:* Department of Mathematics, University of Illinois, Urbana, Ill. 61801, U.S.A. *Telephone:* 217-367-7029.

DOOB, Leonard W., PH.D.; American psychologist; b. 3 March 1909, New York; s. of William and Florence Doob; m. Eveline Bates 1936; three s.; ed. Dartmouth Coll., Duke Univ., Univ. of Frankfurt, and Harvard Univ.; Dept. of Psychology, Yale University 1934-77, Prof. of Psychology 1950-77, Emer. 1977-, Sr. Research Scientist 1978-; Psychologist, War Dept., 1942-43; Policy Co-ordinator, Overseas Branch, Office of War Information 1944-45; Chair. Council of African Studies, Yale Univ. 1961-67, 1972-; Visiting Research Prof. Univ. Coll. of Dar es Salaam, Tanzania 1967-68, Univ. of Ghana 1971; Dir. of Social Sciences, Yale 1963-66; Ed. Journal of Social Psychology 1965-; Fellow John Simon Guggenheim Foundation 1960-61. *Publications:* Propaganda 1935, Frustration and Aggression 1939, The Plans of Men 1940, Public Opinion and Propaganda 1948, Social Psychology 1952, Becoming More Civilised 1960, Communication in Africa 1961, Patriotism and Nationalism 1964, Ants Will Not Eat Your Fingers 1966, A Crocodile Has Me by the Leg 1967, Resolving Conflict in Africa 1970, Patterning of Time 1972, Pathways to People 1975, Ezra Pound Speaking 1978, Panorama of Evil 1978, The Pursuit of Peace 1981, Personality, Power and Authority 1983, Slightly Beyond Skepticism 1987, Inevitability 1988. *Leisure interests:* music, cycling, gardening. *Address:* Department of Psychology, Box 11A, Yale Station, New Haven, Conn. 06520, U.S.A. *Telephone:* (203) 387-2266.

DOOGE, James Clement Ignatius, M.E., M.SC.; Irish engineer and politician; b. 30 July 1922, Birkenhead, England; s. of Denis Patrick and Veronica Catherine (née Carroll) Dooge; m. Veronica O'Doherty 1946; two s. three d.; ed. Christian Brothers' School, Dún Laoghaire, Univ. Coll., Dublin, Iowa, U.S.A.; Jr. Civil Engineer, Irish Office of Public Works 1943-46; Design Engineer, E.S.B. 1946-58; Prof. of Civil Eng., Univ. Coll., Cork 1958-70, Univ. Coll., Dublin 1970-81, 1982-84; Minister for Foreign Affairs 1981-82; Leader Irish Senate 1983-87; Pres. Royal Irish Acad. 1987-; mem. Exec. Bureau Int. Union for Geodesy and Geophysics 1979-; Hon. Agric. Science Degree 1978, Hon. D.Tech. 1980, Hon. D.Sc. (Birmingham), Hon. Sc.D. (Dublin) 1988; Horton Award, American Geophysical Union 1959; Kettle Premium and Plaque 1948 and Mullins Medal 1951, 1962 (Irish Inst. of Civil Engineers). *Address:* University College, Earlsford Terrace, Dublin 2 (Office); 2 Belgrave Road, Monkstown, Ireland (Home).

DOO KINGUE, Michel, DR. SC.; Cameroonian diplomatist and United Nations official; b. 10 Jan. 1934, Cameroon; s. of Samuel Kingue; m. Constance Epanya 1958; five s. three d.; ed. Univ. of Paris (Sorbonne); Perm. Sec., Ministry of Educ., Cameroon 1961-63; Special Adviser for Africa to Dir.-Gen. UNESCO 1963-68; Dir. Div. of Int. Orgs. and Programmes UNESCO, Paris 1968-71; Asst. Admin. UN Devt. Programme (UN Asst. Sec.-Gen.) and Dir. Regional Bureau for Africa 1971-82; UN Under-Sec.-Gen. and Exec. Dir. UNITAR 1983-; Chevalier des Arts et Lettres (France). *Publications:* several political and econ. studies and reports. *Leisure interests:* swimming, music, dance. *Address:* 801 United Nations Plaza, New York, N.Y. 10017 (Office); 211 East 70th Street, New York, N.Y. 10021, U.S.A. (Home); B.P. 550 Douala, Cameroon. *Telephone:* (212) 963-8621 (Office in New York).

DOOLITTLE, Gen. James H., M.SC., D.SC.; American aviator and business executive; b. 14 Dec. 1896, Alameda, Calif.; s. of Frank H. and Rosa C. (née Shephard) Doolittle; m. Josephine Daniels 1917; two s.; ed. Univ. of California, and Mass. Inst. of Tech.; enlisted in U.S. Army Signal Corps as aviation cadet 1917; commissioned as Second Lieut.; flight and gunnery instructor; served in Army as Second and First Lieut. 1917-30; est. a number of air records, including the following (1) first flight across U.S. in less than 24 hours, (2) won Schneider Cup Race 1925, (3) first man to do outside loop, (4) first man to fly over 300 m.p.h. in a land plane; retd. from Army with a reserve commission to become Man. of Aviation for Shell Oil Co. 1930; est. new transcontinental flight record 1931; new world speed record for land planes 1932; recalled to active duty with U.S. Army 1940; as Lieut.-Col. led famous Tokyo raid April 1942; later commanded 12th and 15th Air Forces, and, in Jan. 1944, 8th Air Force, retd. Air Force 1959; rank of Gen. 1985; Vice-Pres. Shell Oil Co. 1946-58, Dir. 1946-67; Chair. Exec. Cttee., Vice-Chair. Bd. of Trustees Aerospace Corpn. 1965-70; Chair. Bd., Space Technology Laboratories 1959-62, Consultant 1962-66; Dir. TRW Inc. 1962-69, Mutual of Omaha Insurance Co. 1961-, United Benefit Life Insurance Co. 1964-, Tele-Trip Co., Inc. 1966-84, Companion Life Insurance Co. 1968-83, Mutual of Omaha Growth and Income Funds 1968-82; adviser to govt. bds.; decorations include Congressional Medal of Honor, D.F.C., and D.S.M. with Oak-Leaf Clusters, Air Medal with three Oak-Leaf Clusters, Silver Star, Bronze Star, and many foreign awards, including Hon. K.C.B. (U.K.); awarded Harmon trophy of Ligue Internationale des Aviateurs for pioneering work in blind flying 1931. *Leisure interests:* hunting, fishing. *Address:* 8545 Carmel Valley Road, Carmel, Calif. 93923, U.S.A. *Telephone:* (408) 625-1896.

DORAZIO; Italian artist; b. 1927, Rome; ed. Rome, Paris; played major role in the revival of Italian Futurist and Abstractionist tradition, published manifesto Forma I 1947; has exhibited throughout Europe, U.S.A., S. America and Australia; est. Fine Arts Dept. of School of Fine Arts, Univ. of Pa. 1960-61, Prof. 1960-69; included in main avant-garde exhbns. of 1950s and 1960s; one-man exhbns. mainly in Venice Biennale 1960, 1966, Düsseldorf 1961, San Marino Int. 1967, Bennington, U.S.A., Cologne, Berlin 1969, Museum of Modern Art, Belgrade 1970, and at Marlborough

Galleries in Rome 1964, 1968, 1972, New York 1965, 1969, London 1966; Venice Biennale Prize 1960, Paris Biennale Prize 1961, Prix Kandinsky 1961, Premio Int. Lissone 1965, Int. Prize, Cracow 1970. *Address:* c/o Marlborough Galleria d'Arte, Rome, Italy.

DORE, Ronald Philip, C.B.E., B.A.; British university professor; b. 1 Feb. 1925, Bournemouth; s. of Philip H. B. Dore and Elsie C. King; m. Nancy MacDonald 1957; one s. one d.; ed. School of Oriental and African Studies, London Univ.; Asst. Prof. then Assoc. Prof., Univ. of B.C. 1956-60; Reader, L.S.E. 1961; Prof., L.S.E. and S.O.A.S. 1964-69; Prof. and Fellow, Inst. of Devt. Studies, Sussex Univ. 1970-81; Tech. Change Centre, London 1982-86; Dir. Japan-Europe Industry Research Centre, Imperial Coll., London 1986-; Visiting Prof. of Sociology, Harvard Univ. 1987-; mem. British Acad. 1975-; Japan Foundation Prize 1977; Foreign Hon. Fellow, American Acad. of Arts and Sciences 1978-, Hon. Foreign Fellow Japan Acad. 1986-. *Publications:* City Life in Japan 1958, Land Reform in Japan 1959, Education in Tokugawa Japan 1965, British Factory/Japanese Factory 1973, The Diploma Disease 1976, Shinohata Portrait of a Japanese Village 1978, Flexible Rigidities, Industrial Policy and Structural Adjustment in Japanese Economy 1986, Taking Japan Seriously: A Confucian Perspective on Leading Economic Issues 1987, Japan and World Depression, Then and Now (Essays) (Jt. Ed.) 1987. *Address:* Japan-Europe Industry Research Centre, Imperial College, Mechanical Engineering Building, Exhibition Road, London, SW7 2BX; 157 Surrenden Road, Brighton, Sussex, England. *Telephone:* 01-589 5111 (Office); (0273) 501 370 (Home).

DORIN, Françoise Andrée Dorée; French actress, novelist and playwright; b. 23 Jan. 1928, Paris; d. of late René Dorin and of Yvonne Guilbert; m. Jean Poiret (b. Poiré) (divorced); one d.; at Théâtre des Deux-Ânes, then du Quartier Latin (Les Aveux les plus doux 1957), then La Bruyère (Le Chinois 1958); Presenter TV programme Paris-Club 1969; playwright and author 1967-. *Publications:* novels include Virginie et Paul, La Seconde dans Rome, Va voir Maman, Papa travaille 1976, Les lits à une place 1980; *songs include:* Que c'est triste Venise, N'avoue jamais, Faisons l'humour ensemble, les Miroirs truqués 1982; *plays include:* Comme au théâtre 1967, la Facture 1968, Un sale égoïste, les Bonshommes 1970, le Tournant 1973, le Tube 1974, l'Autre Valse 1975, Si t'es beau, t'es con 1976, le Tout pour le tout 1978, l'Intoxe 1980; lyrics for Vos gueules les mouettes 1971, Monsieur Pompadour 1972, l'Etiquette 1983, Les jupes-culottes 1984, La valise en carton (musical comedy) 1986, L'age en question 1986; Chevalier, Légion d'honneur, ordre nat. du Mérite, Arts et Lettres; trophée Dussane 1973. *Address:* 23 rue Simon-Dereure, 75018 Paris, France.

DORIVAL, Bernard, D. ES. L.; French professor and writer; b. 14 Sept. 1914; s. of André Dorival and Suzanne Beurdeley; m. Claude de la Brosse 1944; three s. one d.; ed. Lycées Carnot and Condorcet, Paris and Ecole normale supérieure; Prof. Ecole du Louvre 1941-; Curator Musée Nat. de l'Art Moderne, Paris 1941-65, Chief Curator 1967-68; Curator Musée Nat. des Granges de Port-Royal 1955-68; Chargé de recherches at Centre Nat. de la Recherche Scientifique 1968-72; Prof. Univ. of Paris 1972-83, Prof. Emer. 1983-. *Publications:* La peinture française 1942, Les étapes de la peinture française contemporaine 1943-46, Du côté de Port-Royal 1946, Les peintres du XXe siècle 1955, L'école de Paris au Musée National de l'Art Moderne 1961; Robert Delaunay 1975, Sonia Delaunay 1980; monographs on Cézanne, Philippe de Champaigne and Rouault, 2 vols. (with Isabelle Ronalt), numerous works on painting. *Address:* 78 rue Notre-Dame-des-Champs, 75006 Paris, France.

DORMAN, Sir Maurice Henry, G.C.M.G., G.C.V.O., D.L., M.A.; British administrator (retd.); b. 7 Aug. 1912, Stafford; s. of the late John Ehrenfried Dorman and Madeleine Bostock; m. F. Monica Churchward Smith 1937; one s. three d.; ed. Sedbergh School, Magdalene Coll., Cambridge; Admin. Officer, Tanganyika Territory 1935, Clerk of Council 1940-45; Asst. to Lieut.-Gov. Malta 1945; Prin. Asst. Sec., Palestine 1947; seconded to Colonial Office as Asst. Sec., Social Services Dept. 1948; Dir. Social Welfare and Community Devt., Gold Coast 1950; Chief Sec., Trinidad and Tobago 1952, Acting Gov., Trinidad 1954, 1955; Gov., C.-in-C. and Vice-Adm. of Colony and Protectorate of Sierra Leone 1956-61, Gov.-Gen. Independent State of Sierra Leone 1961-62; Gov. and C.-in-C. State of Malta 1962-64, Gov.-Gen. 1964-71; Deputy Chair. Pearce Comm. on Rhodesia 1972; Deputy Chair. Ramsbury Bldg. Soc. 1981-83, Chair. West of England Building Soc. 1983-87, Wiltshire Area Health Authority 1974-82, Swindon Health Authority 1982-88; a Trustee, Imperial War Museum, Lambeth 1972-85; Pres. Anglo-Sierra Leone Soc.; Chief Commdr., St. John Ambulance 1975-80, Lord Prior, Venerable Order of St. John 1980-86; Bd. of Govs., Badminton School, Bristol; Deputy-Lieut., Wiltshire; Hon. D.C.L. (Durham), Hon. LL.D. (Royal Univ. of Malta), G.C.St.J. 1978; Gran Croce al Merito Melitense (Sov. Ordine Militare di Malta) 1966. *Leisure interests:* house, garden, golf, reading. *Address:* The Old Manor, Overton, Marlborough, Wiltshire, England. *Telephone:* (067) 286-600.

DORMANDY, John Adam, M.D., F.R.C.S.; British surgeon; b. 5 May 1937, Hungary; s. of Paul Dormandy and Clara Dormandy; m. Klara Dormandy 1982; one s. one d.; ed. St. Paul's School, London and London Univ.; Resident in Surgery, St. George's Hosp. Medical School 1963-65, Lecturer in Applied Physiology 1970-74, Sr. Lecturer in Surgery 1975-80, Consul-

tant Vascular Surgeon, St. James' and St. George's Hosp. 1973-; Pres. of Section of Clinical Medicine, Royal Soc. of Medicine 1978; Pres. Venous Forum 1984; Chair. Int. Soc. of Haemorrheology 1982; Examiner in Physiology, Royal Coll. of Surgeons 1984-, Huntarian Prof. 1970; Hamilton Bailey Prize in Surgery 1973; Frahreus Medal 1983. *Publications:* numerous articles in books and scientific journals. *Leisure interests:* squash, skiing, roulette. *Address:* Department of Vascular Surgery, St. George's Hospital, London SW17, England. *Telephone:* (01) 767-8346.

DORN, Dieter; German actor and theatre director; b. 31 Oct. 1935, Leipzig; ed. Theaterhochschule, Leipzig and Max-Reinhardt-Schule, Berlin; actor, producer and dir. in Hannover 1958-68; dir. in Essen and Oberhausen 1968-70; Dir. at Deutsches Schauspielhaus, Hamburg 1971, Burgtheater, Vienna 1972, 1976; Dir. at Staatliche Schauspielbühnen, Berlin 1972-75, Salzburg Festival 1974, 1982, 1986; Chief Dir. Münchner Kammerspielen (producing works by Lessing, Goethe, Büchner, Shakespeare etc.) 1976-83, Man. (Intendant) 1983-; has also dir. opera productions in Vienna, Munich, Kassel and at Salzburg and Ludwigsburg festivals. *Address:* Münchner Kammerspielen, 8000 Munich, Federal Republic of Germany.

DORODNITSYIN, Anatoliy Alekseyevich; Soviet geophysicist; b. 2 Dec. 1910, Bashino, Tula Region; ed. Grozny Petroleum Inst.; Instructor, higher educational and research establishments, Moscow, Leningrad 1936-41; Cen. Aerodynamics Inst. Moscow 1941-55; Mathematics Inst. U.S.S.R. Acad. of Sciences 1945-55; Prof. Moscow Physics-Tech. Inst. 1947-; mem. U.S.S.R. Acad. of Sciences 1953-; Dir. Computing Centre, U.S.S.R. Acad. of Sciences 1955-; State Prizes 1946, 1947, 1951; Hero of Socialist Labour 1970; Order of Lenin (five times), Hammer and Sickle Gold Medal and other decorations. *Publications:* The Boundary Layer in Compressible Gas 1942, The Effects of the Earth's Surface Topography on Air Currents 1950, Asymptotic Laws of Distribution of Proper Meanings for Some Special Types of Second Order 1952, Solution of Mathematical and Logical Problems with Help of Fast Electronic Computers 1956, Laminar Border Layer in Compressible Gas 1957, Some Cases of Axial Symmetric Supersonic Current of Gas 1957, A Contribution to Solution of Mixed Problems of Transonic Aerodynamics 1959, A Method of Solution of Equation of Laminar and Border Layer 1960. *Address:* 117333 Moscow, Vavilova str. 40, U.S.S.R.

DORONINA, Tatyana Vasiliyevna; Soviet actress; b. 12 Sept. 1933, Leningrad; d. of Vasiliy Ivanovich Doronin and Anna Ivanovna Doronina; m. Robert Dimitrievich Takhnenko; ed. Studio School of Moscow Art Theatre; Leningrad Lenin Komsomol State Theatre 1956-59; Leningrad Maxim Gorky State Bolshoi Drama Theatre 1959-66; Moscow Art Theatre 1966-71; Moscow Mayakovski Theatre 1971-83; Moscow Arts Theatre 1983-; People's Artist of the U.S.S.R., Honoured Artist of R.S.F.S.R. *Main roles include:* theatre: Zhenka Shulzhenko (Factory Girl by Volodin), Lenochka (In Search of Happiness by Rozov), Sophia (Wit Works Woe by Griboyedov), Nadya Rozoyeva (My Elder Sister by Volodin), Nadezhda Polikarpovna (The Barbarians by Gorky), Lushka (Virgin Soil Upturned by Sholokov), Nastasya Filippovna (The Idiot by Dostoyevsky), Valka (Irkutsk Story by Arbuzov), Oxana (Loss of the Squadron by Korneichuk), Masha (Three Sisters by Chekhov), Grushenka (Brothers Karamazov by Dostoyevsky), Arkadina (The Seagull by Chekhov); films: Nadya (Elder Sister by Volodin), Natasha (Again about Love by Radzuiskiy), Zoya (First Echelon), Klava (Horizon), Nika (Roll Call), Shura (Stepmother); also acted in TV films. *Address:* Moscow Arts Theatre (MKhAT), 22 Tverskoi Boulevard, Moscow, U.S.S.R.

DOROSZKIEWICZ, Bazyli; Polish priest; b. 15 March 1914, Cisy; ed. Warsaw Univ., Moscow Theological Acad.; parish priest of Polish Autocephalous Orthodox Church, Michałowo 1940-46; parish priest, Gródek nr. Białystok 1946-60; Bishop of Wrocław and Szczecin Diocese 1960-70; Metropolitan of Warsaw and of Poland 1970-; mem. Nat. Unity Front 1960; Commdr.'s Cross with Star, Officer's Cross, Kt.'s Cross of Order of Polonia Restituta, Order of the Holy Agnus Dei (Finnish Orthodox Church) and numerous other Polish and foreign awards. *Publications:* religious and historical articles in ecclesiastical press, including Cerkiewny Wiestnik, Wiadomości; Pastoral letters and occasional messages to congregation. *Leisure interests:* collecting old prints and icons, building and restoration of sacred buildings including Cathedral in Wrocław. *Address:* Al. Świerczewskiege 52 m. 6, 03-402 Warsaw, Poland. *Telephone:* 19-34-09.

DORR, Noel, M.A., B. COMM.; Irish diplomatist; b. 1 Nov. 1933, Limerick; s. of John Dorr and Bridget Clancy; m. Caitriona Doran 1983; ed. St. Nathy's Coll., Ballaghderreen, Nat. Univ. of Ireland, Georgetown Univ., Washington, D.C.; Third Sec., Dept. of Foreign Affairs, Dublin 1960-62, Embassy, Brussels 1962-64, First Sec. Embassy, Washington, D.C. 1964-70, Dept. of Foreign Affairs, Dublin 1970-72, Counsellor (Press and Information) 1972-74, Asst. Sec. and Political Dir. 1974-77, Deputy Sec. and Political Dir. 1977-80, Perm. Rep. to UN 1980-83; Amb. to U.K. 1983-87; Sec. Dept. of Foreign Affairs 1987-. *Leisure interests:* reading, swimming. *Address:* Department of Foreign Affairs, 80 St. Stephen's Green, Dublin 2, Ireland.

DORRANCE, John Thompson, Jr.; American business executive; b. 7 Feb. 1919, Cinnaminson, N.J.; m. Diana Dripps 1979; three s. one d.; ed. St. George's School, Princeton Univ.; mem. Bd. of Dirs. Campbell Soup Co. 1947-, Asst. Treas. 1950-55, Asst. to the Pres. 1955-62, Chair. of Bd.

1962–84, Chair. of Exec. Cttee. 1984–; mem. Bd. of Dirs., Morgan Guaranty Trust Co. 1955–, Penn. Mutual Life Insurance Co., Carter Hawley Hale Stores Inc. *Address:* 230 S. Broad Street, 9th Floor, East Philadelphia, Pa. 19102 (Office); Monk Road, Gladwyne, Pa. 19035, U.S.A. (Home).

DORSEY, Bob Rawls; American oil executive; b. 27 Aug. 1912, Rockland, Texas; m. Angelina Johnapelus 1941; two s. one d.; ed. Univ. of Texas; with Gulf Oil Corpn., Port Arthur Refinery 1934–38; Univ. of Texas 1938–40; Port Arthur Refinery, Gulf Oil Corpn. 1940–48; Man. Venezuela Gulf Refining Co., Puerto la Cruz, Venezuela 1948–55; Gen. Office, Gulf Oil Corpn. 1955–58, Admin. Vice-Pres. 1958–61, Sr. Vice-Pres. 1961, Exec. Vice-Pres. 1961–65, Pres. 1965–72, Dir. 1964–76, Chair. of the Bd. and C.E.O. 1973–76; Charter Trustee, Univ. of Pittsburgh; Oil and Gas Consultant, Austin, Tex. 1976–78; Chair. and Chief Operations Resource Drilling, Inc., Houston, Tex. 1978–; Dir. The Superior Oil Co., Canadian Superior Oil Ltd., Falconbridge Nickel Mines Ltd., mem. Univ. of Tex. Devt. Bd.; Hon. D.Sc. (Tampa); Distinguished Graduate Award in Engineering, Univ. of Texas 1965, Distinguished Alumnus of Univ. of Texas 1968. *Leisure interests:* hunting, fishing, modern art, horticulture, football, baseball, reading (especially geography). *Address:* 5151 San Felipe Street, Suite 1380, Houston, Tex. 77056, U.S.A.

DORST, Jean P(ierre), DR.SC.; French biologist and philosopher; b. 7 Aug. 1924, Brunstatt, Haut-Rhin; s. of Victor J. Dorst and Gabrielle Rusch; m. Emmanuelle Munier 1985; ed. Univ. of Paris; Asst. Muséum national d'histoire naturelle 1947, Master of Confs. 1949, Prof. and Dir. of Lab. of Zoology (Birds and Mammals) 1964, Deputy Dir.-Gen. 1971, Dir.-Gen. 1976–85; Past Pres. Charles Darwin Foundation for the Galapagos; Trustee, Inst. océanographique, Conservatoire nat. des Arts et Métiers; mem. Acad. des Sciences, Inst. de France, Acad. des sciences d'outre-mer, Acad. d'Alsace, Acad. de Bordeaux and numerous scientific socs. in France, Europe and rest of world; Officier, Légion d'honneur; Officier, Ordre Nat. du Mérite; Order of the Golden Ark (Netherlands). *Publications:* The Migrations of Birds 1962, Before Nature Dies 1965, Field Guide to the Larger African Mammals 1967, The Life of Birds 1971, L'Univers de la Vie 1975, La Force du Vivant 1979, Asia Sub-orientale 1987, Amazonica 1987. *Leisure interests:* fine arts, painting, philately, horse-riding. *Address:* 14 quai d'Orléans, 75004 Paris, France (Home). *Telephone:* (43) 31 8956 (Office); (43) 29 52 22 (Home).

DORST, Tankred; German author; b. 19 Dec. 1925, Sonneberg; s. of Max and Elisabeth Dorst; mem. German PEN Centre, Bayerische Akad. der schönen Künste, Deutsche Akad. der darstellenden Künste, Deutsche Akad. für Sprache und Dichtung; several prizes including Gerhart Hauptmann Prize. *Works include:* around 20 plays for stage and television including Toller, Eiszeit, Merlin oder das wüste Land; several opera libretti; author and dir. of films including Klaras Mutter, Mosch, Eisenhans. *Address:* Schleissheimerstrasse 182, D-8000 Munich 40, Federal Republic of Germany. *Telephone:* 3006432.

DOSHI, Balkrishna Vithaldas, A.R.I.B.A.; Indian architect; b. 26 Aug. 1927, Pune (Poona); s. of Vithaldas Gokuldas and Radhaben Vithaldas; m. Kamala Savailal Parikh 1955; three d.; ed. Sir J.J. Coll. of Arts, Bombay; Sr. Designer, Le Corbusier Studio, Paris 1951–55; Prin., Vastu-Shilpa Architecture and Planning Firm, Ahmedabad 1956–77; f. mem. and First Hon. Dir. School of Architecture, Ahmedabad 1962–72, School of Planning, Ahmedabad 1972–81; Dean, Centre for Environmental Planning and Tech. 1972–79; Vice-Pres. Council of Architecture, Govt. of India 1974–79; mem. Advisory Bd., Architecture and Urbanism Publishing Co., Tokyo 1972–, Bldg. Inst., London 1972–76, Int. Jury Panel, Competition for Urban Environment in Developing Countries, Manila 1975–76; Partner, Messrs. Stein Doshi & Bhalla, New Delhi, Ahmedabad 1977; f. mem.-trustee and Dir. Vastu-Shilpa Foundation for Studies and Research in Environmental Design, Ahmedabad 1978–; Chair. Centre for Environmental Planning and Tech., Study Cell 1978–; Fellow, Indian Inst. of Architects; Hon. Fellow, A.I.A. 1971; Padmashree award, Govt. of India 1976; Pan Pacific Architectural Citation award, Hawaii Chapter of A.I.A. 1981. *Major works include:* townships for Gujarat State Fertilizer Co. Ltd., Baroda 1964–65, Electronics Corpn. of India Ltd., Hyderabad 1968, Dept. of Atomic Energy, Govt. of India, Kota 1972, Indian Farmers' Fertilizer Co-op., Kalol 1973, L.D. Inst. of Indology, Ahmedabad 1959, Campus for Centre for Environmental Planning and Tech., Ahmedabad 1967, Indian Inst. of Man., Bangalore 1977. *Publications:* numerous articles and contributions to architectural journals. *Leisure interests:* photography, studies of philosophy. *Address:* "Sangath", Thaltej Road, Ahmedabad 380 054 (Office); 5 Sundarnagar, New Delhi 110 003 (Office); 14 Shri Sadma Society, Navrangpura, Ahmedabad, 380 009, India (Home). *Telephone:* 443173/445670 (Ahmedabad Office); 618236/618237 (New Delhi Office); 442444 (Home).

DOSHI, Vinod, M.SC. (ENG.); Indian business executive; b. 20 March 1932; ed. Albion Coll., Mich., U.S.A. and Univ. of Mich.; man. trainee, Cooper Eng. Ltd. (now amalgamated with Walchandnagar Industries Ltd.) 1958, Dir. in charge of operations 1960, Man. Dir. 1970–75; Vice-Chair. and Man. Dir. Walchandnagar Industries Ltd. 1975, now Chair.; mem. Bd. of Dirs. The Premier Automobiles Ltd. 1972, Chair. of Bd. 1982; Chair. and Dir. numerous cos.; mem. or fmr. mem. of numerous govt. bodies etc. *Leisure interests:* colour photography, music and sound recording, amateur theatre and commercial cinema. *Address:* Walchandnagar Industries Ltd., Con-

struction House, Walchand Hirachand Marg, Ballard Estate, Bombay 400038, India. *Telephone:* 268091.

DOS SANTOS, H.E. Cardinal Alexander José Maria, O.F.M.; Portuguese ecclesiastic; b. 18 March 1924, Inhambane; ordained 1953, elected to Church in Lourenço Marques, (now Maputo) 1974, consecrated Bishop 1975; cr. Cardinal 1988. *Address:* Paço Arquiepiscopal, Avenida Eduardo Mondlane 1448, C.P. 258, Maputo, Mozambique. *Telephone:* 21.873.

DOS SANTOS, José Eduardo; Angolan politician; b. 28 Aug. 1942, Luanda; s. of Eduardo Avelino dos Santos and Jacinta José Paulino; ed. Liceu Salvador Correia; joined Movimento Popular de Libertação de Angola (MPLA) 1961; went into exile 1961 and was a founder mem. and Vice-Pres. of MPLA Youth based in Léopoldville, Congo (now Kinshasa, Zaire); first Rep., MPLA, Brazzaville 1961; sent with group of students for training in Moscow 1963; graduated as Petroleum Engineer, Inst. of Oil and Gas, Baku 1969; then military course in telecommunications; returned to Angola and participated in war against Portuguese 1970–74; Second in Command of Telecommunications Services, MPLA Second Politico-Military Region, Cabinda; mem. Provisional Readjustment Cttee., Northern Front 1974; mem. MPLA Cen. Cttee. and Political Bureau 1974–; Chair. MPLA; Minister of Foreign Affairs, Angola 1975; Co-ordinator, MPLA Foreign Relations Dept. 1975; Sec. Cen. Cttee. for Educ., Culture and Sport, then for Nat. Reconstruction, then Economic Devt. and Planning 1977–79; First Deputy Prime Minister, Minister of Planning and Head of Nat. Planning Comm. 1978–79; Pres. of Angola and Chair. of Council of Ministers Sept. 1979–; C.-in-C. of FAPLA (Armed Forces of MPLA). *Address:* Gabinete do Presidente, Luanda, Angola.

DOS SANTOS, Manuel, B.SC.; Mozambican diplomatist; b. 7 May 1944; mem. Mozambique Liberation Front Exec. Cttee. 1967; fmr. Nat. Treasurer; mem. Cen. Cttee.; Sec. for Econ. Affairs; Public Relations Officer to Prime Minister 1974; Dir. Foreign Trade at Ministry for Industry and Trade 1975–76; Gen. Sec. Ministry of Foreign Affaris 1977–78; Minister for Internal Trade 1978–80; Amb. to Tanzania 1980–83; Perm. Rep. of Mozambique to UN 1982–; Pres. Econ. and Soc. Council UN 1986–. *Address:* Permanent Mission of Mozambique to the United Nations, 70 East 79th Street, New York, N.Y. 10021, U.S.A. *Telephone:* (212) 517-4550.

DOS SANTOS, Marcelino; Mozambique poet and nationalist leader; b. 1931, Lourenço Marques; ed. Lisbon and Paris; Sec. of External Affairs, Presidential Council of Frente de Libertação de Moçambique (FRELIMO) 1969–75; Vice-Pres. FRELIMO (now Frelimo Party) 1970–78, mem. Political Bureau FRELIMO, Sec. for Econ. Affairs April 1980–; Minister of Devt. and Econ. Planning 1975–78, for the Nat. Comm. of the Plan 1978–80; fmr. Gov. Sofala Province; audience with Pope Paul VI, Rome July 1970. *Address:* FRELIMO, Maputo, Mozambique.

DOST, Shah Mohammad; Afghan politician; b. 1929, Kabul; ed. Kabul Univ.; mem. People's Democratic Party of Afghanistan 1963, mem. Cen. Cttee. 1979; fmr. Deputy Foreign Minister and Foreign Minister of the Democratic Rep. of Afghanistan; mem. Revolutionary Council; Minister of State for Foreign Affairs 1986–88; Order of People's Friendship. *Address:* c/o Ministry of Foreign Affairs, Shah Mahmoud Ghazi Street, Shar-i-Nau, Kabul, Afghanistan. *Telephone:* (93) 25441.

DOTRICE, Roy; British actor; b. 26 May 1925, Guernsey, Channel Islands; s. of Louis Dotrice and Neva Wilton; m. Kay Newman 1946; three d.; ed. Dayton and Intermediate Schools, Guernsey; air gunner, R.A.F. 1940; P.O.W. 1942–45; acted in repertory 1945–55; formed and directed Guernsey Theatre Co. 1955; Royal Shakespeare Co. 1957–65 (playing Caliban, Julius Caesar, Hotspur, Firs, Puntila, Edward IV, etc.); World War 2½, New Theatre, London 1966; Brief Lives (one-man play), Criterion (over 400 performances, world record for longest-running solo performance) 1969, toured England, Canada, U.S.A. 1973, Mayfair (over 150 performances) 1974; Broadway season 1974; Australian tour 1975; Peer Gynt, Chichester Festival 1970; One At Night, Royal Court 1971; The Hero, Edinburgh 1970; Mother Adam, Arts 1971; Tom Brown's Schooldays, Cambridge 1972; The Hollow Crown, seasons in U.S.A. 1973 and 1975, Sweden 1975; Gomes, Queen's 1973; The Dragon Variation, Duke of York's 1977; Australian tour with Chichester Festival 1978; Passion of Dracula, Queen's 1978; Oliver, Albery 1979; Mr. Lincoln (one-man play), New York 1980, Fortune 1981, A Life, New York 1981, Henry V, Stratford, Conn. 1981, Falstaff (American Shakespeare Co.) 1982, Kingdoms, Broadway 1982, Churchill, Washington and Los Angeles 1983, The Genius, Los Angeles 1983, Enemy of the People, New York 1985, Hay Fever, New York and Washington 1985–86. *Films include:* The Heroes of Telemark 1965, A Twist of Sand 1968, Lock up Your Daughters 1969, Buttercup Chain, Tomorrow, One of Those Things 1971, Nicholas and Alexandra 1971, Amadeus, The Corsican Brothers 1983, The Eliminators 1985, Shaka Zulu 1985, Young Harry Houdini 1986. *TV appearances include:* Dear Liar, Brief Lives, The Caretaker (Emmy Award), Imperial Palace, Misleading Cases, Clochemerle, Dickens of London, Stargazy on Zummerdown; numerous American TV appearances including Remington Steel, Hart to Hart, Family Reunion, Magnum P.I., Fairy Tale Theatre, Tales from Darkside, A Team, The Wizard, Tales of Gold Monkey; TV Actor of the Year Award 1968. *Leisure interests:* baseball, fishing, riding. *Address:* Leading Players, 31 Kings Road, London,

S.W.3 (Agent); 98 St. Martin's Lane, London, W.C.2, England. *Telephone:* 01-730 9411; 01-836-7054.

DOTY, Paul Mead, B.S., M.A., PH.D.; American biochemist and specialist in science policy and arms control; b. 1 June 1920; ed. Pennsylvania State Coll., Columbia and Cambridge Univs.; Instructor and Research Assoc. Polytechnic Inst., Brooklyn 1943-45, Asst. Prof. Chemistry 1945-46; Asst. Prof. Chemistry, Univ. de Notre Dame 1947-48; Asst. Prof. Harvard 1948-50, Assoc. Prof. Chemistry 1950-56, Prof. 1956-; Pres. Science Advisory Cttee. 1961-65; Mallinckrodt Prof. of Biochemistry 1968-88; Consultant to the Arms Control and Disarmament Agency, Nat. Security Council; Dir. of Center for Science and Int. Affairs, Harvard Univ. 1973-85; mem. Gen. Advisory Cttee. on Arms Control 1977-81; Sr. Fellow, Aspen Inst., Fellow, American Acad. of Arts and Science, Nat. Acad. of Sciences, Philosophical Soc., Rockefeller Fellow, Cambridge Univ. 1946-47. *Address:* Center for Sciences and International Affairs, John F. Kennedy School of Government, Harvard University, 79 Boylston Street, Cambridge, Mass. 02138, U.S.A. *Telephone:* 617-495-1401.

DOUGLAS, Charles Primrose, M.A., M.B., F.R.C.O.G.; British professor and consultant obstetrician; b. 17 Feb. 1921, Ayr; s. of Charles Douglas and Rhoda (née Patrick) Douglas; m. Angela Francis 1948; three s. one d.; ed. Loretto School, Cambridge and Edinburgh Univs.; William Waldorf Astor Foundation Fellow, U.S.A. 1957; Visiting Fellow, Duke Univ. 1958; Sr. Lecturer Univ. of West Indies 1959-66; Prof. Obstetrics and Gynaecology Royal Free Hosp., Univ. of London 1966-75, Univ. of Cambridge 1976-88; Hon. F.A.C.O.G.; mem. Council Royal Coll. of Obstetricians and Gynaecologists 1980-86, Hon. Fellow 1983. *Publications:* Diseases of the Vulva 1972, numerous professional articles. *Leisure interests:* horse racing and breeding, holidays. *Address:* Old Mill House, Linton Road, Balsham, Cambs., CB1 6HA, England. *Telephone:* 0223-336871.

DOUGLAS, Donald Willis, Jr.; American businessman; b. 3 July 1917, Washington D.C.; s. of Donald Willis Douglas and Charlotte (Ogg) Douglas; m. 1st Molly McIntosh 1939 (deceased), 2nd Jean Cooper 1950; two d.; ed. Stanford Univ. and Curtiss-Wright Tech. Inst.; joined Douglas Aircraft Co. Inc., Santa Monica, Calif. 1939, Chief, Flight Test Group in charge of testing models 1943-, Dir. Contract Admin. 1948, in charge, Research Laboratories, Santa Monica Div. 1949, Vice-Pres. Mil. Sales 1951-57, Pres. 1957-67; Corporate Vice-Pres., McDonnell Douglas Corpn. 1967-71, Sr. Corp. Vice-Pres. 1971-72; Pres. and C.E.O. Douglas Devt. Co. 1972-74; Chair. of Bd., Capistrano Nat. Bank 1975-82, Capistrano Bancorp 1981-; Chair. of Bd., Biphase Energy Systems 1975-80, DCOR Partners Real Estate 1979-80, Biphase Energy Systems, Jt. Venture of Research—Cottrell and Transamerica Delaval 1980—82, Sr. Consultant, Market Devt. 1982-; Chair. of Bd. of Trustees, Donald Douglas Museum and Library 1974-, Govt. Aerospace Industries Asscn., Air Force Asscn.; Dir. Partners Real Estate Inc. 1978-; Trustee Air Force Museum Foundation; mem. Asscn. of the U.S. Army, Conquistadores del Cielo, Nat. Defense Transportation Asscn., American Inst. of Aeronautics and Astronautics; Dir. Hilton Hotels Corpn. 1966-; Chevalier, Légion d'honneur 1961, Officer of the Order of Merit (Italy) 1962; mem. various clubs and yachting clubs. *Leisure interests:* hunting, fishing, yachting. *Address:* P.O. Box 8788, Trenton, N.J. 08650, U.S.A.

DOUGLAS, Kirk, A.B.; American actor; b. 9 Dec. 1916, Amsterdam, N.Y.; s. of Harry and Bryna (née Sanglel) Danielovitch; m. 1st Diana Dill (divorced 1950), two s.; m. 2nd Anne Buydens 1954, two s.; ed. St. Lawrence Univ., and American Acad. of Dramatic Arts; Pres. Bryna Productions 1955-; Dir. Los Angeles Chapter, UN Asscn.; Acad. Awards 1948, 1952, 1956; New York Film Critics Award, Hollywood Foreign Press Award, Commdr., Ordre des Arts et Lettres 1979, Presidential Medal of Freedom 1981, etc.; Hon. Dr. of Fine Arts (St. Lawrence) 1958. *Broadway stage appearances:* Spring Again, Three Sisters, Kiss and Tell, The Wind is Ninety, Alice in Arms, Man Bites Dog, The Boys of Autumn (not on Broadway). *Films include:* The Strange Love of Martha Ivers, Letter to Three Wives, Ace in the Hole, The Bad and the Beautiful, 20,000 Leagues under the Sea, Ulysses, Lust for Life, Gunfight at O.K. Corral, Paths of Glory, The Vikings, Last Train from Gun Hill, The Devil's Disciple, Spartacus, Strangers When We Meet, Seven Days in May, Town without Pity, The List of Adrian Messenger, In Harms Way, Cast a Giant Shadow, The Way West, War Waggon, The Brotherhood, The Arrangement, There Was a Crooked Man, Gunfight 1971, Light at the Edge of the World, Catch Me a Spy, A Man to Respect 1972, Cat and Mouse, Scalawag (dir.) 1973, Once Is Not Enough 1975, Posse (prod., actor) 1975, The Moneychangers (TV) 1976, Holocaust 2000 1977, The Fury 1977, Villain 1978, Saturn 3 1979, The Final Countdown 1980, The Man from Snowy River, Tough Guys 1986, Queenie (TV miniseries) 1987. *Publication:* The Ragman's Son: An Autobiography 1988. *Address:* The Bryna Company, 141 El Camino Drive, Beverly Hills, Calif. 90212; 805 N. Rexford Drive, Beverly Hills, Calif. 90210, U.S.A. *Telephone:* (213) 274-5294 (Office).

DOUGLAS, Michael Anthony, J.P., M.P.; Dominican politician; b. 26 April 1940, Dominica; s. of Robert Bernard Douglas and Bernadette Douglas; m. Olivia Elemena Bryan 1962; five s. two d.; ed. Dominican Grammar School, Mount St. Benedict Coll., Trinidad, N.E. Gloucestershire Coll. of Art and Tech., England, Gloucester City Tech. Coll.; Councillor Portsmouth Town Council 1970-87; Minister for Agric., Trade and Co-operatives 1975-

76, for Communications and Works 1976-78, for Finance and Deputy Prime Minister 1979-80; Leader of Opposition 1985-; Leader Labour Party 1985-; Gov. IMF, IBRD and Caribbean Devt. Bank 1979-80. *Leisure interests:* swimming, playing dominoes. *Address:* Indian River Inn, Bay Street, Portsmouth, Dominica, West Indies. *Telephone:* (809) 44-55289; (809) 44-82401.

DOUGLAS, Michael Kirk, B.A.; American actor and film producer; b. 25 Sept. 1944, New Brunswick, N.J.; s. of Kirk Douglas (q.v.) and Diana Douglas; m. Diandra Mornell Luker 1977; one s.; Acad. Award for Best Actor (for Wall Street) 1988. *Film appearances:* It's My Turn, Hail Heroll 1969, Summertime 1971, Napoleon and Samantha 1972, Coma 1978, Running 1979, Star Chamber 1983, Romancing the Stone 1984, A Chorus Line 1985, Jewel of the Nile 1985, Fatal Attraction 1987, Wall Street 1987, Heidi 1989, Black Ruin 1989. *Films produced:* One Flew Over the Cuckoo's Nest (Academy Award for Best Film 1975), The China Syndrome, Sarman (exec. producer), Romancing the Stone, Jewel of the Nile; appeared in TV series Streets of San Francisco. *Address:* 1888 Century Park East, Suite 1400, Los Angeles, Calif. 90067, U.S.A.

DOUGLAS, Roger Owen; New Zealand accountant and politician; b. 5 Dec. 1937, Auckland; s. of Norman V. and Jenny Douglas; m. Glennis June Anderson 1961; one s. one d.; ed. Auckland Grammar School, Auckland Univ.; entered House of Reps. as Labour mem. for Manukau 1969 (now Manurewa); Minister of Broadcasting 1973-75, of the Post Office 1973-74, of Housing (with State Advances, Housing Corpn.) 1974-75; Minister of Finance and Minister in Charge of the Inland Revenue Dept. and of Friendly Socs. 1984-87, of Finance 1987-88; fmr. Pres. Auckland Labour Regional Council, Manukau Labour Cttee. *Publications:* There's Got to be a Better Way 1980, Towards Prosperity 1987; several papers on int. and econ. affairs. *Leisure interests:* cricket, rugby, reading. *Address:* 15 Wheturangi Road, Green Lane, Auckland, New Zealand (Home). *Telephone:* 545-603 (Home).

DOUGLAS, William Wilton, M.D., F.R.S.; British professor of pharmacology; b. 15 Aug. 1922; s. of T. H. J. Douglas and Catherine Dorward (née Wilton); m. Jeannine M. H. Dumoulin 1954; two s.; ed. Glasgow Acad. and Univ. of Glasgow; Resident House Surgeon, Glasgow Western Infirmary 1946, Law Hosp. Carluke 1947; Demonstrator in Physiology, Univ. of Aberdeen 1948; served R.A.M.C. 1949-50; mem. staff, Nat. Inst. of Medical Research, Mill Hill 1950-56; Prof. of Pharmacology, Albert Einstein Coll. of Medicine, New York 1956-68; Prof. of Pharmacology, Yale Univ. School of Medicine 1968-. *Publications:* papers in scientific journals. *Leisure interests:* yachting, skiing. *Address:* 76 Blake Road, Hamden, Conn. 06517, U.S.A. *Telephone:* (203) 776-8696.

DOUGLAS-HOME, Hon. William, B.A.; British playwright; b. 3 June 1912, Edinburgh; s. of 13th Earl of Home, Kt.; m. Rachel Brand 1951; one s. three d.; ed. Eton and New Coll., Oxford; fmr. Capt. in R.A.C.; professional playwright 1937-. *Plays:* Great Possessions 1937, Passing By 1940, Now Barabbas 1947, The Chiltern Hundreds 1947, Ambassador Extraordinary 1948, Master of Arts 1949, The Thistle and the Rose 1949, Caro William 1952, The Bad Samaritan 1953, The Manor of Northstead 1954, The Reluctant Debutante 1955, The Iron Duchess 1957, Aunt Edwina 1959, Up a Gum Tree 1960, The Bad Soldier Smith 1961, The Cigarette Girl 1962, The Drawing Room Tragedy 1963, The Reluctant Peer 1964, Two Accounts Rendered 1964, Betzi 1965, A Friend in Need 1965, A Friend Indeed 1966, The Secretary Bird 1968, The Queen's Highland Servant 1968, The Grouse Moor Image 1968, The Bishop and the Actress 1968, The Jockey Club Stakes 1970, Uncle Dick's Surprise 1970, The Douglas Cause 1971, Lloyd George Knew My Father 1972, At the End of the Day 1973, The Bank Manager 1974, The Dame of Sark 1974, The Lord's Lieutenant 1974, In The Red, The Kingfisher, Rolls Hyphen Royce, The Perch, The Consulting Room 1977, The Editor Regrets 1978, You're All Right: How am I? 1981, Four Hearts Doubled 1982, Her Mother Came Too 1982, The Golf Umbrella 1983, David and Jonathan 1984, After the Ball is Over 1985, Portraits 1987. *Publications:* Mr Home Pronounced Hume (autiobiography) 1979, Sins of Commission 1985. *Leisure interests:* golf, politics. *Address:* Derry House, Kilmeston, nr. Alresford, Hants., England. *Telephone:* (096 279) 256.

DOUNTAS, Mihalis; Greek diplomatist; b. 1932, Athens; ed. Univ. of Athens; entered Greek Diplomatic Service 1958; Cyprus and Turkish Desk in Ministry of Foreign Affairs 1958-60; took part in bilateral Greek-Turkish negotiations 1959; mem. Del. to UN Gen. Assembly 1960-66; Consul in Toronto, Canada 1960-63; First Sec. Embassy in Nicosia 1963-66; First Sec., Washington, D.C. 1966-69; Counsellor, Nicosia 1969-71; Counsellor, Perm. Greek Del. to NATO 1971-73; Head of Greek Del. to talks on Mutual and Balanced Force Reductions (MBFR), Vienna 1973-74; Diplomatic Adviser to Constantine Karamanlis, Prime Minister Aug. 1974; Amb. to Cyprus 1974-79, to Norway 1980-82; Amb. to UN 1982-88; Officer, Order of Phoenix, Commdr., Order of the Holy Sepulchre; Officer, Order of Merit (Egypt). *Address:* c/o Ministry of Foreign Affairs, Odos Zalokosta 2, Athens, Greece.

DOURS, Jean, L. ES D.; French administrator; b. 14 Jan. 1913; s. of Simeon Dours and Mathilde Cieutat; ed. Lycée d'Auch, Coll. de Saint-Gaudens and Faculté de Droit, Paris; Adviser, Council of Prefecture of Rouen 1939;

Asst. Prefect, Albertville 1943; Asst. Chief, Office of Cen. Admin. 1945; Asst. Dir. Private Office, Prefect of Seine 1947-57; Technical Adviser, Private Office of René Billères, Minister of Educ.; Adviser, Head Office of Nat. Defence 1958, Dir. 1959; Prefect, Bône 1961-62; Dir. Pvt. Office of Christian Fouchet, High Commr. of France in Algeria April-June 1962, Pvt. Office of Christian Fouchet, Minister of Information 1962, of Nat. Educ. 1962-66; Dir.-Gen. Sûreté Nationale 1967; Dir.-Gen. of Nat. Police 1969-72; Dir.-Gen. Groupement des Industries Françaises Aéronautiques et Spatiales 1973-80; Mayor of Auch 1968-; Pres. Dir.-Gen. Société d'études Commerciales de Casino 1974-; Conseiller gen. Canton de Miélan 1973-; Commdr., Légion d'honneur, Croix de guerre, Commdr. des Palmes Académiques, and other awards. *Address:* 4 rue de Galilée, 75116 Paris (Office); 64 rue de Longchamp, Neuilly-sur-Seine; Domaine de Sainte-Livrade, 32170 Miélan, France (Homes).

DOUVILLE, Raymond, F.R.S.C., B.SC.; Canadian journalist and historian; b. 17 Sept. 1905, La Pérade, Quebec; s. of Alphonse Douville and Alice Chavigny Douville; m. Bella Beaulac 1937; three d.; ed. Univ. of Montreal; fmr. Deputy Minister and Registrar, Quebec Prov. *Publications:* Premiers Seigneurs et Colons de la Pérade 1948, Visages du Vieux Trois-Rivières 1956, La vie quotidienne en Nouvelle-France 1964, La vie quotidienne des Indiens du Canada 1967, Daily Life in Early Canada (trans.) 1967, Na Nova França O Canada (trans.) 1970; Ed. La Vie d'Arthur Buies 1933, Bien Public Aaron Hart 1938; Collaborator for the Biographical Dictionary of Canada. *Leisure interests:* historical research, travel. *Address:* 3309 rue L'Heureux, Apt. 6, Ste-Foy, Quebec G1X 1Y7, Canada. *Telephone:* (418) 651-7942.

DOVER, Sir Kenneth James, Kt., M.A., D.LITT., F.R.S.E., F.B.A.; British classical scholar; b. 11 March 1920, Croydon; s. of Percy Henry James and Dorothy Valerie Anne (Healey) Dover; m. Audrey Ruth Latimer 1947; one s. one d.; ed. St. Paul's School, Balliol and Merton Colls., Oxford; served Royal Artillery 1940-45; Fellow and Tutor of Balliol Coll., Oxford 1948-55; Prof. of Greek, Univ. of St. Andrews 1955-76, Chancellor 1981-; Pres. Corpus Christi Coll. Oxford 1976-86, Hon. Fellow 1986-; Visiting Lecturer, Harvard Univ. 1960; Visiting Prof. Univ. of Calif., Berkeley 1967; Prof.-at-Large Cornell Univ. 1983-88; Prof. Stanford Univ. 1987-; F.B.A. 1966-, Pres. 1978-81; Hon. Fellow, Balliol Coll. 1977-, Merton Coll. 1980-, Pres. Hellenic Soc. 1971-74, Classical Asscn. 1975; Foreign mem. Royal Netherlands Acad. 1979-; Foreign hon. mem. American Acad. of Arts and Sciences 1979-; Hon. LL.D. (Birmingham) 1979, Hon. D.Litt. (Bristol and London) 1980, (Liverpool) 1983, (Durham) 1984, Hon. LL.D. and D. Litt. (St. Andrews) 1981, Hon. D.H.L. (Oglethorpe) 1984. *Publications:* Greek Word Order 1960, Clouds (Aristophanes) 1968, Lysias and the Corpus Lysiacum 1968, (with A. W. Gomme and A. Andrewes) Historical Commentary on Thucydides, vol. IV 1970, vol. V 1981, Theocritus, Select Poems 1971, Aristophanic Comedy 1972, Greek Popular Morality in the Time of Plato and Aristotle 1974, Greek Homosexuality 1978, The Greeks 1980, Ancient Greek Literature (with M. L. West and others) 1980, Greek and the Greeks 1987, The Greeks and their Legacy 1989. *Leisure interests:* rough and lonely country and hill walking, historical and comparative linguistics. *Address:* 49 Hepburn Gardens, St. Andrews, Fife, KY16 9LS, Scotland. *Telephone:* St. Andrews 73589.

DOVLATYAN, Frunzik Vaginakovich; Soviet (Armenian) actor and film director; b. 1927; ed. Moscow All-Union Inst. of Cinema; fmr. stage actor; has worked in films since 1944; mem. CPSU 1951-; ed. Moscow All-Union Inst. of Cinema; Sec. of Armenian Cinema Union 1969-; Armenian State Prize 1950; People's Artist of U.S.S.R. 1983. *Acting roles include:* Melik-Mansur in David-bek 1944, Vagachan in Anait 1947, Manoukian in The Noise of the River 1959; *Films include:* The Career of Dima Gorin 1961, Morning Trains 1963, Hello, it's Me! 1966, Birth 1978, Live Long 1980.

DOW, (John) Christopher (Roderick), F.B.A., B.SC. (ECON.); British economist; b. 1916, Harrogate; s. of Warrender Begernie and Amy Dow; m. Clare Keegan 1960; one s. three d.; ed. Bootham School, York, Brighton, Hove and Sussex Grammar School, and Univ. Coll., London; Drummond-Fraser Research Fellow, Dept. of Economics Univ. of Manchester 1938-39; R.A.F. 1940-43; Ministry of Aircraft Production 1943-45; Econ. Section, Cabinet Office, later Treasury successively Econ. Asst., Econ. Adviser, Sr. Econ. Adviser 1945-54, 1962-63; Research in Man. of British Economy, Cambridge Univ. 1954-55; Nat. Inst. of Econ. and Social Research, London 1955-62, Deputy Dir. 1957-62; Asst. Sec.-Gen. (Econ. and Statistics) OECD 1963-73; Exec. Dir. Bank of England 1973-81, Adviser to Gov. 1981-84; Visiting Fellow Nat. Inst. of Econ. and Social Research. *Address:* NIBSR, 2 Dean Trench Street, London, S.W.1, England.

DOWELL, Anthony James, C.B.E.; British ballet dancer; b. 16 Feb. 1943, London; s. of Arthur H. Dowell and late Catherine E. Dowell; ed. Royal Ballet School; Prin. dancer, The Royal Ballet 1966, Sr. Prin. dancer 1967-; joined American Ballet Theatre 1978; created the following ballets: The Dream 1964, Benvolio in Romeo and Juliet 1965, Shadow Play 1967, Monotones 1969, Triad 1972, Manon 1974; narrator in Oedipus Rex, Metropolitan Opera House, New York 1981; created role of Prospero in Nureyev's The Tempest, Royal Opera House, London 1982; Asst. to Dir. Royal Ballet 1984-85, Dir. 1986-. *Address:* c/o The Royal Ballet, Covent Garden, London, WC2E 7QA, England. *Telephone:* 01-240 1200.

DOWELL, John Derek, PH.D., C.PHYS., F.INST.P., F.R.S.; British professor of elementary particle physics; b. 6 Jan. 1935, Ashby de la Zouch; s. of William E. Dowell and Elsie D. Dowell; m. Patricia Clarkson 1959; one s. one d.; ed. Coalville Grammar School, Leics. and Univ. of Birmingham; Research Fellow, Univ. of Birmingham 1958-60; Research Assoc. CERN, Geneva 1960-62; Lecturer, Univ. of Birmingham 1962-70, Sr. Lecturer 1970-74, Reader 1974-80, Prof. of Elementary Particle Physics 1980-; Visiting Scientist, Argonne Nat. Lab. U.S.A. 1968-69; Scientific Assoc. CERN 1973-74, 1985-87; Chair. SERC Particle Physics Cttee. 1981-85; mem. CERN Scientific Policy Cttee. 1981-; mem. American Physical Soc.; Rutherford Medal and Prize, Inst. of Physics 1988. *Publications:* numerous papers in physics journals. *Leisure interests:* piano, amateur theatre, skiing, squash. *Address:* 57 Oxford Road, Moseley, Birmingham, B13 9ES, England. *Telephone:* (021) 449-3332.

DOWIYOGO, Bernard; Nauru politician; b. 14 Feb. 1946; ed. local schools and Australian Nat. Univ.; Lawyer; M.P. 1973-; Sec. Nauru Gen. Hosp. and Gen. Man. Nauru Co-operative Soc.; Pres. of Nauru 1976-78; Minister of Justice Dec. 1983-; Chair. Bank of Nauru 1985-; Leader Nauru Party. *Address:* c/o Parliament House, Nauru, Central Pacific.

DOWLING, John Elliott, PH.D.; American professor of biology and neurobiologist; b. 31 Aug. 1935, Rhode Island; s. of Joseph Leo Dowling and Ruth W. (Tappan) Dowling; m. 1st Susan Kinney (divorced 1974), two s.; m. 2nd Judith Falco 1975, one d.; ed. Harvard Univ.; Instructor, Harvard Univ. 1961, Asst. Prof. 1961-64; Assoc. Prof., Johns Hopkins Univ. 1964-71; Prof. of Biology, Harvard Univ. 1971-, Assoc. Dean 1980-84, Master, Leverett House 1981-; mem. N.A.S., American Acad. of Arts and Sciences; Hon. M.D. (Lund, Sweden) 1982; Friedenwald Medal 1979, Retinal Research Award 1981. *Publications:* 160 publs. in professional journals (1986) and ed. of 5 vols; The Retina: An Approachable Part of the Brain 1987. *Leisure interests:* sailing, squash and music. *Address:* The Biological Laboratories, 16 Divinity Avenue, Cambridge, Mass. 02138 (Office); Master's Lodgings, Leverett House, Harvard University, Cambridge, Mass. 02138, U.S.A. (Home).

DOWLING, Vincent, D.F.A.; American (b. Irish) actor, director, producer and playwright; b. 7 Sept. 1929, Dublin; s. of Mai Kelly Dowling and William Dowling; m. Olwen Patricia O'Herlihy 1975; one s. four d.; ed. St. Mary's Coll., Rathmines, Dublin, Brendan Smith Acad. of Acting; with Standard Life Insurance Co., Dublin 1946-50; Brendan Smith Productions, Dublin 1950-51; Roche-David Theatre Productions 1951-53; actor, dir., Deputy Artistic Dir., Lifetime Assoc., Abbey Theatre, Dublin 1953-76; Producing Dir. Great Lakes Shakespeare Festival, Cleveland, Ohio 1976-84; Artistic and Producing Dir. Solvang Theaterfest 1984-86; Prof. of Theatre, Coll. of Wooster, Ohio 1986-87; Artistic Dir., Abbey Theatre 1987-; Outstanding Producer, Cleveland Critics Circle Award 1982 for The Life and Adventures of Nicholas Nickelby; Irishman of the Year 1982; TV Emmy Award, for Playboy of the Western World 1983. *Original plays:* Do Me A Favorite, or The Fit-Ups 1978, Acting is Murder 1986. *Leisure interests:* fly fishing, collecting paintings and sculpture. *Address:* Abbey Theatre, Lower Abbey Street, Dublin 1, Ireland; Stepaside House, Box 30A, East River Road, Huntington, Mass. 01050, U.S.A. *Telephone:* (01) 748-741 (Dublin).

DOWN, Sir Alastair Frederick, Kt., O.B.E., M.C., T.D., C.A.; British oil executive; b. 23 July 1914, Kirkcaldy, Fife, Scotland; s. of Frederick Edward Down and Margaret Isobel Hutchison; m. Bunny Mellon 1947; two s. two d.; ed. Marlborough Coll.; British Petroleum (then Anglo-Iranian Oil Co.) 1938-; Army Service 1940-45; with BP in Iran 1945-47, London 1947-54; Chief Rep. of BP, Canada 1954, later Pres. The British Petroleum Co. of Canada Ltd., BP Canada Ltd., BP Refinery Canada Ltd., BP Exploration Co. of Canada Ltd.; Man. Dir. The British Petroleum Co. Ltd. 1962-75, Deputy Chair. 1969-75; Chair., Burmah Oil Co. Ltd. 1975-83, Chief Exec. 1975-80; Chair. British-North American Research Asscn. 1980-84, London American Energy, N.V., 1981-; Dir. TRW Inc., Ohio 1977-, Scottish American Investment Co. Ltd., Edinburgh 1980-, Royal Bank of Canada, Montreal, 1981-; mem. Soc. of Chartered Accountants of Scotland; Chair., Council of Marlborough Coll.; Fellow, British Inst. of Man., Businessman of the Year Award 1980; Cadman Memorial Medal, Inst. of Petroleum 1981. *Leisure interests:* golf, fishing, shooting. *Address:* Brieryhill, Hawick, Roxburghshire TD9 7LL, Scotland.

DOWNES, Ralph (William), C.B.E., K.S.G., M.A., B.MUS., F.R.C.M.; British organist; b. 16 Aug. 1904, Derby; s. of James and Constance Downes; m. Agnes Rix 1929 (died 1980); one s.; ed. Derby Municipal Secondary School, Royal Coll. of Music, Keble Coll., Oxford, and Pius X School of Liturgical Music, New York; Dir. of Music, Univ. Chapel, Princeton Univ. 1928-35; Prof. of Organ, Royal Coll. of Music 1954-75; Concert Organist and Organist, the London Oratory 1936-77, Emer. 1977-; Organ Consultant to L.C.C., Royal Festival Hall 1949-53, Govt. of Malta 1960-62, Corpn. of Croydon 1961-64, Cardiff City Council (St. David's Hall) 1978-; Curator of Organs, Royal Festival Hall 1954-, and Fairfield Hall, Croydon 1964-77; Jury-mem. Int. Organ Festivals, Amsterdam, Haarlem, Munich, St. Albans, Manchester; designer of organs (Royal Festival Hall, London Oratory, Paisley Abbey, Gloucester Cathedral, St. Albans Cathedral, S. Giovanni Cathedral, Valetta (Malta), St. David's Hall, Cardiff, Lancaster Univ., etc.); organ, choral and piano compositions and articles on organ design and its musical significance.

Publication: Baroque Tricks 1983; Hon. R.A.M., Hon. F.R.C.O. *Address:* c/o The Oratory, London, S.W.7, England. *Telephone:* 01-567 6330 (Home).

DOWNEY, Sir Gordon (Stanley), K.C.B., B.SC.ECON.; British public servant; b. 26 April 1928, London; s. of Stanley William and Winifred Downey; m. Jacqueline Goldsmith 1952; two d.; ed. Tiffin's School, London School of Econs.; served Royal Artillery 1946–48; Ministry of Works 1951; entered Treasury 1952; Asst. Private Sec. to Chancellor of Exchequer 1955–57; Asst. Sec. 1965, Under-Sec. 1972; Head of Cen. Unit., Treasury 1975; Deputy Sec. 1976; Deputy Head of Cen. Policy Review Staff (on secondment) 1978–81; Comptroller and Auditor-Gen. 1981–87; Special Adviser to Ernst and Whinney 1988–. *Leisure interests:* reading, tennis, visual arts. *Address:* Chinley Cottage, Eaton Park Road, Cobham, Surrey, England. *Telephone:* Cobham 67878.

DOWNIE, Leonard, Jr., M.A.; American newspaper editor and author; b. 1 May 1942, Cleveland, Ohio; s. of Leonard and Pearl M. (Evenheimer) Downie; m. 1st Barbara Lindsey 1960 (divorced 1971); m. 2nd Geraldine Rebach 1971; three s. one d.; ed. Ohio State Univ.; reporter, ed., Washington Post 1964–74, metropolitan ed. 1974–79, London corresp. 1979–82, Nat. Ed. 1982–84, Man. Ed. 1984–. *Publications:* Justice Denied 1971, Mortgage on America 1974, The New Muckrakers 1976. *Leisure interest:* travel. *Address:* Washington Post, 1150 15th Street, N.W., Washington, D.C. 20071, U.S.A. *Telephone:* (202) 334-7512.

DOWNIE, Robert Silcock, M.A., B.PHIL., F.R.S.E.; British professor of moral philosophy; b. 19 April 1933, Glasgow; s. of Robert M. Downie and Margaret M. Brown; m. Eileen Dorothea Flynn 1958; three d.; ed. Glasgow Univ., Queen's Coll., Oxford; Tutor, Worcester Coll., Oxford 1958–59; Lecturer in Moral Philosophy, Glasgow Univ. 1959–68, Sr. Lecturer 1968–69, Prof. 1969–; Visiting Prof. Syracuse Univ., U.S.A. 1963–64, Dalhousie Univ., Nova Scotia 1976. *Publications:* Government Action and Morality 1964, Respect for Persons 1969, Roles and Values 1971, Education and Personal Relationships 1974, Caring and Curing 1980, Healthy Respect 1987. *Leisure interest:* music. *Address:* Department of Philosophy, Glasgow University, Glasgow, G12 8QQ, Scotland. *Telephone:* (041) 339 8855 Ext. 4273.

DOWNS, Sir Diarmuid, C.B.E., F.R.S., F.ENG.; British chartered engineer; b. 23 April 1922, Kilburn, Middx.; s. of John Downs and Ellen McMahon; m. Mary C. Chillman 1951; one s. three d.; ed. Gunnersbury Catholic Grammar School and Univ. of London; joined Ricardo Consulting Engineers 1942, Dir. 1957, Man. Dir. 1967, Chair. and Man. Dir. 1976, Chair. Ricardo Consulting Engineers PLC 1984–87; Pres. Inst. of Mechanical Engs. 1978–79, Fed. Int. des Socs. d'Ingénieurs des Techniques de l'Automobile 1978–80; mem. Advisory Council for Applied Research and Devt. 1976–80, Science and Eng. Research Council 1981–84, Design Council 1981–; mem. Bd. of Dirs. Soc. of Automotive Engs. Inc. 1983–86, British Council 1988; Foreign Assoc. Nat. Acad. of Eng., U.S.A.; Dir. Universe Publs. Ltd.; Chair. Council of Surrey Univ.; Hon. mem. Hungarian Acad. of Sciences 1988; J. A. Ewing Medal (Inst. of Civil Engs.). *Publications:* papers on internal combustion engines in British and int. journals. *Leisure interests:* theatre, literature. *Address:* 143 New Church Road, Hove, Sussex, England. *Telephone:* (0273) 419357.

DOWSETT, Charles James Frank, PH.D., D.PHIL., F.B.A.; British orientalist; b. 2 Jan. 1924, London; s. of the late Charles Aspinall Dowsett and Louise Stokes; m. Friedel Lapuner 1949 (died 1984); ed. Owen's School, Islington, St. Catherine's Soc., Oxford and Peterhouse, Cambridge, Ecole des Langues Orientales Vivantes, Paris and Inst. Catholique, Paris; Lecturer, then Reader, in Armenian, S.O.A.S., London Univ. 1954–65; Calouste Gulbenkian Prof. of Armenian Studies, Oxford Univ. and Fellow of Pembroke Coll., Oxford 1965–; Visiting Prof., Chicago Univ. 1976; mem. of Council, Royal Asiatic Soc. 1972–76, Philological Soc. 1973–77; mem. Bd. of Man., Marjory Wardrop Fund for Georgian Studies 1966–, Chair. 1983–86; mem. Ed. Bd., Revue des études arméniennes, Paris 1978–. *Publications:* Russian Tales and Legends 1956, The History of the Caucasian Albanians by Movses Dasxuranci 1961, The Penitential of David of Ganjak 1961, Tales of the Hodja 1964, Armenian Folktales and Fables 1972, Kütahya Armenian Tiles, vol. 1, The Inscribed Tiles (with J. Carswell) 1972; contribs. to Iran and Islam: Vladimir Minorsky Memorial Volume 1971, Hayg Berberian Memorial Volume 1985 and to several learned journals; trans. from Flemish (Felix Timmermans' Driekoningentryptiek, A Christmas Triptych 1955, Ernest Claes' De Witte, Whitey 1970. *Leisure interests:* thar and ud; caricature and comic verse. *Address:* Oriental Institute, Pusey Lane, Oxford (Office); 21 Hurst Rise Road, Cumnor Hill, Oxford, OX2 9HE, England (Home).

DOWSON, Duncan, PH.D., F.ENG., F.I.MECH.E., F.R.S.; British professor of mechanical engineering; b. 31 Aug. 1928; s. of Wilfrid Dowson and Hannah Dowson; m. Mabel Strickland 1951; one s. (and one s. deceased); ed. Lady Lumley's Grammar School, Pickering and Univ. of Leeds; research eng. Sir W.G. Armstrong Whitworth Aircraft Co. 1953–54; lecturer in Mechanical Eng. Univ. of Leeds 1954, Sr. Lecturer 1963, Reader 1965, Prof. of Eng. Fluid Mechanics and Tribology 1966–, Dir. Inst. of Tribology, Dept. of Mech. Eng. 1967–, Head, Dept. of Mech. Eng. 1987–; Pro-Vice-Chancellor, Univ. of Leeds 1983–85; Foreign mem. Royal Swedish Acad. of Eng. Sciences; Fellow, American Soc. of Mechanical Eng. (ASME), American

Soc. of Lubrication Engs. (ASLE); recipient of numerous awards from Inst. of Mech. Eng., ASME, ASLE etc.; Hon. D. Tech. (Chalmers Univ. of Tech. Göteborg); James Clayton Fund Prize, Thomas Hawksley Gold Medal. *Publications:* Elastohydrodynamic Lubrication: the fundamentals of roller and gear lubrication (jointly) 1966, History of Tribology 1979, An Introduction to the Biomechanics of Joints and Joint Replacement (jtly.) 1981, Ball Bearing Lubrication: The Elastohydrodynamics of Elliptical Contacts (jtly.) 1981; papers in professional journals. *Leisure interests:* travel, astronomy. *Address:* 23 Church Lane, Adel, Leeds, LS16 8DQ, England. *Telephone:* (0532) 678933.

DOWSON, Graham Randall; British business executive; b. 13 Jan. 1923, Southend; s. of late Cyril James and late Dorothy Celia Dowson (née Foster); m. 1st Fay Valerie Weston 1954 (dissolved 1974), two d.; m. 2nd Denise Joy Shurman 1975; ed. City of London School, Ecole Alpina, Switzerland; war service 1939–45, Pilot, Squadron Leader R.A.F. 1941–46; Sales, U.S. Steel Corpn. (Columbia Steel), Los Angeles 1946–49; Mid-South Network (MBS), Radio U.S.A. 1949–52; Dir. A. C. Nielsen Co., Oxford 1953–58, Southern T.V. Ltd., London 1958–74; Dir. Rank Org. 1960, Deputy Chief Exec. 1972, Chief Exec. 1974–75; Chair. Mooloya Investments 1975–78, Erskine House Investments 1975–83, Pincus Vidler Arthur Fitzgerald 1979–83; Chair. and Chief Exec., Teltech Marketing Services Ltd. 1984–; Dir. Carron Holdings Ltd. 1976–82, Carron Investments Ltd. 1976–82, Nimslo Ltd. 1978, (Deputy Chair. 1979-), PPR Securities Ltd. 1976–82, RCO Holdings PLC 1979–, Filmbond PLC 1985–; Deputy Chair. Nimslo Int. Ltd., Nimslo European Holdings Ltd., Nimslo Corpn. 1979–88; Nat. Playing Fields Assen. 1974–; Jt. Pres. British Section, European League for Econ. Co-operation 1972–83, Jt. Pres. 1983; Chair. Migraine Trust 1985–88, Dowson Salisbury ASS Ltd. 1988; Nash Industries PLC 1988–; Dir. Fairhaven Int. 1988–. Royal London Yacht Club. *Leisure interest:* sailing. *Address:* 193 Cromwell Tower, Barbican, London, EC2Y 8DD, England. *Telephone:* 01-588 0396.

DOWSON, Sir Philip (Manning), Kt., C.B.E., R.A., R.I.B.A.; British architect; b. 16 Aug. 1924, Johannesburg, S. Africa; s. of Robert Dowson and Ina Cowen; m. Sarah Crewdson 1950; one s. two d.; ed. Gresham's School, Univ. Coll., Oxford, Clare Coll., Cambridge; Lieut. R.N.V.R. 1943–47; Cambridge 1947–50; Architectural Assen. 1950–53; joined Ove Arup & Partners 1953; Founder, Architectural Partner, Arup Assocs. 1963; Sr. Partner, Ove Arup 1969–; mem. Royal Fine Art Comm. 1971–, Craft Advisory Cttee. 1972–75; Gov. St. Martin's School of Art 1975–80; Trustee, Thomas Cubitt Trust 1978–, Royal Botanic Gardens, Kew 1983–, The Armouries, HM Tower of London 1984–; Royal Gold Medal for Architecture 1981. *Works include:* univ. devt. and coll. buildings: Oxford, Cambridge, Birmingham, Leicester; housing; new uses for old buildings; industrial and office devts. *Publications:* articles in technical press. *Leisure interest:* sailing. *Address:* 2–4 Dean Street, London, W1V 6QB; 1 Pembroke Studios, Pembroke Gardens, London, W.8, England.

DOYLE, Brian André, B.A., LL.B.; British (later Zambian) judge; b. 10 May 1911, Moulmien, Burma; m. Nora Slattery 1937; one s. one d.; ed. Douai School and Trinity Coll., Dublin; Magistrate, Trinidad and Tobago 1937; Resident Magistrate Uganda 1942; Solicitor-Gen. Fiji 1948, Attorney-Gen. 1949; Attorney-Gen. N. Rhodesia 1956, Attorney-Gen. and Minister of Legal Affairs 1959–65; Justice of Appeal, Zambia 1965; Chief Justice of Zambia 1969–75; Dir. Law Devt. Comm. 1975–79; Judge Botswana Court of Appeal 1973–79, 1988–; Chair. Delimitation Comm., Botswana 1981–82. *Address:* c/o 41 Choumert Square, Peckham Rye, London, SE15 4RE, England.

DOYLE, Frederick Bernard, B.SC., M.B.A., C.ENG., F.I.C.E., C.B.I.M.; British civil engineer; b. 17 July 1940, Manchester; s. of James Hopkinson and Hilda Mary (née Spotsworth) Doyle; m. Ann Weston 1963; two s. one d.; ed. St. Bede's Coll., Manchester, Victoria Univ. of Manchester, Harvard Business School; Resident Civil Engineer, British Rail 1961–65; Man. Consultant, Arthur D. Little Inc. 1967–72; with Booker McConnell Ltd. 1973–81, Sec. to Exec. Cttee. 1973, Dir. Eng. Div. 1974, Chair. Gen. Eng. Div. 1976, Chair. and Chief Exec. Booker McConnell Eng. Ltd. Jan. 1979, Dir. of parent co. Jan. 1979; Chief Exec. Social Democratic Party Sept. 1981–83, Welsh Water Authority 1983–87; Operations Dir. F. J. C. Lilley PLC June–Dec. 1987; Man. Consultant 1988–; NATO Fellowship 1965. *Leisure interests:* sport, theatre, reading, travel. *Address:* 12 Conway Street, Brecon, Powys, LD3 7HP, Wales.

DOYLE, William, PH.D., F.B.I.M.; American business executive; b. 15 Feb. 1932, Seattle, Wash.; s. of James W. and Lillian I. (née Kime) Doyle; m. Judith Ann Gosha 1957; two s. one d. (and one s. deceased); ed. O'Dea High School, Seattle Univ., Oregon State Univ.; Research Chemist, Texaco Inc. 1959–64, Research Supervisor 1964–68, Asst. to Vice-Pres. Petrochemicals 1968–70, to Sr. Vice-Pres. Refining/Marketing 1970–71, Asst. Div. Man. Producing 1971–73, Asst. Regional Man. Marketing 1973–77, Deputy Man. Dir. Texaco Ltd. 1977–81, Man. Dir. Exploration and Production 1981–, Vice-Pres. 1987–, Pres. Texaco North Sea U.K. Co. 1981–; Vice-Pres. U.K. Offshore Operators Assen. (England) 1984, Pres. 1985–; mem. Inst. of Dirs. *Leisure interests:* motor racing, squash, tennis, art, music. *Address:* 1 Knightsbridge Green, London, S.W.1, England; 2000 Westchester Avenue, White Plains, New York, N.Y. 10650, U.S.A. *Telephone:* 01-584 5000.

DRABBLE, Bernard J., B.A.; Canadian international financial official; b. 20 May 1925, Portsmouth, England; s. of James C. W. Drabble and Mary Buchanan Simpson; ed. Portsmouth Grammar School and McGill Univ.; joined Bank of Canada 1947, various posts including Deputy Chief, Research Dept. 1964, Assoc. Adviser 1966, Adviser 1971, Deputy Gov. 1974; Exec. Dir. for Canada, Ireland etc., IMF 1974–81; Assoc. Deputy Minister, Dept. of Finance 1981–; Alt. Gov. IMF 1982–, Inter-American Devt. Bank 1984–, Asian Devt. Bank 1984–, AfDB 1984–; Allan Oliver Gold Medal, McGill Univ. *Leisure interests:* tennis, swimming, music. *Address:* L'Esplanade Laurier, 20th Floor, East Tower, 140 O'Connor Street, Ottawa, Ont. K1A 0G5, Canada (Office). *Telephone:* (613) 996-1963 (Office); (613) 238-4127 (Home).

DRABBLE, Margaret, C.B.E.; British author; b. 5 June 1939, Sheffield; d. of the late J. F. and Kathleen (née Bloor) Drabble; m. 1st Clive Swift 1960 (divorced 1975), two s. one d.; m. 2nd Michael Holroyd (q.v.) 1982; ed. Newnham Coll., Cambridge; Chair., Nat. Book League 1980–; Ed. The Oxford Companion to English Literature 1979–84; Hon. D.Litt. (Sheffield) 1976, (Bradford) 1988; Hon. Fellow, Regents Coll., London 1988; E. M. Forster Award, American Acad. of Arts and Letters 1973. *Publications:* A Summer Bird-Cage 1963, The Garrick Year 1964, The Millstone 1965 (John Llewelyn Rhys Memorial Prize 1966), Jerusalem the Golden 1967, The Waterfall 1969, The Needle's Eye 1972, Arnold Bennett: A Biography 1974, The Realms of Gold 1975, The Genius of Thomas Hardy (Editor) 1976, The Ice Age 1977, For Queen and Country: Britain in the Victorian Age 1978, A Writer's Britain 1979, The Middle Ground (novel) 1980, The Oxford Companion to English Literature (Ed.) 1985, The Radiant Way (novel) 1987, A Natural Curiosity 1989. *Address:* c/o Peters, Fraser and Dunlop, Fifth Floor, The Chambers, Chelsea Harbour, Lots Road, London SW10, England. *Telephone:* (01) 376-7676.

DRACH, Ivan Fyodorovich; Soviet (Ukrainian) author and poet; b. 1936, Telizhentsy, Kiev Dist.; ed. Dept. of Philology, Kiev Univ.; Advanced Course in Theatre and Drama, Moscow Univ.; mem. CPSU 1959–; Leader Narodni Rykh, Kiev 1989–. *Publications include:* Sun Flower 1962, Ballads of Everyday Life 1967, I Come to You 1970, Poems 1972, The Kievan Sky 1976, The Sun and the Word (poetry) 1978. *Address:* U.S.S.R. Union of Writers, Ul. Vorovskogo 52, Moscow, U.S.S.R.

DRĂGAN, Dr. Joseph Constantin; Romanian industrialist (lives in Italy); b. 20 June 1917, Lugoj, Timiş County; ed. Univs. of Bucharest and Rome; Pres. and Man. Dir. Propangas A.G., Drachen-Propangas GmbH, Petrogaz S.A., Dragofina S.A.H., Butan-Gas S.P.A., Paso S.P.A., Dacia Sr.1., Drago-Butano S.A., Dragon-Gas S.A. all controlled by Dragofina Investment Trust and Euro-Fina S.A.; founded Romanian Catholic Monitor and European Bulletin 1949, Eastern Europe Monitor 1954, Europa si Neamul Romanesc and Noi Tracii 1974; fmr. Chair. N. Italy Marketing Asscn., fmr. Pres. Int. Marketing Fed.; mem. Int. Chamber of Commerce. *Publications:* works on management, marketing and history. *Address:* Via Larga 11, 20122 Milan, Italy. *Telephone:* (02) 87.04.87; (02) 805.63.77.

DRĂGĂNESCU, Emil; Romanian politician (retd.); b. 18 Dec. 1919, Galaţi; m. Ofelia Drăgănescu; one s. one d.; ed. Polytechnic School, Bucharest; Eng. in Bucharest 1942–48; Deputy Man. Romanian Railways, Bucharest 1950–51; Deputy Minister of Building and of Building Materials Industry 1952–55; Vice-Chair., State Control Cttee. 1955–61; Vice-Chair. State Planning Cttee. 1961–65; Minister of Electric Power 1965–68; Vice-Chair. Council of Ministers 1968–78; Minister of Transport and Telecommunications 1972–74; Chair. Nat. Council for Physical Educ. and Sports 1973–74; Chair. State Planning Cttee. 1974–75; Minister of Sports and Tourism 1978–82; mem. of RCP 1946–; mem. Central Cttee. of RCP 1965–84; alt. mem. Exec. Political Cttee. 1968–69, mem. Exec. Political Cttee. 1969–79; mem. Grand Nat. Assembly 1969–, Nat. Council Front of Socialist Democracy and Unity 1980–; Order of Labour 1969. *Address:* c/o Marea Adunare Naţională, Bucharest, Romania. *Telephone:* 16-21-50.

DRAKE, Sir (Arthur) Eric (Courtney), Kt., C.B.E., M.A., F.C.A., D.L.; British business executive; b. 29 Nov. 1910, Rochester, Kent; s. of Dr. A. W. Courtney Drake and Ethel Davidson; m. 1st Rosemary Moore 1935; two d.; m. 2nd Margaret E. Wilson 1950; two s.; ed. Shrewsbury School and Pembroke Coll., Cambridge; British Petroleum Co. Ltd. (fmrly. Anglo-Iranian Oil Co.) 1935–75; Man. Dir. The British Petroleum Co. Ltd. 1958–75, Deputy Chair. 1962–69, Chair. 1969–75; Pres. Chamber of Shipping of U.K. 1964; Hon. Petroleum Adviser to British Army 1971–; mem. Cttee. on Invisible Exports (resigned 1975), Gen. Cttee., of Lloyd's Register of Shipping (retd. 1981), Gov. Body of Shrewsbury School (retd. 1983); Chair. Mary Rose Trust 1979–83, Vice-Pres. 1983–; Deputy Lieut. for Hampshire 1983–; Hon. D.Sc. (Cranfield) 1971; Hon. Fellow, Manchester Inst. of Science and Tech. 1974, Hon. Fellow, Pembroke Coll., Cambridge 1975; Freeman of City of London 1974; one of H.M. Lieuts. for City of London; Hambro Award for Businessman of the Year 1971, Commdr. Ordre de la Couronne (Belgium), Kt. Grand Cross, Order of Merit (Italy), Officier, Légion d'honneur (France), Order of Homayoun II (Iran) 1974, Commdr. Order of Leopold (Belgium) 1975, Cadman Memorial Medal of Inst. of Petroleum 1976; Elder Brother, Trinity House; Hon. Co. Master Mariners. *Leisure interests:* sailing, shooting. *Address:* The Old Rectory, Cheriton, Alresford, Hants, England. *Telephone:* (096) 279-334.

DRAKE, Frank Donald, B.ENG.PHYS., M.A., PH.D.; American astronomer; b. 28 May 1930, Chicago; s. of Richard C. Drake and Winifred Thompson Drake; m. 1st Elizabeth B. Bell 1953 (divorced 1976); three s.; m. 2nd Amahl Shakhashiri 1978; two d.; ed. Cornell and Harvard Univs.; U.S.N. 1952–55; Harvard Radio Astronomy Project 1955–58; Ewen-Knight Corpn. 1957–58; Scientist, Head Scientific Services and Telescope Operations on Nat. Radio Astron. Observatory 1958–63; Chief, Lunar and Planetary Science Section, Jet Propulsion Laboratory 1963–64; Prof. of Astronomy, Cornell Univ. 1964–85, Goldwin Smith Prof. of Astronomy 1976–85; Dir. Arecibo Ionospheric Observatory 1966–68; Assoc. Dir. Center for Radio-physics and Space Research, Cornell Univ. 1967–75; Chair. Dept. of Astronomy, Cornell Univ. 1968–71; Dir. Nat. Astronomy and Ionosphere Center 1971–81; Prof. of Astronomy, Univ. of Calif., Santa Cruz 1984–, Dean Div. of Natural Sciences 1984–88; Pres. Astronomical Soc. of the Pacific 1988–90; mem. A.A.A.S., N.A.S. 1972–, The Explorers Club, Advisory Bd. The World Book Encyclopedia, Int. Astronomical Union, Int. Scientific Radio Union, American Astronomical Soc.; Fellow, American Acad. of Arts and Sciences; Pres. SETI Inst.; Vice-Pres. CETI Foundation; mem. Bd. of Dirs. The Planetary Soc., Extrasolar Planetary Foundation, Assoc., Univ. for Research in Astronomy. *Publications:* Intelligent Life in Space 1962, and over 135 papers and articles. *Leisure interests:* snorkelling, horticulture, lapidary. *Address:* Lick Observatory, Univ. of California, Santa Cruz, Calif. 95064, U.S.A. *Telephone:* (408) 429 4885.

DRAKE, Stillman, A.B., F.R.S.C.; Canadian (b. American) university professor; b. 24 Dec. 1910, Berkeley, Calif., U.S.A.; s. of Bryant S. Drake and Flora Frickstad (Drake); m. 1st Eda Salzman 1936 (divorced), two s.; m. 2nd Lucille Jarrell 1950 (divorced); m. 3rd Florence Selvin 1967; ed. Marin Junior Coll., Univ. of California at Berkeley; Calif. Municipal Statistics, Inc., San Francisco 1936–40; U.S. Govt. agencies 1940–45; Heller, Bruce & Co., San Francisco 1946–56; Banco Gubernamental de Fomento, San Juan, Puerto Rico 1956–58; Blyth & Co. Inc., San Francisco 1958–67; Prof. of History of Science, Univ. of Toronto 1967–77, Emer. Prof. 1977–; Fellow American Acad. of Arts and Sciences; mem. Int. Acad. of History of Science, Paris; Fellow, John Simon Guggenheim Memorial Foundation 1971–72, 1976–77; Hon. LL.D. (Calif., Berkeley) 1968, (Toronto) 1979; Premio Galileo Galilei, Pisa 1984, George Sarton Medal 1988. *Publications:* Galileo: Dialogue (trans.) 1953, Discoveries and Opinions of Galileo 1957, Controversy on the Comet of 1618 1960, Mechanics in 16th-Century Italy 1969, Galileo Studies 1970, Galileo: Two New Sciences (trans.) 1974, Galileo Against the Philosophers 1974, Galileo at Work 1978, Galileo 1980, Cause, Experiment and Science 1981, Telescopes, Tides and Tactics 1983. *Leisure interest:* music. *Address:* 219 Glen Road, Toronto, Ont., Canada. *Telephone:* (416) 922-0497.

DRAPEAU, Jean, C.C., Q.C., LL.B.; Canadian lawyer and politician; b. 18 Feb. 1916, Montreal; s. of late Joseph-Napoléon Drapeau and Berthe Martineau; m. Marie-Claire Boucher 1945; three s.; ed. Jean-de-Brébeuf and Le Plateau Schools, Montreal, and Univ. of Montreal; admitted to Montreal Bar 1943; practised law in Criminal and Civil Courts, specializing in commercial and corpn. law; Mayor of Montreal 1954–57, 1960–86; founded Montreal Civic Party 1960; Senior Canadian rep. at the Int. Bureau of Exhbns., Paris 1967–71; mem. Admin. Council, BTM Int. 1980–; Hon. degrees from Univs. of Moncton 1956, Montreal 1964, McGill 1965, Boswell Inst., Loyola Univ. 1966, Sir George Williams Univ. and Laval Univ. 1967; Hon. mem. American Bar Asscn.; Gold Medal, Royal Architectural Inst. of Canada 1967; Commdr. Légion d'honneur.

DRAPICH, Wit, M. ECON. SC.; Polish politician; b. 23 Jan. 1924, Świątniki Górne, Cracow Voivodship; ed. Higher School of Economics, Szczecin; served in Home Army during German occupation; Asst., Higher School of Econs., Szczecin 1951–55; Lecturer, Tech. Univ., Szczecin 1955–56; mem. Polish Socialist Party (PPS) 1945–48, Polish United Workers' Party (PZPR) 1948–; Sec. PZPR Voivodship Cttee., Szczecin 1956–65, First Sec., Voivodship Cttee., Cracow 1975–77; Deputy mem. PZPR Cen. Cttee. 1971–75, mem. 1975–81; mem. Chief Council, Union of Fighters for Freedom and Democracy (ZBoWiD); Deputy Chair. All-Poland Cttee. Nat. Unity Front (OK FJN) 1977–83; Dir. of Dept., Ministry of Education and Higher Education 1966–69, Deputy Minister 1969–72; Chair. of Presidium, Voivodship Nat. Council, Cracow 1972–73, Voivode, Cracow 1973–75; Deputy to Seym (Parl.) 1957–65, 1976–85; mem. Presidium Provisional Nat. Council of Patriotic Movt. for Nat. Rebirth 1982–83, mem. Presidium Nat. Council 1983–87; Cross of Valour 1945, Gold Cross of Merit 1955, Kt.'s Cross of Order Polonia Restituta 1958, Commdr.'s Cross with Star 1983, Order of Banner of Labour (2nd Class) 1969, (1st Class) 1974, Medal of 30th Anniversary of People's Poland 1974, Gold Medal for Merits for Country's Defence 1975, Partisan Cross 1976.

DRAWICZ, Andrzej; Polish writer, critic and essayist; b. 20 May 1932, Warsaw; ed. Univ. of Warsaw; published works 1950; led Koła Młodych ZLP, Warsaw 1953–54; dir. Student Theatre of Satire 1954–64; asst. dir. of Polish Literary Inst., Warsaw 1955–58. *Publications include:* Polish Literature 1917–67, 1968, Konstanty Paustowski 1972, Zaproszenie do podróży 1974, and numerous articles on Russian literature.

DRAY, William Herbert, M.A., D.PHIL., LL.D., F.R.S.C.; Canadian professor of philosophy; b. 23 June 1921, Montreal, P.Q.; s. of William J. Dray and Florence E. Jones; m. Doris K. Best 1943; one s. one d.; ed. Univ. of

Toronto and Balliol and Nuffield Colls. Oxford; R.C.A.F. 1941–46, Active Reserve 1956–66; lecturer in Philosophy, Univ. of Toronto 1953–55, Asst. Prof. to Prof. 1955–68; Prof. Trent Univ. 1968–76, Chair. Dept. of Philosophy 1968–73; Prof. of Philosophy with cross-appt. to History, Univ. of Ottawa 1976–86; visiting appts. at Ohio State Univ. 1959, Case Inst. 1966, Harvard Univ. 1967, 1973, Stanford Univ. 1962, Duke Univ. 1973; several awards including Molson Prize of the Canada Council 1986. *Publications:* Laws and Explanation in History 1957, Philosophy of History 1964, Perspectives in History 1980; Substance and Form in History (ed., with L. Pompa) 1981; articles in professional journals. *Address:* Apt. 1403, 100 Observatory Lane, Richmond Hill, Ont., L4C 1T4, Canada.

DREES, Willem, DR.ECON.; Netherlands politician; b. 24 Dec. 1922, The Hague; s. of the late Dr. Willem Drees and Catharina Hent; m. Anna E. Gescher 1947; one s. four d.; ed. grammar school, The Hague and Netherlands School of Econs., Rotterdam; Economist, IMF, Washington, D.C. 1947–50; Financial Counsellor, Netherlands Embassy, Jakarta 1950–53; Deputy Dir. Cen. Planning Bureau, The Hague 1955; Dir. of the State's Budget, Ministry of Finance, 1956–69; Treas.-Gen. Ministry of Finance 1969–71; Prof. of Public Finance, Netherlands School of Econs. 1963–71; mem. Second Chamber of States-Gen. (Parl.) May-July 1971, 1972–77; Minister of Transport and Public Works 1971–72; mem. Int. Inst. of Public Finance, Bd. of Gen. Chamber of Audit 1977–83; Knight, Order of Netherlands Lion 1961, Commdr. Order of Orange-Nassau 1972. *Publications:* On the Level of Government Expenditure in the Netherlands after the War 1955, Moving the Capital City 1959, Efficiency in Government Spending 1966, Financing Higher Education 1966, Dutch Public Expenditure 1985. *Leisure interest:* animal watching. *Address:* Wildhoeflaan 35, The Hague, Netherlands. *Telephone:* 070-680118.

DREIER, Ralf, DR.JUR.; German professor of law; b. 10 Oct. 1931, Bad Oeynhausen; s. of Heinrich and Martha (née Volkmann) Dreier; unmarried; ed. legal studies; Asst. Lecturer, Kommunalwissenschaftliches Inst., Univ. of Münster 1963–70; Lecturer, later Prof. Univ. of Münster 1970–73; Prof. of Gen. Legal Theory, Univ. of Göttingen 1973–; mem. Akad. der Wissenschaften, Göttingen. *Publications:* Zum Begriff der 'Natur der Sache' 1965, Das kirchliche Amt 1972, Recht-Moral-Ideologie 1981. *Address:* Juristisches Seminar der Universität Göttingen, Platz der Göttinger Sieben 6, 3400 Göttingen, Federal Republic of Germany. *Telephone:* 0551-397384.

DREIMANIS, Aleksis, D.SC.; Canadian (b. Latvian) geologist, university professor and consultant; b. 13 Aug. 1914, Valmiera, Latvia; s. of Peteris Dreimanis and Marta Eleonora Leitis; m. Anita Kana 1942; two d.; ed. Latvian Univ., Univs. of Waterloo and Western Ontario, Canada; Asst. then Lecturer, Inst. of Geology, Univ. of Latvia 1937–44; Consultant, Inst. of Mineral Resources of Latvia 1942–44; Mil. Geologist, Latvian Legion 1944–45; Assoc. Prof., Baltic Univ., Hamburg and Pinneberg, Germany 1946–48; lecturer, later Prof., Dept. of Geology, Univ. of Western Ont., Canada 1948–80, Prof. Emer. 1980–; Chair. Council, Latvian Nat. Fed. in Canada 1953–71; mem. Canadian Nat. Cttee. on Research in Geological Sciences (Chair. Sub-cttee. on Quaternary Geology) 1967–72; Pres. Int. Union for Quaternary Research Comm. on Genesis and Lithology of Quaternary Glacial Deposits 1973–87; Pres. American Quaternary Assn. 1980–82; consultant various Canadian and U.S. govt. institutions and pvt. cos. 1949–; numerous prizes and awards including Centennial Medal of Canada 1967, Queen Elizabeth II Silver Jubilee Medal 1977, Logan Medal, Geological Assn. of Canada 1978. *Publications:* about 200 scientific papers, mainly on glacial geology and on the last ice age in N. America and Northern Europe. *Leisure interests:* photography, gardening. *Address:* Department of Geology, University of Western Ontario, London, Ont., N6A 5B7 (Office); 287 Neville Drive, London Ont., N6G 1C2, Canada (Home). *Telephone:* (519) 661-3197 (Office); (519) 672-6865 (Home).

DRELL, Sidney David; American professor of physics; b. 13 Sept. 1926, Atlantic City, N.J.; s. of Tulla and Rose White Drell; m. Harriet Stainback 1952; one s. two d.; ed. Princeton Univ. and Univ. of Illinois; Research Assoc. Univ. of Illinois 1949–50; Physics Instructor Stanford Univ. 1950–52; Research Assoc. M.I.T. 1952–53, Asst. Prof. 1953–56; Assoc. Prof. Stanford Univ. 1956–60, Prof. of Physics 1960–63, Lewis M. Terman Prof. and Fellow 1979–84; Prof. Stanford Linear Accelerator Center 1963–, Deputy Dir. 1969–, Exec. Head of Theoretical Physics 1969–86; Visiting Scientist and Guggenheim Fellow, CERN 1961–62; Visiting Prof. and Loeb Lecturer, Harvard Univ. 1962, 1970; Consultant to Los Alamos Scientific Lab. 1956–, Office of Science and Tech., Exec. Office of the Pres. 1960–73, President's Science Advisory Cttee. 1966–70, Arms Control and Disarmament Agency 1969–81, Office of Tech. Assessment, U.S. Congress 1975–, Office of Science and Tech. Policy 1977–82, Nat. Security Council 1973–81; Consultant, Senate Select Cttee. on Intelligence 1978–83; Co-Dir. Stanford Centre for Int. Security and Arms Control 1984–; mem. High Energy Physics Advisory Panel to DOE 1974–86 (Chair. 1974–82); mem. JASON Div. (Mitre Corpn.) 1960–; mem. Bd. The Arms Control Assn., Washington 1978–; mem. Council on Foreign Relations 1980–; mem. Advisory Cttee. M.I.T. Physics Dept. 1974–; Visiting Schrodinger Prof., Theoretical Physics, Univ. of Vienna 1975; mem. Bd. of Trustees, Inst. for Advanced Study, Princeton, N.J. 1974–83; Bd. Gov. Weizmann Inst. of Science, Rehovoth, Israel 1970–; Bd. Dir. Annual Reviews Inc. 1976–; mem. numerous advisory cttees., and

editorial boards; mem. N.A.S., American Acad. of Arts and Sciences, American Philosophical Soc. 1987–, M.I.T. Lincoln Lab. Advisory Bd. 1985–, Aspen Strategy Group 1984–; Fellow American Physical Soc. (Pres. 1986); Guggenheim Fellow, Rome 1972; Richtmeyer Memorial Lecturer to American Assn. of Physics Teachers 1978; Visiting Fellow, All Souls Coll., Oxford Univ. 1979; Danz Lecturer, Univ. of Washington 1983; I. I. Rabi Visiting Prof. Columbia Univ. 1984; Hon. D.Sc. (Univ. of Ill., Chicago Circle) 1981; E. O. Lawrence Memorial Award 1972, Univ. of Ill. Alumni Award for Distinguished Service in Engineering 1973, Leo Szilard Award for Physics in the Public Interest 1980, Macarthur Fellowship Award 1984, Univ. of Ill. Achievement Award 1988, Hans Betne Lecturer, Cornell Univ. 1988. *Publications:* Relativistic Quantum Mechanics, Relativistic Quantum Fields (both with J. D. Bjorken), Facing the Threat of Nuclear War 1983 and numerous articles in The Physical Review and other professional journals. *Leisure interest:* music. *Address:* Stanford Linear Accelerator Center, P.O. Box 4349, Stanford, Calif. 94309 (Office); 570 Alvarado Row, Stanford, Calif. 94305, U.S.A. (Home).

DRENTH, Pieter Johan Diederik, PH.D.; Netherlands professor of work and organisational psychology; b. 8 March 1935, Appelscha; s. of Gerrit Drenth and Froukje Wouda; m. Maria Annetta Elizabeth de Boer 1959; three s.; ed. Vrije Univ., Amsterdam; served in Royal Dutch Navy 1955–60; Research Fellow Social Science Research Div., Standard Oil Co., New York 1960–61; Sr. lecturer in Psychometrics and Industrial Psychology, Vrije Univ., Amsterdam 1962–67, Prof. of Work and Organisational Psychology 1967–; Vice-Chancellor 1983–87; Visiting Prof. Washington Univ. St. Louis 1966, Univ. of Washington, Seattle 1977; Sec.-Treasurer Royal Netherlands Acad. of Arts and Sciences 1987–; mem. Royal Netherlands Acad. of Arts and Sciences 1980; Heymans Award for Outstanding Contrib. to Psychology 1986; Dr. h.c. (Ghent). *Publications:* Mental Tests and Cultural Adaptation (Ed.) 1972, Inleiding in de testtheorie 1976, New Handbook Work and Organizational Psychology (Ed.) 1983, Decisions in Organizations 1988, Advances in Organizational Psychology (Ed.) 1988, numerous scientific papers and psychological tests. *Leisure interests:* athletics, tennis, bridge. *Address:* Vrije Universiteit, Department of Work and Organizational Psychology, De Boelelaan 1089, 1081 HV Amsterdam; Royal Netherlands Academy of Arts and Sciences, Kloveniersburgswal 27-29, 1000 GC Amsterdam (Office); Pekkendam 6, 1081 HR Amsterdam, The Netherlands (Home). *Telephone:* (020) 548 5502; (020) 222902 (Office); (020) 420 885 (Home).

DRESE, Claus Helmut, DR.PHIL.; German theatre director; b. 25 Dec. 1922, Aachen; s. of Karl Drese and Helene Drese; m. Helga Lautz 1950; two c.; studied German studies, philosophy and history in Cologne, Bonn and Marburg; Theatre Literary Man., Mannheim 1952–59; Theatre Dir. Heidelberg 1959–62, Wiesbaden 1962–68, Cologne 1968–75, Zurich 1975–; Dir. Vienna State Opera 1986–(91). *Publications:* various contributions to newspapers, radio and television. *Address:* Seehaldenstr. 16, 8802 Kilchberg; Opernhaus Zürich, Falkenstrasse 1, 8008 Zürich, Switzerland.

DREW, Jane Beverly, F.R.I.B.A., F.I.ARB., F.S.I.A.; British architect; b. 24 March 1911, Thornton Heath, Surrey; d. of Harry Guy Radcliffe Drew and Emma Spering Jones; m. 2nd Edwin Maxwell Fry (q.v.) 1942; two d. by 1st marriage; ed. Croydon High School, Architectural Assn.; in partnership with J. T. Alliston 1934–39; pvt. practice 1939–45; Partner, Fry, Drew & Partners 1946–73, Fry, Drew, Knight & Creamer 1973–; Asst. Town Planning Adviser to Resident Minister, West African Colonies 1944–45; Sr. Architect Capital Project of Chandigarh, Punjab, India 1951–54; Beamis Prof. M.I.T. 1961; Visiting Prof. of Architecture Harvard Univ. 1970; Bicentennial Prof., Utah Univ. 1976; mem. Council R.I.B.A.; mem. Council, Pres. Architectural Assn. 1969; Hon. Fellow, A.I.A., Nigerian Inst. of Architects; Hon. LL.D. (Ibadan), Dr. h.c. (Open Univ.), Hon. Dr. Lit. (Newcastle) 1987; major work includes housing, hospitals, schools, colls. in U.K., West Africa, Middle East, India; town planning, housing and amenity bldgs. in Iran, West Africa, India; a section of Festival of Britain 1951, The Open University. *Publications:* Architecture for Children (with Maxwell Fry) 1944, Village Housing in the Tropics (with Maxwell Fry and Harry Ford) 1945, Founder Ed. Architects' Year Book 1945–, Architecture in the Humid Tropics (with Maxwell Fry), Tropical Architecture 1956, Architecture and the Environment 1976. *Address:* West Lodge, Cotherstone, Barnard Castle, Co. Durham, DH12 9PF, England. *Telephone:* (Teesdale) 50217.

DREWS, Juergen, M.D.; German physician and research director; b. 16 Aug. 1933, Berlin; m. Helga Eberlein 1963; three d.; ed. Berlin, Innsbruck, Frankfurt and Yale Univs.; Head, Dept. of Chemotherapy, Sandoz Research Inst., Vienna 1976–79, Dir. 1979–81; Dir. Pharmacology R. and D. Sandoz, Basel 1982–84; Dir. Pharmacology Research Roche, Basel; Dir. Corp. Research and mem. Exec. Cttee., F. Hoffmann La Roche and Co. Ltd., Basel 1986–. *Publications:* Chemotherapie 1979, Immunpharmakologie 1986; 160 scientific papers. *Leisure interests:* skiing, climbing, literature, piano. *Address:* F. Hoffmann La Roche and Co. Ltd., P.O. Box, CH-4002, Basel, Switzerland. *Telephone:* (061) 688-58-66.

DREYFUS, George; composer; b. 22 July 1928, Wuppertal, Germany; m.; two s. one d.; ed. Vienna Acad. of Music; Composer-in-residence, Tienjin, China 1983, Shanghai 1987. *Compositions include:* Garni Sands, The Gilt-Edged Kid (operas): Symphonies Nos. 1 & 2; Symphonie Concertante 1977;

Jingles . . . & More Jingles; Reflections in a Glasshouse; The Illusionist; The Grand Aurora Australis Now Show; Galgenlieder; Songs Comic & Curious; Music in the Air; From within Looking out; The Seasons; Ned Kelly Ballads; Quintet after the Notebook of J.-G. Noverre; Sextet for Didjeridu & Wind Instruments; Old Melbourne; several pieces for young people; Lifestyle 1988, Song of Brother Sun 1988 (choral pieces); Henry Lawson Award 1972; Prix de Rome 1976; Mishkenot Sha'ananim, Jerusalem 1980, The Sentimental Bloke (musical) 1985. *Publication:* The Last Frivolous Book (autobiog.) 1984. *Leisure interests:* swimming, gardening. *Address:* 3 Grace Street, Camberwell, Vic. 3124, Australia.

DREYFUS, Lee Sherman, M.A., PH.D.; American teacher and politician; b. 20 June 1926, Milwaukee, Wis.; s. of Woods Orlow Dreyfus and Clare Bluett Dreyfus; m. Joyce M. Unke 1947; one s. one d.; ed. Milwaukee public schools, Washington High School and Univ. of Wisconsin (Madison); war service, U.S.N., 1944–46; Instructor, Univ. of Wis. (Madison) 1949–52; Instructor, Asst. Prof., Assoc. Prof. and Assoc. Dir. of Mass Communications, Wayne State Univ., Detroit, Mich. 1952–62; Prof. of Speech and Radio-Television educ., Univ. of Wis. (Madison) 1962–67, Chair. Radio-Television-Film Div. 1965–67; Chair. State ETV Cttee., Wis. 1962–65; Pres. Wisconsin State Univ. (Stevens Point) 1967–72, Chancellor 1972–78; Educ. Adviser to U.S. Sec. of Army 1970–73; Gov. of Wisconsin 1979–83; Pres. C.O.O. Sentry Worldwide Insurance Group Jan. 1983–84, Pres. Lee Sherman Dreyfus Inc. 1984–; Pres.'s Gold Medal, Distinguished Public Service Medal Sec. of Defense; Republican. *Publications:* numerous articles and co-author of a book on the role of the media in educ. *Address:* Box 1776, Waukesha, Wis. 53188, U.S.A. *Telephone:* (414) 544-1221.

DREYFUS, Pierre, D.EN.D.; French business executive; b. 18 Nov. 1907; s. of Emmanuel and Madeleine (née Bernard) Dreyfus; m. Laure Ullmo 1936; one d.; Insp.-Gen. of Industry and Commerce, Chief of Gen. Inspectorate, and Dir. of Cabinet to Minister of Industry and Commerce 1947–49; Pres. Houillères de Lorraine 1950, Charbonnages de France 1954; Pres. of Energy Comm. of the Plan, and Dir. of Cabinet to Minister of Industry and Commerce 1954; Vice-Pres. Régie nat. des usines Renault 1948–55, Pres., Dir.-Gen. 1955–76; Pres. Soc. des Aciers fins de l'Est 1955–76, Société Financière et Foncière, Soc. Renault-Finance, Lausanne 1976–80; Minister of Industry 1981–82; Chargé de mission auprès du Pres. de la République May–June 1981, 1982–; Grand Officier, Légion d'honneur. *Address:* 12 rue Duroc, 75007 Paris, France (Home).

DREYFUS, Pierre; French industrialist; b. 2 Nov. 1907, Mulhouse; m. Colette Schwob 1933; three c.; ed. Lycée de Mulhouse, Ecole de Filature et Tissage, Mulhouse; joined Etablissement Dreyfus Frères, Mulhouse 1929, Admin. Dir. 1933, Man. Dir. 1949–65; Président-directeur-général, P. Dreyfus et Cie., Mulhouse 1965–; Président du Directoire de Schaeffer-Impression, Vieux-Thann; Chevalier, Légion d'honneur. *Address:* 62 blvd. Leon Gambetta, 68100 Mulhouse, France.

DREYFUSS, Richard Stephan; American actor; b. 29 Oct. 1947, New York; s. of Norman Dreyfuss and Gerry D. Student; ed. San Fernando Valley State Coll.; alternative mil. service Los Angeles County Gen. Hosp. 1969–71; mem. American Civil Liberties Union Screen Actors Guild, Equity Asscn., American Fed. of TV and Radio Artists, Motion Picture Acad. Arts and Sciences; Golden Globe Award 1978, Acad. Award for Best Actor in The Goodbye Girl 1978. *Stage appearances include:* Julius Caesar 1978, The Big Fix (also producer) 1978, Othello 1979. *Films include:* American Graffitti 1972, Dillinger 1973, The Apprenticeship of Duddy Kravitz 1974, Jaws 1975, Inserts 1975, Close Encounters of the Third Kind 1976, The Goodbye Girl 1977, The Competition 1980, Whose Life Is It Anyway? 1981, Down and Out in Beverly Hills 1986, Stakeout 1988, Moon over Parador, Let it Ride; Dir. producer Nuts 1987. *Address:* 2355 Benedict Canyon Drive, Beverly Hills, Calif. 90210-1434, U.S.A.

DRICKAMER, Harry George, B.S.E., M.S., PH.D.; American professor of chemistry, physics and chemical engineering; b. 19 Nov. 1918, Cleveland, Ohio; s. of George H. and Louise S. Drickamer; m. Mae Elizabeth McFillen 1942; two s. three d.; ed. Univ. of Michigan; Pan American Refining Corpn., Texas City 1942–46; Asst. Prof. of Chemical Eng., Univ. of Illinois 1946–49, Assoc. Prof. 1949–53, Prof. 1953–, Head, Div. of Chemical Eng. 1955–58, mem. Center for Advanced Study 1963–; mem. Nat. Acad. of Eng., N.A.S., American Acad. of Arts and Sciences, American Philosophical Soc.; numerous awards including Allan P. Colburn Award, American Inst. of Chemical Engineers 1947, Ipatieff Prize, American Chem. Soc. 1956, Oliver E. Buckley Solid State Physics Award, American Physical Soc. 1967, William Walker Award, American Inst. of Chemistry 1972, Langmuir Award in Chemical Physics, American Chemical Soc. 1974, P. W. Bridgman Award, Int. Asscn. for the Advancement of High Pressure Research and Tech. 1977, Michelson-Morley Award, Case-Western Reserve Univ. 1978, John Scott Award, City of Philadelphia 1984, A. von Humboldt Award, Fed. Repub. of Germany 1986, W. K. Lewis Award, American Inst. of Chemical Engs. 1986, Peter Debye Award in Physical Chem., American Chemical Soc. 1987, Welch Award in Chem., R.A. Welch Foundation 1987, Distinguished Professional Achievement Award, Univ. of Mich. 1987, Elliot Cresson Medal (Franklin Inst.) 1988. *Publications:* Over 300 papers in scientific journals. *Leisure interests:* reading of Roman, medieval and 18th century history, walking. *Address:* School of Chemical Sciences, University of Illinois, 1209 W. California Street, Urbana, Ill. 61801, (Office); 304 East Pennsylvania Street, Urbana, Ill. 61801, U.S.A. (Home). *Telephone:* (217) 333-0025 (Office).

DRINAN, Robert F., M.A., LL.M., TH.D.; American politician, professor and writer; b. 15 Nov. 1920, Boston; s. of James J. Drinan and Ann Flanagan; ed. Boston Coll., Georgetown Univ. and Gregorian Univ., Rome; ordained Jesuit Priest 1953; Dean Boston Coll. Law School 1956–70; mem. U.S. Congress from Mass. 1971–81; Prof. Georgetown Univ. Law Center 1981–; mem. A.B.A.; Fellow, American Acad. of Arts and Sciences; 17 hon. degrees from American univs. *Publications:* Religion, the Constitution and Public Policy 1969, Vietnam and Armaggedon 1970, Honor the Promise 1976, Beyond the Nuclear Freeze 1983, Cry of the Oppressed 1987. *Address:* Georgetown University Law Center, 600 New Jersey Avenue, N.W., Washington, D.C. 20001, U.S.A. *Telephone:* (202) 662-9073.

DRING, (Dennis) William, R.A.; British artist; b. 26 Jan. 1904; s. of William H. Dring; m. Grace E. Rothwell 1931; one s. two d.; ed. Slade School of Fine Art; portrait and landscape painter; official war artist to Ministry of Information, Admiralty and Air Ministry during World War II. *Address:* Windy Ridge, Compton, Winchester, Hants., England. *Telephone:* (0962) 712181.

DRINKALL, John, C.M.G., M.A.; British diplomatist (retd.); b. 1 Jan. 1922, Maymo, Burma; m. Patricia Ellis; two s. two d.; ed. Haileybury Coll. and Brasenose Coll., Oxford; entered diplomatic service 1947; Nanking (now Nanjing), China 1948; Tamsui, Taiwan 1949; Foreign Office 1951; Cairo 1953; Foreign Office 1957; Brasília 1960; Foreign Office 1962; Cyprus 1965; Brussels 1967; Head, W. European Dept., Foreign Office 1970; Canadian Nat. Defence Coll. 1971; Amb. to Afghanistan 1972–76; High Commr. in Jamaica, concurrently Amb. to Haiti 1976–81. *Leisure interests:* sports, mountain walking. *Address:* Bolham House, Tiverton, Devon, EX16 7RA, England. *Telephone:* 0884 254333.

DRISS, Rachid; Tunisian journalist and diplomatist; b. 27 Jan. 1917, Tunis; m. Jeanine Driss 1953; one s.; ed. Sadiki Coll., Tunis; joined Neo-Destour party 1934; journalist exiled in Cairo, and with Pres. Bourguiba founder mem. Bureau du Maghreb Arabe; returned to Tunisia 1955; Ed. El Amal; Deputy, Constitutional Assembly 1956; Sec. of State Post Office and Communications 1957–64; mem. Nat. Assembly 1958, 1969; Amb. to the U.S.A. and Mexico 1964–68; mem. Political Bureau of Council of the Repub. 1969–; Perm. Rep. to UN 1970–76; Vice-Pres. Econ. and Soc. Council 1970, Pres. 1971; Founder, Pres. Asscn. des Etudes Internationales 1981–, Arab Bd. for Child Devt.; Dir. Etudes Int. (quarterly); Grand Cordon de l'Ordre de l'Indépendance de la République Tunisienne and many foreign decorations. *Publications:* From Bab Souika to Manhattan 1980, Diaries from the Maghreb Office in Cairo 1981, A l'aube la lanterne 1981, From Djakarta to Carthage 1985. *Address:* rue St. Cyprien, 2016 Carthage, Tunisia.

DRIVER, William J., B.B.A., LL.B.; American government official; b. 9 May 1918; s. of John J. Driver and Bridget A. Farrell; m. Marian R. McKay 1947; two s.; ed. Niagara Univ., Rochester, N.Y., and George Washington Univ., Washington, D.C.; Exec. and Admin. Officer, H.Q., Adjutant-Gen., European Theatre of Operations, U.S. Army 1942–46; Office of Asst. Chief of Staff, U.S. Army 1951–53; Chief Benefits Dir., Veterans Admin. 1959–61; Deputy Admin., Veterans Admin. 1961–65, Admin. of Veterans Affairs 1965–69; Pres. Mfg. Chemists Asscn. 1969–78; Commr. Social Security Admin. 1980–82; Vice-Chair. Save Our Security Coalition; Chair. Gov.'s Advisory Bd. on Ageing, Va. 1982–; numerous awards. *Address:* 215 West Columbia Street, Falls Church, Virginia 22046, U.S.A.

DRIZULIS, Aleksandrs; Soviet historian and state official; b. 29 June 1920, Pskov; ed. Moscow Historical Archival Inst.; mem. CPSU 1950–; Deputy Dir. Inst. of History Acad. of Sciences, Latvian SSR 1949–63, Dir. and Academic Sec. Dept. of Social Sciences, 1963–70; mem. Latvian Acad. of Sciences 1963–, Vice-Pres. 1975–; cand. mem. Cen. Cttee. of Latvian CP 1961–66, mem. 1966–; Sec. of Cen. Cttee. of Latvian CP 1970–75; mem. Presidium of Latvian Supreme Soviet 1967–71, Deputy Chair. 1975–85; Chair. Latvian Supreme Soviet 1985–; Latvian State Prize 1967, various orders. *Address:* Latvian Academy of Sciences, Ul. Turgeneva 19, Riga, Latvian S.S.R., U.S.S.R.

DROGHEDA, 11th Earl of, cr. 1661; **Charles Garrett Ponsonby Moore,** K.G., K.B.E.; b. 23 April 1910; British newspaper executive and arts administrator; ed. Eton and Trinity Coll., Cambridge; joined staff of Financial News 1932–; worked for Ministry of Production 1942–45; Man. Dir. Financial Times 1945–70, Chair. and Chief Exec. 1971–75; Deputy Chair. Economist Newspaper Ltd.; Chair. Royal Opera House, Covent Garden Ltd. 1958–74, Newspaper Publrs.' Asscn. Ltd. 1968–70; Dir. Times Newspapers Holdings 1981–, Earls Court and Olympia Ltd.; Gov. The Royal Ballet, Chair. Royal Ballet School 1978–82; Pres. Inst. of Dirs. 1975–76; Chair. London Celebrations Cttee. Queen's Silver Jubilee 1977; Chair. Henry Sotheran 1981–, Clifton Nurseries 1979–86; Hon. D.Litt. (City Univ.) 1979, Hon. D.C.L. (Durham) 1982; Commdr. Légion d'honneur 1960, Ordine al Merito (Italy) 1968, Grand Officer Order of Léopold II (Belgium) 1974. *Address:* Parkside House, Wick Lane, Englefield Green, Surrey, England.

DROIT, Michel; French journalist and writer; b. 23 Jan. 1923, Vincennes; s. of Jean Droit and Suzanne Plisson; m. Janine Bazin 1947; one s. one d.; ed. Lycée Louis le Grand, Paris, Univ. of Paris, and Ecole Libre des

Sciences Politiques; Resistance Movement 1942–44; War Correspondent and Reporter for press, radio and TV 1944–56; Foreign Affairs Commentator, French TV 1956–60; Ed.-in-Chief Tribunes et Débats, French TV 1960–61, Le Figaro Littéraire 1961–71; Advisory Ed. to La Librairie Plon 1968; Reporter France-Inter 1969–81; Man. Adviser to Le Figaro 1971–; Producer TV Programme A propos 1962–74; writer and dir. Ces Années Là 1975, Cela s'appelait l'Empire 1980; co-produced Le XIXe siècle ou la peinture en liberté 1981; mem. Académie française 1980–; Prix Max Barthou 1955, Prix Carlos de Lazerme 1961, Grand Prix du Roman de l'Académie Française (for Le retour) 1964; Chevalier, Légion d'honneur, Médaille militaire, Croix de guerre, Officier, Ordre nat. du Mérite. *Publications include:* novels: L'écorché, Pueblo, Le retour, Les compagnons de la Forêt-Noire, L'Orient perdu, La ville blanche, La mort du connétable, Les Feux du crépuscule, La rivière de la guerre; travel: Jours et nuits d'Amérique du sud, J'ai vu vivre le Japon, Panoramas mexicains, Les clartés du jour, Les lueurs de l'aube, Une plume et un micro; Ordres et décorations de France; essays: André Maurois, La Camargue; biography: De Lattre Maréchal de France, L'homme du destin (5 vols.); short stories: La fille de l'ancre bleue; film: Un Français libre. *Leisure interests:* big game hunting, karate, skin-diving. *Address:* 76 rue Spontini, 75116 Paris, France.

DROMER, Jean; French banker; b. 2 Sept. 1929, Paris; s. of Henri Dromer and Fortunée Sayag; m. Eliane Dhombres 1952; one s. four d.; ed. Ecole Libre des Sciences Politiques and Ecole Nationale d'Administration; Insp.-Gen. des Finances; Sec.-Gen. Rueff-Armand Cttee. on econ. expansion 1958; Tech. Counsellor, Office of Minister of Foreign Affairs 1961–64; Counsellor for Financial, Econ. and Social Affairs to Pres. de Gaulle 1964–67; Sec.-Gen. responsible for Econ. and European Co-operation 1967; Exec. Vice-Pres. then Vice-Chair. of Int. Cttee., Banque Nationale de Paris 1968; Pres. Cie. Financière France-Afrique 1973–; Chair. Banque Internationale pour l'Afrique Occidentale 1975–; Pres. C.I.C. de Paris 1986, Compagnie Financière du C.I.C. 1986, Banque de l'Union Européene 1986, L'Union des Assurances de Paris 1987–88, UAP-INT. 1987, French Asscn. of Banks; mem. numerous councils etc.; Chevalier, Légion d'honneur; Officier, Ordre nationale du Mérite. *Address:* 9 Place Vendôme, 75001 Paris (Office); 39 boulevard de Montmorency, 75016 Paris (Home); 18 rue La Fayette, 75009 Paris, France. *Telephone:* 42.60.33.40 (Office); 525.72.73 (Home).

DRONKE, (Ernst) Peter (Michael), M.A., F.B.A.; British medieval Latin scholar and author; b. 30 May 1934; s. of A. H. R. Dronke and M. M. Dronke (née Kronfeld); m. Ursula Miriam Brown 1960; one d.; ed. Victoria Univ., N.Z. and Magdalen Coll. Oxford; Research Fellow, Merton Coll. Oxford 1958–61; Lecturer in Medieval Latin, Cambridge Univ. 1961–79, Reader in Medieval Latin Literature 1979–, Fellow of Clare Hall 1964–; Visiting Prof. of Medieval Studies, Westfield Coll. London 1981–86; Corresp. Fellow, Real Academia de Buenas Letras; Hon. Pres., Int. Courtly Literature Soc.; Co-Ed. Mittellateinisches Jahrbuch 1977–. *Publications:* Medieval Latin and the Rise of European Love-Lyric (2 vols.) 1965–66, The Medieval Lyric 1968, Poetic Individuality in the Middle Ages 1970, Fabula 1974, Abelard and Heloise in Medieval Testimonies 1976, Barbara et antiquissima carmina (with Ursula Dronke) 1977, Bernardus Silvestris, Cosmographia (Ed.) 1978, Introduction to Francesco Colonna, Hypnerotomachia 1981, Women Writers of the Middle Ages 1984, The Medieval Poet and his World 1984, Dante and Medieval Latin Traditions 1986, Introduction to Rosvita, Dialoghi Drammatici 1986, Ed. A History of Twelfth-Century Western Philosophy 1988; essays in learned journals and symposia. *Leisure interests:* music, film and Brittany. *Address:* 6 Parker Street, Cambridge, England. *Telephone:* Cambridge 359942.

DROOGLEEVER FORTUYN, Jan, M.D., M.SC.; Netherlands neurologist; b. 12 April 1906; ed. Univs. of Utrecht, Amsterdam; Dept. of Neurology, Amsterdam 1939–51; Montreal Neurological Inst. 1946–47; Dutch Central Inst. for Brain Research 1947–51; Prof. Emer. of Neurology, Groningen 1951–. *Publications:* Experimental Study on Cortico-Thalamic Relationships 1938, Studies in Epilepsy 1947, Studies on Topographical Relationships in the Brain 1956, Petit Mal 1957, Geometrical properties of the neurons in general and of the lateral geniculate body of the rabbit in particular 1964, Forms of Muscle Fatigue 1970, On the State of the Nervous System and Related Subjects 1971–73, Hyperventilation Syndrome 1976, Neurology of Perception 1979, Perception of Pitch 1980, The Nervous System as Regulator, Computer and Symbolizer 1983, On Neuro-Informatics 1988. *Address:* Department of Neurology, University Hospital, Oostersingel 59, Groningen, Netherlands. *Telephone:* 050-619111.

DROSSOYIANNIS, Anthony; Greek politician and former army officer; b. 1922, Athens; m.; one s.; ed. Mil. Acad.; during 2nd world war, active service with Ieros Lochos (Sacred Battalion) in Middle East under Allied Command, took part in liberation of Samos 1943, of islands of Aegean and Dodecanese as Commdr. of commando units of Ieros Lochos 1944; subsequently in Third Army Corps, and Instructor, Mil. Acad. until 1947, Co. Commdr. of Tactical Staff and Deputy Commdr. of a commando unit, Civil War 1947–50, served with commando and infantry units 1950–67 rank of Bn. Commdr.; banished, and imprisoned several times during mil. dictatorship; promoted to rank of Maj.-Gen. after return to democracy; Minister of Public Order 1986–88; Gold Medal of Bravery with Mil. Cross,

Medal of Merit (several times). *Address:* c/o Ministry of Public Order, Odos 3rd September 1948, Athens, Greece.

DROZ, Georges André Léopold, D. EN D.; French international official; b. 4 May 1931, Algiers; s. of Albert Droz and Denise (née Dupré); m. Danièle Frison-Roche 1952; one s. three d.; ed. Algiers and Paris; mil. service, French Air Force 1955–57; Sec. Hague Conf. on Private Int. Law 1957, First Sec. 1965, Deputy Sec.-Gen. 1968, Sec.-Gen. 1978–; Assoc. Prof., Paris I, Panthéon-Sorbonne Univ. 1975–76; Lecturer, Hague Acad. of Int. Law 1974, 1980; Officer, Nat. Order of Merit of Luxembourg. *Publications:* Compétence judiciaire et effets des jugements dans le Marché Commun 1972, Pratique de la Convention de Bruxelles du 27 septembre 1968 1973, Les Régimes matrimoniaux en droit international privé comparé 1974; one hundred articles in French and foreign legal publs. *Leisure interests:* mountaineering. *Address:* Hague Conference on Private International Law, Javastraat 2c, 2585AM The Hague, Netherlands. *Telephone:* (70)-633303.

DROZD, Mikhail Filippovich; Soviet official; mem. Cen. Cttee. Latvian CP 1971–; First Sec. of a Regional Cttee. of Latvian CP, Elgava–1978; Minister of the Interior, Latvian S.S.R. 1978–. *Address:* Ministry of the Interior, Riga, Latvian S.S.R., U.S.S.R.

DROZDOVA, Margarita Sergeyevna; Soviet ballerina; b. 1948; ed. Moscow Choreographic Inst. danced with Stanislavsky Musical Theatre Ballet Co., Moscow 1967–; mem. CPSU 1980–; U.S.S.R. Peoples' Artist 1986. *Roles include:* Odette-Odile, Gayané, The Commissar (M. Bronner's 'Optimistic Tragedy'), Medova (A. Adam's 'Corsaire'), Swanilda (Delibes' 'Coppélia'). *Address:* Stanislavsky Musical Theatre, Moscow, U.S.S.R.

DRUCKER, Daniel Charles, PH.D.; American engineer; b. 3 June 1918, New York; s. of Moses Abraham Drucker and Henrietta Weinstein; m. Ann Bodin 1939; one s. one d.; ed. Columbia Univ., New York; Instructor Cornell Univ., Ithaca, N.Y. 1940–43; Supervisor Armour Research Foundation 1943–45; Asst. Prof. Ill. Inst. of Tech., Chicago 1946–47; Assoc. Prof., then Prof. Brown Univ., Providence, R. I. 1947–64, Chair. Div. of Eng. 1953–59, L. Herbert Ballou Univ. Prof. Brown Univ. 1964–68; Pres. Soc. for Experimental Stress Analysis 1960–61, American Acad. of Mechanics 1972–73, American Soc. of Mechanical Eng. 1973–74, Int. Union of Theoretical and Applied Mechanics 1980–84, Vice-Pres. 1984–88; Pres. American Soc. for Eng. Educ. 1981–82; Dean of Eng., Univ. of Ill. at Urbana-Champaign 1968–84; Graduate Research Prof. of Eng. Sciences, Univ. of Florida 1984–; mem. Nat. Acad. of Eng.; Foreign mem. Polish Acad. of Sciences; mem. Nat. Science Bd. 1988–94; Hon. mem. Ill. Soc. of Professional Engineers; Fellow American Acad. of Arts and Sciences, American Acad. of Mechanics, American Soc. of Civil Engineers, American Soc. of Mechanical Engineers (also Hon. mem.); Fellow, A.A.A.S. (mem. Council); Guggenheim Fellow 1960–61, NATO Sr. Science Fellow 1968, Charter Fellow, American Soc. for Eng. Educ. 1983; Murray Lecturer, Soc. for Experimental Stress Analysis 1967, Marburg Lecturer, American Soc. for Testing and Materials 1966; Hon. D.Eng. (Lehigh, Univ. Bethlehem, Pa.) 1976; Dr. h.c. Technion, Israel Inst. of Tech. 1983; Hon. Dr. Sc. (Brown Univ.) 1984, (Northwestern Univ.) 1985; M. M. Frocht Award, Soc. for Experimental Stress Analysis, 1971, Illig Medal, Columbia Univ. 1938, Lamme Medal, American Soc. for Eng. Educ. 1967, von Karman Medal, American Soc. of Civil Eng. 1966, Thomas Egleston Medal, Columbia Univ. School of Eng. and Applied Science 1978, Gustave Trasenster Medal, Univ. of Liège, Belgium 1979, William Prager Medal, Soc. of Eng. Science 1983, Timoshenko Medal, American Soc. of Mechanical Engineers 1983, John Fritz Medal, Nat. Medal of Science 1988, Founder Eng. Socs. 1985, 1986 Thurston Lecturer and Distinguished Lecturer 1987–89, American Soc. of Mechanical Engineers. *Publications:* Introduction to the Mechanics of Deformable Bodies 1967, and over 150 technical articles. *Address:* 231 Aerospace Engineering Building, University of Florida, Gainesville, Fla. 32611, U.S.A. *Telephone:* (904) 392-0961.

DRUCKER, Peter Ferdinand, LL.D.; American management consultant and teacher; b. 19 Nov. 1909, Vienna, Austria; s. of Adolph and Caroline Drucker; m. Doris Schmitz 1937; one s. three d.; ed. Gymnasium, Vienna and Univ. of Frankfurt; Prof. of Political Philosophy, Bennington Coll., Bennington, Vt. 1942–49; Prof. of Management, Graduate School of Business Admin., New York 1950–72; Clarke Prof. of Social Science, Claremont Grad. School, Claremont, Calif. 1971–; Prof. and Lecturer in Oriental Art, Pomona Coll., Claremont 1980–; Man. Consultant (own firm) 1945–; Fellow, A.A.A.S., American Acad. of Management, Int. Acad. of Man.; Hon. Fellow, British Inst. of Management; 16 hon. degrees from univs. in U.S.A., U.K., Japan, Belgium and Switzerland; Britannica Award 1987. *Publications:* The End of Economic Man 1939, The Future of Industrial Man 1942, Concept of the Corporation 1946, The New Society 1950, The Practice of Management 1954, America's Next Twenty Years 1957, Landmarks of Tomorrow 1959, Managing for Results 1964, The Effective Executive 1966, The Age of Discontinuity 1969, Technology, Management and Society 1970, The New Markets and other essays 1971, Management: Tasks, Responsibilities, Practices 1974, The Unseen Revolution; How Pension Fund Socialism came to America 1976, People and Performance 1977, Management, an Overview 1978, Adventures of a Bystander 1979, Song of the Brush, Japanese Paintings 1979 (co-author), Managing in Turbulent Times 1980, Toward the Next Economics and other essays 1981, The Changing World of the Executive 1982, The Last of All Possible

Worlds (fiction) 1982, The Temptation to Do Good (fiction), Innovation and Entrepreneurship 1985, Frontiers of Management 1986, The New Realities 1989, and educational films. *Address:* Claremont Graduate School, Claremont, Calif. 91711 (Office); 636 Wellesley Drive, Claremont, Calif., U.S.A. (Home). *Telephone:* (714) 621-1488 (Home).

DRUON, Maurice Samuel Roger Charles; French author; b. 23 April 1918, Paris; m. Madeleine Marignac 1968; ed. Lycée Michelet, Ecole des Sciences Politiques, Faculté des Lettres de Paris; War Corresp. Allied Armies 1944–45; mem. Académie Française 1966–, Perpetual Sec. 1985–; Minister for Cultural Affairs 1973–74; mem. French Parl. 1978–81, mem. European Parl. 1979–80, mem. Académie Royale du Maroc 1980, assoc. mem. Académie d'Athènes 1981; mem. Franco-British Council 1972–; Dr. h.c. (York Univ., Ont.) 1987; Prix Goncourt for novel Les grandes familles 1948, Prix de Monaco 1966; Commdr., Légion d'honneur, Commdr. des Arts et Lettres, Commdr., Order of Phoenix (Greece), Commdr. Ordre de la Républíque de Tunisie, Grand Cross of Merit (Italy), Grand Officier ordre du Lion du Sénégal, Grand Cross of the Aztec Eagle (Mexico), Grand Officier, Order of Merit (Malta), Ordre du Mérite culturel (Monaco), Ordre de l'Honneur de Grèce, du Ouissam Alaouite. *Publications:* Lettres d'un Européen 1943, La dernière brigade 1946, La fin des hommes (3 vols. Les grandes familles 1948, La chute des corps 1950, Rendez-vous aux enfers 1951), La volupté d'être 1954, Les rois maudits 1955–77 (7 vols. Le roi de fer, La reine étranglée, Les poisons de la couronne, La loi des mâles, La louve de France, Le lis et le lion, Quand un Roi perd la France), Tistou les pouces verts 1957, Alexandre le Grand 1958, Des seigneurs de la plaine à l'hôtel de Mondez 1962, Les mémoires de Zeus (2 vols. L'aube des dieux 1963, Les jours des hommes 1967), Bernard Buffet 1964, Paris, de César à Saint Louis 1964, Le pouvoir 1965, Les tambours de la mémoire 1965, Le bonheur des uns ... 1967, Discours de réception à l'Académie française 1968, L'avenir en désarroi 1968, Vézelay, colline éternelle 1968, Nouvelles lettres d'un européen 1943–70, Une église qui se trompe de siècle 1972, La parole et le pouvoir 1974, Oeuvres complètes 1974–79, Attention la France 1981, Réformer la démocratie 1982; plays: Mégarée 1942, Un voyageur 1953, La Contessa 1962. *Leisure interests:* riding, travel. *Address:* 73 rue de Varenne, 75007 Paris (Home); Abbaye de Faise, Les Artigues de Lussac, 33570 Lussac, France (Home).

DRURY, Allen Stuart, B.A.; American writer; b. 2 Sept. 1918, Houston; ed. Stanford Univ.; Ed. Tulare Bee 1940–41; County Ed. Bakersfield Californian 1942; army service 1942–43; Senate Staff, United Press 1943–45; freelance corresp. Washington 1946–47; Nat. Ed. Pathfinder Magazine 1947–52; Nat. Staff, Washington Evening Star 1952–54; Senate Staff, New York Times 1954–59; contrib. Readers' Digest 1959–62; mem. Nat. Council on the Arts 1983–; Pulitzer Prize for novel Advise and Consent 1960. *Publications:* Advise and Consent 1959, A Shade of Difference 1962, A Senate Journal 1963, That Summer 1965, Three Kids in a Cart 1965, Capable of Honor 1966, A Very Strange Society 1967, Preserve and Protect 1968, The Throne of Saturn 1971, Courage and Hesitation 1972, Come Nineveh, Come Tyre 1973, The Promise of Joy 1975, A God Against the Gods 1976, Return to Thebes 1977, Anna Hastings 1977, Mark Coffin, U.S.S. 1979, Egypt: The Eternal Smile 1980, The Hill of Summer 1981, Decision 1983, The Roads of Earth 1984, Pentagon 1986. *Address:* c/o The Lantz Office, 888 Seventh Avenue, New York, N.Y. 10106, U.S.A.

DRURY, Hon. Charles Mills, P.C., O.C., C.B.E., D.S.O., E.D.; Canadian politician; b. 17 May 1912; m. Jane Ferrier Counsell (deceased); two s. two d.; ed. McGill Univ., Royal Military Coll., Kingston, Ontario, and Univ. of Paris; Chief, UNRRA Mission, Poland 1945–47; Deputy Minister, Dept. of Nat. Defence 1949–55; Pres. Provincial Transport Co. 1956–60; Pres. Avis Transport of Canada Ltd. 1958–63, Needco Frigistors Ltd. 1960–63; Dir. Livingstone Range Syndicate Ltd. 1961–63; Minister of Defence Production and Industry 1963–68; Pres. of Treasury Bd. 1968–74; Minister of Science and Tech. and of Public Works 1974–76; Special Rep. for Constitutional Devt. in N.W. Territories 1977; resigned seat in House of Commons Jan. 1978; Chair. Nat. Capital Comm. Feb. 1978–; Chevalier, Légion d'honneur, Order of Polonia Restituta (Poland); Liberal. *Leisure interest:* sport. *Address:* 161 Laurier Street W., Ottawa, Ont. (Office); 71 Somerset Street W., Apt. 1002, Ottawa, Ont. K2P 2G2, Canada (Home).

DRUZHININ, Mikhail Ivanovich; Soviet military official; b. 1920; ed. Higher Mil. Pedagogical Inst. and Mil. Acad. of Gen. Staff; entered Soviet Army 1939; mem. CPSU 1943–; Chief of political dept. of a div. 1955–60; political party work in army 1962–63; first deputy chief of political directorate of a mil. dist. 1969–73; Chief of Political Work in Armed Forces 1973–; cand. mem. Cen. Cttee. CPSU 1981–; Hero of Soviet Union 1945. *Address:* The Kremlin, Moscow, U.S.S.R.

DRYER, Douglas Poole, PH.D., F.R.S.C.; Canadian professor of philosophy; b. 27 Nov. 1915, Toronto; s. of William Dryer and Mabel McLeod; m. 1st Pegeen Synge 1946, 2nd Ellice Baird 1965; one s. three d.; ed. Harvard Univ., U.S.A.; Instructor, Union Coll. 1939–41, Harvard Coll. 1943–45; lecturer, Tufts Coll. 1944–45; lecturer, Univ. of Toronto 1945–63, Prof. 1963–81, Prof. Emer. 1981–; mem. editorial staff Kant-Studien 1975–; fmr. mem. editorial staff Dialogue; mem. Editorial Cttee., Collected Works of J. S. Mill. *Publications:* Kant's Solution for Verification in Metaphysics 1966, Introduction to J. S. Mill, Collected Works, Vol. X 1969; numerous articles on Kant and Mill. *Leisure interests:* hiking, Scottish dancing.

Address: 61 Lonsdale Road, Toronto, M4V 1W4, Canada. *Telephone:* (416) 924-4208.

D'SOUZA, Most Rev. Eugene, B.A., B.ED.; Indian ecclesiastic; b. 15 Nov. 1917, Nagpur; s. of Ignatius Charles D'Souza; mem. Congregation of Missionaries of St. Francis de Sales 1935; ordained priest 1944; consecrated first native Bishop of Nagpur 1951, first Archbishop 1953; est. St. Francis de Sales Coll. of Arts & Science and St. Charles Seminary, Nagpur 1956; Archbishop of Bhopal 1963–; est. Bhopal School of Social Sciences, Univ. Coll., Univ. of Bhopal 1965; est. Asha Niketan, Rehabilitation Centre for handicapped and deaf children 1967; mem. Catholic Bishops' Conf. of India, mem. Standing Cttee. 1953–; mem. Governing Bd. St. John's Medical Coll., Bangalore; active participant Vatican Council II and several int. conventions; Nat. Award for Distinguished Service in Educ. and Rehabilitation of the Handicapped 1976. *Address:* Archbishop's House, 33 Ahmedabad Palace Road, Bhopal, M.P. 462 001, India. *Telephone:* 73619.

DU DAOZHENG; Chinese journalist; b. Nov. 1923, Shanxi; s. of Du Xixiang and Qi Luaying; m. Xu Zhixian 1950; one s. four d.; ed. Middle School, Dingxiang, Shanxi and Beijing Marx-Lenin Coll.; Chief of Hebei and Guangdong Bureau, Xinhua News Agency 1949–56; Ed.-in-Chief Yangchen Wanbao 1956–69; Dir. Home News Dept., Xinhua News Agency 1977–82; Ed.-in-Chief Guangming Daily 1982; Dir. Press and Publs. Admin. 1987–; winner of the Nat. News Prize 1979. *Publications:* Explore Japan (co-author), Interviews with Famous Chinese Journalists. *Leisure interest:* photography. *Address:* 106 Yong An Road, Beijing, People's Republic of China. *Telephone:* 338561-328.

DU GONG; Chinese diplomatist; Amb. to Italy 1986–. *Address:* Embassy of the People's Republic of China, Via Bruxelles 56, 00198 Rome, Italy.

DU PENGCHENG; Chinese writer; b. 1921, Shaanxi; war correspondent pre-1949; joined New China News Agency 1951. *Publications:* Defend Yanan, In Days of Peace, Young Friends; *Address:* Xian Branch, Chinese Writers' Association, Xian, Shaanxi, People's Republic of China.

DU PING; Chinese military officer; b. 1908, Wan Zai County, Jiangxi Province; Red Army Cadre during Long March; Dir. Political Dept. Chinese People's Volunteers 1950; Dir. Political Dept. PLA Northeast Mil. Region 1954; Deputy Political Commissar PLA Shenyang Units 1955; Lieut.-Gen. PLA 1955; Political Commissar PLA Nanjing Units 1963–; mem. Presidium CCP 9th Nat. Congress 1969 (re-elected to CCP 10th Nat. Congress 1973); mem. CCP 9th Cen. Cttee. 1969 (re-elected to 10th Cen. Cttee. 1973); alt. mem. CCP 11th Cen. Cttee. 1977; mem. CCP Cen. Consultative Cttee. at CCP 12th Nat. Congress 1982, mem. Cen. Advisory Comm. 1982–; mem. Calligraphers Asscn. of China. *Leisure interest:* calligraphy. *Address:* People's Liberation Army, Nanjing Units Headquarters, People's Republic of China.

DU RUNSHENG; Chinese politician and economist; b. 8 Aug. 1913, Taigu, Shanxi; ed. Beijing Teachers Univ.; involved in revolutionary activities in early 1930s; commdr. guerrilla forces Taihang Mountains; mem. of a border region govt., Deputy Gov. Taihang Pref. 1937–45; Sec.-Gen. Cen.-Plains Bureau, CPC 1946–49; Sec.-Gen. Cen.-South Bureau, CPC, Vice-Chair. Land Reform Cttee. of Cen.-South Region 1949; Sec.-Gen. Cen. Dept. of Rural Work, CPC and Deputy Dir. Agric. and Forestry Office of State Council 1953; Sec.-Gen. Acad. of Sciences 1956; in disgrace during Cultural Revolution 1967–76; Deputy Dir. State Agric. Comm. in charge of Policy Study on Rural Reform 1979; Dir. Rural Policy Research Office of Secr., CPC and Pres. Rural Devt. Research Centre, State Council; in charge of Policy Study on Rural Econ. Reform and Devt. 1982–; mem. Cen. Advisory Cttee., CPC 1983–, Deputy Head Leading Group for Educ. of Cadres, CCP Cen. Cttee. 1985–, Deputy to NPC, mem. Finance and Econ. Cttee., NPC 1983–; Vice-Chair. Nat. Agricultural Zoning Cttee. 1983–; Deputy Head Leading Group for Devt. of Rural Energy 1984–; Hon. Prof. Beijing Agricultural Univ. 1949–, especially since 1979. *Publications:* Rural Economic Reform in China (collection of articles) 1985, many articles on rural devt. in China. *Leisure interest:* tennis. *Address:* Rural Development Research Centre, State Council, Beijing (Office); No. 9 Xihuangchenggen Nanjie, Beijing, People's Republic of China. *Telephone:* 665254 (Office).

DU YI; Chinese diplomatist; Chargé d'affaires a.i., Embassy, Burundi 1972; Counsellor, Algeria 1977–78; Amb. to Mali 1979–84, to the Congo 1984–. *Address:* Embassy of the People's Republic of China, B.P. 213, Brazzaville, The Congo. *Telephone:* 81-11-20.

DU YIDE; Chinese military official; b. 1912, Hubei. Vice-Commdr. PLA Navy 1961; Deputy Political Commissar PLA Navy 1965; purged 1967; rehabilitated 1972; Deputy Political Commissar PLA Navy 1975; Political Commissar PLA Navy 1978; mem. 11th Cen. Cttee. 1977; Commdr. Lanzhou Mil. Region 1980–83, mem. Cen. Advisory Cttee. 1983–. *Address:* Peoples' Liberation Army Headquarters, Lanzhou Military Region, Peoples' Republic of China.

DU YUZHOU; Chinese government official; Vice-Minister of Textiles Nov. 1985–. *Address:* Ministry of Textile Industry, Beijing, People's Republic of China.

DUA, Indardev, B.A., LL.B.; Indian judge; b. 4 Oct. 1907, Mardan (now in Pakistan); s. of Amirchand and Parbati Devi; m. Sheila Dua 1951; one s.;

ed. Christian Coll., Lahore, Law Coll., Punjab and Punjab Univ.; practised at the Bar, Lahore High Court 1933–47; Punjab High Court 1947–58; Judge, Punjab High Court 1958, Delhi High Court 1966; Chief Justice, Delhi High Court 1967–69; Judge of the Supreme Court 1969–73; mem. Int. Law Assen., Regional Branch (India), Ombudsman Advisory Bd., Int. Bar Assen., Allentown, Pa., U.S.A.; Lokayukta (Ombudsman), State of Rajasthan 1973–78; now Arbitrator, Legal Adviser; Chair. Human Rights Sub-Cttee., Int. Law Assen.; mem. Ombudsman Advisory Bd., Int. Bar Assen., Senate, Gurukul Kangri Univ., Man. Cttee. P. G. Dav Coll., New Delhi. *Leisure interests:* studies in development of rule of law and liberal-democratic movement, human rights, promotion of egalitarian system of society. *Address:* 5-C, Sagar Apartments, 6 Tilak Marg, New Delhi, India. *Telephone:* 387537.

DUAN JUNYI; Chinese politician; b. 1913, Shandong; ed. School of Tech., Jinan Univ.; Responsible person, Nat. Fed. of Students, and rep., Peking (now Beijing) Fed. of Students 1937; Sec. CCP Hebei-Henan Region Cttee., before 1949; mem., S.W. Mil. and Admin. Cttee. 1950; Dir., Industry Dept. S.W. Mil. and Admin. Cttee. 1950; Vice-Chair. Financial and Econ. Cttee., S.W. Mil. and Admin. Cttee. 1950–54; Vice-Minister Ministry of Machine Building 1952–60; Deputy for Shandong to 1st Nat. People's Congress 1954; mem. Nat. Cttee., All China First Machine Building Trades Union 1955; Minister First Ministry of Machine Building 1960; CCP del. to Nat. Cttee., 4th CPPCC 1964; mem. Pres. CCP 11th Nat. Congress 1977–; mem. CCP 11th Cen. Cttee. 1977–82, Cen. Advisory Comm. 12th CCP Nat. Congress 1982–; Minister of Railways 1978; First Sec. Henan Prov. CCP Cttee. 1978–81; Chair. Henan CCP Prov. People's Govt. (fmrly. Revolutionary Cttee.) 1978–79; First Political Commissar PLA Henan Mil. Dist. 1978–81, PLA Garrison, Beijing 1981–83, CCP First Sec. Beijing 1981–83; Adviser Nat. Cttee. of Ageing 1984–; Hon. Vice-Pres. Beijing Social Welfare Foundation 1984–; mem. Standing Cttee. of Cen. Advisory Comm. 1987–. *Address:* Office of the First Secretary, Zhongguo Gonchan Dang, Beijing, People's Republic of China.

DUARTE, José Napoleón; Salvadorean civil engineer and politician; b. 23 Nov. 1925; m. Inés Durán de Duarte; six c.; ed. Univ. of Notre Dame, South Bend, Ind.; practising civil engineer until 1964; Mayor, San Salvador 1964 (twice re-elected); a founder and first Gen. Sec. Christian Democratic Party 1960s; elected Pres. of El Salvador 1972; not allowed to serve term; imprisoned then exiled; in exile, Venezuela 1972–79; returned to El Salvador after coup Oct. 1979; mem. ruling junta 1980–82; Pres. of El Salvador 1980–82, 1984–89. *Publication:* My Story 1986. *Address:* c/o Partido Demócrata Cristiano, 3A Calle Poniente 836, San Salvador, El Salvador.

DUBAI, Ruler of (see Maktum, Rashid al-).

DU BAIN, Myron; American business executive; b. 3 June 1923, Cleveland, Ohio; m. Alice Elaine Hilliker 1944, one s. one d.; ed. Univ. of Calif. at Berkeley, Stanford Univ., Calif.; Officer, U.S.N. 1943–46; joined Fireman's Fund Insurance Co., San Francisco, in Marine Dept. 1946, Man. Pacific Inland Marine Dept. 1957–59, Asst. Vice-Pres. 1959–61, Vice-Pres. with Sr. Exec. responsibility for Inland Marine Operations 1961–68, Sr. Vice-Pres. with Sr. Exec. Responsibility for Property, Liability and Multiple Line Operations 1968–73, Exec. Vice-Pres. 1973–74, Pres., C.E.O. and Dir. 1974–82, Chair. of Bd. 1975–; Pres., C.E.O. Amfac Inc. 1983–85; Chair. SRI Int'l., Calif. 1985–; Dir. and Vice-Chair. American Express Co.; Dir. Amfac Inc., Honolulu, Potlach Corpn., San Francisco, Pacific Telephone & Telegraph Co., San Francisco, First Interstate Bank, Calif. Roundtable, Crusader Insurance Co., Reigate, Terra Nova Insurance Co., London; Chair. and Trustee AFIA Worldwide Insurance; mem. Exec. Cttee Nat. Assen. of Casualty and Surety Execs., Advisory Council for Stanford Univ. Graduate School of Business, Advisory Council Nat. Alliance of Business, Advisory Cttee. The Advertising Council Inc.; Dir. San Francisco Opera; mem. Nat. Support Council U.S. Cttee. for UNICEF, and many other social and commercial cttees. *Leisure interests:* tennis, travel. *Address:* SRI International, 333 Ravenswood Avenue, Menlo Park, Calif. 94025, U.S.A.

DUBČEK, Alexander, RN.DR.; Czechoslovak politician; b. 27 Nov. 1921, Uhrovec; ed. Communist Party Coll., Moscow, and Law Faculty, Comenius Univ., Bratislava; Chief Sec. of Regional Cttee. of CP of Slovakia in Banská Bystrica 1953–55; Chief Sec. Regional Cttee. of CP of Slovakia, Bratislava 1958–60; mem. Presidium and Sec. of Cen. Cttee. of CP of Slovakia 1962–68; mem. Presidium Cen. Cttee. of CP of Czechoslovakia 1963–69; First Sec. Cen. Cttee. of CP of Slovakia 1963–68; First Sec. Cen. Cttee. CP of Czechoslovakia 1968–69; Chair. Cen. Cttee. of Slovak Nat. Front 1963–68; mem. Presidium of Cen. Cttee. of Nat. Front; Deputy to Nat. Assembly 1948, 1960, 1964–69, and to Slovak Nat. Council 1964–70; mem. Exec. Cttee. of Presidium Cen. Cttee. CP of Czechoslovakia 1968–69; Deputy to House of the People 1967–70; Chair. Fed. Assembly April-Oct. 1969; Amb. to Turkey 1969–70; appointed Inspector, Forestry Admin., Bratislava 1970, (now retd.); Order of 25 Feb. 1948, 1949, Award for Merits in Construction 1958, Czechoslovak Peace Prize 1968; Dr h.c. (Bologna) 1988. *Address:* c/o Forestry Enterprise, Bratislava, Czechoslovakia.

DUBERSTEIN, Kenneth Marc, M.A.; American politician; b. 21 April 1944, Brooklyn; s. of Aaron D. Duberstein and Julie C. Falb; m. Sydney

M. Greenberg 1982; two s.; one d. from previous m.; ed. Franklin and Marshall Colls. and American Univ.; Research Asst. to Congressman Rooney of Pa. 1965–66, to Senator Javits of New York 1966–67; Co-Dir. Campaign Operations 1968; Admin. Asst. to Pres. Franklin and Marshall Coll. Lancaster, Pa. 1967–70; Congressional Liaison Officer, Gen. Services Admin. Washington 1970–71, Deputy Dir. for Congressional Liaison 1971–72, Dir. Congressional Affairs 1972–76; Deputy Under-Sec. of Legis. Affairs, Dept. of Labor 1976–77; Vice-Pres., Dir. Business and Govt. Relations, Comm. for Econ. Devt. 1977–81; Deputy Asst. to Pres. Ronald Reagan, Washington 1981–83, Asst. to Pres. for Legis. Affairs 1982–83; Vice-Pres. Timmons & Co., Wash., 1983–87; Deputy Chief of Staff to Pres. Reagan 1987–88, Chief of Staff 1988–89. *Address:* c/o The White House, 1600 Pennsylvania Avenue, N.W., Washington, D.C. 20500, U.S.A.

DUBININ, Mikhail Mikhailovich; Soviet physical chemist; b. 1 Jan. 1901, Moscow; ed. Moscow Higher Tech. School; in Moscow Higher Tech. School 1921–32, Prof. 1933–; Head of Laboratory of Sorbtion Processes, Inst. of Physical Chemistry, U.S.S.R. Acad. of Sciences 1946–; mem. U.S.S.R. Acad. of Sciences 1943–; Pres. Mendeleyev Chemical Soc. 1946–50; Head Chemical Section U.S.S.R. Acad. of Sciences 1948–57; Ed.-in-Chief Bulletin of U.S.S.R. Acad. of Sciences, Chemical Series; Hon. mem. Hungarian Acad. of Sciences; State Prize 1942, 1950, Hero of Socialist Labour, Order of Lenin (twice), Order of the Patriotic War, Order of the Red Star (twice), Hammer and Sickle Gold Medal, Order of the October Revolution and other decorations. *Publications:* Fiziko-khimicheskie osnovy sortsionnoi tekhniki 1935, 1939, Theory of Volume Filling for Vapor Adsorption 1966, Porous Structure and Adsorption Properties of Active Carbons 1966, Adsorption in Micropores 1967, Porous Structure of Adsorbents and Catalysts 1967, Surface of Non-Porous and Porous Adsorbents 1970, 1973, 1974, Physical Adsorption of Gases and Vapors in Micropores 1975. *Address:* c/o U.S.S.R. Institute of Physical Chemistry, Academy of Sciences, Leninsky Prospekt 31, Moscow 117071, U.S.S.R.

DUBININ, Nikolay Petrovich; Soviet geneticist; b. 4 Jan. 1907, Kronstadt; s. of Pyotr Fedorovich and Anna Gerasimovna Dubinin; m. Lydia Georgievna Dubinina 1962; one d.; ed. Moscow Univ.; at Moscow Zootechnical Inst. 1928–32; at Inst. of Cytology, Histology and Embryology, U.S.S.R. Acad. of Sciences 1932–48; at Inst. of Forestry 1949–55, Inst. of Biophysics 1955–58; Dir. Inst. of Cytology and Genetics, Siberian Dept., U.S.S.R. Acad. of Sciences 1958–60; Dir. Inst. of Gen. Genetics, U.S.S.R. Acad. of Sciences 1966–; mem. CPSU 1969–; Presidium mem. Siberian Dept., U.S.S.R. Acad. of Sciences 1958; Corresp. mem. U.S.S.R. Acad. of Sciences 1946–66, mem. 1966–; Chair. of "Man and Environment" Section of State Cttee. for Science and Tech. of U.S.S.R. Council of Ministers; Darwin Medal 1950, Lenin Prize 1966, Order of October Revolution 1975, 30th Anniversary of Victory Medal, Order of Lenin 1986. *Publications:* General Genetics 1970, Horizons of Genetics 1970, Vesnoe Dvizhenie 1973. *Leisure interests:* fishing, hunting. *Address:* Institute of General Genetics, U.S.S.R. Academy of Sciences, 7 Profsoyuznaya Street, 117312 Moscow, U.S.S.R. *Telephone:* 135-62-13.

DUBININ, Yuri Vladimirovich, CAND. HIST. SC.; Soviet diplomatist; b. 1930; ed. Moscow Inst. for Int. Relations; Asst. in Embassy to France trans. with UNESCO; mem. Diplomatic Service 1955–; ed. Moscow Inst. for Int. Relations; mem. Apparat U.S.S.R. Ministry of Foreign Affairs 1960–63, 1968–78; First Sec., Embassy Counsellor, Embassy in France 1963–68; Amb. to Spain Oct. 1978–86, to U.S.A. May 1986; Perm. Rep. to UN Jan. 1987–. *Address:* Permanent Mission of the U.S.S.R. to the United Nations, Palais des Nations, 1211 Geneva 10, Switzerland.

DuBOIS, G. Macy, M.ARCH; Canadian architect; b. 20 Dec. 1929, Baltimore, Md., U.S.A.; s. of Benjamin V. and Lilly DuBois; m. 1st Sarah Buchanan 1957, 2nd Helga Plumb 1975; one s. one d.; ed. Tufts and Harvard Univs.; designer, The Architects Collaborative 1957–58; architect-designer, John B. Parkin 1958–59; architect, Robert Fairfield Architects 1959–61; architect, Fairfield & DuBois, Architects 1961–75; Partner DuBois Plumb & Assocs. 1975–; Hon. Fellow, American Inst. of Arch.; hon. mem. Physics Soc., Eng. Soc.; Massey Medal 1964, 1968, Low Energy Bldg. Design Award 1980, Gov.-Gen.'s Medal 1983. *Address:* DuBois Plumb & Associates, 76 Richmond Street East, Toronto, Ont., M5c 1P1, Canada. *Telephone:* (416) 363-1103.

DUBOIS, Jacques-Emile, D.SC.; French university professor; b. 13 April 1920, Lille; s. of Paul Dubois and Emilienne Chevrier; m. Bernice Claire Shaaker 1952; one s. one d.; ed. Univs. of Lille and Grenoble; Mem. Liberation Cttee., Isère 1944; Ramsay Fellow, Univ. Coll., London 1948–50; Scientific Adviser to French Cultural Counsellor, London 1948–50; Prof. of Physical Chemistry and Petrochemistry, and Dir. of Chemistry Inst., Univ. of Saar 1949–57, Dean of Science Faculty 1953–57; Prof. of Physical Organic Chemistry, Univ. of Paris 1957–; Research Fellow, Columbia Univ., New York 1956; Guest Prof. of Physical Chemistry, Univ. of Saar 1958; Scientific Adviser to French Minister of Educ. 1962–63; Joint Dir. of Higher Educ. 1963–65; Dir. of Research for Ministry of Defence 1965–77; Co-Dir. Curie Foundation 1977–80; Dir. French Nat. Univ. Agency for Scientific and Tech. Documentation and Information (AUDIST) 1978–81; Scientific Dir. Cie. Générale d'Electricité 1979–83; Chair. IUPAC Interdivisional Cttee. on Machine Documentation 1970–77; Founding Pres., Assen. for Research and Devt. in Chem. Informatics (ARDIC) 1971–; Vice-

Pres. French Physical Chem. Soc. 1972–74, Pres. 1974–76; Vice-Pres. CNIC (Nat. Centre for Chemical Information) 1972–; French Nat. Del. to Codata, Vice-Chair. 1980–; mem. Directorate Nat. Research Council 1963–71, 1976–; mem. Council French Chemical Soc. 1965–67, Faraday Soc.; Officier, Légion d'honneur, Commdr. Ordre national du Mérite, Médaille de la Résistance, Commdr. des Palmes académiques, Jecker Prize and Berthelot Medal (Acad. of Sciences), Le Bel and Ancel Prizes (French Chemical Soc.), Stas Medal (Belgian Chemical Soc.), Grand Prix Technique, City of Paris 1975, Bruylants Chair. and Medal (Louvain Univ.) 1982. *Publications:* works in field of kinetics, fast reaction rates, electro-chemistry, automation applied to chemistry and author of the DARC topological system used for on-line information systems and for computer-assisted design in chemistry. *Leisure interest:* skiing. *Address:* 100 rue de Rennes, 75006 Paris, France. *Telephone:* 4222-45-16.

Du BOULAY, Francis Robin Houssemayne, M.A., F.B.A.; British academic (retd.); b. 19 Dec. 1920, Kent; s. of the late Philip Du Boulay and Mercy Friend; m. Cecilia (Celia) Burnell Matthews 1948; two s. one d.; ed. Christ's Hospital, Horsham, Phillips Acad., Andover Mass., Balliol Coll., Oxford; during World War II served in Friends Ambulance Unit, then as jr. officer in R.A.; appointed lecturer in History, Bedford Coll., London 1947–60; Prof. of Medieval History 1960–82, Emer. Prof. 1982–; Hon. Sec. Royal Historical Soc. 1960–65. *Publications:* The Lordship of Canterbury 1966, An Age of Ambition 1970, Germany in the later Middle Ages 1983, Legion and other poems 1983, and numerous articles on English and German history. *Leisure interest:* poetry. *Address:* Broadmead, Riverhead, Sevenoaks, Kent, TN13 3DE, England.

DUBOWITZ, Victor, M.D., PH.D., F.R.C.P., D.C.H.; British professor of pediatrics; b. 6 Aug. 1931, Beaufort West, S. Africa; s. of late Charley Dubowitz and Olga Schattel; m. Lilly M. S. Sebok 1960; four s.; ed. Central High School, Beaufort West and Univs. of Cape Town and Sheffield; intern, Groote Schuur Hospital, Cape Town 1955; Sr. House Officer, Queen Mary's Hosp. for Children 1957–59; Research Assoc. Royal Postgraduate Medical School 1958–59; Lecturer in Clinical Pathology, Nat. Hosp. for Nervous Diseases, London 1960; Lecturer in Child Health, Univ. of Sheffield 1961–65, Sr. Lecturer 1965–67, Reader 1967–72; Research Assoc. Inst. for Muscle Disease and Asst. Pediatrician, Cornell Medical Coll., New York 1965–66; Prof. of Pediatrics, Royal Postgraduate Medical School 1972–; Consultant Pediatrician, Hammersmith Hosp. 1972–; Dir. Jerry Lewis Muscle Research Centre; recipient of several awards etc. *Publications:* The Floppy Infant 1969, Muscle Biopsy: A Modern Approach (with M. H. Brooke) 1973, Gestational Age of the Newborn (with L. M. S. Dubowitz) 1977, Muscle Disorders in Childhood 1978, The Neurological Assessment of the Pre-term and Full-term Newborn Infant (with L. M. S. Dubowitz) 1981, A Colour Atlas of Muscle Disorders in Childhood 1989. *Leisure interests:* sculpting, hiking, antique glass. *Address:* Department of Pediatrics, Hammersmith Hospital, Ducane Road, London, W.12, England. *Telephone:* 01-740 3295.

DuBRIDGE, Lee Alvin, M.A., PH.D.; American physicist and educator; b. 21 Sept. 1901, Terre Haute, Indiana; s. of Frederick A. and Elizabeth (née Browne) DuBridge; m. Doris M. Koht 1925 (died 1973), one s. one d.; m. 2nd Arrola Bush Cole 1974; ed. Cornell Coll., and Univ. of Wisconsin; Instructor in Physics, Univ. of Wisconsin 1925–26; Fellow Nat. Research Council at Calif. Inst. of Tech. 1926–28; Asst. Prof. of Physics, Washington Univ. St. Louis, Mo. 1928–33; Assoc. Prof. 1933–34; Prof. of Physics and Chair. of Dept., Univ. of Rochester 1934–46; Dean of Faculty of Arts and Science 1938–42; on leave of absence, Univ. of Rochester, for war service as Dir. of Radiation Lab. at M.I.T., under the Nat. Defense Research Cttee. 1940–45; Pres. of Calif. Institute of Tech. 1946–69; Scientific Adviser to Pres. Nixon 1969–70; mem. Scientific Advisory Cttee., Gen. Motors 1971–76; mem. Gen. Advisory Cttee. U.S. Atomic Energy Comm. 1946–52; Chair. Science Advisory Cttee., Office of Defense Mobilisation 1952–56; mem. Nat. Academy of Sciences, American Philosophical Society; Pres. American Physical Society 1947; mem. Governing Bd., American Inst. of Physics 1941–46; Fellow, A.A.A.S.; mem. Bd. of Trustees, Carnegie Endowment for Int. Peace 1951–57, Nat. Science Foundation Bd. 1950–54, 1958–64; mem. Bd. of Trustees, Rockefeller Foundation 1956–67; mem. Bd. of Trustees Mellon Inst. 1958–67; Trustee, U.S. Churchill Foundation 1960–68, Thomas Alva Edison Foundation, Inc. 1960–68, Henry E. Huntington Library and Art Foundation, San Marino, Calif.; various directorships, Benjamin Franklin Fellow, Royal Soc. of Arts, London, England 1962–; Research Corpn. award 1947, Medal for Merit 1948, King's Medal for Service in Cause of Freedom 1946, Hon. Fellow and Gold Medal award American Coll. of Cardiology 1966, Vannevar Bush Award (Nat. Science Foundation) 1982; numerous hon. degrees. *Publications:* Photoelectric Phenomena (with A. L. Hughes) 1932, New Theories of the Photoelectric Effect 1935, Introduction to Space 1960. *Address:* 1730 Homet Road, Pasadena, Calif. 91106, U.S.A. (Home). *Telephone:* (818) 793-1683.

DUBY, Georges Michel Claude; French professor of history; b. 7 Oct. 1919, Paris; s. of Louis Duby and Marguerite Dimanche; m. Andrée Combier 1942; one s. two d.; ed. Lycée de Mâcon and Univ. of Lyon; Prof. of Medieval History, Faculty of Letters, Besançon 1950, Aix-Marseille 1951–; Prof. of History of Medieval Socs., Collège de France, Paris 1970–; Dir. of revue Etudes Rurales; mem. Inst. de France 1974–; mem. Academie

française; assoc. mem. British Acad., Acad. Royale de Belgique, Royal Historical Soc., Medieval Acad. of America; Foreign mem. Accad. Nazionale dei Lincei, Hungarian Acad. of Sciences, American Philosophical Soc.; Pres. Comité Scientifique de la Fondation de France; Dr. h.c. (Catholic Univ. of Louvain, Free Univ., Amsterdam, Univ. de Liège, Univ. of Montreal); Ordre du Mérite Agricole, Commdr., Légion d'honneur, Commdr. Arts et Lettres, and several prizes for works on history. *Publications:* La société aux XIe et XIIe siécles dans la région mâconnaise, 1953, Histoire de la civilisation française (with R. Mandrou) 1958, L'An Mil 1967, Guerriers et Paysans, essai sur la première croissance économique de l'Europe 1973, Le Dimanche de Bouvines 1973, Les procès de Jeanne d'Arc (with A. Duby) 1973, Saint Bernard: L'Art Cistercien 1976, Le Temps de Cathédrales, L'Art dans la société 980–1420 1976, Medieval Marriage 1978, Les Trois Ordres ou l'Imaginaire du féodalisme 1978, L'Europe au Moyen Age, Art roman, Art Gothique 1979, Dialogues, Georges Duby—Guy Lardreau 1980, le chevalier, la femme et la prêtre 1981, Guillaume le Maréchal 1984, Histoire de la vie privée 1985, Histoire de France: Le Moyen Age 1987. *Address:* Collège de France, 11 place Marcelin Berthelot, 75005 Paris (Office); Beaurecueil, Le Tholonet, 13100 Aix-en-Provence, France (Home). *Telephone:* Paris 329-12-11.

DUBY, Jean Jacques, PH.D.; French mathematician and scientist; b. 5 Nov. 1940, Paris; s. of Jean Duby and Lucienne (née Lacomme) Duby; m. Camille Poli 1963; one d.; ed. Ecole Normale Supérieure, Paris; research staff mem., Thomas J. Watson Research Center, U.S.A. 1963–64; Systems Engineer IBM France 1965–66, Br. Office Man. 1977–78, Dir. of Science and Tech. 1986–88; Man. Grenoble Scientific Centre 1967–69; Assoc. Prof., European Systems Research Inst. and Univ. of Geneva 1970–71; Project Man. Paris Stock Exchange 1972–73; Man. Application Systems, IBM Mohansic Lab 1974–75; Exec. Asst. to Vice-Chair., IBM Corp. 1975–76; Special Assignment, IBM Communications Div. 1979; Dir. Switching Systems, IBM Europe 1980–82, now Group Dir. Science and Tech.; Scientific Dir. C.N.R.S. 1982–86; Chevalier ordre nat. du Mérite (France), ordre nat. de la Côte d'Ivoire. *Leisure interests:* skiing, mountaineering. *Address:* IBM Europe, Tour Pascal, Cedex 40, 92075 Paris la Défense, France.

du CANN, Col. the Rt. Hon. Sir Edward Dillon Lott, P.C., K.B.E., M.A., M.P., F.R.S.A.; British politician and banker; b. 28 May 1924, Beckenham; s. of late C. G. L. du Cann and Janet (née Murchie) du Cann; m. Sallie Murchie 1962; one s. two d.; ed. Woodbridge School, Suffolk, and St. John's Coll., Oxford; M.P. 1956–87; Founder and Chair. Unicorn Group of Unit Trusts 1957–62, 1964–72, 87; Founder mem. Asscn. Unit Trust Mans. 1961; Econ. Sec. to the Treasury 1962–63; Minister of State, Bd. of Trade 1963–64; Chair. of Conservative Party 1965–67, Pres. 1981–82; Chair. 1922 Cttee. 1972–84; First Chair. Select Cttee. on Public Expenditure 1970–72, Public Accounts Cttee. 1972–79; First Chair. Treasury and Civil Service Cttee. 1979–83, Liaison Cttee. of Select Cttee. Chairs. 1979–83; Vice-Chair. British-American Parl. Group 1975–79; Pres. of Conservative Parl. European Community Reform Group 1985–87; Founder Chair. All-Party Maritime Affairs Parl. Group 1984–87; First Chair. Public Accounts Comm. 1984–87; Chair. Keyser Ullmann Ltd. 1972–75, Cannon Assurance Ltd. 1972–80, Lonrho PLC 1984– (Dir. 1972–); Visiting Fellow, Univ. of Lancaster Business School 1970–82; Patron, Asscn. of Insurance Brokers 1973–77, Human Ecology Foundation 1987; Gov. Hatfield Coll., Durham Univ. 1988; Renter Warden Fruiterers Co. 1988, Upper Warden 1989; Pres. Inst. of Freight Forwarders 1988–89; Hon. Vice-Pres. British Insurance Brokers Asscn. 1978; mem. Cttee. of Privileges 1974–, Panel of Judges, Templeton Foundation 1984; mem. of Man. Council of the G.B.-Sasakawa British-Japanese Foundation 1984–; First Hon. Freeman Borough of Taunton Dean 1977; led first British Parl. del. to China 1982; Hon. Col. 155 Regiment (Wessex) Volunteers 1972–82, Hon. Life mem. of the Inst. of RCT; Admiral, House of Commons Yacht Club. *Publication:* Investing Simplified 1959, How to Bring Government Expenditure under Parlimentary Control 1979, A New Competition Policy 1984, Hoist the Red Ensign 1987. *Address:* 9 Tufton Court, Tufton Street, London, S.W.1, England.

DUCCI, Roberto, LL.D.; Italian fmr. diplomatist and professor of diplomacy; b. 8 Feb. 1914, Florence; s. of Adm. of the Fleet Gino Ducci and Virginia Boncinelli; m. Wanda Matyjewicz 1951; two s.; ed. Rome Univ.; entered Foreign Service 1937; served Ottawa 1938, Newark N.J. 1940; Italian Del. to Peace Conf. 1946, Warsaw 1947, Rio de Janeiro 1949, Italian Del. to N.A.T.O. and O.E.E.C. 1950–55; mem. Del. Brussels Six-Power Conf. 1955–57; Chair. Drafting Cttee. Rome Treaties 1956–57; Asst. Dir.-Gen. Econ. Affairs 1955–57; Amb. to Finland 1958–62; Head, Italian Del. to Brussels U.K.-EEC Conf. 1961–63; Deputy Dir.-Gen. for Political Affairs 1963–64, Dir.-Gen. 1970–75; Amb. to Yugoslavia 1964–67, to Austria 1967–70, to U.K. 1975–80; State Councillor 1980–84; Prof. of Political Science, Rome Univ. 1982–; mem. Bd., European Investment Bank 1958–68; Vice-Pres. Mattiotti Foundation; Grand Cross, Italian Order of Merit. *Publications:* Prima età di Napoleone 1933, Questa Italia 1948, L'Europa Incompiuta 1971, D'Annunzio Vivente 1973, I Contemporanei 1976, L'Innocenza (poems) 1978, Libro di Musica (poems) 1980, I'Capintesta 1982, Candidato a Morte 1983 and numerous political essays and articles. *Leisure interests:* riding, collecting antique glass. *Address:* Consiglio di Stato, Palazzo Spada, Rome (Office); Via Belsiana 35, 00187, Rome, Italy (Home). *Telephone:* (06) 678 0183.

DUCKMANTON, Sir Talbot Sydney, Kt., C.B.E.; Australian broadcasting executive; b. 26 Oct. 1921, South Yarra, Victoria; s. of S. J. Duckmanton; m. 1st Florence Simmonds 1947 (deceased), one s. three d.; ed. Newington Coll., Stanmore, N.S.W., Sydney Univ. and Australian Administrative Staff Coll.; Australian Army and Air Force Service; Australian Broadcasting Comm. 1939–82, Man. for Tasmania 1953–57, Controller of Admin. 1957–59, Asst. Gen. Man. (Admin.) 1959–64, Deputy Gen. Man. 1964–65, Gen. Man. 1965–82; Vice-Pres. Asian Broadcasting Union 1970–73, Pres. 1973–77; Pres. Commonwealth Broadcasting Assen. 1975–82; Trustee, Visnews Ltd. 1965–82, Int. Inst. of Communications; mem. Council, Australian Admin. Staff Coll. 1969–82, Australian Film Devt. Corpn. 1970–75, Australian Council for the Arts 1973–75. *Address:* P.O. Box E148, St. James, Sydney 2000, N.S.W., Australia.

DUCREUX, Louis Raymond; French theatrical and operatic manager; b. 22 Sept. 1911, Marseilles; s. of Jean and Jeanne (née Pieri) Ducreux-Picon; m. Madeleine Cheminat 1931 (divorced), one s.; Artistic Man. Theatrical Company Le Rideau Gris, Marseilles 1931–35; Co-Dir. with André Roussin 1935–40; Stage Dir. Cie. Claude Dauphin, Cannes 1940–42; Actor-Man. La Comédie de Lyon 1942–43; playwright, actor, composer and stage dir. in Paris 1944–61; Man. Opéra de Marseille 1961–65, 1968–72, Opéra de Monte Carlo 1965–72, Grand Théâtre de Nancy 1973–77; Dir. first part of film A Sunday in the Country 1984, Officier, Légion d'honneur, Officier des Arts et Lettres. *Publications include:* Plays: La part du feu, Un souvenir d'Italie, French version of The Heiress and Bell, Book and Candle; Musical Plays: L'amour en papier, Le Square du Pérou; novel: La Porte tournante du café Riche. *Address:* 10 rue Hégésippe-Moreau, 75018 Paris, France; 20 Boulevard Princesse Charlotte, Monte-Carlo, Monaco. *Telephone:* Paris 43-87-05-85.

DUDA, Edward, M.A.; Polish politician; b. 27 Dec. 1922, Podedworze, Włodawa district; ed. Higher School of Social Sciences, Warsaw; Mem. of Peasant Battalions (BCh) and later of People's Army (AL) during Nazi occupation 1940–45; mem. Civic Militia, later mem. Łódź Voivodship Board, Union of Fighters for Freedom and Democracy (ZBoWiD) during post-war years; active mem. youth orgs.; Ed.-in-Chief Walka Młodych 1951–55; Deputy Chair. of Presidium, Warsaw Voivodship Nat. Council 1955–58; Head of Propaganda Dept., Cen. Cttee. of United Peasant Party (ZSL) 1958–59, 1962–65; Chair. of Presidium, Rzeszów Voivodship Nat. Council 1965–69; mem. Exec. Council of ZSL 1949, mem. Cen. Cttee. 1959–84, Sec. of Cen. Cttee. 1969–80, mem. Presidium of Cen. Cttee. 1971–80; Deputy to Seym 1961–85; Chair. Seym Comm. for Admin., Local Econ. and Environmental Protection 1976–80; mem. Presidium of Gen. Bd., Polish-Soviet Friendship Soc. (TPPR) 1974–84; mem. State Council 1976–80, Sec. 1980–83; Deputy Chair. Gen. Bd. ZBoWiD 1979–85; numerous decorations incl. Order of Banner of Labour (First and Second Class), Grunwald cross (Third Class), Kt.'s Cross, Commdr. Cross with Star of Order of Polonia Restituta, Partisan Cross.

DUDAS, Koloman; Czechoslovak politician; b. 2 Dec. 1934, Cata, Levice Dist.; ed. Teacher Training Coll.; teacher, Deputy Head, then Head, Secondary School, Samorin 1965–70; political official West Slovak Regional CPSL Cttee. 1970–81; Chair. Dist. Nat. Cttee. at Dunajska Streda 1981–88; Leading Sec. Dist. Party Cttee. 1988–; mem. CPSL Presidium 1988–. *Address:* Communist Party of Slovakia, Hlboká 2, 883 33 Bratislava, Czechoslovakia.

DUDBRIDGE, Glen, PH.D., F.B.A.; British university teacher; b. 2 July 1938, Clevedon, Somerset; s. of George Victor Dudbridge and Edna Kathleen Dudbridge (née Cockle); m. Sylvia Lo Fung-young 1965; one s. one d.; ed. Bristol Grammar School, Magdalene Coll. Cambridge (Scholar, then Bye-Fellow) and New Asia Inst. of Advanced Chinese Studies, Hong Kong; Research Fellow, Magdalene Coll. 1965; Lecturer in Modern Chinese, Oxford Univ. 1965–85; Prof. of Chinese, Cambridge Univ. 1985–89; Prof. of Chinese, Oxford Univ. 1989–; Fellow, Wolfson Coll. Oxford 1966–85, Emer. Fellow 1985–; Fellow, Magdalene Coll. Cambridge 1985–89; Fellow, Univ. Coll. Oxford 1989–; Visiting Prof., Yale Univ., U.S.A. 1972–73, Univ. of Calif., Berkeley, U.S.A. 1980. *Publications:* The Hsi-yu chi (a study of antecedents to the sixteenth-century Chinese novel) 1970, The Legend of Miao-shan 1978, The Tale of Li Wa (study and critical edition of a Chinese story from the ninth century) 1983. *Address:* Oriental Institute, Pusey Lane, Oxford, OX2 1LE, England. *Telephone:* Oxford 278200.

DUDINSKAYA, Natalya Mikhailovna; Soviet ballerina; b. 21 Aug. 1912, Kharkov, U.S.S.R.; d. of Mikhail Dudinskiy and Natalya Grippenberg; m. Konstantin Sergeyev 1947; ed. Leningrad School of Choreography; Prima Ballerina Kirov Academic Opera and Ballet Theatre, Leningrad; theatre coach in the Kirov Theatre 1951–; lecturer Vaganova Choreographical Inst., Leningrad 1964–. *Principal parts include:* all ballets by Tchaikovsky, Raimonda by Glazunov, Giselle, Les Sylphides, Don Quixote and The Bayadere by Mincous; has created leading roles in: Laurencia by Krein, Gayane by Khachaturyan, Cinderella by Prokofiev, The Bronze Horseman by Gliere, Shuralé by Yarullin, the Polish Maiden in Taras Bulba by Soloviev-Sedoy 1956, Sarie in The Path of Thunder by Kara Karayev 1958, Baroness Strahl in The Masquerade by Laputin 1960, Titania in A Midsummer Night's Dream 1963, The Wicked Fairy in the film The Sleeping Beauty 1964, The Spanish Suite by Viana López Gerardo 1966, Miniature by Krein 1967, Pacquita 1968; choreographic work (with K.

Sergeyev): Hamlet 1970, Le Corsair 1973, The Left-Hander 1976, Beethoven Apassionata 1977, Class-Concert 1981; guest artist in many foreign countries; People's Artist of U.S.S.R.; State Prizewinner 1941, 1947, 1949, 1951; Order of Esteem 1939, Order Red Banner of Labour 1940, 1972, 1983, 1988, Medal for Defence of Leningrad, Order Friendship of Peoples 1982, and other decorations. *Leisure interests:* swimming, diving. *Address:* 2 Gogol Street, Apartment 13, Leningrad 191065, U.S.S.R. *Telephone:* 3147172.

DUDINTSEV, Vladimir Dmitriyevich; Soviet writer; b. 29 June 1918, Kupyansk, Ukraine; s. of Claudia and Dmitry Dudintsev; m. Natalia Gordeeva 1942; one s. three d.; ed. Moscow Legal Inst.; Soviet Army 1941–45; Feature Writer of Komsomolskaya Pravda 1946–51; mem. Union of Soviet Writers. *Publications:* With Seven Brothers (collected stories) 1952, In His Place 1954, Not By Bread Alone 1956, 1968, Tales and Stories 1959, A New Year's Tale 1960, Stories 1963; trans. Suvra Golovanivsky's Poplar on the other Bank 1967 and twenty other books 1957–74, White Vestments 1988. *Leisure interest:* sailing. *Address:* Lomonosovsky Prospekt 19, KW 74, Moscow W311; U.S.S.R. Union of Writers, Ul. Vorovskogo 52, Moscow, U.S.S.R. *Telephone:* 130-21-68 (Home).

DUDLEY, Hugh Arnold, C.B.E., CH.M., F.R.C.S., F.R.A.C.S.; British professor of surgery; b. 1 July 1925, Dublin, Eire; s. of Walter Dudley and Ethel Smith; m. Jean Bruce Lindsay Johnston 1947; two s. one d.; ed. Edinburgh and Harvard Univs.; Lecturer in Surgery, Edin. Univ. 1954–58; Sr. Lecturer in Surgery, Aberdeen Univ. 1958–63; Foundation Prof. of Surgery, Monash Univ., Melbourne 1963–72; Prof. of Surgery, St. Mary's Hosp., London 1973–88, Prof. Emer. 1988–; Pres. of Surgical Research Soc. of Australasia, and of G.B. and Ireland, of Biological Eng. Soc. and of British Journal of Surgery Soc.; Hon. Fellow American Surgical Assen. 1986, S.A. Coll. of Surgeons 1987. *Publications:* Principles of General Surgical Management 1958, Communication in Medicine and Biology 1977; Ed. Emergency Surgery 1979, 1986, Operative Surgery 1976–, Guide for House Surgeons 1974, 1982, 1987. *Leisure interests:* shooting, surgical history. *Address:* Academic Surgical Unit, St. Mary's Hospital, London, W2 1NY, England. *Telephone:* 01-725 6246.

DUE, Ole; Danish politician; b. 10 Feb. 1931, Korsør; s. of H. P. Due and Jenny (née Jensen) Due; m. Alice Maud Halkier Nielsen 1954; three s. one d.; ed. Univ. of Copenhagen; civil servant Ministry of Justice Copenhagen 1955, Head of Div. 1970, Head of Dept. 1975, Acting Appeal Court Judge 1978; Judge Court of Justice, EEC 1979, Pres. 1988–; Kt., Order of Dannebrog. *Publications include:* articles on Community law, private int. law and legal technique. *Address:* Court of Justice of the European Community, Bd. Konrad Adenauer, 2925 Luxembourg. *Telephone:* 4303-2200.

DUERR, Hans-Peter Emil, PH.D.; German physicist; b. 7 Oct. 1929, Stuttgart; s. of Dr. Rupert and Eva (née Kraepelin) Duerr; m. Carol Sue Durham 1956; two s. two d.; ed. Univs. of Stuttgart and California, Berkeley; Research Asst. Dept. of Physics, Berkeley 1956–57, Max-Planck Inst. für Physik, Göttingen and Munich 1958–62; Visiting Assoc. Prof., Berkeley and Inst. of Mathematical Sciences, Madras, India 1962–63; Visiting Prof., Berkeley 1968–69; Prof. Univ. of Munich 1969; mem. Directorate Max-Planck Inst., Munich 1971–, Chair. 1977–80; Man. Dir. Max-Planck Inst. für Physik und Astrophysik 1978–80; mem. Exec. Cttee. Greenpeace Germany 1984–; mem. Pugwash Council 1987–(92); Chair. Bd. Global Challenges Network 1987–, Werner-Heisenberg-Institut für Physik, Advisory Cttee. Wissenschafts-Zentrum München 1984–; mem. Deutschen Akademie der Naturforscher Leopoldina, Halle, G.D.R.; mem. Bd. Vereinigung Deutscher Wissenschaftler, mem. Bd. Int. Foundation for the Survival and Devt. of Humanity 1988–. *Publications:* more than 90 publications on nuclear physics, elementary particle physics and gravitation. *Address:* Max-Planck Institut für Physik und Astrophysik, Föhringer Ring 6, D 8000 Munich 40, Federal Republic of Germany. *Telephone:* 089 32308 280.

DUESENBERRY, James Stembel, B.A., M.A., PH.D.; American economist; b. 18 July 1918; ed. Univ. of Michigan; Teaching Fellow in Econs., Univ. of Michigan 1939–41; in U.S.A.F. 1942–45; Instructor, M.I.T. 1946; Teaching Fellow in Econs., Harvard Univ. 1946–48, Asst. Prof. of Econs. 1948–53, Assoc. Prof. 1953–57, Prof. 1957–; Fulbright Research Prof., Cambridge Univ. 1954–55; Ford Foundation Research Prof. 1958–59; Consultant, Cttee. of Econ. Devt. 1956; mem. President's Council of Econ. Advisers 1966–68. *Publications:* Income, Saving and the Theory of Consumer Behavior 1949, Business Cycles and Economic Growth (with Lee Preston) 1958, Cases and Problems in Economics 1959, Money and Credit: Impact and Control 1964, Capital Needs in the Seventies (with T. Mayer and Robert Alber), Money, Banking and the Economy 1981. *Address:* 25 Fairmont Street, Belmont, Mass. 02178, U.S.A.

DUFF, Rt. Hon. Sir (Arthur) Antony, G.C.M.G., C.V.O., D.S.O., D.S.C.; British diplomatist (retd.); b. 1920; m. Pauline Marion (née Bevan) Duff 1944; one s. two d.; Amb. to Nepal 1964–65; with Commonwealth Office and subsequently with FCO 1965–69; Deputy High Commr., Kuala Lumpur 1969–72; High Commr. to Kenya 1972–75; Deputy Under-Sec. FCO 1975–79; Perm. Rep. to WEU 1977–78; Deputy Gov. of Southern Rhodesia 1979–80, Deputy Sec. Cabinet Office 1980–87. *Address:* c/o National Westminster Bank Ltd., 17 The Hard, Portsea, PO1 3DU, England.

DUFF, George Francis Denton, M.A., PH.D., F.R.S.C.; Canadian professor of mathematics; b. 28 July 1926, Toronto; s. of George H. Duff and Laura Denton Duff; m. Mary E. Wood 1951 (divorced 1985); two s. three d.; ed. Univ. of Toronto and Princeton Univ.; Instr. Mass. Inst. of Tech. 1951-52; Asst. Prof. of Math. Univ. of Toronto 1952-57, Assoc. Prof. 1957-61, Prof. 1961-, Chair. Dept. of Math. 1968-75; Pres. Canadian Math. Soc. 1971-73. *Publications:* Partial Differential Equations 1956, Differential Equations of Applied Mathematics (with D. Naylor) 1966, Calculus (with J. DelGrande) 1972; various mathematical papers in journals. *Leisure interests:* reading (history, biography, science), astronomy, travel. *Address:* Department of Mathematics, University of Toronto, Toronto, Ont., M5S 1A1 (Office); 20 Buckingham Avenue, Toronto, Ont., M4N 1R2, Canada (Home). *Telephone:* (416) 978-4804 (Office); (416) 481-0169 (Home).

DUFFY, Michael John, B.L.; Australian politician; b. 2 March 1938, Mildura, Vic.; m.; three c.; ed. Christian Brothers' Coll., Albury, N.S.W., Newman Coll., Univ. of Melbourne; worked as solicitor; mem. House of Reps. for Holt, Vic. 1980-; Minister for Communications and Minister assisting the Minister for Defence 1983-87, for Trade Negotiations, Minister Assisting the Minister for Industry, Tech. and Commerce and Minister Assisting the Minister for Primary Industries and Energy 1987-; del. to Victoria Labor Party State Conf. 1982, 1984; mem. Labor Party Victorian Branch Admin. Cttee. 1973-76; mem. House of Reps. Jt. Cttee. of Public Accounts 1980-83. *Leisure interests:* cricket, football, horse racing, reading and music. *Address:* Parliament House, Canberra, A.C.T. 2600, Australia.

DUFOIX, Georgina, D.ÈS SC. ECON.; French politician; b. 14 Feb. 1943, Paris; m. Antoine Dufoix 1963; two s. two d.; ed. Lycée de Nîmes and Univs. of Montpellier and Paris; mem. Man. Cttee. Parti Socialiste 1979; Sec. of State for Family Affairs 1981-83, for Family Affairs, Population and Immigrant Workers 1983-84; Minister for Social Affairs and Nat. Solidarity 1984-86; Socialist Deputy for Gard March 1986-. *Address:* Assemblée nationale, 75355 Paris; 264 chemin des Écoliers, 30000 Nîmes, France (Home).

DUFOURCQ, Norbert, D. ÈS L.; French musicologist and organist; b. 21 Sept. 1904, Saint Jean de Braye, Loiret; s. of Albert Dufourcq; m. Odette Latron 1926; one s. five d.; ed. Collège Stanislas and Lycée Henri IV, Paris, Sorbonne and Ecole Nationale des Chartes; teacher of History, Coll. Stanislas, Paris 1935-45; Prof. of History of Music and Musicology at Paris Conservatoire 1941-75; Organist Eglise Saint-Merry 1923-; Sec.-Gen., then Vice-Pres. then Pres. of Soc. of Friends of Organ 1927-; mem. of Comm. for Historic Organs 1933-85; Ed.-in-Chief review L'Orgue 1929-; Prof. Sweet Briar Coll. (Paris) 1949-78; Pres. Société Française de Musicologie 1956-58; Prof. Ecole Normale de Musique de Paris 1958-63; Pres. Soc. de l'Ecole des Chartes 1975-76; Dir. Conservatoire Municipal J.-P. Rameau Paris 1974-80; in charge of course in Modern Western Civilization, Sorbonne; Dir. Orgue et Liturgie, les Grandes Heures de l'Orgue, L'Orgue, Cahiers et Mémoires de l'Orgue, Les Dossiers de l'Orgue; Lecturer, Jeunesses Musicales de France 1942-68; Visiting Prof., Univs. of Lisbon and Ottawa; Grand Prix Nat. du Patrimoine 1983. *Publications:* Essai d'une bibliographie de l'histoire de l'orgue en France (with R. Fallou) 1929, Le grand orgue de Pézenas 1933, Documents inédits relatifs à l'orgue français, XIVe-XVIIIe siècles 1934-35, Esquisse d'une histoire de l'orgue en France du XIIIe au XVIIIe siècles 1935, La musique d'orgue française de J. Titelouze à J. Alain 1941-49, Le grand orgue et les organistes de St. Merry de Paris 1947, Orgues comtadines et provençales 1935, Les Clicquot 1942, César Franck, Le Clavecin 1949-81, L'Orgue 1948-82, Petite histoire de la musique en Europe 1960-88, Bach, génie allemand, génie latin? 1947-49, Bach, le maître de l'orgue 1948-84, La musique française 1948-70, Autour de Coquard, Nicolas Lebègue 1954, Notes et références ... sur Michel R. Delalande 1957, Jean de Joyeuse et la pénétration de la facture parisienne dans le Midi de la France au XVIIe siècle 1958, J. B. de Boesset 1962, Le grand orgue du prytanée militaire de la Flèche 1964, Le livre de l'orgue française, Vol. II: Le buffet 1969, Vol. I: Les sources 1971, Vol. IV: La musique 1972, Vol. III: La facture (Parts I and II) 1975-78, Vol. V: Miscellanea 1983; César Franck et la genèse des premières oeuvres d'orgue 1973, Eugène Gigout 1982, Les grands orgues de St. Merry de Paris à travers l'histoire 1983; preface to organ compositions of P. Dandrieu, G. Jullien, N. de Grigny, A. Raison, Clérembault, G. C. Nivers (3 vols.), F. Couperin (2 vols.), A. Dornel, M. Lanes, M. Corrette (3 vols.), A. Boely (6 vols.); Pièces de Clavecin de N. Lebègue 1957, L'orgue parisien sous le règne de Louis XIV 1957, Nobles et Seigneurs aux confins du Haut Maine et de l'Anjou, La Seigneurie des D'Espeigne de Venerelles à Luché-Pringé 1987, Préfaces aux livres de clavecin de J. F. Dandrieu 1973; Le Manuscrit 172 de la Bibliothèque Municipale de Toure 1988; edited La musique, des origines à nos jours 1948, Histoire de France, Vol. I 1954, Larousse de la Musique 1957-58 (2 vols.), La Vie musicale en France sous les Rois Bourbons (30 vols.), Recherches sur la musique classique française (25 vols.) 1960-87, musical section of Que Sais-Je? (60 vols.), La Musique, les Hommes, les Instruments, les Oeuvres 1965-81 (2 vols.); Gen. Ed. Le lys d'or, Les neuf muses (30 vols.). *Leisure interests:* archaeology, travel. *Address:* 14 rue Cassette, 75006 Paris, France. *Telephone:* 42-22-53-29.

DÜGERSÜREN, Mangalyn; Mongolian diplomatist; b. 15 Feb. 1922, Galuut Somon, Bayanhonger Aymag (Province); ed. Inst. of Int. Relations, Moscow; schoolmaster 1941-44; studies in Moscow 1946-51; Deputy Head, later Head of Dept., Ministry of Foreign Affairs, Mongolia 1951-53; Sec. of Cen. Cttee. of Mongolian Revolutionary Youth League 1953-54; Deputy Minister of Justice 1954-56, of Foreign Affairs 1956-58; Amb. to India 1958-62; First Deputy Minister of Foreign Affairs 1962-63, Minister of Foreign Affairs 1963-68; Perm. Rep. to UN 1968-72, 1988-; Perm. Rep., UN Office at Geneva and other int. orgs. 1972-76, Minister for Foreign Affairs 1976-88; mem. Cen. Cttee. of Mongolian People's Revolutionary Party; Deputy to People's Great Hural (Parl.) 1963-69, 1977-; Order of Friendship Among Peoples 1982. *Address:* Permanent Mission of the Mongolian People's Republic to the United Nations, 6 East 77th Street, New York, N.Y. 10021, U.S.A. *Telephone:* (861) 9460, 9464.

DUGGER, John Scott; American artist and designer; b. 18 July 1948, Los Angeles, Calif.; s. of Dr. James Attwood Dugger, M.D. and Julian Marie Riddle; unmarried; ed. Loy Norrix High School, Kalamazoo, Mich., Gilmore Inst. of Art, Mich., School of the Art Inst. of Chicago, Ill.; created Perennial (first Ergonic Sculpture), Paris 1970; Delegation Leader, Soc. for Anglo-Chinese understanding Delegation to China 1972; Founder-Dir. Banner Arts, London 1976; mem. Exec. Cttee. Art Services Grants Ltd. (Artists' Housing Charity) 1980-85; Chair. Assen. of Space Artists, London 1984, 1985; Vice-Chair. Int. Artists Asscn., U.K. Cttee. 1986-87; maj. works include Documenta 5, People's Participation Pavilion, Kassel, Fed. Repub. of Germany 1972, Monumental Banner Installation, Trafalgar Square, London 1974, Sports Banner Exhbn., Inst. of Contemporary Arts, London 1980; Major Award, Arts Council of G.B. 1978, Calouste Gulbenkian Foundation Awards 1979, 1980, Original Art Banners commissioned for H.M. the Queen's 60th Birthday, Buckingham Palace 1986; works on display at Arts Council of G.B., Tate Gallery, London. *Leisure interests:* oriental art, mountaineering, martial arts. *Address:* 96 Ockendon Road, London, N1 3NW, England; 3101 Margarita Avenue, Burlingame, Calif., U.S.A. 94010. *Telephone:* 01-226 5600 (U.K.); 415-347-6291 (U.S.A.).

DUISENBERG, Willem Frederik, D.ECONS.; Netherlands economist; b. 9 July 1935, Heerenveen; m. Tine Stelling 1960; two s. one d.; ed. State Univ. of Groningen; Scientific Asst., State Univ., Groningen 1961-65; with I.M.F. 1966-69; Special Adviser De Nederlandsche Bank N.V. 1969-70; Prof. of Macro-econs., Univ. of Amsterdam 1970-73; Minister of Finance 1973-77; Dir. BIS; Pres. De Nederlandsche Bank Jan. 1982-. *Publications:* Economic Consequences of Disarmament 1965, The IMF and the International Monetary System 1966, The British Balance of Payments 1969, Some Remarks on Imported Inflation 1970. *Leisure interests:* sailing, tennis, photography. *Address:* De Nederlandsche Bank, Westeinde 1, P.O.B. 98, 1000 AB Amsterdam (Office); Gentsestraat 108, Scheveningen, Netherlands (Home). *Telephone:* (020) 5249111 (Office); (070) 555988 (Home).

DUKAKIS, Michael Stanley; American politician; b. 3 Nov. 1933, Brookline, Mass.; s. of Dr. Panos Dukakis and Euterpe Dukakis; m. Katharine Dickson; one s. two d.; ed. Brookline High School, Swarthmore Coll., Harvard Law School; Army service in Korea 1955-57; mem. Town Meeting, Brookline 1959, Chair. Town Cttee. 1960-62; Attorney Hill & Barlow, Boston 1960-74; alt. Del. Democratic Nat. Convention 1968; mem. Mass. House of Reps. for Brookline 1962-70, later Chair. Cttee. on Public Service and mem. Special Comm. on Low Income Housing; founded a research group for public information 1970; moderator of television public affairs debate programme The Advocates; Gov. of Massachusetts 1975-79, 1983-90; Democratic Cand. for Pres. 1988; lecturer and Dir. of Inter-Governmental Studies, John F. Kennedy School of Govt., Harvard Univ. 1979-82. *Address:* Executive Department, State House, Boston, Mass. 02133 (Office); 85 Perry Street, Brookline, Mass. 02146, U.S.A. (Home).

DUKE, Angier Biddle; American diplomatist and university chancellor; b. 30 Nov. 1915, New York City; s. of Cordelia Drexel Biddle and Angier B. Duke; m. Robin Chandler Lynn 1962; three s. one d.; ed. St. Paul's School, Concord, N.H., and Yale Univ.; Maj. U.S.A.A.F., Second World War; entered American Foreign Service 1949, Sec. and Consul, Buenos Aires 1949-51; Special Asst. to Amb. in Madrid 1951-52; Amb. to El Salvador 1952-53; Pres. Int. Rescue Cttee. 1954-61; Vice-Pres. CARE 1955-58; Chair. Exec. Cttee. American Friends of Viet-Nam 1957-60; Chief of Protocol, Dept. of State, Washington, D.C. 1961-65, and Chief of Protocol for White House with rank of Amb. 1961-65, 1968; Amb. to Spain 1965-68, to Denmark 1968-69, to Morocco 1979-81; Commr. of Civic Affairs, New York 1974-77; Pres., Spanish Inst., New York 1977-79; Pres. American Immigration and Citizenship Conf. 1959-64; Chair. New York State Council on Ethnic Affairs 1978-79, U.S.-Japan Foundation 1981-86, Appeal of Conscience Foundation 1972-, World Affairs Council of Long Island 1981-; Pres. Moroccan-American Foundation 1982-86; Dir. Foreign Policy Asscn., Statue of Liberty Centennial Comm., Four Freedoms Foundation; special adviser, Aspen Inst.; Trustee, Long Island Univ.; Hon. C.B.E., Hans J. Morgenthau Memorial Award 1981, Ordre nat. du Mérite (France), Royal Order of Danneborg (Denmark), Isabel La Católica (Spain), Commdr. Order of George I (Greece) and numerous other foreign decorations, Gold Medal, Spanish Inst. New York 1988; Hon. L.H.D. (Long Island Univ.), Hon. LL.D. (Iona Coll, Duke Univ.). *Leisure interests:* skiing, golf. *Address:* Chancellor's Office, Long Island University, Southampton, New York, N.Y. 11968 (Office); 435 East 52nd Street, New York 10022, U.S.A. (Home). *Telephone:* (516) 283-4000, (212) 759-9145 (Office).

DUKES, Alan M., M.A.; Irish politician; b. 22 April 1945, Dublin; s. of James Dukes and Margaret Moran; m. Fionnuala Corcoran 1968; two d.; ed. Scoil Colmcille and Colaiste Mhuire, Dublin, and Univ. Coll., Dublin; Chief Econ., Irish Farmers Assen. 1967–72; Dir. Irish Farmers Assen., Brussels 1973–76; Personal Adviser to Commr. of EEC 1977–80; mem. Dáil Eireann for Kildare 1981–; Opposition Spokesperson on Agric. March–Dec. 1982; Minister of Agric. 1981–82, for Finance 1982–86, for Justice 1986–87; Leader Fine Gael March 1987–; Pres. Irish Council of the European Movt.; Vice-Pres. European Peoples Party; mem. Council of State. *Address:* Dáil Eireann, Dublin, Ireland.

DULBECCO, Renato; American virologist; b. 22 Feb. 1914, Cantanzaro, Italy; s. of Leonardo and Maria Dulbecco; m. 1st Guiseppina Salva 1940 (divorced 1963); m. 2nd Maureen Muir 1963; two d. (one s. deceased); ed. Università degli Studi, Turin; Asst. Prof. of Pathology, Univ. of Turin 1940–46, of Experimental Embryology 1947; Research Assoc. Dept. of Bacteriology, Indiana Univ. 1947–49; Senior Research Fellow Calif. Inst. of Tech. 1949–52, Assoc. Prof. 1952–53, Prof. 1954–63; Senior Fellow, Salk Inst. for Biological Studies 1963–72; Asst. Dir. of Research, Imperial Cancer Research Fund Labs. (London) 1972–74, Deputy Dir. 1974–77; Sr. Clayton Foundation Investigator, Salk Inst. for Biological Studies, Univ. of California 1977–; Chair. Int. Physicians for Prevention Nuclear War Inst., American-Italian Foundation for Cancer Research; mem. American Assen. for Cancer Research, N.A.S., American Acad. of Arts and Sciences; Foreign mem. Royal Soc., London 1974, Accad. Nazionale dei Lincei; Hon. mem. Accademia Ligure di Scienze e Lettere; Trustee, La Jolla County Day School; Hon. LL.D. (Glasgow) 1970, Hon. D.Sc. (Yale) 1968, Dr. h.c. (Vrije Univ., Brussels) 1968; several awards, including Ehrlich Prize, Ludovic Gross Horwitz Prize 1973, Selman A. Waksman Award in Microbiology, N.A.S., 1974, Nobel Prize in Medicine (Physiology) 1975; Mandel Gold Medal (Czechoslovak Acad. of Sciences) 1982. *Address:* The Salk Institute, 10010 North Torrey Pines Road, La Jolla, Calif. 92037 (Office); 7525 Hillside Drive, La Jolla, Calif., U.S.A. (Home).

DULTZIN, Leib (Leon Aryeh); Israeli business executive; b. 31 March 1913, Minsk, Russia; m. Annette Gutman Hanow 1962; one s. (by previous marriage), one d.; lived in Mexico 1928–56, Israel 1965–; mem. of the exec. Jewish Agency, Treas. 1968–78, Chair. Exec. Cttee. 1973–74, 1978–; Minister without Portfolio, Govt. of Israel 1970–73; Gov. Pal Land Devt. Co. Ltd., Bank Leumi Le Israel; Dir. Rassco Ltd., Yakhim Hakal Co. Ltd., Otzar Hataasiya; mem. World Directorate, Keren Hayesod; mem. Exec. Likud Party; mem. of numerous Zionist orgs. *Publications:* The Economic Role of the Middle Class, The Middle Classes and Their Role in the Productive Absorbtion of New Immigrants. *Address:* The Jewish Agency for Israel, P.O. Box 91920, Jerusalem; and 11 Mapu Street, Tel-Aviv, Israel.

DUMAS, Pierre, L. ÈS D.; French politician; b. 15 Nov. 1924; ed. Ecole Libre des Sciences Politiques; Sales Man. Box Co., La Rochette; Deputy 1958–62, 1967, 1968, 1969–73; Sec. of State for Public Works April–Oct. 1962, Sec. of State for Relations with Parl., responsible for Tourism 1962–67; Sec. of State to Prime Minister, in charge of Tourism 1967–68; Sec. of State for Social Affairs 1968–69; Chair. Comm. on Foreign Affairs, Nat. Ass. 1986; Senator Sept. 1986–; Pres. Soc. française pour le Tunnel Routier du Fréjus 1962–; Pres. Office Nat. des Forêts 1973–84; Mayor of Chambéry 1959–77, 1983–; Chevalier, Légion d'honneur; Rassemblement pour la République. *Address:* 17 rue de Boigne, 73000 Chambéry, France (Home).

DUMAS, Rhetaugh Etheldra Graves, M.S., PH.D., R.N., F.A.A.N.; American health and higher education administrator and nurse; b. 26 Nov. 1928, Natchez, Miss.; d. of Rhetaugh Graves and Josephine (Clemmons) Graves Bell; m. A. W. Dumas, Jr. 1950; one d.; ed. Dillard Univ., New Orleans, Yale Univ. School of Nursing and Union Graduate School, Yellow Springs, Ohio; Dir. Student Health Center, Dillard Univ. 1957–59; Yale-New Haven Hosp. 1960; Instr. in Psychiatric Nursing, Dillard Univ. 1961; Research Asst. and Instr. Yale Univ. School of Nursing 1962–65, Asst. Prof. 1965–66, Assoc. Prof. 1966–72; Dir. of Nursing, Conn. Medical Health Center, Yale-New Haven Medical Center 1966–72; Chief, Psychiatric Nursing Educ. Branch, Div. of Manpower and Training 1972–75; Deputy Dir. Div. of Manpower and Training Programs, Nat. Inst. of Mental Health 1976–79; Deputy Dir. Nat. Inst. of Mental Health, Alcohol, Drug Abuse and Mental Health Admin., U.S. Public Health Service 1979–81; Dean and Prof., Univ. of Mich. School of Nursing, Ann Arbor 1981–; Pres. American Acad. of Nursing 1987–89; mem. N.A.S. Inst. of Medicine; several awards and hon. degrees. *Publications:* numerous articles in professional journals and book chapters. *Leisure interests:* reading, music, singing. *Address:* The University of Michigan School of Nursing, 1325 Catherine Road, Ann Arbor, Mich. 48109-0604 (Office); 6 Eastbury Court, Ann Arbor, Mich. 48105, U.S.A. (Home). *Telephone:* (313) 764-7185 (Office); (313) 668-6103 (Home).

DUMAS, Roland, L. EN D.; French lawyer, journalist and politician; b. 23 Aug. 1922, Limoges; s. of Georges and Elisabeth (née Lecanuet) Dumas; m. 2nd Anne-Marie Lillet 1964; two s. one d.; ed. Lycée de Limoges, Univs. of Paris and London; called to the Bar, Paris 1950, and has practised as a lawyer ever since; journalist with Socialiste Limousin, La Corrèze républicaine et socialiste 1967–; mem. Nat. Assembly 1956–58, 1967–68, 1981–83, 1986–88; Minister for European Affairs 1983–84, for Foreign

Affairs 1984–86, May 1988–; Govt. Spokesman July-Dec. 1984; Pres. Nat. Ass. Comm. on Foreign Affairs 1986–88; Chevalier, Légion d'honneur. *Publications:* J'ai vu vivre la Chine, Les Avocats, Le Droit de l'information et de la presse, Plaidoyer pour Roger-Gilbert Lecomte. *Address:* 37 quai d'Orsay, 75700 Paris; 4 place du Général Leclerc, 24000 Périgueux; 28 rue de Bièvre, 75005, France.

DUMAS-DUBOURG, Françoise Thérèse Bernadette Marie; French museum curator; b. 14 Oct. 1932, Bordeaux; d. of Jean Dubourg and Anne-Marie Vignes; m. Etienne Dumas 1957; three s. one d.; ed. Lycée Fénelon, Lycée Henri IV and Ecole des Chartes; Curator, Bibliothèque nationale, Paris 1957, Cabinet des Médailles 1958, Chief Curator in charge of research and publs. 1979, Chief Curator, Library of Institut de France 1981–; Chair. Société française de numismatique 1975–77; several awards including Prix de la Sauvegarde de l'Art français. *Publications:* Le Trésor de Fécamp et le Monnayage en France occidentale pendant la seconde moitié du Xe siècle 1971; about 100 articles on munismatics. *Address:* 25 quai de Conti, 75006 Paris, France. *Telephone:* 43-26-85-40.

du MAURIER, Dame Daphne (Lady Browning), D.B.E.; British writer; b. 13 May 1907; d. of the late Sir Gerald du Maurier and of Muriel Beaumont; m. Sir Frederick Browning 1932 (died 1965); one s. two d.; ed. privately, Paris. *Publications:* The Loving Spirit 1931, I'll Never be Young Again 1932, The Progress of Julius 1933, Gerald, a Portrait 1934, Jamaica Inn 1936, The du Mauriers 1937, Rebecca 1938, Frenchman's Creek 1941, Hungry Hill 1943, The Years Between (play) 1945, The King's General 1946, September Tide (play) 1948, The Parasites 1949, My Cousin Rachel 1951, The Apple Tree 1952, Mary Anne 1954, The Scapegoat 1957, The Breaking Point 1959, The Infernal World of Branwell Brontë 1960, Castle Dor (continuation of MS. left by late Sir A. Quiller-Couch) 1962, The Glass-Blowers 1963, Flight of the Falcon 1964, Vanishing Cornwall 1967, The House on the Strand 1969, Not After Midnight 1971, Rule Britannia 1972, Golden Lads 1975, The Winding Stair: Francis Bacon, His Rise and Fall 1976, Growing Pains (autobiog.)1977 (title in U.S.A. Myself When Young), The Rendezvous and other stories, The Rebecca Notebook and Other Memories 1981. *Leisure interests:* walking, swimming. *Address:* Kilmarth, Par, Cornwall, England. *Telephone:* Par 2766.

DUMBADZE, Nodar Vladimirovich; Soviet author; b. 14 July 1928, Tbilisi, Georgia; ed. Univ. of Tbilisi. *Publications include:* Me, Grandmother, Iliko and Ilarion 1960, A Night of Sun 1967, Don't be Afraid, Mum! 1971. *Address:* U.S.S.R. Union of Writers, Ulitsa Vorovskogo 52, Moscow, U.S.S.R.

DUMBUTSHENA, Enoch, B.A., B.ED.; Zimbabwean judge; b. 25 April 1920, Chegutu; s. of the late Job Dumbutshena and Sarah Chendzira Dumbutshena; m. 1st Alphosina Mahlangu 1948 (deceased); m. 2nd Miriam Masango 1964; two s. three d.; ed. Adams Coll., Natal, South Africa, Univ. of South Africa, Gray's Inn, London; worked as teacher, journalist and legal practitioner; Legal Adviser to African Nat. Congress (ANC), Vic. Falls Constitutional Negotiations, S. Rhodesia 1975, to UANC, Geneva Constitutional Conf. 1976, Int. Constitutional Conf. 1978; M.P. for Zimbabwe Democratic Party 1979; Judge 1980–; mem., Judicial Service Comm. 1980–; Judge Pres., High Court of Zimbabwe 1983–; Chief Justice of Zimbabwe March 1984–; Chair. Law Review Comm. 1988–; Hon. Vice-Pres. Zimbabwe Law and Population Studies Project; Chair., Omay Devt. Trust; Chair., Art Printers Employees' Trust; fmr. Dir., Merchant Bank of Cen. Africa; Trustee, Prince Edward School; mem., Bd. of Trustees, Chisipite Jr. School, Bd. of Govs., Arundel School; Hon. Citizen of Atlanta, Ga. 1981. *Publication:* Zimbabwe Tragedy 1976. *Leisure interests:* reading, writing, walking, climbing not-very-high mountains. *Address:* P.O. Box CH 70, Chisipite, Harare (Office); 6 Colne Brook Lane, Highlands, Harare (Official Residence); 11 Cromlet Road, Valleydale Township, Arcturus, Zimbabwe (Home). *Telephone:* 724778 (Office); 884147 (Official Residence); 27620 (Home).

DUMMETT, Prof. Michael Anthony Eardley, M.A.; British professor of philosophy; b. 27 June 1925, London; s. of George Herbert Dummett and Mabel Iris Dummett (née Eardley-Wilmot); m. Ann Chesney 1951; three s. two d.; ed. Sandroyd School, Winchester Coll., Christ Church, Oxford; served army 1943–47; Asst. lecturer in Philosophy, Univ. of Birmingham 1950–51; Harkness Foundation Fellow, Univ. of Calif., Berkeley 1955–56; Reader in Philosophy of Mathematics, Oxford Univ. 1961–74; Sr. Research Fellow, All Souls Coll., Oxford 1974–79, Sub-Warden 1974–76; Visiting lecturer Univ. of Ghana 1958, Stanford Univ., Calif., U.S.A. 1960–66, Univ. of Minn. 1968, Princeton Univ. 1970, Rockefeller Univ., New York 1973; William James Lecturer in Philosophy, Harvard Univ. 1976; Wykeham Prof. of Logic, Univ. of Oxford 1979–; Fellow, New College, Oxford 1979–; Fellow, British Acad. 1967–84 (resgnd.); Emer. Fellow, All Souls College, Oxford 1980–; Chair. Joint Council for the Welfare of Immigrants 1970–71; unofficial cttee. of enquiry into events in Southall, 1979–80; Shadow Bd. Barclays Bank 1981. *Publications:* Frege: Philosophy of Language 1973, The Justification of Deduction 1973, Elements of Intuitionism 1977, Truth and other Enigmas 1979, Immigration: where the Debate goes wrong 1978, Catholicism and the World Order 1979, The Game of Tarot 1979, Twelve Tarot Games 1980, The Interpretation of Frege's Philosophy 1981, Voting Procedures 1984, The Visconti-Sforza Tarot Cards 1986. *Leisure interests:*

history of card games and playing cards. *Address:* 54 Park Town, Oxford, OX2 6SJ, England. *Telephone:* Oxford 58698.

DUMON, Bernard Claude Jean-Pierre, M.SC.; French business executive; b. 16 July 1935, Paris; s. of Jean-Baptiste Dumon and Denise Marchal; m. Claude Gaillochet 1967; two s.; ed. Ecole Polytechnique and Stanford Univ. Sec.-Gen. Union Sucrière de l'Aisne 1963, Asst. Dir.-Gen. 1968, Dir.-Gen. 1971; Asst. Dir.-Gen. Generale Sucrière 1974, Pres. Dir.-Gen. 1980–; Pres. Dir.-Gen. Saint Louis group 1980–; Légion d'honneur. *Leisure interests:* tennis, squash, wind-surfing, skiing, hunting. *Address:* 32 boulevard Victor Hugo, 92200 Neuilly-sur-Seine, France. *Telephone:* (1) 47 57 41 46.

DUMONT, René; French agronomist; b. 13 March 1904, Cambrai; s. of Rémy and Françoise (née Busque) Dumont; m. Suzanne Philippon 1928; one d.; ed. Institut National Agronomique, Ecole Supérieure d'Agriculture Tropicale; adviser in agronomy, rural economy and agricultural planning to numerous govts. throughout the world, to UN, UNESCO, FAO, etc.; Prof. of Agriculture, Inst. Nat. Agronomique 1933–74; Prof., Institut d'études politiques de Paris 1946–66, Institut du développement économique et social 1958–74; candidate, French Presidential election 1974; Dr. h.c. (Laval Univ., Quebec; Univ. of Ottawa). *Publications:* 29 works including: Terres vivantes 1961, L'Afrique noire est mal partie 1962, Nous allons à la famine 1966, Développement et socialisme 1969, Cuba, est-il socialiste? 1970, Paysanneries aux abois 1972, L'utopie ou la mort 1973, Agronome de la faim 1974, La croissance de la famine 1975, La Chine, révolution culturale 1976, Nouveaux voyages dans les campagnes françaises, Seule une écologie socialiste 1977, Paysans écrasés, terres massacrées 1978, l'Afrique étranglée (in collection) 1980, le Mal développement en Amérique latine (in collection) 1981, Finis les lendemains qui chantent 1983, Pour l'Afrique j'accuse 1986, Taiwan, le prix de la réussite 1987. *Address:* 1 rue Clos d'Orléans, 94120 Fontenay-sous-Bois, France. *Telephone:* 48-73-34-61.

DUNANT, Yves, DR.CHEM.; Swiss chemicals and pharmaceuticals executive; b. 8 Sept. 1912, Emmen; s. of Georges Dunant and Denyse (née Schumacher); m. 1st Chantal de Rivoyre 1949 (deceased), 2nd Claudine Guyonnet 1974; two d.; ed. Eidgenössische Technische Hochschule, Zürich, Inst. Pasteur, Univ. of Paris; joined Sandoz Ltd., Basel 1938; Asst. mem. Bd. of Man. Laboratoires Sandoz, Paris 1946, mem. Bd. of Man. 1948; Head of Marketing Dept. of Pharmaceutical Div., Sandoz Ltd. 1963, Head of Pharmaceutical Div., mem. Exec. Cttee. 1967, Man. Dir. 1969, Vice-Chair. and Man. Dir. 1973–76, Chair. and Man. Dir. 1976–81, Chair. Bd. 1981–85, Hon. Chair. and mem. of Bd. 1985–88. *Leisure interests:* travel, modern art, literature, music, sports. *Address:* 15 rue Raynonard, 75016 Paris, France (Home).

DUNAWAY, Dorothy Faye; American actress; b. 14 Jan. 1941, Bascom, Florida; d. of John and Grace Dunaway; m. 1st Peter Wolf 1974; m. 2nd Terry O'Neill 1982 (divorced 1987); ed. Univs. of Florida and Boston; spent three years with Lincoln Center Repertory Co. in New York, appearing in A Man For All Seasons, After the Fall and Tartuffe; Off-Broadway in Hogan's Goat 1965; appeared at the Mark Taper Forum, L.A. in Old Times, as Blanche du Bois in A Streetcar Named Desire 1973, The Curse of an Aching Heart 1982; *films include:* Hurry Sundown 1967, The Happening 1967, Bonnie and Clyde 1967, The Thomas Crown Affair 1968, A Place For Lovers 1969, The Arrangement 1969, Little Big Man 1970, Doc 1971, The Getaway 1972, Oklahoma Crude 1973, The Three Musketeers 1973, Chinatown 1974, Three Days of the Condor 1975, The Towering Inferno 1976, Voyage of the Damned 1976, Network 1976, The Eyes of Laura Mars 1978, The Champ 1979, The First Deadly Sin 1981, Mommie Dearest 1981, The Wicked Lady 1982, Supergirl 1984, Barfly 1987, Burning Secret 1988. *Television includes:* After the Fall 1974, The Disappearance of Aimee 1976, Hogan's Goat, Mommie Dearest 1981, Evita!—First Lady 1981, 13 at Dinner 1985, Beverly Hills Madame 1986; Academy Award Best Actress for Network. *Address:* c/o I.C.M. 8899 Beverly Boulevard, Los Angeles, Calif. 90048, U.S.A.

DUNBAR, Maxwell John, M.A., PH.D., F.R.S.C.; Canadian professor of oceanography; b. 19 Sept. 1914, Edinburgh, Scotland; s. of William Dunbar and Elizabeth Robertson; m. 1st Joan Jackson (died 1959), 2nd Nancy Wosstroff 1960; three s. three d.; ed. Fettes Coll., Edin., Oxford Univ., Yale Univ., McGill Univ., Canada; Canadian Consul to Greenland 1941–46; Asst. Prof. of Zoology, McGill Univ. 1946–48, Assoc. Prof. 1948–59, Prof. 1959–82, Prof. Emer. 1982–, Chair. Marine Sciences Centre 1963–77; Gov. Arctic Inst. of N. America 1963–75; Dir. Eastern Arctic Investigations (Canada) 1947–55; Expeditions: W. Greenland 1935, 1936, Alaska 1938, Ungava Bay 1947, 1949, 1950, 1951, Hudson Bay 1954; Guggenheim Fellowship, Denmark 1952–53; Organizer and Chair. first Polar Oceans Conf. (SCOR, SCAR) 1974; Int. Convenor, Int. Biological Programme 1971–75; Fellow Arctic Inst. of N. America, A.A.A.S., Linnean Soc. of London; Hon. Fellow American Geographical Soc. of New York; Hon. D.Sc. (Memorial Univ. of Newfoundland) 1979; Bruce Memorial Medal Polar Exploration (Edin.) 1950, Fry Gold Medal, Canadian Soc. of Zoology 1979, N. Slope Bourough Arctic Science Prize (Alaska) 1986, Canadian Arctic Science Award 1987, J. P. Tully Medal in Oceanography (Canadian Meteology and Oceanography Soc.) 1989. *Publications:* Eastern Arctic Waters 1951, Marine Distributions 1964, Ecological Development in Polar Regions 1968, Environment and Good Sense 1971, Polar Oceans 1977, Marine Production Mechanisms 1980; over 100 scientific papers. *Leisure interests:* music (piano, guitar, folk music, composition), tree-farming. *Address:* Climate Research Group, Dept. of Meteorology, McGill University, 805 Sherbrooke Street West, Montréal, H3A 2K6 (Office); 488 Strathcona Avenue, Westmount, Québec, H3Y 2X1, Canada (Home). *Telephone:* (514) 398-4407 (Office); (514) 935-3120 (Home).

DUNCAN, Archibald Alexander McBeth, M.A., F.R.S.E., F.B.A.; British professor of history; b. 17 Oct. 1926, Pitlochry; s. of Charles George Duncan and Christina Helen McBeth; m. Ann Hayes Sawyer 1954; two s. one d.; ed. George Heriot's School, Edinburgh, Univ. of Edinburgh, Balliol Coll., Oxford; Lecturer, Balliol Coll. 1950–51, Queen's Univ., Belfast 1951–53, Univ. of Edin. 1953–62; Prof. of Scottish History, Univ. of Glasgow 1962–, Clerk of Senate 1978–83. *Publications:* Scotland, The Making of the Kingdom 1975, ed. and revised W. C. Dickinson, Scotland from the Earliest Times to 1603 1977, Ed. Acts of Robert I, 1306–29, vol.V, Regesta Regum Scottorum 1988. *Address:* Department of Scottish History, 9 University Gardens, Glasgow, G12 8QH; 17 Campbell Drive, Bearsden, Glasgow, G61 4NF, Scotland (Home). *Telephone:* (041) 339 8855 (Office); (041) 942 5023 (Home).

DUNCAN, Admiral Charles Kenney; American naval officer; b. 7 Dec. 1911, Nicholasville, Kentucky; s. of late Charles W. Duncan and late May Kenney; m. 1st Sheila A. Taylor 1941 (deceased 1985); m. 2nd Jean (née Keyser) Duncan 1986; ed. Univ. of Kentucky, U.S. Naval Acad. and Armed Forces Staff Coll.; Exec. Officer, U.S.S. Hutchins 1942; Commdg. Officer U.S.S. Wilson 1943; Dir. of Naval Officer Procurement, Bureau of Naval Personnel 1944; Exec. Officer, U.S.S. Wisconsin 1946; Commdr. Destroyer Div. 62, 1951; Admin. Aide to Chief of Naval Personnel 1953; Commdg. Officer, U.S.S. Chilton 1955; Commdr. Amphibious Group One 1958, Amphibious Training Command, Pacific 1959; Commdr. Naval Base, Subic Bay, Philippines 1961; Asst. Chief of Naval Personnel 1962; Commdr. Cruiser-Destroyer Force Atlantic 1964, Amphibious Force Atlantic 1965, Second Fleet and NATO Striking Fleet Atlantic 1967; Chief of Naval Personnel and Deputy Chief of Naval Operations (Manpower and Naval Reserve) 1968; C.-in-C. Atlantic 1970–72; C.-in-C. U.S. Atlantic Fleet 1970–72; Supreme Allied Commdr. Atlantic 1970–72; mem. Sec. Navy's Advisory Bd. on Educ. and Training 1976–83; Bd. of Trustees, San Diego Museum of Art 1981–; Assoc. Foreign mem. Acad. Française de Marine 1984; Hon. Officer, Greek Nat. Org. Encouraging NATO's Aims 1973–; Distinguished Service Medal, Legion of Merit, Grand Cross of Order of Orange-Nassau, and many other awards. *Leisure interests:* travel, reading. *Address:* 813 First Street, Coronado, Calif. 92118, U.S.A. *Telephone:* (619) 435-4244.

DUNCAN, Charles William, Jr.; American company executive and former government official; b. 9 Sept. 1926, Houston, Tex.; s. of Charles William and Mary Lillian (née House) Duncan; m. Anne Smith 1957; one s. one d.; ed. Rice Univ., Univ. of Texas; served U.S.A.A.F. 1944–46; Duncan Coffee Co. 1948 (later Duncan Foods Co., rising to Vice-Pres. 1957, Pres. 1958; merged with Coca-Cola Co. 1964; Chair. Coca-Cola Co. in Europe 1967–70; Exec. Vice-Pres. Coca-Cola Co. 1970–71, Pres. 1971–74; Chair. Duncan, Cook and Co. 1985–; Chair. and Dir. Robertson Distribution Systems and Rotan Mosle Financial Corpn. 1974–76; U.S. Deputy Sec. of Defense 1977–79; Sec. of Energy 1979–81; Dir. American Express Co., Coca Cola Co., Chemical Banking Corpn., Cameron Iron Works, Inc., Texas Eastern Corpn., Texas Commerce Bancshares Inc., United Technologies Corpn.; Chair. Bd. Govs. Rice Univ.; mem. Council on Foreign Relations; Trustee Brookings Inst. *Leisure interests:* tennis, hunting, fishing, ranch. *Address:* 50th Floor, Republic Bank Center, 700 Louisiana, Houston, Tex. 77002 (Office); 9 Briarwood Court, Houston, Tex. 77019, U.S.A. (Home).

DUNCAN, James Francis, O.B.E., M.A., D.PHIL., M.SC., F.R.S.N.Z.; British (New Zealand citizen) professor and technological and futures consultant (retd.); b. 25 July 1921, Liverpool; m. Margaret Lingard 1946; one s. one d.; ed. Liverpool Collegiate School and Jesus Coll., Oxford; Prin. Scientific Officer Atomic Energy Research Establishment, Harwell, U.K. 1946–52; Reader in Radiochemistry Univ. of Melbourne 1952–62; Prof. of Inorganic and Theoretical Chemistry Univ. of Wellington, N.Z. 1962–87; Chair. Wellington Science Fair 1964–78, N.Z. Science Fair Bd. 1978–84, Patron 1984–; Chair. Comm. for the Future 1976–82, Chair. N.Z. Futures Trust 1982–; mem. Inventions Devt. Authority 1964–69; N.Z. UNESCO Comm. 1966–69; Nat. Devt. Council 1969–75; Hon. Fellow N.Z. Inst. of Chemistry; Trustee Nat. Library 1968–78; Dwyer Medal, Univ. of N.S.W. *Publications:* about 200 scientific publs. including three books and about 60 publs. on N.Z.'s future including: Options for New Zealand's Future 1965. *Leisure interests:* music and farming. *Address:* 6/304 Karori Road, Wellington (Home); New Zealand Futures Trust, Box 12008, Wellington, New Zealand (Office). *Telephone:* (04) 736644 (Office); (04) 769190 (Home).

DUNCAN, John Spenser Ritchie, C.M.G., M.B.E., M.A.; British diplomatist; b. 26 July 1921, Glencarse, Scotland; s. of late Rev. J. H. Duncan, D.D., and Sophia Playfair Ritchie; m. Sheila Grace Fullarton Conacher 1950; ed. George Watson's Boys' Coll., Glasgow Acad., Dundee High School, Edinburgh Univ.; Sudan Political Service 1941–56; Deputy Dir.-Gen. British Information Services, U.S.A. 1959–63; Consul-Gen. Muscat 1963–65; Head of Personnel, FCO 1965–69; Minister, Canberra 1969–71; High Commr. in Zambia 1971–74; Amb. to Morocco 1975–78; High Commr. in Bahamas 1978–81. *Publications:* The Sudan: A Record of Achievement 1952, The

Sudan's Path to Independence 1957. *Address:* 9 Blackford Road, Edinburgh, EH9 2DT, Scotland.

DUNCAN, Stanley Frederick St. Clare, C.M.G.; British diplomatist (retd.); b. 13 Nov. 1927, London; s. of Stanley Gilbert Scott Duncan and Louisa Elizabeth (née Brown) Duncan; m. Jennifer Jane Bennett 1967; two d.; ed. Latymer Upper School; India Office 1946–47; Pvt. Sec. to Parl. Under-Sec. of State, Commonwealth Relations Office 1954; Second Sec., High Comm., Ottawa 1954–55; British Govt. Information Officer, Toronto 1955–57; Second Sec., Wellington, N.Z. 1958–60; Commonwealth Relations Office 1960; seconded to Cen. African Office 1962–64; First Sec., Nicosia 1964–67; Head of Chancery, Embassy, Lisbon 1970–73; Consul-Gen. and subsequently Chargé d'Affaires, Lourenço Marques (now Maputo), Mozambique 1973–75; Counsellor (Political), Embassy, Brasilia 1976–77; Head of Consular Dept., FCO 1977–80; Canadian Nat. Defence Coll. 1980–81; Amb. to Bolivia 1981–85; High Commr. to Malta 1985–87. *Address:* Tucksmead, Longworth, Oxon, OX13 5ET, England.

DUNDAS, Sir Hugh Spencer Lisle, Kt., C.B.E., D.S.O., D.F.C.; British business executive; b. 22 July 1920, Barnborough, nr. Doncaster; s. of late Frederick James Dundas and Sylvia Mary (née March-Phillipps) Dundas; m. Enid Rosamund Lawrence 1950; one s. two d.; ed. Stowe School; joined S. Yorks. Squadron, Auxiliary Air Force 1939, Fighter Commdr. 1939–43, in N. Africa, Malta, Sicily, Italy 1943–50; Ed. and Man. Beaverbrook Newspapers 1948–60; Exec. Rediffusion 1961, Man. Dir. 1970–74, Chair. 1978–85; Dir. Wembley Stadium Ltd. 1978; Dir., then Chair. B.E.T. Leisure Holdings PLC 1973–85; Chair. A-R TV PLC 1978–85; Chair. Thames TV Ltd. 1981–87; Chair. The British Electric Traction Co. PLC 1982–87. *Address:* 55 Iverna Court, London, W8 6TU; The Schoolroom, Dockenfield, Farnham, Surrey, England (Homes). *Telephone:* 01-937 0773, Frensham 2331.

DUNHAM, Katherine; American dancer and choreographer; ed. Chicago and Northwestern Univs.; début, Chicago World's Fair 1934; with Chicago Opera Co. 1935–36; Julius Rosenwald Travel Fellowship 1936–37; Dance Dir. Labor Stage 1939–40; has appeared in numerous films 1941–; founded Katherine Dunham School of Cultural Arts and Katherine Dunham Dance Co. 1945; numerous tours and personal appearances in North and South America and Europe. *Publications:* Journey to Accompong, Form and Function in Primitive Dance, Form and Function in Educational Dance, etc. *Address:* c/o Performing Arts Training Center, St. Louis, Ill. 62201, U.S.A.

DUNHAM, Sir Kingsley C., Kt., PH.D., F.R.S., F.ENG., F.R.S.E., S.D.; British geologist; b. 2 Jan. 1910, Sturminster Newton, Dorset; s. of Ernest Pedder and Edith Agnes Dunham; m. Margaret Young 1936; one s.; ed. Johnston School, Durham, Univ. of Durham and Harvard Univ.; Temp. Geologist, New Mexico Bureau Mines 1935; Geologist, Geological Survey of Great Britain 1935–45, Head of Petrographical Dept. 1946–50; Prof. of Geology and Head of Dept. Univ. of Durham 1950–66, Sub-Warden 1959–61, Prof. Emer. 1968; Consulting Geologist, Laporte Industries Ltd. 1953–66, Consolidated Gold Fields Ltd. 1954–66; Geological Adviser ICI Ltd. 1961–66; Dir. Inst. of Geological Sciences (Natural Environment Research Council) 1966–75; Chair. Council for Environmental Science and Eng. 1972–75; Pres. Yorks. Geological Soc. 1958–60, British Asscn. for the Advancement of Science (Section C 1961, Assoc. 1972–73), Inst. of Mining and Metallurgy 1963–64, Geological Soc. of London 1966–68, Int. Union of Geological Sciences 1969–72, Mineralogical Society 1976–78; Dir. Weardale Holdings Ltd., Weardale Minerals Ltd. 1982–86; mem. Council, Royal Soc. 1964–66, Foreign Sec., Vice-Pres. 1971–76; Chair. Int. Geological Correlation Project of IUGS/UNESCO 1972–76; mem. Council for Scientific Policy, Dept. of Educ. and Science 1964–66; U.K. mem. Council Int. Inst. for Applied Systems Analysis 1973–77, Hon. Scholar 1977; Fellow of Imperial Coll. 1976, D.Sc. h.c. (Durham, Liverpool, Birmingham, Illinois, Leicester, Michigan, Kent, Edinburgh, Exeter, Hull), Hon. Sc.D. (Cambridge), D.Univ. (Open Univ.); Bigsby Medal of Geological Soc. 1954, Gold Medal of Inst. of Mining and Metallurgy 1968, Murchison Medal of Geological Soc. 1966, Royal Medal of the Royal Soc. 1970, Wollaston Medal 1976, Haidinger Medal, Austrian Geological Survey 1976; Leopold von Buch Medal, German Geological Soc. 1981, Aberconway Medal, Inst. of Geology 1986. *Publications:* Geology of the Organ Mountains of New Mexico 1936, Geology of the Northern Pennine Orefield (Vol. I) 1949, (Vol. II with A. A. Wilson) 1985, Fluorspar 1952, Geology of North Skye (with F. W. Anderson) 1966, Geology and Hematite Deposits of South Cumbria (with W. C. C. Rose) 1977; Ed. Symposium on the Paragenesis and Reserves of the Ores of Lead and Zinc 1948. *Leisure interests:* music, gardening. *Address:* Charleycroft, Quarryheads Lane, Durham, DH1 3DY, England. *Telephone:* 091-384 8977.

DUNITZ, Prof. Jack David, F.R.S.; British professor of chemistry; b. 29 March 1923, Glasgow, Scotland; s. of William (Wulfi) Dunitz and Mildred Dunitz; m. Barbara Steuer 1953, two d.; ed. Hutcheson's Grammar School, Glasgow, Univ. of Glasgow; Research Fellowships at Univ. of Oxford 1946–48, 1951–53; at Calif. Inst. of Tech. 1948–51, 1953–54; Visiting Scientist, U.S. Nat. Insts. of Health 1954–55; Sr. Research Fellow, Davy-Faraday Research Lab., Royal Inst., London 1956–57; Visiting appointments at Ia. State Univ. 1965, Univ. of Minn. 1966, 1983, Tokyo Univ. 1967, Technion, Haifa 1970, Cornell Univ. 1976; Overseas Fellow, Churchill Coll., Univ. of Cambridge 1968; Prof. of Chemical Crystallography, Eidg-

enössische Technische Hochschule (Swiss Fed. Inst. of Tech.), Zürich 1957–; mem. and fellow, several foreign acads.; Centenary Medal, Chem. Soc., London 1977, Havinga Medal, Leiden Univ. 1980, Tishler Prize, Harvard Univ. 1985, Paracelsus Prize, Swiss Chemical Soc. 1986. *Publications:* X-Ray Analysis and the Structure of Organic Molecules 1979; about 250 papers on various aspects of crystal and molecular structure. *Address:* Laboratory of Organic Chemistry, ETH-Zentrum, CH-8092 Zürich (Office); Obere Heslibachstrasse 77, CH-8700 Küsnacht, Switzerland (Home). *Telephone:* 01-256-2892 (Office).

DUNKEL, Arthur, B.SC.ECON.; Swiss international civil servant; b. 28 Aug. 1932, Lisbon, Portugal; m. Christiane Muller-Serda 1957; one s. one d.; ed. French Lycée, Lisbon, Business School, Lausanne, Coll. St. Michel, Fribourg, Univ. of Lausanne; joined Swiss Fed. Office for Foreign Econ. Affairs, Bern 1956, Head, section for OECD matters 1960–64, for co-operation with developing countries 1964–71, for world trade policy 1971–73; Perm. Rep. to GATT with rank of Minister Plenipotentiary 1973–76; Del. of Fed. Council for Trade Agreements with rank of Amb. 1976–80; Dir.-Gen. GATT 1980–; Vice-Chair. and Rapporteur UNCTAD Inter-Governmental Group on Supplementary Financing 1968; Rapporteur UNCTAD Bd. 1969; Chair. GATT Cttee. on Balance-of-Payments Restrictions 1972–75; Chair. UN Conf. on New Wheat Agreement 1978; Asst. Lecturer, Inst. of Journalism, Univ. of Fribourg 1974–; Sr. Lecturer, Faculty of Econ. Social Sciences, Univ. of Geneva 1983–; Hon. Dr. of Political Science (Univ. of Fribourg 1980). *Address:* GATT, Centre William Rappard, 154 rue de Lausanne, CH-1211, Geneva 21, Switzerland. *Telephone:* 022-31.02.31.

DUNLOP, Sir Ernest Edward, A.C., K.B., O.B.E., C.M.G., M.S., F.R.C.S., F.R.A.C.S., F.A.C.S.; Australian consultant surgeon; b. 12 July 1907, Wangaratta; s. of James H. Dunlop and Alice E. M. Payne; m. Helen L. R. Ferguson 1945; two s.; ed. Benalla High School, Victorian Coll. of Pharmacy, Melbourne Univ., St. Bartholomew's Hosp., London, and British Postgraduate School, Hammersmith; Registrar, Royal Melbourne Hosp., Royal Victoria Eye and Ear Hosp. and British Postgraduate Medical School 1934–39; specialist surgeon, St. Mary's Hosp., Paddington, London 1939; served with Royal Australian Army Medical Corps 1939–46; Hon. surgeon, Royal Melbourne Hosp., Royal Victoria Eye and Ear Hosp., and consultant surgeon, Peter MacCullum Clinic for Cancer 1946–67; consultant, Royal Melbourne Hosp. 1967–; Chief Medical Officer, British Phosphate Comm. 1974–80; mem. Titulaire Int. Soc. of Surgeons 1963–, Int. Medical Sciences Acad. 1981–; launched Sir Edward Dunlop Research Foundation 1985; Hon. mem. Assen. of Surgeons of India; Hon. Fellow, American Medical Assen.; Hon. D.Sc. (Punjab). *Publications:* Medical Experiences in Japanese Captivity 1946, Carcinoma of the Oesophagus 1960, The War Diaries of Sir Edward ("Weary") Dunlop 1986. *Leisure interests:* farming, travelling, rugby football, golf. *Address:* 14 Parliament Place, Melbourne 3002 (Office); 605 Toorak Road, Toorak, Melbourne 3142; Smith's Gully Road, Smith's Gully, Vic., Australia (Home).

DUNLOP, John T., A.B., PH.D., LL.D.; American economist and industrial relations expert; b. 5 July 1914, Placerville, Calif.; s. of John and Antonia Dunlop (née Forni); m. Dorothy Webb 1937; two s. one d.; ed. Univs. of California and Cambridge, England; Instructor Harvard Univ. 1938, Assoc. Prof. 1945, Chair. Wertheim Cttee. on Industrial Relations 1945–, Prof. 1950–, Chair. Dept. of Econs. 1961–66, Dean Faculty of Arts and Sciences 1970–73; Chair. Bd. for Settlement of Jurisdictional Disputes 1948–57; mem. Atomic Energy Labor Relations Panel 1948–53; mem. Sec. Labor's Advisory Cttee. on Labor-Management Relations in Atomic Energy Installations 1954–57; mem. Kaiser Steelworkers' Commission 1960–68, Presidential Railroad Comm. 1960–62, Missiles Sites Labor Comm. 1961–67; Chair. Nat. Manpower Policy Task Force 1968–69; mem. President's Nat. Comm. on Productivity 1970–73, Chair. 1973–75; Chair. Manpower Inst. 1970–; Dir. Cost of Living Council 1973–74; Co-ordinator President's Labor-Man. Cttee. 1974–76; U.S. Sec. of Labor 1975–76; Chair. Construction Industry Joint Conf. 1959–68; mem. Construction Industry Collective Bargaining Comm. 1969–71; Chair. U.S. Labor Man. Group 1976–; Chair. Construction Industry Stabilization Cttee. 1971–73, mem. 1973–74; Pres. Industrial Relations Research Assen. 1960, Int. Industrial Relations Research Assen. 1973–76; mem. American Acad. of Arts and Sciences, American Philosophical Soc., Inst. of Medicine; Louis K. Comstock Award, Nat. Electrical Contractors' Assen. 1974. *Publications:* Wage Determination under Trade Unions 1944, Cost Behaviour and Price Policy 1943, Collective Bargaining: Principles and Cases (with James J. Healy) 1949, The Wage Adjustment Board. (with Arthur D. Hill) 1950, The Theory of Wage Determination (Editor) 1957, Industrial Relations Systems 1958, Industrialism and Industrial Man 1960, Potentials of the American Economy (Editor) 1961, Economic Growth in the United States (Editor) 1961, Automation and Technological Change (Editor) 1962, Frontiers of Collective Bargaining (Editor) 1967, Labor and the American Community (with Derek Bok) 1970, Inflation and Incomes Policies: the Political Economy of Recent U.S. Experience 1974, Industrialism and Industrial Man Reconsidered 1975, The Lessons of Wage and Price Controls—The Food Sector 1978, Business and Public Policy 1980, Dispute Resolution, Negotiation and Consensus Building 1984. *Leisure interest:* walking. *Address:* 509 Pleasant Street, Belmont, Mass. 02178, U.S.A. (Home). *Telephone:* (617) 484-2958.

DUNN, Douglas Eaglesham, F.R.S.L.; British poet; b. 23 Oct. 1942; s. of William D. Dunn and Margaret McGowan; m. 1st Lesley B. Wallace 1964 (died 1981); m. 2nd Lesley Jane Bathgate 1985; one s.; ed. Univ. of Hull; full-time writer since 1971; Writer-in-residence Duncan of Jordanstone Coll. of Art and Dundee Dist. Libraries 1987–; Hon. Visiting Prof. Dundee Univ. 1987–; Hon. LL.D. (Dundee) 1987. *Publications:* Terry Street 1969 (Somerset Maugham Award 1972), The Happier Life 1972, New Poems 1972–73 (ed.) 1973, Love or Nothing 1974 (Faber Memorial Prize 1976), A Choice of Byron's Verse (ed.) 1974, Two Decades of Irish Writing (criticism) 1975, The Poetry of Scotland (ed.) 1979, Barbarians 1979, St. Kilda's Parliament 1981 (Hawthornden Prize 1982), Europa's Lover 1982, A Rumoured City: New Poets from Hull (ed.) 1982, To Build a Bridge: A Celebration of Humberside in Verse (ed.) 1982, Elegies 1985 (Whitbread Poetry Award and Whitbread Book of the Year 1986), Secret Villages (short stories) 1985, Selected Poems 1986, Northlight 1988. *Leisure interests:* playing the clarinet and saxophone, listening to jazz, gardening. *Address:* c/o Faber & Faber Ltd., 3 Queen Square, London, WC1N 3AU, England; Braeknowe, 44 Gray Street, Tayport, Fife, DD6 9HU, Scotland.

DUNN, Hugh Alexander, A.O., B.A.; fmr. Australian diplomatist, now professor; b. 20 Aug. 1923, Rockhampton; s. of James M. Dunn and Mary E. Miller; m. Margaret J. Anderson 1968; one d.; ed. Brisbane Boys' Coll., Queensland Univ., Univ. of Oxford; journalist, Brisbane Courier-Mail 1953; Lecturer, East Asiatic Studies, Toronto Univ., Canada 1953–54; joined foreign service 1952, served in Japan, Repub. of Korea, U.S.A., India and Viet-Nam; Amb. to Repub. of China (Taiwan) 1969–72, to Argentina (also accred. to Uruguay and Paraguay) 1973–76; High Commr. in Kenya (also accred. to Uganda, Seychelles and Ethiopia) 1978–80; Amb. to People's Repub. of China 1980–84; Hon. Prof. Griffith Univ. 1984–; mem. Australia-China Council 1985–. *Publication:* Cao Zhi, The Life and Works of a Royal Chinese Poet 1983, Sino-Australian Relations: The Record 1972–85, Co-Ed. 1985–; The Shaping of a Sinologue of Sorts 1987, The Teaching of Chinese Language and its Application (Co-Ed.) 1987–. *Leisure interests:* golf, trout fishing, writing. *Address:* c/o Department of Modern Asian Studies, Griffith University, Nathan, Queensland 4111, Australia.

DUNN, Dame Lydia Selina, C.B.E., J.P., M.L.C., B.S.; Hong Kong business executive; b. 29 Feb. 1940; d. of Yenchuen Yeh Dunn and Dunn Chen Yin-chu Bessie; m. Michael Thomas 1988; ed. St. Paul's Convent School and Univ. of California, Berkeley, U.S.A.; Exec. Trainee, Swire & Maclaine 1963, Dir. 1973, Man. Dir. 1976, Chair. 1982–; Dir. John Swire & Sons (HK) Ltd. 1978–; Exec. Dir. Swire Pacific Ltd. 1982–; Chair. Swire Loxley Ltd. 1982–, Swire Marketing Ltd. 1986–, Camberley Enterprises Ltd. 1986–; Dir. Cathay Pacific Airways Ltd. 1985–, Hong Kong and Shanghai Banking Corpn. 1981–; mem. Legis. Council 1976– (Sr. mem. 1985–); mem. Finance Cttee. 1976–; mem. Exec. Council 1982–, (Sr. mem. 1988–; mem. Council, Chinese Univ. of Hong Kong 1978–, Clothing Inst. 1974–, Hong Kong/Japan Business Co-operation Cttee. 1983–, Hong Kong/U.S. Econ. Co-operation Cttee. 1984–, Hong Kong Branch, Hong Kong Assen., 1983–; Chair. Hong Kong Trade Devt. Council 1983–; mem. Council, Trade Policy Research Centre, London 1980–, Volvo Int. Advisory Bd. 1985–, Int. Council of Asia Soc. 1986–. *Publication:* In the Kingdom of the Blind 1983. *Leisure interest:* collection of antiques. *Address:* John Swire & Sons (Hong Kong) Ltd., 5th Floor, Swire House, 9 Connaught Road C, Hong Kong.

DUNNETT, Alastair MacTavish; British journalist; b. 26 Dec. 1908, Kilmacolm; s. of David Sinclair Dunnett and Isabella Crawford MacTavish; m. Dorothy Halliday 1946; two s.; ed. Overnewton School and Hillhead High School, Glasgow; entered Commercial Bank of Scotland Ltd. 1925; co-founder, The Claymore Press 1933–34; with Glasgow Weekly Herald 1935–36, The Bulletin 1936–37, Daily Record 1937–40; Chief Press Officer, Sec. of State for Scotland 1940–46; Ed. Daily Record 1946–55, The Scotsman 1956–72; Man. Dir. Scotsman Publications Ltd. 1962–70, Chair. 1970–74; Chair. Thomson Scottish Petroleum Ltd., Edinburgh 1972–79, Dir. 1979–87; mem. Exec. Bd. Thomson Org. Ltd. 1973–78; Dir. Scottish Television 1975–79; Gov. Pitlochry Festival Theatre; mem. Press Council 1959–62, Scottish Tourist Bd. 1962–70, Council of Nat. Trust for Scotland 1962–70, Scottish Int. Educ. Trust, Scottish Theatre Ballet Cttee.; Hon. LL.D. (Strathclyde) 1978. *Publications:* Treasure at Sonnach 1935, Heard Tell 1946, Quest by Canoe 1950, Highlands and Islands of Scotland 1951, The Duke's Day 1970, No Thanks to the Duke 1978; Plays: The Original John Mackay 1956, Fit to Print 1962; Among Friends (autobiog.) 1984, The Scottish Highlands (with David Paterson and Dorothy Dunnett) 1988. *Leisure interests:* sailing, riding, walking. *Address:* 87 Colinton Road, Edinburgh EH10 5DF, Scotland (Home). *Telephone:* 031-337 2107.

DUNROSSIL, 2nd Viscount (cr. 1959); **John William Morrison,** C.M.G.; British diplomatist (retd.); b. 22 May 1926, London; s. of 1st Viscount Dunrossil, G.C.M.G., M.C., P.C., Q.C.; m. 2nd Diana M. Cunliffe 1969, two d.; ed. Fettes Coll., Edinburgh, and Oriel Coll., Oxford; joined Commonwealth Service 1951, served in Canberra, Dhaka, Pretoria, Cape Town; External Relations Officer, IMCO 1968–70; Counsellor and Head of Chancery, Ottawa 1970–74; Counsellor, Brussels 1974–78; High Commr. in Fiji 1978–82, concurrently accred. to Nauru and Tuvalu, and alt. U.K. del. to S. Pacific Comm.; High Commr. in Barbados 1981–83, concurrently accred. to Grenada, Saint Lucia, Dominica, Saint Vincent and the Grenadines, later to Antigua and

Barbuda, and British Govt. Rep. to St. Christopher and Nevis; Gov. and Commdr.-in-Chief of Bermuda 1983–88; K.St.J. *Address:* c/o House of Lords, London, SW1, England.

DUNSTAN, (Andrew Harold) Bernard, R.A.; British artist; b. 19 Jan. 1920; s. of late Dr. A. E. Dunstan; m. Diana M. Armfield 1949; three s.; ed. St. Paul's School, Byam Shaw School and Slade School; has exhibited at Royal Acad. since 1945; exhibits regularly at Agnews, London; numerous one-man exhbns.; works in many public and pvt. collections including Museum of London, Nat. Portrait Gallery, Nat. Gallery of New Zealand; mem. New English Art Club; Hon. Sec. Artists' Gen. Benevolent Inst. *Publications:* Learning to Paint 1970, Painting in Progress 1976, Painting Methods of the Impressionists 1976. *Leisure interests:* music, walking in London. *Address:* 10 High Park Road, Kew, Richmond, Surrey, TW9 4BH, England. *Telephone:* 01-876 6633.

DUNSTAN, Donald Allan, A.C., Q.C., LL.B., M.P.; Australian solicitor and politician; b. 21 Sept. 1926, Fiji; s. of Vivian Dunstan and Ida May Hill; m. 1st Gretel Ellis 1949 (divorced 1975), two s. one d.; m. 2nd Adele Koh 1976 (died 1978); ed. Collegiate School of St. Peter, Adelaide, and Univ. of Adelaide; Labour mem. of Parl. 1953–79; Attorney-Gen., Minister of Aboriginal Affairs and Social Welfare of South Australia 1965, Premier, Treas. and Minister of Housing of South Australia 1967–68, Leader of Opposition 1968–70, Premier, Treas. 1970–79, also Minister of Devt. and Mines 1970–73; Chair. Victorian Tourism Comm. 1982–; Nat. Pres. Australian Freedom from Hunger Campaign 1982–; Freeman of City of George-town, Penang 1973. *Address:* c/o Victorian Tourism Commission, World Trade Centre, Cnr. of Spencer and Flinders Streets, Melbourne, Vic. 3005 (Office); 59 Gipps Street, East Melbourne, Vic. 3002, Australia (Home).

DUNSTAN, Gordon Reginald, M.A., F.S.A.; British university professor (retd.); b. 25 April 1917, Plymouth; s. of Frederick John Menhennet Dunstan and Winifred Amy Orchard; m. Ruby Maud Fitzer 1949; two s. one d.; ed. Leeds Univ.; Minor Canon, St. George's Chapel, Windsor Castle 1955–59; Minor Canon, Westminster Abbey 1959–67; Canon Theologian, Leicester Cathedral 1966–82; Prof. of Moral and Social Theology, King's Coll., London Univ. 1967–82, Prof. Emer. 1982–; Chaplain to H.M. the Queen 1976–87; Hon. D.D. (Exeter) 1973, Hon. LL.D. (Leicester) 1986, Hon. Research Fellow, Exeter Univ. 1982–; Hon. Fellow Royal Soc. of Medicine, 1984, Hon. mem. Royal Coll. of Physicians 1987. *Publications:* The Family Is Not Broken 1962, The Register of Edmund Lacy, Bishop of Exeter 1420–1455, 5 vols. 1963–72, A Digger Still 1968, Not Yet the Epitaph 1968, The Sacred Ministry 1970, The Artifice of Ethics 1974, A Moralist in the City 1974, (Co-Ed.) with M. J. Seller) Consent in Medicine 1983, The Moral Status of the Human Embryo 1988, Co. Ed. (with D. Callahan) Biomedical Ethics: An Anglo-American Dialogue 1988, Co. Ed. (with E.A. Shinebourne) Doctors Decisions: Ethical Conflicts In Medical Practice 1989. *Leisure interests:* small islands, *domus* and *rus. Address:* 9 Maryfield Avenue, Pennsylvania, Exeter, EX4 6JN, Devon, England. *Telephone:* (0392) 214 691.

DUNWORTH, John Vernon, C.B., C.B.E.; British scientist; b. 24 Feb. 1917; s. of late John Dunworth and Susan Ida (née Warburton); m. Patricia Noel Boston 1967; one d.; ed. Manchester Grammar School and Clare Coll., Cambridge; Twisden Studentship and Fellowship, Trinity Coll., Cambridge 1941; War Service with Ministry of Supply on Radar Devt. 1939–44; Nat. Research Council of Canada, on Atomic Energy Devt. 1944–45; Univ. Demonstrator in Physics, Cambridge 1945; joined A.E.R.E., Harwell 1947; Dir. Nat. Physical Laboratory 1964–76; Alt. Mem., Organizing Cttee. of UN Atoms for Peace Conf., Geneva 1955, 1958; Vice-Pres. Int. Cttee. of Weights and Measures 1968–75, Pres. 1975–85, Hon. mem. 1985–; Fellow, American Nuclear Soc. 1960; Chair. British Nuclear Energy Soc. 1964–70; Commdr. with Star, Order of Alfonso X el Sabio (Spain) 1960. *Address:* The Warbuck, Kirk Michael, Isle of Man. *Telephone:* Kirkmichael 878359 and Ramsey 813003.

DU PLESSIS, Barend Jacobus, B.SC.; South African politician; b. 1 Jan. 1940, Johannesburg; m.; three s. one d.; ed. Voortrekker High School, Boksburg, Potchefstroom Univ. for Christian Higher Educ., Potchefstroom Coll. of Educ.; teacher 1962, joined S. A. Broadcasting Corpn., then worked in pvt. sector; elected to Roodepoort City Council 1972, subsequently became Deputy Mayor, then Mayor; M.P. for Florida 1974–; served on numerous cttees. and select groups; Deputy Minister of Foreign Affairs 1982; Minister for Educ. and Training 1983, Minister of Finance 1984–86, of Finance and Econ. Advisory Services in Office of State Pres. Nov. 1986–. *Address:* House of Assembly, Cape Town, South Africa.

DU PLESSIS, Christian; British freelance opera singer; b. 2 July 1944, Vryheid, South Africa; ed. Potchefstroom and Bloemfontein Univs.; début in Pretoria 1967; British début in Andrea Chenier at Theatre Royal, Drury Lane 1970; prin. baritone, English Nat. Opera 1973–81; U.S.A. début in Les Pecheurs de Perles, Texas 1984; Covent Garden début in Rigoletto 1984; recipient, Ernest Oppenheimer Bursary 1968, 1969, 1970; maj. roles with cos. in U.K., U.S.A., France, Holland, Hong Kong, Ireland; major recordings for Orera Rara, EMI, Decca and ABC Dunhill. *Leisure interest:* Dir. of Fine Arts gallery. *Address:* c/o Performing Arts, 1 Hinde Street, London, W1M 5RH, England.

DU PLESSIS, Daniel Jacob, M.B., CH.B., M.CH., F.R.C.S.; South African surgeon and university vice-chancellor; b. 17 May 1918, Paarl; s. of Daniel J. du Plessis and Louisa M. (Carstens) du Plessis; m. Louisa S. Wicht 1946; two s.; ed. Paarl Boys' High School, Univs. of Cape Town and the Witwatersrand; Capt. S. African Medical Corps 1942–46; postgraduate studies, Cape Town, Johannesburg, Oxford and London 1946–52; Surgeon, Univ. of Cape Town and Groote Schuur Hosp. 1952–58; Prof. of Surgery, Univ. of the Witwatersrand, Johannesburg 1958–77, Vice-Chancellor 1978–83; Nuffield Scholarship 1951–52, Carnegie Fellowship 1963; Hon. Fellowship American Coll. of Surgeons 1974, American Surgical Asscn. 1981, Asscn. of Surgeons of G.B. and Ireland 1979, Coll. of Surgeons of S.A. 1982; Pres. Southern Transvaal Br., Medical Asscn. of S.A. 1986–87; mem. Advisory Council for Univs. and Technikons 1984–; Hon. Life Vice-Pres. Surgical Research Soc. of S.A., Asscn. of Surgeons of S.A. 1984; Chair. of Council, B. G. Alexander Nursing Coll. 1985–; Natalspruit Nursing Coll. 1986–; mem. Council, Medical Univ. of Southern Africa 1986-, Johannesburg Coll. of Educ. 1986–; Council, Univ. of Transkei, Bd. of Govs., American Coll. of Surgeons 1988–(1991); Trustee, S.A. Blood Transfusion Service 1985–; Hon. LL.D. (Witwatersrand) 1984; Hon. M.D. (Cape Town) 1986; Paul Harris Rotary Award 1983. *Publications:* Principles of Surgery 1968, Synopsis of Surgical Anatomy 1975 and articles in professional journals. *Leisure interests:* walking, reading. *Address:* 17 Chateau Road, Richmond, Johannesburg 2092, South Africa (Home).

DU PLESSIS, Frederick Johannes, M.COM., D.ECON.; South African business executive; ed. Potchefstroom Univ. and Vrije Univ. Amsterdam; Prof. of Money and Banking, Pretoria Univ. 1964–71; Dir. S.A. Inst. for Business Cycle Research 1970–79; now Chair. Sanlam, Trustbank, Santambank, Senbank, Federale Mynbou, Bankorp, Sankorp; Dir. of many cos. including American S.A. Investment Co., Messina, Trust Bldg. Soc., Urban Foundation, Small Business Devt. Corpn., Sasol, Federale Volksbeleggings, Gencor, Santam Insurance Ltd., Nissan-Magnis Holdings, Murray & Roberts; mem. Econ. Council of State Pres. and other affiliations. [*Deceased*]

DU PLESSIS, Pieter Christiaan, M.SC.; South African politician and farmer; b. 19 May 1935, Nebo, Sekhukuneland, Transvaal; ed. Hoër Volkskool, Heidelberg, Transvaal, Univ. of Pretoria; at Agricultural Research Inst., Univ. of Pretoria 1958–66, concurrently farmer and mem. numerous agricultural bds.; elected mem. Prov. Council, Lydenburg/Barberton Constituency 1966; M.P. for Lydenburg 1970–; Chair. Youth Action Group of Nat. Party, Transvaal 1972; Deputy Minister of Finance 1979; Minister of Agric. and Fisheries 1980, of Mineral and Energy Affairs 1980–83, of Manpower 1983–86, of Manpower and Public Works 1986–88; National Party. *Address:* c/o House of Assembly, Cape Town, South Africa.

DU PLOOY, Robert Abraham, B.ECON., D.JUR.; South African diplomatist; b. 5 July 1921; s. of Jacob Bester du Plooy and Eileen Beryl Wicks; m. Giulia Vera Bonino 1945; one s.; ed. Grey Coll., Bloemfontein, Univ. of South Africa, Univ. of Cologne, Fed. Repub. of Germany; mil. service 1941–46; Dept. of Mines 1946–49; diplomatic service 1950–; Head Office, Dept. of Foreign Affairs 1950–53; Vice-Consul, Hamburg 1954–55; Embassy Sec., Cologne 1955–60; Head Office, Dept. of Foreign Affairs 1960–67; Envoy Extraordinary, Rio de Janeiro, Brazil 1967–70; Amb. to Argentina (also accred. to Chile and Bolivia) 1970–74; Head Office, Dept. of Foreign Affairs 1975–78; in Namibia 1978–79; Amb. to Transkei 1979–81, to France 1981–87. *Publication:* Treaties and Intergovernmental Agreements with Commonwealth States 1958. *Leisure interest:* golf. *Address:* Ministry of Foreign Affairs, Union Bldgs., Private Bag X152, Pretoria, South Africa.

DUPONG, Jean; Luxembourg lawyer and politician; b. 18 May 1922, Luxembourg; ed. Athenée de Luxembourg, Loyola Coll., Montreal, Canada, and Univs. of Lausanne and Paris; Lawyer at Court of Appeal, Luxembourg 1948–; Deputy for S. Constituency 1954–; Minister of Justice, Nat. Educ., Family Affairs and Population 1967–69, of Nat. Educ., Labour and Social Security 1969–72, of Nat. Educ., Youth, Labour and Social Security 1972–74; Pres. Christian Social Party 1965–72, Counsellor of State 1979; Bronze Star (U.S.A.), Croix de guerre, Luxembourg. *Address:* P.B. 472, Luxembourg, Grand Duchy of Luxembourg.

DUPONT, Jacques-Bernard; French inspector of finances and diplomatist; b. 5 April 1922, Castelnau-Magnoac; s. of Louis Dupont and Alice Perisse; m. Marianne Ederle 1952; two s. one d.; ed. Univ. of Toulouse and Ecole Nationale d'Administration, Paris; lecturer, Tübingen Univ. 1946–49; with French High Comm., Germany 1949–52; Ecole Nat. d'Administration 1952–54; Asst. Insp. of Finances 1954, 3rd Class 1955, 2nd Class 1957, Head of Gen. Inspection 1956; with Financial Counsellor, Saarbrücken 1957, Tech. Adviser, Ministry of Foreign Affairs 1958, Head office, Insp.-Gen. of Finances 1961; Amb. to Dahomey (now Benin) 1961–63; Asst. Dir.-Gen. O.R.T.F. 1963, Dir.-Gen. 1964–68; Vice-Pres. European Broadcasting Union 1966–67; Dir.-Gen. Man., Cie. Int. des Wagons-Lits et du Tourisme 1969–; Pres. Groupement des Industries du Transport et du Tourisme 1975–; Vice-Pres. French-Canadian Chamber of Commerce 1977–; Pres. Société d'étude et de promotion hôtellière 1977–; P.L.M. 1982–; Dir. Banque Nationale de Paris 1979; Officier, Légion d'honneur, Officier, Ordre national du Mérite. *Address:* 40 rue de l'Arcade, 75008 Paris (Office); 1 rue du Maréchal-de-Lattre-de-Tassigny, 92200 Neuilly-sur-Seine, France (Home).

du PONT, Pierre Samuel, IV, LL.D.; American lawyer and politician; b. 22 Jan. 1935, Wilmington, Del.; s. of Pierre S. du Pont III (q.v.) and Jane (née Holcomb) du Pont; m. Elise R. Wood 1958; three s. one d.; ed. Philips Exeter Acad., Princeton Univ., and Harvard Univ.; mem. Delaware House of Reps. 1968–70; U.S. House of Reps. 1970–76, serving on Int. Relations Cttee. and Merchant Marine and Fisheries Cttee.; Gov. of Delaware 1977–85; Assoc. Richards, Layton and Finger 1985–; "Watchdog of the Treasury" Award; Republican. *Address:* Richards, Layton and Finger, One Rodney Square, P.O. Box 551, Wilmington, Del. 19899 (Office); Patterns, Rockland, Del. 19732, U.S.A. (Home).

DU PUIS, George Bonello, LL.D., M.P.; Maltese notary and politician; b. 24 Jan. 1928; m. Iris Gauci Maistre; three c.; ed. St. Catherine's High School, Sliema, the Lyceum and Univ. of Malta; mem. Parl. 1971–; Treasurer, Nationalist Party 1973–; Minister of Finance 1987–. *Address:* Ministry of Finance, Auberge de Castille, Valletta, Malta. *Telephone:* 225231.

DURAFOUR, Michel André François; French writer and politician; b. 11 April 1920, Saint-Etienne, Loire; s. of Antoine Durafour and Olga (née Gaillard); m. Maryse Forissier 1973; one s. one d.; ed. Lycée de St. Etienne and Law Faculty of Paris Univ.; assignment in office of Minister of Information 1944–46; journalist, writer, Deputy Mayor 1947–65, Mayor of St.-Etienne 1965–77; mem. Senate for Loire, Independent 1965–67; Deputy to Nat. Assembly for St.-Etienne N.-E., N.-W. 1967–68, 1973–74, 1978–81; Minister of Labour 1974–76, Minister attached to PM with responsibility for Econ. and Finance 1976–77, of the Civil Service and Admin. Reform May 1988–, of State Feb. 1989–; mem. Secretariat Parti Radical-Socialiste; mem. Nat. Bureau of Mouvement Réformateur 1971–; Chair. Groupe des Réformateurs (social democratic group) in Nat. Assembly 1973–74; Pres. Comm. de la Production et des échanges de l'Assemblée Nat.; Assoc. Prof. Univ. of Paris IX 1980–81; Prof. Univ. de Lyon III 1981–; Pres. Conseil Régional (Rhône-Alpes) 1980–81, Regional Councillor and Gen. Chair. Budget 1986–; mem. Senate for Loire, Social Democratic group 1983–; Vice-Prés. de la Commission des Affaires Culturelles du Sénat 1985, de la Commission des Finances du Sénat 1986; Grand Prix du Théâtre for Les Démoniaques 1950, Grand Prix du Roman d'Aventure for Agnès et les vilains Messieurs 1963. *Publications:* Les Démoniaques 1950, Notre rêve qui êtes aux cieux (film entitled Les fruits sauvages), Bettina Colonna, Les hommes sont comme ça, Le juif du ciel, Les moutons du ciel, Agnès et les vilains Messieurs (under pseudonym Pierre Jardin), Dites-le avec des pastèques, Pascaline and others. *Address:* 70 bis rue Bonaparte, 75006 Paris, France.

DURÁN, Roberto; Panamanian boxer; b. 16 June 1951, Chorrillo; m. Felicidad Durán; four c.; ed. primary school; professional boxer March 1967–; won world lightweight title from Ken Buchanan June 1972; made record number of championship defences (12) before relinquishing title to box as welterweight from Feb. 1979; won World Boxing Council version of world welterweight title from Ray Leonard (q.v.), Montreal June 1980: lost it to Leonard, New Orleans Nov. 1980, retained it 1989; 79 fights, 75 wins; exempt from all taxes, receives monthly pension for life from Govt. *Leisure interest:* cars. *Address:* Nuevo Reperto El Carmen, Panama.

DURAND-RIVAL, Pierre J. H.; French steel industry executive; b. 1 July 1930, Chambéry; s. of Eugène and Marie (née Callet) Durand-Rival; m. Nicole Guyot 1953; three d.; ed. Ecole Polytechnique, Ecole Nat. des Ponts et des Chaussées; mil. service 1951–52; Engineer Ministry of Public Works, Corsica 1954–58, Bas-Rhin 1958–61; Engineer Ministry of Public Health 1961–63; iron and steel engineer SACILOR steel makers, constructing and operating new mills 1963–66, Man., then Gen. Man. 1966–70, Chair. and Man. Dir. 1976–80; Gen. Man. and mem. Bd. SOLMER steel makers 1971–76; Admin. Marine-Wendel 1977; Chair. and Man. Dir. Cie. générale d'automatismes (CGA-Alcatel) 1983–; Chair. Chief Exec. Carnaud-Basse Indre; Deputy Chief Exec. and Dir. Eurotunnel 1986–89, Tech. Adviser Jan. 1989–. *Leisure interests:* skiing, walking. *Address:* Eurotunnel SA, tour Franklin, cedex 11, 92081 Paris-la-Défense (Office); 12 rue Lota, 75016 Paris; Le Pradon, 83320 Carqueiranne, France (Homes).

DURAS, Marguerite; French writer; b. 4 April 1914, Giadinh, Indo-China; d. of Henri Donnadieu and Marie Legrand; ed. Sorbonne; graduated in law; Sec., Colonies Ministry 1935–41; writer 1943–. *Publications:* Les impudents 1943, La vie tranquille 1944, Un barrage contre le Pacifique 1950, Le marin de Gibraltar 1952, Les petits chevaux de Tarquinia 1953, Des journées entières dans les arbres 1954 (short stories, Prix Jean Cocteau), Le square 1955, Moderato Cantabile 1958, Les viaducs de la Seine-et-Oise 1960, Hiroshima mon amour (film), Dix heures et demie du soir en été 1960 (film 1967), L'après-midi de Monsieur Andesmas 1962, Le ravissement de Lol. V. Stein, Des journées entières dans les arbres (play) 1964, Les eaux et les forêts (play) 1965, Le vice-consul 1966, L'amante anglaise 1967, Yes, peut-être and Le Shaga (two plays) 1968, Détruire, dit-elle 1969, Susanna Andler (play) 1969, Abaha Sabana David 1971, L'amour 1972, Jaune le soleil (film) 1971, Nathalie Granger (film) 1972, India Song (film, Grand Prix, Acad. du cinéma) 1973, La femme du Gange (film) 1974, L'amant (novel, Prix Goncourt 1984, Ritz Paris Hemingway Award 1986), Baxter Vera Baxter 1977, Abahn Sabana David 1976, La Musica, Yes peut-être 1976 (plays); writer and dir. les Eaux et les Forêts 1978, Aurelia Steiner (film) 1979, l'Homme assis dans le couloir (film) 1980, Savannah Bay, La maladice de la mort 1983, L'amant (prix Goncourt, prix Ritz Paris

Hemingway 1986) 1984, Les Enfants 1984, La Douleur (autobiog. stories) 1986, Les yeux bleus cheveux noirs, La pute de la côte normande 1986, Emily L. 1989. *Address:* 5 rue St. Benoît, 75006 Paris, France.

DURENBERGER, David Ferdinand, J.D.; American politician; b. 19 Aug. 1934, St. Cloud, Minn.; s. of George G. Durenberger and Isabelle M. Cebulla; m. Gilda Beth (Penny) Baran 1971; four s. by previous m.; ed. St. John's Univ. and Univ. of Minnesota; admitted Minn. Bar 1959; mem. firm, LeVander, Gillen, Miller & Durenberger, South St. Paul 1959-66; Exec. Sec. to Gov. Harold LeVander 1967-71; Counsel for Legal and Community Affairs, Corporate Sec., H. B. Fuller Co., St. Paul 1971-78; Senator from Minnesota 1978-; mem. numerous public bodies, community orgs. etc.; Republican. *Address:* U.S. Senate, 154 Russell Senate Building, Washington, D.C. 20510, U.S.A.

DUREY, Peter Burrell, B.A., F.L.A.; New Zealand (b. British) university librarian; b. 29 Aug. 1932, Sunderland, England; s. of Preston Burrell and Doris (née Marshall) Durey; m. Patricia Mary Antill 1965 (divorced 1984); two d.; ed. Washington Grammar School, Co. Durham, Durham Univ. and Loughborough Coll.; Sr. Asst. Librarian, Reading Univ. 1957-63; Sub-Librarian, Sussex Univ. 1963-66; Deputy Librarian, Univ. of Keele 1966-70; Librarian, Univ. of Auckland, N.Z. 1970-; Fellow, N.Z. Library Asscn., Pres. 1981. *Publications:* The Purpose and Practice of Medicine (ed.) 1960, Staff Management in University and College Libraries 1976 and numerous articles in the professional press. *Leisure interests:* swimming, painting and toy theatres. *Address:* University of Auckland Library, Private Bag, Auckland, New Zealand (Office); 21 Wimbledon Way, Remuera, Auckland 5, New Zealand (Home). *Telephone:* (09) 737-999 (Office); (09) 542-954 (Home).

DURHAM, Sir Kenneth, Kt., B.SC., C.B.I.M.; British company director; b. 28 July 1924, Blackburn, Lancs.; s. of George and Bertha (née Aspin) Durham; m. Irene Markham 1946; one s. one d.; ed. Queen Elizabeth Grammar School, Blackburn, Univ. of Manchester; Flight Lieut. in R.A.F. 1943-46; joined Atomic Research Establishment, Harwell, then Unilever Research Lab., Port Sunlight 1950, Head of Lab. 1961; Head of Lab., Colworth 1965; Chair. BOCM Silcock Ltd. 1971; Dir. Unilever Ltd. and Unilever NV 1974-; Vice-Chair. Unilever Ltd. (now Unilever PLC) 1978-82, Chair. 1982-86; Dir. British Aerospace Ltd. Sept. 1980-, Deputy Chair. 1986-; Dir. Woolworth Holdings 1985-, Chair. 1986-, Morgan Grenfell Holdings 1986-; Chair. Trade Policy Research Centre 1982; Vice-Pres. Liverpool School of Tropical Medicine 1982-; Gov. London Business School 1982; Advisory Council Chase Manhattan Bank NA 1983; mem. Int. Advisory Cttee. of United Technologies Corpn. 1983; Chair. Econ. and Financial Policy Cttee., CBI 1983-86; Trustee Leverhulme Trust 1974. *Publications:* Surface Activity and Detergency 1960, various scientific papers. *Leisure interests:* walking, golf. *Address:* c/o Woolworth Holdings PLC, North West House, 119 Marylebone Road, London, NW1 5PX, England. *Telephone:* 01-724 7749.

DURKIN, John Anthony, B.A., LL.B.; American politician; b. 29 March 1936, Brookfield, Mass.; s. of Joseph Durkin and Charlotte Dailey; m. Patricia Moses 1965; one s. two d.; ed. Holy Cross Coll., Worcester, Mass., Georgetown Univ. Law Center, Washington, D.C.; served in U.S.N. 1959-61, Lieut.-Commdr. in Corps Reserve; Asst. to Admin. of Nat. Banks, Washington, D.C. 1963-66; Asst. Attorney-Gen., New Hampshire 1966-68; New Hampshire Insurance Commr. 1968-73; mem. Exec. Cttee. of Nat. Assen. of Insurance Commrs. 1970-73; Senator from New Hampshire 1975-81; firm Perito, Duerk, Carlson & Pinco, Washington 1981-. *Leisure interests:* reading, travelling.

DURKÓ, Zsolt; Hungarian composer; b. 10 April 1934, Szeged; s. of Dr. Gábor Durkó and Irén Patkós; m. Rita Gerencsér 1970; two s.; ed. Music Acad. of Budapest, under F. Farkas, and Accad. Santa Cecilia, Rome, under G. Petrassi; Prof. of 20th Century Composition, Music Acad. of Budapest 1970-80; mem. Bd., Fed. of Hungarian Musicians 1969-; Premio d'Atri, Rome 1963, First Prize, Int. Tribune of Composers, Paris 1975, Critics' Prize (Hungarian Radio) twice, Listeners' Prize (Hungarian Radio) twice, Special Citation of Int. Koussewitzky Award, Kossuth Prize 1978, Eminent Artist's title 1987. *Compositions:* vocal: Altamira 1968, Colloids 1969, two Cantatas 1971, 1972, Halotti Beszéd (Burial prayer) 1972, Moses (opera) 1977; instrumental: Organismi 1964, Psicogramma for piano 1964, Una Rapsodia ungherese 1965, Fioriture 1966, String Quartets, no. 1 1966, no. 2 1970, Iconographies, no. 1 1970, no. 2 1971, Chamber Music 1973, Fire Music, Turner Illustrations 1976, Refrains 1978, Quattro Dialoghi 1979, Son et Lumière 1980, Andromeda 1980, Piano Concerto 1981, Essay for Clarinet and Piano 1982, Ornamenti for orchestra 1985, Széchenyi Oratorio 1985, Midsummernight's Music (for guitar) 1986, Clarinet-Sextet 1987, Octet 1988. *Address:* Attila u. 103, 1012 Budapest I, Hungary. *Telephone:* 753-946.

DUROSELLE, Jean-Baptiste, D. ES. L.; French historian; b. 17 Nov. 1917, Paris; s. of Albert Duroselle and Jeanne Péronne; m. Christiane Viant 1940; three s. one d.; ed. Lycée Louis-le Grand, Paris and Ecole Normale Supérieure; teacher Lycées of Orleans, Chartres and Versailles 1943-45; Asst. Prof. Sorbonne 1945-49, Prof. 1964-83, Prof. Emer. 1983-; Prof. Univ. of Saarbrücken, 1950-57; Univ. of Lille 1957-58; Fondation Nat. des Sciences Politiques 1958-64; Visiting Prof. at numerous univs. in Europe

and America; mem. Académie des Sciences Morales et Politiques 1975; foreign mem. American Philosophical Soc.; Royal Acad. of Belgium; Hon. mem. American Historical Assen.; Dr. Hon. (Univ. of Notre Dame, Ind.), (Univ. of Liège); Prix int. Balzan 1982; Officier Légion d'honneur, Grande Uff. del Merito Italiano. *Publications:* 22 books, including Les débuts du catholicisme social en France 1822-70 1953, Histoire diplomatique de 1919 à nos jours 9th ed. 1986, Le conflit de Trieste 1963, La France et les Français (2 vols.) 1970-72, La décadence 1980, Tout empire perira 1982, L'Abîme 1985, Clemenceau 1988, 300 articles. *Leisure interests:* collecting books. *Address:* 5 rue de Naples, Rocquencourt, 78150 Le Chesnay, France. *Telephone:* (1) 39-54-43-16.

DÜRR, Heinz; German industrialist; b. 16 July 1933, Stuttgart; s. of Otto Dürr; m. Heide Dürr; three d.; ed. Tech. Hochschule, Stuttgart; Man. and Man. Dir. Dürr GmbH (fmrly. Otto Dürr GmbH), Stuttgart 1957-80; Chair. Bd. of Dirs. AEG Aktiengesellschaft, Berlin and Frankfurt 1980-; mem. Bd. of Dirs. Daimler-Benz AG, Stuttgart 1986-; Chair. Supervisory Bd. Olympia AG, Wilhelmshaven 1980-; mem. Supervisory Bd. Frankfurter Allianz-AG, Frankfurt 1981-; Pres. Metal Industry Asscn., Stuttgart 1975-80; mem. Advisory Council Dresdner Bank, Frankfurt 1980-. *Leisure interests:* tennis, golf, theatre. *Address:* AEG Aktiengesellschaft, Theodor-Stern-Kai 1, D-6000 Frankfurt 70, Federal Republic of Germany.

DURRANI, Shakirullah; Pakistani investment banker and airline executive; b. 20 Sept. 1928, Sheikh-Kale, Tehsil Charsadda, Peshawar; s. of late Maj. Mohd. Zaman Khan; m. Samina Hayat 1951; one s. five d.; ed. Government Coll., Lahore, Indian Military Acad., Dehradun, and Pakistan Military Acad., Kakul; Regular Officer Pakistan Army until 1951; Lloyds Bank Ltd., training in U.K. and service in Karachi, Rawalpindi, Lahore and Dacca branches 1952-60; Chief of Operations, Pakistan Industrial Credit and Investment Corpn. 1960-63, Deputy Man. Dir. 1963-66; Man. Dir. Investment Corpn. of Pakistan 1966-68; Man. Dir. Pakistan Int. Airlines Corpn. 1968-71; Gov. State Bank of Pakistan 1971; under house arrest Dec. 1972; Pres. Commercial Devt. Finance Corpn. 1983-; Sitara-e-Khidmat 1965, Sitara-e-Quaid-e-Azam 1969, Grand Cordon, Order of Independence First Class (Jordan) 1970. *Address:* c/o State Bank of Pakistan, P.O. Box 4456, McLeod Road, Karachi, Pakistan.

DURRANT, Jennifer Ann; British artist and painter, b. 17 June 1942, Brighton; d. of Caleb John Durrant and Winifred May Wright; m. William A. H. Henderson 1964 (divorced 1976); ed. Varndean Grammar School for Girls, Brighton, Brighton Coll. of Art and Crafts, Slade School of Fine Art, Univ. Coll., London; part-time art teacher various colls. 1965-74; part-time Lecturer on Painting, St. Martin's School of Art, London 1974-87, R.C.A. 1979-; Chelsea School of Art 1987-; Exhbn. Selector, Northern Young Contemporaries, Whitworth Gallery, Manchester, TV S.W. Arts; Painting Faculty mem. The British School at Rome 1979-83; Newham Hosp. Comm. (in assen. with Greater London Arts Asscn. and King Edward's Hosp. Fund); Towner Art Gallery, Eastbourne; Abbey Minor Travelling Scholarship 1964; Arts Council Award 1976; Arts Council Maj. Award 1978; Artist-in-Residence, Somerville Coll., Oxford 1979-80; Greater London Arts Asscn. Award 1980; one-person exhbns. at Univ. of Surrey, Guildford 1975, Arnolfini Gallery, Bristol 1979, Museum of Modern Art, Oxford 1980, Nicola Jacobs Gallery, London 1982, 1985, Arcade Gallery, Harrogate 1983, Northern Centre for Contemporary Art, Sunderland 1986; Serpentine Gallery, London 1987, Newlyn-Orion, Newlyn Art Gallery, Penzance, Cornwall 1988; numerous group exhbns. in London, Liverpool, Reykjavik, Boston, U.S.A., Edmonton, Canada, New York, Aachen, Fed. Repub. of Germany, Pittsburg, U.S.A., Birmingham, Stoke-on-Trent, Sheffield 1988, Newcastle 1989; works in collections of Arts Council of G.B., British Council, Contemporary Art Soc., Tate Gallery, London, Museum of Fine Arts, Boston, U.S.A., Neue Gallery, Aachen etc. and in pvt. collections; Athena Art Award 1988. *Leisure interests:* classical music, including opera, archaeology, visiting museums, looking at paintings and sculpture. *Address:* 9-10 Holly Grove, London, SE15 5DF, England. *Telephone:* 01-639 6424.

DURRELL, Gerald Malcolm, O.B.E., F.R.S.L., F.R.G.S., F.Z.S.; British zoologist and writer; b. 7 Jan. 1925, Jamshedpur, India; s. of Lawrence Samuel and Louisa Florence (née Dixie) Durrell; brother of Lawrence Durrell (q.v.); m. 1st Jacqueline Sonia Rasen 1951 (divorced), 2nd Lee Wilson McGeorge 1979; ed. pvt. tutors; student keeper, Whipsnade Park 1945-46; zoological collecting expeditions: British Cameroons 1947 and 1948, British Guiana 1949, Argentina and Paraguay 1953, British Cameroons 1956, Trans-Argentine 1958, New Zealand, Australia and Malaysia 1961, Sierra Leone 1964, Mexico 1968, Mauritius 1976, 1977, India/Assam 1978, Madagascar 1978, Mexico 1979, Mauritius and Madagascar 1981; established own zoo in Jersey 1959, founded Jersey Wildlife Preservation Trust 1964; contributes to many magazines and dailies; numerous lectures, B.B.C. broadcasts and 5 major T.V. series on animals; Fellow Int. Inst. of Arts and Letters, Inst. of Biology; mem. British Ornithologists Union; Hon. L.H.D. (Yale), Hon. D.Sc. (Durham). *Publications include:* The Overloaded Ark 1952, Three Singles to Adventure 1953, The Bafut Beagles 1953, The Drunken Forest 1955, My Family and Other Animals 1956, Encounters with Animals 1959, A Zoo in My Luggage 1960, The Whispering Land 1962, Menagerie Manor 1964, Two in the Bush 1966, Rosy is My Relative (novel) 1968, Birds, Beasts and Relatives 1969, Fillets of Plaice 1971, Catch Me a Colobus 1972, Beasts in My Belfrey 1973, The Stationary Ark 1976, Golden

Bats and Pink Pigeons 1977, The Garden of the Gods 1978, The Picnic and Suchlike Pandemonium 1979, The Mockery Bird 1981, Amateur Naturalist 1982, How to Shoot an Amateur Naturalist 1984, Durrell in Russia 1986; Childrens' Books: The New Noah 1956, Island Zoo 1961, Look at Zoos 1961, My Favourite Animal Stories 1963, The Donkey Rustlers 1968, The Talking Parcel 1974, The Fantastic Flying Journey 1987. *Leisure interests:* reading, photography, drawing, swimming, history and maintenance of zoological gardens. *Address:* Jersey Wildlife Preservation Trust, Les Augres Manor, Trinity, Jersey, Channel Islands. *Telephone:* (0534) 61949.

DURRELL, Lawrence George, F.R.S.L.; British author; b. 27 Feb. 1912, Julundur, India; s. of Lawrence Samuel and Louisa Florence (née Dixie) Durrell; brother of Gerald Durrell (q.v.); m. Ghislaine de Boysson 1973; two d. (one deceased); ed. Coll. of St. Joseph, Darjeeling, India, and St. Edmund's Coll., Canterbury, England; fmrly. Foreign Service Press Officer (Athens and Cairo), Press Attaché (Alexandria and Belgrade), Dir. of Public Relations (Dodecanese Islands), Dir. of British Council Institutes (Kalamata, Greece, and Cordoba, Argentina), and Dir. of Public Relations (Govt. of Cyprus); Duff Cooper Memorial Prize 1957, James Tait Black Memorial Prize 1974. *Publications:* Poetry: A Private Country 1943, Cities, Plains and People 1946, On Seeming to Presume 1948, The Tree of Idleness 1955, Selected Poems 1956, Collected Poems 1960, 1968, 1979, The Ikons 1966, The Red Limbo Lingo 1971, Vega and Other Poems 1973, New Selected Poems 1978; Verse drama: Sappho 1950, Acte 1962, An Irish Faustus 1964; Prose: Panic Spring 1937, The Black Book 1938, Prospero's Cell 1945, Cefalu (The Dark Labyrinth) 1947, Reflections on a Marine Venus 1953, Bitter Lemons 1957, The Alexandria Quartet: Justine 1957, Balthazar 1958, Mountolive 1958, Clea 1960; Tunc 1968, Spirit of Place 1969, Nunquam 1970, The Big Supposer 1973, Monsieur 1974, Sicilian Carousel 1977, Livia 1978, The Greek Islands 1978, A Smile in the Mind's Eye 1981, Constance 1982, Sebastian 1983, The Avignon Quincunx 1984–85; Humour: Esprit de corps 1957, Stiff Upper Lip 1958, Sauve qui peut 1966; Juvenile: White Eagles Over Serbia 1957; Trans. Four Greek Poets 1946, Pope Joan 1948; Letters: A Private Correspondence (with Henry Miller) 1962. *Address:* 13 St. James's Square, London, S.W.1, England.

DÜRRENMATT, Friedrich; Swiss writer; b. 5 Jan. 1921, Konolfingen; s. of Reinhold and Hulda (née Zimmermann) Dürrenmatt; m. Lotti Geissler 1946 (died 1983), one s. two d.; m. 2nd Charlotte Kerr 1984; ed. Univs. of Berne and Zürich. *Publications:* Plays: Es steht geschrieben, Der Blinde, Romulus der Grosse, Die Ehe des Herrn Mississippi, Ein Engel kommt nach Babylon, Der Besuch der alten Dame, Frank V, Die Physiker, Herkules und der Stall des Augias, Der Meteor, Die Wiedertäufer, König Johann (after Shakespeare), Play Strindberg, Titus Andronicus (after Shakespeare), Portrait eines Planeten, Der Mitmacher, Die Frist, Die Panne, Dichterdämmerung, Urfaust, Woyzeck, Achterloo, Rollenspiele, Protokoll, Einer Fiktiven Lurzenierung (with Charlotte Kerr) Achterloo IV. *Plays for radio:* Der Doppelgänger, Der Prozess um des Esels Schatten, Nächtliches Gespräch mit einem verachteten Menschen, Stranitzky und der Nationalheld, Herkules und der Stall des Augias, Das Unternehmen der Wega, Abendstunde im Spätherbst, Der Gerettete, Der Erfinder. *Fiction:* Der Richter und sein Henker, Der Verdacht, Das Versprechen, Justiz. *Prose:* Pilatus, Der Nihilist, Der Hund, Der Theaterdirektor, Der Tunnel, Grieche sucht Griechin, Im Coiffeurladen, Das Bild des Sisyphos, Mister X macht Ferien, Nachrichten über den Stand des Zeitungswesens in der Steinzeit, Aufenthalt in einer kleinen Stadt, Abuis Chanifa, und Anan Ben David, Smithy, Das Sterben der Pythia, Die Wurst, Der Sohn, Der Alte, Aus den Papieren eines Wärters, Der Sturz, Der Mitmacher, Die Stadt, Stoffe I-III, Minotaurus, eine Ballade, Der Auftrag. *Essays:* Theaterprobleme, Theaterschriften und Reden, Monstervortrag über Gerechtigkeit und Recht, Zusammenhänge, Essay über Israel, Friedrich Schiller, Sätze aus Amerika, Lesebuch, Die Heimat im Plakat (artwork in book form, with essay), Der Rest ist Dank, Meine Russlandreise, Friedrich Dürrenmatt zu Varlin, Theater, Versuche. *Criticism:* Kritiken und Zeichnungen, Literatur und Kunst. *Essays:* numerous essays and speeches; Bilder und Zeichnungen (artwork in book form). *Leisure interests:* painting, astronomy. *Address:* Pertuis du Sault 74, 2000 Neuchâtel, Switzerland.

DÜRRENMATT, Peter Ulrich; Swiss journalist; b. 29 Aug. 1904; ed. Univs. of Berne and Geneva; began career as teacher; mem. staff Schweizer Mittelpresse 1934; Ed. Swiss Section Basler Nachrichten 1943–49, Chief Ed. 1949–73; mem. Nat. Council 1959. *Publications:* Die Bundesverfassung, ihr Wert und ihre Bewährung 1948, Kleine Geschichte der Schweiz im zweiten Weltkrieg 1949, Zerfall und Wiederaufbau der Politik 1951, Schweizergeschichte 1957, Die Welt zwischen Krieg und Frieden 1959, Europa will leben 1960, 50 Jahre Weltgeschichte 1962, In die Zeit gesprochen 1965. *Address:* Pfaffenlohweg 60, Riehen, Switzerland.

DUTILLEUX, Henri; French composer; b. 22 Jan. 1916, Angers; s. of Paul and Thérèse (née Koszul) Dutilleux; m. Geneviéve Joy 1946; ed. Conservatoire Nat. de Musique, Paris; career devoted to music 1945–; Dir. service Créations Musicales Radiodiffusion française 1945–63; Prof. of Composition Ecole Normale de Musique, Paris 1961–, Pres. 1969–74; Assoc. Prof. Conservatoire Nat. Supérieur de Musique, Paris 1970–71; Vice-Pres. Syndicat Nat. des Auteurs et Compositeurs 1962–; fmr. mem. UNESCO Music Council; Hon. mem. American Acad. and Inst. of Arts and Letters, New York; 1st Grand Prix de Rome 1938, Grand Prix du Disque 1957,

1958, 1966, 1968, 1976, 1978 and 1984, Grand Prix National de la Musique 1967, Prix de la Ville de Paris 1974, Koussevitzky Int. Recording Award 1976, World Record Award (Montreux) 1983; Prix Int. Maurice Ravel 1987; Commdr., Légion d'honneur. *Compositions:* Sonata for Piano 1948, First Symphony 1951, Le Loup (Ballet) 1953, Second Symphony (Le Double) 1959, Métaboles (for orchestra) 1964, Cello Concerto: Tout un monde lointain 1970, Figures de Résonances (for two pianos) 1971, Preludes for Piano 1974, Ainsi la Nuit (for string quartet) 1976, Timbres, Espace, Mouvement (for orchestra) 1978, 3 Strophes sur le nom de Sacher (for cello) 1981, Violin Concerto 1985, For Aldeburgh 85 (for oboe, harpsichord and percussion) 1985, L'Arbre des Songes. *Address:* 12 rue St.-Louis-en-l'Isle, 75004 Paris, France. *Telephone:* 43-26-39-14.

DUTOIT, Charles E.; Swiss conductor and music director; b. 7 Oct. 1936; s. of Edmond Dutoit and Berthe Dutoit (Laederman); m. Marie-Josée Drouin 1982; one s. one d.; ed. Conservatory of Lausanne, Accademia Musicale Chigiana, Siena, Italy, Conservatorio Benedetto Marcello, Venice, Italy and Berks. Music Center, Tanglewood, U.S.A.; Conductor Berne Symphony Orchestra (Assoc. Conductor 1964, Music Dir. 1966–68), Radio Zurich Orchestra, Nat. Symphony Orchestra of Mexico (Music Dir.), Gothenberg Symphony Orchestra, Sweden (Music Dir.) Montreal Symphony Orchestra (Music Dir.) 1977–, Minn. Orchestra (Prin. Guest Conductor 1983–84, 1985–86); Artistic Dir. and Prin. Conductor Philadelphia Orchestra 1990, 1991; many recordings including 24 for Decca since 1980; début Royal Opera House Covent Garden (conducting Faust) 1983; D.Mus. h.c. (Montreal) 1984, (Laval) 1985; Grand Prix de l'Académie du disque français, High Fidelity Int. Record Critics' Award, Montreux Record Award, Grand Prix du Prés. de la République (France), Japan Record Acad. Award, Artist of the Year (Canada Music Council) 1982. *Address:* Orchestre Symphonique de Montréal, 85 St. Catherine Street West, Suite 900, Montreal, Quebec H2X 3P4, Canada. *Telephone:* (514) 842-3402.

DUTT, James L., B.A.; American business executive; b. 11 Feb. 1925, Topeka, Kan.; ed. Washburn Univ., Topeka, and Univ. of Dayton, Ohio; joined Beatrice Foods Co., Kan. dairy plant 1947, Man. dairy plant, Dayton, Ohio 1961–67, Asst. Gen. Sales Man. Dairy Div. 1967–68; Asst. Dir. Marketing and Man. Services and New Products 1968–74, Corp. Vice-Pres. and Exec. Vice-Pres. Dairy and Soft Drink Div. 1974, Dir Int. Dairy Operations 1974–75, Pres. Int. Food Operations 1975, Exec. Vice-Pres. 1975–77, Dir. 1976–, Pres. and C.O.O. 1977–79, Chair. and C.E.O. 1979–84; Pres. Esmark Inc. 1984–; mem. bd. numerous cos. and insts. *Address:* Beatrice Foods Co., 2 N. LaSalle Street, Chicago, Ill. 60602, U.S.A.

DUTT, Utpal, B.A.; Indian director, actor and playwright; b. 29 March 1929, Shillong; s. of Girijaranjan Dutt and Shailabala Dutt; m. Sova Sen 1961; one d.; ed. St. Xavier's Coll., Calcutta Univ.; toured India and Pakistan with Shakespeareana Co. 1947–48, 1953–54; f. Little Theatre Group 1947, producing Shakespeare in English and Bengali before producing Dutt's own plays Angaar 1959, Kallol 1965, Manusher Adhikarey 1968; f. People's Little Theatre 1971, producing his own plays Tiner Talwar 1971, Suryashukar 1971, Barricade 1972 etc.; wrote and dir. plays for several Jatra cos. 1968–82; has acted in about 200 films, winning nat. award for best film actor for film Bhuvan Shome 1969; Dir. of films Megh 1961, Ghumbhangar Gaan 1965, Jhor 1980, Baishakhi Megh 1981, Mother (from novel by Gorky) 1984; toured G.D.R. 1986, with his play Mahavidroho; Ed. journal Epic Theatre; Nat. Acad. of Dance, Drama and Music Award. *Publications:* Invincible Vietnam 1967, Hunting the Sun 1972, Towards a Revolutionary Theatre 1982, The Great Rebellion 1986 and about 40 plays in Bengali. *Leisure interests:* cricket, chess, music, books. *Address:* 140/24 Netaji Subhas Bose Road, Calcutta 700 040, India. *Telephone:* 46-8329.

DUTTON, Geoffrey Piers Henry, A.O.; Australian writer; b. 2 Aug. 1922, Anlaby, S. Australia; s. of Henry Hampden Dutton and Emily Dutton (née Martin); m. 1st Ninette Clarice Florence Trott 1944 (divorced 1985), two s. one d.; m. 2nd Robin Lucas 1985; ed. Geelong Grammar School, Vic., Univ. of Adelaide, Magdalen Coll., Oxford; Pilot, R.A.A.F. 1941–45; Sr. Lecturer in English, Univ. of Adelaide 1954–62; Commonwealth Fellow, Univ. of Leeds, England 1960; Visiting Prof., Kansas State Univ., U.S.A. 1962; Founding Ed. Australian Letters, Australian Book Review, Penguin Australia 1955–65; Co-founder and Dir. Sun Books 1965–; Ed. The Bulletin Literary Supplement 1980–85, Ed. The Australian Literary Magazine 1985–88; mem. Australian Council for the Arts, Commonwealth Literary Fund, Literature Bd., Australia Council 1968–78; mem. Council, Australian Nat. Univ. 1976–80. *Publications:* 42 books of poetry, biography, fiction, literary and art criticism, travel, children's; they include Nightflight and Sunrise 1944, Antipodes in Shoes 1958, Walt Whitman 1961, Patrick White 1961, Russell Drysdale 1964, The Literature of Australia 1964, Poems Soft and Loud 1967, Tamara 1969, Australia's Censorship Crisis (with M. Harris) 1970, Findings and Keepings 1970, New Poems to 1972, Australian Verse from 1805–1976, A Body of Words 1978, Patterns of Australia 1980, The Australian Heroes 1981, T. Gill's Australia 1981, The Eye-Opener 1982, In Search of Edward John Eyre 1982, The Prowler 1982, Snow on the Saltbush 1984, The Australian Collection 1985, The Innovators 1986. *Leisure interest:* swimming. *Address:* c/o Curtis Brown Ltd., P.O. Box 19, Paddington, N.S.W. 2021, Australia. *Telephone:* 02-331 5301.

DUŢU Alexandru, PH.D.; Romanian historian and author; b. 2 Sept. 1928, Bucharest; s. of Nicolae Duţu and Elisabeta Negoescu; m. Angela Dăscălescu 1958 (died 1986); one d., one s.; ed. Coll. of Modern Philology and Coll. of Law; researcher of the Inst. for South East European Studies 1963–; ed. Revue des études sud-est européennes; Deputy Ed. Synthesis; Deputy Ed. Mentalities 1984–; Prize of the Romanian Acad., of the Int. Asscn. for South-East European Studies; IREX grant; Fellowship Great Britain 1968–69, U.S.A. 1986; corresp. mem. Romanian Acad. of Social and Political Sciences (1970–); Vice-Chair. of the Int. Asscn. for Comparative Literature 1979–85; mem. French, Austrian, Spanish socs. for the study of the 18th century culture; mem. Romanian Writers' Union, American Historical Asscn. *Works include:* Shakespeare in Romania, 1964, Les livres de sagesse dans la culture roumaine 1971, Romanian Humanists and the European Culture 1977, European Intellectual Movements and the Modernization of the Romanian Culture 1981, Humanisme, baroque, lumières—l'exemple roumain 1984, The Human Dimension of History. Trends in the History of Mentalities 1986. *Leisure interests:* skiing, travelling. *Address:* Bd. Republicii 13, Bucharest (Office); Str. Arieşului 6, 78144 Bucharest, Romania (Home).

DUVAL, Sir (Charles) Gaëtan, Kt., BAR.-AT-LAW; Mauritius politician; b. 9 Oct. 1930, Rose Hill; s. of Charles R. and Rosina M. Duval; divorced; one s.; ed. Royal Coll., Curepipe, Lincoln's Inn, London and Faculty of Law, Univ. of Paris; entered politics 1958; mem. Town Council, Curepipe 1960, re-elected 1963, Legis. Council, Curepipe 1960, re-elected 1963; mem. Municipal Council, Port Louis 1969–; Chair. Town Council, Curepipe 1960–61, 1963–68; Minister of Housing, Lands and Town and Country Planning 1964–65; attended London Constitutional Conf. 1965; Leader, Parti Mauritien Social Démocrate (PMSD) 1966–; first M.L.A. for Grand River North-west and Port Louis West 1967; Leader of the Opposition 1967–69; Minister of External Affairs, Tourism and Emigration 1969–73; Mayor, City of Port Louis 1969–71; Lord Mayor of Port Louis 1971–74, 1981–; Mayor of Curepipe 1976–79; Pres. Asscn. Touristique de l'Océan Indien (A.T.O.I.) 1973; Chair. S. African Regional Tourism Council 1973; Deputy Prime Minister 1983–88; Minister of Justice 1983–86, of Employment and Tourism 1986–88; Grand Officier, Ordre national du Tchad, Ordre du Lion du Sénégal; Médaille de l'Assemblée National Française, Médaille de la République Française; Commdr. Légion d'honneur, Ordre National du Centre-Afrique. *Leisure interests:* horse-riding, farming. *Address:* Parti Mauricien Social Démocratique, Place Foch, Port Louis, Mauritius.

DUVAL, H.E. Cardinal Léon-Etienne, D.THEOL.; Algerian (b. French) ecclesiastic; b. 9 Nov. 1903, Chenex, Haute-Savoie, France; s. of François Duval and Joséphine Saultier; ed. Petit Séminaire, Roche-sur-Foron, Grand Séminaire Annecy, Séminaire français Rome, and Pontificia Universitas Gregoriana; ordained priest 1926, Prof. Grand Séminaire Annecy 1930–42; Vicar-Gen. and Dir. of works, Diocese of Annecy 1942–46; consecrated Bishop of Constantine and Hippo 1946; Archbishop of Algiers 1954–; created Cardinal 1965; Officier, Légion d'honneur. *Publications:* Paroles de paix 1955, Messages de paix 1955–1962 1962, Laïcs, prêtres, religieux dans l'église 1967, Evêque en Algérie (in collab.) 1984. *Address:* Notre-Dame d'Afriques, 4, Avenue Gurak Ali, Bologhine-Alger, Algeria. *Telephone:* (62) 35-89.

DUVALIER, Jean-Claude; Haitian politician; b. 3 July 1951, Port-au-Prince; s. of late Pres. François Duvalier and Simone (née Ovide) (q.v.); m. Michele Bennett 1980; one s.; ed. Coll. of St. Louis de Gonzague, Port-au-Prince and faculty of law, Univ. of Haiti; named political heir to Pres. François Duvalier Jan. 1971; Life Pres. 1971–86 (overthrown in coup); now living in Grasse, France.

DUVALIER, Simone; fmr. First Lady of Haiti; b. 19 March 1913, Léogane, Port-au-Prince; d. of Jules Faine; m. late Pres. François Duvalier 1939; one s. (Jean-Claude, q.v.) three d.; ed. secondary school, Port-au-Prince; trained as nurse; First Lady of Haiti 1957–81; now living in Grasse, France.

DUVERGER, Maurice; French political scientist; b. 5 June 1917, Angoulême; s. of Georges and Anne (née Gobert) Duverger; m. Odile Batt 1949; ed. Bordeaux Univ; contrib. to Le Monde 1946–; Prof. of Political Sociology, Paris Univ. 1955–85, Prof. Emer. 1985–; f. and Dir. of Centre d'Analyse comparative des systèmes politiques, Sorbonne; worked on Nouvel Observateur 1966–70; mem. American Acad. of Arts and Sciences; Commandeur, Légion d'honneur. *Publications:* Les partis politiques 1951, Demain, la république ... 1959, De la dictature 1961, La Sixième république et le régime présidentiel 1961, Introduction to the Social Sciences 1964, Introduction à la politique 1964, La démocratie sans le peuple 1967, Institutions politiques 1970, Janus: les deux faces de l'Occident 1972, Sociologie de la politique 1973, La monarchie républicaine 1974, Lettre ouverte aux socialistes 1976, L'autre coté des choses 1977, Echec au roi 1978, Les orangers du lac Balaton 1980, La République des Citoyens 1982, Bréviaire de la cohabitation 1986, La Cohabitation des Français 1987. *Leisure interest:* theatre. *Address:* La Sorbonne, 17 rue de la Sorbonne, 75005 Paris (Office); 24 rue des Fossés-Saint-Jacques, 75005 Paris, France (Home).

DUVILLARD, Henri; French politician; b. 3 Nov. 1910, Luxeuil-les-Bains; s. of Benoit Duvillard and Emilie Mougenot; m. Germaine Grandjean 1933; journalist; Dir. La Dépêche du Loiret 1947–52; on staff of Gen. Koenig (Minister of Nat. Defence) 1954–55; on staff of Henri Ulver (Minister of Industry and Commerce) 1955–56; on staff of Maurice Lemaire (Sec. of

State for Industry and Commerce) 1956–58; Deputy for Loiret 1958–63, 1963–67, 1973–78; fmr. Vice-Pres. U.N.R. Group in Nat. Assembly; fmr. Public Relations Officer, Papeteries de France; Minister for Ex-Servicemen 1967–72; Pres. Comité Nat. du Mémorial du Gen. de Gaulle; mem. Inst. Charles du Gaulle; Hon. Deputy; Légion d'honneur, Médaille militaire, Croix de guerre (1939–45), Médaille de la Résistance. *Address:* 12 rue du Grenier à Sel, 45000 Orléans, France.

DUYSENS, Louis N.M., PH.D.; Netherlands professor of biophysics; b. 15 March 1921, Heerlen; m. Wilhelmina A. Kesler 1952; two s. one d.; ed. Univ. of Utrecht; Fellow, Carnegie Inst. of Washington, Stanford, Calif. 1952–53; Research Assoc. Univ. of Illinois 1953–54; Biophysical Research Group, Univ. of Utrecht 1954–56; Prof. of Biophysics, Univ. of Leiden 1956–86; studies on prevention of nuclear war 1986–; mem. Netherlands and U.S. acads. etc.; C.F. Kettering Award 1964. *Publications:* numerous articles in learned journals. *Address:* Charlotte de Bourbonlaan 2, 2341 VD Oegstgeest, The Netherlands (Home). *Telephone:* 71-171764 (Home).

DUYSHEYEV, Arstanbek; Soviet politician; b. 1932, Kirghiz S.S.R.; mem. CPSU 1957–; ed. K. I. Skryabin Kirghiz Agric. Inst.; worked as a vet on a state farm in the Djumgal Region, as chief vet on a state farm in the Tonsk Region and subsequently as the dir. of the Djumgal state farm; party work 1960–; Party Sec. of the Djumgal Region, Chief Organizer of the Cen. Cttee. of the Kirghiz CP, then First Sec. of the Uzgensk Regional Cttee. of the Kirghiz CP, then Sec. of Cen. Cttee., Kirghiz CP 1968–71; First Sec. of Issyk-Kul Dist. Cttee. 1971; mem. Presidium, Supreme Soviet of Kirghiz S.S.R. 1971–75, Pres. Presidium 1979–81; mem. Politburo, Cen. Cttee. of Kirghiz CP 1978–; Chair. Council of Ministers, Kirghiz S.S.R. 1981–86; Deputy to Presidium, Supreme Soviet of the U.S.S.R. 1979. *Address:* c/o Council of Ministers, Frunze, Kirghizia, U.S.S.R.

DVORSKÝ, Peter; Czechoslovak opera singer; b. 25 Sept. 1951, Partizánske, Topol'čany Dist.; s. of Vendelín Dvorský and Anna Dvorská; m. Marta Varšová 1975; two d.; ed. State Conservatoire, Bratislava; studied with R. Carossi and M. di Luggo, Milan 1975–76; opera soloist, Slovak Nat. Theatre, Bratislava 1972; sang at Metropolitan Opera, New York 1977, Covent Garden, London 1978, Bolshoi Theatre, Moscow 1978, La Scala, Milan 1979; regularly at Vienna State Opera, also in Munich, Sofia, Kiev, Budapest, Geneva, Chicago, Bonn, Paris, Monte Carlo, Prague, etc.; awards include Tchaikovsky Competition, Geneva (5th Prize 1974, 1st Prize 1975), Klement Gottwald State Prize 1979, Giuseppe Verdi Medal 1979, Artist of Merit 1981, Nat. Artist 1984, Kammersänger, Vienna 1986. *Leisure interests:* hunting, music, piano, family. *Address:* Slovenské národné divadlo, Gorkého 4, 815 86, Bratislava, Czechoslovakia.

DY, Francisco Justiniano, M.D., M.P.H.; Philippine public health administrator; b. 17 Sept. 1912, Manila; m. Fé L. de la Fuente 1941; two s. two d.; ed. Univ. of Philippines and School of Hygiene and Public Health, Johns Hopkins Univ., U.S.A; Research Asst. and Instructor, Inst. of Hygiene, Univ. of Philippines 1938–41; U.S. Army 1942–45; Sr. Surgeon, U.S. Public Health Service 1945–46; Consultant and Chief of Malaria Division, U.S. Public Health Service Rehabilitation Programme in Philippines 1946–50; Prof. of Malariology and Chair. Dept. of Parasitology, Inst. of Hygiene, Univ. of Philippines 1950–52; Deputy Chief, Malaria Section, World Health Org. (WHO), Geneva 1950–51; Regional Malaria Adviser, WHO, for W. Pacific Region 1951–57; Dir. of Health Services, WHO Regional Office for W. Pacific 1958–66, Regional Dir. of WHO for W. Pacific 1966–79, Regional Dir. Emer. 1979–; Prof. of Community Medicine, Univ. of Philippines 1969–; mem. Nat. Research Council of Philippines; mem. WHO Expert Advisory Panel on Malaria 1979–; Distinguished Service Star (Philippines), Legion of Merit, with Oak Leaf Cluster (U.S.A.), Distinguished Order of Diplomatic Service Heung-in Medal (Republic of Korea) 1979, Ancient Order of Sikatuna Medal (Philippines) 1979, and other decorations. *Leisure interest:* cooking. *Address:* Regional Office for the Western Pacific, World Health Organization, P.O. Box 2932, Manila (Office); 901 E. de los Santo Avenue, Quezon City, Philippines (Home). *Telephone:* 521-8421 (Office); 98-47-39 (Home).

DYBENKO, Nikolai Kirillovich, CAND. ECON. SC.; Soviet politician and diplomatist; b. 1928; ed. Siberian Mining and Metallurgical Inst., CPSU Cen. Cttee. Higher Party School; engineer, sr. foreman in number of factories 1952–55; mem. CPSU 1951–; Head of section, Sec., Pres., First Sec. Regional Cttee. 1955–64; First Sec. Novosibirsk City Cttee. of CPSU 1964–66; Sec. of Novosibirsk Dist. Cttee. of CPSU 1966–73; work on CPSU Cen. Cttee. 1973–78; Second Sec. of Cen. Cttee. of Lithuanian CP 1978–86; Amb. to Mozambique 1986–; Deputy to U.S.S.R. Supreme Soviet 1981–; cand. mem. of CPSU Cen. Cttee. 1986–. *Address:* U.S.S.R. Embassy, Maputo, Mozambique.

DYBKJAER, Lone; Danish politician; b. 23 May 1940, Copenhagen; ed. Tech. Univ. of Denmark; Sec., Acad. of Tech. Sciences 1964–66, Medico-Tech. Cttee. 1966–70; Head Information Secr., Tech. Univ. of Denmark 1970–77; Adviser, Geotechnical Inst. 1978–79; Chair. Parl. Energy Policy Cttee. 1984–87, Parl. nine-mem. Cttee. on Tech. Bds. 1986–; Radical Liberal Party Spokesperson on Energy, Labour Market and Environmental Questions; Minister of the Environment 1988–. *Address:* Ministry of the Environment, Slotsholmsgade 12, 1216 Copenhagen K, Denmark. *Telephone:* (01) 12-76-88.

DYLAN, Bob; American composer and singer; b. Robert Zimmerman 24 May 1941, Duluth, Minn.; ed. Univ. of Minnesota; best known for composition and interpretation of pop, country and folk music; self-taught on harmonica, guitar, piano, autoharp; performer numerous tours and concerts 1960–66, 1971, 1974, 1975, 1976, 1978–80, 1981; devised and popularized folk-rock 1965; f. new group The Travelling Wilburys 1988. *Numerous songs include:* Blowin' in the Wind, Don't Think Twice It's All Right, A Hard Rain's A-gonna Fall, She Belongs to Me, It's All over Now Baby Blue, The Times They Are A-changing, Just Like a Woman, I'll Be Your Baby Tonight, I Shall Be Released, Lay, Lady, Lay, If Not for You, Mr. Tambourine Man, Like a Rolling Stone, Simple Twist of Fate, Forever Young, Mozambique, Hurricane, Knockin' on Heaven's Door, Gotta Serve Somebody, etc.; albums include: Blonde on Blonde, The Freewheelin' Bob Dylan, Highway 61 Revisited, Nashville Skyline, New Morning, Blood on the Tracks, Desire, Slow Train Coming, Infidels, Empire Burlesque, Knocked out Loaded, Down in the Groove 1988, Dylan and the Dead (with Grateful Dead) 1989; has acted in films, Eat the Document, Pat Garrett and Billy the Kid, Renaldo and Clara (also directed), Hearts of Fire 1986 and Concert for Bangladesh; Hon. D. Mus. (Princeton) 1970. *Publications:* Tarantula 1966, 1971, Writings and Drawings 1973, The Songs of Bob Dylan 1966–1975, Lyrics 1962–1985. *Address:* P.O. Box 870, Cooper Station, New York, N.Y. 10276-0870, U.S.A.

DYMSHYTS, Venyamin Emmanuilovich; Soviet engineer and politician; b. 28 Sept. 1910; ed. Higher Tech. School, Moscow; Mem. CPSU 1937–; in metallurgical construction 1931–50; Deputy Minister construction enterprises in metallurgical and chemical industries 1950–57; Chief Engineer (Construction), Bhilai Steel Plant, India 1957–59; Chief of Dept., State Planning Cttee. 1959–61, First Deputy Chair. 1961–62, Chair. 1962; Chair. Econ. Council U.S.S.R. 1962–65; Chair. U.S.S.R. State Cttee. for Material and Tech. Supplies 1965–76; a Vice-Chair., U.S.S.R. Council of Ministers 1962–86; mem. Cen. Cttee. CPSU 1961–; Deputy to Supreme Soviet 1962–; State Prize 1946, 1950, Order of Lenin (four times), Order of the Red Banner of Labour (twice), Hero of Socialist Labour (U.S.S.R.) and seven other decorations. *Address:* c/o State Cttee. for Material and Technical Supplies, 5 Orlikov pereulok, Moscow, U.S.S.R.

DYREMOSE, Henning, M.B.A.; Danish politician; b. 22 Dec. 1945, Holstebro; s. of Christian Dyremose; ed. Copenhagen School of Econs. and Business Admin.; fmr. teacher, Copenhagen School of Polytechnics; fmr. man. consultant; joined NOVO pharmaceutical group 1974; mem. Folketing (Parl.) 1979–84; Policy Spokesman, Conservative Parl. Group 1982–84; Marketing Dir. NOVO Enzymes Div. 1984–86; Minister of Labour 1986–. *Address:* Ministry of Labour, Laksegade 19, 1063 Copenhagen K, Denmark. *Telephone:* (01) 92-59-00.

DYSON, Freeman John, F.R.S.; American physicist; b. 15 Dec. 1923, Crowthorne, England; s. of late Sir George Dyson and Lady Mildred (Atkey) Dyson; m. 1st Verena Huber 1950 (divorced 1958), 2nd Imme Jung 1958; one s. five d.; ed. Cambridge and Cornell Univs; Fellow of Trinity Coll., Cambridge 1946; Warren Research Fellow, Birmingham Univ. 1949;

Prof. of Physics, Cornell Univ. 1951–53; Prof., Inst. for Advanced Study, Princeton 1953–; Chair. Fed. of American Scientists 1962; mem. U.S. Nat. Acad. of Sciences 1964–; Hon. D.Sc. (City Univ., U.K.) 1981; Gifford Lecturer, Aberdeen 1985; Heineman Prize, American Inst. of Physics 1965, Lorentz Medal, Royal Netherlands Acad. 1966, Hughes Medal, Royal Soc. 1968, Max Planck Medal, German Physical Soc. 1969, Harvey Prize, Israel Inst. of Tech. 1977, Wolf Prize (Israel) 1981. *Publications:* Disturbing the Universe 1979, Weapons and Hope 1984, Origins of Life 1986, Infinite in All Directions 1988; papers in The Physical Review, Journal of Mathematical Physics, etc. *Address:* Institute for Advanced Study, Princeton, N.J. 08540, U.S.A. *Telephone:* (609)734-8055.

DYSON, James, M.A., SC.D., F.INST.P., F.R.S.; British scientific officer (retd.); b. 10 Dec. 1914; s. of George Dyson and Mary G. (Bateson) Dyson; m. 1st Ena L. Turner (dissolved 1948), one d.; m. 2nd Marie F. Chant 1948 (died 1967); m. 3rd Rosamund P. G. Shuter 1975; ed. Queen Elizabeth School, Kirkby Lonsdale and Christ's Coll. Cambridge; student apprentice BT-H Co. Rugby 1936–39, Research Eng. 1939–46; Consultant (Optics), AEI Research Labs. Aldermaston 1946–63; Supt. Div. of Mechanical and Optical Metrology, Nat. Physical Lab. 1963–74, Deputy Chief Scientific Officer 1975–76; Hon. Fellow, Royal Microscopial Soc. *Publications:* Interferometry 1969; papers on applied optics in learned journals. *Address:* 6 Rectory Close, Tadley, Basingstoke, Hants., RG26 6PH, England.

DZHELEPOV, Venedikt Petrovich; Soviet nuclear physicist; b. 1913, Moscow; ed. Leningrad Polytech. Inst; mem. CPSU 1949–; mem. of staff at U.S.S.R. Acad. of Sciences Inst. of Physics and Tech. 1941–43; at Inst. of Atomic Energy 1943–48; Deputy Dir. of U.S.S.R. Acad. of Sciences Inst. of Nuclear Problems 1948–56; Dir. of a lab. at Jt. Inst. for Nuclear Research, Dubna 1956–; work on applications of nuclear physics to medicine 1965–; Corresp. mem. of U.S.S.R. Acad. of Sciences 1966–; U.S.S.R. State Prize 1961, 1963, Order of Lenin, Order of Red Banner of Labour. *Address:* Academy of Sciences of U.S.S.R., Moscow V-71, Leninsky Pr. 14, U.S.S.R.

DZHIGARKHANIAN, Armen Borisovich; Soviet stage and film actor; b. 1935, Armenia; ed. Yerevan Theatre Inst.; actor with Stanislavsky Russian Drama Theatre in Yerevan 1955–67; with Moscow Lenin Komsomol Theatre 1967–69, with Mayakovsky Theatre 1969–; Armenian S.S.R. State Prize 1975, 1979. *Roles include:* Levinson in Fadeev's Thunder, Stanley in Tennessee Williams's Streetcar Named Desire, Socrates and Nero in Radzinsky's Chats with Socrates and the Theatre in the time of Nero and Seneca; has also starred in a number of films. *Address:* Mayakovsky Theatre, Moscow, U.S.S.R.

DZYUBA, Ivan Mikhailovich; Soviet literary critic; b. 26 July 1931, Mykolavka, Ukraine; ed. Donetsk Pedagogical Inst., research at Shevchenko Inst. of Literature; about 100 articles published since 1950; Ed. various journals published by Ukrainian State Publishing House; published An Ordinary Man or a Petit-Bourgeois as well as numerous Samizdat articles in 1960s; expelled from Writers' Union 1969 after publication of Internationalism or Russification? (Amsterdam 1973, New York 1974); sentenced to 5 years' imprisonment 1973; recanted and released Nov. 1973.

E

EABORN, Colin, F.R.S.; British scientist and professor of chemistry; b. 15 March 1923, Cheshire; s. of Tom Stanley Eaborn and Caroline Eaborn; m. Joyce Thomas 1949; ed. Ruabon Grammar School, Clwyd, Univ. Coll. of N. Wales, Bangor; worked at Univ. of Leicester 1947–62 (Asst. Lecturer 1947–50, Lecturer 1950–57, Reader in Chem. 1957–62); at Univ. of Sussex 1962–, Prof. of Chem. 1962–, Dean of School of Molecular Sciences 1964–68, 1978–79, Pro-Vice Chancellor (Science) 1968–73; Research Assoc., Univ. of Calif. at Los Angeles 1950–51; Robert A. Welch Visiting Scholar, Rice Univ., Tex. 1961–62, Erskine Fellow, Univ. of Canterbury, N.Z. 1965; Distinguished Prof. of Chem., New Mexico State Univ. 1973, Commonwealth Fellow and Visiting Prof. of Chem., Univ. of Victoria, B.C., Canada 1976; Hon. Sec., Chemical Soc. 1964–71; mem. Council Royal Soc. 1978–80, 1988–; Regional Ed., Journal of Organometallic Chem. 1963–; Award for Organometallic Chem. 1974, Ingold Medal 1976 (both Royal Soc. of Chem.). *Publications:* Organosilicon Compounds 1960, The Synthesis and Reactions of the Carbon-Silicon Bond (in Organometallic Compounds of the Group IV Elements, Pt. 1) 1968, over 440 research papers in scientific journals. *Address:* School of Chemistry and Molecular Sciences, University of Sussex, Brighton, BN1 9QJ, England (Office). *Telephone:* (0273)-606755.

EAGLE, Harry, A.B., M.D.; American researcher in cell biology; b. 13 July 1905, New York; s. of Louis and Sadie (née Kushnoy) Eagle; m. Hope Whaley 1928; one d.; ed. Johns Hopkins Univ. and Johns Hopkins Medical School; Asst. Instructor Dept. Medicine, Johns Hopkins Medical School 1928–32; Nat. Research Fellow, Harvard 1932–33; Asst. Prof. Microbiology, Univ. of Pa. Medical School 1933–36; U.S. Public Health Service 1936–61; Dir. Venereal Disease Research Lab. and Lab. of Experimental Therapeutics, Johns Hopkins School of Hygiene and Public Health, and the Public Health Service 1936–48, Adjunct Prof. of Bacteriology, Johns Hopkins School of Hygiene and Public Health 1946–48; Scientific Dir., Research Branch, Nat. Cancer Inst. 1947–49; Chief, Section on Experimental Therapeutics at Nat. Microbiological Inst., Nat. Inst. of Health 1949–59, Laboratory of Cell Biology at Nat. Inst. of Allergy and Infectious Diseases 1959–61; Prof. and Chair., Dept. of Cell Biology, Albert Einstein Coll. of Medicine, N.Y. 1961–71, Div. of Biological Sciences 1968–71, Univ. Prof. 1971–, Dir. Cancer Research Center 1972–86, Deputy Dir. 1986–, Assoc. Dean for Scientific Affairs 1974–; Harvey Lecturer 1959; Trustee, Microbiological Foundation (Waksman); mem. numerous advisory cttees.; mem. numerous socs. including Nat. Acad. of Sciences, American Acad. of Arts and Sciences, Soc. of American Microbiologists (Pres. 1957–58), American Acad. of Microbiology, American Asscn. of Immunologists (Pres. 1964–65), American Asscn. of Cancer Research (on Bd. of Dirs. 1963–66); Hon. M.Sc. (Yale), Hon. D.Sc. (Wayne), (Duke Univ.) 1981, (Rockefeller Univ.) 1982; Eli Lilly Award in Microbiology 1936, Presidential Certificate of Merit 1948, Borden Award, American Asscn. of Medical Colls. 1964, Albert Einstein Commemorative Award 1968, Modern Medicine Award 1972, Louisa Gross Horwitz Award 1973, Sidney Farber Medical Research Award 1974, Johns Hopkins Soc. of Scholars Award 1975, Einstein Hon. Alumnus Award 1976, Hubert H. Humphrey Cancer Research Centre Award 1982, Waterford Int. Biomedical Science Award 1983, E. B. Wilson Award 1984, Nat. Medal of Science 1987. *Publications:* studies relating to: Bacterial physiology; Immunochemistry: serodiagnosis of syphilis, blood coagulation; Chemotherapy: syphilis, trypanosomiasis and tropical diseases; Detoxification of metal poisoning; Mode of action of antibiotics; Cell and tissue culture. *Address:* Albert Einstein College of Medicine, Eastchester Road and Morris Park Avenue, New York, N.Y. 10461 (Office); 370 Orienta Avenue, Mamaroneck, N.Y. 10543, U.S.A. (Home). *Telephone:* (212)430-2302 (Office); (914)OW 8-8218 (Home).

EAGLEBURGER, Lawrence Sidney, M.S.; American government official; b. 1 Aug. 1930, Milwaukee, Wis.; s. of late Dr. Leon S. and Helen M. Eagleburger; m. Marlene Ann Heinemann 1966; three s.; ed. Univ. of Wisconsin; joined U.S. foreign service 1957; Third Sec., Tegucigalpa, Honduras 1957–59; Dept. of State 1959–62; Second Sec., Belgrade, Yugoslavia 1962–65; Dept. of State 1965–66; mem. Nat. Security Council staff 1966–67; Special Asst. to Under-Sec. of State 1967–68; Politicial Adviser, U.S. Mission to NATO 1969–71; Dept. Asst. Sec. of Defense, Internal Security Affairs 1971–72, Acting Asst. Sec. of Defense, Internal Security Affairs 1973, Exec. Asst. to Sec. of State 1973–77; Deputy Asst. to Pres. for Nat. Security Operations 1973; Deputy Under-Sec. of State for Man., Exec. Asst. to Sec. of State 1975–77; Amb. to Yugoslavia 1977–81; Asst. Sec. of State for European Affairs 1981–82, Under-Sec. of State for Political Affairs 1982–84; Deputy Sec. of State March 1989–; Prof. (part-time) Univ. of S. Carolina 1984– (Distinguished Visiting Prof. of Int. Studies 1984); Pres. Kissinger Assocs. Inc. July 1984–; mem. Bd. ITT Corpn. 1984–, Josephson Int. Mutual Life Insurance Co. of N.Y., LBS Bank; President's Award for Distinguished Civil Service, Dept. of Defence Distinguished Service Medal. *Address:* Kissinger Associates Inc., 350 Park Avenue, New York, N.Y. 10022, U.S.A.

EAGLETON, Thomas Francis, LL.B.; American lawyer and politician; b. 4 Sept. 1929; ed. Amherst Coll. and Harvard Univ.; admitted to Mo. Bar 1953; pvt. law practice, St. Louis 1953–56; Circuit Attorney, St. Louis 1957–60; Attorney-Gen., State of Mo. 1961–65, Lieut.-Gov. 1965–68; Senator from Missouri 1969–87; selected as candidate for Vice-Presidency but later resigned 1972; Democrat. *Address:* c/o SD-197, Dirksen Senate Office Building, Washington, D.C. 20510, U.S.A.

EALES, Lennox, M.D., F.R.C.P.; South African professor of medicine; b. 16 May 1918, Plumstead, Cape; s. of William Clarence Eales and Hilda Mary Webber; m. Irene Grace (née Gee) Eales 1946; one s. two d.; ed. Rondebosch and Univ. of Cape Town; Assoc. Prof. of Clinical Medicine, Univ. of Cape Town 1957–64, Prof. 1964–83, Emer. Prof. 1983–, Dir. U.C.T./CSIR Renal Metabolic Research Group 1957–67, U.C.T./MRC Porphyria Research Group 1967–83; Nuffield Dominion Medical Fellowship 1946, Rockefeller Fellowship 1956, U.C.T. Fellowship for Distinguished Research 1963. *Publications:* scientific publs. on clinical nutrition, porphyria and renal diseases. *Leisure interests:* reading, fishing, growing dahlias, indigenous trees, proteas and ericas. *Address:* Silvermine Village, Private Bag 1, Noordhoek 7985, South Africa. *Telephone:* (021) 89-1738.

EAMES, Most Rev. Robert Henry Alexander, PH.D.; British ecclesiastic; b. 27 April 1937; s. of William E. Eames and Mary E. T. Eames; m. Ann C. Daly 1966; two s.; ed. Methodist Coll., Belfast, Queen's Univ., Belfast and Trinity Coll., Dublin; Research Scholar and Tutor, Faculty of Laws, Queen's Univ., Belfast 1960–63; Curate Asst., Bangor Parish Church 1963–66; Rector, St. Dorothea's, Belfast 1966–74; Examining Chaplain to Bishop of Down 1973; Rector, St. Mark's, Dundela 1974–75; Bishop of Derry and Raphoe 1975–80; Bishop of Down and Dromore 1980–86; Archbishop of Armagh and Primate of All Ireland 1986–; Select Preacher, Oxford Univ. 1986–87, Cambridge Univ. 1989; Irish Repub., Anglican Consultative Council 1984, mem. Standing Cttee. 1985; Chair. Archbishop of Canterbury's Comm. on Communion and Women in the Episcopate. *Publications:* A Form of Worship for Teenagers 1965, The Quiet Revolution—Irish Disestablishment 1970, Through Suffering 1973, Thinking through Lent 1978, Through Lent 1984 and contributions to New Divinity, Irish Legal Quarterly, Criminal Law Review, Northern Ireland Legal Quarterly, Univ. Review and The Furrow. *Address:* The See House, Cathedral Close, Armagh, BT61 7EE, Northern Ireland.

EANES, Gen. António dos Santos Ramalho; Portuguese army officer and politician; b. 25 Jan. 1935, Alcains; s. of Manuel dos Santos Eanes and Maria do Rosario Ramalho; m. Maria Manuela Duarte Neto Portugal 1970; two s.; ed. High School, Castelo Branco, Higher Inst. of Applied Psychology, Lisbon Faculty of Law; enlisted in Army School 1953; Commissioned to Portuguese India 1958–60, Macau, Mozambique 1962–66, Operations Officer of Light Infantry Battalion, Mozambique 1966–67, Information Officer, Portuguese Guinea (Guinea-Bissau) 1969–73, Angola 1973–74; Physical Education Instructor, Mil. Acad. 1968; Dir. of Dept. of Cultural and Recreational Affairs 1973; rank of Second Lieut. 1957, Lieut. 1959, Capt. 1961, Major 1970, Gen. 1978; involved in leadership of mil. movements finally contesting mil. apparatus and colonial wars 1968–74; after April Revolution named to first 'Ad-hoc' Cttee. for mass media June 1974; Dir. of Programmes of Portuguese TV June-Sept. 1974, Chair. of Bd. of Dirs. of TV co., resigned after accusation of 'probable implication' in abortive counter-coup March 1975, cleared after inquiry; rank of Lieut.-Col.; mem. Cttee. restructuring 5th Div., Gen. Staff Armed Forces; Army Chief of Staff (with temporary rank of Gen.) 1975–76; mem. of Mil. Cttee. of Council of Revolution; responsible for Constitutional Law approved Dec. 1975; Col. 1976; Pres. of Portugal 1976–86; Chair. of Council of Revolution; C.-in-C. of Armed Forces 1976–80, 1980–81; Leader, Portuguese Democratic Renewal Party 1986–87; War Cross 2nd class, Silver Medal for Distinguished Services with Palm, Silver Medal for Exemplary Behaviour, Commemorative Medal of the Portuguese Armed Forces, Degree of Knight of Mil. Order of Avis. *Address:* c/o Partido Renovador Democrático, Travessa do Fala Só 9, 1200 Lisbon, Portugal. *Telephone:* 323997.

EARLE, Arthur Frederick, PH.D.; Canadian economist and management consultant; b. 13 Sept. 1921, Toronto, Ont.; s. of Frederick Charles Earle and Hilda Mary (née Brown); m. Vera Domini Lithgow 1946; two s. one d.; ed. Univ. of Toronto and London School of Economics; Royal Canadian Navy 1939–46; Canada Packers Ltd. 1946–48; Aluminium Ltd. in British Guiana, West Indies and Canada 1948–53; Treas. Alumina Jamaica Ltd. 1953–55; Sales Exec., Aluminium Union, London 1955–58; Vice-Pres. Aluminium Ltd. Sales Inc., New York 1958–61; Deputy Chair. Hoover Ltd. 1961–65, Man. Dir. 1963–65, Dir. 1961–74; Prin., London Graduate School of Business Studies 1965–72; Pres. Int. Investment Corpn. for Yugoslavia 1972–74, Boyden Consulting Group Ltd. 1974–82, Assoc., Boyden Associates 1974–82; Adviser to Pres., Canadian Devt. Investment Corpn. 1983–86; Man. and Econ. Consultant 1983–; Chair. Canadian Assen. of Friends of L.S.E.; mem. The Consumer Council 1963–68; Gov. and mem. of Council of Man. of Ditchley Foundation; Gov. Nat. Inst. of Econ. and Social

Research 1968–74; Dir. Nat. Ballet of Canada 1982–86, Rio Algom Ltd. 1983–; Gov. and Hon. Fellow, L.S.E.; Fellow, London Business School. *Publications:* numerous economic and management publs. *Leisure interest:* hill climbing. *Address:* P.O. Box 752, Niagara-on-the-Lake, Ontario, L0S 1J0, Canada (Home). *Telephone:* (416) 468-3119 (Home).

EARLE, Ion, B.A., T.D.; British discount banker (retd.); b. 12 April 1916, Neath, Glamorgan; s. of the late Stephen Earle and of Beatrice (née Blair White); m. Elizabeth Dain Stevens 1946; one s. one d.; ed. Stowe School, Univ. Coll., Oxford and Univ. of Grenoble; Head of Regional Org., Fed. of British Industries 1952–60; Chief Exec., Export Council for Europe 1960–64; Dir. British Nat. Export Council 1964–66, Deputy Dir.-Gen. 1966–71; joined Kleinwort Benson Ltd. 1972; Clive Discount Co. Ltd. 1973–81. *Leisure interests:* golf, gardening, travel. *Address:* Mackers, 69 Sea Avenue, Rustington, West Sussex, BN16 2DP, England. *Telephone:* 0903-773350.

EASON, Henry, C.B.E., J.P., B.COM., F.I.B.; British banking administrator; b. 12 April 1910, Middlesbrough; s. of late H. and F.J. Eason; m. Florence Isobel Stevenson 1939; one s. two d.; ed. Yarm and King's Coll., Univ. of Durham; barrister; Lloyds Bank Ltd. until 1939; R.A.F. (Wing Commdr.), Second World War; Sec.-Gen. Inst. of Bankers 1959–71, Vice-Pres. 1969–75, Hon. Fellow 1971. *Leisure interests:* golf, travel, reading. *Address:* 12 Redgate Drive, Hayes Common, Bromley, Kent, BR2 7BT, England.

EASTCOTT, Harry Hubert Grayson, M.S., F.R.C.S., F.R.C.O.G.; British surgeon; b. 17 Oct. 1917, Montreal, Canada; s. of Henry George Eastcott and Gladys (née Tozer) Eastcott; m. Doreen Joy Mittell 1941; four d.; ed. Latymer School, London and Medical Schools at St. Mary's Hosp., London, Middlesex Hosp., London and Harvard; jr. resident appointments 1941–43; Surgeon Lieut. R.N.V.R. 1944–46; Sr. Surgical Registrar St. Mary's Hosp., London 1947–50, Asst. Dir. Surgical Unit of Medical School 1950–54, Consultant Surgeon 1955–82, Emer. 1982–; Consultant Surgeon Royal Masonic Hosp., London 1964–80; King Edward VII Hosp. for Officers, London 1965–87; in Surgery and Vascular Surgery R.N. 1957–82; Pres. Medical Soc., London 1976 (Sec. 1963, Trustee 1987), Section of Surgery, Royal Soc. of Medicine 1977 (Sec. 1963), United Services Section 1980–82, Int. Vascular Symposium, London 1981; Sr. Vice-Pres. Royal Coll. of Surgeons 1982 (mem. Ct. of Examiners 1964–70, mem. Council 1971–83, Jr. Vice-Pres. 1981–82); fmr. Examiner in Surgery Univs. of London, Cambridge, Lagos and Queen's, Belfast; Hunterian Professorship R.C.S. 1953; Editorial Sec. British Journal of Surgery 1972–78; Hon. mem. Soc. for Vascular Surgery, U.S.A. 1974, Purkinje Soc., Czechoslovakia 1984; Hon. F.A.C.S. 1977, Hon. F.R.A.C.S. 1978, Hon Fellow American Surgical Asscn. 1981; several memorial lectures. *Publications:* Arterial Surgery 1969, A Colour Atlas of Operations upon the Internal Carotid Artery 1984; contrib. to Lancet. *Leisure interests:* music, travel and aeronautics. *Address:* 6 Upper Harley Street, Regent's Park, London, NW1 4PS (Office); 47 Chiltern Court, Baker Street, London, NW1 5SP, England (Home). *Telephone:* (01) 935 2020

EASTMAN, Dean Eric, PH.D.; American physicist, science policy consultant, and data processing executive; b. 21 Jan. 1940, Oxford, Wis.; m. Ella Mae Staley 1979; Research Staff mem. IBM, Yorktown Heights, N.Y. 1963–74, Man. Surface Physics and Photo-emission 1971–82, Dir. Advanced Packaging Tech. Lab. and Sr. Man. III-V Semi-conductor Packaging Tech. & Systems Dept. and GaAs Devices and Tech. Dept. 1982–85, STD Dir. of Devt. and Product Assurance 1985–86, IBM Research Vice-Pres. of Logic, Memory and Packaging 1986–; Govt. Adviser to numerous science orgs.; mem. N.A.S., Nat. Acad. of Eng.; APS Oliver E. Buckley Prize 1980; Fellow American Physical Soc. *Publications:* numerous articles on solid state physics in professional journals. *Address:* IBM T. J. Watson Research Center, Yorktown Heights, N.Y. 10598 (Office); 806 Pines Bridge Road, Ossining, N.Y. 10562, U.S.A. (Home).

EASTMAN, Ernest, M.I.A.; Liberian diplomatist and politician; b. 27 March 1930, Monrovia; s. of H. Nathan Eastman and Adeliue Payne; m. Salma Mohammedali; four s. five d.; ed. Coll. of West Africa, Oberlin Coll., Ohio, Columbia Univ., New York; Dir. Bureau of Afro-Asian Affairs (Dept. of State) 1957–64; Under-Sec. of State for Admin. 1964–67; Under Sec. of State 1968–72; Amb. to East Africa (Kenya, Lesotho, Madagascar, Tanzania, Uganda, Zambia) 1972–74; Amb. to the Far East (Japan, Repub. of Korea, Democratic People's Repub. of Korea, Philippines, Indonesia, India) 1974–77; Sec.-Gen. Mano River Union (Economic and Customs Union for the Repubs. of Liberia, Sierra Leone and Guinea) 1977–83; Minister of Foreign Affairs 1983–85; mem. special missions to the Presidents of Dahomey, Niger, Guinea, Ivory Coast, Gambia, and U.S.A.; mem. official del. to several int. confs. of the O.A.U., U.N. and Non-Aligned Movement; several decorations including Knight Great Band, Humane Order of African Redemption, several European and African decorations. *Publications:* A History of the State of Maryland in Liberia 1957, many newspaper articles on international affairs. *Address:* c/o Ministry of Foreign Affairs, P.O.B. 9002, Monrovia, Liberia.

EASTMAN, Harry Claude MacColl, PH.D., F.R.S.C.; Canadian professor of economics; b. 29 July 1923, Vancouver; s. of Samuel Mack and Antonia Françoise (née Laribe) Eastman; m. Sheila MacQueen 1949; three d.; ed,

Int. School, Geneva, Dauntsey's School, Wiltshire, Humberside Coll. Inst., Toronto and Univs. of Toronto, Sask. and Chicago; served with Royal Canadian Air Force 1943–45; Prof. of Econs., Univ. of Toronto 1963–, Vice-Pres. (Research and Planning) 1977–81; Chair. (Fed.) Comm. of Inquiry on the Pharmaceutical Industry; mem. Canadian Nat. Comm. for UNESCO 1957–60, Canadian Political Science Asscn. (Sec. and Treas. 1955–65), Int. Econ. Asscn. (mem. Exec. Cttee. 1968–74), Canadian Econs. Asscn. (Pres. 1971–72). *Address:* 11 Maclennan Avenue, Toronto, Ont. M4W 2Z1 (Home); 150 St. George Street, Toronto, Ont. M5S 1A1, Canada (Office).

EASTON, David, B.A., PH.D., F.R.S.C.; Canadian professor of political science; b. 24 June 1917, Toronto; s. of Albert Easton and Mary Easton; m. Sylvia Johnstone 1942; one s.; ed. Univ. of Toronto and Harvard Univ.; Teaching Fellow Dept. of Govt. Harvard Univ. 1944–47; Asst. Prof. Dept. of Political Science Univ. of Chicago 1947–53, Assoc. Prof. 1953–55, Prof. 1955–, Andrew MacLeish Distinguished Service Prof. 1969–82, Prof. Emer. 1982–; Sir Edward Peacock Prof. of Political Science Queen's Univ., Kingston, Ont. 1971–80; Distinguished Prof. of Political Science Univ. of Calif., Irvine 1981–; Pres. American Political Science Asscn. 1968–69; Int. Cttee. on Social Science Documentation 1969–71; Chair. Bd. of Trustees Acad. of Ind. Scholars 1979–81; Co-Chair. Western Center, American Acad. of Arts and Sciences 1984–, Vice-Pres. of Acad. 1984–; Fellow Center for Advanced Study in the Behavioral Sciences, Stanford 1957–58, American Acad. of Arts and Sciences 1962–; Ford Prof. of Governmental Affairs 1960–61; Hon. LL.D. (McMaster) 1970, (Kalamazoo) 1972. *Publications:* The Political System: An Inquiry into the State of Political Science 1953, A Framework for Political Analysis 1965, A Systems Analysis of Political Life 1965, Varieties of Political Theory (Ed.) 1966, Children in the Political System: Origins of Political Legitimacy (with J. Dennis) 1969, plus several reports of educ. cttees. chaired by him. *Address:* University of California, School of Social Sciences, Irvine, Calif. 92717, U.S.A. *Telephone:* (714) 856-6132.

EASTWOOD, Clint; American actor and film director; b. 31 May 1930, San Francisco; s. of Clinton and Ruth Eastwood; m. Maggie Johnson 1953 (divorced); one s. one d.; ed. Los Angeles City Coll.; worked as lumberjack, Ore.; army service; appeared in TV series Rawhide 1959–65; owner Malpaso Productions 1969–; mem. Nat. Arts Council 1973; Mayor of Carmel 1986–88; Legion d'honneur. *Films appeared in include:* Revenge of the Creature 1955, Francis in the Navy 1955, Lady Godiva 1955, Tarantula 1955, Never Say Goodbye 1956, The First Travelling Saleslady 1956, Star in the Dust 1956, Escapade in Japan 1957, Ambush at Cimarron Pass 1958, Lafayette Escadrille 1958, A Fistful of Dollars 1964, For a Few Dollars More 1965, The Good, the Bad and the Ugly 1966, The Witches 1967, Hang 'Em High 1968, Coogan's Bluff 1968, Where Eagles Dare 1969, Paint Your Wagon 1969, Kelly's Heroes 1970, Two Mules for Sister Sara 1970, The Beguiled 1971, Play Misty for Me (also dir.) 1971, Dirty Harry 1971, Joe Kidd 1972, High Plains Drifter (also dir.) 1973, Magnum Force 1973, Thunderbolt and Lightfoot 1974, The Eiger Sanction (also dir.) 1975, The Outlaw Josey Wales (also dir.) 1976, The Enforcer 1976, The Gauntlet (also dir.) 1978, Every Which Way But Loose 1978, Escape from Alcatraz 1979, Bronco Billy (also dir.) 1980, Any Which Way You Can 1980, Firefox (also dir.) 1982, Honky Tonk Man (also dir.) 1982, Sudden Impact (also dir.) 1983, Tightrope 1984, City Heat 1984, Pale Rider 1985 (also dir.), Heartbreak Ridge 1986 (also dir.), dir. film Breezy 1973, Bird 1988 (Golden Globe Award for Best Dir. 1989), The Dead Pool 1988. *Address:* Warner Brothers Studio, Burbank, Calif. 91522; Carmel, Calif., U.S.A. (Home).

EASUM, Donald B., M.P.A., PH.D.; American diplomatist; b. 27 Aug. 1923, Culver, Ind.; s. of Chester and Norma Brown Easum; m. Augusta Pentecost 1954; three s. one d.; ed. Univ. of Wisconsin, Princeton and London Univs.; Reporter New York Times 1949; joined Foreign Service 1953; held diplomatic posts in Nicaragua 1955–57, Indonesia 1957–59, Office of Sec. of State 1959–61, Senegal 1963–66, Niger 1966–67; Exec. Sec. Agency for Int. Devt., Dept. of State 1961–63; Staff Dir. Interdept. Group for Inter-American Affairs 1969–71; Amb. to Upper Volta 1971–73; Asst. Sec. of State for African Affairs 1974–75; Amb. to Nigeria March 1975–79; Pres. African-American Inst., New York 1979–. *Publications:* articles on Argentina and U.S.-African relations. *Leisure interests:* music, tennis, table tennis, gardening. *Address:* African-American Institute, 833 United Nations Plaza, New York, N.Y. 10017, U.S.A.

EATON, George, F.C.A.; Irish management consultant; b. 11 Jan. 1942, Cork; s. of Thomas J. V. Eaton and Catherine Hannon; m. Ellen Patricia O'Grady 1966; one d.; ed. Christian Brothers Coll., Cork, The Inst. of Chartered Accountants, Ireland; with Touche Ross, Chartered Accountants, Cork 1964–66; Chief Accountant, Seafield Fabrics, Youghal 1966–67; Deputy Man. Dir. Gen. Fabrics Ltd., Athlone 1967–75; Sr. Partner Eaton Dowd, Man. Consultants 1976–; Chair. Portuguese Irish Econ. Asscn. 1987–; Pres. The Chambers of Commerce of Ireland 1985–87. *Publication:* Introducing Ireland 1989. *Leisure interests:* history, genealogy, reading, writing. *Address:* 2 Fitzwilliam Place, Dublin 2; 15 Custume Place, Athlone, Ireland. *Telephone:* 353.1.611911 (Dublin); 353.902.78531 (Athlone).

EBAN, Abba, M.A.; Israeli politician; b. (as Aubrey Solomon) 2 Feb. 1915, Cape Town, South Africa; s. of Avram Solomon and Alida Solomon; m. Susan Ambache 1945; one s. one d.; ed. Queens' Coll., Cambridge; Research Fellow and Tutor for Oriental Languages, Pembroke Coll. 1938; apptd. Liaison Officer of Allied H.Q. with the Jewish population in Jerusalem for training volunteers 1942; Chief Instructor at the Middle East Arab Centre in Jerusalem 1944; entered service of Jewish Agency 1946; apptd. Liaison Officer with UN Special Comm. on Palestine 1947; apptd. by the Provisional Govt. of Israel as its rep. in the UN 1948, Perm. Rep. 1949-59, Vice-Pres. Gen. Assembly 1953; Amb. to U.S.A. 1950-59; mem. Knesset 1959-88; Minister without Portfolio 1959-60, Minister of Educ. and Culture 1960-63, Deputy Prime Minister 1963-66, Minister of Foreign Affairs 1966-74; Guest Prof. Columbia Univ. 1974; on-screen Commentator and Chief Consultant, TV series Civilization and the Jews 1984; Pres. Weizmann Inst. of Science 1958-66; Vice-Pres. UN Conf. on Science and Tech. in Advancement of New States 1963, mem. UN Advisory Cttee. on Science and Tech. for Devt.; mem. Inst. for Advanced Study, Princeton Univ. 1978; Fellow World Acad. of Arts and Sciences, Fellow American Acad. of Arts and Sciences, Hon. L.H.D., Hon. Ph.D., Hon. Dr. (Univs. of New York, Boston, Maryland, Cincinnati, Temple, Brandeis, Yeshiva, etc.). *Publications:* The Modern Literary Movement in Egypt 1944, Maze of Justice 1946, The Toynbee Heresy 1955, Voice of Israel 1957, Tide of Nationalism 1959, Chaim Weizmann: A Collective Biography 1962, Reality and Vision in the Middle East (Foreign Affairs) 1965, My People 1968, My Country 1973, Autobiography 1978, The New Diplomacy 1983, Heritage, Civilization and the Jews 1985; numerous articles in English, French, Hebrew and Arabic. *Address:* c/o The Knesset, Jerusalem, Israel.

EBEN, Petr; Czechoslovak composer; b. 22 Jan. 1929, Žamberk; s. of Vilém Eben and Marie Ebenová-Kahlerová; m. Šárka Ebenová (née Hurníková) 1953; three s.; ed. Acad. of Music Arts, Prague; Music Dir., TV, Prague 1954; Début as pianist, Prague 1954; lecturer, Inst. for Musicology, Charles' Univ., Prague 1955-; mem. Union of Composers, Prague; Chair. Creative Section of Czech Music Soc.; numerous prizes for compositions. *Compositions include:* Sunday Music for organ, Apologia Sokratus (oratorio), Vox Clamatis (for orchestra), Pragensia (cantata), Bitter Earth (cantata for choir and organ), Landscapes of Pathmos (for organ and percussion), Desire of Ancient Things (madrigals for choir on texts by A. Symons). *Publications:* Score-Reading and Playing (co-author), contributions to journals. *Address:* El. Peškové 11, 150 00 Prague 5, Czechoslovakia. *Telephone:* 533179.

EBERHARD, Wolfram, PH.D.; American professor of sociology (retd.); b. 17 March 1909, Potsdam, Germany; s. of Prof. Gustav and Gertrud (née Müller) Eberhard; m. 1st Alide Roemer 1934 (divorced 1981), two s.; m. 2nd Dr. I. D. Raacke 1982 (died 1983); m. 3rd Irene Ohnesorge; ed. School of Oriental Languages, Berlin, and Univ. of Berlin; Prof. of Chinese History and Language Ankara Univ., Turkey 1937-48; Prof. of Sociology, Univ. of Calif. (Berkeley) 1948-76 (Prof. Emer. 1976-); Guggenheim Fellow; Corresp. mem. Acad. of Sciences and Literature, Mainz, Bavarian Acad. of Sciences, Munich, and the China Acad., Taiwan; Fellow American Folklore Asscn. *Publications:* Settlement and Social Change in Asia 1967, Moral and Social Values of the Chinese 1971, The Chinese Silver Screen 1972, Studies in Hakka Folktales 1974, History of China (revised edition) 1976, 1980, Lexikon Chinesischer Symbole 1982, China's Minorities, Yesterday and Today 1982. *Leisure interest:* ranching. *Address:* 3933 Harrison Street 204, Oakland, Calif. 94611, U.S.A. (Home). *Telephone:* (415) 654-1937 (Home).

EBERHART, Richard, M.A., LITT.D.; American poet; b. 5 April 1904, Austin, Minn.; s. of the late Alpha La Rue Eberhart and Lena Lowenstein; m. Helen Elizabeth Butcher 1941; one s. one d.; ed. Univ. of Minnesota, Dartmouth Coll., St. John's Coll., Cambridge, England and Harvard Univ.; U.S.N.R. World War II, rose to Lieut.-Commdr.; Asst. Man. Butcher Polish Co. 1946, now Hon. Vice-Pres. and mem. of Bd. of Dirs.; Master of English, St. Mark's School, Southborough, Mass. 1933-41, Cambridge School, Kendal Green, Mass. 1941-42; Visiting Prof. of English and Poet in residence, Univ. of Washington 1952-53; Prof. of English, Univ. of Connecticut 1953-54; inaugural Visiting Prof. of English, Poet in residence, Wheaton Coll., Norton, Mass. 1954-55; Resident Fellow in Creative Writing, Christian Gauss Lecturer, Princeton 1955-56; Prof. of English, Poet in residence, Dartmouth 1956-, Class of 1925 Prof. 1968-70, Emer. 1970-; Distinguished Visting Prof., Univ. of Fla., Gainesville 1974, Visiting Prof. 1975-86; Adjunct Prof., Colombia Univ. 1975; Regents' Prof., Univ. of Calif., Davis 1975; Hon. Fellow, St. John's Coll. Cambridge 1986; mem. Advisory Cttee. on Arts for Nat. Cultural Center, Washington (now John F. Kennedy Center for Performing Arts) 1959; Consultant in Poetry, Library of Congress 1959-61; mem. Nat. Inst. Arts and Letters (now American Acad. and Inst. of Arts and Letters) 1960 (mem. American Acad. 1982), Peace Corps Mission to Kenya Aug. 1966, American Acad. Arts and Sciences 1967; Founder and Pres. Poets' Theatre Inc., Cambridge, Mass. 1951; Fellow of Acad. of American Poets 1969; Consultant in American Letters 1963-66; Hon. Pres. Poetry Society of America 1972-, London Poetry Int. 1973, Third World Congress of Poets, Baltimore 1976; D.Lit. (Dartmouth) 1954, (Skidmore) 1966, (Wooster) 1969, (Colgate) 1974, D.H.L. (Franklin Pierce) 1978, (St. Lawrence Univ.) 1985; Harriet Monroe Memorial Prize 1950, Shelley Memorial Prize 1951, Bollingen Prize 1962, Pulitzer Prize 1966, Nat. Book Award 1977, Pres.'s Medallion, Univ. of Fla. 1977; Poet Laureate of New Hampshire 1979; New York quarterly Poetry Award 1980, Diploma of World Acad. of Arts and Culture, Repub. of China 1981, Sarah Jolepha Hale Award 1982; honoured by proclamation of Richard Eberhart Day (Rhode Island 14 July 1982, Dartmouth Coll. 14 Oct. 1982).

Publications: A Bravery of Earth 1930, Reading the Spirit 1937, Song and Idea 1942, Poems New and Selected 1944, Burr Oaks 1947, Brotherhood of Men 1949, An Herb Basket 1950, Selected Poems 1951, Undercliff 1953, Great Praises 1957, Collected Poems 1930-60 1960, Collected Verse Plays 1962, The Quarry 1964, Selected Poems 1930-65 1965, New Directions 1965, Thirty One Sonnets 1967, Shifts of Being 1968, Fields of Grace 1972, Collected Poems 1930-1976 1976, Collected Poems 1930-1986 1986, Poems to Poets 1976, To Eberhart from Ginsberg 1976, Survivors 1979, Of Poetry and Poets (criticism) 1979, Ways of Light 1980, New Hampshire/Nine Poems 1980, Four Poems 1980, A Celebration 1980, Chocorua 1981, Florida Poems 1981, The Long Reach 1984, Negative Capability 1986, Maine Poems 1988. *Leisure interests:* cruising on coast of Maine and swimming. *Address:* 5 Webster Terrace, Hanover, New Hampshire 03755, U.S.A. *Telephone:* (603) 643-2938.

EBERLE, Adm. Sir James Henry Fuller, G.C.B.; British naval officer (retd.); b. 31 May 1927, Bristol; s. of Victor F. Eberle, M.C.; m. Ann P. Thompson (died 1988); one s. two d.; ed. Clifton Coll. and Royal Naval Coll., Dartmouth; served in Second World War at home, East Indies and Pacific 1944-45; served in Korean War, H.M.S. Belfast and Fleet Staff Officer 1952-53; sr. officer, 100 Minesweeping Squadron 1958-59; Capt. H.M.S. Intrepid 1968-70; Defense Fellow, Univ. Coll., Oxford 1970; Flag Officer, Carriers and Amphibious Ships, and Commdr. NATO Striking Group Two 1975-76; mem. Admiralty Bd. 1977-78; Commdr.-in-Chief Fleet, Allied C.-in-C. Eastern Atlantic, C.-in-C. Channel 1979-80; C.-in-C. Naval Home Command 1981-82; retd. 1983; Dir. Royal Inst. of Int. Affairs Jan. 1984-; Freeman of Bristol 1946, London 1982. *Leisure interests:* tennis, field sports. *Address:* Royal Institute of International Affairs, Chatham House, 10 St. James's Square, London, SW1Y 4LE, England.

EBERLE, William Denman; American business executive; b. 5 June 1923, Boise, Ida.; s. of J. Louis and Clare (née Holcomb) Eberle; m. Jean C. Quick 1947; three s. one d.; ed. Stanford Univ., Harvard Univ. Graduate School of Business and Harvard Law School; admitted Ida. bar 1950; partner Richards, Haga and Eberle (law firm) 1950-60; Dir. Boise Cascade Corpn. 1952-68; mem. Ida. House of Reps. 1955-61, Speaker 1959-61; Pres., C.E.O. and Dir. American Standard Inc. 1966-71; Special Rep. of U.S. Govt. for Trade Negotiations 1971-75; Exec. Dir. Cabinet Council on Int. Econ. Policy 1974-75; Pres., C.E.O. Motor Vehicle Mfrs. Assn. 1975-77; Pres. Manchester Assocs. Ltd., SERH Inc. 1975-; Chair. EBCO Inc. 1975-, Holders Capital Corpn. 1975-; Dir. or fmr. Dir. Atlantic Group of Insurance Cos., PPG Industries, Fed. Reserve Bank of New York, Nat. Industrial Conf. Board, Hewlett Packard; Dir. Mitchell Energy and Devt. Corp., ADPACS Inc., Tertiary Inc., Vectron Inc., Engenics Inc.; Trustee Cttee. for Econ. Devt., Overseas Devt. Council, Stanford Univ.; Chair. U.S.-Japan Foundation; Vice-Chair. U.S. Council, Int. Chamber of Commerce, U.S.-Canadian Foundation; mem. UNA of U.S.A. *Address:* 53 Mount Vernon Street, Boston, Mass. 02108 (Office); 36 Masconomo Street, Manchester, Mass. 01944, U.S.A. (Home).

EBERT, James David, PH.D.; American embryologist; b. 11 Dec. 1921, Bentleyville, Pa.; s. of Alva Charles Ebert and Anna Frances Brundege; m. Alma Christine Goodwin 1946; one s. two d.; ed. Washington and Jefferson Coll. and Johns Hopkins Univ.; Faculty, M.I.T. 1950-51, Indiana Univ. 1951-55; Dir. Dept. of Embryology at Carnegie Inst. of Washington 1956-76; Hon. Prof. of Biology at Johns Hopkins Univ. and Hon. Prof. of Embryology at Johns Hopkins Univ. School of Medicine 1956-; Dir. Marine Biological Lab. 1970-75, 1977-78, Pres. 1970-78; Pres. Carnegie Inst. of Washington 1978-87; Dir. Chesapeake Bay Inst., Johns Hopkins Univ. 1987-; Chair. Assembly of Life Sciences 1973-77; Trustee, Jackson Lab.; mem. N.A.S. (Vice-Pres. 1981-); mem. Philosophical Soc.; Fellow, American Acad. of Arts and Sciences; Hon. Sc.D. (Yale, Indiana and Washington and Jefferson Coll.), Hon. LL.D. (Moravian Coll.); First Distinguished Service Award, Washington and Jefferson Coll. 1965, Eminent Scientist Award, Japan Soc. for the Promotion of Science 1972, Pres. Medal, American Inst. of Biological Sciences 1972; *Publications:* The Biology of Ageing (Co-ed.) 1960, Interacting Systems in Development (Co-author) 1965, 1970, Biology (Co-author) 1973, Tests of Teratogenicity in Vitro (Co-ed.) 1976, Mechanisms of Cell Change (Co-ed.) 1979, professional articles. *Address:* Office of the Director, Chesapeake Bay Inst., The Johns Hopkins University, Shadyside Campus, 4800 Atwell Road, Shadyside, Md. 20764-0037 (Office); Winthrop House, 4100 North Charles Street, Baltimore, Md. 2128, U.S.A. (Home). *Telephone:* (301) 867-7550 (Office).

EBERT, Peter; British (naturalized) opera director; b. 6 April 1918, Frankfurt-am-Main, Germany; s. of late Carl Ebert and Lucie Oppenheim; m. 1st Kathleen Havinden 1944, two d.; m. 2nd Silvia Ashmole 1951, five s. three d.; ed. Salem School, Germany, and Gordonstoun, Scotland; Intendant, Stadttheater Bielefeld, Germany 1973-75, Wiesbaden State Theatres 1975-77; Dir. of Productions, Scottish Opera 1965-76, Gen. Admin. 1977-80; Producer, Guild Opera Co., Los Angeles 1962-76; Hon. D.Mus. (St. Andrew's) 1979. *Leisure interest:* raising a family. *Address:* Ades House, Chailey, East Sussex, BN8 4HP, England. *Telephone:* (082572) 2441.

EBERT, Robert Higgins, D.PHIL., M.D.; American academic physician; b. 10 Sept. 1914, Minneapolis, Minn.; s. of Lilian Gilbertson and Michael H. Ebert; m. 1939; two s. one d.; ed. Univs. of Chicago and Oxford Univ.;

Prof. of Medicine, Univ. of Chicago 1955–56; Hanna Payne Prof. of Medicine, Western Reserve Univ. 1956–58; Dir. of Medicine, Univ. Hosps., Cleveland 1956–58; John H. Hord Prof. of Medicine, Western Reserve Univ. 1958–64; Chief of Medical Services, Mass. Gen. Hosp. 1964–65; Jackson Prof. of Clinical Medicine, Harvard Univ. 1964–65, Dean of Faculty of Medicine 1965–77, Dean Harvard Medical School 1965–77, Pres. Harvard Medical Center 1965–77, Caroline Shields Walker Prof. of Medicine (Emer.) 1973–77; Pres. Milbank Memorial Fund, New York 1978–84; Special Adviser to Pres., The Robert Wood Johnson Foundation, Princeton, N.J. 1985–, Special Adviser, The Commonwealth Fund, New York; Chair. The Population Council 1977–; Rhodes Scholar 1936–39. *Publications:* scientific articles on inflammation and tuberculosis. *Leisure interests:* fishing, walking. *Address:* The Robert Wood Johnson Foundation, P.O. Box 2316, Princeton, N.J. 08540, U.S.A. *Telephone:* (609) 452-8701.

EBOO PIRBHAI, Diwan Sir, Kt., O.B.E.; company director; b. 25 July 1905, Bombay; s. of Pirbhai, by his wife Kuvarbai; m. Kulsumbai, d. of Karmali Nathoo, 1925; three s. (one deceased) three d.; ed. Duke of Gloucester School, Nairobi; Rep. of the Aga Khan, Chair., H.H. Prince Aga Khan Shia Imami Ismaili Leader's Int. Forum; fmr. Pres. Muslim Assen.; mem. Nairobi City Council 1938–43; mem. Legis. Council, Kenya 1952–60, and other official bodies; granted title Count 1954 and title of Diwan 1983 by Aga Khan, Brilliant Star (Zanzibar) 1956, Order of the Crescent Cross (Comoros) 1966. *Address:* P.O. Box 40898, Nairobi; 12 Naivasha Avenue, Muthaiga, Nairobi, Kenya.

EBTEHAJ, Abol Hassan; Iranian banker and administrator; b. 29 Nov. 1899, Rasht, Iran; s. of Ebrahim and Fatima Ebtehaj; m. 1st Mariam Nabavi 1929, 2nd Azarnoosh Sani 1956; one s. one d.; ed. Paris and Beirut; joined Imperial Bank of Iran 1920; Govt. Inspector Agricultural Bank and Controller of State-owned Cos. 1936; Vice-Gov. Bank Melli Iran (Cen. Bank) 1938; Chair. and Man. Dir. Mortgage Bank 1940; Gov. Bank Melli Iran, Cen. Bank of Iran 1942–50; Chair. Persian Del. Middle East Financial and Monetary Conf., Cairo 1944; Chair. Persian Del. Bretton Woods Conf. 1944; Amb. to France 1950–52; Adviser to Man. Dir. I.M.F. 1952; Dir. Middle East Dept., I.M.F. 1953; Man. Dir. Plan Organization (Devt. Bd.), Teheran 1954–59; Chair. Econ. Comm. Baghdad Pact 1956, mem. High Econ. Council 1954–59; Founder, Chair. and Pres. Iranians' Bank (private bank, associated with Citibank, New York 1968) 1959–72, Chair. 1972–77; imprisoned under Shah's regime Nov. 1961, charges dropped and released June 1962; Founder and Chair. Iran America Int. Insurance Co. 1974–79. *Leisure interests:* reading, walking. *Address:* 4 Cumberland House, Kensington Court, London, W8 5NX, England. *Telephone:* 01-937 9922.

EBURNE, Sir Sidney (Alfred William), Kt., M.C.; British banker; b. 26 Nov. 1918, Highgate, London; s. of Alfred Edmund Eburne and Ellen Francis Eburne; m. Phoebe Freda Beeton Dilley 1942; one s. one d.; ed. Downhills School; Capt., R.A. 1939–46; joined Morgan Grenfell & Co. Ltd. 1946, Dir. 1968–75, Morgan Grenfell Holdings Ltd. 1971–75, Morgan Grenfell (Jersey) Ltd. 1972–75; Dir. of Finance, Crown Agents for Overseas Govts. and Admins. 1975, Chair. 1978–83; Man. Dir. Crown Agents 1976–77; Crown Agent 1977; Chair. Senior Crown Agent 1978–83; Dir. Abbey Capital Property Group 1978–82 and other subsidiary property cos. *Leisure interests;* golf, travelling. *Address:* Motts Farm, Eridge, Nr. Tunbridge Wells, BN3 9LJ, England.

ECCLES, 1st Viscount (cr. 1964), of Chute, 1st Baron (cr. 1962); **David McAdam Eccles,** C.H., K.C.V.O., P.C., M.A.; British politician; b. 18 Sept. 1904, London; s. of William McAdam Eccles M.S., F.R.C.S. and Anna Coralie Anstie; m. 1st Hon. Sybil Frances Dawson 1928 (died 1977); two s. one d.; m. 2nd Mary Grapo Hyde 1984; ed. Winchester and New Coll., Oxford; mem. staff Cen. Mining and Investment Corpn. 1923–39; joined Ministry of Econ. Warfare 1939; Econ. Adviser to H.M. Ambs. in Madrid and Lisbon 1939–42; Ministry of Production 1942–43; Conservative M.P. for Chippenham Div. of Wilts. 1943–62; Minister of Works 1951–54, of Educ. 1954–57; Pres. Bd. of Trade 1957–59; Minister of Educ. 1959–62; Paymaster-Gen. with responsibility for the Arts 1970–73; Chair. Trustees of British Museum 1968–70, of British Library 1973–78; Pres. World Crafts Council 1974–78. *Publications:* Wages on the Farm, 1945, Half-Way to Faith 1966, Life and Politics 1967, On Collecting 1968, The Letters of Sybil and David Eccles 1982. *Address:* 6 Barton Street, London, S.W.1; Dean Farm, Chute, nr. Andover, Hampshire, England; Four Oake Farm, Somerville, N.J., U.S.A. *Telephone:* 01-222 1387; (026) 470 210; (201) 725 0966.

ECCLES, Sir John Carew, Kt., C.H., M.B., B.S., D.PHIL., F.R.A.C.P., F.R.S.N.Z., F.A.A., F.R.S.; Australian research physiologist; b. 27 Jan. 1903, Melbourne; s. of William James and Mary (née Carew) Eccles; m. 1st Irene Frances Miller 1928 (divorced 1968), four s. five d.; m. 2nd Helena Táboříková 1968; ed. Melbourne Univ., Magdalen Coll., Oxford; Rhodes Scholar 1925; Jr. Research Fellow, Exeter Coll., Oxford 1927–32, Staines Medical Fellow 1932–34; Fellow and Tutor, Magdalen Coll., Oxford, lecturer in physiology 1934–37; Dir. Kanematsu Memorial Inst. of Pathology, Sydney, Australia 1937–43; Prof. of Physiology, Otago Univ., New Zealand 1944–51, Australian Nat. Univ., Canberra 1951–66; AMA/ERF Inst. for Biomedical Research, Chicago 1966–68; at State Univ. of N.Y. at Buffalo 1968–75; Waynflete Lecturer, Oxford 1952; Herter Lecturer, Johns Hopkins Univ., Baltimore 1955; Ferrier Lecturer, Royal Soc. 1960; Gifford Lecturer, Edinburgh University 1977–79; Foreign Hon. mem. American Acad. of

Arts and Sciences, Accad. Nazionale dei Lincei, Deutsche Akad. der Naturforscher (Leopoldina); mem. Pontifical Acad. of Sciences, American Philosophical Soc., National Acad. of Sciences, Indian Acad. of Sciences, Royal Acad. of Belgium, Max-Planck-Inst. für Biophysikalische, Chemie, Göttingen; Pres. Australian Acad. of Science 1957–61; Hon. Fellow Exeter Coll. and Magdalen Coll. Oxford, Hon. Fellow New York Acad. of Sciences; Hon. Sc.D. (Cambridge, Tasmania, Univ. British Columbia, Gustavus Adolphus Coll., Marquette, Loyola, Yeshiva, Oxford, Fribourg, Georgetown, Sukuba), Hon. M.D. (Charles Univ., Prague, Univ. of Turin), Hon. LL.D. (Melbourne); Cothenius Medal, Royal Medal, Royal Soc. 1962, Nobel Prize for Medicine 1963; Order of the Rising Sun, 2nd Class 1986. *Publications:* Reflex Activity of the Spinal Cord (in collaboration) 1932, Neurophysiological Basis of Mind 1953, Physiology of Nerve Cells 1957, Physiology of Synapses 1964, The Cerebellum as a Neuronal Machine 1967, Inhibitory Pathways of the Central Nervous System 1969, Facing Reality 1970, The Understanding of the Brain 1973, The Self and its Brain (with Sir Karl Popper) 1977, Molecular Neurobiology of the Mammalian Brain 1978, Ze. 1987 (with P. and E. McGeer), The Human Mystery 1979, Sherrington, His Life and Thought (with W. C. Gibson) 1979, The Human Psyche 1980, The Wonder of Being Human: Our Brain, Our Mind (with D. N. Robinson) 1984, Evolutionary Pinnacle: mammalian brain to human brain 1988. *Leisure interests:* philosophy, art, European travel. *Address:* Ca' a la Gra', CH 6611 Contra, Ticino, Switzerland.

ECEVIT, Bülent, B.A.; Turkish journalist and politician; b. 28 May 1925, Istanbul; s. of late Prof. Fahri Ecevit, M.P. and Nazli Ecevit; m. Rahşan Ecevit 1946; ed. Robert Coll., Istanbul, Ankara, London and Harvard Univs.; govt. official 1944–50, Turkish Press Attaché's Office, London 1946–50; Foreign News Ed., Man. Ed., later Political Dir. Ulus (Ankara) 1950–61, Political Columnist, Ulus 1956–61; M.P. (Republican People's Party) 1957–60, 1961–80; mem. Constituent Assembly 1961; Minister of Labour 1961–65; Political Columnist Milliyet 1965; Prime Minister Jan.-Nov. 1974, June–July 1977, 1978–79 (resigned Oct. 1979); Sec.-Gen. Republican People's Party 1966–71, Chair. 1972–80; detained after coup Sept. 1980, released Oct. 1980, imprisoned by mil. régime Dec. 1981–Feb. 1982 rearrested April 1982, imprisoned again Aug.–Oct. 1982; elected Chair. Democratic Left Party Jan. 1989; mem. Turkish Philosophical Soc., Turkish Language Assen., Ankara Journalists' Assen. *Publications:* Ortanin Solu (Left of Centre) 1966, Bu Düzen Değismelidir (The System Must Change) 1968, Atatürk ve Devrimcilik (Atatürk and Revolution) 1970, Sohbet (conversations), Demokratik Sol (Democratic Left) 1974, Dis Politika (Foreign Policy) 1975, Işçi-Köylü Elele (Workers and Peasants Together) 1976, Şiirler (Poems) (German, Russian, Serbian, Danish and Romanian trans.) 1976; Translations into Turkish: Gitanjali (R. Tagore) 1941, Straybirds (R. Tagore) 1943, Cocktail Party (T. S. Eliot) 1963. *Leisure interests:* art and literature. *Address:* Or-an Şehri 69/5, Ankara, Turkey (Home).

ECHANDI JIMÉNEZ, Mario, LL.D.; Costa Rican diplomatist and politician; b. 1915; ed. Univ. de Costa Rica; legal career 1938–47; Sec.-Gen. Partido Unión Nacional 1947; Amb. to U.S.A. 1950–51, 1966–68; Minister for Foreign Affairs 1951–53; Pres. of Costa Rica 1958–62; defeated candidate in Pres. election Feb. 1970. *Address:* San José, Costa Rica.

ECHEVERRÍA ALVAREZ, Lic. Luis; Mexican lawyer and politician; b. 17 Jan. 1922, Mexico, D.F.; m. Maria Esther Zuno de Echeverria; five s. two d.; ed. Univ. Nacional Autónoma de México; Pvt. Sec. to Pres. of Exec. Cttee. of Partido Revolucionario Institucional (PRI) 1940–52, also Dir. of Press and Propaganda, PRI 1949–52; Dir. of Accounts and Admin., Sec. of Marine 1952–54; Sr. Official, Sec. of Public Educ. 1954–57; Sr. Official, Cen. Exec. Cttee. of PRI 1957; Under-Sec. of Interior 1958–63, Sec. of Interior 1963–70; Asst. Prof. of Law, Univ. Nac. Autónoma de México; Pres. of Mexico 1970–76; Gen. Dir. Centre for Econ. and Social Studies of the Third World 1976–86; mem. Exec. Council UNESCO 1977, Amb. at Large 1977–78, to Australia (also accred. to New Zealand) 1979–80. *Address:* Porfirio Diaz No. 50, San Jeronimo Lídice, Magdalena Contreras, C.P. 10200 Mexico.

ECKHARDT, Sándor; Hungarian oncologist; b. 14 March 1927, Budapest; s. of Sándor Eckhardt and Irén Huszár; m. Mária Petrányi; three s.; ed. Semmelweis Medical Univ. Budapest; specialist in internal medicine 1955; training course of malignant diseases in children, Villejuif, France 1969; MRC Fellow, Chester Beatty Inst., London, 1961; Eleanor Roosevelt Cancer Research Fellow, Bethesda 1964–65; Chair. Drug Devt. Program, Hungary 1966–70; Dir. Nat. Inst. of Oncology, Budapest 1971–; Prof. Clinical Oncology, Postgraduate Univ. Medical School, Budapest 1977–; mem. Hungarian Acad. of Sciences 1984–; Chair. Trial Centre of East European countries and Program Co-ordinator of drug research 1979–; mem. Union Int. Contre le Cancer (UICC) Exec. Cttee. 1978–86, Treasurer 1986–; Sec. Gen. 14th Int. Cancer Congress 1982–86; adviser WHO Cancer Unit 1971–; mem. Medical Advisory Cttee. WHO Euro Office, Copenhagen 1974–82; mem. Scientific Council Int. Agency for Research on Cancer 1976–80, Chair. 1979–; mem. American Assen. of Cancer Research 1976–, Medical Acad. of Moscow 1979–, American Soc. of Clinical Oncology 1987–, European Soc. of Medical Oncology 1985–; Chief ed. Antitumour Drug Therapy, Budapest 1977–; Clinical ed. Oncology 1978–, Onkologie 1987–; Labour Order of Merit 1975, State Prize 1980. *Publications:* include Drug Therapy of Cancer (WHO Geneva) 1973; Dibromodulcitol 1982; Drug Development in Eastern Europe 1987; co-ed. Proceedings of the 14th

International Cancer Congress, Budapest (13 vols.) 1986. *Address:* National Institute of Oncology, 1525 Budapest, Ráth György utca 7/9, Hungary. *Telephone:* 36/1/554-411.

ECO, Umberto; Italian university professor; b. 5 Jan. 1932; s. of Giulio Eco and Giovanna Bisio; m. Renate Ramge 1962; two c.; ed. Univ. degli Studi, Turin; with Italian Television 1954-59; Asst. Lecturer in Aesthetics, Univ. of Turin 1956-63, Lecturer 1963-64; Lecturer Faculty of Architecture, Univ. of Milan 1964-65; Prof. of Visual Communications, Univ. of Florence 1966-69; Prof. of Semiotics, Milan Polytechnic 1970-71, Univ. of Bologna 1971-; Visiting Prof. New York Univ. 1969-70, 1976, Northwestern Univ. 1972, Yale Univ. 1977, 1980, 1981, Columbia Univ. 1978, 1984; Columnist on L'Espresso 1965; Ed. VS 1971-; Medicis Prize 1982, McLuhan Teleglobe Prize 1985. *Publications:* Il Problema Estetico in San Tommaso 1956, Sviluppo dell'Estetica Medioevale 1959 (as Art and Beauty in the Middle Ages 1986), Opera Aperta 1962, Diario Minimo 1963, Apocalittici e Integrati 1964, L'Oeuvre Ouverte 1965, La Struttura Assente 1968, Il Costume di Casa 1973, Trattato di Semiotica Generale 1975, A Theory of Semiotics 1976, The Role of the Reader 1979, Il Nome della Rosa (novel) 1981, Semiotics and the Philosophy of Language 1984, Sette anni di desiderio 1977-83 1984, Il pendolo di Foucault 1988. *Address:* Via Melzi d'Eril 23, Milan, Italy. *Telephone:* 34-78-06.

EDBERG, Rolf; Swedish journalist, diplomatist and administrator; b. 14 March 1912, Lysvik; s. of C. F. and Mandis Edberg; m. Astrid Persson 1937; one s. two d.; Chief Ed. Oskarshamns Nyheter 1934-37; Asst. Ed. Östgöten, Linköping 1938-40, Chief Ed. 1941-45; Chief Ed. Ny Tid, Gothenburg 1945-56; mem. Parl. 1941-44 and 1949-56; Del. to UN 1952-61; Amb. to Norway 1956-67; Gov. Province of Värmland 1967-77; Rep. to Council of Europe 1949-52, to Scandinavian Council 1953-56; Pres. Swedish Press Club 1951-53; Del. Disarmament Conf. 1962-65; Pres. Stockholm Int. Peace Inst. 1973-78; Environmental Cttee., Acad. of Sciences 1974; Hon. Ph.D. 1974. *Publications:* On the Shred of a Cloud 1966, At the Foot of the Tree 1972, Letters to Columbus 1973, On Earth's Terms 1974, A House in the Cosmos 1974, Dream of Kilimanjaro 1976, Shadows across the Savanna 1977, Land of Glistening Waters 1980, Drops of Water Drops of Life 1984, ... and they always sailed 1985, Born with the Pleiades 1987, (with Alexey Yablokov) Sunday Is Too Late, East-West dialogue 1988; and several other works on political and ecological subjects. *Address:* Hagtornsgatan 3, 652 30, Karlstad, Sweden. *Telephone:* 054-154525.

EDBERG, Stefan; Swedish tennis player; b. 19 Jan. 1966, Vastervik; won Jr. Grand Slam 1983, Milan Open 1984, San Francisco, Basle and Memphis Opens 1985, Gstaad, Basle and Stockholm Opens 1986, Australian Open 1986, 1987, Wimbledon 1988; Winner (with Anders Jarryd) Masters and French Open 1986, Australian and US Opens 1987; semi-finalist in numerous tournaments; mem. Swedish Davis Cup Team 1984, 1987.

EDDINGTON, Paul, C.B.E.; British actor; b. 18 June 1927, London; s. of Albert Clark Eddington and Frances Mary Roberts; m. Patricia Scott 1952; three s. one d.; ed. The Friends School, Sibford, Oxon., Royal Acad. of Dramatic Art with Entertainments Nat. Service Assen. (ENSA) 1944-45; repertory, Birmingham 1945-47, Sheffield 1947-52, Ipswich 1953-55; Hon. M.A. (Sheffield) 1988. *Stage appearances include:* The Tenth Man (West End début), Thark, Present Laughter 1961, War and Peace, Brand, Becket, Julius Caesar, All's Well That Ends Well, All Things Bright and Beautiful, The Fire Raisers, A Severed Head (all at Bristol Old Vic) 1962-63, also appeared in A Severed Head in New York 1964, Portrait of a Queen 1965, Jorrocks 1966, Queenie 1967, Forty Years On 1968, Long Day's Journey into Night, Journey's End 1973, Absurd Person Singular 1974, Donkeys Years, Ten Times Table, Middle Age Spread, Who's Afraid of Virginia Woolf 1981, Noises Off 1982, Lovers Dancing 1983, Forty Years On 1984, Jumpers 1985, H.M.S. Pinafore (Sir Joseph Porter) 1987, Harlequinade 1988, The Browning Version 1988, Australian tour with the Victoria State Capella; numerous TV appearances since 1955, including: The Spread of the Eagle, Gigolo and Gigolette, Quartet, Frontier, Special Branch, the Good Life (Good Neighbors in U.S.A.), Outside Edge, Hay Fever, Yes Minister, Yes Prime Minister; mem. Council, British Actors' Equity Asscn. 1972-75; Gov. Bristol Old Vic Theatre Trust 1975-84; Clarence Derwent Award for a Musical (Jorrocks) Variety Club of G.B. award for Actor of the Year (40 Years On) 1984; A.C.E. Award for actor in Comedy Series (Yes Prime Minister). *Leisure interests:* reading, listening to music, thinking about gardening. *Address:* c/o I.C.M. Ltd., 388/396 Oxford Street, London, W1N 9HE, England. *Telephone:* 01-629 8080.

EDEL, (Joseph) Leon, M.A., D. ES L.; American writer and teacher; b. 9 Sept. 1907, Pittsburgh, Pa.; s. of Simon Edel and Fanny Malamud; m. 1st Bertha Cohen 1935 (divorced 1950), m. 2nd Roberta Roberts 1950 (divorced 1979); m. 3rd Marjorie P. Sinclair 1980; ed. Yorkton Collegiate Inst., Saskatchewan, McGill Univ. and Univ. of Paris; Graduate Asst. in English, McGill Univ. 1927-28; Asst. Prof. Sir George Williams Univ., Montreal 1932-34; journalism and broadcasting 1934-43; U.S. Army 1943-47; Adjunct Prof., New York Univ. 1950-53, Assoc. Prof. 1953-55, Prof. of English 1955-66; Henry James Prof. of English and American Letters 1966-73, Prof. Emer. 1973-; Citizens Prof. of English, Hawaii Univ. 1972-78, Prof. Emer. 1978-; Visiting Fellow Humanities Research Centre, Canberra 1976; Vernon Prof. of Biography, Dartmouth Coll. 1977; Pres. U.S. PEN 1957-59; F.R.S.L. 1970, American Acad. of Arts and Sciences 1959; Sec. Nat. Inst.

of Arts and Letters 1965-67; Pres. Authors' Guild 1969-71, mem. Council Authors' Guild 1966-68; Soc. of American Historians, Modern Humanities Research Asscn., Educational Advisory Bd. Guggenheim Foundation 1967-80, Advisory Cttee. Metropolitan Museum Centenary 1969-70; Hon. mem. William Alanson White Psychoanalytic Soc. 1967-, American Acad. of Psychoanalysis; Hon. D.Litt. (Union Coll., Schenectady, N.Y., Saskatchewan Univ., McGill Univ. and Hawaii Lea Coll., Honolulu); Bronze Star Medal (U.S. Army), Pulitzer Prize (biography) 1963, Nat. Book Award (non-fiction) 1963, Nat. Inst. of Arts and Letters Gold Medal for Biography 1976, Hawaii Writers Award 1977, Nat. Arts Club Medal (for literature) 1981, Nat. Book Critics' Circle Award for Biography 1986. *Publications:* The Life of Henry James (I The Untried Years 1953, II The Conquest of London 1962, III The Middle Years 1962, IV The Treacherous Years 1969, V The Master 1972), Willa Cather (with E. K. Brown) 1953, The Psychological Novel 1955, Literary Biography 1957; Editor: The Complete Plays of Henry James 1949, Selected Letters of Henry James 1955, The Complete Tales of Henry James (12 vols.) 1962-65, The Diary of Alice James 1964, Literary History and Literary Criticism 1964, The American Scene 1968, Henry D. Thoreau 1970, Henry James: Letters (I and II) 1974-75, (III) 1980, (IV) 1984, Selected Letters 1987, Edmund Wilson: The Twenties 1975, The Thirties 1980, The Forties 1983, The Fifties 1986, Bloomsbury: A House of Lions 1979, Stuff of Sleep and Dreams (essays) 1982, Writing Lives 1984, Ed. two vols of Henry James criticism and essays 1984, Henry James, A Life 1985, The Complete Notebooks of Henry James (with Lyall H. Powers) 1986; over 450 articles and reviews. *Leisure interests:* music, book collecting, swimming. *Address:* 3817 Lurline Drive, Honolulu, Hawaii 96816, U.S.A. *Telephone:* 808-737-0766.

EDELMAN, Gerald Maurice, M.D., PH.D.; American molecular biologist; b. 1 July 1929, New York; s. of Edward and Anna Freedman Edelman; m. Maxine Morrison 1950; two s. one d.; ed. Ursinus Coll., Univ. of Pennsylvania, and The Rockefeller Univ.; Medical House Officer, Mass. Gen. Hospital 1945-55; Capt., U.S. Army Medical Corps. 1955-56; Asst. Physician, Hospital of The Rockefeller Univ. 1957-60; Asst. Prof. and Asst. Dean of Graduate Studies, The Rockefeller Univ, 1960-63, Assoc. Prof. and Assoc. Dean of Graduate Studies 1963-66, Prof. 1966-74; Vincent Astor Distinguished Prof. 1974-; Assoc. Neurosciences Research Program, Scientific Chair. 1980; Dir. Neurosciences Inst., Neurosciences Research Program 1981; mem. Biophysics and Biophysical Chemistry Study Section, Nat. Inst. of Health 1964-67, Scientific Council, Centre for Theoretical Studies 1970-72, The Harvey Society 1974-, Pres. 1975-76; mem. Nat. Acad. of Sciences, American Acad. of Arts and Sciences, American Philosophical Soc., Genetics Soc., American Chem. Soc., American Soc. of Biological Chemists, American Assen. of Immunologists, American Soc. for Cell Biology, Soc. for Developmental Biology, Alpha Omega Alpha Hon. Medical Soc., Council on Foreign Relations, A.A.A.S.; Hon. mem. Japanese Biochemical Soc., Pharmaceutical Soc. of Japan; Foreign mem. Acad. des Sciences; Fellow, N.Y. Acad. of Sciences; Trustee, Rockefeller Brothers Fund 1972-82; Non-res. Fellow and mem. Bd. of Trustees, Salk Inst. for Biological Studies; Fellow, New York Acad. of Medicine; mem. Bd. of Overseers Faculty of Arts and Sciences, Univ. of Pa.; mem. Bd. Scientific Overseers, The Jackson Laboratory; mem. Bd. of Trustees, Carnegie Inst. of Washington, mem. Advisory Cttee.; mem. Advisory Bd., The Basel Inst. for Immunology 1970-77, Chair. 1975-77; mem. Bd. of Governors, Weizmann Inst. of Science, Israel; Hon. D.Sc. (Univ. of Pa.) 1973; (Adolphus Coll., Minn.) 1975; Hon. Sc.D. (Ursinus Coll.) 1974, (Williams Coll.) 1976; Hon. M.D. (Univ. of Siena) 1974; Annual Alumni Award, Ursinus Coll. 1969, Eli Lilly Award in Biological Chem., American Chemical Soc. 1965, Spencer Morris Award, Univ. of Pa. 1954, Nobel Prize for Physiology or Medicine 1972 (with R. Porter q.v.), Albert Einstein Commem. Award of Yeshiva Univ. 1974, Buchman Memorial Award, Calif. Inst. of Tech. 1975, Rabbi Shai Shaknai Mem. Prize in Immunology and Cancer Research, Hebrew Univ.-Hadassah Medical School, Jerusalem 1977, Regents Medal of Excellence, New York 1984. *Publications:* about 325 articles in professional journals. *Leisure interests:* violin, chamber music. *Address:* The Rockefeller University, 1230 York Avenue, New York, N.Y. 10021 (Office); 35 East 85th Street, N.Y. 10028, U.S.A. (Home).

EDELMANN, Otto Karl; Austrian opera singer; b. 5 Feb. 1917, Vienna; m. Ilse-Maria Straub 1960; two s. one d.; ed. Realgymnasium and State Acad. of Music, Vienna; first opera appearances 1938; P.O.W. in U.S.S.R. two years during Second World War; mem. Vienna State Opera 1948-; with Salzburg Festival 1948-; perm. mem. Metropolitan Opera New York 1954-; took part in first Bayreuth Festival 1951; world-famous as Sachs in Die Meistersinger; Kt. Order of Dannebrog, Austrian Gold Cross of Honour for Sciences and Arts. *Leisure interests:* painting and boxing. *Address:* Wien-Kalksburg 1238, Breitenfurterstrasse 547, Austria.

EDELSTEIN, Victor; British couturier; b. 10 July 1945, London; m. Anna Maria Succi 1974; trainee designer Alexon 1962, Asst. Designer and Pattern Cutter to Biba 1967, designer Salvador 1971, Christian Dior 1975; f. Victor Edelstein Ltd. 1978-. *Leisure interests:* opera, gardening, collecting old master drawings. *Address:* 49 Princes Gate, London, S.W.7, England.

EDEN OF WINTON, Baron (Life Peer), cr. 1983, of Rushyford in the County of Durham; **John Eden,** Bt., P.C.; British politician; b. 15 Sept 1925; M.P. for Bournemouth West 1954-83; Minister of State, Ministry of

Technology July-Oct. 1970; Minister for Industry, Dept. of Trade and Industry 1970-72; Minister of Posts and Telecommunications 1972-74; Dir. Assoc. Book Publishers PLC, Cen. and Sheerwood PLC 1984-87; Del. to Council of Europe and WEU 1960-62, NATO Parliamentarians' Conf. 1962-66; mem. House of Commons Expenditure Cttee. 1974-76; Pres. Wessex Area Conservatives 1974-77, Wessex Area Young Conservatives 1978-80; Chair. House of Commons Select Cttee. on European Legislation 1976-79; Chair. Select Cttee. on Home Affairs 1981-83; Chair. Wonder World PLC 1982-, Gamlestaden PLC 1987-, Bd. of Trustees of Royal Armouries 1986-; Pres. Independent Schools' Asscn. 1969-71; Conservative. *Address:* 41 Victoria Road, London, W.8; Knoyle Place, East Knoyle, Salisbury, Wilts., England.

EDGERTON, Harold Eugene, B.S., M.S., D.SC.; American scientist, inventor and teacher; b. 6 April 1903, Fremont, Neb.; s. of Frank Eugene Edgerton and Mary (Coe) Edgerton; m. Esther May Garrett 1928; two s. one d.; ed. Univ. of Nebraska and Massachusetts Inst. of Tech.; Research Asst. M.I.T. 1927-28, Instructor 1928-32, Asst. Prof. of Electrical Eng. 1932-38, Assoc. Prof. 1938-48, Prof. 1948-66, Inst. Prof. Emer. 1966-; Inventor of electronic flash (strobe) 1931; Co-Founder, E.G. & G. (fmrly. Edgerton, Germeshausen and Grier), Vice-Pres. 1947, Chair. of Bd. 1955-66, Hon. Chair. of Bd. 1966-75; three expeditions to Einewetok for Atomic Energy Comm.; underwater camera devt. for Nat. Geographic Soc., Capt. Jacques Y. Cousteau, and Bathyscaphes FNRS 111, Trieste and Archimede; Fellow, Inst. of Electrical and Electronic Engineers, Photographic Soc. of America, Royal Photographic Soc. of Great Britain, Soc. of Motion Pictures and T.V. Engineers; mem. of numerous scientific insts. including American Acad. of Applied Science, Acad. of Underwater Arts and Sciences, American Acad. of Arts and Sciences, Nat. Acad. of Sciences, Nat. Acad. of Engineering, Woods Hole Oceanographic Inst.; Hon. Dr. Eng. (Univ. of Nebraska), Hon. LL.D. (Doane Coll., Univ. of S. Carolina) 1969, Hon. D.Sc. (Washington Univ. in St. Louis) 1979, Hon. Dr. h.c. of Humane Letters (Univ. of Lowell, Mass.) 1984, Hon. Fellowship (Univ. of Haifa) 1984; 48 awards including U.S. Camera Achievement Gold Medal 1951, E. I. duPont Gold Medal of Soc. of Motion Picture and TV Engineers 1962, Richardson Medal of Optical Soc. of America 1968, John Oliver LaGorce Gold Medal of Nat. Geographic Soc. 1968, Holley Medal, American Soc. of Mechanical Engineers 1973, Nat. Medal of Science 1973, Lockheed award for Marine Science, Marine Tech. Soc. 1978, Nikon Special Achievement Award 1979, Eastman Kodak Gold Medal, Soc. of Motion Piture and T.V. Engineers 1983, Founders Award (18th), Nat. Acad. of Eng. 1983, Outstanding Alumnus Award (Coll. of Eng., Univ. of Nebraska) 1988, Nat. Medal of Tech. 1988, Pathfinder Award, Freemont, Neb. 1988, Centennial Award (Nat. Geographic Soc.) 1988. *Publications:* Flash, Seeing The Unseen (with J. R. Killian) 1954, Electronic Flash, Strobe 1970, Moments of Vision (with J. R. Killian) 1979, Sonar Images 1985, Stopping Time: The Photographs of Harold Edgerton (Ed. Gus Kayafas) 1987, and 186 tech. articles. *Leisure interests:* nature photography (particularly humming-birds), deep-sea studies, guitar music, sonar searches for wrecks, geology. *Address:* Massachusetts Institute of Technology, Room 4-405, Cambridge, Mass. 02139, U.S.A. (Office). *Telephone:* (617) 494-8783 (Office).

EDGLEY, Michael Christopher, M.B.E.; Australian entrepreneur; b. 17 Dec. 1943, Melbourne; s. of the late Eric Edgley and of Edna Edgley (née Luscombe); m. Jeni King 1972; one s. two d.; ed. Trinity Coll., Perth; Chair. Michael Edgley Int. Pty. Ltd. 1962-, promoting a wide range of cultural, artistic and sporting events; Citizens of the Year Award for W.A. 1976. *Leisure interests:* jogging, horse racing, tennis. *Address:* Suite 6, 424 St. Kilda Road, Melbourne, Vic. 3004, Australia.

EDINBURGH, H.R.H. The Prince Philip, Duke of, Earl of Merioneth and Baron Greenwich of Greenwich in the County of London (all titles cr. 1947), created Prince of the United Kingdom of Great Britain and Northern Ireland 1957, K.G., K.T., O.M., G.B.E.; b. 10 June 1921, Corfu; s. of H.R.H. the late Prince Andrew of Greece and Denmark, G.C.V.O. and of H.R.H. the late Princess (Victoria) Alice Elizabeth Julia Marie, R.R.C., elder d. of 1st Marquess of Milford Haven, G.C.B., G.C.V.O., K.C.M.G.; ed. Cheam School, Salem (Baden), Gordonstoun School and Royal Naval Coll., Dartmouth; served 1939-45 war with Mediterranean Fleet in Home Waters and with British Pacific Fleet in S.E. Asia and Pacific; renounced right of succession to the Thrones of Greece and Denmark and was naturalized a British subject 1947, adopting the surname of Mountbatten; m. 20 Nov. 1947 H.R.H. Princess Elizabeth (now H.M. Queen Elizabeth II), elder daughter of H.M. King George VI; Personal A.D.C. to H.M. King George VI 1948-52; P.C. 1951-; Chancellor, Univ. of Wales 1948-76, Univ. of Edinburgh 1952-, Univ. of Cambridge 1977-, Salford Univ.; Admiral of the Fleet, F.M. and Marshal of the R.A.F. 1953-, of R.N.Z.A.F. 1978, Marshal of N.Z. Army 1978; Patron and Chair. of Trustees, Duke of Edinburgh's Award Scheme 1956-; P.C. of Canada 1957-; Visitor, R.C.A. 1967-; Pres. numerous bodies, including English-Speaking Union of the Commonwealth 1952-, R.S.A. 1952-, Commonwealth Games Federation 1955-, Royal Agricultural Soc. of the Commonwealth 1958-, B.M.A. 1959-60, Wildlife Trust 1960-65, 1972-77, World Wildlife Fund British Nat. Appeal 1961-81, Council for Nat. Academic Awards 1965-75, Scottish Icelandic Assn. 1965-, The Maritime Trust 1969-79, Nat. Council of Social Service 1970-73, Australian Conservation Foundation 1971-76, David Davies Memorial Inst. of Int. Studies 1979-, World Wildlife Fund for Nature Int. 1981-; Hon. LL.D.

(Wales, London, Edinburgh, Cambridge, Karachi and Malta), Hon. D.C.L. (Durham and Oxford), Hon. D.Sc. (Delhi, Reading, Salford, Southampton and Victoria), Hon. Degree (Eng. Univ., Lima, Peru); Hon. Dr. of Law (Univ. of Calif. at Los Angeles), numerous awards and decorations from many countries. *Publications:* Birds from Britannia 1962, Wildlife Crisis (with late James Fisher) 1970, The Environmental Revolution: Speeches on Conservation 1962-77 1978, Men, Machines and Sacred Cows (speeches and essays) 1984, Down to Earth 1988, Living off the Land 1989. *Address:* Buckingham Palace, London, S.W.1, England.

EDLÉN, Bengt, DR.PHIL.; Swedish university professor; b. 2 Nov. 1906, Gusum; s. of Gustaf and Maria Edlén (née Rundberg); m. 1st Ruth E. Grönwall 1935, 2nd Elfriede I. Mühlbach 1940; one s. three d.; ed. Uppsala Univ.; Asst. Physics Dept., Uppsala Univ. 1928, Asst. Prof. 1934; Prof. of Physics, Lund Univ. 1944-73, Emer. Prof. 1973-; mem. Swedish, Danish, Norwegian Acads. of Sciences, Académie des Sciences, Paris, American Acad. of Arts and Sciences, etc.; Commdr. de l'Ordre des Palmes académiques; Hon. D.Sc.(Kiel); awards in recognition of research on atomic spectra with applications to astrophysical problems, including the solar corona, include: Arrhenius Gold Medal of Swedish Acad. of Sciences, Gold Medal of Royal Astronomical Soc., London, H. N. Potts Medal of Franklin Inst., Pa., Mees Medal of Optical Soc. of America, Henry Draper Medal of N.A.S., Washington. *Leisure interests:* spectroscopy, gardening. *Address:* Physics Department, University of Lund, Lund, Sweden. *Telephone:* 046-111037.

EDMOND, John Marmion, PH.D., F.R.S.; American professor of marine geochemistry; b. 27 April 1943; s. of Andrew J. S. Edmond and late Christina M. Edmond; m. Massoudeh Vafai 1978; two s.; ed. Univ. of Glasgow, Univ. of Calif. at San Diego and Scripps Inst. of Oceanography; Asst. Prof. Mass. Inst. of Tech. 1970, Assoc. Prof. 1975, Prof. of Marine Geochemistry 1981-; Mackelwane Award, American Geophysical Union 1976. *Publications:* more than 80 scientific papers in professional journals. *Leisure interests:* reading, gardening. *Address:* 21 Robin Hood Road, Arlington, Mass. 02174, U.S.A. *Telephone:* 617-253-5739.

EDMUND-DAVIES, Baron (Life Peer), cr. 1974; **Herbert Edmund Edmund-Davies,** LL.D., B.C.L.; British judge; b. (as Herbert Edmund Davies) 15 July 1906, Mountain Ash, Glam.; s. of Morgan John and Elizabeth Maud Davies (née Edmunds); m. Eurwen Williams-James 1935; three d.; ed. Mountain Ash Grammar School, King's Coll., London and Exeter Coll., Oxford; Lecturer and Examiner, London Univ. 1930-31; Army Officers' Emergency Reserve 1938, Infantry OCTU, later commissioned Royal Welch Fusiliers 1940; Q.C. 1943, Bencher 1948, Treas. 1965, 1966; Asst. Judge Advocate-Gen. 1944-45; Recorder Merthyr Tydfil 1942-44, Swansea 1944-53, Cardiff 1953-58; Judge of High Court of Justice, Queen's Bench Div. 1958-66; Lord Justice of Appeal 1966-74; Lord of Appeal in Ordinary 1974-81; Chair. Lord Chancellor's Cttee. on Limitation of Actions 1961, Tribunal of Inquiry into Aberfan Disaster 1966, Council of Law Reporting 1967-72, Home Sec.'s Criminal Law Revision Cttee. 1969-77, Home Office Cttee. of Inquiry into Police 1977-79; Life mem. Canadian Bar Assn.; Trustee, CIBA Foundation 1974-81; Hon. Life mem. Royal Soc. of Medicine; Pres. Univ. Coll. of Swansea 1965-75; Pro-Chancellor Univ. of Wales 1974-84; Pres. London Welsh Assn. and Trust 1982-; Life Gov. and Fellow, King's Coll., London; Hon. Fellow, Exeter Coll., Oxford; LL.D. (London), Hon. LL.D. (Wales), B.C.L. (Oxford). *Address:* House of Lords, London, S.W.1; 5 Gray's Inn Square, London, WC1R 5EU, England. (Home).

EDMUNDS, Joseph Edsel, PH.D.; St. Lucia diplomatist; b. 1 July 1935, Barbados; m.; two c.; ed. Puerto Rico and Cornell Univs.; Teacher, St. Mary's Coll. 1950-55; Research Fellow, Regional Research Centre, West Indies Univ. 1965-66; joined Windward Islands Banana Research Scheme (WINBAN) 1966, Deputy Dir. of Research 1970-71, Dir. 1971-84; founder mem. Org. of Tropical American Nematologists, Pres. 1969-70; Dir. Nat. Devt. Corpn. 1972-79; Chair. Cttee. on Educ. Priorities 1975-80; fmr. Chair. Nat. Advisory Cttee. on Educ. and Adviser to Minister of Educ. 1982; Senator, St. Lucia Govt. 1979-84; Perm. Rep. of St. Lucia to the UN 1984-. *Address:* Permanent Mission of St. Lucia to the United Nations, 41 East 42nd Street, Suite 315, New York, N.Y. 10017, U.S.A. *Telephone:* 697-9360.

EDSALL, John Tileston, A.B., M.D.; American professor of biological chemistry; b. 3 Nov. 1902, Philadelphia; s. of David Linn Edsall and Margaret Harding Tileston; m. Margaret Dunham 1929 (deceased 1987); three s. (one deceased); ed. Harvard Coll., Harvard Medical School and Cambridge Univ.; Asst. Prof. of Biological Chem., Harvard Univ. 1932-38, Assoc. Prof. 1938-51, Prof. 1951-73, Prof. Emer. 1973; Guggenheim Fellow, Calif. Inst. of Tech. 1940-41; Ed.-in-Chief Journal of Biological Chemistry 1958-67; Visiting Fulbright Lecturer, Cambridge 1952, Tokyo 1964; Visiting Prof., Coll. de France, Paris 1955; Spiers Memorial Lecturer, Faraday Soc., Cambridge 1952; Visiting Lecturer, Australian Nat. Univ., Canberra 1970; Scholar Fogarty Int. Center, Nat. Insts. of Health, Bethesda, Md. 1970-71; Pres. American Soc. of Biological Chemists 1957-58, Sixth Int. Congress of Biochemistry, New York 1964; Chair. Survey of Sources for the History of Biochemistry and Molecular Biology 1975-80; Visiting Prof., Univ. of Calif., Los Angeles 1977, Univ. of Calif., Riverside 1980; mem. Interunion Biothermodynamics Comm. 1973-78, Nat. Acad. of Sciences,

American Philosophical Soc., American Acad. of Arts and Sciences, Deutsche Akad. der Naturforscher (Leopoldina), Royal Danish Acad. of Sciences; mem. Cttee. on Scientific Freedom and Responsibility, American Asscn. for the Advancement of Science 1976–82, Chair. 1979–81; Foreign mem. Royal Swedish Acad. of Sciences; Hon. Dr. Phil. Univ. of Göteborg 1972, Hon Sc.D. (Western Reserve Univ., New York Medical Coll. and Univs. of Chicago and Mich.); Passano Foundation Award for Medical Research 1966, Willard Gibbs Medal (American Chemical Soc.) 1972, Philip Hauge Abelson Award (A.A.A.S.) 1989. *Publications:* Proteins, Amino Acids and Peptides (with E. J. Cohn) 1943, Biophysical Chemistry (with J. Wyman) Vol. 1 1958, Aspects actuels de la biochimie des acides aminés et des proteines 1958, Advances in Protein Chemistry (Co-Editor) Vols. 1-39, Archival Sources for the History of Biochemistry and Molecular Biology (Co-Editor) 1980, Biothermodynamics (with H. Gutfreund) 1983; numerous papers on chemistry of amino acids, proteins, and enzymes in Journal of American Chemical Soc., Journal of Biological Chemistry, etc. *Leisure interests:* travel, photography, walking. *Address:* Biochemistry and Molecular Biology, 7 Divinity Avenue, Harvard University, Cambridge, Mass. 02138 (Office); 985 Memorial Drive, Cambridge, Mass. 02138, U.S.A. (Home). *Telephone:* (617) 495-2314 (Office); (617) 876-5007 (Home).

EDWARD, David Alexander Ogilvy, C.M.G., M.A., LL.B., Q.C.; British public servant; b. 11 Nov. 1934, Perth; s. of John O. C. Edward and Margaret I. MacArthur; m. Elizabeth Young McSherry 1962; two s. two d.; ed. Sedbergh School, Univ. Coll., Oxford and Edinburgh Univ.; advocate 1962–, Clerk Faculty of Advocates 1967–70, Treasurer 1970–77; Pres. Consultative Cttee., Bars and Law Socs. of the EEC 1978–80; Salvesen Prof. of European Insts. and Dir. Europa Inst., Univ. of Edinburgh 1988–; Specialist Adviser to House of Lords Select Cttee. on the EEC; Chair. Continental Assets Trust PLC, Hopetoun House Preservation Trust, Scottish Council for Arbitration; Dir. Adam & Co. PLC, Harris Tweed Assoc. Ltd.; Trustee Nat. Library of Scotland 1966–; mem. Law Advisory Cttee. 1976–88, Panel of Arbitrators, Int. Centre for Settlement of Investment Disputes. *Leisure interest:* gardening. *Address:* Europa Institute, University of Edinburgh, Old College, South Bridge, Edinburgh, EH8 9YL (Office); 32 Heriot Row, Edinburgh EH3 6ES, Scotland (Home). *Telephone:* 031-667 1011, Ext. 4215 (Office); 031-225 7153 (Home).

EDWARDES, Sir Michael Owen, Kt., B.A., F.B.I.M.; British company executive; b. 11 Oct. 1930, South Africa; s. of Denys Owen Edwardes and Audrey Noel (née Copeland); m. Mary Margaret Finlay 1958; three d.; ed. St. Andrew's Coll., Grahamstown, S.A., Rhodes Univ., S.A.; joined Chloride Group in S.A. as management trainee 1951, mem. Man. Bd. 1969, Chief Exec. 1972, Exec. Chair. 1974–77, non-Exec. Deputy Chair. 1977–82, Chair. (non-exec.) 1982–88 (acting Chief Exec. 1985–87); Chair. and Chief Exec. BL PLC 1977–82; Dir. (non-exec.) Hill Samuel Group PLC 1980–87, Standard Securities 1984–87, Minerals and Resources Corpn. 1984–; Chair. Mercury Communications Ltd. 1982–83, ICL PLC 1984; Chair. and Chief Exec. Dunlop Holdings 1984–85; Chair. Stabilization Ltd., 1984–, Tryhorn Investments Ltd. 1987–, Flying Pictures Ltd. 1987–; C.E.O. Minorco 1989–; Deputy Chair. R. K. Carvill Int. Holdings Ltd.; Dir. (non-exec.) Int. Man. Devt. Inst., Washington 1978–; Pres. Comité des Constructeurs d'Automobile du Marché Commun 1979–80; mem. Nat. Enterprise Bd. 1975–77, CBI Council 1974 (mem. President's Cttee. 1981–), Review Cttee. for Queen's Award for Industry; Young Businessman of the Year 1975; Hon. D.Iur. Rhodes Univ., S.A. 1980; Hon. Fellow, Inst. of Mechanical Engineers. *Publication:* Back From the Brink 1983. *Leisure interests:* water skiing, sailing, squash, tennis.

EDWARDS, Blake; American film director; b. (as William Blake McEdwards) 26 July 1922, Tulsa, Okla.; m. Julie Andrews (q.v.) 1969; ed. high school; wrote for radio shows Johnny Dollar, Line-Up; writer and creator of Richard Diamond; creator TV shows Dante's Inferno, Peter Gunn, Mr. Lucky; writer and co-producer of films: Panhandle 1947, Stampede 1948; writer of films: All Ashore 1952, Sound Off 1952, Cruisin' Down the River 1953, Drive a Crooked Road 1954, My Sister Eileen (musical version) 1955, Operation Mad Ball 1957, Notorious Landlady 1962; writer and dir. of films including: Bring Your Smile Along 1955, He Laughed Last 1955, Mr. Cory 1956, This Happy Feeling 1958; *films directed:* Operation Petticoat 1959, High Time 1960, Breakfast at Tiffany's 1961, Days of Wine and Roses 1962, The Carey Treatment 1972; producer, co-writer, dir.: The Soldier in the Rain 1963, The Pink Panther 1964, A Shot in the Dark 1964, What Did You Do in the War, Daddy? 1966, Peter Gunn 1967, The Party 1968, Darling Lili 1969, Wild Rovers 1971, The Tamarind Seed 1974, The Return of the Pink Panther 1975, The Pink Panther Strikes Again 1976, Revenge of the Pink Panther 1978, 10 1979, S.O.B. 1980, Victor/Victoria 1981, Trail of the Pink Panther 1982, Curse of the Pink Panther 1983, The Man Who Loved Women 1983, Micki and Maude 1984, That's Life 1986, Sunset 1988; producer, dir. Experiment in Terror 1962; co-writer, dir. The Great Race 1964. *Address:* c/o Creative Artists Agency Inc., 1888 Century Park E. Suite, 1400 Los Angeles, Calif. 90067, U.S.A.

EDWARDS, Edwin Washington, LL.D.; American politician; b. 7 Aug. 1927, Marksville, La.; s. of Clarence W. Edwards and Agnes Brouillette Edwards; m. Elaine Schwartzenburg 1949; two d. two s.; ed. Louisiana State Univ.; naval cadet 1945–46; practised law in Crowley, La. 1949–, sr. partner in law firm of Edwards, Edwards and Broadhurst; practised in Baton Rouge, La. 1980–; mem. Crowley City Council 1954–62, La. State

Senate 1964–66; House of Reps. 1965–72, Public Works Cttee. 1965–68, Whip to La. and Miss. Dels., Judiciary Cttee. and Cttee. on Internal Security; Gov. of Louisiana 1972–79, 1984–88; Chair. Interstate Oil Compact Comm. 1974–, Ozarks Regional Comm. 1974–, Educ. Comm. of Task Force on State, Institutional and Fed. Responsibilities May 1975–; mem. Nat. Resources and Environmental Man. Cttee. of Southern Govs.' Conf., Rural and Urban Devt. Cttee. of Nat. Govs.' Conf.; mem. Crowley Chamber of Commerce, Crowley Industrial Foundation, American Legion; Democrat.

EDWARDS, Sir George Robert, Kt., O.M., C.B.E., F.R.S.; British aeronautical designer and executive; b. 9 July 1908; m. Marjorie Annie Thurgood 1935; one d.; ed. London Univ.; design staff, Vickers Armstrong, Weybridge 1935, Experimental Man. 1940, Chief Designer 1945, Gen. Man. and Chief Engineer 1953; Man. Dir. British Aircraft Corpn. Ltd. 1960–75; Pro-Chancellor Univ. of Surrey 1964–79, Pro-Chancellor Emer. Sept. 1979–; mem. Royal Inst. 1971–; Hon. F.R.Ae.S., Hon. F.A.I.A.A.; Trustee R.A.F. Museum; Hon. D.Sc. (Southampton) 1962, (Salford) 1967, (Cranfield Inst. of Tech.) 1970, (City Univ.) 1975, (Stirling) 1979, (Surrey) 1979; Hon. D.Sc.(Eng.) (London) 1970; Hon. LL.D. (Bristol) 1973; British Gold Medal for Aeronautics 1952, Daniel Guggenheim Medal 1959, Taylor Gold Medal, Albert Medal 1972, Royal Soc. Royal Medal 1974, D.L. Surrey 1981. *Address:* Albury Heights, White Lane, Guildford, Surrey, England.

EDWARDS, Iorwerth Eiddon Stephen, C.M.G., C.B.E., LITT.D., F.B.A.; British Egyptologist (retd.); b. 21 July 1909, London; s. of the late Edward Edwards and Ellen Jane Higgs; m. Annie Elizabeth Lisle 1938; one s. (deceased) one d.; ed. Merchant Taylors' School, Gonville and Caius Coll., Cambridge; Asst. Keeper, Dept. of Egyptian and Assyrian Antiquities British Museum 1934–50, Deputy Keeper 1950–55, Keeper Dept. of Egyptian Antiquities 1955–74; Foreign Assoc. mem. Académie Française. *Publications:* Hieroglyphic Texts in the British Museum, Vol. VIII 1939, The Pyramids of Egypt (many trans. and edns.) 1947, Hieratic Papyri in the British Museum, 4th series, Oracular Amuletic Decrees of the Late New Kingdom 1960, Treasures of Tutankhamun (Catalogue of the London Exhibition) 1972, Tutankhamun, His Tomb and its Treasures 1976, Jt. Ed. and contrib. The Cambridge Ancient History, Vols. I-III 1970–87. *Leisure interests:* gardening, cricket. *Address:* Dragon House, Bull Ring, Deddington, Oxford, OX5 4TT, England. *Telephone:* (0869) 38481.

EDWARDS, James Burrows, D.M.D., F.A.C.D., F.I.C.D.; American oral surgeon and university president; b. 24 June 1927, Hawthorne, Fla.; s. of O. M. Edwards; m. Anne Norris Darlington 1951; one s. one d.; ed. Coll. of Charleston, Univ. of Louisiana and Univ. of Pa. Graduate Medical School; oral surgery residency, Henry Ford Hosp., Detroit, Mich. 1958–60; dentistry practice, specializing in oral and maxillofacial surgery, Charleston, S.C. 1960–; Clinical Assoc. in Oral Surgery, Coll. of Dental Medicine, Medical Univ., S.C. 1967–77, Clinical Prof. of Oral Surgery and Community Dentistry 1977–82, Prof. of Oral and Maxillofacial Surgery 1982–, Pres. of Univ. 1982–; Fellow American Coll. of Dentists, Int. Coll. of Dentists; mem. Federation Dentaire Internationale, British Assoc. of Oral and Maxillofacial Surgeons, Int. Soc. of Oral and Maxillofacial Surgeons and numerous dental orgs. in U.S.; Chair. of Charleston County Republican Cttee. 1964–69; Chair. of First Congressional District Republican Cttee. 1970; mem. S.C. Statewide Steering Cttee. for Republican Party; mem. S.C. State Senate 1972–74; Governor of South Carolina 1975–78; U.S. Sec. of Energy 1981–82; mem. Bd. of Dirs. S.C. Nat. Bank, J. P. Stevens & Co. Inc., Phillips Petroleum Co., Burris Chemical Inc., William Benton Foundation, Brendle's Inc., SCANA Corpn., Encyclopaedia Britannica Inc., Imo Delaval Inc., Harry Frank Guggenheim Foundation; several hon. degrees. *Leisure interests:* hunting, fishing, sailing, water skiing. *Address:* Medical University of South Carolina, 171 Ashley Avenue, Charleston, S.C. 29340, U.S.A.

EDWARDS, John Hilton, M.B., B.CHIR., F.R.S., F.R.C.P.; British professor and consultant in genetics; b. 23 March 1928, London; s. of Harold Clifford Edwards and Ida Margaret (Phillips) Edwards; m. Felicity Clare Toussaint 1953; two s. two d.; ed. Univ. of Cambridge, Middlesex Hospital, London; Medical Officer, Falklands Islands Dependancy Survey 1952–53; with MRC Unit on Population Genetics, Oxford 1958–60; Geneticist, Children's Hospital of Philadelphia, Pa. 1960–61; Lecturer, Univ. of Birmingham, subsequently Sr. Lecturer and Reader, 1961–67; Prof. of Human Genetics 1969–79; Investigator, New York Blood Center 1967–68; Consultant in Human Genetics, Univ. of Iceland 1967–, in Clinical Genetics, Nat. Health Service; Prof. of Genetics, Univ. of Oxford 1979–; Visiting Prof. of Paediatrics, Cornell Univ., Ithaca, N.Y., U.S.A. 1967–68; Hon. Consultant Paediatrician, Birmingham Regional Bd. 1967–79. *Publications:* numerous publications on paediatrics, clinical genetics and mathematical genetics; Human Genetics 1978. *Leisure interests:* gliding, skiing, *Address:* Genetics Laboratory, Department of Biochemistry, South Parks Road, Oxford, OX1 3QU; 78 Old Road, Headington, Oxford, England (Home). *Telephone:* (0865) 275317 (Office); (0865) 60430 (Home).

EDWARDS, Kenneth John Richard, PH.D.; British university vice-chancellor; b. 12 Feb. 1934; s. of John Edwards and Elizabeth M. Edwards; m. Janet M. Gray 1958; two s. one d.; ed. Market Drayton Grammar School, Univ. of Reading and Univ. Coll. of Wales, Aberystwyth; Fellow, Univ. of Calif. 1961–62; A.R.C. Fellow, Welsh Plant Breeding Station, Aberystwyth 1962–63, Sr. Scientific Officer 1963–66; Lecturer in Genetics, Univ. of Cambridge 1966–84, Head, Dept. of Genetics 1981–84; Lecturer, St. John's

Coll. Cambridge 1971–84, Fellow 1971–87, Tutor 1981–84; Sec.-Gen. of Faculties, Univ. of Cambridge 1984–87; Vice-Chancellor, Univ. of Leicester 1987–; Visiting Lecturer, Birmingham 1965; Visiting Prof., Buenos Aires 1973; Leverhulme Research Fellow, Univ. of Calif. 1973. *Publications:* Evolution in Modern Biology 1977; articles on genetics in scientific journals. *Leisure interests:* music, gardening. *Address:* Knighton Hall, Leicester, England. *Telephone:* Leicester 706677.

EDWARDS, Philip Walter, PH.D., F.B.A.; British professor of English Literature; b. 7 Feb. 1923, Barrow-in-Furness; s. of the late R. H. Edwards and B. Edwards; m. 1st Hazel Valentine 1947 (died 1950), 2nd Sheila Wilkes 1952; three s. one d.; ed. King Edward's High School, Birmingham, Univ. of Birmingham; Lecturer in English, Univ. of Birmingham 1946–60, Prof. of English Literature, Trinity Coll. Dublin 1960–66, Visiting Prof., Univ. of Mich. 1964–65, Prof. of Literature, Univ. of Essex 1966–74, Visiting Prof., Williams Coll., Mass. 1969, Visiting Fellow, All Souls Coll., Oxford 1970–71, King Alfred Prof. of English Literature, Univ. of Liverpool 1974–, Visiting Prof., Univ. of Otago, New Zealand 1980. *Publications:* Sir Walter Ralegh 1953, The Spanish Tragedy (ed.) 1959, Shakespeare and the Confines of Art 1968, Massinger, Plays and Poems (ed. with C. Gibson) 1976, Pericles Prince of Tyre (ed.) 1976, Threshold of a Nation 1979, Hamlet Prince of Denmark (ed.) 1985, Shakespeare: A Writer's Progress 1986, Last Voyages 1988. *Leisure interest:* hill-walking. *Address:* 12 South Bank, Oxton, Birkenhead, Merseyside, L43 5UP, England. *Telephone:* 051-652 6089.

EDWARDS, Robert John, C.B.E.; British journalist; b. 26 Oct. 1925, Farnham, Surrey; s. of Gordon and Margaret (née Grain) Edwards; m. 1st Laura Ellwood 1952 (dissolved 1972), two s. two d.; m. 2nd Brigid Segrave 1977; ed. Ranelagh School; Ed. Tribune 1951–55; Deputy Ed. Sunday Express 1957–59; Ed. Daily Express 1961–62, 1963–65; Ed. Evening Citizen (Glasgow) 1962–63; Ed. Sunday People (fmrly. The People) 1966–72; Ed. Sunday Mirror 1972–84; Dir. Mirror Group Newspapers 1976–, Sr. Group Ed. 1984–, Non-Exec. Deputy Chair. 1985–. *Leisure interest:* boating. *Publication:* Goodbye Fleet Street 1988. *Address:* 74 Duns Tew, Oxford, OX5 4JL, England. *Telephone:* (0869) 40417.

EDWARDS, (Roger) Nicholas (see Crickhowell, Baron).

EDWARDS, Sir Sam(uel Frederick), Kt., F.R.S., F.INST.P., F.I.M.A., F.R.S.C., C.CHEM.; British physicist and administrator; b. 1 Feb. 1928, Swansea; s. of Richard and Mary Jane Edwards; m. Merriell E. M. Bland 1953; one s. three d.; ed. Swansea Grammar School, Gonville and Caius College, Cambridge, Harvard Univ.; member, Inst. for Advanced Study, Princeton 1952–53; staff mem. Birmingham Univ. 1953–58, Manchester Univ. 1958–72; Prof. of Theoretical Physics, Manchester Univ. 1963–72; John Humphrey Plummer Prof. of Physics, Cambridge Univ. 1972–84, Cavendish Prof. 1984–; mem. Council, Inst. of Physics 1967–73, Vice-Pres. of Inst. 1970–73, Chair. Publ. Div. 1970–73; mem. Science Bd., Science Research Council 1970–73, mem. Physics Cttee. 1968–70, Polymer Science Cttee. 1968–73, Chair. Physics Cttee. 1970–73, Science Research Council 1973–77; Dir. Lucas Industries 1981–; mem. Council European Physical Soc. 1969–71, Univ. Grants Cttee. 1971–73, Scientific Advisory Council, Min. of Defence 1973–81, 1988– (Chair. 1978–81), Advisory Bd. for the Research Councils, Dept. of Ed. and Science 1973–77, Metrology and Standards Requirements Bd., Dept. of Industry 1974–77, Advisory Council on Research and Devt., Dept. of Energy 1974–77 (Chair. 1983–), U.K. Del. NATO Science Cttee. 1974–78, Senatsausschuss für Forschungspolitik und Forschungsplanung der Max Planck Gesellschaft 1975–77, Council Inst. of Mathematics and its Applications 1976– (Pres. 1980–81), European Council for Research and Devt. 1975–79, Scientific Advisory Cttee. Allied Corpn. 1980–84; Chair. Council British Assen. for Advancement of Science 1977–82, Pres. 1988–89, Council Royal Soc. 1981–83 (Vice-Pres. 1982–83); Chief Scientific Adviser, Dept. of Energy 1983–; Fellow Gonville and Caius Coll., Cambridge 1972–; Hon. D.Tech., (Loughborough) 1975, Hon. D.Sc. (Edinburgh, Salford, Bath, Birmingham, Wales, Strasbourg); Maxwell Medal and Prize, Inst. of Physics 1974, American Physical Soc. Prize for High Polymer Physics 1982, Davy Medal, Royal Soc. 1984, Gold Medallist, Inst. of Math. 1986. *Address:* The Cavendish Laboratory, Madingley Road, Cambridge, CB3 0HE, England. *Telephone:* 0223-33-7423.

EDWARDS, William Philip Neville, C.B.E., M.A.; British industrialist; b. 5 Aug. 1904; ed. Rugby, Corpus Christi Coll., Cambridge, and Princeton Univ. (Davison Scholar); Public Relations Officer, London Passenger Transport Bd. 1939–41; Asst. to Chair. of Supply Council, Ministry of Supply 1941–43; Head of Industrial Information Div., Ministry of Production, and alt. Dir. of Information, British Supply Council, Washington 1943–45; Dir. Overseas Information Div., Bd. of Trade, London 1945–46; Counsellor, British Embassy, Washington, D.C., in charge of British Information Services 1946–49; Deputy Overseas Dir. Fed. of British Industries (F.B.I.) 1949–51, Dir. Promotion and Information, F.B.I. 1951–65, Confederation of British Industry (C.B.I.) 1965–66; Dir. of British Overseas Fairs Ltd. 1953–66, Chair. 1966–68; U.K. Assoc. Dir. Business Int. S.A. 1969–75; Chair. Burton Sheen Ltd. 1971–75; Dir. P.R.I. Group 1968–77. *Address:* Four Winds, Kithurst Lane, Storrington, Sussex, England. *Telephone:* (090 66) 4507.

EELSEN, Pierre Henri Maurice, L. END.; French company executive and administrator; b. 12 July 1933, Montmorency, Val-d'Oise; s. of Maurice

Eelsen and Jacqueline Robert; m. 1st, two s. one d.; m. 2nd Danièle Mesle, 1980, one s.; ed. Lycée Jacques-Decour, Paris, Univ. de Paris; at Renault 1958–84, responsible for econ. studies Renault Eng. 1959, attached to Dir. of Relations 1965, Head Dept. Agric. Machinery 1967, attached to Gen. Secretariat 1969, Asst. to Sec.-Gen. 1971, Jt. Sec.-Gen. 1975, Gen. Del. 1979, mem. Exec. Cttee. 1981; Head Dept. Int. Affairs Chambre syndicale des constructeurs d'automobiles 1962; mem. European Econ. and Social Cttee. 1982; Pres. Nat. Asscn. for devt. of Overseas depts. 1982; Admin. Ecole nat. d'admin. 1983; Pres.-Dir.-Gen. Air Inter 1984–; Pres. Agence Nationale pour le Développement de l'Education Permanente (ADEP) 1985–, Chambre Syndicale des Transporteurs Aériens; Chevalier, ordre nat. du Mérite, Chevalier, Légion d'honneur. *Address:* 33 rue Lhomond, 75005 Paris; la Mare Hermier, Amfreville sur Iton, 27400 Louviers, France (Homes).

EFFERT, Sven, DR.MED.; German professor of medicine; b. 31 March 1922, Aachen; s. of Edgar Effert and Else Philips; m. Ilse Tutscheck 1946; two s. one d.; ed. Univs. of Bonn, Freiburg and Düsseldorf; Asst. Prof. Univ. of Düsseldorf, Faculty of Medicine 1964–66; Prof. of Internal Medicine, Faculty of Medicine, Rheinisch-Westfälische Technische Hochschule Aachen 1966–, Head of Dept. for Internal Medicine I 1966–, Dir. Helmholtz-Inst. for Biomedical Eng. 1971–; Pres. Soc. of German Natural Researchers and Physicians 1979; German Soc. of Cardiology 1981–; mem. Deutsche Akad. der Naturforscher (Leopoldina); Int. Fellow of the Council of the American Heart Asscn.; Award Verdienstkreuz (North-Rhine-Westphalia) 1st Class. *Publications:* 460 publs. and 25 contribs. to books since 1948. *Address:* Abteilung Innere Medizin I, Medizinische Fakultät d. RWTH Aachen, Pauwelsstrasse-D-5100 Aachen (Office); Rotbendenstrasse 14, D-5100 Aachen, Federal Republic of Germany (Home). *Telephone:* 0241-80 89 300 (Office); 0241-6 10 58 (Home).

EFHOLM, Mogens; Danish business executive; b. 20 May 1910, Copenhagen; s. of Christian Christensen and Ingeborg (née Ohlsson); m. Birgitte Jensen 1947; ed. univ., and commercial studies in England, Germany and France; Copenhagen trade agencies 1930–45; Man. Dir. Emil Warthoe & Soenner A/S 1945–50, Nordisk Andelsforbund (Scandinavian Co-operative Wholesale Soc.) 1951–64, "National" Co. 1953–57, Nordisk Andels-Eksport (Scandinavian Co-operative Export) 1954–64; mem. Cen. Cttee. Int. Co-operative Alliance, London 1961–64; mem. the "Maritime and Commercial Court" 1961–81; Chair. Nordisk Andelsforbund, Calif., Inc., San Francisco 1962–64; Sec.-Gen. European Co-operative Wholesale Cttee. for Developments in Production and Marketing Fields 1963–64; Commercial Adviser 1964–; Kt., first rank Order of Dannebrog. *Leisure interests:* literature and philosophy. *Address:* 65B Strandvejen, Copenhagen Ø, Denmark. *Telephone:* 01-29-36-46.

EFI, The Hon. Taisi Tupuola Tufuga; Western Samoa politician; b. 1938; s. of Tupua Tamasese Mea'ole; ed. St. Joseph's Coll., Apia, Western Samoa and Victoria Univ., Wellington, N.Z.; elected to Western Samoan Parl. 1965; Minister of Works, Civil Aviation, Marine and Transport 1970–73; Prime Minister 1976–82, fmr. Minister of Foreign Affairs, Local and Dist. Affairs and Police. *Address:* Apia, Western Samoa.

EFIMOV (see Yefimov).

EGAL, Mohamed Ibrahim; Somali politician; b. 1928, Berbera; s. of Haji Ibrahim Egal and Hajia Khadija Mohamed Osman; m. Aasha Saeed Abby 1946; three s. two d.; ed. Koranic School, Sheikh Intermediate School, and in U.K.; Sec. Berbera Branch, Somali Nat. League Party 1956; Sec.-Gen. Somali Nat. League Party 1958–60; Prime Minister of Somaliland 1960; Minister of Defence, Somali Repub. 1960–62, of Educ. 1962–63; resgnd. from cabinet 1963; f. SNC Party 1963; re-elected to Parl. March 1964; Leader of Parl. Opposition 1963–65; resgnd. leadership 1965; mem. Somali Youth League Party 1966; Prime Minister and Minister of Foreign Affairs, Somali Repub. 1967–69; in detention following coup 1969, released Oct. 1975; apptd. Amb. to India July 1976, rearrested Oct. 1976, released Feb. 1982; then Chair. Chamber of Commerce, Industry and Agric. *Leisure interests:* golf, reading and films. *Address:* P.O. Box 27, Via Asha, Mogadishu, Somalia.

EGDAHL, Richard H., M.D., PH.D.; American professor of surgery; b. 13 Dec. 1926, Eau Claire, Wis.; m. Cynthia H. Taft 1983; three s. one d. (by previous m.); ed. Dartmouth Coll., Harvard Medical School and Univ. of Minnesota; Prof. of Surgery and Dir. of Research Labs. Medical Coll. of Va. 1957–64; Chair. Div. of Surgery, Boston Univ. Medical Center 1964–73; Prof. of Surgery, Boston Univ. School of Medicine 1964–, Prof. of Public Health 1983–; Dir. Boston Univ. Medical Center 1973–; Academic Vice-Pres. for Health Affairs, Boston Univ. 1973–, Dir. Health Policy Inst. 1975–, Dir. Center for Industry and Health Care 1976–. *Publications:* 250 publs. *Leisure interest:* tennis. *Address:* Office of the Director, Boston University Medical Center, 720 Harrison Avenue, Suite 1107, Boston, Mass. 02118, U.S.A. *Telephone:* 617-638-8100.

EGEBERG, Roger Olaf, M.D.; American physician; b. 13 Nov. 1903, Chicago, Ill.; s. of Hans Olaf and Ulrikka Rostrup (née Nielsen) Egeberg; m. Margaret McEchron Chahoon; one s. two d.; ed. Cornell and Northwestern Univs.; Intern, Wesley Hospital, Chicago; Resident, Univ. Hospital, Ann Arbor, Mich.; practised medicine (specializing in internal medicine) Cleveland, Ohio 1932–1942; Chief Medical Service, Veterans' Admin. Hospital,

Los Angeles 1946-56; Medical Dir. Los Angeles County Hospital 1956-58; Los Angeles County Dept. Charities 1958-64; mem. staff Los Angeles County Gen. Hospital, and Rancho Los Amigos Hospital, Downey, Calif.; Prof. of Medicine Univ. of Calif. at Los Angeles (U.C.L.A.) 1948-64, Coll. of Medical Evangelists 1956-64; Prof. of Medicine Univ. of S. Calif. 1956-69, Dean School of Medicine 1964-69; Scholar in residence, Inst. of Medicine, N.A.S. 1983-; Chair. Calif. Regional Planning Programs 1967-69; mem. Nat. Advisory Cancer Council, Special Medical Advisory Group to the Veterans' Admin., Calif. Bd. of Public Health; Asst. Sec. for Health, Educ. and Welfare 1969-71, Special Asst. to Sec. for Health Policy 1971-77; Chief Medical Officer Medicare Bureau 1977-78; Co-Chair. U.S.-U.S.S.R. Comm. for Health Co-operation 1972-75; Dir. Office of Professional and Scientific Affairs, Health Care Financing Admin. 1978-83; Fellow, American Coll. of Physicians; mem. American Medical Asscn., American Clinical and Climatological Asscn., Calif. Bd. of Public Health 1961-67 (Pres. 1964-67); Bronze Star, Legion of Merit, St. Olaf's Medal (Norway). *Publications:* numerous articles in professional journals. *Address:* Institute of Medicine, 2101 Constitution Avenue, Suite JH 716, Washington, D.C. 20418, U.S.A.

EGELAND, Leif, M.A.(OXON), B.C.L.; South African diplomatist and businessman; b. 19 Jan. 1903, Durban; s. of the late J. J. and Ragnhild (née Konsmo) Egeland; m. Marguerite Doreen de Zwaan 1942 (deceased 1984); one d.; ed. Durban High School, Natal Univ. Coll., and Trinity Coll., Oxford; Rhodes Scholar for Natal 1924, Harmsworth Scholar Middle Temple 1927; Barrister 1930; Fellow Brasenose Coll. 1927-30; Advocate Supreme Court S. Africa 1931; M.P. Durban 1933-38, Zululand 1940-43; with 6th S. African Armoured Div., Middle East 1943; Union Minister to Sweden 1943-46, to Neths. and Belgium 1946-48; High Commr. for Union of South Africa in London 1948-50; S. African Del. to San Francisco Conf. 1945; leader of S. African Del. to Final Assembly L.N., Geneva 1946; S. African Del. to First and Third Gen. Assemblies of UN, Paris, to Paris Peace Conf. 1946 and Pres. Comm. for the political and territorial questions in the draft Peace Treaty with Italy at that Conf.; Chair. Smuts Memorial Trust; Life Trustee of the South Africa Foundation; Pres. South African Guide Dogs Asscn.; Hon. Pres. South African Inst. for Int. Affairs; Hon. Bencher Middle Temple; F.R.S.A. 1948; Hon. LL.D. (Cambridge); Hon. Fellow, Brasenose Coll. (Oxford); Knight Commdr. with Star of St. Olav (Norway), Knight Grand Cross of the North Star (Sweden); Order of Meritorious Service, Class I (Gold), S. Africa 1987. *Publications:* Bridges of Understanding (autobiog.) 1977. *Leisure interests:* tennis, gardening, bridge. *Address:* 11 Fricker Road, Illovo, Johannesburg, South Africa.

EGERTON, Sir Stephen Loftus, K.C.M.G., M.A.; British diplomatist; b. 21 July 1932, Indore, India; s. of William Egerton and Angela D. (née Bland) Egerton; m. Caroline Cary-Elwes 1958; one s. one d.; ed. Eton Coll., Trinity Coll., Cambridge; served with 60th Rifles 1951-53; joined Foreign Office 1956; served in Lebanon, Kuwait, Baghdad, New York, Tripoli, Rio de Janeiro; Amb. to Iraq 1980-82; Asst. Under-Sec. of State for Middle Eastern Affairs FCO 1982-86; Amb. to Saudi Arabia April 1986-; First Class, Order of Feisal bin Abdul Aziz 1987. *Leisure interests:* conversation, topiary. *Address:* British Embassy, P.O. Box 94351, Riyadh 11693, Saudi Arabia; c/o Foreign and Commonwealth Office, King Charles Street, London, S.W.1., England.

EGGAN, Fred Russell, PH.D.; American anthropologist; b. 12 Sept. 1906, Seattle, Wash.; s. of Alfred J. Eggan and Olive M. Smith; m. 1st Dorothy Way 1938 (deceased), 2nd Joan Rosenfels 1969; no. c.; ed. Univ. of Chicago; Instructor, Univ. of Chicago 1935-40, Asst. Prof. 1940-44, Assoc. Prof. 1945-48, Prof. of Anthropology 1948-, Chair. Dept. of Anthropology 1948-52, 1961-63; Dir. Philippine Studies Program 1953-; Harold H. Swift Distinguished Service Prof. 1963-74, Prof. Emer. 1974-; Research Scholar in Residence, School of American Research, Santa Fe, N.M. 1979-80; mem. Pacific Science Bd., Sr. Advisory Comm. Encyclopaedia Britannica 1953-; Fellow Centre for Advanced Study in The Behavioural Sciences, Stanford Univ. 1958-59; Visiting Fellow, All Souls' Coll., Oxford 1970; Hon. F.R.A.I.; Corresponding Fellow British Acad.; mem. Nat. Acad. of Sciences, American Philosophical Soc., American Acad. of Arts and Sciences; mem. Bd. of Trustees, Museum of the American Indian, Heye Foundation, New York 1982; Viking Fund Medal, L. H. Morgan Lecturer; Frazer Lecturer 1971. *Publications:* Social Organization of the Western Pueblos 1950, The American Indian 1968; Ed. of Social Anthropology of North American Tribes 1937 (2nd edn. 1955), Essays in Social Anthropology and Ethnology 1975. *Leisure interests:* travel, photography. *Address:* Department of Anthropology, 1126 East 59th Street Chicago, Ill. 60637 (Office); 974 Old Santa Fe Trail, Santa Fe, N.M. 87501, U.S.A. (Home). *Telephone:* 962 7001 (Office); (505) 988-3425 (Home).

EGILSSON, Ólafur; Icelandic lawyer and diplomatist; b. 20 Aug. 1936, Reykjavik; s. of Egill Kristjánsson and Anna Margrjet Thurídur Ólafsdóttir Briem; m. Ragna Sverrisdóttir Ragnars 1960; one s. one d.; ed. Commercial College of Iceland and Iceland Univ.; journalist with newspapers Vísir 1956-58, Morgunblaðið 1959-62; Publishing Exec. 1963-64; Head, NATO Regional Information Office, Reykjavik 1964-66; Gen.-Sec. Icelandic Asscn. for Western Co-operation 1964-66; Political Div., Icelandic Foreign Ministry 1966-69; First Sec., then Counsellor, Icelandic Embassy, Paris 1969-71; Deputy Perm. Rep. OECD, UNESCO and Council of Europe 1969-71; Deputy Perm. Rep. N. Atlantic Council, Deputy Head, Icelandic Del. to

EEC, Counsellor, Embassy in Brussels 1971-74; Counsellor, then Minister Counsellor, Political Div. of Foreign Ministry 1974-80; Chief of Protocol (with rank of Amb.) 1980-83; Acting Prin. Pvt. Sec. to Pres. of Iceland 1981-82; Deputy Perm. Under Sec. and Dir.-Gen. for Political Affairs, Foreign Ministry 1983-87; Amb. to U.K. (also accred. to Ireland, Netherlands and Nigeria) 1986-; Chair., Bd. of Govs. Icelandic Int. Devt. Agency 1982-87; Exec. mem. Bible Soc. of Iceland 1977-87, History Soc. 1982-; Commdr. Icelandic Order of the Falcon and decorations from Finland, France, Norway, Spain, Sweden and Luxembourg. *Publications:* Coauthor: Iceland and Jan Mayen 1980, NATO's Anxious Birth—The Prophetic Vision of the 1940's 1985; Ed. Bjarni Benediktsson 1983. *Leisure interests:* history, skiing, music (classical), opera). *Address:* Icelandic Embassy, 1 Eaton Terrace, London, S.W.1; 101 Park Street, London, W.1, England (Home). *Telephone:* 01-730 5131 (Embassy); 01-629 8660 (Home).

EGLI, Alphons, D.JUR.; Swiss politician; b. 8 Oct. 1924, Lucerne; s. of Gotthard Egli; m.; three c.; ed. legal studies in Zurich, Berne and Rome; private legal practice in Lucerne 1952-82; mem. Lucerne Municipal Council 1963-67, Lucerne Cantonal Parl. 1967-75; mem. Council of States 1975, Leader, Christian Democratic Group 1979; Fed. Councillor 1982-; Head, Fed. Dept. of the Interior 1982-85, 1986, Pres. of Swiss Confed. and Head of State Jan.-Dec. 1986. *Address:* c/o Federal Chancellery, Bundeshaus-West, Bundesgasse, 3003 Berne, Switzerland.

EGLIN, Colin Wells; South African politician and quantity surveyor; b. 14 April 1925, Cape Town; s. of Carl Eglin and Elsie Mary Wells; m. Joyce Cortes 1949; three d.; ed. De Villiers Graaff High School and Univ. of Cape Town; army service in Egypt and Italy 1943-45; mem. Pinelands Municipal Council 1951-54, Cape Prov. Council 1954-58; mem. Parl. for Pinelands Constituency 1958-61, for Sea Point Constituency 1974-; Chair. Progressive Party of S.A. for Cape Province 1959-66, Chair. Nat. Exec. 1966-70, Nat. Leader 1970-75; Nat. Leader S.A. Progressive Reform Party 1975-77, Progressive Federal Party 1977-79; Nat. Chair. Progressive Fed. Party 1979-86, Nat. Leader 1986-88; (Official Opposition Leader 1977-79, 1986-87); Partner, Bernard James and Partners (Quantity Surveyors) 1952-. *Publications:* Betrayal of Coloured Rights, Forging Links in Africa, Priorities for the Seventies, New Deal for the Cities, Africa—A Prospect of Reconciliation, Pacesetter for Political Change, Security Through Negotiation. *Leisure interests:* tennis, golf, travel. *Address:* Progressive Federal Party, P.O. Box 1475, Cape Town 8000 (Office); 2 Cassandra, 42 Victoria Road, Clifton, Cape, South Africa (Home). *Telephone:* 48-7278 (Home).

EGLINTON, Geoffrey, PH.D., D.SC., F.R.S.; British professor of organic geochemistry; b. 1 Nov. 1927, Cardiff; m. Pamela J. Coupland 1955; two s. one d.; ed. Sale Grammar School and Univ. of Manchester; Post-doctoral Fellow, Ohio State Univ. 1952; Lecturer in Organic Chem., Univ. of Glasgow 1954-64; Visiting Fellow, Univ. of Calif. (Berkeley) 1964; Sr. Lecturer in Organic Chem., Univ. of Glasgow 1964-67, Reader 1967; Sr. Lecturer in Organic Geochem. and Head, Organic Chem. Unit, Univ. of Bristol 1967, Reader in Organic Geochem. 1968-73, Prof. and Head of Organic Geochem. Unit 1973-; NASA Gold Medal 1973, Hugo Muller Silver Medal (Chem. Soc.) 1974, Alfred E. Treibs Medal 1981, Melvin Calvin Lectureship (Univ. of Calif., Berkeley) 1985, Major Edward Fitzgerald Coke Medal of the Geological Soc. 1986, H. Burr Skinbach Visiting Scholar, Woods Hole Oceanographic Inst. 1986. *Publications:* over 350 articles and books. *Leisure interests:* hiking, sailing. *Address:* Organic Geochemistry Unit, University of Bristol, School of Chemistry, Cantock's Close, Bristol, BS8 1TS (Office); 7 Redhouse Lane, Westbury-on-Trym, Bristol, BS9 3RY, England (Home). *Telephone:* (0272) 303671 (Office); (0272) 683833 (Home).

EGUCHI, Teiji; Japanese business executive; b. 18 June 1926, Fukuoka Pref.; ed. Keio Univ.; joined Bridgestone 1950, Man. Overseas Admin. Dept. 1967, Man. Corporate Admin. Dept. 1969, Man. of Tire Finance Dept. 1971, Dir. and Gen. Man. Finance Div. 1973, Man. Dir. and Gen. Man. of Corporate Admin. and Finance Div. 1975, Sr. Man. Dir. Corporate Admin. Operations 1978-81, Sr. Man. Dir. Purchasing and Gen. Affairs Operations 1981-84, Exec. Vice-Pres. Bridgestone Corpn. 1984-85, Chair. 1985-. *Address:* Bridgestone Corpn., 10-1 Kyobashi 1-Chome, Chuo-ku, Tokyo 104, Japan.

EHLERMANN, Claus-Dieter, DR. IUR.; German lawyer; b. 15 June 1931, Scheessel; s. of Kurt Ehlermann and Hilde (née Justus) Ehlermann; m. Carola Grumbach 1959; two d.; ed. Univs. of Marburg/Lahn and Heidelberg, Univ. of Michigan Law School, Ann Arbor; Research Asst. Fed. Constitutional Court, Karlsruhe 1959-61; Legal Adviser, Legal Service of the Comm. of European Communities 1961-73, Dir. and Deputy Financial Controller 1973-77, Dir.-Gen. of the Legal Service 1977-87; Spokesman of the Comm. of the European Communities and of its Pres. Jacques Delors (q.v.) 1987-; Hon. Prof. Univ. of Hamburg. *Publications:* numerous documents on the European Community and its legal order. *Leisure interests:* reading, skiing, gardening. *Address:* Commission of the European Communities, 200 rue de la Loi, B-1049 Brussels, Belgium. *Telephone:* 00/32/2/235 21 78, 235 49 03.

EHMKE, Horst Paul August; German lawyer and politician; b. 4 Feb. 1927, Danzig; s. of Dr. med. Paul Ehmke and Hedwig (née Hafften); m. 1st Theda Baehr, 2nd Maria Hlavacova 1972; one s. two d.; ed. High

School, Danzig, Univ. of Göttingen and Princeton Univ., U.S.A; Research Assoc., Law School, Berkeley, U.S.A. 1958; graduated in Bonn 1960; Prof. of Law Univ. of Freiburg 1961-67, Dean of Law and Govt. Faculty 1966-67; Deputy of Fed. Minister of Justice 1967-69, Fed. Minister of Justice March-Oct. 1969; mem. Bundestag 1969-; Head of Fed. Chancellor's Office and Minister 1969-72; Fed. Minister for Research and Tech., Posts and Telecommunications 1972-74; Deputy Chair. Parl. Group 1977; Social Democrat. *Publications:* Grenzen der Verfassungsänderung 1953, "Ermessen" und "Unbestimmter Rechtsbegriff" im Verwaltungsrecht 1960, Wirtschaft und Verfassung 1961, Prinzipien der Verfassungsinterpretation 1963, Politik der praktischen Vernunft 1969, Politik als Herausforderung 1974, (II) 1979, Fristenregelung und Grundgesetz 1975, Das Portrait 1980, Die Macht der Großen und der Kleinen Tiere 1980, Beiträge zur Verfassungstheorie und Verfassungspolitik 1981. *Leisure interests:* history, modern literature, modern art, gardening. *Address:* Bundeshaus, 5300 Bonn 1, Federal Republic of Germany. *Telephone:* Bonn 163429 and 164834.

EHRENBERG, Herbert, DR.RER. POL.; German politician; b. 21 Dec. 1926, Collnischken, East Prussia; m. Ilse Borreck 1963; two d.; ed. Hochschule für Arbeit, Politik und Wirtschaft and Göttingen Univ; Lecturer in social sciences; econ. dept. of Bau-Steine-Erden trade union; Fed. Civil Service 1968-72, rising to Sec. of State in Ministry of Labour and Social Affairs; mem. Bundestag (lower house of Parl.) 1973-; Minister of Labour and Social Affairs 1977-82; mem. SPD 1955-, mem. Nat. Exec. 1975-84, Vice-Pres. Parl. Group 1983-, Chair. Econ. and Finance Policy Comm. of Nat. Exec. *Publications:* Lohnpolitik heute 1963, Die Erhard-Saga 1965, Vermögenspolitik für die siebziger Jahre 1971, Zwischen Marx und Markt 1973, Blick zurück nach vorn 1975, Sozialarbeit und Freiheit (with A. Fuchs) 1980. *Address:* Göresstrasse 15, Bundeshaus, 5300 Bonn; 2940 Wilhelmshaven, Kolkweg 31A, Federal Republic of Germany. *Telephone:* 02225-2688.

EHRENBERGER, Vlastimil, ING., C.Sc; Czechoslovak politician; b. 16 Feb. 1935, Svojanov, Svitavy Dist.; ed. Mining Coll., Ostrava; technician, Ostrava-Karviná Coal Mines 1955-61; mem. North Bohemia C.P. Regional Cttee., Cen. Cttee. of Czechoslovakia C.P., Sec. for Industry 1970-73, mem. Cen. Cttee. 1976-; scientific worker, Research Inst. for Fuel Economy 1968-69; Deputy Dir. of Construction of Ostrava-Karviná Coal Mines 1969-70; Vice-Premier of Czechoslovakia 1973-74; Minister of Fuel and Energy 1974-88; Head of Czechoslovak del. to the Perm. Comm. for the Coal Industry of CMEA; Deputy of Fed. Assembly 1974-89; mem. Scientific Council of the Mining Coll., Ostrava, Head of Inst. of Systems Analysis and Modelling of Raw Material Systems; Order of Merit for Construction 1975, Commdr.'s Cross with the Star of the Order for Services to Poland. *Publications:* numerous publs. on modelling of fuel-energy complexes. *Address:* c/o Ministry of Fuel and Energy, Vinohradská 8, 120 70 Prague 2, Czechoslovakia.

EHRET, Robert, DR. JUR.; German banker; b. 19 July 1925, Mannheim; fmr. mem. of Supervisory Bd., Deutsche Bank AG; Deputy Chair. Supervisory Bd. Otto AG für Beteiligungen (Hamburg); mem. Supervisory Bd. BASF AG (Ludwigshafen-Rhein), Dyckerhoff AG (Wiesbaden), Gruner + Jahr AG (Hamburg). *Address:* c/o Deutsche Bank AG, Postfach 10 06 01, 6000 Frankfurt am Main 1, Tanusanlage 12, Federal Republic of Germany.

EHRLICH, Paul Ralph, M.A., PH.D.; American population biologist; b. 29 May 1932, Philadelphia, Pa.; s. of William and Ruth (Rosenberg) Ehrlich; m. Anne Fitzhugh Howland 1954; one d.; ed. Univs. of Pennsylvania and Kansas; Assoc. investigator, U.S.A.F. research project, Alaska and Univ. of Kansas 1956-57; Research Assoc. Chicago Acad. of Sciences and Univ. of Kansas Dept. of Entomology 1957-59; mem. Faculty, Stanford Univ. 1959-, Prof. of Biology 1966-, Bing Prof. of Population Studies 1976-; Fellow A.A.A.S.; mem. N.A.S.; Hon. D.Hum.Litt. (Univ. of the Pacific) 1970. *Publications:* How to Know the Butterflies 1961, Population Resources, Environment 1970, 1972 (both with A. H. Ehrlich); The Population Bomb 1968, 1971; How to be a Survivor (with R. L. Harriman) 1971; co-editor: Man and the Ecosphere (with J. P. Holdren and R. W. Holm) 1971; Global Ecology (with J. P. Holdren) 1971, Human Ecology (with A. H. Ehrlich and J. Holdren) 1973, Ark II (with D. Pirages) 1974, The Process of Evolution (with R. W. Holm and D. R. Parnell) 1974, The End of Affluence (with A. H. Ehrlich) 1974; Biology and Society (with R. W. Holm and I. Brown) 1976, The Race Bomb (with S. Feldman) 1977, Ecoscience: Population, Resources, Environment (with A. H. Ehrlich and J. P. Holdren) 1977, Introduction to Insect Biology and Diversity (with H. V. Daly and J. T. Doyen) 1978, The Golden Door: International Migration, Mexico and the U.S. (with D. L. Bilderback and A. H. Ehrlich) 1979, Extinction: The Causes and Consequences of the Disappearance of Species (with A. H. Ehrlich) 1981, Machinery of Nature 1986, Earth (with A. H. Ehrlich) 1987, The Birder's Handbook (with D. Dobkin and D. Whage) 1988, New Words/New Mind (with R. Ornstein) 1989 and other books; over 500 scientific and popular articles. *Leisure interest:* collecting primitive art. *Address:* Department of Biological Sciences, Stanford University, Stanford, Calif. 94305, U.S.A. *Telephone:* 415-723-3171.

EHRLICH, S. Paul, Jr., M.P.H., M.D.; American physician; b. 4 May 1932, Minn.; s. of S. Paul Ehrlich and Dorothy E. Fiterman; m. Geraldine McKenna 1959; three d.; ed. Univs. of Minnesota and Calif.; Staff Physician, Grants and Training Branch, Nat. Heart Inst., Nat. Insts. of Health,

Bethesda 1959-60; Chief, Epidemiology Field Training Station, Heart Disease Control Program, Wash., D.C. 1961-66, Deputy Chief Heart Disease Control Program 1966-67; Lecturer in Epidemiology, School of Public Health, Univ. of Calif. 1963-; Clinical Assoc. Prof., Dept. of Community Medicine and Int. Health, Georgetown Univ. School of Medicine, Wash., D.C. 1967-; Adjunct Prof. of Int. Health, Univ. of Texas; Deputy Dir. Pan American Health Org., Washington 1979-; Assoc. Dir. for Bilateral Programs, Office of Int. Health, 1967-68; Deputy Dir. Office of Int. Health 1968-69; Acting Dir. Office of Int. Health, Dept. of Health, Educ. and Welfare Dec. 1969-70, Dir. 1970-77; Asst. Surgeon-Gen., USPHS 1970, Acting Surgeon-Gen. 1973-77, Deputy Surgeon-Gen. 1976-77; U.S. Rep. to World Health Org. (WHO) 1969-72, 1973-76; Diplomate, American Bd. of Preventive Medicine; Chair. Exec. Bd. of WHO 1972; Sr. Adviser American Asscn. of World Health 1984-86, Health Consultant 1986-. *Publications:* Articles on Chronic Disease Control, Coronary Disease Risk Factors, and the Relationship of the Stroke to Other Cardiovascular Diseases. *Address:* 6512 Lakeview Drive, Falls Church, Va. 22041, U.S.A.

EHRLICHMAN, John Daniel, B.A., J.D.; American attorney and writer; b. 20 March 1925, Tacoma, Wash.; s. of late Rudolph I. Ehrlichman and Lillian Danielson; m. 1st Jeanne Fisher 1949 (divorced), three s. two d.; m. 2nd Christy McLaurine 1978, one s.; ed. Univ. of Calif. (Los Angeles) and Stanford Univ.; served with U.S. Army Air Corps during Second World War; fmrly. with Hullin Ehrlichman Roberts and Hodge (law firm) Seattle; Dir. of Convention Activities subsequently Tour Dir. Presidential Campaign 1968; Counsel to Pres. Nixon Nov. 1968-69; Asst. to Pres. for Domestic Affairs Nov. 1969-March 1973 (resigned over the Watergate case); convicted for Watergate related charges July 1974, Feb. 1975 (sentenced to prison term, released April 1978); Radio Commentator MBS 1978-80. *Publications:* The Company 1976, The Impact of Elections 1977, The Whole Truth 1979, Witness to Power 1982, The China Card 1986, Sketches and Notes 1987, and numerous magazine articles. *Address:* P.O. Box 5559, Santa Fe, N.M. 87502, U.S.A.

EHRMAN, John Patrick William, M.A., F.B.A., F.S.A., F.R.HIST.S.; British historian; b. 17 March 1920, London; s. of Albert Ehrman and Rina Ehrman; m. Elizabeth Susan Anne Blake 1948; four s.; ed. Charterhouse and Trinity Coll. Cambridge; served R.N. 1940-45; Fellow of Trinity Coll. 1947-52; Historian, Cabinet Office 1948-56; Lees Knowles Lecturer, Cambridge Univ. 1957-58; James Ford Special Lecturer, Oxford Univ. 1976-77; Hon. Treas. Friends of the Nat. Libraries 1960-77; Trustee, Nat. Portrait Gallery 1971-85; mem. Reviewing Cttee. on the Export of Works of Art 1970-76, Royal Comm. on Historical Manuscripts 1973-; Chair. Advisory Cttee. to British Library Reference Div. 1975-84, Panizzi Foundation Selection Council 1983-. *Publications:* The Navy in the War of William III 1953, Grand Strategy 1943-45 (2 vols.: U.K. Official Military Histories of the Second World War) 1956, Cabinet, Government and War 1890-1940 1958, The British Government and Commercial Negotiations with Europe 1783-1793 1962, The Younger Pitt (Vol. I) 1969, (Vol. II) 1983. *Address:* The Mead Barns, Taynton, Nr. Burford, Oxon, England.

EIBL-EIBESFELDT, Irenäus, DR.PHIL.; Austrian professor of zoology; b. 15 June 1928, Vienna; s. of Anton and Maria (von Hauninger) Eibl-Eibesfeldt; m. Eleonore Siegel 1950; one s. one d.; ed. Univs. of Vienna and Munich; Research Assoc., Biol. Station, Wilhelminenberg, nr. Vienna 1946-49, Max Planck Inst. of Behavioural Physiology 1951-69; Head of ind. research unit on human ethology, Max Planck Inst. 1970-; Prof. Univ. of Munich 1963-; corresp. mem. Deutsche Akad. der Naturforscher Leopoldina; Wilhelm Bölsche Gold Medal 1971, Burda Prize for Communications research 1980. *Publications:* Galapagos, die Arche Noah im Pacific 1960, Im Reich der tausend Atolle 1964, Grundriss der vergleichenden Verhaltensforschung 1967, Liebe und Hass 1970, Der vorprogrammierte Mensch 1973, Menschenforschung auf neuen Wegen 1976, Der Hai: Legende eines Mörders (with H. Hass) 1977, Die Maldiven. Paradies im Indischen Ozean 1982, Die Biologie des menschlichen Verhaltens, Grundriss der Humanethologie 1984. *Address:* Fichtenweg 9, 813 Starnberg 2, Federal Republic of Germany. *Telephone:* (08151) 6607.

EICHER, Lawrence D., PH.D.; American scientist and administrator; b. 3 Nov. 1938, Colorado; m. Nancy Darby 1960; two s. one d.; ed. Univ. of Northern Colorado, Univ. of California (Berkeley), Texas A & M Univ.; science teacher 1960-64; Sr. Data Analyst, Thermodynamics Research Center, Texas A & M Univ. 1967-72; Program Man., Scientific and Tech. Data Systems, Nat. Science Foundation 1972-74; Asst. to Dir., Inst. for Applied Tech., Nat. Bureau of Standards 1974-76, Chief, Office of Standards Information, Analysis and Devt., Nat. Eng. Lab., NBS 1975-79, Dir. Office of Eng. Standards, NBS 1979-80; Asst. Sec.-Gen., Int. Org. for Standardization (ISO), Geneva 1980-86, Sec.-Gen. 1986-. *Publications:* Finding and Building Agreement for the Technology of a Better World (ISO) 1984, Standards for Expanding Markets—the ISO/IEC Approach (review) 1987, Technical Regulations and Standards (World Bank Handbook) 1987, over forty scientific and educational papers. *Address:* International Organization for Standardization, Case Postale 56, CH-1211 Geneva 20, Switzerland (Office); Joli Crêt C, 1261 Chéserex, Switzerland (Home). *Telephone:* (022) 34 12 40 (Office); (022) 69 24 49 (Home).

EICHLER, Irena; Polish actress; b. 19 April 1908, Warsaw; ed. Theatrical School, Warsaw, student of Aleksander Zelwerowicz; began career in

Vilnius, Lvov, Krakow and Łódź; later with Polish and Nat. Theatres in Warsaw; abroad 1939–45; went to Brazil, helped organize Brazilian Nat. Theatre and Dramatic School; Warsaw theatres 1945–; Rozmaitości, Nowy, Współczesny, Ludowy; Teatr Narodowy 1958–; State Prize (1st Class) 1955, Order of Banner of Labour (1st Class) 1959, Minister of Culture and Arts Prize 1965, 1977; Officer's Cross, Order of Polonia Restituta. *Roles include:* Salome (Wilde), Cleopatra (Norwid), Chimène (Corneille), Judith (Giraudoux), Balladyna (Słowacki), Mrs. Warren (Shaw), Rosita (Lorca), Maria Stuart (Schiller), Phèdre (Racine), Maria Tudor (V. Hugo), Mutter Courage (Brecht), Mewa (Chekhov), Jocasta (Sophocles), Klytemnestra (Aeschylus), Gabriella Zapolska (own play). *Publication:* Gabriella Zapolska. *Address:* ul. Odolańska 20 m. 1, 02-562 Warsaw, Poland.

EICK, Jürgen, DR.RER.POL.; German journalist; b. 24 March 1920, Dresden; s. of Professor Heinrich Eick and Hedwig Jürgens; m. Elisabeth Durchleuchter 1947; one s. one d.; ed. econ. studies; joined Wirtschaftszeitung, Stuttgart 1946, Allgemeine Zeitung, Mainz 1948; Dir. econ. section, Frankfurter Allgemeine Zeitung 1949, Jt. Ed. FAZ 1963–86; Bundesverdienstkreuz 1976, Grosses Ehrenzeichen für Verdienste um die Republik Österreich 1977; Ludwig Erhard Prize 1977. *Publications:* Angina Temporis 1955, Wenn Milch und Honig fliessen 1958, Das Jahrhundert des kleinen Mannes 1960, So nutzt man den Wirtschaftsteil einer Tageszeitung 1971, Wie man eine Volkswirtschaft ruinieren kann 1974, Das Regime der Ohnmächtigen 1976, Als noch Milch und Honig flossen 1982. *Leisure interests:* golf, hunting, books. *Address:* Frankfurter Allgemeine Zeitung, Hellerhofstrasse 2–4, Postfach 100808, D-6000 Frankfurt (Office); Kurt-Schumacher-Ring 72, D-6072 Dreieich, Federal Republic of Germany (Home). *Telephone:* 0691/75910 (Office); 06103/33140 (Home).

EIDEM, Bjarne Mørk; Norwegian politician b. 4 Oct. 1936, Vega; m.; fmr. teacher; mem. Vega Municipal Council 1963–71; mem. Storting 1969, Vice-Chair. Standing Cttee. on Shipping and Fisheries 1985; mem. Nordic Council 1972–; Minister of Fisheries May 1986–. *Address:* Ministry of Fisheries, P.O. Box 8118, Dep., Oslo 1, Norway. *Telephone:* (2) 56-36-80.

EIGEN, Manfred, DR. RER. NAT.; German physical chemist; b. 9 May 1927, Bochum; s. of Ernst Eigen and Hedwig Feld; m. Elfriede Müller; one s. one d.; ed. Georg-August-Univ. zu Göttingen; Max-Planck Inst. of Physical Chem., Göttingen, as Asst., later as Prof. and Head of Dept. 1953–, Dir. 1964; Hon. Prof. Technical Univ., Göttingen 1971–; Pres. Studienstiftung des Deutschen Volkes 1983–; Otto Hahn Prize 1962, Nobel Prize for Chem. (with Norrish and Porter) for investigation of extremely rapid chemical reactions by means of disturbing the (molecular) equilibrium by the action of very short energy pulses 1967; mem. Akad. der Wissenschaften, Göttingen; Foreign hon. mem. American Acad. of Arts and Sciences, Foreign Assoc. mem. Nat. Acad. of Sciences, U.S.A.; Foreign mem. Royal Soc., U.K., Acad. Française 1978; Hon. Dr. Univ. of Washington, St. Louis Univ., Harvard Univ. and Cambridge Univ. and numerous other hon. degrees. *Address:* Max-Planck-Institut für biophysikalische Chemie, Karl-Friedrich-Bonhoeffer-Institut, Am Fassberg, Georg-Dehio-Weg 14, 3400 Göttingen-Nikolausberg, Federal Republic of Germany. *Telephone:* 0551-20-14-32.

EIKA, Hallvard; Norwegian farmer and politician; b. 5 Dec. 1920, Torquay, Sask., Canada; s. of Ketil and Kari (née Landsverk) Eika; m. Aslaug Vethe 1959; two s. one d.; ed. Agricultural Coll. of Norway and abroad; Scientific Asst., Inst. for Agricultural Economy, Agricultural Coll. of Norway 1946–48; Consultant, Norwegian Farmers' Union 1948–50, Royal Soc. for Rural Devt. of Norway 1950–52; Farmer, Bø 1952–; Chair. Norwegian Farmers' Union 1955–66; mem. Bd. Norwegian Forest Owners Fed. 1955–65, Bøndernes Bank A/S 1962–87, Fokús Bank A/S 1987–, Forenede Liv Insurance Comp. 1956–79; mem. Presidium, Cen. Council of Nordic Agricultural Orgs. 1956–66; Vice-Pres. Int. Fed. of Agricultural Producers 1964–67; Mayors of Bø 1967–70; mem. Parl 1969–77; Minister of Agric. 1970–71; Minister of Commerce and Shipping 1972–73; Chair. Bø Hotel A/S 1968–; Chair. Telemark Distrikts högskole 1971–76; Dir. Telemark Agric. Soc. 1977–85; Pres. Agric. Credit Asscn. 1981–89. *Address:* Bø, Telemark, Norway. *Telephone:* (03) 950083.

EILENBERG, Samuel, PH.D.; American mathematician; b. 30 Sept. 1913; ed. Univ. of Warsaw; Instructor, Univ. of Michigan 1940–41, Asst. Prof. 1941–45, Assoc. Prof. 1945–46; Prof. Indiana Univ. 1946–47; Prof. Columbia Univ. 1947–84; Visiting Prof. Univ. of Paris 1950–51, and 1966–67; mem. N.A.S., American Acad. of Arts and Sciences; hon. mem. London Math. Soc.; fmr. Vice-Pres. American Math. Soc.; Hon. Dr. (Brandeis) 1980, (Pennsylvania) 1985, (Columbia) 1987, (Louvain) 1987; Hon. Life mem. New York Acad. of Science; Wolf Prize 1985/86; Steele Prize (American Math. Soc.) 1987. *Publications:* Foundations of Algebraic Topology (with N. E. Steenrod) 1952, Homological Algebra (with H. Cartan) 1956, Recursiveness (with C. C. Elgot) 1970, Automata, Languages and Machines, vol. A 1974, vol. B. 1976; numerous articles in professional journals. *Leisure interest:* Indian and S.E. Asian art. *Address:* Department of Mathematics, Columbia University, New York, N.Y. 10027, U.S.A.

EILTS, Hermann Frederick, M.A., LL.D.; American (b. German) diplomatist (retd.); b. 23 March 1922, Germany; m. Helen Brew Eilts 1948; two s.; ed. Ursinus Coll., Johns Hopkins Univ., Univ. of Pennsylvania; several diplomatic posts in Teheran 1947–48, Jeddah 1948–51, Aden 1951–54,

Baghdad 1954–56, Washington, D.C. 1956–61; First Sec., American Embassy, London 1962–64; Counsellor, Deputy Head of Mission, American Embassy, Tripoli 1964–65; Amb. to Saudi Arabia 1965–70; Diplomatic Adviser to U.S. Army War Coll. 1970–73; Amb. to Egypt 1973–79; Prof. of Int. Relations, Boston Univ. 1979–, Dir. Center for Int. Relations 1982–, Chair. Dept. of Political Science 1982–87; Arthur Fleming Award for Distinguished Govt. Service, U.S. Army Decoration for Distinguished Civilian Service, Joseph C. Wilson Award for Achievement in International Affairs 1979, Dept. of State Distinguished Service Award 1979, Egyptian Collar of The Nile (First Class) 1979. *Leisure interests:* coins, stamps, reading, hiking, tennis. *Address:* Boston University, 152 Bay State Road, Boston, Mass. 02115 (Office); 67 Cleveland Road, Wellesley, Mass. 02181, U.S.A. (Home).

EINAUDI, Giulio; Italian publisher; b. 2 Jan. 1912, Turin; s. of Prof. Luigi Einaudi and Ida Pellegrin; m. Renata Aldrovandi 1950; three s. three d.; ed. Liceo Massimo d'Azeglio and Univ. of Turin; Founder Publishing House, Giulio Einaudi Editore 1933, Gen. Man. 1954–. *Leisure interests:* mountaineering, paintings, rare books. *Address:* Via Umberto Biancamano 1, C.P. 245, 10121 Turin, Italy. *Telephone:* 533653.

EINEM, Gottfried von; Austrian professor and composer; b. 24 Jan. 1918, Berne, Switzerland; s. of William and Gerta Louise von Einem; m. Lotte Ingrisch; one s.; ed. Gymnasium at Ratzeburg and musical studies with Boris Blacher; Coach, State Opera in Berlin 1939–44; Musical Adviser to Dir. of Dresden State Opera, Coach Bayreuth Festival 1938–39; mem. Bd. of Salzburg Festival 1948–51; mem. Acad. of Arts, Berlin (West and East), Vienna Konzerthaus Gesellschaft 1963–; Emer. Prof. Hochschule für Musik, Vienna; numerous awards and prizes including Austrian State Prize 1965. *Compositions:* Operas: Death of Danton (Büchner), The Trial (Kafka), Der Zerrissene (Nestroy), Visit of the Old Lady (Dürrenmatt), Kabale und Liebe (Schiller), Jesu Hochzeit (Lotte Ingrisch); Cantatas: Stunden Lied (Brecht), An die Nachgeborenen (various poets); also five ballets and various other works for orchestra including two piano concertos, a violin concerto, songs and four string quartets. *Leisure interest:* cooking. *Address:* Vienna A1010, 1/2/5 Nikolaigasse, Austria. *Telephone:* 523443.

EISEN, Herman N(athaniel), A.B., M.D.; American immunologist and microbiologist; b. 15 Oct. 1918, Brooklyn, N.Y.; s. of Joseph M. Eisen and Lena M. (Karush) Eisen; m. Natalie Aronson 1948; three s. two d.; ed. New York Univ.; Prof. of Medicine (Dermatology), Washington Univ., St. Louis 1955–61, Prof. of Microbiology and Head of Dept. 1961–73; Prof. of Immunology, Mass. Inst. of Technology 1973–; mem. Bd. Scientific Advisors Mass. Gen. Hospital, Boston 1977–, Boston Children's Hospital 1976–, Howard Hughes Medical Inst., Miami 1978–, Merck, Sharp & Dohme Research Laboratories, Rahway 1976–; Harvey Lecturer 1964; Consultant to Surgeons-Gen. of Public Health Service, Dept. of the Army; Chair. Study Section for Allergy and Immunology, Nat. Insts. of Health 1964–68; mem. editorial boards of Journal of Immunology, Bacteriological Reviews, Physiological Reviews, Proceedings of the Nat. Acad. of Sciences of U.S.A.; mem. Bd. of Scientific Advisors, Mass. Gen. Hosp., Boston; mem. Bd., Merck, Sharpe and Dohme, Howard Hughes Medical Inst.; mem. American Soc. for Clinical Investigation (Vice-Pres. 1963–64), American Asscn. of Immunologists (Pres. 1968–69), American Soc. for Biological Chemists, American Asscn. of Physicians, N.A.S., Inst. of Medicine, American Acad. of Arts and Sciences; New York Univ. Medical Science Achievement Award 1978. *Publications:* Methods in Medical Research Vol. 10 (Ed.) 1964, Microbiology (co-Author) 1967, 1973, Immunology 1974, Contemporary Topics in Molecular Immunology Vol. 5 (Ed.) 1976; about 150 scientific articles. *Leisure interests:* reading, tennis. *Address:* E-17-128 Center for Cancer Research, Massachusetts Institute of Technology, Cambridge, Mass. 01239 (Office); 9 Homestead Street, Waban, Mass. 02168, U.S.A. (Home). *Telephone:* 617-253-6406.

EISENBERG, Leon, M.D., M.A.; American physician and professor of psychiatry; b. 8 Aug. 1922, Philadelphia; s. of Morris Eisenberg and Elizabeth Sabreen; m. 1st Ruth Bleier 1947 (divorced 1967), 2nd Carola Guttmacher 1967; one s. one d.; ed. Univ. of Pennsylvania, Mt. Sinai Hosp., New York, Sheppard Pratt Hosp., Baltimore, Johns Hopkins Hosp., Baltimore; Capt. U.S. Army Medical Corps 1948–50; Instructor in Psychiatry and Pediatrics, Johns Hopkins Medical School 1954, Asst. Prof. 1955–58, Assoc. Prof. 1958–61, Prof. of Child Psychiatry 1961–67; Chief of Psychiatry Massachusetts Gen. Hosp. 1967–74; Prof. of Psychiatry, Harvard Medical School 1967–, Chair. of Exec. Cttee. of Psychiatry 1974–80, Presley Prof. and Chair., Dept. of Social Medicine and Health Policy 1980–; Royal Soc. of Medicine Visiting Prof. 1983; Queen Elizabeth II Lecturer, Canadian Pediatric Soc. 1986; Consultant, Div. of Mental Health, WHO 1980; Liliy Lecturer, Royal Coll. of Psychiatrists 1986; Dir. WHO/Harvard Collaborating Center for Research and Training in Psychiatry 1986–; mem. Inst. of Medicine N.A.S. 1974–, expert advisory panel on Mental Health 1984–; Hon. Sc.D. (Manchester) 1973; Theobald Smith Award 1979, Aldrich Award 1980, Samuel T. Orton Award 1980, Hon. Fellow Royal Coll. of Psychiatrists 1985. *Publications:* many medical publications. *Leisure interests:* classical music, theatre, reading. *Address:* Harvard Medical School, 25 Shattuck Street, Boston, Mass. 02115; 9 Clement Circle, Cambridge, Mass. 02138, U.S.A. *Telephone:* (617) 732-1710 (Office); (617) 868-0112 (Home).

EISENHOWER, John Sheldon Doud, B.S., M.A.; American author and diplomatist; b. 3 Aug. 1922, Denver, Colo.; s. of late Gen. Dwight D. Eisenhower (President of the U.S.A. 1953-61) and Mamie (Doud) Eisenhower; m. Barbara Jean Thompson 1947 (divorced 1986); one s. three d.; ed. Stadium High School, Tacoma, Wash., U.S. Military Acad., West Point, Columbia Univ. and Armored Advance Course and General Staff Coll., U.S. Army; assigned to First Army, Second World War; Instructor in English, U.S. Mil. Acad., West Point 1948-51; served as Battalion Operations Officer, Div. Asst. Operations Officer and Div. Intelligence Officer, Korea; Joint War Plans Div., Army Staff, Pentagon 1957-58; Asst. Staff Sec. in White House 1958-61; researcher and editor on Eisenhower memoirs The White House Years; Amb. to Belgium 1969-71; Consultant to President Nixon; Chair. Interagency Classification Review Cttee. 1972-73; Brig.-Gen. U.S. Army Reserve 1974; mem. Nat. Archives Advisory Cttee. 1974-77; Chair. Pres.'s Advisory Cttee. on Refugees 1975; Legion of Merit, Bronze Star, Army Commendation Ribbon, Combat Infantry Badge, Grand Cross, Order of the Crown (Belgium). *Publications:* The Bitter Woods 1969, Strictly Personal 1974, Allies 1981. *Leisure interest:* aviation. *Address:* P.O. Box 278, Kimberton, Pa. 19442, U.S.A. (Home).

EISENSTADT, Shmuel N., M.A. PH.D.; Israeli professor of sociology; b. 10 Sept. 1923, Warsaw, Poland; s. of Michael Eisenstadt and Rosa Baruchin; m. Shulamit Yaroshevski 1948; two s. one d.; ed. Hebrew Univ., Jerusalem and London School of Econs. and Political Science; Chair. Dept. of Sociology, Hebrew Univ., Jerusalem 1951-69, Prof. of Sociology 1959-, Dean, Faculty of Social Sciences 1966-68; Visiting Prof., Univ. of Oslo 1958, Univ. of Chicago 1960, Harvard Univ. 1966, 1968-69, 1975-80, Michigan 1970, Chicago 1971, Zürich 1975, Stanford 1984, 1986, 1987, 1988; Carnegie Visiting Prof., Mass. Inst. of Technology 1962-63, Simon Visiting Prof., Univ. of Manchester 1977; Research Fellow, Hoover Inst. 1986; Hon. Research Fellow, Australian Nat. Univ. 1977; Chair. Council on Community Devt., Israel 1962-66, Israeli Sociological Soc. 1969-72; Fellow, Center for Advanced Studies in the Behavioral Sciences, Stanford Univ. 1955-56; Hon. Fellow, London School of Econs.; Foreign Fellow American Anthropological Asscn.; Fellow Netherlands Inst. of Advanced Studies 1973; Dr. h.c. (Helsinki) 1986; mem. Israel Acad. of Sciences and Humanities, Int. Sociological Soc., American Sociological Asscn.; Foreign mem.American Philosophical Soc.; Foreign Hon. mem. American Acad. of Arts and Sciences; Foreign Assoc. N.A.S.; mem. Advisory Bd. International Encyclopedia of the Social Sciences; McIver Award, American Sociological Asscn. 1964, Rothschild Prize in the Social Sciences 1969, Israel Prize in the Social Sciences 1973, Balzan Award in Sociology 1988. *Publications:* The Absorption of Immigrants 1954, From Generation to Generation 1956, Essays on Sociological Aspects of Economical and Political Development 1961, The Political Systems of Empires 1963, Essays on Comparative Institutions 1965, Modernization, Protest and Change 1966, Israeli Society 1968, The Protestant Ethic and Modernization 1968, Political Sociology of Modernization (in Japanese) 1968, Comparative Perceptives on Social Change (Ed.) 1968, Charisma and Institution Building: Selections from Max Weber (Ed.) 1968, Ensayos sobre el Cambio social y la Modernización (Spanish) 1969, Modernizicão e Mudança Social (Portuguese) 1969, Political Sociology (Ed.) 1970, Social Differentiation and Stratification 1971, Collection of Essays in Japanese 1971, Tradition, Change and Modernity 1973, Collection of Essays in Spanish 1973, Post-traditional Societies (Ed.) 1974, The Form of Sociology: Paradigms and Crises (with M. Curelaru) 1976, Macrosociology (with M. Curelaru) 1977, Revolutions and Transformation of Societies 1978, Patrons, Clients and Friends (with L. Roniger) 1984, Transformation of Israeli Society 1985, Origins and Diversity of Axial Age Civilizations (Ed.) 1986, Society, Culture and Urbanisation (with A. Shachar) 1987, The Origins of the State Reconsidered (with M. Abitbol and N. Chazan) 1986, European Civilization in Comparative Perspective 1987, Center Formation, Protest Movements and Class Structure in Europe and the U.S. (with L. Roniger and A. Seligman) 1987, Patterns of Modernity I and II 1987, Kulturen der Achsenzeit (trans.) 1987, Die Transformation der Israelichen Gesellschaft (trans.) 1987, The Early State in African Perspective 1988, Knowledge and Society: Studies in the Sociological Culture, Past and Present 1988. *Address:* The Hebrew University, Mount Scopus, Jerusalem (Office); 30 Radak Street, Jerusalem, Israel (Home). *Telephone:* 632467.

EISENSTAEDT, Alfred; American photographer; b. 6 Dec. 1898, Dirschau, Germany; s. of Joseph and Regina Eisenstaedt; m. Kathy Eisenstaedt (died 1972); ed. Hohenzollern Gymnasium Berlin; emigrated to U.S.A. 1935; with Time Inc. 1936-, staff photographer Life magazine 1936-72, People magazine 1972-; freelance work including advertising, promotion and giving lectures throughout U.S.A.; Photographer of the Year 1951, Culture Prize in Photography (German Soc. of Photographers), Int. Understanding Award 1967, Clifton Edom Award, Univ. of Missouri Joseph Sprague Award, and many others. *Publications:* Witness to our Time, Martha's Vineyard, The Eye of Eisenstaedt, Witness to Nature, Wimbledon: A Celebration, People, Eisenstaedt's Album, Eisenstaedt's Guide to Photography, Eisenstaedt—Germany, Eisenstaedt—Aberdeen, Eisenstaedt on Eisenstaedt. *Leisure interests:* music, hiking, greenhouse gardening. *Address:* Time Inc., Time & Life Building, Room 2850, Rockefeller Centre, New York, N.Y. 10020, U.S.A. *Telephone:* (212) 556-2342.

EISNER, Thomas, B.A., PH.D.; American professor of biology; b. 25 June 1929, Berlin, Germany; s. of Hans E. Eisner and Margarete Heil-Eisner; m. Maria L. R. Löbell 1952; three d.; ed. High School and Preparatory School, Montevideo, Uruguay, Champlain Coll., Plattsburgh, N.Y. and Harvard Univ.; Research Fellow in Biology, Harvard Univ. 1955-57; Asst. Prof. of Biology, Cornell Univ. 1957-62, Assoc. Prof. 1962-66, Prof. of Biology 1966-76, Jacob Gould Schurman Prof. of Biology 1976; Consultant, World Environmental Research Programme MacArthur Foundation 1987-; Lalor Fellow 1954-55, Guggenheim Fellow 1964-65, 1972-73; mem. Nat. Council for Nature Conservancy 1969-74, Council Fed. American Scientists 1977-81; Dir. National Audubon Soc. 1970-76; Pres. American Soc. of Naturalists 1988; mem. N.A.S. 1969, American Philosophical Soc., Akademie Naturforscher Leopoldina; Fellow, American Acad. of Arts and Sciences, Royal Soc. of Arts, Animal Behaviour Soc., American Entomological Soc., Club of Earth, Zero Population Growth (Dir. 1969-70); Chair. Biology Section, A.A.A.S. 1980-81, mem. Cttee. for Scientific Freedom and Responsibility 1980-87, Chair. Subcttee. on Science and Human Rights 1981-87; mem. Steering Cttee. on Consequences of Nuclear War 1983-; Scientific Advisory Council, World Wildlife Fund 1983-, N.A.S. Cttee. on Human Rights 1987-, Advisory Council, Monell Chemical Senses Inst. 1988-; World Resources Inst. 1988-; Hon. Ph.D. (Univ. Würzburg, Univ. Zürich); Newcomb-Cleveland Prize (with E. O. Wilson) of A.A.A.S. 1967, Founders Memorial Award of Entomological Soc. of America 1969, Outstanding Teacher Award, Cornell Univ. 1973, Archie F. Carr Medal 1983, four awards for film Secret Weapons, BBC TV 1984; Proctor Prize 1986, Karl Ritter von Frisch Medal 1988. *Publications:* over 200 technical papers and five books on animal behaviour, chemical ecology, comparative physiology, chemical communication in animals. *Leisure interests:* orchestra conducting, piano, conservation, photography. *Address:* Section of Neurobiology and Behaviour, Division of Biological Sciences, W347 Mudd Hall, Cornell University, Ithaca, N.Y. 14853, U.S.A. *Telephone:* (607) 255-4464.

EITAN, Lieut.-Gen. Raphael; Israeli army officer; b. 1929, Tel Adashim; m.; four c.; ed. Tel-Aviv and Haifa Univs.; joined Palmach when 17; Deputy Co. Commdr. 1948; various posts with paratroops 1950-53; Commdr. Paratroop Unit, Sinai campaign 1956; Deputy Commdr. Paratroop Brigade 1958, Commdr. 1964-67; Commdr. Jordan Valley Brigade 1967-68; Chief Paratroop and Infantry Officer, rank of Brig.-Gen. 1968-73; Commdr. Div. on Golan Heights, rank of Maj.-Gen., Yom Kippur War 1973-74; C.O. Northern Command 1974-77; Chief of Gen. Staff Branch 1977-78; Chief of Gen. Staff 1978-83. *Address:* c/o Israeli Defence Forces, General Staff, Tel-Aviv, Israel.

EKANDEM, H.E. Cardinal Dominic Ignatius, O.B.E.; Nigerian ecclesiastic; b. 1917, Obio Ibiono, Cross River State; s. of Chief Paul Eno Ekandem Ubo and Nwa Ibong Umana Essien; ed. St. Paul's Major Seminary, Enugu and Okpala, Owerrinta; ordained priest 1947; Asst. Priest, Ifuho and Afaha Obong; Rector of Minor Seminary; consecrated auxiliary Bishop of Calabar 1954; Bishop of Ikot Ekpene 1963-; Apostolic Admin. Port Harcourt Diocese 1970-73; Pres. Episcopal Conf. of Nigeria 1973-79; cr. Cardinal 1975; mem. Sacred Congregation for the Evangelization of the Peoples; Pres. Asscn. of Episcopal Confs. of Anglophone W. Africa 1977; Hon. D.D. 1954; Hon. O.B.E. 1960; Commdr. Order of the Niger 1965. *Publications:* Shepherd among Shepherds 1979 and Annual Addresses to Episcopal Conferences 1973-78. *Leisure interests:* reading and cultural exercises such as drama. *Address:* Cardinal's House, Library Avenue, P.O. Box 70, Ikot Ekpene, Cross River State, Nigeria. *Telephone:* Ikot Ekpene 21.

EKANGAKI, Nzo; Cameroonian politician; b. 22 March 1934, Nguti; ed. Bali Coll., Hope Waddle Training Inst., Calabar, Nigeria and Univs. of Ibadan, Nigeria, London, Oxford and Bonn; served in several posts in Cameroon Admin. 1959-60; Deputy Minister of Foreign Affairs 1962-64; Minister of Public Health and Population 1964-65, of Labour and Social Welfare 1965-72; Sec.-Gen. Org. of African Unity 1972-74; Adviser to Presidency, Yaoundé 1985-; Sec.-Gen. Kamerun Nat. Democratic Party (KNDP) 1962-66; mem. of Political Bureau, Cameroon Nat. Union Party (CNU) 1966-75; mem. Parl. S. Cameroon 1961-62, mem. first Nat. Federal Assembly 1962-65, 1965-71; del. to many int. confs., to WHO Conf., Geneva 1964, to several Int. Labour Confs.; rep. on many missions abroad. *Publications:* An Introduction to East Cameroon 1956, To the Nigerian People 1958. *Address:* c/o Presidency of the Republic, Yaoundé, Cameroon.

EKE, Abudu Yesufu, B.SC., M.A.; Nigerian educational administrator; b. 7 Sept. 1923, Benin City; s. of Yesufu O. and Barikisu A. Eke; m. Clara Noyogiere Eke 1956; three s. three d.; ed. Higher Coll., Yaba, Univ. Coll., Ibadan and Sidney Sussex Coll., Cambridge; various posts in Public Relations Dept. 1948-54; Information Officer, Fed. Information Services 1954-55; Asst. Registrar, Univ. Coll., Ibadan 1955-58; Principal Information Officer, subsequently Chief Information Officer, Western Nigeria Information Services 1959-61; Registrar, Univ. of Ife 1961-62; Commr. for Information, W. Region Govt. June-Aug. 1962; Registrar, Univ. of Lagos 1962-71; Commr. for Finance and Economic Development, Midwest State Govt. 1967-71; Fed. Commr. for Educ. 1971-74; Educ. and Econ. Consultant 1975-82; Amb. to U.S.A. 1982-83; Hon. LL.D. (Nigeria and Wayne State Univs.). *Publications:* History of Group Divergence in Physical Anthropology, One Nigeria (one-act play), Problems of Decolonization in

Africa, The Future of the OAU, A New Policy on Education in Nigeria, The Eradication of Illiteracy in Nigeria. *Address:* c/o Ministry of Foreign Affairs, NTA Building, Awolowo Road, Ikoyi Island, Lagos, Nigeria.

EKER, Bjarne Reidar, DR. MED.; Norwegian doctor; b. 26 Nov. 1903, Oslo, Norway; m. 1953; ed. Universitet i Oslo; Scientific Asst., Anatomy Inst., Oslo Univ. 1932-36; Pathologist, Univ. Hospital 1936-39; Chief Pathologist, Norwegian Radium Hospital 1939-74, Dir. 1947-75; Dir. Norsk Hydro's Inst. for Cancer Research 1953-75; Pres. Norwegian Cancer Soc. 1950-66; Chair. Radiation Hygiene Advisory Council 1956-74. *Publications:* about 50 scientific publications in the field of genetics, radiobiology and tumour pathology. *Leisure interests:* fishing, skiing. *Address:* The Norwegian Radium Hospital, Montebello, Oslo 3, Norway.

EKLUND, (Arne) Sigvard, D.S.; Swedish nuclear physicist; b. 19 June 1911, Kiruna; s. of Severin Eklund and Vilhelmina Pettersson; m. Anna-Greta Johansson 1941; one s. two d.; ed. Univ. of Uppsala; Nobel Inst. for Physics 1937-45; Asst. Prof. of Nuclear Physics, Royal Inst. of Technology, Stockholm 1946, Senior Scientist, Research Inst. for Nat. Defence Stockholm 1946-50; Dir. of Research AB Atomenergi, Stockholm 1950-56, Deputy to Man. Dir. 1950-61, Dir. of Reactor Devt. Div. 1957-61; Sec.-Gen. Second UN Conf. on Peaceful Uses of Atomic Energy 1958; Dir.-Gen. Int. Atomic Energy Agency (IAEA) 1961-81; Dir.-Gen. Emer. 1981-; mem. Royal Swedish Acad. of Eng. Sciences 1953, Royal Swedish Acad. of Sciences 1972; Fellow, American Nuclear Soc. 1961; Hon. mem. British Nuclear Eng. Soc. 1963; Foreign Assoc. Nat. Acad. of Engineering (U.S.A.) 1979; Atoms for Peace Award 1968; Gold Medal, Province of Vienna 1971; Dr. h.c. (Graz) 1968, (Acad. Mining and Metallurgy, Cracow) 1971, (Bucharest) 1971, (Chalmers Inst. of Tech., Gothenburg, Sweden) 1974, (Moscow State Univ.) 1977, (Columbia) 1977, (Buenos Aires) 1977, (Budapest Tech. Univ.), (Tech. Univ. Dresden) 1978, (Yon-Sei Univ., Seoul) 1978, (National Agrarian Univ., La Molina, Peru) 1979, (Royal Inst. of Tech., Stockholm) 1980; Hon. Senator (Vienna Univ.) 1977. *Address:* International Atomic Energy Agency, c/o Vienna International Centre, P.O. Box 200, A-1400 Vienna (Office); Krapfenwaldgasse 48, 1190 Vienna, Austria (Home). *Telephone:* 2360-1515 (Office); 32-24-24 (Home).

EKSTEEN, Jacobus Adriaan, M.A.; South African diplomatist (retd.), broadcasting executive and consultant; b. 31 Oct. 1942, Volksrust; s. of Jacobus Adriaan and Helena Barendina Hendrika (née Baard) Eksteen; m. Jeannette Emmarentia Swanepoel 1968; three s.; ed. Univs. of Pretoria and South Africa; entered Civil Service 1961; mem. S.A. legal team at Int. Court of Justice in South West Africa (Namibia) cases 1966; Third Sec., Second Sec., then First Sec., Embassy, U.S.A. 1968-73; served in Head Office of Dept. of Foreign Affairs as Head of UN and S.W.A. sections 1973-76; Counsellor and Deputy Perm. Rep. at S.A. Perm. Mission to UN 1976, Minister 1978, Acting Perm. Rep. 1977-79, Perm. Rep. and Amb. 1979-81; Head of Planning Div., Ministry of Foreign Affairs 1981-83; mem. S.A. Del. to Patent Cooperation Treaty, Washington 1970, to INTELSAT Conf., Washington 1971, to UN Gen. Assembly 1972, 1979, 1981; involved in all discussions on Namibia 1977-83; presented South Africa's case in UN Security Council Aug. 1981; Dir.-Gen. (desig.) South African Broadcasting Corp. 1983, Dir.-Gen. 1984-88. *Leisure interests:* reading, walking, stamp collecting, hunting. *Address:* P.O. Box 20027, Alkantrant 0005, South Africa. *Telephone:* (012) 473288.

EKWENSI, Cyprian; Nigerian pharmacist and author; b. 26 Sept. 1921, Minna, Northern Nigeria; ed. Govt. Coll., Ibadan, Achimota Coll., Ghana, School of Forestry, Ibadan, Higher Coll., Yaba, Chelsea School of Pharmacy, Univ. of London, Iowa Univ.; Lecturer in Biology, Chem. and English, Igbobi Coll., Lagos 1947-49; Lecturer, School of Pharmacy, Lagos 1949-56; Pharmacist, Nigerian Medical Service 1956; Head of Features, Nigerian Broadcasting Corpn. 1956-61; Dir. of Information, Fed. Ministry of Information, Lagos 1961-66; Dir. of Information Services, Enugu 1966; Chair. East Cen. State Library Board, Enugu 1971-75; Man. Dir. Star Printing and Publishing Co. Ltd. 1975-79, Niger Eagle Press 1981-; Visiting Lecturer, Iowa Univ.; mem. Pharmaceutical Socs. of Great Britain and Nigeria, Nigerian Arts Council, Soc. of Nigerian Authors, Inst. Public Relations Nigeria and U.K.; Dag Hammarskjöld Int. Award for Literary Merit 1968. *Publications:* When Love Whispers, Ikolo the Wrestler 1947, The Leopard's Claw 1950, People of the City 1954, Passport of Mallam Ilia, The Drummer Boy 1960, Jagua Nana 1961, Burning Grass, An African Night's Entertainment, Yaba Round about Murder 1962, Beautiful Feathers 1963, Great Elephant Bird, Rainmaker 1965, Lokotown, Juju Rock, Trouble in Form VI, Iska, Boa Suitor 1966, Coal Camp Boy 1973, Samankwe in the Strange Forest 1974, Samankwe and the Highway Robbers, Restless City, Christmas Gold 1975, Survive the Peace 1976, Divided We Stand 1980, Motherless Baby 1980, Jaguanana's Daughter 1986, For a Roll of Parchment 1986, Beneath the Convent Wall 1987. *Leisure interests:* photography, Adire Tie-Die. *Address:* Hillview Crescent, Independence Layout, P.O. Box 317, Enugu, Nigeria (Home).

EKWUEME, Alex Ifeanyichukwu, PH.D.; Nigerian architect and politician; b. 21 Oct. 1932, Oko; ed. King's Coll., Lagos, Univ. of Washington, Seattle, Univ. of Strathclyde, Glasgow; est. Ekwueme Associates (architects) 1960; fmr. Pres. Architectural Registration Council of Nigeria; Vice-Pres. candidate with Alhaji Shehu Shagari (q.v.) in Presidential elections Aug. 1979;

Vice-Pres. of Nigeria 1979-83; arrested 1984, released August 1986; banned from political activity or holding public office; Nat. Party of Nigeria.

ELATH, Eliahu, B.A., M.A., PH.D.; Israeli diplomatist; b. 30 July 1903, Snovsk, Russia; s. of Menahem and Rivka Epstein; m. Zehava Zalel 1931; ed. Hebrew Univ. of Jerusalem and American Univ. of Beirut; Jewish Agency 1934; Jewish Agency Observer to San Francisco Conf. 1945; Head of Jewish Agency's Political Office in Washington, D.C. and Special Rep. of Provisional Council of Govt. of Israel 1948; Israel Amb. to U.S.A. 1948-50; Minister to Great Britain 1950-52, Amb. 1952-59; Adviser, Ministry of Foreign Affairs 1959-60; Pres. Hebrew Univ., Jerusalem 1961-67, now Pres. Emer.; Pres. Israel Oriental Soc.; Vice-Pres. Jewish Colonization Asscn. (ICA); Chair. Afro-Asian Inst., Tel-Aviv; Hon. Ph.D. *Publications:* Bedouin, Their Life and Manners 1934, Trans-Jordan 1935, Israel and Her Neighbours 1959, San Francisco Diary 1971, Britain's Routes to India 1971, Zionism and the Arabs 1974, Zionism at the UN, a Diary of the First Days 1976, The Struggle for Statehood 1979. *Leisure interests:* music and reading. *Address:* 17 Bialik Street, Beth Hakerem, Jerusalem, Israel. *Telephone:* 524615.

ELDEM, M. Necat; Turkish politician; b. 1928, Mardin; m.; two c.; ed. Erzurum Lycée, Faculty of Political Sciences, Istanbul Univ.; Jr. Gov. in various towns in Anatolia; Admin. Insp. 1961-74; Gov. of Çankin 1974, Burdur and Yozgat -1978; Minister of Justice 1983-86. *Address:* c/o Adalet Bakanliği, Bakanliklar, Ankara, Turkey. *Telephone:* (41)185260.

ELDER, Mark Philip, M.A.; British music director; b. 2 June 1947; s. of John Elder and Helen Elder; m. Amanda Jane Stein 1980; one d.; ed. Bryanston School and Corpus Christi Coll., Cambridge; music staff Wexford Festival 1969-70; Chorus Master and Asst. Conductor Glyndebourne 1970-71; music staff Covent Garden 1970-72, Staff Conductor Australian Opera 1972-74, English Nat. Opera 1974, Assoc. Conductor 1977, Music Dir. 1979-; Prin. Guest Conductor London Mozart Players 1980-83; BBC Symphony Orchestra 1982-85; Music Dir., Rochester Philharmonic Orchestra, N.Y. 1989-. *Address:* c/o London Coliseum, St. Martin's Lane, London, W.C.2, England.

ELDIN, Gérard; French civil servant and banker; b. 21 March 1927, Cannes; s. of Charles and Elise Eldin; m. Marie-Cécile Bergerot 1960; two s. two d.; ed. Univ. d'Aix-en-Provence and Ecole Nationale d'Administration; Insp. of Finances 1954-58; served in the Treasury 1958-63; Adviser to Minister of Finance and Econ. Affairs 1963-65; Deputy Dir. Dept. of Planning 1965-70; Deputy Sec.-Gen. OECD 1970-80; Deputy Gov. Crédit Foncier de France 1980-86; Chair. Foncier-Investissement 1982, Crédit-Logement 1986; Chevalier, Légion d'honneur; Officier, Ordre national du Mérite. *Leisure interests:* tennis, music, local history, archaeology. *Address:* Crédit Foncier de France, 19 rue des Capucines, 75001 Paris (Office); 63 bis rue de Varenne, 75007 Paris, France (Home). *Telephone:* 42.44.80.00 (Office); 45.51.51.86 (Home).

ELEY, Daniel Douglas, O.B.E., SC.D., F.R.S.; British professor of physical chemistry; b. 1 Oct. 1914, Wallasey, Cheshire; s. of Daniel Eley and Fanny Allen Eley (née Ross); m. Brenda May Williams 1942; one s.; ed. West Bridgford County Secondary School, Nottingham, Christ's Coll., Finchley, Manchester Univ. and St. John's Coll. Cambridge; wartime research (for Ministry of Supply) and lecturing, Colloid Science Dept., Cambridge Univ. 1939-45; lecturer in Colloid Chem., Bristol Univ. 1945-51, Reader in Biophysical Chem. 1951-54; Prof. of Physical Chem., Nottingham Univ. 1954-80, Emer. Prof. 1980-. *Publications:* Catalysis and the Chemical Bond 1954, Adhesion (Ed.) 1961. *Leisure interests:* gardening, walking, motoring, skiing, music and literature. *Address:* Chemistry Department, Nottingham University, University Park, Nottingham, NG7 2RD (Office); Brooklands, 35 Brookland Drive, Chilwell, Nottingham, NG9 4BD (Home). *Telephone:* Nottingham 506101 (Ext. 2348) (Office); Nottingham 255701 (Home).

ELEY, Sir Geoffrey (Cecil Ryves), Kt., C.B.E.; British (retd.) company director; b. 18 July 1904, East Bergholt, Suffolk; s. of Charles Cuthbert Eley and Ethel Maxwell Eley; m. Penelope Hughes Wake-Walker 1937; two s. two d.; ed. Eton, Trinity Coll., Cambridge and Harvard Univ.; on editorial staff of Financial News 1926-28; int. banking and finance in England, France, Switzerland and U.S.A. 1928-32; London Man. of Post and Flagg N.Y. 1932-39; Naval Intelligence Div. Admiralty 1939-40; Capital Issues Cttee. 1940-41; Dir. of Contracts Ministry of Supply 1941-46, Dir. of Overseas Disposals 1946-47; Dir. Thomas Tilling Co. Ltd. 1949-76, Chair. 1965-76; Leader of U.K. Trade Mission to Egypt, Sudan and Ethiopia 1955; Dir. BOC Int. Ltd. 1959-76, Vice-Chair. 1964-76; Dir. British Bank of the Middle East 1948-77, Deputy Chair. 1952-77; Dir. Bank of England 1949-66; mem. London Electricity Bd. 1948-58; Chair. British Drug Houses Ltd. 1948-65, Brush Group Ltd. 1953-58, Richard Thomas and Baldwins Ltd. 1959-64, Heinemann Group of Publishers Ltd. 1965-76; Dir. Equity and Law Assurance Soc. 1948-80, Airco Inc. 1974-76; mem. Council Royal U.K. Benevolent Asscn. 1957-85, Council, Friends of the Tate Gallery 1977-85; Vice-Pres. Middle East Asscn. 1962-84; High Sheriff Co. of London 1954-55, High Sheriff of Greater London 1966-67. *Leisure interests:* gardening, the arts, foreign travel. *Address:* The Change House, Great Yeldham, Essex, CO9 4PT, England. *Telephone:* Great Yeldham 237 260.

ELFVING, Gösta; Swedish journalist and politician; b. 2 Sept. 1908, Ludvika; s. of Oscar E. Signe Jonsson-Elfving; m. A. L. Ljungkvist 1933; one d.; on staff of Värmlands Folkblad 1925, Ed. 1934-40; Editor-in-Chief Västgöta-Demokraten Borås 1940-44; Editor-in-Chief Morgon-Tidningen Stockholm (leading Swedish Labour daily) 1944-57; mem. Exec. Social Democratic Party 1944-58, State Youth Cttee. 1939-51, State Tourist Cttee. 1948-51, of Parl. 1954-57; Chair. or mem. of several Royal Comms.; Gov. Kopparbergs (Län) 1957-73. *Address:* Kyrkogårdsgatan 39A, 752 24 Uppsala, Sweden.

ELGEE, Neil Johnson, M.D.; American professor of medicine; b. 3 April 1926, Nova Scotia, Canada; s. of William Harris Elgee and Lucile Nevers Elgee; m. Leona Karlson 1951; one s. four d.; ed. New Brunswick and Rochester Univs.; Intern in Medicine, Peter Bent Brigham Hosp., Boston 1950-51; Asst. Resident in Medicine, Strong Memorial Hosp., Rochester 1951-52; Research Fellow in Endocrinology, Univ. of Wash. 1952-54, Chief Resident in Medicine 1954-55, Clinical Faculty 1957-, Clinical Prof. of Medicine 1968-; Gov. American Coll. of Physicians 1965-71, Regent 1974-78; Inst. of Medicine 1978-; Master American Coll. of Physicians. *Publications:* several scientific journals. *Leisure interests:* squash, writing. *Address:* 1229 Madison Ave., Suite 1500, Seattle, Washington 98104 (Office); 3621 72nd Avenue S.E., Mercer Island, Washington 98040, U.S.A. *Telephone:* 206 292-6200 (Office); 206 232 2994 (Home).

ELIADES, Elias; Cypriot politician; b. 24 Oct. 1947, Paphos; m. Irene Chalkiadaki; one d.; ed. Athens Univ., Greece; practised as lawyer, Paphos 1973-82; Chair. Paphos Greek Co-operative Savings Bank 1973-; mem. Bd. of Dirs. Land Devt. Org.; Minister of Defence 1985-88. *Address:* c/o Ministry of Foreign Affairs, Nicosia, Cyprus.

ELIAS, H.E. Judge Taslim Olawale, Q.C., B.A., LL.M., PH.D., LL.D.; Nigerian lawyer; b. 11 Nov. 1914, Lagos, Nigeria; s. of Momolesho Elias and Ibidun Elias; m. Ganiat Yetunde Elias 1959; three s. two d.; ed. C.M.S. Grammar School, Lagos, Igboli Coll., Lagos, Univ. Coll., London and Inst. of Advanced Legal Studies, London; Yarborough Anderson Scholar of Inner Temple 1946-49; called to the bar 1947; Legal Counsel 1949-60; Simon Research Fellow, Univ. of Manchester 1951-53; Oppenheim Research Fellow, Inst. of Commonwealth Studies, Nuffield Coll. and Queen Elizabeth House, Oxford 1954-60; Visiting Prof. in Politicial Science, Delhi Univ. 1956; mem. Del. to Nigerian Constitutional Conf., London 1958; Minister of Justice, Nigeria 1960-66, Attorney-Gen. 1960-72, mem. Fed. Exec. Council 1966-71; Commr. for Justice 1967-72, Chief Justice of Supreme Court 1972-75; Judge Int. Court of Justice 1976- (Vice-Pres. 1979-82, Acting Pres. 1981-82, Pres. 1982-85); Gov. SOAS, London Univ. 1957-60; mem. Gov. Council, Univ. of Nigeria 1959-66; mem. UN Int. Law Comm. 1961-75, Gen. Rapporteur 1965-66, Chair. 1970; Chair. UN Cttee. of Constitutional Experts to draft Congo Constitution 1961, 1962; mem. Expert Cttee. drafting OAU Charter 1963; led Nigerian del. to Conf. on Settlement of Investment Disputes and to Special Cttee. on Prins. of Int. Law concerning Friendly Relations and Co-operation among States 1964, Chair. drafting Cttee., Protocol of Mediation, Conciliation and Arbitration 1964; Prof. of Law and Dean of Faculty of Law, Univ. of Lagos, Nigeria 1966-72; Chair. Cttee. of the Whole at UN Conf. on Law of Treaties 1968, 1969; mem. Exec. Inst. of Human Rights, Strasbourg 1969; Leading Counsel in Namibia Case, ICJ 1971; Ed. Nigerian Law Journal 1968-73; Ed. Nigerian Annual and Annual Proc. of Nigerian Soc. of Int. Law; Chair. Advisory Judicial Cttee. of Nigeria 1972-75; Chair. Sixth Commonwealth Law Conf., Lagos 1980; Vice-Pres. World Bank Admin. Tribunal 1980-81; Pres. Court, final round Philip C. Jessup Int. Law Moot Court Competition 1981; mem. Advisory Bd. for Law Reports of the Commonwealth 1984-; Chair. Governing Council, Nigerian Inst. of Int. Affairs 1972-; Pres. Asian-African Legal Consultative Cttee. 1972; mem. Exec. Int. Comm. of Jurists 1975-; Pres. Nigerian Soc. of Int. Law; Chair. African Inst. of Int. Law; Assoc. mem. Inst. of Int. Law 1962, mem. 1983; Hon. mem. American Soc. of Int. Law 1973; Pres. World Asscn. of Judges 1975; mem. Int. Law Asscn., Curatorium of The Hague Acad. of Int. Law; Hon. Fellow Nigerian Inst. Advanced Legal Studies (Univ. of Lagos), Nigerian Inst. of Architects; Hon. mem. Soc. of Public Teachers of Law, U.K.; Corresp. mem. Gov. SOAS (London Univ.) 1970-; Foreign Hon. mem. American Acad. of Arts and Sciences; Assoc. mem. Int. Acad. Comparative Law; Pres. World Asscn. for Int. Relations 1984-; Titular mem. Int. Maritime Law Asscn.; mem. Council of Man. of British Inst. of Int. and Comparative Law; World Jurist Award 1973; Hon. LL.D. (Dakar) 1969, (Ahmadu Bello) 1972, (Ife) 1974, (Howard) 1975, (Jodhpur) 1976, (Hull) 1980, (Dalhousie) 1983, (Nairobi) 1983, (Manchester) 1984, (Buckingham) 1986, (Lagos State Univ.) 1987, (Jos) 1987; Hon. D.Litt. (Ibadan) 1969, (Nsukka) 1973, (Lagos) 1974; Hon. D.Sc. (London) 1983; Hon. Bencher of the Inner Temple 1982; Fellow of Univ. Coll. (London) 1982; Nigerian Nat. Merit Award; Commdr. of Fed. Repub. of Nigeria; Distinguished Fellow of the Delian Inst. of Int. Relations 1986; Distinguished Prof. Emer. of Lagos State Univ. 1987; Gold Medallist of Univ. of Lagos 1987. *Publications:* Nigerian Land Law and Custom 1951, Nigerian Legal System 1954, Makers of Nigerian Law 1956, The Impact of English Law upon Nigerian Customary Law 1960, Nigerian Land Law (4th edn.) 1962, Ghana and Sierra Leone: Development of their Laws and Constitutions 1962, British Colonial Law: A Comparative Study 1962, Government and Politics in Africa 2nd ed. 1963, Nature of African Customary Law 2nd edn. 1962 (transl. into French and Russian), The

Nigerian Legal System 1963, Nigeria: Development of its Laws and Constitution 1967, Problems Concerning the Validity of Treaties 1971, Problems concerning the Validity of Treaties (Hague Acad. of Int. Law lecture, in Recueil des cours) 1971, Nigerian Magistrate and the Offender 1972, Law and Social Change in Nigeria 1972, Africa and the Development of International Law 1972, Law in a Developing Society 1973, Modern Law of Treaties 1974, Judicial Process in Commonwealth Africa 1976, New Horizons in International Law 1979, Africa Before the World Court 1981, The International Court of Justice and Some Contemporary Problems 1983; Co-author of British Legal Papers 1958, International Law in a Changing World 1963, Sovereignty Within the Law 1965, African Law: Adaptation and Development 1965, Law, Justice and Equity 1967, Nigerian Prison System 1968, Nigerian Press Law 1969, Essays in International Law in Honour of Judge Manfred Lachs 1984, Essays on Third World Perspectives in Jurisprudence, Africa and the West 1986; Contrib. to Encyclopaedia of Public International Law No. 7 1984; many articles. *Address:* c/o International Court of Justice, Peace Palace, 2517 KJ The Hague, Netherlands (Office); 20 Ozumba Mbadiwe Street, Victoria Island, Lagos, Nigeria (Home). *Telephone:* 612389.

ELIAS, Peter, PH.D.; American professor of electrical engineering; b. 26 Nov. 1923, New Brunswick; s. of Nathaniel Mandel Elias and Ann Wahrhaftig Elias; m. Marjorie Forbes 1950; two s. one d.; ed. Massachusetts Institute of Technology and Harvard Univ.; war service U.S.N. 1944-46; Jr. Fellow, Soc. of Fellows, Harvard Univ. 1950-53; Asst. Prof. of Electrical Eng., M.I.T. 1953-56, Assoc. Prof. 1956-60, Prof. 1960-, Head of Dept. 1960-66, Cecil H. Green Prof. 1970-72, Edwin S. Webster Prof. 1974-; Visiting Prof. at various univs.; mem. American Acad. of Arts and Sciences, N.A.S. and Nat. Acad. of Eng. *Publications:* numerous scientific articles. *Leisure interests:* reading, travel. *Address:* Department of Electrical Engineering, Massachusetts Institute of Technology, 77 Massachusetts Ave., Cambridge, Mass. 02139; 102 Raymond Street, Cambridge, Mass. 02140, U.S.A.

ELIASSON, Jan, M.A.; Swedish international official and diplomatist; b. 17 Sept. 1940, Gothenburg; s. of John H. Eliasson and Karin (née Nilsson) Eliasson; m. Kerstin Englesson 1967; one s. two d.; ed. School of Econs., Gothenburg; entered Swedish Foreign Service 1965; Swedish OECD Del., Paris 1967; at Swedish Embassy, Bonn 1967-70; First Sec. Swedish Embassy, Washington 1970-74; Head of Section, Political Dept., Ministry for Foreign Affairs, Stockholm 1974-75; Personal Asst. to the Under-Sec. of State for Foreign Affairs 1975-77; Dir. Press and Information Div., Ministry for Foreign Affairs 1977-80, Asst. Under-Sec., Head of Div. for Asian and African Affairs, Political Dept. 1980-82; Foreign Policy Adviser, Prime Minister's Office 1982-83; Amb., Under-Sec. for Political Affairs, Stockholm 1983-87; Amb. Perm. Rep. of Sweden to UN, New York 1988-; Sec. to Swedish Foreign Policy Advisory Bd. 1983-87; Expert, Royal Swedish Defence Comm. 1984-86; Chair. UN Trust Fund for S.A. 1988-; Personal Rep. to Sec.-Gen. on Iran-Iraq 1988-. *Leisure interests:* literature, tennis. *Address:* Permanent Mission of Sweden to the United Nations, 825 Third Avenue, 39th Floor, New York, N.Y. 10022 (Office); 117 East 64th Street, New York, N.Y. 10021, U.S.A. (Home). *Telephone:* (212) 751-5900 (Office); (212) 737-9178 (Home).

ELICKER, Paul Hamilton, B.A., M.B.A.; American business executive; b. 5 April 1923, New York; s. of Paul E. Elicker and Elizabeth M. Elicker; ed. Yale Univ. and Harvard Business School; Lieutenant in U.S. Navy 1942-46; Systems Staff, Murray Corpn., Detroit 1948-49; financial analyst, Ford Motor Co. 1949-51; consultant, McKinsey & Co. 1951-56; Treasurer, SCM Corpn. 1956, Vice-Pres. Finance 1957-59, mem. Bd. 1959-, Exec. Vice-Pres. 1970-72, Pres. and C.E.O. 1972-79, Chair., Pres. and C.E.O. 1979-85, Chairman and C.E.O. 1985-. *Leisure interests:* skiing and tennis. *Address:* 50 Sutton Place South PH-H, New York, N.Y. 10022, U.S.A. (Home). *Telephone:* (212) 319 6545 (Home).

ELIEL, Ernest L., PH.D.; American professor of chemistry; b. 28 Dec. 1921, Cologne, Germany; s. of Oskar Eliel and Luise Tietz; m. Eva Schwarz 1949; two d.; ed. Univs. of Edinburgh, Havana and Illinois; Asst. Laboratorios Vieta-Plasencia 1943-46; Instructor, later Assoc. Prof., Univ. of Notre Dame 1948-60, Prof. 1960-72, Head Dept. of Chem. 1964-66; W. R. Kenan Jr. Prof. of Chem., Univ. of N. Carolina, Chapel Hill 1972-; Summer Consultant, Standard Oil of Indiana Inc. 1956; Nat. Science Foundation Senior Post-doctoral Fellow, Harvard Univ. 1958, Calif. Inst. of Technology 1958-59, Eidgenössische Technische Hochschule, Zürich 1967-68; Guggenheim Fellow 1975-76, 1983-84; mem. Nat. Acad. of Sciences, American Acad. of Arts and Sciences, American Chemical Soc. (Chair. 1987-); Hon. D.Sc. Duke Univ. 1983; Lavoisier Medal 1968, N. Carolina Award in Science 1986 and other awards. *Publications:* Stereochemistry of Carbon Compounds 1962, Conformational Analysis (co-author) 1965, Elements of Stereochemistry 1969 and over 360 articles in professional journals; co-editor: Topics in Stereochemistry 1967-. *Leisure interests:* photography, travel, swimming, hiking. *Address:* Department of Chemistry, University of North Carolina, Chapel Hill, N.C. 27514 (Office); 725 Kenmore Road, Chapel Hill, N.C. 27514, U.S.A. (Home). *Telephone:* 919-962-6197 (Office); 919-929-7966 (Home).

ELINSON, Jack, PH.D.; American professor of sociomedical sciences; b. 30 June 1917, New York; s. of Sam Elinson and Rebecca Block Elinson; m.

May Gomberg 1941; three s. one d.; ed. Coll. of the City of New York and George Washington Univ.; scientific aide, U.S. Govt. Food and Drug Admin., Soil Conservation Service, Nat. Bureau of Standards 1937–41; statistician, War Dept. 1941–42; Social Science Analyst, Dept. of Defense, Armed Forces Information and Educ. Div., Attitude Research Br. 1942–51; Sr. Study Dir. Nat. Opinion Research Center, Univ. of Chicago 1951–56; Prof. of Sociomedical Sciences, Columbia Univ. 1956–86, Emer. 1986–; Visiting Prof. of Behavioral Sciences, Univ. of Toronto 1969–75, Distinguished Visiting Prof., Inst. for Health Care Policy, Rutgers Univ. 1986–, Visiting Prof. Graduate Program in Public Health, Robert Wood Johnson Medical School 1986–; numerous professional appts., honours and distinctions. *Publications:* Chronic Illness in a Rural Area (with R. E. Trussell) 1959, Family Medical Care under Three Types of Health Insurance (with J. J. Williams and R. E. Trussell) 1962, Public Image of Mental Health Services (with E. Padilla and M. E. Perkins) 1967, Health Goals and Health Indicators (with A. E. Siegmann) 1979, Assessment of Quality of Life in Clinical Trials of Cardiovascular Therapies (with N. K. Wenger, M. E. Mattson and C. D. Furberg) 1984; articles in professional journals. *Address:* Columbia University, 600 West 168 Street, New York, N.Y. 10032 (Office); 1181 E. Laurelton Parkway, Teaneck, N.J. 07666, U.S.A. *Telephone:* (201) 836-9222.

ELION, Gertrude Belle, M.S.; American pharmacologist; b. 23 Jan. 1918, New York; d. of Robert Elion and Bertha Cohen; ed. Hunter Coll. and New York Univ.; Lab. Asst. Biochem. New York Hosp. School of Nursing 1937; Research Asst. Denver Chemical Manufacturing Co., New York 1938–39; schoolteacher, New York 1940–42; food analyst, Quaker Maid Co. 1942–43; Research Asst. Johnson & Johnson, New Brunswick, N.J. 1943–44; Biochemist, Wellcome Research Labs., Tuckahoe, New York 1944–50, Sr. Research Chemist 1950–, Head of Experimental Therapy 1966–83, Scientist Emer. 1983–; Adjunct Prof. of Pharmacology and Experimental Medicine, Duke Univ. 1970, Research Prof. of Pharmacology 1983–; Adjunct Prof. Pharmacology Univ. of N.C., Chapel Hill 1973; consultant, U.S. Public Health Service 1960–64; mem. Bd. of Scientific Counselors, Nat. Cancer Inst. 1980–84; mem. Council, American Cancer Soc. 1983–86; Fellow, New York Acad. of Sciences; mem. American Chem. Soc., A.A.A.S., Chem. Soc. (London), American Soc. of Biological Chemists, American Assen. for Cancer Research etc.; Garvan Medal 1968, President's Medal, Hunter Coll. 1970; Judd Award Memorial Sloan-Kettering Cancer Center 1983; Hon. D.Sc. (George Washington Univ.) 1969, (Univ. of Mich.) 1983; Hon. D.M.S. (Brown) 1969. *Publications:* articles in professional journals. *Address:* 3030 Cornwallis Road, Research Triangle Park, N.C. 27709 (Office); 1 Banbury Lane, Chapel Hill, N.C. 27514, U.S.A. (Home).

ELISSAR, Eliaju Ben, PH.D.; Israeli diplomatist and politician; b. 2 Aug. 1932, Radom, Poland; s. of Eliezer Israel Gottlieb and Haja Dobrzynski; m. Nitza Efrony 1979; one s.; ed. Sorbonne, Paris, and Univ. of Geneva; escaped from Poland to Palestine 1942; returned to Europe as student 1950; Govt. service Israel and abroad until 1965; Corresp. for L'Aurore and Le Journal de Genève in Israel; active mem. of Herut Movement; elected to Cen. Cttee. of Herut 1970, Party Spokesman 1971, Herut Exec. Cttee. 1972, Herut Directorate 1978; in charge of Information Dept. during Likud nat. election campaigns 1973, 1977; Dir.-Gen. Prime Minister's Office 1977–80; Israel's First Amb. to Egypt 1980–81; mem., Knesset 1981–; Chair. Foreign Affairs and Defence Cttee. 1982–84; Grand officier, Ordre de l'Ethiopie 1964, Grand Cruz Extraordinaria, Orden de la Democracia (Colombia) 1980. *Publications:* La Politique Etrangère du IIIème Reich et les Juifs, La Guerre israélo-arabe. *Address:* The Knesset, Jerusalem, Israel. *Telephone:* (02) 554111.

ELIZABETH II (Elizabeth Alexandra Mary); Queen of Great Britain and Northern Ireland and of Her other Realms and Territories (see under Reigning Royal Families at front of book for full titles); b. 21 April 1926, London; d. of H.R.H. Prince Albert, Duke of York (later H.M. King George VI), and Duchess of York (now H.M. Queen Elizabeth The Queen Mother, q.v.); succeeded to The Throne following Her father's death, 6 Feb. 1952; married, 20 Nov. 1947, H.R.H. The Prince Philip, Duke of Edinburgh, b. 10 June 1921; children: Prince Charles Philip Arthur George, Prince of Wales (heir apparent), b. 14 Nov. 1948; Princess Anne Elizabeth Alice Louise, The Princess Royal, b. 15 Aug. 1950; Prince Andrew Albert Christian Edward, Duke of York, b. 19 Feb. 1960; Prince Edward Antony Richard Louis, b. 10 March 1964. *Address:* Buckingham Palace, London; Windsor Castle, Berkshire, England; Palace of Holyroodhouse, Edinburgh, Scotland; Balmoral Castle, Aberdeenshire, Scotland; Sandringham, Norfolk, England.

ELIZABETH ANGELA MARGUERITE; H.M. Queen Elizabeth the Queen Mother, Lady of the Order of the Garter, Lady of the Order of the Thistle, C.I., G.C.V.O., G.B.E., Lord Warden of the Cinque Ports; member of the British Royal Family; b. 4 Aug. 1900; d. of the 14th Earl of Strathmore and Kinghorne; m. 1923 H.R.H. The Duke of York, later H.M. King George VI (died 1952); reigned as Queen 1936–52. *Address:* Clarence House, London, S.W.1; Royal Lodge, Windsor Great Park, Berks., England; Castle of Mey, Caithness, Scotland.

ELJASIEWICZ, Józef, M.ENG.; Polish politician; b. 18 March 1935, Białystok; ed. Warsaw Polytechnic; own electrical installations service 1957–; mem. Democratic Party (SD) 1967–; mem. Nat. Crafts Council, Chair.

Crafts Chamber Council in Białystok 1976–; Deputy Chair. SD Voivodship Cttee., Białystok 1981–, Deputy Chair. SD Cen. Cttee. March 1981–85; Commdr.'s Cross, Order of Polonia Restituta, Gold Cross of Merit, Jan Kiliński Medal. *Address:* c/o Centralny Komitet SD, ul. Rutkowskiego 9, 00-021 Warsaw, Poland. *Telephone:* 26-10-01.

ELKES, Joel, M.B., CH.B., M.D.; American physician; b. 12 Nov. 1913, Koenigsberg, Germany; s. of Elkanan and Miriam Elkes; m. 1st Dr. Charmian Bourne 1943; one d.; m. 2nd Josephine Rhodes 1975; ed. Univ. of London and Birmingham Medical School, England; Sir Halley Stuart Research Fellow in Pharmacology, Univ. of Birmingham 1942–45, Lecturer in Pharmacology 1945–48, Senior Lecturer and Act. Dir. Dept. of Pharmacology 1948–50, Prof. and Chair. Dept. of Experimental Psychiatry 1951–57; Consultant Psychiatrist, Birmingham Hospitals and Scientific Dir. Birmingham Regional Psychiatric Early Treatment Centre 1953–57; Chief, Clinical Neuropharmacology Research Center, Nat. Inst. of Mental Health (U.S. Nat. Insts. of Health) 1957–63; Dir. of Behavior and Clinical Studies Center, St. Elizabeth's Hospital 1957–63, Clinical Prof. of Psychiatry, George Washington Univ. School of Medicine 1957–63; Henry Phipps Prof. and Dir. Dept. of Psychiatry and Behavioral Sciences, The Johns Hopkins Univ. School of Medicine, Psychiatrist-in-Chief, The Johns Hopkins Hospital 1963–74; Distinguished Service Prof. Emer. The Johns Hopkins Univ. 1975–; Samuel McLaughlin Visiting Prof.-in-Residence, McMaster Univ., Ont. 1975; Dir. Dept. of Behavioral Medicine, Univ. of Louisville 1981; Prof. Emer., McMaster Univ. and Univ. of Louisville 1985–; Ed. Psychopharmacologia, Assoc. Ed. Journal of Psychiatric Research; Org. Sec. 1st Int. Neurochemical Symposium; fmr. mem. Central Council Int. Brain Research Org. Research Cttee.; mem. Mental Health Research Fund, Bd. of Dirs. and Scientific Advisory Cttee. Inst. for the Advancement of Health 1983; Fellow, American Acad. of Arts and Sciences, American Psych. Assen., American Coll. of Psychiatry, Royal Coll. of Psychiatry, U.K., American Coll. Neuropsychopharmacology, Royal Coll. of Physicians, Canada, Acad. of Behavioral Medicine; Benjamin Franklin Fellow, Royal Soc. Arts; Harvey Lecturer 1962, Salmon Lecturer 1964, Jacob Bronowski Lecturer 1978; First Pres. American Coll. of Neuropsychopharmacology; Pres. American Psychopathological Assen. 1968, etc.; mem. Bd. of Trustees Univ. of Jerusalem and Haifa Univ.; Hon. Chair. Wellness Forum, Kentucky 1980; mem. Foundations Fund Award Bd., Chair. 1976; Taylor Award 1969. *Publications:* Effects of Psychosomimetic Drugs in Animals and Man 1956, Drug Effects in Relation to Receptor Specificity within the Brain 1958, Ataractic and Hallucinogenic Drugs in Psychiatry 1958, Psychopharmacology: The Need for some Points of Reference 1959, Schizophrenic Disorder in Relation to Levels of Neural Organisation: The Need for Some Conceptual Points of Reference 1961, Subjective and Objective Observation in Psychiatry 1962, Behavioral Pharmacology in relation to Psychiatry 1967, Towards a Science of Health on Brain, Behavior and Well-Being 1983. *Leisure interests:* painting, music, clubs. *Address:* c/o Department of Psychiatry and Behavioral Sciences, Health Sciences Center, Univ. of Louisville, Louisville, Ky. 40292, U.S.A. *Telephone:* (502) 588-5387.

ELKIN, Alexander, C.M.G., DR.JUR., LL.M.; British international law consultant; b. 2nd Aug. 1909, St. Petersburg (now Leningrad); s. of Boris Elkin and Anna Elkin; m. Muriel Solomons 1937; ed. Grunewald Gymnasium, Russian Academic School, Berlin and Univs. of Berlin, Kiel and London; called to Bar, Middle Temple 1937; practised at English Bar 1937–39; B.B.C. Monitoring Service 1939–42; govt. service 1942–45; UN Service 1945–48 (Assoc. Chief, Legal Service, Interim Secr., Asst. Dir. UN European Office, Geneva); Deputy Legal Adviser, later Legal Adviser OEEC (later OECD), Paris 1949–61; Legal Consultant, formation of AfDB 1962–64; Acting Gen. Counsel AfDB 1964–65; UNDP Legal Consultant, formation of Caribbean Devt. Bank 1967–68; Special Adviser on European Community Law, FCO 1970–79; other legal consultancies for int. orgs.; Ford Foundation Leadership Grant 1960; lecturer at int. seminars etc. and Univ. of Bradford 1979–84, Univ. of Bath 1979–. *Publications:* articles in yearbooks, professional journals etc. *Leisure interests:* reading, visiting art collections, travel. *Address:* 70 Apsley House, Finchley Road, London NW8 0NZ, England *Telephone:* (01) 483-2475.

ELKIN, Stanley Lawrence, PH.D., L.H.D.; American author; b. 11 May 1930, New York; s. of Philip Elkin and Zelda Feldman; m. Joan M. Jacobson 1953; two s. one d.; ed. Univ. of Illinois; mem. Faculty, Washington Univ. 1960, Prof. of American Literature 1969–, Merle Kling Prof. of Modern Letters 1983–; Visiting Lecturer, Smith Coll. 1964–65; Visiting Prof. Univs. of Calif. at Santa Barbara 1967, Wis. 1969, Ia. 1974, Yale Univ. 1975, Boston Univ. 1976; Guggenheim Fellow 1966–67; Rockefeller grantee 1968–69; mem. American Acad. of Arts and Letters; numerous awards including Richard and Hinda Rosenthal Award 1980, Nat. Book Critics Circle Award 1982, Creative Arts Award, Brandeis Univ. 1986. *Publications:* Boswell 1964, Criers and Kibitzers, Kibitzers and Criers 1966, A Bad Man 1967, The Dick Gibson Show 1971, Stories from the Sixties (ed.) 1971, The Making of Ashenden 1972, Searches and Seizures 1973, The Franchiser 1976, The Living End 1979, Best American Short Stories of 1980 1980, Stanley Elkin's Greatest Hits 1980, George Mills 1982, The Magic Kingdom 1985, Early Elkin 1985, The Rabbi of Lud 1987, The Six-Year-Old Man 1987, The Coffee Room 1988. *Address:* Washington University, Duncker Hall, St. Louis, Mo. 63130, U.S.A.

ELLEMANN-JENSEN, Uffe, M.A.; Danish journalist and politician; b. 1 Nov. 1941; s. of Jens Peter Jensen; m. Alice Vestergaard 1971; two s. two d.; ed. Univ. of Copenhagen; Danish Defence staff 1962-64; Sec. Meat Producers' Asscn. 1964-67; journalist on Berlingske Aftenavis 1967-70; Econ. and political corresp. Danish television 1970-75; Ed.-in-Chief and mem. Bd. daily newspaper Borsen 1975-76; mem. Parl. 1977- (Liberal); Party spokesperson, political affairs 1978-82; Chair. Parl. Market Cttee. 1978-79; mem. Exec. Cttee. Liberal Party 1979, Chair. 1985-; mem. Bd. Cen. Bank 1978-81, Index Figures' Bd. 1979-81, Inter-Parl. Union 1979-; Minister of Foreign Affairs, Sept. 1982-; Robert Schuman Prize 1987. *Publications:* De nye millionaerer (The New Millionaires) 1971, Det afhaengige samfund (The Dependant Society) 1972, Hvad gør vi ved Gudenåen (We ought to do something about Gudenåen) 1973, Den truede velstand (The Threatened Wealth) 1974, Økonomi (Economy) 1975, Da Danmark igen sagde ja til det falles (When Denmark Repeated its Yes to Europe) 1987; numerous articles in newspapers and periodicals. *Leisure interests:* fishing, hunting. *Address:* Ministry of Foreign Affairs, Asiatisk Plads 2, 1448 Copenhagen, Denmark.

ELLICOTT, Robert James, Q.C.; Australian lawyer and politician; b. 15 April 1927, Mooree, N.S.W.; s. of John James Ellicott and Ruby Violet Doney; m. Colleen Betty Turton 1950; two s. two d.; ed. Fort Street Boys' High School and Univ. of Sydney; admitted to Bar in N.S.W. 1950, Victoria 1960; appointed Q.C. 1964; Commonwealth Solicitor-Gen. 1969-73; mem. House of Reps. for Wentworth, N.S.W. 1974-80; Opposition spokesman on Consumer Affairs and Commerce 1974-75; Attorney-Gen. 1975-77; Minister for Home Affairs and for the Capital Territory 1977-79, for Home Affairs and the Environment 1979-81, for Cultural and Sporting Affairs 1978-79; Judge, Fed. Courts March 1981-83. *Leisure interests:* tennis, fishing. *Address:* Onslow Avenue, Elizabeth Bay, N.S.W. 2011, Australia.

ELLINGHAUS, William M.; American communications executive (retd.); b. 19 April 1922, Baltimore, Md.; m. Erlaine Dietrich 1942; six s. two d.; Commercial Man., Chesapeake and Potomac Telephone Co. (CPTC) of Maryland 1950-51; Public Officer Man. CPTC of Virginia 1951-52, Dist. Commercial Man. 1952-55; Gen. Commercial Supervisor, CPTC of West Virginia 1955-57, Div. Commercial Man. 1957, Gen. Accounting Supervisor 1957-58, Comptroller 1958-60, Vice-Pres. and Dir. 1960-62; Vice-Pres. (Accounts), Chesapeake and Potomac Telephone Cos. 1962, Vice-Pres. (Personnel) 1962-65; Asst. Vice-Pres. (Planning), American Telephone and Telegraph Co. (ATT) 1965-66, Asst. Vice-Pres. (Marketing and Rate Plans) 1966-67, Vice-Pres. 1967-70, Exec. Vice-Pres. 1970, Vice-Chair. 1976-79, Pres. and C.O.O. 1979-84; Exec. Vice-Chair. New York Stock Exchange 1984-86; Pres. New York Telephone Co. 1970-76; Hon. LL.D. (Iona Coll.) 1974, Hon. L.H.D. (Manhattan Coll.) 1975, Hon. LL.D. (St. John's Univ.) 1976, Hon. LL.D. (Pace Univ.) 1976, Hon. D.Sc. (Washington Coll.) 1979, Hon. D.C.S. (New York) 1981, Hon. D.Hum.Litt. (Union Coll.) 1982. *Address:* 550 Madison Avenue, New York, N.Y. 10022 (Office); 55 Crow's Nest Road, Bronxville, N.Y. 10708, U.S.A. (Home).

ELLIOTT, Brian Robinson, M.A., D.LITT., D.UNIV.; Australian university teacher; b. 11 April 1910, Adelaide; s. of Arthur J. Elliott and Esther R. (née Macclesfield) Elliott; m. Patricia S. Williams 1939 (died 1986); two s. one d.; ed. Univ. of Adelaide; apptd. to Dept. of English, Univ. of Adelaide 1940, Reader in Australian Literary Studies after War, retd. 1975; Rockefeller award for study in U.S.A. *Publications:* Leviathan's Inch (novel) 1946, Marcus Clarke (biography) 1958, The Landscape of Australian Poetry 1967, jt. compiler Bards in the Wilderness: Australian Colonial Poetry to 1920, St. Lucia, Queensland 1979, trans. Lévy-Bruhl Lucien's La Mythologie Primitive 1985. *Leisure interests:* music, gardening. *Address:* 25 Glenunga Avenue, Glenunga, S. Australia. *Telephone:* 79 2084.

ELLIOTT, Rev. Prebendary Charles Middleton, M.A., D.PHIL.; British ecclesiastic; b. 9 Jan. 1939, Wakefield; s. of Joseph W. Elliott and Mary E. Elliott; m. Hilary M. Hambling 1962; three s.; ed. Repton, Lincoln and Nuffield Colls. Oxford and Scholae Cancellarii, Lincoln; lecturer in Econs. Univ. of Nottingham 1962-65; Reader in Econs. Univ. of Zambia 1965-69; Asst. Sec. Jt. Cttee. on Soc., Devt. and Peace, Vatican/WCC, Geneva 1969-72; Sr. Lecturer in Econs. Univ. of E. Anglia 1972-77; Prof. of Devt. Studies, Univ. of Wales 1977-82; Dir. Christian Aid 1982-84; Benjamin Meakin Prof. Univ. of Bristol 1985-86; Visiting Prof. King's Coll. London 1987-88; Sec. Inst. of Contemporary Spirituality 1988-; Collins Religious Book Prize 1985. *Publications:* Patterns of Poetry in the Third World 1975, Praying the Kingdom 1985, Praying through Paradox 1987, Comfortable Compassion 1987, Signs of Our Times 1988, Sword and Spirit: Christianity in a Divided World 1989. *Leisure interests:* walking, gardening, fly-fishing, sailing. *Address:* 119 Fentiman Road, London, SW8 1JZ, England. *Telephone:* 01-582 1743.

ELLIOTT, James Philip, PH.D., F.R.S.; British professor of theoretical physics; b. 27 July 1929; s. of James Elliott and Dora K. Smith; m. Mavis R. Avery 1955; one s. two d.; ed. Univ. Coll. Southampton; Sr. Scientific Officer, Atomic Energy Research Est. Harwell 1951-58; Visiting Assoc. Prof. Univ. of Rochester, U.S.A. 1958-59; Lecturer in Math. Univ. of Southampton 1959-62; Reader in Theoretical Physics, Univ. of Sussex 1962-69, Prof. 1969-. *Publications:* Symmetry in Physics 1979; papers in learned journals. *Leisure interests:* gardening, sport, music. *Address:* 36

Montacute Road, Lewes, Sussex, BN7 1EP, England. *Telephone:* Lewes 474783.

ELLIOTT, Prof. John Huxtable, F.B.A.; British professor of history; b. 23 June 1930, Reading, Berks.; s. of Thomas Charles Elliott and Janet Mary Payne; m. Oonah Sophia Butler 1958; ed. Eton Coll. and Trinity Coll., Cambridge; Asst. Lecturer in History, Univ. of Cambridge 1957-62, Lecturer 1962-67; Prof. of History, King's Coll., Univ. of London 1968-73; Prof., School of Historical Studies, Inst. for Advanced Study, Princeton, N.J. 1973-; Fellow, Trinity Coll., Cambridge 1954-67, Royal Acad. of History, Madrid, British Acad., American Acad. of Arts and Sciences, American Philosophical Soc; Dr. h.c. (Universidad Autónoma de Madrid) 1983, Visitante Ilustre of Madrid 1983; Wolfson Literary Award for History and Biography 1986; Commdr. of the Order of Alfonso X El Sabio 1984; Medal of Honour, Universidad Int. Menéndez y Palayo 1987; Commdr. Order of Isabel la Católica 1987, Grand Cross of the Order of Alfonso X, El Sabro 1988. *Publications:* Imperial Spain, 1469-1716 1963, The Revolt of the Catalans 1963, Europe Divided, 1559-1598 1968, The Old World and the New, 1492-1650 1970, Ed. (with H. G. Koenigsberger) The Diversity of History 1970, A Palace for a King (with J. Brown) 1980, Memoriales y Cartas del Conde Duque de Olivares 1978-80, Richelieu and Olivares 1984, The Count-Duke of Olivares 1986, Spain and Its World 1500-1700 1989. *Address:* School of Historical Studies, Institute for Advanced Study, Olden Lane, Princeton, N.J. 08540, U.S.A.; 73 Long Road, Cambridge, CB2 2HE, England. *Telephone:* Cambridge 841332.

ELLIOTT, Michael, C.B.E., D.SC., C.CHEM., PH.D., F.R.S.C., F.R.S.; British organic research chemist; b. 30 Sept. 1924, London; s. of Thomas W. and Isobel C. (Burnell) Elliott; m. Margaret O. James 1950; two d.; ed. The Skinners' Co. School, Tunbridge Wells, Univ. of Southampton and King's Coll., London; Scientific Officer Dept. of Insecticides and Fungicides, Rothamsted Experimental Station 1948-53, Sr. Scientific Officer 1953-61, Prin. Scientific Officer 1961-70, Sr. Prin. Scientific Officer 1970-79, Deputy Chief Scientific Officer 1979-84, Head of Dept. of Insecticides and Fungicides and Deputy Dir. Rothamsted Experimental Research Station 1979-84; Visiting Lecturer, Univ. of Calif. (Berkeley) 1969, 1974; Visiting Prof., Imperial Coll., London 1979-; Fellow, King's Coll., London 1984-; consultant on chem. of insecticides 1984-; Visiting Research Scientist, Pesticide Chem. and Toxicology Lab., Univ. of Calif. (Berkeley) 1985-88; Hon. D.Sc. (Southampton) 1985; Mullard Medal, Royal Soc. 1982, Prix de la Fondation de la Chimie 1989, and other awards and prizes. *Publications:* more than 200 scientific articles. *Leisure interest:* photography. *Address:* 9 Long Ridge, Aston, Stevenage, Herts. SG2 7EW, England. *Telephone:* (043) 888328.

ELLIOTT, Sir Norman Randall, Kt., C.B.E., M.A.; British electricity executive; b. 19 July 1903, London; s. of William Randall Elliott and Catherine Dunsmore; m. Phyllis Clarke 1963; ed. privately and St. Catharine's Coll., Cambridge; called to Bar, Middle Temple, London 1932; Col. Deputy Dir. of Works, 21 Army Group 1939-44; mem. North of Scotland Hydro Electric Board, London Passenger Transport Board, London and Home Counties Joint Electricity Authority; Chair. South-Eastern Electricity Authority, South-Eastern Electricity Bd. 1948-62, South of Scotland Electricity Bd. 1962-67, The Electricity Council 1968-72; Dir. James Howden & Co. Ltd. 1967-68, Chair. Howden Group 1973-83; Dir. Newarthill & McAlpine Group 1972-; Dir. and Consultant Schlumberger Ltd. 1977-; Chair. British Nat. Cttee., Union Int. des Producteurs et Distributeurs d'Energie Electrique. *Publications:* Electricity Statutes, Orders and Regulations 1951, 1967. *Leisure interests:* ball games, theatre. *Address:* 3 Herbrand Walk, Cooden, East Sussex, England.

ELLIOTT, Osborn, A.B.; American journalist; b. 25 Oct. 1924, New York City; s. of John and Audrey N. (Osborn) Elliott; m. 1st Deirdre M. Spencer 1948 (divorced 1972), three d.; m. 2nd the fmr. Mrs. Inger A. McCabe, two step d., one step s.; ed. The Browning School (N.Y.), St. Paul's School (Concord) and Harvard Univ.; Reporter N.Y. Journal of Commerce 1946-49; Contributing Ed. Time 1949-52, Assoc. Ed. 1952-55; Senior Business Ed. Newsweek 1955-59, Man. Ed. 1959-61, Ed. 1961-69, 1972-75, Editor-in-Chief 1969-72, 1975-76, Vice-Chair. 1970, Pres. 1971, Chief Exec. Officer 1971-76, Chair. of Bd. 1972-76; Deputy Mayor for Econ. Devt., New York 1976-77; Dean Graduate School of Journalism, Columbia Univ., New York 1979-86; Prof. Columbia Univ.; fmr. Dir. Washington Post Co.; Trustee, American Museum of Natural History, Asia Soc., Lincoln Centre Theatre, New York Public Library 1968-72; St. Paul's School 1969-73, Winston Churchill Foundation of the U.S. Ltd. 1970-73; mem. Council on Foreign Relations, Pulitzer Prize Bd. 1979-86; mem. Bd. of Overseers of Harvard Coll. 1965-71; Fellow American Acad. of Arts and Sciences; served with U.S. Naval Reserve 1944-46. *Publications:* Men at the Top 1959, The World of Oz 1980; Ed. The Negro Revolution in America 1964. *Address:* Journalism Building, Columbia University, New York, N.Y. 10027, U.S.A. (Office).

ELLIOTT, Sir Roger (James), Kt., M.A., D.PHIL., F.R.S.; British physicist; b. 8 Dec. 1928, Chesterfield; s. of James Elliott and Gladys Elliott (née Hill); m. Olga Lucy Atkinson 1952; one s. two d.; ed. Swanwick Hall School, Derbyshire and New Coll., Oxford; Research Assoc. Univ. of Calif., Berkeley 1952-53; Research Fellow, Atomic Energy Research Est., Harwell 1953-55; lecturer, Univ. of Reading 1955-57; Lecturer, Oxford

Univ. 1957–65, Reader 1965–74, Fellow, St. John's Coll. 1957–74, Wykeham Prof. of Physics 1974–79; Sec. and Chief Exec., Oxford Univ. Press 1988–; Visiting Prof. Univ. of Calif., Berkeley 1960–61; Miller Visiting Prof. Univ. of Ill., Urbana 1966; Visiting Distinguished Prof. Fla. State Univ. 1981; Del. OUP 1971–78, Chair. Computer Bd. 1983–87; Physical Sec. and Vice-Pres. Royal Soc. (London) 1984–88; Hon. D.Sc. (Paris) 1983; Maxwell Medal (Physical Soc.) 1968. *Publications:* Magnetic Properties of Rare Earth Metals 1972, Solid State Physics and its Applications 1973, articles in learned journals. *Address:* Oxford University Press, Walton Street, Oxford, England. *Telephone:* Oxford 56767.

ELLIS, Elmer, B.A., A.M., PH.D.; American historian; b. 27 July 1901, McHenry County, N. Dakota; s. of Thomas Clarkson and Lillie Jane (Butterfield) Ellis; m. Ruth Clapper 1925; ed. Univ. of N. Dakota and State Univ. of Iowa; Instructor N. Dakota State Teachers' Coll. 1925–28; Lecturer in History, State Univ. of Iowa 1928–30; Asst. Prof., Assoc. Prof. and Prof. of History, Univ. of Missouri 1930–71; Acting Dean of Graduate School, Univ. of Missouri, summers 1936, 1939, 1941, Vice-Pres. in charge of Extra Divisional Educational Activities 1945–46, Dean of Faculty Coll. of Arts and Science 1946–55, Acting Pres. 1954–55, Pres. 1955–66; Pres. Emer. Univ. of Missouri 1966–; Pres. Nat. Council for Social Studies 1937; U.S. Army History Branch, War Dept. Gen. Staff 1943–45, mem. History Advisory Cttee., U.S. Army and Chair. 1957–59; Pres. Miss. Valley Hist. Asscn. 1950; mem. Bd. of Editors Mississippi Valley Historical Review 1947–50, Bd. of Dirs. Social Science Research Council 1946–51; Fulbright Visiting Lecturer, Univ. of Amsterdam 1951–52; Pres. Bd. of Dirs. Harry S. Truman Inst. for Nat. and Int. Affairs 1957–77; mem. Bd. of Foreign Scholarships, U.S. Dept. of State 1958–61, Civil Rights Advisory Cttee. U.S. Dept. of Agriculture 1965–68; Pres. Nat. Comm. on Accrediting 1962–64; Pres. Nat. Asscn. State Univs. and Land-Grant Colls. 1964–65; Consultant Educ. Comm. of States 1967–71, Rockefeller Foundation 1967; Educational Consultant on Admin., Univ. of Del Valle, Cali, Colombia 1967, Texas Technological Univ. 1968–69; mem. Bd. of Curators, Stephens Coll. 1967–73; Chair. Missouri Arthritis Council 1971–84; Consultant on Admin. Structure, Orissa Agric. and Tech. Univ., Bhubaneswar, India 1970; Pres. Mo. State Historical Soc. 1974–77; Hon. LL.D. (Univ. of N. Dakota 1946, Central Coll. Fayette, Missouri 1955, Drury Coll., Springfield, Missouri 1956, Washington Univ. 1960), Hon. Litt.D. (Culver-Stockton Coll., Canton, Mo. 1961), D.Litt. (St. Louis Univ. 1966); Distinguished Service Award, Org. of American Historians 1982; Missouri, The American Legion Distinguished Service Award 1983. *Publications:* Education Against Propaganda 1937, Mr. Dooley at his Best 1938, Henry Moore Teller, Defender of the West 1941, Mr. Dooley's America, a Life of Finley Peter Dunne 1941, Toward Better Teaching in College 1954. *Address:* 323 Jesse Hall, University of Missouri, Columbia, Mo. 65211 (Office); 107 W. Brandon Road, Columbia, Mo. 65203, U.S.A. (Home). *Telephone:* (314) 882-4269 (Office).

ELLIS, George Francis Rayner, F.R.A.S., PH.D.; British/South African professor of astrophysics and applied mathematics; b. 11 Aug. 1939, Johannesburg; s. of George Rayner Ellis and Gwen Hilda (née MacRobert) Ellis; m. 1st Sue Parkes 1963, 2nd Mary Wheeldon 1978; one s. one d.; ed. Michaelhouse, Univ. of Cape Town and Cambridge Univ.; Fellow Peterhouse, Cambridge 1965–67; Asst. Lecturer, lecturer Cambridge 1967–73; Prof. of Applied Math., Univ. of Cape Town 1974–88; Prof. of Cosmic Physics, SISSA, Trieste 1988–; G.C. MacVittie Visiting Prof. of Astronomy, Queen Mary Coll., London 1987–; Chair. Quaker Service, West Cape 1976–86, Quaker Peacework Cttee. 1978–86, S.A. Inst. of Race Relations, West Cape 1985–87, S.A. Yearly Meeting of Quakers 1986–88, ORIZ Scientific Cttee. 1988; Fellow Inst. of Maths and its Applications; mem. Int. Cttee. on Gen. Relativity and Gravitation; Fellowship of Univ. of Cape Town; Herschel Medal of Royal Soc. of S.A.; Gravity Research Foundation 1st Prize 1979. *Publications:* The Large Scale Structure of Space-Time (with S.W. Hawking q.v.) 1973, The Squatter Problem in the Western Cape (with J. Maree, D. Hendric) 1976, Low Income Housing Policy (with D. Dewar) 1980, Flat and Curved Space-Times (with R. Williams) 1988. *Leisure interests:* climbing, gliding. *Address:* SISSA, Strada Costiera 11, Mivamore, Trieste 34014, Italy; 3 Marlow Road, Cape Town 7700, South Africa. *Telephone:* 224-118; 712313.

ELLIS, Howard S., B.A., M.A., PH.D., LL.D.; American economist; b. 2 July 1898, Denver, Colo.; s. of Sylvester B. Ellis and Nellie B. Young; m. Hermine Hoerlesberger 1935; three d.; ed. Univs. of Iowa, Michigan, Harvard, Heidelberg and Vienna; Instructor and later Prof., Univ. of Michigan 1920–22, 1924–38, of Calif. 1938–43, 1946–50 and 1951–65; Visiting Prof., Columbia 1944–45, 1949–50, Tokyo 1951, Wisconsin 1972; econ. analyst, Fed. Reserve Board, Washington 1943–44; Asst. Dir. of Research and Statistics 1944–45; Econ. Policy Cttee., U.S. Chamber of Commerce 1945–46; Dir. Marshall Aid Research Project Council on Foreign Relations 1949–59; Pres. American Econ. Asscn. 1949; Pres. Int. Econ. Asscn. 1953–56, mem. Exec. Cttee. 1956–62; Visiting Prof., Univ. of Bombay 1958–59; Head, UNESCO Mission on Econs. in Latin America 1960, Econ. Research Center, Athens 1963, U.S. Aid Mission, Rio de Janeiro 1965–67, IV Semana Económica Internacional, Barcelona 1973. *Publications:* German Monetary Theory 1905–1933 1934, Exchange Control in Central Europe 1941, The Economics of Freedom: The Progress and Future of Aid to Europe 1950, Approaches to Economic Development 1955, Private

Enterprise and Socialism in the Middle East 1970; Ed. The Economy of Brazil 1969, Fact and Fancy about the Oil Industry 1978, Notes on Stagflation 1978. *Leisure interests:* music, garden. *Address:* 936 Cragmont Avenue, Berkeley, Calif. 94708, U.S.A. *Telephone:* 525-2734.

ELLIS, John Tracy, M.A., PH.D.; American professor of church history; b. 30 July 1905, Seneca, Ill.; s. of Elmer L. Ellis and Ida C. Ellis; ed. St. Viator Coll. and Catholic Univ. of America, Washington D.C.; Prof. of History St. Viator Coll. 1930–32; Coll. of St. Teresa 1932–34; Instructor, Asst. Prof., Assoc. Prof., then Full Prof. of Church History Catholic Univ. of America 1935–63; Professorial Lecturer 1976–; Prof. of Church History Univ. of San Francisco 1964–76; Visiting Prof. Brown Univ., R.I. 1967, Univ. of Notre Dame, Ind. 1970, Gregorian Univ., Rome 1974, Angelicum Univ. 1976; ordained Priest 1938; named Domestic Prelate of Pope Pius XII 1955; 22 Hon. Degrees (1988) including Univs. of Notre Dame, Fla., Southern Calif., Georgetown; Laetare Medal 1978. *Publications:* The Life of James Cardinal Gibbons 1952, American Catholicism 1956 (revised 1969), American Catholics and the Intellectual Life 1956, Catholic Bishops: A Memoir 1983. *Leisure interests:* reading biography and history, walking. *Address:* The Catholic University of America, Washington D.C., 20064, U.S.A. (Office). *Telephone:* (202) 635-5640.

ELLIS, Osian Gwynn, C.B.E., F.R.A.M.; British harpist; b. 8 Feb. 1928, Ffynnongroew, Flintshire, Wales; s. of Rev. T. G. Ellis; m. Rene Ellis Jones 1951; two s.; ed. Denbigh Grammar School, Royal Acad. of Music; fmr. Prin. Harpist London Symphony Orchestra; mem. Melos Ensemble; Prof. of Harp Royal Acad. of Music 1959–; recitals and concerts worldwide; radio and TV broadcasts; works written for him include harp concertos by Hoddinott 1957, Mathias 1970, Jersild 1972, Gian Carlo Menotti 1977, William Schuman 1978 and Harp Suite in C, Op. 83 by Britten; Hon. D.Mus. (Wales) 1970; Grand Prix du Disque, French Radio Critics' Award and other awards. *Address:* 90 Chandos Avenue, London, N.20, England. *Telephone:* 01-445 7896.

ELLIS, Reginald John, PH.D., F.R.S.; British professor of biological sciences; b. 12 Feb. 1935, Newcastle-under-Lyme; s. of Francis Gilbert Ellis and Evangeline Gratton Ellis; m. Diana Margaret Warren 1963; one d.; ed. Highbury Grove Grammar School, London and King's Coll., Univ. of London; Agricultural Research Council Fellow, Dept. of Biochemistry, Univ. of Oxford 1961–64; Lecturer, Depts. of Botany and Biochemistry, Univ. of Aberdeen 1964–70; Sr. Lecturer, Univ. of Warwick 1970–73, Reader 1973–76, Prof. of Biological Sciences 1976–; Sr. Research Fellow, Science and Eng. Research Council 1983–88; Tate & Lyle Award 1980. *Publications:* 100 papers on plant and microbial biochemistry in the scientific literature; Chloroplast Biogenesis (Ed.) 1984. *Address:* Department of Biological Sciences, University of Warwick, Coventry, West Midlands, CV4 7AL (Office); 44 Sunningdale Avenue, Kenilworth, Warwicks., CV8 2BZ, England (Home). *Telephone:* 0203-523509 (Office); 0926-56382 (Home).

ELLIS, Sir Ronald, Kt., B.SC. TECH., F.ENG.; British company director and consultant; b. 12 Aug. 1925, Colne, Lancs; s. of William Ellis and Bessie Brownbill; m. 1st Cherry H. Browne 1956 (died 1978), 2nd Myra Ann Royle 1979; one s. one d.; ed. Preston Grammar School, Harris Inst., Preston, Univ. of Manchester; Apprentice Leyland Motors Ltd. 1941–46, Sales Eng. 1949–54; Gen. Man. British United Traction 1954–60; Gen. Sales and Service Man., Leyland 1960–64; Dir. Overseas Mfg. 1964–66, Gen. Man. 1966–68; Man. Dir. Truck and Bus Div. British Leyland 1968–76, Dir. 1970–76; H.M. Govt. Head of Defence Sales 1976–81; Dir. Wilkinson Sword 1981–86, Consultant 1981–; Chair. EIDC Ltd. Consultants 1981–, TIP Europe 1986–, Home Rouxl Ltd. 1986–, Brooklands Aerospace Group 1987–; Gov. UMIST 1970–, Vice-Pres. 1983–, Hon. Fellow 1981–. *Leisure interests:* fishing, sailing, reading. *Address:* 12 Seaton Close, Putney, London, SW15 3TJ; Allenview Cottage, Witchampton, Dorset, BH21 5AQ, England.

ELLISON, Rt. Rev. and Rt. Hon. Gerald Alexander, K.C.V.O., P.C., M.A., D.D.; British ecclesiastic; b. 19 Aug. 1910, Windsor, Berks; s. of John Henry Joshua Ellison and Sara Dorothy Graham Crum; m. Jane Elizabeth Gibbon 1947; one s. two d.; ed. Westminster School, New Coll., Oxford and Westcott House, Cambridge; Curate Sherborne Abbey 1935–37; Domestic Chaplain to Bishop of Winchester 1937–39, to Archbishop of York 1943–46; Chaplain to R.N.V.R. (mentioned in despatches) 1939–43; Domestic Chaplain to Portsea 1946–50; Examining Chaplain to Bishop of Portsmouth 1949–50; Canon of Portsmouth 1950; Bishop of Suffragan of Willesden 1950–55; Bishop of Chester 1955–73; Bishop of London 1973–81; Vicar-General of Archbishop of Canterbury in Bermuda 1983–84; Dean of the Chapels Royal 1973–81; Prelate of the Order of the British Empire and of Imperial Soc. of Knights Bachelor 1973–81; Episcopal Canon of Jerusalem 1977; Select Preacher Oxford Univ. 1940, 1961, 1972, Cambridge Univ. 1957; Chaplain Master Mariners' Co. 1946–73, Glass Sellers' Co. 1951–73; Chaplain and Sub-Prelate Order of St. John 1973–; Chair. Bd. of Governors Westfield Coll., London Univ. 1953–67; mem. Council of King's Coll., London Univ. 1973–80, Vice-Chair. newly constituted Council 1980–; mem. Archbishop's Comm. on Women and Holy Orders 1963–66, Archbishop's Comm. on Church and State 1967; Pres. Actors' Church Union; Chair. Oxford Soc.; Fellow King's Coll., London Univ. 1968; Hon. Fellow Westfield Coll., London Univ., New Coll., Oxford Univ.; Hon. Bencher Middle Temple

1976; Hon. Chaplain R.N.R.; a steward of Henley Royal Regatta; Order of St. John. *Publications:* The Churchman's Duty 1957, The Anglican Communion 1960. *Leisure interests:* oarsmanship, walking. *Address:* Billeys House, 16 Long Street, Cerne Abbas, Dorset, DT2 7JF, England.

ELLISON, Ralph (Waldo); American writer; b. 1 March 1914, Okla.; m. Fanny McConnell 1946; ed. Tuskegee Inst.; writer of reviews, short stories, articles and criticism 1939–; Fellow, American Acad. Rome 1955–57; subsequently taught at Bard Coll. 1958–61; Alexander White Visiting Prof., Univ. of Chicago 1961; Visiting Prof. of Writing, Rutgers Univ. 1962–64; Albert Schweitzer Prof. in Humanities, N.Y. Univ. 1970–79; mem. Nat. Inst. of Arts and Letters, American Acad. of Arts and Sciences, American Acad. of Arts and Letters, and others; Rosenwald Fellowship; Nat. Book Award and Russwurm Award for first novel Invisible Man; lecturer on American culture and literature and Negro folklore at several American universities and at Salzburg Seminar 1954; several hon. degrees; Medal of Freedom 1969; Chevalier de l'Ordre des Arts et Lettres 1970, Nat. Medal of Arts 1985. *Publications:* Invisible Man 1952, Shadow and Act (essays) 1964, Going to the Territory (essays) 1986. *Address:* 730 Riverside Drive, New York, N.Y. 10031, U.S.A.

ELLSWORTH, Ralph E., PH.D.; American librarian and professor; b. 22 Sept. 1907; Forest City, Iowa; s. of Wallace and Helma Ellsworth; m. Theda Chapman 1931; two s.; ed. Oberlin Coll., Western Reserve Univ., Chicago Univ.; Librarian, Adams State Coll. 1931–34; Dir. Libraries, Colorado Univ.; Dir. Libraries, Iowa Univ. 1944–58; Dir. Libraries and Prof. of Library Science, Colorado Univ. 1958–72, Prof. Emer. 1972–. *Publications:* (with D. E. Bean) Modular Planning for College and Small University Libraries 1948, Library Buildings 1960, The American Right Wing 1960, Planning College and University Buildings 1960, The School Library: Facilities for Independent Study 1964, The School Library 1965, The Economics of Book Storage 1969, Academic Library Buildings 1973, Manual for Planning Academic Library Buildings 1975, Ellsworth On Ellsworth 1980, George Norlin as His Friends Knew Him 1980. *Leisure interests:* travel, angling, music, library architecture. *Address:* 860 Willowbrook Road, Boulder, Colo. 80302, U.S.A. *Telephone:* (303) 443-2592.

ELMANDJRA, Mahdi, PH.D.; Moroccan university professor; b. 13 March 1933, Rabat; s. of M'Hamed Elmandjra and Rabia Elmrini; m. Amina Elmrini 1956; two d.; ed. Lycée Lyautey, Casablanca, Putney School, Vermont, U.S.A., Cornell Univ., London School of Economics and Faculté de Droit, Univ. de Paris; Head of Confs., Law Faculty, Univ. of Rabat 1957–58; Adviser, Ministry of Foreign Affairs, and to Moroccan Del. to UN 1958–59; Dir.-Gen., Radiodiffusion Télévision Marocaine 1959–60; Chief of African Div., Office of Relations with Mem. States, UNESCO 1961–63; Dir. Exec. Office of Dir.-Gen. of UNESCO 1963–66; Asst. Dir.-Gen. of UNESCO for Social Sciences, Human Sciences and Culture 1966–69; Visiting Fellow, Centre of Int. Studies, London School of Econs. and Political Science 1970; Asst. Dir.-Gen. of UNESCO for Pre-Programming 1971–74; Special Adviser to Dir.-Gen. of UNESCO 1975–76; Prof. Univ. Mohamed V, Rabat 1977–; Co-ordinator, Conf. on Tech. Co-operation between Developing Countries (UNDP) 1979–80; Senior Adviser, UN Int. Year of Disabled Persons 1980–81; Pres. Futuribles Int.; Consultant, Intergovernmental Bureau for Informatics 1981–; mem. Club of Rome, Acad. of the Kingdom of Morocco; Vice-Pres. Asscn. Maroc-Japon; mem. World Acad. of Art and Science, Exec. Cttee., Soc. for Int. Devt., Exec. Cttee., African Acad. of Sciences, Pugwash Conferences, Founding Pres. Moroccan Asscn. of Human Rights; Officier, Ordre des Arts et Lettres (France); Prix de la vie économique (France) 1981, Medal of the French Acad. of Architecture 1984, Order of the Rising Sun (Third Class), Japan 1986, Master Jury Aga Khan Award for Architecture 1986. *Publications:* The League of Arab States 1957, Nehru and the Modern World 1968, Relations between Japanese and Western Arts 1968, Economie et Culture (in Economie et Société Humaine) 1972, Informatics in Government (IBI World Conf. on Informatics) 1972, Globalidad Interdisciplinaria y Exigencias Sociales Cualitativas 1972, The United Nations System: An Analysis 1973, Global Co-operation as an Operational Concept (with John E. Fobes) 1975, Alternatives for a New International Economic Order 1976, The Future of the Socio-Cultural Values of the Mediterranean 1977, International Organization and Development 1977, Political Facets of the North-South Dialogue, 1978, Architects and National Development 1978, No Limits to Learning: A Report to the Club of Rome 1979, Africa 2000 1980, The New Age of Culture and Communication 1981, The Future of Humor 1982, Maghreb 2000 1982, L'Interpellation du Tiers Monde 1982, Les Aspects économiques du dialogue Euro-Arabe 1982, Information and Sovereignty 1983, The Conquest of Space: Political, Economic and Socio-Cultural Implications 1984, Casablanca 2000 1984, Development and Automation 1985, Communications, Information and Development 1985, Tomorrow's Habitat 1985, Learning Needs in a Changing Society 1986, Media and Communications in Africa 1986, The Future of International Cooperation 1986, The Financing of Research and Development in the Third World 1986, Development Aid as an Obstacle to Development 1987, The Place and Role of Science and Technology 1987, For a Better Life for All in the Metropolis 1987, Culture, Arts and Traditions: Vision Prospective 1987, Nouvelles Tendances des Recherches en Sciences Sociales 1987, Present and Potential Uses of Informatics and Telematics in Health 1987, Le Sommet Francophone: Instrument de Relations Internationales? 1987,

Maghreb et Francophonie 1988, Three Scenarios for The Future of International Cooperation 1988, The Place of Arab Culture in the World of Tomorrow 1988, Social Change and Law 1988. *Leisure interests:* reading, skiing. *Address:* B.P. 53, Rabat, Morocco. *Telephone:* Rabat 742 58.

ELSÄSSER, Hans Friedrich, DR.RER.NAT.; German astronomer; b. 29 March 1929, Aalen/Württemberg; s. of Jakob Elsässer and Margarete Elsässer-Vogelsang; m. Ruth Abele 1953; two s. one d.; ed. Univ. of Tübingen; Asst. Prof., Univ. of Tübingen 1957, Univ. of Göttingen 1959; Prof. of Astronomy, Univ. of Heidelberg 1962–; Dir. State Observatory, Heidelberg-Königstuhl 1962–75; Dir. Max Planck Inst. for Astronomy, Heidelberg-Königstuhl 1968–; mem. Acad. of Sciences of Heidelberg, Halle and Vienna; Comendador de la Orden de Isabel la Católica (Spain). *Publications:* about 100 articles in astronomical journals and three textbooks, two with H. Scheffler. *Leisure interest:* tennis. *Address:* Max-Planck-Institut für Astronomie, D-69 Heidelberg-Königstuhl, Federal Republic of Germany. *Telephone:* 06221/528 200.

ELSLANDE, Renaat van; Belgian lawyer, university professor and politician; b. 21 Jan. 1916, Boekhoute; m. Ghislaine Van Acker 1945; one s. three d.; Professor, Univ. of Louvain; mem. Chamber of Reps. 1949–81; Minister, Under-Sec. of State for Cultural Affairs 1960–61, Deputy Minister of Nat. Educ., Minister of Cultural Affairs 1961–63; Minister of Cultural Affairs, Deputy Minister of Educ. 1963–65; Minister of European Affairs and Flemish Culture 1966–68; Minister of Home Affairs 1972; Minister of Foreign Affairs 1973; Minister of Foreign Affairs and Devt. 1974–77; Minister of Justice 1977–80; Vice-Prime Minister and Minister of Justice 1978–79; Christian Social Party. *Publications:* Europa's Toekomst 1975, Belgie en de Derde Wereld 1977. *Address:* Van Elslande Renaat, Kerkstraat 39, 1660 Beersel-Lot, Belgium *Telephone:* 02 376 32 39.

ELTIS, Walter Alfred, M.A.; British economist; b. 23 May 1933, Warnsdorf, Czechoslovakia; s. of Rev. Martin Eltis and Mary Schnitzer; m. Shelagh M. Owen 1959; one s. two d.; ed. Wycliffe Coll., Emmanuel Coll. Cambridge and Nuffield Coll. Oxford; Research Fellow in Econs. Exeter Coll., Oxford 1958–60; lecturer in Econs., Univ. of Oxford 1961–88; Fellow and Tutor in Econs., Exeter Coll. Oxford 1963–88, Fellow Emer. 1988–; Econ. Dir. Nat. Econ. Devt. Office 1986–88, Dir.-Gen. 1988–; Visiting Reader in Econs., Univ. of W. Australia 1970–71; Visiting Prof. Univ. of Toronto 1976–77, European Univ. Florence 1979; Adam Smith Prize, Cambridge 1956. *Publications:* Growth and Distribution 1973, Britain's Economic Problem: Too Few Producers (with R. Bacon) 1976, The Classical Theory of Economic Growth 1984. *Leisure interests:* chess, music, *Address:* National Economic Development Office, Millbank Tower, 21/41 Millbank, London, SW1P 4QX (Office); Danesway, Jarn Way, Boars Hill, Oxford, OX1 5JF, England (Home). *Telephone:* 01-211 5386 (Office); (0865) 735440 (Home).

ELTON, 2nd Baron, cr. 1934, of Headington; **Rodney Elton,** M.A., T.D.; British politician and company director; b. 2 March 1930, Oxford; s. of Godfrey Elton, 1st Baron and Dedi Hartmann; m. 1st Anne Frances Tilney 1958 (dissolved), 2nd Susan Richenda Gurney 1979; one s. three d.; ed. Eton Coll. and New Coll., Oxford; fmr. Capt. Qualified Officer Warwicks. and Worcs. Yeomanry; fmr. Maj. Leics. and Derbyshire Yeomanry; farming 1957–73; Asst. Mastership in History Loughborough Grammar School 1962–67, Fairham Comprehensive School for Boys 1967–69; contested Loughborough div. of Leics. 1966, 1970; Lecturer Bishop Lonsdale Coll. of Educ. 1969–72; Opposition Whip House of Lords 1974–76; an Opposition Spokesman 1976–79; Parl. Under-Sec. of State for N. Ireland 1979–81, Dept. of Health and Social Security 1981–82, Home Office 1982–84, Minister of State 1984–85; Minister of State Dept. of Environment 1985–86; Chair. Financial Intermediaries' Mans.' and Brokers' Regulatory Assen. (FIMBRA) 1987–; Dir. Andry Montgomery Ltd. 1977–79, Deputy Chair. 1987–; Dir. Overseas Exhbns. Ltd. 1977–79, Bldg. Trades Exhbn. Ltd. 1977–79; mem. Panel on Takeovers and Mergers 1987; Conservative. *Leisure interest:* painting. *Address:* House of Lords, London, S.W.1, England. *Telephone:* 01-219 3165.

ELTON, Charles Sutherland, F.R.S.; British zoologist; b. 29 March 1900, Manchester; s. of late Oliver Elton and Letitia Maynard MacColl; m. 1st Rose Montague 1928, no c.; m. 2nd Edith J. Scovell 1937, one s. one d.; ed. Liverpool Coll. and New Coll., Oxford; Ecologist, Oxford Univ. Expedition to Spitsbergen 1921, Merton Coll. Arctic Expedition 1923, Oxford Univ. Arctic Expedition 1924, Oxford Univ. Lapland Expedition 1930; Dir. Bureau of Animal Population, Dept. of Zoological Field Studies, Oxford Univ. 1932–67; Reader in Animal Ecology, Oxford Univ. and Senior Research Fellow, Corpus Christi Coll. 1936–67; Hon. Fellow, Corpus Christi Coll., Oxford 1967–; mem. Nature Conservancy 1949–56; Foreign Hon. mem. American Acad. of Arts and Sciences 1968; Gold Medal, Linnean Soc. 1967; Darwin Medal, Royal Soc. 1970, Tyler Ecology Award 1976, Edward W. Browning Award (Conservation) 1977. *Publications:* Animal Ecology 1927, Animal Ecology and Evolution 1930, The Ecology of Animals 1933, Exploring the Animal World 1933, Voles, Mice and Lemmings 1942, The Ecology of Invasions by Animals and Plants 1958, The Pattern of Animal Communities 1966. *Leisure interests:* natural history, reading, gardening. *Address:* 61 Park Town, Oxford, OX2 6SL, England. *Telephone:* Oxford 57644.

ELTON, Prof. Sir Geoffrey (Rudolph), PH.D., LITT.D., F.B.A.; British professor of history; b. 17 Aug. 1921, Tübingen, Germany; s. of Victor and

Eva Ehrenberg; m. Sheila Lambert 1952; no c.; ed. Grammar School, Prague, Rydal School, Colwyn Bay and Univ. of London; served army (Infantry and Intelligence) 1943–46; Asst., Univ. of Glasgow 1948–49; Asst. lecturer, lecturer and reader, Univ. of Cambridge 1949–67, Prof. of English Constitutional History 1967–83, Regius Prof. of Modern History 1983–88; Fellow, Clare Coll., Cambridge 1954; Founder and Pres. List and Index Soc. 1965–; Fellow British Acad. 1967 (Publications Sec. 1981), Royal Historical Soc. 1954, Pres. 1973–76, Fellow Univ. Coll. London; Foreign mem. American Acad. of Arts and Sciences 1975; Hon. D.Litt. (Glasgow) 1979, (Newcastle) 1981, (Bristol) 1981, London (1985), Göttingen (1987). *Publications:* The Tudor Revolution in Government 1953, England under the Tudors 1955, Reformation Europe 1963, Practice of History 1967, Policy and Police 1972, Reform and Renewal 1973, Studies in Tudor and Stuart Politics and Government, 3 vols., Reform and Reformation: England 1509–58 1977, F. W. Maitland 1984, The Parliament of England 1559–1581 1986, Ed. New Cambridge Modern History vol. 2 1958. *Leisure interests:* squash rackets, gardening, malt whisky. *Address:* Clare College, Cambridge; Faculty of History, West Road, Cambridge, England. *Telephone:* 335326 (Faculty of History).

ELVIN, Herbert Lionel, M.A.; British educationalist; b. 7 Aug. 1905, Buckhurst Hill, Essex; s. of Herbert Henry Elvin (Pres. T.U.C. 1938) and Mary Jane Elvin; m. Mona Bedortha Dutton 1934; one s.; ed. Trinity Hall, Cambridge, and Yale Univ; Fellow of Trinity Hall, Cambridge, and mem. of Faculty of English, Cambridge, 1930–45; temporary civil servant, Air Ministry 1940–42, Ministry of Information (American Div.) 1942–45; Principal, Ruskin Coll., mem. Faculty of English, Oxford 1945–50; mem. Univ. Grants Cttee. 1946–50; Dir. Dept. of Education, UNESCO 1950–56; Prof. Education (Tropical Areas) London Univ., Inst. of Education 1956–58; Dir. Inst. of Education, London Univ. 1958–73; Chair. Commonwealth Educ. Liaison Cttee. 1965–73; mem. Govt. of India Educ. Comm. 1965–66; Hon. Fellow, Trinity Hall, Cambridge 1979; Emer. Prof. of Educ. (London). *Publications:* Men of America 1941, An Introduction to the Study of Poetry 1949, Education and Contemporary Society 1965, The Place of Commonsense in Educational Thought 1977, The Educational Systems in the European Community (Ed.) 1982, Encounters with Education 1987. *Leisure interests:* reading, golf. *Address:* 4 Bulstrode Gardens, Cambridge, England. *Telephone:* 358309.

ELVIN, Violetta (Violetta Prokhorova); British ballerina; b. 3 Nov. 1925, Moscow; d. of Vassili Prokhorov and Irena T. Grimusinskaya; m. 1st Harold Elvin 1944 (divorced 1952); m. 2nd Siegbert J. Weinberger 1953; m. 3rd Fernando Savarese 1959; one s.; ed. Bolshoi Theatre School, Moscow; Mem. Bolshoi Theatre Ballet 1942, evacuated to Tashkent 1943; ballerina, Tashkent State Theatre; rejoined Bolshoi Theatre as soloist 1944; joined Sadler's Wells Ballet, Royal Opera House, Covent Garden (now the Royal Ballet) as guest soloist 1946, and later as regular mem., prima ballerina 1951–56; guest artist, Stanislavsky Theatre, Moscow 1944, Sadler's Wells Theatre 1947; guest prima ballerina, La Scala 1952–53; guest artist, Cannes 1954, Copenhagen 1954, Teatro Municipal, Rio de Janeiro 1955, Festival Hall 1955; guest prima ballerina, Royal Opera House, Stockholm 1956; Royal Opera House, Covent Garden 1956 (concluded her stage career); Dir. Ballet Co. San Carla Opera, Naples 1985–87; film appearances: The Queen of Spades, Twice Upon a Time, Melba. *Leisure interests:* reading, walking, swimming. *Address:* Marina di Equa, 80066 Seiano, Bay of Naples, Italy. *Telephone:* 081-8798520.

ELWORTHY, Baron (Life Peer), cr. 1972; **Marshal of the Royal Air Force (Samuel) Charles Elworthy**, K.G., G.C.B., C.B.E., D.S.O., D.F.C., A.F.C.; British air force officer; b. 23 March 1911, Timaru, New Zealand; s. of late Percy Elworthy; m. Audrey Hutchinson 1936 (died 1986); three s. one d.; ed. Marlborough Coll. and Trinity Coll., Cambridge; Reserve of Air Force Officers 1933; Called to Bar (Lincoln's Inn) 1935 (Bencher 1970); R.A.F. 1936–, Bomber Command 1939–45, Commandant R.A.F. Staff Coll. 1957–59; Deputy Chief of Air Staff 1959–60; C.-in-C. Middle East 1960–63; Chief of Air Staff Sept. 1963–67; Chief of Defence Staff 1967–71; Constable and Gov. of Windsor Castle 1971–78; H.M. Lieut. for Greater London 1973–78. *Leisure interests:* travel, fishing. *Address:* Gordons Valley, R.D.2, Timaru, South Canterbury, New Zealand. *Telephone:* (056) 24702.

ELWYN-JONES, Baron (Life Peer) cr. 1974, of Llanelli in the County of Carmarthen and of Newham in Greater London; **(Frederick) Elwyn Elwyn-Jones**, Kt., P.C., C.H., M.A., Q.C.; British lawyer and politician; b. 24 Oct. 1909, Llanelli; s. of Frederick and Elizabeth Jones; m. Pearl Binder 1937; one s. two d.; ed. Llanelli Grammar School, Univ. Coll. of Wales, Aberystwyth, and Gonville and Caius Coll., Cambridge; called to Bar, Gray's Inn 1935; Deputy Judge Advocate 1943–45; mem. British War Crimes Exec. Nuremberg 1945; M.P. 1945–74; Q.C. 1953; Q.C. Northern Ireland 1958; Recorder of Merthyr Tydfil 1949–53, of Swansea 1953–60, of Cardiff 1960–64, of Kingston-upon-Thames 1964–70; Parl. Pvt. Sec. to Attorney-Gen. 1946–51; Attorney-Gen. 1964–70; Lord Chancellor 1974–79; Lord of Appeal 1979–; Pres. Univ. Coll., Cardiff; Fellow of King's Coll., London, Gonville and Caius Coll., Cambridge; mem. Bar Council 1956–59, Inter-Departmental Cttee. on Court of Criminal Appeal 1964; Chair. of Soc. of Labour Lawyers 1957–60; Treas. of Justice, British Section, Int. Comm. of Jurists 1959–64, 1970–74; U.K. Observer Malta Referendum 1964; Bencher Gray's Inn 1960, Treas. 1980; Pres. Mental Health Foundation 1982–; Major R.A., T.A.; Freeman of Llanelli and London; Hon. LL.D. (Wales, Columbia, Ottawa, Law Soc. of Upper Canada, Warsaw, Philippines, Sussex Univ.); Labour. *Publications:* Hitler's Drive to the East 1937, The Battle for Peace 1938, The Attack from Within 1939, In My Time 1983. *Leisure interests:* travelling, walking. *Address:* House of Lords, London, SW1A 0PW, England. *Telephone:* 01-219 5410.

ELYTIS, Odysseus; Greek poet and essayist; b. 2 Nov. 1911, Heracleion, Crete; s. of Panayiotis and Maria Alepoudelis; ed. Univs. of Athens and Paris; contributed first to review Nea Grammata 1935; rank of 2nd Lieut. in World War II service; became expounder of surrealism; art critic for newspaper Kathimerini 1946–48; Broadcasting and Programme Dir. Hellenic Nat. Broadcasting Inst. 1945–46 and 1953–54; represented Greece at Rencontres Int. de Genève 1948, Congrès de l'Association des Critiques d'Art 1949 and Incontro Romano della Cultura 1960; mem. Nat. Theatre Admin. Council, Consultative Cttee. of the Greek Nat. Tourist Org. on the Athens Festival; Dr. h.c. phil. (Thessaloniki) 1975, Dr. h.c. (Paris) 1980; Hon. D.Litt. (London) 1981; First State Poetry Prize 1960, Nobel Prize for Literature 1979; Benson Silver Medal (R.S.L.) 1981; Hon. Citizen of Mytilene; Order of the Phoenix 1965; Grand Commdr. Order of Honour 1979. *Publications:* Clepsydras of the Unknown 1937, Sporades 1938, Orientations 1940, Sun the First 1943, An Heroic and Funeral Chant for the Lieutenant Lost in Albania 1946, To Axion Esti—It Is Worthy 1959, Six Plus One Remorses for the Sky 1960, The Light Tree and the Fourteenth Beauty 1972, The Sovereign Sun 1972, The Trills of Love 1973, The Monogram 1973, The Painter Theophilos 1973, Step-poems 1974, Offering My Cards to Sight 1974, Second Writing 1976, The Magic of Papadiamantis 1976, Signalbook 1977, Maria Nefeli 1978, Selected Poems 1981, Three Poems 1982, Journal of an Unseen April 1984, Saphfo 1984. *Leisure interests:* trying home painting and collage. *Address:* 23 Skoufa Street, Athens, Greece. *Telephone:* 3626458.

EMAN, J. H. A. (Henny); Aruban lawyer and politician; leader Arubaanse Volkspartij (AVP); Prime Minister of Aruba and Minister of Gen. Affairs 1986–89. *Address:* c/o Office of the Prime Minister, Oranjestad; Arubaanse Volkspartij, Oranjestad, Aruba.

EMANUEL, Nikolay Markovich; Soviet physical chemist; b. 1 Oct. 1915, Tim, Kursk Region; s. of Mark and Olga Emanuel; m.Tatyana Yevgenyevna Pavlovskaya; one d.; ed. Leningrad Industrial (Polytechnical) Inst.; Scientific worker at Inst. of Chemical Physics, U.S.S.R. Acad. of Sciences 1938–; Asst. Prof. Moscow Univ. 1944–50, Prof. 1950–; mem. C.P.S.U. 1948–; Corresp. mem. U.S.S.R. Acad. of Sciences 1958–66, mem. 1966–, Head, Dept. of Kinetics of Chemical and Biological Processes at Inst. of Chemical Physics, U.S.S.R. Acad. of Sciences 1960–, Academician-Sec. Dept. of General and Technical Chemistry 1975–; Chair. Nat. Cttee. of Soviet Chemists 1972–; Editor-in-Chief of Journal Uspekhi Khimii 1973–; Foreign mem. Royal Swedish Acad. of Sciences 1974, Acad. of Sciences of German Democratic Republic 1970, Polish Acad. of Sciences; mem. New York Acad. of Sciences 1974–, Leopoldina 1977–; Hon. mem. Hungarian Acad. of Sciences 1976; Dr. h.c. Szeged Univ. (Hungary) 1974, Uppsala Univ. (Sweden) 1977; Lenin Prize for research into properties and particular features of chain reactions 1958; Order of Red Banner of Labour 1965 and 1971, Order of Lenin 1975, Order of Peace and Friendship (Hungary) 1975, State Prizes for Research 1981, 1983, Hero of Socialist Labour 1982, and other decorations. *Publications:* Intermediate products of complex gaseous reactions 1946, The inhibition of fat oxidation processes 1967, Liquid Phase Oxidation of Hydrocarbons 1967, Clinical oncology—a quantitative approach 1972, Chemical Kinetics, Homogeneous Reactions 1962, 1969, 1974, Kinetics of Experimental Tumor Processes 1977. *Address:* Inst. of Chemical Physics, U.S.S.R. Academy of Sciences, Kosygin Street 4, Moscow 117334, U.S.S.R. *Telephone:* 137-64-20 (Office).

EMBUREY, John Ernest; British cricketer; b. 20 Aug. 1952, Peckham, London; s. of John Emburey and Rose Emburey; m. Susie Emburey 1980; two d.; ed. Peckham Manor Secondary School; right-hand batsman, off-break bowler, slip or gully fielder; plays for Middx.; county début 1973, county cap 1977; Test debut 1978; toured with England team to Australia 1978–79, 1979–80, West Indies 1981, 1986, India 1981–82; Captain of England June-July 1988; played in World Cup, Pakistan, Australia and N.Z. 1987–88. *Leisure interests:* golf, squash, reading. *Address:* c/o Middlesex County Cricket Club, Lord's, London N.W.1, England.

EMELEUS, Harry, D.SC., C.B.E., F.R.S.; British professor of chemistry; b. 22 June 1903, London; s. of Karl H. and Ellen Emeleus; m. Mary C. Horton 1931; two s. two d.; ed. Imperial Coll., London, Technische Hochschule, Karlsruhe and Princeton Univ.; mem. staff, Imperial Coll., London 1931–45; Prof. of Inorganic Chem., Cambridge Univ. 1945–70, now Prof. Emer.; Fellow Sidney Sussex Coll., Cambridge, Imperial Coll., London; Davey Medal (Royal Soc.), Lavoisier Medal (French Chem. Soc.), Stock Medal (German Chem. Soc.). *Publications:* Modern Aspects of Inorganic Chemistry (with J. S. Anderson) 1938; scientific papers in chemical journals. *Leisure interests:* fishing, gardening *Address:* 149 Shelford Road, Trumpington, Cambridge, CB2 2ND, England. *Telephone:* Cambridge 840374.

EMENEAU, Murray Barnson, M.A., PH.D.; American professor; b. 28 Feb. 1904, Lunenburg, Nova Scotia, Canada; s. of Archibald and Ada Emeneau; m. Katharine Fitch Venter 1940; two stepdaughters; ed. Dalhousie, Oxford and Yale Univs.; Instructor in Latin, Yale Univ. 1926–31; Fellowships, Yale Univ. and American Council of Learned Socs. 1931–40; research in India 1935–38; Asst. Prof. of Sanskrit and Gen. Linguistics, Univ. of Calif., Berkeley 1940–43, Assoc. Prof. 1943–46, Prof. 1946–71, Prof. Emer. 1971–, Faculty Research Lecturer 1955–56, Chair. Dept. of Linguistics 1953–58, Chair. Dept. of Classics 1959–62; Guggenheim Fellowship 1949, 1956–57, 1958; Vice-Pres. Linguistic Soc. of America 1949, Pres. 1950; Assoc. Ed. American Oriental Soc. 1940–47, Ed. 1947–52, Pres. 1954–55, Western Branch 1964–65; Hermann Collitz Prof. of Indo-European Comparative Linguistics, Indiana Univ. 1953; mem. American Philosophical Soc. 1952; Hon. mem. Nat. Inst. of Humanistic Sciences, Vietnam 1957, Linguistic Soc. of India 1964, Linguistic Research Group of Pakistan 1971; Hon. Fellow Royal Asiatic Soc. 1969; mem. American Acad. of Arts and Sciences 1970; Vice-Pres. Int. Asscn. for Tamil Research 1966; Hon. Pres. 6th World Sanskrit Conf. 1984; Presented with Studies in Indian Linguistics by Centres of Advanced Study in Linguistics, Deccan Coll. and Annamalai Univ., and Linguistic Soc. of India 1968; Hon. L.H.D. (Chicago) 1968, Hon. LL.D. (Dalhousie) 1970, Hon. D. Litt (Hyderabad) 1987; Berkeley Citation 1971; Lucius Wilbur Cross Medal Yale Graduate School Asscn. 1969. *Publications:* Jambhaladatta's Version of the Vetālapañcaviṅśati 1934, A Union List of Printed Indic Texts and Translations in American Libraries 1935, Kota Texts 1944–46, Studies in Vietnamese (Annamese) Grammar 1951, Kolami, a Dravidian Language 1955; Vedic Variants Vol. III (with M. Bloomfield & F. Edgerton) 1934; A Dravidian Etymological Dictionary (with T. Burrow) 1961, 1984, Dravidian Borrowings from Indo-Aryan (with T. Burrow) 1962, Brahui and Dravidian Grammar 1962, Kālidāsa's Sakuntalā translated from the Bengali Recension 1962, Dravidian Linguistics, Ethnology and Folktales (collected papers) 1967, A Dravidian Etymological Dictionary: Supplement (with T. Burrow) 1968, Toda Songs 1971, Ritual Structure and Language Structure of the Todas 1974, Language and Linguistic Area 1980, Toda Grammar and Texts 1984, Sanskrit Studies 1988. *Leisure interests:* ballet, opera, travel. *Address:* Department of Linguistics, University of California, Berkeley, Calif. 94720 (Office); 909 San Benito Road, Berkeley, Calif. 94707, U.S.A. (Home).

EMERTON, Rev. John Adney, M.A., D.D., F.B.A.; British ecclesiastic and academic; b. 5 June 1928, Winchmore Hill; s. of Adney S. Emerton and Helena M. (née Quin) Emerton; m. Norma E. Bennington 1954; one s. two d.; ed. Minchenden Grammar School, Southgate, Corpus Christi Coll., Oxford and Wycliffe Hall, Oxford; ordained deacon 1952, priest 1953; Asst. lecturer in Theology, Birmingham Univ. 1952–53; curate, Birmingham Cathedral 1952–53; lecturer in Hebrew and Aramaic, Univ. of Durham 1953–55; lecturer in Divinity, Univ. of Cambridge 1955–62; Fellow, St. Peter's Coll. and Reader in Semitic Philology, Univ. of Oxford 1962–68; Regius Prof. of Hebrew, Univ. of Cambridge 1968–; Fellow St. John's Coll. Cambridge 1970–; Sec., Int. Org. for Study of Old Testament 1971–; Hon. Canon, St. George's Cathedral, Jerusalem 1984–; Hon. D.D. (Edinburgh); Visiting Fellow, Inst. for Advanced Studies, Hebrew Univ. of Jerusalem 1983; visiting professorships at various overseas univs. etc. *Publications:* The Peshitta of the Wisdom of Solomon 1959, The Old Testament in Syriac—The Song of Songs 1966; articles in journals. *Address:* St. John's College, Cambridge, CB2 1TP; 34 Gough Way, Cambridge, CB3 9LN, England.

EMERY, Alan Eglin Heathcote, M.D., PH.D., D.SC., F.R.C.P., F.L.S., F.R.S.E.; British physician and professor of human genetics; b. 21 Aug. 1928, Manchester; s. of Harold Heathcote Emery and Alice Eglin; ed. Manchester Grammar School, Manchester Univ. and Johns Hopkins Univ., U.S.A.; Postdoctoral Research Fellow, Johns Hopkins Univ., Baltimore 1961–64; Lecturer, then Reader in Medical Genetics, Manchester Univ. 1964–68; Foundation Prof. and Chair., Dept. of Human Genetics, Edin. Univ. 1968–83, Prof. Emer. and Univ. Fellow 1983–; Visiting Fellow, Green Coll., Oxford 1985–; Pres. British Clinical Genetics Soc. 1980–83; Vice-Pres. Genetical Soc. 1985–; Int. Award for Genetic Research (U.S.A.) and other awards. *Publications:* Elements of Medical Genetics (7th edn.) 1987, Principles and Practice of Medical Genetics 1983, Psychological Aspects of Genetic Counselling 1984, Introduction to Recombinant DNA 1985, Methodology in Medical Genetics, (2nd edn.) 1986, Duchenne Muscular Dystrophy 1987; 200 scientific papers. *Leisure interests:* marine biology, oil painting, writing poetry. *Address:* Medical School, Teviot Place, Edinburgh, EH8 9AG; 1 Eton Terrace, Edinburgh, EH4 1QE, Scotland (Home). *Telephone:* (031) 667-1011 Ext. 2505 (Office); (031) 343-2262 (Home).

EMERY, Kenneth O., PH.D.; American oceanographer; b. 6 June 1914, Saskatchewan, Canada; s. of Clifford A. and Agnes B. Emery; m. Caroline Alexander 1941 (died 1984); two d.; m. Phyllis Z. Williams 1985; ed. N. Texas Agricultural Coll., Arlington, Univ. of Illinois and Scripps Inst. of Oceanography; Assoc. Geologist, Ill. State Geological Survey 1941–43; Assoc. Marine Geologist, Univ. of Calif. Div. of War Research 1943–45; Asst., Assoc. and Prof. of Geology, Univ. of S. Calif. 1945–62; Geologist, U.S. Geological Survey (summer only) 1946–60; Senior Scientist, Woods Hole Oceanographic Inst. 1962–79, Emer. 1979–, Dean of Educ. 1967, Henry Bryant Bigelow Chair., Oceanography 1975; Guggenheim Fellowship 1959; mem. Nat. Acad. of Sciences, American Acad. of Arts and Sciences, American Asscn. of Petroleum Geologists, Geological Soc. of America, Royal Swedish Acad. of Sciences; Shepard Prize in Marine Geology 1969, Médaille Commémorative du Prince Albert Ier de Monaco, Compass Distin-

guished Achievement Award 1974, A.A.A.S.—Rosenstiel Award in Oceanography 1975, Illini Achievement Award (Univ. of Ill.) 1977, Maurice Ewing Award for Oceanography 1985. *Publications:* Bikini and Adjacent Atolls 1954, The Sea off Southern California 1960, The Dead Sea 1967, Oyster Pond 1970, The Western North Atlantic Ocean (with Elazar Uchupi) 1972, The Geology of the Atlantic Ocean (with Elazar Uchupi) 1984, Eighteenth-century Gunflints from Fort Michilimackinac and other colonial sites (with T. M. Hamilton) 1987, Mediterranean Coasts of Israel and Sinai: Holocene Tectonism from Geology, Geophysics and Archaeology (with D. Neer and N. Bakler) 1987. *Leisure interest:* stock market. *Address:* 74 Ransom Road, Falmouth, Mass. 02540, U.S.A.

EMILIANI, Vittorio; Italian journalist; b. 1 Dec. 1935, Predappio, Forlì; s. of Nicola Emiliani and Lina Bartoletti; m. Silvana Forni 1960; one s. one d.; ed. High School and Univ.; began reporting career with Olivetti journal Comunità; then contributor to Il Mondo and L'Espresso; Sub-Ed. and Special Corresp. of Milan daily Il Giorno with emphasis on social and econ. matters and devt. of urban environment mid-1960s–1974; Special Corresp., then Chief Political Commentator of Rome daily Il Messaggero 1974–80, Ed.-in-Chief 1980–86. *Publications:* Ravenna, una capitale 1965, Gli anarchici 1973, L'Italia mangiata 1977 and contributions to Enciclopedia europea Garzanti; wrote inquiry for TV on Italian minor industries. *Leisure interests:* cycling, tennis, skiing, cooking and wine tasting. *Address:* Il Messaggero, Via del Tritone 152, Rome 00187 (Office); Viale delle Medaglie d'Oro, Rome, Italy (Home).

EMILIO (see Pucci di Barsento, Marchese Emilio).

EMIN, Gevork (pseudonym of Karlen Grigorovich Muradyan); Soviet (Armenian) poet; b. 30 Oct. 1919, Ashtarak, Armenia; mem. CPSU 1953–; ed. Dept. of Hydrotechnology, Yerevan Polytechnic Inst.; served in Soviet Army 1941–45; first works published 1935; Chief Ed. of Literaturnaya Armenia 1969–72; *works include:* Predtropye 1940, The New Road (collection of verse) 1949 (Russian trans. 1950), Searchings 1955, Until This Day 1959, Two Roads 1962, At This Age 1968 (Russian trans. 1972), The Twentieth Century 1970, Seven Songs about Armenia 1974, Century. Earth. Love. 1974 (Russian trans. 1976); trans. in many languages, including English; two Soviet orders.

EMİROĞLU, Metin; Turkish politician; b. 1943, Arapkir; m.; two c.; ed. Faculty of Law, Univ. of Istanbul; fmr. practising lawyer; later mem. staff, State Planning Org.; mem. Parl. for Malatya; mem. Motherland Party; Minister of Educ., Youth and Sport 1986–87. *Address:* c/o Ministry of Education, Milli Egition, Genclik ve Spor Bakonlıgı, Ankara, Turkey.

EMMENS, Clifford Walter, PH.D., D.SC., F.S.S., F.BIOL., F.A.A.; Australian university professor; b. 9 Dec. 1913, London; s. of Walter J. Emmens and Narcissa L. Pugh; m. Muriel E. Bristow 1937; two s. two d.; ed. Purley County School and Univ. Coll., London; demonstrator in Zoology, Univ. Coll., London 1936–37; research biologist MRC 1937–48, seconded to Ministry of Home Security and R.A.F. 1941–46; Head Dept. of Veterinary Physiology, Univ. of Sydney 1948–78, seconded part-time as officer-in-charge, CSIRO Sheep Biology Lab., later Div. of Animal Physiology 1952–54; Chair. various cttees. of CSIRO, Nat. Health and Medical Research Council etc.; mem. numerous professional socs.; Oliver Bird Medal and Prize (U.K.) 1961; Istituto Spallanzani Medal (Italy) 1964; Hon. D.V.Sc. *Publications:* author and co-author of numerous books and more than 200 scientific papers. *Leisure interests:* aquarium keeping, history of science. *Address:* 603/22 Sutherland Street, Cremorne, N.S.W. 2090, Australia. *Telephone:* (02) 909 1607.

EMMET, Dorothy Mary, M.A., D.LITT.; British university professor; b. 29 Sept. 1904, London; d. of late Rev. Cyril W. Emmet and late Gertrude Julia (née Weir); ed. Lady Margaret Hall, Univ. of Oxford; adult education work Maesyrhaf Settlement 1927–28, 1931–32; Commonwealth Fellowship in U.S. 1928–30; Research Fellow, Somerville Coll., Oxford 1930–31; Lecturer in Philosophy, King's Coll., Newcastle-on-Tyne 1932–38; Lecturer in Philosophy of Religion, Univ. of Manchester 1938–45, Reader in Philosophy 1945–46; Sir Samuel Hall Prof. of Philosophy, Univ. of Manchester 1946–66, Emer. Prof. 1966–; Hon. Fellow Lady Margaret Hall, Oxford; Emer. Fellow Lucy Cavendish Coll., Cambridge; Hon. D.Litt. (Glasgow, Leicester). *Publications:* Whitehead's Philosophy of Organism 1932, Philosophy and Faith 1936, The Nature of Metaphysical Thinking 1945, Function, Purpose and Powers 1958, Rules, Roles and Relations 1966; Ed. (with A. MacIntyre) Sociological Theory and Philosophical Analysis 1970, The Moral Prism 1979, The Effectiveness of Causes 1984. *Leisure interests:* walking, gardening, reading. *Address:* 11 Millington Road, Cambridge, England. *Telephone:* Cambridge 350822.

EMMETT, Martin Frederick Cheere, B.SC., M.B.A.; Canadian business executive; b. 30 Aug. 1934, Johannesburg; s. of Cecil Frederick Cheere and Thelma Maria (Ford) Cheere; m. Alice Ellen Lavers 1956; one s. two d.; ed. Univ. of Witwatersrand, Queen's Univ., Ontario; market research, planning and gen. man. in mfg. plants for Alcan Canada Products Ltd. until becoming Vice-Pres. Consumer Products 1962–72; Group Vice-Pres. Wines and Spirits Div. Standard Brands Ltd., Montreal, then Vice-Pres. and Chief Financial Officer 1972–73, Pres. and C.E.O. 1973–76; Pres. Int. Standard Brands Inc. 1976–80; Pres. and C.O.O. Standard Brands Inc. 1980–81; Exec. Vice-Pres. Nabisco Brands Inc. 1981–82, Sr. Exec. Vice-

Pres. 1982–83; Chair. Int. Nabisco Brands Inc. 1982–83, Vice-Chair. (Toronto) 1985–; Vice-Chair. Burns, Fry Hoare Govett Inc. 1983–85, Chair. 1985–. *Leisure interests:* golf, tennis, skiing. *Address:* Burns Fry Hoare Govett Inc., 40 East 52nd Street, 8th Floor, New York, NY 10022. *Telephone:* (212) 980-3415.

EMMONS, Howard Wilson, M.E., M.S., SC.D.; American professor of mechanical engineering; b. 30 Aug. 1912, Morristown, N.J.; s. of Peter Emmons and Margaret Lang Emmons; m. Dorothy Allen 1937; two s. one d.; ed. Stevens Inst. of Technology and Harvard Univ.; Research Eng., Westinghouse Electric and Manufacturing Co. 1938–39; Prof., Univ. of Pa. 1939–40; Prof., Harvard Univ. 1940–83, Prof. Emer. 1983–; Chair. Fire Research Cttee., Nat. Acad. of Sciences 1968–70, *ad hoc* Fire Panel, Nat. Bureau of Standards 1971–75, Engineering Evaluation Panel; mem. Nat. Acad. of Sciences, Nat. Acad. of Engineering; Hon. mem. American Soc. of Mechanical Eng.; Hon. Dr. Eng. (Stevens Inst. of Technology), Dr. h.c. (Worcester Polytechnic Inst.); Gold Medal Int. Combustion Symposium; Centenary Award Stevens Inst. of Technology; Timoshenko Medal ASME, Fluid Dynamics Award, American Physical Soc., Man of the Year Award, Soc. of Fire Protection Engineers 1982, Guise Award 1986. *Publications:* numerous articles in scientific journals. *Leisure interests:* tennis, town government. *Address:* Division of Applied Science, 308 Pierce Hall, Harvard University, Cambridge, Mass. 02138 (Office); 233 Concord Road, Sudbury, Mass. 01776, U.S.A. (Home). *Telephone:* (617) 495-2847 (Office); (617) 443-6623 (Home).

EMOVON, Emmanuel Uwumagbuhunmwun, PH.D.; Nigerian professor of chemistry and government minister; b. 24 Feb. 1929, Benin City; s. of Gabriel A. Emovon and Oni Emovon; m. Adesuwa C. Akenzua 1959; three s. three d.; ed. Baptist School, Benin City, Edo Coll., Benin City, Univ. Coll., Ibadan, Univ. Coll., London Univ., U.K.; Lecturer in Chem., Univ. Coll. Ibadan 1959; Prof. of Chem., Univ. of Benin 1971; Vice-Chancellor Univ. of Jos 1978; Fed. Minister of Science and Tech. 1985–; fmr. mem. numerous Govt. Cttees. and Bds.; fmr. external examiner; Fellow Science Asscn. of Nigeria, Nigerian Acad. of Science. *Publications:* numerous scientific papers. *Address:* 9 Kofo Abayomi Street, Victoria Island, P.M.B. 12793, Lagos, Nigeria. *Telephone:* 01-613506 (Office); 01-682564 (Home).

EMSLIE, Rt. Hon. Lord; George Carlyle Emslie, M.B.E., M.A., LL.B., F.R.S.E.; British judge; b. 6 Dec. 1919, Glasgow; s. of late Alexander Emslie and Jessie B. Carlyle; m. Lilias A. M. Hannington 1942; three s.; ed. High School of Glasgow and Univ. of Glasgow; mil. service 1940–46; Advocate 1948; Advocate-Depute (Sheriff Courts) 1955–57; Q.C. (Scotland) 1957; Sheriff of Perth and Angus 1963–66; Dean, Faculty of Advocates 1965–70; Senator, Coll. of Justice in Scotland 1970–72; Lord Justice-Gen. of Scotland and Lord Pres. Court of Session 1972–; Chair. Scottish Agric. Wages Bd. 1969–73; mem. Council on Tribunals (Scottish Cttee.) 1962–70; Hon. Bencher, Inner Temple 1974; Inn. of Court of N. Ireland 1981; Hon. LL.D. (Glasgow) 1973. *Leisure interests:* golf, reading. *Address:* 47 Heriot Row, Edinburgh, EH3 6EX, Scotland. *Telephone:* 031-225 3657.

ENAHORO, Chief Anthony; C.F.R.; Nigerian politician, journalist, newspaper publisher and company director; b. 22 July 1923, Uromi Ishan, Bendel State; s. of late Chief Okotako Enahoro and Princess Inibokun Okoje; m. Helen Ediae 1954; four s. one d.; ed. Govt. Schools Uromi and Owo, King's Coll. Lagos; journalist 1942–52; Ed. Southern Nigerian Defender 1944–45, Daily Comet 1945–49; Assoc. Ed. West African Pilot; Ed.-in-Chief Nigerian Star 1950–52; foundation mem. Action Group Party, later Acting Gen. Sec. and Fed. Vice-Pres.; Chair. Uromi Dist. Council and Ishan Div. Council; mem. Western House of Assembly and Fed. House of Reps. and Party Chief Whip 1951–54; Dir. Nat. Coal Bd. 1953–56; Minister of Home Affairs, Transport, Information and Midwest Affairs and Leader of the House (Western Region) 1954–59; Fed. M.P. and Opposition Spokesman on Foreign Affairs, Internal Affairs and Legislature Affairs 1959–63; moved motion for self-govt. and attended all constitutional talks preceding independence in 1960; detained during Emergency period Western Region 1962, fled to Britain, extradited and imprisoned in Nigeria for treasonable felony; released by Mil. Govt. 1966; Leader, Midwest State del. to Constitutional Conf. and mem. Constitutional Cttee. 1966; Fed. Commr. for Information, Culture, Youth, Sports, Co-operatives and Labour 1967–75; Fed. Commr. for Special Duties 1975; Pres. World Black and African Festival of Arts and Culture 1972–75; State Chair. Nat. Party of Nigeria 1978–80; Chair. Cttees. Edo State Movt. 1981–, Nigerian Shippers Council 1982; Hon. D.Sc. (Benin) 1972. *Publication:* Fugitive Offender (autobiography). *Leisure interests:* golf, reading, travel. *Address:* Rainbow House, 144 Upper Mission Road, P.M.B. 1425, Benin City, Nigeria. *Telephone:* 20080-3 (Office); 052-243770 (Home).

ENDELEY, E. M. L., O.B.E.; Nigerian medical doctor and politician; b. 10 April 1916, Buea (then in Nigeria); s. of late Chief Mathias Liffafe Endeley and of Mariana Mojoko Liombe; m. 1st Ethel Mina Green (divorced 1961), 2nd Fanny Ebenye Njoh 1965; nine s. three d.; ed. Buea Govt. School, Catholic Mission, Bojongo, Govt. Coll. Umuahia, Higher Coll., Yaba; qualified as doctor 1942; entered Govt. service 1943; served Lagos, Port Harcourt, etc.; in charge of Cottage Hospital, Buea; trade union leader 1947; formed Cameroons Nat. Fed. (afterwards Kamerun Nat. Congress) 1949; mem. House of Reps. and Council of Ministers 1952–54, Minister

without Portfolio, Minister of Labour; First Premier, Southern Cameroons 1955–59; Pres. Bakweri Co-op. Marketing Union 1955; led South Cameroons Del. to Constitutional Conf., London 1957; first Premier of South Cameroons 1958–59; Leader of the Opposition 1959–61; Leader Nat. Convention Party (later Cameroon People's Nat. Convention Party), West Cameroon 1961–66; Asst. Treas. and mem. Cameroon Nat. Union (now Cameroon People's Democratic Movt.) Political Bureau 1966–74, mem. Cen. Cttee. 1975–; mem. Nat. Ass., Yaoundé 1973–; Chair. House Cttee. on Production, Town Planning, Agriculture, Stockfarming, Rural and Civil Engineering. *Leisure interests:* mountaineering, gardening, wild game hunting, farming. *Address:* P.O. Box 5, Buea, Southwest Province, Cameroon. *Telephone:* Buea 32-42-26.

ENDERBY, Keppel Earl, Q.C., LL.M.; Australian lawyer and politician; b. 25 June 1926, Dubbo, N.S.W.; s. of Alfred Charles and Daisy Kathleen Enderby; m.; two c.; ed. Dubbo High School, Univs. of Sydney and London; N.S.W. singles and Australian foursomes amateur golf champion 1946; practising barrister 1955–62, 1976–82; Lecturer, Examiner in Commercial Law, Sydney Technical Coll. 1955–62; Senior Lecturer in Law, Australian Nat. Univ. 1963–65; mem. Nat. Exec. Australian Labor Party 1971–75; M.P. for A.C.T. 1970–74, for Canberra 1974–75; Minister for A.C.T. and Northern Territory 1972–73; Minister for Supply and for Secondary Industry 1973–74, for Mfg. Industry 1974–75; Attorney-Gen. Feb.–Nov. 1975, Minister for Customs and Excise Feb.–June 1975; Judge Supreme Court, N.S.W. 1982–; mem. Privileges Cttee. of House of Representatives 1973–75, Chair. 1975; Councillor, N.S.W. Branch, Australian Inst. of Int. Affairs (Pres. 1983–85), Nat. Pres. Australia-U.S.S.R. Soc. 1986–, Vice. Pres. Australian Esperanto Assen. 1988–. *Publications:* articles in Federal Law Review 1964, Australian Quarterly 1976. *Leisure interests:* reading, farming, flying, golf, sailing. *Address:* 2 Phoebe Street, Balmain, Sydney, Australia. *Telephone:* 8104227.

ENDERS, Thomas O., M.A.; American economist; b. 28 Nov. 1931, Hartford, Conn.; m. Gaetana Marchegiano; one s. three d.; ed. Yale, Paris and Harvard Univs.; with Dept. of State 1959–; Research Specialist, Div. of Research and Analysis for Far East 1959–60; Econ. Officer, Stockholm 1960–63; Supervisory Int. Economist, Bureau of European Affairs 1963–66; Special Asst. Office of Under Sec. of State for Political Affairs 1966–68; Deputy Asst. Sec. of State for Int. Monetary Affairs 1968–69; Deputy Chief of Mission, Belgrade 1969–71, Phnom-Penh 1971–74; Asst. Sec. of State for Econ. and Business Affairs 1974–75; Amb. to Canada 1975–79, to EEC, Brussels 1979–81, to Spain 1983–86; Asst. Sec. of State for Inter-American Affairs 1981–83; Man. Dir. Int. Corp. Finance Dept., Salomon Bros Inc. 1986–; Arthur S. Flemming Award 1970. *Address:* Salomon Bros. Inc., 2, New York Plaza, 14th Floor, New York, N.Y. 10004, U.S.A.

ENDO, Kaname; Japanese politician; b. 31 Oct. 1915; previous posts include: Parl. Vice-Minister of Finance; Chair. Prime Minister's Office Cttee. and Cttee. on Rules and Admin., House of Councillors; Sec.-Gen., Liberal Democratic Party (LDP) Miyagi Prefectural Fed. of Party Brs. Deputy Chair., LDP Diet Affairs Cttee.; Minister of Justice 1986–87; (resgnd.); Liberal Democratic Party. *Address:* 211 Sangi-in Kaikan, 2-2-1 Nagata-cho, Chiyoda-ku, Tokyo 100, Japan.

ENGEL, Albert Edward, PH.D.; American professor of geology; b. 17 June 1916, St. Louis, Mo.; s. of Louis and Louise Engel; two s.; ed. Univ. of Missouri and Princeton Univ.; Geologist, U.S. Geol. Survey 1942–47; Prof. of Geology, Calif. Inst. of Technology 1948–58; Prof. of Geology and Environmental Sciences, Univ. of Calif. at San Diego and Scripps Inst. of Oceanography; mem. Nat. Acad. of Sciences, American Acad. of Arts and Sciences etc.; Guggenheim Fellow 1953. *Publications:* approximately 200 articles and three books discussing the origin and evolution of the Earth and its life. *Leisure interests:* horticulture, architecture, archaeology, ecology, painting, politics. *Address:* Division of Geological Research, Scripps Institution of Oceanography, University of California, San Diego, A-020, La Jolla, Calif. 92093, U.S.A.

ENGEL, Johannes, K.; German journalist and editor; b. 29 April, 1927, Berlin; s. of Karl and Anna (née Helke) Engel; m. Ruth Moter 1951; one s. one d.; journalist Int. News Service and Der Spiegel magazine 1946–, Office Man., Frankfurt-am-Main 1948, Dept. Head 1951, Ed.-in-Chief, Hamburg 1961–. *Address:* Kirchenredder 7, 2000 Hamburg 63, Federal Republic of Germany. *Telephone:* 3007-1 (Office).

ENGELHARDT, Klaus, D.THEOL.; German ecclesiastic; b. 11 May 1932, Schillingstadt; s. of Wilhelm and Therese (née Nell) Engelhardt; m. Dorothea Schlink 1960; two s. one d.; ed. Univs. of Göttingen, Basel, Heidelberg; curate, Evangelische Landeskirche (Protestant Church), Baden 1960–62, Bishop of the Protestant Church of Baden 1980–; student priest, Karlsruhe 1962–65; Prof. of Theology, Päd. Hochschule 1965–80. *Address:* Blumenstrasse 1, 7500 Karlsruhe, Federal Republic of Germany.

ENGELL, Hans; Danish politician; b. 8 Oct. 1948, Copenhagen; s. of Knud Engell Anderson; journalist for Berlingske newspaper consortium; Head of Press Service of Conservative People's Party; M.P. 1984–, Minister for Defence 1982–87; Conservative. *Address:* Copenhagen K, Denmark.

ENGEN, René Léopold Alexis; Belgian civil engineer; b. 13 Dec. 1918, Brussels-Etterbeek; s. of Léopold Engen and Louise Etienne; m. Madeleine

Lekeu 1942; one d.; ed. Free Univ. of Brussels; Eng. with ACEC 1942-45; Eng. Verreries de Momignies 1945, Chief Eng. 1949, Dir. 1950; Dir. Verreries Réunies Val St. Lambert et Momignies 1954; Gen. Man. Verlica-Momignies 1960, Man. Dir. 1961, Admin. Del. 1968-81; Dir. Bouteilleries Belges Réunies 1963, Special Projects 1966, Vice-Pres. 1968-73; Gen. Man. Electrorail 1969-81, Schneider 1972-80 (Vice-Pres. and Gen. Man. 1979-81); Vice-Pres. Cofibel 1973; fmr. Dir. Spie-Batignolles, Jeumont-Schneider, Jeumont-Industrie, Cie. Financière pour le Développement des Entreprises, Creusot-Loire (Pres. 1975-81), Arbed, Salem, Banque de l'Union Européenne, Intercom, Merlin Gerin, Interrelax (Pres. 1969), Fondation Industrie Université, Marine Schneider, CFUE, Ceca, Elican Devt. Co., Arbed, etc.; Pres. Exec. Cttee. Creusot-Loire; Officier, Ordre de la Couronne, Ordre de Léopold, Officier Légion d'honneur, Citoyen d'honneur de Momignies, Médaille de la Résistance, Médaille Civique (1st Class), Insigne d'honneur d'or de lauréat de travail de Belgique and numerous other decorations. *Address:* Villa L'Aulnaie, Avenue François Pelletier, F-83990 Saint-Tropez, France.

ENGGAARD, Knud; Danish politician; b. 4 June 1929, Odder, East Jutland; s. of Jens Enggaard; service in the Air Force; Nat. Chair. Liberal Youth 1959-62; M.P. 1964-77, 1979-81, 1984-; twice Chair. Liberal Parl. Group; Minister for the Interior 1978-79, for Energy 1982-86, for the Interior 1986-87, for Econ. Affairs 1987-88, of Defence June 1988-; Liberal. *Address:* Ministry of Defence, Slotsholmsgade 10, 1216 Copenhagen K, Denmark. *Telephone:* (01) 92-33-20.

ENGHOLM, Björn, DIPL.-POL.; German politician; b. 9 Nov. 1939, Lübeck; m.; two c.; ed. Acad. of Econs. and Politics, Hamburg, and Univ. of Hamburg; apprentice printer 1959-62, Journeyman's Certificate 1962; joined SPD 1962, mem. governing bd. 1984-; lecturer and freelance journalist 1964-69; mem. Bundestag 1969-82; Parl. State Sec. Ministry of Educ. and Science 1977-81, Minister 1981-82, Opposition leader Landstag of Schleswig-Holstein 1983-, Minister-Pres. May 1988-. *Address:* Jürgen-Wullenwever-Strasse 9, 2400 Lübeck, Federal Republic of Germany.

ENGL, Walter L., DR.RER.NAT., F.I.E.E.E.; German professor of engineering; b. 8 April 1926, Regensburg; ed. Technical Univ. of Munich; Siemens Instrument and Control Div. 1950-63, latterly Head of Research Div.; Prof. Tech. Univ. of Aachen 1963-, Dean Faculty of Eng. 1967-69; Visiting Prof. Univ. of Arizona 1967, Stanford Univ. 1970, Univ. of Tokyo 1972, 1980; mem. Acad. of Science of North Rhine-Westphalia; mem. Int. Union of Radio Science. *Publications:* 80 publs. *Address:* Institut für Theoretische Elektrotechnik, Rheinisch-Westfälische Technische Hochschule Aachen, Kopernikusstrasse 16, 5100 Aachen, Federal Republic of Germany. *Telephone:* 0241-803900.

ENGLAND, Glyn, F.ENG., F.I.E.E., F.I.MECH.E., C.B.I.M., J.P.; British engineer and administrator; b. 21 April 1921, Tonyrefail, South Wales; s. of Charles Thomas and Alice England; m. Tania Reichenbach 1942; two d.; ed. Queen Mary Coll. and London School of Econs., London Univ.; Research Asst. 1939-40; war service in R.E.M.E. 1942-47; variety of field work in electricity supply industry 1947-58; Devt. Eng. (Policy), Cen. Electricity Generating Bd. (CEGB) 1958-66, Chief Operations Eng. 1966-71, Dir.-Gen. of S.-W. Region 1971-73; Chair. of S.-W. Electricity Bd. 1973-77; Chair. CEGB 1977-82; Chair. Council for Environmental Conservation 1983-88; Dir. U.K. Centre for Econ. and Environmental Devt. 1984; Vice-Pres. Int. Union of Producers and Distributors of Electrical Energy; fmr. Labour mem. Hertfordshire County Council, Council of Magistrates' Assscn.; Freeman of the City of London; Dir. F. H. Lloyd (Holdings) 1982-87, Triplex Lloyd PLC 1987-; Chair. Dartington Inst. 1985-; Hon. D.Sc. (Bath). *Publications:* The Electricity Supply Industry and Economic Growth 1964, Security of Supply in the Design and Operation of the Grid System in England and Wales 1968, Efficiency Audit and Public Enterprise, Landscape in the Making (jointly). *Leisure interest:* active enjoyment of the countryside. *Address:* Woodbridge Farm, Ubley, Bristol, BS18 6PX, England. *Telephone:* (0761) 62479.

ENGLISH, Sir David, Kt.; British journalist; b. 26 May 1931; m. Irene Mainwood 1954; one s. two d.; ed. Bournemouth School; Feature Ed. Daily Sketch 1956; Foreign Corresp. Sunday Dispatch 1959; Washington Corresp. Daily Express 1961-63, Chief American Corresp. 1963-65, Foreign ed. 1965-67, Assoc. Ed. 1967-69; Ed. Daily Sketch 1969-71, Daily Mail 1971-; Mail on Sunday 1982-; mem. Bd. Assscn. of British Ed. 1985-. *Publication:* Divided They Stand (a British view of the 1968 American Presidential Election) 1969. *Leisure interests:* reading, skiing, boating. *Address:* Daily Mail, London, EC4 0JA, England (Office). *Telephone:* 01-353 6000.

ENGLISH, Joseph Thomas, M.D.; American psychiatrist; b. 21 May 1933, Philadelphia, Pa.; s. of Thomas J. English and Helen Gilmore English; m. Ann Carr Sanger 1969; two s. one d.; ed. Jefferson Medical Coll.; Resident in Psychiatry, Inst. of Pa. Hospital, Philadelphia 1959-61, Nat. Inst. of Medical Health, Bethesda, Md. 1961-62; Chief Psychiatrist, U.S. Peace Corps. 1962-66; Asst. Dir. Office of Econ. Opportunity, Office of the Pres. 1966-68; Admin., Health Services and Mental Health Admin. U.S. Dept. of Health, Educ. and Welfare 1968-70; Pres. New York City Health and Hosps. Corpn. 1970-73; Adjunct Prof. Cornell Univ. School of Medicine 1975-; Assoc. Dean and Prof. of Psychiatry, New York Medical Coll. 1979-;

Dir. Dept. of Psychiatry, St. Vincent's Hosp. and Medical Center, New York 1973-; Visiting Fellow, Woodrow Wilson Nat. Fellowship Foundation. *Address:* St. Vincent's Hospital and Medical Center, 203 West 12 Street, New York, N.Y. 10011, U.S.A. *Telephone:* (212) 790-8252.

ENGLISH, Terence Alexander Hawthorne, M.B., F.R.C.S.; British surgeon; b. 3 Oct. 1932, Pietermaritzburg, South Africa; s. of Arthur Alexander English and the late Mavis Eleanor Lund; m. Ann Margaret Smart Dicey 1963; two s. two d.; ed. Witwatersrand Univ. and Guy's Hosp. Medical School, London; Intern, Demonstrator in Anatomy, Junior Surgical Registrar, Guy's Hosp. 1962-65; Resident Surgical Officer, Bolingbroke Hosp. 1966; Surgical Registrar, Brompton Hosp. 1967; Sr. Surgical Registrar, Nat. Heart and London Chest Hosps. 1968-72; Research Fellow, Cardiac Surgery, Ala. Univ. 1969; Consultant Cardiothoracic Surgeon to Papworth and Addenbrooke Hosps. 1973-; Dir. British Heart Foundation Heart Transplant Research Unit, Papworth Hosp. 1980-; Consultant Cardiac Advisor, Humana Hosp. Wellington, London 1983-; Pres. Int. Soc. for Heart Transplantation 1984-85; mem. Council, Royal Coll. of Surgeons 1981-(89); Man. of the Year, Royal Assscn. for Disability and Rehabilitation 1980, Clement Price Thomas Award, Royal Coll. of Surgeons 1986. *Publications:* over 60 articles in scientific journals. *Leisure interests:* reading, hill walking, South African history. *Address:* 19 Adams Road, Cambridge, CB3 9AD, England. *Telephone:* (0223) 68744.

ENGMAN, Lewis August, A.B., LL.B.; American lawyer and government official; b. 6 Jan. 1936, Grand Rapids, Mich.; s. of H. Sigurd and Florence C. Lewis Engman; m. 2nd Patricia L. Hanahan 1978; three s. by previous marriage; ed. Univ. of Michigan, Univ. Coll., London, London School of Econs. and Harvard Law School; Assoc. Warner, Norcross & Judd, law firm, Grand Rapids 1961-65, Partner 1965-70, 1976-79; Counsel Winston & Strawn, Washington 1985-; Dir. of Legis. Affairs, President's Cttee. on Consumer Interests 1970; Gen. Counsel Office of Consumer Affairs 1970-71; Asst. Dir. Domestic Council 1971-73; Chair. Fed. Trade Comm. 1973-75; mem. Council, Admin. Conf. of U.S. 1974-75, Public mem. 1986-; mem. Council Int. Fed. of Pharmaceutical Mfrs. Assscns. 1979-84; Pres. Pharmaceutical Manufacturers Assscn. 1979-84, Nat. Drug Trade Conf. 1980; Dir. Dyers-Ives Foundation 1964-. *Address:* 2550 M. Street, Suite 500, Washington, D.C. 20037, U.S.A.

ENGO, Paul Bamela; Cameroon diplomatist; b. 5 Oct. 1931, Ebolowa; m.; seven c.; ed. Middle Temple Inn, London; Crown Counsel, Legal Depts. of Nigeria and Cameroon 1959-61; Magisterial Bench for Southern Cameroon 1961-63; mem. Cameroon's Fed. Judicial Comm. 1961-64; Minister Counsellor, Embassy in Bonn, Fed. Repub. of Germany 1964-65, in Washington D.C. 1965-68, of the Cameroon Perm. Mission to the UN 1968, Minister Plenipotentiary 1969; Vice-Chair. Sixth Cttee. UN Gen. Ass. 1969, Chair. 1970; Perm. Rep. of Cameroon to the UN 1984-; Tech. Adviser to Minister for Foreign Affairs 1973-84; Personal Rep. of Pres. for Law of the Sea and Chair. of its Nat. Comm. 1973-84; Lecturer, English Common Law, Nat. School of Admin. and Magistrature 1973-84. *Address:* Permanent Mission of Cameroon to the United Nations, 22 East 73rd Street, New York, N.Y. 10021, U.S.A. *Telephone:* 794-2295.

ENGSETH, William; Norwegian politician; b. 1 Aug. 1933, Målselv, Troms; m.; ed. Norwegian Coll. of Physical Educ.; served as officer in Air Force 1953-67, apptd. Head, Bardufosstun training centre 1967; mem. Målselv Municipal Council 1967, 1971; Co. Gov., Troms 1983; Chair. Regional Cttee. for N. Norway 1983-; Minister of Local Govt. and Labour 1987-88, of Transport and Communications 1988-; mem. N. Norwegian Oil Council, Nordkalott Cttee. *Address:* Ministry of Transport and Communications, Møllergt. 1-3, POB 8119 Dep., Oslo 1, Norway. *Telephone:* (2) 11-90-90.

ENNALS, Baron (Life Peer), cr. 1983, of Norwich in the County of Norfolk; **David Hedley Ennals,** P.C., M.P.; British politician; b. 19 Aug. 1922, Walsall; s. of Arthur Ford Ennals and Jessie Ennals; m. 1st Eleanor Caddick 1950 (divorced 1977), three s. one d.; m. 2nd Gene Tranoy 1977; ed. St. Mary's Grammar School, Loomis Inst.; war service; Labour Party Overseas Sec. 1957-64; M.P. for Dover 1964-70, for Norwich North 1974-83; Minister of State, Dept. of Health and Social Security 1968-70, Foreign and Commonwealth Office 1974-76; Sec. of State for Social Services 1976-79; mem. Council Ockenden Venture 1972-76, 1979-; Chair. UN Assscn. 1984-, Nat. Assscn. for Mental Health (MIND) 1984-, Gandhi Foundation 1984-; Labour. *Publications:* Strengthening the United Nations 1957, Middle East Issues 1958, United Nations Peace Force 1960, United Nations on Trial 1962, Out of Mind 1973. *Address:* 47 Brookfield, Highgate West Hill, London, N.6, England.

ENRIGHT, Dennis Joseph, D.LITT.; British teacher and writer; b. 11 March 1920, Leamington Spa, Warwicks.; s. of George and Grace (née Cleaver) Enright; m. Madeleine Harders 1949; one d.; ed. Leamington Coll., and Downing Coll., Cambridge; Lecturer in English, Farouk I Univ. Alexandria 1947-50; Org. Tutor, Birmingham Univ. Extra-Mural Dept. 1950-53; Visiting Prof. Konan Univ. (Japan) 1953-56; Gastdozent, English Seminar, Berlin Free Univ. 1956-57; British Council Prof. Chulalongkorn Univ. Bangkok 1957-59; Johore Prof. of English, Univ. of Singapore 1960-70; Co-editor Encounter Magazine 1970-72; Editorial adviser, Chatto and Windus 1972-74, Dir. 1974-82; contributor to Scrutiny, Observer, New

York Review of Books, Times Literary Supplement, Encounter, Listener; Queen's Gold Medal for Poetry 1981; Dr. h.c., Univ. of Surrey, Univ. of Warwick. *Publications:* poetry: The Laughing Hyena and Other Poems 1953, Bread rather than Blossoms: Poems 1956, The Poetry of Living Japan: An Anthology 1957, Some Men are Brothers: Poems 1960, Addictions: Poems 1962, The Old Adam 1965, Unlawful Assembly 1968, Selected Poems 1969, The Typewriter Revolution and Other Poems 1971, Daughters of Earth 1972, The Terrible Shears 1973, Rhyme Times Rhyme 1974, A Choice of Milton's Verse 1975, Sad Ires 1975, Paradise Illustrated 1978, A Faust Book 1979, Collected Poems 1981, Instant Chronicles 1985, Collected Poems 1987; essays and literary criticism: The Apothecary's Shop: Essays on Literature 1957, Conspirators and Poets: literary criticism 1966, Man is an Onion 1972, A Mania for Sentences 1983, The Alluring Problem: An Essay On Irony 1986, Fields of Vision: Essays On Literature, Language and Televison 1988; children's novels: The Joke Shop 1976, Wild Ghost Chase 1978, Beyond Land's End 1979; also: Academic Year 1955, The World of Dew: Aspects of Living Japan 1956, Heaven Knows Where 1957, Insufficient Poppy 1960, Figures of Speech 1965, Memoirs of a Mendicant Professor 1969, Shakespeare and the Students 1970; Editor: Samuel Johnson: The History of Rasselas, Prince of Abyssinia 1976, Oxford Book of Contemporary Verse 1945–1980 1980, Oxford Book of Death 1983, Fair of Speech: The Uses of Euphemism 1985. *Address:* 35A Viewfield Road, London, SW18 5JD, England. *Telephone:* (01) 874 8908.

ENRILE, Juan Ponce (see Ponce Enrile, Juan).

ENRIQUE Y TARANCÓN, H.E. Cardinal Vicente; Spanish ecclesiastic; b. 14 June 1907, Burriana, Castellón; s. of Manuel E. Urios and Vincenta T. Fandos; ed. Seminario Conciliar Rortosa, Tarragona and Universidad Pontificia Valencia; Admin. Asst. of Vinaroz 1930–33, Archpriest 1938–43; Archpriest, Villarreal 1943–46; Bishop of Solsona 1946–64; Gen. Sec. Spanish Bishopric 1956–64; Archbishop of Ovopie 1964–69; Archbishop of Toledo, Primate of Spain 1969–71; Archbishop of Madrid 1971–83; Cardinal de Tit. de S. Juan Crisóstomo, Monte Sacro 1969–; mem. Sacred Congregations for Bishops, Divine Worship, and Reform of Canon Law; mem. Spanish Acad. 1969. *Publications:* La Renovación Total de la Vida Cristiana 1954, Los Seglares en la Iglesia 1958, Sucesores de los Apóstoles 1960, La Parroquia, Hoy 1961, El Misterio de la Iglesia 1963, Ecumenismo y Pastoral 1964, La Iglesia en el Mundo de Hoy 1965, El Sacerdocio a la Luz del Concilio Vaticano II 1966, La Iglesia del Posconcilio 1967, La Crisis de Fe en el Mundo Actual 1968, Unidad y pluralismo en la Iglesia 1969, Liturgia y lengua del pueblo 1970, El magisterio de Santa Teresa 1970. *Leisure interests:* musical composition, listening to classical music, particularly Bach. *Address:* c/o Palacio Arzobispal, S. Justo 2, Madrid 12, Spain.

ENRIQUEZ SAVIGNAC, Antonio, M.A.; Mexican politician; b. Aug. 1931, Mexico City; loan official, IDB 1960–63; Adviser to Dir.-Gen., Bank of Mexico 1964–73; Dir.-Gen. Nat. Fund for Devt. of Tourism 1969–76; Under-Sec. of Planning, Ministry of Tourism 1976–77; Dir. Industrial Devt., Nat. Bank of Mexico 1977–81; Asst. Dir. of Finance, Petroleos Mexicanos 1981–82; Under-Sec. Ministry of Finance 1982; Minister of Tourism Dec. 1982–. *Address:* Avenida Presidente Masaryk No. 172, CP 11587, México, D.F., Mexico.

ENTREMONT, Philippe; French pianist and conductor; b. 7 June 1934, Reims; s. of Jean and Renée (Monchamps) Entremont; m. Andrée Ragot 1955; one s. one d.; ed. Institution Notre-Dame à Reims, Conservatoire National Supérieur de Musique de Paris; has performed with all major orchestras of world 1953–; Pres. of Acad. Int. de Musique Maurice Ravel, Saint-Jean-de-Luz 1973–80; Musical Dir. and Permanent Conductor, Wiener Kammerorchester 1976–; Dir. New Orleans Symphony Orchestra 1980–86; Principal Conductor Denver Symphony Orchestra 1986–88, Paris Orchestre Colonne (1988–); Officier de l'Ordre nat. du Mérite, Chevalier, Légion d'honneur; Österreicheisches Ehrenkreuz für Wissenschaft und Kunst; Harriet Cohen Piano Medal 1951, Grand Prix International Concours Marguerite Long-Jacques Thibaud 1953, 4 Grand Prix du Disque Awards, Edison Award 1968; Grammy Award 1972. *Leisure interest:* golf. *Address:* Schwarzenbergplatz 10/7, A-1040 Vienna, Austria.

ENUKIDZE, Guram Nikolayevich; Soviet administrator and politician; Sec. Tbilisi City Cttee., Georgian CP 1973–75; cand. mem. Cen. Cttee. of Georgian CP 1976–78, Deputy Sec. 1978–; Chair. State Cttee. on Television and Radio Broadcasting 1976–79; mem. Politburo, Cen. Cttee. of Georgian CP 1978–; Party Sec. for Ideology and Propaganda 1979–. *Address:* Central Committee of Communist Party of the Georgian S.S.R., Tbilisi, Georgian S.S.R., U.S.S.R.

ENWONU, Benedict Chuka, M.B.E.; Nigerian sculptor; b. 1921; ed. Holy Trinity School, Onitsha, Govt. Colls. Umu-Ahia and Ibadan, Univ. Coll., London; first One-Man Show, Lagos 1942; on the strength of this he was given a special scholarship by Shell-Mex to study in England; rep. UNESCO Exhbn., Paris 1946; first One-Man Exhbn., London 1948, subsequent exhbns. 1950, 1952, 1955; exhbns. U.S. 1950; commissioned to execute statue of H.M. Queen Elizabeth, doors, panels and Speaker's Chair, Lagos House of Representatives, and the group The Risen Christ for the Chapel, Univ. Coll., Ibadan; Art Adviser to the Federal Govt. of Nigeria 1968–72; fmr. Prof. of Fine Arts, Univ. of Ife; his works have been purchased by

H.M. Queen Elizabeth II, the late Sir Jacob Epstein and others; R. B. Bennett Empire Art Prize 1957.

ENZENSBERGER, Hans Magnus, DR. PHIL.; German poet and writer; b. 11 Nov. 1929, Kaufbeuren; m. 3rd Katharina Bonitz; two d.; ed. Univs. of Erlangen, Freiburg im Breisgau, Hamburg and Paris; Third Programme Editor, Stuttgart Radio 1955–57; Lecturer, Hochschule für Gestaltung, Ulm 1956–57; Literary Consultant to Suhrkamp's (publishers), Frankfurt 1960–; mem. "Group 47", Ed. Kursbuch (review) 1965–75, Publisher 1970–; Ed. TransAtlantik (monthly magazine) 1980–82; Publisher and Ed., Die Andere Bibliothek 1985–; Hugo Jacobi Prize 1956, Kritiker Prize 1962, Georg Büchner Prize 1963, Premio Pasolini 1982, Heinrich Böll Prize 1985. *Publications:* poetry: Verteidigung der Wölfe 1957, Landessprache 1960, Blindenschrift 1964, Poems for People Who Don't Read Poems (English edn.) 1968, Gedichte 1955–1970 1971, Mausoleum 1975; essays: Clemens Brentanos Poetik 1961, Einzelheiten 1962, Politik und Verbrechen 1964; also: Deutschland, Deutschland unter Anderen 1967, Das Verhör von Habana (play) 1970, Freisprüche 1970, Der kurze Sommer der Anarchie (novel) 1972, Gespräche mit Marx und Engels 1973, Palaver 1974; Edited Museum der Modernen Poesie 1960, Allerleirauh 1961, Andreas Gryphius Gedichte 1962, Edward Lears kompletter Nonsense (translation) 1977, Raids and Reconstruction (essays, English edn.), Der Untergang der Titanic (epic poem) 1978, Die Furie des Verschwindens 1980, Politische Brosamen 1982, Critical Essays 1982, Der Menschenfreund 1984, Ach Europa! 1987, Mittelmass und Wahn 1988, Requiem für eine romantische Frau 1988. *Address:* c/o Suhrkamp Verlag, Fach 2446, 6000 Frankfurt/Main, Federal Republic of Germany.

EÖRSI, Gyula; Hungarian lawyer and university official; b. 19 Sept. 1922, Budapest; m. Marianna Hajou 1949; two c.; ed. Pázmány Péter Univ., Budapest; staff mem., later Head, Legislation Dep't., Ministry of Justice 1945–57; Assoc. Prof. Eötvös Loránd Univ., Budapest 1950, Prof. 1956–; Corresp. mem. Acad. of Sciences 1962–73, mem. 1973–, Pres. Section IX (Econs. and Law) 1973–79; Rector, Eötvös Loránd Univ., Budapest 1978–84; Visiting Prof., Int. Faculty of Comparative Law, Luxembourg 1963, 1964, 1966, 1967; Visiting Prof., Univ. of Dar es Salaam, Tanzania 1968, 1970; Corresp. mem. Gesellschaft für Rechtsvergleichung, Fed. Repub. of Germany 1969; Assoc. mem. Acad. int. de droit comparé, Brussels 1970; Visiting Prof., Stockholm and Lund Univs., Sweden 1973; Dr. h.c. (Univ. of Stockholm); specializes in trade and comparative law; State Prize 1978; Labour Order of Merit (twice). *Publications:* A tulajdon fejlődése (The Development of Property) 1951, A tervszerződések (Planned Contracts) 1957, A jogi felelősség alapproblémái (Fundamentals of Tort Liability) 1961, Összehasonlító polgári jog (Comparative Civil Private Law) 1974, Private and Government Liability of the Torts of Employees and Organs (in International Encyclopaedia of Comparative Law) 1975. *Address:* 1026 Budapest, Szilágyi Erzsébet fasor 81, Hungary. *Telephone:* 565-535.

EÖTVÖS, Peter; German composer and conductor; b. 2 Jan. 1944, Székelyudvarhely, Hungary; s. of László Eötvös and Ilona Szücs; m. 1st Piroska Molnár 1968, 2nd Pi-Hsien Chen 1976; two c.; ed. Acad. of Music, Budapest (composition) and Musikhochschule, Cologne, Fed. Repub. of Germany (conducting); composed numerous works for theatre, cinema and TV 1960–; Répétiteur Cologne Opera 1967–68; producer and composer at WDR Electronic Music Studio, Cologne 1971–79; Musical Dir. Ensemble. Intercontemporain, Paris 1979–; Prin. Guest Conductor BBC Symphony Orchestra, London 1985–. *Compositions include:* Moro Lasso 1963/72, Hochzeitsmadrigal 1963/76, Endless Eight 1981, Fairy-Tale 1968, Cricketmusic 1979, Intervalles-intérieurs 1981, Sequences of the Wind 1975, Chinese Opera 1986. *Leisure interests:* pipe, jazz, walking. *Address:* D-5275 Bergneustadt 2, Attenbach, Federal Republic of Germany. *Telephone:* (02763) 6525.

EPHRAM, George; Lebanese business executive and politician; b. 1934; Chair. Indefco; mem. Bd. Industrialists' Soc.; Minister of Posts, Telecommunications, Industry and Oil 1982–84; Maronite. *Address:* c/o Office du Président du Conseil des Ministres, Place de l'Etoile, Beirut, Lebanon.

EPLEY, Marion Jay, LL.B.; American business executive; b. 17 June 1907; s. of Marion Jay and Eva (née Quin) Epley; m. Dorris Glenn Ervine 1934; one s. one d.; ed. Tulane Univ. and Tulane Law School, New Orleans, Louisiana; private law practice, New Orleans 1930–43, 1945–47; U.S. Navy 1942–45; Gen. Attorney, Texaco Inc. Louisiana and New York 1948–57, Asst. to Chair. of Bd. of Dirs. 1958–60, Vice-Pres. 1958–60, Senior Vice-Pres. 1960–61, Exec. Vice-Pres. 1961–65, Pres. 1965–70, Chair. 1970–71; Chair. Dormar Ltd. 1983–. *Address:* 340 South Ocean Boulevard, Palm Beach, Fla. 33480, U.S.A. *Telephone:* (305) 655-2345.

EPP, Jake, B.A., B.ED., M.P.; Canadian politician; b. 1 Sept. 1939, St. Boniface, Man.; m. Lydia Martens; one c.; ed. Univ. of Manitoba; teacher Steinbach Coll. Inst., Man.; mem. House of Commons 1972–; Minister of Indian Affairs and Northern Devt. 1979; Minister of Nat. Health and Welfare 1984–89, of Energy, Mines and Resources Jan. 1989–; Chair. Caucus Cttee. on Fed. Prov. Relations 1980, of Health and Welfare 1983; mem. House Standing Cttee. on Labour, Manpower and Immigration and of Special Jt. Cttee. on Immigration; mem. Canadian Parl. Asscn., Canada-U.S.A. Interparl. Group; Town Councillor, Steinbach 1970–72; Progressive Conservative

Party. *Address:* House of Commons, Ottawa, K1A 0A2; 391 Southwood Drive, Steinbach, Man. R0A 2A0, Canada (Home).

EPSTEIN, Emanuel, PH.D.; American professor of plant nutrition and plant physiologist; b. 5 Nov. 1916, Duisburg, Germany; s. of Harry Epstein and Bertha Epstein (née Löwe); m. Hazel M. Leask 1943; two c. (one deceased); ed. Univ. of California (Davis and Berkeley); Plant Physiologist, U.S. Dept. of Agric., Beltsville, Md. 1950–58; Lecturer and Assoc. Plant Physiologist, Univ. of California (Davis) 1958–65, Prof. of Plant Nutrition and Plant Physiologist 1965–87, Prof. Emer. 1987–; Prof. of Botany 1974–87, Prof. Emer. 1987–; Consultant to Govt. agencies, private orgs. and publrs. at various times; Guggenheim and Fulbright Fellowships; mem. N.A.S.; Gold Medal, Pisa (Italy) Univ. 1962; Charles Reid Barnes Life Membership Award, American Soc. of Plant Physiologists 1986. *Publications:* Mineral Nutrition of Plants: Principles and Perspectives 1972, The Biosaline Concept: An Approach to the Utilization of Underexploited Resources (Co-ed.) 1979, research papers, reviews and articles. *Leisure interests:* hiking, photography and history. *Address:* Department of Land, Air and Water Resources, University of California, Davis, Calif. 95616, U.S.A. *Telephone:* (916) 752-0197.

EPSTEIN, Gabriel, F.R.I.B.A., S.A.D.G.; British architect and planning consultant; b. 25 Oct. 1918, Duisburg, Germany; s. of Dr. Harry Epstein and Bertha Loewe; m. Josette A. Glonneau 1955; two s. one d.; ed. schools in Germany, Switzerland and Israel and Architectural Assćn. School of Architecture, London; Partner, Shepheard, Epstein & Hunter 1955–86; Prof. of Architecture and Dir. of Inst. of Public Bldgs. and Design, Univ. of Stuttgart 1978–88; Prof. Centre for Infrastructure Planning, Univ. of Stuttgart 1984–; Pres. Architectural Assćn., London 1963–64, Franco-British Union of Architects 1976–77; mem. Berlin Acad. of Arts and Letters; Dr.h.c. (Lancaster). *Works include:* master plan and bldgs., Univ. of Lancaster; master plans for Open Univ. (U.K.), Univ. of Tlemcen (Algeria) and Univ. of Ghana; town-planning consultant for London Docks (Wapping) 1976–81. *Publications:* Planning Forms for Twentieth Century Cities 1976, Well-Being In Cities: The Low Energy City 1979, Energy Use and City Form 1981. *Leisure interest:* painting. *Address:* 3 rue Mazet, 75006 Paris, France. *Telephone:* 43.25.89.59.

EPSTEIN, Michael Anthony, C.B.E., M.D., D.SC., PH.D., F.R.C.PATH., F.R.S.; British virologist; b. 18 May 1921, London; ed. St. Paul's School, London, Trinity Coll., Cambridge, and Middlesex Hosp. Medical School, London; House Surgeon, Middlesex Hosp. and Addenbrooke's Hosp., Cambridge 1944; commissioned R.A.M.C. 1945–47; Asst. Pathologist, Bland Sutton Inst., Middlesex Hosp. Medical School 1948–65; Berkeley Travelling Fellow and French Govt. Exchange Scholar, Inst. Pasteur, Paris 1952–53, Visiting Investigator, Rockefeller Inst., New York 1956; Reader in Experimental Pathology, Middlesex Hosp. Medical School, and Hon. Consultant in Experimental Virology, Middlesex Hosp. 1965–68; Prof. of Pathology, Univ. of Bristol 1968–85, Head of Dept. and Hon. Consultant Pathologist, Avon Area Health Authority (Teaching) 1968–82; Emer. Prof. of Pathology, Univ. of Bristol at Nuffield Dept. of Clinical Medicine, Univ. of Oxford 1985–; Extraordinary Fellow, Wolfson Coll., Oxford 1986–; mem. MRC Cell Bd. 1979–84, Chair. 1982–84; Chair. CRC/MRC Jt. Cttee. for Inst. of Cancer Research 1982–87; mem. MRC 1982–86, Chair. MRC Tropical Medicine Research Bd. 1985–88, Medical and Scientific Advisory Panel, Leukaemia Research Fund 1982–85, Council of Royal Soc. 1983–85; mem. UK Co-ordinating Cttee. on Cancer Research 1983–87, Scientific Advisory Cttee., The Lister Inst. of Preventive Medicine 1984–86; Scientific Adviser, Charing Cross Medical Research Centre 1984–87; Foreign Sec. and Vice-Pres. Royal Soc. 1986–, MRC Assessor 1987–; mem. Expert Working Party on Bovine Spongiform Encephalopathy, Dept. of Health 1988–; Hon. Prof. Zhongshan Medical Univ., People's Repub. of China 1981, Chinese Acad. of Preventive Medicine 1988; Hon. Fellow Queensland Inst. of Medical Research 1983; Hon. mem. Belgian Soc. for Study of Cancer 1979, FRCP 1986, Pathological Soc. 1987; Hon. MD (Edin.) 1986; Leeuwenhoek Prize Lecturer, Royal Soc. 1983; Markham Skerritt Prize (Univ. of Bristol) 1977, Paul Ehrlich and Ludwig Darmstaedster Prize and Medal (Frankfurt) 1973, Bristol-Myers Award (New York) 1982, Prix Griffuel (Paris) 1986, Gairdner Foundation Int. Award (Toronto) 1988, S. Weiner Distinguished Visitor Award (Univ. of Manitoba) 1988. *Publications:* over 200 scientific papers in international journals. *Address:* Nuffield Department of Clinical Medicine, University of Oxford, John Radcliffe Hospital, Headington, Oxford, OX3 9DU, England. *Telephone:* (0865) 817 623.

EPSTEIN, William, B.A., LL.B., LL.D.; Canadian international administrator; b. 10 July 1912, Calgary; s. of Harry Louis Epstein and Bella Geffen Epstein; m. Edna Hyman 1946; one s.; ed. Calgary High School, Univ. of Alberta, L.S.E.; called to Bar, Alberta 1936; served in Canadian Army, reaching rank of Capt., Second World War; Sec., Canadian Claims Comm., Canadian Mil. HQ, London 1945; apptd. to Secr., Preparatory Comm. of the UN, London 1945; Chief, Middle East Section of the Political and Security Council Affairs Dept., UN Secr. 1946–50, Chair., UN Staff Cttee. 1949–50, Dir., Disarmament Div. and Chief, Disarmament Group 1950–72; Sr. Political Officer, UN Palestine Comm. 1948; rep. UN Sec.-Gen. at: five-power Sub-Cttee. on Disarmament, London 1954–57, Conf. on the Discontinuance of Nuclear Tests, Geneva 1959, Ten Nation Cttee. on Disarmament, Geneva 1960, Conf. of the Eighteen Nation Cttee. on

Disarmament 1962–73, Conf. of the Cttee. on Disarmament, Geneva 1962–73; Tech. Consultant, Comm. for the Denuclearization of Latin America 1965–67; Sr. Fellow, UN Inst. for Training and Research 1973–; Special Consultant on Disarmament to Sec.-Gen. of UN 1973–; Rockefeller Foundation Fellowship in "Conflict in Int. Affairs" 1973–75; Visiting Prof., Univ. of Vic. 1974–78; Cecil H. and Ida Greene Visiting Prof., Univ. of B.C. 1975; Visiting Prof., Carleton Univ. 1977–78; Chair., Canadian Pugwash Group 1978–; mem. Canadian del. to six sessions of UN Gen. Ass. 1978–82; mem. Bd. of Dirs. Canadian Inst. for Int. Peace and Security 1984–86; Sr. Special Fellow UN Inst. for Training and Research 1973–; special lecturer UN fellowship programme in disarmament; Hon. LL.D. (Univ. of Calgary) 1971, (Univ. of Alberta) 1984, Commdr., Mexican Order of the Aztec Eagle 1977, Peace Award (World Federalists of Canada) 1978, Rolex Award for Enterprise 1978, MacArthur Foundation research 1987. *Publications:* The United Nations and Disarmament, 1945–70, (Ed.) 1970, Disarmament: Twenty-Five Years of Effort 1971, The Last Chance: Nuclear Proliferation and Arms Control 1976, A New Design for Nuclear Disarmament (Co-ed.) 1977, New Directions in Disarmament (Co-ed.), We Can Avert a Nuclear War (Co-ed.) 1983, The Prevention of Nuclear War: a United Nations Perspective 1983; numerous articles on arms control, disarmament, int. security and Canadian policies in these fields. *Leisure interests:* walking, reading, sculpting, art. *Address:* United Nations Institute for Training and Research, 801 UN Plaza, New York, N.Y. 10017 (Office); 400 East 58th Street, New York, N.Y. 10022, U.S.A. (Home). *Telephone:* (212) 963-8649 (Office); (212) 758-3320 (Home).

ERB, Richard David, PH.D.; American government official; b. 15 April 1941, New York; s. of David and Margaret Erb; m. Joanna R. Shelton 1980; ed. W.C. Mepham High School, State Univ. of N.Y., Buffalo, Stanford Univ., Calif.; Asst. to Gov. Sherman Maisel, Bd. of Govs. of Fed. Reserve System 1967–69; Consultant, Arthur D. Little Inc. 1969–71; Money and Capital Market Economist, Salomon Brothers 1971; Staff Asst. to Pres., The White House 1971–74; Council on Foreign Relations Int. Affairs Fellow and Resident Economist, American Enterprise Inst. 1974–76; Deputy Asst. Sec. of Treasury for Developing Nations Finance 1976–77; Professorial Lecturer, Johns Hopkins School of Advanced Int. Studies 1975–78; Resident Fellow, American Enterprise Inst. 1977–80; Consultant to U.S. Comptroller of the Currency 1977–80, to U.S. Sec. of the Treasury 1981; Exec. Dir. IMF 1981–84, Deputy Man. Dir. 1984–; Woodrow Wilson Fellow, mem. Council on Foreign Relations. *Publications include:* Federal Reserve Policies and Public Disclosure 1978, International Resource Transfers: The International Financial System and Foreign Aid 1979, The Arab Oil Producing Economies of the Gulf 1979, contributions to journals and numerous articles. *Leisure interests:* tennis, skiing, cooking, gardening. *Address:* International Monetary Fund, 700 19th Street, N.W., Washington, D.C. 20431, U.S.A. (Office). *Telephone:* 202-623-4607 (Office).

ERBAKAN, Necmettin; Turkish politician; b. 1926, Sinop; ed. Inst. of Mechanics, Technical Univ. of Istanbul and Technische Universität, Aachen, Germany; Asst. lecturer, Inst. of Mechanics, Technical Univ. of Istanbul 1948–51; Engineer, Firma Deutz 1951–54; Prof. Technical Univ. of Istanbul 1954–66; Chair. Industrial Dept., Turkish Assćn. of Chambers of Commerce 1966–68, Chair. of Assćn. 1968; mem. Nat. Assembly 1969–80; f. Nat. Order Party 1970 (disbanded 1971); Chair. Nat. Salvation Party Oct. 1973 (disbanded 1981); Deputy Prime Minister and Minister of State Jan.–Sept. 1974; Deputy Prime Minister 1975–77, July–Dec. 1977; detained 1980–81. *Address:* c/o National Salvation Party, Ankara, Turkey.

ERBE, Johannes, M.B.A.; Dutch business executive; b. 1 Feb. 1927, Amsterdam; m. B. H. Klein Kranenberg 1952; two s. one d.; ed. Univ. of Amsterdam, Univ. of Wisconsin, U.S.A.; with Unilever 1951–, Commercial Dir., Turkey 1958–62, Man. Dir., Turkey 1962–67, Chair. Nat. Management, Fed. Repub. of Germany 1967–69, Food and Drinks Co-ordination 1969–71, Head Corporate Devt. 1971–72, Dir. 1972–75, Frozen Products Co-ordinator 1975–85, Chair. Overseas Cttee. 1985–86, mem. Special Cttee. 1986–, Vice-Chair. Unilever NV 1983–; Chair. Industry Council for Devt., New York 1982–86; mem. Bd. Banque Paribas Nederland N.V., Hollandsche Beton Groep N.V. (Chair. desig. 1988–); Kt. Order of the Dutch Lion 1985. *Leisure interest:* golf. *Address:* Unilever PLC, Unilever House, P.O. Box 68, London, EC4P 4BQ, England. *Telephone:* 01-822 6317.

ERBEN, Heinrich Karl, PH.D.; German professor of geology and paleontology; b. 19 May 1921, Prague; s. of Emil Erben and Eugenie (née Seckl) Erben; m. Ursula Jonas 1946; one s. one d.; ed. German Real-Gymnasium Prague II, Univs. of Berlin and Tübingen; Asst. Prof., Univ. of Tübingen 1949–50; Sr. Lecturer, Univ. of Würzburg 1951–53; Research Prof., Univ. of Mexico 1953–56; Assoc. Prof., Univ. of Bonn 1956–62; Faculty of Science, Univ. of Kabul 1962–63; Prof. of Geology and Paleontology, Univ. of Bonn 1964–86, Emer. Prof. 1986–; Dir. Paleontology Inst. 1964–86; Pres. German Paleontological Soc. 1968, Nat. Cttee. of Int. Union of Geological Sciences 1972–76, German Nat. Cttee. for UNESCO 1986–88; mem. Acad. of Science and Literature (Mainz), German Acad. of Sciences Leopoldina (Halle), Sudetic Acad. of Science and Arts (München), Acad. Europea (London). *Publications:* Die Entwicklung der Lebewesen 1975, Leben heisst Sterben 1981, Se extinguirá la raza humana? 1982, Intelligenzen im Kosmos? 1984, Estamos solos en el cosmos? 1985, Evolution-sieben Jahrzehnte nach Ernst Haeckel 1988, numerous geoscientific and biological publs. *Leisure inter-*

ests: Pre-Columbian art, art of the Far East, epistemological philosophy. *Address:* Kastanienweg 14, 5307 Wachtberg-Adendorf, Federal Republic of Germany.

ERDÉLYI, Miklós; Hungarian conductor; b. 9 Feb. 1928, Budapest; s. of Ernő Erdélyi and Ida Friedrich; m. Kata Miklós 1952; ed. Music Acad. of Budapest under János Ferencsik; started career as conductor in 1947; helped found Hungarian Radio chorus 1949, acted as their second conductor 1951; joined staff of Hungarian State Opera 1951–; conductor, touring throughout Europe 1951–, and in U.S.A. 1972; concerts with Berlin Philharmonic Orchestra 1974, 1975, 1978; concerts in Japan 1986 1987, 1988; Perm. Guest Conductor Netherlands Radio Orchestra 1982–86, Nat. Opera, Finland 1986–; toured with Bamberg Symphony Orchestra to Festivals of Ascona, Montreux, Besançon and Ludwigsburg 1976, 1978; gave first performance of numerous Hungarian 20th-century works; has conducted everything from 17th-century opera (Monteverdi: The Coronation of Poppaea) to contemporary oratorio (E. Petrovics: The Book of Jonah); Kossuth Prize 1975, Eminent Artists' Distinction 1985. *Publications:* Franz Schubert (biography) 1963, numerous studies in musical journals. *Leisure interests:* travel, architecture. *Address:* H-1115 Budapest, Tétényi ut 7A, Hungary. *Telephone:* 655-160.

ERDEM, Kaya; Turkish government official; b. 1928, Zonguldak; s. of Hilmi and Pakize Erdem; m. Sevil Şibay 1956; two d.; ed. High School of Commerce, Univ. of Marmara; mem. faculty, Anatolian Univ. 1959–65; Finance Dir. Sugar Corpn. 1960–62; Asst. Dir.-Gen. State Treasury 1963–72; mem. Cttee. for Reorganization of State Econ. Enterprises 1971–72; Dir.-Gen. State Treasury 1972–73; Chief Financial Counsellor, Turkish Embassy, London 1973–76; Sec.-Gen. Ministry of Finance 1978–80; Minister of Finance 1980–82, Deputy Prime Minister, Minister of State 1983–89; prominent in drafting and implementation of econ. stabilization programme 1980. *Publications:* State Economic Enterprise 1966, and numerous articles on cost and managerial accountancy. *Leisure interests:* bridge, tennis. *Address:* c/o Office of the Deputy Prime Minister, Basbakan yard. ve Devlet Bakani, Bakanlikar, Ankara, Turkey.

ERDMANN, Karl Dietrich, DR.PHIL; German professor of history; b. 29 April 1910, Cologne; s. of Wilhelm Erdmann and Louise Schmitz; m. Sylvia Pieh 1938; ed. Univs. of Cologne, Marburg, Paris and London; school teacher, Cologne 1934; worked in industry 1938–39; mil. service 1939–45; Asst. Prof. Dept. of History, Univ. of Cologne 1947–50; Prof. 1953–78, now Prof. Emer.; Rector, Univ. of Kiel 1966–67; Gen. Sec. German UNESCO Comm. 1951–52; Chair. Verband der Historiker Deutschlands 1962–67; Pres. Deutscher Bildungsrat 1966–70, Comité Int. des Sciences Historiques 1975–80; mem. Göttingen Acad., Royal Danish Acad. of Sciences, Historical Comm. of Bavarian Acad. of Sciences; Hermann Ehlers Prize 1977; Medal of Int. Council on Archives; Cultural Prize of the City of Kiel 1982. *Publications:* Volkssouveränität und Kirche 1949, Adenauer in der Rheinlandpolitik 1966, Deutsche Geschichte: die Zeit der Weltkriege 1976, Die Ökumene der Historiker 1987. *Leisure interests:* travel, swimming, walking. Address: Ernestinenweg 18, 2312 Mönkeberg/Kiel, Federal Republic of Germany. *Telephone:* 0431-231083.

ERDŐS, Paul, PH.D.; Hungarian professor of mathematics; b. 26 March 1913, Budapest; s. of Louis Erdős and Ann Wilhelm; unmarried; ed. Univs. of Budapest and Manchester; Visiting Prof. of Maths., Hungarian Acad. of Sciences and Technion, Haifa; travels constantly in U.S.A., Canada, Hungary, U.K., France and Israel; Cole Prize, American Maths. Soc. 1951; Kossuth State Prize 1958; shared Wolf Foundation Prize (Israel) 1983. *Publications:* about 1,000 research papers in number theory and other branches of pure mathematics. *Leisure interests:* history, politics. *Address:* Mathematical Institute, Hungarian Academy of Sciences, Reáltanoda u. 13-15, Budapest, Hungary; c/o Dr. R. L. Graham, Bell Laboratories, Murray Hill, N.J. 07974, U.S.A.

EREDIAUWA, Omo N'Oba N'Edo Uku-Akpolokpolo, B.A.; Oba of Benin; Nigerian traditional monarch; b. 2 June 1923; ed. Edo Coll., Benin, Govt. Coll., Ibadan, Yaba Coll., Lagos, Cambridge Univ., England; followed career in Civil Service; retd. 1973 as Perm. Sec. in Fed. Ministry of Health; Civil Commr. for Bendel State 1975–77; succeeded to throne of Benin March 1979; mem. Council of State 1979–. *Address:* The Palace, Box 1, Benin City, Bendel State, Nigeria.

ERICKSON, Arthur Charles, C.C., B.ARCH., F.R.A.I.C., A.R.C.A.; Canadian architect; b. 14 June 1924, Vancouver; s. of late Oscar and of Myrtle Erickson; ed. Univ. of British Columbia, McGill Univ.; travel study in Mediterranean countries and N. Europe 1950–53; private practice 1953–62; Asst. Prof. Univ. of Oregon 1955–56; Instructor and Asst. Prof. Univ. of British Columbia 1957–60, Assoc. Prof. 1961; Canada Council Fellowship for architectural research in Asia 1961; with Erickson, Massey 1963–72; Prin. Arthur Erickson Architects 1972–; mem. many architectural insts., asscns.; mem. Science Council of Canada Cttee. on Urban Devt. 1971, Bd. Canadian Conf. of the Arts 1972, Canadian Council on Urban Research, Bd. of Trustees, Inst. for Research on Public Policy, fmr. mem. Design Council of Portland Devt. Comm.; mem. Int. Cttee. of Museums of Modern Art, Americas Soc.; Life mem. Vancouver Art Gallery; Hon. Fellow, American Inst. of Architects 1978; Hon. D. Eng., (Nova Scotia Technical Coll.) 1971, Hon. LL.D. (Simon Fraser Univ.) 1973, (McGill Univ.) 1975,

(Univ. of Manitoba) 1978; Hon. D.Litt. (British Columbia) 1985; Hon. F.A.I.A.; Hon. M.R.I.B.A.; won First Prize in competition for Simon Fraser Univ., First Prize for design of Canadian Pavilion at Expo '70, Osaka, Pan Pacific Citation, American Inst. of Architects, Hawaiian Chapter 1963, Molson Prize, Canada Council for the Arts 1967, Architectural Inst. of Japan Award for Best Pavilion Expo '70, Royal Bank of Canada Award 1971, American Architectural Fraternity 1973, Auguste Perret Award, Int. Union of Architects 1974, Canadian Housing Design Council Awards for Residential Design 1975, President's Award of Excellence, American Soc. of Landscape Architects 1979, Grande Medaille d'Or Académie d'Architecture de France 1984, Gold Medal Royal Architectural Inst. of Canada 1984, Gold Medal, American Inst. of Architects 1986. *Publications:* The Architecture of Arthur Erickson 1975, Seven Stones by Edith Iglaner, The Architecture of Arthur Erickson 1988. *Address:* Arthur Erickson Architects, 2412 Laurel Street, Vancouver, B.C. and 80 Bloor Street West, Toronto M5S 2V1, Ont., Canada (Offices). *Telephone:* 879-0221 (Office, Vancouver); 416 967-4477 (Toronto).

ERICKSON, Richard John, J.D., PH.D.; American officer, lawyer and educator; b. 21 June 1943, Alexandria, Va.; s. of Theodore John and Helen Anita (née Whisnant) Erickson; m. Joan Kathryn Harmony 1970; one d.; ed. Florida State Univ., Univ. of Michigan Law School and Univ. of Virginia; Graduate Asst. Fla. State Univ. 1964–65; Visiting Prof. Univ. of Detroit 1970; Asst. Staff Judge Advocate, Headquarters Air Univ., Maxwell Air Force Base 1971–73; Project Researcher, Office of The Judge Advocate-Gen., U.S.A.F. 1971–75; U.S. Expert at Geneva Conf. on the Reaffirmation and Devt. of Int. Humanitarian Law in Armed Conflict 1972; Editor-in-Chief Air Force Law Review 1973–75; Faculty mem., The Judge Advocate-Gen's School, U.S.A.F., Maxwell Air Force Base 1973–75; Deputy Dir. and Chief Int. Law Div. HQ U.S.A.F., Europe, Ramstein Air Base, Fed. Repub. of Germany 1975–77, Chief 1977–78; Judge Advocate, Int. Law Div. HQ, U.S.A.F., Washington, D.C. 1978–82; Chief Fiscal Law Branch, Gen. Law Div., HQ, U.S.A.F., Washington, D.C. 1982–83; Staff Judge Advocate, Hellenikon Air Base, Athens, and Legal Adviser to Chief, U.S. Mil. Aid Group Greece 1983–84; U.S. rep., First Latin American Seminar on Int. Humanitarian Law, Bogotá, Colombia 1979; U.S. mem. and first legal adviser U.S.–Greek Jt. Comm. on Defence and Econ. Co-operation; U.S. mem. U.S.–Greek labour negotiations 1984–; mem. American Bar Assen., Fed. Bar Assen., Int. Law Assen. of Brussels, Inter-American Bar Assen., American Inst. of Aeronautics and Astronautics, American Assen. for Advancement of Slavic Studies, Southern Political Science Assen., Air Force Assen., fellow Thomas Jefferson Foundation; American Jurisprudence Awards in Admiralty and Legislation, Meritorious Service Medal with two Oak Leaf Clusters. *Publications:* International Law and the Revolutionary State 1972; articles in Air University Review, Air Force Law Review, Alabama Lawyer, Virginia Journal of International Law. *Leisure interests:* bridge, chess, bowling.

ERIKSON, Erik Homburger; American psychoanalyst; b. 15 June 1902, Frankfurt am Main, Germany; m. Joan Mowat Serson; two s. one d.; ed. Vienna Psychoanalytic Inst., Univ. of Vienna, Harvard Univ.; Research Fellow, Harvard Medical School 1935–36; Research Asst., Instructor, Asst. Prof. in Psychoanalysis Yale School of Medicine 1936–39; Research Assoc. Child Devt., lecturer in Psychiatry, Prof. of Psychology Univ. of Calif. 1939–51; training psychoanalyst, San Francisco 1942; Senior Staff mem. Austen Riggs Center, Stockbridge, Mass. 1951–60; Visiting Prof. Psychiatry Univ. of Pittsburgh Medical School 1951–60; Visiting Prof. Int. Studies M.I.T. 1958–60; Prof. of Human Devt., lecturer in Psychiatry Harvard Univ. 1960–70, Prof. Emer. 1970–, Distinguished Visiting Prof. Erikson Centre 1983–; Sr. Consultant in Psychiatry Mount Zion Hosp., San Francisco 1972–; mem. Int. Psychoanalytic Assen. (Vienna) 1933, American Psychoanalytic Assen. (Boston) 1934 (Life mem. 1964), Nat. Acad. of Educ. (now mem. Emer.), American Acad. of Arts and Sciences; Fellow Center for Advanced Studies in the Behavioural Sciences, Stanford, Calif. 1962, 1965, Davie Lecturer (Cape Town) 1968, Godkin Lecturer (Harvard) 1972, Jefferson Lecturer Nat. Endowment for the Humanities 1973; Hon. M.A. (Harvard), LL.D. (Brown, Harvard, Calif.), Sc.D. (Loyola), Soc. Sc. D. (Yale); Fil. dr. h.c. (Lund) 1980; Foneme Prize (Milan) 1969, Nat. Book Award 1970, Pulitzer Prize 1970, Melcher Award 1970, Aldrich Award American Acad. of Pediatrics 1971, Research Award Nat. Assoc. For Mental Health 1974. *Publications:* Childhood and Society 1950, 1963, Young Man Luther: A Study in the Psychoanalysis and History 1958, Insight and Responsibility 1964, Identity: Youth and Crisis 1968, Gandhi's Truth: On the Origins of Militant Non-Violence 1969, Dimensions of a New Identity (1973 Jefferson Lectures) 1974, Life History and the Historical Moment 1975, Toys and Reasons 1976, Vital Involvement in Old Age (with Joan Erikson and Helen Kivnick) 1986; Ed. Youth: Change and Challenge 1963, Adulthood 1978. *Address:* 329 San Rafael Avenue, Belvedere, Calif. 94920, U.S.A.

ERIKSSON, Per-Olof, M.SC.ENG.; Swedish business executive; b. 1 March 1938, Seglora; s. of Gunhild Eriksson and Herbert Eriksson; m. Helena Eriksson Joachimsson 1962; two s. one d.; ed. Royal Inst. of Tech., Stockholm; Dir. and Head of Production and Materials Control, Sandvik Coromant 1975; Pres. Seco Tools AB 1976; Pres. and C.E.O. Sandvik AB 1984–. *Leisure interests:* orienteering, skiing, tennis and sailing. *Address:*

Sandvik AB, S-811 81 Sandviken; 57 Hedåsvägen 57, S-811 61 Sandviken, Sweden (Home). *Telephone:* 26 26 41 14 (Office); 26 27 02 02 (Home).

ERKMEN, Hayrettin, D.ECON.S.; Turkish economist and politician; b. 19 April 1915, Giresun; s. of Ali and Rahime Erkmen; m. Münire Babaoglu 1955; two s.; ed. Ankara School of Political Sciences, Geneva School of Econs. and Lausanne School of Law; Reporter, Bd. of Financial Research, Ministry of Finance 1948; Asst. Prof. of Econs. Univ. of Istanbul 1949; Minister of Labour 1953-55, 1957-58, of Commerce 1958-60, of Reconstruction (acting) 1959-60, of Foreign Affairs 1979-80; mem. Nat. Assembly (Dem. Party) before 1960; mem. Senate (Justice Party) 1975-80; Chair. Bd. Import-Export Bank of Turkey 1984; arrested after mil. coup 1960, found guilty on political charges 1961. *Publication:* La participation des salariés à la gestion de l'entreprise 1948. *Address:* Arifi Paşa Korusu 11/5 Bebek, Istanbul, Turkey.

ERLANDE-BRANDENBURG, Alain; French museum curator; b. 2 Aug. 1937, Luxeuil les Bains; s. of Gilbert Erlande and Renée Pierra; m. Anne-Bénédicte Mérel 1980; two s. one d.; Curator musée de Cluny and musée d'Ecouen 1967, Chief Curator 1981; Dir. of Studies école pratique des hautes études 1975; Prof. école du Louvre; Asst. Dir. musées de France 1987-; Pres. Soc. française d'archéologie; Chevalier ordre nat. du mérite, Légion d'honneur, Officier des arts et lettres. *Publications:* Paris monumental 1974, Le roi est mort 1975, Les rois retrouvés 1977, La Dame à la licorne 1978, La cathédrale d'Amiens 1982, L'abbaye de Cluny 1982, L'art gothique 1984, Chartres 1986, La conquête de l'Europe 1260-1380 1987. *Address:* 10 Bis, rue de Pré aux Clercs, 75007 Paris; Impasse de l'abbaye, 77120 Beautheil, France. *Telephone:* 45 44 95 38; 64 03 41 94.

ERLANGER, Philippe; French writer and international art organizer; b. 11 July 1903, Paris; s. of late Camille Erlanger; ed. Lycée Janson de Sailly, Université de Paris à la Sorbonne and Ecole libre des sciences politiques; organizer of about 500 exhbns. and over 1,000 theatrical and musical presentations; Dir. French Assen. for Artistic Affairs 1938-68; Head, Artistic Exchange Dept., Ministry of Foreign Affairs 1946-68; Inspector-Gen. Ministry of National Education 1960-67; Minister Plenipotentiary 1968; Founder and Hon. Pres. Cannes Int. Film Festival 1946; Grand Prix du Rayonnement Français 1962, Grand Prix Littéraire du Département de la Seine 1963, Prix des Ambassadeurs 1966, Grand Prix Gobert (Acad. Française) 1969, Grand Prix Littéraire de la Ville de Paris 1977; Commdr. Légion d'honneur, Hon. C.B.E., and numerous other French and foreign decorations. *Publications include:* Henri III 1935, Le Régent 1938, Monsieur, Frère de Louis XIV 1953, Diane de Poitiers 1955, L'étrange mort de Henry IV 1957, Le massacre de la Saint-Barthélemy 1960, Cinq Mars 1962, Louis XIV 1965, Clemenceau 1968, Richelieu 1969, Margaret d'Anjou 1970, La Reine Margot 1972, La France sans étoile 1974, La vie de Madame de Longueville 1977, Philippe V d'Espagne 1978, Charles Quint 1980, Henri VIII, Le dernier age d'or de la monarchie 1984, Le Crépuscule des Rois 1985, Ninon de Lenclos 1986. *Address:* Résidence du Grand Hôtel, 45 La Croisette, Cannes 06400, France (Home). *Telephone:* (93) 48-56-19.

ERNEMANN, André; Belgian diplomatist; b. 31 Aug. 1923, Antwerp; s. of Joseph Jean Ernemann and Marthe Janssens; m. Kristin Diaz 1977; entered Foreign Service 1947; served Rome, Teheran, Paris; Consul-Gen. in New York 1969; mem. del. to Conf. on Security and Co-operation in Europe 1973; Dir. Int. Orgs. Service in Ministry of Foreign Affairs; Perm. Rep. to UN Sept. 1976-81; Amb. to Austria 1981-86, to Spain 1986-. *Leisure interest:* tennis. *Address:* Belgian Embassy, Paseo de la Castellana 18°, 6°, 28046 Madrid, Spain.

ERNI, Hans; Swiss painter; b. 21 Feb. 1909, Lucerne; m. Doris Kessler 1949; one s. two d.; ed. Académie Julien, Paris and Vereinigte Staatsschulen für freie und angewandte Kunst, Berlin; mem. Groupe Abstraction-Création, Paris; mem. S.W.B.; exhbns. Lucerne, Paris, Basel, Oxford, Liverpool, London, Cambridge, Leicester, Zürich, Milan, Rotterdam, Prague, Stockholm, Chicago, New York, Rome, Copenhagen, Tokyo, San Francisco, Los Angeles, Washington, Mannheim, Cologne; abstract mural picture Swiss section Triennale Milan, frescoes Lucerne; great mural Switzerland for Swiss Nat. Exhbn. Zürich 1939; Great Murals Exposition internationale de l'Urbanisme et de l'Habitation Paris 1947, Mural in Bernese hospital Montana; mem. Alliance Graphique Int.; Int. Prize at the Biennale del Mare 1953; great mural at the Musée Ethnographique, Neuchâtel 1954; has illustrated bibliophile edns. of classics by Plato, Pindar, Sophocles, Virgil, Buffon, Renard, Valéry, Homer (Odyssey), Albert Schweitzer (La Paix), Voltaire (Candide), Paul Eluard, etc.; murals for Int. Exhbn. in Brussels 1958; mosaics for the Abbey of St. Maurice 1961, for Swiss T.V. and Radio Building, Berne 1964; Engraved glass panels "Day and Night" and "Towards a Humanistic Future" for the Société des Banques Suisses, Geneva, 1963; exhbns. in Japan and Australia 1963, 1964, Pro Juventute stamps 1965; murals in Rolex Foundation, Union de Banques Suisses, Sion 1966, for Swissair Zürich, and La Placette Geneva 1967; exhbns. in Chicago, New York, Geneva 1966-68. *Publications:* Wo steht der Maler in der Gegenwart? 1947, Erni en Valais 1967, Israel Sketchbook 1968. *Leisure interest:* art. *Address:* 6045 Meggen, Lucerne, Switzerland. *Telephone:* 041-371382.

ERROLL OF HALE, 1st Baron (cr. 1964) of Kilmun in the County of Argyll; **Frederick James Eroll,** P.C., M.A. C.ENG., F.I.E.E., F.I.MECH.E.; British

politician; b. 27 May 1914, London; s. of late George Murison Erroll; m. Elizabeth Sowton Barrow 1950; ed. Oundle School and Trinity Coll., Cambridge; served in engineering industry 1936-39; war service, Tank Div., reached rank of Col. 1939-45; M.P. for Altrincham and Sale 1945-64; Parl. Sec. Ministry of Supply 1955-56, Bd. of Trade 1956-58; Econ. Sec. Treasury 1958-59; Minister of State, Bd. of Trade 1959-60; Privy Counsellor 1960-; Pres. Bd. of Trade 1961-63; Minister of Power 1963-64; mem. Nat. Econ. Development Council 1962-63; Chair. Bowater Corpn. 1973-84, Consolidated Gold Fields 1976-83, Pres. 1982-; Chair and Dir. of several other cos. 1965-; Pres. London Chamber of Commerce 1966-69, Vice-Pres. 1969; mem. of the Council of Inst. of Dirs. 1949-55, 1965, Chair. 1973-76, Pres. 1976-84, Chancellor 1984-87; Deputy Chair. Decimal Currency Bd. 1966-71; Pres. of the British Export Houses Assen. 1968-72, Hispanic and Luso-Brazilian Councils 1969-73, U.K.-S.A. Trade Assen. 1979-84; Chair. Cttee. on Liquor Licensing 1971-72, Automobile Assen. 1974-86, Vice-Pres. 1986-; Conservative. *Address:* House of Lords, London, S.W.1, England.

ERSHAD, Lieut.-Gen. Hossain Mohammad; Bangladesh fmr. army officer and politician; b. 1 Feb. 1930, Rangpur; s. of the late Maqbul Hussain and of Begum Majida Khatun; m. Raushan Ershad 1956; one s. one adopted d.; ed. Univ. of Dacca, Officers' Training School, Kohat, Pakistan; first appointment in 2nd East Bengal Regt. 1952; several appointments in various units including Adjutant, East Bengal Regt. Centre, Chittagong 1960-62; completed staff course, Quetta Staff Coll. 1966; promoted Lieut.-Col. 1969; Commdr. 3rd East Bengal Regt. 1969-70, 7th East Bengal Regt. 1971-72; Adjutant-Gen. Bangladesh Army; promoted Col. 1973; attended Nat. Defence Coll., New Delhi, India 1975; promoted Brig. 1975, Maj.-Gen. 1975; Deputy Chief of Army Staff 1975-78, Chief 1978-86; rank of Lieut.-Gen. 1979; led mil. takeover in Bangladesh March 1982; Chief Martial Law Administrator and Pres. Council of Ministers 24 March 1982, adopted title of Prime Minister Oct. 1982, of Pres. of Bangladesh Dec. 1983, elected Pres. of Bangladesh Oct. 1986; also Minister of Defence 1986-, of Information 1986-88; fmrly. in charge of several ministries including Home Affairs; Chief Adviser Bangladesh Freedom Fighters' Assen.; Chair. Bangladesh Olympic Assen., Bangladesh Lawn Tennis Fed.; UN Population Award 1987. *Leisure interests:* golf, writing poems, art, literature and oriental music. *Address:* Bangabhaban, Dhaka, Bangladesh.

ERSIN, Gen. Nurettin; Turkish army officer; b. 1918, Gelibolu; m.; two c.; ed. Army Mil. Acad. and Staff Coll.; Commdr. Turkish Peace Force, Cyprus 1974; full gen. 1974; Commdr. First Army 1977; Commdr. Turkish (Ground Forces) 1978-. *Address:* c/o Ministry of National Defence, Milli Savunma Bakanlığı, Bakanlıklar, Ankara, Turkey.

ERSKINE, Ralph, C.B.E., A.R.I.B.A., A.M.T.P.I., S.A.R.; British architect; b. 24 Feb. 1914, Mill Hill, London; s. of George and Mildred (née Gough) Erskine; m. Ruth Monica Francis 1939; one s. two d.; ed. Friends' School, Saffron Walden, Essex, Regent Street Polytechnic, London, and Konst. Akad., Stockholm; own practice in Sweden since 1940, branch office in Byker, Newcastle upon Tyne 1969-; engaged in city renewals plans, new library for Stockholm Univ., town planning, designs for flats, private houses, housing estates, industrial buildings, churches, shopping centres, and homes for the elderly; designed Hall of Residence, Clare Coll., Cambridge, England; studies and research in architectural problems on building in subarctic regions; sketches: town site, Resolute, N.W.T., Canada; Guest Prof. at Technical School, Zürich; lectures in Netherlands, Japan, Canada, Sweden, Finland, Poland, Denmark, Switzerland, Austria, Germany, Norway, Russia, England, France, Italy and America; has participated in exhbns. in Sweden, Canada, Netherlands, Denmark, Norway and Switzerland; foreign mem. Royal Swedish Acad. of Arts; Hon. A.I.A., Dr.Tech. (Lund Univ.) 1970; Hon. D.Litt. (Heriot Watt Univ., Edinburgh) 1982; Kasper Salin Prize (Sweden), Ytong Prize 1974; medal: litteris et artibus 1980; Gold Medal (Royal Architecture Inst. of Canada) 1982; Wolf Prize for Architecture 1984; Royal Gold Medal (Royal Inst. of British Architects) 1987. *Publications:* contrib. to architectural magazines, etc. *Leisure interests:* skiing, skating, sailing. *Address:* Gustav III's väg, 170 11 Drottningholm, Sweden. *Telephone:* 7590352, 7590050 (Office).

ERTL, Josef; German politician; b. 7 March 1925, Oberschleissheim; s. of Adolf Ertl and Magdalena Wagner; m. Paula Nicklas 1953; three s.; ed. Technical Univ. of Munich; nat. labour service, mil. service as pilot in support aviation wing (cadet); agric. labourer and apprentice; joined Bavarian State Ministry of Food, Agric. and Forests 1952; Dir. Youth Advisory Service until 1959; Head, Agricultural School, Miesbach 1959; Dir., Office of Agric., Miesbach 1960; Sr. Agricultural Counsellor 1960; mem. Bundestag 1961-; Land Vice-Chair. 1963; Fed. Minister of Food, Agric. and Forestry 1969-83; Vice-Chair. Parl. Free Democrats 1971-83 (retd.), Hon. Pres. 1983-; Pres. German Skiing Assen. 1978-, German Agricultural Soc. 1984-; Chair. Bavarian FDP 1971-83; Hon. Chair. 1983-; Hon. Senator Univ. of Soil Culture, Vienna; Dr. h.c. (Tokyo); Grosskreuzverdienstorden; numerous foreign decorations; Free Democrat. *Publications:* 1000 Fragen für den jungen Landuirt, Agrarpolitik Ohne Illusionen. *Leisure interests:* skiing, hunting, sailing, swimming, historical literature and biographies, classical music, painting. *Address:* Auerstrasse 20, 8182 Bad Wiessee/Obb, Federal Republic of Germany. *Telephone:* (0228) 5291.

ESAKI, Leo, PH.D.; Japanese scientist; b. 12 March 1925, Osaka; s. of Soichiro Esaki and Niyoko Ito; m. 1st Masako Araki 1959; one s. two d.; m. 2nd Masako Kondo 1986; ed. Univ. of Tokyo; with Sony Corpn. 1956-60, conducted research on heavily-doped Ge and Si which resulted in the discovery of tunnel diode; with IBM Corpn., U.S.A. 1960-, IBM Fellow 1967-, IBM T. J. Watson Research Center, New York, 1960-, Man. Device Research 1962-; Dir. IBM-Japan 1976-, Yamada Science Foundation 1976-; Sir John Cass Sr. Visiting Research Fellow, London Polytechnic 1981; major field of research is nonlinear transport and optical properties on semiconductors, junctions, thin films, etc., currently involved on a man-made semiconductor lattice grown by a computer-controlled molecular-beam epitaxy; mem. Japan Acad. 1975; Foreign Assoc. N.A.S. 1976, American Nat. Acad. of Engineering 1977; Nishina Memorial Award 1959, Asahi Press Award 1960, Toyo Rayon Foundation Award 1961, Morris N. Liebmann Memorial Prize 1961, Stuart Ballantine Medal, Franklin Inst. 1961, Japan Acad. Award 1965, Nobel Prize for Physics 1973, Order of Culture, Japanese Govt. 1974, U.S.-Asia Inst. Science Achievement Award 1983, American Physical Soc. Int. Prize for New Materials (with others) 1985. *Publications:* numerous articles in professional journals. *Address:* IBM T. J. Watson Research Center, P.O. Box 218, Yorktown Heights, N.Y. 10598; Young Road, RFD No. 4, Katonah, N.Y. 10536, U.S.A. (Home). *Telephone:* (914) 945-2342 (Office).

ESAKI, Masumi; Japanese politician; b. 1915; mem. House of Reps. for Aichi prefecture; fmr. Parl. Vice-Minister for Construction; fmr. Deputy Sec.-Gen. and Chair. Liberal-Democratic Party (LDP) Diet Policy Cttee.; Dir.-Gen. Defence Agency July-Dec. 1960, 1971-72; Minister of Home Affairs and Chair. Nat. Public Safety Comm. 1972-73; Minister of Int. Trade and Industry 1978-79; Chair. LDP Exec. Council 1976-77; Dir. Gen. Man. and Co-ordination Agency 1985-86. *Leisure interest:* yachting. *Address:* House of Representatives, Tokyo, Japan.

ESCHENBACH, Christoph; German conductor and concert pianist; b. 20 Feb. 1940, Breslau (now Wrocław, Poland); ed. Musikhochschulen, Cologne and Hamburg; Musical Director of Philharmonic Orchestra, Ludwigshafen 1979-83; Leader and Chief Artistic Dir. Tonhalle Orchestra, Zürich 1982-86; 1st Prize, Steinway Piano Competition 1952, Munich Int. Competition 1962, Clara Haskil Competition 1965; has appeared with Vienna Symphony, London Philharmonic, Royal Philharmonic and Tonhalle Orchestras, Radio Orchestras of Hamburg, Munich, Stuttgart, Israel Philharmonic and Israel Chamber Orchestras, NHK Orchestra Tokyo, Houston Symphony, Atlanta Symphony and Houston Opera Orchestras, Musical Dir. Houston Symphony Orchestra 1988-. *Address:* Houston Symphony Orchestra, 615, Louisiana Street, Houston, Tex. 77002, U.S.A. *Telephone:* (713) 2244240.

ESCHENMOSER, Albert, DR. SC. NAT.; Swiss chemist; b. 5 Aug. 1925, Erstfeld; s. of Alfons and Johanna (née Oesch) Eschenmoser; m. Elizabeth Baschnonga 1954; two s. one d.; ed. Collegium Altdorf, Kantonsschule St. Gallen, Swiss Federal Inst. of Technology, Zürich; Privatdozent, Organic Chemistry, Swiss Fed. Inst. of Technology 1956, Assoc. Prof. of Organic Chemistry 1960, Prof. Organic Chemistry 1965; Foreign Hon. mem. American Acad. of Arts and Sciences 1966; Foreign Assoc. Nat. Acad. of Sciences, U.S.A. 1973; mem. Deutsche Akademie der Naturforscher Leopoldina (Halle) 1976; Hon. Fellow, Royal Soc. Chem. (London) 1981; Foreign mem. Royal Soc. 1986, Pontifical Acad. (Vatican) 1986, Akad. der Wissenschaften (Göttingen) 1986, Acad. Europaea 1988; Hon. Dr. rer. nat. (Fribourg) 1966, Hon. D.Sc. (Chicago) 1970, (Edinburgh) 1979; Kern Award, Swiss Fed. Inst. of Technology 1949, Werner Award, Swiss Chemical Soc. 1956, Ruzicka Award, Swiss Fed. Inst. of Technology 1958, Fritzsche Award, American Chemical Soc. 1966, Marcel Benoist Prize (Switzerland) 1973, R. A. Welch Award in Chemistry (Houston, Texas) 1974, Kirkwood Medal (Yale) 1976, A.W.V. Hofmann-Denkmünze, GDCh 1976, Dannie-Heinemann Prize (Akademie der Wissenschaften, Göttingen) 1977, Davy Medal (Royal Soc., London) 1978; Tetrahedron Prize (Pergamon Press) 1981, G. Kenner Award (Univ. of Liverpool) 1982, Arthur C. Cope Award (American Chemical Soc.) 1984, Wolf Prize in Chemistry (Israel) 1986. *Publications:* numerous articles on organic synthesis in professional journals. *Address:* Bergstrasse 9, 8700 Küsnacht (ZH), Switzerland. *Telephone:* 9107392.

ESCHERICH, Rudolf Johann, DR.RER.POL; German business executive; b. 27 Oct. 1923, Wegscheid, Bavaria; m. Helga Koch 1959; one s. one d.; ed. Univ. of Munich; Chair. Man. Bd. Vereinigte Aluminium-Werke AG 1976-85, Chair. Supervisory Bd. Jan. 1986-, Man. Bd. VIAG 1975-. *Leisure interests:* flying, golf, tennis, skiing. *Address:* Vereinigte Aluminium-Werke AG, 5300 Bonn, Georgvon-Boeselager-Strasse 25 (Office); 5205 St. Augustin 2, Drachenfelsstrasse 13, Federal Republic of Germany (Home). *Telephone:* 5522215 (Office); St. Augustin 22596 (Home).

ESCOBAR, María Luisa; Venezuelan composer; b. 5 Dec. 1909; ed. Curaçao and Paris; Founder and Pres. until 1943 Ateneo de Caracas; founder and Dir-Gen. Asociación Venezolana de Autores y Compositores (A.V.A.C.) 1947; Artistic Dir. the Ballet-Theatre of Caracas; rep. Venezuela at Int. Congress on Musical Education, Paris 1937, Int. Conf. of Society Authors and Composers, Buenos Aires 1948, Rome 1962, 25th Int. Congress Nat. Fed. of Music Clubs, U.S.A. 1949, First Inter-American Music Conf., U.S.A. 1949; awarded medals and diplomas of honour by Venezuela,

France, Cuba, Mexico, U.S.A., and India. *Works include:* Orquideas azules (symphony and ballet), La Princesa Girasol (operetta), Guaicaipuro (ballet), Vals Sentimental (piano and orchestra), El Rey Guaicaipuro (opera), Canaimé (musical drama), Concierto Sentimental (piano and orchestra), Pajaro de Siele Colores (violin and piano) and many folksongs, etc. *Leisure interests:* journalism, radio and T.V. announcing. *Address:* Guaicaipuro, Calle Baruta, Bello Monte (Notre), Caracas, Venezuela (Home).

ESCOBAR CERDA, Luis; Chilean economist; b. 1927; m. 2nd Helga Koch 1973; four c.; ed. Univ. de Chile and Harvard Univ.; Dir. School of Econs., Univ. de Chile 1951-55, Dean of Faculty of Econs. 1955-64; Minister of Econ. Devt. and Reconstruction 1961-63; mem. Inter-American Cttee. for Alliance for Progress 1964-66; Exec. Dir. Int. Monetary Fund 1964-66, 1968-70, IBRD 1966-68; Special Rep. for Inter-American Orgs. IBRD 1970-75; Trustee of Population Reference Bureau 1968-73; mem. Advisory Cttee. on Population and Devt. OAS 1968-73, Council Soc. for Int. Devt. 1969-72; Deputy Exec. Sec. Joint Bank/Fund Devt. Cttee. 1975-; Prof. Georgetown Univ. 1975-, George Washington Univ. 1977, Dept. of Econs., American Univ. 1978-. *Publications:* The Stock Market 1959, Organization for Economic Development 1961, A Stage of the National Economic Development 1962, Considerations on the Tasks of the University 1963, Organizational Requirements for Growth and Stability 1964, The Role of the Social Sciences in Latin America 1965, The Organization of Latin American Government 1968, Multinational Corporations in Latin America 1973, International Control of Investments 1974, External Financing in Latin America 1976, 1978. *Address:* International Bank for Reconstruction and Development, 1818 H Street, N.W., Washington, D.C. 20433, U.S.A.; Los Tulipanes 2979, Santiago, Chile.

ESCOLAR SOBRINO, Hipólito; Spanish librarian; b. 29 May 1919, Naval-manzano; s. of Emiliano and Amparo Escolar Sobrino; m. Concepción Franco 1947; two s.; ed. Univ. of Madrid; Prof. Univ. of Madrid 1942; Dir. public library at Avila 1944, Toledo 1945, Almería 1947; Sec., Gen. Man. of Archives and Libraries 1952; Pres. Int. Soc. of Librarians 1958; Dir. Centre for Co-ordination of Madrid Libraries 1969; Dir. Nat. Library 1975-86; Cruz de Alfonso X, Medalla Militar and decorations from Bulgaria and France. *Publications:* Marquetin para bibliotecarios 1970, Planeamiento bibliotecario 1971, El lector, la lectura y la comunicación 1972, Historia social del libro (4 vols.) 1974, 1975, Dos mil años de pensamiento bibliotecario español 1982, Los editores y el cambio 1982, Historia del libro 1984, Historia de las bibliotecas 1985; annotated editions and translations of Caesar and Cicero. *Leisure interest:* golf. *Address:* Juan de Urbieta 63, 3° izda, Madrid, Spain. *Telephone:* 4-33-05-28.

ESCOVAR SALOM, Ramón; Venezuelan politician; b. 1926, Lara State; mem. Nat. Congress 1947; Minister of Justice; Rep. to Lara State Legis. Assembly; mem. Senate; Sec.-Gen. of the Presidency 1974-75; Minister of Foreign Affairs 1975-77. *Address:* c/o Ministerio de Relaciones Exteriores, Carmelitas a Santa Capilla, Caracas, Venezuela.

ESER, Günter O., DR.; German international air transport official; b. 10 Sept. 1927, Bad Godesberg; s. of Ernst Eser and Martha Siering; m. Florida Huisman 1976; two s.; ed. Bonn Univ., Fed. Acad. of Finance and Harvard Man. Program; Auditor, Fed. German Ministry of Finance 1953-55; various posts with Deutsche Lufthansa AG 1955-84, latterly mem. Chief Exec. Bd.; mem. Advisory Bd. Europäische Reiseversicherung, American Univ.; Pace Univ. New York; Dir.-Gen. Int. Air Transport Asscn. (IATA) 1985-; Bundesverdienstkreuz (Germany), Commendatore Officiale (Italy). *Leisure interests:* trekking, ocean-fishing, literature, music. *Address:* c/o IATA, P.O. Box 160, CH 1216 Cointrin-Geneva, Switzerland; IATA, 2000 Peel Street, Montreal, P.Q. H3A 2R4, Canada.

ESHPAI, Andrei Yakovlevich; Soviet composer; b. 1925; ed. Moscow Conservatory; studied with E. K. Golubev; First Sec. of R.S.F.S.R. Composers' Union 1973-79; *Compositions include:* Angara (ballet), Lenin is with us (cantata); 3 symphonies; 2 concertos for piano and orchestra; concerto for violin and orchestra; also film music and songs; R.S.F.S.R. People's Artist 1975; U.S.S.R. State Prize 1976; U.S.S.R. People's Artist 1981.

ESKENAZI, Gérard André, M.B.A.; French business executive; b. 10 Nov. 1931, Paris; s. of Roger Eskenazi and Léone Blanchard; m. Arlette Gravelin 1964; three s. one d.; ed. studies in law and business admin.; joined Banque de Paris et des Pays-Bas (now Banque Paribas) 1957, Pres. Cie Financière de Paribas 1978-82; Deputy Chair. and Pres. Groupe Bruxelles Lambert S.A. 1982-; Chair. of Bd., Paribas (Suisse) S.A. 1980-; Chair. Cometra Oil Co. 1982-; Chair. Exec. Cttee., Lambert Brussels Corpn. 1983-; mem. Bd. Schneider S.A., Chargeurs S.A., Power Corpn. of Canada Ltd., Electrobel, Cobepa, Drexel Burnham Lambert, Banque Internationale à Luxembourg, Banque Paribas Belgique, Banque Paribas N.V., La Royale Belge; Chevalier, Ordre Nat. du Mérite. *Leisure interest:* horse riding. *Address:* Groupe Bruxelles Lambert S.A., 24 avenue Marnix, 1050 Brussels, Belgium (Office); 7 rue Maurice Ravel, 92210 Saint Cloud, France (Home). *Telephone:* (2) 517.21.11 (Office).

ESKOLA, Antti Aarre, PH.D.; Finnish professor of social psychology; b. 20 Aug. 1934, Urjala; m. Riti Laakso 1958; one s. one d.; ed. Univ. of Helsinki; Prof. of Sociology, Univ. of Turku 1965; Prof. of Social Psychology, Univ. of Tampere 1966-; Research Prof., Acad. of Finland 1982-87. *Publications:* Social Influence and Power in Two-Person Groups 1961, Blind

Alleys in Social Psychology 1988, several other studies, textbooks, essay collections and a novel. *Address:* University of Tampere, Department of Sociology and Social Psychology, P.O. Box 607, 33101 Tampere, Finland. *Telephone:* (358) 31 156111.

ESMENARD, Francis; French publisher; b. 8 Dec. 1936, Paris; s. of Roland Esmenard and Andrée Michel; one s.; Pres.-Dir.-Gen. Éditions Allin Michel 1982–, Paris. *Address:* Éditions Allin Michel, 22 rue Huyghens, 75014 Paris, France (Office). *Telephone:* 43 20 12 20.

ESPINASSE, Jacques Paul, M.B.A.; French business executive; b. 12 May 1943, Ales; s. of Gustave Espinasse and Andrée Bernadel; m. Daniele Samat 1964; one s. one d.; ed. Univ. of Michigan; financial analyst, London and Brussels 1967–70; Consultant, Science Man. Int. 1970–73; Head, Control Dept. Renault Véhicules Industriels 1973–78, Commercial Man. in charge of export in Europe 1979; Head, Int. Treasury Dept. Régie Renault 1980; Financial Officer, Sommer Allibert 1981–82; Chief Financial Officer, CEP Communication 1982–85; Chief Financial Officer, Havas 1985–87, Exec. Vice-Pres. 1987–. *Leisure interest:* golf. *Address:* Havas, 136 avenue Charles de Gaulle, 92200 Neuilly-sur-Seine (Office); 29 boulevard Suchet, 75016 Paris, France (Home). *Telephone:* 47 47 37 51 (Office).

ESQUEA GUERRERO, Emmanuel T., LL.D.; Dominican lawyer and diplomatist; b. 25 July 1944, Santo Domingo; s. of Ana Leonor Guerrero and Fidias Estanislao Esquea; m. Miriam Mota de Esquea 1974; two s.; ed. Autonomous Univ. of Santo Domingo, Univ. of Toulouse and in Italy, Spain and the Netherlands; Prof. of Law and Legal Practice, Univ. Nacional Pedro Henríquez Ureña, Santo Domingo 1971–83; Perm. Rep. to UN 1978–80; mem. Bd. of Trustees of INSTRAW 1979–82; Legal Advisor to Exec. Power 1982–86; mem. House of Reps. *Publications:* Mundo Juridico 1987, articles in several journals. *Leisure interests:* reading, sailing. *Address:* Apt. 201, Abraham Lincoln Ave. No. 852, Santo Domingo, Dominican Republic. *Telephone:* (809) 565-6714, (809) 567-8126.

ESQUIVEL, Manuel, P.C.; Belize teacher and politician; b. 2 May 1940, Belize City; s. of John and Laura Esquivel; m. Kathleen Levy 1971; one s. two d.; ed. Loyola Univ., U.S.A., Univ. of Bristol, England; teacher at St. John's Junior Coll., Belize City–1984; f. United Democratic Party 1973, Chair. 1976–82; fmr. Councillor, Belize City Council; mem. Senate 1979–; Prime Minister of Belize Dec. 1984–; Dr. h.c. (Loyola Univ., U.S.A.) 1986. *Address:* Office of the Prime Minister, Belmopan, Belize. *Telephone:* (08) 22346.

ESSAAFI, M'Hamed; Tunisian diplomatist; b. 26 May 1930, Kelibia; m. Hedwige Klat 1956; one s. one d.; ed. Sorbonne, Paris; First Sec., London 1956; Counsellor, then Minister plenipotentiary, Ministry of Foreign Affairs 1960–64; Amb. to U.K. 1964–69; Sec.-Gen. Ministry of Foreign Affairs 1969–70, 1976–78; Amb. to U.S.S.R. 1970–74, to Fed. Germany 1974–76, to Belgium, Luxembourg and EEC 1978–79; Perm. Rep. to UN Jan.–Aug. 1980; UN Sec.-Gen.'s Special Rep. for Humanitarian Affairs in S.E. Asia 1980–81; Chef de Cabinet of UN Sec.-Gen. Jan.–June 1982; UN Under Sec.-Gen. and Disaster Relief Co-ordinator July 1982–; Grand Officier, Ordre de la République tunisienne; Chevalier, Ordre de l'Indépendance. *Address;* UNDRO, Palais des Nations, 1211 Geneva, Switzerland.

ESSBERGER, Ruprecht; German television director and writer; b. 8 March 1923, Berlin; s. of Eduard and Hedwig Essberger; m. 1st Alexandra Massenberg 1949 (divorced 1962), two s.; m. 2nd Merle Insanali 1969, one d.; ed. Univs. of Hamburg and Göttingen; asst. television dir. North German Rundfunk 1950, television dir. 1953; freelance television dir. and writer 1957–. *television series include:* Familie Schölermann, Das Fernsehgericht tagt 1960–78, Ehen vor Gericht 1970–83, 1989–, Verkehrsgericht 1983–, Bundesverdienstkreuz 1989; Golden Screen, Golden Rose and Golden Camera awards. *Leisure interests:* music, sailing. *Address:* Agnesstrasse 2, 2000 Hamburg 60, Federal Republic of Germany. *Telephone:* 040/470519; 089/3597728.

ESSELENS, Maurits; Belgian financial official; b. 17 Oct. 1916; m.; three c.; served Belgian Ministry of Finance until 1975, latterly Dir.-Gen. Treasury; fmr. Govt. Commr. Banque Nat. de Belgique, Inst. de Réescompte et de Garantie; fmr. Chair. Comité du Fonds et des Rentes; fmr. Dir. Caisse Autonome des Dommages de Guerre, Inst. Belgo-Luxembourgeois du Change; fmr. mem. Conseil Supérieur des Finances, Conseil des Insts. de Crédit Public; Vice-Pres. European Investment Bank (EIB) and Vice-Chair. Bd. of Dirs. 1976–82.

ESSER, Otto; German business executive; b. 1 June 1917; Partner and Man. E. Merck, Darmstadt; Vice-Chair. Fed. of Employers, German Chem. Industry; Pres. Confederation of German Employers' Asscns. (BDA) 1977–86. *Address:* 8765 Erlenbach, Am Forstweg 1, Federal Republic of Germany.

ESSEX, David; British singer, actor and composer; b. 23 July 1947, London; s. of Albert and Doris Cook; m. Maureen Neal; one s. one d.; started in music industry 1965; TV debut on Five O'Clock Club; has since made numerous TV appearances in U.K., Europe and U.S.A., including own BBC series 1977, The River BBC1 Series 1988; appeared on stage in repertory and later in Godspell 1971, Evita 1978, Childe Byron, Mutiny! (also wrote music) 1985; albums include: Rock On 1974, All the Fun of the Fair 1975, Out on the Street 1976, Gold and Ivory 1977, Imperial Wizard

1979, Hot Love 1980, Be Bop the Future 1981, Stage Struck 1982, The Whisper 1983, This One's For You 1984 (all solo); War of the Worlds (with Jeff Wayne, Richard Burton and others), From Alpha to Omega (with Cat Stevens) 1978, Silver Dream Racer (film soundtrack: composer/producer) 1979; first concert tour of U.K. 1974, subsequent tours 1975 (including Europe, U.S.A. and Australia), 1976, 1977, 1978, 1979 (including Europe and U.S.A.), 1980, 1987, 1988; films include: Assault, All Coppers Are . . . 1971, That'll Be The Day (Variety Club Award) 1973, Stardust 1974, Silver Dream Racer 1979; numerous gold and silver discs for LP and single records in Europe and U.S.A.; voted Best Male Singer and Outstanding Music Personality in Daily Mirror poll 1976; Variety Club of G.B. Award for Show Business Personality of the Year (joint) 1978. *Leisure interests:* motorcycling, horse-riding, flying, tennis. *Address:* c/o Derek Bowman, 109 Eastbourne Mews, London, W.2, England. *Telephone:* 01-402 5169.

ESSONGHE, Jean-Baptiste; Gabonese diplomatist; b. 1927, Setté-Cama, Gabon; m.; two c.; ed. Ecole Nat. de la France d'Outre-Mer, Paris; entered civil service, later Sec.-Gen. Nat. Assembly; First Counsellor, Embassy in France 1967–68, later in U.S.A., Perm. Mission to UN Office, Geneva, and Embassy in Canada; Amb. to Tunisia 1974–75; Perm. Rep. UN 1975–77; Amb. to Spain 1978–83. *Address:* c/o Ministry of Foreign Affairs, Libreville, Gabon.

ESSWOOD, Paul Lawrence Vincent, A.R.C.M.; British counter-tenor singer; b. 6 June 1942, Nottingham; s. of Alfred W. Esswood and Freda Garatt; m. Mary L. Cantrill 1966; two s.; ed. West Bridgford Grammar School and Royal Coll. of Music; Lay Vicar, Westminster Abbey 1964–71; Prof. Royal Coll. of Music 1971–74; co-founder, Pro Cantione Antiqua—A Cappella 1967; opera debut, L'Erismena, Univ. of Calif., Berkeley 1968; debut at La Scala, Milan with Zürich Opera in L'Incoronazione di Poppea and Il Ritorno d'Ulisse 1978; Scottish opera debut in Dido and Aneas 1978; world premiere, Penderecki's Paradise Lost, Chicago Lyric Opera 1979, Philip Glass's Akhnaton, Stuttgart 1984; has appeared at many maj. int. festivals; specialist in performance of baroque music and has made many recordings of works by Bach, Handel, Purcell, Monteverdi, Cavalli etc. *Leisure interests:* sports, aquariology, gardening. *Address:* 6 Gowan Avenue, London, SW6 6RF, England. *Telephone:* 01-736 3141.

ESSY, Amara; Côte d'Ivoire diplomatist; b. 20 Dec. 1943, Bouake; four c.; head, Div. of Econ. Relations 1970; First Counsellor, Ivory Coast Embassy, Brazil 1971–73, Ivory Coast Mission to the UN 1973–75; Perm. Rep. to the UN Office, Geneva 1975–81, to UNIDO, Vienna 1975–81; Amb. to Switzerland 1978–81; Perm. Rep. to the UN, New York 1981–; participated in the following UN confs.: Law of the Sea (Caracas, Geneva, New York), Int. Women's Year (Mexico City), Econ. Co-operation among Developing Countries, UNCTAD (Nairobi, Manila) and of the codification of int. law; meetings of the Econ. and Social Council and Comm. on Human Rights. *Address:* Permanent Mission of Côte d'Ivoire to the United Nations, 46 East 47th Street, New York, N.Y. 10021, U.S.A.

ESTANG, Luc; French writer; b. 12 Nov. 1911, Paris; s. of Lucien Achille Marie Bastard and Marie Eugénie Peyroux; m. Suzanne Madeleine Bouchereau-Boisgontier 1939; one d.; ed. Artois and in Belgium; journalist and literary and dramatic critic, La Croix (Paris) 1934–55; Editorial Advisor to Editions du Seuil, Paris, weekly collaboration on radio; mem. jury of Prix Renaudot; Grand Prix de la Société des Gens de Lettres 1959; Grand prix de Littérature de l'Académie Française 1962, Prix Guillaume Apollinaire 1968, Grand Prix de la Société des Poètes français 1978, Chevalier de la Légion d'honneur, Officier des Arts et des Lettres, Officier de l'Ordre national du mérite. *Publications:* novels: Les stigmates, Cherchant qui dévorer, Les fontaines du grand abîme, L'interrogatoire, L'horloger du cherche-midi, Le bonheur et le salut, Que ces mots répondent, L'apostat, La fille à l'oursin, Il était un p'tit homme, Boislevent, Les déicides, Les Femmes de M. Legouvé, Le loup meurt en silence, Le démon de pitié, Celle qui Venait du Rêve 1989; poetry: Les quatre éléments, Les béatitudes, D'une nuit noire et blanche, La laisse du temps; Corps à Coeur; essays: Le passage du Seigneur, Présence de Bernanos, Saint-Exupéry par lui-même, Ce que je crois, Invitation à la poésie; play: Le jour de Caïn. *Address:* 28 rue de l'Université, 75007 Paris, France. *Telephone:* 42.61.23.61.

ESTES, William K., PH.D.; American behavioural scientist; b. 17 June 1919, Minneapolis, Minn.; s. of Dr. George D. Estes and Mona Kaye; m. Katherine Walker 1942; two s.; ed. Univ. of Minnesota; Medical admin. officer U.S. Army 1944–46; Faculty mem. Indiana Univ. 1946–62; Prof. of Psychology Stanford Univ. 1962–68; Ed. Journal of Comparative and Physiological Psychology 1962–68, Psychological Review 1977–82; Prof., Rockefeller Univ. 1968–79; Prof., Harvard Univ. 1979–; Pres. Experimental Div., American Psychological Assen. 1958; Chair. Office of Scientific and Eng. Personnel, Nat. Research Council 1982–85; Chair., Cttee. on Contribs. of the Behavioral and Social Sciences to the Prevention of Nuclear War, N.A.S. 1985–; Guggenheim Fellow 1985–86; Chair. Psychonomic Soc. 1972, Soc. for Math. Psychology 1984; mem. Soc. of Experimental Psychologists, N.A.S., American Acad. of Arts and Sciences, etc.; Distinguished Scientific Contribution Award of American Psychological Assen. 1962, Warren Medal for Psychological Research 1963. *Publications:* An Experimental Study of Punishment 1944, Modern Learning Theory (with S. Koch and others) 1954, The Statistical Approach to Learning Theory 1959, Studies in Mathematical

Learning Theory (with R. R. Bush) 1959, Stimulus Sampling Theory (with E. Neimark) 1967, Learning Theory and Mental Development 1970, Handbook of Learning and Cognitive Processes (ed.) 1975, Models of Learning, Memory, and Choice 1982. *Leisure interest:* music. *Address:* William James Hall, Harvard University, Cambridge, Mass. 02138, U.S.A. *Telephone:* 617-495-3899.

ESTEVE-COLL, Elizabeth, B.A., F.R.S.A.; British museum director; ed. Birkbeck Coll., Univ. of London; librarian, London Borough of Merton, Kingston Coll. of Art, Kingston Polytechnic 1968-77; Head, Dept. of Learning Resources, Kingston Polytechnic 1977-82; Univ. Librarian Univ. of Surrey, Chair. Arts Cttee. 1982-85; Chief Librarian, Nat. Art Library, Victoria & Albert Museum 1985-87; Dir. Victoria & Albert Museum Jan. 1988-; Assoc. Library Asscn. *Address:* Victoria & Albert Museum, South Kensington, London, SW7 2RL, England. *Telephone:* 01-938 8361/3/4.

ESTIER, Claude; French journalist and politician; b. 8 June 1925, Paris; s. of Henri Ezratty and Luice Bernerbe; m. Denyse Abeille 1947; one d.; ed. Lycée Carnot, Paris; Political Ed. Le Populaire 1947; Ed. L'Observateur, France-Observateur, then le Nouvel Observateur 1950-; Ed. Le Monde 1955-58; Ed.-in-Chief Libération 1958-64, Dire 1968; mem. Nat. Assembly 1967-68, 1981-86; Pres. Comm. for Foreign Affairs 1983-86; mem. Paris City Council 1971-; Nat. Press Sec. Socialist Party 1971-79; Editorial Dir. L'Unité (Socialist Party Weekly) 1972-; mem. European Parl. 1979-81; Senator Sept. 1986-, Pres. Socialist Group 1988. *Publications:* Pour l'Algérie 1963, L'Egypte en révolution 1965, Journal d'un Fédéré 1969, La plume au poing 1977, Mitterrand Président 1981, Veridique histoire d'un Septennat (with Veronique Neiertz). *Address:* Palais du Luxembourg, 75291 Paris cedex 06; 12 rue Cortot, 75018 Paris, France (Home).

ETAIX, Pierre; French film director and actor; b. 23 Nov. 1928, Roanne; s. of Pierre and Berthe (née Tacher) Etaix; m. 2nd Annie Fratellini 1969; ed. lycée; apprenticed as stained-glass designer; Asst. film producer 1949-55; small part in Robert Bresson's Pickpocket 1959; leading role in Jacques Tati's Jour de Fête, Paris Olympia 1960; Chevalier, Ordre nat. du Mérite, Ordre des Arts et des Lettres; directed first short film Rupture 1961; other short films; Heureux anniversaire 1962 (Acad. Award ("Oscar") for best short film 1963), Insomnie (First Prize, Oberhausen Festival 1965); full-length films: Le soupirant 1963 (Prix Louis Delluc, Prize for best humorous film, Moscow Festival 1963), Yoyo 1964 (Grand Prix de l'O.C.I.C., Grand Prix pour la Jeunesse, Cannes 1965), Tant qu'on a la santé 1966 (Coquille d'Argent, Saint-Sebastian Festival), Le grand amour 1969 (Grand Prix du Cinéma Français, Grand Prix de l'O.C.I.C. 1969), Les clowns 1970, Pays de cocagne 1971, Sérieux comme le plaisir 1975, Max mon amour 1986. *Publications:* Vive la pub. 1984, Stars System 1986 (both jtly.). *Address:* 8 passage Lepic, 75018 Paris, France.

ETAYO MIQUEO, José Javier; Spanish professor of mathematics; b. 28 March 1926, Pamplona; s. of Nicolás Etayo and María Miqueo; m. Laura Gordejuela 1956; four s.; ed. Univs. of Valladolid, Zaragoza and Madrid; Prof. Univ. of Madrid 1952-61; Full Prof. Univ. of Zaragoza; Full Prof. of Math. Univ. Complutense of Madrid 1963-; Vice-Dean Faculty of Sciences, Univ. of Madrid 1971-75; Pres. Real Soc. Matemática Española 1976-82; mem. Consejo Superior de Investigaciones Científicas 1969, Spanish Cttee. Int. Math. Union 1979-85; mem. Real Acad. de Ciencias de Madrid 1983-. *Publications:* Gen. math. and geometry textbooks, various math. research papers. *Leisure interests:* reading, music, theatre, cinema. *Address:* Facultad de Ciencias Matemáticas, Universidad Complutense, 28040 Madrid (Univ.); Av. Reina Victoria, 70, 4 B, 28003 Madrid, Spain (Home). *Telephone:* 4490053 (Univ.); 2541173 (Home).

ETCHEGARAY, A. E. Cardinal Roger, D.IUR.UTR.; French ecclesiastic; b. 25 Sept. 1922, Espelette; s. of Jean-Baptiste Etchegaray and Aurélie Dufau; ed. Petit Séminaire, Ustaritz, and Grand Séminaire, Bayonne; ordained priest 1947, served diocese of Bayonne 1947-60; Asst. Sec., then Sec.-Gen. French Episcopal Conf. 1961-70, Pres. 1975-81; Archbishop of Marseilles 1970-84; Pres. Council of European Episcopal Confs. 1971-79; Prelate, Mission of France 1975-81; cr. Cardinal 1979; Pres. Comm. Justice and Peace 1984-; Pres. Council Cor Unum 1984-; Officier, Légion d'honneur. *Publications:* Dieu à Marseille 1976, J'avance comme un âne 1984. *Address:* Piazza San Calisto, Città del Vaticano, Italy. *Telephone:* 698 71 91.

ETCHEVERRY, Michel Adrien; French actor; b. 16 Dec. 1919, Saint-Jean-de-Luz; s. of Paul and Marie (née Manton) Etcheverry; m. Jacqueline Hebel 1947; one s. one d.; ed. Teacher Training Coll., Gironde, Conservatoire d'Art Dramatique, Bordeaux, Conservatoire National Supérieur d'Art Dramatique; began career as teacher, Saint-Sulpice-de-Faleyrens 1940; actor with Louis Jouvet 1945-51, appearing in productions including L'école des femmes, Knock, Le Diable et le bon Dieu, Pygmalion, L'alouette, Le journal d'Anne Frank, L'annonce faite à Marie; assoc. mem. Comédie-Française 1961-63, mem. 1963-, appearing in productions including Nicomède, Cinna, Polyeucte, L'avare, Marie Stuart, Le maître de Santiago, Le Cardinal d'Espagne, La reine morte, Le Cid, Le carrosse du Saint Sacrement, La Rabouilleuse, La soif et la faim, L'otage, L'école des femmes, Dom Juan, Malatesta, Le bourgeois gentilhomme, Georges Dandin, Un fil à la patte, L'impromptu de Marigny, C'est la guerre Monsieur Gruber, La nostalgie, Camarade, Le légataire universel, Le médecin malgré

lui, La Célestine, La nuit des rois, Cinna, Monsieur le Trouhadec saisi par la débauche, La poudre aux yeux, On ne badine pas avec l'amour, Meurtre dans la cathédrale, Met en scène les Fausses Confidences. *Films include:* Le fils de Caroline Chérie, Notre-Dame de Paris, Le salaire du péché, C'est arrivé à Aden, Michel Strogoff, Recours en grâce, Vers l'extase, Le passage du Rhin, Le puits aux 3 vérités, Le petit garçon de l'ascenseur, Amours célèbres, Mathias Sandorf, Le tigre se parfume à la dynamite, Paris brûle-t-il?, Perceval le Gallois, I ... comme Icare; numerous TV appearances including Les loups, La dévotion à la croix, Quatre-vingt treize, L'île mystérieuse, Un bourgeois de Calais, Cinna, Le Cid, Le roi Lear, Le fil rouge, Un bourgeois de Paris, Georges Dandin, Le Maître de Santiago, Le deuil sied à Electre, Le légataire universel, Le jeu de l'amour et du hasard 1976; Pres. French Actors' Union 1959, Membre du Droit 1963; Chevalier de la Légion d'honneur, Officier des Arts et des Lettres. *Address:* 47 rue de Borrego, 75020 Paris, France.

ETEKI MBOUMOUA, William-Aurélien, LIC. EN DROIT; Cameroonian politician; b. 20 Oct. 1933, Douala; s. of Joseph Mboumoua and Mana Katta; m. Naimi Betty Eyewe; one s. one d.; ed. Ecole Nat. de la France d'Outremer, Paris; Prefect for Nkam 1959; for Sanage Maritime 1960-61; Minister of Educ., Youth and Culture 1961-68; mem. Exec. Council, UNESCO 1962-68, Pres. of Conf., UNESCO 1968-70; Special Adviser, with rank of Minister, to Pres. of United Republic of Cameroon 1971-74, 1978-80; Minister charged with Special Functions at the Presidency 1978; Co-Minister in charge of Missions 1980-84, Minister of Foreign Affairs 1984-87; Sec.-Gen. OAU 1974-78; Commdr. des Palmes académiques, and many other decorations. *Publications:* Un certain humanisme 1970, Démocratiser la culture 1974, and many articles on education and African culture. *Leisure interests:* literature, poetry, painting, tennis, football, swimming. *Address:* c/o National Assembly, Yaoundé, Cameroon. *Telephone:* Yaoundé 22-13-28.

ETEMADI, Nour Ahmad; Afghan diplomatist and politician; b. 22 Feb. 1921, Qandahar; ed. Istiqlal Lyceum and Kabul Univ.; fmr. diplomatic posts in London and Washington; Econ. Section, Ministry of Foreign Affairs 1953-64, Deputy Minister of Foreign Affairs 1963, Minister 1965-71; Amb. to Pakistan 1964; Prime Minister 1967-71; Amb. to Italy 1972-73, to U.S.S.R. (also accred. to Finland and Romania) 1973-74, 1975-76, to Pakistan 1976-78; arrested 1978. *Address:* Pule Charchi Prison, Kabul, Afghanistan.

ETHERINGTON, Edwin Deacon, B.A., LL.B.; American attorney and executive; b. 25 Dec. 1924, Bayonne, N.J.; s. of late Charles Kenneth Etherington and Ethel Bennett; m. Katherine Colean 1953; three s.; ed. Lawrenceville School, N.J., Wesleyan Univ. and Yale Law School; Instructor and Asst. to Dean, Wesleyan Univ. 1948-49; Law Clerk, Hon. Henry W. Edgerton, U.S. Court of Appeal, Washington, D.C. 1952-53; Attorney, Wilmer and Broun, Washington, D.C. 1953-54, Milbank, Tweed, Hadley, New York 1954-56; Sec. New York Stock Exchange 1956-58, Vice-Pres. 1958-61; Partner, Pershing Co., New York 1961-62; Trustee, National Urban Coalition, Alfred P. Sloan Foundation 1969-76; Dir. American Express Co., American Express Int. Bank, American Can Co., Automatic Data Processing, Inc., United States Trust Co. of New York; Pres. American Stock Exchange 1962-66; Pres. Wesleyan Univ. 1967-70, now Pres. Emer.; Pres. Nat. Center for Voluntary Action, Washington, D.C. 1971-72, Chair. 1972-; Counsel, Reid and Reige, P.C., Hartford, Conn. (law firm); Chair. Nat. Advertising Review Bd. 1973-74; Chair. Governor's Comm. on Services and Expenditures (for State of Conn.) 1971; mem. and official of several civic socs. and orgs.; Hon. LL.D. (Wesleyan Univ. and Amherst Coll. Mass.) 1965, (Trinity) 1967, (Amherst) 1968; Hon. L.H.D. (American Int. Coll.) 1967; Citizen of the Year Award, Conn. 1972. *Publications:* numerous articles. *Leisure interest:* golf. *Address:* 102 Bassett Creek Trail, Hobe Sound, Fla. 33455, U.S.A.

ETIANG, Paul Orono, B.A.; Ugandan diplomatist; b. 15 Aug. 1938, Tororo; s. of Kezironi Orono and Mirabu Adacat Adeke; m. Zahra A. Foum 1967; two s. two d.; ed. Busoga Coll. and Makerere Univ. Coll.; District Officer, Provincial Admin. 1962-64; Asst. Sec., Ministry of Foreign Affairs 1964-65, Third Sec. 1965-66; Second Sec., Uganda Embassy, Moscow 1966-67; First Sec. Uganda Mission to UN 1967-68; First Sec. 1968; High Commr. to U.K. 1969-71; Chief of Protocol and Marshal of Diplomatic Corps, Uganda 1971-; Perm. Sec. Ministry of Foreign Affairs 1971-73, Acting Minister of Foreign Affairs May-Oct. 1973; Minister of State for Foreign Affairs 1973-74; of State 1974-76, of Transport and Communications 1976-78, of Transport 1978-79, for Regional Co-operation 1988-; Asst. Sec.-Gen. OAU 1978-87. *Leisure interests:* billiards, badminton, music, theatre. *Address:* Ministry for Regional Co-operation, P.O. Box 4411, Kampala, Uganda.

ETIEMBLE, René, D. ÈS L.; French professor emeritus of literature and writer; b. 26 Jan. 1909, Mayenne; m. Jeannine Kohn 1963; one d.; ed. Lycée de Laval, Lycée Louis le Grand, Ecole Normale Supérieure and Fondation Thiers; Faculté de droit, Ecole des langues orientales; Prof. Univ. of Chicago 1937-43, Univ. of Alexandria, Egypt 1944-48, Univ. of Montpellier 1949-55; Prof. of Gen. and Comparative Literature, Univ. of Paris (Sorbonne) 1956-78, Hon. Prof. 1979; mem. Istituto Veneto di Scienze, Lettere ed Arti; Prix de la Première Pièce 1948, Prix de l'Essai, Acad. Française, Prix Int. du Livre 1981, Prix de l'Union Rationaliste 1982,

Grand prix 1982, Ecrivain de 1986, P.E.N. Club français. *Publications include:* Rimbaud (with Y. Gauclère) 1936, L'enfant de choeur 1937, Peaux de couleuvre 1948, Le mythe de Rimbaud (3 vols. 1952–61—Prix Sainte-Beuve de la Critique), Supervielle 1960, Blason d'un corps 1961, Parlez-vous franglais? 1964, Hygiène de lettres (5 vols.) 1952–67, Le nouveau singe pèlerin 1958, Le jargon des sciences 1966, Le sonnet des voyelles 1968, Retours du monde 1969, Mes contre-poisons 1974; on China: Confucius 1956, Le nouveau singe filérin 1958, Connaissons-nous la Chine 1964, Les Jésuites en Chine 1966, Yun Yun, l'érotique chinoise 1969, Essais de littérature (vraiment) générale 1974, Quarante ans de mon maoïsme 1976, Colloque sur la traduction poétique 1978, Philosophes Taoïstes 1980, Comment lire un roman japonais 1980, Trois femmes de race 1981, Quelques essais de litterature universelle 1982, Rimbaud: système solaire ou trou noir 1983, Le coeur et la cendre, soixante ans de poésie 1984, Racismes 1986, Confucius 551–1985, 1986, Goliath ou la mache on fascisme (trans.) 1986, L'Europe chinoise 1987, Romanciers du XVIIIe siècle (ed.) 1988. *Address:* 4 rue de la Paletière, Vigny 28500 Vernouillet, France.

ETIENNE-MARTIN, (pseudonym of Martin, Etienne); French sculptor; b. 4 Feb. 1913, Loriol; s. of Etienne Martin Greffier and Marie Tagliazucelli-Corneau; m. 1st Annie Talboutier, three s.; m. 2nd Marie-Thérèse Le Balc'h; ed. Lycée de Valence, Ecole des Beaux Arts, Lyons, Acad. Ranson, Paris and atelier of sculptor Charles Malfray; Prof. Ecole des Appliqués 1958–60, Ecole Américaine de Fontainebleau 1958–, Ecole Nat. Supérieure des Beaux Arts, Atelier d'Art Monumental, Paris 1967–; exhbns. at Salon de Mai et des Réalités Nouvelles; numerous exhbns. in France, Europe and U.S.A.; retrospective exhbns. at Musée Rodin 1972, Centre Georges Pompidou 1984; mem. Inst. de France (Acad. des Beaux Arts); numerous awards including First Prize Venice Biennale 1966, Grand Prix Nat. des Arts 1967, Copley Foundation Prize 1967, Grand Prix des Arts de la Ville de Paris 1977; Chevalier, Légion d'honneur; Officier, Ordre Nat. du Mérite, Commdr. des Arts et des Lettres. *Address:* 7 rue du Pont de Fer, 75005 Paris (Office); 49 quai de Bourbon, 75004 Paris, France (Home).

ETKIND, Efim Grigorievich; literary scholar; b. 26 Feb. 1918, Petrograd (now Leningrad); s. of Grigori Etkind and Polina Spivak; m. Katherina Zvorykina 1940; two d.; ed. Leningrad Univ.; served in Soviet army in Second World War on Karelian and Ukrainian fronts; Candidate of Philol. Sc. 1947 (dissertation on Novels of Zola in 1860s); taught in Faculty of Romance Langs., Leningrad Pedagogical Inst. 1947–74; Dr. Philol. Sc. 1965 (dissertion on Theory of Translation); degrees and title of Prof. removed and expelled from U.S.S.R. Union of Writers for defence of various poets 1974; left U.S.S.R. Oct. 1974; Docteur d'État 1975 (Sorbonne; dissertation on Theory of Poetic Translation); now lives in Paris, and teaches at Université de Paris X; Corresp. mem. Bayerischen Akademie der Schönen Künste, Akad. der Wissenschaften und der Literatur zu Mainz, Deutschen Akad. für Sprache und Dichtung, Darmstadt. *Publications include:* Poetry and Translation 1963; Russian Poet-Translators from Trediakovsky to Pushkin 1973, The Substance of Verse and the Problems of the Theory of Translation 1974, Notes of a Non-Conspirator 1977 (Paris), Form as Content (articles) 1977 (Würzburg); Un art en crise (Essai d'une poétique de la traduction poétique) 1981; Russische Lyrik aus drei Jahrhunderten 1981, Anna Achmatowa 1982, Poésie russe (anthology) 1983, Russische Lyrik des 20. Jahrhunderts 1984. *Address:* Université de Paris X, 200 Avenue de la République, 92000 Nanterre, Paris (Office); 31 Jardins Boieldieu, 92800 Puteaux, France (Home). *Telephone:* 47 76 34 86.

ETO, Takami; Japanese politician; b. 1925; fmr. mem. Miyazaki Prefectural Ass., elected mem. House of Reps. for 1st Constituency Miyazaki Prefecture 1969; fmrly. Dir. House of Reps. Rules and Admin. Cttee., Parl. Vice-Minister of Agric., Forestry and Fisheries; Deputy Chair. Liberal Democratic Party Policy Research Council, Chair. Diet Affairs Cttee. Oct. 1984–; Minister of Construction 1985–86; Liberal Democratic Party. *Address:* House of Representatives, Tokyo, Japan.

ETOUNGOU, Simon Nko'o; Cameroonian diplomatist and politician; b. 14 Feb. 1932; ed. secondary and post-secondary schools, and diplomatic training in France; Head of Office in Ministry of Econ. Planning 1956–57; Cabinet Attaché, Ministry of Finance 1958–59; First Sec., Cameroon Embassy, Paris 1960; Minister-Counsellor 1960–61; Amb. to Tunisia 1961–64; led numerous Cameroon dels. 1963–64; concurrently Amb. to Algeria July-Nov. 1964, to U.S.S.R. 1964–65; Minister of Foreign Affairs 1965–66, 1968–70, Minister of Finance 1966–68; Amb. to Belgium, Netherlands and Luxembourg and Perm. Rep. to EEC 1971–79; Amb. to Algeria 1985–88, to France 1988–; Kt. of Nat. Order of Merit (Cameroon), and decorations from Senegal, Tunisia, Fed. Repub. of Germany and Gabon. *Address:* c/o Ambassade du Cameroun, 73 rue d'Auteuil, 75016 Paris, France. *Telephone:* (1) 47 43 4833.

ETROG, Sorel; Canadian sculptor; b. 29 Aug. 1933, Jassy, Romania; ed. Jassy High School and Tel Aviv Art Inst.; Brooklyn Museum Art School Scholarship 1958; first one-man show 1958; Canadian rep. Venice Biennale 1966; commissions include Los Angeles Co. Museum 1966, Canadian Pavilion, Expo 67, Olympic Centre, Toronto 1972, Bow Valley Square, Calgary 1975, SunLife Canada. Toronto 1984; works now in numerous public collections including Nat. Gallery of Canada, Tate Gallery, London, Musée d'Art Moderne, Paris, Museum of Modern Art, New York etc.; one-man exhbns. in Montreal, Toronto, New York, Paris, London, Chicago, Los Angeles, Geneva, Amsterdam, Venice, Milan, Rome; designer and illustrator of books; wrote and dir. film Spiral (CBC) 1975; mem. Royal Canadian Acad., Arts and Letters Club. *Publications include:* Dream Chamber 1982, Hinges (play) 1983, The Kite 1984. *Address:* Box 5943, Station A, Toronto, Ont. M5W 1P3, Canada.

ETZDORF, Hasso von, LL.D.; German diplomatist; b. 2 March 1900; ed. Univs. of Berlin, Göttingen and Halle; held various posts at Foreign Office and diplomatic appointments in Tokyo, Rome, Genoa, etc.; Chief of German Del. to Interim Cttee. for European Defence Community (EDC), Paris 1953; Deputy Sec.-Gen. Western European Union (WEU), London 1955; Amb. to Canada 1956–58; Deputy Under-Sec. of State, Foreign Office 1958–61; Amb. to U.K. 1961–65; Hon. G.C.V.O. *Address:* Eichtling, 8018 Grafing, München, Federal Republic of Germany. *Telephone:* 08093-1402.

ETZWILER, Donnell Dencil, B.A.; American pediatrician; b. 29 March 1927, Mansfield, Ohio; s. of Donnell S. Etzwiler and Berniece J. Etzwiler; m. Marion Grassby Etzwiler 1952; one s. three d.; ed. Indiana and Yale Univs.; Intern, Yale-Grace New Haven Community Hosp. 1953–54; Resident, New York Hosp., Cornell Medical Center 1954–55, N.I.H. Fellowship in Metabolism 1956–57; Instructor, Cornell Univ. Medical Coll., New York 1956–57; Clinical Prof., Univ. of Minn. School of Medicine 1957–; Pediatrician, Park Nicollet Medical Center, Minn. 1957–; Medical Dir., Camp Needlepoint 1960–85; Pediatrician, Project Hope, Peru 1962; Dir. Int. Diabetes Center 1967–, Vice-Pres. Int. Diabetes Fed. 1979–85; Commr., Nat. Comm. on Diabetes 1975–76; Pres. American Diabetes Asscn. 1976–77; Convenor, Int. Diabetes Fed. 1980–; Dir. Diabetes Collaborating Center, WHO 1985–; Banting Medal 1977, Upjohn Award 1983, Beckton Dickinson Camp Award 1979, Diabetes in Youth Award 1976, American Diabetes Asscn.; Fellow, All India Inst. of Diabetes, Bombay 1979; Fellow, Inst. of Medicine, N.A.S. 1981. *Publications:* Education Management of the Patient with Diabetes 1973, Diabetes Manual; Health Education for Living Program 1976, Living Well With Diabetes 1985; Ed. First International Workshop on Diabetes and Camping 1974; over 90 scientific articles in medical journals. *Leisure interests:* tennis, photography, travel. *Address:* International Diabetes Center, 5000 West 39th Street, Minneapolis, Minn. 55416, U.S.A. *Telephone:* (612) 927-3393.

EURICH, Richard Ernst, O.B.E., R.A.; British painter; b. 14 March 1903, Bradford, Yorks.; s. of F. W. Eurich and Gwendolen Carter-Squire; m. Mavis Pope 1934; four c. (two deceased); ed. Bradford Grammar School, Bradford School of Arts and Crafts and Slade School, London; one-man exhbn. (drawings) Goupil Gallery, London 1929; subsequent exhbns.: 16 exhbns. of paintings, Redfern Gallery, London 1932–60, three exhbns. of paintings, Tooth's Gallery, London 1968–75; Retrospective, Cartwright Hall, Bradford 1950, 1976; Ash Barn, Petersfield 1984; Fine Art Soc. "Eurion at 80" 1983; Hunting Group Prize 1980. *Address:* c/o Fine Art Society, 148 New Bond Street, London, W1Y 0JT; Appletreewick, 4 West Road, Dibden Purlieu, Southampton, Hants., SO4 5RJ, England (Home). *Telephone:* (0703) 842291 (Home).

EUSTACE, Sir Joseph Lambert; St. Vincent and the Grenadines politician; b. 1908; teacher, then politician; became govt. minister; retd., then apptd. Gov.-Gen. of St. Vincent and the Grenadines 1985–. *Address:* Governor General's Residence, Kingstown, Saint Vincent and the Grenadines.

EVANS, Daniel Jackson, M.S.; American politician; b. 16 Oct. 1925, Seattle, Wash.; s. of Daniel Lester and Irma (Ide) Evans; m. Nancy Ann Bell 1959; three s.; ed. Roosevelt High School, Seattle, and Univ. of Washington; U.S.N.R. 1943–46; Lieut. on active duty Korean War 1951–53; Asst. Man. Mountain Pacific Chapter, Assoc. Gen. Contractors 1953–59; State Rep. King County 1956–64; Partner, Gray and Evans, structural and civil engineers 1959–64; Gov. Washington State 1965–77; Chair. Western Govs. Conf. 1968–69, Nat. Govs. Conf. 1973–74; Senator from Washington 1983–89; mem. Advisory Comm. on Intergovernmental Relations 1972, Trilateral Comm. 1973; Keynote Speaker Republican Nat. Convention 1968; mem. Pres.'s Vietnamese Refugee Comm. 1974; mem. Nat. Center for Productivity and Quality of Working Life 1975–76; mem. Carnegie Council on Policy Studies in Higher Educ. 1977; Trustee Urban Inst. 1977, The Carnegie Foundation for the Advancement of Teaching 1977; Pres. Evergreen State Coll. 1977–83; several hon. degrees; Nat. Municipal League Distinguished Citizen Award 1977; Republican. *Leisure interests:* skiing, sailing, mountain climbing.

EVANS, David Stanley, F.R.S.S.A., F.R.A.S., PH.D.; British professor of astronomy (retd.); b. 28 Jan. 1916, Cardiff; s. of Arthur Cyril Evans and Kate (née Priest) Evans; m. Betty Hall Hart 1948; two s.; ed. Cardiff High School, King's, Coll., Cambridge; Research Asst., Univ. Observatory, Oxford 1938–46; Second Asst. Radcliffe Observatory, Pretoria, S.A. 1946–51; Chief Asst. Royal Observatory, Cape 1951–68; Prof. of Astronomy, Univ. of Tex. at Austin 1968, Jack Josey Centennial Prof. 1966–68, 1986–; Assoc. Dir. for Research McDonald Observatory 1968–81; mem. American Astronomical Soc., Int. Astronomical Union; Fellow British Inst. of Physics; Hon. Citizen (Texas); Tyson Medal 1938, Macintyre Award, Astronomical Soc. S.A. 1972, Gill Medal, Astronomical Soc. S.A. 1988. *Publications:* Teach Yourself Astronomy 1952, Observation in Modern Astronomy 1968, Ed. (with others) Herschel at the Cape 1968, Big and Bright (with D.

Mulholland) 1986, Under Capricorn 1988, Frontiers of Astronomy 1944, 200 scientific papers. *Leisure interests:* gardening, squash, history of astronomy. *Address:* 6001 Mountainclimb Drive, Austin, Tex. 78731, U.S.A. *Telephone:* (512) 454-9496.

EVANS, David Wyke, M.A.; Australian diplomatist; b. 13 March 1934, Adelaide; s. of Dr Mervyn W. Evans and Phyllis E. Evans; m. Pamela R. Stratmann 1959; two s. one d.; ed. Prince Alfred Coll., Adelaide, and Univs. of Adelaide and Oxford; joined Australian Commonwealth Public Service 1959; Third (later Second) Sec., Embassy in Jakarta 1962-65; First Sec. Australian Mission to UN, New York 1968-70; Counsellor, Belgrade 1970-72; High Commr. in Ghana (and Amb. to Senegal and Ivory Coast) 1974-77; Head of Information Branch, Dept. of Foreign Affairs 1977-79, Head of Europe, Americas and N.Z. Div. 1980; Amb. to U.S.S.R. (also accred. to Mongolia) 1981-83; High Commr. in Malaysia 1984-87; Deputy High Commr. in U.K. 1987-; Rhodes Scholar 1957. *Leisure interests:* tennis, golf. *Address:* Australia House, Strand, London, WC2B 4LA, England. *Telephone:* 01-438 8211.

EVANS, Dennis Frederick, F.R.S.; British professor of chemistry; b. 27 March 1928, Nottingham; s. of George Frederick and Gladys Martha Evans; ed. Nottingham High School and Lincoln Coll., Oxford; ICI Research Fellow, Oxford 1952-53, 1954-56; Research Assoc., Univ. of Chicago, U.S.A. 1953-54; lecturer in Inorganic Chem. Imperial Coll., London 1956-63, Sr. lecturer 1963-64, Reader 1964-81, Prof. of Inorganic Chem. 1981-. *Publications:* articles in various scientific journals. *Leisure interests:* wine, travel, ornithology, marathon-running and homicide. *Address:* Department of Chemistry, Imperial College of Science, London, S.W.7 (Office); 64 Cathcart Road, London, S.W.10, England (Home). *Telephone:* 01-589 5111, Ext. 4579 (Office); 01-352 6540 (Home).

EVANS, Earl Alison, Jr., PH.D.; American biochemist; b. 11 March 1910, Baltimore, Md.; s. of Earl Alison and Florence (Lewis) Evans; ed. Baltimore Polytechnic Inst., Johns Hopkins and Columbia Univs.; Asst. Pharmacology, School of Medicine, Johns Hopkins Univ. 1931-32, Asst. endocrine research 1932-34; Univ. Fellow in Biochemistry, Columbia Univ. 1934-36; Instructor in Biochemistry, Chicago Univ. 1937-39, Asst. Prof. 1939-41, Assoc. Prof. and Act. Chair. of Dept. 1941-42, Prof. 1942-, Chair. of Dept. 1942-72; Reserve Officer, U.S. Foreign Service, Chief Scientific Officer, American Embassy, London 1947-48; Consultant to Sec. of State 1951-53; mem. Bd. of Scientific Counsellors, Nat. Inst. of Arthritis and Metabolic Diseases, Nat. Insts. of Health 1960-63; mem. Div. Cttee. for Biological and Medical Sciences, Nat. Science Foundation 1963-66; Chair. Postdoctoral Fellowship Cttee., Div. of Biology and Agriculture, N.A.S., Nat. Research Council 1963-65; mem. Air Force Office of Scientific Research Fellowship Bd. 1966-, Advisory Bd. American Foundation for Continuing Educ. 1962-; Rockefeller Fellow, Univ. of Sheffield, England 1940-41; Fellow, All Souls Coll., Oxford 1968-69; Fellow, Pierpont Morgan Library 1969-, Welch Lecturer (Houston) 1972; mem. A.C.S. Soc. for Experimental Biology and Medicine, British Biochemical Soc., American Soc. of Biological Chemists, American Soc. of Bacteriologists; Hon. mem. Asociación Química Argentina; Fellow A.A.A.S.; Eli Lilly Medal of A.C.S. 1941. *Publications:* Biochemical Studies of Bacterial Viruses 1952; co-author: Biological Symposia V 1941, Symposium of Respiratory Enzymes 1942; Editor: Biological Action of The Vitamins 1942. *Address:* 1120 N. Lake Shore Drive, Chicago, Ill. 60611, U.S.A. *Telephone:* 312-753-3960 (Office).

EVANS, Edwin C., B.S., M.D.; American physician; b. 30 June 1917, Milledgeville, Ga.; s. of Watt Collier and Bertha (Chambers) Evans; m. Marjorie Wood 1945; one s. five d.; ed. Univ. of Georgia, Johns Hopkins Univ. School of Medicine; Intern Hartford (Connecticut) Hosp. 1940-42; Medical Corps, U.S. army 1942-46; Chief Resident in Medicine, Baltimore City Hosp. 1946-47; Fellow in Pathology, Hosp. of Univ. of Pa. 1947-48; private practice of Internal Medicine in Atlanta, Georgia 1948-87; Clinical Assoc. Prof. of Medicine, Emory Univ. School of Medicine, Atlanta 1972-, Prof. Emer. 1987-; Adjunct Prof. of Medicine, Mercer Univ. School of Pharmacy, Atlanta 1980-; Dir. of Geriatrics, Georgia Baptist Medical Center 1987-; mem. N.A.S. Inst. of Medicine, and numerous medical asscns. *Publications:* a number of contributions to medical journals. *Leisure interest:* photography. *Address:* Georgia Baptist Medical Center, 300 Boulevard, N.E., Atlanta, Ga. 30312 (Office); 500 Westover Drive, N.W., Atlanta, Ga. 30305, U.S.A. (Home). *Telephone:* (404) 653-3591 (Office); (404) 355-2203 (Home).

EVANS, Gareth John, Q.C., M.A., LL.B.; Australian politician; b. 5 Sept. 1944, Melbourne; s. of late Allan O. Evans and of Phyllis Evans (née Le Boeuf; m. Merran Anderson 1969; one s. one d.; ed. Melbourne High School, Univ. of Melbourne, Magdalen Coll., Oxford; lecturer and Senior lecturer in Law, Univ. of Melbourne 1971-76; mem. Australian Reform Comm. 1975; Barrister-at-Law 1977-78; Senator for Victoria 1978-; 'Shadow' Attorney-Gen. 1980-83; Attorney-Gen. 1983-84; Minister for Resources and Energy, Minister Assisting the Prime Minister and Minister Assisting the Minister for Foreign Affairs 1984-87; Minister for Transport and Communications 1987-88, for Foreign Affairs and Trade 1988-; Deputy Leader of Govt. and Man. of Govt. Business in the Senate 1987-. *Publications:* Labor and the Constitution 1972-75 (Ed.) 1977, Law, Politics and the Labor Movement (Ed.) 1980, Labor Essays 1980, 1981, 1982 (Co-Ed.), Australia's Constitution—Time for Change? 1983 (Co-author). *Leisure interests:* read-

ing, tennis, travel, food. *Address:* Parliament House, Canberra, A.C.T. 2600; 4 Treasury Place, Melbourne, Vic. 3000, Australia.

EVANS, Sir Geraint Llewellyn, Kt., C.B.E.; British opera singer; b. 16 Feb. 1922, Pontypridd, Wales; m. Brenda Evans Davies 1948; two s.; ed. Guildhall School of Music; prin. baritone, Royal Opera House, Covent Garden 1948-84; has sung leading roles at: Glyndebourne Festival Opera, Vienna State Opera, La Scala (Milan), Metropolitan Opera (New York), San Francisco Opera, Lyric Opera (Chicago), Salzburg, Edinburgh Festival, Paris Opera, Teatro Colon (Buenos Aires), Mexico City, Welsh Nat. Opera, Scottish Opera, Berlin Opera, Teatr Wielki (Warsaw); Dir. Harlech TV; F.G.S.M. 1960; Hon. R.A.M. 1969; Hon. D.Mus. (Wales) 1965, (Leicester), F.R.C.M. 1981, Hon. D.Mus. (London) 1982, Council for Nat. Academic Awards (C.N.A.A.) 1980, Fellow, Univ. Coll., Cardiff 1976, Royal Northern Coll. of Music 1978, Royal Coll. of Music 1981, Univ. Coll of Wales 1987; Hon. Fellow, Jesus Coll., Oxford 1979; Dr. h.c. (Oxford) 1985; Worshipful Co. of Musicians Sir Charles Santley Memorial Award 1963, Harriet Cohen Int. Music Award (Opera Medal) 1967, Fidelio Medal 1980, San Francisco Opera Medal 1980. *Publication:* Sir Geraint Evans: a Knight at the Opera (with Noël Goodwin) 1984. *Address:* 17 Highcliffe, 32 Albemarle Road, Beckenham, Kent, England. *Telephone:* 01-650 3039.

EVANS, Gwynfor, M.A., LL.D.; Welsh politician; b. 1 Sept. 1912, Barry; s. of Dan and Catherine (née Richard) Evans; m. Rhiannon Prys Thomas 1940; four s. three d.; ed. Barry County School, Univ. Coll. of Wales, Aberystwyth, St. John's Coll., Oxford; qualified as solicitor 1939; Hon. Sec. Heddychwyr Cymru (Welsh Pacifist Movement) 1939-45; Chair. Union of Welsh Independents 1954; M.P. (Plaid Cymru), Carmarthen 1966-70, 1974-79; Pres. Plaid Cymru (Welsh Nationalist Party) 1945-81; mem. Carmarthen County Council 1949-74; mem. Court of Govs., Univ. of Wales and Univ. Coll., Aberystwyth; past mem. Welsh Broadcasting Council; Hon. LL.D. (Univ. of Wales) 1973; Hon. Pres. Plaid Cymru. *Publications:* Plaid Cymru and Wales 1950, Rhagom i Ryddid 1964, Aros Mae 1971, Wales can Win 1973, Land of My Fathers 1974, A National Future for Wales 1975, Diwedd Prydeindod, Bywyd Cymro 1982, Seiri Cenedl y Cymry 1986, Welsh Nation Builders 1988, Pe Bai Cymru'n Rhydd 1989. *Address:* Talar Wen, Pencarreg, Llanybydder, Dyfed, Wales. *Telephone:* Llanybydder 480907.

EVANS, Harold J., PH.D.; American plant physiologist; b. 19 Feb. 1921, Franklin, Ky.; s. of James H. and Allie Evans; m. Elizabeth Dunn 1946; two d.; ed. Univ. of Kentucky and Rutgers Univ.; Asst. Prof., Assoc. Prof., Prof. of Botany, N. Carolina State Univ. 1950-60; Post-doctoral Fellow, Johns Hopkins Univ. 1952; Prof. of Plant Physiology, Oregon State Univ. 1961-, Dir. Lab. for Nitrogen Fixation 1978-; Visiting Prof. Univ. of Sussex 1967; George A. Miller Visiting Prof. Univ. of Illinois 1973; Pres. American Soc. of Plant Physiologists 1971-, mem. Bd. of Trustees 1977; mem. Nat. Acad. of Sciences, 1971-; Hoblitzelle Nat. Award 1965, Oregon State Univ. Alumni Distinguished Prof. Award 1973, Milton Harris Research Award, George Ferguson Distinguished Prof. Award 1983; Univ. of Kentucky Distinguished Alumnus award 1975, Charles Ried Barnes Award, American Soc. of Plant Physiologists 1985, Distinguished Prof. of Plant Physiology, Oregon State Univ. 1988. *Publications:* Nitrogen Fixation Research Progress (Co-ed.) 1985; numerous articles in professional journals. *Address:* 2939 Mulkey Street, Corvallis, Ore. 97330, U.S.A. *Telephone:* (503) 752 3227.

EVANS, Harold Matthew, M.A.; British newspaper editor and writer; b. 28 June 1928, Manchester; s. of Fred and Mary Evans; m. 1st Enid Parker 1953 (divorced), one s. two d.; m. 2nd Tina Brown 1981, one s.; ed. Durham Univ.; Commonwealth Fund Fellow, Univ. of Chicago 1956-57; Ed. Sunday Times, London 1967-81, The Times 1981-82; mem. Bd. Times Newspapers Ltd., Dir. 1978-82; Int. Press Inst. 1974-80; Dir. Goldcrest Films and Television 1982-85; Ed.-in-Chief Atlantic Monthly 1984-86, Contributing Ed. 1986-; Ed. Dir. U.S. News and World Report 1984-86, Contributing Ed. 1986-; Adviser to Chair. Condé Nast Publications 1986-; Ed.-in-Chief, Condé Nast Traveler 1987-; Fellow, Soc. Industrial Artists, Inst. of Journalists; Dr. h.c. (Stirling); Journalist of the Year Prize 1973, Int. Ed. of the Year Award 1975, Inst. of Journalists Gold Medal Award 1979; Design and Art Dir., Pres.'s Award 1981, Ed. of Year Award, Granada 1982, Hord Medal, Royal Photographic Soc. 1981, Press Photographers of G.B. Award 1986. *Publications:* Active Newsroom 1964, Editing and Design, Newsman's English 1970, Newspaper Design 1971, Newspaper Headlines 1973, Newspaper Text 1973, We Learned to Ski (co-author) 1974, Freedom of the Press 1974, Pictures on a Page 1978, Suffer the Children (co-author), How We Learned to Ski 1983, Good Times, Bad Times 1983. *Leisure interests:* music, table tennis, skiing. *Address:* Condé Nast's Traveler, 360 Madison Avenue, New York, N.Y. 10017, U.S.A. *Telephone:* (212) 880 2120.

EVANS, John James, M.B.A.; American management consultant; b. 12 Aug. 1923, New York; s. of James J. Evans and Mary Galan; ed. Univ. of Nebraska, City Coll. of New York and New York Univ.; Man. Roman Silversmiths 1946-49; systems, Addressograph-Multigraph Corpn. 1949-53; Man. Consultant, Vice-Pres. Fairbanks Assocs. Greenwich Conn., Fairbanks Assocs. New York and Washington 1953-59, Pres. 1959-. *Publications:* articles in professional journals. *Address:* P.O. Box 1009, Alamo, Calif. 94507, U.S.A.

EVANS, John Robert, C.C., M.D., D.PHIL., F.R.C.P.; Canadian university administrator; b. 1 Oct. 1929; s. of William Watson (deceased) and Mary Evelyn Lucille (née Thompson) Evans (deceased); m. Jean Gay (née Glassco) 1954; four s. two d.; ed. Univ. of Toronto and Univ. Coll., Oxford; Resident in clinical medicine and Hon. Registrar, Nat. Heart Hosp., London, England 1955–56; Asst. Resident in medicine, Sunnybrook Hosp., Toronto 1956–57; Asst. Resident in medicine, Toronto Gen. Hosp. 1957–58, Chief Resident in medicine 1959–60; Ontario Heart Foundation Fellow, Hosp. for Sick Children, Toronto 1958–59; Research Fellow, Baker Clinic Research Lab., Harvard Medical School 1960–61; Markle Scholar in Academic Medicine, Univ. of Toronto 1960–65, Assoc. Dept. of Medicine 1961–65, Pres. Univ. of Toronto 1972–78, Prof. Dept. of Medicine 1978–; Dean, Faculty of Medicine and Prof. Dept. Medicine McMaster Univ. 1965–72, Vice-Pres. (Health Sciences) 1967–72; Chair. Nat. Health Grants, Dept. of Nat. Health and Welfare 1969–74; Dir. Population, Health and Nutrition Dept., World Bank 1979–83, WHO Adviser, Cttee. Medical Research 1976–80; Chair. and C.E.O. Allelix Inc. (Biotechnology), Mississauga, Ont. 1983–; Pres. Assoc. of Canadian Medical Colls. 1971; Dir. Alcan Aluminium Ltd., Dofasco Inc., Royal Bank of Canada, Southam Inc., Torstar Ltd.; Fellow, Royal Coll. of Physicians and Surgeons of Canada, Royal Coll. of Physicians (London), Inst. of Medicine, N.A.S. 1972–80, American Council on Clinical Cardiology; Master, American Coll. of Physicians; mem. numerous medical cttees. and socs.; 14 hon. degrees; Trustee, Rockefeller Foundation. *Leisure interests:* farming, conservation. *Address:* 58 Highland Avenue, Toronto, Ontario M4W 2A3, Canada.

EVANS, Lloyd Thomas, A.O., M.AGR.SCI., D.PHIL., D.SC.; Australian botanist; b. 6 Aug. 1927, Wanganui, New Zealand; s. of Claude Evans and Gwendolyn Fraser; m. Margaret Newell 1954; two s. two d. (one deceased); ed. Wanganui Collegiate School, Univ. of Canterbury, New Zealand, and Brasenose Coll., Oxford; Rhodes Scholar 1951–54; Commonwealth Fund Fellow, Calif. Inst. of Tech. 1954–56; Research Scientist, Div. of Plant Industry, Commonwealth Scientific and Industrial Research Org. (CSIRO) 1956–, Chief 1971–78; N.A.S. Pioneer Research Fellow, U.S. Dept. of Agric., Beltsville, U.S.A. 1963–64; Overseas Fellow, Churchill Coll., Cambridge 1969–70; Visiting Fellow, Wolfson Coll., Cambridge 1978; Pres. Australian Soc. of Plant Physiologists 1971–73, Australian and New Zealand Assen. for Advancement of Science 1976–77, Australian Acad. of Science 1978–82 (Fellow); mem. Bd. of Trustees, Int. Foundation for Science, Stockholm 1982–, Int. Rice Research Inst., Philippines 1984–; Hon. mem. Royal Soc., N.Z., Royal Agric. Soc., England; Hon. LL.D. (Canterbury) 1978; Fellow, Royal Soc., U.K.; Bledisloe Medal 1974, Farrer Medal 1979, other awards and prizes. *Leisure interests:* windsurfing, chopping wood, Charles Darwin. *Publications:* Environmental Control of Plant Growth 1963, The Induction of Flowering 1969, Crop Physiology 1975, Day-length and the Flowering of Plants 1975, Wheat Science—Today and Tomorrow 1981, Policy and Practice 1987, over 150 research papers. *Address:* 3 Elliott Street, Campbell, Canberra, A.C.T. 2601, Australia. *Telephone:* (062) 477815.

EVANS, Matthew, B.SC.(ECONS.); British publishing executive; b. 7 Aug. 1941; s. of George Ewart and Florence E. Evans; m. Elizabeth A. (née Mead) 1966; two s.; ed. Friends' School, Saffron Walden and London School of Econs.; bookselling 1963–64; with Faber & Faber 1964–, Man. Dir. 1972–, Chair. 1981–; Chair. Nat. Book League 1982–84, English Stage Co. 1984–; mem. Council, Publishers' Assen. 1978–84, Franco-British Soc. 1981–; Gov. B.F.I. 1982–. *Leisure interest:* cricket. *Address:* 3 Canonbury Place, London, N1 2NQ, England. *Telephone:* 01-226 0320.

EVANS, Maurice; American actor-manager; b. 3 June 1901, Dorchester, Dorset, England; s. of Alfred Herbert and Laura Evans; ed. Grocers' Company School, London; in America 1936–; U.S. Army 1942–45; Artistic Supervisor, New York City Center Theatre 1949–51; Hon. degrees from Univ. of Hawaii, Lafayette Coll., Penn., Brandeis Univ.; Pulitzer and Critics Prizes for production of Teahouse of the August Moon 1953, Legion of Merit 1945. *Plays acted in include:* Richard II, Hamlet 1938–39, Henry IV, Part I 1939, Twelfth Night 1940–41, Macbeth 1941–42, Hamlet 1945–47; produced and acted in Man and Superman 1947–49, The Browning Version 1949, The Devil's Disciple 1950, Richard II 1951, Dial "M" for Murder 1952–54, The Apple Cart 1956–57, Heartbreak House 1959–60, Tenderloin (musical) 1960–61, The Aspern Papers 1961–62, Shakespeare Revisited, A Program for Two Players (with Helen Hayes) 1962–63, Holiday 1980, On Golden Pond 1981. *Films include:* Kind Lady 1950, Androcles and the Lion, Gilbert and Sullivan, Macbeth 1960, Warlord 1965, Jack of Diamonds, Planet of the Apes 1967, Rosemary's Baby, Thin Air 1968, Beneath the Planet of the Apes 1970. [*Died 12 April 1989*].

EVANS, Mostyn (Moss); British trade unionist; b. 13 July 1925; m. Laura Bigglestone 1947; three s. (one deceased) three d.; ed. Church Road Secondary Modern School, Birmingham; Union Official, Transport and Gen. Workers' Union: District Officer, Chemical and Eng. Industries, Birmingham 1956; Regional Officer, Midlands 1960, Nat. Officer, Eng. 1966; Nat. Sec. Chemical, Rubber and Oil Industries 1969, Eng. Industries 1969, Automotive Section 1969–73; Nat. Organizer T.G.W.U. 1973–78, Gen. Sec. T.G.W.U. 1978–85; Vice-Pres. Int. Chemical Workers Fed. (ICEF) 1980–82, Pres. ICEF 1982–; mem. TUC Gen. Council 1977–85, Int. Cttee.

of TUC 1978–82, Chair. 1982–85; British Overseas Trade Bd. 1978–79; mem., Royal Inst. of Int. Affairs 1978–, A.C.A.S. 1982–85; Dir. Unity Trust 1984–. *Address:* 6 Highland Drive, Hemel Hempstead, Herts., England. *Telephone:* Hemel Hempstead 157503.

EVANS, Sir Richard Mark, K.C.M.G., K.C.V.O., B.A.; British diplomatist (retd.); b. 15 April 1928, British Honduras (now Belize); s. of late Edward Walter Evans and Anna Margaret Kirkpatrick Evans; m. Rosemary Grania Glen Birkett 1973; two s.; ed. Dragon School, Oxford, Repton School, and Magdalen Coll., Oxford; Third Sec., Peking 1955–57, Second Sec., London 1958–62, First Sec., Peking 1962–64, First Sec. (Commercial), Berne 1964–68, First Sec., London 1968–70, Head of Nr. Eastern Dept., FCO 1970–72 and Far Eastern Dept. 1972–74, Counsellor (Commercial), Stockholm 1975–77, Minister (Econ.), Paris 1977–79, Asst., then Deputy Under-Sec., FCO 1979–83, Amb. to People's Repub. of China 1984–88; Sr. Research Fellow, Wolfson Coll., Oxford; mem. Int. Bd. of Advice, ANZ Banking Group. *Leisure interests:* music, reading, travel. *Address:* Sevenhampton House, Sevenhampton, Highworth, Wilts., SN6 7QA, England.

EVANS, Robert, C.B.E., C.ENG., F.I.GAS, M.I.MECH.E., F.I.GAS.E., M.INST.E.; British engineer; b. 28 May 1927, Liverpool; s. of Gwilym Evans and Florence May Evans; m. Lilian Ward 1950; one s. one d.; ed. City of Liverpool Coll. and Univ. of Liverpool; with North Western Gas Bd. 1950–56; Burmah Oil Co. 1956–62; Dir. of Eng., Southern Gas 1962–72; Deputy Dir. (Operations), Gas Council 1972; Dir. (Operations), British Gas Council 1972–75; Deputy Chair. North Thames Gas 1975–77; Chair. East Midlands Gas 1977–82; Man. Dir. for Supplies, British Gas PLC 1982–83, Chief Exec. 1983–, Chair. July 1989–. *Leisure interest:* golf. *Address:* c/o British Gas PLC, Rivermill House, 152 Grosvenor Road, London, SW1V 3JL (Office); 165 The Albany, Manor Road, East Cliff, Bournemouth, BH1 3EL, England (Home). *Telephone:* 08277 5518 (Nuneaton); 0202 294108 (Home).

EVANS, Sir Robert Charles, Kt., B.M., F.R.C.S.; British climber, surgeon and academic (retd.); b. 19 Oct. 1918, Liverpool; s. of R. C. Evans and E. Evans; m. Denise Nea Morin; three s.; ed. Shrewsbury School and Oxford Univ.; served R.A.M.C., S.E. Asia (despatches) 1943–46; Surgical Registrar etc. United Liverpool and Liverpool Regional Hosps. 1947–57; Prin. Univ. Coll. of N. Wales 1958–84; Vice-Chancellor Univ. of Wales 1965–67, 1971–73; Deputy Leader Mt. Everest Expedition 1953; Leader Kangchenjunga Expedition 1955; Hunterian Prof. Royal Coll. of Surgeons 1954; Hon. D.Sc. (Wales) 1956; Founder's Medal Royal Geographical Soc. 1956. *Publications:* Kangchenjunga, The Untrodden Peak 1956, On Climbing 1956. *Address:* Ardincaple, Capel Curig, Betws y Coed, N. Wales.

EVANS, Robert John Weston, PH.D., F.B.A.; British historian; b. 7 Oct. 1943, Leicester; s. of T. F. Evans and M. Evans; m. Kati Róbert 1969; one s. one d.; ed. Dean Close School, Cheltenham and Jesus Coll., Cambridge; Research Fellow, Brasenose Coll. Oxford 1968–; Univ. Lecturer in Modern History of East-Central Europe, Oxford 1969–; ed. English Historical Review 1985–; Wolfson Literary Award for History 1980, Austrian Anton Gindely-Preis 1986. *Publications:* Rudolf II and his World 1973; The Making of the Habsburg Monarchy 1979. *Address:* Brasenose College, Oxford, OX1 4AJ; 83 Norreys Road, Cumnor, Oxon, England (Home). *Telephone:* Oxford 277890 (Coll.).

EVANS, Russell Wilmot, M.C., LL.B.; British business executive; b. 4 Nov. 1922, Birmingham; s. of William Henry Evans and Ethel Williams Wilmot; m. Pamela Muriel Hayward 1956; two s. one d.; ed. King Edward's School, Birmingham, Univ. of Birmingham; infantry co. commdr. in Italy during war service; qualified as solicitor 1949; Asst. Sec. at Harry Ferguson 1951, Sec. of Massey-Ferguson (Holdings) and its U.K. subsidiaries after merger of Ferguson and Massey-Harris, resgnd. 1962; on Parent Bd. of group of private companies in construction industry; joined Rank Org. 1967, Deputy Sec. 1967–68, Sec. 1968–72, Dir. 1972–, Man. Dir. 1975–82, Deputy Chair. 1981–82, Chair. 1982–83; Dir. of principal subsidiary and assoc. cos., incl. Rank Xerox, Fuji Xerox and Southern Television; Dir. Eagle Star Holdings PLC 1982–87, Eagle Star Insurance Co. 1982–85, Roehampton Club Ltd. 1971–88 (Chair. Bd. of Dirs. 1984–88); Chair. Butlin's 1975–83, Rank City Wall 1976–83, Oxford Econ. Forecasting Ltd. 1986–. *Leisure interests:* tennis, squash, photography, golf. *Address:* Walnut Tree, Roehampton Gate, London, S.W.15, England.

EVENO, Bertrand; French publishing executive; b. 26 July 1944, Egletons; s. of Jean-Jacques Eveno and Suzanne Gavoille; m. Brigitte Pery 1984; five d.; ed. Lycée Condorcet and Law Faculty, Paris; Treasury Inspector 1973–77; Tech. Consultant to Health Minister 1977–78; Cabinet Dir. for Minister of Culture and Communication 1978–81; mem. Atomic Energy Comm. Control Bd. 1981–83; Deputy Gen. Man. André Shoe Co. 1984–86; Pres. Gens d'Images 1986; Chair. Editions Fernand Nathan 1987–; Zellidja Scholarship 1961. *Publication:* monograph on Willy Ronis in Les grands photographes 1983. *Address:* Editions Nathan, 9 rue Méchain, 75014 Paris, France.

EVENSEN, Jens, LL.D.; Norwegian lawyer and politician; b. 5 Nov. 1917, Oslo; s. of Jens Evensen and Victoria Bjerkaas; m. Sylvei Brun Lie 1943; two s.; ed. law schools and Harvard Univ., U.S.A.; Jr. partner, law firm 1942–45; Legal Counsel to Solicitor-Gen. 1948–49; Advocate, Supreme Court 1951; Rockefeller Fellowship 1952–53; Dir.-Gen. Legal Dept., Ministry of Foreign Affairs 1961–73; Chair. Norwegian Petroleum Council

1965–75, Fishery Limits Comm. 1967–69, many other cttees.; Amb. for negotiating Trade Agreement with European Communities 1972; Minister of Commerce 1973–74, of Law of the Sea 1974–79; Chair. Norwegian Del. to Third UN Law of the Sea Conf. 1973–, Vice Pres. UN Law of the Sea Conf.; Amb., Int. Law Adviser, Ministry of Foreign Affairs 1979–; Ad hoc Judge, Int. Court of Justice 1980–82, Judge 1985–; Assoc. mem. Inst. de Droit International 1971; mem. Perm. Court of Arbitration 1978, Int. Law Comm. 1979. *Leisure interests:* sailing, skiing. *Address:* c/o The International Court of Justice, The Peace Palace, The Hague, Netherlands (Office); Linlandvn. 15, 1390 Vollen Asker, Oslo, Norway (Home). *Telephone:* Oslo 798515 (Home).

EVERDING, August; German theatre manager; b. 31 Oct. 1928, Bottrop, Westphalia; s. of August and Gertrude (née Elbers) Everding; m. Gustava v. Vogel 1963; four s.; ed. Univs. of Bonn and Munich; fmrly. production asst. Münchner Kammerspiele and asst. to Kortner and Schweikart; Chief Stage Man. Münchner Kammerspiele 1959, Producer 1960, Intendant 1963; Intendant, Hamburg State Opera 1973; Bavarian State Opera 1977; Generalintendant, Bavarian State Theatre 1982–; Prof. Univ. of Munich and Musikhochschule, Munich; mem. Presidium, Goethe Inst.; mem. Rundfunkrat; Vice-Pres. Deutschen Bühnenvereins; Pres. Internationale Theaterinstitut in Deutschland; Bundesverdienstkreuz; Commendatore nell'ordine al merito della Repubblica Italiana. *Address:* Burg, 8022 Grünwald bei München; Generalintendanz der Bayerischen Staatstheater, Prinzregententheater, Prinzregentenplatz, D-8000 Munich 80, Federal Republic of Germany. *Telephone:* 2185-1.

EVERED, David Charles, M.D., F.R.C.P., F.I.BIOL.; British physician and scientific administrator; b. 21 Jan. 1940, Beaconsfield; s. of Thomas C. Evered and Enid C. Evered; m. Anne Lings 1964; one s. two d.; ed. Cranleigh School, Surrey and Middlesex Hosp. Medical School; jr. hospital appts. London and Leeds 1964–70; First Asst. in Medicine, Wellcome Sr. Research Fellow and Consultant Physician, Univ. of Newcastle-upon-Tyne and Royal Vic. Infirmary 1970–78; Dir. The Ciba Foundation, London 1978–88; Second Sec., MRC, London 1988–; mem. numerous cttees., socs. and other professional bodies. *Publications:* Diseases of the Thyroid 1976, Atlas of Endocrinology (with R. Hall and R. Greene) 1979, Collaboration in Medical Research in Europe (with M. O'Connor) 1981; numerous papers in professional journals. *Leisure interests:* reading, history, tennis, sailing. *Address:* The Medical Research Council, 20 Park Crescent, London, W1N 4AL, England. *Telephone:* 01-636 5422.

EVERETT, Douglas Hugh, D.SC., F.R.S., F.R.S.E., F.R.S.C., M.B.E.; British academic; b. 26 Dec. 1916, Hampton; s. of Charles and Jessie Everett; m. Frances Elizabeth Jessop 1942; two d.; ed. Hampton Grammar School, Univs. of Reading and Oxford; Research Asst. Univ. Coll., Dundee 1938–39; Ramsay Fellow, Balliol Coll., Oxford 1939–41; Maj., Special Duties, War Office 1942–45; ICI Fellow, Oxford Univ. 1945–47; Fellow and Lecturer, Exeter Coll., Oxford 1947–48; Prof. of Chemistry Univ. Coll. Dundee, St. Andrews Univ. 1948–54; Unilever Prof. of Physical Chemistry, Univ. of Bristol 1954–82, Prof. Emer. 1982–, Dean of Faculty of Science 1966–68; Pro-Vice-Chancellor 1973–76; Vice-Pres. and Gen. Sec. B.A.A.S. 1983–88; Pres. Int. Asscn. of Colloid and Interface Scientists 1988–(90); Tilden Lecturer, Chemical Soc., London, Award in Surface and Colloid Chemistry. *Publications:* Introduction to the Study of Chemical Thermodynamics 1959, Surface Tension and Adsorption (with others) 1965, Basic Principles of Celloid Science 1988, and many scientific papers. *Leisure interests:* walking, painting. *Address:* Department of Physical Chemistry, School of Chemistry, University of Bristol, Cantock's Close, Bristol, BS8 1TS (Office); 35 Downleaze, Bristol, BS9 1LX, England (Home). *Telephone:* 0272 303030 (Office); 0272 682990 (Home).

EVERETT, Rupert; British actor; b. 1960, Norfolk; ed. Ampleforth School and Cen. School for Speech and Drama, London; apprenticed with Glasgow Citizen's Theatre 1979–82; *Stage appearances include:* Another Country 1982, The Vortex 1989. *Films include:* Another Country 1984, Dance with a Stranger 1985, The Right Hand Man 1985, Duet for One, Chronicle of Death Foretold 1987, Hearts of Fire 1987, Haunted Summer 1988. *TV includes:* The Far Pavilions 1982, Princess Daisy 1983. *Address:* c/o Duncan Heath, 162 Wardour Street, London, W1 4AB, England.

EVERINGHAM, Douglas Nixon, M.B., B.S.; Australian politician and medical practitioner; b. 25 June 1923, Wauchope, N.S.W.; s. of Herman Clifford and Hilda Mary Everingham; m. Beverly May Withers 1948; one s. two d.; ed. Fort Street School, Univ. of Sydney; Resident Medical Officer in gen. and mental hospitals 1946–53; gen. practice 1953–67, 1976–77; Medical Asst., pvt. fertility control clinic 1987–; mem. House of Reps. 1967–75, 1977–84; Minister for Health 1972–75; Opposition spokesman on Aboriginal Affairs and Northern Australia 1977–79, on Veterans' Affairs and the Capital Territory 1979–80; Vice-Pres. World Health Assembly 1975; Opposition Del. UN 1982; Sec. Govt. Sub-Cttee. on Disarmament 1980–84. *Publications:* Chemical Shorthand for Organic Formulae 1943, Critique of Bliss Symbols 1956, Braud Inglish Speling 1966, Convivial Carnage 1977. *Leisure interests:* semantics, interlinguistics, pasigraphy, spelling reform, humanism, world federalism. *Address:* 58 Raeside Street, Westlake, Queensland 4074, Australia. *Telephone:* (07) 376 7763.

EVERLING, Ulrich, DR.JUR.; German judge; b. 2 June 1925, Berlin; s. of Emil Everling; m. Lore Schwerdtfeger 1953; two s. two d.; ed. Zehlendorfer Gymnasium, Berlin and Univ. of Göttingen; lawyer, Fed. Ministry of Econs. 1953–80, Head of Dept. of European Policy 1970–80; Lecturer, Hon. Prof. of European Law, Univ. of Münster 1971–75, Univ. of Bonn 1985–; Judge, Court of Justice of the European Communities 1980–88; Pres. Third Chamber 1985–. *Publications:* Die europäische Wirtschaftsgemeinschaft: Kommentar zum Vertrag (co-author) 1960, Das Niederlassungsrecht im Gemeinsamen Markt 1964; numerous articles on European law and policy. *Address:* Dahlienweg 5, 5307 Wachtberg-Pech, Federal Republic of Germany. *Telephone:* 324177.

EVERT, Chris(tine) Marie: American lawn tennis player; b. 21 Dec. 1954, Fort Lauderdale, Fla.; d. of James Evert; m. 1st John Lloyd 1979 (divorced 1987); m. 2nd Andy Mill 1988; ed. St. Thomas Aquinas High School, Fort Lauderdale; amateur player 1970–72; professional since 1972; Wimbledon Singles Champion 1974, 1976, 1981; French Champion 1974, 1975, 1979, 1980, 1982, 1985, 1986; U.S.A. Champion 1975, 1976, 1977, 1978, 1980, 1982; Italian Champion 1974, 1975, 1980; South African Champion 1973; Colgate Series Champion 1977, 1978; World Champion 1979; played Wightman Cup for U.S.A. 1971–73, 1975–82 and has unbeaten record in singles; won 1000th singles victory Dec. 1984; played Federation Cup for U.S.A. 1977–82; Pres. Women's Tennis Assocn. 1975–76. *Publication:* Lloyd on Lloyd (with John Lloyd) 1985. *Address:* c/o International Management Group, 1 Ereview Plaza, Cleveland, Ohio 44114, U.S.A.

EVERT, Militiades; Greek politician; b. 1939; m. Lisa Evert; Mayor of Athens 1986–; New Democracy Party. *Address:* Office of the Mayor, City Hall, Athens, Greece.

EVREN, Gen. Kenan; Turkish army officer; b. 1918; m.; three c.; ed. Military Acad., War Coll.; Artillery Officer 1938; served in Korea; promoted to Gen. 1964; Commdr. 1st Army Corps.; Chief of Staff of Commdr. of the Land Forces, then Deputy Chief of Staff of the Armed Forces; Commdr. Fourth Army (Aegean Army), Izmir 1976; rank of Gen. 1974; Chief of the Land Forces 1977; Chief of Staff of the Armed Forces 1978–; led coup deposing civilian govt. Sept. 1980; Head of State and Chair. Nat. Security Council Sept. 1980–, Pres. of Turkey 1982–; Head, Turkish mil. del. to U.S.S.R. 1975. *Address:* The Presidency, Ankara, Turkey.

EVRON, Ephraim; Israeli diplomatist; b. 12 June 1920, Haifa; m. Rivka Passman 1943; one s. one d.; ed. Haifa Reali School, Hebrew Univ., Jerusalem; served with British Army in Middle East 1941–46, Israel Defence Force 1948–49; Political Sec. to Foreign Minister 1949–51; Sec. to Prime Minister 1951–52; Second Sec., Washington Embassy 1953, Exec. Asst. to Defence Minister 1954–55; with Israeli Fed. of Labour 1957–61; Counsellor, then Minister, Embassy to London 1961–65, Washington 1965–68; Amb. to Stockholm 1968–69, to Ottawa 1969–71; Asst. Dir. Gen., Ministry of Foreign Affairs 1972–73, Deputy Dir. Gen. 1973–77, Dir. Gen. 1977–78; Amb. to U.S.A. 1978–82. *Address:* c/o Ministry of Foreign Affairs, Tel-Aviv, Israel.

EWALDSEN, Hans Lorenz, DIPL.SC.POL.; German business executive (retd.); b. 6 Sept. 1923, Lunden, Schleswig Holstein; s. of Lorenz and Marie (née Kröger) Ewaldsen; m. Marianne Paulsen 1951; two s.; ed. Univ. of Kiel; mem. Man. Bd., Deutsche Babcock AG 1960, Pres. and C.E.O. 1967, Chair. Supervisory Bd. 1984; Chair. Supervisory Bd. Balcke-Dürr AG, Ratingen, Borsig GmbH, Berlin, Gerling-Konzern Lebensversammlung AG, Cologne, Vereinigte Kesselwerke AG, Düsseldorf; mem. Supervisory Bd. numerous cos. *Leisure interests:* hunting, tennis. *Address:* c/o Deutsche Babcock AG, 4200 Oberhausen, Duisburgerstrasse 375, Federal Republic of Germany.

EWANS, Sir Martin Kenneth, K.C.M.G., M.A.; British diplomatist; b. 14 Nov. 1928; s. of late John Ewans; m. Mary Tooke 1953; one s. one d.; ed. St. Paul's School and Corpus Christi Coll. Cambridge; joined Commonwealth Relations Office 1952; served Karachi 1954–55, Ottawa 1958–61, Lagos 1962–64, Kabul 1967–69, Dar es Salaam 1969–73; Head, E. African Dept. FCO 1973–77; Minister, New Delhi 1978–82; Sr. civilian instr. Royal Coll. of Defence Studies 1982–83; High Commr. in Zimbabwe 1983–85, in Nigeria 1986–. *Leisure interest:* bird-watching. *Address:* Foreign and Commonwealth Office, King Charles Street, London, S.W.1, England.

EWART, Gavin Buchanan, M.A., F.R.S.L.; British poet and freelance writer; b. 4 Feb. 1916, London; s. of George Arthur Ewart and Dorothy Hannah Turner; m. Margaret Adelaide Bennett 1956; one s. one d.; ed. Wellington Coll. and Christ's Coll., Univ. of Cambridge; Salesman 1938–39; war service with R.A. 1940–46; in publishing 1946; with British Council 1946–52; Advertising Copywriter 1952–71; freelance writer 1971–; Cholmondeley Award for Poetry 1971; Travelling Scholarship 1978. *Publications:* The Collected Ewart 1933–80 1980, The New Ewart (Poems 1980–1982) 1982, More Little Ones 1982, The Ewart Quarto 1984, The Young Pobble's Guide to His Toes 1985, The Learned Hippopotamus (verse for children) 1986, The Complete Little Ones of Gavin Ewart 1986, The Gavin Ewart Show 1986, Late Pickings 1987, Selected Poems 1988, Penultimate Poems 1989. *Leisure interests:* music, theatre, reading. *Address:* 57 Kenilworth Court, Lower Richmond Road, London, SW15 1EN, England.

EWEN, Paterson; Canadian artist and teacher of fine art; b. 7 April 1925, Montreal, Quebec; four s.; ed. Montreal Museum of Fine Arts, School of Art and Design, McGill Univ., Montreal; solo exhbns. in Ont. 1969, 1972–74,

1977, 1978, 1980, 1982, 1984, Vancouver, B.C. 1977, 1978; exhbns. in New Brunswick 1975, New Jersey, U.S.A. 1975, Calgary, Alberta 1980, Basel, Switzerland 1978, Denmark 1980–81, Fed. Repub. of Germany 1981, Luxembourg 1981, Belgium 1981, Japan 1981, Venice, Italy 1982, London, 1982; Asst. Prof. Univ. of W. Ont. 1972–; Award, Montreal Museum of Fine Arts, Sr. Canada Council Award 1971, Purchase Prize 1977. *Publications:* Carmen Lamanna at the Owens Art Gallery 1975, contrib., Paterson Ewen: Recent Works 1977. *Address:* University of Western Ontario, Visual Arts Dept., London, Ont. N6A 5B7; c/o Carmen Lamanna Gallery, 840 Yonge Street, Toronto, Ont. M4W 2H1, Canada.

EWERTSEN, Harald Wind; Danish ear, nose and throat specialist; b. 17 April 1913, Hjorring; m. Bodil Knipschildt 1942; three s. two d.; ed. Københavns Universitet; Doctor's dissertation, Univ. of Copenhagen 1946; Ear, nose and throat specialist 1949; Dir. State Hearing Rehabilitation Centre of Copenhagen 1951–83; Asst. Prof. Danmarks Larerhojskole 1965–76; Vice-Pres. Int. Soc. of Audiology 1962–66; Pres. Danish Medical Audiological Soc. 1967–72; Danish rep. in EEC working group on deafness 1973–76; Co-ed. International Audiology 1962–66; mem. Bd. of Danish physicians' group, Amnesty Int. 1983–84; mem. Bd. of Danish physicians for the prevention of nuclear war; Adviser to WHO European Region on world-wide prevention of hearing impairment 1985–88; Hon. mem. Int. Asscn. Physicians in Audiology 1983; Vald. Klein Prize 1974; Kt. of Dannebrog; Finnish Liberty Cross in Silver and Gold; many specialist publs. *Leisure interests:* magic conjuring tricks, photography. *Address:* 208 Virum Stationsvej, Virum, Denmark. *Telephone:* 02-85-6100.

EWING, Maria Louise; American opera singer; b. 27 March 1950, Detroit; d. of Norman I. Ewing and Hermina M. Veraar; m. Sir Peter Hall (q.v.) 1982; one d.; ed. Cleveland Inst. of Music; début at Metropolitan Opera, New York singing Cherubino in The Marriage of Figaro 1976, closely followed by débuts with major U.S. orchestras including New York Philharmonic and at La Scala Milan; performs regularly at Glyndebourne including Sir Peter Hall's productions of the Barber of Seville, L'Incoronazione di Poppea and Carmen 1985; repertoire also includes Pelléas et Mélisande, The Dialogues of the Carmelites, Così fan Tutte, La Perichole, La Cenerentola, Marriage of Figaro (Susanna), Chicago Lyric Opera 1987; Salome, Covent Garden 1988; also appears as concert and recital singer; début Promenade Concèrts, London 1987. *Leisure interests:* home and family. *Address:* c/o Harold Holt Ltd., 31 Sinclair Road, London, W14 0NS; 33 Bramerton Street, London, S.W.3, England.

EWING, Winifred Margaret, M.A., LL.B.; British solicitor and politician; b. 10 July 1929, Glasgow; d. of George Woodburn and Christina B. Anderson; m. Stewart Martin Ewing 1956; two s. one d.; ed. Queen's Park School, Univ. of Glasgow, Peace Palace, The Hague; practising solicitor 1956–; mem. Parl. for Hamilton 1967–70, for Moray and Nairn 1974–79, 1987–; mem. European Parl. 1975–, for the Highlands and Islands of Scotland 1979–; Pres. Scottish Nat. Party; Vice-Pres. European Democratic Alliance 1984–; Chair. Cttee. on Youth, Culture, Educ., Information and Sport, European Parl. 1984–; Sec. Glasgow Bar Asscn. 1961–67, Pres 1970–71. *Leisure interests:* hill walking, collecting paintings. *Address:* Goodwill, Lossiemouth, Morayshire; 52 Queen's Drive, Glasgow, G42 8DD, Scotland. *Telephone:* 041-423 1765 (Glasgow).

EXLEY, Charles Errol, Jr., M.A., M.B.A.; American business executive; b. 14 Dec. 1929, Detroit, Mich.; s. of Charles Errol and Helen Margaret (Greenizen) Exley; m. Sara Elizabeth Yates 1952; one s. two d.; ed. Wesleyan Univ., Middletown, Conn., Graduate School of Business, Columbia Univ., New York, N.Y.; Financial Analysis Dept., Burroughs Corpn. 1954–56, Asst. to Controller 1956–57, Supervisor of Operations Analysis 1957–60, Controller of Office Products Group 1960–63, Controller 1963–66, Vice-Pres. and Group Exec., Office Products Group 1966–71, Vice-Pres. Finance 1971–73, Exec. Vice-Pres. Finance, and Dir. 1973–76; Pres. NCR Corpn., Dir. and mem. Exec. Cttee. 1976–, C.E.O. 1983–, Chair. April 1984–. *Leisure interest:* sailing. *Address:* NCR Corporation, 1700 Patterson Boulevard, Dayton, Ohio 45479 (Office); 3720 Ridgeleigh Road, Dayton, Ohio 45479, U.S.A. (Home).

EXON, John James; American politician; b. 9 Aug. 1921, Geddes, S. Dakota; s. of John J. and Luella (Johns) Exon; m. Patricia Pros 1943; one s. two d.; ed. Univ. of Omaha; Vice-Chair., Neb. State Democratic Cen. Cttee. 1964–68; mem. Neb. Democratic Party Exec. Cttee. 1964–; Neb. Democratic Nat. Cttee. Man 1968–70; Gov. of Nebraska 1971–79; Senator from Nebraska 1978–; mem. Democratic Nat. Cttee., American Legion, Veterans of Foreign Wars. *Address:* 340 Dirksen Senate Office Building, Washington, D.C. 20510, U.S.A. *Telephone:* 202-224-4224.

EYADÉMA, Gen. (Etienne) Gnassingbe; Togolese army officer and politician; b. 26 Dec. 1937, Pya, Lama Kara District; served with French Army 1953–61 in Indo-China, Dahomey, Niger and Algeria; commissioned 1963; Army Chief of Staff (Togo) 1965–; led army coup Jan. 1967; Pres. of Togo April 1967–, and Minister of Defence 1967, 1981–; f. Rassemblement du Peuple Togolais, Paris 1969, Pres. 1969, mem. Political Bureau; Chair. ECOWAS 1980–81; Grand Officier, Ordre National de Mono, Mil. Cross, Chevalier, Légion d'honneur (France). *Leisure interest:* hunting. *Address:* Présidence de la République, Lomé, Togo.

EYCKMANS, Luc A.F., M.D., PH.D.; Belgian professor of medicine; b. 23 Feb. 1930, Antwerp; s. of Robert Eyckmans and Alice van Genechten; m. Godelieve Cornelissen 1957; four s. three d.; ed. Univ. of Leuven; Fellowship in Tropical Medicine, Antwerp 1956–57; Hospital Physician, Kisantu (fmr. Belgian Congo) 1957–60; Fellowship in Infectious Diseases, Dallas and Cornell, New York 1961–64, in Tropical Medicine, Bahia, Brazil 1964; Lector in Infectious Diseases and Physician, Univ. of Leuven 1965–72; Prof. of Medicine (Infectious Diseases), Univ. of Antwerp 1973–, Dir. Inst. of Tropical Medicine "Prince Leopold" 1976–; Visiting Prof. Univ. of Leuven 1977–; Bd. mem. Franqui Foundation; Dr. h.c. (Lille). *Publications:* 130 contributions to professional journals. *Leisure interest:* hiking. *Address:* Institute of Tropical Medicine, Nationalestraat 155, B 2000 Antwerp (Office); Wildenhoge 26, B 3009 Winksele, Belgium (Home). *Telephone:* 03-237.67.31 (Office).

EYRAUD, Francis-Charles, L. EN D., D.E.S.; French business executive; b. 16 Aug. 1931, Saint-Bonnet, Hautes Alpes; s. of Charles Eyraud and Francine Villaron; m. Simone Desmé 1967; two s. one d.; ed. Coll. du Rondeau Montfleury, Grenoble, Faculté de Droit, Lettres, I.E.P., Paris; E.N.A. promotion, Alexis de Tocqueville 1958; civil admin. of finance 1960; Prof. Centre de Formation des Finances 1961; in charge of practical studies, Faculté de Droit 1962; special mission fo U.S.A. 1965; Chef de Bureau 1967; civil admin. 1968; Deputy Dir. 1973; judicial agent of Treasury 1979; Pres. Dir.-Gen. Société Nationale d'Exploitation Industrielle des Tabacs et Allumettes (SEITA) 1981–; Administrateur Délégué du CORE-STA 1982–, Vice-Pres. 1984–86, Pres. 1986–; Officier, Légion d'honneur, Ordre Nationale du Mérite; Officier des Palmes académiques; Commdr. des Arts et des Lettres, and other decorations. *Publications:* Cours de Legislation Financière 1965. *Address:* 53 quai d'Orsay, 75007 Paris (Office); 33 rue Saint-Augustin, 75008 Paris, France (Home). *Telephone:* 45.55.91.50 (Office); 47.42.50.67 (Home).

EYRE, Ivan; Canadian artist and university professor; b. 15 April 1935, Tullymet, Sask.; s. of Thomas and Kay Eyre; m. Brenda Fenske 1957; two s.; mem. Faculty, Univ. of Manitoba, Winnipeg 1959–, Head, Drawing Dept. 1974–78, Prof. of Drawing and Painting 1975–; one-man shows at Montreal Museum of Fine Arts, Winnipeg Art Gallery, Nat. Gallery of Canada, Ottawa, Frankfurter Kunstkabinett, W. Germany, Canada House, London, Canadian Cultural Centre, Paris, France; has participated in group shows in all the major cities of Canada, Colombia and Spain; works represented in permanent collections at Winnipeg Art Gallery, Nat. Gallery, Ottawa, Vancouver Art Gallery, Montreal Museum of Fine Arts etc.; Canada Council Sr. Fellow 1966–77; mem. Royal Canadian Acad. of Arts; Queen's Jubilee Medal 1977; Academic of Italy with Gold Medal 1980; Jubilee Award, Univ. of Manitoba Alumni Asscn. 1982. *Address:* 1098 Trappistes Street, Winnipeg, Manitoba R3V 1B8, Canada. *Telephone:* (204) 261-8171.

EYRE, Richard; British theatre, film and television director; b. 28 March 1943; m. Sue Birtwistle 1973; one d.; ed. Sherborne School and Cambridge Univ.; Assoc. Dir. Royal Lyceum, Edinburgh 1967–70; Artistic Dir. Nottingham Playhouse 1973–78; Producer-dir. Play for Today for BBC 1978–80; Assoc. Dir. Nat. Theatre (now called Royal Nat. Theatre) 1980–86, Artistic Dir. 1988–. *Plays directed include:* Hamlet (Royal Court) 1980, Guys and Dolls, The Beggar's Opera, Schweyk in the Second World War (Nat. Theatre) 1982, The Government Inspector (Nat. Theatre) 1985, Futurists (Nat. Theatre) 1986, Kafka's Dick (Royal Court) 1986, High Society (W. End) 1987, Bartholomew Fair 1988, A Walk in the Woods (W. End) 1988. *Films:* The Ploughman's Lunch (Evening Standard Award for Best Film) 1983, Laughterhouse (Venice TV Prize) 1984. *Television:* The Imitation Game 1980, Pasmore 1981, The Cherry Orchard, Country 1982, Past Caring, The Insurance Man (Tokyo Prize) 1986, Tumbledown 1987, STV Award for Best Dir. 1968, 1969, 1970, Evening Standard Award for Best Dir. 1982, SWET Award for Best Dir. 1982, Time Out Award Best Dir. 1986, Vittorio de Sica Award 1986, Special Award, Evening Standard Drama Award, RAI Prize 1988 (Tumbledown). *Address:* c/o Curtis Brown, 162-168 Regent Street, London, W1R 5TA, England.

EYSENCK, Hans Jurgen, PH.D., D.SC.; British psychologist; b. 4 March 1916, Berlin, Germany; s. of Eduard Eysenck and Ruth Werner; m. Sybil Bianca Giuletta Rostal 1950; four s. one d.; ed. Univ. of Dijon, Exeter and London; Research Psychologist, Mill Hill Emergency Hosp. 1942–45; Psychologist, Maudsley Hospital, London 1945; Reader and Dir., Psychological Dept., Inst. of Psychiatry, Univ. of London 1950–55, Prof. of Psychology 1955–84, Emer. 1984–. *Publications:* Dimensions of Personality 1947, The Scientific Study of Personality 1952, The Structure of Human Personality 1953, Uses and Abuses of Psychology 1953, The Psychology of Politics 1954, Sense and Nonsense in Psychology 1956, The Dynamics of Anxiety and Hysteria 1957, Perceptional Processes and Mental Illness 1957, Manual for the Maudsley Personality Inventory 1959, Experiments in Personality (2 vols.) 1960, Behaviour Therapy and the Neuroses 1960, Handbook of Abnormal Psychology 1960, Manual for the Eysenck Personality Inventory 1963, Experiments with Drugs 1963, Crime and Personality 1964, Experiments in Motivation 1964, Causes and Cures of Neuroses 1965, Experiments in Behaviour Therapy 1965, Fact and Fiction in Psychology 1965, Smoking, Health and Personality 1965, The Biological Basis of Personality 1967, Structure and Measurement of Personality 1969, The Structure of Human Personality 1970, Readings in Intro- version/Extra-version 1971, Race, Intelligence and Education 1971, Psychology is about People 1972, Encyclopaedia of Psychology (ed.) 1972-, Measurement of Intelligence 1973, Experimental Study of Freudian Theories 1973, The Inequality of Man 1973, Eysenck on Extraversion 1973, Case Histories in Behaviour Therapy 1975, Know Your Own Personality (with Glenn Wilson) 1975, Textbook of Human Psychology 1976, Sex and Personality 1976, The Measurement of Personality 1976, Psychoticism as a Dimension of Personality 1976, Reminiscience 1977, You and Neurosis 1977, Sex, Violence and the Media (with D. K. Nias) 1978, The Structure and Measurement of Intelligence 1979, A Model for Personality 1980, The Causes and Effects of Smoking 1980, Mindwatching (with M. Eysenck) 1981, A Model for Intelligence 1982, Astrology—Science or Superstition (with D. Nias) 1982, Explaining the Unexplained (with C. Sargent) 1982, For Better, for Worse—A Guide to Happy Marriage 1983, Personality and Individual Differences (with M. W. Eysenck) 1985, Decline and Fall of the Freudian Empire 1986. *Leisure interests:* tennis, squash, photography. *Address:* Department of Psychology, Institute of Psychiatry, Maudsley Hospital, Denmark Hill, London, S.E.5; 10 Dorchester Drive, London, S.E.24, England (Home).

EYTAN, Walter; M.A.; Israeli political consultant; b. 24 July 1910, Munich, Germany; s. of Dr. Maurice Leon Ettinghausen and Hedwig Kahn; m. Beatrice Levison; two s. one d.; ed. St. Paul's School, London, and Queen's Coll., Oxford; Lecturer in German, Queen's Coll., Oxford 1934–46; Prin., Public Service Coll., Jerusalem 1946–48; Dir.-Gen. Ministry Foreign Affairs, Israel 1948–59; Amb. to France 1960–70; Political Adviser to Foreign Minister 1970–72; Chair. Israel Broadcasting Authority 1972–78; Trustee, Chair. Bd. of Man. Museum of Islamic Art, Jerusalem; mem. Bd. of Govs., Haifa Univ.; Hon. Fellow, Hebrew Union Coll. 1983; Commdr., Légion d'honneur 1976. *Publication:* The First Ten Years 1958. *Address:* 18 Rehov Balfour, Jerusalem, Israel. *Telephone:* 02-631268.

EYTON, Anthony John Plowden, R.A., A.R.W.S., R.W.A.; British artist; b. 17 May 1923, Teddington, Middx.; s. of Capt. John S. Eyton and Phyllis A. Tyser; m. Frances M. Capell 1960 (divorced); three d.; ed. Twyford School, Canford School and Camberwell School of Art; part-time teacher, Camberwell Art School 1955–86, Royal Acad. Schools 1963–; one-man exhbns. St. George's Gallery 1955, New Art Centre 1959, 1961, 1968, New Grafton Gallery 1973, William Darby Gallery 1975, Browse & Darby 1978, 1981, 1985, 1987, South London Art Gallery (retrospective) 1980, Imperial War Museum 1983; Hon. mem. Pastel Soc.; Hon. R.O.I.; several awards and prizes. *Address:* 166 Brixton Road, London, SW9 6AU, England. *Telephone:* 01-735 9859.

EZRA, Baron (Life Peer), cr. 1983, of Horsham in the County of West Sussex; **Derek Ezra,** Kt., M.B.E.; British business executive; b. 23 Feb. 1919; s. of David and Lillie Ezra; m. Julia Elizabeth Wilkins 1950; ed. Monmouth School and Magdalene Coll., Cambridge; mil. service 1939–47; rep. of Nat. Coal Bd. at Cttees. of OEEC and ECE 1948–52; mem. U.K. Del. to High Authority of European Coal and Steel Community 1952–56; Regional Sales Man. Nat. Bd. 1958–60, Dir.-Gen. of Marketing 1960–65; mem. Nat. Coal Bd. 1965, Deputy Chair. 1965–71, Chair. 1971–82; Chair. British Inst. of Man. 1976–78, Vice-Chair. 1978; Chair. British Coal Int.; Chair. British Nationalised Industries Chairmen's Group 1980–81, Pres. Nat. Materials Handling Centre 1978; Pres. Coal Industry Soc. 1981–86, British Standards Inst. 1983–, Econ. Research Council 1985–, Inst. of Trading Standards Admin. 1987–; Dir. Redland PLC 1982–; Chair. Associated Heat Services PLC 1966–, British Iron and Steel Consumers Council 1983–86, Petrolex PLC 1982–85; Industrial Adviser to Morgan Grenfell 1982–88; Chair. Throgmorton Trust 1984–; mem. British Overseas Trade Bd. 1972–82, Bd., Solvay, Belgium; Hon. Fellow Inst. of Civil Engineers 1986; Hon. LL.D. (Leeds) 1982; Order of Merit, Italy, Commdr. Order of Merit, Luxembourg, Officier, Légion d'honneur. *Publications:* Coal and Energy 1978, The Energy Debate 1983. *Address:* House of Lords, Westminster, London, S.W.1; 2 Salisbury Road, Wimbledon, London, SW19 4EZ, England. *Telephone:* 01-946 2122 (Office).

F

FABBRI, Fabio; Italian politician, lawyer and journalist; b. 15 Oct. 1933, Ciano d'Enza, Reggio Emilia; s. of Nello Fabbri and Gisella Brechi; m. Minnie Manzini 1959; one s. one d.; ed. Univ. of Parma; fmr. journalist with Il Mondo and contrib. to Nord e Sud, Itinerari, Mondo Operario; now contrib. to L'Avanti and other political and cultural magazines; Chair. Parma Provincial Transport Authority 1968–70; Socialist Senator for Borgotaro Salsomaggiore, Emilia Romagna 1976–; fmr. Under-Sec., Ministry of Agric. and Forestry; Minister for Regional Affairs 1982–83, for EEC Affairs 1986–87; Chair. of Socialist Parl. Group; Pres. Istituto per il dialogo e la cooperazione internazionale. *Leisure interests:* reading, trekking, skiing. *Address:* Piazza Garibaldi 17, 431000 Parma, Italy. *Telephone:* 30121.

FABER, Georges, D.JUR.; Luxembourg business executive; b. 4 Dec. 1926; m. Josée Carosati 1949; one s. two d.; ed. Univs. of Freiburg, Paris, Geneva and The Hague; joined ARBED S.A. 1952, Deputy Man. Legal Dept. 1972, Man. 1973, mem. Bd. Dirs. 1977, C.E.O. 1986–; Dir. Soc. Gen. de Belgique, Banque Int. Luxembourg S.A., Fed. of Luxembourg Industrialists; Pres. Asscn. of Iron and Steel Industry; mem. Int. Fiscal Asscn., Council of State of Luxembourg, Inst. Grand-Ducal; Grand Officier Ordre de la Couronne de Chêne. *Publications:* numerous articles in econ., legal and fiscal publs. *Leisure interests:* literature, music, walking. *Address:* ARBED S.A., 19 Avenue de la Liberté, 2930 Luxembourg (Office); 10 Boulevard Emmanuel Servais, 2535 Luxembourg (Home). *Telephone:* 27422 (Home).

FABIAN, (Andrew) Paul, M.A.; British diplomatist; b. 23 May 1930, Mitcham, Surrey; s. of Andrew T. Fabian and Edith M. Whorwell; m. 1st Elizabeth V. Chapman 1957 (divorced 1983), one s. two d.; m. 2nd Eryll F. Dickinson 1983; ed. St. Paul's School and Wadham Coll., Oxford; Served Singapore Engineer Regt. 1952–54; H.M. Overseas Civil Service, Tanganyika 1955–64; seconded to Foreign Office as Vice-Consul (later Second Sec.) at Usumbura, Ruanda-Urundi 1961–64; diplomatic postings to Lusaka 1964, Ankara 1967, FCO 1969, New Delhi 1973, FCO 1977, Islamabad 1979, Karachi 1982, FCO 1986; High Commr. in Tonga 1987–. *Leisure interests:* chess, catching up on my reading. *Address:* British High Commission, P.O. Box 56, Nuku'alofa, Tonga.

FABIANI, Dante Carl; American industrialist; b. 13 Aug. 1917, Waterbury, Conn.; s. of Rosato Fabiani and Barbara Poscente; m. Virginia Parnham 1944; one s. two d.; ed. Tri-State Coll. and Purdue Univ.; Auburn Rubber Corpn., Ind. 1938–42; Gen. Electric Co., Ind. 1942–45; Continental Can Co., Ohio 1945–47; Controller, Asst. Man. Standard Products Co., Ohio 1948–51; Dir., Sec.-Treas. Townsend Co., Pa. 1951–59; Vice-Pres. Finance, H. K. Porter Co. Inc. 1959–60; Dir., Vice-Pres. Finance, McDonnell Aircraft Corpn., Missouri 1960; Dir. Crane Co., New York 1960–, Chair. 1960–80; Chair. Pirelli Cable Corpn. 1983–; Dir. Huttig Sash & Door Co., St. Louis, Kearney Nat. Corpn., Textron Inc., C.F.I. Steel Corpn. 1970–, Medusa Corpn., Cleveland, Ohio, Pirelli Enterprises. *Address:* 15 North Avenue, Westport, Conn. 06880, U.S.A. (Home).

FABIANI, Simonetta (see Simonetta).

FABIUS, Laurent; French politician; b. 20 Aug. 1946, Paris; s. of André Fabius and Louise Mortimer; m. Françoise Castro 1981; two s.; ed. Lycées Janson-de-Sailly and Louis-le-Grand, Paris, Ecole normale supérieure, Ecole Nat. d'Admin.; Auditor, Council of State 1973–; First Deputy Mayor of Grand-Quevilly 1977–81; Deputy (Seine-Maritime) to Nat. Assembly 1978–81, 1986– Pres. June 1988–; Nat. Sec. Parti Socialiste, in charge of press 1979–81; Minister-Del. for the Budget, attached to Minister of Econ. and Finance 1981–83; Minister of Industry and Research March 1983–84, Prime Minister 1984–86; Pres. Regional Council, Haute Normandie 1981–; Grand Croix de l'ordre nat. du Mérite. *Publication:* La France inégale 1975. *Address:* 15 place du Panthéon, 75005 Paris, France (Home).

FABREGA, Jorge, M.L.; Panamanian attorney and professor of law; b. 19 April 1922, Santiago; m. Gloria de Fabrega 1960; two s. two d.; ed. Univ. of Southern California, Univ. of Pennsylvania, Univ. of Panama; Alt. Justice Court of Appeals 1960–68, Supreme Court of Panama 1970–80; Prof. of Law, Univ. of Panama 1967–; Pres. Govt. Comm. drafting Labour Code 1969–71, Constitutional Comm. 1983, Panamanian Bar Asscn. 1983–85; mem. Govt. Comm. drafting new Judicial Code 1970–74; Hon. mem. Spanish Bar, Brasilian Labour Judicial Order. *Publications:* Enriquecimiento sin causa 1960, Institutes of Civil Procedure 1972, Casacion 1978, Estudios Procesales 1984, Código de Trabajo Anotado 1970, 1971, 1986, Estudios Procesales 1988. *Leisure interests:* reading, travel. *Address:* Edificio Bank of America, Calle 50, P.O. Box 7274, Panama 5, Republic of Panama. *Telephone:* 69-6412, 69-6601.

FÁBRI, Zoltán; Hungarian film director; b. 15 Oct. 1917, Budapest; s. of Mihály Furtkovics and Olga Gröber; m. Noémi Apor; one s.; ed. grammar school, Acad. of Fine Arts, Budapest, and Acad. of Dramatic Art, Budapest; fmr. painter, later·actor at Nat. Theatre 1941; army service, Second World War; joined Artists' Theatre, Budapest, after Second World War; later Head of Youth Theatre; joined State Film Production Org. 1950, film dir.

1952–; Chair. Union of Hungarian Film Artists; Grand Prix, Carlovy-Vary Film Festival for Professor Hannibal 1956; Grand Prix, Moscow Film Festival for Twenty Hours 1965, Kossuth Prize 1953, 1955, 1970. *Films:* The Storm 1952, Fourteen Lives Saved 1954, Merry-Go-Round 1955, Professor Hannibal 1956, Summer Clouds 1959, Anna 1958, The Brute 1960, Two Half-Times in Hell 1961, Darkness in Daytime 1963, Twenty Hours 1965, Late Season 1966, Boys of Pál-Street 1968,The Tot Family 1969, Ants' Nest 1971, One Day More or Less 1972, The Unfinished Sentence 1974, The Fifth Seal 1976, Hungarians 1977, Bálint Fábián Meets God 1980, Requiem 1981, Name-day Guests 1984. *Address:* c/o Hungarofilm, H-1054 Budapest 5/5, Báthory-utca 10, Hungary. *Telephone:* 116-650.

FABRICIUS, Fritz, DR. JUR.; German professor of law; b. 18 May 1919, Fedderwardergroden; s. of Martin Fabricius and Helene (née Ehmen) Fabricius; m. Gisela Nagel 1948; one s.; ed. Münster Univ.; naval officer 1940–45; Asst. Münster Univ. 1956–61, lecturer 1961–64; Full Prof. of Commercial, Company and Labour Law Bochum Univ. 1964–84, Prof. Emer. 1984–; Man. Dir. Verwaltungs- und Wirtschaftsakademie Industriebezirk 1967–84; mem. Cttee. of Ind. Experts for the European Social Charter with the European Council, Strasbourg 1976–82, 1982–88, 1988–; Bundesverdienstkreuz (First Class). *Publications:* Relativität der Rechtsfähigkeit 1963, Mitbestimmung in der Wirtschaft 1970, Markwirtschaft und Mitbestimmung 1978, Unternehmens-rechtsreform und Mitbestimmung in einer sozialen Marktwirtschaft 1982, Rechtsprobleme gespaltener Arbeitsverhältnisse im Konzern 1982, Streik und Aussperrung im Internationalen Recht 1988, Kommentar zum betriebsverfassungsgesetz 1988. *Leisure interest:* music. *Address:* Dahlhauserstrasse 71/4320 Hattingen 1, Federal Republic of Germany. *Telephone:* 02324- 829 83.

FACIO, Gonzalo J.; Costa Rican lawyer and diplomatist; b. 28 March 1918, San José; s. of Gonzalo D. Facio and María Teresa Segreda de Facio; m. Ana Franco de Facio 1953; one s. five d.; ed. Univ. de Costa Rica, New York Univ. School of Law, and Inst. of Inter-American Law, New York; founding mem. Facio & Cañas (law firm); Prof. Philosophy of Law, Univ. de Costa Rica 1944–47, Prof. Admin. Law 1947–51, 1959–62, Prof. Econ. and Social Org. 1959–61; founder mem. Partido de Liberación Nacional 1948, mem. Exec. Cttee. 1948–56, Chair. Planning Bd. 1959–62; Amb., Rep. to OAS 1956–58, 1962, Vice-Chair. Council 1957–58, Chair. 1963–64; Amb. to U.S.A. 1962–66; Minister of Foreign Affairs 1970–78; Head del. to 12 UN Gen. Assemblies; Pres. Security Council, UN Jan. 1974, March 1975; mem. Admin. Tribunal of the Inter-American Devt. Bank, Washington, D.C.; Ed. Surco (Magazine) 1942–45, Acción Democrática (weekly) 1945–48, La República (daily) 1955–56; *Publications:* The Living Constitution 1976, Meditations on the Bicentennial Celebration 1976, Our Voice in the World 1977, Economic and Social Human Rights 1979. *Address:* c/o Facio & Cañas, P.O.Box 5173, San José; 3155 Avenida 13, San José, Costa Rica (Home).

FADEYECHEV, Nikolay Borisovich; Soviet ballet dancer; b. 27 Jan. 1933; ed. Bolshoi Theatre Ballet School; Bolshoi Theatre Ballet Co., 1952–; People's Artist of R.S.F.S.R. and of U.S.S.R. (1976); Order of the Red Banner of Labour. *Chief roles:* Siegfried (Swan Lake), Albert (Giselle), Jean de Brien (Raimonde), Harmodius (Spartacus), Frondoso (Laurensia), Danila (Stone Flower), Romeo (Romeo and Juliet), Prince Desire (Sleeping Beauty). *Address:* State Academic Bolshoi Theatre of U.S.S.R., 1 Ploshchad Sverdlova, Moscow, U.S.S.R.

FADEYEV, Dr Ludvig Dmitriyevich; Soviet mathematician and physicist; b. 1934, Leningrad; ed. Leningrad Univ.; Sr. Research Fellow, Leningrad Branch, Inst. of Math., U.S.S.R. Acad. of Sciences 1965–; mem. staff, Leningrad State Univ. 1967–, Prof. at Mathematical-Mechanical Faculty 1969–; Pres. Int. Mathematical Union 1986–; specialist in quantum mechanics; State Prize 1971. *Address:* Leningrad A. A. Zhdanov State University, Universitetskaya nab. 7/9, Leningrad, U.S.S.R.

FAGIN, Claire Mintzer, PH.D.; American professor, dean and academic; b. 25 Nov. 1926, New York; d. of Harry Fagin and Mae (Slatin) Mintzer; m. Samuel Fagin 1952; two s.; ed. Wagner Coll., Teachers' Coll., Columbia Univ. and New York Univ.; Staff Nurse, Sea View Hosp., Staten Island, New York 1947, Clinical Instructor 1947–48; Bellevue Hosp., New York 1948–50; Psychiatric Mental Health Nursing Consultant, Nat. League for Nursing 1951–52; Asst. Chief, Psychiatric Nursing Service Clinical Center, Nat. Inst. of Health 1953–54, Supt. 1955; Research Project Co-ordinator, Children's Hosp., Dept. of Psychiatry, Washington, D.C. 1956; Instructor in Psychiatric-Mental Health Nursing, New York Univ. 1956–58, Asst. Prof. 1964–67, Dir. Graduate Programs in Psychiatric-Mental Health Nursing 1965–69, Assoc. Prof. 1967–69; Prof. and Chair. Nursing Dept., Herbert H. Lehman Coll. 1969–77; Dir. Health Professions Inst., Montefiore Hosp. and Medical Center 1975–77; Dean, School of Nursing, Univ. of Pa., Philadelphia 1977–; mem. Task Force Jt. Cttee. on Mental Health of Children 1966–69, Gov.'s Cttee. on Children, New York 1971–75, Inst. of Medicine, N.A.S. (Governing Council 1981–83), American Acad. of Nursing (Governing Council 1976–78), Expert Advisory Panel on Nursing, WHO

1974-, Nat. Advisory Mental Health Council, Nat. Inst. of Mental Health 1983-(87); Pres. American Orthopsychiatric Asscn. 1985; Consultant to many foundations, public and private univs., health care agencies; speaker on radio and TV; Fellow The Coll. of Physicians of Philadelphia 1986; Hon. D.Sc. (Lycoming Coll., Cedar Crest Coll., Univ. of Rochester); numerous awards and distinctions. *Address:* Nursing Education Building, University of Pennsylvania, Philadelphia, Pa. 19104; 1311 Remington Road, Wynnewood, Pa. 19096, U.S.A. (Home).

FAHD IBN ABDUL AZIZ; King of Saudi Arabia; b. 1923, Riyadh; s. of King Abdul Aziz ibn Saud; Minister of Educ. 1953, of the Interior 1962-1975; Second Deputy Prime Minister 1967-75, First Deputy Prime Minister 1975-82, Prime Minister June 1982-; became Crown Prince 1975; succeeded to the throne on the death of his brother 13 June 1982; assumed title "Servant of the Two Shrines" 1986. *Address:* Royal Diwan, Riyadh, Saudi Arabia.

FAHMY, Ismail; Egyptian diplomatist and politician; b. 2 Oct. 1922, Cairo; s. of Mohammed Fahmy and Fayka Noshy; m. Afaf Hamed Mahmoud 1947; two s. one d.; ed. Cairo Univ.; joined Foreign Office 1946; Vice-Consul, Paris 1947-49; mem. Perm. Mission to UN 1949-57, adviser to Egyptian del. to Gen. Assembly 1949-64, alt. Rep. Gen. Assembly 1965-66, mem. del. UN Security Council 1949-50, 1962-63, Rep. Technical Assistance Cttee. 1951-56, alt. Rep. Econ. and Social Council 1951-56, alt. Rep. Collective Measures Cttee., Adviser to Del., alt. Rep. and Rep. Political Cttee. 1949-56, Vice-Chair. (21st session), Chair. (22nd session); Rep. Exec. Bd. UNIDO 1969-71; Rep. Prep. Comm. IAEA 1956-57, Perm. Rep. to IAEA 1957-60, mem. Bd. of Govs. 1957-60, 1971, Vice-Pres. Bd. 1959-60, mem. del. 1st-4th Annual Conf. of IAEA 1958-61, Chair. del. 1968-71; Dir. Dept. of Int. Orgs. and Confs., Ministry of Foreign Affairs 1964-68; Amb. to Austria 1968-71; Under-Sec. of State for Foreign Affairs 1971-73, Minister of Tourism April-Oct. 1973, of Foreign Affairs 1973-77, Deputy Premier 1975-77, resgnd. Nov. 1977; mem. Higher Council of Nuclear Energy 1975-77. *Publication:* Negotiating for Peace in the Middle East 1983. *Leisure interest:* reading. *Address:* 22 Saraya El Gueira Zamalek, Cairo, Egypt. *Telephone:* 418458.

FAHMY, Col.-Gen. Mohamed Ali; Egyptian armed forces officer; b. 11 Oct. 1920, Cairo; s. of Ali Fahmy and Hanem El Gabry; m. Nadia Abaza 1959; two s. one d.; ed. Eng. Faculty of Cairo Univ., Mil. Acad., Staff Coll., Air Defence Acad. in Kalinin, U.S.S.R.; Instructor, Sr. Officers' Studies Inst. 1952-63; Army Operations Dept. 1952-58; Commdr. 2nd Light A/A Regt. 1958, 14th A/A Regt. 1958-59, 64th A/A Regt. 1959-61, 6th Artillery Group 1961-63; Chief of Staff, 5th Artillery Div. 1963-66, Commdr. 1966-68; Air Defence Chief of Staff 1968-69; C.-in-C. Air Defence Forces 1969-75; C.-in-C. Armed Forces 1975-78; fmr. Mil. Adviser to the Pres.; rank of Maj.-Gen. 1965, Lieut.-Gen. 1973, Col.-Gen. (4-star Gen.) 1979; Order of Liberation 1952, Memorial Order of Founding of U.A.R. 1958; Mil. Star 1971; Star of Honour (PLO) 1974; Yugoslav Star with Gold Belt, First Class 1974; Order of King Abdul-Aziz, First Class (Saudi Arabia) 1974; numerous ribbons and medals. *Publications:* Two books on the Palestinian Campaign, Germany, a Threat to Peace, Germany between East and West (in two parts), book on African unity, book on African nationalism, The Fourth Service: The History of the Egyptian Air Defence Force.

FAILLARD, Hans, D. PHIL; German professor of biochemistry; b. 2 April 1924, Cologne; s. of Hermann and Elisabeth (née Kühn) Faillard; m. Maria Scholl 1952; one s.; ed. Univ. of Cologne; Prof. of Physical Chem., Ruhr Univ., Bochum 1964-, Rector 1969-72; Vice-Pres. West German Rectors' Conf. 1970-76; Prof. of Biochem., Univ. of the Saarland, Saarbrücken 1973-, Pres. of Univ. 1973-79; Chair. Cttee. for Int. Contacts of the Alexander von Humboldt Foundation 1973-; mem. Cen. Cttee. W. German Conf. of Ministers for Cultural Affairs 1978-, Cttee. for Research, W. German Rectors' Conf. 1980-; Hochhaus Award, Univ. of Cologne; medals from Hebrew Univ., Israel, and Seoul Nat. Univ., Korea. *Publications:* more than 80 publs. in the field of glycoproteins and more than 30 papers on educational topics. *Address:* Universität des Saarlandes, D6600 Saarbrücken (Office); Richard-Wagner Strasse 87, 6602 Dudweiler; 35 An der Wallburg, D-5060 Bensberg-Refrath, Federal Republic of Germany (Home). *Telephone:* (0681) 3022440 (Office); (06897) 761660; (02204) 63437.

FAIRBANKS, Douglas Elton, Jr.; American actor, writer and producer; b. 9 Dec. 1909, New York; s. of late Douglas Elton and of Anna Beth (Sully) Fairbanks; m. Mary Lee Epling 1939 (died 1988); three d.; ed. Pasadena Polytechnic, Harvard Mil. School, Los Angeles, Collegiate Mil. Schools, New York, tutored London and Paris; began film career 1923, stage career 1927; acted in more than 75 films and 20 plays in U.S. and U.K. (produced or co-produced 15); produced 160 one-act TV plays 1953-58; organized own production co., Criterion Films Corp. (U.K.) 1934; fmr. Chair. Dougfair Corp. and subsidiaries; Chair. The Fairbanks Co. (Calif.) 1946, Douglas Fairbanks Ltd. (U.K.) and associated cos. 1952-58; Pres. Fairtel Corp. (N.Y.) 1969; Dir./Consultant various int. cos. 1950-75; Gov. Ditchley Foundation; Trustee Edwina Mountbatten Trust; mem. Council on Foreign Relations, New York; mem. Mountbatten Memorial Trust (U.S.A.); mem. Bd. of Govs., Exec. Cttee. Royal Shakespeare Theatre, Stratford-on-Avon; Nat. Vice-Chair. Cttee. Defend America by Aiding Allies 1940-41, Vice-Pres. Franco-British War Relief Asscn. 1939-41, Pre-

sidential Envoy, Special Mission to Latin America 1940-41; Chair. Share Through C.A.R.E. Comm. 1946-50, American Relief for Korea 1951-55; rank of Capt., U.S.N. Reserve 1954; Nat. Vice-Pres., American Asscn. for UN 1946-55; Sr. Churchill Fellow (Westminster Coll.); Visiting Fellow, St. Cross Coll., Oxford, Hon. D.F.A. (Westminster Coll.), Hon. LL.D. (Denver Univ.), Hon. M.A. (Oxford Univ.); Hon. K.B.E., D.S.C., K.St.J.; Officier de la Légion d'honneur, Croix de guerre avec palmes (France), U.S. Silver Star, Legion of Merit with Valor attachment, other military and diplomatic honours from Italy, West Germany, Belgium, Greece, Netherlands, Brazil, Chile, South Korea etc.; also professional awards from U.S., Germany and Italy. *Publications:* screenplays, short stories, poems, articles, political essays. *Films include:* Stella Dallas 1926, The Dawn Patrol 1930, Outward Bound 1930, Little Caesar 1930, Morning Glory 1933, Catherine the Great 1934, The Amateur Gentlemen, The Prisoner of Zenda 1937, The Young in Heart 1938, Gunga Din 1939, The Corsican Brothers 1941, The Exile 1946, Sinbad the Sailor 1946, Lady in Ermine 1947, The Fighting O'Flynn 1948, State Secret 1950, Ghost Story 1981; *Plays include:* Moonlight is Silver, My Fair Lady, The Pleasure of His Company, The Secretary Bird, Present Laughter, Out on a Limb, My Fair Lady, Sleuth, etc. *Leisure interests:* swimming, tennis, golf, travel. *Publication:* The Salad Days (autobiog.) 1988. *Address:* Inverness Corpn., 545 Madison Avenue, New York, N.Y. 10022; 575 Park Avenue, New York, N.Y. 10021; The Vicarage, 448 North Lake Way, Palm Beach, Fla. 33480, U.S.A.

FAIRCLOUGH, Anthony John, M.A., F.R.S.A.; British government official; b. 30 Aug. 1924; m. Patricia Monks 1957; two s.; ed. St. Philip's Grammar School, Birmingham and St. Catharine's Coll., Cambridge; Ministry of Aircraft Production and Ministry of Supply 1944-48; Colonial Office 1948; Sec. Nyasaland Comm. of Inquiry 1959; Private Sec. to Minister for Commonwealth Relations and for the Colonies 1963-64; Head, Pacific and Indian Ocean Dept. Commonwealth Office 1964-68; Head, W. Indian Dept. FCO 1968-70; Head, New Towns 1 Div. Dept. of Environment 1970-72, Head of Planning, Minerals and Countryside Directorate 1973-74; Dir. Cen. Unit on Environmental Pollution 1974-78; Dir. Int. Transport, Dept. of Transport 1978-81; Dir. for the Environment, EEC 1981-85; Acting Dir.-Gen. for the Environment, Consumer Protection and Nuclear Safety, Comm. of the European Communities 1985-86, Deputy Dir.-Gen. for Devt. 1986-. *Address:* 12 rue Balderic, 32 quai aux Briques, 1000 Brussels, Belgium.

FAIRFAX, Sir Vincent Charles, Kt., C.M.G.; Australian business executive; b. 26 Dec. 1909, Cambooya, Queensland; s. of the late John H. F. Fairfax and of Ruth B. Dowling; m. Nancy Heald 1939; two s. two d.; ed. Geelong Grammar School, Victoria and Brasenose Coll., Oxford; mil. service 1940-46; Royal Flying Doctor Service 1954-71; Dir. Bank of N.S.W. 1953-82, John Fairfax Ltd. 1956-87; Dir. Australian, Mutual Provident Soc. 1956, Chair. 1966-82; Chair. Stanbroke Pastoral Co. Pty. Ltd. 1964-82, Australian Section, Commonwealth Press Union 1950-73, Boys Brigade 1950 (Pres. 1973); Chief Commr. Scout Asscn. N.S.W. 1958-68, for Australia 1969-73, Nat. Pres. 1977-86; mem. Council Royal Agricultural Soc., N.S.W. 1950-, Treas. 1959, Pres. 1970-79, Vice-Patron 1979; Deputy Pres. Royal Agricultural Soc. of Commonwealth 1966; mem. Church of England Property Trust 1950-71, Council Art Gallery Soc. of N.S.W. 1953-69, Glebe Admin. Bd. 1962-73; Trustee, Walter and Eliza Hall Trust 1953. *Leisure interests:* tennis, golf, trout fishing. *Address:* 50 Bridge Street, Sydney, N.S.W. 2000 (Office); Elaine, 550 New South Head Road, Double Bay, N.S.W. 2028, Australia (Home). *Telephone:* 232 5960 (Office); 327 1416 (Double Bay).

FAITH, Adam (pseudonym of Terence Nelhams); British singer and actor; b. 1940, London; worked in cutting rooms, Pinewood Studios 1956; Asst. Editor, Beaconsfield Studios 1958; TV début as singer in Oh Boy 1959. *Television appearances include:* Drumbeat, The Adam Faith Show, Boy Meets Girls, Budgie, Just Another Little Blues Song, Alfie, Minder on the Orient Express, etc.; London stage appearances include: Night Must Fall, Alfie, Billy Liar, City Sugar, Budgie 1989. *Films include:* Beat Girl, Never Let Go, What A Whopper!, Stardust, McVicar, Foxes.

FAIVRE d'ARCIER, Bernard, L. ÈS L.; French civil servant; b. 1944, Abertville; s. of Guy Faivre d'Arcier and Geneviève Teilhard de Chazelles; m. Sylvie Dumont 1966; one s.; ed. Hautes études commerciales and Inst. d'études politiques; Civil Admin. Ministry of Culture 1972-79; Dir. Festival d'Avignon 1979-84; Tech. Adviser to the Prime Minister's Cabinet 1984-86; Pres. la SEPT (TV Channel) 1986; Consultant, UNESCO 1987-88; Adviser to the Pres. of the Nat. Ass. 1988-; Officier des Arts et des Lettres. *Leisure interests:* art, theatre. *Address:* 6 rue Saint-Bon, 75004 Paris, France. *Telephone:* 42 72 84 38.

FAJĘCKI, Jan, M.ECON.SCI.; Polish economist and politician; b. 30 June 1922, Warsaw; ed. Cen. School of Planning and Statistics, Warsaw; exec. posts in State Bonds Press, Warsaw 1945-53; Asst. Industrial Econs. Dept., Cen. School of Planning and Statistics, Warsaw 1949-55; managerial posts in Cen. Publishing Office, Ministry of Culture and Art 1954-59; lecturer in printing tech., Warsaw Polytechnic 1960-63; Dir., subsequently Pres. of Bd. and Ed.-in-Chief, Epoka Publrs. of Democratic Party, Warsaw 1961-86; mem. Democratic Party (SD) 1962-, Capital Cttee., Warsaw; mem. SD Cen. Cttee. 1973-85, Presidium of SD Cen. Cttee. 1976-85 (Deputy Chair. 1981-85), mem. Secr. of SD Cen. Cttee. April 1981-85;

mem. Seym (Parl.) 1980-85, fmr. Chair. SD Deputies' Club; mem. Co-ordinating Council for Information System in Social Sciences of Polish Acad. of Sciences, Polish Economic Soc. and Polish Soc. of Book Publrs.; numerous Polish decorations.

FAJKOWSKI, Józef, PH.D.; Polish political and social worker; b. 4 July 1927, Szczuczyn; m. Maria Chojnowska 1955; one s. one d.; ed. Nicholas Copernicus Univ., Toruń, and Coll. of Social Sciences, Warsaw; teacher 1952-58; mem. Man. Cttee. Prov. and Nat. Assen. of Rural Youth 1958-61; Head of Dept. of Culture and Art, Olsztyn Prov. Council 1961-65; research worker, Polish Acad. of Science, mem. editorial staff United Peasants' Party publishing houses 1965-71; mem. Parl. (Seym) and Vice-Chair. Seym Comm. of Culture and Art 1971-76; Deputy Minister of Culture and Art 1973-81; Amb. to Finland 1982-83; Dir. Museum of Peasants' Movement History 1984-; Silver Cross of Merit, Gold Cross of Merit, Officers' and Commdrs.' Cross, Order of Polonia Restituta and many other awards. *Publications:* Ruch ludowy na Mazurach i Warmii 1945-1949 1968, Wieś w ogniu, Eksterminacja wsi polskiej w latach okupacji hitlerowskiej 1971, Zarys historii ruchu ludowego 1972, Zbrodnie hitlerowskie na wsi polskiej 1939-1945 1981, and many articles on the rural movement and history of Polish peasants. *Leisure interests:* reading, gardening. *Address:* Mokotowska 46a m. 14, 00-543 Warsaw, Poland. *Telephone:* 219812.

FAKHOURY, Rachid: Lebanese diplomatist; m.; two c.; with diplomatic corps 1952-, Attaché, Lebanese Embassy, Belgium 1952-54, Sec., Saudi Arabia 1956-60, Greece 1960-64, Counsellor, Pakistan 1965-66, Minister-Counsellor, France 1966-71, Amb. to Saudi Arabia 1972-78; Dir. Int. Orgs., Conferences and Cultural Relations, Ministry of Foreign Affairs 1978-83, Perm. Rep. to UN, New York June 1983-. *Address:* Permanent Mission of the Lebanon to the United Nations, Room 533-535, 866 United Nations Plaza, New York, N.Y. 10017, U.S.A.

FALCÃO, Dr. Armando Ribeiro; Brazilian lawyer and politician; b. 1920, Ceará State; Leader Chamber of Deputies 1959; Minister of Justice 1960-61, 1974-79. *Address:* c/o Ministério de Justiça, Palácio da Justiça, Brasília, D.F., Brazil.

FALCONER, Douglas Scott, SC.D., F.R.S., F.R.S.E.; British geneticist; b. 10 March 1913, Aberdeenshire, Scotland; s. of Gerald S. Falconer and Lillias Douglas; m. Margaret Duke 1942; two s.; ed. Edinburgh Acad. and St. Andrews Univ.; joined Scientific Staff of Agric. Research Council 1947, Prof. of Genetics and Dir. of the Council's Unit of Animal Genetics, Dept. of Genetics, Univ. of Edin. 1968-80. *Publications:* Introduction to Quantitative Genetics 1960, 1981, 1989 and 91 research papers (1986), mainly on mouse genetics and quantitative genetics. *Address:* Department of Genetics, University of Edinburgh, Edinburgh, EH9 3JN, Scotland.

FALCUCCI, Franca; Italian politician; b. 22 March 1926, Rome; active in Christian Democrat party (D.C.) 1944-; Deputy Political Sec. of D.C. 1975-76; Chair. of European Union of Christian Democrat Women 1978-; Senator for Rome VII, subsequently for Cerreto Sannita (Campania) 1968-; fmr. Under-Sec. of State, Ministry of Educ.; Minister of Educ. 1986-87. *Address:* Camera del Deputati, Rome, Italy.

FALETAU, 'Inoke Fotu; Tongan diplomatist; b. 24 June 1937, Neiafu; s. of 'Akau'ola (Siosateki Faletau) and Sisilia Lyden; m. Evelini Ma'ata Hurrell; three s. three d.; ed. St. Peter's School, Cambridge, N.Z., Tonga High School, Auckland Grammar, N.Z., Univ. of Wales (Swansea) and Manchester Univ., England; joined Tonga Civil Service, Treasury Dept. 1958; Asst. Sec. to Govt., Prime Minister's Office 1965, Sec. 1969; Resources and External Relations Officer, Univ. of the South Pacific 1971-72; High Commr. to the U.K. 1972-82; Amb. to France (also accred to Fed. Repub. of Germany, U.S.S.R., U.S.A., Luxembourg, Belgium and Denmark) 1972-82; Dir. Man. Devt. Programme, Commonwealth Secretariat 1983-84; Dir. Commonwealth Foundation 1985-; Grand Cross, Order of Merit, Fed. Repub. of Germany, Luxembourg. *Leisure interests:* rugby football, tennis and bridge. *Address:* Commonwealth Foundation, Marlborough House, Pall Mall, London, SW1Y 5HY, England. *Telephone:* 01-930 3783/4.

FALICOV, Leopoldo Maximo, PH.D., SC.D.; American (b. Argentinian) physicist; b. 24 June 1933, Buenos Aires; s. of Isaias Felix Falicov and Dora Samoilovich; m. Marta Alicia Puebla 1959; two s.; ed. Buenos Aires Univ., Cuyo Univ., Univ. of Cambridge; Research Assoc. Dept. of Physics, Inst. of Metal Study, Univ. of Chicago 1960-61, instructor in Physics 1961-62, Asst. Prof. 1962-65, Assoc. Prof. 1965-68, Prof. 1968-69; Prof. of Physics Univ. of Calif., Berkeley 1969-, Miller Research Prof. 1979-80, Chair. Dept. of Physics 1981-83; fmr. Visiting Fellow Fitzwilliam Coll., Univ. of Cambridge, U.K., Fulbright Fellow 1969; OAS Visiting Prof., Argentina 1970; Nordita Visiting Prof., Univ. of Copenhagen 1971-72, 1987; Fulbright Lecturer, Spain 1972, Guggenheim Fellow 1976-77; Visiting Fellow Clare Coll., Univ. of Cambridge, U.K. 1976-77; Exchange Prof. Univ. of Paris 1977, 1984; Assoc. Fellow, Third World Acad. of Sciences; mem. N.A.S; Foreign mem. Danish Acad. of Sciences and Letters. *Publications:* Group Theory and its Physical Applications 1966, La Estructura Electrónica de los Sólidos 1967, numerous articles in professional journals. *Address:* University of California, Berkeley, Calif. 94720 (Office); 90 Avenida Drive, Berkeley, Calif. 94708, U.S.A. (Home).

FALIN, Valentin Mikhailovich; Soviet diplomatist; b. 3 April 1926, Leningrad; ed. Moscow State Inst. of International Relations; official in Soviet Control Comm. in Germany 1950-52; mem. staff U.S.S.R. Ministry of Foreign Affairs 1952-56; Head, Second European Dept., Ministry of Foreign Affairs 1966-68, Third European Dept. 1968-71; Amb. to Fed. Repub. of Germany 1971-78; Deputy Dir. Int. Information Dept., Cen. Cttee. CP 1978-83, Head Int. Dept. Oct. 1988-; Political Commentator, Izvestia 1983-86, Pres. Novosti March 1986-; mem. Cen. Audit Comm. of CPSU; cand. mem. CPSU Cen. Cttee. 1986-. *Address:* Novosti, Zubovsky bul. 4, Moscow, U.S.S.R.

FALKNER, Sir (Donald) Keith, Kt., F.R.C.M., F.R.S.A.; British musician; b. 1 March 1900, Sawston, Cambs.; s. of John Charles Falkner; m. Christabel Margaret Fullard 1930; two d.; ed. New Coll. School, Oxford, Perse School, Cambridge and Royal Coll. of Music, London; Pilot R.N.A.S. 1917-18; professional singer 1923-46; Sqdn. Ldr. R.A.F.V.R. 1940-45; Music Officer, British Council in Italy 1946-50; Visiting Prof. Cornell Univ. 1950-51, Assoc. Prof. 1952, Prof. 1956-60; Dir. Royal Coll. of Music 1960-74; Jt. Artistic Dir. Kings Lynn Festival 1981-83; Hon. R.A.M., Hon. F.G.S.M., Hon. Fellow Trinity Coll. of Music, London, Hon. D. Mus. (Oxford); Hon. mem. Assen. Européenne des Conservatoires de Musique. *Publication:* Voice (in Menuhin series of guide books for young musicians) 1983. *Leisure interests:* golf, cricket, squash racquets, walking, reading. *Address:* Low Cottages, Ilketshall St. Margaret, Bungay, Suffolk, England. *Telephone:* Bungay 2573.

FALL, Ibrahima; Senegalese politician and educator; b. 1942, Tivaouane, Thies; s. of Momar Khoudia Fall and Seynabou (Diakhate) Fall; m. Déguène Fall; four c.; ed. Univ. of Dakar, Inst. of Political Science, Paris, Faculty of Law, Univ. of Paris; Prof. of Int. Law and Int. Relations, Dean of Faculty of Law, Univ. of Dakar 1975-81; Minister of Higher Educ. 1983-84, of Foreign Affairs 1984-; Adviser, Supreme Court of Senegal; Consultant, UNESCO; mem. African Council for Higher Educ. *Publications:* articles in professional journals. *Address:* Ministry of Foreign Affairs, P.O. Box 4044, Dakar; Sicap Fenêtre Mermoz, Dakar, Senegal (Home). *Telephone:* 21.34.31 (Office).

FALL, Médoune; Senegalese diplomatist and politician; b. 21 July 1919, St. Louis, Senegal; ed. Ecole supérieure, Dakar; Sec., Territorial Assembly, Senegal 1952-56; Dir. of Social Insurance, Louga 1956-59; Dist. Chief, Podor and Bambey 1959-60; Head, Diourbel Regional Devt. Assistance Centre 1960-61; Gen. Dir. Nat. Bd. for Farm Produce Purchases, later Gov. of Diourbel Region 1961-63; Amb. to France 1964-66, concurrently to Spain, and Rep. to UNESCO 1965-66; Amb. to Belgium and Perm. Rep. to EEC 1966-68; Amb. to U.S.S.R. 1968-71; Perm. Rep. to UN 1971-79; Amb. to Japan 1979-80; Minister of the Interior 1980-83, of Defence 1983-; Minister of Defence, Confed. of Senegambia 1982-. *Address:* c/o Ministry of Defence, Dakar, Senegal.

FALLACI, Oriana; Italian writer and journalist; b. 29 June 1930, Florence; d. of Edoardo and Tosca (Cantini) Fallaci; ed. Liceo Classico 'Galileo Galilei', Florence, and medical school; entered journalism 1946, special corresp. 1950, war corresp. since 1967 (Viet-Nam, Indo-Pakistan war, Middle East, insurrections in South America); Hon. D.Litt. (Columbia Coll., Chicago); St. Vincent Prize for Journalism (twice), Bancarella Prize for Best Seller, numerous other prizes. *Publications:* The Useless Sex 1960, The Egotists 1965, If the Sun Dies 1968, Interview with History 1974; novels: Penelope at War 1963, Nothing and So Be It 1969, Letter to a Child Never Born 1975, A Man 1979 (Premio Viareggio 1979); numerous articles in Life, Look, New York Times Magazine, Washington Post, New Republic, etc., and in Europe, Asia and South America. *Address:* c/o Rizzoli Editore Corporation, 355 Lexington Avenue, New York, N.Y. 10016, U.S.A. (Office).

FÄLLDIN, (Nils Olof) Thorbjörn; Swedish farmer and politician; b. 24 April 1926, Högsjö; s. of N. J. and Hulda (Olsson) Fälldin; m. Solveig Oberg 1956; two s. one d.; ed. secondary school; mem., Second Chamber of Parl. 1958-64, First Chamber 1967-70; mem. Parl. (Riksdag) 1971-85; Chair. Centre Party 1971-85; Prime Minister 1976-78, 1979-82. *Leisure interests:* fishing, athletics. *Address:* Ås, 870 16 Ramvik, Sweden (Home). *Telephone:* 0612/43097 (Home).

FALLE, Sir Samuel, K.C.M.G., K.C.V.O., D.S.C.; British diplomatist (retd.); b. 19 Feb. 1919, London; s. of Theodore de Carteret Falle and Hilda Beatrice Falle; m. Merete Rosen 1945; one s. three d.; ed. Victoria Coll., Jersey, Channel Islands; served in Royal Navy 1937-48; Diplomatic Service 1948; Consul-Gen., Gothenburg, Sweden 1961-63; Head of UN Dept., Foreign Office 1963-67; Deputy High Commr. in Malaysia 1967-69; Amb. to Kuwait 1969, to Sweden 1974-77; High Commr. in Singapore 1970-74, in Nigeria 1977-78; Del. of Comm. of European Communities, Algiers 1979-82; carried out evaluation of EEC aid to Zambia 1983-84; Kt. Grand Cross, Order of Polar Star, Sweden 1975. *Leisure interests:* jogging, swimming, cross-country skiing, languages. *Address:* Slättna, S-57030 Mariannelund, Sweden; 1 Oakwood Nook, Leeds, West Yorkshire, LS8 2JA, England. *Telephone:* (44) 532-403253.

FALUVÉGI, Dr. Lajos; Hungarian economist and politician (retd.); b. 22 Oct. 1924, Mátraderecske; s. of György Faluvégi and Vilma Ádám; m. Ilona Szász 1947; one s.; ed. Univ. of Econ. Sciences; joined the working-class movement 1947, Hungarian Socialist Workers' Party 1962; held various posts at Ministry of Finance; Deputy Minister of Finance 1968–71, Minister 1971–80; Deputy Chair. Council of Ministers 1980–86; mem. State Planning Cttee. 1973–86, Nat. Planning Office 1980–86; Hon. Prof. Univ. of Econ. Sciences 1985; mem HSWP Cen. Cttee. 1974–; fellow mem. Int. Bankers Asscn. 1979–; Labour Order of Merit; Socialist Hungary and Labour medals; Red Banner Order of Labour 1986. *Publications:* State Finance and Economic Management 1973, 1977, Our Economic Work of Construction and the Finance Policy 1979, Our Financial Affairs during the 1970s 1980 (in Hungarian), The Present Value of Planning 1983 (in Hungarian) and numerous articles on economic policy. *Leisure interest:* nature appreciation. *Address:* National Planning Office, H-1370 Budapest V, Roosevelt tér 7–8, P.O. Box 610, Hungary. *Telephone:* 110-200.

FALWELL, Jerry L., B.A.; American ecclesiastic; b. 11 Aug. 1933, Lynchburg, Va.; s. of Cary H. Falwell and Helen V. Beasley; m. Macel Pate 1958; two s. and one d.; ed. Baptist Bible Coll., Springfield, Missouri; ordained American Baptist minister; founder and pastor Thomas Road Baptist Church, Lynchburg 1956–, now sr. pastor; founder and Pres. Moral Majority Inc. (now Liberty Foundation) 1979–87; fmr. Chair. Praise the Lord Ministry; host TV show Old Time Gospel Hour (nat. syndication); public lecturer; founder Liberty Univ., Lynchburg 1971; Hon. D.D. (Tennessee Temple Univ.), Hon. LL.D. (California Grad. School of Theology), (Central Univ.), Seoul, Korea); Clergyman of the Year Award (Religious Heritage) 1979, Jabotinsky Centennial Medal 1980, and numerous other awards. *Publications:* Church Aflame (co-author) 1971, Capturing a Town for Christ (co-author) 1973, Listen, America! 1980, The Fundamentalist Phenomenon 1981, Finding Inner Peace and Strength 1982, When It Hurts Too Much to Cry 1984, Wisdom for Living 1984, Stepping Out on Faith 1984, Strength For the Journey (autobiog.) 1987. *Address:* Thomas Road Baptist Church, Lynchburg, Va. 24514, U.S.A.

FALZON, Michael, B.ARCH., M.P.; Maltese architect and politician; b. 17 Aug. 1945, Gzira; m. Mary Anne Aquilina; one s.; ed. the Lyceum and Univ. of Malta; fmrly. in practice as architect; mem. Nat. Exec. Nationalist Party 1975–; Ed. The Democrat (weekly paper) 1975; mem. Parl. 1976–; Minister for Devt. of Infrastructure 1987–. *Publications:* newspaper articles. *Address:* Ministry for Development of Infrastructure, Valletta, Malta.

FAN WEITANG; Chinese academic; Pres. Coal Mining Research Inst. 1981–. *Address:* Chinese Academy of Sciences, Beijing, People's Republic of China.

FAN ZENG; Chinese artist; b. 1938, Nantong, Jiangsu Prov.; ed. Nankai Univ., Cen. Acad. of Fine Arts; Prof. in Oriental Arts Dept., Nankai Univ., Tianjin; work displayed in U.S.A., W. Europe and Japan. *Address:* Oriental Arts Department, Nankai University, Tianjin, People's Republic of China.

FAN ZHILUN; Chinese government official; b. 29 Oct. 1935, Sichuan Prov.; s. of Ximing and Zhongshi Fan; m. Xin Ding 1966; one s. one d.; ed. Nanjing Military Acad., Nat. Defence Univ.; joined PLA 1951; rose through ranks to Battalion Cmmdr. 1951–68; Deputy Dir. Operational Dept. 1968–71, Dir. 1971–78; Deputy Divisional Cmmdr. 1978–81, Divisional Cmmdr. 1981–83; Deputy Chief of Staff Nanjing Military Area 1983–85; Deputy Cmmdr. and Chief of Staff People's Armed Police Force 1985–87, Deputy Cmmdr. 1987–; First, Second and Third Class Merits. *Publications:* The Growth of a Tankman 1960, and numerous articles on mil. training and admin. of armed forces. *Leisure interests:* swimming, mountain-climbing, shooting, Chinese chess. *Address:* 3 Jiao Yu St., Xi Dan, Beijing, People's Republic of China. *Telephone:* 655931.

FAN ZIYU, Maj.-Gen.; Chinese politician; b. 1914, Dayong Co., Huhan Prov.; joined CCP and Red Army 1935; on Long March in Dept. of Supplies, 2nd Front Army 1934–35; Champion of Swimming Contest for Generals in People's Liberation Army Units 1960; Maj.-Gen., Gen. Logistics Dept., PLA 1964, Deputy Dir. 1978–; Minister of Commerce 1971–78. *Address:* People's Republic of China.

FANFANI, Amintore; Italian economist and politician; b. 6 Feb. 1908; Fellow, Catholic Univ. of Milan 1932, Titular Prof. in Econ. History 1936, later Prof. Univ. of Rome 1954; mem. Constituent Assembly for XVI Dist. 1946, M.P. for same dist. 1948–68; Minister of Labour and Social Security in 4th, 5th and 6th De Gasperi Cabinets 1947–50; Minister of Agric. and Forestry, 8th De Gasperi Cabinet July 1951, Minister of the Interior 1953, 1987–88, of Budget April 1988–, and Prime Minister Jan. 1954; Sec. Christian Democrat Party 1954–59, 1973–75, Chair. April-Oct. 1976; Prime Minister 1958–59, 1960–63, 1982–83; Minister of Foreign Affairs 1965, 1966–68; Pres. of Senate 1968–73, 1976–82, 1985; Life Senator 1972–; Pres. UN Gen. Assembly 1965–66; numerous hon. degrees. *Publications:* Le origini dello spirito capitalistico 1932, Cattolicesimo e protestanesimo nella formazione storica del capitalismo 1934, Storia delle dottrine economiche 1938–71, Indagini sulla rivoluzione dei prezzi 1939, Storia economica 1940–71, Storia del lavoro 1943, Colloqui sui poveri 1941, Persona, beni, società 1945, Le tre città 1946, Poemi Omerici ed Economia Antica 1960, Una Pieve in Italia 1964, Strategia della Sopravvivenza 1975, ONU 1965–66, 1976, Capitalismo, Socialità, Partecipazione 1976. *Address:* Via XX Settembre 97, 00187 Rome, Italy.

FANG Li Zhi; Chinese astrophysicist; b. 12 Feb. 1936, Hangzhou; s. of Cheng Pu and Peiji (née Shi) Fang; m. Shuxian Li 1961; two s.; ed. Univ. of Peking; Asst. teacher Univ. of Science and Tech. of China 1958–63, Lecturer 1963–78, Prof. of Physics 1978–87, Vice-Pres. of Univ. 1984–87; Prof. and Head Theoretical Astrophysics Group, Beijing Astronomical Observatory, Chinese Acad. of Sciences 1987–; Sr. Visiting Fellow Inst. of Astronomy, Cambridge Univ. 1979–80; Visiting Prof. Research Inst. of Fundamental Physics, Kyoto Univ. 1981–82, Physics Dept. Univ. of Rome 1983; mem. Inst. for Advanced Study, Princeton 1986; Assoc. mem. Int. Centre for Theoretical Physics, Trieste 1984–; mem. Chinese Acad. of Sciences 1981–, N.Y. Acad. of Sciences 1986–; mem. of Council Chinese Soc. of Physics 1982–87, Chinese Soc. of Astronomy 1982–85, Asscn. pro Centro Int. de Fisica 1983–87, Int. Centre for Theoretical Physics 1984–, Int. Centre for Relativistic Astrophysics 1985–, Chinese Soc. of History of Science and Tech. 1987–; Pres. Chinese Soc. of Gravitation and Relativistic Astrophysics 1983–; Vice-Pres. Chinese Soc. of Astronomy 1985–; mem. various IAU and IUPAP comms., etc.; Ed. Scientia Sinica 1978–, Acta Physica Sinica 1979–, Acta Astronomica Sinica 1980–83, Acta Astrophysica Sinica 1982–83, Journal of Modern Physics, etc.; Nat. Award for Science and Tech. 1978, Chinese Acad. of Sciences Award 1982, New York Acad. of Sciences Award 1988, etc. *Publications:* Modern Cosmology Review (ed.) 1978, Astrophysics Today (ed.) 1980, Basic Concepts in Relativistic Astrophysics (with R. Ruffini) 1981, English ed. 1987, Cosmology of the Early Universe (ed. with R. Ruffini) 1984, Galaxies, Quasars and Cosmology (ed. with R. Ruffini) 1985, Advances in Science of China: Physics (ed. with others) 1986, Introduction to Mechanics (with S.X. Li) 1986, Observational Cosmology (ed. with others) 1987, Creation of the Universe (with S.X. Li) 1987, Quantum Cosmology (ed. with R. Ruffini) 1987, Collection of History of Sciences (ed.) 1987, Philosophy as a Tool of Physics 1988, Origin, Structure and Evolution of Galaxies (ed.) 1988. *Leisure interest:* swimming. *Address:* Beijing Astronomical Observatory, Chinese Academy of Sciences, Beijing, People's Republic of China. *Telephone:* 2566978.

FANG QIANG; Chinese party and government official; Vice-Gov. Jiangxi Prov. 1979–81; Adviser Jiangxi Prov. People's Govt. 1983–86; mem. Cen. Advisory Cttee. of CCP Cen. Cttee. 1987–. *Address:* Central Advisory Committee of the Central Committee of the Chinese Communist Party, Zhongnanhai, Beijing, People's Republic of China.

FANG WEIZHONG; Chinese state official; b. 11 March 1928, Dongfeng County, Jilin Prov.; Vice-Chair., State Planning Comm. 1977–; alt. mem. 12th CCP Cen. Cttee. 1982; mem. 13th CCP Cen. Cttee. 1987; mem. Council of People's Bank of China 1974–. *Address:* State Planning Commission, Beijing (Office); 38 S. Yuetan Street, Sanlihe Beijing, People's Republic of China (Home).

FANG YI; Chinese politician; b. 1916, Xiamen, Fujian Prov.; ed. Commercial Press, Shanghai 1930; on Long March 1934; Sec.-Gen. N. China People's Govt. 1948; Vice-Gov. of Shandong 1949, of Fujian 1949–52; Deputy Mayor of Shanghai 1952–53; Vice-Minister of Finance 1953–54; with Embassy of People's Repub. of China, Hanoi 1954–61; alt. mem. 8th Cen. Cttee. of CCP 1956; Dir. of Bureau for Econ. Relations with Foreign Countries, State Council 1961–64; Chair. Comm. for Econ. Relations with Foreign Countries 1964–68; alt. mem. 9th Cen. Cttee. of CCP 1969; Minister of Econ. Relations with Foreign Countries 1969–76, for State Science and Tech. Comm. 1978–84; Vice-Premier, Council of State 1978–82, State Councillor 1982–; Deputy Dir. leading Group for Co-ordinating Nat. Scientific Work 1973–; Vice-Pres. Chinese Acad. of Sciences 1977–79, Pres. 1979–81; Deputy for Fujian 5th NPC 1978; mem. 10th Cen. Cttee. of CCP 1973, mem. Politburo, 11th Cen. Cttee. CCP 1977–82; mem. Politburo, 12th Cen. Cttee. CCP 1982–84; Sec. Secr. CCP Cen. Cttee. 1980–82; Deputy Head Leading Group for Scientific Work 1983–; Hon. Pres. Soc. of Nonferrous Metals 1984–. *Address:* c/o The State Council, Beijing, People's Republic of China.

FANGIO, Juan Manuel; Argentine racing driver; b. 24 June 1911, Balcarce; s. of Loreto Fangio; began motor sporting career as riding mechanic in long-distance road races at age of 11; drove himself six years later; aged 37 when left Argentina to commence European Grand Prix racing in 1948; World Champion a record five times (1951, 1954, 1955, 1956 and 1957), runner-up 1950 and 1953; *Grand Prix wins:* 1950 Monaco (Alfa Romeo), 1950 Belgian (Alfa Romeo), 1950 French (Alfa Romeo), 1951 Swiss (Alfa Romeo), 1951 French (Alfa Romeo, with Luigi Fagioli), 1951 Spanish (Alfa Romeo), 1953 Italian (Maserati), 1954 Argentine (Maserati), 1954 Belgian (Maserati), 1954 French (Mercedes-Benz), 1954 German (Mercedes-Benz), 1954 Swiss (Mercedes-Benz), 1954 Italian (Mercedes-Benz), 1955 Argentine (Mercedes-Benz), 1955 Belgian (Mercedes-Benz), 1955 Dutch (Mercedes-Benz), 1955 Italian (Mercedes-Benz), 1956 Argentine (Ferrari, with Luigi Musso), 1956 British (Ferrari), 1956 German (Ferrari), 1957 Argentine (Maserati), 1957 Monaco (Maserati), 1957 French (Maserati), 1957 German (Maserati); retd. 1958; now Pres. Mercedes-Benz Argentina, Buenos Aires.

FANO, Ugo, SC.D.; American professor of physics; b. 28 July 1912, Turin; s. of Gino Fano and Rosa (Cassin) Fano; m. Camilla V. Lattes 1939; two d.; ed. Univ. of Turin; lecturer, Univ. of Rome 1937–38; Fellow, Resident Investigator, Carnegie Inst. of Washington, Cold Spring Harbor, N.Y. 1940–46, consultant and ballistician, U.S. Army Ordnance 1944–45; Physicist, Nat. Bureau of Standards 1946–49, Chief, Radiation Theory Section 1949–60, Sr. Research Fellow 1960–66; Prof. of Physics, James Franck Inst. Univ. of Chicago 1966–82, Prof. Emer. 1982–; Hon. D.Sc. (Queen's, Belfast) 1978, (Paris) 1979; Rockefeller Public Service Award 1956 and other distinctions. *Publications:* Irreducible Tensorial Sets (with G. Racah) 1959, Basic Physics of Atoms and Molecules (with L. Fano) 1959, Physics of Atoms and Molecules 1972, Atomic Collisons and Spectra (with A. R. P. Rau) 1986; articles in scientific journals. *Address:* 5801 S. Dorchester Avenue, Chicago, Ill. 60637, U.S.A. *Telephone:* (312) 702-7010 (Office); (312) 643-8487 (Home).

FANTIS, Akis; Cypriot politician; b. 15 Dec. 1944, Nicosia; m. Athina Constantinou; three d.; ed. Pancyprian Gymnasium; studied law in Moscow; postgraduate studies, London; fmr. Special Sec., then Sec. for Int. Relations, Pancyprian Workers' Fed. (PEO); Sec. WFTU 1975–79; fmr. Dir. Monday's issue, Haravghi, Co-Ed. and Dir. Athlitiko Vima, Co-Ed. Embros; Govt. Spokesman 1988–. *Address:* Prime Minister's Office, Nicosia, Cyprus.

FARAFONOV, Georgiy Nikolayevich; Soviet diplomatist; b. 1919; entered diplomatic corps 1946; Counsellor, Embassy, Sweden 1961–63; with U.S.S.R. Ministry of Foreign Affairs 1963–66; Counsellor, Embassy, Finland 1966–72; sr. posts in Ministry of Foreign Affairs 1972–75; Amb. to Iceland 1975–79; Head of Scandinavian Div., Ministry of Foreign Affairs 1979–. *Address:* Ministry of Foreign Affairs, Smolenskaya-Sennaya pl. 32134 Moscow, U.S.S.R.

FARAH, fmr. Empress of Iran (see Pahlavi).

FARAH, Abdulrahim Abby; Somali diplomatist; b. 22 Oct. 1919, Cardiff, U.K.; m. Sheila Arthur Farrel 1950; ed. Univ. of Exeter and Balliol Coll., Oxford; Amb. to Ethiopia 1961–65; Perm. Rep. of Somalia to UN 1965–72; UN Commr. for Tech. Co-operation 1972–73; UN Asst. Sec.-Gen. for Special Political Questions 1973–79; Co-ordinator UN Special Econ. Assistance Programme; Under Sec.-Gen. for Special Political Questions 1979–86; Under Sec.-Gen., Dept. for Special Political Questions, Regional Co-operation and Decolonization and Trusteeship Affairs 1987–. *Address:* Office of the Under Secretary-General, United Nations Secretariat, New York, N.Y. 10017 (Office); 1453 Midland Avenue, Bronxville, New York 10708, U.S.A. (Home). *Telephone:* (914) 237-7675 (Home).

FARAH DIRIR, Saleh Hadji, M.SC.; Djibouti diplomatist and scientist; b. 6 May 1937, Djibouti; m.; one s. one d.; ed. Univ. of London and Kansas State Teachers' Coll.; held following positions 1964–77: lecturer in physical sciences and adviser, Ministry of Educ. and Higher Educ., Somalia; Chair. of Sciences and Math. Div., Assoc. Dean of Academic Affairs, Asst. Dean and Dean of Coll. Educ., Nat. Univ. of Somalia; mem., later Chair. Nat. Science Cttee.; Chief, Perm. Mission of Djibouti to UN 1977–79; Perm. Rep. to UN 1979–. *Address:* Permanent Mission of Djibouti to the United Nations, 866 United Nations Plaza, Suite 4011, New York, N.Y. 10017, U.S.A.

FARELL CUBILLAS, Arsenio, PH.D.; Mexican politician; b. June 1921, Mexico City; ed. Nat. Univ of Mexico; lecturer in Civil Law and Gen. Theory of Process, Nat. Univ. of Mexico and in Civil Law, Iberoamerican Univ., Mexico City; Pres. Nat. Chamber of Sugar and Alcohol Industries 1973; Dir.-Gen. Fed. Electricity Comm. 1973–76; Dir.-Gen. Social Security Inst. 1976–82; Sec. of State for Employment 1982–85, for Labour and Social Security May 1985–. *Publications:* essays and articles on legal matters. *Address:* Secretaría del Trabajo y Prevision Social, Dr. Vértiz y Dr Río de la Loza, México, D.F., Mexico.

FARIS, Mustapha, DIPL.ING.; Moroccan economist; b. 17 Dec. 1933, Casablanca; s. of Abdelkader and Fatima (née Labdi) Faris; m. 1958; two s.; ed. Ecole nat. des Ponts et Chaussées, Paris; Govt. Civil Engineer, Dept. of Public Works 1956–61; Dir. of Supply, Nat. Irrigation Office 1961–65; Dir.-Gen. of Hydraulic Eng. 1965–69; Sec. of State for Planning attached to Prime Minister's Office 1969–71; Minister of Finance 1971–72; Pres., Dir.-Gen. Banque nationale pour le Développement économique 1972–77, Chair. and Gen. Man. 1984–; fmr. Vice-Pres. Int. Comm. on Large Dams; Gov. IBRD (World Bank), African Devt. Bank; Gen. Man. B.A.I.I., Paris; fmr. Vice-Chair. and Man. Dir. Banque arabe et internationale d'Investissement –1981; Vice-Pres. World Food Council; Ordre du Trône. *Leisure interests:* music, literature. *Address:* Banque Nationale pour le Développement Économique, B.P. 407, Rabat, Morocco. *Telephone:* 660.40, 688.44.

FARKAS, Ferenc; Hungarian composer; b. 15 Dec. 1905, Nagykanizsa; s. of Aladár Farkas and Blanka Saly; m. Margit Kummer 1939; one s.; ed. Budapest Music Acad. and Accademia Santa Cecilia, Rome, with Ottorino Respighi; film music composer and conductor in Vienna and Copenhagen 1932–36; Teacher of Composition, Metropolitan Higher Music School, Budapest 1936; State Conservatory of Kolozsvar 1941, Dir. 1943–44; Asst. Dir. of Choir, Hungarian State Opera 1945–46; Dir. State Conservatory of Székesfehérvár 1946–48; Prof. of Composition, Budapest Music Acad. 1949–75, Order of Hungarian Standard (with Laurel Wreath) 1980; Cavaliere dell'Ordine della Repubblica Italiana 1984; Kossuth Prize 1950, Erkel Prize 1960, Eminent Artist title 1970, Herder Prize 1979. *Works include:* Bűvös szekrény (Magic Cupboard), opera 1938–42, Furfangos diákok (Sly Students), ballet 1949, Csinom Palkó, musical play 1950, Vidróczki, opera

1964, Panegyricus, dance play 1972; cantatas: Szent János kutja (Cantata Lyrica) 1945, Cantus Pannonicus 1958, Tavaszvárás (Waiting for Spring) 1967, Bontott zászlók (Flying Flags) 1973, Kőröshegyi Betlehemes (Jeu de Crèches) 1970, Aspirationes Principis (Rákóczi Cantata) 1975, Vita Poetae 1976; Laudatio Szigethiana (oratorio); Psaumes de Fête 1975–77, Vivit Dominus 1981, Omaggio a Pessoa 1985; various works for orchestra and choir; chamber music, song cycles, incidental film and stage music. *Leisure interests:* literature, visual arts. *Address:* Nagyajtai-utca 12, Budapest II, Hungary. *Telephone:* 564643.

FARLEY, Carole, MUS.B.; American soprano opera singer; b. 29 Nov. 1946, Le Mars, Ia.; d. of Melvin and Irene (Reid) Farley; m. Jose Serebrier 1969; one d.; ed. Indiana Univ. and Hochschule für Musik, Munich (Fulbright Scholar); operatic debut in U.S.A. in title role of La Belle Hélène, New York City Opera 1969; debut at Metropolitan Opera as Lulu 1977; now appears regularly in leading opera houses of the world and in concert performances with major orchestras in U.S.A. and Europe; roles include Monteverdi's Poppea, Massenet's Manon, Mozart's Idomeneo, Verdi's La Traviata, Offenbach's Tales of Hoffmann and Strauss's Salome; numerous recordings, including Le Pré aux Clercs, Behold the Sun, French Songs by Chausson, Duparc, Satie, Fauré, and Prokofiev Songs; several awards and prizes. *Leisure interests:* skiing, jogging, swimming, dancing, cooking, entertaining, reading. *Address:* 270 Riverside Drive, New York, N.Y. 10025, U.S.A.; 20 Queen's Gate Gardens, London, SW7 5LZ, England. *Telephone:* 212-662-8073 (New York); 01-584 7626 (London).

FARLEY, Edward A., M.B.A.; American banker; ed. Iona Coll. and New York Univ.; fmr. credit reporter, Dun & Bradstreet Corpn.; man. program, Mfrs. Hanover Trust Co. New York 1951–56, Asst. Man. 1956–58, Asst. Sec. 1958–59, Asst. Vice-Pres. 1959–62, Vice-Pres. 1962–69, Sr. Vice-Pres., Regional Officer 1969–76, Sr. Vice-Pres. and Deputy Gen. Man. Corp. Banking Group Metropolitan Div. 1976–78, Exec. Vice-Pres. Metropolitan Div. 1978, now Vice-Chair. and Dir.; Vice-Chair. Mfrs. Hanover Corpn. *Address:* Manufacturers Hanover Corporation, 270 Park Avenue, New York, N.Y. 10017, U.S.A.

FARLEY, Francis James Macdonald, M.A., PH.D., F.INST.P., F.R.S.; British physicist; b. 13 Oct. 1920, Lucknow, India; s. of Brig. E. L. Farley and Helen C. Pemberton; m. 1st Josephine M. Hayden 1945, 2nd Margaret A. Slee 1977; three s. one d.; ed. Clifton Coll. and Univ. of Cambridge; radar research, Ministry of Supply 1941–45; Chalk River Labs., Canada 1945–46; research student, Cambridge 1946–49; Sr. Lecturer, Auckland Univ. 1950–57; muon (g-2) experiment, CERN, Geneva 1957–67; Dean, Royal Mil. Coll. of Science, Shrivenham 1967–82, now Prof. Emer.; Visiting Prof., Dept. of Eng., Univ. of Reading 1982–86; Hon. Fellow, Trinity Coll., Dublin; Visiting Research Physicist, Yale Univ. 1984–; Visiting Research Prof. Boston Univ. 1989–; Consultant, Centre Antoine Lacassagne, Nice 1986–; Hughes Medal, Royal Soc. 1980. *Publications:* Elements of Pulse Circuits 1955; scientific papers on nuclear physics, cosmic rays, relativity, precise measurement of the gyromagnetic ratio of the muon, ocean wave energy, etc. *Leisure interests:* skiing, gliding, windsurfing, travel. *Address:* Le Masage, chemin de Saint Pierre, 06620 Le Bar sur Loup, France. *Telephone:* 93.42.45.12.

FARLOW, Talmage Holt; American musician; b. 7 June 1921, Greensboro, N.C.; s. of Clarence E. Farlow and Annie B. Holt; m. Tina Zwirlein 1973; jazz guitarist with musical groups Red Norvo, Buddy De Franco, Artie Shaw; formed jazz trio 1956–; numerous guest appearances and tours in U.S.A. and Europe; has recorded more than 25 albums. *Address:* c/o Concord Jazz Records, Box 845, 2888 Willow Road, Concord, Calif. 94522, U.S.A.

FARMER, Frank Reginald, O.B.E., B.A., F.R.S., F.INST.P.; British engineer; b. 18 Dec. 1914; s. of Frank Henry Farmer and Minnie Godson; m. Betty Smart 1939; one s. two d.; ed. St. John's Coll., Cambridge; Kestner Evaporator and Eng. Co. 1936–46; Dir. Safety Reliability Directorate, UKAEA, (fmrly. Dept. of Atomic Energy) 1947–79; Ed. Reliability Eng. 1980–; Hon. F.S.E. Foreign Assoc., Nat. Acad. of Engineers, U.S.A.; Churchill Gold Medal 1974. *Publication:* Nuclear Reactor Safety 1977. *Leisure interests:* golf, books. *Address:* The Long Wood, Lyons Lane, Appleton, Warrington, WA4 5ND, England. *Telephone:* Warrington 62503.

FARMER, James Leonard; American civil rights leader; b. 12 Jan. 1920, Marshall, Texas; s. of late James Leonard Farmer, PH.D. and late Pearl Marion Houston Farmer; m. Lula A. Peterson 1949 (died 1977); two d.; ed. Wiley Coll. and Howard Univ.; fmr. Program Dir., Nat. Assoc. for the Advancement of Colored People (NAACP); fmr. Int. Rep. State, County and Municipal Employees Union; Dir. Congress of Racial Equality 1961–66; Pres. Center for Community Action Educ. 1965–; Prof. of Social Welfare, Lincoln Univ. 1966–68; Adjunct Prof. New York Univ. 1968; Asst. Sec. for Admin., U.S. Dept. of Health, Educ. and Welfare 1969–70; Pres. Council on Minority Planning and Strategy 1973–76; Exec. Dir. Coalition of American Public Employees 1977–82; Virginia Commonwealth Prof., Mary Washington Coll., Fredericksburg, Va.; Visiting Prof., Antioch Univ., Philadelphia, Pa.; Chair. Bd. Fund for an Open Society. *Publication:* Freedom—When? 1966, Lay Bare the Heart (autobiog.). *Leisure interests:* detective stories, fishing. *Address:* Rt. 3 Box 1305, Fredericksburg, Va. 22401, U.S.A. *Telephone:* (703) 898-2917.

FARMER, Sir (Lovedin) George (Thomas), Kt., LL.D., M.A., F.C.A., J.DIP.M.A.; British motor executive; b. 13 May 1908, Bridgnorth, Shropshire; s. of Lovedin Thomas Farmer and Florence Webb; m. 1st Editha Mary Fisher 1938 (died 1980); m. 2nd Muriel Gwendoline Mercer Pinfold 1980; ed. Oxford High School; Chair. Rover Ltd. 1963–73; Deputy Chair. British Leyland Motor Corpn. Ltd. 1972–73; Pres. Birmingham Chamber of Commerce 1960–61, Soc. of Motor Mfrs. and Traders 1962–64, Deputy Pres. 1964–65, Chair. Exec. Cttee. 1968–72; Chair. Zenith Carburettor Co. 1973–77; Dir. Aero Designs (Isle of Man) Ltd.; mem. Livery of Worshipful Co. of Coach and Coach Harness Makers; Gov. Chair. of Exec. Council and Finance Cttee. of Royal Shakespeare Theatre until 1975, Deputy Chair. 1975–77; Pres. Loft Theatre, Leamington Spa; Pro-Chancellor Univ. of Birmingham 1966–75. *Leisure interests:* theatre, golf, fishing. *Address:* Longridge, The Chase, Ballakillowey, Colby, Isle of Man. *Telephone:* Port Erin 832603.

FARMER, Richard Gilbert, M.S., M.D., F.A.C.P.; American physician; b. 29 Sept. 1931, Kokomo, Ind.; s. of Oscar I. Farmer and Elizabeth J. Gilbert Farmer; m. Janice M. Schrank 1958; one s. one d.; ed. Indiana Univ., Univ. of Maryland, Wisconsin County Hosp. (Marquette Univ.), Mayo Foundation, Rochester, Minn. and Univ. of Minnesota; mil. service 1960–62; staff, Cleveland Clinic Foundation and Cleveland Clinic Hosp. 1962–, Chair. Dept. of Gastroenterology 1972–82, Chair. Div. of Medicine 1975–; Asst. and Assoc. Clinical Prof., Case Western Reserve Univ. School of Medicine 1972–; mem. Inst. of Medicine, Nat. Advisory Bd., Nat. Foundation for Ileitis and Colitis, Nat. Comm. on Digestive Diseases 1977–79; Gov. for Ohio, American Coll. of Physicians 1980–84, Regent 1985–; Chair. Health and Public Policy Comm. 1986–; Pres. American Coll. of Gastroenterology 1978–79, Asscn. of Program Dirs. in Internal Medicine 1977–79; Interstate Postgraduate Medical Asscn. 1983–84; mem. Council to assess quality of care in the Medicare program, Gen. Accounting Office, U.S. House of Reps. 1986–; Special Citation, American Coll. of Physicians 1984. *Publications:* author or co-author of approx. 215 publs. in the medical literature, primarily relating to digestive diseases with a specific interest in inflammatory bowel disease; ed. of two books and contrib. to others. *Leisure interests:* squash, tennis, running and reading (history and current events). *Address:* Division of Medicine, Cleveland Clinic Foundation, 9500 Euclid Avenue, Cleveland, Ohio 44106; 150 Hunting Trail, Chagrin Falls, Ohio 44022, U.S.A. (Home). *Telephone:* (216) 444-2335 (Office).

FARNDALE, Gen. Sir Martin Baker, K.C.B.; British army officer (retd.); b. 6 Jan. 1929, Trochu, Alberta, Canada; s. of Alfred Farndale and Margaret Louise Farndale (née Baker); m. Margaret Anne Buckingham 1955; one s.; ed. Yorebridge School, Yorks., R.M.A. Sandhurst and Staff Coll. Camberley; 1st Regt. Royal Horse Artillery, Egypt, Germany 1949–54; HQ 7 Armoured Div., Germany 1954–56, 22 Light Air Defence Regt., U.K. 1957–58; Staff Coll., U.K. 1959; HQ 17 Gurkha Div., Malaya 1960–62; War Office, Mil. Operations, London 1962–64; 1st Regt. Royal Horse Artillery, Command of The Chestnut Troop, Germany and Aden 1964–66; Staff Coll. Instructor 1966–69; 1st Regt. Royal Horse Artillery, in Command 1969–71; Ministry of Defence, Policy Staff, London 1971–73; Command 7th Armoured Brigade, Germany 1973–75; Dir. Public Relations, Ministry of Defence, London 1976–78, Dir. Mil. Operations 1978–80; Command 2nd Armoured Div., Germany 1980–83, Command 1st British Corps 1983–85, Command Northern Army Group/C.-in-C. British Army of the Rhine 1985–87; Master Gunner St. James's Park 1988–; Col. Commdt. Royal Horse Artillery 1988–, Royal Artillery 1982–, Army Air Corps 1980–88; Hon. Col. 1st Regt. Royal Horse Artillery 1983–, 3rd Battalion The Yorkshire Volunteers 1983–. *Publications:* History of the Royal Artillery 1914–1918 in France and Flanders, History of the Royal Artillery 1914–18, The Forgotten Front, and the Home Base. *Leisure interests:* military history and gardening. *Address:* c/o Lloyds Bank, London, S.W.1, England.

FARON, Bolesław, H.H.D.; Polish literary historian and politician; b. 17 Feb. 1937, Czarny Potok; s. of Jan and Anna Faron; m. Barbara Faron 1961; one s.; ed. Higher School of Pedagogics, Cracow; teacher in secondary schools, Cracow 1958–64; Asst. 1959–66, Lecturer 1966–69, Asst. Prof. 1969–78, Extraordinary Prof. 1978– Higher School of Pedagogics, Cracow, Pro-Rector 1971–75, Rector 1975–81; Ed.-in-Chief twice-monthly Ruch Literacki 1977–82; mem. Cttee. of Polish Literature of Polish Acad. of Sciences, Historical-Literary Comm. of Cracow Branch of Polish Acad. of Sciences (Vice-Chair. 1970–76), Adam Mickiewicz Literary Soc.; Minister of Educ. 1981–85; mem. Nat. Council of Culture 1982–86; Dir. Polish Inst., Vienna 1986–; mem. Polish United Workers' Party (PZPR) 1956–, deputy mem. PZPR Cen. Cttee. 1981–86; Prizes from Ministry of Science, Higher Educ. and Technology (1st and 2nd Class), Officer's Cross of Order of Polonia Restituta, Silver Cross of Merit, Nat. Educ. Comm. Medal. *Publications:* Zbigniew Uniłowski 1969, Prozaicy dwudziestolecia międzywojennego. Sylwetki 1972, Stefan Kołaczkowski jako krytyk i historyk literatury 1976, Oświatowe przekroje i zbliżenia 1985. *Leisure interests:* travel, skiing. *Address:* ul. Dobra 29 m. 16, 00-344 Warsaw, Poland. *Telephone:* 26-78-49.

FARQUHAR, John William, A.B., M.D.; American (b. Canadian) physician and professor of medicine; b. 12 June 1927, Winnipeg, Canada; s. of John Giles Farquhar and Marjorie Victoria Roberts; m. Christine Louise Johnson 1968; one s. one d. (and two s. from previous marriage); ed. Univ. of California, Berkeley and San Francisco; intern. Univ. of Calif. Hosp.,

San Francisco 1952–53, Resident 1953–54, 1957–58; Postdoctoral Fellow 1955–57; Resident Univ. of Minn. 1954–55; Research Assoc. Rockefeller Univ., New York 1958–62; Asst. Prof. of Medicine Stanford Univ. 1962–66, Assoc. Prof 1966–73, Prof. 1973–; Dir. Stanford Centre for Research in Disease Prevention 1973–; Dir. Collaborating Centre for Chronic Disease Prevention WHO 1985–; mem. staff Stanford Univ. Hosp.; mem. N.A.S. Inst. of Medicine, American Soc. of Clinical Investigation, Acad. of Behavioral Medicine; James D. Bruce Award 1983; Myrdal Prize 1986. *Publications:* The American Way of Life Need Not Be Hazardous to Your Health 1978; contribs. to professional journals. *Address:* School of Medicine, Stanford University, Stanford, Calif. 94305, U.S.A. *Telephone:* (415) 723-6051.

FARR, Dennis Larry Ashwell, M.A., F.R.S.A., F.M.A.; British art historian and museum director; b. 3 April 1929, Luton, Beds.; s. of Arthur W. Farr and Helen E. Farr; m. Diana Pullein-Thompson 1959; one s. one d.; ed. Luton Grammar School, and Courtauld Inst. of Art, Univ. of London; Asst. Witt Librarian, Courtauld Inst. 1952–54; Asst. Keeper, Tate Gallery, London 1954–64; Curator, Paul Mellon Collection, Washington, D.C. 1965–66; Sr. lecturer and Deputy Keeper Univ. Art Collections, Univ. of Glasgow 1967–69; Dir. City Museums and Art Gallery, Birmingham 1969–80; Dir. Courtauld Inst. Galleries 1980–; Gen. Ed. Clarendon Studies in the History of Art, Oxford Univ. Press 1985–; Pres. Museums Assn. 1979–80; Chair. Assn. of Art Historians 1983–86; Hon. D. Litt. (Birmingham) 1981. *Publications:* William Etty 1958, Tate Gallery Modern British School Catalogue (co-author) 1964, English Art 1870–1940 1978, Lynn Chadwick: Sculptor. A Complete Catalogue (with Eva Chadwick) 1989. *Leisure interest:* avoiding academics. *Address:* 35 Esmond Road, Bedford Park, London, W4 1JG, England. *Telephone:* 01-387 0370 (Office); 01-995 6400 (Home).

FARRAR, Frank L. LL.B.; American politician; b. 2 April 1929, Britton, S. Dak.; s. of Virgil and Venetia Farrar; m. 'Pat Henley; one s. four d.; ed. Univ. of S. Dakota Business School and Univ. of S. Dakota School of Law; service in Korean War, retd. Capt. U.S. Army Reserve; Internal Revenue Agent 1955–57; Marshall Co. Judge; Marshall Co. State Attorney; Attorney-Gen. of S. Dakota 1962–68; Gov. of S. Dakota 1969–71; Chair. Marshall Co.; Republican Party. *Address:* P.O. Box 190, Britton, S. Dak. 57430, U.S.A. *Telephone:* (605) 448-2274.

FARRELL, Eileen; American opera singer; b. 1920, Williamantic, Conn.; d. of Michael Farrell and Catherine Kennedy; m. Robert V. Reagan 1946; one s. one d.; debut with Columbia Broadcasting Co. 1941, own programme for six years; opera debut with San Francisco Opera (Il Trovatore); toured throughout the U.S.A. and in other parts of the world; several hon. degrees; Grammy Award. *Address:* c/o International Creative Management Artists Ltd., 40 West 57th Street, New York, N.Y. 10019, U.S.A.

FARRER-BROWN, Leslie, C.B.E.; British public servant; b. 2 April 1904, London; s. of the late Sydney and Annie Brown; m. Doris Evelyn Jamieson 1928 (died 1986); two s.; ed. London School of Economics; Asst. Registrar, London School of Econs. 1927–28; Admin. Staff, Univ. of London 1928–36; Sec. Cen. Midwives Bd. 1936–44; Ministry of Health 1941–44; Dir. Nuffield Foundation 1944–64; Chair. Overseas Visual Aid Centre 1958–70, Centre for Educational TV Overseas 1964–70, Inst. of Race Relations 1964–68; Cttee. for Research and Devt. in Modern Languages 1965–70; Centre for Information on Language Teaching 1966–72; Nat. Council for Social Service 1960–73; Voluntary Cttee. on Overseas Aid and Devt. 1966–76, Inst. of Child Health (Univ. of London) 1966–76; Vice-Pres. Royal Commonwealth Soc. 1969–; Gov. Commonwealth Foundation; Dir. Alliance Bldg. Soc. 1969–83, Chair. 1975–81; Hon. Fellow, London School of Econs., Chair. of Council and Pro-Chancellor, Univ. of Sussex 1976–80; Hon. LL.D. (Birmingham, Witwatersrand and Sussex), Hon. D.Sc. (Keele), Hon. F.D.S., R.C.S. *Leisure interests:* travel, painting. *Address:* 3 Kennet Court, Woosehill, Wokingham, Berks., England. *Telephone:* Wokingham 771907.

FARROW, Mia Villiers; American actress; b. 9 Feb. 1945, Calif.; d. of John Villiers Farrow and Maureen O'Sullivan; m. 1st Frank Sinatra (q.v.) 1966 (divorced 1968), 2nd André Previn (q.v.) 1970 (divorced 1979); eight c.; Stage début in The Importance of Being Earnest, New York 1963; French Acad. Award for best actress 1969, David Donatello Award (Italy) 1969, Rio de Janeiro Film Festival Award 1969, San Sebastian Award. *Stage appearances in London:* Mary Rose, The Three Sisters, House of Bernarda Alba 1972–73, The Marrying of Ann Leete (R.S.C.) 1975, The Zykovs 1976, Ivanov (R.S.C.) 1976; appeared in Romantic Comedy (Broadway) 1979. *Films include:* Guns at Batasi 1964, Rosemary's Baby 1968, Secret Ceremony 1969, John and Mary 1969, See No Evil 1970, The Great Gatsby 1973, Full Circle 1978, A Wedding 1978, Death on the Nile 1978, The Hurricane 1979, A Midsummer's Night's Sex Comedy 1982, Zelig 1983, Broadway Danny Rose 1984, Purple Rose of Cairo 1985, Hannah and her Sisters 1986, Radio Days 1987, September 1988, Another Woman 1988, Oedipus Wrecks 1989. *TV appearances:* Peyton Place 1964–66; Johnny Belinda 1965, Peter Pan 1975. *Leisure interests:* reading, mind wandering, listening to music and certain people. *Address:* c/o Lionel Larner Ltd., 850 7th Avenue, New York, N.Y. 10019, U.S.A.

FARULLI, Piero; Italian professor of viola; b. 13 Jan. 1920, Florence; s. of Lioniero and Maria (née Innocenti) Farulli; m. Antonia Parisi 1945; ed. Conservatorio Statale Luigi Cherubini, Florence (under Gioacchino

Maglioni); Prof. of Viola 1957–77; for thirty years a mem. of Quartetto Italiano; has also collaborated with Amadeus and Berg Quartets; appeared with Trio de Trieste 1978; has lectured at Accad. Chigiana di Siena and at Salzburg Mozarteum; mem. of judging panel at several int. competitions and has been active in many aspects of musical life and education in Italy, notably at the Scuola di Musica in Fiesole; Medaglia della Cultura e dell'Arte. *Address:* Via G. d'Annunzio 153, Florence, Italy. *Telephone:* 608007.

FASCELL, Dante B., J.D.; American politician; b. 9 March 1917, Bridgehampton, Long Island, N.Y.; s. of Charles and Mary Gulotti Fascell; m. Jeanne-Marie Pelot 1941; one s. (deceased) two d.; ed. Univ. of Miami; legal attaché to State Legis. Del. from Dade County 1947–50; Florida State Rep. 1950, 1952; Rep. from Florida, U.S. Congress 1954–; Chair, U.S. Congressional Cttee. on Foreign Affairs 1984–; Vice-Chair. U.S. del. to Conf. on Security and Co-op. in Europe, Belgrade 1977–78, Madrid 1980–83; Chair. or mem. various congressional sub-cttees., etc.; Benjamin Rosenthal Congressional Leadership Award, Nat. Council of Jewish Women Award; Democrat. *Publications:* articles in newspapers and journals. *Leisure interest:* fishing. *Address:* 2354 Rayburn Building, Washington, D.C. 20515; 7855 S.W. 104 Street, Suite 220 Miami, Fla. 33156, U.S.A. *Telephone:* (202) 225-4506 (Washington Office); (305) 536-5301.

FASI, Mohammed El; Moroccan university rector; b. 2 Sept. 1908, Fez; m. Malika El Fasia 1935; three s. three d.; ed. Al Qarawiyin Univ., Fez, Univ. de Paris à la Sorbonne and Ecole des Langues orientales, Paris; teacher, Inst. des hautes Etudes marocaines 1935–40; Head Arab MSS section, Bibliothèque Gén., Rabat 1940, Tutor to Prince Moulay Hassan 1941–44, 1947–52; Rector Al Qarawiyin Univ. 1942–44, 1947–52; Vice-Pres. Conseil des Uléma 1942–; Founder-mem. Istiqlal Party 1944; under restriction 1944–47, 1952–54; Minister of Nat. Educ. 1955; Rector Mohammed V Univ. until 1970, Al Qarawiyin Univ. 1970–72; Pres. Moroccan Del. to Gen. Conf. of UNESCO 1956, 1958, 1960, 1964, Vice-Pres. 1962, leader of numerous UNESCO Confs. in the Arab World, Chair. Exec. Bd. of UNESCO 1964–66; mem. Exec. Council and Special Cttee., UNESCO 1978–; Minister of State for Cultural Affairs and Nat. Educ. 1968; mem. of Royal Cabinet 1979; Pres. Admin. Council of the Assen. of partially or entirely French-speaking Univs. (AUPELF) 1966, Prix Mohammed El Fasi instituted by AUPELF 1987; Pres. Assen. of African Univs. 1967; Pres. Exec. Bd. of Assen. of Islamic Univs. 1969; Tutor to the Crown Prince and the Royal Princesses 1972–; mem. Acad. of Arabic Language, Cairo 1958, Acad. of Iraq, Royal Acad. of Morocco 1980; Dr. h.c. (Bridgeport) 1965, (Lagos, Jakarta) 1968, (Laval, Quebec) 1986. *Publications:* Numerous works in Arabic and French including L'évolution politique et culturelle au Maroc 1958, La formation des cadres au Maroc 1960, Chants anciens des femmes de Fès 1967, Encyclopaedia of Moroccan poetry (20 vols.) 1986–; Ed. UNESCO's Gen. History of Africa, vol. III. *Leisure interests:* painting (has held exbns.). *Address:* Centre de Coordination entre les Commissions nationales arabes pour l'UNESCO, B.P. 702, Rabat-Agdal; avenue des Muriers, route des Zaërs, Rabat, Morocco. *Telephone:* 705-55 (Office); 523-65 (Home).

FASSBAENDER, Brigitte; German mezzo-soprano; b. 3 July 1939, Berlin; d. of Willi Domgraf-Fassbaender and Sabine Peters; ed. Nuremberg Conservatoire and studied with father; début Bavarian State Opera, Munich 1961; has appeared at La Scala Milan, Vienna State Opera, Covent Garden London, Metropolitan New York, San Francisco and Salzburg. *Address:* c/o Jennifer Selby, Ittisstrasse 57, 8000 Munich 82, Federal Republic of Germany.

FAST, Howard; American writer; b. 11 Nov. 1914, New York; s. of Barney and Ida (née Miller) Fast; m. Bette Cohen 1937; one s. one d.; ed. Nat. Acad. of Design; began writing 1931; translated into 82 languages; film has been made of Spartacus; Bread Loaf Literary Award 1934, Schomburg Award for Race Relations 1944, Newspaper Guild Award 1947, Stalin Int. Peace Prize 1954, Screenwriters Award 1960, Secondary School Book Award 1962, Emmy Award (for The Ambassador) 1974. *Publications include:* Novels: The Children 1935, Place in the City 1937, Conceived in Liberty 1939, The Last Frontier 1941, The Unvanquished 1942, Citizen Tom Paine 1943, Freedom Road 1944, Clarkton 1947, My Glorious Brothers 1948, The Proud and the Free 1950, Spartacus 1951, Silas Timberman 1954, Moses, Prince of Egypt 1958, The Winston Affair 1959, April Morning 1961, Power 1962, Agrippa's Daughter 1964, Torquemada 1966, The Hunter and the Trap 1967, The Hessian 1972, A Touch of Infinity 1973, Time and the Riddle 1975, The Immigrants 1977, The Second Generation 1978, The Establishment 1979, The Legacy 1981, Max 1982, The Outsider 1984, The Immigrant's Daughter 1985, The Dinner Party, The Pledge 1988, The Confession of Joe Cullen 1989; Short stories: Patrick Henry and the Frigate's Keel, Departure and Other Stories, The Last Supper; History: Romance of a People, Peekshill: U.S.A., The American (Biography) 1946, The Passion of Sacco and Vanzetti 1953, The Naked God, The Jews 1969, The Crossing 1970; Plays: The Crossing, The Hill, The Ambassador (for TV) 1974, Citizen Tom Paine 1985, The Novelist 1986; Screenplays: Spartacus 1959, The Hill 1963, Martian Shop 1964, Torquemada 1966, The Hunter and the Trap 1967, The General Zapped an Angel 1970. *Leisure interests:* gardening, working about my country place. *Address:* c/o Houghton Mifflin Co., 2 Park Street, Boston, Mass. 02107, U.S.A.

FATAYI-WILLIAMS, Atanda, M.A., LL.M., F.R.S.A.; Nigerian judge (retd.); b. 22 Oct. 1918, Lagos; s. of late Alhaji Issa Williams and the late Alhaja S. Ashakun Williams; m. Irene Violet Lofts 1948; three s.; ed. Methodist Boys' School, Lagos, Trinity Hall, Cambridge, Middle Temple, London; Private practice, Lagos 1948–50; Crown Counsel, Lagos 1950–55; Deputy Commr. for Law Revision, W. Nigeria 1955–58; Chief Registrar, High Court of W. Nigeria 1958–60, High Court Judge 1960–67; Justice of Appeal, W. State 1967–69; Justice, Supreme Court of Nigeria 1969–79, Chief Justice 1979–83; Chair. Ports Arbitration Bd. 1971, All Nigeria Law Reports Cttee. 1972–75, Bd. of Trustees, Van Leer Nigerian Educ. Trust 1973–85, Body of Benchers 1979–80, Fed. Judicial Service Comm. 1979–83, Legal Practitioners Privileges Cttee. 1979–83, Judiciary Consultative Cttee. 1979–83, Council of Legal Educ. 1984–; Hon. Fellow, Trinity Hall, Cambridge Univ. 1983–; Fellow Nigerian Inst. of Advanced Legal Studies 1988–; Chair. UBA Trustees Ltd. 1986–, Advisory Cttee. of Shareholders, First Interstate Merchant Bank of Nigeria Ltd. 1987–; mem. Nigerian Inst. of Int. Affairs 1972–, Int. Comm. of Jurists, World Council of Judges; Commdr. of the Fed. Repub. 1980, Grand Commdr. Order of the Niger 1983. *Publications:* Revised Laws of Western Nigeria (with Sir John Verity) 1959, Ed. Western Nigeria Law Reports 1955–1958, Sentencing Processes, Practices and Attitudes, as seen by an Appeal Court Judge 1970, Faces, Cases and Places (autobiog.). *Leisure interests:* swimming, walking, reading, travel. *Address:* 8, Adetokumbo Ademola Street, Victoria Island, Lagos, Nigeria. *Telephone:* 611315 (Home).

FATEH, A. F. M. Abul, M.A.; Bangladesh diplomatist; b. 28 Feb. 1926, Mymensingh; s. of Abdul Gafur and Zohra Khatun; m. Mahfuza Banu 1956; two s.; ed. Dhaka Univ. Carnegie Fellow in Int. Peace 1962–63; Pakistan Foreign Service 1949–71; Third Sec. Pakistan Embassy, France 1951–53, High Comm. Calcutta, India 1953–56; Second Sec. Embassy, U.S.A. 1956–60; Dir. Ministry of Foreign Affairs, Karachi 1961–65; First Sec., Czechoslovakia 1965–66; Counsellor, New Delhi, India 1966–67; Deputy High Commr., Calcutta 1968–70; Amb. to Iraq 1971; Adviser to Acting Pres. of Bangladesh Aug. 1971; Foreign Sec. of Bangladesh Jan. 1972; Del. to Commonwealth Youth Ministers Conf., Lusaka 1973; Amb. to France and to Spain and Perm. Del. to UNESCO 1972–75, to Algeria 1977–82; High Commr. in U.K. 1976–77; Leader Bangladesh Del. to Extraordinary Plenary Session, UN Council for Namibia, Algiers 1980 and to Ministerial Meeting of Non-Aligned Countries Co-ordinating Bureau on Namibia, Algiers 1981; Chair. Commonwealth Human Ecology Council Symposium, London 1977, Seminar on Foreign Policy Objectives of Bangladesh, Devt. Research Centre, Dhaka 1984; Hon. Rep. Royal Commonwealth Soc. in Bangladesh 1985–. *Leisure interests:* gardening, angling. *Address:* 21 Dhanmondi Residential Area, Road No. 8, Dhaka, Bangladesh.

FATT, Paul, F.R.S.; British professor of biophysics; Reader in Biophysics, University Coll., London 1956–76, Prof. 1976–, Fellow 1973. *Publications:* papers in various scientific journals. *Address:* Department of Biophysics, University College, Gower Street, London, WC1, England. *Telephone:* 01-387 7050 (Ext. 283).

FATTAL, Dia Allah El-, L.E.N.D.; Syrian diplomatist; b. 1927; m.; two c.; ed. Syrian Univ., Damascus, School of Int. Service, American Univ., Washington, D.C., U.S.A.; with Legation to Holy See, Rome 1952–57; Second Sec., Addis Ababa 1958–61; Second, then First Sec., Washington, D.C. 1962–65, Chargé d'Affaires 1965–67; Counsellor, Mission to UN, New York 1967–72; Amb. to Holy See, Rome 1975–81; Perm. Rep. to UN, Geneva –1981; Perm. Rep. to UN, New York 1981–86. *Address:* Ministry of Foreign Affairs, Damascus, Syria.

FAUCHER, Albert, L.S.SC., M.A.; Canadian professor of economic history; b. 20 July 1915, Beauce, P.Q.; s. of Joseph Faucher and Corinne Tardif; m. Louisette Couture 1946; three s. one d.; ed. Univs. of Montreal and Toronto and Univ. of Laval; Asst. Prof. Univ. of Laval 1945–50, Prof. of Econ. History 1950–82, Prof. Emer. 1983–; Visiting Prof. Toronto 1950, McGill Univ. 1970; Nuffield Fellowship 1953–54; Canada Council Award 1969–70; Gov.-Gen.'s Award 1974; Leon-Gérin Québec Prize 1985. *Publications:* Histoire économique et unité canadienne 1970, Québec en Amérique 1973. *Leisure interests:* hiking, snowshoeing. *Address:* Department of Economics, Université Laval, Québec G1K 7P4; 1246 avenue Forget, Sillery, Quebec, G1S 3Y7, Canada. *Telephone:* 527-6705 (Home).

FAUL, Rev. Denis O'Beirne, B.A. (HONS.), S.T.L.; Irish ecclesiastic; b. 14 Aug. 1932, Dundalk, Co. Louth; s. of Dr. Joseph Faul and Anne F. O'Beirne; ed. Louth Nat. School, St. Mary's Coll. Dundalk, St. Patrick's Coll. Armagh, St. Patrick's Coll., Maynooth and Gregorian Univ., Rome; ordained priest 1956; teacher, St. Patrick's Acad. Dungannon, Co. Tyrone 1958–83, Prin. 1983–. *Publications:* 15 books and 20 leaflets on N. Ireland problems; papers on Patristics and history of Irish Catholic church. *Leisure interests:* books, modern languages. *Address:* St. Patrick's Academy, Dungannon, Co. Tyrone, Northern Ireland. *Telephone:* 22165/22668.

FAULKNER, Sir Eric Odin, Kt., M.B.E., T.D.; British banker; b. 21 April 1914, St. Albans, Herts.; s. of Sir Alfred Edward Faulkner, C.B., C.B.E., and Lady Florence Edith Faulkner; m. Joan Mary Webster 1939; one s. one d.; ed. Bradfield Coll. and Corpus Christi Coll., Cambridge; joined Glyn, Mills & Co. (Bankers) 1936, Local Dir. 1947, Man. Dir. 1950, Deputy Chair. 1959, Chair. 1963–68; Army Service, Royal Artillery (Lt.-Col.) 1939–46;

Dir. Union Discount Co. of London Ltd. 1949–70, Chair. 1953–70; Dir. Hudsons Bay Co. 1950–72, Vickers Ltd. 1957–79; Deputy Chair. Lloyds Bank Ltd. 1968–69, Chair. 1969–77; Dir. Bank of London and South America 1969–71, Lloyds Bank Int. Ltd. 1971–77, Lloyds Bank Ltd. 1968–84, Finance for Industry Ltd. 1977–79; Advisory Dir. Unilever PLC, Unilever N.V. 1978–84; Chair. Cttee. of London Clearing Banks, 1972–74; Pres. British Bankers' Asscn. 1972–73, 1979–84; Warden Bradfield Coll. 1965–83; Hon. Fellow Corpus Christi Coll., Cambridge. *Leisure interest:* fly fishing. *Address:* Farriers Field, Sevenoaks Road, Ightham, Kent, TN15 9AA, England.

FAULKNER, Harry George Basil, B.SC.; British business executive; b. 3 Dec. 1931, Stockholm, Sweden; s. of Harry G. Faulkner and Elin Faulkner; m. Beata Lundgren; two d.; ed. M.I.T. and IMEDE, Switzerland; joined Alfa-Laval AB 1957, Sales Dir. 1966–68, Div. Gen. Man. 1968–71, Exec. Vice-Pres. 1971–72, Exec. Vice-Pres. and Acting Pres. 1972–80, Pres. and C.E.O. 1980–. *Leisure interests:* skiing, fishing, boats, cars. *Address:* Alfa-Laval AB, P.O. Box 12150, S-102-24 Stockholm, Sweden. *Telephone:* (08) 80 99 00.

FAULKNER, Hon. J. Hugh, P.C., M.B.A.; Canadian politician; b. 9 March 1933, Montreal; s. of George V. Faulkner and Elizabeth Baird; m. Jane Meintjies; two s. one d.; ed. Lakefield Coll. School, McGill Univ., Int. Man. Inst. and Carleton Univ.; fmr. teacher, Peterborough; M.P. for Peterborough 1965–79; Chair. Standing Cttee. on Labour and Employment 1966; Deputy Speaker of Parl. 1968; Parl. Sec. to Sec. of State 1970; Sec. of State 1972–76; Minister of State for Science and Tech. 1976–77; Minister of Indian Affairs and Northern Devt. 1977–79; Visiting Prof., Faculty of Admin., Ottawa Univ. 1979–80, Visiting Lecturer, Bronfman School of Man., McGill Univ. 1981; Vice-Pres. Environmental, Occupational Health and Safety, Alcan Aluminium Ltd. 1981–83; Man. Dir. Indian Aluminium Co. Ltd.; mem. Bd. of Govs. Int. Man. Inst., India. *Leisure interests:* skiing, canoeing, tennis. *Address:* Alirajpur House, A9/29 Vasant Vihar, New Delhi 110057, India (Home).

FAURE, Maurice Henri, D. EN D.; French politician; b. 2 Jan. 1922, Azerat (Dordogne); s. of René Faure and Irène Joudinaud; m. Andrée Guillemain 1945; two s.; ed. Lycée de Périgueux, Faculty of Law and Letters, Bordeaux and Toulouse Univs.; Deputy for Lot (Radical-Socialist) 1951 (re-elected to Nat. Assembly 1958, 1962, 1967, 1968, 1973, 1978); Sec. of State for Foreign Affairs (Mollet Cabinet) 1956–57, (Bourgès-Manoury Cabinet) June-Nov. 1957, (Gaillard Cabinet) 1957–58; Minister for European Insts. May-June 1958, for Justice May-June 1981; Minister of State for Employment and Housing May 1988–; mem. Conseil Constitutionnel Feb. 1989–; Pres. French del. Common Market and Euratom Conf., Brussels 1956; mem. del. 11th Session UN Gen. Assembly, New York 1956; Special Asst. Minister for Foreign Affairs on Morocco and Tunisia 1956–57; fmr. mem. European Coal and Steel Community Ass.; mem. European Parl. 1959–67, 1973–81; mem. Senate 1983–; fmr. Mayor of Prayssac (Lot), Mayor of Cahors 1965–; Conseiller Général, Salviac canton (Lot) 1957–58, Montcuq canton 1963–; Pres. Departmental Asscn. of Mayors of Lot, Mouvement européen; Pres. Entente démocratique of the Nat. Assembly 1960–62; Pres., later Leader, Parti republicain radical et radical-socialiste 1961–65, 1969–71; fmr. Pres. Rassemblement démocratique Group, Nat. Assembly; Pres. Econ. Devt. Comm. for Midi-Pyrénées 1964–70; Pres. Conseil général du Lot 1970–; resigned from Rassemblement pour la République May 1977; Vice-Pres. Conseil de la région Midi-Pyrénées 1974–; Commdr. Mérite civil and other awards. *Address:* 45 avenue Georges-Mandel, 75016 Paris; 28 boulevard Raspail, 75007 Paris, France (Home).

FAURE, Roland; French journalist; b. 10 Oct. 1926, Montelimar; s. of Edmond Faure-Geors and Jeanne Gallet; m. Véra Hitzbleck 1956; three s.; ed. Enclos Saint-François, Montpellier and Faculté de Droit, Aix-en-Provence; journalist, Méridional-la France, Marseilles 1947; del. in America, Asscn. de la presse latine d'Europe et d'Amerique 1951; founder and Ed.-in-Chief, Journal français du Brésil, Rio de Janeiro 1952–53; Diplomatic Ed. L'Aurore 1954, Head of Diplomatic Service 1959, Ed.-in-Chief 1962, Dir. and Ed.-in-Chief 1968–78; attached to Cabinet of Minister of Public Works 1957–58; Dir. Toutes les nouvelles de Versailles 1954–; mem. Admin. Bd. Antenne 2 1975–79; Dir. of Information, Radio-France 1979–81; founder and Dir. radio CVS 1982; Pres. Dir.-Gen. Société Nat. de programme Radio France 1986–, Société Nat. de Radiodifffusion; Pres. Université radiophonique et télévisuelle int. (URTI) 1987, Communauté des radios publiques de langue français (CRPLF) 1987; mem. numerous professional asscns. etc.; Chevalier, Légion d'Honneur; Officier, Ordre Nat. du Mérite. *Publications:* Brésil dernière heure 1954; articles in newspapers and journals. *Address:* 116 avenue du Président Kennedy, Paris 16e (Office); 94 boulevard de la Tour Maubourg, Paris 7e, France (Home). *Telephone:* (1) 42 30 20 51 (Office).

FAUROUX, Roger, L. ÉS L.; French business executive; b. 21 Nov. 1926, Montpellier (Hérault); s. of Théo and Rose (née Ségu) Fauroux; m. Marie Le Roy Ladurie 1953; three s. three d.; ed. Lycée de Besançon, Lycée Henri IV, Paris, Ecole normale supérieure, Ecole nationale d'admin.; Asst. Insp. of Finance 1956, Insp. 1958; Office of Minister of Educ. May-Nov. 1960; Admin. Dir. Cie. Pont-à-Mousson 1961, Finance Dir. 1964–69; Finance Dir. Cie. de Saint-Gobain-Pont-à-Mousson 1970, Asst. Dir.-Gen. 1972–75, Admin. Dir.-Gen. 1978–80, Pres. Dir.-Gen. 1980–86; Dir. Ecole nat.

d'administration 1986–88; Pres. Soc. des investisseurs du Monde (newspaper) 1986–; Dir. Certain Teed Products, Fabbrica Pisana (Italy), Cristaleria Española (Spain), Cie. Générale des Eaux, Banque Nationale de Paris, Institut Pasteur, Petrofina (Belgique), SmithKline Beckman (U.S.A.); mem. Supervisory Bd. Vereinigte Glaswerke; Chevalier, Légion d'honneur, Officier, Ordre Nat. du Mérite. *Address:* 101 rue de Grenelle, 75700 Paris, France (Office).

FAUVET, Jacques, L. EN D.; French editor; b. 9 June 1914, Paris; s. of Pierre and Andrée (née Meunier-Pouthot) Fauvet; m. Claude Decroix 1939; five c.; ed. Lycée St. Louis, Paris, and Faculté de Droit, Univ. de Paris; an Ed., l'Est républicain, Nancy 1937–39; joined Le Monde 1945, Head of Domestic Politics Dept. 1948–58, Asst. Ed.-in-Chief 1958–63, Ed.-in-Chief 1963–83, Gen. Ed. 1968, Dir.-Gen. 1969–82; Chair. Nat. Comm. on Data Protection, mem. Interpol Control Comm. 1984–; Commdr. Légion d'honneur, Grand officier d'Ordre Mérite, Croix de guerre (1939–45). *Publications:* Les partis politiques dans la France actuelle 1947, Les forces politiques en France 1951, La France déchirée 1957, La politique et les paysans 1958, La IVe République 1959, La fronde des généraux 1961, Histoire du parti communiste français, Vol. I 1964, Vol. II 1965, combined edn. 1977. *Address:* 5 rue Louis-Boilly, Paris 16e, France. *Telephone:* 45.20-14-57.

FAVIER, Jean, D. ES L.; French historian; b. 2 April 1932, Paris; m. Lucie Calisti 1956; four s.; ed. Faculté des Lettres, Paris, and Ecole nationale des chartes; mem. Ecole française de Rome 1956–58; Master of Confs., Faculté des lettres, Rennes 1964, Rouen 1966–69; Dir. of Studies, Ecole pratique des hautes études 1965–; Prof. of Medieval Econ. History, Univ. of Paris-Sorbonne 1969–; Dir. Inst. of History, Sorbonne 1971–; Dir.-Gen. Archives de France 1975–; Dir. Revue historique 1973–; mem. Acads. of Lyon, Reims and Rouen; hon. mem. Luxembourg Acad.; several prizes including Prix des Ambassadeurs 1978 and Grand Prix Gobert (Acad. française) 1981; Chevalier Légion d'honneur; Officier, Ordre Nat. du Mérite; Commdr. des Arts et des Lettres; Chevalier des Palmes académiques and decorations from Belgium, Luxembourg and Poland. *Publications:* Un conseiller de Philippe-le-Bel: Enguerran de Marigny 1963, Les Finances pontificales à l'époque du grand schisme d'Occident 1966, De Marco Polo à Christophe Colomb 1968, Les contribuables parisiens à la fin de la guerre de cent ans 1970, Finance et fiscalité au bas moyen age 1971, Paris au XVe siècle 1974, Le trafic fluvial dans la région parisienne au XVe siècle 1975, Philippe-le-Bel 1978, La guerre de cent ans 1980, François Villon 1982, Le Temps des principautés 1984. *Leisure interests:* organ, photography. *Address:* 60 rue des Francs Bourgeois, 75141 Paris Cedex 03, France.

FAVRE, Alexandre Jean Auguste; French scientist; b. 23 Feb. 1911, Toulon; s. of Auguste Favre and Annie Mercure; m. Luce Palombe 1939; one s. two d.; ed. Univs. Aix-Marseille and Paris; Asst. Lecturer, Faculty of Science, Univ. of Marseilles 1932–38, Lecturer 1938–41, Asst. Prof. 1941–45, Assoc. Prof. 1945–51, Prof. 1951–; Dir. Inst. of Mechanical Statistics of Turbulence 1960–, Emer. Prof. 1981–; Scientific Asst. Ministry of Air 1932; Scientific Counsellor, Nat. Office of Aerospatial Studies and Research 1947, Atomic Energy Commissariat 1958; mem. Nat. Cttee. for Scientific Research 1963, Nat. Cttee. for Univs. 1972–75, Mathematical Soc. of France, Physical Soc. of France, American Physical Soc., mem. Acad. des Sciences 1977; Pres. Fédération universitaire de Mécanique; mem. Nat. Acad. for Air and Space 1983–; Officier Légion d'honneur, Officier Ordre national du Mérite, Commdr. des Palmes académiques. *Major Research includes:* hypersustentation 1934, hyperconvection 1951; inventor of centrifugal sub-trans-supersonic compressor 1940; inventor of apparatus for statistical measurement of time correlation 1942, and of appliance for detection of random noise 1952; research on turbulence of fluids and space-time correlations 1942–89, and on statistical equations of turbulent compressible gas 1948–89. *Publication:* De la causalité à la finalité à propos de la turbulence (with others). *Leisure interest:* philosophy of sciences. *Address:* Institut de Mécanique Statistique de la Turbulence, 12 avenue Général Leclerc, 13003 Marseille; Le Chambord no. 1, 122 rue Cdt. Rolland, 13008 Marseille, France (Home). *Telephone:* 91-50-54-39 (Office); 91-77-65-86 (Home).

FAVRHOLDT, David Cornaby, DR.PHIL.; Danish professor of philosophy; b. 24 April 1931, Oregon, U.S.A.; s. of Elias Favrholdt and Bertha Cornaby; m. 1st Nina Fønss 1961, 2nd Anne Birch 1968; no c.; ed. Copenhagen Univ.; Asst. Prof. in Philosophy, Copenhagen Univ. 1961–66; Prof. of Philosophy and Head of Dept., Odense Univ. 1966–; mem. Royal Danish Acad. of Science and Letters; mem. Danish Research Council for Humanities 1985–89; Aarhus Univ. Gold Medal 1958; Fyens Stiftstid. Research Prize 1972. *Publications:* An Interpretation and Critique of Wittgenstein's Tractatus 1964, Philosophy and Society 1968, Chinese Philosophy 1971, The List of Sins 1973, Lenin: His Philosophy and World View 1978; trans. of Wittgenstein and John Locke. *Leisure interests:* piano, classical music. *Address:* Department of Philosophy, Odense University, Campusvej 55, 5230 Odense M (Office); Oehlenschlægersvej 57, 5230 Odense M, Denmark (Home). *Telephone:* 09-158600.

FAWCETT, Don Wayne, M.D.; American anatomist; b. 14 March 1917, Springdale, Iowa; s. of Carlos J. Fawcett and Mary Mable Kennedy; m. Dorothy Secrest 1941; two s. two d.; ed. Harvard Coll., Harvard Medical School; Capt., Medical Corps, U.S. Army 1943–46; Research Fellow in Anatomy, Harvard Medical School 1946, Instructor 1946–68, Assoc. 1948–

51, Asst. Prof. 1951-55, Hersey Prof. of Anatomy and Head of Dept. 1959-85, Curator, Warren Anatomical Museum 1961-70, James Stillman Prof. of Comparative Anatomy 1962-85, Sr. Assoc. Dean for Preclinical Affairs 1975-77; scientist Int. Laboratory for Research on Animal Diseases, Kenya 1980-85; Prof. and Chair. Dept. of Anatomy, Cornell Medical Coll. 1955-59; Pres. American Assen. of Anatomists 1965-66, American Soc. for Cell Biology 1961-62, Int. Fed. of Socs. for Electron Microscopy 1976-79; mem. N.A.S. and numerous socs.; numerous hon. degrees. *Publications:* Over 150 papers and two textbooks on histology, cell biology and reproductive biology. *Leisure interests:* photography of wild animals, shell collecting, zoological research. *Address:* 1224 Lincoln Road, Missoula, Mont. 59802, U.S.A. *Telephone:* (406) 549-1415.

FAWCETT, Sir James Edmund Sandford, Kt., D.S.C., Q.C.; British barrister-at-law; b. 16 April 1913, Didcot; s. of Joseph and Edith Fawcett; m. Frances B. Lowe 1937; one s. four d.; ed. Rugby School, and New Coll., Oxford; practised at the Bar 1937-39, 1950-55, 1972-; Asst. Legal Adviser, Foreign Office 1945-50; Gen. Counsel, IMF 1955-60; Fellow, All Souls Coll., Oxford 1938, 1960-69; mem. European Comm. of Human Rights 1962-84, Pres. 1972-81; Dir. of Studies, Royal Inst. of Int. Affairs 1969-73; Chair. British Inst. of Human Rights 1976-81; Prof. of Int. Law, King's Coll., London 1976-80, Prof. Emer. 1980-; mem. Inst. of Int. Law 1973-; Visiting Fellow, Southampton Univ. 1974-. *Publications:* British Commonwealth in International Law 1963, Application of the European Convention on Human Rights 1968, The Law of Nations 1969, International Economic Conflicts 1977, Law and International Resource Conflicts (with Audrey Parry) 1981, Law and Power in International Relations 1981, Outer Space: new perspectives 1984. *Leisure interests:* astronomy, piano. *Address:* 20 Murray Court, 80 Banbury Road, Oxford, England. *Telephone:* Oxford 57821.

FAWZI, Ahmad Muhammad Al-Salem; Jordanian civil engineer and politician; b. 1927, Amman; m.; ed. Baghdad Coll. and in U.S.A.; Engineer, Amman 1950-51; District Engineer, Maa'n 1951-53; Chief of Tech. Section for Bldgs. June-Oct 1953; Asst. Under-Sec., Ministry of Public Works 1953, Under-Sec. 1959; apptd. responsible for all aspects of road design and construction 1955; mem. Devt. Bd. and Chief of Exec. Cttee. of Cen. Water Authority 1959; Govt. Rep. at Potash Co. 1959-61; mem. Exec. Cttee. of Hejaz Railway Redevt. Scheme 1962; Mayor of Amman 1964-; Minister of Municipal and Rural Affairs and Minister of State to Prime Minister 1967-68; Minister of Public Works 1968-69; Sec. Civil Eng. Union; Chair. Housing Corpn. Bd., Hidjaz Railway Reconstruction Cttee.; Al-Istiqlal Order (1st Class), Al Kawkab Medal (1st Class), Al Nahada Medal (2nd Class), Alawi Medal of Morocco. *Address:* c/o Municipality of Amman, Amman, Jordan.

FAYAT, Henri, D.LL.; Belgian lawyer and politician; b. 28 June 1908, Molenbeek-Saint-Jean; ed. Royal Athenaeum, Brussels and Univ. of Brussels; Advocate, Brussels 1935-73; Legal Attaché, Belgian Foreign Office, London 1942-43; Chief Asst. to the Belgian Ministry of the Interior, London 1943, and in Brussels 1944; Chief Asst. to Deputy Prime Minister 1944-45; mem. House of Reps. 1946-71; Prof. Faculty of Law, Univ. of Brussels (Vrije Univ.) 1948-78; mem. Consultative Ass. of the Council of Europe 1949-50, Common Ass. of the European Coal and Steel Community 1954-57; Minister of Foreign Trade 1957-58, 1968-71; Deputy Foreign Minister 1961-66; Sec. of State for Foreign Trade 1972-73, for Ports Policy 1973; Chair. Brussels Conf. on British application for membership of EEC 1963; Chair. Acad. Bd., Programme on Int. Legal Co-operation, Vrije Universiteit, Brussels 1974-78; Chair. Algemeen Nederlands Verbond 1978-87; in 1962 adapted Belgium's Foreign Service to country's bilingual character; successfully negotiated 1963 Treaty between Belgium and Netherlands on Scheldt-Rhine Canal. *Address:* 51A Aarlenstraat, 1040 Brussels, Belgium.

FAYE, Jean Pierre; French writer; b. 19 July 1925, Paris; one s. one d.; ed. Univ. de Paris à la Sorbonne; teacher, Lycée de Reims 1951-54; Exchange Fellow Univ. of Chicago 1954-55; Asst. Prof. Univ. de Lille 1955-56, Univ. de Paris (Sorbonne) 1956-60; Research, Centre nat. de la Recherche scientifique 1960- (now Dir. of Research); Founder of the Collectif Change and Centre d'Analyse et de Sociologie des Langages (C.A.S.L.); Founder and Pres. High Council, Coll. Int. de Philosophie; f. and Pres. The European Philosophical Univ., Paris 1986; Pres. European Univ. of Research; Ed. of the review Change 1968; Prix Renaudot 1964. *Publications:* Novels: Entre les rues 1958, La cassure 1961, Battement 1962, Analogues 1964, L'écluse 1964, Les troyens 1970, Inferno versions 1975, L'ovale 1975, Yumi, visage caméra 1983; Poems: Fleuve renversé 1959, Théâtre 1964, produced in Odéon Théâtre de France by Roger Blin 1965, Couleurs pliées 1965, Verres 1977, Syeeda 1984; Essays: Le récit hunique 1967, Langages totalitaires, Théorie du récit 1972, La critique du langage et son économie 1973, Migrations du récit sur le peuple juif 1974, Les Grandes Journées du Père Duchesne 1981, Dictionnaire Politique, essai de Philosophie Politique 1982. *Address:* Editions Seghers-Laffont, 6 place Saint Sulpice, Paris 6e; European University of Research, 1 rue Descartes, Paris 5e, France.

FAZEKAS, János; Romanian politician (retd.); b. 16 Feb. 1926, Lupeni, Hunedoara County; s. of János and Zsuzsánna Fazekas; m. Erzsébet Fazekas 1949; two s.; mem. Union of Communist Youth 1944, Sec. for Odorheiul-Secuiesc Dist. 1944, for Braşov and then for Mureş 1946-47, mem. of Bureau 1946, Sec. of Cen. Cttee. Union of Communist Youth 1950-54; Deputy to Grand Nat. Assembly 1950; mem. Romanian CP 1954-, mem. Cen. Cttee. 1954-84, Sec. 1954-61; Minister of Food Industry 1961-65; a Vice-Chair. Council of Ministers 1965-82; Minister of Internal Trade 1974-80; Alt. mem. of Exec. Political Cttee. of Cen. Cttee. 1965-67; mem. 1967-82; Chair. Council on Co-ordination and Guidance of Supplies and Services for the Population 1977-79; Chair. Co-ordination Council of Consumer Goods Production 1979-82; mem. Acad. of Social and Political Sciences 1970, Standing Bureau Supreme Council of Econ. and Social Devt. 1980-82; Hero of Socialist Labour. *Leisure interests:* political science, economics, history and literature. *Address:* c/o Consiliul de Ministri, Str. Academiei 34, Bucharest, Romania.

FEAST, Michael William, PH.D., F.R.A.S., F.R.S.S.A., A.R.C.S.; British astronomer; b. 29 Dec. 1926, Deal; s. of Frederick Feast and Dorothy (née Knight) Feast; m. Elizabeth Constance Maskew 1962; one s. two d.; ed. Imperial Coll., London; Postdoctoral Fellow, Nat. Research Council of Canada 1949-51, astronomer Radcliffe Observatory 1952-74, South African Astronomical Observatory 1974-, Dir. 1977-; Pres. Int. Astronomical Union Comm. on Stellar Spectra 1967-70, on Variable Stars 1970-76; Vice-Pres. Int. Astronomical Union 1979-85; Pres. Astronomical Soc. of S.A. 1957-58, 1979-80; Hon. Prof. of Astronomy, Univ. of Cape Town 1983-; Gill Medal, Astronomical Soc. of S.A. 1983. *Publications:* over 200 astronomical and physics papers, mainly in Royal Astronomical Soc. notices. *Address:* South African Astronomical Observatory, P.O. Box 9, Observatory 7935, South Africa. *Telephone:* (2721) 47-0025.

FEBRES CORDERO RIVADENEIRA, León; Ecuadorian businessman, engineer and politician; mem. Partido Social Cristano (PSC); PSC cand. in elections 1978, 1979; Pres. of Ecuador 1984-88. *Address:* c/o Oficina del Presidente, Quito, Ecuador.

FEDERSPIEL, Per T.; Danish barrister; b. 9 April 1905, Berlin, Germany; s. of Holger and Asta (née Nutzhorn) Federspiel; m. Elin Zahle 1934; three s.; ed. Harrow School and Copenhagen Univ.; London corresp. to Danish newspapers 1931-32; Sec. to Danish Counsel in the E. Greenland sovereignty case at the Int. Court at The Hague 1932-33; Counsel at the Danish Courts of Appeal 1937; Hon. Legal Adviser to the British Embassy, Copenhagen 1945-77; Minister of Special Affairs 1945-47; mem. Danish Parl. 1947-73; Del. to the UN Ass. 1946-49; mem. UN Palestine Comm. 1947-48, Consultative Ass., Council of Europe 1949-71, Chair. 1960-63; Chair. Econ. Cttee. 1953-60; mem. European Parl. 1973-74; Patron Liberal Int.; hon. mem. Int. Comm. of Jurists; mem. Exec. Cttee. 1963-77; Hon. Gov. Atlantic Inst. 1963-; Chair. Caratorium of the Robert Schuman Prize 1967-; Hon. K.B.E. *Leisure interests:* history, antiques, gardening. *Address:* 38 Dyrehavegaardsvej, DK-2800, Lyngby, Denmark. *Telephone:* 01-135800 (Office); 02-880009.

FEDERSPIEL, Thomas Holger; Danish lawyer; b. 25 Oct. 1935, Hellerup; s. of Per Torben and Elin (née Zahle) Federspiel; m. Benedicte (née Buhl) Federspiel 1965 (divorced 1984); two s.; ed. Krebs Skole, Rungstead Statsskole, Copenhagen Univ; joined Jonas Bruun 1961-66, Slaughter and May, Davis Polk & Wardell 1966-67; partner Per Federspiel 1968; admitted to Court of Appeal 1964, Supreme Court 1969; Chair. Danish Bar Council Cttee. on private int. law 1971-81; Pres. Int. Bar Assen. 1980-82; mem. Int. Bar Assen. 1971-84, Hon. mem. 1984; Hon. mem. American Bar Assen. 1981. *Leisure interests:* tennis, skiing, shooting. *Address:* Gothersgade 109, 1123 Copenhagen (Office); Bernstorffsvaenget 6, 2820 Gentofte, Denmark (Home). *Telephone:* (01) 13-58-00 (Office); (01) 64-28-14 (Home).

FEDIRKO, Pavel Stefanovich; Soviet official; b. 1932; ed. Rostov Eng. Inst. of Rail Transport, mem. CPSU 1957-; CPSU Cen. Cttee. Party High School; Komsomol posts 1954-58; party posts 1958-62; First Sec. of Igarka City Cttee. CPSU 1962-65; Sr. posts in Krasnoyarsk Regional Cttee. CPSU 1965-70; First Sec. Krasnoyarsk City Cttee. CPSU 1970-72; First Sec. Krasnoyarsk Regional Cttee. CPSU 1972-87; Pres. of Man. of Cen. Union 1987-; Deputy to Supreme Soviet 1974-; mem. Cen. Cttee. CPSU 1976-; Order of Lenin. *Address:* The Kremlin, Moscow, U.S.S.R.

FEDORCHUK, Gen. Vitaliy Vasilyevich; Soviet politician; b. 1918, Zhitomir, Ukraine; higher ed.; served in party orgs. in Zhitomir and Kiev Provs. 1939-; local newspapers 1934-36, mil. school 1936-39, thereafter full-time in security services; served in Soviet Army in World War II; mem. CPSU 1940-; Chair. of State Security Cttee. of Ukrainian S.S.R. 1970-82; mem. Cen. Cttee. of Ukrainian CP 1971-; cand. mem. of Politburo of Cen. Cttee. of Ukrainian CP 1973-76, mem. 1976-82; Deputy mem. of U.S.S.R. Supreme Soviet; mem. of U.S.S.R. Comm. for Legis. Proposals; Chair. of U.S.S.R. State Security Cttee. (KGB) May-Dec. 1982; Minister of Internal Affairs, with rank of Army Gen., and Head of MVD militia Dec. 1982-86. *Address:* Council of Ministers, Moscow, U.S.S.R.

FEDORENKO, Nikolay Prokofiyevich; Soviet economist; b. 28 April 1917, Preobrazhenskoe Village, Zaporozhye Region; m. Dljacina Nina Fedorenko; one d.; ed. Moscow M. V. Lomonosov Inst. of Fine Chemical Tech. and Higher Party School of CPSU Cen. Cttee.; Soviet Army 1942-45; Instructor, Head of Dept., Moscow M. V. Lomonosov Inst. of Fine Chemical Tech. 1946-62; Deputy Academician-Sec. Dept. of Econs., U.S.S.R. Acad. of Sciences 1962-63; Dir. Cen. Econ.-Mathematical Inst., U.S.S.R. Acad.

of Sciences 1963–; Corresp. mem. U.S.S.R. Acad. of Sciences 1962–64, Academician 1964–; Academician-Sec. 1972–; State Prize 1970. *Publications:* numerous works on economics of chemical industry. *Leisure interests:* Russian and foreign painting. *Address:* 117418 ul. Krasikova 32, Moscow, U.S.S.R. *Telephone:* 129-06-33.

FEDORENKO, Nikolay Trofimovich, D.PHIL.; Soviet sinologist and diplomatist; b. 22 Nov. 1912, Pyatigorsk, Stavropol; s. of Matrena and Trofim Fedorenko; m. Alla Fedorenko 1943; three d.; ed. Moscow Inst. of Oriental Studies; Diplomatic service 1939–; Counsellor, Soviet Embassy, Chongqing 1946; Chargé d'Affaires, Nanjing 1948, Beijing 1952; Head, First Far East Dept. (China); mem. Policy Planning Bd., Ministry of Foreign Affairs 1950–55; Deputy Foreign Minister 1955; Amb. to Japan 1958–62; Perm. Rep. to UN 1962–68; on staff of Ministry of Foreign Affairs 1968–69; Sr. Assoc. Inst. of Peoples of Asia, U.S.S.R. Acad. of Sciences 1968–, Dir. Econ. Math. Inst. 1963–85, Head Lab. 1986–; Acad. Sec. 1972–85; Ed.-in-Chief Foreign Literature monthly 1970, Sec. Bd. of Writers' Union of U.S.S.R. 1970; mem. Presidium Acad. of Sciences 1972–88; Counsellor to the Presidium 1988–; Corresp. mem. U.S.S.R. Acad. of Sciences 1958–; Hon. mem. Accad. Fiorentina. *Publications:* 25 books and over 150 articles on Chinese literature. *Address:* Institute of Oriental Studies, Zhdanova 12, Moscow, U.S.S.R. *Telephone:* 233-5147, 4364098.

FEDOROV, Nikolay Aleksandrovich; Soviet haematologist; b. 11 Jan. 1904, Voronezh; ed. Voronezh Univ.; Sr. Research Assoc. Cen. Inst. of Haematology and Blood Transfusion 1929–33; Head of Lab. 1933, Head of Dept., Moscow Stomatology Inst. 1943–; Corresp. mem. U.S.S.R. Acad. of Medical Sciences 1957–63, mem. 1963–; mem. Bd. Int. Soc. of Haematologists; Order of Red Banner of Labour. *Publications:* Over 100 works on blood transfusion and conservation, new blood and plasma substitutes, especially heteroproteoseones; established existence and duration of burn putoantigens thus creating a new trend in haematology (immunochemotherapy). *Address:* Central Institute of Blood Transfusion, U.S.S.R. Ministry of Public Health, 4 Novozykovsky pereulok, Moscow, U.S.S.R.

FEDOROV, Svyatoslav Nikolaevich; Soviet ophthalmologist; b. 1927, Ukraine; ed. Flying Acad., Rostov-on-Don, Rostov Medical Inst.; worked as eye-doctor in Veshenskaya, then in regional hosp.; head of faculty of Eye Inst., Cheboksary, and then Archangel, where he elaborated technique of lens-implant; Dir. of Moscow Research Inst. for Eye Surgery 1967–; elected to Congress of People's Deputies of the U.S.S.R. 1989; mem. CPSU. *Address:* Research Institute for Eye Surgery, Hospital No. 81, Moscow, U.S.S.R.

FEDOROV, Viktor Stepanovich; Soviet politician; b. 1912; ed. Grozny Oil Inst.; mem. CPSU 1939–; Dir. Grozny Oil Inst. 1937–40; in oil industry 1940–46; First Deputy Minister of Oil Industry 1946–57; Chair. of Council for Nat. Economy of Bashkir Econ. Region 1957–58; Chair. of State Cttee. for Oil Refining and Petro-Chemicals for Gosplan U.S.S.R. 1958–64; Minister of Oil Refining and Petro-Chemicals 1965–86; Deputy Supreme Soviet 1958–; cand. mem. Cen. Cttee. CPSU 1961–76, mem. 1976–; Hero of Socialist labour, Order of Lenin (twice), Hammer and Sickle Gold Medal and other awards; State Prize U.S.S.R. *Address:* Ministry of Oil Refining and Petro-Chemicals, 1 Ulitsa Marx-Engels, Moscow, U.S.S.R.

FEDOSEYEV, Vladimir Ivanovich; Soviet musician and conductor; b. 1932; ed. conductors' class of Moscow Musical Pedagogical Inst., Moscow Conservatoire; mem. CPSU 1963–; artistic Dir. and Chief Conductor of orchestra of Russian folk instruments 1959–74, of the Bolshoi Symphony Orchestra of U.S.S.R. Radio Network 1974–; works with Bolshoi Theatre and Kirov Ballet and Opera, Leningrad State Prize (Glinka) 1970, People's Artist of U.S.S.R. 1980. *Address:* c/o Bolshoi Theatre, Ploshchad Sverdlova, Moscow, U.S.S.R.

FEDOSEYEV, Pyotr Nikolayevich, DR. PHIL. S.C.; Soviet philosopher; b. 22 Aug. 1908, Starinskoe Village, Gorky Region; ed. Gorky Teachers' Inst. and Moscow Inst. of History, Philosophy and Literature; Dir. U.S.S.R. Acad. Inst. of Philosophy 1955–62, Dir. Inst. of Marxism-Leninism 1967–73; mem. U.S.S.R. Acad. of Sciences 1960–, Vice-Pres. and Chair. section of Social Sciences 1962–88; mem. CPSU 1939, mem. Cen. Cttee. 1962–; Deputy to U.S.S.R. Supreme Soviet 1961–; mem. U.S.S.R. Parl. Cttee.; mem. Int. Social Services Council 1977–, Inst. Int. de Philosophie; Foreign mem. of G.D.R., Mongolian and Polish Acads. of Sciences; Hon. mem. Hungarian, Bulgarian and Czechoslovakian Acads. of Sciences; Chair. U.S.S.R.-Hungarian Friendship Soc.; Order of Lenin (four times); Order of Patriotic War, Order of Red Banner of Labour (twice), Hero of Socialist Labour 1978, Karl Marx Gold Medal (U.S.S.R. Acad. of Sciences) 1981, Order of the October Revolution 1983. *Publications:* How Did Human Society Appear? 1934, Historical Materialism as a Science About the Laws of Society Development 1954, Productive Forces and Relations of Production of Socialist Society 1955, Socialism and Humanism 1958, Communism and Philosophy 1962, 1972, Marxism in XX Century 1972, 1977, Dialectics of the Contemporary Epoch 1966, 1972, 1978, The Leninist Theory of Socialist Revolution and Modernity 1975, The Philosophy of Fodor Pavlov 1975, Economic Problems of developing the Murmansk Region (ed.). *Address:* U.S.S.R. Academy of Sciences, 17 Leninsky Prospekt, Moscow, U.S.S.R.

FEDOSOV, Yevgeny Aleksandrovich, DR. TECH. SC.; Soviet automation specialist; b. 1929; ed. Bauman Tech. Inst.; post-graduate work at Inst.

1953–56; mem. CPSU 1959; research fellow, head of dept., Deputy Dir. of Inst. 1956–70, Dir. 1970–; simultaneously head of Dept. of Physico-Tech. Inst. 1970–; Prof. 1969; corresp. mem. U.S.S.R. Acad. of Sciences 1979, mem. 1984–; Lenin Prize 1976, Hero of Socialist Labour 1983. *Address:* U.S.S.R. Academy of Sciences, Leninsky Pr. 14, Moscow V-71, U.S.S.R.

FEDOTOV, Feliks Nikolayevich; Soviet diplomatist; b. 1929; diplomatic service 1952–; Counsellor at Embassy in Iraq 1968–69, Counsellor-Envoy 1969–72; sr. post in U.S.S.R. Ministry of Foreign Affairs 1972; Amb. to Sudan 1972–77, to Syria 1985–86. *Address:* Moscow, U.S.S.R.

FEDOTOV, Sergey Aleksandrovich; Soviet geophysicist; b. 19 March 1931, Leningrad; ed. Moscow State Univ.; worked at O. Y. Schmidt Inst. of Earth Physics, Acad. of Sciences, Moscow 1957–71; corresp. mem. Acad. of Sciences 1970–; Dir. Inst. of Vulcanology, Far Eastern Scientific Centre, Acad. of Sciences 1971–; Vice-Pres. Int. Asscn. of Vulcanology; Order of October Revolution; numerous scientific works. *Address:* Institute of Vulcanology, Far Eastern Scientific Centre, Academy of Sciences, Petropavlovsk-Kamchatsky, Karaginskaya 56/4, U.S.S.R.

FEE, Cardinal Thomas (see Ó Fiaich, Cardinal Tomás).

FEHER, George, PH.D.; American professor of physics; b. 29 May 1924, Czechoslovakia; s. of Ferdinand Feher and Sylvia Feher (née Schwartz); m. Elsa Rosenvasser Feher 1961; three d.; ed. Univ. of California, Berkeley; Research Physicist Bell Telephone Labs., N.J. 1954–60; Visiting Assoc. Prof. Columbia Univ., N.Y. 1956–60; Prof. of Physics Univ. of Calif., San Diego Jan. 1960–; Visiting Prof. M.I.T. 1967–68; mem. American Physical Soc., Biophysical Soc. (Nat. Lecturer 1983), mem. Bd. of Dirs. Technion-Israel Inst. of Tech., Haifa, Israel 1968–; mem. N.A.S. 1975–; mem. American Acad. of Arts and Sciences 1977–; mem. Bd. Govs. Weizmann Inst. of Science, Rehovot 1988–; Fellow of American Asscn. for the Advancement of Science 1986–; awards include American Physical Soc. Prize for origination and devt. of Electron Nuclear Double Resonance (ENDOR) technique and for applying it to solid state and nuclear research problems 1960, Biophysics Prize 1982; Oliver E. Buckley Solid State Physics Prize 1976. *Publications:* over 100 articles in numerous specialist scientific journals, reviews, symposia. *Leisure interests:* photography, sports. *Address:* Department of Physics B-019, University of California at San Diego, La Jolla, Calif. 92093, U.S.A. *Telephone:* (619) 534-4389.

FEHRENBACH, Charles Max, L. ÈS SC.; French professor of astronomy; b. 29 April 1914, Strasbourg; s. of Charles Fehrenbach and Alma (née Holtkemper) Fehrenbach; m. Myriam Léonie Graff 1939; two s. one d.; ed. Lycée Fustel-de-Coulanges and Univ. of Strasbourg; Asst. Lecturer Univ. of Strasbourg 1934; Teacher Lycée Saint-Charles, Marseilles 1939; Astronomer Strasbourg Observatory 1941; Asst. Dir. Haute Provence Observatory 1943, Dir. 1948–83; Prof. of Astronomy, Univ. of Marseilles 1948–83, Prof. Emer. 1983–; Dir. Marseilles Observatory 1949–81; Pres. Comm. des instruments, Observatoire européen austral 1969–72, mem. Bd. 1965–72; mem. Bd. Canada France Hawaii Telescope 1975–79, Pres. 1979; mem. Int. Astronomical Union, Vice-Pres. 1973–79; mem. Bureau des Longitudes 1973, Pres. 1987; mem. Rotary Int., Hon. mem. S.A. Astronomical Soc. 1965; Assoc. mem. Royal Astronomical Soc., London 1961; mem. Acad. des Sciences Paris 1968, Int. Astronomical Acad. 1986; Assoc. mem. Acad. Royale des Sciences de Belgique 1973, Acad. of Athens 1980; Corresp. mem. Acad. of Coimbra 1953, Halle 1966, Vienna 1973; Croix de guerre, Commdr. Légion d'honneur, Palmes académiques, ordre de Léopold II, Chevalier du Mérite agricole, Officier Ordre de Léopold de Belgique; Lauréat, Inst. de France, Acad. Royale de Belgique, Grand prix des sciences de la Ville de Paris 1976, Médaille d'or du C.N.R.S. 1978. *Publications:* 280 publs. in int. reviews on astronomy and related topics. *Leisure interests:* gardening, fishing. *Address:* Les Magnaraelles, Lourmarin, 84160 Cadenet, France. *Telephone:* 9068 8028.

FEI SHENGFU; Chinese artist; b. 1927, Shanghai; ed. Dept. of Drawing, Cen. Acad. of Fine Arts. *Address:* People's Republic of China.

FEI XIAOTONG; Chinese social anthropologist; b. 2 Nov. 1910, Wukiang Dist., Jiangsu Prov.; s. of Fei Po-an and Yang Renglan; m. Meng Yin 1939; one d.; ed. Yanjing Univ., Beijing, Qinghua Univ., Beijing, London School of Econs.; Prof. of Social Anthropology, Nat. Yunnan Univ. 1939; Visiting Prof., Harvard Univ. (invited by State Dept.), later Inst. of Pacific Relations, New York 1943; Prof. of Anthropology, Qinghua Univ., Beijing 1945; Visiting Fellow, L.S.E. 1946; Deputy Dean, Qinghua Univ., Beijing 1949; Vice-Pres. Cen. Inst. of Nat. Minorities 1952; Vice-Chair. Nationalities Affairs Comm. (under State Council) 1957; Prof. of Anthropology, Cen. Inst. of Nat. Minorities 1957–1982; Pres. Sociology Soc. of China 1979; Prof. of Sociology, Beijing Univ. 1979; Dir. Inst. of Sociology, Chinese Acad. of Social Sciences 1980, Emer. 1983–; Vice-Chair. Chinese Democratic League 1980–87, Chair. 1987–; Vice-Chair. Standing Cttee. April 1988–; Vice-Pres. Assen. for Int. Understanding 1988–; Vice-Pres. Chinese People's Political Consultative Conf. 1983; Huxley Lecturer, Royal Anthropological Inst. 1981; Hon. Fellow, L.S.E. 1982; Adviser Nationalities Affairs Comm. 1983; Malinowski Award 1980. *Publications include:* Peasant Life in China 1939, Earthbound China 1945, Systems of Child Rearing, Rural China 1947, Rural Reconstruction, Gentry Power and Imperial Power 1948, China's Gentry 1953, Toward a People's Anthropology 1981, Chinese Village Close-up 1983, Collections of Essays on Sociology 1985, Small Town in China 1986. *Leisure interests:* chess, jogging. *Address:* Institute of Sociology, Beijing University, Beijing, People's Republic of China. *Telephone:* 894196.

FEIFFER, Jules; American cartoonist and writer; b. 26 Jan. 1929, New York; s. of David Feiffer and Rhoda Davis; m. 1st Judith Sheftel 1961, one d.; m. 2nd Jennifer Allen 1983, one d.; ed. Art Students League, Pratt Inst.; asst. to syndicated cartoonist Will Eisner 1946–51; cartoonist, author, syndicated Sunday page, Clifford, engaged in various art jobs 1953–56; contributing cartoonist Village Voice, New York City 1956–; cartoons published weekly in The Observer (London) 1958–66, 1972–82, regularly in Playboy (magazine); cartoons nationally syndicated in U.S. 1959–; sponsor Sane; U.S. Army 1951–53; mem. Dramatists Guild Council 1970–; Hon. Fellow Inst. for Policy Studies 1987; Acad. Award for Animated Cartoon, Munro 1961; Special George Polk Memorial Award 1962; Best Foreign Play, English Press (for Little Murders) 1967, Outer Critics Circle Award (Obie) 1969, (The White House Murder Case) 1970, Pulitzer Prize, Editorial Cartooning 1986. *Publications:* books: Sick, Sick, Sick 1959, Passionella and other stories 1960, The Explainers 1961, Boy, Girl, Boy, Girl, 1962, Hold Me! 1962, Harry, The Rat With Women (novel) 1963, Feiffer's Album 1963, The Unexpurgated Memoirs of Bernard Mergendeiler 1965, The Great Comic Book Heroes 1967, Feiffer's Marriage Manual 1967, Pictures at a Prosecution 1971, Ackroyd (novel) 1978, Tantrum 1980, Jules Feiffer's America: From Eisenhower to Reagan 1982, Marriage is an Invasion of Privacy 1984, Feiffer's Children 1986, Ronald Reagan in Movie America 1988, Elliott Loves 1989 (book and play); plays: Crawling Arnold 1961, Little Murders 1966, God Bless 1968, The White House Murder Case 1970, Feiffer on Nixon: The Cartoon Presidency 1974, Knock Knock 1975, Grown Ups 1981, A Think Piece 1982, Feiffer's America 1985, Carnal Knowledge 1988; screenplays: Little Murders 1971, Carnal Knowledge 1971, Popeye 1980, I Want to Go Home 1989. *Address:* c/o Universal Press Syndicate, 4900 Main Street, Kansas City, Miss. 64112, U.S.A.

FEILDEN, Sir Bernard Melchior, Kt., C.B.E., D.UNIV., A.A. DIPL. HONS., F.R.I.B.A., F.S.A., F.R.S.A.; British architect; b. 11 Sept. 1919, London; s. of Robert Humphrey Feilden, M.C., and Olive (née Binyon) Feilden; m. Ruth Mildred Bainbridge 1949; two s. two d.; ed. Bedford School, Univ. Coll., London, Architectural Assn., London; qualified as architect 1949; Sr. Partner, Feilden and Mawson 1954–77, now Consultant; Architect, Norwich Cathedral 1963; Surveyor, York Minster 1965, St. Paul's Cathedral, London 1969; Consultant Architect Univ. of East Anglia 1969, Hyde Park Estate, London 1972; St. Giles Cathedral Project 1975, Conservation Plan for Chesterfield Town Centre 1976–81, R.I.B.A. Rep. on Ancient Monuments Bd. 1962–77, mem. R.I.B.A. Council 1975–77; Pres. Ecclesiastical Architects' and Surveyors' Assn. 1976; Dir. Int. Centre for the Study and Preservation of Cultural Property, Rome (ICCROM) 1977–81, Dir. Emer. 1983; Pres. The Guild of Surveyors 1976; Chair. U.K. Cttee. of Int. Council on Monuments and Sites 1981; Architectural Conservation Consultant; mem. Cathedrals Advisory Comm., Churches Conservation Cttee. 1981–; Hon. F.A.I.A. 1987; Outstanding Conservation Award 1975, Aga Khan Award for Architecture 1986, three Civic Trust Awards and four Commendations. *Publications:* The Wonder of York Minster 1976, An Introduction to Conservation (for UNESCO) 1980, The Conservation of Historic Buildings 1982, Ed. Management Manual for World Cultural Heritage Sites (UNESCO). *Leisure interests:* painting, sailing, fishing, chess. *Address:* Stiffkey Old Hall, Wells-next-the-Sea, Norfolk, NR23 1QJ, England. *Telephone:* 032875 585.

FEILDEN, Geoffrey Bertram Robert, C.B.E., M.A., F.ENG., F.I.MECH.E., F.R.S.; British engineer; b. 20 Feb. 1917, London; s. of Robert H. and Olive (Binyon) Feilden; m. 1st Elizabeth A. Gorton, m. 2nd Elizabeth D. Angier; one s. two d., three step-c.; ed. Bedford School, King's Coll., Cambridge; with Lever Bros. and Unilever Ltd. 1939–40; Power Jets Ltd. 1940–46; Ruston & Hornsby Ltd. 1946–59, Chief Eng. Turbine Dept. 1949, Eng. Dir. 1954; Man. Dir. Hawker Siddeley Brush Turbines Ltd. and Dir. Hawker Siddeley Industries Ltd. 1959–61; Group Tech. Dir. Davy-Ashmore Ltd. 1961–68; Deputy Dir.-Gen. British Standards Inst. 1968–70, Dir.-Gen. 1970–81; Dir Averys Ltd. 1974–79, Plint and Partners Ltd. 1982–; Prin. Consultant, Feilden Assocs. Ltd. 1981–; consultant to Int. Energy Authority; mem. or fmr. mem. various advisory councils, cttees. etc.; Sr. Fellow, R.C.A., London; Hon. F.I. Struct.E.; Hon. F.I.Q.A.; Hon. mem. Foundation for Science and Tech.; Hon. D.Sc. (Queen's Univ., Belfast); Hon. D.Tech. (Loughborough). *Publications:* books, papers and articles on engineering subjects. *Leisure interests:* sailing, skiing, photography. *Address:* Verlands, Painswick, Gloucestershire, GL6 6XP, England. *Telephone:* 0452-812112.

FEIN, Rashi, PH.D.; American professor of economics; b. 6 Feb. 1926, New York; s. of Isaac M. Fein and Clara (née Wertheim) Fein; m. Ruth Breslau 1949; two s. two d.; ed. The Johns Hopkins Univ.; with U.S.N. 1944–46; mem. Dept. of Econ., Univ. of North Carolina 1952–61; Sr. Staff, Council of Econ. Advisers 1961–63; Sr. Staff, Econ. Studies Div., Brookings Inst. 1963–68; Prof. of Econ. of Medicine, Harvard Medical School, Dept. of Social Medicine and Health Policy 1968–; John M. Russell Medal, Markel Scholars, Heath Clark Lecturer, London School of Hygiene and Tropical Medicine. *Publications:* Economics of Mental Illness 1958, The Doctor Shortage: An Economic Diagnosis 1967, Financing Medical Education: An

Analysis of Alternative Policies and Mechanisms (with Gerald I. Weber) 1971, A Right to Health: The Problem of Access to Primary Medical Care (with Charles Lewis and David Mechanic) 1978, Alcoholism in America: The Price We Pay 1984, Medical Care, Medical Costs: The Search for a Health Insurance Policy 1986, numerous articles. *Address:* 205 Commonwealth Avenue, Boston, Mass. 02116, U.S.A. *Telephone:* 617-536 4888.

FEINBERG, E. L. (see Feinberg, Yevgeniy Lvovich).

FEINBERG, Nathan, DR.JUR.UTR.; Israeli emeritus professor; b. 6 June 1895, Kovno, Russia; s. of Leon and Henia (née Ratner) Feinberg; m. 1st Judith Ostrovsky-Mevorach 1925 (deceased), 2nd Anna Hirshowitz 1974; ed. Univ. of Zürich and Graduate Inst. of Int. Studies, Geneva; Head of Dept., Ministry of Jewish Affairs, Lithuania 1919–21; Sec. Cttee. of Jewish Dels., Paris 1922–24; law practice in Palestine 1924–27 and 1934–45; Lecturer, Univ. of Geneva 1931–33; Lecturer, Hebrew Univ., Jerusalem 1945–49, Assoc. Prof. 1949–52, Prof. of Int. Law and Relations 1952–66, Emer. Prof. 1966–, Dean of Faculty of Law 1949–51; mem. Perm. Court of Arbitration; Hon. mem. Inst. Int. Law, Bd. of Govs. Hebrew Univ., Israel Historical Soc.; Worthy of Jerusalem; Dr. Philosophiae h.c. (Hebrew Univ., Jerusalem). *Publications:* La question des minorités à la Conférence de la paix de 1919–1920 et l'action juive en faveur de la protection internationale des minorités 1929, La juridiction de la Cour Permanente de Justice Internationale dans le système des mandats 1930, La juridiction de la Cour Permanente de Justice dans le système de la protection internationale des minorités 1931, La pétition en droit international 1933, Some Problems of the Palestine Mandate 1936, L'admission de nouveaux membres à la Société des Nations et à l'Organisation des Nations Unies 1952, The Jewish Struggle against Hitler in the League of Nations—the Bernheim Petition (in Hebrew) 1957, The Legality of a 'State of War' after the Cessation of Hostilities 1961, Palestine under the Mandate and the State of Israel—Problems in International Law (in Hebrew) 1963, The Jewish League of Nations Societies (in Hebrew) 1967, The Arab-Israel Conflict in International Law 1970, On an Arab Jurist's Approach to Zionism and the State of Israel 1971, Studies in International Law, with Special Reference to the Arab-Israel Conflict 1979, Essays on Jewish Issues of our Time (in Hebrew) 1980, Reminiscences (in Hebrew) 1985; co-editor The Jewish Year Book of International Law 1949; editor Studies in Public International Law in Memory of Sir Hersch Lauterpacht (in Hebrew) 1962. *Address:* 6 Ben Labrat Street, Jerusalem 92307, Israel. *Telephone:* 633345.

FEINBERG, Yevgeniy Lvovich; Soviet physicist; b. 27 June 1912, Baku; s. of Dr. L. B. Feinberg and T. A. Feinstein; m. Valentine Konen 1932; one d.; ed. Moscow Univ.; Postgraduate, Moscow Univ., 1935–38; Research Assoc., Lebedev Inst. of Physics U.S.S.R. Acad. of Sciences 1938–, Head of Sector 1952–88, Councillor and Dir. 1988–; lecturer, Asst. Prof. Moscow Power Inst. 1935–39; Prof. Gorky Univ. 1944–45; Prof. Moscow Eng. Physics Inst. 1946–54; Corresp. mem. U.S.S.R. Acad. of Sciences 1966–. *Publications:* Art in the Science Dominated World 1987; works on radiophysics, nuclear physics, cosmic rays, statistical acoustics and elementary particles, philosophy of science and art. *Leisure interests:* chess. *Address:* P. N. Lebedev Institute of Physics, 53 Leninsky Prospekt, 117924 Moscow B-333, U.S.S.R. *Telephone:* 132-29-29 (Office).

FEINENDEGEN, Ludwig E., DR.MED.; German professor of nuclear medicine; b. 1 Jan. 1927, Garzweiler; s. of Ludwig Feinendegen and Rosa Klauth; m. Jeannine Gemuseus 1960; two s.; ed. Univ. of Cologne; Asst. Physician and Scientist, Medical Dept. Brookhaven Nat. Lab., Upton, U.S.A. 1958–63; Scientific Officer, Euratom, Brussels and Paris 1963–67; Dir. Inst. of Medicine Nuclear Research Center Jülich G.m.b.H. and Prof. for Nuclear Medicine, Univ. Hospital, Düsseldorf 1967–; mem. Advisory Council, Fed. Ministry of Health and other professional appts.; mem. Rhine Westfalen Acad. of Sciences (Vice-Pres. 1978–79); Bundesverdienstorden. *Publications:* 450 publs. in nat. and int. scientific journals and books. *Address:* Institute of Medicine, Nuclear Research Center Jülich G.m.b.H., P.O. Box 1913, 5170 Jülich (Office); Wolfshovener Strasse 197, 5170 Jülich-Stetternich, Federal Republic of Germany (Home). *Telephone:* 02461-616443 (Office); 02461-7528 (Home).

FEINSTEIN, Alvan Richard, M.D.; American professor of medicine and epidemiology; b. 4 Dec. 1925, Philadelphia, Pa.; ed. Univ. of Chicago; Intern, then Resident, Yale New Haven Hosp. 1952–54; Research Fellow, Rockefeller Inst. 1954–55; Resident, Columbia-Presbyterian Medical Center, New York 1955–56; Clinical Dir. Irvington House, Irvington-on-Hudson, New York 1956–62; Instructor then Asst. Prof., New York Univ. School of Medicine 1956–62; Chief, Clinical Pharmacology, West Haven Va. Hosp. 1962–64, Chief, Clinical Biostatistics 1964–74, Chief, Eastern Research Support Center 1967–74; mem. Faculty of School of Medicine, Yale Univ. 1962–, Prof. of Medicine and Epidemiology 1969–; Francis Gilman Blake Award (Yale Univ.) 1969, Distinguished Service Award (Chicago Univ.) 1975, Ludwig Heilmeyer Soc. Gold Medal Award 1981, Richard and Hinda Rosenthal Foundation Award (American Coll. of Physicians) 1982, Charles V. Chapin Medal Award 1983, Yale Science and Eng. Assn. Annual Award 1986, Robert J. Glaser Annual Award (Soc. for Gen. Internal Medicine) 1987, J. Allyn Taylor Int. Prize in Medicine 1987. *Publications:* Clinical Judgment 1967, Clinical Biostatistics 1977, Clinical Epidemiology 1985, Clinimetrics 1987. *Leisure interests:* guitar, folk songs.

Address: Yale University School of Medicine, 333 Cedar Street, P.O. Box 3333, New Haven, Conn. 06510-8025, U.S.A. *Telephone:* (203) 785-4145.

FEINSTEIN, Charles Hilliard, B.COM., PH.D., C.A. (S.A.), F.B.A.; British professor of economic and social history; b. 18 March 1932, Johannesburg, S. Africa; s. of Louis Feinstein and Rose Feinstein; m. 1st Ruth Loshak 1958, 2nd Anne Digby 1980; one s. three d.; ed. Parktown Boys' High School, Johannesburg, Univs. of Witwatersrand and Cambridge; Research Officer, Dept. of Applied Econs. Univ. of Cambridge 1958-63, Lecturer, Faculty of Econs. 1963-78; Fellow, Clare Coll., Cambridge 1963-78, Sr. Tutor 1969-78; Prof. of Econ. and Social History, Univ. of York 1978-87, Head, Dept. of Econs. and Related Studies 1981-86; Reader in Recent Social and Econ. History, Univ. of Oxford; Professorial Fellow, Nuffield Coll., Oxford 1987-; Man. Ed. Economic Journal 1980-86; mem. Council and Exec. Cttee. Royal Econ. Soc. 1980-; mem. Council, Econ. History Soc. 1980-; mem. Econ. Affairs Cttee., Econ. and Social Research Council 1982-86; Visiting Scholar, Dept. of Econs., Harvard Univ. 1986-87. *Publications:* Domestic Capital Formation in the United Kingdom 1920-38 1965, Socialism, Capitalism and Economic Growth (essays, ed.) 1972, National Income, Expenditure and Output of the United Kingdom, 1855-1965, 1972, York 1831-1981 (ed.) 1981, British Economic Growth (with R.C.O. Matthews and J. Odling-Smee) 1982, The Managed Economy, Essays in British Economic Policy and Performance since 1929 (ed.) 1983, Studies in Capital Formation in the United Kingdom, 1750-1920 (with S. Pollard) 1988. *Leisure interests:* reading, theatre, collecting secondhand books. *Address:* Treetops, Harberton Mead, Headington, Oxford, OX3 0DB, England. *Telephone:* (0865) 63993.

FEINSTEIN, Dianne; American politician; b. 22 June 1933, San Francisco, Calif.; d. of Leon and Betty (Rosenburg) Goldman; m. Bertram Feinstein 1962; one d.; ed. Stanford Univ., Calif.; Intern in Public Affairs, Coro Foundation, San Francisco 1955-56; Asst. to Calif. Industrial Welfare Comm., Los Angeles, also San Francisco 1956-57; Vice-Chair. Calif. Women's Bd. Terms and Parole 1962-66; Chair. San Francisco City and County Advisory Comm. for Adult Detention 1967-69; Superintendant City and County of San Francisco 1970-78; Bd. of Govs. Bay Area Council 1972-; Mayor of San Francisco 1978-88; mem. numerous other public bodies etc.; Republican. *Address:* 909 Montgomery Street, San Francisco, Calif. 94133, U.S.A.

FEIT, Christian, DR.JUR.UTR.; German diplomatist (retd.); b. 21 Oct. 1921, Breslau (now Wrocław, Poland); m. Gabriele von Below 1950; two s. two d.; diplomatic service, Fed. Repub. of Germany; Vice-Consul in New York, Detroit, Houston, U.S.A. 1952-54; Commercial Attaché, Valparaíso, Chile 1954-55; at Ministry of Foreign Affairs 1955-58, 1963-68, 1974-83; First Sec., Embassy in Madrid 1958-63; Minister Counsellor (Political Affairs), Paris 1969-74; Amb. to Belgium 1983-87; Officer, Cross of Merit (Fed. Repub. of Germany) and decorations from France, Belgium, Spain, Chile, Peru, Luxembourg, Austria, Monaco and Netherlands. *Address:* Rubensstrasse 19, 53 Bonn 2, Federal Republic of Germany. *Telephone:* 228-374647.

FEJTI, György; Hungarian politician; b. 1946, Sátoraljaujhely; ed. Technical Univ., Budapest; Asst. Tech. Univ. Budapest; various posts in Communist Youth Fed., Sec. Cen. Cttee. 1976-79, First Sec. 1980-86; First Sec. HSWP Co. Borsod Cttee. 1985-87; deputy dept. head HSWP Cen. Cttee.; mem. Party Cen. Cttee. 1980-, Sec. Cen. Cttee. 1987-. *Address:* Hungarian Socialist Workers Party, Central Committee, 1387 Budapest, Széchenyi rakpart 19, Hungary. *Telephone:* 111-400.

FEKETE, János; Hungarian banker and economist; b. 1918, Budapest; m. Ilona Freska; one d.; ed. Univ. of Econs., Budapest; fmrly. served in Nat. Savings Bank, Szarvas; joined Nat. Bank of Hungary 1948, then worked at Ministry of Finance and Ministry of Foreign Affairs; rejoined Nat. Bank of Hungary 1953, Deputy Chair. 1968, First Deputy Chair. 1980-88; Chair. Hungarian Int. Bank Ltd., London; Deputy Chair. Cen. European Int. Bank, Budapest; mem. of Bd. of Int. Bank of Econ. Cooperation and Int. Investment Bank, Moscow, and Zentral Wechsel- und Kreditbank AG, Vienna; mem. of the Consultative Group on Int. Econ. and Monetary Affairs Inc. 1978-; Gov. IMF 1982-; mem. Parl. 1985-; State Prize of the Hungarian People's Republic. *Publication:* Back to Realities 1982. *Leisure interest:* sport. *Address:* National Bank of Hungary, H-1850, Budapest, Szabadság tér 8, Hungary. *Telephone:* 327-963.

FELCH, William Campbell, M.D.; American physician; b. 14 Nov. 1920, Lakewood, Ohio; s. of Don H. W. Felch and Beth Campbell; m. Nancy Cook Dean 1945; two s. one d.; ed. Phillips Exeter Acad., Princeton Univ. and Columbia Coll. of Physicians and Surgeons; served U.S. Army 1942-48; in private practice, internal medicine 1951-88; Chief of Staff, United Hosp., Port Chester, New York 1975-77; Ed. The Internist 1975-86; Medical Dir. Osborn Home, Rye 1979-88; Exec. Vice-Pres. Alliance for Continuing Medical Educ. 1979-; mem. Inst. of Medicine, N.A.S.; Fellow American Coll. of Physicians; Ed. Acme Almanac 1978-; Award of Merit, New York State Soc. of Internal Medicine 1976; Internist of Distinction, Soc. of Internal Medicine of New York 1973. *Publications:* Aspiration and Achievement 1981, Primer, Continuing Medical Education (Co.-Ed.) 1986. *Leisure interests:* sailing, golf. *Address:* 26337 Carmelo Street, Carmel, Calif. 95923, U.S.A. *Telephone:* (408) 625-6593.

FELDBAEK, Ole, M.A., DR.PHIL.; Danish professor of economic history; b. 22 July 1936, Copenhagen; s. of Commdr. Henri Feldbaek and Kathy Feldbaek; m. Inge Kjaergaard 1976; one s. one d.; ed. Univ. of Copenhagen; Lecturer in Econ. History, Univ. of Copenhagen 1968, Prof. 1981-; Fellow, Royal Danish Acad. *Publications:* books and articles on 18th century European and Asian history (econ., political and mil.). *Address:* 15 Efteraarsvej, 2920 Charlottenlund, Denmark.

FELDBERG, Wilhelm Siegmund, C.B.E., M.D., F.R.C.P., F.R.S.; British physiologist; b. 19 Nov. 1900, Hamburg, Germany; s. of Emil Daniel and Amalie (née Bacharach) Feldberg; m. 1st Katherine Scheffler 1925 (deceased); one s. (deceased) one d.; m. 2nd Kim O'Rourke 1977 (deceased); ed. Univ. of Berlin; Reader in Physiology, Cambridge Univ. until 1949; Head of Physiology and Pharmacology Div., Nat. Inst. for Medical Research, London 1949-65, Hon. Head 1965-66; Head, Lab. of Neuropharmacology, Nat. Inst.for Medical Research 1966-74, Grant Holder 1974-; Hon. Lecturer, Univ. of London 1950-; Fellow, Royal Soc. 1947-; Ferrier Lecturer 1974, Sherrington Lecturer 1980, Charnock Bradley Memorial Lecturer 1980; Hon. mem. Physiological Soc., British Pharmacological Soc., Royal Soc. of Medicine, Soc. française d'allergie, German Physiological Soc., German Pharmacological Soc., Berliner Medizinische Gesellschaft, Berliner Physiologische Gesellschaft 1980; Hon. M.D. (Freiburg, Berlin, Cologne, Würzburg, Liège, Heidelberg); Hon. D.Sc. (Bradford Univ.) 1973, (Univ. of London) 1979, (Univ. of Cambridge) 1987; Hon. LL.D. (Glasgow Univ.) 1976, (Aberdeen Univ.) 1977; Hon. Foreign mem. Acad. royale de Médicine de Belgique (1982); Grand Cross, Order of Merit (Federal Republic of Germany) 1961; Baly Medal 1963; Schmiedeberg Plakette 1969, Philip Stöhr Medal 1970, Royal Medal (Royal Soc.) 1983. *Publications:* Histamin (with E. Schilf), A Pharmacological Approach to the Brain from its Inner and Outer Surface 1963, Fifty years on: Looking Back on some Developments in Neurohumoral Physiology 1982; numerous articles in medical and scientific journals. *Leisure interests:* women's fashions, collecting antique furniture. *Address:* National Institute for Medical Research, Mill Hill, London, NW7 1AA; Lavenham, 74 Marsh Lane, Mill Hill, London NW7 4NT, England (Home). *Telephone:* 01-959 3666 (Office); 01-959 5545 (Home).

FELDMAN, Jerome Myron, M.D.; American physician and medical scientist; b. 27 July 1935, Chicago, Ill.; s. of Louis Feldman and Marian (Swichkow) Feldman; m. Gaye Arleen Friedman 1960; one s. two d.; ed. Northwestern Univ., Michael Reese, Chicago, and Duke Univ.; Chief, Endocrinology and Metabolism, Durham Veteran's Admin. Hospital 1971-; Assoc. Prof. of Medicine, Duke Univ. 1972-, Dir. Clinical Research Unit Core Lab. 1984-; mem. Duke Comprehensive Cancer Center 1982-; Ed. Journal of Clinical Endocrinology and Metabolism 1983-89. *Publications:* 203 research articles, book chapters and reviews dealing with hormone-secreting tumours, endocrinology and metabolism. *Leisure interests:* music, art. *Address:* Duke University Medical Center, Box 2963, Durham, N.C. 27710, U.S.A. *Telephone:* 919-286-0411 Ext. 7329.

FELDMAN, Myer, B.S. (ECON.), LL.B.; American lawyer and politician; b. 22 June 1917, Philadelphia, Pa.; s. of Israel and Bella Kurland Feldman; m. 1st Silva Moskovitz 1941, 2nd Adrienne Arsht 1980; one s. one d.; ed. Univ. of Pennsylvania; Gowen Fellow, Univ. of Pennsylvania 1938-39, Prof. of Law 1940-42; Served U.S.A.A.F. 1942-46; Special Counsel, SEC, Exec. Asst. to Chair., SEC 1949-53; Counsel, Senate Banking and Currency Cttee. 1955-57; Prof. of Law, American Univ. 1956-59; Legislative Asst., Senator John F. Kennedy 1958-61; Dir. of Research, Democratic Nat. Cttee. 1960; Deputy Special Counsel to Pres. of the U.S. 1961-64, Counsel 1964-65; Gov. Weizmann Inst., Israel 1962-84; Overseer Coll. of the Virgin Islands 1963-; Trustee, Eleanor Roosevelt Foundation 1963-76, United Jewish Appeal 1965-, Jewish Publication Soc. 1965-78; Chair. Bd. Speer Publs., Capital Gazette Press Ind., Bay Publs. 1968-77; Contributor to The Saturday Review 1965-71; partner Ginsburg and Feldman 1965-; Dir. Flying Tiger Line 1966-82, Flame of Hope, Inc. 1967-; Del. to Democratic Nat. Convention 1968; Chair. Bd. of Dirs. of WWBA Inc., WLLH Inc. and WADK Inc., Financial Satellite Corpn. 1984-; mem. Exec. Cttee., Bd. of Dirs., Nat. Savings and Trust Co. 1976-; Vice-Chair. Congressional Leadership for the Future 1970; Pres. New York Int. Art Festival 1973-77; Pres. McGovern for Pres. Cttee. 1972; Chair. and Treas. Birch Bayh for Pres. Cttee. 1975-76; Dir. Special Olympics Inc. 1983-, Henry M. Jackson Found. 1984-; John F. Kennedy Library 1983-; Pres. Radio Assoc. Inc. 1959-81; Democrat. *Publications:* Standard Pennsylvania Practice (4 vols.). *Leisure interests:* tennis, swimming. *Address:* 1250 Connecticut Avenue, N.W., Washington, D.C. 20036, U.S.A. *Telephone:* (202) 637-9025.

FELDSTEIN, Martin Stuart, M.A., D.PHIL.; American economist; b. 25 Nov. 1939, New York; s. of Meyer and Esther (Gevarter) Feldstein; m. Kathleen Foley 1965; two d.; ed. Harvard and Oxford Univs.; Research Fellow, Nuffield Coll., Oxford 1964-65, Official Fellow 1965-67, Lecturer in Public Finance 1965-67; Asst. Prof. of Econs., Harvard Univ. 1967-68, Assoc. Prof. 1968-69, Prof. 1969-, George F. Baker Prof. 1984-; Pres. Nat. Bureau of Econ. Research 1977-; Chair. Pres.'s Council of Econ. Advisers 1982-84; Dir. American Int. Group, Great Western Financial, TRW Inc., Hosp. Corpn. of America, Int. Advisory Council of The Morgan Bank; Econ. Adviser, Dean Witter Reynolds, Data Resources Inc.; columnist, Wall Street Journal, Washington Post; Fellow, American Acad. of Arts and Sciences, Econometric Soc., Nat. Asscn. of Business Economists; mem.

American Econ. Asscn. (John Bates Clark Medal 1977), Vice-Pres. 1988; mem. Inst. Medicine, Nat. Acad. of Sciences, Council on Foreign Relations, Trilateral Comm.; Hon. Dr. of Laws (Univ. of Rochester) 1984, (Marquette) 1985. *Address:* 147 Clifton Street, Belmont, Mass. 02178, U.S.A.

FELDT, Kjell-Olof, PH.D.; Swedish politician; b. 18 Aug. 1931, Holmsund; m. Birgitta von Otter; ed. Univs. of Uppsala and Lund; Under-Sec., Ministry of Finance 1967-70, 1982; Minister of Trade 1970-75, of Finance 1983-; Minister without Portfolio 1975-76; M.P. 1971-; Social Democratic Labour Party. *Address:* Ministry of Finance, Rodbodgatan 6, S-10333 Stockholm, Sweden.

FELICI, H.E. Cardinal Angelo; Italian ecclesiastic; b. 26 July 1919, Segni; ordained Catholic priest 1942, elected Archbishop of Cesariana, Numidia 1967, consecrated Bishop 1967; cr. Cardinal 1988; Apostolic Nuncio in France. *Address:* c/o The Vatican, Vatican City, Rome, Italy.

FELL, Robert, C.B., C.B.E., F.R.S.A.; British trade official; b. 6 May 1921; s. of Robert Fell and Mary Ann Fell; m. Eileen Wicks 1946; two s. one d.; ed. Whitehaven Grammar School; War Office 1939; mil. service 1940-46; Bd. of Trade 1947; Trade Commr., Queensland, Australia 1954-59; Asst. Sec., Tariff Div., Bd. of Trade 1961; Commercial Counsellor, Delhi 1961-66; Under-Sec. in charge of Export Promotion 1967-71; Sec. Export Credits Guarantee Dept. 1971-74; Chief Exec. The Stock Exchange 1975-82; Commr. for Securities and Commodities Trading, Hong Kong 1981-84, for Banking and Deposit-taxing Cos. 1984-87; mem. British Overseas Trade Bd. 1972-75; Pres., City Branch, B.I.M. 1976-82; Commr. of Banking, Hong Kong 1984-87. *Leisure interests:* Rugby football (watching) and gardening. *Address:* Dalegarth, Guildown Avenue, Guildford, Surrey, England. *Telephone:* Guildford 572204.

FELLGETT, Peter Berners, PH.D., F.R.S.; British professor of cybernetics; b. 22 April 1922, Ipswich; s. of Frank Ernest Fellgett and Rowena Wagstaff; m. Janet Mary Briggs; one s. two d.; ed. The Leys School, Cambridge and Cambridge Univ.; Sr. Observer, the Observatories, Cambridge Univ. 1952-59; Prin. Scientific Officer, Royal Observatories, Edinburgh 1959-65; Prof. of Cybernetics, Reading Univ. 1965-87; R. W. Wood Prize (Optical Soc. of America) 1977. *Address:* Department of Cybernetics, 3 Earley Gate, P.O. Box 238, Whiteknights, Reading, Berks. RG6 2AL (Office); Little Brighter, St. Kew Highway, Bodmin, Cornwall PL30 3DU (Home). *Telephone:* (0208) 850-337.

FELLINI, Federico; Italian film director; b. 20 Jan. 1920; m. Giulietta Masina (q.v.) 1943; screen writer: Quarta pagina 1942, Roma città aperta 1944-45, Paisa 1946, Il delitto di Giovanni Episcopo 1947, In nome della legge 1948-49, La città si difende 1951, Il brigante di Tacca di Lupo 1953, etc.; Dir. Lo sceicco bianco 1952, I vitelloni 1953, La strada (Oscar) 1954, Il bidone 1955, Le notti di Cabiria (Oscar) 1957, Fortunella 1958, La Dolce Vita (Cannes 1st Prize) 1960, The Temptation of Dr. Antonio (from Boccaccio 70) 1962, 8½ (Oscar) 1963, Giulietta degli spiriti (Golden Globe, Hollywood) 1964, Satyricon 1969, Never Bet the Devil Your Head (from Spirits of the Dead) 1969, I Clowns (television film) 1971, Roma 1972, Amarcord (New York Film Critics' Circle Award 1974) 1973, Casanova 1976, La Cité des Femmes 1979, Orchestra Rehearsal 1979, And the Ship Sails On 1984, Ginger and Fred 1985, Intervista 1987; has always written scripts for his own films. *Publications:* Amarcord 1974, Quattro film 1975. *Address:* 141a Via Margutta 110, Rome, Italy.

FELTS, William Robert Jr., M.D.; American professor of medicine; b. 24 April 1923, Judsonia, Ark.; s. of Wylie R. Felts and Willie E. Lewis; m. 1st Jeanne E. Kennedy 1954 (divorced 1971), 2nd Lila Mitchell Dudley 1987; three s. one d.; ed. Univ. of Arkansas; Asst. Chief, Arthritis Research Unit, Veteran's Admin. Hosp., Washington, D.C. 1953-54, Adjutant Asst. Chief 1954-58, Chief 1958-62; Consultant in Rheumatology, U.S. Naval Hosp., Bethesda, Md. 1957-70; Instructor, now Prof. of Medicine, George Washington Univ. 1958-, Dir. Div. of Rheumatology 1970-79; mem. numerous advisory bds., professional orgs. etc. *Publications:* over 100 articles on medical socioeconomics, rheumatology and internal medicine. *Leisure interests:* photography, fishing, travel. *Address:* 2150 Pennsylvania Avenue, N.W., Washington, D.C. 20037 (Office); 1492 Hampton Hill Circle, McLean, Va. 22101, U.S.A. (Home). *Telephone:* 202-994-4377 (Office); 703-356-6233 (Home).

FENBY, Eric William, O.B.E., D.MUS., D.LITT., F.R.C.M., F.T.C.L.; British musician, author and teacher; b. 22 April 1906, Scarborough; s. of Herbert H. Fenby and Ada Brown; m. Rowena C. T. Marshall 1944; one s. one d.; ed. Municipal School, Scarborough, private tuition in music but largely self-taught; Amanuensis to Frederick Delius as he composed A Song of Summer, Idyll, Violin Sonata No. 3, Songs of Farewell 1928-34; Musical Adviser, Boosey & Hawkes, Publishers, London 1936-39; Capt. Royal Army Educ. Corps 1941-45; Musical Dir. North Riding Training Coll. 1948-62; Artistic Dir. Delius Centenary Festival, Bradford 1962; Pres. Delius Soc. 1964-; Prof. of Composition, Royal Acad. of Music 1963-77 (Hon. mem. 1965); Hon. mem. Royal Philharmonic Soc.; conducted recording of all works taken down at Delius' dictation in album The Fenby Legacy 1983; Dr. h.c. (Jacksonville, Bradford and Warwick Univs.). *Publications:* Delius as I Knew Him 1936, A Song of Summer (film script) 1968; numerous arrangements of Delius' works. *Leisure interests:* reading, chess. *Address:*

1 Raincliffe Court, Stepney Road, Scarborough, N. Yorks., YO12 5BT England. *Telephone:* (0723) 372988.

FENCHEL, Tom Michael, D.PHIL.; Danish professor of marine biology; b. 19 March 1940, Copenhagen; s. of W. Fenchel and Käte (née Sperling); m. 1st Anne Thane 1964, 2nd Hilary Adler 1978; one s. one d.; ed. Univ. of Copenhagen; lecturer in marine biology, Univ. of Copenhagen 1964-70; Prof. of Ecology and Zoology, Univ. of Aarhus 1970-87; Prof. of Marine Biology, Univ. of Copenhagen 1987-; Gold Medal, Univ. of Copenhaghen 1964, Ecology Prize 1987, Huntzmann Award for Oceanography 1987. *Publications:* Theories of Populations in Biological Communities (with F. B. Christiansen) 1977, Bacteria and Mineral Cycling (with T. H. Blackburn) 1979, Ecology of Protozoa 1987. *Address:* Marine Biological Laboratory, University of Copenhagen, Strandpromenaden 5, 3000 Helsinger, Denmark. *Telephone:* 452213344.

FENDALL, Neville Rex Edwards, M.D., D.P.H., F.F.C.M.; British professor of public health and int. health consultant; b. 9 July 1917, Auckland, N.Z.; s. of late Francis Alan Fendall and Ruby Inez (née Matthews) Fendall; m. Margaret Doreen Beynon 1942; ed. Univ. Coll. and Hosp. London; joined Colonial Medical Services Nigeria, Malaya, Singapore, Kenya 1944-64; Staff mem. Rockefeller Foundation 1964-66; Regional Dir., Population Council Inc., New York 1966-71; Middlemass Hunt Prof. Int. Community Health 1971-81; Visiting Lecturer Tropical Public Health, Harvard 1966; Visiting Prof. of Public Health, Boston Univ. 1982-; Adjunct Prof. Community Health Sciences, Univ. of Calgary 1983-; Prof. Emer. Univ. of Liverpool 1981-; mem. Panel of Experts WHO 1960-85; Int. Health Consultant 1958-; Langley Memorial Prize 1963, Mrigendra Gold Medal Nepal 1983, corresp. mem. Acad. of Medical Sciences, Guatemala 1986. *Publications:* Auxiliaries in Health Care 1972, Paramedicals for PHC in the Commonwealth (jt. author) 1979, Health Planning, Manpower, Epidemiology, Primary Health Care 1948-1986. *Leisure interests:* travel, gardening. *Address:* Primcare, Berwyn, North Close, Bromborough, Wirral, L62 2BU, England. *Telephone:* 051-334 2193.

FENECH-ADAMI, Edward, LL.D.; Maltese politician, lawyer and journalist; b. 7 Feb. 1934, Birkirkara; s. of Luigi Fenech Adami and Josephine Pace; m. Mary Sciberras 1965; four s. one d.; ed. St. Aloysius Coll., Univ. of Malta; entered legal practice 1959; Ed. Il-Poplu (weekly) 1962-69; mem. Nat. Exec. Nationalist Party 1961, Asst. Gen. Sec. 1962-75, Chair. Gen. and Admin. Councils 1975-77, Leader April 1977-; mem. Parl. 1969-; Leader of Opposition 1977-82, 1983-87; Prime Minister May 1987-; Vice-Pres. European Union of Christian Democrat Parties 1979-. *Address:* Auberge de Castille, Valletta, Malta. *Telephone:* (356) 623026.

FENG HE; Chinese sculptor; b. 12 Nov. 1931, Peixian, Jiangsu Prov.; s. of Feng Zigu and Chen Jiechen; m. Zhou Ji 1965; one s.; ed. Cen. Inst. of Fine Arts; mem. Sculpture Research Studio Inst. of Fine Arts, Deputy Dir. 1981-84, Vice-Dir. 1988-; specialized in ceramics and animal sculpture; exhibited work China Art Gallery 1979, 1981, also in France and Burma; *works include:* Woman's Head 1958, The Master of the Land 1964, Doe 1964, Bellicose Goat 1978, Buffalo 1979, You are always in our hearts dear Premier Zhou 1979, Ah Bing the blindman 1979, Buffalo and the Leopard 1985, Moonlight 1985, Winter 1986, Monument of Juvenile Heroes. *Address:* Central Institute of Fine Arts, East Beijing, People's Republic of China. *Telephone:* 55-4731 (Ext. 387).

FENG JINSONG; Chinese artist; b. March 1934, Huangpei, Hubei Prov.; s. of Feng Xuren and Feng Chunbao; m. Wang Guanghui 1958; two s.; Pres. Hubei Acad. of Fine Arts 1985-; Vice-Pres. Hubei br. Chinese Fine Artists' Asscn.; Sr. Bd. mem., Art Cttee. of Hubei Prov. *Publications:* six paintings, including A Breath of Spring, reproduced in New Schools of Chinese Painting and Collected Works of Chinese Middle-aged and Young Artists; five paintings, including A Little Bird, in English edn. of Chinese Literature in Summer 1988. *Leisure interests:* Chinese calligraphy, Taijiquan (traditional Chinese shadow boxing). *Address:* Hubei Academy of Fine Arts, Wuhan, People's Republic of China. *Telephone:* 877129.

FENG JINWEN; Chinese jurist; Deputy Mayor Fuzhou Municipality 1964; Deputy Procurator-General 1982-; Head Chinese Procurator Del. to Japan 1986-. *Address:* Supreme People's Procuratorate, Beijing, People's Republic of China.

FENG JIXIN; Chinese politician; Chair. Control Cttee., People's Govt., Heilongjiang Prov. 1953; Sec. CCP Cttee., Heilongjiang 1953-64; Vice-Gov. Jiangsu Prov. 1964-, Cultural Revolution; mem. Standing Cttee. CCP Cttee., Jiangsu 1965-, Cultural Revolution; Vice-Chair. Provincial Revolutionary Cttee., Gansu Prov. 1977-79; Sec. CCP Cttee., Gansu 1978-79; Gov. Gansu 1979-81; First Political Commissar, PLA Gansu Mil. Dist. 1981-83; Acting First Sec. CCP Cttee., Gansu 1981-82, First Sec. 1982-83, mem. Cen. Advisory Comm. 1983-; Adviser State Econ. Comm. 1984-. *Address:* Chinese Communist Party Provincial Committee, Lanzhou, Gansu Province, People's Republic of China.

FENG KANG; Chinese mathematician and computer scientist; b. 9 Sept. 1920, Suzhou, Jiangsu; s. of Feng Zhu-Pei and Feng-Yan Su Qin; m. 1st Li Kai-De 1960 (divorced 1965), 2nd Shi Yu-Ming 1987; ed. Nanjing Univ., U.S.S.R. Acad. of Sciences Math. Inst.; fundamental research contribs. to finite element methods and symplectic geometric methods in scientific and engineering computing; Dir. Chinese Acad. of Sciences Computing Centre 1978-87, Hon. Dir. 1987-; Prof. of Math. Chinese Acad. of Sciences Graduate School 1978-; Vice-Pres. Chinese Computer Soc. 1978-86; mem. Chinese Acad. of Sciences; Pres. Chinese Soc. of Computational Math. 1985-; Chief Ed. Journal of Computational Math. 1983-; Max Planck Gesellschaft Visiting Prof., Univ. of Stuttgart and Tech. Hochschule 1987-88; Int. Scientific Adviser, Sir George Cayley Inst. of Computational and Information Mechanics, London 1988-. *Publications:* numerous math. papers. *Leisure interests:* classical art and music. *Address:* P.O. Box 2719, Beijing 100080, People's Republic of China (Office). *Telephone:* 289001 (Office); 285203 (Home).

FENG LANRUI; Chinese economist; b. 16 Sept. 1920, Guiyang, Guizhou Province; d. of Feng Shaotang and Xie Guangyu; m. Li Chang 1946; two s. two d.; Sr. Research Fellow, Inst. of Marxism-Leninism and Mao Zedong Thought, Chinese Acad. of Social Sciences 1980-, Deputy Dir. 1980-82, Adviser 1983-; mem. Editorial Cttee., Encyclopedia of People's Repub. of China, for vol. Scientific Socialism 1980-, A Comprehensive Dictionary of Economics, for vol. Population, Labour and Consumption 1983-, Sun Yefang Prize for econ. article of 1984; Sec.-Gen. China Council of Econ. Asscns. 1981-; mem. Standing Cttee. Chinese People's Friendship Asscn. 1986-. *Publications:* Labour: Payment and Employment (collected articles) 1982, Regarding the Principle—To Each According to his Work, Chinese Research on Employment Theory 1982, Urban Employment and Wages in China (co-author) 1982, On the Relationship between Employment and Economic Growth (co-author) 1983, The Worldwide New Industrialization and China's Socialist Modernization (co-author) 1984, On Letting Some People Get Rich Ahead of Others 1984, The Incomplete Form of Distribution according to Work at the Initial Stage of Socialism 1985, Overcome Egalitarianism and Let Some People Get Rich Ahead of Others 1985, More on Letting Some People Get Rich Ahead of Others 1986, The Double Hundred Policy Cannot be Separated from Democracy and Freedom 1986, The Double Hundred Policy and Science Associations 1986, Distribution According to Work, Wage and Employment 1988, and articles. *Address:* Institute of Marxism-Leninism and Mao Zedong Thought, Chinese Academy of Social Sciences, Jianguomennei Dajie, Beijing, People's Republic of China. *Telephone:* 508265; 5137744, Ext. 3043.

FENG WENBIN; Chinese politician; b. 1911, Hunan; joined CCP 1928; Head, Youth Dept., CCP 1947-53; in political disgrace 1953-77; Vice-Pres. Cen. Party School 1979-; Chair. Comm. for Collecting Party Historical Documents 1981-; First Sec. Provisional Party Cttee. of Organs under Cen. Cttee. of CCP 1982-; mem. Cen. Advisory Cttee. 1982-. *Address:* Central Party School, Bejing, People's Republic of China.

FENG YOULAN, PH.D.; Chinese philosopher; b. 4 Dec. 1895, Tanghe, Honan; m. Ren Zaikun 1918; two s. two d.; ed. China Inst., Shanghai, Beijing Univ. and Columbia Univ., U.S.A.; Prof. of Philosophy Zhongzhou Univ., Kaifeng 1923-25, Yenching Univ. 1926-28, Qinghua Univ. 1928-52; Dean, Coll. of Arts, Head of Philosophy, Qinghua Univ. 1933-52; Dean, Coll. of Arts, Southwestern United Univs. 1939-46; Visiting Prof. Univ. of Pennsylvania, U.S.A. 1946-47; Chief, Div. Chinese Philosophy, Research Inst. of Philosophy, Acad. Sinica 1954-66; Prof. Beijing Univ. 1952-; Hon. degrees from Princeton Univ., Columbia Univ. (U.S.A.), Univ. of Delhi (India). *Publications:* A Comparative Study of Life Ideals 1924, A Conception of Life 1924, A History of Chinese Philosophy (2 vols.) 1930-1936, A New Treatise on Neo-Confucianism 1938, China's Road to Freedom 1939, A New Treatise on the Way of Living 1939, A New Treatise on the Nature of Man 1942, The Spirit of Chinese Philosophy 1942, A New Treatise on the Methodology of Metaphysics 1948, Collected Essays in Wartime 1948, A Short History of Chinese Philosophy 1948, A New History of Chinese Philosophy, vols. 1-3 1983-85, My Memoirs 1984, The Collected Works of Feng Yulan (vol. 1) 1985, (vols. 4, 5) 1987, (vols. 2, 3) 1988, A New History of Chinese Philosophy (vol. 4) 1987. *Address:* Department of Philosophy, Beijing University, People's Republic of China.

FENG YUJIU; Chinese diplomatist; b. 1912; Deputy Dir., General Bureau of Highways, Ministry of Communications 1950-56; Asst., Ministry of Communications 1960-65; Dir. Bureau of Shipping 1960-65; Amb. to Norway 1965-67, to Mauritania 1969-73, to Nigeria 1973-79, to Hungary 1979-83. *Address:* c/o Ministry of Foreign Affairs, Beijing, People's Republic of China.

FENG ZHISHAN; Chinese diplomatist; Amb. to Burkina Faso 1973, 1984-88; Counselor Embassy, Cameroon 1973-77. *Address:* c/o Embassy of the People's Republic of China, Ouagadougou, Burkina Faso.

FENG ZHISHAO; Chinese operatic artist; b. 1939. *Address:* Beijing Opera Company, No. 1 Troupe, Beijing, People's Republic of China.

FENGER MØLLER, Grethe, B.LL.; Danish politician; b. 6 Nov. 1941, Frederiksberg, nr. Copenhagen; d. of Torben Fenger Møller; ed. Univ. of Copenhagen; Sec. in Ministries of Labour and Social Affairs; Pres. Soc. of Danish Women (Dansk Kvindesamfund); M.P. 1977-; Minister of Labour 1982-86; Conservative. *Address:* c/o Ministry of Labour, Lakesgade 19, 1063 Copenhagen K, Denmark. *Telephone:* 16-48-00.

FENN, Ingemund; Norwegian newspaper editor; b. 18 Sept. 1907, Stryn, Nordfjord; m. Elsa Reinertsen 1941; one s.; univ. educ.; journalist 1928-; on staff of Bergens Tidende 1936-, Ed. Oslo office and parl. corresp. 1946-56, Chief Ed. 1956; Pres. Parl. Corresp. Asscn. 1951-56; Chair. Norwegian Liberal Press Asscn. 1959-71; mem. Bd. Norwegian Editors' Asscn., Norwegian Press Asscn., Chair. Bd. Norwegian News Bureau; mem. Town Council; Liberal. *Address:* Bergens Tidende, P.O. Box 873, 5001 Bergen (Office); Starefossvei 58B, 5000 Bergen, Norway (Home). *Telephone:* 317266.

FENN, Sir Nicholas M., K.C.M.G., M.A.; British diplomatist; b. 19 Feb. 1936, London; s. of Rev. Prof. J. E. Fenn and Kathleen (née Harrison) Fenn; m. Susan C. Russell 1959; two s. one d.; ed. Kingswood School, Bath and Peterhouse, Cambridge; Flying Officer, R.A.F. 1954-56; Third Sec. Mandalay, then Rangoon 1959-63, Asst. Pvt. Sec. to Sec. of State for Foreign Affairs 1963-67, First Sec. British Interests Section, Swiss Embassy, Algiers 1967-69, First Sec. and Spokesman, U.K. Mission to the UN, New York 1969-72, Deputy Head Energy Dept. FCO 1972-75, Counsellor British Embassy, Beijing 1975-79, Head of News Dept. and Foreign Office Spokesman 1979-82; Amb. to Burma 1982-86, to Ireland 1986-. *Leisure interest:* sailing. *Address:* British Embassy, 33 Merrison Road, Dublin 4, Ireland; FCO, King Charles Street, London, SW1A 2AH, England.

FENNER, Frank John, C.M.G., M.B.E., M.D., F.A.A., F.R.S., F.R.A.C.P., F.R.C.P.; Australian research biologist; b. 21 Dec. 1914, Ballarat, Vic.; s. of Dr. and Mrs. Charles Fenner; m. E. M. Roberts 1943; one d.; ed. Thebarton Tech. High School, Adelaide High School, Adelaide Univ.; Medical Officer, Hospital Pathologist, Australian Forces 1940-43, Malariologist 1943-46; Francis Haley Research Fellow, Walter and Eliza Hall Inst. for Medical Research, Melbourne 1946-48; Travelling Fellow, Rockefeller Inst. for Medical Research 1948-49; Prof. of Microbiology, Australian Nat. Univ. 1949-73, Dir. John Curtin School of Medical Research 1967-73, Dir. Centre for Resource and Environmental Studies 1973-79; F.R.S. 1958; Foreign Assoc., U.S. Nat. Acad. of Sciences 1977; Chair. Global Comm. for the Certification of Smallpox Eradication, WHO 1977-80; Univ. Fellow, Australian Nat. Univ. 1980-82; Visiting Fellow, John Curtin School of Medical Research 1983-; Harvey Lecturer, Harvey Soc. of New York 1958; Overseas Fellow, Churchill Coll., Cambridge 1961-62; David Syme Prize, Melbourne Univ. 1949; Mueller Medal 1964; ANZAAS Medal 1980; Britannica Australia Award 1967; ANZAC Peace Prize 1980; Leeuwenhoek Lecture 1961; Flinders Lecture 1967, David Lecture 1973, Florey Lecture 1983, Burnet Lecture 1985; Stuart Mudd Award 1986, Japan Prize 1988. *Publications:* about 200 scientific papers, mainly on acidfast bacili, pox viruses, viral classification and environmental problems, The Production of Antibodies (with F. M. Burnet) 1949, Myxomatosis (with F. N. Ratcliffe) 1965, The Biology of Animal Viruses 1968, Medical Virology (with D. O. White) 1970, Classification and Nomenclature of Viruses, Second Report 1976, The Australian Academy of Science: the First Twenty-five Years (ed. with A. L. G. Rees) 1980, Veterinary Virology (with others) 1987, Smallpox and its Eradication (with others) 1988, Human Monkeypox (with Z. Jezek) 1988, The Orthpoxviruses (with others) 1988, Portraits of Viruses (ed. with A. Gibbs) 1988. *Leisure interests:* gardening, tennis. *Address:* 8 Monaro Crescent, Red Hill, Canberra, A.C.T. 2603, Australia. *Telephone:* 95-9176.

FENWICK, Millicent; American politician and diplomatist; b. 25 Feb. 1910, New York; d. of Ogden and Mary Stevens Hammond; m. Hugh McL. Fenwick 1932; one s. one d.; ed. Columbia Univ. and New School for Social Research; mem. Bd. of Educ. Bernardsville, N.J. 1936-41, Bernardsville Borough Council 1958-63, Gen. Assembly of N.J. 1969-73; mem. U.S. House of Reps. 1975-83; Amb. to FAO, Rome 1983-87; several hon. degrees. *Publication:* Speaking Up 1982. *Address:* Bernardsville, N.J., U.S.A. (Home).

FERENCZY, Oto, PH.DR.; Czechoslovak composer; b. 30 March 1921, Brezovica nad Torysou, Prešov Dist.; s. of Gejza and Irena Ferenczy; m. Viera Kotuliak 1957 (died 1980); one d.; ed. Faculty of Arts, Slovak Univ., Bratislava 1939-45; Head of Musical Dept., Library of Comenius Univ., Bratislava 1945-51; teacher, Coll. of Musical Arts, Bratislava 1951, Dean 1953-55, Docent 1953-66, Sub-Dean and Pro-Rector 1956-62, Rector 1962-66, Prof. 1966-; cand. mem. Cen. Cttee., CP of Slovakia 1968-71, mem. 1971-; Pres., Union of Slovak Composers 1970-72, 1982-87; Laureate Bartók Competition, Budapest 1948; Klement Gottwald State Prize 1981, Order of Labour 1981, Nat. Artist 1983. *Works include:* Music for four String Instruments 1947, Concertino for Chamber Orchestra 1949, Serenade for Strings, Harp and Wind Instruments 1955, Finale 1958, Elegy 1958, Sonata for Violin and Piano 1962, Partita 1964, Sonnets from Shakespeare 1965, The Northern Star 1960, An Uncommon Humoresque 1966, Symphonic Prologue 1973, Concerto for Piano and Orchestra 1978. *Publications:* Experience and Apprehension of Music 1947 and numerous articles on music aesthetics, philosophy of music, music education. *Leisure interest:* history. *Address:* Matusova 27, 811-04 Bratislava, Czechoslovakia. *Telephone:* 374192.

FERENSZTAJN, Bogumil, D.TECH.; Polish politician; b. 20 April 1934, Radom; m.; ed. Mining Faculty of Silesian Tech. Univ., Gliwice; worked at Mining Design Bureau, Gliwice 1956-69, then at Main Bureau of Mining Research and Design, Katowice 1969-76; Gen. Dir., Studies and Classification Bureau, Katowice 1976-82; mem. Polish United Workers' Party (PZPR) 1961-; Sec. for Econ. Matters, PZPR Voivodship Cttee., Katowice 1982-83; First Sec. PZPR Voivodship Cttee., Katowice 1983-87;

alt. mem. PZPR Cen. Cttee. 1985–86, mem. 1986–, alt. mem. Political Bureau of PZPR Cen. Cttee. 1986–87; Minister of Regional Planning and Construction 1987–; mem. Econ. Cttee. Council of Ministers KERM 1988–; Deputy to Seym (Parl.) 1985–, mem. Seym Comm. of Mining and Power Industry; Knight's and Officer's Cross, Order of Polonia Restituta and other awards and decorations. *Publications:* numerous scientific works on mining tech. *Address:* Ministerstwo Gospodarki Przestrzennej i Budownictwa, ul. Wspólna 2, 00-926 Warsaw, Poland.

FERGANI, Yacine; Algerian politician; b. 19 Jan. 1946, Jijel; ed. Ecole des Mines, Paris and Stanford Univ., U.S.A.; Asst. Dir.-Gen. SNTR 1970–72; Asst. Pres. Dir.-Gen. SONATRACH 1976–78, Vice-Pres. 1978–83; Sec. Gen. Ministry of Post and Telecommunications 1983–86; Deputy Minister of Chemical and Petrochemical Industries Feb. 1986–88; Minister of Post and Telecommunications 1988–. *Address:* 4 blvd Salah Bouakouir, Algiers, Algeria. *Telephone:* (2) 61-12-20.

FERGUSON, C. David; American business executive; ed. Marietta Coll.; joined Engine Parts Div. Gould Inc. 1963, Foil Div. 1967; subsequently Group Vice-Pres. (Materials and Components); Exec. Vice-Pres. (Materials and Components); Chair., Pres. and C.E.O. Gould Inc. 1988–; Pres. and Gen. Man. Foil Div., Gould Inc., Eastlake, O.; mem. Bd. Gould Foils Ltd., Nikko Gould Foil Co., Ltd., Gould Electronics (Canada) Ltd. *Address:* 10 Gould Center, Rolling Meadows, Ill. 60008, U.S.A. (Office).

FERGUSON, Glenn Walker, B.A., M.B.A., J.D.; American administrator; b. 28 Jan. 1929, Syracuse, N.Y.; s. of Forrest E. and Mabel W. Ferguson; m. Patricia Lou Head 1950; two s. one d.; ed. Cornell Univ., Univ. of Santo Tomas (Manila), Univ. of Chicago and Univ. of Pittsburgh; U.S. Air Force 1951–53; Staff Assoc. Governmental Affairs Inst., Washington, D.C. 1954–55; Asst. Ed. and Asst. Sec.-Treas., American Judicature Soc., Chicago 1955–56; successively Admin. Asst. to Chancellor, Asst. Dean and Asst. Prof. Graduate School of Public and Int. Affairs, Assoc. Dir., Co-ordinated Educ. Center, Univ. of Pittsburgh 1956–60; Man. Consultant, McKinsey and Co., Washington, D.C. 1960–61; Special Asst. to Dir., U.S. Peace Corps 1961, Peace Corps Dir. in Thailand 1961–63, Assoc. Dir. 1963–64; Dir. Vista Volunteers, Office of Econ. Opportunity, Washington, D.C. 1964–66; Amb. to Kenya 1966–69; Pres. Clark Univ. 1970–73, Univ. of Connecticut 1973–78; Pres. Radio Free Europe and Radio Liberty 1978–82; Pres. Lincoln Center 1983–84, Equity for Africa, Inc. 1985–; mem. Pres. Task Force on Poverty 1964, Fed. Bar Asscn., Council on Foreign Relations, American Bar Assen.; Bd. of Trustees, Cornell Univ. 1972–76; Assoc. Fellow Yale Univ.; mem. Nat. Press Club; fmr. Dir. Foreign Policy Assen. and Private Export Funding Corpn.; Arthur Flemming Award 1968. *Address:* Wagner Road, Shelter Harbour, R.I. 02891, U.S.A.

FERGUSON, James L.; American business executive; b. 16 March 1926, Evanston, Ill.; s. of J. Larnard Ferguson and Justine Dickson Ferguson; m. 2nd Esther Baskin 1981; two s. one d.; ed. Hamilton Coll. and Harvard Business School; served U.S. Army Corps of Engineers in Pacific Theater, World War II; Assoc. Advertising Man. Procter & Gamble Co.; joined Gen. Foods Corpn. 1963, Gen. Man. Bird's Eye Div. 1967, Vice-Pres. 1968, Group Vice-Pres. 1970, Exec. Vice-Pres. 1972, C.O.O. and Dir. 1972, Pres. 1972, C.E.O. 1973, Chair., Pres. and C.E.O. 1974, Chair. and C.E.O. 1977–86, now Chair. Exec. Cttee.; Vice-Chair. Philip Morris Inc. (after merger with Gen. Foods Corpn. 1985); Dir. Union Carbide Corpn., Chase Manhattan Bank, Sawyer-Ferguson-Walker Co., Trustee, Hamilton Coll. *Leisure interests:* sports, music. *Address:* 812 Park Avenue, New York, N.Y. 10021 (Home); c/o General Foods Corporation, 250 North Street, White Plains, N.Y. 10625, U.S.A. (Office). *Telephone:* (914) 335-2500 (Office).

FERGUSON, Paul; South African stockbroker; b. 23 August 1943, Johannesburg; s. of Ray and Joy Ferguson; trained as chartered accountant; Dir. Fergusson Bros., Hall Stewart & Co. Inc. 1973–, Chair. 1983–; Pres. Johannesburg Stock Exchange 1982–84, Cttee. mem. 1979–, Chair. 1988–; Dir. of various cos. *Leisure interest:* squash. *Address:* P.O. Box 691, Johannesburg 2000 (Office); 60 Kent Road, Dunkeld, Johannesburg 2196, South Africa (Home). *Telephone:* (011) 833 5740 (Office); (011) 788 2227 (Home).

FERGUSON-SMITH, Malcolm Andrew, M.B., CH.B., F.R.C.PATH., F.R.S., F.R.S.E.; British professor of medical genetics; b. 5 Sept. 1931; s. of John Ferguson-Smith and Ethel May Ferguson-Smith (née Thorne); m. Marie Eva Gzowska 1960; one s. three d.; ed. Stowe School, Univ. of Glasgow; Registrar in Lab. Medicine, Dept. of Pathology, Western Infirmary, Glasgow 1958–59; Fellow in Medicine and Instructor, Johns Hopkins Univ. School of Medicine 1959–61; Lecturer, Sr. Lecturer, then Reader in Medical Genetics, Univ. of Glasgow 1961–73, Prof. 1973–87; Prof. of Pathology, Univ. of Cambridge 1987–; Fellow Peterhouse Coll., Cambridge 1987–; Dir. W. of Scotland Medical Genetics Service 1973–87, East Anglian Regional Clinical Genetics Service 1987–; Hon. Consultant in Medical Pediatrics, Royal Hosp. for Sick Children, Glasgow 1966–73, in Clinical Genetics, Yorkhill and Assoc. Hosps. 1973–87; Pres. Clinical Genetics Soc. 1979–81; Ed. Prenatal Diagnosis 1980–; mem. Johns Hopkins Univ. Soc. of Scholars; Bronze Medal, Univ. of Helsinki 1968. *Publications:* Early Prenatal Diagnosis (Ed.) 1983, Essential Medical Genetics (Co-Author) 1984; papers on cytogenetics, gene mapping, human genetics and prenatal diagnosis in medical journals. *Leisure interests:* swimming, sailing, fishing.

Address: c/o Department of Pathology, University of Cambridge, Tennis Court Road, Cambridge, CB2 1QP, England. *Telephone:* 333691.

FERGUSSON, Sir Ewen Alastair John, K.C.M.G., M.A.; British diplomatist; b. 28 Oct. 1932, Singapore; s. of late Sir Ewen MacGregor Field Fergusson and Lady (Winifred Evelyn) Fergusson; m. Sara Carolyn Montgomery Cuninghame, née Gordon Lennox 1959; one s. two d.; ed. Rugby and Oriel Coll., Oxford; 2nd Lieut. 60th Rifles (KRRC) 1954–56; Foreign (Diplomatic) Service 1956–; Asst. Private Sec. to Minister of Defence 1957–59; British Embassy, Addis Ababa 1960; Foreign and Commonwealth Office 1963; British Trade Devt. Office, New York 1967; Counsellor and Head of Chancery, Office of U.K. Perm. Rep. to European Communities 1972–75; Private Sec. to Foreign and Commonwealth Sec. 1975–78, Asst. Under-Sec. of State 1978–82; Amb. to South Africa 1982–84, to France 1987–; Deputy Under-Sec. of State 1984–87. *Address:* British Embassy, 35 rue du Faubourg Saint Honoré, 75008 Paris, France. *Telephone:* 42-66-91-42.

FERLINGHETTI, Lawrence, M.A., DR.UNIV.; American writer; b. 4 March 1920, Yonkers, New York; s. of Charles Ferlinghetti and Clemence Mendes-Monsanto; m. 1951; one s. one d.; ed. Columbia Univ., Univ. of Paris. *Publications include:* Pictures of the Gone World (poems), Selections from Paroles by Jacques Prévert, A Coney Island of the Mind (poems), Her (novel), Starting from San Francisco (poems), Unfair Arguments with Existence (7 plays), Routines (plays), The Secret Meaning of Things (poems), Tyrannus Nix? (poem), Back Roads to Far Places (poems), Open Eye, Open Heart (poems), The Mexican Night (travel journal), Who are We Now? 1976, Landscapes of Living and Dying (poems) 1979, Endless Life: Selected Poems 1981; Literary San Francisco: A Pictorial History from the Beginnings to the Present (with Nancy J. Peters) 1980, Leaves of Life: Drawings from the Model 1983, Over All the Obscene Boundaries (poems) 1984, Seven Days in Nicaragua Libre 1984, Love in the Days of Rage (ed. with Nancy J. Peters) 1988; Ed. City Lights Books; also translations, film-scripts and phonograph records. *Address:* c/o City Lights Bookstore, 261 Columbus Avenue, San Francisco, Calif. 94133, U.S.A. *Telephone:* (415) 362-8193.

FERM, Anders; Swedish diplomatist; b. 1938, Ockeldo; m.; one c.; ed. Stockholm School of Econs.; Special Political Asst. to Minister of Transport 1965–69, Prime Minister's Chef de Cabinet 1969–73; Exec. Sec. of Ind. Comm. of Disarmament and Security Issues, Vienna 1980–83; Perm. Rep. to UN, New York 1983–88; exec. man. publishing 1973–80, fmr. mem. numerous cttees. and bds. including PEN Club, Publrs. Assen., Swedish Television Corpn. *Address:* c/o Ministry for Foreign Affairs, Gustav Adolfs torg 1, P.O. Box 16121, 103 23 Stockholm, Sweden.

FERNANDES, Most Rev. Angelo Innocent, D.D., S.T.L.; Indian ecclesiastic; b. 28 July 1913, Karachi; s. of John Ligorio Fernandes and Evelyn Sabina Fernandes; ed. St. Patrick's, Karachi, St. Joseph's Seminary, Mangalore, Papal Univ., Kandy, Sri Lanka; Archbishop of Delhi 1967–; Sec. Gen. Catholic Bishops' Conf. of India 1960–72, Chair. Justice, Devt. and Peace Comm. 1968–76, 1986–; mem. Vatican Justice and Peace Acad. 1966–76; Exec. Pres. World Conf. on Religion and Peace, New York and Geneva 1970–84, Pres. Emer. 1984–; attended five World Synods of Catholic Bishops and mem. of Synod Secr. 1971–74, 1980–83; Chair. Office of Ecumenical and Inter-religious Affairs of Fed. of Asian Bishops' Confs. 1985–. *Publications:* Apostolic Endeavour 1962, Religion, Development and Peace 1971, Religion and the Quality of Life 1974, Religion and a New World Order 1976, Towards Peace with Justice 1981, God's Rule and Man's Role 1982, Summons to Dialogue 1983, The Christian Way Today 1987. *Address:* Archibishop's House, Ashok Place, New Delhi 110 001, India. *Telephone:* (011) 343457.

FERNANDES, George; Indian trade unionist and politician; b. 3 June 1930, Bangalore, Karnataka; s. of John and Alice Fernandes; m. Leila Kabir 1971; one s.; ed. St. Peter's Seminary, Bangalore; joined Socialist Party of India 1949; Ed. Konkani Yuvak (Konkani Youth) monthly in Konkani language 1949, Raithavani weekly in Kannada language 1949, Dockman weekly in English 1952–53, also New Society; fmr. Chief Ed. Pratipaksha weekly in Hindi; trade union work in South Kanara 1949, 1950, in Bombay and Maharashtra 1950–58; founding Pres. All-India Radio Broadcasters and Telecasters Guild, Khadi Comm. Karmachari Union, All-India Univ. Employees' Confed.; Pres. All-India Railwaymen's Fed. 1973–74; organized nat. railways strike 1974; Treas. All-India Hind Mazdoor Sabha 1958; formed Hind Mazdoor Panchayat 1958, Gen. Sec. for over 10 years; Convenor, United Council of Trade Unions; fmr. mem. Gen. Council of Public Services Int. (PSI), Int. Transport Workers' Fed. (ITF); Founder Chair. New India Co-operative Bank Ltd. (fmrly. Bombay Labour Co-operative Bank Ltd.); mem. Nat. Cttee. of Socialist Party of India 1955–77, Treas. 1964, Chair. 1973–77; Gen. Sec. Samyukta Socialist Party of India 1969; mem. Bombay Municipal Corpn. 1961–68; mem. for Bombay City, Lok Sabha 1967–77; went underground on declaration of emergency 1975; arrested and charged in the Baroda Dynamite Case June 1976, case withdrawn March 1977; mem. Lok Sabha for Muzaffarpur, Bihar (elected while in prison) 1977–79; Minister for Communications March–July 1977, for Industry 1977–79; mem. Janata Party 1977, a Gen. Sec. 1985–86; resigned from Govt. July 1979; Deputy Leader Lok Dal 1980–, mem. Nat. Exec.; Chair. Nat. Campaign Cttee., Janata Party; Pres. Hind Mazdoor Kisan Panchayat, Schumacher Foundation, India; Editor Pratipaksha

(Hindi monthly), The Other Side (English-language monthly). *Publication:* What Ails the Socialists. *Leisure interests:* music, reading. *Address:* 6/105 Kaushalya Park, Haus Khas, New Delhi 110016, India.

FERNÁNDEZ MALDONADO SOLARI, Gen. Jorge; Peruvian army officer and politician; b. 29 May 1922, Ilo, Moquegua; s. of Arturo Fernandez Maldonado Soto and Amelia Solari de Fernandez Maldonado; m. Estela Castro Faucheux; two s. two d.; ed. Chorillos Mil. School; Head of Army Intelligence Service; Dir. of Army Intelligence School, also of Mariscal Ramon Castilla Mil. School, Trujillo; Mil. Attaché, Argentina; mem. Pres. Advisory Cttee. (COAP); Minister of Energy and Mines 1968-75; Army Chief of Staff 1975-76; Prime Minister, Minister of War, Commdr.-Gen. of Army Feb.-July 1976; Senator 1985-. *Address:* c/o The Senate, Lima, Peru. *Telephone:* 361362.

FERNÁNDEZ-MURO, José Antonio; Argentine painter; b. 1 March 1920; Dir. Nat. School of Fine Arts, Buenos Aires 1957-58; travelled and studied in Europe and America on UNESCO Fellowship of Museology 1957-58; lives in New York 1962-; one-man exhbns. in Buenos Aires, Madrid, Washington, New York, Rome and Detroit; represented in numerous Group Shows including 50 ans de Peinture Abstraite, Paris and The Emergent Decade, Guggenheim Museum 1965; prizes include Gold Medal, Brussels World Fair 1958, Guggenheim Int. and Di Tella Int. awards. *Major works:* Superimposed circles 1958, In Reds, Di Tella Foundation, Buenos Aires 1959, Horizonte terroso, Museum of Modern Art, Caracas 1961, Circulo azogado, Museum of Modern Art, New York 1962, Lacerated Tablet, Rockefeller, New York 1963, Elemental Forms, M.I.T. 1964, Silver Field, Guggenheim Museum 1965, Summit, Bonino Gallery, New York.

FERNÁNDEZ ORDÓÑEZ, Francisco; Spanish lawyer, politician and banker; b. 22 June 1930, Madrid; m. María Paz García Mayo; ed. Harvard Univ., U.S.A., Univ. of Madrid; Technical Gen.-Sec. Ministry of Finance 1973-74; Minister of Finance 1977-79, of Justice 1980-81; founded Partido de Acción Democrática (PAD) 1981; Pres. Inst. Nacional de Industria (I.N.I.) 1974; Chair. Banco Exterior de España 1983-85; Minister for Foreign Affairs 1985-; Gran Cruz de Carlos III, Gran Cruz de Mérito Civil, Hon. Cruz de San Raimundo de Penafort. *Publications:* Introducción en España sobre el IVA, La España Necesaria 1980, Palabras en Libertad 1982. *Address:* Ministry for Foreign Affairs, Plaza de Santa Cruz, Madrid (Office); Guisando 28, Madrid, Spain (Home). *Telephone:* 266.68.09 (Office).

FERNÁNDEZ RETAMAR, Roberto, DR. EN FIL.; Cuban writer; b. 9 June 1930, Havana; s. of José M. Fernández Roig and Obdulia Retamar; m. Adelaida de Juan 1952; two d.; ed. Univ. de la Habana, Univ. de Paris à la Sorbonne and Univ. of London; Prof. Univ. de la Habana 1955-; Visiting Prof. Yale Univ. 1957-58; Dir. Nueva Revista Cubana 1959-60; Cultural Counsellor of Cuba in France 1960; Sec. Union of Writers and Artists of Cuba 1961-65; Dir. of Review Casa de los Américas 1965-; Visiting lecturer Columbia Univ. 1957, Univ. of Prague 1965; Nat. Prize for Poetry, Cuba 1952. *Publications:* Poetry: Elegía como un Himno 1950, Patrias 1952, Alabanzas, Conversaciones 1955, Vuelta de la Antigua Esperanza 1959, Con las Mismas Manos 1962, Poesía Reunida 1948-1958 1966, Buena Suerte Viviendo 1967, Que veremos arder 1970, A quien pueda interesar 1970, Cuaderno paralelo 1973; studies: La poesía Contemporánea en Cuba 1954, Idea de la Estilística 1958, Papelería 1962, Ensayo de otro mundo 1967, Introducción a Cuba: la historia 1968, Caliban 1971, Lectura de Martí 1972, El son de Vuelo popular 1972. *Leisure interests:* reading, swimming.

FERNANDO, Most Rev. Nicholas Marcus; B.A., PH.L., D.D.; Sri Lankan ecclesiastic; b. 6 Dec. 1932; s. of W. Severinus Fernando and M. M. Lily Fernando; Ordained priest 1959; Rector, St. Aloysius Minor Seminary 1965-73; Archbishop of Colombo May 1977-; Chair. Episcopal Comm. for Clergy, Religions, and Seminaries, Sri Lanka. *Address:* Archbishop's House, Gnanarthapradeepaya Mawatha, Colombo 8, Sri Lanka. *Telephone:* 595471.

FERNANDO, Thusew Samuel, C.B.E., Q.C., LL.B.; Ceylonese judge; b. 5 Aug. 1906, Ambalangoda; s. of late T. O. Fernando; m. Malini Wickramasuriya 1943; one s.; ed. Royal Coll., Colombo, Univ. Coll., Colombo, Univ. Coll., London, and Lincoln's Inn, London; Crown Counsel 1936-52; Solicitor-Gen. Ceylon 1952-54; Attorney-Gen. 1954-56; Justice of Supreme Court of Ceylon 1956-68; mem. Judicial Service Comm. 1962-68; Pres. Int. Comm. of Jurists, Geneva 1966-77, Vice-Pres. 1977-; mem. Int. Cttee. of Inst. on Man and Science, New York; Pres. Asian-African Legal Consultative Cttee. 1971; Pres. Court of Appeal 1971-73; mem. Constitutional Court 1972; High Commr. in Australia and N.Z. 1974-77. *Leisure interests:* social services, human rights. *Address:* 3 Cosmas Avenue, Barnes Place, Colombo 7, Sri Lanka.

FERNEYHOUGH, Brian John Peter; British composer and professor of composition; b. 16 Jan. 1943, Coventry; s. of Frederick G. Ferneyhough and Emily M. (née Hopwood) Ferneyhough; m. 1st Barbara J. Pearson 1967, 2nd Elke Schaaf 1980, 3rd Carolyn Steinberg 1984; ed. Birmingham School of Music, Royal Acad. of Music, Sweelinck Conservatorium, Amsterdam and Basle Conservatorium; Composition teacher, Musikhochschule, Freiburg, Germany 1973-78, Prof. of Composition 1978-86; Prin. Composition Teacher, Royal Conservatory of The Hague 1986-; leader of Master Class in Composition, Civica Scuola di Musica, Milan 1985-; Visiting Artist, Berlin 1976-77; Guest Prof. Musikhögskolan, Stockholm 1980, 1981, 1982,

1985; Visiting Prof. Univ. of Chicago 1986; Lecturer in Composition, Darmstadt Int. Courses 1976, 1978, 1980, 1982, 1984, 1986; Koussevitsky Prize 1979, Grand Prix du Disque 1978, 1984, Chevalier des Arts et des Lettres 1984, and other awards and prizes. *Works include:* Sonatas for String Quartet 1967, Firecycle Beta 1969-71, Transit 1972-74, Time and Motion Study III 1974, La Terre Est Un Homme 1976-79, Second String Quartet 1979-80, Lemma-Icon-Epigram 1981, Carceri d' Invenzione 1981-86. *Publications:* various articles published separately. *Leisure interests:* reading, cats, wife, wine (not in that order). *Address:* Urbanstrasse 14, 7800 Freiburg, Federal Republic of Germany. *Telephone:* (0)761-3 54 18.

FERNIOT, Jean; French journalist; b. 10 Oct. 1918, Paris; s. of Paul and Jeanne (née Rabu) Ferniot; m. 1st Jeanne Martinod 1942 (divorced), 2nd Christiane Servan-Schreiber 1959; three s. two d.; ed. Lycée Louis-le-Grand; Head, Political Dept., France-Tireur 1945-57; Political Columnist, L'Express 1957-58; Chief Political Correspondent France-Soir 1959-63; Ed. L'Express 1963-66; on staff Radio Luxembourg 1967-; Political Commentator France-Soir 1967-70, Asst. Chief Ed. 1969-70; Dir. at éditions Grasset, in charge of Collection Humeurs 1978-83; Dir. then Adviser Cuisine et vins de France 1981; mem. jury, Prix interallié 1970-; Prix Interallié 1961; Commdr. des Arts et des Lettres; Croix de Guerre. *Publications:* Les ides de mai 1958, L'ombre porté 1961, Pour le pire 1962, Derrière la fenêtre 1964, De Gaulle et le 13 mai 1965, Mort d'une révolution 1968, Paris dans mon assiette 1969, Complainte contre X 1973, De de Gaulle à Pompidou 1972, Ça suffit! 1973, Pierrot et Aline 1973, La petite légume 1974, Les vaches maigres (with Michel Albert) 1975, Les honnêtes gens 1976, C'est ça la France 1977, Vous en avez vraiment assez d'être français 1979, Carnet de croûte 1980, le Pouvoir et la sainteté 1982, Le Chien-loup 1983, Saint Judas 1984, Un mois de juin comme on les aimait 1986. *Address:* 11 bis rue d'Orléans, 92200 Neuilly-sur-Seine, France.

FERRARO, Geraldine Anne, J.D.; American politician; b. 26 Aug. 1935, Newburgh, N.Y.; d. of Dominick and Antonetta L. (Corrieri) Ferraro; m. John Zaccaro 1960; one s. two d.; ed. Marymount Manhattan Coll., Fordham Univ.; lawyer in New York Bar 1961, U.S. Supreme Court 1978; practised law in New York 1961-74, Asst. Dist. Attorney, Queens County, New York 1974-78; mem. House of Reps. 1979-84; first woman from a major party to be a cand. for U.S. Vice-Pres. (with Walter Mondale, q.v.) in 1984 presidential election; Fellow Harvard Univ., Kennedy School of Govt., 1988; Pres. Int. Inst. of Women Political Leaders; mem. Nat. Democratic Inst. for Int. Affairs; Democrat. *Publication:* My Story (with Linda Bird Francke) 1985. *Address:* 218 Lafayette Street, New York, N.Y. 10012, U.S.A. (Office).

FERRAZZI, Ferruccio; Italian painter; b. 15 March 1891, Rome; m. Orizia Randone 1922; three s.; Titular Prof. of Decoration, Inst. of Fine Arts, Rome 1929-; Instructor, American Acad., Rome 1935-36; Dir. Scuola Vaticana del Mosaico 1967; mem. Acad. d'Italie 1932, Accad. del Disegno Firenze 1935-, Accad. Nazionale S. Luca 1925, Accad. Pontificia Virtuosi al Pantheon 1950; First Int. Prize Carnegie Inst. 1926. *Works include:* Focolare (Rome Modern Art Gallery) 1910, Genitrice (Rome) 1912, Presagio (Bologna Municipal Gallery) 1914, Vita gaia (Galleria Capitolina, Rome) 1921, Festa notturna, Adolescente 1922, Horitia (Florence Modern Art Gallery) 1923, Caratteri della famiglia (New York) 1923, Viaggio tragico (Pittsburgh), Idolo (Coll. Wedekind) 1925, Tempesta (Jeu de Paume, Paris) 1925, La Monta 1929, Il toro romano (Rome Modern Art Gallery) 1930, Seven tapestries (Palace of Corpns., Rome) 1932, Sabaudia (mosaic) 1935, Clemenza di Traiano (Palace of Justice, Milan) 1938, Fabiola e Ninetta che parlano (Art Gallery, Bucharest) 1933; frescoes for churches: S. Eugenio, Rome, S. Rita, Cascia 1951, Univ. of Padua, etc.; encaustic paintings for S. Benedetto Church, Rome 1949; mosaic Dell' Apocalisse 1927-54, Acqui; frescoes: Risurrezione, Amatrice 1953-55; l'Ultima Cena di Cristo, Assisi 1956, Le Opere e i Giorni, Mausoleo Acqui 1954-60; four sculptures Nella Villa di S. Liberata 1959-65; mosaic, Propaganda Fide Coll., Rome 1965-66; mosaic, apse of the Church of S. Antonio, Taranto 1970; seven paintings on Illuminazione della Memoria 1972. *Leisure interests:* poetry, sculpture. *Address:* Strada del Pianone 15, "Giardino delle Sculture", Santa Liberata, Grosseto 58010 (Studio); Piazza delle Muse, Via G. G. Porro 27, Rome 00197, Italy. *Telephone:* Santa Liberata 814327; Rome 801270.

FERRER, José; American actor and director; began career as opera singer; operatic début in title role, Gianni Schicchi, Santa Fe Opera; sang Amonasro in Aida, Beverly Hills Opera; Dir. Don Giovanni, Dallas, Tex.; has directed ballet in several cities. *Films:* Joan of Arc (Acad. Award nomination for Best Supporting Actor) 1948, Whirlpool 1950, Crisis 1950, Cyrano de Bergerac (Acad. Award for Best Actor) 1950, Anything Can Happen 1952, Moulin Rouge (Acad. Award nomination for Best Actor) 1952, Miss Saidie Thompson 1953, The Caine Mutiny 1954, Deep in my Heart 1954, The Shrike (also Dir.) 1955, Cockleshell Heroes (also Dir.) 1956, The Great Man (also Dir. and Screenwriter) 1957, The High Cost of Loving (Dir.) 1958, I Accuse (also Dir.) 1958, Return to Peyton Place (Dir.) 1961, State Fair (Dir.) 1962, Lawrence of Arabia 1962, Nine Hours to Rama 1963, Stop Train 349 From Berlin 1964, A Midsummer Night's Sex Comedy 1982, To Be Or Not To Be 1983, The Evil that Men Do 1984, Dune 1984, Bloody Birthday 1986. *Plays include:* Cyrano de Bergerac, The Silver Whistle, Twentieth Century (also Dir.; Tony Award for Direction), Stalag 17 (Producer and Dir.; Tony Award for Direction), The Four

Poster (also Dir.; Tony Award for Direction), The Shrike (also Dir..; Tony Awards and three Critics' Circle Awards), My Three Angels (Dir.), The Andersonville Trial (Dir.), The Girl Who Came to Supper, Man of La Mancha, A Life in the Theater. *Television:* many appearances, including Cyrano de Bergerac, The Marcus-Nelson Murders, Fame, Evita, Berlin Tunnel 21. *Address:* P.O. Box 616 Coconut Grove, Fla. 33133, U.S.A.

FERRIER, Johan Henri Eliza; Suriname politician; b. 12 May 1910, Paramaribo; Mem. Suriname Parl. 1946–48; Dir. Dept. of Educ., Paramaribo 1951–55; Prime Minister, Minister of Gen. Affairs, of Home Affairs 1955–58; Counsellor, Ministry of Educ., Arts and Science, Netherlands 1959–65; Man. Dir. Billiton Mining Co., Suriname 1966–67; Gov. of Suriname 1968–75; Pres. Repub. of Suriname 1975–80; Dr. of Arts and Philosophy, Netherlands 1950. *Address:* c/o Office of the President, Paramaribo, Suriname.

FERRY, John Douglass, PH.D.; American professor of chemistry; b. 4 May 1912, Dawson, Canada (of U.S. parents); s. of Douglass Hewitt Ferry and Eudora Beaufort Bundy; m. Barbara Norton Mott 1944; one s. one d.; ed. Stanford Univ. and Univ. of London; Instructor, Harvard Univ. 1936–38, Soc. of Fellows, Harvard 1938–41, Research Assoc. 1942–45; Assoc. Chemist, Woods Hole Oceanographic Inst. 1941–45; Asst. Prof., Univ. of Wisconsin 1946, Assoc. Prof. 1946–47, Prof. 1947–82, Farrington Daniels Research Prof. 1973–82, Prof. Emer. 1982–, Chair. Dept. of Chem. 1959–67; Pres. Soc. of Rheology 1961–63; Chair. Int. Cttee. on Rheology 1963–68; mem. Nat. Acad. of Sciences; Fellow, American Acad. of Arts and Sciences, Hon. mem. Groupe français de Rhéologie, Soc. of Rheology, Japan; Special Lecturer, Kyoto Univ., Japan 1968, Univ. de Grenoble (Ecole d'Eté) 1973; Eli Lilly Award, A.C.S. 1946; Bingham Medal, Soc. of Rheology 1953; Kendall Award, A.C.S. 1960; High Polymer Physics Prize, American Physical Soc. 1966; Colwyn Medal, Inst. of the Rubber Industry (London) 1971; Witco Award, A.C.S. 1974, Tech. Award, Int. Inst. of Synthetic Rubber Producers 1977, Goodyear Medal, Rubber Div. A.C.S. 1981, Div. of Polymer Chem. Award, A.C.S. 1984. *Publication:* Viscoelastic Properties of Polymers 1961, 1970, 1980. *Leisure interest:* travel. *Address:* Department of Chemistry, University of Wisconsin, Madison, Wis. 53706; 137 N. Prospect Avenue, Madison, Wis. 53705, U.S.A. (Home). *Telephone:* (608) 262-1485 (Office); (608) 233-4936 (Home).

FERSHT, Alan Roy, M.A., PH.D., F.R.S.; British professor of organic chemistry; b. 21 April 1943, London; s. of Philip and Betty Fersht; m. Marilyn Persell 1966; one s. one d.; ed. Sir George Monoux Grammar School, Walthamstow and Gonville and Caius Coll., Cambridge; Research Fellow, Brandeis Univ. Waltham, Mass. 1968–69; Fellow, Jesus Coll., Cambridge 1969–72; mem. scientific staff, MRC Lab. of Molecular Biology, Cambridge 1969–77; Eleanor Roosevelt Fellow, Stanford Univ., Calif. 1978–79; Wolfson Research Prof. of Royal Soc. 1978–89; Prof. of Biological Chem., Imperial Coll., London 1978–88; Herschel Smith Prof. of Organic Chem., Cambridge Univ. 1988–; Fellow Gonville and Caius Coll., Cambridge 1988–. *Publications;* Enzyme Structure and Mechanism 1977; papers in scientific journals. *Leisure interests:* chess, horology. *Address:* University Chemical Laboratory, Lensfield Road, Cambridge CB2 1EW (Office); 82 Mill End Road, Cambridge CB1 4JP, England (Home). *Telephone:* (0223) 336341 (Office); (0223) 212377 (Home).

FERY, John Bruce, M.B.A.; American business executive; b. 16 Feb. 1930, Bellingham, Wash.; s. of Carl S. and Margaret Fery; m. Delores Carlo 1953; three s.; ed. Univ. of Washington and Stanford Univ. Graduate School of Business; Asst. to Pres., Western Kraft Corpn. 1955–56, Production Man. 1956–57; Asst. to Pres., Boise Cascade Corpn. 1957–58, Gen. Man. Paper Div. 1958–60, Vice-Pres. 1960–67, Exec. Vice-Pres. and Dir. 1967–72, Pres. 1972–78, C.E.O. 1978–, Chair 1978–. *Address:* Boise Cascade Corporation, One Jefferson Square, Boise, Idaho 83728 (Office); 609 Wyndemere Drive, Boise, Idaho 83702, U.S.A. (Home). *Telephone:* (208) 384-7560 (Office).

FESHBACH, Herman, PH.D.; American professor of physics; b. 2 Feb. 1917, New York, N.Y.; s. of David and Ida Feshbach; m. Sylvia Harris 1940; two s. one d.; ed. City Coll., New York, N.Y. and M.I.T.; Tutor in Physics, City Coll., New York 1937–38; Asst. Prof. M.I.T. 1945–47, Assoc. Prof. 1947–54, Prof. of Physics 1954–, Cecil and Ida Green Prof. 1976–83, Inst. Prof. 1983–87, Inst. Prof. Emer. 1987–, Dir. Center for Theoretical Physics 1967–73, Head, Dept. of Physics 1973–83; Guggenheim Fellow 1954–55, Ford Foundation Fellow 1962–63; Vice-Pres. American Acad. of Arts and Science 1973–76, Pres. 1982–86; Ed. Annals of Physics 1977–, Contemporary Concepts in Physics; Chair. DOE/NSF (Nat. Science Foundation) Nuclear Science Advisory Cttee. 1979–82; Pres. American Physical Soc. 1980–81; mem. Nat. Acad. of Sciences; mem. Bd. of Govs. Weizmann Inst. of Science; Trustee, Associated Univs. Inc. 1974–87; Chair. Elect. Section B (Physics), A.A.A.S. 1986–(87); Navy Ordnance Award 1943; Bonner Prize, American Physical Soc. 1973, Humboldt Sr. U.S. Scientist Award 1982–83, Nat. Medal of Science 1986. *Publications:* Methods of Theoretical Physics (with Philip M. Morse) two vols. 1953, Theoretical Nuclear Physics (with Amos de Shalit) 1974, Reaction Dynamics (with F. S. Levin) 1973. *Address:* Department of Physics, Room 6-307, Massachusetts Institute of Technology, 77 Massachusetts Avenue, Cambridge, Mass. 02139 (Office); 5 Sedgwick Road, Cambridge, Mass. 02138, U.S.A. (Home). *Telephone:* (617) 253-4821 (Office); (617) 354-2721 (Home).

FETSCHER, Iring, DR. PHIL.; German political scientist; b. 4 March 1922, Marbach; s. of Prof. Rainer Fetscher; m. Elisabeth Götte 1957; two s. two

d.; ed. König-George-Gymnasium, Dresden, Eberhard-Karls-Universität, Tübingen, Université de Paris, and Johann Wolfgang Goethe-Univ., Frankfurt; Ed. Marxismusstudien 1956–; radio commentator on political, philosophical and sociological questions; Prof. of Political Science, Johann Wolfgang Goethe-Univ., Frankfurt 1963–; Theodor-Heuss Prof. New School for Social Research, New York 1968–69; Guest Prof. Tel-Aviv Univ. 1972; Fellow, Netherlands Inst. for Advanced Study in the Humanities and Social Sciences 1972–73; Inst. for Advanced Studies, Australian Nat. Univ., Canberra; Extraordinary Prof. for Social and Political Philosophy, Catholic Univ. of Nijmegen 1974–75. *Publications include:* Von Marx zur Sowjetideologie 1956, Uber dialektischen und historischen Materialismus (Commentary of Stalin) 1956, 1962, Rousseaus politische Philosophie 1960, 1968, 1975, Der Marxismus, seine Geschichte in Dokumenten Vol. I 1962, Vol. II 1964, Vol. III 1965, 4th edn. in one vol. 1983, Marx-Engels Studienausgabe (4 vols.) 1966, Introduction to Hobbes' Leviathan 1966, Karl Marx und der Marxismus 1967, Der Rechtsradikalismus 1967, Der Sozialismus 1968, Der Kommunismus 1969, Hegel: Grösse und Grenzen 1971, Modelle der Friedenssicherung 1972, Wer hat Dornröschen wachgeküsst?—das Märchenverwirrbuch 1972, 1974, Marxistische Porträts Vol. I 1975, Herrschaft und Emanzipation 1976, Terrorismus und Reaktion 1981, Analysen zum Terrorismus, Ideologien und Strategien 1981, Vom Wohlfahrtsstaat zu neuen Lebensqualität, die Heransforderungen des demokratischen Sozialismus 1982, Der Nulltarif der Wichtelmänner, Märchen- und andere Verwirrspiele 1982, Arbeit und Spiel (essays) 1983, Hanbuch der politischen Ideen (Co-ed. with H. Münkler), Vols. 1, 3, 4, 5 1985–88, Überlebensbedingungen der Menschheit zur Dialektik des Fortschritts 1986, Die Wirksamkeit der Träume, literarische Skizzen eines Sozialwissenschaftlers 1987. *Leisure interests:* collects autographed letters and manuscripts. *Address:* J. W. Goethe Universität, Senckenberganlege 31, 6000 Frankfurt-am-Main; Ganghoferstrasse 20, 6000 Frankfurt-am-Main, Federal Republic of Germany (Home). *Telephone:* 52-15-42.

FETTEROLF, Charles Frederick, B.S.; American business executive; b. 18 July 1928, Huntington, Pa.; s. of Harry B. and Beryl Unangst Fetterolf; m. Frances S. Fetterolf 1953; two s.; ed. Grove City Coll.; joined Aluminum Co. of America 1952, Gen. Man. Marketing 1975, Vice-Pres. for Operations, Mill Products 1977, Vice-Pres. Alcoa Smelting Process Project 1978, Vice-Pres. for Operations, Primary Products 1979, Vice-Pres. for Science and Tech. 1981, Exec. Vice-Pres. for Mill Products 1981, Dir. and Pres. Aluminum Co. of America 1983–, C.O.O. 1985–; Dir. Mellon Bank, Provident Life and Accident Insurance Co.; Trustee Univ. of Pittsburg, Grove City Coll.; mem. of Bd. of Overseers, Univ. of Pa. *Leisure interests:* golf, skiing, tennis; work with under-privileged. *Address:* Aluminum Company of America, 1501 Alcoa Bldg., Pittsburgh, Pa. 15219 (Office); 213 Creek Drive, Sewickley, Pa. 15143, U.S.A. (Home). *Telephone:* (412) 553-4881 (Office); (412) 741-8398 (Home).

FETTWEIS, Alfred Leo Maria, D. ÈS SC.; German professor of communication engineering; b. 27 Nov. 1926, Eupen, Belgium; s. of Paul Fettweis and Helene (née Hermanns) Fettweis; m. Lois J. Piaskowski 1957; two s. three d.; ed. Catholic Univ. of Louvain, Columbia Univ., Polytechnic Inst. of Brooklyn; Devt. engineer with Int. Telephone and Telegraph Corpn. (ITT), Belgium 1951–54, 1956–63 and U.S.A. 1954–56; Prof. of Theoretical Electricity, Eindhoven Univ. of Tech. 1963–67; Prof. of Communication Eng. Ruhr Univ. of Bochum 1967–; Prix Acta Technica Belgica 1963, Darlington Prize Paper Award 1980, I.E.E.E. Centennial Medal 1984, Tech. Achievement Award of I.E.E.E Circuits and Systems Soc. 1987, Karl-Küpfmüller-Preis of Informationstechnische Gesellschaft 1988, and other prizes; Dr. h.c. (Linköping) 1986, (Mons) 1988, (Leuven) 1988; mem. Rheinisch-Westfälische Akad. der Wissenschaften. *Publications:* many tech. papers on circuits, systems and related areas, about 30 patents. *Leisure interests:* hiking, music. *Address:* Lehrstuhl für Nachrichtentechnik, Ruhr-Universität Bochum, P.O. Box 102148, D-4630 Bochum (Office); Im Königsbusch 18, D-4630 Bochum 1, Federal Republic of Germany (Home). *Telephone:* 0234-7003063 (Office); 0234-797922 (Home).

FETTWEIS, Günter Bernhard Leo, DR. ING.; Austrian mining engineer and university professor; b. 17 Nov. 1924, Düsseldorf, Germany; s. of Ewald I. Fettweis and Aninhas M. (née Leuschner-Fernandes) Fettweis; m. Alice Y. Fettweis; one s. three d.; ed. Univ. of Freiburg and Technical Univ. of Aachen; Jr. Mining Inspector Nordrhein-Westfalen 1953–54; Ruhr coal-mining industry, then Production Man. of the Osterfeld, Sterkrade and Hugo Haniel coal mines, B.A.G. Neue Hoffnung, Oberhausen/Ruhr 1955–59; Prof. and Head Dept. of Mining Eng. and Mineral Econs., Montan Univ. Leoben, Austria 1959–, Rector (Vice-Chair.) 1968–70; Vice-Pres., later Pres. Mining Soc. of Austria 1963–; Vice-Pres. Austrian Soc. of Rock Mechanics 1968–81, Int. Organizing Cttee. World Mining Congress 1976–; mem. Supervising Bd. ÖBAG (Austrian State Mining Industry) 1988–; Corresp. mem. Austrian Acad. of Sciences 1977, mem. 1983–, Chair. Bd. Inst. for Research about Mineral Resources 1983–87; Dr. h.c. (Aachen), (Miskolc, Hungary); Austrian State Award of Energy Research; nat. and int. medals. *Publications:* World Coal Resources, Methods of Assessment and Results 1976–79, Atlas of Mining Methods (co-author) 1963–66, Ed.: Mining in the Process of Change 1988. *Leisure interests:* history, philosophy, Africa, sailing. *Address:* Institut für Bergbaukunde der Montanuniversität Leoben, Franz-Josef-Strasse 18, A-8700 Leoben (Office);

Gasteigergasse 5, A-8700 Leoben, Austria (Home). *Telephone:* (03842) 42555/230 (Office); (03842) 21190 (Home).

FEUILLÈRE, Edwige; French actress; b. 29 October 1910, Vesoul; m. Pierre Feuillère (divorced); ed. Conservatoire national de Paris; appeared for two years at the Comédie française, at Théâtre nat. populaire 1965; has played leading parts in La dame aux camélias, Sodome et Gomorrhe, L'aigle à deux têtes, Partage de midi, La parisienne, Phèdre, Constance, Rodogune, La liberté est un dimanche, Pour Lucrèce, Lucy Crown, Eve et Line, La folle de Chaillot, A Delicate Balance, Les bonshommes, Sweet Bird of Youth, La visite de la vieille dame, Le bateau pour Lipaia, Cher Menteur 1980, Leocadia 1984-85. *Films include:* Sans lendemain, De Mayerling à Sarajevo, J'étais une aventurière, L'idiot, Olivia, Cap de l'espérance, Adorables créatures, Le blé en herbe, Les fruits de l'été, En cas de malheur, La vie à deux, Les amours célèbres, Le crime ne paie pas, Si la vie nous sépare, La chair de l'orchidée, Cher Menteur 1980. *TV appearances:* Les dames de la côte, Le Chef de Famille, Le Tueur Triste; Officier Légion d'honneur, Commdr. des Arts et Lettres. *Publications:* Les feux de la mémoire, Moi, La Clairon. *Leisure interest:* reading. *Address:* 19 rue Eugène Manuel, Paris 16e, France.

FEYIDE, Chief Meshach Otokiti, A.C.S.M., D.I.C., C.ENG., F.I.M.M., F.INST.PET.; Nigerian chartered engineer; b. 31 March 1926, Ipele, Ondo State; s. of Chief Samuel and Juliana Elebe (née Adeola) Otokiti; m. Christiana Oluremi 1954; one s. two d.; ed. Govt. Coll., Ibadan, Camborne School of Mines, U.K., Imperial Coll. of Science and Tech., London; Insp. of Mines 1954-59; Petroleum Engineer, Ministry of Mines and Power 1960, Chief Petroleum Engineer 1964, Dir. Petroleum Resources 1970; Sec.-Gen. OPEC 1975-76; Chief Exec. Petroleum Inspectorate, Nigerian Nat. Petroleum Corpn. 1977-78; Petroleum Consultant 1979-; Publr. and Man. Ed. Nigerian Petroleum News 1984-; Austrian Grand Decoration of Honour 1978; Officer Order of the Fed. Repub. (OFR) 1982; Nigerian American Chamber of Commerce Award to Leading Businessmen 1983. *Leisure interests:* music, reading. *Address:* P.O. Box 1790, Lagos, Nigeria. *Telephone:* Lagos 636999.

FEYZIOĞLU, Turhan, LL.D.; Turkish university professor and government official; b. 19 Jan. 1922, Kayseri; s. of Sait Azmi and Neyyire Feyzioğlu; m. Leyla Firdevs 1949; one s.; ed. Galatasaray Lycée, Istanbul Univ., and Ecole nationale d'Administration, Paris; Asst. Prof. Ankara Political Science School 1945-47, Assoc. Prof. 1947-54; Research, Nuffield Coll., Oxford 1954; Co-ed. Forum 1954-58; Prof. Ankara Univ. 1955; Dean, Political Science School, Ankara 1956; Participant Harvard Int. Seminar 1956; M.P. 1957, 1961, 1965-80; mem. Nat. Exec. Cttee. Republican People's Party 1957-61, Vice-Pres. 1965, 1966; Pres. Middle East Tech. Univ. 1960; mem. Constituent Ass. 1960; Minister of Educ. 1960; Minister of State 1961; Deputy Prime Minister 1962-63; mem. Turkish High Planning Council 1961-63, 1975-78; Turkish Rep. Consultative Assembly Council of Europe 1964-66, 1972; Leader Republican Reliance Party 1967-; Deputy Prime Minister 1975-77, Deputy Prime Minister and Minister of State Jan.-Sept. 1978, mem. Ataturk Research Centre 1983; Dr. h.c. (Kayseri Univ.) 1985. *Publications;* Administrative Law 1947, Judicial Review of Unconstitutional Laws 1951, Les partis politiques en Turquie 1953, The Reforms of the French Higher Civil Service 1955, Democracy and Dictatorship 1957, Communist Threat 1969, In the Service of the Nation 1975, Kemal Ataturk, Leader de la Libération Nationale 1981, Ataturk's Way 1982, Chypre, Mythes et Réalités 1984, Ataturk and Nationalism 1986, The Crux of the Cyprus Problem 1987. *Leisure interest:* gardening. *Address:* Ataturk Research Center, Ataturk Bulvarı, 217 Ankara (Office); Çevre sokak, 54/9, Çankaya, Turkey (Home). *Telephone:* 1270619 (Home).

FFORDE, John Standish, M.A.; British banker; b. 16 Nov. 1921, Broadstone, Dorset; s. of late F. C. Fforde; m. Marya Retinger 1951; three s. one d.; ed. Rossall School and Christ Church, Oxford; Asst. Prime Minister's Statistical Branch 1951-53; Fellow in Econs., Nuffield Coll., Oxford 1953-56; Adviser Bank of England 1957-59, Deputy Chief Cen. Banking Information Dept. 1959-64, Adviser to Govs. 1964-66, 1982-84, Chief Cashier 1966-70, Dir. 1970-82, official historian 1984-; Dir. Mercantile House Holdings 1984-, Halifax Bldg. Soc. 1984-; Dir. The Jt. Mission Hosp. Equipment Bd. Ltd. 1981-, Chair. 1985-; Dir. CL-Alexanders Laing and Cruikshank Ltd. 1987-. *Publications:* The Federal Reserve System 1945-49 1953, An International Trade in Managerial Skills 1957. *Leisure interests:* travel, walking. *Address:* Mercantile House, 66 Cannon Street, London, EC4N 6AE, England.

FFRENCH-DAVIS, Ricardo, PH.D.; Chilean economist; b. 27 June 1936; s. of H. L. Ffrench-Davis and G. Muñoz; m. Marcela Yampaglia 1966; ed. Catholic Univ. of Chile, Univ. of Chicago; Researcher and Prof. of Econs., Econ Research Cen., Catholic Univ. 1962-64; Prof. of Econs., Univ. of Chile 1962-73; Deputy Man. Research Dept., Cen. Bank of Chile 1964-70; Research Dir. Cen. on Planning Studies, Catholic Univ. 1970-75; Vice-Pres. and Dir. Corpn. for Latin American Econ. Research (CIEPLAN), Santiago 1976-; mem. Acad. Council, Latin American Program, The Woodrow Wilson Centre, Washington, D.C. 1977-80; Visiting Fellow, Univ. of Oxford 1974; Visiting Prof., Boston Univ. 1976; Pres. Acad. Circle, Acad. de Humanismo Cristiano, Chile 1978-81; Co-ordinator Working Group on Econ. Issues of Inter-American Dialogue 1985-86; mem. Editorial Bds. Latin American Research Review, El Trimestre Economico and Colección Estudios Cieplan. *Publications:* Políticas Económicas en Chile: 1952-70 1973, El cobre en el desarrollo nacional (co-ed.) 1974, Economía internacional: teorías y políticas para el desarrollo 1979, Latin America and a New International Economic Order (co-ed.) 1981, 1985, The Monetarist Experiment in Chile 1982, Relaciones financieras externas y la economía latinoamericana (ed.) 1983, Debt Financial Liberalization and Crisis in Chile 1985, Debt Renegotiation Frameworks and Development in Latin America 1986; Development and External Debt (co-ed.) 1988, Notes on Neostructuralism 1988, Debt-equity swaps in Chile 1989; over 70 articles on int. econs., Latin-American econ. devt., and Chilean econ. policies. *Address:* Corporation for Latin American Economic Research, Colón 3494, Casilla 16496, Santiago 9, Chile. *Telephone:* 2283262.

FIALA, (Josef Herbert) Ernst; Austrian business executive; b. 2 Sept. 1928, Vienna; s. of Josef and Anna Fiala; m. Friederike Huber 1955; two s. one d.; ed. Tech. Hochschule, Vienna; Asst., Inst. für Verbrennungskraftmaschinen und Kraftfahrwesen, Tech. Hochschule, Vienna 1952-54; research engineer, Daimler Benz AG, Sindelfingen, later Head of Research, PKW-Aufbauten 1954-63; Prof., Tech. Hochschule, Berlin, Inst. für Kraftfahrzeuge, and Dir. Tech. Testing Centre for Motor Vehicles 1963-70; Dir. of Research, Volkswagenwerk AG 1970, mem. Admin. Bd. for Research and Devt. 1973-88; mem. Supervisory Bd. Adlerwerke, Frankfurt, Audi AG, Deutsche Automobilgesellschaft, Hoesch Stahl AG, Triumph Werke Nürnberg AG; mem. Bd. of Dirs. Volkswagen of America; mem. Consultative Council, Volkswagen do Brasil; Chair. Research Advisory Council, Forschungsvereinigung Automobiltechnik e.V.; mem. Bd. of Man., Forschungsvereinigung Verbrennungskraftmaschinen; recipient of several awards. *Publications:* articles in professional journals. *Leisure interests:* skiing, sailing, surfing, swimming, cycling, classical music. *Address:* Volkswagenwerk AG, D-3180 Wolfsburg 1; Walfischgasse 5, A-1010, Vienna, Austria. *Telephone:* 05361/92 0821 (Office); 0222/5131420 (Homes).

FIALKA, Ladislav; Czechoslovak mime, choreographer and director; b. 22 Sept. 1931, Prague; ed. Conservatoire dance dept., Prague 1951-56; mime, dir., choreographer, artistic man. of pantomime ensemble, Balustrade Theatre, Prague 1958-; mem. Union of Czech Dramatic Artists; tours abroad since 1959 to U.S.S.R., U.S.A., Canada, Denmark, Poland, G.D.R., U.K., Sweden, Finland, Algeria, Belgium, Italy, Romania, Pakistan, Switzerland, Fed. Repub. of Germany, Mexico, Cuba, Costa Rica; State Prize of Klement Gottwald 1962, City of Prague Prize 1962, Medal for Exemplary Work 1968, Artist of Merit 1972, National Artist 1979; pantomimes: Cassander and Pierrot 1956, The Shipwrecked 1956, The Flower-girl 1956, At the Crossroads 1956, Pantomime on the Balustrade 1956, If a Thousand Clarinets 1959, Glass Fairy Tale for Czechoslovak glass exhibition in Moscow 1959, Nine Hats on Prague 1960, Fair Pantomime 1960, Etudes 1961, The Road 1962, The Madmen 1965, The Button 1968, Caprichos 1971, Funambules '77 1977, The Nose 1981; also films and television films. *Address:* Balustrade Theatre, Prague, Czechoslovakia.

FICHTENAU, Heinrich, PH.D.; Austrian professor of medieval history; b. 10 Dec. 1912, Linz; m. Anna Widl 1954; two d.; ed. Univ. of Vienna, Austrian Inst. for Historical Research; Research Asst. Univ. of Vienna 1936-50, Assoc. Prof. 1950-62, Prof. of Medieval History and Auxiliary Sciences 1962-83, Emer. Prof. 1983-; Dir. Austrian Inst. for Historical Research 1968-83; Corresp. Fellow British Acad.; Corresp. Fellow Medieval Acad. of America; Fellow Austrian Acad. of Sciences. *Publications:* Mensch u. Schrift im Mittelalter 1946, Babenberger-Urkundenbuch (with E. Zoellnor), (Vol. 1) 1950, (Vol. 2) 1955, (Vol. 3) 1968, Arenga 1957, Carolingian Empire 1957, Urkundenwesen in Österreich 1971, Beiträge zur Mediaevistik, (Vol. 1) 1975, (Vol. 2) 1977, (Vol. 3) 1986, Lebensordnungen des 10. Jahrhunderts (2 vols.) 1984. *Leisure interests:* bookworm. *Address:* 1A Mariahilfer Strasse, Vienna 1060, Austria.

FICHTNER, Kurt, DR.RER.OEC.; German politician; b. 16 Aug. 1916 Breslau (now Wrocław, Poland); Deputy Chair. Econ. Council of G.D.R. 1964-65; Minister of Iron Ore Mining and Metallurgy 1965-67; Deputy Chair. Council of Ministers 1967-74; Deputy Chair. State Planning Comm. 1974-; cand. mem. Cen. Cttee. Sozialistische Einheitspartei Deutschlands (SED) 1971-, Council of Ministers; Vaterländischer Verdienstorden in Bronze, Silver and Gold and other decorations. *Address:* Ministerrat, Berlin, German Democratic Republic.

FIEDLER, Leslie A., PH.D.; American professor of English and literary critic; b. 8 March 1917, Newark, N.J.; s. of Jacob Fiedler and Lillian Rosenstrauch; m. 1st Margaret Shipley 1939 (divorced 1972), three s. three d.; m. 2nd Sally Andersen 1973, two step-s.; ed. Univ. of Wisconsin and New York Univ. (Heights); mem. of Staff, Montana State Univ. 1941-63, Chair. Dept. of English 1954-56; Prof. of English, State Univ. of New York at Buffalo 1964, Chair. Dept. of English 1974-77; Assoc. Fellow, Calhoun Coll., Yale Univ.; Samuel Clemens Prof., SUNY Distinguished Prof.; teaches at vacation courses at univs. in many parts of Europe and U.S.A.; Rockefeller Fellow 1946-47, Fulbright Fellow 1951-53, 1961-62; Kenyon Review Fellowship in Criticism and Christian Gauss Fellowship, Princeton Univ. 1956; Guggenheim Fellowship 1970-71; mem. American Acad. and Inst. of Arts and Letters 1988; Furioso Poetry Prize 1957, Award of Nat. Inst. of Arts and Letters 1957. *Publications include:* An End to Innocence: Essays on Culture and Politics 1955, The Art of the Essay 1958, Love and Death in the American Novel 1960, 1966, No! In Thunder: Essays on Myth and Literature 1960, Pull Down Vanity and

Other Stories 1962, The Second Stone: A Love Story 1963, Waiting for the End 1964, Back to China 1965, The Last Jew in America 1966, The Return of the Vanishing American 1968, Nude Croquet and Other Stories 1969, Being Busted 1970, Collected Essays 1971, The Stranger in Shakespeare 1972; The Messengers Will Come No More 1974, In Dreams Awake 1975, Freaks 1977, Reader 1977, The Inadvertent Epic 1979, Olaf Stapledon 1982, What Was Literature? 1982. *Leisure interests:* swimming and/or meditation. *Address:* Department of English, Clemens Hall, Amherst Campus, Buffalo, N.Y. 14260; 154 Morris Avenue, Buffalo, N.Y. 14214, U.S.A. (Home). *Telephone:* (716) 636-2573 (Office); (716) 838-4105 (Home).

FIELDHOUSE, Adm. Sir John (David Elliott), G.C.B., G.B.E.; British naval officer; b. 12 Feb. 1928; s. of Sir Harold Fieldhouse; m. Margaret Ellen Cull 1953; one s. two d.; ed. Royal Naval Coll., Dartmouth; Midshipman, E. Indies Fleet 1945–46; entered Submarine Service 1948; Commdr. H.M.S. Acheron 1955; C.O. H.M.S. Dreadnought 1964–66; Exec. Officer H.M.S. Hermes 1967; Capt. SM10 (Polaris Squadron) 1968–70; Capt. H.M.S. Diomede 1971; Commdr. Standing Naval Force Atlantic 1972–73; Dir. Naval Warfare 1973–74; Flag Officer, Second Flotilla 1974–76; Flag Officer Submarines, Commdr. Submarine Force E. Atlantic 1976–78; Controller of Navy 1979–81; C.-in-C. Fleet and Allied C.-in-C., Channel and E. Atlantic 1981–82; First Sea Lord and Chief of Naval Staff 1983–85; Chief of Defence Staff 1985–88; mem. Inst. of Nuclear Engineers, Worshipful Co. of Glovers. *Address:* Ministry of Defence, Main Building, Whitehall, London, SW1A 2HB, England. *Telephone:* 01-218 2214.

FIELDSEND, John Charles Rowell, B.A., LL.B.; British judge; b. 13 Sept. 1921, Lincoln; s. of Charles and Phyllis Fieldsend; m. Muriel Gedling 1945; one s. one d.; ed. Michaelhouse, Natal, Rhodes Univ. Coll., Grahamstown, S.A.; served Royal Artillery 1943–45; called to the Bar, S. Rhodesia 1947, Q.C. 1959; Advocate in private practice 1947–63; Pres. Special Income Tax Court for Fed. of Rhodesia and Nyasaland 1958–63; High Court Judge, S. Rhodesia 1963–68 (resigned); Asst. Solicitor, Law Comm. for England and Wales 1968–78; Sec. Law Comm. 1978–80; Chief Justice of Zimbabwe 1980–83; Chief Justice, Turks and Caicos Islands 1985–87; Judge, Court of Appeal, St. Helena, Ascension, Falkland Islands and British Antarctic Territory 1985–, Court of Appeal, Gibraltar 1985–; Prin. Legal Adviser, British Indian Ocean Territory 1984–87, Chief Justice 1987–. *Leisure interests:* travel, home-making. *Address:* Great Dewes, Ardingly, Sussex, England.

FIENNES, Sir Ranulph Twisleton-Wykeham-, 3rd Bt., cr. 1916; British travel writer, lecturer and explorer; b. 7 March 1944, Windsor; s. of Lieut.-Col. Sir Ranulph Twisleton-Wykeham-Fiennes, D.S.O., 2nd Bt., and Audrey Newson; m. Virginia Pepper 1970; ed. Eton; Lieut. Royal Scots Greys 1966, Capt. 1968, retd. 1970; attached 22 SAS Regt. 1966, Sultan of Muscat's Armed Forces 1968; Leader, British Expdns. to White Nile 1969, Jostedalsbre Glacier 1970, Headless Valley, B.C. 1971, (Towards) North Pole 1977; Leader, Transglobe Expdn. (1st polar circumnavigation of world on its polar axis) 1979–82; Exec. Consultant to Chair. of Occidental Petroleum Corpn. Sept. 1984–; Hon. D.Sc. (Loughborough Coll.) 1986; Dhofar Campaign Medal 1969, Sultan's Bravery Medal 1970; Livingstone Medal, Royal Scottish Geographical Soc., Gold Medal of Explorers Club of N.Y. 1983, Founders Medal Royal Geographical Soc. 1984, Polar Medal 1986. *Publications:* A Talent for Trouble 1970, Ice Fall in Norway 1972, The Headless Valley 1973, Where Soldiers Fear to Tread 1975, Hell on Ice 1979, To the Ends of the Earth 1983, Bothie—The Polar Dog (with Virginia Twisleton-Wykeham-Fiennes) 1984, Living Dangerously 1987. *Leisure interests:* langlauf, photography. *Address:* Greenlands, Exford, Minehead, West Somerset, England. *Telephone:* 064 383 350.

FIGG, Sir Leonard Clifford William, K.C.M.G.; British diplomatist; b. 17 Aug. 1923; s. of late Sir Clifford and Lady Eileen (née Crabb) Figg; m. Jane Brown 1955; three s.; ed. Charterhouse, Trinity Coll., Oxford; R.A.F. 1942–46; Diplomatic Service 1947–; served Addis Ababa 1949–52, Foreign Office 1952–58, Amman 1958–61, Foreign Office 1961–67; Counsellor 1965; Deputy Consul-Gen., Chicago 1967–69; Dept. of Trade and Industry 1970–73; Consul-Gen. and Minister, Milan 1973–77; Asst. Under-Sec. of State, FCO 1977–80; Amb. to Ireland 1980–83; Vice-Chair. British Red Cross Soc. 1983–; Pres. Aylesbury Conservative and Unionist Asscn. 1985–; mem. Council, Co-operation Ireland 1985–. *Leisure interest:* field sports.

FIGGIS, Brian Norman, PH.D., D.SC., F.A.A.; Australian professor of inorganic chemistry; b. 27 March 1930, Sydney; s. of John N. E. Figgis and Dorice B. M. (née Hughes) Figgis; m. Jane S. Frank 1968; one s. one d.; ed. Univ. of Sydney, Univ. of New South Wales; Research Fellow, then Lecturer, Univ. Coll. London 1957–62, Visiting Prof. Univ. of Texas 1961, Reader, then Prof. Inorganic Chemistry, Univ. of W. Australia 1963–, Visiting Prof. Univ. of Ariz. 1968, Univs. of Florence and Sussex 1975, Visiting Scientist Institut Laue-Langevin, Brookhaven Nat. Lab. and Argonne Nat. Lab. 1984; Burrows Award Royal Australian Chemical Inst. 1985, Walter Burfitt Prize, Royal Soc. of N.S.W. 1986. *Publications:* Introduction to Ligand Fields, Interscience 1966, Ed. Transition Metal Chemistry, Vols. 8 & 9, 1984–85. *Leisure interest:* building construction. *Address:* School of Chemistry, University of Western Australia, Nedlands, W.A. 6009 (Office); 9 Hamersley Street, Cottesloe, W.A. 6011, Australia (Home). *Telephone:* 09-3803157 (Office); 09-3843032 (Home).

FIGGURES, Sir Frank, K.C.B., C.M.G.; British civil servant (retd.); b. 5 March 1910; ed. Oxford and Yale Univs.; called to Bar 1936; Mil. Service (R.A.) 1940–46; Treasury 1946–71; Dir. Trade and Finance, OEEC 1948–51; Under-Sec. Treasury 1955–60; Sec.-Gen. EFTA 1960–65; Third Sec. Treasury 1965–68; Second Perm. Sec. (Finance Group) 1968–71; Dir.-Gen. Nat. Econ. Devt. Office 1971–73; Chair. Pay Bd. 1973–74; BBC Consultative Group on Industrial and Business Affairs 1976–80, Chair. BBC Gen. Advisory Council 1978–82; Dir. Julius Baer Int. 1975–84. *Address:* 7A Spring Lane, Glaston, Uppingham, Rutland, LE15 9BX, England. *Telephone:* Uppingham 822777.

FIGUEIREDO, Elisio de; Angolan diplomatist; b. 13 June 1940; ed. studies in political science and int. affairs; mem. People's Movement for the Liberation of Angola (MPLA), active in independence campaign; worked at UN Secr., later spokesman of MPLA in various countries; MPLA rep. in U.S.A. 1974–76; Perm. Rep. to UN 1976–88; Amb. to U.K. 1988–. *Address:* 87 Jermyn Street, London, S.W.1, England.

FIGUEIREDO, Gen. João Baptista de; Brazilian army officer and politician; b. 15 Jan. 1918, Rio de Janeiro; s. of Euclydes and Valentina de Oliveira Figueiredo; m. Dulce Maria Guimarães de Castro 1942; two s.; ed. Mil. Acad., Advanced Training School for Officers, and Army Staff Coll.; became instructor at these establishments; with Brazilian Mil. Mission, Paraguay 1955–57; mem. Armed Forces Gen. Staff; Head Fed. Intelligence and Counter-Intelligence Service; Commdr. Public Security Force of State of São Paulo 1966–67, Horse Guards Regt. 1967–69; promoted to Brig.-Gen. 1969; Head of the Mil. Household 1969–74, of Nat. Information Service; Maj.-Gen. 1974, Gen. 1978; Pres. of Brazil 1979–85; Aliança Renovadora Nacional. *Address:* Av. Prefeito Mendes de Moraes 1400/802, S. Conrado, Rio de Janeiro, Brazil.

FIGUERES FERRER, José; Costa Rican politician; b. 25 Sept. 1906; m. 2nd Karen Olsen; six c.; ed. Univ. de Costa Rica, Univ. de México; coffee planter and rope maker in Costa Rica until 1942; exiled to Mexico 1942–44; became Pres. of ruling junta of the Repub. after 1948, resgnd. 1949; worked on econ. problems 1949–52; Pres. 1953–58, 1970–74; Visiting Prof., Harvard Univ. 1963–64; Pres. Partido de Liberación Nacional; Theodore Brent Prize. *Publications:* Cartas a un Ciudadano, La Pobreza de las Naciones 1973, and numerous articles. *Address:* Apartado 4820, San José, Costa Rica. *Telephone:* 25-16-68.

FIGUEROA, Adolfo, PH.D.; Peruvian professor of economics; b. 14 April 1941, Carhuaz; s. of Jose Manuel and Modesta Figueroa; m. Yolanda Vásquez 1965; one s. one d.; ed. Colegio Guadalupe (High School), Lima, San Marcos Univ., Lima, Vanderbilt Univ., Nashville, Tenn., U.S.A; Prof. of Econs., Catholic Univ. of Lima 1970–, Head Dept. of Econs. 1976–79; Dir. Research Project on Productivity and Educ. in Agric. in Latin America, ECIEL Program 1983–85; Consultant to ILO, FAO, Inter-American Foundation; Visiting Prof. Univ. of Pernambuco, Brazil 1973, St. Antony's Coll., Oxford 1976, Univ. of Ill., U.S.A. 1980, Econs. Dept., Univ. of Nicaragua 1985. *Publications:* Estructura del Consumo y Distribución de Ingresos en Lima 1968–1969 1974, Distribución del Ingreso en el Peru 1975, Capitalist Development and the Peasant Economy in Peru 1984; articles in econ. journals. *Address:* Departamento de Economía, Universidad Católica del Perú, Apartado 12514, Lima 21, Peru. *Telephone:* 622540.

FIIL, Niels Peter, PH.D.; Danish business executive; b. 8 Feb. 1941; s. of Svend Rasmussen and Gerda Fiil Rasmussen; m. Berthe M. Willumsen 1978; one d.; ed. Univ. of Copenhagen; Assoc. and Asst. Prof. Univ. of Copenhagen 1970–81; Visiting Prof. Harvard Medical School 1978–79; Man. Molecular Biology R&D, Novo Industri A/S 1980–86, Vice-Pres. 1987–; mem. European Molecular Biology Org. 1979, Royal Danish Acad. of Science and Letters 1982, Royal Swedish Acad. of Eng. Science 1988. *Publications:* scientific papers in the field of microbial genetics and biotechnology. *Address:* Novo Industri A/S, Molecular Biology R&D, Novo Alle, 2880 Bagsvaerd (Office); Fuglebakkevej 5, 2000 Frederiksberg, Denmark (Home). *Telephone:* 45 2 98 23 33 (Office); 45 1 34 53 32 (Home).

FIJAŁKOWSKI, Stanisław; Polish graphic artist; b. 4 Nov. 1922, Zdolbunov; m. Waleria Walicka 1951; one s.; ed. Acad. of Fine Arts, Łódź; main exhibitions: *Graphic arts:* Biennial, Krakow 1966–78, Ljubljana 1967–79, Tokyo 1968, Bradford 1970–74, Florence 1969, 1976, Xylon 1969–87, Lugano 1972, Frechen 1976–80, Jyväskylä 1978–, Heidelberg 1979–, 2nd Canadian, Edmonton 1980, 'Artists 79' UNO New York 1979, Int. Impact Art Festival, Kyoto 1981, Poland in Perspective, World Print Council in San Francisco 1985, Edinburgh, Bois Pluriel, Evry, Ashley Gallery, Epsom, Schloss Schwetzingen, Tampere, Padiglione d'Arte Contemporanea, Milan 1986, Galerie Marina Dinkler, W. Berlin, Surrealismi, Punkaharju, Finland, Graphika Atlantica, Reykjavik 1987. *Paintings:* Biennial, São Paulo 1969, Venice 1972, New Delhi 1973, 1975, Menton 1972, 1974; 'Presences polonaises', Centre Georges Pompidou, Paris 1983; several one-man exhibitions abroad; mem. Int. Asscn. Xylographers 'Xylon' 1986–; Prizes: Kraków 1968, 1970, Cyprian Kamil Norwid Critics Reward 1971, Lugano 1972, Ljubljana 1977, Frechen 1978, Heidelberg 1979, Cagnes-sur-Mer 1986, State Prize 1988. *Leisure interest:* film making. *Address:* Zachodnia 12 m. 59, 91-058 Łódź, Poland. *Telephone:* 57 75 51.

FIKENTSCHER, Wolfgang, D.JUR.; German professor of law; b. 17 May 1928, Nuremberg; s. of Erich Fikentscher and Elfriede (née Albers)

Fikentscher; m. Irmgard (née van den Berge) Fikentscher 1956; three s. one d.; ed. Univs. of Erlangen, Munich and Ann Arbor, Mich.; teacher of Labour Law, Trade Union Schools 1952–56; Prof. of Law, Univ. of Münster 1958–65, Univ. of Tübingen 1965–71, Univ. of Munich 1971–; legal adviser Wacker-Chemie GmbH 1951–56; Fellow Netherlands Inst. for Advanced Study in the Social Sciences 1971–72. *Publications:* Methoden des Rechts in vergleichender Darstellung, (5 vols.) 1975–77, Wirtschaftsrecht, (2 vols.) 1983, Schuldrecht 1985, numerous books and articles on civil and commercial law, antitrust law, int. law. *Leisure interest:* anthropology. *Address:* Institut für internationales Recht der Universität München, Ludwigstr. 29/11, 8000 München 22 (Univ.); Mathildenstr. 8a 8130 Starnberg, Federal Republic of Germany (Home). *Telephone:* (089) 2180-2443 (Univ.); (08151) 13454 (Home).

FIKRE-SELASSIE, Wogderess; Ethiopian politician; mem. Shengo; fmr. Deputy Chair. Provisional Mil. Admin. Council, now mem.; Prime Minister of Ethiopia Sept. 1987–. *Address:* Office of the Prime Minister, Addis Ababa, Ethiopia.

FILALI, Abdellatif; Moroccan diplomatist; b. 26 Jan. 1928, Fez; m.; ed. Univ. of Paris; joined Ministry of Foreign Affairs, rank of Amb. 1957; Perm. Rep. to the UN 1958–59; Chief of Royal Cabinet 1959–61; Chargé d'affaires, Embassy to France 1961–62; Amb. to Belgium, the Netherlands and Luxembourg 1962–63, to People's Repub. of China 1965–67, to Algeria 1967–68, to Spain 1970–71 and 1972–78; Minister of Higher Educ. 1968–70, of Foreign Affairs 1971–72; Perm. Rep. to the UN 1978–80; Amb. to U.K. 1980–81; Minister of Foreign Affairs, Co-operation and Information 1985–86, of Foreign Affairs and Co-operation Oct. 1986–; Perm. Sec. Acad. of Kingdom of Morocco 1981. *Address:* Ministry of Foreign Affairs, Quartier Administratif, Rabat, Morocco.

FILARET (see Philaret).

FILATOV, Aleksandr Pavlovich; Soviet government official and industrial specialist official; b. 24 June 1922; ed. Novosibirsk Inst. of Rail Transport Engineers 1947, Moscow Higher Party School, CPSU; engineer with Construction Trust, Novosibirsk 1947–48; mem. CPSU 1947–; political work in Novosibirsk, then Tomsk 1948–60; Head of Industrial Dept. of Novosibirsk Dist. Cttee. CPSU 1960–61; Sec., Novosibirsk City Cttee. CPSU 1961–63; First Deputy Chair. of Exec. Cttee. of Novosibirsk City Workers' Soviet 1963–66; First Sec., Novosibirsk City Cttee. CPSU 1966–73; Deputy to R.S.F.S.R. Supreme Soviet 1967–79; cand. mem. Cen. Cttee. CPSU 1971–81, mem. 1981–; Second Sec., Novosibirsk Dist. Cttee. CPSU 1973–78, First Sec. 1978–; mem. Mil. Council, Siberian Mil. Dist. 1978–; Deputy to Council of Union, U.S.S.R. Supreme Soviet 1979–; Order of Lenin 1982. *Address:* Central Committee of the Communist Party of the Soviet Union, Staraya pl. 4, Moscow, U.S.S.R

FILATOVA, Ludmila Pavlovna; Soviet opera-singer (mezzo-soprano); b. 6 Oct. 1935, Ozenburg; d. of Filatov Pavel and Valentina Semoylova; m. Rudakos Igor 1971; ed. Faculty of Mathematics, Leningrad Univ.; mem. CPSU 1969–; began singing in choir; mem. of Kirov Opera choir 1958–60; soloist with Kirov Opera 1960–; teacher of singing, Leningrad Conservatoire 1973–; gives chamber concerts: Shostakovich, Tchaikovsky, Rachmaninov, Glinka etc.; Glinka Prize 1960; People's Artist of U.S.S.R. 1983. *Major roles include:* Lyubasha in A Bride for the Tsar, Marfa in Khovanshchina, Carmen, Marta-Ekaterina in Petrov's Peter I. *Address:* Flat 13, Ryleyeva-strasse N6, Leningrad, U.S.S.R.

FILBINGER, Hans Karl, D. IUR.; German lawyer and politician; b. 15 Sept. 1913, Mannheim; m. Ingeborg Breuer 1950; one s. four d.; ed. Albert-Ludwigs-Univ., Freiburg im Breisgau, Ludwig-Maximilians-Univ., Munich, and Univ. de Paris; teacher, Univ. of Freiburg 1937–40; war service and P.O.W. 1940–46; lawyer, Freiburg 1946–60; mem. Landtag of Baden-Württemberg 1960; Minister of Interior, Baden-Württemberg 1960–66; Minister-Pres. of Baden-Württemberg 1966–78; Pres. Bundesrat (Upper House) 1973–74; mem. Comm. on Decartelization Questions 1947; Founder mem. German-French Soc., Freiburg, Soc. for Supra-national Co-operation; mem. NATO Parl. Conf.; Chair. Baden-Württemberg Democrat (CDU) Fed.; Pres. Studienzentrum Weikersheim e.V.; Dr.rer.nat. h.c.; Grosskreuz des Bundesdienstkreuzes and other awards. *Publications:* Die Schranken der Mehrheitsherrschaft im Aktienrecht und Konzernrecht 1942, Entscheidung zur Freiheit 1972, Hans Filbinger—der Fall und die Fakten 1980, Hans Filbinger—ein Mann in unserer Zeit 1983. *Leisure interests:* mountain climbing, skiing. *Address:* 7800 Freiburg-im-Breisgau, Riedbergstrasse 29, Federal Republic of Germany. *Telephone:* 0711-603530 (Office).

FILER, John H.; American insurance executive; b. New Haven, Conn.; m. Marlene A. Klick 1977; four d.; ed. De Pauw and Yale Univs.; joined Gumbart, Corbin, Tyler and Cooper (law firm), New Haven 1951; mem. Connecticut Senate 1957–58; Chair. Farmington Bd. of Educ. 1961–67; Asst. Counsel Aetna Life and Casualty Co. 1958, Gen. Counsel 1966, Admin. Asst. to Chair. and Pres. 1967, Exec. Vice-Pres. 1968, Vice-Chair. Jan. 1972, Chair. and C.E.O. 1972–84; Dir. U.S. Steel Corpn., Vice-Chair. Conn. Business and Industry Assen., Dir. Insurance Assen. of Conn., Inst. of Life Insurance, Greater Hartford Chamber of Commerce, Aetna Life and Casualty Co., Samuel Montague Co. (Holdings) 1982–; Partner Tyler, Cooper and Alcorn 1984–. *Address:* City Place, Hartford, Conn. 06103 (Office); West Hartford, Conn. 06107, U.S.A. (Home).

FILGUEIRA VALVERDE, José, D. EN FILOS. Y LET., L. EN D.; Spanish professor emeritus; b. 28 Oct. 1906, Pontevedra; s. of José and Araceli (née Valverde) Filgueira; m. María Teresa de Oscáriz 1938; five c.; ed. Univs. Santiago, Zaragoza, Madrid; Prof. Emer. Spanish Language and Literature; Dir. Emer. Museo de Pontevedra; mem. Real Acad. de la Historia, Real Acad. Gallega; Hon. Counsellor Consejo Superior de Investigaciones Científicas; Gold Medal City and Province of Pontevedra; Gold Medal of Fine Arts. *Publications:* 320 books, pamphlets and papers on history, art and archaeology of Galicia, including El Libro de Santiago 1953, Camoens 1958, Cantigas de Santa María de Alfonso X 1979. *Telephone:* Pontevedra 986-85 21 40.

FILIPOV, Grisha; Bulgarian politician; b. 13 July 1919, Kadiyevka, Ukraine; ed. Moscow Univ., USSR; returned to Bulgaria 1936; mem. Bulgarian CP 1940–; arrested for political activities and sentenced to 15 years' imprisonment 1941; released after coup 1944; various posts in party, including Head of Inspectorate in Ministry of Industry 1947; Counsellor, Deputy Head and Deputy Chair. of Cttee. on Planning 1951–58; Deputy Head of a Dept., Cen. Cttee. of Bulgarian CP 1958; cand. mem. Cen. Cttee. of Bulgarian CP 1962–66, mem. 1966–, Sec. Cen. Cttee. 1971–82, March 1986–; Deputy Chair. State Planning Comm. 1962–66; mem. Politburo 1974–; mem. State Council 1986–; Chair. Council of Ministers 1981–86; mem. Nat. Assembly. *Address:* Ministerski Suvet, Sofia, Bulgaria.

FILLIOUD, Georges, L. EN D.; French journalist and politician; b. 7 July 1929, Lyon; s. of Marius Fillioud and Camille Metifiot; m. Aimée Dieunet 1949; one s. one d.; ed. Ecole nationale professionnelle de Lyon, Univs. of Paris and Lyon; Journalist, Chief Reporter, then Sr. Ed., Europe No.1 radio station 1956–66; Deputy (Drôme) to Nat. Assembly 1967–68, 1973–81; Asst. Sec.-Gen. Convention des institutions républicaines 1970; Councillor, Romans 1970–77, Mayor 1977–81; Press Sec. Parti socialiste 1971–; Sec.-Gen. Féd. des élus socialistes et républicains 1972–; mem. Parl. Del. for French broadcasting 1974; Vice-Pres. Nat. Ass. Socialist Group 1978–79; Minister of Communication 1981–83, Sec. of State 1983–86; Conseiller d'État 1986. *Publications:* Le dossier du Vercors 1965, L'affaire Lindemans 1966. *Address:* 31 avenue Mac-Mahon, 75017 Paris (Home); 1 rue de Mars, 26100 Romans-sur-Isère, France (Home).

FINAISH, Mohamed, PH.D.; Libyan banking executive; b. 13 March 1936; m. Hind Deen 1963; one s. three d.; ed. Cairo Univ. and Univ. of Southern California; Asst. & Public Relations Man. Shell Co., Tripoli 1960; Sec.-Gen. Bank of Libya 1963; Dir. Research Dept., Central Bank of Libya 1972–73, Econ. Advisor 1977–78; Alt. Exec. Dir. IMF 1973–77, Exec. Dir. 1978–, Alt. Gov., Libya 1977–; Exec. Dir. UBAF, New York 1977–84. *Address:* 700 19th Street, N.W., Washington, D.C. 20431 (Office); 6419 Woodridge Road, Alexandria, Va. 22312, U.S.A. (Home).

FINCH, Jon Nicholas; British actor and film director; b. 2 March 1942, Caterham, Surrey; s. of Arthur Leonard Finch and Nancy Karen Houghton; m. Catriona MacColl 1981; ed. Caterham School; served 21 Special Air Service (SAS) Regt. (Artists) Reserve 1960–63; theatre technician and dir. etc. 1963–67, actor in TV 1967–70; Hon. Dr. of Metaphysics; Most Promising Newcomer, Variety Club of G.B. 1972; feature films since 1971 include lead role in Roman Polanski's Macbeth, Alfred Hitchcock's Frenzy, Lady Caroline Lamb, Une Femme Fidele, Death on the Nile, Breaking Glass, Girocity, Doktor Faustus, Riviera, Paradiso, Plaza Real, Streets of Yesterday, The Voice; TV films: The Rainbow, Unexplained Laughter; Theatre: Les Liaisons Dangereuses. *Leisure interests:* reading, parachuting. *Address:* Neasrader Ltd., 135 New King's Road, London, SW6 4SL, England.

FINCH, William G. H.; American radio engineer; b. 28 June 1895, Birmingham, England; m. 1st Elsie Grace George 1916 (died 1967), one d.; m. 2nd Helen Stork Ambler 1969; ed. Woodward High School, Cincinnati, Marconi Inst., New York and Columbia Univ.; with Cleveland Illuminating Co. 1916–17, Nat. District Telegraph Co., New York 1917–19 and Royal Indemnity Co. 1919–21; Radio Eng. and Ed. Int. News Service 1921–; established first radiotypewriter press circuit between New York and Chicago 1932, between New York and Havana 1933; Chief Radio Consulting Engineer and Tech. Dir. Hearst Newspapers; Chief Eng. Sec. American Radio News Corpn. 1929–34; Asst. Chief Fed. Communications Comm. 1934–35; Founder and Pres. Finch Telecommunications Inc. 1935–41; Chief Engineer 74th Congress Investigation Cttee.; served U.S.N. 1941–44 and 1949, now Special Asst. Electronics to Asst. Chief Bureau of Shipping for Electronics; inventor automatic highspeed radio printing system, radio relay and recorder, and high fidelity transmission system; holds 160 patents; mem. Int. Radio Consulting Cttee., Tech. Comm. on radio and cable communications to American Publishers Assen. 1924–; Fellow A.I.E.E., etc.; Legion of Merit, Wisdom Award 1971, etc. *Address:* 3025 Morningside Boulevard, Port St. Lucie, Fla. 33452; 1913 Stuart Avenue, Richmond, Va. 23220, U.S.A. (Homes).

FINCHAM, John Robert Stanley, PH.D., F.R.S.; British professor of genetics; b. 11 Aug. 1926, Southgate, Middx.; s. of Robert Fincham and Winifred Western; m. Ann Katherine Emerson 1950; one s. three d.; ed. Peterhouse and Botany School, Univ. of Cambridge; Lecturer in Botany, Univ. Coll. Leicester 1950–54, Reader in Genetics, Univ. of Leicester 1954–60; Head, Dept. of Genetics, John Innes Inst. 1960–66; Prof. and Head, Dept. of

Genetics, Univ. of Leeds 1966–76, Univ. of Edinburgh 1976–84, Univ. of Cambridge 1984–; Emil Christian Hansen Medal (Copenhagen) 1977. *Publications:* Fungal Genetics (with P. R. Day, later edns. also with A. Radford) 1963, Microbial and Molecular Genetics 1965, Genetic Complementation 1966, Genetics 1983. *Address:* Department of Genetics, Downing Street, Cambridge, CB2 3EH (Office); 10 Guest Road, Cambridge, CB1 3AL, England (Home). *Telephone:* (0223) 333988 (Office); (0223) 355630 (Home).

FINDLAY, Ian Herbert Fyfe; British insurance broker; b. 5 Feb. 1918, Aberystwyth, Wales; s. of Prof. Alexander and Alice Mary (de Rougemont) Findlay; m. Alison Mary Ashby 1950; two s. one d.; ed. Fettes Coll., Edinburgh; served as Capt., R.A. 1939–45; Dir. Price, Forbes & Co. Ltd. 1953, Chair. 1967–72; Deputy Chair. Sedgwick Forbes (Holdings) Ltd. 1972–74, Chair. 1974–77; Chair. Lloyds Insurance Brokers Asscn. 1969–70, Cttee. of Lloyds 1971–74, 1976–79, Deputy Chair. Lloyds 1977, Chair. 1978–79; Chair. British Insurance Brokers' Asscn. 1980–82, Chair. Guide Dogs for the Blind Asscn. 1981–87; Trustee, St. George's English School, Rome 1980–; Gov. Brighton Coll. 1980–88. *Leisure interest:* golf. *Address:* 24 Forest Ridge, Keston Park, Kent, England. *Telephone:* Farnborough (Kent) 52993.

FINE, Donald I., A.B.; American publishing executive; b. 19 April 1922, Ann Arbor, Mich.; s. of late Morris S. Fine and Kathleen Perlis; m. Diana Northam 1946 (divorced); one s.; ed. Harvard Coll. and Columbia Graduate School; Man. Ed. Dell First Editions, Western Printing and Lithographing Co. 1951–58; Ed.-in-Chief Popular Library Books 1958–60; Vice-Pres. and Ed.-in-Chief Dell Books 1960–68; f., Vice-Pres. and Ed.-in-Chief Delacorte Press 1960–68; Exec. Vice-Pres. Coward - McCann Inc. 1968–69; f., Pres., Publisher Arbor House Publishing Co. Inc. 1969–83; f., Pres., Owner Donald I. Fine Inc. 1983–; Presidential citation with two oak leaf clusters. *Publications:* contrib. to The American Reading Public (R. R. Bowker). *Address:* 128 East 36th Street, New York, N.Y. 10016, U.S.A. *Telephone:* (212) 696-1838.

FINI, Leonor; Italian painter; b. 30 Aug. 1918, Buenos Aires, Argentina; d. of Erminio Fini and Malvina Braun; ed. Trieste; numerous one-man exhbns. in Paris, Rome, London, New York; retrospective exhbns. Knokke-le-Zoute, Belgium 1965, Galleria d'Arte Moderna, Ferrara 1983, Yokohama, Osaka, Kitakyushyu and Sapporo, Japan 1985–86, Musée du Luxembourg, Paris 1986; created numerous décors for La Scala, Milan, Paris Opera, Comédie française, Compagnie Madeleine Renaud, Jean-Louis Barrault, etc.; has participated in numerous group exhbns. including Venice Biennale and Salon de Mai, Paris; has illustrated numerous books; mem. Acad. Royale de Belgique 1977; Dott. h.c. Free Univ. of Trieste. *Publications:* Le Livre de Leonor Fini 1975, Miroir des chats 1976, Fêtes secrètes 1978, Fruits de la passion 1980, Carmilla (Sheridan le Fanu) 1983, Oeuvres complètes Baudelaire 1986, Contes (Edgar Alan Poe) 1987, Chats d'Atelier, Photos Tana Kaleya, Texte Leonor Fini 1988. *Address:* 8 rue de la Vrillière, 75001 Paris, France.

FINK, Gerald R., PH.D.; American professor of genetics; b. 1 July 1940, Brooklyn, New York; s. of Rebecca Fink and Benjamin Fink; m. Rosalie Lewis 1961; two d.; ed. Amherst Coll., Yale Univ.; Postdoctoral Fellow, Nat. Insts. of Health 1965–66, 1966–67; Instructor, Nat. Insts. of Health Graduate Program 1966; Instructor, Cold Spring Harbor Summer Program 1970–; Asst. Prof. of Genetics Cornell Univ. 1967–71, Assoc. Prof. 1971–76, Prof. 1976–79, Prof. of Biochemistry 1979–82; Prof. of Molecular Genetics, M.I.T. 1982–; American Cancer Soc. Prof. of Genetics 1982–; mem. Whitehead Inst. for Biomedical Research 1982–; Assoc. Ed. Genetics 1970–74, Journal of Bacteriology 1973–78; Ed. Gene 1978–, Molecular and General Genetics 1979–; Sec. Genetics Soc. of America 1977–80, Vice-Pres. 1986–87, Pres. (elect) (1988-89); mem. N.A.S., American Acad. of Arts and Sciences; Hon. D.Sc. (Amherst Coll.) 1982; N.A.S.—U.S. Steel Prize in Molecular Biology 1981, Genetics Soc. of America Medal 1982, Yale Science and Eng. Award 1984, Emil Christian Hansen Foundation Award for Microbiological Research 1986. *Publications:* numerous scientific publs. *Address:* Whitehead Institute, 9 Cambridge Center, Cambridge, Mass. 02142 (Office); 40 Aston Road, Chestnut Hill, Mass. 02167, U.S.A. (Home).

FINLAY, Frank, C.B.E.; British actor; b. 6 Aug. 1926, Lancs.; s. of Josiah Finlay; m. Doreen Joan Shepherd 1954; two s. one d.; ed. St. Gregory the Great, Farnworth, Royal Acad. of Dramatic Art, London; repertory 1950–52, 1954–57; Clarence Derwent Best Actor Award (for Chips with Everything) 1962, Best Actor Award, San Sebastian (for Othello) 1966, Soc. of Film and TV Arts Awards (for The Lie and Don Quixote), Best Actor Award (for Bouquet of Barbed Wire). *Stage appearances include:* Belgrade, Epitaph for George Dillon 1958, Sugar in the Morning, Sergeant Musgrave's Dance, Chicken Soup with Barley, Roots, I'm Talking About Jerusalem, The Happy Haven, Platonov, Chips with Everything 1958–62 (all at Royal Court), St. Joan, The Workhouse Donkey, Hobson's Choice 1963, Othello, The Dutch Courtesan 1964, The Crucible, Much Ado About Nothing, Mother Courage 1965, Juno and the Paycock, The Storm 1966 (all at Nat. Theatre), After Haggerty (Aldwych, Criterion), Son of Man (Leicester Theatre, Round House) 1970, Saturday Sunday Monday, The Party 1973, Plunder, Watch It Come Down, Weapons of Happiness 1976, Amadeus 1982 (all at Nat. Theatre), Kings and Clowns (Phoenix), Filumena (Lyric) 1978, The Girl in Melanie Klein 1980, The Cherry Orchard 1983,

Mutiny (Piccadilly) 1985, Beyond Reasonable Doubt 1987. *Film appearances include:* The Longest Day, Private Potter, The Informers, A Life for Ruth, Loneliness of the Long Distance Runner, Hot Enough for June, The Comedy Man, The Sandwich Man, A Study in Terror, Othello, The Jokers, I'll Never Forget What's 'Is Name, The Shoes of the Fisherman, Deadly Bees, Robbery, Inspector Clouseau, Twisted Nerve, Cromwell, The Molly Maguires, Assault, Victory for Danny Jones, Gumshoe, Shaft in Africa, Van Der Walk and the Girl, Van Der Walk and the Rich, Van Der Walk and the Dead, The Three Musketeers, The Ring of Darkness, The Wild Geese, The Thief of Baghdad, Sherlock Holmes—Murder by Decree, Enigma, Return of the Soldier, The Ploughman's Lunch, A Christmas Carol, The Key, Life Force, Sakharov. *TV appearances include:* Julius Caesar, Les Misérables, This Happy Breed, The Lie, Casanova, The Death of Adolf Hitler, Don Quixote, Voltaire, Merchant of Venice, Bouquet of Barbed Wire, 84 Charing Cross Road, Saturday Sunday Monday, Count Dracula, The Last Campaign, Napoleon in Betzi, Dear Brutus, Tales of the Unexpected, Tales from 1001 Nights, Aspects of Love—Mona, In the Secret State, Verdict on Erebus. *Address:* c/o Al Parker Ltd., 55 Park Lane, London, W.1, England.

FINLAY, Thomas Aloysius, B.A.; Irish lawyer; b. 17 Sept. 1922; s. of Thomas A. Finlay and Eva Finlay; m. Alice Blayney 1948; two s. three d.; ed. Xavier School, Dublin, Clongowes Wood Coll., University Coll.; called to the Bar, Dublin, King's Inn 1944; mem. Dail Eireann 1954–57; Sr. Counsel 1961; Bencher 1972; Judge of the High Court 1972, Pres. 1974; Chief Justice 1985–; Hon. Bencher (Inn of Court, N. Ireland) 1985, (Middle Temple) 1986. *Leisure interests:* fishing, shooting, conversation. *Address:* 22 Ailesbury Drive, Dublin 4, Ireland. *Telephone:* 693395.

FINLAYSON, Jock Kinghorn; Canadian banker (retd.); b. 27 May 1921, Nanaimo, B.C.; s. of John Archibald and Elizabeth (Lister) Finlayson; m. 1st Jean Clancy Clark 1947 (divorced 1975), 2nd Madeleine Victoria Coussement 1976; two s. one d.; joined Royal Bank of Canada, Nanaimo 1939; served Royal Canadian Air Force, World War II; managerial posts Royal Canadian Bank, Alta. and main branch, Montreal 1960–64, Asst. Gen. Man. Head Office 1964–67, Gen. Man. Int. 1967–69, Chief Gen. Man. 1969–72, Dir. 1970–, Vice-Pres. 1970–72, Deputy Chair. and Exec. Vice-Pres. 1972–77, Vice-Chair. 1977–83, Vice-Chair. with responsibility for worldwide corporate banking activities 1980–83, Pres. 1980–83; Dir. Royal Bank and Trust Co., New York, Canadian Reynolds Metals Co., RJR-Macdonald Inc., Miron Inc., M.I.C.C. Investments Ltd., Orion Royal Bank Ltd., London, PanCanadian Petroleum Ltd., Royal Insurance Group (also Chair.), Sun Life Assurance Co., Canada, United Corpn. Ltd. *Leisure interests:* fishing, shooting, golf. *Address:* P.O. Box 369, Station A, Montreal, Que. H3C 2T1, Canada.

FINNBOGADÓTTIR, Vigdís; Icelandic teacher and politician; b. 15 April 1930, Reykjavík; d. of Finnbogi Rutur Thorvaldsson and Sigridur Eiriksdóttir; m. (divorced); one adopted d.; ed. Junior Coll., Menntaskólinn i Reykjavík, Univs. of Grenoble and Sorbonne, France, Univ. of Iceland; taught French, Junior Colls., Menntaskólinn i Reykjavík, Menntaskólinn vid Hamrahlid; Iceland Tourist Bureau, Head Guide Training; Dir. Reykjavík Theatre Co. 1972–80; taught French drama, Univ. of Iceland; worked for Icelandic State TV; fmr. Chair. Alliance Française; mem. Advisory Cttee. on Cultural Affairs in Nordic Countries 1976–, Chair. 1978–; Pres. of Iceland Aug. 1980–; Hon. G.C.M.G. 1982. *Leisure interest:* theatre. *Address:* Office of the President, Reykjavík, Iceland.

FINNEY, Albert; British actor; b. 9 May 1936; m. 1st Jane Wenham (dissolved), one s.; m. 2nd Anouk Aimée 1970 (divorced 1978); ed. Salford Grammar School and Royal Acad. of Dramatic Art; Birmingham Repertory Co. 1956–58; Shakespeare Memorial Theatre Co. 1959; Nat. Theatre 1965, 1975; formed Memorial Enterprises 1966; Assoc. Artistic Dir. English Stage Co. 1972–75; Dir. United British Artists 1983–86; Hon. Litt.D. (Sussex) 1966; Lawrence Olivier Award 1986; London Standard Drama Award for Best Actor 1986. *Plays acted in include:* Julius Caesar, Macbeth, Henry V, The Beaux' Stratagem, The Alchemist, The Lizard on the Rock, The Party 1958, King Lear, Othello 1959, A Midsummer Night's Dream, The Lily-White Boys 1960, Billy Liar 1960, Luther 1961, 1963, Much Ado About Nothing, Armstrong's Last Goodnight 1965, Miss Julie 1965, Black Comedy 1965, Love for Love 1965, A Flea in her Ear 1966, A Day in the Death of Joe Egg 1968, Alpha Beta 1972, Krapp's Last Tape 1973, Cromwell 1973, Chez Nous 1974, Hamlet 1976, Tamburlaine the Great 1976, Uncle Vanya 1977, Present Laughter 1977, The Country Wife 1977–78, The Cherry Orchard 1978, Macbeth 1978, Has "Washington" Legs? 1978, The Biko Inquest (Dir.) 1984, Sergeant Musgrave's Dance (Dir.) 1984, Orphans 1986, J. J. Farr 1987; Dir. Loot 1975. *Films acted in include:* The Entertainer 1959, Saturday Night and Sunday Morning 1960, Tom Jones 1963, Night Must Fall 1963, Two for the Road 1967, Scrooge 1970, Gumshoe 1971, Murder on the Orient Express 1974, Wolfen 1979, Loophole 1980, Looker 1980, Shoot the Moon 1981, Annie 1982, Life of John Paul II 1983, The Dresser 1983, Under the Volcano 1983, The Endless Game (TV) 1989; Directed and acted in Charlie Bubbles 1968, Orphans 1987. *Address:* c/o International Creative Management, 388-396 Oxford Street, London, W1N 9HE, England. *Telephone:* 01-629 8080.

FINNEY, David John, C.B.E., M.A., SC.D., F.R.S., F.R.SE.; British professor of statistics, b. 3 Jan. 1917, Latchford, Warrington; s. of Robert George

Stringer Finney and Bessie Evelyn Finney (née Whitlow); m. Mary Elizabeth Connolly 1950; one s. two d.; ed. Univs. of Cambridge and London; statistician, Rothamsted Experimental Station 1939–45; Lecturer in the Design and Analysis of Scientific Experiment, Univ. of Oxford 1945–54; Reader in Statistics, Univ. of Aberdeen 1954–64, Prof. of Statistics 1964–66; Prof. of Statistics, Univ. of Edinburgh 1966–84; Dir. Agricultural and Food Research Council's Unit of Statistics 1954–84; Dir. Research Centre, Int. Statistical Inst., Netherlands 1987–88; Pres. Biometric Soc. 1964–65; Chair. Computer Bd. for Univs. 1970–74; Pres. Royal Statistical Soc. 1973–74; Visiting Scientist Int. Rice Research Inst. 1984–85; FAO "Key Consultant" to Indian Agricultural Statistics Research Inst. 1983–; Hon. D. ès Sciences agronomiques (Gembloux), D.Sc. (City Univ., Heriot-Watt Univ.). *Publications:* Probit Analysis 1947, 1952, 1971, Biological Standardization (with J.H. Burn and L.G. Goodwin) 1950, Statistical Method in Biological Assay 1952, 1964, 1978, Introduction to Statistical Science in Agriculture 1953, 1962, 1972, Experimental Design and its Statistical Basis 1955, Técnica y Teoría en el Diseño de Experimentos 1957, Introduction to the Theory of Experimental Design 1960, Statistics for Mathematicians 1968, Statistics for Biologists 1980; about 230 papers. *Leisure interests:* music, travel, statistics. *Address:* 43 Cluny Drive, Edinburgh EH10 6DU, Scotland (Home). *Telephone:* 031-447 2332 (Home).

FINNIS, John Mitchell, LL.B., D.PHIL.; Australian university teacher and barrister; b. 28 July 1940, Adelaide; s. of Maurice M. S. Finnis and Margaret McKeller Stewart; m. Marie Carmel McNally 1964; three s. three d.; ed. St. Peter's Coll., Adelaide, Univ. of Adelaide, Oxford Univ.; Fellow and Praelector in Jurisprudence, Univ. Coll., Oxford 1966–; Lecturer in Law, Oxford Univ. 1966–72, Rhodes Reader in the Laws of the British Commonwealth and the United States 1972–, mem. Philosophy Sub-Faculty 1984–; Prof. and Head of Dept. of Law, Univ. of Malawi 1976–78; Barrister, Gray's Inn 1972–; Gov., Plater Coll., Oxford 1972–; Consultor, Pontificia Commissio Iustitia et Pax 1977–; Special Adviser, Foreign Affairs Cttee., House of Commons, on role of UK Parl. in Canadian Constitution 1980–82; mem. Catholic Bishops' Jt. Cttee. on Bio-ethical Issues 1981–, Int. Theological Comm. (Vatican) 1986–; Gov., Linacre Centre for Medical Ethics 1981–. *Publications:* Halsbury's Laws of England, 4th edn., vol. 6 (Commonwealth and Dependencies) 1974, Natural Law and Natural Rights 1980, Fundamentals of Ethics 1983, Nuclear Deterrence, Morality and Realism (with Joseph Boyle and Germain Grisez) 1987; articles on constitutional law, legal philosophy, ethics and moral theology. *Address:* University College, Oxford, OX1 4BH; 12 Gray's Inn Square, London, WC1R 5JP; 12 Staverton Road, Oxford, OX2 6XJ, England (Home). *Telephone:* (0865) 276602 (Univ. Coll.); 01-405 8654 (Gray's Inn); (0865) 58660 (Home).

FINNISTON, Sir (Harold) Montague, Kt., B.SC., F.ENG., PH.D., F.R.S., F.R.S.A., F.R.S.E., F.I.C.; British metallurgist; b. 15 Aug. 1912, Glasgow, Scotland; s. of Robert Finniston and Esther (née Diamond) Finniston; m. Miriam Singer 1936; one s. one d.; ed. Allen Glen's School, Glasgow, Glasgow Univ. and Royal Coll. of Science and Tech., Glasgow; joined Stewarts & Lloyds 1934; Chief Research Officer, Scottish Coke Research Cttee. 1937; metallurgist, Atomic Energy of Canada, Chalk River 1945–46; U.K. Atomic Energy Authority, Harwell 1948–58; Research Dir. C.A. Parsons & Co. and Man. Dir. Int. Research and Devt. Co. Ltd. 1959–67; Deputy Chair. British Steel Corpn. 1967–73, C.E.O. 1971–73, Chair. 1973–76; Group C.E.O. and Dir. Sears Holdings Ltd. 1976–79; Dir. Cluff Oil 1976–, GKN 1976–83, Blandburgh 1980–84, Bodycote Int. Ltd. 1980–84, (and Chair.) Anderson Strathclyde 1980–83, Butterfield-Harvey 1981–84 (Deputy Chair. 1984–), Barmel Assocs. Ltd. 1981–84; Chair. Drake and Scull Holdings Ltd. 1980–83, H. M. Finniston Ltd. 1980–, Sherwood Int. 1984–, Taddale Investments PLC (also Chief Exec.) 1983–; Future Tech. Systems Ltd. 1981–, KCA Drilling 1983–, Gen. Sec. B.A.A.S. 1970–73; mem. Bd. Nat. Research Devt. Corpn. 1963–73; Chair. Int. Research Devt. Co. Ltd. 1968–77, Political and Econ. Planning (now Policy Studies Inst.) 1975–84, Redpath, Dorman, Long 1972–74, Council, Scottish Business School 1976–, Metal Sciences (Holdings) PLC 1983–, Industrial Tech. Securities 1984–; Pres. Metals Soc. 1974–75, Inst. of Man. Services 1977–82, Ironbridge Gorge Museum Devt. Trust 1977–, Design Industries Asscn. 1978–; Vice-Pres. Royal Soc.; Vice-Pres. Iron and Steel Inst., Vice-Pres. A.S.L.I.B. 1974–76, Pres. 1976–78; Pres. Asscn. of British Chambers of Commerce 1980–83, British Industrial and Scientific Film Asscns. 1980–, British Export Houses 1984–, Eng. Industries Asscn. 1984–, Asscn. of Project Mans. 1984–; Vice-Pres. Inst. of Marketing 1980–; Chair. Cttee. of Inquiry into Eng. 1977; Chair. Prison Reform Trust 1981–88, Report to the Nation 1982 (Channel 4); Dir. British Nutrition Found. 1982–88, Eng. Council Award Co. 1984–; Pro-Chancellor, Surrey Univ. 1977–, Chancellor, Stirling Univ. Aug. 1978–; Chair. Bd. of Govs. Carmel Coll. 1980–82; Assoc. of Royal Coll. of Science and Tech.; mem. Nat. Econ. Devt. Council 1974–76; Liveryman, Worshipful Co. of Tinplate Workers 1972; mem. British Asscn. 1974, Royal Inst. of G.B. 1978 (mem. Cttee. of Mans.); Hon. mem. Materials Science Club, American Iron and Steel Inst., Iron and Steel Inst. of Japan, Inst. of Chemical Eng. 1975, Indian Inst. of Metals, Smeatonian Soc. of Civil Eng. 1977; Fellow, Inst. of Metallurgists, Pres. 1975–76; Fellow, British Inst. of Man. 1972, Univ. of Manchester (UMIST) 1973, R.S.A. 1975, Royal Soc. of Edinburgh 1978, Inst. of Physics; Hon. Fellow Sunderland Polytechnic, Inst. of Sheet Metal Eng. 1975; Hon. D.Sc. (Strathclyde) 1968, (Birmingham) 1971, (City Univ.) 1974, (Cranfield Inst. of Tech.) 1976, (Bath) 1977, (Sussex) 1981; Hon.

D.Univ. (Surrey) 1969, (Stirling) 1979, (Open Univ.) 1982; Hon. D.C.L. (Newcastle) 1976; Hon. D.Eng. (Liverpool) 1978, Hon. LL.D. (Glasgow) 1978, (Hull); Dr. h.c. (Open Univ.) 1982; Bessemer Medal, Tawara Gold Medal (Japan) 1975, A.A. Griffiths Silver Medal 1976, Eichner Medal (France) 1976, Glazebrook Medal 1976. *Leisure interests:* walking, reading, spectator sports. *Address:* 6 Manchester Square, London, W1M 1AU; Flat 72, Prince Albert Court, 33 Prince Albert Road, St. John's Wood, London, N.W.8, England (Home). *Telephone:* 01-486 3658 (Office).

FINOGENOV, Pavel Vasilyevich; Soviet official; b. 1919; mem. CPSU 1943–; graduated Leningrad Military-Mechanical Inst. 1953; various posts including Dir. of a plant 1941–60; Deputy Dir. Soviet of Nat. Economy, Vladimir 1960–65; USSR Deputy Minister 1965–73, First Deputy Minister 1973–79, Minister of Defence Industry 1979–; mem. Supreme Soviet; Head Socialist Labour; Lenin Prize, U.S.S.R. State Prize. *Address:* Council of Ministers, The Kremlin, Moscow, U.S.S.R.

FIOLET, Herman Antonius, D.THEOL.; Netherlands ecclesiastic and writer; b. 15 Aug. 1920, Amsterdam; ed. High School, Katwijk and R. C. Univ., Nijmegen; ordained Priest 1946; Dir. Inst. for Lay Educ. 1953–59; Prof. of Dogmatical and Ecumenical Theol. 1959–73; Gen. Sec. Council of Churches in the Netherlands 1970–85; mem. Bd. of Ecumenical Devt. Co-operative Soc. 1974–83; many nat. and int. study comms.; Coebergh Prize for best ecumenical book in Netherlands (1960-68) 1968. *Publications:* 15 books including: Een kerk in onrust om haar belijdenis dissertation 1953, Verdeelde christenen in gesprek 1960, Onvermoed perspectief op de oecumene 1964, Dilemma doorbroken 1965, Vreemde Verleiding 1968, Tweede Reformatie 1969, and many articles in nat. and int. theological periodicals. *Leisure interests:* music, chess and skiing. *Address:* 's-Gravelandseweg 86 A 21, 1217 EW Hilversum, Netherlands. *Telephone:* 035-12530.

FIRESTONE, Leonard Kimball, B.A.; American business executive and diplomatist; b. 10 June 1907, Akron, Ohio; s. of Harvey S. Firestone and Idabelle Smith; brother of Raymond Christy Firestone (q.v.); m. 1st Polly Curtis (deceased), 2nd Barbara K. Heatley 1966 (died 1985); two s. one d.; ed. Hill School, Pottstown, Pa., Princeton Univ.; Sales Dept., Firestone Tire & Rubber Co. 1931–41, Vice-Pres. 1932–35, Sales Man., Akron 1935–39, Dir. 1939–73; Pres. Firestone Aviation Products Co. 1941–43; Pres., Gen. Man. Firestone Tire & Rubber Co. of Calif. 1943–70; Lieut. U.S.N. 1941–43; Amb. to Belgium 1973–77; Dir. Nat. Council on Alcoholism Inc.; mem. Nat. Bd. of Assocs., Smithsonian Inst.; Hon. Chair. Deafness Research Foundation; Past Pres. World Affairs Council; mem., Past Chair. Bd. of Trustees, Univ. of S. California; Hon. LL.D. (S. Calif.) 1965, (Pepperdine) 1971, Hon. D. Hum. (Okla. Christian Coll.) 1970; Grand Band, Order of the Star of Africa 1969. *Address:* 515 South Flower Street, Suite 4470, Los Angeles, Calif. 90071, U.S.A. *Telephone:* (213) 680-28-85.

FIRESTONE, Raymond Christy, B.A.; American businessman (retd.); b. 6 Sept. 1908, Akron, Ohio; s. of Harvey S. Firestone and Idabelle Smith; brother of Leonard Kimball Firestone (q.v.); m. 1st Laura Lisk 1935 (deceased 1960), 2nd Jane Allen Messler 1962; two d.; ed. Princeton Univ.; joined Sales Div., Firestone Tire and Rubber Co. 1933; Gen. Man., Memphis, Tenn. plant 1936–37; Pres. Firestone Tire and Rubber Co. of Tenn. 1937–49; Dir., Firestone Tire and Rubber Co. 1942–77, Vice-Pres. (Research and Devt.) 1949–54, Exec. Vice-Pres. 1954–57, Pres. 1957–64, Chair. Exec. Cttee. and C.E.O. 1964–73, Chair. of the Bd. 1966–76, C.E.O. 1966–73; mem. numerous civic and business orgs.; Hon. LL.D. (Akron), Hon. D.Hum. (Univ. of Liberia); several awards. *Leisure interests:* foxhunting, golf. *Address:* Lauray Farms, Bath, Ohio 44210, U.S.A.

FIRKUŠNÝ, Rudolf; pianist; b. 11 Feb. 1912, Napajedla, Czechoslovakia; m. Tatiana Nevolova 1965; one s. one d.; ed. Conservatoires of Music, Brno and Prague; first appeared with Czech Philharmonic Orchestra 1922; world-wide concert tours including tours of Europe 1930–39, S. America 1943–, annual tours of Europe and U.S.A. since 1943, tours of Australia, N.Z. 1959, 1967, Japan 1978, 1983, 1985, 1987; mem. of Faculty Juilliard School, New York. *Address:* Staatsburg, New York 12580, U.S.A.

FIRNBERG, Hertha, DR. PHIL.; Austrian politician; b. 18 Sept. 1909, Vienna; d. of Dr. Josef and Anna Firnberg; m. 1932; ed. Univs. of Vienna and Freiburg i. Br.; employed by Prokura (publishers) 1941–45; Asst. Inst. for Econ. and Cultural History, Univ. of Vienna 1946; Head of Statistical Dept., Chamber for Blue- and White-Collar Workers, Lower Austria 1948–69; mem. Bundesrat 1959, Nationalrat 1963; Chair. Socialist Party's Fed. Women's Cttee. 1966–; Deputy to Chair. Fed. Socialist Party 1966–83; Minister without Portfolio April 1970; Minister for Science and Research 1970–84; Körnerpreis; Förderungspreis der Stadt Wien. *Publications:* various sociological studies. *Leisure interests:* reading, swimming, walking. *Address:* 1100 Vienna, Altdorferstrasse 5, Austria.

FIRTH, Peter; British actor; b. Oct. 1953, Bradford; has appeared with Nat. Theatre in Equus, Romeo and Juliet, Spring Awakening; Broadway appearances include role of Mozart in Amadeus; has appeared in several TV films, plays and series. *Films include:* Brother Sun and Sister Moon, Daniel and Maria, Diamonds on Wheels, Aces High, Joseph Andrews, Equus, When You Coming Back Red Ryder?, Tess, Lifeforce, Letter to Brezhnev, A Tree of Hands. *Address:* c/o Plant & Froggatt Ltd., 3 Windmill Street, London, W.1, England.

FIRTH, Sir Raymond William, Kt., M.A., PH.D., F.B.A.; British social anthropologist; b. 25 March 1901, Auckland, N.Z.; s. of Wesley Hugh Bourne Firth and Marie Elizabeth Jane Firth (née Cartmill); m. Rosemary Upcott 1936; one s.; ed. Auckland Univ. Coll. and London School of Econs.; field research in anthropology, Tikopia, British Solomon Islands Protectorate 1928–29; Lecturer in Anthropology, Univ. of Sydney 1930–31, Acting Prof. 1931–32; Lecturer in Anthropology, London School of Econs. (L.S.E.) 1932–35, Reader 1935–44, Prof. 1944–68; Emer. Prof. Univ. of London 1968–; Prof. Pacific Anthropology, Hawaii Univ. 1968–69; Visiting Prof. Univ. of British Columbia 1969, Cornell Univ. 1970, Univ. of Chicago 1955, 1970–71, Graduate Center City Univ. of New York 1971–72, Australia Nat. Univ., Canberra 1972–73, Univ. of Calif., Davis 1974, Berkeley 1977, Univ. of Auckland 1978; Hon. Sec. Royal Anthropological Inst. 1936–39, Pres. 1953–55; research in peasant econs. and anthropology in Malaya as Leverhulme Research Fellow 1939–40; served with Naval Intelligence Div. Admiralty 1941–44; Sec. of Colonial Social Science Research Council, Colonial Office 1944–45; research surveys in W. Africa 1945, Malaya 1947, New Guinea 1951; field research in Tikopia 1952, 1966, in Tikopia settlements 1973; Life Pres. Assen. of Social Anthropologists of the Commonwealth; Hon. Life mem. N.Z. Assen. of Social Anthropologists; Fellow, Center for Advanced Study in the Behavioral Sciences, Stanford, Calif. 1959; Hon. Fellow, L.S.E. and School of Oriental and African Sciences, London Univ.; Foreign Hon. mem. American Acad. of Arts and Sciences, American Philosophical Soc., Royal Soc. of N.S.W., Royal Soc. of N.Z., Royal Danish Acad. of Sciences and Letters; Hon. Ph.D. (Oslo) 1965, (Jagiellonian Univ., Cracow) 1984, Hon. LL.D. (Michigan) 1967, Hon. D.Litt. (East Anglia) 1968, (Australian Nat. Univ.) 1969, (Exeter) 1972, (Auckland) 1978, Hon. D.Hum. Letters (Chicago) 1968, Hon. D.Sc. (British Columbia) 1970, Hon. D.Sc. Econ. (London) 1984; Viking Fund Medal 1959, Huxley Memorial Medal 1959. *Publications:* The Kauri Gum Industry 1924, Primitive Economics of the New Zealand Maori 1929, Art and Life in New Guinea 1936, We, The Tikopia: A Sociological Study of Kinship in Primitive Polynesia 1936, Human Types 1938, Primitive Polynesian Economy 1939, The Work of the Gods in Tikopia 1940, Malay Fishermen: Their Peasant Economy 1946, Elements of Social Organization 1951; Ed. Two Studies of Kinship in London 1956, Ed. Man and Culture: An Evaluation of the Work of Malinowski 1957, Social Change in Tikopia 1959, History and Traditions of Tikopia 1961, Essays on Social Organization and Values 1964, Ed. Themes in Economic Anthropology 1967, Tikopia Ritual and Belief 1967, Rank and Religion in Tikopia 1970, Families and their Relatives (with Jane Hubert and Anthony Forge) 1970, The Sceptical Anthropologist, Social Anthropology and Marxist Views of Society 1972, Symbols Public and Private 1973, Tikopia-English Dictionary 1985. *Leisure interests:* Romanesque art, 15th-18th century music. *Address:* 33 Southwood Avenue, London, N.6, England. *Telephone:* 01-348 0768.

FISCHER, Annie; Hungarian pianist; b. 1914; m. Aladár Tóth (deceased); ed. Budapest Acad. of Music; studies with Arnold Székely and Ernő von Dohnányi; concert debut in Beethoven's C Major Concerto 1922; numerous concerts, tours and recordings 1926–; 1st Prize, Int. Liszt Competition, Budapest 1933; Kossuth Prizes 1949, 1955 and 1965; Hon. Prof. of Acad. of Music, Budapest 1965; decorated Eminent Artist; Red Banner Order of Labour 1974. *Address:* Szent István Park 14, H-1137 Budapest XIII, Hungary. *Telephone:* 297-282.

FISCHER, Edmond H., D. ÉS SC.; American professor of biochemistry; b. April 1920, Shanghai, China; s. of Oscar Fischer and Renee C. (née Tapernoux) Fischer; m. Beverley B. Bullock; two s.; ed. Faculty of Sciences, Univ. of Geneva, Asst. Labs. of Organic Chem. Univ. of Geneva 1946–47; Fellow, Swiss Nat. Foundation 1948–50; Research Fellow, Rockefeller Foundation 1950–53; Privat-dozent, Univ. of Geneva 1950; Research Assoc. Div. of Biology, Calif. Inst. of Tech. 1953; Asst. Prof. Univ. of Washington 1953–56, Assoc. Prof. 1956–61, Prof. of Biochem. 1961–; mem. numerous cttees., professional orgs. etc.; mem. N.A.S., A.A.A.S., American Acad. of Arts and Sciences, Swiss Chem. Soc., British Biochem. Soc.; several awards and honours; Dr. h.c. (Montpellier) 1985, (Basel) 1988. *Leisure interests:* classical piano, flying (private pilot). *Address:* Biochemistry Department SJ-70, University of Washington, Seattle, Wash. 98195 (Office); 5540 N.E. Windermere Road, Seattle, Wash., U.S.A. (Home). *Telephone:* 206-543-1741 (Office); 206-523-7372 (Home).

FISCHER, Erik, M.A.; Danish art historian; b. 8 Oct. 1920, Copenhagen; s. of Adolf Fischer and Ellen Henius; ed. Univ. of Copenhagen; Asst. Keeper of Prints and Drawings, Royal Museum of Fine Arts, Copenhagen 1948–57, Keeper of Prints and Drawings 1957–; Asst. Prof. of Art History, Univ. of Copenhagen 1964–; Chair. Danish State Art Foundation 1965–67; Pres. Int. Advisory Cttee. of Keepers of Public Collections of Graphic Art 1971–76; Hon. mem. Bd. of Dirs. Germanisches Nationalmuseum, Nuremberg 1977; Fellow, Royal Danish Acad.; Assoc. Ateneo Veneto; Kt., Order of Dannebrog, Order of Nordstjernen, Klein Prize 1973; Amalienborg Medal 1983. *Publications:* Moderne dansk Grafik 1957, Melchior Lorck Drawings 1962, Tegninger af C.W. Eckersberg 1983, Von Abildgaard bis Marstrand 1985, Billedtekster (anthology) 1988. *Leisure interests:* nursing my arboretum, playing my piano. *Address:* Knabrostraede 13, 1210 Copenhagen; Agergårdsvej 5, Ammendrup, DK-3200 Helsinge, Denmark. *Telephone:* 33-149328 (Copenhagen); 48-794404 (Helsinge).

FISCHER, Ernst Otto, DR.RER.NAT., DIPL.CHEM.; German professor of chemistry, b. 10 Nov. 1918, Müchen-Solln; s. of late Prof. Dr. Karl Tobias Fischer and Valentine Danzer; ed. Theresiengymnasium and Tech. High School, Munich; Lecturer in Chem. (now Tech. Univ.) 1954–57, Prof. of Inorganic Chem. 1964–; Prof. of Inorganic Chem., Munich Univ. 1957–64, Univ. of Jena 1959, Univ. of Marburg 1960, 1964; Firestone Lecturer, Univ. of Wisconsin 1969; Visiting Prof., Univ. of Florida 1971; Inorganic Chem. Pacific West Coast Lecturer, U.S.A., Canada 1971; Arthur D. Little Visiting Prof., M.I.T. 1973; Visiting Distinguished Lecturer, Univ. of Rochester 1973; mem. Bayerische Akad. der Wissenschaften 1964, Deutsche Akad. der Naturforscher Leopoldina 1969; corresp. mem. Austrian Acad. of Sciences 1976, Acad. of Sciences Göttingen 1977; foreign mem. Accad. Naz. dei Lincei 1976; foreign hon. mem. American Acad. of Arts and Sciences 1977; Hon. Dr.rer.nat. (Univs. of Munich 1972, Erlangen, Nuremberg 1977, Veszprém 1983), Hon. D.Sc. (Strathclyde) 1975; American Chem. Soc. Centennial Fellow 1976; Göttinger Acad. Prize for Chem. 1957, Alfred-Stock-Gedächtnis Prize 1959, Nobel Prize for Chem. 1973. *Publications:* 500 scientific publs., Fe$(C_5H_5)_2$ Structure 1952, Cr$(C_6H_6)_2$ 1955, Übergangsmetall-Carben-Komplexe 1964, Übergangsmetall-Carbin-Komplexe 1973, Metal-Complexes Vol. I (with H. Werner) 1966. *Leisure interests:* history, arts, mountaineering. *Address:* Sohnckestrasse 16, 8 Munich 71, Federal Republic of Germany. *Telephone:* 794623.

FISCHER, Gerhard Karl-Johan; German diplomatist; b. 20 Sept. 1921, Oslo, Norway; m. Ann F. Lohman 1952; one s. one d.; ed. Univ. of Munich; war service, P.O.W. 1940–47; Ministry of Foreign Affairs 1953–54, 1964–70, 1974–77; served Addis Ababa 1954–57, Hong Kong 1957–60; Head of Consulate, Madras, India 1960–64; Amb. to Malaysia 1970–74, to Ireland 1977–80, to the Netherlands 1980–83, to Switzerland 1983–85. *Address:* Westerbuchberg, Madergasse 35, 8212 Übersee, Federal Republic of Germany.

FISCHER, Gottfried Bermann, DR.MED., DR.PHIL. h.c.; American publisher; b. 31 July 1897, Gleiwitz, Silesia, Germany (now Gliwice, Poland); m. Brigitte Fischer 1926; three d.; ed. Univs. of Breslau, Freiburg and Munich; Asst. Surgeon in Berlin hosp. 1923–25; with S. Fischer Verlag 1925–, Owner and Pres. 1934, firm moved to Vienna 1936, to Stockholm 1938; emigrated to U.S.A. 1940, founded L.B. Fischer Corpn., New York; re-established S. Fischer Verlag in Frankfurt/Main 1950, later Chair. of Bd. S. Fischer Verlag GmbH, retd. 1968; founded Fischer Bücherei, Frankfurt (paperback publrs.) 1952; Ed. Neue Rundschau (literary periodical); Ehrensenator Frankfurt/Main Univ. 1980; Dr. Phil. h.c. (Berne Univ.) 1972; Goethe Plakette (Frankfurt) 1957, Grosses Bundesverdienstkreuz 1958, with Star 1984. *Publications:* Autobiography Bedroht-Bewahrt, Fischer Verlag 1967; Correspondence with Thomas Mann 1932–1955 1973, Lebendige Gegenwart, Reden und Aufsätze 1977. *Leisure interests:* sculpturing, tennis. *Address:* Casa Fischer, 1-55041 Camaiore (Lucca), Italy; *Telephone:* Camaiore 584 989088 (Italy).

FISCHER, Ivan; Hungarian-Dutch conductor; b. 20 Jan. 1951, Budapest; s. of Sándor Fischer and Éva Boschán; m. Anneke Boeke; two d.; ed. B. Bartók Music Conservatory, Budapest and Wiener Hochschule für Musik under Hans Swarowsky, Mozarteum, Salzburg under Nikolaus Harnoncourt; Jt. Music Dir. Northern Sinfonia of England, Newcastle 1979–82; Music Dir. Kent Opera 1982–; founder and Music Dir. Budapest Festival Orchestra 1983; debut in London with Royal Philharmonic Orchestra 1976; concert tours with London Symphony Orchestra to Spain 1981, U.S.A. 1982, world tour 1983; main performances in U.S.A.: Los Angeles Philharmonic, San Francisco Symphony and Chicago Symphony Orchestras; Premio Firenze 1974; Rupert Foundation Award, BBC, London 1976. *Operas:* Idomeneo, Don Giovanni, Julius Caesar, La Bohème, La Clemenza di Tito; recordings with Decca, Philips, CBS, Hungaroton. *Address:* 8 Bracknell Gardens, London, N.W.3, England, and 1061 Budapest, Népköztársaság utja 27, Hungary. *Telephone:* 01-794 8595 (London); 426-061 (Budapest).

FISCHER, Dr. Karl Ingmar Roman; Austrian diplomatist; b. 1922; ed. Volkschule, Realgymnasium, univ.; Fed. Ministry of Foreign Affairs 1949–53; Second Sec., Lisbon 1953–55, First Sec., Washington, D.C. 1955–59; Counsellor Ministry of Foreign Affairs 1954–63; Embassy, Paris 1963–70; in charge of Bilateral Econ. Relations, Ministry of Foreign Affairs 1970–74; Amb. to Sweden 1974–79; Chef de Cabinet, Deputy Sec.-Gen. for Foreign Affairs, Fed. Ministry of Foreign Affairs 1979–82; Amb. to Liechtenstein (resident in Vienna) 1981–84; Perm. Rep. of Austria to UN 1982–88. *Address:* Margaretenstrasse 6/14, A-1040 Vienna, Austria.

FISCHER, Oskar; German diplomatist; b. 19 March 1923, Asch, Czechoslovakia; m.; one c.; ed. elementary school, Coll. of Cen. Cttee. of CPSU (1962–65); mem. Socialist Unity Party (SED) 1946–; tailor 1946–47; Chair. Spremberg Dist. Exec. 1947–48, Land Exec. of Brandenburg, G.D.R. 1949–50; Sec. Cen. Council Free German Youth, World Fed. of Democratic Youth 1951–55; mem. World Youth Council 1952–55; G.D.R. Amb. to Bulgaria 1955–59; head of section, Cen. Cttee. of SED 1960–62, mem. Cen. Cttee. 1971–; Deputy Minister of Foreign Affairs 1965–73, State Sec. and Perm. Deputy Minister 1973–75, Minister Jan. 1975–; Deputy of Volkskammer 1976–; Karl Marx Order, Vaterländischer Verdienstorden in Gold, Banner of Labour, Medal of Merit and other awards. *Address:* Ministerium für Auswärtige Angelegenheiten, Marx-Engels-Platz 2, Berlin, German Democratic Republic.

FISCHER, Paul Henning, D.IUR.; Danish diplomatist; b. 24 March 1919, Copenhagen; s. of Ernst Fischer and Ellen Dahl; m. Jytte Kalckar 1945; one s.; ed. Lyceum Alpinum, Zuoz, Switzerland and Univ. of Copenhagen; Foreign Service 1944–, Stockholm, The Hague, Ministry of Foreign Affairs 1944–60; Asst. Prof. Univ. of Copenhagen 1948–52; Del. Gen. Ass., UN 1959, 1961; Amb. to Poland 1960–61; Perm. Under-Sec. of State for Foreign Affairs 1961–71; Amb. to France 1971–80, to Fed. Repub. of Germany 1980–89; mem. UN register for fact-finding experts in internal disputes; mem. Perm. Court of Arbitration, The Hague 1982; Judge ad hoc Int. Court of Justice, The Hague 1988; Commdr. Order of Dannebrog (1st Class) and foreign decorations. *Publications:* European Coal and Steel Community, International Law Studies on International Co-operation; numerous articles. *Leisure interests:* literature, music. *Address:* Straedet 8, Borsholm, DK-3100 Hornbaek, Denmark. *Telephone:* 2 24 01 51.

FISCHER, Robert James (Bobby); American chess player; b. 9 March 1943, Chicago, Ill.; s. of Gerard and Regina (Wender) Fischer; started to play chess aged 6; mem. Manhattan Chess Club 1955; U.S. Junior Chess Champion 1956, 1957; winner, U.S. Open Championship 1957, 1959, 1960, 1962, 1963; participated in Interzonal Tournament, Portoroz, Yugoslavia 1958; named Int. Grand Master (the youngest ever) 1958; has participated in numerous int. chess tournaments 1958–; defeated Boris Spassky (q.v.) to become World Chess Champion 1972–75; City of New York Gold Medal 1972. *Publications:* Games of Chess 1959, My Sixty Memorable Games 1969, Bobby Fischer Teaches Chess 1972. *Address:* c/o United States Chess Federation, 186 Route 9W, New Windsor, N.Y. 12550, U.S.A.

FISCHER, Stanley, M.SC., PH.D.; American economist; b. 15 Oct. 1943, Lusaka, Zambia; s. of Philip Fischer and Ann Kopelowitz; m. Rhoda Keet 1965; three s.; ed. Univ. of London and M.I.T.; Postdoctoral Fellow Univ. of Chicago 1969–70, Asst. Prof. of Econs. 1970–73; Assoc. Prof. M.I.T. 1973–77, Prof. 1977–; Vice-Pres. and Chief Economist World Bank, Washington D.C. 1988–; Visiting Sr. Lecturer Hebrew Univ., Jerusalem 1972, Fellow Inst. for Advanced Studies 1976–77, Visiting Prof. 1984; Visiting Scholar Hoover Inst. Stanford Univ. 1981–82; Fellow Econometric Soc., American Acad. of Arts and Sciences. *Publications:* Rational Expectations and Economic Policy (Ed.) 1980, Indexing, Inflation, and Economic Policy 1986, Macroeconomics and Finance: Essays in Honor of Franco Modigliani (Ed.) 1987, Macroeconomics (with Dornbusch) 1987, Economics (with Dornbusch and Schmalensee) 1988, Ed. NBER Macroeconomics Annual and work on int. economic and macroeconomic issues. *Address:* World Bank, 1818 H. Street N.W., Washington, D.C. 20433, U.S.A. (Office). *Telephone:* (202) 473 3774.

FISCHER-APPELT, Peter, DR.THEOL.; German university administrator; b. 28 Oct. 1932, Berlin; s. of Hans Fischer-Appelt and Margret née Appelt; m. Hildegard Zeller 1959; two s. one d.; ed. Schubart-Oberschule, Aalen and Univs. of Tübingen, Heidelberg and Bonn; Scientific Asst., Protestant Theology Faculty, Univ. of Bonn 1961–70; Pastor, Köln-Mülheim 1964–65; co-founder and Chair. Bundesassistentenkonferenz, Bonn 1968–69; Pres. Univ. of Hamburg 1970–, teaching assignment in Systematic Theology 1972–; Deputy Chair. Inst. für Friedensforschung und Sicherheitspolitik, Univ. of Hamburg 1970–, Chair. Bd. of Trustees, Hans-Bredow Inst. für Rundfunk und Fernsehen 1970–; mem. Exec. Cttee. Inter-Univ. Centre for Postgrad. Studies, Dubrovnik 1971–, Chair. 1981–; mem. Bd. of Trustees, Deutscher Akad. Austauschdienst and various other student comms., etc.; H.L.D. h.c. (Temple Univ.); Gold Medal, Bulgarian Acad. of Sciences, Pro Cultura Hungarica Medal. *Publications:* Metaphysik im Horizont der Theologie Wilhelm Herrmanns 1965, Albrecht Ritschl und Wilhelm Herrmann 1968, Rechtfertigung 1968, Wissenschaft und Politik 1971, Zum Gedenken an Ernst Cassirer 1975, Integration of Young Scientists into the University 1975, Wilhelm Herrmann 1978, Hiob oder die Unveräusserlichkeit der Erde 1981, The Future of the University as a Research Institution 1982, Was darf ich hoffen? Erwartungen an das Musiktheater 1982, Die Oper als Denk- und Spielmodell 1983, Die Kunst der Fuge: Ein deutsches Forschungsnetz im Aufbau 1984, Dialogue and Co-operation for World Peace Today 1985, Die Universität zwischen Staats einfluss und Autonomie 1986, Die Universität im Prozess der Humanisierung der Gesellschaft 1987, The University in the 21st Century 1988. *Leisure interests:* chess, skiing, music, opera, theatre. *Address:* University of Hamburg, Edmund-Siemers-Allee 1, D-2000 Hamburg 13; Waldweg 22, D-2085 Quickborn-Heide, Federal Republic of Germany. *Telephone:* 040/4123-4475 (Office); 04106-71212 (Home).

FISCHER-DIESKAU, Dietrich; German baritone; b. 28 May 1925, Berlin; s. of Dr. Albert Fischer-Dieskau and Dora Klingelhöffer; m. 1st Irmgard Poppen 1949 (died 1963), three s., 2nd Ruth Leuwerik 1965 (divorced 1967), 3rd Kristina Pugell 1968, 4th Julia Varady 1978; ed. high school in Berlin, singing studies with Prof. Georg Walter and Prof. Hermann Weissenborn; mil. service 1943–45; P.O.W. in Italy until 1947; First Lyric and Character Baritone, Berlin State Opera 1948–; mem. Vienna State Opera Co. 1957–; Prof. Hochschule der Künste Berlin 1981–; numerous concert tours in Europe, U.S.A. and Asia; has appeared at a number of festivals: Bayreuth, Salzburg, Lucerne, Montreux, Edinburgh, Vienna, Holland, Munich, Berlin, Coventry, etc.; best-known roles in Falstaff, Don Giovanni, The Marriage of Figaro, etc.; first performances of contemporary composers Britten, Henze, Tippett, etc.; mem. Akad. der Künste, Bayerische Akademie der Schönen Künste, Munich, Int. Mahler-Gesellschaft (Vienna) and German Section, Int. Music Council; Hon. mem. Wiener Konzerthausgesellschaft 1963, Royal Acad. of Music (London), Royal Acad. (Stockholm), Deutschen Oper, Berlin 1978, Royal Philharmonic Soc.; Hon. D.Univ. (Oxford) 1978, Hon. D.Mus. (Paris-Sorbonne) 1980, (Yale) 1980; Int. Recording Prizes almost every year since 1955; Berlin Kunstpreis 1950, Mantua Golden Orpheus Prize 1955; Bundesverdienstkreuz, 1st Class 1958; Edison Prize 1960, 1962, 1964, 1965, 1967, 1970; President's Prize, Charles Gros Acad., Paris 1980, Förderungspreis der Ernst-von-Siemens-Stiftung 1980; Mozart Medal 1962, Golden Orpheus 1967; Grosses Verdienstkreuz des Verdienstordens der Bundesrepublik Deutschland 1974; Grammy Award (more than once); Prix Mondial Montreux (more than once), etc. *Publications:* Texte deutscher Lieder 1968, Auf den Spuren der Schubert-Lieder 1971, Wagner und Nietzsche, der Mystagoge und sein Abtrünniger 1974, Franz Schubert, ein Portrait 1976, Robert Schumann-Wort und Musik 1981, Töne sprechen, Worte klingen-Zur Geschichte und Interpretation des Gesanges 1985, Nachklang 1987. *Leisure interest:* painting. *Address:* Lindenallee 22, D-1000 Berlin 19, Germany.

FISHER, Hon. Sir Henry Arthur Pears, Kt., M.A.; British lawyer, businessman and college principal; b. 20 Jan. 1918, Repton, Derbyshire; s. of late Lord Fisher of Lambeth (Archbishop of Canterbury, 1945–61) and of Lady Fisher of Lambeth; m. Felicity Sutton 1948; one s. three d.; ed. Marlborough Coll., Christ Church, Oxford; served in Leics. Regt. (rank of Hon. Lieut.-Col.) 1940–46; Barrister-at-law 1947–68, Q.C. 1960, Judge of the High Court 1968–70; Dir. J. Henry Schroder Wagg and Co. Ltd. 1970–75, Thomas Tilling Ltd. 1970–83, Equity and Law Life Assurance Soc. Ltd. 1975–88; conducted inquiry into the Confait Case 1976–77; Chair. Bd. of Govs. Imperial Coll. 1975–88, of Council, Marlborough Coll. 1977–82, Cttee. of Inquiry into self-regulation at Lloyd's 1979–80, Appeal Cttee. of City Takeover Panel 1981–, Investment Man. Regulatory Org. 1986–; Pres. Wolfson Coll., Oxford 1975–85, Hon. Fellow 1985; Trustee, Pilgrim Trust 1965–, Chair. 1979–83; Fellow, All Souls Coll., Oxford 1946–73, Emer. 1973–; Hon. mem. Lloyd's 1983; Hon. Fellow, Darwin Coll., Cambridge 1984; Hon. LL.D. (Hull) 1979. *Leisure interest:* music. *Address:* 1 Hare Court, Temple, London, E.C.4, England. *Telephone:* 01-353 3171.

FISHER, Joel, B.A.; American sculptor; b. 6 June 1947, Ohio; s. of James R. and Marye (née Giffin) Fisher; m. Pamela Robertson-Pearce 1977 (separated); one s.; ed. Kenyon Coll. Ohio; numerous one-man exhbns. in U.S.A. and Europe 1961–; numerous group exhbns. 1962–; Kress Foundation Art History Award 1967, Gast der Berliner Kunstler Program des DAAD 1973–74. *Address:* The Astral, 184 Franklin Street 19-D, Brooklyn, N.Y. 11222, U.S.A.

FISHER, Max Henry; British merchant banker; b. 30 May 1922, Berlin; s. of Friedrich Fischer and Sophia Baks; m. Rosemary Margaret Maxwell 1952; two s. one d.; ed. Rendcomb Coll. and Lincoln Coll., Oxford; army service 1942–46; German War Documents Project, Foreign Office Library 1949–56; Visiting lecturer, Melbourne Univ. 1956; Financial Times, successively Diplomatic Corresp., Foreign Ed., Asst. Ed., Deputy Ed. 1957–73; Ed., Financial Times 1973–80; Dir. S. G. Warburg & Co. Ltd., Commercial Union Assurance plc PLC 1981–, Booker McConnell PLC 1981–; Gov. L.S.E. 1981–. *Publications:* With Prof. N. Rich, ed. The Holstein Papers (4 vols.). *Leisure interests:* music, history. *Address:* 16 Somerset Square, Addison Road, London, W.14, England.

FISHER, Michael Ellis, PH.D., F.R.S.; British professor of chemistry, physics and mathematics; b. 3 Sept. 1931; s. of Harold Wolf Fisher and Jeanne Marie Fisher (née Halter); m. Sorrel Castillejo 1954; three s. one d.; ed. King's Coll., London; London Univ. Postgraduate Studentship 1953–56; DSIR Sr. Research Fellow 1956–58; Lecturer in Theoretical Physics, King's Coll., London 1958–62, Reader in Physics 1962–64, Prof. 1965–66; Prof. of Chem. and Math., Cornell Univ., U.S.A. 1966–73, Horace White Prof. of Chem., Physics and Math. 1973–87, Chair. Dept. of Chem. 1975–78; Wilson H. Elkins Prof., Inst. for Science and Tech., Univ. of Maryland 1988–; Guest Investigator, Rockefeller Inst., New York 1963–64; Visiting Prof. of Applied Physics, Stanford Univ., U.S.A. 1970–71; Walter Ames Prof., Univ. of Wash. 1977; Visiting Prof. of Physics, M.I.T. 1979; Visiting Prof. of Theoretical Physics, Oxford 1985; John Simon Guggenheim Memorial Fellow 1970–71, 1978–79; Fellow American Acad. of Arts and Sciences; Foreign Assoc., N.A.S., U.S.A., Irving Langmuir Prize in Chemical Physics, American Physical Soc. 1970, Award in Physical and Math. Sciences, New York Acad. of Sciences 1978, Guthrie Medal, Inst. of Physics 1980, Wolf Prize in Physics, Israel 1980, Michelson-Morely Award, Case-Western Reserve Univ. 1982, James Murray Luck Award, N.A.S. U.S.A. 1983, Boltzmann Medal, Int. Union of Pure and Applied Physics 1983. *Publications:* Analogue Computing at Ultra-High Speed (with D. M. MacKay) 1962, The Nature of Critical Points 1964; contribs. to scientific journals. *Leisure interests:* Flamenco guitar, travel. *Address:* Institute for Physical Science and Technology, University of Maryland, College Park, Md. 20742, U.S.A. *Telephone:* (301) 454 7779 (Office).

FISIAK, Jacek, H.H.D.; Polish philologist and politician; b. 10 May 1936, Konstantynów Łódzki; m.; ed. Warsaw Univ.; scientific worker Łódź Univ. 1959–67, Asst. Prof. 1962–67; staff mem. Adam Mickiewicz Univ., Posnań 1965–, Head English Philology Dept. 1965–69, Dir. English Philology Inst. 1969–, Extraordinary Prof. 1971–77, Prof. 1977–, Rector 1985–88; Chair.

Comm. on Modern Languages and Literature, Ministry of Higher Educ. 1974–; Minister of Educ. 1988–; Visiting Prof. Univ. of Calif., L.A. 1963–64, Univ. of Kan. 1970, Univ. of Fla. 1974, State Univ. of New York 1975, American Univ., Washington, D.C. 1979–80, Univ. of Kiel 1979–, Vienna Univ. 1983; Ed. Studia Anglica Posnaniensia 1967–, Papers and Studies in Contrastive Linguistics 1972–, Ed.-in-Chief Folia Linguistic Historia 1978–; mem. Polish United Worker's Party; Chair. Neophilological Cttee., Polish Acad. of Sciences 1981–; mem. editorial bds. of numerous foreign and int. philological journals, numerous scientific socs.; Commdr.'s Cross of Polonia Restituta Order, Nat. Educ. Comm. Medal, Commdr.'s Cross of lion of Finland Order and numerous other decorations. *Publications include:* Morphemic Structure of Chaucer's English 1965, A Short Grammar of Middle English 1968, Recent Developments in Historical Phonology 1978 (ed.), Historical Phonology (ed.) 1980, Historical Syntax (ed.) 1983. *Leisure interests:* history, sport. *Address:* Ministerstwo Edukacji, Narodowej, Al. I Armii Wojska Polskiego 25, 00-918 Warsaw, Poland.

FISTOULARI, Anatole; British (naturalized) conductor; b. 20 Aug. 1907, Kiev; s. of Gregor and the late Sophie Fistoulari; m. 1st Anna Mahler 1942 (dissolved), one d.; m. 2nd Mary Elizabeth Lockhart 1957; ed. Kiev, Berlin and Paris; first symphony concert, Kiev 1914, later conducted all over Russia; concerts in Western Europe 1920; conducted Grand Opera Russe, Paris, with Chaliapin 1931; conducted Ballet de Monte Carlo with Massine in England, France, Italy and U.S.A.; first symphony concert with London Symphony Orchestra 1942, Prin. Conductor, London Philharmonic Orchestra 1943–44, now guest conductor; Founder and Prin. Conductor of London Int. Orchestra 1943, now guest conductor; numerous engagements in Europe, Israel, South Africa and the Americas; numerous recordings. *Address:* Flat 4, 65 Redington Road, London, N.W.3, England.

FISZBACH, Tadeusz, DR.TECH.SC.; Polish politician; b. 4 Nov. 1935, Dobraczyn, Lwów (Lvov) Voivodship (now in U.S.S.R.); s. of Rudolf and Bronisława Fiszbach; m. Hanna Fiszbach 1960; one s. one d.; ed. Higher School of Agric., Olsztyn, Higher School of Social Sciences, Warsaw, and Main School of Planning and Statistics, Warsaw; foreman, then technologist and chief engineer, Regional Co-operative Creamery, Elbląg 1957–62; fmr. activist in Polish Youth Union (ZMP); mem. PZPR 1958–, work in party apparatus 1963–, also Instructor, Town and Dist. Cttee, PZPR, Elbląg, Instructor, Voivodship Cttee. PZPR, Gdańsk, and First Sec., PZPR Dist. Cttee., Tczew 1968–70; Sec. of Propaganda, then Organizational Sec. of Voivodship Cttee. PZPR, Gdańsk 1971–75, First Sec. Voivodship Cttee., Gdańsk 1975–81; mem. PZPR Cen. Cttee. 1976–82, deputy mem. Political Bureau of Cen. Cttee. 1980–82; Counsellor Embassy, Helsinki 1982–86; Minister's Adviser, Ministry of Foreign Affairs 1987–; Deputy to Seym 1976–85; Order of Banner of Labour (2nd class), Kt.'s Cross, Order of Polonia Restituta, other decorations. *Leisure interests:* sport, books, theatre. *Address:* Ministerswo Spraw Zagranicznych, 00-580 Warsaw, al. I Armii Wojska Polskiego 23, Poland.

FITCH, Val Logsdon, B.ENG., PH.D.; American physicist; b. 10 March 1923, U.S.A.; s. of Fred B. and Frances M. (née Logsdon) Fitch; m. 1st Elise Cunningham 1949 (died 1972), 2nd Daisy Harper 1976; two s.; ed. McGill and Columbia Univs.; U.S. Army 1943–46; Instructor, Columbia Univ. 1953–54, Princeton Univ. 1954, rising to Prof., Princeton Univ. 1960–, Chair. Dept. of Physics 1976–, Cyrus Fogg Brackett Prof. of Physics 1976–; Sloan Fellow 1960–64; mem. N.A.S., American Acad. of Arts and Sciences, President's Science Advisory Cttee. 1970–73; Research Corpn. Award 1968; Ernest Orlando Laurence Award 1968, John Witherill Medal, Franklin Inst. 1976; Nobel Prize for Physics jointly with J. W. Cronin (q.v.) for work on elementary particles 1980. *Publications:* Major publs. in area of elementary particles. *Leisure interest:* conservation. *Address:* Joseph Henry Laboratories, P.O. Box 708, Princeton University, Princeton, N.J. 08544, U.S.A. *Telephone:* 609-452-4374.

FITCHEW, Geoffrey Edward, M.A., M.SC.; British international civil servant; b. 22 Dec. 1939, Manchester; s. of Stanley Edward Fitchew and Elizabeth Scott; m. Mary Theresa Spillane 1966; two s.; ed. Uppingham School, Magdalen Coll., Oxford and London School of Econs.; Pvt. Sec. to Perm. Sec., Dept. of Econ. Affairs, 1966–67, Pvt. Sec. to Minister of State, H.M. Treasury 1967–68; Financial Counsellor, U.K. Perm. Rep. to EEC 1978–80; Under-Sec. European Communities Group 1983–85, Under-Sec. External Finance Group 1985–86, Dir. Gen., Financial Insts. and Co. Law, Comm. of the European Communities 1986–; mem. Bd. of Dirs., European Investment Bank 1983–85; Gwilym Gibbon Research Fellow, Nuffield Coll., Oxford 1973–74; Oxford Univ. Ancient History Prize 1962. *Leisure interests:* golf, tennis, squash, reading. *Address:* Room 119/R2, EEC Commission, 8 Square de Meeus, Brussels 1040, Belgium. *Telephone:* 235-37-19.

FITERMAN, Charles; French politician; b. 28 Dec. 1933, Saint-Etienne; s. of Moszek Fiterman and Laja Rozenblum; m. Jeannine Poinas 1953; Departmental Sec. Jeunesse Communiste 1952; Sec. CGT, Saint-Etienne S.F.A.C. 1958–62; Dir. Cen. School, Parti communiste français (PCF) 1963–65; elected to PCF Cen. Cttee. 1972, to Political Bureau and Cen. Cttee. Sec. 1976; Gen. Councillor, Head, econ. section and PCF Rep. to liaison cttee. of signatory parties to Common Programme of the Left 1977; Deputy (Val-de-Marne) to Nat. Assembly 1978–81; Minister of State, Minister of Transport 1981–84; Deputy for Rhône 1986. *Address:* 2 place

du Colonel-Fabien, 75019 Paris (Office); 251 avenue Jean Jaurès, 69007 Lyon, France (Office).

FITOURI, Mohamed, L. EN D.; Tunisian politician; b. 4 April 1925, Kairouan; m. two c.; ed. Lycée Carnot, Tunis, Inst. des hautes études, Tunis and Faculté de Droit, Paris; called to the bar 1952; mem. Council Nat. Asscn. of Lawyers 1960; Advocate, Court of Cassation 1962; mem. Econ. and Social Council; City Counsellor, Tunis 1969; Deputy to Nat. Ass. Nov. 1969–; Minister of Justice 1970–71, of Finance 1971–77, of Foreign Affairs 1977–80; Grand Cordon, Ordre de la République, Ordre de l'Indépendance. *Address:* 17 rue Slaheddine, El Ayoubi, Tunis, Tunisia.

FITT, Baron (Life Peer), cr. 1983, of Bell's Hill in the County of Down; **Gerard Fitt;** British politician; b. 9 April 1925, Belfast; s. of George Patrick Fitt and Mary Ann Fitt; m. Susan Doherty 1947; five d. (and one d. deceased); entered local politics in Belfast 1955; mem. Northern Ireland Parl., Stormont, for Dock Constituency 1962–72; mem. U.K. Parl., Westminster, for Belfast West 1966–83; Deputy Chief Exec., N. Ireland Assembly 1974–1975; Leader, Social Democratic and Labour Party (SDLP), resigned Nov. 1979; M.P. 1979–83. *Address:* 85 Antrim Road, Belfast, BT15 2BJ, Northern Ireland; Irish Club, 82 Eaton Square, London, S.W.1; House of Lords, London, SW1A 0PW, England.

FITTIPALDI, Emerson; Brazilian racing driver; b. 12 Dec. 1946, São Paulo; s. of Wilson and Juze Fittipaldi; m. Maria Helena Dowding 1970; one s. two d.; ed. scientific studies; Brazilian Champion Formula V and Go-Kart 1967; Formula 3 Lombard Championship 1969; World Champion 1972, 1974; Second in World Championship 1973, 1975. *Leisure interests:* tennis, radio control aeroplanes and all kinds of sports. *Address:* Fittipaldi Representações Ltda., Alameda Amazonas, 282 Alphaville, Barueri 064500, São Paulo, Brazil.

FITZGERALD, Charles Patrick, D.LITT.; British professor of Far Eastern History (retd.); b. 5 March 1902, London; s. of J. Sauer Fitzgerald and Josephine Fitzpatrick; m. Pamela Sara Knollys 1941; three d.; ed. Clifton Coll., Bristol and School of Oriental and African Studies, London; commercial employment, writing and travelling in China 1923–39; Foreign Office, London 1939–45; British Council, N. China 1945–51; Prof. of Far Eastern History Australian Nat. Univ., Canberra 1951–69, Emer. Prof. 1969–; Visiting Prof. Univ. of Melbourne 1970–72; Leverhulme Fellowship 1936–39. *Publications:* Son of Heaven: a biography of Tang Tai Zung 1927, China: A Short Cultural History 1935, Revolution in China, Floodtide in China, Barbarian Beds: Origins of the Chair in China, Ancient China, Mao Tsetong and China, The Empress Wu, History of China, Why China?: Recollections of China 1923–51. *Address:* 4 St. Paul's Street, Randwick, N.S.W. 2031, Australia.

FITZGERALD, Edmund B., B.S.E.; American business executive; b. 5 Feb. 1926, Milwaukee; s. of Edmund and Elizabeth Bacon Fitzgerald; m. Elisabeth McKee Christensen 1947; two s. two d.; ed. Univ. of Michigan; fmr. Chair. and C.E.O. Cutler-Hammer Inc., Milwaukee; then Vice-Chair. and C.O.O., Industrial Products, Eaton Corpn. (following merger with Cutler-Hammer); Pres. Northern Telecom Inc., U.S.A. (subsidiary of Northern Telecom Ltd.) 1980, C.E.O. and Chair. 1982–, C.E.O. Northern Telecom Ltd. 1984–, Chair. 1985–; Dir. Bell Canada Enterprises, Inc., Northern Telecom Ltd., STC, PLC; mem. Pres. Reagan's Nat. Telecommunications Security Advisory Council; Trustee, Cttee. for Econ. Devt., Washington, D.C.; fmr. Pres. Nat. Electrical Mfrs. Asscn.; fmr. Vice-Chair. Industry Advisory Council, Dept. of Defense. *Address:* Northern Telecom Limited, 3 Robert Speck Parkway, Mississauga, Ont., Canada; Northern Telecom Inc., 127 Woodmont Boulevard, Nashville, Tenn. 37205, U.S.A. *Telephone:* (416) 897-9000 (Mississauga).

FITZGERALD, Ella; American singer; b. 25 April 1918, Newport News, Va.; m. Ray Brown (divorced 1953); one s.; sang with Chick Webb Band 1934–39; toured with Jazz at the Philharmonic troupe in U.S., Japan, and Europe 1948; appeared in film Pete Kelly's Blues 1955; numerous night club and television and concert appearances 1956–; toured with An Evening of Jazz troupe in Sweden, Norway, Denmark, France, Belgium, Germany, Italy, Switzerland 1957; Dr. h.c. (Yale) 1986; eight Grammy Awards; many awards from musicians' polls and Downbeat and Metronome magazines; recordings for Decca 1936–55, Verve 1956–, now Pablo Records. *Records include:* Mack the Knife 1960, Ella Fitzgerald 1965, Things Ain't What They Used To Be 1965, Tribute to Porter 1965, Whisper Not 1966, Côte d'Azur (with Duke Ellington) 1967, Best 1967, Watch What Happens 1972, Take Love Easy 1975, Ella in London 1975, Montreux Ella. *Address:* c/o Norman Granz, 451 North Canon Drive, Beverly Hills, Calif. 90210, U.S.A.

FITZGERALD, Frances; American author; b. 1940; d. of Desmond Fitzgerald and Marietta Peabody Fitzgerald Tree; ed. Radcliffe Coll.; author of series of profiles for Herald Tribune magazine; freelance author of series of profiles, Vietnam 1966; Overseas Press Club Award 1967; Nat. Inst. of Arts and Letters Award 1973; Pulitzer Prize 1973; Nat. Book Award 1973; Sydney Hillman Award 1973; George Polk Award 1973; Bancroft Award for History 1973. *Publications:* Fire in the Lake: The Vietnamese and the Americans in Vietnam 1972, America Revised 1979; articles in magazines. *Address:* c/o Simon and Schuster Inc., 1230 Avenue of the Americas, New York, N.Y. 10020, U.S.A.

FITZGERALD, Dr. Garret; Irish economist and politician; b. 9 Feb. 1926, Dublin s. of late Desmond Fitzgerald and Mabel McConnell; m. Joan O'Farrell 1947; two s. one d.; ed. Belvedere Coll., Univ. Coll. and King's Inns, Dublin; called to the Bar 1946; Research and Schedules Man. Aer Lingus 1947-58; Rockefeller Research Asst., Trinity Coll., Dublin 1958-59; Lecturer in Political Econ. Univ. Coll., Dublin 1959-73; mem. Nat. Univ. of Ireland Senate; Econs. Corresp. and Hon. Sec. Inst. of Transport; mem. Seanad Éireann 1965-69; mem. Dáil Éireann for Dublin South-East 1969-, Leader and Pres. Fine Gael 1977-87; Minister for Foreign Affairs 1973-77; Taoiseach (Prime Minister) of Repub. of Ireland 1981-82, 1982-87; Pres. Council of Ministers of EEC Jan.–June 1975, Irish Council of European Movement; Vice-Pres. European People's Party, European Parl.; fmr. Man. Dir. Economist Intelligence Unit of Ireland; Dir. GPA Group 1987-; fmr. Irish Corresp. BBC, Financial Times, Economist and Economic Corresp. Irish Times; Hon. LL.D. (New York, St. Louis); Hon. D.C.L. (St. Mary's Univ., Halifax, Nova Scotia) 1985, (Oxford) 1987. *Publications:* State-sponsored Bodies 1959, Planning in Ireland 1968, Towards a New Ireland 1972, Unequal Partners (UNCTAD) 1979, Estimates for Baronies of Minimum Level of Irish Speaking Amongst Successive Decennial Cohorts 1771-1781 to 1861-1871 1984. *Address:* Leinster House, Kildare Street, Dublin 2, Ireland.

FITZGERALD, Penelope Mary, B.A.; British teacher and writer; b. 17 Dec. 1916, Lincoln; d. of E. V. Knox and Christina Hicks; m. Desmond Fitzgerald 1942; one s. two d.; ed. Somerville Coll., Oxford; English Tutor, Westminster Tutors, London 1965-; Booker McConnell Prize for Fiction 1979, Rose Mary Crawshay Prize for Charlotte Mew and her Friends 1984. *Publications:* (biography) Edmund Burne-Jones 1975, The Knox Brothers 1977; (novels) The Golden Child 1978, The Bookshop 1978, Offshore 1979, Human Voices 1980, At Freddies 1982, Charlotte Mew and her Friends 1984, Innocence 1986, The Beginning of Spring 1988; ed. William Morris's unpublished Novel on Blue Paper 1982. *Leisure interests:* cooking, growing orange trees, travelling, boats, lino-cuts and graphics. *Address:* c/o William Collins, 8 Grafton Street, London, W1X 3LA, England.

FITZGERALD, Peter Hanley, PH.D., D.SC., F.R.C.PATH., F.R.S.N.Z.; New Zealand director of cancer research; b. 10 Oct. 1929, Gore; s. of John J. Fitzgerald and Nora Eileen (née Hanley) Fitzgerald; m. Kathleen O'Connell 1955; three s. two d.; ed. St. Bede's Coll., Christchurch, Univ. of Canterbury, Univ. of New Zealand and Univ. of Adelaide; Dir. Cancer Soc. of N.Z. Cytogenetic and Molecular Oncology Unit, Christchurch Hosp. 1967-; Pres. N.Z. Genetics Soc. 1978, N.Z. Soc. for Oncology 1973-74; mem. Nat. Scientific Cttee. Cancer Soc. of N.Z. 1981-85, Int. Scientific Advisory Bd. Cancer Congress, Seattle 1982, Canterbury Museum Trust Bd. 1985-, Royal Soc. of N.Z. Council 1986-; Hon Cytogeneticist Canterbury Hosp. Bd. 1967-; Hon. Lecturer in Botany and Zoology Univ. of Canterbury 1971-, in Pathology Christchurch Medical School, Univ. of Otago 1979-; Sir George Grey Scholarship 1952; N.Z. Nat. Research Fellowship 1955-57. *Publications:* over 125 publs. on cancer-related topics. *Leisure interests:* gardening and hiking. *Address:* Cancer Society of New Zealand Cytogenetics Unit, Christchurch Hospital, Christchurch (Office); 60 Middlepark Road, Christchurch 4, New Zealand (Home). *Telephone:* (64)3 640890 (Office); (64)3 480057 (Home).

FITZGERALD, Stephen Arthur, A.O., B.A., PH.D.; Australian scholar and diplomatist; b. 18 Sept. 1938, Hobart, Tasmania; s. of F. G. FitzGerald; m. Helen Overton; one s. two d.; ed. Tasmania Univ., Australian Nat. Univ.; Dept. of Foreign Affairs 1961-66; Research Scholar, Australian Nat. Univ. 1966-69, Research Fellow 1969-71, Fellow 1972-73, Professorial Fellow 1977-,Head Dept. of Far Eastern History 1977-79, Head Contemporary China Centre, Research School of Pacific Studies 1977-79; Amb. to People's Repub. of China (also accred. to Democratic People's Repub. of Korea) 1973-76; Ed. Australian Journal of Chinese Affairs; Deputy Chair. Australia-China Council 1979-; mem. Australian Acad. of Science Sub-Cttee. on Relations with China; Trustee, Australian Cancer Foundation 1985-; Chair. Asian Studies Council 1986-; Chair. and Man. Dir. Stephen Fitzgerald and Co. Ltd. *Publications:* China and the Overseas Chinese 1972, Talking with China 1972, China and the World 1977. *Address:* P.O. Box 1937, Canberra City, A.C.T. 2601, Australia.

FITZHARDINGE, Laurence Frederic, F.A.H.A., M.A.; Australian university reader (retd.); b. 6 July 1908, Chatswood, N.S.W.; s. of J. F. (Eric) Fitzhardinge and Florence Marion (née Rutherford) Fitzhardinge; m. Hope Verity Hewitt 1936; two s.; ed. Univ. of Sydney and New Coll., Oxford; Research Officer in charge of Australian collections Nat. Library of Australia, Canberra 1934-44; Lecturer in Classics Univ. of Sydney 1945-50; Reader in Australian History, A.N.U., Canberra 1950-74; Commonwealth Fellow St. John's Coll., Cambridge 1968-69; Fellow Library Assen. Australia; Royal Australian Historical Soc. *Publications:* Sydney's First Four Years by Watkin Tench (Ed.) 1961, William Morris Hughes: a political biography (Vol. I) 1964, (Vol. II) 1979, The Spartans 1980. *Leisure interests:* bibliography, typography, ancient history. *Address:* River View, Oaks Estate, Queanbeyan, N.S.W. 2620, Australia. *Telephone:* (062) 972158.

FITZPATRICK, Gen. Sir (Geoffrey Richard) Desmond, G.C.B., D.S.O., M.B.E., M.C.; British army officer (retd.); b. 14 Dec. 1912, Ash Vale, Hants; s. of late Brig.-Gen. Sir Richard Fitzpatrick and Lady Fitzpatrick; m. Mary Campbell 1944; one s. one d.; ed. Eton Coll. and Royal Mil. Coll.,

Sandhurst; commissioned 1932; served in Palestine 1938-39, in Middle East, Italy and N.W. Europe 1939-45; ADC to H.M. The Queen 1959; Asst. Chief of Defence Staff, Ministry of Defence 1959-61; Dir. Mil. Operations, War Office 1962-64; Chief-of-Staff, British Army of the Rhine (B.A.O.R.) 1964-65; GOC-in-C., N. Ireland 1965-66; Vice-Chief of Gen. Staff 1966-68; promoted Gen. 1968; C.-in-C. B.A.O.R. and Commdr. Northern Army Group 1968-70; Deputy Supreme Allied Commdr., Europe 1970-73; ADC (Gen.) to the Queen 1970-73; Lieut.-Gov. and C.-in-C. of Jersey 1974-79; Col. The Blues and Royals, and Gold Stick to the Queen 1979-. *Leisure interests:* sailing and shooting. *Address:* Belmont, Otley, Ipswich, Suffolk, IP6 9PF, England.

FITZPATRICK, Thomas J.; Irish politician and solicitor; b. 14 Feb. 1918, Scotshouse, Co. Monaghan; s. of John Fitzpatrick and Jennie Markey; m. 1st Betty Cullen 1946 (died 1951), two d.; m. 2nd Carmel McDonald 1973, one s.; ed. St. Macartan's coll., Monaghan, and Univ. Coll., Dublin; solicitor 1939-; Councillor, Cavan Urban Council 1950-, Chair. 1960-73, fmr. mem. various local authority cttees.; mem. Seanad Éireann 1961-65; mem. Dáil Éireann 1965-; fmr. mem. Fine Gael Front Bench and Nat. Exec.; Fine Gael Spokesman on Local Govt. 1969-73; Minister for Lands 1973-76, of Transport and Power 1976-77. *Address:* Dáil Éireann, Leinster House, Kildare Street, Dublin 2; Rathanna, Drumelis, Cavan, Ireland.

FIXMAN, Marshall, PH.D.; American chemist and teacher; b. 21 Sept. 1930, St. Louis, Mo.; s. of Benjamin Fixman and Dorothy Finkel; m. 1st Marian Beatman 1959 (died 1969), 2nd Branka Ladanyi 1974; one s. two d.; ed. Univ. City High School, Mo., Washington Univ., Mo. and M.I.T.; Postdoctoral Fellow, Yale Univ. 1953-54; served U.S. Army 1954-56; Instructor in Chem., Harvard Univ. 1956-59; Sr. Fellow, Mellon Inst., Pa. 1959-61; Dir. Inst. of Theoretical Science, Univ. of Ore. 1961-64, Prof. of Chem. 1961-65; Sloan Visiting Prof. of Chem., Harvard Univ. 1965; Prof. of Chem., Yale Univ. 1965-79; Prof. of Chem. and Physics, Colo. State Univ. 1979-; Fellow American Acad. of Arts and Sciences, American Physical Soc.; mem. N.A.S.; Alfred P. Sloan Fellowship 1962-64; American Chemical Soc. Award in Pure Chem. 1964; American Physical Soc. High Polymer Physics Prize 1980; Assoc. Ed. of Journal of Chemical Physics, Macromolecules, Journal of Physical Chem., Accounts of Chemical Research. *Leisure interests:* hiking and photography. *Address:* Department of Chemistry, Colorado State University, Fort Collins, Colo. 80523, U.S.A. *Telephone:* (303) 491-6037.

FLAHIFF, H.E. Cardinal George Bernard, C.C.; Canadian ecclesiastic; b. 26 Oct. 1905, Paris, Ontario; s. of John J. Flahiff and Eleanor Fleming; ed. Univs. of Toronto and Strasbourg; ordained 1930; Prof. of Medieval History, Univ. of Toronto Graduate School and Pontifical Inst. of Medieval Studies 1935-54; Superior Gen. Basilian Fathers 1954-61; Archbishop of Winnipeg 1961-82; cr. Cardinal 1969; numerous hon. degrees. *Address:* St. Michael's College, 81 St. Mary Street, Toronto, Ont. M5S 1J4, Canada. *Telephone:* (416) 926-1300.

FLAMAND, Paul Henri; French publisher; b. 25 Jan. 1909; s. of Henri Flamand and Marie Dufour; m. Marguerite Olivier 1937 (deceased); two s. three d.; ed. Coll. Saint-Paul, Angoulême; Founder and Dir. of Editions du Seuil, Paris 1938-79; mem. Conseil de développement culturel 1971-73, Conseil supérieur des lettres 1974-; Pres. Gazette du Palais 1979-. *Address:* 9 avenue de Dourdan, 91530 Saint-Chéron, France.

FLAMMARION, Charles-Henri, L. ÈS L.; French publishing executive; b. 27 July 1946, Boulogne-Billancourt; s. of the late Henri Flammarion and of Pierrette Chenelot; m. Marie-Françoise Mariani 1968; one s. two d.; ed. Lycée de Sèvres, Paris Sorbonne and Columbia Univ., U.S.A.; Asst. Man. Edns. Flammarion 1972-81, Gen. Man. 1981-85, Pres. Flammarion Group 1985-, Pres. Flammarion Bookshop; Pres. Edns. J'ai Lu 1982-; mem. Bureau du Syndicat Nat. de l'Edition 1979-. *Leisure interests:* cooking, travel, skiing, walking. *Address:* 26 rue Racine, 75006 Paris (Office); 5 avenue Franco-Russe, 75007 Paris, France (Home).

FLAMSON, Richard J., III; American banker; b. 2 Feb. 1929, Los Angeles, Calif.; s. of Richard J. Flamson and Mildred Jones Flamson; m. Arden Black 1951; three s. one d.; ed. Claremont Men's Coll., Univ. of Washington; joined Security Pacific Nat. Bank 1955, Vice-Pres. Admin., Instalment Loan Div. 1962, Nat. Banking Dept. 1965, Int. Banking Dept 1968, Sr. Vice-Pres. 1969, Exec. Vice-Pres. 1970, Vice-Chair. of Bd. 1973-80; Pres. Security Pacific Corpn. 1973-80; Pres. and C.E.O. Security Pacific Bank 1978-80, Chair. Jan. 1981-; Chair., C.E.O. Security Pacific Corpn. 1980-; Dir. and Officer several subsidiary cos. *Leisure interests:* boating, tennis, golf, reading. *Address:* Security Pacific Corp., 333 South Hope Street, Los Angeles, Calif. 90071 (Office); 2000 Kewamee Drive, Corona del Mar, Calif. 92625, U.S.A. (Home). *Telephone:* (213) 613-6526 (Office); (714) 673-8593 (Home).

FLANAGAN, Barry; British sculptor; b. 1941, Prestatyn, N. Wales; ed. Mayfield Coll., Sussex, Birmingham Coll. of Arts and Crafts and St. Martin's School of Art, London; one-man exhbns. at Rowan Gallery, London (several, 1966-94) Waddington Galleries, London (several, 1980-85), Serpentine and Whitechapel Art Galleries, London, Centre Georges Pompidou, Paris, Museum of Modern Art, New York and many others in Europe, U.S.A., Argentina and Japan; works in public collections including Art Inst., Chicago, Kunsthaus, Zurich, Museum of Modern Art, New York,

Nagaoka Museum, Tokyo, Nat. Gallery of Canada, Ottawa, Stedelijk Museum, Amsterdam, Tate Gallery and Victoria and Albert Museum, London and Walker Art Gallery, Liverpool; outdoor sculpture commissioned by City of Ghent and by Camden Borough Council, London for Lincoln's Inn Fields, London; mem. Zoological Soc. of London. *Address:* 87 Wardour Street, London W.1, England. *Telephone:* 01-437 5947.

FLANAGAN, James Loton, SC.D; American research engineer: b. 26 Aug. 1925, Greenwood, Mass.; s. of Hanks G. and Wilhelmina B. Flanagan; m. Mildred E. Bell 1958; three s.; ed. Massachusetts Inst. of Tech. and Mississipi State Univ.; mem. Research Div., AT&T Bell Labs., Murray Hill, N.J. 1957-, Head, Speech and Auditory Research Dept. 1961-67, Head, Acoustics Research Dept. 1967-85, Dir., Information Prins. Research Lab. 1985-; mem. Nat. Acad. of Eng., N.A.S.; L. M. Ericsson Int. Prize; IEEE/ASSP Soc. Award. *Publications:* about 150 tech. papers in archival journals; 45 U.S. patents; two books. *Leisure interests:* salt-water fishing, swimming, jogging. *Address:* AT&T Bell Laboratories, 600 Mountain Avenue, Murray Hill, N.J., U.S.A. *Telephone:* (201) 582-3945.

FLANNERY, Joseph Patrick, B.S., M.B.A.; American business executive; b. 20 March 1932, Lowell, Mass.; s. of Mary Agnes Egan Flannery; m. Margaret Barrows 1957; three s. three d.; ed. Lowell Tech. Inst., Harvard Grad. School of Business Admin.; Pres. Uniroyal Chemical Co. 1975-77; Exec. Vice-Pres. Uniroyal Inc., Middlebury, Conn. 1977; Pres. of parent co. and mem. Bd. of Dirs. and Exec. Cttee. 1977-, C.E.O. Feb. 1980-, Chair. Feb. 1982-, Chair., Pres. and C.E.O. Uniroyal Holding, Inc. 1986-; Partner Clayton & Dubilier, Inc.; Dir. Newmont Mining Corpn., K Mart Corpn., Ingersoll-Rand Co., Amstar Corpn., O.M. Scott & Sons, Irish American Partnership. *Address:* 455 Chase Parkway, Waterbury, Conn. 06708-3392, U.S.A. *Telephone:* (203) 757-9471 (Office).

FLAVIN, Dan; American artist; b. 1 April 1933, New York; s. of Daniel Nicolas and Viola Marion Bernzott Flavin; m. Sonja Sverdija 1961 (divorced 1976); one s.; ed. Cathedral Coll. of Immaculate Conception Preparatory Seminary, Brooklyn; fluorescent light artist; numerous one-man exhbns. in U.S.A. 1961-; exhibits in collections in U.S.A. and Europe; Guest Lecturer in Design, Univ. of N. Carolina 1967; Guest Prof. Univ. of Bridgeport 1973; founded Dan Flavin Art Inst., New York 1983; Skowhegan Medal for Sculpture 1965. *Address:* Dan Flavin Art Institute, P.O. Box 1286, Bridgehampton, Long Island, New York 11932 (Office); P.O. Box 1210, Wainscott, N.Y. 11975, U.S.A. (Home). *Telephone:* 516-537-1476 (Office).

FLECHTHEIM, Ossip K., D.JUR., D.PHIL.; German professor of political science (retd.) and writer; b. 5 March 1909, Nikolayev, Russia; s. of Hermann Flechtheim and Olga Farber; m. Lili Faktor 1942; one d.; ed. Univs. of Freiburg, Paris, Heidelberg, Berlin, Cologne, Graduate Inst. of Int. Studies, Geneva; Asst. Research Assoc. Columbia Univ., New York 1939-40; Instructor Atlanta Univ., Ga. and Bates Coll., Lewiston, Maine 1940-46; Prof. Colby Coll., Waterville, U.S.A. 1946-51; Visiting Prof. Free Univ. of Berlin 1951-52; Prof. Deutsche Hochschule für Politik, Berlin 1952-59; Prof. of Political Science Free Univ. of Berlin 1959-74; Section and Branch Chief Office of U.S. War Crimes Attorney 1946-47; mem. PEN. *Publications:* Hegels Strafrechtstheorie 1936, 1976, Die KPD in der Weimarer Republik 1948, 1986, Fundamentals of Political Science 1952, Von Hegel zu Kelsen 1963, Eine Welt oder keine? 1964, Weltkommunismus im Wandel 1965, 1977, History and Futurology 1966, Bolschewismus 1917-1967: Von der Weltrevolution zum Sowjetimperium 1967, Zeitgeschichte und Zukunftspolitik 1974, Von Marx bis Kolakowski-Sozialismus oder Untergang in der Barbarei? 1978, Der Kampf um die Zukunft-Grundlagen der Futurologie 1980, Marx heute-pro und contra 1983, Rosa Luxemburg zur Einführung 1984, Karl Liebknecht zur Einführung 1985, Ist die Zukunft noch zu retten? 1987, Marx zur Einführung (with H.-M. Lohmann) 1988. *Address:* Rohlfsstrasse 18, D-1000 Berlin 33, Federal Republic of Germany. *Telephone:* (030) 823 20 51.

FLECKENSTEIN, Günther; German theatre director; b. 13 Jan. 1925, Mainz; m. Heike Haase 1965; two d.; ed. Realgymnasium, Mainz, and Univ. Mainz; producer of plays and operas; Dir. Deutsches Theater, Göttingen 1966-86; freelance producer 1986-; Guest Dir. for theatres in Berlin, Hamburg and Stuttgart; Guest Dir. TV in Munich, Stuttgart and Berlin; Dir. Hersfelde Festspiele 1976-81; has dramatized for stage and TV Der Grosstyrann und das Gericht (Bergengruen); stage production in German of Les jeux sont faits (Sartre), Im Räderwerk (Sartre); productions for children's and young people's theatre; Zückmayer Medal for services to the German language 1979, Hon. Plaque, Bad Hersfeld 1982, Hon. Plaque, Göttingen 1984, Polish Medal for Cultural Service 1986. *Address:* Sonnenstr. 8a, D-8034 Unterpfaffenhofen, Federal Republic of Germany.

FLEGEL, Manfred; German economist and politician; b. 3 June 1927, Magdeburg; ed. Univs. of Rostock and Berlin; mem. and Sec. Cen. Cttee. Nat.-Demokratische Partei Deutschlands 1948-; mem. Volkskammer 1950-; mem. Econ. Cttee. 1950-54, Chair. Finance Cttee. 1954-67; Deputy Chair. Council of Ministers of G.D.R. 1961-, Minister for Materials Supply 1971-74; mem. Presidium Nat. Council of Nat. Front 1971-; Chair. State Contract Court 1974-; Chair. Nat. Arbitration Bd.; Vaterländischer Verdienstorden in Bronze; Ernst-Moritz-Arndt Medaille. *Address:* Ministerrat, Berlin, German Democratic Republic.

FLEISCHER, Ezra; Israeli professor and poet; b. 7 Aug. 1928, Romania; m. Anat Rappaport 1955; two s.; ed. Univ. of Bucharest and Hebrew Univ., Jerusalem; political prisoner in Romania 1952-55; emigrated to Israel 1960; Dir. Geniza Research Inst. for Hebrew Poetry, Israel Nat. Acad. of Sciences and Humanities 1967-; Prof. of Medieval Hebrew Poetry, Hebrew Univ., Jerusalem 1973-; mem. Israel Acad. of Sciences and Humanities 1984-; Israel Prize for Poetry 1959, Bialik Prize for Judaic Studies 1986. *Publications:* Poetry: Fables 1957, The Burden of Gog 1959, At Midnight 1961; research: The Poems of Shelomo Ha-Bauli 1973, The Pizmonim of Anonymus 1974, Hebrew Liturgical Poetry in the Middle Ages 1975, The Yozer, its Emergence and Development 1984, Eretz Israel Prayer and Prayer Rituals as Portrayed in the Geniza Documents 1988, numerous articles in periodicals. *Address:* 5 Radak Street, Jerusalem 9 01, Israel. *Telephone:* (02) 630 660.

FLEISCHHAUER, Carl-August, DR.JUR.; German lawyer; b. 9 Dec. 1930, Düsseldorf; s. of Kurt and Leonie (née Schneider-Neuenburg) Fleischhauer; m. Liliane Sarolea 1957; two d.; ed. Univs. of Heidelberg, Grenoble, Paris and Chicago; Research Fellow, Max-Planck Inst. for Comparative Foreign Public Law and Int. Law, Heidelberg 1960-62; with Foreign Service of Fed. Repub. of Germany 1962-83, Legal Adviser to Fed. Foreign Office 1975, Legal Adviser and Dir.-Gen. Legal Dept. 1976; Under-Sec.-Gen. for Legal Affairs, Legal Counsel, UN 1983-; Bundesverdienstkreuz and foreign decorations. *Publications:* various legal publications. *Leisure interests:* modern history, literature. *Address:* Secretariat, Room 3427, United Nations, UN Plaza, New York, N.Y. 10017 (Office); 420 East 54th Street, New York, N.Y.10022, U.S.A. (Home). *Telephone:* (212) 754 5338 (Office); (212) 758 0517 (Home).

FLEISCHMANN, Martin, PH.D., F.R.S., F.R.S.C.; British professor of chemistry; b. 29 March 1927; s. of Hans Fleischmann and Margarethe Srb; m. Sheila Flinn 1950; one s. two d.; ed. Worthing High School, and Imperial Coll. London; ICI Fellow, Univ. of Durham 1952-57; lecturer, then Reader, Univ. of Newcastle-upon-Tyne 1957-67; Electricity Council Faraday Prof. of Electrochem. Univ. of Southampton 1967-77; Sr. Fellowship, Science and Eng. Research Council 1977-82; Pres. Int. Soc. of Electrochemistry 1970-72; Research Prof. Dept. of Chem. Univ. of Southampton 1982-. *Publications:* numerous papers and book chapters. *Leisure interests:* skiing, walking, music, cooking. *Address:* Bury Lodge, Duck Street, Tisbury, Wilts., SP3 6LJ, England. *Telephone:* (0747) 870384.

FLEISCHMANN, Rudolf, DR.RER.NAT.; German physicist; b. 1 May 1903, Erlangen; s. of Dr. Albert and Franziska Fleischmann (née Kiefl); m. Marianne Müller 1963; ed. Univs. of Erlangen, Munich; Inst. of Physics, Göttingen 1930-32, Heidelberg 1932-34; Kaiser Wilhelm Physical Inst., Heidelberg 1934-41; Extraordinary Prof. of Physics, Univ. of Strasbourg 1941-44; Prof. of Physics, Univ. of Hamburg, and Dir. of State Physical Inst. 1947-53; Prof. of Physics, Head of Physics Dept., Univ. of Erlangen 1953-69, Emer. 1970-. *Address:* 9 Langemarckplatz, 852 Erlangen, Federal Republic of Germany. *Telephone:* 09131 26221.

FLEMING, John Marley, M.B.A.; American business executive; b. 4 April 1930, Massachusetts; s. of Dr. David A. Fleming and Mary L. Marley; m. Jeanne C. Retelle 1961; one s. two d.; ed. Harvard Coll. and Harvard Graduate School of Business Admin.; Deck Officer, U.S. Navy 1952-55; Frigidaire Div., Gen. Motors Corpn. 1957-63; Sales Promotion Man. Ford Motor Co. 1963-68; Vice-Pres. J. Walter Thompson Co. 1968-70; Marketing Dir. Oldsmobile Div., Gen. Motors Corpn. 1970-77; Dir. of Sales, Adam Opel A.G., Germany 1977-80; Dir. Commercial Vehicle Operations, Vauxhall 1980-82; Chair. and Man. Dir. Vauxhall Motors Ltd. 1982-86; Vice-Pres. Sales, Gen. Motors Europe 1986-. *Leisure interests:* golf, skiing, sailing. *Address:* Aircenter, Stelzenstrasse 4, 8152 Glattbrugg, Switzerland. *Telephone:* 01-828 2200.

FLEMING, Robben Wright, LL.D.; American educator; b. 18 Dec. 1916; s. of Edmund P. and Jeanette Wheeler Fleming; m. Aldyth L. Quixley 1942; one s. two d.; ed. Beloit Coll., Wis. and Univ. of Wisconsin; Attorney, Securities and Exchange Comm., Washington, D.C. 1941-42; Mediator, Nat. War Labor Bd. 1942; Dir. Industrial Relations Center, Univ. of Wis. 1947-52; Prof. of Law, Univ. of Ill. 1958-64; Dir. Inst. of Labor and Industrial Relations, Univ. of Ill. 1952-58; Prof. of Law and Chancellor, Univ. of Wis. 1964-67; Prof. of Law, Pres. Univ. of Mich., Ann Arbor 1968-78, Pres. Emer. 1982-, Interim Pres. Jan.-Sept. 1988; Pres. Corpn. for Public Broadcasting 1979-81; Sr. Educ. Consultant, Kellog Foundation, Annenberg Corpn. for Public Broadcasting Project; mem. of Bd. Nat. Inst. for Dispute Resolution, Johnson Foundation, Recine, Wis.; mem. East-West Center, Univ. of Hawaii; numerous hon. degrees. *Publications:* The Politics of Wage Price Decisions (with M. Edelman) 1965, The Labor Arbitration Process 1965. *Leisure interests:* sports, reading. *Address:* 339 Hutchins Hall, The Law School, University of Michigan, Ann Arbor, Mich. 48109 (Office); 2108 Vinewood Avenue, Ann Arbor, Mich. 48104, U.S.A. (Home). *Telephone:* (313) 763-9868 (Office).

FLEMING, Scott, J.D.; American lawyer; b. 17 Oct. 1923, Twin Falls, Idaho; m. 1st Barbara Stayton 1943; m. 2nd Jenny Skinner 1954; two d.; ed. Reno High School, Univ. of Calif. Berkeley, Univ. of Chicago and Harvard Business School; legal practice, San Francisco 1949-52; Attorney, Henry J. Kaiser Co. Legal Dept. 1952-55; various positions, Kaiser Foundation Health Plan 1955–71, Sr. Vice-Pres. 1973–; Deputy Asst. Sec. for Health Policy Devt. Dept. of Health, Educ. and Welfare 1971–73; Dir. and Vice-Pres. Orcon Corpn. Union City, Calif. 1983–; Dir. Fisher Berkeley Corpn., Oakland, Calif. 1988–; mem. Inst. of Medicine of N.A.S. *Leisure interests:* white water kayaking, skiing, backpacking, windsurfing, scuba diving, photography. *Address:* Kaiser Foundation Health Plan, 1 Kaiser Plaza, Oakland, Calif. 94612, (Office); 2750 Shasta Road, Berkeley, Calif. 94708, U.S.A. (Home). *Telephone:* 415-271-6471 (Office); 415-848-3455.

FLEMING, Rt. Rev. William Launcelot Scott, K.C.V.O., M.S., D.D., F.R.S.E.; British ecclesiastic and explorer; b. 7 Aug. 1906; s. of late Robert Alexander Fleming; m. Jane Agutter 1965; ed. Rugby School, Trinity Hall and Westcott House, Cambridge, and Yale Univ. (Commonwealth Fund Fellow 1929–31); ordained 1933; Fellow and Chaplain Trinity Hall 1933–49, Dean 1937–49; expeditions to Iceland and Spitzbergen 1932–33; Chaplain and Geologist, British Graham Land Expedition 1934–37; Chaplain, R.N.V.R. 1940–44; Dir. Service Ordination Cands. 1944–46; Dir. Scott Polar Research Inst., Cambridge 1946–49; Bishop of Portsmouth 1949–59; Bishop of Norwich 1959–71; Dean of Windsor, Domestic Chaplain to H.M. Queen Elizabeth II, Register Order of the Garter 1971–76; Chair. Church of England Youth Council 1950–61; Chair. Archbishops' Advisers on Needs and Resources of the Church of England 1963–76; Vice-Chair. Parl. Group for World Govt. 1970–76; mem. Royal Comm. on Environmental Pollution 1970–73; Pres. Young Explorers Trust 1976–78; Hon. Chaplain R.N.V.R. (now R.N.R.) 1950; Hon. Fellow, Trinity Hall, Cambridge 1956; Hon. Vice-Pres. Royal Geographical Soc. 1961; Gov. United World Coll. of the Atlantic 1960–; Trustee, The Prince's Trust 1974–85; Visitor Bryanston School; Hon. D.C.L. (East Anglia) 1970; Polar Medal 1936–37. *Address:* Tithe Barn, Poyntington, Dorset, DT9 4LF, England. *Telephone:* Corton Denham 479.

FLEMMING, Arthur Sherwood, A.M., LL.B.; American educator and government official; b. 12 June 1905; s. of Harry H. and Harriet (Sherwood) Flemming; m. Bernice Virginia Moler 1934; three s. two d.; ed. Ohio Wesleyan, American and George Washington Univs.; Instructor, American Univ. 1927–30, Dir. School of Public Affairs 1934–39, Exec. Officer 1938–39; mem. U.S. Civil Service Comm. 1939–48, Int. Civil Service Advisory Bd. 1950–64, Nat. Advisory Cttee. of Peace Corps 1961–65; Pres. Ohio Wesleyan Univ. 1948–58 (on leave 1953–57); Asst. to Dir. Office of Defense Mobilization 1951–53, Dir. 1953–57; statutory mem. Nat. Security Council, participating by invitation of the Pres. of the U.S. in Cabinet meetings 1953–57; Sec. of Health, Educ. and Welfare 1958–61; Pres. Univ. of Oregon 1961–68; Pres. Macalester Coll., St. Paul 1968–71; Chair. Bd. of Trustees, Citizenship Clearing House 1959–62; Pres. Nat. Council of Churches in America 1967–70; Fed. Commr. on Ageing 1963–78; mem. U.S. Comm. on Civil Rights, Chair. 1974–81; numerous hon. degrees; Republican. *Address:* c/o Commission on Civil Rights, 1121 Vermont Avenue, N.W., Washington, D.C. 20425, U.S.A.

FLEMMING, John Stanton, M.A.; British economist; b. 6 Feb. 1941, Reading, Berks.; s. of Sir Gilbert Nicolson Flemming and Virginia (née Coit); m. Jean Briggs 1963; three s. one d.; ed. Rugby School and Trinity and Nuffield Colls., Oxford; Lecturer and Fellow in Econs. Oriel Coll., Oxford 1963–65; Official Fellow in Econs. Nuffield Coll., Oxford 1965–80, Bursar 1970, Fellow Emer. 1980–; Ed. Economic Journal 1976–80; Chair. Econ. Affairs Cttee. Social Science Research Council 1980–84; Chief Adviser and Head of Econs. Div. Bank of England 1980–84, Econ. Adviser to Gov. 1984–88, Exec. Dir. 1988–; mem. Council, Royal Econs. Soc., Inst. for Fiscal Studies, Advisory Bd. on Research Councils (U.K.) 1986–; Council European Econ. Asscn. 1985–88; Harkness Fellow, Harvard Univ. 1978–79. *Publications:* articles in academic journals. *Address:* c/o Bank of England, Threadneedle Street, London EC2R 8AH, England. *Telephone:* 01-601 4444.

FLEROV, Georgiy Nikolayevich; Soviet physicist; b. 2 March 1913, Rostov-on-Don; ed. Leningrad Industrial Inst.; scientific work, Leningrad Inst. of Physics and Tech. 1938, later Chief Lab. of Multicharged Ions, Kurchatov Inst. of Atomic Energy, Moscow; Dir. Nuclear Reaction Laboratory, Jt. Inst. for Nuclear Research, Dubna 1960–; mem. CPSU 1954–; Corresp. mem. U.S.S.R. Acad. of Sciences 1953–68, Academician 1968–; Hero of Socialist Labour, State Prize (three times), Lenin Prize 1967, etc. *Publications:* The Absorption of Slow Neutrons by Cadmium and Mercury 1939, The Spontaneous Fission of Uranium (with K. A. Petrzhak) 1940, Experiments on the Fission of Uranium (with L. I. Russinov) 1940, On the Proton Decay of Radioactive Nuclei (with others) 1964, Synthesis of transuranic elements (with others): element 102 (1957–66), 103 1966, 104 1964, 105 1970, 106 1974, 107 1977, Elements of the Second Hundred (with I. Zvara) 1971, Experiments on the Synthesis of and Search for Transuranic Elements at the JINR 1971, Superheavy elements 1977. *Address:* Laboratory of Nuclear Reactions, Joint Institute for Nuclear Research, Dubna, Moscow Region, U.S.S.R.

FLETCHER, Hugh Alasdair, M.COM., M.B.A.; New Zealand business executive; b. 28 Nov. 1947, Auckland; s. of Sir James Muir Cameron Fletcher and Margery V. (née Gunthorp) Fletcher; m. Sian Seerpoohi Elias 1970; two s.; ed. Auckland Univ. and Stanford Univ.; C.E.O. Fletcher Holdings Ltd. 1980, Man. Dir. Fletcher Challenge Ltd. 1981, C.E.O. Oct. 1987–; Chair. Air New Zealand Ltd. 1985–; Harkness Fellowship 1970–72. *Leisure interest:* horse riding/hunting. *Address:* Fletcher Challenge Ltd., Private Bag, Auckland (Office); 79 Penrose Road, Auckland, New Zealand (Home). *Telephone:* 0649 594 300 (Office); 0649 594 226 (Home).

FLETCHER, James Chipman, PH.D.; American scientific administrator; b. 5 June 1919, Millburn, N.J.; s. of Harvey and Lorena (Chipman) Fletcher; m. Fay Lee 1946; one s. three d.; ed. Columbia Univ. and Calif. Inst. of Tech.; Research physicist, U.S.N. Bureau of Ordnance 1940; Special Research Assoc., Cruft Lab. of Harvard Univ. 1941; Teaching Fellow, Princeton Univ. 1942, later Instructor and Research Physicist; Teaching Fellow, Calif. Inst. of Tech. 1945; instructor, Univ. of Calif., Los Angeles 1948; Dir. Theory and Analysis Lab., Electronics Div., Hughes Aircraft Co. 1948; Assoc. Dir. Ramo Woolridge Corpn. 1954, subsequently Dir. of Electronics, Guided Missile Div. (later became Space Tech. Laboratories); organized Space Electronics Corpn. (with F. W. Lehan) 1958, subsequently Pres. Space Gen. Corpn. (following merger of Space Electronics Corpn. and Aerojets Gen. Corpn.) 1961, Chair. of Bd. 1961–64, 1985–; Pres. Univ. of Utah 1964–71; Admin. NASA 1971–77, 1986–89; Whiteford Prof. Univ. of Pittsburgh 1977–84, Distinguished Prof. of Public Service 1984–86; consultant engineer 1977–; Bd. of Dirs. Burroughs Corpn., Standard Oil Co., Indiana, COMARCO Inc., Astrotech Int. 1984–86, Fairchild Industries 1985–86; Dir. Defensive Technologies Study (SDI) 1983–; Bd. of Trustees, The Rockefeller Foundation 1978–85; Trustee, Univ. Corpn. for Atmospheric Research 1981–, Argonne Lab. 1984–; U.S.A.F. Exceptional Civilian Service Medal 1978, NASA Distinguished Service Medal 1978, 1981; Hon. D.Sc. (Utah) 1971, (Brigham Young) 1977, Dr. h.c. (Lehigh) 1978. *Address:* 7721 Falstaff Road, McLean, Va. 22102, U.S.A. (Home).

FLETCHER, Neville Horner, PH.D., D.SC., F.T.S., F.A.A.; Australian physicist; b. 14 July 1930, Armidale, N.S.W.; s. of A. H. Fletcher; m. Eunice M. Sciffer 1953; one s. two d.; ed. Armidale High School, New England Univ. Coll., Univ. of Sydney, Harvard Univ.; Research Engineer, Clevite Transistor Products, U.S.A. 1953–55; Researcher, CSIRO Radiophysics Lab. 1956–59, Dir. Inst. of Physical Sciences 1983–88; Chief Research Scientist 1988–; at Univ. of New England 1960–83, Sr. Lecturer in Physics 1960–63, Prof. of Physics 1963–83, Dean, Faculty of Science 1963–65; mem. Univ. Council 1968–72, Chair. Professional Bd. 1970–72, Pro Vice-Chancellor 1969–72, Prof. Emer. 1983–; mem. Australian Research Grants Cttee. 1974–78, Sec. Physical Sciences, Acad. of Science 1980–84, Pres. Inst. of Physics 1981–83; mem. Govt. Meteorology Policy Cttee. 1981–84, Int. Comm. on Acoustics 1985–; Edgeworth David Medal (Royal Soc. of N.S.W.) 1963; Fellow, Australian Acad. of Tech. Sciences and Eng.; Visiting Prof. and Fellow to various insts. *Publications:* The Physics of Rainclouds 1962, The Chemical Physics of Ice 1970, Physics and Music 1976, over 100 papers in scientific journals. *Leisure interests:* music (flute and organ). *Address:* Dept. of Electronic Materials Engineering, Research School of Physical Sciences, Australian National University, Canberra, A.C.T. 2601 (Office), 30 Rosebery Street, Fisher, A.C.T. 2611, Australia (Home). *Telephone:* (062) 49-4406 (Office); (062) 88-8988 (Home).

FLETCHER-COOKE, Sir John, Kt., C.M.G., M.A.; British colonial official (retd.) and writer; b. 8 Aug. 1911, Burnham, Bucks; s. of the late Charles Arthur Fletcher-Cooke and Gwendolen May (née Bradford); m. 1st Louise Brander 1936, one s.; m. 2nd Alice Egner 1949 (dissolved), one s. one d.; m. 3rd Marie-Louise, Vicomtesse de la Barre 1977; ed. Malvern Coll., Paris and Oxford Univs.; Colonial Office, Pvt. Sec. to Perm. Under-Sec. 1934–37; Malayan Civil Service 1937–42; Served in R.A.F. and taken P.O.W. by Japanese 1942–46; Sec. to Constitutional Comm. Malta 1946; Under-Sec. to Palestine Govt. 1946–49; Counsellor, U.K. Del. to UN 1949–51; Colonial Sec., Cyprus 1951–55; Minister for Constitutional Affairs, Tanganyika 1956–59; Chief Sec. to Govt. 1959–60; Deputy Gov. of Tanganyika 1960–61; M.P. (Southampton Test) 1964–66; Commonwealth Parl. Assen. Del. to Nigeria 1965; Visiting Prof. Colorado Univ. 1961–62, 1966, 1973, 1974; mem. Kenya Constituencies Delimitation Comm. 1962; Adviser to Ottoman Bank 1962–64; mem. Exec. Cttee. Overseas Employers' Fed. 1963–65; Vice-Chair. Int. team to review structure and org. of FAO, Rome 1967; Dir. Programmes in Diplomacy, Carnegie Endowment, New York 1967–68; Official Mission for British Govt. to New Hebrides 1969; Chair. various Civil Service Selection Bds. 1971–80. *Publications:* Parliament as an Export (co-author) 1966, The Emperor's Guest 1971 (many editions including a Talking Book Edition for the Blind 1982); numerous articles on the United Nations, Commonwealth, Middle East and African affairs; short stories. *Address:* c/o Lloyds Bank, Stock Exchange Branch, 111 Old Broad Street, London, EC2N 1AU; 4 North Court, Great Peter Street, London, S.W.1, England.

FLEXNER, James Thomas; American author; b. 13 Jan. 1908, New York; s. of Simon Flexner and Helen Thomas Flexner; m. Beatrice Hudson 1950; one c.; ed. Lincoln School of Teachers Coll. and Harvard Univ.; Reporter, New York Herald Tribune 1929–31; Exec. Sec. Noise Abatement Comm. of New York City Bd. of Health 1931–33; Pres. American Center PEN 1954–55, Soc. of American Historians 1975–77; mem. American Acad. and Inst. of Arts and Letters; Parkman Prize 1962, Pulitzer Prize 1972, Nat. Book Award 1972. *Publications:* Doctors on Horseback 1937, America's Old Masters 1938, Steamboats Come True 1944, History of American Painting, 3 vols. 1947, 1954, 1962, The Traitor and the Spy 1953, George Washington, (4 vols.) 1965, 1967, 1970, 1972, Washington, The Indispensable Man 1974, The Young Hamilton 1978, An American Saga: The Story of

Helen Thomas and Simon Flexner 1983. *Address:* 530 East 86th Street, New York, N.Y. 10028, U.S.A.

FLIMM, Jürgen; German theatre director; b. 17 July 1941, Giessen; s. of Dr. Werner Flimm and Dr. Ellen Flimm; early work at the Munich Kammerspielen (studio theatre); Dir. Nationaltheater, Mannheim 1972-73; Prin. Dir. Thalia Theater, Hamburg 1973-74; directed plays in Munich, Hamburg, Bochum and Frankfurt 1974-79; Dir. Cologne Theatre 1979-85, Thalia Theatre, Hamburg 1985-. *Address:* Osterleystrasse 72, D-2000 Hamburg 55, Federal Republic of Germany.

FLINDT, Flemming Ole; Danish ballet dancer and choreographer; b. 30 Sept. 1936; m. Vivi Gelker 1967; three d.; ed. Royal Danish Ballet School; ballet dancer 1955-; solo dancer Royal Theatre, Copenhagen 1957-60; Danseur Etoile Théâtre Nat. de l'Opéra, Paris 1960-65; Artist Dir. Royal Danish Ballet 1966-78, Dallas Ballet 1981-; guest artist Royal Ballet Covent Garden 1963; guest choreographer Metropolitan Opera House, New York and la Scala, Milan 1965; Grand Prix Italia (La Leçon) 1963. *Choreography:* La leçon, (Ionesco) 1963, Jeune homme à marier, (Ionesco) 1964, The Three Musketeers 1966, The Miraculous Mandarin 1966, The Triumph of Death, Dreamland 1974; choreography and libretto: Felix Luna 1973. *Address:* Dallas Ballet Asscn. Inc., 1925 Elm Street, Suite 300, Dallas, Tex. 75201, U.S.A.

FLIRI, Franz, DR.PHIL.; Austrian professor of geography; b. 9 Feb. 1918, Baumkirchen; s. of Franz J. Fliri and Maria Plank; m. 1st Anna Loidl 1940, 2nd Katharina Salzmann 1975; one s. three d.; mil. service 1937-45; farmer 1946-59; teacher 1959-63; Docent 1963; Extraordinary Prof. of Geography, Univ. of Innsbrück 1964-68, Prof. 1968-87, Prof. Emer. 1987-, Dean, Faculty of Philosophy 1973-74, Rector 1977-79; mem. Austrian Acad., Akad. Leopoldina; Dr. h.c. (Vienna). *Publications:* Klima der Alpen (Tirol) 1975, Synoptische Klimatographie der Alpen 1984, Dorfbuch Baumkirchen 1985; several articles in research journals. *Leisure interest:* farming. *Address:* 6121 Baumkirchen (Tirol), Dorfstrasse 13, Austria. *Telephone:* 05224-2957.

FLITNER, Andreas, DR. PHIL., M.A.; German educationist; b. 28 Sept. 1922, Jena; s. of Wilhelm Flitner and Elisabeth Czapski; m. Sonia Christ 1950; one s. six d.; ed. Gymnasium "Christianeum", Hamburg, and Univs. of Hamburg, Heidelberg, Basel and Oxford; Lecturer in German, Univ. of Cambridge 1950-51; Tutor, Leibniz-Kolleg, Tübingen and High School Teacher 1951-54; Dozent in Educ., Tübingen 1955; Extraordinary Prof. of Educ., Erlangen 1956-58; Prof. of Educ., Univ. of Tübingen 1958-; Visiting Prof. Evanston, Ill. 1967, London 1976. *Publications:* Erasmus im Urteil seiner Nachwelt 1952, Die politische Erziehung in Deutschland—Geschichte und Probleme 1957, Wege zur pädagogischen Anthropologie (with T. Ballauff) 1963, Die Jugend und die überlieferten Erziehungsmächte (with G. Bittner) 1965, Soziologische Jugendforschung — Darstellung und Kritik aus pädagogischer Sicht 1963, Goethe an W. von Humboldt, Goethe—Jb. 1965, Brennpunkte gegenwärtiger Pädagogik, Studien zur Schul- und Sozialerziehung 1969, Das Basler Winckelmann-Porträt 1971, Spielen-Lernen, Praxis und Deutung des Kinderspiels 1972, Missratener Fortschritt, Pädagogische Anmerkungen zur Bildungspolitik 1977, Konrad, sprach die Frau Mama—Über Erziehung und Nicht-Erziehung 1985, Lernen mit Kopf und Hand (jt. author) 1983, Für das Leben oder für die Schule? Pädagogische und politische Essays 1987; Ed. Erasmus, Briefe 1956, J. A. Comenius, Grosse Didaktik 1954, Wilhelm v. Humboldt, works in 5 vols. (with K. Giel) 1960-81, Einführung in pädagogisches Sehen und Denken (with H. Scheuerl) 1984, Erziehung in Wissenschaft und Praxis (30 vols.) 1967-79, Das Kinderspiel, Texte 1978, Der Numerus clausus und seine Folgen 1976, Abitur-Normen gefährden die Schule (with D. Lenzen) 1977; Co-Ed. Sozialpädagogik (10 vols.) 1968-75, Zeitschrift für Pädagogik 1962- (Chair. 1969-80). *Address:* Im Rotbad 43, 7400 Tübingen, Federal Republic of Germany. *Telephone:* 292407.

FLOHN, Hermann, DR.RER.NAT.; German meteorologist; b. 19 Feb. 1912, Frankfurt/Main; s. of Jacob Flohn and A. (née Burckhard) Flohn; m. Elisabeth Hobe 1937; one d.; ed. Univs. of Frankfurt, Innsbruck and Würzburg; staff mem. Dept. of Meteorology, Berlin 1935-39; officer in Luftwaffe 1939-45; at Cen. Office for Meteorology, Bad Kiningen 1946-52, German Meteorological Office, Offenbach 1952-61; Prof. of Climatology Univ. of Würzburg 1953, Ordinary Prof. Univ. of Bonn and Dir. Meteorological Inst. 1961-77, Prof. Emer. 1977-; Cothenius Medal (Gold), A. Wegener Medal, Int. Meteorilogical Org. Prize 1986; mem. Acad. Leopoldina, Halle, also Acads. of Munich, Düsseldorf and Brussels. *Publications:* Climate and Weather (trans. into 6 languages) 1969, Jt. Ed. The Climate of Europe: Past, Present and Future 1984, Das Problem der Klimaänderungen in Verganenheit und Zukunft, XVIII 1985. *Address:* Manserglerweg 19, 5300 Bonn 1, Federal Republic of Germany. *Telephone:* 0228-735104.

FLORAKIS, Charilaos Ioannoy; Greek politician; b. 20 July 1914, Rahoula; ed. Coll. of Telegraph, Telephone, Post Office and Public Utility, law school; fmr. Sec. Exec. Cttee., Fed. of Telegraphists; joined CP of Greece (KKE) during war; partisan during occupation; Commdr. unit of First Div. of Democratic Army of Greece during civil war; mem. Cen. Cttee. KKE 1949, First Sec. 1973, Gen. Sec. 1978-; M.P. for Athens 1974, 1977, 1981-; Friendship of the People Award (U.S.S.R.), Karl Marx

Decoration (G.D.R.), Dimitrov Decoration (Bulgaria), Elas Decoration, Decoration of Military Valour, (Democratic Army of Greece), Order of Lenin 1984. *Address:* Odos Kapodistriou 16, Athens 147, Greece. *Telephone:* 36 39 788/36 34 334.

FLORES TORRES, Gen. Jorge; Peruvian army officer and government minister; b. 11 April 1929, Tacna; began mil. career as soldier in Cavalry School 1947; cadet at Chorrillos Mil. School 1948-52; fmr. Instructor at School of Equitation, Dir. of Cavalry School, Chief of Nat. Defence Secr., Maj.-Gen. First Mil. Region, Piura; rank of Gen. 1984; Minister of Defence (Army) 1985. *Address:* Ministry of Defence (Army), Avenida Boulevar s/n, Lima, Peru. *Telephone:* 359567.

FLORIN, Peter; German diplomatist; b. 2 Oct. 1921, Cologne; s. of Wilhelm Florin; m.; three c.; ed. Karl-Liebknecht-Schule and Mendeleyev Coll. of Chem., Moscow; Asst., later Ed., Nat. Cttee. for a Free Germany weekly magazine, Moscow; mem. CP (KPD) 1945; Vice-Pres. Wittenberg dist. 1945; Ed.-in-Chief, Halle 1946-48; Head of Dept., Ministry of Foreign Affairs, G.D.R. 1949-52; Head of Foreign Affairs and Int. Relations Dept., Cen. Cttee. SED 1953-66, cand. mem. Cen. Cttee. 1954-58, mem. Cen. Cttee. 1958-; mem. Volkskammer 1953-; Amb. to Czechoslovakia 1967-69; State Sec., First Deputy Minister of Foreign Affairs 1969-73; Perm. Rep. to UN 1973-82; Order of the Red Star (U.S.S.R.), Vaterländischer Verdienstorden in Silver, in Gold (twice), and other decorations. *Address:* c/o Ministry of Foreign Affairs, Berlin, German Democratic Republic.

FLOWERS, Baron (Life Peer) cr. 1979, of Queen's Gate in the City of Westminster; **Brian Hilton Flowers;** M.A., D.SC., F.INST.P., F.R.S.; British physicist; b. 13 Sept. 1924, Blackburn, Lancs.; s. of late Rev. Harold J. Flowers and of Marion V. (née Hilton) Flowers; m. Mary Frances Behrens 1951; two step s.; ed. Gonville and Caius Coll., Cambridge, and Univ. of Birmingham; Anglo-Canadian Atomic Energy Mission (Tube Alloys) at Montreal and Chalk River, Canada 1944; Atomic Energy Research Establishment, Harwell 1946, Head of Theoretical Physics Div. 1952, Chief Research Scientist 1958; Prof. Theoretical Physics, Manchester Univ. 1958-61, Langworthy Prof. of Physics 1961-72; Pres. Inst. of Physics 1972-74, European Science Foundation 1974-80, Nat. Soc. for Clean Air 1977-79; Fellow, Physical Soc. 1956, mem. Council 1960, 1961; mem. Council Inst. of Physics 1961, Vice-Pres. 1962-66; mem. Advisory Council on Scientific Policy 1962-64, Council on Scientific Policy 1965-67, Advisory Bd. for the Research Councils 1972-73; Del. Pugwash Conf. Cambridge 1962, Dubrovnik 1963, Karlovy Vary 1964, Venice 1965, Oxford 1972; Chair. Steering Cttee. of the Nat. Physical Lab. 1965-68; Chair. Computer Bd. for Univs. and Research Councils 1966-70, Science Research Council 1967-73, Cttee. of Vice-Chancellors and Principals 1983-85, Nuffield Foundation Sept. 1987-; Council, Royal Coll. of Art 1980-85; part-time mem. UKAEA 1976-81; Rector, Imperial Coll., Univ. of London 1973-85; Vice-Chancellor Univ. of London Sept. 1985-; Chair. Royal Comm. on Environmental Pollution 1973-76, Standing Comm. on Energy and the Environment 1978-81, Univs. Industry Advisory Cttee. 1984-85; Sr. Fellow, Royal Coll. of Art 1983; Hon. Fellow (Gonville and Caius Coll., Cambridge) 1974, (Newcastle Polytechnic) 1984, (Univ. of Manchester Inst. of Science and Tech.) 1985; Hon. D.Sc. (Sussex) 1968, (Wales) 1972, (Leicester) 1973, (Manchester) 1973, (Liverpool) 1974, (Bristol) 1982, Hon. Sc. D. (Dublin) 1984; Hon. LL.D. (Dundee, Oxford) 1985, (Glasgow) 1987; Hon. D.Eng. (Nova Scotia) 1983; Chevalier Légion d'honneur 1975, Officier 1981; Corresp. mem. Swiss Acad. of Eng. Sciences 1986; Founder-mem. SDP 1981. *Publications:* numerous scientific papers in the journals of learned societies on nuclear reactions and the structure of atomic nuclei, on science policy and on energy and the environment. *Leisure interests:* music, painting, walking. *Address:* Senate House, University of London, Malet Street, London, WC1E 7HU, England. *Telephone:* 01-636 8000.

FLYNN, John Gerrard, M.A.; British diplomatist; b. 23 April 1937, Greenock; s. of the late Thomas Flynn and Mary (née Chisholm) Flynn; m. Drina Anne Coates 1973; one s. one d.; ed. Univ. of Glasgow; entered Foreign Office 1965, Second Sec. Lusaka 1966, First Sec. Foreign Office 1968; Head of Chancery Montevideo, 1971; FCO 1976; Chargé d'Affaires Luanda 1978; Counsellor Brasilia 1979, Madrid 1982; High Commr. in Swaziland 1987-. *Leisure interests:* golf, walking, music. *Address:* c/o Foreign and Commonwealth Office, (Mbabane), King Charles Street, London, SW1A 2AH, England.

FLYNN, Padraig; Irish politician; b. 9 May 1939, Castlebar; m. Dorothy Tynan; one s. three d.; ed. St. Patrick's Teacher Training Coll., Dublin; fmr. school teacher and publican; mem. Mayo County Council 1967-86; mem. Dail. 1977-; Minister of State, Dept. of Transport and Power 1980-81; Minister for the Gaeltacht March-Oct. 1982; Minister for Trade, Commerce and Tourism Oct.-Dec. 1982; Minister for Environment 1987-; Fianna Fail. *Address:* Newtown Street, Castlebar, Co. Mayo, Republic of Ireland. *Telephone:* 094 22686.

FO, Dario; Italian actor, clown and playwright; m. Franca Rame 1954; Comedian teatro di rivista; theatre group La Comune. *Publications:* Accidental Death of an Anarchist, Can't Pay? Won't Pay!, Manuale et minimo dell attore 1987, Mistero Buffo and other political dramas.

FOBES, John Edwin; American diplomatist and international official; b. 16 March 1918, Chicago, Ill.; s. of Wilfred Franklin Fobes and Mabel

Skogsberg; m. Hazel Ward Weaver 1941; one s. one d.; ed. Northwestern Univ., Fletcher School of Law and Diplomacy and School for Advanced Int. Studies, Johns Hopkins Univ. U.S.; Army Air Force 1942–45; UN Secr., London and New York 1945–46; Admin. Analyst, U.S. Bureau of the Budget 1947–48; Asst. Dir. Tech. Assistance, U.S. Marshall Plan, Washington 1948–51; Deputy Dir. Org. and Planning, Mutual Security Agency, Washington 1951–52; Adviser, U.S. Del. to NATO and European Regional Orgs., Paris 1952–55; Dir. Office of Int. Admin., Dept. of State 1955–59; (elected) mem. UN Advisory Cttee. on Admin. and Budgetary Questions 1955–60; Sr. Adviser, U.S. Del. to the 10th–14th sessions of UN Gen. Assembly; Special Adviser to Asst. Sec. of State, Washington 1959–60; Program Officer and Deputy Dir. U.S. Agency for Int. Devt. Mission to India 1960–64; Asst. Dir.-Gen. (Admin.), UNESCO, Paris 1964–70, Deputy Dir.-Gen. 1971–77, Chair. U.S. Nat. Comm. for UNESCO 1980–81, Vice-Chair. 1982–83; Pres. Americans for Universality of UNESCO 1984–, Econ. Devt. Foundation 1985–; Chair. U.S. Assen. for the Club of Rome 1982–87; mem. Club of Rome 1983–; Pres. American Library in Paris 1968–70; Visiting Scholar Indiana and Harvard Univs. 1970, D. H. Bucknell Univ. 1973; Visiting Scholar and Adviser on Int. Studies Duke Univ. 1978–82, Univ. of North Carolina, Adjunct Prof. of Political Science Western Carolina Univ. 1982–. *Leisure interests:* community service, walking, reading, writing. *Address:* 28 Beaverbrook Road, Asheville, N.C. 28804, U.S.A. *Telephone:* (704) 253-5383.

FOCCART, Jacques; French civil servant; b. 31 Aug. 1913, Ambrières; s. of Guillaume Foccart and Elmire de Courtemanche de la Clémandière; m. Isabelle Fenoglio 1939; ed. Coll. de l'Immaculée Conception, Laval; exporter 1935–; Adviser, Rassemblement du Peuple français (RPF) Group, Council of the Repub. 1952–58; Sec.-Gen. RPF 1954; Tech. Adviser, Gen. de Gaulle's office (Pres. of the Council) 1958–59; Tech. Adviser in Secr.-Gen. of Presidency of Repub. 1959; Sec.-Gen. Presidency for French Community and African and Malagasy Affairs 1960–69, 1969–74; Adviser to Prime Minister Jacques Chirac 1986–88; Dir. Société R. Gonfreville 1975–; Commdr. Légion d'honneur, Croix de guerre 1939–45, Rosette de la Résistance. *Address:* 57 rue de Varenne, 75700, Paris (Office); Villa Charlotte, 95270 Luzarches, France (Home).

FOCK, Jenő; Hungarian politician; b. 17 May 1916, Budapest; Mechanic; Nat. Youth Cttee. CP 1937, Deputy Minister, Metallurgy and Eng. 1951–54; Sec. Nat. Council of Trade Unions 1955–57; Sec. Cen. Cttee. Hungarian Socialist Workers' party 1957–61, mem. Political Cttee. 1957–80; a Deputy Chair. Council of Ministers 1961–67, Chair. 1967–75; Co-Pres. Fed. of Tech. and Scientific Socs.; Hero of Socialist Labour 1975. *Leisure interests:* literature, fine arts, watching football, playing tennis. *Publication:* A szocializmus épitésének gazdaságpolitikája (Political Economy of Socialism in the State of Construction) 1972. *Address:* Federation of Technical and Scientific Societies, 1055 Budapest, Kossuth Lajos tér 6/8, Hungary. *Telephone:* 533-333.

FOCKE, Katharina, DR.PHIL.; German journalist and politician; b. 1922, Bonn; d. of Ernest Friedlander and Dr. Franziska (née Schulz) Friedlander; m. Dr. Ernst Günter Focke 1954 (died 1961); ed. Hamburg Univ.; journalist 1946–54; joined Social Democratic Party 1964; mem. North Rhine Westphalia Diet 1966; mem. Bundestag 1969–80; Parl. State Sec. of Fed. Chancellor 1969–72; Fed. Minister for Youth, Family Affairs and Health 1972–76; mem. Cttee. for Devt. of Deutscher Bundestag 1976–79, European Parl. 1979, Cttee. for Devt. and Cooperation of European Parl. 1979; Social Democrat. *Publications:* Europa über den Nationen 1962, Europäer in Frankreich 1965. *Address:* 5300 Bonn 1, Bundeshaus H.T. 210, Federal Republic of Germany. *Telephone:* 16-38-82.

FOGEL, Robert William, PH.D.; American historian, university professor and economist; b. 1 July 1926, New York; s. of Harry Gregory and Elizabeth (Mitnik) Fogel; m. Enid Cassandra Morgan 1949; two s.; ed. Cornell, Columbia, Cambridge, Harvard and Johns Hopkins Univs.; Instructor, Johns Hopkins Univ. 1958–59; Asst. Prof., Univ. of Rochester 1960–64; Assoc. Prof., Univ. of Chicago 1964–65, Prof. 1965–75; Prof., Harvard Univ. 1975–81; Prof. of Econs. and Business, Univ. of Chicago 1981–, Dir. Center for Population Econs. 1981–; Chair. History Advisory Cttee. of the Math. Social Science Bd. 1965–72; Pres. Econ. History Assen. 1977–78; Social Science History Assen. 1980–81; Nat. Bureau of Econ. Research Assoc.; Fellow Nat. Soc., American Acad. of Arts and Sciences, N.A.S., Royal Historical Soc., A.A.A.S.; Arthur H. Cole Prize 1968, Schumpeter Prize 1971, Bancroft Prize in American History 1975. *Publications:* The Union Pacific Railroad 1960, Railroads and American Economic Growth 1972, Time on the Cross 1974, Ten Lectures on the New Economic History 1977, Which Road to the Past?: Two Views of History 1983. *Leisure interests:* carpentry, photography. *Address:* Center for Population Economics, University of Chicago, Graduate School of Business, 1101 East 58th Street, Chicago, Ill. 60637 (Office); 5321 S. University Avenue, Chicago, Ill. 60615, U.S.A. (Home).

FOGG, Gordon Elliott, C.B.E., B.SC., PH.D., SC.D., LL.D., F.I.BIOL., F.R.S.; British botanist; b. 26 April 1919, Langar, Notts.; s. of Rev. Leslie Charles Fogg and Doris Mary Fogg (née Elliott); m. Elizabeth Beryl Llechid Jones 1945; one s. one d.; ed. Dulwich Coll., Queen Mary Coll., Univ. of London, and St. John's Coll., Cambridge; Asst. for Seaweed Survey of Britain, Marine Biological Assen. 1942; Plant Physiologist, Pest Control Ltd. 1943–45; Asst.

Lecturer, Dept. of Botany, Univ. Coll. London 1945–47, Lecturer 1947–53, Reader 1953–60; Prof. of Botany in Univ. of London at Westfield Coll. 1960–71; Prof. of Marine Biology, Univ. Coll. of N. Wales 1971–85, Prof. Emer., Univ. of Wales 1985–; Rockefeller Fellow 1954; Hon. Sec. Inst. of Biology 1953–56, Vice-Pres. 1961–62, Pres. 1976–77; Botanical Sec., Soc. for Experimental Biology 1957–60; Pres. British Phycological Soc. 1962–63, Int. Phycological Soc. 1964; Jt. Hon. Sec. Xth Int. Botanical Congress, Edinburgh 1964; Visiting Research Worker, British Antarctic Survey 1966, 1974, 1979; Gen. Sec. British Assen. 1967–72; Royal Soc./Leverhulme Visiting Prof. Univ. of Kerala 1970; Chair. of Council, Freshwater Biol. Assen. 1974–85; Trustee, British Museum (Natural History) 1976–85, Royal Botanic Gardens, Kew 1983–; mem. Royal Comm. on Environmental Pollution 1979–85, Natural Environment Research Council 1981–82; Leverhulme Emer. Fellowship 1986–88. *Publications:* the Metabolism of Algae 1953, The Growth of Plants 1963, Algal Cultures and Phytoplankton Ecology (with B. A. Thake) 1987, Photosynthesis 1968, The Blue-Green Algae (with W. D. P. Stewart, P. Fay and A. E. Walsby) 1973. *Leisure interests:* water-colour painting, walking, listening to music, photography. *Address:* Marine Science Laboratories, Menai Bridge, Anglesey, Gwynedd, LL59 5EY, Wales. *Telephone:* 0248712-641.

FOGH-ANDERSEN, Poul, M.D., DR.MED.; Danish plastic surgeon; b. 7 Dec. 1913, Copenhagen; s. of late Vagn Fogh-Andersen and Lili Fogh-Andersen (née Nielsen); m. Birgit Duelund 1943; one s. two d.; ed. St. Jörgen's High School and Copenhagen Univ.; Scientific Asst., Univ. Inst. of Human Genetics, Copenhagen 1939–40; Asst., various Copenhagen hospitals 1941–45; Asst. Surgeon, Copenhagen Municipal Hosp. 1946–49; First Asst. surgeon, Univ. Hosp. 1950–53, Deaconess Hosp. 1954–55; Chief Surgeon, Dept. of Surgery A (Plastic Surgery), Deaconess Hosp. Copenhagen 1956–84; Consultant Plastic Surgeon, Univ. Hosp. 1956–62; Plastic Surgeon, Dronning Louise's Children's Hosp. Copenhagen 1959–71; Consultant Surgeon, State Inst. for Defective Speech 1956–84; Danish Ed. Scandinavian Journal of Plastic and Reconstructive Surgery 1967–; Co-founder and Pres. Danish Soc. of Plastic and Reconstructive Surgery 1964–69; Pres. Org. Danish Plastic Surgeons 1966–84, Scandinavian Assen. of Plastic Surgeons 1966–68; Corresp. mem. American Soc. of Plastic and Reconstructive Surgery 1955–, Swedish Assen. of Plastic Surgeons 1966–, British Assen. of Plastic Surgeons 1973–; Hon. mem. Japan Soc. of Plastic and Reconstructive Surgery 1975–; Gen. Sec. 2nd Int. Congress on Cleft Palate, Copenhagen, Aug. 1973; Honors Award, American Cleft Palate Assen. 1973; Repub. of Korea Plaque of Appreciation 1980. *Publications:* Inheritance of Harelip and Cleft Palate (Thesis) 1942, chapters in textbooks and articles in scientific periodicals on surgery and plastic surgery. *Leisure interest:* history of plastic surgery. *Address:* 16 Carl Feilbergs Vej, 2000 Copenhagen F, Denmark. *Telephone:* 866516.

FOIGHEL, Isi, D.LL.; Danish professor of jurisprudence and politician; b. 21 Dec. 1927, Chemnitz, Germany; s. of Hania Foighel; emigrated to Denmark in early 1930s; Prof. of Jurisprudence, Univ. of Copenhagen 1964–80, Prof. of Tax Law 1980–; Chair. of Comm. for Home Rule for Greenland; M.P. 1984–, Minister for Fiscal Affairs 1984–87; Conservative. *Address:* Ministry of Finance, Christiansborg Slotsplads 1, 1218 Copenhagen K, Denmark. *Telephone:* (01) 92-65-00.

FOJTÍK, Jan, PHDR., CSC.; Czechoslovak politician; b. 1 March 1928, Milotice nad Bečvou; ed. Charles Univ. Prague and Acad. of Social Sciences of Cen. Cttee. of CPSU Moscow; Ed. of journal Soviet Science-Philosophy, Czechoslovak-Soviet Inst. 1950–51; Ed. Rudé právo 1951–68; Ed.-in-Chief of Nová mysl (New Thought); Rector of School of Political Studies Cen. Cttee., CP of Czechoslovakia 1969; Alt. mem. Cen. Cttee., CP of Czechoslovakia 1966–69, mem. 1969–, Sec. 1969–; mem. Cen. Cttee. Secr. 1970–; Deputy to House of People, Fed. Assembly 1969–71; Chair. Cultural Cttee., House of the People 1969; Deputy to House of Nations, Fed. Assembly 1971–; Cand. mem. Presidium Cen. Cttee. of CP of Czechoslovakia 1982–88, mem. 1988–; Chair. CP of Czechoslovakia Educ. Comm. 1988–; Award for Merits in Construction 1963, State Journalists' Prize 1965, Friendship Medal (Mongolia) 1972, Order of Victorious February 1973, Order of Republic 1978. *Address:* Central Committee of CP of Czechoslovakia, Prague 1, nábr. Kyjevské brigády 12, Czechoslovakia (Office).

FOLDES, Andor; American concert pianist; b. 21 Dec. 1913, Budapest, Hungary; s. of Emil Foldes and Valerie Ipolyi; m. Lili Rendy 1940; ed. Classical Gymnasium, Budapest, and under Dohnányi, Liszt Acad. of Music, Budapest; Debut with Budapest Philharmonic Orchestra 1921; First Prize, Int. Franz Liszt Piano Competition, Budapest 1933; Head Piano Master Class, Conservatory, Saarbrücken 1957–65; numerous world tours; first Western pianist to play in Peking (1978) since Cultural Revolution; resident in U.S. 1939–61, Switzerland 1961–; Grosses Bundesverdienstkreuz (Fed. Repub. of Germany), Ordre du Mérite culturel et artistique (France), Médaille d'argent (City of Paris) 1970. *Publications:* Keys to the Keyboard 1950, Gibt es einen zeitgenössischen Beethoven-Stil? 1963. *Leisure interests:* art collecting, literature, hiking, swimming, theatre, people. *Address:* 8704 Herrliberg, Zürich, Switzerland.

FOLEY, Maurice; British politician; b. 9 Oct. 1925; s. of Jeremiah and Agnes Foley; m. Catherine O'Riordan 1952; three s. one d.; ed. St. Mary's Coll., Middlesbrough; worked as electrical fitter; mem. Electrical Trades Union 1941–46, Transport and Gen. Workers' Union 1948–; M.P. 1963–73;

Jt. Parl. Under-Sec. Home Office 1966–67; Minister of State, Foreign Office 1968–70; EEC Deputy Dir.-Gen. for Devt. 1973–86. *Address:* Gillingham House, Gillingham Street, London, S.W.1, England.

FOLEY, Thomas Stephen, B.A., LL.B.; American politician; b. 6 March 1929, Spokane, Wash.; s. of Ralph E. Foley and Helen Marie Higgins; m. Heather Strachan 1968; ed. Washington Univ.; Partner Higgins and Foley 1957–58; Deputy Prosecuting Attorney, Spokane Co. 1958–60; Instructor of Law, Gonzaga Univ. 1958–60; Asst. Attorney Gen., Wash. State 1960–61; Interior and Insular Affairs Cttee., U.S. Senate, Washington 1961–64; mem. 89th–100th Congresses from 5th Dist. Wash.; Chair. Agric. Cttee. 1975–81, Vice-Chair. 1981–; Chair. House Democratic Caucus 1976–80, House Majority Whip 1981–87, Majority Leader Jan. 1987–; Democrat. *Address:* c/o House of Representatives, H148 Capitol Building, Washington, D.C. 20515, U.S.A.

FOLKERS, Karl, PH.D.; American professor of chemistry; b. 1 Sept. 1906, Decatur, Ill.; s. of August W. Folkers and Laura Black Folkers; m. Selma Johnson 1932; one s. one d.; ed. Univs. of Ill. and Wisconsin and Yale Univ.; with Merck and Co. Inc., Rahway, N.J. 1934–62, in Lab. of Pure Research 1934, Asst. Dir. of Research 1938, Dir. of Organic and Biochemical Dept. 1945, Assoc. Dir. of Research and Devt. Div. 1951, Dir. of Organic and Biological Chemical Research 1953, Exec. Dir. of Fundamental Research 1956, Vice-Pres. for Exploratory Research 1962; Pres. and C.E.O. Stanford Research Inst., Menlo Park, Calif. 1963; Prof. of Chem. and Dir. of Inst. for Biomedical Research, Univ. of Tex. 1968–; Harrison-Howe Recipient and Lecturer 1949; Pres. A.C.S. 1962; mem. N.A.S., A.C.S., A.A.A.S. and other socs.; Foreign mem. Royal Swedish Acad. of Eng. Sciences; mem. Bd. of Trustees Gordon Reseach Confs. 1971–77; mem. Council of Bd. of Trustees Stanford Research Inst. 1971–74, Int. Advisory Bd. for Comprehensive Medicinal Chem. 1987, A.C.S. Council Steering Cttee. 1987; Hon. mem. Soc. Italiana di Scienze Farmaceutiche; Hon. D.Phar. (Uppsala, Sweden), Hon D.Sc. (Wisconsin and Illinois, and Philadelphia Coll. of Pharmacy and Science); numerous awards including Mead Johnson Co. Award (co-recipient) 1940, Presidential Certificate of Merit 1948, Perkins Medal 1960, Nichols Medal 1967, Von Meter Prize of American Thyroid Asscn. (co-recipient), first Robert A. Welch Award and Medal for research in the life processes 1972, Acad. of Pharmaceutical Sciences Research Achievement Award in Pharmaceutical and Medicinal Chem. 1974, Priestley Medal 1986, Univ. of Ill. Alumni Achievement Award 1986. *Publications:* Vitamins and Coenzymes (with Arthur F. Wagner and K. Folkers) 1964; and 882 publs. in the field of vitamins, antibiotics, hormones and drugs, 348 of which are on Coenzyme Q. *Address:* Institute for Biomedical Research, The University of Texas at Austin, Austin, Tex. 78712; 6406 Mesa Drive, Austin, Tex. 78731, U.S.A. (Home). *Telephone:* (512) 471-7174 and (512) 471-7292 (Office).

FOLTINEK, Herbert, DR. PHIL.; Austrian literary historian; b. 29 April 1930, Vienna; s. of Helmut Foltinek and Elisabeth Foltinek (née Jaeschke); m. Elisabeth Sengstschmid 1964; ed. Univ. of Vienna and Univ. of London; lecturer in German, Univ. of Cambridge 1957–59; Asst., English Dept., Univ. of Vienna 1959–66, Docent 1966, Prof. of English and American Language and Literature 1966–; mem. Austrian Acad. of Sciences. *Publications:* Arthur Schnitzler: Grosse Szene (Ed.) 1959, Vorstufen zum Viktorianischen Realismus: Der englische Roman von Jane Austen bis Charles Dickens 1968, Susan Ferrier: Marriage (Ed.) 1971, Fielding's Tom Jones und das österreichische Drama 1976, George Eliot 1982, Dramatische Ansätze in der englischen Romanliteratur des achtzehnten Jahrhunderts 1983, Charles Dickens und der Zwang des Systems 1987. *Address:* Institut für Anglistik und Amerikanistik, A-1010 Vienna, Universitätsstrasse 7 (Office); Ferrogasse 48/7, A-1180 Vienna, Austria (Home). *Telephone:* 43 00 2564 (Office).

FOMICHENKO, Konstantin Yefimovich; Soviet party official and diplomatist; b. 1927; mem. CPSU 1948–; party work 1945–58; graduated from Party High School of Cen. Cttee. of CPSU 1958; mem. Chelyabinsk Dist. Cttee. of CPSU 1955–70, Sec. 1970–73; mem. Cen. Cttee. of CPSU 1973–77; Sec. Cen. Cttee. of Kirghiz CP 1977–81; Amb. to Ethiopia 1981–86; mem. Supreme Soviet. *Address:* The Kremlin, Moscow, U.S.S.R.

FONCHA, John Ngu; Cameroonian politician; b. 21 June 1916, Nkwen, N.W. Prov.; s. of Foncha and Magdalene Ngebi; m. Anna Atang 1945; four s. three d.; ed. Bamenda Govt. School, St. Michael's School, Delta Pastoral Church, Buguma, St. Charles' Coll. Onitsha, Agric. Coll., Moore Plantation, Ibadan; Probationary teacher and teacher 1934–56; Co-founder Kamerun United Nat. Congress (KUNC) 1952; mem. Eastern Regional Ass., Nigeria 1951–53; mem. S. Cameroons Quasi-Regional Ass. 1954–65; Founder-Pres. Kamerun Nat. Democratic Party (KNDP) 1955–66; Prime Minister and Minister of Local Govt., Southern Cameroons 1959–61, Prime Minister W. Cameroon 1961–65; Vice-Pres. Fed. Repub. of Cameroon 1961–70; Co-founder and Vice-Pres. Cameroon Nat. Union (CNU) 1966; Vice-Pres. Political Bureau 1970–75, Cen. Cttee. 1975; Grand Chancellor of Cameroon Nat. Orders 1979. *Publication:* Farewell to Prime Minister and People of West Cameroon. *Leisure interest:* gardening. *Address:* P.O. Box 157, Bamenda, N.W. Province, United Republic of Cameroon.

FONDA, Jane; American actress; b. 21 Dec. 1937; d. of the late Henry Fonda and of Frances (née Seymour); m. 1st Roger Vadim (q.v.) 1967 (dissolved 1973), one d.; m. 2nd Tom Hayden 1973, one s.; ed. Vassar Coll. *Films include:* Tall Story 1960, A Walk on the Wild Side 1962, Period of Adjustment 1962, Sunday in New York 1963, The Love Cage 1963, La Ronde 1964, Histoires extraordinaires 1967, Barbarella 1968, They Shoot Horses Don't They? 1969, Klute 1970, Steelyard Blues 1972, Tout va bien 1972, A Doll's House 1973, The Blue Bird 1975, Fun with Dick and Jane 1976, Julia 1977, Coming Home 1978, California Suite 1978, The Electric Horseman 1979, The China Syndrome 1979, Nine to Five 1980, On Golden Pond 1981, Roll-Over 1981, Agnes of God 1985, The Morning After 1986, Old Gringo, Union Street; TV: The Dollmaker (ABC-TV) 1984 (Emmy Award); Acad. Award for Best Actress 1972, 1979; Golden Globe Award 1978. *Publications:* Jane Fonda's Workout Book 1982, Women Coming of Age 1984, Jane Fonda's new Workout and Weight Loss Program 1986. *Address:* Fonda Films, P.O. Box 491355, Los Angeles, Calif. 90049, U.S.A.

FONG, Hiram, LL.B., LL.D.; American attorney and politician; b. 1 Oct. 1907, Honolulu; s. of Lum Fong and Chai Ha Lum; m. Ellyn Lo; three s. one d.; ed. Kalihi Waena Grammar School, St. Louis Coll. and McKinley High School, Univ. of Hawaii and Harvard Law School; served in U.S. Army Air Corps 1942–44; Deputy City Attorney, Honolulu 1935–38; Vice-Speaker Hawaii Territorial House of Reps. 1944–48, Speaker 1948–54; Founder of law firm of Fong, Miho, Choy and Robinson; Chair. Finance Factors, Finance Investment Co., Finance Factors Foundation, Finance Enterprises, Ocean View Cemetery, Highway Construction and Market City Ltd.; U.S. Senator from Hawaii 1959–77; Hon. LL.D. (Univ. of Hawaii) 1953, (Tufts Univ., Lafayette Coll.) 1960, (Lynchberg Coll.) 1970, (Lincoln Univ.) 1971, (Univ. of Guam) 1974, (St. John's Univ.) 1975, (Calif. Western School of Law) 1976, (Tung Wu Univ. and China Acad., Taiwan) 1978; Hon. L.H.D. (Long Island Univ.) 1968; Order of Brilliant Star with Grand Cordon (Taiwan) 1976, Order of Diplomatic Service Merit (Repub. of Korea), Gwanghwan Medal 1977; Republican. *Address:* 1102 Alewa Drive, Honolulu Hawaii 96817, U.S.A.

FONTAINE, André; French journalist; b. 30 March 1921, Paris; s. of Georges Fontaine and Blanche Rochon-Duvignaud; m. Isabelle Cavaillé 1943; two s. one d.; ed. Coll. Ste. Marie de Monceau, Paris, Sorbonne and Faculty of Law, Paris Univ.; journalist 1946–, joined Le Monde 1947, Foreign Ed. 1951–69, Chief Ed. 1969–85, Ed.-in-Chief and Dir. Jan. 1985–; mem. Bd. French Inst. of Int. Relations, Bank Indosuez 1983–85; Chair. Group on Int. Strategy for the Ninth French Plan 1982; Atlas international Ed. of the Year 1976. *Publications:* L'alliance atlantique à l'heure du dégel 1960, History of the Cold War (two vols.) 1965, 1967, La guerre civile froide 1969, Le dernier quart du siècle 1976, La France au bois dormant 1978, Un seul lit pour deux rêves 1981, Sortir de l'hexagonie (with others) 1984. *Address:* Le Monde, 5 rue des Italiens, 75427 Paris Cédex 09, France. *Telephone:* 42.47.97.27.

FONTAINE, Maurice Alfred, D. ÈS SC.; French physiologist; b. 28 Oct. 1904, Savigny-sur-Orge; s. of Emile Fontaine and Lea Vadier; m. Yvonne Broca 1928; one s.; ed. Lycée Henri IV, Paris, and Faculty of Sciences and Faculty of Pharmacy, Univ. of Paris; various posts at Faculty of Sciences, Paris and Faculty of Pharmacy, Paris; Dir. Lab. at Ecole pratique des hautes études 1946–; Dir. Inst. Océanographique, Paris 1957–68, 1975–; Pres. Soc. Européenne d'Endocrinologie comparée 1969–; Dir. of Museum Nat. d'Histoire naturelle, Paris 1966–71; lectures on comparative and ecological physiology, particularly of marine animals; specializes in comparative endocrinology and fish migration; Dir. of Research in these fields and also the study of ectocrine substances in sea water and marine pollution; fmr. Pres. Acad. des Sciences; mem. Acad. nat. de Médecine, Acad. d'Agric., New York Acad. of Sciences; Commdr. Légion d'honneur, Commdr. Ordre de Sahametrei (Cambodia), Commdr. Ordre de St. Charles (Monaco). *Publication:* Physiologie (collection La Pléiade) 1969. *Leisure interest:* the sea. *Address:* 195 rue Saint-Jacques, 75005 Paris (Office); 25 rue Pierre Nicole, 75005 Paris, France (Home).

FONTEYN, Margot (see Arias, Señora Doña Margot Fonteyn de).

FOOT, Rt. Hon. Michael Mackintosh, P.C., M.P.; (brother of Lord Caradon, q.v.); British journalist and politician; b. 23 July 1913; s. of the late Isaac Foot; m. Jill Craigie 1949; ed. Forres School, Swanage, Leighton Park School, Reading, and Wadham Coll., Oxford; Pres. Oxford Union 1933; contested Monmouth 1935; Asst. Ed. Tribune 1937–38, Jt. Ed. 1948–52, Ed. 1952–59, Man. Dir. 1952–74; mem. staff Evening Standard 1938, Acting Ed. 1942–44; political columnist Daily Herald 1944–64; M.P. for Plymouth, Devonport 1945–55, for Ebbw Vale 1960–83, for Blaenau Gwent 1983–; fmr. Opposition spokesman on European Policy; Sec. of State for Employment 1974–76; Lord Pres. of Council, Leader of House of Commons 1976–79, Shadow Leader 1979–80; Deputy Leader of Labour Party 1976–80, Leader 1980–83; Hon. Fellow, Wadham Coll., Oxford 1969; Hon. mem. N.U.J. 1985; Hon. D.Litt. (Univ. of Wales) 1985; Spanish Republican Order of Liberation 1973; Labour. *Publications:* Armistice 1918–1939 1940, Trial of Mussolini 1943, Brendan and Beverley 1944, part author Guilty Men 1940 and Who Are the Patriots? 1949, Still At Large 1950, Full Speed Ahead 1950, The Pen and the Sword 1957, Parliament in Danger 1959, Aneurin Bevan Vol. I 1962, Vol. II 1973, Harold Wilson: A Pictorial Biography 1964, Debts of Honour 1980, Another Heart and Other Pulses 1984, Loyalists and Loners 1986, The Politics of Paradise 1988. *Address:* House of Commons, London, S.W.1, England.

FOOT, Philippa Ruth, M.A., F.B.A.; British university professor; b. 3 Oct. 1920, Owston Ferry, Lincs,; d. of W. S. B. Foot and Esther Cleveland Bosanquet; m. M. R. D. Foot 1945 (dissolved 1960); no. c.; ed. Somerville Coll. Oxford; Lecturer in Philosophy, Somerville Coll. Oxford 1947–50, Fellow and Tutor 1950–69, Vice-Prin. 1967–69, Sr. Research Fellow 1970–; Prof. of Philosophy, Univ. of Calif. Los Angeles 1974–, Griffin Prof. 1988–; fmr. Visiting Prof. Cornell Univ., M.I.T., Univ. of Calif. (Berkeley), Princeton Univ., City Univ. of New York; Pres. Pacific Div. American Philosophical Asscn. 1983–84; mem. American Acad. of Arts and Sciences. *Publications:* Theories of Ethics (ed.) 1967, Virtues and Vices 1978; articles and reviews in professional journals. *Leisure interests:* reading, walking, gardening. *Address:* 15 Walton Street, Oxford, OX1 2HG, England; Department of Philosophy, University of California, Los Angeles, Calif. 90024, U.S.A. *Telephone:* Oxford 57130.

FOOTS, Sir James (William), Kt., B.M.E., I.M.M.; Australian mining engineer and company director; b. 12 July 1916; m. Thora H. Thomas 1939; one s. two d.; ed. Coburg and Univ. High Schools, Melbourne and Melbourne Univ.; mining engineer, with North Broken Hill Ltd. 1938–43, Allied Works Council 1943–44, Lake George Mines Ltd. 1944–45, Zinc Corpn. Ltd. 1946–54; Asst. Gen. Man. Zinc Corpn. and New Broken Hill Consolidated Ltd. 1952–54; Gen. Man. Mount Isa Mines Ltd. 1955–66, Dir. 1956–, Man. Dir. 1966–70, Chair. 1970–81; Chief Exec. M.I.M. Holdings Ltd. 1970–81, Chair. 1970–83, Deputy Chair. 1983–87; Dir. Westpac Banking Corpn. 1971–, Chair. 1987–, ASARCO Inc. 1985–87, Castlemaine Tooheys Ltd. 1983–85; mem. Senate Queensland Univ. 1970–, Chancellor 1985–; Chair. Queensland Univ. Foundation Ltd. 1982–85, Gov. 1985–; Pres. Australian Mining Industry Council 1974, 1975; Pres. Australasian Inst. of Mining and Metallurgy 1974; Pres. 1986 Congress, Council of Mining and Metallurgical Insts.; Hon. M.Aus., Hon. D.Eng. *Address:* G.P.O. Box 2236, Brisbane, Queensland 4001, Australia. *Telephone:* 228 1852.

FORBES, Hon. Alexander James, M.C., D.PHIL.; Australian politician; b. Dec. 1923, Hobart, Tasmania; m. Margaret Allison Blackburn 1952; two s. three d.; ed. Knox Grammar School, Sydney, St. Peter's Coll., Adelaide, Royal Mil. Coll., Duntroon, and Univs. of Adelaide and Oxford; served with 2nd Australian Mountain Battery, New Guinea and Bougainville 1942; mem. British Occupation Forces, Japan 1946, on attachment to British Army 1946–47; student, Adelaide Univ. 1947–50; a resident tutor, St. Mark's Coll., Adelaide 1951; travelling scholarships until 1954; lecturer in Political Science, Univ. of Adelaide 1954–56; Liberal M.P. for Barker 1956–; Minister for the Army and Minister Assisting the Treas., also responsible for Navy 1963–64; Minister for Health 1966–71, for Immigration 1971–72; Opposition spokesman for Defence 1973–75; mem. Council, Australian Nat. Univ. 1961–63; Pres. Australian Inst. of Int. Affairs (S. Australian Branch) 1960–62; State Pres. Liberal Party (S. Australian Div.) 1979–82; Pres. Fed. Liberal Party 1982–85; mem. Council of Nat. Library 1979–, Chair. 1982–.

FORBES, Sir Archibald Finlayson, G.B.E., Kt.; British chartered accountant and business executive; b. 6 March 1903, Johnstone, Renfrewshire; s. of the late Charles Forbes and of Elizabeth (née Robertson) Forbes; m. Angela Gertrude Ely 1943 (died 1969); one s. two d.; ed. Paisley and Glasgow Univ.; Chartered accountant 1927; fmr. mem. firm of Thomson McLintock & Co.; mem. various Govt. Cttees. and Comms. 1931–65; Exec. Dir. Spillers Ltd. 1935–73; Dir. of Capital Finance, Air Ministry 1940; Deputy Sec. Ministry of Aircraft Production 1940–43; Controller of Repair, Equipment and Overseas Supplies for R.A.F. 1943–45; mem. Aircraft Supply Council 1943–45; Chair. Iron and Steel Bd. 1946–49; Chair. The Debenture Corpn. 1949–79; Deputy Chair. British Millers' Mutual Fund Ltd. 1940–52, Chair. 1952–62; Pres. Fed. of British Industries 1951–53; Chair. Iron and Steel Bd. 1953–59; Chair. Cen. Mining and Investment Corpn. 1959–64; Chair. Midland Bank 1964–75, Pres. 1975–83; Chair Midland and Int. Banks (MAIBL) 1964–76; Chair. Spillers Ltd. 1965–68, Pres. until 1980; Chair. Cttee. of London Clearing Banks 1970–72; Pres. British Bankers' Assen. 1970–72, Epsom Coll. 1964–; fmr. Dir. Shell Transport and Trading Co., Dunlop Holdings, English Electric Co.; fmr. Deputy Chair. Finance Corpn. for Industry; Hon. Treas. Nat. Assen. Leagues of Hospital Friends, British Wireless for the Blind Fund; mem. Governing Body Imperial Coll. of Science and Tech. 1959–75; Chair. Council for Arthritis and Rheumatism 1983–. *Leisure interests:* golf, fishing. *Address:* 40 Orchard Court, Portman Square, London, W1 9PB, England. *Telephone:* 01-935 9304.

FORBES, Bryan; British film executive, director and screenwriter; b. 22 July 1926, Stratford, London; m. Nanette Newman 1955; two d.; ed. West Ham Secondary School; studied at Royal Acad. Dramatic Art, first stage appearance 1942; served in Intelligence Corps 1944–48; entered films as actor 1948; wrote and co-produced The Angry Silence 1959; Dir. Whistle Down the Wind 1961; Writer and Dir. The L-Shaped Room 1962, Seance on a Wet Afternoon 1963, King Rat 1964; Writer Only Two Can Play 1962; Producer and Dir. The Wrong Box 1965; Writer, Producer and Dir. The Whisperers 1966, Deadfall 1967, The Madwoman of Chaillot 1968, The Raging Moon (Long Ago Tomorrow in U.S.A.) 1970; Dir. Macbeth 1980, Killing Jessica 1986; Writer, Producer and Dir. filmed biography of Dame Edith Evans for Yorkshire TV 1973; filmed documentary on life style of Elton John for ATV 1974; wrote and dir. The Slipper and the Rose 1975, Menage à trois (Better Late than Never in U.S.A.) 1981, The Endless

Game 1988; Dir. British segment of The Sunday Lovers 1980; Dir. The King in Yellow (for LWT Television) 1982, The Naked Face 1983; produced, wrote and dir. International Velvet 1977; Head of Production, Assoc. British Picture Corpn. 1969–71, subsequently became EMI Film Productions Ltd.; mem. Gen. Advisory Council of BBC 1966–69, Experimental Film Bd. of British Film Acad.; Govt. Nominee BBC Schools Broadcasting Council 1972–; Pres. Beatrix Potter Soc. 1982–, Nat. Youth Theatre 1984–; Trustee, Writers' Guild of G.B.; Dir. Capital Radio Ltd.; Dr. h.c. (Council for Nat. Academic Awards) 1987; British Film Acad. Award for The Angry Silence; Best Screenplay Awards for Only Two Can Play, Seance on a Wet Afternoon; UN Award for The L-Shaped Room; many Film Festival prizes. *Publications:* Truth Lies Sleeping (short stories) 1951, The Distant Laughter (novel) 1972, Notes for a Life (autobiog.) 1974, The Slipper and the Rose 1976, Ned's Girl (biography of Dame Edith Evans) 1977, International Velvet (novel) 1978, Familiar Strangers (novel, U.S. title Stranger) 1979, That Despicable Race—a History of the British Acting Tradition 1980, The Rewrite Man (novel) 1983, The Endless Game 1986. *Leisure interests:* collecting books, running a bookshop, landscape gardening, collecting Napoleonic relics, avoiding bores. *Address:* c/o The Bookshop, Virginia Water, Surrey, England. *Telephone:* Wentworth 2463.

FORBES, James; British chartered accountant and business executive; b. 2 Jan. 1923, Farnborough, Hants; s. of Major and Mrs. D. Forbes; m. Alison Mary Moffat 1948; two s.; ed. Christ's Hospital, Officers' Training School, Bangabu, India; served with 15th Punjab Regt., Indian Army 1942–45, Deputy Asst. Dir. Ordnance Services, Gen. HQ (India), Hon. Maj. 1945–46; Chartered Accountant with Peat, Marwick, Mitchell and Co., London 1952–58; with Schweppes Ltd. (now Cadbury Schweppes PLC) 1964–78, Group Chief Accountant and Dir. Main Subsidiaries 1964–69, Sec. and Financial Adviser on Formation, then Financial Dir. 1969–78; joined Tate and Lyle PLC 1978, Dir. and Chair. Pension Fund Service 1978–80, Vice-Chair. 1980–84; Treasurer Inst of Chartered Accountants 1984–86; Treasurer, Chair. Council of Almoners, Christ's Hosp. 1987- (Gov. 1983–); Dir. British Rail Investments Ltd. 1980–84, Steetley PLC 1984–, Compass Hotels 1984–, Lautro Ltd. 1986–; Forestry Commr. 1982–; mem. various bds., cttees. and socs. *Leisure interest:* golf. *Address:* Centre Point, 103 New Oxford Street, London, WC1A 1QH, England (Office).

FORBES, Malcolm Stevenson, D.SC., L.H.D., LL.B., LITT.D., D.F.A., LL.D., D.ECON.; American author and publisher; b. 19 Aug. 1919, New York; s. of Bertie Charles and Adelaide (née Stevenson) Forbes; m. Roberta Remsen Laidlaw 1946 (divorced 1985); four s. one d.; ed. Lawrenceville Acad., Princeton, Nasson Coll., Okla., Christian Coll., Milliken Univ., Ball State Univ., Franklin Pierce Coll., American Graduate School of Int. Man., Pace Univ., Potomac School of Law, Kean Coll., N.J., Westminster Coll., Seton Hill Coll. and Lakeland Coll.; Owner and Publr. Fairfield Times (weekly), Lancaster, Ohio 1941; served with U.S. army 1942–45; f. Lancaster Tribune (weekly) 1942; Assoc. Publr. Forbes Magazine Business, New York 1946–54, Publr. and Ed.-in-Chief 1957–; Vice-Pres. Forbes Inc., New York 1947–64, Pres. 1964–80, Chair. and C.E.O. 1980–; f., Pres. and Publr. Nation's Heritage 1948–49; State Senator 1952–58; N.J. Del.-at-large 1960; Chair. N.J. Rhodes Scholarship Cttee. 1976, 1978, 1979; Chair. Bd. 60 Fifth Ave. Corpn., Chair. Bd. and Pres. Slegers-Forbes Inc., Pres. Forbes Trinchera Inc., Chair. Fiji Forbes, Chair. Bd. Sangre de Cristo Ranches Inc. (all divs. of Forbes Inc.); mem. numerous balloonist socs.; 47 hon. degrees; several medals and awards. *Publications:* Fact and Comment 1974, The Sayings of Chairman Malcolm 1978, The Further Sayings of Chairman Malcolm 1986. *Leisure interests:* ballooning, motorcycling, collecting. *Address:* Timberfield, Far Hills, New Jersey 07931 (Home); 60 Fifth Ave., New York, N.Y. 10011, U.S.A. (Office).

FORCHHAMMER, Jes, D.SC., M.D.; Danish cancer research scientist; b. 5 April 1934, Aarhus; s. of Nels B. Forchhammer and Margrethe Høgstrøm; m. Anne Jette Edinger (née Balle); two s. one d.; ed. Copenhagen Univ.; Research Fellow, Dept. of Antibiotics, State Serum Inst. 1961–63; lecturer, Dept. of Microbiology, Copenhagen Univ. 1963–73; Visiting Asst. Prof. Dept. of Biochem. Pittsburgh Univ. Medical School 1969–70; EMBO Sr. Research Fellow, Dept. of Biological Sciences, Stanford Univ. 1970–71; Dept. of Molecular Oncology, The Fibiger Inst. Danish Cancer Soc. 1973–, Head Dr. 1986–; mem. Royal Danish Acad. *Publications:* co-author: Cancer and Chemicals 1981–85, Viral Carcinogenesis 1987. *Leisure interests:* hockey, tennis, skiing, music. *Address:* The Fibiger Institute, Danish Cancer Society, Ndr. Frihavnsgade 70, 2100 Copenhagen Ø, Denmark.

FORD, Charles Edmund, D.SC., F.R.S., F.L.S., F.Z.S.; British scientist; b. 24 Oct. 1912; s. of Charles Ford and Ethel Eubornia Ford (née Fawcett); m. Jean Ella Dowling 1940; four s.; ed. Slough Grammar School, King's Coll., Univ. of London; Demonstrator, Dept. of Botany, King's Coll. 1936–38; Geneticist, Rubber Research Scheme, Ceylon 1938–41, 1944–45; served R.A. 1942–43; Dept. of Atomic Energy, Ministry of Supply at Chalk River Labs., Ont., Canada 1946–49; Head of Cytogenetics Section, MRC, Radiobiology Unit, Harwell 1949–71; mem. MRC's External Staff, Sir William Dunn School of Pathology, Oxford 1971–78; Boerhaave Visiting Prof., Medical Faculty, Univ. of Leiden, 1978–80. *Publications:* papers on cytogenetics in scientific journals. *Leisure interests:* travel, friends. *Address:* 156 Oxford Road, Abingdon, Oxfordshire, England. *Telephone:* Abingdon 20001.

FORD, David Robert, L.V.O., O.B.E.; British government official; b. 22 Feb. 1935; s. of William E. Ford and Edna Ford; m. 1st Elspeth A. Muckart 1958 (divorced 1987), two s. two d.; m. 2nd Gillian Petersen (née Monsarrat) 1987; ed. Tauntons School; officer, R.A. 1955–72 retd. from army, rank of Maj.; seconded to Hong Kong Govt. 1967; Deputy Dir. Hong Kong Govt. Information Service 1972–74, Dir. 1974–76; Deputy Sec. Hong Kong Govt. Secr. 1976; Under-Sec. Northern Ireland Office 1977–79; Sec. for Information, Hong Kong Govt. 1979–80; Hong Kong Commr. in London 1980–81; Royal Coll. of Defence Studies 1982; Dir. of Housing, Hong Kong Govt. 1983–84, Sec. for Housing 1985, for the Civil Service 1985–86; Chief Sec., Hong Kong 1986–. *Leisure interests:* tennis, fishing, photography, theatre. *Address:* Government Secretariat, Hong Kong.

FORD, Gerald Rudolph, Jr.; American politician and lawyer; b. 14 July 1913, Omaha, Neb.; s. of Gerald R. Ford, Sr. and Dorothy Gardner Ford; m. Elizabeth (Betty) Bloomer 1948; three s. one d.; ed. Univ. of Michigan and Yale Univ. Law School; partner, law firm Ford and Buchen 1941–42; U.S.N. service 1942–46; mem. law firm Butterfield, Keeney and Amberg 1947–49; mem. U.S. House of Reps. 1949–73; House Minority Leader 1965–73; Vice-Pres. of U.S.A. 1973–74, Pres. of U.S.A. 1974–77; Visiting Prof. in Govt., Univ. of Mich.; Chair. Bd. of Acad. for Educational Devt. 1977–; mem. Interparl. Union, Warsaw 1959, Brussels 1961, Belgrade 1963; mem. U.S.-Canadian Interparl. Group, Chair. House of Repub. Conf. 1963; mem. Bd. Shearson, Loeb, Rhoades Inc.; Dir. 20th Century Fox 1981–84; Adviser American Express Co. 1981– (Dir. 1982–); mem. Warren Comm., American Enterprise Inst.; American Political Science Distinguished Congressional Service Award; Republican. *Publications:* Portrait of the Assassin (with John R. Stiles), A Time to Heal (memoirs) 1979. *Address:* P.O. Box 927, Rancho Mirage, Calif. 92270, U.S.A.

FORD, Harrison; American actor; b. 1942, Chicago; m. 1st Mary Ford; two s.; m. 2nd Melissa Ford; ed. Ripon Coll.; numerous TV appearances. *Films include:* Dead Heat on a Merry-Go-Round 1966, Luv 1967, The Long Ride Home 1967, Getting Straight 1970, Zabriskie Point 1970, The Conversation 1974, American Graffiti 1974, Star Wars 1977, Heroes 1977, Force 10 from Navarone 1978, Hanover Street 1979, Frisco Kid 1979, The Empire Strikes Back 1980, Raiders of the Lost Ark 1981, Blade Runner, Return of the Jedi 1983, Indiana Jones and the Temple of Doom, Witness, The Mosquito Coast 1986, Working Girl 1988, Frantic 1988. *Address:* 146 North Almont Drive, Suite 8, Los Angeles, Calif. 90048, U.S.A.

FORD, Sir Hugh, Kt., F.R.S., PH.D., D.SC., F.ENG.; British professor and engineering consultant; b. 16 July 1913, Thornby, Northants.; s. of Arthur Ford and Constance Mary Ford; m. Wynyard Scholfield 1942; two d.; ed. Northampton School and Imperial Coll., Univ. of London; served apprenticeship Great Western Railway 1931–36; Research engineer Imperial Coll. 1936–39, Imperial Chemical Industries 1939–42; Chief Tech. Officer British Iron and Steel Fed. 1942–47; Tech. Dir. Paterson Eng. 1947–48; Reader, then Prof. Imperial Coll. 1948–65, Prof. of Mechanical Eng. and Head of Dept. 1965–78, Prof. Emer. 1978–; Dir. Davy Ashmore, Alfred Herbert Ltd., etc. 1965–78; Chair. Ford and Dain Partners 1972–82, Sir Hugh Ford and Assocs. 1981–; Pres. Inst. of Mechanical Engineers 1976–77, The Welding Inst. 1983–85, Inst. of Metals 1985–87; Hawkesley Gold Medal 1948, Sir James Ewing Medal, James Watt Int. Gold Medal, Dr. h.c. (Belfast, Sheffield, Aston, etc.). *Publications:* Advanced Mechanics of Materials 1962, 100 scientific papers. *Leisure interests:* music, gardening, model engineering. *Address:* 18 Shrewsbury House, Cheyne Walk, London, S.W.3; Shamley Cottage, Stroud Lane, Shamley Green, Surrey, England (Home). *Telephone:* 01-352-4948, 0483 898012 (Home).

FORD, Sir John Archibald, K.C.M.G., M.C., M.A. (OXON.); British diplomatist (retd.); b. 19 Feb. 1922, Newcastle-under-Lyme; s. of Ronald Mylne Ford and Margaret Jessie Ford (née Coghill); m. Emaline Burnett 1956; two d.; ed. St. Michael's Coll., Tenbury, Sedbergh School, Oriel Coll., Oxford; served in R.A., rank of Major 1942–46; joined Foreign Service (later Diplomatic Service) 1947; Third Sec. British Legation, Budapest 1947–49, Third Sec. and Resident Clerk Foreign Office 1949–52, Private Sec. to Perm. Under-Sec. of State, Foreign Office 1952–54; Consul, San Francisco 1954–56; seconded to H.M. Treasury 1956–59; attended course at Admin. Staff Coll., Henley 1959; First Sec. and Head of Chancery British Residency, Bahrain 1959–61; Asst., Foreign Office Personnel Dept. 1961–63, Head of Establishment and Org. Dept., Diplomatic Service 1964–66; Counsellor (Commercial), British Embassy, Rome 1966–70; Asst. Under-Sec. FCO 1970–71; Consul-Gen. New York and Dir.-Gen. British Trade Devt. in U.S. 1970–75; Amb. to Indonesia 1975–78; High Commr. in Canada 1978–81; Lay admin. Guildford Cathedral 1982–84; mem. Exec. Cttee. V.S.O. 1982–86; Chair. Voluntary and Christian Service 1985–88. *Publication:* Honest to Christ 1988. *Leisure interests:* walking, gardening, reading, writing. *Address:* Guildown, Guildford, Surrey, GU2 5EN, England and 633 Admiral Block 8750, South A1A, Jensen Beach, Fla. 34957, U.S.A.

FORD, Robert Arthur Douglass, C.C., M.A., D.LITT.; Canadian diplomatist; b. 8 Jan. 1915, Ottawa; s. of Arthur Rutherford Ford and May Lavinia Scott; m. Maria Thereza Gomes 1946 (died 1983); ed. Univ. of Western Ontario and Cornell Univ.; Instructor, History Dept., Cornell Univ. 1939–40; Dept. of External Affairs 1940–, served Rio de Janeiro, Moscow, London 1940–51; Chargé d'Affaires, Moscow 1951–54; Head of European

Div., Dept. of External Affairs 1954–57; Amb. to Colombia 1957–58, to Yugoslavia 1959–61, to U.A.R. 1961–63, to U.S.S.R. 1964–80; Special Adviser on East-West Relations 1980; Founder mem. Int. Inst. of Geopolitics; mem. Palme Comm. on Disarmament and Security Issues; Hon. Pres. Asscn. France-Canada du Bourbonnais; Hon. D.Litt. (Western Ontario) 1965; Hon. LL.D. (Toronto) 1987; Gov.-Gen.'s Award for Poetry 1956, Gold Medal of Professional Inst. of Public Service of Canada 1971. *Publications:* Poetry: A Window on the North 1956, The Solitary City 1969, Holes in Space 1979, Needle in the Eye 1983, Doors, Words and Silence 1985, Dostoyevsky and Other Poems 1988; Russian Poetry: A Personal Anthology 1984, A Diplomat's Reflections on The Soviet Union 1988 and articles on foreign affairs. *Leisure interests:* travel, poetry, translations (Russian, Portuguese). *Address:* la Poivrière, St. Sylvestre-Pragoulin, 63310 Randan, France. *Telephone:* (70) 59-01-47.

FORD, Wendell Hampton; American politician; b. 8 Sept. 1924, Owensboro, Ky.; s. of E. M. and Irene (Schenck) Ford; m. Jean Neel 1943; one s. one d.; ed. Daviess County High School, Univ. of Kentucky, Maryland School of Insurance; served U.S. Army, Ky. 1944–46, Nat. Guard 1949–62; Chief Asst. to Gov. of Kentucky 1959–61; mem. Ky. Senate 1966–67; Lieut.-Gov. Kentucky 1967–71, Gov. 1971–74; U.S. Senator from Kentucky Dec. 1974–; mem. Senate Energy and Natural Resources Cttee., Commerce, Science, Transportation Cttee. (Chair. Consumer Sub-Cttee.); mem. Democratic Steering Cttee., Chair. Democratic Nat. Campaign Cttee. 1976, Head of Democratic Senatorial Campaign Cttee.; Chair. Nat. Democratic Govs. 1973–74; fmr. mem. Nat. Democratic Party Advisory Council; fmr. Chair. common law enforcement, justice and public safety, Southern Govs.' Conf.; mem. U.S. Chamber of Commerce, Pres. 1956–57; Int. Vice-Pres. Jaycees. *Leisure interests:* fishing, hunting. *Address:* 2017 Fieldcrest Drive, Owensboro, Ky. 42301, U.S.A. (Home). *Telephone:* (502) 685-5158 (Home).

FORD, William Clay, B.S.(ECON.); American businessman; b. 14 March 1925, Detroit; s. of Edsel Ford and Eleanor Clay Ford; brother of Henry Ford II (q.v.); m. Martha Firestone 1947; one s. three d.; ed. Yale Univ.; Dir. Ford Motor Co. 1948–; mem. of Sales and Advertising Staff 1948 and of the Industrial Relations Staff 1949; quality control Man. Lincoln-Mercury Div. Jet Engine Defence Project 1951; Man. Special Product Operations 1952; Vice-Pres. Ford Motor Co. and Gen. Man. Continental Div. 1953, Group Dir. Continental Div. 1955, Vice-Pres. Product Design 1956–80, Chair. Design Cttees., of Exec. Cttee. 1978–, Vice-Chair. of Bd. 1980–89, Chair. Company Finance Cttee. 1987–; Pres./Owner Detroit Lions Professional Football Team; Chair. Edison Inst.; Trustee Eisenhower Medical Center, Thomas A. Edison Foundation; mem. Bd. of Dirs. Nat. Tennis Hall of Fame, Boys Club of America. *Address:* Ford Motor Co., The American Road, Dearborn, Mich. 48121, U.S.A.

FORDE, Henry deBoulay, LL.B., Q.C.; Barbadian lawyer and politician; b. 20 March 1933, Christ Church, Barbados; adopted s. of late Courtley Ifill and of Elise Ifill; m. Cheryl Wendy Roach; four s.; ed. Harrison Coll., Barbados, Christ's Coll., Cambridge, Middle Temple, London; Research Asst., Dept. of Criminology, Univ. of Cambridge 1958, Research Student, Int. Law, worked on British Digest of Int. Law, Univ. of Cambridge 1958–59, Supervisor and Tutor in Int. Law, Emmanuel Coll., Cambridge 1958–59; called to English Bar 1959, to Barbadian Bar 1959; Lecturer, Extra-Mural Programme, Univ. of West Indies 1961–68, Part-time Lecturer, Caribbean Studies, 1964–69; mem. House of Ass. for Christ Church West 1971–; Minister of External Affairs and Attorney-Gen. 1976–81; Leader of the Opposition 1986–; mem. Int. Comm. of Jurists; mem. Privy Council; Leader Barbados Dels. to UN, OAS and other int. orgs. 1976–81; mem. Commonwealth Cttee. on Vulnerability of Small States 1985. *Leisure interests:* reading, walking, gardening. *Address:* Juris Chambers, Suite 205, Kays House, 13–14 Roebuck Street, Bridgetown (Office); Codrington Court, Society, St. John, Barbados, West Indies (Home). *Telephone:* (809) 429-2203, 429-2208 (Office); (809) 433-3388 (Home).

FORGEOT, Jean; French business executive; b. 10 Oct. 1915, Paris; s. of P. E. Forgeot and Aydée Lefebvre; m. Sylviane Busck 1948; one d.; ed. Faculté de Droit, Paris; Insp., Ministry of Finance 1942–55; Adviser to the Cabinet of Vincent Auriol; Sec.-Gen. to Pres. of Repub. 1947–54; fmr. Pres. Dir.-Gen. Schneider S.A., now Hon. Pres. 1970–, now Vice-Pres. Chrysler-France (fmrly. Soc. des Automobiles Simca) 1955–; Pres. Dir.-Gen. Cie. Financière de l'Union européenne 1971, Dir. 1976–; Dir. Esso-Standard, Cie. Maritime des Chargeurs réunis, Imprimerie Georges Lang; Pres. Dir.-Gen. Creusot-Loire 1972–; Officier Légion d'honneur, Croix de guerre (1939–45), Officier du Mérite maritime. *Leisure interests:* tennis, golf. *Address:* 20 boulevard Suchet, 75116 Paris, France.

FORLANI, Arnaldo; Italian politician; b. 8 Dec. 1925, Pesaro; s. of Luigi and Caterina Forlani; m. Alma Ioni 1956; three s.; ed. Univ. of Urbino; mem. Chamber of Deputies 1958–; Deputy Sec. of Christian Democrat Party 1962–69, Political Sec. (Leader) 1969–73, Feb. 1989–; Minister of State Undertakings 1969–70, of Defence 1974–76, of Foreign Affairs 1976–79; Prime Minister 1980–81, Deputy Prime Minister 1983–87; Pres. Christian Democratic Party 1986. *Leisure interest:* journalism. *Address:* Piazzale Schumann 15, Rome, Italy. *Telephone:* 6784109 (Home).

FORMAN, Sir John Denis, Kt, O.B.E.; British company director; b. 13 Oct. 1917, Beattock, Scotland; s. of the late Rev. Adam Forman and of Flora (née Smith) Forman; m. Helen de Mouilpied 1948; two s.; ed. Loretto Pembroke Coll., Cambridge; war service with Argyll and Sutherland Highlanders 1940–45 (Commdt. Orkney and Shetland Defences Battle School 1942, wounded, Cassino 1944); Chief Production Officer, Cen. Office of Information Films 1947; Dir. British Film Inst. 1948–55, Chair. Bd. of Govs. 1971–73; Jt. Man. Dir., Granada TV Ltd. 1965–81, Chair. 1974–87; Dir. Granada Group 1964–, Deputy Chair. 1984–; Chair. Novello & Co. 1971–; Dir. Royal Opera House, Covent Garden 1981–, Deputy Chair. 1983–; mem. Council Royal Northern Coll. of Music (RNCM) 1975–84, Hon. mem. 1981; several hon. degrees; Fellow, British Acad. of Film and TV Arts 1977; Ufficiale dell' ordine al Merito della Repubblica Italiana. *Publication:* Mozart's Piano Concertos 1971. *Leisure interests:* music, shooting. *Address:* Granada Group Ltd., 36 Golden Square, London, W1R 4AH, England. *Telephone:* 01-734 8080.

FORMAN, Miloš; American (b. Czechoslovak) film director; b. 18 Feb. 1932, Čáslav; ed. Film Faculty, Acad. of Music and Dramatic Art, Prague; Dir. Film Presentations, Czechoslovak TV 1954–56; of Laterna Magika, Prague 1958–62; mem. Artistic Cttee., Šebor-Bor Film Producing Group; Czechoslovak Film Critics' Award for Peter and Pavla 1963, Grand Prix 17th Int. Film Festival, Locarno, for Peter and Pavla 1964, Prize Venice Festival 1965, Grand Prix of French Film Acad. for A Blonde in Love 1966, Klement Gottwald State Prize 1967, Acad. Award (Best Dir.) for One Flew Over the Cuckoo's Nest 1976, Acad. Award, also César Award for Amadeus 1985. *Films include:* Talent Competition, Peter and Pavla 1964, The Knave of Spades, A Blonde in Love 1965, Episode in Zruč, Like a House on Fire (A Fireman's Ball) 1968, Taking Off 1971; Co-Dir. Visions of Eight 1973, One Flew Over the Cuckoo's Nest 1975, Hair 1979, Ragtime 1980, Amadeus 1983, Valmont 1988. *Address:* c/o Robert Lantz, 888 7th Avenue, New York, N.Y. 10106, U.S.A.

FORMICA, Gianni, PH.D.; Italian space research administrator; b. 23 March 1922, Milan; s. of Aldo Formica and Angioletta Veggi; m. Emma Saracchi 1958; one d.; ed. Milan Polytechnic; Dir. G.E.C.—Gen. Electric, Milan 1959–69; Prof. of Hydraulics Faculty of Agronomy, Catholic Univ. of Milan 1962–70; Dir. Soc. Italiana Sistemi Informativi Elettronici 1969–73, Head, Milan office 1970–73; Prof. of Hydraulics, Faculty of Eng., Univ. of Ancona 1971–73; Dir. European Space Operations Centre 1973; *Publications:* numerous works on digital computing, the scientific applications of computers and related subjects, satellite operations. *Leisure interests:* skiing, boating, classical music, literature.

FORMICA, Salvatore; Italian politician; b. 1 March 1927, Bari; Senator, Milan VI 1979–83; Socialist (P.S.I.) M.P. for Bari 1983–; Minister of Transport in second Cossiga Govt. and Forlani Govt.; fmr. Minister of Finance; Minister for Foreign Trade 1986–87, for Labour 1987–88, April 1988–; mem. Parl. Comm. of Inquiry into Masonic Lodge P2. *Address:* Via Flavia 6, 00187 Rome, Italy.

FORMIGONI, Roberto; Italian politician; b. 30 March 1947, Lecco; s. of Emilio Formigoni and Doralice Formigoni; Leader Movimento Popolare (political arm of Catholic Movt. Comunione e Liberazione); mem. Christian Democratic Party governing directorate; Vice-Pres. European Parl. *Address:* Movimento Pololare, Via Copernico 7, 20125 Milan, Italy. *Telephone:* (02) 606641.

FORREST, Sir James Alexander, Kt., F.A.A.; Australian lawyer and industrialist; b. 10 March 1905, Kerang, Victoria; s. of John and Mary Gray Forrest; m. Mary Christina Armit 1939; three s.; ed. Caulfield Grammar School, Melbourne Univ.; Partner, Hedderwick Fookes & Alston, Solicitors 1933–70, Consultant 1970–73; served R.A.A.F. and Dept. Aircraft Production 1942–45; Dir. Victoria Branch Bd., Australian Mutual Provident Soc. 1945–57, Chair. 1957–77; Dir. Australian Mutual Provident Soc. 1961–77; Dir. Australian Consolidated Industries Ltd. 1950–53, Chair. 1953–77; Dir. Nat. Bank of Australasia Ltd. 1950–59, Chair. 1959–78; Chair. Chase-N.B.A. Group Ltd. 1979–80, Alcoa of Australia Ltd. 1970–78; Dir. Western Mining Corpn. Ltd. 1970–77; mem. Council, Boy Scouts Asscn. of Australia 1949–73, Scout Educ. and Training Cttee., 1976–, Council, Scotch Coll. 1959–71, Royal Children's Hosp. Research Foundation 1960–78, Council, Monash Univ. 1961–71, Victoria Law Foundation 1969–75, Bd. Art Foundation of Victoria 1977–80; Fellow Australian Acad. of Science 1977; Hon. LL.D. (Monash) 1979. *Leisure interests:* golf, fishing, gardening. *Address:* 11 Russell Street, Toorak, Vic. 3142, Australia (Home).

FORREST, John Samuel, M.A., D.SC., F.R.S., F.INST.P., F.ENG.; British director of research; b. 20 Aug. 1907, Hamilton; s. of Samuel Forrest and Elizabeth Forrest; m. 1st Ivy M. Olding 1940 (died 1985), 2nd Joan M. Downie 1985; one s.; ed. Hamilton Acad. and Univ. of Glasgow; physicist, Cen. Electricity Bd. (CEB), Glasgow 1930, London 1931; in charge of CEB research lab. 1934–40; Dir. and founder, Cen. Electricity Research Labs., Leatherhead 1940–73; Sec. Electricity Supply Research Council 1949–72; Visiting Prof. of Electrical Eng. Univ. of Strathclyde 1964–; Foreign Assoc. Nat. Acad. of Eng., U.S.A.; several awards and hon. degrees. *Publications:* papers on electrical power transmission and insulation. *Address:* Arbores, Portsmouth Road, Thames Ditton, Surrey, KT7 0EG, England. *Telephone:* 01-398 4389.

FORSTER, Isaac; Senegalese international judge; b. 14 Aug. 1903; ed. Lycée Hoche, Versailles, and Univ. of Paris; Gen. State Counsel's Dept. for French W. Africa 1930; Deputy Judge, Dakar 1933; Deputy to Prosecutor,

Conakry, Guinea 1933; Judge, St. Denis, Réunion, then Madagascar 1941; Judge of Court, Guadeloupe 1945, French W. Africa 1947; Pres. of Chamber, Dakar 1957; Sec.-Gen. of Govt., Senegal 1958–60; Prosecutor-Gen., Dakar 1959; First Pres. Supreme Court of Senegal 1960–64; Judge, Int. Court of Justice, The Hague 1964–82; assoc. mem. Inst. of Int. Law; numerous decorations. *Address:* c/o Ministry of Foreign Affairs, Dakar, Senegal.

FORSTER, Margaret, B.A.; British writer; b. 25 May 1938, Carlisle; d. of Lilian Hind and Arthur Gordon Forster; m. Edward Hunter Davies 1960; one s. two d.; ed. Carlisle County High School and Somerville Coll., Oxford. *Publications:* 14 novels since 1964; The Rash Adventurer; the rise and fall of Charles Edward Stuart 1973, work on Thackeray, and Significant Sisters: History of Active Feminism 1839–1940 1984, Elizabeth Barrett Browning: A Life 1988, Elizabeth Barrett Browning; selected poems (ed.) 1988. *Leisure interests:* fell walking and reading contemporary fiction. *Address:* 11 Boscastle Road, London, N.W.5, England. *Telephone:* 01-485 3785.

FORSTER, Sir Oliver Grantham, K.C.M.G., L.V.O.; British diplomatist; b. 2 Sept. 1925, London; s. of Norman and Olive Forster; m. Beryl Evans 1953; two d.; ed. Hurstpierpoint and King's Coll., Cambridge; H.M. Forces 1944–48; Commonwealth Relations Office (CRO) 1951; Pvt. Sec. to Parl. Under-Sec. of State 1953; Second Sec., Karachi 1954; First Sec. CRO 1956–59, Madras 1959–62, Washington 1962–65; Pvt. Sec. to Sec. of State for Commonwealth Affairs 1965–67; Counsellor and Head of Chancery, Manila 1967–70; Counsellor (Commercial/Economic) later Minister (March 1975), New Delhi 1970; Asst. Under-Sec. of State and Deputy Chief Clerk, FCO 1975–79; Amb. to Pakistan 1979–84; HQA (Pakistan) 1984. *Address:* 71 Raglan Road, Reigate, Surrey, RH2 0HP, England.

FORSTER, Raymond Robert, D.SC., Q.S.O., F.R.S.N.Z.; New Zealand museum director and research scientist (retd.); b. 19 June 1922, Hastings; s. of Robert C. Forster and Winifred M. Forrest; m. Lyndsay McLaren Clifford 1948; two s. two d.; ed. Hastings primary and high schools and Vic. Univ. Wellington; entomologist, Dominion Museum of N.Z. (interrupted by wartime naval service) 1941–48; Zoologist, Asst. Dir. Canterbury Museum, Christchurch 1948–57; Dir. Otago Museum 1957–87; Fulbright Research Scholar and Research Fellow, Harvard Univ. 1956–57; Hon. Research Fellow, Bishop Museum Hawaii 1964–, American Museum of Natural History 1976–; Thorne Fellow, American Museum of Natural History 1989; Sr. Research Fellow, Smithsonian Inst. Washington June 1989–; Fellow, Art Galleries and Museums Assn.; Hutton Medal 1971, Queen's Silver Jubilee Medal 1977, Hector Medal 1983; Hon. D.Sc. (Otago) 1978. *Publications:* Spiders of New Zealand, Otago Museum Bulletins Vols. I-IV 1967–88; co-author with wife: Small Land Animals of New Zealand 1970, New Zealand Spiders 1973; more than 80 scientific publs. on arachnids. *Leisure interests:* natural history photography. *Address:* c/o Entomology Department, American Museum of Natural History, Central Park West at 79th Street, New York, N.Y. 10021 (Office); 100 Norfolk Street, St. Clair, Dunedin, New Zealand (Home). *Telephone:* (212) 769-5612 (Office); (024) 871-065 (Home).

FORSYTH, Bill; British film-maker; b. 1947, Glasgow; ed. Nat. Film School, Beaconsfield; Hon. D.Litt. (Glasgow) 1984. *Films:* That Sinking Feeling 1979, Gregory's Girl 1980, Local Hero 1982, Comfort and Joy 1984, Housekeeping 1987, Breaking In 1988. *Address:* c/o A. D. Peters, 10 Buckingham Street, London, W.C.2, England.

FORSYTH, Elliott Christopher, B.A., DIP.ED., D. UNIV.; Australian professor of French; b. 1 Feb. 1924, Mount Gambier; s. of Samuel Forsyth and Ida Muriel (née Brummitt) Forsyth; m. Rona Lynette Williams 1967; two d.; ed. Prince Alfred Coll., Adelaide, Univ. of Adelaide and Univ. of Paris; teacher Friends' School, Hobart, Tasmania 1947–49; Lecturer, Sr. Lecturer in French Univ. of Adelaide 1955–66; Visiting Lecturer Univ. of Wisconsin, Madison 1963–65; Foundation Prof. of French La Trobe Univ., Melbourne 1966–87, Emer. Prof. 1987–; Fellow Australian Acad. of Humanities 1973, Australian Coll. of Educ. 1977; Commdr. Ordre des Palmes Académiques. *Publications:* La Tragédie française de Jodelle à Corneille (1553–1640): le thème de la vengeance 1962, Saül le furieux/La Famine (tragédies de Jean de la Taille) (ed.) 1968, Concordance des 'Tragiques' d'Agrippa d'Aubigné 1984, Baudin in Australian Waters (ed. with J. Bonnemains and B. Smith) 1988. *Leisure interests:* music, photography, bushwalking and church activities. *Address:* 25 Jacka Street, N. Balwyn, Vic. 3104, Australia. *Telephone:* (03) 857 4050.

FORSYTH, Frederick; British author; narrated Soldiers (TV) 1985. *Publications:* The Biafra Story 1969, The Day of the Jackal 1971, The Odessa File 1972, The Dogs of War 1974, The Shepherd 1975, The Devil's Alternative 1979, No Comebacks 1982, The Fourth Protocol 1984, The Negotiator 1988. *Leisure interests:* sea angling, reading.

FORTE, Baron (Life Peer), cr. 1982, of Ripley in the County of Surrey; **Charles Forte,** Kt., F.H.C.I.; British hotelier and caterer; b. 26 Nov. 1908, Monteforte Casalattico, Frosinone, Italy; s. of Rocco and Maria Luigia Forte; m. Irene Mary Chierico 1943; one s. five d.; ed. Alloa Acad., Dumfries Coll., and Mamiani, Rome; came to London and opened first milk bar 1935; acquired Criterion Restaurant 1953, Monico Restaurant, Café Royal, Slater and Bodega chain 1954, Hungaria Restaurant 1956,

Waldorf Hotel 1958, Fuller's Ltd. 1959; Chair. Forte's (Holdings) Ltd., Les Grands Hôtels Associés Ltd., Paris, Hôtel George V, Paris; Deputy Chair. Trust Houses Forte Ltd. 1970–78, C.E.O. 1971–75, Joint Chief Exec. 1975–78, Chair. 1982–; Chair. Snamprogetti 1978–80; Dir. TraveLodge Int. Inc., TraveLodge Australia; Dir. Forte's and Co. Ltd., Nat. Sporting Club, Theatre Restaurants Ltd., etc.; Consul-Gen. of San Marino in London; Pres. Italian Chamber of Commerce for G.B. 1952–, Westminster Chamber of Commerce 1983–; mem. British Inst. of Florence, Italy; Bd. mem. British Travel Asscn.; Hon. Ph.D. (Stirling) 1983; Free Enterprise Award from Aims of Industry 1981; Grand Officer of the Order of the Italian Repub., Cavaliere di Gran Croce della Repubblica Italiana; Knight of Magistral Grace of Sovereign and Mil. Order of Malta; Grande Médaille de Vermeil de la Ville de Paris 1979. *Publications:* Forte (autobiography). *Leisure interests:* literature, music, fishing, shooting. *Address:* 166 High Holborn, London, WC1V 6TT, England. *Telephone:* 01-836 7744.

FORTIER, Most Rev. Jean-Marie; Canadian ecclesiastic; b. 1 July 1920, Quebec; s. of Joseph Fortier and Alberta Jobin; ed. Petit Séminaire de Québec, Laval Univ., Univ. of Louvain, Belgium, Univ. Gregorienne, Rome; History Teacher, Grand Séminaire de Québec 1950–60; Auxiliary Bishop of Ste.-Anne-de-la-Pocatière 1960; Bishop of Gaspé 1965; Archbishop of Sherbrooke 1968–; mem. Vatican's Sacred Congregation of Sacraments and Divine Worship 1975–84; Vice-Pres. of A.E.Q. 1981–85, Pres. 1985–; mem. Comité du Laïcat 1985–. *Address:* 130 de la Cathédrale, Sherbrooke, Que. J1H 4M1, Canada.

FOSS, Lukas; American composer, conductor, pianist and professor of music; b. 15 Aug. 1922, Berlin, Germany; s. of Martin Fuchs and Hilda Schindler; m. Cornelia B. Brendel 1950; one s. one d.; ed. Lycée Pasteur, Paris, Curtis Inst. of Music, Yale Univ. Music School; Prof. of Conducting and Composition, Univ. of Calif. at Los Angeles 1951–62; Founder Dir. Center for Creative and Performing Arts, Buffalo Univ. 1963–; Musical Dir. Conductor Buffalo Philharmonic Orchestra 1962–70; Musical Dir. Conductor Brooklyn Philharmonic Orchestra 1971–, Jerusalem Symphony Orchestra 1972–76, Milwaukee Symphony Orchestra 1981–; Dir., Conductor Ojai Festival, Calif. 1955, 1956, 1957, Festival of the Arts Today, Buffalo Philharmonic 1960–67, Franco-U.S. Festival (New York Philharmonic Orchestra) 1964, Stravinsky Festival (New York Philharmonic Orchestra) 1965; Visiting Prof. Harvard Univ. 1969–70, Manhattan School of Music 1972–73, Carnegie Mellon Univ. 1987–; mem. Nat. Inst. of Arts and Letters, Acad. of Arts and Letters; Dr. h.c. (Brandeis Univ.) 1983; New York Music Critics' Circle Award; Prix de Rome; Guggenheim Fellowship; Ditson Award 1973, and nine composition awards. *Compositions include:* Time Cycle, Echoi, Baroque Variations, Paradigm, Geod, three operas, Orpheus, Map, Percussion Concerto, String Quartets, American Cantata, Night Music for John Lennon, Thirteen Ways of Looking at a Blackbird, Solo Observed. *Address:* 17 East 96th Street, New York, N.Y. 10128, U.S.A. *Telephone:* (212) 534-4832.

FOSSET, André; French politician and fmr. newspaper publisher; b. 13 Nov. 1918, Paris; s. of Emile and Suzanne (Brunel) Fosset; m. Geneviève Richard 1941; three s. two d,; mem. Municipal Council, Paris, and Gen. Council, Seine 1945–59; mem. Senate 1958–76, 1977–; Minister for the Quality of Life Jan.–Aug. 1976; mem. Econ. and Social Council 1977, European Parl. 1977–78; Pres. Comité français des expositions 1977–; Hon. Pres. Le Parisien Libéré; Chevalier Légion d'honneur. *Address:* Comité Français des Expositions, 22 avenue Franklin D. Roosevelt, 75008 Paris (Office); Palais du Luxembourg, 75291 Paris cedex 06; 25 avenue de l'Europe, 92310 Sèvres, France (Home). *Telephone:* (1) 92.25.70.94 (Office); 626-42-06 (Home).

FOSTER, Brendan, M.B.E., B.SC.; British athlete; b. 12 Jan. 1948, Hebburn, Co. Durham; s. of Francis and Margaret Foster; m. Susan Margaret Foster 1972; one s. one d.; ed. Sussex Univ., Carnegie Coll., Leeds; competed Olympic Games, Munich 1972, 5th in 1,500 m.; Montreal 1976, won bronze medal in 10,000 m., 5th in 5,000 m., Moscow 1980, 11th in 10,000 m.; competed Commonwealth Games, Edinburgh 1970, won bronze medal at 1,500 m.; Christchurch 1974, won silver medal at 5,000 m.; Edmonton 1978, won gold medal at 10,000 m. and bronze medal 5,000 m; European champion at 5,000 m. 1974 and bronze medallist at 1,500 m. 1971; has held World record at 3,000 m. and 2 miles; European record holder at 10,000 m., Olympic record holder at 5,000 m.; Dir. Recreation, Gateshead March 1982; Man. Dir. Nike Int. 1982–86, Vice-Pres. Marketing (Worldwide) and Vice-Pres. (Europe) 1986–87; Man. Dir. Nova Int. 1987–; BBC TV Commentator 1981–; Hon. Master of Educ. (Newcastle Univ.); Hon. Fellow (Sunderland Polytechnic); Hon. D.Litt. (Sussex Univ.) 1982. *Publication:* Brendan Foster with Cliff Temple 1978. *Leisure interests:* sport and running every day. *Address:* Whitegates, 31 Meadowfield Road, Stocksfield, Northumberland, England. *Telephone:* (0661) 843143.

FOSTER, Sir Christopher David, Kt., M.A.; British economist; b. 30 Oct. 1930, London; s. of George C. Foster; m. Kay S. Bullock 1958; two s. three d.; ed. Merchant Taylors School and King's Coll. Cambridge; Fellow and Tutor, Jesus Coll. Cambridge 1964–66; Dir.-Gen. of Econ. Planning, Ministry of Transport 1966–70; Head, Unit for Research in Urban Econs., L.S.E. 1970–76, Prof. of Urban Studies and Econs. 1976–78, Visiting Prof. 1978–86; Gov. Centre for Environmental Studies 1967–70, Dir. 1976–78; Visiting Prof. of Econs. M.I.T. 1970; Head of Econ. and Public Policy Div. Coopers

& Lybrand Assocs. 1978–84, Public Sector Practice Leader and Econ. Adviser 1984–86, Dir. and Head Econs. Practice Div. 1988–; Commercial Adviser to Bd. of British Telecommunications PLC 1986–. *Publications:* The Transport Problem 1963, Politics, Finance and the Role of Economics: The Control of Public Enterprise (with R. Jackman and M. Perlman) 1972, Local Government Finance 1980; papers in various econ. and other journals. *Leisure interests:* theatre, reading. *Address:* 6 Holland Park Avenue, London, W.11, England. *Telephone:* 01-727 4757.

FOSTER, Lawrence; American conductor; b. 23 Oct. 1941, Los Angeles; m. Angela Foster 1972; one d.; studied with Fritz Zweig and Karl Böhm and at Bayreuth Festival Master Classes; Music Dir. Young Musicians Foundation, Los Angeles 1960–64; Conductor San Francisco Ballet 1960–64; Asst. Conductor L.A. Philharmonic Orchestra 1965–68; Chief Guest Conductor Royal Philharmonic Orchestra, London 1969–74; Music Dir. Houston Symphony Orchestra 1971–78; Music Dir. Orchestre Philharmonique, Monte Carlo 1978–; Music Dir. Duisburg Orchestra, Fed. Repub. of Germany 1982–86; Music Dir. Chamber Orchestra of Lausanne 1985–; Koussevitsky Memorial Conducting Prize, Tanglewood 1966. *Leisure interests:* reading history and biographies, films. *Address:* c/o Harrison Parrott Ltd., 12 Penzance Place, London, W.11, England.

FOSTER, Norman Robert, DIP.ARCH., M.ARCH., R.I.B.A.; British architect; b. 1 June 1935, Reddish; s. of Robert Foster and Lilian Smith; m. Wendy Ann Cheesman 1964; two s.; ed. Manchester Univ. School of Architecture and Dept. of Town and Country Planning, Yale Univ. School of Architecture; Urban Renewal and City Planning Consultants work 1962–63; pvt. practice, as "Team 4 Architects" (with Wendy Cheesman, George Wolton, Richard Rogers q.v.) London 1963–67, Foster Associates (now Foster Assocs. Ltd.) 1967–, Dir. (with Wendy Foster) Foster Assocs. (Hong Kong) 1984, Dir. Foster Assocs. Japan 1987; Collaboration with Buckminster Fuller 1968–83; Consultant Architect to Univ. of E. Anglia 1978–87; fmr. External Examiner R.I.B.A. Visiting Bd. of Educ.; fmr. mem. Architectural Asscn. Council (Vice-Pres. 1968); fmr. teacher Univ. of Pa., Architectural Asscn., London, London Polytechnic, Bath Acad. of Arts; F.S.I.A.D. 1975; IBM Fellow, Aspen Design Conf. 1980; Council mem. R.C.A. 1981–; Hon. F.A.I.A. 1980; Hon. Litt.D. (Univ. of E. Anglia) 1980; Hon. D.Sc. (Bath) 1986; Assoc. of Royal Acad.; Architectural Design Projects Awards 1964, 1965, 1966, 1969; Financial Times Industrial Architecture Awards 1967, 1974, 1984, citations 1970, 1971, 1981; R.I.B.A. Awards 1969, 1972, 1977, 1978, commendation 1981; R.S.A. Business and Industry Award 1976; Int. Design Awards (Brussels) 1976, 1980; R. S. Reynolds Int. Memorial Awards (U.S.A.) for Willis Faber HQ 1976, Salisbury Centre for Visual Arts 1979; Finniston Award 1978, Structural Steel Awards 1972, 1978, 1984, 1986, citation 1980, Ambrose Congreve Award 1980 and winner of numerous competitions, including BBC new Radio Competition Centre 1983, Arts Centre, Nîmes, France 1984; Royal Gold Medal for Architecture 1983, Constructa-European Award Program for Industrial Architecture 1986, Premio Compasso d'Oro Award 1987, Japan Design Foundation Award 1987, PA Innovations Award 1988, Annual Interiors Award (U.S.A.) 1988, Kunstpreis Award, Berlin 1989. *Major works include:* Pilot Head Office for IBM, Hampshire 1970, Tech. Park for IBM, Greenford 1975, Sainsbury Centre for Visual Arts, Norwich 1977, Head Office for Willis, Faber and Dumas, Ipswich 1979, Devt. project, Whitney Gallery, New York 1979, Students Union Project, Univ. Coll., London 1979, Third London Airport Terminal and Master Planning Studies 1980, Centre for Renault Car Co. U.K. 1980, Hong Kong and Shanghai Banking Corpn. HQ, Nat. German Indoor Athletics Stadium, Frankfurt, Radio Centre for BBC, London, Arts Centre, Nimes 1984, Century Tower, Tokyo 1987, Barcelona Telecommunications Tower 1988, Bilbao Metro System 1988, Kings Cross London Master Plan 1988; work exhibited in Museum of Modern Art, New York 1979, Parma 1979, Copenhagen 1979; exhbns. in Barcelona 1976, London 1979; work in perm. collection of Museum of Modern Art, New York. *Publications:* The Work of Foster Assocs. RIBA, Hong Kong Bank: The Building of Norman Foster's Masterpiece and numerous contributions to the architectural and tech. press. *Leisure interests:* gen. aviation (sailplanes, light aircraft, helicopters), running. *Address:* Foster Associates Ltd., 172–182 Great Portland Street, London, W1N 5TB, England; Foster Associates Japan, Sansei Ogawamachi Building, 2-6-3 Kanda Ogawa-machi, Chijoda-ku, Tokyo, Japan (Office). *Telephone:* 01-637 5431 (London); 3 293 6071 (Japan).

FOSTER, Sir Robert Sidney, G.C.M.G., K.C.V.O., K.ST.J.; British official (retd.); b. 11 Aug. 1913, London; s. of the late Sidney Charles Foster and Jessie Edith (née Fry) Foster; m. Margaret Walker 1947; ed. Eastbourne Coll. and Peterhouse, Cambridge; Cadet, Northern Rhodesia Admin. Service 1936–38, Dist. Officer 1938–40; Mil. Service 1940–43; Dist. Officer, N. Rhodesia 1943–53, Sr. Dist. Officer 1953–57, Prov. Commr. 1957–60, Sec., Native Affairs 1960–61; Chief Sec., Nyasaland 1961–63, Deputy Gov. 1963–64; High Commr., W. Pacific 1964–68; Gov. and C.-in-C. Fiji 1968–70, Gov.-Gen. 1970–72; Trustee, The Beit Trust; Officier Légion d'honneur 1966. *Leisure interest:* do-it-yourself. *Address:* "Kenwood", 16 Ardnave Crescent, Southampton, Hants., SO1 7FJ, England. *Telephone:* Southampton 769412.

FOSTER-SUTTON, Sir Stafford William Powell, Kt., K.B.E., C.M.G., O.B.E. MIL., Q.C.; British lawyer; b. 24 Dec. 1898, Philadelphia, Pa., U.S.A.; s. of

G. W. Foster-Sutton and Florence Mary Sutton; m. Linda Dorothy Allwood 1919; one s. (deceased) one d.; ed. St. Mary Magdalen School and pvt. tutor; served in army 1914-26; active service R.F.C. and R.A.F. First World War 1914-18; called to the Bar (Gray's Inn) 1926; pvt. practice 1926-36; Solicitor-Gen. Jamaica 1936; Attorney-Gen. Cyprus 1940; Col. Commdg. Cyprus Volunteer Force and Insp. Cyprus Forces 1941-44; mem. for Law and Order and Attorney-Gen. Kenya 1944-48, Acting Gov. Aug.-Sept. 1947; Attorney-Gen. Malaya 1948-50; Chief Justice Fed. of Malaya 1950; Officer Administering the Govt., Fed. of Malaya Sept.-Dec. 1950; Pres. West African Court of Appeal 1951-56; Chief Justice, Fed. of Nigeria 1956-58; Act. Gov.-Gen. May-June 1957; Pres. Pensions Appeal Tribunals for England and Wales 1958-73; Chair. Zanzibar Comm. of Inquiry 1961, Regional Boundaries and Constituencies Delimitation Comms., Kenya 1962, Referendum Observers, Malta 1964; Vice-Pres. Council of Britain/Nigeria Asscn. 1982-, Exec. Cttee. Overseas Service Pensioners' Asscn.; mem. Court, Worshipful Company of Tallow Chandlers, Master 1981-. *Address:* 7 London Road, Saffron Walden, Essex, England. *Telephone:* Saffron Walden 22246 (Home).

FOSTERVOLL, Alv Jakob; Norwegian (fmr.) politician and civil servant; b. 20 Jan. 1932, Kristiansund; s. of Alv Kr. and Astrid Fostervoll; m. Gerd Klinge 1967; two s.; ed. Teachers' Coll. of Norway; teacher, Gomalandet School, Kristiansund 1956-57, Headmaster 1967; mem. Kristiansund Municipal Council, Alderman 1960-, Deputy Chair. 1967-69; mem. Møre and Romsdal County Council 1967; mem. Bd. Møre and Romsdal County Steamship Co. 1967; mem. Storting 1969-77; Chair. Nordmøre Labour Party 1965-69; Minister of Defence 1971-72, 1973-76; Cttee. of Municipal Affairs and Environment Protection 1976-77; County Gov. of Møre and Romsdal 1977-; Chair. Co. Ass. Horten Verft A/S 1978-; mem. Co. Ass. A/S Wichmann 1980-, Statoil (Norway) 1982-; Pres. Norwegian Defence Asscn. 1981-. *Address:* Møretun, 6400 Molde, Norway. *Telephone:* (072) 54111 (Office); (072) 51560 (Home).

FOU TS'ONG; Chinese pianist; b. 10 March 1934; m. 1st Zamira Menuhin 1960 (dissolved 1970), one s.; m. 2nd Hijong Hyun 1973 (dissolved 1978); m. 3rd Patsy Toh 1987; one s.; ed. Shanghai and Warsaw; first performance, Shanghai 1953, concerts in Eastern Europe and U.S.S.R. 1953-58; London debut 1959, concerts in Europe, N. and S. America, Australia and Far East. *Address:* 62 Aberdeen Park, London, N5 2BL, England. *Telephone:* 01-226 9589.

FOUCHET, Paul Jacques; French diplomatist (retd.); b. 25 Jan. 1913, Nogent-sur-Marne; m. Lisette Caprioli 1946; one d.; ed. Lycée Condorcet and Faculty of Law, Paris; French Consulate, Addis Ababa 1938-39, Third Sec. Ankara 1941, French Consulate, Baghdad 1941-42, resgnd. 1942; recalled by Vichy Govt. 1943, Civil and Mil. Command, Algeria 1943; Allied Mil. Govt., Italy 1943-44, mem. French Del. to Consultative Council on Italian Affairs 1944-45, Consul, Milan 1945-46; Office of Foreign Affairs, Paris 1946-47; First Sec. New Delhi 1947-49; mem. French Del. to UN Special Comm. on Balkans 1949-50; First Sec. Athens 1950-52, Second Counsellor, Vienna 1954-59; Head of Dept. for Tech. Co-operation 1959-62; Amb. to Niger 1962-64, to Dominican Repub. 1964-66, to Libya 1966-69; Deputy Gen. Dir., Cultural, Scientific and Tech. Dept., Ministry of Foreign Affairs 1969-71; Amb. to Brazil 1972-75, to Sweden 1975-78; Consultant to Thompson C.S.F. and Entreprise Jean Lefèvre 1978-82; Officier Légion d'honneur; Commdr. Ordre national du Mérite. *Leisure interests:* sailing, swimming. *Address:* 2 rue de Noisiel, 75116 Paris, France.

FOULKES, Sir Nigel Gordon, Kt., M.A., C.B.I.M., F.R.S.A.; British business executive; b. 29 Aug. 1919, London; ed. s. of Louis Augustine and Winifred Foulkes; m. Elisabeth Walker 1948; ed. Gresham's School and Balliol Coll., Oxford; Production Man., H. P. Bulmer & Co., Ltd. 1947-51; Man. Consultant, P.E. Consulting Group Ltd. 1951-56; Sr. Personnel Officer, Birfield Ltd. 1957-58; Dir. Greaves and Thomas Ltd. 1959-61; Exec. Asst. to Chair., Int. Nickel Ltd. 1961-64; Man. Dir. Rank Xerox Ltd. 1964-70; Chair. F.O.B.A.S. Ltd. 1970-76, British Airports Authority 1972-77, Civil Aviation Authority 1977-82, Equity Capital for Industry 1983-86, Equity Capital Trustee Ltd. 1983-; Chair. ECI Man. (Jersey) Ltd. 1986-, ECI Int. Man. Ltd. 1987-; Dir. Imagic Holdings 1971-77, Charterhouse Group 1972-85, Bekaert Group (Belgium) 1973-85, Council, British Inst. of Man. 1972-77, Stone-Platt Industries 1975-82; mem. CBI Pres.'s Cttee. 1976-77; mem. Court, Brunel Univ., London 1975. *Address:* c/o ECI Ventures, Brettenham House, Lancaster Place, London, W.C.2, England. *Telephone:* 01-895 1000.

FOURASTIÉ, Jean, D. EN D., ING.; French academic (retd.); b. 17 April 1907, St. Benin d'Azy; s. of Honoré Fourastié and Eulalie (née Mouly) Fourastié; m. Melle F. Moncány de Saint-Aignan 1935; four c.; ed. Collège de Juilly, Paris, Ecole Centrale des Arts et Métiers; Commr.-in-Charge Insurance Ministry of Finance 1934-46; Prof. Conservatoire Nat. des Arts et Métiers 1940-78, Inst. d'Etudes Politiques, Paris 1945-78; Dir. of Studies Ecole Pratique des Hautes Etudes 1946-77; Econ. and Tech. Counsellor Commissariat Général au Plan 1946-53, Pres. of Comm. of Main d'Oeuvre 1953-67; journalist l'Express 1968-78, Figaro 1966-; Prix Gouverneur Général Cornez 1965, Médaille d'Or de la Société d'Encouragement à l'Industrie 1976. *Publications:* La Civilisation de 1975, le Grand Espoir du XXe siécle 1949, L'Economie Française dans le Monde, La Productivité 1958, Les Ecrivains témoins du Peuple (with F. Fourastié), Les 40 000

heures 1965, Comment mon Cerveau s'informe 1974, La Réalité Economique 1978, Ce que je crois 1981, Le Rire Suite 1983, Pourquoi les prix baissent 1984, D'une France à une Autre 1986. *Address:* 24 rue Lecourbe, 75015 Paris, France.

FOURCADE, Jean-Pierre; French politician: b. 18 Oct. 1929, Marmande; s. of Raymond and Germaine (née Raynal) Fourcade; m. Odile Mion 1958; one s. two d.; ed. Coll. de Sorèze, Bordeaux Univ. Faculté de Droit, Inst. des Etudes politiques; student, Ecole Nat. d'Admin. 1952-54; Insp. des Finances 1954-73; Chargé de Mission to Sec. of State for Finance (later Minister of Finance) 1959-61, Conseiller technique 1962, Dir. adjoint du Cabinet 1964-66; Asst. Head of Service, Inspection gén. des Finances 1962; Head of Trade Div., Directorate-Gen. of Internal Trade and Prices 1965, Dir.-Gen. 1968-70; Asst. Dir.-Gen. Crédit industriel et commercial 1970, Dir.-Gen. 1972-74, Admin. 1973-74; Admin., later Pres. and Dir.-Gen. Soc. d'Epargne mobilière 1972-74; Admin. Banque transatlantique 1971-74, Soc. commerciale d'Affrètement et de Combustibles 1972-74; Minister of Econ. and Finance 1974-76, of Supply 1976-77, of Supply and Regional Devt. 1977; Mayor of Saint-Cloud 1971-; Conseiller-Gén., canton of Saint-Cloud 1973-; Conseiller Régional, Ile de France 1976, Vice-Pres. 1982-; Senator, Hauts de Seine 1977; Pres. Comité des Finances Locales 1980-, Comm. des Affaires Sociales du Sénat 1983-; Pres. Clubs Perspectives et Réalités 1975-82; Vice-Pres. Union pour la Démocratie française (U.D.F.) 1978-85, mem. 1985-; Officier, Ordre national du Mérite. *Address:* Sénat, Palais du Luxembourg, 75006 Paris; 8 Parc de Bearn, 92210 Saint-Cloud, France (Home).

FOUREST, Henry-Pierre; French ceramist; b. 22 Dec. 1911, Paris; s. of Georges Fourest and Valentine Fourest (née Noe); m. Françoise Labayle-Pararnaud 1946; one s. three d.; ed. Ecole du Louvre and Inst. d'Art et Archéologie; Asst. Dept. of Paintings, Musée du Louvre; Asst. in Musée nat. Céramique de Sèvres; Chief Curator of Musée nat. Céramique de Sèvres, Musée nat. Adrien Dubouché; Lecturer Ecole nat. supérieure Céramique de Sèvres; fmr. Prof. Ecole du Louvre; Pres. Asscn. de l'Ecole du Louvre; Chevalier Légion d'honneur, Commdr. des Arts et des Lettres, Officier Ordre nationale du Mérite. *Leisure interests:* music, ichthylogy. *Address:* 16 rue de Liège, Paris 9e, France. *Telephone:* 48-74-19-81.

FOURIE, Bernardus Gerhardus, M.A., B.COM.; South African diplomatist and broadcasting executive; b. 13 Oct. 1916, Wolmaransstad; s. of N. P. Fourie; m. Daphne Madeleine Doyle 1962; one s. one d.; ed. Pretoria and New York Univs; served in Berlin, Stockholm and Brussels 1934-38; London High Comm. 1940-47; Del. to San Francisco Conf. 1945, UN Prep. Comm. and 1st Gen. Assembly 1946; with Dept. of External Affairs Int. Orgs. Div. 1952-58, Asst. Sec. African Div. 1957-58; Perm. Rep. to UN 1958-62; Under Sec. African Div., Dept. of Foreign Affairs 1962-63; Sec. of Information 1963-66; Sec. Foreign Affairs 1966-80; Dir.-Gen. Dept. of Foreign Affairs and Information 1980-82; Amb. to U.S.A. 1982-85; Chair. of Bd. S.A.B.C. 1985-89; Hon. LL.D. (Rand Afrikaans Univ.) 1977; Decoration for Meritorious Service 1980, Grand Cross Order of Good Hope 1980. *Leisure interests:* tennis, gardening. *Address:* S.A.B.C., P.O. Box 91123, Auckland Park, 2006, Johannesburg; Highstreet 164, Ashlea Gardens, Pretoria 0181, South Africa (Home).

FOURNIER, Jacques, L. EN D.; French lawyer; b. 5 May 1929, Épinal; s. of Léon Fournier and Ida Rudmann; m. 1st Jacqueline Tazerout (deceased); three s.; 2nd Michèle Dubez 1980; ed. Inst. for Political Studies, Paris and Nat. School of Admin.; Civil Servant, French State Council 1953, Master of Petitions 1960, State Councillor 1978; Legal Adviser, Embassy in Morocco 1961-64; Head of Dept. of Social Affairs, Gen. Planning Office 1969-72; Asst. Sec.-Gen. to Pres. of France 1981-82; Sec.-Gen. of the Govt. 1982-86; Pres. of Admin. Council of Gaz de France 1986-88; Pres. S.N.C.F. Aug. 1988-; Chevalier Ordre Nat. du Mérite; Officier, Légion d'Honneur. *Publications:* Politique de l'Education 1971, Traité du social, situations, luttes politiques, institutions 1976, Le Pouvoir du social 1979. *Address:* 88 rue Saint Lazarre, 75436, Paris Cedex 09 (Office); 85 rue d'Assas, 75006, Paris, France (Home). *Telephone:* 47 54 22 24 (Office); 43 29 67 86 (Home).

FOURNIER-ACUÑA, Fernando, LL.D.; Costa Rican lawyer and diplomatist; b. 13 Sept. 1916, San José; ed. Univ. de Costa Rica and Harvard Univ.; founding mem. Facio, Fournier & Cañas (law firm), San José 1942-; Prof. of History of Law, Univ. de Costa Rica 1947-48; Prof. of Roman Law 1959; mem. Constituent Ass. 1949-; Deputy Minister of Foreign Affairs 1953-54; Minister 1955; Amb. to U.S.A. and Perm. Rep. to OAS 1955-56; Del. Inter-American Council of Jurists 1961; mem. Exec. Cttee. Inter-American Fed. of Lawyers 1961-69, Pres. 1967; mem. Int. Acad. of Trial Lawyers 1969-. *Address:* Facultad de Derecho, Universidad de Costa Rica, Apartado 3979, San José, Costa Rica.

FOURQUET, Gen. Michel Martin Léon; French air force officer and administrator; b. 9 June 1914, Brussels, Belgium; m. Micheline Roger 1939; three s. two d.; ed. Lycée Louis-le-Grand and Ecole Polytechnique, Paris; Air Force Officer 1943-44; Commdt. First Tactical Air Group 1960-61, 5th Air Region, Algiers 1961-62; Chief Commdt. Forces in Algeria 1962; Sec.-Gen. of Nat. Defence 1962-66; Perm. Under-Sec. for Armaments 1966-68; Chief of Staff of Armed Forces 1968-71; mem. Higher Air Council 1962-68; mem. Atomic Energy Cttee. 1966-71; Pres. Supervisory Council Soc. Nat. Industrielle Aérospatiale 1973-75; Pres. and Dir. Gen. Soc. des Autoroutes

Paris-Est-Lorraine 1972-81; Pres. Groupement pour le Financement de Fos 1972-78; Pres., Dir.-Gen. Office Gén. de l'Air 1978-84, Hon. Pres. 1984-; Dir. Soc. gén. de surveillance, Geneva 1972-, Sommer Alibert 1973-; Grand Croix Légion d'honneur, Compagnon de la Libération, Croix de guerre, Croix de la Valeur militaire, Médaille de l'Aéronautique, D.F.C. (U.K.), etc. *Leisure interests:* riding, hunting. *Address:* 5 Villa Sainte-Foy, 92200 Neuilly-sur-Seine, France (Home).

FOWDEN, Sir Leslie, Kt., PH.D., F.R.S.; British plant chemist; b. 13 Oct. 1925, Rochdale, Lancs.; ed. Univ. Coll., London; mem. Scientific Staff, Human Nutrition Research Unit, Medical Research Council 1947-50; Lecturer in Plant Chem., Univ. Coll., London 1950-55, Reader 1956-64, Prof. of Plant Chem. 1964-73 and Dean of Faculty of Science 1970-73; Dir. Rothamsted Experimental Station 1973-86; Dir of Arable Crops Research, Agricultural and Food Research Council 1986-88; mem. Council of Royal Soc. 1970-72; Scientific Advisory Panel Botanical Gardens, Kew 1977- (Trustee 1983-); Consultant Dir. Commonwealth Bureau of Soils 1973; Chair. Agricultural and Veterinary Advisory Cttee., British Council 1987-. *Address:* 31 Southdown Road, Harpenden, Herts., AL5 1PF, England.

FOWKE, Philip Francis, L.R.A.M., A.R.C.M., A.R.A.M.; British concert pianist; b. 28 June 1950, Gerrards Cross; s. of Francis H. V. Fowke and Florence L. (née Clutton) Fowke; winner, Royal Acad. of Music Scholarship 1967, Nat. Fed. of Music Socs. Award 1973, BBC Piano Competition 1974; Wigmore Hall début 1974; U.K. concerto début with Royal Liverpool Philharmonic 1975; Winston Churchill Fellowship for study in New York 1976; BBC Promenade Concert début 1979; U.S. début 1982; débuts in Denmark, Bulgaria, France, Switzerland, Hong Kong, Belgium and Italy 1983; Austrian début at Salzburg Mozart week 1984; German début 1985; now appears regularly with all the leading orchestras in U.K. and gives regular recitals and concerto performances for BBC Radio; Prof. Royal Acad. of Music 1984-, recordings of Tchaikovsky, Rachmaninoff, Chopin; Professors Memorial Prize 1968, Albanesi Prize 1969, Countess of Munster Musical Trust Award 1972, City Livery Club Prize 1973, and numerous other awards and prizes. *Leisure interests:* architecture, travel, monasticism. *Address:* Kaye Artists Management, Kingsmead House, 250 King's Road, London, SW3 6NR, England. *Telephone:* 01-352 4494.

FOWLER, Sir (Edward) Michael (Coulson), Kt., M.ARCH., F.N.Z.I.A., A.R.I.B.A.; New Zealand architect; b. 19 Dec. 1929, Marton; s. of William Coulson and Faith Agnes Fowler (née Netherclift); m. Barbara Hamilton Hall 1953; two s. one d.; ed. Christ's Coll., Christchurch, Auckland Univ.; with Ove Arup & Partners, London 1954-55; Partner, Gray Young, Morton Calder & Fowler, Wellington 1959; Sr. Partner, Calder, Fowler & Styles 1960-; travelled abroad to study cen. banking systems security methods; work includes Overseas Terminal, Wellington, Reserve Bank, Wellington, Dalmuir House, Wellington Club, office bldgs., factories, houses, churches; Dir. Robert Jones Investments Ltd., N.Z. Sugar Co., Southern Cross TV Ltd., CIGNA Insurance (N.Z.) Ltd.; mem. Wellington City Council 1968-74; Chair. NZIA Educ. Cttee. 1967-73; Mayor of Wellington 1974-83; Chair. Queen Elizabeth II Arts Council of N.Z. 1983-86; Pres. N.Z. Youth Hostel Asscn. 1983-86. *Publications:* Country Houses of New Zealand 1972, Wellington Sketches: Folios I, II 1973, The Architecture and Planning of Moscow 1980, Eating Houses in Wellington 1980, Wellington-Wellington 1981, Eating Houses of Canterbury 1982, Wellington Celebration 1983, The New Zealand House 1983, Buildings of New Zealanders 1984. *Leisure interests:* sketching, writing. *Address:* Calder, Fowler, Styles & Turner, P.O. Box 2692, Wellington, (Office); Apt. 1, Michael Fowler Hotel, Cable Street, Wellington, New Zealand (Home). *Telephone:* 726916 (Office); 856676 (Home).

FOWLER, Henry Hamill, A.B., LL.B., J.S.D.; American lawyer, investment banker and government official; b. 5 Sept. 1908, Roanoke, Va.; s. of Mack Johnson Fowler and Bertha (née Browning) Fowler; m. Trudye Pamela Hathcote 1938; one s. (deceased) two d.; ed. Roanoke Coll. and Yale Univ. Law School; admitted to Va. Bar 1933, D.C. Bar 1946; Counsel Tenn. Valley Authority 1934-38, Asst. Gen. Counsel 1939; Asst. Gen. Counsel Office of Production Man. 1941, War Production Bd. 1942-44; Econ. Adviser, U.S. Mission Econ. Affairs, London 1944; served Foreign Econ. Admin. 1945; Admin. Nat. Production Authority 1951-52; Admin. Defense Production Admin.; Dir. Office of Defense Mobilization and mem. Nat. Security Council 1952-53; sr. mem. law firm, Fowler, Leva, Hawes and Symington, Washington D.C., 1946-51, 1953-61, 1964-65; Under-Sec. U.S. Treasury 1961-64, Sec. 1965-68; Gen. Partner Goldman, Sachs, New York 1969-81; Chair. Goldman Sachs Int. Corpn. 1969-84, U.S. Treasury Advisory Comm. on Int. Monetary Affairs 1974-84; Chair. Atlantic Council of the U.S. 1972-77; Co-Chair. Cttee. on Present Danger 1976-, Bretton Woods Cttee. 1985-, Citizens' Network for Foreign Affairs 1987-; Trustee, Lyndon B. Johnson Foundation; Councillor, Conf. Bd., Roanoke Coll.; mem. Council, Miller Center of Public Affairs, Univ. of Va.; Democrat. *Leisure interests:* tennis, bridge, books. *Address:* c/o Goldman, Sachs & Co., 85 Broad Street, New York, N.Y. 10004 (Office); 209 South Fairfax Street, Alexandria, Va. 22314, and 200 East 66th Street, New York, N.Y. 10021, U.S.A. (Homes). *Telephone:* (212) 676-8322 (Office).

FOWLER, Norman (see Fowler, Peter Norman).

FOWLER, Peter Howard, D.SC., F.R.S.; British physicist; b. 27 Feb. 1923, Cambridge; s. of Sir Ralph Howard Fowler, F.R.S. and Eileen Rutherford;

m. Rosemary Hempson (née Brown) 1949; three d.; ed. Winchester Coll. and Univ. of Bristol; Flying Officer in R.A.F., Radar and Tech. Officer 1942-46; Asst. Lecturer in Physics, Univ. of Bristol 1948, Lecturer 1951, Reader 1961, Royal Soc. Research Prof. 1964-88, Emer. Prof. 1988-; Visiting Prof. Univ. of Minn. 1956-57; Hughes Medal, Royal Soc. 1974. *Publication:* co-author: The Study of Elementary Particles by the Photographic Method 1959. *Leisure interests:* gardening, meteorology. *Address:* H. H. Wills Physics Laboratory, Tyndall Avenue, Bristol, BS8 1TL; 320 Canford Lane, Westbury on Trym, Bristol, England (Home). *Telephone:* Bristol 303605 (Office).

FOWLER, Rt. Hon. (Peter) Norman, P.C., M.A.; British politician; b. 2 Feb. 1938; s. of the late N. F. Fowler and Katherine Fowler; m. Fiona Poole 1979; two d.; ed. King Edward VI School, Chelmsford, Trinity Hall, Cambridge; Nat. Service Comm., Essex Regiment 1956-58; joined The Times 1961, Special Corresp. 1962-66, Home Affairs Corresp. 1966-70; mem. Council, Bow Group 1967-69, Editorial Bd., Crossbow 1962-69; Vice-Chair. N. Kensington Conservative Asscn. 1967-68; Chair. E. Midlands Area, Conservative Political Centre 1970-73; M.P. for Nottingham South 1970-74, for Sutton Coldfield Feb. 1974-; mem. Parl. Select Cttee. on Race Relations and Immigration 1970-74; Jt. Sec. Conservative Parl. Home Affairs Cttee. 1971-72, Vice-Chair. 1974; Parl. Pvt. Sec. N. Ireland Office 1972-74; Opposition Spokesman on Home Affairs 1974-75; Chief Opposition Spokesman on Social Services 1975-76, on Transport 1976-79; Minister of Transport 1979-81, Sec. of State for Transport 1981, for Social Services 1981-87, for Employment June 1987-; mem. Lloyds 1989-. *Publications:* After the Riots: The Police in Europe 1979, and political pamphlets. *Address:* c/o The House of Commons, London, SW1A 0AA, England.

FOWLER, William Alfred, B.ENG., PH.D.; American professor of physics; b. 9 Aug. 1911, Pittsburgh, Pa.; s. of late John McLeod and Jennie Summers (née Watson) Fowler (deceased); m. Ardiane Foy Olmsted 1940 (deceased); two d.; ed. Ohio State Univ. and Calif. Inst. of Tech.; Research Fellow in Nuclear Physics, Calif. Inst. of Tech. 1936-39, Asst. Prof. of Physics 1939-42, Assoc. Prof. 1942-46, Prof. 1946-70; Inst. Prof. of Physics 1970-82, Inst. Prof. of Physics Emer. 1982-; Research Staff mem., Section T, and Div. 4, Nat. Defense Research Cttee. (N.D.R.C.) 1941, Asst. Dir. of Research, Section L, Div. 3, N.D.R.C. 1941-45; Tech. Observer, Office of Field Services and New Devts. Div., War Dept. in S. and S.W. Pacific Theaters 1944; Act. Supervisor, Ord. Div., R and D NOTS 1945; Science Dir., Project Vista, Dept. of Defense 1951-52; Visiting Prof. of Physics, M.I.T. 1966; Fulbright Lecturer and Guggenheim Fellow, Univ. of Cambridge 1954-55, Guggenheim Fellow, St. John's Coll. and Dept. of Applied Maths. and Theoretical Physics, Univ. of Cambridge 1961-62, Visiting Fellow, Inst. of Theoretical Astronomy, Univ. of Cambridge 1968, 1969, 1970, 1971, 1972; Lecturer at numerous univs. and socs. in U.S. and abroad; Chair. Jt. Discussion on Nucleogenesis 10th Gen. Assembly in Int. Astronomical Union, Moscow 1958; Chair. Office of Physical Science, Nat. Acad. of Science 1981-(84); del. to numerous int. confs. on astronomy, nuclear physics, astrophysics and cosmology; mem. Int. Astronomical Union, A.A.A.S., American Astronomical Soc., American Asscn. of Univ. Profs. (Pres. Calif. Inst. of Tech. Chapter 1963-67), Nat. Acad. of Sciences (Chair. Physics Section 1971-74), B.A.A.S., R.S.A., etc.; mem. Nat. Science Bd., Nat. Science Foundation 1968-74, Space Science Bd. 1971-74, 1977-80; Corresp. mem. Soc. royale des Sciences de Liège; Fellow, American Physical Soc. (mem. Bd. of Eds. 1953-55, of Council 1958-61, Vice-Pres. 1975, Pres. 1976), American Acad. of Arts and Sciences, Royal Astronomical Soc., London, Assoc. 1975; Hon. mem. The Naturvetenskapliga Foreningen 1984; Hon. D.Sc. (Univ. of Chicago) 1976, (Ohio State Univ.) 1978, (Denison Univ.) 1982, (Ariz. State Univ.) 1985, (Univ. of Mass.) 1987, (Williams Coll.) 1988; Dr. h.c. (Univ. of Liège) 1981, (Observatoire de Paris) 1981; shared Nobel Prize for Physics 1983; Naval Ordnance Devt. Award 1945, Medal for Merit 1948, Lamme Medal, Ohio State Univ. 1952, Liège Medal, Univ. of Liège 1955, Calif. Co-Scientist of the Year 1958, Barnard Medal of Meritorious Service to Science, Columbia Univ. 1965, Apollo Achievement Award, NASA 1969, Bonner Prize, American Physical Soc. 1970; G. Unger Vetlesen Prize, Columbia Univ. 1973, Nat. Medal of Science 1974, Eddington Medal, Royal Astronomical Soc. 1978, Bruce Gold Medal, Astronomical Soc. of the Pacific 1979, Sullivant Medal, Ohio State Univ. 1985. *Publications:* Contributions to numerous scientific books and journals. *Address:* Kellogg Radiation Laboratory, (106-38), California Institute of Technology, 1201 East California Boulevard, Pasadena, Calif. 91125, U.S.A. *Telephone:* (818) 356-4272.

FOWLER, William Wyche, Jr., J.D.; American politician; b. 6 Oct. 1940, Atlanta; s. of William Wyche Fowler and Emelyn Barbre; one d.; ed. Davidson Coll. and Emory Univ.; Chief Asst. to U.S. Congressman 1965; mem. Atlanta Bd. Aldermen 1969-73; Pres. Atlanta City Council 1973-77; mem. 95th-99th Congresses from 5th Ga. Dist.; Senator from Ga. Jan. 1987-; mem. American Bar Asscn.; Myrtle Wreath Award 1972; Democrat. *Address:* U.S. Senate, Washington, D.C. 20510, U.S.A.

FOWLES, John; British author; b. 31 March 1926, Essex; s. of Robert J. Fowles and Gladys M. Richards; m. Elizabeth Whitton 1954; no c.; ed. Bedford School and Univ. of Oxford; PEN Silver Pen Award 1969, W. H. Smith Literary Award (for The French Lieutenant's Woman) 1969; Hon. D.Litt. (Exeter) 1983. *Publications:* The Collector 1963, The Aristos 1964,

The Magus 1965, The French Lieutenant's Woman 1969, Poems 1973, Shipwreck 1974, The Ebony Tower 1974, Daniel Martin 1977, Islands (with Fay Godwin) 1978, The Tree 1979, The Enigma of Stonehenge 1980, Mantissa 1982, Thomas Hardy's England 1984, Land 1985, A Maggot 1985. *Leisure interests:* local and natural history. *Address:* c/o Anthony Sheil Assocs., 45 Doughty Street, London, WC1N 2LF, England.

FOX, Edward; British actor; b. 13 April 1937; s. of Robin and Angela Fox; m. 1st Tracy Pelissier, one d.; m. 2nd Joanna Fox, one d.; ed. Ashfold School, Harrow School and Royal Acad. of Dramatic Art; actor since 1957; started in provincial repertory theatre 1958 and has since worked widely in films, stage plays and television; recipient of several awards for television performance as Edward VIII in Edward and Mrs Simpson 1978; *stage appearances include:* Knuckle 1973, The Family Reunion 1979, Anyone for Denis 1981, Quartermaine's Terms 1981, Hamlet 1982, The Dance of Death 1983, Interpreters 1986, The Admirable Crichton 1988. *Films include:* The Go-Between 1971, The Day of the Jackal, A Doll's House 1973, Galileo 1976, A Bridge Too Far, The Duellists, The Cat and the Canary 1977, Force Ten from Navarone 1978, The Mirror Crack'd 1980, Gandhi 1982, Wild Geese, The Bounty 1984, The Shooting Party, Return from the River Quai 1989. *Leisure interest:* playing the piano. *Address:* c/o Leading Artists, 60 St. James's Street, London, S.W.1.

FOX, Sir (Henry) Murray, G.B.E., M.A., D.LITT., F.R.I.C.S.; British chartered surveyor; b. 7 June 1912; s. of the late Sir Sidney Fox; m. Helen Isabella Margaret Crichton 1941 (died 1986); one s. two d.; ed. Malvern and Emmanuel Coll., Cambridge; Chair. Trehaven Trust Group 1962–; Pres. City and Metropolitan Bldg. Soc. 1985–, Chair. 1976–85; Dir. Toye, Kenning and Spencer Ltd., City of London Sinfonia 1979; Man. Trustee, Municipal Mutual Insurance Ltd. 1977–; Sheriff, City of London 1971–72; Lord Mayor of London 1974–75. *Leisure interests:* golf, walking, reading. *Address:* 80 Defoe House, Barbican, London, E.C.2, England. *Telephone:* 01-588 8306.

FOX, Maurice Sanford, PH.D.; American professor of molecular biology; b. 11 Oct. 1924; s. of Albert Fox and Ray Fox; m. Sally Cherniavsky 1955; three s.; ed. Stuyvesant High School, Univ. of Chicago; Instructor, Univ. of Chicago 1951–53; Asst., Rockefeller Univ. 1953–55, Asst. Prof. 1955–58, Assoc. Prof. 1958–62; Assoc. Prof., M.I.T. 1962–66, Prof. 1966–79, Lester Wolfe Prof. of Molecular Biology 1979–, Head, Dept. of Biology 1985–; mem. Bd. Council for a Liveable World 1962–; Breast Cancer Task Force 1977–80; mem. Inst. of Medicine, N.A.S.; Fellow A.A.A.S., Nuffield Research Fellow 1957. *Publications:* numerous learned papers. *Leisure interest:* ancient history. *Address:* Department of Biology, Massachussets Institute of Technology, Cambridge, Mass., 02139 (Office); 195 Tappan Street, Brookline, Mass. 02146, U.S.A. (Home). *Telephone:* 617-253 4703 (Office); 617-738 0860 (Home).

FOX, Paul Leonard, C.B.E.; British television executive; b. 27 Oct. 1925; m. Betty R. Nathan 1948; two s.; ed. Bournemouth Grammar School; Parachute Regt. 1943; reporter, Kentish Times 1946, The People 1947; scriptwriter, Pathe News 1947; BBC TV scriptwriter 1950; Ed. Sportsview 1953, Panorama 1961; Head, BBC TV Public Affairs Dept. 1963, Current Affairs Group 1965; Controller, BBC 1 1967–73; Dir. of Programmes, Yorkshire TV 1973–74, Man. Dir. Yorkshire TV 1977–, Dir. of Programmes 1973–84; Dir. Independent Television News 1977–86, Chair. 1986–; Chair. ITV Network Programme Cttee. 1978–80, Council, Independent Television Cos. Asscn. Ltd. 1982–84; mem. Royal Comm. on Criminal Procedure 1978–80; Pres. Royal TV Soc. 1985–; Dir. Channel Four 1985–, World TV News 1986–; Hon. LL.D. (Leeds) 1984. *Leisure interests:* television, attending race meetings. *Address:* Yorkshire Television, The Television Centre, Leeds, LS3 1JS, England.

FOX, Peter Kendrew, M.A.; British university librarian; b. 23 March 1949, Beverley, Yorks.; s. of Thomas Kendrew Fox and Dorothy Wildbore; m. Isobel McConnell 1983; one d.; ed. Baines Grammar School, Poulton-le-Fylde, Lancs., King's Coll. London and Univ. of Sheffield; Asst. Library Officer, Cambridge Univ. Library 1973–77, Asst. Under-Librarian 1977–78, Under-Librarian 1978–79; Deputy Librarian, Trinity Coll. Dublin 1979–84, Librarian 1984–; mem. British Library Project on Teaching and Learning Skills for Librarians 1978–79, SCONUL Advisory Cttee. on Information Services 1979– (Chair. 1987–), An Chomhairle Leabharlanna 1982–, Cttee. on Library Co-operation in Ireland 1984–, Nat. Preservation Advisory Cttee. (British Library) 1984–; Jt. Ed. An Leabharlann: The Irish Library 1982–; Assoc. King's College, Library Asscn. *Publications:* Reader Instruction Methods in Academic Libraries 1974, User Education in the Humanities in US Academic Libraries 1979, Trinity College Library Dublin 1982; Ed.: Library User Education—Are New Approaches Needed? 1980, Second (and Third) Int. Conf. on Library User Educ. Proc. 1982 (and 1984), Treasures of the Library—Trinity College Dublin 1986; articles and reviews in librarianship journals. *Leisure interests:* music and gardening. *Address:* Trinity College Library, College Street, Dublin 2, Ireland. *Telephone:* (01) 772941.

FOX, Renée Claire, A.B., PH.D.; American academic; b. 15 Feb. 1928, New York; d. of Paul Fox and Henrietta Gold; ed. Smith Coll., Northampton, Mass., Radcliffe Coll., Harvard Univ.; Research Asst. and Assoc., Bureau of Applied Social Research, Columbia Univ. 1953–58; lecturer, Asst. and Assoc. Prof., Barnard Coll., Columbia Univ. 1955–66; lecturer in Sociology,

Harvard Univ. 1967–69, Research Assoc., Program on Tech. and Soc. 1968–71; Prof. of Sociology, Univ. of Pa. 1969– (Chair. Dept. 1972–78), Prof. of Psychiatry, School of Medicine 1972–, Prof. of Sociology, School of Nursing 1978–, Annenberg Prof. of Social Sciences 1978–; Assoc. Ed. Journal of Health and Social Behaviour 1985–87; numerous prizes, awards and honours. *Publications:* numerous articles and essays on sociology and medicine. *Address:* Department of Sociology, University of Pennsylvania, 507 McNeil Building/CR, Philadelphia 19104 (Office); The Wellington, 135 South 19th Street, Philadelphia, Pa. 19103, U.S.A. (Home). *Telephone:* (215) 898-7933 (Office); (215) 563-4912 (Home).

FOXLEY, Alejandro, M.SC., PH.D.; Chilean economist; b. 26 May 1939, Viña del Mar; s. of Harold Foxley (Chapman) and Carmen Rioseco; m. Gisela Tapia 1963; two c.; ed. Univ. of Wisconsin, Harvard Univ. and Catholic Univ., Valparaíso; Dir. Global Planning Div., Nat. Planning Office, Govt. of Chile 1967–70; Dir. Center for Nat. Planning Studies, Catholic Univ. of Chile 1970–76; mem. Exec. Council, Latin-American Social Science Council (CLACSO) 1975–81; mem. Joint Cttee. Latin-American Studies, Social Science Research Council, New York 1975–78; Pres. Corpn. for Latin-American Econ. Research (CIEPLAN), Santiago 1976–; Helen Kellogg Prof. of Econs. (part-time) and Int. Devt., Univ. of Notre Dame 1982–; Assoc. Ed. Journal of Development Economics 1977–; Visiting Fellow, Univ. of Sussex 1973, Oxford 1975, M.I.T. 1978; Ford Int. Fellow 1963–64, Daugherty Foundation Fellow 1965–66; Ford Foundation Fellow 1970; mem. Exec. Cttee. Interamerican Dialogue, Wash., Int. Advisory Bd. Journal Latin American Studies. *Publications:* Redistributive Effects of Government Programmes, Income Distribution in Latin-America, Estrategia de Desarrollo y Modelos de Planificación, Legados del Monetarismo: Argentina y Chile, Para una Democracia Estable 1985, Chile y su futuro: un país posible 1989, Chile puede más 1989, numerous articles and working papers. *Address:* CIEPLAN, Colón 3494, Santiago (Office); Golfo de Darien 10236, Santiago (Las Condes), Chile (Home). *Telephone:* 228-3262 (Office); 20 79 24 (Home).

FOYER, Jean, D. EN D.; French politician; b. 27 April 1921; m. Gisèle Penin 1946; Prof., Paris Univ.; Deputy for Maine-et-Loire, Mayor of Contigné; Sec. of State for Relations with Mem. States of the French Community (Debré Cabinet) 1960; Minister of Co-operation 1961–62, of Justice 1962–67; Pres. Nat. Assembly Comm. on Constitutional Laws of Legislation and Gen. Admin. of the Repub. 1968–72, 1973–81; Minister of Public Health 1972–73; Pres. Conseil Supérieur de la Propriété Industrielle 1976–; mem. Inst. de France; Chevalier du Mérite agricole; Grand Cross Order of St. Gregory the Great, Grand Cross of Merit Order of Sovereign of Malta. *Address:* Assemblée nationale, 75355 Paris (Office); Contigné, 49330 Châteauneuf-sur-Sarthe, France (Home).

FOYLE, Christina Agnes Lilian; British bookseller; b. 1911; d. of the late William Foyle; m. Ronald Batty 1938; ed. Parliament Hill School and Aux Villas Unspunnen, Switzerland; entered book trade 1928; began Foyle's Literary Luncheons 1930; Man. Dir. W. & G. Foyle Ltd., Foyle's Libraries Ltd. 1963–, Dir. John Gifford Ltd., Foyle's Gallery, The Book Club, Foyle's Literary Luncheons; Hon. D.Univ. (Essex) 1975. *Publication:* So Much Wisdom (Ed.) 1984. *Address:* W. & G. Foyle Ltd., 119 Charing Cross Road, London, W.C.2; Beeleigh Abbey, Maldon, Essex, England. *Telephone:* 01-437 5660 (Office).

FOZARD, John William, O.B.E., D.C.AE., C.ENG., F.ENG., F.R.S., F.R.AE.S., F.I.ME-CH.E., F.A.I.A.A., F.R.S.A.; British engineer; b. 16 Jan. 1928, Liversedge, Yorks.; s. of John Fozard and Eleanor Paulkit; m. 1st Mary Ward 1951 (divorced 1985), two s.; m. 2nd Gloria D. S. Roberts 1985; ed. Leeds Coll. of Technology, Hull Municipal Tech. Coll., Univ. of London (external) and Coll. of Aeronautics, Cranfield; apprentice, Blackburn Aircraft Ltd. 1943–48; joined Hawker Aircraft Ltd., Kingston-upon-Thames 1950, Head of Project Office 1961, Chief Designer P1154 1963, Chief Designer Harrier 1965, Deputy Chief Engineer (Hawker Siddeley Aviation Ltd.) 1968, Exec. Dir. 1971; Divisional Marketing Dir. Kingston-Brough Div. British Aerospace 1978, Divisional Dir. Special Projects, Weybridge Div. 1984, Mil. Aircraft Div. 1986–88; Lindbergh Prof. of Aerospace History, Smithsonian Inst., Nat. Air and Space Museum, Washington, D.C. 1988–; Pres. Royal Aeronautical Soc. 1986–87; Simms Gold Medal, London Soc. of Engs. 1971; British Silver Medal for Aeronautics 1978; Clayton Prize (Inst. of Mech. Engs.) 1984; Mullard Award, Royal Soc. (with R. S. Hooper) 1984; Hon. D.Sc. (Strathclyde) 1983; Hon. Fellow, Inst. of Engs. of Pakistan 1987. *Publications:* some 100 articles in learned journals and technical press. *Address:* National Air and Space Museum, Smithsonian Institution, Washington, D.C. 20560; 306 North Columbus Street, Alexandria, Va. 22314, U.S.A. (Home). *Telephone:* 202-357-2515 (Office); 703-549-5142 (Home).

FRAENKEL-CONRAT, Heinz, M.D., PH.D.; American professor of molecular biology; b. 29 July 1910, Breslau; s. of Prof. Ludwig Fraenkel and Lili Conrat; m. 1st Jane Opermann 1939 (divorced 1964), two s.; 2nd Beatrice Singer 1964; ed. Breslau, Vienna, Munich, Geneva and Univ. of Edinburgh; Rockefeller Inst. 1936–37; Instituto Butantan, São Paulo 1937–38; Inst. of Experimental Biology, Univ. of Calif. (Berkeley) 1938–42; Western Regional Lab., Albany, Calif. 1942–49; Rockefeller Fellow working with Linderstrøm-Lang (Copenhagen), F. Sanger (Cambridge), R. R. Porter (London) 1950; Dept. of Virology, Dept. of Molecular Biology, Univ. of Calif. (Berkeley) 1951–, Prof. 1955–81, Prof. Emer. 1981–; Lasker Award

1958; Humboldt Award 1985, and other distinctions. *Publications:* five books and 310 articles in scientific journals. *Leisure interests:* reading, hiking, swimming, bridge. *Address:* Department of Molecular Biology, W. M. Stanley Hall, University of California, Berkeley, Calif. 94720 (Office); 870 Grizzly Peak Blvd., Berkeley, Calif. 94708, U.S.A. (Home). *Telephone:* 415-642-5212 (Office).

FRAGA IRIBARNE, Manuel: Spanish writer, diplomatist and politician; b. 23 Nov. 1922, Villalba, Lugo; m. María del Carmen Estévez 1948; two s. three d.; ed. Santiago and Madrid Univs.; Prof. of Political Law, Valencia Univ. 1945; Diplomatic Service 1945-; Prof. Theory of State and Constitutional Law, Madrid Univ. 1948-; Gen. Sec. Inst. of Hispanic Culture 1951; Gen. Sec. Nat. Educ. Ministry 1955; Dir. Inst. of Political Studies 1961; Minister of Information and Tourism 1962-69; also Sec.-Gen. of Cabinet 1967-69; Amb. to U.K. 1973-75; Minister of the Interior and Deputy Premier for Internal Affairs 1975-76; f. Alianza Popular 1976, Leader 1979-86, Jan. 1989-; mem. Cttee. for Defence of Christian Civiliz-ation, Union of Family Orgs. *Publications:* thirty books on press, art, constitutional and social subjects. *Leisure interests:* hunting, fishing. *Address:* Joaquín María López 72, Madrid 15; c/o Marqués de la Ensenada, 14, Piso 3, Oficina 25 (Centro Colón), 28004 Madrid, Spain. *Telephone:* 419 59 08/04 (Office).

FRAME, Sir Alistair Gilchrist, Kt., M.A., B.SC., F.ENG.; British company executive; b. 3 April 1929, Dalmuir, Dumbartonshire; s. of Alexander and Mary (Fraser) Frame; m. Sheila Mathieson 1953; one d.; ed. Univs. of Glasgow and Cambridge ; Dir. Reactor and Research Groups, UKAEA 1963-68; joined Rio Tinto-Zinc Corpn. 1968, later Dir. and Deputy C.E.O. 1976, C.E.O. and Jt. Deputy Chair. 1978-82, Deputy Chair. 1982-84, Chair. March 1985-; Dir. Plessey Telecommunications Ltd., 1978-, Nat. Enterprise Bd. 1978-79, Vickers 1981-, Toronto Dominion Bank 1981-, Glaxo 1985-; Chair. Council of Mining and Metallurgic Insts. 1983-; mem. Eng. Council 1981-; Dir. Britoil 1983-84; Royal Soc. Esso Energy Award 1978. *Publications:* some papers to learned insts. *Leisure interests:* walking, watching rugby, gardening. *Address:* Pine Cottage, Holmbury St. Mary, Surrey, England (weekend).

FRAME, Janet, C.B.E.; New Zealand writer; b. 1924, Dunedin; ed. Oamaru North School, Waitaki Girls' High School, Dunedin Training Coll. and Otago Univ.; Hubert Church Award for N.Z. Prose; N.Z. Scholarship in Letters 1964, Burns Fellow, Otago Univ., Dunedin. *Publications:* Lagoon 1951, Owls do Cry 1957, Faces in the Water 1961, The Edge of the Alphabet 1962, Scented Gardens for the Blind 1963, The Reservoir (stories), Snowman, Snowman (fables), The Adaptable Man 1965, A State of Siege 1967, The Pocket Mirror (poetry), Yellow Flowers in the Antipodean Room 1968, Mona Minim and the Smell of the Sun (children's book) 1969, Intensive Care (novel) 1971, Daughter Buffalo (novel) 1972, Living in the Maniototo (novel) 1979, The Carpathians 1988.

FRANÇA, José-Augusto, D. ÉS L., D.HIST.; Portuguese writer and art his-torian; b. 16 Nov. 1922, Tomar; s. of José M. França and Carmen R. França; m. 2nd Marie-Thérèse Mandroux; one d. (by previous marriage); ed. Lisbon Univ., Ecole des Hautes Etudes and Univ. of Paris; travels in Africa, Europe and Americas 1945-; Ed. Lisbon literary review Unicornio 1951-56, Co-ed. Cadernos de Poesia 1951-53; Founder-Dir. Galeria de Marco, Lisbon 1952-54; art critic 1946-; film critic 1948-; lexicographical publr. 1948-58; lived in Paris 1959-63; Ed. Pintura & Näo 1969-70; Ed. Cólóquio Artes 1970-; Prof. Cultural History and History of Art, Dir. Dept. of Art History, New Univ. of Lisbon 1974-, Dir. Faculty of Social Sciences 1982; Dir. Fondation C. Gulbenkian, Centre Culturel Portugais, Paris 1983-89; Visiting Prof. Univ. of Paris III 1985-86; Vice-Pres. Int. Asscn. of Art Critics 1970-73, Pres. 1985-87, Pres. of Honour 1987-; Vice-Pres. Acad. Européenne de Sciences, Arts et Lettres; Pres. Acad. Nacional de Belas Artes, Lisbon 1974-80; City Councillor, Lisbon 1974-75; Pres. Inst. Cultura Portuguesa 1976-80; mem. Int. Asscn. of Art Critics, Int. Cttee. of Art History, PEN Club, Soc. Européenne de Culture, Soc. de l'Histoire de l'Art français, Acad. Nacional de Belas Artes, Acad. das Ciencias de Lisboa, Acad. Portuguesa de História, Acad. Européenne de Sciences, Arts et Lettres, World Acad. of Arts and Science, Acad. Nat. Sciences, Arts et Lettres de Bordeaux; Officier Ordre national du Mérite; Chevalier Ordre des Arts et Lettres (France); Commdr. Ordem Rio Branco (Brazil). *Publications:* Natureza Morta (novel) 1949, Azazel (play) 1957, Despedida Breve (short stories) 1958; Essays: Charles Chaplin—the Self-Made Myth 1952, Amadeo de Souza-Cardoso 1957, Situação da Pintura Ocidental 1959, Da Pintura Portuguesa 1960, Dez Anos de Cinema 1960, Une ville des lumières: La Lisbonne de Pombal 1963, A Arte em Portugal no Século XIX 1967, Oito Ensaios sobre Arte Contemporânea 1967, Le romantisme au Portugal 1972, Almada, o Português sem Mestre 1972, A Arte na Sociedade Portuguesa no Século XX 1972, Antonio Carneiro 1973, A Arte em Portugal no século XX 1974, Zé Povinho 1975, Manolo Millares 1977, Lisboa: Urbanismo e Arquitectura, O Retrato na Arte Portuguesa, Rafael Bordalo Pinheiro, o Português tal e qual 1980, Malhoa & Columbano, Historia da Arte Ocidental 1780-1980 1987. *Leisure interests:* travel and detective stories. *Address:* Mailing address: Rua Escola Politecnica 49/4 Lisbon 2; Fondation C. Gulbenkian, 51 avenue d'Iéna, 75116 Paris, France. *Telephone:* 362028 (Lisbon); 47-20-85-83 (Paris).

FRANÇAIS, Jean; French diplomatist; b. 31 Oct. 1920, Paris; s. of Emile and Lucile (née Caressa) Français; m. 1st Eliane Nicoletis, three s. one d.; m. 2nd Ildiko Tiborc 1964, two s.; ed. Lycée Condorcet, Law School of Paris Univ., Ecole Libre des Sciences Politiques; Attaché at Press Dept., Ministry of Foreign Affairs 1944; attached to Gen. Commissariat for German and Austrian Affairs 1946; Embassy Attaché, Rio de Janeiro 1949, Sec., Madrid 1953; attached to Gen. Secr., Ministry of Foreign Affairs 1956; Pvt. Counsellor to Defence Minister 1958-60, to Minister Asst. to the Prime Minister 1960, to Sec. of State for Foreign Affairs 1962; Gen. Consul in Nairobi 1960-62; Dir. Office of Sec. of State for Foreign Affairs 1963-65; Amb. to Cen. African Repub. 1965-66, to Nepal 1967, to Uruguay 1971-75, to Zambia (also accred. to Botswana) 1975, to Venezuela 1979-83; Master of Conferences, Law School, Univ. of Paris 1956; Officier Légion d'honneur, Officier Ordre national du Mérite, Croix de guerre. *Publication:* Le rouge et l'or (novel) 1983. *Address:* 18 rue du Général Niox, 75016 Paris, France. *Telephone:* 224-12-31 (Paris).

FRANCESCATTI, Zino; French concert violinist; b. 9 Aug. 1902, Mar-seilles; m. Yolande Potel de la Brière 1930; ed. privately; has played with most of the world's leading orchestras; frequently mem. of jury in int. musical contests; Hon. mem. Paris Conservatoire Orchestra, Philadelphia Orchestra, etc.; Pres. Fondation Zino Francescatti; annual Zino Frances-catti Int. Violin Competition launched Aix en Provence 1987; Commdr. Ordre de Léopold de Belgique 1967, Commdr. Légion d'honneur 1975, Ordre des Arts et des Lettres, Grand Officier Ordre Nat. du Mérite 1985. *Leisure interests:* chess problems, stamp collecting, driving, gardening. *Address:* Villa les Cigales, 13600 La Ciotat, France.

FRANCIS, Dick (see Francis, Richard Stanley).

FRANCIS, Harold Huyton; New Zealand diplomatist; b. 1 May 1928, Auckland; m.; three c.; ed. Univ. Coll., Oxford, and Auckland Univ.; joined Dept. of External Affairs 1954; Third Sec., High Comm. in London 1954-57, Second Sec. 1957-60; Head of S. Pacific and Antarctic Div. of External Affairs Dept. 1960-62; First Sec., later Counsellor, Embassy in Washing-ton, D.C. 1962-65; Head, Asian Div. of Ministry of Foreign Affairs, as Counsellor then Minister 1966-70; High Commr. in Singapore 1970-73; Asst. Sec., Ministry of Foreign Affairs, in charge of Admin. 1974-78; Perm. Rep. to the UN 1978-83. *Address:* Ministry of Foreign Affairs, Auckland, New Zealand.

FRANCIS, Richard (Dick) Stanley, O.B.E.; British author; b. 31 Oct. 1920, Tenby, S. Wales; s. of George V. and Catherine M. Francis; m. Mary M. Brenchley 1947; two s.; fighter and bomber pilot, R.A.F. 1940-46; amateur steeplechase jockey (Nat. Hunt racing) 1946-48; professional steeplechase jockey 1948-57; champion steeplechase jockey 1953-54; racing columnist, Sunday Express 1957-73; author and novelist 1957-; Edgar Allan Poe Awards 1970, 1980 and Gold Dagger Award 1980, all for best crime novel of year. *Publications:* The Sport of Queens (autobiog.) 1957, Dead Cert (novel) 1962, Lester (biog. of Lester Piggott) 1986, The Edge, and over 26 novels of adventure and risk. *Leisure interests:* horses, travel, boats. *Address:* 5100 North Ocean Blvd. No. 609, Sea Ranch Lakes, Fort Lauder-dale, Fla. 33308, U.S.A.

FRANCIS, Richard Trevor Langford, M.A., F.R.S.A., C.B.I.M.; British broad-casting executive and administrator; b. 10 March 1934, Harrogate; s. of late Eric Roland Francis and Esther Joy Todd; m. 1st Beate Ohlhagen 1958 (dissolved), 2nd Elizabeth Penelope Anne Fairfax Crone 1974; four s.; ed. Uppingham School and Univ. Coll., Oxford; BBC Trainee 1958-60, TV Production Asst. 1960-62, Producer Afternoon Programmes 1962-63, Panorama 1963-65, Asst. Ed. Panorama 1965-66, 24 Hours 1966-67, Pro-jects Ed. Current Affairs 1967-70, Head Special Projects, Current Affairs 1970-71, Asst. Head Current Affairs Group 1971-73, Controller BBC Northern Ireland 1973-77, Dir. News and Current Affairs BBC 1977-82, Man. Dir. BBC Radio 1982-86; Head EBU Operations for US Elections and Apollo 1968-69, Head for Elections 1972; Dir.-Gen. British Council 1987-; Dir. Visnews 1978, Deputy Chair. 1979-82; mem. British Exec. Int. Press Inst. 1978-82, Deputy Chair. 1979-82; mem. Media Law Group; fmr. mem. 'D' Notice Cttee.; Hon. Pres. Radio Acad. 1986-. *Leisure interests:* offshore sailing, photography and the children. *Address:* c/o The British Council, 10 Spring Gardens, London, SW1A 2BN, England. *Telephone:* 01-389 4879.

FRANCIS, Sam, M.A.; American artist; b. 1923, San Mateo, Calif.; m. Mako Ioemitsu; one c.; ed. Univ. of California at Berkeley; first exhbn. 1947; subsequent exhbns. include San Francisco 1948, Paris 1951, 1955, 1956, New York 1956, London, Berne, Tokyo, Osaka 1957, Brussels 1958, Dunn Int. Exhbn., London 1963, Centre for Nat. Contemporary Arts, Paris 1969, Tokyo Prize for American Artists in Japan; rep. in perm. collections of Museum of Modern Art and Guggenheim Foundation, New York, Tate Gallery, London; three mural panels, Kunsthalle, Basle, Swit-zerland 1956-57, mural, Söfu School Tokyo 1957. *Address:* c/o Galerie Smith Anderson, 200 Homer Street, Palo Alto, Calif. 94301, U.S.A.

FRANCISCI DI BASCHI, Marco, D.IUR.; Italian diplomatist b. 3 Feb. 1920, Angleur, Belgium; s. of Francesco Francisci and Berthe Berlemont; m. Franca Angelini 1974; three c.; ed. Rome Univ.; entered diplomatic service 1948; Sec., Washington Embassy 1950-51; mem. Perm. Del. to UN, New York 1951-55; Consul, Klagenfurt, Austria 1955-58; Dir. Int. Orgs.

Branch, Gen. Econ. Affairs Directorate, Foreign Ministry 1958–75; Amb. to People's Repub. of China 1975–80; Amb. and Perm. Rep. to OECD, Paris 1980–83, Amb. and Perm. Rep. to FAO, Rome 1983–. *Address:* Via Cesalpino 10, 00161 Rome, Italy. *Telephone:* (06) 860019.

FRANCO DA COSTA DE OLIVEIRA FALCÃO, H.E. Cardinal Manuel; Portuguese ecclesiastic; b. 10 Nov. 1922, Lisbon; ordained 1951, elected to the titular Church of Telepte 1966, consecrated Bishop 1967, succeeded to Beja 1980; cr. Cardinal 1988. *Address:* Bispado, Apdo. 94, Rua D. Manuel I, 7801 Beja, Almemtejo, Portugal. *Telephone:* (084) 26.518.

FRANÇOIS-PONCET, Jean André, PH.D.; French diplomatist; b. 8 Dec. 1928, Paris; s. of André François-Poncet and Jacqueline Dilais; m. Marie-Thérèse de Mitry 1959; two s. one d.; ed. Wesleyan Univ., Fletcher School of Law and Diplomacy at Tufts Univ., Paris Law School, Nat. School of Public Admin., Paris and Stanford Univ. Graduate School of Business; joined Ministry of Foreign Affairs 1955; worked in office of Sec. of State 1956–58; Sec.-Gen. of Del. to Negotiations for Treaties for EEC and EURATOM 1956–57; Head of European Institutions section in Ministry 1958–61; Prof., Institut d'études politiques de Paris 1960–; Head of Assistance and Co-operation Mission in Morocco 1961–63; in charge of African Affairs in Ministry 1963–68; Counsellor, Embassy in Iran 1968–70; Chair. of Bd., Pres. and C.E.O., Etablissements J. J. Carnaud & Forges 1971–75; Sec. of State for Foreign Affairs Jan.-July 1976; Sec.-Gen. to Presidency of French Repub. 1976–78; Minister of Foreign Affairs 1978–81; Conseiller Général, Lot-et-Garonne 1967–, Pres. Conseil Général 1978–; Dir. FMC Corpn. 1982–; Senator, Lot-et-Garonne Sept. 1983–; First Vice-Pres., Conseil régional d'Aquitaine 1985–; Chevalier Légion d'honneur; Ordre nationale du Mérite. *Publication:* The Economic Policy of Western Germany 1970. *Address:* 6 boulevard Suchet, 75116 Paris, France (Home). *Telephone:* 504-13-37 (Home).

FRANJIEH, Suleiman; Lebanese politician; b. 14 June 1910, Zgharta; m.; five c.; ed. coll. at Antoura, near Beirut; elected to Parl. as Ind. mem. 1960 and 1964; Minister of Posts, Telegraphs and Telephones and of Agric. 1960–61, of the Interior 1968, of Justice, Econ., of Public Works and of Nat. Econ. 1969–70; head, trade del. to negotiate Soviet-Lebanese trade and payments agreement; Pres. of Lebanon 1970–76. *Address:* rue de la Patriarchat, Beirut, Lebanon.

FRANK, Sir (Frederick) Charles, Kt., O.B.E., D.PHIL., F.INST.P., F.R.S.; British professor of physics (retd.); b. 6 March 1911, Durban, S. Africa; s. of Frederick Frank and Medora Celia Emma (née Read) Frank; m. Maia Maita Asché 1940; ed. Thetford Grammar School, Ipswich School and Lincoln Coll., Oxford; Kaiser Wilhelm Inst. für Physik, Berlin-Dahlem 1936–38; Colloid Science Lab., Cambridge 1939–40; Chemical Defence Research Establishment, Porton 1940; Air Ministry, A.D.I. (Science) 1940–46; H. H. Wills Physics Lab., Univ. of Bristol 1947–76, Research Fellow 1948–51, Reader 1951–54, Prof. 1954–69, Henry Overton Wills Prof. and Head of Dept. 1969–76, Emer. Prof. 1976–; Visiting Prof. Univ. of Calif., San Diego 1964–65; Raman Visiting Prof., Raman Research Lab., Bangalore 1979–80; Vice-Pres. Royal Soc. 1967–69, Fellow 1954; Foreign Assoc. U.S. Nat. Acad. of Eng. 1980, Royal Soc. of S.A. 1986; Hon. Fellow Lincoln Coll., Oxford 1968, Inst. of Physics 1977, Bristol Univ. 1986; Bakerian Lecturer 1973; Hon. D.Sc. (Ghent) 1955, (Bath) 1974, (Trinity Coll. Dublin) 1968, Hon. D. Univ. (Surrey) 1977, (Warwick) 1981; Dr. h.c. (Univ. de Paris-Sud) 1986; Holweck Prize 1963; Crystal Growth Award, American Asscn. for Crystal Growth 1978, Gregori Aminoff Medal, Royal Swedish Acad. of Sciences 1981, Guthrie Medal and Prize, Inst. of Physics 1982, Fellow, Indian Acad. of Sciences. *Publications:* articles in various learned journals, mostly dealing with dielectrics, the physics of solids, crystal growth, crystal dislocations, liquid crystals, polymers and geophysics. *Leisure interests:* gardening, walking. *Address:* Orchard Cottage, Grove Road, Coombe Dingle, Bristol BS9 2RL, Avon, England (Home). *Telephone:* 0272-681708 (Home).

FRANK, Ilya Mikhailovich; Soviet physicist; b. 23 Oct. 1908, Leningrad; ed. Moscow Univ; Asst. to Prof. S. I. Vavilov 1928; worked at Leningrad Optical Inst. (Lab. of Prof. A. N. Terenin) 1930–34, at Lebedev Inst. of Physics (U.S.S.R. Acad. of Sciences) 1934–; Prof. of Physics, Moscow Univ. 1944–, Head of Lab. 1957–; Corresp. mem. U.S.S.R. Acad. of Sciences 1946–48, Academician 1968–; Nobel Prize for Physics (with Tamm and Cherenkov) 1958, State Prize 1946, Order of Lenin (thrice), Order of the Red Banner of Labour, Order of the October Revolution 1978, Vavilov Gold Medal 1979 etc. *Publications:* Function of Excitement and Curve of Absorption in Optic Dissociation of Tallium Ioclate 1933, Coherent Radiation of Fast Electron in a Medium 1937, Pair Formation in Krypton under Gamma Rays 1938, Doppler Effect in Refracting Medium 1942, Neutron Multiplication in Uranium-Graphite Systems 1955, On Group Velocity of Light in Radiation in Refracting Medium 1958, Vavilov-Cherenkov Radiation 1960, Optics of Light Sources 1960, On Some Peculiarities of Elastic Deceleration of Neutrons 1964. *Address:* Joint Institute for Nuclear Research, Head Post Office, P.O. Box 79, Moscow, U.S.S.R.

FRANK, Paul, DR. RER. POL.; German foreign office official; b. 4 July 1918, Hilzingen; s. of Josef and Anna Frank; m. Irma Sutter 1950; two s.; ed. Volksschule, Realgymnasium and Univs. of Freiburg i. Br., Zürich and Fribourg (Switzerland); Vice-Consul, Paris 1950, First Sec. 1955; Chief,

West European Desk, Foreign Office, Bonn 1957; Counsellor, Observer Mission to UN, New York 1960; mem. Planning Staff, Foreign Office 1963, Dir. W. European Dept. 1965, Dir. of Political Affairs 1968, Co-ordinator for German-French Co-operation 1981–82; fmr. Sec. of State 1970, Chief of the President's Office 1974–79; various decorations. *Publications:* Die Entschlüsselte Botschaft 1981, Die senile Gesellschaft 1984, Cézanne—Eine Biographie 1986. *Leisure interests:* painting, architecture. *Address:* Weisstannenweg 20, 7821 Breitnau, Federal Republic of Germany.

FRANKE, Egon; German politician; b. 11 April 1913, Hannover; co-founder of S.P.D.; in charge of Org. Dept. of Party Exec. until 1952; Dist. Chair., Hannover; Land Chair., Lower Saxony; mem. Bundestag for Hannover 1951–; mem. Party Exec. 1964–73; Alderman, Hannover 1945–47; mem. Landtag Hannover 1946–47, Lower Saxony 1947–51; Chair. All-German Cttee. 1967–69; Minister of Intra-German Affairs 1969–82. *Address:* Marienburger Weg 32, 3000 Hannover-Buchholz, Federal Republic of Germany.

FRANKE, Herbert, PH.D., LL.D.; German university professor; b. 27 Sept. 1914, Cologne; s. of Max and Berta (née Maase) Franke; m. Ruth Freiin von Reck 1945; one s.; ed. Univs. of Cologne, Bonn and Berlin; Reader Cologne Univ. 1949; British Council Fellow, Cambridge 1951; Prof. of Far Eastern Studies Univ. of Munich 1952, Dean Faculty of Letters 1958–59, now Emer. Prof.; Sec.-Gen. XXIVth Int. Congress of Orientalists 1957; Deutsche Morgenländische Gesellschaft Sec. 1953, Pres. 1965–71; Ed. of its Zeitschrift 1960–65; Vice-Pres. Deutsche Forschungsgemeinschaft 1974–80; Visiting Prof. Univ. of Washington 1964–65, 1969–70; mem. Bavarian Acad. of Sciences, Pres. 1980–85; Hon. Fellow, Jesus Coll., Cambridge 1980; Corresp. mem. Austrian Acad. of Sciences 1984; Hon. mem. Royal Irish Acad. 1985, Soc. Asiatique, Paris 1985; Prix Stanislas Julien (Acad. des Inscriptions et Belles-Lettres, Paris) 1953. *Publications:* Beiträge zur Wirtschaftsgeschichte Chinas unter der Mongolenherrschaft 1949, Sinologie 1953, Beiträge zur Kulturgeschichte Chinas unter der Mongolenherrschaft 1956 etc. *Leisure interest:* chamber music. *Address:* Institut für Ostasienkunde, Universität München, Munich (Office); Fliederstrasse 23, 8035 Gauting, Federal Republic of Germany (Home). *Telephone:* Munich 850-29-07.

FRANKEL, Max, M.A.; American journalist; b. 3 April 1930, Gera, Germany; s. of Jacob A. Frankel and Mary (Katz) Frankel; m. 1st. Tobia Brown 1956 (deceased 1987); two s. one d.; m. 2nd Joyce Purnick 1988; ed. Columbia Univ., New York; mem. staff, The New York Times 1952–, Chief Washington Corresp. 1968–72, Sunday Ed. 1973–76, Editorial Pages Ed. 1977–86, Exec. Ed. 1986–; Pulitzer Prize for Int. Reporting 1973. *Address:* The New York Times, 229 West 43rd Street, New York, N.Y. 10036, U.S.A.

FRANKEL, Sir Otto Herzberg, Kt., D.SC., D.AGR., F.R.S., F.A.A., F.R.S.N.Z.; Australian geneticist; b. 4 Nov. 1900, Vienna; m. Margaret Anderson 1939; ed. Agricultural Univ. of Berlin; geneticist, later Dir., Wheat Research Inst., N.Z. 1929–49; Dir. Crop Research Div., Dept. of Scientific and Industrial Research, N.Z. 1949–51; Chief, Div. of Plant Industry, Commonwealth Scientific and Industrial Research Org. 1951–62, mem. of Exec. 1962–66, Hon. Research Fellow 1966–; Hon. mem. Japan Acad. 1983; Foreign Assoc. mem. N.A.S. 1988. *Publications:* articles in New Zealand, Australian, British and American journals; co-ed: Plant Genetic Resources 1970, Crop Genetic Resources 1975, Conservation and Evolution 1981 (co-author), The Use of Plant Genetic Resources 1988. *Leisure interests:* skiing, fishing, gardening. *Address:* C.S.I.R.O., P.O. Box 1600, Canberra City, A.C.T. 2601 (Office); 4 Cobby Street, Campbell, A.C.T. 2601, Australia (Home).

FRANKEL, Sally Herbert, M.A., PH.D., D.SC.; British economist; b. 22 Nov. 1903, Johannesburg, S. Africa; s. of late Jacob and Mathilde (née Buxbaum) Frankel; m. Ilse J. Frankel 1928; one s. one d.; ed. St. John's Coll., Johannesburg, Univ. of the Witwatersrand and London School of Economics; Prof. of Econs. and Head of Dept. of Econs. and Econ. History, Univ. of Witwatersrand 1931–46; Chair. Comm. to report on Rhodesia Railways Ltd. 1942–43; Chair. Comm. of Enquiry into Mining Industry of S. Rhodesia 1945; mem. Royal Comm. on East Africa 1953–55; Emer. Prof. in Econs. of Underdeveloped Countries, Oxford; Emer. Fellow, Nuffield Coll. (Prof. and Professorial Fellow 1946–71); Visiting Prof. Univ. of Va. 1967, 1968, 1970, 1971, 1972, 1973; Hon. D.Litt. (Rhodes Univ.), Hon. D.Sc.(Econ.) (Witwatersrand). *Publications:* Co-operation and Competition in the Marketing of Maize in South Africa 1926, The Railway Policy of South Africa 1928, Coming of Age: Studies in South African Citizenship and Politics 1938, Capital Investment in Africa: Its Course and Effects 1938, The Concept of Colonisation 1949, The Economic Impact on Under-Developed Societies 1953, Investment and the Return to Equity Capital in the South African Gold Mining Industry 1887-1965: An International Comparison 1967, Gold and International Equity Investment 1969, Money: Two Philosophies, the Conflict of Trust and Authority 1977, Money and Liberty 1980. *Leisure interests:* gardening, chess. *Address:* 62 Cutteslowe House, Park Close, Oxford, OX2 8NP, England. *Telephone:* Oxford 514748.

FRANKENTHALER, Helen, B.A.; American artist; b. 1928, New York; m. Robert Motherwell 1958 (divorced 1971); ed. Bennington Coll., Vt.; Trustee Bennington Coll. 1967; Fellow Calhoun Coll., Yale Univ. 1968;

one-woman exhbns. throughout U.S.A. and Europe, particularly at André Emmerich Gallery 1959-, Whitney Museum of American Art, and Metropolitan Museum of Art, New York 1951-73, Guggenheim Museum, New York 1975, retrospective 1985 (exhbn. travelled U.S.A., Canada 1986), Corcoran Gallery, Washington, D.C. 1975, Museum of Fine Arts, Houston 1976, U.S.I.A. (United States Information Agency) exhbn., Janie C. Lee Gallery, Dallas 1973, 1975, 1976, 1978, 1980, Knoedler Gallery, London 1978, 1981, 1983, 1985, Sterling & Francine Clark Art Inst., Williamstown, Mass. 1980; mem. American Acad. and Inst. of Arts and Letters 1974, NEA Council on the Arts 1975, Corpn. of Yaddo 1973-78; Trustee Bennington Coll. 1967-; Fellow, Calhoun Coll., Yale Univ. 1968-; travelled to Far East, Australia, Latin America 1978-79; Hon. D.Hum.Litt. (Skidmore Coll.) 1969, Hon. D.F.A. (Smith Coll.) 1973, (Moore Coll. of Art) 1974, (Bard Coll.) 1976, Hon. Dr. of Art (Radcliffe Coll.) 1978, (Amherst Coll.) 1979; Hon. D.F.A. (Pa. Coll. of Art, Williams Coll., Harvard Univ.) 1980, (Yale Univ.) 1981, (Brandeis Univ.) 1982, (Univ. of Hartford) 1983, (Syracuse Univ.) 1985; First Prize, Paris Biennale 1959; Joseph E. Temple Gold Medal Award, Pennsylvania Acad. of Fine Arts 1968, Spirit of Achievement Award, Albert Einstein Coll. of Medicine 1970, Gold Medal of the Commune of Catania, Florence 1972, Garrett Award, Art Inst. of Chicago 1972, Creative Arts Award, American Jewish Congress 1974, Art and Humanities Award, Yale Women's Forum 1976, Extraordinary Woman of Achievement Award, Nat. Conf. of Christians and Jews 1978; Mayor's Award of Honor for Art and Culture, New York City 1986. *Address:* c/o Andre Emmerich, 41 East 57th Street, New York, N.Y. 10022, U.S.A.

FRANKEVICH, Yevgeniy Leonidovich, DR. PHYS.-MATH. SC.; Soviet scientist; b. 1930; ed. Kalinin Polytechnic, Leningrad; postgrad. jr. then sr. researcher 1957-71; mem. CPSU 1961-; head of lab. U.S.S.R. Acad. of Sciences Inst. of Chemical Physics 1971-; Prof. 1972; Lenin Prize 1986. *Address:* U.S.S.R. Academy of Sciences, Leninsky Prospekt 14, Moscow, U.S.S.R.

FRANKFURT, Stephen Owen, B.A.; American advertising executive; b. 17 Dec. 1931; ed. New York Univ. and Pratt Inst.; joined Young & Rubicam 1955, Art and Copy Supervisor 1957, Vice-Pres. and Dir. of Special Projects 1960, Sr. Vice-Pres. and Co-Creative Dir. of Agency 1964, Creative Dir. 1967-74, Pres. 1968-, with Kenyon & Eckhardt (now Bozell, Jacobs, Kenyon & Eckhardt) 1974-; Gold Medal, N.Y. Art Dirs. Club 1958, 1959, 1961, 1962, 1963; Special Gold Medal Outstanding TV Advertising 1961, Winner TV Category Venice Film Festival 1964, Achievement Award, N.Y. Art Dirs. Club 1968. *Address:* Bozell, Jacobs, Kenyon and Eckhardt Inc., 40 W. 23rd Street, New York, N.Y. 10010, U.S.A.

FRANKL, Peter; British concert pianist; b. 2 Oct. 1935, Budapest, Hungary; s. of Tibor and Laura Frankl; m. Annie Feiner 1958; one s. one d.; ed. High School, Franz Liszt Music Acad., Budapest; regular concert tours with leading orchestras and conductors throughout the world; numerous festival appearances including Edinburgh, Windsor, Cheltenham, Lucerne, Flanders, Aldeburgh, Adelaide; mem. chamber trio with György Pauk (q.v.) and Ralph Kirshbaun; winner of int. competitions at Paris 1957, Munich 1957, Rio de Janeiro 1959; Franz Liszt Award, Budapest 1958; Hon. Citizen, Rio de Janeiro 1960. *Numerous recordings including:* complete works for piano of Schumann and Debussy, orchestral and chamber pieces. *Leisure interests:* football, opera, theatre. *Address:* 5 Gresham Gardens, London, NW11 8NX, England. *Telephone:* 01-455 5228.

FRANKLIN, Aretha; American singer; b. 25 March 1942, Memphis; d. of Rev. C. L. Franklin; made first recordings at father's Baptist church, Detroit; toured as gospel singer; moved to New York, signed contract with Columbia Records 1960, with Atlantic 1966, with Arista 1980. *Recordings include:* Aretha 1961, The Electrifying Aretha Franklin 1962, Laughing on the Outside, The Tender, the Moving, the Swinging Aretha Franklin 1963, Running out of Fools, The Gospel Sound of Aretha Franklin 1964, Soul Sister 1966, I Never Loved a the Way I Love You 1967, Lady Soul, Aretha Now, Aretha in Paris 1968, Aretha's Gold 1969, This Girl's in Love with You, Spirit in the Dark 1970, Live at Fillmore West 1971, Young, Gifted and Black, Amazing Grace 1972, Hey Now Hey, The Best of Aretha Franklin, The First Twelve Sides 1973, Let Me in Your Life, With Everything I Feel in Me 1974, You 1975, Sparkle, Ten Years of Gold 1976, Sweet Passion 1977, Almighty Fire 1978, La Diva 1979, Aretha 1980, Love All the Hurt Away 1981, Jump to It 1982, Get It Right 1983.

FRANKLIN, John Hope, A.M., PH.D.; American writer and university professor; b. 2 Jan. 1915, Bentiesville, Okla.; s. of Buck Colbert and Mollie (née Parker) Franklin; m. Aurelia E. Whittington 1940; one s.; ed. Fisk Univ., Harvard Univ.; Instructor in History Fisk Univ. 1936-38; Prof. of History St. Augustine's Coll. 1939-43, N.C. Coll., Durham 1943-47, Howard Univ. 1947-56; Chair. Dept. of History Brooklyn Coll. 1956-64; Prof. of American History Univ. of Chicago 1964-82, Chair. Dept. of History 1967-70, John Matthews Manly Distinguished Service Prof. 1969-; James B. Duke Prof. of History Duke Univ. 1982-; Pitt Prof. of American History and Institutions Cambridge Univ. 1962-63; Visiting Prof. Harvard, Wis., Cornell, Hawaii, Calif. and Cambridge Univs., and Salzburg Seminar; Chair. Bd. of Foreign Scholarships 1966-69, Nat. Council on Humanities 1976-79; Dir. Ill. Bell Telephone Co. 1972-80; Edward Austin Fellow 1937-38, Rosenwald Fellow 1937-39, Guggenheim Fellow 1950-51, 1973-74; Pres.'s Fellow, Brown Univ. 1952-53, Center for Advanced Study in

Behavioural Science 1973-74; Sr. Mellon Fellow, Nat. Humanities Center 1980-; Fulbright Prof., Australia 1960; Jefferson Lecturer in Humanities 1976; mem. Bd. of Dirs. Salzburg Seminar, Museum of Science and Industry 1968-80; mem. American Historical Asscn. (Pres. 1978-79), Southern Historical Asscn. (Pres. 1970-71), Org. of American Historians (Pres. 1970-75), Assn. for Study of Negro Life and History, American Studies Assn., American Philosophical Soc., American Assn. of Univ. Profs.; numerous hon. degrees. *Publications:* Free Negro in North Carolina 1943, From Slavery to Freedom: A History of Negro Americans 1947, 6e. 1987, Militant South 1956, Reconstruction After the Civil War 1961, The Emancipation Proclamation 1963, Land of the Free (with others) 1966, Illustrated History of Black Americans 1970, A Southern Odyssey 1976, Racial Equality in America 1976, George Washington Williams: A Biography 1985; Ed. Civil War Diary of James T. Ayers 1947, A Fool's Errand (by Albion Tourgee) 1961, Army Life in a Black Regiment (by Thomas Higginson) 1962, Color and Race 1968, Reminiscences of an Active Life (by John R. Lynch) 1970. *Leisure interests:* cultivating orchids, fly fishing, classical music. *Address:* Department of History, Duke University, Durham, N.C. 27708 (Office); 208 Pineview Road, Durham, N.C. 27707, U.S.A. (Home).

FRANKLIN, Warwick Orlando; Barbados land surveyor and politician; b. 9 Oct. 1938; m. Grace King; two s. one d.; ed. Combermere School, Trinidad Dept. Survey School and Waltham Forest Technical Coll., U.K.; teacher; surveyor, Waterworks Dept. 1965-67, Lands and Surveys Dept. 1967; Deputy Commr. of Valuations 1970, Commr. 1971-76; Man Dir. Dan Homes Co. Ltd.; Dir. Franklin & Franklin; First Vice-Pres. Democratic Labour Party 1983-; mem. Parl. for St. Philip North 1981-; Minister of Agric., Food and Fisheries 1986-. *Address:* Ministry of Agriculture, Food and Fisheries, Graeme Hall, Christ Church; Oughtlands, St. Philip, Barbados, (Home).

FRANKS, Baron (Life Peer), cr. 1962, of Headington in the County of Oxford; **Oliver Shewell Franks,** P.C., O.M., G.C.M.G., K.C.B., K.C.V.O., C.B.E., M.A., F.B.A.; British college principal (retd.); b. 16 Feb. 1905, Birmingham; s. of Rev. S. Franks and Katharine Shewell; m. Barbara Mary Tanner 1931 (died 1987); two d.; ed. Bristol Grammar School and Queen's Coll., Oxford; Fellow and Praelector in Philosophy, Queen's Coll. Oxford 1927-37; Prof. of Moral Philosophy Univ. of Glasgow 1937-45; Civil Servant (temporary) Ministry of Supply 1939-46, Perm. Sec. 1945-46; Provost Queen's Coll. Oxford 1946-48; Hon. Fellow of Queen's Coll., Oxford 1948, Wolfson Coll., Oxford, Worcester Coll., Oxford, Lady Margaret Hall, Oxford, St. Catherine's Coll., Cambridge; British Amb. to U.S.A. 1948-52; Chair. Lloyds Bank 1954-62; Chair. Friends' Provident and Century Life Office 1955-62; Chair. Cttee. of London Clearing Bankers 1960-62; Chair. Cttee. of Inquiry into events leading to Argentine invasion of the Falkland Islands 1982; mem. Nat. Econ. Devt. Council (NEDC) 1962-64; Provost, Worcester Coll., Oxford 1962-76; Chancellor, Univ. of E. Anglia 1965-84; mem. Political Honours Scrutiny Cttee. 1977-87; Hon. D.C.L. (Oxford) and other hon. degrees. *Address:* Blackhall Farm, Garford Road, Oxford, OX2 6UU, England. *Telephone:* Oxford 511286.

FRANTZ, Justus; pianist; b. Hohensalza; ed. under Prof. Eliza Hansen in Hamburg and Wilhelm Kempf in Positano; prizewinner, Int. Music Competition, Munich 1967; since 1969 has appeared at all maj. European concert venues and toured U.S.A., Far East and Japan; has made many tours and recordings in piano duo with Christoph Eschenbach and received Edison Int. Award for their recording of Schubert marches 1983; co-founder and dir. Schleswig-Holstein Music Festival; Prof. Hamburg Musik-hochschule; recordings include works by Scarlatti, Beethoven, Mozart and concertos for two, three and four pianos by J. S. Bach. *Address:* c/o Musikhochschule, Hamburg, Federal Republic of Germany.

FRANZ, Herbert, DR. PHIL., DR. SC. AGRIC., DIPL. ING.; Austrian professor of agriculture; b. 23 Jan. 1908, Sopron, Hungary; s. of Carl Franz and Josefine Franz (née Holschek); m. Gertrude Hubatsch 1935; one s. three d.; ed. Univ. of Vienna; Head of Dept. of Soil and Environment Research, Inst. of Agric. Admont, Seiermark 1939-51; Assoc. Prof. for Soil Science, Univ. of Agric., Vienna 1952-56, Prof. 1956-77, Prof. Emer. 1977-; Corresp. mem. Austrian Acad. of Sciences 1971, mem. 1975; Hon. mem. Hungarian Acad. of Sciences 1983; Dr. h.c. (Gödöölö Univ.); Bronze Medal Univs. of Helsinki, Hiroshima, Gödöölö. *Publications:* Die Landtierwelt der mittleren Hohen Fauern, Denkschrift 1943, Bodenzoologie als Grundlage der Bodenpflege 1950, Feldbodenkunde 1960, Die Bodenfauna der Erde in biozönotischer Betrachtung, (2 vols.) 1975, Ökologie der Hochgebirge 1979. *Address:* A2340 Mödling, Jakob-Thomastr. 38, Austria. *Telephone:* (02236) 88 92 04.

FRANZ JOSEF II, Prince of Liechtenstein, Duke of Troppau and of Jägerndorf, Count of Rietberg; b. 16 Aug. 1906, Schloss Frauenthal; s. of Prince Alois and Princess Elisabeth of Liechtenstein; m. Georgine (Gina), Gräfin von Wilczek 1943; four s. one d.; ed. Schottengymnasium and Forestry and Agricultural Univ., Vienna; Ruler and Head of State, Principality of Liechtenstein July 1938-; handed over exec. power to son, Prince Hans Adam, Aug. 1984. *Address:* Schloss Vaduz, Principality of Liechtenstein. *Telephone:* 075-21212.

FRANZEN, Ulrich J., B.A., B.ARCH.; American architect; b. 15 Jan. 1921, Germany; m. 1st Joan Cummings 1942 (divorced 1962), two s. one d.; m.

2nd Laura Hughes 1980; ed. Williams Coll., and Harvard Univ.; Head of Ulrich Franzen and Assocs., New York 1955-; Lecturer Yale and Cornell Univs., Univs. of Cincinnati and Illinois, etc.; Visiting Prof. Yale, Harvard and Washington Univs. and Carnegie Inst. of Tech.; Chair. Architectural Bd. of Review, City of Rye 1958-63, Urban Design Review Bd., City of Cincinnati 1964-65, Nat. Council on Schoolhouse Construction and U.S.N. Review and Advisory Panel on Architecture 1965; Pres. Architectural League of New York 1966; mem. A.I.A.; numerous awards for design and construction including Brunner Memorial Prize, Nat. Inst. of Arts and Letters 1962, Thomas Jefferson Award 1970, 1971, 1972. *Works include:* Barkin Levin Co., Long Island City 1958, Philip Morris Research Center, Richmond, Va. 1959, Plans for Helen Whiting Inc., Pleasantville, N.Y. 1962, Philip Morris Operations Center 1963, Agronomy Building for Cornell Univ. and New Alley Theatre, Houston, Texas, Residence and Dining Halls, Univ. of N.H., housing for elderly, Torrington, Conn. 1972, First City Nat. Bank of Binghamton, N.Y. 1973. *Address:* Ulrich Franzen and Assocs., 228 E. 45th Street, New York, N.Y. 10017, U.S.A.

FRAPPIER, Armand, C.C., O.B.E., M.D., L.SC., F.R.S.C.; Canadian professor emeritus of medicine and microbiology, b. 26 Nov. 1904, Salaberry-de-Valleyfield, Que.; s. of Arthur-Alexis Frappier and Bernadette Codebecq; m. Thérèse Ostiguy 1929; one s. three d.; ed. Valleyfield Seminary and Univ. of Montreal; postgraduate studies in U.S.A. and Europe including Pasteur Inst., Paris; Prof. of Microbiology and Preventive Medicine, Univ. of Montreal until 1974, now Prof. Emer.; f. and fmr. Dir. Inst. of Microbiology and Hygiene of Montreal (now Armand Frappier Inst.); f. and fmr. Dir. Laboratories St. Luc Hosp., Montreal, retd. 1975, Consultant to the Dir. 1975-; participated in work of several public health and health research orgs. in Canada and elsewhere; fmr. mem. WHO panel of experts on tuberculosis; mem. numerous nat. and int. socs.; Thomas W. Eadie Prize (Royal Soc. of Canada, F. N. G. Starr Medal (Canadian Medical Asscn.) and other awards; five hon. degrees. *Publications:* numerous articles in medical and scientific journals. *Leisure interests:* hunting, fishing, gardening, making jam, music. *Address:* 6150 avenue du Boisé, App. K7, Montreal, Que. H3S 2V2, Canada. *Telephone:* 735-9569.

FRASER, Lady Antonia, M.A., F.R.S.L.; British author; b. 27 August 1932, London; d. of the Earl and Countess of Longford (q.v.); m. 1st Hugh Fraser (died 1984) 1956 (divorced 1977), three s. three d.; m. 2nd Harold Pinter (q.v.) 1980; ed. Dragon School, Oxford, St. Mary's Convent, Ascot and Lady Margaret Hall, Oxford; mem. Cttee. English PEN 1979- (Pres. 1987-), Crimewriters Assn. 1980-86; Hon. D.Litt. (Hull) 1986. *Publications:* King Arthur 1954, Robin Hood 1955, Dolls 1963, History of Toys 1966, Mary, Queen of Scots 1969 (James Tait Black Memorial Prize), Cromwell: Our Chief of Men 1973, King James VI and I 1974, Scottish Love Poems, A Personal Anthology 1974, Kings and Queens of England (Ed.) 1975, Love Letters (anthology) 1976, Quiet as a Nun 1977, The Wild Island 1978, King Charles II 1979, Heroes and Heroines (Ed.) 1980, A Splash of Red 1981, Cool Repentance 1982, Oxford In Verse (Ed.) 1982, The Weaker Vessel 1984 (Wolfson History Prize), Oxford Blood 1985, Your Royal Hostage 1987, Boadicea's Chariot: The Warrior Queens 1988; television adaptations of Quiet as a Nun 1978, Jemima Shore Investigates 1983. *TV plays:* Charades 1977, Mister Clay 1985. *Address:* c/o Curtis Brown, 162-168 Regent Street, London, W1 52B, England. *Telephone:* 01-262 1011.

FRASER, Sir Campbell (see Fraser, Sir (James) Campbell).

FRASER, Douglas Andrew; American labour official; b. 18 Dec. 1916, Glasgow, Scotland; s. of Douglas and Sara (Andrew) Fraser; m. Winifred Davis 1967; two d.; ed. Chadsey High School, Detroit, Mich.; Admin. Asst. to Pres. United Auto Workers 1951-59, Regional Dir. 1959-62, mem.-at-large Exec. Bd. 1962-70, Vice-Pres. 1970-77, Pres. 1977-83, Pres. Emer. 1983-; mem. Bd. Chrysler 1979-82. *Leisure interests:* reading, some spectator sports. *Address:* 8000 East Jefferson, Detroit, Mich. 48214, U.S.A. (Office). *Telephone:* (313) 926-5201.

FRASER, Sir (James) Campbell, Kt., B.COM., F.R.S.E., C.B.I.M.; British business executive; b. 2 May 1923, Dunblane, Scotland; s. of Alexander Ross and Annie McGregor Fraser; m. Maria Harvey (née McLaren) 1950; two d.; ed. Glasgow Univ. and Dundee School of Econs.; served in R.A.F. 1941-45; Raw Cotton Comm. 1950-52; Economist Intelligence Unit 1952-57; with Dunlop Rubber Co. Ltd. 1957-; Exec. Dir. Dunlop Holdings Ltd. 1969, Man. Dir. 1972-78, Chair. 1978-83, Pres. 1983-84; Chair. Scottish TV 1975-; fmr. Pres. Soc. of Business Economists; Dir. British Petroleum PLC, BAT Industries PLC, Bridgewater Paper Co. 1984-, Tandem Computers Ltd., Alexander Proudfoot PLC; Pauline Hyde & Assocs. Ltd., Britoil PLC; Vice-Pres. Scottish Opera; Chair. Green Park Health Care PLC; Deputy Pres. CBI 1981-82, Pres. 1982-84; mem. Council Confed. of British Industry, CBI Pres. Comm., Council of SMMT, Visiting Prof. Univ. of Stirling; Trustee of The Economist; Hon. Dr. Univ. (Stirling), Hon. LL.D. (Strathclyde) 1979. *Leisure interests:* athletics, reading, theatre, cinema, gardening, walking. *Address:* 114 St. Martin's Lane, London, WC2N 4AZ, England (Office).

FRASER, John Allen, P.C., Q.C., M.P., LL.B.; Canadian politician; b. 15 Dec. 1931, Yokohama, Japan; m. Catherine Findlay; three c.; ed. Univ. of British Columbia; called to Bar, B.C. 1955-; mem. House of Commons 1972-; Minister of the Environment and Postmaster Gen. 1979; Minister of Fisheries and Oceans 1984-85 (resgnd.), elected Speaker of the House of Commons 1986; fmr. Caucus Spokesperson for Post Office, Labour and Environment; fmr. mem. Parl. Special Cttee. on acid rain; fmr. Chair. of Progressive Conservative Party Cttee. on Pollution, Environment and Fisheries; Chair. Environmental Law Subsection of Canadian Bar Assn. *Address:* Room 222-N, House of Commons, Ottawa, Ont., KIA OA6, Canada. *Telephone:* (613) 992-5042.

FRASER, Rt. Hon. (John) Malcolm, A.C., C.H., P.C., M.A.; Australian politician; b. 21 May 1930, Melbourne; s. of the late J. Neville Fraser and of Una Fraser; m. Tamara Beggs 1956; two s. two d.; ed. Melbourne Grammar School and Oxford Univ.; mem. Parl. for Wannon 1955-83; mem. Jt. Parl. Cttee. of Foreign Affairs 1962-66; Chair. Govt. Mems.' Defence Cttee.; Sec. Wool Cttee.; mem. Council of Australian Nat. Univ., Canberra 1964-66; Minister for the Army 1966-68, for Educ. and Science 1968-69, for Defence 1969-71, for Educ. and Science 1971-72; Parl. Leader of Liberal Party 1975-83; Prime Minister 1975-83; Co-Chair. Commonwealth Eminent Persons Group (EPG) 1985-86; Distinguished Visiting Prof. Inst. for Advanced Studies in the Humanities, Edin. Univ. 1988-; Hon. Fellow Magdalen Coll., Oxford 1982; Hon. Vice-Pres. Oxford Soc. 1983; Sr. Adjunct Fellow, Center for Strategic and Int. Studies 1983; Distinguished Int. Fellow, American Enterprise Inst. for Public Policy Research 1984; Fellow for Int. Council of Assocs. at Claremont Univ. 1985; mem. Byrnes Int. Advisory Bd., Univ. of S. Carolina, U.S.A. 1985, InterAction Council for Fmr. Heads of Govt., American Enterprise Inst., ANZ Int. Bd. of Advice 1987; Consultant, Alexanders Laing & Cruickshank Holdings Australia Pty. Ltd. 1987-; Hon. LL.D. (S. Carolina) 1981; B'nai B'rith Gold Medal 1980. *Leisure interests:* fishing, photography, vintage cars, motorcycles. *Address:* 44th Floor, ANZ Tower, 55 Collins Street, Melbourne, Vic. 3000, Australia. *Telephone:* (03) 654 1822.

FRASER, Baron (Life Peer), cr. 1989, of Carmyllie in the District of Angus; Peter Lovat, B.A., LL.B., Q.C., M.P.; British politician and lawyer; b. 29 May 1945; s. of Rev. George Robson Fraser and Helen Jean Meiklejohn; m. Fiona Macdonald Mair 1969; one s. two d.; ed. St. Andrew's Prep. School, Grahamstown, S.A., Loretto School, Musselburgh, Gonville and Caius Coll., Cambridge, Edinburgh Univ.; called to Scottish Bar 1969; Lecturer in Constitutional Law, Heriot-Watt Univ. 1972-74; Standing Jr. Counsel in Scotland to FCO 1979; Chair. Scottish Conservative Lawyers Law Reform Group 1976; Conservative M.P. for S. Augus 1979-83, for Angus East 1983-87; Parl. Pvt. Sec. to Sec. of State for Scotland 1981-82; Solicitor Gen. for Scotland 1982-, Lord Advocate Jan. 1989-. *Leisure interests:* skiing, golf, wind-surfing. *Address:* Slade House, Carmyllie, by Arbroath, Angus, Scotland. *Telephone:* Carmyllie 215.

FRASER, Peter Marshall, M.C., M.A., F.B.A.; British classical scholar; b. 6 April 1918; s. of Archibald Fraser; m. 1st Catharine Heaton-Renshaw 1949 (marriage dissolved), one s. three d.; m. 2nd Ruth Elsbeth Renfer 1955, two s.; m. 3rd Barbara Ann Stewart Norbury 1973; ed. City of London School and Brasenose Coll. Oxford; served Seaforth Highlanders 1941-45, Mil. Mission to Greece 1943-45; Sr. Scholar, Christ Church Oxford 1946-47; Lecturer in Hellenistic History, Oxford Univ. 1948-64, Reader 1964-; Fellow of All Souls Coll. Oxford 1954-, Domestic Bursar 1962-65, Sub-Warden 1980-82, Acting Warden 1985-87; Jr. Proctor, Oxford Univ. 1960-61; Dir. British School at Athens 1968-71; Chair. Man. Cttee., Soc. of Afghan Studies 1972-82; Ordinary mem. German Archaeological Soc.; Corresp. Fellow, Archaeological Soc. of Athens; Gen. Ed. and Chair., British Acad. Cttee., Lexicon of Greek Personal Names 1973-; Chair. Man. Cttee. of Afghan Studies 1972-82 (Vice-Chair. 1985-); Hon. D.Phil. (Trier) 1984. *Publications:* The Rhodian Peraea and Islands (with G. E. Bean) 1954, Boeotian and West Greek Tombstones (with T. Rönne) 1957, Samothrace, The Inscriptions (Vol. II, Excavations of Samothrace) 1960, The Wares of Autolycus; Selected Literary Essays of Alice Meynell (Ed.) 1965, Ptolemaic Alexandria 1972, Rhodian Funerary Monuments 1977, A Lexicon of Greek Personal Names (Vol. 1) 1987; trans. of works from Swedish; articles in learned journals. *Address:* All Souls College, Oxford, England.

FRASER, Robert Donald Bruce, PH.D.; Australian physicist; b. 14 Aug. 1924, Ickenham, England; s. of D. F. Fraser and M. W. (née Addie) Fraser; m. Mary Jean Nicholls 1950; one s. two d.; ed. King's Coll., London; MRC Studentship King's Coll. 1948-51, Nuffield Foundation Fellowship 1951-52; CSIRO Div. of Protein Chemistry 1952-87, Chief of Div. 1983-; F.A.A. 1978; Royal Soc. of Victoria Science Medal 1982; S. G. Smith Memorial Medal, Textile Inst. (England) 1984; Fogarty Scholar N.I.H. (U.S.A.). *Publications:* Keratins (jointly) 1972, Conformation in Fibrous Proteins (jointly) 1975, and 162 publs. in journals. *Address:* 36 Thomson Street, Essendon, Vic. 3040, Australia.

FRASER, Sir William Kerr, G.C.B., M.A., LL.D., F.R.S.E.; British civil servant; b. 18 March 1929, Glasgow; s. of late Alexander M. Fraser and of Rachel Fraser; m. Marion Anne Forbes 1956; three s. one d.; ed. Eastwood School, Clarkston and Univ. of Glasgow; Flying Officer R.A.F. 1952-55; joined Scottish Office, Edin. 1955, Perm. Under-Sec. of State 1978-88; Prin. and Vice-Chancellor Univ. of Glasgow Oct. 1988-. *Leisure interests:* reading, doing nothing. *Address:* 14 Braid Avenue, Edinburgh, EH10 6EE, Scotland. *Telephone:* 031-447 375.

FRASER, William, C.B.E., B.S.C., C.ENG., F.I.E.E.; British business executive; b. 15 July 1911, Glasgow; m. Kathleen Mary Moore 1938 (died 1971); two s. two d.; ed. Glasgow High School and Univ. Coll. London; joined Joseph Lucas Ltd. and rose to Production Engineer 1937; joined Scottish Cables Ltd. 1937, Dir. 1938, Man. Dir. 1948, Chair. 1958; Chair. Scottish Cables (South Africa) Ltd. 1957; Chair. Scottish Council Fed. British Industries 1959–61; Exec. Dir. British Insulated Callender's Cables Ltd. (now BICC Ltd.) 1959, Deputy Chair. and C.E.O. 1971–73, Chair. 1973–76; Vice-Chair. Phillips Cables (Canada) 1961–70, Exec. Dir. Overseas Cos. 1962–70; Deputy Chair. Metal Manufactures Ltd. (Australia) 1963–70, Man. Dir. Overseas 1964–68, Man. Dir. Overseas and Construction Group 1968–70; Chair. BIC Construction Co. Ltd. 1968–69, Balfour Beatty & Co. Ltd. 1969–70; Dir. Clydesdale Bank Ltd. 1974–84, Anglesey Aluminium Ltd. 1971–74. *Leisure interests:* fishing, shooting, golf. *Address:* Fenwick Lodge, Ewenfield Road, Ayr, Scotland.

FRASER OF KILMORACK, Baron (Life Peer), cr. 1974, of Rubislaw in the County of the City of Aberdeen; **(Richard) Michael Fraser,** Kt., C.B.E.; British politician, businessman and consultant; b. 28 Oct. 1915, Nottingham; s. of the late Dr. Thomas Fraser, C.B.E., D.S.O. and the late Maria-Theresia Kayser; m. Elizabeth Chloë Drummond 1944; two s. (one deceased); ed. Aberdeen Grammar School, Fettes Coll., Edinburgh, and King's Coll., Cambridge; Royal Artillery 1939–46 (rank of Lieut.-Col.); Conservative Research Dept. 1946–64, Head of Home Affairs Section 1950–51, Joint Dir. 1951–59, Dir. 1959–64; Sec. Conservative Party's Advisory Cttee. on Policy 1951–64, Deputy Chair. Conservative Party 1964–75; Sec. to Conservative Leader's Consultative Cttee. 1964–70, 1974–75; Chair. Conservative Research Dept. 1970–74; Dir. Glaxo Holdings PLC 1975–85, Glaxo Group Ltd. 1975–85, Glaxo Enterprises Inc. (U.S.A.) 1983–85, Glaxo Trustees Ltd. 1975–86, Whiteaway Laidlaw Bank Ltd. 1981–; Smith-Mundt Fellowship, U.S.A. 1952; M.B.E. (Mil.) 1945. *Publications:* Ruling Performance—British Governments from Attlee to Thatcher (contrib.) 1987; articles in historical and political journals. *Leisure interests:* reading, music, opera, ballet, travel. *Address:* 18 Drayton Court, London, SW10 9RH, England. *Telephone:* 01-370 1543.

FRATINI, Georgina Carolin; British fashion designer; b. 22 Sept. 1931, Kobe, Japan; d. of The Hon. Somerset Butler C.I.E. and Mrs Somerset Butler; m. 1st Renato Fratini 1961, 2nd Jimmy Logan 1967; ed. in Toronto, Simla, Rangoon, Hathrop Castle, Glos. and Royal Coll. of Art; Asst. Costume and Set. Designer, Katherine Dunham Dance Group 1951–53; freelance designer 1953–63; founder, Designer and Dir. Gina Fratini Ltd. 1964–. *Leisure interests:* gardening, horse-racing. *Address:* Marvic House, Bishops Road, London, S.W.6 (Office); Wandle Road, London, S.W.17, England (Home). *Telephone:* 01-386-8759.

FRAYN, Michael; British author and playwright; b. 8 Sept. 1933; s. of late Thomas A. Frayn and Violet A. Lawson; m. Gillian Palmer 1960 (divorced 1988); three d.; ed. Kingston Grammar School and Emmanuel Coll., Cambridge; reporter, The Guardian 1957–59, columnist 1959–62; columnist, The Observer 1962–68; stage plays: The Two of Us 1970, The Sandboy 1971, Alphabetical Order 1975, Donkeys' Years 1976, Clouds 1976, Balmoral 1978, Liberty Hall (new version of Balmoral) 1980, Make and Break 1980, Noises Off 1982, Benefactors 1984; has also written plays and documentaries for television, including: Jamie, on a Flying Visit (BBC) 1968, Birthday (BBC) 1969 (plays); Second City Reports (with John Bird—Granada) 1964, Beyond a Joke (with John Bird and Eleanor Bron—BBC) 1972, Making Faces (BBC) 1975 (series); One Pair of Eyes 1968, Laurence Sterne Lived Here 1973, Imagine a City Called Berlin 1975, Vienna: The Mask of Gold 1977, Three Streets in the Country 1979, The Long Straight (Great Railway Journeys of the World) 1980, Jerusalem 1984 (all BBC documentaries); trans. plays, including The Cherry Orchard, Three Sisters, The Seagull, Uncle Vanya, Wild Honey (Chekhov), The Sneeze, The Fruits of Enlightenment (Tolstoy), Exchange (Trifonov), Number One (Anouilh); recipient of numerous drama awards. *Publications:* novels: The Tin Men 1965, The Russian Interpreter 1966, Towards the End of the Morning 1967, A Very Private Life 1968, Sweet Dreams 1973; non-fiction: Constructions (philosophy) 1974; several vols. of collections of columns and translations; *film:* Clockwise 1985. *Address:* c/o Elaine Green Ltd., 31 Newington Green, London, N.16, England.

FRAYSSE, Jean-Pierre; French banker; b. 18 Nov. 1930, Casablanca, Morocco; m. (divorced); one s. one d.; started banking career with Société Générale 1954–62; with Int. Div. of Banque Louis Dreyfus 1962–71; Exec. Dir. Lloyds Bank Int. Ltd. 1971–76; Exec. Deputy Chair. Guinness Mahon & Co. Ltd., London 1976–. *Leisure interests:* swimming, reading, tennis. *Address:* Guinness Mahon & Co. Ltd., 32 St. Mary at Hill, London, E.C.3, England (Office). *Telephone:* 01-623 9333 (Office).

FRAZÃO, Sérgio Armando, B.A., LL.D.; Brazilian diplomatist; b. 26 Feb. 1917, Rio de Janeiro; s. of Félix Armando de Morais Frazão and Zelia Halbout de Amorin Carrão; m. Lice de Faria Frazão 1939; one s.; ed. Colégio Pedro Segundo, Univ. of Brazil Law School; entered diplomatic service 1942; served in Paris, Vienna, with Perm. Mission to UN, New York, Santiago, Lisbon and Washington, D.C. 1946–61; Amb. to Egypt 1964–66, to Uruguay 1966–69; Head Brazilian Del. to UN, Geneva 1969; Amb. to Fed. Repub. of Germany 1969–71; Perm. Rep. to UN 1971–75; Amb. to Spain 1975–82; Pres. Brazilian Coffee Inst. 1961; mem. Del. to

UN Gen. Assembly 1953, 1954, 1971–74; Pres. ECOSOC 1973, and rep. to numerous other int. confs.; Grand Officer of Mil. Merit, Grand Officer Ordem de Cristo (Portugal), Order of Merit (Argentina), Grand Cross, Ordem do Rio Branco, Commdr. Order of Merit (Italy). *Publications:* The Autonomy of the Will; many articles on political and econ. subjects. *Address:* Ministério das Relações Exteriores, Esplanada dos Ministérios 70170, Brasília, D.F., Brazil.

FRAZEE, Rowland C., O.C., B.COMM.; Canadian banker; b. 12 May 1921, Halifax, N.S.; s. of Rowland Hill and Callie Jean (née Cardwell) Frazee; m. Marie Eileen Tait 1949; one s. one d.; ed. King's Coll. and Dalhousie Univ., Halifax; joined Royal Bank of Canada 1939, Asst. Gen. Man., Montreal 1964–65, Dist. Gen. Man., Winnipeg 1965–68, Gen. Man. Canadian Dists. 1968–70, Vice-Pres., Toronto 1970–72, Vice-Pres. and Chief Gen. Man., Montreal 1972–73, Dir., Exec. Vice-Pres. and Chief Gen. Man. 1973–77, Pres. 1977–80, C.E.O. 1979–86, Chair. 1980–86; Dir. Continental Corpn., Power Corpn. of Canada, Int. Minerals & Chemical Corpn., BCE Inc., IMC Fertilizer Group, Inc., Ganong Bros. Ltd., Newfoundland Capital Corpn. Ltd., Noranda Forest Inc., The Royal Bank of Canada, Montreal Children's Hosp. Foundation, Roosevelt Int. Park Comm.; Trustee, Sports Fund for the Physically Disabled; Gov. McGill Univ.; Past Chair., Jr. Achievement of Canada. *Leisure interests:* golf, swimming, reading. *Address:* The Royal Bank of Canada, 1 Place Ville Marie, Montreal, Que. H3C 3A9, Canada.

FRECCIA, Massimo; American (b. Italian) conductor; b. 19 Sept. 1906; ed. Cherubini Royal Conservatoire, Florence; guest conductor New York Philharmonic Orchestra 1938, 1939, 1940; Musical Dir. and Conductor, Havana Philharmonic Orchestra 1939–43, New Orleans Symphony Orchestra 1944–52, Baltimore Symphony Orchestra 1952–59; Chief Conductor Rome (R.A.I.) Orchestra 1959–; frequent appearances as guest conductor of famous orchestras in Europe and U.S.; tours in Australia 1963, Japan 1967, South Africa 1969; appeared at various int. festivals, including Vienna, Prague, Berlin, Lisbon, Montreux; Hon. D.Mus. Tulane Univ., New Orleans; Order of the Star of Italian Solidarity. *Address:* c/o Ibbs and Tillett, 124 Wigmore Street, London, W1H 0AX; 25 Eaton Square, London, S.W.1, England (Home).

FREDERICK, Robert Rice, A.B.; American business executive; b. 12 Jan. 1926, Elkhart, Ind.; s. of Vard W. Frederick and Beryl C. Rice; m. Carolyn N. Smith 1949; two d.; ed. DePauw Univ.; with General Electric Co. 1948–82, Sr. Vice-Pres. Corporate Strategic Planning 1977–79, Exec. Vice-Pres. Int. Sector 1979–82; Pres. and C.O.O. RCA Corpn. 1982–, C.E.O. 1985–87. *Address:* RCA Corporation, 30 Rockefeller Plaza, New York, N.Y. 10020, U.S.A.

FREDGA, Arne, DR.CHEM.; Swedish organic chemist; b. 18 July 1902, Uppsala; s. of Dr. Carl Fredga and Elin (née Cassel) Fredga; m. Brita Öhlin 1931; two s. two d.; ed. Univ. of Uppsala; Asst. at the Chemical Inst. Uppsala Univ. 1930–35, Asst. Prof. of Chem. 1935–39, Prof. of Organic Chem. 1939–69, Prof. Emer. 1969–; mem. Swedish Royal Acad. of Sciences 1943–, Nobel Cttee. of Chem. 1944–75, Nat. Science Research Council 1952–54, Nat. Cttee. for Chem. 1956–62; Pres. Swedish History of Science Soc. 1967–81, Nobel Cttee. of Chem. 1972–75, Bd. of Trustees of Nobel Foundation 1972–75, Nat. Cttee. History of Science 1974–81; Hon. mem. Soc. Chimique Belge, Finska Kemistsamfundet. *Publications:* about 200 papers on stereo-chemistry, organic compounds of sulphur and selenium, plant growth regulators and chemical biography. *Leisure interests:* botany, history of science. *Address:* Börjegatan 3 A, 752 24 Uppsala, Sweden. *Telephone:* 018-135734.

FREDRICKSON, Donald Sharp, M.D., D.SC., F.R.C.P.; American physician and scientist; b. 8 Aug. 1924, Canon City, Colo.; s. of Charles Arthur Fredrickson and Blanche (Sharp) Fredrickson; m. Henriette Priscilla Dorothea Eekhof 1950; two s.; ed. Univs. of Colorado and Michigan; House Officer, Peter Bent Brigham Hosp. 1949–50, Asst. in Medicine 1950–52; Research Fellow in Medicine, Harvard 1950–51; Research Fellow in Medicine, Mass. Gen. Hosp. 1952–53; Clinical Assoc., Nat. Heart Inst., Nat. Insts. of Health 1953–55, mem., Sr. Resident Staff, Lab. of Cellular Physiology and Metabolism 1955–61, Clinical Dir. Nat. Heart Inst. 1961–66, Head, Section on Molecular Diseases, Lab. of Metabolism 1962–66, Dir. Nat. Heart Inst. 1966–68; Chief, Molecular Disease Branch, Nat. Heart and Lung Inst. 1966–74, Dir. Intramural Research 1969–74; Pres. Inst. of Medicine, N.A.S. 1974–75; Dir. Nat. Insts. of Health 1975–81; Scholar-in-Residence N.A.S. 1981–83; Vice-Pres. Howard Hughes Medical Inst. 1983–84, Pres., C.E.O. and Trustee 1984–87; numerous lectureships in U.S.A. and Europe 1964–; mem. Advisory Bd. Health Affairs; Ed. The Metabolic Basis of Inherited Disease, Edns. I–V; Chair. Nat. Advisory Cttee. Nat. Insts. of Health Centennial; mem. White House Science Council, Bd. of Dirs. Corange Ltd., Greater Minnesota Corpn.; mem. A.A.A.S., American Acad. of Arts and Sciences, American Philosophical Soc., American Heart Asscn., American Soc. for Clinical Investigation, American Soc. of Human Genetics, Asscn. of American Physicians, Int. Soc. of Cardiology, N.A.S. and many other professional bodies; Corresp. mem. British Cardiac Soc, Deutsche Gesellschaft für Inntere Medizine, Medical Soc. of Sweden; Fellow American Coll. of Cardiology, American Coll. of Physicians; numerous awards and hon. degrees. *Leisure interests:* skiing, tennis. *Address:* 6615 Bradley Boulevard, Bethesda, Md. 20817, U.S.A.

FREEDBURG, Sydney Joseph, O.B.E., A.M., PH.D.; American museum curator and professor of fine arts; b. 11 Nov. 1914, Boston; s. of Samuel Freedburg and Lillian (née Michelson) Freedburg; m. 1st Anne Blake 1942 (divorced 1950); one s.; m. 2nd Susan Pulitzer 1954 (died 1965); one s. one d.; m. 3rd Catherine Blanton 1967; one s.; ed. Harvard Univ.; mem. Faculty Harvard Univ. 1938-40, 1953-, Prof. of Fine Arts 1960-83, Arthur Kingsley Porter Prof. 1979-83, Prof. Emer. 1983-, Chair. Dept. 1959-63, Prof. in residence Harvard Univ. Center for Renaissance Studies 1973-74, 1980-81, mem. Faculty Council Harvard Univ. 1974-77, Chair. Univ. Museums Council 1977-80; Chief Curator Nat. Gallery, Washington 1983-88; Asst. Prof. Art, then Assoc. Prof. Wellesley Coll. 1946-54; Visiting Lecturer Inst. of Modern Art, Boston 1947; mem. Advisory Council Guggenheim Foundation 1978-; Vice-Chair. Nat. Exec. Cttee. for Rescue of Italian Art 1966-74; mem. Bd. Dirs. Save Venice, Inc.; Fellow American Council of Learned Socs. 1958-59, 1966-67; Nat. Endowment Humanities Sr. Fellow 1973-74; Grand Officer, Order of Star of Italian Solidarity; Grand Officer, Order of Merit of Italian Repub.; Nat. Medal of Arts; Fellow American Acad. of Arts and Sciences; mem. Coll. Art Asscn. *Publications:* Parmigianino, His Works in Painting 1950, Painting of the High Renaissance 1961, Andrea del Sarto 1963, Painting in Italy 1500-1600 1971, Circa 1600 1983. *Address:* 3328 Reservoir Road, Washington, D.C. 20007, U.S.A.

FREEDMAN, Ronald, PH.D.; American sociologist-demographer; b. 8 Aug. 1917, Winnipeg, Canada; s. of Ada Freedman and Issadore Freedman; m. Deborah Selin 1941; one s. one d.; ed. Univs. of Michigan and Chicago, U.S.A.; Instructor to Prof. of Sociology, Univ. of Michigan 1946-79, Roderick D. McKenzie Distinguished Prof. of Sociology 1979-87, Emer. 1987-; Founder and Dir. Population Studies Center 1962-71, Assoc. Dir. 1971-; Study Dir. Nat. Survey on Growth of American Families 1954-55; Co-Dir. Taiwan Population Studies Center 1962-64; Tech. Adviser and Consultant World Fertility Survey 1972-84; Pres. Population Asscn. of America 1964-65; mem. President's Cttee. on Population and Family Planning 1968; Chair. Tech. Advisory Cttee., Demographic Health Surveys 1985-; Consultant Leading Group on Birth Planning, People's Repub. of China, Taiwan Prov. Inst. of Family Planning, World Bank, Rockefeller Foundation, Ford Foundation, WHO, Hewlett Foundation, Population Council, East-West Population Inst. and nat. family planning programmes in Malaysia, Korea, India, Indonesia, Hong Kong; Guggenheim Fellow and Fulbright Fellow 1957-58; mem. N.A.S.; Fellow Center for Advanced Study in Behavioral Sciences; awards include Taeuber Award 1981. *Publications:* Recent Migration to Chicago 1950, Principles of Sociology (with others) 1952, Family Planning, Sterility and Population Growth (with others) 1959, World Population: The Vital Revolution (Ed.) 1964, The Sociology of Human Fertility: An Annotated Bibliography 1975, The Contribution of Social Science to Population Policy 1987, Local Area Variations in Reproductive Behaviour in the People's Republic of China 1973-1982 (with others) 1988 and many others. *Address:* Population Studies Center, University of Michigan, 1225 South University, Ann Arbor, Mich. 48109 (Office); 1404 Beechwood Road, Ann Arbor, Mich. 48103, U.S.A. (Home). *Telephone:* (313) 763-7280 (Office); (313) 663-8327 (Home).

FREEMAN, H.E. Cardinal James Darcy, K.B.E.; Australian ecclesiastic; b. 19 Nov. 1907, Sydney; s. of Robert Freeman and Margaret Smith; ed. Christian Brothers' High School, Sydney, St. Columba's Coll., Springwood and St. Patrick's Coll., Manly; Ordained Priest 1930; Pvt. Sec. to H.E. Cardinal Gilroy, Archbishop of Sydney 1941-46; Auxiliary Bishop of Sydney 1957; Bishop of Armidale 1968; Archbishop of Sydney 1971-83; cr. Cardinal by Pope Paul VI 1973; Kt. of the Holy Sepulchre. *Address:* P.O. Box 246, Randwick, N.S.W. 2031, Australia. *Telephone:* 3998564.

FREEMAN, Rt. Hon. John, P.C., M.B.E.; British journalist, diplomatist and businessman (retd.); b. 19 Feb. 1915; s. of Horace Freeman; m. 1st Elizabeth Johnston 1938 (divorced 1948) 2nd Margaret Kerr 1948 (died 1957), 3rd Catherine Dove 1962 (divorced 1976), 4th Judith Mitchell 1976; two s. three d. and one adopted d.; ed. Westminster School and Brasenose Coll., Oxford; Advertising Consultant 1937-40; active service in North Africa, Italy and North-West Europe 1940-45; M.P. (Lab.) Watford 1945-55; Financial Sec. to the War Office 1946-47; Under-Sec. of State for War 1947-48; Parl. Sec. to the Ministry of Supply 1948-51 (resgnd.); retd. from politics 1955; Deputy Ed. New Statesman 1958-61, Ed. 1961-65; British High Commr. in India 1965-68; Amb. to U.S.A. 1969-71; Chair. London Weekend Television 1971-84, C.E.O. 1971-76; Chair. and C.E.O. LWT (Holdings) 1977-84; Visiting Prof. of Int. Relations, Univ. of Calif. (Davis) 1985-; mem. Bd., ITN (Ind. Television News) 1971-76, Chair. 1976-81; mem. Bd., Ind. Television Publs. 1971-76; Chair. Bd. of Govs., British Film Inst. 1976-77; Vice-Pres. Royal Television Soc. 1975-84; Chair. Communications and Marketing Foundation 1977-79; Chair. Page and Moy (Holdings) Ltd. 1979-84; mem. (fmr. Chair.) Hutchinson Ltd. 1978-84; Trustee Reuters 1984-88; Gold Medal (Royal Television Soc.) 1981. *Address:* c/o Political Science Department, University of California, Davis, Calif. 95616, U.S.A.

FREEMAN, Michael Alexander Reykers, B.A., M.B., B.CH., M.D., F.R.C.S.; British orthopaedic surgeon; b. 17 Nov. 1931, Surrey; s. of Donald G. Freeman and Florence J. Elms; m. Patricia Gill 1968; one d., two s. two d. by previous marriages; ed. Corpus Christi Coll. Cambridge and London Hosp. Medical Coll.; Intern, London Hosp.; resident in Orthopaedic Surgery, Westminster Hosp. and Middx. Hosp. 1962-68; Consultant, London

Hosp. 1968-; co-founder/Dir. Biomechanics Unit, Imperial Coll. London 1956-75; ed. Adult Articular Cartilage 1973-79; mem. Bd. MRC; inventor prostheses and surgical procedures for replacement of hip, knee, ankle and joints of the foot; mem. numerous professional socs. etc.; awards include Robert Jones Medal (British Orthopaedic Asscn.) 1964. *Publications:* The Scientific Basis of Joint Replacement 1977, Arthritis of the Knee 1980. *Leisure interests:* gardening, reading. *Address:* London Hospital, Whitechapel, London, E.1; 149 Harley Street, London, W.1 (Offices); 79 Albert Street, London, N.W.1, England (Home). *Telephone:* 01-377 7766; 01-935 4444 (Offices); 01-387 0817 (Home).

FREEMAN, Orville Lothrop, LL.B.; American lawyer and politician; b. 9 May 1918, Minneapolis, Minn.; s. of Orville E. Freeman and the late Frances (née Schroeder) Freeman; m. Jane C. Shield 1942; one s. one d.; ed. Cen. High School, Minneapolis, Minnesota Univ. Law School; Chair., Civil Service Comm., Minn. 1946-48; admitted to Minn. Bar 1947; partner in law firm 1947-55; Gov. State of Minn. 1955-61; nominated John F. Kennedy at Democratic Nat. Convention, Los Angeles 1960; U.S. Sec. of Agric. 1961-69; Pres. EDP Tech. Int. Inc. 1969-70; Pres. Business Int. Corpn. 1970-81, C.E.O. 1971-81, Chair. 1981-86; Sr. Partner int. law firm, Popham, Haik, Schnobrich, Kaufman and Doty Ltd., Washington 1985-; Chair. U.S. Group, India-U.S. Business Council, U.S. Group, U.S.-Nigerian Joint Agric. Consultative Comm., Bd. of Govs. UN Asscn. of U.S.A., Sime-Derby Int. Plant Research Inst. 1982-; mem. Exec. Cttee. Advisory Council on Japan-U.S. Econ. Relations; mem. Bd. of Dirs. Cttee. for the Future, Natomas Corpn., Franklin Mint, UNA of U.S.A., Multinational Agribusiness Systems Inc.; mem. Council on Foreign Relations, Int. Club of Washington, D.C., Univ. Club of New York City; Faculty mem. Salzburg Seminar 1974, 1977; Hon. mem. Soil Conservation Soc. of America; Hon. Ph.D. (Univ. Seoul, American Univ., Washington, D.C., Fairleigh Dickinson Univ., Rutherford, N.J., St. Joseph's Coll., Philadelphia, Pa.). *Publications:* World Without Hunger and many articles. *Leisure interests:* skiing, squash, swimming, sailing. *Address:* 1101 S. Arlington Ridge Road, Arlington, Va., U.S.A.

FREEMAN, Sir Ralph, Kt., C.V.O., C.B.E., M.B.E. (MIL.), M.A., F.ENG., F.I.C.E., F.R.S.A., F.C.I.T., F.A.S.C.E.; British chartered engineer; b. 3 Feb. 1911, London; s. of late Sir Ralph Freeman and Mary Lines; m. Joan E. Rose 1939; two s. one d.; ed. Uppingham School and Worcester Coll., Oxford; Construction Engineer, Dorman Long and Co., South Africa, Rhodesia and Denmark 1932-36, 1937-39, Braithwaite and Co. 1936-37; on staff of Freeman, Fox & Partners 1939-46, Partner 1947-62, Sr. Partner 1963-79, Consultant 1979-; served with Royal Engineers, Experimental Bridging Est. 1943-45, later bridging adviser to Chief Engineer 21 Army Group H.Q., N.W. Europe Campaign; mem. Council, Inst. of Civil Engineers 1951-55, 1957-61, Vice-Pres. 1962-66, Pres. 1966-67; mem. Nat. Consultative Council to Ministry of Works 1952-56, Bd. of Govs., Westminster Hosp. 1963-69, Advisory Council on Scientific Research and Devt. 1966-69, Defence Scientific Advisory Council 1969-72, Royal Fine Art Comm. 1968-85; Consulting Engineer to H.M. the Queen for Sandringham Estate 1949-76; Chair. Asscn. Consulting Engineers 1975-76; Pres. Welding Inst. 1975-77; mem. gov. body, Imperial Coll. of Science and Tech. 1975-83; Hon. Fellow, Rhodesian (now Zimbabwe) Inst. of Engineers 1969, Inst. of Mechanical Engineers 1970, Worcester Coll., Oxford 1980; Hon. D.Univ. (Surrey); Kt. Order of Orange-Nassau 1945. *Publications:* several papers in Proceedings Inst. of Civil Engineers. *Leisure interests:* all kinds of "Do-It-Yourself". *Address:* Freeman, Fox & Partners, 25 Victoria Street (South Block), London, SW1H 0EX (Office); Ballards Shaw, Ballards Lane, Limpsfield, Oxted, Surrey, RH8 0SN, England (Home). *Telephone:* 01-222 8050 (Office); Oxted 723284 (Home).

FREEMAN, Raymond, M.A., D.PHIL., D.SC., F.R.S.; British research scientist; b. 6 Jan. 1932; s. of late Albert and Hilda F. Freeman; m. Anne-Marie Périnet-Marquet 1958; two s. three d.; ed. Nottingham High School and Lincoln Coll., Oxford; Engineer, French Atomic Energy Comm., Centre d'Etudes Nucléaires de Saclay 1957-59; Sr. Scientific Officer, Nat. Physical Lab. 1959-63; Man. NMR Research, Instrument Div., Varian Assocs., Palo Alto, Calif. 1963-73; Univ. Lecturer in Physical Chem. and Fellow, Magdalen Coll., Oxford 1973-87, Aldrichian Praelector in Chem. 1982-87; John Humphrey Prof. of Magnetic Resonance, Univ. of Cambridge 1987-, Fellow Jesus Coll., Cambridge. *Publications:* A Handbook of Nuclear Magnetic Resonance 1987; several scientific papers on nuclear magnetic resonance spectroscopy in various journals. *Leisure interests:* swimming, traditional jazz. *Address:* Department of Physical Chemistry, Lensfield Road, Cambridge, CB2 1EP (Office); Jesus College, Cambridge, CB5 8BL; 29 Bentley Road, Cambridge, CB2 2AW, England (Home). *Telephone:* (0223) 336450 (Office); (0223) 323958 (Home).

FREERKSEN, Enno, D.PHIL., D.MED.; German medical research scientist; b. 11 Sept. 1910, Emden; m.; one s. two d.; ed. Univs. of Rostock, Giessen, Zürich and Marburg; Asst. Prof., Giessen 1939, Full Prof. of Experimental Medicine, Kiel 1945-; Dir. of Borstel Research Inst. 1950-. *Publications:* contributions to scientific journals in Germany and abroad on experimental medicine and biology (morphology, immunology, mycobacteria, chemotherapy, leprosy, tuberculosis) medical history and scientific theory. *Address:* Sterleyerstrasse 44, 2410 Mölln/Holst, Federal Republic of Germany.

FREETH, Sir Gordon, K.B.E., LL.B.; Australian politician; b. 6 Aug. 1914, S. Australia; s. of Rt. Rev. Evelyn and Gladys M. (née Snashall) Freeth; m. Joan C. C. Baker 1939; one s. two d.; ed. Univ. of Western Australia; Barrister and Solicitor W. Australia 1938–; Solicitor Katanning, W. Australia 1939–49; R.A.A.F. 1942–45; mem. Parl. 1949–69; Minister for Interior and Works 1958–63 and Minister assisting the Attorney-Gen. 1962–64, for Shipping and Transport 1963–68, for Air and Minister assisting the Treas. 1968, for External Affairs Feb.–Oct. 1969; Amb. to Japan 1970–73; practised law, Perth 1973–77; High Commr. in U.K. 1977–80; Chair. Australian Consolidated Minerals 1981–; Liberal. *Leisure interests:* golf, reading. *Address:* Tingrith, 25 Owston Street, Mosman Park, W.A. 6012, Australia.

FREI, Ephraim Heinrich, D.PHIL.; Israeli professor of electronics; b. 2 March 1912, Vienna, Austria; s. of the late Dr. Siegmund Frei and Franziska (Wiener) Frei (both killed in Nazi concentration camp); m. Yael Fanny Rosenfeld 1948 (deceased); two c.; ed. Vienna and Hebrew Univs.; Broadcasting Engineer, British Army; attached to British Embassy, Athens 1944–46; mem. staff Scientific Dept., Ministry of Defence 1948–50; Prof. and Head Dept. of Electronics, Weizmann Inst. of Science 1960–77, Prof. Emer. Medical Physics, Dept. of Electronics 1977–; Visiting Prof. Hebrew Univ., Jerusalem 1982–; mem. Inst. for Advanced Study, Princeton, N.J. 1952; Int. Research Fellow, Stanford Research Inst. Calif. 1960; mem. Bd. of Dirs. Yeda 1963–82, Chair. 1975–79; mem. Editorial Bd., Journal of Cardiovascular Ultrasonography; Chair. XII Int. Conf. Medical and Biological Eng., and V Int. Conf. Medical Physics; Del., Int. Union of Radio Science (URSI), Chair. Israel Cttee. on Bio-Effects 1985–; Fellow, I.E.E.E. 1967, Life mem. 1982; Hon. Life mem. Magnetics Soc. 1979; Hon. Fellow, Israel Soc. Medical and Biological Eng. 1981; Jubilee Dr. Phil. (Vienna) 1986; Computer Pioneer NCC 1975; Weizmann Prize 1957. *Publications:* scientific papers on electronics, physics and biomedical engineering. *Leisure interests:* hiking, archeology. *Address:* Weizmann Institute, P.O. Box 26, Rehovot, Israel.

FREITAS DO AMARAL, Prof. Diogo (see do Amaral, Prof. Diogo Freitas).

FRÉJACQUES, Claude, D. ES SC.; French scientist; b. 1 Aug. 1924, Paris; s. of Maurice and Thérèse (née Bernard) Fréjacques; m. Nicole Duisit 1949; eight c.; ed. Lycée Henri IV, Paris, Ecole Polytechnique; Dir. of Research, Laboratoire Central des Poudres 1946–57; Lecturer Ecole Polytechnique 1956–69; Head Dept. of Physical Chem., Commissariat à L'Energie Atomique 1959–70, Dir. Chemistry Div. 1971–80; Dir. Délégation Générale à la Recherche Scientifique et Technique 1980–81; mem. Comité Energie Atomique 1981–; Admin. Thomson/CSF 1983–, AFME 1983–, Elf Aquitaine 1984–; Pres. Centre Nat. de la Recherche Scientifique (CNRS) Nov. 1981; Pres. Admin. Council 1983–; Pres. Comité Consultatif de la recherche scientifique 1975–77, Société de Chimie-Physique 1976–78, Bureau Nat. de Métrologie 1978–80, French Chemical Soc. (SFC) 1984–86, French Nuclear Energy Soc. (SFEN) 1984–85; Commdr. Légion d'honneur; Commdr. Ordre nationale du Mérite, Ordre des Palmes académiques. *Publications:* on chemistry, physical chemistry, separation of isotopes. *Leisure interests:* skiing, mountaineering. *Address:* 15 quai Anatole France, Paris (Office); 54 avenue de Saxe, Paris, France (Home).

FRELEK, Ryszard, PH.D.; Polish politician; b. 30 May 1929, Parysów near Garwolin; ed. Cen. School of Foreign Service, Warsaw; mem. Peasant Youth Union, then Polish Youth Union to 1950, Polish United Workers' Party (PZPR) 1950–; Corresp. in India, PAP (Polish Press Agency) 1957–59, Deputy Ed.-in-Chief of Foreign Dept. 1959–62, Deputy Ed.-in-Chief of PAP 1968–69; worked at PZPR Cen. Cttee. 1962–68; Head of Polish Inst. of Int. Affairs 1969–71, Chair. Scientific Council 1978–81; Docent, Warsaw Univ. for many years, Prof. Extraordinary of Political Sciences 1976–; mem. Cen. Cttee. 1971–81; Head of Foreign Dept. of Cen. Cttee., PZPR 1971–78, mem. Secr. of Cen. Cttee. 1971–75, Sec. Cen. Cttee. 1975–80; Perm. Rep. to UN 1980–81; Deputy to Seym 1972–80; Chair. Seym Cttee. of Foreign Affairs 1976–80; Prof. Politics and Propaganda Centre, Social Sciences Acad. PZPR Cen. Comm., Warsaw 1986–; Chair. Scientific Council of Silesian Scientific Inst.; mem. Polish Cttee. of Pugwash; mem. SEC; Order of Banner of Labour (1st Class), Kt.'s Cross, Order of Polonia Restituta, Order of the Builders of People's Poland. *Publication:* Historia zimnej wojny (History of Cold War) 1971, novels, plays, screenplays.

FRÉMAUX, Louis Joseph Felix; French orchestral conductor; b. 13 Aug. 1921, Air-sur-Lys; ed. Conservatoire National Supérieur de Musique, Paris; Musical Dir. and Perm. Conductor of Orchestre Nat. de l'Opéra de Monte-Carlo, Monaco 1955–66; Prin. Conductor, Rhones-Alpes Philharmonic Orchestra, Lyons 1968–71; Prin. Conductor and Musical Dir., City of Birmingham Symphony Orchestra 1969–78; Chief Conductor, Sydney Symphony Orchestra 1979–81; Prin. Guest Conductor 1982–85; 8 Grand Prix du Disque Awards; Koussevitsky Award, Notturni ed Alba of McCabe 1973. *Address:* 25 Edencroft, Wheeleys Road, Birmingham, B15 2LW, England. *Telephone:* (021) 440 4683.

FRENCH, Alfred, M.A.; British and Australian university teacher; b. 12 July 1916, Wolverhampton; s. of Percy French and Susan (née Parsonage) French; m. 1st Lidmila Štollová 1939 (deceased); one s.; m. 2nd Alleeta Garson 1980; ed. Wolverhampton Grammar School, Selwyn Coll., Cambridge; Lecturer Caroline Univ. of Prague 1938–39; served in British Army

1940–46; Classics Master at Newington Coll., Sydney, N.S.W. 1947–50; Sr. Lecturer, then Reader in Classics, Univ. of Adelaide, S.A. 1950–81; Visiting Research Fellow, Univ. of Adelaide 1982; Czech Military Medal 1943, Fellow of Australian Acad. of the Humanities 1977. *Publications:* A Book of Czech Verse 1958, The Growth of the Athenian Economy 1964, The Poets of Prague 1969, The Athenian Half Century 1972, Czech Poetry, Vol. 1 1973, Czech Writers and Politics 1984, The Poet's Lamp 1987, Sixth-Century Athens 1987, trans. Sunset Over Atlantis (from Czech) 1960. *Leisure interests:* travel, writing, translation. *Address:* 27 Woodfield Avenue, Fullarton, South Australia 5063. *Telephone:* 272 0183.

FRENCH, Charles Stacy, S.B., M.A., PH.D.; American scientist; b. 13 Dec. 1907, Lowell, Mass.; s. of Charles Ephraim French and Helena Stacy French; m. Margaret Wendell Coolidge 1938; one s. one d.; ed. Loomis School and Harvard Univ.; Research Fellow, Biology, Calif. Inst. of Tech.; Pasadena, Calif. 1934–35; Guest Worker, Kaiser Wilhelm Inst. Berlin-Dahlem 1935–36; Austin Teaching Fellow, Biochem., Harvard Medical School, Boston 1936–38; Instructor (Research), Chem., Univ. of Chicago 1938–41; Asst., Assoc. Prof. Botany, Univ. of Minn. 1941–47; Dir. Dept. of Plant Biology, Carnegie Inst. 1947–73, Dir. Emer. 1973–; Prof. (by courtesy) Biology, Stanford Univ.; Chair. Western Section, American Soc. Plant Physiologists 1954 (Charles Ried Barnes Life Membership Award 1971); mem. Nat. Acad. of Sciences, American Acad. of Arts and Sciences, Deutsche Akad. der Naturforscher Leopoldina, Soc. Gen. Physiologists (Pres. 1955–56), Harvard Club of the Peninsula (Pres. 1973–75), Botanical Soc. of America (Award of Merit 1973); Hon. Ph.D. (Göteborg) 1974. *Publications:* Numerous articles and reviews in tech. journals on photosynthesis and the spectroscopy and functions of plant pigments; annual reports in Carnegie Inst. of Washington Year Book 1948–. *Leisure interests:* mountaineering, conservation of natural areas, development of instruments for plane table plotting for maps. *Address:* Carnegie Institution, Stanford, Calif. (Office); 11970 Rhus Ridge Road, Los Altos Hills, Calif., U.S.A. (Home). *Telephone:* (415) 325-1521 (Office); (415) 948-8318 (Home).

FRENCH, Marilyn, M.A., PH.D.; American author and critic; b. 21 Nov. 1929, New York; d. of E. C. Edwards and Isabel Hazz; m.; two s.; ed. Hofstra Coll. and Harvard Univ.; secretarial and clerical work 1946–53; Lecturer, Hofstra Coll. 1964–68; Asst. Prof. Holy Cross Coll. Worcester, Mass. 1972–76; Mellon Fellow, Harvard Univ. 1976–77. *Publications:* The Book as World-James Joyce's Ulysses 1976, The Women's Room (novel) 1977, The Bleeding Heart (novel) 1981, Shakespeare's Division of Experience 1981, Beyond Power: On Women, Men and Morals 1985. *Address:* c/o Summit Books, 1230 Avenue of the Americas, New York, N.Y. 10020, U.S.A.

FREND, Rev. William Hugh Clifford, T.D., D.PHIL., D.D., F.R.S.E., F.B.A.; British clergyman and professor of ecclesiastical history; b. 11 Jan. 1916, Shotterhill, Surrey; s. of Edwin George Clifford Frend and Edith Frend (née Bacon); m. Mary Grace Crook 1951; one s. one d.; ed. Haileybury Coll., Keble Coll. Oxford, Sorbonne, Paris and Berlin Univs.; served in War Office and War Cabinet Offices and as Intelligence Officer, Political Warfare Exec. 1940–47; full-time mem. Editorial Bd., German Foreign Ministry Documents 1947–51; Research Fellow, Nottingham Univ. 1951–52; S. A. Cook Bye-Fellow, Gonville and Caius Coll. Cambridge 1952–54; Asst. Lecturer, then Lecturer in Church History and Doctrine, Cambridge Univ. 1953–69, Fellow of Gonville and Caius Coll. 1956–69, Dir. of Studies in Archaeology and Anthropology 1961–69; Prof. of Ecclesiastical History, Glasgow Univ. 1969–84, Prof. Emer. 1984–; Priest in Charge of Barnwell and Thurning with Luddington 1984–; T.A., rank of Capt. 1947–67; ordained Church of England 1982; Pres. Comité Int. d'Histoire Ecclésiastique Comparée 1980–83; Vice-Pres. Asscn. Int. d'Etudes Patristiques 1983–87; Hon. D.D. (Edin.) 1974. *Publications:* The Donatist Church 1952, Martyrdom and Persecution in the Early Church 1965, The Early Church 1965, The Rise of the Monophysite Movement (2nd edn.) 1979, The Rise of Christianity 1984, Saints and Sinners in the Early Church 1985, History and Archaeology in the Study of Early Christianity 1988. *Leisure interests:* amateur Romano-British archaeology, golf, collecting old stamps and coins, gardening. *Address:* The Rectory, Barnwell, Peterborough, PE8 5PG, England. *Telephone:* Oundle 72374.

FRENI, Mirella; Italian opera singer; b. 27 Feb. 1935, Modena; d. of Ennio Freni and Gianna (née Arcelli) Freni; m. Leone Magiera 1955; one d.; debut 1955, debut at La Scala, Milan 1962, Glyndebourne Festival 1961, Royal Opera House, Covent Garden 1961, Metropolitan Opera, N.Y. 1965; has sung at Vienna State Opera and at Salzburg Festival and leading opera houses throughout the world. *Major roles include:* Nanetta in Falstaff, Mimi in La Bohème, Zerlina in Don Giovanni, Susanna, Adina in L'elisir d'amore, Violetta in La Traviata, Desdemona in Otello. *Address:* c/o Herbert H. Breslin Inc., 119 W. 57th Street, New York, N.Y. 10019, U.S.A.

FRÈRE, Jean; Belgian diplomatist and banker; b. 1919, Chatou, Seine-et-Oise, France; s. of Maurice Frère; m. Marie-Rose Vanlangenhove 1949; one s. three d.; ed. Germany, Austria, Brussels Univs.; with Solvay & Cie. (Chemical Industries), Brussels 1941–46; entered diplomatic service 1946, Attaché (Commercial and Econ.), Belgian Legation, Prague 1948–51; Political Div., Ministry of Foreign Affairs 1951–52; First Sec. (Econ.), Belgian Embassy, Rome 1952–58; Gen. Sec. EIB 1958–; mem. Belgian Del. Conf.

between EEC mem. countries and Britain 1962; Conseiller Banque Lambert 1962-, Man. Partner 1967-; Conseiller Général Banque Bruxelles Lambert S.A. 1975-81, Conseiller Général Honoraire 1981-; mem. of Bd., Banco di Roma (Belgique) S.A.; Chair. BBL-Australia, Merchant Bankers, Melbourne; many Belgian and foreign decorations. *Leisure interests:* violin, painting, photography, electronics. *Address:* 3315 San Marco, 30124 Venice, Italy. *Telephone:* (041) 5222647.

FRERE, Sheppard Sunderland, C.B.E., D.LITT., F.B.A.; British professor of the archaeology of the Roman Empire; b. 23 Aug. 1916, Graffham, Sussex; s. of Noel Gray Frere and Barbara Sunderland; m. Janet Cecily Hoare 1961; one s. one d.; ed. Lancing Coll. and Magdalene Coll. Cambridge; Asst. Master, Epsom Coll. 1938-40; Nat. Fire Service 1941-46; Asst. Master, Lancing Coll. 1946-54; Lecturer in Archaeology, Manchester Univ. 1954-55; Reader in the Archaeology of the Roman Provs., London Univ. 1955-61, Prof. 1961-66, Prof. of the Archaeology of the Roman Empire 1966-83, Emer. Prof. 1983-; Fellow of All Souls, Oxford, now Emer. Fellow; Pres. Royal Archaeological Inst. 1978-80, Soc. for the Promotion of Roman Studies 1983-86; Ed. Britannia 1970-79, Britannia Monograph Series 1980-. *Publications:* Britannia, A History of Roman Britain 1967, Verulamium Excavations (Vol. I) 1972, (Vol. II) 1983, (Vol. III) 1984, Roman Britain From the Air (with J. K. St. Joseph) 1983. *Address:* Netherfield House, Marcham, Abingdon, Oxon, OX13 6NP, England.

FRESNO LARRAIN, H.E. Cardinal Juan Francisco; Chilean ecclesiastic; b. 26 July 1914; ordained 1937; consecrated Bishop of Copiapó 1958; Archbishop of La Serena 1967, of Santiago de Chile 1983; created Cardinal 1985. *Address:* Avenida Simón Bolívar 2843, Santiago de Chile, Chile.

FRETWELL, Sir (Major) John Emsley, G.C.M.G., M.A.; British diplomatist; b. 15 June 1930, Chesterfield; s. of F. T. Fretwell; m. Mary Ellen Eugenie Dubois 1959; one s. one d.; ed. Chesterfield Grammar School, Lausanne Univ., King's Coll., Cambridge; H.M. Forces 1948-50; entered diplomatic service 1953, Third Sec., Hong Kong 1954-55, Second Sec., Embassy in Beijing 1955-57, Foreign Office 1957-59, 1962-67, First Sec., Moscow 1959-62, First Sec. (Commercial), Washington 1967-70, Commercial Counsellor, Warsaw 1971-73, Head of European Integration Dept. (Internal), FCO 1973-76, Asst. Under-Sec. of State 1976-79, Minister, Washington 1980-81; Amb. to France 1982-87; Political Dir. and Deputy to Perm. Under-Sec. of State, FCO 1987-. *Leisure interests:* skiing, walking. *Address:* c/o Foreign and Commonwealth Office, King Charles Street, London, SW1, England.

FREUD, Lucian, C.H.; British painter; b. 8 Dec. 1922; s. of the late Ernst and Lucie Freud; m. 1st Kathleen Epstein 1948 (divorced 1952); two d.; m. 2nd 1953 Lady Caroline Maureen Blackwood (divorced 1957); ed. Cen. School of Art, E. Anglian School of Painting and Drawing; Teacher at Slade School of Art, London 1948-58; first one-man exhbn. 1944, subsequently 1946, 1950, 1952, 1958, 1963, 1968, 1972, 1978; retrospectives, Hayward Gallery 1974, 1988, 1989; works included in public collections: Tate Gallery, Nat. Portrait Gallery, Victoria and Albert Museum, Arts Council of Great Britain, British Council, British Museum, Fitzwilliam Museum, Cambridge, Nat. Museum of Wales, Cardiff, Scottish Nat. Gallery of Modern Art, Edinburgh, Walker Art Gallery, Liverpool, Ashmolean Museum of Art, Oxford, etc.; in Australia at Brisbane, Adelaide, Perth; in France at Musée Nat. d'Art Moderne, Centre Georges Pompidou, Paris; in U.S.A. at The Art Inst. of Chicago, Museum of Modern Art, New York, Cleveland Museum of Art, Ohio, Museum of Art, Carnegie Inst., Pittsburgh, Achenbaach Foundation for Graphic Arts and Fine Arts, San Francisco, The St. Louis Art Museum, Hirshhorn Museum and Sculpture Garden, Smithsonian Inst., Wash. *Address:* c/o James Kirkman, 46 Brompton Square, London, SW3 2AF, England.

FREUND-ROSENTHAL, Miriam Kottler (Mrs. Harry Rosenthal), M.A., PH.D.; American Zionist leader; b. 17 Feb. 1906, New York; d. of Harry Kottler and Rebecca Zindler; m. 1st Milton Freund 1927 (died 1968), two s.; m. 2nd Harry Rosenthal 1974; ed. Hunter Coll., New York Univ.; Teacher public high schools, New York to 1943; mem. Nat. Bd. Hadassah (Women's Zionist Org.) 1940-, Chair. Youth Activities 1943-48, Vocational Educ. 1948-53, Nat. Youth Aliyah 1953-56; Vice-Pres. Hadassah 1953-56, Pres. 1956-60; Ed. Hadassah Magazine 1966-71; Del. to American Jewish Conf. 1943, to 21st Orientalist Congress, Moscow 1960; Co-chair. American Zionist Youth Comm. 1944-49; Founding charter mem. Brandeis Youth Foundation 1944; mem. Actions Cttee., World Zionist Org. 1956-; mem. Presidium, World Zionist Congress 1960-64; Chair. Exec. Cttee., American Zionist Council 1960-65; mem. Nat. Board, Jewish Nat. Fund, Vice-Pres. 1960-; mem. Bd. United Israel Appeal (UIA) 1960-; mem. Exec., World Council Synagogues 1966-; mem. Nat. Council, Nat. Planning Assen. 1970; mem. Assembly, Jewish Agency June 1971-; Vice-Pres. American Zionist Fed. 1970-72, Women's Cttee., Brandeis Univ.; Chair. Israel Seminars Foundation, Nat. Liaison with Yaal; Nat. Vice-Pres. Mercaz 1978-83; mem. Cabinet, State of Israel Bonds, Chair. Women's Div., State of Israel Bonds 1983-; mem. American Assen. Univ. Women, American Jewish Hist. Soc., Bd. of Trustees, American Friends of the Hebrew Univ. 1978; Henrietta Szold Centennial Lectures for Hebrew Univ. and American Jewish Hist. Soc.; recipient citation of Jewish Book Council, America 1954; Hunter Coll. Hall of Fame 1972. *Publications:* Jewish Merchants in Colonial America 1936, Jewels for a Crown 1963; Israel's Services to Arab Citizens 1982

(Ed.); articles in various journals. *Leisure interests:* travel, painting, writing. *Address:* 50 West 58th Street, New York, N.Y. 10019 (Office); 515 South Lexington, St. Paul, Minn. 55116, U.S.A. (Home). *Telephone:* (212) 355-7900 (Office); (612) 426-3576 (Home).

FREYMOND, Jacques, D. ÈS L.; Swiss professor of history; b. 5 Aug. 1911, Lausanne; s. of Arthur Freymond and Jeanne Heubi; m. Antoinette Cart 1940; two s. one d.; ed.Univs. of Lausanne, Munich and Paris; Teacher in various secondary schools 1935-42; Prof. of Modern and Contemporary History, Univ. of Lausanne 1943-55; Prof. of Diplomatic History, Ecole des Sciences sociales et politiques, Univ. of Lausanne 1946-55; Diplomatic Chronicler, Gazette de Lausanne 1946-55; Rockefeller Fellow in U.S. for studies, especially Yale and Columbia Univs. 1949-50; Prof. of History, Graduate Inst. of Int. Studies, Geneva 1951-81, Dir. 1955-78; Prof. History of Int. Relations, Univ. of Geneva 1958-77; Pres. European Cultural Centre, Geneva 1986-; corresp. mem. Acad. des Sciences morales et politiques 1961; mem. Int. Red Cross Cttee. 1959-72, Vice-Pres. 1965-66, 1969-70; Pres. Int. Political Science Assen. 1964-67; Assoc. Prof. Inst. d'Etudes politiques, Paris 1978-79; Dr. h.c. (Geneva, Bucharest). *Publications:* La politique de François Ier à l'égard de la Savoie 1939, Lénine et l'impérialisme 1951, De Roosevelt à Eisenhower: la politique étrangère américaine 1953, Le conflit Sarrois 1959, La Première Internationale, recueil de documents (Ed.) vols. 1 and 2 1962, vols. 3 and 4 1971, Etudes et documents sur la Première Internationale en Suisse (Ed.) 1964, Western Europe since the War 1964, Contributions à l'étude du Comintern (Ed.) 1965, Guerres, Révolutions, Croix-Rouge 1976, La Suisse et la diplomatie multilatérale (Ed.) 1976, Les hommes d'état célèbres 1920-1970 (Ed. and author) 1977, Documents Diplomatiques Suisses 1848-1945 vol. 6 1914-18 (Ed.) 1982, La paix dangereuse 1986. *Address:* 1294 Genthod, Geneva, Switzerland (Home). *Telephone:* 741195.

FREYNDLIKH, Alisa Brunovna; Soviet actress; b. 8 Dec. 1934; ed. Leningrad Theatre Inst.; worked with Komissarzhevskaya Theatre, Leningrad 1957-61; then with Lensoviet Theatre, Leningrad 1961-83, Gorky Theatre 1983-; worked in films 1958-; R.S.F.S.R. State Prize 1976, U.S.S.R. People's Artist 1981. *Films include:* Family Happiness 1970, My Life 1973, The Princess and the Pea 1977, An Everyday Novel 1977, Always With Me 1977, Stalker 1980, An Old-Fashioned Comedy 1980, Agony 1981, The Canary Cage 1984. *Address:* c/o Gosudarstvennyi Akademicheskii Bolshoi Teatr im. M. Gorkogo, Leningrad, U.S.S.R.

FRICK, Alexander; Liechtenstein politician; b. 1910, Schaan, Liechtenstein; s. of Alexander and Theresia Frick-Wanger; m. Hildegard Kranz 1939; five s. four d.; ed. Training Coll. for Teachers; began career as teacher 1929; official in Tax Dept. 1930-36, Chief of Dept. 1936; Head of Govt. 1945-62; Pres. of the Diet 1969; Hon. Dr. (Freiburg); Grand Cross of Liechtenstein Order of Merit, Great Silver Insignia of Honour (Bande der Republik Österreich), Grosskreuz des Piusordens; mem. Bürgerpartei. *Address:* Im Ganser 121, Schaan, Principality of Liechtenstein. *Telephone:* 2-18-02.

FRICK, Gottlob; German bass opera signer; b. 1906; ed. Stuttgart Opera Chorus and under Neudörfer-Opitz; first small part in Bayreuth Festival 1930; with Coburg Opera 1934, then Freiburg-im-Breisgau and Königsberg Opera; with Dresden Opera 1940-50; joined West Berlin City Opera 1950; regular appearances with Vienna State Opera, Bavarian State Opera and guest artist at Covent Garden and Metropolitan, New York; chiefly known for Wagnerian roles including Daland, Hermann, King Heinrich, King Mark, Pogner, Gurnemanz and bass parts in The Ring especially Fasolt, Hunding and Hagen; also sings in Oratorio; Verdienstkreuz (1st Class), Grosses Bundesverdienstkreuz, Österreichisches Ehrenkreuz für Wissenschaft und Kunst (1st Class). *Address:* Enzkieis-Pforzheim, Eichelberg-Haus Waldfrieden, 7531 Olbronn-Dürrn, Federal Republic of Germany. *Telephone:* 07043-6508.

FRICKER, Peter Racine, F.R.C.O., A.R.C.M.; British musician; b. 5 Sept. 1920, London; s. of Edward Racine and Deborah Alice Fricker (née Parr); m. Helen Clench 1943; ed. St. Paul's School and Royal Coll. of Music; served R.A.F. 1939-45; worked in London as composer, conductor and music admin. 1946-64; Dir. of Music, Morley Coll. 1952-64; Prof. of Music, Univ. of Calif. 1964-; Hon. mem. R.A.M., Hon. Prof. Fellow, Univ. of Wales, Cardiff; Hon. D.Mus. (Leeds) 1958; Order of Merit (Fed. Repub. of Germany) 1965. *Works:* First String Quartet 1948, First Symphony 1949, First Violin Concerto 1950, Violin Sonata 1950, Second Symphony 1951, Viola Concerto 1953, Second String Quartet 1953, Second Violin Concerto 1953, Piano Concerto 1954, Dance Scene for Orchestra 1954, Horn Sonata 1955, Litany for Double String Orchestra 1955, Musick's Empire (Chorus and Orchestra) 1955, 'Cello Sonata 1956, The Vision of Judgement (Oratorio) 1957, Octet 1958, Comedy Overture 1958, Toccata for Piano and Orchestra 1959, Serenade No. 1 for Six Instruments 1959, Serenade No. 2 for Flute, Oboe and Piano 1959, Third Symphony 1960, 12 Studies for Piano 1961, Cantata for Tenor and Chamber Ensemble 1962, O Longs Désirs (song cycle for soprano and orchestra) 1963, Ricercare for Organ 1965, Four Dialogues for Oboe and Piano 1965, Four Songs, Voice and Piano, Texts by Andreas Gryphius (also with Orchestra) 1965, Fourth Symphony 1966, Fantasy for Viola and Piano 1966, Three Scenes for Orchestra, The Day and the Spirits (soprano and harp) 1967, Seven Counterpoints for Orchestra 1967, Ave Maris Stella (male voices and piano) 1967, Refrains for Solo

Oboe 1968, Magnificat for Soloists, Chorus and Orchestra 1968, Episodes for Piano 1968, Concertante No. 4 for Flute, Oboe, Violin and Strings 1968, Set No. 1 for organ 1968, Toccata Gladius Domini for organ 1968, Some Superior Nonsense for Tenor and Chamber Ensemble 1969, Serenade No. 3 for Four Saxophones 1969, Episodes II for Piano 1969, Praeludium for Organ 1969, Paseo for Guitar 1970, The Roofs for Soprano and Percussionist 1970, Concertante No. 5 for Piano and String Quartet 1971, Intrada for Organ 1971, Nocturne for Orchestra 1971, Ballade for Flute and Piano 1972, Seven Little Songs (Hölderlin) for Chorus 1972, Introitus for Orchestra 1972, The Groves of Dodona for Six Flutes 1973, Two Petrarch Madrigals for Chorus 1974, Spirit Puck for Clarinet and Percussions 1974, Trio Sonata for Organ 1974, Third String Quartet 1976, Fifth Symphony, for Organ and Orchestra 1976, Sinfonia for Wind Instruments 1977, Anniversary for Piano 1977, Sonata for Two Pianos 1977, Serenade No. 4 for Three Clarinets and Bass Clarinet 1977, Laudi Concertati for Organ and Orchestra 1979, Serenade No. 5 for Violin and Cello 1979, In Commendation of Music (for soprano, recorder, viola da gamba and harpsichord) 1980, Five Short Pieces for Organ 1980, Six Mélodies de François Jammes (for tenor, violin, cello and piano) 1980, Two Spells for Solo Flute 1980, Bagatelles for Clarinet and Piano 1981, For Three (for oboes) 1981, Two Expressions for Piano 1981, Rondeaux for Horn and Orchestra 1982, Rejoice in the Lord (anthem) 1982, Whispers at these Curtains (Oratorio) 1984, Madrigals for Brass Quintet 1984, Aspects of Evening for Cello and Piano, Concertino for Orchestra, Recitative Impromptu and Procession for Organ 1985, Concerto for Orchestra 1986, Second Sonata for Violin and Piano 1987, Diversions for Piano 1987, Second Piano Concerto 1989, A Dream of Winter for Baritone and Piano 1989. *Leisure interest:* travel. *Address:* Department of Music, University of California, Santa Barbara, California 93106 (Office); 5423 Throne Court, Santa Barbara, Calif. 93111, U.S.A. (Home). *Telephone:* (805) 964-3737.

FRIDAY, William Clyde, B.S., LL.B., LL.D., D.C.L.; American educator; b. 13 July 1920, Raphine, Va.; s. of David Latham and Mary Elizabeth Rowan Friday; m. Ida Willa Howell 1942; three d.; ed. Wake Forest Coll., N. Carolina State Coll. and Univ. of N. Carolina Law School; Asst. Dean of Students, Univ. of N. Carolina at Chapel Hill 1948-51, Acting Dean of Students 1950-51, Admin. Asst. to Pres. 1951-54, Sec. of Univ. 1954-55, Acting Pres. 1956, Pres. 1956-86; Pres. The William R. Kenan, Jr. Fund 1986-; Hon. LL.D. (Wake Forest Coll., Belmont Abbey, Duke Univ., Princeton Univ., Elon Coll., Davidson Coll. Kentucky and Mercer Univs.), Hon. D.C.L. (Univ. of the South) 1976, (St. Augustine's Coll.) 1986, Hon. D.P.S. (Univ. of N.C. at Charlotte) 1986, Hon. D.F.A. (N. Carolina School of Arts) 1987, Hon. L.H.D. (Univ. of North Carolina at Greensboro) 1988. *Leisure interests:* gardening, golf, reading. *Address:* The William R. Kenan, Jr. Fund, P.O. Box 3808, Chapel Hill, N.C. 27515-3808, U.S.A.

FRIDERICHS, Hans, DR.RER.POL.; German politician and banker; b. 16 Oct. 1931, Wittlich; m. Erika Wilhelm; two d.; Man., Rhineland-Hesse Chamber of Industry and Trade 1959-63; Deputy Business Man. FDP 1963-64, Business Man. 1964-69; mem. Bundestag 1965-69, 1976-77; Sec. of State, Ministry of Agric., Viniculture and Protection of the Environment for Rhineland Palatinate 1969-72; Fed. Minister of Econs. 1972-77; Dir. Dresdner Bank 1977-85, Chair. Bd. Man. Dirs. 1978-85; Deputy Chair. FDP 1974-77; mem. Supervisory Bd. AEG Telefunken Dec. 1979-, Chair. 1980-84. *Leisure interests:* art, sport. *Address:* Kappelhofgasse 2, 6500 Mainz, Federal Republic of Germany.

FRIDH, Gertrude; Swedish actress; b. 26 Nov. 1921; ed. Gothenburg School of Dramatic Art; Gothenburg Theatre 1944-49; Intima Theatre, Stockholm 1950; Allé Theatre, Stockholm 1955-57; Royal Dramatic Theatre, Stockholm 1958-. *Plays acted in include:* Ett Dockhem 1953, Som ni behagar 1954, Le Misanthrope 1957, Anna Karenina 1958, Hedda Gabler 1964 (London 1968). *Films acted in include:* Skepp till indialand 1947, Tvd trappor över gåaden 1949-50, Hjärter Knekt 1950, Smultrunstället (Wild Strawberries) 1957, Ansiktet (The Face) 1958, Djävulens Öga 1960.

FRIDLENDER, Georgy Mikhailovich; Soviet academic; b. 1915, Kiev; s. of Mikhail Fridlender and Angèle (Hesse) Fridlender; m. Petrunina Nina Nikolajeune 1958; ed. Leningrad Univ.; editorial and scholarly work for the Inst. of Russian Literature 1955-; full Prof. 1964; Hon. Pres. Int. Dostoevsky Soc. 1983; State Prize in Literature of U.S.S.R. 1983; has participated in the preparation of Acad. Edns. of Belinsky, Gogol, Turgenev and Dostoevsky; Ed.-in-Chief of Acad. publs.: History of the Russian Novel 1962-64 (Vols. I & II); Dostoevsky and his Time 1971, Dostoevsky: Materials and Research 1974-88, vols. 1-7, Dostoevsky and Foreign Literatures 1978. *Publications include:* Lessing 1957, Lessing's Laocoon 1957, Marx and Engels and Problems of Literature 1964, Dostoevsky's Realism 1964, The Poetics of Russian Realism 1971, Dostoevsky and World Literature 1979, 1983, Literature in the Movement of Time 1983, Aesthetics and Literary History 1976, Methodological Problems of Literary Science 1983, The Classical Aesthetical Heritage and Marxism 1983. *Address:* c/o Institut russkoi literatury (Pushkinsky dom), Naberezhnaya Makarova 4, Leningrad; Vtoraja linija, No. 29, logem. 5, 199053 Leningrad, U.S.S.R. (Home). *Telephone:* 213-29-04 (Home).

FRIDOVICH, Irwin, PH.D.; American biochemist; b. 2 Aug. 1929, New York; s. of Louis Fridovich and Sylvia Applebaum Fridovich; m. Mollie D. Finkel 1951; two d.; ed. City Coll. of New York, Duke Univ. Medical

Center, Durham; Instructor in Biochem., Duke Univ. 1956-58, Assoc. in Biochem. 1958-62, Asst. Prof. of Biochem. 1961-66, Assoc. Prof. of Biochem. 1966-71, Prof. 1971-76, James B. Duke Prof. 1976-; Visiting Research Assoc., Harvard Univ. 1961-62; mem. N.A.S.; Herty Award, Georgia Section of American Chem. Soc. 1980; Founders' Award for Outstanding Research in Toxicology 1980; Cressy A. Morrison Award, New York Acad. of Sciences; North Carolina Award in Science 1986; Sr. Passano Foundation Laureate 1987; Hon. D.Sc. (Paris) 1980. *Publications:* approximately 294 articles in major scientific journals. *Leisure interests:* hiking, canoeing, gardening. *Address:* Department of Biochemistry, Duke University Medical Center, Durham, N.C. 27710, U.S.A. (Office). *Telephone:* (919) 684-5122.

FRIED, Charles, M.A., LL.B.; American lawyer; b. 15 April 1935, Prague, Czechoslovakia; s. of Anthony Fried and Marta (Wintersteinova) Fried; m. Anne Sumerscale 1959; one s. one d.; ed. Princeton, Oxford and Columbia Univs.; law clerk to Assoc. Justice John M. Harlan, U.S. Supreme Court 1960; mem. Faculty, Harvard Law School 1961-, Prof. of Law 1965-, Carter Prof. of Gen. Jurisprudence 1981-; Deputy Solicitor-Gen. and Counsellor to Solicitor-Gen. 1985, Solicitor-Gen. of U.S.A. 1985-. *Publications:* An Anatomy of Values 1970, Medical Experimentation: Personal Integrity and Social Policy 1974, Right and Wrong 1978, Contract as Promise: A Theory of Contractual Obligation 1981; contributions to legal and philosophical journals. *Address:* Office of the Solicitor-General, U.S. Department of Justice, Room 5143, Washington, D.C. 20530, U.S.A. *Telephone:* 202-633-2201.

FRIED, Josef, PH.D.; American organic chemist; b. 21 July 1914, Przemysl, Poland; s. of Abraham and Frieda Fried; m. Erna M. Werner 1939; one d.; ed. Univs. of Leipzig, Zürich and Columbia; Research Assoc., Squibb Inst. for Medical Research, New Brunswick, N.J. 1944-47, Head of Dept. 1947-49, Dir. Div. of Organic Chem. 1959-63; Prof. Depts. of Chem., Biochem., and Ben May Laboratory for Cancer Research, Univ. of Chicago 1963-, Louis Block Prof. 1973-, Chair. Dept. Chem. 1977-80; mem. Nat. Acad. of Sciences, American Acad. of Arts and Sciences, A.C.S., American Soc. Biol. Chemists, British and Swiss Chem. Socs.; Fellow, A.A.A.S., New York Acad. of Sciences; A.C.S. Award in Medical Chem. 1974. *Publications:* concerning chemistry and bio-chemistry of steroids, prostaglandins, carcinogenic hydrocarbons. *Leisure interests:* violin (chamber music), skiing, sailing, growing orchids. *Address:* Department of Chemistry, University of Chicago, 5735 S. Ellis Avenue, Chicago, Ill. 60637, U.S.A. *Telephone:* (312) 702-7264.

FRIEDAN, Betty; American feminist leader; b. 4 Feb. 1921, Peoria, Illinois; d. of Harry and Miriam (Horwitz) Goldstein; m. Carl Friedan 1947 (divorced 1969); two s. one d.; ed. Smith Coll.; f. Nat. Org. for Women 1966, first Pres. 1966-70, Chair. 1970-72; Organizer Nat. Women's Political Caucus 1971, Int. Feminist Congress 1973, First Women's Bank & Trust Co. 1973; Visiting Prof. of Sociology, Temple Univ. 1972, Yale Univ. 1974, Queen's Coll. 1975; Contributing Ed., McCalls Magazine 1971-74; Jt. Chair. Nat. Comm. for Women's Equality; numerous lectures in U.S.A. and Europe; mem. PEN; American Humanist Award 1975. *Publications:* The Feminine Mystique 1963, It Changed My Life: Writings on the Women's Movement 1976, The Second Stage 1982, The Fountain of Age; articles in McCall's, Harper's, etc. *Address:* 1 Lincoln Place, 40K, New York, N.Y. 10023, U.S.A.

FRIEDEL, Jacques; French physicist; b. 11 Feb. 1921, Paris; s. of Edmond Friedel and Jeanne Friedel (née Bersier); m. Mary Winifred Horder 1952; two s.; ed. Ecole Polytechnique, Ecole des Mines de Paris, Bristol Univ.; Mining engineer, Ecole des Mines de Paris 1948-56, Maître de Conférences, Univ. de Paris 1956-59; Prof. of Solid State Physics, Univ. de Paris (later Paris Sud) 1959-, Dir. Third Cycle: Exact and Nat. Sciences 1974-77; Pres. Section 21, Consultative Cttee. on Univs. 1975-80; Pres. Consultative Comm. of Scientific and Tech. Research 1978-80; mem. Acad. of Sciences 1977-; Hon. mem. Royal Soc., London, American Acad. of Sciences and Letters, Swedish Acad. of Sciences, Leopoldina, American Physical Soc., Inst. of Physics; Hon. D.Sc. (Bristol) 1977, (Lausanne) 1979; Officier, Légion d'honneur, Commdr. Ordre du Mérite. *Publication:* Dislocations 1956. *Leisure interest:* gardening. *Address:* 2 rue Jean-François Gerbillon, 75006 Paris, France. *Telephone:* 42-22-25-85.

FRIEDKIN, William; American film director; b. 29 Aug. 1939; s. of Louis Friedkin and Rae Green; m. Lesley-Anne Down (divorced); one s. *Films directed include:* Good Times 1967, The Night They Raided Minsky's 1968, The Birthday Party 1968, The Boys in the Band 1970, The French Connection 1971 (Acad. Award for Best Picture, 1971), The Exorcist 1973, Sorcerer 1977, The Brinks Job 1979, Cruising 1980, Deal of the Century 1983, To Live and Die in L.A. 1985, C.A.T. Squad 1986.

FRIEDLANDER, Frederick Gerard, PH.D., F.R.S.; British university teacher of mathematics; b. 25 Dec. 1917, Vienna; ed. Univ. of Cambridge; Fellow, Trinity Coll. Cambridge 1940-42, 1945-46; temporary Experimental Officer, Admiralty 1943-45; Faculty Asst. Lecturer, Cambridge 1945-46; Lecturer, Univ. of Manchester 1946-54; Lecturer, Univ. of Cambridge 1954-79, Reader in Partial Differential Equations 1979-82, Reader Emer. 1982-; Hon. Research Fellow, Univ. Coll. London 1984-. *Publications:* Sound Pulses 1958, The Wave Equation on a Curved Space-Time 1975, Introduction to the Theory of Distributions 1982; papers in mathematical journals. *Address:* Department of Mathematics, University College London, Gower Street, London, WC1E 6BT; 43 Narcissus Road, London, NW6 1TL, England (Home). *Telephone:* 01-387 7050; 01-794 8665 (Home).

FRIEDMAN, Irving S., PH.D.; American economist; b. 31 Jan. 1915; s. of Sigmund Friedman and Sara Tobor; m. Edna Friedman 1938; two s. one d. (deceased); ed. Columbia Univ., N.Y.; mem. Office of U.S. Sec. of Treasury 1941–46; Asst. Dir. of Monetary Research 1945–46; Div. Chief IMF 1946–48, Asst. for Policy Matters to Deputy Man. Dir. 1948–50, Dir. Exchange Restrictions Dept. 1950–64; The Econ. Adviser to Pres. of Int. Bank for Reconstruction and Devt. (World Bank) 1964–70; Chair. Econ. Cttee.; Vice-Pres. President's Council (for Econ. Research and Policy); Fellow, All Souls Coll., Oxford and Visiting Prof. Yale Univ. 1970–71; Adviser to Pres. and Prof. in Residence, World Bank 1971–74; Sr. Vice-Pres. and Sr. Adviser for Int. Operations, Citibank, New York 1974–80; Sr. Int. Adviser First Boston Corpn., mem. of Int. Advisory Bd. 1980–85; Adviser and Consultant Inter-American Devt. Bank 1980–82, Security Pacific Bank 1981–82, Asian Devt. Bank 1982–, African Devt. Bank 1982–, Nordic Devt. Bank 1982–, Banco de Talca, Chile 1980–82, American Security Bank 1982–86, Energy Devt. Int. 1983–; Chair. Washington Capital Markets Group 1984–; Chair. I. S. Friedman Inc.; Visiting Prof. Univ. of Va. 1980–, Fordham Univ. 1986–; Sr. Fellow, Centre for Int. Banking Studies, Univ. of Virginia; Chair. Center of Concern 1971–, Population Resource Center 1982–; Paul Hoffman Awards Trust Fund 1975–85; Pres. and Treas. Soc. for Int. Devt. 1960–75; mem. Council SID 1975–; mem. American Econ. Soc., Council on Foreign Relations; mem. North-South Round Table 1980–; Dir. numerous cos.; Hon. M.A. (Oxford), Hon. LL.D. (American Coll. of Switzerland); Order of Sacred Treasure, Japan, Commdr. of Falcon, Iceland 1980, Medal of Honour, World Business Council 1983. *Publications:* Inflation: A Worldwide Disaster 1973 (new edition 1980), The Emerging Role of Private Banks in the Developing World 1977, The World Debt Dilemma: Managing Country Risk 1983, Toward World Prosperity: Reshaping the Global Monetary System 1986, and numerous articles on international economics. *Leisure interests:* music, literature, golf, sailing, tennis, astronomy. *Address:* 6620 Fernwood Court, Bethesda, Md.; and 860 UN Plaza, New York, N.Y. (Home); 1015 18th Street, N.W. Suite 802, Washington, D.C. 20036, U.S.A. (Office). *Telephone:* (202) 822-8482 (Office); (301) 365 5023 (Home).

FRIEDMAN, Milton, PH.D.; American economist; b. 31 July 1912, New York; s. of Jeno Saul and Sarah Esther Friedman; m. Rose Director 1938; one s. one d.; ed. Rutgers Univ., Chicago and Columbia Univs.; Assoc. Economist, Nat. Resources Cttee. 1935–37, Nat. Bureau of Econ. Research 1937–45 (on leave 1940–45), 1948–81; Prin. Economist, Div. of Tax Research, U.S. Treasury Dept. 1941–43; Assoc. Dir. Statistical Research Group, Div. of War Research, Columbia Univ., New York 1943–45; Prof. of Econs., Univ. of Chicago 1948–83, Prof. Emer. 1983–; Sr. Research Fellow, Hoover Inst. of Stanford Univ., Calif. 1976–; Bd. of Eds. Econometrica; mem. Advisory Bd., Journal of Money, Credit and Banking 1968–; Pres. American Econ. Asscn. 1967; mem. President's Comm. on All-Volunteer Armed Force 1969–70, on White House Fellows 1971–73, President's Econ. Policy Advisory Bd. 1981–; Pres. Mont Pelerin Soc. 1970–72, Western Econ. Assn. 1984–85; mem. Nat. Acad. of Sciences 1973–; numerous hon. degrees; Nobel Prize for Econ. Science 1976; Grand Cordon of the Sacred Treasure (Japan) 1986; Nat. Medal of Science (U.S.) 1988; Presidential Medal of Freedom (U.S.) 1988. *Publications:* Income from Independent Professional Practice (with Simon Kuznets) 1946, Sampling Inspection (with others) 1948, Essays in Positive Economics 1953, A Theory of the Consumption Function 1957, A Program for Monetary Stability 1960, Capitalism and Freedom 1962, Price Theory; a provisional text 1962, A Monetary History of the United States 1867-1960 (with Anna J. Schwartz) 1963, Inflation: Causes and Consequences 1963, The Balance of Payments: Free Versus Flexible Exchange Rates (with Robert V. Roosa) 1967, Dollars and Deficits 1968, Optimum Quantity of Money and Other Essays 1969, Monetary Statistics of the United States (with Anna J. Schwartz) 1970, A Theoretical Framework for Monetary Analysis 1972, Social Security: Universal or Selective (with Wilbur J. Cohen) 1972, An Economist's Protest 1972, Money and Economic Development 1973, Milton Friedman's Monetary Framework 1974, Price Theory 1976, Tax Limitation, Inflation and the Role of Government 1978, Free to Choose (with Rose D. Friedman) 1980, Monetary Trends in the United States and the United Kingdom (with Anna J. Schwartz) 1982, Bright Promises, Dismal Performance: An Economist's Protest (with William R. Allen) 1983, Tyranny of the Status Quo (with Rose D. Friedman) 1984. *Leisure interests:* tennis, carpentry, talk. *Address:* Hoover Institution, Stanford University, Stanford, Calif. 94305, U.S.A.

FRIEDMANN, Jacques Henri, L. EN D., DIPL.; French business executive; b. 15 Oct. 1932, Paris; s. of André Friedmann and Marie-Louise (née Bleiweiss) Friedmann; m. Cécile Fleur 1962; two s. one d.; ed. Law Faculty, Sorbonne, Inst. d'Etudes Politiques de Paris, Ecole Nat. d'Administration; Inspector of Finance 1959, Special Asst. 1964, then Tech. Adviser Ministry of Finance 1965–66; Acting Deputy Sec.-Gen. Int. Cttee. on European Econ. Co-operation 1966–67; Head Finance Dept. French Planning Org. 1967–70; Chief Exec. Sec. to Sec. of State for Econ. Affairs and Finance 1969–70, to Minister for Liaison with Parl. 1971; Head of Cen. Dept. of Gen. Inspectorate for Nat. Economy 1971–72; Adviser, Econ. and Financial Affairs, then Chief Exec. Sec. to Prime Minister 1972–74, Special Asst. to

Prime Minister 1974; Chair. Compagnie Générale Maritime 1974–82; Chair. and Man. Dir. Compagnie Parisienne de Chauffage Urbain 1983–87; Chair. Bd. Caisse d'Epargne de Paris 1985–; Special Asst. Minister of Econ. Affairs, Finance and Privatisation 1986–87; Chair. of Bd. and C.E.O. Air France 1987–88; Chevalier Légion d'Honneur, Chevalier Ordre Nat. du Mérite. *Address:* 80 Avenue de Breteuil, 75015 Paris, France (Home). *Telephone:* 43.23.83.19.

FRIEL, Brian; British writer; b. 9 Jan. 1929; s. of Patrick Friel and Christina MacLoone; m. Anne Morrison 1954; one s. four d.; ed. St. Columb's Coll., Derry, St. Patrick's Coll., Maynooth, St. Joseph's Training Coll., Belfast; taught in various schools 1950–60; full-time writer 1960–; mem. Irish Acad. of Letters, Aosdana 1983–; Hon. D.Litt. (Nat. Univ. of Ireland) 1983. *Publications:* collected stories: The Saucer of Larks 1962, The Gold in the Sea 1966; *plays:* Philadelphia, Here I Come! 1965, The Loves of Cass McGuire 1967, Lovers 1968, The Mundy Scheme 1969, Crystal and Fox 1970, The Gentle Island 1971, The Freedom of the City 1973, Volunteers 1975, Living Quarters 1976, Aristocrats 1979, Faith Healer 1979, Translations 1981 (Ewart-Biggs Memorial Prize, British Theatre Asscn. Award), Three Sisters (trans.) 1981, The Communication Cord 1983, Fathers and Sons 1987, Making History 1988. *Leisure interests:* reading, trout-fishing, slow tennis. *Address:* Drumaweir House, Greencastle, County Donegal, Ireland.

FRIENDLY, Fred W., H.L.D.; American broadcaster and journalist; b. 30 Oct. 1915, New York City; s. of Samuel Wachenheimer and Therese Friendly; m. 1st Dorothy Greene, two s. one d.; m. 2nd Ruth W. Mark 1968, three step-s.; ed. Cheshire Acad., Connecticut, and Nichols Coll., Dudly, Massachusetts; began broadcasting career writing, producing and narrating series Footprints in the Sands of Time on local radio station 1938; U.S. Army 1941–45 as lecturer in Educ. section and corresp. for China, Burma and India on Army newspaper Roundup; commenced long professional partnership with Edward R. Murrow with historical gramophone record I Can Hear It Now; then CBS Radio Series Hear It Now and TV series See It Now 1951, Exec. Producer CBS Reports 1959–64, Pres. CBS News 1964–66; Edward R. Murrow Prof. of Journalism, Columbia Univ. 1966; Adviser on Television to Ford Foundation 1966–; Chair. Mayor Lindsay's Task Force on CATV and Telecommunications 1968; mem. Rhode Island Heritage Hall of Fame; Hon. D. Hum. Litt. (Grinnell Coll., Iowa and Brown Univ., Rhode Island); Soldier's Medal of Heroism, Legion of Merit with four battle stars, George Foster Peabody Awards (ten). *Publications:* See It Now (co-author) 1955, Due to Circumstances Beyond Our Control 1967, The Good Guys, The Bad Guys and the First Amendment 1976, Minnesota Rag 1981; articles in the New York Times Magazine: What's Fair on the Air? 1975, A Crime and its Aftershock 1976. *Address:* 4614 Fieldston Road, Riverdale, N.Y. 10471, U.S.A.

FRIIS, Henning Kristian; Danish social research executive; b. 11 Oct. 1911, Copenhagen; s. of Prof. Aage Friis and Benedicte Blichfeldt; m. Inge Holm 1986; two s. one d.; ed. Københavns Univ.; Social Science Adviser, Ministry of Social Affairs 1941–58; Sec.-Gen. Danish Govt. Youth Comm. 1945–52, Cttee. on Scientific and Tech. Personnel 1956–59; Chair. OECD Cttee. for Scientific and Tech. Personnel 1958–65; Exec. Dir. Danish Nat. Inst. of Social Research 1958–79; Dir. EEC Study on Poverty in Denmark 1979–80; WHO Consultant on the Elderly 1980–82; Chair. Future Study on Ageing 1985–, European Social Research Cttee., Int. Gerontological Asscn. 1954–60; Chair. Bd. of Trustees, Danish Schools of Social Work 1966–71; mem. Exec. Cttee. Int. Sociological Asscn. 1959–65; Vice-Chair. Danish Social Science Council 1968–77, European Centre for Co-ordination in the Social Sciences 1968–82; Dir. Study on Social Changes in next 20 years 1982–86; mem. Bd. of Trustees, UN Inst. on Training and Research 1965–76; mem. Exec. Cttee., Int. Social Science Council 1970–73, 1979–; Ed. Scandinavia between East and West 1950, and Family and Society 1964; Hon. mem. Danish Statistical Soc. *Publications:* Social Policy and Social Trends 1958, Longstanding Public Assistance Clients 1960, Development of Social Research in Ireland 1965, Social Policy and Social Research in India 1968, Old People in Three Industrial Societies (co-author) 1968, National and International Policies for Social Research 1972, The Aged in Denmark 1979, Pensions and Retirement up to the year 2000 1980, Poverty and Poverty Policies in Denmark 1980, The Uncertain Future: Denmark at the Year 2000 1985. *Leisure interests:* art, reading, travel. *Address:* Gammel Kongevej 174, Frederiksberg 6, Denmark. *Telephone:* (01) 31 01 20.

FRIMPONG-ANSAH, Jonathan Herbert; Ghanaian banker; b. 22 Oct. 1930, Mampong, Ashanti; s. of Hammond Owusu-Ansah and Elizabeth Achiaa; m. Selina Agyemang 1954; three s. one d.; ed. Univ. of Ghana and L.S.E.; Statistician, Ghana Govt. 1954–59; Bank of Ghana, Dir. of Research 1961–65, Deputy Gov. 1965–68, Gov. 1968–73; Chair. Ghana Diamond Marketing Bd. 1969–72; Dir. Volta River Authority 1972–; Chair. Ashanti Goldfields Corpn. Ltd. 1973–; Vice-Chair. Deputies of the Cttee. of the Bd. of Govs. on Reform of the Int. Monetary System and Related Issues, IMF, Wash. 1973–74; Consultant World Bank 1975; Chair. Standard Bank Ghana, Ltd., Accra 1975–81, Akosombo Textiles Ltd. 1975–; Chair. UN Experts Group on Establishment of African-Caribbean-Pacific Investment and Trade Bank 1978–79 Dir. SIFIDA, Geneva 1981–; Fellow, Center for Int. Affairs, Harvard 1978–, Ghana Acad. of Arts and Sciences 1979–; Hon. Prof. of Finance, Univ. of Ghana 1979–. *Publications:* articles in Economic

Bulletin (Ghana), Bulletin of the Inter Credit Bank (Geneva), Univ. of Ghana journals; contribs. in International Monetary Reform—Documents of the Committee of Twenty 1974, Ghana Who's Who 1977. *Leisure interest:* art. *Address:* Hillhurst, Kewferry Drive, Northwood, Middx., HA6 ZPA, England; 3 Liberation Link, Accra, Ghana. *Telephone:* Northwood 27909; Accra 23314.

FRINK, Dame Elisabeth, D.B.E., R.A.; British sculptor; b. 14 Nov. 1930, Thurlow; m. 1st Michael Jammet 1956 (dissolved 1962), one s.; m. 2nd Edward Pool 1968 (dissolved 1974); m. 3rd Alexander Csáky 1974; ed. Convent of the Holy Family, Exmouth, and Guildford and Chelsea Schools of Art; taught sculpture at Chelsea School of Art 1953-60, St. Martin's School of Art 1955-64; Visiting lecturer, part-time, R.C.A. 1965-67; exhibited regularly at Waddington Galleries 1955-, and also abroad; lived in France 1967-72; now living and working in Dorset; mem. Royal Fine Art Comm. 1976-81; Trustee, British Museum 1975-; Dr. h.c. (Open Univ.) 1983, (Univ. of Exeter) 1988, (Cambridge) 1988, Hon. D.Lit. (Cambridge) 1988. *Publications:* (illustrated) Aesop's Fables 1967, Canterbury Tales 1971, The Odyssey 1974, The Iliad 1975, Children of the Gods 1983, Horace Odes 1987; The Art of Elisabeth Frink 1972, Elisabeth Frink—Catalogue Raisonné 1985. *Leisure interests:* music, riding, outdoor occupations. *Address:* Woolland House, Blanford Forum, Dorset, England. *Telephone:* 025-86 543.

FRISCH, Max Rudolf; Swiss writer and architect; b. 15 May 1911, Zürich; ed. Zürich Univ. and Zürich Inst. of Tech.; worked as foreign corresp. for newspapers throughout Europe and the Near East; diploma in architecture 1941; designs executed include the Zürich Recreation Park; first play published 1945; abandoned architecture for full-time writing 1955; Rockefeller Grant for Drama 1951; mem. American Acad. of Arts and Letters 1974; Dr. h.c. (Bard Coll., New York) 1980, Hon. D.Litt. (Birmingham) 1985; Prize of the German Acad. 1958, Jerusalem Prize, Ehrenpreis des Schillergedächtnispreises des Landes Baden-Württemberg 1965, Grosser Schillerpreis Zürich 1974, Friedenspreis des Deutschen Buchhandels 1976, Commdr. de l'Ordre des Arts et des Lettres 1985; Neustadt Prize 1986. *Publications:* Plays and novels: Blätter aus dem Brotsack 1940, Santa Cruz 1944, J'adore ce qui me brûle oder Die Schwierigen 1945, Bin oder Die Reise nach Peking 1945, Nun singen sie wieder 1945, Die chinesische Mauer 1947, Als der Krieg zu Ende war 1949, Tagebuch 1946-1949 1950, Graf Oederland 1951, Don Juan oder Die Liebe zur Geometrie 1953, Stiller 1954 (translated into 17 languages), Homo faber 1957 (translated into 15 languages), Biedermann und die Brandstifter 1958, Die grosse Wut des Philipp Hotz 1958, Andorra 1961 (translated into 11 languages), Mein Name sei Gantenbein 1964, Biografie: Ein Spiel 1967, Öffentlichkeit als Partner 1968, Wilhelm Tell für die Schule 1971, Tagebuch 1966-71 1972, Dienstbüchlein 1974, Montauk 1975, Werkausgabe 1975, Triptychon—3 szenische Bilder 1976, Der Mensch erscheint im Holozän 1980, Blaubart, eine Erzählung (1982). *Address:* CH-6611 Berzona, Switzerland; c/o Suhrkamp-Verlag, Frankfurt/Main, Federal Republic of Germany.

FRISCHENSCHLAGER, Friedhelm, DR.JUR.; Austrian politician; b. 6 Oct. 1943, Salzburg; m.; two c.; ed. schools in Salzburg and Univ. of Vienna; reader, Univ. of Vienna; municipal councillor and mem. Salzburg City Bd. 1972; mem. Nationalrat 1977-; Fed. Minister for Nat. Defence 1983-86; mem. Austrian Freedom Party (FPÖ) and leader of its Parl. Group. *Leisure interests:* sport, literature. *Address:* c/o Freedom Party of Austria, 28 Kärntnerstr., Vienna, Austria.

FRISINGER, Haakan H. J., M.ENG.; Swedish business executive; b. 8 Dec. 1928, Skoevde; s. of Anna and Anders Johansson; m. Annakarin Lindholm 1953; two s. one d.; ed. Chalmers Univ. of Tech., Gothenburg and Harvard Business School; Head, Man. Unit Product and Production Co-ordination, AB Volvo 1966; Head, Volvo Köping Plant 1971; Head of Volvo Car Production and mem. Corporate Exec. AB Volvo 1975; Head, Volvo Car Industry Div. and Exec. Vice-Pres. AB Volvo 1977; Pres. Volvo Car Corpn. 1978; Pres. and C.O.O., AB Volvo 1983-87. *Leisure interests:* music, art, golf, sport, hunting. *Address:* AB Volvo, S-405 08 Gothenburg, Sweden. *Telephone:* (31) 59 00 90.

FRITZ, Walter Helmut; German writer; b. 26 Aug. 1929, Karlsruhe; s. of Karl T. Fritz and Hedwig Fritz; ed. Univ. of Heidelberg; poetry teacher at the Univ. of Mainz; has lectured in Europe, America and Africa; mem. of Akademie der Wissenschaften und der Literatur, Mainz, Bayerische Akademie der Schönen Künste, Munich, Deutsche Akademie für Sprache und Dichtung, Darmstadt, PEN; Stuttgarter Literaturpreis, Villa Massimo-Stipendium. *Publications:* 20 books containing lyrics and prose, recent works: Gesammelte Gedichte 1979, Wunschtraum Alptraum (poems) 1981, Werkzeuge der Freiheit (poems) 1983, Cornelias Traum, Aufzeichnungen 1985, Immer einfacher immer schwieriger (poems) 1987. *Address:* Kolbergerstrasse 2a, 7500 Karlsruhe 1, Federal Republic of Germany. *Telephone:* 0721-683346.

FRITZHAND, Marek, PH.D.; Polish philosopher; b. 12 Oct. 1913, Buczacz; s. of Schmerl and Frimeta Fritzhand; m. Karolina Gruszczyńska 1948; one d.; ed. Lwów Univ.; Assoc. Prof. Lwów Univ. 1954-66, Prof. 1966-84, Prof. Emer. 1984, Dean, Faculty of Philosophy, Warsaw Univ. 1962-65, Dean, Faculty of Social Sciences 1975-77, Head, Moral Science Dept. 1956-83, Prof. Emer. 1983-; Ed.-in-Chief Etyka 1966-71, mem. of Editorial Staff

1973-; mem. Polish United Workers Party (PZPR) 1948-; mem. Polish Philosophical Soc.; mem. Cttee. of Philosophical Sciences, Polish Acad. of Sciences 1966-72, Chair. 1972-80, 1984-; Corresp. mem. Polish Acad. of Sciences 1973, mem. -1983; mem. Cttee. of Nat. Educ. Comm. Medal 1979-; Gold Cross of Merit (twice), Cross of Valour, Cross of Grunwald (3rd Class), Knight's Cross, Order of Polonia Restituta, Meritorious Teacher of People's Poland 1978, Commdr. Order of Polonia Restituta 1983, State Prize (2nd Class) 1984, Order of Banner of Labour (1st Class) 1984. *Publications include:* Człowiek, humanizm, moralność 1961, 1966, Konieczność a moralność 1961, Myśl etyczna młodego Marksa 1962, W kręgu etyki marksistowskiej 1966, Główne kierunki i zagadnienia metaetyki 1970, O niektórych właściwościach etyki marksistowskiej 1975, Wartości a Fakty 1982, over 160 articles on ethics and philosophy. *Leisure interest:* photography. *Address:* Al. Wyzwolenia 2 m. 3, 00-570 Warsaw, Poland. *Telephone:* 284679.

FRODSHAM, John David, M.A., PH.D., F.A.H.A.; British/Australian university professor and consultant; b. 5 Jan. 1930, Cheshire; s. of J. K. Frodsham and W. E. Frodsham; m. Tan Beng-choo 1964; three s. two d.; ed. Emmanuel Coll., Cambridge, Australian Nat. Univ.; lecturer in English Univ. of Baghdad 1956-58, in Oriental Studies Univ. of Sydney 1960-61, in Far Eastern History Univ. of Malaya 1961-65, Sr. Lecturer in Far Eastern History Univ. of Adelaide 1965-67; Reader in Chinese Australian Nat. Univ. 1967-71; Prof. of Comparative Literature Univ. of Dar-es-Salaam 1971-73, Foundation Prof. English and Comparative Literature Murdoch Univ. 1973-; Visiting Prof. Cornell 1965, Hawaii 1968, American Coll. of Greece 1985, Tamkang Univ. of Taiwan 1985; Visiting Fellow, Inst. of E. Asian Philosophies, Univ. of Singapore 1989; Consultant Ausean Int. Ltd. 1987-; Fellow and Pres. Professors' World Peace Acad. 1983-; Pres. Australasian Soc. of Psychical Research 1978-, mem. Soc. of Psychical Research; mem. Australia-China Council 1979-83; Current Affairs Commentator for ABC 1958-. *Publications:* An Anthology of Chinese Verse, Vol. 1 1967, The Murmuring Stream (2 vols.) 1967, The Poems of Li Ho 1970, New Perspectives in Chinese Literature 1971, The First Chinese Embassy to the West 1973, Foundations of Modernism: Modern Poetry 1980, Goddesses, Ghosts and Demons: The Collected Poems of Li He 1983, Classicism & Romanticism: A Comparative Period Study (4 vols.) 1986, Turning Point 1988. *Leisure interests:* psychical research, sailing. *Address:* School of Humanities, Murdoch University, Murdoch, Western Australia 6150 (Office); 105 Riverton Drive, Rossmoyne, Western Australia 6155 (Home). *Telephone:* (09) 332-2313 (Office); 457-1608 (Home).

FROGGATT, Sir Leslie (Trevor), Kt; Australian business executive; b. 8 April 1920; s. of Leslie Froggatt and Mary H. Brassey; m. Jessie E. Grant 1945; three s.; ed. Birkenhead Park School, Cheshire; joined Asiatic Petroleum Co., Ltd. 1937; Shell Singapore, Shell Thailand, Shell Malaya 1947-54, Shell Egypt 1955-56; Dir. of Finance, Gen. Man. Kalimantan, Borneo and Deputy Chief Rep. PT Shell Indonesia 1958-62; Area Co-ordinator, S. Asia and Australasia, Shell Int. Petroleum Co., Ltd. 1962-63, various assignments in Europe 1964-66; Shell Oil Co. Atlanta, Ga. 1967-69; Dir. Shell Australia Ltd. 1969-; Chair. and C.E.O. Shell Group Australia 1969-80; Chair. Ashton Mining Ltd. 1981-; Dir. Pacific Dunlop Ltd., Australian Industry Devt. Corpn.; Dir. Australian Inst. of Petroleum Ltd. 1983-84; mem. Australian Nat. Airlines Comm. *Leisure interests:* reading, music, racing, golf. *Address:* 20 Albany Road, Toorak, Vic. 3142, Australia. *Telephone:* (03) 20.1357.

FRÖHLICH, Albrecht, PH.D., F.R.S.; British professor of pure mathematics; b. 22 May 1916; s. of Julius Fröhlich and Frida Fröhlich; m. Dr. Evelyn Ruth Brooks 1950; one s. one d.; ed. Realgymnasium, Munich, Germany and Bristol Univ.; Asst. Lecturer in Math., Univ. Coll., Leicester 1950-52; Lecturer in Math., Univ. Coll. of N. Staffs. 1952-55; Reader in Pure Math., King's Coll., Univ. of London 1955-62, Prof. 1962-81, Emer. Prof. 1982-, Head Dept. of Math. 1971-81; Sr. Research Fellow, Imperial Coll., Univ. of London 1982-; Fellow Robinson Coll., Cambridge 1982-84, Emer. Fellow 1984-; Visiting Royal Soc.-Israeli Acad. Research Prof. 1978; George A. Miller Prof., Univ. of Ill., U.S.A. 1981-82; Gauss Prof., Göttingen Acad. of Sciences, Fed. Repub. of Germany 1983; Corresp. mem. Heidelberg Acad. of Sciences 1982; Fellow King's Coll. 1977; Sr. Berwick Prize, London Math. Soc. 1976. *Publications:* Formal Groups 1968, Galoi's Module Structure of Algebraic Integers 1983, Class Groups and Hermitian Modules 1984; papers in mathematical journals. *Leisure interests:* cooking, eating, walking, music. *Address:* 63 Drax Avenue, Wimbledon, London, S.W.20, England. *Telephone:* 01-946 6550.

FRÖHLICH, Prof. Herbert, F.R.S.; British physicist; b. 9 Dec. 1905, Rexingen, Germany; m. Fanchon Aungst 1950; ed. Univ. of Munich; Lecturer and Reader, Univ. of Bristol, then Prof. of Theoretical Physics, Univ. of Liverpool 1948-73, Prof. Emer. 1973-, Hon. Research Fellow 1973; Foreign mem. Max Planck Inst., Germany 1980-; Max Planck Medal 1972, five hon. doctorates. *Publications:* various scientific papers and books. *Address:* Department of Physics, University of Liverpool, P.O. Box 147, Liverpool, L69 3BX, England (Office).

FROLOV, Ivan Timofeyevich, DR.PHIL.SC.; Soviet politician; b. 1929; ed. Moscow Univ.; head of section, chief sec. of journal Voprosy filosofii 1956-62, Ed.-in-Chief 1968-77; mem. CPSU 1960-; consultant ed. deputy chief sec. of journal Problems of Peace and Socialism 1962-65; asst. to sec.

of CPSU Cen. Cttee. 1965–68; Chief Sec. Problems of Peace and Socialism 1977–79; Deputy Dir. of All-Union Inst. of Systems Analysis 1979–80; Pres. of Council of Philosophy with Acad. of Sciences Presidium 1980–86; ed.-in-chief Kommunist 1986–; mem. of CPSU Cen. Cttee. 1986–; Pres. of U.S.S.R. Philosophical Soc. 1987–; Asst. to Gen. Sec. of CPSU Cen. Cttee. 1987–; Deputy to U.S.S.R. Supreme Soviet. *Address:* Kommunist, ul. Pravdy 24, Moscow, U.S.S.R.

FROLOV, Konstantin Vasilevich, D.TECH.SCI.; Soviet machine construction specialist; b. 1932; ed. Bryansk Inst. of Transport and Machine Construction; Prof. 1971–; engineer at Leningrad Metallurgical Plant 1956–58; research work U.S.S.R. Acad. of Sciences Inst. of Machine Construction 1961–63, Head of Lab. 1963–75, Dir. 1975–; Vice-Pres. U.S.S.R. Acad. of Sciences, Acad. Sec. of Mechanics Section 1985–; mem. U.S.S.R. Acad. of Sciences 1984–; concurrently teacher at Moscow Univ. 1960–62, Moscow Inst. of Technology 1962–75, Moscow Bauman Tech. College 1975–; *Address:* c/o Moskovsky vyshiy technologicheskii universitet im. Baumona, Moscow, U.S.S.R.

FROMENT-MEURICE, Henri, L.ÉS.L.; French diplomatist; b. 5 June 1923, Paris; m. Gabrielle Drouilh 1948; three s. one d.; ed. Ecole libre des Sciences Politiques, Ecole Nat. d'Admin.; Sec., Ministry of Foreign Affairs 1950–52, Sec. for Far East, Tokyo 1952–53, Chief of Diplomatic Staff, Commissariat Gén. de France en Indochine 1953–54, Asst. Pvt. Sec. to Sec. of State for Foreign Affairs 1954–56, First Sec. Embassy, Moscow 1956–59, with Cen. Admin. (Europe) 1959–63, Chargé d'Affaires, Embassy, United Arab Repub. (now Egypt) 1963–64, First Counsellor, Cairo Embassy, 1964–65, Chief of Cultural Exchange Service, Cen. Admin. 1965–68, Minister Plenipotentiary 1968, Advisory Minister, Moscow 1968–69, Dir. Cen. Admin., Asia and Pacific Ocean 1969–75, Econ. Affairs 1975–79, Amb. to U.S.S.R. 1979–81, to Fed. Repub. of Germany 1982–83; Ambassadeur de France 1984; Adviser to Chair. Banque Paribas 1985–; Officier Légion d'honneur, Officier Ordre nationale du Mérite. *Publications:* Une puissance nommée Europe 1984 (Adolphe Bentinck Prize), Une éducation politique 1987; several articles in Preuves, Commentaire and Revue des Deux Mondes. *Leisure interests:* music, piano. *Address:* Banque Paribas, 12 boulevard Madeleine, Paris 75009 (Office); 8 avenue Perronet, 92200 Neuilly-sur-Seine, France (Home).

FROMM, Hans Walther Herbert, DR.PHIL.; Finnish/German professor of philology; b. 26 May 1919, Berlin; s. of Rudolf Fromm and Luise (née Hennig) Fromm; m. 1st Lore Sprenger 1950 (divorced 1974); one d.; m. 2nd Beatrice Müller-Hansen 1974; ed. Berlin Univ., Univ. of Tübingen; lecturer and Prof. of Germanic Philology, Univ. of Turku 1952–58; Prof. of German Philology and Finno-Ugric Languages, Univ. of Munich 1960–87, Prof. Emer. 1987–; mem. Bayerische Akademie der Wissenschaften 1971–, Finnish Acad. of Sciences; Chair. Scientific Reviewers' Cttee., Deutsche Forschungsgemeinschaft, Bonn 1972–76, Comm. for Medieval German Literature, Munich 1978–; Dr. phil. h.c. (Turku) 1969, Commdr. Order of Kts. of the Finnish Lion (1st Class) 1985, Brüder-Grimm-Preis 1987. *Publications:* Bibliographie deutscher Übersetzungen aus dem Französischen (6 vols.) 1950–53, Germanistische Bibliographie seit 1945, Theorie u. Kritik 1960, Der deutsche Minnesang (2 vols.) 1961, 1985, Kalevala (2 vols.) 1967, Konrad von Fussesbrunnen (Ed.) 1973, Finnische Grammatik (1982), Esseitä Kalevalasta 1987. *Leisure interest:* chess. *Address:* Roseggerstrasse 35a, D-8012 Ottobrunn, Federal Republic of Germany. *Telephone:* (089) 605882.

FROMME, Friedrich Karl, DR.PHIL.; German journalist; b. 10 June 1930, Dresden; s. of Prof. Dr. med. Albert and Dr. med. Lenka Fromme; m. Traute Kirsten 1961; one d.; ed. studies in science, politics and public law; teaching asst., Univ. of Tübingen 1957–62; Ed. Süddeutscher Rundfunk 1962–64, Frankfurter Allgemeine Zeitung (FAZ) 1964–68; Bonn corresp. FAZ 1968–73; Ed. responsible for internal politics, FAZ 1974–, for Co-ordination 1986–. *Publications:* Von der Weimarer Verfassung zum Bonner Grundgesetz 1962, Der Parlamentarier — ein Freier Beruf? 1978, Gesetzgebung im Widerstreit 1980. *Address:* 6100 Darmstadt, Scheppallee 84, Federal Republic of Germany. *Telephone:* 06151/315324.

FROMSTEIN, Mitchell S.; American business executive; b. 1928; ed. Univ. of Wis.; Krueger Homes Inc. 1948–49; Account Exec. Maultner Advertising Agency 1949–53; former Pres. TV Parts Inc.; Partner, Fromstein Assocs.; Pres., C.E.O. and Dir. The Parker Pen Co., Janesville, Wis. 1985–86; Pres. and C.E.O. Manpower Inc., Milwaukee 1976–; C.E.O. Blue Arrow PLC 1989–. *Address:* Blue Arrow PLC, 16 Finsbury Square, London, E.C.2, England. *Telephone:* 01-256 5011.

FRONDIZI, Arturo, D.IUR.; Argentine lawyer and politician; b. 1908; ed. Univ. de Buenos Aires; formed a resistance movement as a student and imprisoned 1930; in law practice 1932; mem. Metropolitan Convention Radical Party, Prof. Univ. de Buenos Aires 1932; Radical deputy 1946; Pres. Parl. Radical Party 1946–50; cand. for Vice-Presidency 1952; Pres. Nat. Cttee. Radical Party 1954; Pres. of Argentina 1958–62; fmr. leader of Movimiento de Integración y Desarrollo. *Publications:* Petroleum and Politics 1955, Los intereses de los trabajadores y le destino de la nacionalidad 1957, Política económica nacional 1963, Política exterior argentina 1963, Petróleo y nación 1964, Estrategia y táctica del movimiento nacional 1965, El problema agrario argentino 1965, El movimiento nacional funda-

mentos de su estrategia 1975. *Address:* Luis Maris Campos 665, Buenos Aires, Argentina.

FROSSARD, André; French journalist; b. 14 Jan. 1915, Colombièr Chatelot (Doubs); Ed. L'Intransigeant 1934; active in Resistance Movt. in World War II; detained by Gestapo, Lyons 1943; Ed.-in-Chief, Temps Present 1945–48, L'Aurore 1948–62; Editorial Dir. Nouveau Candide 1961; Columnist, Le Figaro 1962–; launched satirical monthly Ça Ira 1965; mem. Acad. Français 1987. *Publications include:* Dieu existe, je l'ai rencontré (Grand Prix Catholique de Littérature 1969), La France en général (Prix Edmond Michelet 1975), N'ayez pas peur (conversations with Pope John Paul II), Le Chemin de la Croix 1986. *Address:* 25 boulevard du Château, 92200 Neuilly sur Seine, France.

FROST, David Paradine, O.B.E.; British television personality and writer; b. 7 April 1939, Beccles, Suffolk; s. of Rev. W. J. Paradine Frost; m. 1st Lynne Frederick 1981 (divorced 1982); m. 2nd Lady Carina Fitzalan Howard 1983; three s.; ed. Gillingham and Wellingborough Grammar Schools, Gonville and Caius Coll., Cambridge; appeared in That Was The Week That Was, BBC Television 1962; other programmes with BBC included A Degree of Frost 1963, 1973, Not So Much A Programme More A Way of Life 1964–65, The Frost Report 1966–67, Frost Over England 1967 (Golden Rose Award, Montreux 1967); appeared in The Frost Programme, ITA 1966–67, 1967–68, 1972; formed London Weekend Consortium with Aidan Crawley 1967; Chair. and C.E.O. David Paradine Ltd. 1966–; Joint Deputy Chair. Equity Enterprises 1973–76 (Chair. 1972–73); NBC current affairs commentator; host in programmes Frost On Friday, Frost On Saturday, Frost On Sunday 1968–69, David Frost Show U.S.A. 1969–72, David Frost Revue, U.S.A. 1971–73, That Was The Year That Was, U.S.A. 1973, The Frost Interview 1974, We British 1975, The Sir Harold Wilson Interviews 1967–77, The Nixon Interviews 1976–77, The Crossroads of Civilisation 1977–78; David Frost Presents the Int. Guiness Book of World Records 1981–; Jt. founder and Dir. TV-am Feb. 1983–; Royal TV Soc's. Award 1967, Richard Dimbleby Award 1967, Emmy Award 1970, 1971, Religious Heritage of America Award 1970, Albert Einstein Award (Communication Arts) 1971. *Publications include:* That Was The Week That Was, How to Live Under Labour, Talking With Frost, To England With Love (with Antony Jay), The Americans, Whitlam and Frost, I Gave Them a Sword, I Could Have Kicked Myself 1982, Who wants to be a Millionaire? 1983, The Rich Tide (jtly.) 1986, The World's Shortest Books 1987. *Address:* David Paradine Ltd., 115–123 Bayham Street, London, N.W.1; 46 Egerton Crescent, London, S.W.3, England.

FROST, Thomas Pearson, F.C.I.B.; British banker; b. 1 July 1933; s. of James Watterston Frost and Enid E.C. Pearson; m. Elizabeth Morton 1958; one s. two d.; ed. Ormskirk Grammar School; joined Westminster Bank 1950; C.E.O. and Vice-Chair. NBNA (now Nat. Westminster Bank U.S.A.) 1980; Gen. Man. Business Devt. Div. Nat. Westminster Bank 1982; Dir. Nat Westminster Bank 1984–, Group Chief Exec. 1987–; mem. British Overseas Trade Bd. 1986–, UK Advisory Bd., British-American Chamber of Commerce; Fellow World Scout Foundation, Freeman, City of London 1978. *Leisure interests:* golf, greenhouse, theatre. *Address:* National Westminster Bank, 41 Lothbury, London, EC2P 2BP, England. *Telephone:* 01-726 1212.

FROWEIN, Jochen Abraham, DR.JUR., M.C.L.; German professor of law; b. 8 June 1934, Berlin; s. of Dr. jur. Abraham Frowein and Hilde Frowein (née Matthis); m. Lore Flume 1962; one s. two d.; ed. Univs. of Kiel, Berlin, Bonn and Univ. of Michigan Law School, Ann Arbor; research fellow, Max-Planck-Inst. for comparative public and int. law 1962–66; Prof. Univ. of Bochum 1967–69, Univ. of Bielefeld 1969–81; Dir. Max-Planck-Inst. and Prof. Univ. of Heidelberg 1981–; mem. European Comm. of Human Rights 1973–; Vice-Pres. German Research Foundation 1977–80. *Publications:* Das de facto-Regime im Völkerrecht 1968, EMRK-Kommentar (with W. Peukert) 1985 and many articles and contributions. *Address:* Max-Planck-Institut für ausländisches öffentliches Recht und Völkerrecht, Berlinerstrasse 48, 6900 Heidelberg, Federal Republic of Germany.

FRUGOLI, Amadeo; Argentine lawyer and politician; b. 26 Feb. 1932, Mendoza; ed. San José Coll., and Univ. of Buenos Aires; Prof., various colls. under Nat. Univ., Cuyo; taught history and civic instruction; Juridical Adviser, Mendoza Prov. Govt. 1965, later Sec.-Gen.; Minister of Govt., Mendoza Prov. 1970; Minister of Social Welfare, Nat. Govt. 1971; Senator and mem. Inst. of Int. Relations 1973–76; Minister of Justice 1981, of Defence Jan.–July 1982. *Address:* c/o Ministerio de Defensa, Paseo Colón No. 255, Buenos Aires, Argentina.

FRÜH, Eugen; Swiss painter and illustrator; b. 22 Jan. 1914, St. Gallen; s. of Huldreich and Teresa Früh; m. Erna Yoshida Blenk (artist) 1934; ed. Zürich School of Art and in Paris and Rome; C. F. Meyer Foundation Fine Arts Prize 1943, Fine Arts Prize, Kanton Zürich 1967. *Works include:* Die kleine Stadt 1941, Pastorale d'été 1946, La comédie et la musique 1947, Capricci 1948, Spanisches Gespräch 1951, Notturno 1957, Château d'artiste 1962, Gartenfest 1964, Bambuswald 1972, Lotus 1973–74; also murals and book illustrations. *Leisure interests:* literature, music, travel. *Address:* Römergasse 9, 8001 Zürich, Switzerland. *Telephone:* 01-478863.

FRÜHAUF, Hans, DR. ING.; German scientist; b. 4 Jan. 1904, Pforzheim, Baden; ed. Eberhard-Ludwigs-Gymnasium, Stuttgart, and Technische Hochschule, Stuttgart; Prof., Tech. Univ. of Dresden 1950, Pro-rector; Dir. of Inst. of High Frequency Tech. and Electronics, Tech. Univ. of Dresden 1950; State Sec. for Research and Tech., and mem. Council of Ministers, G.D.R. 1961–62; mem. German Acad. of Sciences (Vice-Pres. 1957–63), mem. of the Forschungsrat (Vice-Pres. until 1962), mem. Wissenschaftrat; Pres. G.D.R. Nat. Cttee. of the URSI; Ed. and Ed.-in-Chief Elektrische Informations- und Energie-Technik, Leipzig; Ed. Bücherei der Hochfrequenztechnik, Leipzig, Über wissenschaftliche Grundlagen der modernen Technik, Berlin, Elektronisches Rechnen und Regeln, Berlin; mem. Akad. der Wissenschaften der G.D.R. 1984–; Hon. Dr. Ing., E.H.; Nat. Prize, Second Class 1951, First Class 1961, Vaterländischer Verdienstorden in Silver, Gerhard Harig Medaille, Max Planck-Medaille, Johannes Stroux-Medaille der Akad. der Wissenschaften 1981. *Address:* 8027 Dresden, Zeunerstrasse 91/48-99, German Democratic Republic. *Telephone:* Dresden 47-86-92, Berlin 208 03 46.

FRÜHBECK DE BURGOS, Rafael; Spanish conductor; b. 15 Sept. 1933, Burgos; s. of Wilhelm and Stephanie (née Ochs) Frühbeck; m. María Carmen Martínez 1959; one s. one d.; ed. music acads. in Bilbao, Madrid, and Munich, and Univ. of Madrid; Chief Conductor, Municipal Orchestra, Bilbao 1958–62; Music Dir. and Chief Conductor, Spanish Nat. Orchestra, Madrid 1962–79; Music Dir. of Düsseldorf and Chief Conductor Düsseldorf Symphoniker 1966–70; Music Dir. Montreal Symphony Orchestra 1974–76; Prin. Conductor Yomiuri Nippon Symphony Orchestra 1980; Prin. Guest Conductor Nat. Symphony, Washington, D.C. 1980; Gran Cruz al Mérito Civil Orden de Alfonso X, Orden de Isabel la Católica. *Address:* 28007 Madrid, Reyes Magos 20, Spain (Home). *Telephone:* 252-04-16 (Home).

FRUTON, Joseph Stewart, PH.D.; American biochemist; b. 14 May 1912, Czestochowa, Poland; s. of Charles Fruton and Ella Eisenstadt; m. Sofia Simmonds 1936; ed. Columbia Univ.; Assoc., Rockefeller Inst. for Medical Research 1934–45; Assoc. Prof. of Physiological Chem., Yale Univ. 1945–50, Prof. of Biochem. 1950–57, Chair. Dept. of Biochem. 1951–67, Eugene Higgins Prof. of Biochem. 1957–82, Emer. 1982–, Dir. Div. of Science 1959–62, Prof. History of Medicine 1980–82, Emer. 1982–; Exec. Sec. Yale Corpn. Presidential Search Cttee. 1985–86; Assoc. Ed. Journal of Biological Chemistry and Journal of Biochemistry; Harvey Lecturer 1955, Dakin Lecturer 1962; Visiting Prof. Rockefeller Univ. 1968–69; Sarton Lecturer 1976; Xerox Lecturer 1977; Benjamin Franklin Fellow, Royal Soc. of Arts; mem. American Philosophical Soc., N.A.S., American Acad. of Arts and Sciences, Harvey Soc., American Chemical Soc., American Soc. of Biological Chemists, Biochemical Soc., History of Science Soc.; Fellow, Guggenheim Foundation 1983–84; Hon. Sc.D. (Rockefeller Univ.) 1976; Eli Lilly Award in Biological Chem. 1944, Pfizer Award in History of Science 1973. *Publications:* General Biochemistry (with S. Simmonds) 1953, Molecules and Life 1972, Selected Bibliography of Biographical Data for the History of Biochemistry since 1800 1974, a Bio-bibliography for the History of the Biochemical Sciences since 1800 1982; numerous scientific articles in Journal of Biological Chemistry, Biochemistry, Journal of American Chemical Soc., Proceedings of N.A.S., and other journals. *Leisure interests:* history of science, music. *Address:* 123 York Street, New Haven, Conn. 06511, U.S.A. *Telephone:* (203) 624-3735.

FRY, Christopher, F.R.S.L.; British dramatist; b. 18 Dec. 1907, Bristol; s. of Emma Marguerite Hammond and Charles John Harris; m. Phyllis Marjorie Hart 1936; one s.; ed. Bedford Modern School; Actor, Citizen House, Bath 1927; teacher, Hazelwood Preparatory School 1928–31; Dir. Tunbridge Wells Repertory Players 1932–35; Dir. Oxford Repertory Players 1940 and 1944–46; at Arts Theatre, London 1945; Hon. Fellow, Manchester Polytechnic 1988; Hon. Dip. Arts (Manchester) 1962, D.Litt. (Lambeth) 1988; Queen's Gold Medal for Poetry 1962. *Publications:* The Boy with the Cart 1939, The Firstborn 1946, A Phoenix too Frequent 1946, The Lady's Not for Burning 1949, Thor, with Angels 1949, Venus Observed 1950, A Sleep of Prisoners 1951, The Dark is Light Enough 1954, Curtmantle (R. S. L. Heinemann Award) 1962, A Yard of Sun 1970, The Brontës of Haworth (four plays for television) 1973, Can You Find Me 1978; Trans. Ring Round the Moon 1950, The Lark (Anouilh) 1954, Tiger at the Gates 1955, Duel of Angels 1958, Judith (Giraudoux) 1962, Peer Gynt 1970, Cyrano de Bergerac 1975, The Best of Enemies (play for television) 1976, Sister Dora (three-part play for television) 1977, introduction and text Charlie Hammond's Sketchbook 1980, Selected Plays 1985, One Thing More, or Caedmon Construed 1986. *Film Scripts:* The Beggar's Opera, The Queen is Crowned, Ben Hur, Barabbas, The Bible. *Leisure interest:* gardening. *Address:* The Toft, East Dean, nr. Chichester, Sussex, England.

FRY, Donald William, C.B.E., M.SC., C.ENG., F.I.E.E., F.I.E.E.E., F.INST.P.; British physicist; b. 30 Nov. 1910, Weymouth, Dorset; s. of William Joseph and Mary Jane (née Symonds) Fry; m. Jessie Florence Wright 1934; three s.; ed. King's Coll., London Univ.; Research Physicist, G.E.C. Research Laboratories 1932–40; with Air Ministry Research Establishment at Swanage and Malvern 1940–46; on staff of Atomic Energy Research Establishment 1946–49; head, Gen. Physics Div. 1950–54, Chief Physicist 1954–58, Deputy Dir. 1958, A.E.R.E., Harwell; Dir. Atomic Energy Establishment, Winfrith 1959–73; awarded Duddell Medal of the Physical Soc.

1950; Fellow King's Coll., London 1960. *Leisure interests:* travel, photography. *Address:* Coveway Lodge, Overcombe, Weymouth, Dorset, England. *Telephone:* Preston (Weymouth) 833276.

FRYE, Herman Northrop, C.C., M.A.; Canadian university professor; b. 14 July 1912, Sherbrooke, Quebec; s. of Herman and Catherine Frye (née Howard); m. Helen Kemp 1937 (deceased); ed. Univ. of Toronto, Emmanuel Coll., and Univ. of Oxford; Dept. of English, Victoria Coll., Univ. of Toronto 1939–, Chair. of Dept. 1952, Prin. of Coll. 1959, Univ. Prof. and Prof. of English in Victoria Coll. 1967, Chancellor 1978–; Foreign mem. American Philosophical Soc. 1976; Hon. Foreign mem. American Acad. of Arts and Sciences 1969; Hon. mem. American Acad. and Inst. of Arts and Letters 1980; Corresp. Fellow, British Acad. 1975; Hon. Fellow, Merton Coll. 1973; 35 hon. degrees; Molson Prize 1970; Lorne Pierce Medal, Royal Soc. of Canada 1958, Canada Council Medal 1967, Pierre Chauveau Medal, Royal Soc. of Canada 1970, Royal Bank Award 1978, Gov.-Gen.'s Literary Award for Non-Fiction 1987, Toronto Arts Foundation Life Achievement Award 1987. *Publications:* Fearful Symmetry: A Study of William Blake 1947, Anatomy of Criticism 1957, The Well-Tempered Critic 1963, The Educated Imagination 1963, T. S. Eliot 1963, Fables of Identity 1963, A Natural Perspective 1965, The Return of Eden 1965, Fools of Time 1967, The Modern Century 1967, A Study of English Romanticism 1968, The Stubborn Structure 1970, The Bush Garden 1971, The Critical Path 1971, The Secular Scripture 1976, Spiritus Mundi: Essays on Literature, Myth and Society 1976, Northrop Frye on Culture and Literature 1978, Creation and Recreation 1980, The Great Code: The Bible and Literature 1982, Divisions on a Ground 1982, The Myth of Deliverance 1983, Northrop Frye on Shakespeare 1986, Northrop Frye on Education 1988, No Uncertain Sounds 1988. *Address:* University of Toronto, Toronto, Ontario M5S 2E1, Canada. *Telephone:* (416) 978-2631.

FRYE, Richard Nelson, PH.D.; American orientalist; b. 10 Jan. 1920, Birmingham, Ala.; s. of Nels Frye and Lillie Hagman; m. 1st Barbara York 1948 (divorced 1973), two s. one d.; m. 2nd Eden Naby 1975, one s.; ed. Univ. of Illinois, Harvard Univ., and School of Oriental and African Studies, London; Jr. Fellow, Harvard 1946–49; Visiting Scholar, Univ. of Teheran 1951–52; Aga Khan Prof. of Iranian Studies, Harvard 1957–; Visiting Prof., Oriental Seminary, Frankfurt Univ. 1958–59; Visiting Prof., Hamburg Univ. 1968–69; Dir. Asia Inst., Pahlavi Univ., Shiraz 1969–74; Assoc. Ed. Cen. Asian Journal, Bulletin of the Asia Inst.; Corresp. Fellow, German Archaeological Inst. 1966–; Hon. D. Litt. (Oxford) 1987. *Publications:* Notes on the Early Coinage of Transoxiana 1949, History of the Nation of the Archers 1952, Narshakhi, The History of Bukhara 1954, Iran 1956, Heritage of Persia 1962, Bukhara, The Medieval Achievement 1965, The Histories of Nishapur 1965, Persia 1968, Inscriptions from Dura Europos 1969, Excavations at Qasr-i-Abu-Nasr 1973, The Golden Age of Persia 1975; Ed. Vol. 4 Cambridge History of Iran 1975, The Ancient History of Iran 1984. *Leisure interests:* fencing, bookbinding. *Address:* 546 Widener Library, Cambridge, Mass. 02138 (Office); Tower Hill Road, Brimfield, Mass. 01010, U.S.A. (Home). *Telephone:* (617) 495-2684 (Office); (413) 245-3630 (Home).

FRYER, Geoffrey, D.SC., PH.D., F.R.S.; British biologist; b. 6 Aug. 1927; s. of W. Fryer and M. Fryer; m. Vivien G. Hodgson 1953; one s. one d.; ed. Huddersfield Coll. and Univ. of London; colonial research student 1952–53; H.M. Overseas Research Service, Malawi 1953–55, Zambia 1955–57, Uganda 1957–60; Sr., then Prin., then Sr. Prin. Scientific Officer, Freshwater Biological Asscn. 1960–81; Deputy Chief Scientific Officer, Windermere Lab., Freshwater Biological Asscn. 1981–88; Hon. Prof., Univ. of Lancaster 1988–; H. R. Macmillan Lecturer, Univ. of B.C. 1963; Distinguished Visiting Scholar, Univ. of Adelaide 1985; Frink Medal, Zoological Soc. of London 1983, Linnean Medal for Zoology, Linnean Soc. of London 1987. *Publications:* The Cichlid Fishes of the Great Lakes of Africa: their biology and evolution (with T. D. Iles) 1972; numerous articles in scientific journals. *Leisure interests:* natural history, walking, books, photography. *Address:* Elleray Cottage, Windermere, Cumbria, LA23 1AW, England.

FU CHONGBI, Maj.-Gen.; Chinese army officer; b. 1916, Tongjiang Co., Sichuan Prov.; joined Red Army 1932, CCP 1933; political commissar with CCP forces before 1949; Commdr. 63rd Corps, Korea 1952; Deputy Commdr. Beijing Mil. Region 1965–68; in political disgrace 1968–74; Political Commissar, Beijing Mil. Region 1975–; mem. Cen. Advisory Comm. 1985–. *Address:* Beijing PLA Units, People's Republic of China.

FU HAO; Chinese diplomatist; b. April 1916, Li Quan County, Shaanxi Prov.; m. Jiao Ling; two s., one d.; ed. N.W. China Teachers Coll.; served in PLA during the civil war; CPC rep. (Col.) 15th Group of Beiping Exec. HQ of CPC, Kuomintang and U.S.A. in Dezhou, Shandong Prov. 1946; Counsellor, Embassy in Mongolia 1950–53; Deputy Dir. Asian Affairs Dept., Ministry of Foreign Affairs 1952–55; Counsellor, frequently Chargé d'Affaires, Embassy in India 1955–62; Dir. Personnel Dept, Ministry of Foreign Affairs 1963–69; Dir. Gen. Office, Ministry of Foreign Affairs 1969–72; Rep. to 26th UN Gen. Ass. 1971; Vice-Minister of Foreign Affairs 1972–74; Amb. to Democratic Repub. of Viet-Nam 1974–77, to Japan 1977–82; Vice Minister, Advisor of Foreign Affairs 1982; Chair. China-Japan Friendship Group of NPC Jan 1985–; Chinese mem. of 21st Century Cttee. for Sino-Japanese Friendship March 1984–; Deputy of 6th Nat. People's Congress, mem. of NPC Standing Cttee. and Vice-Chair. NPC

Foreign Affairs Cttee. 1983–88; Deputy of 7th Nat. People's Congress, mem. Standing Cttee. and Vice-Chair. NPC Foreign Affairs Cttee. 1988–. *Address:* c/o The Great Hall of the People, Beijing, People's Republic of China. *Telephone:* 66.5764.

FU HENGXUE; Chinese woodcut artist; b. 1933, Pucheng Cty., Shaanxi; d. Cen. Acad. of Fine Arts. *Address:* People's Republic of China.

FU KUIQING; Chinese army officer; Sec. CCP Prov. Cttee., Heilongjiang 1971–74; Vice-Gov., Heilongjiang 1972–74; Deputy Political Commissar, Shenyang Mil. Region, PLA 1977; Political Commissar, Fuzhou Mil. Region, PLA 1981–85; mem. 12th CCP Cen. Cttee. 1982–87; Political Commissar Nanjing Mil. Region, PLA 1985–. *Address:* Nanjing Military Region Headquarters, Nanjing, Jiangsu, People's Republic of China.

FU QIFENG; Chinese acrobat and magician; b. 15 March 1941, Chengdu, Sichuan; d. of Fu Tianzheng; m. Xu Zhuang 1961; one s. one d.; performer, acrobatics troupe, Beijing 1960–70; Founder and Ed. Acrobatics and Magic (journal); mem. Research Dept. Assoc. of Chinese Acrobats 1987–, Council mem., Beijing Branch 1981–. *Publications:* Chinese Acrobatics Through the Ages 1986, The Art of Chinese Acrobatics 1988; (with brother) Acrobatics in China 1983, History of Chinese Acrobatics 1988. *Address:* 5-2-501 Hongmiao Beili, Jintai Road, Beijing 100025, People's Republic of China.

FU QUANYOU; Chinese army officer; Commdr. Chengdu Mil. Region, PLA 1985–; mem. 12th CCP Cen. Cttee. 1985; mem. 13th CCP Cen. Cttee. 1987–; Deputy Sec. CCP Cttee., Chengdu Mil. Region 1985–. *Address:* Chengdu Military Region Headquarters, Chengdu, Sichuan, People's Republic of China.

FU TIANCHOU; Chinese sculptor, environment artist and professor; b. 4 March 1920, Nanhai, Guangdong Prov.; s. of Fu Yue and Yuan Lei-jun; m. Liu Yu-hua 1950; two d.; ed. Sculpture Dept., Nat. Art Acad., Chongqing; two one-man exhbns. Chongqing 1946; jt. exhbn. with Xia Lin, Shanghai 1947; exhbn. of his sculptures and Gu Yuan's paintings, Macao and Hong Kong 1986; Prof., Cen. Acad. of Fine Arts, Beijing; Council mem., Chinese Artists' Asscn.; mem. All-China Urban Sculpture Art Cttee.; Vice-Chair. Art Cttee. of China Co. of Sculptural Murals; Ed. Chinese Sculpture magazine. *Sculptures include:* monument to Wuchang Uprising led by Dr. Sun Yat-sen (white marble sculptures in relief), Beijing 1958; bronze statue of Zhou Enlai, Tianjin 1986; bronze statue of dramatist Ouyang Yuqian, Beijing and of Nu Wa (both first prize winners, All-China Urban Sculpture Competition 1987). *Environment designs include:* The Longevity Mountain, Qinghuangdao (8 km. long). *Publications include:* Collection of Fu Tianchou's Sculptures 1985, The Art That Shifts Feelings 1986; Ed. The Art of the Terracotta Warriors and Horses At Qinshihuang's Tomb (in English, French and German) 1985, The Sculpture of the Qin and Han Dynasties (in Chinese) 1985, (in English) 1988, The Chinese Art Dictionary 1988. *Leisure interests:* study of ancient Chinese sculpture, environmental art. *Address:* Department of Sculpture, The Central Academy of Fine Arts, Beijing, People's Republic of China. *Telephone:* 5004239.

FU TIANLIN; Chinese poet; b. 1946, Zizhang County, Sichuan. *Poems include:* Sparkling Dewdrops in the Night, Sweat, I am an Apple, Fallen Leaves, Blossoms in the Orchard, Orange Grove, The Canary, The Sun River. *Publication:* Green Musical Notes. *Address:* People's Republic of China.

FU ZHONG, Col.-Gen.; Chinese army officer; b. 1900, Xuyong Co., Sichuan Prov.; worker-student in France 1919–22; joined CCP 1921; mem. 5th Cen. Cttee., CCP 1925, 6th Cen. Cttee. 1928; on Long March 1935; Gen. Political Dept., PLA 1947–67; in political disgrace 1967–74; Vice-Chair. All China Sports Guidance Comm. 1978–; Vice-Chair. China Fed. of Art and Literature 1978–; mem. CCP Advisory Comm. 1982–87. *Address:* CCP Central Committee, Beijing, People's Republic of China.

FU ZHUANZUE; Chinese soldier; Divisional Commdr., First Field Army 1949; Deputy Commdr., Wuhan Mil. Region, PLA Air Force 1954, Commdr. 1972; Political Commissar, PLA Air Force 1973. *Address:* People's Republic of China.

FUÀ, Giorgio; Italian professor of economics; b. 19 May 1919, Ancona; s. of Riccardo Fuà and Elena Segre; m. Erika Rosenthal 1943; three s.; ed. Scuola Normale Superiore, Pisa, Univ. of Pisa, Univ. of Lausanne, Switzerland, Graduate Inst. of Int. Studies, Geneva; Jr. Econ. Adviser to Pres. Adriano Olivetti, Olivetti s.p.a. 1941–45; with Istituto Mobiliare Italiano (finance corpn.), Rome 1946–47; Assoc. Prof. of Econ. Statistics, Univ. of Pisa 1947–50; Econ. Affairs Officer, UN Econ. Comm. for Europe, Geneva 1950-54; Chief Econ. Adviser to Pres. Enrico Mattei, Ente Nazionale Idrocarburi (state oil and gas corpn.), Rome 1954–60; Prof. of Econs., Faculty of Econs., Ancona 1960–; Pres. ISTAO (managerial education), Ancona 1967–; Societá Italiana degli Economisti, Genoa 1983–1986, mem. Accademia Nazionale dei Lincei 1986–. *Publications:* Reddito nazionale e politica economica 1957, Idee per la programmazione economica 1963, Lo Stato e il risparmio privato 1970, Occupazione e capacità produttiva 1976, Lo sviluppo economico in Italia: Lavoro e reddito 1981, Problems of Lagged Development in OECD Europe 1980, Industrializzazione senza fratture 1983, Troppe Tasse sui Redditi 1985, Conseguenze economiche della evoluzione demografica 1986. *Address:* ISTAO, Via delle Grazie 67, 60128 Ancona; Faculty of Economics, Università degli studi di Ancona, Palazzo degli Anziani, 60100 Ancona; Via Monte d'Ago 75, 60131 Ancona, Italy (Home). *Telephone:* 071-85769 (ISTAO); 071-5893927 (University); 071-894629 (Home).

FUCHS, Anke, LL.M.; German lawyer and politician; b. 5 July 1937, Hamburg; m.; two c.; ed. Hamburg, Innsbruck and School of Public Admin., Speyer; mem. Regional Exec., Young Socialist Org. 1954; joined Social Democratic Party (SPD) 1956; trainee, regional org. of German Fed. of Trade Unions, Nordmark (Hamburg) 1964–68; Regional Sec. Metal Workers' Union (IG Metall), mem. Reform Comm. on Training for Legal Profession, mem. SPD Regional Exec., mem. Hamburg Judge Selection Cttee. 1968–70; mem. SPD Party Council 1970–, a Deputy Chair. 1984–, Party Man. 1987–; mem. Bundestag 1980–; mem. Hamburg Citizens' Assembly 1970–77; Exec. Sec. IG Metall 1971–77; State Sec. Fed. Ministry of Labour and Social Affairs 1977–80, Parl. State Sec. 1980–82; Fed. Minister for Youth, Family Affairs and Health April-Oct. 1982. *Address:* Ollenhauerstrasse 1, 5300 Bonn 1, Federal Republic of Germany.

FUCHS, Hans; German international finance official; b. 28 July 1926, Danzig (now Gdansk); s. of Dr. Hans and Melanie (née Schaper) Fuchs; m. Dr. Barbara S. Fuchs 1956; one s. two d.; ed. Technische Hochschule, Stuttgart, Escuela Especial de Canales, Puertos y Caminos, Columbia Univ., N.Y.; with Maschinenfabrik Augsburg-Nurnberg A.G.; joined IBRD (World Bank) as engineer 1956; Asst. Chief, Industry Div. 1963, Deputy Asst. Dir. 1964; Deputy Dir., Dept. of Investments, Latin America, Europe, Australasia, Int. Finance Corpn. (IFC) 1965; Dir. Eng. Dept. IFC 1968–69; Dir. Industrial Projects Dept. IBRD 1969–83; Dir. Western Africa Projects Dept., IBRD 1983–. *Leisure interests:* languages, tennis, skiing, history. *Address:* International Bank for Reconstruction and Development, 1818 H Street, N.W., Washington, D.C. 20433 (Office); 6715 Loring Court, Bethesda, Md. 20817, U.S.A. (Home). *Telephone:* (202) 477-6388 (Office); (301) 365-4039 (Home).

FUCHS, Victor Robert, M.A., PH.D.; American professor of economics; b. 31 Jan. 1924, New York; s. of Alfred Fuchs and Frances S. (Schieber) Fuchs; m. Beverly Beck 1948; two s. two d.; ed. New York and Columbia Univs.; Assoc. Prof. of Econs. New York Univ. 1959–60; Program Assoc. Econs. Ford Foundation 1960–62; Research Assoc. Nat. Bureau of Econ. Research 1962–; Prof. of Community Medicine, Mount Sinai School of Medicine 1968–74; Prof. of Econs. City Univ. of New York Graduate Center 1968–74; Prof. of Econs. (in Depts. of Econs. and Family, Community and Preventative Medicine) Stanford Univ. 1974–, Henry J. Kaiser Jr. Prof. 1988–; Fellow, American Acad. of Arts and Sciences; Madden Memorial Award 1982. *Publications:* The Economics of the Fur Industry 1957, Changes in the Location of Manufacturing in the U.S. since 1929 1962, The Service Economy 1968, Production and Productivity in the Service Industries 1969, Who Shall Live? Health, Economics and Social Choice 1975, Economic Aspects of Health (ed.) 1982, How We Live 1983, The Health Economy 1986. *Leisure interest:* hiking. *Address:* National Bureau of Economic Research, 204 Junipero Serra Boulevard, Stanford, Calif. 94305, U.S.A. *Telephone:* (415) 326-7639.

FUCHS, Sir Vivian Ernest, PH.D., F.R.S.; British geologist and explorer; b. 11 Feb. 1908, Freshwater, Isle of Wight; s. of Ernest and Violet Anne Fuchs (née Watson); m. Joyce Connell 1933; one s. one d. (one d. deceased); ed. St. John's Coll., Cambridge; with Cambridge East Greenland Expedition 1929, Cambridge Expedition to East African Lakes 1930–32; Leader, Lake Rudolf Rift Valley Expedition 1933–34; Leader, Lake Rukwa Expedition 1937–38; served Second World War; Commdr. Falkland Islands Dependencies Survey (Antarctica) 1947–50; Dir. Falkland Islands Dependencies Scientific Bureau 1951–60; Dir. British Antarctic Survey 1960–73; Pres. Int. Glaciological Soc. 1961–63, British Assoc. for Advancement of Science 1972, Royal Geog. Soc. 1982–84; Leader, Trans-Antarctic Expedition 1955–58; Hon. Fellow, Wolfson Coll., Cambridge 1970, St. John's Coll., Cambridge 1983; Hon. mem. Chilean Soc. of History and Geography 1982–; Hon. LL.D. (Edinburgh, Birmingham), Hon. D.Sc. (Durham) 1958, (Cambridge) 1959, (Wales) 1971, (Leicester) 1972; Founder's Gold Medal (Royal Geog. Soc.) 1951, Polar Medal 1953, and Clasp, Special Gold Medal (Royal Geog. Soc.) 1958, Silver Medal (R.S.A.), Gold Medal (Royal Scottish Geog. Soc.), Richthofen Gold Medal (Berlin Geog. Soc.), Kirchenpauer Gold Medal (Hamburg Geog. Soc.), Gold Medal (Paris Geog. Soc.) 1958, Hubbard Gold Medal (American Nat. Geog. Soc.), Gold Medal (Royal Netherlands Geog. Soc.) 1959, Hans Egede Medal (Royal Danish Geog. Soc.) 1961, Prestwich Medal (Geological Soc., London) 1960, Medal of Chilean Soc. of History and Geography 1982. *Publications:* The Crossing of Antarctica (with Sir Edmund Hillary) 1958, Antarctic Adventure 1959; Ed. Great Explorers, The Forces of Nature 1976, Of Ice and Men 1982; various geological and geographical papers. *Leisure interests:* gardening, swimming. *Address:* 106 Barton Road, Cambridge, CB3 9LH, England. *Telephone:* 0223-359238.

FUENTES, Carlos; Mexican author and diplomatist; b. 11 Nov. 1928, Mexico City; s. of Rafael Fuentes Boettiger and Berta Macías Rivas; m. 1st Rita Macedo 1959, one d.; m. 2nd Sylvia Lemus 1973, one s. one d.; ed. Univ. of Mexico, Inst. des Hautes Etudes Internationales, Geneva; mem. Mexican Del. to ILO, Geneva 1950–51; Asst. Head, Press Section, Ministry of Foreign Affairs, Mexico 1954; Asst. Dir. Cultural Dissemination, Univ. de Mexico 1955–56; Head Dept. of Cultural Relations,

Ministry of Foreign Affairs 1957–59; Ed. Revista Mexicana de Literatura 1954–58, Co-Ed. El Espectador 1959–61, Ed. Siempre and Politica 1960–; Amb. to France 1974–77; fmr. Prof. of Spanish and Comparative Literature, Columbia Univ., New York; Prof. of Comparative Literature, Harvard Univ. 1984–86, Robert F. Kennedy Prof. of Latin American Studies 1987–; Pres. Modern Humanities Research Asscn. 1989–; fmr. Adjunct Prof. of English and Romance Languages, Univ. of Pennsylvania, Pa.; Fellow, Woodrow Wilson Int. Center for Scholars, Washington, D.C. 1974; Fellow of the Humanities, Princeton Univ.; Virginia Gildersleeve Visiting Prof., Barnard Coll., New York; Edward Leroc Visiting Prof., School of Int. Affairs, Columbia Univ., New York; Norman Maccoll Lecturer, Univ. of Cambridge, England; The Biblioteca Breve Prize (for A Change of Skin) 1967, The Javier Villaurrutia Prize (for Terra Nostra) 1975, Rómulo Gallegos Prize (for Terra Nostra) 1977, Mexican Nat. Award for Literature 1984, Miguel de Cervantes Prize (for Cristobal Nonato) 1987, Ruben Pario Prize 1988, IUA Prize (for The Old Gringo) 1989. *Publications:* Los días enmascarados 1954, La región más transparente 1958, Las buenas conciencias 1959, Aura 1962, La muerte de Artemio Cruz 1962, Cantar de ciegos 1965, Zona sagrada 1967, Cambio de piel (Biblioteca Breve Prize 1967), Paris, La Revolución de Mayo 1968, La Nueva Novela Hispanoamericana 1969, Cumpleaños 1969, Le Borgne est Roi 1970, Casa con Dos Puertos 1970, Todos los gatos son pardos 1970, Tiempo Mexicano 1971, Don Quixote or the Critique of Reading 1974, Terra Nostra 1975, La Cabeza de la Hidra 1978, Orchids in the Moonlight (play) 1982, The Old Gringo 1985, The Good Conscience 1987, Cristobal Nonato (novel) 1987, Myself With Others (Essays) 1988. *Address:* c/o Brandt & Brandt, 1501 Broadway, New York, N.Y. 10036, U.S.A.

FUGARD, Athol; South African actor and playwright; m.; one d.; leading role in Meetings with Remarkable Men (film) 1977, The Guest (BBC production) 1977; acted in and wrote script for Marigolds in August (film); winner Silver Bear Award, Berlin Film Festival 1980, New York Critics Award for A Lesson From Aloes 1981, London Evening Standard Award for Master Harold and the Boys 1983, Commonwealth Award for Contribution to American Theatre 1984; Hon. D.Lit. (Natal and Rhodes Univs.), Dr. h.c. (Univ. of Cape Town, Georgetown Univ., Washington, D.C.). *Plays:* The Blood Knot, Hello and Goodbye, People are Living Here, Boesman and Lena 1970, Sizwe Banzi is Dead 1973, The Island 1973, Statements after an Arrest under the Immorality Act 1974, No Good Friday 1974, Nongogo 1974, Dimetos 1976, The Road to Mecca 1984; The Guest (film script) 1977, A Lesson from Aloes 1979 (author and dir. Broadway production 1980), Master Harold and the Boys 1981, Place with the Pigs (acted and dir.); *film:* Marigolds in August 1981, The Guest 1984; acted in films Gandhi 1982; Hon. D.F.A. (Yale Univ.) 1973, Dr. h.c. (New York, Pennsylvania, City Univ. of New York). *Publications:* Notebooks 1960–77; novel: Tsotsi 1980; plays: Road to Mecca 1985, A Place with the Pigs 1988. *Address:* P.O. Box 5090, Walmer, Port Elizabeth, South Africa.

FUGLEDE, Bent, D.PHIL.; Danish professor of mathematics; b. 8 Oct. 1925, Copenhagen; s. of late Albert Fuglede and Adda (née Fjord Pedersen) Fuglede; m. Olafia Einarsdottir 1954; one s.; ed. Univ. of Copenhagen; Asst. Teacher Tech. Univ. of Denmark 1952–54, Prof. of Math. 1960–64; Asst. Prof. Univ. of Copenhagen 1954–59, Assoc. Prof. 1959–60, Prof. of Math. 1965–; mem. Royal Danish Acad. of Sciences and Letters 1968, Finnish Acad. of Sciences and Letters 1980. *Publications:* Finely Harmonic Functions 1972, numerous scientific articles. *Address:* Trongaardsparken 67, 2100 Lyngby, Denmark. *Telephone:* (02) 88 18 72.

FUHRMANN, Horst, DR.PHIL.; German historian; b. 22 June 1926, Kreuzburg; s. of Karl and Susanna Fuhrmann; m. Dr. Ingrid Winkler-Lippoldt 1954; one s. one d.; collaborator, Monumenta Germaniae Historica 1954–56; Asst., Rome 1957; Asst. and lecturer 1957–62; Prof. Univ. of Tübingen 1962–71; Pres. Monumenta Germaniae Historica, Munich and Prof. Univ. of Regensburg 1971–; Premio Spoleto 1962, Cultore di Roma 1981; Dr.jur. h.c. (Tübingen); Dr.phil. h.c. (Bologna); Ordre Pour le mérite. *Publications:* The Donation of Constantine 1968, Influence and Circulation of the Pseudoisidorian Forgeries (3 vols.) 1972–74, Germany in the High Middle Ages 1978, From Petrus to John Paul II: The Papacy 1980, Invitation to the Middle Ages 1987. *Address:* Ludwigstrasse 16, D-8000 Munich 22 (Office); Sonnenwinkel 10, D-8031 Steinebach, Federal Republic of Germany (Home).

FUJIMORI, Masamichi; Japanese executive; b. 22 Dec. 1921, Osaka; s. of Tatsumaro Fujimori and Kimiko Ono; m. Yoko Sato 1951; two d.; ed. Tokyo Imperial Univ.; lecturer, First Faculty of Tech., Tokyo Univ. 1948; joined Sumitomo Metal Mining Co. Ltd. 1950, Gen. Man. Metallurgy Dept. 1971, Dir. 1972, Man. Dir. 1977, Sr. Man. Dir. 1979, Exec. Vice-Pres. 1981, Pres. 1983–88, Chair. June 1988–; Pres. Japan Mining Industry Asscn. 1987–88; Hon. Fellow Inst. of Mining and Metallurgy 1985; Blue Ribbon Medal 1982. *Leisure interest:* bonsai. *Address:* Sumitomo Metal Mining Co. Ltd., 5-11-3, Shimbashi, Minato-ku, Tokyo (Office); 4-7-25, Shinkawa, Mitaka-City, Tokyo, Japan (Home).

FUJIMORI, Tetsuo, B.LL.; Japanese banker; b. 16 July 1919, Nagano Pref.; s. of Yonezo and Tetsuo Fujimori; m. Mie Fujimori; two s. one d.; ed. Faculty of Law, Tohuku Univ.; joined Dai-Ichi Bank (merged with Nippon Kangyo Bank to become Dai-Ichi Kangyo Bank 1971) 1945, Dir. and Gen. Man. Office Planning Div. 1973, Dir. and Gen. Man. Corporate

Planning Div. 1973–75, Man. Dir. 1975–79, Sr. Man. Dir. 1979–80, Deputy Pres. 1980–82, Chair. 1982–88, Dir. and Adviser June 1988–; Auditor Furukawa Co., Ltd., Tokyo 1983–; Hon. Fellowship Inst. of Mining and Metallurgy, London 1985–. *Leisure interests:* golf, reading. *Address:* Dai-Ichi Kangyo Bank, 1-5, Uchisaiwaicho 1-chome, Chiyoda-ku, Tokyo 100 (Office); 21-17, Kichijoji Higashimachi, 2-chome, Musashino-shi 180, Tokyo, Japan (Home).

FUJIMOTO, Takao; Japanese politician; b. 1931, Kagawa Pref.; m.; one s.; ed. Faculty of Law, Tokyo Univ.; joined Nomura Securities Co. Ltd. 1944; joined Nippon Telegraph and Telephone Public Corpn. 1957; elected House of Reps. for 1st constituency Kagawa Pref. 1963; Parl. Vice-Minister of Science and Tech. Agency 1970; Chair. Liberal Democratic Party (LDP) Science and Tech. Sub-Cttee. of the Policy Research Cttee. 1972; Parl. Vice-Minister of the Environment Agency 1973; Chair. Standing Cttee. on Foreign Affairs 1976, LDP Standing Cttee. on Public Information 1983; Minister of State, Dir.-Gen. Okinawa Devt. Agency 1985; Deputy Sec.-Gen. LDP 1985–86; Minister of Health and Welfare 1987–88. *Leisure interests:* sports (baseball), reading, golf, karaoke singing. *Address:* House of Representatives, Tokyo, Japan.

FUJINAMI, Takao; Japanese politician; b. 3 Dec. 1932; ed. Waseda Univ.; mem. House of Reps. 1967–; Parl. Vice-Minister for Science and Tech. 1972, for Educ. 1973; Minister of Labour 1979–80; Chair. Educational Affairs Div. 1975 and Vice-Chair. Policy Affairs Research Council 1978; Minister of State and Chief Cabinet Sec. 1983–85; Liberal-Democratic Party. *Address:* Cabinet Secretariat, 2-3 Nagato-cho, Chiyoda-ku, Tokyo; Kudan Shukusha, 2-14-3 Fujimi, Chiyoda-ku, Tokyo, Japan.

FUJINO, Hirotake, M.P.A.; Japanese international finance official; b. 18 June 1933, Tokyo; m. Midoriko Eguchi 1963; two d.; ed. Koishikawa High School, Tokyo, Tokyo Univ. and Woodrow Wilson School, Princeton Univ.; Head, S. Gifu Taxation Office 1963–64; Deputy Dir. Int. Finance Bureau, Ministry of Finance 1964–67; First Sec. Japanese Del. to OECD 1967–71; Deputy Dir. Securities Bureau, Ministry of Finance 1971–73, Deputy Dir.-Gen. 1982–84; Dir. Fair Trade Comm. 1973–75; Dir. Financial Bureau, Ministry of Finance 1975–77; Minister-Counsellor, Japanese Del. to OECD 1977–80; Asst. Vice-Minister of Finance 1980–82; Dep. Dir. Securities Bureau, Ministry of Finance 1982–84, Exec. Dir. IMF 1984–87. *Publications:* articles on Tokyo capital market in Banker and other periodicals. *Leisure interests:* Go, golf, travel.

FUJIOKA, Masao; Japanese banker; b. 31 Oct. 1924, Tokyo; m.; two s. one d.; ed. Tokyo Univ. and Univ. of Chicago; Economist, IMF 1960–64; Dir. of Short-Term Capital Div. of Int. Finance Bureau, Ministry of Finance 1964–66; took part in preparatory work at ECAFE to establish Asian Devt. Bank (ADB) 1966; Dir. Admin. Dept., ADB 1966–69; Dir. Co-ordination Dept., Overseas Econ. Co-operation Fund 1969; Deputy Dir.-Gen. Int. Finance Bureau, Ministry of Finance 1970–75, Dir.-Gen. 1975–77; Exec. Dir., Export-Import Bank of Japan 1977–81; Adviser to Minister of Finance 1981; Chair. and Pres. Asian Devt. Bank ADB 1981–; founder Asian Pacific Bankers' Club 1980. *Publications:* Government Loans and Investment 1957, Income Doubling Plan of Japan 1963, Evolving International Finance 1975, New IMF (ed.) 1976, Growing International Finance 1977, Japan's International Finance—Today and Tomorrow 1979; numerous articles and reports on int. finance and econ. co-operation. *Address:* Asian Development Bank, 2330 Roxas Boulevard, P.O. Box 789, Manila 2800, Philippines.

FUJISAKI, Akira, LL.B.; Japanese business executive; b. 1 May 1917, Kagoshima; s. of Kokichi Fujisaki and Misako Morita; m. Sakae Ishida 1951; one d.; ed. Tokyo Imperial Univ.; joined Sumitomo Mining Co. Ltd. (later Sumitomo Metal Mining Co. Ltd.) 1942, Dir. 1967, Man. Dir. 1970, Pres. 1973–83, Chair. 1983–88; Pres. Japan Mining Industry Asscn. 1976–77, 1981–82; Exec. Dir. Fed. of Econ. Orgs. 1977–, Japan Fed. of Employers' Asscns. 1977–; Trustee, Japan Cttee. for Econ. Devt. 1971–; Blue Ribbon Medal 1979; First Order of the Sacred Treasure 1987. *Leisure interests:* golf, reading. *Address:* 2-7-14, Nishi-Kamakura, Kamakura-shi, Kanagawa Prefecture, Japan (Home). *Telephone:* 0467-32-6233 (Home).

FUJITA, Masaaki; Japanese politician; b. 3 Jan. 1922, Hiroshima; s. of Sadaichi and Masano Fujita; m. Jun Ohara 1947; three s. one d.; ed. Waseda Univ.; began career with Fujita Corpn., construction firm, now Adviser; elected three times to House of Councillors from constituency in Hiroshima Pref. 1965–; fmr. Chair. House of Councillors Finance Cttee.; Parl. Vice-Minister of Finance; Chair. Diet Policy Cttee. of Liberal Democratic Party (LDP), Sec.-Gen. LDP in the House of Councillors 1980–83; assoc. of Masayoshi Ohira (q.v.); Minister of State, Dir.-Gen. of Admin. Affairs in Office of Prime Minister, Dir.-Gen. Okinawa Devt. Agency 1976–77. *Leisure interests:* reading, playing Go, golf. *Address:* 17-13 Motoyoyogicho, Shibuyaku, Tokyo, 151 Japan. *Telephone:* (03) 466-0351.

FUJITA, Yoshio, DR.SC.; Japanese astronomer; b. 28 Sept. 1908, Fukui City; s. of Teizo Fujita; m. Kazuko Nezu 1941; two s. one d.; ed. Tokyo Univ.; Asst. Prof. Univ. of Tokyo 1931, Prof. 1951–69, Emer. Prof. 1969–; Visiting Prof. Pa. State Univ. 1971; Guest Investigator Dominion Astrophysical Observatory 1960, Mount Wilson and Palomar Observatories 1972, 1974; mem. Japan Acad. 1965–, Sec.-Gen. 1988–; Foreign mem. Royal Soc. of Sciences, Liège 1969–; Imperial Prize, Japan Acad. 1955; Cultural Merit

Award, Fukui City 1971; Hon. Citizen, Fukui City 1979. *Publication:* Interpretation of Spectra and Atmospheric Strucutre in Cool Stars 1970. *Address:* 6-21-7 Renkoji, Tama-shi 206, Japan. *Telephone:* (0423) 74-4186.

FUJIYAMA, Naraichi; Japanese diplomatist; b. 17 Sept. 1915, Tokyo; m. Shizuko Takagi 1946; ed. Univs. of Tokyo and N. Carolina; Consul, New York 1953-54; Counsellor, Vienna 1959-63, Jakarta 1963-65; Chief of Protocol, Ministry of Foreign Affairs 1965-68, Dir.-Gen. Public Information Bureau 1968-71; Amb. to Austria 1971-75, to Italy 1975-79, to the U.K. 1979-82; Chair. Bd. of Govs., IAEA, Vienna 1973-74; Press Sec. to Emperor Hirohito on his State visit to the U.S.A. 1975; Sr. Consultant in Japan to Scottish Devt. Agency 1982-; Exec. Adviser, Nippon Electric Co. 1982-, Mitsubishi Motor Co. 1982-, Hotel New Otani 1982-; Pres. Japan-Austria Soc., Tokyo 1985; Order of the Sacred Treasure (First Class) 1987. *Publication:* A Country Called Britain (in Japanese) 1984. *Address:* 7-7-19 Koyama, Shinagwa-ku, Tokyo, Japan. *Telephone:* (03) 781-3350.

FUJIYOSHI, Tsuguhide; Japanese business executive; b. 24 Jan. 1913, Fukuoka; s. of late Kiichi and of Haruko Fujiyoshi; m. Yuko 1941; three s. two d.; ed. Tokyo Univ.; joined Toyo Rayon Co. Ltd. (now Toray Industries Inc.) 1935, Hamburg Office 1960-61, Man. Nagoya Plant 1961, Dir. 1962, Man. Dir. 1964, Exec. Vice-Pres. 1966, Pres. 1971-80, Chair. 1980-. *Leisure interest:* golf. *Address:* Toray Industries Inc., 2-chome, Nihonbashi-Muromachi, Chuo-ku, Tokyo 103 (Office); Room 901, Takanawa Sky Mansion 8-6, Takanawa 4-chome, Minato-ku, Tokyo 108, Japan (Home). *Telephone:* 03-445-6511.

FUKUDA, Hajime; Japanese politician; b. 1902; ed. Tokyo Univ.; Reporter, Political Ed., Kyodo News Service; mem. House of Reps. for Fukui Pref. 1949-; fmr. Parl. Vice-Minister of Labour; Minister of Int. Trade and Industry 1962, for Home Affairs 1972-73, 1974-76, of Justice 1976-77; Speaker House of Reps. 1980-83; Supreme Adviser to Pres. Liberal Democratic Party 1984-; Liberal-Democratic Party. *Address:* 10-11, Tairamachi 2-chome, Meguro-ku, Tokyo, Japan.

FUKUDA, Takeo; Japanese politician; b. 14 Jan. 1905; ed. Tokyo Imperial Univ.; with Ministry of Finance 1929-50, Deputy Vice-Minister 1945-46, Dir. of Banking Bureau 1946-47, Dir. Budget Bureau 1947-50; mem. House of Reps. 1952-; Chair. Policy Bd. Liberal-Democratic Party, later Sec.-Gen.; fmr. Minister of Agric. and Forestry; Minister of Finance 1965-1966; Sec.-Gen. Liberal-Democratic Party, Pres. Liberal-Democratic Party 1966-68; Minister of Finance 1968-71, 1973-74, of Foreign Affairs 1971-72; Dir.-Gen. Admin. Man. Agency 1972-73; Deputy Prime Minister, Dir. of Econ. Planning Agency 1974-76 (resgnd.); Prime Minister, Pres. Liberal-Democratic Party 1976-78. *Address:* House of Representatives, Tokyo; 4-20-3 Nozawa, Setagaya-ku, Tokyo, Japan.

FUKUI, Kenichi; Japanese chemist; b. 4 Oct. 1918, Nara; s. of Ryokichi and Chie Fukui; m. Tomoe Horie 1947; one s. one d.; ed. Kyoto Imperial Univ.; research on synthetic fuel chemistry, Army Fuel Lab. 1941-45; Lecturer in Fuel Chem., Kyoto Imperial Univ. 1943, Asst. Prof. 1945, Prof. 1951-82; Sr. Foreign Scientist Fellow, Nat. Science Foundation 1970; mem. Int. Acad. of Quantum Molecular Science, France 1970-; Councillor Kyoto Univ. 1970-73; Dean Faculty of Eng., Kyoto Univ. 1971-73; Chemist U.S.-Japan Eminent Scientist Exchange Programme 1973; Counsellor Inst. for Molecular Science 1976-; Pres. Kyoto Univ. of Industrial Arts and Textile Fibres (renamed Kyoto Inst. of Tech. 1984) 1982-; Vice-Pres. Chemical Soc. of Japan 1978-79, Pres. 1983-84; Chair. Exec. Cttee. 3rd Int. Congress of Quantum Chem., Kyoto 1979; Foreign Assoc. N.A.S. 1981; mem. European Acad. of Arts, Sciences and Humanities 1981; Hon. mem. American Acad. of Arts and Sciences 1983; mem. Japan Acad. 1983; mem. Pontifical Acad. of Sciences 1986-; Nobel Prize for Chemistry 1981; Japan Acad. Medal 1962; Order of Culture 1981; Person of Cultural Merits 1981; Grand Cordon, Order of the Rising Sun 1988. *Publications:* several hundred papers on chemical reactivity, statistical theory of gellation, organic synthesis by inorganic salts, polymerization kinetics and catalysts, reaction engineering, catalytic engineering, etc. *Address:* 23 Kitashirakawa-Hiraicho Sakyo-ku, Kyoto 606, Japan. *Telephone:* 075-781-5785.

FULBRIGHT, (James) William, LL.B., M.A.; American politician; b. 9 April 1905; m. Elizabeth Kremer Williams 1932; two d.; ed. Univ. of Arkansas, Oxford Univ. and George Washington Univ.; Special Attorney Anti-Trust Div., U.S. Dept. of Justice 1934-35; Instructor in Law, George Washington Univ. 1935-36; lecturer in Law Univ. of Arkansas 1936-39, Pres. 1939-41; mem. 78th Congress (1943-45), 3rd Dist., Arkansas; U.S. Senator from Arkansas 1945-74; Chair. Senate Cttee. Foreign Relations 1959-74; counsellor Hogan & Hartson, Washington 1975-; Hon. L.L.D. (Manchester) 1984; Japan Foundation Award 1974, Benjamin Franklin Medal (R.S.A.) 1977, Onassis Int. Prize 1989; Hon. K.B.E. 1975; Democrat. *Publications:* Old Myths and New Realities 1964, Prospects for the West 1965, The Arrogance of Power 1967, The Crippled Giant 1972. *Address:* 555 13th Street, N.W., Washington, D.C. 20004 (Office); Fayetteville, Ark. 72701, U.S.A. (Home).

FULCI, Francesco Paolo, LL.D., M.C.L.; Italian diplomatist; b. 19 March 1931, Messina; s. of Sebastiano Fulci and Enza Sciascia; m. Claris Glathar 1965; three c.; ed. Messina Univ., Columbia Univ., New York, Coll. of Europe, Bruges, and Acad. Int. Law, The Hague, entered Italian Foreign Service 1956; First Vice-Consul of Italy, New York 1958-61; Second

Sec. Italian Embassy, Moscow 1961-63; Foreign Ministry, Rome 1963-68; Counsellor Italian Embassy, Paris 1968-74, Minister Italian Embassy, Tokyo 1974-76; Chief of Cabinet Pres. of Senate, Rome 1976-80; Amb. to Canada 1980-85; Perm. Rep. to NATO, Brussels 1985-; Cross of Merit (Fed. Repub. of Germany); Officer Légion d'Honneur (France); Commdr. Imperial Order of the Sun (Japan), Great Officer Order of Merit (Italy); Hon. Dr. (Windsor Univ., Ont.). *Leisure interest:* swimming. *Address:* 9 Avenue des Sorbiers, 1180 Brussels, Belgium. *Telephone:* 375.62.56.

FULLER, Arthur Orpen, PH.D., F.R.S.SA.; South African geologist; b. 28 Aug. 1926, Cape Town; s. of Thomas Arthur Fuller and Doris Erpingham Orpen; m. Anne Jane Low 1954; two d.; ed. Univ. of Cape Town and Princeton Univ.; geologist Union Corpn. Ltd. 1949-53; Assoc. Prof., Univ. of Cape Town 1957-88; N.S.F. Sr. Fellowship, Mich. Tech. Univ. 1970-71; NASA Consultant 1980; Head of Geology and Mineralogy Dept., Univ. of Cape Town 1988-; Pres. Geological Soc. of S.A. 1985. *Publications:* numerous articles in int. journals, including Nature and Econ. Geology. *Leisure interests:* music, golf, rock angling. *Address:* Department of Mineralogy and Geology, University of Cape Town, Rondebosch C.P. 7700, South Africa.

FULLER, Roy Broadbent, C.B.E., F.R.S.L.; British solicitor, author and poet; b. 11 Feb. 1912, Failsworth, Lancashire; s. of Leopold Charles Fuller and Nellie Broadbent; m. Kathleen Smith 1936; one s.; ed. Asst. Solicitor, Woolwich Equitable Building Soc. 1938, Solicitor 1958-69, Dir. 1969-87; Prof. of Poetry, Oxford Univ. 1968-73; war service in Royal Navy 1941-46; Chair. Building Socs. Asscn. Legal Advisory Panel 1958-69; mem. Arts Council Poetry Panel 1955-59, Bd. Poetry Book Soc. 1960-76, Arts Council 1976-77, Library Advisory Council for England 1977-79; Gov. BBC 1972-79; Duff Cooper Memorial Prize 1968; Queen's Medal for Poetry 1970; Hon. D.Litt. (Kent) 1986. *Publications:* Poetry: The Middle of a War 1942, A Lost Season 1944, Epitaphs and Occasions 1949, Counterparts 1954, Brutus's Orchard 1957, Collected Poems 1962, Buff 1965, New Poems 1968, Seen Grandpa Lately? 1972, Tiny Tears 1973, From the Joke Shop 1975, An Ill-Governed Coast 1976, Poor Roy 1977, The Reign of Sparrows 1980, New and Collected Poems 1934-84, Subsequent to Summer 1985, Consolations 1987, Available for Dreams 1989, Collected Poems for Children 1989; Novels: The Second Curtain 1953, Fantasy and Fugue 1954, Image of a Society 1956, The Ruined Boys 1959, The Father's Comedy 1961, The Perfect Fool 1963, My Child, My Sister 1965, The Carnal Island 1970; Edited: The Building Societies Acts; Criticism: Owls and Artificers 1972, Professors and Gods 1973; Autobiography: Souvenirs 1980; Vamp till Ready 1982, Home and Dry 1983, Memoirs of Childhood and Youth 1989. *Address:* 37 Langton Way, London, S.E.3, England. *Telephone:* 01-858 2334.

FULLERTON, R. Donald, B.A.; Canadian banker; b. 7 June 1931, Vancouver, B.C.; s. of late C. G. and late Muriel E. Fullerton; ed. Univ. of Toronto; joined Canadian Bank of Commerce (now Canadian Imperial Bank of Commerce), Vancouver 1953; Agent, New York 1964; Regional Gen. Man., Regina 1966; Regional Gen. Man., Int. 1967; Deputy Chief Gen. Man. 1971; Exec. Vice-Pres. and Chief Gen. Man. 1973; Dir. Canadian Imperial Bank of Commerce 1974-, Pres. and Chief Operating Officer 1976-80, Vice-Chair. and Pres. 1980-84, Pres. and C.E.O. 1984-85, Chair. 1985-; Dir. North American Life Assurance Co., AMOCO Canada Petroleum Co. Ltd., IBM (Canada) Ltd., Wellesley Hosp.; mem. Bd. of Govs. Corpn. of Massey Hall and Roy Thomson Hall; Hon. Gov. Nat. Ballet Co. of Canada. *Address:* Canadian Imperial Bank of Commerce, Head Office, Commerce Court, Toronto, Ont., M5L 1A2, Canada.

FULLERTON, William Hugh, M.V., M.A.; British diplomatist; b. 11 Feb. 1939, Wolverhampton; ed. Cheltenham Coll. and Queens' Coll., Cambridge; Shell Int. Petroleum Co. Uganda 1963-65; Foreign Office 1965; MECAS, Shemlan, Lebanon 1965-66; Information Officer, Jeddah 1966-67; U.K. Perm. Mission to UN, New York 1967; FCO 1968-70; Head of Chancery, High Comm., Kingston (also accred. to Haiti) 1970-73, Embassy, Ankara 1973-77; FCO 1977-80; Counsellor, Islamabad 1980-83; Amb. to Somalia 1983-87; on loan to Ministry of Defence 1987-88; Gov. Falkland Islands, Commr. for S. Georgia and S. Sandwich Islands and High Commr. for British Antarctic Territory 1988-. *Leisure interests:* travelling in remote places, reading, sailing, music. *Address:* Foreign and Commonwealth Office, Heads of Mission Section, King Charles Street, London, S.W.1; c/o Travellers' Club, 106 Pall Mall, London, S.W.1, England.

FUNAHASHI, Masao; Japanese business executive; b. 3 May 1913, Aichi Pref.; s. of Azuma and Suzu Funahashi; m. Keiko Matsubara 1946; one s. one d.; ed. Tokyo Univ.; Man. Purchasing Dept., Furukawa Electric Co. Ltd. 1959, of Finance and Accounting Dept. 1961, Man. Dir. 1968, Exec. Dir. 1971, Vice-Pres. 1973, Pres. 1974-83, Chair. 1983-; Chair. Japan-Jordan Friendship Asscn. 1981-, Japan-Somalia Friendship Asscn. 1983-. *Leisure interest:* golf. *Address:* c/o Furukawa Electric Co. Ltd., 6-1, Marunouchi 2-chome, Chiyoda-ku, Tokyo, Japan. *Telephone:* Tokyo (03) 286-3010 (Office).

FUNCKE, Liselotte; German politician; b. 20 July 1918, Hagen; d. of Oscar Funcke and Bertha (née Osthaus) Funcke; ed. commercial studies in Berlin; fmrly. in industry and commerce, Hagen and Wuppertal; mem. Diet of North Rhine-Westphalia 1950-61; mem. Bundestag 1961-79, Vice-

Pres. Bundestag 1969–79; Chair. Bundestag Finance Cttee. 1972–79; mem. Presidium, FDP 1968–82, Deputy Chair. FDP 1977–82; Minister of Economy and Transport, North Rhine-Westphalia 1979–80; Govt. Rep. responsible for integration of overseas workers and their families Jan. 1981–; Bundesverdienstkreuz (1973) and other medals. *Address:* 58 Hagen, Stadtgarten-Allee 1, Federal Republic of Germany (Home). *Telephone:* Hagen (02331) 339055.

FUNKE, Gösta Werner, PH.D.; Swedish scientist and administrator; b. 27 Oct. 1906, Stockholm; s. of Oscar Werner Funke and Sofia Carlsson; m. Gunborg Blomqvist 1935; two d.; ed. Univ. of Stockholm, and Tech. Hochschule, Darmstadt; Lecturer in Physics, Univ. of Stockholm 1937–41; Prof. Tech. Coll., Norrköping 1939–43, Bromma Coll. 1943–45; Sec.-Gen. Swedish Atomic Cttee. 1945–59; mem. Swedish Nat. Cttee. for UNESCO 1957–60; Sec.-Gen. Swedish Nat. Science Research Council 1945–72, Swedish Atomic Research Council 1959–72; mem. Joint Cttee. for the Nordic Research Councils 1948–72; Swedish Rep. to CERN 1953–72; Pres. of Finance Cttee. 1961–64, Pres. of Council 1966–69; Swedish Rep., European Southern Observatory (ESO) 1961–72, Pres. of Council 1966–68; Swedish rep. on many cttees. concerning Nordic or int. collaboration in different fields of science; mem. Swedish Acad. of Eng. Sciences 1968–; Riddare av Vasaorden, Kommendör av Nordstjärneorden, Commdr. Ordre nationale du Mérite (France). *Publications:* Text Book of Mathematics 1940, Sverige inför atomåldern 1956, Introduktion till naturvetenskaplig forskning i Sverige 1963; articles in specialized journals. *Leisure interest:* gardening. *Address:* Carrer Viena 1, Alfaz del Pi, Alicante, Spain.

FUNSTON, George Keith; American executive; b. 12 Oct. 1910; m. Elizabeth Kennedy 1939; one s. two d.; ed. Sioux Falls High School, Trinity Coll., Hartford, Conn., and Harvard School of Business Admin.; Asst. to Vice-Pres. in Charge of Sales, American Radiator and Standard Sanitary Corpn. 1935–38, Asst. to Treas. 1938–40; Sales-Planning Dir., later Dir. of Purchases, Sylvania Electric Products, Inc. 1940; War Production Bd. 1941–44; Lieut.-Commdr. U.S. Navy 1944–45; Pres. Trinity Coll., Hartford, Conn. 1944–51; Pres. New York Stock Exchange 1951–67; Chair. Olin Mathieson Chemical Corpn. 1967–72; Dir. Metropolitan Life Insurance Co., and several other companies; 22 hon. degrees from American univs. *Leisure interests:* riding, reading, skiing, tennis. *Address:* 911 Strangler Fig Lane, Sanibel, Fla. 33957, U.S.A.

FÜRER, Arthur Carl Othmar, D.IUR., D.ECON.; Swiss lawyer and business executive; b. 18 Dec. 1920, Gossau; s. of Carl and Clara Fürer (née Staub); m. Bea Hofer 1951; one s.; ed. Gymnasium Feldkirch, Austria, Univs. of Fribourg, Berne and St.-Gall; practised as attorney in St.-Gall 1944–46; joined Société pour le Développement de l'Economie Suisse, Zürich 1946–47; Legal Adviser and Man. Sec. to Georg Fischer AG, Schaffhausen 1947–54; with Nestlé Alimentana S.A. (now Nestlé S.A.), Vevey 1954–84, Gen. Man. 1969, Man. Dir. 1975–82, Chair. 1982–84; Chair. Bank Leu AG Zürich 1984–87; mem. Consultative Comm. for Trade Policy of the Swiss Confed., Bd. Sté Int. Pirelli S.A., Basle, Bd. Georg Fischer AG, Schaffhausen; Int. Counsellor of Conf. Bd. 1977–; mem. Bd. Assocs. Harvard Graduate Business School. *Address:* Chemin des Roches CH-1803 Chardonne, Switzerland (Home). *Telephone:* 021-51-47-94 (Home).

FURET, François; French academic; b. 27 March 1927, Paris; s. of Pierre Furet and Marie-Rose Monnet; m. Deborah Kan 1986; one s. one d.; Researcher C.N.R.S. 1956–61; Jr. Prof. Ecole des Hautes Etudes en Sciences Sociales 1961, Sr. Prof. 1967–, Pres. 1977–85; Pres. Fondation Saint-Simon 1982; Dir. Inst. Raymond Aron 1985–. *Publications:* l'Atélier de l'Histoire 1982, Karl Marx et la Révolution française 1986, La gauche et la révolution au milieu du XIXe siècle 1986, La Révolution (1770–1880) 1988, Le Dictionnaire critique de la Révolution française (with M. Ozouf) 1988. *Address:* Institut Raymond Aron, 6–8 rue Jean Calvin, Paris 75005 (Office); 8 rue Saint-Paul, Paris 75004, France (Home). *Telephone:* 43 31 20 00 (Office); 40 27 00 96 (Home).

FURGLER, Kurt, DR.IUR.; Swiss lawyer and politician; b. 24 June 1924, St.Gall; m. Ursula Stauffenegger; two s. four d.; ed. Univs. of Fribourg, Zürich, Geneva, Grad. Inst. for Int. Studies, Geneva; Lawyer, St.-Gall 1950–71; mem. Nat. Council 1955–71; Leader of Christian Dem. Party Group in Fed. Council; mem. Fed. Council Jan. 1972–, Vice-Pres. Jan.–Dec. 1976, Jan.–Dec. 1980, Jan.–Dec. 1984, Pres. of the Swiss Fed. Jan.–Dec. 1977, Jan.–Dec. 1981, Jan.–Dec. 1985; Head of Fed. Dept. of Justice and Police 1972–83, of Dept. of Public Economy 1983–86; Hon. D.Jur. (Boston Univ.) 1985. *Leisure interests:* sport, music, literature. *Address:* Bundeshaus-Ost, 3003 Berne, Switzerland. *Telephone:* 61-20-01.

FÜRST, Janos Kalman; British orchestral conductor; b. 8 Aug. 1935, Budapest, Hungary; s. of Lajos Fürst and Borbala Spitz; m. 1st Antoinette Reynolds 1962 (divorced 1977), two s.; m. 2nd Ingeborg Nordenfelt; ed. Franz Liszt Acad. of Music, Budapest and Brussels Conservatory; Dir. Irish Chamber Orchestra 1963–66; Resident Conductor Ulster Orchestra 1967–71; Chief Conductor Malmö Symphony Orchestra 1974–78; Music Dir. Marseilles Opera 1981–; Music Dir. Aalborg Symphony Orchestra 1980–83; Dir. Marseilles Philharmonic Orchestra 1985–; Chief Conductor Irish Radio and TV Symphony Orchestra 1987–; Swedish Gramophone Prize 1980. *Leisure interests:* reading and history.

FURTH, Harold Paul, PH.D.; American physicist; b. 13 Jan. 1930, Vienna, Austria; s. of Otto Furth and Gertrude (Harteck) Furth; m. Alice M. Lander 1959 (divorced 1977); one s.; ed. Hill School, Harvard and Cornell Univs.; physicist, Univ. of Calif. Lawrence Radiation Lab., Livermore 1956–65, Group Leader 1965–67; Prof. of Astrophysical Sciences, Princeton Univ. 1967–, Co-Head, Experimental Div., Plasma Physics Lab. 1967–78, Assoc. Dir. and Head, Research Dept. Plasma Physics Lab. 1978–80, Program Dir. Plasma Physics Lab. 1980–81, Dir. Plasma Physics Lab. 1981–; recipient of several awards. *Address:* Princeton Plasma Physics Laboratory, P.O. Box 451, Princeton, N.J. 08543 (Office); 36 Lake Lane, Princeton, N.J. 08540, U.S.A. (Home). *Telephone:* 609-283-3555 (Office).

FURTH, Warren Wolfgang, A.B., J.D.; American lawyer and international official; b. 1 Aug. 1928, Vienna, Austria; s. of John W. Furth and Hedwig von Ferstel; m. Margaretha F. de la Court 1959; one s. one d.; ed. Harvard Coll., and Harvard Law School; Law Clerk, Palmer, Dodge, Gardner, Bickford & Bradford, Boston, Mass. 1951; admitted to New York Bar 1952; Law Clerk to Hon. H.M. Stephens, Chief Judge, U.S. Court of Appeals, Dist. of Columbia Circuit 1952–53; U.S. Army 1954–57; Assoc. Cravath, Swaine & Moore (law firm) 1957–58; with ILO, Geneva 1959–70; Exec. Asst. to Dir.-Gen. 1964–66, Chief of Tech. Co-operation Branch and Deputy Chief, Field Dept. 1966–68, Deputy Chief, later Chief, Personnel and Admin. Services Dept. 1968–70; Asst. Dir.-Gen. WHO (Admin. Services; Co-ordinator, Special Programme for Research & Training in Tropical Diseases and responsibility for Special Programme for Research, Devt. and Research Training in Human Reproduction) 1971–. *Publication:* WHO's Strategy for Meeting the 60% Technical Co-operation Target (WHO Chronicle 31) 1977. *Address:* World Health Organization, avenue Appia, 1211 Geneva (Office); 13 route de Presinge, 1241 Puplinge (Geneva), Switzerland (Home). *Telephone:* 49.72.67.

FURUI, Yoshimi; Japanese politician; Member House of Reps. from Tottori 1960–; fmr. Vice-Minister of Home Affairs; fmr. Health and Welfare Minister; Vice-Chair. Liberal Democratic Party Policy Affairs Research Council; Chair. LDP Research Comm. on Security; Minister of Justice 1978–79. *Publications:* Interpretation of Local Autonomy Law, The Electoral System, Our Electoral Law. *Address:* c/o House of Representatives, Tokyo, Japan.

FURUKAWA, Susumu, B.A.; Japanese banker; b. 19 Aug. 1913, Saga Prefecture; m. Kimiko Furukawa; four s.; ed. Kyoto Univ.; entered Nomura Bank (now Daiwa Bank) 1938, Gen. Man. Business Dept. 1961, Dir. 1961, Man. Dir. 1963, Sr. Man. Dir. 1966, Deputy Pres. 1968, Pres. 1973–77, Chair. 1977. *Leisure interests:* haiku (seventeen-syllabled poem), golf. *Address:* c/o Daiwa Bank Ltd., 21 Bingomachi, 2-chome, Higashiku, Osaka 541 (Office); 13-7, 2-chome, Furuedai, Suita City, Osaka, Japan (Home).

FURUYA, Toru; Japanese politician; b. 6 Jan. 1909; ed. Tokyo Imperial Univ.; joined Ministry of the Interior; mem. House of Reps. 1967–; Deputy Sec.-Gen. Liberal Democratic Party; Parl. Vice-Minister for Home Affairs; Minister of Home Affairs and Chair. Nat. Security Comm. 1984–86. *Publication:* Murder Investigation. *Leisure interests:* go and shogi playing, reading, sports. *Address:* c/o Ministry of Home Affairs, 2–I, Kasumigaseki, Chiyoda-ku, Tokyo 100, Japan.

FUSI, Juan Pablo; Spanish historian and library director; b. 1945, San Sebastian; ed. Universidad Complutense de Madrid and Oxford Univ., England; taught at San Diego, Calif., U.S.A.; Dir. Centre for Iberian Studies, St. Anthony's Coll., Oxford 1976–80; Prof. of Contemporary History, Santander Univ. 1980–; Dir. Nat. Library of Spain 1986–; Dr. h.c. (New York) 1987. *Publications:* Política obrera en el País Vasco 1880–1923 1975, España 1808–1936 (with Raymond Carr), España, de la dictadura a la democracia (with Raymond Carr; Premio Espejo de España 1979), El problema vasco en la II República 1979, El País Vasco; Pluralismo y nacionalidad 1984, Franco; many contribs. to Spanish and foreign magazines on contemporary history. *Address:* Biblioteca Nacional, Paseo de Recoletos 20, 28001 Madrid, Spain.

FUSSELL, Paul, M.A., PH.D.; American university professor; b. 22 March 1924, Calif.; s. of Paul Fussell and Wilhma Wilson Sill; m. 1st Betty Harper 1949 (divorced 1987); one s. one d.; m. 2nd Harriette Behringer 1987; ed. Pomona Coll., Harvard Univ.; Instructor in English, Conn. Coll. 1951–54; Asst. Prof. then Prof. of English, Rutgers Univ. 1955–76, John DeWitt Prof. of English Literature 1976–83; Donald T. Regan Prof. of English Literature, Univ. of Pa. 1983–; Nat. Book Award; Nat. Book Critics Circle Award; Emerson Award; Hon. Litt.D. (Pomona Coll.) 1980, (Monmouth Coll., N.J.) 1985. *Publications:* Theory of Prosody in 18th Century England 1954, Poetic Meter and Poetic Form 1965, The Rhetorical World of Augustan Humanism 1965, Samuel Johnson and the Life of Writing 1971, The Great War and Modern Memory 1975, Abroad: British Literary Travelling between the Wars 1980, The Boy Scout Handbook and Other Observations 1982, Class: A Guide through the American Status System 1983, Sassoon's Long Journey (ed.) 1983, The Norton Book of Travel (ed.) 1987, Thank God for the Atom Bomb and Other Essays 1988. *Leisure interest:* reading. *Address:* Apt. 4-H, 2020 Walnut Street, Philadelphia, Pa. 19103, U.S.A. *Telephone:* (215) 557-0144.

FYFE, William Sefton, PH.D., F.R.S., F.R.S.C.; Canadian professor of chemistry; b. 4 June 1927, N.Z.; s. of Colin and Isabella Fyfe; three c.; ed. Univ.

of Otago, N.Z.; Lecturer in Chemistry, Otago Univ. 1955–58; Prof. of Geology, Univ. of Calif., Berkeley 1958–66; Royal Soc. Prof. Manchester Univ. 1966–72; Prof. of Geology, Univ. of Western Ont. 1972–84, Dean Faculty of Science 1986–; awards include Guggenheim Fellowships, Logen Medal, Holmes Medal, European Union of Geosciences 1989. *Publications:*

5 books, 300 scientific papers. *Leisure interests:* wildlife, swimming, travel. *Address:* Office of the Dean of Science, University of Western Ontario, London, Ont. N6A 5B7; 1197 Richmond Street, London, Canada N6A 3L3 (Home). *Telephone:* (519) 661-3041 (Office).

G

GABLE, Christopher; British actor; m. Carole Needham; one s.; former leading dancer, The Royal Ballet; stage career began in 1967 and has included appearances in Sweet Bird of Youth, Cyrano de Bergerac, The Good Companions; has since appeared with RSC and in various TV series and plays. *Films include:* Women in Love, 1969, The Music Lovers 1970, The Boy Friend 1972, Pianorma, The Slipper and the Rose 1975.

GABLENTZ, Otto von der, PH.B.; German diplomatist; b. 9 Oct. 1930, Berlin; s. of Prof. Otto Heinrich von der Gablentz and Hilda (née Zietlow); m. Christa Gerke 1965; one s. four d.; ed. Univs. of Berlin and Freiburg, Coll. of Europe, Bruges, St. Anthony's Coll. Oxford, and Harvard Univ.; joined foreign service of Fed. Repub. of Germany 1959; served in Australia 1961–64, worked in Bonn on Berlin and Germany 1964–67, German Embassy, London 1967–72, Dept. of European Political Co-operation 1973–78, seconded to Chancellor's Office 1978, Head of Section, Foreign and Defence Policy 1981; Amb. to Netherlands 1983–. *Address:* Embassy of the Federal Republic of Germany, Groot Hertsginnelaan 18–20, 2517 EG, The Hague, Netherlands.

GABRE-SELLASSIE, Zewde, PH.D.; Ethiopian diplomatist; b. 12 Oct. 1926, Metcha, Shoa; ed. Haile Sellassie I Secondary School, Coll. des Frères and St. George School, Jerusalem, Coll. des Frères and American Mission, Cairo, Univ. of Exeter, Oxford Univ. and Lincoln's Inn, London; Econ. Attaché, later Head of Press, Information and Admin. Div., Ministry of Foreign Affairs 1951–53; Dir.-Gen. Maritime Affairs 1953–55; Deputy Minister, Ministry of Public Works, Transport and Civil Aviation 1955–57; Mayor and Gov. of Addis Ababa 1957–59; Amb. to Somalia 1959–60; Minister of Justice 1961–63; Senior mem. St. Antony's Coll., Oxford 1963–71; Perm. Rep. to the UN 1972–74; Minister of Interior March-May 1974, of Foreign Affairs May-Dec. 1974; Deputy Prime Minister July-Sept. 1974; Visiting lecturer, Univ. of Calif., U.S.A. 1965; Vice-Pres. ECOSCO 1974; Officer of Menelik II, Grand Cross of Phoenix (Greece), of Istiqlal (Jordan), Grand Officer Flag of Yugoslavia, Order of Merit (Fed. Repub. of Germany).

GABRIEL, Peter; British rock singer and songwriter; b. 13 May 1950; ed. Charterhouse; co-f. Genesis rock band 1966; left group to start career as soloist 1975; numerous solo albums; financed World of Music, Arts and Dance Festival (WOMAD) featuring music from Third World countries 1982. *Songs include:* Solsbury Hill, D.I.Y., Games Without Frontiers, Shock the Monkey, Big Time, Sledgehammer, Don't Give Up (with Kate Bush), Biko. *Albums:* Chalk Mark in a Rainstorm (co-wrote songs with Joni Mitchell, q.v.), Peter Gabriel I-IV, Peter Gabriel Plays Live, Birdy (soundtrack for the film), several pieces for soundtrack to film Last Temptation of Christ.

GABRIELIDES, Andreas, M.SC.; Cypriot politician; b. 1949, Amiantos; m.; three c.; ed. Higher Commercial Lyceum, Nicosia, Prague Univ., Czechoslovakia, Univ. of Aberdeen, Scotland; served Nat. Guard 1966–67; Agronomist, Dept. of Agric. 1967–70, 1972–81; Gen. Man. Cyprus Dairy Industry Org. 1981–88; Minister of Agric. and Natural Resources 1988–; Fellow Inst. of Econ. Devt., World Bank. *Address:* Ministry of Agriculture and Natural Resources, Nicosia, Cyprus.

GABRIELLI, Adolfo Ricardo Pablo; Argentine judge; b. 30 June 1911, La Plata (Prov. of Buenos Aires); s. of Alejandro and Adela L. Doussinague Gabrielli; m. Ligia Estela Ferro 1939; two s. two d.; ed. Nat. Univ. of Córdoba; Head of Legal Affairs, State Tax Office 1937–43; Sec. Fed. Court of Second Instance 1943–46; Admin. Judge to Capital 1946; Nat. Judge in Litigation 1950; Fed. Judge in Civil and Commercial Affairs 1953; Judge of Fed. Chamber (Admin. Litigation Court) Nov. 1955–; law practice 1973–76; Minister of the Supreme Court of Justice April 1976, Pres. Aug. 1976, retd. 1983; Paul Harris Fellow (Rotary Foundation); Dr. h.c. (Córdoba) 1983; Orden del Sol de Perú, Gran Cruz Orden Nacional de Cruceiro do Sul, Orden de Mérito Jurisdicción de Trabajo en grado de Gran Cruz (Brazil). *Publications:* Derecho Tributario Penal 1946, Procedimiento Tributario 1975, La pena de prisión en materia tributaria 1976, La defraudación fiscal y las penas corporales 1976, La Corte y la opinión pública 1986, The Fiscal Residence of Companies 1987. *Leisure interest:* specializing in taxation law. *Address:* Brown 533, San Isidro, Province of Buenos Aires, Argentina (Home). *Telephone:* 743-2316 (Home).

GABRIELSKI, Jan Stanisław, M.A.; Polish politician; b. 27 March, 1944, Wilczewo, Bydgoszcz Voivodship; ed. Higher School of Agric., Olsztyn; senior asst., Inst. of Economy and Org. of Agric., Higher School of Agric., Kortowo 1970–71; activist in youth groups; Chair. Nat. Students' Council of Rural Youth Union (ZMW), then Sec.-Gen. Bd. ZMW 1971–73; Deputy Chair. Gen. Bd. Socialist Union of Polish Students (SZSP) 1973–75, Chair. Gen. Bd. SZSP 1976–80; Chair. Gen. Bd. Union of Socialist Rural Youth (ZSMW) 1975–76; Deputy Chair. Gen. Bd. of Union of Socialist Polish Youth (ZSMP) 1976; Deputy Chair. Chief Council of Fed. of Socialist Unions of Polish Youth (FSZMP) 1975–81; mem. PZPR 1968–, deputy mem. PZPR Cen. Cttee. 1976–80, mem. Cen. Cttee. Oct. 1980–81, 1986–,

mem. Secr. of PZPR Cen. Cttee. Oct. 1980–81, Head of Social and Professional Dept., PZPR Cen. Cttee. 1981–86, Head, Political and Organizational Dept., PZPR Cen. Cttee. 1986–; Deputy to Seym 1976–85; fmr. Deputy Chair. Seym Comm. of Science and Tech. Progress; Gold Cross of Merit, J. Krasicki Gold Award. *Address:* Komitet Centralny PZPR, Nowy Świat 6, 00-497 Warsaw, Poland.

GACEK, Elżbieta Łucja, M.A.; Polish lawyer and politician; b. 6 July 1938, Wąchock, Kielce Voivodship; ed. Jagellonian Univ., Cracow; apprentice, subsequently Assoc. Judge of Voivodship Court, Kielce 1960–66; Judge of Dist. Court, Kielce 1966–75; Judge of Regional Labour and Social Insurance Court, Kielce 1975–85; Judge of Voivodship Court, Kielce 1985–; Deputy to Seym (Parl.) 1985–; mem. Council of State 1985–88; Vice-Speaker and Marshal of SEYM (Parl.) 1988–; mem. Polish United Workers' Party (PZPR) 1962–; active leader of Patriotic Movt. for Nat. Rebirth (PRON) and Polish Women's League, Kielce; mem. Pres. Municipal Nat. Council, Kielce 1984; Gold and Silver Cross of Merit and other decorations. *Address:* Kancelaria Sejmu PRL, ul. Wiejska 4/6, 00-902 Warsaw, Poland (Office).

GACIC, Radisa; Yugoslav politician; b. 1938, Bajina Basta; ed. teacher training and legal studies; mem. League of Communists of Yugoslavia (LCY) 1957–, Sec. 1986–; Sec. Serbian League of Communists Cen. Cttee. Pres. 1982–86; mem. Republican Conf. of Serbian S.A.W.P. *Address:* League of Communists of Yugoslavia, Belgrade, Yugoslavia.

GADAMER, Hans-Georg, DR.PHIL.; German professor of philosophy; b. 11 Feb. 1900, Marburg; two d.; ed. Univ. of Marburg; Prof. of Philosophy, Univ. of Leipzig 1939, Rector 1946–47; Prof. Univ. of Frankfurt/Main 1947, Univ. of Heidelberg 1949; mem. Sächsische Akad. der Wissenschaften, Leipzig and Acads. of Heidelberg, Darmstadt, Athens, Budapest and Turin; mem. Acad. Nazionale dei Lincei, Rome; Hon. mem. American Acad. of Arts and Sciences, British Acad.; Dr.phil. h.c. (Ottawa) 1977, (Washington) 1979; Orden pour le mérite Grosses Bundesverdienstkreuz mit Stern; Reuchlin Prize (Pforzheim) 1971; Hegel Prize (Stuttgart) 1979. *Publications:* Platos dialektische Ethik 1968, Wahrheit und Methode. Grundzüge einer philosophischen Hermaneutik 1975; essays, studies and articles on philosophy. *Address:* Am Büchsenackerhang 53, 6900 Heidelberg, Federal Republic of Germany.

GADDA CONTI, Piero, LL.D.; Italian writer; b. 13 Feb. 1902, Milan; s. of Giuseppe and Matilde Gadda Conti; m. Anna Maria Castellini 1939; one s.; ed. Pavia Univ.; Novelist and journalist; Italian Literary Prizewinner 1930, Bagutta Prize for Literature for La Paura 1971. *Publications:* L'Entusiastica Estate 1924, Liuba 1926, Verdemare 1927, Mozzo 1930, A Gonfie Vele 1931, Gagliarda 1932, Orchidea 1934, Festa da Ballo 1937, Nuvola 1938, Moti del Cuore 1940, Vocazione Mediterranea 1940, Incomparabile Italia 1947, Beati Regni 1954, Vita e melodie di Giacomo Puccini 1955, Adamira 1956, Vanterie Adolescenti 1960, Cinema e civiltà 1960, Cinema e Giustizia 1961, Cinema e Sesso 1962, Cinema e Libertà 1963, La Milano dei Navigli 1965, Cinema e Società 1965, La Brianza 1966, La Paura 1970, Confessioni di Carlo Emilio Gadda 1974, Concerto d'Autunno 1976; plays: La Veste d'Oro 1924, Dulcinea 1927. *Address:* Piazza Castello 20, Milan, Italy. *Telephone:* 873-771, 80-33-58.

GADDAFI, Col. Mu'ammar Muhammad al-; Libyan army officer and political leader; b. 1942, Serte; s. of Mohamed Abdulsalam Abuminiar and Aisha Ben Niran; m. 1970; four s. one d.; ed. Univ. of Libya, Benghazi; served with Libyan Army 1965–; Chair. Revolutionary Command Council 1969–77; C.-in-C. of Armed Forces Sept. 1969–; Prime Minister 1970–72; Minister of Defence 1970–72; Pres. of Libya March 1977–; Sec.-Gen. of Gen. Secr. of Gen. People's Congress 1977–79; Chair. OAU 1982–83; mem. Pres. Council, Fed. of Arab Republics 1971–; rank of Maj.-Gen. Jan. 1976, retaining title of Col. *Publications:* The Green Book (3 vols.), Military Strategy and Mobilization, The Story of the Revolution. *Address:* Office of the President, Tripoli, Libya.

GADDAFI, Wanis; Libyan politician; Head of Exec. Council in Cyrenaican Prov. Govt. 1952–62; Fed. Minister of Foreign Affairs 1962–63, of Interior 1963–64, of Labour 1964; Amb. to Fed. Repub. of Germany 1964–65; Minister of Planning and Devt. 1966–68, of Foreign Affairs 1968; Prime Minister 1968–69; imprisoned for two years 1971–73.

GADDAM, Encik Kasitah bin, B.A.; Malaysian politician; b. 18 Oct. 1947, Ranau, Sabah; m. Puan Rosnie bte Ambuting; four c.; ed. Sabah Coll., Kota Kinabalu and Univ. of Malaya; Admin. Officer, Chief Minister's Dept. Kota Kinabula, Sabah 1971; Asst. Dir. of Immigration, Sabah 1971–76; Regional Man. K.P.D. for Kundasang, Ranau and Tambunan, Admin. Officer/Purchasing Man. K.P.D. Headquarters, Kota Kinabalu 1977–80; Dir. of Personnel for East Malaysia and Brunei, Inchcape Malaysia Holding Bhd. 1980–83; Chair. Sabah Devt. Bank, Sabah Finance Bd., Soilogen (Sabah) Sdn. Bhd. 1985; mem. Parl. 1986–; Minister, Prime Minister's Dept. 1986–; Vice-Pres. Parti Bersatu Sabah 1984–. *Address:* Prime Minister's Department, Jalau Dato Onn, 50502 Kuala Lumpur, Malaysia.

GADGIL, Vithal Narhar, B.SC.; Indian politician; b. 22 Sept. 1928, Pune; s. of Narhar Vishnu Gadgil and Anandi Gadgil; m. Jahnavi Gadgil; one s. one d.; ed. L.S.E.; Prof. of Econ., Ruparel Coll., Bombay 1955-60; Prof. of Constitutional Law, New Law Coll., Bombay 1960-66; mem. Rajya Sabha 1971; Minister for Defence Production 1975-77, of Communications 1983-84, of Information and Broadcasting 1985-86; Advocate Supreme Court; Consulting Ed. Marathi Encyclopaedia; Gen. Sec. Congress Party; mem. Exec. Cttee. of Maritha Sahitya Parishad; *Address:* 479 Shaniwar Peth, Pune 411030, India (Home).

GADOUREK, Ivan; Netherlands professor of sociology (retd.); b. 11 July 1923, Brno; s. of Josef Gadourek and Milada (née Dostalova) Gadourek; m. J. C. A. Backer 1949; two d.; ed. Masaryk Univ. and Univ. of Leyden; research Assoc., Netherlands Inst. for Preventive Medicine 1948-58; Prof. of Sociology, Univ. of Gröningen 1958-84; mem. Royal Netherlands Acad. of Arts and Sciences 1975-; Dr. h.c. (Utrecht); Kt. Orde van de Nederlandse Leeuw. *Publications:* The Political Control of Czechoslovakia 1953, The Sociology of Knowledge 1956, A Dutch Community 1963, Absences and Well-being of Workers 1965, Social Change as Redefinition of Roles. *Leisure interests:* climbing, music, literature. *Address:* Westerse Drift 88, 92572 LK HAREN, The Netherlands. *Telephone:* (050) 345457.

GADSDEN, Sir Peter Drury Haggerston, G.B.E., M.A., D.SC., F.ENG., F.I.M.M., F.INST.M.; British business executive; b. 28 June 1929, Mannville, Alta., Canada; s. of late Rev. Basil C. and Mabel F. (née Drury) Gadsden; m. Belinda Ann de Marie Haggerston 1955; four d.; ed. Rockport, Belfast, The Elms, Colwall, Wrekin Coll., Wellington and Jesus Coll., Cambridge; dir. of cos. since 1952; marketing economist (mineral sands), UNIDO 1969; Dir. City of London (Arizona) Corpn. 1970-88, Chair. 1985-88, Ellingham Estate Ltd. 1974-, Clothworkers' Foundation 1974-, Provident Assoc. for Medical Care (PPP) 1981-, Chair. 1984-; Dir. William Jacks 1984-, Aitken Hume 1986-; Consultant, Associated Minerals Consolidated Ltd. 1971-; Sheriff of London 1970-71; Alderman of the City of London 1971-, Lord Mayor of London 1979-80; Pres. Metropolitan Soc. for the Blind 1979-, Ironbridge Gorge Museum Devt. Trust; Hon. Pres. Australian Heritage Soc. 1986-; Vice-Pres. Sir Robert Menzies Memorial Trust Blackwood Little Theatre 1986-; Chancellor, The City Univ. 1979-80; Chair. Britain-Australia Soc.; Chair. Britain-Australia Bicentennial Cttee.; Chair. Royal Commonwealth Soc. 1984-; Chair. City of London (Arizona) Corpn. 1985-; Hon. mem. London Metal Exchange; Inst. of Royal Engineers 1986-; Underwriting mem. Lloyds; mem. Crown Agents Holding and Realization Bd. 1981-; Gov. The Hon. The Irish Soc. 1984-; Patron Guild of Rahere 1986-; Vice-Patron Museum of Empire and Commonwealth Trust 1986-; mem. Court Mary Rose Devt. Trust; Trustee Chichester Festival Theatre 1986-; Liveryman, Clothworkers' Co.; Master Worshipful Co. of Engineers 1983-85; Hon. Liveryman, Plaisterers' Co., Marketors' Co., Actuaries' Co.; Officier Etoile Equatoriale (Gabon) 1970; H.M.'s Comm. of Lieutenancy for the City of London 1979-; K. St. J. *Publications:* articles on minerals and the minerals industry in professional journals. *Leisure interests:* skiing, sailing, walking, forestry, farming, photography. *Address:* 606 Gilbert House, Barbican, London, EC2Y 8BD, England. *Telephone:* 01-638 8346 (Office); 01-638 9968 (Home).

GADZHIEV, Rauf Soltan ogly; Soviet composer of popular music; b. 1922, Azerbaizhan; mem. CPSU 1958-; ed. Azerbaizhan Conservatoire (studied composition under K. Karavayev); organizer and Dir. of Azerbaizhan State Popular Orchestra 1955-; Minister of Culture for Azerbaizhan S.S.R. 1965-71; *Compositions include:* musical comedy Romeo is my Neighbour, Cuba—My Love, Don't Hide Your Smile, The Fourth Bell, Mama, I'm Getting Married, The Flame (ballet), Youth Symphony, Algiers Suite (for symphony orchestra), Cantatas: Spring, An Oath to the Party, Poem about a Communist; compositions for chamber and popular orchestras; music for shows and films, and over 80 popular songs; People's Artist of Azerbaizhan 1964; People's Artist of U.S.S.R. 1978. *Address:* Azerbaizhan State Popular Orchestra, Baku, Azerbaizhan, U.S.S.R.

GAEBLER, (Gerhard Otto) Rainer, DR. ING.; German engineer; b. 30 March 1938, Leipzig; s. of Otto Gaebler and Charlotte Fischer; m. Uta Neef 1964; one d.; gas tech. engineer 1959-; Pres. Land Synod of Evangelical-Lutheran Church in Saxony 1983-84, Vice-Pres. 1984-; Pres. Synod of Union of Evangelical Churches in G.D.R. 1986-; mem. Conf. of Evangelical Church Leaders and Bd. of Union of Evangelical Churches in G.D.R. 1986-. *Publication:* Gut gedacht ist halb gelöst. *Address:* Schwantesstrasse 67, 7024 Leipzig, German Democratic Republic *Telephone:* 231 41 53.

GAEHTGENS, Thomas Wolfgang, DR. PHIL.; German professor of the history of art; b. 24 June 1940, Leipzig; m. Barbara Feiler 1969; two s.; ed. Univs. of Bonn, Freiburg and Paris; teacher Univ. of Göttingen 1973, Prof. of Art History 1974-79, Technische Hochschule, Aachen 1979, Freie Univ. Berlin 1979-; awarded bursary for the J. Paul Getty Centers for the History of Art and the Humanities, Santa Monica, Calif. 1985-86; mem. Akademie der Wissenschaften, Göttingen. *Publications:* Napoleon's Arc de Triomphe, Versailles als Nationaldenkmal 1984, Joseph-Marie Vien 1988. *Address:* Kunsthistorische Institut der FU, Morgensternstrasse 2-3, D-1000 Berlin 45 (Office); Peter-Lenné-Strasse 20, D-1000 Berlin 33, Federal Republic of Germany (Home). *Telephone:* 030-772 70 40 (Office); 030-831 14 39 (Home).

GAETANO, Cortesi; Italian industrial executive; b. 8 May 1912, Mesenzana, Varese; s. of late Giuseppe Gaetano and Angela (née Ferrini); m. Fiorella Lello 1946; three s.; ed. Univ. Bocconi, Milan; research at London School of Econs., Berlin Handelshochschule and Yale; joined econ. agency Istituto per la Ricostruzione Industriale (IRI) working in Stabilimenti Tessili Italiana and later in Banca Commerciale Italiana, New York and Italy 1940-45, in Cen. Inspectorate 1945-47; Gen. Dir. of Finmeccanica 1957-60, of IRI 1960-66; Chair. and Gen. Man. Italcantieri (Trieste) 1966-71, Gen. Man. Fincantieri 1971-74; Chair. and Gen. Man. Alfa Romeo S.p.A. 1974-79, and fmrly. to Alfa Romeo Alfasud S.p.A.; Pres. Studi Impianti Consulenze Automotoristiche S.r.l.; mem. Bd. of Dirs. and Exec. Cttee., Assoc. Sindacale Intersind (employers' asscn. for state-controlled firms). *Publication:* Pianificazione Programmazione e Controlli Industriali 1955. *Leisure interest:* mountains. *Address:* c/o Alfa Romeo S.p.A., Via Gattemelata 45, 20149 Milan, Italy. *Telephone:* 02-93391.

GAETE ROJAS, Sergio; Chilean lawyer and government minister; b. 9 Sept. 1939, Santiago; s. of Guillermo Gaete Rojas and Raquel Rojas Errazuriz; m. Carmen Street Ferrier 1963; three s.; practised as lawyer 1964-85; mem. Fourth Legis. Comm. 1981-85; mem. Anti-Monopolies. Comm. Tribunal 1982-85; Titular Prof. of Roman and Civil Law, Pontificia Universidad Católica de Chile 1964-, Vice-Dean Faculty of Law 1970-73, Dean 1973-85; Minister of Public Educ. 1985-87. *Publication:* La Comunicabilidad en torno a los Elementos del Delito. *Leisure interests:* music, chess. *Address:* c/o Avenida Libertador Bernardo O'Higgins No. 1371, 7° Piso, Santiago, Chile.

GAFNY, Arnon, M.A.; Israeli economist and banker; b. 1932, Tel-Aviv; m. Mira Gafny; one s. two d.; ed. Bard Coll., N.Y., U.S.A., and Hebrew Univ., Jerusalem; Falk Inst. for Econ. Research 1954-56; Asst. to Financial Adviser to Chief of Staff, Israel Defence Forces 1957-59; Chief Asst., Budgets Dept., Ministry of Finance 1959-61; Head, Econ. and Commercial Dept. of Ports Authority 1961; Dir. Ashdod Port 1961-70; Dir. of Budgets, Ministry of Finance 1970-75, Dir.-Gen. 1975-76; Gov. Bank of Israel 1977-82; Deputy Chair., Man. Dir. and C.E.O. Israel Gen. Bank Ltd. Oct. 1983-; Chair. Koor Industries Nov. 1986-. *Address:* Israel General Bank Ltd., 38 Rothschild Boulevard, Tel-Aviv 61006 (Office); P.O. Box 677, Tel-Aviv, Israel (Home). *Telephone:* 03-645-645 (Office).

GAGAROV, Dmitri Nikolayevich; Soviet politician; b. 1938; ed. Kuybyshev Tech. Inst. of Soviet Far East, Cen. Cttee. Higher Party School; technician 1962-66; mem. CPSU 1966-; Sr. engineer with 'Dalnergo' 1966-72; First Deputy Pres. Vladivostok City Exec. Cttee. 1972-73; First Sec. Pervorechensky Regional Cttee. of CPSU (Vladivostok) 1973-75; Pres. Vladivostok City Cttee. of CPSU 1975-78; First Sec. 1978-79; Second Sec. of Primorskoy Dist. Cttee. of CPSU 1979-83; work for U.S.S.R. Cen. Cttee. 1983-84; First Sec. Primorskoy Dist. Cttee. of CPSU 1984-; mem. Cen. Cttee. of CPSU 1986-. *Address:* City Committee of Communist Party of the Soviet Union, Vladivostok, U.S.S.R.

GAGE, Harlow W., B.A.; American motor company executive; b. 6 Feb. 1911, Springfield, Mass.; ed. Norwich Univ., Northfield, Vt.; with Gen. Motors Ltd. (starting as Messenger, Overseas Div. in New York) 1934-, Asst. to Man. Dir., Gen. Motors Near East S.A., Alexandria, Egypt 1936-40, Sales Corresp. for Foreign Distributors' Div. of Gen. Motors, New York Jan.-Dec. 1941, at Overseas Operations Div., Washington 1942-45, Sales Man. Gen. Motors New Zealand Ltd., Wellington 1945-54, Man. Dir. GM New Zealand Ltd. 1954-56, Asst. to Man. Dir. of Gen. Motors-Holden's Pty. Ltd., Melbourne 1956-58, Asst. Man. Dir. GM-Holden's June 1958, Man. Dir. 1959-62, Regional Group Exec. GM Overseas Div. 1962-63, Feb.-Oct. 1968, Dir. Opel, Holden's group with responsibility for GM vehicle mfg. subsids. 1963-68, Gen. Man. GM Overseas Div. and Vice-Pres. and mem. of Admin. Cttee. of Gen. Motors Corpn. Oct. 1968-; Trustee, Council for Latin America Inc., U.S. Council of Int. Chamber of Commerce; Dir. American-Australian Asscn.; mem. Bd. of Dirs. of Nat. Foreign Trade Council Inc., The Council on Foreign Relations. *Address:* General Motors Corporation, General Motors Building, Detroit, Mich. 48202, U.S.A.

GAGE, Nathaniel Lees, PH.D.; American professor of education; b. 1 Aug. 1917, Union City, N.J.; s. of Hyman Gewirtz and Rose Lees Gewirtz; m. Margaret E. Burrows 1942; one s. three d.; ed. Univ. of Minnesota and Purdue Univ.; Asst. Prof. Purdue Univ. 1947-48; Asst. Prof. of Educ. Univ. of Ill. 1948-51, Assoc. Prof. 1951-56, Prof. of Educ. 1956-62, of Psychology 1961-62; Prof. of Educ. Stanford Univ. 1962-79, of Psychology 1962-87, Margaret Jacks Prof. of Educ. 1979-87, Prof. Emer. 1987-; Guggenheim Fellow; Fellow, Center for Advanced Study in Behavioural Sciences; mem. Nat. Acad. of Educ.; Thorndike Award, American Educational Research Asscn. Award. *Publications:* Teacher Effectiveness and Teacher Education 1972, Scientific Basis of the Art of Teaching 1978, Educational Psychology (with D. C. Berliner) 1984, Hard Gains in the Soft Sciences: The Case of Pedagogy 1985. *Address:* CERAS, School of Education, Stanford University, Stanford, Calif. 94305, U.S.A. *Telephone:* 415-723-2300.

GAGE, Peter William, M.B., CH.B., PH.D., D.SC.; Australian professor of physiology; b. 21 Oct. 1937, Auckland, New Zealand; s. of John and Kathleen (née Burke) Gage; m. Jillian Shewan 1960; two s. two d.; ed. Univ. of Otago; house surgeon, Auckland Hosp. 1961; research asst. Green

Lane Hosp., Auckland 1962; research scholar, A.N.U., Canberra 1963–65; N.I.H. Int. Postdoctoral Fellow, Dept. of Physiology and Pharmacology, Duke Univ., Durham, N.C. 1965–67, Asst. Prof. 1967–68, Sr. Lecturer, School of Physiology and Pharmacology, Univ. of N.S.W. 1968–70, Assoc. Prof. 1971–76, Prof. 1976–84, Dir. Nerve-Muscle Research Centre 1982–84; Prof. and Chair. Dept. of Physiology, John Curtin School of Medical Research, A.N.U. 1984–; Fellow, Australian Acad. of Science. *Leisure interests:* tennis, bushwalking. *Address:* 10 Harbison Crescent, Wanniassa, A.C.T. 2903, Australia.

GAGNEBIN, Albert P., B.S., M.S.; American mining executive; b. 23 Jan. 1909, Torrington, Conn.; s. of Charles A. and Marguerite E. (Huguenin) Gagnebin; m. Genevieve Hope; two d.; ed. Yale Univ.; Research Engineer, Int. Nickel Co. Inc. 1932–49, Ductile Iron Group Leader 1949–54, Asst. Man. of Nickel Sales 1955–56, Man. 1956–61, Asst. Vice-Pres. 1957–58, Vice-Pres. 1958–64, Vice-Pres. Int. Nickel Co. of Canada Ltd. 1960–64, Exec. Vice-Pres. Int. Nickel Co. of Canada Ltd. and Int. Nickel Co. Inc. 1964–67, Dir. Int. Nickel Co. Inc. 1964–, Int. Nickel Co. of Canada 1965–, Pres. Int. Nickel Co. of Canada Ltd. and Int. Nickel Co. Inc. 1967–72, Chair. and Chair. Exec. Cttee. 1972–74; fmr. Dir. INCO Ltd. (fmrly. Int. Nickel Co. of Canada Ltd.), Abex Corpn.; Dir. American-Swiss Asscn. Inc., N. American Advisory Bd. of Swissair; fmr. Dir. Abex Corpn., Centennial Insurance Co., The Bank of New York, Toronto-Dominion Bank, Ingersoll-Rand Co., Shering-Plough"Corpn.; Dir. Emer. Illinois Cen. Industries; fmr. Trustee Atlantic Mutual Insurance Co.; mem. Yale Eng. Asscn.; co-inventor of Ductile Iron; mem. Nat. Acad. of Eng., Washington, D.C. (Awards 1952, 1965 and 1967); Hon. Life mem. American Foundrymen's Soc.; Officier, Ordre national du Mérite 1976. *Publications:* Fundamentals of Iron and Steel Castings 1957, and numerous articles. *Address:* 143 Grange Avenue, Fair Haven, N.J. 07704, U.S.A. *Telephone:* (201) 747-0139.

GAGNON, H.E. Cardinal Edouard, P.S.S.; Canadian ecclesiastic; b. 15 Jan. 1918, Port-Daniel, Gaspé; ordained 1940; consecrated Bishop of Saint Paul in Alberta 1969, renounced position 1972; Archbishop (Titular See of Iustiniana prima) 1983; cr. Cardinal 1985; Pres. Pontifical Council for the Family May 1985–. *Address:* Via di Porta Angelica 31, 00193, Rome, Italy.

GAGNON, Jean-Marie, PH.D., M.B.A., F.R.S.C.; Canadian professor of finance; b. 7 July 1933, Fabre; m. Rachel Bonin 1959; three s.; ed. Univ. of Chicago and Univ. Laval; chartered accountant, Clarkson, Gordon, Cie. 1957–59; Prof. of Finance, Univ. Laval 1961–; Visiting Prof. Faculté Universitaire Catholique à Mons, Belgium 1972–74, Univ. of Nankai, People's Repub. of China 1985. *Publications:* Income Smoothing Hypothesis 1970, Belgian Experience with Mergers 1982, Taux de rendement et risque 1982, Traité de gestion financière 1987. *Address:* 1340 Corrigan, Sainte Foy, G1W 3E9, Canada.

GAIRY, Rt. Hon. Sir Eric Matthew, Kt., P.C., F.R.S.A.; Grenada politician; b. 18 Feb. 1922, St. Andrew's, Grenada; m. Cynthia Gairy 1949; two d.; ed. St. Andrew's R.C. School.; founder and leader United Labour Party 1950–; mem. Legis. Council 1951–54, 1954–57; Minister of Trade and Production 1956–57; Chief Minister, Minister of Finance to 1962 (dismissed); Premier 1967–74; fmr. Minister of Home and External Affairs, Security and Defence; Prime Minister, Minister of Planning and Devt., Lands and Tourism, Information Service, Public Relations and Natural Resources, independent Grenada 1974–79 (deposed in coup); Hon. Dr. rer. pol. (Ecclesiastical Univ. England) 1974, Hon. Dr. Iur. (Kyung Hee Univ.) 1976; Order of the Liberator (Venezuela) 1971, Kt. Grand Cross Order of the Holy Cross of Jerusalem 1974, Silver Jubilee Medal 1977 and other awards. *Leisure interests:* cricket, tennis, billiards, dancing, music. *Address:* St. Georges, Grenada.

GAJA, Roberto, LL.D.; Italian diplomatist; b. 27 May 1912, Turin; s. of Guido Gaja and Carlotta Pia Galliani; m. Carla Travaglini 1937; one s. two d.; ed. Univ of Turin law faculty.; entered diplomatic service 1937; First Sec. and Chargé d'affaires, Vienna 1946–47; Italian Rep. and later Chargé d'affaires, Tripoli 1949–52; Counsellor, Paris 1955; Asst. Dir. of Personnel, Ministry of Foreign Affairs 1957, Gen. Dir. for Political Affairs 1964–69, Sec.-Gen. of Ministry 1969–75; Minister, Sofia; rank of Amb. 1967; Amb. to U.S.A. 1975–78. *Publications:* Discorsi sul Mondo Oscuro 1937, The Political Consequences of the Atomic Bomb 1959, Foreign Policy and Nuclear Weapons 1969, An Inquiry into Italian Foreign Policy 1970, Introduzione alla politica estera dell'era nucleare 1986, Professione: diplomatico (with others) 1987, Il Marchese d'Ormea 1988. *Address:* Via Francesco Ferrara No. 40, 00191 Rome, Italy. *Telephone:* (06) 3274776.

GAJDUSEK, Daniel Carleton, M.D.; American medical research scientist; b. 9 Sept. 1923, Yonkers, N.Y.; s. of Karl Gajdusek and Ottilia Dobroczki; forty-three adopted s. and d. from Melanesia and Micronesia; ed. Marine Biological Laboratory, Woods Hole, Mass., Univ. of Rochester, Harvard Medical School, Calif. Inst. of Tech.; served in Medical Corps; Babies Hosp. of Columbia Presbyterian Medical Center, N.Y. 1946–47; Cincinnati Children's Hosp. 1947–48; Medical Mission in Germany 1948; Sr. Fellow, Nat. Research Council, Calif. Inst. of Tech. 1948–49; Children's Hosp., Boston, Mass. 1949–51; Research Fellow, Harvard Univ. and Senior Fellow, Nat. Foundation for Infantile Paralysis 1949–52; Walter Reed Army Medical Center 1952–53; Institut Pasteur, Teheran, Iran and Univ. of Md. 1954–55; Visiting Investigator at Walter and Eliza Hall Inst., Australia

1955–57; Lab. Chief Nat. Inst. of Neurological Disorders and Stroke, Nat. Inst. of Health (NIH), Bethesda, Md. 1958–, Chief of Study of Child Growth and Devt. and Disease Patterns in Primitive Cultures, and of Laboratory of Slow, Latent and Temperate Virus Infections 1958–; Chief of Cen. Nervous System Studies Lab. 1971–; Hon. Curator Melanesian Ethnology, Peabody Museum, Salem, Mass.; Hon. Prof. of Virology Hupei Medical Coll., People's Repub. of China 1986, Beijing Medical Univ. 1987; mem. Soc. for Paediatric Research, American Paediatric Soc., N.A.S., American Acad. of Arts and Sciences, American Philosophical Soc., Deutsche Akademie der Naturforscher Leopoldina, American Acad. of Neurology; Hon. mem. Slovak Acad. of Science and Mexican, Colombia and Belgian Acads. of Medicine; Meade Johnson Award, American Acad. of Pediatrics 1961, Dautrebande Prize 1976, Cotzias Prize 1978; shared Nobel Prize in Physiology or Medicine for discoveries concerning new mechanisms for the origin and dissemination of infectious diseases 1976; Huxley Medal, Royal Anthropological Inst. of G.B. and Ireland 1988; several hon. degrees. *Publications:* Hemorrhagic Fevers and Mycotoxicoses 1959, Slow, Latent and Temperate Virus Infections 1965, Correspondence on the Discovery of Kuru 1976, Kuru (with Judith Farquhar) 1980, Research, Travel and Field Expedition Journals (40 vols.) 1954–85; and over 700 papers on microbiology, immunology, pediatrics, neurology and genetics. *Leisure interests:* linguistics, mountaineering. *Address:* Prospect Hill, 6552 Jefferson Pike, Frederick, Md. 21701 (Home); NINDS, National Institutes of Health, Bethesda, Md. 20892, U.S.A. (Office).

GAJEWSKI, Wacław, PROF. DR.; Polish geneticist (retd.); b. 28 Feb. 1911, Kraków; s. of Wacław and Wanda Gajewski; m. Anna Bogdani 1938; one s. one d.; ed. Warsaw Univ.; Doctor 1937–46, Docent 1946–54, Assoc. Prof. 1954–64, Prof. 1964–; Corresp. mem. Polish Acad. of Sciences 1958–69, mem. 1969–, mem. Presidium Polish Acad. of Sciences 1980–; Chair. Comm. of Planning, Budget and Financial Matters of Pres. of Polish Acad. of Sciences 1984–; Chair. Botanical Cttee. 1968–76, Dir. Inst. of Biochem. and Biophysics until 1976; Head, Dept. of Taxonomy and Geography of Plants, Dept. of Genetics, Dept. of Genetics Inst. Biochem. and Prof. Inst. of Botany, Warsaw Univ., now Prof. Emer.; Editor-in-Chief Acta Societatis Botanicorum Poloniae; mem. Editorial Bd. Molecular and General Genetics; Pres. Polish Soc. of Genetics; mem. Int. Asscn. for Plant Taxonomy, Int. Soc. for the Study of Evolution, American Soc. of Naturalists, American Genetics Asscn.; Knight's Cross, Order of Polonia Restituta 1957, Officer's Cross 1973, State Prize (1st Class) 1976. *Publications:* popular scientific books: Symbioza (Symbiosis) 1946, Tajemnica liścia (Secrets of the Leaf) 1949, Jak poznawano prawa dziedziczności (How they Learned the Laws of Heredity) 1958, W poszukiwaniu istoty dziedziczenia (In Search of the Essence of Heredity) 1966, Genetical Engineeering 1980, University Textbook of General and Molecular Genetics 5th edn. 1983, Molecular Biology (Co-author) 1986; numerous articles. *Leisure interests:* skiing, climbing, literature. *Address:* Aleje Ujazdowskie 4, 00-478 Warsaw, Poland.

GALADARI, Abdel-Wahab; United Arab Emirates business executive; b. 1938, Dubai; ed. American Univ., Beirut; Clerk with British Bank of the Middle East, then admin. post with Dubai Electrical Co.; founded re-export business with brothers Abdel-Rahim and Abdel-Latif 1960, real estate co. c. 1962; Dir. Nat. Bank of Dubai 1965–69; left family business 1976; formed Union Bank of the Middle East 1977, Chair. –1983; Chair. A. W. Galadari Holdings and over 20 associated cos.; Propr. Hyatt Regency and Galadari Galleria hotels; sponsored 1980 Dubai Grand Prix motor race. *Address:* A. W. Galadari Group of Companies, P.O. Box 22, Dubai, United Arab Emirates.

GAŁAJ, Dyzma, D.ECON. SCI.; Polish politician and scientist; b. 15 Jan. 1915, Mystkowice, Łowicz district; s. of Kazimierz and Maria Gałaj; m. 1944; one s. one d.; ed. Univ. of Łódź; Teacher 1937–39; combatant in Peasants' Battalions 1942–45; active mem. Rural Youth Union ("Wici") 1938–48; after liberation scientific worker, agric. acads. in Łódz, Olsztyn and Warsaw 1948–70; Editor-in-Chief Wieś Współczesna 1956–64 and Wieś i Rolnictwo; Head, Inst. for Research on Regions being industrialized, Polish Acad. of Sciences 1964–71; Dir. Inst. for Rural and Agric. Devt., Polish Acad. of Sciences, 1971–85, Prof. Emer. 1985–; mem. Peasants' Party 1948–; mem. Cen. Cttee. United Peasants' Party 1956–84, mem. Presidium, Cen. Cttee. 1969–76, Vice-Pres. Cen. Cttee. 1971–72; Deputy to Seym 1960–80, Marshal of Seym 1971–72; mem. State Council 1972–76; Order of Banner of Labour First and Second Class, Commdr. and Knight's Cross of Order Polonia Restituta, Cross of Valour, Partisans' Cross and other decorations. *Publications:* books on agriculture and peasants' political movt.; numerous articles in professional journals. *Address:* ul. Krasińskiego 7, 01-530 Warsaw, Poland (Home). *Telephone:* 39-18-72 (Home).

GALAMBOS, Robert, M.A., PH.D., M.D.; American professor of neurosciences; b. 20 April 1914, Lorain, Ohio; s. of John and Julia Galambos; m. 1st Jeannette Wright 1939, three d.; m. 2nd Carol Armstrong 1971; m. 3rd Phyllis Johnson 1977; ed. Harvard Univ. and Univ. of Rochester School of Medicine; Teaching Fellow, Physiology, Harvard Univ. 1939–41, Tutor in Biochem. 1941–42, 1947–48, Research Fellow, Psycho-Acoustic Lab. 1947–51; Instructor in Physiology, and Jr. Investigator, Office of Scientific Research and Devt., Harvard Univ. Medical School 1942–43; Intern, Emory Univ. Hospital 1946, Asst. Prof. Anatomy, Emory Univ. Medical School 1946–47; Chief, Dept. of Neurophysiology, Walter Reed Army Inst. of

Research 1951–62; Eugene Higgins Prof. of Psychology and Physiology, Yale Univ. 1962–68; Prof. Neurosciences, Univ. of Calif., San Diego 1968, Emer. 1981. *Publications:* The Avoidance of Obstacles by Flying Bats: Spallanzani's Ideas (1794) and later Theories, in Isis (34) 1942, Inhibition of Activity in Single Auditory Nerve Fibers by Acoustic Stimulation, in Journal of Neurophysiology (7) 1944, A Glia-neural Theory of Brain Function, in Proceedings of N.A.S. (47) 1961, An Electroencephalograph Study of Classical Conditioning (with Guy C. Sheatz), in American Journal of Physiology (203) 1962, Suppression of Auditory Nerve Activity by Stimulation of Efferent Fibers to Cochlea, in Journal of Neurophysiology (19) 1965, and 125 others. *Address:* Children's Hospital Research Center, 8001 Frost Street, San Diego, Calif. 92123 (Office); 8826 La Jolla Scenic Drive, La Jolla, Calif. 92037, U.S.A. (Home). *Telephone:* (619) 576-5846 (Office); (619) 453-0151 (Home).

GALANSHIN, Konstantin Ivanovich; Soviet politician; b. 12 March 1912, Gavrilov-Yam, Yauroslav Oblast; ed. Urals Industrial Inst.; Electrical Fitter 1930–37; Engineer, Central Relay Service of "Uralenergo" Power System, Deputy Chief, then Chief of Relay Service of "Permenergo" Power System, Dir. of Perm. Region Hydroelectric Power Station 1937–50; First Sec. Berezniki Town City Cttee. of CPSU 1950–54; Party Official, Sec. 1954–56, 2nd Sec. 1956–60; First Sec. Perm. Regional Cttee. of CPSU 1960–68; First Sec. Perm. Industrial Cttee. CPSU 1963–64; U.S.S.R. Minister of Pulp and Paper Industry 1968–80; Deputy to U.S.S.R. Supreme Soviet 1962–; mem. CPSU 1944–, mem. Cen. Cttee. 1961–; Order of Lenin (3 times), Order of Red Banner of Labour and other decorations. *Address:* c/o U.S.S.R. Ministry of Pulp and Paper Industry, 13/5 Bolshoi Kiselny Pereulok, Moscow, U.S.S.R.

GALBRAITH, J. Kenneth, PH.D.; American economist, diplomatist and writer; b. 15 Oct. 1908, Iona Station, Ont., Canada; m. Catherine Merriam Atwater 1937; three s.; ed. Toronto, California and Cambridge (England) Univs.; Research Fellow, Calif. Univ. 1931–34; Instructor, Harvard Univ. 1934–39, Lecturer 1948–49, Prof. of Econs. 1949–75, Emer. Prof. 1975–; Asst. Prof. Princeton Univ. 1939–42; Asst. then Deputy Admin. Office of Price Admin. 1941–43; mem. Bd. of Editors Fortune Magazine 1943–48; Amb. to India 1961–63; Dir. Office of Econ. Security Policy, State Dept. 1946; BBC Reith Lecturer 1966; mem. Nat. Inst. of Arts and Letters (Pres. Bd. Dirs. 1984–), American Econ. Asscn. (Pres. 1971), American Farm Econs. Asscn., Americans for Dem. Action (Chair. 1967–68); Fellow American Acad. of Arts and Sciences (Pres. Bd. Dirs. 1984–); mem. American Acad., Inst. of Arts and Letters 1984; Commdr. Légion d'honneur; numerous hon. degrees; Freedom Medal 1946. *Publications include:* Theory of Price Control, American Capitalism 1952, The Great Crash, Economics and the Art of Controversy 1955, The Affluent Society 1958, Journey to Poland and Yugoslavia 1959, The Liberal Hour 1960, Made to Last 1964, The New Industrial State 1967, The Triumph (novel) 1968, Ambassador's Journal 1969, Indian Painting (co-author) 1969, A Contemporary Guide to Economics, Peace and Laughter 1971, A China Passage 1973, Economics and the Public Purpose 1974, Money: Whence It Came, Where It Went 1975, The Age of Uncertainty 1976, The Galbraith Reader 1978, Almost Everyone's Guide to Economics 1979, The Nature of Mass Poverty 1979, Annals of an Abiding Liberal 1980, A Life in Our Times (autobiog.) 1981, The Anatomy of Power 1984, A View from the Stands: Of People, Military Power and the Arts 1986, Economics in Perspective: A Critical History 1987, History of Economics: The Past as the Present 1987, Capitalism, Communism and Coexistence (with S. Menshikov) 1988. *TV series:* The Age of Uncertainty (BBC) 1977. *Address:* 207 Littauer Center, Harvard University, Cambridge, Mass. 02138 (Office); 30 Francis Avenue, Cambridge, Mass. 02138, U.S.A. (Home).

GALBRAITH, Nicol Spence, C.B.E., M.B., F.R.C.P., F.F.C.M., D.P.H.; British medical epidemiologist; b. 17 March 1927, Southborough, Kent; s. of Dr. S. N. Galbraith and May Gledhill; m. Zina-Mary Flood 1952; three d.; ed. Rose Hill School, Tunbridge Wells, Tonbridge School, and Guy's Hosp. Medical School, Univ. of London; House Officer, Guy's and Lewisham Hosps. 1950–51; army medical officer 1952–53; Sr. House Officer, Brook Gen. Hosp. 1954–55; Medical Registrar, Lewisham Hosp. 1955–58; Epidemiologist, Research Lab. of Public Health Lab. Service 1958–63; Deputy Medical Officer of Health, later Medical Officer of Health, London Borough of Newham 1963–73; Area Medical Officer, City and East London Area Health Authority 1973–77; Sr. Lecturer in Community Medicine, London School of Hygiene and Tropical Medicine 1973–; Lecturer in Community Medicine, St. Bartholomew's Hosp. 1975–; Dir. Communicable Disease Surveillance Centre, Public Health Lab. Service 1977–88; Past Pres. Section of Epidemiology and Community Medicine, Royal Soc. of Medicine; Past Pres. Infection Control Nurses' Asscn.; Pres. British Soc. for the Study of Infection; Stewart Prize, British Medical Asscn. 1984. *Publications:* a book on infection, chapters in books and over 100 scientific papers on the epidemiology of communicable disease. *Leisure interests:* gardening, public health history. *Address:* Communicable Disease Surveillance Centre, 61 Colindale Avenue, London, NW9 5EQ, England.

GALE, Ernest Frederick, PH.D., SC.D., F.R.S.; British professor emer. of chemical microbiology; b. 15 July 1914, Luton, Beds.; s. of Ernest Francis Edward Gale and Nellie Annie Gale; m. Eiry Mair Jones 1937; one s.; ed. Weston-super-Mare Grammar School and St. John's Coll., Cambridge;

research in chemical microbiology, Cambridge 1937–83; Sr. Student, Royal Comm. for Exhbn. of 1851 1939–41; Beit Memorial Fellow 1941–43; mem. Staff, Medical Research Council 1943–60, Dir. M.R.C. Unit for Chemical Microbiology 1948–60; Prof. of Chemical Microbiology, Univ. of Cambridge 1960–81; Fellow, St. John's Coll., Cambridge 1940–48; Meetings Sec. Soc. for Gen. Microbiology 1952–58, Int. Rep. 1963–67, Pres. 1967–69, Hon. mem. 1978–; Herter Lecturer, Baltimore 1948; Hanna Lecturer, Western Reserve Univ. 1951; Harvey Lecturer, N.Y. 1955; Malcolm Lecturer, Syracuse Univ. 1967; Linacre Lecturer, St. John's Coll., Cambridge Univ. 1973; Squibb Lecturer, Nottingham Univ. 1986; Fellow of Royal Soc. 1953–; Leeuwenhoek Lecturer, Royal Soc. 1956. *Publications:* Chemical Activities of Bacteria 1947, Organisation and Synthesis in Bacteria 1959, Promotion and Prevention of Synthesis in Bacteria 1968, The Molecular Basis of Antibiotic Action 1972, 1981; scientific papers and reviews in journals of biochemistry and microbiology. *Leisure interest:* photography. *Address:* 7 Hazeldene, Sandhills Road, Salcombe, Devon, England. *Telephone:* Salcombe 3426 (Home).

GALEA, Louis, B.A., LL.D., M.P.; Maltese lawyer and politician; b. 2 Jan. 1948; m. Vincienne Zammit 1977; two d.; mem. Gen. Council and Exec. Cttee. Nationalist Party 1972–, Admin. Council 1975–; mem. Parl. 1976–; Minister for Social Policy 1987–. *Address:* Ministry for Social Policy, Valletta, Malta.

GALEYEV, Albert Abubakirovich, DR.PHY.MATH.SC.; Soviet physicist; b. 1940; ed. Univ. of Novosibirsk; worked at U.S.S.R. Acad. of Sciences Inst. of Nuclear Physics 1961–70; sr. researcher at Acad. of Sciences Inst. of High Temperatures 1970–73; mem. CPSU 1976; Head of Section at Acad. of Sciences Inst. of Space Research 1973–; Prof. 1980; Lenin Prize 1984. *Address:* U.S.S.R. Academy of Sciences, Moscow V-71, Leninsky Prospekt 14, U.S.S.R.

GALKIN, Dmitri Prokhovovich; Soviet politician; b. 1926; ed. Magnitorgorsk Mining Inst.; Deputy Sec. Party Cttee., chief engineer 1948–73; mem. CPSU 1949–; Dir. Magnitorgorsk Metallurgical Combine 1973–79; U.S.S.R. First Deputy Min. of Ferrous Metallurgy 1979–81, Minister of Ferrous Metallurgy for Ukranian S.S.R. 1981–; mem. CPSU Cen. Cttee. 1976–81, CPSU Cen. Auditing Comm. 1981–; Deputy to U.S.S.R. Supreme Soviet. Hero of Socialist Labour 1976; State Prize 1974, 1982. *Address:* Communist Party of Soviet Union, Kiev, Ukranian S.S.R., U.S.S.R.

GALL, Joseph Grafton, PH.D.; American professor of biology; b. 14 April 1928, Washington, D.C.; s. of late John C. and Elsie (Rosenberger) Gall; m. 1st Dolores M. Hogge 1955, one s. one d.; m. 2nd Diane M. Dwyer 1982; ed. Yale Univ.; Instructor, Asst. Prof., Assoc. Prof., Prof., Dept. of Zoology, Univ. of Minnesota 1952–64; Prof. of Biology and Molecular Biophysics and Biochem., Yale Univ. 1964–83; mem. staff Dept. of Embryology, Carnegie Inst. 1983–; mem. Cell Biology Study Section, Nat. Insts. of Health 1963–67, Chair. 1972–74; Pres. American Soc. for Cell Biology 1968, Soc. for Developmental Biology 1984–85; mem. Bd. of Scientific Counsellors, Nat. Inst. of Child Health and Human Devt., N.I.H. 1986–; mem. Bd. of Scientific Advisers, Jane Coffin Childs Memorial Fund for Medical Research 1986–; Visiting Prof. St. Andrews Univ. 1960, 1968, Univ. of Leicester 1971; Visiting Scientist Max Planck Inst., Tübingen 1960; mem. N.A.S., A.A.A.S., American Acad. of Arts and Sciences; E. B. Wilson Medal, American Soc. for Cell Biology 1983, Wilbur Cross Medal of Yale Univ. 1988. *Publications:* scientific articles on chromosome structure, nucleic acid biochemistry, cell fine structure, organelles of the cell. *Leisure interest:* collecting books on the history of biology. *Address:* Department of Embryology, Carnegie Institution, 115 West University Parkway, Baltimore, Md. 21210 (Office); 107 Bellemore Road, Baltimore, Md. 21210, U.S.A. (Home).

GALLAGHER, Francis George Kenna, C.M.G., LL.B.; British diplomatist (retd.); b. 25 May 1917, London; s. of George and Joanna Gallagher; ed. London Univ.; entered civil service 1935; active service R.A.F. 1941–45; entered diplomatic service 1945; Vice-Consul, Marseilles 1948; Second-Sec., Paris 1948; First Sec., Western Orgs. Dept., Foreign Office 1950; Head of Chancery, Damascus 1953; Asst. Head, Northern Dept. 1956, Mutual Aid Dept. 1959; Head, European Econ. Orgs. Dept. 1960; Commercial Counsellor, Berne 1963; Head, Western Econ. Dept., C.R.O. 1965; Asst. Under-Sec. of State, Foreign Office 1968; Amb., Head of Del. to OECD 1971–77, Chair. Exec. Cttee. 1976–77; Consultant to CBI on Int. Trade Policy 1978–80. *Leisure interests:* music, chess. *Address:* The Old Courthouse, Kirkwhelpington, Northumberland, NE19 2RS, England. *Telephone:* Otterburn 40373.

GALLAIS, Fernand Georges, DR. ÈS SC., DR. EN PHARMACIE; French professor of chemistry; b. 3 May 1908, Paris; m. Françoise Hine 1941; one s. two d.; ed. Faculté des Sciences, Sorbonne, Faculté de Pharmacie, Paris; research asst. 1934; lecturer Science Faculty, Univ. of Toulouse 1943–50, Prof. 1950; Dir. Ecole Nat. Supérieure de Chimie 1950–65; Vice-Dir. C.N.R.S. 1965–66, Scientific Dir. 1967–73; Prof. Toulouse Univ., Dir. Coordination Chemistry Lab. C.N.R.S. 1973–78; Corresp. mem. Acad. of Science 1966, mem. 1973–; Officier Légion d'Honneur, Commdr. Palmes Académique. *Publications:* more than 150 scientific papers in chemistry, textbooks on gen. and inorganic chemistry 1958–62. *Leisure interests:* yachting, skiing. *Address:* L.A.A.S.-C.N.R.S., 7 avenue du Colonel Roche,

31400 Toulouse (Office); 2 rue de l'Aubisque, 31500 Toulouse, France (Home). *Telephone:* 61.33.62.00 (Office); 61.20.52.63 (Home).

GALLEGO MORELL, Antonio, D.PHIL.; Spanish university rector (retd.); b. 10 Jan. 1923, Granada; s. of Antonio and Eloisa Gallego Morell; m. Matilde Roca Lozada 1952; four c.; ed. Univs. of Granada and Madrid; Prof. of Spanish Literature, Univ. of Granada 1952, Dean, Faculty of Arts 1968–72, Rector 1976–84; Rector, Univ. of Málaga 1972–75; Premio Rivadeneyra, Spanish Acad. 1953; Acad. corresp. Acad. Española, de la Historia y de Bellas Artes de S. Fernando; Premio Nacional de Literatura 1973. *Leisure interest:* travel. *Address:* Plaza Gracia 3-1°, Granada, Spain. *Telephone:* 26 28 26.

GALLEY, Robert; French engineer and politician; b. 11 Jan. 1921, Paris; s. of Léon and André (neé Habrial) Galley; m. Jeanne Leclerc de Hautecloque 1960; two s.; ed. Lycée Louis-le-Grand, Paris, Lycée Hoche, Versailles, Ecole centrale des arts et manufactures and Ecole Nat. Supérieure du pétrole et des moteurs; Compagnie Chérifienne des Pétroles 1950–54; in Commissariat à l'Energie atomique 1955–66; Pres. of Perm. Comm. for Electronics, Dept. of Planning 1966–; mem. Admin. Council de l'Institut de recherche d'informatique et d'automatique (Iria) 1967–; mem. Nat. Ass. 1968–78, 1981–, Senator 1980–81; Minister of Supply and Housing May–July 1968, of Scientific Research and Atomic Energy 1968–69, of Posts 1969–72, of Transport 1972–73, of the Armed Forces 1973–74, of Supply 1974–76, of Co-operation 1976–81, also of Defence 1980–81; Mayor of Troyes 1972–; Treasurer RPR 1984–; Commdr., Légion d'honneur, Compagnon, Ordre de la Libération, Croix de guerre (1939–45). *Address:* Assemblée nationale, 75555 Paris; 18 boulevard Victor Hugo, 10000 Troyes, France.

GALLIKER, Franz, DR.IUR.; Swiss banker; b. 29 May 1926, Basle; m. Susanne Graber 1958; three s.; ed. Basle Univ.; legal counsellor, Swiss Bank Corpn., Basle and London 1954–61, Sub-Man., Basle 1961–65, Deputy Man., Basle 1965–70, Man., Basle 1970–72, Cen. Man. 1972–75, Gen. Man. 1975–84, Chair. 1984–; mem. Bd. of Dirs. Swiss Aluminium Ltd., BBC Brown, Boveri and Co. Ltd., Ciba-Geigy Ltd., Holzstoff Holding Inc., Sulzer Bros. Ltd. *Leisure interests:* tennis, skiing, music, fine arts. *Address:* Swiss Bank Corporation, Aeschenplatz 6, CH-4002, Basle, Switzerland. *Telephone:* (061) 20 20 20.

GALLIMARD, Claude; French publisher; b. 10 Jan. 1914, Paris; s. of Gaston and Yvonne (Redelsperger) Gallimard; m. Simone Cornu 1939; four c.; ed. Faculté de Droit, Paris.; joined Editions Gallimard 1937, Asst. Dir.-Gen. 1966–76, Pres., Dir.-Gen. 1976–. *Address:* Editions Gallimard, 5 rue Sébastien-Bottin, 75007 Paris (Office); 17 rue de l'Université, 75007 Paris, France (Home).

GALLINER, Peter; British publisher; b. 19 Sept. 1920, Berlin, Germany; s. of Dr. Moritz Galliner and Hedwig Isaac; m. Edith Marguerite Goldschmidt 1948; one d.; ed. in Berlin and London.; worked for Reuters, London 1942–45; Foreign Man. Financial Times, London 1945–61; Chair. of Bd. and Man. Dir. Ullstein Publishing Group, Berlin 1961–64; Vice-Chair. and Man. Dir. British Printing Corpn. Publishing Group, London 1967–70; Int. Publishing Consultant 1965–67, 1970–75; Chair. Peter Galliner Assocs. 1970–; Dir. Int. Press. Inst. 1975–; Fed. Cross of Merit, First Class (Fed. Repub. of Germany), Ecomienda, Orden de Isabel la Cathólica (Spain). *Leisure interests:* reading, music. *Address:* 27 Walsingham, St. John's Wood Park, London, NW8 6RH, England; Untere Zäune 15, 8001 Zürich, Switzerland. *Telephone:* 01-722 5502 (London).

GALLO, Robert, M.D.; American biomedical scientist; b. 23 March 1937, Waterbury, Conn.; m. Mary J. Hayes 1961; two s.; ed. Providence Coll., Jefferson Medical Univ., Philadelphia and Yale Univ.; Intern and Resident in Medicine, Univ. of Chicago 1963–65; Clinical Assoc. Nat. Cancer Inst. Bethesda, Md. 1965–68, Sr. Investigator 1968–69, Head, Section on Cellular Control Mechanisms 1969–72, Chief, Lab. of Tumor Cell Biology, Div. of Cancer Etiology 1972–; mem. Bd. of Govs. Franco American AIDS Foundation, World AIDS Foundation 1987; Lasker Award for Basic Biomedical Research 1982; Gen. Motors Cancer Research Award 1984; Armand Hammer Cancer Research Award 1985; Lasker Award for Clinical Research 1986, Gairdner Foundation Award and other awards for cancer research; 9 hon. degrees. *Publications:* over 700 scientific publs. *Leisure interests:* swimming, reading historical novels, tennis, theatre. *Address:* Laboratory of Tumor Cell Biology, National Cancer Institute, 9000 Rockville Pike, Bethesda, Md., U.S.A.

GALMOT, Yves; French judge; b. 5 Jan. 1931, Paris; s. of Jean-Jacques Galmot and Marie Germaine Lengauer; m. Katrine-Marie Nicholson 1958; two s.; ed. Lycée Louis le Grand, Paris, Inst. d'Etudes Politiques de Paris, Ecole Nat. d'Administration; auditor, Council of State 1956; Tech. Adviser, Office of High Commr. for Youth and Sport 1958; Maitre des Requêtes, Council of State 1962; Govt. Commr. Legal Section, Council of State 1964–68; Sec.-Gen. Entreprise Minière et Chimique 1970–74; Councillor of State 1981; Judge, Court of Justice of European Communities 1982–88. *Leisure interest:* golf.

GALPIN, Rodney D., C.B.I.M.; British banker and business executive; b. 5 Feb. 1932; s. of Sir Albert Galpin, C.V.O.; m. Sylvia Craven 1956; one s. one d.; ed. Haileybury and Imperial Service Coll.; joined Bank of England 1952; Sec. to Gov. 1962–66, Deputy Prin. Discount Office 1970–74, Deputy

Chief Cashier Banking and Money Markets Supervision 1974–78, Chief Establishments 1978–80, Chief Corp. Services 1980–82, Assoc. Dir. 1982–84, Dir. 1984–88; Chair. and Group C.E.O. Standard Chartered PLC 1988–; Gov. and Council mem. Haileybury 1973–; mem. Council Scout Asscn. 1972–, mem. Council Foundation for Man. Educ. 1984–86; Freeman City of London Award 1981; Order of St. John. *Leisure interests:* tennis, gardening, music. *Address:* Standard Chartered PLC, 38 Bishopsgate, London, EC2N 4DE, England. *Telephone:* 01-280 7001.

GALSWORTHY, Sir John, K.C.V.O., C.M.G.; British diplomatist (retd.); b. 19 June 1919, London; s. of the late Capt. Arthur Galsworthy and Violet Gertrude (Harrison) Galsworthy; m. Jennifer Ruth Johnstone 1942; one s. three d.; ed. Emanuel School, and Corpus Christi Coll., Cambridge.; served in H.M. Forces 1939–41; Foreign Office 1941–46; Third Sec., Madrid 1946; Second Sec., Vienna 1949; First Sec., Athens 1951; Foreign Office 1954; Bangkok 1958; Counsellor, British Del. to EEC, 1962; Econ. Counsellor, Bonn 1964–67, Paris 1967–70; Minister (European Economic Affairs), Paris 1970–71; Amb. to Mexico 1972–77; Business Consultant 1978–82; U.K. Observer to El Salvador elections March 1982. *Address:* Lanzeague, St. Just in Roseland, Truro, Cornwall, England.

GALTIERI, Lieut.-Gen. Leopoldo Fortunato; Argentine army officer and politician; b. 15 July 1926, Caseros (Prov. of Buenos Aires); m. Lucia Noemi Gentili 1949; one s. two d.; ed. Buenos Aires, Nat. Mil. Coll.; Sub-Lieut., Engineers 1945, Lieut. 1947, First Lieut. 1949, Capt. 1952; joined Batallón 4 de Zapadores (Sappers), 1952–54; became Major 1957, Infantry Div. Commdr. 1962, Lieut.-Col. 1967; Prof. at Escuela Superior de Guerra 1962; Sub.-Dir. Engineers' Training School 1964–67; promoted Col. 1967, Brig.-Gen. commanding 9th Infantry Brigade 1972–73, 7th Brigade 1974–75; Major-Gen. 1975; Deputy Chief of Staff 1975; Commdr. 2nd Army Corps 1976, 1st Army Corps Jan.–Dec. 1979; Lieut.-Gen. Dec. 1979–, C.-in-C. of the Army 1979–82; also mem. ruling military junta 1979–82; Pres. of Argentina 1981–82; seized Falkland Is. April 1982; under arrest 1983–court martialled for conduct during Falklands War (on trial for violations of human rights 1983, acquitted Dec. 1985); sentenced to 12 years in prison for negligence for starting and losing the Falklands conflict 1986; numerous military decorations. *Address:* Magdalena Military Base, Buenos Aires, Argentina.

GALVAO FILHO, Orlando, M.A.; Brazilian business executive; b. 1940; m.; two c.; ed. Navy Acad. and Catholic Univ. of Rio de Janeiro; fmr. lecturer in Industrial Econs. and Org.; joined Petrobrás 1974, Head Finance Dept. 1981–88, C.E.O. Jan. 1989–; mem. Brazilian Asscn. of Professional Economists. *Address:* Petrobrás, Av. Republica do Chile 65, 20.035 Rio de Janeiro, Brazil.

GALVÊAS, Ernane; Brazilian economist and banker; b. 1 Oct. 1922, Cachoeiro do Itapemirim; s. of José Galvêas and Maria de Oliveira; m. Odaléa dos Santos 1948; one s. one d.; ed. Coll. of Economics and Finance, Rio de Janeiro Univ., Centro de Estudios Monetarios Latino-Americanos, Mexico and Yale Univ.; fmrly. Prof. of Banking and Finance, Coll. of Econs. and Finance, Rio de Janeiro, subsequently Prof. of Int. Trade, of Monetary Policy and of Int. Monetary Policy; Assoc. Chief, Econs. Dept., Supervisory Council for Finance and Credit (SUMOC) 1953–61; Econ. Consultant to Minister of Finance 1961–63; Financial Dir. Merchant Marine Comm. 1963–65; Dir. Foreign Trade Dept., Banco do Brasil 1966–68; Pres. Banco Central do Brasil 1968–74, 1979; Minister of Finance 1980–84; Exec. Vice-Pres. Aracruz Celulose S.A. 1974–79. *Publications:* Brazil—Frontier of Development 1974, Development and Inflation 1976, Brazil—Open or Closed Economy? 1978, Apprentice of Entrepreneur 1983, Financial System and Capital Market 1985, The Saga of the Crisis 1985, The Oil Crisis 1985; numerous articles on economic and financial topics. *Address:* Avenida Atlântica, 2492 Apt. 301, Rio de Janeiro, RJ Brazil.

GALVIN, Gen. John Rogers, M.A.; American army officer; b. 13 May 1929, Wakefield, Mass.; s. of John James Galvin and Mary Josephine Logan; m. Virginia Lee Brennan 1961; four d.; ed. U.S. Military Acad., Columbia Univ., Univ. of Pennsylvania, Command and Gen. Staff Coll. and Fletcher School of Law and Diplomacy; commissioned 2nd Lieut. U.S. Army 1954; Military Asst. and ADC to Sec. of U.S. Army 1967–69; Commdr. 1st Bn. 8th Cavalry 1969–70; Mil. Asst. to Supreme Allied Command in Europe (SACEUR) 1974–75; Commdr. Div. Support Command 3rd Infantry Div. 1975–77, Chief of Staff 1977–78; Commanding Gen. 24th Infantry Div. 1981–83; VII (U.S.) Corps 1983–85; Commdr.-in-Chief U.S. Southern Command 1985–87; Supreme Allied Cmmdr. Europe and C.-in-C. U.S. European Command 1987–; Defense Distinguished Service Medal, Silver Star, Legion of Merit, Distinguished Flying Cross, Air Medal with 'V', Soldier's Medal. *Publications:* The Minute Men 1967, Air Assault 1969, Three Men of Boston 1974. *Leisure interests:* reading, writing and jogging. *Address:* SHAPE, 1110 Brussels, Belgium.

GALVIN, Robert W.; American executive; b. 9 Oct. 1922, Marshfield, Wis.; m. Mary Barnes 1944; two s. two d.; ed. Univs. of Notre Dame and Chicago; Motorola, Inc. Chicago 1940–, Pres. 1956–, Chair. of Bd. 1964–, C.E.O. 1984–86; Dir. Harris Trust and Savings Bank, Chicago; Trustee Illinois Inst. of Tech.; Fellow, Univ. of Notre Dame; Dir. Junior Achievement of Chicago; mem. Pres.'s Comm. on Int. Trade and Investment; Electronic Industries Asscn. Medal of Honour 1970. *Leisure interests:*

skiing, water-skiing, tennis, horse-riding. *Address:* 1303 East Algonquin Road, Schaumburg, Ill. 60196, U.S.A. (Office).

GALWAY, James, O.B.E., F.R.C.M.; British flautist; b. 8 Dec. 1939, Belfast; s. of James and Ethel Stewart (née Clarke) Galway; m. 1st 1965; one s.; m. 2nd 1972; one s. two twin d.; m. 3rd Jeanne Cinnante 1984; ed. Mountcollyer Secondary School, Royal Coll. of Music, Guildhall School of Music, Conservatoire National Supérieur de Musique, Paris; first post in Wind Band of Royal Shakespeare Theatre, Stratford-on-Avon; later worked with Sadler's Wells Orchestra, Royal Opera House Orchestra, BBC Symphony Orchestra; Prin. Flute, London Symphony Orchestra and Royal Philharmonic Orchestra; Prin. Solo Flute, Berlin Philharmonic Orchestra 1969–75; int. soloist 1975–; soloist/conductor 1984–; has made numerous recordings; (awarded Grand Prix du Disque 1976); Hon. M.A. (Open Univ.) 1979, Hon. D.Mus. (Queen's Univ., Belfast) 1979, Hon. D.Mus. (New England Conservatory of Music) 1980; Officier Arts et des Lettres 1987. *Publications:* James Galway: An Autobiography 1978, Flute (Menuhin Music Guide) 1982, James Galway's Music in Time 1983. *Leisure interests:* music, walking, swimming, films, theatre, TV, computing, chess, backgammon, talking to people. *Address:* c/o London Artists, 73 Baker Street, London, W1M 1AH, England.

GAMASSI, Gen. Mohamed Abdul Ghani al–; Egyptian army officer and government official; b. 9 Sept. 1921, el-Batanoun, Menoufia Governorate; ed. Mil. Acad., Staff Coll., Nasser Higher Mil. Acad.; Asst. Dir. of Mobilization Dept. 1954–55; Commdr. 5th Reconnaissance Regt. 1955–57; Staff Officer, Armoured Corps 1957–59; Commdr. 2nd Armoured Brigade 1959–61; Commdr. Armour School 1961–66; Chief, Army Operational Branch 1966–67; Chief of Staff, Eastern Mil. Zone 1967–68; Deputy Dir. Reconnaissance and Intelligence Dept. 1968–70; Commdr. Operational Group, Syrian Front 1970–71; Chief, Armed Forces Training Dept. 1971–72; Chief of Operations Dept. and Deputy Chief of Staff of Armed Forces 1972–73; Chief of Staff of Armed Forces 1973–74; Minister of War and C.-in-C. of Armed Forces 1974–78, also a Deputy Prime Minister 1975–78; Mil. Adviser to Pres. 1978; Order of Liberation 1952, Memorial Order of Founding of U.A.R. 1958, Star of Honour 1973, Star of Honour (PLO) 1974, Kt. Order of Mil. Honour (Syria) 1974, Order of Courage (Libya) 1974, Order of the Two Niles, First Class (Sudan) 1974, Order of King Abdel Aziz, First Class (Saudi Arabia) 1974, Order of Homayoun, First Class (Iran) 1975; numerous ribbons and medals. *Address:* Office of the President, Abdeen, Cairo, Egypt.

GAMBIER, Dominique, D.ÉS SC.ECON.; French university teacher; b. 14 Aug. 1947, Rouen; s. of Michel and Yvette Morel; m. Hélène Chatel 1974; two d.; ed. Lycée Corneille, Rouen and Ecole Centrale de Paris; Asst. Univ. of Rouen 1972–81; Prof. Ecole Centrale de Paris 1981–83; special assignment, Commissariat General au Plan 1983–84; Maître de conferences, and Dir. Inst. of Research and Documentation in Social Sciences (I.R.E.D.), Univ. of Rouen 1984–87; expert adviser, EEC, Brussels 1980–81; scientific adviser, Observatoire français des conjonctures économiques (OFCE) 1981–83; Regional Councillor, Haute-Normandie; Pres. Univ. of Rouen 1987–88; Deputy for Seine Maritime 1988–. *Publications:* Analyse conjoncturelle du chômage, Théorie de la politique économique en situation d'incertitude 1980, Le marché du travail 1982, L'emploi en France 1988; numerous articles on economy of work and labour etc. *Leisure interests:* football, tennis, skiing. *Address:* Saint Georges sur Fontaine, 76690 Cleres, France (Home). *Telephone:* 35-34-74-59 (Home).

GAMBLING, William Alexander, PH.D., D.SC., F.ENG., F.R.S.; British professor of optical communication, industrial consultant and company director; b. 11 Oct. 1926, Port Talbot, Glamorgan; s. of George Alexander and Muriel Clara Gambling; m. Margaret Pooley 1952; one s. two d.; ed. Univs. of Bristol and Liverpool; Lecturer in Electric Power Eng., Univ. of Liverpool 1950–55; Fellow, Nat. Research Council, Univ. of B.C. 1955–57; Lecturer, Sr. Lecturer and Reader, Univ. of Southampton 1957–64, Prof. of Electronics 1964–80, Dean of Eng. and Applied Science 1972–75, Head of Dept. 1974–79, British Telecom Prof. of Optical Communication 1980–; Visiting Prof., Univ. of Colo. 1966–67, Bhabha Atomic Research Centre, India 1970, Osaka Univ., Japan 1977; Hon. Prof. Huazhong Univ. of Science and Tech., Wuhan, 1986–, Beijing Inst. of Posts and Telecommunications, Hon. Dir. Beijing Optical Fibres Lab., People's Repub. of China 1987–; Pres. I.E.R.E. 1977–78; Chair. Comm.D, Int. Union of Radio Science 1981–84, Eng. Council 1983–88; mem. Bd., Council of Eng. Insts. 1974–79, Electronics Research Council 1977–80, Nat. Electronics Council 1977–78 and 1984–; mem. Advisory Bd. Optical and Quantum Electronics and Material Letters, British Nat. Cttee. for Radio Science 1978–87, Educational Advisory Council, IBA 1980–82; Hon. Fellow I.E.R.E., I.E.E.; Selby Fellow, Australian Acad. of Science 1982; Foreign mem. Polish Acad. of Sciences 1985; mem. Eng. Industries Training Bd. 1985–88; numerous awards and prizes. *Publications:* papers on electronics and optical fibre communications. *Address:* Department of Electronics and Computer Science, University of Southampton, SO9 5NH, Hants., England.

GAMBON, Michael John; British actor; b. 19 Oct. 1940, Dublin; s. of Edward Gambon and Mary Gambon; m. Anne Miller 1962; one s.; ed. St. Aloysius School for Boys, London; fmr. Mechanical Engineer; first stage appearance with Edwards/Máclimmoir Co., Dublin 1962; Nat. Theatre, Old

Vic 1963–67; Birmingham Repertory and other provincial theatres 1967–69, title roles including Othello, Macbeth, Coriolanus; R.S.C. Aldwych 1970–71; The Norman Conquests 1974, Otherwise Engaged 1976, Just Between Ourselves 1977, Alice's Boys 1978; with Nat. Theatre 1980, appearing in Galileo (London Theatre Critics' Award for Best Actor), Betrayal, Tales from Hollywood; with R.S.C., Stratford and London 1982–83, title roles in King Lear, Antony and Cleopatra, Old Times 1985, A Chorus of Disapproval, Nat. Theatre 1985 (Olivier Award for Best Comedy Performance), A Small Family Business 1987, Uncle Vanya 1988, Mountain Language 1988. *TV:* numerous appearances including: Ghosts, Oscar Wilde, The Holy Experiment, Absurd Person Singular, The Borderers, The Singing Detective. *Films:* The Beast Must Die 1975, Turtle Diary 1985, Paris by Night 1988, The Cook, the thief, his wife and her lover, Dry White Season. *Leisure interests:* flying, gun collecting, clock making. *Address:* 126 Kennington Park Road, London, SE11 4DJ, England.

GAMBRELL, David Henry; American lawyer and politician; b. 20 Dec. 1929, Atlanta, Ga.; s. of E. Smythe Gambrell and Kathleen Hagood; m. Luck Flanders; one s. three d.; ed. Davidson Coll. and Harvard Law School; Practising Lawyer, Atlanta 1952–, Partner Gambrell, Clarke, Anderson and Stolz 1963–; Chair. Georgia Democratic Party 1970–71; Senator from Georgia 1971–73; Pres. Atlanta Bar Asscn. 1965, Georgia Bar Asscn. 1967; Democrat. *Address:* 3600 First Atlanta Tower, Atlanta, Ga. 30383 (Office); 3820 Castlegate Drive, N.W., Atlanta, Ga. 30327, U.S.A. (Home).

GAMEDZE, Dr. A. B., M.A.; Swazi teacher, theologian and diplomatist; b. 3 April 1921, Shiselweni District; s. of Rev. John Mbulawa Gamedze and Sarah Mavosho (née Shongwe) Gamedze; m.; three s. three d.; ed. at Mhlosheni and at Matsapa, Swaziland, at Umphumulo Inst., Natal, Adams Coll., Natal, and Wheaton Coll., Ill., U.S.A.; Head Teacher, Jerusalem School 1942, transferred to Franson Christian High School 1943; Head teacher, Makhonza School 1946–47; started first rural market for Jerusalem and New Haven Farmers Assen.; at Wheaton Coll., Ill., studying educ., Christian educ. and theology 1947–51; Lecturer, Evangelical Teacher Training Coll., Natal 1951–56; Founder and Ed. Africa's Hope 1955–61; Pres. African Teachers' Christian Fellowship 1956; ordained Minister of Evangelical Church 1956; assisted Organizing Insp. of Religious Educ. in Secondary Schools, Transvaal 1958; Lecturer in Divinity and Educ. and Chaplain of Univ. of Fort Hare 1960–61; joined staff of Franson Christian High School 1962; Supt. (Grantee) of all Evangelical Church Schools 1962–65; Vice.-Pres. Evangelical Church; Vice-Pres. Swaziland Conf. of Churches 1964, Pres. 1979–80; Sr. Liaison Officer, Swaziland 1965–67; mem. Senate 1967; Minister of Educ., Swaziland 1967–71; Ed. Imbokodvo Bulletin 1969–70; High Commr. in U.K., concurrently Amb. to France, Belgium and Fed. Repub. Germany 1971–72; Sec. to Swazi Nation 1973–74, then Private Sec. to King Sobhuza II, then Chief of Protocol, Dept. of Foreign Affairs; Ed. Imbokodvo Bulletin 1969–70; Pres. Assen. of Evangelicals 1975–80; Chair. Swaziland Bible Soc. 1980–81; Dir. of Church Extension in northern Swaziland; dir. of various cos.; Hon. LL.D. (Wheaton Coll., U.S.A.) 1968. *Leisure interests:* writing, walking, Evangelical Church in Swaziland, indoor games. *Address:* P.O. Box 868, Mbabane, Swaziland. *Telephone:* 2661 (Office); 2427 (Home).

GAMKRELIDZE, Thomas V.; Soviet linguist; b. 23 Oct. 1929, Kutaisi, Georgia; s. of Valerian and Olimpiada Gamkrelidze; m. Nino Djavakhishvili 1968; one s. one d.; ed. Tbilisi Univ.; post-graduate work 1952–55; Lecturer, Georgian S.S.R. Acad. of Sciences Inst. of Linguistics 1956–60; Head of Dept. 1960–73, Dir., The Oriental Inst. 1973–; Head of Dept. Tbilisi State Univ. 1966–; Deputy to U.S.S.R. Supreme Soviet 1984–; main work in area of theoretical linguistics, Kartvelian Semitic and Indo-European linguistics and semiology; elected to Congress of People's Deputies of the U.S.S.R. 1989; mem. CPSU 1981–; mem. U.S.S.R. Acad. of Sciences 1984; Foreign Hon. mem. American Acad. of Arts and Sciences; Corresp. F.B.A.; mem. Austrian Acad. of Sciences; Foreign mem. Sächsische Akad. der Wissenschaften, Hon. mem. Indogermanische Gesellschaft, Linguistic Soc. of America, Societas Linguistica Europaea (Pres. 1986). *Leisure interests:* music, tennis. *Address:* The Oriental Institute, Georgian Academy of Sciences, Acad. Tsereteli Street 3, 380062 Tbilisi, Georgia U.S.S.R. *Telephone:* 23 38 85.

GAMMELGAARD, Lars P.; Danish politician; b. 9 Feb. 1945, Aarhus; s. of Hans Peter Gammelgaard; ed. Aarhus Univ.; secondary school teacher 1973–79; mem. Folketing (Parl.) 1979–; Policy Spokesman, Conservative Parl. Group 1983–86; Minister of Fisheries 1986–, also of Nordic Affairs 1987–88. *Address:* Ministry of Fisheries, Stormgade 2, 1470, Copenhagen K, Denmark. *Telephone:* (01) 92-65-00.

GAMZATOV, Rasul Gamzatovich; Soviet poet and politician; b. 8 Sept. 1923, Tsadasa, Daghestan, A.S.S.R.; ed. Moscow A. M. Gorky Literary Inst.; National poet of Daghestan; mem. CPSU 1944–; worked on newspaper Bolshevik Gor 1941–51; radio ed. of programmes in Avar language, Dagestan; mem. staff, Maxim Gorky Inst., Moscow 1945–50; Chair. of Bd. of Union of Daghestan Writers 1951–; Deputy of Supreme Soviet of U.S.S.R. 1962–, mem. Presidium; mem. Soviet Cttee. of solidarity with countries of Asia and Africa; State Prize 1952, Stalin Prize, Lenin Prize 1963, Orders of Lenin 1960, 1983, of Red Banner of Labour (twice), Hero of Socialist Labour, State Prize 1980, etc. *Publications:* Hot Love and Burning Hate 1943, My Country 1947, Our Mountains 1947, The Homeland of a Miner 1950, Verse 1950, Tales of my Elder Brother 1952, Poems 1954, Spring in Dagestan 1955, My Heart is in the Mountains 1959, Stars on High 1962, Mountains and Valleys 1963, Zarema 1963, And Star Speaks with Star 1964, Selected Lyrics 1965, Mutlaka 1966, Sick Teeth (poetry) 1967, My Daghestan 1968, The Last Price 1978 (Firdausi Prize), Collected Works (3 vols.) 1968-69, Look after two Mothers. *Address:* Daghestan A.S.S.R. Union of Writers, Makkhachkala, U.S.S.R.

GAN ZHIJIAN; Chinese government official; Vice-Minister for State Planning 1985-88, for Construction May 1988-. *Address:* Baiwahzhuang Street, Beijing, People's Republic of China.

GANAO, David-Charles; Congolese politician; b. 20 July 1928, Djambala; m. Shirley O'Hayes 1964; four s.; ed. Teachers Training Coll.; teacher, then Headmaster; Diplomatic training in France 1960; Head of Political Affairs, Congolese Foreign Ministry 1960-63; Minister of Foreign Affairs 1963-68, of Co-operation, Tourism and Civil Aviation 1966-68; Amb. and Perm. Rep. to the UN, Geneva 1969-73; Amb. to Switzerland 1970-73; Minister of Foreign Affairs 1973-75; Deputy Exec. Sec., UN Econ. Comm. for Africa 1977; Dir. Div. of Conf. Services, Public Information and External Relations, UNIDO 1979-. *Address:* United Nations Industrial Development Organization, P.O. Box 300, A-1400 Vienna, Austria.

GANDAR, Hon. Leslie Walter; J.P., D.SC., F.INST.P.; New Zealand sheep farmer, politician and diplomatist; b. 26 Jan. 1919, Wellington; s. of Max Gandar; m. Monica Justine Smith 1944; four s. two d.; ed. Wellington Coll. and Victoria Univ., Wellington; war service in R.N.Z.A.F. 1940-44; sheep farming 1945-; mem. Pohangina Co. Council 1952-69, Chair. 1959-69; mem. M'tu Catchment Bd. 1956-68; mem. Massey Univ. Council 1963-75, Chancellor 1970-75; M.P. 1966-78; Minister of Energy and Science 1972, Educ., Science and Tech. 1975-78; High Commr. to U.K. 1979-82; Chair. New Zealand Social Advisory Council 1982-86, Social Science Research Council 1983-, Nat. Library 1979, Capital Discovery Place (Children's Museum); Pres. Friends of Turnbull Library; Queen Elizabeth II Nat. Trust 1983-87; Fellow, N.Z. Inst. of Agric. Science. *Leisure interests:* wood-carving, reading. *Address:* 34 Palliser Road, Roseneath, Wellington, New Zealand.

GANDHI, Maneka Anand; Indian politician and fmr. beauty queen; b. 1956, Punjab, India; d. of the late Col. T. S. Anand and of Amteshwar Anand; m. Sanjay Gandhi 1974 (died 1980); one s.; ed. Jawaharlal Univ., New Delhi; fmr. adviser to Sanjay Gandhi; editor of Surya (Sun) newspaper 1977-80; attended Lucknow Convention 1982; founder and leader of Sanjay Vichar Manch (Sanjay Ideas Org.) 1982; founder and leader of political party Rashtriya Sanjay Manch (merged with Janata Party April 1988) 1983; Pres. road haulage firm Rajhani Traders. *Publication:* Sanjay Gandhi 1980. *Leisure interests:* wildlife, books, hospitals for animals and social service. *Address:* c/o Rashtriya Sanjay Manch, New Delhi, India.

GANDHI Rajiv; Indian airline pilot and politician; b. 20 Aug. 1944, Bombay; s. of Firoze Gandhi and Indira Gandhi; m. Sonia Maino 1968; one s. one d.; ed. Trinity Coll., Cambridge; trained as airline pilot, U.K.; pilot with India Airlines; entered politics 1981; contested Lok Sabha by-election and won seat, Amethi, Uttar Pradesh (fmrly. held by younger brother, late Sanjay Gandhi) June 1981; mem. Nat. Exec. Indian Youth Congress June 1981-; Pres. Congress (I) Party 1983-; Prime Minister Oct. 1984-, also Minister of Science and Tech., Planning, Atomic Energy, Space; fmr. Minister of External Affairs. *Address:* Office of the Prime Minister, South Block, New Delhi 110011, India.

GANDOIS, Jean Guy Alphonse; French company executive; b. 7 May 1930, Nieul; s. of Eugène and Marguerite (née Teillet) Gandois; m. Monique Testard 1953; two s.; ed. École Polytechnique, Paris; Civil Engineer, Ministry of Public Works, French Guinea 1954-58; mem. of tech. co-operation missions to Brazil and Peru 1959-60; Asst. to Commercial Dir. Wendel & Cie 1961, Econ. Dir. 1966; Econ. and Commercial Dir. Wendel-Sidelor 1968; Gen. Man. Sacilor 1973; Pres., Dir.-Gen. Sollac 1975; Dir.-Gen. Rhône-Poulenc SA 1976, Vice-Pres. 1977-79, Chair. and C.E.O. 1979-82 (resigned); Chair. and C.E.O. Pechiney 1986-; mem. Bd. of Dirs. BSN, Compagnie Financière de Paribas, Peugeot S.A., Lyonnaise des Eaux, Vallourec, Hewlett-Eurofrance (all in France); Chair. Cockerill-Sambre, Dir. Forges de Clahecq, mem. Advisory Bd. Société Générale de Belgique (all Belgium); Chair. Pechiney Corpn., mem. Bd. of Dirs., Howmet Corpn. (U.S.A.), Philips, France, Europa Metalli, Italy; Chevalier Légion d'honneur; Grand Croix Order de la Couronne (Belgium); Grand Officier, Ordre du Chène (Luxembourg). *Address:* 51 boulevard Suchet, 75016 Paris, France (Home). *Telephone:* 45.61.68.47 (Office).

GANI, Joseph Mark, B.SC., D.I.C., PH.D., D.SC., F.A.A.; Australian statistician; b. 15 Dec. 1924, Cairo, Egypt; s. of Mark Gani and Lucy Israël; m. Ruth Stephens 1955; two s. two d.; ed. Canadian Acad. Kobe, Japan, English School, Cairo, Imperial Coll. London and Australian Nat. Univ., Canberra; lecturer, Sr. Lecturer and Reader, Univ. of W. Australia 1953-60; Sr. Fellow, Australian Nat. Univ. 1961-64; Prof. Michigan State Univ., E. Lansing 1964-65; Prof. Univ. of Sheffield 1965-74; Chief, Div. of Math. and Statistics CSIRO, Australia 1974-81; Chair. Dept. of Statistics, Univ. of Kentucky, Lexington 1981-85; Chair. Statistics Program, Univ. of Calif., Santa Barbara 1985-; founder, Applied Probability Trust (for encouragement of research in mathematical sciences) 1964; Ed. Journal of Applied Probabilities, Advanced Applied Probabilities, Math. Scientist; Nuffield Dominion Travelling Fellow, 1956-57; Fellow, Inst. of Mathematical Stats., American Statistical Asscn.; Hon. Fellow, Royal Statistical Soc.; Hon. life mem. Statistical Soc. of Australia. *Publications:* The Condition of Science in Australian Universities 1963, The Making of Statisticians (ed.) 1982, The Craft of Probabilistic Modelling (ed.) 1986. *Leisure interests:* reading, walking, painting. *Address:* Statistics Program, University of California, Santa Barbara, Calif. 93106, U.S.A. *Telephone:* (805) 961-4274.

GANI, Shafiqul; Bangladesh politician; b. 11 Sept. 1946, Nilphamari; s. of the late Mashiur Rahman; ed. Queen Mary Coll., London and London School of Journalism; Assoc. Ed. The Mashal (weekly) 1968-70; Ed. The Red Dust 1970; Convenor Gonotentric Jubo League 1972; mem. Steering Cttee. Nationalist Front 1977; M.P. 1979; Minister of Youth and Sports 1984-85, Minister of State for Roads and Transport 1985, for Tourism and Civil Aviation 1985-86; Minister of Works 1986-87. *Leisure interests:* painting, writing, hunting. *Address:* c/o Ministry of Works, Bangladesh Secretariat, Main Extension Bldg., 2nd Floor, Dhaka, Bangladesh.

GANILAU, Ratu Sir Penaia Kanatabatu, G.C.M.G., K.C.V.O., K.B.E., D.S.O., E.D.; Fijian politician and administrator; b. 28 July 1918; m. 1st Adi Laisa Delaisomosomo Yavaca (deceased) 1949, five s. two d.; m. 2nd Adi Lady Davila Ganilau 1975 (died 1984); m. 3rd Veniana Bale Cagilaba 1985; ed. Queen Victoria Memorial School, Fiji, and Devonshire Course for Admin. Officers, Wadham Coll., Oxford; served with FIR 1940-46, rank of Capt.; Colonial Admin. Service 1947; Dist. Officer 1948-53; mem. Comm. on Fijian Post-Primary Educ. in the Colony 1953; served with Fiji Mil. Forces 1953-56; Fijian Devt. Officer and Roko Tui Cakaudrove conjoint 1956; seconded to post of Tour Man. and Govt. Rep., Fiji Rugby Football Tour of N.Z. 1957; Deputy Sec. for Fijian Affairs 1961-65; Minister for Fijian Affairs and Local Govt. 1965-70; Leader of Govt. Business and Minister for Home Affairs, Lands and Mineral Resources 1970-72; Minister for Communications, Works and Tourism 1972-75; Deputy Prime Minister 1973-83; Minister for Home Affairs 1975-77, for Fijian Affairs, and Rural Devt. 1977-83; Gov.-Gen. and C.-in-C. of Fiji 1983-87; following 14 May 1987 coup by Lieut. Col. Rabuka (q.v.), declared a State of Emergency and formed own admin. 18 May 1987; apptd. Pres. Dec. 1987-; mem. Council of Ministers; Official mem. Legis. Council; Chair. Fijian Affairs Bd., Fijian Devt. Fund Bd., Native Land Trust Bd., Great Council of Chiefs; Pres. Fiji Rugby Union; represented Fiji against Maori All Blacks 1938 and during rugby tour of N.Z. 1939; Hon. Col., 2nd Battalion (Territorial), FIR 1973, K.St.J. *Leisure interest:* rugby football. *Address:* c/o Government House, Suva, Fiji.

GANSHOF VAN DER MEERSCH, Viscount Walter, LL.D.; Belgian jurist; b. 1900, Bruges; m. Elizabeth Orts 1923; one s. one d.; ed. King's Coll., Wimbledon, England, Royal Athenaeum, Bruges, and Univs. of Paris and Brussels; Prof. of Constitutional Law 1938, European Law 1958, Comparative Law 1960, Univ. of Brussels; Pres. Inst. of European Studies, Brussels, and Inter-Univ. Centre of Public Law; Pres. Inter-Univ. Centre of Comparative Law; Judge Advocate-Gen. 1940; served in Belgian Army in both World Wars; Lieut.-Gen.; High Commr. for Security of the Realm 1943; mem. Supreme Court of Justice 1947-; Minister of Gen. Affairs in Africa 1960; Judge ad hoc, Int. Court of Justice, the Hague 1960-68; Attorney-Gen. 1968; Vice-Pres. European Court of Human Rights, Strasbourg 1973-; lecturer, Hague Acad. of Int. Law 1975; Francqui Chair., Univ. Louvain 1975; Hon. Bencher Gray's Inn, London; mem. Acad. Int. de Droit comparé, Acad. Royale des Sciences d'Outremer, Acad. Royale des Lettres et des Sciences de Belgique (Pres.); Dr. h.c. (Strasbourg); Hon. C.B. (U.K.), Grand Cross Order of Crown (Belgium), Grand Cross Order of Léopold (Belgium), Commdr. Legion of Merit (U.S.A.), Commdr. Légion d'honneur, Grand Officier Order Crown of Oak (Luxembourg), Belgian and French Croix de guerre and other war medals. *Publications:* Pouvoir de fait et règle de droit dans le fonctionnement des institutions politiques 1956, Fin de la souveraineté belge au Congo 1963, Le droit des organisations européennes 1964, Le droit des communautés européennes 1969. *Address:* 33 avenue Jeanne, 1050 Brussels, Belgium. *Telephone* 02-6472914.

GANTIN, H.E. Cardinal Bernardin; Benin ecclesiastic; b. 8 May 1922, Toffo; ordained priest 1951; elected to titular Church of Tipasa, Mauritania 1956, consecrated 1957; apptd. to Cotonou, Benin 1960; cr. Cardinal 1977; Prefect, Sacred Congregation of Bishops April 1984-; Pres. Papal Comm. for Justice and Peace; Deacon of the Sacred Heart of Christ the King; Pres. Papal Council "Cor unum"; Cardinalizia di Vigilanza, Inst. per le Opere di Religione. *Address:* Piazza S. Calisto 16, 00153 Rome, Italy.

GANTZ, Marvin Everett, Jr.; American business executive (retd.); b. 28 Oct. 1918, Denver, Colo.; m. Mary Louise Bash; one s. (deceased); ed. Colorado School of Mines; joined Alcoa 1940; Vice-Pres. Fabricating Div. 1968-69, Mill Products, Mfg. 1969-74, Vice-Pres. Operations, Mill Products 1974-75; Exec. Vice-Pres. Mill Products 1975-81; Vice-Chair. and Dir. Aluminium Co. of America (Alcoa) 1981-85; Distinguished Achievement Medal, Colorado School of Mines 1981. *Leisure interests:* golf, skiing, running. *Address:* RD 1-Box 320G, Ligonier, Pa. 15658, U.S.A. (Home). *Telephone:* (412) 238-4280 (Home).

GANTZ, Wilbur H. III., M.B.A.; American business executive; b. 5 Dec. 1937, York, Pa.; s. of Wilbur H. Gantz and Flora Kashner; m. Linda Theis

1962; three c.; ed. Princeton Univ. and Harvard Business School; Dir. Baxter Travenol Labs. Inc. 1981–, Exec. Vice-Pres. and C.O.O. 1983–87, Pres. 1987–; Dir. W. W. Grainger Inc., Zenith Electronics Inc., Harris Bankcorp, Harris Banking & Trust Co. *Address:* Baxter Travenol Labs. Inc., 1 Baxter Parkway, Deerfield, Ill. 60015, U.S.A.

GANZURI, Kamal Al-, M.A., PH.D.; Egyptian politician; b. 1933; ed. Cairo Univ. and Michigan Univ.; Gov. of Beni Suef and Under-Sec. Ministry of Planning 1975; fmr. consultant for planning and devt. at UN; fmr. Head, Nat. Planning Inst., Minister of Planning 1982–85; Deputy Prime Minister and Minister of Planning 1985–, Int. Co-operation 1985–87. *Address:* Ministry of Planning, Sharia Salah Salem, Cairo (Nasr City), Egypt.

GAO DEZHAN; Chinese senior engineer and state official; b. 6 Aug. 1932; worked in chemical, petrochemical and light industries; alt. mem. 12th CCP Cen. Cttee.; Dir. Jilin Prov. Econ. Comm. Vice-Gov., Jilin 1983–85, Gov. 1985–87; Deputy Sec. CCP Prov. Cttee., Jilin 1985; Minister of Forestry 1987–; Vice-Chair. All-China Greening Cttee. March 1988–; Deputy Head Cen. Forest Fire Prevention Aug. 1988–; alt. mem. 13th CCP Cen. Cttee. 1987. *Address:* Hepingli, Dongchang District, Beijing, People's Republic of China.

GAO DI; Chinese party official; b. 1927; Sec. CCP Cttee., Jilin Prov. 1983–; mem. CCP Cen. Cttee. 1985–; Vice-Pres Cen. Party School April 1988–. *Address:* Jilin Provincial Chinese Communist Party, Changchun, Jilin, People's Republic of China.

GAO FENGLIAN; Chinese athlete; b. 1964, Inner Mongolia; Bronze Medal, Fukuoka Invitation Judo Tournament 1983; Silver Medal, Third World Women's Judo Championship, Vienna 1984. *Address:* Chinese Judo Institute, Beijing, People's Republic of China.

GAO HOULIANG, Maj.-Gen.; Chinese army officer; b. 1915, Xinxian Co., Henan Prov.; joined Red Army 1932, CCP 1933; Maj.-Gen. Nanjing Mil. Region 1964; Deputy Political Commissar, PLA Air Force 1976, First Political Commissar 1977–; alt. mem. 11th Cen. Cttee. CCP 1977, 12th Cen. Cttee. 1982–85; mem. Cen. Advisory Comm. 1987–; Second Sec. CCP Cttee. PLA Air Force 1979–. *Address:* People's Republic of China.

GAO JIANZHONG; Chinese diplomatist; Amb. to Papua New Guinea 1985–. *Address:* Embassy of the People's Republic of China, P.O. Box 1351, Baroko, Papua New Guinea.

GAO JINGDE, D.TECH.SCI.; Chinese professor of electrical engineering; b. 5 Feb. 1922, Shaanxi; ed. Northwestern Inst. of Tech., Leningrad Inst. of Tech.; Prof. of Electrical Eng., Tsinghua Univ., Beijing 1956–, Pres. of Univ. 1983–; mem. Chinese Acad. of Sciences 1980–; Vice-Pres. Chinese Electrical Eng. Soc. 1980–; Pres. Chinese Electrotechnical Soc. 1981–; Fellow, I.E.E.E. (U.S.A.) 1986–. *Address:* Tsinghua University, Beijing, People's Republic of China.

GAO QINGSHI; Chinese computer scientist; b. 18 Aug. 1934; ed. Beijing Univ.; researcher, Inst. of Computing Tech., Academia Sinica 1958–; Deputy, 5th NPC 1978–83; mem. Dept. of Tech. Sciences Academia Sinica 1985–; Deputy 6th NPC 1983–88, 7th NPC 1988–. *Address:* Institute of Computing Technology, Zhong Guan Cun, Beijing 100080, People's Republic of China.

GAO SHANGQUAN; Chinese government official and professor of economics; b. 1929, Jia Ding County, Shanghai; s. of Gao Ruyu and Xiang Shi; m. Cha Peijun 1958; one s.; ed. St. John's Univ., Shanghai; worked as researcher, Deputy Div. Chief, Div. Chief, Bureau for Machine-Bldg. Industry of Ministry of Industry of local North-Eastern People's Govt.; Policy Research Dept., First Ministry of Machine-Bldg. Industry; Research Dept., Ministry of Agricultural Machine-Bldg. Industry; Research Dept., Ministry of Agricultural Machine-Bldg. Industry; Office of Agricultural Mechanization, State Council; Policy Research Dept., State Comm. of Machine-Bldg. Industry; Research Fellow, Research Centre for Agricultural Devt., and Sr. Economist, State Comm. of Machine-Bldg. Industry; State Comm. for Restructuring Econ. System 1982, then Deputy Dir. and Head, Research Inst. of Restructuring the Econ. System; Vice-Minister in charge of State Comm. for Restructuring the Econ. System, Vice-Group-Leader, Leading Group for Restructuring Housing System, under State Council; Vice-Pres. Assen. of China's Urban Economy; mem. Standing Council, Assen. of China's Industrial Economy; Prof., Beijing Univ. and Chinese People's Univ.; Dir. of Editing Cttee., Reforms in China's Econ. System magazine. *Publications:* Enterprises Should Enjoy Certain Autonomy 1956, Follow A Road of Our Own In Agricultural Modernization 1982, Nine Years of Reform in China's Economic System 1987, A Road To Success 1987, Selected Works of Gao Shangquan 1989; also ed. of numerous publications. *Address:* State Commission for Restructuring the Economic System, 22 Xianmen Street, Beijing, People's Republic of China. *Telephone:* 653156.

GAO YANG; Chinese politician; b. Liaoning; Deputy Sec. and concurrently Dir., Org. Dept., CCP Shenyang Municipal Cttee.; Chair., Liaotung 1950–52; Dir. Labour Bureau, Liaotung People's Prov. Govt. 1950; Council mem. N.E. People's Govt. 1951–53; Sec. CCP Liaotung Prov. Cttee. 1953; Deputy 1st NPC 1954, 2nd NPC 1958, 3rd NPC 1964; mem. Control Cttee., CCP Central Cttee 1965–Cultural Revolution; Deputy Dir. Industrial Work

Dept., CCP Cen. Cttee. 1958; Minister of Chemical Industry 1962–Cultural Revolution; Sec., Secr., CCP Cen. Cttee., disappeared during Cultural Revolution; rehabilitated 1978; Minister, State Farms and Land Reclamation Comm. 1980–82; First Sec. Hebei CCP Cttee. 1982; mem. Cen. Advisory Comm. 1982–; Pres. CCP Cen. Cttee. Party School 1987–; Chair. Bd. of Dirs. China Investment Consultants March 1986–; Pres. Cen. Party School March 1987–. *Address:* State Council, Beijing, People's Republic of China.

GAO YANGWEN; Chinese politician; b. 1917, Shandong Prov.; Minister of the Coal Industry 1980–82; Vice-Minister State Energy Comm. 1980–82; Adviser, Energy Research Asscn. 1981–; Chair. Bd. of Dirs., China Southwestern Energy Devt. Corpn. 1982–; Vice-Chair. Kanghua Devt. Corpn. May 1988–; Alt. mem. 12th Cen. Cttee. CCP 1982–87; Adviser Financial and Econ. Leading Group, CCP Cen. Cttee. 1985–. *Address:* c/o Ministry of the Coal Industry, Beijing, People's Republic of China.

GAO YING; Chinese author; b. 25 Dec. 1929, Jiaozuo, Henan; s. of Gao Weiya and Sha Peifem; m. Duan Chuanchen 1954; one s. two d.; Vice-Chair. Sichuan Br., and mem. Council, Chinese Writers' Asscn.; mem. Sichuan Political Consultative Conf. *Publications:* The Song of Ding Youjun, Lamplights around the Three Gorges, High Mountains and Distant Rivers, Cloudy Cliff (long novel), Da Ji and her Fathers (novel and film script), The Orchid (novel), Loving-Kindness of the Bamboo Storey (collection of prose), Mother in my Heart (autobiographical novel), Songs of Da Liang Mountains (collection of poems), Frozen Snowflakes (collection of poems), Reminiscences. *Leisure interests:* painting, music. *Address:* Sichuan Branch of Chinese Association of Literary and Art Workers, Buhou-jie Street, Chengdu, Sichuan, People's Republic of China.

GAO ZHANXIANG; Chinese party official; b. 1935; mem. Communist Youth League Cen. Cttee. 1964, Sec. 1978–82; alt. mem. 12th CCP Cen. Cttee. 1982–87; Sec. CCP Cttee., Hebei Prov. 1983–, Vice-Minister of Culture 1986–. *Address:* Hebei Provincial Chinese Communist Party, Shijiazhuang, Hebei, People's Republic of China.

GAPONOV-GREKHOV, Andrey Viktorovich; Soviet physicist; b. 7 June 1926, Moscow; ed. Gorky State Univ.; postgraduate student, Gorky State Univ. 1949–52; Instructor, Gorky Polytech. Inst. 1952–55; Sr. Scientific Assoc., Head of Dept. of Radio Physics, Research Inst., Gorky State Univ. 1955–; Corresp. mem. U.S.S.R. Acad. of Sciences 1964–68, Academician 1968–; State Prize 1967. *Publications:* numerous theoretical and experimental works in field of inducted cyclotronic radiation, which led to development of a new class of electronic instruments—masers with cyclotronic resonance. *Address:* Gorky State University, Gorky, U.S.S.R.

GAPUROV, Mukhamednazar; Soviet politician; b. 1922, Turkmenia; mem. CPSU 1944–; ed. Chardzhu Teachers' Training Inst.; teacher at secondary school 1941–42, Prin. 1943–44; service in Soviet Army 1942–43; Sec. regional cttee. of Turkmen CP; First Sec. Dist. Turkmen Komsomol Cttee.; Sec. Cen. Cttee. of Turkmen Komsomol; First Sec. Chardzhu Dist. Cttee. of Turkmen CP 1944–62; mem. Turkmen CP Cen. Cttee. 1958–; mem. Presidium of Supreme Soviet, Turkmen S.S.R. 1959–63, 1969–; Deputy to U.S.S.R. Supreme Soviet 1962–; mem. Budget and Planning Comm., Council of U.S.S.R. Supreme Soviet 1974–; Chair. Council of Ministers and Minister of Foreign Affairs of Turkmen S.S.R. 1963–69; cand. mem. Cen. Cttee. of CPSU 1966–71, mem. 1971–86; First Sec. Cen. Cttee. of Turkmen CP 1969–86. *Address:* c/o Central Committee of the Communist Party of the Turkmen S.S.R., Ashkhabad, Turkmen S.S.R., U.S.S.R.

GARABEDIAN, Paul R., PH.D.; American professor of mathematics; b. 2 Aug. 1927, Cincinnati, Ohio; ed. Brown and Harvard Univs.; Nat. Research Council Fellow 1948–49; Asst. Prof. of Math., Univ. of Calif. 1949–50; Asst. Prof. of Math., Stanford Univ. 1950–52, Assoc. Prof. 1952–56, Prof. 1956–59; Scientific Liaison Officer, ONR-London 1957–58; Prof., Courant Inst. of Math. Sciences, New York Univ. 1959–, Dir. Courant Math. and Computing Lab. of U.S. Dept. of Educ. 1972–73, Dir. Div. of Computational Fluid Dynamics 1978–; Sloan Foundation Fellowship 1961–63; Guggenheim Fellowship 1966, 1981–82; Fairchild Distinguished Scholar, Calif. Inst. of Tech. 1975; mem. N.A.S., American Acad. of Arts & Sciences, American Math. Soc., American Physical Soc., American Inst. of Aeronautics and Astronautics, Ed. Bd. Applicable Analysis, Complex Variables and Applications; NASA Public Service Group Achievement Award 1976; NASA Certificate of Recognition 1980; Boris Pregal Award, New York Acad. of Sciences 1980; Birkhoff Prize in Applied Math. 1983. *Publications:* numerous papers in learned journals. *Address:* Courant Institute of Mathematical Sciences, New York University, 251 Mercer Street, New York, N.Y. 10012; 110 Bleecker Street, New York, N.Y. 10012, U.S.A. (Home).

GARAIKOETXEA URRIZA, Carlos; Spanish (Basque) lawyer, politician and economist; b. 2 June 1939, Pamplona; s. of Juan Garaikoetxea and Dolores Urriza; m. Sagrario Mina Apat 1966; three s.; mem. Inst. Príncipe de Viana, org. to protect and promote Basque culture, Navarra Dist. Council 1971; Dist. Councillor, Navarra 1971; Chair. Navarra Chamber of Commerce and Industry 1971; mem. Regional Council of Partido Nacionalista Vasco (Basque Nationalist Party—PNV) 1974, Chair. Nat. Council PNV 1977, re-elected 1978; mem. Navarra Dist. Parl. 1979; Pres. Gen. Council of the Basque Country 1979; elected to Basque Parl. as PNV cand. for Guipuzcoa March 1980; Pres. of Basque Govt. 1980–86; Hon. Pres. and gold medals from many orgs. and asscns. *Leisure interests:* music (especially classical), skiing, Basque pelota, reading (especially political essays and history). *Address:* Palacio de Ajuria-Enea, Vitoria-Gasteiz, Spain. *Telephone:* (945) 23 16 16.

GARANG, John, D.ECON.; Sudanese guerrilla leader; b. 1943, Jonglei; ed. Iowa State Univ.; Sudanese Army 1969-70; trained as Co. Commdr., Fort Benning, U.S.A., later Lieut.-Col. Mil. Research Center, Khartoum; f. and Leader Sudan People's Liberation Movt. and Sudan People's Liberation Army May 1983-.

GARANGO, Capt. Marc Tiémoko, L. EN D.; Burkinâbe army officer and politician; b. 27 July 1927, Gaoua; ed. Univs. of Dakar, Paris, Aix-en-Provence; completed mil. training at Bingerville, Ivory Coast; served in French Army in Indochinese and Algerian campaigns; promoted to Lieut. 1961, Capt. 1963; Supply Officer, Upper Volta (now Burkina Faso) Army 1965-66; Minister of Finance and Commerce 1966-75; Amb. to China (Taiwan) 1966, to Fed. Repub. of Germany (also to Austria and Switzerland) 1977-81, to U.S.A. 1981-83; fmr. Pres. Banque Centrale des Etats de l'Afrique de l'Ouest; Pres. Nat. Monetary Cttee. (BCEAO); Gov. IMF. *Address:* c/o Ministry of Foreign Affairs, Ouagadougou, Burkina Faso.

GARAS, Klára, PH.D.; Hungarian art historian; b. 19 June 1919, Rákosszentmihály; d. of Pál Garas and Irén Strasser; ed. Budapest Univ. of Sciences; joined staff Budapest Museum of Fine Arts 1945, subsequent posts to Gen. Dir. 1964-84; Corresp. mem. Hungarian Acad. of Sciences 1972, mem. 1985-; Labour Order of Merit (golden degree) 1974, 1979. *Leisure interests:* 15th to 18th-century European and Hungarian painting. *Publications:* Magyarországi festészet a XVII. században (Hungarian Painting in the 17th century) 1953, Magyarországi festészet a XVIII. században (Hungarian Painting in the 18th century) 1955, Olasz reneszánsz portrék a Szépmüvészeti Muzeumban (Italian Renaissance Portraits in the Museum of Fine Arts) 1965, 1973, Carlo Innocenzo Carloni (co-author) Milano 1966, A velencei settecento festészete (Venetian Paintings of the 18th Century) 1977, Franz Anton Maulbertsch. Leben und Werk (his Life and Work) with preface by Oskar Kokoschka, Salzburg 1974; A 17. század német és osztrák rajzmüvészete (Deutsche und österreichische Zeichnungen des 18. Jahrhunderts) 1980; several publs. on the Budapest Museum of Fine Arts. *Address:* 1126 Budapest, Kiss János altábornagy utca 48/c, Hungary.

GARBA, Maj.-Gen. Joseph Nanven, M.P.A.; Nigerian army officer (retd.) and politician; b. 17 July 1943, Langtang; m. Evelyn Okon Edem; one s. five d.; ed. Sacred Heart School, Shendam, Nigerian Mil. School, Zairia, Mons Officer Cadet School, Aldershot, Staff Coll., Camberley, England, Harvard Univ.; Platoon Command, 4th Bn. 1963, Co. Command 1963-64, Mortar Platoon Command 1964; Second in Command Fed. Guards 1964-65; Gen. Staff Officer, 3 HQ, Second Brigade 1965; UN Officer, India and Pakistan 1965-66; Officer Commdg. Fed. Guards 1966-68; Commdr. Brigade of Guards 1968-75; mem. Supreme Mil. Council 1975-79; Commr. for External Affairs 1975-78; Commdt. Nigerian Defence Acad. 1978-79; Amb. and Perm. Rep. to UN Jan. 1984-; Fellow Inst. of Politics and Cen. for Int. Affairs Harvard Univ. 1980-83. *Leisure interests:* basketball, photography. *Address:* Permanent Mission of Nigeria to the United Nations, 733 Third Avenue, New York, N.Y. 10017 (Office); 548 South Broadway, Rarrytown, N.Y. 10591, U.S.A. (Home). *Telephone:* (212) 953-9130 (Office); (914) 631-5800 (Home).

GARBERS, Christoph Friedrich, D.PHIL.; South African scientist; b. 21 Aug. 1929, Piet Retief, Transvaal.; s. of Andris Wilhelm Friedrich and Lucy Sophia Carolina (née Wolhuter) Garbers; m. Barbara Z. G. Viljoen 1957; three s. one d.; ed. Pretoria Univ., Zurich Univ.; Research Officer Klipfontein Organic Products 1951; student Zurich Univ. 1951-54; Research Officer Council for Scientific and Industrial Research (CSIR) 1954-58; Sr. lecturer, Stellenbosch Univ. 1958-65, Prof. Organic Chem. 1966-78; Vice-Pres. CSIR 1979, Deputy Pres. 1980, Pres. 1980-; Chair. S. African Acad. for Science and Arts 1983-85; Chair. S. African Inventions Devt. Corpn. 1980-88; Dir. Tech. Finance Corpn. (Pty) Ltd. 1988-; mem. Scientific Advisory Council 1980-87, Water Research Comm. 1980-, Advisory Council for Tech. 1987-; Council mem. Univ. of S.A. 1980-; Trustee Hans Merensky Foundation 1980-; Rep. at ICSU 1980-; Havenga Prize for Chem. 1977, Gold Medal, S.A. Chem. Inst. 1980. *Leisure interest:* tennis. *Address:* P.O. Box 395, Pretoria (Office), 330 The Rand, Lynnwood, Pretoria, South Africa. *Telephone:* 861313 and 841 3761 (Office); 473574 (Home).

GARBO, Greta Lovisa; American (b. Swedish) film actress; b. (as Greta Gustafsson) 18 Sept. 1905; d. of Sven and Louvisa Gustafsson; ed. Royal Dramatic Acad., Stockholm; Nat. Theatre 1924; star of first film Gösta Berlings Saga in Sweden 1924; went to U.S.A. 1925; special Acad. Award 1954; Commdr. Order of the North Star (Sweden) 1983. *Films include:* Joyless Street 1925, The Torrent 1926, The Temptress 1926, Flesh and the Devil 1927, Love 1927, The Divine Woman 1928, The Mysterious Lady 1928, A Woman of Affairs 1929, Wild Orchid 1929, The Single Standard 1929, The Kiss 1929, Romance 1930, Inspiration 1931, Mata Hari 1931, Grand Hotel 1932, Queen Christina 1933, The Painted Veil 1934, Anna Karenina 1935, Camille 1936, Conquest 1937, Ninotchka 1939, Two Faced Woman 1941. *Address:* 450 East 52nd Street, New York, N.Y., U.S.A.

GARCÉS, Francisco, M.A. (ECONS.); Chilean economist; b. 30 Aug. 1934, Santiago; s. of Francisco Garcés and María Garrido; m. María Isabel Echeverría Ruíz-Tagle; one s.; ed. Univ. Católica de Chile, Williams Coll., Williamstown, Mass., and Columbia Univ., New York; Econ. Research Inst., Univ. Católica de Chile 1958; Research Dept., Cen. Bank of Chile 1958-72, Man. Capital Market and Financial Insts. 1975-77; Prof. of Econs., Univ. of Chile 1971-76; Financial Adviser, Ministry of Planning, Govt. of Brazil, OAS 1973; Exec. Sec., Cttee. on Public Sector Securities 1975; Pres. Central Savings and Loan Bank 1977; Alt. Exec. Dir. International Monetary Fund 1977-78, Exec. Dir. 1978-80; Dir. and fmr. Chair. Special Field of Economists of Soc. of Engineers and Economists of Chile; fmr. Dir. Casapropia Savings and Loan Asscn. and Nat. Sugar Industry (IANSA). *Leisure interests:* being a director of sporting and cultural institutions. *Publications:* articles on financial subjects in the Bulletin of the Central Bank of Chile and in specialized journals. *Address:* c/o Banco Central de Chile, Agustinas 1180, Santiago, Chile.

GARCÍA AGUILAR, Horacio; Mexican politician; b. 1919, Salvatierra, Guanajuato; ed. Nat. School of Agric., Chapingo; has worked at Ministry of Agric., Nat. Bank of Rural Credit, Nat. Bank of Foreign Trade, Mexican Insurance Co., Bank of Mexico; Dir.-Gen. Fund for Agrarian Devt. 1965-82; Asst. Dir.-Gen. Bank of Mexico 1981; mem. Admin. Bd. of Rural Credit, Nat. Bank of Fisheries and Ports, Workers' Bank, Nacional Financiera, Centre for Agrarian Research; Minister of Agric. and Hydraulic Resources 1982-86. *Address:* c/o Secretaría de Agricultura, Tacuba No. 7, México, D.F., Mexico.

GARCÍA AÑOVEROS, Jaime, D.IUR.; Spanish lawyer and politician; b. 24 Jan. 1932, Teruel; s. of Jaime and Luisa Garcia Añoveros; m. Elisa Escriña 1960; one s. three d.; ed. Tafalla, Univ. of Valencia, Univ. of Bologna, Italy; Asst. lecturer in Public Finance, Law Faculty, Madrid Univ. 1956-61; lecturer in Economy and Finance, Seville Law Faculty 1961-71, in Financial and Fiduciary Law 1971; Prof. Fiscal Law; Adviser and Head of Study Service, Banco Urquijo, Seville; fmr. Ed. Civitas (law journal); fmr. mem. Unión de Centro Democrático, Congress of Deputies; fmr. Chair. Congress Budget Cttee.; Minister of Finance 1979-82. *Address:* Lagasca 28, 28001 Madrid (Office); Av. República Argentina, 13 Seville, Spain (Home). *Telephone:* 435-20-10 (Office).

GARCÍA DIEZ, Juan Antonio; Spanish politician; b. 4 Aug. 1940, Madrid; m. Ana de Penalosa Zuzquiza; two d.; ed. Complutense Univ. of Madrid; Prof. of Econ. Theory, Univ. of Madrid 1966-68; fmr. Commercial Attaché, Spanish Embassies in Peru and Bolivia; fmr. Vice Sec.-Gen. Ministry of Commerce, later Tech. Sec.-Gen.; Sec.-Gen. RENFE 1976-77; mem. Social Democrat Party (PSD) (subsequently merged with Union of the Democratic Centre-UCD); UCD Deputy for Cadiz; Minister of Trade and Tourism 1977-80, for the Economy and Trade 1980-82; also Second Deputy Prime Minister 1981-82; Dir. Centre for Studies on Current Problems. *Address:* Victor de la Serna 9, 28016 Madrid, Spain.

GARCÍA MÁRQUEZ, Gabriel (Gabo); Colombian writer; b. 1928, Aracataca; m. Mercedes García Márquez; two s.; ed. secondary school and Univ. of Bogotá, Univ. of Cartagena; began writing books 1946; lived in Baranquilla; Corresp. Espectador in Rome, Paris; first novel published while living in Caracas, Venezuela 1957; est. bureau of Prensa Latina (Cuban press agency) in Bogotá; worked for Prensa Latina in Havana, Cuba, then as Deputy Head of New York Office 1961; lived in Spain, contributing to magazines, Mundo Nuevo, Casa de las Américas; went to Mexico; invited back to Colombia by Pres. July 1982; Rómulo Gallegos Prize 1972; Nobel Prize for Literature 1982. *Publications include:* La hojarasca (Leaf Storm) 1955, El coronel no tiene quien le escriba (No One Writes to the Colonel) 1961, La mala hora (In Evil Hour) 1962, Los funerales de la Mamá Grande (Big Mama's Funeral) 1962, Cien años de soledad (One Hundred Years of Solitude) 1967, La increíble y triste historia de la cándida Eréndira (Innocent Erendira and other stories) 1972, El otoño del patriarca (The Autumn of the Patriarch) 1975, Crónica de una muerte anunciada (Chronicle of a Death Foretold) 1981, El Olor de la Guayaba (Fragrance of Guava) 1982, El amor en los tiempos del cólera (Love in the Time of Cholera) 1984, Relato de un naufrago (The Story of a Shipwrecked Sailor) 1986, Miguel Littín's Adventure: undercover in Chile 1986, The General in His Labyrinth 1989. *Address:* c/o Agencia Literaria Carmen Balcelos, Diagonal 580, Barcelona, Spain.

GARCIA NIETO, José; Spanish poet; b. 6 July 1914, Oviedo; Ed. poetry magazines Garcilaso (and founder), Acanto, Poesia Española, Mundo Hispanico; poetry recitals and confs. in Spain and in Lisbon, Rome, London, Ghent, Louvain, Caracas etc.; has run courses in contemporary poetry at Int. Univ. of Santander and Univ. of Valencia; mem. Real Academia Española, Real Academia de Bellas Letras y Ciencias Históricas de Toledo, Instituto de Estudios Madrileños; Hon. mem. and fmr. Pres. Circulo de Bellas Artes; numerous prizes including Premio Nacional de Literatura 1957, Premio Ciudad de Barcelona 1968. *Publications:* numerous vols. of poetry, including Tregua 1951, La Red 1956, Hablando Solo 1968, Sonetos y Revelaciones de Madrid 1976, Suplica por la Paz del Mundo y Otros "Collages" 1977, Los Cristales Fingidos 1978, El Arrabal 1980, Galiana 1986, Carta a la madre 1988; short stories: Donde el Mundo no Cesa de Referir su Historia 1982; Ed. (with F.T. Comes) Antologia de Poetas

Hispanoamericanos 1964, Antologia de Leyendas Hispanoamericanas 1964. *Address:* c/o Real Academia Española, Calle de Felipe IV 4, Madrid, Spain.

GARCÍA PELÁEZ, Raúl, LL.D.; Cuban lawyer, politician and diplomatist; b. 15 Jan. 1922; ed. Univ. of Havana; fmr. mem. July 26th Revolutionary Cttee.; later Prosecutor at Camagüey Court of Appeal, then Chair. Camagüey Municipal Council for Co-ordination and Inspection; then Gen. Treas. Revolutionary Forces in Camagüey Prov., Rep. of Nat. Inst. of Agrarian Reform in Nuevitas, and Gen. Sec. Matanzas Prov. Cttee. of United Party of Cuban Socialist Revolution; mem. Cen. Cttee. of Cuban CP 1965–80, Head of Revolutionary Orientation Comm. of Cent. Cttee. of Cuban CP until 1967; Amb. to U.S.S.R. 1967–74. *Address:* Partido Comunista, Plaza de la Revolución, Havana, Cuba.

GARCÍA-PEÑA, Roberto; Colombian journalist; b. 1910; ed. Externado de Colombia, Bogotá, and Univ. of Chile; Reporter El Tiempo 1929; Private Sec. to Minister of Govt. 1930; Sec. Colombian Embassy, Peru 1934, Chile 1935, Chargé d'affaires 1937; Sec.-Gen. Ministry of Foreign Affairs 1938; Ed. El Tiempo 1939–81; mem. Council of Dirs., Inter-American Press Soc.; Best Journalist Award 1977, Gold Medal 1978. *Address:* Avenida Jiménez 6-77, Apdo. Aéreo 3633, Bogotá, D.E., Colombia.

GARCÍA PÉREZ, Alan; Peruvian politician; b. 23 May 1949, Lima; s. of Carlos García Ronceros and Nyta Pérez de García; m. Pilar Norse; four d.; ed. José Maria Eguren Nat. Coll., Universidad Católica, Lima, Universidad Nacional Mayor de San Marcos (graduated as lawyer), Universidad Complutense, Madrid, Spain, Sorbonne and Inst. of Higher Latin American Studies, Paris, France; mem. of Partido Aprista Peruano since his teens; returned to Peru and elected mem. of Constituent Ass. 1978; subsequently apptd. Org. Sec. and Chair. Ideology of Aprista Party; Parl. Deputy 1980–85; became Sec.-Gen. of Party 1982, now Pres.; nominated Presidential Candidate 1984; obtained largest number of votes, Nat. Presidential Elections April 1985; on withdrawal of Izquierda Unida candidate, Alfonso Barrantes Lingán, proclaimed Pres.-elect June 1985, assuming powers 28 July 1985. *Address:* Oficina del Presidente, Lima, Peru.

GARCÍA RAMÍREZ, Sergio, PH.D.; Mexican lawyer and politician; b. 1938, Guadalajara; ed. Nat. Univ. of Mexico; Research Fellow and teacher of penal law, Inst. of Juridical Research, Nat. Univ. of Mexico 1966–76; Dir. Correction Centre, State of Mexico and Judge, Juvenile Courts; Asst. of Govt. Ministry of Interior; Attorney-Gen. of Fed. Dist.; Under-Sec. Ministries of Nat. Resources, Interior, Education, Industrial Devt.; Dir. Prevention Centre of Mexico City; fmr. Minister of Labour; Attorney-Gen. 1982–88; mem. Mexican Acad. of Penal Sciences, Mexican Inst. of Penal Law, Nat. Inst. of Public Admin., Ibero-American Inst. of Penal Law etc. *Publications include:* Teseo Alucinado 1966, Asistencia a Reos Liberados 1966, El Artículo 18 Constitucional 1967, La Imputabilidad en el Derecho Penal Mexicano, El Código Tutelar para Menores del Estado Michoacán 1969, La Ciudadanía de la Juventud 1970, La Prisión 1975, Los Derechos Humanos y el Derecho Penal 1976, Legislación Penitenciaria y Correccional Comentada 1978, Otros Minotauros 1979, Cuestiones Criminológicas y Penales Contemporáneas 1981, Justicia Penal 1982. *Address:* c/o Oficina del Procurador General, México, D.F., Mexico.

GARCÍA ROBLES, Alfonso, LL.D.; Mexican diplomatist; b. 20 March 1911; s. of Quirino and Theresa Robles García; m. Juana María de Szyszlo 1950; two s.; ed. Univ. Nacional Autónoma de México, Univ. of Paris, and Acad. of Int. Law, The Hague; Foreign Service 1939–, Sweden 1939–41; Head, Dept. of Int. Orgs., later Dir.-Gen. of Political Affairs and Diplomatic Service 1941–46; Dir. of Div. of Political Affairs, UN Secr. 1946–57; Head of Dept. for Europe, Asia and Africa, Mexican Ministry of Foreign Affairs 1957–61; Amb. to Brazil 1962–64; Under-Sec. for Foreign Affairs 1964–71; Perm. Rep. to UN 1971–75; Sec. for Foreign Affairs 1975–76; Pres. Preparatory Comm. for the Denuclearization of Latin America 1964–67; Perm. Rep. to Disarmament Conf., Geneva 1977–; Chair. Mexican Del. to UN Gen. Assembly on disarmament, New York 1978; shared Nobel Peace Prize 1982. *Publications:* Pan-Americanism and the Good Neighbour Policy 1940, The Sorbonne Yesterday and Today 1943, Post-War Mexico 1944, Mexican International Policy 1946, Echoes of the Old World 1946, The Post-War World: From the Atlantic Charter to the San Francisco Conference (2 vols.) 1949, The Geneva Conference and the Extent of Territorial Waters 1959, The Denuclearization of Latin America 1967, The Ilatelolco Treaty 1967, Mexico in the United Nations (2 vols.) 1970, The Prohibition of Nuclear Arms in Latin America 1975, Six Years of Mexican Foreign Policy 1976, The Review Conference of the non-Proliferation Treaty 1977, 338 Days of Ilatelolco 1977, La Asamblea General del Desarme (The Disarmament General Assembly) 1979, El Comité de Desarme 1980. *Address:* 13 Avenue de Budé, Geneva, Switzerland. *Telephone:* 34-57-40.

GARCIA VARGAS, Julian; Spanish politician; b. 1946, Chamberri, Madrid; m.; two s.; economist; fmrly on staff of fmr. Office of Provision and Transport; fmr. Financial Tax Inspector, Ministry of Trade, Deputy Dir.-Gen., Directorate-General of Financial Policy, Man. Consortium of Urban Contrib. of Madrid; Pres. Insituto de Credito Oficial 1982–86; Minister for Health and Consumer Affairs July 1986–; mem. Movt. of Civil Servants of the Admin. *Address:* Ministerio de Sanidad y Consumo, Paseo del Prado 18–20, Madrid 4, Spain. *Telephone:* Madrid 467 2165.

GARCÍA YEBRA, Valentín; Spanish professor of Greek (retd.); b. 28 April 1917, Lombillo de los Barrios, León; m. Dolores Mouton Ibáñez 1946; four d.; ed. Univ. Cen. de Madrid; Ed., Foreign Section of magazine Arbor, Madrid 1948–55; Dir. Inst. Politécnico Español, Tangiers, Morocco 1955–66; Dir. Inst. Calderón de la Barca, Madrid 1966–69; Co-Founder Inst., Univ. de Lenguas Modernas y Traductores, Univ. Complutense, Madrid 1974, Vice-Dir. and Prof. of Theory of Translation 1974–85; Co-Founder Gredos 1944, Co-Dir. 1944–88; mem. Real Acad. Espanola de la Lengua 1985–; Translation Prize, Belgian Ministry of Educ. and Culture 1964, Premio Ibáñez Martín 1971, Premio Nieto López, Real Academia Española 1982; Comendador de las Ordenes de Alfonso X. el Sabio y de Isabel la Católica. *Publications:* trilingual edns. (Greek, Latin and Spanish) of Aristotle's Metaphysics and Poetica; Teoría y práctica de la traducción 1982, Entorno a la traducción. Teoría, Crítica, Historia 1983, Claudicación en el uso de preposiciones 1988; many transls. from Greek, Latin, German and French, some from Italian and Portuguese. *Leisure interests:* farming, gardening. *Address:* Conde de Cartagena 5, 2° A, 28007 Madrid, Spain. *Telephone:* 552 48 26.

GARDELLI, Lamberto; Italian conductor; b. 8 Nov. 1915, Venice; ed. Liceo Musicale Rossini, Pesaro; began career as concert pianist and as repetiteur Rome Opera; opera conductor début (La Traviata), Rome 1944; conductor Stockholm 1944–55; Guest Conductor Danish State Radio Symphony Orchestra, Copenhagen 1955–61; Conductor Budapest Opera 1961–65; Glyndebourne début 1964, Metropolitan New York début 1966, Covent Garden London début 1969; Conductor Royal Opera, Copenhagen 1973–; Prin. Conductor Munich Radio Symphony Orchestra 1983–. *Address:* c/o Allied Artists Agency, 42 Montpelier Square, London, SW7 1JZ, England. *Telephone:* 01-589 6243.

GARDENT, Paul; French mining executive; b. 10 July 1921, Grenoble; s. of Louis and Edith (née Rocher) Gardent; m. Janine Robert 1958; one s.; ed. Ecole Polytechnique; Mining Engineer, Valenciennes 1944–48; Asst. Chief Mining Engineer, Lille 1948–49, Chief Mining Engineer 1950; Tech. Adviser to J.M. Louvel (Minister of Industry and Commerce) 1950–52; Dir. of Gen. Studies, Charbonnages de France 1952–58; Dir. of Gen. Studies and Financial Services, Houillères du bassin de Lorraine 1958–63; Asst. Dir., then Dir.-Gen. Houillères du bassin du Nord et du Pas-de-Calais 1963–68; Dir.-Gen. Charbonnages de France 1968–80; Conseiller d'Etat 1980–; Commdr. Légion d'honneur, Commdr. Ordre nationale du Mérite. *Address:* 5–7 rue de la Chaise, Paris 75007, France (Home). *Telephone:* 45-44-03-43.

GARDINER, Baron (Life Peer) cr. 1963, of Kittisford, in the County of Somerset; **Gerald Austin Gardiner,** P.C., C.H., M.A.; British barrister; b. 30 May 1900; s. of the late Sir Robert Gardiner; m. 1st Lesly Trounson 1925 (died 1966), one d.; m. 2nd Muriel Box 1970; ed. Harrow School and Magdalen Coll., Oxford; Pres. Oxford Union and Oxford Univ. Dramatic Soc. 1924; called to Bar 1925; mem. Cttee. on Supreme Court Practice and Procedure 1947–53; Q.C. 1948; mem. Lord Chancellor's Law Reform Cttee. 1952–63; Master of Bench of Inner Temple 1955; Chair. Gen. Council of the Bar 1958, 1959; Lord Chancellor 1964–70; mem. Int. Comm. of Jurists 1971–; Chancellor The Open Univ. 1972–77; Hon. LL.D. (Birmingham, London, Southampton, Manitoba, Melbourne, Laval, Law Soc. of Upper Canada); Hon. D.Univ. (York) 1966. *Publications:* Capital Punishment as a Deterrent and the Alternative 1956, Law Reform Now (Jt. Ed.) 1963. *Leisure interests;* law reform and the theatre. *Address:* Mote End, Nan Clark's Lane, Mill Hill, London, NW7 4HH, England.

GARDINER, John Eliot, M.A.; British conductor; b. 20 April 1943; s. of late Rolf Gardiner and of Marabel (Hodgkin) Gardiner; m. Elizabeth S. Wilcock 1981; ed. Bryanston School, King's Coll., Cambridge, King's Coll., London and in Paris and Fontainebleau with Nadia Boulanger; formed Monteverdi Choir at Cambridge 1964, Monteverdi Orchestra 1968 and established int. reputation with performance of his own edition of Monteverdi Vespers of 1610 at Henry Wood Promenade Concert, London 1968; founded English Baroque Soloists 1978; U.S. debut with Dallas Symphony Orchestra 1979; Prin. Conductor CBC Van. Orchestra 1981–83; Music Dir. Lyon Opera 1983–; Artistic Dir. Göttingen Handel Festival, Veneto Musica Festival 1981–; is noted particularly for revivals of baroque opera including several operas by Rameau; numerous awards. *Address:* 7 Pleydell Avenue, London, W.6; Gore Farm, Ashmore, Salisbury, Wilts., England (Home). *Telephone:* 01-741 0987.

GARDINER, Robert Kweku Atta, B.SC., M.A.; Ghanaian civil servant and international administrator; b. 29 Sept. 1914, Kumasi; s. of Phillip H. D. Gardiner and Nancy T. Ferguson; m. Linda Charlotte Edwards 1942; one s. two d.; ed. Fourah Bay Coll., Sierra Leone, Selwyn Coll., Cambridge, and New Coll., Oxford; Lecturer in Econs. Fourah Bay Coll. 1943–46; Area Specialist UN Trusteeship Dept. 1947–49; Dir. Dept. of Extra-Mural Studies, Univ. Coll. Ibadan, Nigeria 1949–53; Dir. Dept. of Social Welfare and Community Devt., Ghana 1953–55; Chair. Kumasi Coll. of Tech. Council, Ghana 1954–58; Perm. Sec. Ministry of Housing, Ghana 1955–57; Establishment Sec. and Head of Civil Service 1957–59; Deputy Exec. Sec. UN Economic Comm. for Africa, Addis Ababa 1959–61, Exec. Sec. 1963–75; fmr. Sec. Ghana Presidential Comm. and Council of States; Special Envoy of UN Sec.-Gen. to the Congo 1961; Dir. UN Div. for Public Admin. 1961; Commr. for Econ. Planning, Ghana 1975–78; Chair. Commonwealth

Foundation 1970–73; David Livingstone Visiting Prof. of Econs., Strathclyde Univ. 1970–71; Vice-Chair. Bd. of Dirs. Int. Inst. for Environmental Affairs; UN Special Rep. to the Congo 1962–63; BBC Reith Lecturer 1965; Hon. D.C.L. (East Anglia, Sierra Leone, Tuskegee Inst., Liberia), Hon. LL.D. (Bristol, Ibadan, East Africa, Haile Sellassie I, Strathclyde), Hon. Ph.D. (Uppsala); Hon. D.Sc. (Kumasi, Bradford); Hon. Col. 1977; Order of the Volta. *Publications:* Development of Social Administration (jointly) 1954, A World of Peoples 1965. *Leisure interests:* golf, reading, music, walking. *Address:* c/o Ministry of Finance and Economic Planning, Accra, Ghana.

GARDNER, Ava; American actress; b. 24 Dec. 1922, Smithfield, North Carolina; d. of Jonas B. and Mary Elizabeth Gardner; m. 1st Mickey Rooney 1942; m. 2nd Artie Shaw 1945; m. 3rd Frank Sinatra (q.v.) 1951 (divorced); ed. Atlantic Christian Coll. *Films include:* Lost Angel, Three Men in White, Singapore, One Touch of Venus, Great Sinner, East Side West Side, My Forbidden Past, Show Boat, Love Star, The Snows of Kilimanjaro, Ride Vaquero, Mogambo, The Barefoot Contessa, Bhowani Junction, The Little Hut, The Sun also Rises, Naked Maja, On the Beach, 55 Days to Peking, Night of the Iguana, The Bible, Mayerling, Tam-Lin, The Life and Times of Judge Roy Bean, Earthquake, The Bluebird, The Cassandra Crossing, City on Fire, The Kidnapping of the President, Priest of Love, Regina; *TV includes:* A.D. 1984, The Long Hot Summer 1985, Harem 1985, Knots Landing 1984–85. *Address:* c/o William Morris Agency, 151 El Camino, Beverly Hills, Calif. 90212, U.S.A.

GARDNER, Booth, M.B.A.; American state governor; b. 21 Aug. 1936, Tacoma; m. Jean Gardner; one s. one d.; ed. Univ. of Washington and Harvard Univ.; Asst. to Dean, School of Business Admin. Harvard Univ. 1966; Dir. School of Business & Econs. Univ. of Puget Sound, Tacoma 1967–72; Pres. Laird Norton Co. 1972–80; mem. Washington Senate 1970–73; County Exec. Pierce Co., Tacoma 1981–84; Gov. State of Washington 1985–; Democrat. *Address:* Legislative Building, AS-13, Olympia, Wash. 98504, U.S.A.

GARDNER, John William, PH.D., LL.D.; American writer and consultant; b. 8 Oct. 1912, Los Angeles; s. of William and Marie Flora Gardner; m. Aida Marroquin 1934; two d.; ed. Stanford Univ., and Univ. of Calif.; Teaching Asst. in Psychology, Univ. of Calif. 1936–38; Instructor in Psychology, Conn. Coll. 1938–40; Asst. Prof. Mount Holyoke Coll. 1940–42; Head Latin-American Section, Foreign Broadcasting Intelligence Service, Fed. Communications Comm. 1942–43; served U.S. Marine Corps 1943–46; staff mem. Carnegie Corpn. of New York 1946–47, Exec. Assoc. 1947–49, Vice-Pres. 1949–55, Pres. 1955–65, Consultant 1968–77; Pres. Carnegie Foundation 1955–65; U.S. Secretary of Health, Educ. and Welfare 1965–68; Head of Urban Coalition (Campaign to transform cities of America) 1968–70; Dir. New York Telephone Co. 1961–65, Shell Oil Co. 1962–65, Time Inc. 1968–72, American Airlines 1968–71; Chair. Common Cause (Citizen's Lobby) 1970–77, Chair. Independent Sector 1980–83; Dir. Leadership Studies, Independent Sector 1984–; Fellow, American Psychological Asscn., American Acad. of Arts and Sciences; Chair. Soc. Sciences Panel, Scientific Advisory Bd., U.S.A.F. 1951–55; Dir. New York School of Social Work 1949–55, Metropolitan Museum of Art 1957–65, Stanford Univ. 1968–82, Rockefeller Brothers Fund 1968–77, New York Foundation 1970–76, Sr. Exec. Council, Conf. Bd. 1970–75; mem. Pres. Kennedy's Task Force on Educ. 1960; Chair. U.S. Advisory Comm. on Int. Educ. and Cultural Affairs 1962–64, Pres. Johnson's Task Force on Educ. 1964, White House Conf. on Educ. 1965, Pres.'s Comm. on Agenda for the 1980's, Pres.'s Comm. on White House Fellowships 1977–81; Special Adviser Aspen Inst. for Humanistic Studies 1977–79; Consultant, United Way of America 1977–; mem. Pres.'s Task Force on Private Sector Initiative 1981–82; hon. degrees from numerous American colls. and univs.; U.S.A.F. Exceptional Service Award 1956, Presidential Medal of Freedom 1964, Nat. Acad. of Sciences Public Welfare Medal 1966, UAW Social Justice Award 1968, AFL-CIO Murray Green Medal 1970, Christopher Award 1971, American Inst. for Public Service Award 1973, Robert F. Kennedy Humanitarian Award 1974, Clark Kerr Educ. Award 1974. *Publications:* Excellence 1961 (revised edn. 1984), Self-Renewal 1963 (revised edn. 1981), No Easy Victories 1968, The Recovery of Confidence 1970, In Common Cause 1972, Know or Listen to Those Who Know (with Francesca Gardner Reese) 1975, Ed. To Turn the Tide (by John F. Kennedy), Morale 1978, Quotations of Wit and Wisdom 1980. *Address:* 1828 L Street N.W., Washington, D.C. 20036, U.S.A. (Office).

GARDNER, Kenneth Burslam, B.A., A.L.A.; British orientalist and librarian; b. 5 June 1924, London; s. of Douglas V. Gardner and Dora V. Bowden; m. Cleone Winifred Adams 1949; two s. two d.; ed. Univ. Coll., London and School of Oriental and African Studies, Univ. of London; Asst. Librarian, School of Oriental and African Studies, Univ. of London 1950–54; Asst. Keeper, Dept. of Oriental Printed Books and MSS., British Museum 1955–57, Keeper 1957–70, Prin. Keeper of Printed Books 1970–74; Deputy Keeper of Oriental MSS. and Printed Books, British Library 1974–1986. *Leisure interests:* gardening, reading, mountain walking. *Address:* The Old Stables, 15 Farquhar Street, Bengeo, Hertford, England. *Telephone:* Hertford 583591.

GARDNER, Richard Lavenham, PH.D., F.R.S.; British scientist; b. 10 June 1943, Dorking; s. of the late Allan Constant and Eileen May Gardner; m.

Wendy Joy Cresswell 1968; ed. St. John's School, Leatherhead, N. E. Surrey Col. of Tech., St. Catharine's Coll. Cambridge; Research Asst. Physiological Lab. Cambridge 1970–73; lecturer in Devt. and Reproductive Biology Dept. of Zoology, Oxford 1973–77, research student Christ Church 1974–77, Royal Soc. Henry Dale Research Prof. 1978–; Hon. Dir. Imperial Cancer Research Fund Devt. Biology Unit 1985–; Scientific Medal, Zoological Soc. 1977. *Publications:* various scientific papers. *Leisure interests:* ornithology, music, sailing, gardening, painting. *Address:* Imperial Cancer Fund Developmental Biology Unit, Department of Zoology, South Parks Road, Oxford, OX1 3PS, England.

GARDNER, Richard Newton, D.PHIL.; American diplomatist; b. 9 July 1927, New York; s. of Samuel I. and Ethel E. Gardner; m. Danielle Almeida Luzzatto 1956; one s. one d.; ed. Harvard Univ., Yale Law School, Oxford Univ.; Rhodes Scholar to Oxford Univ. 1951–54; Prof. of Law and Int. Org., Columbia Univ. 1957–61, 1965–76, 1981–; Deputy Asst. Sec. of State for Int. Org. Affairs, U.S. State Dept. 1961–65; U.S. Amb. to Italy 1977–81; Lawyer, Coudert Bros. 1981–; mem. U.S. Advisory Cttee. on Law of the Sea 1971–76; Arthur S. Flemming Award 1963. *Publications:* Sterling-Dollar Diplomacy 1956, In Pursuit of World Order 1964, Blueprint for Peace 1966, The Global Partnership: International Agencies and Economic Development 1968. *Leisure interests:* tennis, classical music, reading. *Address:* Columbia Law School, 435 W. 116 Street, New York (Office); 1150 Fifth Avenue, New York, N.Y. 10028, U.S.A. (Home).

GARDNER, Wilford Robert, M.S., PH.D.; American physicist; b. 19 Oct. 1925, Logan, Utah; s. of Robert Gardner and Nellie Barker Gardner; m. Marjorie L. Cole 1949; one s. two d.; ed. Utah State and Iowa State Univs.; Physicist, U.S. Salinity Lab., Riverside, Calif. 1953–66; Prof. of Soil Physics, Univ. of Wis. 1966–80; Head, Dept. of Soil and Water Science, Univ. of Ariz. 1980–87; Dean. Coll. of Natural Resources, Univ. of Calif., Berkeley 1987–; N.S.F. Sr. Fellow, Univs. of Cambridge and Wageningen 1959–60; Fulbright Fellow Ghent Univ. 1971–72; mem. N.A.S.; Soil Science Soc. of America Research Award. *Publication:* Soil Physics 1972. *Leisure interests:* music, sailing, travel, history. *Address:* College of Natural Resources, University of California, Berkeley, Calif. 94720, U.S.A.

GARETOVSKI, Nikolay, D.ECON.; Soviet banker and politician; b. 1926, Moscow; m. Elena Garetovski 1952; two s.; ed. Moscow Financial Inst.; electrician Aircraft Enterprise 1942–44; joined Ministry of Finance 1950, Deputy Man. Dir. Budgetary Dept. 1966; consultant, Head of Div. CPSU Central Cttee. 1966–81; Deputy Minister of Finance 1981–86, First Deputy Minister 1986–87; Chair. Bd. of Dirs. State Bank 1987–; Orders of Labour Red Banner, Badge of Honour. *Publications:* Finance and Credit under Economic Reform 1969, Financial Vehicles in Stimulating Economic Growth 1972, Instruments of Economic Policy and their Impact on the Efficiency of Production 1980, numerous works on finance. *Leisure interests:* numismatics, philately. *Address:* Neglinnaya 12, Moscow, U.S.S.R. *Telephone:* 292-08-28.

GARFUNKEL, Art, M.A.; American singer and actor; b. 13 Oct. 1941, Forest Hills, New York; m. Kim Cermak 1988; ed. Columbia Univ.; fmrly. mem. singing duo Simon (Paul Simon, q.v.) and Garfunkel 1964–71, now solo performer; *songs with Simon include:* The Sounds of Silence, Dangling Conversation, Homeward Bound, I Am a Rock, At the Zoo, 7 O'Clock News, Silent Night, 59th Street Bridge Song, Scarborough Fair, Parsley, Sage, Rosemary and Thyme, Mrs. Robinson, The Boxer, Bridge Over Troubled Water; *albums with Simon:* Wednesday Morning 3 a.m. 1964, Sounds of Silence 1966, Parsley, Sage, Rosemary and Thyme 1966, The Graduate 1968, Bookends 1968, Bridge Over Troubled Water 1970; solo albums include Angel Clare 1973, Breakaway 1975, Watermark 1978, Fate for Breakfast (Doubt for Dessert) 1979, Art Garfunkel 1979, Scissors Cut 1981, Simon & Garfunkel: The Concert in Central Park 1982; *films include:* Catch-22 1970, Carnal Knowledge 1971, Bad Timing ... A Sensual Obsession 1980, Good to Go 1986, Lefty 1988; recipient two Grammy Awards for songs Mrs. Robinson 1969, six Grammy Awards for album Bridge Over Troubled Water 1970, Grammy Award for film soundtrack of The Graduate.

GARLAND, George David, PH.D., F.R.S.C.; Canadian geophysicist; b. 29 June 1926, Toronto, Ont.; s. of N. L. Garland and Jean McPherson; m. Elizabeth MacMillan 1949; two s. one d.; ed. Univ. of Toronto and St. Louis Univ.; Geophysicist, Dominion Observatory, Ottawa 1950–54; Prof. of Geophysics, Univ. of Alberta, Edmonton 1954–63; Prof. of Geophysics, Univ. of Toronto 1963–; Deputy Gen. Sec. Int. Union of Geodesy and Geophysics 1960–63, Gen. Sec. 1963–73, Pres. 1979; Vice-Pres. Acad. of Science, Royal Soc. 1980–. *Publications:* The Earth's Shape and Gravity 1965, and papers in scientific journals dealing with gravity, terrestrial magnetism, structure of the earth's crust, electrical conductivity of the crust, heat flow from the earth. *Leisure interests:* canoeing, history of Canadian exploration, early maps. *Address:* 194 Owen Boulevard, Willowdale, Ont. M2P 1G7, Canada.

GARLAND, Patrick, B.A.; British television director and writer; b. 10 April 1935; s. of the late Ewart Garland and Rosalind Fell; m. Alexandra Bastedo 1980; ed. St. Mary's Coll., Southampton, St. Edmund Hall, Oxford; actor, Bristol Old Vic 1959, Age of Kings, BBC TV 1961; lived Paris 1961–62; wrote two plays for ITV 1962; Research Asst., Monitor, BBC TV

1963; Dir. and Producer, BBC Arts Dept. 1962–74. *Plays directed:* Forty Years On 1968, 1984, Brief Lives 1968, Getting On 1970, Cyrano 1971, Hair (Israel) 1972, The Doll's House (New York and London) 1975, Under the Greenwood Tree 1978, Look After Lulu 1978, Beecham 1980, York Mystery Plays 1980, My Fair Lady (U.S.A.) 1980, Kipling (London and New York) 1984, Canaries Sometimes Sing 1987; Co-Author of Underneath the Arches 1982–83; Artistic Dir. Chichester Festival Theatre (The Cherry Orchard, The Mitford Girls, On the Rocks, Cavell, Goodbye, Mr Chips, As You Like It, Forty Years On, Merchant of Venice) 1980–84. *Films:* The Snow Goose 1974, The Doll's House 1976; produced: Fanfare for Elizabeth (Queen's 60th birthday gala) 1986, Celebration of a Broadcaster (for Richard Dimbleby Cancer Fund) 1986. *Publications:* Brief Lives 1967, The Wings of the Morning 1989; poetry in London Magazine, New Poems, Poetry West, Encounter; short stories in Transatlantic Review; England Erzählt Gemini, Light Blue Dark Blue. *Leisure interests:* Victorian novels, walking in Corsica. *Address:* 9 Ranulf Road, London, N.W.2, England.

GARLAND, Hon. Sir Victor, K.B.E., B.A., F.C.A.; Australian company director and fmr. politician and diplomatist; b. 5 May 1934, Perth; m. Lynette May Jamieson 1960; two s. one d.; ed. Hale School and Univ. of W. Australia; in practice as chartered accountant 1958–70; mem. Fed. House of Reps. 1969–81; Fed. Exec. Councillor 1971–; Minister for Supply 1971–72; Minister assisting the Treas. 1972, 1975–76; Chief Opposition Whip 1974–75; Chair. House of Reps. Expenditure Cttee. 1976–77; Minister for Special Trade Representations (trade negotiations in Europe, the U.S., Canada and Japan) 1977–79, for Business and Consumer Affairs 1979–80; represented Australian Govt. at numerous int. conferences 1973–79; Chair. Commonwealth Dels. to UNCTAD V, Manila May 1979; High Commr. in the U.K. 1981–83; Dir. Prudential Corpn. PLC 1984–, Throgmorton Trusts PLC 1985–; Deputy Chair. South Bank Bd. 1985–; Freeman City of London 1982. *Address:* 142 Holborn Bars, London, EC1N 2NH, England (Office). *Telephone:* 01-405 9222, Ext. 2137.

GARN, Edwin Jacob (Jake), B.S.; American politician; b. 12 Oct. 1932, Richfield, Utah; s. of Jacob E. Garn and Fern Christensen; m. 1st Hazel R. Thompson 1957 (died 1976), two s. two d.; m. 2nd Kathleen Brewerton 1977, two s. one d.; ed. Univ. of Utah; Special Agent, John Hancock Mutual Life Insurance Co., Salt Lake City 1960–61; Asst. Man. Home Life Insurance Co. New York, Salt Lake City 1961–66; Gen. Agent, Mutual Trust Life Insurance Co., Salt Lake City 1966–68; City Commr. Salt Lake City 1968–72, Mayor 1972–74; Dir. Met. Water Dist. 1968–72; Senator from Utah 1974–; Republican. *Publication:* Night Launch 1989. *Address:* 505 Dirksen Senate Building, Washington, D.C. 20510, U.S.A.

GARN, Stanley Marion, PH.D.; American physical anthropologist and educator; b. 27 Oct. 1922, New London, Conn.; s. of Harry Garn and Sadie Edith (Cohen); m. Priscilla Crozier 1950; one s. one d.; ed. Harvard Coll. and Harvard Univ.; Research Assoc., Chemical Eng., Chemical Warfare Service Devt. Lab., M.I.T. 1942–44; Tech. Ed., Polaroid Co. 1944–46; Consultant in Applied Anthropology 1946–47; Research Fellow, Cardiology, Mass. Gen. Hosp., Boston 1946–52; Instructor in Anthropology, Harvard Univ. 1948–52; Anthropologist, Forsyth Dental Infirmary, Boston 1947–52; Dir. Forsyth Face Size Project, Army Chemical Corps 1950–52; Harvey White Lecturer, Children's Hosp., Chicago; Walker-Ames Visiting Prof., Univ. of Washington; Chair. Dept. of Growth and Genetics, Fels Research Inst., Yellow Springs, Ohio 1952–68; Harvey White Lecturer, Children's Hosp., Chicago; Walker-Ames Visiting Prof., Univ. of Washington; Raymond Pearl Memorial Lecturer, Human Biology Council; Neuhauser Lecturer, Soc. for Pediatric Radiology; Fellow, American Acad. of Arts and Sciences, Center for Human Growth and Devt., Univ. of Mich., Ann Arbor 1968–, Prof. of Nutrition 1968–, Prof. of Anthropology 1972–; Hon. Fellow American Acad. of Pediatrics; mem. N.A.S.; Distinguished Faculty Award, Univ. of Mich. *Publications:* Races 1950, Readings on Race 1960, Human Races 1961, Culture and the Direction of Human Evolution 1964, The Earlier Gain and Later Loss of Cortical Bone 1970, Writing the Biomedical Research Paper 1970, Prenatal Antecedents of Postnatal Growth 1986. *Leisure interests:* photomicrography and culture of succulents. *Address:* Center for Human Growth and Development, 300 North Ingalls Building, Ann Arbor, Mich. 48109-0406; 2410 Londonderry Road, Ann Arbor, Mich. 48104, U.S.A. (Home). *Telephone:* (313) 764-2443 (Office); (313) 665-5235 (Home).

GARNAUT, Ross Gregory, B.A., PH.D.; Australian economist and diplomatist; b. 28 July 1946, Perth, W.A.; s. of late L. Gurnaut and P. W. Gurnaut; m. Jayne Potter 1974; two s.; ed. Perth Modern School, W.A. and Australian Nat. Univ., Canberra; Research Fellow, Sr. Research Fellow and Sr. Fellow Econs. Dept. Research School of Pacific Studies Australian Nat. Univ. 1972–75, 1977–83; First Asst. Sec.-Gen. Financial and Econ. Policy, Papua New Guinea Dept. of Finance 1975–76; Research Dir. Australia Econ. Relations Research Project, ASEAN 1980–83; Sr. Econ. Adviser to Prime Minister Bob Hawke (q.v.) 1983–85; Amb. to People's Repub. of China 1985–87. *Publications:* Irian Jaya: The Transformation of a Melanesian Economy 1974, ASEAN in a Changing Pacific and World Economy 1980, Indonesia: Australian Perspectives 1980, Taxation and Mineral Rents 1983, Exchange Range and Macro-Economic Policy in Independent Papua New Guinea 1984, The Political Economy of Manufacturing Protection: Experiences of ASEAN and Australia 1986, Australian

Protectionism: Extent, Causes and Effects 1987. *Leisure interests:* cricket, tennis and the history of humanity. *Address:* Department of Foreign Affairs and Trade, Canberra A.C.T., Australia.

GARNER, James (James Baumgardner); American actor; b. 7 April 1928, Norman, Okla.; m. Lois Clarke 1956; one s. two d.; ed. New York Berghof School; worked as travelling salesman, oil field worker, carpet layer, bathing suit model; toured with road cos.; Emmy Award; Purple Heart. *TV appearances include:* Cheyenne, Maverick 1957–62, Nichols 1971–72, The Rockford Files 1974–79, Space 1985. *Films include:* Toward the Unknown, Shoot-out at Medicine Bend 1957, Darby's Rangers 1958, Sayonara, Up Periscope 1959, The Americanization of Emily 1964, 36 Hours 1964, The Art of Love 1965, A Man Could Get Killed 1966, Duel at Diablo 1966, Mister Buddwing 1966, Grand Prix 1966, Hour of the Gun 1967, Marlowe 1969, Support Your Local Sheriff 1971, Support Your Local Gunfighter 1971, Skin Game 1971, They Only Kill Their Masters 1972, One Little Indian 1973, Health 1979, The Fan 1980, Victor/Victoria 1982, Murphy's Romance 1985, Promise (made for TV) 1986, Sunset 1987. *Address:* c/o International Creative Management, 8899 Beverly Boulevard, Los Angeles, Calif. 90048, U.S.A.

GARNER, Wendell Richard, PH.D.; American psychologist and university professor; b. 21 Jan. 1921, Buffalo, N.Y.; s. of Richard Charles and Lena Cole Garner; m. Barbara Chipman Ward 1944; one s. two d.; ed. Franklin and Marshall Coll. and Harvard Univ.; Instructor, rising to Prof., Johns Hopkins Univ. 1946–67, Chair. Dept. of Psychology 1954–64; James Rowland Angell Prof. of Psychology, Yale Univ. 1967–, Dir. of Social Sciences 1972–73, 1981–, Chair. Dept. of Psychology 1974–77, Dean of the Graduate School 1978–79; mem. Nat. Acad. of Sciences; Hon. D.Sc. (Franklin and Marshall Coll.) 1979, D.Hum.Litt. (Johns Hopkins Univ.) 1983; Distinguished Scientific Contribution Award, American Psychological Asscn. 1964, Warren Medal, Soc. of Experimental Psychologists 1976. *Publications:* Applied Experimental Psychology (with A. Chapanis and C. T. Morgan) 1949, Uncertainty and Structure as Psychological Concepts 1962, The Processing of Information and Structure 1974, Ability Testing (ed. with A. Wigdor) 1982. *Leisure interests:* gardening, hiking. *Address:* Department of Psychology, Yale University, New Haven, Conn. 06520 (Office); 48 Yowago Avenue, Branford, Conn. 06405, U.S.A. (Home). *Telephone:* (203) 432-4654 (Office); (203) 481-0007 (Home).

GARNHAM, Percy Cyril Claude, C.M.G., M.D., D.SC., F.R.C.P., F.I.BIOL., F.R.S.; British medical protozoologist; b. 15 Jan. 1901, London; s. of late Lieut. P. C. Garnham, R.N.D. and late Edith Garnham; m. Esther Long Price 1924; two s. four d.; ed. St. Bartholomew's Hospital, London; Colonial Medical Service 1925–47; f. Div. of Insect Borne Diseases, Nairobi, Kenya 1944; Reader in Medical Parasitology, London School of Hygiene and Tropical Medicine 1947–51, Prof. of Medical Protozoology and Dir. Dept. of Parasitology, London School of Hygiene and Tropical Medicine 1952–68; Sr. Research Fellow, Imperial Coll. of Science and Tech., London 1968–79; Prof. Emer. (Univ. of London); Visiting Prof. Univ. of Strathclyde 1970–87; Fogarty Int. Scholar 1970; Pres. Royal Soc. of Tropical Medicine and Hygiene 1967–69, British Soc. of Parasitologists 1970–72, European Fed. of Parasitologists 1971–75; Pres. 2nd Int. Conf. on Protozoology; Pontifical Academician, Acad. of Sciences, Vatican; Assoc. mem. Acad. royale de Médecine, Belgium, Acad. Nat. de Médecine, France; Foreign mem. Acad. Royale des Sciences d'Outremer de Bruxelles, Accad. Lancisiana, Rome, Royal Danish Acad. of Sciences and Letters; Hon. mem. Polish, Mexican and British Socs. of Parasitologists, Soc. of Protozoologists, Soc. Pathologie Exotique, Paris, Brazilian, British and American Socs. of Tropical Medicine, Soc. de Protistologues de la Langue française, Soc. de Geografia de Lisboa, Royal Entomological Soc. 1979; Hon. Fellow, London School of Hygiene and Tropical Medicine 1976, Imperial Coll. of Science and Tech. 1979; Hon. F.R.C.P. (Edinburgh); Dr. h.c. (Bordeaux and Montpellier); Kt. of Grace Mil. and Hospitaller Order of St. Lazarus of Jerusalem, Univ. of London Gold Medal 1928, Darling Medal and Prize WHO 1952, Bernhardt Nocht Medal, Hamburg 1958, Gaspar Vianna Medal, Brazil 1962, Manson Medal 1966, Emile Brumpt Prize (Paris) 1970, Médaille d'Or, Soc. de Pathologie Exotique 1971, Médaille de Vermeil, Acad. Nat. de Médecine, France 1972, Mary Kingsley Medal, Liverpool 1973, Rudolf Leuckart Medal (Germany) 1974, Frink Medal, Zoological Soc. London 1985, Linnean Medal, Linnean Soc. London 1986. *Publications:* Immunity to Protozoa (with Pierce and Roitt) 1963, Malaria Parasites 1966, Progress in Parasitology 1971. Catalogue Garnham Collection of Malaria Parasites (with A. J. Duggan) 1986. *Leisure interests:* chamber music, European travel, completing book, The Wake of Poe. *Address:* Southernwood, Farnham Common, Bucks., England (Home). *Telephone:* Farnham Common 3863.

GARNSWORTHY, Most Rev. Lewis Samuel, D.D.; Canadian (Anglican) ecclesiastic; b. 18 July 1922, Edmonton, Alta.; s. of Leonard and Lillian Garnsworthy; m. Jean V. Allen 1954; one s. one d.; ed. Univ. of Alberta and Wycliffe Coll.; ordained priest 1946; Asst. Curate, St. John the Baptist 1946; Rector, St. Nicholas' Church, Birch Cliff 1948, Church of the Transfiguration, Toronto 1956, St. John, York Mills 1960; Suffragan Bishop of Diocese of Toronto 1968, Bishop of Toronto 1972; Archbishop of Toronto 1979–88; Metropolitan of the Ecclesiastical Prov. of Ontario 1979–85; Hon. D.D. (Wycliffe) 1969, (Trinity) 1973, (Huron) 1976. *Leisure interest:* gardening. *Address:* 135 Adelaide Street East, Toronto, Ont. M5C 1L8, Canada. *Telephone:* (416) 363-6021.

GARRARD, Rose, DIP.A.D.; British sculptor and mixed media artist; b. 21 Sept. 1946, Bewdley, Worcs.; d. of Col. W. V. Garrard. M.B.E. and Germaine Garrard; m. (divorced); no c.; ed. Stourbridge, Birmingham and Chelsea Colls. of Art and Acad. des Beaux Arts, Paris; freelance designer, model and prop-maker to magazines, theatres, advertisers and TV 1969–83; arts consultant to architects advising on public works projects including Liverpool Shopping Precinct and Elephant & Castle Shopping Centre 1971–74; Artist in Schools Residency, Cen. Foundation School for Girls, Bow, E. London 1982; Artist-in-Residence, Birmingham City Art Gallery 1983; Sr. Lecturer, half full-time, Art and Social Context, Dartington Coll. of Arts; has held various other part-time teaching and lecturing appts. throughout U.K.; solo exhbns. in Worcester 1967, London 1977, 1983, Cambridge 1983, Birmingham, Liverpool, Bristol, Nottingham and Rochdale 1984, Inst. of Contemporary Art (ICA), London 1984; has participated in numerous group exhbns. in U.K., Europe, U.S.A., Canada, and Australia since 1967; works in many public and pvt. collections including Victoria & Albert Museum, Contemporary Art Soc. and Arts Council of G.B.; mem. numerous selection panels etc.; Int. Multiples Prize Award by Paolozzi 1969; Prix d'Honneur de Paris for Sculpture 1971; Arts Council of G.B. Purchase Award 1979; Greater London Arts Asscn. Major Award 1980. *Address:* Studio 21, 105 Carpenters Road, London, E18, England. *Telephone:* 01-519 6321.

GARRELS, Robert M., B.S., M.S., PH.D.; American professor of geology; b. 24 Aug. 1916, Detroit, Mich.; s. of John C. Garrels and Margaret Anne Garrels; m. 1st Jane M. Tinen 1940 (divorced 1969), one s. two d.; m. 2nd Cynthia A. Hunt 1970; ed. Univ. of Michigan and Northwestern Univ.; Instructor, Asst., Assoc. Prof., Northwestern Univ. 1941–52, Prof. of Geology 1965–69; Chief of Solid State Group, Geochem. and Petrology Branch, U.S. Geological Survey 1952–55; Assoc. Prof., Harvard Univ. 1955–57, Prof. of Geology 1957–63, Chair. Dept. of Geological Sciences 1963–65; Henri Speciale Chair of Applied Science, Univ. of Brussels 1962–63; Prof. of Geology, Scripps Inst. of Oceanography 1969–71; Captain James Cook Prof. of Oceanography, Univ. of Hawaii 1972–74; Prof. of Geology Northwestern Univ. 1972–80; Prof. of Marine Science, Univ. of South Fla. 1980– (St. Petersburg Progress Endowed Chair 1983); mem. Nat. Acad. of Sciences, American Acad. Arts and Sciences; Hon. D.Sc. (Brussels) 1969, (Univ. Louis Pasteur, Strasbourg) 1976; Hon. Ph.D. (Univ. of Michigan) 1980; Petroleum Research Fund of American Chemical Soc. Type C Award 1963, Best Paper Award (with F. T. Mackenzie) in Journal of Sedimentary Petrology 1966, Arthur L. Day Medal of Geological Soc. of America 1966, V. M. Goldschmidt Award, Geochem. Soc. 1973, Penrose Medal of Geological Soc. of America 1978, Roebling Medal, Mineralogical Soc. of America 1981, Wollaston Medal, Geological Soc. of London 1981, Fla. Scientist of the Year Award, Museum of Science and Industry, Tampa 1985; Life mem. Bermuda Biological Station for Research 1985; Hon. Fellow Geological Soc. of America 1988. *Publications:* A Textbook of Geology 1951, Mineral Equilibria at Low Temperature and Pressure 1960, Solution, Minerals and Equilibria (with C. L. Christ) 1965, The Evolution of Sedimentary Rocks (with F. T. Mackenzie) 1971, Water, The Web of Life (with Cynthia Hunt) 1972, Chemical Cycles and the Global Environment (with F. T. Mackenzie and Cynthia Hunt) 1975, Thermodynamic values at low temperature for natural inorganic materials: An Uncritical Survey (with Terri L. Woods) 1987. *Leisure interest:* athletics. *Address:* Department of Marine Science, University of South Florida, 140 Seventh Avenue South, St. Petersburg, Florida 33701, U.S.A. *Telephone:* (813) 893-9538.

GARRETT, Prof. Stephen Denis, F.R.S.; British professor of science; b. 1 Nov. 1906, Leiston, Suffolk; s. of the late Stephen Garrett and Mary Marples; m. Ruth Jane Perkins 1934; three d.; ed. Eastbourne Coll., Univ. of Cambridge, Imperial Coll., Univ. of London; Asst. Plant Pathologist, Waite Agric. Research Inst., Univ. of Adelaide 1929–33; Research Student, Imperial Coll., Univ. of London 1934–35, Leverhulme Fellowship 1935–37; Mycologist, Rothamsted Experimental Station 1937–48; Mycologist, W. Indian Banana Research Scheme 1948; Lecturer, Univ. of Cambridge 1949–61, Reader 1961–71, Prof. 1971–73, Emer. 1973–, Fellow of Magdalene Coll.; Fellow, Inst. of Biology 1964; Hon. Fellow Indian Acad. of Sciences 1973; Hon. mem. British Mycological Soc. 1975, British Soc. for Plant Pathology 1984. *Publications:* include Soil Fungi and Soil Fertility 1963, Pathogenic Root-Infecting Fungi 1970, 80 papers in scientific journals. *Leisure interest:* keeping annotated card index of British and some European florals. *Address:* 315 Lichfield Road, Cambridge, CB1 3SH, England (Home). *Telephone:* 0223-247865.

GARRONE, H.E. Cardinal Gabriel Marie, D.PHIL., D.THEOL.; French ecclesiastic; b. 12 Oct. 1901, Aix-les-Bains, Savoie; s. of Jean Garrone and Joséphine Mathieu; ed. Inst. Notre-Dame de la Villette, Univ. de Grenoble and Pontificia Universitas Gregoriana, Rome; ordained priest 1925; Prof., Grand Seminary, Chambéry 1945; Archbishop Coadjutor, Toulouse 1947; Archbishop, Toulouse and Narbonne, Primate of Narbonne 1956–66; Vice-Pres. Perm. Council of Plenary Assembly of French episcopate 1964–66; Pro-Prefect, Congregation of Seminaries and of Univs., Rome 1966–67; Prefect, Congregation for Catholic Educ. 1968–80; Pres. Comité de Présidence pour les rapports de l'Eglise avec la Culture 1980–; cr. Cardinal by Pope Paul VI 1967; Grand Croix Légion d'honneur, Croix de guerre (1939–45). *Publications:* Psaumes et prières, Invitation à la prière, Leçons

sur la foi, La morale du Credo, La porte des écritures, Panorama du Credo, Sainte Eglise notre Mère, Morale chrétienne et valeurs humaines, Que faut-il croire?, La religieuse présente à Dieu et au monde, Seigneur, dis-moi ton nom, Le Concile, orientations, Qu'est-ce que Dieu?, Ce que croyait Thérèse de Lisieux, Religieuse aujourd'hui? Oui mais ..., L'Eucharistie au secours de la foi, Voilà ta mère, L'action catholique, Foi et pédagogie, L'Eucharistie, Pourquoi prier?, La religieuse, signe de Dieu dans le monde, Les Psaumes, prière pour aujourd'hui, La profession de foi de Paul VI, Ce que croyait Pascal, Le goût de pain, Les écrits spirituels du Cardinal Saliège, Présentation de "Gaudium et spes", Le secret d'une vie engagée: Mgr. Guerry, L'Eglise: 1965–72, Que faut-il faire?, La foi en 1973, Pour vous, qui suis-je?, La foi au fil des jours, Le Credo lu dans l'histoire, le Prêtre, Aller ... jusqu'à Dieu, Ce que croyait Jeanne Jugan, Notre foi tout entière, Marie hier et aujourd'hui, Prédication et Eucharistie, Je suis le Chemin 1981, 50 ans de vie d'Eglise 1982, La communion fraternelle "dernière volonté du Seigneur, Synode 85, Présentation sommaire et ordonneé de la foi. *Address:* Largo del Colonnato 3, 00193 Rome, Italy.

GARTON, George Alan, S.B.ST.J., PH.D., D.SC., F.R.S.E., F.R.S.; British biochemist; b. 4 June 1922, Scarborough, Yorks.; s. of late William E. and Frances M. E. Garton; m. Gladys F. Davison 1951; two d.; ed. Scarborough High School for Boys and Univ. of Liverpool; experimental asst., Ministry of Supply 1942–45; Johnston Research and Teaching Fellow, Univ. of Liverpool 1949–50; Rowett Research Inst., Aberdeen 1950–83, Head, Lipid Biochem. Dept. 1963, Deputy Dir. 1968, Hon. Research Assoc. 1983–; Visiting Prof. of Biochem. Univ. of N. Carolina 1967; Chair. British Nat. Cttee. for Nutritional and Food Services 1982–87; mem. Council, British Nutrition Foundation 1982–; Hon. Research Fellow, Univ. of Aberdeen 1987–; Pres. Int. Confs. on Biochemistry of Lipids 1982–. *Publications:* many papers, reviews and chapters in books on the subjects of lipid biochemistry and nutrition. *Leisure interests:* golf, gardening, philately, foreign travel. *Address:* Ellerburn, 1 St. Devenick Crescent, Cults, Aberdeen, AB1 9LL, Scotland. *Telephone:* (0224) 867012.

GARTON, William Reginald Stephen, D.SC., A.R.C.S., F.R.S.; British professor emeritus of spectroscopy; b. 7 March 1912, London; s. of William and Gertrude (née Thiel) Garton; m. 1st Margarita F. Callingham 1940 (dissolved 1976), 2nd Barbara Lloyd Jones 1976; four d.; ed. Sloane School, London, Chelsea Polytechnic and Imperial Coll., London; Demonstrator in Physics, Imperial Coll., London 1936–39; R.A.F. 1939–45; lecturer in Physics, Imperial Coll. 1946–54, Sr. Lecturer 1954–57, Reader 1957–64, Prof. of Spectroscopy 1964–69, Assoc. Head, Dept. of Physics 1970–79, Sr. Research Fellow 1979–, now Prof. Emer.; Hon. Fellow, Imperial Coll. 1983; Assoc. Harvard Coll. Observatory 1963–; Fellow Optical Soc. of America; Emer. Fellow, Leverhulme Trust 1987–(89); Hon. D.Sc. (York Univ., Toronto) 1976. *Publications:* numerous papers on spectroscopy, atomic physics and astrophysics. *Leisure interests:* oriental history, spelaeology. *Address:* Blackett Laboratory, Imperial College, London, S.W.7 (Office); Chart House, Great Chart, Ashford, Kent, England; 9 calle Tico Medina, Mojacar (Almeria), Spain (Homes). *Telephone:* 01-589 5111 (Office); 0233 21657 (Ashford Home).

GARVIN, Clifton C., Jr.; American business executive; b. 22 Dec. 1921; s. of Clifton and Esther (Ames) Garvin; m. Thelma Volland 1943; one s. three d.; ed. Virginia Polytechnic Inst. Army service until 1947; joined Exxon 1947, Process Engineer, Baton Rouge Refinery, Man. Product Supply and Distribution Exxon Co. U.S.A. (fmrly. Humble Oil & Refinery Co.) 1961, Vice-Pres. Exxon Co. U.S.A. Cen. Region 1963, Pres. Exxon Chemical Co., Exec. Vice-Pres., Dir. Exxon Corpn. 1968, Pres. 1972–75, Chair. of Board and C.E.O. 1975–86; Dir. American Petroleum Inst., Chair. 1982–83; Dir. Citibank, N.A. (fmrly. First Nat. City Bank), Citicorp, PepsiCo, Sperry Corpn.; Chair. The Business Council; mem. The Business Roundtable; mem. Bd. Sloan-Kettering Inst. for Cancer Research; mem. American Chemical Soc., American Inst. of Chemical Engs., Nat. Petroleum Council; mem. The Business Council, Chair. 1983–; Trustee, Vanderbilt Univ., Cttee. for Econ. Devt., Vanderbilt Univ., The Conference Board. *Leisure interest:* golf. *Address:* Room 1250, One Rockefeller Plaza, New York, N.Y. 10020, U.S.A.

GARWIN, Richard L., M.S., PH.D.; American physicist; b. 19 April 1928, Cleveland, Ohio; s. of Robert and Leona S. Garwin; m. Lois E. Levy 1947; two s. one d.; ed. public schools in Cleveland, Case Western Reserve Univ. and Univ. of Chicago; Instructor and Asst. Prof. of Physics, Univ. of Chicago 1949–52; mem. staff, IBM Watson Lab., Columbia Univ. 1952–65, 1966–70; Adjunct Prof. of Physics, Columbia Univ. 1957–; Dir. of Applied Research, IBM T. J. Watson Research Center 1965–66, IBM Fellow 1967–; mem. Defense Science Bd. 1966–69; mem. President's Science Advisory Cttee. 1962–64, 1969–72; mem. IBM Corporate Tech. Cttee. 1970–71; Prof. of Public Policy, Kennedy School of Govt., Harvard 1979–81, Adjunct Research Fellow 1982–; Andrew D. White Prof.-at-Large, Cornell Univ. 1982–; mem. Council on Foreign Relations; mem. Nat. Acad. of Sciences, Inst. of Medicine 1975–81, Nat. Acad. of Eng. 1978–, American Philosophical Soc. 1979–; Fellow, American Physical Soc. American Acad. of Arts and Sciences; Ford Foundation Fellow, CERN, Geneva 1959–60; Hon Dr. (Case Western Reserve Univ.) 1966. *Publications:* Co-Author: Nuclear Power Issues and Choices 1977, Nuclear Weapons and World Politics 1977,

Energy, the Next Twenty Years (co-author) 1979, The Dangers of Nuclear Wars 1979; about 130 published papers and 30 U.S. patents. *Leisure interests:* skiing, military technology, arms control, social use of technology. *Address:* IBM Corporation, Research Division, Thomas J. Watson Research Center, P.O. Box 218, Yorktown Heights, New York, N.Y. 10598, U.S.A. *Telephone:* (914) 945-2555.

GASCAR, Pierre; French writer; b. 13 March 1916, Paris; m. 2nd Alice Simon 1958; two s. (by first marriage); army service in France and Scotland 1939–40; captured, twice escaped, recaptured and sent to Rawa-Ruska concentration camp (Ukraine); fmr. journalist, journeys in Europe, China, S.E. Asia, America and Africa; Prix des Critiques, Prix Goncourt 1953, Grand Prix de Littérature (Acad. Française) 1969, Prix de littérature du Prince Pierre de Monaco 1978. *Publications:* Les meubles 1949, Les bêtes, Le temps des morts 1953, Les femmes 1955, La graine, Chine ouverte 1956, L'herbe des rues, Voyage chez les vivants 1958, La barre de corail, Soleils, Les pas perdus 1959, Le fugitif 1961, Vertiges du présent, Les moutons de feu 1963, Le meilleur de la vie 1964, Les charmes 1965, Auto 1968, Les chimères 1969, L'arche 1971, Le présage 1973, L'homme et l'animal 1974 Les sources 1975, Le bal des ardents 1977, L'ombre de Robespierre 1979, Un jardin de curé 1979, Les secrets de maître Bernard 1980, Le règne végétal 1981, Buffon 1983, Le fortin 1983, Le diable à Paris 1985, Humboldt, L'Explorateur 1986, Du côté de chez Monsieur Pasteur 1986, L'Ange gardien 1987. *Leisure interest:* travel.

GASCON, Jean, C.C., LL.D.; Canadian actor and theatre director; b. 21 Dec. 1920, Montreal; s. of Charles-Auguste and Rose Gascon; m. Marilyn Gardner; ed. Univ. of Western Ont., Queen's Univ. at Kingston, McGill Univ., Bishop's Univ., McMaster Univ., Univ. of Guelph, Univ. de Montréal, Univ. of Ottawa; f. Le Théâtre de Nouveau Monde 1951; co-founder and Dir. (later Gen. Dir.), Nat. Theatre School 1960; Assoc. Dir., Shakespearean Festival Foundation of Canada, Stratford, Ont. 1964; Artistic Dir., Stratford (Ont.) Festival 1967–74; Dir. of Theatre, Nat. Arts Centre, Ottawa 1977–; Molson Award (for promotion of better understanding between French and English cultures in Canada), Canadian Drama Award, Royal Bank Award 1974, Prix du Québec for Theatre 1985. *Leisure interests:* reading, intelligent conversation. *Address:* 227 ave. Clarke, Appt. 2, Westmount, Quebec, Canada. *Telephone:* 933-5776.

GASH, Norman, C.B.E., M.LITT., F.R.S.E., F.B.A., F.R.HIST.S., F.R.S.L.; British historian; b. 16 Jan. 1912, Meerut, India; s. of Frederick Gash and Kate Gash née Hunt; m. Ivy Dorothy Whitehorn 1935; two d.; ed. Reading School and St. John's Coll. Oxford; Lecturer in History, Univ. Coll. London 1936–40; war service in army 1940–46; Lecturer in History, St. Salvator's Coll., St. Andrews 1946–53; Prof. of Modern History, Univ. of Leeds 1953–55; Prof. of History, St. Andrews Univ. 1955–80, now Prof. Emer., Vice-Prin. 1967–71, Dean of Faculty of Arts 1978–80; Hinkley Visiting Prof., Johns Hopkins Univ., U.S.A. 1962; Ford's Lecturer in English History, Oxford Univ. 1963–64; Sir John Neale Lecturer, Univ. Coll. London 1981; Hon. Fellow St. John's Coll., Oxford 1987; Hon. D.Litt. (Strathclyde) 1984, (St. Andrews) 1985. *Publications:* Politics in the Age of Peel 1953, Mr Secretary Peel 1961, Reaction and Reconstruction in English Politics 1832–52 1965, Sir Robert Peel 1973, Aristocracy and People: Britain 1815–65 1979, Lord Liverpool 1984, Pillars of Government 1986. *Leisure interests:* gardening and swimming. *Address:* Old Gatehouse, Portway, Langport, Somerset, TA10 0NQ, England. *Telephone:* (0458) 250334.

GASIS, Andrew; Greek professor of law; b. 17 Oct. 1909, Athens; m. 1st Calliope Nicoloudis 1939 (divorced 1960), 2nd Miranda Lagacos 1961; one s. three d.; ed. Athens Univ., Berlin and Hamburg Univs. and Univ. Coll., London; Asst. Prof. Athens Univ. 1945–61, Prof. 1961–74, Dean, School of Law 1969–70; retd. 1974; Dir. Greek Inst. of Int. and Foreign Law 1974–; Chair. Bd. of Dirs., Nat. Cen. of Social Research 1974–81, Greek Union of Arbitrators 1985–; Pres. Comm. to revise Family Law 1975–79; Dir. Révue Hellénique du Droit Int. 1975–. *Publications:* Breach of Contract 1940, Disposing of Another's Real Property 1942, The New Monetary Laws 1946, Contribution to the Interpretation of the Greek Civil Code 1949–57, Collision of Rights 1959, General Principles of the Civil Law 1970, Equality of Rights and Obligations between Men and Women in Private Law 1979, The New Law on Divorce 1980, Problems of the New Family Law 1983–84, and over 40 articles on civil law, civil procedure, conflict of laws, comparative law. *Address:* 19 Herodotou Street, GR 10674 Athens, Greece. *Telephone:* 7228282.

GASKILL, William; British theatre and opera director; b. 24 June 1930; ed. Salt High School, Shipley, and Hertford Coll., Oxford; Dir., Granada Television 1956–57; Asst. Artistic Dir. Royal Court Theatre, London 1958–60; Dir. Royal Shakespeare Co. 1961–62; Assoc. Dir. Nat. Theatre, London 1963–65, 1979; Artistic Dir. English Stage Co., Royal Court Theatre 1965–72, mem. Council 1978–; Dir. Joint Stock Theatre Group 1974–. Stage productions include: (Royal Court Theatre) Epitaph for George Dillon, One Way Pendulum, Saved, Early Morning, Man is Man, Lear, Big Wolf, The Sea, The Gorky Brigade; (National Theatre) The Recruiting Officer, Mother Courage, Philoctetes, Armstrong's Last Goodnight, The Beaux Stratagem, The Madras House, A Fair Quarrel; (Royal Shakespeare Co.) The Caucasian Chalk Circle, Richard III, Cymbeline; (Joint Stock) The Speakers, Fanshen, Yesterday's News, A Mad World,

My Masters, The Ragged Trousered Philanthropists; other productions include Baal, Love's Labours Lost, King Oedipus and Oedipus at Colonnus (Dubrovnik Festival), The Barber of Seville, and La Bohème (Welsh Nat. Opera). *Address:* 124A Leighton Road, London, N.W.5, England.

GÁSPÁR, Sándor; Hungarian politician; b. 15 April 1917, Pánd; mem. C.P. 1936–, several posts in C.P. 1945–; Asst. Gen. Sec. Cen. Council of Trade Unions 1952, Gen. Sec. 1956–59, 1965–83, Pres. 1983–88; First Sec. Budapest Cttee. of HSWP 1959–61, 1962–65, mem. Cen. Cttee. 1956–88, Sec. 1961, mem. Political Cttee. 1962–88; M.P.; Deputy Pres. Hungarian Presidential Council 1963–88; Pres. WFTU 1978–; Order of Merit, Order of the October Revolution (U.S.S.R.), Golden Medal of the WFTU. *Publications:* A nemzetközi szakszervezeti mozgalom (The International Trade Union Movement) 1980, A munkásosztály szolgálatában (In the Service of the Working Class) 1983. *Address:* Central Council of Trade Unions, H-1415 Budapest VI, Dózsa Gy, ut 84/b, Hungary. *Telephone:* 225-840.

GASPARI, Remo; Italian politician; b. 10 July 1921, Gissi, Chieti; mem. Christian Democrat Party (D.C.) 1945–, Deputy Prov. Sec., Chieti Cttee. 1948, Mayor of Gissi; M.P. for Aquila-Pescara-Teramo-Chieti 1953–, Under-Sec., Ministry of Posts 1960–62, Ministry of Industry and Trade 1962–63, Ministry of Posts 1963–66, Ministry of Interior 1966–68, fmr. posts as Minister of Transport and Civil Aviation, Without Portfolio for Reform of Public Admin., of Health, for Parl. Relations and of Posts and Telecommunications; Minister Without Portfolio for Public Admin. 1986–87, for Civil Protection and Natural Disasters 1987–88, for Southern Italy April 1988–. *Address:* Camera del Deputati, Rome, Italy.

GASS, Ian Graham, D.SC., F.R.S.; British geologist and university professor; b. 20 March 1926, Gateshead, Durham (now Tyne and Wear); s. of late John G. and Lillian R. Gass; m. F. Mary Pearce 1955; one s. one d.; ed. Royal Grammar School, Newcastle upon Tyne, Almondbury Grammar School, Huddersfield and Leeds Univ.; served H.M. forces 1944–48; Geologist, Sudan Geological Survey 1952–55, Cyprus Geological Survey 1955–60; Asst. Lecturer, Univ. of Leicester 1960–61; Lecturer, Sr. Lecturer Univ. of Leeds 1961–69; Prof. of Earth Sciences, Open Univ. 1969–82, Personal Chair. 1982–; Prestwich Medal, Geological Soc. 1979; Murchison Medal 1988; mem. Natural Environment Research Council 1985–87. *Publications:* more than 100 publications on earth sciences research and educ. *Leisure interests:* hill walking, bridge. *Address:* Department of Earth Sciences, The Open University, Walton Hall, Milton Keynes, MK7 6AA (Office); 12 Greenacres, Bedford, MK41 9AJ, England (Home). *Telephone:* (0908) 653751 (Office); (0234) 52712 (Home).

GASSMAN, Vittorio; Italian actor and director; b. 1 Sept. 1922; ed. Law Univ. of Rome and Dramatic Acad. of Rome. *Plays acted in include:* Hamlet, Othello, As You Like It, Troilus and Cressida, Oedipus Rex, Prometheus Bound, Ghosts, Peer Gynt, Orestes, Rosencrantz and Guildenstern are Dead, Richard III, etc.; has directed his own group since 1951. *Films acted in include:* Bitter Rice, Anna, Rhapsody, War and Peace, the Miracle, I Soliti Ignoti, etc.; Dir. Kean 1956 and The Great War, Venice Festival winner; Dir. musical- play Irma la Douce; four awards for the best Italian theatre actor of the year, four for the best film actor; created Teatro Popolare Italiano (mobile theatre, 3,000 seats); dir. and played Agamemnon in production of Aeschylus' Oresteia, Syracuse 1960. *Address:* Piazza S. Alessio 32, 00191 Rome, Italy.

GASSMANN, Rev. Günther, D.THEOL.; German ecclesiastic; b. 15 Aug. 1931, Frankenhausen; s. of Julius Gassmann and Meta Gassmann; m. Ursula Kähler 1958; three s.; ed. Univ. of Heidelberg and Univ. of Oxford; Asst. Prof. Univ. of Heidelberg 1962–69; Research Prof. Inst. for Ecumenical Research, Strasbourg 1969–76; Pres. Cen. Office, Lutheran Churches in Germany, Hanover 1976–82; Ecumenical Officer Lutheran World Fed., Geneva 1982–83; Dir. Comm. on Faith and Order, World Council of Churches, Geneva 1984–. *Publications:* The Historic Episcopate and the Unity of the Church 1964, Confessions in Dialogue (with N. Ehrenstrom) 1974, Concepts of Unity in the Faith and Order Movement 1977, The Unity of the Church 1983, numerous articles in periodicals. *Leisure interests:* trains, stamps. *Address:* World Council of Churches, 150 Route de Ferney, 1211 Geneva, Switzerland. *Telephone:* (22) 91 63 37.

GASTAUT, Henri Jean; French biologist; b. 5 April 1915, Monaco; s. of Jean-Baptiste Gastaut and Marie-Louise Monceau; m. Yvette Reynaud 1935; two s. one d.; ed. Monaco and Nice Lycées, Marseilles Univ.; Head, Nervous Anatomy Lab. 1939, Nervous Diseases Clinic 1944, Tit. Prof. Pathological Anatomy 1952–72, Marseilles Univ. Medical Faculty; Head, Marseilles Hospitals Neurobiological Lab. 1953–, Marseilles region Centre for Epileptic Children 1960–; Dir. Neurobiological Research Unit, Inst. Nat. de la Santé, Marseilles 1961–; Marseilles Hospitals Biologist 1963–; Dir. Medical Tropical Inst., Dean of the Medical Faculty, Marseilles 1967; Rector Acad. of Aix-Marseilles 1971–, Titular Prof. Clinical Neurophysiology 1973–; Dir. Inst. of Neurological Research 1984; Sec., later Pres., Int. Fed. of Socs. for Electroencephalography and Clinical Neurophysiology, Int. League against Epilepsy; Hon. mem. or Corresp., Acad. française de Médecine, Acad. royale belge de Médecine, Acad. Nacional de Medicina de Buenos Aires; Soc. de Neurologie française, American Acad. of Neurology, Royal Coll. of Psychiatrists (U.K.), Royal Soc. of Medicine (U.K.), etc.; Dr. h.c. (Ottawa, Liège, Bologna, Shanghai); Prix Monthyon (French

Acad. des Sciences) 1957; Officier Légion d'honneur, Commdr. Ordre national du Mérite, Ordre des Palmes académiques, Officier Saint Charles de Monaco, Commdr. Ordre National, Ivory Coast. *Publications:* books and monographs on applied neurophysiology. *Leisure interest:* collection of ethnographical art. *Address:* 87 boulevard Périer, 13008 Marseille, France. *Telephone:* (91) 81-44-82.

GASTON, William W., B.S.; American business executive; b. 1926, Fayetteville, N.C.; m.; ed. Clemson Univ.; with Gold Kist Inc. Atlanta 1950-, Sr. Vice-Pres., mem. Man. Exec. Cttee. 1972-77, Exec. Vice-Pres., mem. Man. Exec. Cttee. 1977-78, Pres., Chair. Man. Exec. Cttee. 1978-, C.E.O. 1984-; Dir. Cen. Bank Co-ops, Ga. N. Railway Co., Cotton States Life and Health Insurance Co., Cotton States Mutual Insurance Co., Nat. Council Farmer Co-ops, Southern Bell Telephone & Telecommunications Co. *Address:* Gold Kist Inc., 244 Perimeter Center, Parkway N.E., Box 2210, Atlanta, Ga. 30346, U.S.A.

GAT, Dr. Joel R., M.SC., PH.D.; Israeli professor of isotope research; b. 17 Feb. 1926, Munich, Germany; m.; two c.; ed. Hebrew Univ., Jerusalem. Dept. of Physical Chem., Hebrew Univ. 1949-50; Ministry of Defence Labs., Jerusalem 1950-52; Israel Atomic Energy Comm., Rehovot 1952-59; Fellow, ISNSE, Argonne Nat. Labs. and Enrico Fermi Inst., Univ. of Chicago, Ill. 1955-56; Fellow, Scripps Inst. of Oceanography, Univ. of Calif. San Diego at La Jolla 1964-65; Acting Head, later Head, Isotopes Dept., Weizmann Inst. of Science 1966-70, 1974; Prof. Isotope Research 1971-; Sr. postdoctoral Fellow at N.C.A.R. Boulder, Colo. 1972-73; Walter P. Reuther Chair in the Peaceful Uses of Atomic Energy 1968. *Address:* The Weizmann Institute of Science, P.O. Box 26, Rehovot, Israel.

GATES, Marshall De Motte, Jr.; American professor of chemistry; b. 25 Sept. 1915, Boyne City, Mich.; s. of Marshall D. Gates and Virginia Orton Gates; m. Martha L. Meyer 1941; two s. two d.; ed. Rice and Harvard Univs.; Asst. Prof. of Chem., Bryn Mawr Coll. 1941-46, Assoc. Prof. 1947-49; Tech. Aide, Nat. Defense Research Council 1943-46; Lecturer in Chem., Univ. of Rochester 1949-52, part-time Prof. 1952-60, Prof. 1960-68, Charles Houghton Prof. of Chem. 1968-81; Prof. Emer. 1981-; Visiting Prof. Dartmouth 1982, 1984, 1985; mem. Cttee. on Drugs Addiction and Narcotics, Div. of Medical Sciences, Nat. Research Council 1956-69; mem. Nat. Acad. of Sciences, American Chem. Soc.; Fellow, American Acad. of Arts and Sciences, New York Acad. of Sciences; Asst. Ed. Journal of American Chemical Society 1949-62, Ed. 1963-69; Max Tishler Lecturer, Harvard 1953, Welch Foundation Lecturer 1960; mem. President's Cttee. on Nat. Medal of Science 1968-70, Advisory Bd., Chem. Abstract Services 1974-76; E. P. Curtis Award 1967, Distinguished Alumnus Award, Rice Univ. 1987. *Leisure interests:* skiing, sailing. *Address:* Department of Chemistry, University of Rochester, Rochester, N.Y. 14627 (Office); 41 West Brook Road, Pittsford, New York, U.S.A. (Home).

GATT, Lawrence, B.ARCH., M.P.; Maltese politician; b. 1941, Rabat, Malta; m. Agnes Sammut; one s. one d.; ed. the Lyceum and Univ. of Malta; mem. Parl. 1971-; Asst. Whip., mem. Exec. Council and mem. Gen. Council, Nationalist Party 1971-; Minister of Productive Devt. May 1987-. *Address:* Ministry of Productive Development, 3 Old Mint Street, Valletta, Malta.

GATTAZ, Yvon; French business executive; b. 17 June 1925, Bourgoin; s. of Marceau Gattaz and Gabrielle Brotel; m. Geneviève Beurley 1954; two s. one d.; ed. Coll. of Bourgoin, Lycée du Parc, Lyon, Ecole Centrale des Arts et Manufactures, Paris; with Aciéries du Nord 1948-50; Automobiles Citroën 1950-54; founder Soc. Radiall 1952, Chair. 1952-; Chair. group of commercial and industrial cos., Rosny-sous-Bois 1967-81; Admin. Centre for External Trade 1979-82, Nat. Council for Scientific Research 1979-81; founder Mouvement des entreprises à taille humaine industrielles et commerciales 1976, Pres. 1976-81; Hon. Pres. 1981-; founder Les Quatres Vérités 1974, Co-Ed. 1974-81; mem. Conseil economique et social 1979-; Pres. Conseil national du Patronat français 1981-86, Hon. Pres. 1986; Pres. admin. council Fondation jeunesse et entreprise 1986-; Chevalier Légion d'honneur; Chevalier, Ordre nat. du Mérite. *Publications:* Les hommes en gris 1970, La fin des patrons 1980. *Leisure interest:* skiing. *Address:* c/o Conseil National du Patronat Français, 31 avenue Pierre 1er de Serbie, 75874 Paris, France (Office).

GATTEGNO, Jean, D. ÈS L.; French administrative official; b. 6 June 1935, Paris; ed. Lycée de Blois, Lycée Henri IV, Lycée Louis le Grand and Ecole Normale Supérieure; Research Fellow, C.N.R.S. 1962-65; subsequently Asst. at Sorbonne and Dir. of Educ. in Tunis; Prof. of English Literature Vincennes (Paris VIII) 1968; Univ. Prof. 1974; Head, Higher Educ. Section, Syndicat Général de l'Education Nationale C.F.D.T. 1973-77; Dir. of Literature, Ministry of Culture; Légion d'honneur. *Publication:* 'Que Sais-je' sur la science fiction and two other works.

GATTING, Michael William, O.B.E.; English cricketer; b. 6 June 1957, Kingsbury, Middx.; m. Elaine Gatting; two s.; ed. Wykeham Primary School and John Kelly High School; first class début for Middx. 1975; awarded county cap 1977; Captain of Middx. 1983-; test début 1977; Capt. of England 1986-; Cricket Writers' Club Young Cricketer of 1981. *Publications:* Limited Overs 1986, Triumph in Australia 1987. *Address:* c/o Middlesex County Cricket Club, Lord's Cricket Ground, St. John's Wood Road, London, NW8 8QN, England. *Telephone:* 01-289 1300.

GAUCI, Victor J.; Maltese diplomatist; b. 25 April 1931; s. of Joseph Gauci and Rose Gauci; m. Margaret Seaborn 1958; two d.; ed. St. Michael's Training Coll., Royal Univ. of Malta, Columbia Univ., New York, and Defence Coll., London; Exec. Officer 1951-58; Higher Exec. Officer 1959-65; Counsellor, Ministry of Commonwealth and Foreign Affairs 1966-70, Perm. Mission of Malta to UN 1966-70; Counsellor and Consul-Gen., Embassy of Malta, Rome 1971-73; Perm. Rep. to UN Office at Geneva 1973, to UN 1979-85; C.D.E. Stockholm and Perm. Rep. to UN in Geneva 1986-87; High Commr. in Australia 1987-. *Leisure interests:* reading, tennis, golf, music. *Address:* Malta High Commission, 261 La Perouse Street, Canberra, A.C.T. 2603, Australia. *Telephone:* (062) 951586.

GAUDRY, Roger, C.C., D.S.C.; Canadian chemist and university administrator; b. 1913, Quebec City; s. of Joseph-Marc Gaudry and Marie-Ange Frenette; m. Madeleine Vallée 1941; two s. three d.; ed. Laval Univ.; Rhodes Scholar, Oxford Univ. 1937-39; Lecturer in Organic Chem., Faculty of Medicine, Laval Univ. 1940, Assoc. Prof. 1945-50, Prof. 1950-54; Guest Speaker at La Sorbonne under the auspices of the Inst. Scientifique Franco-Canadien; Asst. Dir. of Research, Research Labs., Ayerst McKenna and Harrison Ltd. 1954, Dir. of Research 1957-65 (and of Ayerst Labs., N.Y.), Vice-Pres. 1963-65; Rector, Univ. de Montréal 1965-75; Vice-Chair. Science Council of Canada 1966-72, Chair. 1972-75; Chair. Council, UN Univ. 1974-76, mem. bd. 1974-80; Fellow, Royal Soc. of Canada 1954; Pres. Chemical Inst. of Canada 1955-56, Canadian Asscn. of Rhodes Scholars 1960-61; mem. Bd. Société de Chimie Industrielle de France 1960-, Bd. of Govs. and Exec. Cttee. Univ. de Montréal 1961-65, Defence Research Bd. of Canada 1962-66, Bd. Nat. Research Council of Canada 1963-68, Nat. Cancer Inst. of Canada 1963-, Bd. Asscn. des Universités partiellement ou entièrement de Langue française 1965-75 (Vice-Pres. 1972-75); mem. Acad. du Monde latin 1967, Inst. de la Vie, Paris 1968-; Pres. Asscn. of Univs. and Colls. of Canada 1969-71; mem. Bd. Int. Asscn. of Univs. 1970-, Pres. 1975-80; Gen. Trust of Canada 1970-75; mem. Econ. Council of Canada 1970-73; Pres. Conf. of Rectors and Principals of Quebec Univs. 1970-72; Hon. Life mem. Corpn. of Professional Chemists of Quebec 1964, Asscn. professionnelle des pharmaciens d'industrie du Québec 1972; Hon. mem. Royal Coll. of Physicians and Surgeons of Canada 1971; and mem. admin. Bd. of many commercial and philanthropic socs.; Pres. Jules & Paul-Emile Léger Foundation 1983-, Science Tech. and Industry Centre 1988-; Chair. Nordic Labs. Inc. 1976-; Dir. St.-Lawrence Starch Co. Ltd. 1984-; Hon. LL.D. (Toronto) 1966, D.Sc. (Royal Mil. Coll. of Kingston) 1966, D.Sc. (Univ. of B.C.) 1967, LL.D. (McGill) 1967, Doctorate (Univ. de Clermont-Ferrand, France) 1967, LL.D. (St. Thomas Univ., Fredericton, N.B.) 1968, LL.D. (Brock Univ., St. Catherines, Ont.) 1969, LL.D. (Bishop's Univ.) 1969, LL.D. (Concordia Univ., Montreal) 1980, D.Sc. (Sask., Regina) 1970, (Western Ont.) 1976; Prov. of Quebec Science Award (three times), Pariseau Medal, Asscn. canadienne-française pour l'avancement des sciences 1958. *Publications:* numerous scientific papers on organic and biological chemistry. *Address:* Université de Montréal, 2910 boulevard Edouard-Montpetit, app. 6, CP 6128, Montreal H3C 3J7, Quebec, Canada.

GAULTIER de LA FERRIÉRE, Jacques Marie Georges, L. EN D.; French diplomatist; b. 18 Dec. 1923, Oran, Algeria; s. of Col. Jean Gaultier de la Ferrière and Marie Thérèse de Larminat; m. Martine Péronne 1946; one s. one d.; ed. Lycée Louis-le-Grand, Faculté de Droit, Univ. de Paris; Admin. Civil Service for Indochina, Commissariat of French Repub., Cambodia 1946-50, Head of Bureau of Cultural Affairs, High Comm., Saigon 1951-53, at Econ. Affairs Directorate of Ministry of Foreign Affairs 1954-55, Directorate of Political Affairs 1955-57, Consul, Sfax 1957, First Sec. Embassy, Pakistan 1959, Consul-Gen. attached to San Francisco 1961-64, Adviser on Foreign Affairs 1964, Press Officer 1965, Head of Cinema-Radio-TV Office, then sub-Dir. at Gen. Directorate of Cultural Relations 1966-69; Adviser, Embassy at Budapest 1969; First Counsellor then Chargé d'affaires, Tel Aviv 1972-75; Perm. Rep. to NATO 1975-77, Head of Pacts and Disarmament Dept., Ministry of Foreign Affairs 1977, Minister 1977, Adjunct Gen. -Sec. of Nat. Defence 1979-82; Amb. to Czechoslovakia 1982-83, to Netherlands 1984-87; Head of Protocol Ministry of Foreign Relations 1983-84; Auditor Inst. of Advanced Study of Nat. Defence 1966-67; Grand Officer, Order of Orange-Nassau, Officier, Légion d'honneur, Commdr. Ordre nat. du Mérite, Chevalier des Arts et des Lettres. *Address:* 6 rue Eugène Delacroix, 75016 Paris, France.

GAUS, Günter; German journalist, diplomatist and politician; b. 23 Nov. 1929, Braunschweig (Brunswick); s. of Willi and Hedwig Gaus; m. Erika Butzengeiger 1955; one d.; ed. Oberrealschule Braunschweig and Munich Univ.; journalist with various daily and weekly newspapers, and Second German TV 1953-65; Programme Dir. Südwestfunk 1965-69; Chief Ed. Der Spiegel 1969-73; Sec. of State, Chancellery of Fed. Repub. of Germany, Bonn 1973; Head of Perm. Representation of Fed. Repub. of Germany, Berlin (G.D.R.) 1974-80; Senator (Minister) for Science and Research, West Berlin Jan.-June 1981; Adolf Grimme Prize, Bronze 1964, Silver 1965; Fr.-Ebert-Stiftung Das Politische Buch des Jahres 1987. *Publications:* Zur Person (two vols.), Bonn ohne Regierung 1965, Gespräch mit Herbert Wehner 1966, Zur Wahl gestellt 1969, Wo Deutschland liegt 1983, Deutschland und die NATO 1984, Die Welt der Westdeutschen 1986, Deutschland im Juni 1988. *Address:* Bahnsenallee 74, 2057 Reinbek, Federal Republic of Germany.

GAUSSEN, Gérard; French diplomatist; b. 17 March 1918, Barcelona, Spain; s. of Edouard and Marthe (née Ferrère) Gaussen; m. Solange Vernes 1946; four s. one d.; ed. Ecole des Roches, Ecole des Sciences politiques, Paris; Vice-Consul Montevideo 1946, Buenos Aires 1947–48; with Ministry of Foreign Affairs 1948–50, 1956–60; Consul to Venice 1950–56; at Centre for Int. Affairs, Harvard Univ. 1961–62; Counsellor, French Embassy, Berne 1962–64, Washington 1964–68; Consul General, Barcelona 1969–72, New York 1972–; Amb. to Sweden 1978–82; Perm. Rep. of France to Economic Comm. for Latin America 1982–84; Pres. Comité français pour la sauvegarde de Venise; Officier Légion d'honneur, Croix de guerre 1939–45, Rosette de la Résistance. *Publication:* De l'Association de l'Afrique au marché commun 1962. *Leisure interests:* golf, skiing. *Address:* 116 avenue Maurice-Barrès, 92200 Neuilly-sur-Seine, France. *Telephone:* 47-47-23-25.

GAUTHERET, Roger, D. ÉS SC.; French professor of biology; b. 29 March 1910, Paris; s. of Fernand Gautheret and Berthe (née Wattiez) Gautheret; ed. Lycée Voltaire, Faculty of Science, Paris Univ.; Asst., Faculty of Science, Paris Univ. 1937–42; Prof. of Cellular Biology, Univ. Pierre et Marie Curie 1942–; mem. Inst. de France (Acad. des Sciences) 1958–, Vice-Pres. 1976, Pres. 1978–80; mem. Agric. Acad. of France; Hon. mem. of numerous foreign socs.; Officier Légion d'honneur, Croix de guerre. *Publications:* La culture des tissus végétaux: principes et réalisation 1959, and many articles on vegetal growth, the culture of vegetable tissue and vegetable hormones in agriculture. *Address:* Irab, 120 avenue Foch, 94000 Créteil (Office); 1 quai aux fleurs, 75004 Paris, France (Home).

GAUVIN, Michel, O.C., C.V.O., D.S.O., B.A.; Canadian diplomatist; b. 7 April 1919, Quebec; s. of Raymond Gauvin and Stella McLean; divorced; m. 2nd Nguyen Thi Minh Huong; two s. one d.; ed. St. Charles Garnier Coll., Laval and Carleton Univs.; Amb. to Ethiopia 1966–69, to Portugal 1969–70, to Greece 1970–76; Head of Canadian del. to Int. Comm. for Control and Supervision, Viet-Nam Jan.-Aug. 1973; Canadian Sec. and Co-ordinator of Royal Visit July 1976 and 1977; Consul-Gen., Strasbourg 1976–78; Amb. to Morocco 1978–80, to People's Repub. of China 1980–85; Special Rep. of UN Human Rights Comm. to Haiti 1986–87; Leader, Canadian Observer Team to Haiti elections Nov. 1987. *Publication:* La geste du régiment de la chaudière. *Leisure interests:* golf, sailing, bridge. *Address:* 706 Echo Drive, Ottawa, Ont., K1S 1P3, Canada.

GAUVIN, William Henry, C.C., M.ENG., PH.D.; Canadian scientist; b. 30 March 1913, Paris; s. of Hector and Albertine Gauvin; m. Dorothy Edna Gauvin 1965; six d.; ed. McGill and Waterloo Univs.; lecturer, Dept. of Chemical Eng., McGill Univ. 1942–44, Assoc. Prof. 1947–62, Research Assoc. 1961–72, Sr. Research Assoc. 1972–, Auxiliary Prof. 1983–; Plant Supt. F. W. Horner Ltd., Montreal 1944–46; Consultant, Paper and Pulp Research Inst. of Canada 1951–57, Head. Chemical Eng. Div. 1957–61; Research Man. Noranda Research Centre 1961–70, Dir. of Research and Devt. Noranda Mines Ltd. 1970–82, Dir. Advanced Tech. Noranda Research Centre 1982–83; Pres. William H. Gauvin Technologies Inc.; Del. Gen. Nat. Research Council of Canada 1970–71; mem. numerous professional socs. in Canada and abroad; D.Sc. h.c. (McGill) and many other awards and prizes. *Publications:* 190 papers in professional journals. *Leisure interests:* tennis, chess, piano. *Address:* 7 Harrow Place, Beaconsfield, Que. H9W 5C7, Canada. *Telephone:* (514) 695-3760.

GAVA, Antonio; Italian politician; b. 30 July 1930, Castellamare di Stabia; Chair. Union of Provs. of Italy 1968, Naples Prov. Sec. 1969, Chair. of First Regional Ass. of Campania, Chair. of Christian Democrat (C.D.) Group in Campania; M.P. for Naples-Caserta 1972–; Minister of Posts and Telecommunications 1986–87, of Finance 1987–88, of the Interior April 1988–. *Address:* Ministry of the Interior, Piazza Viminale, Palazzo Viminale, Via Depretis, 00184 Rome, Italy.

GAVASKAR, Sunil, B.A.; Indian cricketer and business executive; b. 10 July 1949, Bombay; ed. St. Xavier's High School, Bombay, and St. Xavier's College, Bombay Univ.; first-class cricket debut 1967, regular 1970–; Test debut 1971; played for Rest of the World team in Australia 1971–72; Capt. of Bombay 1975–; Capt. India (32 tests) 1978–83; played for Somerset in English Co. Championship 1980; 10,122 runs in Test cricket up to end of 1987 (retd.); including record 34 centuries in Test cricket; over 18,000 runs in first-class cricket –1983; highest score (236 v. Australia Dec. 1983) by Indian in Test match; Arjuna Award 1975, Padma Bhushan 1980, both Govt. of India; first player to score more than 10,000 Test runs 1987; first player to score over 2,000 runs against three countries 1987; only man to play in a hundred successive Tests. *Publications:* Sunny Days—An Autobiography 1976, Idols (autobiog.) 1982, Runs 'n Ruins 1984. *Address:* Nirlon Synthetic Fibres and Chemicals Ltd., Nirlon House, 254-B, Dr. Annie Besant Road, Worli, Bombay-400025; 40-A, Sir Bhalchandra Road, Dadar, Bombay-400014, India (Home).

GAVAZZENI, Gianandrea; Italian musician and writer; b. 1919, Bergamo; ed. Milan Conservatory (under Renzo Lorenzoni) and under Ildebrando Pizzetti and Mario Pilati; conductor 1940–; associated with La Scala, Milan 1948–, Artistic Dir. 1966–68; has participated in many festivals with La Scala including the Edinburgh Festival 1957, World Fair, Brussels 1957, Expo 1967, Montreal and also at the Bolshoi and Kremlin theatres, Moscow 1964; has directed numerous operatic recordings with La Scala; as a music

critic has written studies of Donizetti, Pizzetti, Mascagni, Mussorgsky and guides to the operas of Mozart, Wagner, etc.; *Compositions include:* Concerto bergamasco (for orchestra), Paolo e Virginia (opera, first perf. at Bergamo 1935) and Il furioso nell'isola di San Domingo (ballet, first perf. at San Remo 1940), Il canto di S. Allessandro, Canti d'operai lombardi (for orchestra), three Concerti di Cinquando (for orchestra), violin and 'cello concertos, piano pieces and numerous songs with words by Bacchelli, Cardarelli, Rilke, etc. *Address:* Via Porta Dipinta 5, Bergamo, Italy.

GAVIN, Lieut.-Gen. James M., D.S.O.; American army officer, diplomatist and business executive; b. 22 March 1907, New York; s. of Martin Thomas and Mary (Terrel) Gavin; m. 2nd Jean Emert Duncan 1948; one d. (first marriage), four d. (second marriage); ed. U.S. Mil. Acad., West Point; enlisted as Private 1924, Lieut. 1929, Lieut.-Gen. 1944; commanded 505th Paratroop Combat Team, landing in Sicily and Salerno 1943; Asst. Div. Commdr. 82nd Airborne Div. landing in Normandy 1944, Div. Commdr. 82nd Airborne Div. landing in Nijmegen 1944; Ardennes 1945; Deputy Chief of Staff for Plans and Research 1955; Chief Research and Devt. 1955–59; Amb. to France 1961–62; Pres. Arthur D. Little, Inc. 1960–61, Chair. of the Bd. 1964–77, Dir. and Consultant 1977–; Dir. American Electric Power Co. Inc., John Hancock Life Insurance Co.; Grand Officier Légion d'honneur, Croix de guerre with palm (France), D.S.C. with oak leaf cluster, Purple Heart, Silver Star (U.S.), D.S.O. (U.K.). *Publications:* Airborne Warfare 1947, War and Peace in the Space Age 1958, France and the Civil war in America 1964, Crisis Now 1968, On to Berlin 1978. *Leisure interests:* reading, golf, tennis, painting. *Address:* c/o Arthur D. Little Inc., 25 Acorn Park, Cambridge, Mass. 02140 (Office); 1302 Alberta Road, Winter Park, Fla. 32789, U.S.A. (Home). *Telephone:* (305) 628-3471 (Home).

GAVIN, John, B.A.; American actor and diplomat; b. 8 April 1932, Los Angeles; s. of Herald Ray Gavin and Delia Diana Pablos; m. Constance Mary Towers; one s. three d.; ed. Stanford Univ.; actor in feature films 1956–80; *films include:* A Time to Live, A Time to Die, Psycho, Midnight Lace, Backstreet, Thoroughly Modern Millie, Mad Woman of Chaillot, Seesaw (musical), Broadway; Special Adviser to Sec.-Gen. OAS 1961–74; Vice-Pres. Atlantic Richfield Co. (to head Fed. & Int. Relations Unit) 1986–87; Pres. Univisa Satellite Communications 1987–; Pres. Gamma Services Corpn. 1968–; spokesman Bank of America 1973–80; Amb. to Mexico 1981–86; mem. Screen Actors' Guild (Pres. 1971–73). *Address:* Univisa Inc., 9200 Sunset Boulevard, Suite 824, Los Angeles, Calif. 90069, U.S.A.

GAVISH, Yeshayahu; Israeli business executive; b. 1925, Tel Aviv; m.; two d.; ed. Staff Coll., France; various commands in Israeli Defence Force 1948–62; Officer Commanding, Southern Command 1962–69; Gen. Man. Koor Metals Ltd. 1969; now Gen. Man. Koor Industries and Head, Koor Metals Steel Group. *Address:* Neve Relim 23, Neveh Magen, Israel. *Telephone:* 03-471644.

GAVRILOV, Andrei; Russian pianist; b. 21 Sept. 1955, Moscow; performs regularly throughout Europe, America and Japan, including recitals at Salzburg, Roque d' Antheron, Schleswig Holstein, Istanbul and Chichester Festivals; has performed in England with the Philharmonia, London Philharmonic, Royal Philharmonic, BBC Symphony and London Symphony Orchestras, in America with the Baltimore Symphony, Detroit Symphony, New York Philharmonic, and the Philadelphia Orchestra; disc awards include the French suites of J. S. Bach and the Etudes of Chopin; winner of the Tchaikovsky Competition in Moscow 1974. *Address:* c/o Harold Holt Ltd., 31 Sinclair Road, London, W14 0NS, England. *Telephone:* 01-603 4600.

GAWRYSIAK, Jerzy; Polish politician; b. 1 Sept. 1928, Rybno, near Włocławek; ed. Leningrad Univ.; scientific worker, Poznań Polytechnic till 1958; Sec. Poznań-Wilda Dist. Cttee. of Polish United Workers' Party (PZPR) 1958–61; Deputy Head of Org. Dept., Poznań Voivod Cttee. of PZPR 1961–63, Econ. Sec. 1964–70; Deputy Chair. Praesidium of Poznań Voivod Nat. Council 1963–64; Under-Sec. of State, Ministry of Internal Trade 1971–72; Head of Econ. Dept., Cen. Cttee. of PZPR 1972; First Sec. Rzeszów Voivod Cttee. of PZPR 1972–75; mem. Cen. Cttee. of PZPR 1975–80; Minister of Internal Trade and Services 1975–76; called to diplomatic service 1976, Amb. to G.D.R. 1977–80; Chair. State Price Comm.; Minister, mem. Council of Ministers 1980–81; Knight's and Officer's Cross, Order of Polonia Restituta, Order of Banner of Labour (2nd Class) 1974.

GAY, Geoffrey Charles Lytton, F.R.I.C.S., F.R.G.S., F.R.S.A.; British international real estate consultant; b. 14 March 1914; s. of Charles Gay and Ida Lytton; m. Dorothy Ann Rickman 1947; one s. two d.; ed. St. Paul's School; served World War II, Durham Light Infantry B.E.F. 1940, Staff Coll. Camberley and India; Lieut.-Col., Chief of Staff, Sind Dist. 1943; joined Knight Frank and Rutley 1929, Sr. Partner 1973–75, Consultant 1975–; Consultant Taylor Woodrow Group 1975–; Gen. Commr. for Inland Revenue 1953–; mem. Westminster City Council 1962–71; World Pres. Int. Real Estate Fed. (FIABCI) 1973–75; mem. St. John Council for London; Gov. Benenden School; Gov. Claysemore School; Licentiate Royal Photographic Soc.; Liveryman, Worshipful Co. of Broderers; Chevalier Ordre de l'Economie Nationale 1960, Officer Order of St. John of Jerusalem

1960, K.St.J. 1979; Médaille de Vermeil (Paris) 1975. *Leisure interests:* photography, painting, music, theatre, fishing. *Address:* Brookmans Old Farm, Iwerne Minster, Blandford Forum, Dorset, DT11 8NG, England.

GAY, Peter, PH.D.; American professor of history; b. 20 June 1923, Berlin, Germany; s. of Morris Fröhlich and Helga Fröhlich; m. Ruth Slotkin 1959; three step-d.; ed. Univ. of Denver and Columbia Univ.; left Germany 1939; Dept. of Public Law and Govt., Columbia Univ. 1947–56, Dept. of History 1956–69, Prof. of History 1962–69, William R. Shepherd Prof. 1967–69; Prof. of Comparative European Intellectual History, Yale Univ. 1969–, Durfee Prof. of History 1970–84, Sterling Prof. of History 1984–; Guggenheim Fellow 1967–68; Overseas Fellow, Churchill Coll., Cambridge, England 1970–71; Visiting Fellow, Inst. for Advanced Study, Berlin 1984; mem. American Historical Assen., French Historical Soc.; Hon. D.Hum. Litt. (Denver) 1970, (Md.) 1979, (Hebrew Univ. Coll., Cincinnati) 1983, (Clark Univ., Worcester) 1985; Nat. Book Award 1967, Melcher Book Award 1967. *Publications:* The Dilemma of Democratic Socialism: Eduard Bernstein's Challenge to Marx 1951, Voltaire's Politics: The Poet as Realist 1959, Philosophical Dictionary 1962, The Party of Humanity: Essays in the French Enlightenment 1964, The Loss of Mastery: Puritan Historians in Colonial America 1966, The Enlightenment: An Interpretation, Vols. I, II 1966, 1969, Weimar Culture: The Outsider as Insider 1969, The Bridge of Criticism: Dialogues on the Enlightenment 1970, The Question of Jean-Jacques Rousseau 1974, Modern Europe (with R. K. Webb) 1973, Style in History 1974, Art and Act: On Causes in History—Manet, Gropius, Mondrian 1976, Freud, Jews and Other Germans: Masters and Victims in Modernist Culture 1978, The Bourgeois Experience: Victoria to Freud, Vols. I, II 1984, 1986, Freud for Historians 1985, Freud: A Life for Our Time 1988; also translations and anthologies. *Leisure interests:* reading, listening to music. *Address:* Department of History, P.O. Box 1504A, Yale University, New Haven, Conn. 06520; 105 Blue Trail, Hamden, Conn. 06518, U.S.A. (Home). *Telephone:* (203) 432-21380 (Office); (203) 228-6752 (Home).

GAYAN, Anil Kumarsingh, LL.M.; Mauritian barrister and politician; b. 22 Oct. 1948; m. Sooryankanti Nirsimloo; one s. one d.; ed. Royal Coll., Curepipe, London School of Econs. and Inner Temple, London; Crown Counsel 1974, Sr. Crown Counsel 1977; Rep. of Mauritius to UN Gen. Ass. 1983, 1984, and at numerous int. conferences 1976–; Pres. African Group, New York 1976–78; Municipal Councillor, Curepipe 1982; mem. Parl. 1982–; Minister of External Affairs, Tourism and Emigration 1983–85. *Publications:* articles in Iranian Journal of International Relations, Mauritius Law Review and local newspapers. *Address:* Royal Road, Curepipe, Mauritius (Home). *Telephone:* 66544 (Home).

GAYDON, Alfred Gordon, D.SC., F.R.S.; British physicist; b. 26 Sept. 1911; s. of Alfred Bert Gaydon and Rosetta Juliet Gordon; m. Phyllis Maude Gaze 1940 (died 1981); one s. one d.; ed. Kingston Grammar School, Kingston-on-Thames, Imperial Coll., London; Warren Research Fellow of Royal Soc. 1945–74; Prof. of Molecular Spectroscopy, Imperial Coll. of Science and Tech., London 1961–73, Prof. Emer. 1973–, Fellow 1980; worked on molecular spectra and on measurement of high temperatures, on spectra and structure of flames, and shock waves; Dr. h.c. (Dijon) 1957; Rumford Medal, Royal Soc. 1960, Bernard Lewis Gold Medal, Combustion Inst. 1960. *Publications:* Identification of Molecular Spectra (with R. W. B. Pearse) 1941, Spectroscopy and Combustion Theory 1942, Dissociation Energies and Spectra of Diatomic Molecules 1947, Flames, their Structure, Radiation and Temperature (with H. G. Wolfhard) 1953, The Spectroscopy of Flames 1957, The Shock Tube in High-temperature Chemical Physics (with I. Hurle) 1963. *Leisure interests:* wildlife photography and fmrly. rowing. *Address:* Dale Cottage, Shellbridge Road, Slindon Common, Sussex, England. *Telephone:* Slindon 277.

GAYE, Amadou Karim, D.M.V.; Senegalese politician and international official; b. 8 Dec. 1913, Saint-Louis; ed. Lycée Saint-Louis, Univ. de Paris, Ecole Nat. Vétérinaire, Alfort, France, Ecole de Cavalerie, Saumur, France; served in Senegalese veterinary service 1949–57; Gen. Counsellor of Senegal 1949–52; Deputy of Union Progressiste Sénégalaise (UPS) 1959–75, Asst. Sec. for Propaganda 1960–70; Minister of Educ. and Culture Jan.–April 1959, of Planning, Devt. and Econ. 1959–60; Minister Del. to Presidency charged with Planning and Tech. Co-operation 1961–62; Minister of Labour and Civil Service Nov.–Dec. 1962, of Agric. 1962–65, of Armed Forces 1965–68, of Foreign Affairs 1968–72; Pres. Econ. and Social Council 1972–75; Sec.-Gen. Org. of the Islamic Conf. 1976–79; Nat. Order of the Lion. *Address:* c/o Ministry of Foreign Affairs, place de l'Indépendance, Dakar, Senegal.

GAYOOM, H.E. Maumoon Abdul, M.A.; Maldivian politician; b. 29 Dec. 1937; m. Nasreena Ibrahim; two s. two d.; ed. Al-Azhar Univ., Cairo; Research Asst. in Islamic History, American Univ. of Cairo 1967–69; Lecturer in Islamic Studies and Philosophy, Abdullahi Bayero Coll., Ahmadu Bello Univ., Nigeria 1969–71; Teacher, Aminiya School 1971; Man. Govt. Shipping Dept. 1972–73; Dir. Govt. Telephone Dept. 1974; Special Under-Sec. to Prime Minister 1974–75; Deputy Amb. to Sri Lanka 1975–76; Under-Sec. Dept. of External Affairs 1976; Perm. Rep. to UN 1976; Deputy Minister of Transport 1976–77, Minister of Transport 1977–78; Pres. of Repub. of Maldives Nov. 1978– (and Minister of Defence and Nat. Security); mem. of Constituent Council of Rabitat Al-Alam Al-Islami; Hon. D.Litt. (Aligarh Muslim Univ. of India) 1983. *Leisure interests:* astrology, calligra-phy, badminton, cricket. *Address:* Office of the President, Malé; Muleeaage, Malé, Maldives (Residence).

GAZE, Raymond Michael, D.PHIL., F.R.S.E., F.R.S.; British biologist; b. 22 June 1927; s. of William Mercer Gaze and Kathleen Grace (née Bowhill) Gaze; m. Robinetta Mary Armfelt 1957; one s. two d.; ed. School of Medicine of the Royal Colls., Edinburgh, Oxford Univ.; House Physician, Chelmsford and Essex Hosp. 1949; Nat. Service Medical Officer in R.A.M.C. 1953–55; Lecturer in Physiology, Univ. of Edin. 1955–62; Alan Johnston, Lawrence and Moseley Research Fellow of Royal Soc. 1962–66; Reader in Physiology, Univ. of Edinburgh 1966–70; Head, Div. of Developmental Biology, Nat. Inst. for Medical Research, London 1970–83; Head, MRC Neural Devt. and Regeneration Group, Zoology Dept., Edinburgh Univ. 1984–. *Publications:* The Formation of Nerve Connections 1970, numerous articles on developmental neurobiology in learned journals. *Leisure interests:* music, drawing and hill-walking. *Address:* Department of Zoology, University of Edinburgh, King's Buildings, West Mains Road, Edin., EH9 3JT (Office); 37 Sciennes Road, Edin., EH9 1NS, Scotland (Home). *Telephone:* 031-667 1081 (Office); 031-667 6915 (Home).

GAZENKO, Oleg Georgievich, PH.D., M.D.; Soviet physiologist; b. 12 Dec. 1918, Nikolayevka, Stavropol territory; m.; one s. one d.; ed. Moscow Medical Inst; service in the Army 1941–46; Research Assoc. Kirov Mil. Medical Acad. 1946–47; U.S.S.R. Acad. of Sciences Inst. of Experimental Medicine 1947–69, Dir. Inst. of Medical and Biological Problems 1969; mem. CPSU 1953; Corresp. mem. U.S.S.R. Acad. of Sciences 1966, mem. 1976–; mem. Int. Acad. of Astronautics, Aerospace Medical Assen.; Corresp. mem. American Physiological Soc. 1979–; Pres. U.S.S.R. Nat. Physiological Soc. 1983–; elected to Congress of People's Deputies of the U.S.S.R. 1989; Order of Lenin, Daniel and Florence Guggenheim Int. Astronautics Award 1975. *Publications:* works on experimental physiology and space medicine; Co-ed. Foundations of Space Biology and Medicine (U.S.A.-U.S.S.R. joint publ.). *Leisure interests:* mountaineering, canoeing. *Address:* U.S.S.R. Academy of Sciences, 14 Leninsky Prospekt, Moscow V-71, U.S.S.R.

GAZIER, Albert, L. EN D.; French politician; b. 16 May 1908, Valenciennes; m. 1st Marie-Louise Elter 1945 (died 1978), 2nd Denise Saleur 1980; employed by Presses universitaires de France, Paris; joined Socialist Party; Sec.-Gen. of Chambre des Employés de la Région parisienne; active in Resistance during Occupation; came to England and later returned to France; mem. of CGT Bureau, CGT Del. to provisional Constituent Assemblies Algiers 1943–44, Paris 1944–45, later Sec. to CGT Bureau; Deputy of Seine; Under-Sec. for Nat. Economy in Gouin Govt.; Under-Sec. for Public Works and Transport in Bidault Govt.; Sec. to Presidency of Council in Blum Govt.; Minister of Information in Pleven and Queuille Govts. 1950–51; Minister of Social Affairs 1956–57; Minister of Information May 1958; mem. Cttee. of Dirs., French Socialist Party 1969–75, Del. Gen. to Cttee of Experts 1973–77; Doyen of Conseil supérieur de la Magistrature 1983–88. *Leisure interests:* tourism, classical music, cinema. *Address:* 14 rue du Capitaine Ménard, 75015 Paris, France. *Telephone:* 45-75-35-19.

GAZIT, Maj.-Gen. Shlomo; Israeli army officer and administrator; b. 1926, Turkey; s. of Efrayim and Zippora Gazit; m. Avigayil Gala; one s. two d.; ed. Tel Aviv Univ.; joined Palmach 1944, Co. Commdr. Harel Brigade 1948; Dir. Office of Chief of Staff 1953; Liaison Officer with French Army Del., Sinai Campaign 1956; Instructor Israel Defence Forces Staff and Command Coll. 1958–59; Gen. Staff 1960–61; Deputy Commdr. Golani Brigade 1962; Instructor Nat. Defence Coll. 1962–64; with Intelligence Branch, IDF 1964–67; Dir. Dept. of Mil. Govt., Gen. Staff and Co-ordinator of Activities in Administered Areas, Ministry of Defence 1967–74; rank of Maj-Gen. 1973; Head of Mil. Intelligence 1974–79; Fellow at Center for Int. Affairs, Harvard Univ. 1979–80; Pres. Ben Gurion Univ. of the Negev 1981–85; Dir.-Gen. Jewish Agency, Jerusalem 1985–88; Sr. Research Fellow Jaffee Centre of Strategic Studies, Tel Aviv Univ. 1988–. *Publications:* Estimates and Fortune-Telling in Defence Work 1980, Early Attempts at Establishing West Bank Autonomy 1980, Insurgency, Terrorism and Intelligence 1980, On Hostages' Rescue Operations 1981, The Stick and the Carrot—Israel's Military Govt. in Judea and Samaria (in Hebrew) 1985, The Third Way—The Way of No Solution 1987. *Address:* J.C.C.S., Tel Aviv University, Ramat-Aviv, Tel-Aviv 69978 (Office); 20 Tarpad Street, Ramat Hasharon 47250, Israel (Home). *Telephone:* (03) 477377 (Home).

GAZZAR, Abdel Hadi el; Egyptian artist; b. 1925; ed. Cairo and Rome Acad. of Fine Arts; Prof. of Painting, Cairo Faculty of Fine Arts; rep. at numerous exhbns., including the 28th and 30th Venice Biennale, Brussels Int. Exhbn. 1958 and São Paulo Bienal 1961; exhbns. in Cairo, Alexandria and Rome; First Prize "10 Years of the Revolution" Exhbn. 1962. *Address:* Faculty of Fine Arts, Cairo University, Cairo, Egypt.

GBEHO, James Victor, B.A.; Ghanaian diplomatist; b. 12 Jan. 1935, Ghana; ed. Achimota Secondary School, Univ. of Ghana; Deputy High Commr. in U.K. 1972–76; Supervising Dir. Int. Orgs. and Confs. Bureau, Ministry of Foreign Affairs, Accra 1976–78; Amb. and Perm. Rep. to UN, Geneva and Vienna 1978–80; Perm. Rep. of Ghana to UN 1980–; Chair. First Cttee. (Politics and Security) UN Gen. Ass. 1982, UN Disarmament Comm. 1984. *Address:* Permanent Mission of Ghana to the United Nations, 19 East 47th Street, New York, N.Y. 10017, U.S.A.

GBEZERA-BRIA, Michel, B.L.; Central African Republic politician and diplomatist; b. 1946, Bossongoa, Cen. African Repub.; m.; five c.; ed. Brazzaville School of Law, Caen School of Econs. and Int. Inst. of Public Admin.; with civil service 1973–, Vice-Minister Sec.-in-charge of diplomatic missions 1975; Deputy Minister of Foreign Affairs 1976; Minister of Public Works, Labour and Social Security 1976–77, of Foreign Affairs 1977–78, of Public Works and Social Security 1978–79; State Comptroller 1979–80, Perm. Rep. to UN, Geneva 1980–83, New York June 1983–. *Address:* Permanent Mission of Central African Republic to the United Nations, Room 1614, 386 Park Avenue South, New York, N.Y. 10016, U.S.A.

GE GUILIN; Chinese traditional painter; b. 1941, Beijing; s. of Ge Shizhen and Fan Fengcai; m. Bai Shulan 1968; two s.; studied with Li Kuchan, Bai Xueshi and Wang Xuetao; specializes in painting flowers and birds; lecturer, Arts and Crafts Centre, Beijing; promoted to Arts and Crafts Artist 1981; many works exhibited, and published in art magazines; mem. Chinese Arts and Crafts Assen. 1987–. *Leisure interest:* classical music. *Address:* No. 29, Fourth Floor Dormitory, Beijing Children's Hospital, Beijing, People's Republic of China. *Telephone:* 421.4198.

GE SHA; Chinese artist; b. 1931, Heilongjiang; specializes in woodcuts. *Leisure interests:* sports, literature and drama. *Address:* Jilin Daily, Changchun, Jilin Province, People's Republic of China.

GE TINGSUI, PH.D.; Chinese scientist; b. 3 May 1913; ed. Univ. of California; researcher, Massachusetts Inst. of Tech. 1944–45; Research Fellow, Univ. of Chicago 1945–49; returned to China 1950; Deputy, 3rd NPC 1964–66; Deputy, 5th NPC 1978–83; Research Scholarship, Max-Planck-Inst. for Metals Research in Fed. Repub. of Germany 1979–80; Deputy Dir. Metal Research Inst., Academia Sinica 1980–; corresp. mem. Lyon Inst. for his contrib. to Sino-French academic exchange 1981; Vice-Pres., Hefei br., Academia Sinica. 1983–; mem. Dept. of Math. and Physics, Academia Sinica 1985–. *Address:* Hefei Branch, Academia Sinica, Dongpudao, Hefei City, People's Republic of China.

GE WUJUE; Chinese writer; b. 12 Sept. 1937, Wenzhou, Zhejiang; s. of Ge Luyang and Zhang Wencang; m. Zhao Baoqing 1962; one d.; ed. Beijing Univ.; worked as journalist for over 20 years; published first book 1961; in political disgrace 1963–77; some works translated into English, French and Japanese; Vice-Chair. Fed. of Art and Literature, Ningxia and Ningxia Branch of Union of Chinese Writers. *Publications:* The Wedding, A Journalist and Her Story, An Experience in the Summer, She and her Girl Friend, The Golden Deer, A View of an Ancient Ferry (short stories), Meditate on the Past (novel), Years and Man (novel), Going to the Ancient Ferry on Today (TV Drama), Four Days in All of Life 1988. *Leisure interests:* sports, music, drawing, calligraphy. *Address:* The Ningxia Union of Art and Literature, Yinchuan, Ningxia, People's Republic of China. *Telephone:* 22319.

GĘBALA, Stanisław, M.ECON.SCI.; Polish politician; b. 21 March 1935, Tarnów; ed. Higher School of Econs., Cracow; worked in District Cttee. of Polish Youth Union (ZMP), Tarnów, subsequently Deputy Head of Dept., ZMP Voivodship Bd. Cracow 1952–56; technologist, subsequently Sec. Factory Cttee. of Polish United Workers' Party (PZPR) in Mechanical Plants, Tarnów 1957–65; Sec. PZPR Dist. Cttee., Tarnów 1965–67; Deputy Dir. for econ. matters in F. Dzierżyński Nitrogen Compounds Plants, Tarnów 1967–68; Gen. Dir. Mechanical Plants, Tarnów 1968–73; Econ. Sec. PZPR Voivodship Cttee., Cracow 1973–75; First Sec. PZPR Voivodship Cttee., Tarnów 1975–80; alt. mem. PZPR Cen. Cttee. 1975–81; Head, Trade and Finance Dept. of PZPR Cen. Cttee., subsequently Head, Econ. Dept. of PZPR Cen. Cttee. 1980–84; Minister of Labour, Wages and Social Affairs 1984–87; mem. Govt. Presidium 1985–87; mem. Seym (Parl.) 1976–85; fmr. Chair. Seym Comm. for Econ. Co-operation with Foreign Countries and Maritime Econ.; Kt's. Cross, Order of Polonia Restituta, and other decorations.

GEDDA, Nicolai; Swedish operatic tenor; b. 11 July 1925, Stockholm; s. of Michael Ustinov and Olga (née Gedda) Ustinov; m. Anastasia Caraviotis 1965; one s. one d.; ed. Musical Acad., Stockholm; Debut, Stockholm 1952; Concert appearances Rome 1952, Paris 1953, 1955, Vienna 1955, Aix-en-Provence 1954, 1955; first operatic performances in Munich, Lucerne, Milan and Rome 1953, Paris, London and Vienna 1954; Salzburg Festival 1957–59, Edinburgh Festival 1958–59; with Metropolitan Opera, N.Y. 1957–; world-wide appearances in opera, concerts and recitals; numerous recordings. *Address:* c/o Lee Askonas, 19A Air Street, London W2, England.

GEDDES, Ford Irvine, M.B.E.; British business executive (retd.); b. 17 Jan. 1913; s. of I. C. Geddes; m. Barbara Gertrude Parry-Okeden 1945; one s. four d.; ed. Loretto School and Gonville and Caius Coll., Cambridge; Anderson Green and Co. Ltd., London 1934, Dir. 1947–68; Army Service 1939–45; Man. Dir. P. & O. Steam Navigation Co. 1960–72, Deputy Chair. 1968–71, Chair. 1971–72; Dir. Equitable Life Assurance Soc. 1955–76, Pres. 1963–71; Dir. Bank of New South Wales (London Advisory Board) 1950–81; Dir. British United Turkeys Ltd. 1962–68, Chair. 1976–78; Chair. Technical Cttee., Chamber of Shipping of U.K. 1960–65, British Shipping Fed. 1965–68; Pres. Int. shipping Fed. 1967–69. *Address:* 18 Gordon Place, London, W8 4JD, England.

GEE, Edwin Austin, M.S., PH.D.; American chemist and business executive; b. 19 Feb. 1920, Washington; s. of Edwin S. and Marie (née Junghans) Gee; m. Genevieve Riordan 1944; three s.; ed. George Washington Univ.; Chemist Naval Research Lab., Washington 1941–42; Chemist U.S. Bureau of Mines 1942–44, Engineer 1945–46, Chief Metallurgist 1947–48; with E. I. du Pont de Nemours & Co. Inc., Wilmington, Del. 1948–78, Devt. Dept. 1960–68, Photo Products Dept. 1968–69, Vice-Pres. and mem. Exec. Cttee. 1970–78, Sr. Vice-Pres. and Dir. –1978; Pres. Int. Paper Co., New York 1978–80, Chair. 1980–85; mem. Nat. Acad. of Eng. *Address:* Box 362, Buck Hill Falls, Pa. 18323, U.S.A. (Home).

GEE, Geoffrey, C.B.E., PH.D., F.R.S.; British professor of chemistry; b. 6 June 1910; s. of Thomas Gee and Mary Ann Gee; m. Marion Bowden 1934; one s. two d.; ed. New Mills Grammar School, Univs. of Manchester and Cambridge; Research Chemist ICI (Dyestuffs Group) 1933–38; Research Chemist British Rubber Producers' Research Assen. 1938–47, Dir. 1947–53; Prof. of Physical Chem., Univ. of Manchester 1953–55, Pro-Vice Chancellor 1966–68, 1972–77, Sir Samuel Hall Prof. of Chem. 1955–76, Prof. Emer. 1976–; Pres. Faraday Soc. 1969–70; Hon. Fellow Manchester Polytechnic 1979; Hon. D.Sc. (Manchester) 1983. *Publications:* numerous scientific papers in Transactions of the Faraday Soc. and other journals. *Leisure interest:* gardening. *Address:* 8 Holmfield Drive, Cheadle Hulme, Cheshire, England. *Telephone:* (061) 485 3713.

GEENS, Gaston, M.ECON.SCI., DR.JUR.; Belgian politician; b. 10 June 1931, Kersbeek-Miskom, Brabant; m. Maria Thielman 1959; three s. one d.; ed. Catholic Univ. at Louvain, Johann Wolfgang Goethe Univ., Frankfurt-am-Main, Fed. Repub. of Germany; Demonstrator at Catholic Univ. at Louvain and Sec. of Centre for Econ. Studies 1955–61; Asst. Dir. CEPESS 1961–72, Dir. 1973–; Senator and Sec. of State for Budget and Science Policy 1974–76; Minister of Budget and Science Policy 1976–77, of Finance 1977–80, of the Budget May–Oct. 1980, for Flemish Community Affairs 1980–81, Econs. and Employment 1981–85, 1985–87; Pres. of the Govt. of Flanders 1985–88; Community Minister of Econs. 1988, Finance and the Budget 1988–. *Publications:* Het arrondissement Leuven—een regionaal economisch onderzoek 1959, Basisgegevens voor sociale politiek 1963, De Wet op de universitaire expansie 1965, De Staatshervorming 1971, De Europese begroting 1976; co-author Perspectieven voor de landbouw in de Euromarkt 1958, Op eigen kracht 1987. *Leisure interests:* reading, classical music, gardening. *Address:* Predikherenberg 32, 3009 Winksele (Leuven), Belgium.

GEERTZ, Clifford, PH.D.; American anthropologist; b. 23 Aug. 1926, San Francisco; s. of Clifford James and Lois (née Brieger) Geertz; m. 1st Hildred Storey 1948 (divorced 1981); m. 2nd Karen Blu; one s. one d.; ed. Antioch Coll., Harvard Univ.; Asst. Prof. of Anthropology, Univ. of Calif. 1958–60; Asst. Prof., then Prof. Dept. of Anthropology, Univ. of Chicago 1960–70, mem. Cttee. for Comparative Study of New Nations 1962–70; Prof. of Social Science, Inst. for Advanced Study Princeton Univ. 1970–, Harold F. Linder Prof. of Social Science 1982–; field work in Java 1952–54, 1986, Bali 1957–58, Morocco 1965–66, 1985–86; Fellow N.A.S., American Philosophical Soc., American Acad. of Arts and Sciences. *Publications:* The Religion of Java 1960, Person, Time and Conduct in Bali 1966, Local Knowledge 1983, Works and Lives 1988 (Nat. Book Critics Circle Award for Criticism) and others. *Address:* The Institute for Advanced Study, Princeton, N.J. 08540, U.S.A. *Telephone:* (609) 734-8000.

GEGESI KISS, Pál, M.D.; Hungarian paediatrician; b. 11 Feb. 1900, Nagyszöllös; s. of Ernö Gegesi Kiss and Mariska Nagy; m. Anna Vadnay 1947; two s. three d. two adopted s.; Rector of Budapest Medical Univ. 1955–61; Dir. Budapest Clinic of Paediatrics No. 1 1946–71, Prof. Emer. 1971–; mem. Hungarian Acad. of Sciences; Pres. Hungarian Nat. Red Cross; Hon. mem. Soviet Soc. of Paediatrics 1957, Purkyné Medical Soc. of Czechoslovakia 1963; Senator h.c. Universitatis, 1982; Kossuth Prize 1953; Order of Labour Gold Medal, Liberation Medal, Order of the Red Banner, Gold Medal, Hungarian Acad. of Sciences. *Publications:* Diabetes Mellitus in Newborns and Infants 1956, 1966; (co-author) Cardiac and Circulatory Diseases in Infancy and Childhood 1953, 1960, Disease and Medical Treatment 1965, Personality Disorders in Childhood 1965, Bases of Clinical Psychology 1968, Psychopathology in Childhood 1972. *Leisure interest:* fine arts. *Address:* No. 1 Clinic of Paediatrics, Semmelweis University Medical School, Bókay János-u. 53, H-1083 Budapest VIII, Hungary. *Telephone:* 343-186.

GEGHMAN, Yahya Hamoud; Yemeni diplomatist; b. 24 Sept. 1934, Jahanah; s. of Hamoud and Izzia Geghman; m. Cathya Geghman 1971; one s. one d.; ed. Law Schools, Cairo, Paris, Damascus and Boston and Columbia Univs.; Teacher of Arabic Language and Literature, Kuwait 1957–59; Dir.-Gen. Yemen Broadcasting System, Special Adviser, Ministry of Foreign Affairs 1962–63; Deputy Perm. Rep. to UN 1963–66, 1967–68; Minister Plenipotentiary, Yemen Arab Repub. (Y.A.R.) Embassy to U.S.A. 1963–67; Minister of Foreign Affairs 1968–69; Minister of State, Personal Rep. of the Pres. 1969; Deputy Prime Minister, Pres. Supreme Council for Youth Welfare and Sport 1969–71; Perm. Rep. to UN 1971–73; Amb. to U.S.A. 1973–74; Minister for Foreign Affairs 1974–75; Deputy Prime Minister for Econ. and Foreign Affairs 1975–76; Chief, Bureau of Inter-Yemen Affairs and Re-unification of Yemen 1977–82; Personal Rep. of Pres. of the Repub. 1977–85; Amb. to Switzerland and Perm. Rep. to UN

Office, Geneva and Vienna 1985–; Gov. for Y.A.R., IBRD, IMF 1970–71; mem. of Del. to Conf. of Arab Heads of Govts. 1965, 1969–79, to U.S.S.R. 1968, to UN Gen. Assembly 1962–; has represented Y.A.R. at many int. functions. *Publications:* articles on politics, economics and literature in various Arabic journals. *Leisure interests:* reading, horseback riding, swimming, writing, chess. *Address:* Permanent Mission of the Yemen Arab Republic, 18A chemin François-Lehmann, 1218 Grand-Saconnex, Geneva, Switzerland. *Telephone:* 98-49-21.

GEH, Hans-Peter, DR.PHIL.; German librarian; b. 11 Feb. 1934, Frankfurt-am-Main; ed. Univs. of Frankfurt and Bristol and Library School, Cologne; Dir. Württembergische Landesbibliothek Stuttgart 1970–; Pres. Int. Fed. of Library Asscns. and Insts. (IFLA) 1985–. *Publication:* Tudor Policy in England before the Tudors. *Leisure interest:* travel. *Address:* Württembergische Landesbibliothek, P.O.B. 10 54 41, 7000 Stuttgart 1, Federal Republic of Germany. *Telephone:* 0711-212-5424.

GEHLHOFF, Walter, M.D.; German diplomatist; b. 6 May 1922, Berlin; s. of Kurt Gehlhoff and Elsbeth Legies; m. Dr. Eva Biegel 1949; one s. two d.; held several diplomatic posts in Bonn 1951–53, 1958–60, Cairo 1953–56, Beirut 1956–58, Teheran 1960–66; Dir. Middle East Affairs Desk, Foreign Office, Bonn 1966; Deputy Asst. Sec. of State for Political Affairs 1969, Acting Asst. Sec. of State 1970; Amb. and Perm. Observer of Fed. Repub. of Germany to UN 1971–73, Amb. and Perm. Rep. 1973–74; State Sec., Foreign Office, Bonn 1974–77; Amb. to the Holy See. 1977–84; Special Rep. for Anglo-German Co-operation 1985; mem. Exec. Council of UNESCO; mem. Bd. of Trustees Anglo-German Foundation for the Study of Industrial Soc. 1986–. *Leisure interests:* music, ornithology, astronomy. *Address:* Bundesministerium des Auswärtigen, Adenauerallee 101, 5300 Bonn, Federal Republic of Germany.

GEHRY, Frank Owen; American architect; b. 29 Feb. 1929, Toronto, Canada; s. of Irving Gehry and Thelma Caplan; m. Berta Aguilera 1975; two s.; ed. Univ. of S. Calif. and Harvard Univ.; designer, Victor Gruen Asscn. Los Angeles 1953–54, planning, design and project dir. 1958–61; project designer, planner, Pereira & Luckman, L.A. 1957–58; Prin. Frank O. Gehry & Assocs., Venice, Calif. 1962–; architect for Museum of Contemporary Art 1983, Calif. Aerospace Museum 1984, Loyola Law School 1981–84, Frances Howard Goldwyn Regional Br. Library 1986, Information and Computer Science Eng. Research Facility, Univ. of Calif. Irvine 1986; Fellow, American Inst. of Architects; Charlotte Davenport Chair. Yale Univ. 1982; Eliot Noyes Design Chair. Harvard 1984; Arnold W. Brunner Memorial Architecture Prize 1983. *Address:* Frank O. Gehry & Associates, 11 Brooks Avenue, Venice, Calif. 90291, U.S.A.

GEIDUSCHEK, E(rnest) Peter, PH.D.; American scientist and professor of biology; b. 11 April 1928, Vienna, Austria; s. of Sigmund Geiduschek and Frieda Tauber; m. Joyce B. Brous 1955; two s.; ed. Columbia and Harvard Univs.; Instructor in Chem. Yale Univ. 1952–53, 1955–57; Asst. Prof. of Chem., Univ. of Mich. 1957–59; Asst. Prof. of Biophysics and Research Assoc. in Biochemistry, Univ. of Chicago 1959–62, Assoc. Prof. of Biophysics and Research Assoc. in Biochemistry 1962–64, Prof. of Biophysics and Research Assoc. in Biochemistry 1964–70; Prof. of Biology, Univ. of Calif., San Diego 1970–, Chair. 1981–83; EMBO Lecturer 1977, Hilleman Lecturer, Univ. of Chicago 1978; Lalor Foundation Faculty Fellow, Yale 1957, Guggenheim Fellow, Inst. de Biologie Moléculaire, Geneva 1964–65; Fellow A.A.A.S.; mem. N.A.S., American Acad. of Arts and Sciences. *Address:* University of California, San Diego, Department of Biology, M-034, La Jolla, Calif. 92093, U.S.A. *Telephone:* (619) 534-3029.

GEIGER, Helmut; German banker and lawyer; b. 12 June 1928, Nuremberg; m.; one s. one d.; ed. Univs. of Erlangen and Berlin; legal asst. Deutsche Bundestag and asst. lawyer, Bonn 1957–59; lawyer in Bonn and man. of office of Öffentliche Bausparkassen 1959–66; Man. Dir. Deutsche Sparkassen-und Giroverband 1966–72, Pres. 1972–; Pres. Int. Inst. der Sparkassen (Int. Savings Bank Inst.), Geneva 1978–84; Pres. EEC Savings Banks Group, Brussels 1985–; mem. Bundestag 1965; mem. Admin. Bd. Deutsche Girozentrale Int., Luxembourg, Kreditanstalt für Wiederaufbau, Frankfurt, Landwirtschaftliche Rentenbank, Frankfurt, Rhineland-Westphalian Inst. of Econ. Research, Essen; mem. Cen. Cttee., German Group, ICC; mem. Presidium, German Red Cross; Chair. and mem. of various charitable and professional bodies; Dr. h.c. (Cologne); Grand Fed. Cross of Merit. *Publications:* Herausforderungen für Stabilität und Fortschritt 1974, Bankpolitik 1975, Gespräche über Geld 1986 and numerous publications on banking matters. *Address:* Simrockstrasse 4, 5300 Bonn 1, Federal Republic of Germany. *Telephone:* 0228/204210.

GEIGER, Rupprecht; German artist; b. 26 Jan. 1908, Munich; s. of Willi Geiger and Clara Weiss; m. Monika Bieber; two s.; ed. architectural studies; practised as architect 1932–39; war artist 1940–45; private studies as painter 1945–50; founding mem. Gruppe Zen 1949; Prof. Düsseldorf Acad. 1965–75, Hon. mem. 1979–; mem. Akad. der Künste, Berlin, Bayerische Akad. der schönen Künste. *Publications:* Farbe ist Element 1975, Ein sehr rotes Buch 1981. *Leisure interest:* painting. *Address:* Muttenhalerstrasse 28, 8000 Munich 71, Federal Republic of Germany. *Telephone:* 79 49 48.

GEIJER, (Johan) Lennart, D.IUR.; Swedish lawyer and politician; b. Sept. 1909, Ystad; m. Ninnie Löfgren 1944; two s. two d.; ed. Univs. of Lund

and Stockholm; Sec. and legal adviser, Swedish Union of Clerical and Tech Employees in Industry 1939–57, Cen. Org. of Salaried Employees in Sweden 1957–66; mem. Consultative Assembly, Council of Europe 1964–66; mem. Riksdag (Parl.) 1962–76; Minister without Portfolio 1966–69, Ministe of Justice 1969–76. *Publication:* Employer and Employees as Judges in the Labour Court 1958. *Address:* Armsfeltsgatan 18, 11534 Stockholm Sweden. *Telephone:* 08/664.14.90.

GEISEL, Gen. Ernesto; Brazilian army officer, business executive and politician; b. 3 Aug. 1907, Bento Goncalves, Rio Grande do Sul; s. of Augusto Geisel; brother of Orlando Geisel (q.v.); m. Amália Markus Geisel; one d.; ed. Military Colleges at Realengo, Armas, Estado Major e Superior de Guerra and Army Staff Coll., U.S.A.; served in various army units; numerous appointments included: chief artillery instructor, mil. coll.; Mil. Attaché, Brazilian Embassy, Uruguay; mem. perm. staff, Escola Superior de Guerra; Deputy Chief Mil. Cabinet of the Presidency 1955, Chief 1964–67; Sec.-Gen. Council for Nat. Security; Sec. of Public Works for State of Paraíba; Supt. of Pres. Bernardes Refinery 1955; mem. Nat. Petroleum Council 1957–58, 1959–61; Minister, Supreme Mil. Court 1967–69; Pres. of Petrobrás 1969–73; Pres. candidate, ARENA Party 1973; Pres. of Brazil 1974–79; numerous decorations. *Address:* c/o Palácio do Planalto, Brasília, D.F., Brazil.

GEISS, Johannes, DR.RER.NAT.; Swiss professor of physics; b. 4 Sept. 1926, Stolp, Poland; s. of Hans Geiss and Irene Wilke; m. Carmen Bach 1955; one d.; ed. Univ. of Göttingen; Research Assoc., Enrico Fermi Inst., Univ. of Chicago 1955–56; Assoc. Prof., Marine Lab., Univ. of Miami 1958–59; Assoc. Prof., Univ. of Berne 1960, Prof. of Physics 1964–, Dir. Inst. of Physics 1966–; Visiting Scientist, NASA Goddard Inst. for Space Studies, New York 1965, NASA Manned Spacecraft Center, Houston 1968–69; Chair. Launching Programme Advisory Cttee., European Space Agency, Paris 1970–72; Visiting Prof. Univ. of Toulouse 1975; Chair. Space Science Cttee., European Science Foundation 1979–; Rector, Univ. of Berne 1982–83; Hon. Dr. (Univ. of Chicago); Fellow of the American Geophysical Union; mem. American Acad. of Arts and Sciences, N.A.S.; Foreign mem. Max-Planck-Inst. für Aeronomie, Int. Acad. of Astronautics; NASA Medal for Exceptional Scientific Achievement. *Publications:* over 200 publications on nucleosynthesis, cosmology, the origin of the solar system, geochronology, climatic history of the earth, the age of meteorites and lunar rocks, comets, solar wind, solar terrestrial relations. *Address:* Physics Institute, University of Berne, Sidlerstrasse 5, CH-3012 Berne, Switzerland. *Telephone:* 31/65 44 02.

GEISSLER, Heiner, DR.JUR.; German politician; b. 3 March 1930, Oberndorff; m. Susanne Thunack 1962; three s.; ed. Univs. of Tübingen and Munich; Dir. Office of Minister of Labour and Social Welfare, Baden-Wurttemberg; mem. Bundestag 1965–67, 1980; Minister for Social Welfare, Health and Sport, Rheinland-Pfalz 1967–77; mem. Parl. of Rheinland-Pfalz 1971; Gen. Sec. C.D.U. 1977–; mem. Television Council, Second German Television 1970–82; Fed. Minister for Youth, Family and Health 1982–85; Bundesverdienstkreuz 1970, Bergverlagspreis Deutsches Alpenverein 1983. *Publications:* Die neue soziale Frage 1976, Der Weg in die Gewalt 1978, Sicherheit für unsere Freiheit 1978, Verwaltete Bürger-Gesellschaft in Fesseln 1978, Grundwerte in der Politik 1979, Zukunftschancen der Jugend 1979, Sport—Geschäft ohne Illusionen? 1980, Mut zur Alternative 1981. *Leisure interest:* mountaineering. *Address:* Konrad-Adenauer-Haus, 5300 Bonn 1, Federal Republic of Germany (Office); Unterer Talacker 17, 6741 Burrweiler, Federal Republic of Germany. *Telephone:* 0228/544444 (Office).

GELAGA-KING, George, B.A.; Sierra Leonean lawyer and diplomatist; b. 29 Oct. 1932, Alberta, Belgian Congo (now Zaire); ed. in Freetown, and Univ. of London; taught in schools and colls., London and Freetown 1960–64; private law practice, Freetown 1964–74; Dir. of The Daily Mail 1969–71; Amb. to France (also accred. to Switzerland, Spain, Portugal, and UNESCO) 1974–78; Perm. Rep. to UN 1978–81; Justice of Appeal, Court of Appeal, Freetown; mem. Sierra Leone Bar Asscn., Sec. 1968–71. *Address:* c/o Court of Appeal, Freetown, Sierra Leone.

GELDOF, Bob; Irish rock singer and charity promoter; b. Dublin; m. Paula Yates 1986; one d.; ed. Black Rock Coll.; many casual jobs, lorry-driving, busking, teaching English, working in factory, etc., then journalist on pop music paper, Georgia Strait, Vancouver, Canada; returned Dublin and f. rock group, Boomtown Rats; brought group to London 1977, recorded for Ensign Records, then Phonogram; organized recording of Do They Know It's Christmas? by Band Aid, raising £8 million for African famine relief Nov. 1984, f. Band-Aid Trust to distribute proceeds 1985, Chair.; organized Live Aid concerts Wembley, London and Philadelphia, U.S.A. with int. TV link-up by satellite, raising £48 million July 1985; f. Live Aid Foundation, U.S.A.; organized publ. of Live Aid book The Greatest Show on Earth 1985; *film appearances include:* Number One, Pink Floyd—The Wall; Hon. K.B.E. 1986; Third World Prize 1986; Dr. h.c. (Ghent) 1986; Hon. D.Lit. (London) 1987; Freeman of Ypres 1986; Elder of the Repub. of Tanzania. *Publication:* Is That It? (autobiog.) 1986. *Address:* c/o Band Aid Trust, P.O. Box 4TX, London, W.1; Davington Priory, Kent, England.

GELFAND, Israil Moiseyevich, D.SC.; Russian mathematician and biologist; b. 2 Sept. 1913, Krasnye Okny; m. Zorya Yakovlevna Shapiro 1942;

wo s.; ed. Moscow State Univ.; Asst. Professor, Dept. of Mathematics, Moscow State Univ. 1935–40, Prof. 1940–; Corresp. mem. U.S.S.R. Acad. f Sciences 1953–; Head of Laboratory of Mathematical Methods in Biology, Moscow State Univ.; Foreign mem. Royal Soc., American Nat. Acad. of Sciences, l'Académie des Sciences (France), Royal Swedish Acad. of Sciences, Royal Irish Soc., American Acad. of Arts and Sciences; Hon. mem. Moscow Mathematical Soc., London Mathematical Soc.; Dr. h.c. Univs. of Oxford, Harvard, Uppsala, and Paris); Wolf Prize in Mathematics 978. *Publications:* numerous works including Unitary Representations of Classical Groups 1950, Generalized Functions Vols. I-VI 1958–66, Normed Rings 1960, Automorphic Functions and the Theory of Representations 962, Cohomology of Infinite Dimensional Lie Algebras and Some Questions of Integral Homology 1970, Representations of the Group SL 2R, Where R is a Ring of Functions 1973, Mechanisms of Morphogenesis in Cell Structures 1977. *Address:* Laboratory of Mathematical Methods in Biology, Moscow State University, Moscow 117234, U.S.S.R.

GÉLIN, Daniel Yves; French actor; b. 19 May 1921, Anger; s. of Alfred and Yvonne (née Le Méner) Gélin; m. 1st Danièle Girard 1946 (divorced), one s.; m. 2nd Sylvie Hirsch 1954 (divorced), two s. (one deceased) one d.; m. 3rd Lydie Zaks 1973, one d.; ed. Lycée de St. Malo, Paris Conservatoire; mem. Théâtre Nat. Populaire Co. 1960–; Chevalier, Légion d'honneur, Officier des Arts et des Lettres. *Films and plays include:* La ronde, Dieu a besoin des hommes 1950, Les mains sales, Paris-Canaille, Les amants du Tage 1955, En effeuillant la Marguerite, Mort en fraude, Charmants garçons 1957, Suivez-moi jeune homme, Ce corps tant désiré, Austerlitz, Monsieur Masure, La morte saison des amours, La proie pour l'ombre, Le Testament d'Orphée 1960, Carthage en flammes, Peur panique, Le jour le plus long, Règlements de compte, La bonne soupe 1963, Vacances portuaises, Le soleil noir 1966, Duel à la vodka 1967, Le mois le plus beau 968, Slogan, Hallucinations sadiques, Détruite dit-elle 1969, La servante 970, Le souffle au coeur 1970, Un linceul n'a pas de poches 1975, Dialogue l'exilés 1975, La police au service du citoyen 1975, Nous irons tous au paradis 1977, l'honorable société 1978, Qu'il est joli garçon, l'assassin de Papa, L'oeil du maître 1979, Huis-clos 1981, La nuit de Varennes 1982, Les enfants 1985; has also appeared on TV. *Publications:* poetry: Fatras 950, Dérives 1965, Poèmes à dire 1970, Deux ou trois vies qui sont les miennes 1977, Mon jardin et moi 1984. *Address:* 92 boulevard Murat, 75016 Paris; 28 Boutigny-sur-Opton, 28100 Dreux, France.

GÉLINAS, Gratien, O.C., F.R.S.C.; Canadian actor, playwright and producer; b. 8 Dec. 1909, St.-Tite-de-Champlain, Quebec; s. of Mathias Gélinas and Geneviève Davidson; m. 1st Simone Lalonde 1935 (died 1967), five s. one d.; m. 2nd Huguette Oligny 1973; ed. Coll. de Montréal, School of Higher Commercial Studies, Montreal; after 2 months in first job with Dupuis Frères (Dept. Store), Montreal, joined La Sauvegarde Insurance Co. as accountant 1929–37; casual radio and stage performances, including creation of character of 'Fridolin' in series of monologues at cabaret Mon Paris, Montreal, culminating in appearance in Télévise-moi-ça, St. Denis Theatre, Montreal 1936; radio debut with 'Fridolin' in Carrousel de la gaîté (later Le train de plaisir) 1937, Fridolinons Revue 1938; left radio for theatre 1941; directed, produced and starred in annual reviews, Montreal and Quebec City 1940–46; leading part in St. Lazare's Pharmacy, Chicago 1945, wrote and starred in TV serial Les quat' fers en l'air 1954–55; Fridolinades revue), Orpheum Theatre, Montreal 1956; appeared as Charles VI (Henry V), and Dr. Caius (Merry Wives of Windsor), with Stratford Shakespearean Festival Co., Stratford (Ontario) and Edinburgh Festival 1956; films: La Dame aux Camélias 1942, Tit-Coq 1952, Bonheur d'occasion 1982, Agnes of God 1984, Les Tisserands du Pouvoir 1987; dir. first production L'alouette 1958, played Charles VII in English adaptation The Lark; wrote Bousille et les justes, appearing in title-role at Montreal premiere 1959, then on tour in Canada including Vancouver Int. Festival 1962, Seattle World Fair 1962; wrote, produced, and acted in Le diable à quatre (satirical review) 1964, author and dir. Hier les enfants dansaient, Montreal premiere 1966, appeared in English adaptation Yesterday the Children were Dancing, Charlottetown Summer Festival 1967; wrote and played title role in La Passion de Narcisse Mondoux, Le Théâtre du Petit Bonheur, Toronto 1986, Le Théâtre du Rideau Vert, Montreal 1987; f. La Comédie-Canadienne, Montreal, after taking over Gaiety Theatre 1957, Gen. Dir. 1957–72; mem. Bd. of Govs., Nat. Film Bd. of Canada 1950–52; Vice-Pres. Asscn. Canadienne du Théâtre Amateur 1950–61; Pres. Canada Theatre Inst. 1959–60; founding mem. Nat. Theatre School of Canada 1960; mem. Royal Soc. of Canada 1958–; Chair. Canada Film Devt. Corpn. 1969–78; Hon. D.Litt. (Montreal) 1949, (Toronto) 1951, Hon. LL.D. (Sask) 1966, (McGill) 1968, (New Brunswick) 1969, (Trent) 1970, (Mount Allinson) 1973; Grand Prix (Dramatists Soc.) for Tit-Coq 1949, Film of Year Award for Tit-Coq 1953, Victor Morin Prize for 1967 (St. Jean Baptiste Soc.) 1967. *Publications:* series of ten topical revues starring 'Fridolin', Tit-Coq (play) 1949, Les quat' fers en l'air (TV serial) 1954–55, Fridolinades (revue) 1956, Bousille et les justes 1959, Le diable à quatre (satirical revue) 1964, Hier les enfants dansaient 1966; films: La Dame aux Camélias 1942, Tit-Coq. *Leisure interests:* classical music, boating, tennis, skating, travel. *Address:* 316 Girouard Street, Box 207, OKA, Quebec J0N 1E0, Canada (Home).

GELL-MANN, Murray, PH.D.; American physicist; b. 15 Sept. 1929, New York City; s. of the late Arthur and Pauline (Reichstein) Gell-Mann; m. J. Margaret Dow 1955 (died 1981); one s. one d.; ed. Yale Univ. of Massachu-

setts Inst. of Tech.; mem. Inst. for Advanced Study, Princeton 1951, 1955; Instructor, Asst. Prof., and Assoc. Prof., Univ. of Chicago 1952–55; Assoc. Prof., Calif. Inst. of Tech. 1955–56, Prof. 1956–66, R. A. Millikan Prof. of Theoretical Physics 1967–; Research Assoc. Univ. of Illinois 1951, 1953; Visiting Assoc. Prof. Columbia Univ. 1954; Visiting Prof. Collège de France and Univ. of Paris 1959–60, Mass. Inst. of Tech. 1963; Consultant, Inst. for Defense Analyses, Arlington, Va. 1961–70, Rand Corpn., Santa Monica, Calif. 1956–; mem. N.A.S.A. Physics Panel 1964–, President's Science Advisory Cttee. 1969–72, Council on Foreign Relations 1975–; Consultant to Los Alamos Scientific Laboratory, Los Alamos, N.M. 1956–; Citizen Regent, Smithsonian Inst. 1975–; Chair. Western Center, American Acad. of Arts and Sciences 1970–76; Chair. of Bd. Aspen Center for Physics 1973–79; mem. Bd. Calif. Nature Conservancy 1984–; Dir. J. D. and C. T. MacArthur Foundation 1979–; mem. Science and Grants Cttee., Leakey Foundation 1977–, mem. N.A.S., American Physical Soc., American Acad. of Arts and Sciences; Foreign mem. Royal Soc. 1978–; Hon. Sc.D. (Yale) 1959, (Chicago) 1967, (Illinois 1968, (Wesleyan) 1968, (Utah) 1970, (Columbia) 1977, Dr. h.c. (Turin, Italy) 1969, Hon. Sc.D. (Cambridge Univ.) 1980; Dannie Heineman Prize, American Physical Soc. 1959; Ernest O. Lawrence Award 1966, Franklin Medal 1967, John J. Carty Medal (Nat. Acad. of Sciences) 1968, Nobel Prize in Physics 1969. *Major works:* Developed strangeness theory, theory of neutral K mesons, eightfold way theory of approximate symmetry; current algebra, quark scheme; contributed to theory of dispersion relations, theory of weak interaction and formulation of quantum chromodynamics. *Publication:* (with Yuval Ne'eman q.v.) The Eightfold Way 1964. *Leisure interests:* historical linguistics, wilderness trips. *Address:* 1024 Armada Drive, Pasadena, Calif. 91103; Lauritsen Laboratory of Physics, California Institute of Technology, 452-48 Pasadena, Calif. 91125, U.S.A. *Telephone:* (818) 356-6686.

GELLERT, Natalya Vladimirovna; Soviet politician; b. 1953; ed. Tselinograd Collective Farm Tech. Coll.; in charge of mechanisation of Tselinograd state-farm, Kazakhstan 1969–74; mem. CPSU 1973–; Deputy to U.S.S.R. Supreme Soviet; Pres. of Comm. on Women, Motherhood and Childcare with Council of Naionalities of U.S.S.R Supreme Soviet 1986–; cand. mem. of CPSU Cen. Cttee. 1986–. *Address:* Council of Nationalities, Moscow, U.S.S.R.

GELLHORN, Martha; American writer and war correspondent; b. St. Louis, Mo.; one s.; ed. John Burroughs School and Bryn Mawr Coll.; War Corresp., covering Spanish Civil War, Finnish-Russian War, Sino-Japanese War, Second World War, Java, Vietnam, and Arab-Israeli Wars; now occasional journalism in Europe. *Publications:* The Trouble I've Seen 1936, A Stricken Field 1939, The Heart of Another 1940, Liana 1943, The Wine of Astonishment 1948, The Honeyed Peace 1953, Two by Two 1958, The Face of War 1959, His Own Man 1961, Pretty Tales for Tired People 1965, The Lowest Trees Have Tops 1967, The Weather in Africa 1978, Travels with Myself and Another 1978, The View from the Ground 1988. *Address:* 72 Cadogan Square, London, S.W.1, England.

GELLNER, Ernest André, M.A., PH.D., D.SC., F.B.A.; British academic; b. 9 Dec. 1925, Paris, France; s. of Dr. R. Gellner and the late A. Fant; m. Susan Ryan 1954; two s. two d.; ed. Prague English Grammar School, St. Albans Co. School, Balliol Coll., Oxford; teacher at L.S.E. 1949–84, (full Prof. 1962–); William Wyse Prof. of Social Anthropology, Univ. of Cambridge 1984–. *Publications:* Words and Things 1959, Thought and Change 1965, Saints of the Atlas 1969, Legitimation of Belief 1979, Muslim Society 1981, Nations and Nationalism 1983, The Psychoanalytic Movement 1985, Culture, Identity and Politics 1987. *Address:* King's College, Cambridge, England (Office). *Telephone:* (0223) 66155 (Home).

GELMAN, Aleksandr Isaakovich; Soviet playwright and scenarist; b. 25 Oct. 1933; ed. Kishinev Univ; mem. CPSU 1956–; worked in factories 1956–67; corresp. for daily papers 1967–71; wrote scripts for series of documentary films 1971–74; elected to Congress of People's Deputies of the U.S.S.R. 1989; U.S.S.R. State Prize 1976. *Film scripts include:* Night Shift 1971, Consider me Grown Up 1974, Xenia, Fyodor's Favourite Wife 1974, First Prize 1975, Clumsy Man 1979, We, The Undersigned 1981. *Theatre work includes:* A Man with Connections. *Address:* c/o U.S.S.R. Union of Writers, Ulitsa Vorovskogo 52, Moscow, U.S.S.R.

GELZER, (Carl Otto) Michael, D.IUR.; Swiss diplomatist; b. 23 July 1916, Schaffhausen; s. of Heinrich Gelzer and Charlotte Lüdecke; m. Marie Christiane Sarasin 1964; two s.; ed. Univ. of Basle; Deputy Attorney-Gen. of Canton of Basle City 1943–45; Fed. Political Dept., Berne 1946; Second Sec. Legation in Bucharest 1951, First Sec. Del. in Berlin, Deputy Chief of Mission 1955; Chief of Section, Fed. Political Dept. 1957; Counsellor of Embassy and later Deputy Chief of Mission, Washington, D.C. 1961; Deputy Chief of Div. for Political Affairs, Fed. Political Dept. 1966, Deputy Dir. for Political Affairs (Africa, Asia and Latin America) 1973–75; Amb. to Fed. Repub. of Germany 1975–81. *Address:* Lindenweg 3, CH-4052 Basel, Switzerland.

GEMAYEL, Amin; Lebanese politician; b. 1942, Bikfayya; s. of Pierre Gemayel; ed. St. Joseph Univ., Beirut; M.P. 1970–; Pres. of Lebanon 1982–88; f. The House of the Future, The Amin Gemayel Educational Foundation, Le Reveil newspaper; mem. Kataeb Party (Phalanges

Libanaises). *Address:* Présidence de la République, Palais de Baabda, Beirut, Lebanon. *Telephone:* 387200.

GENDREAU-MASSALOUX, Michèle; French public servant; b. 28 July 1944, Limoges; d. of François Massaloux and Marie-Adrienne Delalais; m. Pascal Gendreau 1970; ed. Ecole Normale Supérieure de Jeunes Filles, Sèvres, Inst. d'Etudes Politiques, Paris; univ. teacher, Sorbonne, Villetaneuse (Paris XIII), then Univ. of Limoges (fmr. Vice-Pres.); Rector Acad. d'Orléans Tours 1981-84; Tech. Adviser to Secr.-Gen. for Nat. Educ. and Univs., Presidency of the Repub., then to Secr.-Gen. for Admin. Reform and Improvement of Relations between Public Services and their Users, Deputy Sec.-Gen. 1985-88, Spokesperson 1986-88, Head of Mission May 1988-; mem. Comm. Nat. de la Communication et des Libertés June 1988-; Chevalier, Ordre Nat. du Mérite. *Publication:* Recherche sur l'Humanisme de Francisco de Quevedo 1977. *Leisure interest:* music. *Address:* Commission Nationale de la Communication et des Libertés, 56 rue Jacob, 75006 Paris, France. *Telephone:* 42.61.83.18.

GENEEN, Harold Sydney, B.S.; American business executive; b. 22 Jan 1910, Bournemouth, England; s. of Alexander and Aida (DeCruciani) Geneen; m. June Elizabeth Hjelm 1949; ed. New York Univ., Harvard Business School; worked for Wall Street brokers 1926-32; Accountant, Mayflower Associates Inc. 1932-34, Lybrand, Ross Bros. & Montgomery 1934-42; American Can Co. 1942-46; Bell & Howell Co., Chicago 1946-50; Jones & Laughlin Steel Corp., Pittsburgh (Vice-Pres. and Controller) 1950-56; Exec. Vice-Pres. and Dir. Raytheon Manufacturing Co., Waltham 1956-59; Pres. and C.E.O., Dir. Int. Telephone and Telegraph Corpn. 1959-73, Chair. 1964-79, Chair. Emer. 1980-, Pres., Chief Operating Officer 1973-77; mem. Nat. Council, Salk Inst. of Biological Studies 1977-; mem. Bd. Int. Rescue Cttee.; U.S. Chair. Advisory Cttee. European Inst. Business Admin.; Doctor of Laws (PMC Colls., Lafayette Coll.); Grand Officer, Order of Merit for Distinguished Service, Peru, Commdr. of Belgian Order of the Crown, Great Cross Civil Merit, Grand Cross of Isabella (Spain). *Address:* 320 Park Avenue, New York, N.Y. 10022, U.S.A.

GENEST, Jacques, C.C., M.D., D.SC., M.A.C.P., F.R.C.P., F.R.S.C.; Canadian physician and medical researcher; b. 29 May 1919, Montreal; s. of Rosario Genest and Annette Girouard-Genest; m. Estelle Deschamps 1953; two s. three d.; ed. Jean de Brébeuf Coll., Univ. of Montreal, Harvard Medical School; resident, Univ. of Montreal Hôtel-Dieu Hosp. 1942-45; Research Fellow, Johns Hopkins Hosp., Baltimore 1945-48, Rockefeller Inst. for Medical Research 1948-51; Dir. Clinical Research Institute and physician, Hôtel-Dieu Hosp. 1952-; consulting practice specializing in hypertension, nephrology and internal medicine; Prof. of Experimental Medicine, McGill Univ. 1960-, of Medicine, Univ. of Montreal 1965-; Consultant Clinical Research Inst. of Montreal 1984-; Dir. Merck & Co., Rahway, N.J. 1972-, Montreal Trust Co. 1980-; John P. Robarts Research Inst., Univ. of W. Ont. 1983-87; Nat. Research Advisory Bd., Cleveland Clinic Foundation 1984-; 12 hon. degrees; several awards and prizes including Gairdner Award 1963, Flavelle Medal, Royal Soc. of Canada 1968, Royal Bank Award 1980, F.N.G. Starr Award, Canadian Medical Asscn. 1982, G. Malcolm Brown Lecture and Prize, Royal Coll. of Physicians and Surgeons of Canada 1984, Distinguished Achievement Award, American Heart Asscn. 1985, Isaac W. Killam Award 1986, R.V. Christie Award 1988 (Canadian Asscn. Profs. of Medicine). *Publications:* 690 publications in scientific journals. *Leisure interests:* reading of classics, history, biography and music. *Address:* Clinical Research Institute of Montreal, 110 Pine Avenue West, Montreal, Que. H2W 1R7, Canada. *Telephone:* (514) 842-1481.

GENG BIAO; Chinese diplomatist, politician and fmr. army officer; b. 1909, Liling, Hunan; ed. North-West Red Army Coll.; Maj.-Gen. 1946; Chief of Staff, Shanxi-Chahar-Hebei Field Army 1947; Asst. Commanding Officer and Chief of Staff, 19th Corps of PLA 1948; Amb. to Sweden 1950-56, concurrently Minister to Denmark 1950-55, to Finland 1951-54; Amb. to Pakistan 1956-59; Vice-Minister of Foreign Affairs 1960-63; Amb. to Burma 1963-67, to Albania 1969-71; Dir. Int. Liaison Dept., CCP 1971-78; mem. 9th (1969), 10th (1973) Cen. Cttee., CCP; mem. Politburo 11th Cen. Cttee. CCP 1977; a Vice-Premier, State Council 1978-82, Minister of Defence 1981-82; mem. Standing Cttee., CCP Cen. Cttee's Mil. Comm. 1979-82; mem. State Council 1982-83; mem. Standing Comm. Cen. Advisory Comm. 1982-; Vice-Chair. Standing Cttee. of Nat. People's Congress (NPC) 1983-. *Address:* c/o State Council, Beijing, People's Republic of China.

GENILLARD, Robert Louis, M.A. (ECON.); Swiss financier; b. 15 June 1929, Lausanne; s. of André E. and Mildred M. (Cornish) Genillard; m. Dirkje H. de Boer 1956; two s. three d.; ed. Collège and Gymnase Scientifique, Lausanne, Univs. of Lausanne and New York; Vice-Chair. and Chair. Supervisory Cttee. TBG Holdings N.V., Netherlands; Vice-Chair. Swiss Aluminum Ltd., Switzerland; Chair. Clariden Bank, Switzerland, Transatlantic Ventures N.V., Netherlands Antilles; Dir. American Express Co., New York, American Express Bank Ltd., New York, Corning Glass Works, New York, Crédit Suisse, Switzerland, Financière Crédit Suisse-First Boston, Switzerland, Sandoz A.G., Switzerland. *Publications:* articles in professional journals. *Address:* 1 quai du Mont-Blanc, 1211 Geneva 1, Switzerland (Office) and 3 rue Louis Aureglia, MC-98000 Monaco (Office).

GENNES, Pierre G. de, PH.D.; French physicist; b. 24 Oct. 1932, Paris; m. Anne-Marie Rouet 1954; one s. two d.; ed. Ecole Normale Supérieure; Research Scientist, Centre d'Etudes Nucléaires de Saclay 1955-59; Prof. of Solid State Physics, Univ. of Paris, Orsay 1961-71; Prof. Coll. de France 1971-, also Dir. Ecole de Physique et Chimie, Paris 1976-; mem. Académie des Sciences, Dutch Acad. of Sciences, Royal Soc., American Acad. of Arts and Sciences, N.A.S.; Hollweck Prize 1968, Prix Cognac-Jay 1970, Prix Ampère 1977, Gold Medal (C.N.R.S.) 1981, Matteuci Medal 1987, Harvey Prize 1988. *Publications:* Superconductivity of Metals and Alloys 1965, The Physics of Liquid Crystals 1973, Scaling Concepts in Polymer Physics 1979. *Leisure interests:* skiing, canoeing, windsurfing. *Address:* 11 place Marcelin-Berthelot, 75005 Paris (Office); 10, Rue Vauquellin, 75005 Paris, France (Home).

GENOVÉS, Juan; Spanish artist; b. 1930, Valencia; ed. Escuela Superior de Bellas Artes, Valencia; has taken part in numerous group exhbns.; one man exhbns. in Spain, Portugal, U.S.A., Italy, Germany, Netherlands, Japan, U.K. and S. America 1956-; took part in Paris Biennale 1961, Venice Biennale 1962, 1966, São Paulo Biennale 1965, etc.; Gold Medal San Marino Biennale 1967, Premio Marzotto 1968. *Address:* c/o Marlborough Fine Art, 6 Albemarle Street, London, W.1, England.

GENSCHER, Hans-Dietrich; German politician; b. 21 March 1927, Reideburg, Saale; s. of Kurt Genscher and Hilda Kreime; m. 1st Luise Schweitzer 1958, 2nd Barbara Schmidt 1969; one d.; ed. Leipzig and Hamburg Univs. Scientific Asst., Parl. Free Democratic Party (FDP) 1956, later Sec. Fed. Party Man. 1962-64, Vice-Chair. 1968-74, Chair. 1974-85; Deputy in Bundestag 1965-; Fed. Minister of the Interior 1969-74; Vice-Chancellor, Minister of Foreign Affairs 1974-; Bundesverdienstkreuz 1973 and other medals. *Publications:* Bundestagsreden 1972, Deutsche Aussenpolitik Reden und Aufsätze aus 10 Jahren, 1974-84, Nach vorn gedacht .. Perspektiven deutscher Aussenpolitik 1986. *Leisure interest:* reading. *Address:* Auswärtiges Amt, Adenauerallee 99-103, 5300 Bonn, Federal Republic of Germany.

GENSOUS, Pierre; French trade union official; b. 25 July 1925; Mont-de-Marsan; s. of Bernard Gensous and Yvonne Lalanne; m. Hannelore Kuhne 1963; one s. one d.; ed. Ecole Nat. Professionnelle, Tarbes; Official, Union départemental des Hautes Pyrenées des syndicats CGT, Sec. Féd. des Métaux CGT 1954; Pres. Int. Union of Metal Workers' Trade Unions 1961-62, Sec.-Gen. 1964; Asst. Sec.-Gen. WFTU 1965-69, Sec.-Gen. 1969-78; a Sec. Conféd. CGT 1978-. *Address:* 213 rue Lafayette, 75480 Paris Cedex 10, France.

GENTILE, Francesco Carlo; Italian diplomatist; b. 15 Oct. 1925, Torre del Greco; m. Samira Sadek Wahba 1963; one s.; ed. Univs. of Naples, Paris, and Louvain, Acad. of Int. Law, The Hague and Yale Univ.; diplomatic service, Emigration Division 1955; Vice-Consul, Cairo 1957, Second Sec., Cairo 1958, UN, Geneva 1960; Econ. Affairs Div., Section I 1960; Consul, Seville 1962; Treaties, Legis. Affairs and Litigation Div 1965; Counsellor, Rabat 1968, Rio de Janeiro 1972; First Counsellor, Brasília 1972; Consul-Gen. Innsbruck 1974; Chief of the Bureau I of Protocol 1978; Amb. to Albania 1981-87, to Ireland 1987-; Grande Ufficiale of the Order of Merit of Italy; numerous other decorations. *Publications:* various publs. on int. law and on foreign policy in magazines. *Address:* Italian Embassy, 63/65 Northumberland Road, Dublin 4; Lucan House, Lucan, Co. Dublin, Ireland. *Telephone:* 601744 (Office).

GENZMER, Harald; German composer; b. 9 Feb. 1909, Blumenthal; s. of Felix and Helen Genzmer; m. Gisela Klein 1949; ed. Hochschule für Musik Berlin; co-repetiteur and dir. of studies, Breslau 1934-37; conservatory and Volkshochschule, Berlin 1938-45; Prof. Musikhochschule, Freiburg im Breisgau 1946-57, Munich 1957-75; Hon. mem. Senate, Musikhochschule Munich; Music Prize of Bavarian Acad. of Arts; Bundesverdienstkreuz; works include: chamber music, organ works, choral music, orchestral pieces and electronic works. *Leisure interests:* philosophy and astronomy. *Address:* Eisensteinstrasse 10, 8000 Munich 80, Federal Republic of Germany. *Telephone:* 980484.

GEORGE, Donald William, A.O., PH.D., F.T.S., F.I.E.E., F.I.MECH.E., F.I.E.AUST., F.A.I.P.; Australian professor of engineering; b. 22 Nov. 1926, Adelaide; s. of late H. W. George; m. Lorna M. Davey 1950; one s. one d.; ed. Canberra High School, Univ. of Sydney; Senior Lecturer, Electrical Eng., Univ. of Sydney 1960-66, Assoc. Prof. 1967-69, P. N. Russell Prof. of Mech. Eng. 1969-74; Vice-Chancellor and Principal, Univ. of Newcastle, N.S.W. 1975-86; Chair. Australian Atomic Energy Comm. May 1976-83; Dir. Australian-American Educ. Foundation 1976-84, Chair. 1977-84; Chair. Australian Vice-Chancellors' Cttee. 1980-81; mem. Bd. of Trustees, Asian Inst. of Tech., Bangkok 1978- (Deputy Chair. 1982-); Dir. Newcastle Newspapers Pty. Ltd. 1985-, Chair. 1986-. *Publications:* various scientific and tech. papers. *Address:* "Shamley Green", Glenning Road, Berkeley Vale, N.S.W. 2259, Australia (Home).

GEORGE, Susan; British actress; b. 26 July 1950; m. Simon MacCorkindale 1984; began acting career 1954. *Films include:* Cup Fever, Davey Jones' Locker, Billion Dollar Brain, Twinky 1969, Spring and Port Wine 1970, Eyewitness 1970, Straw Dogs 1971, Dirty Mary and Crazy Larry 1974, Mandingo 1975, Out of Season 1975, A Small Town in Texas 1977, Tomorrow Never Comes 1978, Venom 1980, A Texas Legend 1981, The

House Where Evil Dwells 1982, The Jigsaw Man 1984, Czechmate 1985, Lightning, The White Stallion 1986, Stealing Heaven (producer) 1987, White Roses (producer) 1988. *TV appearances include:* Swallows and Amazons, Human Jungle, The Right Attitude 1968, Dr. Jekyll and Mr. Hyde 1973, Lamb to the Slaughter 1979, Royal Jelly 1979, The Bob Hope Special 1979, Pajama Tops 1982, Masquerade 1983, Hotel 1985, Blacke's Magic 1986, Jack the Ripper. *Theatre:* The Sound of Music 1962, The Country Girl 1984, Rough Crossing 1987; Dir. Amy Int. Productions Ltd., London. *Publication:* illustrated book of poetry 1987. *Address:* c/o Jean Diamond, London Management, 235 Regent Street, London, W1A 2JT, England. *Telephone:* 01-493 1610.

GEORGE, W. H. Krome; American chemical engineer and business executive; b. 27 March 1918, St. Louis, Mo.; m. Jean Murphy 1946; three s.; ed. Edwardsville Public School, Ill., Virginia Mil. Inst. and Mass. Inst. of Technology (MIT); joined Aluminium Co. of America (Alcoa) 1942, Plant Technical Div., Baton Rouge 1942-44, Cost and Tech. Adviser, East St. Louis 1944-51, Senior Staff Accountant, Pittsburgh 1951-56, Chief Cost Accountant 1956-60, Admin. Asst. Controller's Div. 1960-63, Man. Econ. Evaluation Div. 1963-64, Vice-Pres. Econ. Analysis and Planning 1964-65, Vice-Pres. (Finance) 1965-67, Exec. Vice-Pres. 1967-70, Dir. 1967-88, Pres. 1970-75, Chief Operating Officer 1972-75, Chair. of Bd. and Chief Exec. Officer 1975-83, Chair. of Exec. Cttee. 1977-86; Dir. Int. Primary Aluminium Inst., Norfolk Southern Corpn. 1983-, TRW Inc. 1983-, Todd Shipyards Corpn. 1983-; fmr. Metro Chair. Nat. Alliance of Businessmen; mem. Corpn. Mass. Inst. Tech. (MIT), World Affairs Council of Pittsburgh, Council on Foreign Relations, Management Executives Soc., Corpn. of Woods Hole Oceanographic Inst., The Business Council; mem. Advisory Council Aluminium Asscn.; Trustee Univ. of Pittsburgh, Allegheny Health, Educ. and Research Corpn. *Address:* Aluminum Company of America, 1501 Alcoa Building, Pittsburgh, Pennsylvania, U.S.A.

GEORGI, Rudi, DR.RER.OEC.; German economist and politician; b. 25 Dec. 1927, Bockau; mem. SPD 1945, SED 1946-; Cand. mem. Cen. Cttee. SED 1967-76, mem. Cen. Cttee. SED 1976-; Minister for Machine and Vehicle Construction (now Machine Tools and Processing Machines) 1965-; Orden Banner der Arbeit, Vaterländischer Verdienstorden, and other decorations. *Address:* Ministerrat, Berlin, German Democratic Republic.

GEORGIEV, Vladimir Ivanov; Bulgarian university professor; b. 1908, Gabare; s. of Ivan G. Grazdanina and Janka Zeljazkova; m. Magdalena A. Obreimova 1953; ed. Univs. of Sofia, Vienna, Paris, Berlin and Florence; Prof. Univ. of Sofia since 1931, Dean Faculty of Letters 1947-48, Rector 1951-56; Dir. Inst. for Linguistics Acad. of Science; mem. Presidium then corresp. mem. Bulgarian Acad. of Science; Hon. Pres. Asscn. Int. des Etudes; Vice-Pres. Int. Cttee. of Slavists; foreign mem. Acad. des Inscriptions et Belles Lettres, Paris, Sächsische Akad. der Wissenschaft, Leipzig, Soc. Finno-Ougrienne, Helsinki, Acad. Royale de Belgique, Acad. of Athens; Dr. h.c. (Berlin and Prague). *Publications:* many works, including Vorgriechische Sprachwissenschaft 1941, Issledovanija po sravniteljno-istoricheskomu jezykoznaniyu 1958, Les deux langues des inscriptions crétoises 1963, Vokalnata sistema v røavoja na slavjanskite ezici 1964, Introduzione alla storia delle lingueindeuropee 1966, Osnovni problemi na slavjanskata diahronna morfologija 1969, Trakijskijat ezik 1977 etc. *Address:* c/o Bulgarian Academy of Sciences, 7 Noemvri 1, Bulgaria.

GEPPAART, Chris P. A., D.JUR.; Netherlands professor of law; b. 2 Dec. 1931, Breda; m. Louise Pauline Heÿkoop 1959; one s. two d.; Inspector of Taxes 1959; clerk Netherlands Supreme Court 1960-66; Prof. of Law, Univ. of Tilburg 1966-, Dean of Law Faculty 1984-, Pro-Rector of Univ. 1986-; mem. Royal Netherlands Acad. of Science. *Publications:* Fiscale Rechtsvinding 1965, Vermogensbelasting, (Vol. 1) 1972, (Vol. 2) 1983. *Address:* Arthur Van Schendelpark 39, 5044 LG Tilburg, Netherlands. *Telephone:* 013-672694.

GEPHARDT, Richard Andrew, B.S., J.D.; American politician; b. 31 Jan. 1941, St. Louis; s. of Louis Andrew Gephardt and Loreen Estelle Cassell; m. Jane Ann Byrnes 1966; one s. two d.; ed. Northwestern Univ. and Univ. of Michigan; mem. Mo. Bar 1965; Partner firm Thompson and Mitchell, St. Louis 1965-76; Alderman 14th Ward, St. Louis 1971-76, Democratic Committeeman 1968-71; mem. 96th to 101st Congress from Third Missouri Dist.; Cand. for Democratic nomination to U.S. Presidency 1988; Pres. Children's Hematology Research Asscn., St. Louis Children's Hosp. 1973-76; mem. Bar Asscn., St. Louis, Mo., American Legion, Young Lawyers' Soc. (Chair. 1972-73). *Address:* 218 Cannon House Office Building, Washington, D.C. 20515, U.S.A.

GERARD, Jean Broward Shevlin, J.D.; American diplomatist and lawyer; b. 9 March 1938, Oregon; d. of Edwin L. Shevlin and Ella (Broward) Shevlin; m. James W. Gerard 1959 (died 1987); one s. one d.; ed. Madeira School, Vassar Coll. and Fordham Univ. School of Law; Attorney, Cadwalader, Wickersham & Taft, New York 1977-81; Amb. and Perm. Del. of U.S.A. to UNESCO 1981-84, Vice-Pres. Exec. Bd. of UNESCO 1982-84; Amb. to Luxembourg 1985-; active in many aspects of public and political (Republican) life since 1961; mem. N.Y. County Lawyers' Assn., Assn. of Bar of City of New York etc.; Hon. LL.D. (S. Carolina) 1983 and other honours. *Address:* 22 Bd. Emmanuel Servais, 2535 Luxembourg. *Telephone:* (352) 460123.

GERASIMOV, Anatoliy Nikolayevich; Soviet politician; b. 1931; ed. V.I. Ulyanov Electro-technical Inst., Leningrad; sr. engineer, head of lab., sec. Party Cttee. of Inst. 1955-67; mem. CPSU 1958-; Sec., First Sec. Petrogradsky Regional Cttee. (Leningrad) 1968-75; Section Head. Leningrad Dist. Cttee. 1975-81, Pres. Nat. Control 1981-84, Sec. 1984-86, First Sec. 1986-; mem. of CPSU Cen. Cttee. 1986-. *Address:* Leningrad City Committee of Communist Party, Leningrad, U.S.S.R.

GERASIMOV, Ivan Aleksandrovich; Soviet military official; b. 1921; ed. Mil. Acad. (Tank Forces) and GHQ Mil. Acad.; served in Soviet Army 1938-; active service at front 1941-45; mem. CPSU 1942-; positions of command 1945-; Regt. Commdr. Deputy Div. Commdr., Deputy Commdr., First Deputy Commdr. of Armed Forces 1965-72; Commdr. First Tank Army in G.D.R. 1969-; First Deputy Commdr. Trans-Carpathian Mil. Dist. 1972-, Commdr. Soviet Forces Group North (Poland) 1973-, Commdr. Kiev Mil. Dist. 1975-; mem. Cen. Cttee. of Ukrainian CP 1976-; cand. mem. Politburo of Ukrainian CP 1977-80, mem. 1980-; cand. mem. CPSU Cen. Cttee. 1976-86, mem. 1986-; Deputy to USSR Supreme Soviet. *Address:* Politburo of the Communist Party of the Ukrainian S.S.R., Kiev, Ukrainian S.S.R., U.S.S.R.

GERASIMOV, Pavel Ivanovich; Soviet diplomatist; b. 1915; entered diplomatic service 1945; Deputy Head of Near and Middle East Dept. at Ministry of Foreign Affairs 1953-54; Counsellor at Embassy, Egypt 1954-59; Amb. to Guinea 1959-60; mem. staff of Ministry of Foreign Affairs 1960-61, 1967-70; Amb. to Luxembourg 1961-62, to Belgium 1962-67; mem. Collegium, Head of Personnel Admin. at Ministry of Foreign Affairs 1970-73; Amb. to Switzerland 1973-78. *Address:* c/o Ministry of Foreign Affairs, Moscow, U.S.S.R.

GERBNER, George, PH.D.; American professor of communications; b. 8 Aug. 1919, Budapest, Hungary; s. of Árpád Gerbner and Margaret Muranyi; m. Ilona Kutas 1946; two s.; ed. Eotvos József School, Budapest, Univs. of Calif. and S. Calif.; reporter, asst. financial ed., feature writer, The Chronicle, San Francisco 1942-43; mil. service, U.S.A. 1943-46; Research Asst. to Assoc. Prof. of Communications, Univ. of Ill. 1946-64; Prof. of Communications and Dean, Annenberg School of Communications, Univ. of Pa. 1964-; Ed. Journal of Communications 1974-; Bronze Star; Hon. L.H.D. (LaSalle Coll.). *Publications:* Analysis of Communications Content 1969, Communications Technology and Social Policy 1973, Mass Media Policies in Changing Cultures 1980, World Communications: A Handbook 1984. *Leisure interests:* sailing, tennis, skiing, gardening. *Address:* The Annenberg School of Communications, University of Pennsylvania, Philadelphia, Pa. 19104 (Office); 234 Golf View Road, Ardmore, Pa. 19003, U.S.A. (Home). *Telephone:* (215) 898-7041 (Office); (215) 642-7497 (Home).

GERDENER, Theo J. A.; South African politician (retd.); b. 19 March 1916, Cape Town; s. of late Dr. G. B. A. Gerdener; m. Martha van Rensberg 1943; three c.; ed. Univ. of Stellenbosch; fmr. mem. editorial staff, Die Burger and Die Huisgenoot; freelance writer 1949-; Leader, Nat. Party, Natal Prov. Council 1954; Dir. and Ed. Die Nataller (Afrikaans newspaper), Durban 1954-59; Senator 1961; Administrator of Natal 1961; Deputy Minister of Bantu Devt. May 1970; Minister of the Interior 1970-72 (resgnd.); f. and Dir. Action South and Southern Africa 1972-73; Founder, Leader Dem. Party 1973-77; Hon. Life Pres., New Repub. Party 1977-. *Leisure interests:* reading and writing. *Address:* 5 Crown Mews, 330 Main Street, Waterkloof, Pretoria, South Africa.

GERE, Richard; American actor; b. 31 Aug. 1949; ed. Univ. of Massachusetts; fmrly. played trumpet, piano, guitar and bass and composed music with various groups; stage performances with Provincetown Playhouse and off-Broadway; appeared in London and Broadway productions of The Taming of the Shrew, A Midsummer Night's Dream and Broadway productions of Habeas Corpus and Bent; film debut 1975. *Films include:* Report to the Commissioner 1975, Baby Blue Marine 1976, Looking for Mr Goodbar 1977, Days of Heaven 1978, Blood Brothers 1978, Yanks 1979, American Gigolo 1980, An Officer and a Gentleman 1982, Breathless 1983, Beyond the Limit 1983, The Cotton Club 1984, King David 1985, Power 1986, No Mercy 1986, Miles From Home 1989. *Address:* c/o Pickwick Maslansky et al, 1 Lincoln Plaza, New York, N.Y. 10023, U.S.A.

GERENTZ, Sven; Swedish journalist; b. 3 Sept. 1921, Visby, Sweden; s. of Thure and Elin (née Hemström) Gerentz; m. Kerstin Blix 1945; one s. one d.; ed. Stockholm School of Economics; Sec. to Bd. of Trade 1945-52, Chamber of Commerce 1952-57; Man. Dir. Swedish Automobile Manufacturers' Asscn. 1957-59, Chair. 1960-83; Deputy Man. Dir. Svenska Dagbladet 1960-62, Man. Dir. 1962-73, Chief Ed. 1969-73; Vice-Chair. Board, Tidningarnas Telegrambyrå (Swedish News Agency) 1965-72, Chair. 1972-73, Man. Dir. 1974-86; mem. Board, Stockholm Chamber of Commerce 1965-, Vice-Chair. 1982-; mem. Bd. of Swedish Radio Co. 1980-86; Chair. of Bd. of Nat. Swedish Road Admin. 1982-. *Publications:* The Stockholm Mercantile Marine Office 1748-1948 1948, The Swedish Bd. of Commerce and the Economy 1951. *Address:* Tidningarnas Telegrambyrå, Kungsholmstorg 5, 105 12 Stockholm (Office); Johannesgatan 28, 111 38 Stockholm, Sweden (Home). *Telephone:* 13-26-00 (Office); 11-77-39 (Home).

GEREVICH, Aladár; Hungarian champion fencer; b. 16 March 1910, Jászberény; s. of Aladár Gerevich Sr. and Irén Herczegh; m. Erna Bogáthy

1938; two s.; fmr. Nat. Bank of Hungary supervisor; six times Olympic team gold medallist (Los Angeles, Berlin, London, Helsinki, Melbourne, Rome); individual Olympic gold medallist (London); seven times sabre team World Championship gold medallist; twice individual world champion, four times sabre team European Championships gold medallist; holder of the individual sabre European title (Lausanne) 1935; mem. Bd. Hungarian Fencing Federation; holder of Master Coach title; Order of Knighthood, Order of Merit for Sport, Labour Order of Merit. *Publication:* A korszerü kardvivás (Modern Way of Sabre Fencing) 1979. *Leisure interests:* tennis, table tennis, swimming, reading. *Address:* Budapest I. Attila körut 39, Hungary. *Telephone:* 756-112.

GERGIEV, Valery; Soviet conductor; b. 1953, Moscow; ed. Leningrad Conservatory; prize winner at All-Union Conductors' Competition, Moscow (while still a student), and at Karajan Competition, Berlin; Chief Conductor of Armenian State Orchestra 1981–84; Asst. Conductor (to Yuriy Temirkanov q.v.) of Kirov Opera, Leningrad; Chief Conductor of Kirov Chamber Orchestra 1984–88; Music Dir. Kirov Opera and Ballet Theatre May 1988–; has toured extensively in Eastern Europe, Germany, Italy, Japan, U.S.A. and France with U.S.S.R. State Symphony Orchestra 1987; conducted BBC Philharmonic at Lichfield Festival and London Symphony Orchestra 1988; Royal Philharmonic, Scottish Nat., BBC Philharmonic 1988–89. *Address:* Harold Holt Ltd., 31 Sinclair Road, London, W14 ONS, England. *Telephone:* 01-603 4600.

GERHARDSEN, Tove Strand; Norweigan politician; b. 29 Sept. 1946, Kongsvinger; m.; fmr. Asst. Dir. Gen. Nat. Hospital, Oslo Univ.; Pvt. Sec. to Minister of Trade and Shipping 1975–77, State Sec. to Minister of Finance 1979–81; Minister of Health and Social Affairs May 1986–. *Address:* Ministry of Health and Social Affairs, P.O. Box 8011, Dep., 0030 Oslo 1, Norway. *Telephone:* (2) 11-90-90.

GERISCHER, Heinz, DR.RER.NAT.; German professor of physical chemistry; b. 31 March 1919, Wittenberg; s. of Oskar and Amalie (née Scheuer) Gerischer; m. Dr. Renate Gersdorf 1948; four d.; ed. Univ. of Leipzig; Asst. Prof. Univ. of Berlin 1946–48; Research Assoc. Max Planck Inst. of Physical Chem., Göttingen 1949–53; Sr. Research Fellow, Max Planck Inst. of Metals, Stuttgart 1954–59; Scientific Mem. 1960–62; Prof. of Electrochemistry, Technical Univ., Munich 1962–63, Prof. of Physical Chem. 1964–69; Scientific Mem. and Exec. Dir. Fritz Haber Inst. of Max Planck Soc., Berlin-Dahlem 1970–82, 1985–86, Dir. Emer. 1987–; Bodenstein-Preis 1953 and Bunsen Denkmünze, 1976, Bunsen-Gesellschaft; Palladium Medal, Electrochemical Soc. 1977; DECHEMA Medal 1982; Hon. D.Sc. (Southampton) 1973; Dr.rer.nat. h.c. (Erlangen) 1979, (Free Univ., Berlin) 1986; Luigi Galvani medal (Soc. Chem. Italiana) 1988. *Publications:* 270 publications in various journals. *Leisure interests:* theatre, fine arts. *Address:* Department of Physical Chemistry, Fritz-Haber-Institut der MPG, Faradayweg 4–6, D-1000 Berlin 33 (Office); Thielallee 21b, D-1000 Berlin 33, Germany (Home). *Telephone:* (030) 832 75 95 (Office); (030) 832 76 05 (Home).

GERLACH, Manfred, DR. JUR.; German politician; b. 8 May 1928, Leipzig; joined Liberal-Dem. Party 1945; co-founder F.D.J. (Free German Youth), Leipzig, German Dem. Repub., mem. Cen. Cttee. 1949–59; Mayor of Leipzig 1950–53; Gen. Sec. Liberal-Demokratische Partei Deutschlands (LDPD) 1954–67, Chair. 1967–; mem. Volkskammer 1949–, Nat. Council of Nat. Front 1954–; Deputy Chair. of the State Council (Staatsrat) 1960–; Vice-Pres. GDR-British Soc. 1963–68; decorations include Stern der Völkerfreundschaft in Gold, Vaterländischer Verdienstorden in Gold (twice), Karl-Marx-Orden. *Leisure interests:* literature and gardening. *Address:* LDPD, Johannes-Dieckman-Strasse 48/49, 1086 Berlin, German Democratic Republic. *Telephone:* 22130.

GERLE, Ladislav, ING.; Czechoslovak technician and economist b. 26 Nov. 1936, Kozlovice, Nový Jičín District; ed. Mining Coll., Ostrava; various economic posts, Nová huť Klementa Gottwalda (metallurgical works), Ostrava 1959–66, Production Man. Karviná plant 1966–70; Second Deputy Dir., later Deputy Dir. for Tech. Devt. and Investments, Ostrava 1970–75; Tech. Dir., Gen. Directorate of Hutnictví železa (Ferrous Metallurgy), Prague 1975–78; Deputy Minister of Metallurgy and Heavy Engineering 1978–79, Minister 1979–81, of Metallurgy, Machine Bldg. and Electrical Eng. April-Oct. 1988; Deputy Prime Minister 1981–88; Deputy to House of Nations, Fed. Assembly 1981–; mem. Cen. Cttee. CP of Czechoslovakia 1981–. *Address:* Govt. Presidium of C.S.S.R., Prague 1, nábř. kpt. Jaroše 4, Czechoslovakia.

GERLING, Hans, DR. RER. POL.; German insurance executive; b. 6 June 1915, Cologne; s. of Robert and Auguste (Hoffmeister) Gerling; m. Irene Uhrmacher 1942; one s. three d.; ed. Universität zu Köln; with Gerling-Konzern Versicherungsgesellschaften (insurance cos.) 1937–; Chair. Bd. Gerling-Konzern Rheinische Versicherungs-Gruppe AG, Cologne, Gerling-Konzern Versicherungs-Beteiligungs-AG, Cologne, Gerling-Global Gen. and Reinsurance Co. Ltd., Gerling Insurance Service Co. Ltd., London, Gerling Global Gen. Insurance Co., Reinsurance Co., Life Insurance Co., Toronto, Gerling Global Offices Inc., N.Y., Gerling Global Reinsurance Co. of S. Africa Ltd.; holds top positions in numerous other companies. *Leisure interest:* history of science. *Address:* von Werth-Strasse 14, Theodor-Heuss

Ring 7, 5000 Köln 1, Federal Republic of Germany (Office); Cologne, Gereonshof, Federal Republic of Germany (Home). *Telephone:* 144-1.

GERMAIN, Hubert; French politician; b. 6 Aug. 1920, Paris; s. of Gen. Maxime and Mme Germain; m. Simone Millon 1945; one s. two d.; ed. Lycée Saint-Louis, Paris and Lycée Michel Montaigne, Bordeaux; Sub-Lieut., French Foreign Legion, Libya 1941–42; Attaché to Cabinet of the C.-in-C. Forces of Occupation in Germany 1945; Mayor of Saint-Chéron 1953–65; Chargé de mission, Cabinet of the Minister of Armed Forces 1960–62, Tech. Adviser 1967–68; Deputy for the fourteenth constituency of Paris 1962–67, 1968–73; Founder and Pres. parl. asscn. Présence et Action du Gaullisme 1969–72; Minister of Posts and Telecommunications 1972–74, of Parl. Relations March-May 1974; Chargé de mission of R.P.R. to Eastern France 1974; Pres. Soc. française de télédistribution; Commdr. Légion d'honneur, Croix de guerre, Médaille de la Résistance; Rassemblement pour la République (R.P.R.). *Address:* 1 place du Palais-Bourbon, 75007 Paris, France.

GERMAIN, Paul, D. ÉS SC.; French professor of theoretical mechanics; b. 28 Aug. 1920, Saint-Malo; s. of Paul Germain and Elisabeth Frangeul; m. Marie-Antoinette Gardent 1942; one s. one d.; ed. Ecole Normale Supérieure de Paris and Univ. of Paris; Research Engineer, Office Nat. d'Etudes et de Recherches Aérospatiales (O.N.E.R.A.) 1946–49, Dir. 1962–68; Assoc. Prof. Univ. of Poitiers 1949–54; Prof. Univ. of Lille 1954–58; Prof. of Theoretical Mechanics Univ. of Paris 1958–77, Ecole Polytechnique 1977–85, Univ. Pierre and Marie Curie 1985–87; Visiting Prof., Brown Univ. 1953–54, Stanford Univ. 1969–70; mem. Acad. des Sciences 1970–, Perm. Sec. 1975–; mem. Int. Acad. of Astronautics, Pontifical Acad. of Sciences; Foreign mem. Accad. Nazionale dei Lincei, Rome 1976, Polish Acad. of Sciences 1978; Foreign Assoc. Nat. Acad. of Eng., Washington 1979; Hon. Fellow, A.I.A.A. 1981; Foreign Assoc. Acad.-Royale Belgique des Lettres, des Sciences et des Arts 1984; Dr. h.c. (Louvain) 1961, (Strathclyde) 1975, (Madrid Univ.Iug.) 1980, (Brussels) 1984. *Publications:* Mécanique des milieux continus 1962, Cours de mécanique des milieux continus 1973, Mécanique 1986 and more than 100 papers on theoretical aerodynamics, magnetohydrodynamics, shock wave theory and mechanics of continua. *Leisure interests:* hiking, swimming, skiing. *Address:* Académie des Sciences, 23 quai de Conti 75006, Paris (Office); 3 Avenue de Champaubert, 75015 Paris, France (Home). *Telephone:* 43-26-66-21 (Office); (43) 06-35-53 (Home).

GERMAN, His Holiness; Yugoslav ecclesiastic; b. 1899, Jošanička Banja, Central Serbia; ed. Theological Faculty, Univ. of Belgrade; Bishop of Moravitza 1951, of Budapest 1952, of Žiča 1956; Patriarch, Serbian Orthodox Church 1958–. *Address:* Serbian Patriarchate, P.O. Box 182, 11001 Belgrade, Yugoslavia. *Telephone:* 635699 (Office).

GERMAN, Aleksey Georgievich; Soviet film director; b. 20 July 1938; ed. Leningrad State Inst. of Theatre, Music and Cinema (pupil of late G. M. Kozintsev); works with Lenfilm Studios 1964–; *Films include:* The Seventh Traveller 1968, Twenty Days Without War 1977, My Friend Ivan Lapshin 1984. *Address:* Lenfilm Studios, Leningrad, U.S.S.R.

GERMANI, Fernando; Italian musician; b. 5 April 1906; ed. Rome Conservatoire and Pontifical Inst. of Sacred Music; Prof. of Organ Music at the Rome Conservatoire, Chigiana Music Acad. (Siena), Curtis Inst. (Philadelphia); recitals in the Americas, Australasia, South Africa, Europe; Commdr. Order of St. Gregory the Great, Commdr. Order of St. Sylvester, Kt. Crown of Italy. *Publications:* Revision of works of Girolamo Frescobaldi 1936, A Method of Organ Playing 1942. *Address:* Via delle Terme Deciane 11, Rome, Italy.

GERSHEVITCH, Ilya, PH.D., F.B.A.; British scholar; b. 24 Oct. 1914, Zürich, Switzerland; s. of Arkadi Gershevitch and Mila Gershevitch; m. Lisbeth Syfrig 1951; one d.; ed. Univs. of Rome and London; monitored foreign broadcasts, London 1942–47; lecturer in Iranian Studies, Cambridge Univ. 1948–65, Reader 1965–82, Fellow of Jesus Coll. 1962–; first European to penetrate certain areas of Western Makran, S.E. Iran (dialect field-work) 1956; Visiting Prof. Columbia Univ., New York, U.S.A. 1960–61, 1965–66; Univ. Exchange Visitor, U.S.S.R. 1965; Ratanbai Katrak Lecturer, Oxford Univ. 1968; mem. Danish Acad. 1982; Foreign Fellow, Accademia dei Lincei 1987; Pres. Philological Soc. 1980–84; Hon. Ph.D. (Berne). *Publications:* A Grammar of Manichean Sogdian 1954, The Avestan Hymn to Mithra 1959, Philologia Iranica 1985; articles in specialist journals, encyclopaedias and collective books. *Leisure interest:* music. *Address:* Jesus College, Cambridge; 54 Owlstone Road, Cambridge, CB3 9JH, England (Home). *Telephone:* Cambridge 314552 (Coll.); Cambridge 357996 (Home).

GERSTNER, Louis Vincent, Jr., M.B.A.; American business executive; b. 1 March 1942, New York; s. of Louis Vincent Gerstner and Marjorie Rutan; m. Elizabeth Robins Link 1968; one s. one d.; ed. Dartmouth Coll. and Harvard Univ.; Dir. McKinsey & Co., New York 1965–78; Exec. Vice-Pres. American Express Co., New York 1978–81, Vice-Chair. 1981–85, Pres. 1985–89; C.E.O. RJR Nabisco April 1989–; Dir. American Express Co., American Express Int. Banking Corpn., Warner/Amex Cable Communications Shearson/American Express Jewel Cos. Inc.; mem. Exec. Cttee., Bd. of Trustees Joint Council on Econ. Educ. 1975–, Chair. 1983–; Bd. of Mans. Memorial Sloan Kettering Hospital 1978–; Dir. Int. Golf Asscn. *Address:* RJR Nabisco Inc., Reynolds Blvd., Winston-Salem, N.C. 27102, U.S.A.

GERTYCH, Zbigniew, D.AGRIC.; Polish horticulturist and politician; b. 26 Oct. 1922, Poznań; s. of Tadeusz and Maria Gerstner; m. 1946; one s. two d.; ed. Jagellonian Univ., Cracow; participated Sept. 1939 Campaign, during German occupation in resistance movement, inmate camps and Gestapo prisons, after escape served in Home Army, seriously wounded 1944; scientific worker, Dendrology Research Centre of Polish Acad. of Sciences, Kórnik 1946-53; Dir. Experimental Fruit-growing Research Centre of Pomological Inst., Brzeźna 1953-64; Asst. Prof. 1963-69, Extraordinary Prof. 1969-79, Ordinary Prof. 1979-, Vice-Dir. Vegetable-growing Inst., Skierniewice 1964-73, Dir. 1973-87; Head, Research Centre on Agric. and Forestry Econs. of Polish Acad. of Sciences 1964-73; Corresp. mem. Polish Acad. of Sciences PAN 1977-; Deputy Sec. Agricultural and Forestry Sciences Dept. PAN 1964-73, Sec. 1978-83, First Deputy Gen. Sec. PAN 1981-83; mem. numerous Polish and foreign scientific socs. incl. Supreme Council and Exec. Cttee. of Int. Soc. of Horticultural Sciences; mem. of PAN Presidium; Deputy to Seym 1957-65, 1980-, Chair. Comm. of Econ. Plan, Budget and Finance 1980, Vice-Marshal of the Seym 1982-85; Chair. Nat. Cttee. of Nat. Action for Schools Assistance 1984-87; mem. Polish United Workers' Party (PZPR) 1955-, mem. Cen. Revisional Comm. PZPR 1975-81; Deputy Chair. of Council of Ministers 1985-87; Amb. to U.K. 1987-; Dr. h.c. (Acad. of Agricultural Sciences, Berlin); Officer's Cross Order of Polonia Restituta, Order of Banner of Labour (1st Class), Cross of Valour and other decorations. *Address:* Embassy of the Polish People's Republic, 47 Portland Place, London, WIN 3AG, England.

GERWICK, Ben Clifford, Jr.; American construction engineer; b. 22 Feb. 1919, Berkeley, Calif.; s. of Ben C. Gerwick, Sr., and Bernice Coultrap Gerwick; m. Martelle Beverly 1941; two s. two d.; ed. Univ. of California at Berkeley; served U.S. Navy, Commdr. U.S.S. Scania 1940-45; Construction Engineer and Man., Ben. C. Gerwick Inc. 1945-52, Pres. 1952-70; Exec. Vice-Pres. Santa Fe-Pomeroy Inc. 1967-71; Prof. of Civil Eng., Univ. of Calif. at Berkeley 1971-; Consulting Engineer 1971-; Pres. Int. Fed. of Prestressing 1974-78; projects include marine construction, bridges, off-shore structures, prestressed concrete, deep foundations, all parts of world, Arctic marine structures; Chair. Marine Bd. Nat. Research Council; mem. Nat. Acad. of Engineering, Norwegian Acad. of Tech. Sciences, Royal Swedish Acad. of Tech. Sciences, German Eng. Soc.; Hon. mem. Pre-stressed Concrete Inst., Concrete Soc., U.K., American Concrete Inst., Association Française du Beton, American Soc. of Civil Engineers; Emil Morsch Medal, German Concrete Soc.; Turner Award 1974, Corbetta Award. *Publications:* Construction of Prestressed Concrete Structures 1970, Construction and Eng. Marketing for Major Project Services 1983, Construction of Offshore Structures 1986. *Leisure interests:* fishing, tree farming. *Address:* 500 Sansome Street, San Francisco, Calif. 94111 (Office); 5727 Country Club Drive, Oakland, Calif. 94618, U.S.A. (Home). *Telephone:* (415) 398-8972 (Office).

GESANG DOJE; Chinese (Tibetan) party official; b. Feb. 1936, Qinghai Prov.; s. of Giamucuo and Sangdang Shiji; m. Zenen Namu 1956; one s. three d.; ed. Nat. Middle School, Sining, Qinghai and in Beijing; returned to Sining as a corresp. 1955; apptd. Vice-Gov. Guoluo Tibetan Autonomous Pref. of Qinghai 1957, then Gov.; alt. mem. 12th CCP Cen. Cttee. 1982, 13th CCP Cen. Cttee. 1987; Chair. Literature and Art Union 1985-; started writing poetry 1956. *Publications include:* Legend of Hot Spring, The Childbirth of a New Town at Daybreak, The Name of Maji Snow Mountain, You are an Infant of Daylight. *Leisure interests:* riding, hunting, painting. *Address:* Qinghai Literature and Art Union, Sining, Qinghai, People's Republic of China. *Telephone:* 77179-152.

GESTRIN, (Lars Olof) Kristian, B.L.; Finnish lawyer and politician; b. 10 April 1929, Helsinki; s. of Lars Gestrin and Mary Cabell; m. Monica Eddina Furuhjelm 1962; one s. two d.; ed. Helsinki Univ.; Lawyer, Ane Gyllenberg Banking Co. 1954-65, mem. Bd. 1958-78; mem. Parl. 1962-79; Chair. Swedish People's Party 1973-74; Minister of Defence 1970-71, 1972-74, for Nordic Co-operation 1970-71, 1975-77, of Trade and Industry 1974-75, of Justice 1975-77, of Educ. and in Ministry of Interior 1977-78; mem. Nordic Council 1975; Chief Man. Dir. Savings Bank of Helsinki 1979-; Chair. Finnish Savings Banks Assen. Supervisory Bd. 1982-; mem. High Court of Impeachment 1986-. *Leisure interest:* literature. *Address:* Tammitie 10, Helsinki 33, Finland (Home). *Telephone:* 60921 (Office); 484 816 (Home).

GETTY, Donald; Canadian politician; b. 30 Aug. 1933, Westmount, Quebec; m. Margaret Mitchell; four s.; ed. Univ. of Western Ont.; joined Imperial Oil Ltd. Edmonton 1955; Lands and Contracts Man. Midwestern Industrial Gas Ltd. 1961; Pres. and Man. Dir. Baldonnel Oil and Gas Ltd. 1964-67; Partner, Doherty, Roadhouse & McCuaig Ltd. (investment firm) 1967; mem. Alberta Legis. 1967-79, 1985-; Minister of Fed. and Inter-governmental Affairs, Prov. of Alberta 1971-75, of Energy and Natural Resources 1975-79; Pres. D. Getty Investments Ltd. 1979; Chair. of Bd. Ipsco 1981-85; served as dir. of numerous cos.; Leader Progressive Conservative Party, Alberta 1985-; Premier of Alberta Nov. 1985-. *Leisure interests:* golf, horse-racing, hunting. *Address:* Office of the Premier, Edmonton, Alberta, Canada.

GETZ, Stan; American saxophone player; b. 2 Feb. 1927, Philadelphia; s. of Alexander and Goldie Getz; m. Monica Silfveskiold 1956 (divorced 1989); three s. two d.; mem. bands led by Jack Teagarden, Stan Kenton, Jimmy Dorsey, Benny Goodman and Woody Herman; leader own group 1949-; appeared in films: The Benny Goodman Story 1955, Get Yourself a College Girl 1964, The Hanged Man 1964, Mickey One 1965; Grammy Awards for records Desafinado 1962, Jazz Samba 1962, Big Band Bossa Nova 1962, Getz/Gilberto 1964, Mickey One 1965, Sweet Rain 1967, Stan Getz Gold 1978; numerous American Jazz magazine Downbeat awards. *Address:* c/o United Entertainment Complex Ltd., 1560 Broadway, Apt. 507, New York, N.Y. 10036, U.S.A.

GETZELS, Jacob Warren, M.A., PH.D.; American professor of education; b. 7 Feb. 1912, Poland; s. of Hirsch Getzels and Frieda Solon Getzels; m. Judith Nelson 1949; one s. two d.; ed. Brooklyn Coll., Harvard and Columbia Univs.; Instructor Educ. and Psychology, Univ. of Chicago 1951, Asst. Prof. 1952-54, Assoc. Prof. 1955-57, Prof. of Educ. and Behavioural Sciences 1958-70, R. Wendell Distinguished Service Prof. 1971-84, Prof. Emer. (engaged in independent research and writing) 1985-; mem. Bd. of Dirs. Spencer Foundation 1971-; mem. Council of Scholars, Library of Congress; Columbia Univ. Medal for Philosophy and Educ.; L.H.D. (Hofstra). *Publications:* The Use of Theory in Educational Administration 1955, Creativity and Intelligence: Explorations with Gifted Students 1962, Educational Administration as a Social Process 1968, Perspectives in Creativity 1975, The Creative Vision 1978. *Leisure interests:* art, theatre, music, study of parish and pilgrimage churches. *Address:* University of Chicago, 5835 S. Kimbark Avenue, Chicago, Ill. 60637 (Office); 5704 S. Kimbark Avenue, Chicago, Ill. 60637, U.S.A. (Home). *Telephone:* 312-962-1592 (Office); 312-752-4870. (Home).

GHAFAR BABA, Abdul; Malaysian politician and business executive; b. 1925; Chief Minister for Melaka 1959-67; Deputy Prime Minister, Minister of Nat. and Rural Devt. May 1986-; Vice-Pres. United Malay Nat. Org. (UMNO) May 1987-; Sec.-Gen. Nat. Front; Chair. PEGI, Batang Berjuntai; Dir. (non-exec.) Dunlop Holdings Ltd. 1983-. *Address:* Ministry of National and Rural Development, Bangunan Bank, Rakayat, 1st Floor, Jalan Tangsi, 50606 Kuala Lumpur, Malaysia. *Telephone:* (03) 2910255.

GHAFFARI, Abolghassem, D.SC., PH.D.; Iranian mathematician; b. 1909, Teheran; s. of Hossein Ghaffari and Massoumeh Shahpouri; m. Mitra Meshkati 1967; two d.; ed. Darolfonoun School, Teheran, and Univs. of Nancy, Paris, London and Oxford; Assoc. Prof. Teheran Univ. 1937-42, Prof. of Math. 1942-72; Math. Research Asst. King's Coll. London 1947-48; Research Fellow, Harvard 1950-51, Research Assoc. Princeton Univ. 1951-52; mem. Inst. for Advanced Study, Princeton 1951-52; Senior mathematician, Nat. Bureau of Standards, Washington, D.C. 1956-57; Aeronautical research scientist 1957-64; Aerospace scientist NASA, Goddard Space Flight Center, Greenbelt, Md. 1964-; Professorial Lecturer in Mathematics and Statistics, American Univ. Washington, D.C. 1958-62, and other American Univs.; Prof. Emer. of Mathematics (Teheran Univ.) 1972; mem. American, French and London Mathematical Socs.; American Astronomical Soc., Philosophical Soc. of Washington; Fellow, New York Acad. of Sciences 1961 and Washington Acad. of Sciences 1963; Chair. Washington Acad. of Science Awards Cttee. for Math., Statistics and Computer Science; American Assen. for Advancement of Science 1965; Orders of Homayoun, Danesh (1st class) and Sepass (1st class), U.S. Special Apollo Achievement Award, Apollo 11 Commemorative Certificate. *Publications:* Sur l'équation fonctionnelle de Chapman-Kolmogoroff 1936, The Hodograph Method in Gas Dynamics 1950, about 60 research articles on Differential Equations in the Large, Brownian Motion, Transonic and Supersonic Flows, Lunar Flight Optimization, Astrodynamics, General Relativity and Relativistic Cosmology. *Address:* 7532 Royal Dominion Drive, Bethesda, Md. 20817, U.S.A. *Telephone:* 301-469-7372.

GHAI, Om Parkash, B.A.; Indian publisher; b. 1 Oct. 1919, Bedian; s. of the late Bishen Das Ghai and Lakshmi Ghai; m. Vimla Ghai 1940; one s. one d.; ed. Panjab Univ., Lahore; author of text books and Chair. Sterling Publrs. (P) Ltd.; rep. India at Int. Publrs. Congress in Rome, London, Mexico, Paris; mem. Int. Cttee. Int. Publrs. Assen.; Pres. Fed. of Publrs. and Booksellers Assens. India 1972, Fed. of Indian Publrs. 1978; mem. Nat. Book Devt. Council 1972; Ed.-in-Chief Journal of Indian Book Industry. *Publications:* International Publishing Today: Problems and Prospects, Unity in Diversity (published in Indian languages, English, German, French and Polish), three textbooks. *Leisure interests:* reading, music, theatre, promoting religious co-existence and professionalism in publishing. *Address:* L-10, Green Park Extn., New Delhi 110016 (Office); A-1/256, Safdarjang Enclave, New Delhi 110029, India (Home). *Telephone:* 669560, 600904 (Office); 600794 (Home).

GHAIDAN, Gen. Saadoun; Iraqi army officer and politician; b. 1930; m.; five s.; ed. secondary educ. in Aana and Military Coll.; commissioned 2nd Lieut. 1953; Commdr. Repub. Body-Guard Forces 1968; Gen. commanding Baghdad Forces 1969; mem. Revolutionary Command Council 1968; Minister of the Interior 1970-74, of Communications 1974-82; Deputy Prime Minister 1979-82. *Address:* Ministry of Communications, Baghdad, Iraq. *Telephone:* 7766041.

GHANEM, Mohamed Hafez, PH.D.; Egyptian lawyer and government official; b. 28 Sept. 1925; m. Jouman M. Gaafar 1956; two s. one d.; ed. Cairo Univ. and Univ. de Paris; Lecturer, Faculty of Law, Alexandria Univ. 1949; Prof. of Public Int. Law and Vice-Dean, Faculty of Law, Ain

Shams Univ. 1960–68; Minister of Tourism 1968–69, of Educ. 1969–71; Sec.-Gen. Arab Socialist Union 1973–75; Deputy Prime Minister 1975–78, Minister of Higher Educ. 1975–76, for Social Devt. and Services, Presidency Affairs and the Sudan 1976–78; Head of Ministerial Cttee. for Local Govt. 1976; Attorney, Legal and Econ. Consultant 1978–; Prof. of Public Int. Law, Ain Shams Univ. 1978–; fmr. Pres. Egyptian Soc. of Int. Law; mem. Arbitration, Conciliation and Mediation Comm. of Org. of African Unity 1966–71; mem. Legal Consultative Comm. for Afro-Asian Countries 1958–65; State Prize for best publ. in field of Int. Law and Political Science 1960. *Publications:* Public International Law (Arabic) 1964, International Organization 1967, International Responsibility 1972. *Leisure interests:* fishing, reading. *Address:* 26 Mahmoud Bassiouny, Cairo (Office); 3 Sharia El Bergass, Garden City, Cairo, Egypt (Home). *Telephone:* 970431, 976572, 972501 (Office); 980987, 988030 (Home).

GHAREKHAN, Chinmaya Rajaninath; Indian diplomatist; b. 4 July 1937; m.; two c.; joined Indian Foreign Service 1958; posts at Embassies in Cairo, Egypt and Kinshasa, Zaire 1958–63; First Sec. Perm. Mission of India to UN, New York 1965–68, Perm. Rep. 1986–; Counsellor Embassy in Belgrade, Yugoslavia 1971–73; Amb. to Laos 1973–75; Chair. Int. Comm. for Supervision and Control, Laos 1973–75; Amb. to Viet Nam 1975–76; Amb. to UN Office, Geneva 1977–80; Head Int. Orgs. Div. at Ministry of External Affairs 1980–81; Additional Sec. and Advisor on Foreign Affairs to Prime Minister 1981–86. *Address:* Permanent Mission of India to the United Nations, 750 Third Ave., 21st Floor, New York, N.Y. 10017, U.S.A. *Telephone:* (212) 661-8020.

GHASIMI, Mohammad Reza, PH.D.; Iranian banker; b. 5 June 1947, Teheran; s. of Reza Ghasimi and Akhtar Ghasimi; m. Shahrbanoco Nawabi 1980; one d.; ed. Univ. of Cambridge, L.S.E., Univ. of Lancaster; Deputy Dir. Econ. Research Dept., Cen. Bank of Iran 1976–78, Dir. 1979–86; Dir.-Gen. Econ. Policy Dept., Ministry of Econ. Affairs and Finance 1978–79; Asst. to Exec. Dir., World Bank 1986–88, Advisor to Exec. Dir. 1988; Exec. Dir. IMF Nov. 1988–. *Publications:* Boosting Non-Oil Exports 1975, A Marketing Strategy for Exports 1975, An Investigation of the Instruments of Monetary Policy 1985, A Textbook on Macroeconomics 1986, numerous articles. *Leisure interests:* reading, tennis. *Address:* c/o International Monetary Fund, 700-19th Street, N.W., Washington, D.C. 20431, U.S.A. *Telephone:* (202) 623-7370.

GHAZALA, Lieut.-Gen. Mohamed Abdel Halim Abu- (see Abdel Halim Abu-Ghazala, Lieut.-Gen. Mohamed).

GHENIMA, Mohamed; Tunisian banker; b. 15 May 1929, Akouda; m. Anissa Smida 1961; three c.; mem. Destour Socialist Party; fmr. Asst. Dir.-Gen. Nat. Bank of Tunisia, Pres., Dir.-Gen.; then Gov. Central Bank of Tunisia until 1980. *Address:* c/o Banque Centrale de Tunisie, 7 place de la Monnaie, Tunis, Tunisia.

GHEORGHIU, Ion (Alin), Romanian painter and sculptor; b. 29 Sept. 1929, Bucharest; s. of Emil Gheorghiu and Chiriachiţa Gheorghiu; m. Anamaria Smigelschi 1970; ed. N. Grigorescu Fine Arts Coll.; mem. Fine Arts Union, Sec. 1978–; creator of extensive cycles: "Suspended Gardens" (paintings), "Chimeras" (sculpture); has held exhbns. in Romania, Helsinki, Moscow, London, Paris, Warsaw, Rome, Philadelphia, Washington, Glasgow, Tokyo, Venice, Szczecin; Romanian Acad. Award 1966, Yomiuri Shimbun Award Tokyo 1971, Italian Acad. Award and Gold Medal 1980, The Trionfo '81 Prize 1981, The Homage to Picasso Medal 1981. *Leisure interests:* hunting and fishing. *Address:* Romanian Fine Arts Union, 21 Nicolae Iorga Street, 1 Bucharest, Romania.

GHEORGHIU, Mihail Mihnea, PH.D., D.LITT.; Romanian government official and university professor; b. 5 May 1919, Bucharest; m. Anda Boldur 1953; one d.; ed. Univ. of Bucharest and studies in France, Italy and U.K.; Chief Ed. Scînteia Tineretului (newspaper) 1944–45; Ed. and Founder, Secolul 20 (monthly int. literary review) 1960–64; Chair. of Bd. Social Future (sociology and political sciences bi-monthly), Luceafărul (literary weekly), Studies in the History of Art 1975–; Univ. Prof. 1946–72; Pres. Council of Cinematography 1962–65; Deputy Minister of Culture and Arts 1965–67; Pres. Inst. for Cultural Rels. 1967–72, Acad. of Social and Political Sciences 1972–88, Nat. Centre for Co-operation and Friendship with other Peoples 1978–; Adviser UNESCO European Centre for Higher Educ.; Nat. State Prize; Special Prize, Int. Film Festivals 1964, 1966; Ordre des Arts et des Lettres (France); Italian Order of Merit; Grosskreuz des Verdienstordens (Fed. Repub. of Germany); Order of Orange-Nassau (Netherlands); Acad. Award 1972; mem. Club of Rome, Société Européenne de Culture, Académie Mondiale de Prospective Sociale (Geneva), New York Acad. of Sciences; Ordine al Merito (Italy); Grand Croix des Verdienstorder (Fed. Repub. of Germany). *Publications:* Orientations in World Literature 1957, Scenes of Shakespeare's Life 1958, Dionysos 1969, Letters from Neighbourhood 1971, Scenes of Public Life 1972, The Last Landscape (poems) 1974, Five Worlds as Spectacle (collection of plays) 1980, Tobacco Flowers (essays) 1984; translations from Shakespeare, W. Whitman, Burns, etc. *Address:* Oneşti 11, Bucharest (Office); Dionisie Lupu 74, Bucharest, Romania (Home). *Telephone:* 147228 (Office); 130303 (Home).

GHERAB, Mohamed Habib; Tunisian diplomatist; b. 8 May 1926, Tunis; s. of Tijani Gherab and Hanifa Gorgi; m. Fawzia Ladjimi 1958; two s. one d.; ed. School of Law, Paris; Amb. to Spain 1965–67; Special Adviser to

Tunisian Sec. of State for Foreign Affairs 1967–69; mem. del. to XXIII Session of UN Gen. Assembly; Asst. Sec.-Gen. of UN and Dir. of Personnel 1969–79; Sec.-Gen. UN Conf. on New and Renewable Sources of Energy 1979-81; Amb. to U.S.S.R. 1981–86. *Leisure interests:* history, politics, administration. *Address:* c/o Ministry of Foreign Affairs, Moscow, U.S.S.R.

GHERSON, Adolph Randolph Albert, B.SC.ECON.; Canadian diplomatist; b. 9 Jan. 1928, Cairo, Egypt; m. Joan Evelyn Slater 1951; one s. one d.; ed. London School of Econs. and Acad. of Int. Law, The Hague; Research Asst. The Economist Intelligence Unit, London 1949–50; Econ. Research Div., Econ. Co-operation Admin. (Marshall Plan) 1950–52; Economist and Asst. to Chair. Int. Wheat Council, London 1952–58; joined Dept. of Trade and Commerce, Ottawa 1958; Head Commodity Trade Policy Div. 1963–64; Gen. Relations and Int. Orgs. Div. 1964–66, U.S. Div. 1966–68; Deputy Head of Mission to EEC, Brussels 1968–72, Acting Head 1970–71; Minister-Counsellor (Econ.), Washington, D.C. 1972–76; Dir.-Gen. Western Hemisphere Bureau, Dept. of Industry, Trade and Commerce 1976–80; Amb. and Perm. Rep. to OECD, Paris 1980–83; Dir.-Gen. European Summit Countries and European Community Bureau, Dept. of External Affairs, Ottawa 1983–86; Chief Air Negotiator, Dept. of External Affairs, Ottawa 1986–. *Leisure interests:* bird watching, 17th and 18th Century maps and engravings. *Address:* Department of External Affairs, 125 Sussex Drive, Ottawa, Ont. K1A 0G2, Canada (Office); Marl Rigours, Larrimac, Quebec, Canada (Home).

GHEZAL, Ahmed; Tunisian diplomatist; b. 1930, M'saken; m.; two c.; ed. Coll. Sadiki, Tunis and Univ. of Toulouse; fmr. lecturer, Nat. School of Admin., Tunis; served with Tunisian Embassy, Belgrade 1959–62, Embassy to EEC and BENELUX countries, Brussels 1962–67; Head European Desk, Ministry for Foreign Affairs 1967–69; Deputy Dir. Political Affairs 1969–70; with Embassy in Washington, D.C. 1970–74; Prin. Pvt. Sec. to the Foreign Minister March 1974, promoted to Dir. Political Affairs Dec. 1974; Amb. to Austria and Hungary, Perm. Rep. to UN Office and IAEA, Vienna 1977–85; Diplomatic Adviser Oct. 1985; Sec.-Gen. Ministry for Foreign Affairs; Perm. Rep. to UN Dec. 1987–; Commdr. Order of the Tunisian Repub., Kt. Order of Independence. *Address:* Permanent Mission of Tunisia to the United Nations, 405 Lexington Avenue, 65th Floor, New York, N.Y. 10174, U.S.A. *Telephone:* (212) 557-3344.

GHIAUROV, Nicolai; Bulgarian singer; b. 13 Sept. 1929, Velingrad; m. Zlatina Ghiaurov; two c.; ed. Sofia Music Acad., Moscow Conservatoire; played violin, piano and clarinet from an early age; debut at Sofia Opera House as Don Basilio in Barber of Seville 1955, debut in Bologna 1958, debut at La Scala, Milan as Varlaam in Boris Godunov 1959; regular appearances at La Scala, Metropolitan Opera, New York, Vienna State Opera; major roles include title role in Boris Godunov, Mephistopheles in Faust. *Address:* c/o John Coast Concerts, 1 Park Close, London S.W.1, England.

GHIKA, Nicolas; Greek painter and designer; b. 1906; s. of Adm. Alexander Hadjikyriacos and Helen Ghika; m. Barbara Warner (née Hutchinson) 1961; ed. Athens and Acad. Ranson, Paris; rep. at numerous group exhbns., museums and art galleries in Europe, U.S.A. and Australia; nineteen one-man exhbns. in Europe and U.S.A., and three retrospectives (British Council, Athens 1946, Whitechapel Gallery, London 1961, Nat. Pinacotheka, Athens 1973); has given lectures, designed décors, costumes and masks for plays and ballets, including Stravinsky's Persephone, Covent Garden, London 1961; Prof. School of Architecture, Athens; mem. Acad. of Athens 1972; First Prize Acad. of Athens. *Publications:* lithographs, engravings, articles on art, etc.; has illustrated books. *Address:* 27 Blomfield Road, London W.9, England; and 3 Kriezotou Street, Athens, Greece.

GHIUSELEV, Nicola; Bulgarian bass opera singer; b. 17 Aug. 1936, Pavlikeni; s. of Nicolai Ghiuselev and Elisareta Ghiuseleva; ed. Acad. of Art, Sofia and singing studies under Christo Brumbarov; m. 1st Roumiana Ghiuselev 1960, 2nd Anamaria Ghiuselev 1984; two s. one d.; joined State Opera Co., Sofia; debut as Timur in Puccini's Turandot, State Opera, Sofia 1961; has since appeared at most of the maj. opera houses of the world and is noted for Russian roles such as Boris Godunov, Dositheus, Prince Igor, Ivan the Terrible and the Verdi bass repertoire; records for EMI, Decca and Philips. *Address:* Villa Elpida, Sofia 1616, Bulgaria. *Telephone:* 3592-562929.

GHIZ, Joseph Atallah, B.COM., LL.B., LL.M., M.L.A., Q.C.; Canadian politician; b. 27 Jan. 1945, Charlottetown, P.E.I.; s. of Atallah J. Ghiz and Marguerite F. (McKarris) Ghiz; m. Rose Ellen McGowan 1972; one s. one d.; ed. Prince of Wales Coll. and Dalhousie and Harvard Univs.; Sr. Partner, Scales, Ghiz, Jenkins & McQuaid 1970–81; Crown Prosecutor, Queens County 1970–72; Fed. Narcotics Drug Prosecutor 1970–79; pvt. law practice 1981; Leader Liberal Party of P.E.I. 1981–; mem. Legis. Ass. 1982–; Leader of Opposition 1982–86; Premier of P.E.I. 1986–. *Publications:* Towards a New Canada (co-author) 1978, final chapter of thesis, Constitutional Impasse over Oil and Gas, in Univ. of N.B. Law Journals 1982. *Address:* P.O. Box 2000, Charlottetown, P.E.I., C1A 7N8 (Office); 122 North River Road, Charlottetown, P.E.I., C1A 3K8, Canada (Home). *Telephone:* 902-368-4400 (Office); 902-892-3065 (Home).

GHIZIKIS, Gen. Phaidon; Greek army officer; b. 16 June 1917, Volos; widower; one s.; ed. Mil. Acad., War Coll. and Nat. Defence Coll.; Lieut.-

Col. 1957, Col. 1966, Brig.-Gen. 1968, Maj.-Gen. 1969, Lieut.-Gen. 1971, Gen. 1973, Commdr. of Raiding Force, Dept. of Hellenic Army Command 1970; Deputy Commdr. of Hellenic Army Command 1971; Commdr. C Corps 1972; Commdr. of First Army 1973; Pres. of Repub. of Greece 1973-74; Kt. Commdr. Royal Order of George I, Grand Cross of the Redeemer. *Address:* c/o Office of the President, Athens, Greece.

GHORBAL, Ashraf, PH.D.; Egyptian diplomatist; ed. Cairo and Harvard Univs.; joined Egyptian Del. to UN 1949; Head Egyptian Interests Section, Indian Embassy, Washington 1968-73; Press Adviser to the Pres. Feb.-Nov. 1973; Amb. to U.S.A. 1973-84. *Address:* 2 Shafik Mansour, Zamalek, Cairo, Egypt.

GHOUSSEIN, Talat al-; Kuwaiti diplomatist; b. 16 May 1924; s. of Yacoub Ghoussein and Soraya Ghoussein; m. 1953; three s.; ed. American Univ. of Cairo; Foreign News Ed. As-Shaab (Jaffa, Palestine) 1946-47; Controller, Arab Nat. Bank Ltd., Jaffa, Palestine 1947-48; Ed. Foreign News and Dir. of English Section, Broadcasting Station of Jordan 1948-49; Dir. Press and Public Information, Ministry of Foreign Affairs, Yemen 1949-53; Sec.-Gen. Devt. Board, Kuwait 1953-60; Deputy Private Sec. to Emir of Kuwait 1960-61; Minister-Counsellor, Kuwait Embassy, Washington 1962-63, Amb. to U.S.A. 1963-70, to Morocco 1970-71, to Japan 1971-78, also accred. to Australia, Indonesia, and Malaysia, to Yemen Arab Repub. 1978-81, to Yugoslavia 1981, also accred. to Hungary and G.D.R. *Publications:* Five Nationalities but one Homeland 1981. *Address:* c/o Ministry of Foreign Affairs, Kuwait City, Kuwait.

GHOZALI, Sid Ahmed; Algerian petroleum executive; b. 31 March 1937, Marnia; ed. Ecole des Ponts et Chaussées, Paris; fmr. Dir. of Energy, Ministry of Industry and Energy; Adviser, Ministry of the Economy 1964; Under-Sec., Ministry of Public Works 1964-65; Pres., Dir.-Gen. Société nationale pour la recherche, la production, le transport, la transformation et la commercialisation des hydrocarbures (SONATRACH) 1966-84, Chair., Man. Dir.; Minister of Hydraulics March-Oct. 1979; Amb. to Belgium 1987-; fmr. mem. Political Bureau, Front de Libération National; mem. Org. technique de mise en valeur des richesses du sous-sol saharien 1962. *Address:* Algerian Embassy, 209 ave. Molière, 1060 Brussels, Belgium.

GHRIB, Mohamed; Algerian politician; b. 24 May 1943, Ahfir; m.; four c.; teacher Ecole Normale d'Oran 1966-67; Asst. Teacher, Faculté des Sciences, Univ. of Algiers 1969-70; Engineer SONELEC, Head of Electronic Project at Sidi Bel Abbes, Dir. Electronic Complex 1970-82; Dir.-Gen. Enterprise Nat. des Industries Electroniques (ENIE) 1982-88; Minister of Heavy Industry 1988-. *Address:* 6 rue Ahmad Bey, Immeuble le Colisee, Algiers, Algeria. *Telephone:* (2) 60-11-14.

GIACCO, Alexander Fortunatus, B.S.CHEM.; American (b. Italian) business executive; b. 24 Aug. 1919, St. John, Italy; s. of Salvatore J. Giacco and Marie Concetta de Maria; m. Edith Brown 1946; two s. three d.; ed. Va. Polytechnic Inst. and Harvard Univ.; Gen. Man. Polymers Dept., Hercules Inc. 1968-73, Operating Dept., Hercules Europe 1973, Vice-Pres. Hercules Inc. 1974-76, mem. Exec. Cttee. 1974, Exec. Vice-Pres. 1976-77, Pres., C.E.O. and Chair. Exec. Cttee. 1977-, Chair. Bd. 1980-87; Chair. Bd. HIMONT Inc. 1983-, C.E.O. 1987-; Vice-Pres. Montedison 1988-; Hon. Dr. Bus. (William Carey Coll.) 1980, (Goldey Beacom Coll.) 1984, Hon. Dr. Laws (Widener Univ. Delaware Law School) 1984. *Leisure interests:* music, golf. *Address:* HIMONT Inc., 3 Little Falls Centre, 2801 Centreville Rd, Wilmington, Del. 19850-5439, U.S.A.

GIACCONI, Riccardo, PH.D.; American astrophysicist; b. 6 Oct. 1931, Genoa, Italy; s. of Antonio Giacconi and Elsa Giacconi Canni; m. Mirella Manaira 1957; one s. two d.; ed. Univ. of Milan; Asst. Prof. of Physics, Univ. of Milan 1954-56; Research Assoc. Indiana Univ. 1956-58, Princeton Univ., 1958-59; joined American Science & Eng. Inc. 1959-73, mem. Bd. of Dirs. 1966, Exec. Vice-Pres. 1969-73; Assoc. Harvard Coll. Observatory 1970-72; Assoc. Dir. Center for Astrophysics 1973-81; Prof. of Astrophysics, Harvard Univ. 1973-81; Prof. of Astrophysics, Johns Hopkins Univ. 1981-; Dir. Space Telescope Science Inst. 1981-; mem. NASA's Space Science Advisory Cttee. 1978-79, NASA's Advisory Council's Informal Ad Hoc Advisory Subcommittee for the Innovation Study 1979-, N.A.S. (mem. Space Science Bd. and High Energy Astrophysics Panel of the Astronomy Survey Cttee. 1979-), American Acad. of Arts and Sciences, A.A.A.S., American Astron. Soc., American Physical Soc. (Fellow 1976), Italian Physical Soc., Int. Astron. Union; Vice-Chair. COSPAR, I.S.C.E.-1 1980; Astronomy Rep. to I.A.U. 1979-81; mem. High Energy Astrophysics Division of the American Astron. Soc., Chair. 1976-77, Fachbeirat, Max-Planck Institut für Physik und Astrophysik, Comitato Scientifico del Centro Internazionale di Storia dello Spazio e del Tempo; Foreign mem. Accademia Nazionale dei Lincei; Laurea Honoris Causa in Astronomy, Univ. of Padua, 1984; mem. various scientific panels etc.; Fulbright Fellow 1956-58; Hon. D.Sc. (Chicago) 1983; Helen B. Warner Award, American Astron. Soc. 1966, Como Prize, Italian Physical Soc. 1967, Röntgen Prize in astrophysics, Physikalisch-Medizinische Gesellschaft, Würzburg 1971, NASA Distinguished Public Service Award 1972, Space Science Award, A.I.A.A. 1976, NASA Medal for Exceptional Scientific Achievement 1980, Elliott Cresson Medal, Franklin Inst. of Philadelphia 1980, Catherine Wolfe Bruce Gold Medal of the Astronomical Soc. of the Pacific 1981, Dannie Heineman Prize for Astrophysics AAS/AIP 1981, Henry Norris Russel

Lecturer of the American Astronomical Soc. 1981, Gold Medal, Royal Astronomical Soc. 1982, A. Cressy Morrison Award in Natural Sciences, New York Acad. of Sciences 1982, Wolf Prize 1987. *Publications:* X-ray Astronomy (co-editor) 1974, Physics and Astrophysics of Neutron Stars and Black Holes (co-editor) 1978, A Face of Extremes: The X-ray Universe (co-ed.) 1985, also numerous articles in professional journals. *Leisure interests:* skiing, scuba diving, painting. *Address:* Space Telescope Science Institute, 3700 San Martin Drive, Baltimore, Md. 21218 (Office); 203 Lambeth Road, Baltimore, Md. 21218, U.S.A. (Home). *Telephone:* 301-338-4711 (Office); 301-366-7005 (Home).

GIACOMELLI, Giorgio, M.A.; Italian diplomatist and international civil servant; b. 25 Jan. 1930, Milan; s. of Gino Giacomelli and Maria Van der Kellen; one s. one d.; ed. Padua Univ., Cambridge, Univ., England and Geneva Inst. of Higher Int. Studies, Switzerland; joined diplomatic service 1956, Second Sec., Madrid 1958, Second Sec., NATO Del. 1961, First Sec. 1962, Chargé d'affaires, Léopoldville (now Kinshasa) 1964, Counsellor, New Delhi 1966, Ministry of Foreign Affairs, Rome: Personnel 1969, Cultural Dept. 1971, Head of Service for Tech. Co-operation 1972, Amb. to Somalia 1973, to Syria 1976; Deputy Dir.-Gen., Emigration Dept., with Ministry of Foreign Affairs, Rome 1980, Dir.-Gen. 1981, Dir.-Gen. Devt. Co-operation Dept. 1981; Commr.-Gen. UNRWA 1985-; Silver Medal for Civil Bravery (Italy); Légion d'honneur (France); Kt. Order of Merit (Italy). *Leisure interests:* music, literature, mountaineering, hunting and riding. *Address:* United Nations Relief and Works Agency for Palestine Refugees in the Near East, P.O. Box 700, Vienna International Centre, A-1400 Vienna, Austria.

GIAEVER, Ivar, PH.D.; American physicist; b. 5 April 1929, Bergen, Norway; s. of John A. Giaever and Gudrun M. Skaarud; m. Inger Skramstad 1952; one s. three d.; ed. Norwegian Inst. of Tech., Rensselaer Polytechnical Inst., N.Y.; Norwegian Army 1952-53; Patent Examiner, Norwegian Patent Office 1953-54; Mechanical Engineer, Canadian Gen. Electric Co. 1954-56; Applied Mathematician, Gen. Electric Co. 1956-58; Physicist, Gen. Electric Research and Devt. Center 1958-; mem. N.A.S. 1974-; Oliver E. Buckley Prize 1965, Guggenheim Fellowship 1970, Nobel Prize for Physics 1973. *Publications in Physics Review Letters:* Energy Gap in Superconductors Measured by Electron Tunneling 1960, Study of Superconductors by Electron Tunneling 1961, Detection of the AC Josephson Effect 1965, Magnetic Coupling Between Two Adjacent Superconductors 1965, The Antibody-Antigen Reaction: A Visual Observation 1973. *Leisure interests:* skiing, sailing, tennis, hiking, camping. *Address:* Research and Development Center, P.O. Box 1088, Schenectady, N.Y. 12301 (Office); 2080 Van Antwerp Road, Schenectady, N.Y. 12309, U.S.A. (Home). *Telephone:* 518-FR4-9708 (Home).

GIAMATTI, A. Bartlett, B.A., PH.D.; American university administrator; b. 4 April 1938, Boston; m. 1960; three c.; Instructor in Italian and Comparative Literature, Princeton Univ. 1964-65, Asst. Prof. 1965-66; Asst. Prof. of English, Yale Univ. 1966-69, Assoc. Prof. 1969-71, Prof. of English and Comparative Literature 1971-86, Master Ezra Stiles Coll. 1970-72, John Hay Whitney Prof. of English 1977-78, Pres. of Yale 1978-86; Visiting Prof. of Comparative Literature New York Univ. summer 1966; mem. Faculty Bread Loaf School (English) summers 1972-74; Fellow, American Acad. of Arts and Sciences, American Assen. for the Advancement of Science; mem. Modern Language Assen., Renaissance Soc. of America, Dante Soc. of America, American Comparative Literature Assen., Nat. Council on Humanities, Medieval Soc. of America, Council on Foreign Relations, Nat. Comm. on Excellence in Educ., American Philosophical Soc., Council for U.S.A. and Italy; Guggenheim Fellow 1969-70; Pres. Nat. League Professional Baseball Clubs 1986-89; Commr. Major League Baseball April 1989-; Trustee, Mount Holyoke Coll., Ford Foundation; Commdr., Order of Merit (Italy); Hon. LL.D. (Princeton) 1978, (Harvard) 1978, (Notre Dame Univ.) 1982, (Coll. of New Rochelle) 1982, (Dartmouth Coll.) 1982; Hon. D.H. (Oberlin Coll.) 1983; Hon. Litt.D. (American Int. Coll.) 1979, (Jewish Theological Seminary of America) 1980, (Atlanta Univ.) 1981; Americanism Award, Bna'i Brith 1986, Barnard Coll. Medal of Distinction 1986, Distinguished Public Service Award, Conn. Bar Assen. 1986, Ellis Island Medal of Honour 1986, Leonardo da Vinci Award 1986. *Publications:* The Earthly Paradise and the Renaissance Epic 1966, Play of Double Senses: Spenser's Faerie Queene 1975, The University and the Public Interest 1981, Exile and Change in Renaissance Literature 1984, co-ed.: The Songs of Bernart de Ventadorn 1962, Ludovico Ariosto's Orlando Furioso 1968, A Variorum Commentary on the Poems of John Milton, Vol. I 1970, ed. Western Literature (3 vols.) 1971, Dante in America: The First Two Centuries 1983. *Address:* National League of Professional Baseball Clubs, 350 Park Ave., New York, N.Y. 10022, U.S.A.

GIANVITI, François Paul Frédéric, D. EN D.; French professor of law; b. 2 Aug. 1938, Paris; s. of Dominique Gianviti and Suzanne Fournier; m. Barbara Zawadsky 1965; one s. two d.; ed. Lycées Henri IV and Louis-le-Grand, Paris, Faculté des Lettres et de Droit, Paris and New York Univ. School of Law; Asst. Faculté de Droit, Paris 1963-67; Dir. of Studies, Faculté de Droit, Nancy 1967-68, Caen 1968-69; Maître de conférences, Faculté de Droit, Besançon, on secondment to IMF 1970-74; Maître de conferences, Univ. of Paris XII 1974-75, Prof. of Law 1975-, Dean 1979-85; Dir. of Legal Affairs, IMF 1986-; Chevalier, Ordre Nat. du Mérite;

Chevalier des palmes académiques. *Publication:* Les Biens. *Address:* International Monetary Fund, Legal Department, Washington, D.C. 20431, U.S.A.

GIAP, Gen. Vo Nguyen (see Vo Nguyen Giap, Gen.).

GIBB, Sir Francis Ross, Kt., C.B.E., F.ENG., F.R.S.A., C.B.I.M.; British civil engineer; b. 29 June 1927, London; s. of Robert Gibb and Violet M. Gibb; m. Wendy M. Fowler 1950; one s. two d.; ed. Loughborough Coll.; Joint Man. Dir. Taylor Woodrow PLC 1979–85, Jt. Deputy Chair. 1983–85, Chair. and Chief Exec. 1985–; Man. Dir. Taylor Woodrow Construction Ltd. 1970–78, Chair. 1978–85, Pres. 1985–; Dir. Taylor Woodrow Int. Ltd. 1969–85; Chair. Taywood Santa Fe Ltd. 1975–85; Deputy Chair. Seaforth Maritime Ltd. 1978–; Chair. Nat. Nuclear Corpn. Ltd. 1981–; mem. Group of Eight 1979–81; mem. Bd. British Nuclear Associates 1980–; Chair. Agrément Bd. 1980–82; mem. Council of CBI 1979–80, 1985–; Chair. Fed. of Civil Eng. Contractors 1979–80, Pres. 1984–87; Hon. B.Sc.; Hon. FINucE. *Leisure interests:* ornithology, gardening, walking, music. *Address:* 10 Park Street, London, W1Y 4DD, England. *Telephone:* 01-578 2366.

GIBBONS, Ian Read, PH.D., F.R.S.; British professor of biophysics; b. 30 Oct. 1931, Hastings, Sussex; s. of Arthur A. Gibbons and Hilda R. Cake; m. Barbara R. Hollingworth 1961; one s. one d.; ed. Faversham Grammar School and King's Coll., Cambridge; Research Fellow, Univ. of Pa. 1957, Harvard Univ. 1958; Asst. Prof. of Biology, Harvard Univ. 1963; Assoc. Prof. of Biophysics, Univ. of Hawaii 1967, Prof. 1969–; Visiting Prof., Univ. of Siena 1981–82; Guggenheim Fellowship 1973. *Publications:* numerous articles in learned journals related to cell motility, especially that of cilia, flagella and other microtubule organelles. *Leisure interests:* gardening, music, computer programming. *Address:* Kewalo Laboratory, 41 Ahui Street, Honolulu, Hawaii 96813 (Office); 3875 Lurline Drive, Honolulu, Hawaii 96816, U.S.A. (Home). *Telephone:* (808) 531-3538 (Office).

GIBBONS, James; Irish politician; b. 3 Aug. 1924, Kilkenny; s. of Martin Gibbons and Agnes Bowe; m. Margaret O'Neill 1950; five s. six d.; ed. Univ. Coll., Dublin; mem. Kilkenny County Council 1954–57; Parl. Sec. to Minister of Finance 1965–69; Minister for Defence 1969–70, Agric. 1970–73, 1977–79; mem. European Parl. 1973–77; mem. Fianna Fáil. *Address:* Dunmore, Ballyfoyle, Co. Kilkenny, Ireland (Home).

GIBBONS, Hon. Sir John David, K.B.E., B.A., J.P., C.B.I.M.; British (Bermudian) politician; s. of the late Edmund G. Gibbons and Winifred G. Gibbons; m. Lully Lorentzen 1958; three s. one d.; ed. Saltus Grammar School, Bermuda, Hotchkiss School, Lakeville, Conn., U.S.A., Harvard Univ., U.S.A.; Government service in Bermuda with Social Welfare Bd. 1948–58, Bd. of Civil Aviation 1958–60, Bd. of Educ. 1956–59, Chair. 1973–74, Dept. of Educ. 1956–59; mem. Governing Body and later Chair. Bermuda Tech. Inst. 1956–70; Trade Devt. Bd. 1960–74; Minister of Health and Welfare 1974–75, of Finance 1975–84; M.P. 1972–84; Prime Minister 1977–82; Chair. Bermuda Monetary Authority 1984–86, Bank of N. T. Butterfield & Son Ltd. 1986–, Econ. Council 1984–, N. T. Butterfield & Son Ltd.; mem. Law Reform Cttee. 1966–72. *Leisure interests:* tennis, golf, skiing, swimming. *Address:* Edmund Gibbons Ltd., 21 Reid Street, Hamilton, Bermuda (Office); Leeward, Point Shares, Pembroke, Bermuda (Home). *Telephone:* 809-29-52396 (Home).

GIBBONS, Stella Dorothea, F.R.S.L.; British poet and novelist; b. 5 Jan. 1902, London; d. of C.J.P.T. Gibbons, M.D. and Maude Phoebe Standish Gibbons; m. Allan Charles Webb 1931 (died 1959); one d.; ed. North London Collegiate School and Univ. Coll., London; Journalist 1922–33, British United Press, Evening Standard, The Lady. *Publications:* The Mountain Beast (poems) 1930, Cold Comfort Farm (Femina Vie Heureuse Prize 1933) 1932, Bassett 1934, The Priestess (poems) 1934, Enbury Heath 1935, The Untidy Gnome 1935, Miss Linsey and Pa 1936, Roaring Tower (short stories) 1937, Nightingale Wood 1938, The Lowland Venus (poems) 1938, My American 1939, Christmas at Cold Comfort Farm (short stories) 1940, The Rich House 1941, Ticky 1943, The Bachelor 1944, Westwood 1946, The Matchmaker 1949, Conference at Cold Comfort Farm 1949, Collected Poems 1950, The Swiss Summer 1951, Fort of the Bear 1953, Beside the Pearly Water (short stories) 1954, The Shadow of a Sorcerer 1955, Here Be Dragons 1956, White Sand and Grey Sand 1958, A Pink Front Door 1959, The Weather at Tregulla 1962, The Wolves were in the Sledge 1964, The Charmers 1965, Starlight 1967, The Snow Woman 1969, The Woods in Winter 1970. *Leisure interests:* listening to classical music, reading.

GIBBS, Anthony Matthews, M.A., F.A.H.A.; Australian professor of English; b. 21 Jan. 1933, Victoria; s. of J. F. L. Gibbs and S. T. Gibbs; m. 1st Jillian Irving Holden 1960, 2nd Donna Patricia Lucy 1983; two s. one step d.; ed. Ballarat Church of England Grammar School, Univ. of Melbourne and Oxford Univ.; lecturer in English, Univ. of Adelaide 1960–66, Univ. of Leeds 1966–69; Prof. of English, Univ. of Newcastle, N.S.W. 1969–75, Macquarie Univ. 1975–; mem. Exec. Cttee. Int. Assen. for the Study of Anglo-Irish Literature 1973–78, Exec. Cttee. English Assen. (Sydney Br.) 1975–; Rhodes Scholarship 1956; Vice-Pres. Australian Acad. of Humanities 1988–89. *Publications:* Shaw 1969, Sir William Davenant 1972, The Art and Mind of Shaw 1983. *Leisure interests:* tennis, sailing. *Address:* School of English and Linguistics, Macquarie University, N.S.W. 2109 (Univ.); 4 Acacia Close, S. Turramurra, N.S.W. 2074, Australia (Home).

GIBBS, Rt. Hon. Sir Harry (Talbot), P.C., G.C.M.G., A.C., K.B.E., B.A., LL.M.; Australian lawyer; b. 7 Feb. 1917, Sydney; s. of Harry Victor Gibbs and Flora MacDonald Gibbs; m. Muriel Ruth Dunn 1944; one s. three d.; ed. Ipswich Grammar School, Queensland and Univ. of Queensland; admitted to Queensland Bar 1939; war service 1939–45 (despatches); Judge, Supreme Court, Queensland 1961, Fed. Court of Bankruptcy and Supreme Court of Australian Capital Territory 1967–70; Justice, High Court, Australia 1970–81; Chief Justice of Australia 1981–87; Hon. LL.D.; Hon. Bencher, Lincoln's Inn. *Leisure interests:* reading, tennis, swimming. *Address:* 99 Elizabeth Street, Sydney, N.S.W. 2000 (Office); 27 Stanhope Road, Killara, N.S.W. 2071, Australia (Home).

GIBBS, Rt. Hon. Sir Humphrey Vicary, P.C., G.C.V.O., K.C.M.G., K.ST.J., O.B.E.; British farmer and fmr. governor; b. 22 Nov. 1902; m. Dame Molly Peel Nelson 1934, five s. (incl. Timothy Gibbs, q.v.); ed. Eton Coll. and Trinity Coll., Cambridge; Farmer, Bulawayo 1928–; Gov. Rhodesia (fmrly. S. Rhodesia, now Zimbabwe) 1960–69; Acting Gov.-Gen. Fed. of Rhodesia and Nyasaland 1963; Dir. of cos.; Hon. LL.D. (Birmingham) 1969, Hon. D.C.L. (E. Anglia) 1969. *Address:* 22 Dornie Road, P.O. Borrowdale, Harare, Zimbabwe. *Telephone:* Harare 88 3281.

GIBBS, Lancelot Richard; Guyanese cricketer and sports organizer; b. 29 Sept. 1934; s. of Ebenezer and Marjorie Gretna (Archer) Gibbs; m. Joy Roslyn Margarete Rogers 1963; one s. one d.; ed. St. Ambrose Anglican Primary School and Day Commercial Standard High School; Right-arm off-spin bowler; first played for British Guyana v M.C.C. at Bourda 1954; played for West Indies in 79 Test Matches 1958–76; played for Warwickshire 1968–73, S. Australia 1970; has taken 309 Test wickets (world record); has taken over 1,000 wickets in First Class Cricket; has taken 103 wickets against Australia and 100 wickets against England (world record); now a sports organizer; several decorations. *Leisure interests:* reading, all sport. *Address:* 276 Republic Park, Peter's Hall, E.B.D., Guyana.

GIBBS, Oswald Moxley, C.M.G., B.SC.; Grenadian diplomatist and consultant; b. 15 Oct. 1927, Snug Corner; s. of Michael 'McKie' Gibbs and Emelda Mary Cobb; m. Dearest Agatha Mitchell 1955; two s. two d.; ed. Grenada Boys' Secondary School and City of London Coll.; Solicitor's Clerk 1948–51; Refinery Operator, Curaçao 1951–55; Civil Servant 1955–57; Welfare Officer, E. Caribbean Comm., London 1965–67, Trade Sec. 1967–72, Deputy Commr. 1972–73, Acting Commr. 1973–74; High Commr. in U.K. (also accred. to European Communities) 1974–78; Consultant, Centre for Independent Devt., Lomé Convention, Brussels 1979–80; Community Devt. Officer, London 1980–83; Business Devt. Man., U.K.-Caribbean Chamber of Commerce 1983–84; High Commr. in U.K. 1984–, Amb. to EEC (Brussels) 1985–; Trustee, Commonwealth Foundation; Chair. Notting Hill Carnival Cttee. 1981–84; Grenada's Del. to signing of Lomé II Treaty. *Leisure interests:* photography, coin collecting, fishing. *Address:* Grenada High Commission, 1 Collingham Gardens, London, S.W.5; 7A Woodside Green, London, S.E.25, England.

GIBBS, R. Darnley, M.SC., PH.D.; British botanist; b. 30 June 1904, Ryde, Isle of Wight; s. of Ernest Gibbs and Edith Beatrice (Wills) Gibbs; m. Avis Patricia Cook 1961; one s.; ed. Univ. Coll., Southampton and McGill Univ.; mem. McGill Univ. staff, Demonstrator to Assoc. Prof. of Botany 1925–55, Prof. of Botany 1955–65, Macdonald Prof. of Botany 1965–71, Prof. Emer. 1971–; fmr. Pres. Fraser-Hickson Inst. Montreal; Fellow, Royal Soc. of Canada (Pres. Section V 1953–54); Fellow, Linnean Soc. of London. *Publications:* A Modern Biology (with E.J. Holmes) 1937, Botany, An Evolutionary Approach 1950, Chemotaxonomy of Flowering Plants 1974; approx. 40 scientific papers. *Leisure interest:* gardening. *Address:* 32 Orchards Way, Southampton, SO2 1RD, England. *Telephone:* 554452.

GIBBS, Field-Marshal Sir Roland Christopher, G.C.B., C.B.E., D.S.O., M.C.; British army officer; b. 22 June 1921, Barrow Gurney; s. of Guy Melvil Gibbs and Margaret Olivia St. John; m. Davina Jean Merry 1955; two s. one d.; ed. Eton Coll. and Royal Mil. Coll., Sandhurst; commissioned into 60th Rifles 1940; served in N. Africa, Italy, N.W. Europe 1939–45; commanded Parachute Bn. 1960–62; British Army Staff, Washington, D.C. 1962–63; commanded Parachute Brigade 1963–66; Chief of Staff, HQ Middle East 1966–67; Commdr. British Forces, Gulf 1969–71, British First Corps 1972–74; C.-in-C. U.K. Land Forces 1974–76; Chief of Gen. Staff 1976–79; Regional Dir. Lloyds Bank 1979–; Constable of H.M. Tower of London 1985–; Chair. Nat. Rifle Assen. *Leisure interests:* pictures, country pursuits. *Address:* Patney Rectory, Devizes, Wilts. SN10 3QZ, England. *Telephone:* Chirton 733.

GIBBS, Stephen, C.B.E.; British business executive; b. 12 Feb. 1920, Birmingham; s. of Arthur Edwin Gibbs and Anne Gibbs; m. Louie Pattison 1941; one s. one d.; ed. Oldbury Grammar School and Univ. of Birmingham; Dir. British Industrial Plastics Ltd. and Chair. subsidiary cos. 1956–68; Dir. Turner and Newall Ltd. 1968–, Man. Dir. 1972–76, Deputy Chair. 1976–79, Chair. 1979–82; Chair. Gibbs Assocs. Ltd. 1984–; Fellow, Plastics and Rubber Inst. *Leisure interests:* gardening, photography. *Address:* Corner House, 11 Dodderhill Road, Droitwich, Worcs., WR9 8ON, England. *Telephone:* (021) 456 1466 (Office).

GIBBS, Timothy Durant; Zimbabwean farmer, miner and politician; b. 27 Dec. 1938, Nyamandhlovu; s. of Sir Humphrey Gibbs (q.v.) and Dame

Molly Gibbs; m. Susan Rankine 1978; two s. two d.; ed. Ruzawi, Marandellas, Diocesan Coll., Rondebosch, S. Africa; Pres. Matabeleland branch, Rhodesian Nat. Farmers' Union (RNFU) 1969-71; Pres. The Rhodesia Party 1974-76; founder Trustee of Modern Farming Publications Trust. *Leisure interests:* family, philately, reading. *Address:* Silver Street House, South Cerney, Cirencester, Glos. GL7 5TP, England. *Telephone:* Cirencester 860218.

GIBIŃSKI, Kornel, PROF.DR.MED.; Polish physician (retd.); b. 7 Sept. 1915, Cracow; s. of Stanisław Gibiński and Anna Pedenkowska; m. Wanda Ostrowska 1941; three c.; ed. Medical Dept. of Jagellonian Univ., Cracow; held in Gross Rosen concentration camp during World War II; Assoc., 3rd Clinic of Internal Diseases in Wrocław 1945-49, Docent 1949-54, Prof. of Clinical Medicine 1954-; Organizer and Dir. Inst. of Internal Medicine, Silesian Medical Acad. in Katowice 1971-85; Corresp. mem. Polish Acad. of Sciences 1964-73, mem. 1973-, Presidium mem. 1975-83, 1987-, Chair. Cttee. of Experimental Therapy, Pres. Polish Soc. of Gastroenterology 1975-85; Vice-Pres. European Soc. of Digestive Endoscopy 1980-84, World Org. of Gastroenterology 1982-86; mem. Bd. Int. Soc. for Chronobiology 1980-87; mem. Int. Soc. of Internal Medicine, New York Acad. of Sciences, Polish Soc. of Physicians, Polish Soc. of Internal Medicine; affil. mem. Royal Soc. of Medicine; Hon. mem. Purkyne Soc. (Czechoslovakia), Gastroenterology Soc. of G.D.R., Gastroenterology Soc. of France, Polish Soc. of Radiologists, Polish Soc. of Internal Medicine; Dr. h.c. (Poznań Medical Acad.) 1975, (Wrocław Medical Acad.) 1976, (Silesian Medical Acad.) 1984; Meritorious Teacher of People's Poland; Alfred Jurzykowski Foundation Award 1978; Meritorious Physician of People's Poland 1979; State Prize (2nd class); Gold Cross of Merit 1955, Kt.'s Cross, Order of Polonia Restituta 1958, Officer's Cross 1964, Order of Banner of Labour, 2nd Class 1973, Order of Builders of People's Poland 1974. *Publications:* over 350, mainly on physiology and gastroenterology, many in translations. *Leisure interests:* travel, painting, sport. *Address:* Ròżana 13A, 40-045 Katowice, Poland. *Telephone:* 58-43-17 (Home); 52-77-80 (Office).

GIBLETT, Eloise R., M.D.; American immunohaemotologist; b. 17 Jan. 1921, Tacoma, Wash.; d. of William Richard Giblett and Rose (Godfrey) Giblett; ed. Univ. of Washington; Clinical Assoc. in Medicine, Univ. of Wash. School of Medicine 1955-57, Clinical Instructor 1957-58, Clinical Asst. Prof. 1958-61, Clinical Assoc. Prof. 1961-66, Clinical Prof. 1966-67, Research Prof. of Medicine 1967-87, Prof. Emer. 1987-; Assoc. Dir. King County Cen. Blood Bank 1955-79, Head of Immunogenetics (Puget Sound Blood Center) 1955-79, Acting Dir. 1979-80, Exec. Dir. 1980-87, Exec. Dir. Emer. 1987-; mem. N.A.S.; Karl Landsteiner Memorial Award, American Assen. of Blood Banks 1976, Philip S. Levine Award, American Soc. of Clinical Pathologists 1978. *Publications:* Genetic Markers in Human Blood 1969; author and co-author of 194 scientific publs. *Address:* Puget Sound Blood Center, Terry and Madison Streets, Seattle, Wash. 98104; 6533 53rd Street, N.E., Seattle, Wash. 98115, U.S.A. (Home). *Telephone:* (206) 292-6574 (Office); (206) 522-6380 (Home).

GIBSON, Baron (Life Peer), cr. 1975, of Penn's Rocks in the County of East Sussex; **Richard Patrick Tallentyre Gibson;** British company director; b. 5 Feb. 1916, London; s. of Thornely Carbutt Gibson and Elizabeth Anne Augusta Wetzlar-Coit; m. Elisabeth Dione Pearson 1945; four s.; ed. Eton Coll., Magdalen Coll., Oxford; Vice-Chair. Westminster Press Ltd. 1953-76; Chair. Pearson Longman Ltd. 1967-79; Deputy Chair. S. Pearson & Son Ltd. 1969-75, Exec. Deputy Chair. 1975-77, Chair. 1978-83; Chair. Arts Council of Great Britain 1972-77, Financial Times Ltd. 1975-78, Nat. Trust 1977-86 (mem. Exec. Cttee. and Council 1966-86). *Leisure interests:* music, architecture, gardening. *Address:* Penn's Rocks, Groombridge, Sussex; and 4 Swan Walk, London, S.W.3, England. *Telephone:* Groombridge 244; 01-351 0344.

GIBSON, Sir Alexander Drummond, Kt., C.B.E., L.R.A.M., A.R.C.M., A.R.C.O.; British conductor; b. 11 Feb. 1926, Motherwell; s. of James McClure Gibson and Wilhelmina Gibson (née Williams); m. Ann Veronica Waggett; three s. one d.; ed. Dalziel School, Glasgow Univ., Royal Scottish Acad. of Music, Royal Coll. of Music, London, Mozarteum, Salzburg, and Accad. Chigiano, Siena. Royal Corps of Signals 1944-48; studied Royal Coll. of Music 1948-51; Asst. Conductor BBC Scottish Orchestra 1952-54; Répétiteur and Asst. Conductor Sadler's Wells Opera 1951-52, Staff Conductor 1954-57; Musical Dir. 1957-59; Guest Conductor Royal Opera House, Covent Garden 1957-58; Musical Dir. and Principal Conductor Scottish Nat. Orchestra 1959-84, Hon. Pres. 1985-; Founder, Artistic Dir. of Scottish Opera 1962-85, Dir. of Music 1985-87, Conductor Laureate 1987-; Guest Conductor all major symphony orchestras of Great Britain and many in Europe and America; Freeman of the Burgh of Motherwell and Wishaw 1964; F.R.S.E. 1978; F.R.S.A. 1980; Hon. F.R.C.M. 1973; Hon. F.R.S.A.M. 1973; Hon. Dr. (Open University) 1978; Hon. LL.D. (Aberdeen and Stirling), Hon. D.Mus. (Glasgow), Hon. R.A.M. 1969; Hon. R.S.A. 1975; Order of St. John of Jerusalem 1975; Arnold Bax Memorial Medal for Conducting 1959; St. Mungo Prize 1970, ISM Musician of the Year Award 1976; Sibelius Medal 1978; British Music Year Book—Musician of the Year 1980. *Address:* 15 Cleveden Gardens, Glasgow, G12 0PU, Scotland. *Telephone:* 041-339 6668.

GIBSON, Eleanor Jack, M.A., PH.D.; American psychologist; b. 7 Dec. 1910, Peoria, Ill.; d. of William and Isabel Grier Jack; m. James Gibson 1932; one s. one d.; ed. Smith Coll. and Yale Univ.; Instructor, Smith Coll.,

Northampton, Mass. 1933-40, Asst. Prof. 1940-49; Research Assoc. in Psychology, Cornell Univ. 1949-65, then Prof. of Psychology; Visiting Prof. M.I.T. 1973, Univ. of Pa. 1984, Univ. of S.C. 1987, Emery Univ. 1988, Univ. of Conn. 1988; Montgomery Fellow, Dartmouth Coll. 1985; Pres. Eastern Psychology Assen. 1968, Experimental Div., American Psychological Assen. 1977; Chair. Division J, American Assen. for the Advancement of Science 1982-83; mem. N.A.S., American Acad. of Arts and Sciences; Hon. D.Sc. (Smith Coll., Mass.) 1972, (Rutgers) 1973, (Trinity Coll.) 1982, (Bates Coll., Maine) 1985, (S.C.) 1987; D.Hum.Litt. (Albany) 1984; Distinguished Scientist Award, American Psychological Assen. 1968, G. Stanley Hall Medal, American Psychological Assen. 1971, Guggenheim Fellow 1972-73, Wilbur Cross Medal, Yale 1973, Howard Crosby Warren Medal 1977, Distinguished Scientific Contribution Award (S.R.C.D.) 1981, Gold Medal, American Psychological Foundation 1986; Hon. D.S.M. (Columbia Univ.) 1983. *Publications:* Principles of Perceptual Learning and Development 1969, Psychology of Reading (with Harry Levin) 1975; articles in all psychological journals. *Address:* Department of Psychology, Cornell University, Ithaca, N.Y. 14853 (Office); RD1 Box 215A, Middlebury, Vt. 05753, U.S.A. (Home). *Telephone:* (607) 255-6303 (Office); (802) 388-6340 (Home).

GIBSON, Frank William Ernest, D.PHIL., D.SC., F.A.A., F.R.S.; Australian professor of biochemistry; b. 22 July 1923, Melbourne; s. of John William and Alice Ruby (née Hancock) Gibson; m. 1st Margaret Burvill 1949 (divorced 1979), two d.; m. 2nd Robin Barker (née Rollason) Gibson 1980, one s.; ed. Collingwood Tech. Coll., Univs. of Queensland, Melbourne and Oxford; Research Asst. Melbourne and Queensland Univs. 1938-47, Sr. Demonstrator Melbourne Univ. 1948-49, Sr. Lecturer 1953-58, Reader in Chemical Microbiology 1959-65, Prof. 1965-66; Australian Nat. Univ. Scholar, Oxford 1950-52; Research Assoc. Stanford Univ. 1959; Dir. of John Curtin School and Howard Florey Prof. of Medical Research Australian Nat. Univ. 1977-80, Prof. of Biochemistry 1967-88; Visiting Prof. and Fellow Lincoln Coll., Oxford 1982-83; Fellow A.N.U. 1989-; Pres. Australian Biochemical Soc. 1978-79, Gowland Hopkins Medallist Biochem. Soc. 1982. *Publications:* many scientific papers and reviews on biochemistry and microbial metabolism. *Leisure interests:* tennis, skiing, music. *Address:* Biochemistry Department, John Curtin School of Medical Research, P.O. Box 334, Canberra, A.C.T. 2601 (Office); 7 Waller Crescent, Campbell, A.C.T., 2601, Australia (Home). *Telephone:* (062) 492550 (Office); (062) 470760 (Home).

GIBSON, Joseph David, C.B.E., B.A.; Fijian diplomatist (retd.); b. 26 Jan. 1928, Rotuma, Fiji; s. of late Charles and Mamao Lavenia Gibson; three s. two d.; ed. Levuka Public School, Marist Brothers High School, Suva, Auckland Teachers' Coll. and Auckland Univ., N.Z.; Teacher, Fiji 1952-62; Principal, Queen Victoria School 1961-62; Secondary School Inspector 1964-65; Asst. Dir. of Educ. 1966-69, Deputy Dir. 1970-71, Dir. and Perm. Sec. for Educ. 1971-74; Deputy High Commr. in U.K. 1974-76, High Commr. 1976-81; High Commr. in New Zealand 1981-83; Amb. to Japan 1984-87; Dir. Feeders Seafoods Ltd., Rotuma Fisheries. *Leisure interests:* fishing, golf. *Address:* 15 Naimawi Street, Lami, Suva, Fiji.

GIBSON, Mel; Australian actor and producer; b. 1956, Peekskill, N.Y., U.S.A.; s. of Hutton Gibson and Anne Gibson; m. Robyn Moore; four s. one d.; ed. Nat. Inst. for Dramatic Art, Sydney. *Films include:* Summer City, Mad Max 1979, Tim 1979, Attack Force Z, Gallipoli 1981, The Road Warrior (Mad Max II) 1982, The Year of Living Dangerously 1983, The Bounty 1984, The River 1984, Mrs. Soffel 1984, Mad Max Beyond Thunderdome 1985, Lethal Weapon, Tequila Sunrise, Lethal Weapon II. *Plays include:* Romeo and Juliet, Waiting for Godot, No Names No Pack Drill, Death of a Salesman. *Address:* c/o Shanahan Management Pty. Ltd., 129 Bourke Street, Woolloomooloo, N.S.W., 2011, Australia.

GIBSON, Hon. Sir Peter (Leslie), Kt., **Hon. Mr Justice Peter Gibson;** British judge; b. 10 June 1934; s. of Harold Leslie Gibson and Martha Lucy Diercking; m. Katharine Mary Beatrice Hadow 1968; two s. one d.; ed. Malvern Coll., Worcester Coll., Oxford; nat. service R.A. 1953-55; called to Bar, Inner Temple 1960; Bencher, Lincoln's Inn 1975; Second Jr. Counsel to Inland Revenue (Chancery) 1970-72; Jr. Counsel to the Treasury (Chancery) 1972-81; Judge of the High Court of Justice, Chancery Div. 1981-; a Judge of the Employment Appeal Tribunal 1984-86. *Address:* Royal Courts of Justice, Strand, London, WC2A 2LL, England.

GIBSON, Quentin Howieson, PH.D., F.R.S.; American (b. British) professor of biochemistry; b. 9 Dec. 1918, Aberdeen, Scotland; s. of William H. Gibson, O.B.E., D.SC.; m. Audrey J. Pinsent 1951; one s. three d.; ed. Repton School and Queen's Univ. Belfast; Demonstrator in Physiology, Queen's Univ., Belfast 1941-47; lecturer in Physiology, Univ. of Sheffield 1947-55, Prof. and Head of Dept. of Biochemistry 1955-63; Prof. of Biophysical Chem., Johnson Foundation, Univ. of Pa. 1963-65; fmr. Prof. of Biochemistry, Cornell Univ.; mem. Physiological Soc. (London), American Soc. of Biological Chemists, N.A.S.; Fellow American Acad. of Arts and Sciences; Ed. Biochemical Journal 1953-59; Ed. Journal of Biological Chemistry 1965-70, Assoc. Ed. 1975-. *Publications:* Rapid Mixing and Sampling Methods in Biochemistry (Editor) 1964. *Leisure interest:* sailing. *Address:* Department of Biochemistry and Molecular Biology, Cornell University, Ithaca, N.Y. 14853 (Office); 98 Dodge Road, Ithaca, New York 14850, U.S.A. (Home).

GIBSON, Rex; South African journalist; b. 11 Aug. 1931, Salisbury; s. of Arthur David Gibson and Mildred Joyce Adams; three d.; ed. King Edward VII School, Johannesburg; articled clerk 1948–52; entered journalism 1952, joined Rand Daily Mail 1959, Chief Sub-Ed. 1962, Arts Ed. 1969, Asst. Ed. then Chief Asst. Ed. 1969–72, Deputy Ed. 1973–76, Ed. 1982–85; Deputy Ed. The Star, Johannesburg 1985–; Founding Ed. Mining News 1967; Ed. The Northern Reporter (first local suburban newspaper) 1968–69; Ed. The Sunday Express 1976–82; Bursar Imperial Relations Trust 1960; Atlas World Review Joint Int. Ed. of the Year Award 1979, Pringle Award for Journalism 1979. *Leisure interests:* reading, tennis, golf. *Address:* P.O. Box 1014, Johannesburg 2000, South Africa.

GIBSON, Roy; British space administrator; b. 4 July 1924, Manchester; m. Inga Elgerus 1971; one s. one d. (by previous marriage); ed. Chorlton Grammar School, Wadham Coll., Oxford, London School of Econs. Colonial Admin. Service, Malaya 1948–58; U.K. Atomic Energy Authority, London 1959–67; Deputy Dir. Technical Centre, European Space Research Org. (ESRO) 1967–71, Dir. of Admin. ESRO 1971–74, Acting Dir.-Gen. 1974–75; Dir.-Gen., European Space Agency 1975–81, Aerospace Consultant 1981–85; Dir.-Gen. British Nat. Space Centre 1985–87; Special Adviser to Dir.-Gen., Int. Maritime Satellite Org. 1987–. *Leisure interests:* music, languages, bridge, walking. *Address:* 8 Battersea Bridge Road, London, S.W.11, England.

GIBSON-BARBOZA, Mário, G.C.M.G.; Brazilian diplomatist; b. 13 March 1918, Olinda, Pernambuco; s. of Oscar Bartholomeu Alves Barboza and Evangelina Gibson Barboza; m. Julia Blacker Baldessarri Gibson-Barboza 1975; ed. Faculdade de Direito de Recife, Superior War Coll. 1951; joined diplomatic service 1940; Vice-Consul, Houston; Sec., Washington, Brussels; Minister-Counsellor, Buenos Aires 1956–59; Deputy Perm. Rep. to UN 1959–60; Amb. to Austria 1962–66, to Paraguay 1967–68; Sec.-Gen. for Foreign Affairs 1968–69; Amb. to U.S.A. 1969; Minister of Foreign Affairs 1969–74; Amb. to Greece 1974–77, to Italy 1977–82, to U.K. 1982–86; recipient of Grand Cross of Order of Brazil and other decorations. *Leisure interests:* riding, reading, theatre. *Address:* c/o Ministerio des Asuntos Exteriores, Palácio do Hamaraty, Esplanada dos Ministérios, 70.170 Brasília, DF, Brazil.

GIELEN, Michael Andreas; Austrian conductor and composer; b. 20 July 1927, Dresden, Germany; m. Helga Augsten 1957; one s. one d.; ed. Univ. of Buenos Aires; studied composition under E. Leuchter and J. Polnauer; Pianist in Buenos Aires; on music staff of Teatro Colón 1947–51; with Vienna State Opera 1951–60, Perm. Conductor 1954–60; First Conductor, Royal Swedish Opera, Stockholm 1960–65; conductor and composer in Cologne 1965–69; Musical Dir. Nat. Orchestra of Belgium 1969–73; Chief Conductor Netherlands Opera 1973–75; Music Dir. and Gen. Man. Frankfurt Opera House Sept. 1977–87; Music Dir. Cincinnati Symphony 1980–86; Prin. Conductor SWF Radio Orchestra, Baden-Baden 1986–; Chief Guest Conductor, BBC Symphony Orchestra 1979–82. *Address:* c/o Ingpen and Williams Ltd., 14 Kensington Court, London, W8 5DN, England.

GIELGUD, Sir (Arthur) John, Kt., C.H., D.LITT. (brother of the late Val Gielgud); British actor and theatrical producer; b. 14 April 1904, London; s. of Frank Gielgud and Kate Lewis; unmarried; ed. Westminster; first stage appearance at Old Vic 1921; Pres. Shakespeare Reading Soc. 1958–, RADA 1977–; New Standard Special Award 1982; Dr. h.c. (Brandeis); Chevalier, Légion d'honneur 1960. *Plays acted in include:* Shakespeare's plays, Restoration comedies, The Constant Nymph, The Good Companions, Richard of Bordeaux, The Potting Shed, Ivanov, Forty Years On, The Battle of Shrivings, Home, Caesar and Cleopatra, Veterans, Bingo, No Man's Land, Half-Life 1977, The Best of Friends 1988. *Productions include:* Shakespeare, Restoration drama, The Importance of Being Earnest, The School for Scandal, The Three Sisters, Dear Brutus, The Circle, The Heiress, The Lady's not for Burning, Ivanov. *Plays directed include:* A Day by the Sea, The Chalk Garden, Nude with Violin, Five Finger Exercise, The Last Joke, Big Fish, Little Fish, School for Scandal, Halfway Up the Tree, Private Lives, The Constant Wife. *Films played in include:* The Barretts of Wimpole Street, St. Joan, Julius Caesar, Richard III, Becket, The Loved One, Chimes at Midnight, Mister Sebastian, The Charge of the Light Brigade, The Tempest, Eagle in a Cage, Lost Horizon, 11 Harrowhouse, Murder on the Orient Express, Providence, Joseph Andrews, Caligula, Portrait of the Artist as a Young Man, Aces High 1976, Romeo and Juliet (TV) 1978, Richard II (TV) 1978, Le Chef d'orchestre 1980, The Formula 1980, Brideshead Revisited (TV) 1980, Arthur 1981, Priest of Love 1981, Sphinx 1981, Richard Wagner 1982, Inside the Third Reich 1982, The Shooting Party 1984, Plenty 1985, The Whistle Blower 1985, Appointment with Death 1987, Arthur 2: On the Rocks 1988. *Operas directed:* The Trojans (Berlioz), A Midsummer Night's Dream (Britten); Shakespeare recital: Ages of Man in Europe, America and Australasia; Hon. LL.D. (St. Andrews) 1950; Hon. D.Litt. (Oxford) 1953, (London) 1977; Companion, Légion d'honneur; Best Supporting Actor (Arthur) 1981, Soc. of Film and TV Arts 1974. *Publications:* Early Stages 1938, Stage Directions 1963, 1964, Distinguished Company 1972, An Actor and his Time (with John Miller and John Powell) (autobiog.) 1979, Backward Glances (essays) 1989. *Leisure interests:* reading, music. *Address:* South Pavilion, Wotton Underwood, Aylesbury HP18 0SB, England.

GIENOW, Herbert Hans Walter, DR.JUR.; German business executive; b. 13 March 1926, Hamburg; s. of Günther and Margarethe Gienow; m. Imina Brons 1954; one s. one d.; ed. Hamburg Univ.; Head Clerk Deutsche Warentreuhand AG, mem. Bd. of Man. 1959; mem. Hamburg Bar; chartered accountant 1961; mem. Bd. of Man. Klöckner-Werke AG 1962, Chair. Oct. 1974–; Chair. Supervisory Bd. for Holstein und Kappert AG, Dortmund, Vereinigte Schmiedewerke GmbH; Deputy Chair. Supervisory Bd. ALZNV; mem. Supervisory Bd. Albingia Versicherungs AG Hamburg; Chair. Consultative Cttee. Deutsche Bank AG Essen. *Leisure interests;* books, sailing, model soldiers. *Address:* Klöckner-Werke AG, 41 Duisburg, Klöcknerstr. 29 (Office); 4030 Ratingen 6, Am Adels 7; and 2 Hamburg 52, Charlotte-Niese-Strasse 17, Federal Republic of Germany (Home). *Telephone:* (0203) 3961 (Office); (02102) 60692 (Home).

GIEREK, Edward; Polish politician; b. 6 Jan. 1913, Porąbka, Będzin district; m. Stanisława Gierek; two s.; ed. Cracow Acad. of Mining and Metallurgy; lived in France 1923–34 and in Belgium 1937–48; one of the organizers and leaders of Belgian resistance movement during German occupation in World War II; after the war Chair. Nat. Council of Poles in Belgium and one of the organizers of the PPR and Union of Polish Patriots in Belgium; returned to Poland 1948; mem. Polish United Workers' Party (PZPR) 1948–81, Sec. Voivodship Cttee. Katowice 1949–54, First Sec. 1957–70; mem. Cen. Cttee. 1954–80, Head Dept. of Heavy Industry, Cen. Cttee. 1954–56, mem. Politburo Cen. Cttee. 1956–80, Sec. Cen. Cttee. 1956–64, First Sec. Cen. Cttee. 1970–80; Deputy to Seym (Parl.) 1952–80; mem. Presidium All-Polish Cttee. of Nat. Unity Front 1971–80; mem. Council of State March 1976–80; internee Dec. 1981, released Dec.1982; Order of Banner of Labour First Class, Order of Builders of People's Poland, Order of Lenin 1973, Order of Great Yugoslav Star 1973, Frédéric Joliot-Curie Gold Medal 1974, José Marti Nat. Order (Cuba) 1975, Great Ribbon of Leopold's Order with Swords (Belgium) 1977, Great Cross of Order Polonia Restituta 1978, Order of October Revolution (U.S.S.R.) 1978, Order of Old Planina with Ribbon (Bulgaria) 1979, Grand Croix Légion d'honneur, and other decorations. *Leisure interests:* poetry, football. *Address:* Ustronie, Silesia, Poland.

GIEROWSKI, Stefan; Polish painter; b. 21 May 1925, Częstochowa; s. of Józef and Stefania (Wasilewska) Gierowski; m. Anna Golka 1951; one s. one d.; ed. Acad. of Fine Arts, Cracow; Docent, Acad. of Fine Arts, Warsaw, Dean of Painting Dept. 1975–80, Extraordinary Prof. 1976–; mem. Polish Asscn. of Plastic Artists, Sec.-Gen. 1957–59, Pres. of Painting Section 1959–61, 1963–66; Knight's and Officer's Cross, Order of Polonia Restituta; Silver Medal, Third Festival of Fine Arts, Warsaw 1978, Prize of Chair. Council of Ministers (1st class) 1979, Jan Cybis Prize 1980. *One-man shows:* Warsaw 1955, 1957, 1960, 1967, 1972, 1974, 1978, 1986, K. Pułaski Museum, Warka 1973, Galerie la Cloche, Paris 1961, 1965, Auverrier Galerie Numaga, Neuchâtel 1967, 1976, 1987, Galerie Simone Von Dormoel, Brussels 1977, Teatr Studio, Warsaw 1983; exhibited in group shows: Contemporary Art Exhbn., Warsaw 1957, Carnegie Inst., Pittsburgh 1964, 1967, Biennale Int. d'arte, San Marino 1965, 34th Biennale, Venice 1968, Triennale of India, New Delhi 1968, Mexico 1975, Lisbon 1976, Madrid 1977, Naples 1986, Kleinjassen 1987. *Address:* Ul. Gagarina 15 m. 97, 00-753 Warsaw, Poland. *Telephone:* 411633.

GIERSCH, Herbert, DR.RER.POL.; German economist; b. 11 May 1921, Reichenbach; s. of Hermann and Helene (née Kleinert) Giersch; m. Dr. Friederike Koppelmann 1949; two s. one d.; ed. Univ. of Münster; Asst. to Prof. Walther Hoffmann, Univ. of Münster 1948, 1950 British Council Fellow, London School of Econs. 1948–49; Admin., Econs. Directorate, OEEC, also Privatdozent, Univ. of Münster 1950–52; Counsellor and Head of Div., Trade and Finance Directorate, OEEC 1953–54; in charge of Econs. Chair. Tech. Hochschule, Brunswick 1954; Prof. of Econs. Univ. of Saarbrücken 1955–65; Visiting Prof. of Econs., Yale Univ. 1962–63, Dean Acheson Visiting Prof. at Yale Univ. 1977–78; Prof. of Econs., Univ. of Kiel, and Pres. Inst. of World Econs., Kiel 1969–; Chair. Asscn. of German Econ. Research Insts. 1970–82; mem. German Econ. Expert Council 1964–70, Council and Exec. Comm. Int. Econ. Asscn. 1971–83, Treas. 1974–83, Hon. Pres. 1983–; Hon. mem. American Econ. Asscn.; Hon. Fellow, London School of Econs.; Corresp. Fellow, British Acad. 1983; Foreign mem. Swedish Acad. of Eng. Sciences, Stockholm 1987; Dr. h.c. (Erlangen) 1977, (Basle) 1984; Grosskreuz des Verdienstordens 1977. *Publications:* Acceleration Principle and Propensity to Import 1953, The Trade Optimum 1957, Allgemeine Wirtschaftspolitik, Vol. I Grundlagen 1960, Vol. II Konjunktur- und Wachstumspolitik 1977, Growth, Cycles and Exchange Rates—The Experience of West Germany (Wicksell Lecture) 1970, Kontroverse Fragen der Wirtschaftspolitik 1971, Indexation and the Fight against Inflation 1973–74, The European Community and the World Economy (Spaak Lecture) 1976, Current Problems of the West German Economy, AEI 1976, Im Brennpunkt: Wirtschaftspolitik- Kritische Beiträge von 1967–77, 1978, A European Look at the World Economy (MacInally Lecture) 1978, Deutsche Wirtschaft wohin 1980, Aspects of Growth, Structural Change and Employment—A Schumpeterian Perspective 1979, Die Rolle der reichen Länder in der wachsenden Weltwirtschaft 1980, Problems of Adjustment to Imports from Less-Developed Countries 1981, Rationality in Political Economy 1981, Wachstum durch dynamischen Wettbewerb 1982, Schumpeter and the Current and Future Development of the World Economy 1982, Arbeit, Lohn und Produktivität 1983, Towards an Explanation of the Productivity Slowdown: an acceleration-deceleration hypothesis (with Frank Wolter) 1983, Wirtschaft, Wachstum und Kommunikation 1984, The Age of Schumpeter 1984, Löhne, Zinsen und Beschäftigung im Wirtschaftswachstum (with Harmen Lehment) 1984, Wirtschaftswachstum und Kommunikation 1985, Real Exchange Rates and Economic Development 1985, Eurosklerose—europäische Wirtschaftsschwäche und ihre Behebung 1986, Perspectives on the World Economy 1986, Elemente einer Theorie weltwirtschaftlicher Entwicklung 1986, Weltwirtschaftliches Wachstum durch Liberalisierung 1986, Die Ethik der Wirtschaftsfreiheit 1986, Freer Trade for Faster Growth 1986, Economic Policies in the Age of Schumpeter 1987, Internal and External Liberalisation for Faster Growth 1987. *Address:* 2300 Kiel, Düsternbrooker Weg 120 (Office); 2300 Kiel, Preusserstrasse 17–19, Federal Republic of Germany. *Telephone:* 0431/884236 (Office); 0431/561872 (Home).

GIERSTER, Hans; German musical director; b. 12 Jan. 1925; ed. Musikhochschule, Munich, and Mozarteum, Salzburg; fmrly. Musical Dir. Freiburg-im-Breisgau Municipal Theatres; Gen. Musical Dir. of Nuremburg 1965; Dir. Musiktheater, Nuremburg 1971; currently Conductor Munich Staatsoper; guest conductor at State operas of Hamburg, Munich and Vienna; guest appearances at festivals in Munich 1964, Edinburgh (with Bavarian State Opera, Così Fan Tutte) 1965, Glyndebourne (presented The Magic Flute) 1966, Zürich 1971, Vienna 1972; concerts with Philharmonic Orchestras of Bamberg, Berlin, Munich, Vienna, London, Mexico City. *Address:* Hallerwiese 4, 8500 Nürnberg, Federal Republic of Germany.

GIESBERT, Franz-Olivier; French journalist and author; b. 18 Jan. 1949, Wilmington, Del., U.S.A.; m. Christine Fontaine 1974; two s. one d.; journalist at Le Nouvel Observateur 1971, sr. corresp. in Washington 1980, Political Ed. 1981, Ed.-in-Chief 1985–88; Ed.-in-Chief Le Figaro 1988–; Aujourd'hui Best Essay Prize 1975. *Publications:* François Mitterrand ou la tentation de l'Histoire (essay) 1977, Monsieur Adrien (novel) 1982, Jacques Chirac (biography) 1987. *Address:* Le Figaro, 25 ave Matignon, 75398 Paris Cedex 08, France. *Telephone:* (1) 42-56-80-80.

GIETZELT, Arthur Thomas; Australian politician; b. 28 Dec. 1920, San Francisco, U.S.A.; m.; two s. one d.; ed. Hurstville High School, Sydney; served in army (rank of sergeant) 1941–46; Councillor (including nine terms as Pres.), Sutherland Shire Council 1956–71; elected to Senate for N.S.W. 1970; Minister for Veterans' Affairs 1983–87; mem. Nat. Exec. of Australian Labor Party (ALP) 1971–, now Sr. Vice-Pres.; mem. Exec. of Local Govt. Asscn. of N.S.W. 1967–71. *Leisure interests:* swimming, reading. *Address:* Parliament House, Canberra, A.C.T. 2600, Australia.

GIEYSZTOR, Aleksander; Polish historian; b. 17 July 1916, Moscow; s. of Alexander and Barbara (Popiel) Gieysztor; m. Irena Czarnecka 1938; one s. one d.; ed. Warsaw Univ.; Adjunct and Docent Warsaw Univ. 1945–49, Prof. 1949–86, Prof. Emer. 1986–, Dir. of Research into origins of Polish State 1949–53, Pro-Rector 1956–59, Dir. Historical Inst. 1955–75; Pres. Univ. Comm. of State Educ. Council 1960–69; mem. Bureau Int. Cttee. of Historical Sciences 1965– (Vice-Pres. 1975–80, Pres. 1980–85); Assoc. Prof. Coll. de France 1968; Corresp. Fellow, Medieval Acad. of America 1968–; Assoc. Royal Historical Soc. 1981–; Visiting Fellow, All Souls Coll., Oxford 1968–69; Visiting Prof., Harvard Univ. 1977–78; Chair. Scientific Council of Historical Inst., Polish Acad. of Sciences 1972–80, Nat. Cttee. ICOM 1981–; Chair. Scientific Council of Nat. Library 1972–77; Dir. Royal Castle Warsaw 1980–; mem. Consultative Council attached to Chair. of Council of State 1986–; Vice-Chair. Polish Club of Int. Relations 1988–; mem. Comité Int. de Paléographie; mem. Polish Acad. of Sciences 1972– (Pres. 1980–83), Warsaw Learned Soc. 1952– (Pres. 1986–), Koninklijke Akad. voor Wetenschappen, Brussels 1972, Acad. Royale de Belgique 1976, Acad. Nat. des Sciences, Belles-Lettres et Arts de Bordeaux, Acad. Belles Lettres 1981, Royal Swedish Acad. 1982, British Acad. 1985; Dr. h.c. (Aix-Marseille, Bordeaux, Paris IV-Sorbonne, Budapest, Moscow and Oxford Univs.); State Prize (1st class) 1953, 1988; Silver Cross Virtuti Militari, Knight's and Commdr. Crosses of Order Polonia Restituta, Officier, Légion d'honneur, Gold Cross of Merit 1953, 1987, Commdr., Ordine al Merito della Repubblica Italiana 1975, Order of Banner of Labour (1st Class) 1977. *Publications:* Władza Karola Wielkiego (Rule of Charles the Great) 1938, Genesis of the Crusades 1950, History of Poland (co-author) 1968, Zarys dziejów pisma łacińskiego (Outline of the History of Latin Alphabet) 1973, Thousand Years of Poland (with S. Herbst and B. Leśnodorski) 1976, Mitologia Słowiańska (Slav Mythology) 1982, numerous articles on medieval history. *Address:* Ul. Wilcza 8 m. 20, 00-532 Warsaw, Poland. *Telephone:* 28-41-38.

GIFFORD, Charles Henry, M.A., F.B.A.; British professor of English; b. 17 June 1913, Blackheath, London; s. of Walter Stanley Gifford and Constance Lena Gifford (née Henry); m. Mary Rosamond van Ingen 1938; one s. one d.; ed. Harrow School and Christ Church, Oxford; war service in R.A.C. (Palestine and N.W. Europe) 1940–46; on teaching staff, English Dept., Univ. of Bristol 1946–76, Prof. of Modern English Literature 1963, Winterstoke Prof. of English 1967, Prof. of English and Comparative Literature 1975, Emer. Prof. 1976–; Ed. Cambridge Studies in Russian Literature 1980–85; Clark Lecturer, Trinity Coll. Cambridge 1985. *Publications:* The Novel in Russia 1964, Comparative Literature 1969, Pasternak: A Critical Study 1977, Tolstoy (Past Masters) 1982, Poetry in a Divided World (1985 Clark Lectures) 1986. *Leisure interests:* visual arts and travel in Europe.

Address: 10 Hyland Grove, Bristol, BS9 3NR, England. *Telephone:* (0272) 502504.

GILASHVILI, Pavel Georgievich; Soviet politician; b. 1918, Georgia; mem. CPSU 1939–; ed. Party High School at CPSU Cen. Cttee.; locksmith 1934–38; First Sec. of a Komsomol Regional Cttee. 1938–39; served in Soviet Army 1939–45; Head of a Dept. of Cen. Cttee. of the Georgian Komsomol, First Sec. of a Regional Cttee. of the Georgian CP, Sec. of Tbilisi City Cttee. of the Georgian CP 1945–58, First Sec. 1972–76; mem. staff of Georgian CP 1958–67, mem. Cen. Cttee. 1956–58, 1971–, mem. Politburo of Cen. Cttee. 1972–; Chair. Council of Ministers of the Abkhazian A.S.S.R. 1967–72; Chair. Presidium of Supreme Soviet of Georgian S.S.R. 1976–; mem. Cen. Auditing Comm. of CPSU 1976–; Vice-Chair. and mem. Presidium, Supreme Soviet of U.S.S.R. 1977–. *Address:* Central Committee of Communist Party of Georgian S.S.R., Tbilisi, Georgian S.S.R., U.S.S.R.

GILBERT, Felix, PH.D.; American professor of history; b. 21 May 1905, Baden-Baden, Germany; s. of William Henry Gilbert and Cécile Gilbert (née Mendelssohn Bartholdy); m. Mary Raymond Gilbert 1955; no c.; ed. Gymnasium, Berlin, Univs. of Heidelberg, Munich and Berlin; worked at Office of Strategic Studies, Washington, D.C. 1943–45, at Dept. of State, Washington, D.C. 1945–46; Prof. of History, Bryn Mawr Coll., Pa. 1946–62; Prof. School of Historical Studies, Institute for Advanced Study, Princeton 1962–75, Prof. Emeritus and Fellow 1975–; mem. American Acad. of Arts and Sciences 1963, American Philosophical Soc. 1969, British Acad. 1973, Istituto Veneto 1985, Pour le mérite 1981; Guggenheim Fellow 1952–53; Hon. D.Phil. (Freie Univ. Berlin); Hon. D.Hum.Let. (Middlebury Coll.), (Yale Univ.) 1987; Hon. D. Jur. (Harvard) 1987; Hon. D.Hist. (Bologna Univ.); Bancroft Prize 1962, Marraro Prize 1981. *Leisure interest:* chess. *Publications:* To the Farewell Address 1961, Machiavelli and Guicciardini 1965, The End of the European Era 1970, History: Choice and Commitment 1977, The Pope, His Banker and Venice 1980, The Makers of Modern Strategy (Co-ed.) 1986. *Address:* Institute for Advanced Study School of Historical Studies, Princeton, N.J. 08540 (Office); 266 Mercer Street, Princeton, N.J. 08540, U.S.A. (Home). *Telephone:* (609) 734 8306 (Office); (609) 921 2944 (Home).

GILBERT, Geoffrey Alan, M.A., PH.D., F.R.S.; British professor of biochemistry (retd.); b. 3 Dec. 1917, Watford, Middx.; s. of Arthur C. and Miriam M. (née Cull) Gilbert; m. Lilo Czigler de Egerszalok 1948; two s.; ed. Kingsbury County School, Middx., and Emmanuel Coll., Cambridge; lecturer, Dept. of Chem., Univ. of Birmingham 1946–47; Research Fellow, Harvard Univ. Medical School 1946–47; Sr. Lecturer, Dept. of Chem., Univ. of Birmingham 1947–61, Reader 1961–69, Prof. of Biochem. 1969–85, Prof. Emer. 1985. *Publications:* articles in scientific journals. *Leisure interests:* travel, photography, watching urban foxes. *Address:* 194 Selly Park Road, Birmingham, B29 7HY, England. *Telephone:* 021-472 0755.

GILBERT, Ian H. G.; British business executive; b. 25 Nov. 1910, Chingford, Essex; s. of Claude Edward Gilbert and Ethel Mary Dolleymore; m. Violet Edith Heelas 1938; one s. two d.; ed. Bradfield Coll., Berkshire; Deloitte, Plender, Griffiths & Co. (Chartered Accountants) 1930–38; Accountant and later Sec. The Leopoldina Railway Co. Ltd., London 1938–51; Dir. Bryant & May Ltd. 1951–55, Man. Dir. 1955–64, Chair. 1964–72; Dir. British Match Corpn. Ltd. 1953–64, Deputy Chair. 1964–72, Chair. 1972–75; Chair. Bryant & May (Latin America) Ltd. 1964–73, Airscrew-Weyroc Ltd. 1965–72; Dir. Baker Perkins Holdings Ltd. 1972–75, Chair. 1975–79; Chair. Anglo-Brazilian Soc. 1970–76. *Leisure interests:* golf, reading. *Address:* Adams Cottage, Bramshott, Liphook, Hants., England. *Telephone:* Liphook 72-3075.

GILBERT, J. Freeman, PH.D; American professor of geophysics; b. 9 Aug. 1931, Vincennes, Ind.; s. of James Freeman Gilbert and Gladys (Paugh) Gilbert; m. Sally Bonney 1959; one s. two d.; ed. Massachusetts Inst. of Technology; Research Assoc., M.I.T., Cambridge, Mass. 1956–57; Asst. Research Geophysicist, Inst. of Geophysics and Planetary Physics, U.C.L.A. 1957, Asst. Prof. of Geophysics, 1958–59, Prof. 1961, Assoc. Dir. 1976–; Sr. Research Geophysicist, Texas Instruments, Dallas, Tex. 1960–61; Consultant, AMOCO, Tulsa, Okla. 1980–; Guggenheim Fellow 1964–65, 1972–73; Overseas Fellow, Churchill Coll., Cambridge, England 1972–73; Fellow American Geophysical Union, N.A.S.; mem. American Acad. of Arts and Sciences, Seismology Soc. of America, Soc. of Exploration Geophysicists, American Math. Soc., Royal Astronomical Soc.; Foreign Hon. Fellow European Union of Geosciences; Gold Medal, Royal Astronomical Soc. 1981, Arthur L. Day Medal, Geological Soc. of America 1985. *Publications:* numerous book chapters and articles in scientific journals. *Address:* Institute of Geophysics and Planetary Physics, Mail Code A-025, University of California, San Diego, La Jolla, Calif. 92093, U.S.A. *Telephone:* (619) 534-2470.

GILBERT, Kenneth Albert, O.C., D.MUS.; Canadian harpsichordist; b. 16 Dec. 1931, Montreal; s. of Albert George Gilbert and Reta M. (Welch); unmarried; ed. Conservatoire de Musique, Montreal and Conservatoire de Paris; Prof. Conservatoire de Musique, Montreal 1965–72; Assoc. Prof. Laval Univ. 1970–76; Guest Prof. Royal Antwerp Conservatory 1971–73; Dir. Early Music Dept. Conservatoire de Strasbourg 1981–85; Prof. Staatliche Hochschule für Musik, Stuttgart 1981–, Hochschule Mozarteum, Salzburg 1984–; Instructor at other music acads., summer schools etc.;

Fellow, Canada Council 1968, 1974, Calouste Gulbenkian Foundation 1971; has recorded complete harpsichord works of Couperin, Scarlatti and Rameau, suites and partitas of J. S. Bach, Well-tempered clavier of Bach and concertos for 2, 3, 4 harpsichords by Bach. *Publications:* editions of complete harpsichord works of Couperin, Scarlatti and Rameau and Bach's Goldberg Variations. *Address:* 23 Cloître Notre-Dame, F-28000 Chartres, France. *Telephone:* 37.21.57.82.

GILBERT, Lewis; British film director; b. 6 March 1920, London; m. Hylda Henrietta Tafler; two s.; entered films as child actor; joined R.A.F. and became Asst. Dir. to William Keighley on Target for Today, etc. 1939; joined G.B. Instructional (G.B.I.) 1944, for whom wrote and dir. The Ten Year Plan, Sailors Do Care, Arctic Harvest, etc. 1946-47; wrote and dir. The Little Ballerina 1947-48, worked on series of documentaries for G.B.I.; Producer/ Dir. Int. Realist 1948; numerous awards. *Films directed include:* The Little Ballerina 1947, Once a Sinner 1950, Scarlet Thread 1951, There is Another Sun 1951, Time Gentlemen Please 1952, Emergency Call 1952, Cosh Boy, Johnny on the Run 1953, Albert R.N. 1953, The Good Die Young 1954, The Sea Shall Not Have Them 1954, Cast a Dark Shadow 1955, Reach for the Sky 1956, The Admirable Crichton 1957, Carve Her Name With Pride 1957, A Cry From the Streets 1958, Ferry to Hong Kong 1959, Sink the Bismarck 1960, Light Up The Sky 1960, The Greengage Summer 1961; co-produced Spare The Rod 1959-60; dir. H.M.S. Defiant 1962, The Seventh Dawn 1964, Alfie 1966, You Only Live Twice 1967, Paul and Michelle (also producer) 1973, Seven Men at Daybreak 1975, Seven Nights in Japan 1976, The Spy Who Loved Me 1977, Moonraker 1978, Dubai (also producer), Educating Rita 1982. *Address:* c/o Baker Rooke, Clement House, 99 Aldwych, London, WC2 BJY, England; 19 blvd. de Suisse, Monaco.

GILBERT, Martin (John), M.A., F.R.S.L.; British historian; b. 25 Oct. 1936; s. of Peter and Miriam Gilbert; m. 1st Helen Robinson 1963, one d.; m. 2nd Susan Sacher, two s.; ed. Highgate School and Magdalen Coll., Oxford; Sr. Research Fellow, St. Antony's Coll., Oxford 1960-62, Fellow, Merton Coll., Oxford 1962-; Visiting Prof. Univ. of S. Carolina 1965, Tel-Aviv 1979, Hebrew Univ. of Jerusalem 1980-; official biographer of Sir Winston Churchill 1968-; Gov., Hebrew Univ. of Jerusalem 1978-; has lectured on historical subjects throughout Europe and U.S.A.; adviser to BBC and ITV for various documentaries; script designer and co-author, Genocide (Acad. Award for best documentary feature film) 1981; Recent History Corresp. Sunday Times 1967; Hon. D.Litt. Westminster Coll., Fulton 1981. *Publications:* The Appeasers (with R. Gott) 1963, Britain and Germany between the Wars 1964, The European Powers 1900-1945 1965, Plough My Own Farrow: The Life of Lord Allen of Hurtwood 1965, Servant of India: A Study of Imperial Rule 1905-1910 1966, The Roots of Appeasement 1966, Recent History Atlas 1860-1960 1966, Winston Churchill 1966, British History Atlas 1968, American History Atlas 1968, Jewish History Atlas 1969, First World War Atlas 1970, Winston S. Churchill, Vol. III, 1914-16 1971, companion vol. 1973, Russian History Atlas 1972, Sir Horace Rumbold: Portrait of a Diplomat 1973, Churchill: a photographic portrait 1974, The Arab-Israeli Conflict: its history in maps 1974, Winston S. Churchill, Vol. IV, 1917-22 1975, companion vol. 1977, The Jews in Arab Lands: their history in maps 1975, Winston S. Churchill, Vol. V, 1922-39, 1976, companion vols. 1980, 1981, 1982, The Jews of Russia: Illustrated History Atlas 1976, Jerusalem Illustrated History Atlas 1977, Exile and Return: The Emergence of Jewish Statehood 1978, Children's Illustrated Bible Atlas 1979, Final Journey, the Fate of the Jews of Nazi Europe 1979, Auschwitz and the Allies 1981, Atlas of the Holocaust 1982, Winston S. Churchill, Vol. VI, 1939-41 1983, The Jews of Hope: A study of the Crisis of Soviet Jewry 1984, Jerusalem: Rebirth of a City 1985, Shcharansky: Hero of our Time 1986, Winston S. Churchill, Vol. VII, 1941-45 1986, The Holocaust, The Jewish Tragedy 1986, Winston Churchill, Vol. VIII 1945-65 1988, Second World War 1989. *Leisure interest:* drawing maps. *Address:* Merton College, Oxford, England.

GILBERT, Stephen; British painter and sculptor; b. 15 Jan. 1910, Fife, Scotland; s. of F. G. W. and Cicely (née Kellett) Gilbert; m. Jocelyn Chewett 1935 (died 1979); one s. one d.; ed. Univ. Coll. School and Slade School of Art, London; one-man exhbns. in London, Dublin, Paris, Amsterdam, Copenhagen, Sheffield, Hull, Cardiff and The Hague 1938-84; has participated in many group exhbns. in Paris and elsewhere; work exhibited in Tate Gallery, London, and Stedelijk Museum, Amsterdam; Gulbenkian Foundation Award 1962; Tokyo Biennale First Award in Sculpture 1965; Welsh Arts Council Award for Sculpture 1966. *Address:* 13 rue Rambuteau, 75004 Paris; 7 Impasse du Rouet, 75014 Paris, France. *Telephone:* 48-87.99.39; 45-42.6942.

GILBERT, Walter, PH.D.; American scientist and molecular biologist; b. 21 March 1932, Boston, Mass.; s. of Richard V. Gilbert and Emma (née Cohen) Gilbert; m. Celia Stone 1953; one s. one d.; ed. Harvard and Cambridge Univs.; Nat. Science Foundation Postdoctoral Fellow, Harvard 1957-58, lecturer in physics 1958-59, Asst. Prof. of Physics 1959-64, Assoc. Prof. of Biophysics 1964-68, Prof. of Molecular Biology 1968-81; American Cancer Soc. Prof. of Molecular Biology 1972-81, Prof. of Biology 1985-86; H. H. Timken Prof. of Science 1986-87; Carl M. Loeb Univ. Prof. 1987-; Chair. Dept. of Cellular and Developmental Biology, Harvard Univ. 1987-; Chair. Scientific Bd., Biogen NV 1978-83, Co-Chair. Supervisory Bd.

1979-81, Chair. Supervisory Bd. and C.E.O. 1981-84; Foreign mem. Royal Soc.; mem. N.A.S., American Physical Soc., American Soc. of Biological Chemists, American Acad. of Arts and Sciences; Guggenheim Fellowship, Paris 1968-69; V. D. Mattia Lectureship, Roche Inst. of Molecular Biology 1976; Smith, Kline and French Lecturer, Univ. of Calif. at Berkeley 1977; Hon. D.Sc. (Univ. of Chicago) 1978, (Columbia Univ., New York and Univ. of Rochester) 1979; U.S. Steel Foundation Award in Molecular Biology (N.A.S.) 1968; Ledlie Prize, Harvard Univ. (with M. Ptashne) 1969; Warren Triennial Prize, Mass. Gen. Hosp. (with S. Benzer, q.v.) 1977; Louis and Bert Freedman Award, New York Acad. of Sciences 1977; Prix Charles-Léopold Mayer, Acad. des Sciences, Inst. de France, (with M. Ptashne and E. Witkin) 1977; Harrison Howe Award of the Rochester br. of the American Chem. Soc. 1978; Louisa Gross Horwitz Prize, Columbia Univ. (with F. Sanger, q.v.) 1979; Gairdner Foundation Annual Award 1979; Albert Lasker Basic Medical Research Award (with F. Sanger) 1979; Prize for Biochemical Analysis, German Soc. for Clinical Chem. (with A. M. Maxam, F. Sanger and A. R. Coulsen) 1980; Sober Award, American Soc. of Biological Chemists 1980; Nobel Prize for Chemistry 1980 with F. Sanger (q.v.) for work on deoxyribonucleic acid (DNA). *Address:* Biological Laboratories, 16 Divinity Avenue, Cambridge, Mass. 02138 (Office); 107 Upland Road, Cambridge, Mass. 02140, U.S.A. (Home). *Telephone:* 617-495-0760 (Office).

GILCHRIST, Sir Andrew Graham, K.C.M.G.; British diplomatist (retd.); b. 19 April 1910, Lesmahagow, Scotland; s. of late J.G. Gilchrist; m. Freda Grace Slack 1946 (deceased); two s. one d.; ed. Edinburgh Acad., and Exeter Coll., Oxford; Siam Branch, British Consular Service 1933-36, 1938-41, also served Paris, Marseille, Morocco; Army service, S.E. Asia 1944-46; Foreign Office 1946-51; Consul-Gen., Stuttgart 1951-54; Foreign Office Counsellor, Staff of U.K. Commr.-Gen. for S.E. Asia, Singapore 1954-56; Amb. to Iceland 1956-59; Consul-Gen., Chicago 1960-63; Amb. to Indonesia 1963-66; Asst. Under-Sec. Commonwealth Office 1966-67; Amb. to Ireland 1967-70; Chair. British Highlands and Islands Devt. Board, Inverness 1970-76. *Publications:* Bangkok Top Secret 1970, Cod Wars and How to Lose Them 1978, The Russian Professor 1984, The Watercress File 1985, The Ultimate Hostage 1986, South of Three Pagodas 1987, Death of an Admiral 1988. *Address:* Arthur's Crag, Hazelbank, by Lanark, Scotland. *Telephone:* Crossford 263.

GILIOMEE, Hermann Buhr, M.A., D.PHIL.; South African university professor and publisher; b. 4 April 1938, Sterkstroom; m. Annette van Coller; two d.; ed. Porterville High School and Univ. of Stellenbosch; lecturer in History, Univ. of Stellenbosch 1967-83; Prof. of Political Studies Univ. of Cape Town 1983-; recipient of Fellowships to Yale Univ. 1977-78, Cambridge Univ. 1982-83, Hebrew Univ. of Jerusalem 1987; political columnist for Die Suid-Afrikaan. *Publications:* The Shaping of South African Society 1652-1820 1979, Ethnic Power Mobilized: Can South Africa Change? 1979, The Parting of the Ways 1982, Afrikaner Political Thought 1750-1850 1983, Up Against the Fences: Poverty, Passes and Privilege 1985. *Address:* P.O. Box 7010, Stellenbosch 7610, South Africa.

GILL, Anthony Keith, F.ENG., B.SC.(ENG.), F.C.G.I., F.I.MECH.E., F.I.PROD.E.; British business executive; b. 1 April 1930, Colchester; s. of Frederick W. Gill and Ellen Gill; m. Phyllis Cook 1953; one s. two d.; ed. Colchester High School and Imperial Coll. London; Production Engineer, Bryce Berger Ltd. 1956, Dir. 1960, Gen. Man. 1965; Dir. Lucas CAV Ltd. 1967; Gen. Man. Fuel Injection Equipment 1972, Gen. Man. 1974; Dir. Joseph Lucas Ltd. 1974, Div. Man. Dir. 1978; Dir. Lucas Industries PLC 1978, Jt. Group Man. Dir. 1980, Group Man. Dir. 1984, Deputy Chair. 1986-87; Chair. and C.E.O. March 1987-; Pres. Inst. of Production Eng. 1986; mem. Council I. Mech. E. 1986-, Advisory Council on Science and Tech. 1985-; Dept. of Trade and Industry's Tech. Requirements Bd. 1985-88, Eng. Council 1988; Chair. EEC Standing Cttee. on Industry 1988; mem. Council of Industry and Higher Educ., NEDO Eng. Industry Sector Gp., Court of Warwick Univ., U.K. Advisory Bd. of INSEAD; Vice-Pres. Eng. Employers Fed. *Leisure interest:* music. *Address:* Mockley Close, Gentleman's Lane, Ullenhall, Henley in Arden, Warwicks., B95 5PT, England. *Telephone:* Tanworth in Arden 2337.

GILLAM, Patrick John, B.A.; British business executive; b. 15 April 1933, London; s. of the late Cyril B. Gillam and of Mary J. Gillam; m. Diana Echlin 1963; one s. one d.; ed. L.S.E.; Foreign Office 1956-57; joined British Petroleum (BP) 1957; Vice-Pres. BP North America Inc. 1971-74; Gen. Man. Supply Dept. 1974-78; Dir. BP Int. Ltd. 1978-82; Chair. BP Shipping Ltd. 1981-88, BP Minerals Int. Ltd. 1982-; Man. Dir. BP Co. 1981-, Chair. BP Africa Ltd. 1982-88, BP Coal Inc. 1986-, Standard Chartered PLC 1988-. *Leisure interest:* gardening. *Address:* The British Petroleum Company PLC, Britannic House, Moor Lane, London, EC2Y 9BU, England.

GILLARD, Francis (Frank) George, C.B.E., B.SC., F.R.S.A.; British broadcasting and communications consultant; b. 1 Dec. 1908, Tiverton, Devon; s. of Francis Henry and Emily Jane Gillard; ed. St. Luke's Coll., Exeter; Schoolmaster 1931-41; BBC War Corresp. 1941-45; BBC W. Region Programme Dir. 1945-55; Chief Asst. Dir. of Sound Broadcasting 1955-56; Controller W. Region 1956-63; Dir. of Sound Broadcasting 1963-69, Man. Dir. Radio 1969; Gov. Wellington School, Somerset 1960-, Chair. 1974-80; mem. Council, Educational Foundation for Visual Aids 1964-87, Chair.

1977–86; mem. Finance Cttee., Univ. of Exeter 1966–86; Consultant EMI Ltd. 1970–80, Corpn. for Public Broadcasting, U.S.A. 1970–80, Cttee. of Enquiry into ABC Australia 1979–81; Hon. LL.D. (Exeter). *Leisure interests:* country life, reading, travel. *Address:* Trevor House, Poole, Wellington, Somerset, TA21 9HN, England. *Telephone:* Wellington (082 347) 2890.

GILLELS, Elizaveta; Soviet violinist; b. 30 Sept. 1919, Odessa; sister of Emil Gillels, m. Leonid Kogan; studied under P. Stalyarsky, A.Yampolsky; numerous prizes at int. competitions, many recordings in U.S.S.R. *Address:* Moscow Conservatory, Moscow, U.S.S.R.

GILLÈS, Daniel; Belgian writer; b. 1917, Bruges; m. Simone Lambinon 1948; one d.; ed. law studies; Prix Rossel (Belgium); Grand Prix de la critique littéraire (France) 1967, Prix Triennal du Roman. *Publications include:* Jetons de présence, Le coupon 1944, Les brouillards de Bruges, L'état de grâce, La termitière, Mort-la-douce, La rouille (stories), Le festival de Salzbourg, Nés pour mourir, La tache de sang, Le spectateur Brandebourgeois; biographies: Tolstoi, D. H. Lawrence ou le puritain scandaleux, Tchékhov. *Leisure interests:* travel, tennis, painting. *Address:* 161 avenue Churchill, 1180-Brussels, Belgium. *Telephone:* 343-71-55.

GILLESPIE, Hon. Alastair William, P.C., M.A., M.COM.; Canadian business executive and politician; b. 1 May 1922, Victoria, B.C.; s. of Errol Pilkington Gillespie and Catherine Beatrice (née Oliver) Gillespie; m. Diane Christie Clark 1947; one s. one d.; ed. Univs. of British Columbia, McGill, Oxford and Toronto; served Canadian Fleet Air Arm, World War II; fmr. Pres. Welmet Industries Ltd., Welland, Canada Chromalox Co., Rexdale; Vice-Pres. and Dir. Canada Corporate Man. Co. Ltd., Toronto; Chair. Exec. Cttee. Canadian Inst. of Public Affairs 1962–64 (Dir. 1954–65); Dir. Richardson, Bond & Wright Ltd., Owen Sound, Int. Equipment Co. Ltd., Montreal, Cashway Lumber Co. Ltd., Malton, Mechanics for Electronics Ltd., Cambridge, Mass., and other cos.; M.P. 1968–79; Vice-Chair. Exec. Cttee. of Commons Finance, Trade and Econ. Affairs Cttee. 1968–70; Parliamentary Sec. to Pres. of Treasury Bd. 1970–71; Minister of State for Science and Tech. 1971–72; Minister of Industry, Trade and Commerce 1972–75, of Energy, Mines and Resources 1975–79, Minister of State for Science and Tech. 1978–79; Pres. Alastair Gillespie & Assocs. Ltd.; Liberal. *Leisure interests:* tennis, golf, skiing and squash. *Address:* 175 Heath Street, W., Toronto, Ont. M4V 1V1, Canada (Office).

GILLESPIE, Iain E., M.D., M.SC., F.R.C.S.; British professor of surgery; b. 4 Sept. 1931, Glasgow; s. of John Gillespie and Flora MacQuarie; m. Muriel McIntyre 1957; one s. one d.; ed. Hillhead High School, Glasgow and Univ. of Glasgow; various appts. Univs. of Glasgow and Sheffield 1953–70; nat. service R.A.M.C. 1954–56; U.S.P.H.S. Postdoctoral Fellow 1961; Prof. of Surgery, Univ. of Manchester and Hon. Consultant in Surgery to Manchester Royal Infirmary 1970–; Dean, Manchester Medical School 1983–86; Rorer Prize for Gastroenterology 1962. *Publications:* articles in professional journals. *Leisure interests:* golf, reading, music. *Address:* University Department of Surgery, Manchester Royal Infirmary, Manchester, M13 9WL (Office); 27 Athol Road, Bramhall, Cheshire, SK7 1BR, England (Home). *Telephone:* 061-276 1234 (Office).

GILLESPIE, John Birks (Dizzy); American musician and composer; b. 21 Oct 1917, Cheraw, S.C.; s. of James and Lottie (Poe) Gillespie; m. Lorraine Wills 1940; ed. High School, Laurinburt Inst.; N.C. Jazz trumpet player 1930–; toured with Teddy Hill Band 1937–39, Earl Hines, Billy Eckstine and others 1939–44; led band 1946–50, combo 1950–56; rep. U.S. Dept. of State on culture tour to Iran, Pakistan, Lebanon, Syria, Turkey, Yugoslavia, Greece, S.A. 1956–58; leader quintet 1958–; toured Argentina 1961; appeared at Jazz Workshop, San Francisco, Monterey Jazz Festival (Calif.), and Juan-les-Pins Festival (France) 1962; numerous other tours, festivals, night club, TV appearances; apptd. African Chief in Iperu 1989–, Hon. King of Entertainers; first prize for soundtrack, Berlin Film Festival 1962; Hon. D.Mus. (Rutgers) 1970; Handel Medallion 1972, Musician of Year Inst. of High Fidelity 1975. *Publications:* Dizzy: To be or Not to Bop 1980 (autobiog.). *Leisure interests:* chess, pool, swimming. *Numerous recordings include:* At Village Vanguard 1969, My Way 1969. *Address:* 477 North Woodland, Eaglewood, N.J. 07631, U.S.A. (Home).

GILLESPIE, Rhondda, B.MUS.; British concert pianist; b. 3 Aug. 1941, Sydney, Australia; d. of David Gillespie and Marie Gillespie; m. Denby Richards 1972; no c.; ed. N.S.W. Conservatorium with Alexander Sverjensky and in London with Louis Kentner and Denis Matthews; debut on Australian radio aged 8 1949; first public recital 1953; winner N.S.W. Concerto Competition, Sydney 1959; European debut in London with Tchaikovsky Piano Concerto 2 1960; since then has played with major orchestras throughout U.K., Netherlands, Germany, Scandinavia, Far East and U.S.A. and made many festival appearances. *Leisure interests:* golf, languages, exotic cooking. *Address:* 2 Princes Road, St. Leonards-on-Sea, East Sussex, TN37 6EL, England. *Telephone:* 0424 712214.

GILLESPIE, Ronald James, PH.D., D.SC., F.R.S., F.R.S.C., F.R.S.C. (U.K.), F.C.I.C.; Canadian (b. British) professor of chemistry; b. 21 Aug. 1924, London; s. of James A. Gillespie and Miriam Gillespie (née Kirk); m. Madge Ena Garner 1950; two d.; ed. London Univ.; Asst. Lecturer, Dept. of Chem., Univ. Coll. London 1948–50, Lecturer 1950–58; Commonwealth Fund Fellow, Brown Univ., R.I., U.S.A. 1953–54; Assoc. Prof., Dept. of Chem., McMaster Univ., Hamilton, Ont., Canada 1958–60, Prof. 1960–, Chair. Dept.

of Chem. 1962–65; Professeur Associé, Univ. des Sciences et Techniques de Languedoc, Montpellier, France 1972–73; Visiting Prof. Univ. of Geneva, Switzerland 1976, of Göttingen, Fed. Rep. of Germany 1978; mem. Chem. Soc., American Chem. Soc.; Hon. LL.D. (Concordia) 1988, (Dalhousie) 1988; numerous medals and awards. *Publications:* Molecular Geometry 1972, Chemistry (jtly.) 1986; papers in scientific journals. *Leisure interests:* skiing, sailing. *Address:* Department of Chemistry, McMaster University, Hamilton, Ont., L8S 4M1; 150 Wilson Street West, Anchaster, Ont. L9G 4E7, Canada (Home). *Telephone:* (416) 648-8895 (ext. 3304).

GILLET, Guillaume; French architect; b. 20 Nov. 1912, Fontaine-Chaâlis; s. of the late Louis Gillet and Suzanne Doumic; m. Rose Gaeremynck; one s. one d.; ed. Ecole Nat. Supérieure des Beaux-Arts, Paris; Premier Grand Prix de Rome 1946, Chief Architect, Bâtiments Civils et Palais Nationaux 1952–; Prof., Ecole Nat. Supérieure des Beaux-Arts 1953–73; Consulting Architect to Ministry of Building; Head Architect, French Section, Brussels Int. Exhbn. 1958; Head of UNESCO Town-Planning Mission to Israel; mem. Acad. des Beaux-Arts 1968, Vice-Pres. 1982, Pres. 1983; mem. Acad. d'architecture 1957–, Pres. 1970–73; mem. Cercle d'études architecturales; Commdr. Ordre des Arts et des Lettres 1966, Ordre de la Couronne (Belgium) 1958, Officer, Légion d'honneur, Commdr. Ordre nat. du Mérite, Officer, Italian Order of Merit, Chevalier de l'Economie nationale, Croix de guerre 1939–45. *Address:* 30 rue d'Armaillé, 75017 Paris (Office); 11 rue Saint-Simon 75007 Paris, France (Home).

GILLET, Renaud; French industrialist; b. 14 Dec. 1913, Lyon; s. of Charles Gillet; m. Marie Colcombet 1939 (deceased); two s. one d.; ed. Ecole Supérieure de Chimie Industrielle, Lyon; with Soc. Rhodiaceta 1935, Cie. Industrielle des Textiles Artificiels et Synthétiques (CTA) 1942; Gen. Man. Textil 1961; Pres. Dir.-Gen. Pricel 1966–73, Hon. Pres. 1973–82; Vice-Pres. Rhône-Poulenc S.A. 1972, Pres. Dir.-Gen. 1973–79, Hon. Pres. 1980–. *Address:* Les Lauzes, 1885 Chésières, Switzerland (Home).

GILLETT, Sir Robin Danvers Penrose, Bt., G.B.E.; British company executive; b. 9 Nov. 1925, London; s. of Sir (Sydney) Harold Gillett, Bt., M.C. (Lord Mayor of London 1958–59), and Audrey Isobel Penrose Gillett (née Wardlaw); m. Elizabeth Marion Grace Findlay 1950; two s.; ed. Nautical Coll., Pangbourne; served Canadian Pacific Steamships 1943–60, Master Mariner 1951, Staff Commdr. 1957; Consultant, Sedwick Ltd.; Underwriting Mem. of Lloyd's; Common Councilman for Ward of Bassishaw, City of London 1965–69, Alderman 1969–, Sheriff 1973–74, Lord Mayor of London 1976–77; Chancellor of The City Univ. 1976–77; Liveryman and past Master of the Hon. Co. of Master Mariners; Chair. of local Civil Defence Cttee. 1967–68; Pres. Nat. Waterways Transport Assen. 1978–83; U.K. Pres. Royal Life Saving Soc. 1978–82, Deputy Commonwealth Pres. June 1982–; Vice Pres. City of London Centre, St. John Ambulance Assen.; Vice-Chair. Port of London Authority 1979–84; Vice-Pres. City of London District Red Cross; Chair of Govs. Pangbourne Coll.; Founder mem. and Fellow, Nautical Inst.; Fellow, Inst. of Admin. Man., Pres. 1980–84; R.N.R. Decoration (RD) 1965, Hon. Commdr. R.N.R. 1971; H.M. Lieut. for City of London 1975; Elder Brother of Trinity House; Trustee, Nat. Maritime Museum 1982–; Gentleman Usher of the Purple Rod 1985–; Institutes Medal 1982; K. St. J.; Hon. D.Sc.(City Univ.) 1976; Officer, Order of the Leopard (Zaire), Commdr., Royal Order of Dannebrog (Denmark), Order of Johan Sedia Makhota (Malaysia), Grand Cross of Municipal Merit (Lima, Peru) 1977, Admin. Management Soc. Gold Medal (U.S.A.) 1983. *Leisure interests:* sailing, photography. *Address:* 4 Fairholt Street, Knightsbridge, London, SW7 1EQ; and Elm Cottage, Biddestone, Wiltshire, England. *Telephone:* 01-589 9860 (Home); 024-971 2445 (Wiltshire).

GILLIAM, Terry Vance, B.A.; American animator, film director, actor, illustrator, writer; b. 22 Nov. 1940, Minn.; s. of James Hall and Beatrice (Vance) Gilliam; m. Margaret Weston; two d.; ed. Occidental Coll.; Assoc. Ed. HELP! magazine 1962–64; freelance illustrator 1964–65, advertising copywriter/art dir. 1966–67; with Monty Python's Flying Circus (U.K.) 1969–76; animator, And Now For Something Completely Different (film); co-dir. and actor, Monty Python and the Holy Grail; dir. Jabberwocky; designer, actor, animator, Monty Python's Life of Brian; co-author, producer, dir. Time Bandits; actor and dir. Monty Python Live at the Hollywood Bowl 1982; co-writer Monty Python's Meaning of Life (film) 1983; co-writer and dir. Brazil 1985, The Adventures of Baron von Munchausen 1988. *Publications:* Monty Python's Big Red Book, Monty Python's Papperbook 1977, Monty Python's Scrapbook 1979, Animations of Mortality 1979, Monty Python's The Meaning of Life. *Address:* The Old Hall, South Grove, Highgate, London, N6 6BP, England.

GILLIATT, Penelope, F.R.S.L.; British author and film critic; b. London; d. of Cyril and Mary (Douglass) Conner; m. 1st Prof. R. W. Gilliatt (divorced); m. 2nd John Osborne (q.v.) 1963 (divorced); one d.; ed. Queen's Coll. Univ. of London, Bennington Coll. Vt., U.S.A.; film critic, The Observer 1961–67, theatre critic 1965; guest film critic, The New Yorker 1967, regular film critic 1968–79, fiction writer 1967–; awards for fiction, American Acad., Nat. Inst. of Arts and Letters 1972; awards for screenplay Sunday Bloody Sunday, Winner Best Original Screenplay, from Writers' Guild of America, Writers' Guild of England, Nat. Soc. of Film Critics (New York), New York Film Critics' Soc. etc. *Publications:* Novels: One by One 1965, A State of Change 1968, The Cutting Edge 1979, Mortal

Matters 1983, A Woman of Singular Occupation 1988; Short stories: What's It Like Out? 1968 (Come Back if it Doesn't Get Better, U.S.A. 1967), Nobody's Business 1972, Penguin Modern Short Stories 1970, Splendid Lives 1977, Quotations From Other Lives 1983, They Sleep Without Dreaming 1985, 22 stories 1986; plays, films: Property 1970, Sunday Bloody Sunday (screenplay) 1971 (reprint with new essay by author 1986), Cliff Dwellers 1981, Property 1983, Nobody's Business 1983, But When All's Said and Done 1985; TV plays: Living on the Box, The Flight Fund 1974, In the Unlikely Event of Emergency 1979; non-fiction: Unholy Fools: Film and Theatre 1972, Jean Renoir, Essays, Conversations, Reviews 1975, Jacques Tati 1976, Three-Quarter Face 1980; Beach of Aurora, opera libretto commissioned by English Nat. Opera Co. 1973-83. *Address:* c/o New Yorker Magazine, 25 West 43rd Street, New York, N.Y. 10036, U.S.A.; 31 Chester Square, London, SW1W 9HT, England.

GILLMORE, David Howe, C.M.G., M.A.; British diplomatist; b. 16 Aug. 1934, Swindon; s. of Air Vice-Marshal A.D. Gillmore and K. V. Gillmore (née Morris); m. Lucile S. Morin 1964; two s.; ed. Trent Coll. and King's Coll., Cambridge; with Reuters Ltd. 1958-60; Asst. to Dir.-Gen., Polypapier S.A. 1960-65; schoolmaster, Inner London Educ. Authority 1965-69; with F.C.O. 1970-; First Sec., British Embassy, Moscow 1972-75; Counsellor, U.K. Del., Mutual & Balanced Force Reductions, Vienna 1975-78; Head of Defence Dept., F.C.O. 1979-81; Asst. Under-Sec. of State 1981-83; High Commr. to Malaysia 1983-86, Deputy Under-Sec. of State 1986-. *Publication:* A Way from Exile (novel) 1967. *Leisure interests:* books, music, exercise. *Address:* c/o Foreign and Commonwealth Office, King Charles Street, London, S.W.1, England. *Telephone:* 01-270 3000.

GILLON, Mgr. Luc-Pierre-A., D.SC.; Belgian ecclesiastic and scientist; b. 15 Sept. 1920, Rochefort; research physicist, Inst. Interuniversitaire des Sciences Nucléaires 1948; guest staff mem. Brookhaven Nat. Lab., New York 1953; Rector Lovanium Univ. 1954; Prof. of Nuclear Eng., Catholic Univ. of Louvain 1972; Trustee Nuclear Research Centre (Mol, Belgium). *Leisure interest:* flying (private aeroplane). *Address:* c/o Nuclear Research Centre, Mols, Belgium.

GILMOUR, Rt. Hon. Sir Ian (Hedworth John Little), Bt., P.C., M.P.; British politician; b. 8 July 1926; s. of Lieut.-Col. Sir John Little Gilmour and Hon. Victoria Laura; m. Lady Caroline Margaret Montagu-Douglas-Scott 1951; four s. one d.; ed. Eton Coll., Balliol Coll., Oxford; Served with Grenadier Guards 1944-47, rank of Second Lieut. 1945; called to the Bar, Inner Temple 1952; Ed. The Spectator 1954-59; M.P. for Norfolk Central 1962-74, for Chesham and Amersham 1974-87; Parl. Under-Sec., Ministry of Defence 1970-71, Minister of State for Defence Procurement 1971-72, for Defence 1972-74, Sec. of State for Defence 1974; Lord Privy Seal 1979-81; Chair. Conservative Research Dept. 1974-75. *Publications:* The Body Politic 1969, Inside Right, A Study of Conservatism 1977, Britain Can Work 1983. *Address:* The Ferry House, Old Isleworth, Middx., England.

GILMOUR, Mavis Gwendolyn, M.D., F.R.C.S., M.P.; Jamaican politician; b. 13 April 1926, St. Elizabeth; d. of Isaac and Adelaide Holness; m.; ed. Howard Univ., Washington, D.C., and Univ. of Edinburgh; medical officer, Kingston Public Hosp. 1951, consultant surgeon 1960-72; mem. Parl. for West Rural St. Andrew 1976-; Minister of Educ. 1980-86, of Social Security and Consumer Affairs 1986-89; Jamaica Labour Party. *Leisure interests:* sewing, horticulture, reading. *Address:* c/o Ministry of Social Security and Consumer Affairs, 14 National Heroes Circle, Kingston 4, Jamaica. *Telephone:* 92-26439; 92-24299.

GILRUTH, Robert Rowe, M.S.; American engineer; b. 8 Oct. 1913, Nashwauk, Minn.; s. of Henry A. Gilruth and Frances M. (Rowe) Gilruth; m. 1st Esther Jean Barnhill 1937 (died 1972), 2nd Georgene Hubbard Evans 1973; one s. one d.; ed. Univ. of Minnesota; with Nat. Advisory Cttee. for Aeronautics (later NASA) 1937-, Dir. Space Task Group (project Mercury) 1958; Dir. NASA Manned Spacecraft Center (Projects Mercury, Gemini and Apollo) 1961-72; Dir. Key Personnel Devt. NASA 1972-73, retd. 1973; Consultant to NASA Administrator 1974-83; Dir. of Space Industries Inc., Houston 1983-; Fellow, American Rocket Soc., Inst. of Aerospace Sciences, American Astronautical Soc.; Gov. Nat. Rocket Club; Sylvanus Albert Reed Award 1950, Outstanding Achievement Award (Univ. of Minn.) 1954, Louis W. Hill Space Transportation Award 1962, NASA Distinguished Service Medal 1962, U.S. Chamber of Commerce Great Living American Award 1962, Dr. Robert J. Goddard Memorial Award of American Rocket Soc. 1962; Hon. Fellow, Inst. of Aerospace Sciences 1963; Spirit of St. Louis Medal by American Soc. of Mechanical Engineers 1965; Americanism Award by China-Burma-India Veterans Asscn. 1965; mem. Int. Acad. of Astronautics 1965-; mem. Houston Philosophical Soc. 1966-; Daniel Florence Guggenheim Award, Int. Acad. of Astro-nautics Soc.; mem. Nat. Acad. of Eng. 1968, Nat. Acad. of Sciences 1974, Int. Space Hall of Fame 1976; four hon. degrees; NASA Distinguished Service Medal 1969; Rockefeller Public Service Award 1969; Hon. Fellow, Royal Aeronautical Soc.; U.S. Nat. Space Hall of Fame Award 1969, American Soc. of Mech. Engineers Medal 1970, Inst. of Mechanical Engineers James Watt Int. Medal 1971, Nat. Aviation Club Award for Achievement 1971, Robert J. Collier Trophy (Nat. Aeronautic Assen. and Nat. Aviation Club) 1972, Nat. Air and Space Museum Trophy for Outstanding Achievement in Aerospace Tech. 1985. *Leisure interests:* boating and boat building. *Address:* Route 1, Box 1486, Kilmarnock, Virginia 22482, U.S.A.

GIMFERRER, Pere; Spanish writer and literary manager; b. 22 June 1945, Barcelona; s. of Pere Gimferrer and Carmen Torrêni; m. María Rosa Caminals 1971; no c.; ed. Univ. of Barcelona; Head Literary Dept. Editorial Seix Barral 1970, Literary Consultant 1973, Literary Man. 1981-; Academician Real Acad. Espanola 1985-; Nat. Prize for Poetry 1966, Critic's Prize 1983. *Publications:* Arde el Mar 1966, L'Espai Desert 1977, Dietari 1981, Fortuny 1983. *Leisure interests:* cinema, travel. *Address:* Editorial Seix Barral, Córcega 270, Barcelona 08008 (Office); Rambla de Cataluna 113, Barcelona 08008, Spain (Home). *Telephone:* 2186204 (Office).

GINSBERG, Allen; American poet; b. 3 June 1926, Newark, N.J.; s. of Louis Ginsberg and Naomi Levy; ed. Grammar High School, Paterson, N.J. and Columbia Coll.; travelled to Mexico and Europe during fifties; interest in Gnostic-mystical poetry and politics led to residence in Far East 1962-63; experiments with poetic effects of psychedelic drugs 1952-, Cambridge experiments with Dr. Timothy Leary 1961; visited Africa and Arctic, South America 1960, Russia and E. Europe 1965; elected Kral Majales (King of May), Czechoslovakia 1965; participated in college poetry readings and conventions 1958-61, also Flower Power marches and anti-war rallies; Contributing Editor, Black Mountain Review, Advisory Guru, The Marijuana Review; attended first Human Be-in, San Francisco 1967, Yippie Life Festival, Chicago 1968; arrested several times during various anti-war protests; Co-Dir. Jack Kerouac School of Disembodied Poetics, Naropa Inst., Colo. (Buddhist Studies Inst.); mem. Nat. Inst. of Arts and Letters 1974; has recorded Songs of Innocence and of Experience by William Blake, Tuned by Allen Ginsberg, First Blues (produced by John Hammond Sr.) 1983; Writer in Residence, Cheltenham Festival of Literature 1979; appeared in film Heavy Petting 1988. *Publications:* Poetry: Howl and Other Poems 1956, Kaddish and Other Poems 1961, Empty Mirror 1961, Reality Sandwiches 1963, Ankor Wat 1968, Airplane Dreams 1968, Planet News 1968, The Fall of America 1973, Mind Breaths 1977, Poems all over the Place 1978, Mostly Sitting Haiku 1978, Straight Hearts Delight 1980, Howl: Annotated by Author 1980, Collected Poems 1947-80 1985, White Shroed, Poems 1980-1985 1986; prose: Yage Letters (with William Burroughs, q.v.) 1963, Indian Journals 1970, Gay Sunshine Interview 1973, Allen Verbatim 1974, The Vision of the Great Rememberer 1974, Journals 1977, Collected Poems 1947-80 1988; songs: First Blues 1975; also many contributions to anthologies. *Leisure interests:* photography, meditation, blues music, drugs. *Address:* c/o City Lights, 261 Columbus Avenue, San Francisco, Calif. 94133, U.S.A.

GINZBERG, Eli, PH.D.; American economist; b. 30 April 1911, New York; s. of Louis Ginzberg and Adele Katzenstein; m. Ruth Szold 1946; one s. two d.; ed. Columbia Univ.; Faculty, School of Business 1935-, Prof. of Econs. -1979, now Special Lecturer; Dir., Conservation of Human Resources 1950-; Chair. Nat. Manpower Advisory Cttee. 1962-73; Chair. Nat. Comm. for Employment Policy 1974-81; Consultant to various govt. depts.; Special Lecturer, Barnard Coll., Columbia Univ. 1981-; Hon. D.Litt. (Jewish Theological Seminary of America) 1966, (Columbia) 1982; Hon. LL.D. (Loyola) 1969; Hon. L.H.D. (Rush) 1985; Medal, Int. Univ. of Social Studies, Rome 1957. *Publications:* The House of Adam Smith 1934, The Unemployed 1943, Occupational Choice 1951, The Ineffective Soldier: Lessons for Management and the Nation (3 vols.) 1959, The Troublesome Presence: American Democracy and the Negro 1964, Men, Money and Medicine 1969, The Human Economy 1976, American Medicine: The Power Shift 1985, Beyond Human Scale: The Large Corporation at Risk 1985, Understanding Human Resources: Perspectives, People and Policy 1985, From Physician Shortage to Patient Shortage: The Uncertain Future of Medical Practice 1986, Technology and Employment: Concepts and Clarifications 1986, Medicine and Society: Changing Relations 1950-2000 1987, The Skeptical Economist 1987, Executive Talent: Developing and Holding Leaders 1988, The Financing of Biomedical Research 1989, My Brother's Keeper 1989. *Leisure interests:* walking, swimming. *Address:* 525 Uris Hall, Columbia University, New York, N.Y. 10027; 845 West End Avenue, New York, N.Y. 10025, U.S.A. (Home). *Telephone:* (212) 280-3410; (212) 864-1857 (Home).

GINZBURG, Aleksandr Ilyich (b. Chizov); Soviet journalist; b. 1936, Moscow; s. of L. I. Ginzburg; m. I. S. Zholkovskaya 1969; two c.; studied journalism, Moscow Univ. 1956-60 and at Moscow Historical Archive Inst. 1966-67; numerous jobs; ed. 3 issues of samizdat poetry for "Sintaksis" 1959-60; expelled from univ. 1960 and sentenced to 2 years imprisonment in camps 1960-62; participated in dissident demonstrations; wrote The White Book (English translation On Trial. The Case of Sinyavsky and Daniel) 1966; sentenced to 5 years imprisonment 1968, released 1972; founded (with Solzhenitsyn (q.v.)) aid-scheme for families of dissidents 1974.

GINZBURG, Lidia Yakovlevna; Soviet writer, critic and literary historian-scholar; b. 1902, St. Petersburg (now Leningrad); ed. Leningrad Univ. *Publications include:* Lermontov 1940, My Past and Thoughts by Herzen 1957, On Lyric Poetry 1964, The History of the Art of the Cello 1965, On Psychological Prose 1977, About the Literary Hero 1979, Old and New 1982, Literature in Search of Reality 1987.

GINZBURG, Natalia; Italian writer; b. 1916, Palermo; m. 1st L. Ginzburg, 2nd Gabriele Baldini; first short stories published at age 18; works now translated into several languages; mem. of Parl. (Communist Party) 1983-;

Strega Prize (for Lessico familiare) 1963; Marzotto Prize (for L'Inserzione). *Publications:* novels include: La Strada che va in Città 1942, E'stato cosi, Valentino, Sagittario, Le voci della sera, Le Piccole Virtù 1962, Lessico familiare 1963, Tutti i nostri ieri, Caro Michele 1973; dramatic works include: Ti ho sposato per allegria, L'Inserzione; other writings include Mai devi domandarmi. *Address:* Piazza Camp Marzio 3, Rome, Italy.

GINZBURG, Vitaly Lazarevich, DR.SC.; Soviet physicist; b. 4 Oct. 1916, Moscow; s. of Lazar and Augusta Ginzburg; m. Nina Ginzburg 1946; one d.; ed. Moscow Univ.; at P. N. Lebedev Physical Inst., U.S.S.R. Acad. of Sciences 1940–; Prof. Gorky Univ. 1945–68, Moscow Tech. Inst. of Physics 1968–; mem. C.P.S.U. 1944–; Corresp. mem. U.S.S.R. Acad. of Sciences 1953–66, mem. 1966–; mem. Inst. Acad. of Astronautics 1969; Assoc. Royal Astronomical Soc., London 1970; Foreign Hon. mem. American Acad. of Art and Science 1971; Foreign mem. Royal Danish Acad. of Sciences and Letters 1977; Hon. Fellow, Indian Acad. of Science 1977; Foreign Fellow, Indian Nat. Science Acad. 1981; Foreign Assoc., N.A.S., U.S.A. 1981; Foreign mem. Royal Soc., London 1987; Hon. D.Sc. (Sussex) 1970; Lomonosov Prize 1962, U.S.S.R. State Prize 1953, Lenin Prize 1966, Order of Lenin, etc. *Publications:* works on theoretical physics (superconductivity, etc.), astrophysics and radiophysics. *Address:* P. N. Lebedev Physical Inst., U.S.S.R. Academy of Sciences, Leninsky Prospect 53, Moscow B-333, U.S.S.R.

GINZTON, Edward Leonard, M.S.E.E., PH.D.; American electrical engineer; b. 27 Dec. 1915, Ukraine, Russia; s. of Leonard Louis and Natalie (Philipova) Ginzton; m. Artemas A. McCann 1939; two s. two d.; ed. Univ. of Calif. at Berkeley and Stanford Univ.; during Second World War developed art of microwave measurements and high-power klystron; later directed construction of several large linear accelerators including the design of the two-mile long SLAC; Teaching and research, Stanford Univ. 1946–61, Trustee 1977–; Co-Founder Varian Assocs., Palo Alto, Calif. 1948, mem. of Bd. 1948–, Chair. of Bd. 1959–, C.E.O. 1984–, Pres. 1964–68; mem. Bd. of Dirs. Mid-Peninsula Housing Devt. Corpn. 1970–, Stanford Hospital 1975–80; Dir. Nat. Bureau of Econ. Research 1981–; mem. Nat. Acad. of Eng. Council 1974–80, NRC Comm. on Nuclear and Alternative Energy Systems 1975–80, mem. Nat. Acad. of Eng., N.A.S.; mem. American Acad. of Arts and Sciences; Inst. of Electrical and Electronic Engineers awards: Morris Liebmann Memorial Prize, Medal of Honor 1969; Calif. Mfr. of the Year Award 1974. *Publications:* Microwave Measurements 1957, numerous papers, technical articles and patents. *Leisure interests:* photography, skiing, sailing, hiking, restoring old motor-cars. *Address:* Varian Associates, 611 Hansen Way, Palo Alto, Calif. 94303 (Office); 28014 Natoma Road, Los Altos Hills, Calif., U.S.A. (Home). *Telephone:* 493-4000 (Office); 948-5362 (Home).

GIOLITTI, Antonio; Italian politician; b. 12 Feb. 1915, Rome; s. of Giuseppe and Maria Tami Giolitti; m. Elena D'Amico 1939; three c.; ed. Univ. of Rome; active in Resistance 1943–44; Communist mem. Constituent Assembly 1946; Under-Sec. of Foreign Affairs June-Oct. 1946; mem. Chamber of Deputies 1948–76, Pres. Comm. for Industry and Trade Chamber of Deputies 1963, 1964–70; joined Italian Socialist Party 1957, mem. Cen. Cttee. 1958–; Minister of the Budget and Econ. Planning 1963–64, 1970–72, 1973–74; Commr. for Co-ordination of Community Funds, Regional Policy, EEC Comm. 1977–85. *Publications:* Riforme e rivoluzione 1957, Il Comunismo in Europa 1960, Un socialismo possibile 1967. *Leisure interests:* walking, reading, music. *Address:* c/o Commission of the European Communities, 200 rue de la Loi, 1040 Brussels, Belgium.

GIORDANO, H.E. Cardinal Michele; Italian ecclesiastic; b. 26 Sept. 1930, Tursi-Lagonegro; ordained 1953, elected to the titular Church of Lari Castello 1971, consecrated bishop 1972, prefect at Matera e Irsina 1974, transferred to Naples 1987; cr. Cardinal 1988. *Address:* Largo Donnaregina 22, 80138 Naples, Italy. *Telephone:* (081) 44.91.18.

GIORDANO, Richard Vincent, B.A., LL.B., PH.D.; American business executive; b. 24 March 1934, New York; s. of Vincent and Cynthia (née Cardetta) Giordano; m. Barbara Claire Beckett 1956; one s. two d.; ed. Stuyvesant School, New York, Harvard Univ. and Columbia Univ. Law School; admitted New York Bar 1961; Assoc. Shearman and Sterling (law firm), New York 1969–63; Asst. Sec. Air Reduction Co. Inc., New York 1963–64, Vice-Pres. Distribution of Products Div. 1964–65, Exec. Vice-Pres. 1965–67, Group Vice-Pres. 1967–71, Pres. and C.O.O. 1971–74, C.E.O. 1977–79; Dir. BOCI 1974; Man. Dir. and C.E.O. BOC Group 1979–84, Chair. and C.E.O. Jan. 1985–; Dir. Cen. Electricity Generating Bd. 1982–; Hon. D.C.S. (St. John's Univ., U.S.A.). *Address:* BOC Group PLC, Chertsey Road, Windlesham, Surrey, GU20 6HJ, England. *Telephone:* 01-352 0037.

GIOSAN, Nicolae, D.SC.; Romanian politician and scientist; b. 30 Dec. 1921, Drîmbar, Alba County; s. of Ioachim Giosan and Maria Giosan; m. Lucia Giosan 1969; two s.; ed. Faculty of Agronomy, Cluj; Prof. Faculty of Agric. Cluj 1948–53; Prof. Agronomics Inst. Nicolae Bălcescu, Bucharest 1953–; Dir. Agronomics Research Station, Cluj 1955–57; Man. Dir. Inst. for Maize Farming Research, Fundulea, Bucharest 1957–62; Deputy Minister of Agric. and Forestry 1953–55; First Deputy Minister and Minister 1962–69; Corresp. Romanian Acad. 1963–74, mem. 1974–; Pres. Acad. of Agronomics and Forestry 1969–81; alt. mem. Cen. Cttee. Romanian Communist Party (RCP) 1955–60, mem. 1960–; alt. mem. Exec. Political Cttee. Cen. Cttee. RCP 1974–; mem. Grand Nat. Assembly 1957–; mem. State Council 1972–74; mem. Exec. Bureau Nat. Council Front of Socialist Democracy and Unity 1974–; Pres. Grand Nat. Assembly 1974; mem. Acad. for Agric. Sciences of U.S.S.R., France and Italy; State Prize, Romanian and other orders and medals. *Address:* Aleea Marii Adunări Naţionale nr. 5, Bucharest, Romania. *Telephone:* 16-21-50.

GIRARD, René Noël, PH.D.; French/American professor and author; b. 25 Dec. 1923, Avignon; s. of Joseph Girard and Thérèse Fabre; m. Martha Virginia McCullough 1952; two s. one d.; ed. Lycée d'Avignon, Ecole des Chartes and Indiana Univ.; Instructor of French, Indiana Univ. 1947–51, Duke Univ. 1952–53; Asst. Prof. Bryn Mawr Coll. 1953–57; Assoc. Prof. The Johns Hopkins Univ. 1957–61, Prof. 1961–68, Chair. Romance Languages 1965–68, James M. Beall Prof. of French and Humanities 1976–80; Prof. Inst. d'études françaises Bryn Mawr, Avignon 1961–, Dir. 1969; Distinguished Faculty Prof. of Arts and Letters, State Univ. of New York at Buffalo 1971–76; Andrew B. Hammond Prof. of French Language, Literature and Civilization, Stanford Univ. 1981–, Prof. of Religious Studies and Comparative Literature 1986–, Dir. Program of Interdisciplinary Research, Dept. of French and Italian 1986–; Chevalier, Ordre Nat. de la Légion d'Honneur 1984, Officier, Ordre des Arts et Lettres 1984; Fellow American Acad. of Arts and Sciences 1979–, Guggenheim Fellow 1960, 1967; Hon. D.Lit. (Vrije Univ.) 1985, Hon. D.Theol. (Innsbruck) 1988; Modern Language Assen. Prize for best article 1964, Acad. Francaise Prize 1973. *Publications include:* Mensonge romantique et vérité romanesque 1961, Dostoïevski: du double à l'unité 1963, La violence et le sacré 1972, Des choses cachées depuis la fondation du monde 1978, Le bouc émissaire 1982, La route antique des hommes pervers 1985, Violence et vérité: autour de René Girard (ed. by Paul Dumouchel) 1985. *Address:* Department of French and Italian, Building 260, Stanford University, Stanford, Calif. 94305, U.S.A. *Telephone:* (415) 723-1356.

GIRARD DE CHARBONNIÈRES, Guy de. L. EN D.; French diplomatist; b. 7 Jan. 1907; m. Countess Marianne de Rumerskirch 1948; one s. one d.; ed. Lycée Janson de Sailly, Ecole des Sciences politiques; Àttaché French Embassy, Brussels 1930; Third Sec. London 1933, Second Sec. 1938, First Sec. 1941; joined Gen. de Gaulle's Comité Nat. 1943, Second Counsellor 1943, Dir. du Cabinet, Commissariat, later Ministry of Foreign Affairs 1943; First Counsellor 1944; Minister to Copenhagen 1945, Amb. 1947–51, to Argentina 1951–55, to Greece 1957–64, to Switzerland 1964–65; Diplomatic Counsellor to the French Govt. 1966–72; retd. 1973; Commdr. Légion d'honneur, Grand Cross Order of Dannebrog (Denmark), etc. *Publications:* Le Duel Giraud-De Gaulle 1984, La plus evitable de toutes les guerres 1985, Les derniers Rois 1985, Les Quatres Saisons 1988. *Address:* Villa Mirette, 06290 Saint Jean, Cap Ferrat, France.

GIRARDOT, Annie Suzanne; French film actress; b. 25 Oct. 1931, Paris; m. Renato Salvatori 1962; one d.; ed. Centre d'art dramatique, Paris, Conservatoire nat. d'art dramatique; with Comédie-Française 1954–57; Suzanne-Bianchetti Prize 1956, Prize for Best Actress, Venice Film Festival (for Trois chambres à Manhattan) 1965, Courteline Prize (for Déclics et des claques) 1965, Prize for Best Actress, Mar del Plata Festival (for Vivre pour vivre) 1968, Best Actress of the Year (for Docteur Françoise Gailland) 1976; Commdr. des Arts et des Lettres. *Plays acted in:* La tour Eiffel qui tue, la Paix chez soi, le Jeu de l'amour et du hasard, la Machine à écrire, les Amants magnifiques, Aux innocents les mains pleines, Une femme trop honnête, Deux sur une balançoire, l'Idiote, Après la chute 1965, le Jour de la tortue 1965, Seule dans le noir 1966, Persephone (speaking part, La Scala, Milan) 1966, Madame Marguerite (1974–75), Marguerite et les autres 1983, L'avare 1986. *Films include:* Treize à table 1955, l'Homme aux clefs d'or 1956, Le rouge est mis, Maigret tend un piège, le Désert de Pigalle 1957, La Corde raide, Recours en grâce 1959, la Française et l'Amour, la Proie pour l'ombre, Rocco et ses frères 1960, le Rendez-vous, les Amours célèbres, le Bateau d'Emile 1961, le Vice et la Vertu 1962, l'Autre Femme 1963, Déclics et des claques, Trois Chambres à Manhattan, l'Or du duc 1965, Vivre pour vivre 1967, Les gauloises bleues, la Bande à Bonnot 1968, Il pleut dans mon village, Erotissimo, Un homme qui me plaît 1969, Dillinger est mort, l'Histoire d'une femme, Elle boit pas, elle fume pas, elle drague pas, mais . . . elle cause, Disons un soir à dîner, les Novices, le Clair de terre 1970, Mourir d'aimer, la Vieille Fille, la Mandarine 1971, les Feux de la chandeleur, Elle cause plus . . . elle flingue 1972, Traitement de choc, Jessua 1973, Il n'y a pas de fumée sans feu 1972, Ursule et Grelu 1973, Juliette et Juliette, la Gifle 1974, Il faut vivre dangereusement, le Gitan, Il pleut sur Santiago 1975, Docteur Françoise Gailland, le Soupçon, D'amour et d'eau fraîche, Cours après moi . . . que je t'attrape 1976, A chacun son enfer 1977, le Dernier Baiser, jambon d'Ardenne, le Point de mire 1977, la Zizanie, la Clé sur la porte, l'Amour en question 1978, Vas-y maman 1978, Cause toujours . . . tu m'intéresses 1979, Bobo, Jacco, le Grand embouteillage 1979, la Vie continue, une Robe noire pour un tueur, la Revanche 1981, Partir, Revenir 1985, Adieu Blaireau 1985. *Television appearance:* le Pain de ménage 1966.

GIRAUD, André Louis Yves; French mining engineer and politician; b. 3 April 1925, Bordeaux; s. of René and Marie Thérèse (Gamet) Giraud; m. Claudine Mathurin-Edme 1949; two s. one d.; ed. Lycée de Bordeaux, l'Ecole Polytechnique, l'Ecole nat. supérieure du pétrole et des moteurs; Engineer with Ministry of Industry 1949; Head of Dept., Inst. français du pétrole 1951, Technical Dir. 1955, Deputy Gen. Dir. 1958–64, mem. Consultative Cttee. for Scientific and Technical Research 1960–64; Dir. of Motor Fuels, Ministry of Industry 1964–69; Vice-Pres. Régie nat. des Usines Renault 1965–71; Dir. Nat. Centre for Exploitation of Oceans 1967–69; Dir. Dept. of Educ. 1969–70; Admin.-Gen. (Govt. delegate), Commissariat for Atomic Energy 1970–78; Minister of Industry 1978–81, of Defence 1986–88; Assoc. Prof. Univ. of Paris-Dauphine 1981–; Dir. Electricité de France 1970–78; Gen. Eng. of Mines 1973–; Pres. Admin. Council, l'Ecole Polytechnique 1974; Pres. Cie. Générale des matières nucléaires 1976–78; Officier Légion d'honneur, Officier Ordre nat. du Mérite; Commdr. des Palmes académiques. *Address:* Université Paris-Dauphine, place de Lattre-de-Tassigny, 75775 Paris Cedex 16; 104 avenue Kléber, 75116 Paris, France.

GIRAUD, Michel; French business executive and politician; b. 14 July 1929, Pontoise, Val d'Oise; s. of Jean Giraud; m. Simone Wietzel; two s. (one deceased) one d.; ed. secondary school at Saint-Martin de France-Pontoise, Lycée Louis le Grand and Sorbonne, Paris; Dir. Société Centrale des Bois 1951–57, Société A. Charles & Fils 1957–72; Pres. Dir.-Gen. SONIBAT 1972–; Pres. Dir.-Gen. Société d'Economie Mixte d'Aménagement et de Gestion du Marché d'Intérêt Nat. de la Région Parisienne 1975–77; Conseiller-Gén. Val de Marne 1967–85; mem. Conseil d'Admin. Parisian Regional Dist. 1967–, Pres. 1972–73; Pres. Conseil Regional, Ile-de-France 1976–; Mayor of Perreux-sur-Marne 1971–; Pres. Assen. of Mayors of France 1983–; Chevalier, Légion d'Honneur, Ordre Nat. du Mérite, des Palmes Académiques, Médaille d'Argent de la Jeunesse et des Sports. *Publications:* Nous tous la France 1983, Raconte-moi Marianne 1984, Notre Ile-de-France Région Capitale 1985. *Leisure interests:* sport, history, music. *Address:* Conseil Régional d'Ile-de-France, Cabinet du President, 33 rue Barbet de Jouy, 75700 Paris, France.

GIRAUDET, Pierre; French civil engineer and airline executive; b. 5 Dec. 1919, Koléa, Algeria; s. of Pierre Giraudet and Irma Basset-Villéon; m. Mireille Bougourd 1947; one s. two d.; ed. Coll. Notre Dame d'Afrique, Lycée Bugeaud, Science Faculty, Algiers. Head of Hydraulic Eng. Services, Moyen Cheliff, Algeria 1946–53; Head of Technical Service, Algerian Dept. of Hydraulic Eng. 1954–56; Head of Algiers Port Devt. 1956–60; Dir. of Works, Ind. Port of Le Havre 1961–67; Dir. of Investments, Deputy Gen. Man. Paris Airport 1967–71; Gen. Man. Régie Autonome des Transports Parisiens (R.A.T.P.), 1972–75; Chair. Air France 1975–84; Pres. IATA 1980–81; Chair. Fondation de France 1983–, Pres., Board of Ecole Nationale des Ponts et Chaussées 1983–; Pres., Dir.-Gen. Flammarion 1984, Schneider SA 1986–; Commdr., Légion d'honneur, Commdr., Ordre national du Mérite. *Leisure interest:* yachting. *Address:* 78 avenue de Suffren, 75015 Paris, France (Home).

GIRAY, I. Safa: Turkish politician; b. 1931, Izmir; m.; three c.; ed. in Ankara, Erzurum, Adana, Faculty of Construction, Istanbul Tech. Univ.; planning engineer at Gen. Directorate of Electricity Works Study Dept. 1963; worked on project studies of Keban and Oymapinar Dams; adviser at Gen. Directorate of Electrical Works; with Black Sea Copper Enterprises 1964–74; Minister of Public Works and Housing 1983–89, of Defence 1989–. *Address:* Bayindirlik ve Iskan Bakanligi, Ankara, Turkey.

GIRDWOOD, Ronald Haxton, C.B.E., M.D., PH.D., F.R.C.P.E., F.R.C.P., F.R.C.P.I., F.R.C.PATH., F.R.S.E.; British university clinical professor and consultant physician (retd); b. 19 March 1917, Arbroath; s. of late Thomas Girdwood and Elizabeth (Haxton) Girdwood; m. Mary E. Williams 1945; one s. one d.; ed. Daniel Stewart's Coll. Edin. and Univ. of Edinburgh; officer, R.A.M.C. 1942–46; Lecturer in Medicine, Univ. of Edin. 1946–51, Sr. Lecturer, then Reader in Medicine 1951–62, Prof. of Therapeutics and Clinical Pharmacology 1962–82, Dean, Faculty of Medicine 1975–79; Rockefeller Research Fellow, Univ. of Mich. 1948–49; Pres. British Soc. for Haematology 1963–64; Pres. Royal Coll. of Physcians of Edin. 1982–85; Chair. Scottish Nat. Blood Transfusion Asscn. 1980–, Medico-Pharmaceutical Forum 1985–87; Hon. F.R.C.A.P., Hon. F.A.C.P.; Leslie Gold Medal in Medicine (Univ. of Edin.) 1939, Suniti Panja Gold Medal (Calcutta School of Tropical Medicine) 1980; awarded Freedom of the township of Sirajgury, Bangladesh 1984; mem. numerous charitable cttees. *Publications:* Malabsorption 1969, Textbook of Medical Treatment 1987, Blood Disorders due to Drugs and other Agents 1973, Clinical Pharmacology 1984; about 300 papers in medical books and journals. *Leisure interests:* photography, painting in oils, writing, gardening. *Address:* 2 Hermitage Drive, Edinburgh, EH10 6DD, Scotland. *Telephone:* (031) 447 5137.

GIRENKO, Andrey Nikolayevich; Soviet politician; b. 1936; ed. Krivorozhsky Mining Inst. and CPSU Cen. Cttee. Higher Party School; engineer in lab., mining mechanic 1958–63; mem. CPSU 1963–; First Sec. Krivorog City Cttee.; First Sec. Dnepropetrovsk Dist. Cttee. Komsomol 1963–70; Second, then First Sec. of Cen. Cttee. of Ukrainian Komsomol 1970–75; Second, then First Sec. of Khevson Dist. Cttee. of Ukrainian CP 1980–87; First Sec. of Crimean Dist. Cttee. of Ukrainian CP 1987–; cand. mem. of CPSU Cen. Cttee. 1981–; Deputy to U.S.S.R. Supreme Soviet. *Address:* Crimean District Committee of Ukrainian Communist Party, Kiev, U.S.S.R.

GIRI, Dr. Tulsi; Nepalese politician; b. Sept. 1926. Deputy Minister of Foreign Affairs 1959; Minister of Village Devt. 1960; Minister without

Portfolio 1960; Minister of Foreign Affairs, the Interior, Public Works and Communications 1961; Vice-Chair. Council of Ministers and Minister of Palace Affairs 1962; Chair. Council of Ministers and Minister of Foreign Affairs 1962–65; mem. Royal Advisory Cttee. 1969–74; Adviser to the King 1974–; Prime Minister, Minister of Palace Affairs and Defence 1975–77. *Address:* Jawakpurdham, District Dhanuka, Nepal.

GIROLAMI, Sir Paul, Kt., B.COM., F.C.A.; British chartered accountant and business executive; b. 25 Jan. 1926, Italy; m. Christabel Mary Gwynne Lewis 1952; two s. one d.; ed. London School of Economics; with Chantrey and Button (Chartered Accountants) 1950–54, Coopers and Lybrand, 1954–65; joined Glaxo as Financial Controller 1965, mem. of Bd. and Finance Dir. 1968, Chief Exec. 1980–86, Deputy Chair. April-Dec. 1985; Chair. Glaxo Holdings Dec. 1985–; Dir. Inner London Bd. of Nat. Westminster Bank PLC 1974–; mem. CBI Council 1986–, Open Univ. Visiting Cttee. 1987; Dir. American Chamber of Commerce (U.K.) 1983; mem. Appeal Cttee. of Inst. of Chartered Accountants 1987, Stock Exchange Listed Cos. Advisory Cttee. 1987, Court of Assts. of The Worshipful Company of Goldsmiths 1986; Grande Ufficiale, Ordine al Merito della Republica Italiana 1987; City and Guilds Insignia Award in Tech. (h.c.) 1988; Freeman, City of London Liveryman 1980. *Leisure interest:* golf. *Address:* 6 Burghley Road, Wimbledon, London, SW19 5BH, England. *Telephone:* 01-946 0608.

GIROUD, Françoise; French journalist and politician; b. 21 Sept. 1916, Geneva, Switzerland; d. of Salih Gourdji and Elda Faragi; one s. (deceased), one d.; ed. Lycée Molière, Coll. de Groslay; began in cinema as script-girl 1932, Asst. Dir. 1937; Ed. Elle 1945–52; Co-founder L'Express 1953, Ed. 1953–71, Dir. 1971–74; Pres. Express-Union 1970–74; mem. Gov. Bd. of Express Group 1971–74; Sec. of State for Women's Affairs 1974–76, for Culture 1976–77; Vice-Pres. Parti Radical 1975–76, Union pour la Démocratie française 1978–; Pres. Action Int. contre la Faim 1984–; Columnist on Le Nouvel Observateur; Hon. Dr. (Ann Arbour Univ.) 1976, (Goucher Coll.) 1977; Chevalier Légion d'honneur 1983. *Publications:* Le tout Paris 1952, Nouveaux portraits 1953, La nouvelle vague: portrait de la jeunesse 1958, Si je mens 1972, Une poignée d'eau 1973, La comédie du pouvoir 1977, Ce que je crois 1978, Une femme honorable 1981, Le Bon Plaisir 1983, Alma Mahler ou l'art d'être aimée 1988; *films:* Antoine et Antoinette 1947, La belle que voilà 1950, L'amour, madame 1951, Julietta 1953, Le bon plaisir 1984, Le quatrième pouvoir 1985. *Address:* Editions Fayard, 75 rue des Saints Pères, 75006 Paris, France.

GISCARD D'ESTAING, François, L. EN D.; French civil servant; b. 17 Sept. 1926; ed. Ecole Nat. d'Admin., Inst. d'Etudes Politiques; Deputy Insp. of Finance 1952, Insp. 1954; Technical Adviser to Minister of Agriculture 1955–56, 1958–59, to Sec. of State for the Budget 1956–57; Head of Cen. Admin. Ministry of Agriculture 1957; Dir. Banque Cen. des Etats d'Afrique Equatoriale et du Cameroun 1959–68; Dir. Banque Française du Commerce Extérieur 1970, Dir.-Gen. 1974, Chair. 1977–82; Inspecteur-Gén. des Finances 1976–; Chair. American Express Bank (France) S.A.; Mayor of Saint-Amant-Tallende 1965–71; Croix de guerre, Officier, Légion d'honneur, Officier, Ordre nat. du Mérite. *Publications:* Financement et garantie du commerce international 1977, Notre-Dame de Paris—les rois retrouvés (with Michel Fleury and Alain Erlande-Brandenburg). *Leisure interests:* big-game hunting, archaeology. *Address:* 12–14 boulevard Point du Champs Elysées, Paris 08 (Office); 3 rue Louis Boilly, 75016 Paris, France (Home). *Telephone:* 42-25-15-16 (Office); 45-20-50-94 (Home).

GISCARD D'ESTAING, Valéry, K.C.B.; French politician and civil servant; b. 2 Feb. 1926, Koblenz, Germany; s. of the late Edmond Giscard d'Estaing and May Bardoux; m. Anne-Aymone de Brantes 1952; two s. two d.; ed. Ecole Polytechnique, Ecole Nat. d'Admin.; Official, Inspection des Finances 1952, Insp. 1954; Deputy Dir. du Cabinet de Prés. du Conseil June-Dec. 1954; Deputy for Puy de Dôme 1956–58, re-elected for Clermont 1958, for Puy du Dôme 1962, 1967, 1984, 1986, 1988. Sec. of State for Finance 1959, Minister for Finance and Econ. Affairs 1962–66, 1969–74; Pres. Comm. des Finances, de l'Economie général et du plan 1967–68; Pres. Cttee. des Affaires Etrangères 1987; Pres. of the French Repub. 1974–81; Founder-Pres. Fed. Nat. des Républicains, Indépendants (from May 1977 Parti Républicain) 1965; Del. to UN Gen. Assembly 1956, 1957, 1958; Chair. OECD Ministerial Council 1960; mem. Conseil Constitutionnel 1981–; Conseiller gen., Puy-de-Dome 1982–88; Pres. Regional Council of Auvergne 1986–; Pres. U.D.F. July 1988–; Grand Maître, Ordre de la Légion d'honneur, Grand Maître, Ordre national du Mérite, Croix de guerre, Chevalier, Ordre de Malte, Grand Cross, Order of Isabel la Católica, Nansen Medal 1979, etc. *Publications:* Démocratie française 1976, Deux français sur trois 1984, Le Pouvoir et La Vie 1988. *Leisure interests:* shooting, skiing. *Address:* Assemblée nationale, 75355 Paris; 11 rue Bénouville, 75016 Paris, France.

GISH, Lillian Diana; American actress; b. (as Lillian de Guiche) 14 Oct. 1899, Ohio; began acting at the age of five, in the theatre, and has appeared in many plays and films; long collaboration with D. W. Griffith; lecture tours of Europe and America 1969, 1970, 1971. *Plays include:* Camille, Dear Octopus, Hamlet (as Ophelia), Crime and Punishment, Life with Father, The Curious Savage, The Trip to Bountiful, The Chalk Garden, The Family Reunion, All the Way Home, A Passage to India, Too True to be Good, Romeo and Juliet (nurse) 1965, Anya (musical) 1965, I Never Sang for My Father 1968, Uncle Vanya, New York 1973, A Musical

Jubilee (musical comedy) 1975; *films include:* An Unseen Enemy 1912, The Mothering Heart 1913, Judith of Bethulia 1913, Home Sweet Home 1914, The Birth of a Nation 1914, Intolerance 1916, Hearts of the World 1918, The Great Love 1918, Broken Blossoms 1918, The Greatest Question 1919, True Heart Susie 1919, Remodelling Her Husband (also dir.) 1920, Way Down East 1920, Orphans of the Storm 1922, The White Sister 1923, Romola 1924, La Bohème 1926, The Scarlet Letter 1926, Annie Laurie 1927, The Wind 1928, His Double Life 1934, The Commandos Strike at Dawn 1943, Miss Susie Slagle's 1946, Duel in the Sun 1946, Portrait of Jennie 1948, The Cobweb 1955, The Night of the Hunter 1955, Orders to Kill 1958, The Unforgiven 1959, Follow Me Boys 1966, Warning Shot 1966, The Comedians 1967, Love Boat 1980, Thin Ice 1980, Arsenic and Old Lace (television) 1969, A Wedding 1978, Infinity in an Hour (television) 1978, Hambone and Hillie 1984, Sweet Liberty 1986, The Whales of August 1987 (Nat. Review Bd. Award for Best Actress 1987). *Publications:* Lillian Gish: an Autobiography 1968, The Movies, Mr. Griffith and Me 1969, Dorothy and Lillian Gish 1973, An Actor's Life for Me! 1987. *Leisure interests:* travel, reading. *Address:* 430 East 57th Street, New York, N.Y. 10022, U.S.A.

GISLASON, Gylfi Th., DR. RER. POL.; Icelandic economist and politician; b. 7 Feb. 1917, Reykjavík; s. of Thorsteinn Gislason and Thórunn Pálsdóttir; m. Gudrún Vilmundardóttir 1939; three s.; ed. Reykjavik Coll., Univs. of Frankfurt am Main and Vienna; Lecturer of Econs., Univ. of Iceland 1941-46, Prof. 1946-56; mem. of Parl. 1946-78; Minister of Educ. and Industries 1956-58, of Educ. and Commerce 1958-71; Prof. of Econs. 1972-; mem. Cen. Cttee. Social-Democratic Party 1942, Sec. 1946-65, Vice-Chair. 1965-68, Chair. 1968-74; Chair. Social-Democratic Parl. Group 1974-78; Pres. of Parl. 1974; Gov. for Iceland, IMF 1956-65; Gov. for Iceland Int. Bank for Reconstruction and Devt. 1965-71; mem. Bd. of Govs. Iceland Bank of Devt. 1953-66, Devt. Fund of Iceland 1966-71, Nat. Theatre 1954-; Chair. State Research Council 1965-71; mem. Icelandic Science Soc.; mem. Nordic Council 1971-78, Chair. Cultural Cttee. 1971-78; Dr. Oecon. h.c. *Publications:* General Business Theory 1941, Bookkeeping 1942, Finance of Private Business Enterprises 1945, Management of Industrial Enterprises 1953, Accountancy 1955, The Marshall Plan 1948, Socialism 1949, Capitalism, Socialism and the Co-operative Movement 1950, The Foreign Policy of Iceland 1953, The Problem of Being an Icelander 1973, Enterprise and Society 1974, Fishery Economics 1975, Essays on Business Administration 1975, Book-keeping 1976, Book-keeping and Balance Sheets 1976, Essays on Commercial Law 1976, Social Democracy 1977, Economics 1981, Business Administration Vol. I 1986, Vols. II, III 1987; 20 songs arranged by Jon Thorarinsson 1985. *Leisure interest:* music; has composed songs for four LP records. *Address:* University of Iceland, Reykjavík 25088 (Office); Aragata 11, Reykjavík, 15804, Iceland (Home). *Telephone:* (91) 25088 (Office); (91) 15804 (Home).

GITALOV, Aleksandr Vasilyevich; Soviet official and politician; b. 1915, Ukraine; tractor-driver 1929-41; served in Soviet Army 1941-45; brigadier of tractor brigades on tractor stations and collective farms 1946-58; Deputy to U.S.S.R. Supreme Soviet 1950-; mem. of Cen. Cttee. of Ukrainian CP 1956-; mem. of Draft Bills Comm. of the Council of Nationalities 1962-74; mem. of Presidium of U.S.S.R. Supreme Soviet 1974-; mem. of Cen. Cttee. of CPSU 1982-; Order of Lenin. *Address:* The Kremlin, Moscow, U.S.S.R.

GIUFFRIDA, Elio; Italian diplomatist; b. 23 Oct. 1919, Catania; s. of late Roberto Giuffrida and Amalia Finocchiaro; m. Stefania Bruno 1945; one s. three d.; with Italian Embassy, Paris 1955-60; Minister-Counsellor and Sec.-Gen. Italian Del., OECD 1967-68; Head, UN Dept. Ministry of Foreign Affairs 1968-69; Sec.-Gen. Italian Del. to UN Gen. Assembly 1968, 1969, 1970; mem. Italian Del., Conf. of Law and Treaties, Vienna 1969, Conf. of Disarmament Cttee., Geneva 1971-72, Conf. on Security and Co-operation in Europe, Geneva 1973-74; Deputy Dir.-Gen. for Emigration and Social Affairs, Ministry of Foreign Affairs 1975-76; Gen. Insp. Ministry of Foreign Affairs 1976; Amb. to Tunisia 1977-80, to Egypt 1980-85; Croce al Merito di Guerra, Chevalier, Légion d'honneur, Cavaliere di Gran Croce al Merito della Repubblica Italiana, Order of Arab Repub. of Egypt. *Leisure interests:* microphysics, philosophy. *Address:* Via Niccolò Piccinni 87, Rome, Italy. *Telephone:* 860 1842.

GIULINI, Carlo Maria; Italian conductor; b. 9 May 1914; m.; three s.; ed. Accad. S. Cecilia, Rome; debut as conductor, Rome 1944; fmr. Dir., Italian Radio Orchestra; fmr. Prin. Conductor, Philharmonia Orchestra (London), Vienna Symphony Orchestra; Music Dir. Los Angeles Philharmonic Orchestra 1978-84; Hon. D.Hum.Litt. (DePaul Univ.) 1979, Gold Medal, Bruckner. Soc. 1978. *Address:* c/o Robert Leslie, 121C King's Avenue, London, S.W.4, England.

GIURANNA, Bruno; Italian viola player; b. 6 April 1933, Milan; ed. Coll. S. Giuseppe and Conservatorio di Musica Santa Cecilia, Rome, and Conservatorio di Musica S. Pietro a Maiella, Naples; Founder mem. I Musici 1951-61; Prof. Conservatorio G. Verdi, Milan 1961-65, Conservatorio S. Cecilia, Rome 1965-78, Prof. Acad. Chigiana, Siena 1966-; Prof. Nordwest-deutsche Musikakademie, Detmold, Germany 1969-83; Prof. Hochschule der Künste, Berlin 1981-; mem. Int. Music Competition jury, Munich 1961-62, 1967, 1969, Geneva 1968, Budapest 1975; soloist at concerts in festivals including Edinburgh Festival, Holland Festival and with orchestras including Berlin Philharmonic Orchestra, Amsterdam Concertgebouw

Orchestra and Teatro alla Scala, Milan; Academician of Santa Cecilia 1974; Artistic Dir. of Orchestra de Camera di Padova 1983. *Address:* Via Misurina 71, 00135 Rome, Italy.

GIURESCU, Dinu C., PH.D.; Romanian historian; b. 15 Feb. 1927; s. of Constantin and Maria S. Giurescu; m. Anca Elena Dinu 1960; two d.; ed. Univ. Bucharest; museographer Bucharest Art Museum 1956-64; with Ministry of Foreign Affairs 1964-68; Prof. of European Civilization, Nicolae Grigorescu Fine Arts Inst. Bucharest 1968-87; lectured in Switzerland, France, Bulgaria, Hungary, Fed. Repub. of Germany, U.S.A.—Dallas 1977, Washington 1980, Univs. of Columbia, Ind., Ill., Ariz., Calif. (Berkeley), Kan., Colo., Ore., Neb., Ohio, Rochester and Huntington Coll. 1982-85; mem. Romanian Nat. Cttee. of Historians; mem. Romanian Nat. Comm. of Mil. History; Prize of the Romanian Acad. *Publications:* Ion Vodă cel Viteaz 1966, Pagini din trecutul diplomaţiei rômâneşti (Pages from the History of Romanian Diplomacy) 1966 (in collaboration), Istoria românilor din cele mai vechi timpuri pînă astăzi (History of the Romanians from Ancient Times Until Today) 1971 (in collaboration); Ţara Românească în secolele XIV-XV (Wallachia in the 14th-15th Centuries) 1971; Istoria Românilor I-II, Din cele mai vechi timpuri pînă la finele sec. XVI (History of the Romanians I-II. From Ancient Times to the end of the XVI century) 1974-76 (in collaboration); Illustrated History of the Romanian People (in Romanian, English, French, German, Russian, Spanish) 1981-82. *Leisure interests:* walking, visiting sites and museums, jazz music. *Address:* Institute of Fine Arts Nicolae Grigorescu, General Budisteanu 19, 70744 Bucharest 12 (Office); 58 Cobălcescu Street, Bucharest 12, Romania (Home). *Telephone:* 15-11-61 (Home).

GIZOULI, Dafallah (see Dafallah, Gizouli).

GJAEREVOLL, Dr. Olav; Norwegian politician and scientist; b. 24 Sept. 1916, Tynset; s. of Gunnar and Kristine Gjaerevoll; m. Astri Skaar 1944; one s. one d.; ed. Uppsala Univ. and in U.S.A. and Canada; Teacher; Curator, Royal Scientific Soc. Museum 1947; joined staff, Teachers Training Coll., Trondheim 1947; Prof. of Botany Univ. of Trondheim 1958-86; Minister of Social Affairs 1963-65; Rep. to Storting 1965-69; Minister of Prices and Wages 1971-72; Minister of the Environment 1972; mem. Trondheim City Council 1952-67, 1980-, Deputy Mayor 1955-58, Lord Mayor 1958-63, 1980-81; Chair. Trondheim United Labour Party 1949-51, 1977-78; mem. State Nature Conservation Council 1958-86, Chair. 1960-86; Chair. Norwegian Inst. for Air Research 1974-80, Steering Comm., UNESCO project Man. and Biosphere 1974-85, Trondheim Univ. Bd. 1976-79; mem. Royal Scientific Soc. 1951-, Acad. of Sciences 1958-. *Leisure interests:* mountain walking and skiing. *Address:* Jonsvannsvn 36, Trondheim, Norway.

GJERDE, Bjartmar; Norwegian politician; b. 6 Nov. 1931, Sande Sunnmøre; s. of Astrid Gjerde and Hjalmar Gjerde; m. Anna Karin Hoel 1954; three s.; Journalist Sunnmøre Arbeideravis 1948-53; Ed. Fritt Slag 1953-58; Chair. Labour League of Youth 1958-61; mem. State Youth Council; Sec. Labour Parl. Group 1961-62; Chief. Sec. Workers' Educ. League 1962-71; mem. Council on Broadcasting 1963-74, UNESCO Comm. 1964-66, Norwegian Cultural Council 1965-85, Council on Adult Educ. 1966-71; Minister of Church and Educ. 1971-72, 1973-76, for Industries 1976-78, for Petroleum and Energy 1978-80; mem. Labour Party Nat. Exec. 1973-81; Dir.-Gen. Norwegian Broadcasting Corpn. (NRK) 1981-, Directorat of Labour 1989-. *Address:* Holbergs pl.7, 0166 Oslo 1, Norway.

GJERTSEN, Astrid; Norwegian politician; b. 14 Sept. 1928, Tyrsted, Horsens, Denmark; played active role in local Conservative party politics and many aspects of community life in Tvedestrand, including health services and consumer affairs; mem. Tvedstrand municipal council 1967-75; mem. Nat. Exec. Norwegian Housewives Asscn. 1968-74; mem. Consumer Council 1973; Proxy mem. Storting 1970-73, mem. 1973-; del. to UN Gen. Assembly 1974; mem. Nordic Council 1977-; Minister of Consumer Affairs and Government Admin. 1981-86. *Address:* c/o The Royal Ministry of Consumer Affairs and Government Administration, Akersgaten 42, Pb 8004 Dep, Oslo, Norway.

GLADILIN, Anatoliy Tikhonovich; Soviet writer; b. 1935, Moscow; ed. Gorky Literary Inst., Moscow; fmr. mem. of U.S.S.R. Writers' Union; literary activity started 1956; one of main contributors (with V. Aksyonov, q.v.) to Katayev's journal Youth 1960-65; one of founders of "Youth Prose" movement in early 1960s; signed letter of 80 writers in support of Solzhenitsyn's letter on abolition of censorship 1967; expelled from Union of Writers 1972; left U.S.S.R. 1976; settled in France. *Publications include:* Chronicle of the Times of Viktor Podgursky 1956, Prognosis for Tomorrow 1972, The Paris Fair 1980, A Big Race Day 1983, F.S.S.R. The French Soviet Socialist Republic Story 1985, As I Was Then: Tales 1986.

GLADKY, Ivan Ivanovich; Soviet politician; b. 2 Nov. 1930, Marinovskoe, Voroshilovgrad Oblast; ed. Kharkov Polytech. Inst.; engineer, technologist mem. CPSU 1953-; cand mem. CPSU Cen. Cttee. 1986-; Deputy to U.S.S.R. Supreme Soviet; worker agricultural state co-operative 1949; army service 1950-54; fitter, worker, sr. apparator; deputy head workshop Severodonezk Chemical Plant 1954-64; Chair. of plant's trade union; Sec. Ukrainian Rep., Council of Trades Unions 1964-70, 1970-81; Sec. All-Union Cen. Council of Trades Unions 1981-86; Chair. State Cttee. for Labour and Social Affairs 1986-; Hero of Socialist Labour, Order of Lenin, Order of Red Banner of Labour (twice) and other decorations. *Address:* 103706, K-12, Kujbyshev Square, 1, State Committee for Labour and Social Affairs, Moscow, U.S.S.R.

GLADSTONE, David Arthur Stewart, M.A.; British diplomatist; b. 1 April 1935, Calcutta; s. of Thomas S. Gladstone and Muriel I. H. Day; m. M. E. April Brunner 1961; one s. one d.; ed. Christ Church, Oxford; joined Foreign Office 1960; served Lebanon, Bahrain (Political Agency) 1962–63, Bonn 1965–69, Cairo 1972–75, British Mil. Govt., Berlin 1976–79, Marseilles (Consul-Gen.) 1983–87; High Commr. to Sri Lanka 1987–. *Leisure interests:* reading, writing, music, squash. *Address:* c/o Foreign & Commonwealth Office, King Charles Street, London, SW1A 2AH, England.

GLADSTONE, Sir (Erskine) William, Bt., J.P., M.A.; British scout and former schoolmaster; b. 29 Oct. 1925, Eton; s. of Charles A. and Isla M. (née Crum) Gladstone; m. Rosamund A. Hambro 1962; two s. one d.; ed. Eton and Christ Church, Oxford; Royal Navy 1943–46; Asst. Master, Shrewsbury School 1949–50, Eton Coll. 1951–61; Headmaster, Lancing Coll. 1961–69; Deputy Lieut. of Flintshire 1969, Clwyd 1974, Lord-Lieut. 1985; Chief Scout, U.K. and Overseas branches 1972–82; Chair. World Cttee. of the Scout Org. 1979–81; Chair. Council of Glenalmond Coll. 1981–86; Lord Lieut. of Clwyd 1985–; Chair. Rep. Body, Church in Wales 1977–. *Leisure interests:* reading history, gardening, shooting. *Address:* Fasque, Laurencekirk, Kincardineshire, Scotland; Hawarden Castle, Deeside, Clwyd, Wales (Home). *Telephone:* Hawarden 520210; Fettercairn 341.

GLADUSH, Ivan Dmitrievich; Soviet party official and politician; Minister for the Interior of Ukrainian S.S.R. 1982–. *Address:* Ministry of the Interior, Kiev, Ukrainian S.S.R., U.S.S.R.

GLADWYN, 1st Baron (cr. 1960), of Bramfield; **Hubert Miles Gladwyn Jebb,** G.C.M.G., G.C.V.O., C.B.; British diplomatist; b. 25 April 1900; s. of Sydney and Rose (née Chichester) Jebb; m. Cynthia Noble 1929; one s. two d.; ed. Eton and Magdalen Coll., Oxford; entered Diplomatic Service 1924; served in Teheran and Rome; Private Sec. to Parl. Under-Sec. of State 1929–31; Private Sec. to Permanent Under-Sec. of State 1937–40; appointed to Ministry of Econ. Warfare 1940; Acting Counsellor in Foreign Office 1941; Head Reconstruction Dept., Foreign Office 1942–45; Counsellor 1943; appointed Exec. Sec. of Preparatory Comm. of UN Aug. 1945; Acting Sec.-Gen. of UN 1946; Asst. Under-Sec. of State in Foreign Office, 1946–49; Deputy Under-Sec. of State 1949–50; UK Rep. on Permanent Comm. of Treaty of Brussels, 1948; Permanent Rep. of U.K. to UN 1950–54; Amb. to France 1954–60; Deputy Leader Liberal Party, House of Lords 1967–1987; Pres. Campaign for a European Political Community; Pres. European Movt. U.K.; mem. European Parl. 1973–76; fmr. Pres. Atlantic Treaty Asscn.; Hon. D.C.L. (Syracuse 1951, Oxford 1954, Essex 1974), Grand Croix, Légion d'honneur 1957; Liberal. *Publications:* The European Idea 1966, Half-Way to 1984 1967, De Gaulle's Europe, or Why the General Says No 1969, Europe After De Gaulle 1970, The Memoirs of Lord Gladwyn 1972. *Address:* 62 Whitehall Court, London, S.W.1; Bramfield Hall, Halesworth, Suffolk, England. *Telephone:* 01-930 3160.

GLAMANN, Kristof, O.B.E.; Danish professor of history, business executive and author; b. 26 Aug. 1923, Kerteminde; s. of Kai Kristof Glamann and Ebba H. K. Glamann (née Madsen); m. Kirsten Jantzen 1954; two s.; ed. Univ. of Copenhagen; Assoc. Prof. of History, Univ. of Copenhagen 1948–60, Prof. of Econ. History 1961–80; Visiting Prof., Univ. of Pa. 1960, Univ. of Wisconsin 1961, Visiting Northern Scholar, London School of Econs. 1966, Visiting Overseas Fellow, Churchill Coll., Cambridge Univ. 1971–72, Visiting Fellow, Toho Gakkai, Tokyo 1977; Master, 4th May and Hassager Coll., Copenhagen; mem. and Chair. Danish Research Council on Humanities 1968–70; mem. Bd. of Dirs., Carlsberg Foundation 1969–, Chair. 1976–; mem. Bd. of Dirs., Carlsberg Ltd. 1970–, Deputy Chair. 1975–77, Chair. 1977–; mem. Bd. of Dirs., Carlsberg Brewery Ltd. 1978–, Royal Copenhagen Ltd. 1978–, Fredericia Brewery 1979–, Politiken Publishers Ltd. 1975–; Chair. Council, Investor and Reinvest Ltd.; Deputy Chair. The Scandinavia-Japan Sasakawa Foundation 1985–; mem. Royal Danish Acad. of Science and Letters 1969, Royal Danish History Soc. 1961, Swedish Acad., Lund 1963, History Soc. of Calcutta 1962, Corresp. mem. French History Soc. 1972; Hon. Pres. Int. Econ. History Asscn. 1974; Hon. F.B.A. 1985; Hon. Dr. Soc. Sci. (Univ. of Gothenburg) 1974. *Publications:* History of Tobacco Industry in Denmark 1875–1950 1981, Prices and Wages 1500–1800 1958, Dutch-Asiatic Trade 1620–1740 1958, Brewing 1962, European Trade 1500–1750 1971, Carlsberg Foundation 1976, Contributed to the Cambridge Economic History of Europe (Vol. V) 1977, Mercantilism 1982, Festschrift 1983; Ed.-in-Chief Scandinavian Econ. History Review 1961–80. *Leisure interests:* painting, walking. *Address:* Carlsberg Foundation, 35 H. C. Andersens Boulevard, 1553 Copenhagen V, Denmark. *Telephone:* 01 14 21 28.

GLASBERGEN, Willem; Netherlands archaeologist; b. 24 July 1923, Noordwijk; s. of Abraham Glasbergen and Hendrika B. Anker; m. Ernestine Duyvis 1952; two s. five d.; ed. State Univ. at Groningen; Asst., Inst. for Biological Archaeology, State Univ. at Groningen 1942–52, Conservator 1953–54, Curator 1955–60; Extra. Prof. Univ. of Amsterdam 1956–60, Ordinarius 1960–; Dir. Inst. of Pre- and Protohistory 1957–72; mem. Royal Netherlands Acad. of Arts and Sciences 1959, Monuments Council 1959.

Publications: Barrow Excavations in the Eight Beatitudes 1954, De Voorgeschiedenis der Lage Landen 1959, Beaker types and their distribution in the Netherlands 1955, De urn van Toterfout en de reformatie van de Britse bronstijd 1957, The Vlaardingen Culture 1962–63, Nogmaals HVS/DKS 1969, De Romeinse castella te Valkenburg Z.H. 1972, The Pre-Flavian garrisons of Valkenburg Z.H. 1974, Aartswoud 1978. *Leisure interest:* forestry. *Address:* Saxa Iuxta, Groningerweg 3, Diever (Dr.), Netherlands.

GLASER, Donald Arthur, PH.D.; American physicist; b. 21 Sept. 1926, Cleveland, Ohio; s. of William Joseph and Lena Glaser; one s. one d.; ed. Case Inst. of Technology, California Inst. of Technology; Univ. of Mich. 1949–59; Univ. of Calif. 1960–; Nat. Science Foundation Fellow 1961; Guggenheim Fellow 1961–62; Biophysicist, Univ. of Calif., Berkeley 1962–64; Prof. of Physics and Molecular Biology, Univ. of Calif. 1960–; mem. N.A.S.; Hon. Sc.D.; Henry Russell Award 1955, Charles Vernon Boys Prize (The Physical Soc.) 1958, Nobel Prize 1960; several awards. *Publications:* Some Effects of Ionizing Radiation on the Formation of Bubbles in Liquids 1952, A Possible Bubble Chamber for the Study of Ionizing Events 1953, Bubble Chamber Tracks of Penetrating Cosmic-Ray Particles 1953, Progress Report on the Development of Bubble Chambers 1955, Strange Particle Production by Fast Pions in Propane Bubble Chamber 1957, Weak Interactions: Other Modes, Experimental Results 1958, The Bubble Chamber 1958, Development of Bubble Chamber and Some Recent Bubble Chamber Results in Elementary Particle Physics 1958, Decays of Strange Particles, 1959, Computer Identification of Bacteria by Colony Morphology 1972, Effect of Nalidixic Acid on DNA Replication by Toluene-treated E. coli 1973, The Isolation and Partial Characterization of Mutants of E. coli and Cold-sensitive Synthesis of DNA 1974, Rates of Chain Elongation of Ribosomal RNA Molecules in E. Coli 1974, Chromosomal Sites of DNA-membrane Attachment in E. coli 1974, Effect of Growth Conditions in DNA-membrane Attachment in E. Coli 1975, Characteristics of Cold-sensitive Mutants of E. coli K12 Defective in Deoxyribonucleic Acid Replication 1975; many papers written jointly with other physicists. *Leisure interests:* skiing, sailing, skin diving, music. *Address:* 229 Molecular Biology-Virus Laboratory, University of California, Berkeley, Calif. 94720, U.S.A.

GLASER, Robert, PH.D.; American university professor of psychology and education; b. 18 Jan. 1921, R.I.; m. Sylvia Lotman; two d.; ed. City Coll. of New York and Indiana Univ.; 1948–49; Asst. Prof. of Psychology, Univ. of Ky. 1949–50; Research Asst. Prof., Univ. of Ill. 1950–52; Sr. Research Scientist, American Inst. for Research 1952–56; Assoc. Prof. of Psychology, Univ. of Pittsburgh 1956–57, Prof. 1957–72, Prof. of Educ. 1964–72, Univ. Prof. of Psychology and Educ. 1972–; Dir. Learning Research and Devt. Center 1963–; Visiting Prof. Univ. of Göteborg 1975, Univ. of Heidelberg 1975, Cen. Univ. of Venezuela, Caracas 1981, Japan Soc. for the Promotion of Science 1982, Cen. Inst. of Educational Research, China 1982; Pres. Nat. Acad. of Educ. 1981–85; mem. Exec. Cttee. Int. Asscn. of Applied Psychology 1977–; mem. numerous advisory cttees. and editorial bds.; mem. American Asscn. for Artificial Intelligence, American Educational Research Asscn.; Fellow American Psychological Asscn., Center for Advanced Study in Behavioral Sciences 1969–70; Guggenheim Fellowhip 1975; American Psychological Asscn.'s E.L. Thorndike Award 1981; Distinguished Scientific Award for the Applications of Psychology 1986; Hon. D.Sc. (Leuven, Belgium) 1980, (Indiana) 1984, (Göteborg, Sweden) 1985. *Publications:* Adaptive Education 1977, (Ed.) Advances in Instructional Psychology 1978, Thinking and Learning Skills 1987, On the Nature of Expertise (with others) 1988. *Address:* 833 LRDC Building, University of Pittsburgh, Pittsburgh, Pa. 15260, U.S.A. *Telephone:* (412) 624-4895.

GLASER, Robert Joy, S.B., M.D.; American physician and foundation executive; b. 11 Sept. 1918, St. Louis, Mo.; s. of Joseph and Regina Glaser; m. Helen H. Hofsommer 1949; two s. one d.; ed. Harvard Coll. and Medical School; appointments Instructor to Assoc. Prof., Washington Univ. School of Medicine 1949–57, Assoc. Dean 1955–57; Dean and Prof. of Medicine, Univ. of Colo. School of Medicine 1957–63, Vice-Pres. for Medical Affairs 1959–63; Prof. of Social Medicine, Harvard Univ. 1963–65; Vice-Pres. for Medical Affairs, Dean of the School of Medicine, Prof. of Medicine, Stanford Univ. 1965–70, Acting Pres. 1968, Visiting Prof. of Medicine 1972–73, Consulting Prof. 1973–; Clinical Prof. of Medicine, Columbia Univ. Coll. of Physicians and Surgeons 1971–72; Vice-Pres. The Commonwealth Fund 1970–72; Pres. and C.E.O. The Henry J. Kaiser Family Foundation 1972–83; Dir. for Medical Science, Lucille P. Markey Charitable Trust 1984–; Dir. Hewlett-Packard Co. 1971–, Calif. Water Service Co. 1973–, The Equitable Life Assurance Soc. of the U.S. 1979–86, First Boston Inc. 1982–; several hon. degrees; Centennial Award for Distinguished Service, Univ. of Colo. 1983; Medal for Distinguished Service, Univ. of Calif., San Francisco 1983; Abraham Flexner Award, Asscn. of American Medical Colls. 1984; Hubert H. Humphrey Cancer Research Center Award 1985. *Publications:* 103 papers on experimental streptococcal infections, antibiotics and other topics concerning medicine and medical educ.; numerous chapters in medical books. *Leisure interests:* photography, travel, swimming, reading and music. *Address:* Lucille P. Markey Charitable Trust, 525 Middlefield Road, Suite 130, Menlo Park, Calif. 94025, U.S.A. *Telephone:* (415) 323-6700.

GLASHOW, Sheldon Lee, PH.D.; American physicist; b. 5 Dec. 1932, New York; s. of Lewis Glashow and Bella Rubin; m. Joan Shirley Alexander

1972; three s. one d.; ed. Bronx High School of Science, Cornell and Harvard Univs.; Nat. Science Foundation Post-Doctoral Fellow, Univ. of Copenhagen 1958-60; Research Fellow, Calif. Inst. of Tech. 1960-61; Asst. Prof., Stanford Univ. 1961-62; Assoc. Prof., Univ. of Calif. (Berkeley) 1962-66; Prof. of Physics, Harvard 1967-, Higgins Prof. 1979-; Alfred P. Sloan Foundation Fellowship 1962-66; Visiting Scientist, C.E.R.N. 1968; Visiting Prof., Univ. of Marseille 1970, M.I.T. 1974, 1980-81, Boston Univ. 1983-84; Consultant, Brookhaven Lab. 1966-; Sr. Scientist, Univ. of Houston 1983-; Univ. Scholar, Texas A & M Univ. 1983-; Fellow, American Physical Soc., A.A.A.S.; Pres. Int. Sakharov Cttee. 1980-85; mem. American Acad. of Arts and Sciences, N.A.S.; Sponsor, Fed. of American Scientists (F.A.S.) and Bulletin of the Atomic Scientists; mem. Advisory Council American Acad. of Achievement 1979-, Science Policy Cttee., C.E.R.N. 1979-; Dr. h.c., Univ. of Aix-Marseille 1982; Oppenheimer Memorial Medal 1977; George Ledlie Award 1978; Hon. D.Sc. (Yeshiva Univ.) 1978; shared Nobel Prize for Physics with Abdus Salam and Steven Weinberg (qq.v.) for work on elementary particles 1979. *Publications:* Over 200 articles on elementary particle physics. *Address:* 30 Prescott Street, Brookline, Mass. 02146, U.S.A. (Home). *Telephone:* 617-495-2904 (Office).

GLASS, H(iram) Bentley, PH.D.; American professor of biology; b. 17 Jan. 1906, Laichowfu, Shantung, China; s. of Wiley B. and Eunice (Taylor) Glass; m. Suzanne G. Smith 1934; two c.; ed. Baylor Univ. and Univ. of Texas; teacher, Timpson High School, Timpson Tex. 1926-28, Stephens Coll., Columbia, Mo. 1934-38, Goucher Coll., Baltimore, Md.; Assoc. Prof. of Biology, Johns Hopkins Univ. 1947-52, Prof. 1952-65; Acad. Vice-Pres. (1965-71) and Distinguished Prof. of Biology, State Univ. of New York at Stony Brook 1965-76, Emer. 1976-; Asst. Ed. Quarterly Review of Biology 1945-48, Assoc. Ed. 1949-57, Ed. 1958-86; mem. Advisory Cttee. on Biology and Medicines, Atomic Energy Comm. 1956-63, Chair. 1962-63; mem. Nat. Acad. of Sciences Cttee. on Genetic Effects of Atomic Radiation 1955-64; mem. Continuing Cttee. Pugwash-COSWA Confs. 1958-64; Chair. Biological Sciences Curriculum Study 1959-65, Bd. Chair. Cold Spring Harbor Lab. 1967-73; lecturer at numerous orgs. Pres. American Asscn. for Advancement of Science 1969, Nat. Asscn. Biology Teachers 1971, American Asscn. of Univ. Profs. 1958-60, American Soc. of Naturalists 1965, American Inst. of Biological Sciences 1954-56, American Soc. of Human Genetics 1967; Vice-Pres. Genetic Soc. of America 1960; Chair. Section of Zoology and Anatomy, Nat. Acad. of Sciences 1964-67, Class II (Biological Sciences) 1968-71; mem. N.A.S., American Acad. of Arts and Sciences, American Philosophical Soc.; Foreign mem. Czechoslovak Acad. of Sciences; numerous hon. degrees. *Publications:* Genes and the Man 1943, Science and Liberal Education 1960, Science and Ethical Values 1965, Genetic Continuity: A Laboratory Block 1965, Genetic Continuity: A Laboratory Block, Teacher's Supplement 1965, The Timely and the Timeless 1970, Progress and Catastrophe: The Nature of Biological Science and its Impact on Human Society 1985, A Guide to the Genetics Collections of the American Philosophical Soc. 1988; Ed. of numerous symposia and surveys, and collaborator on other books; numerous articles. *Leisure interests:* music, philately (China). *Address:* P.O. Box 65, East Setanket, New York, N.Y. 11733, U.S.A. *Telephone:* 516-751-8985.

GLASS, Philip; American composer; b. 31 Jan. 1937, Baltimore; s. of Benjamin Glass and Ida (Gouline) Glass; m. 1st JoAnne Akalaitis; m. 2nd Luba Burtyk; one s. one d.; ed. Univ. of Chicago and Juilliard School of Music; Composer-in-Residence, Pittsburgh Public Schools 1962-64; studied with Nadia Boulanger, Paris 1964-66; f. Philip Glass Ensemble 1968, concert tours U.S.A. and Europe 1968-; f. record co. Chatham Square Productions, New York 1972; *Compositions include:* (operas) Einstein on the Beach 1976, Satyagraha 1980, The Photographer 1982, The Civil Wars 1982-84, Akhnaten 1984, The Making of the Representative for Planet 8 1988; (film score) Koyaanisqatsi 1982; (instrumental works) Strung Out 1967, Piece in the Shape of a Square 1968, Music in Similar Motion 1969, Music in Fifths 1970, Music in Changing Parts 1972, Music in 12 Parts 1974, Another Look at Harmony 1974, North Star 1975; Broadcast Music Industry Award 1960, Lado Prize 1961, Benjamin Award 1961, 1962, Young Composer's Award, Ford Foundation 1964-66, Fulbright award 1966-67 and other awards. *Publication:* Opera on the Beach 1988. *Address:* c/o International Production Associates, 853 Broadway, Room 2120, New York, N.Y. 10003, U.S.A.

GLASSER, Georges Charles; French industrialist; b. 24 Aug. 1907, Paris; m. Huguette Farjon 1934 (deceased); three d.; ed. Lycée Janson-de-Sailly, Paris, Ecole polytechnique; Hon. Pres. Soc. Alsthom Atlantique; Hon. Pres. Soc. Nat. Sud-Aviation, Union Syndicale des Industries Aéronautiques, Fédération Industries Electriques et Electroniques; Commdr. Légion d'honneur, Chevalier du Mérite agricole, Grand Officer, Order of Orange-Nassau, Médaille de l'Aéronautique, Commdr. Order of the Lion (Finland), Commdr. du Mérite sportif. *Leisure interests:* tennis, golf. *Address:* 3 rue Dangeau, Paris 75016, France. *Telephone:* 4520-1305.

GLASSPOLE, Sir Florizel Augustus, G.C.M.G., G.C.V.O.; Jamaican politician; b. 25 Sept. 1909, Kingston; s. of Rev. Theophilus A. Glasspole and Florence Glasspole (née Baxter); m. Ina Josephine Kinlocke 1934; one d.; ed. Wolmer's Boys' School, Ruskin Coll., Oxford; Accountant 1932-44; Gen. Sec. Jamaica United Clerks Asscn. 1937-48, Jamaica Trades Union Congress

1939-52, Water Comm. and Manual Workers Asscn. 1941-48, Municipal and Parochial Gen. Workers Union 1945-47, Nat. Workers Union 1952-55; Pres. Jamaica Printers and Allied Workers Union 1942-48; Gen. Hospital and Allied Workers Union 1944-47, Mental Hospital Workers Union 1944-47, Machado Employees Union 1945-52; Dir. City Printery Ltd. 1944-50; mem. House of Reps. 1944-73, Leader 1955-62, 1972-73; Minister of Labour 1955-57, of Educ. 1957-62, 1972-73; Vice-Pres. PNP; Sec. PNP Parl. Group 1944-73; Gov.-Gen. of Jamaica 1973-; mem. Standing Cttee on West Indian Fed. 1953-58, House of Reps. Cttee. preparing Jamaica's independence constitution, mem. Del. finalizing constitution with British Govt. 1962; workers' rep. on several Govt. Bds. 1942-53; mem. Bd. of Govs. Inst. of Jamaica 1944-57, Kingston School Bd.; ex officio mem. K.S.A.C. 1944-55; Hon. LL.D. (Univ. of West Indies) 1982; two Jamaican decorations and Order of Andrés Bello (1st Class) (Venezuela) 1973. *Leisure interests:* sports, gardening. *Address:* Kings House, Kingston 10, Jamaica.

GLAVIN, William F., M.B.A.; American business executive; b. 3 March 1932, Albany, New York; s. of John Glavin; m. Cecily McClatchy; three s. four d.; ed. Coll. of the Holy Cross, Wharton Graduate School of the Univ. of Pennsylvania; fmr. Exec. Int. Business Machines and Vice-Pres. Operations, Service Bureau Corpn. (an IBM subsidiary); Exec. Vice-Pres. Xerox Data Systems 1970, Group Vice-Pres. 1972, Man. Dir. and C.O.O. 1974, Exec. Vice-Pres. Xerox 1980, and Exec. Vice-Pres. for Reprographics and Operations 1982, Pres. Business Equipment Group 1983-, Vice-Chair. Xerox Corpn. 1985-; mem. Bd. of Dirs. Xerox, Fuji Xerox and Rank Xerox, also the Xerox Foundation; mem. Bd. of Dirs. Gould Inc., State Street Boston Corpn., Norton Co.; mem. Bd. of Trustees and Pres.'s Council Coll. of the Holy Cross. *Leisure interests:* golf, reading, art, music. *Address:* P.O. Box 1600, Stamford, Conn. 06904, U.S.A. *Telephone:* 203-968 3055.

GLAZER, Nathan, PH.D.; American educationist; b. 25 Feb. 1923, New York; s. of Louis and Tillie (Zacharevich) Glazer; m. 1st Ruth Slotkin 1943 (divorced 1958), 2nd Sulochana Raghavan 1962; three c.; ed. City Coll. of New York, Univ. of Pennsylvania and Columbia Univ; mem. of staff, Commentary Magazine 1944-53; Ed. and Editorial Adviser, Doubleday Anchor Books 1954-57; Visiting Lecturer, Univ. of Calif., Berkeley 1957-58; Instructor, Bennington Coll., Vermont 1958-59; Visiting Lecturer, Smith Coll. 1959-60; Prof. of Sociology, Univ. of Calif., Berkeley 1963-69; Prof. of Educ. and Social Structure, Harvard Univ. 1969-; Fellow, Center for Advanced Study in the Behavioural Sciences, Stanford, Calif. 1971-72; mem. American Acad. of Arts and Sciences, Library of Congress Council of Scholars; Guggenheim Fellow 1954, 1966; Hon.LL.D. (Franklin and Marshall Coll.) 1971, LL.D. (Colby Coll.) 1972, D.H.L. (Long Island Univ.) 1978, (Hebrew Union Coll.) 1986. *Publications:* American Judaism 1957, 1972, The Social Basis of American Communism 1961, Remembering the Answers 1970, Affirmative Discrimination 1976, Ethnic Dilemmas 1964-1982 1983; co-author: The Lonely Crowd 1950, Faces in the Crowd 1952, Studies in Housing and Minority Groups 1960, Beyond the Melting Pot 1963; co-editor: The Public Interest 1973-. *Address:* Graduate School of Education, Harvard University, Gutman Library, 6 Appian Way, Cambridge, Mass. 02138 (Office); 12 Scott Street, Cambridge, Mass. 02138, U.S.A. (Home). *Telephone:* (617) 495-4671 (Office); (617) 868-5459 (Home).

GLAZUNOV, Ilya; Soviet painter; b. 10 June 1930, Leningrad; ed. Repin Art School (pupil of B. Ioganson); First Prize Int. Art Exhbn., Prague 1956; first one-man show, Moscow 1957; teacher of drawing in Izhevsk, then Ivanovo; returned to Moscow 1960; exhibited in art exhbns. in Warsaw, Rome, Copenhagen, Vietnam, Laos, Paris, Leningrad, Santiago, Stockholm, Berlin (East and West), Leipzig, Fed. Germany 1960-77, London (Barbican) 1987. *Address:* U.S.S.R. Union of Artists, Universitetskaya naberezhnaya, Leningrad, U.S.S.R.

GLAZUR, Adam, M.SC.; Polish engineer and politician; b. 7 Jan. 1933, Kołaczyce near Jasło; ed. Electrical Faculty, Acad. of Mining and Metallurgy, Cracow; Chief Power Engineer, later Chief Engineer, then Dir., Glass Works at Krosno 1954-64; Head of Dept. in Ministry of Construction and Construction Materials Industry 1964-69, Under-Sec. of State 1969-74, First Deputy Minister 1974-75, Minister of Construction and Construction Materials Industry 1975-80; Chief Insp. of Energetic Economy June-Dec. 1980; fmr. mem. Polish United Workers' Party (PZPR) (expelled 1980), deputy mem. Cen. Cttee. PZPR 1975-80; sentenced to seven years' imprisonment for corruption 1982; Special State Prize 1978, Kt.'s Cross, Order of Polonia Restituta, Order of Banner of Labour (1st Class) 1976.

GLEASON, Andrew Mattei, B.S.; American mathematician; b. 4 Nov. 1921, Fresno, Calif.; s. of Henry Allan Gleason and Eleanor Theodalinda Mattei; m. Jean Berko 1959; three d.; ed. Yale Univ; U.S. Navy 1942-46, 1950-52; Junior Fellow of Soc. of Fellows, Harvard Univ. 1946-50, Asst. Prof. of Mathematics 1950-53, Assoc. Prof. 1953-57, Prof. of Mathematics 1957-69, Hollis Prof. of Mathematicks and Natural Philosophy 1969-; mem. N.A.S., American Acad. of Arts and Sciences, American Philosophical Soc.; Pres. American Mathematical Soc. 1981-82; Pres., Int. Congress of Mathematicians 1986; Hon. M.A.; Newcomb-Cleveland Prize of A.A.A.S. 1952. *Publication:* Fundamentals of Abstract Analysis 1966. *Address:* Department of Mathematics, Harvard University, Cambridge, Mass. 02138 (Office); 110 Larchwood Drive, Cambridge, Mass. 02138, U.S.A. (Home). *Telephone:* 495-4316 (Office); 864-5095 (Home).

GLEICH, Walter A.; German business executive and consultant; b. 4 Nov. 1924, Hamburg; s. of Walter H. and Ferdinande (née von Gossler) Gleich; m. Inta Köhn; four d.; ed. High School, Hamburg; joined Norddeutsche Affinerie AG 1942, mem. Man. Bd. 1961-86, Pres. 1976-86; Man. Dir. Ulrich H. Köhn GmbH, Hamburg; numerous other appointments. *Leisure interests:* sailing, tennis. *Address:* Asia Haus, Ost-West-Strasse 49, 2000 Hamburg 11, Federal Republic of Germany. *Telephone:* (32) 17-60.

GLEISSNER, Heinrich, DR.JUR.; Austrian diplomatist; b. 12 Dec. 1927, Linz; unmarried; ed. Univs. of Vienna and Innsbruck, Bowdoin Coll., Brunswick, Maine; at Coll. of Europe, Bruges 1950-51; entered Austrian Foreign Service 1951; at Austrian Embassy, Paris, and Office of the Austrian Observer at Council of Europe, Strasbourg 1952-53, Ministry for Foreign Affairs 1953-55, Austrian Embassy, London 1955-57; Sabbatical at Univ. of Vienna 1957-59; at Ministry for Foreign Affairs 1959-61, Austrian Nat. Bank 1961, Ministry for Foreign Affairs 1961-62, Mission to the Office of the UN, Geneva 1962-65; mem. Consulate-Gen., New York 1965-66, Consul-Gen. 1966-73; Ministry for Foreign Affairs 1973-75, Head of Western Dept. 1974-75; Dir. Security Council and Political Cttees. Div., UN, New York 1975-79; Amb. to U.K. 1979-81; with Ministry of Foreign Affairs 1982-. *Address:* c/o Ministry of Foreign Affairs, Ballhausplatz 2, 1010 Vienna, Austria.

GLEMP, H.E. Cardinal Józef, DR.IUR.UTR.; Polish ecclesiastic; b. 18 Dec. 1929, Inowrocław; s. of Kazimierz and Salomea (née Kośmicka) Glemp; ed. Primatial Spiritual Seminary, Gniezno, and Lateran Univ.; ordained priest, Gniezno 1956; educational work with young and sick, Mielzyn and Witkowo, and catechistic work Wągrowiec, Miasteczko Krajeńskie 1956-58; studied in Rome 1958-64; obtained title Chaplain to His Holiness and Advocate of Sacred Rota, Rome; various posts, Gniezno Curia Tribunal and Lecturer, Higher Seminary, Gniezno 1964-67; joined Secr., Primate of Poland Dec. 1967; Roman Law Lecturer, Acad. of Catholic Theology, Warsaw; fmr. mem. Episcopal Comm. for Revision of Canon Law and Sec. Comm. for Polish Insts. Rome; Ordinary, Diocese of Warmia, Olsztyn March 1979-July 1981; Archbishop-Metropolitan of Gniezno and Warsaw and Primate of Poland July 1981-; cr. Cardinal 1983; Co.-Chair. Working Group for Legis. Affairs, Joint Comm. of Govt. and Episcopate Jan.-July 1981; Chair. Chief Council of Polish Episcopate, Chair. Conf. of Polish Episcopate for Greek Catholic and Armenian Churches in Poland 1981-; Dr. h.c. (Acad. of Catholic Theology, Warsaw) 1982, (Villanova Univ., U.S.A.) 1985, (Lublin Catholic Univ.) 1985, (St. Thomas Univ., Manila) 1988; Culture for Peace Prize (Sardinia) 1986; mem. Congregation for the Eastern Church. *Publications:* De conceptu fictionis iuris apud Romanos 1974, Lexiculum iuris romani 1974, Through Justice in Charity 1982, Człowiek wielkiej wiary 1983, Kościół na drogach Ojczyny 1985, Chcemy z tego sprawdzianu wyjść prawdomówni i wiarygodni 1985, Kościół i Polonia 1986, W tęczy Franków orze i krzyż 1987, O Eucharystii 1987, Nauczaine pasterskie 1988, A wolanie moje niech do Giebie przyjdzie 1988, Let my call come to you 1988, Nauczaine spoleczne 1981-1986, 1989. *Address:* Rezydencja Prymasa Polski, Ulica Miodowa 17, 00-246 Warsaw (Residence); ul. Jana Łaskiego 7, 62-200 Gniezno, Poland (Office). *Telephone:* 31 21 57 (Residence), 21 02 (Office).

GLEMSER, Oskar Max, DR.-ING.; German chemist; b. 12 Nov. 1911, Stuttgart; s. of Karl Glemser and Amalie Gogel; m. Ida-Maria Greiner 1938; one s. one d.; ed. Gymnasium Bad-Canstatt and Technische Hochschule, Stuttgart; Sr. Engineer, Inst. for Inorganic Chemistry and Electro Chemistry, Technische Hochschule, Aachen 1939-41, Dozent 1941-48, Extra-Mural Prof. 1948-52; Prof. and Dir. of the Inst. of Inorganic Chemistry Univ. of Göttingen 1952-80; Pres. of Acad. of Sciences, Göttingen 1962-70; mem. Bureau IUPAC 1973-77; mem. Leopoldina German Acad. for Scientific Research, Halle, Austrian Acad. of Sciences, New York Acad. of Sciences, American Asscn. for the Advancement of Science; Pres. German Chemical Soc. 1976-77; Dr. Ing. e.h., Dr. rer. nat. h.c., Dr. h.c.; Liebig Medal of German Chemical Soc. 1970; Silver Medal of Univ. of Helsinki 1972; Medal of Jozef Stefan Inst., Ljubljana, Henri Moissan Medal of Société Française de Chimie. *Leisure interests:* archaeology, literature, skiing, swimming. *Address:* Tammannstrasse 4, 34 Göttingen (Office); Richard-Zsigmondy Weg 10, 34 Göttingen, Federal Republic of Germany (Home). *Telephone:* 0551-393067 (Office); 0551-57814 (Home).

GLEN, Sir Alexander Richard, K.B.E., D.S.C.; British business executive; b. 18 April 1912; s. of the late R. Bartlett Glen; m. Baroness Zora de Collaert 1947; ed. Fettes Coll., and Balliol Coll., Oxford; Organizer and Leader, Oxford Univ. Arctic Expedition 1933, 1935-36; Banking, New York and London 1936-39; R.N.V.R. 1939-59; Chair. H. Clarkson & Co. Ltd. 1962-72; Deputy Chair. Export Council for Europe 1960-64, Chair. 1964-66; mem. Council Royal Geographical Soc. 1945-47, 1954-57, 1961-62; mem. Council, Mount Everest Foundation 1955-57; Chair. British Tourist Authority 1969-77; Group Chair. Anglo World Travel 1978-81; Deputy Chair. British Transport Hotels 1978-83; Dir. Gleneagles Hotels 1980-83; mem. Historic Bldgs. Council for England 1976-80, Horse-race Totalisator Bd. 1976-84, Advisory Council, Victoria and Albert Museum 1976-, Chair. 1978-84; Pres. BALPA 1982-; numerous medals and decorations. *Publications:* Young Men in the Arctic 1935, Under the Pole Star 1937, Footholds Against a Whirlwind (autobiog.) 1975. *Leisure interests:* travel, skiing, sailing. *Address:* The Dower House, Stanton, Broadway, Worcs., WR12 7NE, England.

GLEN, Robert, O.C., PH.D., F.R.S.C., F.A.I.C.; Canadian entomologist and research administrator; b. 20 June 1905, Paisley, Scotland; s. of James Allison Glen and Jeannie Blackwood Barr; m. Margaret Helen Cameron 1931; two s.; ed. Univs. of Saskatchewan and Minnesota; Jr. and Asst. Entomologist, Dominion Entomological Lab., Saskatoon, Sask. 1928-35, in charge wireworm investigations, Dominion Entomological Lab. 1935-45; Research Co-ordinator, Entomology Div., Canada Dept. of Agriculture, Ottawa 1945-50, Chief, Entomology Div. 1950-57; Assoc. Dir. Science Service, Canada Dept. of Agriculture 1957-59; Dir.-Gen. Research Branch, Canada Dept. of Agriculture 1959-62, Asst. Deputy Minister (Research) 1962-68; Sec. Commonwealth Scientific Cttee. 1968-72; Fellow, Entomological Soc. of Ontario, Entomological Soc. of Canada, Pres. 1957; Pres. E. Ontario Branch, Agricultural Inst. of Canada 1950-51, Entomological Soc. of America 1962; Caleb Dorr Fellowship, Univ. of Minn. 1931-32; Shevlin Fellowship, Univ. of Minn. 1932-33; mem. Science Council of Canada 1966-68; Foreign Assoc. N.A.S. (U.S.A.) 1967; Outstanding Achievement Award, Univ. of Minn. 1960; Hon. LL.D. (Univ. of Sask.) 1959, Hon. D.Sc. (Ottawa) 1960; Gold Medal Entomological Soc. of Canada 1964, Medal of Service Order of Canada 1967, etc.; Hon. mem. Canadian Seed Growers Asscn. 1968 (for life), Entomological Soc. of America 1972, of Canada 1975. *Publications include:* Elaterid larvae of the tribe Lepturoidini 1950, and reports on Canadian entomology and agricultural research. *Leisure interests:* sports, gardening, golf. *Address:* 4523 Juniper Place, Victoria, B.C., V8N 3KI, Canada. *Telephone:* 477-5924.

GLENAMARA, Baron (Life Peer), cr. 1977, of Glenridding in the county of Cumbria; **Edward Watson Short,** P.C., C.H.; British politician; b. 17 Dec. 1912; ed. Bede Coll., Durham; served Second World War and became Capt. in Durham Light Infantry; Headmaster, Princess Louise County Secondary School, Blyth, Northumberland 1947; Leader Labour Group, Newcastle City Council 1950; M.P. for Newcastle upon Tyne Central 1951-76; Opposition Whip (N. Area) 1955-62; Deputy Chief Opposition Whip 1962-64; Parl. Sec. to Treasury and Govt. Chief Whip 1964-66; Postmaster-Gen. 1966-68; Sec. of State for Educ. and Science 1968-70; Deputy Leader of Labour Party 1972-76; Lord Pres. of Council, Leader of House of Commons 1974-76; Chair. Cable and Wireless Co. 1976-80; mem. Council, World Wildlife Fund U.K.; Pres. Finchdale Abbey Training Coll. for the Disabled, Durham; Chancellor Newcastle upon Tyne Polytechnic. *Publications:* The Story of the Durham Light Infantry 1944, The Infantry Instructor 1946, Education in a Changing World 1971, Birth to Five 1974, I Knew My Place 1983, Whip to Wilson: The Crucial Years of Labour Government 1989. *Address:* House of Lords, London S.W.1; 21 Priory Gardens, Corbridge, Northumberland, England.

GLENDINNING, Hon. Victoria, M.A., F.R.S.L.; British author and journalist; b. 23 April 1937, Sheffield; d. of Baron Seebohm of Hertford and Lady Seebohm (née Hurst); m. 1st O. N. V. Glendinning 1959 (divorced 1981), four s.; m. 2nd Terence de Vere White 1981; ed. St. Mary's School, Wantage, Millfield School, Somerville Coll., Oxford and Univ. of Southampton; part-time teaching 1960-69; part-time psychiatric social work 1970-73; Editorial Asst. Times Literary Supplement 1974-78. *Publications:* A Suppressed Cry 1969, Elizabeth Bowen: portrait of a writer 1977, Edith Sitwell: a unicorn among lions 1981, Vita: a biography of V. Sackville-West 1983, Rebecca West: a life 1987; articles in newspapers and journals. *Leisure interest:* gardening. *Address:* c/o David Higham Associates, 5-8 Lower John Street, Golden Square, London, W1R 4HA, England.

GLENN, Sir Archibald (see Glenn, Sir Joseph Robert Archibald).

GLENN, Lt.-Col. John Herschel, Jr., D.F.C. (8 times) and Air Medal with 18 clusters; American politician, aviator and astronaut; b. 18 July 1921, Cambridge, Ohio; s. of John H. Glenn and Clare Sproat; m. Anna Margaret Castor 1943; one s. one d.; ed. Muskingum Coll., Univ. of Maryland; naval aviation cadet 1942; commissioned Marine Corps 1943; Marine Fighter Squadron 155 in Marshall Islands 1944 (59 combat missions); mem. Fighter Squadron 218 North China Patrol; Instructor Corpus Christi, Texas 1948-50; Marine Fighter Squadron Korea (63 missions); Fighter Design Branch, Navy Bureau of Aeronautics, Washington 1956; speed record Los Angeles—New York (3 hr. 23 min.) 1957; training for space flight 1960-61. completed 3 orbits of the earth in Spaceship Friendship VII, 20th Feb. 1962; resigned from U.S. Marine Corps 1965; Dir. Royal Crown Cola Co. 1965-74; Consultant to NASA; U.S. Senator from Ohio Jan. 1975-; NASA Distinguished Service Medal 1962; U.S. Nat. Space Hall of Fame Award 1969; Democrat. *Publication:* (co-author) We Seven 1962. *Address:* SH-503 Hart Senate Office Building, Washington, D.C. 20510, U.S.A.

GLENN, Sir (Joseph Robert) Archibald, Kt, O.B.E., B.C.E. F.I.E. (AUST.), F.I.CHEM.E.; Australian chemicals executive and engineer; b. 24 May 1911, Sale, Victoria; s. of Joseph Robert Glenn; m. Elizabeth M. M. Balderstone 1939; one s. three d.; ed. Scotch Coll., Melbourne, Melbourne and Harvard Univs.; Chief Engineer ICI Australia Ltd. 1947-49, Gen. Man. 1949-53, Man. Dir. 1953-73, Chair. 1963-73; Dir. ICI Ltd. 1970-75; Chair. Fibremakers Ltd. 1963-73; Dir. Bank of New South Wales (now called Westpac Banking Corpn.) 1967-84; Chair. IMI Australia Ltd. 1970-78, Collins Wales Pty. Ltd. 1973-84, Tioxide Australia Ltd. 1973-86, IC Insurance Australia Ltd. 1974-86; Dir. Alcoa Australia Ltd. 1973-86, Hill Samuel Australia Ltd. 1973-83, Westralian Sands Ltd. 1977-86, Newmont Pty. Ltd. (now called Newmont Australia Ltd.) 1976-88; Gov. Atlantic Inst. of Int. Affairs; Chair. Council, Scotch Coll. 1953-82, Ormond Coll. Council 1976-81, Pacific

Inst. Council 1976–; Chancellor, La Trobe Univ., Melbourne 1966–72; Hon. D.Univ. (La Trobe) 1981. *Leisure interests:* tennis, golf, farming. *Address:* 360 Collins Street, Melbourne 3000 (Office); 1A Woorigoleen Road, Toorak, Melbourne, Vic. 3142, Australia (Home). *Telephone:* 6657703 (Office); 03-241 6367 (Home).

GLENNAN, T. Keith, B.S.; American engineer and administrator; b. 8 Sept. 1905, Enderlin, N.D.; s. of late Richard Henry Glennan and Margaret Laing Pauline; m. Ruth Haslup Adams 1931; one s. three d.; ed. Eau Claire (Wis.) High School, Eau Claire State Teachers' Coll., and Yale Univ. Sheffield Scientific School; Western Electric Co. Ltd. 1928–30; Electrical Research Products Co. 1930–35; Paramount Pictures Inc. 1935–41; Studio Man. Samuel Goldwyn Studios 1941–42; Admin., later Dir. U.S. Navy Underwater Sound Lab. (Columbia Univ. Div. of War Research), New London, Conn. 1942–45; exec. with Ansco, Binghamton (New York) 1945–47; Pres. Case Inst. of Tech., Cleveland 1947–66; mem. Atomic Energy Comm. 1950–52; First Admin. NASA 1958–61; Pres. Assoc. Univ. Inc. 1965–68; Dir. Republic Steel Corpn., and other companies; U.S. Rep. (rank of Amb.) to IAEA 1970–73; Consultant, U.S. Dept. of State 1973–; Trustee Rand Corpn. 1963–73, Aerospace Corpn. 1969–70, 1974–77, Case Western Reserve Univ. 1971–78; Fellow, American Acad. of Arts and Sciences, Nat. Acad. of Eng.; Medal for Merit; Hon. LL.D. (Tulane, Miami, Western Reserve Univ., Columbia Univ.); Hon. D.Sc. (Oberlin Coll., Clarkson Coll. of Technology, John Carroll, Akron, Toledo, Muhlenberg Coll., Cleveland State); Hon. D.Eng. (Stevens Inst. of Tech., Case Inst. of Tech., Fenn Coll.); Hon. M.A. (Yale); Univ. Medal of Honor (Rice Univ.), NASA Distinguished Service Medal 1966, U.S. State Dept. Distinguished Honor Award 1973, Univ. Medal (Case Western Reserve Univ., Cleveland) 1980; Benjamin Franklin Fellow (Royal Soc. of Arts, London). *Leisure interests:* woodworking, public service, new towns. *Address:* 11400 Washington Plaza, W., Apartment 903, Reston, Va. 22090, U.S.A. *Telephone:* 703-471-4210.

GLESKE, Leonhard, DR.RER.POL.; German banker; b. 18 Sept. 1921; s. of Gustav Gleske and Lydia Gohl; m. Christa Reimann 1956; one s. three d.; fmr. mem. of the Bd. and mem. Central Bank Council, Deutsche Bundesbank; fmr. Dir. Bank for Int. Settlements; Dr. h.c. (Univ. of Münster) 1985; Hon. Prof. (Mannheim) 1986. *Address:* Wilhelm-Epstein-Strasse 14, D-6000 Frankfurt 50, Federal Republic of Germany.

GLIDEWELL, Rt. Hon. Sir Iain (Derek Laing), Kt., P.C., Q.C., **Lord Justice Glidewell;** British judge; b. 8 June 1924; s. of Charles Norman Glidewell and Nora Glidewell; m. Hilary Winant 1950; one s. two d.; ed. Bromsgrove School, Worcester Coll., Oxford; served R.A.F.V.R. 1942–46; called to Bar, Gray's Inn 1949, Bencher 1977; Q.C. 1969; a Recorder of the Crown Court 1976–80; a Judge of Appeal, Isle of Man 1979–80; a Judge of the High Court of Justice, Queen's Bench Div. 1980–85; Presiding Judge, N.E. Circuit 1982–85; a Lord Justice of Appeal 1985–; mem. Senate of Inns of Court and the Bar 1976–79, Supreme Court Rule Cttee. 1980–84; Chair. Judicial Studies Bd., Panels for Examination of Structure Plans: Worcs. 1974, W. Midlands 1975; conducted Heathrow Fourth Terminal Inquiry 1978. *Leisure interests:* beagling, walking, theatre. *Address:* Royal Courts of Justice, Strand, London, WC2A 2LL, England.

GLIGOROV, Kiro; Yugoslav politician; b. 3 May 1917, Štip; s. of Blagoje and Katarina Gligorov; m. Nada Gligorov; one s. two d.; ed. Faculty of Law, Univ. of Belgrade; mem. Presidium of Antifascist Assembly of People's Liberation of Macedonia, and Antifascist Council People's Liberation of Yugoslavia during Second World War; Deputy Sec.-Gen. to Govt. of Yugoslavia 1946–47; Asst. Minister of Finance 1947–52; Prof. of Econs. Belgrade Univ. 1948–49; Deputy Dir. Exec. Council for Gen. Econ. Affairs 1955–62; Fed. Sec. for Finance 1962–67; Vice-Pres. Fed. Exec. Council 1967–69; mem. League of Communists of Yugoslavia (mem. Exec. Bureau 1969–74); mem. Presidency, Socialist Fed. Repub. of Yugoslavia 1971–72; Pres. Parl. 1974–78; holder of many Yugoslav and foreign honours. *Publications:* many articles and studies in finance and economics. *Leisure interests:* tennis, hunting. *Address:* Bulevar Oktobarske revolucije 14, Belgrade, Yugoslavia. *Telephone:* 640-687.

GLISTRUP, Mogens; Danish lawyer and politician; b. 28 May 1926, Rønne; s. of Lektor Lars Glistrup; m. Lene Borup Svendsen 1950; one s. three d.; ed. Rønne, Copenhagen Univ.; training in American law Univ. of Calif., Berkeley 1951–52; teacher in income tax law Univ. of Copenhagen 1956–63; law practice 1950–81, own firm 1956–82; founded Progress Party 1972; mem. Parl. 1973–83, re-elected 1984, returned to prison Feb. 1984; on trial for alleged tax evasion and fraud since 1974, convicted June 1983 and sentenced to three years in gaol for infringing tax laws, released March 1985; mem. Parl. 1987–. *Publications:* Skatteret 1957, Income Tax—Enemy Number One of Society 1979, Glistrup on Glistrup Case 1983. *Leisure interests:* chess, bicycling, bridge, football. *Address:* c/o Progress Party, Folketinget, Christiansborg, 1218 Copenhagen K, Denmark.

GLITMAN, Maynard Wayne, M.A.; American diplomatist; b. 8 Dec. 1933, Chicago; s. of Ben and Reada (née Kutok Klass) Glitman; m. G. Christine Amundsen 1956; three s. two d.; ed. Univ. of Illinois, Fletcher School of Law and Diplomacy, Univ. of California; with U.S. army 1957; with Foreign Service Dept. of State 1956, 1966–67, Dir. Office of Int. Trade 1973–74, Deputy Asst. Sec. of State for Internal Trade policy 1974–76; economist 1956–59; Vice-Consul Bahamas 1959–61; Econ. Officer Embassy, Ottawa

1961–65; mem. Del. to UN Gen. Ass. 1967, Nat. Security Council Staff 1968; Political Officer, First Sec. Embassy in Paris 1968–73; Deputy Asst. Sec. of Defence for Europe and NATO 1976–77, Deputy Perm. Rep. to NATO 1977–81; Amb. and Deputy Chief U.S. Del. to Intermediate Nuclear Forces Negotiations, Arms Control and Disarmament Agency, Switzerland 1981–84; Amb. and U.S. Rep. Mutual and Balanced Forces Negotiation, Vienna 1985; Amb. and Chief U.S. Negotiator Intermediate Nuclear Forces Negotiation, Geneva 1985–88, Amb. to Belgium 1988–; Public Service Medal (U.S.A. Dept. of Defence) 1981. *Address:* 27 Boulevard du Regent, 1000 Brussels, Belgium; Fletcher Vt., General Delivery, Jeffersonville, Vt. 05464, U.S.A. (Home).

GLOBUS, Yoram; Israeli film producer; b. 7 Sept. 1943; f. Noah Films with Menahem Golan (q.v.) 1963; bought Cannon Films (U.S.A.) with Menahem Golan 1979 and has since produced over 100 motion pictures, including Over the Top, Barfly, Shy People, Dancers, Missing in Action I, II & III, Death Wish IV, The Assault (winner of 1986 Acad. Award for Best Foreign Language Film), Surrender, Runaway Train, Hanna's War, Masters of the Universe, King Lear; now Head Cannon Entertainments. *Address:* The Cannon Group, Inc., 640 San Vicente Boulevard, Los Angeles, Calif. 90048, U.S.A.

GLOCK, Sir William Frederick, Kt., C.B.E.; British musician; b. 3 May 1908, London; s. of William G. Glock and Gertrude Maltby; m. Anne Geoffroy-Dechaume 1952; ed. Christ's Hospital, West Horsham, Gonville and Caius Coll., Cambridge and under Artur Schnabel, Berlin; Music critic, Daily Telegraph 1934, The Observer 1934–45, New Statesman 1958–59; served with R.A.F. 1941–46; Dir. Summer School of Music, Bryanston 1948–52, Dartington Hall, Devon 1953–79; Founder and Ed. The Score 1949–61; Chair. British Section, Int. Soc. of Contemporary Music 1954–58; Controller of Music, BBC 1959–72; mem. Bd. of Dirs. Royal Opera House, Covent Garden 1968–73; Artistic Dir. Bath Festival 1975–84; Chair. London Orchestral Concert Bd. 1975–86; mem. South Bank Bd. 1986–; Ed. Eulenburg books on music 1974–; Hon. mem. Royal Philharmonic Soc. 1971; mem. Arts Council of G.B. 1972–75; Hon. D.Univ. (York); Hon. D.Mus (Nottingham); Hon. Fellowship Royal Northern Coll. of Music 1981, Hon. D.Litt. (Bath); Gold Medal of R.S.A. 1971. *Address:* Vine House, Brightwell-cum-Sotwell, Wallingford, Oxon., England. *Telephone:* 0491-37144.

GLOSSOP, Peter; British opera singer (baritone); b. 6 July 1928, Sheffield; s. of Cyril Glossop and Violet Elizabeth Wright; m. Joyce Blackham 1955 (divorced 1976); m. 2nd Michele Yvonne Amos 1977 (divorced 1987), two d.; ed. High Storrs Grammar School, Sheffield; joined Sadler's Wells Opera 1952; with Covent Garden Opera Co. 1962–66; freelance singer 1966–; First Prize Bulgarian First Competition for Young Opera Singers 1961; debut at La Scala, Milan as Rigoletto 1965; Hon. D.Mus. (Sheffield) 1970; *films:* Pagliacci, Otello. *Leisure interest:* golf. *Address:* End Cottage, 7 Gate Close, Hawkchurch, Near Axminster, Devon, England. *Telephone:* Hawkchurch 266.

GLOUCESTER, H.R.H. The Duke of; Prince Richard Alexander Walter George, G.C.V.O., the Earl of Ulster and the Baron Culloden; b. 26 Aug. 1944; s. of the late Duke of Gloucester (third s. of H.M. King George V) and The Lady Alice Montagu-Douglas-Scott (d. of the 7th Duke of Buccleuch); m. Birgitte van Deurs 1972; one s. (Alexander, Earl of Ulster) two d. (Lady Davina Windsor and Lady Rose Windsor); ed. Wellesley House, Broadstairs, Eton Coll. and Magdalene Coll., Cambridge; Corporate mem. R.I.B.A. 1972; Commdr.-in-Chief St. John Ambulance Brigade 1972–74; Col.-in-Chief Gloucestershire Regt. 1974–, Royal Pioneer Corps 1977–; Hon. Col. Royal Monmouthshire Royal Engineers (Militia) 1977–; Grand Prior Order of St. John 1975–; Royal Trustee, British Museum 1973–; Pres. Inst. of Advanced Motorists 1971, Cancer Research Campaign 1973, Nat. Asscn. of Boys' Clubs 1974, Christ's Hosp. 1975, St. Bartholomew's Hosp. 1975, Royal Smithfield 1975, British Consultants Bureau 1978; Patron of Heritage of London Trust 1982; Deputy Chair. Historic Buildings and Monuments Comm. for England 1983; Sr. Fellow Royal Coll. of Art 1984; as Rep. of H.M. The Queen visited Australia 1963, wedding of Crown Prince of Nepal 1963, seventieth birthday celebrations of King Olav V of Norway 1973, Mexico 1973, Nepal 1975, Saudi Arabia and the Philippines 1975, independence celebrations of Seychelles 1976 and of Solomon Islands 1978, Australia and Holland 1979, independence celebrations of Vanuatu 1980, Philippines, Indonesia and Burma 1981, India, Cyprus and Belgium 1982, France, Repub. of Korea, Canada, Jordan and U.A.E. 1983, U.S.A., Thailand, Brunei, Bahrain, Kuwait and Qatar 1984, New Zealand, Canary Islands, Egypt, Algeria and Tunis 1985, U.S.S.R., Fed. Repub. of Germany, Berlin, Italy 1986; K.St.J. *Publications:* On Public View, The Face of London, Oxford and Cambridge. *Address:* Kensington Palace, London, W.8 and Barnwell Manor, Peterborough, PE8 5PJ, England.

GLOVER, Gen. Sir James (Malcolm), K.C.B., M.B.E.; British fmr. army officer and business executive; b. 25 March 1929; s. of Maj.-Gen. Malcolm Glover; m. Janet Diones De Pree 1958; one s. one d.; ed. Wellington Coll., R.M.A., Sandhurst; commissioned R.A. 1949; Royal Horse Artillery 1950–54; Instructor, R.M.A., Sandhurst 1955–56; transferred to Rifle Brigade 1956; Brigade Maj., 48 Gurkha Brigade 1960–62; Directing Staff, Staff Coll. 1966–68; C.O., 3rd Bn. Royal Green Jackets 1970–71; Col. Gen. Staff, Ministry of Defence 1972–73; Commdr. 19 Airportable Brigade 1974–75;

Brig. Gen. Staff (Intelligence), Ministry of Defence 1977–78; Commdr. Land Forces Northern Ireland 1979–80; Deputy Chief of Defence Staff (Intelligence) 1981–83; Vice-Chief of Gen. Staff, and mem. Army Bd. 1983–85; C.-in-C., U.K. Land Forces 1985–87; has served in Fed. Repub. of Germany, Malaya, Singapore, Hong Kong, Cyprus and Northern Ireland; Dir. British Petroleum PLC; Chair. Delta Data Services Ltd.; Dir. British Petroleum PLC, United Airships Ltd. *Leisure interests:* travel, gardening, shooting, mountain walking. *Address:* c/o Lloyds Bank, Cox's & King's Branch, 6 Pall Mall, London, SW1Y 5NH, England.

GLOVER, Jane Alison, M.A., D.PHIL.; British conductor; b. 13 May 1949; d. of Robert Finlay Glover; ed. Monmouth School for Girls and St. Hugh's Coll., Oxford; Jr. Research Fellow St. Hugh's Coll. 1973–75, Lecturer in Music 1976–84, Sr. Research Fellow 1982–; Lecturer St. Anne's Coll., Oxford 1976–80, Pembroke Coll. 1979–84; mem. Oxford Univ. Faculty of Music 1979–; professional conducting debut at Wexford Festival 1975; operas and concerts for BBC, Glyndebourne, Teatro la Fenice, Venice, London Symphony Orchestra, London Philharmonic Orchestra, Royal Philharmonic Orchestra, Philharmonia English Chamber Orchestra, BBC Welsh Symphony Orchestra, Bournemouth Sinfonietta, etc.; Musical Dir. London Choral Soc. 1983–; Artistic Dir. London Mozart Players 1984–; Prin. Conductor Huddersfield Choral Soc. 1989–; mem. BBC Cen. Music Advisory Cttee. 1981–85, Music Advisory Cttee. Arts Council 1986–88; Gov. R.A.M. 1985–; Hon. D.Mus. (Exeter) 1986, Hon. D.Litt. (Loughborough) 1988; Hon. Dr. (Open Univ.) 1988. *TV:* documentaries and series, and presentation, especially Orchestra 1983, Mozart 1985. *Publications:* Cavalli 1978; contribs. to The New Monteverdi Companion 1986, Monteverdi 'Orfeo' Handbook 1986; articles in numerous journals. *Leisure interests:* The Times crossword puzzle and theatre. *Address:* c/o Lies Askonas Ltd., 186 Drury Lane, London, WC2B 5RY, England. *Telephone:* 01-405 1808.

GŁÓWCZYK, Jan, D.ECON.SC.; Polish journalist and politician; b. 30 May 1927, Grzybów; ed. Jagellonian Univ., Cracow, and Inst. of Social Sciences of Cen. Cttee. of Polish United Workers' Party (PZPR), Warsaw; worked in Finance Dept. of Dist. Nat. Council, Nowy Sącz 1945–47; lecturer Higher School of Econs., Cracow 1951–52, Higher School of Social Sciences of PZPR Cen. Cttee., Warsaw 1957–62; Ed.-in-Chief, weekly Życie Gospodarcze 1957–82; Chair. Trade Union of Book, Press, Radio and TV Employees 1978–79; mem. Presidium Gen. Bd. Polish Econ. Soc. 1971–; mem. Polish Journalists' Assen. 1960–82; mem. PZPR 1951–, mem. PZPR Cen. Cttee. 1981–88, alt. mem. Political Bureau of PZPR Cen. Cttee. 1981–86, mem. Political Bureau 1986–88, Chair. Social Policy Comm. of PZPR Cen. Cttee. 1981–86, Sec. PZPR Cen. Cttee. 1982–, Chair. Comm. for Propaganda of PZPR Cen. Cttee. 1986–88; Chair. Editorial Council of daily Trybuna Ludu 1986–; Chair. Council of Workers' Publishing Cooperative Prasa-Książka-Ruch 1982–88; Commdr.'s Cross of Order of Polonia Restituta and other decorations. *Address:* Komitet Centralny PZPR, ul. Nowy Świat 6, 00-497 Warsaw, Poland.

GLUSHENKO, Yevgeniya Konstatinovna; Soviet film actress; b. 4 Sept. 1952; ed. Shchepkin Theatre School; worked with Maly Theatre 1974–. *Films include:* Unfinished Play for Mechanical Piano 1977, Profile and Front-View 1979, Oblomov 1980, First-Time Married 1980, In Love of One's Own Accord 1982 (Moscow and West Berlin Film Festival Prizes 1983). *Address:* c/o Maly Teatr, Moscow, U.S.S.R.

GLYNN, Ian Michael, M.D., PH.D., F.R.C.P., F.R.S.; British professor of physiology; b. 3 June 1928, London; s. of Hyman and Charlotte Glynn; m. Jenifer Muriel Franklin 1958; one s. two d.; ed. City of London School, Trinity Coll. Cambridge, Univ. Coll. Hosp. London; House Physician Cen. Middlesex Hosp. 1952–53; Nat. Service R.A.F. Medical Branch 1956–57; MRC Scholar Physiological Lab. Cambridge 1956, Fellow Trinity Coll. 1955–, demonstrator in Physiology 1958–63, Lecturer 1963–70, Reader 1970–75, Prof. of Membrane Physiology 1975–86, Prof. of Physiology 1986–, Vice-Master Trinity Coll. 1980–86; Visiting Prof. Yale Univ. 1969; mem. British MRC 1976–80, Council of Royal Soc. 1979–81, Agric. Research Council 1981–86; Chair. Editorial Bd. Journal of Physiology 1968–70; Hon. mem. American Acad. of Arts and Sciences 1984, Hon. M.D. (Univ. of Aarhus) 1988. *Publications:* The Sodium Pump (with J. C. Ellory) 1985 and papers in scientific journals. *Address:* Physiological Laboratory, Downing Street, Cambridge, CB2 3EG (Office); Daylesford, Conduit Head Road, Cambridge, England (Home). *Telephone:* 0223-333869 (Office).

GNATT, Poul Rudolph; New Zealand (b. Danish) dancer, choreographer and producer; b. 24 March 1923, Vienna, Austria; s. of late Kai Gnatt and Kaja (née Olsen); m. Rigmor Strøyberg 1951; four s.; ed. Royal Danish Ballet School; joined Royal Danish Ballet School 1929, Principal Dancer 1949; Principal Dancer, Ballettes des Champs Elysées 1946–49; Metropolitan Ballet 1947–49, Ballet Russe 1950–51, Borovansky Ballet 1951–53; Founder and Artistic Dir. New Zealand Ballet 1953–63, 1969–71; guest performances and short return to Royal Danish Ballet 1963–64; Resident teacher, Australian Ballet School and Producer/Ballet-master. The Australian Ballet 1964; Founder of Dance Theatre, Philippines, Manila 1968; Guest Producer, N.Z. Ballet Co. 15 year birthday season, Basel 1975, N.Z. Ballet 1977, Scottish Ballet July-Aug 1978 (producing Napoli by August Bournonville); staged La Sylphide in Munich 1979, Divertissement by August Bournonville at Budapest State Opera Ballet 1979, Napoli at Oslo 1980, Le Conservatoire at Australian Ballet, La Sylphide at Ballet Metropolitan, Ohio, Act III of Napoli at New Zealand Ballet; La Sylphide and La Ventana at State Ballet, Warsaw 1984, Napoli (jt. production with Kirsten Ralov), Finnish Nat. Ballet 1986; Stage Dir. Norwegian Opera and Ballet 1971–; Companion of the Queen's Service Order 1983. *Leisure interests:* tennis, handicraft, opera. *Address:* Niels Julesgate 40, Oslo 2, Norway. *Telephone:* 44-67-10.

GNEUSS, Helmut Walter Georg, DR. PHIL.; German professor of English; b. 29 Oct. 1927, Berlin; s. of Kurt Gneuss and Margarete (née Grimm) Gneuss; m. Mechthild Gretsch 1974; ed. Freie Universität Berlin, St. John's Coll., Cambridge; lecturer German Dept., Durham Univ. 1955–56, Dept. of English, Freie Univ. Berlin 1956–62, Heidelberg Univ. 1962–65; Prof., English Univ. of Munich 1965–; Visiting Professorial Fellow Emmanuel Coll., Cambridge 1970, Visiting Prof. Univ. of N.C., Chapel Hill 1974; mem. Bayerische Akademie der Wissenschaften; Vice-Pres. Henry Bradshaw Soc. *Publications:* Lehnbildungen und Lehnbedeutungen im Altenglischen 1955, Hymnar und Hymnen im englischen Mittelalter 1968, articles and reviews on Medieval English literature, history of English libraries, history of the liturgy. *Address:* Institut für Englische Philologie, Universität München, Schellingstrasse 3, D-8000 München 40, Federal Republic of Germany. *Telephone:* 89-2180-2369.

GOČÁR, Jiří, ING.; Czechoslovak architect; b. 12 June 1913, Prague; ed. Faculty of Civil and Structural Engineering, Czech Technical Univ.; own practice until 1948; Stavoprojekt, Prague 1944–54; Union of Architects affil. to Union of Czechoslovak Artists 1954–56; Union of Architects of Czechoslovakia 1956–59, Chair. 1959–69; Head of Architects' Atelier 1965; mem. Council for Reconstruction of Prague Castle 1959–68; Deputy Chair. Fed. Cttee. for Tech. Devt. and Investment 1969–70; architect with Investis 1970–; Chair. Union of Czech Architects 1969–70; mem. Exec. Cttee. Union Int. des Architectes, Chair. Czechoslovak Section 1967; Chair. Coordination Cttee., Federal Ministry for Tech. Devt. and Investment, for Housing Environment 1972; work on housing, public and industrial buildings; mem. Cen. Cttee. CP of Czechoslovakia 1966–70; Order of Labour 1963. *Address:* Investis, Prague 1, Břehová 1, Czechoslovakia.

GODARD, Jean-Luc; French film director; b. 3 Dec. 1930, Paris; s. of Paul Godard and Odile Monad; m. 1st Anna Karina 1961 (divorced); m. 2nd Anne Wiazemsky 1967; ed. Lycée Buffon and Faculté des lettres, Paris; journalist and film critic; film director 1958–; Prix Jean Vigo for A bout de souffle 1960, Jury's Special Prize and Prix Pasinetti, Venice Festival 1962, Diploma of Merit, Edinburgh Film Festival 1968 for Weekend, Grand Prix National 1982; Chevalier, Ordre nat. du Mérite. *Films:* Opération Béton 1954, Une femme coquette 1955, Tous les garçons s'appellent Patrick 1957, Charlotte et son Jules 1958, Une histoire d'eau 1958, A bout de souffle 1959, Le petit soldat 1960, Une femme est une femme 1961, Les sept péchés capitaux 1961, Vivre sa vie 1962, RoGoPaG 1962, Les carabiniers 1963, Le mépris 1963, Les plus belles escroqueries du monde 1963, Paris vu par ... 1963, Bande à part 1964, Une femme mariée 1964, Alphaville 1965, Pierrot le fou 1965, Masculin-féminin 1966, Made in U.S.A. 1966, Deux ou trois choses que je sais d'elle 1966, La chinoise 1967, Loin du Vietnam 1967, Weekend 1967, Le plus vieux métier du monde 1967, Vangelo '70 1967, Le gai savoir (TV) 1968, Un film comme les autres 1968, One Plus One 1968, One American Movie-1 a.m. 1969, British Sounds 1969, Le vent d'est 1969, Lotte in Italia 1970, Vladimir et Rosa 1971, Tout va bien 1972, Numéro deux 1975, Ici et ailleurs 1976, Bugsy 1979, Sauve qui peut 1980, Passion 1982, Prénom Carmen 1983, Detective 1984, Je vous salue, Marie 1985, King Lear 1987, Soigne ta droite 1987, Aria (segment) 1987. *Publication:* Introduction à une véritable histoire du cinéma 1980. *Address:* c/o Directors Guild, 7950 Sunset Blvd., Hollywood, Calif. 90046, U.S.A.; 15 rue du Nord, 1180 Rouille, Switzerland.

GODDARD, Leonard, M.A., B.PHIL., F.A.H.A.; British professor of philosophy; b. 13 Feb. 1925, Nottingham; s. of Bertram Goddard and Frances Goddard; m. Phyllis Dunsdon 1945 (divorced 1981); m. 2nd Patricia Johnson 1988; two d.; ed. Univ. of St. Andrews, Univ. of Cambridge; R.A.F. 1943–47; Asst. Lecturer, Univ. of St. Andrews 1952–55; lecturer and then Sr. Lecturer Univ. of New England, Australia 1956–61, Prof. of Philosophy, Univ. of New England 1961–66, Dean of Arts 1964–66; Prof. of Logic and Metaphysics, Univ. of St. Andrews 1966–77, Dean of Arts 1972–74; Boyce Gibson Prof. of Philosophy, Univ. of Melbourne 1977–; Visiting Fellow Australian Nat. Univ. 1974–76. *Publications:* (with R. Routley) The Logic of Significance and Context, Vol. 1 1973, Philosophical Problems 1977, (with B. Judge) The Metaphysics of Wittgenstein's Tractatus 1982. *Leisure interests:* golf, boating. *Address:* Department of Philosophy, University of Melbourne, Parkville, Vic., Australia 3052. *Telephone:* 03-344 5142.

GODDARD, Samuel Pearson, LL.B.; American lawyer and politician; b. 8 Aug. 1919, Clayton, Missouri; s. of Samuel Pearson Goddard Sr. and Florence Goddard; m. Julia Hatch Goddard 1944; three s.; ed. Harvard Coll., and Univ. of Arizona Law School; U.S. Army Air Corps 1941–46; law firm, Goddard and Ahearn; Chair. Tucson United Community Campaign 1959, Pres. 1960–62; Pres. Western Conf. of Community Chests, United Funds and Councils 1961–63; mem. Nat. Bd. Dirs. United Community Funds and Councils of America 1963–69, Exec. Cttee. 1966–69, Vice-Pres. 1968–69; Chair. Democratic Party of Ariz. 1960–62, 1978–; Gov. of Arizona 1965–67; Democratic Nat. Ctteeman. 1972–78; mem. White

House Conf. Cttee., Children and Youth 1959, Phoenix Symphony Bd. 1968-78, Bd. of Govs., United Way of America 1972-78; Chair. Warwick Land Co. 1974-; Chair. Task Force "Making People a Part of the System" 1971, UWA Nat. Acad. for Volunteerism 1973-75; officer of numerous business, civic and academic orgs. *Address:* 4724 East Camelback Canyon Drive, Phoenix, Ariz. 85018, U.S.A.

GODDEN, Rumer (Mrs. Margaret Rumer Haynes Dixon); British author; b. 10 Dec. 1907; d. of Arthur L. Godden and Katherine N. Hingley; m. 1st Laurence S. Foster 1934, 2nd James L. Haynes-Dixon 1949; two d.; ed. privately; *Publications:* Chinese Puzzle 1935, The Lady and the Unicorn 1937, Black Narcissus 1939, Breakfast with the Nikolides 1941, Fugue in Time 1944, The River 1946, A Candle for St. Jude 1948, Kingfishers Catch Fire 1952, An Episode of Sparrows 1955, The Greengage Summer 1959, China Court 1961, The Battle of the Villa Fiorita 1963, In This House of Brede 1969; trans. Prayers from the Ark 1962; Two Under the Indian Sun (autobiography) 1965, Swans and Turtles 1968, The Raphael Bible 1970, Shiva's Pigeons (with Jon Godden) 1972, The Peacock Spring 1975, Five for Sorrow, Ten for Joy 1979, Gulbadan 1980, The Dark Horse 1981, Thursday's Children 1984, A Time To Dance: No Time To Weep (memoirs) 1987, The Story of Holly and Ivy 1987, A House With Four Rooms, Memoirs, Vol. II; poems, children's books, films. *Leisure interests:* family, travel, ballet, Pekinese dogs. *Address:* Ardnacloich, Moniaive, Thornhill, Dumfriesshire DG3 4H2, Scotland.

GODEAUX, Jean, D. EN D.; Belgian banker; b. 3 July 1922, Jemeppe sur Meuse; s. of Léon Godeaux and Claire de Barsy; m. Thérèse Ceron 1950; two s. three d.; ed. Univ. Catholique de Louvain; Bar of Namur 1944-47; Asst., Inst. for Econ. and Social Research 1947; Nat. Bank of Belgium 1947-49; Technical Asst., IMF 1949-50, Alt. Exec. Dir. 1950-54, Exec. Dir. 1954; Man. Banque Lambert 1955-59, Man. Partner 1960-72, Pres. 1973-74; Pres. Banking Comm. 1974-82; Gov. Nat. Bank of Belgium March 1982-; Pres. and Chair. BIS 1985-87; Grand officier de l'Ordre de Léopold; Officier, Légion d'honneur; Commdr., Ordre de St. Grégoire le grand; Grand Croix, ordre du mérite (Luxembourg), (Austria). *Leisure interests:* skiing, tennis. *Address:* c/o National Bank of Belgium, boulevard de Berlaimont 5, 1000 Brussels (Office); rue de la Loi 235, Boite 3, 1040 Brussels, Belgium (Home). *Telephone:* 02.219.4600 (Office); 02.231.0764 (Home).

GODET, Maurice R., D. ÈS SC.; French professor of mechanics; b. 22 Jan. 1930, Geneva, Switzerland; s. of Romain Godet and Silvia Godet; two d.; ed. New York Univ., Yale Univ. and Univ. of Paris; Lab. Asst. Yale Univ. 1951-57, Research Engineer Medical School 1957-58; Research Engineer Div. C. Shell, Calif. 1958-62; Asst. Prof. of Mechanics, Inst. Nat. des Sciences Appliqués de Lyon 1962-67, Prof. 1968-; Chevalier, Ordre du Mérite, Officier, Palmes académiques; Lauréat Willemberg Foundation 1986, Tribology Gold Medal 1988. *Publications:* over 150 papers on tribology. *Leisure interest:* music. *Address:* Laboratoire de Mécanique des Contacts, Institut National des Sciences Appliqués de Lyon, 69621 Villeurbanne; Le Farou, 20 avenue Gambetta, 69450 St. Cyr au Mont d'Or, France (Home).

GODLEY, Georgina, M.A.; British fashion designer; b. 11 April 1955, London; d. of Michael Godley and Heather Godley; m. Sebastian Conran 1988; no c.; ed. Putney High School, Thames Valley Grammar School, London, Wimbledon School of Art, Brighton Polytechnic and Chelsea School of Art; designer, Browns, London and Paris 1979-80; partner and designer, Croalla, London 1980-85; Dir. and sole designer Georgina Godley Ltd. (produces own label collections) 1986-; mem. British Fashion Council Designer Cttee.; Visiting lecturer at various fashion and art colls. in London and elsewhere in U.K.; work included in perm. exhbn. at Victoria & Albert Museum, London and Bath Costume Museum; ICA Young Contemporaries award 1978. *Address:* Georgina Godley London Ltd., 19A All Saints Road, London, W11 1HE, England.

GODREJ, Adi Burjor, M.S.; Indian business executive; b. 3 April 1942; s. of Dr Burjor Pirojsha Godrej and Jai Burjor Godrej; m. Parmeshwar Mader 1966; one s. two d.; ed. St. Xavier's High School & Coll., Bombay and Massachusetts Inst. of Technology; Pres. North Bombay Jaycees 1968; Pres. Indian Soap & Toiletries Makers' Asscn. 1974-77, Indian Vegetable Oil Export Asscn. 1976-80, Cen. Org. for Oil Industry & Trade 1981-83, Solvent Extractors Asscn. of India 1983-85; Chair. Compound Livestock Feeds Mfrs. Asscn. of India 1975-77, Devt. Council for Oils, Soaps & Detergents 1976-78, 1985-, Oils & Seeds Importers Asscn. 1978-80, Noble Soya House Ltd. 1986-; Dir. numerous cos. *Leisure interests:* sailing and motor boating, water-skiing, horse riding, squash, bridge, reading. *Address:* Godrej Soaps Pvt. Ltd., Eastern Express Highway, Vikhroli, Bombay 400079 (Office); Plot No. 2, Military Road, Juna, Bombay 400049, India (Home). *Telephone:* 582177/584461 (Office); 6200489/6200795 (Home).

GODWIN, Fay S.; British photographer; b. 17 Feb. 1931, Berlin, Germany; d. of British father and American mother; two. s.; ed. many schools all over the world; had no photographic training; started photographing her young children 1966; touring exhbns. relating to publ. of The Oldest Road 1975; commissioned by Nat. Trust to photograph the Trust's historic properties and sites in Wessex 1982; British Council's overseas tour of Fay Godwin's Landscape Photographs started 1984; major retrospective landscape exhbn., Serpentine Gallery, London 1985; Land exhbn. at Yale Center for British Art, U.S.A.; teaches at photographic schools and workshops; major award from Arts Council of G.B. to continue landscape work in British Isles 1978; Bradford Fellowship 1986/87; Fellow Nat. Museum of Photography, Bradford 1987; Pres. Ramblers Asscn. 1987-(90). *Publications:* The Oldest Road: An Exploration of the Ridgeway (with J. R. L. Anderson) 1975, The Oil Rush (with Mervyn Jones) 1976, The Drovers' Roads of Wales (with Shirley Toulson) 1977, Islands (with John Fowles) 1978, Remains of Elmet: A Pennine Sequence (with poems by Ted Hughes) 1979, Romney Marsh and the Royal Military Canal (with Richard Ingrams) 1980, Tess: The Story of a Guide Dog (with Peter Purves) 1981, The Whisky Roads of Scotland (with Derek Cooper) 1982, Bison at Chalk Farm 1982, The Saxon Shore Way from Gravesend to Rye (with Alan Sillitoe) 1983, The National Trust Book of Wessex 1985, Land (with an essay by John Fowles) 1985, The Secret Forest of Dean 1986. *Leisure interests:* walking, photography and reading. *Address:* c/o Anthony Sheil Associates, 43 Doughty Street, London, WC1N 2LF, England. *Telephone:* 01-405 9351.

GOEBEL, Walther F., PH.D.; American professor of biochemistry; b. 24 Dec. 1899, Palo Alto, Calif.; s. of Julius Goebel and Kathryn Vreeland; m. 1st Cornelia Van Rensselear Robb 1930 (deceased); m. 2nd Alice Lawrence Behn 1976; two d.; ed. Univs. of Illinois and Munich; Research Asst., Rockefeller Univ. (fmrly. Rockefeller Inst.) 1924-27, Research Assoc. 1927-34, Assoc. mem. 1934-44, mem. 1944-57, Prof. of Biochemistry 1957-70, Prof. Emer. 1970-; mem. N.A.S.; Hon. D.Sc. (Middlebury Coll., Vt., Rockefeller Univ.) 1978, (Connecticut Acad. of Science and Eng.) 1983; Avery-Landsteiner Award, Gesellschaft für Immunologie 1973. *Publications:* numerous scientific articles on biochemistry, microbiology and chemical immunology in Journal of American Chemical Soc., of Experimental Medicine, of Biochemistry and of General Physiology; Annales de Inst. Pasteur, Proceedings of N.A.S., etc. *Leisure interests:* music, photography, painting, reading, gourmet cooking. *Address:* 123 Essex Meadows, Essex, Conn. 06426, U.S.A. (Home). *Telephone:* (203) 767-2726 (Home).

GOEHR, Alexander, M.A.; British composer; b. 10 Aug. 1932, Berlin; s. of Walter Goehr; m. 1st Audrey Baker 1954, 2nd Anthea Felicity Staunton 1972, 3rd Amira Katz; one s. three d.; ed. Berkhamstead School, Royal Manchester Coll. of Music, Paris Conservatoire (with Oliver Messiaen), and privately with Yvonne Loriod; composer, teacher, conductor 1956-; held classes at Morley Coll., London; part-time post with BBC, being responsible for production of orchestral concerts 1960-; works performed and broadcast worldwide; Hon. Fellow Royal Manchester Coll. of Music; awarded Churchill Fellowship 1968; Composer-in-Residence, New England Conservatory, Boston, Mass. 1968-69; Assoc. Prof. of Music, Yale Univ. 1969-70; Prof. West Riding Chair of Music Univ. of Leeds 1971-76; Prof. of Music, Univ. of Cambridge, Fellow of Trinity Hall, Cambridge 1976-; Ruth Lecturer 1987; Hon. D.Mus. (Southampton) 1973, Hon. A.R.C.M. 1976, Hon. F.R.N.C.M. 1980, Hon. F.R.C.M. 1981. *Works include:* Songs of Babel 1951, Sonata 1952, Fantasias 1954, String Quartet 1956-57, Capriccio 1957, The Deluge 1957-58, La belle dame sans merci 1958, Variations 1959, Four Songs from the Japanese 1959, Sutter's Gold 1959-60, Suite 1961, Hecuba's Lament 1959-61, A Little Cantata of Proverbs 1962, Concerto for Violin and Orchestra 1961-62, Two Choruses 1962, Virtutes 1963, Little Symphony 1963, Little Music for Strings 1963, Five Poems and an Epigram of William Blake 1964, Three Pieces for Piano 1964, Pastorals 1965, Piano Trio 1966, Arden muss sterben (Arden Must Die—opera) 1966, Quartet 1967, Romanza 1968, Naboth's Vineyard 1968, Symphony in One Movement, Opus 29 1970, Shadowplay-2 1970, Sonata about Jerusalem 1970, Concerto for eleven instruments 1970, Piano Concerto 1972, Chaconne for wind 1974, Lyric Pieces 1974, Metamorphosis/Dance 1974, String Quartet No. 3 1976, Psalm IV 1976, Fugue on the notes of the Fourth Psalm 1976, Romanza on the notes of the Fourth Psalm 1977, Fugue for Three Clarinets 1978, Das Gesetz der Quadrille 1979, Babylon the Great is Fallen 1979, Sinfonia 1980, Cello Sonata 1984, Behold the Sun 1984, Symphony with Chaconne 1986. *Address:* Faculty of Music, 11 West Road, Cambridge; c/o Schott and Co. Ltd., 48 Great Marlborough Street, London, W.1, England. *Telephone:* Cambridge 61661.

GOENKA, Harsh Vardhan, M.B.A.; Indian industrialist; b. 10 Dec. 1957, Calcutta; s. of Rama Prasad Goenka and Sushila Goenka; m. Mala (née Sanghi) 1977; one s. one d.; ed. St. Xavier's Coll., Calcutta, Int. Man. Inst., Geneva; joined family business, became Dir.-in-Charge Aryodaya Ginning Mills; Man. Dir. CEAT Tyres of India Ltd. 1982-; Dir. numerous cos. *Leisure interests:* sport, theatre. *Address:* CEAT Tyres of India Ltd., CEAT Mahal, 463 Dr. Annie Besant Road, Worli, Bombay 400 025, India. *Telephone:* 493 0621 (Office); 828 0872 (Home).

GOES, Albrecht; German writer; b. 22 March 1908; s. of Eberhard Goes and Elisabeth (née Panzerbieter); m. Elisabeth Schneiter 1933; three d.; ed. Tübingen Univ; Evangelical pastor, Württemberg 1930-52; writer 1953-; mem. Berliner Akad. für Künste, Deutsche Akad. für Sprache und Dichtung; Dr. h.c. Theology (Mainz) 1974; Lessing Prize, Hamburg 1953, Buber-Rosenzweig Medal 1978. *Publications:* Unruhige Nacht, Von Mensch zu Mensch 1949, Gedichte 1950, Das Brandopfer 1953, Freude am Gedicht 1954, Vertrauen in das Wort 1955, Ruf und Echo 1956, Genesis 1957, Hagar am Brunnen 1958, Rede auf Goethes Mutter 1958, Ravenna 1959, Aber im Winde das Wort 1963, Das Löffelchen 1965, Im Weitergehen

1966, Der Knecht macht keinen Lärm 1968, Die guten Gefährten 1969, Kanzelholz 1971, Tagwerk, Prosa und Verse 1976, Lichtschutten Du (poems) 1979. *Address:* 7000 Stuttgart-Rohr, Im Langen Hau 5, Federal Republic of Germany. *Telephone:* 749103.

GOETHE, (Wolf) Hartmut (Giselher), DR. MED.; German physician and scientific director; b. 16 Oct. 1923, Stargard/Pommern; s. of Johannes Goethe and Margarethe (née Grasshoff) Goethe; m. Hildegard Roehrs 1964; one s. three d.; ed. Univ. of Hamburg; medical asst. Tropical Hosp. Bernhard Nocht Inst. (BNI) 1949, Medical Asst., Dir. Medical Chem. Dept. BNI 1952–54; Port Dir. Port Health Authority 1954–55; Ship's Doctor, Fishery Research Vessel 1955–56; Co. Doctor, Esso Shipping Co., then Deputy Medical Dir. Esso AG 1956–64; Scientific Dir. Dept. of Nautical Medicine BNI 1965–. *Publications:* numerous research and scientific papers on ships' medicine and tropical diseases. *Leisure interests:* riding, gardening, writing. *Address:* Bernhard Nocht Institute of Tropical and Nautical Medicine, Zirkusweg 11, D-2000 Hamburg 4 (Office); Otternweg 12, D-2055 Aumuehle, German Federal Republic (Home). *Telephone:* 040-31 102 490 (Office); 04104-2505 (Home).

GOETZE, Roger; French business executive; b. 6 Dec. 1912, Paris; s. of Frédéric Goetze and Eugénie Dupraz; m. Marcelle Charpentier 1935; one s.; ed. Lycée Carnot and Faculté des Lettres et des Sciences de Paris; Insp. of Finances 1937; Dir.-Gen. of Finance, Algeria 1942–49; Dir. of Budget 1949–57; Pres. S.N. Repal 1946–66; Gov. Crédit Foncier de France S.A. 1957, Gov. 1967–77; Pres. CFEC 1978–83, Hon. Pres. 1984, and SACI 1978; mem. Comm. de la privatisation 1986–; Grand Officier, Légion d'honneur, Commdr. Ordre nat. du Mérite, Croix de Guerre, Commdr. du Mérite Saharien. *Address:* 96 ter rue de Longchamp, 92200 Neuilly-sur-Seine, France.

GOEUDEVERT, Daniel; French business executive; b. 31 Jan. 1942, Reims; one s. three d.; ed. Sorbonne, Paris; Sales Man. Citroen, Paris 1965–68; Sales Dir. Citroen, Geneva 1969–71, Gen. Man. 1971–74; mem. Bd., Citroen, Cologne 1974; Gen. Man. Renault 1975–78, Export Sales Dir. 1978–81; Gen. Man. Ford-Werke AG, Cologne 1981–. *Address:* Ottoplatz 2, D-5000 Cologne-21 (Deutz), Federal Republic of Germany.

GOFF, Philip Bruce, M.A., M.P.; New Zealand politician; b. 1953, Auckland; m. Mary Ellen Moriarty 1979; two s. one d.; ed. Papatoetoe High School; Lecturer in political science at Auckland Univ.; field officer in Insurance Workers' Union; fmr. Chair. Labour Youth Council; M.P. for Roskill 1981–; Minister of Housing, for the Environment, responsible for Government Life Insurance Corpn., responsible for State Insurance Office, in charge of the Public Trust Office 1984–87, of Employment, of Youth Affairs and Assoc. Minister of Educ. 1987–, of Tourism 1987–88; Labour. *Leisure interests:* jogging, hiking, gardening, squash. *Address:* House of Representatives, Wellington, New Zealand.

GOFF OF CHIEVELEY, Baron (Life Peer), cr. 1986, of Chieveley in the Royal County of Berkshire; **Robert (Lionel Archibald) Goff,** Kt., P.C., D.C.L., F.B.A.; **Rt. Hon. Lord Goff of Chieveley;** British lawyer; b. 12 Nov. 1926; s. of L. T. Goff; m. Sarah Cousins 1953; two s. (one deceased) two d.; ed. Eton Coll., New Coll., Oxford; served in Scots Guards 1945–48 (Commdr. 1945); called to the Bar, Inner Temple 1951; Bencher 1975; Q.C. 1967; Fellow and Tutor, Lincoln Coll., Oxford 1951–55; in practice at the Bar 1956–75; a Recorder 1974–75; Judge of the High Court, Queen's Bench Div. 1975–82; Judge in charge of Commercial List, and Chair. Commercial Court Cttee. 1979–81; Chair. Council of Legal Educ. 1976–82, Vice-Chair. 1972–76, Chair. Bd. of Studies 1970–76; Chair. Common Professional Examination Bd. 1976–78; Chair. British Inst. of Int. and Comparative Law 1986–, Court of Univ. of London 1986–, Sub-Cttee. E (Law) of House of Lords Select Cttee. on European Communities 1986–; Pres. Bentham Club 1986, Chartered Inst. of Arbitrators 1986–, Holdsworth Club 1988; Hon. Prof. of Legal Ethics, Univ. of Birmingham 1980–81; Maccabean Lecturer 1983; mem. Gen. Council of the Bar 1971–74; mem. Senate of Inns and Court and Bar 1974–82; Chair. Law Reform and Procedure Cttee. 1974–76; Lord Justice of Appeal 1982–86; Lord of Appeal in Ordinary 1986–; Hon. Fellow, Lincoln Coll., Oxford, New Coll., Oxford; Hon. D.Litt. (City) 1977. *Publications:* The Law of Restitution (with Prof. Gareth Jones) 1966. *Address:* House of Lords, Westminster, London, S.W.1, England.

GOGOBERIDZE, Lana Levanovna; Soviet film director; b. 13 Oct. 1928; ed. Tbilisi Univ. and VGIK (S. A. Gerasimov's Studio); mem. CPSU 1965–; Head of a Dir.'s Studio at Rustaveli Theatre School, Tbilisi 1975–; Peoples' Artist of Georgian S.S.R. 1979, Venice Film Festival Prize 1979, U.S.S.R State Prize 1980. *Films include:* Under the Same Sky 1961, I See the Sun 1965, Boundaries 1970, When the Almond Blossomed 1973, Interviews on Personal Problems 1979, A Day Longer than Night 1985, Turnover 1986. *Address:* c/o Teatralnoe uchilishche im Rustaveli, Tbilisi, Georgian S.S.R., U.S.S.R.

GOH CHOK TONG, M.A.; Singapore politician; b. 20 May 1941, Singapore; s. of Goh Kah Khoon (deceased) and Quah Kwee Hwa; m. Tan Choo Leng 1965; one s. one d.; ed. Raffles Inst., Univ. of Singapore and Williams Coll., U.S.A.; worked in Singapore Admin. Service 1964–69, Planning and Projects Man. Neptune Orient Lines (NOL) 1969–73, Man. Dir. 1973–77; fmr. Chair. Nat. Statistical Comm.; fmr. mem. Bd. Port of Singapore

Authority, Post Office Savings Bank, Sembawang Shipyard Ltd., Container Warehousing & Transportation (Pte.) Ltd.; Chair. Singapore Labour Foundation; mem. Parl. 1976–; Sr. Minister of State for Finance 1977–79; Minister for Trade and Industry 1979–81, Minister for Health and Second Minister for Defence 1981–82, for Defence and Second Minister for Health 1982–84; First Deputy Prime Minister and Minister of Defence Jan. 1985–. *Leisure interests:* tennis, golf. *Address:* Ministry of Defence, Tanglin, Singapore 1024.

GOH KENG SWEE, PH.D.; Singapore politician; b. 6 Oct. 1918, Malacca; s. of Goh Leng Inn and Tan Swee; m. Alice Woon 1942; one s.; ed. Anglo-Chinese School, Singapore, and Raffles Coll., London Univ; fmrly. Vice-Chair. People's Action Party; fmr. mem. Legis. Assembly from Kreta Ayer Div. and Minister for Finance 1959–65; initiated Singapore's industrialization plan, the establishment of Econ. Devt. Board; Minister of Defence 1965–67, of Finance 1967–70, of Educ. 1979–81, 1981–84, of Defence 1970–79, concurrently Deputy Prime Minister 1973–80, First Deputy Prime Minister 1980–84 and with responsibility for the Monetary Authority of Singapore 1980–81; Econ. Adviser to Chinese Govt. July 1985–; mem. Governing Council, Asian Inst. for Econ. Devt. and Planning, Bangkok 1963–66; Ramon Magsaysay Award for Govt. Service 1972. *Publications:* Urban Incomes and Housing; a Report on the Social Survey of Singapore, 1953–54 1958, Economics of Modernization and Other Essays 1972, The Practice of Economic Growth 1977. *Address:* c/o Ministry of Foreign Affairs, 2nd Floor, City Hall, St. Andrews Road, Singapore 0617.

GOHEEN, Robert Francis, PH.D.; American educator and public servant; b. 15 Aug. 1919, Vengurla, India; s. of Robert H. H. and Anne (Ewing) Goheen; m. Margaret M. Skelly 1941; two s. four d.; ed. Lawrenceville School and Princeton Univ.; Instructor, Princeton Univ. 1948–50, Asst. Prof. 1950–57, Prof. 1957–72, Pres. 1957–72, Pres. Emer. 1972–; Senior Fellow in Classics, American Acad. in Rome 1952–53; Dir. Nat. Woodrow Wilson Fellowship Programme 1953–56; Sr. Fellow Woodrow Wilson School 1981–; Dir. Mellon Fellowships in the Humanities 1982–; mem. Bd. Asia Soc., Bharatiya Vidya Bhavan (U.S.A.), Carnegie Endowment for Int. Peace, Inst. for Int. Educ., Fund for New Jersey, United Bd. for Christian Higher Educ. in Asia, Midlantic Banks Inc., Thomson Newspapers Inc.; mem. Int. Advisory Bd. Chemical Bank and Advisory Panel, Bureau of Oceans and Int. Scientific and Environmental Affairs, U.S. Dept. of State; Chair. Council on Foundations, Inc. 1972–77; Pres. Edna McConnell Clark Foundation 1977; Amb. to India 1977–80; fmr. Gov. Reza Shah Kabir Univ. (Iran); fmr. Regent, Smithsonian Inst.; fmr. Co-Chair. Indo-U.S. Sub-comm. on Educ. and Culture; fmr. Dir. Equitable Life Assurance Soc. of U.S., Dreyfus Third Century Fund; fmr. mem. Bd. American Acad. in Rome, Rockefeller Foundation, Carnegie Foundation for Advancement of Teaching; mem. Council on Foreign Relations, American Acad. of Arts and Sciences; Hon. LL.D., Litt.D., L.C.D., L.H.D., degrees from 26 univs. and cols. including Harvard, Yale, Madras, North Carolina, Notre Dame. *Publications:* The Imagery of Sophocles' Antigone, The Human Nature of a University. *Leisure interests:* golf, tennis, reading. *Address:* 1 Orchard Circle, Princeton, N.J. 08540, U.S.A.

GOIZUETA, Roberto, B.S.; American business executive; b. 18 Nov. 1931, Havana, Cuba; s. of Crispulo D. and Aida (née Cantera) Goizueta; m. Olga T. Casteleiro; two s. one d.; ed. Yale Univ.; went to U.S.A. 1961 having been processing engineer for Tropics Industrial Corpn., Havana 1953–60; asst. to Sr. Vice-Pres. Coca-Cola Export Corpn., Nassau, Bahamas 1960–64; asst. to Vice-Pres. on research and devt., Coca-Cola Co., Atlanta, Ga. 1964–66, Vice-Pres. Eng. 1966–74, Sr. Vice-Pres. 1974–75, Exec. Vice-Pres. 1975, Vice-Chair. 1979–80, Dir. 1980–, Pres. 1980–81, Chair. and C.E.O. 1981–; Dir. Trust Co. of Ga. and Trust Co. bank (Atlanta); trustee and mem. various bodies. *Leisure interest:* golf. *Address:* Office of the Chairman, The Coca-Cola Co., One Coca-Cola Plaza, N.W., Atlanta, Ga. 30313, U.S.A.

GOL, Jean, D.LL.; Belgian politician and barrister; b. 8 Feb. 1942, Hammersmith, England; s. of Stanislas Gol and Léa Karny; m. Rosita Winkler 1967; one d.; ed. Univ. of Liège; mem. Liège Bar 1964–; research scholarship, Fonds National de la Recherche Scientifique 1964–69; Sr. Asst., Dept. of Public Law, Univ. of Liège 1969–71, lecturer, Faculty of Philosophy and Literature 1974–; mem. Prov. Council of Liège 1968–71, Parl. 1971–, City Council of Liège 1977–; Deputy Minister, Ministry of Regional Economy for Wallonia 1974–77; Chair. Parti Réformateur Libéral (P.R.L.) 1979–81; Deputy Prime Minister, Minister of Justice and Institutional Reforms 1981–88; Officier de l'Ordre de Léopold, Grand Officier, Légion d'honneur. *Publications:* Le monde de la presse en Belgique 1970, Le redressement wallon 1977, L'optimisme de la volonté 1985. *Address:* rue Lebeau, 5, 4000 Liège, Belgium (Home). *Telephone:* 041/23 18 02 (Home).

GOLAN, Menahem; Israeli film director and producer; b. 31 May 1929, Tiberius; ed. Old Vic., London; f. Noah Films with Yoram Globus (q.v.) 1963; Sr. Vice-Pres. Cannon Group Inc. 1979–89; f. 21st Century Production Corpn. Feb. 1989–; *directed films:* Over the Top, Delta Force, Over the Brooklyn Bridge, Enter the Ninja, The Magician of Lublin; films include: Barfly, Surrender, Death Wish IV, Superman IV, Street Smart, Dancers, 52 Pickup, Otello, The Assault, Hanoi Hilton, Cannon Movie Tales, Masters of the Universe, Duet for One, Tough Guys Don't Dance, Shy People, Hanna's War; all have Golan and Globus as exec. producers.

GÖLCÜKLÜ, Ahmet Feyyaz; Turkish judge and academic; b. 4 Oct. 1926, Ula; s. of Zeki and Ruhiye Gölcüklü; m. (divorced 1975) two s.; ed. Univ. of Istanbul and Univ. of Neuchâtel; became Asst. Prof. at Faculty of Political Sciences Univ. of Ankara 1954, Assoc. Prof. 1958, Prof. 1965, Dir. School of Journalism and Broadcasting 1969 and 1972, Dean, Faculty of Political Sciences 1973-76, currently Prof. Faculty Political Sciences; Judge, European Court of Human Rights 1977-; mem. Turkish Consultative Assembly (Constituent Assembly) 1981-82; Chief of Dept. of Public Admin., Faculty of Political Sciences 1985. *Publications:* Examination of the Accused Person in Penal Matters 1952, Personal Liberty of the Accused in Criminal Procedure 1958, A Research on Juvenile Delinquency in Turkey 1963, Turkish Penal System 1965, Mass Communication Law 1973. *Address:* Pilot Sokak 8/4, Çankaya, Ankara, Turkey. *Telephone:* 393008.

GOLD, Jack, B.SC.(ECONS.), LL.B., F.R.S.A.; British film director; b. 28 June 1930; m. Denyse Macpherson 1957; two s. one d.; ed. London Univ.; Asst. Studio Man., BBC radio 1954-55; Ed. Film Dept., BBC 1955-60; Dir. TV and film documentaries and fiction 1960-. *TV films include:* Tonight, Death in the Morning (British Acad. of Film and TV Arts Award) 1964, Modern Millionairess, Famine, Dowager in Hot Pants, World of Coppa (Bafta Award 1967), Mad Jack (Grand Prix, Monte Carlo) 1971, The Resistable Rise of Arturo Ui, Stockers Copper (Bafta Award 1972), Catholics (Peabody Award) 1974, The Naked Civil Servant (Italia Prize, Int. Emmy and Critics Award) 1976, (Desmond Davies Award 1976), Thank You Comrades, A Walk in the Forest, Merchant of Venice, Praying Mantis, Macbeth, L'Elegance 1982, The Red Monarch 1983, The Tenth Man 1988. *Films include:* The Bofors Gun 1968, The National Health 1973, (Evening News Best Comedy Film 1973), Who? 1974, Aces High (Evening News Best Film Award) 1976, The Medusa Touch 1977, The Sailor's Return (Monte Carlo Catholic Award, Monte Carlo Critics Award) 1978, Little Lord Fauntleroy (Christopher Award) 1981, A Lot of Happiness (Int. Emmy Award) 1983, Sakharov 1984, (Ace Award), Me and the Girls 1985, Murrow (Ace Award) 1986, Escape from Sobibor 1987, (Golden Globe Award), Stones for Ibarra 1988; movie masterclass 1988. *Leisure interests:* music, reading. *Address:* 18 Avenue Road, London, N6 5DW, England.

GOLD, Phil, C.C., M.D., PH.D., F.R.C.P.(C.), F.R.S.C., F.A.C.P.; Canadian professor of medicine and physiology; b. 17 Sept. 1936, Montreal; m. Evelyn Katz; three c.; ed. McGill Univ.; postgraduate training and research, The McGill Univ. Medical Clinic of The Montreal Gen. Hosp.; Medical Research Council of Canada Centennial Fellow 1967-68, Assoc. and Career Scientist 1969-80; Lecturer, Teaching Fellow, Asst. and Assoc. Prof., Dept. of Physiology and Dept. of Medicine, McGill Univ. 1965-73, Prof. of Medicine and Clinical Medicine, 1973-, and of Physiology 1974-; Dir. McGill Cancer Centre 1978-80; Dir. McGill Univ. Medical Clinic, The Montreal Gen. Hosp. 1980-; Sr. Physician, The Montreal Gen. Hosp. 1973-, Physician-in-Chief 1980-, Sr. Investigator Hosp. Research Inst.; Hon. Consultant, Royal Victoria Hosp., Montreal 1981-; Chair. Dept. of Medicine, McGill Univ. 1985-, Douglas G. Cameron Prof. of Medicine, McGill Univ. 1987-; mem. numerous professional socs., scientific research bds. and orgs. etc. *Publications:* 130 articles in professional journals (1988). *Address:* Room 648, The Montreal General Hospital, 1650 Cedar Avenue, Montreal, Que. H3G 1A4, Canada (Office).

GOLD, Sir Joseph, Kt., LL.M., S.J.D.; British lawyer; b. 12 July 1912, London; m. Ruth Schechter 1939; one s. two d.; ed. London and Harvard Univs; Lecturer in Law, London Univ. 1937-39; mem. British Govt. Mission to Washington 1942-46; with IMF 1946-79, Gen. Counsel, Dir. Legal Dept. 1960-79; Senior Consultant 1979-; Hon. LL.D, Columbia Univ. medal; A.B.A. Medal in Int. Law. *Publications:* Fund Agreement in the Courts (vol. I) 1962, (vol. II) 1982, (vol. III) 1986, (vol. IV) 1989, The Stand-By Arrangements of the IMF 1970, Voting and Decisions in the IMF 1972, Membership and Nonmembership in the IMF 1974, Aspectos Legales de la Reforma Monetaria 1979, Legal and Institutional Aspects of the International Monetary System: Selected Essays, Vol. 1 1979, Vol. 2 1984, Exchange Rates in International Law and Organization 1988, and contributions to various IMF publs. and to professional journals in various countries. *Address:* International Monetary Fund, 700 19th Street, N.W., Washington, D.C. 20431 (Office); 7020 Braeburn Place, Bethesda, Md. 20817, U.S.A. (Home).

GOLD, Thomas, F.R.S., SC.D.; American (fmrly. British) astronomer; b. 22 May 1920, Vienna, Austria; s. of Max Gold and Josefine Gold; m. 1st Merle Eleanor Tuberg 1947, 2nd Carvel Lee Beyer 1972; four d.; ed. Zuoz Coll., Switzerland, and Trinity Coll., Cambridge; Experimental Officer, British Admiralty (radar research) 1943-46; Fellow, Trinity Coll., Cambridge 1947; Chief Asst. to Astronomer Royal, Royal Greenwich Observatory 1952-56; Prof. of Astronomy, Harvard Univ. 1957-59; Prof. of Astronomy, Cornell Univ. 1971-86, Prof. Emer. 1987-; Dir. Cornell Univ. Center for Radiophysics and Space Research 1959-81; Hon. Fellow, Trinity Coll. Cambridge 1986-; Fellow, Royal Soc., London; mem. N.A.S., American Philosophical Soc; Fellow American Acad. of Arts and Sciences; Gold Medal, Royal Astronomical Soc. 1985. *Publications:* The Steady State Theory of the Expanding Universe 1948, The Alignment of Galactic Dust 1952, The Field of a Uniformly Accelerated Charge 1954, Instability of the Earth's Axis of Rotation 1955, The Lunar Surface 1956, Cosmic Rays from the Sun 1957, Plasma and Magnetic Fields in the Solar System 1959, The Origin of Solar Flares 1960, The Nature of Time 1967, Rotating Neutron Stars

as the Origin of the Pulsating Radio Source 1968, Rotating Neutron Stars and the Nature of Pulsars 1969, Apollo 12 Seismic Signal: Indication of a Deep Layer of Powder 1970, Terrestrial Sources of Carbon and Earthquake Outgassing 1978, Power from the Earth 1987. *Leisure interests:* skiing, water skiing. *Address:* 36 Madingley Road, Cambridge, CB3 0EX, England. *Telephone:* (0223) 312423.

GOLDANSKII, Vitalii Iosifovich; Soviet physicist and chemist; b. 18 June 1923, Vitebsk; s. of Josif Efimovich Goldanskii and Yudif Iosifovna Melamed; m. Lyudmila Nikolayevna Semenova 1947; two s.; ed. Moscow Univ.; mem. CPSU 1950-; mem. of staff of Inst. of Chemical Physics 1942-52, 1961-, sr. positions 1971-, Dir. 1988-; mem. of staff of U.S.S.R. Acad. of Sciences Inst. of Physics 1952-61; Asst. Prof. of Moscow Physical-Tech. Inst. 1947-51, with Inst. of Physical Engineering, Moscow 1951-(posts of Asst. Prof., Prof.); Chair. Soviet Pugwash Cttee., mem. Pugwash Council and Exec. Cttee. 1987-; Ed.-in-Chief High Energy Chemistry journal 1967-87; Chem. Physics (Soviet) journal 1988-; Lenin Prize 1980, Golden Mendeleev Medal 1975, Karpinskii Prize, City of Hamburg FVS Foundation 1983; mem. U.S.S.R. Acad. of Sciences 1981- (Corresp. mem. 1962-81); main work on chemical physics, radiation and nuclear chem.; mem. Royal Danish Acad. of Science and Letters 1977, Deutsche Akad. Naturforsch. Leopoldina 1976, American Acad. of Arts and Sciences 1987, Acad. of Sciences of the D.D.R. 1987; Hon. Life mem. New York Acad. of Sciences 1975; Centenary Foreign Fellow American Chemical Soc. 1976; Fellow American Physics Soc.; Hon. mem. Hungarian Physics Soc. 1974; numerous orders and other decorations. *Publications:* Kinematics of Nuclear Reactions 1959, Counting Statistics of Nuclear Particles 1959, Mössbauer effect and its applications in chemistry 1963, Physical chemistry of positron and positronium 1968, Tunnelling phenemona in chemical physics 1986, Kinematical Methods in High Energy Physics 1987; books, reviews, articles. *Leisure interests:* aphorisms, humour, movies, records. *Address:* Institute of Chemical Physics, U.S.S.R. Academy of Sciences, Ul. Kosygina 4, Moscow 117334, U.S.S.R. *Telephone:* 137-35-45 (Office).

GOLDBERG, Sir Abraham, Kt., M.D., D.SC., F.R.C.P., F.R.S.E.; British professor of medicine; b. 7 Dec. 1923, Edinburgh; s. of the late Julius Goldberg and Rachel Goldberg; m. Clarice Cussin 1957; two s. one d.; ed. George Heriots School, Edin. and Univs. of Edinburgh and Glasgow; Nuffield Research Fellow, Univ. Coll. Hosp., London 1952-54; Eli Lilly Travelling Fellow in Medicine, Univ. of Utah 1954-56; Regius Prof. of Materia Medica, Univ. of Glasgow 1970-78, Regius Prof. of Practice of Medicine 1978-; Chair. Cttee. on Safety of Medicines 1980-86; mem. other medical research cttees. etc.; Sydney Watson Smith Lectureship, Royal Coll. of Physicians (Edinburgh) 1964; Henry Cohen Lectureship, Hebrew Univ. 1973; Alex Fleck Award (Univ. of Glasgow) 1967, Fitzpatrick Lecture, Royal Coll. of Physicians (London) 1988. *Publications:* Diseases of Porphyr in Metabolism (jtly.) 1962, Recent Advances in Haematology (Ed. jtly.) 1971, Clinics in Haematology "The Porphyrias" (jtly.) 1980, Disorders of Porphyrin Metabolism (jt. author) 1987. *Leisure interests:* medical history, literature, writing, walking, swimming. *Address:* University of Glasgow, Gardiner Institute of Medicine, Western Infirmary, Glasgow, G11 6NT (Office); 16 Birnam Crescent, Bearsden, Glasgow, G61 2AU, Scotland (Home). *Telephone:* 041-339 2800 (Office).

GOLDBERG, Arthur Joseph, B.S. IN L., DR.JUR.; American lawyer and diplomatist; b. 8 Aug. 1908, Chicago, Ill.; s. of Joseph Goldberg and Rebecca Perlstein; m. Dorothy Kurgans 1931; one s. one d.; ed. City Coll., Chicago and Northwestern Univ; Private Law Practice 1929-48; Gen. Counsel, Congress of Industrial Workers 1948-55; Gen. Counsel, United Steelworkers 1948-61; Special Counsel, American Fed. of Labor-Congress of Industrial Orgs. 1955-61; Gen. Counsel, Industrial Union Dept., AFL-CIO 1955-61; Sec. of Labor 1961-62; Justice of U.S. Supreme Court 1962-65; Perm. Rep. U.S. to UN 1965-68; Chair. UNA of U.S.A. 1968-70, Hon. Chair. 1970-; Senior partner Paul, Weiss, Goldberg, Rifkind, Wharton and Garrison, New York 1968-71; Law Practice, Washington 1971-; Amb.-at-Large 1977-78; Head of U.S. Del., CSCE, Belgrade 1977-78; Prof. of Law and Diplomacy, American Univ., Washington 1972-73; Charles Evans Hughes Prof., Woodrow Wilson School, Princeton Univ. 1968-69; Distinguished Prof. School of Int. Relations, Columbia Univ. 1969-70; Distinguished Visiting Prof. Hastings Coll. of the Law, Univ. of Calif., San Francisco 1974-; Presidential Medal of Freedom 1978; Democrat. *Publications:* Civil Rights in Labor-Management Relations: a Labor Viewpoint 1951, AFL-CIO—Labor United 1956, Unions and the Anti-Trust Laws 1956, Management's Reserved Rights 1956, Ethical Practices 1958, A Trade Union Point of View 1959, Suggestions for a New Labor Policy 1960, The Role of the Labor Union in an Age of Bigness 1960, The Annals of The American Academy of Political and Social Science (Vol. 339) 1962, The Defenses of Freedom: The Public Papers of Arthur J. Goldberg 1966, Equal Justice: the Warren Era of the Supreme Court 1972. *Address:* 2801 New Mexico Avenue, N.W., Washington, D.C. 20007, U.S.A. *Telephone:* (202) 293-2868.

GOLDBERG, Bertrand, F.A.I.A.; American architect; b. 17 July 1913, Chicago, Ill.; s. of Benjamin R. and Sadie (Getzhof) Goldberg; m. Nancy S. Florsheim 1946; one s. two d.; ed. Harvard College, Bauhaus, Berlin, and Armour Inst. of Tech.; Propr. architectural and eng. office, Bertrand Goldberg Assocs., Chicago 1937-; lecturer in U.S.A., Canada, England,

France and China; principal works include Cinestage Theatre, Chicago 1957, Astor Tower Hotel and Marina City, Chicago 1963, Elgin State Hosp., Ill. 1967, Raymond Hilliard Housing Center, Chicago 1966, Charles Dana Cancer Center, Boston 1973, Prentice Women's Hosp., Chicago 1974, St. Joseph's Hosp., Tacoma 1975, Health Sciences Center, Stony Brook 1976, Brigham Women's Hosp., Boston 1983, Biosciences Research Bldg., Boston 1984, Good Samaritan Hosp., Phoenix 1982, Providence Hosp., Mobile 1985, River City, Chicago 1985, Wright College, Chicago 1988; mem. Exec. Cttee. Chicago Maternity Center, Bd. of Community Associates Northwestern Univ. Center for Urban Affairs and Policy; Dir. of Chicago Architectural Assistance Center, Lincoln Acad., Visiting Cttee. Univ. of Calif. School of Architecture and Urban Planning, Task Force Cttee. on Housing Costs U.S. Dept. of Housing and Urban Devt., Steering Cttee. Innovative City Project, Chicago Mayor's Task Force on High Tech. Devt.; awards include A.I.A. Honor Award 1959, Leading Architect Award (City of Chicago) 1961, Silver Medal (Architectural League, N.Y.) 1965, A.I.A. Distinguished Bldg. Award 1967, American Registered Architect Design Excellence Award 1978, ORT Centennial Award 1979; Trustee St. Xavier College; Officer Ordre des Arts et des Lettres 1985; Fellow American Concrete Inst. *Publications:* numerous articles on urbanism, density, technology and the role of architecture in society. *Address:* Bertrand Goldberg Associates, River City, 800 S. Wells Street, Chicago, Ill. 60610, U.S.A. *Telephone:* (312) 431-5200.

GOLDBERG, Edward David, PH.D.; American professor of chemistry; b. 2 Aug. 1921, Sacramento, Calif.; s. of Edward Davidow Goldberg and Lillian Rothholz Goldberg; one s. three d.; ed. Univ. of California (Berkeley) and Univ. of Chicago; practising marine chemist specialising in marine pollution and wastes of soc.; Prof. of Chem., Scripps Inst. of Oceanography; served as consultant to many nat. and int. bodies (including UNESCO and FAO); has given over 200 scientific papers; Guggenheim Fellow 1960; NATO Fellow 1970; B. H. Ketchum Award 1984; mem. N.A.S. *Publications:* The Health of the Oceans 1976, Black Carbon in the Environment 1985. *Address:* Scripps Institution of Oceanography, La Jolla, Calif. 92093; 750 Val Sereno Drive, Encinitas, Calif. 92024, U.S.A. (Home). *Telephone:* (619) 534-2407 (Office).

GOLDBERG, Samuel Louis, B.A., F.A.H.A.; Australian academic; b. 19 Nov. 1926, Melbourne; s. of Myer Goldberg and Bella Silman; m. Jane Adamson 1978; two s. one d.; ed. Coburg and Univ. High Schools, Melbourne, Univ. of Melbourne and Oxford Univ.; Prof. of English Literature, Univ. of Sydney 1963-66; Prof. of English, Univ. of Melbourne 1966-76; Sr. Fellow History of Ideas Unit, A.N.U. 1976-87, Sr. Fellow Dept. of Philosophy, Research School of Social Sciences 1987-; Visiting Fellow Inst. for Advanced Studies, Univ. of Edinburgh 1972, Clare Hall, Cambridge 1979, Gonville and Caius Coll., Cambridge 1981; Churchill Visiting Prof. Univ. of Bristol 1974; Visiting Prof. A.N.U. 1975; Convenor Acad. of Humanities Project, History of Culture in Australia. *Publications:* The Critical Review (Ed.) 1958, The Classical Temper 1961, Joyce 1962, An Essay on King Lear 1974, Australian Cultural History (Ed.) 1981-88. *Address:* Department of Philosophy, Research School of Social Sciences, Australian National University, Box 4, GPO Canberra, A.C.T., 2601 (Univ.); 23 Kidston Crescent, Curtin, Australian Capital Territory, Australia 2605 (Home). *Telephone:* (062) 82 2278 (Home).

GOLDBERGER, Marvin Leonard, PH.D.; American professor of physics; b. 22 Oct. 1922, Chicago, Ill.; s. of Joseph and Mildred Sedwitz Goldberger; m. Mildred C. Ginsburg 1945; two s.; ed. Carnegie Inst. of Technology and Univ. of Chicago; Research Assoc. Radiation Lab., Univ. of Calif. (Berkeley) 1948-49, M.I.T. 1949-50; Asst. Prof., Prof., Univ. of Chicago 1950-57; Eugene Higgins Prof. of Physics, Princeton Univ. 1957-77, Chair. Physics Dept. 1970-76, Joseph Henry Prof. of Physics 1977-78; Pres. Calif. Inst. of Tech. 1978-87; Dir. Inst. for Advanced Study, Princeton Univ. 1987-; Chair. Fed. of American Scientists 1971-72; mem. N.A.S., American Acad. of Arts and Sciences; Dannie Heineman Prize for Mathematical Physics 1961; Hon. Sc.D. (Carnegie-Mellon Univ. 1979, Univ. of Notre Dame 1979); Hon. LL.D. (Occidental Coll. 1980); Hon. D.H.L. (Hebrew Union Coll. 1980, Univ. of Judaism 1982). *Publication:* Collision Theory (with K. M. Watson) 1964. *Leisure interests:* running, tennis, cooking. *Address:* 97 Olden Lane, Princeton, N.J. 08540, U.S.A. (Home).

GOLDHABER, Gertrude Scharff, PH.D.; American physicist; b. 14 July 1911, Mannheim, Germany; d. of Otto Scharff and Nelly Steinharter; m. Maurice Goldhaber (q.v.) 1939; two s.; ed. Univs. of Freiburg, Zürich, Berlin and Munich; Research Assoc. in Physics, Imperial Coll., London 1935-39; Physicist, Univ. of Ill. 1939-48; Consultant, Argonne Nat. Lab. 1946-50; Asst. Prof., Univ. of Ill. 1948-50; Assoc. Physicist, Brookhaven Nat. Lab. 1950-58, Physicist 1958-62, Senior Physicist 1962-; Consultant, Los Alamos Scientific Lab. 1953-; Adjunct Prof. Cornell Univ. 1980-82, Johns Hopkins Univ. 1982-85; Chair. ad hoc Panel on Nuclear Data Compilations, Nuclear Research Council, N.A.S. 1969-71; Councillor-at-Large, American Physical Soc. 1978-81, mem. of American Physical Soc. Exec. on History of Physics 1983-84; mem. NAS 1972-, Report Review Cttee. 1973-81, Forum Cttee. 1974-80; mem. Cttee. on Problems of Women in Physics 1971-72, Research Advisory Cttee., Nat. Science Foundation 1972-74, Editorial Cttee., Annual Reviews of Nuclear Science 1972-77, Bd. of Trustees, Fermi Nat. Accelerator Lab. 1972-78, Physics

Visiting Cttee., Harvard Univ. 1973-77, President's Cttee. on the Nat. Medal of Science 1977-79, Editorial Bd. for Journal of Physics G, 1978-80, Educ. Advisory Cttee., New York Acad. of Sciences 1982-; mem. NAS-NRC Cttee. on Educ. and Employment of Women in Science and Eng. 1978-82; Consultant Arms Control and Disarmament Agency 1974-77; Fellow, A.A.A.S.; L.I. Achievers Award in Science 1982; mem. Cttee. on Human Rights, N.A.S. 1984-87; mem. Nat. Advisory Cttee. on Pre-Coll. Materials Devt., 1984-; mem. A.A.A.S., mem.-at-large Section B (Physics) 1986-(90); Renewal of Ph.D. (50th Anniversary), Univ. of Munich 1985. *Publications:* author and co-author of many articles on physics subjects. *Leisure interests:* history of science, literature and art, recent results in neuroendocrinology and brain structures and function, tennis, swimming, hiking. *Address:* 1510F Department of Physics, Brookhaven National Laboratory, 510A Upton, N.Y. 11973 (Office); 91 South Gillette Avenue, Bayport, N.Y. 11705, U.S.A. (Home). *Telephone:* 516-282-3912 (Office); 516-HR2-0651 (Home).

GOLDHABER, Maurice, PH.D.; American physicist; b. 18 April 1911, Lemberg, Austria; s. of Charles Goldhaber and Ethel Frisch Goldhaber; m. Gertrude Scharff (Goldhaber q.v.) 1939; two s.; ed. Berlin Univ. and Cambridge Univ., U.K.; Prof. of Physics, Univ. of Ill. 1938-50; Senior scientist, Brookhaven Nat. Lab. 1950-60, Chair. Dept. of Physics 1960-61, Dir. 1961-73; Adjunct. Prof. of Physics, New York State Univ. 1965-; mem. N.A.S., American Philosophical Soc.; Fellow, American Acad. of Arts and Sciences, A.A.A.S., Chair. Section B, Physics 1981, American Physical Soc., Pres. 1982; Tom W. Bonner Prize in Nuclear Physics of American Physical Soc. 1971, Associated Univs. Inc. Distinguished Scientist 1973-; U.S. Atomic Energy Comm. Citation for Meritorious Contributions 1973, J. Robert Oppenheimer Memorial Prize 1982; Hon. Ph.D. (Tel-Aviv) 1974, Hon. Dr. h.c. (Univ. of Louvain-La-Neuve) 1982. *Publications:* numerous articles in professional scientific journals on neutron physics, radioactivity, nuclear isomers, nuclear photo-electric effect, nuclear models, fundamental particles. *Leisure interests:* tennis, hiking. *Address:* 91 South Gilette Avenue, Bayport, N.Y. 11705, U.S.A.

GOLDIN, Nikolay Vasiliyevich; Soviet engineer and politician; b. 20 March 1910; ed. Kharkov Electrical Engineering Inst.; fitter, asst. engine-driver from 1924; sr. dispatch control engineer from 1937; Man of Trust, Dir. of Bd. of Assembly of Electrical Equipment, U.S.S.R. Ministry of Construction of Heavy Industry Plants 1941-50; Head of reconstruction works on many iron and steel plants devastated in Second World War, particularly Zaporozhstal Iron and Steel Works 1943-50; Deputy Minister for Construction of Heavy Industry Plants, then for Construction of Metallurgical and Chemical Industries Plants 1950-57; Chief Engineer, Bhilhai Iron and Steel Works, India 1958-61; First Deputy Chair. of All-Russian Council of Nat. Economy 1961-62; Econ. Counsellor, U.S.S.R. Embassy, Cuba 1962-63; Deputy Minister of Assembly and Special Construction Works 1965-67; Minister for Construction of Heavy Industry Enterprises 1967-86; Deputy to U.S.S.R. Supreme Soviet 1967-; Pres. Soviet-Indian Friendship Soc.; mem. CPSU 1929-, mem. Cen. Cttee. 1971-; Jawaharlal Nehru Prize 1979; U.S.S.R. State Prize; Hero of Socialist Labour, Order of Lenin (five times) and several other decorations *Address:* c/o Ministry for Construction of Plants of Heavy Industry, 19/21, 5 Ulitsa Yamskogo Polya, Moscow, U.S.S.R.

GOLDING, Bruce, B.SC., M.P.; Jamaican politician; b. 5 Dec. 1947, Ginger Ridge, St. Catherine; s. of Tacius and Enid Golding; m.; one s. two d.; mem. Cen. Cttee. Jamaica Labour Party 1969, Gen. Sec. 1974-84, Chair. 1984-; mem. Parl. for West St. Catherine 1972-76, for South Cen. St. Catherine 1983-; Senator 1976-83; Minister of Construction 1980-89. *Leisure interests:* hunting, fishing, motoring. *Address:* P.O. Box 13, Kingston 6, Jamaica. *Telephone:* (809) 927-9091.

GOLDING, Sir William (Gerald), Kt., C.B.E., M.A., F.R.S.L.; British writer; b. 19 Sept. 1911, St. Columb, Cornwall; s. of Alec and Mildred Golding; m. Ann Brookfield 1940; one s. one d.; ed. Marlborough Grammar School, Brasenose Coll., Oxford; Hon. Fellow, Brasenose Coll., Oxford 1966; Hon. D.Litt. (Sussex) 1970, (Kent) 1974, (Warwick) 1981, (Oxford) 1983, (Sorbonne) 1983; C.Lit. 1984. *Publications:* Lord of the Flies 1954 (film 1963), The Inheritors 1955, Pincher Martin 1956, Free Fall 1959, The Spire 1964, The Hot Gates 1965, The Pyramid 1967, The Scorpion God 1971, Darkness Visible 1979, Rites of Passage 1980, A Moving Target 1982, The Paper Men 1984, An Egyptian Journal 1985, Close Quarters 1987, Fire Down Below 1989; Brass Butterfly (play) 1958; Booker McConnell Prize 1980, James Tait Black Memorial Prize 1980, Nobel Prize for Literature 1983. *Leisure interests:* music, water gardens, Greek. *Address:* c/o Faber & Faber Ltd., 3 Queen Square, London, WC1N 3AU, England.

GOLDMAN, Berthold, D. EN D., M. ÈS L.; French international lawyer; b. 12 Sept. 1913, Bucharest, Romania; s. of Nathan and Ernestine (née Trau) Goldman; m. Suzanne Hemy 1939; one s.; Prof., Faculty of Law, Indochina Univ. 1948-49, Univ. of Dijon 1949-60, Univ. of Paris 1960-70; Prof., Paris Univ. of Law, Econs. and Social Sciences 1971-81, Pres. 1974-79, Hon. Pres. and Prof. 1979-81, Prof. Emer. 1981-; mem. Int. Law Inst. 1969-; Ed.-in-Chief Journal du Droit International and Jurisclasseur de Droit International; Hon. Pres. French branch Int. Law Asscn., Comité Français de Droit Int. Privé; Chevalier, Légion d'Honneur; Commdr. Ordre Nat. du Mérite; Commdr. des Palmes Académiques. *Publications:* De la détermination du gardien responsable 1946, Les conflits de lois dans l'arbitrage international en droit privé 1963, Les domaines d'application territoriale des lois de la concurrence 1969, Droit commercial européen 1983. *Leisure interests:* music, theatre, literature. *Address:* 15 rue Clement Marot, 75008 Paris, France. *Telephone:* (1) 47.23.58.67.

GOLDMAN, Sir Samuel, K.C.B.; British fmr. banker and civil servant; b. 10 March 1912, London; s. of late Philip and Sarah Goldman; m. Patricia Rosemary Hodges 1943; one s.; ed. Raines Foundation School, Davenant Foundation School and London School of Econs.; Moody's Economist Services 1934–38; Sebag and Co. 1938–39; Bank of England 1940–47; joined Civil Service as statistician, Central Statistical Office Jan. 1947, transferred to Treasury 1947, Chief Statistician 1948, Asst. Sec. 1952, Under-Sec. 1960, Third Sec. 1962; Second Perm. Sec., Treasury 1968–72; fmr. Man. Dir. Orion Bank Ltd.; fmr. Chair. Henry Ansbacher Holdings Ltd.; fmr. Chair. Covent Garden Market Authority. *Leisure interests:* gardening, music. *Address:* White Gate, Church Lane, Haslemere, Surrey, England. *Telephone:* (0428) 4889.

GOLDREICH, Peter, PH.D.; American professor of planetary science and astronomy; b. 14 July 1939, New York, N.Y.; s. of Paul Goldreich and Edith Rosenfield Goldreich; m. Susan Kroll 1960; two s.; ed. Cornell Univ; Post-Doctoral Fellow Cambridge Univ. 1963–64; Asst. Prof. Astronomy and Physics, Univ. of Calif. (Los Angeles Campus) 1964–66, Assoc. Prof. 1966; Assoc. Prof. Planetary Science and Astronomy Calif. Inst. Tech. 1966–69, Prof. 1969–; mem. N.A.S. 1972–. *Publications:* on planetary dynamics, pulsar theory, radio emission from Jupiter, galactic stability and interstellar masers. *Leisure interests:* competitive athletics. *Address:* 1201 East California Boulevard, Pasadena, Calif. 91109 (Office); 999 San Pasqual, Pasadena, Calif. 91106, U.S.A. (Home).

GOLDS, Anthony Arthur, C.M.G., L.V.O.; British diplomatist; b. 31 Oct. 1919, Macclesfield, Cheshire; s. of the late Arthur O. and Florence (née Massey) Golds; m. Suzanne Macdonald Young 1944; one s. one d.; ed. King's School, Macclesfield and New Coll., Oxford; served Royal Armoured Corps 1939–46; Commonwealth Relations Office (C.R.O.) 1948–51; First Sec., Calcutta and Delhi 1951–53; S. Asia Dept., C.R.O. 1953–56; First Sec. Ankara 1957–59, Karachi 1959–61; Counsellor, Head of Malaysia/Indonesia Dept., Foreign Office/C.R.O. 1961–65; Counsellor, Rome 1965–70; Amb. to Cameroon, Gabon and Equatorial Guinea 1970–72; High Commr. in Bangladesh 1972–74; Senior Civilian Instructor, Royal Coll. of Defence Studies 1975–76; Dir. British Nat. Cttee. of ICC 1977–83. *Leisure interests:* literature, cricket, rugby, golf. *Address:* 4 Oakfield Gardens, London, SE19 1HF, England. *Telephone:* 01-670 7621 (Home).

GOLDSCHMIDT, Berthold; British composer and conductor (retd.); b. 18 Jan. 1903, Hamburg; ed. Univs. of Hamburg and Berlin, State Acad. of Music, Berlin; Asst. Conductor, Berlin State Opera 1925–26; Conductor at Darmstadt Opera 1927–29; Guest Conductor, Leningrad Philharmonic Orchestra 1931; Conductor Berlin on radio, and Artistic Advisor to Carl Ebert, Berlin State Opera 1931–33; Guest Conductor for BBC and most major British orchestras 1933–; Mendelssohn State Prize for composition 1925; British Arts Council Prize for opera 'Beatrice Cenci' 1951. *Works include:* Der gewaltige Hahnrei (opera), chamber music pieces and other compositions. *Address:* 13 Belsize Crescent, London, NW3 5QY, England. *Telephone:* 01-435 0931.

GOLDSCHMIDT, Bertrand, DR. ÈS SC.; French scientist; b. 2 Nov. 1912, Paris; m. Naomi de Rothschild 1947; one s. one d.; ed. Ecole de Physique et de Chimie, Univ. of Paris; Asst. Curie Lab., Paris 1935–40; Section Leader Anglo-Canadian Atomic Project 1942–45, Head, Chemistry Div. 1946; Head, Chemistry Div. Commissariat à l'Energie Atomique 1946–59, Head, External Relations Div. 1953–59, Head, External Relations and Planning 1959–70, Head Int. Relations Div. 1970–77, Adviser 1978–80; Gov. for France IAEA 1957–80, Chair. IAEA 1980; Prof. Inst. d'Etudes Politiques 1960–65; Exec. Vice-Pres. European Atomic Energy Soc. 1955–58; Pres. Soc. Industrielle des Minerais de l'Ouest 1955–61; Commdr. Légion d'honneur; Atoms for Peace Award 1967; mem. Scientific Advisory Cttee. to IAEA 1959; Commdr., Légion d'honneur; Grand Officier, Ordre nat. du Mérite. *Publications:* L'aventure atomique 1962, Les rivalités atomiques 1967, Le complexe atomique 1980, Pionniers de l'atome 1987. *Address:* Commissariat à l'Energie Atomique, 29-33 rue de la Fédération, 75015 Paris (Office); 11 boulevard Flandrin, 75116 Paris, France (Home). *Telephone:* 504-11-93 (Home).

GOLDSCHMIDT, Neil Edward, A.B., LL.B.; American lawyer and politician; b. 16 June 1940, Eugene, Ore.; s. of Lester H. and Annette G. (Levin) Goldschmidt; m. Margaret Wood 1965; one s. one d.; ed. Univs. of Oregon and California; Civil Rights Worker, Miss. 1964; Attorney with Legal Aid Service, Portland, Ore. 1967–70; City Commr., Portland 1971–72; Mayor of Portland 1973–79; U.S. Sec. of Transportation 1979–81; Vice-Pres. Int. Marketing NIKE/BRS Inc., Beaverton, Ore. 1981–; Chair. Standing Cttee. on Housing and Community Devt. 1976–79, Ad Hoc Housing Task Force 1977–79, Energy Task Force of the Nat. League of Cities 1977–79; Trustee, U.S. Conf. of Mayors 1978–79; Gov. of Oregon Jan. 1987–; fmrly. mem. Advisory Cttee. on State and Local Govt. Affairs, Harvard's John F. Kennedy School of Govt.; mem. Bd. of Kaiser Health and Hospital Plan, Oakland, Calif. 1981–, Bd. of Nat. Semiconductor, Santa Clara, Calif., Bd.

of Gelco Corpn., Eden Prairie, Minn. *Leisure interests:* reading, swimming, all spectator sports. *Address:* 3900 South West Murray Boulevard, Beaverton, Ore. 97005 (Home); Governor's Office, State Capitol Building, Salem, Ore. 97310, U.S.A. (Office).

GOLDSMITH, Sir James Michael, Kt.; Franco-British industrialist; b. 26 Feb. 1933, Paris; s. of Frank Goldsmith and Marcelle Mouiller; m. 1st Isabel Patino 1954 (deceased), one d.; m. 2nd Ginette Lery 1958 (dissolved), one s. one d.; m. 3rd Lady Annabel Vane Tempest Stewart, two s. one d.; ed. Eton College; founder and Chair. Cavenham Ltd.; Chair. and founder Générale Occidentale S.A. 1969–, (sold majority of his shares); Gen. Oriental Ltd., Cayman Islands; fmr. Publr. L'Express magazine, Paris. *Address:* Cavenham House, Park Lane, Cranford, Middx., England; 42 Avenue Friedland, 75008 Paris, France. *Telephone:* 01-897 7741 (England), 766-5197 (France).

GOLDSTEIN, Abraham S., M.A.; American professor of law; b. 27 July 1925, New York, N.Y.; s. of Isidore and Yetta (Crystal) Goldstein; m. Ruth Tessler 1947; one s. one d.; ed. City Coll. N.Y. and Yale Law School; Assoc., Cook and Berger, Washington, D.C. 1949; Law Clerk to Circuit Judge David Bazelon (q.v.), U.S. Court of Appeals 1949–51; Partner, Donohue and Kaufman 1951–56; Assoc. Prof., Yale Law School 1956–61, Prof. 1961–, Dean 1970–75, Sterling Prof. of Law 1975–; Visiting Prof. of Law, Stanford Law School 1963; Visiting Fellow, Inst. of Criminology, Cambridge Univ. 1964–65; mem. Faculty, Salzburg Seminar in American Studies 1969; Visiting Prof. Hebrew Univ. Jerusalem 1976, UN Asia and Far East Inst. for Prevention of Crime, Tokyo 1983, Tel Aviv Univ. 1986; mem. Comm. to Revise Criminal Statutes of Conn. 1966–70; Consultant, President's Comm. on the Admin. of Criminal Justice 1966–67; mem. Gov.'s Planning Comm. of Criminal Admin. 1967–71, mem. Conn. Bd. of Parole 1967–69; Vice-Pres. Conn. Bar Foundation 1976–79; Sr. Vice-Pres. American Jewish Congress 1977–84; mem. Exec. Cttee. 1977–; Hon. M.A. (Cambridge, Yale), Hon. LL.D. (New York Law School, Depaul Univ.). *Publications:* The Insanity Defence 1967, Crime, Law and Society (with J. Goldstein) 1971, Criminal Procedure (with L. Orland) 1974, The Passive Judiciary 1981; articles and book reviews in professional journals. *Address:* Yale Law School, New Haven, Conn. 06520, U.S.A. (Office).

GOLDSTEIN, Avram, M.D.; American professor of pharmacology and neurobiologist; b. 3 July 1919, New York; s. of Israel Goldstein and Bertha Markowitz; m. Dora Benedict 1949; four c.; ed. Harvard Coll. and Harvard Medical School; Instructor, then Asst. Prof. in Pharmacology, Harvard 1948–55; Prof. and Chair., Pharmacology, Stanford Univ. 1955–70, Prof. 1970–; Dir. Addiction Research Foundation, Palo Alto, Calif. 1974–87; mem. N.A.S.; Franklin Medal, Sollmann Award, Nathan Eddy Award. *Publications:* Biostatistics 1964, Principles of Drug Action 1968; over 300 articles in the primary scientific journals. *Leisure interests:* aviation and aviation writing. *Address:* Department of Pharmacology, Stanford University, Stanford, Calif. 94305, U.S.A. *Telephone:* (415) 321-8339.

GOLDSTEIN, Joseph Leonard, M.D.; American physician and genetics educator; b. 18 April 1940, Sumter, S.C.; s. of Isadore E. Goldstein and Fannie A. Goldstein; ed. Washington and Lee Univ., Lexington, Va., Univ. of Chicago and Rensselaer Polytechnic Inst.; Intern, then Resident in Medicine, Mass. Gen. Hosp., Boston 1966–68; Clinical Assoc., Nat. Insts. of Health 1968–70; Postdoctoral Fellow, Univ. of Washington, Seattle 1970–72; mem. Faculty, Univ. of Texas Health Science Center, Dallas 1972–, Paul J. Thomas Prof. of Medicine, Chair. Dept. of Molecular Genetics 1977–, Harvey Soc. Lecturer 1977; mem. Advisory Bd. Howard Hughes Medical Inst. 1985–; non-resident Fellow, The Salk Inst. 1983–; mem. Scientific Advisory Bd. Welch Foundation 1986–; Bd. Dirs. Passano Foundation 1985–; mem. Editorial Bd. Cell, Arteriosclerosis and Science; mem. N.A.S., American Acad. of Arts and Sciences, Asscn. of American Physicians, American Soc. of Clinical Investigation (Pres. 1985–86), American Soc. of Human Genetics, American Soc. of Biological Chemists, American Fed. of Clinical Research; Heinrich-Wieland Prize 1974, Pfizer Award in Enzyme Chem., American Chemical Soc. 1976, Passano Award, Johns Hopkins Univ. 1978, Gairdner Foundation Award 1981, Award in Biological and Medical Sciences, New York Acad. of Sciences 1981, Lita Annenberg Hazen Award 1982, Research Achievement Award, American Heart Asscn. 1984, Louisa Gross Horwitz Award 1984, 3M Life Sciences Award 1984, Albert Lasker Award in Basic Medical Research 1985, Nobel Prize in Physiology or Medicine 1985. *Publication:* The Metabolic Basis of Inherited Disease (Co-author) 1983. *Address:* Department of Molecular Genetics, University of Texas Health Science Center at Dallas, 5323 Harry Hines Boulevard, Dallas, Tex. 75235; 3730 Holland Avenue, Apt. H, Dallas, Tex. 75219, U.S.A. (Home).

GOLDSTINE, Herman Heine, M.S., PH.D.; American mathematician; b. 13 Sept. 1913, Chicago, Ill.; s. of Isaac O. Goldstine and Bess (Lipsey) Goldstine; m. 1st Adele Katz 1941 (died 1964), 2nd Ellen Watson 1966; one s. one d.; ed. Univ. of Chicago; research asst. Univ. of Chicago 1936–37, Instructor 1937–39; Instructor Univ. of Mich. 1939–42, Asst. Prof. 1942–50; Asst. Project Dir. Electronic Computer Project, Inst. for Advanced Study, Princeton 1946–55, Acting Project Dir. 1954–57; Perm. mem. Inst. for Advanced Study, Princeton 1952–; Dir. Math. Sciences Dept. IBM Research; Dir. Scientific Devt. IBM Data Processing H.Q., White Plains, New York; Consultant to Dir. of Research, IBM, now IBM Fellow;

consultant to various govt. and mil. agencies; mem. N.A.S., American Philosophical Soc., American Acad. of Arts and Sciences, American Math. Soc., Academic Cttee., Annenberg Research Inst. 1987-, Bd. Nat. Constitution Center 1987-; Exec. Officer, American Philosophical Soc. 1984-; Hon. Ph.D. (Lund) 1974; Hon. D.Sc. (Adelphi) 1978, (Amherst) 1978; Nat. Medal of Science and other honours. *Publications include:* The Computer from Pascal to von Neumann 1972, A History of Numerical Analysis from the 16th to the 19th Century 1977, A History of the Calculus of Variations from the 17th Century through the 19th Century 1980; Ed. Mathematical Papers of John I and James I Bernoulli 1988. *Address:* American Philosophical Society, 104 South Fifth Street, Philadelphia, Pa. 19106 (Office); 1900 Rittenhouse Square, Apt. 13B, Philadelphia, Pa. 19103, U.S.A. (Home). *Telephone:* 215-627-0706 (Office); 215-545-5361 (Home).

GOLDSTONE, Jeffrey, M.A., PH.D., F.R.S.; British physicist; b. 3 Sept. 1933, Manchester; s. Hyman and Sophia Goldstone; m. Roberta Gordon 1980; one s.; ed. Manchester Grammar School and Trinity Coll., Cambridge; Research Fellow, Trinity Coll., Cambridge 1956-60, Staff Fellow 1962-82; Univ. lecturer, Applied Math. and Theoretical Physics, Cambridge 1971-76, Reader in Mathematical Physics 1976; Prof. of Physics, M.I.T. 1977-83, Cecil and Ida Green Prof. of Physics and Dir. Center for Theoretical Physics 1983-; several visiting lectureships; Fellow, American Acad. of Arts and Sciences; Heineman Prize, American Physical Soc. 1981; Guthrie Medal, Inst. of Physics 1983. *Publications:* articles in scientific journals. *Address:* 6-313, Massachusetts Institute of Technology, Cambridge, Mass. 02139 (Office); 18 Orchard Road, Brookline, Mass. 02146, U.S.A. (Home). *Telephone:* 617-253-6263 (Office); (617) 277-5932 (Home).

GOLDSTÜCKER, Eduard, PH.D.; British (born Czechoslovak) university professor; b. 30 May 1913, Podbiel; s. of Jozef Goldstücker and Terezie Altmann; m. Marta Borčová 1937; two d.; ed. Charles Univ., Prague, and Oxford Univ., England; Sec. of League for Human Rights, Prague 1936-38; secondary school teacher 1938-39; in U.K. 1939-45, worked at Czechoslovak Ministry of Foreign Affairs in London 1943-44; Ambassadorial Sec., Paris 1944-45; Deputy Amb. in London 1947-49; Envoy to Tel-Aviv 1950-51; political imprisonment 1951-55; Dept. of German Literature, Faculty of Philosophy, Charles Univ., Prague 1956-69, Prof. 1963-69, Pro-Rector of Charles Univ. 1966-69; Chair. Union of Czechoslovak Writers 1968-69; Deputy to Czech Nat. Council 1968-69; Visiting Prof. of Comparative Literature, Sussex Univ. 1969-71, Prof. 1971-78 now Emer.; Visiting Fellow, Center Study of Democratic Insts., Santa Barbara, Calif. 1972-73; Corresp. mem. Deutsche Akad. für Sprache und Dichtung 1976-; Hon. Ph.D. (Univ. of Constance) 1986; several awards including Goethe Gold Medal of Goethe Inst., Munich 1967, Klement Gottwald Award 1968; deprived of state citizenship of Czechoslovak Socialist Repub. 1974. *Publications:* History of German literature, especially German literature in Prague; Rainer Maria Rilke und Franz Werfel 1960, Franz Kafka 1964 (Prize of Publishing House of Czechoslovak Writers), Libertà e Socialismo 1968, The Czech National Revival, the Germans and the Jews 1972, Da Praga a Danzica 1981. *Address:* 107 Preston Drove, Brighton, Sussex, BN1 6LD, England.

GOLDTHORPE, John Harry, M.A., F.B.A.; British sociologist and academic; b. 27 May 1935, Barnsley; s. of Harry and Lilian Eliza Goldthorpe; m. Rhiannon Esyllt Harry 1963; one s. one d.; ed. Wath-upon-Dearne Grammar School, Univ. Coll. London, London School of Econs.; Asst. Lecturer Dept. of Sociology Univ. of Leicester 1957-60; Fellow, King's Coll. Cambridge 1960-69; Asst. Lecturer then Lecturer in Faculty of Econs. and Politics, Univ. of Cambridge 1962-69; Official Fellow, Nuffield Coll., Oxford 1969-; mem. British Econ. and Social Research Council 1988-; Helsinki Univ. Medal. *Publications:* (with David Lockwood et al.) The Affluent Worker series (3 vols.) 1968-69, (with Keith Hope) The Social Grading of Occupations 1974, (with Fred Hirsch, eds.) The Political Economy of Inflation 1978, Social Mobility and Class Structure 1980; Ed. Order and Conflict in Contemporary Capitalism 1984, Die Analyse soziales Ungleichheit: Kontinuitat, Erneueruing, Innovation (with Hermann Strasser, Ed. and Contrib.) 1985. *Leisure interests:* lawn tennis, bird watching, computer chess. *Address:* Nuffield College, Oxford, OX1 1NF; 32 Leckford Road, Oxford, OX2 6HX, England. *Telephone:* (0865) 278559 (Office); (0865) 56602 (Home).

GOLDWATER, Barry Morris; American politician; b. 1 Jan. 1909; s. of Baron and Josephine (née Williams) Goldwater; m. Margaret Johnson 1934 (died 1985); two s. two d.; ed. Staunton Military Acad., Univ. of Arizona; Republican Senator from Arizona 1952-64, 1969-87; Republican candidate for Pres. of United States 1964; Chair. Senate Select Intelligence Cttee. 1981-85, Armed Services Cttee. 1985-87; Goldwater's Inc. 1929-, Pres. 1937-53, Chair. Bd. 1953-; U.S. Army Air Force 1941-45; Presidential Medal of Freedom 1986. *Publications:* Arizona Portraits 1940, Journey Down the River of Canyons 1940, Speeches of Henry Ashurst: The Conscience of a Conservative 1960, Why Not Victory? 1960, Where I Stand 1964, The Face of Arizona 1964, People and Places 1967, Conscience of a Majority 1970, Delightful Journey 1971, The Coming Breakpoint 1976, Barry Goldwater and the South West 1976, With no Apologies 1979, Goldwater (autobiog.) 1988. *Address:* P.O. Box 1601, Scottsdale, Ariz. 85252, U.S.A.

GÖLLNER, Theodor, PH.D.; German professor of musicology; b. 25 Nov. 1929, Bielefeld; s. of Friedrich Göllner and Paula Brinkmann; m. Marie Louise Martinez 1959; one s. one d.; ed. Univs. of Heidelberg and Munich; lecturer, Univ. of Munich 1958-62, Asst. Prof., Assoc. Prof. 1962-67; Assoc. Prof., then Prof. Univ. of Calif. Santa Barbara 1967-73; Prof., Chair. Inst. of Musicology, Univ. of Munich 1973-; mem., Dir. Comm. of Music History, Bavarian Acad. of Sciences 1982-. *Publications:* Formen früher Mehrstimmigkeit 1961, Die mehrstimmigen liturgischen Lesungen 1969, Die Sieben Worte am Kreuz 1986. *Address:* Institute of Musicology, Univeristy of Munich, 8000 Munich 22, Geschwister-Scholl-Platz 1 (Office); 8031 Seefeld 2, Bahnweg 9, Federal Republic of Germany (Home). *Telephone:* 089-2180-2364 (Office).

GOLOVCHENKO, Ivan Kharitonovich; Soviet politician; mem. of Auditing Comm. of Ukrainian CP 1954-58; Minister for the Maintenance of Public Order 1962-68; Minister of the Interior of Ukrainian S.S.R. 1962, 1968-82; mem. Cen. Cttee. Ukrainian CP 1966-82. *Address:* c/o Ministry of the Interior, Kiev, Ukrainian S.S.R., U.S.S.R.

GOLSONG, Heribert, DR.IUR.; German international lawyer; b. 23 Oct. 1927, Oberhausen; m. Christine Vanneste 1954; two s. one d.; ed. Univs. of Cologne, Würzburg and Bonn, Coll. of Europe, Bruges and Hague Acad. of Int. Law; Court of Appeal, Cologne 1951-54; Council of Europe 1954-79; Sec. European Comm. on Human Rights 1954-56; Sec. Legal Cttee., Assembly 1957-59, Political Cttee. 1959-60; Deputy Registrar, European Court of Human Rights 1963-68; Dir. of Legal Affairs, Council of Europe 1965-77, Dir. of Human Rights 1977-79; Legal Adviser, European Resettlement Fund, Paris 1961-79; Dir. Research Programme, Hague Acad. of Int. Law 1967; Vice-Pres. and Gen. Counsel IBRD (World Bank) 1979-82; Sec.-Gen. Int. Centre for the Settlement of Investment Disputes Oct. 1980-83; Adviser on Int. Financial and Commercial Transactions at Arent, Fox, Kintner, Plotkin and Kahn 1983-87, Sloan, Lehner and Ruiz 1987-, Washington, D.C.; Prof. of Law at the American Univ., Washington, D.C.; Hon. Prof. of Law, Heidelberg; LL.D. h.c. (Edinburgh); Order of Merit, Fed. Repub. of Germany, Grand Commdr. Order of Merit, Liechtenstein; Commdr. Order of King Léopold, Belgium, Commdr. Order of St. Olav, Norway; Commdr. Grand Decoration in Gold for Services to Austria. *Publications:* in German: The System of Judicial Protection of the European Convention on Human Rights 1958, The Legislative History of the Basic Law of the Federal Republic of Germany 1961, International Commentary on the European Convention on Human Rights; in English: The International Protection of Human Rights 1963, and numerous articles in German, French, English and Italian on public int. law. *Leisure interests:* music, history. *Address:* 1920 North Street, N.W., Washington, D.C. 20036, (Office); 7300 Oak Lane, Chevy Chase, Md. 20815, U.S.A. (Home).

GOMA, Col. Louis Sylvain; Congolese army officer and politician; b. 1941; ed. Versailles and Saint-Cyr; Asst. Dir. of Mil. Engineers until 1968; Chief of Staff of Congolese People's Nat. Army 1968-, promoted Capt. 1968; mem. Parti Congolais du Travail (PCT) 1969-, Cen. Cttee. 1970-, Special Gen. Staff of Revolution 1974-, Political Bureau; Sec. of State for Defence 1969-70; Minister of Public Works and Transport 1970-74; promoted Maj. 1973; Chief of Gen. Staff of Armed Forces 1974; Prime Minister 1975-84, responsible for Plan 1975-79; mem. Council of State 1975-77; mem. PCT Mil Cttee. (Second Vice-Pres.) 1977-79. *Address:* c/o Office du Premier Ministre, Brazzaville, Congo People's Republic.

GOMARD, Bernhard, D.JUR.; Danish professor of law; b. 9 Jan. 1926, Karise; s. of C. J. Gomard and Karen (née Magle) Gomard; m. 1974; one s.; ed. Univ. of Copenhagen; Legal Adviser Danish Dept. of Justice 1950-58, Danish Atomic Comm. 1956-76, Danish Insurance Cos. 1958-; Prof. of Law, Univ. of Copenhagen 1958-; Chair. Bd. of Dirs., Kjobenhavns Handelsbank, Byggeriets Realkreditfond; mem. and Chair. numerous govt. cttees.; Hon. Prof. Univ. of Freiburg; mem. Danish Acad. of Sciences 1975; Nordic Jurists Prize 1987. *Publications:* articles and treatises on contract co. law, civil procedure, with particular emphasis on Danish law. *Address:* Institute of Legal Science, 6, Studiestraede, 1455 Copenhagen K (Office); Hyldegaards Tvaervej 10 a, 2920 Charlottenlund, Denmark (Home). *Telephone:* (01) 912166 (Office); (01) 635864 (Home).

GOMBOJAV, Damdingiyn; Mongolian politician; b. 12 April 1919; ed. Inst. of Oriental Studies, Inst. of Foreign Trade, U.S.S.R.; Head of Import Dept., Foreign Trade Board, Deputy Trade Minister 1954-56; Trade Rep. in Moscow 1956-60; Minister of Foreign Trade 1960-65; Deputy Chair. Council of Ministers, Chair. Comm. for CMEA (Comecon) Affairs 1965-77; Sec. Cen. Cttee., Mongolian People's Revolutionary Party (MPRP) 1977-85, Alt. mem. Political Bureau MPRP 1976-81; mem. Political Bureau MPRP Cen. Cttee. 1981-85; Deputy to the Great People's Hural (Assembly). *Address:* c/o Central Committee of the Mongolian People's Revolutionary Party, Ulan Bator, Mongolia.

GOMBRICH, Sir Ernst (Hans Josef), Kt., C.B.E., PH.D., F.B.A., F.S.A., F.R.S.L.; British art historian; b. 30 March 1909, Vienna, Austria; s. of Dr. Karl Gombrich and Prof. Leonie (née Hock); m. Ilse Heller 1936; one s.; ed. Theresianum, Vienna, and Vienna Univ.; Research Asst., Warburg Inst., Univ. of London 1936-39; BBC Monitoring Service, Second World War; Senior Research Fellow, Warburg Inst. 1946-48, Lecturer 1948-54, Reader 1954-56, Special Lecturer 1956-59, Dir. 1959-76; Prof. of History of the Classical Tradition, Univ. of London 1959-76, Prof. Emer. 1976-; Slade Prof. of Fine Art, Univ. of Oxford 1950-53; Durning-Lawrence Prof. of

History of Art, Univ. Coll., London 1956–59; Visiting Prof. Harvard Univ. 1959; Slade Prof. of Fine Art, Univ. of Cambridge 1961–63; Hon. Fellow, Jesus Coll., Cambridge 1963; Prof. at Large, Cornell Univ. 1970–76; Trustee, British Museum 1974–79; mem. Standing Comm. on Museums and Galleries (now Museums and Galleries Comm.) 1976–83; Sr. Fellow, Royal Coll. of Art 1984; Corresp. mem. Turin, Uppsala, Netherlands, Bavarian and Swedish Acads.; Hon. mem. American Acad. of Arts and Sciences; Foreign mem. American Philosophical Soc., American Acad. and Inst. of Arts and Letters; Hon. Fellow, R.I.B.A.; Hon. D.Lit. (Queen's Univ., Belfast), Hon. LL.D. (St. Andrews), Hon. D.Litt. (Leeds, Oxford), Hon. Litt.D. (Cambridge, Manchester), Hon. D.Hum.Litt. (Chicago Univ.) 1975, (Pa. Univ.) 1977, Hon. D.Litt. (Harvard, London) 1976, D.Univ. (Essex) 1977, Hon. L.H.D. (Brandeis Univ.) 1981; W. H. Smith and Son Annual Literary Award 1964; Medal of N.Y. Univ. 1970; Erasmus Prize 1975; Austrian Cross of Honour 1st class 1975; Pour le Mérite 1977; Hegel Prize from City of Stuttgart 1977, Österreiches Ehren Zeichen 1983, Balzan Preis 1985, Preis der Stadt Wien 1986, Ludwig Wittgenstein Preis 1988. *Publications:* Caricature (with E. Kris) 1940, The Story of Art 1950, (14 editions), Art and Illusion 1959, Meditations on a Hobby Horse 1963, Norm and Form 1966, In Search of Cultural History 1969, Aby Warburg 1970, Symbolic Images 1972, Illusion in Nature and Art (ed. with R. L. Gregory) 1973, Art History and the Social Sciences 1974, The Heritage of Apelles 1976, The Sense of Order 1978, Ideals and Idols 1979, The Image and the Eye 1982, Tributes 1984, New Light on Old Masters 1986, Reflections on the History of Art (Ed. R. Woodfield) 1987. *Leisure interest:* music. *Address:* 19 Briardale Gardens, London, NW3 7PN, England. *Telephone:* 01-435 6639.

GOMER, Robert, PH.D.; American professor of chemistry; b. 24 March 1924, Vienna, Austria; s. of Richard Gomer and Mary Gomer; m. Anne Olah 1955; one s. one d.; ed. Pomona Coll. and Univ. of Rochester; Instructor, then Assoc. Prof., James Franck Inst. and Dept. of Chem., Univ. of Chicago 1950–58, Prof. 1958–, Dir. James Franck Inst. 1977–83, Carl William Eisendrath Distinguished Service Prof. of Chem. 1984–; Assoc. Ed. Journal of Chemical Physics 1957–59, Review of Scientific Instruments 1963–65; mem. Editorial Bd. Surface Science 1964–70; Consultant, Pres.'s Science Advisory Bd. 1961–65; Chair. Editorial Bd. Bulletin of the Atomic Scientists 1965–70, mem. Bd. of Dirs. 1960–84; Assoc. Ed. Applied Physics 1974–; Co-Ed. Springer Series in Chemical Physics 1978–; mem. N.A.S., American Acad. of Arts and Sciences and Leopoldina Akademie der Naturforscher; Bourke Lecturer, Faraday Soc. 1959; Kendall Award in Colloid or Surface Science, American Chemical Soc. 1975; Davisson-Germer Prize, American Physical Soc. 1981. *Publications:* about 160 scientific articles; Field Emission and Field Ionization 1961. *Leisure interests:* skiing, music and literature. *Address:* The University of Chicago, The James Franck Institute, 5640 South Ellis Avenue, Chicago, Ill. 60637; 4824 South Kimbark, Chicago, Ill. 60615, U.S.A. (Home). *Telephone:* (312) 962-7191 (Univ.); (312) 536-2182 (Home).

GOMES, Marshal Francisco da Costa; Portuguese army officer; b. 30 June 1914, Chaves; s. of António José Gomes and Idalina Júlia Monteiro da Costa Gomes; m. Maria Estela née Furtado de Antas Varejao 1952; one s.; ed. Military Coll., Cavalry School, Univs. of Coimbra and Oporto and Inst. de Altos Estudos Militares; Chief of Staff, Military Command, Macau 1949–51; mem. H.Q. staff, NATO, Norfolk, U.K., 1954–56; Under-Sec. of Army Staff 1959–61; 2nd-in-Command Mil. Forces, Mozambique 1965–68; C.-in-C. Mil. Forces, Mozambique 1968–69; C.-in-C. Mil. Forces, Angola 1970–72; Chief of Staff, Armed Forces of Portugal 1972–74, 1974–76; mem. Junta Nacional de Salvação 1974–75; Pres. of Portugal 1974–76; mem. Supreme Revolutionary Council of Armed Forces Movt. 1975–76; Grand Officer Ordem Nacional do Cruzeiro do Sul do Brasil, Medalha de Mérito Militar 1st Class, Campaign Medals Mozambique, Angola, and numerous other awards. *Leisure interests:* riding, swimming. *Address:* Av dos Eva 121-9°C, Lisbon, Portugal.

GOMEZ, Alain Michel, LIC. EN DROIT; French businessman; b. 18 Oct. 1938, Paris; s. of Francis Gomez and Simone Blet; m. Francine le Foyer 1967; ed. Univ. of Paris, Ecole nat. d'administration; Inspecteur des Finances 1965–69; Asst. Dir. of Finance, Saint-Gobain S.A. 1970–71, Financial Dir. 1971–72; joined Société Générale pour l'Emballage 1972, Dir.-Gen. 1972, Pres. 1977–; Pres. and Dir.-Gen. Saint-Gobain Desjonquères 1973–, Saint-Gobain Emballage 1974–, Dir. Duralex branch, Saint-Gobain 1978–, Dir. Saint-Gobain Pont à Mousson 1977–; Pres. Thomson SA Feb. 1982–; Chair. and C.E.O. Thomson CSF 1982–; Chevalier, Légion d'honneur. *Publications:* (co-author under name Jacques Mandrin) L'Enarchie 1967, Socialisme ou Social-médiocratie 1968. *Leisure interest:* cycling. *Address:* 173 Boulevard Haussmann, 75008 Paris (Office); 117 rue du Temple, 75003 Paris, France (Home).

GOMEZ, Jill; British opera and concert singer; b. Trinidad; ed. Royal Acad. of Music, Guildhall School of Music; operatic début with Glyndebourne Festival Opera 1969 and has since sung leading roles incl. Mélisande, Calisto and Ann Truelove in The Rake's Progress; has appeared with The Royal Opera, English Opera and Scottish Opera in roles incl. Pamina, Ilia, Fiordiligi, the Countess in Figaro, Elizabeth in Elegy for Young Lovers, Tytania, Lauretta in Gianni Schicchi, and the Governess in The Turn of the Screw; created the role of Flora in Tippett's The Knot Garden, at

Covent Garden and of the Countess in Thea Musgrave's Voice of Ariadne, Aldeburgh 1974; sang title role in Massenet's Thaïs, Wexford 1974 and Jenifer in The Midsummer Marriage with Welsh Nat. Opera 1976; created title role in William Alwyn's Miss Julie for radio 1977, Tatiana in Eugene Onegin with Kent Opera 1977; Donna Elvira in Don Giovanni, Ludwigsburg Festival 1978; title role in BBC world premiere of Prokoviev's Maddalena 1979; Fiordiligi in Così fan tutte, Bordeaux 1979; sang in premiere of the Eighth Book of Madrigals in Zurich Monteverdi Festival 1979; Violetta in Kent Opera's production of La Traviata, Edinburgh Festival 1979; Cinna in Lucio Silla, Zurich 1981; The Governess in The Turn of the Screw, Geneva 1981; Cleopatra in Giulio Cesare, Frankfurt 1981; Teresa in Benvenuto Cellini, Berlioz Festival, Lyon 1982, Leila in Les Pêcheurs de Perles, Scottish Opera 1982–83; Governess in The Turn of the Screw, English Nat. Opera 1984; Helena in Glyndebourne's production of Britten's A Midsummer Night's Dream; Donna Anna in Don Giovanni, Frankfurt Opera 1985 and with Kent Opera 1988; Rosario in Goyescas by Granados 1988. Regular engagements including recitals in France, Austria, Belgium, Netherlands, Germany, Scandinavia, Switzerland, Italy, Spain and the U.S.A.; Festival appearances include Aix-en-Provence, Spoleto, Bergen, Versailles, Flanders, Netherlands, Prague, Edinburgh and BBC Promenade concerts; numerous recordings, including Vespro della Beata Vergine 1610 (Monteverdi), Acis and Galatea (Handel), The Knot Garden (Tippett), three recital discs of French, Spanish and Mozart songs, Quatre Chansons Françaises (Britten), Trois Poèmes de Mallarmé (Ravel), Chants d'Auvergne (Cantreloube), Les Illuminations (Britten), Bachianas Brasileiras No. 5 (Villa Labos), Cabaret Classics with John Constable, Knoxville-Summer of 1915 (Barber). *Address:* 16 Milton Park, London, N6 5QA, England. *Telephone:* 01-348 4193.

GÓMEZ BERGÉS, Víctor; Dominican lawyer and politician; b. 25 Feb. 1940, Santiago de los Caballeros; ed. Univ. Autónoma de Santo Domingo; Asst. legal officer, Dept. of Formal Complaints, Secr. for Admin., Control and Reclamation of Nat. Resources 1962, Head, Dept. of Complaints 1963, Deputy Sec. of State for Admin., Control and Reclamation of Nat. Resources 1963, for Agric. 1964; Sec. of State for Interior and Police 1965; Sec.-Gen. Dominican Municipal League 1966; Sec. of State for Educ., Fine Art and Culture 1970–72; Sec. of State for Foreign Affairs 1972–75; Sec. of State without Portfolio 1975–77; Sec. of State for Finance 1977; Sec. of State for Industry and Commerce 1977–78; mem. Nat. Devt. Comm.; del. to numerous int. confs.; Orden de Duarte, Sánchez y Muella. *Address:* c/o Secretaría de Estado de Finanzas, Calle México, Santo Domingo, D.N., Dominican Republic.

GOMORY, Ralph Edward, PH.D.; American mathematician and business executive; b. 7 May 1929, Brooklyn Heights, N.Y.; s. of Andrew L. Gomory and Marian Schellenberg; m. Laura Secretan Dumper 1954 (divorced 1968); two s. one d.; ed. Williams Coll., King's Coll., Cambridge, and Princeton Univ; Lieut., U.S. Navy 1954–57; Higgins Lecturer and Asst. Prof., Princeton Univ. 1957–59; joined IBM 1959, Fellow 1964, filled various managerial positions including Dir. Mathematical Science Dept., Dir. of Research 1970–86, Vice-Pres. 1973–84, Sr. Vice-Pres. 1985–, mem. Corporate Man. Bd. 1983–, Sr. Vice-Pres. for Science and Tech. 1986–; Andrew D. White Prof.-at-Large, Cornell Univ. 1970–76; Dir. Bank of New York, IBM Asia/Pacific Group, Nova Pharmaceutical Corpn., Industrial Research Inst.; mem. N.A.S., Nat. Acad. of Eng., American Acad. of Arts and Sciences, Council on Foreign Relations, White House Science Council (1986–); Fellow, Econometric Soc., American Acad. of Arts and Sciences 1973; Trustee, Hampshire Coll. 1977–86, Princeton Univ. 1985–; Hon. D.Sc. (Williams Coll.) 1973, (Polytechnic Univ.) 1987; Hon. L.H.D. (Pace Univ.) 1986; Lanchester Prize, Operations Research Soc. of America 1964, John von Neumann Theory Prize 1984, Harry Goode Memorial Award 1984. *Address:* IBM Corporation, Old Orchard Road, Armonk, N.Y. 10504, U.S.A.

GOMRINGER, Eugen; Swiss professor of aesthetics; b. 20 Jan. 1925, Cachuela Esperanza, Bolivia; m. 1st Klara Stöckli 1950, 2nd Nortrud Ottenhausen; five s. one d.; ed. Kantonsschule, Zürich, and Univ. of Berne; Sec. and Docent, Hochschule für Gestaltung, Ulm 1954–58; Art Dir. Swiss Industrial Abrasives 1959–67; Man. Dir. Schweizer Werkbund, Zürich 1961–67; Man. of Cultural Relations, Rosenthal AG, Germany 1967–; Prof. of Aesthetics, Düsseldorf Art School 1976–; mem. Akad. der Künste, Berlin. *Publications:* several books of poetry and monographs in the art field. *Leisure interests:* mountaineering, art collecting, farming, dogs. *Address:* Art Academy, Eiskellerstr.1, D-4000 Düsseldorf; (Offices); Wurlitz 22, D-8673 Rehau; Werresstrasse 71, D-4040 Neuss, Federal Republic of Germany (Homes). *Telephone:* 09287-72276 (Rosenthal AG); 09283-1324 and 02101-35134 (Homes).

GONÇALVES, Gen. Vasco dos Santos; Portuguese army officer; b. 3 May 1921, Lisbon; s. of Victor Candido Gonçalves and Alda Romana dos Santos; m. Aida Rocha Afonso 1950; one s. one d.; ed. Mil. Coll., Army School; joined Portuguese Army 1942; mem. teaching staff, Bridges and Roads Section, Army School; promoted to rank of Lieut. 1946, Capt. 1954, Maj. 1963, Lieut.-Col. 1967, Brig. 1974, Gen. 1975; various commissions in Eng. Branch of Army, later mem. Directorate, Eng. Branch; mem. Armed Forces Movt. 1974–75, Supreme Revolutionary Council March-Sept. 1975; Prime Minister 1974–75; several awards and decorations. *Leisure interests:*

political economy, philosophy, history, natural history. *Address:* Avenida Estados Unidos da America, 86, 5° esq., 1700 Lisbon, Portugal.

GONCERZEWICZ, Maria Irena; Polish paediatrician; b. 28 August 1917, Brzeźnica; m.; two c.; ed. Medical Faculty, Poznań Univ. 1949; Extraordinary Prof. 1972, Ordinary Prof. 1980; Lecturer and researcher, Paediatric Clinic, Medical Acad., Poznań 1949-53, Sr. Asst. 1954, Adjunct 1955-62, Asst. Prof. 1962-72, Head Dept. of Paediatric Propedeutics, Inst. of Paediatrics, Medical Acad., Poznań 1968-76; Vice-Dir. Inst. of Paediatrics, Medical Acad., Poznań 1970-76; Co-founder and first Gen. Dir. Hospital—Monument Child's Health Centre, Warsaw 1976-; mem. Man. Devt. Cttee. Polish Acad. of Sciences; Chair. Devt. Defects Cttee.; Order of Banner of Labour (1st Class); Commdr.'s and Kt.'s Cross Order of Polonia Restituta, Nat. Educ. Comm. Medal, Gold Hon. Award For Merits to Warsaw, other distinctions. *Publications:* numerous medical publications, total of 197 scientific works published in Polish and foreign journals (1987). *Leisure interests:* reading, symphony music, resting at river- and lake-side. *Address:* ul. Karowa 18a m. 5, 00-324 Warsaw, Poland. *Telephone:* 26-18-75 (Home); 15-40-40 (Office).

GONCHAR, Oles' (Aleksandr Terentyevich); Soviet (Ukrainian) writer and official; b. 1918, Sukha, nr. Poltava, Ukraine; contributor to regional newspaper 1933-37; staff mem. of Kharkov Dist. Komsomol newspaper 1937-41; started publishing stories and novels 1938; served in Soviet Army 1941-45; graduated Dnepropetrovsk Univ. 1946; mem. of CPSU 1946-; mem. of U.S.S.R. Writers' Union 1947; Chair. of Ukrainian Writers' Union 1962, 1966 and 1970; elected deputy to U.S.S.R. Supreme Soviet 1970-; Academician, Ukrainian Acad. of Sciences 1978; awards include: Order of Lenin 1960, Order of Glory, Order of Red Star, three medals for bravery, Stalin Prizes 1947, 1948, Shevchenko Prize 1962, Lenin Prize 1964, State Prize 1982 (for book "Your Dawn"). *Publications include:* Spring at the Morava 1938, Man and the Weapon 1962, The Cathedral 1968, The Cyclone 1970, The Brigantine 1973, Your Dawn 1982.

GONDA, Jan, PH.D.; Netherlands Sanskrit scholar; b. 14 April 1905, Gouda; s. of Jan Gonda and Martha J. Derksema; m. Henriette Wijnholt 1962; ed. State Univ. Utrecht and Leiden; Extraordinary Prof. Sanskrit State Univ. Utrecht 1932-41, Prof. Sanskrit and Indo-European Linguistics 1941-76; mem. Royal Dutch Acad. of Sciences; Hon. Fellow Royal Asiatic Soc.; Hon. Foreign Mem. American Acad. of Arts and Sciences; Rabindranath Tagore Medallist. *Publications:* Oud-Javaans Brahmanda Purana (2 vols.) 1932, Similes in Sanskrit Literature 1939, Ursprung und Wesen des indischen Dramas 1940, Sanskrit in Indonesia 1952, Repetition in the Veda 1959, Die Religionen Indiens (Vol. I) 1960, (Vol. II) 1963, Visnuism and Sivaism 1970, Old Indian 1971, The Vision of the Vedic Poets 1963, The Savayajñas 1965, Dual Deities 1974, Vedic Literature 1975, Selected Studies (5 vols.) 1975, Medieval Religious Literature in Sanskrit 1977, The Ritual Sutras 1977, Vedic Hymns Not Employed in the Solemn Ritual 1978, Vedic Ritual 1980, The Vedic Morning Litany 1981, The Haviryajñāh Somāh 1982, Prajapati and the year 1984, Pūsan and Sarasvati 1985, The Ritual Functions of Grasses in the Veda 1985, Prajāpati's Rise to Higher Rank 1986, Rice and Barley Offerings in the Veda 1987, Manka Interpretation in the Satapathe-Bráhmana 1988, Prayer and Blessing 1988, and many other works on Sanskrit and Indo-European linguistics. *Leisure interests:* walking, music. *Address:* 13 van Hogendorpstraat, Utrecht, Netherlands (Home). *Telephone:* 030-516531.

GONG BENYAN; Chinese state official; b. Jan. 1927, Wendeng Co., Shandong Prov.; m. Lin Lezhi; two s. one d.; joined Communist Youth League 1943, Party 1944; Dir. Qiqihar No. 1 Machine Tools Plant 1967, jailed by followers of 'Gang of Four' 1968-72, reinstated 1977; Dir. Fulaerji No. 1 Heavy-duty Machinery Plant 1978; mem. CCP Standing Cttee. Heilongjiang Prov. 1981; Dir. Industry and Communications Office, and Chair. Prov. Econ. Comm., Heilongjiang 1981; alt. mem. 12th CCP Cen. Cttee. 1982-87; Vice-Gov., Heilongjiang 1983-; Mayor of Harbin 1985-. *Leisure interest:* reading works of literature. *Address:* 39 Ashihe Street, Nangang Dist., Harbin, Heilongjiang; Heilongjiang Provincial People's Government, Harbin, Heilongjiang, People's Republic of China.

GONG PUSHENG; Chinese diplomatist; b. 6 Sept. 1913, Shanghai; m. Chang Hanfu (deceased); two d.; Deputy Dir. Int. Orgs. and Confs. Dept., Ministry of Foreign Affairs 1949-58, Dir. 1958-67; mem. 1st-4th Exec. Cttee., All-China Democratic Women's Fed. 1949-84; Vice-Pres. Red Cross Soc. of China 1979-85; Amb. to Ireland 1980-83; mem. of Nat. Cttee., Chinese People's Political Consultative Conf. 1983-; Vice-Pres. China UN Asscn. 1985-; Prof. Foreign Affairs Coll., Beijing 1985-. *Address:* c/o Ministry of Foreign Affairs, Beijing, China.

GONTHIER, Giovinella, M.A.; Seychelles diplomatist; m.; ed. Wheaton Coll. and Harvard University; lecturer Seychelles Coll., Mont Fleuri 1973-75; Dir. Meeting Planning Div. Combined Insurance Co., Chicago 1975-79; Counsellor Ministry of Foreign Affairs, also served at Embassy, France 1979-80, Charge d'affaires, UN Perm. Mission, New York 1980-83, Amb. to U.S.A. and Perm. Rep. to UN, New York 1983-87.

GONZALES POSADA, Luis; Peruvian politician and lawyer; b. 30 July 1945, Pisco; fmr. Legal Adviser, Banco Industrial, Corporacíon Financiera de Desarrollo, Electricidad del Perú and of Social Security Dept.; mem. of Bd. of Dirs., Seguro Social Obrero, Seguro Social del Empleado, Empresa

Nacional de Turismo del Perú, La Crónica, Futura and Visión Peruana publishing cos.; Dir. and Founder of the daily Hoy and the weekly Visión; has been on staff of La Tribuna, La Prensa, Correo and La Crónica; mem. Colegio de Abogados de Lima and of Colegio de Periodistas de Lima; Minister of Justice 1985-86. *Address:* c/o Ministry of Justice, Palacio de Gobierno, Pescaderia, Lima, Peru.

GONZÁLEZ ARIAS, Luis; Paraguayan diplomatist; b. 1938, Carapegua; m.; two c.; ed. Faculty of Law, Nat. Univ. of Asunción, Univ. de la República, Montevideo, Uruguay, Acad. of Int. Law, The Hague; Cultural Affairs Officer, Ministry of Foreign Affairs 1961-63, Dir. Int. Org., Treaties and Conf. Dept. 1965-69; Vice-Consul, Montevideo 1963-65; Minister Counsellor, Washington 1969-71; Alt. Rep. of Paraguay to OAS 1969-71; Del. to Gen. Assembly, OAS 1971-; Minister Plenipotentiary of Mission of Paraguay to UN 1971-79; Perm. Rep. to UN 1979-84; Del. to Third UN Conf. on the Law of the Sea, UN Conf. on Water Resources. *Address:* c/o Ministerio des Asuntos Exteriores, Asunción, Paraguay.

GONZÁLEZ CASANOVA, Pablo; Mexican researcher and professor; b. 11 Feb. 1922, Toluca; s. of Pablo González Casanova and Concepción del Valle; m. Natalia Henríquez Ureña 1947; three s.; ed. El Colegio de México, Escuela Nacional de Antropología, Univ. Nacional Autónoma de México and Univ. de Paris; Asst. Researcher, Inst. de Investigaciones Sociales, Univ. Nacional Autónoma de México (UNAM) 1944-50, Researcher 1950-52, Full-time Researcher 1973-78; Researcher, El Colegio de México 1950-54; Sec. Gen. Asscn. of Univs. 1953-54; Titular Prof. of Mexican Sociology, Escuela Nacional de Ciencias Políticas y Sociales, UNAM 1952-66, of Gen. Sociology 1954-58; Dir. Escuela Nacional de Ciencias Políticas y Sociales 1957-65, Full-time Titular Prof. 1964-65, Titular Prof. of Research Planning 1967-; Dir. Inst. Investigaciones Sociales, UNAM 1966-70; Rector, UNAM 1970-72; Visiting Prof. Cambridge Univ. 1981-82; Pres. Admin. Cttee. Facultad Latinoamericana de Ciencias Sociales, Santiago and Centro Latinoamericano de Investigaciones Sociales, Rio de Janeiro, UNESCO 1959-65; Consultant UN Univ. 1983-87; Dir. Centre Interdisciplinarii Univ. Nacional Autónoma di Mexico 1986-; mem. Asscn. Int. de Sociologues de Langue Française, Comité Int. pour la Documentation des Sciences Sociales, Acad. de la Investigación Científica; Pres. Asociación Latinoamericana de Sociología 1969-72. *Publications:* El misoneísmo y la modernidad cristiana 1948, Satira del Siglo XVIII (with José Miranda) 1953, Una utopia de América 1953, La literatura perseguida en la crisis de la Colonia 1958, La ideología norteamericana sobre inversiones extranjeras 1955, Estudio de la técnica social 1958, La Democracia en México 1965, Las categorías del desarrollo económico y la investigación en ciencias sociales 1967, Sociología de la explotación 1969, América Latina: Historia de Medio Siglo 1925-1975 (2 vols., Editor) 1977, Historia del Movimiento Obrero en América Latina, Siglo XX 1981, El Estado y los Partidos Políticos en México 1981. *Address:* Peña Pobre 28, Tlalpan, Mexico, D.F. 14050, Mexico. *Telephone:* 5506702.

GONZÁLEZ DEL VALLE, Jorge; Guatemalan economist and international official; ed. Univ. of San Carlos, Guatemala, Columbia Univ., New York, Yale Univ., New Haven, Conn.; worked in Bank of Guatemala and Cen. American Bank for Econ. Integration; Exec. Dir. IMF for four years; Exec. Sec. Cen. American Monetary Council for nine years; Head Centre for Latin American Monetary Studies (CEMLA) 1978-. *Address:* CEMLA, Durango 54, México 7, D.F., Mexico.

GONZÁLEZ MÁRQUEZ, Felipe; Spanish lawyer and politician; b. 5 March 1942, Seville; m. Carmen Romero; two s. one d.; ed. lower and high school, school of law, continued studies at Catholic Univ. of Louvaine, Belgium; on graduating from law school, opened first labour law office to deal with workers' problems in Seville 1966; mem. Spanish Socialist Youth 1962; mem. Spanish Socialist Party (Partido Socialista Obrero Español PSOE) 1964-, mem. Seville Provincial Cttee. 1965-69, Nat. Cttee. 1969-70, mem. Exec. Bd. 1970, First Sec. 1974-79, resigned; re-elected Sept. 1979-, now Sec.-Gen.; Prime Minister of Spain and Pres. Council of Ministers Dec. 1982-; Chair. Socialist Parl. Group; Grand Cross of the Order of Mil. Merit 1984. *Publications:* What is Socialism? 1976, P.S.O.E. 1977. *Leisure interest:* reading. *Address:* Ministerio de la Presidencia, Complejo de la Moncloa, Edif. INIA, Madrid; Calle Joaquín García Morato 165, Madrid 3, Spain. *Telephone:* 2544107.

GONZÁLEZ MARTÍN, H.E. Cardinal Marcelo; Spanish ecclesiastic; b. 16 Jan. 1918, Villanubla, Valladolid; ordained 1941; consecrated Bishop of Astorga 1961; titular Archbishop of Case Mediane 1966; auxiliary Archbishop of Barcelona 1967; Archbishop of Toledo and Primate of Spain 1971-; created Cardinal by Pope Paul VI 1973. *Address:* Arco de Palacio 1, Toledo, Spain. *Telephone:* 224 100.

GOOCH, Graham Alan; British cricketer; b. 23 July 1953, Leytonstone; s. of Alfred and Rose Gooch; m.; ed. Norlington Junior High School, Leytonstone; right-hand batsman, right-arm medium bowler; début for Essex 1973; awarded county cap 1975; Test début 1975 (scoring 0 in each innings); toured Australia 1978-79, Australia and India 1979-80, West Indies 1981, India and Sri Lanka 1981-82, India 1987; Capt. unofficial English XI in S.A. tour 1982; banned from representing England for three years for part in S.A. tour 1982-85; shared with K. S. McEwan in second wicket record partnership for Essex, 321 v. Northants., Ilford 1978; record core of 198, not out, for any one-day competition in Benson & Hedges Cup match Essex v. Sussex, Hove 1982; record score of 176 in John Player Sunday League match Essex v. Glamorgan, Southend 1983; Capt. of Essex 1986-, of England July 1988. *Leisure interests:* squash, golf, football. *Address:* c/o Essex County Cricket Club, The County Ground, New Writtle Street, Chelmsford, Essex, CM2 0PG, England.

GOODALL, Sir Reginald, Kt., C.B.E.; British conductor; b. 13 July 1901, Lincoln; s. of Edward Goodall and Adelaide Jones; m. Eleanor Gipps 1932; no c.; ed. Lincoln Cathedral Choir School and Boston, Mass., U.S.A. and Royal Coll. of Music; conductor, English Nat. Opera 1945-47, Royal Opera House, Covent Garden 1947-; Hon. D.Mus. (Oxford, Leeds). *Leisure interest:* gardening. *Address:* 16 Lower Addison Gardens, London, W.14; Barham Court, Barham, Canterbury, Kent, England. *Telephone:* 01-603 7055 (London); Barham 831-392.

GOODE, Anthony William, B.S., M.D., F.R.C.S., F.R.S.M.; British surgeon; b. 3 Aug. 1944, Newcastle-upon-Tyne; s. of William Henry Goode and Eileen Veronica Goode; m. Patricia Josephine Flynn 1987; ed. Corby School and Univ. of Newcastle-upon-Tyne; clinical surgical posts in Newcastle Hosps. Group 1968-76; Univ. of London Teaching Hosps. 1976-; Prin. Investigator in Life Sciences NASA 1968-; Reader in Surgery Univ. of London 1984-; Consultant Surgeon London Hosp., Whitechapel, London 1984-; Asst. Sec. Gen. British Acad. of Forensic Science 1982-87; Hon. Sec. British Asscn. of Endocrine Surgeons 1983-; mem. Int. Soc. of Surgery 1984-, Int. Soc. of Endocrine Surgeons 1984-, New York Acad. of Sciences 1986-. *Publications:* numerous papers and articles on nutrition in surgical patients, endocrine diseases, metabolic changes in manned spaceflight and related topics. *Leisure interests:* cricket, music-especially opera. *Address:* The Surgical Unit, The London Hospital, Whitechapel, London, E1 1BB, England. *Telephone:* 01-377 7000.

GOODENOUGH, Ward Hunt, PH.D.; American anthropologist; b. 30 May 1919, Cambridge, Mass.; s. of Erwin R. Goodenough and Helen M. Lewis; m. Ruth A. Gallagher 1941; two s. two d.; ed. Groton School, Cornell and Yale Univs.; Instructor in Anthropology, Univ. of Wis. 1948-49; Asst. Prof. of Anthropology, Univ. of Pa. 1949-54, Assoc. Prof. 1954-62, Chair. of Dept. 1976-82, Prof. and Curator of Oceanian Ethnology 1962-80, Univ. Prof. 1980-; Visiting Prof. of Anthropology, Cornell Univ. 1961-62, Univ. of Hawaii 1982-83; Fulbright Lecturer, St. Patrick's College, Maynooth, Ireland 1987; Bd. Chair., Human Relations Area Files Inc. 1971-81; mem. Bd. of Dirs. A.A.A.S. 1972-75; Pres. American Ethnological Soc. 1963, Soc. for Applied Anthropology 1964; mem. American Philosophical Soc., American Acad. of Arts and Sciences, Nat. Acad. of Sciences; Ed. American Anthropologist 1966-70. *Publications:* Property, Kin and Community on Truk 1951, Co-operation in Change 1963, Explorations in Cultural Anthropology 1964, Description and Comparison in Cultural Anthropology 1970, Culture, Language and Society 1971, Trukese-English Dictionary 1980, Supplementary vol. 1989. *Leisure interests:* music, stamp collecting. *Address:* University Museum, Philadelphia, Pa. 19104-6398; 204 Fox Lane, Wallingford, Pa. 19086, U.S.A. *Telephone:* 215-898-7461 (Office); 215-565-1084 (Home).

GOODES, Melvin Russell, B.COMM., M.B.A.; Canadian business executive; b. 11 April 1935, Hamilton, Ont.; s. of late Cedric P. Goodes and of Mary M. (Lewis) Goodes; m. Arlene M. Bourne 1963; one s. two d.; ed. Queen's Univ., Kingston, Ont. and Univ. of Chicago; Research Assoc. Canadian Econ. Research Assocs. Toronto 1957-58; Market Planning Coordinator, Ford Motor Co. of Canada 1960-64; Asst. to Vice-Pres. O'Keefe Breweries, Toronto 1964-65; joined Warner-Lambert Co. 1965, Pres. Warner-Lambert Mexico 1970-76, Pres. Pan-Am Zone 1976-77, Pres. Pan-Am (Asia Zone) 1977-79, Pres. Consumer Products Div. 1979-80, Sr. Vice-Pres. then Pres. Consumer Products Group 1981-83, Exec. Vice-Pres. then Pres. U.S. Operations 1984-85, Pres. and C.O.O. 1985-; Ford Foundation Fellow 1958; Sears, Roebuck Foundation Fellow 1959. *Leisure interests:* golf, tennis, racquetball, bridge. *Address:* Warner-Lambert Company, 201 Tabor Road, Morris Plains, N.J. 07950, U.S.A. *Telephone:* (201) 540-3636.

GOODISON, Sir Nicholas Proctor, Kt., PH.D., F.S.A., F.R.S.A.; British stock-broker; b. 16 May 1934, Radlett; s. of Edmund Harold Goodison and Eileen Mary Carrington Proctor; m. Judith Abel Smith 1960; one s. two d.; ed. Marlborough Coll. and King's Coll., Cambridge; joined H. E. Goodison & Co., of The Stock Exchange (now named Quilter, Goodison Co. Ltd.) 1958, Partner 1962, Senior Partner 1975-, Chair. 1985-; mem. Council of The Stock Exchange 1968-, Chair. various standing cttees. 1971-76, Chair. of The Stock Exchange 1976-(88), of Int. Stock Exchange 1987-88; Vice-Pres. Int. Fed. of Stock Exchanges 1982-84, Pres. 1985-86; Chair. Courtauld Inst., TSB Group 1988-; Dir. (non-exec.) British Steel 1989-; Trustee, Nat. Heritage Memorial Fund 1988-; Vice-Chair. Bd. of English Nat. Opera; Chair. Nat. Art-Collections Fund, Bd. Burlington Magazine Publs.; Hon. Keeper of Furniture, Fitzwilliam Museum, Cambridge; Hon. Treas. Furniture History Soc.; Pres. Antiquarian Horological Soc.; Gov. Marlborough Coll.; Hon. D.Litt. (City Univ.). *Publications:* English Barometers 1680-1860 1968, Ormolu: the Work of Matthew Boulton 1974; many papers and articles on the history of furniture, clocks and barometers. *Leisure interest:* history of furniture and decorative arts. *Address:* 25 Milk Street, London, EC2V 8LU, England. *Telephone:* (01) 606-7070.

GOODLAD, John I, PH.D.; American university teacher; b. 19 Aug. 1920, N. Vancouver, B.C., Canada; s. of William Goodlad and Mary Inkster; m. Evalene M. Pearson 1945; one s. one d.; ed. Univs. of British Columbia and Chicago; fmr. school teacher, school principal and dir. of educ. in B.C.; consultant in curriculum, Atlanta (Ga.) Area Teacher Educ. Service 1947-49; Assoc. Prof. Emory Univ. and Agnes Scott Coll. 1949-50; Prof. and Dir. Div. of Teacher Educ. Emory Univ. and Dir. Agnes Scott Coll.—Emory Univ, Teacher Educ. Program 1950-56; Prof. and Dir. Center for Teacher Educ. Univ. of Chicago 1956-60; Dir. Corinne A. Seeds Univ. Elementary School, Univ. of Calif., Los Angeles 1960-84; Prof. Graduate School of Educ., Univ. of Calif. (L.A.) 1960-85, Dean 1967-83; Dir. of Research, Inst. for Devt. of Educ. Activities Inc. 1966-82; Prof. Coll. of Educ. Univ. of Washington 1985-; recipient of nine hon. degrees and other awards. *Publications:* numerous books and articles in educ. journals. *Leisure interests:* boating, fishing, walking. *Address:* University of Washington, College of Education, Area of Policy, Governance and Administration, M203 Miller Hall DQ-12, Seattle, Wash. 98195, U.S.A. *Telephone:* 206-543-6230; 206-543-6162.

GOODMAN, Baron (Life Peer) cr. 1965, of the City of Westminster; **Arnold Abraham Goodman,** C.H., M.A., LL.M.; British solicitor; b. 21 Aug. 1913; ed. Univ. Coll., London, and Downing Coll., Cambridge; Partner, Goodman Derrick & Co., Solicitors; Chair. Arts Council of Great Britain 1965-72, British Lion Films (Holdings) 1965-72; mem. South Bank Theatre Bd. 1968-81, Industrial Reorganization Comm. 1969-71; Fellow, Univ. Coll., London; Chair. Assen. for Business Sponsorship of the Arts, Theatres' Trust; Pres. Theatre Investment Fund 1985; Chair. Newspaper Publishers' Assen. 1970-76; Pres. Nat. Book League 1972-84; mem. Bd. of Dirs. Royal Opera House, Covent Garden 1972-83; Pres. Theatres Advisory Council 1972-; Pres. English Nat. Opera 1986; Chair. Housing Corpn. and Nat. Building Agency 1973-77; Deputy Chair. British Council 1976-; Master of Univ. Coll., Oxford 1976-86, Hon. Fellow 1986-; Dimbleby Memorial Lecture 1974. *Publication:* Not for the Record 1972. *Address:* 9-11 Fulwood Place, Gray's Inn, London, WC1V 6HQ, England. *Telephone:* 01-404 0606.

GOODMAN, Julian; American broadcasting executive; b. 1 May 1922, Glasgow, Ky.; s. of Charles Austin and Clara (Franklin) Goodman; m. Betty Davis 1946; three s. one d.; ed. Western Kentucky and George Washington Univs.; Vice-Pres., NBC News 1961-65; Senior Exec. Vice-Pres. NBC Inc. 1965, Pres. 1966-74, C.E.O. 1970-77, Chair. 1974-79; Dir. NBC, RCA Corpn., Associated Press; Trustee, The Museum of Broadcasting; Hon. LL.D. (William Jewell Coll., Liberty, Mo.), Hon. D. Hum. Litt. (Florida Univ.) 1973; George Foster Peabody Award 1947; Gold Medal, Int. Radio and TV Soc. 1972; Paul White Memorial Award, Int. Conf. of Radio and TV News Dirs. 1973; Distinguished Service Award, Nat. Assen. of Broadcasters 1976. *Leisure interests:* sailing, golf. *Address:* National Broadcasting Co. Inc., 30 Rockefeller Plaza, New York, N.Y. 10020, U.S.A. *Telephone:* 212-664-4444.

GOODMAN, Nelson, PH.D.; American professor of philosophy; b. 7 Aug. 1906, W. Somerville, Mass.; s. of Henry L. Goodman and Sarah (Woodbury) Goodman; m. Katharine Sturgis 1944; no c.; ed. Harvard Coll. and Harvard Graduate School of Arts and Sciences; Instructor Tufts Coll. 1945-46; Assoc. Prof. Univ. of Pa. 1946-51, Prof. of Philosophy 1951-64; H. A. Wolfson Prof. of Philosophy, Brandeis Univ. 1964-67; Research Assoc. in Educ. Harvard Univ. 1967-75, Prof. of Philosophy 1968-77, Prof. Emer. 1977-; Corporator Worcester Art Museum 1984-89; numerous visiting lectureships, fellowships, etc.; Corresp. Fellow, British Acad.; Hon. L.H.D. (Pa.); Hon. L.D. (Adelphi). *Publications:* The Structure of Appearance 1951, Fact, Fiction and Forecast 1954, Languages of Art 1968, Problems and Projects 1972, Ways of Worldmaking 1976, Of Mind and Other Matters 1984, Reconceptions (with Catherine Elgin) 1988. *Leisure interest:* fine arts (study and collecting). *Address:* Emerson Hall, Harvard University, Cambridge, Mass., U.S.A. *Telephone:* (617) 495-2195; (617) 495-2191.

GOODMAN, Raymond John; British international civil servant; b. 26 Oct. 1916, London; s. of J. S. Goodman and Helena Taylor; m. Dorothy Bruchholz 1953; two s. two d.; ed. London School of Econs. and Univs. of Copenhagen and Oslo; War Service, R.N.V.R. 1940-46; Dir. Political and Econ. Planning (P.E.P.), London 1946-53; Asst. to Chair. of Marks and Spencer Ltd. 1953-56; joined World Bank Staff 1956, Asst. Dir. of Admin. 1962-65, Deputy Dir. Far East (later Asia) Dept. 1965-68, Dir. E. Asia and Pacific Dept. 1968-74, Dir. Financial Policy 1975-77, Asst. to Senior Vice-Pres. (Operations) 1977-80; Consultant to World Bank 1982-; Adviser to Fed. Gov. of Nigeria 1981; Team Leader, Ind. Review of Papua New Guinea economy 1985 (published by Australian Nat. Univ. 1985); Chief of Mission to review Netherlands Antilles and Aruba Economies 1986; Team Leader, Special Study on Indonesia 1988; Hon. Vice-Pres. Consumers Assen. of G.B. 1957-; Pres. Group Health Assen. of Washington, D.C. 1962-63. *Address:* 2946 Macomb Street, N.W., Washington, D.C. 20008, U.S.A. (Home). *Telephone:* EM2-2946 (Home).

GOODPASTER, Gen. Andrew Jackson, M.S.E., PH.D.; American army officer (retd.); b. 12 Feb. 1915, Granite City, Ill.; s. of Andrew Jackson Goodpaster and Teresa Mary (Mrovka) Goodpaster; m. Dorothy Anderson 1939; two d.; ed. McKendree Coll., Lebanon, Ill., U.S. Mil. Acad., Command and Gen. Staff School, Fort Leavenworth, Kan., and Princeton Univ.; C.O.

48th Engineer Battalion, Italy 1943; Staff Officer, War Dept. 1944–47; Graduate study, Princeton Univ. 1947–50; Special Asst. to Chief to Staff, Supreme HQ Allied Powers Europe (SHAPE) 1950–54; District Engineer, San Francisco 1954; Staff Sec. to Pres. of U.S.A. 1954–61; Asst. Div. Commdr. 3rd Infantry Div. 1961; Commdg. Gen. 8th Infantry Div., Europe 1961–62; Asst. to Chair. Joint Chiefs of Staff 1962–66; Dir. Joint Staff, Org. of Joint Chiefs of Staff 1966–67; Commandant, Nat. War Coll., Washington, D.C., with added duty as U.S. Army Rep., UN Mil. Staff Cttee. 1967–68; mem. U.S. Del to Paris talks on Viet-Nam April–June 1968; Deputy Commdr. U.S. Mil. Assistance Command, Viet-Nam 1968–69; C.-in-C. U.S. European Command 1969–74; Supreme Allied Commdr. Europe (NATO) 1969–74; Fellow, Woodrow Wilson Int. Center for Scholars, Washington, D.C. 1975–76; Prof., Govt. and Int. Studies, The Citadel, Charleston, S.C. 1976–77; Supt. U.S. Mil. Acad., West Point 1977–81; Chair. American Battle Monuments Comm. 1985–; Distinguished Service Cross, Defense D.S.M. with Oak Leaf Cluster, Army D.S.M. with Three Oak Leaf Clusters, Navy D.S.M.; Air Force D.S.M., Silver Star, Legion of Merit with Oak Leaf Cluster, Purple Heart with Oak Leaf Cluster, Medal of Freedom 1984, numerous other U.S. and foreign decorations from Italy, Repub. of Korea, Netherlands, Belgium, Luxembourg, Fed. Repub. of Germany, Turkey and Portugal. *Publication:* For the Common Defense 1977. *Address:* 409, N. Fairfax Street, Alexandria, Va. 22314; c/o American Battle Monuments Commission, 20 Massachusetts Avenue N.W., Room 5127, Washington, D.C., U.S.A.

GOODWIN, John Forrest, M.D., F.R.C.P., F.A.C.C.; British professor of clinical cardiology; b. 1. Dec. 1918, Ealing; s. of Col. W. R. P. Goodwin and Myrtle Dale Goodwin; m. Barbara Cameron Robertson 1943; one s. one d.; ed. Cheltenham Coll., St. Mary's Hosp. Medical School, Univ. of London; Lecturer, Sr. Lecturer and Prof. of Clinical Cardiology, Royal Postgraduate Medical School, London 1949–84, Prof. Emer. 1984–; Pres. British Cardiac Soc. 1972–76, Int. Soc. and Fed. of Cardiology 1978–80; Second Vice-Pres. Royal Coll. of Physicians of London 1979–80; mem. of Council British Heart Foundation 1975–85, Expert Cttee. on Cardiovascular Disease WHO; Chair. Coronary Prevention Group, U.K. 1985–88, Nat. Forum for Coronary Heart Disease Prevention 1987; Hon. Consulting Cardiologist St. George's Hosp., London 1986; Star of Pakistan, Commdr. of the Icelandic Falcon; Dr. h.c. (Lisbon); Hon. F.A.C.P. *Publications:* numerous scientific papers to medical journals. *Leisure interests:* history, photography, travel. *Address:* Cromwell Hospital, Cromwell Road, London, SW5 0TU (Office); 2 Pine Grove, Lake Road, Wimbledon, London, SW19 7HE, England (Home). *Telephone:* 01-370 4233 (Office); 01-947 4851 (Home).

GOODWIN, Leonard George, C.M.G., B.SC., M.B., B.S., F.R.C.P., F.R.S.; British medical scientist; b. 11 July 1915; s. of Harry George Goodwin and Lois Goodwin; m. Marie Evelyn Coates 1940; no c.; ed. William Ellis School, London, Univ. Coll. London, Univ. Coll. Hosp.; Demonstrator, School of Pharmacy, London 1935–39; Protozoologist, Wellcome Labs. of Tropical Medicine 1939–63, Head of Labs. 1958–63; Dir. Nuffield Labs. of Comparative Medicine, Inst. of Zoology, The Zoological Soc. of London 1964–80, Dir. of Science, Zoological Soc. of London 1966–80; Consultant, Wellcome Trust 1984–; Jt. Hon. Sec. Royal Soc. of Tropical Medicine and Hygiene 1968–74, Pres. 1979–81; Chair. Trypanosomiasis Panel, Overseas Devt. Ministry 1974–77, Filariasis Steering Cttee., WHO Special Programme 1978–82; Chair. Editorial Bd. Parasitology 1980–, Royal Soc./U.F.A.W. Steering Group on Guidelines on Care of Lab. Animals 1985–; Hon. Dir. Wellcome Museum for Medical Science 1984–85, Wellcome Trust Film Unit 1986–; Fellow Univ. Coll. London 1981–; Hon. D. Sc. (Brunel) 1986; Soc. of Apothecaries Gold Medal 1974, Harrison Memorial Medal 1978, Schofield Medal, Guelph Univ. 1979, Silver Medal, Zoological Soc. 1980. *Publications:* Biological Standardization (Jt. Author) 1950, Biochemistry and Physiology of Protozoa (Contrib.) 1955, A New Tropical Hygiene (Jt. Author) 1960, Recent Advances in Pharmacology (contrib.) 1962; many contribs. to scientific journals, mainly on pharmacology and chemotherapy of tropical diseases, especially malaria, trypansomiasis and helminth infections. *Leisure interests:* dabbling in arts and crafts, especially pottery (slipware), gardening and passive participation in music and opera. *Address:* Shepperlands Farm, Park Lane, Finchampstead, Berks., RG11 4QF, England. *Telephone:* Eversley 732153.

GOODWIN, Trevor Walworth, C.B.E., D.SC., F.I.BIOL., F.R.S.C., C.CHEM., F.R.S.; British professor of biochemistry; b. 22 June 1916, Neston, Cheshire; s. of Arthur W. Goodwin and Agnes Goodwin; m. Kathleen S. Hill 1944; three d.; ed. Birkenhead Inst. and Univ. of Liverpool; wartime scientist, Ministry of Food 1940–44; Lecturer in Biochem. Univ. of Liverpool 1944–50, Sr. Lecturer 1950–59; Prof. of Biochem. and Agricultural Biochem. Univ. Coll. of Wales, Aberystwyth 1959–66; Johnston Prof. of Biochem. Univ. of Liverpool 1966–83, Prof. Emer. 1983–; Nat. Science Sr. Foreign Scientist, Univ. of Calif. (Davis) 1964; numerous visiting professorships and lectureships etc.; CIBA medallist, Biochemical Soc. 1970; Roussel Prize 1982 and many other awards and distinctions. *Publications:* six books and over 400 articles in scientific journals. *Leisure interests:* gardening, writing, history of biochemistry. *Address:* Monzar, 9 Woodlands Close, Parkgate, S. Wirral, Cheshire, L64 6RU, England. *Telephone:* (051) 336 4494.

GOOKIN, R(alph) Burt, B.SC., M.B.A.; American business executive; b. 23 June 1914, Chariton, Iowa; s. of Albert Burton and Maude Mary McFarland Gookin; m. Mary Louise Carroll 1948; one s. one d.; ed. Northwestern Univ. and Harvard Business School; with Firestone Tyre and Rubber Co 1935–40, Forest Lawn Co. 1940–41, Los Angeles Shipbuilding and Drydock Co. 1942–43, Consolidated Steel Co. 1944–45, Exec. Accountant H. J. Heinz Co. 1945, Controller 1951, Dir. and Vice-Pres. Finance 1959, Exec. Vice Pres. 1964, Pres. and C.E.O. 1966, Vice-Chair. and C.E.O. 1973–79; mem and fmr. Chair. Bd. of Govs., Uniform Product Code Council; mem. Bd. of Dirs. Bank America Corpn., Westinghouse Electric Corpn., PPG Industries, Allegheny Health, Educ. & Research Corpn., Pittsburgh Br. of Fed Reserve Bank of Cleveland, Grocery Mfrs. of America, Inc. (fmr. Chair.) etc.; mem. Bd. of Visitors, Graduate School of Business, Univ. of Pittsburgh; mem. Business Advisory Council, Graduate School of Industrial Admin., Carnegie-Mellon Univ.; fmr. Pres. of Financial Exec. Research Foundation and Pittsburgh Chapter of Financial Execs. Inst. *Leisure interest:* golf. *Address:* 300 Fox Chapel Road, Pittsburgh, Pa. 15238, U.S.A.

GOONERATNE, Tilak Eranga, B.A.; Ceylonese civil servant and lawyer b. 27 March 1919; s. of Thomas Edwin Gooneratne and Dona Sophia Athulathmudali; m. Pamela Jean Rodrigo 1947; two d.; ed. St. John's Coll. Panadura, Ceylon, Ceylon Univ., and Ceylon Law Coll.; joined Ceylon Civil Service 1943; Asst. Sec. Ministry of External Affairs 1947–51; Controller of Immigration and Emigration 1949–51; Govt. Agent, Trincomalee 1951–54 Matra 1954–56; Registrar Gen. Marriages, Births and Deaths 1956–58 Dir.-Gen. of Broadcasting and Dir. of Information, Ceylon 1958–60; Commr Co-operative Devt. 1960–63; Acting Perm. Sec. Ministry of Commerce and Trade 1963; Dir. of Econ. Affairs 1963; Deputy Sec. to Treasury 1963–65 Pres. Colombo Plan Council for Tech. Co-operation in S. and S.E. Asia 1964–65; Del. to UN Gen. Assembly 1964–65; Deputy Sec.-Gen. Commonwealth Secr. 1965–70; High Commr. to U.K. 1970–77, Amb. to European Communities 1974–78, also Amb. to Belgium, Netherlands Luxembourg 1975–78. *Publications:* An Historical Outline of the Development of the Marriage and Divorce Laws of Ceylon, An Historical Outline of the Development of the Marriage and Divorce Laws Applicable to Muslims in Ceylon, Fifty Years of Co-operative Development in Ceylon *Leisure interests:* tennis, table tennis, travel. *Address:* 17B Warwick Avenue, London, W.9, England.

GOONETILLEKE, Albert, M.D., F.R.C.P.A., M.R.C. PATH.; Ceylonese pathologist; b. 4 Feb. 1936, Colombo; s. of Arlis Goonetilleke (deceased); m Sunanaseele Wijesinghe 1958; one s. one d.; medical officer Sri Lanka Health Dept. 1962–68; lecturer Univ. of Edin. 1968–70, Univ. of Leeds 1970–71; with Charing Cross Medical School, London 1972–; Ananda Coll Gold Medal Sri Lanka 1954; mem. British Asscn. for Forensic Medicine C H. Milburn Award (B.M.A.). *Publications:* Injuries Caused By Falls from Heights, Safety at Work, Safety in the Home, various articles in forensic medicine and pathology. *Leisure interests:* still and video filming, water colour painting. *Address:* 4 Ascott Avenue, Ealing, London, WS 5QB England (Office).

GOORMAGHTIGH, John Victor, D. EN DROIT; Belgian lawyer and public servant; b. 15 March 1919, Ghyverinchove; s. of S. Norbert Goormaghtigh and Mable Lawrence; m. Eliane Weber 1945; two s. one d.; ed. Brussels Univ.; admitted to the Bar 1942; Advocate, Court of Appeal 1945; Dir Belgian Inst. of Int. Affairs 1947–52; Joint Sec. Int. Academic Union 1949; Consultant to UNESCO 1950; Sec.-Gen. Int. Political Science Asscn. 1955–60; Dir. European Centre, Carnegie Endowment for Int. Peace 1950–78; Prof. of Political Science, Univ. of Geneva 1961–62; Chair. Bd. Int. School of Geneva 1961–66; Chair. Int. Baccalaureate Office 1965–81 Dir. Centre for Research on Int. Insts. 1974–79; Sec.-Gen. European Science Foundation, Strasbourg 1980–86; Prof. Grad. Inst. of Int. Studies Geneva 1975–76; Ed. Chronique de Politique Etrangère 1948–52; Chevalier Order of the Crown, Croix de guerre (Belgium and France), Médaille de la Résistance, Chevalier, Ordre de la Valeur du Cameroun. *Publication.* Parliaments and the United Nations: Dissemination of Information to Parliamentarians. *Leisure interests:* painting, gardening. *Address:* Château de Scharrachbergheim, 67310 Wasselonne, France (Home). *Telephone:* (88) 50-66-07 (Home).

GOPAL, Sarvepalli, M.A., D.PHIL., D.LITT.; Indian professor of history; b. 23 April 1923, Madras; s. of late Sir Sarvepalli Radhakrishnan (fmr. Pres. of India); ed. Univs. of Madras and Oxford; lecturer and reader in history Andhra Univ., Waltair, 1948–52; Asst. Dir. Nat. Archives, New Delhi 1952–54; Dir. Historical Div., Ministry of External Affairs, New Delhi 1954–66; reader in S. Asian history, Oxford 1966–71; Fellow, St. Antony's Coll., Oxford 1966–; Prof. of Contemporary History, Jawaharlal Nehru Univ., New Delhi, 1971–83, Prof. Emer. 1983–; Chair. Nat. Book Trust of India 1973–76; mem. Exec. Bd. of UNESCO 1976–80; Hon. D.Litt. (Andhra Univ.) 1975, (Sri Venkateswara Univ., Tirupati) 1979, (Banaras Univ.) 1984; Sahitya Akademi Award 1976; Corresp. Fellow, Royal Historical Soc. 1980. *Publications:* The Viceroyalty of Lord Ripon, The Viceroyalty of Lord Irwin, British Policy in India, Jawaharlal Nehru (Vols. I, II and III) *Address:* St. Antony's College, Oxford, England; 97 Radhakrishna Salai, Mylapore, Madras 600004, India (Home).

GOPALAN, Coluthur, M.D., PH.D., F.R.C.P., F.R.S.; Indian nutritionist; b. 29 Nov. 1918, Salem Town, Tamil Nadu; m. Seetha Gopalan 1944; one s. one d.; ed. Univs. of Madras and London; Dir. Nat. Inst. of Nutrition, Hyderabad 1960–74; Dir.-Gen. Indian Council of Medical Research 1974–79; Pres.

Nutrition Foundation of India 1979–; Pres. Int. Union of Nutritional Sciences 1975–79; Chair. Regional Advisory Cttee. on Medical Research, WHO 1975–80, Global Advisory Cttee. 1977–80; mem. numerous task forces, advisory bodies, cttees. on nutrition; Nuffield Foundation Fellow, IRC 1946–49; Rockefeller Foundation Fellow 1953–54; Fellow, Indian Nat. Science Acad., Indian Acad. of Sciences, Nat. Acad. of Medical Sciences; numerous awards and prizes; Hon. D.Sc. (Banaras Hindu Univ.). *Publications:* over 200 papers in journals in India and abroad and several books on nutrition. *Address:* Nutrition Foundation of India, B-37, Gulmohar Park, New Delhi 110049, India.

GOPPEL, Alfons; German lawyer and politician; b. 1 Oct. 1905, Regensburg; s. of Ludwig and Barbara Goppel; m. Gertrud Wittenbrink 1935; five c.; ed. Humanistisches Gymnasium, Regensburg, and Ludwig Maximilians Univ., Munich; State Attorney 1934, Judge 1938; Vice-Mayor of Aschaffenburg 1952; State Sec. of Justice (Bavaria) 1957; Minister of Interior (Bavaria) 1958–62; Minister-Pres. of Bavaria 1962–78; mem. Bavarian Land Diet 1954–78; mem. European Parl. 1979–84; numerous decorations. *Address:* 8033 Krailling/Obb., Sommerweg 2, Federal Republic of Germany.

GORAI, Rt. Rev. Dinesh Chandra, B.A., B.D., D.D.; Indian ecclesiastic; b. 5 Jan. 1934, West Bengal; s. of Joyram and Sushila Gorai; m. Binapani Gorai 1962; two s.; ed. Calcutta Univ. and Serampore Coll.; ordained Priest as Methodist 1962; consecrated as Church of N. India Bishop 1970; Bishop of Barrackpore 1970–82, of Calcutta 1982–; Moderator Church of North India 1983–86; social worker and rural devt. expert, ecumenical leader. *Address:* Bishop's House, 51 Chowringhee Road, Calcutta 700 071, India. *Telephone:* 44-5259.

GÖRANSSON, Bengt; Swedish politician; b. 25 July 1932, Stockholm; m. Lena Göransson; five c.; ed. Univ. of Stockholm; courier, Reso Ltd. (travel org.) 1960–71; Chair. Manilla School for the Deaf 1970–78; Head, Community Centre Asscn. 1971; Chair. of Bd. Nat. Theatre Centre 1974–82; mem. various official cttees.; Chair. of Bd. Fed. of Workers' Educational Asscns. 1980–82; Minister for Cultural Affairs 1982–. *Address:* Ministry of Education and Cultural Affairs, S-10333 Stockholm, Sweden.

GORAY, Narayan Ganesh, B.A., LL.B.; Indian politician; b. 15 June 1907, Hindala, Maharashtra; s. of Ganesh Govind Gore and Saraswati; m. Sumati Kirtane 1935; one d.; ed. Fergusson Coll., Poona; Congress Socialist Party 1930, mem. Nat. Exec. 1934, Mayor of Poona; imprisoned for political activities before independence; Joint Sec. Socialist Party 1948; Gen. Sec. Praja Socialist Party 1949–54, 1954–65, Chair. 1965–71; Mayor, Pune Municipal Corpn. 1967–68; led first wave of Satyagrahis against Portuguese Govt. in Goa; mem. Lok Sabha 1957–62, Rajya Sabha 1970–76; High Commr. to U.K. 1977–79; ed. Janata Weekly 1971–. *Publications:* History of the United States of America 1959, etc. *Leisure interests:* music, painting, writing. *Address:* 1813 Sadashiv Peth, Poona 30, Maharashtra State, India. *Telephone:* 56614.

GORBACHEV, Mikhail Sergeyevich; Soviet politician; b. 2 March 1931, Privolnoye, Krasnogvardeisky Dist.; m. Raisa Gorbacheva (q.v.) 1956; one d.; ed. Faculty of Law, Moscow State Univ. and Stavropol Agricultural Inst.; began work as machine operator 1946; joined CPSU 1952; First Sec. Stavropol Komsomol City Cttee. 1955–58, later Deputy Head, Dept. of Propaganda, Second, then First Sec. Komsol Territorial Cttee.; Party Organizer, Stavropol Territorial Production Bd. of Collective and State Farms 1962–66; Head, Dept. of party bodies of CPSU Territorial Cttee. 1962–66; First Sec. Stavropol City Party Cttee. 1966–68; Second Sec. Stavropol Territorial CPSU Cttee. 1968–70, First Sec. 1970–78; mem. CPSU Cen. Cttee. 1971–, Sec. for Agric. 1978–85, alt. mem. Political Bureau CPSU, Cen. Cttee. 1979–80, mem. Oct. 1980–, Gen. Sec. CPSU Cen. Cttee. March 1985–; Deputy Supreme Soviet of U.S.S.R. 1970– (Chair. Foreign Affairs Comm., Soviet of the Union 1984–85), mem. Presidium 1985–88, Chair. Oct. 1988–, Supreme Soviet of R.S.F.S.R. 1979–; elected to Congress of People's Deputies of the U.S.S.R. 1989; del. to CPSU Congress 1961, 1971, 1976, 1981, 1986; Order of Lenin (three times), Orders of Red Banner of Labour, Badge of Honour and other medals. *Publications:* A Time for Peace 1985, The Coming Century of Peace 1986, Speeches and Writings 1986, Peace has no Alternative 1986, Moratorium 1986, Perestroika: New Thinking for Our Country and the World 1987. *Address:* Central Committee of the Communist Party of the Soviet Union, Staraya Pl. 4, Moscow, U.S.S.R.

GORBACHEVA, Raisa Maksimovna (née Titorenko), CAND. PHIL. SC.; Soviet politician; b. 1934, Stavropol; m. Mikhail Gorbachev (q.v.) 1956; one d.; ed. Stavropol Teachers' Training Coll.; teacher in Stavropol; sociologist at Stavropol Teacher Training Inst. 1957–61; Pres. of Cultural Heritage Comm. 1987–. *Address:* The Kremlin, Moscow, U.S.S.R.

GORCE, Pierre; French diplomatist; b. 17 June 1917, Limoges; m. Ruth Correll 1945, (divorced 1977); m. 2nd. Leila Abbosh; ed. École Nationale de la France d'Outre-Mer; High Comm. Cambodia 1955–56, Amb. 1956–61; Directeur des Études, l'Institut des Hautes Études d'Outre-Mer 1961–63; Amb. to Albania 1963–67, to Iraq 1967–70, to Indonesia 1970–76, to Denmark 1976–82; Pres. of France-Denmark Asscn., Paris; Officier de la Légion d'honneur; Commdr. Ordre national du Mérite; Croix de guerre. *Address:* 35 rue du Général Delestraint, 75016 Paris, France.

GORCHAKOV, Pyotr Andreyevich; Soviet military official; b. 1917; mem. CPSU 1939–; ed. Lenin Mil. Political Acad.; served in Soviet Army 1938–; Party Sec. of a regt.; Commdr. of a regt. (political affairs); head of political dept. of a rifle div. on the Bryansk, Cen. and Fourth Ukrainian Front 1941–45; political admin. of various orgs.; mem. Mil. Council and Head of the Political Admin., Mil. Dist. of Baltic Provs. 1945–70; mem. Cen. Cttee. of Latvian CP 1966–71; Head of Political Admin. of Strategic Missile Units 1970–; Deputy to U.S.S.R. Supreme Soviet 1970–; cand. mem., later mem., Cen. Cttee. of CPSU 1971–; Hero of the Soviet Union. *Address:* The Kremlin, Moscow, U.S.S.R.

GORDEY, Michel; French journalist and writer; b. 17 Feb. 1913, Berlin, Germany; s. of Samuel Rapaport and Eugenia Gourvitch; m. Beverly Bronstein 1950; one s. one d.; ed. Lycée Janson de Sailly, Law Faculty of Sorbonne and Ecole des Sciences Politiques, Paris; Lawyer, Paris 1933–37; French Army 1937–40; U.S. Office of War Information, French Editor, Voice of America 1941–45, Chief Ed. 1944–45; U.S. Corresp. Paris-Presse 1945; U.S. and UN Corresp., Agence France-Presse, New York and Washington 1945–46; Roving Foreign and Diplomatic Corresp. France-Soir, Paris 1945–56, Chief Foreign Corresp. 1956–73; assignment to China 1971–72; Roving Foreign and Diplomatic Corresp., L'Express, Paris 1973–77; Special Corresp., Europe, Newsday, New York 1977–; articles have been published in magazines and newspapers in U.K., U.S.A., Federal Repub. of Germany, Japan, Italy and Switzerland; TV and radio broadcasts in U.K., U.S.A., Canada and Federal Repub. of Germany; several journalistic awards. *Publication:* Visa pour Moscou 1951. *Leisure interests:* reading, high mountains, walking. *Address:* 16 rue de Savoie, 75006 Paris, France. *Telephone:* 43-54-7982.

GORDEYEV, Vyacheslav Mikhailovich; Soviet ballet dancer; b. 1948; ed. Moscow Choreographic School; work with State Acad. of Ballet and Theatre 1968–; mem. CPSU 1977–; First Prize Moscow Int. Ballet Competition 1973, U.S.S.R. People's Artist 1984. *Roles include:* Prince, Désiré (Tchaikovsky's Nutcracker, Sleeping Beauty), Romeo (Prokofiev's Romeo and Juliet), Spartacus, Ferhat (Melnikov's Legend of Love), Albert (Giselle), Basile (Minkus's Don Quixote). *Address:* State Academy of Ballet and Theatre, Moscow, U.S.S.R.

GORDIENKO, Aleksey Fyodorovich; Soviet official; b. 1917; First Sec. of Dneprodzerzhinsk City Cttee., Dnepropetrovsk Dist. Cttee. of Ukrainian CP; mem. of Cen. Auditing Comm. of CPSU 1976–81; mem. of Cen. Cttee. of CPSU 1980–; mem. of Supreme Soviet of U.S.S.R. 1980–. *Address:* The Kremlin, Moscow, U.S.S.R.

GORDIMER, Nadine, F.R.S.L.; South African writer; b. 20 Nov. 1923; d. of Isidore Gordimer and Nan Myers; m. Reinhold Cassirer 1954; one s. one d.; ed. convent school; Hon. mem. American Acad. and Inst. of Arts and Letters, American Acad. of Arts and Sciences; Vice-Pres. American PEN, Officier Ordre des Arts et des Lettres 1987; recipient of W. H. Smith Literary Award 1961 and Thomas Pringle Award (English Acad. of S.A.) 1969, James Tait Black Memorial Prize 1971, Booker Prize (co-winner) 1974, Grand Aigle d'Or Prize (France) 1975, CNA Literary Award (S. Africa) 1974, 1979, 1981, Scottish Arts Council Neil M. Gunn Fellowship 1981, Modern Language Asscn. Award (U.S.A.) 1981, Premio Malaparte (Italy) 1985, Nelly Sachs Prize (Germany) 1985, Bennett Award (U.S.A.) 1987. *Publications:* The Soft Voice of the Serpent (stories), The Lying Days (novel) 1953, Six Feet of the Country (stories) 1956, A World of Strangers (novel) 1958, Friday's Footprint (stories) 1960, Occasion for Loving (novel) 1963, Not For Publication (stories) 1965, The Late Bourgeois World (novel) 1966, A Guest of Honour (novel) 1970, Livingstone's Companions (stories) 1972, The Black Interpreters (literary criticism) 1973, The Conservationist (novel) 1974, Selected Stories 1975, Some Monday for Sure (stories) 1976, Burger's Daughter 1979, A Soldier's Embrace (stories) 1980, July's People (novel) 1981, Something Out There (novella) 1984, Six Feet of Country (short stories) 1986, A Sport of Nature (novel) 1987, The Essential Gesture (essays) 1988; co-editor South African Writing Today 1967. *Address:* 7 Frere Road, Parktown, Johannesburg, South Africa.

GORDIS, Robert, PH.D.; American rabbi and biblical scholar; b. 6 Feb. 1908, Brooklyn, N.Y.; m. Fannie Jacobson 1928; three s.; ed. Coll. of City of New York, The Dropsie Coll., Philadelphia and Jewish Theological Seminary; Mayer Sulzberger Fellow in Biblical Philology, Dropsie Coll. 1926–29; Instructor in Bible and Jewish History, Hebrew Teachers' Training School for Girls 1928–30; Instructor, Teachers' Inst. of Jewish Theological Seminary 1930–31; Rabbi, Temple Beth-El, Rockaway Park, L.I. 1931–68, Rabbi Emer. 1968–; Seminary Prof. of Bible, Jewish Theological Seminary 1937; Pres. Rabbinical Assembly of America 1944–46; Vice-Pres. Synagogue Council of America 1946–48, Pres. 1948–49; Adjunct Prof. in Religion, Columbia Univ. 1949–57; lecturer in Old Testament, Union Theological Seminary 1953–54; Prof. of Bible, Jewish Theological Seminary of America 1961–69; Consultant to Center for Study of Democratic Insts. of Fund for Repub. 1960–79; Prof. of Religion, Temple Univ. 1967–74; Rappaport Prof. of Philosophies of Religion, Jewish Theological Seminary 1974–81, Prof. Emer. 1981–; Fellow American Acad. of Jewish Research and mem. Exec. Bd. 1970–; Assoc. Ed. Dept. of the Bible and contrib. to Universal Jewish Encyclopaedia; Chair. Bd. of Editors Judaism, Ed. 1968–; Guggenheim Fellow 1976; Hon. D.D. (Jewish Theological Seminary) 1950, Hon. D.H.L. (Spertus Coll.). *Publications:* Biblical Text in the Making

1937, The Jew Faces a New World 1941, The Wisdom of Ecclesiastes 1945, Conservative Judaism—An American Philosophy 1945, Koheleth—The Man and His World 1951, Song of Songs 1954, Judaism and the Modern Age 1955, A Faith for Moderns 1960, The Root and the Branch—Judaism and the Free Society 1962, The Book of God and Man: A Study of Job 1965, Judaism in a Christian World 1966, Sex and the Family in Jewish Tradition, Leave a Little to God 1967, Poets, Prophets and Sages—Essays in Biblical Interpretation 1971, Faith and Reason, Essays in Judaism 1973, The Book of Esther 1974, Song of Songs—Lamentations 1974, The Word and the Book (Studies in Biblical Language and Literature) 1976, Love and Sex—A Modern Jewish Perspective 1978, The Book of Job: Commentary, New Translation and Special Studies 1978, Understanding Conservative Judaism 1978, Judaic Ethics for a Lawless World 1986. *Leisure interests:* music, theatre, chess, swimming. *Address:* 15 East 84th Street, New York City, N.Y. 10028 (Office); 150 West End Avenue (Apt. 24M), New York, N.Y. 10023, U.S.A. (Home). *Telephone:* 212-TR7-4500 (Office); 212-877-1484 (Home).

GORDON, Donald; South African business executive; b. 24 June 1930, Johannesburg; s. of Nathan and Sheila Gordon; m. Peggy Cowan 1958; one d. two s.; ed. King Edward VII School, Johannesburg; C.A. and auditor Kessel Feinstein 1955-58; founder Liberty Life Asscn. of Africa Ltd., Chair. and C.E.O. 1958-; Founder Guardbank Growth Fund, Chair. 1970-; Chair. Guardian Nat. Insurance Co. Ltd. 1974-; Chair. First Union Gen. Investment Trust Ltd. 1977-, Liberty Life Group 1978-, Continental and Industrial Trust PLC 1986-; Dir. Guardian Royal Exchange Assurance Group 1971-, United Bldg. Soc. 1972-, Bd. Standard Bank Investment Corpn. 1979-; Founder and Chair. TransAtlantic Holdings PLC 1981; mem. Bd. Capital and Counties PLC 1982-, The S. African Breweries Ltd. 1982-, Plate Glass and Shatterprufe Industries Ltd. 1982-, Premier Group Holdings Ltd. 1983-; Businessman of the Year 1965, Sunday Times Man of the Year 1969, Business Statesman Award (Harvard Business School). *Leisure interest:* tennis. *Address:* Liberty Life Association of Africa Ltd., P.O. Box 10499, Johannesburg, South Africa 2000. *Telephone:* 011-712-2100.

GORDON, Isidor, M.B., CH.B., F.R.S.S.A.; South African pathologist; b. 11 April 1913, Cape Town; m. Jean Erskine Dick 1937; one s. two d.; ed. South African Coll. School, Cape Town, Univs. of Cape Town and Natal; Asst. Pathologist and lecturer, subsequently Sr. lecturer, Depts. of Pathology and Forensic Medicine, Univ. of Cape Town 1938-45; served S.A. Medical Corps; Sr. State Pathologist, Durban 1946-53; apptd. Prof. of Pathology, Univ. of Natal, Durban 1953, Dean Faculty of Medicine 1955-71, Prof. of Pathology and Forensic Medicine 1962-78, Emer. Prof. of Forensic Medicine 1979-; Univ. of Natal's mem. S.A. Medical Council 1955-74, mem. 1975-79; mem. Council, Coll. of Medicine of S.A. 1981-83, Royal Soc. of S.A. 1987-88; represented S.A. Medical-Legal Soc., Univ. of Natal and State Health Dept. at numerous int. meetings; Hon. Fellow in Forensic Pathology, Coll. of Medicine of S.A.; Hon. M.D. (Natal) 1982; Hon. LL.D. (Univ. of S.A.) 1982; Silver Medal, Medical Assen. of S.A. 1974. *Publications:* Co-author Medical Jurisprudence 1942, 1953, Medico-Legal Mythology 1975, Forensic Medicine: A Guide to Principles 3rd edn. 1988; World Health Manpower Shortage 1971-2000 1971, The medico-legal aspects of rapid deaths initiated by hypoxia and anoxia, in Legal Medical Annual (ed. by C. H. Wecht) 3rd edn. 1988. *Leisure interests:* reading and the study of science topics in molecular biology, cosmology and palaeo-anthropology. *Address:* 18 Jesmond Court, 69 Berea Park Road, Durban, 4001, South Africa. *Telephone:* 031-217419.

GORDON, Rt. Hon. John Bowie (Peter), P.C.; New Zealand politician (retd.); b. 1921, Stratford; s. of Dr. William P. Gordon, C.B.E. and Dr. Doris C. Gordon, M.B.E.; m. Dorothy Morton 1943; two s. one d.; ed. St. Andrew's Coll., Christchurch, Lincoln Coll.; served as pilot in R.N.Z.A.F. 1941-44, mentioned in despatches; Past Pres. West Otago Branch Federated Farmers; mem. first Nat. Hydatids Council; Chair. Dir. of Heriot Transport 1951-54; Dir. Farmers' Mutual Insurance 1951-60, N.Z. Bd. Shaw Savill 1956-60; toured Britain, Scandinavia and U.S. under Nuffield Scholarship 1954; visited U.S. under U.S. State Dept. Foreign Leadership Award 1964; M.P. for Clutha 1960-78; Minister of Transport for Railways and Civil Aviation 1966-72, of Marine and Fisheries 1972, of Labour and of State Services 1975-78; Otago Univ. Council 1978-88; mem. Nat. Transition Cttee. Local Govt. Reform; Dir. several cos. including Nat. Bank of N.Z., South Pacific Tyres, Gen. Accident Corpn. *Leisure interests:* golf, cooking, gardening. *Address:* Tapanui, Otago, New Zealand.

GORDON, Lincoln, D.PHIL.; American political economist and diplomatist; b. 10 Sept. 1913, New York; s. of Bernard and Dorothy (née Lerned) Gordon; m. Allison Wright 1937; two s. two d.; ed. Harvard Univ. and Balliol Coll., Oxford; Instructor in Govt., Harvard Univ. 1936-40; Prof. of Govt. and Admin. Harvard Business School and Graduate School of Public Admin. 1946-50; Govt. service with Nat. Resources Planning Bd. 1939-40; Nat. Defense Advisory Cttee. 1940-41; W.P.B. 1942-45; Deputy Programme Vice-Chair., W.P.B. 1944, Programme Vice-Chair. 1945; Consultant, Dept. of State in development of European Recovery Programme 1947-48; Dir. Programme Div. ECA in Office of Special Rep. in Europe 1949-50; Economic Adviser to Special Asst. to the Pres. (W. A. Harriman) 1950-51; Asst. Dir. for Programme, Office of Dir. for Mutual Security 1951-52; Minister for Econ. Affairs and Chief of MSA Mission to U.K.

1952-55; William Ziegler Prof. of Int. Econ. Relations, Harvard Univ Graduate School of Business Admin. 1955-61; Amb. to Brazil 1961-66 Asst. Sec. of State for Inter-American Affairs 1966-67; Pres. The Johns Hopkins Univ. 1967-71; Visiting Prof. of Political Econs., Johns Hopkins School of Advanced Int. Studies 1971-72; Fellow Woodrow Wilson Int Center for Scholars, Washington 1972-75; Senior Fellow Resources for the Future, Washington 1975-80; Chair. Nat. Acad. of Eng. Cttee. on Future Energy Alternatives for Puerto Rico 1978-80; Nat. Intelligence Officer-at Large CIA 1980-83; Guest Scholar, Brookings Inst. 1984-; seven hon degrees. *Publications:* The Public Corporation in Great Britain 1938 Government and the American Economy (with M. Fainsod) 1941; Ed International Stability and Progress: United States Interests and Instru ments 1957; United States Manufacturing Investment in Brazil (with E L. Grommers) 1961, O Progresso Pela Aliança 1962, A New Deal for Latin America 1963, edited From Marshall Plan to Global Interdependence 1978 Growth Policies and the International Order 1979, co-author (with Joy Dunkerley and others) Energy Strategies in Developing Nations 1981 Eroding Empire: Western Relations with Eastern Europe (with J. F Brown and others) 1987. *Leisure interests:* music ('cellist), woodworking *Address:* 3069 University Terrace, N.W., Washington D.C., 20016, U.S.A (Home). *Telephone:* 202-797-6259 (Office); 202-244-1315 (Home).

GORDON, Richard F., Jr.; American football manager and former astronaut; b. 5 Oct. 1929, Seattle, Wash.; m. Barbara Field; four s. two d.; ed. Univ. of Washington; entered U.S. Navy 1951; received naval aviator wings 1953; attended All-Weather Flight School; later at Naval Air Station, Jacksonville, Fla.; attended Navy's Test Pilot School, Patuxent River 1957; first project test pilot for F4H Phantom II; won Bendix Trophy Race 1961; selected by NASA as astronaut Oct. 1963; pilot of backup crew for Gemini VIII flight; pilot of Gemini XI mission Sept. 1966; Command module pilot, Apollo XII Nov. 1969; retd. USN/NASA 1972; Exec. Vice-Pres. New Orleans Saints professional football team 1972-; NASA Exceptional Service Medal, NASA Distinguished Service Medal, USN Distinguished Service Medal.

GORDON, William Edwin, PH.D.; American radio physicist; b. 8 Jan. 1918 Paterson, N.J.; s. of William and Mary Scott Gordon; m. Elva Freile 1941; one s. one d.; ed. Montclair State Coll., N.J. and New York and Cornell Univs.; Assoc. Prof. Cornell Univ. 1953-59, Prof. 1959-65, Walter R. Read Prof. of Eng. 1965-66; Dir. Arecibo Ionospheric Observatory, Puerto Rico 1960-66 (conceived and directed construction of world's largest antenna reflector); Prof. of Electrical Eng. and Space Physics and Astronomy, Rice Univ. 1966-, Dean of Eng. and Science 1966-75, Vice-Pres. 1969-72, Dean, School of Natural Sciences 1975-80, Provost and Vice-Pres. 1980-86; Foreign Sec., N.A.S. 1986-; Chair. Bd. of Trustees, Upper Atmosphere Research Corpn. 1971-72, 1973-78; Vice-Pres. Int. Union of Radio Science 1975-78; Senior Vice-Pres. 1978-81, Pres. 1981-85; mem. N.A.S. Cttee. on Solar Terrestrial Research 1967-74, 1979-81, NSF Panel on Atmospheric Sciences 1967-74, NAS Panel on Jicamarca Radio Observatory 1969-74, NSF Research Advisory Cttee. 1973-76; Bd. of Trustees and Exec. Cttee. Univ. Corpn. for Atmospheric Research 1975-81, Vice-Chair. Bd. of Trustees 1977-78, Chair. 1978-81, Trustee 1975-81, 1986-; Bd. of Trustees, Cornell Univ. 1976-80; mem. Arecibo Observatory Advisory Bd. 1977-80; mem. N.A.S., A.A.A.S., Nat. Acad. of Eng., Foreign Assoc. Acad. of Eng. Japan; mem. Int. Council of Scientific Unions Advisory Cttee. 1981-, Vice-Pres. 1988-; Councillor American Meteorological Soc.; Fellow, American Geophysical Union, Inst. of Electrical and Electronic Engineers, Guggenheim Fellow 1972-73; Hon. D.S. (Austin Coll.) 1978; Balth Van der Pol Gold Medal for distinguished research in radio sciences 1966, 50th Anniversary Medal of American Meteorological Soc. 1970, Arktowski Medal 1984, U.S.S.R. Medal Geophysics 1985. *Publications:* numerous articles in learned journals. *Leisure interests:* sailing, swimming, music. *Address:* Rice University, P.O. Box 1892, Houston, Tex. 77251, U.S.A. *Telephone:* (713) 527-6020.

GORDON LENNOX, Lord, Nicholas Charles, K.C.M.G., L.V.O., B.A.; British diplomatist; b. 31 Jan. 1931, London; s. of Duke and Duchess of Richmond and Gordon; m. Mary Williamson 1958; one s. three d.; ed. Eton Coll. and Worcester Coll. Oxford; served in Army (Greenjackets) 1949-51; entered H.M. Foreign Service 1954, served in Washington, Santiago, Paris and London; Amb. to Spain 1984-. *Address:* c/o Foreign and Commonwealth Office, London, S.W.1, England.

GORDON-SMITH, Ralph; British business executive; b. 22 May 1905; m. Beryl Mavis Cundy 1932; ed. Bradfield Coll.; Smiths Industries Ltd. 1927-; Dir. 1933, Group Man. Dir. 1947-, Chair. 1951-73, Chief Exec. 1967-, non-exec. Chair. 1968-, Pres. 1973-; Dir. EMI Ltd. 1951-75. *Address:* 23 Kingston House East, Princes Gate, London, S.W.7; Brook House, Quay Meadow, Old Bosham, West Sussex, England. *Telephone:* 01-584 9428.

GORE, Albert, Jr.; American politician; b. 31 March 1948; s. of Albert and Pauline (LaFon) Gore; m. Mary E. Aitcheson 1970; one s. three d.; ed. Harvard and Vanderbilt Univs.; investigative reporter, editorial writer, The Tennessean 1971-76; home-builder and land developer, Tanglewood Home Builders Co. 1971-76; livestock and tobacco farmer 1971-; mem. House of Reps. 1977-79; Senator from Tennessee Jan. 1985-; Democrat. *Address:* The Senate, Washington, D.C. 20510, U.S.A.

GORE, Frederick John Pym, C.B.E., R.A.; British painter; b. 8 Nov. 1913; s. of Spencer Frederick Gore and Mary Joanna (née Kerr) Gore; ed. Lancing Coll. and Trinity Coll., Oxford, Ruskin, Westminster and Slade Schools of Art; war service 1939-45; taught at Westminster School of Art 1937, Chelsea and Epsom 1947, St. Martin's 1946-79, Head of Painting Dept. 1951-79, Vice-Prin. 1961-79; one-man exhbns. at Galerie Borghèse, Paris 1938, Redfern Gallery 1937, 1949, 1950, 1953, 1956, 1962, Mayor Gallery 1958, 1960, Juster Gallery, New York 1963; Chair. R.A. exhbns. cttee. 1976-87; Trustee Imperial War Museum 1967-84. *Publications:* Abstract Art 1956, Painting, Some Principles 1965, Piero della Francesca's 'The Baptism' 1969. *Leisure interest:* Russian folk dancing. *Address:* Flat 3, 35 Elm Park Gardens, London, S.W.10, England. *Telephone:* 01-352 4940.

GORE, Madhav, PH.D.; Indian university administrator; b. 15 Aug. 1921, Hubli, Karnataka State; s. of the late S. R. Gore; m. Phyllis Marr 1949; one s. one d.; ed. Bombay Univ., Tata Inst. of Social Sciences, Columbia Univ., New York; Sr. lecturer, Delhi School of Social Work 1948-53, Prin. 1953-62; Dir. Tata Inst. of Social Sciences 1962-82; Vice-Chancellor Univ. of Bombay 1983-86; Chair. Indian Council of Social Science Research 1971-77; mem. Cttee. on Police Training 1972-77; Homi Bhabha Fellow 1982; Padma Bhushan Award 1975, Silver Jubilee Award for Social Science 1974. *Publications:* Social Work and Social Work Education 1965, Education and Modernisation in India 1982 and various other books and papers. *Leisure interests:* photography, literature, listening to Indian classical music. *Address:* N-16, Sector 7, Vashi, New Bombay 400 703, India. *Telephone:* 551 0400 (office); 683 799 (Home).

GÓRECKI, Henryk Mikołaj; Polish composer; b. 6 Dec. 1933, Czernica, near Rybnik; s. of Otylia Górecki and Roman Górecki; m. Jadwiga Górecki 1959; two c.; studied composition in Katowice State Higher School of Music under B. Szabelski; Docent, Faculty of Composition, State Higher School of Music, Katowice, Rector 1975-79, Extraordinary Prof. 1977-79; First Prize, Young Composers' Competition, Warsaw, for Monologhi 1960, Paris Youth Biennale, for 1st Symphony 1961; Prize, UNESCO Int. Tribune for Composers for Refrain 1967, for Ad Matrem 1973; First Prize, Composers' Competition, Szczecin, for Kantata 1968; Prize of Union of Polish Composers 1970, of Cttee. for Polish Radio and TV 1971, of Minister of Culture and Arts 1965, 1969, 1973; State Prize 1st class for Ad Matrem and Nicolaus Copernicus Symphony 1976. *Address:* Ul. Feliksa Kona 4, m.1, 40-133 Katowice, Poland *Telephone:* 58-17-58.

GOREN, Maj.-Gen. Shlomo; Israeli rabbi; b. 1917, Poland; m.; one s. two d.; ed. Hebrew Univ.; settled in Palestine 1925; Co-founder Kfar Hassidim; Chief Chaplain, Israel Defence Forces; Chief Rabbi of Tel-Aviv (elected June 1968); Ashkenazi Chief Rabbi of Israel Oct. 1972-83; Rabbi Kook Prize. *Publications:* Nezer Hakodesh (on Maimonides), Shaarei Tahara, Talmud Yerushalmi Meforash, Torath Ha Moadim, etc., as well as works on religion in military life, prayers for soldiers etc. *Address:* Chief Rabbinate, Hechal Shlomo, Jerusalem, Israel.

GORETTA, Claude; Swiss film director; b. 23 June 1929, Geneva. *Films include:* Le fou 1970, Le jour des noces 1971, L'invitation 1973, The Wonderful Crook 1976, The Lacemaker 1977, Bonheur toi-même 1980, The Girl from Lorraine 1981, The Death of Mario Ricci 1983, Orpheus 1985. *Address:* Swiss Film Centre, Muenstergasse 18, CH-8001 Zürich, Switzerland. *Telephone:* 01-472-860.

GOREV, Nikolay Nikolayevich; Soviet pathologist; b. 21 April 1900, Kazan; ed. Irkutsk Univ.; Asst. of Pathological Chair, Irkutsk Univ. 1926-31; Head of Chair, Khabarovsk Med. Inst. 1931-34; Head of Dept. Inst. of Experimental Biology and Pathology 1934-53; Corresp. mem. U.S.S.R. Acad. of Medical Sciences 1945-53, mem. 1953-; Head of Chair. Kiev Stomatological Inst. 1945-55; Head of Lab., Kiev Inst. of Physiology 1953-60, Kiev Inst. of Tuberculosis 1955-58; Dir. Inst. of Gerontology and Experimental Pathology 1958-61, Head of Lab. 1961-; Head of Experimental Cardiology Dept. 1969-74, Consultant 1974-; mem. of Board, U.S.S.R. Socs. of Pathophysiologists, Gerontologists, Cardiologists; has participated in congresses and symposia in Norway, Britain, Czechoslovakia, Hungary, etc.; Order of Lenin, Order of Red Banner of Labour, Badge of Honour, Merited Scientist of Ukrainian S.S.R. *Publications:* about 140 works and 5 monographs on pathology of cardiovascular system, shock, hypertension, atherosclerosis, myocardial infarction, gerontology. *Address:* Institute of Gerontology, 67 Vyshgorodskaya Street, Kiev, U.S.S.R. *Telephone:* 430-41-94.

GORIA, Giovanni; Italian politician; b. 30 July 1943, Asti; m.; two c.; Prov. Sec. Christian Democrat (D.C.) Party in Asti 1975-76; Dir. Cassa di Risparmio di Asti 1974-76; M.P. for Cuneo-Alessandria-Asti 1976-; fmr. Under-Sec. of State for Budget and Econ. Planning; Minister for Treasury 1982-87, Prime Minister of Italy 1987-88. *Address:* Camera del Deputati, Rome, Italy.

GORING, Marius; British actor; b. 23 May 1912, Newport, Isle of Wight; ed. Perse School, Cambridge and Univs. of Frankfurt, Munich and Paris; studied for the stage under Harcourt Williams and Old Vic Dramatic School; first London stage appearance 1927; joined Old Vic and appeared in many leading Shakespearian and other classical roles; has appeared throughout Europe and acted in German and French; founded the company of Shakespeare Comedians 1957, subsequently undertook Arts Council tour of Paris, Netherlands, Finland and India with them; now appears frequently in the London theatres, at the Royal Shakespeare Theatre, Stratford-upon-Avon and other theatres in U.K.; Vice-Pres. British Actors' Equity Assen. 1975-; recent stage appearances include: The Apple Cart (Cambridge), The Devil's Disciple (Yvonne Arnaud Theatre), The Bells (Derby and London), Sleuth (London and Liverpool), The Wisest Fool (Yvonne Arnaud Theatre), Habeas Corpus (Liverpool, Edinburgh and on tour), Jubilee Gaieties (Windsor and on tour), Lloyd George Knew My Father (national tour), Peer Gynt (Nottingham), Dame of Sark (nat. tour), Metamorphoses (Royal Coll. Music), The Winslow Boy 1984 (nat. tour), Beyond Reasonable Doubt (Queens Theatre, London) 1988, Towards Zero (Churchill Theatre, Bromley and Nat. Tour) 1989; television: The Expert, Year of the Crow, The Gamekeeper, Fall of Eagles, Saul Bellow 1975, The Holocaust 1977, Wilde Alliance 1977, Edward VIII 1978, William and Mary 1978, Girl in Yellow Dress 1979, Levkas Man 1979, Charlie Boy 1980, Hammer House of Horror 1980, Cymbeline 1982, The Old Men at the Zoo 1982, Gnostics (series) 1987, autobiographical documentary 1987. *Films include:* The Red Shoes, A Matter of Life and Death, So Little Time, Up from the Beach, Subterfuges 1968, First Love 1969, The Girl in Blue Velvet 1978, Meetings with Remarkable Men 1978, The Holocaust 1978, Year of the French 1982, Hammer House of Horror 1983, The Late Nancy Irving 1984, The Moviemakers, Loser Takes All 1988; numerous radio and TV plays. *Leisure interests:* riding, skating. *Address:* c/o Film Rights Ltd., 4 New Burlington Place, Regent Street, London, W1X 2AS; Middle Court, The Green, Hampton Court, Surrey, England. *Telephone:* 01-437 7151.

GORIZONTOV, Pyotr Dmitriyevich; Soviet pathophysiologist; b. 3 Sept. 1902, Petropavlovsk; m. 1928; one d.; ed. Omsk Medical Inst.; Junior Research Assoc., Omsk Medical Inst. 1927-30; Senior Research Assoc., Lenin Acad. of Agricultural Sciences 1930-32; Head of Lab., Deputy Dir. Inst. of Public Health, Magnitogorsk 1932-34; Junior Research Assoc., Asst. Prof., Head of Chair, First Moscow Medical Inst. 1934-52; Head of Chair, Cen. Inst. of Postgraduate Medical Training 1953-60; Head of Lab., Deputy Dir. 1952-, Dir. Inst. of Biophysics, U.S.S.R. Ministry of Public Health 1962-68; mem. CPSU 1957-; Corresp. mem. U.S.S.R. Acad. of Medical Sciences 1952-62, mem. 1962-; mem. of Hon. U.S.S.R. Soc. of Röntgenologists and Radiologists; mem. Bd. U.S.S.R. Soc. of Pathophysiologists; Order of Lenin (three times), Red Banner of Labour, Badge of Honour, Lenin Prize 1963. *Publications:* about 200 works, including Homeostasis and monographs Effect of Brain on Cholesterine Metabolism, Pathological Physiology of Acute Radiation Sickness Resulting from External Ionizing Radiation. *Leisure interest:* nature photography. *Address:* Institute of Biophysics, U.S.S.R. Ministry of Public Health, 46 Zhivopisnaya ulitsa, Moscow; Apartment 120, 24 Kutuzovsky prospekt, Moscow, U.S.S.R. *Telephone:* 249-31-18 (Home).

GORMAN, Joseph Tolle, B.A., LL.B.; American business executive; b. 1937, Rising Sun, Ind.; m. Bettyann Gorman; ed. Kent State Univ. and Yale Univ.; Assoc. Baker, Hostetler & Patterson, Cleveland 1962-67; Legal Dept. TRW Inc., Cleveland 1968-69, Asst. Sec. 1969-70, Sec. 1970-72, Vice-Pres. Sr. Counsel, Automotive Worldwide Operations 1972-73, Vice-Pres. Asst. Gen. Counsel 1973-76, Vice-Pres. Gen. Counsel 1976-80, Exec. Vice-Pres. Industrial and Energy Sector 1980-84, Exec. Vice-Pres., Asst. Pres. 1984-85, Pres. and C.O.O. 1985-; mem. Bd. of Dirs. Soc. Corpn., Soc. Nat. Bank, Cleveland, Standard Oil Co.; mem. Council on Foreign Relations and other public appts. *Address:* TRW Inc., 1900 Richmond Road, Cleveland, O. 44124, U.S.A.

GORMAN, William Moore, B.A., F.B.A.; British academic economist; b. 17 June 1923, Kesh, Northern Ireland; s. of the late Richard Gorman and Sarah Crawford Gorman (née Moore); m. Dorinda Maud Scott 1950; ed. Mount Temple School, Dublin, Foyle Coll., Derry and Trinity Coll. Dublin; Rating, then Petty Officer, R.N. 1943-46; Asst. Lecturer, Lecturer then Sr. Lecturer in charge, Dept. of Econometrics and Social Statistics, Birmingham Univ. 1949-61; Prof. of Econs., Oxford Univ. and Prof. Fellow of Nuffield Coll. 1962-67; Prof. of Econs., L.S.E. 1967-79; Official Fellow, Nuffield Coll., Oxford 1979-84, Sr. Research Fellow 1984-; Visiting Prof. at various U.S. univs. between 1956 and 1980; Hon. D.Soc.Sc. (Birmingham) 1973, Hon. D.Sc. (Southampton) 1974, Hon. D.Econ.Sc. (Nat. Univ. of Ireland) 1986; Fellow Econometric Soc. (Pres. 1972); Hon. Foreign mem. American Acad. of Arts and Sciences 1986. *Publications:* articles in various econ. periodicals. *Leisure interests:* talking and reading. *Address:* Nuffield College, Oxford, OX1 1NF (Office); 32 Victoria Road, Oxford, OX2 7QD, England and Moorfield, Fountainstown, Myrtleville, Co. Cork, Republic of Ireland (Homes). *Telephone:* (0865) 278579 (Office); (0865) 56087 (Oxford), (021) 831174 (Myrtleville).

GORMLEY, Antony, M.A., D.F.A.; British sculptor; b. 30 Aug. 1950, London; s. of Arthur J. C. Gormley and Elsbeth Brauninger; m. Vicken Parsons 1980; two s. one d.; ed. Ampleforth Coll., Trinity Coll., Cambridge, Cen. School of Arts and Crafts, London, Goldsmiths' Coll., Univ. of London and Slade School of Fine Arts, London; one-man exhbns. Whitechapel Art Gallery, London 1981, Coracle Press Gallery London 1983, Salvatore Ala, New York, Riverside Studios, London and Chapter Gallery, Cardiff 1984; Salvatore Ala, New York, Frankfurt Kunstverein, Regensburg Städtisches

Museum, Salvatore Ala, Milan 1985, Victoria Miro, London 1986, Serpentine Gallery, London, Salvatore Ala, New York, Seibu Contemporary Arts, Tokyo, Le Criée, Rennes 1987; has participated in several group exhbns. including Venice Biennale 1982, 1986, Prospect '86, Frankfurt, Between Object and Image (British Sculpture Since the '60s) in Madrid, Barcelona, Bilbao, Documenta 8, Kassel, Fed. Repub. of Germany and in London, Tokyo, New York, Brazil, Australia and N.Z. *Leisure interests:* walking, talking, stillness and silence. *Address:* 49 Talfourd Road, London, SE15 5NN, England.*Telephone:* 01-701-7718.

GORMLEY, Baron (Life Peer), cr. 1982, of Ashton-in-Makerfield in Greater Manchester; **Joseph Gormley,** O.B.E.; British trade unionist; b. 5 July 1917, Ashton-in-Makerfield, Lancs; m. Sarah Ellen Mather 1937; one s. one d.; ed. St. Oswald's Roman Catholic School, Ashton-in-Makerfield; mem. of Nat. Exec. Cttee. of Nat. Union of Mineworkers (NUM) 1958–82, Gen. Sec. of N.-W. Area 1961, Pres. of NUM 1971–82; mem. Nat. Exec. Cttee. of Labour Party 1963–73, mem. Org. Cttee.; mem. Bureau, Socialist Int.; mem. Gen. Council of TUC 1973–80; Dir. British Investment Trust 1978–; mem. British Overseas Trade Bd. 1979–80; Dir. United Racecourses Ltd. 1982–; J.P., Lancs. until 1963; Hon. Fellow (Manchester Univ. Science and Tech. Inst.) 1980; Commdr's. Cross Order of Merit (Fed. Repub. of Germany) 1981. *Publication:* Battered Cherub 1982 (autobiog.). *Leisure interest:* rugby football. *Address:* 1 Springfield Grove, Sunbury-on-Thames, Middx., England (Home).

GORSE, Georges; French diplomatist; b. 15 Feb. 1915; s. of Maurice and Esilda (Duclos) Gorse; m. Nadine Gelat 1942; one s. two d.; ed. Lycée Louis-le-Grand and Ecole Normale Supérieure (Agrégé de Lettres); Prof. French Lycée at Cairo 1939–40; Prof. Fouad I Univ. 1940; joined Gen. de Gaulle 1940; Deputy Chief Cabinet of Gen. de Gaulle at Algiers 1944 and at Paris 1945; mem. of the Consultative and Constituent Assemblies; Socialist Deputy (for la Vendée) Nat. Assembly 1945–51, re-elected Deputy (for Hauts-de-Seine) 1967, 1968, 1973, 1978, 1986; Under-Sec. of State for Moslem Affairs 1946; Under-Sec. of State for French Territories Overseas 1949; mem. Council, Union Française 1952–58; Del. UN sessions at San Francisco and New York; Amb. to Tunisia 1957–59, Perm. Rep. to European Community 1959–61; Sec. of State for Foreign Affairs (relations with francophone African States) 1961–62; Minister of Co-operation May-Nov. 1962; Amb. to Algeria 1963–67; Minister of Information 1967–68, of Labour, Employment and Population 1973–74; Mayor of Boulogne-Billancourt 1971–; Pres. Hesnault Soc. 1983–; Officier, Légion d'honneur; Rassemblement pour la République. *Address:* Assemblée nationale, 75355 Paris, France.

GORSHKOV, Leonid Aleksandrovich; Soviet politician; b. 1930; ed. Siberian Mining and Metallurgical Inst.; engineer, chief mining engineer 1952–54; mem. CPSU 1952–; sec. party org. in mine 1954–57; Second, First Sec. Kiselvo City Cttee. of CP (Kemerovo Dist) 1957–64; Section Head, sec., second, first sec. of Kemerovo Dist. Cttee. of CPSU 1964–85; mem. of CPSU Cen. Cttee. 1976–; Deputy Pres. of U.S.S.R. Council of Ministers of R.S.F.S.R. 1985–; Deputy to U.S.S.R. Supreme Soviet. *Address:* The Kremlin, Moscow, U.S.S.R.

GORTON, Rt. Hon. Sir John Grey, P.C., G.C.M.G., C.H., M.A.; Australian fmr. politician; b. 9 Sept. 1911, Melbourne; s. of J. R. Gorton; m. Bettina Brown 1935; two s. one d.; ed. Geelong Grammar School and Brasenose Coll., Oxford; served R.A.A.F. during Second World War, severely wounded; Councillor Kerang Shire 1947–52, and Pres. of Shire; Senator for State of Victoria 1949–68, Govt. Leader in Senate 1967–68; Minister for Navy 1958–63; Minister Assisting Minister for External Affairs 1960–63; Minister-in-Charge CSIRO 1962–68; Minister for Works and under-Prime Minister, Minister-in-Charge of Commonwealth Activities in Educ. and Research 1963–66; Minister for Interior 1963–64, for Works 1966–67; Minister for Educ. and Science 1966–68; Prime Minister of Australia 1968–71; Minister of Defence and Deputy Leader of Liberal Party March-Aug. 1971; mem. Parl. Liberal Party Exec.; Spokesman on Environment and Conservation, Urban & Regional Devt.; Deputy Chair. of Jt. Parl. Cttee. on Prices 1973–74; mem. House of Reps. 1968–75; fmrly. Liberal; Independent May-Nov. 1975. *Leisure interests:* reading, swimming. *Address:* Suite 3, 9th Floor, Qantas House, 197 London Circuit, Canberra City, ACT 260, Australia.

GORTON, Slade; American lawyer and politician; b. 8 Jan. 1928, Chicago, Ill.; m. Sally Clark 1958; one s. two d.; ed. Evanston High School, Ill., Dartmouth Columbia Univ. Law School; U S Army 1945–46, U.S.A.F. 1953–56, presently Col. U.S.A.F. Reserve; admitted to Bar, Wash. State 1953; mem. Wash. State House of Reps. 1958–68, Majority Leader 1967–68; Wash. State Attorney-Gen. 1968–80; Senator from Washington State 1981–87; Partner Davis, Wright and Jones, Seattle 1987–; mem. Wash. State Law and Justice Comm. 1969–80 (Chair. 1969–70), State Criminal Justice Training Comm. 1969–80 (Chair. 1969–76), Pres.'s Consumer Advisory Council 1975–77, Nat. Asscn. of Attorneys-Gen. 1969–80 (Pres. 1976–77); Wyman Award 1980; Republican. *Address:* 2600 Century Square, Seattle, Washington, D.C. 98101, U.S.A.

GORYUNOV, Dmitriy Petrovich; Soviet journalist and diplomatist; b. 30 Sept. 1915, Kovrov, Vladimir; s. of Pyotr Gerasimovich Goryunov and Aleksandra Fyodorovna; m. Veronika Gavrilovna Lomovaya 1947; one d.; ed. Higher Party School; worked as lathe-turner and journalist in Kovrov

1930–40; mem. CPSU 1940–; Ed. youth paper Leninetz and Leader, Ivanovo Region Komsomol Cttee. (youth org.) 1940–42; in charge of propaganda, Cen. Cttee. HQ of Komsomol, Moscow 1942–46; training at Party School 1946–49; Ed. Komsomolskaya Pravda 1949–57; Asst. Ed. Pravda 1957–60; Dir.-Gen. Tass Agency 1960–67; Amb. to Kenya 1967–73, to Morocco 1975–78; Deputy to Supreme Soviet U.S.S.R. until 1970; mem. Cen. Auditing Comm. and Alt. mem. of CPSU Cen. Cttee. until 1971; Order of Lenin and of Red Banner of Labour. *Leisure interest:* history of Russian literature. *Address:* c/o Ministry of Foreign Affairs, Moscow, U.S.S.R.

GORYWODA, Manfred, D.ECON.SC.; Polish economist and politician; b. 31 Aug. 1942, Łany, near Koźle; ed. econ. studies; scientific worker, Main School of Planning and Statistics, Warsaw, till 1970; worked at Cen. Cttee. of Polish United Workers' Party (PZPR) 1971–80, Deputy Head, Econ. Dept. 1975–77, Head, Dept. of Planning and Econ. Analyses 1977–79; Head of Econ. Advisers Team of Prime Minister 1980–82; mem. PZPR 1961–, deputy mem. PZPR Cen. Cttee. 1980–81, mem. Cen. Cttee. July 1982–, Sec. PZPR Cen. Cttee. July 1982–84; Chair. Planning Comm. attached to Council of Ministers 1983–87; 1st Sec. PZPR Voivodship Cttee., Katowice 1987–; alt. mem. Political Bureau PZPR Cttee. 1987; Deputy to Seym 1985–; Kt.'s Cross of Order of Polonia Restituta and other decorations. *Address:* Komitet Wojv PZPR, Pl. Dzierżyńskiego 1, 40-929 Katowice, Poland.

GOSKIRK, William Ian Macdonald, C.B.E., M.A.; British petroleum executive; b. 2 March 1932, Carlisle; s. of William Goskirk and Flora Macdonald; m. Hope Ann Knaizuk 1969; one d.; ed. Carlisle Grammar, Queen's Coll., Oxford; with Shell Int. Petroleum 1956–74, Shell Condor, Colombia 1958, Shell, Venezuela 1959–67, 1971–73, Asiatic Petroleum, N.Y. 1967–71; Anschutz Corpn. 1974–76; with BNOC 1976–85, Chief Exec. 1982–85; Dir. Coopers and Lybrand Assocs. Ltd. 1986–. *Leisure interests:* gardening, philately. *Address:* c/o Naval and Military Club, 94 Piccadilly, London, W.1, England. *Telephone:* 01-499 5163.

GOSS, Richard John; South African chartered accountant; b. 8 July 1928, Cape Town; s. of John Archer Goss; m. Myrtle Atherstone 1955; one s. two d.; ed. Rondebosch Boys' High School; joined S.A. Breweries as Man. Accountant, Head Office, Johannesburg 1952, Chief Accountant 1954–57, Asst. Admin. Man. 1957–60, Group Commercial Man. 1960–64; attended Harvard Business School, U.S.A. 1964; Gen. Man., Beer Div., S.A. Breweries 1965–67, Group Man. Dir. 1967–83; Chair. Kersaf Investments Ltd. 1983–, Sun Hotels Ltd. 1983–; Bd. mem. of all major cos. of S.A. Breweries Group; Dir. Nedbank Group and Barlow Rand. *Leisure interest:* tennis. *Address:* P.O. Box 784487, Sandton 2146, South Africa.

GOSSE, Edmund Barr, M.A.; Australian company director; b. 14 July 1915, Perth; s. of late Sir James Gosse and Joanna Gosse (née Barr Smith); m. Christel Gebhardt 1939; one s. one d.; ed. St. Peter's Coll., Adelaide, Trinity Hall, Cambridge; Man. Lysaght's Works, Newcastle 1953–63; Chair, John Lysaght (Aust.) Ltd. 1967–80; Dir. Perpetual Trustees of Australia Ltd., Amalgamated Wireless Australia Ltd.; mem. Iron & Steel Inst., U.K. *Leisure interests:* ornithology, golf. *Address:* 27 Sutherland Crescent, Darling Point, NSW 2027, Australia.

GOSTEV, Boris Ivanovich; Soviet politician; b. 16 Sept. 1927; ed. Moscow Technological Inst. for Light Industry; engineer 1951–53; various posts in U.S.S.R. Ministry of Light Industry, U.S.S.R. State Econ. Council, and U.S.S.R. State Planning Cttee. 1953–63; mem. CPSU 1954–; various posts in Cen. Cttee. CPSU 1963–66; First Deputy Chief of Planning and Finance Dept. of Cen. Cttee. CPSU 1966–75; mem. Cen. Auditing Comm. CPSU 1971–76; cand. mem. Cen. Cttee. CPSU 1976–81, mem. 1981–; Deputy to Council of the Union U.S.S.R. Supreme Soviet 1979–; First Deputy Head of Econ. Inst. of Cen. Cttee. CPSU 1982–85, Head 1985–; U.S.S.R. Minister of Finance 1985–; Order of October Revolution 1977. *Publications:* include a book on agriculture 1980. *Address:* Central Committee of the Communist Party of the Soviet Union, Staraya pl. 4, Moscow, U.S.S.R.

GOTLIEB, Allan Ezra, O.C., B.C.L., M.A., LL.B.; Canadian diplomatist; b. 28 Feb. 1928, Winnipeg; s. of David Phillip and Sarah (née Schiller) Gotlieb; m. Sondra Kaufman 1955; one s. two d.; ed. Univ. of Calif., Univ. of Oxford, Harvard Univ.; joined Dept. of External Affairs 1957; Second Sec. Mission to UN, Geneva 1960–62; First Sec. Del. to 18th Int. Disarmament Conf. 1962–64; Head of Legal Div., Dept. of External Affairs, Ottawa 1965–66; Asst. Under-Sec. of State for External Affairs and Legal Adviser 1967–68; Deputy Minister of Communications 1968–73, of Manpower and Immigration 1973–76; Chair. Employment and Immigration Comm. 1976–77; Under-Sec. of State for External Affairs 1977–81; Amb. to U.S.A. 1981–88; Visiting Prof. of Canadian Studies, Harvard Centre for Int. Affairs 1989–; Addison-Browne Prize in Private Int. Law, Harvard Law School 1954; Deak Prize, American Soc. of Int. Law 1974, Elise and Walter A. Haas Int. Award 1985. *Publications:* Disarmament and International Law 1965, Canadian Treaty-Making 1968, Human Rights, Federalism and Minorities 1970, Impact of Technology on International Law 1982. *Address:* Harvard Centre for Int. Affairs, Cambridge, Mass. 02138, U.S.A.

GOTO, Yasuo; Japanese business executive; b. 6 March 1923, Ehime Pref.; s. of Hideki Goto and Torayo (née Miyaoka) Goto; m. Nobuko Shimomura 1951; one d.; ed. Hosei Univ.; joined Yasuda Fire and Marine

Insurance Co. Ltd. 1948, Br. Gen. Man. Fukuoka Br. 1971-73, Dir. 1973-74, Dir., Gen. Man. Pres. Staff Office, Research Dept. 1974-76, Man. Dir. 1976-78, Sr. Exec. Man. Dir. 1978-80, Exec. Vice-Pres. 1980-83, Pres. Feb. 1983-; Blue Ribbon Medal. *Leisure interests:* go, golf. *Address:* 4-32-16, Minami-Ogikubo, Suginami-ku, Tokyo, Japan.

GOTODA, Masaharu; Japanese politician; b. 9 Aug. 1914; ed. Tokyo Univ.; mem. House of Reps. 1976-; with Ministry of Home Affairs 1939; Chief Sec., Home Affairs Ministry, 1959, Dir., Local Tax Bureau 1959-62; Sec.-Gen. Nat. Police Agency 1962-63, Dir. of Security Bureau 1963-65, Dir.-Gen. 1969-72; Deputy Chief Cabinet Sec. 1972-73; Minister of Home Affairs 1979-80; Chief Cabinet Sec. 1982-83, 1985-87; Dir.-Gen. Nat. Public Safety Comm. 1979-80, Hokkaido Devt. Agency 1979-80, Admin. Man. Agency 1983-84, Man. Co-ordination Agency 1984-85. *Address:* c/o House of Representatives, Tokyo, Japan.

GOTT, Karel; Czechoslovak singer; b. 14 July 1939, Plzeň; ed. Prague Conservatory (studied under Prof. Karenin); mem. Semafor Theatre, Prague 1963-65; mem. Apollo Theatre, Prague, 1965-67; freelance artist 1967-; numerous foreign tours; co-operation with foreign record companies; prizes and awards: Golden Nightingale trophy (annual pop singer poll 1963-66, 1968-81, 1983), MIDEM Prize, Cannes 1967, MIDEM Gold Record 1969, Polydor Gold Record 1970, Supraphon Gold Record 1972, 1973, 1979, 1980, Music Week "star of the year 1974" (UK) 1975, awarded title Artist of Merit 1982, "Gold Aerial 1983", radio station BRT (Belgium, 1984).

GÖTTE, Klaus, DR.JUR.; German business executive; b. 22 April 1932, Diepholz; s. of Heinrich and Anneliese (née Engel) Götte; m. Grazia Michaela Elsaesser 1958; one s. two d.; ed. Göttingen; Man. Bankhaus C.G. Trinkhaus, Düsseldorf 1955-68, Fried. Krupp GmbH, Essen 1968-72; mem. Bd. of Man., Allianz Versicherungs-AG, Munich, and Allianz Lebensversicherungs-AG, Stuttgart 1972-80; Man. Partner, Friedrich Flick Industrieverwaltung KGaA, Düsseldorf 1980-82; Chair. Bd. Man. Dirs. MAN Aktiengesellschaft (fmrly. Gutehoffnungshütte Aktienverein), Munich 1983-. *Address:* Ungererstrasse 69, 8000 Munich 40, Federal Republic of Germany.

GÖTTING, Gerald; German politician; b. 9 June 1923, Halle; s. of Werner Götting and Corisande von Galléra; m. Sabine Richter 1952; one s. one d.; ed. August-Hermann-Francke-Stiftung, Halle, Martin Luther Univ., Halle; war service 1942-45; mem. CDU 1946-, Sec.-Gen. 1949-66, Chair. 1966-; Deputy Pres. Volkskammer 1950-58; Pres. CDU in Volkskammer 1958-63; Deputy Chair. State Council GDR 1960-; Deputy Chair. Volkskammer Nat. Defence Cttee. 1960-69; Chair. Volkskammer Foreign Affairs Cttee. 1963-69; Pres. Volkskammer 1969-76, Deputy Pres. 1980-; Pres. League for Int. Friendship 1976-; Ehrenspange zum Vaterländischen Verdienstorden 1969,Stern der Völkerfreundschaft 1973, Held der Arbeit 1983, Karl Marx Order 1988 and other decorations. *Publications include:* The Christian says Yes to Socialism 1960, Land under Kilimanjaro 1964, Albert Schweitzer—Pioneer of Humanity 1970, Christian Democrats and their Contributions to the Advanced Socialist Society of the German Democratic Republic 1977, Beitrag christlicher Demokraten zu Gegenwart und Zukunft 1987. *Address:* Otto-Nuschke-Strasse 59/60, 1080 Berlin, German Democratic Republic. *Telephone:* 22 88 0.

GOTTLIEB, Robert Adams, B.A.; American editor; b. 29 April 1931, New York; s. of Charles Gottlieb and Martha (née Kean) Gottlieb; m. 1st Muriel Higgins 1952, 2nd Maria Tucci 1969; two s. one d.; ed. Columbia Coll. and Cambridge Univ.; employee Simon and Schuster 1955-65, Ed.-in-Chief 1965-68; Ed.-in-Chief Alfred A. Knopf 1968-87, Pres. 1973-87; Ed.-in-Chief The New Yorker 1987-. *Leisure interests:* ballet, movies, reading. *Address:* The New Yorker, 25 W. 43rd Street, New York, N.Y., U.S.A. *Telephone:* (212) 840-3800.

GOTTMANN, Jean-Iona, F.B.A., D. ÈS L., D.E.S.; French professor of geography; b. 10 Oct. 1915, Kharkov, U.S.S.R.; s. of late Elie Gottmann and Sonia G. (née Ettinger) Gottman; m. Bernice Adelson 1957; ed. Lycée Montaigne and St. Louis, Paris, and Sorbonne Univ.; mem. Inst. for Advanced Study, Princeton 1942-65; Consultant U.S. Govt. Wartime Agencies, Washington D.C. 1942-44; Chargé de Mission, Cabinet Ministre Economie Nat., Paris 1945-46; Dir. of Studies and Research, UN Secr. New York, 1946-47; Assoc. Prof. Johns Hopkins Univ. Baltimore 1944-48; Prof. Inst. d' Etudes Politiques, Univ. of Paris 1948-56, Chargé de Recherche C.N.R.S. Paris 1948-51; Research Dir. Twentieth Century Fund, New York 1956-61; Dir. d' Etudes, Ecole des Hautes Etudes, Paris 1960-83, Prof. of Geography, Univ. of Oxford 1968-83, Prof. Emer. 1983-; Fellow Hertford Coll., Oxford 1968-; Chevalier, Légion d' Honneur et Palmes Academiques, Hon. mem. of American Acad. of Arts and Sciences and other scientific socs.; Hon. D.Litt., Hon. D.Sc., Hon. LL.D. *Publications:* L'Amerique 1949, A Geography of Europe 1950, La Politique des Etats et Leur Géographie 1952, Virginia at Mid Century 1955, Les Marches des Matières Premières 1957, Megalopolis 1961, The Significance of Territory 1973, The Coming of the Transactional City 1983, La Città Invincibile 1983, Megalopolis Revisited 1987 and numerous articles. *Leisure interests:* travel, reading. *Address:* c/o Hertford College, Oxford OX1 3BW (Office); 19 Belsyre Court, Woodstock Road, Oxford, OX2 6HU, England (Home). *Telephone:* 0865-57076 (Home).

GOTTSCHALK, Carl William, M.D.; American professor of medicine; b. 28 April 1922, Salem, Va.; s. of Carl and Lulu (Helbig) Gottschalk; m. Helen M. Scott 1947; two s. one d.; ed. Roanoke Coll. and Univ. of Virginia; Research Fellow in Physiology, Harvard Medical School 1947-50; Asst. Resident and Resident (Medicine), Mass. Gen. Hosp. 1950-52; Fellow in Cardiology, Instr., Asst. Prof., Assoc. Prof., Prof. of Medicine and Physiology, Univ. of N.C. at Chapel Hill 1952-69, Kenan Prof. of Medicine and Physiology 1969-; Established Investigator, American Heart Asscn. 1957-61, Career Investigator 1961-; Hon. Sc.D. (Roanoke Coll.) and other awards. *Publications:* papers on physiology and the kidney. *Address:* Department of Medicine, (226H), School of Medicine, University of North Carolina at Chapel Hill, Chapel Hill, N.C. 27514, U.S.A.

GOTTSCHALK, Gerhard, PH.D.; German professor of microbiology; b. 27 March 1935, Schwedt/Oder; s. of Gerhard Gottschalk and Irmgard Gottschalk; m. Ellen-Marie Hrabowski 1960; two s. one d.; ed. Univs. of Berlin and Göttingen; Research Assoc. Dept. of Biochem., Univ. of Calif. Berkeley 1964-66; Dozent, Univ. of Göttingen 1967-70, Prof. of Microbiology 1970-, Rector 1975-76. *Publication:* Bacterial Metabolism 1986. *Address:* Institute of Microbiology, University of Göttingen, Grisebachstrasse 8, 3400 Göttingen, Federal Republic of Germany. *Telephone:* 0551/393781.

GÖTZ, Alexander, DIPL. ING. DDr.; Austrian public servant and politician; b. 27 Feb. 1928, Graz; s. of Alexander Götz (mother deceased); m. Elisabeth Götz 1956; one s. two d.; ed. Tech. High School, Graz; joined Freiheitliche Partei Österreich (FPÖ) 1955-, Chair. Graz Town Party 1955-, Chair. Provincial Party 1964-73, Del. Styrian Prov. Council 1965-74, Chair. and Leader of Parl. Group of FPÖ 1978-79; elected to Graz Town Council 1958, Alderman 1958, Deputy Mayor of Graz 1964-73, Mayor 1973-; Dr. h.c. (Montclair State Coll. N.J., U.S.A.) 1980; Grosses Ehrenzeichen für die Verdienste um die Rep. Österreich 1970, Grosses Verdienstkreuz des Verdienstordens (Fed. Repub. of Germany) 1973, Grosses Goldenes Ehrenzeichen 1978, Grand Officer of the Order of Stella della Solidarieta Italiana; mem. 50 cultural and sport orgs. *Publications:* numerous articles and pamphlets. *Leisure interests:* films, tennis, swimming. *Address:* Rathaus, A-8010, Graz, Austria (Office). *Telephone:* 73-1-91 (Office).

GÖTZE, Heinz, DR. PHIL.; German publisher; b. 8 Aug. 1912, Dresden; ed. Univs. of Leipzig, Munich and Naples; Partner (Co-Proprietor) Springer-Verlag, Berlin, Heidelberg, New York, Tokyo 1957-, J. F. Bergmann Verlagsbuchhandlung, Munich 1957-; Lange & Springer, Scientific Bookshop, Berlin 1957-; Pres. of Springer-Verlag New York Inc. 1964-, Chair. 1983-; mem. Bd. of Dirs. Universitätsdruckerei H. Stürtz A.G., Würzburg 1965-; Corresp. mem. German Archaeological Inst. 1956-; Dr. med. h.c. Univs. of Heidelberg and Erlangen 1972. *Address:* Springer-Verlag, D-69 Heidelberg, Tiergartenstrasse 17 (Office); Ludolf Krehl-Strasse 41, D-69 Heidelberg, Federal Republic of Germany (Home). *Telephone:* 06221-487225 (Office).

GOUDEV, Vladimir Victorovich; Soviet diplomatist; b. 1940; sr. posts in Ministry of Foreign Affairs at home and abroad 1963-75; Embassy First Sec. in Iraq 1975-79; Chief of Section, Deputy Chief of Near East Dept. of Ministry of Foreign Affairs 1979-86; Deputy Dir., Chief of Dept. in Directorate of Near East and North Africa of Ministry of Foreign Affairs 1986-87; Amb. to Iran 1987-. *Address:* U.S.S.R. Embassy, Neauphle-le-Chateau Avenue, Tehran, Iran.

GOUGH, Rt. Rev. Hugh Rowlands, C.M.G., O.B.E., T.D., M.A., D.D.; British ecclesiastic; b. 19 Sept. 1905, Pakistan; s. of Rev. Charles Massey Gough; m. Madeline Elizabeth Kinnaird 1929; one d.; Ed. Cambridge Univ., London Coll. of Divinity; Deacon 1928, Priest 1929; Curate St. Mary Islington 1928-31; Perpetual Curate St. Paul, Walcot, Bath 1931-34; Vicar St. James Carlisle 1934-39, St. Matthew Bayswater 1939-46, of Islington and Rural Dean 1946-48; Prebendary St. Paul's Cathedral 1948; Archdeacon West Ham 1948-58; Suffragan Bishop of Barking 1948-59; Archbishop of Sydney 1959-66, Primate of Australia 1959-66; retd. 1972; Deputy Lieut. Co. of Essex 1952-59; mem. Council London Coll. of Divinity, Clifton, Theological Coll., Haileybury Coll., Monkton Combe School, St. Lawrence Coll., Chigwell School, Stowe School, Kingham Hill Trust; war service 1939-45, O.B.E. (Mil.), mentioned in despatches; Hon. Chaplain to the Forces 2nd Class; Hon. D.D. (Lambeth and Wycliffe Coll., Toronto), Hon. Th.D. (Australia); Sub-Prelate, Order of St. John 1959. *Address:* The Forge, Over Wallop, Stockbridge, Hants., England. *Telephone:* (0264) 781315.

GOUGH, Michael; British actor; b. 1917, Malaya; numerous film and TV appearances. *Films include:* Women in Love, Velvet House, Julius Caesar, Trog, The Go Between, Henry VIII and his Six Wives, Horror Hospital, Boys from Brazil, Memed, Out of Africa, Caravaggio, Machenka. *Address:* c/o Plunkett Greene Management, Ltd., 91 Regent Street, London, W.1, England.

GOUHIER, Henri Gaston; French university professor and writer; b. 5 Dec. 1898, Auxerre; m. Marie-Louise Dufour; one d.; ed. Ecole Normale Supérieure and Faculté des lettres de Paris; Prof., Faculty of Literature, Lille Univ. 1929-41, Univ. of Paris 1941-68; mem. Acad. des Sciences morales et politiques 1961-, Acad. Française 1979-, Royal Acad. of Belgium, Acad. dei Lincei 1981; Commdr., Légion d'honneur; Grand Prix de littérature de l'Acad. Française 1965, Grand Prix littéraire de la Ville de Paris 1976, Prix Mondial Ciro del Duca 1988. *Publications:* La pensée

religieuse de Descartes 1924, La vocation de Malebranche 1926, La philosophie de Malebranche et son expérience religieuse 1926, Notre ami Maurice
Barrès 1928, La vie d'Auguste Comte 1931, L'essence du théâtre 1943,
La jeunesse d'Auguste Comte et la formation du positivisme (3 vols.) 1933,
1936, 1941, Les conversions de Maine de Biran 1947, La philosophie et son
histoire 1944, L'histoire et sa philosophie 1952, Le théâtre et l'existence
1952, Les premières pensées de Descartes 1958, L'oeuvre théâtrale 1958,
Bergson et le Christ des Evangiles 1961 (Prix Lecomte de Nouy 1962), La
pensée métaphysique de Descartes 1962, Pascal, Commentaires 1966,
Benjamin Constant 1967, Les méditations métaphysiques de J.-J. Rousseau
1970, Le combat de Marie Noel 1971, Renan, auteur dramatique 1972,
Pascal et les Humanistes Chrétiens: L'affaire Saint-Ange 1974, Antonin
Artaud et l'essence du théâtre 1974, Fénelon philosophe 1977, Cartésian-
isme et Augustinisme au XVIIe siècle 1978, Rousseau et Voltaire: Portraits
dans deux miroirs 1983, Pascal, Conversion et apologétique 1986, L'anti-
humanisme au XVIIe Siècle 1987. *Leisure interest:* theatre. *Address:* c/o
Académie Française, 23 quai de Conti, 75006 Paris; 60 boulevard Emil
Augier, 75116 Paris, France.

GOUKOUNI Oueddei (see Oueddei, Goukouni).

GOULD, Beatrice Blackmar, M.S.; American magazine editor and writer;
b. 27 Oct. 1898, Emmetsburg, Iowa; d. of H. E. Blackmar and Mary K.
Fluke; m. Charles Bruce Gould 1923; one d.; ed. State Univ. of Iowa and
Columbia Univ.; Newspaper reporter and woman's Ed. N.Y. Sunday World
1926–29; writer for magazines 1929–35; Ed. (with husband) Ladies' Home
Journal 1935–62; various journalistic awards (with husband). *Publications:*
Man's Estate 1927, The Terrible Turk 1934, American Story 1968 (two
plays and autobiography, with husband). *Leisure interests:* theatre, books,
sailing, swimming, dancing. *Address:* Bedensbrook, Box 188, Hopewell,
N.J. 08525, U.S.A. *Telephone:* 609-466-0170.

GOULD, Bryan Charles, LL.M. (N.Z.), M.A., B.C.L. (OXON), M.P.; British politician;
b. 11 Sept. 1939, Hawera, N.Z.; s. of Charles T. and Elsie M. (née Driller)
Gould; m. Gillian A. Harrigan 1967; one s. one d.; ed. Victoria and Auckland
Univs., N.Z. and Balliol Coll., Oxford; in diplomatic service, British
Embassy Brussels 1964–68; Fellow and Tutor in Law, Worcester Coll.,
Oxford 1968–74; M.P. for Southampton Test 1974–79, Dagenham 1983–;
presenter and reporter Thames TV 1977–83; Opposition Spokesman on
Trade 1983–86, on Trade and Industry 1987–; mem. of Shadow Cabinet,
Labour's Campaign Co-ordinator 1986–. *Publications:* Monetarism or Pros-
perity? 1981, Socialism and Freedom 1985. *Leisure interests:* food, wine,
gardening. *Address:* House of Commons, London, S.W.1 (Office); 53 Vanbrugh Court, Wincott Street, London, S.E.11, England (Home).

GOULD, Elliott; American actor; b. 29 Aug. 1938, Brooklyn, New York;
s. of Bernard and Lucille (née Raver) Goldstein; m. 1st Barbra Streisand
(q.v.) 1963 (divorced 1971), one s; m. 2nd Jenny Bogart 1973 (divorced
1975, remarried 1978), one s. one d.; made Broadway début in Rumple
1957; other appearances include Say Darling 1958, Irma La Douce 1960, I
Can Get It For You Wholesale 1962, Drat! The Cat 1965, Harry in Little
Murders 1967 and 1971; toured in The Fantastiks with Liza Minnelli.
Films include: The Confession 1966, The Night They Raided Minsky's
1968, Bob and Carol and Ted and Alice 1969, Getting Straight 1970,
M*A*S*H 1970, The Touch 1971, Little Murders 1971, The Long Good-
Bye 1972, Nashville 1974, I Will . . . I Will . . . For Now 1976, Harry and
Walter Go to New York 1976, A Bridge Too Far 1977, The Silent Partner
1979, The Lady Vanishes 1979, Escape to Athens 1979, The Muppet Movie
1979, Falling in Love Again 1980, The Devil and Max Devlin 1981, Over
the Brooklyn Bridge 1984, The Naked Face 1984, Act of Betrayal 1988.
Address: c/o William Morris Agency, 151 El Camino, Beverley Hills, Calif.
90212, U.S.A.

GOULD, Kingdon, Jr., A.B., LL.B.; American diplomatist; b. 3 Jan. 1924,
N.Y.; s. of Kingdon and Annunziata (Lucci) Gould; m. Mary Bunce Thorne
1945; four s. five d.; ed. High School in Millbrook, N.Y., Yale Univ. and
Yale Law School; Dir. Consolidated Coal Co. 1945–69; Organizer and Prin.,
A & G Partnership, Parking Man. Inc. 1953–69; Amb. to Luxembourg
1969–72, to the Netherlands 1973–76; Founder and Chair. Glenelg Country
School 1954–; Dir. Butler Bros. 1955–57; Incorporator and Dir. State Bank
of Laurel, Md. 1956–63; Organizer White Mountain Nat. Bank 1962;
Organizer and Dir. Madison Nat. Bank 1963–69; Chair. Murray Corpn.
1964–69; mem. Md. Board of Natural Resources 1968–69. *Leisure interests:*
riding, swimming, fly fishing, tennis, golf, skiing, chess. *Address:* Overlook
Drive, Laurel, Md. 20810, U.S.A. (Home).

GOULD, Morton; American composer and conductor; b. 10 Dec. 1913,
New York; s. of James H. Gould and Frances Arkin; m. (separated); two
s. two d.; ed. Richmond Hill High School, New York; pianist, composer,
conductor, arranger, recording artist; conductor on radio programmes
over many years, guest conductor of maj. symphony orchestras; many
commissioned compositions for ballet, TV, films, etc.; Pres. American Soc.
of Composers, Authors and Publrs. 1986–; Grammy Award, ASOL Gold
Baton; mem. American Acad. and Inst. of Arts and Letters. *Published
compositions:* Spirituals for Orchestra, Latin American Symphony, Interplay (Robbins ballet), Fall River Legend (DeMille ballet), American Salute,
Pavanne, Jekyll and Hyde Variations, Holocaust Suite, Symphony of

Spirituals, Derivations, etc. *Address:* 231 Shoreward Drive, Great Neck,
N.Y. 11021, U.S.A.

GOULD, Samuel Brookner, A.M.; American university administrator; b.
11 Aug. 1910, New York; s. of Nathaniel Gould and Lina Brookner; m.
Laura J. Ohman 1936; one s.; ed. Bates Coll., New York Univ., Oxford,
Cambridge and Harvard Univs.; Instructor, William Hall High School, W.
Hartford, Conn. 1932–38; Head Dept. of Speech, Brookline, Mass. Schools
1938–47; Prof. of Radio, Speech, Dir. of Div. of Radio, Speech and Theatre,
Boston Univ. 1947–50; Asst. to Pres., Boston Univ. 1950–53; Senior Assoc.,
Cresap, McCormick & Paget 1953–54; Pres. Antioch Coll. 1954–59; Chancel-
lor, Univ. of Calif. at Santa Barbara 1959–62; Pres. Educational Broadcast-
ing Corpn. 1962–64; Chancellor, State Univ. of New York 1964–70, Emer.
1970–; Dir. McKinsey and Co. Inc. 1970–71; Vice-Pres. Educ. Testing
Service and Pres. Inst. for Educ. Devt. 1971–74; Educ. Consultant 1975–;
Chancellor, Conn. Comm. for Higher Educ. 1976–77; mem. numerous
educational and civic cttees.; Hon. LL.D. (Bates Coll., Wilberforce Univ.,
Union Coll., New York Univ., Univ. of Akron, Univ. of Pittsburgh, Univ.
of Calif., Colgate Univ., State Univ. of N.Y.), Hon. L.H.D. (Alfred Univ.,
Hamilton Coll.), Hon. Litt.D. (Colgate Univ.), Hon. D.Sc. (Albany Medical
Coll.). *Publications:* Knowledge is Not Enough 1959, Training the Local
Announcer (with S. A. Diamond) 1950, Explorations in Non-Traditional
Study (co-editor) 1972, Diversity by Design (co-author) 1973. *Leisure inter-
est:* golf. *Address:* 4822 Ocean Boulevard, Sarasota, Fla. 33581, U.S.A.

GOULD, Stephen Jay, PH.D.; American professor of geology; b. 10 Sept.
1941, New York; s. of the late Leonard and of Eleanor (née Rosenberg)
Gould; m. Deborah Lee Gould 1965; two s.; ed. Antioch Coll., Columbia
Univ.; Asst. Prof. of Geology and Asst. Curator of Invertebrate Paleontol-
ogy, Harvard Univ. 1967–71, Assoc. Prof. and Assoc. Curator 1971–73,
Prof. of Geology and Curator 1973–, Alexander Agassiz Prof. of Zoology
1982–; mem. Cttee. of Profs. Dept. of Biology, Adjunct mem. Dept. of
History of Science; D. Hum. Litt. (Marlboro Coll.) 1982, D.S. (Bucknell
Univ.) 1982, (MacAlester Coll.) 1983, D.Jur. (Antioch Coll.) 1983, D.S.
(Denison, Colgate, Md. and Pace Univs.) 1984; Fellow, A.A.A.S., American
Acad. of Arts and Sciences; numerous medals and awards; mem. various
socs. *Publications:* Ontogeny and Phylogeny 1977, Ever Since Darwin
1977, The Panda's Thumb 1980, The Mismeasure of Man (Nat. Book
Critics Circle Award 1982) 1981, Hen's Teeth and Horse's Toes 1983, The
Flamingo's Smile 1985, Time's Arrow, Time's Cycle 1987, An Urchin in
the Storm 1987 and numerous articles. *Leisure interests:* baseball, choral
singing. *Address:* Museum of Comparative Zoology, Harvard University,
Cambridge, Mass. 02138, U.S.A. *Telephone:* (617) 495 2470.

GOULDING, Marrack Irvine, C.M.G.; British diplomatist and international
civil servant; b. 2 Sept. 1936; s. of Hon. Sir Irvine Goulding; m. Susan
Rhoda D'Albiac 1961; two s. one d.; ed. St. Paul's School and Magdalen
Coll. Oxford; joined H.M. Foreign (later Diplomatic) Service 1959; with
Middle East Centre for Arab Studies 1959–61; Kuwait 1961–64; Foreign
Office 1964–68; Tripoli, Libya 1968–70; Cairo 1970–72; Private Sec. Minister
of State for Foreign and Commonwealth Affairs 1972–75; seconded to
Cabinet Office 1975–77; Counsellor, Lisbon 1977–79; Counsellor and Head
of Chancery, U.K. Mission to UN, New York 1979–83; Amb. to Angola
and concurrently to São Tomé and Principe 1983–85; UN Under Sec.-Gen.,
Special Political Affairs, 1986–. *Leisure interests:* travel and birdwatching.
Address: 40 E. 61st Street, Apt. 18, New York, N.Y. 10021, U.S.A.; 82
Claverton Street, London, SW1V 3AX, England. *Telephone:* (212) 935-
6157; 01-834 3046.

GOULED APTIDON, Hassan; Djibouti politician; b. 1916, Djibouti; Rep.
of French Somaliland (now Repub. of Djibouti) to French Govt. 1952–58;
Vice-Pres. Territorial Ass. 1958–59; Deputy to French Nat. Ass. 1959–62;
Minister of Educ. 1963–67; mem. (later Pres.) Ligue Populaire Africaine
pour l'Indépendance—LPAI (fmrly. Ligue Populaire Africaine) 1967–79;
Pres. Council of Govt., responsible for Co-operation May–June 1977; Chair.
Rassemblement Populaire pour le Progrès (RPP) March 1979–; Pres.
Repub. of Djibouti, C.-in-C. of the Armed Forces June 1977–. *Address:*
Présidence de la République, Djibouti, Republic of Djibouti.

GOULIAN, Mehran, A.B., M.D.; American physician; b. 31 Dec. 1929,
Weehawken, N.J.; s. of Dicran Goulian and Shamiram Mzrakjian; m. Susan
Hook 1961; three s.; ed. Columbia Coll. and Columbia Coll. of Physicians
and Surgeons; Fellow in Medicine (Hematology). Yale Univ. School of
Medicine 1959–60; Research Fellow in Medicine (Hematology), Harvard
Univ. July–Dec. 1960, 1962–63, Instructor in Medicine 1963–65; Clinical and
Research Fellow in Medicine (Hematology), Mass. Gen. Hosp. July–Dec.
1960, 1962–63, Asst. in Medicine, 1963–65; Fellow in Biochem., Stanford
Univ. School of Medicine 1965–67; Research Assoc. in Biochem., Univ. of
Chicago and Argonne Cancer Research Hospital 1967–69, Assoc. Prof. of
Medicine 1967–70, Assoc. Prof. of Biochem. 1969–70; Prof. of Medicine,
Univ. of Calif., San Diego 1970–. *Leisure interest:* music. *Address:* Depart-
ment of Medicine, University of California, San Diego, La Jolla, Calif.
92093-0613, U.S.A. *Telephone:* (619) 534-3016.

GOULLI, Slaheddine El, PH.D.; Tunisian diplomatist; b. 22 June 1919,
Sousse; m. M. J. Zineb-Larré 1958; one d.; ed. Coll. de Sousse, Coll. Sainte
Barbe, Sorbonne and Univ. de Paris; in private industry 1947–56; active
in Tunisian Nat. Liberation Movement, Europe 1947–56; Consul-Gen. Mar-

seilles 1956–57; Counsellor, Washington 1958, Minister, Washington 1959–61; Alt. Exec. Dir. World Bank 1961; Amb. to Belgium, also accred. to Netherlands and Luxembourg 1962–69, concurrently Perm. Rep. to EEC; Perm. Rep. to UN 1969; Amb. to U.S.A. 1969–73, also accred. to Mexico 1970–73 and Venezuela 1972–73; Special Adviser to Foreign Minister 1974–76; Amb. to the Netherlands 1976–78; Adviser Foreign Ministry 1979; Chair. Philips Electronics (Tunisia) 1980–; mem. Bd. W.T.C. Asscn., Brussels, Rotary Int.; Grand Cordon de l'Ordre de la République Tunisienne 1966, also decorations from Belgium, Netherlands and Luxembourg. *Leisure interests:* golf, swimming, reading. *Address:* 2 rue des Roses, La Marsa, Tunisia. *Telephone:* 01-271 307.

GOUNELLE DE PONTANEL, Hugues; French professor of medicine; b. 27 Feb. 1903, Chateauroux; m. Jeanne Gamas 1940; one s. two d.; ed. Lycée de Chateauroux and Univ. of Strasbourg; Intern and Head of Clinic, Faculté de Médécine, Strasbourg 1925–32; Prof. Agrégé, Val de Grace, Paris 1938; founder, Foch Research Centre for Human Nutrition 1940; Pres. Acad. Nat. de Médécine 1983; Officier Légion d'honneur; Commdr. Ordre nat. du Mérite, du Mérite agricole, etc. *Publications:* 300 scientific publications. *Address:* 5 rue Auguste Maquet, 75016 Paris, France (Home).

GOURAD HAMADOU, Barkad; Djibouti politician; fmr. mem. of French Senate; fmr. Minister of Health; Prime Minister of Djibouti Sept. 1978–, Minister of Ports 1978–87, Minister of Planning and Land Devt. 1987–; mem. Rassemblement Populaire pour le Progrès (RPP). *Address:* Office du Premier Ministre, Djibouti, Republic of Djibouti.

GOURDON, Alain; French lawyer and author; b. 16 Oct. 1928, Paris; s. of Raymond and Marguerite (née Thuret) Gourdon; m. 2nd Claudine Cruz; one s. one d. (from previous marriage); ed. Lycée Carnot, Univ. of Paris, Ecole Nat. de l'Admin.; Auditeur, Cour des Comptes 1952; Adviser to the Royal Khmer Govt. 1957–60; High Counsellor, mem. Supreme Court, Morocco 1961–63; Consultant OECD 1964; Conseiller-Maître, Cour des Comptes 1981–84; Admin. Général, Bibliothèque Nat. 1981–84; mem. Jt. Inspection Unit, UNO, Geneva 1985–; Chevalier, Légion d'honneur, Chevalier Ordre nat. du mérite, Commdr. des Arts et des Lettres. *Publications* (as Julien Cheverny): Eloge du colonialisme 1961, Le carnaval des régents 1963, Les cadres 1967, Le temps des obsèques 1970, Sexologie de l'Occident 1976, Mendès-France ou le rêve français 1976, les Matriarches 1978. *Leisure interests:* travel, books. *Address:* Route des Gravannes, Veigy-Foncenex 74140, France. *Telephone:* 50.94.83.88.

GOURISSE, Daniel, D. ÈS SC.; French professor of chemical engineering and administrator; b. 13 March 1939, Charleville; s. of Robert Gourisse and Marie-Marguerite Lalle; m. Michèle Maës 1961; three s.; ed. Ecole Centrale des Arts et Manufactures; Laboratory head, Commissariat à l'Energie Atomique (Atomic Energy Comm.) 1964–73, Tech. adviser to the Gen. Admin. 1973–76, Head, Chem. Eng. Dept. 1976–84; Prof. of Chem. Eng., Ecole Centrale des Arts et Manufactures 1969–76, of Gen. and Ind. Sciences 1977–78, Dir. Ecole Centrale 1978–; Pres. Conf. des Grandes Ecoles 1985–, Office de robotique et de productique du Commissariat à l'énergie atomique 1985–; Chevalier, Ordre nat. du Mérite, Officier, Palmes académiques. *Leisure interests;* music, gardening, tennis and cycling. *Publications:* many articles in international journals. *Address:* Ecole Centrale des Arts et Manufactures, Grande Voie des Vignes, 92295 Chatenay-Malabry; Cedex; C.E.N. Fontenay aux Roses BP6, 9220 Fontenay aux Roses; 12 avenue de la Cure d'Air, 91400 Orsay, France (Home). *Telephone:* (1) 46.83.62.54 (Ecole Centrale); (1) 46.54.97.61 (C.E.N. Fontenay); 69.07.83.05.

GOUTARD, Noel; French business executive; b. 22 Dec. 1931, Casablanca, Morocco; s. of F. Antoine Goutard and M. Edmée (née Lespinasse) Goutard; m. Dominique Jung 1964; one s. one d.; ed. Lycée Louis le Grand, Paris, Univ. of Bordeaux and Pace Coll., New York; Vice-Pres. Frenville Co., New York 1954–60; Finance Exec. Warner Lambert Int., Morris Plains, N.J. 1960–62; African Area Man. Pfizer Inc., New York 1962–66; Exec. Vice-Pres. Gevelot S.A. Paris 1966–71; Pres. and C.O.O. Compteurs Schlumberger S.A., Paris 1971–76; Exec. Vice-Pres. and mem. Bd. of Dirs. Chargeurs S.A., Paris 1976–83; Exec. Vice-Pres. and C.O.O. Thomson S.A., Paris 1983–84, Pres. and C.O.O. 1984–; Pres.-Dir. Gen. Valéo SA 1987–; Pres. la Sev 1987–; mem. Bd. Thomson CSF, Banque Thomson, Thomson-Brandt Armements, etc. *Leisure interests:* tennis, travel. *Address:* Valéo SA, 64 avenue de la Grande Armée, 75848 Paris cedex 17, France.

GOUYON, H.E. Cardinal Paul; French ecclesiastic (retd.); b. 24 Oct. 1910, Bordeaux; s. of Louis Gouyon and Jeanne Chassaing; ed. Inst. Catholique de Paris, Gregorian Univ., Rome; ordained priest 1937; consecrated Bishop 1957; Bishop of Bayonne 1957; Titular Archbishop of Pessinonte 1963; Archbishop of Rennes 1964–85; cr. Cardinal 1969; Nat. Pres. Pax Christi 1966–82; mem. Secretariat for non-believers; Officier, Légion d'honneur, Commdr., ordre nat. du Mérite, Croix de guerre 1939–45. *Publications:* Introduction de la reforme disciplinaire tridentine dans la diocèse de Bordeaux 1582–1624 1957, L'intercommunion-est elle possible? 1976, Marcel Callo, témoin d'une génération 1981. *Address:* Ma Maison, 181 rue Judaïque, 33000 Bordeaux Cedex, France.

GOUYOU BEAUCHAMPS, Xavier; French television executive; b. 25 April 1937, Paris; two s.; ed. Lycée Janson de Sailly, Inst. d'études politiques and Ecole nat. d'admin.; Dir. of Staff Loiret Pref. 1964–66; Asst.

Head of Staff, Minister of Agric. 1966–68, Minister of Educ. 1968–69; Official Staff Rep., Minister of Econ. and Finance 1969–74; Tech. Adviser to Gen. Secr. of the Pres. 1974–76; Prefect of Ardèche 1976–77; Pres. and Dir.-Gen. SOFIRAD 1977–81; Pres. Télédifffusion de France Dec. 1986–; Chevalier ordre nat. du Mérite, Mérite agricole, Croix de la Valeur militaire. *Publication:* Le ministère de l'économie et des Finances, un Etat dans l'Etat? 1976. *Address:* 38 rue Lacépède, 75005 Paris, France.

GOVOROV, Vladimir Leonidovich; Soviet army officer; b. 18 Oct. 1924, Odessa; s. of the late Marshal L. A. Govorov; ed. Special Artillery School, Moscow, Frunze Mil. Acad., Military Acad. of General Staff, Moscow; served in Soviet Army 1942–; commdr. of artillery section and battery, Leningrad and Second Baltic Fronts 1943–45; mem. CPSU 1946–; Deputy Commdr., Commdr. of a regt.; Chief of Staff of a div. 1946–58; sr. positions in Soviet Army 1958–69; First Deputy C.-in-C. of Group of Soviet Troops in Germany 1969–71; Commdr., Baltic Mil. Dist., 1971–72; Deputy of Supreme Soviet of Latvian S.S.R. 1971–75; Commdr. of Moscow Mil. Dist., Chief of Moscow Garrison 1972–80; rank of Gen. 1977; Deputy to Council of the Union, U.S.S.R. Supreme Soviet 1972–84; cand. mem. of Cen. Cttee. CPSU 1976–81, mem. 1981–; mem. of Comm. on Foreign Affairs 1979–84; U.S.S.R. Deputy Minister of Defence 1984–; Deputy to Council of Nationalities, U.S.S.R. Supreme Soviet 1984–; Order of Lenin Order of Red Banner (twice), Hero of Soviet Union 1984, many other medals, Soviet and foreign. *Address:* Ministry of Defence, Moscow, U.S.S.R.

GOW, Gen. Sir (James) Michael, G.C.B.; British army officer (retd.); b. 3 June 1924, Sheffield, Yorks.; s. of late J. C. Gow and late Mrs. Alastair Sanderson; m. Jane Emily Scott 1946; one s. four d.; ed. Winchester Coll.; commissioned Scots Guards 1943; served N.W. Europe 1944–45; Malayan Emergency 1949; Equerry to H.R.H. Duke of Gloucester 1952–53; graduated Staff Coll. 1954; Brigade Maj. 1955–57; Regimental Adjt. Scots Guards 1957–60; Instructor Army Staff Coll. 1962–64; commanded 2nd Bn. Scots Guards, Kenya and England 1964–66; G.S.O.1 HQ, London Dist. 1966–67; Commdr. 4th Guards Brigade 1968–70; at Imperial Defence Coll. 1970; Brig.-Gen. Staff (Int.) HQ, British Army of the Rhine (BAOR), and Asst. Chief of Staff G2 HQ, Northag 1971–73; G.O.C. 4th Armoured Div., BAOR 1973–75; Col. Commandant Intelligence Corps 1973–86; Dir. Army Training 1975–78; G.O.C. Scotland 1979–80; Gov. Edinburgh Castle 1979; Commdr. Northern Army Group and C.-in-C. BAOR, 1980–83; Commandant, Royal Coll. of Defence Studies 1984–86; A.D.C. Gen. to H.M. The Queen 1981–83; Commr. British Scouts W. Europe 1980–83; Brig. Queen's Bodyguard for Scotland (Royal Co. of Archers); Vice-Pres. Royal Caledonian Schools, Bushey 1983–, Royal Patriotic Fund Corpn. 1983–; Pres. Royal British Legion Scotland and Earl Haig Fund Scotland 1986–; Sec.-Gen. The Prince's Youth Business Trust 1986; Freeman City of London, Freeman and Liveryman Painters and Stainers Co. *Publications:* Trooping The Colour—A History of the Sovereign's Birthday Parade 1980; articles in military and historical journals. *Leisure interests:* sailing, music, travel, reading. *Address:* Long Vere House, Loxhill, Hascombe, by Godalming, Surrey, England. *Telephone:* 048-632-230.

GOWANS, Sir James Learmonth, Kt., C.B.E., M.D., D.PHIL., F.R.C.P., F.R.S.; British medical scientist and administrator; b. 7 May 1924, Sheffield; s. of John Gowans and Selma Josefina Ljung; m. Moyra Leatham 1956; one s. two d.; ed. Trinity School, Croydon, King's Coll. Hospital Medical School, Oxford Univ.; Fellow, St. Catharine's Coll., Oxford Univ. 1961–; Sr. Scientific Adviser, Celltech Ltd. 1988–; Consultant, WHO Global Programme on AIDS 1987–88; Henry Dale Research Prof. of Royal Soc. 1962–77; Dir. MRC Cellular Immunology Unit 1963–77, mem. MRC 1965–69, Sec. and Deputy Chair. 1977–87; Chair. MRC Biological Research Bd. 1967–69; mem. Advisory Bd. for the Research Councils 1977–87; mem. Council and a Vice-Pres. Royal Soc. 1973–75; Hon. ScD. (Yale) 1966, Hon. D.Sc. (Chicago) 1971, (Birmingham) 1978, (Rochester, N.Y.) 1987, Hon. M.D. (Edin.) 1979, Hon. LL.D. (Glasgow) 1988; Hon. D.M. (Southampton) 1987; Gairdner Award, Ehrlich Prize, Feldberg Award, Royal Medal of Royal Soc., Wolf Prize; Foreign Assoc. N.A.S. (U.S.A.). *Publications:* articles in scientific journals. *Address:* 75 Cumnor Hill, Oxford, OX2 9HX, England.

GOWER, David Ivon; British cricketer; b. 1 April 1957, Tunbridge Wells, Kent; s. of Richard Hallam Gower and Sylvia Mary Gower; ed. King's School, Canterbury and Univ. Coll. London; début for Leics. 1975; début for England, Test Matches against Pakistan and N.Z. 1978; Capt. of England in one Test against Pakistan 1982, in two Tests against Pakistan 1984; apptd. Capt. of Leics. 1984; Capt. of England 1984–86, Aug. 1988, 1989–; Capt. of England in Tests against India and Australia and West Indies, became ninth English player to pass 5,000 runs in Tests 1985, passed 6,000 1987, reached 7,000 test runs in 100th Test Match in 1988; played in 96 test matches, 6th highest scorer of test runs for England. *Publications:* articles in Wisden Cricket Monthly. *Leisure interests:* Cresta run, skiing, tennis, golf, photography. *Address:* c/o Leicestershire County Cricket Club, Grace Road, Leicester, LE2 8AD, England.

GOWING, Margaret Mary, C.B.E., B.SC., F.B.A.; British professor of history; b. 26 April 1921, London; d. of Ronald Elliott and Mabel Elliott (née Donaldson); m. Donald Gowing 1944 (deceased); two s.; ed. Christ's Hosp. and L.S.E.; civil servant, Bd. of Trade 1942–45; Historical Section of Cabinet Office 1945–59; mem. of Inquiries into Public Records, Grigg

1952–54, Wilson 1978–81; Historian and Archivist of UKAEA 1959–66; Reader in Contemporary History, Univ. of Kent at Canterbury 1966–72; Prof. of the History of Science, Oxford Univ. 1972–86; Dir. Contemporary Scientific Archives Centre 1973–86; mem. Lord Chancellor's Advisory Council on Public Records 1974–82, BBC Archives Advisory Cttee. 1976–79; Trustee Nat. Portrait Gallery 1978–, Imperial War Museum 1986–87; Hon. D.Litt. (Leeds and Leicester), Hon. D.Sc. (Manchester), (Bath) 1987. *Publications:* British War Economy (with Sir Keith Hancock) 1949, Civil Industry and Trade (with E. L. Hargreaves) 1952, Britain and Atomic Energy 1939–1945 1964, Independence and Deterrence, Vol. I: Policy Making, Vol. II: Policy Execution 1974. *Address:* 5 Northmoor Place, Oxford, OX2 6XB, England. *Telephone:* (0865) 55564.

GOWON, Gen. Yakubu, B.A., PH.D; Nigerian army officer; b. 19 Oct. 1934, Garam, Pankshin Div., Plateau State; s. of Yohanna and Saraya Gowon; m. Victoria Hansatu Zakari 1969; one s. two d.; ed. St. Bartholomew's School, Wusasa, Zaria, Govt. Coll. (Barewa), Zaria, Royal Military Acad., Sandhurst, Staff Coll., Camberley and Jt. Services Staff Coll., Latimer, England; Adjutant, Nigerian Army March 1960; with UN peacekeeping force, Congo 1960–61, Jan.-June 1963; promoted Lieut.-Col. and appointed Adjutant-Gen. Nigerian Army June 1963; Chief of Staff 1966; Maj.-Gen. June 1967; promoted Gen. Oct. 1971; Head of Fed. Mil. Govt. and C.-in-C. of Armed Forces of Fed. Repub. of Nigeria 1966–75 (deposed in coup); studying at Warwick Univ. 1975–83, Postgraduate 1978–82; Chair. Assembly of Heads of State, OAU 1973–74; returned to Nigeria 1983, to Togo Jan. 1984; Hon. LL.D., Hon. D.Sc., Hon. D.Litt. *Leisure interests:* squash, tennis, photography, pen-drawings. *Publication:* Faith in Unity 1970. *Address:* Lomé, Togo.

GOWRIE, Rt. Hon. The Earl of, Alexander Patrick Greysteil Hore-Ruthven, P.C., B.A., A.M.; British company director and parliamentarian; b. 26 Nov. 1939, Dublin, Eire; s. of The Hon. A. H. P. Hore-Ruthven and Pamela Margaret Fletcher; m. 1st Xandra Bingley 1962, one s. (divorced 1973); m. 2nd Adelheid Gräfin von den Schulenburg 1974; ed. Eton Coll., Balliol Coll. Oxford and Harvard Univ., U.S.A.; Fellow and Tutor, Lowell House, Harvard Univ. 1965–68; Asst. Prof., Emerson Coll., Boston 1967–68; Lecturer in English and American Literature, Univ. Coll. London 1969–72; a U.K. del. to UN 1971; a Lord-in-Waiting to H.M. the Queen 1972–74; Govt. Whip, House of Lords 1972–74; Consultant, Thomas Gibson Fine Art 1974–79; Opposition Spokesman on Econ. Affairs and Adviser to Margaret Thatcher 1977–79; Minister of State, Dept. of Employment 1979–81; Minister of State and Deputy to the Sec. of State, Northern Ireland Office 1981–83; Minister of State, Privy Council Office and Minister for the Arts 1983–84; mem. of Cabinet as Chancellor of the Duchy of Lancaster (retaining portfolio as Minister for the Arts) 1984–85; Chair. Sotheby's Int. 1985–86, The Really Useful Group 1985–, Sotheby's 1986–; Provost R.C.A. 1986–. *Publications:* A Postcard from Don Giovanni (poems) 1972, The Genius of British Painting: The Twentieth Century 1975, Derek Hill: An Appreciation 1987. *Leisure interests:* reading, writing, looking at pictures, walking and wine. *Address:* c/o Sotheby's, 35 New Bond Street, London, W.1, England. *Telephone:* 01-493 8080.

GOYER, Hon. Jean-Pierre, P.C., Q.C., B.A., LL.B.; Canadian lawyer and fmr. politician; b. 17 Jan. 1932, St. Laurent, Quebec; s. of Gilbert and Marie-Ange Goyer; m. 1960; three d.; ed. Univ. of Montreal; Called to the Bar of Quebec and Ont.; M.P. for Montreal-Dollard 1965, re-elected 1968, 1972, 1974; Parl. Sec. to Sec. of State for External Affairs 1968–70; mem. Cabinet and Solicitor-Gen. of Canada 1970–72; Minister of Supply and Services and Receiver Gen. of Canada 1972–78; practises law in Montreal; partner, Clarkson, Tétrault, Montreal 1979–; Chair. Bd. and Dir. Canada Lands Co. (Mirabel) Ltd; Vice-Chair. Bd. and Dir. Canadair Ltd.; Dir. Lavalin Int. Inc., Bombardier Inc.; Pres. Arts Council of Montreal Urban Community; mem. Bd. Trustees, Heritage Montreal Foundation; Liberal. *Leisure interests:* tennis, skiing, squash. *Address:* 22nd Floor, 630 Dorchester Boulevard West, Montreal, H3B 1V7 (Office); Apartment 518, Habitat 67, Montreal, H3C 3R6, Canada (Home).

GRAAFF, Sir de Villiers, Bart., M.B.E., M.A.; South African fmr. politician; b. 8 Dec. 1913; s. of Sir D. P. de Villiers Graaff; m. Helena le Roux Voigt 1939; two s. one d.; ed. Univs. of Cape Town, Oxford and Leiden (Netherlands); served Second World War; M.P. 1948–58, 1958–77; Chair. United Party, Cape Province 1956–58; Leader of the Opposition (United S. African Nat. Party) 1956–77; participated in formation of New Repub. Party, Interim Leader 1977; Hon. LL.D. (Rhodes Univ.); Decoration for Meritorious Service (S.A.) 1979. *Address:* De Grendel, Tygerberg, Private Bag G.P.O. Cape Town, Cape Province, South Africa.

GRABAR, André, D. ès L.; French art historian and archaeologist; b. 26 July 1896, Kiev, U.S.S.R.; s. of Nicolas Grabar and Elizabeth Baronne Prittwitz; m. Julie Ivanova 1923 (deceased); two s.; Prof. of History of Art, Strasbourg Univ. 1928–37, Ecole pratique des Hautes Etudes 1937–66; Prof. of Early Christian and Byzantine Archaeology, Coll. de France 1946–66; founded Cahiers Archéologiques; mem. Acad. des Inscriptions et Belles Lettres 1955–, Dumbarton Oaks Inst., Deutsches Archäologisches Inst. and of other Acads. in U.K., U.S.A., Austria, Bulgaria, Denmark, Norway, Serbia, Italy; Dr. h.c. (Princeton, Edinburgh and Uppsala); Officier, Légion d'honneur, Officier, Ordre des Palmes académiques. *Publications:* La peinture religieuse bulgare 1928, L'empereur dans l'art byzan-

tin 1936, Martyrium 1946, La peinture byzantine 1954, Le haut Moyen-Age 1957, La peinture romane 1958, L'iconoclasme byzantin 1958, Sculptures byzantines de Constantinople 1963, Byzance 1964, Le premier art chrétien 1967, Le siècle d'or de Justinien 1967, L'art du Moyen Age en Europe orientale, L'art de la fin de l'Antiquité et du Moyen Age 1968, Christian Iconography, a Study of its Origins 1968, Les manuscrits grecs illuminés de provenance italienne 1973, Les voies de la création en iconographie chrétienne 1980. *Leisure interest:* painting. *Address:* 2 avenue Dode de la Brunerie, 75016 Paris, France.

GRABER, Pierre; Swiss politician; b. 6 Dec. 1908, La Chaux-de-Fonds; s. of Paul and Blanche (née Vuilleumier) Graber; ed. Gymnasiums in Neuchâtel and Berne and Univs. of Neuchâtel and Vienna; Lawyer, Lausanne 1933–46; mem. Lausanne Legis. Council 1933–46; mem. Great Council of Vaud 1937–46; Mayor of Lausanne 1946–49; mem. Lausanne City Council and Dir. Dept. of Finance, Lausanne 1949–62; mem. Council Canton Vaud, Dir. Dept. of Finance 1962–70, Pres. 1968; mem. Nat. Council 1942–69, Pres. 1966; Leader of Socialist Group in Fed. Ass. 1967–69; mem. Fed. Council 1970–77, Head of Fed. Political (Foreign Affairs) Dept. 1970–77; Vice-Pres. Fed. Council Jan.-Dec. 1974; Pres. of Swiss Confed. Jan.-Dec. 1975; Social Democrat. *Address:* c/o Social-Democratic Party, Postfach 4084, 3001 Berne, Switzerland.

GRABOWSKI, Zbigniew, D.TECH.SC.; Polish civil engineer and politician; b. 8 March 1930, Warsaw, m.; one s. one d.; ed. Civil Eng. Faculty of Warsaw Technical Univ. 1954; scientific worker of Warsaw Tech. Univ. 1953–, Asst. Prof. 1967–70, Extraordinary Prof. 1970–75, Prof. 1975–, Head, Geotechnics and Underground Bldgs. Research Centre 1970–88, organizer and Dir. Roads and Bridges Inst. of Civil Eng. Faculty 1970–85, Rector 1985–88; scientific consultant, Geoprojekt design office, Warsaw 1970–78; mem. Civil Eng. Cttee. of Polish Acad. of Sciences; Chair. Polish Geotechnics Cttee.; mem. Cen. Qualifying Comm. for Scientific Workers attached to Chair. of Council of Ministers, Chair. Tech. Sciences Section 1973–85; Chair. three scientific councils of research insts.; mem. Cttee. for Science and Technological Progress attached to Council of Ministers 1987–88; mem. College of Ministry of Nat. Educ.; mem. Consultative Council attached to Chair. of Council of State 1986–; Minister, Head of Office for Scientific-Technological Progress and Implementation 1988–; mem. Econ. Cttee. of Council of Ministers 1988–, Int. Soc. of Soil Mechanics and Foundation Eng., Polish United Workers' Party (PZPR) 1950–; Officer's Cross of Polonia Restituta Order, Meritorious Teacher of Polish People's Repub., Nat. Educ. Comm. Medal and other decorations. *Address:* Urząd Postępu Naukowo-Technicznego i Wdrożeń, ul. Wspólna 1/3, 00-921 Warsaw, Poland. *Telephone:* 21 75 57 (Office).

GRACE, J. Peter; American business executive; b. 25 May 1913, Manhasset, N.Y.; s. of Joseph P. and Janet Macdonald Grace; m. Margaret Fennelly 1941; ed. Yale Univ.; joined W. R. Grace & Co. 1936, Sec. 1942–43, Dir. 1943–, Vice-Pres. 1945, Pres. and C.E.O. 1945–81, Chair. and C.E.O. 1981–, Pres. 1986–; Dir. Kennecott Copper Corpn., Citibank N.A., Ingersoll-Rand Co., Citicorp., Milliken and Co., Brascan Ltd., Stone & Webster Inc.; Chair. of Bd. Chemed Corpn.; Trustee, Atlantic Mutual Insurance Co.; Trustee, U.S. Council for Int. Chamber of Commerce; active in many fields of public service; Hon. LL.D. from several colls. and univs.; many foreign decorations. *Address:* W. R. Grace & Co., Grace Plaza, 1114 Avenue of the Americas, New York, N.Y. 10036-7794, U.S.A. (Office). *Telephone:* (212) 764-5555 (Office).

GRACQ, Julien; French professor and writer; b. 27 July 1910, St. Florent le Vieil, Maine et Loire; ed. Ecole Normale Supérieure and Ecole des Sciences Politiques, Paris (Prof. agrégé d'histoire); Prof. d'histoire 1935–47; Prof. d'histoire Lycée Claude Bernard, Paris 1947–70; retd. *Publications:* Au château d'Argol 1939, Un beau ténébreux 1945, Le roi pêcheur 1947, Liberté grande 1947, André Breton 1947, La littérature à l'estomac 1950, Le rivage des Syrtes 1951, Un balcon en forêt 1958, Préférences 1961, Lettrines 1967, La presqu'île 1970, Lettrines 2 1974, Les eaux étroites 1976, En lisant, En écrivant 1981, La forme d'une ville 1985, Autour des Sept Collines 1988. *Leisure interest:* chess. *Address:* 61 rue de Grenelle, 75007 Paris, France.

GRAD, Harold, PH.D.; American professor of mathematics; b. 14 Jan. 1923, New York; s. of Herman Grad and Helen Selinger; m. Betty J. Miller 1949; one s. one d.; ed. Cooper Union and New York Univ.; Asst. Prof., New York Univ. 1948, Assoc. Prof. 1952, Prof. of Math. 1957–, Founder and Dir. MHD Div., Courant Inst. of Math. Sciences 1956–80; Chair. Fluid Dynamics Div. 1963, Plasma Physics Div. 1969, American Physical Soc.; mem. Bd. of Govs. N.Y. Acad. of Sciences 1978–81; mem. N.A.S., American Math. Soc., American Physics Soc., Soc. of Industrial Applied Math., Nat. Philosophical Soc., Soc. of Eng. Sciences; Distinguished Prof. Faculty of Sciences, Nagoya Univ. 1981, Guggenheim Fellow 1981–82; New York Acad. of Science award in Nuclear Physics and Eng. 1970, Soc. of Eng. Sciences Eringen Medal 1982. *Publications:* articles and chapters in books on kinetic theory of gases, plasma physics, controlled thermonuclear research. *Address:* Courant Institute of Mathematical Sciences, 251 Mercer Street, New York, N.Y. 10012 (Office); 248 Overlook Road, New Rochelle, N.Y. 10804, U.S.A. (Home). *Telephone:* 212-460-7204 (Office); 914-636-7969 (Home).

GRADE, Baron (Life Peer), cr. 1976, of Elstree in the county of Hertfordshire; **Lew Grade,** Kt.; British television executive; b. 25 Dec. 1906; s. of the late Isaac and Olga Winogradsky; brother of Baron Delfont (q.v.); m. Kathleen Sheila Moody 1942; one s.; ed. Rochelle Street School; Jt. Man. Dir. theatrical agents—Lew and Leslie Grade Ltd. 1955; Deputy Man. Dir. Assoc. Television Ltd. 1955–; Chair. and Man. Dir. Inc. Television Co. Ltd.; Chief Exec. and Deputy Chair. Assoc. Communications Corpn. Ltd. (fmrly. Assoc. Television Corpn.), Chief Exec. and Chair. 1973–82; Deputy Chair. and Man. Dir. ATV Network Ltd. until 1973, Chair. 1973–77, Pres. 1977–82; Chair. Stoll Theatres Corpn., Moss Empires 1973–82; A. P. Films Ltd., Assoc. Film Distributors 1978–; ACC Enterprises Inc.; Chair. and Chief Exec. Embassy Communications Int. 1982–85; Dir. Assoc. Television Corpn. (Int.) Ltd., Independent Television Corpn. (U.S.A.), Canastel Broadcasting Corpn. (Canada), New World Music Ltd., Ambassador Bowling Ltd., Planned Holdings Ltd., Bermans (Holdings) Ltd., Pye Records Ltd. *Publication:* Still Dancing 1987. *Address:* Embassy House, 3 Audley Square, London, W1Y 5DR, England.

GRADE, Michael Ian; British broadcasting executive; b. 8 March 1943, London; s. of Leslie Grade; m. Hon. Sarah Lawson 1982; one s. one d.; ed. St. Dunstan's Coll., London; trainee journalist Daily Mirror 1960, Sports Columnist 1964–66; Theatrical Agent Grade Org. 1966; Jt. Man. Dir. London Man. and Representation 1969–73; Deputy Controller of Programmes (Entertainment) London Weekend TV 1973–77, Dir. of Programmes and mem. Bd. 1977–81; Pres. Embassy TV 1981–84; Controller BBC 1 1984–86; Dir. of Programmes BBC TV 1986–88; C.E.O. Channel Four TV 1988–; Head Ind. Inquiry into Fear of Crime; mem. Council London Acad. of Music and Dramatic Art 1981–, B.A.F.T.A. 1986–. *Leisure interests:* entertainment. *Address:* Wycombe End House, Wycombe End, Beaconsfield, Bucks, HP9 1NE, England. *Telephone:* 743-8000.

GRADIN, Anita; Swedish politician; b. 12 Aug. 1933, Hörnefors, Västerbotten Co.; m. Lieut.-Col. Bertil Kersfelt; one d.; ed. Coll. of Social Work and Public Admin. Stockholm; journalist 1950–63; Social Welfare Planning Cttee. Stockholm 1963–67; Sr. Admin. Officer, Cabinet Office 1967–68; mem. Stockholm City Council 1966–68; mem. Parl. 1968; Chair. District Branch, Fed. of Social Democratic Women, Stockholm 1968–82; Chair. Council for Int. Adoptions 1973–82; Vice-Chair. Nat. Fed. of Social Democratic Women in Sweden 1975–; Chair. Council of Europe Cttee. on Migration, Refugees and Demographic Questions 1978–82; Minister at Ministry of Labour with special responsibility (for Immigrant and Equality Affairs) 1982–85; Minister with special responsibility for Foreign Trade, Ministry of Foreign Affairs 1986–. *Address:* Ministry of Foreign Affairs, Trade Department, Fredsgatan 8, 103 33 Stockholm, Sweden.

GRAF, Hans, DR.ING.; German business executive; b. 5 Oct. 1931, Bad Marienberg; mem. Exec. Bd. Krupp Stahl AG, Bochum, Krupp Stahl AG, Siegen. *Address:* Krupp Stahl AG, P.O. Box 10 12 20, 5900 Siegen (Office); Baumgartenstrasse 1, 4630 Bochum 6, Federal Republic of Germany (Home). *Telephone:* 0271/801-2541 (Office).

GRAF, Steffi; German tennis player; b. 14 June 1969, Bruehl; d. of Peter Graf; coached by her father, trained by Pavel Slozil; won Orange Bowl 12s 1981, European 14-and under and European Circuit Masters 1982, Olympic demonstration event, L.A.; winner German Open 1986, French Open 1987, 1988, Australian Open 1988, 1989, Wimbledon 1988 (runner-up 1987), US Open 1988 (runner-up 1987), numerous Women's Doubles Championships with Gabriela Sabatini (q.v.); Olympic Champion 1988; ranked No. 1 Aug. 1987–; named Official World Champion 1988; Grand Slam winner 1988, 1989.

GRAFFMAN, Gary; American pianist; b. 14 Oct. 1928; s. of Vladimir and Nadia (Margdin) Graffman; m. Naomi Helfman 1952; ed. Curtis Inst. of Music, Philadelphia under Mme. Isabelle Vengerova; Professional début with Philadelphia Orchestra 1947; concert tours all over the world; appears annually in America with major orchestras; teacher Curtis Inst. and Manhattan School of Music 1980–, Artistic Dir. Curtis Inst. 1986–; year offstage to correct finger injury 1980–81; gramophone recordings for Columbia Masterworks and RCA Victor including concertos of Tchaikovsky, Rachmaninoff, Brahms, Beethoven, Chopin and Prokofiev; Leventritt Award 1949. *Publication:* I Really Should be Practising (autobiog.) 1981. *Address:* Harry Beall Management, 119 West 57th Street, New York, N.Y. 10019; Curtis Institute of Music, 1726 Locust Street, Philadelphia, Pa. 19103, U.S.A.

GRAHAM, Alastair, D.SC., F.Z.S., F.R.S.; British professor of zoology; b. 6 Nov. 1906; ed. Edinburgh and London Univs.; Prof. of Zoology, Univ. of Reading, until 1972, Prof. Emer. 1972–; Frink Medal, Zoological Soc. 1976. *Publications:* British Prosobranch Molluscs (Jt. Author) 1962, Other Operculate Gastropod Molluscs 1971. *Address:* 207 Wokingham Road, Reading, Berks., England. *Telephone:* (0734) 62276.

GRAHAM, Angus Charles, M.A., PH.D., F.B.A.; British professor of Classical Chinese (retd.); b. 8 July 1919, Penarth; s. of Charles H. Graham and Mabelle Graham; m. Der Pao Chang 1955; one d.; ed. Ellesmere Coll., Salop., Corpus Christi Coll., Oxford and S.O.A.S. London; Lecturer in Classical Chinese, S.O.A.S. 1950, Reader 1966, Prof. 1971–84; Visiting Fellow, Hong Kong Univ. 1954–55; Visiting Prof. Yale Univ. 1966–67, Univ. of Mich. 1970, Tsing Hua Univ. 1987, Brown Univ. 1988, Univ. of

Hawaii 1989; Fellow Soc. of Humanities, Cornell Univ. 1972–73; Sr. Research Fellow, Inst. of E. Asian Philosophies, Singapore 1984–86. *Publications:* Two Chinese Philosophers 1958, The Book of Lieh-tzŭ 1960, The Problem of Value 1961, Poems of the Late T'ang 1965, Later Mohist Logic, Ethics & Science 1978, Chuang-tzŭ: the Seven Inner Chapters 1981, Reason and Spontaneity 1985, Studies in Chinese Philosophy and Philosophical Literature 1986. *Address:* P.O. Box 84, Borehamwood, Herts., WD6 3AX, England.

GRAHAM, Billy (see Graham, William Franklin).

GRAHAM, Christopher Forbes, D.PHIL., F.R.S.; British biologist; b. 23 Sept. 1940; ed. Oxford Univ.; fmrly. Jr. Beit Memorial Fellow in Medical Research, Sir William Dunn School of Pathology; Lecturer, Dept. of Zoology, Univ. of Oxford 1970–85, Prof. of Animal Devt. 1985–; Professorial Fellow St. Catherine's Coll., Oxford 1985–; mem. British Soc. for Cell Biology, British Society for Developmental Biology, Soc. for Experimental Biology, Genetical Soc. *Publication:* Developmental Control in Plants and Animals 1984. *Address:* Department of Zoology, University of Oxford, South Parks Road, Oxford, OX1 3PS, England.

GRAHAM, Daniel Robert, B.A., LL.D.; American farmer and politician; b. 9 Nov. 1936, Coral Gables, Fla.; s. of Ernest R. Graham and Hilda Simmons; m. Adele Khoury 1959; four d.; ed. Univ. of Florida and Harvard Univ.; Vice-Pres. Sengra Devt. Corpn. 1963–79; Florida State Rep. from Coral Gables 1966–70; Florida State Senator from Coral Gables 1970–78; Gov. of Florida 1979–87, Senator 1987–; Audubon Soc. Conservation Award 1974; Democrat. *Leisure interests:* golf, tennis and reading. *Address:* 241 Dirksen Senate Building, Washington, D.C. 20510, U.S.A.

GRAHAM, Donald Edward, B.A.; American newspaper publisher; b. 22 April 1945, Baltimore, Md.; s. of late Philip L. Graham and of Katharine Meyer Graham (q.v.); m. Mary L. Wissler 1967; one s. three d.; ed. Harvard Univ.; joined the Washington Post 1971, Asst. Man. Ed./Sports 1974–75, Asst. Gen. Man. 1975–76, Exec. Vice-Pres. and Gen. Man. 1976–79, Publr. Jan. 1979–; fmrly. reporter and writer for Newsweek. *Address:* The Washington Post, 1150 15th Street, N.W., Washington, D.C. 20071, U.S.A. *Telephone:* (202) 334 7138.

GRAHAM, Sir John Alexander Noble, Bart., G.C.M.G., M.A.; British diplomatist (retd.); b. 15 July 1926, Calcutta, India; s. of late Sir Reginald Graham, Bart., V.C., O.B.E.; m. Marygold E.G. Austin 1956; two s. one d.; ed. Eton Coll., Trinity Coll., Cambridge; served with British Army 1944–47; entered diplomatic service 1950, serving in Lebanon, Bahrain, Kuwait and Jordan; Asst. Private Sec. to Foreign Sec. 1954–57; First Sec., Belgrade 1957–60, Benghazi 1960–61; Foreign Office 1961–66, Kuwait 1966–69; Principal Private Sec. to Foreign Sec. 1969–72; assigned to Washington, D.C. 1972–74; Amb. to Iraq 1974–77, to Iran 1979–80; Deputy Under-Sec., FCO 1977–78, 1980–81; Rep. N. Atlantic Council 1982–86; Dir. The Ditchley Foundation 1987–. *Address:* The Ditchley Foundation, Ditchley Park, Enstone, Oxon., OX7 4ER, England. *Telephone:* (060 872) 346.

GRAHAM, Katharine Meyer; American newspaper executive; b. 16 June 1917, New York; d. of Eugene and Agnes Meyer; m. Philip L. Graham 1940 (died 1963); three s. (incl. Donald E. Graham, q.v.) one d.; ed. Madeira School, Vassar Coll., and Univ. of Chicago; Reporter San Francisco News 1938–39; various depts. The Washington Post 1939–45; Pres. The Washington Post Co. (owns The Washington Post, Washington, Newsweek magazine, several TV stations and over 50 cable TV systems) 1963–73, Chair. of Bd. and C.E.O. 1973–; Publr., The Washington Post 1969–79; Co-Chair. of Bd. of Int. Herald Tribune 1983–; Trustee, The Conf. Bd., The Urban Inst., Fed. City Council, George Wash. Univ., Univ. of Chicago; mem. Ind. Comm. on Int. Devt. Issues (Brandt Comm.) Conf. Bd. 1982–, Reuters 1989–; mem. Bd. Newspaper Advertising Bureau, Inc., American Newspaper Publrs. Assen., Assoc. Press; mem. American Soc. of Newspaper Eds.; John Peter Zenger Award 1973. *Address:* 1150 15th Street, N.W., Washington, D.C. 20071 (Office); 2920 R Street, N.W., Washington, D.C. 20007, U.S.A. (Home).

GRAHAM, Martha, LL.D.; American dancer and choreographer; b. 11 May 1894, Pittsburgh, Pa.; d. of George Greenfield Graham and Jane Hamilton Beers; m. Erick Hawkins 1948; ed. Bard Coll.; studied with Ruth St. Denis; Soloist Denishawn Co. 1920, Greenwich Village Follies 1923; choreographer-dancer 48th Street Theatre, New York 1926; Founder, Artistic Dir. Martha Graham Dance Co., Martha Graham School of Contemporary Dance; solo performances with leading orchestras of U.S.A.; toured with co. abroad; Guggenheim Fellow 1932, 1939, Capezio Award 1959, Aspen Award 1965, Creative Arts Award, Brandeis Univ. 1968, Distinguished Service to Arts Award, Nat. Inst. of Arts and Letters 1970, Handel Medallion of New York 1970, New York State Council on Arts Award 1973; Presidential Medal of Freedom 1976; Légion d'honneur 1983, Nat. Medal of the Arts 1985. Hon. mem. American Acad. of Arts and Letters 1983; Hon. LL.D. (Mills Coll., Brandeis Univ., Smith Coll., Harvard, etc.). *Works include:* Appalachian Spring, Letter to the World, Cave of the Heart, Diversion of Angels, Acrobats of God, Dark Meadow, Night Journey, Clytemnestra, Phaedra, Legend of Judith, Errand into the Maze, Seraphic Dialogue, Mendicants of the Evening, Myth of a Voyage, Holy Jungle, Stone of Destiny, Dream 1974, Lucifer 1975, Scarlet Letter 1975, Point of Crossing 1975, Acts of Light 1981, Andromache's Lament 1982,

Phaedra's Dream 1983, City of Florence Gold Florin 1983, The Rite of Spring 1984, Song 1985. *Publication:* The Notebooks of Martha Graham 1937. *Address:* Martha Graham School of Contemporary Dance Inc., 316 East 63rd Street, New York, N.Y. 10021, U.S.A. *Telephone:* (212) 832-9166.

GRAHAM, Patricia Albjerg, PH.D.; American educator; b. 9 Feb. 1935, Lafayette, Ind.; d. of Victor L. Graham and Marguerite Hall Albjerg; m. Loren R. Graham 1955; one d.; ed. Purdue and Columbia Univs.; Teacher Deep Creek and Maury High Schools, Norfolk, Va. 1955–58; Chair. History Dept., St. Hilda's and St. Hugh's School, New York 1958–60, Part-time Coll. Adviser 1961–63, 1965–67; Lecturer, Ind. Univ., School of Educ., Bloomington 1964–65; Asst. Prof., Barnard Coll. and Columbia Teacher's Coll., New York 1965–68, Assoc. Prof. 1968–72, Prof. 1972–74; Prof., Harvard Univ. Graduate School of Educ., Cambridge, Mass. 1974–79, Warren Prof. 1979–, Dean Graduate School of Educ. 1982–; Dean Radcliffe Inst. and Vice-Pres. for Institutional Planning, Radcliffe Coll., Cambridge, Mass. 1974–76, Dean Radcliffe Inst. and Vice-Pres. Radcliffe Coll. 1976–77; Dir. Nat. Inst. of Educ. 1977–79; Charles Warren Prof. of History of Educ., Harvard Univ. 1979–; Vice-Pres. for Teaching, American Historical Asscn. 1985–; Pres. Nat. Acad. of Educ. 1985–; Dir. Spencer Foundation 1983–, Johnson Foundation 1983–. *Publications:* Progressive Education: From Arcady to Academe, A History of the Progressive Education Association 1967, Community and Class in American Education, 1865–1918 1974, Women in Higher Education (co-ed. with Todd Furniss) 1974. *Address:* Harvard University Graduate School of Education, Longfellow Hall, Appian Way, Cambridge, Mass. 02135, U.S.A. *Telephone:* (617) 496-3401.

GRAHAM, Sir Peter Alfred, Kt., O.B.E., F.I.B., C.B.I.M.; British banker; b. 1922; m.; two s. two d.; ed. St. Joseph's Coll.; war service in Fleet Air Arm; joined Chartered Bank of India, Australia and China 1947, serving throughout Far East 1947–62, Chief Man., Hong Kong 1962–70, Gen. Man., London 1970–75, Deputy Man. Dir. of Standard Chartered Bank PLC (now Standard Chartered PLC) 1975–77, Group Man. Dir. 1977–83, Sr. Deputy Chair. 1983–87, Chair. 1987–88; Chair. Standard Chartered Merchant Bank PLC 1977–82, Mocatta and Goldsmid Ltd. 1983–87, Crown Agents for Overseas Govts and Admins. Oct. 1983–; Deputy Chair. Council Inst. of Bankers 1980–81, Chartered Trust PLC 1983–85, ICC United Kingdom; Chair. Advisory Cttee. City Business School 1981–; Pres. Inst. of Bankers 1981–83; Hon. D.Sc. (City Univ.) 1985. *Leisure interests:* golf, tennis, fruit farm. *Address:* 33 Kelso Place, London, W.8, England.

GRAHAM, William B., B.S., J.D.; American lawyer and business executive; b. 14 July 1911, Chicago, Ill.; s. of William Graham and Elizabeth Burden Graham; m. 1st Edna Kanaley 1940 (died 1981); two s. two d.; m. 2nd Catherine Van Duzer Gaubin 1984; ed. Univ. of Chicago; Patent Lawyer 1936–39; Partner Dawson and Ooms 1940–45; Vice-Pres. and Gen. Man. Baxter Travenol Labs., Deerfield 1945–53, Pres., C.E.O. 1953–71, Chair., C.E.O. 1971–80, Chair. 1980–85, Sr. Chair. 1985–; Dir. First Nat. Bank of Chicago, Northwest Industries, Deere and Co.; Pres., Dir. Lyric Opera of Chicago, Dir. Nat. Park Foundation, Washington, D.C., Botanic Garden Skokie, Ill.; Trustee Univ. of Chicago, Evanston Hosp. and Orchestral Assoc.; Ill. St. Andrew Award 1974; Weizman Inst. Professional Chair. 1978; HIMA Pioneering Award, Nat. Kidney Foundation First Award, Achievement Award, Medical Technical Services 1983, Chicago Civil Award, De Paul Univ. 1986. *Address:* Baxter Travenol Laboratories Inc., 1 Baxter Parkway, Deerfield, Ill. 60015 (Office); 40 Devonshire Lane, Kenilworth, Ill. 60043, U.S.A. (Home).

GRAHAM, William Franklin (Billy), A.B., B.TH.; American evangelist; b. 7 Nov. 1918, Charlotte, N.C.; s. of William Franklin and Morrow Graham; m. Ruth M. Bell 1943; two s. three d.; ed. Florida Bible Seminary, Tampa and Wheaton Coll.; ordained to Baptist Ministry 1939; Minister First Baptist Church, Western Springs, Ill. 1943–45; First Vice-Pres. Youth for Christ Int. 1945–48; Pres. Northwestern Schools, Minneapolis 1947–52; founder World Wide Pictures, Burbank, Calif.; worldwide evangelistic campaigns 1949–; speaker weekly Hour of Decision radio programme 1950–; also periodic crusade telecasts; founder, Billy Graham Evangelistic Assoc.; Hon. Chair. Lausanne Congress on World Evangelization 1974; Hon. Dr. (Hungarian Calvinist Church) (Christian Acad. of Theol.) 1981; numerous awards including Bernard Baruch Award 1955, Humane Order of African Redemption 1960, Gold Award, George Washington Memorial Inst. 1963, Horatio Alger Award 1965, Int. Brotherhood Award Nat. Conf. of Christians and Jews 1971, Sylvanus Thayer Award, Assoc. of Graduates of U.S. Mil. Acad. 1972, Franciscan Int. Award 1972; Man of South Award 1974, Liberty Bell Award 1975, Templeton Prize 1982, Pres. Medal of Freedom 1983, A Biblical Standard for Evangelicals 1984, Approaching Hoofbeats 1985. *Publications:* Peace with God 1953 (revised edn. 1985), The Secret of Happiness 1955, My Answer (book) 1954, World Aflame 1965, The Challenge, The Jesus Generation 1971, Angels—God's Secret Agents 1976, How to be Born Again 1977, The Holy Spirit 1978, Till Armageddon 1981, Approaching Hoofbeats: The Four Horsemen of the Apocalypse 1983, A Biblical Standard for Evangelists 1984, Unto The Hills 1986, Facing Death and the Life After 1987, Answers to Life's Problems 1988. *Address:* 1300 Harmon Place, Minneapolis, Minn. 55403 (Office); Montreat, N. Carolina 28757, U.S.A. (Home). *Telephone:* 612-338-0500 (Office).

GRAHAM-DIXON, Anthony Philip, Q.C., M.A.; British barrister (retd.); b. 5 Nov. 1929, London; s. of Leslie C. Graham Dixon, Q.C. and Dorothy Rivett; m. Suzanne Villar 1956; one s. one d.; ed. Westminster School and Christ Church, Oxford; served, R.N.V.R. 1953–55; called to Bar, Inner Temple 1956; Q.C. 1973; retired from practice at Bar 1986; Chair. London Concertino Ltd. 1982–; Trustee, Soc. for Promotion of New Music 1988–; Deputy Chair. Public Health Lab. Service Bd. 1988–. *Leisure interests:* music, gardening, tennis, pictures. *Address:* 31 Hereford Square, London, SW7 4NB; Masketts Manor, Nutley, Uckfield, E. Sussex, England. *Telephone:* 01-370 1902; Nutley 2719.

GRAHL-MADSEN, Atle, DR.JUR.; Norwegian professor of international law; b. 31 Aug. 1922, Bergen; s. of Mads Madsen and Ragnhild Marie Grahl-Madsen (née Grahl-Nielsen); m. 1st Aasa E. Skurtveit 1955 (divorced); m. 2nd Elisabeth Kjaergaard 1987; four s.; ed. Fayes Skole, Bergen, Bergens Katedralskole, Univ. of Oslo and Acad. of Int. Law, The Hague; Asst. judge, city courts, Oslo and Drammen 1947–48; Resettlement Officer, Int. Refugee Org., British Zone of Germany 1948–49; Asst. judge, county courts, Idd og Marker and Onsøy 1949–50; Assoc. Holm, Rode & Christophersen (law firm), Oslo 1951–52; Attorney-at-law (advocate) Oslo 1952–53, Bergen 1953–72; Research Fellow, Norwegian Research Council for Science and the Humanities 1960–67; Special Consultant to UN High Commr. for Refugees, Geneva 1962–63; Prin. Lecturer in Law, Norwegian School of Econs. and Business Admin. 1967–76; Prof. of Int. Law, Uppsala Univ. and Dir. Swedish Inst. of Int. Law, Uppsala 1976–81; Prof. of Law, Univ. of Bergen 1980–; mem. UN Comm. of Inquiry on Reported Massacres in Mozambique 1974; Royal Order of the North Star (Sweden), Commdr. "pro Merito Melitensi", Sovereign Mil. Order of Malta and other decorations; Plaquette of Honour, Norwegian Refugee Council; Golden Fridtjof Nansen Ring. *Publications:* Menneskerett og sunt vett 1959, The Status of Refugees in International Law, Vol. I 1966, Vol. II 1972, Européisk Fellesskap 1972, Territorial Asylum 1980, Norsk fremmedrett i Støpeskjeen 1985, The Emergent International Law relating to Refugees 1985, Bergen i verden (ed.) 1985, Scangrid 1986, The Spirit of Uppsala (ed.) 1984, Ny utlendingslav 1987 and numerous articles on legal, social, military and other matters. *Leisure interests:* flags, heraldry, hiking, skiing, boating. *Address:* Department of Public and International Law, University of Bergen, Allégaten 34, N-5007 Bergen, Norway.

GRAINVILLE, Patrick; French novelist; b. 1 June 1947, Villers-sur-mer; s. of Jacques and Suzanne (née Laquerre) Grainville; m. Françoise Lutgen 1971; ed. Lycée Deauville, Sorbonne; Teacher, Lycée de Sartrouville 1971–; Prix Goncourt for Les flamboyants 1976. *Publications:* La toison 1972, La lisière 1973, L'abîme 1974, Les flamboyants 1976, La Diane rousse 1978, Le dernier viking 1980, Les fortresses noires 1982, La caverne céleste 1984, Le paradis des orages 1986. *Address:* Lycée Evariste Gallois, 87 avenue de Tobrouk, 78500 Sartrouville (Office); 10 avenue Lafayette, 78600 Maisons-Lafitte, France (Home).

GRAMM, William Philip, PH.D.; American politician; b. 8 July 1942, Fort Benning, Ga.; s. of Kenneth M. and Florence (Scroggins) Gramm; m. Wendy Lee 1970; two s.; ed. Univ. of Georgia; mem. Faculty, Dept. of Econs. Tex. A. and M.U. Coll. Station 1967–78, Prof. 1973–78; Partner Gramm & Assocs. 1971–78; mem. House of Reps. 1979–85; Senator from Texas Jan. 1985–; Democrat. *Publications:* articles in professional journals. *Address:* United States Senate, Washington, D.C. 20510, U.S.A.

GRAMOV, Marat Vladimirovich, CAND HIST. SC.; Soviet politician; b. 1927; ed. Saratov Higher Party School; Saratov Army 1944–47; komsomol work in Saratov District 1948–53; mem. CPSU 1951–; head of section of Molodoy Leninets newspaper 1953–59; Ed. of regional newspaper Znamya Oktobrya 1959–60; Second Sec. Kursavo Regional Cttee. of CPSU 1960–61; Section Head, Deputy, First Deputy Chief Ed. dist. newspaper Stavropolskaya Pravda 1961–64; Deputy Section Head of Stavropol Dist. Cttee. of CPSU 1964–67; work for CPSU Cen. Cttee. 1967–83; Pres. of Cttee. of Physical Culture and Sport with U.S.S.R. Council of Ministers 1983–; Pres of U.S.S.R. Olympic Cttee.; Deputy to U.S.S.R. Supreme Soviet; cand. mem of U.S.S.R. Cen. Cttee. 1986. *Address:* U.S.S.R. Olympic Committee, Moscow, U.S.S.R.

GRANADO, Donald Casimir; Trinidadian trade unionist, politician and diplomatist; b. 4 March 1915, Trinidad; s. of Gregorio and Octavia Granado (née Auguste); m. Anne-Marie Lombard 1959; one s. two d.; fmr. school teacher; Sec. Union of Commercial and Industrial Workers 1950–54 Sec./Treas. Trinidad and Tobago Fed. of Trade Unions 1953–54; Pres C.G.A. Credit Union 1954–56; Sec./Treas. People's Nat. Movement 1956 Minister of Labour and Social Services 1956–61; Minister of Health and Housing and Deputy Leader of House of Reps. 1961–63; Trinidad and Tobago Amb. to Venezuela 1963–64; High Commr. to Canada 1964–69 Amb. to Brazil and Argentina 1965–69; High Commr. to U.K. 1969–71 Perm. Rep. to EEC 1969–71; fmr. Amb. to France, Germany, Italy Belgium, Luxembourg, Netherlands, Switzerland; Pres. Nat. Golf Club Vice-Pres. Trinidad and Tobago Golf Assoc.; Pres. Save Our Student Assoc.; awarded Trinity Cross (Trinidad and Tobago's highest honour) Nat. Father of the Year Award 1983. *Leisure interests:* golf, bridge football (training), gardening, community activities. *Address:* 20 Grove Road, Valsayn North, Trinidad. *Telephone:* 662-5905.

GRANDY, Marshal of the R.A.F. Sir John, G.C.B., G.C.V.O., K.B.E., D.S.O.; British air force officer; b. 8 Feb. 1913, Northwood, Middx.; s. of the late Francis Grandy and Nellie Grandy (née Lines); m. Cecile Elizabeth Florence Rankin 1937; two s.; ed. Univ. Coll. School, London; Pilot Officer 1931; served Second World War; Deputy Dir. Operational Training, Air Ministry 1946–49; Air Attaché, Brussels 1949–50; Commdr. Northern Sector Fighter Command 1950; Air Staff H.Q. Fighter Command 1952–54; Commdt. Cen. Fighter Establishment 1954–57; Imperial Defence Coll. 1957; Commdr. Task Force Grapple 1957–58; Asst. Chief of Air Staff 1958–61; C.-in-C. R.A.F. Germany, Commdr. 2nd Allied Tactical Air Force 1961–63; A.O.C.-in-C. Bomber Command 1963–65; C.-in-C. British Forces Far East and U.K. Mil. Rep. to SEATO 1965–67; Air Commodore 1956; Air Vice-Marshal 1958; Air Marshal 1961; Air Chief Marshal 1965; Marshal of the R.A.F. 1971; Chief of Air Staff 1967–71; Gov. and Commdr.-in-Chief of Gibraltar 1973–78; Constable and Gov. Windsor Castle 1978–88; Dir. Brixton Estate Ltd. 1971–73, 1978–83; Sr. Pres. The Officers Asscn. 1980–82, Disablement in the City, Berkshire Branch BLESMA; Deputy Chair. R.A.F. Benevolent Fund 1980–; Patron Polish Air Force Asscn., G.B. 1979–; Hon. Panglima Mangku Negara; Hon. Liveryman of the Haberdashers' Co.; Freeman of City of London; Chair. Trustees Imperial War Museum 1978–; Trustee R.A.F. Church, St. Clement Danes, Shuttleworth Trust, RAF Trustee, Burma Star Asscn., The Prince Philip Trust Fund; Pres. The Air League 1984–87; a Vice-Pres. Nat. Asscn. of Boys Clubs; mem. Cttee. Royal Humane Soc., Life Pres. RNLI; Kt.St.J. *Address:* c/o Whites', St. James's Street, London SW1, England.

GRANE, Leif, DR. THEOL.; Danish professor of church history; b. 11 Jan. 1928, Lyngby; s. of Jens Grane and Emma (née Christensen) Grane; m. Vreni Welti 1968; two s. one d.; ed. Univ. of Copenhagen, studies at Univs. of Lund and Tübingen; church minister, Brønshøj 1954–56; Prof. of Religion and History, Teachers' Training School 1956–60; Sr. Scholar Univ. of Copenhagen 1960–64, Prof. of Church History 1964–; Head Coll. Domus Regiae, Copenhagen 1979–; Chair. Steering Cttee. Int. Congresses for Lutheran Research 1975–83; Dean and mem. Steering Bd. Univ. of Copenhagen 1967–72, 1978–83; mem. Royal Acad. of Sciences and Letters 1981–; Dr. Theol. h.c. (Munich) 1980, (Oslo) 1986. *Publications:* Confessio Augustana 1959, Contra Gabrielem 1962, Peter Abelard 1964 (German and English), Protest og Konsekvens 1968 (Finnish), Modus loquendi theologicus: Luthers kampf um die Erneuerung der Theologie 1975, Det teoliske Fakultet 1830–1979, 1980, Kirken i det 19. århundrede 1982 (German), Evangeliet for folket: Drøm og virkelighed i Martin Luthers liv 1983. *Leisure interests:* friendships and carpentry. *Address:* St. Kannikestræde 2, DK-1169, Copenhagen K. (Home); Institute of Church History, Købmagergade 44-46, DK-1150, Copenhagen K., Denmark (Office). *Telephone:* (01) 15 28 11 (Office); (01) 15 99 16 (Home).

GRANELLI, Luigi; Italian politician; b. 1 March 1929, Lovere, Milan; Christian Democrat (D.C.) M.P. for Milan-Pavia 1968–79; Senator for Cantù 1979–1983, for Vimercate 1983–; Minister without Portfolio for Scientific and Tech. Research 1986–87. *Address:* Camera del Deputati, Rome, Italy.

GRANFIL, Toma; Yugoslav diplomatist; b. 31 Aug. 1913, Vršac; s. of Dr. Djoka and Jelena Granfil; m. Anica Aldan 1940; ed. Belgrade Law School; practising lawyer 1936–41; participated in Nat. Liberation Struggle 1941–45; Minister for Trade and Supplies, Serbia 1948–49; Chair. Yugoslav Section ICC, Paris 1954–65; Man. Dir. and Pres., Yugoslav Bank for Foreign Trade 1955–65; Vice-Pres. Exec. Council of Serbia 1965–67; Pres. Yugoslav-Italian Econ. Comm. 1967–71; mem. Fed. Exec. Council in charge of econ. relations with foreign countries 1967–71; Chief of Yugoslav del. for negotiations with EEC 1968–71; Amb. to U.S.A. 1971–75; Dir. Gen. of Export Credit & Insurance Fund 1978–79; Pres. Man. Bd. Yugoslav Bank for Int. Econ. Cooperation 1979–83; mem. Fed. Council 1983; several Yugoslav and foreign decorations. *Publications:* several articles and studies in econ. policy. *Address:* c/o Federal Government Buildings, Belgrade; (Office); Lackovićeva 1, Belgrade, Yugoslavia (Home). *Telephone:* 681-148 (Office); 663-967 (Home).

GRANIER DE LILLIAC, René; French business executive; b. 27 Oct. 1919, Nantes; s. of René and Marie-Ange (née Le Guennan) Granier de Lilliac; m. Paule de Rodellec du Porzic 1947; one s.; ed. Ecole Polytech.; joined Cie. Française des Pétroles 1954, responsible for Middle East Operations 1954, Sec.-Gen. 1960, Man. 1963, Dir. 1968, Vice-Pres. 1970, Asst. Dir.-Gen. 1971, Pres., Dir.-Gen. 1971–84 (retd.), Hon. Pres., Dir. 1984–; Dir.-Gen. Compagnie Française de Raffinage 1966–71, Vice-Pres. 1972–84, Dir. 1984–; Pres. Total-Chimie 1968–71, now Dir.; Officier, Légion d'honneur, Commdr., Ordre nat. du Mérite. *Address:* Compagnie Française des Pétroles, 5 rue Michel-Ange, 75016 Paris (Office); 71 rue Perronet, 92200 Neuilly-Sur-Seine, France (Home).

GRANIN, Daniil; Soviet short-story writer and novelist; b. 1918; ed. Leningrad Polytechnic Inst.; engineer 1940–50; first publs. 1949. *Publications:* Second Variant 1949, Those Who Seek 1955, The House on Fontanka 1958, After the Wedding 1958, I Challenge the Storm 1962, Selected Works 1978, The Leningrad Catalogue 1984, Buffalo 1987. *Address:* U.S.S.R. Union of Writers, U1. Vorovskogo 52, Moscow, U.S.S.R.

GRANIT, Ragnar Arthur, MAG. PHIL., M.D.; Swedish neurophysiologist; b. 30 Oct. 1900, Helsinki, Finland; s. of Arthur W. Granit and Albertina H.

Malmberg; m. Baroness Marguerite Bruun 1929; one s.; ed. Swedish Normallyceum, Helsinki, and Helsinki Univ.; Dozent, Helsinki Univ. 1929–37, Prof. of Physiology 1937–40; Fellow, Univ. of Pa. 1929–31; Invited Royal Caroline Inst., Stockholm 1940, Prof. of Neurophysiology 1946–67; Dir. Nobel Inst. for Neurophysiology 1945–67; Visiting Prof. Rockefeller Inst. 1956–66, St. Catherine's Coll., Oxford 1967, Fogarty Int. Cen., Nat. Inst. of Health, Bethesda, U.S.A. 1971–72, 1975, Univ. Düsseldorf 1974, Max-Planck Inst., Bad Nauheim 1976; Pres. Royal Swedish Acad. of Science 1963–65; foreign mem. Royal Soc., London, N.A.S., Wash., Accad. dei Lincei, Rome, and several other acads.; hon. mem. American Acad. of Arts and Sciences; several prizes and hon. degrees; Nobel Prize for Physiology or Medicine 1967. *Publications:* Ung Mans Väg till Minerva 1941, Sensory Mechanisms of the Retina 1947, Receptors and Sensory Perception 1955, Charles Scott Sherrington, An Appraisal 1966, Basis of Motor Control 1970, Mechanisms Regulating the Discharge of Motoneurons 1972, The Purposive Brain 1977, Hur det kom sig (Memories of Research and Motivations) 1983. *Leisure interest:* gardening. *Address:* 14 Eriksbergsgatan, 114 30 Stockholm, Sweden. *Telephone:* (08) 213728 (Home).

GRANÖ, Olavi Johannes, PH.D.; Finnish professor of geography; b. 27 May 1925, Helsinki; s. of Prof. Dr. J. Gabriel Granö and Hilma Ekholm; m. Eeva Kaleva 1953; two d.; ed. Turku, Helsinki and Copenhagen Univs.; Asst. Prof. of Geography, Helsinki Univ. and Helsinki School of Econs. 1948–57; Assoc. Prof. of Geography, Turku Univ. 1958–61, Prof. 1962–88, Chancellor 1984–; Pres. Archipelago Research Inst. 1965–84; Pres. Finnish Nat. Research Council for Sciences 1964–69; Pres. Cen. Bd. of Research Councils (Acad. of Finland) 1970–73; mem. Science Policy Council 1964–74; Pres. Advisory Cttee. for Research of Nordic Council of Ministers 1976–82; Academician, Acad. of Finland 1980; mem. Finnish Acad. of Science and Letters 1970; Visiting Fellow, Clare Hall, Cambridge Univ. 1982; Hon. Corresp. mem. Royal Geographical Soc. (London) 1980; Hon. mem. Geographical Soc. of S. Sweden 1981, mem. Royal Swedish Acad. of Sciences 1985; Dr. h.c. (Toruń, Poland) 1980; Finnish Geographical Soc. Fennia Medal 1988. *Publications:* scientific publications on geography, geology, history of science and science policy. *Address:* Department of Geography, Turku University, 20500 Turku (Office); Sirppitie 1A, 20540 Turku, Finland (Home). *Telephone:* 645100 (Office); 370640 (Home).

GRANT, Allan Kerr, M.B., B.S., F.R.A.C.P., F.R.C.P., F.R.C.P. (E); Australian consultant physician (gastroenterologist); b. 29 Oct. 1924, Adelaide; s. of Kerr Grant and Kate Moffatt; m. Mary Raymond Hone 1949; three s. one d.; ed. St. Peter's Coll., Adelaide, Univ. of Adelaide; Hon. Asst. Physician, Royal Adelaide Hosp. 1956–59, Queen Elizabeth Hosp. 1960–64, Dir. Gastroenterology Unit 1960–84; Visiting Gastroenterologist, Adelaide Children's Hosp. 1964–84; Physician (Lieut.-Col.), Australian Field Force, Vietnam 1968–69; Sr. Visiting Specialist, Flinders Medical Centre, S. Australia 1984–; Assoc. Clinical Prof., Flinders Univ. of S. Australia 1984–; Assoc. Dean, Postgraduate Medical Studies, Univ. of Adelaide 1984–; Consulting Physician, Queen Elizabeth Hosp., South Australia 1985–; Pres. Gastroenterological Soc. of Australia 1974–76, Australian Postgraduate Fed. in Medicine 1986–; mem. Medical Bd. of S. Australia 1982–, Medical Advisory Cttee., Univ. of Adelaide 1978–83; Medical Dir., S. Australian Postgraduate Medical Educ. Asscn. 1983–; Travelling Scholar, Royal Australasian Coll. of Physicians 1952. *Publication:* Clinical Diagnosis of Gastrointestinal Disease (with A. P. Skyring) 1981. *Leisure interests:* horticulture, ornithology, photography, opera, ballet, fishing. *Address:* 33 Hackney Road, Hackney, South Australia 5000 (Office); 296 South Terrace, Adelaide, South Australia 5000 (Home). *Telephone:* (08) 362 8288 (Office); (08) 223 7085 (Home).

GRANT, Bruce Alexander, B.A.; Australian author and government official; b. 4 April 1925, Perth; s. of Leslie John Grant and Myrtle Rapson Williams; m. 1st Enid Walters 1947 (dissolved 1961), one s. two d.; m. 2nd Joan Pennell 1962, two s.; ed. Perth Modern School, Univ. of Melbourne, Harvard Univ., served Royal Australian Navy 1943–45; with The Age 1950–65, Film, Theatre Critic and Literary Ed. 1950–53, Foreign Corresp., Europe 1954–57, Asia 1959–63, Wash. 1964–65; Fellow in Political Science Univ. of Melbourne 1965–68, Visiting Fellow 1976; columnist 1968–72; High Comm. to India (also accred. to Nepal) 1973–76; Research Assoc. Int. Inst. for Strategic Studies., London 1977; Dir. Inst. Political Science 1979–; Dir. then Chair. Australian Dance Theatre 1979–82; Writer-in-Residence Monash Univ. 1981; Adviser on Arts Policy State Govt. of Victoria 1982–86; Visiting Fellow, Australian Nat. Univ., Canberra 1983; Pres. Melbourne Spoleto Festival of Three Worlds 1984–87; Chair. Victorian Premier's Literary Awards 1984–86, Victorian Australian Bicentennial Authority 1985–86; Consultant to Minister for Foreign Affairs and Trade 1988–. *Publications:* Indonesia 1964, The Crisis of Loyalty 1972, Arthur and Eric 1977, The Boat People 1979, Cherry Bloom 1980, Gods and Politicians 1982, The Australian Dilemma 1983, Australia and the 21st Century (1988); numerous short-stories, articles and chapters in books on int. affairs. *Address:* c/o Curtis Brown (Australia) Pty. Ltd., 19 Union Street, Sydney, N.S.W. 2021, Australia.

GRANT, Cedric Hilburn, PH.D.; Guyanese professor and diplomatist; b. 23 April 1936; m. Lorene Grant; four d.; ed. Univs. of Leicester and Edinburgh; Resident Tutor, Inst. of Adult Education, Univ. of Ghana 1963–65; Research Fellow, Inst. of Social and Econ. Research, Univ. of the W. Indies 1965–67; Ford Foundation Fellow, Univ. of Edin. 1967–69; Asst. Prof., Univ. of Waterloo, Canada 1969–71, Assoc. Prof. 1971–78; Consultant to Govt. of Guyana 1968–71, 1974; High Commr. in Zambia 1975–77, in U.K. (also accred. to France, Fed. Repub. of Germany, the Netherlands, Yugoslavia) 1977–81; Amb. to U.S.A. 1982–. *Leisure interest:* music. *Publication:* The Making of Modern Belize: Politics, Society and British Colonialism in Central America 1976. *Address:* Embassy of Guyana, 2490 Tracy Place, Washington, D.C. 20008, U.S.A.

GRANT, James Pineo, B.A., J.D.; American international civil servant; b. 12 May 1922, Beijing, China; s. of John B. Grant,M.D., and Charlotte Hill; m. Ethel Henck 1943; three s.; ed. Univ. of California at Berkeley, Harvard Univ. Law School; served U.S. army 1943–45; with UN Relief and Rehabilitation Admin. 1946–47; Acting Exec. Sec. to Sino-American Jt. Cttee. on Rural Reconstruction 1948–50; Law Assoc., Covington and Burling, Wash., D.C. 1951–54; Regional Legal Counsel, New Delhi, U.S. aid programmes for S. Asia 1954–56; Dir. U.S. aid mission, Ceylon (now Sri Lanka) 1956–58; Deputy to Dir. Int. Co-operation Admin. (U.S. foreign aid programme) 1959–62; Deputy Asst. Sec. of State, Near East and S. Asian Affairs 1962–64; Dir. U.S. aid mission, Turkey (rank of Minister) 1964–67; Asst. Admin. Agency for Int. Devt. (AID) 1967–69; Pres. Overseas Devt. Council (ODC), Wash., D.C. 1969–80; Exec. Dir. UN Children's Fund (UNICEF) Jan. 1980–; mem. Bd. of Dirs. Overseas Devt. Council, Johns Hopkins Univ., Int. Voluntary Services; Hon. Dr. Iur., Hon LL.D. (Notre Dame Univ., Maryville Coll.), Hon. D.Sc. (Hacettepe Univ., Ankara); Bronze Star with oak leaf cluster; Breast Order of Yun Hui (China); Distinguished Public Service Award 1961, Rockefeller Public Service Award 1980, Boyaca Award (Colombia) 1984, Gold Mercury Int. Award 1984. *Publications:* several articles in journals. *Address:* UNICEF, 3 United Nations Plaza, New York, N.Y. 10017 (Office); 331 East 38th Street, New York, N.Y. 10016, U.S.A. (Home). *Telephone:* (212) 754-7848 (Office).

GRANT, Keith Frederick, A.R.C.A.; British artist, painter, muralist and lecturer; b. 10 Aug. 1930, Liverpool; s. of Charles Grant and Gladys Emma Grant; m. Gisèle Barka Djouadi 1964; one s. one d.; ed. Bootle Grammar School, Willesden School of Art and R.C.A., London; State Scholarship to Norway 1960; Head of Fine Art Dept., Maidstone Coll. of Art, Kent 1968–71; Gulbenkian Award Artist-in-Residence, Bosworth Coll., Leics. 1973–75; Head of Painting Dept., Newcastle Polytechnic 1979–81; Head of Dept. of Art, The Roehampton Inst. of Higher Educ., London 1981–; one-man shows in London, Iceland, Norway, France and Italy 1960–; recorded volcanic eruption, Iceland 1973; painted launch of Ariane Rocket 1982; visited Sarawak 1984 and 1985; designed prints for use in Earthlife Foundation's Rainforest Campaign; designed book covers for 6 Peter Mattheissen works 1988–89; One man exhbns. London 1988–89; Guest Visiting Artist, Ben Gurion Univ. of the Negev and British Israel Art Foundation 1988; works in many public collections including Arts Council of G.B., Nat. Gallery of N.Z., Nat. Gallery of S. Australia, Hamilton Art Gallery, Ontario, Trondheim Art Gallery, Norway, Contemporary Art Soc., Fitzwilliam Museum, Cambridge; mural/mosaics Charing Cross Hosp., London, Gateshead Metro Station; painting, Guildhall School of Music and Drama, London; sculpture, Shaw Theatre, London; Silver Medal, Mural Painting, R.C.A. 1958. *Leisure interests:* walking, music, travel and writing. *Address:* Department of Art, The Roehampton Institute of Higher Education, Grove House, Roehampton Lane, London, SW15 5PJ (Office); 15 St. John's Terrace, Lewes, East Sussex, BN7 2DL, England (Home). *Telephone:* 01-876 2242 (Office); (0273) 474797 (Home).

GRANT, Peter James; British business executive; b. 5 Dec. 1929; s. of late Lieut-Col. P. C. H. Grant and Mrs. Grant (née Gooch); m. 1st Ann Pleydell-Bouverie, one s. one d.; m. 2nd Paula Eugster, one s. two d.; ed. Winchester Coll. and Magdalen Coll. Oxford; Lieut. Queens Own Cameron Highlanders; joined Edward de Stein & Co. 1952, merged with Lazard Brothers & Co., Ltd. 1960; Dir. Standard Industrial Group 1966–72, Charrington, Gardner, Lockett & Co., Ltd. 1970–74, Walter Runciman PLC 1973–; Dir. Sun Life Assurance Soc. PLC 1973–, Vice-Chair. 1976, Chair. 1983–; mem. Industrial Devt. Bd. 1985–. *Leisure interests:* shooting, golf, gardening. *Address:* Vinehall Manor, Robertsbridge, Sussex, England; Letter Kilmuir, North Kessock, Inverness, Scotland. *Telephone:* (042 487) 279; (046 373) 275.

GRANT, Peter Raymond, B.A., PH.D., F.R.S.; British professor of biology; b. 26 Oct. 1936, London; s. of Frederick Thomas Charles Grant and Mavis Irene Grant; m. Barbara Rosemary Matchett 1962; two d.; ed. Cambridge Univ. and Univ. of British Columbia; Postdoctoral Fellowship Yale Univ. 1964–65; Asst. Prof. of Biology McGill Univ., Canada 1965–68, Assoc. Prof. 1968–73, Prof. 1973–78; Prof. Univ. of Michigan 1978–85; Prof. Princeton Univ. 1985–; F.L.S.; Fellow American Asscn. for Advancement of Science; Hon. Ph.D. (Uppsala). *Publication:* Ecology and Evolution of Darwin's Finches 1986. *Leisure interests:* camping, hiking, music and reading. *Address:* Biology Department, Princeton University, Princeton, N.J. 08544, U.S.A.

GRANT, Verne E., PH.D.; American biologist; b. 17 Oct. 1917, San Francisco, Calif.; s. of Edwin E. and Bessie C. (Swallow) Grant; m. 1st Alva Day 1946, 2nd Karen S. Alt 1960; one s. two d.; ed. Univ. of California (Berkeley); Visiting Investigator, Carnegie Inst. of Washington, Stanford,

Calif. 1949–50; Geneticist and experimental taxonomist, Rancho Santa Ana Botanic Garden, Claremont, Calif. 1950–67; Prof. of Biology, Inst. of Life Science, Texas A. & M. Univ. 1967–68; Prof. of Biological Sciences, Univ. of Ariz. 1968–70; Dir. Boyce Thompson Arboretum, Ariz. 1968–70; Prof. of Botany, Univ. of Tex. 1970–87, Prof. Emer. 1987–; Nat. Research Council Fellowship 1949–50; Phi Beta Kappa Award in Science 1964; Certificate of Merit, Botanical Soc. of America 1971; mem. N.A.S.; Fellow American Acad. of Arts and Sciences. *Publications:* Natural History of the Phlox Family 1959, The Origin of Adaptations 1963, The Architecture of the Germplasm 1964, Flower Pollination in the Phlox Family (with Karen Grant) 1965, Hummingbirds and Their Flowers (with Karen Grant) 1968, Plant Speciation 1971, 1981, Genetics of Flowering Plants 1975, Organismic Evolution 1977, The Evolutionary Process 1985; numerous papers on plant genetics and plant evolution. *Leisure interests:* hiking, railroading, classical music. *Address:* Department of Botany, University of Texas at Austin, Austin, Tex. 78712 (Office); 2811 Fresco Drive, Austin, Tex. 78731, U.S.A. (Home). *Telephone:* 512-471-5858 (Office).

GRANT, Walter Lawrence, PR.ENG., D.SC., M.SC., C.E. and M.I.MECH.E., A.F.R.AE.S., M.(S.A.)I.M.E.; South African engineer; b. 22 Aug. 1922, Potchefstroom, Transvaal; s. of Walter W. Grant and Petronella Peters; m. Anna Catharina Christina van Deventer; ed. Witwatersrand Tech. Coll., Univs. of the Witwatersrand and Pretoria; Head, Thermodynamic Div., Nat. Mechanical Eng. Research Inst. (N.M.E.R.I.), S. African Council for Scientific and Industrial Research (C.S.I.R.) 1952–57, Dir. N.M.E.R.I. 1957–59; Chief Engineer, S.A. Atomic Energy Bd. 1959–64, Deputy Dir.-Gen. and Dir. of Reactor Eng. 1964–67; Dir.-Gen. S.A. Atomic Energy Bd. 1967–70, Deputy Pres. 1970–71; Gen. Man. Uranium Enrichment Corpn. of S.A. Ltd. 1971–79, Man. Dir. July 1979–86; Exec. Gen. Man. Nuclear Research and Devt. Group 1986–87; Chief Systems Engineer, Integrators of System Tech. (Pty) Ltd. (IST) Pretoria; Hon. D.Sc. (Pretoria) 1974; Hon. Prof. Mechanical Eng., Univ. of Pretoria 1983; Gold Medal, Inst. of Mechanical Eng. 1958, Havenga Prize 1966, Co-recipient Hendrik Verwoerd Award 1971, Claude Harris Leon Foundation Annual Award 1981 (for work on uranium enrichment process), Gold Medal of S.A. Inst. of Mechanical Engineers 1983 and other awards. *Publications:* 29 scientific publs. 1953–78. *Leisure interests:* photography, target shooting. *Address:* IST, P.O. Box 1848, Pretoria, 0001 (Office); Vergesig, The Old Fort Road 9, Lynwood, Pretoria, 0081, South Africa (Home). *Telephone:* 322-6671/8, Ext. 175 (Office).

GRANVILLE, Sir Keith, Kt., C.B.E., M.INST.T.; British airline executive; b. 1 Nov. 1910, Faversham; m. 1st Patricia Capstick 1933, 2nd Truda Belliss 1946; two s. five d.; ed. Tonbridge School; Trainee, Imperial Airways 1929, served in Italy, Tanganyika, Southern and Northern Rhodesia, Egypt, India; then Man. African and Middle East Div., BOAC 1947, Commercial Dir, BOAC 1954, Deputy Man. Dir. 1958–60; Chair. BOAC Associated Companies Ltd. 1960–64; Deputy Chair BOAC 1964–71, Deputy Chair. and Man. Dir. Jan. 1969, Chair. 1971–72; mem. Exec. Cttee. IATA 1972–74, Pres. 1972–73; Deputy Chair. British Airways Bd. 1972–74; mem. Maplin Devt. Authority 1973–74; Hon. F.R.Ae.S. *Address:* Speedbird, 1837 Chateau-D'Oex, Switzerland. *Telephone:* 029 47603 (Home).

GRAPPELLI, Stéphane; French musician; b. 26 Jan. 1908, Paris; s. of Ernest and Anna (née Hanocke) Grappelli; one d.; ed. Conservatoire Nat. Supérieur de Musique; pianist and jazz violinist; f. mem. Quintet of the Hot Club of France 1934 (with the late Django Reinhardt); composed musical accompaniments for silent films and theatre; numerous int. tours and recordings, including six records with Yehudi Menuhin (q.v.); Officier, Légion d'honneur; Officier Ordre Nat. du Mérite; Officier des Arts et des Lettres; Médaille de Vermeil, Paris. *Leisure interests:* walking, travel. *Address:* 87 rue de Dunkerque, 75009 Paris, France.

GRASS, Günter; German artist and writer; b. 16 Oct. 1927, Danzig (now Gdańsk, Poland); m. 1st Anna Schwarz 1954, three s. one d.; m. 2nd Utte Grunert 1979; ed. art school; Dr.h.c. (Kenyon Coll.) 1965, (Harvard) 1976; Lyric Prize, Süddeutscher Rundfunk 1955, Group 47 Prize 1959, Literary Prize, Asscn. of German Critics 1960, Georg-Büchner Prize 1965, Theodor-Heuss Prize 1969, Int. Feltrinelli Prize 1982. *Publications:* Die Vorzüge der Windhühner (poems and drawings) 1955, Die Blechtrommel 1959 (film The Tin Drum 1979), Gleisdreieck (poems and drawings) 1960, Katz und Maus 1961 (film 1967), Hundejahre 1963, Ausgefragt (poems) 1967, Über das Selbstverständliche 1968, Örtlich betäubt 1969, Aus dem Tagebuch einer Schnecke 1972, Dokumente zur politischen Wirkung 1972, Die Bürger und seine Stimme 1974, Der Butt 1976, Denkzettel 1978, Das Treffen in Telgte 1979, Kopfgeburten 1980, Aufsätze zur Literatur 1980, Zeichnen und Schreiben Band I 1982, Widerstand lernen-Politische Gegenreden 1980–83 1984, Band II 1984, On Writing and Politics 1967–83 1985, The Rat 1987, Zünge Zeigen 1988, Werkansgabe, 10 vols. 1988; plays: Hochwasser 1956, Noch 10 Minuten bis Buffalo 1958, Onkel, Onkel 1958, Die bösen Köche 1961, Die Plebejer proben den Aufstand 1965, Davor 1968. *Address:* Niedstrasse 13, 1 Berlin 41, Federal Republic of Germany.

GRASSBERGER, Roland, LL.D.; Austrian criminologist; b. 1905, Vienna; s. of Dr. Roland Grassberger and Mathilde Rabl; m. Isabella Hiess 1933; two s.; ed. High School and Univ. of Vienna; practice at Criminal Court 1929–30, at Police Office 1931–32; Asst. Lecturer in Criminology, Univ. of Vienna 1930, lecturer 1931–46, Dir., Inst. of Criminology, Univ. of Vienna

1946-75, Prof. of Criminal Law and Criminology 1948-75, Dean, Faculty of Law 1954-55, 1960-61, Rector of Univ. of Vienna 1962-63; Sworn Expert for Criminology at Austrian Courts 1931-. *Publications:* Die Brandlegungs-kriminalität 1928, Die Strafzumessung 1932, Gewerbs- und Berufsverbrech-ertum in den U.S.A. 1933, Die Lösung kriminalpolitischer Probleme durch die mechanische Statistik 1946, Psychologie des Strafverfahrens 1950, 1968, Die Kriminalität des Wohlstandes 1962, Die Unzucht mit Tieren 1968. *Leisure interest:* history. *Address:* Tendlergasse 17, 1090 Vienna, Austria. *Telephone:* 42-50454.

GRASSLEY, Charles E., M.A.; American farmer, teacher and politician; b. 17 Sept. 1933, New Hartford, Ia.; m. Barbara Ann Speicher; five c.; ed. Univs. of Northern Iowa and Iowa; farmer; Instructor Political Science, Drake Community Coll. 1962, Charles City Coll. 1967-68; mem. Ia. House of Reps. 1959-75; mem. House of Reps. 1975-81 from 3rd Dist., Ia.; Senator from Iowa 1981-; Republican; mem. Nat. Farm Bureau. *Address:* Hart Senate Office Building, Washington, D.C. 20510 (Office); Rural Route 1, New Hartford, Ia. 50660, U.S.A. (Home).

GRATZ, Leopold; Austrian politician; b. 4 Nov. 1929, Vienna; m.; ed. Faculty of Law, Univ. of Vienna; served in Fed. Ministry for Social Admin. 1952-53; mem. Secr. Socialist Parl. Party 1953, Sec. 1957; Sec. Socialist Party Exec. 1963; mem. Bundesrat 1963-66, Nationalrat 1966-; Chair. Educational Policy Comm. of Exec. of Socialist Party 1968; Minister of Educ. 1970-71; Mayor of Vienna 1973-84; Minister of Foreign Affairs 1984-86; Pres. Nat. Council 1986-89. *Address:* Parliament Building, 1017 Vienna, Austria.

GRATZIOS, Agamemnon; Greek army officer; b. 1922, Elafotopos-Epirus; s. of Constantine Gratzios; m.; two s.; ed. Artillery Special Airborne Forces School (U.S.A.-Fed. Repub. of Germany) War Coll., Nat. Defence Coll.; war service 1940-41; Nat. Resistance during World War II; engaged in guerrilla warfare 1946-49; Mil. Acad. 1939, 2nd Lieut. 1942, 1st Lieut. 1946, Capt. 1948, Maj. 1952, Lieut.-Col. 1960, Col. 1967, Brig.-Gen. 1971, Maj.-Gen., Commdr. XII Div. 1972, Lieut.-Gen. 1974, Commdr. HMCII, 'C" Army Corps, Commdr. 1975, Chief Hellenic Army Gen. Staff 1976, Gen. 1980, Chief Hellenic Nat. Defence Gen. Staff 1980-; Golden Order of Merit for Gallant Actions (twice), War Cross "C" Class (twice), Golden Cross, Order of Phoenix, with Swords, Medal for Mil. Valour "A" Class, Medal of Helleno-Italo-German War 1940-41, Medal of Nat. Resistance 1941-45, Golden Cross Order of King George "A", Kt. Commdr. Cross Order of Phoenix, Kt. Commdr. Cross of King George (2nd Class), Kt. Commdr. Order of Honour, Medal for Mil. Merit (Yugoslavia), Legion of Merit Order of Commdr. (U.S.A.), Commdr., Légion d'honneur, Grande Ufficiale dell'Ordine al Merito (Italy). *Address:* Ministry of National Defence, Holargos (Pentagon), Athens, Greece. *Telephone:* 644 2917.

GRAUR, Alexandru; Romanian philologist; b. 9 July 1900, Botoşani, Romania; m. Neaga Sion; one s.; ed. Bucharest Univ., and the Sorbonne, Paris; Prof. of Philology, Univ. Bucharest (Dean of Philological Faculty 1954-56); mem. of Praesidium of Acad. of Socialist Repub. of Romania; Gen. Man. Publishing House of the S.R.R. Acad. 1955-74; State Prize 1953, Star of Socialist Repub. of Romania, Fourth Class, Order of Labour, First Class. *Publications include:* Les consonnes géminées en latin 1929, I et V en latin 1929, Nom d'agent et adjectif en roumain 1929, Incercare asupra fondului principal lexical al limbii române 1954, Studii de linguistică generală 1960, Etimologii româneşti 1963, The Romance Character of Romanian 1967, Tendinţele actuale ale limbii române 1968, Alte etimologii româneşti 1975; contributions to Gramatica Limbii române (Vols. I-II) 1963; numerous articles in newspapers and learned periodicals in Romania, France, U.S.S.R., U.K., China, etc. *Address:* Academia R.S.R., Calea Victoriei 125, Bucharest (Office); Boul. A. Ipătescu 12, Bucharest (22), Romania (Home). *Telephone:* 50.52.08.

GRAVE, Walter Wyatt, C.M.G., PH.D.; British educationist; b. 16 Oct. 1901, King's Lynn; s. of the late Walter and Annie Grave; m. Kathleen Margaret Macpherson 1932; two d.; ed. Emmanuel Coll., Cambridge; Fellow of Emmanuel Coll., Cambridge 1926-66, 1972-, Tutor 1936-40; Lecturer in Spanish, Cambridge Univ. 1936-40, Sr. Proctor 1938-39; Admin. Officer Ministry of Labour and Nat. Service 1940-43; Univ. Registrary, Cambridge 1943-52; Prin. Univ. Coll. of West Indies 1953-58; Censor Fitzwilliam House, Cambridge, 1959-66; Master Fitzwilliam Coll., Cambridge 1966-71, Hon. Fellow 1971-; Hon. LL.D. (Cambridge and McMaster Univs.). *Publication:* Fitzwilliam College, Cambridge 1869-1969 1983. *Address:* 16 Kingsdale Court, Great Shelford, Cambridge, CB2 5AT, England. *Telephone:* 0223) 840722.

GRAVEL, Mike; American politician; b. 13 May 1930, Springfield, Mass.; s. of Alphonse and Maria Gravel; m. Rita Martin 1959; one s. one d.; ed. Columbia Univ.; Real estate developer; mem. Alaska House of Reps. 1962-66; Speaker, Alaska House of Reps. 1965; U.S. Senator from Alaska 1969-81; f. Mike Gravel Resource Analysts, Anchorage, Alaska 1981-; Democrat. *Publications:* Jobs and More Jobs, Citizen Power, The Pentagon Papers (editor). *Address:* 512 1/2 G Street, S.E., Washington, D.C. 20022, U.S.A.

GRAVES, Harold N., Jr., A.B., M.S.; American journalist; b. 20 Jan. 1915, Manila, Philippines; s. of Harold N. Graves and Florida Tolbert; m. Alta F. Judy 1937; three s.; ed. Princeton and Columbia (School of Journalism)

Univs.; Editorial Research Asst. for Literary Digest 1936; Assoc. Ed. Pathfinder 1936-39; Dir. Princeton Listening Center 1939-41; Asst. to Dir. Foreign Broadcast Intelligence Service, Fed. Communications Comm., Wash. 1941-43; attached to U.S. Navy, Office of Strategic Services, Wash., Ceylon and Thailand 1943-45; Wash. corresp. Providence (R.I.) Evening Bulletin 1946-50; Dir. of Information, IBRD 1950-67, IDA 1959-67, Int. Finance Corpn. 1960-67; Assoc. Dir. Devt. Services Dept. IBRD and IDA 1967-73; Exec. Sec. Consultative Group on Int. Agricultural Research 1972-75; Chair. Cttee. to Establish Int. Center for Agricultural Research on the Dry Areas 1975-77; Consultant to the Cholera Research Lab., Dacca 1977-80; Trustee Int. Inst. for Social Research 1974-80. *Leisure interest:* golf. *Address:* 4816 Grantham Avenue, Chevy Chase, Maryland 20015, U.S.A. *Telephone:* OLiver 4-1694.

GRAY, E. George, PH.D., F.R.S.; British professor of anatomy (retd.); b. 11 Jan. 1924, Pontypool, Monmouth (now Gwent); s. of William Gray and Charlotte Atkinson; m. May Rautiainen 1953; two s.; ed. Univs. of Wales, Aberystwyth; Reader in Anatomy, Univ. Coll., London 1962-67, Prof. 1967-77; Head, Dept. of Biological Ultrastructure, Medical Research Council 1977-83; now Hon. Research Assoc., Dept. of Anatomy, Univ. Coll., London; Hon. mem. American Assen. of Anatomists. *Publications:* numerous papers on the nervous system in journals and books. *Leisure interests:* violin playing, water colour painting. *Address:* 58 New Park Road, Newgate Street Village, Hertford, SG13 8RF, England. *Telephone:* (0707) 872891.

GRAY, George William, PH.D., C.CHEM., F.R.S.C., F.R.S.; British professor of chemistry; b. 4 Sept. 1926, Edinburgh; s. of John William Gray and Jessie Colville (née Hunter); m. Marjorie Mary Canavan; three d.; ed. Univs. of Glasgow and London; mem. staff, Dept. of Chem., Univ. of Hull 1946-, Sr. Lecturer 1960, Reader 1964, Prof. of Organic Chem. 1978-84, G. F. Grant Prof. of Chem. 1984-; Sr. Ed. Molecular Crystals and Liquid Crystals; mem. Planning and Steering Cttee. for Int. Liquid Crystal Confs.; Queen's Award for Technological Achievement 1979; Rank Prize for Optoelectronics 1980; Leverhulme Medal of Royal Soc. 1987. *Publications:* Molecular Structure and the Properties of Liquid Crystals 1962, Liquid Crystals and Plastic Crystals (Ed. and jtly. with P. A. Winsor) 1974, The Molecular Physics of Liquid Crystals (Ed. and jtly. with G. R. Luckhurst) 1979, Smectic Liquid Crystals—Textures and Structures (with J. W. Goodby) 1984; Thermotropic Liquid Crystals (Ed.) 1987; 180 papers on liquid crystals in scientific journals. *Leisure interests:* gardening, philately. *Address:* Department of Chemistry, University of Hull, Hull, HU6 7RX (Office); Glenwood, 33 Newgate Street, Cottingham, HU16 4DY, England (Home). *Telephone:* (0482) 465485 (Office); (0482) 844853 (Home).

GRAY, H.E. Cardinal Gordon Joseph, M.A.; British ecclesiastic; b. 10 Aug. 1910, Leith, Edinburgh, Scotland; s. of Francis W. Gray and Angela Gray; ed. Holy Cross Acad., Edinburgh, St. Joseph's Coll., Mark Cross, St. John's Seminary, Wonersh and St. Andrews Univ., Scotland; ordained 1935; Curate St. Andrews 1935-41; Parish Priest Hawick 1941-47; Rector Blairs Coll., Aberdeen (Nat. Jr. Seminary for Scotland) 1947-51; Archbishop of St. Andrews and Edin. 1951-85 (retd.); Apostolic Admin. of Diocese of Aberdeen 1963-65; cr. Cardinal 1969; Hon. Fellow Educational Inst. of Scotland 1970; Hon. D.D. (St. Andrews) 1967, Hon. D.Univ. (Heriot-Watt) 1981. *Leisure interests:* gardening, carpentry, liturgy. *Address:* The Hermitage, St. Margaret's Convent, Whitehouse Loan, Edinburgh, EH9 1BB, Scotland.

GRAY, Harry Barkus, PH.D; American chemist; b. 14 Nov. 1935, Kentucky; m. Shirley Barnes 1957; two s. one d.; ed. Univ. of W. Kentucky, Northwestern Univ. and Univ. of Copenhagen; Asst. Prof. of Chem., Columbia Univ. 1961-63, Assoc. Prof. 1963-65, Prof. 1965-66; Prof. of Chem. Calif. Inst. of Tech. 1966-, now Arnold O. Beckman Prof.; mem. N.A.S., American Acad. of Arts and Sciences; Foreign mem. Royal Danish Soc. of Science and Letters; Franklin Award 1967, Fresenius Award 1970, American Chem. Soc. Award in Pure Chem. 1970, Harrison Howe Award 1972, MCA Award 1972, Guggenheim Fellow 1972-73, American Chem. Soc. Award in Inorganic Chem. 1978, Remsen Award 1979, Tolman Award 1979, Centenary Medal 1985, Nat. Medal of Science 1986, Pauling Medal 1986, Calif. Scientist of the Year 1988. *Publications:* Electrons and Chemical Bonding 1965, Molecular Orbital Theory 1965, Ligand Substitution Processes 1966, Basic Principles of Chemistry 1967, Chemical Dynamics 1968, Chemical Principles 1970, Models in Chemical Science 1971, Chemical Bonds 1973, Electronic Structure and Bonding 1981, Molecular Electronic Structures 1981. *Leisure interests:* tennis, music. *Address:* Noyes Laboratory of Chemical Physics, California Institute of Technology, Pasadena, Calif. 91125 (Office); 1415 East California Boulevard, Pasadena, Calif. 91106, U.S.A. (Home). *Telephone:* (818) 356-6500 (Office); (818) 793-1978 (Home).

GRAY, Harry J., M.S., LL.D.; American business executive; b. 1919, Milledgeville Crossroads, Georgia; m.; two c.; ed. Univ. of Illinois; served as Capt. in Army in 2nd World War; fmrly. Sr. Exec. Vice-Pres. Litton Industries; Pres. and Chief Admin. Officer and Dir., United Technologies Corpn. 1971-79, C.E.O. 1972-85, Chair. and Pres. 1974-86, also Chair. Finance Cttee., Pres. 1981-83; Dir. Union Carbide, Citicorp., Citibank, N.A., of New York; mem. Business Council, Wash., D.C., Conf. Bd., New York, I.E.E.E. Silver Star and Bronze Star for gallantry in action. *Address:*

United Technologies Corporation, United Technologies Building, Hartford, Conn. 06101 U.S.A.

GRAY, Hon. Herbert E.; Canadian politician; b. 25 May 1931, Windsor, Ont.; s. of Harry and Fannie Gray; m. Sharon Sholzberg 1967; one s. one d.; ed. Victoria Public School, Kennedy, Coll. Inst. Windsor, McGill Univ. and Osgoode Hall Law School, Toronto; M.P. 1962–; Chair. of House of Commons Standing Cttee. on Finance, Trade and Econ. Affairs 1966–68; Parl. Sec. to Minister of Finance 1968–69; Minister without Portfolio 1969–70, Minister of Nat. Revenue 1970–72, of Consumer and Corporate Affairs 1972–74, of Industry, Trade and Commerce 1980–82, of Regional Industrial Expansion Jan.–Oct. 1982; Pres. of Treasury Bd. 1982–84; Opposition House Leader 1984–; Govt. Observer Inter-American Conf. of Ministers of Labour, Bogotá 1963; Vice-Chair. Del. to NATO Parl. Conf., Paris 1963; mem. Del. to Canada-France Interparl. Conf. 1966; mem. Canadian Del. to IMF and IBRD meeting 1967, Canada-U.S. Interparl. Conf. 1967–68; Liberal. *Address:* 1253 Victoria Avenue, Windsor, Ontario, Canada.

GRAY, Sir John Archibald Browne, M.A., M.B., B.CHIR., SC.D., F.R.C.P., F.R.S.; British physiologist and administrator (retd.); b. 30 March 1918, London; s. of Sir Archibald Gray, K.C.V.O., C.B.E.; and Elsie Cooper; m. Vera K. Mares 1946; one s. and d.; ed. Cheltenham Coll., Clare Coll., Cambridge and Univ. Coll. Hospital London; Service Research for MRC 1943–45; Surgeon Lieut., R.N.V.R. 1945–46; MRC Scientific Staff, Nat. Inst. for Medical Research 1946–52; Reader in Physiology, Univ. Coll. London 1952–58, Prof. of Physiology 1958–66; Second Sec. MRC 1966–68, Sec. 1968–77; mem. Scientific Staff MRC 1977–83; Hon. Fellow Clare Coll., Cambridge 1976; Pres. Freshwater Biological Assen. 1983–88; mem. Council, Marine Biological Assen. 1964–68; Hon. D.Sc. (Exeter) 1985. *Publications:* numerous papers on sensory receptors and sensory nervous system. *Leisure interests:* sailing, painting. *Address:* Seaway, North Rock, Kingsand, Nr. Torpoint, Cornwall, England. *Telephone:* Plymouth 822745.

GRAY, Louis Patrick, B.SC., JU.D.; American lawyer and civil servant; b. 18 July 1916, St. Louis, Mo.; m.; four c.; ed. U.S. Naval Acad. Annapolis, Md. and George Washington Univ. Law School, Washington, D.C.; served U.S. Navy World War II, Korean War, rose to Capt. and post of Mil. Asst. to Chair., Jt. Chiefs of Staff and Asst. to Sec. of Defence for Legal and Legis. Affairs; retd. from Navy 1960; admitted to bar, D.C. 1949, Conn. 1958, and has practised before U.S. Court of Mil. Appeals, Supreme Court, Court of Claims, Court of Appeals for D.C. Circuit; joined Suisman, Shapiro & Wool 1961, Partner Suisman, Shapiro, Wool, Brennan & Gray 1967–69, 1970, Suisman, Shapiro, Wool & Brennan 1973–; Founded Capital for Tech. Corpn.; Exec. Asst. to Sec. of Health, Educ. and Welfare 1969–70; Special Consultant to President's Cabinet Cttee. on Educ. 1970; Asst. Attorney Gen. for Civil Div. of Justice Dept. 1970, Head of Civil Div. 1971; Acting Dir. FBI 1972–73 (resgnd. over Watergate case); indicted April 1978 for alleged conspiracy; indictment dismissed at request of prosecution in Dec. 1980; mem. American Bar Assen.; active in numerous civil and community affairs; Distinguished Service Award; Navy Commendation Medal with combat "V", American Defense Service Medal with bronze "A", UN Service Medal, Submarine Combat Pin (3 stars). *Address:* 325 State Street, New London, Conn. 06320, U.S.A.

GRAY, Peter, F.R.S.; British professor of physical chemistry; b. 25 Aug. 1926, Newport, Monmouth (now Gwent); s. of the late Ivor Hicks Gray and Rose Ethel Gray; m. Barbara Joan Hume 1952; two s. two d.; ed. Newport High School, Gonville and Caius Coll., Cambridge; Univ. Demonstrator in Chemical Eng., Univ. of Cambridge 1951–55; Lecturer, Physical Chem. Dept., Univ. of Leeds 1955–59, Reader 1959–62, Prof. 1962–88; Master Gonville and Caius Coll., Cambridge 1988–; Visiting Prof., Univ. of B.C. 1958–59, Univ. of W. Ont. 1969, Univ. of Göttingen 1979, Macquarie Univ. 1980, Univ. of Paris VI 1986, Univ. of Gottingen 1986; Mc'dola Medal, Royal Inst. of Chem. 1956, Lewis Medal 1978, Marlow Meda', Faraday Soc. 1983. *Publications:* numerous papers in scientific journals. *Address:* The Master's Lodge, Gonville and Caius Coll., Cambridge, CL? 12A; 4 Ancaster Road, Leeds, LS16 5HH, England (Home). *Telephone:* 0532-752826 (Home).

GRAY, Robin Trevor, D.D.A.; Australian politician; b. 1 March 1940, Victoria; s. of Rev. W. J. Gray; m. Judith F. Boyd 1965; two s. one d.; ed. Box Hill High School, Dookie Agric. Coll. and Univ. of Melbourne; teacher, Victoria Educ. Dept. 1961, Middx. County Council, U.K. 1964; agric. consultant Colac, Victoria 1965, Launceston, Tasmania 1965–76; part-time lecturer in Agric. Econs. Univ of Tasmania 1970–76; Deputy Leader of Opposition, Tasmania 1979–81, Leader of Opposition 1981–82, Premier 1982–, Minister for Racing and Gaming 1982–84, Energy and Treas. 1982–, for Forests 1984–86, for State Devt. 1984–; Liberal. *Leisure interests:* cricket, golf, reading. *Address:* 11 Beech Road, Launceston, Tasmania 7250, Australia. *Telephone:* 003-444858.

GRAY, Simon James Holliday, M.A.; British teacher and writer; b. 21 Oct. 1936; s. of Dr. James Davidson Gray and Barbara Cecelia Mary Holliday; m. Beryl Mary Kevern 1965; one s. one d.; ed. Westminster School, Dalhousie Univ., Halifax, N.S., Univ. of Cambridge; Supervisor in English, Univ. of B.C. 1960–63, Sr. Instructor 1963–64; lecturer in English, Queen Mary Coll., Univ. of London 1965–84; Hon. Fellow, Q.M.C., Univ. of London. *Publications:* Novels: Colmain 1963, Simple People 1965, Little

Portia 1967, A Comeback for Stark 1968, non-fiction: An Unnatural Pursuit and Other Pieces 1985; Plays: Wise Child 1968, Sleeping Dog 1968, Dutch Uncle 1969, The Idiot 1971, Spoiled 1971, Butley 1971 (Evening Standard Award), Otherwise Engaged 1975 (Best Play, New York Drama Critics' Circle, Evening Standard Award), Plaintiffs and Defendants 1975, Two Sundays 1975, Dog Days 1976, Molly 1977, The Rear Column 1978, Close of Play 1979, Quartermaine's Terms 1981, Tartuffe 1982, Chapter 17 1982, Common Pursuit 1984, An Unnatural Pursuit and Other Pieces (non-fiction) 1985, Melon 1987. Television: After Pilkington 1987. *Publication:* How's That for Telling 'Em, Fat Lady (memoirs) 1988. *Leisure interests:* squash, watching cricket and football, tennis, swimming. *Address:* c/o Judy Daish Associates, 83 Eastbourne Mews, London, W2 6LQ, England.

GRAYLIN, John Cranmer, C.M.G.; British (Zimbabwean) lawyer and politician; b. 12 Jan. 1921, Stow Maries, Essex; s. of George John and Evelyn Gertrude (née Hull) Graylin; m. Sibella Margaretha Alheit 1946; two s. three d.; ed. Mid-Essex Technical Coll., Chelmsford, England, and Law Society School of Law, London; R.A.F., Second World War; Solicitor 1949; settled in Rhodesia (now Zimbabwe) 1950; law practice, Livingstone 1951–; Livingstone Municipal Councillor 1952; mem. Fed. House of Parl. 1953–63; Deputy Chair. of Cttees. 1954; Minister of Agric. 1959–63 (resgnd.); Chair. Tobacco Export Promotion Council of Rhodesia 1964–67; Chair. Nat. Export Council 1967–69, Transportation Comm. 1969; Chief Exec. Assen. Rhodesian Industries 1969–74; Exec. Chair. Manpower Devt. 1978; Man. Dir. Bikita Minerals 1979–; mem. Exec. Cttee. Zimbabwe Scientific Assen.; fmr. mem. of Bd. Agricultural Finance Corpn., Agricultural Research Council. *Leisure interests:* golf, bird watching, growing orchids, raising pheasants. *Address:* Box CH226, Chisipite, Salisbury, Zimbabwe. *Telephone:* 23941 (Office); 47858 (Home).

GRAYSON, Cecil, M.A., F.B.A.; British professor of Italian studies; b. 5 Feb. 1920, Batley, Yorks.; s. of John M. Grayson and Dora Hartley; m. Margaret Jordan 1947; one s. three d.; ed. Batley Grammar School and St. Edmund Hall Oxford; Univ. Lecturer in Italian, Oxford 1948–57; Serena Prof. of Italian Studies, Oxford Univ. and Fellow of Magdalen Coll. 1958–87; Pres. Modern Humanities Research Assen. 1988; Serena Medal for Italian Studies, British Acad.; Premio Galileo (Pisa). *Publications:* Early Italian Texts (with C. Dionisotti) 1949, 1965, L. B. Alberti, Opusculi Inediti 1954, L. B. Alberti, Opere Volgari (3 vols.) 1960, 1966, 1973, V. Calmeta, Prose e Lettere 1959, Cinque Saggi su Dante 1972, L. B. Alberti, On Painting and Sculpture 1972, The World of Dante (ed.) 1980. *Leisure interests:* music, walking. *Address:* 11 Norham Road, Oxford, OX2 6SF, England (Home). *Telephone:* (0865) 57045 (Home).

GREATBATCH, Sir Bruce, Kt., K.C.V.O., C.M.G., M.B.E.; British colonial administrator; b. 10 June 1917, Warwicks.; ed. Malvern Coll. and Brasenose Coll., Oxford; appointed to Colonial Service, N. Nigeria 1940; war service with Royal W. African Frontier Force 1940–45; resumed colonial service, N. Nigeria 1945, Resident 1956, Sec. to Gov. and Exec. Council 1957, Sr. Resident, Kano 1958; Sec. to Premier of N. Nigeria and Head of Regional Civil Service 1959; Deputy High Commr. in Kenya 1964; Gov. and C.-in-C. of the Seychelles and Commr. for the British Indian Ocean Territory 1969–73; Head of British Devt. Div. in the Caribbean 1974–78; Consultant 1978–; K. St. J. 1969. *Address:* Greenleaves, Painswick, Stroud, Glos., GL6 6TX, England. *Telephone:* (0452) 813517.

GREAVES, Derrick, A.R.C.A.; British artist; b. 5 June 1927, Sheffield; s. of Harry Greaves and Mabel Greaves; m. Mary Margaret Johnson 1951; two s. one d.; ed. R.C.A., London and British School at Rome; part-time teacher St. Martins School of Art 1954–64, Maidstone Coll. of Art and Royal Acad. Schools 1960; Head of Printmaking, Norwich Coll. of Art 1983–; first one-man exhbn., Beaux Arts Gallery 1953; subsequent one-man exhbns. at Zwemmer Gallery 1958, 1960, 1962, 1963, Inst. of Contemporary Arts (ICA), London 1969, 1971, Bear Lane Gallery, Oxford 1970, 1973, Belfast 1972, Dublin 1972, Whitechapel Gallery 1973, Monika Kinley 1973–, City Gallery, Milton Keynes 1975–, Cranfield Inst. of Tech. 1978, Exposicion Int. de la Plastica, Chile 1978; group exhbns. include Contemporary Arts Soc. 1956, Venice Biennale 1956, Pushkin Museum, Moscow 1957, Whitechapel Gallery 1963, Carnegie Int. Exhbn., Pa. 1964, Haymarket Gallery 1974, Royal Acad. 1977, Graves Art Gallery, Sheffield 1980, Fischer Fine Art 1980, Mall Galleries, London 1981, Mappin Art Gallery 1986, Leeds Art Gallery 1986, Philadelphia Museum of Art 1986, Walker Art Gallery; Prize John Moore's Exhbn. 1957, Belfast Open Painting Exhbn. purchase prize 1962. *Publications:* Derrick Greaves. Paintings 1958–80, numerous catalogues.

GREBENSHCHIKOV, Boris; Soviet rock musician and pop star; b 1954, Leningrad; ed. Leningrad Univ.; worked for a time as a computer programmer; lead singer and guitarist of rock-group Akvarium; recordings include Akvarium (U.S.S.R.) 1987. *Address:* c/o Melodiya, Leningrad, U.S.S.R.

GRECH, Joe Debono; Maltese politician; b. 17 Sept. 1941, Birkirkara; m. Edith Vella; two c.; ed. St. Aloysius Coll.; mem. Gen. Workers, Union Rep. for Gozo 1971; Sec. Petrol and Chemicals Section 1973–76; fmr. Pres. Nat. Exec. Socialist Youth Movt., Gen. Sec. 1967–76; fmr. mem. Nat. Exec. Labour Party, Propaganda Sec. 1971–88; Man. Nat. Cargo Handling Co. Interprint; M.P. 1976–; Minister of Parastatal and People's Investments

May–Sept. 1983, of Agric. and Fisheries 1983–87; Deputy Leader Labour Party Aug. 1988–. *Address:* 51 Fleur-de-Lys Road, Birkirkara, Malta. *Telephone:* 443712.

GRECH ORR, Charles; Maltese solicitor and journalist; b. 27 Nov. 1927; s. of John Grech and Martha Orr; m. Grace Ganado 1960; one s. two d.; ed. Lyceum and Univ. of Malta; practising solicitor 1948–52; law reporter, Allied Newspapers Ltd. 1947, subsequently night ed., chief sub-ed., features ed., asst. ed. The Times, Ed. 1965–. *Leisure interests:* tennis, gardening. *Address:* The Times, 341 St. Paul Street, Valletta (Office); 111 Dingli Street, Sliema, Malta (Home). *Telephone:* 224032/6 (Office); 330232.

GRECO, Emilio; Italian sculptor; b. 11 Oct. 1913, Catania; m. Anna Greco 1969; one s. one d.; ed. Accad. di Belle Arti, Palermo; Prof. of Sculpture Accad. di Belle Arti, Rome; mem. Accad. Nazionale di San Luca; first sculpture exhbn., Catania 1933; one-man exhbns. in Rome, Milan, Naples, London, San Francisco; Rhode Island; represented in numerous group exhbns. in Italy and abroad including 4th Rome Quadriennale, 28th Venice Biennale, Bienal São Paulo 1957, Palazzo Barberini 1958, Zwerge Garden Salzburg 1959; works in public and private collections in Rome, Milan, Venice, Florence, Trieste, Città del Capo, London, Leeds, Monaco, Hamburg, Cologne, St. Louis, Leningrad and Pinacoteca Vaticana; engaged on monument to Pope John XXIII 1965–67; Greco Garden (180 sq. m. perm. exhbn. space), Hakone, Japan; perm. room, Hermitage, Leningrad 1980; Emilio Greco Museum, Sabaudia 1984; Medaglia d'Oro of Italian Pres. 1961, Comune di Venezia prize, Venice Biennale 1956. *Major works:* Monumento a Pinocchio in Collodi 1953–56, Grande Bagnante I (Tate Gallery, London) 1956, Grande Bagnante 3 (Musée National d'Art Moderne, Paris) 1957, Testa di Donna (Pinacoteca Vaticana) 1957, Grande Figura Accoccolata (Museum of Modern Art, Kyoto, Japan) 1961, three bronze doors, Cathedral of Orvieto 1961–64, Monument to Pope John XXIII 1965–67, Self-portrait (Galleria degli Uffizi, Florence) 1982. *Leisure interest:* music. *Address:* Viale Cortina d'Ampezzo 132, Rome, Italy. *Telephone:* 32 841 48.

GREEN, Albert Edward, PH.D., SC.D., F.R.S.; British professor of natural philosophy; m. Gwendoline May Rudston 1939; ed. Jesus Coll., Cambridge; Fellow, Jesus Coll., Cambridge 1936–39; Lecturer in Math., Durham Colls., Univ. of Durham 1939–48; Prof. of Applied Math., Univ. of Newcastle upon Tyne 1948–68; Sedleian Prof. of Natural Philosophy, Univ. of Oxford 1968–77, Emer. 1977–; Fellow, The Queen's Coll., Oxford 1968–77, Supernumerary Fellow 1977–; Hon. D.Sc. (Durham) 1969, (Nat. Univ. of Ireland) 1977; Hon. LL.D. (Glasgow) 1975; Timoshenko Medal, A.S.M.E. 1974; Theodore von Karmen Medal, American Soc. of Civil Engineers 1983. *Address:* 20 Lakeside, Oxford, England.

GREEN, Anthony Eric Sandall, DIP. FINE ART, R.A.; British artist; b. 30 Sept. 1939, Luton; s. of Frederick Sandall and Marie Madeleine (née Dupont) Green; m. Mary Louise Cozens-Walker 1961; two d.; ed. Highgate School, Slade School of Fine Art, Univ. Coll. London; Asst. Art Master, Highgate School 1961–67; Harkness Fellowship U.S.A. 1967–69; held over 35 one-man exhbns.; works in public and private collections worldwide; French Govt. Scholarship, Paris 1960, Exhibit of the Year R.A. Summer Exbhn. 1977. *Publication:* A Green Part of the World (with Martin Bailey) 1984. *Leisure interests:* family, travel. *Address:* 17 Lissenden Mansions, Highgate Road, London, NW5 IPP, England. *Telephone:* 01-485 1226.

GREEN, Rev. Bernard, M.A., B.D.; British ecclesiastic; b. 11 Nov. 1925, Walgrave, Northants.; s. of George Samuel Green and Laura Agnes Annie (née Holliday) Green; m. Joan Viccars 1952; two s. one d.; ed. Wellingborough School, Bristol Univ., Bristol Baptist Coll., St. Catherine's Coll., Oxford and Regent's Park Coll., Oxford; nat. service in coal mines 1944–47; ordained 1952; Minister Yardley Baptist Church, Birmingham 1952–61; Mansfield Road Baptist Church, Nottingham 1961–76, Horfield Baptist Church, Bristol 1976–82; Baptist Chaplain Nottingham Univ. 1961–66; Gen. Sec. Baptist Union of G.B. 1982–; Moderator Free Church Fed. Council 1988–89; frequent broadcaster and mem. religious advisory panels BBC Radio Nottingham and Bristol 1970–82; Chair. Mansfield Road Baptist Housing Assen. 1968–76, Horfield Housing Assen. 1976–82; Dir. Baptist Times Ltd. 1982–, Baptist Holiday Fellowship Ltd. 1982–, Baptist Union Corpn. Ltd. 1982–, Baptist Insurance PLC 1982–, London Baptist Property Bd. 1982–. *Leisure interests:* reading, music, gardening, walking. *Address:* Baptist Union of Great Britain and Ireland, Baptist Church House, 4 Southampton Row, London, WC1B 4AB, England (Office). *Telephone:* 01-405 9803 (Office).

GREEN, Dan, B.A.; American book publishing executive; b. 28 Sept. 1935, Passaic, N.J.; s. of Harold Green and Bessie Roslow; m. Jane Oliphant 1959; two s.; ed. Syracuse Univ., N.Y.; Publicity Dir. Dover Press 1957–58; Station WNAC-TV 1958–59; Bobbs-Merrill Co. 1959–62; Simon & Schuster Inc. 1962–85, Assoc. Publr. 1976–80, Vice-Pres., Publr. 1980–84; Pres. Trade Publishing Group 1984–85; Founder, Publr., Kenan Press 1979–80; C.E.O. Wheatland Corpn. 1985–, Grove Press 1985–; Publr., Weidenfeld & Nicolson 1985–. *Address:* Weidenfeld & Nicolson, 10 East 53rd Street, New York, N.Y. 10022, U.S.A. *Telephone:* (212) 207-6900.

GREEN, The Hon. Sir Guy Stephen Montague, K.B.E., LL.B.; Australian judge; b. 26 July 1937, Launceston, Tasmania; s. of Clement Francis Montague and of the late Beryl Margaret Jenour (née Williams) Green; m.

Rosslyn Marshall 1963; two s. two d.; ed. Launceston Church Grammar School and Univ. of Tasmania; admitted to Bar 1960; Partner Ritchie & Parker Alfred Green & Co. 1963–71; Pres. Tasmanian Bar Assen. 1968–70; Magistrate 1971–73; Chief Justice of Tasmania 1973–; Lieut.-Gov. of Tasmania 1982–; mem. Faculty of Law Tasmania Univ. 1974–85, Chair. Sir Henry Baker Memorial Fellowship Cttee. 1973–; Chair. Council of Law Reporting 1978–85; Chair. Tasmanian Cttee., Duke of Edin.'s Award in Australia 1975–80; Dir. Winston Churchill Memorial Trust 1975–85, Deputy Nat. Chair. 1980–85; Chancellor, Univ. of Tasmania 1985–; Pres. St. John Council 1984–; Deputy Chair. Council Australian Inst. of Judicial Admin. 1986–88; Priory Exec. Officer, Order of St. John in Australia 1984–; Kt. of Grace, Most Venerable Order of the Hosp. of St. John of Jerusalem, Hon. LL.B. *Address:* Chief Justice's Chambers, Supreme Court of Tasmania, Salamanca Place, Hobart, Tasmania 7000, Australia. *Telephone:* 002-303442.

GREEN, Hamilton; Guyanese politician; b. 9 Nov. 1934, Georgetown; s. of Wilfred Amelius Green and Edith Ophelia Dorothy Green; m. Shirley Field-Ridley 1970 (died 1982); four s. three d.; ed. Queen's Coll.; fmrly. Gen. Sec., People's Nat. Congress, Minister of Works, Hydraulics and Supply, of Public Affairs, of Co-operatives and Nat. Mobilization, of Health, Housing and Labour; fmrly. Vice-Pres. with responsibility for Public Welfare, Vice-Pres. with responsibility for Production; Vice-Pres. and Prime Minister of Guyana 1985–. *Publication:* From Pain to Peace—Guyana 1953–1964 (series of lectures at Cyril Potter Coll. of Educ. 1986). *Leisure interest:* reading (history and philosophy), table tennis, boxing and fitness training. *Address:* Office of the Prime Minister, Parliament Buildings, Georgetown (Office); Plot 'D' Lodge, Georgetown, Guyana (Home). *Telephone:* 58821 (Office).

GREEN, Howard, M.D., M.SC.; American scientist and medical school professor; b. 10 Sept. 1925, Toronto, Canada; s. of Benjamin Green and Rose M. Green; m. Rosine Kauffmann; ed. Univ. of Toronto and Northwestern Univ., U.S.A.; Research Asst., Dept. of Physiology, Northwestern Univ. 1948–50; Research Assoc. (Instructor), Dept. of Biochemistry, Univ. of Chicago 1951–53; Instructor, Dept. of Pharmacology, New York Univ. School of Medicine 1954; Capt., M.C., U.S. Army Reserve, Immunology Div., Walter Reed Army Inst. of Research 1955–56; Dept. of Pathology, New York Univ. School of Medicine 1956–68, Prof. and Chair., Dept. of Cell Biology 1968–70; Prof. of Cell Biology, M.I.T. 1970–80; Higgins Prof. of Cellular Physiology and Chair. Dept. of Physiology and Biophysics, Harvard Medical School 1980–86, George Higginson Prof. of Physiology 1986–, Chair. Dept. of Cellular and Molecular Physiology 1988–; Mr and Mrs J. N. Taub Int. Memorial Award for Psoriasis Research 1977; Selman A. Waksman Award in Microbiology 1978; Lewis S. Rosenstiel Award in Basic Medical Research 1980, Lila Gruber Research Award, American Acad. of Dermatology 1980, The Passano Award 1985. *Publications:* numerous articles on cell biology, genetics, growth and differentiation. *Address:* Department of Cellular and Molecular Physiology, Harvard Medical School, 25 Shattuck Street, Boston, Mass. 02360; 82 Williston Road, Brookline, Mass. 02146, U.S.A. (Home).

GREEN, Julian; American novelist; b. 6 Sept. 1900, Paris, France; s. of Edward Moon Green and Mary-Adelaide Hartridge; one s.; ed. Lycée Janson de Sailly and Univ. of Virginia; mem. Acad. Française 1971–, Acad. Royale de Belgique, American Acad., etc.; prizes include Prix Nat. des Lettres (France) 1966, Grand Prix de l'Acad. Française 1970, Harper Prize, Bookman Prize; Grand Prix Littérature de Pologne; Commdr. Légion d'honneur. *Publications:* Complete Works in La Pléiade, vol. I 1972, vols. II and III 1973, vols. IV and V 1974; *novels include:* L'apprenti-psychiâtre 1920, Le voyageur sur la terre 1924, Mont-Cinère 1926, Adrienne Mesurat 1927, Léviathan 1929, L'autre sommeil 1931, Epaves 1932, Le visionnaire 1934, Minuit 1936, Varouna 1940, Si j'étais vous 1947, Moira 1950, Le malfaiteur 1956 (revised 1974), Chaque homme dans sa nuit 1960, L'autre 1971, Le Mauvais Lieu 1978, Histoire de vertige 1983, Les pays lointains 1987; *Journal:* Les années faciles (1928–34), Derniers beaux jours (1935–39), Devant la porte sombre (1940–43), L'oeil de l'ouragan (1943–45), Le revenant (1946–50), Le miroir intérieur (1950–54), Le bel aujourdhui (1955–58), Vers l'invisible (1958–66), Ce qui reste de jour (1967–72), La bouteille à la mer (1972–76), La Terre est si belle (1976–78), La Lumière du monde (1978–81), L'arc-en-ciel (1981–88); Villes: journal de voyage; *autobiographical works:* Partir avant le jour 1963, Mille chemins ouverts 1964, Terre lointaine 1966, Jeunesse 1974; *plays:* Demain n'existe pas 1979, L'Automate 1980, Le Grand Soir 1981, Sud 1953, L'ennemi 1954, L'ombre 1956; *biography:* Frère François 1983; numerous essays. *Address:* Editions de la Pléiade, 5 rue Sebastien-Bottin, 75007 Paris, France.

GREEN, Marshall, B.A., LL.D.; American diplomatist (retd.); b. 27 Jan. 1916, Holyoke, Mass.; s. of Addison Loomis Green and Gertrude Metcalf; m. Lispenard Seabury Crocker 1942; three s.; ed. Groton School, and Yale Univ.; Pvt. Sec. to American Amb. to Japan 1939–41; Lieut. U.S. Navy 1942–45; U.S. Foreign Service 1945–; Third Sec., Wellington, N.Z. 1946–47; Japanese Desk Officer, State Dept., Washington 1947–50; Second, later First Sec., Stockholm 1950–55; Nat. War Coll. 1955–56; Policy Planning Adviser, Far East, State Dept. 1956–59; Minister-Counsellor, Seoul 1959–61; Consul-Gen., Hong Kong 1961–63; Deputy Asst. Sec. of State, Far East 1963–65; Amb. to Indonesia 1965–69; Asst. Sec. of State for E. Asian and Pacific Affairs 1969–73; Amb. to Australia 1973–75; Coordinator of

Population Affairs 1975–79; Chief Del. to UN Population Comm. 1977, 1979; Chair. U.S. Govt. Task Force on Int. Population Issues 1976–; Senior Fellow Nat. Defense Unit. 1979–; Consultant to State Dept. on Refugees and Population 1979–; Dir. Population Crisis Cttee. 1979–, Nat. Cttee. U.S.-China relations 1981–; Pres. Japan-American Soc. of Wash. 1983–; Meritorious Service Award, Nat. Civil Service League Career Service Award, Distinguished Service Award, Order of Rising Sun (Japan). *Leisure interests:* music, travel, conservation, sports. *Address:* 5063 Millwood Lane, Washington, D.C. 20016, U.S.A. *Telephone:* (202) 244-5474.

GREEN, Norman Michael, PH.D., F.R.S.; British biochemist; b. 6 April 1926; s. of Ernest Green and Hilda Margaret Carter; m. Iro Paulina Moschouti 1953; two s. one d.; ed. Dragon School, Oxford, Clifton Coll., Bristol, Magdalen Coll., Oxford, and Univ. Coll. Hosp. Medical School, London; Research Student, Univ. of Wash., Seattle 1951–53; Lecturer in Biochemistry, Univ. of Sheffield 1953–55; Research Fellow and Lecturer in Chem. Pathology, St. Mary's Hosp. Medical School, London 1956–62; Visiting Scientist, N.I.H., Md. 1962–64; Research Staff, Div. of Biochem., Nat. Inst. for Medical Research 1964–. *Publications:* research papers in scientific journals on the structure of proteins and of membranes. *Leisure interests:* mountain climbing, pyrotechnics. *Address:* 57 Hale Lane, Mill Hill, London, NW7 3PS, England.

GREEN, Sir Peter James Frederick, Kt.; British underwriter; b. 28 July 1924, London; s. of J. E. Green and M. B. Holford; m. 1st A. P. Ryan 1950 (died 1985), m. 2nd J. M. Whitehead 1986; no c.; ed. Harrow School and Christ Church, Oxford; Lloyd's underwriter 1947–; mem. Cttee. of Lloyd's 1974–77, 1979–83, Deputy Chair. of Lloyd's 1979–80, Chair. 1980–83; Chair. Janson Green Ltd. 1966–86, Janson Green Holdings Ltd. 1986–; Lloyd's Underwriters' Assen. 1973, Jt. Hull Cttee. 1977; Gold Medal (Lloyds) 1983. *Leisure interests:* shooting, fishing, sailing, and working. *Address:* Janson Green, 10 Crescent, Minories, London E.C.3, England. *Telephone:* 01-480 6440.

GREEN, Roger Curtis, PH.D., F.R.S.N.Z.; American/New Zealand professor of prehistory; b. 15 March 1932, Ridgewood, N.J.; s. of Robert J. Green and Eleanor Richards; m. 1st Kaye Chandler Smith 1959, m. 2nd Valerie J. Sallen 1984; two c.; ed. Univ. of New Mexico and Harvard Univ.; Research Assoc. American Museum of Natural History 1959; Sr. Lecturer in Prehistory, Univ. of Auckland 1961–66, Assoc. Prof. 1966–67, Prof. in Prehistory 1973–, Head, Dept. of Anthropology 1980–84; Anthropologist, B.P. Bishop Museum 1967–73, Research Assoc. 1973–; Assoc. Prof. in Anthropology, Univ. of Hawaii 1967–70, James Cook Visiting Prof. 1981–82; mem. U.S. Nat. Acad. of Sciences and numerous other learned socs.; Fulbright Scholar 1958–59; Elsdon Best Medal, Polynesian Soc. 1973; Maharaia Winiata Memorial Prize 1974. *Publications:* numerous articles in historical, anthropological, archaeological journals etc. *Leisure interests:* music, travel, walking. *Address:* Department of Anthropology, University of Auckland, Private Bag, Auckland; P.O. Box 60-054 Titirangi, Auckland 7, New Zealand. *Telephone:* 737-999 (Ext. 8567); 817-7608.

GREENAWAY, Peter; British film director; b. 1942; trained as painter and first exhibited pictures at Lord's Gallery 1964; film ed. Cen. Office of Information 1965–76; began making own films in 1966. *Films include:* Train, Tree 1966, Revolution, Five Postcards from Capital Cities 1967, Intervals 1969, Erosion 1971, H is for House 1973, Windows, Water, Water Wrackets 1975, Goole by Numbers 1976, Dear Phone 1977, 1-1CO, A Walk Through H, Vertical Features Remake 1978, The Falls 1980, Act of God, Zandra Rhodes 1981, The Draughtsman's Contract 1982, Four American Composers 1983, Making a Splash, A TV Dante-Canto 5 1984, Inside Rooms-The Bathroom, 1985, A Zed & Two Noughts 1985, Belly of An Architect 1986, Drowning by Numbers 1988, The Cook, the Thief, his Wife and her Lover 1989.

GREENBERG, Bernard, PH.D.; American professor of biological sciences; b. 24 April 1922, New York; s. of Isidore Greenberg and Rose Gordon; m. Barbara Muriel Dickler 1949; two s. two d.; ed. Brooklyn Coll. and Univ. of Kansas; Prof. of Biological Sciences, Univ. of Ill. at Chicago 1966–; Visiting Scientist, Istituto Superiore di Sanità, Rome, Italy 1960–61, 1967–68, Instituto de Salubridad y Enfermedades Tropicales 1962, 1963; Fulbright-Hays Sr. Research Scholar, Rome 1967–68; Consultant and Expert Witness in Forensic Entomology; Scientific Gov. Chicago Acad. of Sciences; Fellow A.A.A.S.; numerous research grants and contracts from Nat. Science Foundation, Nat. Insts. of Health and other bodies. *Publications:* over 90 scientific publs. including Flies and Disease (2 vols.) 1971, 1973. *Leisure interests:* antiquities, art, archaeology and travel. *Address:* 1463 East 55th Place, Chicago, Ill. 60637, U.S.A. *Telephone:* (312) 996-3103 (Univ.); (312) 667-5380 (Home).

GREENBERG, Joseph Harold, PH.D.; American professor of anthropology; b. 28 May 1915, Brooklyn, N.Y.; s. of Jacob Greenberg and Florence Pilzer Greenberg; m. Selma Berkowitz 1940; ed. Columbia Coll. and Northwestern Univ.; Army service in Signal Intelligence Corps 1940–45; Instructor and Asst. Prof. of Anthropology, Univ. of Minn. 1946–48; Asst., Assoc., then Prof., Columbia Univ. 1948–62; Dir. West African Languages Survey 1959–66; Prof. of Anthropology, Stanford Univ. 1962–, Ray Lyman Wilbur Distinguished Prof. of Social Sciences 1971; First Distinguished Lecturer, American Anthropological Assen. 1970; mem. N.A.S., American Acad. of Arts and Sciences 1972–, American Philosophical Soc. 1975; Pres. Linguistic Soc. of America 1977; Guggenheim Fellow 1955, 1982; Fellow Stanford Humanities Center 1982; Hon. D.Sc. (Northwestern Univ.) 1982; Haile Sellassie I Prize for African Research 1967, N.Y. Acad. of Sciences Award for Behavioral Sciences 1980. *Publications:* The Languages of Africa 1963, Universals of Language (Ed.) 1963, Anthropological Linguistics: An Introduction 1968, Language Universals—A Research Frontier (in Science) 1969, The Indo-Pacific Hypothesis (in Current Trends in Linguistics Vol. 8, Ed. Thomas Sebeok) 1970, Language, Culture and Communication 1971, New Invitation to Linguistics 1977, Universals of Human Language (4 vols.) 1978, Language in the Americas 1987. *Leisure interest:* playing the piano. *Address:* Stanford University, Stanford, Calif. 94305 (Office); 860 Mayfield Street, Stanford, Calif. 94305, U.S.A. (Home).

GREENBOROUGH, Sir John Hedley, K.B.E., C.B.I.M., F.INST.PET.; British oil executive; b. 7 July 1922, Kingston-upon-Thames; s. of William and Elizabeth Marie Greenborough (née Wilson); m. Gerta Ebel 1951; one s.; ed. Wandsworth School and U.S. Navy, Pensacola, Florida, U.S.A.; joined Asiatic Petroleum Co., London 1939; with Shell Oil Calif., U.S.A. 1946–47; with Shell Brazil 1947–57; Exec. Vice-Pres. Shell Argentina 1960–66; Far East Area Coordinator, Shell Int., London 1966–69; Man. Dir. of Marketing, Shell-Mex and B.P. Ltd. 1969–71, Chief Exec., Man. Dir. 1971–75; Deputy Chair. Shell U.K. Ltd. 1976–80, Man. Dir. 1976–78; Vice-Chair. British Chamber of Commerce, Argentina 1962–66, British Road Fed. 1969–75; Chair. U.K. Oil Pipelines Ltd. 1971–77, U.K. Oil Industry Emergency Cttee. 1971–78, U.K. Petroleum Industry Advisory Cttee. 1971–77; Non-Exec. Dir. Bowater Industries PLC 1979–, Deputy Chair. (non-exec.) 1984–88; Gov. Ashridge Man. Coll. 1972–, Chair. Govs. 1977–; mem. CBI Council 1972–, Deputy Pres. 1977, Pres. of CBI 1978–80, mem. Finance and Gen. Purposes Cttee. 1982–, Chair. 1984–; Pres. Inst. of Petroleum 1976–78, Inc. Soc. of British Advertisers 1976–78; mem NEDC July 1977–80; Chair. Newarthill PLC (Sir Robert McAlpine Group) 1980–; Dir. Lloyds Bank PLC 1980– (Deputy Chair. 1985–), Hogg-Robinson & Gardner Mountain PLC 1980–, Laporte Industries (Holdings) PLC 1983–86; Pres. Nat. Council for Voluntary Orgs. 1980–86; Vice-Pres. Inst. of Marketing 1980–; Chair. Nursing Staff, Midwives, Health Visitors and Professions Allied to Medicine Pay Review Body 1983–86; Pres. Strategic Planning Soc. 1986–; Hon. LL.D. (Birmingham) 1983; Liveryman Co. of Distillers 1975; Freeman City of London. *Leisure interests:* golf, travel, music. *Address:* 40 Bernard Street, London, WC1N 1LG (Office); 30 Burghley House, Oakfield, Somerset Road, Wimbledon Common, London, SW19 5JB, England (Home). *Telephone:* 01-837 3377 (Office).

GREENE, Graham, O.M., C.H.; British writer; b. 2 Oct. 1904; ed. Berkhamsted School and Balliol Coll., Oxford; Sub-Ed. The Times 1926–30; Lit. Ed. Spectator 1940–41; Foreign Office 1941–44; Dir. Eyre and Spottiswoode (Publishers) Ltd. 1944–48; Dir. of The Bodley Head 1958–68; mem. Panamanian del. to Washington, D.C. for signing of Canal Treaty 1977; Hon. Litt.D. (Cambridge) 1962, (Oxford) 1979, Hon. D.Litt. (Edinburgh) 1967, Dr. h.c. (Moscow State Univ.) 1988; Hon. Fellow, Balliol Coll., Oxford 1963; Chevalier Légion d'honneur 1969, Grand Cross Order of Vasco Núñez de Balboa (Panama) 1983; Hon. Citizen Anacapri 1978; Shakespeare Prize (Hamburg) 1968, Dos Passos Prize 1980; Jerusalem Prize 1981; C.Lit. 1984; Commdr. des Arts et des Lettres 1984, Ruben Dario Cultural Independence Order. *Publications:* Babbling April 1925, The Man Within 1929, The Name of Action 1930, Rumour at Nightfall 1931, Stamboul Train 1932, It's a Battlefield 1934, England Made Me 1935, Journey without Maps, A Gun for Sale 1936, Brighton Rock 1938, The Lawless Roads, 1939, The Confidential Agent 1939, The Power and the Glory 1940 (Hawthornden Prize), British Dramatists 1942, The Ministry of Fear 1943, Nineteen Stories 1947, The Heart of the Matter 1948, The Lost Childhood and Other Essays 1951, The End of the Affair 1951, Essais Catholiques 1953, Twenty-one Stories 1954, Loser Takes All 1955, The Quiet American 1955, Our Man in Havana 1958, A Burnt-Out Case 1961, In Search of a Character: Two African Journals 1961, A Sense of Reality 1963, The Comedians 1966, May We Borrow Your Husband? And Other Comedies of the Sexual Life (short stories) 1967, Collected Essays 1969, Travels with my Aunt 1969, A Sort of Life (autobiography) 1971, The Honorary Consul 1973, Lord Rochester's Monkey (biography) 1974, The Human Factor 1978, Dr. Fischer of Geneva or The Bomb Party 1980, Ways of Escape (autobiog.) 1980, J'Accuse 1982, Monsignor Quixote 1982, Getting to know the Generals 1984, The Tenth Man 1985, The Captain and the Enemy 1988. *Plays:* The Living Room 1953, The Potting Shed 1957, The Complaisant Lover 1959, Carving a Statue 1964, The Return of A. J. Raffles 1975, For Whom the Bell Chimes 1980, Yes & No 1980. *Screenplays:* Brighton Rock 1948, The Fallen Idol 1948, The Third Man 1949, Our Man in Havana 1960, The Comedians 1967. *Children's Books:* The Little Train 1947, The Little Fire Engine 1950, The Little Horse Bus 1952, The Little Steamroller 1953. *Address:* c/o Reinhardt Books Ltd., 27 Wright's Lane, London, W8 5T2, England.

GREENE, Graham Carleton, C.B.E., M.A.; British publisher; b. 10 June 1936, Berlin, Germany; s. of Sir Hugh Carleton Greene and Helga Mary Connolly; m. 1st Judith Margaret Gordon-Walker 1957 (divorced), 2nd Sally Georgina Horton 1976; one s.; ed. Eton and Univ. Coll., Oxford; Dir. Jonathan Cape Ltd. 1962–, Man. Dir. 1966–68; Dir. Chatto, Virago, Bodley Head and Cape Ltd. 1969–88, Jt. Chair. 1970–87; Dir. Book Reps (N.Z.)

Ltd. 1971–88, CVBC Services 1972–88, Australasian Publishing Co. Ltd. (Chair. 1978–) 1969–88, Guinness Peat Group 1973–88, Triad Paperbacks 1975–88, Greene, King and Sons PLC 1979–, Statesman and Nation Publishing Co. (Chair. 1981–85) 1980–85, Statesman Publishing Co. Ltd. (Chair. 1981–85) 1980–85, Random House Inc. 1987–88; Chair. Random House UK Ltd. 1988–, British Museum Publs. Ltd. 1988–; Chair. Nation Pty. Co. Ltd. 1981–86, New Society 1984–86; mem. Bd. of British Council 1977–, mem. Council of Publishers Assen. (Pres. 1977–79) 1969–, Trustee, British Museum 1978–, Int. Cttee. of Int. Publishers Assen. 1977–, Groupe des Editeurs de Livres de la CEE (Pres. 1984–86) 1977–86; Chevalier, Ordre des Arts et des Lettres. *Address:* 11 Lord North Street, Westminster, London, SW1P 3LA, England.

GREENE, Jack Phillip, PH.D.; American professor of history; b. 12 Aug. 1931, Lafayette, Ind.; s. of Ralph B. Greene and Nellie A. (Miller) Greene; m. Sue L. Neuenswander 1953; one s. one d.; ed. Univ. of N.C., Indiana Univ. and Duke Univ., Durham, N.C.; History Instructor Mich. State Univ., E. Lansing 1956–59; Asst. Prof. of History Western Reserve Univ., Cleveland, Ohio 1959–62, Assoc. Prof. 1962–65; Visiting Assoc. Prof. and Visiting Ed. William and Mary Quarterly Coll. of William and Mary in Va., Williamsburg 1961–62; Assoc. Prof. of History Univ. of Mich., Ann Arbor 1965–66; Visiting Assoc. Prof. of History Johns Hopkins Univ., Baltimore, Md. 1964–65, Prof. 1966–75, Chair. Dept. of History 1970–72, Andrew W. Mellon Prof. in Humanities 1975–; Harmsworth Prof. of American History Oxford Univ. 1975–76; Visiting Prof. Hebrew Univ. of Jerusalem 1979, Ecole des Hautes Etudes en Science Sociale 1986–87; mem. Inst. for Advanced Study 1977–81, 1985–86; Fellow, Woodrow Wilson Int. Center for Scholars 1974–75, Center for Advanced Study in Behavioural Sciences 1979–80, Churchill Coll., Cambridge 1986–, Nat. Humanities Center 1977–78, Guggenheim Fellow 1964–65. *Publications:* ten books, including Quest for Power 1963, Diary of Colonel Landon Carter of Sabine Hall (2 vols.) 1965, Settlements to Society 1966, Colonies to Nation 1967, Reinterpretation of American Revolution 1968, All Men are Created Equal 1976, Colonial British America 1983, Encyclopedia of American Political History 1984, Peripheries and Center 1986, Political Life in Eighteenth Century Virginia 1986, Intellectual Heritage of the Constitutional Era 1986, Magna Carta for America 1986, American Revolution 1987, Pursuits of Happiness 1988, Selling the New World 1988. *Leisure interest:* travel. *Address:* Department of History, The Johns Hopkins University, Baltimore, Md., U.S.A. *Telephone:* (301) 338 7596.

GREENE OF HARROW WEALD, Baron (Life Peer), cr. 1974, of Harrow in Greater London; **Sidney Francis Greene,** Kt., C.B.E.; British trade unionist; b. 12 Feb. 1910, London; s. of Frank J. Greene and Alice Kerrod; m. Masel E. Carter 1936; three d.; ed. in London; Gen. Sec. Nat. Union of Railwaymen 1957–74; mem. Gen. Council, TUC 1957–75, Chair 1969–70; Chair. TUC Econ. Cttee. 1968–75; mem. N.E.D.C. 1962–75; mem. Advisory Council, Export Credits Guarantee Dept. 1967–70; Dir. Bank of England 1970–78, Times Newspapers Holdings Ltd. (fmrly. Times Newspapers Ltd.) 1974–82, Rio Tinto Zinc Corpn. 1975–80, Nat. Freight Corpn. 1973–77, Southern Electricity Bd. 1964–77, Industry and Parl. Trust Ltd. 1977, Trades Union Unit Trust 1970–80. *Leisure interests:* cricket, gardening. *Address:* 26 Kynaston Wood, Boxtree Road, Harrow Weald, Middx., HA3 6UA, England.

GREENEWALT, Crawford Hallock, B.S.; American executive; b. 16 Aug. 1902, Cumington, Mass.; s. of Frank Lindsay and Mary Hallock Greenewalt; m. Margaretta Lammot du Pont 1926; two s. one d.; ed. William Penn Charter School, Philadelphia and Massachusetts Inst. of Tech.; joined E. I. du Pont de Nemours and Co. 1922; Pres. du Pont de Nemours 1948–62, Chair. of Bd. 1962–67, Chair. of Finance Cttee. 1967–74; Dir. Morgan Guaranty Trust Co. 1963–72, Boeing Co. 1964–74; Fellow, American Acad. of Arts and Sciences; mem. N.A.S., American Philosophical Soc., M.I.T. Corpn.; Trustee Emer., Carnegie Inst. Wash., D.C.; Regent, Smithsonian Inst. 1956–74, Regent Emer. 1974–; many hon. degrees; Chemical Industry Award 1952, William Proctor Prize (A.A.A.S.) 1957, Medal for Advancement of Research (American Soc. of Metals) 1958. *Publications:* The Uncommon Man 1959, Hummingbirds 1960, Bird Song: Acoustics and Physiology 1969. *Address:* Greenville, nr. Wilmington, Del. 19807, U.S.A. (Home).

GREENFIELD, James Lloyd; American newspaper executive; b. 16 July 1924, Cleveland; m. Margaret Ann Schwertley; ed. Harvard Univ.; Cleveland Press 1939–41; Voice of America 1949–50; Corresp. for Time Magazine, Korea and Japan 1951–55, Bureau Chief, New Delhi 1956–57, Deputy Bureau Chief, London 1958–61; Chief Diplomatic Corresp. Time-Life, Wash., D.C. 1961–62; Deputy Asst. Sec. of State, Public Affairs 1962–64; Asst. Sec. of State, Public Affairs 1964–66; Asst. Vice-Pres. Continental Air Lines, L.A., Vice-Pres. Westinghouse Broadcasting Co. 1968–69; Foreign Ed. New York Times 1969–77, Asst. Man. Ed. 1977–. *Address:* 850 Park Ave., New York, N.Y. 10021, U.S.A. (Home).

GREENFIELD, Julius Macdonald, C.M.G., Q.C., LL.B., B.C.L.; British (Rhodesian) retd. lawyer and politician; b. 13 July 1907, Boksburg, Transvaal, S. Africa; s. of Rev. C. E. and Mrs. Greenfield; m. Florence M. Couper 1935; two s. one d. (deceased); ed. Milton School, Bulawayo, and Univs. of Cape Town and Oxford; Rhodesian Rhodes Scholar 1929; admitted to practise as advocate of High Court of S. Rhodesia 1933, practised at Bulawayo till

1950; elected to S. Rhodesia Parl. (United Party) 1948; Minister of Justice and Internal Affairs 1950–53; elected to Parl. of Fed. of Rhodesia and Nyasaland (Fed. Party) 1953; Minister of Home Affairs and Educ. 1953–55; Minister of Educ. and Law 1955–58; Minister of Law 1958–62, of Law and Home Affairs 1962–63; returned to law practice 1964; Puisne Judge of High Court of Rhodesia 1968–74. *Publications:* Instant Crime 1976, Testimony of a Rhodesian Federal 1978. *Leisure interest:* politics of southern Africa. *Address:* 17 Alder Way, West Cross, Swansea, SA3 5PD, Wales. *Telephone:* 403585.

GREENHILL OF HARROW, Baron (Life Peer), cr. 1974, of the Royal Borough of Kensington and Chelsea; **Denis Arthur Greenhill,** G.C.M.G., O.B.E.; British diplomatist; b. 7 Nov. 1913, Woodford, Essex; s. of James and Susie Greenhill; m. Angela McCulloch 1941; two s.; ed. Bishop's Stortford Coll. and Christ Church, Oxford; served in Second World War in Egypt, N. Africa, Italy, India and S.E. Asia, demobilized with rank of Col.; in British Foreign Service 1946–73, in Sofia 1947–49, Washington, D.C. 1949–52; at Foreign Office 1952–54; at Imperial Defence Coll. 1954; U.K. Del. to NATO, Paris 1955–57, to Singapore 1957–59; Counsellor, Washington, D.C. 1959–62, Minister 1962–64; Asst. Under-Sec. of State, Foreign Office 1964–66; Deputy Under-Sec. of State 1966–69; Perm. Under-Sec. of State for Foreign and Commonwealth Affairs 1969–73; Gov. BBC 1973–78; led British mission to Rhodesia Feb. 1976; Dir. S. G. Warburg and Co. 1974–, Clerical, Medical and Gen. Assurance, Wellcome Foundation 1974–85, BAT Industries Ltd. 1974–83, Hawker Siddeley Group 1974–84, British Petroleum 1973–78, BL Int. 1977–82; Gov. BUPA 1978–83, S.O.A.S. 1978–85; Chair. King's Coll. Hosp. Medical School 1977–83; Trustee Rayne Foundation; mem. Security Comm. 1977–82, Int. Advisory Cttee., First Nat. Bank of Chicago 1976–81; Fellow King's Coll., London 1984–; Grand Cross Lion of Finland 1984. *Address:* 33 King William Street, London, EC4R 9AS (Office); 25 Hamilton House, Vicarage Gate, London, W.8, England (Home). *Telephone:* 01-280 2222 (Office), 01-937 8362 (Home).

GREENSPAN, Alan, M.A., PH.D.; American economist; b. 6 March 1926, N.Y.; s. of Herbert Greenspan and Rose Goldsmith; ed. New York and Columbia Univs.; Pres., Townsend-Greenspan & Co. Inc., econ. consultants 1954–74, 1977–; mem. Nixon for Pres. Cttee. 1968–69; mem. Task Force for Econ. Growth 1969, Comm. on an All-Volunteer Armed Force 1969–70, Comm. on Financial Structure and Regulation 1970–71; Consultant to Council of Econ. Advisers 1970–74, to U.S. Treasury 1971–74, to Fed. Reserve Bd. 1971–74; Chair. Council of Econ. Advisers 1974–76, Nat. Comm. on Social Security Reform 1982–83; Chair. Fed. Reserve Bd. of Govs. 1987–; Dir. Council on Foreign Relations; mem. Sec. of Commerce's Econ. Comm.'s Cen. Market System Cttee. 1972, G.N.P. Review Cttee. of Office of Man. and Budget, Time Magazine's Bd. of Economists 1971–74, 1977–, President's Econ. Policy Advisory Bd. 1981–89, President's Foreign Intelligence Advisory Bd. 1982–89, Exec. Cttee. Trilateral Comm.; Sr. Adviser Brookings Inst. Panel on Econ. Activity 1970–74, 1977–; Adjunct Prof. Graduate School of Business Man., New York 1977–87; Past Pres., Fellow, Nat. Assen. of Business Economists; Dir. Trans World Financial Co. 1962–74, Dreyfus Fund 1970–74, Gen. Cable Corpn. 1973–74, 1977–78, Sun Chemical Corpn. 1973–74, Gen. Foods Corpn. 1977–, J. P. Morgan & Co. 1977–, Mobil Corpn. 1977–, Aluminium Co. of America (ALCOA) 1978–; Jefferson Award 1976; William Butler Memorial Award 1977. *Leisure interest:* golf. *Address:* 120 Wall Street, New York, N.Y. 10005, U.S.A.

GREENSTEIN, Jesse Leonard, PH.D.; American astronomer; b. 15 Oct. 1909, New York; s. of Maurice Greenstein and L. Feingold; m. Naomi Kitay 1934; two s.; ed. Horace Mann School for Boys and Harvard; engaged in real estate and investments 1930–34; Nat. Research Fellow 1937–39; Assoc. Prof., Yerkes Observatory, Univ. of Chicago 1939–48; Research Assoc. McDonald Observatory, Univ. of Tex. 1939–48; Mil. Researcher under Office of Scientific Research and Devt. (optical design), Yerkes 1942–45; Prof. and Exec. Officer for Astronomy 1948–72, Calif. Inst. of Tech.; Lee A. DuBridge Prof. 1970–80, Prof. Emer. 1980–; staff mem. Mount Wilson and Palomar Observatories 1948–80, Palomar Observatory 1980–; mem. Owens Valley Radio Observatory staff; Chair. Faculty of Inst. 1965–67; Visiting Prof. Inst. for Advanced Studies, Princeton 1964 and 1968–69, Princeton Univ., Univ. of Hawaii, Nordisk Inst. for Teoretisk Atomfysik, Copenhagen, Bohr Inst., Univ. of Delaware; mem. N.A.S., American Acad. Achievement, American Philosophical Soc., Int. Astronomical Union, Bd. of Overseers, Harvard Coll. 1965–71, Bd. of Trustees, Pacific Asia Museum, Editorial Bd. Astrophysical Letters, Astrophysical Journal; Chair. Bd. Assoc. Univs. Research in Astronomy 1974–77; Consultant to Nat. Science Foundation, Nat. Aeronautics and Space Admin.; Chair. N.A.S. Survey of Astronomy; Astronomy for the '70s; Russell Lecturer, American Astronomical Soc.; Hon. D.Sc. (Arizona) 1987; Calif. Scientist of Year Award 1964; Bruce Medal, Astronomical Soc. of Pacific; Distinguished Public Service Medal of NASA; Gold Medal, Royal Astronomical Soc. *Publications:* Stellar Atmospheres (Editor), 400 technical papers. *Leisure interests:* Japanese art, travel, wine. *Address:* California Institute of Technology, Pasadena, California, U.S.A. *Telephone:* 818-356-4006.

GREENWALD, Gerald, M.A.; American business executive; b. 11 Sept. 1935, St. Louis, Mo.; s. of Frank and Bertha Greenwald; m. Glenda Lee Gerstein 1958; three s. one d.; ed. Princeton Univ., Wayne State Univ.,

Detroit; U.S.A.F. 1957-60; with Ford Motor Co. 1957-79, Pres. Ford Venezuela, Dir. Non-Automative Operations, Europe; Vice-Chair. Chrysler Corpn., Highland Park, Mich. 1979-85; Chair. Chrysler Motors 1985-. *Address:* Chrysler Corporation, Chrysler Center, Detroit, Mich. 48288, U.S.A.

GREENWALT, Tibor Jack, M.D.; American medical director; b. 23 Jan. 1914, Budapest, Hungary; s. of late Bela Greenwalt and Irene Greenwalt; m. 1st Margaret Hirschfeld (died 1948), 2nd Shirley Johnson (died 1970), 3rd Pia Glas 1971; one s.; ed. Washington Square Coll. and New York Univ.; various hosp. appointments 1937-41; Maj., U.S. Army Medical Corps. 1942-46; Asst. Chief of Medicine, Station Hosp., Ft. Leavenworth, Kan. 1942-46; Chief of Lab. Services, 181st Gen. Hospital, Karachi 1944-46; Medical Dir. Milwaukee Blood Center 1947-66; Medical Dir. (Dir. 1976), Blood Program, American Nat. Red Cross 1967-78; Dir. Hoxworth Blood Center 1979-87; Prof. of Medicine, Univ. of Cinn. Medical Center 1979-87, Deputy Dir. for Research 1987-; Emer. Prof. of Medicine and Pathology 1987-; Sr. mem. Inst. of Medicine. *Publications:* several books and numerous articles in scientific journals. *Leisure interests:* literature, music, Mesopotamian Archaeology. *Address:* Hoxworth Blood Center, 3231 Burnet Avenue, Cincinnati, Ohio 45267 (Office); 328 Compton Hills Drive, Cincinnati, Ohio 45215, U.S.A. (Home). *Telephone:* 513-569-1337 (Office); 513-521-1659 (Home).

GREENWOOD, Allen Harold Claude, C.B.E., J.P.; British business executive; b. 4 June 1917, London; ed. Cheltenham Coll. and Coll. of Aeronautical Engineering; joined Vickers-Armstrongs Ltd. 1939; R.N.V.R. (Fleet Air Arm) 1942-46; Service Man., Vickers-Armstrongs (Aircraft) Ltd. 1953, Dir. 1960; Sales and Service Man., British Aircraft Corpn. Ltd. 1961, Deputy Chair. 1972-75, Chair. 1976-77; Deputy Chair. British Aerospace 1977-83; one of Airframe Dirs. for Concorde 1961; Dir. British Aircraft Corpn. (Operating) Ltd. 1964, British Aircraft Corpn. (U.S.A.) Inc. 1964 (Chair. 1976-), SEPECAT S.A. 1966, Panavia Aircraft G.m.b.H. 1969-81 (Chair. 1969-72), British Aerospace Australia Ltd. 1972, REMPLOY Ltd. 1968-79 (Chair. 1976-79); Europlane Ltd. 1973, Industrial Advisers to the Blind 1974; Pres. Soc. of British Aerospace Cos. Ltd. 1970-72, Deputy Pres. 1981-82, Asscn. Européenne des Constructeurs de Matériel Aérospatiel 1974; Deputy Chair. Eng. Employers' Asscn. 1982. *Address:* 2 Rookcliff, Park Lane, Milford-on-Sea, Hants., England. *Telephone:* (0590) 42893.

GREENWOOD, Norman Neill, PH.D., D.SC., SC.D., C.CHEM., F.R.I.C., F.R.S.; British professor of inorganic and structural chemistry; b. 19 Jan. 1925, Melbourne, Australia; s. of late Prof. J. Neill Greenwood and late Gladys Uhland; m. Kirsten M. Rydland; three d.; ed. Univs. of Melbourne and Cambridge; Resident Tutor and Lecturer, Trinity Coll., Univ. of Melbourne 1946-49; Sr. Harwell Research Fellow, A.E.R.E. 1951-53; Lecturer, then Sr. Lecturer in Inorganic Chem. Univ. of Nottingham 1953-61; Prof. and Head, Dept. of Inorganic Chem. Univ. of Newcastle-upon-Tyne 1961-71; Prof. and Head, Dept. of Inorganic and Structural Chem. Univ. of Leeds 1971-; Visiting Prof. at univs. in Australia, U.S.A., Canada and Denmark since 1966; Tilden Lectureship and Medal (Chem. Soc.) 1966; R.S.C. Medal for Main Group. Element Chem. 1974; Gold Medal of City of Nancy (France) 1977; D. de l'Univ. h.c. (Nancy) 1977, A. W. von Hofmann Lectureship (Gesellshaft Deutscher Chemiker) 1983; Liversidge Lectureship and Medal (R.S.C.) 1984; and other awards and distinctions. *Publications:* several books and some 400 original research papers in journals. *Leisure interests:* music, skiing. *Address:* School of Chemistry, University of Leeds, Leeds, LS2 9JT, England. *Telephone:* 0532 33640.

GREER, David Steven, M.D.; American specialist; b. 12 Oct. 1925, Brooklyn, New York; s. of Jacob Greer and Mary (Zaslawsky) Greer; m. Marion Clarich 1950; one s. one d.; ed. Univs. of Notre Dame and Chicago; Intern, Yale-New Haven Medical Center 1953-54; Resident in Medicine, Univ. of Chicago Clinics 1954-57; specialist in internal medicine, Fall River, Mass. 1957-74; Chief of Staff, Dept. of Medicine, Fall River Gen. Hosp. 1959-62; Medical Dir. Earle E. Hussey Hosp., Fall River 1962-72; Chief of Staff, Dept. of Medicine, Truesdale Clinic and Truesdale Hosp., Fall River 1971-74; Faculty mem. Tufts Univ. Coll. of Medicine, Boston, Mass. 1969-78; Faculty mem. Brown Univ. Program in Medicine 1973-, Dean 1981-; mem. N.A.S. Inst. of Medicine; various public appts.; Cutting Foundation Medal for Service to Religion and Medicine 1976 and other awards. *Publications:* numerous articles on chronic disease, geriatrics, long-term care and health-care evaluation. *Leisure interest:* squash. *Address:* Brown University Program in Medicine, Box G, Providence, R.I. 02912, U.S.A. *Telephone:* (401) 863-3330.

GREER, Germaine, PH.D.; Australian feminist and author; b. 29 Jan. 1939, Melbourne; d. of Eric Reginald and Margaret May (Lafrank) Greer; ed. Melbourne and Sydney Univs. and Cambridge Univ., England; Lecturer in English, Warwick Univ. 1968-73; Instructor in Poetry and Dir. Cen. for Study of Women's Literature, Univ. of Tulsa 1979-82; numerous television appearances and public talks including discussion with Norman Mailer (q.v.) in The Theatre of Ideas, New York. *Publications:* The Female Eunuch 1970, The Obstacle Race 1979, Sex and Destiny: The Politics of Human Fertility 1984, Shakespeare 1985, The Madwoman's Underclothes 1986, Fortune's Maggot 1987, Kissing the Rod: An Anthology of 17th Century Verse 1988, Daddy, We Hardly Knew You (autobiog.) 1989; articles for Listener, Spectator, Esquire, Harper's Magazine, Playboy,

Private Eye and other journals. *Leisure interest:* gardening. *Address:* c/o Aitken and Stone, 29 Fernshaw Road, London, SW10 0TG, England.

GREET, Rev. Dr. Kenneth Gerald; British minister of religion; b. 17 Nov. 1918, Bristol; s. of Walter and Renée Greet; m. Mary Eileen Edbrooke 1947; one s. two d.; ed. Cotham Grammar School, Bristol, Handsworth Coll., Birmingham; Cwm and Kingstone Methodist Church 1940-42; Ogmore Vale Methodist Church 1942-45; Tonypandy Cen. Hall 1947-54; Sec. Dept. of Christian Citizenship of Methodist Church and Social Responsibility Div. 1954-71; Sec., Methodist Conf. 1971-84, Pres. 1980-81; mem. British Council of Churches 1955-84 (Chair. Exec. 1977-80), World Methodist Council 1957- (Chair. Exec. Cttee. 1976-81); Chair. Exec. Temperance Council of Christian Churches 1961-71; Moderator, Free Church Fed. Council 1982-83; Co-Chair. World Disarmament Campaign 1982-86, Vice-Pres. 1986-; Rep. to Cen. Cttee., WCC, Addis Ababa 1971, Nairobi 1975; Beckly Lecturer 1962, Willson Lecturer, Kansas City 1966, Cato Lecturer, Sydney 1975; Chair. of Govs., Southlands Coll. 1986-; Hon. D.D. (Ohio, U.S.A.). *Publications:* The Mutual Society 1962, Man and Wife Together 1962, Large Petitions 1962, Guide to Loving 1965, The Debate About Drink 1969, The Sunday Question 1969, The Art of Moral Judgement 1970, When the Spirit Moves 1975, A Lion from a Thicket 1978, The Big Sin: Christianity and the Arms Race 1982, Under the Rainbow Arch 1984, What Shall I Cry 1986. *Leisure interests:* tennis, photography. *Address:* 89 Broadmark Lane, Rustington, Sussex, BN16 2JA, England.

GREEVY, Bernadette; Irish mezzo-soprano concert singer; b. Dublin; d. of Patrick J. Greevy and Josephine F. Miller; m. Peter A. Tattan 1965 (died 1983); one s.; ed. Convent of the Holy Faith, Clontarf, Dublin; London début, Wigmore Hall 1964; has since appeared on maj. concert platforms in Europe, U.S.A., Canada and Far East; recordings of works by Brahms, Handel, Haydn, Bach, Berlioz, Britten, Elgar and Mahler; Harriet Cohen Int. Music Award; Order of Merit (Order of Malta); Dame of the Holy Sepulchre; Pro Ecclesia et Pontifice (Vatican). *Leisure interests:* gardening, cooking, painting. *Address:* Melrose, 672 Howth Road, Dublin 5, Ireland.

GREGG, Judd, J.D., LL.M.; American politician; b. 14 Feb. 1947, Nashua, N.H.; m. Kathleen MacLellan 1973; one s. one d.; ed. Columbia and Boston Univs.; admitted N.H. Bar 1972; law practice, Nashua, N.H.; mem. 97th-100th Congresses from 2nd N.H. Dist. 1981-89; mem. N.H. Gov.'s Exec. Council 1978-80; Gov. of New Hampshire 1989-; Republican. *Address:* Office of the Governor, State Capitol, Concord, N.H., U.S.A.

GRÉGOIRE, Henri; Belgian classical and Byzantine scholar; Prof. of Greek and Byzantine History, Brussels Univ.; Sather Prof. Univ. of Calif. 1938; Co-Founder Ecole Libre des Hautes Etudes N.Y.; Vice-Dean Faculty of Letters 1941-45, Pres. 1944; Asst. Prof. of History, New School for Social Research, N.Y.; Pres. Asscn. Int. des Byzantinistes; Ed. Byzantion, Corpus Bruxellense Historiae Byzantine, La Nouvelle Clio, Ta Kyprin; Co-Founder and Jt. Ed. of Le Flambeau 1918-; Renaissance 1942-; Pres. Centre Nat. de Recherches Byzantines, and Ed. of its publs.; assoc. mem. Acad. des Inscriptions et Belles Lettres, Paris, and Accad. Nazionale dei Lincei, Rome; mem. Brussels, Bucharest, Copenhagen, Mainz, Munich and Palermo Acads., Medieval Acad. of America, Slav Insts. of Prague and of Belgrade; Chair. Acad. of Mythological and Religious Research, Bulgarian Historical Society, Byzantine Insts. of Providence, R.I., Paris and Istanbul, etc.; Dr. h.c. (Paris, Athens, Thessalonika, Algiers, Sofia, Cairo). *Publications:* Digenis Akritas, the Byzantine Epic in History and Poetry (with P. Morphopoulos) 1942, Dans la montagne grecque 1948, Asklepios, Apollon Smintheus et Rudra (with R. Goossens and M. Mathieu), La base historique de l'épopée médiévale 1950, Les Persécutions dans l'Empire romain (with P. Orgels, J. Moreau and A. Maricq) 1951, Euripides Tragédies III-VII, Les perles de la poésie slave 1960.

GRÉGOIRE, H.E. Cardinal Paul; Canadian ecclesiastic; b. 24 Oct. 1911, Montreal; ordained 1937, elected to the titular Church of Curubi 1961, consecrated bishop 1961; prefect to Montreal 1968; cr. Cardinal 1988. *Address:* The Archbishopric, 2000 rue Sherbrooke Ouest, Montreal, Quebec Province, H3H 1G4, Canada. *Telephone:* (514) 931-7311.

GRÉGOIRE, Pierre; Luxembourg politician; b. 9 Nov. 1907; s. of Aloyse Grégoire and Catherine Maas; m. Octavie Schmit 1932; one s.; ed. secondary and higher education, Luxembourg; Admin. career 1929-33; Editorial staff Luxemburger Wort 1933-59; Minister of the Interior and Transport 1959-64, of Nat. Educ. and Public Service 1964-67, of Cultural and Religious Affairs 1964-68, of Foreign Affairs and Defence 1967-69; Pres. Asscn. of Catholic Writers; in concentration camp 1940-45; mem. Chamber of Deputies, Pres. until 1974; numerous Luxembourg and foreign decorations. *Publications:* Drucker, Gazettisten und Zensoren (5 vols.) 1964, Le baiser d'Europe 1967, and about sixty other works (literary, poetry, history, criticism, etc.). *Leisure interests:* gardening and walking. *Address:* Strassen, 177A route d'Arlon, Luxembourg. *Telephone:* Strassen 31598.

GREGOR, Ján, ING.; Czechoslovak economist; b. 10 May 1923, Turčianska Štiavnička; ed. School of Economics, Bratislava; Head of Dept., Commr.'s Office for Light Industry 1951-52; Deputy Commr. of Trade 1953-54; Deputy Commr. of Consumer Goods Industry 1956-60; Head of Dept., Slovak Planning Comm. 1960-63, Deputy Chair. 1963-69; Deputy Minister of Planning, Slovak Socialist Repub. 1969-70; Minister of Industry, Slovak

Socialist Repub. 1970–71; Deputy Prime Minister of Č.S.S.R. 1971–76; Deputy to House of Nations, Fed. Ass. 1971–76; Chair. Czechoslovak-Romanian Govt. Comm. for Econ. and Scientific Tech. Co-operation 1973–76; Chair. Czechoslovak section of Czechoslovak-Vietnamese Cttee. for Econ. and Scientific Tech. Co-operation 1974–76; Vice-Premier Slovak Socialist Repub. 1976–83; Deputy of Slovak Nat. Council 1976–, Deputy Chair. 1983–, Chair. Club of Deputies 1983–86; mem. Cen. Cttee. CP of Slovakia 1981–; Order of Labour 1970, Order of Victorious February 1973, Order of Repub. 1983. *Address:* c/o Slovak National Council, Októbrové nám 12, 812 80 Bratislava, Czechoslovakia.

GREGORIAN, Vartan, M.A., PH.D.; American professor of history; b. 8 April 1934, Tabriz, Iran; s. of Samuel B. Gregorian and Shushanik G. (née Mirzaian) Gregorian; m. Clare Russell 1960; three c.; ed. Coll. Armenien, Stanford Univ.; Instructor, Asst. Prof., Assoc. Prof. of History San Francisco State Coll. 1962–68; Assoc. Prof. of History Univ. of Calif., Los Angeles 1968, Univ. of Texas, Austin 1968–72, Dir. Special Programs 1970–72; Tarzian Prof. Armenian and Caucasian History Univ. of Pennsylvania 1972–80, Dean 1974–79, Provost 1978–80; Prof. of History and Near Eastern Studies, New York City 1984–; Pres. New York Public Library 1981–; Pres. Browns Univ. 1988–; mem. Nat. Humanities Faculty 1970, Silver Cultural Medal Italian Ministry of Foreign Affairs 1977, Gold Medal of Honour City and Province of Vienna 1976, Cactus Teaching Award 1971; John Simon Guggenheim Fellow 1971–72; mem. Historical Asscn., Asscn. for Advancement of Slavic Studies. *Publications:* The Emergence of Modern Afghanistan 1880–1946 1969, numerous articles for professional journals. *Address:* New York Public Library, 42nd Street and Fifth Avenue, New York, N.Y. 10018 (Office); 408 Drew Avenue, Swarthmore, Pa. 19081, U.S.A. (Home).

GREGORIOS, Metropolitan Paulos, M.DIV., S.T.M., D.TH., F.I.I.C.S. (formerly Verghese, Rev. Thadikkal Paul); Indian ecclesiastic, educationist and writer; b. 9 Aug. 1922, Tripunithura, India; s. of T. P. Piely and Aley Piely; ed. Goshen Coll., Oklahoma and Yale Univs., Princeton Theological Seminary, Keble Coll., Oxford, Serampore Univ.; journalist 1937–42; with Indian Posts and Telegraphs Union 1942–47; taught in govt. schools in Ethiopia 1947–50; Assoc. Sec. Indian Posts and Telegraphs Union of India for Travancore and Cochin 1945–47; studied in U.S.A. 1950–54; Gen. Sec. Orthodox Christian Student Movement of India 1955–57; Hon. lecturer in Religion, Union Christian Coll., Alwaye 1954–56; Special Staff Asst. H.I.M. Haile Sellassie I 1956–59; Chief Adviser Haile Sellassie Foundation 1959; Assoc. Gen. Sec. and Dir. of the Div. of Ecumenical Action, WCC, Geneva 1962–67; Prin., Syrian Orthodox Theological Seminary, Kottayam, Kerala 1967–; consecrated as Bishop 1975; Chair. Church and Soc. Working Group, WCC, Kerala Study Group, Oriental Orthodox Curriculum Cttee.; Metropolitan of Delhi 1976–; Vice-Chair. Kerala Philosophers' Congress; Vice-Pres. M.O.C.M.M. Hospital, Kolencheri, Christian Peace Conf., Prague; mem. various WCC and Christian Peace Conf. comms. and cttees.; mem. Presidium WCC 1983–; Vice-Pres. Indo-G.D.R. Friendship Soc. 1983–; mem. Comparative Education Soc. in Europe, London, Societas Liturgica (Int.), Gregory of Nyssa Soc. (Int.), Indian Philosophical Congress, Int. Soc. of Metaphysics, Asscn. of Human Psychologists (Int.), Asscn. of Christian Philosophers of India; Chief Ed. Star of the East (quarterly, Kottayam); Ed. New Frontiers in Higher Education (quarterly, Delhi); fmr. leader WCC del. to UNESCO; mem. Senate Kerala Univ. 1972–76, Serampore Univ. 1970–74; Fellow, Int. Inst. of Community Service, Int. Biographical Asscn.; Hon. TH.D. Leningrad Theological Acad., Lutheran Theological Acad., Budapest; Order of St. Vladimir (U.S.S.R.), etc. *Publications:* Joy of Freedom 1967, The Gospel of the Kingdom 1968, The Freedom of Man 1970, Be Still and Know 1971, Koptisches Christentum 1973, Die Syrischen Christen in Indien 1974, Freedom and Authority 1974, The Quest for Certainty 1975, The Human Presence 1978, Truth without Tradition? 1978, Cosmic Man 1980, Science for Sane Societies 1980. *Leisure interests:* boating, mountain hikes. *Address:* Orthodox Seminary, P.O. Box 98, Kottayam, Kerala 686001; Delhi Orthodox Centre, 2 Tughlakabad Inst. Area, New Delhi 110062, India. *Telephone:* (011) 643-6417.

GREGORY, Roderic Alfred, C.B.E., M.SC., PH.D., D.SC., F.R.C.P., F.R.S.; British physiologist; b. 29 Dec. 1913, London; s. of Alfred and Alice Gregory; m. Alice Watts 1939; one d.; ed. George Green's School, London, and Univ. Coll. and Hospital, Univ. of London; Sharpey Scholar, Univ. Coll., London 1936–39; Rockefeller Travelling Medical Fellow 1939–41; Lecturer in Physiology, Univ. Coll., London 1941–45; Sr. Lecturer in Physiology, Univ. of Liverpool 1945–48; George Holt Prof. of Physiology, Univ. of Liverpool 1948–81, Prof. Emer. 1981–; mem. MRC 1967–71; Hon. mem. American Gastroenterological Asscn. 1967, British Soc. of Gastroenterology 1974, British Physiological Soc. 1981, American Physiological Soc. 1981; Foreign Hon. mem. American Acad. of Arts and Sciences 1980; Vice-Pres., Royal Soc. 1972–73; Fellow, Univ. Coll., London; Hon. D.Sc. (Univ. of Chicago); Baly Medal Royal Coll. of Physicians, London; Feldberg Prize; Anniversary Medal, Swedish Medical Soc.; Hunter Medal and Triennial Prize, Royal Coll. of Surgeons of England 1969; Beaumont Prize, American Gastroenterological Asscn. 1976, Royal Medal, Royal Soc. 1978, Feltrinelli Prize for Medicine, Academia dei Lincei, Rome 1979. *Publications:* Various articles in journals of physiology and gastroenterology. *Leisure interest:* music. *Address:* Department of Physiology, University of Liverpool, P.O. Box 147, Liverpool, L69 3BX, England. *Telephone:* 051-709-6022.

GREIG, Henry Louis Carron, C.V.O., C.B.E.; British businessman; b. 21 Feb. 1925, London; s. of Sir Louis and Lady Greig; m. Monica Stourton 1955; three s. one d.; ed. Eton Coll. and Royal Military Coll., Sandhurst; Scots Guards 1943–47, attained rank of Capt.; joined Horace Clarkson and Co. Ltd. 1948, Dir. 1954, Man. Dir. 1962, Chair. 1973–85; Chair. Horace Clarkson Holdings PLC 1976–; Dir. James Purdey and Sons Ltd. 1972–, Baltic Exchange Ltd. 1978–82, Vice-Chair. 1982, Chair. 1983–85; Dir. Williams and Glyn's Bank 1983–85, Royal Bank of Scotland 1985–; Gentleman Usher to H.M. the Queen 1962–. *Address:* Brook House, Fleet, Hants., England; Binsness, Forres, Moray, Scotland. *Telephone:* (0252) 617596; (0309) 72334.

GREINDL, Josef; German singer; b. 23 Dec. 1912; studied with Paul Bender and Anna Bahr-Mildenburg 1932–36; with Krefeld Stadttheater 1936, Städtische Bühnen, Düsseldorf 1938, Berlin State Opera 1942, Deutsche Oper Berlin 1948–, Vienna State Opera 1956–59, 1965–; sang at Bayreuth Festival 1943, 1944, 1952–70, Salzburg Festival 1949–52, Lucerne Festival 1951, Zürich Festival 1951–54, Easter Festival (Salzburg) 1969–70; Dir. Opera and Music School, Saarbrücken 1961–; has frequently sung at foreign opera houses, including Metropolitan Opera, New York, La Scala, Milan and in Rome, Naples, Venice, Paris, Lisbon, Amsterdam, Chicago, Tokyo, Buenos Aires, San Francisco and Mexico City; numerous European concert tours and recordings; Berlin Art Prize 1955; Bundesverdienstkreuz (1st Class).

GREINER, Walter Albin Erhard, M.SC., PH.D.; German physicist; b. 29 Oct. 1935, Neuenbau/Thür; s. of Albin and Elsa (Fischer) Greiner; m. Bärbel Chun 1960; two s.; ed. Univs. of Darmstadt and Freiburg; Research Asst., Univ. of Freiburg 1961–62; Asst. Prof., Univ. of Md., U.S.A. 1962–64; Prof. and Dir. Inst. of Theoretical Physics, Univ. of Frankfurt am Main 1965–; Guest Prof. , Nat. Bureau of Standards, Wash., D.C. 1965, Univ. of Melbourne, Australia 1966, Univ. of Va., U.S.A. 1967–68, Univ. of Calif., Berkeley 1972, 1974, Yale Univ. 1973, 1975, 1980; Adjunct Prof., Vanderbilt Univ., Nashville, Tenn., U.S.A., and Oak Ridge Nat. Lab., Tenn. 1978, 1979, 1981; Perm. Consultant, Gesellschaft für Schwerionenforschung, Darmstadt 1976–; Max Born Prize, Inst. of Physics, U.K. 1974; Otto Hahn Prize, Frankfurt 1982; Dr.sc h.c. (Univ. of the Witwatersrand, S. Africa) 1982. *Publications:* Nuclear Theory (with Eisenberg) (3 vols.) 1972, Lectures on Theoretical Physics (7 vols.), Dynamics of Heavy-Ion Collisions (with Cindro and Ricci), Quantum Electrodynamics of Strong Fields (jtly.) 1985; over 350 papers in nat. and int. journals. *Leisure interests:* mycology, music, fishing, walking. *Address:* Institut für Theoretische Physik, Johann Wolfgang Goethe Universität, Robert Mayer Strasse 8–10, D-6000 Frankfurt am Main (Office); Gundelhardtstrasse 44, D-6233 Kelkheim/Taunus, Federal Republic of Germany (Home). *Telephone:* (0611)-7982332 (Office); (06195)-3468 (Home).

GREISEN, Kenneth Ingvard, PH.D.; American physicist (retd.); b. 24 Jan. 1918, Perth Amboy, N.J.; s. of Ingvard C. Greisen and Signa (Nielsen) Greisen; m. 1st Elizabeth C. Chase 1941 (died 1975), one s. one d.; m. 2nd Helen A. Leeds 1976; ed. Perth Amboy High School, Wagner Coll., Franklin & Marshall Coll. and Cornell Univ.; Instructor, Cornell Univ. 1942–43, Asst. Prof. of Physics and Nuclear Studies 1946–48, Assoc. Prof. 1948–50, Prof. 1950–84, Prof. Emer. 1984–, Chair. Astronomy Dept. 1976–79, Univ. Ombudsman 1975–77, Dean of Univ. Faculty 1978–83; Scientist, Manhattan Project, Los Alamos, N.M. 1943–46; Fellow American Physical Soc.; mem. N.A.S. *Publications:* The Physics of Cosmic X-Ray, Gamma-Ray and Particle Sources 1971; numerous articles on cosmic rays and high energy astrophysics; chapters in various review books. *Address:* 336 Forest Home Drive, Ithaca, N.Y. 14850, U.S.A. *Telephone:* (607) 257-1650.

GREKOV, Leonid Ivanovich; Soviet government official and diplomatist; b. 1928; mem. CPSU 1949–; served in Soviet Army 1943–44; ed. Kharkov Aviation Inst.; engineer, Deputy Sec., Sec. of CPSU Cen. Cttee. of Moscow Inst. of Aircraft Engine Construction 1954–63; Sec., then First Sec. of Kalinin Regional Cttee. CPSU 1966–71; mem. Cen. Cttee. CPSU 1971–; mem. of Moscow City Cttee. CPSU 1971–75; mem. Politburo of Cen. Cttee. of Uzbek CP 1976–85; Amb. to Bulgaria 1985–. *Address:* Soviet Embassy, Blvd. Bulgaro-suvetska druzhba 28, Sofia, Bulgaria.

GREKOVA, Irina Nikolaevna (pseud. of Elena Sergeevna Venttsel); Soviet author; b. 1907, Reval (Talinn); ed. Moscow Univ. Prof. of Cybernetics, Moscow Air Force Acad. 1955–67; published first story 1957. *Publications include:* Beyond the Entryway 1962, The Lady's Hairdresser 1963, Under the Streetlight 1966, During the Tests 1967, Little Garnsov 1970, The Landlady 1976, Life at the Department: Tales 1981, The Rapids (novel) 1984, A Legendary Figure 1987.

GRENFELL, 3rd Baron, cr. 1902, of Kilvey; Julian Pascoe Francis St. Leger Grenfell, Bt.; British international civil servant; b. 23 May 1935, London; s. of late 2nd Baron Grenfell of Kilvey; m. 1st Loretta Reali 1961 (dissolved 1970), one d.; m. 2nd Gabrielle Raab 1970, two d.; m. 3rd Elizabeth Porter Scott 1987; ed. Eton Coll., King's Coll., Cambridge; Second Lieut., Kings Royal Rifle Corps 1954–56; Pres. Cambridge Union 1959; Capt. Queen's Royal Rifles (Territorial Army) 1963; television journalist 1960–64; joined IBRD 1965, Chief of Information and Public Affairs in Europe 1969–72, Deputy Dir. European Office 1973–74, Special Rep. ·of

IBRD to the UN Orgs. 1974-81, Special Adviser IBRD HQ 1983-87, Sr. Adviser 1987-; Labour. *Publication:* Margot (novel) 1984. *Leisure interests:* diplomatic history, writing fiction. *Address:* c/o World Bank, 1818 H Street, N.W., Washington, D.C. 20433, U.S.A. *Telephone:* (202) 477-8844 (Office).

GRENIER, Jean-Marie René, LIC. EN DROIT; French business executive; b. 27 June 1926, Paris; s. of Henri Grenier and Germaine Pissary; m. Marie-Alix Bonnet de Paillerets 1958; three s. one d.; ed. Lycée Fustel-de-Coulanges, Strasbourg, Ecole Bossuet, Lycée Louis-le-Grand, Faculté de Droit, Paris and Ecoles des Hautes Etudes Commerciales, Paris; Deputy Dir. Soc. des Usines Chimiques Rhone-Poulenc 1962, Dir. 1970, Commercial Dir. 1971; Dir. Rhone-Poulenc S.A. 1977-82; Pres. Syndicat de l'industrie chimique organique de synthèse et biochimie 1975-84, Hon. Pres. 1984-; Adviser Foreign Trade 1975-; Chevalier ordre nat. du Mérite, Croix de la valeur militaire. *Leisure interests:* tennis, skiing. *Address:* Le Moulin Pocancy (Marne), 51130 Vertus; 74 rue Claude Bernard, 75005 Paris, France (Home). *Telephone:* (33) 26709315; (33-1) 47 07 79 82 (Home).

GRESFORD, Guy Barton, B.SC., F.R.A.C.I.; Australian science administrator; b. 7 March 1916, Sydney; m. Bettine Attiwill 1948; one s. two d.; ed. Hobart High School, Royal Melbourne Technical Coll., Trinity Coll., Univ. of Melbourne, and School of Admin., Harvard Univ.; Officer in Charge, Australian Scientific Liaison Office, London 1942-46; Asst. Sec. (Australian) Commonwealth Scientific and Industrial Research Org. 1947-52, Sec. (Physical Sciences) 1952-59, Sec. 1959-66; Dir. for Science and Tech., UN 1966-73; Sec. UN Advisory Cttee. for Application of Science and Tech. to Devt. 1966-73, mem. 1975-77; Sr. Adviser on Science, Tech. and the Environment, Australian Dept. of Foreign Affairs 1973-78; Deputy Sec.-Gen., UN Conf. on Science and Tech. for Devt. 1978-79; Consultant 1980-; Harkness Fellow, Commonwealth Fund of New York 1957. *Leisure interests:* books, walking, gardening. *Address:* 19 Summerhill Road, West Hobart, Tasmania 7000, Australia. *Telephone:* (002) 347257.

GREY, Dame Beryl Elizabeth, D.B.E.; British prima ballerina; b. 11 June 1927, London; d. of Arthur Ernest and Annie Elizabeth Groom; m. Dr. Sven Gustav Svenson 1950; one s.; ed. Dame Alice Owens School, London, Madeline Sharp School, Royal Ballet School, and de Vos School of Dance; début Sadler's Wells Co. 1941; Prima Ballerina with Royal Ballet until 1957; freelance int. prima ballerina since 1957; first full-length ballet Swan Lake on 15th birthday; has appeared since in leading roles of classical and numerous modern ballets including Giselle, Sleeping Beauty, Sylvia, Casse Noisette, Les Sylphides, Checkmate, Donald of the Burthens, Dante Sonata, Three Cornered Hat, Ballet Imperial, Lady and the Fool, Les Rendezvous; American, Continental, African, Far Eastern tours with Royal Ballet since 1945; guest artist European Opera Houses in Norway, Finland, Sweden, Denmark, Belgium, Romania, Germany, Italy, etc.; guest artist South and Central America, Middle East, Union of South Africa, Rhodesia, Australasia; first foreign guest artist ever to dance with the Bolshoi Ballet in Russia 1957-58 (Moscow, Leningrad, Kiev, Tiflis) and first to dance with Peking Ballet and Shanghai Ballet 1964; Dir.-Gen. of Arts Educational Trust, London 1966-68; Artistic Dir. of London Festival Ballet 1968-79; produced and staged Giselle, Perth, Australia 1984, Sleeping Beauty, Royal Swedish Ballet, Stockholm 1985; Pres. Dance Council for Wales 1982-; Vice-Pres. Royal Acad. of Dancing; Chair. Imperial Soc. Teachers of Dancing; Trustee of Royal Ballet Benevolent Fund, Dance Teachers' Benevolent Fund (Vice-Chair. 1987-), London City Ballet; Vice-Pres. Fed. of Music Festivals, Keep-fit Soc.; Patron Dancers Resettlement Trust, Benesh Inst.; Fellow Imperial Soc. of Teachers of Dancing 1966-; Hon. D.Mus. (Leicester), Hon. D.Litt. (City Univ.). *Publications:* Red Curtain Up 1958, Through the Bamboo Curtain 1965; edited My Favourite Ballet Stories 1981. *Leisure interests:* piano playing, painting, swimming. *Address:* Fernhill, Priory Road, Forest Row, East Sussex, RH18 5JE, England. *Telephone:* (034282) 2539.

GREY OF NAUNTON, Baron (Life Peer), cr. 1968; **Ralph Francis Alnwick Grey,** G.C.M.G., G.C.V.O., O.B.E., LL.B.; British civil servant (retd.); b. 15 April 1910, Wellington, New Zealand; s. of Francis A. Grey and Mary W. Spence; m. Esmé Burcher 1944; two s. one d.; ed. Wellington Coll., Auckland Univ. Coll., Pembroke Coll., Cambridge; Barrister and Solicitor, Supreme Court of N.Z. 1932, Judge's Assoc. N.Z. 1932-36; Cadet, Colonial Admin. Service, Nigeria 1937, Asst. Financial Sec. 1948, Admin. Officer (First Class) 1951, Devt. Sec. 1952, Sec. to the Gov.-Gen. and Council of Ministers 1954; Chief Sec. Fed. of Nigeria 1955-57, Deputy Gov.-Gen. 1957-59; mem. Council of Ministers, Fed. of Nigeria 1955-57, and mem. Council of Ibadan Univ. Coll.; Gov. and C.-in-C. British Guiana 1959-64; Gov. and C.-in-C. Bahamas 1964-68, also Gov. Turks and Caicos Islands 1965-68; Gov. of N. Ireland 1968-73; Deputy Chair. Commonwealth Devt. Corpn. 1973-79, Chair. 1979-80; Bristol Regional Bd., Lloyds Bank Ltd. 1973-81; Chair. Royal Overseas League 1976-81, Pres. 1981-; mem. Council, Cheltenham Ladies' Coll. 1975-87; Pres. Scout Council, Northern Ireland 1969-, Britain-Nigeria Asscn. 1983-, Overseas Service Pensioners Asscn. 1983-; Chancellor, New Univ. of Ulster 1980-84; Chancellor Univ. of Ulster 1984-; Hon. LL.D. (Queen's Univ., Belfast, Nat. Univ. of Ireland); Hon. D.Litt. (New Univ. of Ulster); Hon. D.Sc. (Univ. of Ulster); Hon. Bencher, Inn of Court Northern Ireland; Bailiff of Egle 1975-87, Chancellor 1987-88; Grand Cross Order of St. John 1975; Lord Prior of the Order of St. John 1988; Hon. Freeman, City of Belfast, Borough of Lisburn; Freeman, City of London. *Leisure interests:* golf, reading. *Address:* Overbrook, Naunton, Glos., England. *Telephone:* (04515) 263.

GRÉZEL, Pierre Louis Charles, L.EN D.; French business executive; b. 1 Dec. 1901, Tunis; s. of Jean and Marguérite (née Tribolet) Grézel; m. Henriette du Cailar 1928; one s. three d.; ed. Ecole Polytech. and Ecole des Mines, Paris; Dir., subsequently Asst. Dir.-Gen. Electricité de France 1946-55; Pres. Cie. Gén. d'Electro-Céramique, Soc. des Accumulateurs Fixes et de Traction 1955; Assoc. Man. MM. Lazard Frères et Cie. 1957; Hon. Pres., Pechiney Ugine Kuhlmann; Admin. Forges de Gueugnon, and other companies; Officier, Légion d'honneur. *Address:* c/o Lazard Frères et Cie., 121 boulevard Haussmann, 75008 Paris, France (Office); 34 rue Guynemer, 75006 Paris, France (Home).

GRIBACHOV, Nikolay Matveyevich; Soviet poet and journalist; b. 19 Dec. 1910, Lopush Village, Bryansk Region; two s.; ed. Coll. of Land Reclamation, Gorky Literary Inst.; Land Surveyor in Northern regions; Ed.-in-Chief Soviet Union 1950-54, 1956-; mem. CPSU 1943-; Sec. of Bd., U.S.S.R. Union of Writers 1953-54, 1959-; alternate mem. Cen. Cttee. CPSU 1961-, mem. 1986-; Deputy R.S.F.S.R. Supreme Soviet 1967-; State Prizewinner 1948, 1949; Lenin Prize 1960, Order of Lenin (twice), Hero of Socialist Labour, Hammer and Sickle Gold Medal, Red Banner, Red Star (twice), Oct. Revolution, Patriotic War 1st Class. *Publications:* The Bolshevik Collective Farm 1947, Spring in the Pobeda 1948, Poems and Verses 1951, After Thunderstorm 1952, My Dear Fellow-Countrymen 1954, Thoughtful Mood 1955, Face to Face with America 1961, Orbit of Century 1961, Selected Works (3 vols.) 1961, America, America 1961, I am Going 1962, Forward, Sergeant! 1963, Night Thunderstorm (novel) 1964, White-Black (poetry) 1965, Love and Anxiety and Battle (poetry) 1967, White Angel in the Field (fiction) 1967, Lyrics of Reflexion 1971, Collected Works (5 vols.) 1971-73; Hail, Combat! 1976. *Address:* U.S.S.R. Union of Writers, Ulitsa Vorovskogo 52, Moscow, U.S.S.R.

GRIBKOV, Gen. Anatoliy Ivanovich; Soviet army officer; b. 23 March 1919, Dukhovoye, Voronezh Oblast; mem. CPSU 1941-; ed. Kharkov Tank College, Military Acad. of the Gen. Staff; joined Soviet Army 1938, rose from Platoon Commdr. to Company Commdr. 1939-41; on staff of mil. districts and Gen. Staff 1942-65; First Deputy Commdr. 1968-73, Commdr. of a mil. dist. 1973-76, Chief of Staff and First Deputy Commdr.-in-Chief, Warsaw Pact Forces 1976-89; rank of Gen. 1976; Cand. mem. Cen. Cttee., CPSU 1976-81, mem. 1981-; Deputy to Supreme Soviet 1970-; Order of Lenin, Order of Oct. Revolution, Order of Red Flag (twice) and various decorations.

GRIERSON, Philip, M.A., LITT.D., F.B.A., F.S.A.; British historian; b. 15 Nov. 1910, Dublin; s. of Philip Henry Grierson and Roberta Ellen Jane Pope; ed. Marlborough Coll., Gonville and Caius Coll., Cambridge; Univ. Lecturer in History, Cambridge 1945-59; Reader in Medieval Numismatics, Cambridge 1959-71; Prof. of Numismatics, Univ. of Cambridge 1971-78, Emer. Prof. 1978-; Prof. of Numismatics and History of Coinage, Univ. of Brussels 1948-81; Ford's Lecturer in History, Univ. of Oxford 1956-57; Fellow, Gonville and Caius Coll., Cambridge 1935-, Librarian 1944-69, Pres. 1966-76; Literary Dir. Royal Historical Soc. 1945-55; Hon. Keeper of the Coins, Fitzwilliam Museum, Cambridge 1949-; Adviser in Byzantine Numismatics to Dumbarton Oaks Library and Collection, Harvard Univ., Washington, D.C., U.S.A. 1955-; Pres. Royal Numismatic Soc. 1961-66; Corresp. mem. Koninklijke Vlaamse Acad. 1955; Assoc. mem. Acad. Royale de Belgique 1968; Corresp. Fellow, Medieval Acad. of America 1972; Hon. Litt.D. (Ghent) 1958, (Leeds) 1978. *Publications:* Les Annales de Saint-Pierre de Gand 1937, Books on Soviet Russia 1917-42 1943, Sylloge of Coins of the British Isles, Vol. I (Fitzwilliam Museum: Early British and Anglo-Saxon Coins) 1958, Bibliographie numismatique 1966, English Linear Measures: a study in origins 1973, Catalogue of the Byzantine Coins in the Dumbarton Oaks Collection and in the Whittemore Collection, Vols. I, II and III (with A. R. Bellinger) 1966-73, Numismatics 1975, Monnaies du Moyen Age 1976, The Origins of Money 1977, Les monnaies 1977, Dark Age Numismatics 1979, Later Medieval Numismatics 1979, Byzantine Coins 1982, Medieval European Coinage, 1: The Early Middle Ages (5th-10th Centuries) (with M. Blackburn) 1986; Ed.: C. W. Previté-Orton, The Shorter Cambridge Medieval History 1952; H. E. Ives, The Venetian Gold Ducat and its Imitations 1954, Studies in Italian History presented to Miss E. M. Jamison 1956; trans. Feudalism (F. L. Ganshof) 1952. *Leisure interests:* squash, science fiction. *Address:* Gonville and Caius College, Cambridge, CB2 1TA, England. *Telephone:* (0223) 332450.

GRIERSON, Ronald Hugh, M.A.; British banker (retd.); b. 6 Aug. 1921, Nuremberg, Germany; s. of Ernest Grierson and Gerda Grierson; m. Elizabeth Heather, Viscountess Bearsted 1966; one s.; ed. Realgymnasium, Nuremberg, Lycée Pasteur, Paris, Highgate School, London and Balliol Coll. Oxford; Dir. S.G. Warburg & Co. Ltd. 1948-86; Deputy Chair. and Chief Exec. Industrial Reorganization Corpn. 1966-68; Chair. Orion Bank 1970-73; Dir.-Gen. for Industry and Tech., Comm. of the European Communities 1973-74; Dir. RJR Nabisco Inc., Chrysler Corpn., W. R. Grace, Inc. 1987; Dir. General Electric Co. PLC 1968-, Vice-Chair. 1983-; Exec. Chair. South Bank Centre 1985-; Hon. D.C.L. (Grove City Coll., Pa.) 1986. *Address:* The General Electric Company PLC, 1 Stanhope Gate, London, W1A 1EH, England. *Telephone:* 01-493 8484.

GRIFFIN, Admiral Sir Anthony (Templer Frederick Griffith), G.C.B.; British naval officer and shipbuilding executive; b. 24 Nov. 1920, Peshawar, India (now Pakistan); s. of Col. Forrester Metcalfe Griffith Griffin, M.C., and Beryl Alice Beatrix Griffith Griffin; m. Rosemary Ann Hickling 1943; two s. one d.; ed. Royal Naval Coll., Dartmouth; entered Royal Navy 1934; war service H.M.S. Gloucester, Fury, Talybont, Implacable, Empress 1939–45, mentioned in despatches 1944, 1945; Lieut.-Commdr. 1949, Commdr. 1951; Application Commdr., H.M.S. Mercury II 1952–54; Exec. Officer H.M.S. Eagle 1955–56; Capt. 1956; Deputy Dir. of Navigation and Direction, Admiralty 1957–59; Command H.M.S. Woodbridge Haven and Capt. Inshore Flotilla 1959–60; Deputy Dir. of Plans 1960–62, Imperial Defence Coll. 1963; Command H.M.S. Ark Royal 1964–65; Rear-Adm. 1966; Naval Sec. 1966; Asst. Chief of Naval Staff (Warfare) 1966–68; Vice-Adm. 1968; Flag Officer Second-in-Command, Far East Fleet 1968–69; Flag Officer, Plymouth, Adm. Supt., Devonport, Commdr. Cen. Sub Area, E. Atlantic, Commdr. Plymouth Sub Area, Channel 1969–71; Controller of the Navy 1971–75; Adm. 1971; Rear-Adm. of the U.K. 1986, Vice-Adm. 1988; Chair. Organizing Cttee. and Chair. Designate of British Shipbuilders 1975–77, Chair. 1977–80; Pres. Royal Inst. of Naval Architects 1981–84; Vice-Pres. The Wellington Coll. 1980–; Co-f. and Exec. British Maritime League 1982–. *Leisure interest:* sailing. *Address:* Moat Cottage, The Drive, Bosham, Sussex, PO18 8JG, England. (Home). *Telephone:* (0243) 573373 (Home).

GRIFFIN, Donald (Redfield), PH.D.; American biologist; b. 3 Aug. 1915, Southampton, N.Y.; s. of late Henry F. Griffin and Mary W. Redfield; m. 1st Ruth Castle 1941 (dissolved 1965), 2nd Jocelyn Crane 1965; one s. three d.; ed. Harvard Coll. and Graduate School of Arts and Sciences, Harvard Univ.; Jr. Fellow, Harvard Univ. 1940–46, Research Assoc. 1942–45; Asst. Prof. of Zoology, Cornell Univ. 1946–47, Assoc. Prof. 1947–52, Prof. 1952–53; Prof. of Zoology, Harvard Univ. 1953–65, Chair. Dept. of Biology 1962–65; Prof. The Rockefeller Univ. 1965–86, Trustee 1973–76; Pres. Harry Frank Guggenheim Foundation, New York 1979–83; mem. N.A.S., American Philosophical Soc.; Elliott Medal 1960. *Publications:* Listening in the Dark 1958, Echoes of Bats and Men 1959, Animal Structure and Function 1962, Bird Migration 1964, The Question of Animal Awareness 1976, 1981, Animal Thinking 1984. *Leisure interest:* sailing. *Address:* The Rockefeller University, 1230 York Avenue, New York, N.Y. 10021-6399 (Office); 471 Walnut Lane, Princeton, N.J. 08540, U.S.A. (Home). *Telephone:* 212-570-8656 (Office).

GRIFFIN, James Bennett, PH.D.; American anthropologist and archaeologist; b. 12 Jan. 1905, Atchison, Kan.; s. of Charles Bennett and Maude (Bostwick) Griffin; m. Ruby Fletcher 1936; three s.; ed. Univs. of Chicago and Michigan; Research Assoc. Museum of Anthropology, Univ. of Mich. 1936–41, Asst. Curator, Archaeology 1936–42, Assoc. Curator 1942–45, Curator 1945–76, Dir. 1946–75, Sr. Research Scientist; Assoc. Prof. of Anthropology, Univ. of Mich. 1945–49, Prof. 1949–76, Prof. Emer. 1976–, Henry Russel Lecturer 1971–72; Chair. Dept. of Anthropology 1972–75; mem. Perm. Council, Int. Union of Prehistoric and Protohistoric Sciences 1948–76, mem. Exec. Cttee. 1962–76; Pres. Cttee. on Anthropology, Pan American Inst. of Geography and History 1954–59; Fellow, American Asscn. for the Advancement of Science, American Anthropological Assen.; mem. Soc. for American Archaeology (Asst. Ed. 1936–46, Assoc. Ed. 1946–50, First Vice-Pres. 1945–46, mem. Exec. Cttee. 1945–46, 1950–53, Pres. 1951–52), N.A.S., Sociedad Mexicana de Antropología; Sec. American Quarternary Assen. 1970–72; mem. Exec. Cttee. Assen. of Field Archaeology 1971–78; Regents Fellow Smithsonian Inst. 1984; Viking Fund Medal and Award in Archaeology 1957; Hon. D.S. (Indiana Univ.) 1971; Fryxell Award for Interdisciplinary Research, Soc. for American Archaeology 1980, Distinguished Service Award 1984. *Publications:* The Fort Ancient Aspect 1943, Archaeological Survey in the Lower Mississippi Alluvial Valley 40–47 (Co-Author) 1950, Archaeology of Eastern United States 1952; and over 250 professional articles. *Leisure interest:* travel. *Address:* Department of Anthropology, Museum of Natural History, 112, S.I. Washington, D.C. 20560 (Office); 8104 Maple Ridge Road, Bethesda, Md. 20814, U.S.A. (Home). *Telephone:* (202) 357-4729 (Office); (301) 656-0509 (Home).

GRIFFIN, Jasper, M.A., F.B.A.; British classical scholar; b. 29 May 1937, London; s. of Frederick William Griffin and Constance Irene Cordwell; m. Miriam Tamara Dressler 1960; three d.; ed. Balliol Coll., Oxford; Jackson Fellow, Harvard Univ. 1960–61; Dyson Research Fellow, Balliol Coll., Oxford 1961–63, Fellow and Tutor in Classics 1963–; T. S. Eliot Memorial Lectures, Univ. of Kent 1984. *Publications:* Homer on Life and Death 1980, Snobs 1982, Latin Poets and Roman Life 1985, The Mirror of Myth 1985, Virgil 1986; Ed. The Oxford History of the Classical World 1986, Homer: The Odyssey 1987. *Leisure interests:* music, wine. *Address:* Balliol College, Oxford, England. *Telephone:* (0865) 277782.

GRIFFIN, Robert P., A.B., B.S., J.D.; American lawyer and politician; b. 6 Nov. 1923, Detroit, Mich.; s. of J. A. and Beulah M. Griffin; m. Marjorie J. Anderson 1947; three s. one d.; ed. Central Michigan Univ., and Univ. of Michigan Law School; admitted to Mich. Bar; mem. law firm Williams, Griffin, Thompson and Coulter, Traverse City 1950–56; mem. U.S. House of Reps. 1956–66; Co-author of Landrum-Griffin Act 1959; U.S. Senator from Michigan 1966–79; Minority Whip in Senate 1969–77; Counsel Miller, Canfield, Paddock and Stone, Traverse City 1979–87; Assoc. Justice, Michigan Supreme Court 1987–; mem. Senate Commerce, Foreign

Relations and Rules and Admin. Cttees.; mem. American Bar Assen.; Chair. Bd. of Trustees of Gerald R. Ford Foundation 1981–; Hon. LL.D. (Univ. of Mich., Detroit Coll. of Law, Cen. Mich., Eastern Mich., Albion Coll., Western Mich., Grand Valley State Coll., Detroit Coll. of Business); Hon. L.H.D. (Hillsdale Coll.); Hon. J.C.D. (Rollins Coll.); Hon. ED.D. (Northern Mich.); Republican. *Leisure interests:* golf, camping. *Address:* Suite 2300, 13561 W. Bay Shore Road, Traverse City, Mich. 49684, U.S.A. *Telephone:* (616) 922-2122.

GRIFFIN, Victor Gilbert Benjamin, M.A., D.THEOL.; Irish ecclesiastic; b. 24 May 1924, Carnew, Co. Wicklow; s. of Gilbert Benjamin Griffin and Martha Violet Crowe; m. Daphne Elizabeth Mitchell 1958; two s.; ed. Mountjoy School, Dublin, Kilkenny Coll., and Trinity Coll., Dublin; Curate St. Augustine's, Londonderry 1947–50; Christchurch, Londonderry 1950–57, Rector 1957–69; Dean St. Patrick's Cathedral, Dublin 1969–; Lecturer in Philosophy, Magee Univ. Coll., Londonderry 1950–69; Scholar and Prizeman Trinity Coll.; Irish People of the Year Award 1979. *Publications:* Trends in Theology (1870-1970) 1970, Anglican and Irish 1976, Pluralism and Ecumenism 1983. *Leisure interests:* golf, walking and music. *Address:* The Deanery, St. Patrick's Cathedral, Dublin 8, Ireland. *Telephone:* 752451 or 754817.

GRIFFITH, Thomas, A.B.; American writer and editor; b. 30 Dec. 1915, Tacoma, Wash.; s. of Thomas Griffith and Anne O'Reilly; m. Caroline Coffman 1937; ed. Univ. of Washington; Reporter, then Asst. City Ed. Seattle Times (Wash.) 1936–41; Nieman Fellow, Harvard 1942; Contrib. Ed., then Assoc. Ed. Time magazine 1943–46, Sr. Ed. 1946, Nat. Affairs Ed. 1949–51, Foreign Ed. 1951–60, Asst. Man. Ed., Time 1960–63; Sr. Staff Ed., all Time Inc. Publs. 1963–67; Ed. Life magazine 1968–73; Press columnist, Time magazine 1973–; Staff contrib. Fortune magazine; columnist, Atlantic Monthly 1974–81. *Publications:* The Waist-High Culture 1958, How True?—a Sceptic's Guide to Believing the News 1974. *Address:* Time & Life Building, Rockefeller Center, New York, N.Y. 10020 (Office); 25 East End Avenue, New York, N.Y. 10028, U.S.A. (Home). *Telephone:* 841-3733 (Office); RE4-7625 (Home).

GRIFFITH JOYNER, Florence; American athlete; d. of Robert Griffith; m. Alfrederick Alphonzo Joyner 1987; ed. Jordan High, Cal State-Northridge and Westwood; NCAA 200 metres champion; 200 metres Olympic silver medallist 1984; worked for Anheuscher-Busch 1987; Olympic Gold Medallist in the 100 and 200 metres, Seoul 1988; 100-metre and 200-metre world records.

GRIFFITHS, Baron (Life Peer), cr. 1985, of Govilon in the county of Gwent; **William Hugh Griffiths**, Kt., M.C., P.C.; British judge; b. 26 Sept. 1923; s. of late Sir Hugh Griffiths, C.B.E.; m. Evelyn Krefting 1949; one s. three d.; ed. Charterhouse and St. John's Coll. Cambridge; called to Bar, Inner Temple 1949, Q.C. 1964; Treas. Bar Council 1968–69; Recorder of Margate 1962–64, Cambridge 1964–70; Judge, Queen's Bench Div., High Court of Justice 1971–80; a Lord Justice of Appeal 1980–85; a Lord of Appeal in Ordinary 1985–; Chair. Security Comm. 1985–; Judge, Nat. Industrial Relations Court 1973–74; mem. Advisory Council on Penal Reform 1967–70; Vice-Chair. Parole Bd. 1976–77; mem. Chancellor's Law Reform Cttee. 1976–. *Leisure interests:* golf, fishing. *Address:* c/o Royal Courts of Justice, London, W.C.2, England.

GRIFFITHS, Bede, B.A.; British Benedictine monk; b. 17 Dec. 1906, Walton-on-Thames; s. of Walter Griffiths and Lilian Griffiths; ed. Christ's Hosp. and Magdalen Coll. Oxford; received into Roman Catholic Church 1932; entered Prinknash Abbey 1933; professed as monk 1937; ordained priest 1940; Prior of Farnborough Abbey 1947–51; novice-master, Pluscarden Abbey, Scotland 1951–55; founded Nirmala Ashram, Bangalore, India 1955; assisted in foundation of Kurisumala Ashram, Kerala 1958–68; Acharya (Prior) of Saccidananda Ashram, Shantivanam 1968–; Gold Medal for ecumenical work (Catholic Art Assen.) 1963. *Publications:* The Golden String 1954, Christian Ashram 1966, Christ in India 1966, Vedanta and Christian Faith 1968, Return to the Centre 1976, Marriage of East and West 1982, Cosmic Revelation 1983, River of Compassion 1987. *Leisure interests:* science, art, philosophy, theology, Indian culture. *Address:* Saccidananda Ashram, Shantivanam, Tannirpalli, Kulittalai, Tvinchviapalli, Tamil Nadu, S. India.

GRIFFITHS, Brian, M.SC.; British professor of banking and international finance; b. 27 Dec. 1941; s. of Ivor Winston Griffiths and Phyllis Mary Griffiths (née Morgan); m. Rachel Jane Jones 1965; one s. two d.; ed. Dynevor Grammar School and L.S.E.; Asst. Lecturer in Econs., L.S.E. 1965–68, Lecturer 1968–76; Dir. Centre for Banking and Int. Finance, City Univ., London 1977–82, Prof. of Banking and Int. Finance 1977–85, Dean, City Univ. Business School 1982–85; Dir. Bank of England 1984–86; mem. Panel of Acad. Consultants 1977–; Head of Prime Minister's Policy Unit 1985–86. *Publications:* Is Revolution Change? (Ed. and Contrib.) 1972, Mexican Monetary Policy and Economic Development 1972, Invisible Barriers to Invisible Trade 1975, Inflation: The Price of Prosperity 1976, Monetary Targets (Ed. with G. E. Wood) 1980. *Leisure interests:* the family and reading. *Address:* c/o 10 Downing Street, London, S.W.1, England.

GRIFFITHS, Philip A., PH.D.; American professor of mathematics; b. 18 Oct. 1938, Raleigh, N.C.; Miller Fellow, Univ. of Calif. (Berkeley) 1962–64,

1975–76, Faculty mem. 1964–67: Visiting Prof. Princeton Univ. 1967–68, Prof. 1968–72; Prof. Harvard Univ. 1972–83, Dwight Parker Robinson Prof. of Math. 1983–84; Provost and James B. Duke Prof. of Math. Duke Univ. 1984–; Guest Prof. Univ. of Beijing 1983; mem. N.A.S.; hon. degrees from Wake Forest, Angers and Beijing Univs.; Guggenheim Fellow 1980–82; other awards and distinctions. *Publications:* some 90 articles in professional journals. *Address:* Office of the Provost, Duke University, Durham, N.C. 27706, U.S.A.

GRIFFITHS, Trevor, B.A.; British playwright; b. 4 April 1935; s. of Ernest Griffiths and Anne Connor; m. Janice Elaine Stansfield 1961 (died 1977); one s. two d.; ed. Manchester Univ.; taught English language and literature 1957–65; Educ. Officer, BBC 1965–72; Writer's Award, British Acad. of Film and TV Artists 1981. *Publications:* Occupations 1972, Sam Sam 1972, The Party 1974, Comedians 1976, All Good Men, and Absolute Beginners 1977, Through the Night, and Such Impossibilities 1977, Thermidor and Apricots 1977, Deeds (Jt. Author) 1978, The Cherry Orchard (trans.) 1978, Country 1981, Oi for England 1982, Sons and Lovers (TV version) 1982, Judgement Over the Dead 1986, Fatherland 1987, Real Dreams 1987. *Address:* c/o A. D. Peters, 10 Buckingham Street, London WC2, England.

GRIGNASCHI, Giancarlo, B.ENG.; Italian industrial executive; b. 30 Oct. 1926, Acqui Terme, Alessandria; s. of Giuseppe Grignaschi and Ninetta Caffa di Cortemilia; m. Ada Rapetti 1957; one s. two d.; ed. Genoa Univ.; with Esso Standard Italiana 1956–67, Vice-Man. Augusta Refinery, Sicily 1967–68, Man. Econ. Studies Office 1968, then Man. Programming and Control for refining sector, Man. Augusta refinery 1970–71, Gen. Man. logistic operations for Italy, Esso Italiana 1971–72, Div. Man. Programming logistic operations for Europe, London 1972, then Man. of operations and logistic programming for Exxon's European affiliates; headed commercial operation of Esso Italiana 1975–76, responsible for logistic operations 1977; Founding partner ENECO S.p.A. specializing in ecological energy 1978; mem. Supervisory Cttee. for extraordinary admin. procedure Liquigas group cos.; Vice-Pres. Ente Nazionale Idrocarburi (ENI) Nov. 1982–; Grande Ufficiale of Republic of Italy. *Leisure interests:* piano playing, twentieth-century poetry. *Address:* ENI, Piazzale Enrico Mattei 1, Rome, Italy. *Telephone:* 06 59001.

GRIGORESCU, Dan, M.A., PH.D.; Romanian critic and historian of culture; b. 13 May 1931, Bucharest; s. of Vasile Grigorescu and Tomescu (Grigorescu) Ecaterina; m. Petrovan Valentina; one s. one d.; ed. Bucharest Univ.; ed. State Publishing House for Art and Literature 1954–58; museographer Nat. Museum of Art, Bucharest 1958–63; chief ed. Meridiane Publishing House 1963–68; Dir. Fine Arts Dept. for Culture and Arts, State Cttee. 1968; Dir. Romanian Library New York 1971–74; Prof. in Comparative Literature Bucharest Univ. 1963–; Visiting Prof. Univ. of Wash., Seattle 1970–71, UCLA 1970; Vice-Pres. Int. Soc. for the History of Culture 1973–; Prize of the Romanian Acad.; R. W. Emerson Award; mem. Romanian Fine Arts Union, Romanian Writers' Union, Int. Assoc. of Art Criticism, Int. Asscn. of Comparative Literature, Int. Asscn. for the History of Culture. *Works include:* Shelley, a monograph 1962; Three Romanian Painters in the 1848 Revolution 1965, Expressionism 1969, Cubism 1971, Pop Art 1972, American Art—a History 1974, Tendencies in 20th Century Poetry 1975, Shakespeare and the Romanian Modern Culture 1975, A Chronological Dictionary of American Literature 1977, The Buffalo's Song, an anthology of Indian American verse and prose 1978, The Adventures of the Image 1979, History of a Lost Generation—The Expressionists 1980, Brancusi 1982, Reality, Myth, Symbol: A Portrait of James Joyce 1984, North of Rio Grande 1986, Primitive and Modern Art 1988. *Address:* Edgar Quinet 7, Bucharest 70118 (Office); Vasile Conta 3-5, Bucharest 70138, Romania (Home).

GRIGOROVICH, Yuriy Vaganov Nikolayevich; Soviet ballet-master; b. 2 Jan. 1927, Leningrad; m. Natalya Igorevna Bessmertnova (q.v.); ed. Leningrad Choreographic School and Lunarcharski Inst. of Theatrical Art, Moscow; Troupe of Kirov Theatre 1946, Soloist until 1964, Ballet-Master, Kirov Theatre 1962–64; Chief Ballet Master, Bolshoi Theatre, Moscow 1964–; Prof. 1973–; People's Artist of U.S.S.R.; Lenin Prize 1970; Ballets include Spartacus, Ivan The Terrible. *Address:* State Academic Bolshoi Theatre, 1 Ploshchad Sverdlova, Moscow, U.S.S.R.

GRIGULL, Ulrich DR. ING.; German professor, editor and consultant; b. 12 March 1912, Gallingen; s. of Wilhelm Grigull and Anna Wormit; m. Lydia Freiheit 1937; two d.; ed. Technische Hochschule, Danzig and Brunswick; Air Transport Research Establishment, Brunswick 1937–45; Farbenfabriken Bayer, Leverkusen 1952–60; Prof. Technische Univ. Munich 1960–80, Prof. Emer. 1980–, Rector, later Pres. 1972–80; Pres. Ass. of Int. Heat Transfer Confs. 1970–74, 1982–86, Int. Assen. for Properties of Steam 1977–79, 1986–88, Int. Centre for Heat and Mass Transfer 1982–86; mem. Bayerische Akad. der Wissenschaften; Max Jakob Award 1973; Arnold Eucken Medaille 1979; Bayerischer Maximiliansorden 1984; Dr. Ing. h.c. (Stuttgart) 1982. *Publications:* several textbooks and 130 scientific papers. *Leisure interest:* mountaineering. *Address:* Heinrich-Vogl-Strasse 1, D-8000 Munich 71, Federal Republic of Germany. *Telephone:* (089) 79 65 57 (Home); (089) 2105 3447 (Institute).

GRILICHES, Zvi, PH.D.; American educator and economist; b. 12 Sept. 1930, Kaunas, Lithuania; m. Diane Asseo 1952; one s. one d.; ed. Hebrew Univ., Jerusalem and Univs. of California (Berkeley) and Chicago; served with Israeli Army 1948–49; naturalized U.S. citizen 1960; Asst. Prof. of Econs. Univ. of Chicago 1956–59, Assoc. Prof. 1960–64, Prof. 1964–69; Prof., Harvard Univ. 1969–78, Nathaniel Ropes Prof. of Political Economy 1979–87, Paul M. Warburg Prof. of Econs. 1987–; Chair. Dept. of Econs. 1980–83; Research Assoc. Nat. Bureau of Econ. Research 1959–60, 1978–, Dir. Programme on Productivity 1978–; Consultant Rand Corpn., Brookings Inst.; mem. Bd. of Govs., Fed. Reserve System, Ford Foundation; mem. American Econ. Assen. (Vice-Pres. 1984); Fellow, A.A.A.S., N.A.S., American Statistical Assen., Econometric Soc. (Pres. 1975), American Statistical Assen. *Publications:* Price Indexes and Quality Change 1971, Economies of Scale and the Form of the Production Function 1971, Handbook of Econometrics (Ed.) 1984, R & D, Patents and Productivity (Ed.) 1984, articles in professional journals. *Address:* 89 Dorset Road, Waban, Mass. 02168, U.S.A.

GRIMES, Don, M.B., B.S.; Australian politician and doctor; b. 4 Oct. 1937, Albury, N.S.W.; s. of Walter John Grimes and Annie Mildred Grimes; two s. two d.; ed. N.S.W. High Schools, Univ. of Sydney; Medical Practitioner 1962–74; Senator for Tasmania 1974–, Opposition Spokesman for Social Security 1976–83, for Repatriation and Compensation 1976–77, for Veterans' Affairs and Compensation 1977, 1980–83, Deputy Leader of the Opposition 1980–83; Deputy Chair. Asia-Pacific Socialist Org. 1981–; Minister for Social Security 1983–84, and Deputy Leader of Govt. in Senate 1983–; Minister for Community Services 1984–87; mem. Labour Party, Pres. Tasmanian Branch 1982–. *Leisure interests:* jazz, reading, bushwalking. *Address:* Parliament House, Canberra, A.C.T. 2600, Australia.

GRIMES, Joseph Rudolph, B.A., M.I.A., J.D., LL.D.; Liberian lawyer, diplomatist and politician; b. 31 Oct. 1923, Monrovia, Liberia; s. of Louis Arthur and Victoria Elizabeth Grimes; m. Doris Delicia Duncan 1954; two d.; ed. Coll. of West Africa, Liberia Coll., Law School Harvard Univ. and Columbia Univ.; Cadet, Bureau of Public Health and Sanitation 1938–42; Clerk, Exec. Mansion 1942–47; Counsellor, Dept. of State 1951–56; Dir. Louis Grimes School of Law, Liberia Univ. 1954–58; Under-Sec. of State 1956–60, Sec. of State 1960–72; Consultant, Liberia Tractor and Equipment 1972–76, Pres. 1976–78, Chair. 1978–88; Dir. W. African Explosives and Chemical Co., Liberia Tractor and Equipment Co., Monrovia Breweries, Elias Bros. Co. 1983–, Nat. Bank of Liberia 1976–84; Chair., Bd. of Dirs., P.T.P. Timber Industries Ltd. 1978–87, Stevfor, Denco Shipping Lines Inc.; Chancellor Episcopal Diocese of Liberia 1976–; Vice-Pres. Bd. of Trustees, Univ. of Liberia 1977–80; Vice-Moderator Church Comm. on Int. Affairs (WCC) 1976–83; mem. Liberian Nat. Constitution Comm., Chair. of its Drafting Cttee. 1981–83, Bd. of Trustees, Monrovia Coll. and Coll. of W. Africa; mem. Liberian Del. to Asian Conf., Bandung 1955, to Heads of African States Conf. 1961, to 15th–26th Sessions of UN Gen. Ass.; Grand Officier, Légion d'honneur, Most Venerable Order of the Pioneers, Kt. Great Band, Humane Order of the African Redemption, Hon. K.B.E., and other honours; Hon. LL.D. (Columbia Univ.) 1971. *Publications:* African Developments in Historical Perspective 1980, Arms Race and Development in Africa 1980 (for Churches' Comm. on Int. Affairs of WCC). *Leisure interests:* reading, croquet. *Address:* P.O. Box 1588, Monrovia, Liberia. *Telephone:* 225 572.

GRIMOND, Baron (Life Peer), cr. 1983, of Firth in the County of Orkney; **Joseph Grimond,** P.C., M.P., LL.D., T.D.; British politician; b. 29 July 1913, St. Andrews, Scotland; s. of Joseph B. Grimond and Helen L. Richardson; m. Laura Bonham Carter 1938; three s. (one deceased) one d.; ed. Eton and Balliol Coll., Oxford; Barrister; served Fife and Forfar Yeomanry 1939–45; fmr. Dir. of Personnel, European Office of UNRRA; Sec. Nat. Trust for Scotland 1947–49; Liberal M.P. for Orkney and Shetland 1950–83; Liberal Chief Whip 1951–57, Leader of Parl. Party 1957–67, May-July 1976; Rector, Edin. Univ. 1961–64; Rector, Aberdeen Univ. 1969–72; Chancellor, Univ. of Kent 1970–; Trustee, Manchester Guardian and Evening News 1967–83; Chubb Fellow of Yale Univ.; Dr. h.c. (Stirling) 1984; Hon. D.C.L. (Kent), Hon. LL.D. (Edinburgh, Aberdeen, Birmingham, Buckingham). *Publications:* The Liberal Future 1959, The Liberal Challenge 1963, The Referendum (with Brian Neve) 1975, The Common Welfare 1978, Memoirs 1979, A Personal Manifesto 1983. *Address:* Old Manse of Firth, Kirkwall, Orkney, Scotland.

GRIMWADE, Sir Andrew (Sheppard), Kt., C.B.E., M.A., F.A.I.M.; Australian industrialist; b. 26 Nov. 1930; s. of Frederick Grimwade and Gwendolen Grimwade; m. Barbara Kater 1959; one s.; ed. Church of England Grammar School, Melbourne, Trinity Coll., Melbourne Univ., Oriel Coll. Oxford, England; Chair. Australian Consolidated Industries Ltd. 1977–82, Kemtron Ltd. Group 1964–; Dir. Nat. Bank of Australasia, Commonwealth Industrial Gases, Nat. Mutual Life Assen., IBM (Australia), Sony (Australia), AHI (N.Z.), Pilkington ACI Ltd.; mem. Australian Govt. Remuneration Tribunal 1976–; Pres. Walter and Eliza Hall Inst. of Medical Research 1978–; Deputy Pres. Australiana Fund 1978–; Pres. Nat. Gallery of Vic. 1976–; Trustee Victorian Arts Centre 1980–; mem. Council for Order of Australia; Fellow Inst. of Dirs. *Publication:* Involvement: The Portraits of Clifton Pugh and Mark Strizic 1969. *Leisure interests:* skiing, Santa Gertrudis cattle breeding, Australian art and books. *Address:* 500 Bourke Street, Melbourne, Vic. 3000, Australia.

GRINDROD, Most Rev. John Basil Rowland, K.B.E., M.A.; Australian ecclesiastic; b. 14 Dec. 1919, Aughton; s. of Edward B. Grindrod and Dorothy G. (née Hunt) Grindrod; m. 1st Ailsa W. Newman 1949 (died 1981); m. 2nd Dell Judith Cornish 1983; two d.; ed. Repton School, Univ. of Oxford and Lincoln Theological Coll.; Archdeacon of Rockhampton, Queensland 1960-65; Vicar of Christ Church, S. Yarra, Melbourne 1965-66; Bishop of Riverina, N.S.W. 1966-71; Bishop of Rockhampton 1971-80; Archbishop of Brisbane 1980-, Primate of Anglican Church of Australia 1982-. *Address:* Bishopsbourne, 39 Eldernell Avenue, Hamilton 4007, Brisbane, Queensland, Australia. *Telephone:* (07) 268-2706; (07) 839-4766.

GRISEZ, Germain, M.A., PH.L., PH.D.; American professor of Christian ethics; b. 30 Sept. 1929, University Heights, Ohio; m. Jeannette Selby 1951; four c.; ed. John Carroll Univ., Univ. Heights, Ohio, Dominican Coll. of St. Thomas Aquinas, River Forrest, Ill. and Univ. of Chicago; Asst. Prof. to Prof. Georgetown Univ. Washington, D.C. 1957-72; part-time Lecturer in Medieval Philosophy, Univ. of Va., Charlottesville 1961-62; Special Asst. to Cardinal O'Boyle, Archbishop of Washington 1968-69; consultant (part-time) Archdiocese of Washington 1969-72; Prof. of Philosophy, Campion Coll. Univ. of Regina, Canada 1972-79; Rev. Harry J. Flynn Prof. of Christian Ethics, Mount Saint Mary's Coll. Emmitsburg, Md. 1979-; mem. Catholic Theol. Soc. of America, American Catholic Philosophical Assen., Fellowship of Catholic Scholars, American Philosophical Assen.; Pro ecclesia et pontifioe medal 1972; Cardinal Wright Award for service to the Church 1983 and other awards. *Publications:* Beyond the New Morality: The Responsibilities of Freedom (with R. Shaw) 1980, The Way of the Lord Jesus, Vol. I, Christian Moral Principles (with others) 1983, Nuclear Deterrence, Morality and Realism (with J. Finnis and Joseph M. Boyle) 1987; numerous articles in learned journals. *Address:* Mount Saint Mary's College, Emmitsburg, Md. 21727-7799, U.S.A. *Telephone:* 301-447-5771.

GRISHIN, Viktor Vasiliyevich; Soviet politician; b. 18 Sept. 1914; ed. Moscow Railway Inst.; fmr. railway engine driver and locomotive depot chief; mem. CPSU 1939-; Sec. Serpukhov City Cttee. CPSU 1942-50; Sec. Moscow Region Cttee. CPSU 1950-56, mem. Cen. Cttee. CPSU 1952-59, 1961-86, Cand. mem. Presidium Cen. Cttee. CPSU 1961-66, Cand. mem. Politburo 1966-71, mem. 1971-86; Chair. All-Union Cen. Council of Trade Unions 1956-67; First Sec. Moscow City Cttee. CPSU 1967-86; Deputy to Supreme Soviet 1950-87; mem. Presidium U.S.S.R. Supreme Soviet; mem. Soviet Parl. Del. to U.K. 1956; Order of Lenin (three times), Badge of Honour, Hammer and Sickle Gold Medal, and other decorations. *Address:* c/o Moscow City Committee of CPSU, 6 Staraya Ploshchad, Moscow, U.S.S.R.

GRISHKIAVICHUS, Pvatras Pyatrovich; Soviet politician; b. 1924; ed. CPSU Cen. Cttee. Higher Party School; Soviet Army 1942-43; partisan div. 1943-44; mem. CPSU 1945-; Ed. of local Lithuanian newspaper 1944-48; work for Cen. Cttee. of Lithuanian CP 1948-50, 1964-71; Ed. of Lithuanian newspapers 1950-55; Sec., Second, First Sec. of Vilnius City Cttee. 1955-74; First Sec. of Cen. Cttee. of Lithuanian CP 1974-; mem. of CPSU Cen. Cttee. 1974-; Deputy of U.S.S.R. Supreme Soviet 1976-. *Address:* Central Committee of Lithuanian Communist Party, Vilnius, Lithuanian S.S.R., U.S.S.R.

GRIST, Norman Roy, M.B., CH.B., F.R.C.P. (E.), F.R.C. PATH.; British professor of infectious diseases; b. 9 March 1918, Doncaster; s. of Walter Reginald Grist and Florence Goodwin (née Nadin) Grist; m. Mary Stewart MacAlister 1943; ed. Shawlands Acad., Univ. of Glasgow; army officer 1943-46; Resident Physician, Ruchill Hosp., Glasgow 1947-48; Research Asst. Dept. of Infectious Diseases, Univ. of Glasgow 1948-52, Lecturer in Virus Diseases, 1952-59, Sr. Lecturer 1959-62, Reader in Viral Epidemiology, Dept. of Virology 1962-65, Prof. of Infectious Diseases 1965-83, Emer. 1983-; Head of Regional Virus Lab., Glasgow 1958-83; mem. Expert Advisory Panel of WHO (Virus Diseases); Bronze Medal (Univ. of Helsinki) 1972, Orden Civil de Sanidad (Spain) 1974. *Publications:* Diagnostic Methods in Clinical Virology (jt. author) 1966, Infections in Current Medical Practice (jt. author) 1986, Diseases of Infection (jt. author) (1988), numerous papers in learned journals. *Leisure interests:* music, gardening, bird watching. *Address:* 5A Hyndland Court, 6A Sydenham Road, Glasgow, G12 9NR, Scotland. *Telephone:* 041-339 5242.

GRISWOLD, Erwin Nathaniel, LL.D., S.J.D., L.H.D., D.C.L.; American lawyer; b. 14 July 1904, East Cleveland, Ohio; s. of James H. Griswold and Hope Erwin; m. Harriet A. Ford 1931; one s. one d.; ed. Oberlin Coll., and Harvard Law School; worked in the office of the Solicitor Gen. 1929-34; Asst. Prof. of Law, Harvard Law School 1934-35, Prof. of Law 1935-46, Dean and Langdell Prof. of Law 1946-67; mem. U.S. Civil Rights Comm. 1961-67; Pres. Assen. American Law Schools 1957-58; Dir. American Council of Learned Socs. 1962-68; Solicitor Gen. of the U.S. 1967-73; Pres. American Bar Foundation 1971-74; Partner, Jones, Day, Reavis & Pogue, Washington 1973-; mem. American Philosophical Soc., Corresp. F.B.A., Hon. Bencher Inner Temple, etc.; many hon. degrees. *Publications:* Spendthrift Trusts 1936, Cases on Federal Taxation 1940-66, Cases on Conflict of Laws (with others) 1964 (5th edn.), The Fifth Amendment Today 1954, Law and Lawyers in the United States 1964. *Leisure interests:* golf, reading. *Address:* 1450 G Street, N.W., Suite 600 Washington, D.C.

20005-2088 (Office); 3900 Watson Place N.W., Washington, D.C. 20016, U.S.A. (Home). *Telephone:* 202-879-3898.

GRITSAI, Alexei Michailovich; Soviet painter; b. 1914, Leningrad; s. of Michail A. Gritsai and Nadezhda A. Gritsai; m. Valentina S. Gritsai 1940; one s.; ed. All-Russian Acad. of Arts (now I.E. Repin Art Inst. Leningrad) 1932-39; taught at Moscow Surikov Inst. of Art 1948-74, Prof. of Art 1966; corresp. mem. U.S.S.R. Acad. of Arts 1954, mem. 1964; People's Artist of U.S.S.R. 1974; awarded U.S.S.R. and R.S.F.S.R. State Prizes; Bronze Medal of Int. Exhbn. Brussels 1958. *Leisure interest:* music. *Address:* Kropotkinskaya 21, 119034 Moscow, U.S.S.R.

GROCHAL, Eugeniusz, M.ECON.SC.; Polish trades union activist and politician; b. 1 March 1920, Jasło; m.; two c.; ed. Tech. Univ., Szczecin; worked as railwayman during German occupation, Tarnów; after liberation participated in rebuilding railway junction, Lubań Śląski 1945; organizer of regional circle Railwaymen's TU, Lubań Śląski, Sec., Chair. 1945-49; attended TU School, Bydgoszcz; Asst. Railwaymen's TU Training Centre, Instructor, Head of Organizational Dept. and Sec. of Gen. Bd., Railwaymen's TU 1950-57, Chair. Gen. Bd. 1957-71; Deputy Chair. Cen. Council of TU (CRZZ) 1971-80; Minister, mem. Council of Ministers and Chair. State Bd. of Prices 1977-80; mem. Polish Socialist Party (PPS) 1946-48, Polish United Workers' Party (PZPR) 1948, mem. PZPR Cen. Cttee. 1971-80, mem. Cen. Revisional Cttee. 1980-81; Deputy to Seym (Parl.) 1965-80; Chair., Seym Comm. of Transport and Communication 1969-78; decorations include Order of Banner of Labour (1st and 2nd classes), Officer's Cross of Order Polonia Restituta, Gold Cross of Merit, Hon. Meritorious Railwayman of People's Poland. *Leisure interests:* fishing, yachting.

GROEBE, Hans, DR. JUR.; German business executive; b. 29 Sept. 1916, Breslau; m. Ruth Racke; one s. one d.; ed. Univ. of Freiburg and Kiel; commercial apprenticeship AEG, Erfurt 1935-37; mil. service 1937-45; rejoined AEG 1950, Commercial Man., Münster 1955-58, Hanover 1958-64, Man. Tech. Products Group 1964, mem. Man. Bd., AEG-Telefunken 1966, Chair. 1970-76, mem. Supervisory Bd. 1976-79; mem. Supervisory Bd. Norex GmbH, Munich, Deutsche Planungs-Gesellschafte G, Munich, Gastrobona AG, Wädenswill and others. *Address:* c/o MCG Management Consultant GmbH, Rehkopfweg 20, 6100 Darmstadt, Federal Republic of Germany. *Telephone:* (06151) 41373.

GROEBEN, Hans von der, DIP.JUR.; German European Community commissioner (retd.); b. 14 May 1907, Langheim, Ostpreussen; s. of Georg von der Groeben and Eva von Mirbach; m. Ilse von ünd zü Gilsa, 1974; ed. Charlottenburg Eng. Coll., Berlin, Bonn and Göttingen Univs.; with Ministry of Agric., Berlin 1933-39; mil. service 1939, 1942-45; Lower Saxony Ministry of Finance 1945-52; Dir. ECSC Div., Fed. Ministry of Econ. Affairs 1952-58; Co-rapporteur Spaak Report (on setting up of EEC); Chair. working party for drawing up EEC Treaty 1956; mem. Comm. of EEC 1958-67; mem. Comm. European Communities 1967-70; Dr. h.c. rer pol.; Prix Jean Monnet 1987, Grosses Bundesverdienstkreuz mit Schulterband und Stern, and other decorations. *Publications:* Europa-Plan und Wirklichkeit 1969, Ziele und Methoden der Europäischen Integration 1972, Kommentar zum Europäischen Wirtschafts-Gemeinschafts Vertrag 1974, 1982/83, Die Europäische Gemeinschaft zwischen Föderation und Nationalstaat 1977, Die Erweiterung der Europäischen Gemeinschaft durch Beitritt der Länder Griechenland, Spanien und Portugal 1979, Möglichkeiten und Grenzen einer Europäischen Union 1980, Aufbaujahre der Europäischen Gemeinschaft (Foundation Years of the EEC) 1982, Die Europaische Gemeinschaft und die Herausturverungen unserer Zeit 1987, Legitimationsprobleme der Europaïscher Gemeinschaft 1987, Eine Ordnungspolitik für Europa 1987. *Leisure interests:* sociology, philosophy, music. *Address:* 5308 Rheinbach, Federal Republic of Germany. *Telephone:* 02226-2525.

GROENMAN, Sjoerd, LITT.D., PHIL.D.; Netherlands sociologist; b. 28 Nov. 1913, Roosendaal; s. of Berend Groenman and Anna Margaretha Joustra; m. Lucie Limborgh Meijer 1939; three s. one d.; ed. Gymnasium Winschoten and Universiteit van Amsterdam; sociologist, Community at Emmen 1938, Northern Econ. Technological Org. 1940, Econ. Technological Inst., Overijssel 1941, Bd. of North-Eastern Polder (Zuiderzeeworks) 1943; Prof. of Sociology, Utrecht State Univ. 1948, Dean, Faculty of Social Sciences 1963-67; Prof., Applied Sociology, Univ. of Leiden 1956-60; Chair. Int. Social Science Council 1960-70; mem. Int. Cttee. on Documentation of Social Sciences 1964-70; mem. Bd. of Dirs. European Centre for Coordination and Documentation in Social Sciences, Vienna 1963-70; Chair. Advisory Cttee. Ministry of Social Work 1956-66; Rector (Magnificus), Utrecht Univ. 1971-76; Hon. Dr. (Univ. of Florida) 1977; Officer, Order of Orange-Nassau, Knight of the Dutch Lion. *Publications:* Methoden der Sociografie (Methods of Social Research) 1950, Kolonisatie op nieuw land (Colonisation on New Land) 1953, Ons deel in de ruimte (Our Part in Space) 1959, Sociaal gedrag en omgeving (Social Behaviour and Surroundings) 1971, Vrijmetselarij in Twente (Freemasonry in Twente) 1979, Met vallen en opstaan (With ups and downs), 200 jaar Vrijmetselarij in Deventer (200 years of Freemasonry in Deventer), Gedenkboek Loge "Le Préjugé Vaincu" (Memorial Lodge "L.P.V.") 1983. *Leisure interest:* publishing in different journals and newspapers. *Address:* Stobbenkamp 33, 7631 CM, Ootmarsum, Netherlands. *Telephone:* 05419-1946.

GRÖER, H.E. Cardinal Hans Hermann, O.S.B.; Austrian ecclesiastic; b. 13 Oct. 1919, Vienna; ordained 1942, elected bishop of Vienna 1986, consecrated 1986; cr. Cardinal 1988; Ordinand for the faithful in the Byzantine Rite resident in Austria. *Address:* Wollzeile 2, A-1010, Vienna, Austria. *Telephone:* (0222) 51.552.

GROLLET, Louis Jean Alfred, M.D.; French physician; b. 14 July 1899; s. of Charles and Louise (née Daval) Grollet; m. Jacqueline Istace 1945; one s. two d.; ed. Univ. de Paris à la Sorbonne; fmr. urologist, Faculty of Medicine, Paris, and Medical Asst., Hôpital Broca; Medical Supt.; Ecole Nat. Vétérinaire d'Alfort (Seine); Sec.-Gen. Soc. of Comparative Pathology; and Int. Cttee. of Congress of Comparative Pathology; Founder Sec.-Gen. of Assen. for Clean Air 1956; Founder Sec.-Gen. of Medical Centre specializing in biological and electronic research; Ed.-in-Chief Revue de pathologie comparée 1931– (Revue de pathologie comparée et de médecine expérimentale since 1967); mem. New York Acad. of Sciences; Officier, Légion d'honneur and other decorations. *Address:* 4 rue Théodule-Ribot, 75017 Paris, France. *Telephone:* (1) 46-22-53-19.

GROMYKO, Anatoly Andreyevich, DR.HIST.Sc.; Soviet political scientist; b. 15 April 1932, Borisov; s. of Andrey Gromyko (q.v.) and Lidia Dmitrievna Gromyko; m.; two s. one d.; ed. Moscow Inst. of Int. Rels.; First Sec., U.S.S.R. Embassy in London 1961–65; Head of Int. Rels. section, Africa Inst. of U.S.S.R. Acad. of Sciences 1966–68; Head of Section for U.S. Foreign Policy, Inst. of the United States and Canada (U.S.S.R. Acad. of Sciences) 1968–73; Minister Plenipotentiary Wash. Embassy 1973–74, Berlin 1974–76; Dir. Africa Inst. (U.S.S.R. Acad. of Sciences) 1976–. *Publications:* U.S. Congress: Elections, Organization, Powers 1957, The 1,036 Days of President Kennedy 1968, The Foreign Policy of the U.S.A.: Lessons and Reality the 60's and 70's 1978, The Conflict in the South of Africa: international aspects 1979, Africa: Progress, Problems, Prospects 1981, Masks and Sculpture of Sub-Saharan Africa 1984. *Leisure interest:* lawn tennis. *Address:* Africa Institute, U.S.S.R. Academy of Sciences, 30–31 Alexey Tolstoy, Moscow 103001, U.S.S.R. *Telephone:* 290-63-85.

GROMYKO, Andrey Andreyevich, D.ECON.; Soviet politician and diplomatist; b. 18 July 1909, Starye Gromyky, Byelorussia; m. Lidia Dmitrievna Gromyko; one s. (Anatoly Gromyko, q.v.); ed. Minsk Agricultural Inst. and Moscow Inst. of Econs.; Member CP 1931–; worked as sr. research scientist at Acad. of Sciences 1936–39; in charge of American Div. of Nat. Council of Foreign Affairs 1939; Counsellor at Wash. Embassy 1939–43; Amb. to U.S.A. and Minister to Cuba 1943–46; Soviet Rep. on UN Security Council 1946–49; Deputy Minister of Foreign Affairs 1946–49; First Deputy Minister 1949–52, 1953–57, Minister of Foreign Affairs 1957–85; a First Deputy Chair. Council of Ministers 1983–85; Amb. to U.K. 1952–53; mem. U.S.S.R. Supreme Soviet 1946–50, 1958–; Cand. mem. CPSU Cen. Cttee. 1952–56, mem. 1956–; mem. Politburo 1973–88; Deputy to U.S.S.R. Supreme Soviet of 2nd, 5th, 6th, 7th, 8th, 9th and 10th Convocations; First Vice-Chair. U.S.S.R. Council of Ministers 1983–86; Chair. Presidium of Supreme Soviet of U.S.S.R. 1985–88; took part in Teheran, Yalta and Potsdam Confs., Chair. Del. to Dumbarton Oaks Conf. on Post-War Security 1944; Chair. Comm. for Publ. of Diplomatic Documentation; Dmitrov Prize (Bulgaria) 1980, Hero of Socialist Labour (twice), Order of Lenin (eight times), Hammer and Sickle Gold Medal (twice), Karl Marx Order 1984, U.S.S.R. State Prize 1984, and other decorations. *Publication:* Memories 1989. *Address:* The Kremlin, Moscow, U.S.S.R.

GRØNDAHL, Kirsti Kolle; Norwegian politician. b. 1 Sept. 1943, Oslo; m.; mem. Royken Municipal Council and Municipal Exec. Bd. 1972–77; mem Storting 1977–, mem. Standing Cttee. on Foreign Affairs and the Constitution 1985–; Minister of Church and Educ. 1986–88, of Devt. and Co-operation; Head, Labour Party Cttee. on Educational Affairs. *Address:* P.O. Box 8119, Dep., Oslo 1, Norway.

GRÖNDAL, Benedikt, B.A.; Icelandic politician and diplomatist; b. 7 July 1924, Önundarfjördur; m. Heidi Gröndal; ed. Reykjavík Coll., Harvard Univ., Univ. of Oxford; journalist with Althydubladid 1938–43, News Ed. 1946–50, Ed. 1959–69; Ed. Samvinnan and Dir. of Div. of Education of Fed. of Icelandic Co-operative Socs. 1951–58; mem. Althing (Parl.) 1956–82; Minister for Foreign Affairs 1978–80, Prime Minister 1979–80; Amb. to Sweden 1982–87, Amb.-at-Large Asia Pacific Area 1987–; Dir. State Educational Library 1969–78; mem. Standing Cttee. N. Atlantic Ass. 1956–59; mem. State Radio Council 1956–71, Chair. 1957–59 and 1960–71; mem. Bd. of Dirs., Nat. Econ. Inst. 1971–78; Chair. Social Democratic Party 1974–80. *Publications:* books include The United States of America 1954, Iceland, from Neutrality to NATO Membership 1971. *Address:* Hjallaland 28, 108 Reykjavik, Iceland.

GRONOUSKI, John Austin, PH.D.; American economist and government official; b. 26 Oct. 1919, Wisconsin; s. of late John A. and Mary R. Gronouski; m. Mary Louise Metz 1948; two d.; ed. Oshkosh State Teachers Coll., Oshkosh, Wis., and Univ. of Wisconsin; U.S. Army Air Corps 1942–45; Prof. Univ. of Maine 1948–50; Research Assoc. Fed. Tax Admins. 1952–56; Research Assoc. Univ. of Wis. 1956–57; Prof. Wayne State Univ. 1957–59; Research Dir. Wis. Dept. of Taxation and Univ. of Wis. Tax Impact Study 1959; Exec. Dir. Revenue Survey Comm., Wis. 1959–60; Commr. of Taxation, Wis. 1960–63; Postmaster-Gen. 1963–65; Amb. to Poland 1965–68; Dean, Lyndon B. Johnson School of Public Affairs, Univ.

of Texas, Austin 1969–74, Prof. of Econ. and Public Affairs 1974–; mem. Nat. Acad. of Public Admin; mem. Presidential Comm. on Int. Radio Broadcasting 1972–73; Chair. Bd. for Int. Broadcasting (Radio Free Europe and Radio Liberty) 1977–81, Consultant to B.I.B. 1981–83; Pres. Polish Inst. of Arts and Sciences 1974–88, Austin Urban League 1981–84; Chair. Austin and Travis County Jt. Comm. on Metropolitan Govt. 1985–87; mem. Austin Private Industry Council 1985–. *Leisure interests:* swimming, golf, politics. *Address:* Lyndon B. Johnson School of Public Affairs, University of Texas, Austin. Tex. 78713 (Office); 700 South First Street, 206 Austin, Tex. 78704; U.S.A. (Home). *Telephone:* 512-471-4962 (Office); 512/447-8319 (Home).

GROOT, Per Søltoft, D.IUR.; Danish diplomatist; b. 21 Nov. 1924, Copenhagen; s. of Henrik and Caroline Groot; m. Inger Sorensen 1974; one s. one d.; ed. Univ. of Copenhagen; entered Danish Foreign Service 1949, seconded to NATO Int. Staff, Paris 1954–57, Prin. in Foreign Ministry 1957–61; Deputy Perm. Rep., Danish NATO Del., Paris 1962–64; Head of Dept., Political Affairs, Foreign Ministry 1964–67; Deputy Under-Sec. of State, Econ. Affairs, Foreign Ministry 1967–73; Amb. to German Democratic Repub. 1973–76, to Japan 1976–84; Govt. Adviser on Arms Control and Disarmament 1984–86; Amb. to Netherlands 1984–; Del. to UN Gen. Assembly 1966, 1974, 1975, 1980, 1984, 1985; Chair. OECD Drafting Group (New Treaty) 1960; Head of Del. to UN Habitat Conf., Vancouver 1976, Non-Proliferation Treaty Review Conf., Geneva 1985; Pres. Danish Lawyers and Economists Asscn. 1970–73; Commdr. Order of Dannebrog, Commdr. Italian Order of Merit, 1st Class Order of Rising Sun (Japan). *Leisure interests:* golf, international security studies. *Address:* Royal Danish Embassy, Sophialaan 11, NL-2514 JR The Hague, Netherlands. *Telephone:* 70-655830 (Office).

GROOTHAERT, Jacques, M.A.; Belgian banker and fmr. diplomatist; b. 25 Nov. 1922, Heist; m. Madeleine Williot 1945; two s.; ed. Univs. of Brussels and Ghent; served in Prague, Moscow, Paris and San Francisco (Consul-Gen.) 1961–64; Minister, London 1964–67, Amb. to Mexico 1967–72, to People's Repub. of China 1972–76; Dir.-Gen. Foreign Econ. Relations, Ministry of Foreign Affairs 1976–80; Chair. Bd. of Dirs. Generale Bank, Brussels 1980–, S.A.B.C.A. 1980–; Dir. Tractebel; Pres. Transurb Consult; Vice-Pres. Fabrimetal; mem. Bd. E.B.E.S. (Electricity) and many other public appts.; Grand Officier de l'Ordre de Léopold II; Commdr. Order de la Couronne; decorations from Mexico, Spain, Denmark, Iceland and France. *Address:* Generale Bank, 3 Montagne du Parc, 1000 Brussels, Belgium.

GROS, André; French judge at International Court of Justice; b. 19 May 1908, Douai; s. of Maurice Gros and Adèle Berr; m. Dulce Simoes-Correa 1940; two s.; ed. Univs. of Lyon and Paris; Asst., Law Faculty Paris 1931, Asst. Prof. Univ. Nancy 1935, Toulouse 1937, Univ. Prof. Public Law 1938–63; seconded to Ministry of Foreign Affairs 1939; Prof. Political Science Rio de Janeiro Univ. 1939, 1941–42; served France 1940; legal Counsellor to French Embassy in London; French Rep. on War Crimes Comm., London 1943; legal adviser to French Del. Council of Foreign Ministers and Peace Conf. Paris 1946; Legal Adviser Ministry of Foreign Affairs 1947; mem. Perm. Court of Arbitration, The Hague 1950; del. to Comm. for the Rhine 1950; Agent to Int. Court of Justice 1950–60; Conseiller d'Etat 1954–; Judge, Int. Court of Justice, The Hague 1964–; mem. Chamber of Court for delimitation maritime boundary Canada-U.S.A. 1982; mem. Inst. of Int. Law 1959, Vice-Pres. 1977–79; mem. UN Int. Law Comm. 1961; mem. Court of Arbitration in Beagle Channel case between Argentina and Chile 1977; mem. Court of Arbitration between France and U.K. (continental shelf delimitation) 1977; mem. Court of Arbitration between Senegal and Guinea-Bissau (delimitation of maritime boundary) 1986; Commdr., Légion d'honneur, Croix de guerre (1939–45) Hon. Mem. of the Bench (Inner Temple) 1972. *Publications:* Survivance de la raison d'état 1932, Problèmes politiques de l'Europe 1942–44 (Spanish trans. 1943), La Convention de Genève sur les pécheries 1959, Traités et documents diplomatiques (with Paul Reuter) 1960, La protection diplomatique (in Encyclopédie française) 1964. *Leisure interests:* reading, golf. *Address:* Palais de la Paix, The Hague, Netherlands (Office); Beau-Rivage, Lausanne, 6 Ouchy, CH-1000, Switzerland (Home).

GROS, François; French biochemist; b. 24 April 1925, Paris; s. of Alexandre Gros and Yvonne Haguenauer; m. 1st Françoise Chasseigne (divorced 1963), 2nd Danièle Charpentier 1964; three c.; ed. Lycée Pasteur, Neuilly, Univs. of Toulouse and Paris, Rockefeller Inst., Univ. of Illinois, U.S.A.; joined C.N.R.S. 1947; Researcher, Lab. Prof. J. Monod 1955; Head of Dept., Inst. de Biologie Physico-chimique 1963; Prof., Faculté des Sciences de Paris 1968, Inst. Pasteur 1972, Collège de France (Chair in Cellular Biochemistry) 1973–; Dir. Inst. Pasteur 1976–81, Head of Biochemistry Unit 1981–; Adviser to Prime Minister 1981–85; mem. EEC's CODEST 1984–; Pres. Asscn. Franco-Israélienne pour la recherche scientifique et tech. 1983–, Scientific Council of Asscn. Française contre la myopathie 1986–; mem. N.A.S., Acad. of Athens; Assoc. mem. Acad. Royale de Belgique; Dr. h.c. (Weizmann Inst., Israel); Gold Medal, Pontifical Acad. of Sciences 1964, Fondation Lacassagne Prize 1968, Charles Léopold Mayer Prize, Acad. des Sciences 1969; Officier Légion d'honneur; Officier Ordre Nat. du Mérite; several foreign decorations. *Publications:* Initiation à la Biochimie (with others); Sciences de la Vie et Société (with others) 1979, Les Secrets du Gène 1986. *Leisure interests:* music, drawing. *Address:* 102 rue de la Tour, 75016 Paris, France. *Telephone:* 45.04.80.63.

GROSHENS, Jean-Claude; French professor and academic administrator; b. 20 Nov. 1926, Strasbourg; s. of Henry and Louise (née Lehr) Groshens; m. Marie-Claude Meunier 1953; three d.; ed. Lycée Fustel-de-Coulanges, Strasbourg, Lycée Henri-Poincaré, Nancy, Lycée Blaise-Pascal, Clermont-Ferrand, Lycée Champollion, Grenoble, and Univ. of Strasbourg; Asst. governmental Sec.-Gen. 1953; Head of Lectures, attached to faculties of law, Grenoble and Dijon Univs. 1958; Prof. Law Faculty, Strasbourg Univ. 1962, Asst. to Dean 1967; Dir. Inst. of Political Studies, Strasbourg 1968; Tech. Advisor for Higher Educ., Ministry of Nat. Educ. 1968, Dir. of Planning 1970; Rector Nancy Acad. 1969, Lille Acad. 1972–75; Dir. Office of Sec. of State for Culture May-Aug. 1976; Dir. of dept, State Sec. for Culture and Pres. Nat. Centre for Literature 1976–80; Prof. Paris II Univ. 1979; Pres. Georges Pompidou Centre 1980–83; head of R.P.R. for Cultural Affairs and Dir. of Office of Sec.-Gen. of R.P.R 1983–, Nat. Sec. R.P.R. for Cultural Affairs 1984; Conseiller d'Etat 1987; Officier, Légion d'honneur; Officier, ordre nat. du Mérite, Commdr. des Palmes Acadé-miques et des Arts et des Lettres; Médaille de vermeil (for tech. educ.); Grand Prix du rayonnement français (Acad. Française). *Publications:* Les institutions et le régime juridique des cultes protestants 1953 and numerous articles on administrative science and politics of culture. *Address:* Conseil d'Etat Palais-Royal, 75100 Paris (Office); 13 rue des Orchidées, 73013 Paris, France (Home).

GROSS, Bernhard, DIPL.ING., DR. RER. NAT.; Brazilian physicist; b. 22 Nov. 1905, Stuttgart, Germany; s. of Wilhelm and Sophie Gross; m. Gertrud Gunz 1935; two s.; ed. Tech. Univ. Stuttgart, and Univ. of Berlin; Research Asst. Dept. of Physics, Stuttgart 1931–33; staff mem. Nat. Inst. of Tech., Rio de Janeiro 1934–46, Dir. Electricity Div. 1946–67; Dir. Physics Div. Brazilian Nat. Research Council 1951–54; Prof. of Physics Univ. of Fed. District, Brazil 1934–37; Prof. of Electrical Measurements Catholic Univ., Rio de Janeiro 1955; fmr. mem. Scientific Advisory Cttee. I.A.E.A. 1957–60; UN 1957–60; Brazilian Rep. to U.N. Scientific Advisory Cttee. 1958–60; mem. Brazilian Del. to UN Scientific Cttee. on Effects of Atomic Radiation 1957–59; Dir. Div. of Scientific and Tech. Information, I.A.E.A., Vienna 1961–67; Dir. of Research, Nat. Nuclear Energy Comm. of Brazil 1967–69; Visiting Prof., Tech. Univ., Karlsruhe, Fed. Repub. of Germany 1969; Scientist, Laboratoire Recherches Physiques, Veyrier, Switz. 1970; Research Prof. Inst. of Physics and Chem. of São Carlos, Univ. of São Paulo 1972–; Visiting Prof. Tech. Univ., Darmstadt, Germany 1978, 1984–86; Consultant, Bell Lab., Murray Hill, N.J. 1972–83; Dr. h.c. (São Paulo) 1975, (Tech. Univ., Darmstadt) 1985. *Publications:* Mathematical Structure of Theories of Viscoelasticity 1953, Singularities of Linear System Functions 1961, Charge Storage Effects in Solid Dielectrics 1964, and over 200 papers on cosmic radiation, radiation effects and dosimetry, electrets, viscoelasticity, electrical network theory. *Address:* Instituto de Fisica de São Carlos, C.P. 369, CEP 13.560 São Carlos, S.P. (Office); R. Padre Teixeira 2498, CEP 13.560, São Carlos, S.P. Brazil (Home). *Telephone:* 162 715365 (Office); 162 710467 (Home).

GROSS, Johannes; German journalist and author; b. 6 May 1932, Neunk-hausen; s. of Albert and Martha Gross; m. Elisabeth Gotthardt 1961; one s. one d.; ed. Univs. of Marburg and Bonn; Bonn corresp. Deutsche Zeitung 1959, Political Ed. 1961; Head, Political Dept. Deutschlandfunk, Cologne 1962; Dir. of Programmes and Dep. Dir.-Gen. Deutsche Welle 1968; Ed. Capital 1974; Editorial Dir. Capital and Impulse 1980; Dir. Gruner und Jahr AG & Co. 1983–; Commentator and host of political talk-show, Second German Nat. Television (ZDF); Columnist, Frankfurter Allgemeine Zeitung; contributor to Encounter (London) and Business Week, New York. *Publications:* Lauter Nachworte 1965, Absagen an die Zukunft, Festschrift für Ludwig Erhard (ed. and co-author) 1972, Unsere letzten Jahre 1980. *Address:* 70 Eupener Strasse, D-5000 Cologne 41, Federal Republic of Germany. *Telephone:* 0221-4908213.

GROSS, John Jacob, M.A.; British author, editor and publisher; b. 12 March 1935, London; s. of late Abraham and Muriel Gross; m. Miriam May 1965; one s. one d.; ed. City of London School, Wadham Coll., Oxford; Ed. with Victor Gollancz Ltd. 1956–58; lecturer, Queen Mary Coll., Univ. of London 1959–62, Hon. Fellow 1988; Fellow of King's Coll., Cambridge 1962–65; Asst. Ed. Encounter 1963–65; Literary Ed. New Statesman 1972–73; Ed. Times Literary Supplement 1974–81; Literary Ed. Spectator 1983–; journalist, New York Times 1983–; Dir. Times Newspapers Holdings Ltd. (fmrly. Times Newspapers Ltd.) 1982; editorial consultant The Wei-denfeld Publishing Group 1982; a Trustee Nat. Portrait Gallery 1977–84; Fellow Queen Mary Coll. 1987; Duff Cooper Memorial Prize 1969. *Publi-cations:* The Rise and Fall of the Man of Letters 1969, James Joyce 1971; Ed. The Oxford Book of Aphorisms 1983. *Address:* 24A St. Petersburgh Place, London W.2, England.

GROSS, Ludwik, M.D.; American research professor of medicine; b. 11 Sept. 1904, Cracow, Poland; s. of Dr. Adolf and Augusta Gross; m. Dorothy L. Nelson 1943; one d.; ed. Jagellon Univ., Cracow; Intern and Resident St. Lazar Hosp., Cracow 1929–32; clinical training, Salpêtrière Hosp., Univ. de Paris à la Sorbonne 1932–39; cancer research, Pasteur Inst., Paris 1932–39, Christ Hosp., Cincinnati, Ohio, U.S.A. 1941–43; Capt. to Major, Medical Corps, U.S. Army 1943–46; Chief, Cancer Research Unit, Veterans Admin. Hosp., New York 1946–; Consultant, Sloan-Kettering Inst. 1953–56, Assoc. Scientist 1957–60; Research Prof., Mount Sinai School of Medicine,

City Univ. of New York 1971–73, Emer. 1973–; Dir. American Asscn. for Cancer Research 1973–76; Distinguished Physician of the Veterans Administration 1977–82; mem. N.A.S., American Medical Asscn., American Soc. of Haematology and other socs.; F.A.C.P., New York Acad. of Sciences, A.A.A.S., Int. Soc. of Haematology; Diplomate, American Bd. of Internal Medicine; awards include Prix Chevillon, Acad. Médecine, Paris 1937, R. R. de Villiers Int. Award for Leukaemia Research 1953, Walker Prize, Royal Coll. Surgeons, England 1962, Pasteur Silver Medal, Pasteur Inst., Paris 1962, L. W. James Award, James Ewing Soc., New York 1962, WHO UN Prize 1962, Bertner Foundation Award, Univ. of Texas 1963, Albert Einstein Centennial Medal, Philadelphia 1965, Albion O. Bernstein M.D. Award, N.Y. State Med. Soc. 1971, Special Virus Cancer Program Award, Nat. Cancer Inst. 1972, William S. Middleton Award, Veterans Admin. 1974, Albert Lasker Basic Medical Research Award, New York 1974; Award for Cancer Immunology, Cancer Research Inst., New York 1975, Prin. Paul Ehrlich-Ludwig Darmstaedter Prize, Frankfurt 1978, Prix Griffuel (Paris) 1978, Katherine Berken Judd Award, Memorial Sloan-Kettering Cancer Center, New York 1985, Alfred Jurzykowski Foundation Award, New York 1985; Légion d'honneur, Hon. D.Sc. (Mount Sinai School of Medicine) 1983. *Publications:* Oncogenic Viruses 1961 (revised 1970, 1983) and over 200 papers on experimental cancer and leukaemia. *Leisure interests:* music, piano. *Address:* Veterans Administration Medical Center, 130 West Kingsbridge Road, Bronx, New York 10468, U.S.A. *Telephone:* (212) 579-1601.

GROSSER, Alfred, D. ES. L.; French professor, author and journalist; b. 1 Feb. 1925, Frankfurt; s. of the late Paul Grosser and Lily (née Rosenthal) Grosser; m. Anne-Marie Jourcin 1959; four s.; ed. Univs. of Aix en Provence and Paris; Asst. Dir. UNESCO Office in Germany 1950–51; Asst. Prof. Univ. of Paris 1951–55; lecturer, later Prof. Inst. d'études politiques 1954–; Dir. Studies and Research, Fondation nat. des Sciences politiques 1956–; Political Columnist La Croix 1955–65, 1984–, Le Monde 1965–, L'Expansion 1979–; Pres. Centre d'information et de recherche sur l'Allemagne contem-poraine 1982–, Euro-création 1986–; Peace Prize, Union of German Publrs. 1975; Chevalier Légion d'honneur. *Publications:* L'Allemagne de l'Occident 1953, La Démocratie de Bonn 1958, Hitler, la presse et la naissance d'une dictature 1959, La Quatrième Republique et sa politique extérieure 1961, La Politique extérieure de la ve Republique 1965, Au nom de quoi? Fondements d'une morale politique 1969, L'Allemagne de notre temps 1970, L'Explication politique 1972, Les Occidentaux: Les pays d'Europe et les Etats Unis depuis la guerre 1978, Le Sel de la Terre. Pour l'engagement moral 1981, Affaires extérieures: La politique de la France 1944–84, 1984, L'Allemagne en Occident 1985, Mit Deutschen streiten 1987, Vernunft und Gewalt. Die französische Revolution und das deutsche Grundgesetz heute 1989. *Leisure interest:* music. *Address:* 27 rue Saint Guillaume, 75007 Paris (Office); 8 rue Dupleix, 75015 Paris, France (Home). *Telephone:* 45 49 50 50 (Office); 43 06 41 82 (Home).

GROSSU, Semyon Kuzmich; Soviet politician; b. 1934, Moldavian S.S.R.; mem. CPSU 1961–; ed. Agricultural Inst., Kishinev; chief agronomist, head of a collective farm 1959–64; mem. Cen. Cttee. of Moldavian CP 1963–; Head Administrator of Suvorov Regional Agric. Production 1964–67; Sec. and mem. Politburo, Cen. Cttee. of Moldavian CP 1976–, First Sec. 1980–; Chair. Council of Ministers and Minister of Foreign Affairs of Moldavian S.S.R. 1978–82; Deputy to USSR Supreme Soviet; Order of Lenin (twice), Order of the October Revolution, Order of the Red Banner of Labour (twice), four medals of U.S.S.R. *Address:* Council of Ministers, Kishinev 277033, Moldavian S.S.R., U.S.S.R.

GRÓSZ, Károly; Hungarian politician; b. 1930, Miskolc; started as printer; graduated teacher Eötvös Loránd Univ., Budapest; successively Secr. Hungarian Young People's Fed., County Borsod; section leader County Borsod Party Cttee.; chief Ed. daily "North Hungary"; Secr. Party Cttee. Hungarian Radio and TV 1961; Deputy leader (HSWP Cen. Cttee. Agi-tation and Propaganda Dept.) 1968–73, leader 1974–79; first Sec. HSWP County Fejér Cttee. 1973–74, Gen. Sec. HSWP 1987; first Sec. County Borsod Party Cttee. 1979–84; first Sec. Budapest Party Cttee. 1984–87, Prime Minister 1987–88; mem. HSWP Political Cttee. 1985–, Gen. Sec. April 1989–; Medal of Merit for Socialist Hungary 1983. *Publication:* Szocializmus és korszerüség—Nemzeti és történelmi felelösség (Socialism and Modernity: National and Historic Responsibility). *Address:* Office of the Prime Minister, Parliament Building, 1357 Budapest, Kossuth Lajos tér 1, Hungary. *Telephone:* 123-500.

GROTOWSKI, Jerzy; Polish theatre director and teacher of acting; b. 11 Aug. 1933, Rzeszów; s. of Marian Grotowski and Emilia Kozlowska; ed. Faculty of Acting of Panstwowa Wyzsza Szkola Teatralna (Nat. Theatrical Acad.) Cracow, Faculty of Stage-directing in Moscow and Cracow; one of the leading exponents of audience involvement, has directed at Stary Teatr (Old Theatre), Cracow 1957–59; Lecturer Nat. Theatrical Acad., Cracow 1959; Dir. Teatr 13 Rzedów (Theatre Lab.), Opole 1959–64, later called Inst. for Research on Actor's Method-Lab. Theatre, moving to Wroclaw 1965–84; worked with R.S.C., London 1966, and at New York Univ.; Dir. Prof. Ecole Supérieure d'Art Dramatique, Aix-en-Provence 1968–70; Prof. h.c. (Pittsburg) 1973, (Chicago Univ.) 1985; has run Pan-Scandinavian courses for actors at Odin Teatret, Holstebro, Denmark 1966, 1967, 1968, 1969, and at Stockholm 1966–; at Centre de Stages Grotowski 1976, De la

Jenaille, France 1976; Dir. Univ. of Explorations of Theatre of the Nations, Wrocław 1975; emigrated Dec. 1982; Prof. Univ. degli Studi di Roma 1982, Columbia Univ. 1983, Univ. of Calif. at Irvine 1983–86; manages travelling drama study group (productions and lectures all over the world); Golden Prize, Int. Festival of Theatres in Belgrade 1967, Ministry of Culture of Poland Award for Research into Pedagogics 1967; Drama Desk Award, N.Y. for Apocalypsis cum Figuris 1969–70, Award of Polish Ministry of Foreign Affairs 1970, State Prize (1st class) for Apocalypsis cum Figuris 1972, Smithsonian Inst. Dipl. 1973, Kt.'s Cross of Order Polonia Restituta 1974, Officer's Cross of Polonia Restituta 1979. *Productions include:* Cain 1960, Dziady 1961, Kordian 1962, Acropolis 1962, Faustus 1963, Hamlet 1964, The Constant Prince 1965, Apocalypsis cum Figuris/collage 1968–69, 1972 (version II), 1974 (version III), Special Project (Holidays), Staże-Doświadczenia (Song of Myself), Undertaking Mountain 1977, Undertaking Earth (Part I: Vigil, Part 2: Acting, Part 3: Village) 1977–78. *Publications:* Towards A Poor Theatre 1968, Le Jour Saint et les autres textes 1974. *Leisure interest:* travelling. *Address:* Via Manzoni 22, 56025 Pontedera, Italy (Office); 115 Central Park West, Apartment 50, New York, N.Y. 10023, U.S.A. (Home).

GROUÈS, Henri (called **Abbé Pierre**); French ecclesiastic and philanthropist; b. 5 Aug. 1912, Lyons; s. of Antoine Grouès and Eulalie Perra; ed. Collège des Jésuites and Univ. of Lyons; entered Capuchin Order 1930; left for health reasons 1938; ordained priest 1938; almoner at the hosp. of La Mure and in charge of the Groupements de Jeunesse and the Orphanage of the Côte Ste. André 1940, vicar of Grenoble Cathedral 1941; f. an escape org. through the Alps and the Pyrenees, f. the cttee. against forced labour; joined Free French Forces in Algiers as Almoner to the Fleet 1944; Deputy for Meurthe-et-Moselle 1946–51; organized help for the destitute and the homeless in France and abroad, and cr. the Centre d'Emmaüs through an appeal to public opinion; f. the revue Faims et Soifs 1954; Officer, Légion d'honneur 1981, Croix de guerre (2 citations avec palmes), Médaille de la Résistance, Médaille des Evadés, Médaille des Combattants Volontaires, Médaille des Maquisards Belges, Médaille Albert Schweitzer 1975. *Publications:* 23 mois de vie clandestine, Vers l'homme, Feuilles éparses (poems), L'Abbé Pierre vous parle, Emmaüs 1959, Pleine vie, Le scandale de la faim interpelle l'église, Abbé Pierre Emmaüs ou Venger l'homme 1979, Revue 'Faims et Soifs' des hommes. *Address:* Monastère de Saint Wandrille, 76490 Caudebec en Caux, France. *Telephone:* 35.96.23.11.

GROUSSARD, Serge, L. ÈS L.; French writer and journalist; b. 18 Jan. 1921, Niort; s. of Col. Georges Groussard and Vera Bernstein; m. 3rd Monique Berlioux 1956; two d. (of previous marriages); ed. Lycée La Rochelle and Lycée Gouraud, Rabat, Ecole Nat. d'Administration, Ecole Libre des Sciences Politiques, and Univ. de Paris; Chief Reporter Le Figaro 1954–62, L'Aurore 1962–69; Special Contrib. Le Figaro 1969–75; Chevalier des Arts et des Lettres, Officier, Légion d'honneur, Croix de guerre, Médaille de la Résistance, Croix de la Valeur Militaire; Prix Claude Blanchard 1948, Prix International du Grand Reportage 1948, Prix du Roman populiste 1949, Prix Fémina 1950, Grand Prix de la Nouvelle 1957. *Publications:* Crépuscule des vivants 1946, Pogrom 1948, Solitude espagnole 1948, Des gens sans importance 1949, La femme sans passé 1950, Talya 1951, La ville de joie 1952, Un officier de tradition 1954, Une chic fille 1956, La belle espérance 1958, Quartier chinois 1958, La passion du Maure 1959, Jeunesse sauvage 1960, Une espionne doit mourir 1962, Les chacals 1964, Mektoub 1968, Tu es soleil 1970, Taxi de nuit 1971, l'Algérie des adieux 1972, La médaille de sang 1973, La guerre oubliée 1974, and others. *Leisure interests:* sport, painting. *Address:* 9 rue Sébastien Bottin, 75007 Paris, France. *Telephone:* 4825-17-43.

GROVÉ, Engelbertus Leonardus, M.SC., D.COMM.; South African civil servant and transport administrator; b. 23 Jan. 1925; m. Monica Spoelstra 1952; one s. two d.; ed. Potchefstroom Univ., Columbia Univ., New York, Pretoria Univ.; civil service 1947–55; Statistician, Transport Services' Head Office 1955–61, Rates Section 1961; studied rail tariff policy, U.S.A., Canada, Europe 1963; Chief Rates Officer, S.A. Transport Services 1964–69, Asst. System Man., Durban Jan.–July 1969, System Man., Kimberley 1969–70, Johannesburg 1970–76, Financial Man. 1976–80, Deputy Dir.-Gen. 1980–83, Dir.-Gen. Feb. 1983–; mem. S.A. Acad. for Arts and Science. *Leisure interests:* jogging and tennis. *Address:* Private Bag X47, Johannesburg 2000 (Office); 47 Third Street, Linden, Johannesburg, South Africa (Home). *Telephone:* 773-5082 (Office); 782-4634 (Home).

GROVE, Henning, B.VET.SC.; Danish politician; b. 7 April 1932, Svoldrup, North Jutland; s. of Peder Grove; ed. Royal Veterinary and Agricultural Coll., Copenhagen; practised as veterinarian; M.P. 1977–; Minister for Fisheries 1985–86; Conservative. *Address:* c/o Ministry of Fisheries, Stormgade 2, 1470 Copenhagen K, Denmark. *Telephone:* (01) 92-65-00.

GROVER, Amar Nath, M.A., LL.B.; Indian judge; b. 15 Feb. 1912, Shwebo (British Upper Burma); s. of G. L. and S. D. Grover; m. Mrs. Kanta Grover 1937; three s. one d.; ed. Univs. of Punjab, Lahore, Christ's Coll., Cambridge and Middle Temple, London; called to Bar 1936; Barrister, High Court, Lahore 1936–47, later at High Court of E. Punjab, Simla and Chandigarh; Judge, High Court, Punjab 1957–68; mem. Punjab Bar Council 1954–57, Law Comm. (Punjab) 1957; Judge, Supreme Court of India 1968–73; Chair. Cen. Comm. of Inquiry into State Ministers of Karnataka 1978; Chair. Press Council of India 1979–85; mem. World Peace Through

Law Centre; mem. Int. Bar Assen; Consulting Jurist; mem. numerous gov. bodies of educ. insts. *Publications:* several articles on various branches of law and the press. *Leisure interests:* golf, reading, fine arts, music (Indian and Western), comparative laws. *Address:* 132 Sunder Nagar, New Delhi 3, India. *Telephone:* 690118.

GROVES, Sir Charles, Kt., C.B.E., F.R.C.M.; British musician and conductor; b. 10 March 1915, London; s. of Frederick Groves and Annie Whitehead; m. Hilary Barchard 1948; one s. two d.; ed. St. Paul's Cathedral Choir School, Sutton Valence School, Kent and Royal Coll. of Music; Conductor, BBC Northern Symphony Orchestra 1944–51; Bournemouth Symphony Orchestra 1951–61, Welsh Nat. Opera Co. 1961–63; Conductor, Dir. of Music, Royal Liverpool Philharmonic Orchestra 1963–77, Conductor Laureate 1985–; Assoc. Conductor Royal Philharmonic Orchestra 1967–; Music Dir. Leeds Philharmonic Soc. 1988–; has toured Europe, U.S.A., S. America, Australia, S. Africa, Japan; numerous TV and radio recordings; conducts all major orchestras in U.K. including opera; Pres. Nat. Fed. of Music Socs. 1972–80, Incorporated Soc. of Musicians 1972–73, 1982–83, Nat. Youth Orchestra of G.B. 1977–; Dir. of Music, English Nat. Opera, Coliseum, London 1978–80; first to conduct complete cycle of Mahler's symphonies in U.K.; Companion of the Royal Northern Coll. of Music; Hon. Fellow Liverpool Polytechnic 1987; Hon. D.Mus. (Liverpool), Hon. R.A.M.; Hon. Dr. (Open Univ.), D.Litt. (Salford Univ.). *Leisure interests:* reading, cricket. *Address:* 12 Camden Square, London, NW1 9UY, England.

GROVES, Wallace, M.A., LL.M.; American financier; b. 20 March 1901, Norfolk, Va.; s. of James S. Groves and Lillie Edwards; m. Georgette Cusson (deceased); three s. two d.; ed. Georgetown Univ., Washington, D.C.; admitted Maryland Bar 1925; pvt. legal practice 1925–31; fmr. Pres. and Chair. Phoenix Securities Corpn.; Founder of Freeport, Bahamas, Wallace Groves Aquaculture Foundation; fmr. Chair. Grand Bahama Port Authority, Hon. LL.D (Ursinus Coll., Pa.), L.H.D. (Georgetown Univ.) 1981. *Leisure interests:* yachting, tennis. *Address:* P.O. Box 140939, Coral Gables, Fla. 33114, U.S.A.

GROZA, Maria; Romanian professor and politician (retd.); b. 1 Sept. 1918, Deva, Hunedoara County; ed. Bucharest Acad. of Econs.; Civil Servant, Ministry of Foreign Affairs 1948–55; Asst. Acad. of Econs., Bucharest 1949–55, lecturer in Social Sciences 1955–; Deputy, Grand Nat. Ass. 1965–80, Vice-Pres. 1965–75; Vice-Chair. Constitutional and Legal Perm. Cttee. of Grand Nat. Ass. 1975–80; Sec. Nat. Council of Women 1958–64, Vice-Pres. 1964–74, 1978–85, mem. Bureau 1974–78; Deputy Minister of Foreign Affairs 1980–87; mem. Nat. Council of Front of Socialist Democracy and Unity 1968–, Cen. Auditing Comm., Romanian 1979–84; Del. to numerous women's int. congresses, UNESCO and UN congresses, confs. and seminars on social and educational problems, World Conf. of Int. Women's Year (Rapporteur General) 1975; mem. Romanian del. to several UN Gen. Assembly Sessions. *Address:* c/o Ministerul Afacerilor Externe, Piata Victoriei 1, Bucharest, Romania. *Telephone:* 14 34 00.

GRÜBEL, Albert, DR.IUR.; Swiss lawyer; b. 22 March 1918, Basel; s. of Wilhelm and Clara Grübel (née Baumann); m. Jona Bach 1951; ed. High School, Basel and Basel Univ.; Commerce Div., Fed. Dept. of Econs. 1943–51; Swiss Fed. of Trade and Industry 1951–66; Amb., Del. of Swiss Fed. Council for trade agreements 1966–67; Dir. Fed. Office for Industry and Labour 1968–74; Perm. Rep. to OECD 1974–83. *Address:* Voltastrasse 43, 8044 Zurich, Switzerland.

GRUBER, Karl J., DR.JUR; Austrian retired politician; b. 3 May 1909, Innsbruck; s. of Peter and Maria (née Runggatscher) Gruber; m. Helga Ahlgrimm 1939; ed. Univs. of Innsbruck and Vienna; Austrian resistance leader 1938–45; Gov. of the Tyrol May-Oct. 1945; State Sec. for Foreign Affairs 1945–46; Minister of Foreign Affairs 1946–53; Amb. to U.S.A. 1954–57; M.P. 1946; lecturer in Econs., Vienna Univ. 1946–61; fmr. Vice-Pres. OEEC; Special Adviser to I.A.E.A 1958–60; Amb. to Spain 1961–66, to Fed. Repub. of Germany 1966; Sec. of State 1966–69; Amb. to U.S.A. 1970–73, to Switzerland 1973–75; Pres. Austro-Latin-American Inst., Vienna; mem. Energy Cttee., Vienna; fmr. Gov. European Cultural Foundation, Amsterdam; Hon. LL.D. (S. Calif.) 1946; Austrian People's Party. *Publications:* Die Politik der Mitte 1945, Voraussetzungen der Vollbeschäftigung 1946, Zusammenhang zwischen Grösse, Kosten und Rentabilität industrieller Betriebe 1948, Zwischen Befreiung und Freiheit 1953, Die Letzte Chance der Freien 1964, Ein Politisches Leben, Österreichs Weg zwischen den Diktaturen 1976, Die Welt im Konflikt 1982, Meine Partei ist Osterreich 1988. *Leisure interests:* sports, underwater photography, reading. *Address:* Rennweg 6A, A-1030 Vienna, Austria (Home). *Telephone:* 78 71 11.

GRUBER, Max, PH.D.; Netherlands professor of biochemistry; b. 9 Nov. 1921, Dresden; s. of Hermann Gruber and Gisella Schnek; m. Susanne Heynemann 1952; ed. Univ. of Utrecht; Asst. Univ. of Utrecht 1946–59, Chief Asst. 1949–52; Prof. of Biochem. Bandung, Indonesia 1952–55; Sr. Research Fellow, The Rockefeller Foundation, Yale Univ. 1955–56; Prof. of Biochem. Rijksuniversiteit Groningen 1956–86; Koninklijke Shell Prize for Chem. 1962; Diplôme d'honneur, Fed. of European Biochemical Socs. 1979. *Publications:* several hundred articles in biochemical journals; chapters and sections in books. *Address:* Biochemisch Laboratorium, Rijksuniversiteit Groningen, Nijenborgh 16, 9747 AG Groningen (Office); Emmalaan 19, 9752 KS Haren (Groningen), The Netherlands (Home). *Telephone:* (0) 50-634164 (Office); (0) 50-344709 (Home).

GRUDZIEŃ, Gen. Mieczysław, M.A.; Polish politician; b. 9 Jan. 1922, Majki, Płock district; ed. Coll. of Political Officers and Military Political Acad.; lived in France and Belgium 1922-47; during World War II activist in French Resistance; returned to Poland 1947 and joined the Polish People's Army 1949; various posts in the mil. party-political machine; recently First Asst. Chief, Political HQ of Polish Army 1971-72; div. Gen. Oct. 1971-; deputy mem. Cen. Cttee. PZPR/Polish United Workers' Party 1971-75, mem. Cen. Cttee. 1975-81; Minister for Combatants' Affairs 1972-81; Chief Combatants' Office (acting) 1981-82, Pres. 1982-87; Vice-Pres. Chief Council of Union of Fighters for Freedom and Democracy, ZBoWiD 1974-; mem. Presidium Cen. Bd., Soc. for Polish-Soviet Friendship 1974-84; Order of Builders of People's Poland 1979 and other decorations. *Address:* Rada Naczelna ZBoWiD, Al. Ujazdowskie 6A, 00-028 Warsaw, Poland.

GRUENBERG, Erich, F.R.C.M., F.G.S.M.; British violinist and music teacher; b. 12 Oct. 1924, Vienna, Austria; s. of Herman and Kathrine Gruenberg; m. Korshed Madan 1956; two d.; ed. in Vienna, Jerusalem and London; Leader, Philomusica of London 1954-56, Stockholm Philharmonic Orchestra 1956-58, London Symphony Orchestra 1962-65, Royal Philharmonic Orchestra 1972-76; leader of London String Quartet and mem. Rubbra-Gruenberg-Pleeth Piano Trio in 'fifties; now appears as soloist with leading orchestras in Britain and abroad; taught at Royal Coll. of Music 1960-65; Prof. Guildhall School of Music and Drama 1981-; winner, Carl Flesch Int. Violin Competition. *Leisure interests:* family, garden, sport. *Address:* 80 Northway, Hampstead Garden Suburb, London, NW11 6PA, England. *Telephone:* 01-455 4360.

GRUIJTERS, Johannes Petrus Adrianus; Netherlands politician; b. 30 June 1931, Helmond; m. Jannetje Mol 1936; one s.; ed. Augustinianum, Eindhoven, Municipal Univ. of Amsterdam; Co. Sec. de Wit's Textiel Nijverheid, Helmond (now incorporated in Hatema Texoprint/Gamma) 1953-58; studied 1958-60; Chief Foreign Ed. Algemeen Handelsblad 1960-67; Councillor Amsterdam Municipal Council 1962-66; Co-Founder Democraten 1966; mem. State Advisory Cttee. for the Constitution and Electoral Law 1967-71; mem. Provincial States of N. Holland 1970-71; Ed.-in-Chief, Het Spectrum, Publrs. 1971-72; mem. Second Chamber 1972-73; Minister of Housing and Physical Planning 1973-77; mem. first Chamber States-Gen. 1977-. *Publications:* De doortrekking van het Wilhelminakanaal-Daarom D'66, Experimenten in democratie, Nixon-McGovern. *Address:* Van Alkemadelaan 85, The Hague, Netherlands. *Telephone:* 070-246524.

GRUMBACH, Melvin Malcolm, M.D.; American physician and university professor; b. 21 Dec. 1925, New York; s. of Emanuel Grumbach and Adele (Weil) Grumbach; m. Madeleine F. Butt 1951; three s.; ed. Columbia Coll. and Columbia Univ. Coll. of Physicians and Surgeons; Resident in Pediatrics, Babies' Hosp., Presbyterian Hosp., New York, 1949-51; Visiting Fellow, Oak Ridge Inst. of Nuclear Studies 1952; Post-doctoral Fellow, Asst. in Pediatrics, Johns Hopkins School of Medicine 1953-55; mem. Faculty, Columbia Univ. Coll. of Physicians and Surgeons 1961-65; Asst. Attending Pediatrician, subsequently Assoc., Head of Pediatric Endocrine Div. and Postdoctoral Training Programme in Pediatric Endocrinology, Babies' Hosp. and Vanderbilt Clinic, Columbia-Presbyterian Medical Center 1955-65; Prof. of Pediatrics, Chair. Dept., Univ. of Calif. School of Medicine, San Francisco 1966-86, Edward B. Shaw Prof. of Pediatrics 1983-, Acting Dir. Lab. of Molecular Endocrinology 1987-; Dir. Pediatric Service Univ. of Calif. Hosps. 1966-86; Pres. Asscn. of Pediatric Dept. Chairman 1973-75, Lawson Wilkins Pediatric Endocrine Soc. 1975-76, Western Soc. for Pediatric Research 1978-79, Endocrine Soc. 1981-82; Exec. Cttee. Int. Soc. of Endocrinology 1984-; mem. Inst. of Medicine, N.A.S., Royal Soc. of Medicine, London, etc.; Joseph M. Smith Prize, Columbia Univ. 1962, Career Scientist Award, Health Research Council, New York 1961-66, Silver Medal, Bicentenary Columbia Coll. of Physicians and Surgeons 1967, Borden Award, American Acad. of Pediatrics 1971, Robert H. William Distinguished Leadership Award, Endocrine Soc. 1980. *Publications:* numerous scientific and clinical papers and monographs. *Leisure interests:* tennis, gardening, literature. *Address:* University of California School of Medicine, San Francisco, Calif. 94143, U.S.A. *Telephone:* (415) 476-2244.

GRÜMMER, Elisabeth: German soprano opera singer; b. 1921; ed. drama school, Meiningen and musical studies in Aachen; engaged at Stadttheater, Aachen 1941, Städtische Oper, Duisburg 1941, Staatsoper, Berlin 1948, Deutsche Oper, Berlin, W. Berlin 1961-; has made appearances at many foreign opera houses; Prof. Staatliche Hochschule für Musik und Darstellende Kunst, Berlin; awarded title of Kammersängerin; Berliner Kunstpreis 1965.

GRUNBERG-MANAGO, Marianne, PH.D.; French biochemist; b. 6 Jan. 1921, Leningrad, U.S.S.R.; d. of Vladimir Grunberg and Catherine Riasanoff; m. Armand Manago 1948; one s. one d.; ed. Univ. of Paris; Research Asst., subsequently Researcher then Sr. Researcher, Nat. Centre for Scientific Research, (CNRS) 1946-61, Head Dept. of Biochemistry, Inst. of Physico-Chemical Biology 1959, Dir. of Research, CNRS 1961-, Head Biochemistry Div. 1967-; Assoc. Prof., Univ. of Paris VII 1972-; Ed.-in-Chief Biochimie; Pres.-elect Int. Union of Biochemistry 1983, Pres. 1985; Vice-Pres. Comm. for Sciences and Tech., UNESCO 1985; mem. Soc. de Chimie Biologique, American Soc. of Biological Chemists, Int. Council of Scientific Unions Gen. Cttee., Acad. des Sciences; Foreign mem. American Acad. of Arts and Sciences, New York Acad. of Sciences; Foreign Hon. mem. N.A.S. (U.S.A.); Charles-Léopold Mayer Prize 1955, 1966, Fogarty Fellow 1977-82; Chevalier, Légion d'honneur. *Publications:* Polynucleotide phosphorylase, in Journal of American Chemical Soc. (with S. Ochoa) 1955, Biosynthèse des acides nucléïques (with F. Gros) 1974, :threonine tRNA ligase gene in *Escherichia coli*, in P.N.A.S. (with others) 1986, Escherichia coli and Salmonella typhimurium 1987; more than 300 scientific articles. *Leisure interest:* paintings. *Address:* Institut de Biologie Physico-chimique, 13 rue P. et M. Curie, 75995 Paris, France. *Telephone:* (1) 43.25.26.09.

GRUNDIG, Max; German business executive; b. 7 May 1908, Nuremberg; s. of Max Emil Grundig and Maria Grundig (née Hebeisen); m. Chantal Rubert; two d.; Chair. Supervisory Bd. Grundig AG -1984, Grundig Bank GmbH -1984; Chair. Bd. of Dirs. Max-Grundig-Stiftung, Fürth; Grosses Bundesverdienstkreuz mit Stern und Schulterband and numerous other decorations from Portugal, Mexico, Italy, Austria and Monaco; Dr.rer.pol. h.c. (Erlangen-Nuremberg). *Address:* 8510 Fürth, Am Europakanal 5, Federal Republic of Germany.

GRUNDY, Vincent Arthur; British company director; b. 6 Dec. 1931, Windermere; s. of Cecil Frederick Grundy and Elizabeth Agnes Grundy; m. 1957; one d.; ed. Worksop Coll.; involved in maj. overseas contracts in Middle E. and Africa for Cementation 1953-70, Man. Dir. Cementation Piling and Foundations Ltd. 1970-74, Cementation Specialist Holdings Ltd. 1974-, joined main Trafalgar Bd. 1977. *Leisure interests:* boating, gardening. *Address:* Camelford, Bradcutts Lane, Cookham Dean, Maidenhead, Berks., England.

GRUNERT, Horst, DR.RER.POL.; German diplomatist; b. 10 April 1928, Berlin; ed. German Acad. of Law; Official in G.D.R. Ministry of Foreign Affairs 1951-; Head (general Consul) in Syria 1965-68; Dir. of Information and Documentation of Ministry 1968-72; Perm. Rep. to UN 1972-74; Deputy Minister of Foreign Affairs 1974-78; Amb. to U.S. and Canada 1978-83, to Austria 1983-86; mem. SED; Vaterländischer Verdienstorden in Silver, Verdienstmedaille der DDR and other decorations. *Address:* c/o Ministry of Foreign Affairs, 102 Berlin, Marx-Engels-Platz 2, German Democratic Republic.

GRUNFELD, Henry; British (b. German) banker; b. 1 June 1904; m. Berta Lotte Oliven 1931; one s.; Chair. S. G. Warburg & Co. Ltd. 1969-74, Pres. 1974-87, Pres. S.G. Warburg Group PLC 1987-. *Address:* 2 Finsbury Avenue, London, EC2M 2PA, England. *Telephone:* 01 606-1066.

GRUNWALD, Ernest, PH.D.; American professor of chemistry; b. 2 Nov. 1923, Wuppertal, Germany; ed. Univ. of California, L.A.; Research Chemist, Portland Cement Assen. 1947; Research Fellow, Columbia Univ. 1948; Assoc. Prof., later Prof., Florida State Univ. 1949-60; Research Chemist, Bell Telephone Labs. 1960; Prof. of Chem., Brandeis Univ. 1964-89, Prof. Emer. 1989-; mem. N.A.S.; Fellow, American Acad. of Arts and Sciences; Chaim Weizmann Fellowship 1955, Alfred P. Sloan Fellowship 1958-60, Guggenheim Fellowship 1975-76; A.C.S. Award in Pure Chem. *Publications:* Co-author: Atoms, Molecules and Chemical Change 1960-80, Rates and Equilibria of Organic Reactions 1963-; Infrared Laser Chemistry 1976-. *Address:* Department of Chemistry, Brandeis University, Waltham, Mass. 02254, U.S.A.

GRUNWALD, Henry Anatole, L.H.D.; American editor and author; b. 3 Dec. 1922, Vienna; s. of Alfred Grunwald and Mila Loewenstein; m. Beverly Suser 1953 (died 1981); one s. two d.; ed. New York Univ.; mem. editorial staff, Time Magazine 1945-87, Sr. Ed. 1951-87, Foreign Ed. 1961-87, Asst. Man. Ed. 1966-68, Man. Ed. 1968-77; Corp. Ed., Time Inc. 1977-79, Ed.-in-Chief 1979-87, Consultant 1987-; Amb. to Austria 1987-; Dir. World Press Freedom Comm., Metropolitan Opera Guild; mem. Council on Foreign Relations; Hon. LL.D. (Iona Coll.) 1981; Hon. L.H.D. (Bennett Coll.) 1983. *Publications:* Salinger, a Critical and Personal Portrait 1962, Churchill, The Life Triumphant 1965, The Age of Elegance 1966; contribs. to Life and Horizon magazines. *Address:* US Embassy, 16 Boltzmanngasse, 1091 Vienna, Austria.

GRÜTZNER, Erich; German chemical worker, social scientist and politician; b. 30 July 1910, Pirna; mem. CP 1932-46, S.E.D. 1946-; mem. Volkskammer 1958-; Chair. Leipzig District Council 1959-74; Chair. Bezirk Leipzig Cttee. of Resistance Fighters June 1974-; mem. Council of State 1960-76; Vaterländischer Verdiensторden in Gold, Order "Banner der Arbeit" and other decorations. *Address:* Leipzig, German Democratic Republic.

GRZYB, Zofia; Polish politician; b. 18 Aug. 1928, Radom; worked in Radom Tobacco Plants, Radom 1947-49, in Walter Metal Works, Radom 1951-53; foreman, Radoskór Leather Industry Works, Radom 1953-; mem. Polish United Workers' Party (PZPR) 1948-, mem. Plenum, Town and Voivodship Cttee., Radom 1953-; mem. Exec. Radoskór Factory PZPR Cttee.; mem. Cen. Party Control Comm. 1980-81, PZPR Cen. Cttee. 1980-, mem. Political Bureau of PZPR Cen. Cttee. 1981-86, Chair. Health and

Environmental Protection Comm. of PZPR Cen. Cttee. 1981-, Comm. Women's Matters of PZPR Cen. Cttee. 1982-; mem. Nat. Council of Patriotic Movt. for Nat. Rebirth (PRON) 1983-87; Kt.'s Cross, Order of Polonia Restituta. *Address:* Komitet Centralny PZPR, ul. Nowy Świat 6, 00-497 Warsaw, Poland.

GRZYWA, Edward Jan, D.SC.TECH.; Polish chemist and politician; b. 8 Feb. 1933, Graboszyce; s. of Jan and Bronisława Grzywa; m. Zdzisława Szymanek-Grzywa 1961; two d.; ed. Moscow M.V. Lomonosov Inst. of Chemical Tech., U.S.S.R., and Nat. Coll. of Rubber Tech., London; scientific worker, then Head of Research Centre, Oświęcim Chemical Plant, Oświęcim 1957-66; Dir. Inst. of Heavy Organic Synthesis, Blachownia Śląska 1966-72; Dir. Dept. for Tech. Progress, Ministry of Chemical Industry 1972-75; Lecturer, Warsaw Tech. Univ. 1974-, Extraordinary Prof. 1973-78, Ordinary Prof. 1978-; Dir. Organic Industry Inst., Warsaw 1973-78; Dir. Industrial Chem. Inst., Warsaw 1978-80; Under-Sec. of State, Ministry of Chemical Industry 1980-82; Minister of Chemical and Light Industry 1982-87; Chair. Chemical Industry Cttee., ECE, UN 1982-84; mem. Chemical Research for World Needs (CHEMRAWN) Cttee., Int. Union of Pure and Applied Chem. 1985-; assoc. mem. Plastic and Rubber Inst., London; mem. Polish United Workers' Party (PZPR) 1951-; State Prize (2nd Class) four times. *Publications:* over 50 scientific works, 110 patents, numerous works on chemical technology. *Address:* ul. Wiktorii Wiedeńskiej 2m. 6, 02-954 Warsaw, Poland.

GSCHEIDLE, Kurt; German engineer and politician; b. 16 Dec. 1924, Stuttgart; s. of Georg and Emma Maria Gscheidle (née Schloz); m. Elisabeth Scharnhorst 1953; one s.; ed. REFA Inst., Sozialakademie; telecommunications technician, Fed. Postal Service 1948; Head, Secr. for Tech. and Econs., Postal Workers' Union 1953-57, Vice-Pres. Postal Workers' Union 1957-69; mem. SPD 1956-; mem. Bundestag (Parl.) 1961-; Sec. of State, Fed. Ministry of Posts 1969-74; Fed. Minister of Traffic 1974-80, Posts and Telecommunications 1980-82; Grosses Bundesverdienstkreuz 1976. *Publications:* books on industrial organization and personnel management. *Leisure interests:* cooking, tennis. *Address:* Görresstrasse 15, Bundeshaus, 5300 Bonn 1, Federal Republic of Germany.

GU CHANGHE; Chinese cartographer and engineer; b. 23 Feb. 1938, Jiang Su province; s. of Cou Lai Yang and Cou Cheng Shi; m. Zhao Jin Bao 1967; two s. one d.; mapped Sino-Pakistan border 1987, Sino-Nepal border 1979. *Address:* Room 206, Unit 1, Che Dao Cron No. 10, Hai Dian District, Beijing, China. *Telephone:* 899 2170.

GU CHAOHAO; Chinese mathematician; b. 15 May 1926; ed. Fudan Univ. and U.S.S.R.; Prof. Dept. of Math. at Fudan Univ., Shanghai 1960; Deputy, 3rd NPC 1964-66; mem. Scientific Council of Academia Sinica 1981; Deputy, 6th NPC 1983-88; Vice-Pres. Fudan Univ. 1984-; mem. Dept. of Math. and Physics, Academia Sinica 1985-; Vice-Chair. China-Brazil Friendship Group of NPC 1986-. *Address:* Room 37, Building 9, Fudan University, Shanghai, People's Republic of China. *Telephone:* 480906 (Shanghai).

GU GENGYU; Chinese politician and businessman; ed. St. Johns Univ. Shanghai; Man. China Animal Products Export Co. 1956; del. for China Democratic Nat. Construction Assen. to 3rd CPPCC 1959; mem. CPPCC 1959-67; disappeared during Cultural Revolution; mem. Standing Cttee. 5th CPPCC 1978; Dir. of Bd. of Dirs., China Int. Trust and Investment Corpn. 1979-; Vice-Chair. of Exec. Cttee., Fed. of Industrialists and Businessmen; Vice-Chair., China Industry, Commerce and Econ. Devt. Corpn. 1987-. *Address:* China International Trust and Investment Corporation, 2 Qianmen St. E., Beijing, People's Republic of China.

GU GONGXU, M.SC.; Chinese geophysicist; b. 5 July 1908, Jiashan Co., Zhejiang Prov.; ed. Shanghai Datong Univ., Colorado Univ., U.S.A.; researcher, Calif. Inst. of Tech. 1936-38; researcher, Inst. of Physics, Peiping (now Beijing) 1938-49; Deputy Dir., Inst. of Geophysics, Academia Sinica 1950-79; Deputy, First NPC 1954-58, 2nd NPC 1958-64, 3rd NPC 1964-66, 5th NPC 1978-83, 6th NPC 1983-88; mem. Standing Cttee. Dept. of Earth sciences, Pres. Geophysics Soc. 1958-; Head, Chinese geophysical study group visiting Iran 1976; mem. UNESCO Int. Advisory Cttee. on Earthquake Risks 1977; Pres. Soc. of Seismology 1979-; Dir. Geophysics Inst. 1980-; mem. Dept. of Math. and Physics, Academia Sinica 1985-. *Address:* Room 212, Bldg. 15, Zhong Guan Cun, Beijing 100080, People's Republic of China. *Telephone:* 284497 (Beijing).

GU GUANGMING; Chinese footballer; b. 1959, Guangdong Prov.; fmr. nat. team capt., capped 105 times; player for Darmstadt 98, Fed. Germany 1987-. *Address:* China Sports Federation, Beijing, People's Republic of China.

GU HUA (born Luo Hongyu); Chinese short story writer; b. 1942, Jiahe County, Hunan; ed. Chenzhou Agricultural School; research worker, Chenzhou Agricultural Research Inst. 1961-75; mem. writing staff, Chenzhou Song and Dance Ensemble 1975-79; Chenzhou Assen. of Literary and Art Workers 1979-; *Publications include:* A Log Cabin Overgrown with Creepers, A Small Town Called Hibiscus. *Address:* Chenzhou Association of Literary and Art Workers, Chenzhou, Peoples Republic of China.

GU HUI; Chinese soldier and party official; Deputy Commdr. Jinan Mil. Region 1985-; alt. mem. CCP Cen. Cttee. 1987-. *Address:* Central

Committee of the Chinese Communist Party, Zhongnanhai, Beijing, People's Republic of China.

GU JIAJI; Chinese diplomatist; Amb. to Zambia 1985-87, to Ethiopia Aug. 1987-. *Address:* Embassy of the People's Republic of China, P.O. Box 5643, Addis Ababa, Ethiopia.

GU JINCHI; Chinese party and government official; Vice-Gov. Sichuan Prov. 1982-86; mem. CCP Cen. Cttee. 1987-; Deputy Sec. Sichuan Provincial Cttee. Jan. 1988-. *Address:* Central Committee of the Chinese Communist Party, Zhongnanhai, Beijing, People's Republic of China.

GU MU; Chinese politician; b. 1914, Roncheng City, Shandong Prov.; joined CP 1932; Mayor of Jinan 1950-52; Deputy Sec. CCP Shanghai 1953-54; Vice-Chair. State Construction Comm. 1954-56, State Econ. Comm. 1956-65; Chair. State Capital Construction Comm. 1965-67; criticized and removed from office during Cultural Revolution 1967; Minister of State Capital Construction Comm. 1973-81, of Foreign Investment Comm. 1979-82, of Import-Export Comm. 1979-82; Political Commissar, PLA Capital Construction Engineering Corps 1979-; Vice-Premier, State Council 1975-82; mem. 11th Cen. Cttee. CCP 1977, Deputy for Shandong, 5th NPC 1978, mem. Secr. 1980-82, 1982-85, State Councillor, State Council 1982-; mem. 12th Cen. Cttee. CCP 1982-87, Exec. Chair. 1988-; Head Co-ordination Group for Tourist Industry 1986-, for Econ. Devt. of Ningbo 1985-; Hon. Pres. Soc. for Study of Econs. of Capital Construction 1980-, Confucius Foundation 1986-, China Assen. for Promotion of Int. Science and Tech. 1988-; Pres. China Econ. Law Research Soc. 1984-; Hon. Chair. China Tourism Assen. 1986-. *Address:* People's Republic of China.

GU XINER; Chinese diplomatist; Amb. to Ghana 1985-. *Address:* Embassy of the People's Republic of China, 7 Agostinho Neto Road, P.O. Box 3356, Accra, Ghana.

GU XIULIAN; b. 1935, Jiangsu Prov.; Chinese party and government official; cadre, State Council 1970; Vice-Minister State Planning Comm., State Council 1973-83; alt. mem., Cen. Cttee., CCP 1977; Vice-Chair. Cen. Patriotic Sanitation Campaign Cttee., Cen. Cttee. 1981-; mem. 12th Cen. Cttee., CCP 1982-; Deputy Sec. CCP Prov. Cttee., Jiangsu 1982-; Gov. of Jiangsu 1983-. *Address:* Office of the Governor, Jiangsu Province, People's Republic of China.

GU YINGQI; Chinese politician; Vice-Minister of Public Health 1984-; Pres. China Rural Hygiene Assen. 1986-. *Address:* Ministry of Public Health, Beijing, People's Republic of China.

GU YUAN; Chinese woodcut artist; b. 1919, Guangdong Prov.; ed. Lu Xun Acad. of Literature and Art, Yanan 1938-40; leader of movement to merge western and traditional techniques. *Address:* People's Republic of China.

GU ZHUOXIN; Chinese party official; b. 1910, Liaoning Prov.; Sec. Finance Dept., Govt. of Shanxi-Hebei-Shandeng-Henan Border Region 1941; Vice-Gov. Nuenjiang Prov. 1948; Dir. Financial Dept., N.E. People's Govt. 1949, Vice-Chair. People's Econ. Cttee. 1950; Vice-Chair. North East Admin. Cttee. (NEAC) 1953; Chair. Financial and Econ. Cttee., NEAC; Vice-Chair. State Planning Comm., State Council 1954; mem. Nat. Cttee. 3rd CPPCC 1959; Sec. Secr. North East Bureau 1963; purged 1968; Sec. CCP Cttee., Anhui 1977; Vice-Chair. Prov. Revolutionary Cttee., Anhui 1978; Chair. Prov. People's Congress, Anhui 1979-83; 2nd Sec. CCP Cttee., Anhui 1981-; mem. Cen. Advisory Comm., Cen. Cttee. 1982, Leading mem. Working Party for Streamlining Party and Govt. Orgs. 1983. *Address:* Office of the Central Advisory Committee, Beijing, People's Republic of China.

GUAN GUANGFU; b. 1931; Chinese commercial and party official; Man. Hubei Br. People's Bank of China; Sec. Hubei Prov. CCP Cttee. 1983-86; First Sec., Political Cttee. Hubei Prov. Mil. Dist. 1983, Chair. Armament Cttee. 1984-; mem. 12th Cen. Cttee. 1985. *Address:* People's Bank of China, Wuhan, Hubei Province, People's Republic of China.

GUAN JUNTING; Chinese government official; mem. Standing Cttee., Zhejiang Province CCP Cttee. 1978-; Sec.-Gen. Cttee. Zhejiang 1978; Commdr. Zhejiang Mil. District 1978-82; Deputy for PLA to 5th NPC 1978. *Address:* People's Republic of China.

GUAN SHANYUE; Chinese artist; b. 1912, Huangdong Prov.; exponent of Lingnan School of painting; studied with Gao Jinafu, Chun Shui Art School; followed Gao Jianfu to Macau 1938; mem. Progressive People's Art Soc., Hong Kong 1948; Vice-Chair. Chinese Artists' Assen. 1979-. *Address:* People's Republic of China.

GUAN WEIYAN; Chinese physicist; b. 18 Aug. 1928, Rudong Co., Jiangsu Prov.; ed. Harbin Polytechnical Inst., Beijing Univ., Moscow Univ.; researcher, Inst. of Physics, U.S.S.R. 1957-60; researcher, Beijing Physics Inst., Academia Sinica 1960-; Deputy Dir. Beijing Physics Inst. 1978-83; Visiting Scholar, Low-temperature Research Center in Grenoble, France 1980; Dir. Beijing Physics Inst. 1983-85; Pres. Univ. of Science and Tech., Hefei 1985-87; mem. Dept of Math. and Physics, Academia Sinica 1985-. *Address:* Room 203, Bldg. 96, Zhong Guan Cun, Beijing 100080, People's Republic of China. *Telephone:* 284060 (Beijing).

GUARNIERI, Roberto; Venezuelan economist and international official; b. Florence, Italy; s. of Raffaello Guarnieri and Livia Cammilli; m. Silene Fernández Colmenter 1963; one s. one d.; ed. Univ. Cen. de Venezuela, Yale Univ., Pembroke Coll., Oxford Univ.; Economist, Banco de Venezuela 1963-67, Adviser to Pres. 1967-72; Dir. of Econ. Research, Ministry of Finance 1972-74; Adviser to Minister of Mines and Hydrocarbons 1971-74; Exec. Dir. IBRD 1974; Alt. Exec. Dir. IMF 1974-76, Exec. Dir. 1976-78; Minister, Embassy in U.S.A. 1974-; Comendador, Orden del Libertador. *Address:* Ministerio de Relaciones Exteriores, Casa Amarilla, Esq. Principal, Caracas, Venezuela.

GUAZZUGLI MARINI, Giulio, DR.PH.; Italian atomic energy administrator; b. 1914; m. Maria Fantozzi 1940; one s. one d.; ed. Rome Univ.; Asst. Prof. of Phil., Rome Univ. 1937-47; Personal Sec. to Signor Carlo Sforza, Ministry of Foreign Affairs 1947-49; official at Council of Europe, Strasbourg 1949-53; Dir., Secr., Council of Coal and Steel Community 1953-57; Exec. Sec. EURATOM Comm. 1958-67; Dir.-Gen. European Community Jt. Research Centre 1968-71; Special Adviser to the Comm. of the European Communities 1971-80. *Leisure interest:* sailing. *Address:* 19 Passeggiata di Ripetta, Rome, Italy.

GUBENKO, Nikolai; Soviet actor and theatrical director; b. 1941; fmr. actor at the Taganka Theatre, Moscow; Dir. of several films including The Orphans (Soviet entry at the Cannes Film Festival 1977), The Life of Holiday-Makers (based on a story by Ivan Bunin), Life . . . Tears . . . Love; Artistic Dir. Taganka Theatre March 1987-. *Address:* c/o Taganka Theatre, Moscow, U.S.S.R.

GUCWA, Stanisław; Polish politician; b. 18 April 1919, Przybysławice; s. of Jan Gucwa and Maria Opta; m. Wiesława Podrygallo 1945; two d.; ed. Acad. of Political Science, Warsaw; Man. posts in Cen. Bd. of Flour Milling Industry and in Ministry of Food 1948-56; Under-Sec. of State Ministry of Agric. 1957-68; Minister of Food Industry and Purchases 1968-71; Vice-Chair. State Council 1971-72; mem. Peasant Party 1945-49, United Peasant Party 1949-; mem. Presidium Cen. Cttee. 1959-81, Chair. Presidium and Secr. of Cen. Cttee. 1971-81; Deputy to Seym (Parl.) 1961-, Marshal of Seym 1972-85; Vice-Chair. Nat. Defense Comm., mem. Foreign Affairs Comm., Seym; mem. Presidium All-Polish Cttee. of Nat. Unity Front 1971-81; numerous decorations including Order of Builders of People's Poland, Commdr.'s Cross of Polonia, Restituta, Order of Banner of Labour (First Class). *Publications:* over 100 papers on economic policy and agric. *Leisure interests:* history, hunting. *Address:* Frascati 8/10m5, 00-902, Warsaw, Poland. *Telephone:* 288264.

GUDMUNDSSON, Albert; Icelandic politician; b. 5 Oct. 1923, Reykjavík; m. Brynhildur H. Jóhannesdóttir; three c.; ed. Cooperative Commercial Coll., Reykjavík and Skerry's Coll., Glasgow; fmr. professional soccer player with Glasgow Rangers, Arsenal (London), F.C. Nancy, A.C. Milan, R.C.P. Paris and O.G.C.N. Nice; established Albert Guðmundsson Ltd. (wholesale co.) 1956; Pres. Alliance Française 1960-67; Hon. Consul of France 1964-; mem. Reykjavík City Council 1970-83, Pres. 1982-83; mem. Parl. 1974-; mem. Cen. Cttee. of Independence Party 1976-; presidential cand. 1980; Chair. Icelandic Football Asscn. 1968-74; hon. mem. of various sports asscns.; Minister of Finance 1983-85, of Energy and Industry 1985-87. *Address:* c/o Ministry of Energy and Industry, Reykjavík, Iceland.

GUDMUNDSSON, Finnbogi, DR.PHIL.; Icelandic teacher and librarian; b. 8 Jan. 1924, Reykjavík; s. of Dr. Gudmundur Finnbogason and Laufey Vilhjálmsdóttir; m. Kristjana P. Helgadóttir 1955; one d.; ed. Univ. of Iceland; Assoc. Prof. of Icelandic Language and Literature, Univ. of Manitoba, Canada 1951-56; lecturer in Icelandic, Univs. of Oslo and Bergen 1957-58; teacher, Reykjavík Gymnasium 1959-64; Docent, Univ. of Iceland 1962-64; Nat. Librarian 1964-; Chair. Asscn. of Icelandic Studies 1962-64, Div. of Icelandic Research Librarians 1966-73, Icelandic Patriotic Soc. 1967-84; hon. mem. Icelandic Nat. League, Winnipeg, Canada. *Publications:* Hómersthýðingar Sveinbjarnar Egilssonar (S. Egilsson's Translations of Homer) 1960, Ad vestan og heiman (collection of speeches and articles) 1967, Stephan G. Stephansson in Retrospect 1982, Ord og daemi (collection of articles) 1983; ed. of several vols. including Nat. Library Yearbook. *Leisure interest:* writing. *Address:* National Library, Reykjavík; Setbergsvegur 1, Hafnarfjördur, Iceland (Home). *Telephone:* 13375 (Office); 50928 (Home).

GUDMUNDSSON, Gudmundur I., CAND.IURIS; Icelandic lawyer and politician; b. 17 July 1909, Hafnarfjordur; m. Rosa Ingolfsdóttir 1942; five s.; ed. Reykjavík Coll., and Univ. of Iceland; law practice 1934-45; Supreme Court Attorney 1939-45; District Judge, Hafnarfjordur 1945-56; mem. Althing 1942-65; Minister for Foreign Affairs 1956-65, Minister of Finance 1958-59; Amb. to U.K., Netherlands, Spain and Portugal 1965-71, to Nigeria 1971, to U.S.A., Canada, Mexico, Brazil, Argentina, Cuba 1971-73, to Sweden, Finland, Austria, Yugoslavia 1973-77, to Belgium, Luxembourg, the EEC and NATO 1977-79; Hon. K.B.E., and many other decorations; Labour. *Address:* Sólvallagata 8, 101 Reykjavík, Iceland.

GUEDES, Prof. Amancio d'Alpoim Miranda, B.ARCH.; Portuguese professor of architecture; b. 13 May 1925, Lisbon; s. of Amilcar José de Miranda Guedes and Maria Soledad Francisca d'Alpoim; m. Dorothy Ann Phillips 1947; two s. two d.; ed. Univ. of Witwatersrand, Johannesburg, S.A., and Escola Superior de Belas Artes, Oporto; self-employed, Lourenço

Marques (now Maputo), Mozambique 1949-75; Prof. and Head of Dept. of Architecture, Univ. of Witwatersrand 1975-; Visiting Prof., Univ. of Queensland 1980, Univ. of Calif. 1980 and 1981; mem. Inst. of S.A. Architects; Commdr. Order of Santiago and Espada, Inst. of S.A. Architects Gold Medal. *Publications:* Architects As Magicians, Conjurers, Dealers In Magic Goods, Promises, Spells —Myself As Witchdoctor 1965, Buildings Grow Out Of Each Other Or How My Own Sagrada Familia Came To Be 1967, Fragments From An Ironic Autobiography 1977, Amancio Guedes (exhibition catalogue) 1980, Vitruvius Mozambicanus 1985. *Leisure interests:* painting, sculpture. *Address:* Department of Architecture, University of the Witwatersrand, 1 Jan Smuts Avenue, Johannesburg; 17 Ninth Avenue, Melville 2092, Johannesburg, South Africa (Home). *Telephone:* 716 2740 (Office); 726 1968 (Home).

GUEILER TEJADA, Dra. Lidia; Bolivian politician and diplomatist; b. Cochabamba; active role in revolution of 1952; became Pvt. Sec. to Pres. Paz Estenssoro (q.v.) 1952; mem. Chamber of Deputies 1956; left Movimiento Nacional Revolucionario and joined Partido Revolucionario de la Izquierda Nacional (PRIN) 1964; f. PRIN-Gueiler as part of Alianza Democrática de la Revolución Nacional 1979; Pres. Chamber of Deputies July-Nov. 1979; Pres. Congress Aug.-Nov. 1979; interim Pres. of Bolivia 1979-80 (overthrown in coup); in exile in Paris, France 1980-82; Amb. to Colombia 1983-86. *Address:* Ministry of Foreign Affairs, Cancellería de la República de Bolivia, Plaza Murillo esq. Ingarí, La Paz, Bolivia.

GUÉNA, Yves René Henri; French politician; b. 6 July 1922, Brest; m. Oriane de la Bourdonnaye 1945; five s. two d.; ed. Ecole Nat. d'Administration; mem. Free French Forces 1940-45; Official in Morocco 1947, Maître des Requêtes, Conseil d'Etat 1957, Dir. de Cabinet to M. Debré (Minister of Justice) 1958-59, Deputy Dir. de Cabinet to M. Debré (Prime Minister) Jan.-July 1959; High Commr. Ivory Coast 1959-60, Envoy Extraordinary (Dean of Diplomatic Corps) 1960-61; elected Deputy for Dordogne, Nat. Ass. 1962, 1967, 1968, 1973, 1974, 1978, lost seat 1981, re-elected 1986, lost seat 1988; Minister of Posts and Telecommunications 1967-68, 1968-69, of Information May-July 1968, of Transport 1973-74, of Industrial and Scientific Devt., March-May 1974; Deputy Sec.-Gen. UDR 1974, Sec.-Gen. 1976-; Political Adviser and Nat. Treasurer, Rassemblement pour la République 1977-79; Mayor of Périgueux (Dordogne) March 1971, re-elected March 1977, March 1983; Conseiller d'Etat 1972; Commdr., Légion d'honneur, Croix de guerre, Médaille de la Résistance. *Publications:* Historique de la communauté 1962, Maintenir l'état 1970, L'enjeu (in collaboration) 1975, Le temps des certitudes 1940-69 1982, Catilina ou la gloire dérobée 1984, Les cents premiers jours (co-author) 1985. *Address:* 96 avenue Victor Hugo, 75116 Paris, France.

GUENÉE, Bernard Marie Albert, D. ÈS L.; French university teacher; b. 6 Feb. 1927, Rennes; s. of Ernest Guenée and Antoinette (née Caisso) Guenée; m. Simonne Lucas 1955; ed. Ecole Nat. des Sciences, Paris, Fondation Thiers; Prof. Univ. de Strasbourg 1958-65, Sorbonne 1965-; Dir. of Studies Ecole Pratique des Hautes Etudes 1980-; mem. of Institut Français (Académie des Inscriptions et Belles Lettres) 1981-. *Publications:* Tribunaux et Gens de Justice dans le bailliage de Senlis à la fin du Moyen Age (vers 1380-vers 1550) 1963, Les Entrées royales françaises de 1328 à 1515, 1968, L'Occident aux XIVe et XVe siècles: Les Etats 1971, Histoire et Culture historique dans l'Occident médiéval 1980, Politique et Histoire au Moyen Age: Recueil d'articles sur l'histoire politique et l'historiographie médiévales (1956-81) 1981, Entre l'Eglise et l'Etat: Quatre vies de prélats français à la fin du Moyen Age 1987. *Address:* 8 Rue Huysmans, 75006 Paris, France. *Telephone:* 45.48.44.40.

GUENIN, Marcel André, PH.D.; Swiss university rector; b. 17 July 1937, Geneva; s. of Léandré André and Isabelle Guenin-Bontempo; m. Ingrid Marina Selbach 1962; three s.; ed. Edgenössische Technische Hochschule Zürich, Univ. of Geneva and Harvard Univ., U.S.A.; Asst. and Master Asst., Univ. of Geneva 1960-64; Research Assoc., Princeton Univ. 1964-66; Lecturer, Graduate Programme, Univs. of Lausanne, Neuchâtel and Geneva 1966-68; Asst. Prof., Univ. of Geneva 1968-70, Professeur extraordinaire 1970-73, Professeur ordinaire 1973-, Dir. Dept. of Theoretical Physics 1974-77; Vice-Rector Univ. of Geneva 1980-83, Rector 1983-87; Pres. PBG Pvt. Bank, Geneva 1987-; mem. Bd. Brown Boveri & Cie. 1987-; Sec.-Gen. European Physical Soc. 1974-79, Fellow 1980; Sec. Swiss Physical Soc. 1975-79; Founding mem. Int. Asscn. of Math. Physicists; mem. American Physical Soc. *Publications:* three books and about 40 scientific publs. *Leisure interests:* skiing, sailing, and music. *Address:* 2B chemin des Manons, 1218 Grand-Saconnex (GE), Switzerland (Home).

GUÉRIN, André Paul; French journalist; b. 1st Dec. 1899, Flers; m. Monique Berger 1951; one d.; ed. Collège de Flers, Lycée de Rennes, Caen Univ., and Ecole Normale Supérieure, Univ. of Paris; on staff of L'Oeuvre 1922-39; Ed. L'Aurore 1946-68, Political Dir. 1969-75; Pres. Club Henri-Rochefort 1963-; Commdr., Légion d'honneur, Croix de guerre; Médaille de vermeil, Paris; Grand Prix Littéraire des Yvelines 1974; Prix Européen du Journalisme. *Publications:* Manuel des Partis politiques en France 1928, Normandie champ de bataille de la libération 1954, Opération Bergère 1961, "1871" La Commune 1966, La folle guerre de 1870 1970, La vie quotidienne en Normandie au temps de Madame Bovary 1975, La vie quotidienne au Palais-Bourbon à la fin de la IIIe République 1978, Des chevaux de guerre hurlant et mordant 1983, La bataille de 1106 à Tinchebray entre les fils de Guillaume le Conquérant. *Leisure interest:* rugby. *Address:* 8 place de l'Abreuvoir, 78160 Märly-le-Roi, France.

GUÉRON, Jules; French atomic scientist; b. 2 June 1907; Tunis; s. of Lazare Guéron and Louise Bornstein; m. Geneviève Bernheim; three s.; ed. Lycée Charlemagne, Paris, and Univ. de Paris à la Sorbonne; Lecturer, Univ. of Strasbourg 1938, Asst. Prof. 1946-69 (on leave since 1947); with Tube Alloys 1941-46; Head of Service Commissariat of Atomic Energy 1946-49, Dir. Commissariat of Atomic Energy 1949-58, Dir. Centre de Saclay 1951-54, Dir. of Gen. Programme 1954-58 Head Physical-Chem. Dept. 1949-58; Dir.-Gen. Research EURATOM 1958-68; Lecturer, Conservatoire Nat. des Arts et Métiers 1951-61; Prof. Faculté des Sciences d'Orsay 1969-76; mem. and Sec. Comm. on Atomic Weights, Int. Union of Pure and Applied Chem. 1960-69; Prix Adrian, Chemical Soc. of France 1935; Officier, Légion d'honneur. *Publications:* about 100 scientific and gen. publications. *Address:* 15 rue de Siam, 75116 Paris, France. *Telephone:* 45.04.09.89.

GUERRA GONZÁLEZ, Alfonso; Spanish politician; b. 31 May 1940, Seville; m.; one s.; tech. engineer; joined Juventudes Socialistas (Socialist Youth) 1958 and Partido Socialista Obrero Español (PSOE) 1964; Gen. Sec. Andalusian section, PSOE; mem. Nat. Cttee. of PSOE until 1970, elected Press Sec. of Exec. Comm. 1970, Organizing Sec., Asst. Gen. Sec. 1979; mem. Congress of Deputies for Seville 1977-; Deputy Prime Minister Dec. 1982-; fmr. mem. Constitutional Comm. in Congress of Deputies; fmr. Vice-Pres. Socialist Parl. Group and mem. Standing Cttee. in Congress of Deputies; contrib. (and fmr. Dir.) El Socialista; Dir. Antonio Machado bookshop, Seville. *Address:* Pedro Pérez Fernández 1, 4°, Sevilla-11, Spain. *Telephone:* 27 97 24.

GUERRI, H.E. Cardinal Sergio; Italian ecclesiastic; b. 25 Dec. 1905, Tarquinia; ordained Roman Catholic priest 1929; cr. Cardinal 1969; fmr. Pro-Pres. Pontifical Comm. for the State of the Vatican City. *Address:* 00120 Stato Città del Vaticano, Rome, Italy.

GUEST, Douglas, C.V.O., M.A., MUS.D., F.R.C.M., F.R.C.O., F.R.S.C.M.; British organist and conductor; b. 9 May 1916, Mortomley, Yorkshire; s. of Harold and Margaret Guest; m. Peggie Falconer 1941; two d.; ed. Reading School, Royal Coll. of Music and King's Coll., Cambridge (Organ Scholar); War Service as Major, R.A. (Battery Commdr.) 1939-45 (mentioned in despatches); Dir. of Music, Uppingham School 1945-50; Organist and Master of Choristers, Salisbury Cathedral 1950-57, Worcester Cathedral 1957-63; Conductor of The Three Choirs Festival 1957-63; Organist and Master of Choristers Westminster Abbey 1963-81, Organist Emer. 1981-; Prof. Royal Coll. of Music 1963-81; Hon. R.A.M. *Composition:* Missa Brevis 1957. *Leisure interest:* fly-fishing. *Address:* The Gables, Minchinhampton, Gloucestershire, GL6 9JE, England. *Telephone:* 0453 883191.

GUEST, George Howell, C.B.E., M.A., MUS.D., F.R.C.O., F.R.S.C.M.; British (Welsh) musician; b. 9 Feb. 1924, Bangor; s. of Ernest Joseph and Gwendolen Guest; m. Nancy Mary Talbot 1959; one s. one d.; ed. Friars' School, Bangor, King's School, Chester, St. John's Coll., Cambridge; Chorister, Bangor Cathedral 1933-35, Chester Cathedral 1935-39; served R.A.F. 1942-46; Organ Student, St. John's Coll., Cambridge 1947-51, Fellow and Organist 1951-, Univ. Lecturer in Music 1956-82; Prof. of Harmony and Counterpoint, R.A.M. 1960-61; mem. of Council, Royal School of Church Music; Examiner, Assoc. Bd. of Royal Schools of Music; Pres. Royal Coll. of Organists 1978-80, Cathedral Organists' Assen. 1979-81; Pres. Inc. Assen. of Organists 1987-; Hon. mem. of Gorsedd of Nat. Eisteddfod of Wales; Hon. R.A.M.; Dir. The Arts Theatre, Cambridge; conducting and adjudicating tours in U.S.A., Canada, Japan, Australia, the Philippines, S. Africa, Greece and most Western European countries; Hon. R.A.M. *Publications:* various articles in musical journals. *Leisure interest:* Yr iaith Gymraeg. *Address:* St. John's College, Cambridge; 9 Gurney Way, Cambridge, England (Home). *Telephone:* (0223) 338683 (College); (0223) 354932 (Home).

GUEST, John Rodney, D.PHIL., F.R.S.; British professor of microbiology; b. 27 Dec. 1935, Leeds; s. of Sidney R. Guest and Kathleen (Walker) Guest; m. Barbara Dearsley 1962; one s. two d.; ed. Campbell Coll., Leeds Univ. and Trinity Coll. Oxford; Guinness Research Fellow, Oxford Univ. 1960-65; Research Assoc. and Fulbright Scholar, Stanford Univ. 1963, 1964; Lecturer in Microbiology, Univ. of Sheffield 1965-68, Sr. Lecturer and Reader 1968-81, Prof. of Microbiology 1981-; Science and Eng. Research Council Sr. Fellowship 1981-86. *Publications:* research papers in scientific journals. *Leisure interests:* hill walking, squash, beekeeping. *Address:* Department of Microbiology, University of Sheffield, Western Bank, Sheffield, S10 2TN, England. *Telephone:* 0742 768555.

GUEVARA ARZE, Walter; Bolivian politician and diplomatist; b. 1911; mem. Nat. Revolutionary Movt. (MNR); unsuccessful presidential and vice-presidential cand. 1960, 1978; fmr. Minister of Interior and fmr. Minister of Foreign Affairs; fmr. rep. at OAS and UN; in exile in 1974; Pres. of Senate Aug. 1979; Acting Pres. of Bolivia Aug.-Nov. 1979 (deposed); Amb. to Venezuela 1983-. *Address:* Embassy of Bolivia, Avda. Luis Roche con Transversal 6, Altamira, Caracas, Venezuela.

GUHA, Mrs. Phulrenu, D.LITT.; Indian social worker; b. 13 Aug. 1911, Calcutta; d. of the late Surendra Nath Datta and Abala Bala Datta; m.

the late Dr. Bireshchandra Guha 1943; ed. Calcutta Univ. and Univ. de Paris à la Sorbonne; participated in Freedom Movement since early days; social worker, W. Bengal, for over fifty years, actively associated with relief, social and children's welfare, family planning, defence aid, social health; undertook relief work during Bengal famine 1943, Noakhali 1946, Calcutta 1947-; Sec. United Council of Relief and Welfare, W. Bengal 1950-63; Chair. W. Bengal Social Advisory Bd. 1959-67, Cttee. on Status of Women in India 1971-74, Assoc. for Social Health in India, W. Bengal, Centre for Women's Devt. Study; Gen. Sec. and Vice-Pres. All India Women's Conf.; mem. Rajya Sabha 1964-70, Union Minister of State for Social Welfare 1967-70; Pres. Indian Council for Child Welfare, Sevak Sangh, W. Bengal 1970-73, Bharatiya Adimjati; Adviser Indian Inst. of Social Welfare and Business Man.; mem. Cen. Social Welfare Bd. 1970-76, All India Congress Cttee.; Pres. Indo-Korea Friendship Assen., Karma Kutir; Chair. Indo-G.D.R. Friendship Soc., W. Bengal, Working Chair. Indo-Soviet Cultural Soc., W. Bengal 1975-82, Vice-Chair. 1982-, Working Chair. Council for Nat. Integration and Democratic Rights; mem. Nat. Cttee. of Women, Govt. of India; Vice-Chair. Int. Year of the Child (non-Govt.), Int. Year of the Child (Govt. of W. Bengal); Working Pres. Nirakshrata Durikaran Samity (eradication of illiteracy); Gov. Bodies of Colls. in Delhi, Calcutta; Padma Bhusan 1977. *Leisure interests:* Rabindra songs, artefacts. *Publications include:* Participation of Women in India's Economy, Rammohan to Vivekanda, Role of Voluntary Organizations in Promoting Nutrition to Pre-school Children. *Leisure interests:* travelling, music, handicrafts, reading. *Address:* 55/5 Purna Das Road, Calcutta 700 029, W. Bengal, India. *Telephone:* 46-4884.

GUI, Luigi; Italian politician; b. 26 Sept. 1914, Padova; s. of Corinto Gui and Angelina Pinzan; m. Alessandra Volpi 1947; three s; war service, Italy and Russia 1941-43; Christian Democrat underground movement 1943-45; elected to Constituent Ass. 1946, re-elected 1948, 1953, 1958, 1963, 1968, 1972, 1976, 1979; fmr. Sec. of the Parl. Comm. on Agric. and Under-Sec. Ministry of Agric. and Forestry; Minister of Labour 1957-58; of Educ. 1962-68, of Defence 1968-70, of Health 1973-74, of Civil Service Reform March-Nov. 1974, of Interior 1974-76; Pres. Christian Democrat Deputies Parl. Group 1958-62; Senate 1976-79, Chamber of Deputies 1979-83, Pres. 1st Comm. on Constitutional affairs; mem. European People's Party, Paduan Acad. of Sciences, Letters and Arts, Council of European Soc. of Culture; Pres. Nat. Petrarch Soc., Casa di Dante, Rome. *Publications:* works on history of philosophy, political history, education and travel. *Address:* Via Bomporti 11, Padua, Italy. *Telephone:* 06/6793381.

GUIBERT, Roger, D. EN D.; French railways executive; b. 15 April 1907, Paris; s. of André Guibert and Louise née Hallopeau; m. Yvonne Thillaye 1928; two s. four d.; ed. Ecole Polytechnique; Engineer for Roads and Bridges, Highways Dept., Strasbourg 1931-34; Prin. Engineer, Chemins de fer du Nord 1935; Chief Engineer, Commercial Service of Soc. Nat. des Chemins de fer Français (SNCF) 1944; Dir. Western Region, SNCF 1958; Deputy Dir.-Gen. SNCF 1958, Dir.-Gen. 1966-74; Hon. Pres. SCETA; Pres. Cercle des Transports; Commdr., Légion d'honneur. *Publications:* Le nouveau statut des transports routiers 1939. Service public et productivité 1956, La SNCF: cette inconnue 1969. *Address:* 1 rue Villebois Mareuil, 75017 Paris, France. *Telephone:* 45.74.67.95.

GUICHARD, Baron Olivier Marie Maurice; French politician; b. 27 July 1920, Néac; s. of Baron Louis Guichard and Madeleine Brisson; Suzanne Vincent 1944 (deceased); three d.; ed. Univ. de Paris and Ecole libre des sciences politiques; mem. Rassemblement du peuple français, and Prin. Sec. to Gen. de Gaulle 1947-54; Press Officer Atomic Energy Commissariat 1955-58; Asst. Dir. Office of Gen. de Gaulle 1958, Tech. Adviser to the Pres. 1959-60; Del. Gen. of Org. des régions sahariennes 1960-62; Gen. Asst. Office of the Prime Minister 1962-67; Del. for Regional and Territorial Affairs 1963-67; elected Deputy for Loire-Atlantique, Nat. Ass. 1967, 1968, 1973, 1974, 1978, 1981, 1986; Minister of Industry 1967-68, of Econ. Planning 1968-69, of Educ. 1969-72, of Supply 1972-73, of Supply, Housing, Tourism and Territorial Devt. 1973-74, of Transport March-May 1974; Minister of State, Keeper of the Seals, and Minister of Justice 1976-77; Mayor of La Baule 1971-; Pres. Conseil régional des Pays de la Loire 1974-; Conseiller d'Etat 1978-; Dir. Cie. nat. du Rhône 1966-67; mem. Council of Admin. Radiodiffusion-Télévision française 1964-67; Pres. Mouvement pour l'indépendance de l'Europe 1975-; Pres. Admin. Council Conservatoire de l'espace littoral et des rivages lacustres 1986-; Médaille militaire; Officier, Légion d'honneur, Croix de guerre. *Publications:* Aménager la France 1965, Education nouvelle 1971, Un chemin tranquille 1975, Mon Général 1980 (Prix des Ambassadeurs). *Address:* Assemblée nationale, 75355 Paris, France.

GUIGNABODET, Liliane, L. ÈS L.; French author; b. 26 March 1939, Paris; d. of Moïse and Olympia N. Graciani; m. Jean Guignabodet 1961; one s. two d.; ed. primary school in Sofia (Bulgaria), Lycée Jules Ferry, Paris, Sorbonne and Univ. of London; Prof. of French, San José, U.S.A. 1961-62; Prof. of Arts and Culture, Ecole Technique d'IBM France 1966-69; author 1977-; mem. PEN Club Français; Prix George Sand 1977; Grand Prix du Roman, Acad. Française 1983. *Publications:* L'ecume du silence 1977, Le bracelet indien 1980, Natalia 1983, Le livre du vent 1984, Dessislava 1986, L'Eternel Printemps 1989. *Leisure interests:* piano, travel, decorating, skiing. *Address:* 55 rue Caulaincourt, 75018 Paris; La Bâste, 77230 Plessis aux Bois, France.

GUILFOYLE, Dame Margaret Georgina Constance, D.B.E.; Australian accountant and politician; b. 15 May 1926, Belfast, Northern Ireland; d. of William and Elizabeth McCartney; m. Stanley Martin Leslie Guilfoyle 1952; one. s. two d.; Chartered Sec. and Accountant 1947–; Liberal mem. Senate for Victoria 1971–87; Minister for Educ. Nov.–Dec. 1975, for Social Security 1975–80, for Finance 1980–83; Fellow, Australian Soc. of Accountants; Assoc. Chartered Inst. of Secs. and Administrators. *Leisure interests:* reading, gardening. *Address:* 21 Howard Street, Kew, Victoria, Australia (Home).

GUILHAMON, (Gaston) Jean (Clément); French business executive; b. 18 April 1922, Paris; s. of Antoine Guilhamon and Marguerite Trabet; m. Nicole Paste 1949; ed. Lycée Montaigne, Lycée Saint-Louis and Ecole Polytechnique; engineer of roads and bridges, Finistère 1946–48; Asst. Dir.-Gen. Electricité et Gaz d'Algérie 1948–62; Head of Commercial Services, Electricité de France 1963–, of Thermal Production 1966–67, Dir. of Equipment 1967–72, Asst. Dir.-Gen. 1972–81, Dir.-Gen. 1982–87; Admin. Del. Org. des Producteurs d'Energie nucléaire 1988–; Commdr., Ordre nat. du Mérite, Légion d'honneur. *Address:* 68 rue de Faubourg St. Honoré, 75008 Paris (Office); 8 allée Bernadotte, 92330 Sceaux, France (Home). *Telephone:* 47.64.22.09 (Office); 43.50.07.13 (Home).

GUILLABERT, André; Senegalese lawyer, politician and diplomatist; b. 15 June 1918; ed. Lycée Faidherbe, St. Louis-du-Sénégal, Faculté des Lettres, Bordeaux, and Faculté de Droit, Toulouse; Lawyer, Dakar Court of Appeal 1945–; Vice-Pres. Conseil Général du Sénégal 1947–52; First Vice-Pres. Territorial Ass., Senegal 1952; Counsellor, Ass. of French Union 1957–58; Senator (France) 1958–59, Senator (French Community) 1959–61; Vice-Pres. Constituent Ass., Senegal 1958–59, First Vice-Pres. Legis. Ass. 1959, Nat. Ass. 1960–62; Amb. to France (also accred. to Denmark, Finland, Norway, Sweden and Spain) 1960–62, 1966–77; Minister of Foreign Affairs, Senegal 1962; Keeper of the Seals and Minister of Justice 1962–63; Deputy and Vice-Pres. Nat. Ass., Senegal 1963–66; mem. Political Bureau and Asst. Sec.-Gen. Parti Socialiste Sénégalais Feb. 1978–; Grand Officier, Légion d'honneur and many other decorations. *Address:* 47 avenue de la République, Dakar, Senegal.

GUILLAUD, Jean Louis; French news agency executive; b. 5 March 1929, Caen; ed. Inst. d'Etudes Politiques, Paris; political journalist, Soc. Générale de Presse 1953–58, Paris-Jour 1958–60, France-Soir and Nouveau Candide 1961–63; Ed.-in-Chief, ORTF 1963, Dir. of TV news 1968–69; special assignment at Secr.-Gen. of Presidency of Repub. 1970–72; Dir. of Regional Stations and Third Channel, ORTF 1972–74; Dir.-Gen. TFI 1975–78, Pres. Dir.-Gen. 1978–81 ; later TV Dir. Hachette Group; Pres. Dir.-Gen. Agence France Presse (AFP) Jan. 1987–; Officier, Légion d'honneur, Officier, ordre nat. du Mérite, Chevalier des Arts et des Lettres. *Address:* Agence France Presse, 11–15 place de la Bourse, 75002 Paris, France.

GUILLAUMAT, Pierre L. J.; French company executive and fmr. civil servant; b. 5 Aug. 1909; ed. Prytanée Militaire, La Flèche and Ecole Polytechnique; Chef du Service des Mines, Indochina 1934–39, Tunisia 1939–43; Dir. of Carburants 1944–51; Admin.-Gen. Atomic Energy Comm. 1951–58; Pres. Petroleum Research Bureau 1945–58; Minister of the Armies, de Gaulle Cabinet, 1958–59, Debré Cabinet 1959–60; Minister attached to Prime Minister's Office 1960–62; Minister of Educ. (*a.i.*) 1960–61; Pres. Union Gén. des Pétroles 1962–65, Electricité de France 1964–66, Entreprise de Recherches et d'Activités Pétrolières 1966–77, Soc. Nat. des Pétroles d'Aquitaine 1966–76, Soc. Nat. ELF-Aquitaine 1976–77; Pres. Conseil d'Admin. de l'Ecole Polytechnique 1971–74, Conseil de l'Université de Technologie de Compiègne 1980–83 (mem. 1983–), Ligue Nationale Française contre le Cancer 1981–; Pres. Comité des relations industrielles, Centre nat. de la recherche scientifique 1981–; Grand Croix Légion d'honneur, Croix de guerre. *Address:* 15 boulevard Richard-Wallace, 92200 Neuilly-sur-Seine, France.

GUILLAUME, Gilbert, L. EN D.; French judge; b. 4 Dec. 1930, Bois-Colombes; ed. Univ. of Paris, Paris Inst. of Political Studies and Ecole Nat. d'Administration; Commr. of Audit, Council of State 1957, Rapporteur 1963, Councillor of State 1981; Legal Adviser, State Secr. for Civil Aviation 1968–79; French Rep. Legal Cttee. of ICAO 1968–69, Chair. of Cttee. 1971–75; Chair. Conciliation Comm. OECD 1973–78; Dir. of Legal Affairs, OECD 1979; mem. European Space Agency Appeals Bd. 1975–78; French Rep. Central Comm. for Navigation of the Rhine 1979–87, Chair. 1981–82; Dir. of Legal Affairs, Ministry of Foreign Affairs 1979–87; Counsel/agent for France in int. arbitration proceedings, numerous cases before European Courts etc.; mem. Perm. Court of Arbitration 1980–; del. to numerous int. legal and diplomatic confs.; Prof. Inst. of Political Studies, Univ. of Paris and other lecturing appts.; mem. various legal assocns., insts. etc.; Judge, Int. Court of Justice 1987–. *Publications:* numerous books and articles. *Address:* International Court of Justice, Peace Palace, 2517 KJ The Hague, The Netherlands. *Telephone:* 92 44 41.

GUILLAUMONT, Antoine Jean-Baptiste, D. ÈS L.; French professor; b. 13 Jan. 1915, L'Arbresle (Rhône); s. of Pierre Guillaumont and Cécile (née Gallon) Guillaumont; m. Claire Boussac 1948; three c.; ed. Faculté des Lettres, Montpellier, Ecole pratique des Hautes Etudes, Paris; teacher at the Lycée de Monaco 1943–45; Researcher C.N.R.S. 1946–51; Dir. of Studies, Ecole pratique des Hautes Etudes, Hebrew and Aramaic 1952–74, Oriental Christianity 1957–81; Prof. in Christian Studies, Collège de France 1977–86, Prof. Emer. 1986–; mem. Institut de France, Acad. des Inscriptions et Belles lettres 1983–; Dr. h.c. Uppsala, Louvain and Liège; Croix de guerre, Palmes académiques. *Publications:* L'Asceticon copte de l'abbé Isaïe 1956, Les Six Centuries des 'Képhalaia Gnostica' d'Evagre le Pontique 1958, Les 'Kephalaia Gnostica' d'Evagre le Pontique et l'histoire de l'origénisme chez les Grecs et chez les Syriens 1962, Aux origines du monachisme chrétien, Abbaye de Bellafontaine 1979. *Address:* 164 rue de Vaugirard, F75015 Paris, France. *Telephone:* (1) 47.34.38.73.

GUILLEM, Sylvie; French ballet dancer; b. 23 Feb. 1965, Le Blanc Mesnil; joins Ecole de Danse, Paris Opera 1976; Ballet de l'Opéra as Quadrille 1981, promoted to Coryphée 1982, to Sujet 1983, Première Danseuse, later Etoile 1984; joins Royal Ballet, London as Prin. Guest Artist Feb. 1989. *Leading roles in:* Romeo and Juliet, Don Quixote, Raymonda, Swan Lake, Giselle, Notre Dame de Paris. *Created roles include:* Cendrillon, In the Middle, somewhat elevated, Magnificat, Le Martyre de Saint-Sébastien; Commdr. des Arts et Lettres 1988; Prize for Excellence and Gold Medal, Varna Int. Dance Competition 1983, Prix Carpeau 1984, Hans Christian Andersen Award 1988. *Address:* c/o Royal Ballet, Royal Opera House, London, WC2E 9DD, England.

GUILLEMIN, Henri; French writer and fmr. university professor; b. 19 March 1903, Mâcon; s. of Philippe Guillemin and Louise Thenoz; m. Jacqueline Rödel 1928; two s. two d.; ed. Ecole Normale Supérieure, Paris; teaching posts, various lycées, France 1928–36; Prof. of French Literature, Univ. of Cairo, Egypt 1936–38; Prof. of French Language and Literature, Univ. of Bordeaux 1938–42; Cultural Counsellor, French Embassy, Berne 1945–62; Prof., Univ. of Geneva 1963–73; Officier, Légion d'honneur; Grand Prix de la Critique, Paris 1965. *Publications:* over 30 volumes of literary history and history. *Address:* 58 faubourg de l'Hôpital, Neuchâtel, Switzerland; La Cour-des-Bois, 71460 Saint-Gengoux-le-National, France. *Telephone:* 038-25-40-51 (Switzerland); 85.50.01.69 (France).

GUILLEMIN, Roger Charles Louis, M.D., PH.D.; American professor of medicine; b. 11 Jan. 1924, Dijon, France; s. of Raymond and Blanche Guillemin; m. Lucienne Jeanne Billard 1951; one s. five d.; ed. Univs. of Dijon, Lyons, Montreal; Prosector of Anatomy, Univ. of Dijon Medical School 1946–47; Research Asst., Inst. of Experimental Medicine and Surgery, Univ. of Montreal 1949–51, Assoc. Dir. and Asst. Prof. of Experimental Medicine 1951–53; Asst. Prof. of Physiology, Coll. of Medicine, Baylor Univ., Houston, Tex. 1953, Assoc. Prof. 1957, Prof. of Physiology and Dir. Laboratories for Neuroendocrinology 1963–70, Prof. of Physiology (Adjunct) 1970–; Consultant in Physiology, Veterans' Admin. Hosp., Houston 1954–60, 1967–70; Lecturer in Experimental Endocrinology, Dept. of Biology, W. M. Rice Univ., Houston 1958–60; Assoc. Prof., Dept. of Experimental Endocrinology, Coll. de France, Paris, as jt. appointment with Coll. of Medicine, Baylor Univ. 1960–63; Consultant in Biochem., M. D. Anderson Hosp. and Tumor Inst., Houston 1967–; Resident Fellow and Research Prof., The Salk Inst. for Biological Studies, San Diego, Calif. 1970–, Dean 1972–73, 1976–77; Prof. of Medicine (Adjunct), Univ. of Calif., San Diego 1971–; mem. N.A.S. 1974–, American Acad. of Arts and Sciences, American Physiological Soc., Soc. for Experimental Biology and Medicine, Int. Brain Research Org., Int. Soc. for Research in Biology and Reproduction, Swedish Soc. of Medical Sciences, Acad. Nat. de Médecine, France, Acad. des Sciences, France, Acad. Royale de Médecine de Belgique, Belgium; Pres. The Endocrine Soc. 1986; Hon. degrees (Univ. of Rochester, Rochester, N.Y.) 1976, (Univ. of Chicago, Ill.) 1977, (Baylor Coll. of Medicine, Houston, Tex.) 1978, (Univ. of Ulm, Ulm/Donau, W. Germany) 1978, (Univ. of Dijon, France) 1978, (Univ. Libre de Bruxelles) 1979, (Univ. de Montréal) 1979, (Univ. of Man., Canada) 1984, (Univ. of Turin, Italy) 1985; Bonneau and La Caze Awards in Physiology (Acad. des Sciences) 1957, 1960, Gairdner Award (Toronto) 1974, Officier, Légion d'honneur, Lasker Foundation Award 1975, co-recipient of Nobel Prize in Physiology or Medicine with Andrew V. Schally (q.v.) for discoveries relating to peptide hormones 1977, Nat. Medal of Science 1977, Barren Gold Medal 1979, Dale Medallist, U.K. Soc. for Endocrinology 1980; numerous int. awards and lectureships. *Address:* The Salk Institute for Biological Studies, P.O. Box 85800, San Diego, Calif. 92138, U.S.A. *Telephone:* (619) 453-4100 (Office).

GUILLÉN, Nicolás; Cuban poet; b. 10 July 1902, Camagüey; s. of Nicolás Guillén and Argelia Batista; ed. Camagüey Inst.; legal studies 1921; poet and author 1922–; Spanish war corresp. for Mediodía magazine 1937–38; Mayoral Cand. for Camagüey 1940 (Popular Socialist, later Cuban CP); Cand. for Senate, La Habana Province 1948; Pres. Cuban Union of Writers and Artists (UNEAC); Amb. of Cuba; Dr. h.c. (Bordeaux) 1977; Lenin Peace Prize 1954; Order of Merit of Haiti, Order of Cyril and Methodius (1st Class), Bulgaria. *Poetry:* Motivos de son 1930, Sóngoro cosongo 1931, West Indies Ltd. 1934, España 1937, Cantos para soldados y sones para turistas 1937, El son entero 1947, La paloma de vuelo popular 1958, Elegías 1958, Tengo 1964, Poemas de Amor 1964, El Gran Zoo 1967, La rueda dentada 1972, El diario que a diario 1972, Por el Mar de las Antillas anda un Barco de Papel 1977; essays on violinist Brindis de Salas 1935; chronicles: Prosa de Prisa 1962. *Address:* Unión de Escritores y Artistas de Cuba, Calle 17, No. 351, Vedado, Havana; Calle O, 22°, No. 2, Edificio Someillán, Vedado, Havana, Cuba. *Telephone:* 32-4551 (Office); 32-1079 (Home).

GUILLERMIN, John; British film director; b. 11 Nov. 1925, London. *Films include:* Torment 1949, Smart Alec 1951, Two on the Tiles 1951, Four Days 1951, Bachelor in Paris 1952, Miss Robin Hood 1952, Operation Diplomat 1953, Adventure in the Hopfields 1954, The Crowded Day 1954, Dust and Gold 1955, Thunderstorm 1955, Town on Trial 1957, The Whole Truth 1958, I Was Monty's Double 1958, Tarzan's Greatest Adventure 1959, The Day they Robbed the Bank of England 1960, Never Let Go 1960, Waltz of the Toreadors 1962, Tarzan Goes to India 1962, Guns at Batasi 1964, Rapture 1965, The Blue Max 1966, P.J. 1968, House of Cards 1969, The Bridge at Remagen 1969, El Condor 1970, Skyjacked 1972, Shaft in Africa 1973, The Towering Inferno 1974, King Kong 1976, Death on the Nile 1978, Mr Patman 1980, Sheena 1984, King Kong Lives 1986. *Address:* c/o ICM, Los Angeles, U.S.A. *Telephone:* 213-550-4000.

GUILLERY, Rainer W., PH.D., F.R.S.; British university teacher, anatomist and neurobiologist; b. 28 Aug. 1929, Greifswald, Germany; s. of Eva Hackel and Hermann Guillery; m. Margot Cunningham Pepper 1955; three s. one d.; ed. Univ. Coll. London; Asst. Lecturer, Anatomy Dept., Univ. Coll. London 1953–56, Lecturer 1956–63, Reader 1963–64; Assoc. Prof., Dept. of Anatomy, Univ. of Wis., Madison, U.S.A. 1964–68, Prof. 1968–77; Prof., Dept. of Pharmacological and Physiological Sciences and Chair. Cttee. on Neurobiology, Univ. of Chicago, U.S.A. 1977–84; Dr. Lee's Prof. of Anatomy, Oxford Univ., England 1984–; Ed.-in-Chief European Journal of Neuroscience 1988–; Fellow, Univ. Coll. London 1987. *Publications:* contribs. to Journal of Comparative Neurology, Journal of Neuroscience, Neuroscience, Brain Research, etc. *Address:* Department of Human Anatomy, South Parks Road, Oxford, OX1 3QX, England. *Telephone:* (0865) 272179.

GUINIER, Prof. André Jean, D. ÈS SC.; French professor of physics; b. 1 Aug. 1911, Nancy; s. of Philibert and Lucie (née Le Monnier) Guinier; m. Claire Chasse 1934; one d.; ed. Lycée de Nancy, Ecole Normale Supérieure, Paris; Prof. of Physics, Univ. of Paris 1949–77; Visiting Prof., Harvard Univ. and Univ. of Ill., U.S.A. 1952–53, American Univ., Cairo 1965; Dir. Lab. of Solid State Physics, Paris 1960–71; Pres. Soc. française de minéralogie et cristallographie 1960, Soc. française de physique 1962, Teaching Comm., Int. Union of crystallography 1966–69, mineral and crystallography section of Nat. Cttee., C.N.R.S. 1966–70, Pres. Int. Union of crystallography 1969–72; mem. Acad. des Sciences; Chevalier, Légion d'honneur, Officier, Ordre nat. du Mérite; Dr h.c. Eth (Zurich); several awards and prizes for physics. *Publications:* Radiocristallographie 1945, Théorie et Technique de la radiocristallographie 1956, X-Ray Diffraction 1963, La Structure de la Matière 1980, Les Rayons X 1984, La Matière à l'état solide 1987. *Address:* 87 avenue Denfert-Rochereau, 75014 Paris, France. *Telephone:* 46.33.38.05.

GUINNESS, Sir Alec, Kt., C.B.E.; British actor; b. 2 April 1914, London; m. Merula Salaman 1938; one s.; ed. Pembroke Lodge, Southbourne and Roborough, Eastbourne; entered Advertising Agency as Copywriter 1933; Scholarship to Fay Compton Studio of Dramatic Art 1934; First Stage appearance April 1934; played in seasons for John Gielgud and Old Vic Theatre Co.; Hamlet in modern dress 1938; served R.N.V.R. 1940–44; began film career 1945; Acad. Award for services to film 1980; Hon. Dr. Fine Arts (Boston Coll) Hon. D.Litt. (Oxford) 1977, BAFTA Award 1980, 1983, Shakespeare Prize 1985, Soc. of West End Theatres Special Award 1989, BAFTA Fellowship 1989. *Films include:* Great Expectations 1946, Oliver Twist 1947, Kind Hearts, and Coronets 1948, The Lavender Hill Mob 1951, The Man in the White Suit 1951, The Bridge on the River Kwai 1957, (Oscar 1958), The Horse's Mouth 1958, Our Man in Havana 1959, Tunes of Glory 1960, Lawrence of Arabia 1962, Dr. Zhivago 1966, The Comedians 1967, Cromwell 1969, Murder by Death 1975, Star Wars 1976, Little Lord Fauntleroy 1980, Lovesick 1982, A Passage to India 1984, Little Dorrit 1986, A Handful of Dust 1987. *Plays include:* The Prisoner 1954, Hotel Paradiso 1956, Ross 1957, Exit the King, Dylan 1963, Macbeth 1965, Wise Child 1967, 1968, A Voyage Round My Father 1971, Habeas Corpus 1973, A Family and a Fortune 1975, Yahoo 1976, The Old Country 1977, The Merchant of Venice 1984, A Walk in the Woods 1988. *TV includes:* Tinker, Tailor, Soldier, Spy 1979, Smiley's People 1981, Edwin 1983, Monsignor Quixote 1985. *Publication:* Blessings in Disguise 1985. *Address:* 235/241 Regent Street, London, W1A 2JT, England.

GUINNESS, James Edward Alexander Rundell, C.B.E.; British banker; b. 23 Sept. 1924, London; s. of the late Sir Arthur Guinness, K.C.M.G., and Lady Frances Patience Guinness (née Wright), M.B.E; m. Pauline Vivien Mander 1953; one s. four d.; ed. Eton and Oxford Univ.; joined family banking firm of Guinness Mahon & Co. 1946, Partner 1953–, Dir. 1953–; Chair. Guinness Mahon Holdings Ltd. 1968–72; Jt. Chair. Guinness Peat Group Ltd. 1973–77, Deputy Chair. 1977–84; Commr., Public Works Loan Bd 1960, Deputy Chair. April 1977–79, Chair. April 1979–, Provident Mutual Managed Pension Funds 1983–; Deputy Chair. Provident Mutual Life Assurance Asscn. 1983–. *Leisure interest:* fishing. *Address:* Coldpiece Farm, Mattingley, Basingstoke, Hants., RG27 8LQ, England.

GUISE, Sir John, G.C.M.G., K.B.E.; Papua New Guinea politician (retd.); b. 29 Aug. 1914, Milne Bay; m.; five s. four d.; ed. Anglican School, Dogura, Milne Bay Province; Gen. Labourer Burns Phil 1927–42; Sergeant-Major, Royal Papua New Guinea Constabulary 1946–55; mem. Legis. Council and mem. Admin.'s Exec. Council 1961–63, House of Ass. 1964–75; Speaker 1968–71; Leader various foreign parl. delegations 1962–81; Deputy Chief Minister and Minister of the Interior 1972–74, Minister of Agric. 1974–75, 1st Gov.-Gen. of Papua New Guinea 1975–77; mem. Nat. Parl. 1977–; unsuccessful cand. for Prime Minister Aug. 1977; Chair. Nat. Emergency Cttee. 1979; Deputy Chair. Public Accounts Cttee. 1978–81; Chair. Nat. Tourist Authority 1982–; Hon. LL.D.; K.St.J. 1976; Independent, later United Party. *Address:* House of Assembly, Port Moresby (Office); Lalaura Village, Cape Rodney, Central Province, Papua New Guinea.

GUITTON, Henri; French professor of economics; b. 5 July 1904, Saint-Etienne; s. of Auguste and Gabrielle (née Bertrand) Guitton; m. Yvonne Loriot de Rouvray 1929; five s. one d.; ed. Lycée de Saint-Etienne and Faculties of Law and Science, Paris; Prof., Law Faculty, Dijon 1938–52; Prof. of Statistics, Faculty of Law and Econ. Science, Univ. of Paris 1952–63, Prof. of Political Economy 1964, Prof. of Econ. Analysis 1971–74, Prof. Emer. 1979; mem. Acad. des sciences morales et politiques, Inst. de France 1971–; mem. Accademia nazionale dei Lincei, Rome 1968–; Hon. Dr. (Liège), (Verune); Commdr., Légion d'honneur. *Publications:* Les fluctuations économiques 1951, Maîtriser l'économie 1967, A la recherche du temps économique 1970, Entropie et Gaspillage 1975, De l'imperfection en économie 1979 Le sens de la durée 1985; Ed. La revue d'économie politique. *Leisure interest:* painting. *Address:* 5 rue des Feuillantines, 75005 Paris, France. *Telephone:* 43.26.41.66.

GUITTON, Jean Marie Pierre; French university professor; b. 18 Aug. 1901; s. of Auguste Guitton and Gabrielle Bertrand; m. Marie-Louise Bonnet (deceased); ed. Ecole Normale Supérieure; fmr. teacher in schools at Troyes, Moulins, Lyon, and Univs. of Montpellier and Dijon; Prof. of Phil. and History of Phil., Univ. of Paris 1955–68; mem. Programmes Cttee. Radiodiffusion et Télévision Française (ORTF) 1965–; Observer at 2nd Vatican Council 1963; mem. Acad. Française 1961–; Foreign mem. Acad. of Athens 1986–, Sofia Acad. of Sciences 1986–; Commdr., Légion d'honneur, Commdr. Ordre national du Mérite, Ordre des Arts et des Lettres, Grand-Croix de St. Grégoire-le-Grand; Grand Prix de Littérature, Acad. Française 1954, Grand Médaille, Bordeaux Acad. of Arts, Sciences and Belles-Lettres 1969, Prix Osiris, Inst. de France 1972. *Publications:* Le temps et l'éternité chez Plotin et Saint Augustin, La philosophie de Newman, L'existence temporelle, Essai sur l'amour humain, Le problème de Jésus, Le nouvel art de penser, Le travail intellectuel, Portrait de Monsieur Pouget, Jésus, Apprendre à vivre et à penser, Le Cardinal Saliège, La vocation de Bergson, L'église et l'évangile, Problème et mystère de Jeanne d'Arc, Journal oecuménique, Le clair et l'obscur vers l'unité, Dialogues avec Paul VI, Profiles parallelles, Histoire et destinée, Oeuvres completes (6 vols.), Ce que je crois, la famille et l'amour, Paul VI secret, le temps d'une vie 1980, Crise dans l'Eglise: le Christ écartelé 1981, Portrait de Marthe Robin, Silence sur l'Essential, etc. *Leisure interest:* painting. *Address:* 1 rue de Fleurus, 75006 Paris; La Pensée, Champagnat, 23190 Bellegarde-en-Marche, France.

GUJRAL, Inder Kumar, M.A.; Indian politician; b. 4 Dec. 1919, Jhelum (now in Pakistan); s. of Shri Avtar Narain Gujral and Shrimati Pushpa Gujral; m. Shrimati Sheila Gujral 1944; two s.; ed. Forman Christian Coll. and Hailey Coll. of Commerce in Lahore, Punjab Univ.; jailed for participation in freedom movement 1930–31 (and again during Quit India movement 1942); Pres. Lahore Students' Union; Gen.-Sec. Punjab Students' Fed.; migrated to India 1947; helped nat. effort for rehabilitation of displaced persons; Vice-Pres. New Delhi Municipal Cttee. 1959–64; M.P. 1964–76; Alt. Leader Indian Del. Inter-Parl. Union Conf., Canberra 1966; mem. Council of Ministers, Govt. of India 1967–76 holding portfolios for Communications and Parl. Affairs 1967–69, for Information, Communications and Broadcasting 1969–71, Minister of State for Works, Housing and Urban Devt. 1971–72, for Information and Broadcasting 1972–75, for Planning 1975–76; Amb. to U.S.S.R. (with ministerial rank) 1976–80; mem. Rajya Sabha 1970–76; Vice-Pres. New Delhi Municipal Cttee. 1959–64; helped organize Citizens Cttee. for Civil Defence; mem. All India Cen. Citizens Council, Sec. Resources Sub-Cttee.; mem. All India Congress Cttee.; Rep. India at Inter-Parl. Union Conf. in Canberra 1966; Alt. Leader Indian Dels. to UNESCO 1970, 1972, 1974, to UN session on Environment, Stockholm 1972; Chair. UNESCO seminar on Man. and Current Communications Systems, Paris 1973; Leader Indian Del. UNESCO session on Environment and Educ., Tbilisi 1977; Founder-Pres. Delhi Arts Theatre; Treas. Fed. of Film Socs. of India; Vice-Pres. Lok Kalyan Samiti; Co-Chair. Asian Regional Conf. of Rotary Int. 1958. *Leisure interests:* theatre, poetry, painting, ecological problems. *Address:* c/o Ministry of External Affairs, New Delhi, India.

GULBINOWICZ, H.E. Cardinal Henryk Roman, D.THEOL.; Polish ecclesiastic; b. 17 Oct. 1928, Szukiszki, Vilna; s. of Antoni Gulinowicz and Waleria Gajewska; ed. Catholic Univ. Lublin; ordained 1950; Titular Bishop, Apostolic Admin. Archdiocese of Białystok 1970–76, Archbishop of Wrocław 1976–; mem. Congregation for Eastern Churches, Congregation Clergy Affairs; cr. Cardinal 1985. *Address:* ul. Katedralna 13, 50-328 Wrocław, Poland. *Telephone:* 225.081.

GULDBERG, Ove; Danish civil engineer, lawyer and politician; b. 2 Dec. 1918, Nysted; s. of Frede and Else Guldberg (née Richter); m. Else Guldberg (née Christiansen) 1942; three s.; employed by Vejle City Admin. 1942; with Civil Eng. Contractor, K. Hindhede 1943; Copenhagen City

Engineer's Office 1944; at Research Lab., Ministry of Fisheries 1946–47; mem. Cen. Cttee., Inst. of Danish Engineers 1946–48, Sec. 1948, Dir. 952–65; Sec. Asscn. of Consultant Engineers 1956, Dir. 1965; Man. of the ldg. of the Inst. of Danish Engineers 1957; mem. Folketing (Parl.) 1964–77; Minister for Transport and Communications 1968–71; mem. European Parl. 973–77, Vice-Pres. 1975–77; Minister for Foreign Affairs 1973–75; Sec. Conf. of Reps. from Eng. Socs. of W. Europe and U.S.A. (EUSEC) 1955–58; Pres. Civil Defence Union 1962–65; mem. Civil Defence Council 1962–68; Commdr., Order of Dannebrog (First Class), Knight Grand Cross St. Michael and St. George, Grand Cross (Fed. Repub. of Germany), Grand Cross St. Olav (Norway), Grand Cross of the Yugoslav Flag, Encomienda le Numero, Orden del Mérito Civil (Spain); Liberal Party.

GÜLEK, Kasim, PH.D.; Turkish politician, economist and farmer; b. 20 Dec. 1910, Adana; s. of Mustafa Rifat and Tayyibe; m. Nilufer Devrimel 967; one s. one d.; ed. Robert Coll., Ecole des Sciences Politiques, Paris, nd Columbia, Cambridge, London, Berlin and Hamburg Univs.; M.P. 940; Chair. Cttee. on Commerce 1943; Minister of Public Works 1947; Minister of Communications 1948; Minister of State 1949; Del. to Council of Europe 1949, 1950, 1951, 1958, 1960, 1961, 1962; Chair. UN Comm. on Korea; fmr. Sec.-Gen. People's Republican Party 1951–59; mem. Constituent Ass. 1960; Vice-Pres. Council of Europe 1961–62; expelled from Republican People's Party for one year Dec. 1962; Pres. N. Atlantic Ass. 1968; Gov. Atlantic Inst. 1969; Senator 1969. *Publications:* Development of Economically Backward Countries 1932, Development of Banking in Turkey 1933, Democracy Takes Root in Turkey 1951. *Leisure interests:* archaeology, photography. *Address:* B. Evler, 50 Sosak no. 3, Ankara, Turkey. *Telephone:* 13-25-63 (Ankara); 45-30-46 (Istanbul).

GULLOTTI, Antonino Pietro; Italian politician; b. 14 Jan. 1929, Ucria, Messina; s. of Benedetto Gullotti and Angela Piccolo; m. Maria Fernanda Germano; Provincial Sec., Partito Democrazia Cristiana (Christian Democrats), Messina 1951, then Regional Sec., Sicily; Nat. Councillor, PDC 1954–, mem. Cen. Cttee. 1960, Vice-Sec. PDC; mem. Chamber of Deputies 1958–; Vice-Pres. Comm. of Enquiry investigating the Mafia; Minister of Public Works 1972–73, for State participation 1973–74, of Health 1974–76, of Public Works 1976–78, of Post and Telecommunications 1978–79, of the Cultural Heritage 1983–87; Christian Democrat.

GULYÁS, Dénes; Hungarian opera singer; b. 31 March 1954; s. of Dénes Gulyás and Mária Szitár; m. Judit Szekeres; two s., one d.; ed. Liszt Ferenc Acad. of Music, Budapest; joined State Opera, Budapest 1978; debut as Rinuccio in Gianni Schicchi; debut in USA, Carnegie Hall and Avery Fisher Hall, New York: concert performances; numerous tours in the USA. *Repertoire includes:* Faust, des Grieux (Manon), Werther, Hoffman, Titus (La Clemenza di Tito), Percy (Anne Boleyn), Ernesto (Don Pasquale), Duke of Mantua (Rigoletto), Fenton (Falstaff), Ferrando (Cosi fan tutte), Don Ottavio, Tamino, Alfredo (La Traviata), Edgardo (Lucia), Nemorino, Rodolfo (La Bohème), Tom Rakewell (The Rake's Progress); 1st prize Parma 1979, won Luciano Pavarotti singing competition, Philadelphia 1981; Holder of Liszt Prize, titled Merited Artist. *Leisure interests:* riding, sailing, viticulture. *Address:* Hungarian State Opera, Budapest 1062, Népköztársaság utja 22, Hungary. *Telephone:* 36/1/312-550.

GUMBARIDZE, Givi; Soviet politician; b. c. 1954, Georgia; Head KGB of Georgian S.S.R.; First Sec. Cen. Cttee. Georgian CP April 1989–. *Address:* Communist Party of the Georgian S.S.R., Tbilisi, Georgian S.S.R., U.S.S.R.

GUMEDE, Josiah, M.B.E.; Zimbabwean fmr. Head of State; b. 19 Sept. 1919, Bubi District, S. Rhodesia; s. of Zion Mhlanjana and Regina Gumede; m. Esther Gasela 1948; three s.; fmr. schoolmaster; worked for Cen. African Fed. in Kenya and U.K.; served in Housing Ministry, London 1965–67, returned to Rhodesia 1967; served in local Govt., Njube Township, Bulawayo 1967–79; Pres. of Zimbabwe Rhodesia May-Dec. 1979; on Bd. of Dirs. of TILCORA and ARDA (Govt. Corpns.). *Leisure interests:* gardening, reading.
[Died 28 March 1989.]

GUMMER, Rt. Hon. John Selwyn, M.A., M.P.; British politician, b. 26 Nov. 1939, Stockport; s. of Canon Selwyn Gummer and Sybille (née Mason); m. Penelope J. Gardner 1977; two s. two d.; ed. King's School, Rochester and Selwyn Coll., Cambridge; Ed., Business Publs. 1962–64; Ed.-in-Chief, Max Parrish and Oldbourne Press 1964–66; Special Asst. to Chair. BPC Publishing 1967; Dir. Shandwick Publishing Co. 1966–81; Dir. Siemssen Hunter Ltd. 1973–80, Chair. 1979–80; Man. Dir. EP Group of Cos. 1975–81; Chair. Selwyn Shandwick Int. 1976–81; M.P. for Lewisham W. 1970–74, Eye, Suffolk (now Suffolk Coastal) 1979–; Parl. Pvt. Sec. to Minister of Agric. 1972; Vice-Chair. Conservative Party 1972–74, Chair. 1983–85; Asst. Govt. Whip 1981, Lord Commr. Treasury (Whip) 1982; Under-Sec. of State for Employment Jan.-Oct. 1983, Minister of State for Employment 1983–84, Paymaster-Gen. 1984–85; Minister of State at Ministry of Agric., Fisheries and Food 1985–88; Minister for Local Govt., Dept. of Environment 1988–; mem. Gen. Synod of Church of England. *Publications:* When the Coloured People Come 1966, To Church with Enthusiasm 1969, The Permissive Society 1970, The Christian Calendar (with L. W. Cowie) 1971, Faith in Politics (with Alan Beith and Eric Heffer) 1987. *Leisure interests:* gardening, Victorian buildings. *Address:* House of Commons, London, SW1A 0AA (Office); 25 Creffield Road, London, W.5; Winston Grange, via Stowmarket, Suffolk, England. *Telephone:* 01-219 4591 (Office); (0728) 860522 (Home).

GUMUCIO-GRANIER, Jorge, LL.D.; Bolivian diplomatist; m.; four c.; ed. Univ. of San Andrés, La Paz, Latin American School of Social Sciences, Chile, Univ. of Pittsburgh; Consultant for Foreign Ministry 1966–67; Chief of Social Devt. Mining Corpn. of Bolivia (COMIBOL) 1968–71; Pres. Social Cttee. Nat. Comm. for Strategy of Devt. 1970–71; served with Dept. of Int. Econ. and Social Affairs Div, UN 1974–78, Dept. of Tech. Co-operation for Devt. Programming and Implementation Div., Americas Br. 1978–82, Dept. of Public Information, UN Secr. 1982–83; Perm. Rep. to UN June 1983–88. *Address:* c/o Ministry of Foreign Affairs, Edif. BCB, 6° piso, La Paz, Bolivia.

GUNA-KASEM, Pracha, PH.D.; Thai diplomatist; b. 29 Dec. 1934, Bangkok; s. of Jote and Rabieb Guna-Kasem; m. Sumanee Chongcharoen 1962; one s.; ed. Dhebsirinda School, Bangkok, Marlborough Coll., Hertford Coll., Oxford and Yale Univ.; joined Ministry of Foreign Affairs 1959, Chief of Section, Political Div. of Dept. of Int. Org. 1960–61, Second Sec. SEATO Div. 1962–63, Alt. Mem. for Thailand, SEATO Perm. Working Group 1962–63, Embassy in Egypt 1964–65, Chief of Foreign News Analysis Div. of Information Dept. and concurrently in charge of Press Affairs 1966–69, Chief of Press Div. 1970–71, Consul-Gen. in Hong Kong 1971–73, Dir.-Gen. of Information Dept. 1973–75; Perm. Rep. to UN 1975–80, UN (Geneva) 1980–82; Dir.-Gen. ASEAN-Thailand 1982; Dir-Gen. Dept. of Econ. Affairs, Foreign Ministry 1984–85; Amb. to France and Algeria 1985–; Perm. Del. to UNESCO 1985–; Dir.-Gen. Dept. of Econ. Affairs, Bangkok 1988–; Special Lecturer, Thammasat Univ., Thai Nat. Defence Coll.; mem. del. to UN Gen. Ass. 1962, 1968, 1970, 1974, to 2nd Afro-Asian Conf., Algeria 1965, to SEATO Council 1966; Kt. Grand Cordon of Order of White Elephant, Grand Cordon (Highest Class) of the Order of the Crown of Thailand, Commdr. Order of Chula Chomklao. *Leisure interests:* golf, bridge, tennis, swimming. *Address:* Department of Economic Affairs, Ministry of Foreign Affairs, Bangkok, Thailand. *Telephone:* 245 5442.

GUNARATNE, Victor Thomas Herat, L.M.S., D.T.M. & H., D.P.H., M.R.C.P.(E.), F.R.C.P.(E.); Ceylonese international health official; b. 11 March 1912, Madampe; s. of the late H. M. G. Herat Gunaratne; m. Clarice Gunaratne 1937; one s. two d.; ed. Ceylon Medical College, London School of Hygiene and Tropical Medicine, and Univ. of Edinburgh Medical School; Deputy Dir. Public Health Services, Ceylon 1959–61; Deputy Dir. Ceylon Medical Services 1961–64; Dir. Health Services, Govt. of Ceylon 1964–67; Pres. World Health Ass. 1967; Dir. WHO Regional Office for S.E. Asia 1968–81, now Regional Dir. Emer., Consultant and Adviser to Minister of Indigenous Medicine, Sri Lanka; Hon. Fellow Indian Acad. of Medical Sciences 1975; Hon. Fellow, Ceylon Coll. of Physicians 1976, Indian Soc. of Malaria and other Communicable Diseases, Sri Lanka Public Health Assn.; Hon. Dr. of Public Health (Mahidol) 1977, Hon. D.S. (Univ. of Sri Lanka) 1978, Hon. D.Med. (State Medical Inst., Mongolia) 1978, Hon. D.Sc. (Benares Univ., India). *Publications:* A History of Medicine and Public Health in Sri Lanka, Challenge Faced by the Medical Profession in Tropical Developing Countries, Challenges and Response, Voyage Towards Health, Selected Addresses and articles in professional journals. *Address:* c/o WHO Programme Co-ordinator and Representative, 16/6 Cambridge Place, Colombo 7, Sri Lanka.

GUNDERSEN, O. C., CAND. JUR; Norwegian lawyer and politician; b. 17 March 1908, Oslo; s. of Hans Christian Gundersen and Hilda Gjeruldsen; m. Ragna Lorentzen 1937; one d.; ed. Oslo Univ.; qualified as solicitor 1931, High Court barrister 1939; Town Councillor, Trondheim 1938, dismissed by Nazis 1941; escaped to Sweden, attached to Norwegian Legation, Stockholm; summoned to London 1942 and apptd. Dir. of State Insurance Office and Chair. Insurance Council; Town Councillor and Alderman Trondheim; Minister of Justice 1945–53; Chair. Norwegian Del. to UN 1949, 1951, 1952; Chair. UN Observer Group (Hungarian Question) 1956; Justice of the Supreme Court; Chair. UN Special Advisory Bd. 1957–; Amb. to U.S.S.R. 1958–61; Minister of Commerce and Shipping 1962–63, of Justice 1963–65; Chair. EFTA Ministerial Council 1953; Judge of Supreme Court 1967–77; Chair. Norwegian State Bank Comm. 1977–80. *Address:* Olav Kyrresgate 11B, Oslo 2, Norway (Home). *Telephone:* 56-51-19.

GUNGAADORJ, Sharavyn; Mongolian politician; b. 1935; ed. Acad. of Agriculture, U.S.S.R.; Chief Agronomist, "Amgalan" State farm; agronomist, Dept. of State Farms 1959–67; Instructor at the Mongolian People's Revolutionary Party (MPRP) Cen. Cttee. 1967–68; Deputy Minister for Agric.; Head of fodder farm in Zabhan Aimak (Prov.); Head of group, Ministry of Agric. 1968–80; First Deputy Minister for State Farms 1980–81; First Sec. Party Cttee. of Selenge Aimak (Prov.) 1981–86; Minister for Agric. 1986–; Deputy Chair. Council of Ministers 1987–; Alt. mem. MPRP Cen. Cttee. 1981–86, mem. 1986–; Deputy to Great People's Hural (Assembly) 1981–. *Address:* Government Palace, Ulan Bator, Mongolia.

GUNGWU, Wang, Dr.; Hong Kong historian and university vice-chancellor; b. Indonesia; ed. in Malaysia, Nanking Univ. and School of Oriental & African Studies, London; fmr. univ. teacher in Malaysia; later Prof. of History, Research School of Pacific Studies, Australian Nat. Univ., Canberra; Vice-Chancellor, Hong Kong Univ. 1986–. *Address:* Hong Kong University, Pokfulam Road, Hong Kong.

GUNN, John Charles, M.D., F.R.C.PSYCH.; British psychiatrist; b. 6 June 1937; m. Celia Willis 1959 (divorced 1986); one s. one d.; ed. Brighton,

Hove and Sussex Grammar School, Reigate Grammar School, Birmingham Univ Medical School; Consultant Psychiatrist, Bethlem Maudsley Hosp. 1971-; Dir. Special Hosps. Research Unit 1975-78; Prof. of Forensic Psychiatry, Univ. of London 1978-; Chair. Research Cttee., Royal Coll. of Psychiatrists 1976-80; Chair. Academic Bd., Inst. of Psychiatry 1980-85; Chair. Forensic Specialist Cttee., Jt. Cttee. on Higher Psychatric Training 1982-85; mem. Ont. Govt. Enquiry in Oakridge, Ont., Canada 1984-85, Home Sec.'s Advisory Bd. on Restricted Patients 1982-, Bethlem Maudsley Special Health Authority 1986-; RMPA Bronze Medal 1970, H. B. Williams Travelling Professorship to Australasia 1985. *Publications:* Violence 1973, Epileptics in Prison 1977, Psychiatric Aspects of Imprisonment 1978, Current Research in Forensic Psychiatry and Psychology, (Vols 1-3) 1982-85. *Leisure interests:* theatre, cinema, opera, walking, photography. *Address:* Institute of Psychiatry, De Crespigny Park, Denmark Hill, London, SE5 8AF, England. *Telephone:* 01-703 5411.

GUNN, Robert Norman, M.A., C.B.I.M., F.I.D., F. INST. M.; British business executive; b. 16 Dec. 1925, Edinburgh; s. of Donald M. and Margaret (née Pallister) Gunn; m. Joan Parry 1956; one d.; ed. Royal High School, Edinburgh, Worcester Coll., Oxford; joined The Boots Co. 1951, Merchandise Buyer 1962-70, Head of Warehousing and Distribution 1971-73, Dir. of Property 1973-78, Dir. Industrial Div. 1979-83 (Man. Dir. 1980-83), Vice-Chair, and Chief Exec. The Boots Co. PLC 1983-85, Chair. and C.E.O. 1985-87, Chair. 1987-; Dir. Foesco Minsep PLC 1984-; mem. Council, CBI, Business in the Community, Scottish Business in the Community, Polytechnics and Colls. Funding Council. *Leisure interests:* gardening, theatre. *Address:* Tor House, Pinfold Lane, Elston, Nr. Newark, Notts., England.

GUNN, Thom(son William), M.A.; British poet; b. 29 Aug. 1929, Gravesend; s. of Herbert Smith Gunn and Ann-Charlotte Gunn; ed. Trinity Coll., Cambridge; taught English at Univ. of Calif., Berkeley 1958-66; Visiting Lecturer in English, Univ. of Calif., Berkeley 1977-; Levinson Prize 1955, Somerset Maugham Prize 1959; grants from Nat. Inst. of Arts and Letters 1964, Rockefeller Foundation 1966, Guggenheim Foundation 1972; Sara Teasdale Prize 1988; Robert Kirsch Award 1988. *Publications:* Fighting Terms 1954, The Sense of Movement 1957, My Sad Captains 1961, Positives (with Ander Gunn) 1966, Touch 1967, Moly 1971, Jack Straw's Castle 1976, Selected Poems 1979, The Passages of Joy 1982, The Occasions of Poetry (prose) 1982 (expanded edn. 1985).
[*Deceased.*]

GUNN, Sir William Archer, K.B.E., C.M.G.; Australian grazier and company director; b. 1 Feb. 1914, Goondiwindi, Queensland; s. of the late Walter Gunn and Doris Isabel Gunn; m. Mary Phillipa Haydon 1939; one s. two d.; ed. The King's School, Parramatta, New South Wales; Chair. Australian Wool Bd. 1963-72, Int. Wool Secr. Bd. 1961-73, Queensland Advisory Bd., Devt. Finance Corpn. 1962-72; Chair. Gunn Devt. Pty. Ltd., Eagle Corpn. Ltd., Cattle Investments Ltd., Livestock Man. Pty. Ltd., Moline Pastoral Co. Pty. Ltd., Roper Valley Pty. Ltd., Coolibah Pastoral Co. Pty. Ltd., Mataranka Pty. Ltd., Unibeef Australia Pty. Ltd.; Dir. Rothmans of Pall Mall (Australia) Ltd., Grazcos Co-operative Ltd., Clausen Steamship Co. (Australia) Pty. Ltd., Walter Reid & Co. Ltd., Gunn Rural Man. Pty. Ltd.; mem. Commonwealth Bank Bd. 1952-59, Faculty of Veterinary Science, Univ. of Queensland 1953-, Reserve Bank Bd. 1959-, Australian Meat Bd. 1953-66, Australian Wool Bureau 1951-63 (Chair. 1958-63), Australian Woolgrowers Council 1947-60 (Chair. 1955-58), Graziers Fed. Council of Australia 1950-60 (Pres. 1951-54), Australian Woolgrowers and Graziers Council 1960-65, Export Devt. Council 1962-65, Exec. Council, United Graziers Assocn. of Queensland 1944-69 (Vice-Pres. 1947-51, Pres. 1951-59), Australian Wool Testing Authority 1958-63, C.S.I.R.O. State Cttee. 51-68, Australian Wool Corpn. 1973; Chair. The Wool Bureau Inc. New York 1962-69, etc.; Trustee Queensland Cancer Fund; Golden Fleece Achievement Award (Nat. Assn. of Wool Manufacturers of America) 1962; Award of the Golden Ram (Nat. Wool Growers' Assocn. of S. Africa) 1973. *Address:* 98 Windermere Road, Ascot, Brisbane, Queensland 4007, Australia (Home). *Telephone:* Brisbane 268-2688 (Home).

GUNNARSSON, Birgir Ísleifur; Icelandic politician; b. 19 July 1936, Reykjavík; s. of Gunnar Espólín Benediktsson and Jorunn Ísleifsdóttir; m. Sonja Bachmann 1956; ed. Univ. of Iceland; Advocate to lower courts 1962, Supreme Court 1967; Leader Heimdallur Youth Soc. 1959-62; Sec.-Gen. Youth Fed. of Independence Party 1959-62; mem. Reykjavík City Council 1962-82; Mayor of Reykjavík 1972-78; M.P. for Reykjavík 1973-; Second Deputy Speaker of Althing 1983-87; Minister for Culture and Educ. July 1987-; Chair. Cttee. on Heavy Industry 1983-87; mem. Bd. Nat. Power Co. 1965-, Civil Aviation Bd. 1984-. *Address:* Ministry of Education, Hverfisgötu 6, 150 Reykjavík, Iceland.

GUNNENG, Arne, LL.B.; Norwegian diplomatist; b. 1 Dec. 1914, Oslo; m. Ingrid Fleischer 1939; three d.; ed. Oslo Katedralskole, Oslo Univ.; First Sec. Embassy, Washington 1945-48; Ministry of Foreign Affairs, Oslo 1948-50; Chargé d'affaires, Warsaw 1950-51; Counsellor, Stockholm 1951-52; Deputy Perm. Rep. N. Atlantic Council, Paris 1952-55; Amb. to Canada 1955-59; Dir.-Gen. of Political Affairs, Ministry of Foreign Affairs, Oslo 1959-62; Amb. to Sweden 1962-66, to USA 1966-73, to Italy (also accred. to Greece) 1973-78, to the Netherlands 1978-83. *Address:* Ministry of Foreign Affairs, 7 juni plassen 1, Pb 8114 Dep., Oslo, Norway.

GUNNESS, Robert Charles, D.SC.; American oil executive; b. 28 July 1911 Fargo, North Dakota; m. Beverly Osterberger; two s. one d.; ed. Univ. of Massachusetts and M.I.T.; Asst. Dir. of Research, Standard Oil Co. (Indiana) 1943-45, Assoc. Dir. 1945-47, Man. of Research 1947-52, Asst. Gen Man. of Mfg. 1952-54, Dir. 1953-75, Gen. Man. Supply and Transportation 1954-56, Exec. Vice-Pres. 1956-65, Pres. 1965-74, Vice-Chair. 1974-75 Vice-Chair. Research and Devt. Bd. Dept. of Defense, Washington, D.C 1951; Dir. Inland Steel Co., Champion Int. Corpn., Consolidated Food Corpn., Paxall Inc., Oakbrook Consolidated Inc., Foote Cone and Belding Communications Inc., Halcon Int. Inc.; Trustee, Univ. of Chicago. St Luke's Hosp., The John Crerar Library; life mem. of Corpn., M.I.T.; mem Nat. Acad. of Eng., American Chem. Soc., American Acad. of Arts and Sciences. *Leisure interests:* golf, skiing. *Address:* P.O. Box 538, Rancho Santa Fe, Calif. 92067; 111 E. Chestnut, Apartment 41-H, Chicago, Ill 60611, U.S.A. (Home).

GUNNING, Brian Edgar Scourse, PH.D., F.R.S., F.A.A.; Australian biologist b. 29 Nov. 1934; s. of William Gunning and Margaret (Scourse) Gunning m. Marion Sylvia Forsyth 1964; two s.; ed. Methodist Coll., Belfast, and Queen's Univ., Belfast; Lecturer in Botany, Queen's Univ. Belfast 1957 Reader 1965; Prof. of Developmental Biology, A.N.U. 1974-. *Publications* Ultrastructure and the Biology of Plant Cells (with M. Steer) 1975 Intercellular Communication in Plants: studies on Plasmodesmata (with A Robards) 1976. *Leisure interests:* hill walking, photography. *Address:* 29 Millen St., Hughes, A.C.T. 2605, Australia. *Telephone:* (062) 812879.

GUNSALUS, Irwin Clyde, PH.D.; American biochemist and author; b. 29 June 1912, Sully Co., S. Dak.; s. of I. C. and Anna (Shea) Gunsalus; m. 1st Merle La Mont 1935, four s. one d.; m. 2nd Carolyn F. Foust 1951 (died 1970) two d.; m. 3rd Dorothy Clark 1970 (died 1982); ed. Cornell Univ. Asst. Bacteriologist, Cornell Univ. 1935-37, Instructor 1937-40, Asst Prof. 1940-44, Assoc. Prof. 1944-46, Prof. 1946-47; Prof. Univ. of Indiana 1947-50; Prof. Univ. of Ill. 1950-55, Prof. of Biochem. 1955-82, Prof. Emer 1982-, Head of Dept. 1955-66; Asst. Sec. Gen. for UN; Dir. Int. Centre for Genetic Eng. and Biotech. 1986; Fogarty Scholar, Nat. Insts. of Health Bethesda, Md. 1980-; Consultant, Scholar, Salk Inst., La Jolla, Calif. 1982- Ed., The Bacteria, Vols. I-V (with R. Stainer), Vol. VI and VII, Biochemica and Biophysical Research Communications, Bacteriological Reviews; mem Advisory Bds. Analytical Biochem., Biochem.; Guggenheim Memorial Foun dation Fellow 1949, 1959, 1968; mem. N.A.S., Foreign Assoc. Acad. des Sciences (France) 1984; American Chem. Soc., American Soc. of Biological Chemists; Mead Johnson Award 1946, Selman A. Waksman Award 1982 Hon. D.Sc. (Indiana Univ.) 1984. *Publications:* over 400 scientific papers *Leisure interests:* gardening, music, art, viniculture. *Address:* Biochemistry Department, 420 Roger Adams Laboratory, University of Illinois, 1209 W California, Urbana, Ill. 61801 (Office); 716 W. Iowa, Urbana, Ill. 61801 U.S.A. (Home). *Telephone:* 217-333-2010 (Office).

GUNSON, Ameral Blanche Tregurtha; British classical singer; b. 25 Oct 1948, London; d. of Charles Cumbria and Auriol Cornwall; m. 1st Maurice Powell 1969 (divorced 1974); m. 2nd Philip Kay 1979; two s.; ed. Convent of Jesus and Mary, London, and Guildhall School of Music and Drama freelance singing career 1972-74, with BBC Singers 1976-80; solo singing career in Britain and abroad, Proms Seasons 1979, 1985; Assoc. Guildhall School of Music and Drama. *Leisure interests:* gardening, reading, walking Russian music, relaxation. *Address:* 3 Charman Road, Redhill, Surrey RH1 6AG, England. *Telephone:* (0737) 762726.

GÜNTHER, Eberhard, D.IUR.; German economist and international official b. 25 Dec. 1911, Freienwalde; s. of Alfred Günther and Elfriede (née Volprecht); m. Edelgard Wujetz 1942; one s. one d. (deceased); ed. Univs of Munich, Kiel, Freiburg im Breisgau, Berlin; mem. of Bd., Nitrogene Syndicate 1938-46; Chair. Bd. of Coal Processing Plant 1946-48; Section Chief in Bizonal Econ. Admin. 1948-50, in Econ. Ministry of Fed. Repub of Germany 1950-58; Pres. of Fed. Cartel Authority 1958-76; Chair. Expert Cttee. for Restrictive Business Practices OECD, Paris 1973-78, German del. to UN Conf. on Trans-nat. Corpns. 1976-78; Hon. Prof. of Law, Berlin Tech. Univ. 1962; Hon. Prof. of Law (Freiburg) 1978; Guest Prof., Univs. of Phila., Berkeley, Georgetown, Keio Daigaku, Tokyo; Great Cross, Spanish Civil Order of Merit; Alexander Rüstow Plakette; Hermann-Lindrath Prize 1982; Grosses Verdienstkreuz mit Stern des Verdienstordens der Bundesrepublik Deutschland. *Publications:* Wirtschaftsordnung und Rechtsordnung 1965, Wege zur Europäischen Wettbewerbsordnung 1968 Ludwig Erhard 1971, Wettbewerb im Wandel 1976, and over 200 articles on cartel law. *Leisure interest:* sailing. *Address:* Taunushöhe 19, 6233 Kelkheim, Federal Republic of Germany. *Telephone:* (06195) 2613.

GUO FENG; Chinese party official; First Sec. CCP, Liaoning Prov. Cttee. 1980-85; 1st Pol. Commissar Liaoning PLA Mil. Dist. 1980-; mem. Cen. Advisory Comm. 1982-. *Address:* c/o Provincial Committee, Zhongguo Gongchan Dang, Shenyang, Liaoning Province, People's Republic of China.

GUO LINXIANG, Gen.; Chinese party official; b. 1914, Yongfeng Co. Jiangxi Prov.; joined Red Army 1930, CCP 1933; Council mem. N. Sichuan Admin. Office 1950-52; Deputy Political Commissar, PLA, North Sichuan Mil. Dist. 1950; Maj.-Gen. 1955; Deputy Political Commissar PLA, Chengdu Units 1959, Second Political Commissar, Chengdu Units 1960; Responsible Person, Chengdu Units 1965; mem. Standing Cttee. Southwest Bureau

CCP 1965; criticized and removed from office during Cultural Revolution 1967; Responsible Person PLA Gen. Logistics Dept. 1973, Political Commissar 1974; Second Political Commissar PLA Xinjiang Units 1978-80; mem. Standing Cttee. CCP, Xinjiang-Uygur Autonomous Regional Cttee. 1978-80; First Political Commissar PLA Nanjing Mil. Region 1980-; mem. Cen. Advisory Comm. 1985-, Presidium 6th NPC 1986-; Sec. Comm. for Discipline Inspection, CCP Cen. Military Comm. 1985-; Deputy Head Leading Group of All-Army Financial and Econ. Discipline Inspection, CCP Cen. Military Comm. 1986-; Deputy Dir.-Gen. Political Dept., PLA, 1985-; Vice-Chair. PLA Literary Awards Examination Cttee. 1986-; mem. Standing Cttee. of Discipline Inspection Comm. 1987-. *Address:* People's Liberation Army Headquarters, Nanjing Military Region, People's Republic of China.

GUO LIWEN; Chinese politician; Sec. Chinese Women's Fed. 1980-82, First Sec. 1982-; mem. 12th CCP Cen. Cttee. 1982-87. *Address:* Chinese Women's Federation, Beijing, People's Republic of China.

GUO MUSUN (Mooson Kwauk); Chinese academic; b. 9 May 1920, Hangyang; s. of Zung-Ung Kwauk and Za-Nan Chow; m. Huichun Kwei Kwauk 1950; two s. one d.; ed. Univ. of Shanghai, Princeton Univ., U.S.A.; Prof. Inst. of Chemical Metallurgy, Chinese Acad. of Sciences 1956, Dir. 1982-86, Emer. Dir. 1986-; Vice-Pres. Chemical, Industrial and Eng. Soc. of China 1978-; Davis-Swindin Memorial Lecturer, Loughborough Univ., England 1985; Visiting Prof. Virginia Polytechnic Inst. and State Univ. 1986-87; mem. Chinese Acad. of Sciences 1981-; Pres. Chinese Soc. of Particuology 1986-; Distinguished Scholar, CSCPRC Program, U.S. Nat. Acad. of Science 1984. *Leisure interest:* kites. *Address:* Institute of Chemical Metallurgy, Chinese Academy of Sciences, Beijing, People's Republic of China. *Telephone:* 28-4241 (Office); 28-4050 (Home).

GUO WEICHENG; Chinese politician; b. 1912, Liaoning Prov.; ed. Shanghai Fudan Univ.; Minister of Railways 1978-81; mem. Presidium, CPPCC 6th Nat. Comm. 1983-. *Address:* People's Republic of China.

GUO YUEHUA; Chinese table tennis player; b. 4 Feb. 1956, Fujian; s. of Guo Leng Ran and Lin Ming Li; m. Shen Yan 1984; one c.; Deputy Dir. Fujian Prov. Comm. of Physical Culture and Sports; World No. 1 Ranked Table Tennis Player 1981, 1982, 1983. *Address:* Tugiang Road, Haus 2, Zimmer 404, Xia Men, Vr. China. *Telephone:* (0592) 32428.

GUO ZHENQIAN; Chinese party and government official; b. 1932; ed. Trade Dept. Beijing People's Univ.; Vice-Gov. Hubei Prov. 1983-84, Acting Gov. Jan. 1986, Gov. May-Oct. 1986; Deputy Sec. Hubei Prov. CCP Cttee. 1985-86; Dir. Hubei Branch People's Construction Bank of China 1986-; Gov. Hubei Provincial People's Govt. 1986-. *Address:* People's Construction Bank of China, Wuhan, People's Republic of China.

GUPTA, Sunil Kumar; Bangladesh politician; b. 1928, Sihipasha; ed. Brajo Mohan Coll., Barisal; mem. East Pakistan Democratic Party 1950, Vice-Pres. Barisal Dist. Cttee.; mem. Nat. Awami Party, then Vice-Pres. Barisal Dist. Cttee. 1957-73, Vice-Pres. Cen. Cttee. 1973; fmr. mem. Cen. Cttee. Bangladesh Nationalist Party; Minister of State for Petroleum and Mineral Resources 1979, 1985, for Ministry of Communications 1985-86, Minister of Textiles 1986-88, of Youth and Sports March-Dec. 1988. *Address:* c/o Ministry of Jute and Textiles, Dhaka, Bangladesh.

GUR, Lieut.-Gen. Mordechai; Israeli army officer; b. 6 May 1930, Jerusalem; s. of Moshe Gur and Tova Gur; m. Rita Gur 1958; two s. two d.; ed. Hebrew Univ., Jerusalem; served in Haganah; Co. Commdr. during Independence War 1948-49; Paratroop Battalion Commdr., Sinai Campaign 1956; Deputy Commdr. Paratroop Forces 1957; Instructor, Command and Staff Coll. 1958; studies at Ecole de Guerre, Paris 1958-60; C.O. Golani Brigade 1961-63; Chief of Command Operations 1964-65; in charge of Command and Staff Coll. 1965-66; Staff and Command 1966-67; C.O. Paratroop Brigade during Six-Day War 1967; mem. Israeli Del. to UN Emergency Session 1967; C.O. Israeli Forces in Gaza and N. Sinai 1967-69, Northern Command 1970-72; Mil. Attaché, Washington 1972-73; C.O. Northern Command during Yom Kippur War Oct. 1973; Chief Mil. Negotiator at Geneva Peace Conf. Dec. 1973; Chief of Staff 1974-78; Head, Koor Mechanics, Koor Industries 1979-; mem. Knesset (Parl.) July 1981-; Minister of Health 1984-86, Without Portfolio Dec. 1988-; Chair. of Bd. Solel Boneh Ltd. 1987; Medal of Valour 1955. *Publications:* The Lion's Gate, Company D, The Templemount is in our Hands; several children's books. *Address:* 25 Mishmeret Street, Afeka, Tel-Aviv 69694, Israel.

GURCHENKO, Ludmila Markovna; Soviet actress; b. 1935; ed. Moscow All-Union Inst. of Cinema; has worked in films since 1956; People's Artist of U.S.S.R. 1983. *Major roles include:* Lena in Night of Revelry, Sonya in Baltic Sky, Anna Georgevna in Old Walls (R.S.F.S.R. State Prize 1976), Nanny-Goat in Mother, Tamara Vasilevna in Five Evenings, Rita in Mechanic Gavrilov's Favourite Woman, Vera in Station for Two (Best Actress Award, 16th All-Union Cinema Festival Leningrad 1983). *Publication:* My Grown-up Childhood 1980.

GURDON, John Bertrand, D.PHIL., F.R.S.; British cell biologist; b. 2 Oct. 1933, Hampshire; s. of W. N. Gurdon and E. M. Gurdon (née Byass); m. Jean Elizabeth Margaret Curtis 1964; one s. one d.; ed. Edgeborough School, Eton Coll., Univ. of Oxford; Beit Memorial Fellow 1958-61; Gosney Research Fellow, Calif. Inst. of Tech., U.S.A. 1961-62; Research Fellow,

Univ. of Oxford 1962-72, Departmental Demonstrator 1963-64, Lecturer, Dept. of Zoology 1966-72; Visiting Research Fellow, Carnegie Inst., Baltimore, Md., U.S.A. 1965; mem. Scientific Staff, Medical Research Council, Molecular Biology Lab., Univ. of Cambridge 1973-83, Head of Cell Biology Div. 1979-83, John Humphrey Plummer Prof. of Cell Biology 1983-; Fellow of Churchill Coll., Cambridge 1973-; Croonian Lecturer, Royal Soc. 1976; Dunham Lecturer, Harvard Medical School 1974; Carter-Wallace Lecturer, Princeton Univ. 1978; Fellow Eton Coll. 1978-; Hon. Student, Christ Church, Oxford 1985; Fullerian Prof. of Physiology and Comparative Anatomy, Royal Inst. 1985-; Hon. Foreign mem. American Acad. of Arts and Sciences 1978; Foreign Assoc., N.A.S., U.S.A. 1980, Belgian Royal Acad. of Science, Letters and Fine Arts 1984; Foreign mem. American Philosophical Soc. 1983; Hon. D.Sc. (Univ. of Chicago) 1978, (Oxford) 1988, (Birbeck Coll., Univ. of London) 1988; Hon. Dr. (Univ. of Paris) 1982; Albert Brachet Prize (Belgian Royal Acad.) 1968, Scientific Medal of Zoological Soc. 1968, Feldberg Foundation Award 1975, Paul Ehrlich Award 1977, Nessim Habif Prize (Univ. of Geneva) 1979, CIBA Medal, Biochem. Soc. 1981, Comfort Crookshank Award for Cancer Research 1983, William Bate Hardy Triennial Prize (Cambridge Philosophy Soc.) 1983, Charles Léopold Mayer Prize (Acad. des Sciences, France) 1984, Ross Harrison Prize (Int. Soc. for Devt. Biology) 1985, Royal Medal (Royal Soc.) 1985, Emperor Hirohito Int. Biology Prize 1987, Wolf Prize for Medicine (jtly. with Edward B. Lewis, q.v.) 1989. *Publications:* Control of Gene Depression in Animal Development 1974. *Leisure interests:* skiing, horticulture, lepidoptera. *Address:* Whittlesford Grove, Whittlesford, Cambridge, CB2 4NZ, England. *Telephone:* (Cambridge) 833518.

GUREVICH, G. I.; Soviet writer; b. 1917, Moscow; first works appeared 1937; Deputy Chair. of Comm. on Science-Fiction Writing in R.S.F.S.R.; author of scientific articles; numerous TV appearances as writer and author of scientific articles. *Publications:* The Soaring Poplar, Frost on the Palm-trees, The Birth of the Sixth Ocean, Captives of the Asteroid, We Are From the Solar System. *Address:* U.S.S.R. Union of Writers, ul. Vorovoskugo, 52, Moscow, U.S.S.R.

GURGULINO de SOUZA, Hector, B.SC., LIC.; Brazilian scientist and educator; b. 1 Aug. 1928, Sao Lourenco, Minas Gerais; s. of Arthur Gurgulino de Souza and Catarina Sachser de Souza; m. Lillian Maria Quilici; ed. Univ. of Mackenzie, São Paulo, Aeronautics Inst. of Tech., Univ. of Kansas, U.S.A., Univ. of São Paulo; Program Specialist, Interamerican Science Program, Pan American Union, Wash. D.C. 1962-64; Head, Unit of Educ. and Research, Dept. of Scientific Affairs, OAS, Wash. D.C. 1964-69; Rector, Fed. Univ. of Sao Carlos, State of São Paulo 1970-74; Dir., Dept. of Univ. Affairs (DAU), Ministry of Educ. and Culture, Brasilia 1972-74; Chair. Interamerican Cttee. on Science and Tech. (CICYT) of the Council for Educ., Culture, OAS, Wash. D.C. 1974-77; Dir. CNP (Nat. Council for Scientific and Tech. Devt.), Brasilia 1975-78, Special Adviser to Pres. 1979-80; Vice Pres., Int. Asscn. Univ. Pres. (IAUP) 1985-87; Pres., Grupo Universitario Latinoamericano (GULERPE), Caracas 1985-87; Vice-Pres. Fed. Council of Educ. of Brazil (CFE), mem. 1982-88; mem. Order of Educational Merit, MEC, Brasilia 1973, Order of Rio Branco, MRE, Brasilia 1974. *Publications:* Gamma-rays from the proton bombardment of Natural Silicon 1957, Computers and Higher Education in Brazil 1984 (articles); (co-ed.) Science Policy 1974; author of chapter on Brazil in International Encyclopedia of Higher Education 1978. *Leisure interests:* sailing, swimming, music. *Address:* United Nations University, Toho Seimei Building, 15-1 Shibuya 2-chome, Shibuya-ku, Tokyo 150 (Office); Aobadai Homes Apt. 204, 4-7 Aobadai 1-chome, Meguro-ku, Tokyo 153, Japan (Home). *Telephone:* 499-2811 (Office); 476-0416 (Home).

GÜRLER, Gen. Faruk; Turkish army officer; b. 1913, Üsküdar, Istanbul; War School, War Acad. for Land Forces; Commdr., Artillery and Infantry Units; Staff Officer, High Defence Council; Instructor War School and War Acad., later Acting Commdr.; Intelligence Officer, NATO; Deputy Chief of Staff of Army Corps., Deputy Artillery Commdr. of Div. and Army Corps., later Army Corps. Commdr.; Chief of Staff of Land Forces Command; Acting Under-Sec. of State, then Under-Sec. of State, Ministry of Nat. Defence; promoted to rank of Gen. 1968; Deputy Chief of Gen. Staff, Commdr. of Land Forces 1968-72; Chief of Gen. Staff 1972-73; fmr. Senator; unsuccessful Presidential cand. 1973.

GURLEY BROWN, Helen; American author and editor; b. 18 Feb. 1922, Green Forest, Ark.; d. of Ira M. and Cleo (Sisco) Gurley; m. David Brown 1959; ed. Texas State Coll. for Women, Woodbury Coll.; Exec. Sec. Music Corpn. of America 1942-45, William Morris Agency 1945-47; Copywriter Foote, Cone & Belding advertising agency, Los Angeles 1948-58; advertisement writer and account exec. Kenyon & Eckhard advertising agency, Hollywood 1958-62; Ed.-in-Chief Cosmopolitan magazine 1965-, Editorial Dir. Cosmopolitan Int. Edns.; mem. Authors League of America, American Soc. of Magazine Eds., AFTRA; Francis Holm Achievement Award 1956-59, Univ. of S. Calif. School of Journalism 1971, Special Award for Editorial Leadership of American Newspaper Woman's Club 1972, Distinguished Achievement Award in Journalism, Stanford Univ. 1977, New York Women in Communications Inc. Award 1985; establishment of Helen Gurley Brown Research Professorship at Northwestern Univ. 1985. *Publications:* Sex and the Single Girl 1962, Sex and the Office 1965, Outrageous Opinions 1966, Helen Gurley Brown's Single Girl's Cook Book 1969, Sex and the

New Single Girl 1971, Having It All 1982. *Address:* Cosmopolitan, 224 West 57th Street, New York, N.Y. 10019 (Office); 1 West 81st Street, New York, N.Y. 10024, U.S.A. (Home).

GURNEY, Oliver Robert, M.A., D.PHIL., F.B.A.; British Assyriologist (retd.); b. 28 Jan. 1911, London; s. of Robert Gurney and Sarah Gamzu Garstang; m. Diane Hope Grazebrook (née Esencourt) 1957; ed. Eton Coll., New Coll., Oxford; during World War II served in R.A. and Sudan Defence Force 1939–45; Reader in Assyriology, Oxford Univ. 1945–65, Prof. 1965–78, Emer. Prof. 1978–; Pres. British Inst. of Archaeology, Ankara 1982–. *Publications:* The Hittites 1952, Some Aspects of Hittite Religion 1977, The Middle Babylonian Legal and Economic Texts from Ur 1983. *Leisure interest:* golf. *Address:* Bayworth Corner, Boars Hill, Oxford, England.

GÜRÜN, Kâmuran; Turkish diplomatist; b. 1924, Çengelköy (Istanbul); m. 1967; studied political science; entered diplomatic service 1948; posted to Turkish Embassy, Bonn 1951; subsequently held various posts at Ministry of Foreign Affairs and diplomatic missions abroad; Dir.-Gen. Dept. for Admin. Affairs 1961, subsequently Perm. Sec. to the Inter-Ministerial Cttee. on External Econ. Relations, Dir.-Gen. Dept. for Econ. and Commercial Affairs, Deputy Sec.-Gen. for Econ. Affairs and Sec.-Gen. Inter-Ministerial Econ. Council; Amb. to Romania 1967–70; Perm. Rep. of Turkey at OECD 1970–72; Amb. to Greece 1974–76; Sec.-Gen. CENTO 1978–79, of Ministry of Foreign Affairs 1980–83. *Address:* c/o Ministry of Foreign Affairs, Ankara, Turkey.

GUSAU, Sarkin Malamai Ibrahim; Nigerian politician; b. 25 Jan. 1925, Sokoto; ed. Gusua Elementary School, Sokoto Cen. Elementary School, Sokoto Middle School, Clerical Training Coll. at Ahmadu Bello Univ., Zaria; Asst. Ed. local newspaper 1943–44; worked for Sokoto Native Authority, as Clerical Officer 1944–46, Sr. Accountant 1946–48, Chief Accountant 1948–50, Supervisor-in-Chief Adult Educ., Public Enlightenment and Community Devt. 1951–60, Asst. Chief Scribe 1960–63, Registrar Sultan's Court 1963–64; mem. Northern Nigeria House of Ass. 1953–56; M.P. 1957–66; Minister of State 1964–66; Commr. 1967–75; mem. Constituent Ass. 1977–78; Chair. Nigerian Grains Bd. 1977–79; Minister of Agric. 1979–82, of Industries 1982; Chair. Savannah Bank of Nigeria 1982–83, Wagritech Co. (Nigeria) Ltd. 1985–; Deputy Chair. Service, Supply and Parts Ltd. 1985–. *Address:* Sultan Bello Road, P.O. Box 1225, Sokoto, Sokoto State, Nigeria (Home).

GUSEV, Vladimir Kuzmich; CAND. TECH. SC.; Soviet politician; b. 1932; ed. Saratov Univ. Saratov Economics Inst.; engineer in Saratov Dist. 1957–70; mem. CPSU 1963–; Dir. of Engels Chemical Combine 1970–75; First Sec. of Engels City Cttee. of CPSU 1975–76; Second, then First Sec. of Saratov Dist. Cttee. of CPSU 1976–85; mem. of CPSU Cen. Cttee. 1981; First Deputy Pres. of R.S.F.S.R. Council of Ministers 1985–86, Deputy Pres. of U.S.S.R. Council of Ministers 1986–; Deputy to U.S.S.R. Supreme Soviet; mem. of CPSU Cen. Cttee. 1986–; elected to Congress of People's Deputies of the U.S.S.R. 1989. *Address:* The Kremlin, Moscow, U.S.S.R.

GUSTAFSON, Torsten, PH.D.; Swedish physicist; b. 8 May 1904, Falkenberg; s. of Albin Gustafson and Hulda Bramstång; m. Karin Lindskog 1935; one s. three d.; ed. Lund, Göttingen and Copenhagen Univs.; Prof., Lund Univ. 1939–70, (of Theoretical Physics 1961–70) now Prof. Emer.; mem. Swedish Atomic Energy Research Council 1945–64, Swedish Atomic Energy Del. 1956–70; Del. European Org. for Nuclear Research, CERN 1953–64; Dir. Nordic Inst. for Theoretical Atomic Physics 1957–58, Chair. 1963–69; Govt. Advisory Del. on Research 1963–68; mem. of numerous Scandinavian Acads. of Science; Dr. h.c. (Helsinki) 1969, (Copenhagen) 1985. *Publications:* papers on flow round airfoil-like bodies 1927–36, on inertia currents in the oceans 1936, on divergencies in quantum electrodynamics 1937–47, on atomic nuclei 1946–, on high-flight altitudes of birds. *Leisure interest:* bird-watching. *Address:* c/o Department of Physics, Lund University, Sölvegatan 14, 223 62 Lund, Sweden. *Telephone:* (046) 113989.

GUSTAFSSON, Carl Åke Torsten, PH.D.; Swedish geneticist; b. 8 April 1908, Stockholm; s. of Emil and Anna Gustafsson; m. Madeleine Berggren 1932; two s. three d.; ed. Lunds Universitet, and in Stockholm and U.S.; Docent, Univ. of Lund 1935, Research Assoc., 1944; Prof. and Head, Inst. of Forest Genetics 1947–68, Prof. Emer. 1974–; Royal Coll. of Forestry, Stockholm 1947, Prefect 1967–68, Head, Inst. of Genetics, Lund Univ. 1968, Prefect 1968; Guest Lecturer at various institutes and universities throughout Europe, and in U.S.A., Thailand, India, Philippines, etc.; mem. Royal Physiographic Soc., Royal Acad. of Forestry and Agriculture, Royal Acad. of Sciences (all in Sweden), and Leopoldina Acad. of Natural Sciences (Germany), Acads. of Sciences and Letters (Denmark and Finland), N.A.S. (U.S.A.), etc. *Publications:* 200 scientific articles; books of prose and poetry. *Address:* Lund University, Sölvegatan 29, 223 62 Lund, Sweden.

GUSTAFSSON, Hans; Swedish politician; b. 21 Dec. 1923, Kvidinge, Kristianstad county; ed. Wendelsberg Folk High School, School of Social Work and Public Admin., Lund; bookbinder 1936–47, Chair. Kvidinge branch, Swedish Bookbinders' Union, and active mem. Swedish Municipal Workers' Union; accountant, Nottebäcks municipality 1952–56; municipal Man. Åstorp borough 1956–58; Deputy Dir. Nat. Asscn. of Community Centres 1958–60; Man. Kallinge municipality 1960–67; City Man. Ronneby

1967–73; Chair. Admin. Cttee., Blekinge County Council 1970–73; mem. Bd. Swedish Asscn. of County Councils 1971–73; Chair. Blekinge Dist. Socialdemokratiska Arbetarepartiet (Social Democratic Labour Party—SDLP) 1973, mem. Bd. SDLP 1975; Minister of Local Govt. 1973–76, of Housing Oct. 1982–; mem. Riksdag (Parl.) 1976–; leader of SDLP Parl. Group 1979–; Chair. Nat. Asscn. of Local Insurance Offices 1977; mem. Bd. Swedish Broadcasting Corpn. and Swedish Radio Co. 1978. *Address:* Bostadsdepartementet, Jakobsg. 26, S-10320, Stockholm, Sweden.

GUSTAFSSON, Lars Erik Einar, D.PHIL.; Swedish author; b. 17 June 1936, Västerås; s. of Einar Gustafsson and Margaretha Carlsson; m. Dena Alexandra Chasnoff 1982; two s. one d.; ed. Uppsala Univ.; Editor-in-Chief, Bonniers Litterara Magasin 1966–72; Research Fellow, Blekfeld Inst. of Advanced Studies 1980–81; Adjunct Prof. Univ. of Texas at Austin 1983–; Prix Charles Veillon; Heinrich Steffen Preis; Övverlids priset. *Publications:* The Death of a Beekeeper 1978, Language and Lie 1978, Stories of Happy People 1981, Bernard Foy's Third Castle 1986, The Silence of the World before Bach (poems) 1988, Fyra Poeter 1988. *Leisure interests:* painting, tennis. *Address:* 2312 Tower Drive, Austin, Tex. 78203, U.S.A.

GUT, Rainer Emil; Swiss banker; b. 24 Sept. 1932, Baar; s. of Emil Anton and Rosa (Müller) Gut; m. Josephine Lorenz 1957; two s. two d.; ed. Cantonal School of Zug.; undertook professional training periods, France and England; N. American Rep. Union Bank of Switzerland, N.Y. 1963; Gen. Partner Lazard Frères & Co., N.Y. 1968; Chair. and C.E.O., Swiss American Corpn. (Crédit Suisse's U.S. investment banking affiliate) 1971; Deputy Gen. Man., Head Office Crédit Suisse, Zürich 1973, Gen. Man. 1975, Spokesman of Gen. Man. 1977–82, Man. Dir. 1982, Chair. March 1983–; Dir. Sulzer Bros. 1983–; Chair. Elektrowatt AG 1981–; Chair. Financière Crédit Suisse, First Boston 1979, Centralschweizerische Kraftwerke 1983; Ordre des Arts et des Lettres 1986, Commdr. Verdienstkreuz (Germany) 1988. *Address:* Crédit Suisse, Paradeplatz 8, 8021 Zurich, Switzerland. *Telephone:* 01-215-11-11.

GUTFREUND, Herbert, PH.D., F.R.S.; British academic; b. 21 Oct. 1921, Vienna, Austria; s. of Paul and Clara (née Pisko) Gutfreund; m. Mary Kathelen Davies 1958; two s. one d.; ed. Vienna and Cambridge Univs.; Research Fellow, Univ. of Cambridge 1947–57; with Agricultural Research Council, Univ. of Reading 1957–64; Visiting Prof., Univ. of Calif. 1965, Max Planck Inst., Germany 1966, Dir. Molecular Enzymology Lab. and Prof. of Physical Biochem., Univ. of Bristol 1967–86, Prof. Emer. 1986–; part-time Scholar in Residence, Nat. Insts. of Health, Bethesda, U.S.A. 1986–89; Scientific mem. (external) Max Planck Inst. for Medical Research 1987–; Fogarty Scholar, Nat. Insts. of Health, Washington 1987. *Publications:* An Introduction to the Study of Enzymes 1965, Enzymes: Physical Principles 1972, Molecular Evolution 1981, Biothermodynamics 1983. *Leisure interests:* hill walking, reading. *Address:* 12a The Avenue, Bristol, BS9 1PA, England. *Telephone:* (0272) 684453.

GUTH, Alan Harvey, PH.D.; American physicist; b. 27 Feb. 1947, New Brunswick, N.J.; s. of Hyman Guth and Elaine Cheiten; m. Susan Tisch 1971; one s. one d.; ed. Mass. Inst. of Tech.; Instructor Princeton Univ. 1971–74; Research Assoc. Columbia Univ. New York 1974–77, Cornell Univ. 1977–79, Stanford Linear Accelerator Center, Calif. 1979–80; Assoc. Prof. of Physics, M.I.T. 1980–86, Prof. 1986–; Physicist, Harvard-Smithsonian Center for Astrophysics 1984–; Alfred P. Sloan Fellow 1981; Fellow, American Physics Soc. *Address:* Center for Theoretical Physics, Massachusetts Institute of Technology, Cambridge, Mass. 02139, U.S.A.

GUTH, Paul; French author, journalist and radio and television broadcaster; b. 5 March 1910, Ossun; s. of Joseph and Maria Guth; m. Juliette Loubère 1936; ed. Coll. de Villeneuve-sur-Lot, Lycée Louis le Grand; teacher of French, Latin and Greek, Lycée de Dijon, Lycée de Rouen, then Lycée Janson de Sailly; journalist, contributor to several newspapers and journals including Spectator, Figaro Littéraire, L'Album du Figaro, La Gazette des Lettres, La Revue de Paris, etc. contrib. to numerous radio programmes; regular appearance on TV programme, Premières Nouvelles; Grand Prix du Théâtre 1946, Grand Prix littéraire, Paris 1964, Grand Prix littéraire, Monaco 1973, Grand Prix de littérature, Acad. Française 1978; Officier, Légion d'honneur, Commdr. des Arts et Lettres. *Publications:* Quarante contre un, Autour des dames du bois de Boulogne, Les sept trompettes, Le Pouvoir de Germaine Calban, Naïf series including, Les mémoires d'un naïf (Prix Courteline 1953), Le naïf locataire (Grand Prix du Roman, Académie Française 1956), Jeanne la mince series; Le naïf dans la littérature, Comment j'ai crée le personnage du naïf, Une bombe littéraire au temps des années folles: dadaïsme, Saint Louis roi de France, Henri IV, Histoire de la littérature française 2 vols. 1967, Lettre ouverte aux idoles 1968, L'histoire de la douce France 1968–70, Mazarin 1972, Le chat beauté, Lettres à votre fils qui en a ras le bol, Notre drôle d'époque comme si vous y étiez; childrens books: La locomotive Joséphine, Le mot de l'histoire, Moustique et le marchand de sable, Moustique et Barbe Bleue, Moustique dans la lune, Si ces grands hommes étaient morts à vingt ans, Moi, Joséphine, impératrice, Lettre ouverte aux futurs illettrés 1980, Le ce que je crois du naïf (essay) 1982, L'aube de la France 1982, Une enfance pour la vie 1984 (Chateaubriand Prize), La tigresse 1985, Si j'étais le Bon Dieu 1987, Discours de déception à l'Académie française 1987, Oui, Le Bonheur! 1988. *Leisure interests:* dreaming, listening to

Mozart, admiring art, talking to my wife. *Address:* 24 rue Desbordes-Valmore, 75016 Paris, France. *Telephone:* (45) 04-98-82.

GUTH, Wilfried, DR.RER.POL.; German banker (retd.); b. 8 July 1919; Chair. Supervisory Bd., Deutsche Bank AG, Metallgesellschaft AG, Frankfurt; Deputy Chair. Supervisory Bd., Allianz Versicherungs AG, Munich/Berlin, Siemens AG, Berlin/Munich. *Address:* Deutsche Bank AG, Taunusanlage 12, 6000 Frankfurt/Main, Federal Republic of Germany.

GUTHARDT, Helmut; German banking executive; b. 8 June 1934, Breuna; s. of Wilhelm and Sophie (née Schmale) Guthardt; m. 1st Margret Weymann 1956; one s. two d.; m. 2nd Marga Ackermann 1984; studied Frankfurt Banking Acad. 1958-60; Man. Dir. Raiffeisen-Rechenzentrum GmbH, Kassel 1963-70, Raiffeisenbank Kurhessen eG, Kassel 1964-65, Raiffeisen-Zentralbank Kurhessen AG, Kassel 1965-70; Man. Dir. Deutsche Genossenschaftsbank 1970-73, Vice-Chair. Bd. of Man. Dirs. 1973-81, Chair. 1981-; Dir. several other cos. *Address:* DG Bank Deutsche Genossenschaftsbank, Am Platz der Republik, P.O. Box 10 06 51, Frankfurt am Main 1, Federal Republic of Germany. *Telephone:* (69) 74 47 01.

GUTHRIE, Randolph Hobson, B.S., LL.B.; American lawyer and business executive; b. 1905, Richmond, Va.; s. of Mr. and Mrs. Joseph H. Guthrie; m. Mabel E. Welton 1934; two s. one d.; ed. The Citadel, Charleston and Harvard Law School; Sr. Partner of Mudge, Rose, Guthrie and Alexander and predecessor firms since 1943; Chair. Bd. of Studebaker-Worthington Inc. 1963-71, Chair. Exec. Cttee. 1971; Chair. Bd. of UMC Industries Inc. 1969-76, Chair. Exec. Cttee. 1976-81. *Leisure interest:* golf. *Address:* 20 Broad Street, New York, N.Y. 10005 (Office); 43 South Beach Lagoon Road, Sea Pines Plantation, Hilton Head, S.C. 29928, U.S.A. (Home). *Telephone:* 212-422-6767.

GUTIERREZ, Carlos Jose, D.JUR.; Costa Rican diplomatist; b. 26 Feb. 1927, Costa Rica; m.; six c.; ed. Costa Rica, Pennsylvania and Texas Univs.; Lecturer in Law, Univ. of Costa Rica 1952, Dean of Faculty of Law 1966-72; Dir. Nat. Insurance Inst. of Costa Rica 1953-58; Pres. Costa Rica Union of Lawyers 1962; Pres. Asscn. of Literary, Artistic and Scientific Writers 1962-63; Dir. for Costa Rica, Stanford Univ. research project on law and devt. 1972-74; teacher, School of Int. Relations, Nat. Univ. of Costa Rica 1976-80; mem. Legis. Ass. 1966-70; Amb. to Fed. Repub. of Germany 1982-83; Minister of Justice 1982-83, for Foreign Affairs and Worship 1983-86; Perm. Rep. of Costa Rica to UN 1986-. *Address:* Permanent Mission of Costa Rica to the United Nations, 211 East 43rd Street, Room 903, New York, N.Y. 10017, U.S.A. *Telephone:* 986-6373.

GUTIERREZ, Gustavo, D.THEOL.; Peruvian ecclesiastic; b. 8 June 1928, Lima; ed. Univ. Nacional Mayor de San Marcos, Lima, Univ. Catholique de Louvain, Univ. de Lyon, Univ. Gregoriana and Inst. Catholique de Paris; ordained priest 1959; Adviser, Nat. Union of Catholic Students 1960-; Prof. Catholic Univ. of Lima 1960-; mem. Pastoral-Theological team, Latin American Conf. of Catholic Bishops (CELAM) 1967-68; Bd. Dir. Inst. Bartolomé Las Casas-Rímac 1974-; Assoc. Vicar, Rímac, Lima 1980-; Visiting Prof. and lecturer at univs., colls. and seminaries in U.S.A. and elsewhere; mem. EATWOT (Ecumenical Asscn. of Third World Theologians); Dr. h.c. (Nijmegen) 1979, (Tübingen) 1985. *Publications:* A Theology of Liberation 1971, The Power of the Poor in History 1980, El Dios de la Vida 1982, We Drink from Our Own Wells: the Spiritual Journey of a People 1983, On Job, God-talk and the Suffering of the Innocent 1986, La verdad los hará libres 1986. *Leisure interests:* swimming, literature. *Address:* Instituto Bartolomé Las Casas-Rímac, Apartado 3090, Lima 100, Peru. *Telephone:* 814704; 814663.

GUTIÉRREZ, Julio César, DR. ECON.; Paraguayan economist and banker; b. 11 Feb. 1920; s. of Emilio and Amalia Gutiérrez; m. Beatriz Ferrari 1963; three s. and two d.; ed. Escuela Nacional de Comercio, Asunción, Universidad Nacional, Asunción, and Centro de Estudios Monetarios Latinamericano, Mexico; Supt. of Banks, Paraguay 1950-56; Financial Adviser to Ministry of Finance 1957-58; Nat. Financial Controller, Paraguay 1959-62; Dir. of Seminary, Faculty of Econ. Sciences, Asunción 1957-60, Univ. Prof. 1960-62; Econ. Counsellor, Paraguayan Embassy, Wash. 1962-69; Exec. Dir. Inter-American Devt. Bank (IDB) 1964-70; Rep. of the IDB in Lima, Peru 1971-73; Exec. Dir. IDB and Minister of Paraguayan Embassy, Washington 1974-76, Exec. Dir. IBRD 1976-78; Exec. Dir. IMF 1978-80; Pres. Petróleos Paraguayos (PETROPAR) 1981-85. *Leisure interests:* fishing and golf. *Address:* Oliva 299, 4° piso, Asunción, Paraguay. *Telephone:* 95-117/8/9.

GUTIÉRREZ, Mario R.; Bolivian politician and diplomatist; b. 19 Oct. 1917, Santa Cruz de la Sierra; s. of Julio A. and Luisa Gutiérrez; m. Mary Sensano 1951; two s. three d.; ed. Univ. Católica de Chile and Gabriel René Moreno Univ., Santa Cruz; mem. Bolivian Socialist Falange; Minister for Foreign Affairs 1971-73; six times interim Pres. of Bolivia; served as Deputy and Senator for La Paz in Nat. Congress; Amb. to UN 1975-78. *Publications:* Alegato Histórico de los Derechos de Bolivia al Pacífico, Predestinación Histórica de Bolivia, Sangre y Luz de Dos Razas, Soberania y Entreguismo, Presencia Internacional de Bolivia. *Address:* P.O. Box 830, La Paz, Bolivia.

GUTIÉRREZ MELLADO, Lieut.-Gen. Manuel; Spanish army officer and government official; b. 30 April 1912, Madrid; s. of Manuel and Carmen Gutiérrez Mellado; m. Carmen Blasco 1939; two s. two d.; ed. Gen. Mil. Acad.; Lieut. in Artillery 1933; took part in civil war, Capt. 1938; Major 1944; Prof. School of Artillery 1944; Lieut.-Col. 1957, Col. 1965; Command, 13 Artillery Regt.; Brig.-Gen. 1970; Prof., Higher Centre of Nat. Defence Studies (CESEDEN), then worked at Supreme Mil. Command 1970-73; Chair. various comms. and inter-ministerial councils 1970-73; Div.-Gen. and mem. Supreme Army Command 1973-75; Commdt.-Gen. and Govt. Rep. in Ceuta 1975-76; Lieut.-Gen. March 1975-; Capt.-Gen. of 7th Mil. Region March-Sept. 1976; Chief of Gen. Staff June-Sept. 1976; First Deputy Prime Minister (for Defence Affairs) 1976-81; Grand Cross of Order of San Hermenegildo, of Order of Mil. Merit and of Order of Aeronautical Merit; Order of Isabel la Católica; Medal of Merit (First Class) Portugal. *Address:* 51 Fortuny Street, Madrid, Spain.

GUTMAN, Natalia; Soviet cellist; b. 14 Nov. 1942; studied at Moscow Conservatory under Prof. Kozolupova and Mstislav Rostropovich; prizes at Vienna Student Festival and Dvořák Competition; has played all over the world and toured U.S.A. with U.S.S.R. State Symphony Orchestra and Svetlanov (q.v.), Russia and Italy with BBC Symphony under Temirkanov (q.v.); recordings with RCA. *Address:* c/o Harold Holt Ltd., 31 Sinclair Road, London, W14 0NS, England. *Telephone:* 01-603 4600.

GUTMANN, Francis Louis Alphonse Myrtil; French government official; b. 4 Oct. 1930, Paris; s. of Robert and Denise (née Coulom) Gutmann; m. Chantal de Gaulle 1964; two s. one d.; ed. Lycée Pasteur, Neuilly-sur-Seine; Head of dept., Ministry of Foreign Affairs 1951-57; Asst. Head Office of Sec. of State for Econ. Affairs 1955, mem. French del. to Econ. and Social Council and to UN Gen. Ass. 1952-55, to Common Market Conf., Brussels 1956-57; Adviser Pechiney Co. 1957-59, Sec.-Gen. 1963, Dir. 1970-71; Sec.-Gen. Fria 1960-62; Pres. Alucam 1968-72; Dir. (chemical div.) Pechiney-Ugine-Kuhlmann group; Pres.-Dir.-Gen. Ugine-Kuhlmann 1971-76, mem. governing bd. Pechiney-Ugine-Kuhlmann group in charge of social affairs 1975-78; Pres. Frialco and Vice-Pres. Friguia 1977-81; Dir.-Gen. French Red Cross 1980-81; Sec.-Gen. Ministry for External Relations 1981-85; Admin. representing the State, Parisbas 1982-84, Gaz de France 1984-85, St. Gobain 1982-85; Amb. to Spain 1985-; Chevalier, Légion d'honneur; Officier, Ordre nat. du Mérite. *Publication:* Les chemins de l'effort. *Address:* Saint-Gobain, Les Miroirs, 18 avenue d'Alsace, 92400 Courbevoie, France (Office).

GUTMANN, Viktor, DIP. ING., DR. TECH., DR. PHIL., SC.D.; Austrian chemist; b. 10 Nov. 1921, Vienna; s. of Viktor Gutmann and Margarete Lehmann; m. Elisabeth Schuster 1968; two s. two d.; ed. Tech. Univ. of Vienna; Asst. in research, Tech. Univ. of Vienna 1946-48, 1950-52, Dozent 1953-57, Prof. of Inorganic Chem. 1957, Head of Dept. 1960; Post-Doctoral Fellow, Cambridge 1948-50; Prof. of Inorganic and Analytical Chem., Baghdad Univ. 1952-53; mem. Göttingen Acad. of Science, Austrian Acad. of Science, Leopoldina Acad. of Science (Halle); Hon. mem. Hungarian Acad. of Science; Dr. Rer. Nat. (h.c.); Dr. Sc. (h.c.); J. Heyrovsky Medal; Carl Friedrich Gauss Medal, Schrödinger Prize, Willhelm Exner Medal, Hon. Medal of the City of Vienna in Gold, Science Prize of the City of Vienna. *Publications include:* Halogen Chemistry (Ed.) 1968, Coordination in non-Aqueous Solutions 1968, Chemical Functionality 1971, General and Inorganic Chemistry 1971, Wissenschaftliche Grundlagen der Homoeopathie 1986, The Donor-Acceptor Approach to Molecular Interactions 1978 and numerous articles; 400 research papers. *Leisure interests:* mountaineering, skiing, gardening. *Address:* Trinksgeltgasse 16, A 2380 Perchtoldsdorf, Austria (Home). *Telephone:* 0222-864570 (Home).

GUTOWSKY, Herbert Sander, PH.D.; American physical chemist; b. 8 Nov. 1919, Bridgman, Mich.; s. of Otto Gutowsky and Hattie Meyers; m. 1st Barbara Joan Stuart 1949 (divorced 1981); three s.; m. 2nd Virginia A. Warner 1982; ed. Indiana and Harvard Univs. and Univ. of Calif. (Berkeley); served in U.S. Army 1941-45; Instructor, Univ. of Ill. 1948, Asst. Prof. 1951-55, Assoc. Prof. 1955-56, Prof. of Chem. 1956-, Head, Div. of Physical Chem. 1956-62, Head, Dept. of Chem. and Chemical Eng. 1967-70, Dir. School of Chemical Sciences, Head, Dept. of Chem. 1970-83, Assoc. mem. Center for Advanced Study, Univ. of Ill. 1962-63; mem. Center for Advanced Study, Univ of Ill. 1983-; Guggenheim Fellow 1954-55; Walker Ames Visiting Prof. at Univ. of Wash. 1957; mem. N.A.S., American Acad. of Arts and Sciences, American Philosophical Soc.; A.C.S. awards: unrestricted grant for petroleum research 1965, Irving Langmuir Award in Chemical Physics 1966, Mid-west Award of St. Louis Section 1973, Peter Debye Award in Physical Chem. 1975; Award of the Int. Soc. of Magnetic Resonance 1974; G. N. Lewis Memorial Lecturer, Univ. of Calif. (Berkeley) 1976; Nat. Medal of Science 1977; G. B. Kistiakowsky Lecturer, Harvard Univ. 1980; Wolf Foundation Prize 1983/84, Hon. D.Sc. (Indiana Univ.) 1983. *Publications:* Scientific articles, mainly in Journal of American Chemical Soc., Journal of Chemical Physics, Physical Review, Discussions of Faraday Soc., Journal of Physical Chemistry. *Leisure interests:* gardening, bicycling, science fiction, philately. *Address:* Department of Chemistry, University of Illinois, 505 South Mathews Street, Urbana, Ill. 61801, U.S.A. *Telephone:* 217-333-7621.

GUTTON, André Henry Georges; French architect and town planner; b. 8 Jan. 1904, Fontenay-sous-Bois; s. of Henry B. Gutton; m. Elisabeth

Lafargue 1927; two s. one d.; ed. Ecole nationale supérieure des beaux arts and Inst. d'Urbanisme de l'Univ. de Paris; Architect for pvt. bldgs. and nat. palaces 1936-; Prof. Inst. of Town Planning 1946-63; Prof. of Theory of Architecture, Nat. School of Fine Arts 1949-58, of Town Planning 1958-74; Tech. Counsellor, Govt. of Syria 1951; mem. Exec. Cttee. Int. Union of Architects 1949-57, Pres. Town Planning Comm. 1951; Consultant Town-Planner Canton of Geneva 1960-70, Bilbao 1962, Brasilia 1967, Bratislava 1967, Belgrade 1986; Hon. Pres. Order of Architects; Vice-Pres. Congress of Architects 1965; mem. Acad. of Architecture, Royal Acad. of Belgium; Hon. Fellow A.I.A.; Int. Prize for Anvers (I.M.A.L.S.O.) 1933; Int. Prize for plan for Place des Nations, Geneva 1958; Officier, Légion d'honneur, Polar Star (Sweden), Kt., Order of Orange-Nassau, of Dannebrog; Officier des Palmes académiques, des Arts et des Lettres. *Major works:* Architectural Plans for Institut de France 1943, Post Office Buildings, Paris 1944, The Opera 1950, Post Office Buildings at Versailles, Nancy, Besançon, Chateauroux, Roanne, Neuilly-sur-Marne, Lyons, Chambéry and schools and offices in France, Town Planning: Plans for Nancy 1938, Dakar (Senegal), Boulogne, Issy 1945, Aleppo (Syria) 1952, Sihanoukville (Cambodia) 1960. *Publications:* Charte de l'urbanisme 1941, Conversations sur l'architecture: (L'édifice dans la cité, La maison des hommes, Les églises et les temples, Les écoles, lycées, universités, L'urbanisme au service de l'homme), De la nuit á l'aurore 1985. *Address:* 3 avenue Vavin, 75006 Paris, France (Home). *Telephone:* 46-33-72-76.

GUTZWILLER, Peter Max, DR.IUR., LL.M.; Swiss lawyer; b. 30 April 1941, Basle; s. of Max and Helly Gutzwiller; m. 1st Vreny Lüscher 1971 (divorced); one s.; m. 2nd Barbara Menzel; ed. Univs. of Basle and Geneva and Harvard Law School; Assoc. Staehelin Hafter & Partners 1970-76, Partner 1977-; mem. Bd. of Int. Law Assen. (Swiss Branch) 1975-; Sec. Swiss Assen. of Int. Law 1976; Major, Swiss Army 1979. *Publications:* Swiss International Divorce Law 1968, Von Ziel und Methode des IPR 1968, Arbeitsbewilligungen für Ausländer 1975, 1976, Grundriss des schweizerischen Privat- und Steuerrechtes (co-author) 1976. *Leisure interests:* art collection (cartoons), music, travel. *Address:* Bleicherweg 58, 8027 Zurich (Office); Sonnenrain 15, 8700 Küsnacht, Switzerland (Home). *Telephone:* 201 45 40 (Office); 910-9988 (Home).

GUY, Michel; French horticulturist and politician; b. 28 June 1927, Paris; s. of late Georges Guy and Aline Charon; ed. Ecole Bossuet, Paris; Man. Dir. Etablissements Guy-Charon (horticulture firm) 1950-70; Artistic Adviser, Int. Festival of Dance 1964-71; Founder and Dir.-Gen. Festival d'Automne, Paris 1972-74, 1978-; Sec. of State for Culture 1974-76; Pres. Bd. of Dirs., French Cinemathèque 1980-81; Vice-Pres. Festival of Avignon 1983; Vice-Pres. 'LA SEPT' (Société d'Ed. de Programmes de Télévision) 1987. *Leisure interest:* collecting modern paintings. *Address:* 156 rue de Rivoli, 75001 Paris, France (Home). *Telephone:* 42-96-12-27.

GUYARD, Marius-François, D.ÈS L.; French university professor; b. 18 March 1921, Paris; s. of Marius Guyard and Jeanne Chabrillat; m. Françoise Bordier 1947; two s. two d.; ed. Ecole Normale Supérieure and the Sorbonne; Prof., Univ. of Athens 1955-57, Strasbourg Univ. 1957-63; Cultural Counsellor, French Embassy, U.K. 1963-65; Prof. of French Literature, Sorbonne 1965-67, 1980-; Vice-Chancellor, Univ. of Montpellier 1967-69, of Amiens 1969-70, of Strasbourg 1970-76, of Lyon 1976-80; Chair. Conf. des Recteurs Français 1975-78; mem. Franco-British Council 1972-; Officier, Légion d'honneur, Commdr. Ordre nat. du Mérite, Commdr. Ordre des Palmes académiques, Chevalier des Arts et Lettres, Commdr. Orange-Nassau, Officier Mérite Italien. *Publications:* La Grande-Bretagne dans le roman français 1954, Recherches Claudéliennes 1964, editions of Lamartine and Hugo, numerous contributions to revues and critical anthologies. *Address:* 13 avenue Trudaine, 75009 Paris, France.

GUYER, Roberto E., LL.D.; Argentine diplomatist; b. 10 March 1923, Buenos Aires; m. María Julia Mackinlay 1962; ed. Buenos Aires School of Law, Acad. of Int. Law, The Hague, and Oxford and Columbia (N.Y.) Univs.; entered Argentine Foreign Service 1956; served in Washington, Bonn, The Hague (as Amb.) and as mem. of Argentine del. to UN and OAS; also held various sr. posts in Argentine Ministry of Foreign Affairs; fmr. Prof. of Int. Law, Univ. de Buenos Aires and Colegio Nacional de Guerra; UN Under-Sec.-Gen. for Political Affairs 1971-78; Amb. to Fed. Repub. of Germany 1978-86; Personal Rep. of Sec.-Gen. to Geneva Peace Conference on Middle East. *Address:* c/o Ministry of Foreign Affairs, Buenos Aires, Argentina.

GUYOT, H.E. Cardinal Louis Jean, D.THEOL.; French ecclesiastic; b. 7 July 1905, Bordeaux; s. of Joseph Guyot and Marie Videau; ed. Univ. of Bordeaux, Grand Séminaire and Collegium Angelicum, Rome; ordained Priest 1932; Priest, Bordeaux 1932; served as Diocesan Chaplain, Coll. St.-Genès and later in youth insts. for eight years; Founder, Séminaire Saint-Maurice pour les Vocations d'Afnés 1938; Vicar-Gen. 1944-49; Coadjutor to Bishop of Coutances 1949; Bishop of Coutances 1950-67; Pres. Comm. épiscopale du Clergé et des Séminaires and mem. Bd., Conseil Perm., Gen. Synod 1964; Archbishop of Toulouse 1966-79; created Cardinal by Pope Paul VI 1973; Keeper Acad. des Jeux Floraux de Toulouse; Officier, Légion d'honneur; Grand Croix Ordre de Malte. *Address:* 181 rue Judaïque, 33081 Bordeaux, France.

GUZE, Samuel Barry, M.D.; American psychiatrist, educator and university official; b. 18 Oct. 1923, New York; s. of Jacob Guze and Jenny (Berry)

Guze; m. Joy Lawrence Campbell 1946; one s. one d.; ed. Washington Univ., St. Louis, Mo.; Intern in Medicine, Barnes Hosp. 1945-46, Fellow in Medicine, Barnes Hosp. and Washington Univ. School of Medicine 1946 and 1948-49, Fellow in Psychiatry 1950-51; Resident in Medicine, Newington Veterans' Admin. Hosp., Conn. 1949-50; Instructor in Medicine, Washington Univ. School of Medicine, St. Louis, Mo. 1951-53, Asst. Prof. 1953-55, Lecturer in Social Work, George Warren Brown School of Social Work 1954-60, Asst. Prof. of Psychiatry and Asst. Prof. of Medicine 1955-59, Assoc. Prof. of Psychiatry and Assoc. Prof. of Medicine 1959-64, Prof. of Psychiatry and Assoc. Prof. of Medicine 1964-, Asst. to Dean 1965-71, Vice-Chancellor for Medical Affairs 1971-, Co-Head, Dept. of Psychiatry 1974-75, Spencer T. Olin Prof. of Psychiatry 1974-, Head of Dept. of Psychiatry 1975-, Pres. Washington Univ. Medical Center 1971-; Asst. Physician, Barnes Hosp. 1951-; Consulting Psychiatrist, Jewish Hosp. of St. Louis 1975-; Psychiatrist-in-Chief, Barnes, Renard and St. Louis Children's Hosps. 1975-; Samuel Hamilton Medal of the American Psychopathological Assen. 1982 and the Paul Hoch Medal 1986; Achievement Award, American Acad. of Clinical Psychiatrists 1987, Distinguished Public Service Award, Dept. of Health and Human Services 1987. *Publications:* Psychiatric Diagnosis (with others) 1974 (several trans.), Criminality and Psychiatric Disorders 1976, Childhood Psychopathology and Development (Ed. with others) 1983, Schizophrenia, Affective Disorders, and Organic Mental Disorders (Ed. with others) in Psychiatry (Ed. Cavenar) 1985. *Address:* Department of Psychiatry, Washington University School of Medicine, 4940 Audubon Avenue, St. Louis, Mo. 63110, U.S.A. *Telephone:* (314) 362-7005.

GUZMÁN NEYRA, Alfonso; Mexican politician and judge; b. 1906, Pánuco, Ver.; s. of Alfonso Victor Guzmán Rodríguez; m. Adelaida Rodríguez Quiroz de Guzmán 1936; one s.; ed. Univ. Nacional Autónama de México; Pres., Supreme Tribunal of Justice, Veracruz; Deputy for First Dist., Veracruz; Pres. Fed. Cttee. for Conciliation and Arbitration; Dir. Govt. Works in Fed. District; Pres. Regional Cttee. of Partido Revolucionario Institucional (PRI); Pres. Supreme Court of Justice 1959-64; Judge Fourth Chamber 1965-69; Pres. Supreme Court of Justice 1969-74. *Leisure interest:* shooting. *Address:* Alejandro Dumas 15, Colónia Polanco, México 5, D.F., Mexico. *Telephone:* 5-20-04-79.

GVISHIANI, Jermen Mikhailovich, D.PHIL.; Soviet philosopher and sociologist; b. 24 Dec. 1928, Akhaltsikhe, Georgia; s. of Mikhail Maksimovich and Irma Khristophorovna Gvishiani; m. Lyudmila Alekseyevna Kosygina (d. of the late Aleksey Kosygin, Chair. of U.S.S.R. Council of Ministers 1964-80) 1948; one s. one d.; ed. Moscow State Inst. of Int. Relations, Moscow State Univ., Inst. of Philosophy, U.S.S.R. Acad. of Science; navy service 1951-55; State Cttee. for Science and Tech., Int. Relations Dept. 1955-65, Deputy Chair. 1965-; Prof. of Philosophy, Moscow State Univ. 1960-71; Chair. Cttee. for Systems Analysis, Presidium of Acad. of Sciences 1971-, Int. Inst. for Applied Systems Analysis 1972, Int. Research Inst. for Man. Problems 1977-, Int. Council for New Initiatives in East-West Co-operation (Vienna Club) 1979-; Co-Chair. U.S.A.-U.S.S.R. Trade and Econ. Council, Sub-cttee. for Science and Tech. 1974-; Dir. Inst. for Systems Studies 1976-; Vice-Chair. Jt. Perm. U.S.S.R.-France Comm. 1967-, Soviet Div., U.S.S.R.-Fed. Repub. of Germany Comm. for Econ. and Tech. Co-operation 1972-; mem. Presidium, Soviet Sociologists' Assen. 1972-; mem. U.S.S.R. Acad. of Sciences, Int. Man. Acad., Sweden Royal Acad. of Eng. Sciences, American Man. Assen., American Man. Acad., Foreign mem. Finnish Acad. Tech. Sciences; mem. Club of Rome; State award, Order of October Revolution, three Orders of Labour Red Banner, Gold Mercury Int. Award, and various medals; Dr h.c. (Prague High Econ. School). *Publications:* Sociology of Business, Organization and Management, Social Function of Science and Science Policy, Scientific and Technological Revolution and Social Progress, etc. *Leisure interests:* music, sport. *Address:* U.S.S.R. State Committee for Science and Technology, Gorki Street 11, Moscow 103009, U.S.S.R. (Office). *Telephone:* 229-85-03 (Office).

GWIAZDA, Władysław, M.ECON.; Polish economist and politician; b. 12 March 1935, Starogard Gdański; ed. Main School of Planning and Statistics, Warsaw; worked in Motoimport Foreign Trade Office, Warsaw 1957-60; Head of Section Office of the Commercial Counsellor, Moscow, U.S.S.R. 1960-64; managerial posts in Ministry of Foreign Trade, including Dir. of Dept. 1964-71; Commercial Counsellor and Minister Plenipotentiary attached to Embassy, Moscow, U.S.S.R. 1971-73; Deputy Minister of Foreign Trade 1973-74, of Foreign Trade and Maritime Economy 1974-81, of Foreign Trade 1981-85; Deputy Chair. Council of Ministers 1985-87; Minister of Foreign Econ. Relations 1987-88; mem. Presidium of Govt. 1987-88; Perm. Rep. of the Polish People's Repub. to the CMEA, Moscow 1988-; mem. Polish United Workers' Party (PZPR) 1957-; Commdr.'s Cross of Order of Polonia Restituta and other decorations. *Address:* Polish Permanent Representation to CMEA, Prosp. Kalinina 56, Moscow, U.S.S.R.

GYENES, András; Hungarian politician; b. 1923, Kisbecskerek; ed. Communist Party Acad., Moscow; started as food industry worker; joined CP 1945; held various TU positions 1944-58; Vice-Pres. Hungarian Council for Physical Training and Sports until 1962; Deputy Head, Foreign Dept., Cen. Cttee., Hungarian Socialist Workers' Party (HSWP) 1962-69, Head 1969-70, 1971-74; Deputy Minister of Foreign Affairs 1970-71; Amb. to

German Democratic Repub. 1974-75; Sec. Cen. Cttee., HSWP 1975-82, Pres. HSWP Supervisory Cttee. 1982-; M.P.; Order of the Hungarian People's Repub. *Address:* Hungarian Socialist Workers' Party, Central Supervisory Committee, 1387 Budapest, Széchenyi rakpart 19, Hungary. *Telephone:* 111-400.

GYLL, John Sören; Swedish company executive; b. 26 Dec. 1940, Skorped; s. of Josef and Gertrud Gyll; m. Lilly Margareta Hellman 1974; two s. one d.; Marketing Dir. and Vice-Pres. Rank Xerox 1963-77; Head of Uddeholm Sweden, Uddeholm AB 1977-79, Exec. Vice-Pres. 1979-81, Pres. and C.E.O. 1981-84; Pres. and C.E.O. Procordia AB 1984-. *Leisure interests:* hunting, skiing. *Address:* Procordia AB, P.O. Box 2278, 103 17 Stockholm, Sweden. *Telephone:* 7913100.

GYLLENHAMMAR, Pehr Gustaf, B.LL.; Swedish business executive; b. 28 April 1935, Gothenburg; s. of Pehr Gustaf Victor Gyllenhammar and Aina Dagny Kaplan; m. Eva Christina Engellau 1959; one s. three d.; ed. Univ. of Lund, studied int. law in England, vocational studies in maritime law, U.S.A., Cen. d'Etudes Industrielles, Geneva; employed by Mannheimer & Zetterlöf (Solicitors), Gothenburg 1959, Haight, Gardner, Poor & Havens (Admiralty Lawyers), New York 1960, Amphion Insurance Co., Gothenburg 1961-64; Asst. Admin. Man. Skandia Insurance Co., Stockholm 1965-66, Vice-Pres. Corporate Planning 1966-68, Exec. Vice-Pres. 1968, Pres. and C.E.O. 1970; joined AB Volvo, Gothenberg 1970, Man. Dir. and C.E.O. 1971-83, Chair. of Bd. and C.E.O. 1983-; Chair. Bd. of Dirs. Swedish Ships' Mortage Bank 1976-, Pharmacia AB 1987-; mem. numerous Bds. of Dirs., incl. Skandinaviska Enskilda Banken 1979-, United Technologies Corpn. 1981-, Kissinger Assocs., Inc. 1982-, Pearson PLC 1983-, Reuters Holdings PLC 1984-, and mem. Bd. numerous cos. and manufacturing orgs.; mem. Royal Swedish Acad. of Eng. Sciences 1974; Dr. Med. h.c. (Gothenburg Univ.) 1981; Hon. D.Tech. (Brunel) 1987; Hon. D.Eng. (Nova Scotia) 1988; Officer (1st Class) Royal Order of Vasa 1973; Commdr. Order of the Lion of Finland 1977, Commdr. Ordre nat. du Mérite 1980; Golden Award, City of Gothenburg 1981; King's Medal (12th Size) with ribbon of Order of the Seraphim 1981; Commdr. St. Olav's Order 1984; Commdr. Order of the Lion of Finland (1st Class) 1986; Commdr. Légion d'honneur 1987; Knight Grand Officier of the Repub. of Italy's Order of Merit 1987. *Publications:* Mot sekelskiftet på måfå (Towards the Turn of the Century at Random) 1970, Jag tror på Sverige (I Believe in Sweden) 1973, People at Work 1977, En industripolitik för människan (Industrial Policy for Human Beings) 1979, and numerous articles for domestic and int. press, incl. contributions to several books. *Leisure interests:* tennis, sailing, skiing, riding. *Address:* AB Volvo, S-40508, Gothenburg, Sweden.

GYNGELL, Bruce; Australian broadcasting executive; b. 8 July 1929; m. 1st Ann Gyngell, one s. two d.; m. 2nd Kathy Rowan, one s.; ed. Sydney Grammar School, Sydney Univ. and Columbia Univ., New York; trainee radio announcer Australian Broadcasting Corpn. 1950; joined Channel Nine TV 1956, first person to appear on Australian TV 16 Sept. 1956, Programme Dir. 1956-64, Man. Dir. 1964-69; Deputy Man. Dir. Anglia TV, England 1972-76; Deputy Man. Dir. ITC Entertainment 1972-75; Chair. Network Planning Cttee. 1974-76; Chair. Australian Broadcasting Tribunal 1977-80; Chief Exec. Special Broadcasting Service (TV Service for ethnic minorities) 1980; Consolidated Media Projects 1983; mem. Bd. TV-am, London Jan.-May 1984, Man. Dir. and Dir. of Programmes May 1984-. *Address:* TV-am, Breakfast Television Centre, Hawley Crescent, London, NW1 8EF, England.

GYSI, Klaus; German journalist and diplomatist; b. 3 March 1912; Joined Communist Party (KPD) 1931; Chief Ed. Aufbau 1945-48, Fed. Sec. Kulturbund 1948-50; Head of Aufau publrs., 1957-66; mem. Volkskammer, German Democratic Repub. 1949-54, 1967-; Minister of Culture 1966-73; State Sec. for Church Affairs 1979-; Amb. to Italy 1973-78; Vaterländischer Verdienstorden in Silver and Gold, Order "Banner der Arbeit". *Address:* c/o Ministry of Foreign Affairs, Berlin, German Democratic Republic.

H

HA VAN LAU; Vietnamese diplomatist; b. 9 Dec. 1918, Thua Thien; m. with three c.; served with Viet-Nam People's Army 1945-54; a del. of Democratic Repub. of Viet-Nam to Geneva Conf. on Indochina 1954, Paris Conf. on Viet-Nam 1968; Asst. Minister of Foreign Affairs 1973; Amb. to Cuba 1974-78; Perm. Rep. to UN 1978-82, Deputy Minister for Foreign Affairs 1982-84; Amb. to France (also accred. to Belgium, The Netherlands and Luxembourg) 1984-. *Address:* Embassy of Viet-Nam, 62 rue Boileau, 75016 Paris, France. *Telephone:* (1) 45.24.50.63.

HAACK, Dieter; German lawyer and politician; b. 9 June 1934, Karlsruhe; s. of Dr. Albrecht H. and Irmgard (Faber) Haack; m. Ursula Dostert 1959; two s. two d.; ed. grammar school, Erlangen and Bonn Univs.; served as Assessor, Bavarian Civil Service 1962-63; in Fed. Ministry for Intra-German Relations 1963-69, Dir. and Adviser, Office of Ministers; mem. Social Democratic Party (SPD) 1961-, mem. SPD Dist. Council, Siegkreis 1964-69, Chair. 1966-68, Chair. SPD Exec. Cttee., Franconia, Deputy Chair. Bavaria; mem. Bundestag (Parl.) 1969; Sec. of State to Minister of Regional Planning, Housing and Urban Devt. 1972-78, Minister 1978-82. *Address:* Wahlkreis 228, Erlangen, Federal Republic of Germany.

HAACKE, Hans Christoph Carl; German artist and professor of art; b. 12 Aug. 1936, Cologne; s. of Dr. Carl Haacke and Antonie Haacke; m. Lynda Snyder 1965; two s.; ed. State Acad., Kassel; Asst. Prof. Cooper Union, 1971-75, Assoc. Prof. 1975-79; Prof. 1979-; Guest Prof. Hochschule für Bildende Künste, Hamburg 1973, Gesamthochschule, Essen 1979; solo exhbns. include Galerie Schmela, Düsseldorf 1965, Howard Wise Gallery, New York 1966, 1968, 1969, Galerie Paul Maenz, Cologne 1971, 1974, 1981, Museum Haus Lange, Krefeld 1972, John Weber Gallery, New York, 1973, 1975, 1977, 1979, 1981, 1983, 1985, Kunstverein, Frankfurt 1976, Galerie Durand-Dessert, Paris 1977, 1978, Museum of Modern Art, Oxford 1978, Stedelijk van Abbemusem, Eindhoven 1979, Tate Gallery, London 1984, Neue Gesellschaft für Bildende Kunst, Berlin 1985, Kunsthalle, Berne 1985, Le Consortium, Dijon 1986, The New Museum of Contemporary Art, New York 1986; group exhbns.: Nul at Stedelijk Museum, Amsterdam 1965, The Machine as seen as the end of the mechanical age, Museum of Modern Art, New York 1968, When Attitudes Become Form, Kunsthalle, Berne 1969, Tokyo Biennale 1970, Information, Museum of Modern Art, New York 1970, Documenta 5, Kassel 1972, Venice Biennale 1976, 1978, Kunst in Europa na '68, Museum van Hedendaagse Kunst, Ghent 1980, '60-'80—attitudes/concepts/images, Stedelijk Museum, Amsterdam 1982, Documenta 7, Kassel 1982, Content: A Contemporary Focus, 1974-1978, Hirshhorn Museum, Washington, D.C. 1984, Time—the Fourth Dimension in Art, Palais des Beaux-Arts, Brussels 1984, Sydney Biennale, Sydney 1984, São Paulo Bienal, São Paulo 1985, Kunst in der Bundesrepublik Deutschland, Nationalgalerie, Berlin 1985, L'Epoque, la mode, la morale, la passion, Centre Georges Pompidou, Paris 1987, Documenta 8, Kassel 1987. *Publications:* (with Edward F. Fry) Werkmonographie 1972, Framing and Being Framed (jtly.) 1975, Nach allen Regeln der Kunst 1984, Unfinished Business (with others) 1987; numerous articles and interviews in int. art magazines. *Address:* c/o Cooper Union for the Advancement of Science and Art, Cooper Square, New York, N.Y. 10003, U.S.A.

HAAG, Rudolf, DR.RER.NAT.; German professor of theoretical physics; b. 17 Aug. 1922, Tubingen; s. of Albert Haag and Anna (née Schaich) Haag; m. Kaethe Fues 1948; three s. one d.; ed. Tech. Univ., Stuttgart and Univ. of Munich; Prof. of Physics, Univ. of Ill., U.S.A 1960-66; Prof. of Theoretical Physics, Hamburg Univ. 1966-87, Prof. Emer. 1987-; Dr. h.c. (Aix-Marseille) 1979; Max-Planck-Medal 1970. *Publications:* over 40 original papers on quantum theory of fields. *Address:* Oeltingsallee 20, D-2080 Pinneberg, Federal Republic of Germany.

HAAK, Jan Friedrich Wilhelm; South African lawyer and politician; b. 20 April 1917, Prince Albert; s. of Klaas D. Haak; m. Maria Theron 1944; one s. two d.; ed. Prince Albert School and Univ. of Stellenbosch; Attorney, Bellville, Cape Town and Pretoria 1945-48 and Pretoria 1977-86; Advocate, Cape Bar 1960; Mayor of Bellville 1949-51; M.P. 1953-; Deputy Minister of Econ. Affairs 1961-64, Deputy Minister of Mines 1962-64, of Planning 1962-64; Minister of Mines and Planning 1964-67, of Econ. Affairs 1967-70; mem. Chief Council of Nat. Party 1951, Prime Minister's Econ. Advisory Council 1975-76; Pres. Afrikaans Handelsinstituut 1975-76; Dir. Electricity Supply Comm. *Address:* 8 Goewerneur Street, Welgemoed, Bellville 7530, Republic of South Africa. *Telephone:* 021-953 1682.

HAAN, Pieter de, M.A.; Netherlands academic; b. 4 Nov. 1927, Augustinusga; m. F. A. Zijlstra 1956; two s.; ed. Univ. of Groningen; Asst. Sec. Landbonnschap, The Hague 1956; Scientific Asst. Landbonnhogeschool 1956-61; Prof. of Land Law, Delft Univ. of Tech. 1961-88; Prof. of Admin. Law and Land Law, Free Univ. Amsterdam 1974-88; Pres. Inst. voor Bonnrecht 1972-; mem. Advisory Council for Physical Planning 1976-, Royal Netherlands Acad. of Sciences 1979-. *Publications:* Land Law, 3 Vols. 1983, 1984, 1988, Bestuusrecht in de sociale rechtstraat, 3 Vols. 1986. *Address:* Ranonkelstraat 159, 2565 BC Den Haag; Schuilenburgerweg 12,

9261 XB Oostermeer, The Netherlands (Home). *Telephone:* 05129 1455 (Home).

HAARDER, Bertel, B. POL. SC.; Danish politician; b. 7 Sept. 1944, Rønshoved, South Jutland; s. of Hans Haarder; ed. Århus Univ.; Instructor at Alborg Teacher Training Coll.; M.P. 1975-; Minister of Educ. 1986-, of Research 1987-; Liberal. *Address:* Ministry of Education, Frederiksholms Kanal 21-25, 1220 Copenhagen K, Denmark. *Telephone:* (01) 92-50-00.

HAAS, Peter E., M.B.A.; American business executive; b. 20 Dec. 1919, San Francisco; s. of Walter A. Haas and Elise Stern; m. 1st Josephine Baum 1945, 2nd Mimi Lurie 1981; two s. one d.; ed. Deerfield Acad., Univ. of Calif. and Harvard Univ.; joined Levi Strauss & Co., San Francisco 1945, Exec. Vice-Pres. 1958-70, Pres. 1970-81, C.E.O. 1976-81, Chair. 1981-; Dir. AT&T 1966-; various public and charitable appts. *Address:* Levi Strauss & Co., P.O. Box 7215, San Francisco, Calif. 94120, U.S.A.

HAASEN, Peter, DR. RER. NAT.; German physicist; b. 21 July 1927, Gotha; s. of Herbert Haasen and Ingeborg Haasen; m. Barbara Kulp 1958; three d.; ed. Univ. of Göttingen, Univ. of Chicago; Research assoc. Max Planck Inst., Stuttgart 1956-58; Prof. of Metal Physics, Univ. of Göttingen 1959-; awarded Heyn Medal, R.F. Mehl Medal. *Publications:* Physical Metallurgy 1974, Physical Metallurgy (ed. R. W. Calm and P. Haasen) 1983. *Address:* Institut für Metallphysik, Universität Göttingen, Hospitalstr. 3-5, D-3400 Göttingen, Federal Republic of Germany. *Telephone:* (0551) 395001.

HAAVIKKO, Paavo Juhani, PH.D.; Finnish writer and publisher; b. 25 Jan. 1931, Helsinki; s. of Heikki Adrian Haavikko and Rauha Pyykönen; m. 1st Marja-Liisa Vartio (née Sairanen) 1955 (died 1966), one s. one d.; m. 2nd Ritva Rainio (née Hanhineva) 1971; ed. Univ. of Helsinki; worked in real estate concurrently with career as writer 1951-67; mem Bd., Finnish Writers' Asscn. 1962-66; mem. State Cttee. for Literature 1966-67; mem. Bd. of Yhtyneet Kuvalehdet magazine co. and Suuri Suomalainen Kirjakerho (Great Finnish Book Club) 1969; Literary Dir. Otava Publishing Co. 1967-83; Dir. Arthouse Publishing Group 1983-; six state prizes for literature; Pro Finlandia Medal; Neustadt Int. Prize for Literature 1984. *Publications:* Tiet etäisyyksiin 1951, Tuuliöinä 1953, Synnyinmaa 1955, Lehdet lehtiä 1958, Talvipalatsi 1959, Runot 1962, Puut, kaikki heidän vihreytensä 1966, Neljätoista hallitsijaa 1970, Puhua vastata opettaa 1972, Runoja matkalta salmen ylitse 1973, Kaksiky m mentä ja yksi 1974, Runot 1949-1974 1975, Runoelmat 1975, Viiniä, Kirjoitusta 1976, Toukokuu, ikuinen 1988 (poems); Poésie 1965, Jahre 1967, Gechichte 1967, Selected Poems 1968, The Superintendent 1973, Le palais d'hiver 1976 (translations); Münchhausen, Nuket 1960, Ylilääkäri 1968, Sulka 1973, Mommilan veriteot 1917 1973, Harald Pitkäikäinen 1974 (plays); Ratsumies 1974 (libretto); Yksityisiä Asioita 1960, Toinen taivas ja maa 1961, Vuodet 1962, Lasi Claudius Civiliksen salaliittolaisten pöydällä 1964 (prose), Kansakun nan linja 1977, Yritys omaksikuvaksi 1987. *Address:* Bulevardi 19C, 00120 Helsinki, Finland.

HABAKKUK, Sir Hrothgar John, Kt., M.A., F.B.A.; British economic historian; b. 13 May 1915, Barry, Glam.; s. of Evan Guest Habakkuk and Anne Bowen; m. Mary Richards 1948; one s. three d.; ed. Barry County School, Univ. Coll., Cardiff, St. John's Coll., Cambridge; Fellow, Pembroke Coll., Cambridge 1938-50, Dir. of Studies in History 1946-50; Lecturer, Faculty of Econs., Cambridge 1946-50; Chichele Prof. of Econ. History, Fellow, All Souls Coll., Oxford 1950-67; Prin. Jesus Coll., Oxford 1968-84; Vice-Chancellor Univ. of Oxford 1973-77; Pres. Univ. Coll. of Swansea 1975-84; Pres. Royal Historical Soc. 1976-80; Chair. Cttee. of Vice-Chancellors and Prins. 1976-77; Chair. Advisory Group on London Health Services 1979-80, Oxon. Health Authority 1982-84; mem. Royal Comm. on Historical Manuscripts 1978-; Fellow, All Souls Coll. 1988-; Rhodes Trustee 1977-85; Hon. Fellow, St. John's and Pembroke Colls., Cambridge, Jesus Coll., Oxford; Foreign mem. American Acad. of Arts and Sciences, American Philosophical Soc.; Hon. D.Litt. (Cambridge, Wales, Pa., Kent, Ulster). *Publications:* American and British Technology in the Nineteenth Century 1962, Population Growth and Economic Development since 1750 1971, Editor, Cambridge Economic History of Europe Vol. VI. *Address:* 28 Cunliffe Close, Oxford, OX2 7BL, England. *Telephone:* (0865) 56583.

HABASH, George, M.D.; Palestinian nationalist leader; b. 1925, Lydda, Palestine; ed. American Univ. of Beirut; mem. Youth of Avengeance 1948 and Arab Nationalists' Movement early 1950s; practised as doctor 1950s; leader of Popular Front for the Liberation of Palestine Nov. 1967- (introduced Marxist-Leninist thought to the Palestinian cause); leader Arab Nationalists' Movt.

HABBEL, Wolfgang R., DR.JUR.; German lawyer and executive; b. 25 March 1924, Dillenburg; s. of Werner and Dorothea Habbel; m. Susan Roedter 1951; two s.; Asst. to Bd. of Man., Auto Union GmbH 1951-59; Personnel Man., European Labour Relations Co-ordinator, Ford of Europe 1960-69; mem. Man. Bd., Boehringer, Ingelheim 1970-71, Audi NSU 1971-78; Chair. Man. Bd., Audi NSU (Audi AG from Jan. 1985) 1979-87; mem. Man. Bd., Volkswagen 1979-, des Landesverbandes der Bayerischen

Ind.; mem. Bd. of Dirs., Gerresheimer Glas AG, Triumph Adler Werke AG; Pres. Gesellschaft für Sicherheitswissenschaft. *Leisure interest:* golf. *Address:* Höhenstrasse 5, 8068 Pfaffenhofen 1, Federal Republic of Germany. *Telephone:* 08441/22 33.

HABECK, Fritz, DR.IUR.; Austrian writer; b. 8 Sept. 1916, Neulengbach; s. of late Dr. Karl and Marianne H. (née Adelsmayr) Habeck; m. Gerda Vilsmeier 1951; two s. two d.; ed. Univ. of Vienna; served in German Army during Second World War; Asst. Man. Josefstadt Theatre, Vienna 1946; radio producer in Vienna 1953–77; Pres. of Austrian PEN Centre 1978; Goethe Award of City of Vienna, City Prize of Vienna, Austrian State Prize, Handel-Mazzetti Prize, Vienna Children's Book Prize 1960, 1961, 1963, 1967, 1970, 1973, State Children's Book Prize 1963, 1967, Wildgans Prize of Austrian Industry 1964, Stifter Prize 1973, Prize of City of Vienna. *Publications:* Novels: Der Scholar vom linken Galgen 1941, Der Tanz der sieben Teufel 1950, Das Boot kommt nach Mitternacht 1951, Das zerbrochene Dreieck 1953, Ronan Gobain 1956, Der Ritt auf dem Tiger 1958, Der Kampf um die Barbacane 1960, Die Stadt der grauen Gesichter 1961, Der verliebte Oesterreicher 1961, Der einäugige Reiter 1964, In eigenem Auftrag (Selections) 1963, Der Piber 1965, Die Insel über den Wolken 1965, König Artus 1965, Aufstand der Salzknechte 1967, Salzburg-Spiegel 1967, Marianne und der wilde Mann 1968; François Villon 1969, Doktor Faustus 1970, Johannes Gutenberg 1971, Schwarzer Hund im goldenen Feld 1973, Der schwarze Mantel meines Vaters 1976, Wind von Südost 1979, Der Gobelin 1982, Der General und die Distel 1985, Die drei Kalendar 1986; Plays: Zwei und zwei ist vier 1948, Baisers mit Schlag 1950, Marschall Ney 1954. *Leisure interests:* gardening, chronicle of the family. *Address:* Grillparzerstrasse 6, 2500 Baden, Austria. *Telephone:* 02252-86-258.

HABERER, Jean-Yves; French government official; b. 17 Dec. 1932, Mazagan, Morocco; m. Anne du Crest 1959; two c.; ed. Inst. d'Etudes politiques, Ecole Nat. d'Admin.; Insp. des Finances 1959, Insp. Gen. 1980; Tech. Adviser to Finance Ministry 1966–68; an Asst. Dir. of Treasury 1967–69, in charge of Intervention Service, Treasury 1969, of Financial Activities 1970, of Int. Business 1973; Dir. of Treasury 1978–82; Head of Office of Minister of Foreign Affairs 1968, of Minister of Defence 1969, of Minister of Econ. and Finance 1976; Prof. Inst. d'Etudes politiques 1970–; Chair. Monetary Cttee. of the EEC 1980–; Pres. and Dir.-Gen. Bank Paribas and Cie. Financière de Paribas 1982–86, Chair. of Bd. Paribas Belgique, and of Supervisory Bd. Compagnie Bancaire 1982; Chair. Credit Lyonnais Sept. 1988–; Dir. Club Mediterranée, Crédit Nat., Cie. Française des Petroles, Crédit du Nord, Crédit Foncier de France, Banque Ottomani, Fives Lille, Power Corpn., Cie. Luxembourgeoise de Télédiffusion, S. G. Warburg, Mercury Securities, Paribas Suisse, Paribas Nederland; Chevalier, Légion d'honneur 1978, Officier Ordre nat. du Mérite 1981. *Address:* Credit Lyonnais, 19 boulevard des Italiens, Paris 2eme (Office); 10 rue Rémusat, 75016 Paris, France (Home).

HABERMAS, Jürgen, DR.PHIL.; German professor of philosophy; b. 18 June 1929, Düsseldorf; m. Ute Habermas-Wesselhöft 1955; three c.; ed. Univs. of Bonn and Göttingen; Research Asst., Inst. für Sozial Forschung, Frankfurt 1956; Prof. of Philosophy, Univ. of Heidelberg 1961, of Philosophy and Sociology, Univ. of Frankfurt 1964; Dir. Max Planck Inst., Starnberg, Munich 1971; Prof. of Philosophy, Univ. of Frankfurt 1983–; Hon. D.D. (New School for Social Research) 1984; Foreign mem. American Acad. of Arts and Sciences 1984; Hegel Prize 1972, Sigmund Freud Prize 1976, Adorno Prize 1980, Geschwister Scholl Prize 1985, Leibniz Prize 1986, Sonning Prize 1987. *Publications:* Strukturwandel der Öffentlichkeit 1962, Theorie und Praxis 1963, Erkenntnis und Interesse 1968, Legitimationsprobleme im Spätkapitalismus 1973, Theorie des kommunikativen Handelns 1981, Moralbewusstsein und Kommunikatives Handeln 1983, Der Philosophische Diskürs ober Moderne 1985, Eine Art Schadens ab wicklüng 1987. *Address:* Department of Philosophy, University of Frankfurt, Dantestrasse 4–6, D-8000 Frankfurt am Main, Federal Republic of Germany.

HABERMEIER, Walter O.; German international finance official; b. 24 Jan. 1931, Heilbronn; m.; two s.; ed. Univs. of Tübingen and Munich; with German Fed. Bank, Dept. of Int. Orgs. and Agreements 1957–60; mem. German Perm. Del., OEEC, Paris 1960–61; Asst. to Pres. European Monetary Agreement 1960–61; Alt. Exec. Dir. IMF 1962–65; Special Adviser, German Fed. Bank 1966; Deputy Treas., IMF 1966, Treas. 1969–87. *Address:* c/o International Monetary Fund, 700 19th Street, N.W., Washington, D.C. 20431, U.S.A.

HABGOOD, Most Rev. Dr. John Stapylton, D.D., M.A., PH.D.; British ecclesiastic; b. 23 June 1927, Stony Stratford; s. of Arthur Henry Habgood and Vera Chetwynd-Stapylton; m. Rosalie Mary Anne Boston 1961; two s. two d.; ed. Eton Coll., King's Coll. Cambridge Univ. and Cuddesdon Coll. Oxford; Demonstrator in Pharmacology, Cambridge Univ. 1950–53; Fellow, King's Coll. Cambridge Univ. 1952–55; Curate, St. Mary Abbott's Church, Kensington 1954–56; Vice-Prin. Westcott House, Cambridge 1956–62; Rector, St. John's Church, Jedburgh, Scotland 1962–67; Prin. Queen's Coll., Birmingham 1967–73; Bishop of Durham 1973–83; Archbishop of York 1983–; Pres. (U.K.) Council on Christian Approaches to Defence and Disarmament 1976–; Chair. World Council of Churches' Int. Hearing on Nuclear Weapons 1981–; mem. Council for Science and Society 1975–, Council for Arms Control 1981–; Moderator of Church and Soc. Sub-Unit,

World Council of Churches; Hon. D.D. (Durham) 1975, (Cambridge) 1984, (Aberdeen) 1988; Hon. Fellow King's Coll., Cambridge 1984. *Publications:* Religion and Science 1964, A Working Faith 1980, Church and Nation in a Secular Age 1983, Confessions of a Conservative Liberal 1988. *Leisure interests:* carpentry, painting. *Address:* Bishopthorpe, York, YO2 1QE, England. *Telephone:* (0904) 707021.

HABIB, Philip Charles, B.S., PH.D.; American diplomatist; b. 25 Feb. 1920 New York; s. of Alexander and Mary (Spiridon) Habib; m. Majorie Slightam 1942; two d.; ed. Univ. of Idaho, and Univ. of California (Berkeley); served U.S. army 1942–46 (rank of Capt.); entered Foreign Service 1949; Third Sec. U.S. Embassy, Canada 1949–51; Second Sec. New Zealand 1952–54; Research specialist, Dept. of State, Washington 1955–57; U.S. Consulate-Gen., Trinidad 1958–60; Foreign Affairs Officer, Dept. of State 1960–61; Counsellor for Political Affairs U.S. Embassy, Repub. of Korea 1962–65; Repub. of Viet-Nam 1965–67; rank of Minister 1966–67, Amb. 1969–71; Deputy Asst. Sec. of State for East Asian and Pacific Affairs 1967–69; Adviser U.S. Del. to meetings on Viet-Nam, Paris 1968–71; Amb. to Repub. of Korea 1971–74; Asst. Sec. of State for East Asian and Pacific Affairs 1974–75; Under-Sec. of State for Political Affairs 1976–78; Diplomat-in-Residence, Stanford Univ. 1978–79; Sr. Research Fellow Hoover Inst. 1980–, American Enterprise Inst. 1983–; Special Pres. Envoy to Middle East 1981–83, to Cen. America 1986–87; Consultant Bechtel Corpn.; Rockefeller Public Service Award 1969, Nat. Civil Service League Award 1970. *Address:* 1606 Courtland Road, Belmont, Calif. 94002, U.S.A.

HABIB-DELONCLE, Michel, L. ÈS L., L. EN D.; French lawyer and politician; b. 26 Nov. 1921, Neuilly-sur-Seine; s. of Louis Habib and Jeanne Deloncle; m. Colette Sueur 1944; three s. (one deceased) two d.; ed. Ecole libre des Sciences Politiques, Paris and Faculties of Law and Letters (Sorbonne), Univ. of Paris; Resistance Movement 1941–45; Journalist, France Catholique 1945–53; Sec.-Gen. Parl. Group Rassemblement du Peuple Français 1948–54; barrister, Cour d'Appel, Paris 1955–; Deputy, Nat. Assembly 1958–63, 1967–73; Sec. of State to the Ministry of Foreign Affairs 1962–66, to the Ministry of Educ. 1966–67; mem. European Parl. 1967–73, Vice-Pres. 1972; mem. del. UN Gen. Assembly 1967–72; Int. Relations Del., Exec. Cttee. Union des Démocrates pour la République 1968–74; Deputy Sec.-Gen. UDR 1971; mem. Cen. Cttee. RPR 1977–; Political Ed. La Nation 1968–74; Pres. Chambre de Commerce Franco-arabe 1970–; Croix de guerre. *Leisure interests:* shooting. *Address:* 46 avenue d'Iéna, 75116 Paris, France.

HABICHT, Werner, DR. PHIL.; German professor of English; b. 29 Jan. 1930, Schweinfurt; s. of Wilhelm Habicht and Magda (née Muller) Habicht; ed. Univ. of Munich, Johns Hopkins Univ., Univ. of Paris; Asst. Freie Universität, Berlin 1957–60, Univ. of Munich 1960–65; Prof. of English, Univ. of Heidelberg 1966–70, Univ. of Bonn 1970–78, Univ. of Würzburg 1978–; Visiting Prof. Univ. of Texas at Austin 1981, Univ. of Colorado, Boulder 1987, Ohio State Univ., Columbus 1988; mem. Akademie der Wissenschaften und der Literatur, Mainz 1982–; Pres. Deutsche Shakespeare-Gesellschaft West 1976–. *Publications:* Die Gebärde in englischen Dichtungen des Mittelalters 1959, Studien zur Dramenform vor Shakespeare 1968, Ed. English and American Studies in German 1968–82; Ed. Jahrbuch, Deutsche Shakespeare-Gesellschaft West 1982–; Co-ed. Literatur Brockhaus, 3 vols. 1988; numerous articles on English literature and drama. *Address:* Institut für Englische Philologie, Universität Würzburg, Am Hubland, D-8700 Würzburg, Federal Republic of Germany.

HABRÉ, Hissène; Chad politician and former opposition leader; formerly one of the leaders of the Front de Libération Nationale du Tchad (FROLINAT); head of Northern Armed Forces Command Council –1977; held the French archaeologists M. and Mme Claustre captive 1974–77; Leader of Forces Armées du Nord 1977–; negotiated with Govt. of Brig.-Gen. Félix Malloum 1978; Prime Minister Aug. 1978–March 1979; resigned after Kano peace agreement with FROLINAT forces led by Goukouni Oueddei March 1979; Minister of State for Defence and War Veterans in Provisional Govt. April–May 1979; Minister of Defence 1979 (in conflict with Goukouni Oueddei in civil war, reported in exile 1980); Minister of Nat. Defence, Veterans and War Victims Dec. 1986–; Pres. of Chad (desig.) June–Oct. 1982, Pres. Oct. 1982– (ousted Gov. of Pres. Goukouni Oueddei (q.v.) in coup). *Address:* Présidence de la République, N'Djamena, Chad.

HABSBURG-LOTHRINGEN, Otto von, DR.POL.SC.; Austrian/German politician and author; b. 20 Nov. 1912, Reichenau, Austria; s. of late Archduke Charles, later Emperor of Austria and King of Hungary, and Zita (née Princess of Bourbon-Parma); m. Regina, Princess of Sachsen-Meiningen 1951; two s. five d.; ed. Univ. of Louvain, Belgium; mem. Pan-European Union 1936–, rep. in Washington 1940–46, Vice-Pres. 1957, Pres. 1973–; mem. for Bavaria (on list of Christian Social Union), European Parl. 1979–84, 1984–; lectures throughout the world on int. affairs and is author of weekly column appearing in 21 daily papers in 5 languages since 1953; mem. Acad. des Sciences Morales et Politiques, Paris, Inst. de France, Real Acad. de Ciencias Morales y Politicas, Madrid, Acad. da Cultura Portuguesa, Acad. Mejicana de Derecho Internacional, Acad. of Morocco, etc.; numerous awards and decorations, including Bayerischer Verdienstorden, Order of Gregory the Great (Vatican), etc.; Robert Schuman Gold Medal 1977, Gold Medal of City of Paris; Konrad Adenauer Prize 1977. *Publications:* 26 books in seven languages on history, politics, world affairs and especially European politics. *Address:* Hindenburgstrasse 15, D-8134 Pöcking-Starnberg, Federal Republic of Germany. *Telephone:* 08157-7015.

HABY, René Jean, D. ÈS L.; French educator and politician; b. 9 Oct 1919, Dombasle; s. of René Haby and Marguerite (née Demangeon); m. Paulette Masson 1945; one s. two d.; ed. Ecole Normale d'Instituteurs de Nancy, Faculté des Lettres de Nancy; History teacher, Lycées of Lons-le-Saumier 1947, Toul 1949, Nancy 1952; Headmaster, Lycées of St. Avold 1954, Avignon 1958, Metz 1960, Montgeron 1962; Dir. of Teaching, Ministry of Nat. Educ. 1962-64; Insp. Gén. de l'Instruction Publique 1963-; Asst. Dir.-Gen. of Teacher Training 1964-65; lecturer, Faculty of Letters and Human Sciences, Nancy 1965, Paris IV 1970; Dir. du Cabinet to Minister of Youth and Sports 1966-68; Rector, Acad. de Clermont-Ferrand 1972-74; Minister of Educ. 1974-78; elected Deputy for Meurthe-et-Moselle, Nat. Ass. 1978-86, UDF Deputy replacing André Rossinot 1986-; Chevalier, Légion d'honneur, Commdr., Ordre nat. du Mérite, Officier des Palmes académiques; Union pour la Démocratie Française. *Publications:* La région des houillères lorraines 1965, Déformations rocheuses au-dessus des excavations souterraines 1970, Combat pour les Jeunes Français 1981; many articles on the economy of N.E. France and on education. *Leisure interest:* tennis. *Address:* Le Nouzet, 4 chemin du Dessus-des-Vignes, 91230 Montgeron, France.

HABYARIMANA, Maj.-Gen. Juvénal; Rwandan army officer and politician; b. 3 Aug. 1937, Gasiza, Gisenyi; s. of Jean-Baptiste Ntibazilikana and Suzanne Nyirazuba; m. Agathe Kanziga 1963; seven c.; ed. Coll. St. Paul, Bukavu, Zaire, Lovanium Univ., Kinshasa and Officers' School, Kigali; joined Nat. Guard as Platoon Leader, became Co. Commdr. and later Asst. Staff Officer to Commdr. of Nat. Guard; Chief of Staff 1963-65; Minister for the Nat. Guard and Chief of Staff of Police 1965-73; promoted to Maj. 1964, Lieut.-Col. 1967, Col. 1970, Maj.-Gen. April 1973; led coup to depose Pres. Grégoire Kayibanda July 1973; Pres. of Rwanda July 1973-, Minister of Nat. Defence 1973-, Prime Minister 1974-; Pres. Comité pour la Paix et l'Unité Nat. 1973-75; Founder and Pres. Mouvement révolutionnaire national pour le développement 1975-; Chair. OCAM Conf. of Heads of State and Govt. 1975; Golden Heart of Kenya 1981 and numerous foreign decorations. *Address:* Présidence de la République, Kigali, Rwanda.

HABYMANA, Bonaventure; Rwandan politician; Minister of Justice 1973-77; Sec.-Gen. of Mouvement Révolutionnaire Nat. pour le Développement. *Address:* c/o Mouvement Révolutionnaire National pour le Développement, B.P. 1055, Kigali, Rwanda.

HACHETTE, Jean-Louis, L. EN D.; French publisher; b. 30 June 1925, Paris; s. of Louis and Blanche (née Darbou) Hachette; m. Y. de Bouillé 1954; one s. two d.; ed. Collège Stanislas, Paris, and Faculté de Droit, Paris; joined Librairie Hachette (founded by great-grandfather in 1826) 1946; entire career spent with Librairie Hachette, Admin. Dir. 1971-; Pres. Librairie Gén. Française 1954-. *Leisure interests:* polo, golf, skiing. *Address:* 79 boulevard Saint-Germain, 75006 Paris (Office); 8 rue de Presbourg, 75116 Paris, France (Home). *Telephone:* 325-22-11 (Office); 704-64-75 (Home).

HACKERMAN, Norman, PH.D.; American university president (retd.); b. 2 March 1912, Baltimore, Md.; s. of Jacob Hackerman. and Anna R. Hackerman; m. Gene A. Coulbourn 1940; one s. three d.; ed. Johns Hopkins Univ.; Asst. Prof. of Chem. Univ. of Texas, Austin 1945, Pres. 1967-70; Pres. Rice Univ. 1970-85, Pres. Emer. and Distinguished Prof. Emer. of Chem. 1985-; Chair. Scientific Advisory Bd. Robert A. Welch Foundation 1982-; mem. N.A.S., American Philosophical Soc., American Acad. of Arts and Sciences and numerous scientific orgs.; recipient of many awards and medals. *Publications:* 211 articles. *Leisure interest:* squash. *Address:* The Robert A. Welch Foundation, 4605 Post Oak Place, Suite 200, Houston, Tex. 77027, U.S.A.

HACKETT, Gen. Sir John Winthrop, G.C.B., C.B.E., D.S.O. AND BAR, M.C., D.L., B.LITT., M.A.; retd. British army officer; b. 5 Nov. 1910, Perth, Australia; s. of Sir John Winthrop Hackett; m. Margaret Frena 1942; three d.; ed. Geelong Grammar School (Australia) and New Coll. Oxford; commissioned 1931; Palestine 1936; Transjordan Frontier Force 1937-40, Syria 1941; Sec. Comm. of Control, Syria and Lebanon; G.S.O. 2, 9th Army; Western Desert 1942; G.S.O. 1, Raiding Forces, GHQ, Middle East Land Forces; Commdr. 4th Parachute Brigade 1943; Italy 1943; Arnhem 1944; Commdr. Transjordan Frontier Force 1947; D.Q.M.G., British Army of the Rhine (B.A.O.R.) 1952; Commdr. 20th Armoured Brigade 1954; G.O.C. 7th Armoured Div. 1956-58; Commdt., Royal Mil. Coll. of Science 1958-61; GOC-in-C, Northern Ireland Command 1961-63; Deputy Chief of Imperial Gen. Staff 1963-64; Deputy Chief of Gen. Staff, Ministry of Defence 1964-66; C.-in-C. B.A.O.R. and Commdr. Northern Army Group 1966-68; Col. Queen's Royal Irish Hussars 1971-78; Hon. Col. 10th Para. Batallion T.A. 1965-73; Hon. Col. Oxford Univ. Officer Training Corps 1970-78; Lees Knowles Lecturer, Cambridge 1961; Kermit Roosevelt Lecturer, U.S.A. 1967; Harmon Memorial Lecturer, U.S.A.F. 1970; Prin. King's Coll., London 1968-75; Visiting Prof. in Classics 1977-; Pres. Classical Asscn. of U.K. 1970-71, English Asscn. of U.K. 1973-74; Fellow, King's Coll., London; Hon. Fellow, St. George's Coll., Univ. of Western Australia, New Coll., Oxford; Hon. LL.D. (Queen's Univ., Belfast, Univ. of Western

Australia, Exeter Univ., Univ. of Buckingham); Chesney Gold Medal, Royal United Services Inst. 1985. *Publications:* many articles and reviews; I was a Stranger 1977, A History of the Third World War (August 1985) (with others) 1978, The Third World War: The Untold Story (with others) 1982, The Profession of Arms 1983. *Leisure interests:* travel, fishing, books, wine and music. *Address:* Coberley Mill, Cheltenham, Glos., GL53 9NH, England. *Telephone:* Coberley 207.

HACKMAN, Gene; American actor; b. 30 Jan. 1931, San Bernardino, Calif.; s. of Eugene Ezra Hackman; m. Fay Maltese 1956; one s. two d.; studied acting at the Pasadena Playhouse. *Films include:* Lilith 1964, Hawaii 1966, Banning 1967, Bonnie and Clyde 1967, The Split 1968, Downhill Racer 1969, I Never Sang For My Father 1969, The Gypsy Moths 1969, Marooned 1970, The Hunting Party 1971, The French Connection 1971, The Poseidon Adventure 1972, The Conversation 1973, Scarecrow 1973, Zandy's Bride 1974, Young Frankenstein 1974, The French Connection II 1975, Lucky Lady 1975, Night Moves 1976, Domino Principle 1977, Superman 1978, Superman II 1980, All Night Long 1980, Target 1985, Twice in a Lifetime 1985, Power 1985, Bat 21, Superman IV 1987, No Way Out 1987, Another Woman 1988, Mississippi Burning 1988, The Package 1989, The Von Metz Incident 1989; Dir. The Science of Lambs; television includes many guest appearances on US series; also My Father, My Mother, CBS Playhouse 1968, and Shadow on the Land 1971; *Stage plays include:* Children From Their Games 1963, Cass Henderson in Any Wednesday 1964, Poor Richard, 1964; Academy Award for Best Actor, New York Film Critics' Award, Golden Globe Award, British Acad. Award, The French Connection, British Acad. Award, The Poseidon Adventure, Cannes Film Festival Award, Scarecrow, Nat. Review Bd. Award, Mississippi Burning 1988, Berlin Film Award 1989. *Address:* 9595 Wiltshire Blvd., Suite 700, Beverly Hills, Calif. 90212, U.S.A.

HACKNEY, Roderick Peter, PH.D., P.R.I.B.A.; British architect and developer; b. 3 March 1942, Liverpool; s. of William Hackney and Rose (Morris) Hackney; m. Christine Thornton 1964; one s.; ed. John Bright's Grammar School, Llandudno, School of Architecture, Manchester Univ.; Job Architect, Expo '67, Montreal, for monorail stations 1967; Housing Architect for Libyan Govt., Tripoli 1967-68; Asst. to Arne Jacobsen, working on Kuwait Cen. Bank, Copenhagen 1968-71; established practice of Rod Hackney Architect, Macclesfield 1972, architectural practices in Birmingham, Leicester, Belfast, Cleator Moor, Workington, Carlisle, Millom, Clitheroe, Manchester, Stirling, Burnley, Chesterfield and Stoke on Trent 1975-88; est. bldg. firm of Castward Ltd.; Council mem. R.I.B.A., including Vice-Pres. for Public Affairs and Vice-Pres. for Overseas Affairs 1978-84, Pres. 1987-; Council mem. Union of Int. Architects 1981-85, Pres. 1987-; Hon. Fellow American Inst. of Architects, Fed. de Colegios de Arquitectos de la Repúb. Mexicana, United Architects of the Philippines; Patron Llandudno Museum and Art Gallery; mem. Editorial Bd., UIA Journal of Architectural Theory and Criticism; Jury mem. Cembureau Award for Low Rise Housing in France 1982, for Prix Int. d'Architecture de l'Institut Nat. du Logement 1983; Chair. Jury for Herouville Town Centre Competition, France 1982-83; Pres. Young Architects Forum, Sofia 1985, Building Communities (Int. Community Architecture Conf.), London 1986; presentation of case for Int. Year of Shelter for the Homeless to all 4 party confs. 1986; Chair. Times/R.I.B.A. Community Enterprise Scheme 1985-87, Trustees of Inner City Trust 1986-; Special Prof. in Architecture, Univ. of Nottingham 1987; mem. Chartered Inst. of Building 1987-; Hon. D. Litt. (Keele) 1989; Dept. of Environment Good Design in Housing Award 1975, 1980; First Prize, for St Ann's Hospice, Manchester 1978; Prix Int. d'Architecture de l'Institut Nat. du Logement 1979-80, RICS/Times Conservation Award 1980, Civic Trust Award of Commendation 1980, 1981, 1984, Sir Robert Matthews Award (Honourable Mention) 1981, Manchester Soc. of Architects Pres.'s Award 1982, Otis Award 1982, Gold Medal, Bulgarian Inst. of Architects 1983, Gold Medal, Young Architect of the Year, Sofia 1983, Grand Medal of Federación de Colegios de Arquitectos de la República Mexicana 1986; TV features: Build Yourself a House 1974, Community Architecture 1977, BBC Omnibus 1987. *Publication:* Highfield Hall, A Community Project 1982. *Leisure interests:* outdoor pursuits, walking, Butterfly Society, fossils, geology, travelling, ballooning, looking at buildings, talking at conferences. *Address:* St. Peter's House, Windmill Street, Macclesfield, Cheshire, SK11 7HS, England.

HADDAD, Sulaiman Ahmed el; Kuwaiti banker and politician; b. 1930; ed. Kuwait Aazamieh Secondary School, and Cairo Univ.; Sec. of Educ. Council of Kuwait; fmr. Financial Asst., Ministry of Educ. and mem. Constituent Assembly for formation of Kuwaiti Constitution; mem. Nat. Ass. 1963; fmr. Chair. and Man. Dir. Arab African Bank; Chair. ARTOC Bank Ltd., Int. Resources and Finance Bank, Arab Investment Co. in Asia and Kuwait; mem. Bd. Arab African Bank, Cairo; Deputy Chair. and Man. Dir. ARTOC (S.A.K.). *Address:* ARTOC, El Sour Street, Arab Gulf Building, P.O. Box 23074, Safat, Kuwait.

HADDIDI, Helmi El-; Egyptian politician; b. Oct. 1925; Prof. of Bone Diseases, Faculty of Medicine, Univ. of Cairo; Asst. Sec.-Gen. Cttee. for Social Affairs, Nat. Democratic Party; fmr. mem. People's Ass.; mem. Shoura Council 1984-; Minister of Health 1985-86. *Address:* c/o Ministry of Health, Sharia Magles El Shaab, Cairo, Egypt.

HADDON-CAVE, Sir (Charles) Philip, K.B.E., C.M.G., M.A.; British overseas administrator; b. 6 July 1925, Hobart, Tasmania; m. Elizabeth Alice Simpson 1948; two s. one d.; ed. Univ. of Tasmania, King's Coll., Cambridge; entered Overseas Admin. Service 1952; successively posted in Kenya, Seychelles and Hong Kong; Financial Sec. Hong Kong 1971-81, Chief Sec. 1981-85; Non-exec. Dir. Kleinwort Benson Group 1986-; Non-exec. Chair. Fleming Overseas Investment Trust PLC 1986-. *Publication:* Air Transport in Australia (with D. M. Hocking) 1951. *Leisure interest:* golf. *Address:* The Old Farmhouse, Nethercote Road, Tackley, Oxon., England.

HADITHI, Murtada al- (see Abdul Baqi, Murtada Said).

HADIWIJAYA, Toyib; D.AGR.SC.; Indonesian agriculturist and politician; b. 12 May 1919, Ciamis, W. Java; ed. Middelbare Landbouwschool Bogor, Faculty of Agriculture, Univ. of Indonesia Bogor, and special studies in U.S.A., Europe and Asia; Asst. plant pathologist, Inst. for Plant Diseases, Dept. of Agriculture, Bogor 1939-48; Student and Instructor of Plant Pathology, Faculty of Agric., Univ. of Indonesia, Bogor 1948-55, Asst. Prof. 1955-56, Prof. 1956-78; Dean of Faculty of Agric. 1957-62; mem. Regional Rep. Council, W. Java 1960-62; Minister of Higher Educ. and Science 1962-64; Amb. to Belgium and Luxembourg 1965-66; Pres. Bogor Agric. Univ. 1966-70; Minister of Plantations 1967-68, of Agric. 1968-78; mem. Supreme Advisory Council and Nat. Assembly 1978-84, mem. Bd. of Trustees Int. Rice Research Inst. Los Baños, Philippines 1970-74; Pres. 19th Session, FAO Conf., Rome 1977; Chair. and mem. of numerous advisory cttees.; chief del. to several int. confs, numerous medals, awards and prizes. *Publications:* over 90 scientific publications and papers on agric. and higher education. *Address:* 9Jl. Perdatan, Jakarta Selantan, Indonesia (Home). *Telephone:* 792400, 794252 Jakarta.

HADLEE, Richard John, M.B.E.; New Zealand cricketer; b. 3 July 1951, Christchurch; s. of W. A. Hadlee (New Zealand cricketer); m. Karen Hadlee; ed. Christchurch Boys High School; left-handed batsman, right-arm medium-fast bowler; played for Canterbury 1972-85, Tasmania 1979-80; debut for Nottinghamshire (England) 1978; test debut for New Zealand 1972; highest test score 103 v West Indies, Christchurch 1979-80; best test bowling performance 9-52 v Australia, Brisbane 1985-86; completed double (scored 1,000 runs and took 100 wickets) in England 1984; toured England 1973, 1978, 1983, 1986, Australia 1972-73, 1973-74, 1980-81, 1985-86, West Indies 1984-85, India and Pakistan 1976-77, Sri Lanka 1983-84; has taken a record number of test wickets (396). *Address:* c/o Nottinghamshire County Cricket Club, Trent Bridge, Nottingham, NGZ 6AG, England.

HAEBLER, Ingrid; Austrian pianist; b. 20 June 1926, Vienna; ed. Vienna, Salzburg and Geneva; won 1st Prize, Int. Competition Munich 1954; specializes in Haydn, Mozart, Schubert and Schumann; mem. Faculty, Salzburg Mozarteum 1969-; Mozart Medal, Vienna 1971. *Address:* c/o Ibbs & Tillett Ltd., 450-452 Edgware Road, London, W2 1EG, England. *Telephone:* 01-258 0525.

HAENDEL, Ida; British (b. Polish) violinist; b. 15 Dec. 1928, Chelm, Poland; ed. Warsaw Conservatoire, pvt. tuition in Paris and London; studied with Carl Flesch and Georges Enesco; first public appearance in G.B., Queen's Hall, London 1938; performances throughout world with many noted conductors including tour with London Philharmonic Orchestra to first Hong Kong Festival of Arts, and China and three tours of U.S.S.R.; participated in centenary anniversary Festival of Bronislav Huberman, Tel-Aviv 1982; celebrated 50th anniversary of debut at Promenade Concerts, London 1987; numerous recordings; Hon. mem. R.A.M. 1982-; Sibelius Medal (Finland) 1982. *Publication:* Woman with Violin (autobiog.) 1970. *Leisure interests:* swimming, horse riding, table tennis, drawing, reading. *Address:* c/o Harold Holt Ltd., 31 Sinclair Road, London, W14 0NS, England. *Telephone:* 01-603 4600.

HAEUSGEN, Helmut; German banker and executive; b. 11 Feb. 1916, Alexandria, Egypt; m. Annelene Krohn; one s. one d.; joined Dresdner Bank AG 1933, elected to Bd. of Man. Dirs. 1964, becoming full mem. 1967, and Chair. 1977; Chair. Supervisory Bd. of Dresdner Bank AG 1978-88; Bd. mem. of various German and int. corpns. and financial insts. *Address;* Lerchersbergring 118, 6000 Frankfurt am Main, Federal Republic of Germany.

HAFERKAMP, Wilhelm; German international official and politician; b. 1 July 1923, Duisburg; m. Ursula Bartz 1951; ed. Univ. of Cologne; Head of Social Policy Dept. of Deutscher Gewerkschaftsbund (German Trade Union Fed.) 1950, mem. Exec. Cttee. and Head of Econ. Dept. 1962-67; Socialist mem. Landtag of North Rhine-Westphalia 1958-66, 1967; Commr. for Energy, Comm. of European Communities 1967-73, Vice-Pres. 1970-, Commr. for Econ. Affairs and Statistical Office 1973-77, Commr. for External Relations (including nuclear affairs) 1977-84. *Address:* 200 rue de la Loi, Brussels, Belgium.

HAFEZ, Maj.-Gen. Amin El; Syrian army officer and politician; b. 1911; fmr. Mil. Attaché in Argentina; took part in the revolution of March 1963; Deputy Prime Minister, Mil. Gov. of Syria and Minister of Interior March-Aug. 1963; Minister of Defence and Army Chief of Staff July-Aug. 1963; Pres. of Revolutionary Council and C.-in-C. of Armed Forces 1963-64; Prime Minister Nov. 1963-May 1964, Oct. 1964-Sept. 1965; Chair. of

Presidency Council 1965-66; sentenced to death *in absentia* Aug. 1971; living in exile.

HAFTMANN, Werner, DR. PHIL.; German art historian and writer; b. 28 April 1912, Glowno; ed. Univs. of Berlin and Göttingen; First Asst. Inst. of History of Art, Florence 1935-40; Dozent in Art History, State High School for Fine Arts, Hamburg 1951-55; Freelance writer 1956-66; Dir. Nat. Gallery, Berlin 1967-74; Lessing Prize, City of Hamburg 1962; Goethe-Plakette (Hesse) 1964; Reuter-Plakette (Berlin) 1974. *Publications:* Das italienische Säulenmonument 1939, Paul Klee: Wege bildnerischen Denkens 1950, 1961, Malerei im XX. Jahrhundert (2 vols.) 1954, Emil Nolde 1958, E. W. Nay 1960, Skizzenbuch: Zur Kultur der Gegenwart 1961, Nolde-Ungemalte Bilder 1963, Wols-Aufzeichnungen 1963, Guttuso, Autobiographische Bilder 1970, Marc Chagall 1972, Jorge Castillo 1975, Marc Chagall, Gouachen, Zeichnungen, Aquarelle 1975, Hans Uhlmann 1975, Klaus Fussmann 1976, Baumeister, Gilgamesch 1976, Der Bildhauer Ludwig Kasper 1978, Der Mensch und seine Bilder 1980, Horst Antes: 25 Votive 1984, Verfemte Kunst 1986. *Address:* Schaftlacherstrasse 21, 8176 Waakirchen, Federal Republic of Germany. *Telephone:* 08021 8562.

HAGEDORN, Jürgen, DR. RER. NAT.; German professor of geography; b. 10 March 1933, Hankensbüttel; s.of Ernst Hagedorn and Dorothea Schulze; m. Ingeborg A. Carl 1965; one d.; ed. Hermann-Billung-Gymnasium, Celle, Tech. Hochschule Hannover and Univ. of Göttingen; Asst. Lecturer Univ. of Göttingen 1962-69, Dozent 1969-70, Prof. 1970-72, Prof. of Geography and Dir. Inst. of Geography 1972-; mem. Göttingen Acad. *Publications:* Geomorphologie des Uelzener Beckens 1964, Geomorphologie griechischer Hochgebirge 1969, Geomorphologische Beiträge (ed.) 1987. *Address:* 3400 Göttingen, Jupiterweg 1, Federal Republic of Germany. *Telephone:* 0551/21323.

HAGEN, Uta Thyra; American actress; b. 12 June 1919, Göttingen, Germany; d. of Oskar F. L. Hagen and Thyra Leisner; m. 1st José V. Ferrer 1938, 2nd Herbert Berghof 1951; one d.; ed. Univ. of Wisconsin High School, Royal Acad. of Dramatic Art, London, and Univ. of Wisconsin; début as Ophelia in Hamlet, Dennis, Mass. 1937; Teacher (and Co-Founder) Herbert Berghof Studio (School of Acting) 1947-; Critics Award 1951, 1963, Tony Award 1951, 1963, Donaldion Award 1951, London Critics Award 1964; Hon. D.F.A. (Smith Coll.) 1978, Hon. Dr. (De Paul Univ., Chicago) 1980, Hon. D.Hum.Litt. (Worcester Coll.) 1982. *Plays acted in include:* The Seagull, Arms and the Man, The Latitude of Love, The Happiest Days, Key Largo, Othello, The Master Builder, Angel Street, A Streetcar Named Desire, The Country Girl, Saint Joan, Tovarich, In Any Language, The Lady's not for Burning, The Deep Blue Sea, Cyprienne, A Month in the Country, The Good Woman of Setzuan, The Affairs of Anatol, The Queen and the Rebels, Who's Afraid of Virginia Woolf?, The Cherry Orchard, Charlotte 1980, Mrs. Warren's Profession (with Roundabout Theatre, New York) 1985, You Can't Tell (Broadway) 1987. *Films:* The Other 1972, The Boys from Brazil 1978. *Publications:* Respect for Acting 1973, Love for Cooking 1976, Sources (memoirs) 1983. *Leisure interests:* gardening, cooking, needlework. *Address:* Herbert Berghof Studio, 120 Bank Street, New York City, N.Y. 10014, U.S.A.

HAGER, Kurt; German politician; b. 24 July 1912, Bietigheim; ed. Ober-realschule, Stuttgart; mem. Kommunistische Partei Deutschlands (KPD) 1930-45, Sozialistische Einheitspartei Deutschlands (SED) 1946-; fmr. journalist; fought in Spanish Civil War 1937-39, Dir. of Radio Madrid; interned in U.K. in Second World War; posts in SED 1945-54; Prof. of Phil., Humboldt Universität zu Berlin 1949; cand. mem. SED Cen. Cttee. 1950-54, mem. 1954-, Sec. for Propaganda of Cen. Cttee 1955-, cand. mem. Politburo 1958-63, mem. 1963-, Sec. and Leader of Ideological Comm., Politburo 1963-; mem. Council of State 1976-; mem. Volkskammer 1958-; Vaterländischer Verdienstorden in Silver and Gold, Karl-Marx Goldmedaille (U.S.S.R.) 1979 and 1980, other decorations. *Address:* Sozialistische Einheitspartei Deutschlands, 102 Berlin Am Mark-Engels-Platz 2, German Democratic Republic.

HÄGG, Gunnar, DR. PHIL.; Swedish university professor; b. 14 Dec. 1903, Stockholm; s. of Erik and Hertha Hägg (née Trägårdh); m. Gunnel Margareta Silfwerbrand 1934; four s. one d.; ed. Univs. of Stockholm, London and Jena; Lecturer, Univ. of Stockholm 1929-36; Prof. of Gen. and Inorganic Chem., Univ. of Uppsala 1936-69; mem. Royal Swedish Acad. of Science 1942, Royal Soc. of Science of Uppsala 1940, Royal Physiographical Soc. of Lund 1943, Royal Neths. Acad. of Science 1950, Royal Danish Soc. of Science 1956, Royal Swedish Acad. of Eng. Sciences 1957, Leopoldina German Acad. of Scientists 1960, Norwegian Acad. of Science 1961; Vice-Pres. Int. Union of Crystallography 1960; mem. Nobel Cttee. for Chemistry, Royal Swedish Acad. of Science 1965, Chair. 1975; Dr. h.c. (Oslo) 1976. *Publications:* Kemisk Reaktionslära 1940, Die Theoretischen Grundlagen der Analytischen Chemie 1950, Teoría de la Reacción Química 1962, Allmän och Oorganisk kemi 1963, General and Inorganic Chemistry 1969; and numerous works mainly dealing with X-ray crystallography and its applications to inorganic chemistry. *Address:* Institute of Chemistry, The University, S-75121 Uppsala; Home: Thunbergsvägen 24, S-75238 Uppsala, Sweden. *Telephone:* 018-183772 (Office); 018-136989 (Home).

HAGGART, Rt. Rev. Alastair Iain MacDonald, M.A.; British ecclesiastic (retd.); b. 10 Oct. 1915, Glasgow; s. of Alexander MacDonald Haggart and Jessie Mackay Haggart; m. 1st Margaret Agnes Trundle 1945 (died 1978),

2nd Mary Elizabeth Scholes 1983; two d.; ed. Durham Univ. and Edin. Theological Coll.; ordained Deacon 1941; Priest 1942; Curate St. Mary's Cathedral, Glasgow 1941-45, Canon 1958-59; Curate St. Mary's, Hendon 1945-48; Precentor St. Ninian's Cathedral, Perth 1948-57; Rector St. Oswald's, Glasgow 1951-59; Synod Clerk 1958-59; Provost St. Paul's Cathedral, Dundee 1959-71; Prin. Edinburgh Theological Coll. 1971-75; Bishop of Edinburgh 1975-86; Primus of Episcopal Church 1977-86; Hon. LL.D. (Dundee) 1970. *Leisure interests:* walking, reading, music, asking questions. *Address:* 19 Eglinton Crescent, Edinburgh, EH12 5BY, Scotland. *Telephone:* 031-337 8948.

HAGIWARA, Susumu, M.D., PH.D.; American professor of physiology; b. 6 Nov. 1922, Hokkaido, Japan; m. Satoko Hagiwara 1953; one s.; ed. Tokyo Univ.; Research Assoc. Dept. of Physiology, Tokyo Univ. Medical School 1946; Asst. Prof. Tokyo Univ. Physiological Inst. 1947-48; Research Fellow, Japanese Pharmacological Inst., Tokyo 1948-50; Assoc. Prof. of Physiology, Tokyo Medical and Dental Univ. 1950-59, Prof. of Physiology 1959-62; Research Zoologist, Univ. of Calif., Los Angeles 1961-64, Prof. of Zoology in Residence 1964-65; Prof. of Physiology and Head of Marine Neurobiology Facility, Scripps Inst., Univ. of Calif. (San Diego) 1965-69; Prof. of Physiology, Univ. of Calif. (L.A.) 1969-, Eleanor I. Leslie Prof. of Neuroscience, Brain Research Inst. 1978-; mem. N.A.S., A.A.A.S., American Acad. of Arts and Science; K. Cole Award, Biophysical Soc. 1976; Ralph Gerard Award, Neuroscience Soc. 1984; Hon. Ph.D. (Univ. of Pierre and Marie Curie, Paris) 1983. *Publication:* Ion Channels in Cell Membrane: Phylogenetic and Developmental Approaches 1983. *Leisure interest:* lepidopteran taxonomy. *Address:* Department of Physiology, School of Medicine, University of California, Los Angeles, Calif. 90024, U.S.A. *Telephone:* 213-825-7621.

HAGLER, Marvelous Marvin; American boxer; b. 23 May 1954, Newark; s. of Robert James Sims Hagler and Ida Mae Lang; m. Bertha Joann Dixon 1980; five c.; undisputed World Middleweight Champion 1980-87; won Championship from Alan Minter and defended it successfully 11 times before losing WBC version to Sugar Ray Leonard (q.v.) April 1987; stripped of other versions of title for agreeing to fight unranked Leonard March 1987; 63 professional fights, 57 wins, 2 draws, 4 defeats. *Address:* Marvelous Marvin Hagler, 1360 Washington Street, Route 53, Hanover, Mass. 02339, U.S.A.

HAGRAS, Dr. Kamal M.; Oman diplomatist; b. 15 Jan. 1927; m. two c.; ed. Cairo, Paris and New York Univs.; joined diplomatic service 1951, served in France, then Colombia, New York, London; also in various depts. of Foreign Office; Chief of Cabinet of Under-Sec.; Amb. to France and Switzerland, Perm. Rep. to UNESCO until 1975; Amb. and Perm. Rep. to UN 1975-77; Rockefeller Foundation Fellowship 1963-65; fmr. Chair. London Diplomatic Asscn.; Oman Wissam First Class; Commdr., Légion d'honneur.

HAGRUP, Knut, D.ECON., D.TECH.; Norwegian airline executive; b. 13 Nov. 1913, Bergen; s. of Henry Lie-Svendsen and Ebba Hagerup; m. Ester Skaugen 1943 (died 1976); two d.; ed. Technische Hochschule, Darmstadt, Commercial Coll., Royal Norwegian Air Force Coll., Hochschule für Verkehrswesen, Dresden, Kungl. Tekniska Høgskolan, Stockholm; Chief Engineer, Norwegian Civil Aeronautics Bd. 1945; Chief Engineer SAS 1946, Vice-Pres. (Operations) 1951, Vice-Pres. (Eng.) 1956, Vice-Pres. (Tech. and Operations) 1960, Exec. Vice-Pres. (Tech. and Operations) 1962, Pres. 1969-79; mem. IATA Exec. Cttee. 1969-78, Pres. IATA 1974-75; Pres. Asscn. European Airlines 1975-76; mem. of Bd. Thai Airways Int. 1969-76, Linjeflyg AB; Chair. SAS Catering A/S, Scanair A/S -1978, Transair Sweden AB 1969-78; Chair. Bd. Comm. on Air Transport (Int. Chamber of Commerce, Paris) 1969-85; mem. Bd. SAAB-SCANIA Flygdivisjon 1979-, Hennes & Mauritz 1979-; Consultant Prof. Pacific Lutheran Univ. (U.S.A.) 1980-; Prof. Northrop Univ. (U.S.A.) 1981-; Consultant to Investor AB, Sweden 1980-, Fortvaltningsbolaget Providentia, Sweden 1980-; Chair. Bd. Saab-Fairchild Airliner programme 1980-; mem. Bd.of Trustees, Northrop Univ. 1981-; Hon. LL.D. (Pacific Univ., U.S.A.), Hon. D.S. (Univ. Northrop, U.S.A.); Commdr., Order of the Northern Star (Sweden) 1976, Order of St. Olav (Norway) 1976, Order of Orange-Nassau (Netherlands) 1979, Légion d'honneur 1979, Order of the White Elephant (Thailand) 1982; British Defence Medal, Norwegian War Medal. *Publications:* La Bataille du Transport Aérien, Die heutige Weltluftfarth, Flygutan Återvändo, Flyet i Fare, How the Aerospace Industry in Western Europe Will Survive. *Leisure interests:* golf, hunting. *Address:* 14 rue Saint Jean, 1260 Nyon, VD, Switzerland. *Telephone:* (022) 61.17.59.

HAGSTRUM, Homer Dupre, B.E.E., M.S., PH.D.; American research physicist (retd.); b. 11 March 1915, St. Paul, Minn.; s. of Andrew Hagstrum and Sadie Hagstrum; m. Bonnie D. Cairns 1948; one s. one d.; ed. Univ. of Minnesota; mem. tech. staff, AT & T Bell Laboratories 1940-85, Head, Surface Physics Research Dept. 1954-78; mem. N.A.S.; Fellow, American Physical Soc., A.A.A.S.; Hon. Sc.D. (Univ. of Minnesota) 1986; recipient of two awards. *Publications:* 110 scientific research articles. *Leisure interests:* astronomy, music. *Address:* 30 Sweetbriar Road, Summit, N.J. 07901, U.S.A.

HAGURA, Nobuya, B.ECON.; Japanese banker; b. 17 Jan. 1919, Kyoto Pref.; m. Toshiko Hagura; one s. one d.; ed. Keio Univ.; joined Nippon Kangyo Bank 1941 (merged with Dai-Ichi Bank to become Dai-Ichi Kangyo Bank 1971), Dir. and Gen. Man., Osaka Branch 1970-71, Man. Dir. and Gen. Man. 1971-73; Man. Dir. of Dai-Ichi Kangyo Bank 1973-75, Sr. Man. Dir. 1975-76, Deputy Pres. 1976-82, Pres. 1982-88, Dir. and Adviser June 1988-. *Leisure interests:* reading, golf. *Address:* Dai-Ichi Kangyo Bank, 1-5, Uchisaiwaicho 1-chome, Chiyoda-ku, Tokyo 100 (Office); 17-10, Shoan 1-chome, Suginami-ku, Tokyo 167, Japan (Home).

HAHN, Carl Horst, DR.RER.POL.; German business executive; b. 1 July 1926, Chemnitz (now Karl-Marx-Stadt, G.D.R.); m. Marisa Traina 1960; three s. one d.; Chair. of Bd., Continental Gummi-Werke AG 1973-81; Chair. Man. Bd., Volkswagenwerk AG 1981-; Chair. Supervisory Bd., Audi NSU Auto Union AG, Neckarsulm, Gerling-Konzern Speziale Kreditversicherungs-AG, Cologne; Deputy Chair. Supervisory Bd., AG für Industrie und Verkehrswesen, Frankfurt am Main, Gerling-Konzern Vertriebs-AG, Cologne; mem. Supervisory Bd., Gerling-Konzern Allgemeine Versicherungs-AG, Cologne, Wilhelm Karmann GmbH, Osnabrück, Deutsche Messe- und Austellungs-AG, Hanover, Deutsche BP AG, Erste Allgemeine Versicherung, Vienna; mem. Man. Bd. Founders' Asscn. of German Science; mem. Foreign Trade Advisory Bd., Fed. Ministry of Trade, Int. Advisory Cttee., Salk Inst., Calif., Consultants' Group, Deutsche Bank AG, Exec. Cttee. VDA, Exec. Cttee. BDI; mem. Bd. Dirs. Deutsche Automobilgesellschaft mbH, Hanover. *Address:* Volkswagenwerk AG, Postfach, 3180 Wolfsburg 1, Federal Republic of Germany.

HAHN, Erwin Louis, PH.D.; American professor of physics; b. 9 June 1921, Sharon, Pa.; s. of Israel Hahn and Mary Weiss; m. 1st Marian Ethel Failing 1944 (deceased), one s. two d.; m. 2nd Natalie Woodford Hodgson 1980; ed. Juniata Coll. and Univ. of Illinois; Asst., Purdue Univ. 1943-44; Research Asst., Univ. of Illinois 1950; Nat. Research Council Fellow, Stanford Univ. 1950-51, Instructor 1951-52; Research Physicist, Watson IBM Lab., New York 1952-55; Assoc. Columbia Univ. 1952-55; Assoc. Prof. Miller Inst. for Basic Research, Berkeley 1958-59, Prof. 1966-67; Univ. of Calif., Berkeley 1955-, Prof. of Physics 1961-; Visiting Fellow, Brasenose Coll., Oxford 1960-61, 1981-82; Eastman (Visiting) Prof., Balliol Coll., Oxford (1988-89); mem. Nat. Acad. of Sciences, American Acad. of Arts and Sciences; Assoc. mem. Slovenian Acad. of Sciences 1981-; Miller Prof. Univ. of Calif. 1985-86; Guggenheim Fellow, 1961, 1970; Buckley Prize 1971, Int. Soc. of Magnetic Resonance Prize 1971; Hon. D.Sc. (Juniata Coll.) 1966, (Purdue Univ., Indiana) 1975; Alexander Humboldt Foundation Award (Fed. Repub. of Germany) 1976-77; Hon. mem. Brasenose Coll., Oxford 1984; co-winner Wolf Foundation Prize 1983/84. *Publication:* Nuclear Quadrupole Resonance Spectroscopy (with T.P. Das) 1958. *Leisure interests:* violin, chamber music. *Address:* Department of Physics, University of California, Berkeley, Calif. 94720, U.S.A. *Telephone:* 415-642-2305.

HAHN, Frank, PH.D., F.B.A.; British university professor; b. 26 April 1925, Berlin, Germany; s. of Arnold and Maria Hahn; m. Dorothy Salter 1946; ed. Bournemouth Grammar School, London School of Econs.; Asst. Lecturer, then Reader in Mathematical Econs., Univ. of Birmingham 1948-60; Lecturer in Econs., Univ. of Cambridge 1960-67; Prof. of Econs., L.S.E. 1967-72; Prof. of Econs., Univ. of Cambridge 1972-; Frank W. Taussig Resident Prof., Harvard Univ. 1975-76; Visiting Prof., M.I.T. 1956-57, Univ. of Calif., Berkeley 1959-60; Fellow of Churchill Coll., Cambridge 1960-; Fellow of British Acad., American Acad. of Arts and Sciences; Pres. Econometric Soc. 1968-69; Man.-Ed. Review of Economic Studies 1965-68; Pres. Royal Econ. Soc. 1986-; Hon. mem. American Econ. Asscn. 1986; Foreign Assoc. N.A.S. 1988; Hon. D.Soc.Sc. (Univ. of Birmingham) 1981; Hon. D.Litt. (Univ. of East Anglia) 1984; Dr. h.c. (Univ. Louis Pasteur, Strasbourg) 1984; Hon. D.Sc. (Econ.) (London) 1985. *Publications:* General Competitive Analysis (with K. J. Arrow, q.v.) 1971, The Share of Wages in National Income 1972, Money and Inflation 1981, Equilibrium and Macroeconomics 1984, Money, Growth and Stability 1985; also more than 80 articles in learned journals. *Leisure interests:* reading, gardening. *Address:* 16 Adams Road, Cambridge, England. *Telephone:* (0223) 352560.

HAHN, Heinz W., D.ENG.; German engineering executive; b. 13 Feb. 1929, Rüsselsheim; m. Lisel Hummel 1955; one d.; ed. Tech. Univ. Darmstadt, Tech. Univ. Karlsruhe; diesel engine engineer Motoren-Werke, Mannheim 1958-61; Chief Eng. Hanomag-Henschel, Hanover 1961-69; Dir. and mem. Bd. Klöckner-Humboldt-Deutz AG, Cologne 1970-74; Pres. and C.E.O. Magirus-Deutsch AG, Ulm 1975-81; Exec. Vice-Pres. and Deputy Chair. IVECO 1981-. *Address:* Schillerstrasse 2, 7900 Ulm (Office); Ginsterweg 31, 7910 Neu-Ulm/Pfuhl, Federal Republic of Germany (Home).

HAHN, Thomas Marshall Jr., PH.D., LL.D.; American corporation executive; b. 2 Dec. 1926, Lexington, Ky.; s. of the late Thomas Marshall and of Mary Elizabeth Boston Hahn; m. Margaret Louise Lee 1948; two d.; ed. Univ. of Kentucky, M.I.T.; Teaching Asst. Univ. of Kentucky 1944-45; U.S.N.R. 1945-46; Physicist, U.S. Naval Ordinance Lab. 1946-47; Research Asst., M.I.T. 1947-50; Assoc. Prof., Univ. of Kentucky 1950-52, Prof. and Head of Dept. of Physics, Va. Polytechnic Inst. and State Univ. 1954-59; Dean of Arts and Sciences, Kansas State Univ. 1959-62; Pres. Va. Polytechnic Inst. and State Univ. 1962-75; Exec. Vice-Pres. Georgia Pacific Corpn. 1975-76, Pres. 1976-82, Pres. and C.E.O. 1983-84, Chair. of the Bd., Pres. and C.E.O. 1984-85, Chair. of Bd. and C.E.O. 1985-; mem. Pres.'s Export Council; mem. Bd. of Dirs. Norfolk Southern Corpn., Coca-Cola Enterprises, API, Sun Trust Banks, Trust Co. of Ga.; Chair. N.Y. Stock

Exchange Listed Co. Advisory Comm., American Paper Inst. 1982–83; Chair. Va. Metropolitan Study Comm. 1966–68; mem. Nat. Science Bd. 972–78; Fellow, American Physical Soc; Hon. LL.D. (Seton Hall Univ.) 976. *Publications:* various scientific research publications. *Leisure interests:* cattle breeding, fishing. *Address:* 133 Peachtree Street, N.E., Atlanta, Ga. 30303, U.S.A.

HAÏDALLA, Lieut.-Col. Mohamed Khouna Ould; Mauritanian army officer and politician; Chief of Staff of Mauritanian Army July 1978–April 979; Minister of Defence April–May 1979, 1980, Prime Minister 1979–80, Pres. of Mauritania 1980–84 (overthrown in coup); Chair. Mil. Cttee. for Nat. Recovery (now Cttee. for Nat. Salvation) 1978–84; arrested Dec. 1984.

HAIG, Gen. Alexander Meigs, Jr.; American army officer and politician; b. 2 Dec. 1924, Philadelphia, Pa.; s. of Alexander M. and Regina Murphy Haig; m. Patricia Fox 1950; two s. one d.; ed. U.S. Mil. Acad., Naval War Coll. and Georgetown Univ.; joined U.S. Army 1947, rising to Brig.-Gen. 1969, Maj.-Gen. 1972, Gen. 1973; Deputy Special Asst. to Sec. and Deputy Sec. of Defence 1964–65; Battalion and Brigade Commdr. 1st Infantry Div., Repub. of Viet-Nam 1966–67; Regimental Commdr. and Deputy Commdt. U.S. Mil. Acad. 1967–69; Sr. Mil. Advisor to Asst. to Pres. for Nat. Security Affairs, the White House 1969–70; Deputy Asst. to Pres. for Nat. Security Affairs 1970–73; Vice-Chief of Staff, U.S. Army Jan.-July 1973; special emissary to Viet-Nam Jan. 1973; retd. from U.S. Army Aug. 1973; Asst. to Pres. and White House Chief of Staff Aug. 1973–Oct. 1974; recalled to active duty, U.S. Army Oct. 1974; C.-in-C., U.S. European Command 1974–79; Supreme Allied Commdr. Europe, NATO 1974–79; Pres., C.O.O. and Dir. United Technologies Corpn. 1980–81; Sec. of State 1981–82; Chair. Atlantic and Pacific Advisory Councils of United Technologies 1982–; Dir. Leisure Tech. Inc. 1983–, Allegheny Int. Inc. 1983–, Commodore Int. Ltd. 1984–; mem. Presidential Comm. on Strategic Forces 1983–84; Sr. Fellow, Hudson Inst. for Policy Research 1982–84; Pres. Worldwide Associates Inc. 1984–; Hon. LL.D. (Utah and Niagara); Gold Medal Nat. Inst. of Social Sciences 1980; numerous medals and awards. *Leisure interests:* golf, tennis, squash, horse-riding. *Address:* Suite 800, 1155 15th Street, N.W., Washington, D.C. 20005, U.S.A.

HAIKEL, Ahmed Abd al Maksoud, PH.D.; Egyptian politician; b. April 1922; ed. Faculty of Dar El-Uloom; Dean, Faculty of Dar El-Uloom for six years; Head, Educ. Cttee. of People's Ass.; mem. Supreme Council of Culture; Deputy Rector for Postgraduate Studies, Univ. of Cairo; Cultural Counsellor, Spain 1973; Minister of Culture 1985–87; State Award for Prominence in the Arts 1985. *Address:* c/o Ministry of Culture, 110 Sharia Galaa, Cairo, Egypt. *Telephone:* 971995.

HAILEY, Arthur; Canadian author; b. 5 April 1920, Luton, Beds., England; s. of George and Elsie Hailey (née Wright); m. Sheila Dunlop 1951; one s. two d. and three s. by previous marriage. *Publications:* Runway Zero Eight (with John Castle) 1958, The Final Diagnosis 1959, In High Places 1962, Hotel 1965, Airport 1968, Wheels 1971, The Moneychangers 1975, Overload 1979, Strong Medicine 1984, The Evening News 1989; novels published in 35 languages; collected plays: Close-Up 1960. *Films:* Zero Hour, Time Lock, The Young Doctors, Hotel, Airport, The Moneychangers, Wheels 1982, Overload 1983, Strong Medicine. *Leisure interests:* reading, music, fishing, swimming, wine. *Address:* Seaway Authors Ltd., First Canadian Place-6000, P.O. 130, Toronto, Ont. M5X 1A4, Canada (Office); Lyford Cay, P.O. Box N-7776, Nassau, Bahamas (Home).

HAILSHAM OF ST. MARYLEBONE, Baron (Life Peer), cr. 1970, of Herstmonceux in the County of Sussex; **Quintin McGarel Hogg,** K.G., P.C., C.H., F.R.S., D.C.L., LL.D.; British politician; b. 9 Oct. 1907, London; s. of the late Douglas McGarel Hogg, 1st Viscount Hailsham, and Elizabeth Brown; m. Mary Evelyn Martin 1944 (died 1978); two s. three d.; m. Deirdre Shannon 1986; ed. Eton Coll. and Christ Church, Oxford; Fellow, All Souls Coll., Oxford 1931–38, 1961–; Barrister, Lincoln's Inn 1932, Bencher 1956, Treas. 1975; Q.C. 1953; M.P. 1938–50, 1963–70; mem. House of Lords 1950–63, 1970–; served war 1939–45; Parl. Under-Sec. to Air Ministry 1945; First Lord of Admiralty 1956–57; Minister of Educ. 1957; Lord Pres. of Council 1957–59, 1960–64; Chair. Conservative Party 1957–59; Lord Privy Seal 1959–60; Minister for Science and Tech. 1959–64; Leader of House of Lords 1960–63; Sec. of State for Educ. and Science April–Oct. 1964; Lord Chancellor 1970–74, 1979–87; Minister responsible for dealing with unemployment in the North East 1963–64; succeeded his father as 2nd Viscount Hailsham 1950, disclaimed title 1963; Rector, Glasgow Univ. 1959–62; Chancellor, Univ. of Buckingham 1983–; Hon. LL.D. (Leeds) 1982. *Publications:* The Law of Arbitration 1935, One Year's Work 1944, The Law and Employer's Liability 1944, The Times We Live In 1944, Making Peace 1945, The Left was never right 1945, The Purpose of Parliament 1946, The Case for Conservatism 1947, The Law Relating to Monopolies, Restrictive Trade Practices and Resale Price Maintenance 1956, The Conservative Case 1959, Interdependence 1961, Science and Politics 1963, The Devil's Own Song 1968, The Door Wherein I Went 1975, Elective Dictatorship 1976, The Dilemma of Democracy: Diagnosis and Prescription 1978, Law, Ethics and Authority 1979, Hamlyn Revisited—The British Legal System 1983. *Address:* The House of Lords, London, SW1A 0PW; The Corner House, Heathview Gardens, London, SW15 3SZ, England (Home). *Telephone:* 01-788 2256.

HAINWORTH, Henry Charles, C.M.G.; British diplomatist (retd.); b. 12 Sept. 1914, Tampico, Mexico; s. of Charles Samuel Hainworth and Emily Laycock; m. Mary Ady 1944; two d.; ed. Blundells School and Cambridge Univ.; British Consular Service, Tokyo 1939; Ministry of Information, New Delhi 1942–46; service in Tokyo, London, Bucharest, Paris, Nicosia 1946–57; Head of Atomic Energy and Disarmament Dept., Foreign Office 1958–61; Del. Sec. for Negotiating with EEC, Brussels 1961–63; Minister Counsellor and H.M. Consul-Gen., British Embassy, Vienna 1963–68; Amb. to Indonesia 1968–70; Amb. and Perm. U.K. Del. to Disarmament Conf., Geneva 1971–74. *Publication:* A Collector's Dictionary 1980. *Address:* 23 Rivermead Court, Ranelagh Gardens, London, SW6 3RU, England.

HAITHEM, Muhammad Ali; Yemeni politician; b. 1940, Dathina, Southern Arabia; fmr. school teacher; Minister of Interior 1967; mem. Presidential Council of S. Yemen 1969–71; Chair. Council of Ministers 1969–70; mem. Nat. Front Gen. Command. Now living in Cairo, Egypt.

HAITINK, Bernard; Netherlands conductor; b. 4 March 1929, Amsterdam; Conductor Netherlands Radio Philharmonic Orchestra 1955–61; appeared regularly as Guest Conductor for Concertgebouw Orchestra, Amsterdam 1956–61, Joint Conductor 1961–64, Perm. Conductor and Musical Dir. 1964–88; Prin. Conductor London Philharmonic Orchestra 1967–79, Artistic Dir. 1970–78, tours with Concertgebouw in Europe, N. and S. America, Japan, with London Philharmonic in Europe, Japan, U.S.A.; Guest Conductor Los Angeles Philharmonic, Boston Symphony, Cleveland, Chicago Symphony, New York Philharmonic, Berlin Philharmonic, Vienna Philharmonic and other orchestras; Musical Dir. Glyndebourne Festival Opera 1978–88; Musical Dir. Royal Opera House, Covent Garden 1987–; records for Philips and EMI; Royal Order of Orange-Nassau (Netherlands) 1969, Medal of Honour, Bruckner Soc. of America 1970; Hon. D. Mus. (Oxford) 1988, (Leeds) 1988; Hon. mem. Int. Gustav Mahler Soc., Gold Medal 1971, Chevalier, Ordre des Arts et des Lettres (France) 1972, Hon. mem. R.A.M. 1973, Hon. K.B.E. 1977, Officer, Order of the Crown (Belgium) 1977. *Address:* c/o Harold Holt Ltd., 31 Sinclair Road, London, W14 0NS, England.

HÁJEK, Jiří, J.U.DR., DR.SC.; Czechoslovak diplomatist and politician; b. 6 June 1913, Krhanice; ed. Charles Univ., Prague; Imprisoned 1939–45; Lecturer, Coll. of Political and Social Science, Prague 1947–48, Prof. 1948–52; Prof. of Int. Relations, Charles Univ. 1952–55; Deputy to Nat. Assembly 1945–54, Chair. Foreign Relations Cttee. 1952–54; Amb. to U.K. 1955–58; Deputy Minister of Foreign Affairs 1958–62, Perm. Rep. to UN 1962–65; Minister of Educ. and Culture 1965–67, Minister of Educ. 1967–68, Minister of Foreign Affairs April–Sept. 1968; mem. Cen. Cttee. CP of Czechoslovakia 1966–68; Corresp. mem. Czechoslovak Acad. of Sciences 1965–76; Dir. Inst. of Political Science, Czechoslovak Acad. of Sciences 1969; scientific worker, Inst. of State and Law, Czechoslovak Acad. of Sciences 1970–73; spokesman Charter 77 (civil rights manifesto); arrested May 1981; Order of the Repub. 1961; Klement Gottwald Order 1968. *Publication:* Dix ans après 1978.

HAJNAL, John, M.A., F.B.A.; British university teacher of statistics; b. 26 Nov. 1924, Darmstadt, Germany; s. of Kalman and Eva Hajnal-Konyi; m. Nina Lande 1950; one s. three d.; ed. Univ. Coll. School, Hampstead, London, England and Balliol Coll. Oxford; Research Asst., Royal Comm. on Population, London 1944–48; Statistician, UN, New York 1948–51; Research Worker, Princeton Univ., N.J., U.S.A. 1951–53; Simon Research Fellow, Univ. of Manchester, England 1953–54, lecturer in Medical Statistics 1954–57; successively Lecturer and Reader in Demography, Reader in and Prof. of Statistics, L.S.E., London Univ. 1957–86. *Publications:* The Student Trap 1972; articles in learned journals on demography, statistics, math., etc. *Address:* 95 Hodford Road, Golders Green, London, NW11 8EH, England.

HÅKANSSON, Lars-Ove, M.ENG.; Swedish business executive; b. 30 April 1937, Lund; s. of Nils Håkansson and Anna-Lisa Håkansson; m. Brita Jönsson 1961; two s.; ed. Chalmers Univ. of Tech. and Harvard Univ.; Design Eng., Skanska, Malmö 1961–65, Head of Bldg. Block Dept. 1965–68, Chief. Eng. Tech. Dept. Stockholm 1968–72, Chief Eng. of Bldg. Dept. Malmö 1972–77, Vice-Pres., Stockholm 1977–80, Exec. Vice-Pres. 1980–86, Pres. and C.E.O. 1986–; Sr. Master, Tech. High School, Malmö 1963–66; mem. Bd. Skanska AB, Investment AB Cardo, Graningeverkens AB, Industri AB Euroc, JM Byggnads & Fastighets AB, Svenska Handelsbanken, Stockholms Läns Stadshypoteks-förening, Svenska Arbetsgivare föreningen and others. *Leisure interests:* golf, tennis, bridge. *Address:* Skanska AB, S-182 25, Danderyd, Stockholm (Office); Strandvägen 23, S-182 62, Djursholm, Sweden (Home). *Telephone:* 08-753 80 00 (Office); 08-755 07 76 (Home).

HAKIM, George, M.A., L. EN D.; Lebanese diplomatist and politician; b. 19 April 1913, Tripoli; s. of John Hakim and Victoria Antakli; m. Laura Zarbock 1951; one s. one d.; ed. American Univ., Beirut, and Univ. of St. Joseph; Adjunct Prof. of Econs., American Univ., Beirut 1943; mem. of several advisory govt. cttees, on econ. and financial questions 1942–46; apptd. alt. del. of Lebanon to Econ. and Social Council of UN 1946; Chief Del. 1949; Counsellor Lebanese Legation, Washington, D.C. 1946–52; Chargé d'affaires 1948 and 1951; Minister of Finance, of Nat. Economy and of Agriculture 1952–53; Minister of Foreign Affairs and of Economy

1953; Deputy Sec.-Gen. Ministry of Foreign Affairs March–July 1955; Minister to Fed. Repub. of Germany 1955–58; concurrently Minister of Nat. Economy March-June 1956; rep. Lebanon at numerous int. confs.; Bd. of Govs. of the Int. Bank for Reconstruction and Devt. and IMF 1947–50; Vice-Chair. Econ. and Financial Cttee. 1949; Chair. Group of Experts on econ. devt. of underdeveloped countries, apptd. by Sec.-Gen. of UN Feb.-May 1951; Amb. to German Fed. Repub. 1958; Perm. Rep. to UN 1959–65; Minister of Foreign Affairs 1965–67; Vice-Pres. American Univ. of Beirut. 1968–76. *Leisure interests:* reading, travelling, swimming.

HAKSAR, Ajit Narain, B.A., M.B.A.; Indian business executive; b. 11 Jan. 1925, Gwalior, Madhya Pradesh; s. of Iqbal Narain Haksar and Shyampati Mulla; m. Madhuri Sapru 1948; one s. one d.; ed. Allahabad and Harvard Univs.; training period with J. Walter Thompson Co., New York 1945–46; joined India Tobacco Co. Ltd. (frmly. The Imperial Tobacco Co. of India Ltd.) as Asst. Marketing 1948; on secondment to British-American Tobacco Co. Ltd., London 1948–50; Marketing Dir. Bd. of India Tobacco 1966, Deputy Chair. 1968, Chair. 1969–83, Chair. Emer. 1983–; Chair. Local Bd., Indian Leaf Tobacco Devt. Co. Ltd.; Chair. Bd. of Govs. Indian Inst. of Tech.; Gov. Indian Inst. of Man.; Non.-Exec. Chair. Webstar Ltd.; Dir. Reserve Bank of India 1977–85, Chair. Local Bd. (Eastern Area) 1977–; mem. Industrial Advisory Cttee., Industrial and Commercial Dept., Govt. of Jammu and Kashmir Dec. 1977–, Gen. Assembly Indian Council for Cultural Relations July 1978–; Past Pres. Bengal Chamber of Commerce and Industry; mem. Bd. of Govs. Indian Inst. of Man. 1971–. *Publications:* Politic Economic Management of India, by India, for India 1988, numerous articles on man. and tourism. *Leisure interest:* golf. *Address:* Virginia House, 37 Chowringhee, Calcutta 700071 (Office); Sai Kuti, 33 Ishwar Nagar, Mathura Road, New Delhi 110065, India (Home). *Telephone:* 24-8141 (Office); 631554, 632266 (Home).

HAKSAR, Parmeshwar Narain, M.SC.; Indian government official and former diplomatist; b. 4 Sept. 1913, Gujranwala, Punjab; s. of the late Jagdish Narain Haksar and of Dhanraj Haksar; m. Urmila Sapru; two d.; ed. Univ. of Allahabad, Univ. Coll., London, London School of Econs., Lincoln's Inn; Joint Sec. in charge of Admin., Ministry of External Affairs 1959–60; served as Amb. and High Commr. in various countries 1960–67; Prin. Sec. to Prime Minister 1967–73; Chief Negotiator, India-Pakistan-Bangladesh 1972–73; Deputy Chair. Planning Comm. with Cabinet rank 1975–77; Pres. CRESSIDA 1978–; Chair. Giri Inst. 1976–, Devt. Centre, Chandigarh 1978–; Chair. Nat. Council of Science and Tech., Indian Statist-ical Inst., Nat. Labour Inst., Nat. Science Foundation, Nat. Inst. of Public Finance and Policy; Co-Chair. Indo-Soviet Comm.; Dir. Press Trust of India; Vice-Pres. Krishna Menon Memorial Soc.; del. to Diplomatic Conf. for Revision of Red Cross Conventions 1949; del. and alt. del. to UN Gen. Assembly 1951, 1966, 1968, 1970; mem. UN Int. Civil Service Comm. 1975–80; mem. Atomic Energy Comm. of India, Space Comm. UGC Stand-ing Advisory Cttee. on Area Studies Programme, Nehru Foundation; Hon. LL.D. (Patiala and Kashmir Univs.). *Publications:* Premonitions 1979, Reflections of our Times 1982. *Leisure interests:* photography, cooking. *Address:* 4/9 Shanti Niketan, New Delhi 110021, India. *Telephone:* 671149.

HALABI, Mohammed Ali el–; Syrian politician; b. 1937, Damascus; ed. Teachers Training School and Damascus Univ.; Teacher 1954–62; mem. Regional Command of Baath Party, Damascus; Mayor of Damascus; mem. Arab Fed. Assembly; mem. People's Council, Speaker 1973–78; Prime Minister 1978–80; Pres. Arab Parl. Union 1974–76. *Address:* c/o Office of the Prime Minister, Damascus, Syria.

HALAWI, Ibrahim; Lebanese politician; b. 1938, Nabatiya; ed. Beirut Arab Univ.; mem. Supreme Shi'ite Islamic Council; Minister of Economy and Tourism 1982–84. *Address:* c/o Conseil des Ministres, Place de l'Etoile, Beirut, Lebanon.

HALBRITTER, Walter; German economist and politician; b. 17 Nov. 1927, Hoym; m.; three c.; Joined Sozialistische Einheitspartei Deutschlands (SED) 1946; Section leader Dept. Planning and Finance of Cen. Cttee. 1954–61; G.D.R. Deputy Minister of Finance 1961–63; Deputy Chair. of State Planning Comm. 1963–65, Chair. Cttee. on Labour and Wages 1963–65; Head Bureau of Prices, rank of Minister 1965–; mem. Cen. Cttee. 1967–; cand. mem. Politburo 1967–73; mem. Presidium of Council of Ministers 1967–80, Deputy Chair. 1980–; Order "Banner der Arbeit", Vaterländischer Verdienstorden in Gold 1977. *Address:* 102 Berlin, Am Marx-Engels-Platz 2, German Democratic Republic.

HALDEMAN, Harry R., B.S.; American business executive; b. 27 Oct. 1926, Los Angeles; s. of Harry F. Haldeman and Katherine Robbins; m. Jo Horton 1949; two s. two d.; ed. Redlands and Los Angeles Univs.; Accounts Exec., J. Walter Thompson Co., Los Angeles and New York 1949–59, Vice-Pres., Man. Los Angeles Office 1960–68; Chief of Staff, Nixon Pres. Campaign 1968; Chief White House Staff 1969–73; Sr. Vice-Pres. Murdock Devt. Co. 1979–85, Pres. Murdock Hotels Corpn. 1984–86; Dir. Haldeman Inc., Family Steak Houses of Miami Inc., Wedgwood Investment Corpn., Los Angeles; Chair. of Bd. Calif. Inst. of Arts 1968; mem. Comm. of White House Fellows 1969–73. *Publication:* The Ends of Power 1978.

HALE, John Hampton, M.A.; Canadian business executive; b. 8 July 1924, London, England; s. of John and Elsie (Coles) Hale; m. 1st Linda Hodgson

1950 (divorced 1979), 2nd Nancy R. Birks 1980; one s. two d.; ed. Eton Coll., Magdalene Coll., Cambridge and Harvard Grad. School of Business Admin.; Alcan Aluminium Ltd., Montreal 1949–60, New York 1960–63 London (Man. Dir. Alcan Booth Industries Ltd.) 1964–70, Exec. Vice-Pres (Finance), Montreal 1970–83; Chair. Aluminium Co. of Canada Ltd. 1979–83 Dir. Alcan Aluminium Ltd. 1970–85, Scovill Inc. (U.S.) 1978–85, Ritz Carlton Hotel, Montreal 1981–83, Bank of Montreal 1985–; Chair. Fairey Holdings Ltd. 1983–86; Man. Dir. Pearson PLC 1983–86; Dir. The Econom ist Newspaper 1984–, SSMC Inc. (U.S.) 1986–; Lay mem. Council of the Int. Stock Exchange, London 1987–. *Leisure interests:* shooting, sailing skiing, gardening, old Canadian books. *Address:* 17th Floor, Millbank Tower, London, SW1P 4QZ (Office); 71 Eaton Terrace, London, SW1W 8TN, England (Home). *Telephone:* 01-828 9020 (Office); 01-730 2929 (Home)

HALE, Sir John Rigby, Kt., M.A., D.LITT., F.B.A., F.S.A., F.R.HIST.S.; British historian; b. 17 Sept. 1923, Ashford, Kent; s. of Dr. E. R. S. Hale and Hilda Birks; m. 1st Rosalind Williams 1953, one s. two d.; m. 2nd Sheila Haynes 1965, one s.; ed. Jesus Coll., Oxford, Johns Hopkins and Harvard Univs.; Fellow and Tutor in Modern History, Jesus Coll., Oxford 1949–64 Visiting Prof. Cornell Univ. 1959; Prof. of History, Univ. of Warwick 1964–69; Prof. of Italian, Univ. Coll., London 1970–88; Visiting Prof. Univ of Calif., Berkeley; Chair. British Soc. for Renaissance Studies 1973–78 Chair. Trustees of the Nat. Gallery, London 1975–81 (Trustee 1973–80) mem. Royal Mint Advisory Cttee. 1979–; Public Orator, Univ. of London 1980–83; Trustee, Victoria and Albert Museum 1983–86, British Museum 1985–; Commr. Museums and Galleries Comm. 1983–; Pres. British Assen of Friends of Museums; mem. Princeton Inst. for Advanced Study 1983–84 Chair. Advisory Cttee. Govt. Art Collection 1984–; Hon. Fellow, Regent's Coll. 1988; Socio Straniero, Accad. Arcadia (Rome) 1972, Academicus ex classe (bronze award), Acad. Medicea (Florence) 1980, Commendatore Ordine al Merito della Repubblica Italiana 1981, Bolla Prize (Services to Venice) 1982, Serena Medal for Italian Studies 1987, Socio Straniero Ateneo Veneto 1987. *Publications:* England and the Italian Renaissance 1954, The Italian Journal of Samuel Rogers 1956, Machiavelli and Renaiss ance Italy 1961, The Literary Works of Machiavelli 1961, The Evolution of British Historiography 1964, Ed. Certain Discourses Military by Sir John Smyth 1964, Renaissance Europe 1480-1520 1971, Ed. Renaissance Venice 1973, Italian Renaissance Painting 1977, Florence and the Medici the Pattern of Control 1977, Renaissance Fortification: Art or Engineering? 1977, The Italian Journal of Antonio de Beatis 1979, Renaissance War Studies 1983, Venice: The Military Organization of a Renaissance State (with M. E. Mallet) 1983, War and Society in Renaissance Europe 1984 *Leisure interest:* Venice. *Address:* 26 Montpelier Row, Twickenham Middlesex, England. *Telephone:* 01-892 9636.

HALEFOĞLU, Vahit M., K.C.V.O., M.A.; Turkish diplomatist; b. 19 Nov. 1919, Antakya; s. of Mesrur and Samiye Halefoğlu; m. Zehra Bereket 1951; one s. one d.; ed. Antakya Coll. and Univ. of Ankara; Turkish Foreign Service 1943–, served Vienna, Moscow, Ministry of Foreign Affairs, London 1946–59; Dir.-Gen., First Political Dept., Ministry of Foreign Affairs 1959– 62; Amb. to Lebanon 1962–65, concurrently accred. to Kuwait 1964–65 Amb. to U.S.S.R. 1965–66, to Netherlands 1966–70; Deputy Sec.-Gen. of Political Affairs, Ministry of Foreign Affairs 1970–72; Amb. to Fed. Repub. of Germany 1972–82, to U.S.S.R. 1982–83; Minister of Foreign Affairs 1983–87; re-elected M.P. 1986; Lebanese, Greek, Italian, German, Spanish, Finnish and British decorations. *Leisure interests:* literature, music, walk ing, swimming. *Address:* c/o Dışişleri Bakanlığı, Müdafaa Cad. Bakanlıkar Ankara, Turkey.

HALEY, John C., B.A., M.S.; American banker; b. 24 July 1929, Akron Ohio; s. of Arthur Reed Haley and Kathryn Moore; m. Rheba Hopkins 1951; two s. two d.; ed. Miami and Columbia Univs.; Asst. Treas., Chase Manhattan Bank N.A. 1959, Second Vice-Pres. 1962, Vice-Pres. 1964, Sr Vice-Pres. 1971; Chief Exec. Orion Banking Group 1970–73; Sr. Vice-Pres. Chase Manhattan Overseas Corpn. 1970–73; Exec. Vice-Pres. Corporate and Institutional Relations, Chase Manhattan Bank N.A. 1973–84, mem. Policy Advisory Cttee.; Deputy Chair. Kissinger Associates 1984–85; Chair. and C.E.O. Business Int. Corpn. 1986–87; Dir. Armco Steel Corpn. 1975– Chair. Nat. Corpn. Fund for Dance Inc.; Trustee, Siemens Foundation, Pace Univ. *Address:* Business International Corporation, 1 Dag Ham marskjold Plaza, New York, N.Y. 10017 (Office); 146 Lambert Road, New Canaan, Conn. 06840, U.S.A. (Home). *Telephone:* (212) 750-6300 (Office) 203 966-5904 (Home).

HALL, Alfred Rupert, M.A., PH.D., LITT.D., F.B.A.; British science historian b. 26 July 1920, Stoke-on-Trent; s. of Alfred Dawson Hall and Margaret Catherine Ritchie; m. 1st Annie Shore Hughes, 2nd Marie Boas; two d.; ed. Alderman Newton's School, Leicester, Christ's Coll., Cambridge; served Royal Corps of Signals 1940–45; Fellow, Christ's Coll., Cambridge 1949–59, Univ. Lecturer, Cambridge 1950–59; posts at Univs. of Calif. and Indiana 1959–63; Prof. History of Science and Tech., Imperial Coll., London 1963–80; Consultant, Wellcome Trust 1980–85; Pres. Int. Acad. of the History of Science 1977–81; Emer. Prof. of History of Science and Tech. Univ. of London 1980–; Allen Scholar, Cambridge 1948, Sarton Medal, Royal Soc. Wilkins Lecturer 1973, Leeuwenhoek Lecturer 1988. *Publi-cations:* various books and articles on History of Science and Tech. includ ing Philosophers at War 1980, The Revolution in Science 1500-1750 1983, hysic and Philanthropy: a history of the Wellcome Trust 1986. *Leisure interests:* walking, gardening. *Address:* 14 Ball Lane, Tackley, Oxford,)X5 3AG, England. *Telephone:* (086) 983 257.

IALL, Anthony Vincent, PH.D., F.L.S., F.R.S.S.A.; British professor of botany, ystematist and conservationist; b. 22 April 1936, Bedford; s. of Alfred 'mith Hall and Lucy Vincentia Wynniatt; m. Grizelda Purdie (née Gray); hree s.; ed. Univ. of Cape Town; Research Asst. (Limnology), Rhodes Jniv. 1956; Lecturer in Botany, Asst. Curator Bolus Herbarium, Univ. of 'ape Town 1963-85, Sr. lecturer 1970-82, Assoc. Prof. 1982-, Keeper Bolus Herbarium 1988-; Gen. Sec. Royal Soc. of S.A. 1968-85; Chair. Co-rdinating Council for Nature Conservation in the Cape 1970-85, Cape 'eninsula Conservation Trust 1980-85; Pres. The Athenaeum Trust 1985-7; Fellow Explorers Club New York; Hon. Life Forest Officer; Merit Award, S. African Council for Council for Conservation and Anti-Pollution 976; Cape Times Centenary Medal 1986. *Publications:* over 70 scientific ubls., including Studies of the South African Species of Eulophia 1965, 'hreatened Plants of Southern Africa 1980, Revision of the Southern African Species of Satyrium 1982, South African Red Data Book: Plants–'ynbos and Karoo Biomes 1985, Joint Phenetic and Cladistic Approach or Systematics 1988. *Leisure interests:* photography, dinghy sailing, travel, estoration of classic cars. *Address:* Bolus Herbarium, University of Cape 'own, Rondebosch 7700 (Office); 29 Barmbeck Avenue, Newlands 7700, outh Africa (Home). *Telephone:* (021) 650-3772 (Office); (021) 64-4637 Home).

IALL, Sir Arnold Alexander, Kt., M.A., F.R.S., D.ENG., D.SC., C.ENG.; British viation and electrical engineer and administrator; b. 23 April 1915, Liver-ool; s. of Robert Alexander Hall; m. 1st Moira Constance Dione Sykes 946 (deceased), three d.; m. 2nd Iola Mary Hall; ed. Alsop High School, Liverpool and Clare Coll., Cambridge; Research Fellow in Aeronautics at Co. of Armourers and Braziers 1936-38; Royal Aircraft Establishment, 'arnborough 1938-45; Zaharoff Prof. of Aviation, Univ. of London 1945-51; Dir. Royal Aircraft Establishment, Farnborough 1951-55; Dir. Hawker Siddeley Group Ltd. 1955-86, Lloyds Bank PLC 1966-85, Lloyds Bank J.K. Man. Ltd. 1979-84, Rolls-Royce Ltd. 1983-88; Man. Dir. Bristol Siddeley Engines Ltd. 1958-63; Vice-Chair. and Man. Dir. Hawker Siddeley Group Ltd. 1963-67, Chair. and Man. Dir. 1967-81, Chair. Hawker Siddeley Group PLC 1977-86; Pro-Chancellor, Univ. of Warwick 1964-70; mem. Advisory Council on Tech. (Ministry of Tech.) 1964, Electricity Supply Research Council 1963-71; Pres. British Electrical and Allied Mfrs. Assch. March 1967-68; Dir. Phoenix Assurance PLC 1969-85, ICI PLC 1970-85, Onan Corpn. 1976-80; Chair. Industrial Policy Group 1972-74; Vice-Pres. Soc. British Aerospace Cos. Ltd. 1971-72, Pres. 1972-73; Chair. Fasco Industries Inc. 1980-81; Dir. Royal Ordnance PLC 1984-87; Vice-Pres. Eng. Employers' Fed. 1984-87; Chancellor Univ. of Loughborough 1980-89; Chair. Trustees of the Science Museum 1983-85; Fellow, Imperial Coll. of Science and Tech., Hon. Fellow Clare Coll., Cambridge; Hon. F.R.Ae.S., Hon. F.A.I.A.A., Hon. A.C.G.I., Hon. F.I.Mech.E., Hon. F.I.E.E., Hon. D.Tech. Foreign Assoc. of U.S. Nat. Acad. of Eng., Hon. mem. A.S.M.E., . Fellow of Eng. Council of Eng. Insts.; British Inst. of Man. Gold Medal 1981; Hon. Sc.D. (Cambridge) 1986; Albert Medal, R.S.A. 1983. *Leisure interest:* sailing. *Address:* Wakehams, Dorney, Nr. Windsor, Berks., SL4 QD, England.

IALL, David, PH.D., F.R.S.N.Z.; New Zealand chairman of university grants ommittee; b. 15 Feb. 1928, N.Z.; s. of John William Hall and Theodora Helen Hall; m. Joan Heward 1950; two s. one d.; ed. Whangarei High chool and Univ. of Auckland; Jr. Lecturer in Chemistry Auckland Univ. Coll. (now Univ. of Auckland) 1950-53, Lecturer 1953-54, Sr. Lecturer 958-63, Assoc. Prof. 1963-65, Prof. 1965-66, 1968-84, Head of Dept. 965-66, 1981-84; Sr. Research Fellow A.E.R.E., Harwell, England 1954-66; Prof. of Chemistry and Chair. Div. Physical Chemistry Univ. of Alberta 966-68; Visiting Research Prof. in Crystallography Univ. of Pittsburgh, 'a. 1961-62; Visiting Scientist MRC Lab. for Molecular Biology, Cambridge 978; Chair. N.Z. Univ. Grants Cttee. 1984-; Fellow Inst. Chemistry, N.Z. *Publications:* 120 scientific works. *Leisure interests:* walking, gardening, hess. *Address:* P.O. Box 12348, Wellington (Office); 23 Rawhiti Terrace, Wellington, N.Z. (Home). *Telephone:* (04) 728-600 (Office); (04) 750-002 Home).

IALL, Donald, L.H.D., D.LITT.; American writer; b. 20 Sept. 1928, New Haven; s. of Donald A. Hall and Lucy (née Wells) Hall; m. 1st Kirby Thompson 1952 (divorced 1969), one s. one d.; m. 2nd Jane Kenyon 1972; ed. Harvard Univ., Oxford Univ., Stanford Univ.; Jr. Fellow Harvard Univ. 1954-57; Asst. Prof. Univ. of Michigan 1957-61, Assoc. Prof. 1961-66, Prof. 1966-77; Poetry Ed. Paris Review 1953-61; Consultant Harper & Row 1964-81; Newdigate Prize for Poetry from Oxford Univ. 1952, Lamont Poetry Selection, Acad. of American Poets 1955, and other awards; Gug-genheim Fellow 1963, 1972; mem. Authors Guild. *Publications: poems:* Exiles and Marriages 1955, The Dark Houses 1958, A Roof of Tiger Lilies 1963, The Alligator Bride 1969, The Yellow Room 1971, The Town of Hill 1975, A Blue Wing Tilts at the Edge of the Sea 1975, Kicking the Leaves 1978, The Toy Bone 1979, The One Day (Nat. Book Circle Critic's Award 1989) 1988; as Ed.: Harvard Advanced Anthology (with L. Simpson and R. Pack) 1950, The New Poets of England and America (with R. Pack) 1957, Second Selection 1962, A Poetry Sampler 1962, Contemporary Amer-

ican Poetry (with W. Taylor) 1962, Poetry in English (with S. Spender) 1963, A Concise Encyclopaedia of English and American Poets and Poetry 1963, Faber Book of Modern Verse 1966, The Modern Stylists 1968, A Choice of Whitman's Verse 1968, Man and Boy 1968, Anthology of American Poetry 1969, Pleasures of Poetry (with D. Emblen) 1971, A Writer's Reader 1976, To Read Literature 1981, To Read Poetry 1982, Oxford Book of American Literary Anecdotes 1981, Claims for Poetry 1982. *Address:* c/o North Point Press, 850 Talbot Avenue, Berkeley, Calif. 94706, U.S.A.

HALL, Henry Edgar, PH.D., F.R.S.; British professor of physics; b. 1928; s. of John A. Hall; m. Patricia A. Broadbent 1962; two s. one d.; ed. Latymer Upper School, Hammersmith and Emmanuel Coll. Cambridge; Royal Soc. Mond Lab. Cambridge 1952-58; Sr. Student, Royal Comm. for Exhbn. of 1851, 1955-57; Research Fellow, Emmanuel Coll. Cambridge 1955-58; Lecturer in Physics, Univ. of Manchester 1958-61, Prof. 1961-; has held visiting professorships in Australia, U.S.A. and Japan (1985); Simon Memorial Prize (with W. F. Vinen) 1963. *Publications:* Solid State Physics 1974; papers in scientific journals. *Leisure interest:* mountain walking. *Address:* The Schuster Laboratory, The University, Manchester, M13 9PL, England.

HALL, John R., B.S.CHEM.ENG.; American business executive; b. 30 Nov. 1932, Dallas, Texas; m. Donna Stauffer 1980; one s.; ed. Vanderbilt Univ., Nashville, Tenn.; with Ashland Oil Inc. 1963-; Co-ordinator, United Carbon Div. 1963; Dir. 1968, Admin. Vice-Pres. 1968-70, Sr. Vice-Pres. 1970-71, Pres. Ashland Chemical Co. (div. of Ashland Oil) 1971-74; Exec. Vice-Pres. Ashland Oil Co. 1974-76, Group Operating Officer 1976-78, C.E.O. for Company petroleum and chemical operations 1978-79, Vice-Chair. and C.O.O. 1979-81, Chair. and C.E.O. Sept. 1981-; fmr. Chair. Nat. Petroleum Refiners' Assch. *Leisure interest:* golf. *Address:* Ashland Oil Inc., P.O. Box 391, Ashland, Ky. 41114 (Office); 99 Stoneybrook Drive, Ashland, Ky. 41101, U.S.A. (Home).

HALL, Nigel John, M.A. (R.C.A.); British sculptor; b. 30 Aug. 1943; s. of Herbert John Hall and Gwendoline Mary (née Olsen) Hall; m. Manijeh Yadegar 1986; ed. Bristol Grammar School, West of England Coll. of Art, R.C.A., London; Harkness Fellowship to U.S.A. 1967-69; first one-man exhbn., Galerie Givaudan, Paris 1967; *other one-man exhbns. include:* Robert Elkon Gallery, New York 1974, 1977, 1979, 1983, Annely Juda Gallery, London 1978, 1981, 1985, 1987, Galerie Maeght, Paris 1981, 1983, Staatliche Kunsthalle, Baden-Baden 1982, Nishimura Gallery, Tokyo 1980, 1984, 1988; *group shows include:* Documenta VI, Kassel 1977, British Sculpture in the Twentieth Century, Whitechapel Gallery, London 1981, Aspects of British Art Today, Tokyo Metropolitan Museum 1982, Britannica: Thirty Years of Sculpture, Le Havre Museum of Fine Art 1988. *Represented in the following collections:* Tate Gallery, London, Musée Nat. d'Art Moderne, Paris, Nat. Galerie, Berlin, Museum of Modern Art, New York, Australian Nat. Gallery, Canberra, Art Inst. of Chicago, Kunsthaus, Zurich, Tokyo Metropolitan Museum, Musée d'Art Moderne, Brussels, Louisiana Museum, Denmark, Nat. Museum of Art, Osaka and others. *Address:* 1, Cahill Street, London, EC1 Y8PH, England. *Telephone:* (01) 253-4730; (01) 727-3162.

HALL, Peter Geoffrey; M.A., PH.D., F.B.A.; British professor of geography and planning; b. 19 March 1932, London; s. of Arthur Vickers and Bertha (née Keefe) Hall; m. 1st Carla M. Wartenberg 1962 (dissolved 1967), 2nd Magdalena Mróz 1967; no c.; ed. Blackpool Grammar School and St. Catharine's Coll., Cambridge; Asst. Lecturer, Birkbeck Coll., Univ. of London 1956-60, Lecturer 1960-65; Reader in Geography with special reference to planning, London School of Econs. 1966-67; Prof. of Geography, Univ. of Reading 1968-; Prof. of City and Regional Planning, Univ. of Calif. (Berkeley) 1980-; mem. South East Econ. Planning Council 1966-79, Social Science Research Council 1974-80; Gill Memorial Prize, Royal Geog. Soc. 1968; Adolphe Bentinck Prize 1979. *Publications:* London 2000 1963, The World Cities 1966, The Containment of Urban England 1973, Urban and Regional Planning 1974, Europe 2000 1977, Growth Centres in the European System 1980, Great Planning Disasters 1980, The Inner City in Context 1981, Silicon Landscapes 1985, Can Rail Save the City? 1985, High-Tech America 1986, Western Sunrise 1987, Cities of Tomorrow 1988, The Carrier Wave 1988, London 2001 1988. *Leisure interests:* reading, talking. *Address:* Department of Geography, University of Reading, Whiteknights, P.O. Box 227, RG6 2AB (Office); 5 Bedford Road, London, W4 1JD, England (Home). *Telephone:* 01-994 5950 (Home).

HALL, Peter George, B.SC., F.INST.PET.; British oil industry executive; b. 10 Dec. 1924; s. of Charles Hall and Rosina Hall; m. Margaret Gladys Adams 1949; two s. two d.; ed. Sandown Grammar School, Isle of Wight, Southampton Univ.; Anglo-Iranian Oil Co. 1946-51; various posts at Fawley Refinery, Esso Petroleum Co. Ltd. 1951-63, Man. Milford Haven Refinery 1963-66, Employee Relations Man. 1966-70; Vice-Pres., Gen. Sekiyu Seisei, Tokyo 1971-74; Asst. Gen. Man., Refining, Imperial Oil Ltd., Toronto 1974-76; Refining Man., Exxon Corpn., New York 1976-77; Dir., Esso Petroleum Co. Ltd., London 1977-78, Vice-Pres., Esso Europe Inc., London 1979-81, Man. Dir. Esso Petroleum Co. 1982-84, Pres. Esso Norge 1984-87; Chair. Snamprogetti Ltd. 1988-. *Leisure interests:* opera, classical music, walking, gardening. *Address:* Snamprogetti Ltd., Snamprogetti House, Basing View, Basingstoke, Hants., RG21 2YY (Office); Oakley, Mill Lawn, Burley, Ringwood, Hants., BH24 4HP, England. *Telephone:* (0256) 461211 (Office); (042 53) 2482 (Home).

HALL, Sir Peter Reginald Frederick, Kt., C.B.E., M.A.; British theatre, opera and film director; b. 22 Nov. 1930, Bury St. Edmunds, Suffolk; s. of Reginald and Grace Hall; m. 1st Leslie Caron 1956 (dissolved 1965), one s. one d.; m. 2nd Jacqueline Taylor 1965 (dissolved 1981), one s. one d.; m. 3rd Maria Ewing (q.v.) 1982, one d.; ed. Perse School and St. Catharine's Coll., Cambridge; Produced and acted in over 20 plays at Cambridge; first professional production Windsor 1953; produced in repertory at Windsor, Worthing and Oxford Playhouse; two Shakespearean productions for Arts Council; Artistic Dir. Elizabethan Theatre Co. 1953; Asst. Dir. London Arts Theatre 1954, Dir. 1955-56; formed own producing co., Int. Playwright's Theatre 1957; Man. Dir. Royal Shakespeare Theatre, Stratford-on-Avon and Aldwych Theatre, London 1960-68; mem. Arts Council 1969-72; Co-Dir., Nat. Theatre (now Royal Nat. Theatre) with Lord Olivier (q.v.) April-Nov. 1973, Dir. 1973-88; f. Peter Hall Co. 1988; Artistic Dir. Glyndebourne June 1983-; Assoc. Prof. of Drama, Warwick Univ. 1966-; Chevalier, Ordre des Arts et Lettres 1965; London Theatre Critics' Award for Best Dir. for The Wars of the Roses 1963, The Homecoming and Hamlet 1965; Antoinette Perry Award for Best Dir. for The Homecoming 1966; Hamburg Univ. Shakespeare Prize 1967; Antoinette Perry Award for Best Dir. for Amadeus 1981; Dr. h.c. (York) 1966, (Reading) 1973, (Liverpool) 1974, (Leicester) 1977. *Productions:* Blood Wedding, Immoralist, The Lesson, South, Mourning Becomes Electra, Waiting for Godot, Burnt Flowerbed, Waltz of the Toreadors, Camino Real, Gigi, Wrong Side of the Park, Love's Labours Lost, Cymbeline, Twelfth Night, A Midsummer Night's Dream, Coriolanus, Two Gentlemen of Verona, Troilus and Cressida, Ondine, Romeo and Juliet, Becket, The Collection, Cat on a Hot Tin Roof, The Rope Dancers (on Broadway), The Moon and Sixpence (opera, Sadlers Wells), Henry VI (parts 1, 2 and 3), Richard III, Richard II, Henry IV (parts 1 and 2), Henry V, Eh?, The Homecoming, Moses and Aaron (opera, Covent Garden), Hamlet, The Government Inspector, The Magic Flute (opera), Staircase, Work is a Four Letter Word (film), Macbeth, Midsummer Night's Dream (film), Three into Two Won't Go (film), A Delicate Balance, Dutch Uncle, Landscape and Silence, Perfect Friday (film), The Battle of Shrivings, La Calisto (opera, Glyndebourne Festival 1970), The Knot Garden (opera, Covent Garden) 1970, Eugene Onegin (opera, Covent Garden) 1971, Old Times 1971, Tristan and Isolde (opera, Covent Garden) 1971, All Over 1972, Il Ritorno di Ulysses (opera, Glyndebourne Festival) 1972, Alte Zeiten (Burgtheater, Vienna) 1972, Via Galactica (musical, Broadway) 1972, The Homecoming (film) 1973, Marriage of Figaro (Glyndebourne) 1973, The Tempest 1974, Landscape (film) 1974, Akenfield (film) 1974, No Man's Land 1975, Happy Days 1975, John Gabriel Borkman 1975, Judgement 1975, Hamlet 1975, Tamburlaine the Great 1976, Volpone 1977, Bedroom Farce 1977, The Country Wife 1977, The Cherry Orchard 1978, Macbeth (Nat. Theatre) 1978, Betrayal (Nat. Theatre) 1978, Cosi Fan Tutte (opera, Glyndebourne) 1978, Fidelio (opera, Glyndebourne) 1979, Amadeus (Nat. Theatre) 1979, Betrayal (New York) 1980, Othello (Nat. Theatre) 1980, Amadeus (New York) 1980, Family Voices (Nat. Theatre) 1981, The Oresteia (Nat. Theatre) 1981, A Midsummer Night's Dream (opera, Glyndebourne) 1981, The Importance of Being Earnest (Nat. Theatre) 1982, Other Places (Nat. Theatre) 1982, The Ring (operas, Bayreuth Festival) 1983, Jean Seberg (Nat. Theatre) 1983, L'Incoronazione di Poppea (opera, Glyndebourne) 1984, Animal Farm (Nat. Theatre) 1984, Coriolanus (Nat. Theatre) 1984, Yonadab (Nat. Theatre) 1985, Carmen (opera, Glyndebourne) 1985, and (Metropolitan Opera) 1986, Albert Herring (opera, Glyndebourne) 1985, The Petition (New York and Nat. Theatre) 1986, Simon Boccanegra (Glyndebourne) 1986, Salome (Los Angeles) 1986, Coming in to Land (Nat. Theatre) 1986, Antony and Cleopatra (Nat. Theatre) 1987, Entertaining Strangers (Nat. Theatre) 1987, La Traviata (Glyndebourne) 1987, Falstaff (Glyndebourne) 1988, Salome (Covent Garden) 1988, Cymbeline (Nat. Theatre) 1988, The Winter's Tale (Nat. Theatre) 1988, The Tempest 1988, Orpheus Descending 1988, Salome (opera, Chicago) 1988, Albert Herning 1989, Merchant of Venice 1989; acted in The Pedestrian (film) 1973. *Publications:* The War of the Roses 1970, Shakespeare's three Henry VI plays and Richard III (adapted with John Barton), John Gabriel Borkman (English version with Inga-Stina Ewbank), Animal Farm (stage adaptation), Peter Hall's Diaries: The Story of a Dramatic Battle 1983. *Leisure interest:* music. *Address:* The Peter Hall Company, 18 Exeter Street, London, WC2E 7DU, England.

HALL, Wesley Winfield; Barbados politician and cricketer; b. 12 Sept. 1937; m. (divorced); four c.; ed. Combermere School and Industrial Soc. London (personnel man.); played amateur and professional cricket in England, Australia, N.Z., India, Sri Lanka and throughout W. Indies including 48 Test Matches in which he took 192 wickets and first hat trick by a West Indian 1961-69; Man. W.I. Cricket Team throughout W.I. and abroad 1983-85; trainee telegraphist, Cable and Wireless, Barbados 1955-60; Public Relations Consultant, Esso, Queensland, Australia 1960-63, British American Tobacco Co. Ltd. (Trinidad and Tobago) 1968-78; Personnel and Public Relations Man. Banks Barbados Breweries Ltd. 1975-85; Independent Senator, Barbados Senate 1971-76, Opposition Senator 1981-86; Minister of Employment, Labour Relations and Community Devt. 1986; Minister of Employment, Labour Relations and Community Devt. 1986-88, of Tourism and Sports Oct. 1988-; Life mem. MCC, Hon. Life mem. Barbados Football Asscn.; Humming Bird Gold Medal 1987. *Publications:* Secrets of Cricket 1962, Pace Like Fire 1965. *Address:* Ministry of Tourism and Sports, P.O. Building, Cheapside, Bridgetown (Office).

HALL, William K., B.S.E., M.B.A., PH.D.; American business executive; b. Oct. 1943, Adrian, Mich.; s. of Daniel S. Hall and Jeanne (Isley) Hall; m. Valerie Worth Smith 1964; three s. one d.; ed. Adrian High School, Adrian Mich. and Univ. of Mich.; Prof. of Business Admin. Univ. of Mich., Harvard Business School, European Inst. of Business Admin., France 1970-81; Consultant to AT&T, Chrysler Corpn., Eastman Kodak, Ford Motor Co Gen. Electric Co., Gen. Motors, Mobil Oil Co., Union Carbide Corpn. and other cos.; Exec. Vice-Pres. Cummins Engine Co., Inc. 1981-84; Dir Cummins Engine Foundation; Pres. and C.O.O. Farley Industries 1984-87 Pres. and C.O.O. Eagle Industries, Chicago; Dir. several cos. *Address* Eagle Industries, Suite 1160, 2 N. Riverside Plaza, Chicago, Ill. 60600 (Office); 855 Lamson Drive, Winnetka, Ill. 60093, U.S.A. (Home). *Telephone* (312) 906-8700 (Office).

HALLBERG, Paul Thure, FIL.LIC.; Swedish library director; b. 10 Dec 1931, Gothenburg; s. of late Severin Hallberg and Eva Hallberg (née Theorell); m. Elisabeth Löfgren 1958; one s.; ed. Gothenburg Univ. and Yale Univ., U.S.A.; Asst. Teacher, Dept. of English Language and Literature, Gothenburg Univ. 1958-59; Librarian, Gothenburg Univ. Library 1960-68, Head of Dept. 1968-77, Dir. 1977-; Sec. Main Cttee. for Scandi Plan 1964-65; Sec. Scandinavian Fed. of Research Librarians 1966-69 mem. Bd. 1979-84; mem. and Librarian, Royal Soc. of Arts and Sciences in Gothenburg 1977-; mem. Nat. Bibliographic Council 1983-; Chair. Swedish Cataloguing Cttee. 1979-85; mem. of Bd. NORDINFO (Nordic Council fo. Scientific Information and Research Libraries) 1986-88; mem. Standing Cttee., Int. Fed. of Library Assens. and Insts., Section on Acquisition and Exchange 1977-85, mem. and Sec. Standing Cttee., Section of Univ Libraries and other Gen. Research Libraries 1985-. *Publications:* autho and ed. of numerous books and articles on bibliography and librarianship *Leisure interests:* music and country cottage. *Address:* Gothenburg Univer sity Library, P.O. Box 5096, S-402 22 Gothenburg (Office); Orangerigata 34, S-412 66 Gothenburg, Sweden (Home). *Telephone:* (031) 63 17 60 (Office (031) 40 23 18 (Home).

HALLGRÍMSSON, Geir; Icelandic politician and banker; b. 16 Dec. 1925 Reykjavík; s. of Áslaug Geirsdóttir Zöega and Hallgrímur Benediktsson m. Erna Finnsdóttir 1948; two s. two d.; ed. Univ. of Iceland and Harvar Law School; Pres. Nat. Union of Icelandic Students 1946-47; law practice Dir. of H. Benediktsson 1951-59; mem. Reykjavík City Council 1954-74 Mayor of Reykjavík 1959-72; alt. M.P. (Althing) 1959-70, mem. 1970-83 mem. Cen. Cttee. Independence Party 1965-87, Vice-Chair. Independence Party 1971, Chair. 1973-83; Prime Minister 1974-78; Minister of Foreign Affairs 1983-86; Gov. Cen. Bank of Iceland 1986-; Grand Cross, Order the Falcon (Iceland), Grand Cross, Order of the White Rose (Finland) Grand Cross, Order of the Polar Star (Sweden), Commdr., Order of St Olav (Norway), Commdr. 1st Class, Order of the Lion (Finland), Gran Officier, Ordre du Mérite (Luxembourg), Commdr., Order of Dannebro (Denmark). *Address:* Central Bank of Iceland, Reykjavík (Office); Dyngju vegi 6, 104 Reykjavík, Iceland (Home). *Telephone:* 699 600 (Office); 3335 (Home).

HALLIDAY, Ian Francis, M.A., F.C.A.; British business executive; b. 1 Nov. 1927, Grimsby; s. of Michael and Jean Halliday; m. Mary Busfiel 1952; one s. two d.; ed. Wintringham Grammar School and Lincoln Coll. Oxford; joined Armitage & Norton (chartered accountants) 1951, Partne 1957-69; Finance Dir. Allied Textile Co. Ltd. 1970-74; Deputy Dir. Indus trial Devt. Unit, Dept. of Industry 1974-77; Finance Dir. Leslie & Godwi (Holdings) Ltd. (insurance brokers) 1977-80; Chief Exec. Nat. Enterprise Bd. (NEB) Feb.-Dec. 1980; Group Finance Dir. Lowndes Lambert Grou Ltd. 1981-87; Dir. (non-exec.) Port of London Authority 1984-. *Leisur interest:* gardening. *Address:* 40 Finthorpe Lane, Huddersfield, HD5 8TU England.

HALLIDAY, Michael Alexander Kirkwood, M.A., PH.D.; British professo of linguistics (retd.); b. 13 April 1925, Leeds; s. of Wilfrid J. Halliday an Winifred Kirkwood; m. 1st Patricia Woolf 1952, one s. one d.; m. 2n Brenda P. Stephen 1961, one d.; m. 3rd Ruqaiya Hasan 1967, one s.; ed Rugby School and Univs. of London and Cambridge; grad. studies in China 1947-50; Asst. lecturer in Chinese, Univ. of Cambridge 1954-58; lecturer then Reader, in Linguistics, Univ. of Edinburgh 1958-63; Dir. Communi cation Research Centre, Univ. Coll. London 1963-70, Reader in Gen Linguistics 1963-65, Prof. 1965-70; visiting appts. and fellowships in U.S.A and Kenya 1971-73; Prof. of Linguistics, Univ. of Ill. at Chicago Circl 1973-75, Univ. of Essex 1974-75, Univ. of Sydney 1976-87, Prof. Emer 1988-; numerous visiting appts., consultancies, etc.; mem. Philological Soc (U.K.), Linguistic Soc. of America, Applied Linguistics Asscn. of Australia Linguistic Asscn. of Canada and the U.S., Australian Linguistics Soc.; Dr h.c. (Nancy) 1968, Hon. D.Litt. (Birmingham) 1987 (York Univ., Canada 1988. *Publications include:* Intonation and Grammar in British English 1967, A Course in Spoken English 1970, Explorations in the Functions o Language 1973, Learning How to Mean: explorations in the developmen of language 1975, System and Function in Language 1976, Language a Social Semiotic 1978, An Introduction to Functional Grammar 1985, Spoke and Written Language 1985. *Leisure interests:* railways and rail trave bushwalking, theatre. *Address:* 5 Laing Avenue, Killara, N.S.W. 2071 Australia. *Telephone:* (02) 498-3568.

HALLMAN, Dr Viola; German business executive; b. 8 Dec. 1944, Hagen, North Rhine Westphalia; d. of Werner and Helga Flachmeier; m. Olof J. Hallman 1971; one d.; ed. Univs. of Hamburg, Marburg and Padua; Chief Exec. Theis Group; Chief Exec. Friedrich Gustav Theis Kaltwalzwerke GmbH 1972, Friedrich Gustav Theis GmbH & Co. Flachdraht- und Profilwerk Hagen-Hohenlimburg 1972, Theis Verpackungssysteme GmbH, Packbandwerk Gelsenkirchen 1975, Alte & Schröder GmbH & Co., Stahlund NE-Veredlungswerke Halver und Hagen-Halden 1979; Chair. and C.E.O. Theis Precision Steel Corpn., Bristol, Conn., U.S.A. 1986-; Chair. of Bd. and Pres. Theis of America, Inc., Wilmington, Del., U.S.A. 1986-; mem. Fed. Cttee. of Business Econs. (BBW) of the RKW, Eschborn, VvU Asscn. of Women Entrepreneurs, Cologne, ASU Working Asscn. of Independent Business Entrepreneurs, Bonn; Manager of the Year 1979. *Publication:* Entrepreneur—Profession Without Future? *Leisure interests:* riding, swimming, literature, history. *Address:* Bondstahlstrasse 14-18, 5800 Hagen-Halden, Federal Republic of Germany. *Telephone:* 02331/93-0.

HALLOWES, Odette Marie Céline, G.C., M.B.E.; British (b. French) wartime agent; b. 28 April 1912; d. of Gaston Brailly; m. 1st Roy Sansom (deceased) 1931, three d.; m. 2nd Captain Peter Churchill (deceased) 1947; m. 3rd Geoffrey Macleod Hallowes 1956; ed. Convent of Ste. Thérèse, Amiens, and privately; worked as British agent with Special Forces in France 1942-43 when captured by the Gestapo; sentenced to death 1943; endured imprisonment and torture until 1945 when she left Ravensbruck Concentration Camp; Vice-Pres. Mil. Medallists' League; mem. Cttee. Victoria Cross and George Cross Asscn.; Pres. 282 (East Ham) Squadron, Air Training Corps; Founder Vice-Pres. Women of the Year Luncheon (Greater London Fund for the Blind); Vice-Pres. Women's Transport Services F.A.N.Y.); Hon. mem. St. Dunstan's Ex-Prisoners of War Asscn.; Légion d'honneur 1950. *Leisure interests:* reading, travelling, cooking, trying to learn patience. *Address:* Rosedale, Eriswell Road, Burwood Park, Walton on Thames, Surrey, England.

HALONEN, Tarja Kaarina; Finnish lawyer and politician; b. 24 Dec. 1943; lawyer, Lainvalvonta Oy 1967-68; social welfare officer, organizing Sec. Nat. Union of Finnish Students 1969-70; lawyer, Cen. Org. of Finnish Trade Unions 1970-; Parl. Sec. to Prime Minister Sorsa 1974-75; mem. Parl. 1979-; Minister, Ministry of Social Affairs and Health 1987-; Social Democratic Party. *Address:* Ministry of Social Affairs and Health, Snellmaninkatu 4-6, 00170 Helsinki, Finland. *Telephone:* (90) 1601.

HALPERIN, Bertrand Israel, PH.D.; American professor of physics; b. 6 Dec. 1941, Brooklyn, New York; s. of Morris Halperin and Eva Teplitsky Halperin; m. Helena Stacy French 1962; one s. one d.; ed. George Wingate High School, Brooklyn, Harvard Coll. and Univ. of California (Berkeley); NSF Postdoctoral Fellow, Ecole Normale Supérieure, Paris 1965-66; mem. tech. staff, Bell Labs. 1966-76; Prof. of Physics Harvard Univ. 1976-, Chair. Dept. of Physics 1988-; Assoc. Ed. Reviews of Modern Physics 1974-80; mem. N.A.S., American Acad. of Arts and Sciences; Fellow American Physical Soc.; Oliver Buckley Prize for Condensed Matter Physics 1982. *Publications:* about 100 articles in scientific journals. *Address:* Lyman Laboratory of Physics, Harvard University, Cambridge, Mass. 02138, U.S.A. *Telephone:* (617) 495-4294.

HALPERIN, Tulio, D.PHIL.; Argentine historian; b. 27 Oct. 1926; ed. Univ. de Buenos Aires, Ecole Pratique des Hautes Etudes, Paris; Prof., Univ. Nac. del Litoral (Rosario, Argentina) 1955-61; Prof. Univ. de Buenos Aires 1959-66, Univ. of Oxford 1970-71, Univ. of Calif. (Berkeley) 1971-; Lecturer, History Dept., Harvard Univ. 1967-. *Publications:* El Pensamiento de Echeverría 1951, Un Conflicto Nacional: Moriscos y Cristianos Viejos en Valencia 1955, El Río de la Plata al Comenzar el Siglo XIX 1960, Tradición Política Española e Ideología Revolucionaria de Mayo 1961, Historia de la Universidad de Buenos Aires 1962, Argentina en el Callejón 1964, Historia contemporánea de América Latina 1969, Hispanoamérica después de la Independencia 1972 (in English The Aftermath of Revolution in Latin America 1973), Revolución y guerra 1972 (in English Politics, Economics and Society in Argentina in the Revolutionary Period 1975). *Address:* History Department, University of California, Berkeley, Calif. 94720, U.S.A.

HALPERN, Daniel, M.F.A.; American editor and author; b. 9 Nov. 1945, Syracuse, N.Y.; s. of Irving Halpern and Rosemary Halpern; m. Jean Carter 1983; ed. California State Univ. and Columbia Univ.; Editor-in-Chief, The Ecco Press (Antaeus) 1969-; Adjunct Prof. Columbia Univ. 1975-; Dir. Nat. Poetry Series 1978-; Visiting Prof. Princeton Univ. 1975-76, 1987-88; Nat. Endowment for the Arts Fellowship 1974, 1975, 1987; Robert Frost Fellowship, CAPS, Carey; Thomas Award for Creative Publishing, etc. *Publications include:* poetry: Travelling on Credit 1972, Street Fire 1975, Life Among Others 1978, Seasonal Rights 1982, Tango 1987. *Leisure interest:* cooking. *Address:* 60 Pheasant Hill Road, Princeton, N.J. 08540; 26 West 17th Street, New York, N.Y. 10011, U.S.A. *Telephone:* 609-921-6796; 212-645-2214.

HALPERN, Jack, PH.D., F.R.S.; American university professor; b. 19 Jan. 1925, Poland; s. of Philip Halpern and Anna Sass; m. Helen Peritz 1949; two d.; ed. McGill Univ., Montreal; NRC Postdoctoral Overseas Fellow, Univ. of Manchester 1949-50; Prof. of Chem., Univ. of B.C., Canada 1950-62; Nuffield Fellow, Univ. of Cambridge 1959-60; Louis Block Distinguished Service Prof., Univ. of Chicago 1962-; External Scientific Mem. Max Planck Inst. für Kohlenforschung, Mulheim 1983-; Visiting Prof. at various univs. in U.S.A. and Copenhagen; numerous other lectureships, professional and editorial appointments; Hon. D.Sc.; Hon. Fellow Royal Soc. of Chem. 1987; American Chemical Soc. Award in Inorganic Chem. 1968, Royal Soc. of Chem. Award in Catalysis 1977, Richard Kokes Award 1978, American Chemical Soc. Award for Distinguished Service in the Advancement of Inorganic Chem. 1985, Willard Gibbs Medal 1986, Bailar Medal 1986, German Chemical Soc. August Wilhelm von Hoffman Medal 1988. *Publications:* more than 250 scientific articles in various scientific journals. *Leisure interests:* art, music. *Address:* Department of Chemistry, University of Chicago, 5735 S. Ellis Avenue, Chicago, Ill. 60637 (Office); 5630 S. Dorchester Avenue, Chicago, Ill. 60637, U.S.A. *Telephone:* (312) 702-7095 (Office); (312) 643-6837 (Home).

HALPERN, Sir Ralph (Mark), Kt., C.B.I.M.; British business executive; b. 1938; m. Joan Halpern; one d.; ed. St. Christopher School, Letchworth; former trainee Selfridges; joined Burton Group PLC 1961, Chief Exec. and Man. Dir. 1978-, Chair. 1981-; co-founder, Top Shop 1970; Chair. CBI Marketing and Common Affairs Cttee. 1984-; mem. CBI City-Industry Task Force. *Address:* c/o Burton Group PLC, 214 Oxford Street, London, W1N 9DF, England.

HALSBURY, 3rd Earl of; John Anthony Hardinge Giffard, B.SC., F.R.I.C., F.INST.P., C.ENG., F.I.PROD.E., F.ENG., F.R.S.; British scientific consultant; b. 4 June 1908; s. of 2nd Earl of Halsbury and the late Esme Stewart; m. 1st Ismay C. Crichton-Stuart 1930, one s.; m. 2nd Elizabeth A. Faith (née Godley) 1936 (died 1983), two d.; ed. Eton Coll.; Lever Bros. 1935-42; Brown-Firth Research Labs. 1942-47; Dir. of Research, Decca Record Co. 1947-49; Man. Dir. Nat. Research Devt. Corpn. 1949-59; Consultant and Dir. Joseph Lucas Industries 1959-74, Distillers Co. Ltd. 1959-78, Head-Wrighston Ltd. 1959-78; Chancellor, Brunel Univ. 1966-; mem. numerous advisory cttees. etc.; Hon. F.I.C.E.; Hon. A.R.C.V.S.; Hon. F.R.S.C.; Hon. D.Tech. (Brunel) 1966; Hon. D. Univ. (Essex.) 1968. *Address:* 4 Campden House, 29 Sheffield Terrace, London, W.8, England. *Telephone:* 01-727 3125.

HALSEY, Albert Henry, M.A., PH.D.; British university professor; b. 13 April 1923, St. Pancras; s. of William T. Halsey and Ada Draper; m. Gertrude M. Littler 1949; three s. two d.; ed. London School of Econs.; research worker, Univ. of Liverpool 1952-54; Lecturer, Univ. of Birmingham 1954-62; Fellow, Centre for Advanced Study of Behavioural Sciences, Palo Alto, Calif. 1956-57; Prof. of Sociology, Univ. of Chicago 1959-60; Dir. Barnett House and Fellow, Nuffield Coll., Oxford 1962-; Prof. of Social and Admin. Studies, Univ. of Oxford 1978-; Hon. D.Sc. (Birmingham) 1987. *Publications:* Origins and Destinations 1980, Changes in British Society 1986, English Ethical Socialism (with Norman Dennis) 1988. *Leisure interest:* gardening. *Address:* Nuffield College, Oxford; 28 Upland Park Road, Oxford, OX2 7RU, England. *Telephone:* Oxford 248014 (Office); Oxford 58625 (Home).

HALSTEAD, Eric Henry, C.B.E., E.D., M.A., B.COM., F.C.A.(N.Z.), F.C.I.S., F.N.Z.I.M.; New Zealand diplomatist, politician, company director and chartered accountant; b. 26 May 1912, Auckland; s. of Harry B. Halstead and Alma Emma Newman; m. Millicent Joan Stewart 1940; three s. one d.; ed. Auckland Grammar School, Auckland Univ. and Teachers' Training Coll.; Maj. N.Z.E.F., mentioned in despatches 1939-45; head of Commercial and Accountancy Dept., Seddon Memorial Tech. Coll. 1945-49; M.P. (mem. of National Party) 1949-57; Minister of Social Security and Minister-in-Charge of Tourist and Health Resorts 1954-56; Minister-Asst. to the Prime Minister 1954-57, concurrently Minister of Industries and Commerce and of Customs 1956-57; Partner Mabee, Halstead and Co.; Pres. Auckland Savings Bank; Dir. Air New Zealand Ltd.; Vice-Pres. N.Z. Inst. of Int. Affairs 1970-; Amb. to Thailand and Laos 1970-73, to Italy, also accred. to Egypt, Iraq, Saudi Arabia 1976-80 and Yugoslavia, and High Commr. to Malta 1976-80; Deputy Chair. Asian Inst. of Tech. 1972-74; business consultant and co. dir. 1974-76, 1980-; mem. New Zealand Industries Devt. Comm. 1980-; mem. Council Univ. of Auckland 1961-70, N.Z. Medical Educ. Trust 1974-76; Hon. Dr. Accademia Tiberina; Hon. D.Sc. (Lancaster) 1987. *Publications:* textbooks on accounting and commercial practice; many published articles on economic, political and foreign affairs. *Leisure interests:* tennis, golf, swimming, reading, writing. *Address:* 21 Grandwe Road, Rotorua, New Zealand. *Telephone:* 89-024.

HALSTEAD, John G. H.; Canadian diplomatist (retd.), consultant and educator; b. 27 Jan. 1922, Vancouver; s. of Frank H. Halstead and Minnie W. Horler; m. Jean M. Gemmill 1953; two s.; ed. Univ. of British Columbia and London School of Econs.; joined Dept. of External Affairs 1946; served London 1948-52, Tokyo 1955-58, Perm. Mission to UN, New York 1958-61, Paris 1961-66; Head of European Div., Ottawa 1966-71; Asst. Under-Sec. of State for External Affairs 1971-74; Acting Under-Sec. and Deputy Under-Sec. 1974-75; Amb. to Fed. Repub. of Germany 1975-80; Amb. and Perm. Rep. to NATO 1980-82; Distinguished Visiting Prof. Inst. for Study of Diplomacy, Georgetown Univ. 1983, Distinguished Research Prof. School of Foreign Service, Georgetown Univ., Washington 1984-; Int. Counsellor Inst. for Study Diplomacy 1986-; Chair. Canadian Council for European Affairs; Dir. Atlantic Council for Canada, Canadian Centre for Arms

Control and Disarmament, Canadian Inst. for Int. Peace and Security; mem. Nat. Exec. Cttee. Canadian Inst. of Int. Relations, Editorial Bd. Nato's Sixteen Nations. *Publications:* numerous articles on int. affairs. *Leisure interests:* painting, philately, tennis, swimming, sailing, skiing. *Address:* c/o School of Foreign Service, Georgetown University, Washington, D.C. 20057, U.S.A.; 187 Billings Avenue, Ottawa, Ont. K1H 5K8, Canada. *Telephone:* (202) 625-8213 (U.S.A.); (613) 521-5221 (Canada).

HALSTEAD, Sir Ronald, Kt., C.B.E., M.A., F.R.S.C., F.B.I.M., F.R.S.A.; British business executive; b. 17 May 1927, Lancaster; s. of Richard and Bessie Harrison Halstead; m. Yvonne Cecile de Monchaux 1968 (deceased); two s.; ed. Queens' Coll., Cambridge; Research Chemist H.P. Bulmer & Co. 1948-53; Mfg. Man. Macleans Ltd. 1954-55; Factory Man. Beecham Products Inc. (U.S.A.) 1955-60; Asst. Man. Dir. Beecham Research Lab. Ltd. 1960-62, Pres. Beecham Research Labs., Inc. (U.S.A.) 1962-64; Vice-Pres. Marketing, Beecham Products, Inc. (U.S.A.) 1962-64; Chair. Food and Drink Div. Beecham Group 1964-67; Chair. Beecham Products 1967-84; Man. Dir. (consumer products) Beecham Group 1973-84; Chair. and Chief Exec. Beecham Group PLC 1984-85; Vice-Chair. Proprietary Assen. of G.B. 1968-77; Pres. Nat. Advertising Benevolent Soc. 1978-80; Vice-Pres. Inst. of Packaging 1979-81, Pres. 1981-83; Non-Exec. Dir. British Steel Corpn. 1979-86, Deputy Chair. 1986-; Gov. Ashridge Man. Coll. 1970-, Vice-Chair. 1977-; Pres. Inc. Soc. of British Advertisers 1971-73; Chair. British Nutrition Foundation 1970-73, Council mem. 1967-79; Vice-Chair. Advertising Assen. 1973-81; Vice-Chair. Food & Drink Industries Council 1973-76; Pres. Food Mfrs. Fed. 1974-76; Fellow, Inst. of Marketing Oct. 1975-, Vice-Pres. 1980-, American Cyanamid (U.S.A.) 1986-, Davy Corpn. 1986-; mem. Council, Food Mfrs Fed. Inc. 1966-; mem. CBI 1970-86, B.I.M. 1972-77, Cambridge Univ. Appointments Bd. 1969-73, Agric. Research Council 1978-84; Dir. The Otis Elevator Co. Ltd. 1978-83, Burmah Oil 1983-; Dir. Nat. Coll. of Food Tech. 1977-78, Chair. of Bd. 1978-83; Chair. Knitting Economic Devt. Cttee. NEDC 1978-; Fellow, Inst. of Grocery Distribution 1979-, Marketing Soc. 1981-; Trustee, Inst. of Econ. Affairs 1980-; mem. Monopolies and Mergers Comm. Newspaper Panel; mem. Industrial Devt. Advisory Bd. Dept. of Trade and Industry 1983-, Chair. 1984-; Hon. Treas. and Dir., Centre for Policy Studies 1984-; mem. Priorities Bd. for Research and Devt. in Agric. and Food, Ministry of Agric. Fish and Food 1984-87; Chair. Bd. of Food Studies Univ. of Reading 1983-86; Council mem. Univ. of Buckingham 1973-, Univ. of Reading 1978-86; Hon. Fellow Inst. of Food Science and Tech. 1983-, Inst. of Marketing 1982-; Hon. Fellow, Queens' Coll. Cambridge 1985; Hon. D.Sc. (Reading) 1982. *Leisure interests:* sailing, squash racquets, skiing. *Address:* 37 Edwardes Square, London, W8 6HH, England. *Telephone:* 01-603 9010.

HALVER, John Emil, M.SC., PH.D.; American biochemist and nutritionist; b. 21 April 1922, Washington; s. of John E. Halver and Helen H. Hansen; m. Jane Loren 1944; two s. three d.; ed. Washington State Univ. and Univ. of Washington; Plant Chemist, Assoc. Frozen Foods, Kent, Wash. 1946; Chief, Western Fish Nutrition Lab. U.S. Fish and Wildlife Service (USFWS) 1950-53; Dir. Western Fish Nutrition Labs., USFWS, Cook, Wash. 1953-75; Sr. Scientist, Nutrition, USFWS, Seattle 1975-78; Nutritionist, Medical Service Corps, U.S. Army Reserve 1950-80; Affiliate Prof. Univ. of Oregon Medical School 1960-70, School of Fisheries, Univ. of Wash. 1955-78; Prof. of Nutrition, School of Fisheries, Univ. of Wash. 1978-; Pres. Halver Corpn., Fisheries Devt. Tech., Inc.; Consultant FAO, UNDP, World Bank, IDRC; mem. American Inst. of Nutrition, N.A.S.; Fellow Fishery Research Biologists; numerous awards and distinctions. *Publications:* 180 original publs. on fish nutrition. *Leisure interests:* sports, fishing, hunting, hiking, dancing, music, theatre, opera. *Address:* 16502 41st N.E., Seattle, Wash. 98155; Box 116, Underwood, Wash. 98651; School of Fisheries WH-10, University of Washington, Wash. 98195, U.S.A. *Telephone:* 206-363-2553; 509-493-2553; 206-543-9619, 206-442-5097.

HALVORSEN, Einfrid; Norwegian politician; b. 13 Oct. 1937; m.; mem. Skien Municipal Council 1973-, Municipal Exec. Cttee. 1977-, Chair. of Council 1983-86, 1987-; State Sec., Ministry of Local Govt. and Labour 1986-87; Minister of Consumer Affairs and Govt. Admin. 1988-; mem. Bd. and Exec. Cttee., Norwegian Assen. of Local Authorities, Nat. Bd., Norwegian Nat. Union of Commercial and Office Employees. *Address:* Ministry of Consumer Affairs and Government Administration, Akersgt. 42, POB 8004 Dep., 0030 Oslo 1, Norway. *Telephone:* (2) 11-90-90.

HAM, James Milton, O.C., S.M., SC.D.; Canadian professor of science and technology; b. 21 Sept. 1920, Coboconck, Ont.; s. of James A. and Harriet Boomer (Gandier) Ham; m. Mary C. (Augustine) Ham 1955; one s. two d.; ed. Univ. of Toronto and Massachusetts Inst. of Tech.; Asst. Prof. M.I.T. 1951-52; Assoc. Prof. Univ. of Toronto 1953-59, Prof. of Electrical Eng. 1959-83, Prof. of Science, Tech. and Public Policy 1983-, Dean, Faculty of Applied Science and Eng. 1966-73, Dean, School of Graduate Studies 1976-78, Pres. Univ. of Toronto 1978-83; mem. various comms. and cttees. etc.; Brookings Fellow in Science and Public Policy, Washington, D.C. 1983-84; Dir. Shell Canada 1981-; several awards and hon. degrees. *Publications:* Scientific Basis of Electrical Engineering (with G. K. Slemon) 1961; articles in professional journals. *Leisure interests:* skiing, photography, literature. *Address:* c/o University of Toronto, Toronto, Ont. M5S 141 (Office); 135 Glencairn Avenue, Toronto, Ont. M4R 1N1, Canada (Home). *Telephone:* (416) 483-8374 (Home).

HAMAD, Abdul-Latif Yousef al-, B.A.; Kuwaiti banker, international official and politician; b. 1937; ed. American Univ., Cairo, Claremont Coll. Calif., Harvard Univ.; mem. del. to UN 1962; Acting Dir.-Gen. Kuwai Fund for Arab Econ. Devt. 1962, Dir.-Gen. 1963-81; Dir., then Man. Dir Kuwait Investment Co. 1963-77; Dir. South and Arabian Gulf Soc. 1963-81 Alt. Gov. for Kuwait, World Bank 1964-81; Chair. Kuwait Prefabricated Bldg. Co. 1965-78; Chair. United Bank of Kuwait Ltd., London 1966-80 Dir. Assistance Authority for Gulf and Southern Arabia 1967-81; Exec Dir. Arab Fund for Econ. and Social Devt. 1972-81; Chair. Compagnie Arabe et Internationale d'Investissements, Luxembourg 1973-81; mem Bd. of Trustees, Corporate Property Investors, New York 1975-81; mem Ind. Comm. on Int. Devt. Issues (Brandt Comm.) 1976-79; mem. Bd. Int Inst. for Environment and Devt., London 1976-80; Chair. Kuwait Nat Investment Group 1977-79; Minister of Finance and Planning 1981-83 Gov. for Kuwait, World Bank and IMF 1981-83; Dir.-Gen. Arab Fund fo Econ. and Social Devt. 1985-; mem. World Bank-Fund Devt. Cttee.; Chair Annual Meetings, IMF 1982; Trustee, Arab Planning Inst., Jordan Univ. Amman, Claremont Coll., Calif., World Scout Foundation, Stockholm 1980- Dir. Scandinavian Securities Corpn., New York; mem. Governing Body Inst. of Devt. Studies, Brighton, England; mem. Bd. of Govs. and Dirs H.E. Sabah al-Salem al-Sabah Foundation; mem. Visiting Cttee., Harvard Univ. Center for Middle Eastern Studies. *Address:* Arab Fund for Econ omic and Social Development, P.O. Box 21923, Kuwait City, Kuwait.

HAMANN, Sefton Davidson, PH.D., F.A.A., F.R.A.C.I.; Australian research physical chemist; b. 8 Jan. 1921, New Zealand; s. of Conrad G. Hamann and Margaret E. Wilson; m. Elizabeth W. Boden 1950; one s.; ed. Christ's Coll., N.Z. and Univs. of N.Z. and Manchester; served Royal N.Z. Navy 1941-45; joined staff of CSIRO 1950, Chief, Div. of Physical Chem. 1960-66 Chief, Div. of Applied Chem. 1966-74, Chair. CSIRO Applied Chemistry Labs. 1974-78, Hon. Research Fellow 1979-; Visiting Prof., Kyoto Univ. Japan 1972; Smith Memorial Medal, R.A.C.I. 1969. *Publications:* Physico Chemical Effects of Pressure 1957; numerous scientific papers and patents *Leisure interest:* music. *Address:* CSIRO Division of Chemicals and Poly mers, G.P.O. Box 4331, Melbourne, Vic. 3001 (Office); 1A Victoria Avenue Canterbury, Vic. 3126, Australia (Home). *Telephone:* (03) 647 7259 (Office) (03) 830 4946 (Home).

HAMBIDGE, Most Rev. Douglas Walter, D.D.; British ecclesiastic; b. 6 March 1927, London; s. of late Douglas Hambidge and late Florence Driscoll; m. Denise Colvill 1956; two s. one d.; ed. Univ. of London, London Coll. of Divinity and Anglican Theological Coll.; ordained priest 1954; St Mark & St. Bartholomew, U.K. 1953-56; Cassiar, B.C., Canada 1956-58 Smithers, B.C. 1958-64; Fort St. John, B.C. 1964-69; Rural Dean Tweedsmuir 1960-64; Canon, St. Andrew's Cathedral 1965; Rural Dean o Peace River 1965-69; Bishop of Caledonia 1969; Metropolitan of Ecclesiasti cal Province of B.C. and Archbishop of New Westminster 1981-. *Leisure interests:* cycling, badminton, squash. *Address:* 302-814 Richards Street Vancouver, B.C., V6B 3A7 (Office); 5887 Highbury Street, Vancouver B.C., V6N 1Y9, Canada (Home). *Telephone:* (604) 684-6306 (Office).

HAMBLING, Maggi; British artist; b. 23 Oct. 1945, Sudbury, Suffolk; d of Harry Leonard Hambling and Marjorie Rose Hambling; ed. Hadleigh Hall School and Amberfield School, Suffolk, Ipswich School of Art, Cam berwell School of Art, London, Slade School of Fine Art, London; studied painting with Lett Haines and Cedric Morris 1960-; first solo exhbn. at Hadleigh Gallery, Suffolk 1967; further solo exhbns. in London 1973, 1977 at Nat. Gallery 1981, Nat. Portrait Gallery 1983, Serpentine Gallery 1987, Richard Demarco Gallery, Edinburgh 1988, Arnolfini Gallery, Bristol 1988 Boise Travel Award 1969, Arts Council Award 1977, First Artist in Residence, Nat. Gallery, London 1980-81. *Public collections:* include Arts Council, British Council, British Museum, Chelmsford and Essex Museum Contemporary Art Soc., European Parl. Collection, Imperial War Museum Ipswich Museum, Leicestershire Ed. Cttee., Minories Colchester, Nat. Gallery, Nat. Portrait Gallery, Royal Army Medical Coll., Rugby Museum, Southampton Art Gallery, Tate Gallery, William Morris School, Birm ingham City Art Gallery, Morley Coll. London, Clare Coll. Cambridge, Whitworth Art Gallery, Gulbenkian Foundation, Preston Art Gallery, HTV Bristol, Scottish Nat. Gallery of Modern Art, Scottish Nat. Portrait Gallery. *Address:* 1 Broadhinton Road, London, S.W.4, England (Home).

HAMBRAEUS, Prof. Gunnar Axel, M.ELEC.ENG.; Swedish engineering scientist and administrator; b. 25 May 1919, Orsa; m. Elsa Lindén 1946; one s. two d.; ed. Uppsala Univ., Royal Inst. of Tech., Stockholm; Sec. Swedish Tech. Research Council 1945-50, 1951-53; Tech. Adviser Swedish Embassy, New York 1950-51; Ed.-in-Chief and Publr. Teknisk Tidskrift 1953-68; Consultant IAEA 1968-69; Man. Dir. Swedish Tech. Press 1969-70; Prof. and Pres. Royal Swedish Acad. of Eng. Sciences 1971-82, Chair. 1983-85; Chair. Pharmacia 1985-87; mem. Bd. of Govs. Bofors, Pharmacia, Forsheda, Hasselblad, Volvo, PK Banken and others, mem. Swedish Telecom Admin. Bd; Tech. Adviser Swedish Govt. Ministry of Industry, ASEA, Volvo, and others; Order of the Northern Star 1974, Seraphim Medal of the King of Sweden 1979, Officier, Légion d'honneur 1980, Grand Cross Order of Merit (Fed. Repub. of Germany, France and Spain), Illis Quorum (Swedish Parl.), Honda Discoveries Laureate (Japan) 1980; Dr.Tech. h.c. (Univ. of Gothenberg) 1975; mem. acads. of science and tech. in Sweden, England, Finland, Mexico, Australia and Argentina.

Publications: works on progress in research and technology, energy problems, R & D policy, science and technology. *Leisure interests:* English history, space science. *Address:* Grevturegatan 14, Box 5073, S-102 42 Stockholm, Sweden. *Telephone:* 08-7912917.

HAMBRO, Charles Eric Alexander; British banker; b. 24 July 1930; s. of late Sir Charles Hambro and Pamela Cobbold; m. 1st Rose E. Cotterell 1954 (dissolved 1976), two s. one d.; m. 2nd Cherry Twiss 1976; ed. Eton Coll.; in Coldstream Guards 1949-52; joined Hambros Bank Ltd. 1952, Man. Dir. 1957-65, Deputy Chair. 1965-72, Chair. 1972-83; Chair. Hambros PLC 1983-; Vice-Chair. Guardian Royal Exchange Assurance Co., Taylor Woodrow Ltd.; Chair. Royal Nat. Pension Fund for Nurses 1968; Chair. Sovereign Oil and Gas 1980-; Dir. General Oriental 1984-, Peninsular and Oriental Steam Navigation 1987-; Trustee British Museum 1984-. *Leisure interests:* shooting, racing, flying. *Address:* Dixton Manor, Gotherington, Cheltenham, Glos., GL52 4RB, England. *Telephone:* (024 267) 2011.

HAMBRO, Jocelyn Olaf, M.C.; British banker; b. 7 March 1919; ed. Eton and Trinity Coll., Cambridge; in Coldstream Guards 1939-45; joined Hambros Bank Ltd. 1945; Man. Dir. 1947-72, Chair. 1965-72; Chair. Hambros PLC 1970-83, Pres. 1983-; Gp. Chair. J. O. Hambro & Co. Jan 1987-, Chair. Phoenix Assurance Co. Ltd. 1978-85, Charter Consolidated Ltd. 1982-; Dir. John Jacobs and Co. Ltd., Chichester Diamonds Ltd. *Address:* 101 Eaton Place, London, S.W.1, England.

HAMBRO, Rupert Nicholas; British banker; b. 27 June 1943, London; s. of Jocelyn Olaf Hambro (q.v.) and the late Anne Silvia Muir; m. Mary Robinson Boyer 1970; one s. one d.; ed. Eton Coll., Aix-en-Provence; Man. Dir. J. O. Hambro & Co., with Hambros Bank 1964-86, Chair. 1983-86; Dir. Daily Telegraph PLC, Triton Europe PLC 1988-, Sedgwick Group PLC 1987-; Chair. Asscn. of Int. Bond Dealers 1979-82; Dir. Anglo-American Corpn. of S.A. *Leisure interests:* racing, shooting. *Address:* 30 Queen Anne's Gate, London, SW1H 9AL, England. *Telephone:* 01-222 2020.

HAMBURGER, Christian; Danish doctor; b. 19 Feb. 1904, Copenhagen; s. of Dr. Ove Hamburger and Agnete Barnekow; m. 1st Mary J. Frylensberg 1932; m. 2nd Ilse Levin 1940 (died 1977); two s. one d.; ed. Københavns Universitet; Scientific Asst., Inst. for Gen. Pathology, Univ. of Copenhagen 1932-35; Head, Hormone Dept. Statens Seruminstitut, Copenhagen 1934-74; mem. Advisory Panel Ciba Foundation 1949-73; mem. Advisory Panel on Biological Standardisation, World Health Org. (WHO) 1952-71; Pres. Danish Soc. for Endocrinology 1947-72; Chief Ed. Acta Endocrinologica 1960-73; Alfred Benzon Prize 1960, Pfizer Prize 1964, Thorvald Madsen Prize 1966; Hon. mem. Deutsche Gesellschaft für Endokrinologie 1970, Finnish Soc. for Endocrinology 1970, Danish Soc. for Endocrinology 1972, Swedish Soc. for Endocrinology 1973; Hon. F.R.C.P. Edin.) 1974. *Publications:* Studies on gonadotropic hormones from the hypophysis and chorionic tissue 1933, Hypophyseal, gonadal and adrenal hormones 1950, Hormone Research 1967. *Leisure interests:* literature, painting. *Address:* 62 Slotsvej, DK-2920 Charlottenlund, Copenhagen, Denmark. *Telephone:* (01) 63 31 16.

HAMBURGER, Jean, M.D., PH.D.; French professor of medicine and writer; b. 15 July 1909, Paris; s. of A. Hamburger and M. Marix; m. Catherine Deschamps 1964; two s. one d.; ed. Lycée Carnot and Faculty of Medicine, Sorbonne, Paris; Prof. of Medicine, Univ. of Paris 1956-; Chief of Nephrology Dept., Hôpital Necker, Paris 1958-; Dir. INSERM renal research unit and CNRS lab. for research on graft immunology; Vice-Pres. Foundation for French Medical Research; mem. Inst. de France (Acad. des Sciences) 1974, Nat. Acad. of Medicine 1975, Acad. Française 1985; fmr. Pres. Int. Soc. of Transplantation, Int. Soc. of Nephrology; F.R.C.P. (London, Edinburgh, Canada); Hon. F.R.S.M.; Grand Officier, Légion d'honneur, Prix mondial Cino del Duca 1979. *Publications:* Néphrologie 1966, La transplantation rénale 1970, Structure and Function of the Kidney 1971, La puissance et la fragilité 1972 (translated into 14 languages), L'homme et les hommes 1976, Discovering the Individual 1978, Demain, les autres 1979, Un jour, un homme. ... 1981, Le journal d'Harvey 1983, La raison et la passion 1984, Le dieu foudroyé 1985, Le miel et la ciguë 1986, Monsieur Littré 1988, La plus belle aventure du monde 1988. *Address:* 38 rue Mazarine, Paris 75006, France (Home).

HAMBURGER, Michael Peter Leopold, M.A.; poet and professor of German Literature; b. 22 March 1924, Berlin; s. of late Richard Hamburger and L. (née Hamburg) Hamburger; m. Anne Ellen File 1951; one s. two d.; ed. Westminster School and Christ Church, Oxford; army service 1943-47; freelance writer 1948-52; Asst. Lecturer in German Univ. Coll., London 1952-55; lecturer, then Reader Univ. of Reading 1955-64; Florence Purington Lecturer Mount Holyoake Coll., Mass. 1966-67; Visiting Prof. State Univ. of N.Y., Buffalo 1969, Stony Brook 1971; Visiting Fellow Center for Humanities Wesleyan Univ., Conn. 1970; Visiting Prof. Univ. of S.C. 1973; Regent's Lecturer Univ. of Calif., San Diego 1973; Visiting Prof. Boston Univ. 1975-77; Prof. (part-time) Univ. of Essex 1978; Bollingen Foundation Fellow 1959-61, 1965-66; F.R.S.L. 1972-86; Corresp. mem. Deutsche Akademie für Sprache und Dichtung, Darmstadt 1973, Akademie der Künste, Berlin, Akademie der Schönen Künste, Munich; prizes for translation: Deutsche Akademie für Sprache und Dichtung 1964, Arts Council 1969, Arts Prize, Inter Nationes, Bonn 1976, Medal, Inst. of

Linguists 1977, Schlegel-Tieck Prize, London 1978, 1981, Wilhelm-Heinse Prize (medallion), Mainz 1978, Goethe Medal 1986. *Publications: poetry:* Flowering Cactus 1950, Poems 1950-51 1952, The Dual Site 1958, Weather and Season 1963, Feeding the Chickadees 1968, Penguin Modern Poems (with A. Brownjohn and C. Tomlinson) 1969, Travelling 1969, Travelling I-V 1973, Ownerless Earth 1973, Travelling VI 1975, Real Estate 1977, Moralities 1977, Variations 1981, Collected Poems 1984; *translations:* Poems of Hölderlin 1943, C. Baudelaire, Twenty Prose Poems 1946, L. van Beethoven, Letters, Journals and Conversations 1951, J. C. F. Hölderlin, Selected Verse 1961, G. Trakl, Decline 1952, A. Goes, The Burnt Offering 1956, H. von Hofmannsthal, Poems and Verse Plays (with others) 1961, B. Brecht, Tales from the Calendar 1961, Modern German Poetry 1910-1960 (with C. Middleton) 1962, H. von Hofmannsthal, Selected Plays and Libretti (with others) 1964, G. Büchner, Lenz 1966, H. M. Enzensberger, Poems 1966, G. Grass, Selected Poems (with C. Middleton) 1966, J. C. F. Hölderlin, Poems and Fragments 1967, H. M. Enzensberger, The Poems of Hans Magnus Enzensberger (with J. Rothenberg and the author) 1968, H. M. Enzensberger, Poems for People Who Don't Read Poems 1968, G. Grass, Poems (with C. Middleton) 1969, P. Bischel, And Really Frau Blum Would Very Much Like to Meet the Milkman 1968, G. Eich, Journeys 1968, N. Sachs, Selected Poems 1968, Peter Bischel, Stories for Children 1971, Paul Celan, Selected Poems 1972, East German Poetry (Ed.) 1972, Peter Huchel, Selected Poems 1974, German Poetry 1910-1975 1977, Helmut Heissenbüttel, Texts 1977, Franco Fortini, Poems 1978, An Unofficial Rilke 1981, Peter Huchel, The Garden of Theophrastus 1983, Goethe, Poems and Epigrams 1983; *criticism:* Reason and Energy 1957, From Prophecy to Exorcism 1965, The Truth of Poetry 1970, Hugo von Hofmannsthal 1973, Art as Second Nature 1975, A Proliferation of Prophets 1983, After the Second Flood: essays in modern German Literature 1986; *autobiography:* A Mug's Game 1973. *Address:* c/o John Johnson Ltd., Clerkenwell House, 45/47 Clerkenwell Green, London, EC1R 0HT, England.

HAMBURGER, Viktor, PH.D.; American university professor (retd.); b. 9 July 1900, Landeshut, Germany; s. of Max and Else Hamburger; m. Martha Fricke 1927 (died 1965); two d.; ed. Univs. of Heidelberg, Munich, Freiburg; Instructor, Univ. of Chicago 1932-35; Asst. Prof. of Zoology, Washington Univ., St. Louis 1935-39, Assoc. Prof. 1939-41, Prof. 1941-69, Chair. Dept. of Zoology 1941-66; E. Mallinckrodt Distinguished Service Univ. Prof. 1968-69; Prof. Emer. of Biology 1969-; mem. Nat. Acad. of Sciences; Fellow American Acad. of Arts and Sciences; Hon. Dr. Sc. (Washington); Hon. Ph.D. (Univ. of Uppsala); F. O. Schmitt Medal and Prize in Neuroscience 1976, Wakeman Award in Neurosciences 1978, R. G. Harrison Prize, Int. Soc. of Developmental Biology 1981, Louisa Gross Horwitz Prize 1983, Ralph Gerard Prize 1985, Medal of the Soc. for Neuroscience 1985. *Publications:* A Manual of Experimental Embryology 1942, 1960; over 100 publications in scientific journals. *Address:* Washington University, St. Louis, Mo. 63130; 740 Trinity Avenue, St. Louis, Mo. 63130, U.S.A. (Home).

HAMEED, A. C. S.; Sri Lankan politician; b. 10 April 1929; M.P. for Harispattuwa 1960-; Minister of Foreign Affairs 1977-89, of Educ., Science and Tech. Feb. 1989-; first to hold separate portfolio of foreign affairs; United Nat. Party. *Address:* Ministry of Education, Science and Technology, Colombo, Sri Lanka.

HAMELIN, Louis-Edmond, O.C., M.A., PH.D., D.ÈS L., F.R.S.C.; Canadian researcher and consultant in polar affairs; b. 21 March 1923, St. Didace; m. Colette Lafay 1951; one s. one d.; ed. Laval Univ., Canada and Univs. of Grenoble and Paris, France; Prof. Laval Univ. 1951-78, Dir. Inst. of Geography 1955-61, Founding-Dir. Centre of Northern Studies 1962-72; mem. Legis Ass., Yellowknife, Northwest Territories, Canada 1971-75; Rector Université de Québec, Trois-Rivières 1978-83; Gov. Int. Devt. Research Centre, Ottawa 1984-88; fmr. Visiting Prof. Univs. of Montréal, Ottawa, Toulouse and Abidjan, Côte d'Ivoire; Gov.-Gen. Award 1976; Grand Prix Geography (Paris) 1977; Molson Foundation Prize (Canada) 1982; Human Sciences Prize (Québec) 1987. *Publications:* Illustrated Glossary of Periglacial Phenomena 1967, Atlas du Monde 1967, Canada: A Geographical Perspective 1973, Canadian Nordicity 1979, The Canadian North 1988. *Leisure interests:* travel, mountaineering, photography. *Address:* 1244 Albert-Lozeau, Sillery, Québec, G1T 1H4, Canada. *Telephone:* (418) 6830386.

HAMER, Alan William; Australian business executive; b. 27 Nov. 1917; ed. Oxford Univ.; joined ICI Australia, England 1941, returned to Australia 1942; associated with setting up of new plants; Works Man. Yarraville plant 1950-56; Controller Tech. Dept. 1956-59, Dir. 1959-68; Chair. ICI Group of Cos. India 1968-71, Man. Dir. and Deputy Chair. ICI Australia Ltd. 1971-79; Dir. Tubemakers of Australia, Reckitt and Coleman Australia, Grindlays Australia, EZ Industries, Woodside Petroleum, E.R.A., Rhodes Scholarship 1937. *Leisure interests:* royal and lawn tennis, golf, cricket, skiing, bridge, music. *Address:* Apartment 10A, 29 Queens Road, Melbourne, Vic. 3004, Australia.

HAMER, H.E. Jean Jérôme, O.P.; Belgian ecclesiastic; b. 1 June 1916, Brussels; ordained 1941; consecrated Titular Bishop of Lorium with personal title of Archbishop 1973; cr. Cardinal 1985; Deacon of S. Saba; Prefect of Congregation for Religious and for Secular Insts. 1985-. *Address:* Piazza di S. Uffizio 11, 00193 Rome, Italy. *Telephone:* (06) 698.4121.

HAMER, Hon. Sir Rupert James, K.C.M.G., E.D., LL.M.; Australian solicitor and politician; b. 29 July 1916, Kew, Vic.; m. April Mackintosh 1944; two s. two d.; ed. Melbourne and Geelong Grammar Schools, Univ. of Melbourne; joined Australian Imperial Forces 1940, served 5½ years N. Africa, New Guinea, N.W. Europe; C.O. Vic. Scottish Regt., Citizen Mil. Forces 1954–58; mem. Vic. Legis. Council for E. Yarra 1958–71; Minister for Immigration, Vic. 1962–64, for Local Govt., Vic. 1964–71; mem. Vic. Legis. Assembly for Kew 1971–81; Chief Sec., Deputy Premier, Vic. 1971–72, Premier 1972–81, Treas. and Minister of the Arts 1972–79, Minister of State Devt., Decentralization and Tourism 1979–81; Pres. Victorian Coll. of Arts 1982–; Chair. Vic. State Opera 1982–; Trustee Melbourne Cricket Ground, Yarra Bend Nat. Park 1975–; Hon. LL.D. (Melbourne). *Leisure interests:* tennis, sailing, football, reading, music. *Address:* 39 Monomeath Avenue, Canterbury, Victoria 3126, Australia. *Telephone:* 836-7968.

HAMID, Salah, M.A., PH.D.; Egyptian politician; b. Sept. 1924, Cairo; ed. Univs. of Cairo, Leeds and Edinburgh; Deputy Dir. Nat. Inst. for Admin. and Devt. 1972; Expert, IBRD; Minister of Finance 1976, 1982–86; part-time Prof. of Econs. Faculty of Commerce, Helwan Univ. 1976; consultant, Cen. Bank 1979. *Address:* c/o Ministry of Finance, Sharia Magles El Sha'ab, Lazoughli Square, Cairo, Egypt.

HAMILTON, Richard; British artist; b. 24 Feb. 1922; s. of Peter and Constance Hamilton; m. Terry O'Reilly 1947 (died 1962); one s. one d.; ed. elementary school, evening classes, St. Martin's School of Art, Royal Academy Schools and Slade School of Art; jig and tool draughtsman, Design Unit 1941–42, Electrical & Musical Industries (EMI) 1942–45; exhbn. of Reaper engravings, Gimpel Fils 1950; devised Growth and Form exhbn., Inst. of Contemporary Arts (ICA) 1951; teacher of design, Cen. School of Arts and Crafts 1952–53; mem. Independent Group, ICA 1952–55; Lecturer, Fine Art Dept., King's Coll., Univ. of Durham (later Univ. of Newcastle-upon-Tyne) 1953–66; teacher of Interior Design R.C.A. 1957–61; exhbns. of paintings 1951–55 and 1956–64, Hanover Gallery 1955 and 1964; organized exhbn. of works by Marcel Duchamp, Tate Gallery 1966; exhbn. of Guggenheim reliefs and studies, London 1966; exhbns. in Kassel 1967, New York 1967, Studio Marconi, Milan 1968, Hamburg 1969; exhbn. of Swinging London 1967 and beach scene paintings, London 1969; exhbn. of Cosmetic Studies, Milan 1969, Berlin 1970; retrospective exhbns., Tate Gallery 1970 (seen in Switzerland and Netherlands also), Guggenheim Museum, New York 1973, Nationalgalerie, Berlin 1974, Paintings, Pastels, Prints, London 1975, Amsterdam 1976, Musée Grenoble 1977, Drawings retrospective, Bielefeld 1978, Prints retrospective, Vancouver 1978, Interfaces exhbn., Denmark 1979, Interiors exhbn., London, New York 1980, Paris 1981, Image and Process exhbn., London 1983; William and Noma Copley Foundation award for painting 1960; Joint First Prize, John Moores Liverpool Exhbn. 1969, Talens Prize, Amsterdam 1970, World Print Award 1983. *Publications:* Polaroid Portraits (Vol. I) 1972, (Vol. II) 1977, (Vol. III) 1983, Collected Words 1982, Image and Process 1983, Prints 1939–83 1984. *Address:* Northend Farm, Northend, Oxon., RG9 6LQ, England.

HAMILTON, William Donald, PH.D., F.R.S.; British zoologist; b. 1 Aug. 1936; s. of Archibald M. Hamilton and Bettina M. (Collier) Hamilton; m. Christine A. Friess 1967; three d.; ed. Tonbridge Schools and Univs. of Cambridge and London; Lecturer in Genetics, Imperial Coll. London 1964–77; Prof. of Evolutionary Biology, Museum of Zoology and Div. of Sciences, Biological Univ. of Mich. 1978–84; Royal Soc. Research Prof. Dept. of Zoology and Fellow, New Coll. Oxford 1984–; Foreign mem. American Acad. of Arts and Sciences, Royal Soc. of Sciences of Uppsala; Darwin Medal, Royal Soc. 1988. *Publications:* articles in scientific journals. *Address:* Department of Zoology, South Parks Road, Oxford, OX1 3PS, England.

HAMILTON, Hon. William McLean, P.C., O.C., B.SC.COM.; Canadian executive and politician; b. 23 Feb. 1919, Montreal; m. Ruth Isabel Seeman 1954; ed. Montreal High School and Sir George Williams Univ. (now Concordia Univ.); Gen. Man. Advertising and Sales Executives' Club of Montreal 1949–57; City Councillor, Montreal 1950–57; M.P. 1953–62; Postmaster-Gen. of Canada 1957–62; Pres. Canadian Park & Tilford Distilleries Ltd. 1963–66, British Columbia Int. Trade Fair 1966–67; Chair. Fidelity Life Assurance Co. 1968–85, Dir. 1985–; Chair. Century Insurance Co. of Canada 1968–85; Pres. Vancouver Bd. of Trade 1970–71, Brink-Hamilton Enterprises Ltd. 1970–78; Pres. and C.E.O. Employers' Council of British Columbia 1973–84. *Leisure interest:* boating. *Address:* 5808 Crown Street, Vancouver, B.C. V6N 2B7, Canada (Home).

HAMILTON, William Maxwell, C.B.E., M.AGR.SC., D.SC., F.R.S.N.Z.; New Zealand research scientist; b. 2 July 1909, Warkworth; s. of William Hamilton and Isabella Hamilton; m. Alice A. Morrison 1945; one s. one d.; ed. Warkworth Dist. High School, Auckland Univ., Massey Agric. Coll. and Univ. of N.Z.; appointed to DSIR (Dept. of Scientific and Industrial Research), N.Z. 1936; Asst. Scientific Liaison Officer London 1937–40; Asst. Sec. DSIR 1948, Sec. (title changed to Dir.-Gen. 1963) 1953–71; Commonwealth Foundation Lectureship to E. Africa 1968; Hon. Life mem. Animal Production Soc.; several hon. lectureships; Medal of N.Z. Assen. of Scientists 1970; Hon. D.Sc. (Massey Univ.) 1971. *Publications:* articles in DSIR Bulletin. *Leisure interests:* gardening, music, photography, Little Barrier Island Sanctuary. *Address:* Hamilton Road, R.D.2, Warkworth, New Zealand. *Telephone:* Warkworth 8613.

HAMIYEH, Adel, M.ENG.; Lebanese civil engineer and politician; b. 2? May 1940, Ein-Enoub; s. of Fouad and Jamal Hamiyeh; m. May Bahee Takieddine 1965; two s. one d.; ed. Int. Coll. of Beirut and American Univ of Beirut; Lecturer in Eng., Lebanese Univ. and Beirut Arab Univ.; eng. construction co.; Chair. Bd. State Railways and Public Transpor Authority; Vice-Pres. Arab Union of Railways; mem. Bd. Council fo Devt. and Reconstruction 1977–82; Minister of Finance 1982–84; Prof. o Aluminium Eng., American Univ. of Beirut. *Publication:* Investigation o the Possible Sources of Water Supply in Beirut and the Suburbs 1973 *Address:* Bachir Kassar Street, Tarazi Building, P.O. Box 4591, Beirut Lebanon. *Telephone:* 300345.

HAMLISCH, Marvin, B.A.; American composer; b. 2 June 1944, New York; s. of Max and Lilly (née Schachter) Hamlisch; ed. Queen's Coll. New York; on tour with Groucho Marx 1974–75; made his debut a pianist with Minn. Orchestra 1975. *Compositions include:* Film scores: The Swimmer 1968, Take the Money and Run 1969, Bananas 1971, The Wa We Were 1974, The Sting 1974, Same Time Next Year 1979, Startin Over 1979, Ordinary People 1980, Seems Like Old Times 1980; popula songs: Sunshine, Lollipops and Rainbows 1960, Good Morning Americ 1975, Nobody Does It Better 1977, Starting Over 1979, Sophie's Choic 1982, D.A.R.Y.L. 1985; Broadway musicals: A Chorus Line 1975, They'r Playing Our Song 1979. *Address:* c/o Songwriters' Guild, 276 Fifth Avenue New York, N.Y. 10001, U.S.A.

HAMLYN, Paul Bertrand; British publisher; b. 12 Feb. 1926, Berlin Germany; s. of late Prof. Richard and Mrs. L. (née Hamburg) Hamburger m. 1st Eileen Margaret Watson 1952 (dissolved 1969), 2nd Helen Gues 1970; one s. one d.; ed. St. Christopher's School, Letchworth, Herts.; f Hamlyn Publishing Group; formed Books for Pleasure 1949, Prints fo Pleasure 1960, Records for Pleasure (marketing long-playing classica records), Golden Pleasure Books 1961, Music for Pleasure (EMI) 1965 Paul Hamlyn Group acquired by IPC 1964; joined IPC Bd. with specia responsibility for all book publishing activities; acquired Butterworth an Co. 1968; Dir. IPC 1965–70, Chair. IPC Books, controlling Hamlyn Publish ing Group (fmrly. Chair. Paul Hamlyn Holdings Ltd. and assoc. cos. 1965–70; Joint Man. Dir. News Int. Ltd. 1970–71; f. and Chair. Octopu Publishing Group (now part of Reed Int. PLC.), London, New York Sydney 1971–, Chair. Octopus Books Ltd. 1971–, Mandarin Publishers Hong Kong 1971–; co-f. (with David Frost, q.v.) and Dir. Sundial Publi cations 1973–; co-f. (with Doubleday & Co., New York) and Dir. Octopu Books Int. BV, Netherlands 1973–; Dir. News America, Tigerprint Ltd. News Int. 1971–86, TV-am 1981–83; Co-Chair. Conran Octopus Ltd. 1983– Chair. Heinemann Group of Publishers Ltd. 1985–, Hamlyn Publishing Group 1986–; mem. Council, Inst. of Contemporary Arts 1977; Hon. D Litt. 1988. *Address:* 59 Grosvenor Street, Mayfair, London, W.1, England *Telephone:* 01-493 5841.

HAMMADI, Sadoon; Iraqi economist and politician; b. 22 June 1930 Karbala; m. Lamia Hammadi 1961; five s.; ed. in Beirut, Lebanon and U.S.A.; Prof. of Econs., Univ. of Baghdad 1957; Deputy Head of Econ Research, Nat. Bank of Libya, Tripoli 1961–62; Minister of Agrarian Reform 1963; Econ. Adviser to Presidential Council, Govt. of Syria 1964 Econ. Expert, UN Planning Inst., Syria 1965–68; Pres. Iraq Nat. Oil Co (INOC) 1968–; Minister of Oil and Minerals 1969–74, of Foreign Affairs 1974–83. *Publications:* Towards a Socialist Agrarian Reform in Iraq 1964 Views about Arab Revolution 1969, Memoirs and Views on Oil Issues 1980. *Leisure interests:* swimming, walking, coin collection, reading novels *Address:* c/o Ministry of Foreign Affairs, Baghdad, Karradat Mariam, Iraq

HAMMARSKJÖLD, Knut Olof Hjalmar Akesson, PH.M.; Swedish diplo matist; nephew of the late Dag Hammarskjöld, Sec.-Gen. of the UN; b. 1 Jan. 1922, Geneva, Switzerland; m.; four s.; ed. Stockholm Univ.; entered Foreign Service 1946, served Paris, Vienna, Moscow, Bucharest, Kabul Sofia 1947–55; First Sec. Foreign Office 1955–57; Head of Foreign Relations Dept., Royal Bd. of Civil Aviation, Stockholm 1957–59; Deputy Head Swedish Del. to OEEC, Paris 1959–60; Deputy Sec.-Gen. European Free Trade Assen. (EFTA) 1960–66; Minister Plenipotentiary; Dir.-Gen. of Int Air Transport Assen. (IATA), Montreal 1966–84, Chair. Exec Cttee. 1981–84; Dir.-Gen. Water Inst., Montreal 1985–; mem. Inst of Transport, London; mem. Alexander S. Onassis Public Benefit Foundatior Int. Cttee. for Award of Athens and Olympia Prizes 1977–83; Gov. Atlantic Inst. for Int. Affairs 1983–; Chair. Corporate Bd. SDS Newspaper Con glomerate, Malmö; Hon. Fellow, Canadian Aeronautics and Space Inst. Commdr. Order of the Lion (Finland), Order of the Falcon (1st Class (Iceland), Commdr. Order of Orange-Nassau (Netherlands), Légion d'Honn eur and Order of the Black Star (France), Grand Officer, Order Al-Istiqla (Jordan); Commdr. (1st Class) Order of the North Star (Sweden), NÖR (Sweden), Grand Cross of the Order of Civil Merit (Spain). *Publications* articles on political, economic and aviation topics. *Address:* SDS, Box 145 20121, Malmö, Sweden. *Telephone:* (76) 40-281200.

HAMMEL, Eugene Alfred, PH.D.; American professor of anthropology and demography; b. 18 March 1930, New York; s. of William Hammel and Violet Brookes; m. Joan Marie Swingle 1951; ed. Univ. of Calif., Berkeley field work in archaeology and linguistics, Calif. 1947–51, in ethnography Peru 1957–58, in archaeology and ethnography in New Mexico 1959–61, ir ethnography in Mexico 1963, in Yugoslavia and Greece 1963, 1965–66

Asst. Prof. Univ. of New Mexico 1959-61; Asst. Prof. Univ. of Calif. (Berkeley) 1961-63, Assoc. Prof. 1963-66, Prof. 1966-, Prof. of Anthropology and Demography 1978-, Dir. Quantitative Anthropology Lab. 1974, Chair. Demography 1978-; archival research in Yugoslavia, Hungary, Austria 1983-; mem. N.A.S. *Publications:* Wealth, Authority and Prestige in the Ica Valley, Peru 1962, Ritual Relations and Alternative Social Structures in the Balkans 1968, The Pink Yoyo: Occupational Mobility in Belgrade c. 1915-65 1969, Statistical Studies of Historical Social Structure (with Wachter and Laslett) 1978; approximately 100 articles. *Leisure interests:* hiking, guitar, carpentry, photography. *Address:* Department of Anthropology, University of California, Berkeley, Calif. 94720, U.S.A. *Telephone:* 415-642-3391.

HAMMER, Armand, B.S., M.D.; American petroleum executive; b. 21 May 1898, New York; s. of Dr. Julius Hammer and Rose Robinson; m. 1st Baroness Olga von Root 1927; one s.; m. 2nd Angela Zevely 1943; m. 3rd Frances Barrett 1956; one s.; ed. Columbia Univ.; Mil. Service, U.S. Army Medical Corps 1918-19; Pres. Allied American Corpn., New York 1923-25, A. Hammer Pencil Co. (New York, London, Moscow) 1925-30, Hammer Galleries Inc., New York 1930-, J. W. Dant Distilling Co. 1943-54; Pres. and Chair. of Bd. Mutual Broadcasting System (New York) 1957-58; Chair. of Bd. and C.E.O. Occidental Petroleum Corpn., Los Angeles 1957-; Chair. M. Knoedlers and Co., Inc., New York 1972-; Pres. Foundation of Int. Inst. of Human Rights, Geneva 1977-; mem. Advisory Bd. of Inst. of Peace 1950-54, Bd. of Govs. Eleanor Roosevelt Cancer Foundation 1960-, Bd. of Dirs. City Nat. Bank (Beverley Hills) 1962-71, Bd. of Trustees Eleanor Roosevelt Memorial Foundation 1973-74, Bd. of Dirs. Canadian Occidental Petroleum Ltd. 1964-, Bd. of Dirs. Raffinerie Belge de Pétroles (RBP) 1968-79, Public Advisory Cttee. on U.S. Trade Policy 1968-69, Nat. Petroleum Council 1968-, Exec. Cttee. Econ. Devt. Bd., Los Angeles 1968-73, Exec. Bd. of Dirs. UN Assen. of Los Angeles 1969-, Bd. of Dirs. UN Assen. of U.S.A. 1970- (Bd. of Govs. 1976-), of the U.S.-U.S.S.R. Trade and Econ. Council, Inc. 1973-, of the Assocs. of Harvard Business School 1975-, of the American Petroleum Inst. 1975-, of the Salk Inst. for Biological Studies (mem. Bd. of Trustees and Chair. Exec. Cttee.) 1969-; Dir. Cities Service 1982-, Southland Corpn. 1983-; mem. Advisory Bd., Center for Strategic and Int. Studies, Georgetown Univ. 1981-; Founder and Chair., Armand Hammer Coll. of American West, New Mexico 1981-; Chair. Pres's. Cancer Panel; Founder and mem. Los Angeles Music Center 1969-; mem. Univ. Bd., Pepperdine Univ., Calif. 1979-; mem. Nat. Support Council, U.S. Cttee. for UNICEF, New York 1980-; Hon. mem. Bd. of Dirs. Florida Nat. Bank of Jacksonville 1966-72; Hon. Corresp. mem. Royal Acad. of Arts 1975-; Hon. mem. Royal Scottish Acad. 1981-; Hon. LL.D. (Pepperdine) 1978, (South Eastern Univ.) 1978, (Columbia) 1978, (Aix-en-Provence) 1981; Hon. D.Hum.Litt. (Colorado) 1979; Hon. Dr. of Public Service (Salem Coll.) 1979; Humanitarian Award, Eleanor Roosevelt Cancer Foundation 1962; Commdr., Order of the Crown (Belgium) 1969; Commdr., Order of Andres Bellos (Venezuela) 1975; Order of the Aztec Eagle (Mexico) 1977; Officier, Légion d'honneur 1978; Order of Friendship between Peoples (U.S.S.R.) 1978; Royal Order of Polar Star, Sweden 1979; Grand Officer, Order of Merit (Italy) 1981, Gold Medal of Italy 1983, Commdr.'s Cross, Légion d'honneur 1983, Commdr., Ordre des Arts et des Lettres 1988, numerous other awards. *Publications:* Quest of the Romanoff Treasure 1932, Hammer: Witness to History (autobiog.) 1987. *Address:* Occidental Petroleum Corporation, 10889 Wilshire Boulevard, Suite 1500, Los Angeles, Calif. 90024, U.S.A. (Office). *Telephone:* 213-879-1700 (Office).

HAMMERSHAIMB, Erling, D.PHIL., D.THEOL.; Danish professor (retd.); b. 3 March 1904, Aalberg; s. of Hjalmar Hammershaimb and Margrethe Kerstens; m. Ida Breum 1946; one s. two d.; ed. Univ. of Copenhagen; Asst. Univ. of Copenhagen 1936-41; Prof. of Old Testament, Univ. of Aarhus 1942-63, Prof. of Semitic Philology 1963-74, Rector 1963-67; mem. Royal Danish Acad., Nathan Söderblom sälskapet; Commdr. Order of Dannebrog; Dr. theol. h.c. (Uppsala). *Publications include:* Amos 1946, The Ethiopic Book of Enok 1956, Genesis: Linguistic Analysis 1957, Some Aspects of Old Testament Prophecy from Isaiah to Malachi 1966, Ibn Khaldun 1982. *Address:* Jens Munksvej 25, 8200 Aarhus N, Denmark. *Telephone:* 06-168840.

HAMMERSLEY, John Michael, D.SC., F.R.S.; British mathematician; b. 21 March 1920, Helensburgh, Scotland; s. of Guy Hugh and Marguerite (née Whitehead) Hammersley; m. Shirley Gwendolene (née Bakewell) Hammersley 1951; two s.; ed. Sedbergh School, Emmanuel Coll., Cambridge; Maj. R.A. 1940-46; Prin. Scientific Officer Theoretical Physics Div., A.E.R.E., Harwell 1955-59; Graduate Asst. Design and Analysis of Scientific Experiments, Oxford 1948-55, Sr. Research Fellow Trinity Coll. 1960-69, Sr. Research Officer, Inst. of Econ. 1960-69, Reader in Math. Statistics 1969-87, Emer. Reader 1987-, Professorial Fellow 1969-87, Emer. Fellow 1987-; numerous short appointments in U.S.A. 1952-84; Rouse Ball Lecturer, Cambridge 1980; Fullbright Fellow 1955, Erskine Fellow 1978; Von Neumann Medal (Brussels) 1966, IMA Gold Medal 1984; mem. various socs. *Publications:* Monte Carlo Methods (with D. C. Handscomb) 1964. *Address:* Trinity College, Oxford (Office); 11 Eynsham Road, Oxford, OX2 9BS, England (Home). *Telephone:* 0865-862181 (Home).

HAMMES, Gordon G., PH.D.; American professor of chemistry and university vice-chancellor; b. 10 Aug. 1934, Fond du Lac, Wis.; s. of Jacob Hammes and Betty (Sadoff) Hammes; m. Judith Ellen Frank 1959; one s. two d.; ed. Princeton Univ. and Univ. of Wisconsin; Postdoctoral Fellow Max Planck Inst. für physikalische Chemie Göttingen, Fed. Repub. of Germany 1959-60; instructor, subsequently Assoc. Prof. M.I.T., Cambridge, Mass. 1960-65; Prof., Cornell Univ. 1965-88, Chair. Dept. of Chem. 1970-75, Horace White Prof. of Chem. and Biochemistry 1975-88, Dir. Biotechnical Program 1983-88; Prof., Univ. of Calif., Santa Barbara 1988-, Vice-Chancellor for Academic Affairs 1988-; mem. Physiological Chem. Study Section, Physical Biochemistry Study Section, Training Grant Cttee., Nat. Insts. of Health; mem. Bd. of Counsellors, Nat. Cancer Inst. 1976-80, Advisory Council, Chem. Dept., Princeton 1970-75, Polytechnic Inst., New York 1977-78, Boston Univ. 1977-85; mem. American Chem. Soc., American Soc. of Biochemistry and Molecular Biology, N.A.S., American Acad. of Arts and Sciences. *Publications:* Principles of Chemical Kinetics, Enzyme Catalysis and Regulation, Chemical Kinetics: Principles and Selected Topics (with I. Amdur); articles. *Address:* 1090 Via Los Padres, Santa Barbara, Calif. 93111, U.S.A.

HAMMES, Michael Noel, M.B.A.; American business executive; b. 25 Dec. 1941, Evanston, Ill.; s. of Ferdinand Hammes and Winifred Hammes; m. Lenore Lynn Forbes 1964; three s. two d.; ed. Georgetown Univ., New York Univ.; Asst. Controller, Ford Motor Assembly Div. 1974, Plant Man., Ford Wixom Assembly Plant 1975, Man. Program Planning, Ford Automotive Ass. Div. 1976, Dir. Int. Business Planning, Int. Operations, Ford 1977, Man. Dir. and Pres., Ford Motor Co. of Mexico 1979, Vice-Pres. Truck Operations, Ford of Europe 1983; Vice-Pres., Int. Operations, Chrysler Motors Corpn. 1986-. *Leisure interests:* skiing, tennis, golf, antique cars. *Address:* Chrysler Motors Corporation, 12000 Chrysler Drive, Highland Park, Mo. 48288-1919 (Office); 5105 Franklin Road, Bloomfield Hills, Mo. 48013, U.S.A. (Home).

HAMMOND, George Simms, B.S., M.S., PH.D.; American professor of chemistry; b. 22 May 1921, Auburn, Me.; s. of Oswald K. Hammond and Majorie Thomas; m. 1st Marian Reese 1945 (divorced 1977); three s. two d. two step-d.; m. 2nd Eva Menger 1977; ed. Bates Coll. of Lewiston, Maine and Harvard Univ.; Asst. Prof. of Chem., Iowa State Univ. 1948-52, Assoc. Prof. 1952-56, Prof. 1956-58; Prof. of Organic Chem., Calif. Inst. of Tech. 1958-64, Arthur Amos Noyes Prof. of Chem. 1964-, Chair. Div. of Chem. and Chemical Eng. 1968-72; Vice-Chancellor Sciences, Univ. of Calif., Santa Cruz 1972-74, Prof. of Chemistry 1972-78, Assoc. Dir. for Corporate Research, Allied Corpn. 1978-80, Dir. Integrated Chemical Systems Lab. 1983-85; Exec. Dir. for Bioscience, Metals and Ceramics 1985; Foreign Sec. N.A.S. 1974-78; mem. American Acad. of Arts and Sciences; Hon. D.Sc. (Wittenburg Univ., Springfield, Ohio) 1972; Dr. h.c. (State Univ. of Ghent) 1973, (Bates Coll., Lewiston, Maine) 1973, (Georgetown Univ.) 1985; A.C.S. Award in Petroleum Chem. 1961, Edward Curtis Franklin Memorial Award for Outstanding Contributions to Chem. 1964, James Flack Norris Award in Physical Organic Chem. 1968, E. Harris Harbison Award for Gifted Teaching, Danforth Foundation 1971, A.C.S. Award in Chemical Education 1974; Priestly Medallist 1976, A.C.S. 1976, Golden Plate Award, American Acad. of Achievement 1976. *Publications:* Co-author: Quantitative Organic Analysis 1957, Organic Chemistry 1959, Advances in Photochemistry (Co-editor) 1967, Elements of Organic Chemistry 1967, Chemical Dynamics 1968, Annual Survey of Photochemistry 1969, Models in Chemical Science 1970; and 250 papers and reviews. *Leisure interests:* family, golf, reading. *Address:* Allied Corpn., Box 1021R, Morristown, NJ 07960 (Office); 43 Noe Avenue, Madison, NJ 07940, U.S.A. (Home). *Telephone:* 201 455 2449 (Office); (201) 377-9279 (Home).

HAMMOND, Jay S.; American state governor; b. 21 July 1922, Troy, N.Y.; m. Bella Gardiner; two d.; ed. Scotia, New York High School, Univ. of Alaska; served U.S. Navy 1942-46, Marine Fighter Pilot, Capt.; Bush Pilot 1946-48; Pilot for U.S. Fish and Wildlife Service 1948-56; fisherman, guide and air taxi operator 1956-; mem. Alaska House of Reps. 1959-65, Chair. Resources Cttee., Republican Party Whip; Man. Bristol Bay Borough 1965-67, Mayor 1972; mem. Alaska Senate 1967-72, Majority Whip, Majority Leader, Chair. Rules and Resources Cttees., Pres. of Senate; Gov. of Alaska 1975-83. *Publications:* various poems. *Address:* c/o State Capitol, Juneau, Alaska, U.S.A. *Telephone:* (907) 465-3500.

HAMMOND, Dame Joan, D.B.E., C.M.G.; Australian singer (retd.); b. 24 May 1912, Christchurch, New Zealand; d. of late Samuel H. and Hilda M. Blandford Hammond; ed. Presbyterian Ladies Coll., Pymble, Sydney and Sydney Conservatorium of Music (violin and singing); fmr. mem. Sydney Philharmonic Orchestra and sports writer, Daily Telegraph, Sydney; first public (singing) appearance, Sydney 1929; London début in Messiah 1938; operatic début, Vienna 1939; has appeared as guest artist at Royal Opera House, Covent Garden, Sadlers Wells, Vienna State Opera, Bolshoi Theatre, Moscow, New York City Center, Netherlands Opera, Barcelona Liceo, etc.; world tours have included Europe, U.S.A., Canada, Australasia, India, S. Africa and U.S.S.R.; repertoire includes: Aida, Madame Butterfly, Tosca, Othello, Don Carlos, La Traviata, La Bohème, Turandot, Tannhäuser, Lohengrin, and Die Zauberflöte; Head of Vocal Studies, Victorian Coll. of Arts; records for HMV (fmrly. for Columbia); Hon. D. Mus. (Western Australia) 1979; Coronation Medal 1953; Sir Charles Santley Award, Worshipful Co. of Musicians 1970. *Publication:* A Voice, A Life 1970. *Leisure interests:* golf, yachting, swimming, writing, reading. *Address:* 46 Lansell Road, Toorak, Vic. 3142, Australia.

HAMMOND, Nicholas Geoffrey Lempriere, C.B.E., D.S.O., F.B.A.; British professor of Greek; b. 15 Nov. 1907, Ayr, Scotland; s. of James Vavasor Hammond and Dorothy Hammond; m. Margaret Campbell Townley 1938; two s. three d.; ed. Fettes Coll., Edinburgh, Gonville and Caius Coll., Cambridge, British School of Archaeology, Athens; Fellow of Clare Coll., Cambridge 1930-54, Tutor 1947-54; Headmaster, Clifton Coll., Bristol 1954-62; Prof. of Greek, Univ. of Bristol 1962-73, Prof. Emer. 1973-; Visiting Prof. Reed Coll., St. Olaf Coll., Univ. of Wis. Haverford Coll., Swarthmore Coll., Univ. of Pa., Trinity Coll., Hartford, Univ. of Adelaide, Univ. of Auckland, Univ. of Ioannina, Univ. of Newcastle, N.S.W.; Fellow, Inst. of Advanced Study, Princeton, The Inst. for Research in the Humanities, Madison, The Nat. Humanities Center, The Nat. Hellenic Research Foundation, Carleton Coll., Minn.; Hon. Fellow Clare Coll. 1973-; Hon. D. Litt. (Univ. of Wis., St. Olaf Coll., Carleton Coll.); Officer of the Royal Hellenic Order of the Phoenix. *Publications:* History of Greece to 322 B.C. 1959, Epirus 1967, Studies in Greek History 1973, History of Macedonia I 1972, II 1980, III 1988, The Classical Age of Greece 1975, Migrations and Invasions of Greece 1976, Alexander the Great 1980, Atlas of the Greek and Roman World 1981, Venture into Greece: with the Guerrillas 1943-44 1983, Three Historians of Alexander 1983, The Macedonian State 1989. *Leisure interests:* gardening, walking. *Address:* 3 Belvoir Terrace, Trumpington Road, Cambridge, CB2 2AA, England. *Telephone:* 0223-357151.

HAMMOND INNES, Ralph, C.B.E.; British author; b. 15 July 1913, Horsham, Sussex; s. of late William Hammond and Dora Beatrice Innes; m. Dorothy Mary Lang 1937; Financial News 1934-40; R.A. 1940-46; Hon. D. Litt. *Publications:* Wreckers Must Breathe 1940, The Trojan Horse 1940, Attack Alarm 1941, Dead and Alive 1946, The Lonely Skier 1947, The Killer Mine 1947, Maddon's Rock 1948, The Blue Ice 1948, The White South 1949, The Angry Mountain 1950, Air Bridge 1951, Campbell's Kingdom 1952, The Strange Land 1954, The Mary Deare 1956, The Land God Gave to Cain 1958, Harvest of Journeys 1960, The Doomed Oasis 1960, Atlantic Fury 1962, Scandinavia 1963, The Strode Venturer 1965, Sea and Islands 1967, The Conquistadors 1969, Levkas Man 1971, Hammond Innes Introduces Australia 1971, Golden Soak 1973, North Star 1974, The Big Footprints 1977, The Last Voyage 1978, Solomons Seal 1980, The Black Tide 1982, High Stand 1985, Hammond Innes' East Anglia 1986, Medusa 1988; works translated into most languages; *Films:* Snowbound, Hell Below Zero, Campbell's Kingdom, The Wreck of the Mary Deare, Golden Soak (TV), Levkas Man (TV). *Leisure interests:* cruising and ocean racing, forestry. *Address:* Ayres End, Kersey, Suffolk, England. *Telephone:* (0473) 82 3294.

HÁMORI, Csaba; Hungarian politician; b. 22 Nov. 1948, Budakeszi; ed. Budapest Tech. Univ.; Asst. lecturer 1973-75; Sec. Communist Youth League of Tech. Univ. 1975; Leader CYL Cen. Cttee., Org. Dept. 1976, First Sec. CYL Budapest Cttee. 1977-80; First Sec. Budapest Dist. XIX HSWP Cttee. 1980-84; First Sec. CYL Cen. Cttee. 1984-; mem. HSWP Cen. Cttee. 1984-, mem. Political Cttee. 1985-; M.P. 1985-88, First Sec. HSWP County Pest Cttee. 1988-; Labour Order of Merit 1983. *Address:* Hungarian Communist Youth League, Budapest XIII, Kun Béla rakpart 37/38, Hungary. *Telephone:* 403-940.

HAMPE, Michael, DR.PHIL.; German theatre, opera and television director and actor; b. 3 June 1935, Heidelberg; s. of Hermann and Annemarie Hampe; m. Sibylle Hauck 1971; one d.; ed. Falckenberg Schule, Munich, Univs. of Vienna and Munich and Syracuse Univ., U.S.A.; Deputy Dir. Schauspielhaus, Zürich 1965-70; Intendant, Nat. Theatre, Mannheim 1972-75, Cologne Opera 1975-85; directs opera at La Scala, Milan, Covent Garden, London, Paris Opera, Salzburg and Edinburgh Festivals, Munich, Stockholm, Cologne, Geneva, Brussels, Zürich, San Francisco, Sydney, Los Angeles; directs drama at Bavarian State Theatre, Munich Schauspielhaus, Zürich, etc.; directs and acts in film and TV; Prof. State Music Acad., Cologne and Cologne Univ.; theatre-bldg. consultant; Bundesverdienstkreuz. *Address:* Offenbachplatz 1, 5000 Köln 1, Federal Republic of Germany. *Telephone:* 2076-201.

HAMPSHIRE, Sir Stuart, Kt., F.B.A.; British university professor; b. 1 Oct. 1914, Healing, Lincs.; s. of George N. Hampshire and Marie West; m. 1st Renée Orde-Lees 1962 (died 1980); m. 2nd Nancy Cartwright 1985, two d.; ed. Repton School and Balliol Coll., Oxford; Fellow, All Souls Coll., Oxford 1936-45; service in army and Foreign Office 1940-46; lecturer in Phil. Univ. Coll., London 1947-50; Fellow, New Coll., Oxford 1950-55; Research Fellow, All Souls Coll., Oxford 1955-60; Prof. of Phil., Univ. Coll., London 1960-63; Prof. and Chair. Dept. of Phil., Princeton Univ. 1963-70; Warden of Wadham Coll., Oxford 1970-84; Prof. Stanford Univ. 1985-; Fellow, British Acad., American Acad. of Arts and Sciences; Hon. D.Litt (Glasgow) 1973. *Publications:* Spinoza 1951, Thought and Action 1959, Freedom of the Individual 1965, Modern Writers and Other Essays 1969, Freedom of Mind and Other Essays 1971, Morality and Pessimism 1972, The Socialist Idea (joint ed.) 1975, Two Theories of Morality 1977, Public and Private Morality (ed.) 1978, Morality and Conflict 1983. *Address:* 334 Laurel Avenue, Menlo Park, Calif. 94025, U.S.A.; 79 Old High Street, Headington, Oxford, England.

HAMPSHIRE, Susan; British actress; b. 12 May 1942; d. of George Kenneth Hampshire and June Hampshire; m. 1st Pierre Granier-Deferre 1967 (dissolved 1974), one s. (one d. deceased); m. 2nd Eddie Kulukundis 1981; ed. Hampshire School, Knightsbridge. Hon. D.Litt. (City Univ., London 1984, (St. Andrews) 1986. *Stage roles include:* Expresso Bongo 1958, Follow that Girl 1960, Fairy Tales of New York 1961, Marion Dangerfield in Ginger Man 1963, Kate Hardcastle in She Stoops to Conquer 1966, On Approval 1966, Mary in The Sleeping Prince 1968, Nora in A Doll's House 1972, Katharina in The Taming of the Shrew 1974, Peter in Peter Pan 1974, Jeannette in Romeo and Jeannette 1975, Rosalind in As You Like It 1975, Miss Julie 1975, Elizabeth in The Circle 1976, Ann Whitefield in Man and Superman 1977, Siri Von Essen in Tribades 1978, Victorine in An Audience Called Edouard 1978, Irene in The Crucifer of Blood 1979, Ruth Carson in Night and Day 1979, Elizabeth in The Revolt 1980, Stella Drury in House Guest 1981, Elvira in Blithe Spirit 1986, Marie Stopes in Married Love. *TV roles:* Andromeda, Fleur Forsyte in The Forsyte Saga (Emmy Award for Best Actress 1970), Becky Sharp in Vanity Fair (Emmy Award for Best Actress 1973), Sarah Churchill, Duchess of Marlborough, in The First Churchills (Emmy Award for Best Actress 1971), Glencora Palliser in The Pallisers, Lady Melford in Dick Turpin 1980, Madeline Neroni in The Barchester Chronicles 1982, Martha in Leaving 1984, Martha in Leaving II 1985, Going to Pot 1985. *Films include:* During One Night 1961, The Three Lives of Thomasina 1963, Night Must Fall 1964, Wonderful Life 1964, Paris in August, The Fighting Prince of Donegal 1966, Monte Carlo or Bust 1969, Rogan, David Copperfield, Living Free 1972, A Time for Loving 1972, Malpertius (E. Poe Prizes du Film Fantastique, Best Actress) 1972, Neither the Sea Nor the Sand, Roses and Green Peppers, Bang. *Publications:* Susan's Story (autobiographical account of dyslexia) 1981, The Maternal Instinct, Lucy Jane at the Ballet 1985, Lucy Jane Makes a Film 1989, Trouble Free Gardening 1989. *Leisure interests:* gardening, music, studying antique furniture. *Address:* c/o Midland Bank Ltd., 92 Kensington High Street, London, W8 4SH, England. *Telephone:* 01-937 0962.

HAMPSON, Norman, M.A.; British academic; b. 8 April 1922, Leyland, Lancs.; s. of Frank Hampson and Elizabeth Jane (née Fazackerley); m. Jacqueline Gardin 1948; two d.; ed. Manchester Grammar School and Univ. Coll. Oxford; war service in R.N. and Free French Navy 1941-47; Lecturer and Sr. Lecturer in French History, Univ. of Manchester 1948-67; Prof. of Modern History, Univ. of Newcastle upon Tyne 1967-74; Prof. of History, Univ. of York 1974-; D. de l'Univ. (Paris). *Publications:* La Marine de l'An II 1959, A Social History of the French Revolution 1963, The Enlightenment 1968, The Life and Opinions of Maximilien Robespierre 1974, Danton 1978, Will and Circumstance: Montesquieu, Rousseau and the French Revolution 1983, Prelude to Terror 1988. *Leisure interest:* gardening. *Address:* 305 Hull Road, York, YO1 3LB, England.

HAMPTON, Christopher James, M.A., F.R.S.L. British playwright; b. 26 Jan. 1946, Fayal, the Azores, Portugal; s. of Bernard Patrick and Dorothy Patience (née Herrington) Hampton; m. Laura Margaret de Holesch 1971; two d.; ed. Lancing Coll., New Coll., Oxford; wrote first play When Did You Last See Your Mother? 1964; Resident Dramatist, Royal Court Theatre 1968-70; freelance writer 1970-; Evening Standard Award for best comedy 1970, 1983 and for best play 1986; Plays and Players London Critics' Award for best play 1970, 1973, 1985; Los Angeles Drama Critics Circle Award 1974; Lawrence Olivier Award for Best Play 1986; New York Drama Critic's Circle Award for Best Foreign Play 1987, Writers Guild of America Screenplay Award 1989, Oscar for Best Adapted Screenplay 1989. *Publications:* When Did You Last See Your Mother? 1967, Total Eclipse 1969, The Philanthropist 1970, Savages 1973, Treats 1976, Able's Will (TV) 1978, The History Man (TV adaptation of novel by Malcolm Bradbury, q.v.) 1981, The Portage to San Cristobal of A.H. (play adaptation of novel by George Steiner) 1983, Tales from Hollywood 1983; The Honorary Consul (film adaptation of a novel by Graham Greene, q.v.) 1983, Les Liaisons Dangereuses (adaptation of a novel by Laclos) 1985, Hotel du Lac (TV adaptation of a novel by Anita Brookner, q.v.) 1986, The Good Father (film adaptation of a novel by Peter Prince) 1986, The Wolf at the Door (film) 1986. *Translations include:* Marya (Babel) 1967, Uncle Vanya, Hedda Gabler 1970, A Doll's House 1971 (film 1974), Don Juan 1972, Tales from the Vienna Woods 1977 (film 1979), Don Juan Comes Back from the War 1978, The Wild Duck 1980, Ghosts 1983, Tartuffe 1984. *Leisure interests:* travel, cinema. *Address:* 2 Kensington Park Gardens, London, W.11, England. *Telephone:* 01-229 2188.

HAMRE, Gen. Sverre Ludvig Borgund; Norwegian army officer (retd.); b. 19 Oct. 1918, Bergen; s. of Olav and Borghild (née Borgund) Hamre; m. Elna Kristiansen 1944; one s. one d.; ed. War Academy; served in Norway 1940; Norwegian Brigade Scotland 1941; Platoon Leader and Co. Commdr. 4th Battalion Welsh Regt. in France, Netherlands, Belgium and Germany 1944; Staff Officer, Army Command 1947, Norwegian Brigade in Germany 1949, Northern Norway 1953; Staff Officer, Allied Forces Northern Europe 1955, Planning Staff NATO Standing Group 1958; Commandant Army Staff Coll. 1961; 2nd in Command, The Brigade in Northern Norway 1964; Logistics, Army Command 1965; Dir. Gen. Logistics and Procurement, Ministry of Defence 1967; Commdr. Allied Forces North Norway 1974; Chief of Defence 1977-83; Pres. NATO Mil. Cttee. 1982-83; Consultant 1983-; Commdr. with Star, Order of St. Olav, Grand Commdr. of Victoria Order and several other Norwegian and foreign decorations. *Leisure interests:* fishing, hunting. *Address:* Myrhaùgen 27, Oslo 7, Norway (Home). *Telephone:* 50-19-83 (Home).

HAMZAH, Tengku Tan Sri Datuk Razaleigh (see Razaleigh).

HAMZEH, Zaid, B.SC.; Jordanian doctor and politician; b. 1932, Salt; ed. Univs. of Cairo and London; held many posts in Ministry of Health; Dir. of Ear, Nose and Throat Hospital 1965; ran private clinic 1965–; Minister of Health 1985–. *Address:* Ministry of Health, P.O.B. 86, Amman, Jordan. *Telephone:* 665131.

HAN BOPING; Chinese politician; Deputy Mayor of Beijing; Pres. China Kanghua Devt. Corpn. Dec. 1987–. *Address:* Beijing Municipal Government, Beijing, People's Republic of China.

HAN GUANG; Chinese politician; b. 1912, Jilin Prov; joined CCP *c.* 1930; mem., N.E. China People's Govt. 1949–53; Deputy Sec., Luda (Port Arthur and Dairen) Municipality CCP Cttee. 1949; Mayor of Luda 1950–54; mem. Nat. Econ. Affairs Council (NEAC) 1953–54, Vice-Chair. Financial and Econ. Affairs Cttee., NEAC (abolished 1954) 1954; Chair. Heilongjiang Prov. People's Govt. 1954–55; Deputy Sec. Heilongjiang Prov. CCP Cttee. 1954–55, Second Sec. 1955–56; Gov. of Heilongjiang 1955–56; alt. mem. 8th CCP Cen. Cttee. 1956–Cultural Revolution; Vice-Chair. State Science and Tech. Comm., State Council, and mem. State Scientific Planning Comm., State Council 1957–Cultural Revolution; Chair. Chinese Section, Sino-Soviet Comm. for Tech. and Scientific Co-operation 1959; mem. Standing Cttee., 3rd NPC 1965–Cultural Revolution; disappeared 1967; mem. Standing Cttee., 5th CPPCC 1978–; Vice-Chair. State Capital Construction Comm., State Council (probably in post 1975–) 1978–81, Chair. 1981–; mem. 11th CCP Cen. Cttee., 1978, 12th Cen. Cttee. CCP 1982–87; Pres. Soc. for Study of Econs. of Capital Construction 1980–; Vice-Chair. Cen. Patriotic Sanitation Campaign Cttee., Cen. Cttee. CCP 1981–; Sec. Comm. for Inspecting Discipline CCP 1982–87; mem. Cen. Party Consolidation Guidance Comm. 1983–. *Address:* c/o State Council, Beijing, People's Republic of China.

HAN NINGFU; Chinese politician; Sec.-Gen. People's Govt., Hubei Prov. 1950; Deputy Dir. Wuhan Iron and Steel Complex and Sec. its CCP Cttee. 1957, Dir. of Complex 1961; Vice-Gov. Hubei 1964–Cultural Revolution; Sec. CCP Cttee., Hubei 1973–81; Vice-Chair. Prov. Revolutionary Cttee., Hubei 1973–79; Second Pres. Party School, Hubei 1974–; Gov. of Hubei 1980–82; Second Sec. CCP Cttee., Hubei 1981–83; Chair. Prov. People's Congress, Hubei 1983–86; mem. Cen. Advisory Comm. 1985–, Presidium 6th NPC 1983–. *Address:* Office of the Provincial Governor, Wuhan, Hubei Province, People's Republic of China.

HAN PEIXIN; Chinese politician and party official; b. 1923; Vice-Chair. Prov. Revolutionary Cttee., Jiangsu 1975–77; mem. Standing Cttee., CCP Cttee., Jiangsu Prov. 1976; Sec. CCP Cttee., Jiangsu 1977–81; Vice-Minister of Light Industry 1978–81; Sec. CCP Cttee., Jiangsu 1981– (leading Sec. 1983–); Acting Gov. Jiangsu Prov. 1982–83; mem. Cen. Cttee. of CCP 1982–, Presidium 6th NPC 1983–. *Address:* Office of the Provincial Governor, Nanjing, Jiangsu Province, People's Republic of China.

HAN RUIJIE; Chinese party official; alt. mem. 12th CCP Cen. Cttee. 1982–87. *Address:* c/o Chinese Communist Party Central Committee, Beijing, People's Republic of China.

HAN SHAO GONG; Chinese writer; b. 1 Jan. 1953, Chang Sha; s. of Han Ke Xian and Zhang Jing Xing; m. Liang Yu Li 1980; one d.; ed. Hunan Teacher's Univ.; Council mem. Chinese Writer's Asscn. 1984; Vice-Chair. Hunan Youth Union 1985; Prize for Best Chinese Stories 1980, 1981. *Publications:* Biography of Ren Bi Shi 1979, Selection of Stories: Yue Nan 1981, Flying Across the Blue Sky 1983, New Stories 1986, To Face the Mystical and Wide World (selection of articles) 1985, The Other Shore (selection of prose pieces) 1988; trans: The Unbearable Lightness of Being 1987; also film script, Deaf Mute and His Suona 1984. *Leisure interests:* Chinese handwriting, violin, basketball. *Address:* Hunan Literature Federation, Chang Sha, Hunan, People's Republic of China. *Telephone:* 27275.

HAN SUYIN (Mrs. Elizabeth Comber), M.B., B.S., L.R.C.P., M.R.C.S.; British medical practitioner and author; b. 12 Sept. 1917, China; d. of Y. T. Chow and M. Denis; m. 1st Gen. P. H. Tang 1938 (died 1947), one d.; m. 2nd L. F. Comber 1952 (divorced 1968); ed. Yenching Univ., Peking, Univ. of Brussels, Belgium, Royal Free Hospital, London Univ.; in London 1945–49; employed Queen Mary Hospital, Hong Kong 1948–52, Johore Bahru Hospital, Malaya 1952–55; pvt. medical practice 1955–63; Lecturer in Contemporary Asian Literature, Nanyang Univ., Singapore 1958–60. *Publications:* Destination Chungking 1942, A Many-Splendoured Thing 1952, . . . And the Rain My Drink 1956, The Mountain is Young 1958, Cast but One Shadow 1962, Winter Love 1962, The Four Faces 1963, The Crippled Tree (autobiog.) 1965, A Mortal Flower (autobiog.) 1966, China in the Year 2001 1967, Birdless Summer (autobiog.) 1968, Morning Deluge—Mao Tse-tung and the Chinese Revolution 1972, Wind in the Tower 1976, Lhasa, the Open City 1977, My House has Two Doors 1980, Phoenix Harvest 1980, Till Morning Comes 1982, The Enchantress (novel) 1985, A Share of Loving (autobiog.) 1987. *Leisure interests:* botany, riding, swimming, lecturing. *Address:* c/o Jonathan Cape, 32 Bedford Square, London, W.C.1, England.

HAN TIANSHI; Chinese party official; Sec. Cen. Discipline Inspection Comm., CCP Cen. Cttee. 1982–87. *Address:* People's Republic of China.

HAN XU; Chinese diplomatist; mem. Protocol Dept., Ministry of Foreign Affairs 1959, Deputy Dir. 1969, Dir. 1972–73; Counsellor Chinese Embassy, U.S.S.R. 1964–65; Deputy Head PRC Liaison Office, Washington 1973–79; Dir. American and Oceanian Affairs Dept., Ministry of Foreign Affairs 1979–82; Vice-Minister of Foreign Affairs 1982–85; alt. mem. 12th CCP Cen. Cttee. 1982, 13th CCP Cen. Cttee. 1987; Amb. to U.S.A. 1985–. *Address:* Embassy of the People's Republic of China, Washington, U.S.A.

HANASHI, Nobuyuki; Japanese politician; b. 1928; previous posts include: Pvt. Sec. to Int. Trade and Industry Minister; Parl. Vice-Minister of cLabour; Chair. Cttee. on Social and Labour Affairs and on Educ., House of Reps.; Head, Labour Section, Liberal Democratic Party (LDP) Nat. Org. Cttee. LDP Deputy Sec.-Gen.; Minister of Home Affairs and Dir. Gen. Nat. Public Safety Comm. 1986–87; Liberal Democratic Party. *Address:* c/o Ministry of Home Affairs, 1-2 Kasumigaseki 2-chome, Chiyoda-ku, Tokyo, Japan.

HANCOCK, Langley George; Australian mining prospector and entrepreneur; b. 10 June 1909, Perth; s. of George and Lilian Hancock; m. Hope M. Nicholas 1944 (deceased); one d.; ed. Hale School, Perth; began career as part-time prospector; Asst. man. Mulga Downs Sheep Station 1927, Man. 1934; discovered signs of blue asbestos in Wittenoon Gorge and began to develop asbestos industry in Western Australia 1936; later extended mining activity to gold, tantalite, vanadium, tin, white asbestos and manganese in partnership with E. A. Wright; Asst. Man. Australian Blue Asbestos Ltd. 1943–48; with E. A. Wright joined Izzy Walters in partnership at Whim Creek 1950; discovered iron-ore in the Pilbara 1952; with Wright negotiated Hanwright Iron Ore Agreement with State Govt. 1967 and was subsequently involved in negotiation and renegotiation and exploration in the Pilbara; established National Miner newspaper and f. Westralian Secessionist Movt. 1974; began extensive coal exploration in Hunter Valley, N.S.W. 1977; latterly involved in prospecting for steaming coal in Queensland and oil and gas exploration through Coho Australia Ltd.; Dir. several cos.; Dr. h.c. (Hillsdale Coll., U.S.A.). *Publications:* Wake Up Australia 1979 and many articles on Australian mining and free enterprise. *Leisure interests:* tennis, flying. *Address:* 49 Stirling Highway, Nedlands, West Australia 6009, Australia. *Telephone:* (09) 386 6344.

HAND, Lloyd N., B.A., LL.B.; American lawyer; b. 31 Jan. 1929, Alton, Ill.; s. of Mr. and Mrs. Nelson T. Hand; m. Lucy Ann Donoghue 1952; two s. three d.; ed. Charles M. Hilby High School, Houston and Univ. of Texas; U.S. Naval Officer 1952–55; Asst. to Senator Lyndon B. Johnson 1957–61; Partner Allbritton, McGee and Hand, Houston 1961–; Chief of Protocol of the U.S.A. 1965; Dir. several corpns. in Los Angeles; mem. Bd. of Dirs. Continental Air Services; Sr. Vice-Pres. TRW Inc.; mem. Bd. of Foreign Scholarships; Dir. Continental Air Lines Inc., MTRW (Mitsubishi Electric Co.—TRW, U.S.); mem. Inst. of Int. Educ. S. Calif. Regional Advisory Cttee.; Dir. Los Angeles World Affairs Council. *Leisure interests:* golf, tennis. *Address:* One Space Park, Redondo Beach, Calif. (Office)*Telephone:* 536-1017 (Office).

HANDLEY, Eric Walter, C.B.E., M.A., F.B.A.; British professor of Greek; b. 12 Nov. 1926, Birmingham; s. of Alfred Walter Handley and A. Doris Cox; m. Carol Margaret Taylor 1952; ed. King Edward's School, Birmingham and Trinity Coll. Cambridge; Asst. Lecturer in Greek and Latin, Univ. Coll. London 1946, Lecturer 1949, Reader 1961, Prof. 1967, Prof. of Greek and Head of Greek Dept. 1968–84; Dir. of Inst. of Classical Studies, Univ. of London 1967–84; Regius Prof. of Greek, Cambridge Univ. and Fellow of Trinity Coll. 1984–; Foreign Sec. British Acad. 1979–88; Pres. Classical Asscn. 1984–85; Cromer Greek Prize (jtly.) 1958. *Publications:* The Telephus of Euripides (with John Rea) 1958, The Dyskolos of Menander 1965, edns. of Greek literary papyri, papers in classical journals. *Leisure interests:* walking and travel. *Address:* Trinity College, Cambridge, CB2 1TQ, England. *Telephone:* (0223) 338400.

HANDLEY, Vernon George, B.A., F.R.C.M.; British conductor; b. 11 Nov. 1930; s. of Vernon Douglas and Claudia Lilian Handley; m. Barbara Black 1954 (divorced), one s. one d. (one s. deceased); m. 2nd Victoria Parry-Jones, one s. one d.; ed. Enfield School, Balliol Coll., Oxford, Guildhall School of Music; Conductor, Oxford Univ. Musical Club and Union 1953–54, Oxford Univ. Dramatic Soc. 1953–54, Tonbridge Philharmonic Soc. 1958–61, Hatfield School of Music and Drama 1959–61, Proteus Choir 1962–81; Musical Dir. and Conductor, Guildford Corpn., and Conductor, Guildford Philharmonic Orchestra and Choir 1962–83; Assoc. Conductor, London Philharmonic Orchestra Sept. 1983– (Guest Conductor 1961–83); Prof. for Orchestra and Conducting, Royal Coll. of Music 1966–72, for Choral Class 1969–72; Guest Conductor 1961–: Bournemouth Symphony Orchestra, City of Birmingham Symphony Orchestra, Royal Philharmonic Orchestra, B.B.C. Welsh Orchestra, B.B.C. Northern Symphony (now B.B.C. Philharmonic) Orchestra, Royal Liverpool Philharmonic Orchestra, Ulster Orchestra, B.B.C. Scottish Symphony Orchestra, New Philharmonia (now Philharmonia) Orchestra; conducted London Symphony Orchestra in int. series, London 1971; Prin. Conductor, Ulster Orchestra 1985–, Malmö Symphony Orchestra 1985–; Fellow Goldsmiths' Coll., London 1987; tours of Germany 1966, 1980, S. Africa 1974, Holland 1980, Sweden 1980, 1981, Germany, Sweden, Holland and France 1982–83; numerous recordings; Hon. R.C.M. 1970; Arnold Bax Memorial Medal for Conducting 1962; Conductor of the Year, British Composer's Guild 1974; Hi-Fi News Audio

Award 1982; Hon. D.Univ. (Surrey) 1980. *Address:* Hen Gerrig, Pen-y-Fan, nr. Monmouth, Gwent, Wales. *Telephone:* (0600) 860318.

HANDLIN, Oscar, PH.D., LL.D., L.H.D., D.H.L., LITT.D.; American academic; b. 29 Sept. 1915, Brooklyn; s. of Joseph and Ida (née Yanowitz) Handlin; m. 1st Mary Flug 1937, one s. two d.; m. 2nd Lilian Bombach 1977; ed. Univs. of Harvard, Michigan, Seton Hall, Lowell and Cincinatti; History instructor, Brooklyn Coll. 1936–38, Harvard Univ. 1939–44; Asst. Prof., Harvard Univ. 1944–48, Assoc. Prof. 1948–54, Prof. of History 1954–62, Dir. Cen. for Study of Liberty in America 1958–66, Winthrop Prof. of History 1962–65, Charles Warren Prof. of History 1965–72, Dir. Charles Warren Cen. for Studies in American History 1965–72, Carl H. Pforzheimer Univ. Prof. 1972–, Dir. Univ. Library 1979–83; Harmsworth Prof., Oxford Univ. 1972–73; Carl. M. Loeb Univ. Prof.; Vice-Chair. U.S. Bd. Foreign Scholarships 1962–65, Chair. 1965–66; Trustee New York Public Library 1973–; Guggenheim Fellow 1954, Brandeis Univ. Fellow 1965–; Fellow American Acad. of Arts and Sciences 1983; History Prize, Union League Club 1934, J.H. Dunning Prize, American History Asscn. 1941, Award of Honour, Brooklyn Coll., 1945, Pulitzer Prize for History 1952, Christopher Award 1958, Robert H. Lord Award 1972. *Publications:* Boston's Immigrants 1941, Commonwealth 1947, This was America 1949, The Uprooted, The American People in the Twentieth Century 1954, Adventure in Freedom 1954, Chance or Destiny 1955, Race and Nationality in American Life 1956, Readings in American History, Al Smith and his America 1958, Immigration as a Factor in American History 1959, The Newcomers – Negroes and Puerto Ricans in a Changing Metropolis 1959, American Principles and Issues 1961, The Dimensions of Liberty 1961, The Americans 1963, Fire-Bell in the Night 1964, Children of the Uprooted 1966, Popular Sources of Political Authority 1967, History of the United States 1967, America, a History 1968, The American College and American Culture 1970, Statue of Liberty 1971, Facing Life–Youth and the Family in American History 1971, A Pictorial History of Immigration 1972, The Wealth of the American People 1975, Truth in History 1979, Abraham Lincoln and the Union 1980, The Distortion of America 1981, Liberty and Power 1986, Liberty in Expansion 1989; ed. several publs. *Address:* 18 Agassiz Street, Cambridge, Mass. 02140, U.S.A. (Home).

HANDS, Terence David (Terry) B.A. (HONS); British theatre director; b. 9 Jan. 1941, Aldershot; s. of Joseph Ronald and Luise Bertha (Köhler) Hands; m. 1st Josephine Barstow 1964 (dissolved 1967); m. 2nd Ludmila Mikael (dissolved 1980); one d.; ed. Woking Grammar School, Birmingham Univ., RADA; Founder-Dir. Everyman Theatre, Liverpool 1964–66; Artistic Dir. Theatregoround, R.S.C. 1966; Assoc. Dir. R.S.C. 1967–77, Jt. Artistic Dir. 1978–86, Chief. Exec. 1986–(91), Artistic Dir. 1987–(91); Consultant Dir. Comédie Française 1975; Chevalier, Ordre des Arts et des Lettres 1973; Hon. D.Lit. (Birmingham) 1988; Meilleure Spectacle de l'Année for Richard III 1972, for Twelfth Night 1976; Plays and Players Award for Henry VI 1977, Society of West End Theatre Award 1978 and 1984. *Productions:* over 40 plays with R.S.C., 5 with Comédie Française, 2 with Burgtheater, Vienna, one opera at Paris Opera House, one at Covent Garden, London; Women Beware Women, Teatro Stabile di Genova, Italy; recording: Murder in the Cathedral 1976; transl. (with Barbara Wright), The Balcony (Genet) 1971, Pleasure and Repentance 1976, Henry V (ed. Sally Beauman) 1976. *Address:* Royal Shakespeare Company, Stratford-upon-Avon, Warwicks., CV37 6BB, England. *Telephone:* (0789) 296655.

HANES, Dalibor, JUDR., DR.SC.; Czechoslovak politician; b. 2 Oct. 1914, Tisovec; ed. Faculty of Law, Charles Univ., Prague; Jr. Lawyer, Prešov, Banská Bystrica 1940–44; Govt. Commr. Chamber of Commerce, Bratislava 1945–48; Dir. Regional Admin. for purchase of agricultural products, Bratislava 1948–49, Area Dir. 1949–50; lecturer, School of Econs., Bratislava 1951–53, Asst. Prof. 1953, Prof. 1962; mem. House of Nations, Fed. Assembly 1968–, Chair. House of Nations 1969; Chair. Fed. Assembly 1969–71, Deputy Chair. 1971–; Chair. House of Nations Dec. 1971; mem. Cen. Cttee. CP of Czechoslovakia 1969–87, Alt. mem. of Presidium 1970; Chair. Cen. Cttee. of Czechoslovak Soviet Friendship Union 1970–72, 1st Deputy Chair. 1972–; Deputy to Slovak Nat. Council 1968–71, Chair. Czechoslovak Group Inter-Parl. Union 1969–70, Vice-Chair. 1976–, Czechoslovak-French Cttee. of Czechoslovak Soc. for Int. Relations 1973–; Order of Labour 1969, Order of Victorious February 1974, Klement Gottwald Order 1984 and other awards. *Publications:* scientific studies and articles in economic publication, textbooks, essays, reviews, reports and lectures. *Address:* House of Nations, Prague 1, Vinohradská 1, Czechoslovakia.

HANFT, Ruth, B.S., M.A.; American health policy consultant; b. 12 July 1929; d. of Ethel Schechter and Max Samuels; m. Herbert Hanft 1951; one s. one d.; ed. School of Industrial and Labor Relations, Cornell Univ. and Hunter Coll.; Social Science Analyst, Social Security Admin. 1964–66; Program Analyst, Office of Econ. Opportunity 1966–68, Dept. of Health, Educ. and Welfare 1968–72; Snr. Research Assoc., Inst. of Medicine, N.A.S. 1972–76; Deputy Asst. Sec., U.S. Dept. of Health and Human Services 1977–81; Health Policy Consultant 1981–88; Adjunct Prof., Dartmouth Medical School 1976–; Consultant, Research Prof. Dept. of Health Services and Admin., George Washington Univ. 1988–; mem. Inst. of Medicine, N.A.S.; Fellow, Hastings Inst.; Walter Patenge Medal of Public Service. *Publications:* Hospital Cost Containment (with M. Zubkoff and I. Raskin)

1978, Improving Health Care Management in the Workplace (with J. Rossow and R. Zager) 1985, Physicians and Hospitals: Changing Dynamics, in The Health Policy Agenda (Ed. M. Lewin) 1985; Human in Vitro Fertilization; Political, Legal and Ethical Issues, in Gynecology and Obstetrics Vol. 5 Chapter 98 1984; articles in professional journals. *Leisure interests:* gardening, needlepoint, travel. *Address:* 600 21st Street, N.W., Washington, D.C. 20052 (Office); 3609 Cameron Mills Road, Alexandria, Va. 22305, U.S.A. (Home). *Telephone:* (703) 836-3945 (Home).

HANIEL, Klaus; German business executive; b. 14 Jan. 1916, Munich; m. Johanna von Lutterotti 1949; two s. one d.; ed. Wilhelm-Gymnasium, Munich and in Aachen and Berlin; Chair. Bd. Gutehoffnungshütte Aktienverein; mem. Bd. Kabel und Metallwerke Gutehoffnungshütte AG, Thyssen-Niederrhein AG; mem. advisory and man. bds. of numerous other firms. *Address:* Schlederloh 10, 8191 Dorfen, Federal Republic of Germany. *Telephone:* 08171-1227.

HANIF KHAN, Rana Muhammad; Pakistani politician; b. 1921, Garh Shanker, E. Punjab; ed. Govt. Coll., Ludhiana; called to the Bar, Lincoln's Inn, London 1955; legal practice, Shahiwal 1955–; mem. Pakistan People's Party 1970–; mem. Nat. Assembly 1970; Minister of Labour, Works and Local Bodies 1971–74, of Finance, Planning and Devt. 1974–77, of Commerce and Local Govt. March-July 1977; detained July 1977. *Address:* c/o National Assembly, Islamabad, Pakistan.

HANKE, Brunhilde (née Anweiler); German social scientist and politician; b. 23 March 1930, Erfurt; mem. Sozialistische Einheitspartei Deutschlands (SED) 1946–, mem. Cen. Council of Freie Deutsche Jugend (FDJ) 1952–63, Second. Sec. FDJ, Potsdam District 1952–61; Mayor of Potsdam 1961–84; mem. Volkskammer 1963–; First Deputy Chair. Cttee. for Business Regulations, Volkskammer 1971–84; mem. Council of State 1964–; Vaterländischer Verdienstorden in Bronze and Silver, and other decorations. *Address:* Staatsrat, Marx-Engels-Platz, Berlin 102, German Democratic Republic.

HANKE, Lewis Ulysses, M.A., PH.D.; American professor of history; b. 2 Jan. 1905, Oregon City, Ore.; s. of William Ulysses Hanke and Mamie Stevenson Hanke; m. Kate Ogden Gilbert 1926; two s. two d.; ed. Piqua High School, Ohio, Northwestern Univ., Evanston, Ill., Harvard Univ.; Instructor of History, Univ. of Hawaii 1926–27; Asst. Prof. of History, American Univ., Beirut, Lebanon 1927–30; Tutor and Instructor of History, Harvard Univ. 1934–39; Dir. Hispanic Foundation, Library of Congress 1939–51; Prof. and Dir. Inst. of Latin American Studies, Univ. of Tex. 1951–61; Prof. of History, Columbia Univ., New York 1961–67; Prof. of History, Univ. of Calif. 1967–69; Prof. of Latin American History, Univ. of Mass. 1969–75, Prof. Emer. 1975–; Pres. American Historical Asscn. 1974; Hon. Dr. (Assumption Coll., Mass., Univs. of Bahai, Brazil, La Paz, Bolivia, Seville, Spain, Tomás Frías, Potosí, Bolivia). *Publications:* The Spanish Struggle for Justice in the Conquest of America 1949, Aristotle and the American Indians 1959, Historia de la Villa Imperial de Potosí (editor with G. Mendoza) 1965, All Mankind is One 1974, Los virreyes españoles en América durante el gobierno de la Casa de Austria (12 vols., ed. with Celso Rodríguez) 1976–80, Guide to the Study of United States History Outside the U.S. 1945–80 (5 vols.) 1985. *Leisure interests:* travel, swimming, detective novels. *Address:* 8 Amity Place, Amherst, Mass. 01002, U.S.A. *Telephone:* (413) 549-4051.

HANKEL, Dr. Wilhelm; German banker and professor; b. 10 Jan. 1929, Danzig; s. of Oskar and Jenny (née Schoffmann) Hankel; m. Utu Hankel; three d.; ed. Univs. of Mainz and Amsterdam; worked in Cen. Planning Bureau of Netherlands Govt. 1951; subsequently joined Deutsche Bundesbank; served in Ministry of Econ. Co-operation and later in Foreign Ministry 1954–57; with Berliner Bank, Berlin and Kreditanstalt für Wiederaufbau, Frankfurt-am-Main 1957–68; Dir. Money and Credit Dept., Fed. Ministry of the Economy and Finance 1968–72; Pres. Hessische Landesbank, Girozentrale, Frankfurt-am-Main 1972–74; lecturer, Univ. of Frankfurt 1966–70, Hon. Prof. 1971–; Monetary Adviser EEC, Brussels 1974–76; Visiting Prof., Harvard, Georgetown and Johns Hopkins Univs., U.S.A. and Wissenschaftszentrum, Berlin. *Publications:* Die zweite Kapitalverteilung 1961, Währungspolitik 1971, Heldensagen der Wirtschaft oder schöne heile Wirtschaftswelt 1975, Der Ausweg aus der Krise 1976, Weltwirtschaft 1977, Caesar 1978, Gegenkurs, von der Schuldenkrise zur Vollbeschäftigung 1984, Keynes, Die Entschlüsselung des Kapitalismus 1986; various articles, lectures, etc. *Leisure interests:* literature, music. *Address:* Berghausenerstrasse 190, 5330 Königswinter 21, Federal Republic of Germany. *Telephone:* (02244) 7447.

HANKES-DRIELSMA, Claude Dunbar; British banker; b. 8 March 1949; Manufacturers Hanover 1968–72; Robert Fleming & Co., Ltd. 1972–77, Dir. 1974–77; Chair. The British Export-Finance Advisory Council (BEFAC) 1981–, The Export Finance Co. Ltd. 1982–, Action Resource Centre 1986–; Chair. Man. Cttee. Price Waterhouse & Partners 1983–89, Adviser 1989–; mem. Gov. Council, Business in the Community 1986–, Pres.'s Cttee. 1988–; mem. Target Team Support Group on Voluntary Sector Initiatives 1987–; Chair. Nat. Council, Young Enterprise 1987–; assisted Dr. Fritz Leutwiler (q.v.) in his role as independent mediator between S.A. Govt. and foreign banks 1985. *Publication:* The Dangers of the Banking System: Funding Country Deficits 1975. *Leisure interests:*

gardening, walking, skiing, reading, ancient art. *Address:* Stanford Place, Faringdon, Oxon., England. *Telephone:* (0367) 20547.

HANKEY, 2nd Baron, cr. 1939, of The Chart; **Robert Maurice Alers Hankey,** K.C.M.G., K.C.V.O., B.A.; British diplomatist; b. 4 July 1905, Croydon, Surrey; s. of Rt. Hon. Maurice Pascal Alers, First Baron Hankey of The Chart; m. 1st Frances Bevyl Stuart-Menteth 1930 (died 1957), m. 2nd Joanna Riddall Wright 1962; two s. two d.; ed. Rugby and New Coll., Oxford; travelling Fellow, Queen's Coll., Oxford 1926–27; entered Diplomatic Service 1927; served in Berlin 1927; Paris 1928, Foreign Office, London 1930; Pvt. Sec. to Rt. Hon. Anthony Eden 1933–36, served Warsaw 1936, Bucharest 1939, Cairo 1941, Teheran 1942, Foreign Office 1943–45; Counsellor, British Embassy, Warsaw 1945–46; Head of Northern Dept., Foreign Office 1946–49; British Chargé d'affaires, Madrid 1949–51; Minister to Hungary 1951–53; Amb. to Sweden 1954–60; Perm. Rep. to OEEC and Official Chair. 1960; Perm. Del. to OECD and Chair. of Econ. Policy Cttee. 1961–65; retd. from British Diplomatic Service 1965; Vice-Pres. European Inst. of Business Admin. (INSEAD), Fontainebleau 1962–80; mem. Int. Council of United World Colls., Council of Int. Baccalaureate Foundation Geneva 1967–76; Dir. Alliance Bldg. Soc. 1970–83; Pres. Anglo-Swedish Soc. 1969–75. *Leisure interests:* reading, skiing, tennis, music. *Address:* Hethe House, Cowden, Edenbridge, Kent, TN8 7DZ, England. *Telephone:* (034286) 538.

HANLEY, John Weller, B.S., M.B.A.; American business executive; b. 11 Jan. 1922, Parkersburg, W. Va.; s. of James P. and Ida May (Ayers) Hanley; m. Mary Jane Reel 1948; two s. one d.; ed. Pennsylvania State Univ., Univ. of Harvard; Engineer, Allegheny Ludlum Steel Corpn. 1942–43; with Procter and Gamble 1947–72, Man. Case Soap Products Div. 1961–63, Vice-Pres. Household Soap Products Div. 1963–67, Corpn. Vice-Pres., Group Exec. 1967–70, Exec. Vice-Pres. 1970–72; Pres. Monsanto Co. 1972–80, C.E.O. 1972–83, Chair. 1975–83, Chair. Exec. Cttee. 1983–; Chair. Hanley Hazelden Center at St. Mary's Hosp., W. Palm Beach, Fla.;Dir. Monsanto Co., Citicorp/Citibank, N.A., The May Dept. Stores Ltd., R.J.R. Nabisco Corpn.; Hon. D.Eng. (Missouri) 1974, Hon. D.Laws (Maryville Coll.) 1979, Hon. LL.D. (Univ. of the Pacific) 1980, (Notre Dame Univ.) 1983, (Washington Univ.) 1984, Hon. D.Sc. (Webster Coll.) 1981; Harvard Alumni Achievement Award 1980. *Leisure interests:* golf, hunting, fishing. *Address:* 713 S.W. Thornhill Lane, Piper's Landing, Palm City, Fla. 34990; Sunrise Lane, Roaring Gap, N.C. 28668, U.S.A. (Summer). *Telephone:* (305) 288-3342 (Fla.).

HANNAH, Nicholas; British barrister; b. 19 Dec. 1940; s. of Gerald Hannah and Margaret Hannah; m. Savitri Hannah 1973; two s. one d.; ed. Middle Temple, London; barrister, London and South Eastern Circuit 1966–79; High Court Judge, Botswana 1979–85; Chief Justice, Swaziland 1985–. *Leisure interests:* fishing, golf, reading. *Address:* Chief Justice's Chambers, P.O. Box 19, Mbabane, Swaziland (Office). *Telephone:* 42901.

HANNAY, Sir David Hugh Alexander, K.C.M.G., B.A.; British diplomatist; b. 28 Sept. 1935, London; s. of J. G. Hannay; m. Gillian Rosemary Rex 1961; four s.; ed. Craigflower School, Torryburn, Fife, Scotland, Winchester Coll. and New Coll. Oxford; Second Lieut., King's Royal Irish Hussars 1954–56; Persian language student, Foreign Office and British Embassy, Tehran 1959–61; Oriental Sec., British Embassy, Kabul 1961–63; Second Sec., Eastern Dept., Foreign Office, London 1963–65; Second, then First Sec., U.K. Del. to European Community, Brussels 1965–70, First Sec. U.K. Negotiating Team 1970–72, Chef de Cabinet to Sir Christopher Soames, Vice-Pres. of the European Community Comm. 1973–77; Counsellor, Head of Energy, Science and Space Dept., FCO, London 1977–79, Counsellor, Head of Middle East Dept. 1979, Asst. Under-Sec. of State (E.E.C.) 1979–84; Minister, British Embassy, Washington, D.C. 1984–85; U.K. Perm. Rep. to E.E.C. 1985–. *Leisure interests:* gardening, travel. *Address:* 21 avenue Henri Pirenne, 1180 Brussels, Belgium. *Telephone:* Brussels 345.7604.

HANNAY, N(orman) Bruce, PH.D.; American research director and corporate consultant; b. 9 Feb. 1921, Mount Vernon, Wash.; s. of Norman Bond and Winnie Evans Hannay; m. Joan Anderson 1943; two d.; ed. Swarthmore Coll. and Princeton Univ.; mem. Tech. Staff, Belle Telephone Labs. 1944–82, Vice-Pres. Research and Patents 1973–82; mem. Bd. of Dirs. Rohm & Haas Co., General Signal Corpn., Plenum Publishing Co., Alex. Brown Cash Reserve Fund and others; Chair. Science Advisory Council, Atlantic Richfield Co. 1981–; Foreign Sec. Nat. Acad. of Eng. 1976–84; Consultant to several corpns. and fmr. consultant to many govt. agencies; mem. advisory bds. for several univs.; research interests: molecular structure, electron emission, mass spectroscopy, semiconductors, solid-state chem., superconductors; mem. N.A.S., Nat. Acad. of Eng., American Acad. of Arts and Sciences; Acheson Medal, Electrochemical Soc. 1976; Perkin Medal 1983; Gold Medal, American Inst. of Chemists 1986; Hon. Ph.D. (Tel Aviv) 1978, Hon. D.Sc. (Swarthmore Coll.) 1979, Hon. D.Sc. (Polytechnic Inst. of New York) 1981. *Publications:* 10 scientific and technical books, 100 articles in scientific and technical journals. *Address:* 2219 Fir Lane, Mitchell Point, Friday Harbor, Wash. 98250, U.S.A. *Telephone:* (206) 378-4122.

HANNIBALSSON, Jón Baldvin, M.A.; Icelandic politician; b. 21 Feb. 1939, Ísafjördur; ed. Menntaskólinn í Reykjavík, Univ. of Edinburgh,

Nationalökonomiska Inst., Stockholm, Univ. of Iceland and Harvard Univ.; teacher Hagaskóli Elementary School, Reykjavík 1964–70; journalist Frjáls thjód, Reykjavík 1964–68; Headmaster Menntaskólinn á Isafirdi, Ísafjördur 1970–79; Chief Ed. Althýdubladid, Reykjavík 1979–82; M.P. 1982–; Minister of Finance 1987–88, for Foreign Affairs and Foreign Trade Sept. 1988–; Chair. SDP 1984–. *Address:* Ministry of Foreign Affairs, Hverfisgötu 115, 150 Reykjavík, Iceland.

HANNON, John W., Jr., B.A.; American banker; b. 22 April 1922, New York; s. of John W. Hannon and Leonora King Hannon; m. Vivien Gardner 1944; one s. two d.; ed. Montclair, N.J. Public Schools and St. Lawrence Univ.; with Commercial Nat. Bank 1946–51, Bankers Trust Co. after merger with Commercial Nat. Bank 1951, Dir. 1973–82, Chair. Exec. Cttee. 1973–75, Pres. 1975–82; Dir. Consumers Power Co., Jackson. *Leisure interests:* golf, sailing. *Address:* 280 Park Avenue, New York, N.Y. 10017 (Office); 17 Warfield Street, Upper Montclair, N.J. 07043, U.S.A. (Home).

HANNOVER, Georg Wilhelm, Prinz von, DR.IUR.; German educationist; b. 25 March 1915, Brunswick; s. of the Duke and Duchess of Brunswick; m. Princess Sophie of Greece (sister of H.R.H. the Duke of Edinburgh q.v.) 1946; two s. one d.; ed. Hamelin/Weser High School, Marlborough Coll., Schule Schloss Salem, Univs. of Vienna and Göttingen; Head, Salemer Schulen 1948–59, now mem. Bd. of Dirs.; Chair. Outward Bound Mountain School (Austria), King Edward VII Foundation (German side); mem. Inst. for Town Planning; Pres. Riding Acad. Munich 1959–62; Hon. Vice-Pres. World Asscn. of Building Socs. and Saving for Bldg. Banks; mem. German Soc. for European Educ.; Pres. Int. Olympic Acad. 1966–70; mem. IOC 1966–71; Nat. Olympic Cttee. for Germany 1966–, Organizing Cttee. for Munich Olympic Games 1966–72. *Address:* Georgi-Haus, 8162 Neuhaus bei Schliersee, Upper Bavaria, Federal Republic of Germany. *Telephone:* Schliersee 72 65.

HANON, Bernard, H.E.C., M.B.A., PH.D.; French business executive; b. 7 Jan. 1932, Bois-Colombes; s. of Max and Anne Hanon; m. Ghislaine de Bragelongne 1965; two s.; ed. Columbia Univ., New York; Dir. of Marketing, Renault Inc., U.S.A. 1959–63; Asst. Prof. of Man. Science, Graduate School of Business, New York Univ. 1963–66; Head of Dept. of Econ. Studies and Programming, Renault 1966–69, Dir. Corp. Planning and Information Systems 1970–75, Dir. Automotive Operations 1976, Exec. Vice-Pres. in charge of Automotive Operations 1976–81; Pres. Renault Inc. U.S.A. 1972–81, Group Gen. Man. 1981, Chair. 1981–85; Man. Hanon Associés 1986–; Ordre nat. du Mérite. *Address:* 8 rue du Commandant Schloesing, 75016 Paris (Office); 50 avenue Foch, 75016 Paris, France (Home).

HANS ADAM, Hereditary Prince of Liechtenstein; b. 14 Feb. 1945; s. of Prince Franz Josef II (q.v.) and Princess Gina; m. Countess Marie Aglaë Kinsky von Wchinitz und Tettau 1967; three s. one d.; ed. Schottengymnasium, Vienna, School of Econs. and Social Sciences, St. Gallen, Switzerland; Chief Exec. of Prince of Liechtenstein Foundation 1970–84; took over exec. authority of Liechtenstein Aug. 1984. *Address:* Schloss Vaduz, Principality of Liechtenstein.

HANSBERGER, Robert Vail, A.A., B.M.E., M.B.A.; American business executive; b. 1 June 1920, Worthington, Minn.; s. of Floyd and Edith (née Vail) Hansberger; m. Klara Katherine Kille 1942; two d.; ed. Worthington Jr. Coll., Univ. of Minnesota, Harvard Univ. Graduate School of Business Admin.; Torpedo Devt. Officer, Chief Mechanical Design Naval Ordnance Lab., U.S.N.R. 1942–46, Budget Dir., Asst. to Exec., Chief Engineer and Vice-Pres. Container Corpn. of America 1947–54; Pres. and Dir. Western Sales Co. Inc. and Exec. Vice-Pres. and Dir. Western Kraft Corpn. 1954–56; Pres., Chief Exec. and Dir. Boise Payette Lumber Co. 1956–57, Founder Boise Cascade Corpn. 1957–72; Chair. and Chief Exec. Futura Industries Corpn. 1972–, Futura Communications Corpn.; Dir. and fmr. Dir. of numerous cos.; Visiting Prof. Boise State Univ. 1975–; mem. Exec. Cttee. and Vice-Chair. The Business Council; mem. Stanford Research Inst. Advisory Bd.; fmr. mem. President's Comm. on Urban Housing, on the White House Fellows Program, on Population Growth and the American Future, and numerous State Comms.; fmr. Trustee Acad. for Educational Research and Devt., Calif. Inst. of Tech. *Leisure interests:* hunting, fishing, skiing, golf, camping, reading. *Address:* Futura Corporation, 1412 W. Idaho, Boise, Ida., 83702 (Office); 1305 Harrison Boulevard, Boise, Ida. 83702, U.S.A. (Home). *Telephone:* 208-336-0150 (Office).

HANSEID, Einar; Norwegian journalsit; b. 19 Nov. 1943, Sandefjord; m. Mari Onsrud 1977; two s.; reporter, Sandefjords Blad 1965; News Ed. Dagbladet 1974; Chief Ed. Hjem & Fritid 1982; Man. Ed. Verdens Gang 1984, Chief Ed. 1987–. *Address:* Verdens Gang, Akersgt. 34, P.O. Box 1185 Sentrum, 0107 Oslo 1, Norway.

HANSEN, Barbara C., PH.D.; American university administrator; b. 24 Nov. 1941, Boston, Mass.; d. of Reynold Caleen and Dorothy Caleen; m. Kenneth D. Hansen 1976; one s.; ed. Univ. of Calif., Los Angeles and Univ. of Washington, Seattle; Research Fellow, Univ. of Pa. Inst. of Neurosciences 1966–68; Asst. and Assoc. Prof. Univ. of Washington 1971–76; Prof. and Assoc. Dean Univ. of Michigan, Ann Arbor 1977–83; Assoc. Vice-Pres. of Academic Affairs and Research and Dean of Grad. School, Southern Ill. Univ., Carbondale 1983–85; Vice-Pres. for Grad. Studies and Research, Univ. of Md.-Baltimore 1986–; Pres. Int. Asscn. for Study of

Obesity 1987–(90); mem. several advisory cttees. etc.; mem. N.A.S. Inst. of Medicine. *Publications:* Controversies in Obesity 1983, book chapters and articles in learned journals. *Leisure interests:* sailing, scuba diving, golf, reading. *Address:* University of Maryland-Baltimore Graduate School, 660 W. Redwood, Suite 257, Baltimore, Md. 21201 (Office); 1179 Ballantrae Lane, McLean, Va. 22101, U.S.A. (Home). *Telephone:* (301) 328-7131 (Office).

HANSEN, Bent, FIL. DR.; Danish-born Swedish economist; b. 1 Aug. 1920, Ildved, Denmark; s. of Henrik Poulsen and Anna Louise (Pedersen) Hansen; m. Soad Ibrahim Refaat 1962; two s. four d.; ed. Univs. of Copenhagen and Uppsala; civil servant, State Dept., Copenhagen 1946; Lecturer Uppsala Univ. 1947–48 and 1950–51, Gothenburg 1948–50; Reader, Uppsala 1951–55; Prof. and Head of Konjunkturinst. (Nat. Inst. of Econ. Research), Stockholm 1955–64, Consultant, Inst. of Nat. Planning, Cairo 1962–65; Special Consultant for OECD, Paris 1965–67; Prof. of Political Economy, Stockholm Univ. 1967–68; Prof. of Econs. Univ. of Calif., Berkeley 1967–87, Prof. Emer. 1987–, Chair. Dept. of Econs. 1977–85; Consultant ECAFE Bangkok 1970–73, IMF 1973, U.S. Treasury 1974, Morocco 1976–77, Bogadizi Univ., Istanbul 1978, World Bank 1985–; Chief ILO Employment Mission to Egypt 1980–81. *Publications:* A Study in the Theory of Inflation 1951, The Economic Theory of Fiscal Policy 1958, Foreign Trade Credits and Exchange Reserves 1961, Development and Economic Policy in the UAR (Egypt) 1965, Lectures in Economic Theory, I and II 1967, Long and Short Term Planning 1967, Fiscal Policy in Seven Countries, OECD, 1969, A Survey of General Equilibrium Systems 1970, Exchange Controls and Development: Egypt 1975, Employment Opportunities and Equity: Egypt in the 1980s, 1982. *Address:* University of California, Barrows Hall 250, Berkeley, Calif. (Office); 8336 Terrace Drive, El Cerrito, Calif. 94530, U.S.A. (Home). *Telephone:* 415-525-0704 (Home).

HANSEN, Clifford Peter, B.S.; American rancher and politician; b. 16 Oct. 1912, Zenith, Wyo.; s. of Peter and Sylvia (Wood) Hansen; m. Martha Elizabeth Close 1934; one s. one d.; ed. Univ. of Wyoming; Vice-Pres., Jackson State Bank 1953–74; Trustee Univ. of Wyoming 1946–63, Pres. Bd. 1956–63; fmr. Chair. Advisory Cttee. on Livestock Research and Marketing to Sec. of Agriculture; Gov. of Wyoming 1963–66; Senator from Wyoming 1967–79; Sec. Republican Conf. 1977; mem. Wyoming Stock Growers' Asscn., Pres. 1953–55; mem. American Nat. Cattlemen's Asscn., Second Vice-Pres. 1956–57; mem. Exec. Cttee. Nat. Govs. Conf. and Western Govs. Conf. 1965–71; mem. Bd. Trustees Buffalo Bill Historical Soc., Univ. of Wyoming Foundation, Pres. Reagan's Cttee. on Federalism, Political Economy Research Center; Emer. Dir. Mountain States Legal Foundation; Stockman of the Century (Wyoming); Hon. LL.D. (Wyoming) 1965; Republican; *Leisure interests:* hiking, riding. *Address:* P.O.B. 448, Jackson, Wyo. 83001, U.S.A. (Home). *Telephone:* (307) 733 3423.

HANSEN, Guttorm; Norwegian journalist and politician; b. 3 Nov. 1920, Namsos; s. of Håkon Hansen and Agnes Selnes; m. Karin Johanne Johnsen 1947; ed. Tech. School; Journalist, Ed. 1945–61; Chair., mem. several municipal and public bds. and cttees.; mem. Exec. Cttee. Labour Party; Deputy mem. Storting (Parl.) 1958–61, mem. 1961–; Vice-Chair. Labour Party Parl. Group 1965–71, Chair. 1971–72; Vice-Chair. Cttee. on Foreign Affairs 1969–71; Pres. Storting 1973–81; Chair. Norwegian Atlantic Cttee. 1966–; mem. Nordic Council 1970–, Bd. European Movement in Norway. *Publications:* NATO, Europe and Norway, The Labour Movement in Nord-Trøndelag, Plan-Perspective-Policy. *Leisure interests:* reading, fishing, skiing. *Address:* Stortinget, Oslo (Office); N. Griegs vei 26, 7800 Namsos, Norway (Home).

HANSEN, Irwin Roy; American businessman; b. 16 Aug. 1913; ed. Univ. of Wisconsin; with Haskins & Sells (C.P.A.'s) 1936–44; joined Minn. Mining & Mfg. Co., St. Paul 1944, Gen. Auditor 1944–50, Asst. Controller 1950–54, Asst. Treas. 1954–57, Treas. 1957–63, Vice-Pres. (Finance) 1963–; Dir. and Vice-Pres. Salisbury Cruises Ltd.; Dir. 3M Foundation; Treas. Big Rock Stone and Material Co., Prehler Electric Insulating Co.; Dir. Business Products Sales Inc., Wonework Lodge Inc., First Nat. Bank of St. Paul. *Address:* 3M Center, St. Paul, Minn. 55101, U.S.A.

HANSEN, Kurt, Prof. DR.ING.; German businessman; b. 11 Jan. 1910, Yokohama, Japan; m. Irmi Strähuber 1937; one s. one d.; ed. Technische Hochschule, Munich; with I. G. Farbenindustrie AG/Farbenfabriken Bayer AG, Leverkusen 1936–74; Man. Uerdingen Factory, Farbenfabriken Bayer Jan. 1955, Wuppertal-Elberfeld Factory 1956–57, mem. Bd. of Man. Bayer AG (fmrly. Farbenfabriken Bayer) 1957–61, Chair. 1961–74, Chair. Supervisory Bd. 1974–84, Hon. Chair. Supervisory Bd. 1984–; Hon. mem. Presidential Bd. Fed. of German Industries, Cologne. *Address:* Bayer AG, 509 Leverkusen Bayerwerk, Federal Republic of Germany.

HANSEN, Morgens Herman, D.PHIL.; Danish lecturer in classical philology; b. 20 Aug. 1940, Copenhagen; s. of Herman Hansen and Gudrun Maria (née Heslet) Hansen; m. Birgitte Holt Larsen; one s.; ed. Univ. of Copenhagen; Research Fellow, Inst. of Classics, Univ. of Copenhagen 1967–69, lecturer in Classical Philology 1969–; Visiting Fellow, Wolfson College, Cambridge 1974; Visiting Prof., Melbourne Univ. 1988; mem. Inst. for Advanced Study, Princeton 1983; Fellow Royal Danish Acad. of Sciences and Letters. *Publications include:* The Sovereignty of the People's Court in 4th Century Athens 1974, Aspects of Athenian Society 1975, Apagoge, Endeixis and Ephegesis 1976, The Athenian Ecclesia 1983, Demography and Democracy

1985, The Athenian Assembly 1987 and over 50 articles in int. journals on Athenian democracy and ancient Greek constitutional history. *Leisure interests:* playing the flute, writing poetry, book binding. *Address:* Wilhelm Marstrandsgade 15, 2100 København Ø, Denmark. *Telephone:* (01) 54 22 11 (Univ.); (01) 26 15 88 (Home).

HANSEN, Morris H., M.A., B.S.; American statistician; b. 15 Dec. 1910, Wyoming; s. of Hans C. Hansen and Maud E. Hansen; m. 1st Mildred Latham 1930 (died 1983); two s. two d.; m. 2nd Eleanore Lamb 1986; ed. Univ. of Wyoming, American Univ.; worked on sample survey design and conduct of surveys; Assoc. Dir. Bureau of the Census; Sr. Survey Statistician and Sr. Vice-Pres. Westat 1969–, Chair. of Bd. 1986–; Pres. Inst. of Math. Statistics 1953, American Statistical Assoc. 1960, Int. Assoc. of Survey Statisticians 1973–77; mem. Social Science Research Council 1963–68, Cttee. Nat. Statistics, N.A.S. 1972–76, Advisory Cttee. to Office of Statistical Policy, Office of Man. and Budget 1970–77; Advisor Program for Nat. Assessment of Educ. Progress; mem. Inter-American Statistical Inst., N.A.S.; Hon. mem. Int. Statistical Inst.; Hon. Fellow Royal Statistical Soc.; Hon. D.Law (Univ. of Wyoming); Rockefeller Public Service Award, Dept. of Commerce Gold Medal. *Publications:* Sample Survey Methods and Theory (with W. N. Hurwitz and W. G. Madow) 1953, Measurement Errors in Censuses and Surveys (with W. N. Hurwitz and M. A. Bershad) 1960 and numerous articles. *Leisure interests:* boating, hiking. *Address:* 13532 Glen Mill Road, Rockville, Md. 20850, U.S.A. *Telephone:* (301) 424 2037.

HANSEN, Niels, D. EN D.; German diplomatist; b. 7 Nov. 1924, Heidelberg; s. of late Karl Hansen; m. Barbara Bartels 1959; three d.; ed. Univs. of Göttingen, Hamburg, Heidelberg, Zürich, Geneva; mil. service Germany and Italy 1942–45; Asst., Law Faculty, Geneva Univ., Switzerland 1951–52; joined Foreign Service of Fed. Repub. of Germany 1952, mem. Econ. Del., Vienna 1954–55, mem. Personal Staff Foreign Minister von Brentano 1955–58, Embassy Lisbon 1958–61, Berne 1961–65, Deputy Consul-Gen. New York 1965–68, Head Mediterranean and European Integration Desks, Foreign Office 1968–73, Minister Counsellor, Perm. Mission to UN, New York 1973–75, Minister and Deputy Chief of Mission, Embassy Washington 1975–79, Head of Policy Planning Staff, Foreign Office 1979–81, Amb. to Israel 1981–85, Perm. Rep. to NATO 1985–; Corresp. mem. Sociedade de Geografia, Lisbon; decorations from Austria, Belgium, Fed. Repub. of Germany, Italy, Luxembourg, Netherlands, Portugal, Spain, Vatican. *Publications:* Le délit de violation d'une obligation d'entretien; numerous contribs. to books and periodicals. *Leisure interests:* flute playing, modern painting and sculpture, languages (French, English, Portuguese, Italian, Hebrew). *Address:* Permanent Delegation of Federal Republic of Germany to NATO, Blvd. Léopold III, B-1110 Brussels, Belgium. *Telephone:* Brussels 241.44.80.

HANSEN, P. Gregers, M.SC., D.PHIL.; Danish physicist; b. 11 Jan. 1933, Frederiksberg; m. Bitten Bisbjerg 1957; two s.; ed. Tech. Univ. of Denmark, Copenhagen; Research Scientist, Group. Leader, Atomic Energy Research Inst. 1956–66; Prof. of Physics at the Univ. of Aarhus 1966–; Sr. Research Physicist and Group. Leader, C.E.R.N. Geneva 1969–79; mem. numerous scientific advisory bds., primarily in Germany, France and at C.E.R.N.; mem. Danish Royal Acad. of Sciences and Letters. *Publications:* many research papers and review articles on subjects in nuclear and atomic Physics. *Leisure interests:* skiing, mountaineering, hiking, literature. *Address:* Institute of Physics, University of Aarhus, 8000 Aarhus C, (Office); Søtoften 36, 8250 Ega, Denmark (Home); Carraz, F-74420 Boege (Summer). *Telephone:* (45) 6-128899 (Office); (45) 6-220779 (Home); (33) 50-39-13-28 (Summer Home).

HANSEN, Rodney Harold, LL.B., A.C.A.; New Zealand barrister and solicitor; b. 13 March 1944, Auckland; s. of Harold Leslie Hansen and Beatrice Augusta Hansen; m. Penelope Jane Berghan 1971; three s.; ed. Mt. Roskill Grammar School and Univ. of Auckland; accountant in Pvt. Practice 1969–73; partner Simpson Grierson Butler White 1975–; convener Working Party on Women in the Legal Profession 1975–, Jt. Convener Commonwealth Law Conf. Organising Cttee. 1985–; mem. Council, Commonwealth Law Assoc. 1986–; Law Soc. Prize, Sr. Scholar in Law, various legal prizes. *Leisure interests:* family, music, reading, gardening, sport. *Address:* Simpson Grierson Butler White, 92-96 Albert Street, Auckland (Office); 5 Bellevue Road, Mt. Eden, Auckland, New Zealand (Home). *Telephone:* (09) 770-620 (Office); (09) 600-335 (Home).

HANSEN, Rolf; Norwegian politician; b. 23 July 1920, Oslo; Chair. Underground Cttee. of AUF (Labour League of Youth) 1939–45, mem. AUF Cen. Exec. 1945–55; Political Sec. Ministry of Social Affairs 1956–59; Org. Sec. Oslo Labour Party 1959–67, Sec. 1967–71, Chair. 1972–74; mem. Cen. Exec. of Labour Party 1969–73; Minister of Defence 1976–80, of Environment 1979–81; fmr. mem. Ombudsman's Cttee. for the Armed Forces. *Address:* c/o Folketeaterbygningen, Postboks 8754, 0184 Oslo 1, Norway. *Telephone:* 42 79 69.

HANSENNE, Michel, D. EN D.; Belgian politician; b. 23 March 1940, Rotheux-Rimiere; M.P. 1974–; Minister of French Culture 1979–81, of Employment and Labour Dec. 1981–88; Dir.-Gen. Int. Labour Office, Geneva Feb. 1989–. *Publication:* Emploi, les scenarios du possible. *Address:* International Labour Office, 4 chemin des Morillons, Geneva, Switzerland.

HANSON, Duane, M.F.A.; American sculptor; b. 17 Jan. 1925, Alexandria, Minn.; s. of Dewey O. and Agnes Nelson Hanson; m. 1st Janice Roche 1950, two s. one d.; m. 2nd Wesla Host 1968, two c.; ed. Luther Coll., Decorah, Iowa, Univ. of Washington, Cranbrook Acad. of Art; taught art in U.S.A. and Germany 1951–58; first solo exhbn. Museum of Art, Cranbrook Acad. of Art, Bloomfield Hills, Minn. 1951; subsequent solo exhbns. include Galerie Netzel, Bremen, Fed. Repub. of Germany 1958, O.K. Harris Works of Art 1970, 1972, 1974, 1980, 1984, Museum of Contemporary Art, Chicago 1974, Neue Galerie, Aachen 1974, Univ. Art Museum, Berkeley, Calif. 1977, Corcoran Gallery of Art, Washington, D.C. 1977–78, Jacksonville Art Museum, Fla. 1980–81, Wichita State Univ., Kan. 1984; travelling exhbn. visiting Tokyo, Osaka, Nagoya 1984, Cranbrook Acad. of Art Museum, Bloomfield Hills 1985; numerous group exhbns. including Miami Art Center 1968, Danneberg Gallery, New York 1971, Galerie de Gestlo, Hamburg 1972, Galerie des 4 Mouvements, Paris 1972, 1973, Lunds Konsthall, Sweden 1974, Edinburgh Festival, Scotland 1974, Palazzo Reale, Milan 1974, Centre Pompidou, Paris 1977–78, 11th Int. Sculpture Conf., Washington, D.C. 1980, Whitney Biennial Exhbn., New York 1981, Museum of Modern Art, Saitama, Japan 1983, Contemporary Sculpture Exhbn., Toledo, Ohio 1984, Pop Art 1955–70: Art Gallery of N.S.W., Sydney, Queensland Art Gallery, Brisbane, Nat. Gallery of Victoria, Melbourne 1985, Figure as Subject: The Last Decade, The Whitney Museum of American Art at the Equitable Center, New York 1986; Blair Award, Art Inst. of Chicago 1974, DAAD Grant for work in sculpture, West Berlin 1974; Hon. D.Hum.Litt. (Nova Univ.) 1979, Florida Prize 1985. *Address:* c/o O.K. Harris Gallery, 383 West Broadway, New York, N.Y. 10012, U.S.A.

HANSON, Baron (Life Peer), cr. 1983, of Edgerton in the County of West Yorkshire; **James Edward Hanson,** Kt., F.R.S.A., C.B.I.M.; British business executive; b. 20 Jan. 1922; s. of late Robert Hanson, C.B.E. and Louisa A. (Cis) Rodgers; m. Geraldine Kaelin 1959; two s. one d.; War service 1939–46; Chair. Hanson Trust PLC 1965–, Hanson Transport Group, Ltd. 1965–; Hon. LL.D. (Leeds); Freeman of London. *Address:* 1 Grosvenor Place, London, SW1X 7JH, England.

HANSON, Robert A.; American business executive; b. 13 Dec. 1924, Moline, Ill.; s. of Nels A. Hanson and Margaret Chapman; m. Patricia Ann Klinger 1955; ed. Augustana Coll., Rock Island, Ill.; joined John Deere Intercontinental Ltd. 1950, Gen. Man. John Deere S.A. (Mexico) 1962–64, (Spain) 1964–66, Dir. of Marketing, Europe, Africa, Middle East 1966–70, Man. Dir. Latin America, Australia, Far East Div. 1970–72, Vice-Pres. Overseas Operations 1972–73, Sr. Vice-Pres. Overseas Div. 1973–75, Exec. Vice-Pres. 1975–78, Pres. 1978–85, C.O.O. 1979–82, Chair. and C.E.O. 1982–; mem. Bd. of Dirs. Deere & Co., Dun & Bradstreet Corpn., Augustana Coll. 1975–82, Continental Ill. Nat. Bank & Trust Co. of Chicago 1981–84, Farm and Industrial Equipment Inst., Procter & Gamble Co.; mem. Int. Council of Morgan Guaranty Trust Co. 1979–81 and 1984–, Bd. of Trustees, Cttee. for Econ. Devt., Univ. of Chicago Cttee. on Public Policy Studies 1981–, Business Cttee. for the Arts 1982–85, N.W. Univ. Assocs. 1982–, Mayo Foundation, U.S. Council for Int. Business; Dir. Merrill Lynch and Co. Inc. 1984–. *Address:* Deere & Co., John Deere Road, Moline, Ill. 61265 (Office); 2200 29th Avenue Court, Moline, Ill. 61265, U.S.A. (Home). *Telephone:* (309) 765-8000 (Office).

HANSON, Robert Paul, PH.D.; American university professor and epidemiologist; b. 1918, Sarona, Wis.; m. Martha Goodlet 1946; one s. one d.; ed. Ashland High School, Wis., Northland Coll., Wis., Univ. of Wisconsin-Madison; Asst. Prof., Univ. of Wisconsin-Madison 1949, Assoc. Prof. 1952, Prof. 1957–72, Samuel H. McNutt Prof. 1972–84, Distinguished Sr. Prof. 1984–; Chair. Cttee. on Biologics, U.S. Livestock Sanitary Assen. 1970–72, Sub-cttee. on Poultry Diseases, Nat. Research Council 1963–72; mem. Jt. Argentina-U.S.A. Comm. on Foot and Mouth Disease 1965–75, Bd., Agric. and Renewable Resources, Nat. Research Council 1973–77, Study Section, Tropical Medicine and Parasitology, Nat. Insts. of Health 1967–71, Cttee. on Foreign Animal Disease to U.S. Sec. for Agric. 1975–82; Adviser to Program on Livestock Devt., U.S. Agency for Int. Devt. 1970–79; Consultant to U.S. Dept. of Agric. on Newcastle Disease 1970–79, to Brazil for UNESCO 1983; mem. N.A.S.; Upjohn Award in Avian Medicine. *Publications:* Newcastle Disease Virus, an Evolving Pathogen 1964, Animal Disease Control: Regional Programs 1983; Ed. and Co-Ed. of five books; author or co-author of 250 scientific papers. *Leisure interests:* botany and genealogy. *Address:* 5730 Dogwood Place, Madison, Wis. 53705, U.S.A.

HANUS, Frantisek; Czechoslovak politician; b. 17 Jan. 1943, Kasovice, W. Bohemia; ed. Coll. of Mechanical and Electrical Eng. and Moscow Inst. of Steel and Alloys; fmr. worker, asst. and chief foreman, Kladno Steel Works; mem. CP of Czechoslovakia (CPCZ) 1966–, Sec. Cen. Bohemian Regional Cttee. 1979, Leading Sec. 1985–; mem. Cen. Cttee. CPCZ, mem. Secr. 1988–. *Address:* Central Committee of the Communist Party of Czechoslovakia, nábř. Ludvíka Svobody 12, 125 11 Prague, Czechoslovakia.

HANUSZKIEWICZ, Adam; Polish actor and theatre director; b. 16 June 1924, Lvov, U.S.S.R.; s. of Włodzimierz Hanuszkiewicz and Stanisława Szydłowska; m. 1st Zofia Ryś, one s. two d.; m. 2nd Zofia Kucówna; ed. State High School of Drama, Łódź, and State Higher School of Drama, Warsaw; début as actor 1945, acted in Cracow, Poznań and Warsaw; début as dir. 1953, directed in Poznań and Warsaw; Artistic Dir. Theatre of

Polish TV 1956–63; Dir. and Producer, Teatr Powszechny (Popular Theatre), Warsaw 1963–68, visited, with theatre company, Prague 1964, 1966, Moscow 1965, London, Paris 1966, Helsinki 1967, Bucharest 1968, Stockholm, Oslo 1969; Gen. Man. and Artistic Dir. Teatr Narodowy, Warsaw 1968–82, visited Helsinki, Leningrad, Moscow 1973, Berlin 1975, Bremen, Budapest, Moscow 1976; acted in 50 major roles in theatre; directed 30 plays in theatre, 100 television plays; State Prize (First Class) for TV work, City of Warsaw Award for theatre work, Theatre Critics' Prize 1964, Order of Banner of Labour, 1st Class 1974, Ekran Gold Screen TV Award 1978, Prize of Minister of Foreign Affairs 1979. *Principal roles include:* Hamlet (Hamlet) 1951–59, Tytus (Bérénice) 1962, Prospero (The Tempest) 1963, Raskolnikov (Crime and Punishment) 1964, Don Juan (Don Juan) 1965, Fantazy (Fantazy) 1967, Count Henryk (Un-divine Comedy) 1969, Duncan (Macbeth) 1972, Créon (Antigone) 1973. *Plays directed include:* Wesele (The Wedding, Wyspiański), Crime and Punishment, Coriolanus, Don Juan, Platonov, The Columbus Boys (Bratny), Kordian (Słowacki), St. Joan 1969, Hamlet 1970, Norwid 1970, Beniowski (Słowacki) 1971, Three Sisters 1971, Twelfth Night 1971, Macbeth 1973, Antigone 1973, The Inspector General 1973, Balladyna (Słowacki) 1973, A Month in the Country 1974, Wacława dzieje (Garczyński) 1974, Kartoteka (Różewicz) 1974, Don Juan 1975, Wesele (Wyspiański) 1976, Mickiewicz 1976, Mąż i żona (Fredro) 1977, Phèdre 1977, Peace 1977, Sen srebrny Salomei (Słowacki) 1977, Wyszedł z domu (Różewicz) 1978, Dziady (Mickiewicz) 1978, Białe małżeństwo (Różewicz) 1978, Treny (Kochanowski) 1979, The Brothers Karamazov, The Decameron 1980, As You Like It, Platonov, School of Wires. *Address:* Al. I Armii WP16, 00-582, Warsaw, Poland.

HAO JIANXIU; Chinese politician; b. 1935, Qingdao; worker, State Operated Cotton Factory No. 6, Qingdao; originated Hao Jianxiu Work Method; mem. Exec. Council, Women's Fed. 1953; mem. Cen. Cttee., Communist Democratic Youth League 1953; Deputy Dir. Cotton Factory No. 6, Qingdao 1964; mem. Cen. Cttee. Communist Youth League 1964–Cultural Revolution; mem. Qingdao Municipality Revolutionary Cttee. 1967; mem. Standing Cttee., Cotton Factory No. 6 Revolutionary Cttee. 1968; Vice-Chair. Qingdao Municipality Revolutionary Cttee. 1971, Trade Union, Shandong 1975; Chair. Women's Fed., Shandong 1975; mem. Standing Cttee., Shandong Prov. CCP Cttee. 1977; mem. 11th CCP Cen. Cttee. 1977–; Vice-Minister of Textile Industry 1978–81, Minister 1981–83; mem. Politburo 13th Cen. Cttee. CCP 1985; Vice-Chair. Women's Fed. 1978–; Vice-Chair. State Tourism Cttee. July 1988–; Nat. Model Worker in Industry 1951, mem. 12th Cen. Cttee. CCP 1982–87, 13th Cen. Cttee. CCP 1987–; Alt. Sec. Secr. 1982, Sec. 1985; mem. Financial and Econ. Leading Group, CCP Cen. Cttee. 1986–; Hon. Pres. Factory Dirs'. Study Soc., Acad. of Social Sciences 1985–.

HAO RAN; Chinese writer; b. 25 March 1932, Jixian Co., Hebei Prov.; s. of Liang Zifen and Su Shi; m. Yang Puqiao 1947; three s. one d.; mem. Bd. of Dirs. China Writer's Assen.; Deputy Ed.-in-Chief Oriental Juvenile. *Publications include:* A Magpie on a Branch, Bright Skies, The Golden Road, Sons and Daughters of Xisha, Attachment for the Mountains and Rivers, Collections of Hao Ran, Selections of Hao Ran. *Leisure interests:* book collecting and stamp collecting. *Address:* 1-8, Building 6, Yue Tan Bei Jie Street, Beijing, People's Republic of China. *Telephone:* 866049.

HARA, Bunbei; Japanese politician; b. 29 April 1913, Tokyo; ed. Tokyo Univ.; entered Home Affairs Ministry 1936; Superintendent-Gen. Metropolitan Police Dept. 1961; mem. House of Councillors 1971–, Chair. Standing Cttee. on Local Admin. 1978, Special Cttee. on Election Laws 1978, on Security 1981; Minister of State and Dir.-Gen. Environment Agency 1981–82. *Address:* c/o Liberal-Democratic Party, 7, 2-chome, Hirakawacho, Chiyoda-ku, Tokyo, Japan.

HARA, Kenzaburo; Japanese politician; b. 6 Feb. 1907, Hyogo Pref.; s. of Kenji Hara and Ben Hara; ed. Waseda Univ., Oregon Univ., U.S.A.; mem. House of Reps. 1946–; Parl. Vice-Minister of Transport 1949, Vice-Speaker 1961–63, Minister of Labour 1968–70, 1971–72, Vice-Chair. Liberal Democratic Party (LDP) Gen. Council 1977–78, Minister of State, Dir.-Gen. Nat. Land Agency and Hokkaido Devt. Agency 1980–81; Speaker House of Reps. 1986–. *Leisure interests:* collecting foreign whiskies, brandies etc.; keeping dogs and carp. *Address:* Residence of Speaker of House of Representatives, 2-18-1, Nagata-cho, Chiyoda-ku, Tokyo 100, Japan. *Telephone:* 03-581 5111.

HARA, Sumio; Japanese banker and attorney; b. 7 March 1911, Yokosuka, Kanagawa; s. of Tokuemon and Haru Hara; m. Kazuko Mimura 1939; two s. one d.; ed. Faculty of Law, Tokyo Imperial Univ.; joined Ministry of Finance 1934; Deputy Dir. Budget Bureau 1953–56; Dir.-Gen. of the Tax Bureau 1956–60; Commr. Nat. Tax Admin. Agency 1960–62; Deputy Pres. The Bank of Tokyo Ltd. 1962–65, Pres. 1965–73, Chair. 1973–77, Exec. Adviser 1977–; Exec. Dir. Japan Tax Assen. 1973–; Attorney Hara, Oshima & Uematsu 1982–; mem. Price Stabilization Policy Council, Econ. Planning Agency 1981–; Special Adviser to the Pres. Japan Chamber of Commerce and Industry and Tokyo Chamber of Commerce and Industry 1975–; Trilateral Comm. 1973–, Int. Advisory Bd., Sperry Corpn. New York 1974–, Arbitrator Int. Centre for Settlement of Investment Disputes, Washington, D.C. 1980–. *Leisure interests:* go, calligraphy. *Address:* The Bank of Tokyo Ltd., 6-3 Nihombashi Hongokucho 1-chome, Chuo-ku, Tokyo; Hara, Oshima & Uematsu, Kotohirakaikan Building, 2-8 Toranomon

1-chome, Minato-ku, Tokyo (Offices); 26-14 Tsutsujigaoka, Midori-ku, Yokohama, Kanagawa, Japan (Home). *Telephone:* 045-981-7507 (Home).

HARALDSETH, Leif; Norwegian politician; b. 30 Nov. 1929, Drammen; m.; dist. sec. LO (Norwegian TU fed.) 1964, Second Sec. 1969, First Sec. 1970-77, Vice-Chair. 1977-87, Pres. 1988-; Minister of Local Govt. and Labour 1986. *Address:* Folkets Hus, Youngsgt. 11, 0181, Oslo 1, Norway.

HARBISON, Earle Harrison, Jr., A.B., LL.B.; American business executive; b. 10 Aug. 1928, St. Louis; s. of Earle Harbison and Rose Hensberg; m. Suzanne G. Siegel 1952; two s.; ed. Washington Univ. St. Louis; with CIA, Washington, D.C. 1949-67; Dir. Man. Information Systems Dept., Monsanto Co. 1967-73, Dir. Corporate Org. and Man. Devt. Dept. 1973-75, Gen. Man. Speciality Chem. Div. 1975, Gen. Man. Plasticizers Div. 1976-77, Gen. Man. Detergents and Phosphates Div. and Plasticizers Div. 1977; Vice-Pres., Man. Dir. Monsanto Commercial Products Co. 1977; Group Vice-Pres. and Man. Dir. Monsanto Chem. Co. 1979-84; Exec. Vice-Pres. Monsanto Co. 1981-86, Pres. and C.O.O. 1986-. *Address:* Monsanto Co., Mail Code D1H, 800 N. Lindbergh Avenue, St. Louis, Mo. 63166, U.S.A.

HARCOURT, Geoffrey Colin, M.COM., PH.D., LITT.D.; Australian economist; b. 27 June 1931, Melbourne; s. of Kenneth and Marjorie (née Gans) Harcourt; m. Joan Bartrop 1955; two s. two d.; ed. Univs. of Melbourne and Cambridge; lecturer in econs., Univ. of Adelaide 1958-62, Sr. lecturer 1963-65, Reader 1965-67, Prof. 1967-85; lecturer in econs. and politics, Univ. of Cambridge 1963-66, 1982-, Dir. of Studies in Economics and Fellow of Trinity Hall, Cambridge 1963-66, Fellow and Lecturer in Econs., Jesus Coll., Cambridge 1982-, Pres. 1988-; Visiting Fellow, Clare Hall, Cambridge 1972-73; Visiting Prof., Univ. of Toronto, Canada 1977, 1980; Fellow, Acad. of the Social Sciences in Australia 1971-; Pres. Economics Soc. of Australia and New Zealand 1974-77; Wellington Burnham Lecturer, Tufts Univ., Medford, Mass. 1975, Edward Shann Memorial Lecturer, Univ. of Western Australia 1975, Newcastle Lecturer in Political Economy, Univ. of Newcastle 1977, Acad. Lecturer, Acad. of the Social Sciences in Australia 1978; G. L. Wood Memorial Lecturer, Univ. of Melbourne 1982; John Curtin Memorial Lecturer, A.N.U. 1982, special lecturer in econs., Univ. of Manchester 1984, Lecturer Nobel Conf. XXII, Gustavus Adolphus Coll., Minn. 1986. *Publications:* Economic Activity (with P. H. Karmel and R. H. Wallace) 1967, Readings in the Concept and Measurement of Income (ed., with R. H. Parker) 1969, 2nd edn. (with R. H. Parker and G. Whittington) 1986, Capital and Growth, Selected Readings (ed., with N. F. Laing) 1971, Some Cambridge Controversies in the Theory of Capital 1972, The Microeconomic Foundations of Macroeconomics (ed.) 1977, The Social Science Imperialists, Selected Essays (edited by Prue Kerr) 1982, Keynes and his Contemporaries (ed.) 1985, Controversies in Political Economy, Selected Essays of G. C. Harcourt (edited by Omar Hamouda) 1986, Int. Monetary Problems and Supply-Side Economics: Essays in Honour of Lorie Tarshis (edited with Jon S. Cohen 1986, and articles in journals. *Leisure interests:* running, cricket, squash and Australian Rules football. *Address:* Jesus College, Cambridge, CB5 8BL; 18 New Square, Cambridge, CB1 1EY, England (Home). *Telephone:* (0223) 68611 ext 236 (Office); 60833 (Home).

HARDEN, Donald Benjamin, C.B.E., M.A., PH.D., F.S.A.; British museum official (retd.) b. 8 July 1901, Dublin, Ireland; s. of late Rt. Rev. John Mason Harden and Constance Caroline (née Sparrow); m. 1st Cecil Ursula Harriss 1934 (died 1963), one d.; m. 2nd Dorothy May McDonald 1965; ed. Westminster School, Trinity Coll., Cambridge, and Univ. of Michigan; Sr. Asst., Dept. of Humanity, Univ. of Aberdeen 1924-26; Commonwealth Fund Fellow 1926-28; Asst. Keeper, Dept. of Antiquities, Ashmolean Museum, Oxford 1929-45, Keeper 1945-56; Leverhulme Research Fellowship 1953; Vice-Pres. Soc. of Antiquaries, London 1949-53, 1964-67; Pres. Council for British Archaeology 1950-54, Oxford Architectural and Historical Society 1952-54, Section H, British Asscn. 1955; Dir. London Museum 1956-70; Pres. Museums Asscn. 1960-61, London and Middlesex Archaeological Soc. 1959-64; Royal Archaeological Inst. 1966-69, Int. Asscn. for History of Glass 1967-74; Commr. Royal Comm. on Historical Monuments (England) 1963-71; mem. Ancient Monuments Bd. for England 1959-74; mem. governing body British School of Archaeology in Iraq 1949-84; Pres. Soc. for Medieval Archaeology 1975-77; Hon. F.B.A. 1987; Hon. mem. German Archaeological Inst.; Gold Medal of Soc. of Antiquaries, London 1977. *Publications:* Roman Glass from Karanis 1936, The Anglo-Saxon Cemetery at Abingdon, Berks. (with E. T. Leeds) 1936; Sir Arthur Evans 1851-1941, A Memoir 1951, revised and enlarged 1983, The Phoenicians 1962 (revised 1971, 1980), Catalogue of Greek and Roman Glass in the British Museum (Vol. I) 1981, Ed. Dark-Age Britain 1956, and Medieval Archaeology (annually 1957-73). *Leisure interests:* archaeology and antiquities. *Address:* 12 St. Andrew's Mansions, Dorset Street, London, W1H 3FD, England.

HARDER, Manfred, DR.IUR; German professor of law; b. 15 Nov. 1937, Frankfurt/Main; s. of Karl and Erna (née Kopf) Harder; m. Judis Kalinowski 1966; one s. one d.; ed. Freie Univ., Berlin; part-time asst. Frei Univ., Berlin 1960-63, teaching asst. 1964-70, Asst. Prof. 1970-71, Prof. 1971; Prof. of Roman and Civil Law, Univ. of Mainz 1972-, Pres. of Univ. 1980-84; Justice of the Palatine Supreme Court, Zweibrücken 1987-. *Publications:* Zuwendungen unter Lebenden auf den Todesfall 1968, Die Leistung an Erfüllungs Statt 1976, Grundzüge des Erbrechts 1983, articles

in learned journals and contributions to legal books. *Address:* Johannes-Gutenberg-Universität, Saarstrasse 21, 6500 Mainz; Alfred-Mumbächer-Strasse 36, 6500 Mainz, Federal Republic of Germany (Home). *Telephone:* 06131/39-2777 (Office); 06131/35924 (Home).

HARDIE, Sir Charles Edgar Mathewes, Kt., C.B.E.; British chartered accountant; b. 10 March 1910; s. of Dr. C. F. and Mrs. R. F. Hardie (née Moore); m. 1st Dorothy Jean Hobson (died 1965), one s. three d.; m. 2nd Mrs. Angela Richli 1966 (dissolved 1975); m. 3rd Rosemary Margaret Harwood 1975; ed. Aldenham School; qualified as Chartered Accountant 1932, Partner, Dixon, Wilson & Co., London 1934-75, Sr. Partner 1975-81; War Service (Col.) 1939-44; Chair. BOAC 1969-70, White Fish Authority 1966-73, Metropolitan Estate & Property Corpn. PLC 1964-71, British Printing Corpn. PLC 1969-76, Fitch Lovell PLC 1970-77; Dir. Trusthouse Forte Ltd. (Deputy Chair. Feb. 1983-); Legion of Merit 1944. *Leisure interest:* bridge. *Address:* Pitt House, 25 New Street, Henley-on-Thames, Oxon, RG9 2BP, England. *Telephone:* (0491) 577944.

HARDIN, Clifford Morris, B.S., M.S., DR. AGRIC. ECON.; American business executive; b. 1915, Knightstown, Ind.; s. of J. Alvin and Mabel (Macy) Hardin; m. Martha Love Wood 1939; two s. three d.; ed. Purdue Univ.; Asst. Prof. of Agricultural Econs., Univ. of Wisconsin 1942-44; Assoc. Prof., Prof. and Chair. Agricultural Econs. Dept., Michigan State Univ. 1946-48, Dir. Agric. Experimental Station 1948-53, Dean of Agriculture 1953-54; Chancellor, Univ. of Nebraska 1954-69; U.S. Sec. of Agriculture 1969-71; Vice-Chair. Ralston Purina Co. 1971-80; Dir. and Scholar-in-Residence, Center for Study of American Business, Washington Univ., St. Louis 1981-85; mem. Exec. Cttee. Council of Higher Educ. of the American Repubs. 1963-69; Consultant and Dir. Stifel, Nicolaus & Co., St. Louis 1980-87; Trustee, Rockefeller Foundation 1961-69, 1972-81, Farm Foundation 1973-83, Freedoms Foundation at Valley Forge 1973-; mem. Bd. Nat. Science Foundation 1966-70; Trustee American Assembly, Winrock Int. Inst. for Agricultural Devt. 1975-, Univ. of Nebraska Foundation 1975-. *Address:* 10 Roan Lane, St. Louis, Mo. 63124, U.S.A. (Home).

HARDING, Air Chief Marshal Sir Peter Robin, K.C.B., C.B.I.M., F.R.AE.S.; British air force officer; b. 2 Dec. 1933; s. of Peter Harding and Elizabeth Kezia Clear; m. Sheila Rosemary May 1955; three s. one d.; ed. Chingford High School; joined R.A.F. 1952; Pilot 12 Squadron 1954-57; QFI and Flight Commdr. R.A.F. Coll., Cranwell 1957-60; Pilot 1 Squadron, R.A.A.F. 1960-62; staff coll. 1963; Air Sec.'s Dept., Ministry of Defence 1964-66; Commanding Officer 18 Squadron, Gutersloh and Acklington 1966-69; jt. services staff coll. 1969-70; Sec. and 'C' Team mem. Defence Policy Staff, Ministry of Defence 1970-71, Dir. Air Staff, Briefing 1971-74; Commdr. R.A.F. Brüggen 1974-76; Dir. Defence Policy, Ministry of Defence 1976-78; Asst. Chief of Staff (Plans and Policy) SHAPE 1978-80; Air Commanding Officer Number 11 Group 1981-82; Vice-Chief Air Staff 1982-84, of Defence Staff 1985; Air Officer Commanding-in-Chief, RAF Strike Command, and C.-in-C. U.K. Air Forces 1985-88; Chief of Air Staff Dec. 1988-; ADC to H.M. the Queen 1985. *Publications:* articles for professional journals and magazines. *Leisure interests:* music, piano, bridge, birdwatching. *Address:* Ministry of Defence, Whitehall, London, S.W.1, England.

HARDWICK, Elizabeth, M.A.; American author; b. 27 July 1916, Lexington, Ky.; d. of Eugene Allen Hardwick and Mary (née Ramsey) Hardwick; m. Robert Lowell 1949 (divorced 1972); one d.; ed. Kentucky Univ., Columbia Univ.; Assoc. Prof. Barnard Coll. Guggenheim Fellow 1947; recipient George Jean Nathan award 1966; mem. American Acad., Inst. of Arts and Letters. *Publications: novels:* The Ghostly Lover 1945, The Simple Truth 1955, Sleepless Nights 1979; *essays:* A View of My Own 1962, Seduction and Betrayal 1974, Bartleby in Manhattan 1983; Ed. The Selected Letters of William James 1960; contribs. to New Yorker. *Address:* 15 W. 67th Street, New York, N.Y. 10023, U.S.A.

HARDY, John Philips, M.A., D.PHIL.; Australian professor of English; b. 1 Jan. 1933, Brisbane; s. of E. A. Hardy and N. A. (née Philips) Hardy; m. 1961 (divorced); three s. one d.; ed. Church of England Grammar School, Brisbane, Univ. of Queensland and Univ. of Oxford; Fellow Magdalen Coll., Oxford 1962-65; Asst. Prof. Univ. of Toronto, Canada 1965-66; Prof. of English Univ. of New England 1966-72, Australian Nat. Univ. 1972-87; Foundation Prof. of Humanities and Social Sciences, Bond Univ. 1988-; Queensland Rhodes Scholar 1957. *Publications:* Reinterpretations: Essays on Poems by Milton, Pope and Johnson 1971, Samuel Johnson 1979, Jane Austen's Heroines 1984, Stories of Australian Migration (Ed.) 1988. *Leisure interests:* swimming, fishing. *Address:* Bond University, Private Bag 10, Gold Coast Mail Centre, Queensland 4217, Australia. *Telephone:* (075) 92 0411.

HARDY, Norman Edgar; Canadian business executive; b. 4 Jan. 1917, Toronto; s. of George and Myrtle (Dunsmore) Hardy; m. Dorothy Walter 1939; two d.; ed. Pickering Coll., Newmarket, Ont.; joined Hardy Cartage 1935; Brewers Warehousing Co. 1948; Man. Labatt's Toronto Brewery 1949; Gen. Man. Ont. Div. 1956, Vice-Pres. 1959; Exec. Vice-Pres. John Labatt Ltd. 1962; Pres. Labatt Breweries of Canada Ltd. 1964; Group Exec. Vice-Pres. John Labatt Ltd. 1968, Pres. 1969-73, Vice-Chair. of Bd. 1973-80, Chair. of Bd. 1981-87; Dir. John Labatt Ltd., Brascan Ltd., Unicorpn. Enterprises; Vice-Chair. and C.E.O. Toronto Blue Jays Baseball

Club; mem. Bd. Noma Industries Ltd., Stambax Inc., Brascan Ltd. *Address:* c/o John Labatt Ltd., 451 Ridout Street, N., London, Ont. N6A 2P6, Canada.

HARDY, Robert, C.B.E.; British actor and author; b. 29 Oct. 1925; one s. two d.; theatre appearances include four seasons of Shakespeare at Stratford-on-Avon, two at Old Vic; world tours include Henry V and Hamlet, U.S.A.; numerous appearances London and Broadway theatres 1952-; writer and/or presenter of numerous TV programmes including The Picardy Affair, The History of the Longbow, Heritage, Horses in our Blood, Gordon of Khartoum etc.; other TV appearances have included Prince Hal and Henry V in Age of Kings, Prince Albert in Edward VII, Malcolm Campbell in Speed King, Winston Churchill in the Wilderness Years, Siegfried Farnon in All Creatures Great and Small, Twiggy Rathbone and Russell Spam in Hot Metal, the Commandant in The Far Pavilions. *Films include:* How I Won the War, Yellow Dog, Dark Places, Young Winston, Ten Rillington Place, Le Silencieux, Gawain and the Green Knight, The Spy Who Came In From The Cold, La Gifle, Robin Hood, The Shooting Party, Paris by Night. *Publication:* Longbow 1976. *Leisure interests:* making and shooting longbows, riding, most country pursuits. *Address:* c/o Chatto & Linnit, Ltd., Prince of Wales Theatre, Coventry Street, London, W.1, England.

HARE, David, M.A., F.R.S.L.; British playwright; b. 5 June 1947, Hastings, Sussex; s. of Clifford Theodore Rippon Hare and Agnes Cockburn Gilmour; m. Margaret Matheson 1970 (dissolved 1980); two s. one d.; ed. Lancing Coll., Jesus Coll., Cambridge; Literary Man. and Resident Dramatist, Royal Court 1969-71; Resident Dramatist, Nottingham Playhouse 1973; f. Joint Stock Theatre Group 1975, Greenpoint Films 1983; Assoc. Dir. Nat. Theatre 1984. *Plays:* Slag, Hampstead 1970, The Great Exhibition, Hampstead 1972, Knuckle, Comedy Theatre 1974, Brassneck, Nottingham Playhouse 1973, Fanshen, Jt. Stock Theatre Group 1975, Teeth 'n' Smiles, Royal Court 1975, Plenty, National Theatre 1978, Broadway 1983, A Map of the World, Adelaide Festival 1982, Nat. Theatre 1983, Pravda, Nat. Theatre 1985, The Bay at Nice and Wrecked Eggs, Nat. Theatre 1986, The Secret Rapture, Nat. Theatre 1988. *Films for TV:* Licking Hitler 1978, Dreams of Leaving 1980, Saigon: Year of the Cat 1983. *Films:* Wetherby 1984, Plenty 1985, Paris by Night 1988, Strapless 1989. *Opera:* The Knife, New York Shakespeare Festival 1987; Evening Standard Drama Award 1970, John Llewelyn Rhys Prize 1974, BAFTA Best Play of the Year 1978, New York Critics' Circle Award 1983, Golden Bear Award for Best Film 1985, Evening Standard Drama Award for Best Play 1985, Plays and Players Best Play 1985, City Limits Best Play 1985, Drama Magazine Awards Best Play 1988. *Address:* 33 Ladbroke Rd., London, W.11, England.

HARE, (Frederick) Kenneth, O.C., PH.D., F.R.S.C.; Canadian professor of geography and physics; b. 5 Feb. 1919, Wylye, Wilts., England; s. of Frederick E. Hare and Irene Smith; m. 1st Suzanne A. Bates 1941 (dissolved 1952), 2nd Helen N. Morrill 1953; two s. one d.; ed. Univs. of London and Montreal; Asst., Assoc. and Full Prof. of Geography, McGill Univ. 1945-62, Chair. Geography Dept. 1950-62, Dean of Arts and Science 1962-64; Prof. of Geography King's Coll., London 1964-66; Master of Birkbeck Coll., Univ. of London 1966-68; Pres. Univ. of British Columbia 1968-69; Prof. of Geography and Physics, Univ. of Toronto 1969-85, Prof. Emer. 1985-; Dir. Inst. for Environmental Studies 1974-79, Provost of Trinity Coll. 1979-86; Chancellor Trent Univ. 1988-; Chair. Royal Soc. of Canada Comm. on Lead in the Environment 1984-86; several medals and awards. *Publications:* author and co-author of books and articles on climate, environment etc. *Leisure interests:* music, photography, gardening. *Address:* 301 Lakeshore Road West, Oakville, Ont. L6K 1G2, Canada.

HARE, Raymond Arthur, A.B.; American diplomatist; b. 3 April 1901, Martinsburg, W. Va.; s. of Frank Earhart Hare and Anna Marte Bowers; m. Julia Cygan 1932; two s.; ed. Grinnell Coll.; Instructor, Robert Coll., Constantinople 1924-27; Exec. Sec. American Chamber of Commerce for Levant 1926-27; Clerk, later Vice-Consul, U.S. Consulate-Gen., Constantinople 1927-28; Language Officer, Paris, 1929, 1931, also Vice-Consul 1931; Sec. in Diplomatic Service and Vice-Consul, Cairo 1931; Vice-Consul, Beirut 1932; Third Sec. and Vice-Consul, Teheran 1933; Dept. of State 1935; Second Sec., Cairo 1939, also at Jeddah 1940-44, also Consul, Cairo 1940; Second Sec., later First Sec. and Consul, London 1944; Dept. of State 1946; Nat. War Coll. 1946-47; Chief, Div. of Middle East, Indian and South Asian Affairs 1947; Deputy Dir. Office of Near East and African Affairs 1948; Deputy Asst. Sec. of State for Near East, S. Asian and African Affairs Oct. 1949; Amb. to Saudi Arabia and Minister to Yemen 1950-53; Amb. to the Lebanon 1953-54; Dir.-Gen. U.S. Foreign Service 1954-56; Amb. to Egypt 1956-58, Amb. to U.A.R. 1958-60, also Minister to Yemen 1959; Deputy Under-Sec. of State (Political Affairs) 1960-61; Amb. to Turkey 1961-65; Asst. Sec. of State (Near Eastern and S. Asian Affairs) 1965-66; Pres. Middle East Inst. 1966-69, Nat. Chair. Middle East Inst. 1969-76, Chair. Emer. 1976-. *Leisure interests:* Islamic architecture, studying the Bible, swimming, walking, golf. *Address:* Middle East Institute, 1761 N Street, N.W., Washington, D.C. 20036 (Office); 3214 39th Street, N.W., Washington, D.C. 20016, U.S.A. (Home).

HARE, Richard Mervyn, M.A., F.B.A.; British philosopher; b. 21 March 1919, Backwell, Avon; s. of Charles F. A. Hare and Louise K. Simonds;

m. Catherine Verney 1947; one s. three d.; ed. Rugby School and Balliol Coll., Oxford; Fellow and Tutor, Balliol Coll., Oxford 1947-66; White's Prof. of Moral Philosophy and Fellow, Corpus Christi Coll., Oxford 1966-83; Grad. Research Prof. of Philosophy, Univ. of Fla. 1983-; Hon. Fellow, Balliol and Corpus Christi Colls.; Foreign Hon. mem. American Acad. of Arts and Sciences; Tanner Award (Utah); *Publications:* The Language of Morals 1952, Freedom and Reason 1963, Practical Inferences 1971, Essays on Philosophical Method 1971, Essays on the Moral Concepts 1972, Applications of Moral Philosophy 1972, Moral Thinking 1981, Plato 1982, Hare and Critics 1988. *Leisure interests:* music, gardening. *Address:* Department of Philosophy, University of Florida, Gainesville, Fla. 32611, U.S.A.; Saffron House, Ewelme, Oxford, OX9 6HP, England. *Telephone:* 904-392-2084 (Fla.); 0865 49431 (Oxford).

HARE DUKE, Rt. Rev. Michael Geoffrey, M.A.; British ecclesiastic; b. 28 Nov. 1925, Calcutta, India; s. of A. R. A. Hare Duke and Dorothy Holmes; m. Grace Lydia Frances McKean Dodd 1949; one s. three d.; ed. Bradfield Coll., Berks., Trinity Coll., Oxford, Westcott House, Cambridge; Sub-Lieut. R.N.V.R. 1944-46; ordained Deacon 1952, Priest 1953; Curate St. John's Wood, London 1952-56; Vicar St. Mark's, Bury 1956-62; Pastoral Dir. Clinical Theology Asscn. 1962-64; Vicar St. Paul's, Daybrook 1964-69; Bishop of St. Andrew's, Dunkeld and Dunblane 1969-. *Publications:* Understanding the Adolescent 1969, The Break of Glory 1970, Freud 1972, Good News 1976, Stories, Signs and Sacraments in the Emerging Church 1982. *Leisure interests:* writing and broadcasting. *Address:* Bishop's House, Fairmount Road, Perth, PH2 7AP, Scotland. *Telephone:* (0738) 21580.

HAREWOOD, 7th Earl of, cr. 1812; George Henry Hubert Lascelles, K.B.E.; British musical administrator; b. 7 Feb. 1923, London; s. of the late 6th Earl of Harewood and H.R.H. Princess Mary, The Princess Royal (d. of H.M. King George V); m. 1st Maria Donata Stein 1949 (dissolved 1967), three s. (she m. 1973 the Rt. Hon. Jeremy Thorpe, q.v.); m. 2nd Patricia Tuckwell 1967, one s.; ed. Eton Coll. and King's Coll., Cambridge; Capt. Grenadier Guards 1942-46; P.O.W. 1944-45; A.D.C. to Earl of Athlone, Gov.-Gen. of Canada 1945-46; Counsellor of State during absence of the Sovereign 1947, 1954 and 1956; mem. Bd. of Dirs. Royal Opera House, Covent Garden 1951-53, 1969-72, Admin. Exec. 1953-60; Dir.-Gen. Leeds Musical Festival 1954-74; Artistic Dir. Edinburgh Int. Festival 1961-65; Chair. British Council Music Advisory Cttee. 1956-66, Arts Council Music Panel 1966-72; Artistic Adviser New Philharmonia Orchestra, London 1966-76; Pres. English Football Asscn. 1964-71, Leeds United Football Club; Chancellor, York Univ. 1963-67; mem. Gen. Advisory Council of BBC 1969-77, Gov. of BBC 1985-87; Man. Dir. English Nat. Opera 1972-85, Chair. 1986-; Pres. British Bd. of Film Classification 1985-; Artistic Dir. Adelaide Festival for 1988, 1986-; Ed. Opera 1950-53, Kobbé's Complete Opera Book 1954, 1976, 1987; Austrian Great Silver Medal of Honour 1959, Lebanese Order of the Cedar 1970, Janáček Medal 1978. *Leisure interests:* looking at painting, sculpture, football. *Publication:* The Tongs and the Bones (autobiog.) 1981. *Address:* Harewood House, Leeds, Yorkshire, LS17 9LG, England.

HARHOFF, Preben, O.B.E.; Danish shipowner; b. 29 Nov. 1911, Copenhagen; s. of late C. J. C. Harhoff and Rigmor Hansen; m. Else Harhoff 1937; one s. one d.; ed. Copenhagen Univ. and in Germany, England and France; with A. P. Moller 1930-32; joined C. K. Hansen Ltd. 1932, partner 1950, Propr., Sr. partner -1968; Co-Propr. Copenhagen Stevedoring Co., Copenhagen Bunkercoal Depot Ltd. -1968; mem. Bd. Int. Farvefabrik A/S, Copenhagen 1946- (Chair. 1953-), A/S Copenhagen Bunkercoal Depot 1946-68, Steamship Co. Dannebrog 1950-67, Steamship Co. Dantank 1952-60, Steamship Co. Atalanta (also Chair.) 1952-57, Dansk Transatlantisk Rederi A/S 1957-80, British Import Union, Copenhagen 1958-82, Den Kjøbenhavnske Sø-Assurence Forening Ltd. 1958-68, Orlogsmuseets Venner 1958-, Dansk Radio A/S 1960-68, Elektromekano A/S 1960-68, Danmarks Rederiforenings Assurance Udvalg 1960-68, Danmarks Rederiforenings Fondsbørs Udvalg 1960-68, Steamship Co. Vendila (also Chair.) 1963-67, Harlang & Toksvig Holding A/S 1968-, Whitbread & Co. (Scandinavia) A/S 1969-, Aktivator Spirituosa (Denmark) A/S 1972-82, Diversa Specialiteter A/S 1972-82, Underberg Import A/S (also Chair.) 1972-82; mem. Council Baltic and Int. Maritime Conf., Copenhagen 1951-68, Int. Tanker Owners Asscn., London 1955-67; Hon. Consul-Gen. for Tunisia in Copenhagen 1962-; Council mem. Corps Consulaire; several decorations. *Leisure interests:* fishing, tennis. *Address:* Esperance Alle 10 C, DK-2920 Charlottenlund, Denmark. *Telephone:* 01-62-62-62.

HÄRING, Bernhard, D. THEOL.; German professor of theology; b. 10 Nov. 1912, Böttingen; s. of Johannes N. Häring and Franziska Flad; ed. Theological Faculty, Gars am Inn and Univ. of Tübingen; Prof. Theologische Hochschule, Gars am Inn 1940, 1947-57; Prof. of Moral Theology, Accademia Alfonsiana/Pontifical Lateran Univ., Rome 1957-87, now Prof. Emer.; Visiting Prof. at various ecumenical theological faculties in U.S.A.; Grosskreuz des Verdienstordens; Pietrak Award (Warsaw) 1973; Dr. h.c. (six), etc. *Publications:* more than 70 books, 270 translations and about 1,000 articles in various languages. *Address:* Kirchplatz 10, 8096 Gars am Inn, Federal Republic of Germany. *Telephone:* 08073-1032.

HARIRI, Rafic Bahaa Edine; Saudi Arabian (b. Lebanon) business executive and diplomat; b. 1944, Sidon, Lebanon; emigrated to Saudi Arabia 1965; teacher, then auditor with eng. co.; set up Civil Construction Establishment

(CICONEST) 1970; joined Oger Enterprises to form Saudi Oger 1978; acquired entire Oger Co. Feb. 1979; has carried out several major projects in Saudi Arabia, Lebanon (through Oger Liban), Morocco (through Saudi Oger), U.K. (through Saudi Oger Services U.K.); built a university, school and hospital, Kfar Falous, Lebanon 1983; f. Hariri Foundation for Culture and Higher Educ. 1979; Chevalier, Légion d'honneur 1981, Kt. of the Italian Repub. 1982, Nat. Cedars Medal (Lebanon) 1983, Saint Butros and Saint Boulos Medal 1983, Save the Children 50th Anniversary Award 1983, King Faisal Medal 1983, Médaille de Paris 1983, Beirut Golden Key 1983. *Address:* P.O. Box 1449, Riyadh 11431, Saudi Arabia.

HARKER, David, PH.D.; American scientist; b. 19 Oct. 1906, San Francisco, Calif.; s. of George Asa and Harriette (Buttler) Harker; m. 1st Katherine deSavich 1930 (died 1973), two d.; m. 2nd Deborah Anne Maxwell 1974; ed. Univ. of California (Berkeley), California Inst. of Tech.; Research Asst., Atmospheric Nitrogen Corpn., Solvay, New York 1930-33; Instructor in Chemistry, Johns Hopkins Univ. 1936-39, Assoc. in Chemistry 1939-41; Assoc., Research Lab., Gen. Electric Co., Schenectady, N.Y. 1941-49, Head Crystallography Div. 1949-50; Dir. The Protein Structure Project, Polytechnic Inst. of Brooklyn 1950-59, Adjunct Prof. of Physics 1953-56, Prof. of Crystallography 1956-59; Head Biophysics Dept. Roswell Park Memorial Inst. 1959-76; Research Prof. of Biophysics, State Univ. of N.Y., Buffalo 1960-76, Professorial Lecturer 1959-76; Visiting Prof. of Biophysics, State Univ. Coll. at Buffalo, N.Y. 1966-76; Research Prof., Graduate Faculty, Niagara Univ., Niagara Falls, N.Y. 1968-76; mem. U.S. Nat. Comm. on Crystallography, Nat. Research Council 1951-56, 1958-63, 1964-67, 1968-71, Chair. 1954-55; Research Scientist Emer., Medical Foundation of Buffalo 1977-; Del. to Gen. Assembly Int. Union of Crystallography, Stockholm 1951, Paris 1954, Montreal 1957, Cambridge 1960 and Moscow 1966; consultant on X-ray diffraction to X-ray Dept. of Gen. Electric Co. 1953-73, to Carborundum Co. 1962-75; Advisory Ed. Trans., Russian Journal Crystallography 1958-59; Dir. Center for Crystallographic Research, Roswell Park Div. of Health Research Inc., Buffalo 1965-76; Assoc. Prof., Faculty of Science, Univ. of Bordeaux Jan.-July 1970; mem. Advisory Bd. Russian Trans., American Inst. Physics 1959-78; Chair. Cttee. at several Int. Congresses of Crystallography 1968, 1969; fmr. mem. Electron Microscope Soc. of America (Pres. 1946, 1947); mem. American Soc. for X-ray and Electron Diffraction (Pres. 1946), Société Française de Minéralogie et de Crystallographie, American Crystallographic Asscn. and A.A.A.S.; mem. Nat. Acad. of Sciences 1977-, American Physical Soc.; national awards, Fankuchen Award, American Crystallographic Asscn. 1980; Hon. D.Sc. (State Univ. of New York) 1981; Gregory Aminoff Medal in Gold, Royal Swedish Acad. of Sciences 1984. *Publications:* numerous scientific papers, book reviews and contributions in journals. *Leisure interests:* rifle and pistol shooting, reading detective stories. *Address:* Medical Foundation of Buffalo Inc., 73 High Street, Buffalo, N.Y. 14203 (Office); Apartment 2, 172 Linwood Avenue, Buffalo, N.Y. 14209, U.S.A. (Home). *Telephone:* (716) 886-2666.

HARKIN, Thomas R., J.D.; American politician; b. 19 Nov. 1939, Cumming, Ia.; s. of Patrick and Frances Harkin; m. Ruth Raduenz 1968; two d.; ed. Iowa State Univ. and Catholic Univ. of America; mem. House of Reps. 1975-85; Senator from Iowa Jan. 1985-; Democrat. *Address:* 317 Hart Senate Office Bldg., Washington, D.C. 20510, U.S.A.

HARLAN, Jack Rodney, PH.D.; American professor of plant genetics; b. 7 June 1917, Washington, D.C.; s. of Harry Vaughn Harlan and Augusta Griffing Harlan; m. Jean Yocum 1939; two s. two d.; ed. George Washington Univ. and Univ. of California at Berkeley; Geneticist, U.S. Dept. of Agric. 1942-61; Prof. of Agronomy, Okla. State Univ. 1951-66; Prof. of Plant Genetics, Univ. of Ill. 1966-84, Prof. Emer. 1984-; Botanist, Dept. of Agric. (plant exploration and introduction) Turkey, Syria, Iraq 1948, Iran, Afghanistan, Pakistan, India, Ethiopia 1960; Sr. Staff mem. Iranian Prehistoric Project, Oriental Inst., Univ. of Chicago 1960, Turkish Prehistoric Project 1964; plant exploration and collection in 16 countries in Sub-Saharan Africa 1967-71; mem. Dead Sea Archaeological Project 1977, 1979, 1983; Guggenheim Fellow 1960; mem. N.A.S., A.A.A.S., American Soc. of Agronomy, Crop Science Soc. of America (Pres. 1966); Fellow American Acad. of Arts and Sciences. *Publications:* Theory and Dynamics of Grassland Agriculture 1956, Origins of African Plant Domestication (Co.-Ed.) 1975, Crops and Man 1975; more than 200 articles in journals. *Leisure interests:* sailing, bird watching, nature conservation. *Address:* 1016 North Hagan Street, New Orleans, La. 70119, U.S.A.

HARLAND, Bryce, M.A.; New Zealand diplomatist; b. 11 Dec. 1931; m.; three s.; ed. Victoria Univ., Wellington and Tufts Univ., U.S.A.; with Ministry of Foreign Affairs 1953-, various missions in Singapore, Bangkok, New York 1956-62, Head S. Pacific and Antarctic Div. 1962-64, Counsellor, Washington, D.C. 1965-69, Head Research Div., then Head Asian Affairs Div. 1969-70; Amb. to China (also accred. to Viet-Nam) 1973-76; Asst. Sec. 1976-81, also Dir. of External Aid Div. 1981-82; Perm. Rep. to UN 1982-85; High Commr. in U.K. (also accred. to Ireland) 1985-. *Address:* New Zealand High Commission, Haymarket, London, SW1Y 4TQ, England.

HARLEY, John Laker, C.B.E., M.A., D.PHIL., F.R.S.; British professor of forest science; b. 17 Nov. 1911, Old Charlton; s. of Charles Laker and Edith Sarah (née Smith) Harley; m. Elizabeth Lindsay Fitt 1938; one s. one d.;

ed. Leeds Grammar School and Wadham Coll., Oxford; Departmental Demonstrator in Botany, Univ. of Oxford 1938-40; army service 1940-45; Browne Research Fellow, The Queen's Coll., Oxford 1945-52, Univ. Demonstrator 1945-62, Official Fellow 1952-64; Reader in Plant Nutrition, Oxford 1962-65; Prof. of Botany Sheffield Univ. 1965-69; Prof. of Forest Science, Oxford 1969-79, Emer. Prof. 1979-; Fellow of St. John's Coll., Oxford 1969-79, Emer. Fellow 1979-; Hon. mem. British Mycological Soc. (Pres. 1969), British Ecological Soc. (Pres. 1970-72); Pres. Inst. of Biology 1984-86; Fellow Linnaean Soc. (Medal for Botany 1988); Dr. h.c. (Uppsala) 1981; Hon. Fellow Wadham Coll., Oxford 1972, Wye Coll., Univ. of London 1983. *Publications:* Biology of Mycorrhiza 1959, 1969, Mycorrhizal Symbiosis (with S. E. Smith) 1983. *Leisure interest:* gardening. *Address:* The Orchard, Old Marston, Oxford, OX3 0PQ, England. *Telephone:* (0865) 249068.

HARMAN, Avraham, B.A.; Israeli diplomatist; b. 7 Nov. 1914, London, England; s. of Israel and Zipporah Harman; m. Zena Stern 1940; one s. two d.; ed. Oxford Univ.; emigrated to Israel 1938; held posts in Jewish Agency 1938-48; Deputy Dir. Govt. Information Bureau 1948-49; Consul-Gen. Montreal 1949-50, New York, and Counsellor Del. to UN 1950-53; Consul-Gen. in New York 1953-55; Asst. Dir.-Gen. Ministry of Foreign Affairs 1955-56; Dir. Information Dept. Jewish Agency 1957-59; Amb. to the U.S.A. 1959-68; Pres. Hebrew Univ. of Jerusalem 1968-83; Chancellor 1983-. *Address:* Hebrew University of Jerusalem, Mount Scopus, Jerusalem 91 905, Israel.

HARMEL, Pierre Charles José Marie, D. EN D.; Belgian university professor and politician; b. 16 March 1911, Uccle, Brussels; s. of Charles Harmel and Eusebie André; m. Marie-Claire van Gehuchten 1946; four s. two d.; Prof., Faculty of Law, Univ. of Liège 1947-81; Prof. Emer.; mem. Chamber of Reps. 1946-71; Minister of Public Instruction and Fine Arts 1950-54; Minister of Justice 1958; Minister of Cultural Affairs 1959-60; Minister of Admin. 1960-61; Prime Minister 1965-66; Minister of Foreign Affairs 1966-73; co-opted Senator 1971; Minister of State Feb. 1973; Pres. of Senate 1973-77; mem. Acad. Royale de Belgique 1977-; Croix de guerre avec palmes 1940. *Publications:* Principes non bis in idem et les droits d'enregistrement 1942, La famille et l'impôt en Belgique 1944, Culture et profession 1944, Les sources et la nature de la responsabilité civile des notaires, en droit Belge de 1830 à 1962 1964, Organisation et déontologie du notariat 1977, Droit commun de la Vente 1985, Grandes avenues du droit 1988. *Address:* 8 avenue de l'Horizon, 1150 Brussels, Belgium. *Telephone:* 02-762 4680.

HARMER, Sir Frederic Evelyn, Kt., C.M.G.; British shipping executive (retd.); b. 3 Nov. 1905, Cambridge; s. of late Sir Sidney F. Harmer and late Lady Laura Russell Harmer (née Howell); m. 1st Barbara Susan Hamilton 1931 (died 1972), one s. three d.; m. 2nd Daphne Shelton Agar 1973; ed. Eton and King's Coll., Cambridge; Treasury 1939, Temp. Asst. Sec. 1943-45, served Washington 1944, 1945; Dir. Peninsular and Orient Steam Navigation Co. 1955-57, Deputy Chair. 1957-70; Govt. Dir. British Petroleum Co. Ltd. 1952-70; Dir. Nat. Westminster Bank Ltd.; Vice-Chair. of Govs., London School of Econs. until Dec. 1969; Chair. Int. Chamber of Shipping until 1971; Hon. Fellow, L.S.E. 1970. *Leisure interests:* sailing, golf. *Address:* Tiggins Field, Kelsale, Saxmundham, Suffolk, England. *Telephone:* (0728) 3156.

HARMOKO; Indonesian journalist and politician; b. 7 Feb. 1939, Kertosono, E. Java; ed. Sr. High School, Kediri, E. Java and Inst. of Nat. Defence (LEMHANAS), Jakarta; journalist, Merdeka (magazine and daily) 1960-65; Ed., Api (daily); Man. Ed. Merdeka and Chief Ed. Merdiko 1966-68; Chief Ed. Mimbar Kita 1968-69; Gen. Man., Chief Ed. Pos Kota (daily); mem. Bd. of Film Censors 1974; mem. Press Council 1975; Chief Ed. Warna Sari 1976-83; mem. House of Reps. and People's Consultative Ass. and Head of Information and Mass Media Div. of Functional Group (GOLKAR) 1978; Head of Advisory Bd. of Newspaper Publrs. Asscn. 1979-84; mem. Exec. Bd. Press and Graphics Asscn. 1980-84; Minister of Information 1983-. *Address:* Ministry of Information, Jln. Merdeka Barat 9, Jakarta, Indonesia.

HARMS, Hans Heinrich, DR.THEOL.; German ecclesiastic; b. 4 July 1914, Osterholz-Scharmbeck; s. of Wilhelm and Christine Harms; m. Marianne Kiel 1940; two d.; ed. Göttingen and Bonn Univs. and Princeton Theological Seminary, U.S.A.; Pastor, Duderstadt 1939, Roringen, Herberhausen 1943; Inspector of Studies, Göttingen 1949; Oberkirchenrat Foreign Office of Church 1950-52; Sec., then Assoc. Dir., Div. of Studies, World Council of Churches (WCC) 1952-60; Sr. Pastor in Hamburg 1960-67; mem. Cen. Cttee. WCC 1961-68, 1975-83, mem. Exec. Cttee. 1975-83; teaching assignment Univ. of Göttingen 1946, Univ. of Hamburg 1961; mem. Council, Evangelical Church in Germany 1973-85; Bishop of Evangelical-Lutheran Church in Oldenburg 1967-85; co-ed. Die Kirchen der Welt, Ökumenische Rundschau, Evangelische Missionszeitschrift, Das Wort in der Welt; Dr. h.c. (Göttingen); Winner of the Niedersachsen Landesmedaille 1985. *Address:* Beethovenstrasse 9, 2900 Oldenburg, Federal Republic of Germany (Home). *Telephone:* 1 43 84 (Home).

HARNICK, Sheldon Mayer; American lyricist; b. 30 April 1924, Chicago; s. of Harry M. and Esther (née Kanter) Harnick; m. 1st Mary Boatner 1950 (divorced); m. 2nd Elaine May 1962; m. 3rd Margery Gray 1965; one

s. one d.; ed. Northwestern Univ.; wrote songs for univ. musicals; contributor to revues: New Faces of 1952, Two's Company 1953, John Murray Anderson's Almanac 1954, The Shoestring Revue 1955, The Littlest Revue 1956, Shoestring 1957 1957; with composer Jerry Bock (q.v.) wrote shows Body Beautiful 1958, Fiorello 1959 (Pulitzer Prize), Tenderloin 1960, Smiling the Boy Fell Dead (with David Baker) 1961, She Loves Me 1963, Fiddler on the Roof (Tony Award) 1964, The Apple Tree 1966, The Rothschilds 1970, Captain Jinks of the Horse Marines (opera, with Jack Beeson) 1975, Rex (with Richard Rodgers) 1976, Dr. Heidegger's Fountain of Youth (opera, with Jack Beeson) 1978, Gold (cantata, with Joe Raposo) 1980, translations: The Merry Widow 1977, The Umbrellas of Cherbourg 1979, Carmen 1981, A Christmas Carol 1981 (musical; book and lyrics), Songs of the Auvergne 1982. *Address:* c/o Cogan, Bell and Co., 330 W. 42nd Street, New York, N.Y. 10036, U.S.A.

HARNONCOURT, Nikolaus; Austrian musician and conductor; b. 6 Dec. 1929, Berlin, Germany; s. of Eberhard and Ladislaja (née Meran) Harnoncourt; m. Alice Hoffelner 1953; three s. one d.; ed. Matura Gymnasium, Graz, Acad. of Music, Vienna; mem. of Vienna Symphony Orchestra 1952–69; Prof., Mozarteum and Inst. of Musicology, Univ. of Salzburg 1972–; founder mem. of Concentus Musicus, Ensemble for Ancient Music 1954; Conductor, Zürich Opera and Amsterdam Concertgebouw Orkest; has given numerous concerts in Europe, Australia and the U.S.A.; shared Erasmus Prize 1980; H.G. Nägeli Medal, Zürich 1983; awards for recordings include Prix Mondiale du Disque, Grand Prix du Disque, Deutscher Schallplattenpreis. *Publication:* Musik als Klargrede, Wege 3u einem neuen Musikverstärdnis 1982. *Leisure interests:* cultural history, woodwork. *Address:* 38 Piaristengasse, 1080 Vienna, Austria.

HARPER, Charles Little, B.S.; American business executive; b. 23 March 1930, Evanston, Ill.; s. of H. Mitchell and Margaret (née Little) Harper; m. Alice P. Fall 1955; two s. four d.; ed. Princeton Univ.; Metallurgical Engineer, Production Controller, Cost Controller The H. M. Harper Co., Morton Grove, Ill. 1954–68; with ITT Harper Inc., Morton Grove 1968–, Pres. 1972–78; Vice-Pres. Joslyn Manufacturing 1979–80, ACF Industries, Houston 1981–84, Joy Manufacturing Co., Houston 1984–; Gen. Man. WKM Div. 1984–; mem. American Soc. Metals, American Inst. of Mining Engineers, Newcomen Soc. *Address:* P.O. Box 4334, Houston, Tex. 77210, U.S.A.

HARPER, Charles Michel, M.B.A.; American business executive; b. 26 Sept. 1927, Lansing, Mich.; s. of Charles F. Harper and Alma Michel; m. Joan F. Bruggema 1950; one s. three d.; ed. Purdue Univ. and Univ. of Chicago; Gen. Motors Corpn., Detroit 1950–54; Pillsbury Co., Minneapolis 1954–74, Group Vice-Pres. Poultry, Food Service and Venture Businesses 1970–74; Exec. Vice-Pres., C.O.O., Dir. Conagra Inc., Omaha 1974–76, Pres., C.E.O. 1976–81, Chair. and C.E.O. 1981–; mem. Bd. of Dirs. Norwest Corpn., Valmont Industries, Inc., Peter Kiewit Sons Inc. *Address:* Conagra Inc., 1 Central Park Plaza, Omaha, Neb. 68102, U.S.A.

HARPER, Edward James, B.A., B.MUS., A.R.C.M., L.R.A.M.; British composer; b. 17 March 1941, Taunton, Somerset; m. 1st Penelope Teece 1969 (divorced 1984); m. 2nd Dorothy C. Shanks 1984, one s. one d.; ed. King Edward VI Grammar School, Guildford, Royal Coll. of Music and Christ Church, Oxford; Lecturer in Music, Univ. of Edin. 1964, Sr. Lecturer 1972–; Dir. New Music Group of Scotland 1973–. *Compositions include:* Bartok Games 1972, Fanny Robin (chamber opera) 1975, Ricercari 1975, 7 Poems by E. E. Cummings 1977, Symphony 1979, Clarinet Concerto 1981, Hedda Gabler (opera) 1985, Qui creavit coelum (mass) 1986, The Mellstock Quire (opera) 1987. *Address:* 7 Morningside Park, Edinburgh, EH10 5HO, Scotland.

HARPER, Heather, C.B.E., F.R.C.M.; British soprano; b. 8 May 1930, Belfast; d. of Hugh and Mary Eliza Harper; m. 2nd Eduardo J. Benarroch 1973; ed. Trinity Coll. of Music, London; created soprano role in Britten's War Requiem, Coventry Cathedral 1962; toured U.S.A. with BBC Symphony Orchestra 1965, U.S.S.R. 1967, soloist opening concerts at the Maltings, Snape 1967, Queen Elizabeth Hall 1967; annual concert and opera tours U.S.A. 1967–; prin. soloist BBC Symphony Orchestra on 1982 tour of Hong Kong and Australia; prin. soloist Royal Opera House U.S. visit 1984; also concerts in Asia, Middle East, Australia, European Music Festivals, S. America; principal roles at Covent Garden, Bayreuth Festival, La Scala (Milan), Teatro Colón (Buenos Aires), Edinburgh Festival, Glyndebourne, Sadler's Wells, Metropolitan Opera House (New York), San Francisco, Frankfurt, Deutsche Oper (Berlin), Japan (with Royal Opera House Covent Garden Co.), Netherlands Opera House, New York City Opera; renowned performances of Arabella, Ariadne, Chrysothemis, Kaiserin, Marschallin (Richard Strauss); TV roles include Ellen Orford (Peter Grimes), Mrs. Coyle (Owen Wingrave), Ilia (Idomeneo), Donna Elvira (Don Giovanni), La Traviata, La Bohème; recordings include Les Illuminations (Britten), Symphony No. 8 (Mahler), Don Giovanni (Mozart), Requiem (Verdi) and Missa Solemnis (Beethoven), Seven Early Songs (Berg), Marriage of Figaro, Peter Grimes, 4 Last Songs (Strauss), 14 Songs with Orchestra; 25 consecutive years as prin. soloist at the Promenade concerts; Dir. Singing Studies at the Britten-Pears School for Advanced Musical Studies, Aldeburgh, Suffolk; Prof. of Singing and Consultant Royal Coll. of Music, London 1986–; First Visiting Lecturer in Residence, Royal Scottish Acad. of Music 1987–; retd. from operatic stage 1986 (operatic farewell, Teatro Colon, Buenos Aires 1986); continues concert performances and recordings; Hon.

Fellow Trinity Coll. of Music; Hon. mem. R.A.M., Hon. D.Mus. (Queen's Univ.); Edison Award 1971, Grammy Award 1979, 1984. *Leisure interests:* gardening, painting, cooking, swimming, tennis. *Address:* 20 Milverton Road, London, NW6 7AS, England.

HARPER, John Lander, M.A., D.PHIL., F.R.S.; British research biologist, consultant and author; b. 27 May 1925, Rugby, Warwicks.; s. of John H. and Harriet M. (née Archer) Harper; m. Borgny Lerø 1954; one s. two d.; ed. Magdalen Coll., Oxford; Demonstrator, Dept. of Agric., Univ. of Oxford 1951–52, lecturer 1953–59; Rockefeller Foundation Fellow, Univ. of Calif. (Davis) 1959–60; Prof., Dept. of Agric. Botany, Univ. Coll. of N. Wales, Bangor 1960–67, Prof. of Agric. Botany and Head, School of Plant Biology 1967–78, Prof. of Botany and Head, School of Plant Biology 1978–82, Prof. Emer. and Dir. of Unit. of Population Biology 1982–; Foreign Assoc. N.A.S. (1984), and other learned socs.; Hon. D.Sc. (Sussex) 1984. *Publications:* Population Biology of Plants 1977, Ecology: Individuals, Populations and Communities 1986; numerous papers in scientific journals. *Leisure interest:* gardening. *Address:* Cae Groes, Glan-y-Coed Park, Dwygyfylchi, Penmaenmawr, Gwynedd, North Wales, United Kingdom. *Telephone:* (0492) 622362.

HARPLEY, Sydney Charles, R.A.; British sculptor; b. 19 April 1927; s. of Sydney Frederick Harpley and Rose Isabel Harpley; m. Sally Holliday 1956 (divorced 1968); two s. one d.; ed. Royal Coll. of Art; realist sculptor, portraits and figure; Smuts Memorial, Cape Town 1963; portraits include Edward Heath, for Constitution Club 1973, Lee Kwan Yew, Singapore 1983; sculpture in collections of Nat. Gallery, N.Z., Nat. Gallery, Cape Town, Paul Mellon, U.S.A., Anton Rupert, S.A., the late Princess Grace of Monaco, Fleur Cowles Meyer, London, S. & D. Josefowitz, Geneva, Lady Verulam, Lord Jersey; Visitors' Choice Prize, R.A. Summer Exhbn. 1978, 1979. *Leisure interests:* chess, music. *Address:* Radigan Farm, Ashill, Somerset, TA19 9NL, England. *Telephone:* (0823) 480249.

HARPPRECHT, Klaus Christoph; German author and television producer; b. 11 April 1927, Stuttgart; s. of Christoph and Dorothea (née Bronisch) Harpprecht; m. Renate Lasker 1961; ed. Evangelical Theological Seminary, Blaubeuren, Württemberg and Univs. of Tübingen, Munich and Stuttgart; junior ed. and Bonn corresp. Christ und Welt 1948–53; commentator and corresp., RIAS Berlin (Rundfunk in amerikanischen Sektor), Sender Freies Berlin and Westdeutscher Rundfunk, Cologne 1953–61; America corresp., Zweites Deutsche Fernsehen 1962–65; Publr., S. Fischer Verlag, and ed. Der Monat 1966–71; consultant and chief speech writer to Chancellor Willy Brandt 1972–74; ed. GEO magazine, Hamburg 1978–79; now ind. writer and TV producer; Theodore Wolff and Drexel awards. *Publications:* The East German Rising 1954, Viele Grüse an die Freiheit 1964, Beschädigte Paradiese 1966, Willy Brandt: Portrait 1970, Deutsche Themen 1973, L'Evolution Allemande 1978, Der Fremde Freund 1982, Amerika: Eine Innere Geschichte 1982, Amerikaner: Freunde, Freunde, Ferne Nachbarn 1984, (with Thomas Hoepker) Amerika die Geschichte seiner Eroberung 1986, Georg Forster—oder die Liebe zur Welt 1987, Das Ende der Gemuetlichkeit 1987, Die Lust der Freiheit. Deutsche Revolutionaere in Paris 1989. *Leisure interests:* music, literature, history. *Address:* 16 Clos des Palmeraies, 83420 La Croix-Valmer, France. *Telephone:* 94/79.60.76.

HARRELL, Lynn; American 'cellist; b. 30 Jan. 1944, New York; s. of Mack Harrell and Majorie Fulton; m. Linda Blandford 1976; one s. one d.; ed. Juilliard School of Music, New York, and Curtis Inst. of Music, Philadelphia; principal 'cellist, Cleveland Orch. (under George Szell) 1963–71; now appears as soloist with the world's major orchestras; teacher, Juilliard School; Visiting Piatigorsky Prof. of Cello at Univ. of Southern Calif., L.A. 1978–87, First Piatigorski Prof. of Cello 1987–; exclusive recording artist, Decca Records, London. *Leisure interests:* chess, opera. *Address:* c/o Columbia Artists, 165 West 57 Street, New York, N.Y. 10019, U.S.A.

HARRIES, Rt. Rev. Richard Douglas, M.A.; British ecclesiastic; b. 2 June 1936; s. of Brig. W. D. J. Harries and G. M. B. Harries; m. Josephine Bottomley 1963; one s. one d.; ed. Wellington Coll., Royal Mil. Acad, Sandhurst, Selwyn Coll, Cambridge, Cuddesdon Coll., Oxford; Lieut., Royal Corps of Signals 1955–58; Curate, Hampstead Parish Church 1963–69; Chaplain, Westfield Coll. 1966–69; Lecturer, Wells Theological Coll. 1969–72; Warden of Wells, Salisbury and Wells Theological Coll. 1971–72; Vicar, All Saints, Fulham, London 1972–81; Dean, King's Coll., London 1981–87; Bishop of Oxford 1987–; Vice-Chair. Council of Christian Action 1979–, Council for Arms Control 1982–; Chair. Southwark Ordination Course, Shalom, End Loans to South Africa (ELSTA), Christian Evidence Soc.; Consultant to the Archbishops on Jewish-Christian Relations; mem. Home Office Advisory Cttee. for Reform of Law on Sexual Offences 1981–85. *Publications:* Prayers of Hope 1975, Turning to Prayer 1978, Prayers of Grief and Glory 1979, Being a Christian 1981, Should Christians Support Guerrillas? 1982, The Authority of Divine Love 1983, Praying Round the Clock 1983, Seasons of the Spirit (Co-Ed.) 1984, Prayer and the Pursuit of Happiness 1985, Reinhold Niebuhr and the Issues of Our Time (Ed.) 1986; contrib. to several books; numerous articles. *Leisure interests:* theatre, literature, sport. *Address:* Diocesan Church House, North Hinksey, Oxford, OX2 0NB, England. *Telephone:* (0865) 244566.

HARRIMAN, Leslie Oriseweyinmi; Nigerian diplomatist; b. 9 July 1930, Warri; s. of A. L. Harriman and Mewe Omadeli-Harriman; m. Clara Edewor 1956; four s. one d.; ed. Govt. School, Benin, Edo Coll., Benin, Govt. Coll., Ibadan, Univ. Coll., Ibadan, Pembroke Coll., Oxford, and Imperial Defence Coll., London; Asst. Dist. Officer, Lagos 1955–58; Second Sec. British Embassy, Spain 1958–59; Counsellor and Acting High Commr. for Nigeria in Ghana 1961–63; Deputy Perm. Sec. Ministry of External Affairs 1965–66; High Commr. to Uganda 1966–69, to Kenya 1966–70; Amb. to France 1970–75, also accred. to Tunisia and Perm. Del. to UNESCO 1970–75; Amb. and Perm. Rep. to UN 1975–79; fmr. Chair. UN Special Cttees. on Peace-Keeping Operations, against Apartheid, UN Ad hoc Cttee. to draft a convention against the taking of hostages; Tom Mboya 10th Memorial Lecture, Nairobi 1978; mem. Bd. of Govs. Commonwealth Foundation; Officer of the Order of the Fed. Repub.; Hon. D.H.L. (Moorehouse Coll., Atlanta); Hon. D.C.L. (St. Augustine's Coll., N.C.). *Publications:* UN and Its Peace Keeping Operations, Britain's Thatcher's International Image (essays), U.S.' Ambivalent Policies in Africa (essays). *Address:* 3B Ashabi Adedire Street, Apapa, Nigeria. *Telephone:* 877145.

HARRINGTON, Fred Harvey, PH.D.; American historian and educational administrator; b. 24 June 1912, Watertown, N.Y.; s. of Arthur William and Elsie (Sutton) Harrington; m. Anna Howes 1935; one s. four d.; ed. Cornell and New York Univs.; Instructor in History, Washington Square Coll. of New York Univ. 1936–37, Univ. of Wis. 1937–39, Asst. Prof. 1939–40; Prof. and Chair. of History and Political Science, Univ. of Ark. 1940–44; Assoc. Prof. of History, Univ. of Wis. 1944–47, Prof. 1947–70, Chair. of Dept. 1952–55, Special Asst. to Pres. 1956–58, Vice-Pres. of Academic Affairs 1958–62, Vice-Pres. 1962, Pres. 1962–70, Vilas Research Prof. of American Diplomatic History 1970–82; Pres. Nat. Asscn. State Univs. and Land Grant Colls. 1968–69; Dir. Nat. Asscn. Educational Broadcasters 1965–68; Dir. American Council of Educ. 1966–68; mem. Indo-American sub-cttee. Educ. and Culture 1975–80; Dir. Study of Int. Linkages of Higher Educ. 1976–78; Program Adviser to Ford Foundation in India 1971–77; Visiting Prof. W. Va. Univ. 1942, Cornell Univ. 1944, Univ. of Pa. 1949, Univ. of Colo. 1951, Oxford Univ. 1955, Univ. of Kyoto (Japan) 1962; Frederic Courtland Penfield Fellow in Diplomacy and Int. Relations, New York Univ. 1933–36; Fellow John Simon Guggenheim Memorial Foundation 1943–44; Ford Foundation Faculty Fellow 1955–56; Hon. LL.D. (New York, Drake, Loyola and Calif.), Hon. L.H.D. (Maine, De Paul and Miami and Northland Coll., Wis.), Hon. Litt.D. (Ife, Nigeria). *Publications:* God, Mammon and the Japanese: Dr. Horace N. Allen and Korean-American Relations (1884–1905) 1944, Fighting Politician: Major-General N. P. Banks 1948, An American History (2 vols., with Curti and Shryock and Cochran) 1950, Hanging Judge, Isaac C. Parker and the Indian Frontier 1951, A History of American Civilization 1953, The Future of Adult Education: New Responsibilities for Colleges and Universities 1977. *Address:* 1840 Van Hise Hall, University of Wisconsin, Madison, Wis. 53706 (Office); 87 Oak Creek Trail, Madison, Wis. 53717, U.S.A. (Home). *Telephone:* 608-262-3682 (Office).

HARRIS, Albert Edward, A.O.; Australian business executive; b. 4 May 1927, Melbourne; s. of late A. E. Harris; m. Vicki I. Jarmalavičius 1967; two d.; ed.. The Scots Coll., Sydney; with Macquarie Broadcasting Service 1946–54; joined Ampol Ltd. 1954, Asst. Gen. Man. 1958, Dir. 1959, Gen. Man. 1963, Chief Gen. Man. 1965, Man. Dir. 1970–, C.E.O. 1977–; Man. Dir. Ampol Exploration Ltd. 1971–, C.E.O. 1977–; Dir. Australian Lubricating Oil Refinery Ltd., W. Australian Pty. Ltd., W. Australian Natural Gas Pty. Ltd.; Deputy Chair. Australian Inst. of Petroleum Ltd.; Chair. Zoological Parks Bd. of N.S.W., Oak Systems of Australia Pty. Ltd., Arena Man. Pty. Ltd., Australian Sports Comm.; Commr. Australian Broadcasting Comm. 1974–77; Queen's Silver Jubilee Medal 1977. *Leisure interest:* tennis. *Address:* P.O. Box 456, North Sydney, N.S.W. 2060 (Office) 43 Wentworth Road, Vaucluse, N.S.W. 2030, Australia (Home). *Telephone:* 929-6222 (Office); 337-2223 (Home).

HARRIS, Rt. Rev. Augustine; British ecclesiastic; b. 27 Oct. 1917, Liverpool; s. of Augustine Harris and Louisa Beatrice Rycroft; ed. St. Francis Xavier's Coll., Liverpool and Upholland Coll., Lancs.; ordained 1942; Curacies 1942–52; Prison Chaplain 1952–66; Prin. Roman Catholic Prison Chaplain 1958–66; Auxiliary Bishop of Liverpool 1966–78; Bishop of Middlesbrough 1978–. *Leisure interests:* golf and walking. *Address:* Bishop's House, 16 Cambridge Road, Middlesbrough, Cleveland, TS5 5NN, England.

HARRIS, Chauncy Dennison, PH.D., D.LITT.; American geographer; b. 31 Jan. 1914, Logan, Utah; s. of Franklin S. and Estella S. Harris; m. Edith Young 1940; one d.; ed. Brigham Young Univ., Oxford and Chicago Univs.; Prof. of Geography, Univ. of Chicago 1947–84, Samuel N. Harper Distinguished Service Prof. 1969–84, Prof. Emer. 1984–, Dean, Graduate Div. of Social Sciences 1954–60; Dir. Centre for Int. Studies 1966–84; Asst. to the Pres. 1973–75, Vice-Pres. for Academic Resources 1975–78; mem. Bd. of Dirs., Social Science Research Council 1959–70, Vice-Chair. 1963–65, mem. Cttee. on Programs and Policy 1959–67, Exec. Cttee. 1967–70; mem. Exec. Cttee., Nat. Research Council Div. of Behavioural Sciences 1967–70; mem. Int. Research and Exchanges Bd. 1968–71; mem. Exec. Cttee. ICSU 1969–72; Del. 17th Gen. Conf. UNESCO, Paris 1972; Vice-Pres. Int. Geographical Union 1956–64, Sec.-Gen. 1968–76; mem. Asscn. of American

Geographers (Pres. 1957), American Asscn. for Advancement of Slavic Studies (AAASS) (Pres. 1962), American Geographical Soc. (Vice-Pres. 1969–74), Nat. Council for Soviet and East European Research (Bd. of Dirs. 1977–83); mem. Council of Scholars, Library of Congress 1980–83; Conseil de la Bibliographie Géographique Internationale 1986–; del. to numerous Int. Geographic Congresses 1949–; Hon. mem. Royal Geographical Soc. and geographical socs. of Paris, Berlin, Frankfurt, Rome, Florence, Warsaw, Belgrade and Japan; D.Econ. h.c. (Catholic Univ., Chile), Hon. LL.D. (Indiana Univ.); Honors Award, Asscn. of American Geographers 1976, Lauréat d'honneur, Int. Geographical Union 1976, Alexander Csoma de Kőrösi Memorial Medal, Hungarian Geographical Soc. 1971, Alexander von Humboldt Gold Medal, Gesellschaft für Erdkunde zu Berlin 1978, Award for Distinguished Contributions to Slavic Studies, AAASS 1978, Cullom Geographical Medal, American Geographical Soc. 1985, Master Teacher Award, Nat. Council for Geographic Educ. 1986, Victoria Medal, Royal Geographical Soc. 1987. *Publications:* Economic Geography of the U.S.S.R. 1949, International List of Geographical Serials 1980, Soviet Geography: Accomplishments and Tasks 1962, Cities of the Soviet Union 1970, Annotated World List of Selected Current Geographical Serials 1980, Guide to Geographical Bibliographies and Reference works in Russian or on the Soviet Union 1975, Bibliography of Geography Part I, Introduction to General Aids 1976, Part II, Regional (Vol. 1) United States of America 1984, A Geographical Bibliography for American Libraries 1985, Directory of Soviet Geographers 1946–1987 1988; articles in professional journals. *Address:* Department of Geography, University of Chicago, 5828 University Avenue, Chicago, Ill. 60637, U.S.A.

HARRIS, Harry, M.D., F.R.S.; British professor of genetics; b. 30 Sept. 1919, Manchester; s. of Sol and Sarah Harris; m. Muriel Hargest 1948; one s.; ed. Manchester Grammar School and Univ. of Cambridge; Prof. and Head of Dept. of Biochem., King's Coll., London 1960–65; Galton Prof. and Head of Dept. of Human Genetics, Univ. Coll., London 1965–76; Hon. Dir. Medical Research Council Human Biochemical Genetics Unit 1962–76; Harnwell Univ. Prof., Univ. of Pa. 1976–; Foreign Assoc. N.A.S.; Dr. h.c. (René Descartes, Paris) 1976. *Publications:* Prenatal Diagnosis and Selective Abortion 1975, Handbook of Enzyme Electrophoresis in Human Genetics (with D. A. Hopkinson) 1976, The Principles of Human Biochemical Genetics (3rd edn.) 1981; ed. (with K. Hirschhorn) Advances in Human Genetics (Vols. 1–14) 1970–85; numerous scientific papers. *Address:* Department of Human Genetics, University of Pennsylvania School of Medicine, 195 John Morgan Bldg., 37th and Hamilton Walk, Philadelphia, Pa. 19104; 4050 Irving Street, Philadelphia, Pa. 19104, U.S.A. (Home). *Telephone:* (215) 898-6891 (Office); (215) 387-0245 (Home).

HARRIS, Harwell Hamilton; American architect; b. 2 July 1903, Redlands, Calif.; s. of Frederick Thomas Harris and May (née Hamilton) Harris; m. Jean Murray Bangs 1937; ed. Pomona Coll., Otis Art Inst.; sculptor 1926–29; practising architect with Richard Neutra 1929–32; private practice 1933–, Los Angeles 1933–51, Austin, Tex. 1951–56; Harris and Sherwood, Fort Worth 1956–57; Architect, Dallas 1958–62; Visiting Critic, Columbia Univ. 1943, Yale Univ. 1950, 1952; lecturer, Univ. of Southern Calif. 1945, 1946; Design Consultant, Nat. Orange Show 1949–54; Dir. School of Architecture, Univ. of Tex. 1951–55; Graduate Design Critic, Columbia Univ. 1960, Adjunct Prof. 1961; Prof. of Architecture, N.C. State Univ. 1962–73; Hon. Dr. of Fine Arts 1985; Int. Exec. Service Corps, Sabah, Malaysia 1972, El Salvador 1977, Singapore 1978; one-man exhbns. Univ. of Texas 1985; Fellow, A.I.A. 1965; H.H.H. Fellowship in Architecture, Univ. of Texas 1985; Graham Foundation, Chicago 1987, Columbia Univ., New York 1988; First Prize, Pittsburgh Glass Inst. 1937, 1938; Honar Award, Southern Calif. Chapter of A.I.A. 1937, Tex. Soc. of Architects 1961. *Works include:* Lowe House 1934, Fellowship Park House 1935, Havens House 1941, Birtcher House 1942, R. Johnson House 1948, English House 1950, Chadwick School 1951, Texas State Fair House 1954, J. L. Johnson House 1956, Eisenberg House 1958, Greenwood Mausoleum 1959, Treanor House 1959, Trade Mart Court 1960, Dallas Unitarian Church 1963, H. H. Harris Studio/House 1968, St. Giles Presbyterian Church 1969. *Publications:* H.H.H., Collection of His Writings and Buildings 1965, The Second Generation 1983, H.H.H. (monograph) 1985, Harwell Hamilton Harris: Tracking Life. *Address:* 122-A Cox Avenue, Raleigh, N.C. 27605, U.S.A. *Telephone:* (919) 833-0624.

HARRIS, Henry, F.R.C.P., F.R.C.PATH., F.R.S.; British cell biologist; b. 28 Jan. 1925; s. of Sam and Ann Harris; m. Alexandra Brodsky 1950; one s. two d.; ed. Sydney Boys High School, Univ. of Sydney, Lincoln Coll., Oxford; Dir. of Research, Cancer Research Campaign, Sir William Dunn School of Pathology, Oxford 1954–59; Visiting Scientist, Nat. Inst. of Health, U.S.A. 1959–60; Head Dept. of Cell Biology, John Innes Inst. 1960–63; Prof. of Pathology, Univ. of Oxford 1963–79, Regius Prof. of Medicine 1979–; Head of the Sir William Dunn School of Pathology, Oxford 1963–; Corresp. mem. Australian Acad. of Science; Foreign Hon. mem. American Acad. of Arts and Sciences; Foreign mem. Max Planck Soc.; Foreign Prof. Coll. de France; Hon. mem. American Asscn. of Pathologists, German Soc. of Cell Biology; Hon. Fellow, Cambridge Philosophical Soc.; Hon. F.R.C.Path. (Australia); Hon. D.Sc. (Edinburgh); Hon. M.D. (Geneva, Sydney); Feldberg Foundation Award; Ivison Macadam Memorial Prize; Prix de la Fondation Isabelle Decazes de Nöue for cancer research, Madonnina Prize for Medical Research; Royal Medal of the Royal Soc., Osler Medal of the Royal Coll.

of Physicians. *Publications:* Nucleus and Cytoplasm 1968, Cell Fusion 1970, La fusion cellulaire 1974, The Balance of Improbabilities 1987, papers on cellular physiology and biochemistry in various scientific books and journals. *Leisure interest:* history. *Address:* Sir William Dunn School of Pathology, South Parks Road, Oxford, OX1 3RE. *Telephone:* (0865) 275503.

HARRIS, Julie; American actress; b. 2 Dec. 1925, Mich.; d. of William Picket and Elsie (née Smith) Harris; m. 1st Jay I. Julien 1946 (divorced 1954); 2nd Manning Gurian 1954 (divorced 1967); one s.; 3rd Walter Erwin Carroll 1977 (divorced 1982); ed. Yale Drama School. *Theatre work includes:* Sundown Beach 1948, The Young and Fair 1948, Magnolia Alley 1949, Montserrat 1949, The Member of the Wedding 1950, Sally Bowles in I am a Camera 1951, The Lark 1956, Little Moon of Alban 1960, A Shot in the Dark 1961, Marathon 33 1964, Ready When You Are, C.B. 1964, And Miss Reardon Drinks a Little 1971, Voices 1972, The Last of Mrs. Lincoln 1973, In Praise of Love 1974, The Belle of Amherst, New York 1976, London 1977, Break a Leg, New York 1979, Mixed Couples, New York 1980, Driving Miss Daisy 1988. *Films include:* East of Eden 1955 (Antoinette Perry Award), I Am a Camera 1956, Poacher's Daughter 1960, The Haunting, The Moving Target, Voyage of the Damned 1976, The Bell Jar 1979. *Television:* Knots Landing 1982. New York Drama Critics' Award for I Am a Camera; numerous other awards. *Address:* c/o William Morris Agency, 1350 Avenue of the Americas, New York, N.Y. 10019, U.S.A.

HARRIS, Kenneth, M.A.; British author, journalist and business executive; b. 11 Nov. 1919; s. of David Harris and Kathleen Powell; m. Doris Young-Smith 1949 (died 1970); no c.; ed. Trowbridge High School for Boys and Wadham Coll., Oxford; war service, R.A. 1940–45; Washington Corresp., The Observer 1950–53, Assoc. Ed. 1976–, Dir. 1978–, Chair. Observer Int. 1981–; Chair. George Outram Ltd. 1981–; radio and TV work (mainly for BBC) 1957–. *Publications:* Travelling Tongues: Debating Across America 1949, About Britain 1967, Conversations 1968, Life of Attlee 1982. *Leisure interests:* reading, walking, horse racing. *Address:* The Observer, 8 St. Andrew's Hill, London, E.C.4, England. *Telephone:* 01-236 0202.

HARRIS, Richard R. St. Johns; Irish actor; b. 1 Oct. 1933, Limerick; s. of Ivan Harris; m. 1st Hon. (Joan) Elizabeth Rees-Williams 1957 (divorced 1969); three s.; m. 2nd Ann Turkel 1974; ed. L.A.M.D.A.; made professional theatre début as Micksee in The Quare Fellow, Theatre Royal, Stratford 1956; also appeared in A View From the Bridge 1956, Paulino in Man, Beast and Virtue 1958; toured U.S.S.R. and East Europe with Joan Littlewood's Theatre Workshop 1958; The Ginger Man 1959; Diary of a Madman, Royal Court 1963; Camelot 1981. *Films include:* Alive and Kicking 1958, Shake Hands with the Devil 1959, The Wreck of the Mary Deare 1959, A Terrible Beauty 1960, All Night Long 1961, The Guns of Navarone 1961, Mutiny on the Bounty 1962, This Sporting Life, Major Dundee 1965, The Heroes of Telemark 1965, The Bible 1966, Hawaii 1966, Caprice 1966, Camelot 1967, The Molly Maguires 1969, A Man Called Horse 1969, Bloomfield 1970, Cromwell 1970, Man in The Wilderness 1971, The Deadly Trackers 1973, 99 and 44/100 Dead 1974, Juggernaut 1975, Robin and Marian 1975, The Return of a Man Called Horse 1976, Orca 1977, The Cassandra Crossing 1977, Golden Rendezvous 1977, The Wild Geese 1978, The Sea Wolves 1979, Ravagers 1979, Tarzan and the Ape Man 1981, Triumphs of a Man Called Horse 1983, Highpoint 1984. *Recordings:* MacArthur Park and This Time, The Prophet, In the Membership of My Days. *Television appearances include:* The Iron Harp 1958, The Snow Goose 1971; Cannes Film Festival Best Actor Award for This Sporting Life.

HARRIS, Richard Travis; British company director; b. 15 April 1919, Epsom, Surrey; s. of Douglas Harris and Rose Emmiline Mary Travis; m. 1st June Constance Rundle 1941; two d.; m. 2nd Margaret Sophia Nye (née Aron) 1953; one s. one d.; ed. Charterhouse, R.M.A. Woolwich; commissioned 2nd Lieut. Royal Signals 1939; served World War II 1939–45; twice mentioned in despatches; Lt.-Col. G.S.O.I. Sigs. BAOR 1946; Sudan Defence Force 1947–50; retd. with rank of Lt.-Col. 1950; Management Trainee Rediffusion 1950; Man. Dir. Rediffusion (Nigeria) Ltd. 1951–54; Deputy Gen. Man. Associated Rediffusion Dec. 1954–57; Man. Dir. Coates & Co. (Plymouth) Ltd. 1957–63; Man. Dir. Dollond & Aitchison Ltd. 1964–70; Chair. and Chief Exec. Dollond & Aitchison Group Ltd. 1970–78; Dir. Gallaher Ltd. 1970–87, Deputy Chair. 1978–84; Dir. Burton Group PLC 1984–; Founder Chair. Devon & Cornwall Branch Inst. of Dirs.; mem. Council Inst. of Dirs. 1975–, Chair. 1982–85, Vice-Pres. 1985–; mem. of Policy and Executive Cttee. Inst. of Dirs. 1976–88; mem. Council Birmingham Univ. 1978–; Gov. Royal Shakespeare Theatre. *Leisure interest:* fly fishing. *Address:* 21 Lucy's Mill, Stratford-upon-Avon, Warwicks., CV39 6DE, England. *Telephone:* (0789) 299631.

HARRIS, Stephen, M.S., PH.D.; American professor of electrical engineering and applied physics; b. 29 Nov. 1936, Brooklyn, New York; s. of Henry Harris and Anne Alpern Harris; m. Frances J. Greene 1959; one s. one d.; ed. Rensselaer Polytechnic, Troy, New York and Stanford Univ.; Prof. of Electrical Eng. Stanford Univ. 1963–, of Applied Physics 1979–, Dir. Edward L. Ginzton Lab. 1983–, Kenneth and Barbara Oshman Prof. 1988–; Guggenheim Fellowship 1976–77; mem. N.A.S., Nat. Acad. of Eng.; A. Noble Prize 1965, McGraw Research Award 1973, Sarnoff Award 1978, Davies Medal 1984, C. H. Townes Award 1985. *Publications:* articles in professional journals. *Leisure interests:* skiing, jogging, hiking. *Address:* Edward L. Ginzton Laboratory, Stanford University, Stanford, Calif. 94305, U.S.A. *Telephone:* 415-497-0224.

HARRISON, Bryan Desmond, PH.D., F.R.S., F.R.S.E.; British plant virologist; b. 16 June 1931, Purley; s. of John William Harrison and Norah (née Webster) Harrison; m. Elizabeth Latham-Warde 1968; two s. one d.; ed. Whitgift School, Croydon and Univs. of Reading and London; ARC Postgrad. Studentship, Rothamsted Experimental Station, Harpenden 1952–54, Research Scientist 1957–66; Scottish Horticultural (later Crop) Research Inst., Dundee 1954–57, Head Virology Div. 1966–; Pres. Asscn. of Applied Biologists 1980–81; Hon. Prof. St. Andrew's Univ. 1987–; Hon. Visiting Prof. Dundee Univ. 1988–. *Publications:* Plant Virology: the Principles (with A. J. Gibbs) 1976, and over 150 research papers and reviews on plant viruses and virus diseases. *Address:* Scottish Crop Research Institute, Invergowrie, Dundee, DD2 5DA, Scotland. *Telephone:* 0382-562731.

HARRISON, Sir Ernest Thomas, Kt., O.B.E.; British business executive; b. 11 May 1926, London; s. of Ernest Horace Harrison and Gertrude Rebecca Gibbons Harrison; m. Phyllis Brenda Knight 1960; three s. two d.; ed. Trinity Grammar School; Sec. and Chief Accountant, Racal Electronics Ltd. (now PLC) 1951, Dir. 1958, Deputy Man. Dir. 1961, Chair. and Chief Exec. 1966–; Chair. and Chief Exec. Decca Ltd. 1980–, Racal-Chubb Ltd. 1985–; active in Nat. Savings Movement 1964–76; Hon. D.Sc. (Cranfield) 1981, (City) 1982; Hon. D.Univ. (Surrey) 1981, (Edin.) 1983; Businessman of Year 1981. *Leisure interests:* horse racing (owner), gardening and sport. *Address:* Racal Electronics PLC, Western Road, Bracknell, Berks., RG12 1RG, England. *Telephone:* (0344) 481222.

HARRISON, Sir Geoffrey (Wedgwood), G.C.M.G., K.C.V.O.; former British diplomatist; b. 18 July 1908, Southsea, Hants.; s. of Commdr. Thomas Edmund Harrison and Maud Winifred Godman; m. Amy Katharine Clive 1936; three s. one d.; ed. Winchester and King's Coll., Cambridge; entered Foreign Office 1932, served Tokyo 1935–37, Berlin 1937–39; Pvt. Sec. to Parl. Under-Sec., Foreign Office 1939–41; First Sec., Foreign Office 1941–45; Counsellor, Brussels 1945–47; Minister, Moscow 1947–49; Head of Northern Dept., Foreign Office 1949–51; Asst. Under-Sec., Foreign Office 1951–56; Amb. to Brazil 1956–58, to Iran 1958–63; Deputy Under-Sec. of State, Foreign Office 1963–65; Amb. to U.S.S.R. 1965–68. *Leisure interests:* gardening, music, reading. *Address:* West Wood, Manningsheath, nr. Horsham, Sussex; 6 Ormond Gate, London, S.W.3, England. *Telephone:* Horsham 40409; 01-352 9488.

HARRISON, George, M.B.E.; British songwriter and performer; b. 25 Feb. 1943, Wavertree, Liverpool; m. 1st Patricia (Pattie) Anne Boyd 1966 (divorced 1977); m. 2nd Olivia Arias 1978; one s.; ed. Dovedale Primary School and Liverpool Inst.; had first guitar at age of 14, now plays guitar, organ and a variety of Indian instruments; ran guitar quintet The Rebels 1956–58; joined The Quarrymen 1958; appeared under various titles until formation of The Beatles 1960; appeared with The Beatles in Hamburg 1960, 1961, 1962, The Cavern, Liverpool 1960, 1961; toured Scotland, Sweden, U.K. 1963, Paris, Denmark, Hong Kong, Australia, New Zealand, U.S.A., Canada 1964, France, Italy, Spain, U.S.A. 1965, Germany, Spain, Philippines, U.S.A. 1966; attended transcendental meditation course at Maharishi's Acad., Rishikesh, India Feb.-April 1968; formed Apple Corpn. Ltd., parent org. of The Beatles Group of Cos. 1968; composed, arranged and recorded own music for film Wonderwall 1968; organized and performed at The Concert for Bangladesh 1971, concert, film and record proceeds for refugees to UNICEF; tour of U.S.A. and Canada 1974; Co-founder Hand Made Films; founder of Material World Charitable Foundation. *Recordings by the Beatles include:* Please Please Me, With the Beatles 1963, A Hard Day's Night 1964, Beatles for Sale 1965, Help! 1965, Rubber Soul 1966, Revolver 1966, Sergeant Pepper's Lonely Hearts Club Band 1967, Magical Mystery Tour 1967, The Beatles (White Album) 1968, Yellow Submarine 1969, Abbey Road 1969, Let It Be 1970. *Solo recordings include:* All Things Must Pass, Living in the Material World, Dark Horse, Extra Texture, 33⅓, Somewhere in England, Gone Tropo, Cloud Nine 1987. *Films by The Beatles:* A Hard Day's Night 1964, Help! 1965, Yellow Submarine (animated colour cartoon film) 1968, TV film Magical Mystery Tour 1967, Let it Be 1970; producer Little Malcolm and His Struggle against the Eunuchs 1973, Shanghai Surprise 1986; Co-exec. Producer Mona Lisa 1986; Raga (with Ravi Shankar (q.v.) and Yehudi Menuhin (q.v.)) 1974. *Publication:* I, Me, Mine 1980. *Address:* c/o Orion Classics, 711 Fifth Avenue, New York, N.Y. 10022, U.S.A.

HARRISON, James Merritt, C.C., PH.D., F.R.S.C.; Canadian geologist; b. 20 Sept. 1915, Regina, Saskatchewan; s. of Roland and Vera (Merritt) Harrison; m. Herta Boehmer Sliter 1944; ed. Univ. of Manitoba and Queen's Univ., Kingston, Ontario; Geologist, Geological Survey of Canada 1943–55; lecturer Queen's Univ. 1949–50; Geological Survey of Canada Chief Precambrian Div. 1955–56, Dir. 1956–64; Asst. Deputy Minister (Research), Dept. of Mines and Tech. Surveys 1964–67; Asst. Deputy Minister (Science and Tech.), Dept. of Energy, Mines and Resources 1967–71, Sr. Asst. Deputy Minister 1972; Asst. Dir.-Gen. for Science, UNESCO 1973–76; mem. Int. Council of Scientific Unions (ICSU) 1962, Exec. and Vice-Pres. ICSU 1963–65, Pres. 1966–68; Pres. Int. Union Geological Sciences 1961–64; Pres. Canadian Inst. of Mining and Metallurgy 1969; Pres. Royal Soc. of Canada 1967–68; mem. Scientific Advisory Bd., NWT Legislature 1981, Chair. 1982, consultant on natural resources; Chair. Canadian Comm. for

UNESCO 1984–; several hon. degrees; Kemp Memorial Medal, Columbia Univ., Blaylock Medal, Canadian Inst. of Mining and Metallurgy, Logan Medal, Geological Asscn. of Canada, Outstanding Achievement Award of Public Service of Canada, R. C. Wallace Medal, Univ. of Man., Hon. mem. Eng. Inst. of Canada. *Leisure interests:* colour photography, golf, sailing. *Address:* 4 Kippewa Drive, Ottawa, Ont. K1S 3G4, Canada.

HARRISON, Reginald (Rex) Carey; British actor-director; b. 5 March 1908, Huyton, Lancs.; s. of William and Edith Harrison; m. 1st Marjorie Thomas 1934, one s.; m. 2nd Lilli Palmer 1943 (divorced 1957), one s.; m. 3rd Kay Kendall 1957 (died 1959); m. 4th Rachel Roberts 1962 (divorced 1971); m. 5th Hon. Elizabeth Rees-Williams 1971 (divorced 1975); m. 6th Mercia Tinker 1978; ed. Liverpool Coll.; first professional appearance Liverpool 1924, first film performance 1929; served in R.A.F. 1941–44; Order of Merit (Italy); Hon. Ph.D. (Boston). *Plays include:* French Without Tears, Design for Living, The Cocktail Party, Bell, Book and Candle, Venus Observed, The Love of Four Colonels, Anne of a Thousand Days, Platonov, My Fair Lady, The Lionel Touch, Henry IV, In Praise of Love (New York), Perrichon's Travels (Chichester), Caesar and Cleopatra (New York), The Devil's Disciple (Los Angeles) 1978, The Kingfisher (New York) 1978–79, Heartbreak House 1983/84 (London, New York), Aren't We All (London, New York) 1985/86, The Admirable Crichton 1988. *Films include:* Storm in a Teacup 1937, St Martin's Lane 1938, The Citadel 1938, Over the Moon 1939, Night Train to Munich 1940, Major Barbara 1940, I Live in Grosvenor Square 1945, Blithe Spirit 1945, The Rake's Progress 1946, Anna and the King of Siam 1946, The Ghost and Mrs. Muir 1947, Unfaithfully Yours 1948, Escape 1948, The Fourposter 1952, King Richard and the Crusaders 1954, The Constant Husband 1955, The Reluctant Debutante 1958, Midnight Lace 1960, Cleopatra 1962, My Fair Lady (Acad. Award) 1964, The Yellow Rolls-Royce 1964, The Agony and the Ecstasy 1965, The Honey Pot 1967, Doctor Dolittle 1967, A Flea in Her Ear 1968, Staircase 1969, The Prince and the Pauper 1976, Behind the Iron Mask 1977, Ashanti 1978. *TV appearances include:* Don Quixote 1972, The Kingfisher 1982, Anastasia 1986. *Publications:* Rex (autobiog.) 1974, If Love Be Love (anthology). *Leisure interests:* sailing, golf, writing. *Address:* 5 Impasse de la Fontaine, Monte Carlo, Monaco 98000.

HARRISON, Sir Richard, Kt., M.D., D.SC., F.R.S.; British anatomist; b. 8 Oct. 1920, London; s. of the late Dr. G. A. Harrison; m. Barbara Jean Fuller; ed. Oundle School, Gonville and Caius Coll., Cambridge, St. Bartholomew's Hosp., London; Prof. of Anatomy, London Hosp. Medical Coll., Univ. of London 1954–68; Prof. of Anatomy, Cambridge Univ. 1968–82, Prof. Emer. 1982–; Hon. Fellow Downing Coll., Cambridge 1982; Chair. Farm Animal Welfare Council 1979–, Bd. of Trustees, British Museum (Natural History) 1978–; Pres. Int. Fed. of Assocns. of Anatomists 1985–87. *Publications:* Functional Anatomy of Marine Mammals 1972–77, Handbook of Marine Mammals 1981–89, Research on Dolphins 1986. *Leisure interests:* golf, gardening. *Address:* Downing College, Cambridge, CB2 1DQ (Office); The Beeches, 8 Woodlands Road, Great Shelford, Cambridge, CB2 5LW, England (Home). *Telephone:* 0223-843287 (Home).

HARRISON, Russell Edward, B.COMM.; Canadian banker; b. 31 May 1921, Grandview, Manitoba; s. of Edward and Annie Harrison; m. Nancy Doreen Bell 1944; one s. one d.; ed. Univ. of Manitoba; Mil. Service World War II, with Canadian Bank of Commerce (now Canadian Imperial Bank of Commerce) 1945–, Asst. Man., Hamilton 1953, Toronto 1956, Chief Insp. of the Bank 1956; Head of Operations, Quebec 1956, Exec. Vice-Pres., Chief Gen. Man. 1969–73, Dir. 1970–, Pres. and Chief Operating Officer 1973–76, Chair. and C.E.O. 1976–84; Dir. MacMillan Bloedel Ltd., Canada Life Assurance Co., Campbell Soup Co., Royal Insurance Co. of Canada Ltd., Transcanada Pipelines, Falconbridge Ltd., and other cos. *Leisure interests:* golf, fishing, swimming. *Address:* P.O. Box 235, Commerce Court, Postal Station, Toronto, Ont. M5L 1E8, Canada (Office). *Telephone:* 862-3861 (Office).

HARRISS, Gerald Leslie, M.A., D.PHIL., F.B.A.; British historian and university teacher; b. 22 May 1925, London; s. of W. L. Harriss and M. J. O. Harriss; m. Margaret Anne Sidaway 1959; two s. three d.; ed. Chigwell School, Essex, Magdalen Coll., Oxford; war service in R.N.V.R. 1944–46; Oxford Univ. 1946–53; Lecturer, Durham Univ. 1953–55, Reader 1956–67; Fellow and Tutor in History, Magdalen Coll., Oxford 1967–. *Publications:* King, Parliament and Public Finance in Medieval England 1975, Henry V: the Practice of Kingship (Ed.) 1985, Cardinal Beaufort 1988. *Address:* Dean Court House, 89 Eynsham Road, Botley, Oxford, OX2 9BY, England.

HARRY, Ralph Lindsay, A.C., C.B.E.; Australian diplomatist (retd.); b. 10 March 1917, Geelong, Victoria; s. of the late A. H. Harry; m. Dorothy Sheppard 1944; one s. two d.; ed. Univ. of Tasmania and Lincoln Coll., Oxford; joined Dept. of External Affairs 1941; Pvt. Sec. to Minister of External Affairs; Asst. Official Sec., Ottawa 1943–45; Second Sec., later First Sec., Washington, D.C. 1945–49 (at UN, New York 1947–48); Dept. of External Affairs, Canberra 1949–53; Consul-Gen. in Geneva 1953–56; Rep. in Singapore, Brunei, Sarawak and Borneo 1956–57; seconded to Ministry of Defence 1958–59; Asst. Sec. Ministry of External Affairs 1960–65; Amb. to Belgium and the EEC 1965–68, to Repub. of Viet-Nam 1968–70, to Fed. Repub. of Germany 1971–75, to UN 1975–78; Dir. Australian Inst. of Int. Affairs 1979–81; Visiting Fellow, Univ. of Tasmania 1979; Pres. Australian Esperanto Assocn. 1980–; mem. Nat. Australia Day

Cttee. 1980–84. *Publications:* The Diplomat who Laughed 1983, Australian-Esperanto Dictionary. *Address:* 8 Tennyson Crescent, Forrest, A.C.T. 2603, Australia. *Telephone:* (062) 95 12 64.

HARSCH, Joseph Close, A.B., M.A.; American journalist; b. 25 May 1905, Toledo, Ohio; s. of Paul Arthur and Leila Katherine (Close) Harsch; m. Anne Elizabeth Wood 1932; three s.; ed. Williams Coll., Williamstown, Mass., and Cambridge Univ., England; Corresp. Christian Science Monitor 1929–, Berlin corresp. 1939–41, war corresp. south-west Pacific 1942, Chief, Washington News Bureau 1949–51, Foreign Affairs Columnist 1952, Chief Editorial Writer, Boston 1971–74, Columnist 1974–; Asst. Dir. Inter-governmental Cttee. on Political Refugees 1939; Radio news analyst for Columbia Broadcasting System 1943–49; Commentator for BBC 1943–57; News Commentator, Nat. Broadcasting Co. 1953–57, Senior European Corresp. 1957–65, Diplomatic Corresp., Washington 1965–67; ABC Commentator 1967–71; Hon. C.B.E. *Publications:* Pattern of Conquest 1943, The Curtain Isn't Iron 1950. *Leisure interests:* sailing, gardening. *Address:* 275 Highland Drive, P.O. Box 457, Jamestown, Rhode Island 02835, U.S.A. *Telephone:* (401) 423-0690.

HART, Gary, LL.B.; American politician and lawyer; b. 28 Nov. 1936, Ottawa, Kan.; m. Lee Ludwig 1958; one s. one d.; ed. Bethany Coll., Okla., Yale Univ.; called to bar 1964; Attorney, U.S. Dept. of Justice, and Special Asst. to Sec., U.S. Dept. of Interior 1964–67; legal practice, Denver, Colo. 1967–70, 1972–74; Nat. Campaign Dir., George McGovern Democratic Presidential Campaign 1970–72; Senator for Colorado 1975–86; assisted in John F. Kennedy Presidential Campaign 1960; voluntary organizer, Robert F. Kennedy Presidential Campaign 1968; fmr. mem. of commrs., Denver Urban Renewal Authority; fmr. mem., Park Hill Action Cttee. *Publications:* Right From the Start, A New Democracy 1983, The Double Man (with W. S. Cohen, q.v.) 1985, America Can Win 1986, The Strategies of Zeus 1987.

HART, George Arnold, M.B.E., C.M.; Canadian banker; b. 2 April 1913, Toronto; s. of George S. and Laura M. (Harrison) Hart; m. 1st Jean C. Gilbert 1939 (deceased), one d.; 2nd Patricia I. Plant 1961; ed. Public and High Schools, Toronto, Ontario; Bank of Montreal 1931–41; Canadian Army 1942–46; Bank of Montreal 1946–, Asst. Gen. Man. Head Office 1954–56, Deputy Gen. Man. 1956–57, Gen. Man. 1957–58, Vice-Pres. and Dir. 1958–59, Pres. 1959–67, C.E.O. 1959–74, Chair. of Bd. 1964–75, Chair. Exec. Cttee. 1964–77; Dir. numerous cos. and official of several commercial and other orgs.; Hon. LL.D. (Saskatchewan, Montreal), Hon. D.C.L. (Bishop's Univ., Acadia Univ.), Hon. D.C.Sc. (Sherbrooke). *Leisure interest:* golf. *Address:* R.R.2, Mountain, Ont., K0E 1S0, Canada.

HART, Herbert Lionel Adolphus, M.A., Q.C., F.B.A.; British university professor (retd.); b. 18 July 1907, Harrogate, Yorks.; s. of Simeon Hart and Rose Hart (née Samson); m. Jenifer Margaret Williams 1941; three s. one d.; ed. Bradford Grammar School and New Coll., Oxford; in practice as barrister in Chancery Div., London 1932–40; service in War Office, London 1940–46; Fellow and Tutor in Philosophy, New Coll., Oxford 1946–53; Prof. of Jurisprudence, Oxford Univ. 1953–70; Prin. of Brasenose Coll., Oxford 1973–78; Hon. Fellow of New Coll., Brasenose and Univ. Coll., Oxford; Dr. h.c. (Stockholm, Glasgow, Edin., Kent, Hull, Cambridge, Chicago, Georgetown, Mexico, Tel. Aviv, Harvard and Jerusalem). *Publications:* Causation in the Law (with A. M. Honoré) 1959, The Concept of Law 1961, Law, Liberty and Morality 1963, The Morality of Criminal Law 1965, Punishment and Responsibility 1968, Essays on Bentham 1982, Essays in Jurisprudence and Philosophy 1983. *Leisure interest:* bicycling. *Address:* 11 Manor Place, Oxford, England. *Telephone:* (0865) 242402.

HART, Dame Judith (see Hart of South Lanark).

HART, Michael, PH.D., F.INST.P., C.PHYS., F.R.S.; British professor of physics; b. 4 Nov. 1938; s. of Reuben H. V. Hart and Phyllis M. (née White); m. Susan M. Powell 1963; three d.; ed. Cotham Grammar School, Bristol and Univ. of Bristol; Research Assoc. Dept. of Materials Science and Eng. Cornell Univ. 1963–65; Dept. of Physics, Univ. of Bristol 1965–67, Lecturer in Physics 1967–72, Reader 1972–76; Sr. Resident Research Assoc. Nat. Research Council, NASA Electronics Research Center, Boston, Mass. 1969–70; Special Adviser, Cen. Policy Review Staff 1975–77; Wheatstone Prof. of Physics, King's Coll. London 1976–84; Prof. of Physics, Univ. of Manchester 1984–; Science Programme Coordinator (part-time), Daresbury Lab. Science and Eng. Research Council 1985–. *Publications:* contributions to learned journals. *Leisure interests:* squash, weaving, flying kites. *Address:* 54 Manor Park South, Knutsford, Cheshire, WA16 8AN, England. *Telephone:* (0565) 2893.

HART, Parker T.; American business consultant and diplomatist (retd.); b. 28 Sept. 1910, Medford, Mass.; s. of William P. Hart and Ella L. Thompson; m. Jane C. Smiley 1949; two d.; ed. Dartmouth Coll., Harvard Univ., National War Coll., and Inst. Universitaire des Hautes Etudes Int., Geneva; Translator, Dept. of State 1937–38; Officer, Foreign Service 1938–69, served Vienna, Pará (Brazil), Cairo, Jeddah, Dhahran 1938–47; Dept. of State 1947–49; Consul-Gen. Dhahran 1949–51; Nat. War Coll. 1951–52; Dir. Office of Near Eastern Affairs, Dept. of State 1952–55; Deputy Chief of Mission Counsellor, Cairo 1955–58; Consul-Gen. and Minister, Damascus 1958; Deputy Asst. Sec. of State, Near Eastern, S. Asian Affairs 1958–61; Amb. to Saudi Arabia 1961–65, concurrently accred. to

Kuwait 1962–63, Minister to Yemen 1961–62; Amb. to Turkey 1965–68; Asst. Sec. of State, Near Eastern, S. Asian Affairs 1968–69; Dir. Foreign Service Inst. 1969; mem. Middle East Inst., Pres. 1969–73; Special Rep. Bechtel Corpn. 1973–75, Consultant, Bechtel Group Inc. 1976–; Bd. of Trustees (Emer.), American Univ. of Beirut; Founding Bd. mem., Inst. for the Study of Diplomacy, Georgetown Univ.; mem. Council on Foreign Relations (New York), Washington Inst. of Foreign Affairs, Bd. of Govs. (Emer.), The Middle East Inst.; Treasurer American Acad. of Diplomacy; Vice-Chair. Inst. of Turkish Studies; Chair. Advisory Cttee., American Friends of Turkey. *Publications:* Two NATO Allies at the Threshold of War: A First-Hand Account of Crisis Management, Greece, Turkey and Cyprus 1965–68; several articles in political journals. *Leisure interests:* bird watching, hiking, languages. *Address:* 4705 Berkeley Terrace, N.W., Washington, D.C. 20007, U.S.A. *Telephone:* (202) 965-1781.

HART, Robert Mayes, M.B.A., LL.M.; American lawyer and petroleum company director; b. 27 Aug. 1925, Oklahoma; s. of James Eben Hart and Marthel (née Mayes); m. Joanne Krusen 1948; two s. one d.; ed. Harvard Univ., Univ. of Oklahoma, New York Univ.; admitted to Oklahoma Bar 1949, New York Bar 1953; Clerk to U.S. district Judge 1949–50; joined Shell Oil Co. as an attorney 1950, Treas. 1962, Exec. Vice-Pres. 1968, Supply Co-ordinator, Shell Int. Petroleum Co., London 1973–81; Dir. Shell Transport & Trading Co. Ltd. 1976–79, 1986–, Man. Dir. 1979–82; Man. Dir. Royal Dutch Shell Group (U.K.) 1976–86; Man. Dir. N. V. Koninklijke Nederlandsche Petroleum Maatschappij (Royal Dutch Petroleum Co.) 1982–86; Dir. Shell Petroleum Inc. 1988–. *Address:* c/o Shell Centre, London, SE1 7NA, England.

HART, Stanley Robert, M.S., PH.D.; American professor of geology and geochemistry; b. 20 June 1935, Swampscott, Mass,; s. of Robert Hart and Ruth M. Hart; m. 1st Joanna Smith 1956 (divorced 1976), 2nd Pamela Shepherd 1980; one s. two d.; ed. Mass. Inst. of Technology, Calif. Inst. of Technology; Fellow, Carnegie Inst. of Washington 1960–61, mem. staff 1961–75; Visiting Prof. Univ. of Calif. San Diego 1967–68; Prof. of Geology and Geochem. M.I.T. 1975–; mem. N.A.S.; Fellow, American Geophysical Union, Geological Soc. of America. *Publications:* more than 100 articles in scientific journals. *Leisure interests:* woodworking, fishing, skiing, squash. *Address:* Department of Earth, Atmospheric and Planetary Sciences, Room 54-1126, Massachusetts Institute of Technology, Cambridge, Mass. 02139 (Office); 172 Mason Terrace, Brookline, Mass. 02146, U.S.A. (Home). *Telephone:* 617-731-4922 (Home).

HART OF SOUTH LANARK, Baroness (Life Peer), cr. 1987, of Lanark in the County of Lanark; **(Constance Mary) Judith Hart,** P.C., D.B.E.; British politician; b. 18 Sept. 1924, Burnley, Lancs.; d. of Harry Ridehalgh; m. Dr. Anthony Bernard Hart 1946; two s.; ed. London School of Econs.; Labour M.P. for Lanark (now Clydesdale) 1959–87; Joint Parl. Under-Sec. of State for Scotland 1964–66; Minister of State for Commonwealth Affairs 1966–67; Minister of Social Security 1967–68; Paymaster-Gen. 1968–69; Minister of Overseas Devt. 1969–70, 1974–75, 1977–79; mem. Nat. Exec. Cttee. of Labour Party 1969–83, Chair. of its industrial Policy Sub-Cttee. and Finance and Econ. Sub-Cttee., Chair. Parl. Labour Group for Latin and Cen. America and the Caribbean 1983–87; Chair. Labour Party 1981–82; Chair. Chile Solidarity Campaign, Emergency Cttee. on Sri Lanka of Int. Alert; Hon. Fellow Inst. of Devt. Studies, Univ. of Sussex. *Publications:* Aid and Liberation 1973 and miscellaneous articles. *Leisure interests:* gardening, theatre, spending time with family. *Address:* 3 Ennerdale Road, Kew, Richmond, Surrey, England (Home). *Telephone:* 01-948 1989 (Home).

HARTARTO; Indonesian politician; b. 30 May 1932, Delanggu, Cen. Java; ed. Inst. of Technology, Bandung and Univ. of New South Wales; mem. Man. Bd. state-owned paper factories of Padalarang and Leces 1959; Tech. Dir. Leces paper factory 1961; Man. Dir. of Bd. dealing with paper industries, Dept. of Industry 1965; Dir. Silicate Industry Div., Directorate-Gen. of Basic Chem. Industries, Dept. of Industry 1974, Dir.-Gen. for Basic Chem. Industries 1979; Minister of Industry 1983–. *Address:* Ministry of Industry, Jln. Gatot Subroto, Kav. 52-53, Jakarta Selatan, Indonesia.

HARTFORD, Huntington, B.A.; American financier and art patron; b. 18 April 1911, New York; s. of Edward and Henrietta (Guerard) Hartford; m. 1st Mary Lee Epling (dissolved 1939); 2nd Marjorie Steele 1949 (dissolved 1961), one s. and one d.; 3rd Diane Brown 1962 (dissolved 1970), one d.; 4th Elaine Kay 1974 (divorced 1981), one d.; ed. St. Paul's School, and Harvard Univ.; Co-Chair. Oil Shale Corpn. (New York) 1949; Founder Huntington Hartford Foundation Calif. 1949, Huntington Hartford Theatre Hollywood 1954, Gallery of Modern Art (New York) 1964 (now called New York Cultural Center in asscn. with Fairleigh Dickinson Univ.); fmr. Developer and owner Paradise Island (Nassau, Bahamas) 1959–; Publr. Show Magazine; Adviser Cultural Affairs to Pres. of Borough of Manhattan 1967; Patron Lincoln Center for the Performing Arts; mem. Advisory Council of Columbia Univ. Dept. of Art History and Archaeology, Nat. Council of the Arts 1969, U.S. People's Fund for UN Inc.; Hon. Fellow, Nat. Sculpture Soc., Broadway Asscn. Man. of Year Award; OAS Award 1966. *Publications:* Jane Eyre (play) 1958, Art or Anarchy 1964, You Are What You Write 1973. *Address:* c/o Townsend, Rabinowitz, Pantaleoni and Valente, 535 Fifth Avenue, New York, N.Y. 10017, U.S.A. (Office).

HARTH, Victor, M.D.; German physician; b. 20 Oct. 1914, Frankfurt am Main; s. of Dipl.-Ing. Fritz Harth and Emmy (née Will) Harth; m. Christa Harth, M.D. 1959; two s. two d.; ed. Univs. of Würzburg, Montpellier, Frankfurt am Main; in practice as a specialist in internal medicine; also Pres. Internal Medicine Section of European Union of Medical Specialists (UEMS); First Vice-Pres. European Asscn. of Internal Medicine (AEMIE); mem. Gov. Council of Berufsverband deutscher Internisten; Pres. Congresses for Psychosomatic Medicine; Editor, Internist; Assoc. Ed. Journal of the Royal College of Physicians, London; Chief Editor, Die Heilkunst; First Chair. Schutzgemeinschaft Alt Bamberg e.V. (asscn. for conservation of old Bamberg); Counsel for the Drug Comm.; medical journalist, producer of medical scientific films and documentary films. *Publications:* articles in scientific journals, especially on diet, gerontology, autovaccination; books concerning diet; articles on urban studies, sociological questions, preservation of monuments. *Leisure interests:* painting, photography, sculpture. *Address:* Hainstrasse 9, 8600 Bamberg, Federal Republic of Germany. *Telephone:* 0951-26608, 26609.

HARTIGAN, James J.; American airline executive; b. 1924; served U.S. Navy 1943–45; with United Air Lines Inc., Mt. Prospect, Ill. 1942–, Asst. Man. Sales 1961–63, Sales Man. 1963–67, Asst. Vice-Pres. Sales 1967, Vice-Pres. Passenger Sales and Services Planning 1968–71, Vice-Pres. System Marketing 1971–73, Sr. Vice-Pres., Gen. Man. Western Div. 1973–75, Group Vice-Pres. Operations, Services, then Exec. Vice-Pres. 1975–81, Pres. 1981–87, C.E.O. 1985–87, Chair. 1987–. *Address:* United Air Lines, Inc., P.O. Box 66100, Chicago, Ill. 60666, U.S.A.

HARTKE, Werner, D.PHIL; German university professor; b. 1 March 1907, Eschwege; s. of Lic.Dr. Dr. h.c. Wilhelm Hartke and Tilly Kühne; m. Christa Behrendt 1936; two s. one d.; ed. Berlin Univ.; mem. Communist Party of Germany 1945, Sozialistische Einheitspartei Deutschlands (SED) 1946–; lecturer, Königsberg and Göttingen Univs., Prof. of Classical Philology 1948–55; Dean, Faculty of Philosophy, Rostock Univ. 1949–51, 1953–55; Prof. Latin Language and Literature, Humboldt Univ., Berlin 1955–, Rector 1956–59; Scientific Dir. Goethe Wörterbuch 1967–; Dir. Berlin Inst. for Antiquity Research, Adviser for research in Ancient History and Archaeology 1969–; Ed. Deutsche Literaturzeitung 1972–, Beiträge zur Alexander von Humboldt-Forschung 1973–; mem. Deutsche Akad. der Wissenschaften, Pres. 1958–68, Vice-Pres. 1968–72; Foreign mem. U.S.S.R. Acad. of Sciences 1966–, Hungarian Acad. of Sciences, Bulgarian Acad. of Sciences 1967–, Inst. d'Egypte; Academia Latinitati inter omnes gentes fovendae; D.Phil. h.c. (Rostock); Nat. Prize, gold medallist of Nat. Order of Merit, Order Kyril Methodii, Gold Medal za zásluhy o vědu a lidstvo of Czechoslovak Acad. of Sciences, Winkelmann-Medal, etc. *Publications:* De saeculo IV exeuntis historiarum scriptoribus 1932, Geschichte und Politik im spätantiken Rome 1940, Römische Kinderkaiser 1951. *Leisure interests:* gardening, painting, sailing, meteorology, ornithology, telecommunications, radio-television technics. *Address:* Akademie der Wissenschaften der DDR, Schiffbauerdamm 19, 104 Berlin; Ostendorfstrasse 26, 117 Berlin, German Democratic Republic (Home). *Telephone:* 67-16-431 (Home).

HARTLEY, Brian Selby, PH.D., F.R.S.; British professor of biochemistry; b. 16 April 1926, Rawtenstall; s. of Norman and Hilda Hartley; m. Kathleen Maude Vaughan 1949; three s. one d.; ed. Queens' Coll. Cambridge, Univ. of Leeds; ICI Fellow, Cambridge 1952–58, Fellow and Lecturer in Biochemistry, Trinity Coll. Cambridge 1964–74; Helen Hay Whitney Fellow Univ. of Washington, Seattle 1958–60; mem. scientific staff MRC Lab. of Molecular Biology 1961–74; Prof. of Biochemistry 1974– and Dir. of Centre for Biotechnology, Imperial Coll., Univ. of London 1982–; Hon. mem. American Soc. of Biological Chemists 1961–74, mem. Royal Soc. Council 1981–83; British Drug Houses Medal for Analytical Biochemistry 1969. *Publications:* papers and articles in scientific journals. *Leisure interests:* fishing, gardening. *Address:* 7th Floor Residence, Department of Biochemistry, Imperial College, London, SW7 2AZ (Office); Grove Cottage, 21 Smith Street, Elsworth, Cambridge, CB3 8HY, England (Home). *Telephone:* 01-589 5111 (Office); 09547 271 (Home).

HARTLEY, Frank Robinson, D.SC.; British professor; b. 29 Jan. 1942, Epsom; s. of Sir Frank Hartley and Lydia May England; m. Valerie Peel 1964; three d.; ed. Kings Coll. School, Wimbledon, Magdalen Coll., Oxford; post-doctoral Fellow, Commonwealth Scientific and Industrial Research Org., Div. of Protein Chemistry, Melbourne, Australia 1966–69; ICI Research Fellow and Tutor in Physical Chemistry, Univ. Coll., London 1969–70; Lecturer in Inorganic Chemistry, Univ. of Southampton 1970–75; Prof. of Chemistry and Head of Dept. of Chemistry and Metallurgy, Royal Mil. Coll. of Science, Shrivenham 1975–82, Acting Dean 1982–84, Prin. and Dean 1984–89; Vice-Chancellor Cranfield Inst. of Tech. 1989–; Asscn. of Commonwealth Univs. Sr. Travelling Fellow 1986; Hon. LL.D. (London) 1987. *Publications:* The Chemistry of Platinum and Palladium (Applied Science) 1973, Elements of Organometallic Chemistry (Chemical Soc.) 1974, Solution Equilibria (with C. Burgess and R. M. Alcock) 1980; The Chemistry of the Metal Carbon Bond (vol. 1–4) 1983–86, Supported Metal Complexes 1985, papers in inorganic, co-ordination and organometallic chemistry in major English, American and Australian journals. *Leisure interests:* rugby refereeing, golf, swimming, squash, gardening. *Address:* Cranfield Institute of Technology, Cranfield, Beds., MK43 0AL (Office); 9 Curtis Road, Shrivenham, Swindon, Wilts., SN6 8AY, England (Home). *Telephone:* (0793) 783277 (Office).

HARTLEY, Fred L(loyd), B.SC.; American oil executive; b. 16 Jan. 1917, Vancouver, B.C., Canada; s. of John William Hartley and Hannah (née Mitchell) Hartley; m. Margaret Alice Murphy 1940; one s. one d.; ed. Univ. of British Columbia; went to U.S.A. 1939, naturalized 1950; Eng. Supervisor, Union Oil Co. of Calif. 1939–53, Man. Commercial Devt. 1953–55, Gen. Man. Research Dept. 1955–56, Vice-Pres. (Research) 1956–60, Sr. Vice-Pres. 1960–63, Dir. 1960–, Exec. Vice-Pres. 1963–64, Pres. 1964–85, C.E.O. 1964–, Chair. Feb. 1975–; Dir. American Petroleum Inst. (API), Calif. Chamber of Commerce, Los Angeles Philharmonic Asscn., Exec. Council on Foreign Diplomats, Union Bank, Rockwell Int.; mem. Nat. Petroleum Council; Trustee, Calif. Inst. of Technology, Tax Foundation, Cttee. for Econ. Devt. *Leisure interests:* golf, boating, fishing and music. *Address:* Unocal Corporation, Box 7600, Los Angeles 90051, U.S.A. *Telephone:* (213) 977-7000.

HÄRTLING, Peter; German writer and journalist; b. 13 Nov. 1933, Chemnitz; s. of Rudolf and Erika (Häntzschel) Härtling; m. Mechthild Maier 1959; two s. two d.; ed. Gymnasium (Nürtingen/Neckar); childhood spent in Saxony, Czechoslovakia and Württemberg; journalist 1953–; Literary Ed. Deutsche Zeitung und Wirtschaftszeitung, Stuttgart and Cologne; Ed. of magazine Der Monat 1967–70, also Co-publisher; Ed. and Man. Dir. S. Fischer Verlag, Frankfurt 1968–74, Ed. Die Väter; mem. PEN. Akademie der Wissenschaften und der Literatur Mainz, Akademie der Künste Berlin, Deutsche Akademie für Sprache und Dichtung Darmstadt; Literaturpreis des Deutschen Kritikerverbandes 1964, Literaturpreis des Kulturkreises der Deutschen Industrie 1965, Literarischer Förderungspreis des Landes Niedersachsen 1965, Prix du meilleur livre étranger, Paris 1966, Gerhart Hauptmann Preis 1971, Deutscher Jugendbuchpreis 1976, Stadtschreiber von Bergen-Enkheim 1978–79, Hölderlin-Preis 1987. *Publications:* Yamins Stationen (poetry) 1955, In Zeilen zuhaus (essays) 1957, Palmström grüsst Anna Blume (essays) 1961, Spielgeist-Spiegelgeist (poetry) 1962, Niembsch oder Der Stillstand (novel) 1964, Janek (novel) 1966, Das Familienfest (novel) 1969, Gilles (play) 1970, Ein Abend, Eine Nacht, Ein Morgen (novel) 1971, Zwettl—Nachprüfung einer Erinnerung (novel) 1973, Eine Frau (novel) 1974, Hölderlin (novel) 1976, Anreden (poetry) 1977, Hubert oder Die Rückkehr nach Casablanca (novel) 1978, Nachgetragene Liebe (novel) 1980, Die dreifache Maria 1982, Das Windrad (novel) 1983, Felix Guttmann (novel) 1985, Waiblingers Augen (novel) 1987, Der Wanderer (novel) 1988. *Address:* Finkenweg 1, 6082 Mörfelden-Walldorf, Federal Republic of Germany. *Telephone:* 06105-6109.

HARTLING, Poul; Danish United Nations official (retd.); b. 14 Aug. 1914, Copenhagen; s. of late M. Hartling (fmr. Minister of Education) and late Mathilde Hartling; m. Dr. (medical) Elsebeth Hartling (née Kirkemann) 1940; three s. one d.; Master of Divinity; Sec. to Student Christian Movement 1934–35, to Denmark's Christian Movement of Senior Secondary Students 1939–43, Curate of Frederiksberg Church 1941–45; Chaplain of St. Luke Foundation 1945–50; Prin. of Zahle's Teachers' Training Coll. 1950–68; mem. Folketing 1957–60, 1964–77; Chair. Liberal Party Parl. Group 1965–68; mem. Nordic Council 1964–68, Pres. 1966–73, Vice-Pres. 1977; Minister of Foreign Affairs 1968–71; Prime Minister 1973–75; Chair. Liberal Party 1973–77; UN High Commr. for Refugees 1978–85; Dr. h.c. Valparaiso Univ., Ind. 1981; Grand Cross of Dannebrog and numerous other decorations. *Publications:* Sursum corda (History of Student Christian Movement); Ed. Church, School, Culture 1963, The Danish Church 1964, From 17 years in Danish Politics 1973, I dine haender 1977, Bladet i Bogen 1980, Politisk Udspil 1981, Godt vejr og dårligt vejr 1983, Otte år i FN's flygtningearbejde 1985. *Leisure interest:* music. *Address:* Emilievej 6E, DK 2920 Charlottenlund, Denmark. *Telephone:* 01-63 5312.

HARTMAN, Arthur A., A.B.; American diplomatist (retd.); b. 12 March 1926, New York; m. Donna Van Dyke Ford; three s. two d.; ed. Harvard Univ., Harvard Law School; served in U.S. Army Air Corps 1944–46; Econ. Officer, Econ. Co-operation Admin., Paris 1948–52; Econ. Officer of U.S. del. to European Army Conf., Paris 1952–54; Politico-Mil. officer, U.S. Mission to NATO, Paris 1954–55; Econ. officer, Joint U.S. Embassy/Agency for Int. Devt. Mission, Saigon, Repub. of Viet-Nam 1956–58; Int. Affairs Officer, Bureau of European Affairs, Dept. of State 1958–61; Staff Asst. to Under-Sec. of State for Econ. Affairs 1961–62, Special Asst. 1962–63; Head of Econ. Section, U.S. Embassy, London 1963–67; Special Asst. to Under-Sec. of State 1967–69; Staff Dir. of Sr. Interdepartmental Group 1967–69; Deputy Dir. of Coordination to Under-Sec. of State 1969–72; Deputy Chief of Mission and Minister-Counsellor, U.S. Mission to European Communities, Brussels 1972–74; Asst. Sec. of State for European Affairs 1974–77; U.S. Amb. to France 1977–81, to U.S.S.R. 1981–87; lecturer-consultant 1987–; mem. Bd., Hartford Insurance Group, American Hosp. in Paris, American Coll. in Paris, French-American Foundation, Dreyfus Funds; mem. Advisory Council Elf-Aquitaine, Cie Lyonnaise des Eaux; Hon. degrees (Wheaton Coll., American Coll. in Paris); Presidential Management Improvement Award 1970, Distinguished Honor Award 1972, Veterans of Foreign Wars Medal of Honor 1981, Sec. of State's Distinguished Service Award 1987, Dept. of State Wilbur J. Carr Award 1987, Annual Nat. Conf. on Soviet Jewry Award 1987. *Address:* 2738 McKinley Street, N.W., Washington, D.C. 20520; APCO,

1155 21st Street N.W., Washington, D.C. 20036, U.S.A. *Telephone:* (202) 362-6660.

HARTMANN, Robert Trowbridge, A.B.; American government official (retd.); b. 8 April 1917, Rapid City, S. Dak.; s. of Miner Louis and Elizabeth (Trowbridge) Hartmann; m. Roberta Sankey 1943; one s. one d.; ed. Stanford Univ.; Reporter Los Angeles Times 1939–41, 1945–48, Editorial and Special Writer 1948–54, Chief of Washington Bureau 1954–63, Chief of Mediterranean and Middle East Bureau, Rome 1963–64; FAO Information Adviser, Washington, D.C. 1964–65; Ed. Republican Conf., House of Reps. 1966–69, Minority Sergeant at Arms 1969–73; Chief of Staff to Vice-Pres. Gerald Ford 1973–74; Counsellor to Pres. Gerald Ford, with Cabinet rank 1974–77; mem. Bd. Visitors, U.S. Naval Acad. 1977–80, Gerald R. Ford Foundation 1981–; Sr. Research Fellow, The Hoover Inst. on War, Revolution and Peace, Stanford Univ. 1977–; Naval Officer 1941–45, Capt. U.S.N.R. (retd.); Reid Foundation Fellow in the Middle East 1951; Better Understanding Citation, English Speaking Union, U.S.A. 1958; Overseas Press Club Citation 1961. *Publication:* Palace Politics 1980. *Leisure interests:* photography, snorkelling. *Address:* 5001 Baltimore Avenue, Bethesda, Md. 20816, U.S.A. (Home). *Telephone:* (301) 229-7616.

HARTNACK, Carl Edward; American banker; b. 9 April 1916, Los Angeles, Calif.; s. of Johannes C. Hartnack and Kate Schoneman; m. Roberta DeLuce 1939; two s. one d.; ed. Belmont High School Los Angeles, Pacific Coast Banking School, Seattle, and American Inst. of Banking; with Security First Nat. Bank (now Security Pacific Nat. Bank) Los Angeles 1934–, Vice-Pres. 1959, Senior Vice-Pres. 1968, Pres. 1969–81, Chair. Int. Bd. 1981–; fmrly. Pres., Vice-Chair. Security Pacific Corpn. 1973–78, Chair. 1978–80, Dir. 1981–. *Leisure interests:* boating, gardening, photography. *Address:* Security Pacific National Bank, 333 South Hope Street, Los Angeles, Calif. 90071, U.S.A. *Telephone:* (213) 345-6004.

HARTOG, Harold Samuel Arnold, K.B.E.; Netherlands business executive; b. 21 Dec. 1910, Nijmegen; s. of Jacob and Suzanne Henriette (Elias) Hartog; m. Ingeborg Luise Michael; one s.; ed. Wiedemann Coll., Geneva; joined Unilever 1931; mem. Netherlands forces, Second World War; joined Unilever in France after Second World War, later in charge of Unilever cos. in Netherlands; mem. Bd. Unilever N.V. 1948–71; mem. Unilever Rotterdam Group Management responsible for Unilever activities in Germany, Austria and Belgium 1952–60; mem. Unilever Cttee. for Overseas Interests, London 1960–62; one of two World Coordinators, Unilever's food interests, London 1962–66; Chair. Unilever N.V. 1966–71 (retd.); Knight Order of Netherlands Lion. *Leisure interest:* collecting Chinese ceramics and porcelain. *Address:* Kösterbergstrasse 40b, D-2000 Hamburg 55, Federal Republic of Germany.

HARTOG, Jan de; Netherlands writer; b. 22 April 1914, Haarlem; s. of Arnold and Lucretia de Hartog-Meyjes; m. Marjorie Eleanor Mein; two s. four d. *Publications:* Het Huis met de Handen 1934, Ave Caesar 1936, Oompje Owadi 1938, Holland's Glory 1940, God's Geuzen Vol. I 1947, Vol. II 1948, Vol. III 1949, Stella 1950, Mary 1951, The Lost Sea 1951, Thalassa 1952, Captain Jan 1952, The Little Ark 1954, The Inspector 1961, Waters of the New World (travel) 1961, The Artist 1963, The Hospital 1965, The Captain 1967, The Children 1969, The Peaceable Kingdom 1972, The Lamb's War 1980, Herinneringen aan Amsterdam 1981, The Trail of the Serpent 1983, Star of Peace 1984, The Commodore 1986; *plays:* De Ondergang van de Vrijheid 1937 (Great Nat. Drama Prize 1939), Mist 1938, Skipper Next to God 1946, Death of a Rat 1946, The Fourposter 1946; detective stories under pseudonym of F. R. Eckma: Een Linkerbeen gezocht 1935, Spoken te koop 1936, Ratten op de trap 1937, Drie Dode Dwergen 1937, De Maagd en de Moordenaar 1938. *Leisure interests:* travel, reading. *Address:* c/o Harper and Row, New York, N.Y. 10001, U.S.A.

HARTSHORN, Michael Philip, F.R.S.N.Z., D.PHIL.; British and New Zealand university teacher; b. 10 Sept. 1936, Coventry, England; m. Jacqueline Joll 1963; four s.; ed. Imperial Coll. of Science and Tech., London, University Coll., Oxford; Lecturer in Chem., Univ. of Canterbury, N.Z. 1960–66, Sr. Lecturer 1966–68, Reader 1968–72, Prof. 1972–; Fulbright Visiting Prof., Cornell Univ., New York 1966–67; Fellowship N.Z. Inst. of Chem. 1969, Hector Medal, Royal Soc. of N.Z. 1973. *Publications:* approx. 170 scientific papers, (with D.N. Kirk) Steroid Reaction Mechanisms 1968. *Leisure interests:* reading, music, gardening. *Address:* 1 Repton Street, Christchurch 1, New Zealand. *Telephone:* 556-450 (Christchurch).

HARTUNG, Hans; German-born French painter; b. 21 Sept. 1904, Leipzig; s. of Curt Hartung and Margarete (née Nakonz); m. Anna-Eva Bergman 1929 (divorced 1938), remarried 1957; ed. Leipzig Univ., Leipzig and Dresden Acads. of Fine Art; first exhibition 1931; Foreign Legion in the Second World War; French nationality 1946; rep. at Dunn Int. Exhbn., London 1963, Tate Gallery, London 1964; mem. Berlin and Munich Acads. of Fine Art; Guggenheim Prize 1956, Rubens Prize 1957, Grand Prize, Venice Biennale 1960; Prix d'honneur, Ljubljana Graphic Art Exhbn. 1967, Grand Prix des Beaux-Arts, Paris 1970; works rep. in numerous museums and galleries in Europe, Asia, North and South America; numerous exhbns., Galérie de France, Paris 1956–; Retrospective exhbns. Museo Civico di Torino 1966, City Museum, Birmingham 1968, Musée National d'Art Moderne, Paris 1969, Museum of Fine Arts, Houston 1969, Wallraf-Richartz-Museum, Cologne 1974, Nationalegalerie, Berlin 1975, Städtische

Galerie, Lenbachhaus 1975, Metropolitan Museum of Art, New York 1975; Musée d'Art Moderne de la Ville, Paris 1980, Musée de la Poste, Paris 1980, Städtische Kunsthalle, Düsseldorf 1981, Staatsgalerie Moderner Kunst, Munich 1981–82, Henie-Onstad Foundation, Oslo 1981, Hôtel de Ville, Paris 1985, L'Énac, Nice 1986; mem. Institut, Acad. des Beaux-Arts, Paris 1977; Commdr., Légion d'honneur, Commdr. des Arts et Lettres, mem. Order of Merit (Fed. Repub. of Germany), Médaille militaire, Croix de guerre, Grand prix des Beaux-Arts de la ville de Paris, Médaille de vermeille de la ville de Paris. *Leisure interest:* photography. *Address:* 06600 Antibes; 23 quai de Conti, 75006 Paris, France.

HARTWELL, Baron (Life Peer), cr. 1968, of Peterborough Court in the City of London; (**William) Michael Berry,** M.B.E., T.D.; British newspaper executive; b. 18 May 1911; s. of the late 1st Viscount Camrose and Viscountess Camrose (née Mary Agnes Corns); m. Lady Pamela Smith 1936 (died 1982); two s. two d.; ed. Eton Coll. and Christ Church, Oxford; served 1939–45 war; Ed. Sunday Mail, Glasgow 1934–35; Man. Ed. Financial Times 1937–39; fmr. Deputy Editor-in-Chief The Daily Telegraph, Chair. and Editor-in-Chief 1954–87; Chair. and Editor-in-Chief The Sunday Telegraph 1961–87; Chair. Amalgamated Press Ltd. 1954–59. *Publication:* Party Choice 1948. *Address:* 18 Cowley Street, London, S.W.1; and Oving House, Whitchurch, nr. Aylesbury, Bucks, England. *Telephone:* 01-222 4673; (0296) 641307.

HARTZOG, George B., Jr., M.B.A.; American lawyer and administrator; b. 17 March 1920, Colleton County, S.C.; s. of George B. and Mazell (Steedly) Hartzog; m. Helen Carlson 1947; two s. one d.; ed. The American Univ., Washington, D.C.; Attorney and Administrator, Dept. of the Interior with Bureau of Land Management and Nat. Park Service 1946; principal field assignments with Nat. Park Service; Asst. Supt. Rocky Mountain Nat. Park, Colorado 1955–57, Great Smoky Mountains Nat. Park, N. Carolina-Tennessee 1957–59; Supt. Jefferson Nat. Expansion Memorial, St. Louis, Mo. 1959–62; Assoc. Dir. Nat. Parks Service 1963–64, Dir. 1964–72; Exec. Dir. Downtown St. Louis, Inc. 1962–63; Prof. of Public Admin., Univ. of Southern Calif., Washington Public Affairs Center 1972–; Vice-Pres. Hartzog, Lader & Richards, Hilton Head, S.C. and Arlington, Va. 1975–; recipient of several awards for services; Hon. LL.D. (Washington Univ.). *Address:* 900 17th Street, N.W., Washington, D.C. 20006 (Office); 1643 Chain Bridge Road, McLean, Va. 22101, U.S.A. (Home).

HARVEY, Anthony; British film director; b. 3 June 1931; s. of Geoffrey Harrison and Dorothy Leon; entered film industry, joining Crown Film Unit 1949; edited numerous films including Private Progress, Brothers-in-law, Carlton Brown of the Foreign Office, I'm Alright Jack, The Angry Silence, The Millionairess, Lolita, the L-Shaped Room, Dr. Strangelove, The Spy Who Came in from the Cold, the Whisperers; directed Dutchman 1968, The Lion in Winter 1969, They Might be Giants 1970, The Abdication 1973, The Glass Menagerie 1973, The Disappearance of Aimee (TV) 1978, Eagle's Wing, Players 1979, Richard's Things 1980, The Patricia Neal Story 1981, Svengali 1982. *Leisure interest:* gardening. *Address:* c/o Arthur Greene, 101 Park Avenue, 43rd Floor, New York, 10178, U.S.A.; c/o William Morris, 31 Soho Square, London, W.1, England.

HARVEY, Barbara Fitzgerald, M.A., B.LITT., F.R.HIST.S., F.S.A., F.B.A.; British academic; b. 21 Jan. 1928, Teignmouth, Devon; d. of Richard Henry Harvey and Anne Fitzgerald Harvey née Julian; unmarried; ed. Teignmouth Grammar School, Bishop Blackall School, Exeter and Somerville Coll. Oxford; Asst., Univ. of Edin., Scotland 1951–52; Lecturer, Queen Mary Coll., Univ. of London 1952–55; Tutor, Somerville Coll. Oxford 1955–, Fellow 1956–, Vice-Prin. 1976–79 and 1981–83; Vice-Pres. Royal Historical Soc. 1986–. *Publications:* Westminster Abbey and its Estates in the Middle Ages 1977, The Westminster Chronicle, 1381–94 (Ed. with L. C. Hector) 1982; articles in learned journals. *Address:* Somerville College, Oxford, OX2 6HD, England. *Telephone:* (0865) 270600.

HARVEY-JONES, Sir John (Henry), Kt., M.B.E.; British business executive; b. 16 April 1924, London; s. of Mervyn and Eileen Harvey-Jones; m. Mary Evelyn Bignell 1947; one d.; ed. Tormore School, Deal, Royal Naval Coll., Dartmouth; served with Royal Navy 1937–56, specialising in submarines, later working with Naval Intelligence; resgnd. with rank of Lieut. Commdr. 1956; joined ICI as Work Study Officer 1956, then held various commercial posts at Wilton and with Heavy Organic Chemicals Div. until appointed Techno-Commercial Dir. 1967; Deputy Chair. HOC Div. 1968; Chair., ICI Petrochemicals Div. 1970–73; appointed to Main Bd. ICI 1973, Deputy Chair 1978–82, Chair. 1982–87; Chancellor Bradford Univ. 1986–; mem. Tees and Hartlepool Port Authority 1970–73; Chair. Phillips-Imperial Petroleum 1973–75; Non-Exec. Chair. Burns Anderson 1987–; Chair. Parallax Enterprises Ltd. 1987–; Non-Exec. Chair. Business Int. Bd. Cttee. 1988–; Non-Exec. Dir. Reed Int. PLC 1975–84, Carrington Viyella Ltd. 1974–79 (Dir. 1981–82), Grand Metropolitan PLC 1989–, (Deputy Chair. 1987–), The Economist 1987– (Chair. 1989–), G.P.A. Ltd. 1987–, Trendroute Ltd. 1988–; Pres. Conseil Européen des Fédérations de l'Industrie Chimique 1984–86; Vice-Pres. Industrial Participation Asscn. 1983–, Hearing and Speech Trust 1985–, Heaton Woods Trust 1986–; Pres. Book Trust Appeal Fund 1987–, Wider Share Ownership Council 1988–; Chair. Council, Wildfowl Trust 1987–; Vice-Chair. Policy Studies Inst. 1980–85, B.I.M. 1980–85 (mem. 1978–); Hon. Vice-Pres. Inst. of Marketing 1982–; mem. Court of British Shippers' Council 1982–87, Police Foundation

1983– (Chair. Trustees 1984–88), Advisory Editorial Bd. of New European 1987–; mem. Council, Chemical Industries Assen. Ltd. 1980–82, British-Malaysian Soc. 1983–87, Youth Enterprise Scheme 1984–86; mem. Foundation Bd., Int. Man. Inst., Geneva 1984–87; mem. Advisory Council, Prince's Youth Business Trust 1986–; mem. Int. Council, European Inst. of Business Admin. 1984–87; Trustee Science Museum 1983–87, Conf. Bd. 1984–86; Hon. mem. The City & Guilds of London Inst. 1988–; Patron Cambridge Univ. Young Entrepreneurs Soc. 1987–, Manpower Services Comm. Nat. Training Awards 1987–, Steer Org.; Vice-Patron British Polio Fellowship 1988–; Hon. Consultant, Royal United Services Inst. for Defence Studies 1987–; Gov. English Speaking Union 1987–; Fellow Smallpiece Trust 1988–; mem. R.S.A., Soc. of Chemical Industry; Hon. Fellow, Royal Soc. of Chemistry 1985, The Inst. of Chemical Engineers 1985; Hon. LL.D. (Manchester) 1985, (Liverpool) 1986, (London) 1987, Cambridge (1987); D.Univ. (Surrey) 1985; Hon. D.Sc. (Bradford) 1986, (Leicester) 1986; Hon. D.C.L. (Newcastle) 1988; Jo Hambro British Businessman of the Year 1986; Int. Assen. of Business Communicators Award of Excellence in Communication 1987; Radar Man of the Year 1987; City & Guilds Insignia Award in Tech. (h.c.) 1987; Commdr.'s Cross of Order of Merit (Fed. Repub. of Germany). *Leisure interests:* ocean sailing, swimming, the countryside, donkey driving, cooking, contemporary literature. *Address:* c/o Parallax Enterprises Ltd., P.O. Box 18, Ross-on-Wye, Hertfordshire, HR9 7TL, England.

HARVIE-WATT, Sir George Steven, Bt., Q.C., T.D., F.R.S.A.; British businessman and fmr. politician; b. 23 Aug. 1903, Bathgate, Scotland; s. of James McDougal Watt and Jessie Harvie; m. Jane Elizabeth Taylor 1932; two s. one d.; ed. George Watson's Coll., Glasgow and Edinburgh Univs.; called to Bar Inner Temple 1930; Brevet Major 1935, Lieut.-Col. Commanding 31st Battalion R.E., T.A. 1938–41; Conservative M.P. for Keighley Div. of Yorkshire 1931–35 and for Richmond, Surrey, 1937–59; Parl. Pvt. Sec. to the late Rt. Hon. Euan Wallace when Parl. Sec. to Bd. of Trade 1937–38, and to Rt. Hon. Winston Churchill 1941–45; Asst. Govt. Whip 1938–40; D.L. Surrey 1942, Greater London Council 1966; J.P. County of London 1944–56; fmr. Dir. Midland Bank Ltd., The Clydesdale Bank, Eagle Star Insurance Co., North British Steel Group; Pres. Consolidated Goldfields 1973–80; fmr. Chair. Monotype Corpn. Ltd.; mem. of Queen's Bodyguard for Scotland—The Royal Company of Archers; Commdr. 63rd A.A. Brigade 1948–50; A.D.C. to H.M. the King 1948–51; A.D.C. to H.M. the Queen 1952–59; Hon. Freeman, City of London 1976. *Publication:* Most of My Life 1980. *Address:* Sea Tangle, Earlsferry, Leven, Fife, KY9 1AD, Scotland. *Telephone:* (0333) 330506.

HARWOOD, Elizabeth Jean, G.R.S.M., L.R.A.M. British soprano; b. 27 May 1938, Barton, Seagrave; d. of Sydney and Constance Harwood; m. Julian A. C. Royle 1966; one s.; ed. Royal Manchester Coll. of Music; joined Glyndebourne Opera Co. 1960; joined Sadlers Wells 1961; toured Australia with Sutherland-Williamson Int. Opera Co. 1965; has sung at Covent Garden, London, with Scottish Opera, at La Scala, Milan, Hamburg State Opera, Metropolitan Opera, New York, and at Salzburg and Vienna Festivals; many TV and concert appearances; roles include Constanze in Die Entführung, Countess in Count Ory, Marzellina in Fidelio, Norina in Don Pasquale, Donna Elvira in Don Giovanni, Fiordiligi in Così fan Tutti, Countess in Marriage of Figaro, Violetta in La Traviata, Sophie and The Marschallin in Der Rosenkavalier, all four soprano roles in The Tales of Hoffmann, title role in Lucia di Lammermoor; Australian Broadcasting Co. Recital and Tour 1986; many recordings include The Merry Widow, La Bohème; Fellow, Royal Manchester College of Music; Kathleen Ferrier Memorial Prize 1960, Bussetto-Verdi Prize 1963. *Leisure interests:* swimming, animals, entertaining. *Address:* Masonetts, Fryerning, Ingatestone, Essex, England. *Telephone:* (0277) 353024.

HASAN, Maj.-Gen. Mahmudul, B.SC.; Bangladesh politician and fmr. army officer; b. 1 March 1936, Tangail Dist.; m.; two s. one d.; ed. Dhaka Univ. and Mil. Coll. of Eng., Resalpur; commissioned June 1958; various ranks in army including Area Commdr. and Engineer-in-Chief; rank of Maj-Gen. 1982; Admin. Dhaka Municipal Corpn. 1982; Minister of Home Affairs July-Nov. 1986, Minister without Portfolio 1986–87, of Agric. 1988–89, of Interior March 1989–. *Leisure interests:* games, sports. *Address:* Ministry of the Interior, Bangladesh Secretariat, School Bldg., 2nd and 3rd Floor, Dhaka, Bangladesh.

HASANI, Baqir Husain, B.SC., LL.B.; Iraqi diplomatist and public administrator; b. 12 Feb. 1915, Baghdad; s. of Abdul and Bidoor Husain; ed. Columbia Univ., New York and Baghdad Univ.; Dir. of Commerce and Registrar of Companies, Iraq Ministry of Econs. 1947–51; Dir.-Gen. of Contracts and Econ. Affairs, Development Bd. 1951–54; Dir.-Gen. of Income Tax, Ministry of Finance 1954–55; Dir.-Gen. and Chair. of Bd. of Dirs. Tobacco Monopoly Admin. 1956–59; Minister, later Amb. to Austria 1959–63; Chair. Bd. of Govs. Int. Atomic Energy Agency (IAEA) 1961–62, Special Adviser to Dir.-Gen. IAEA 1963–67, 1970–76; Adviser to Perm. Mission of Saudi Arabia, Vienna 1978–81; mem. Iraqi and later IAEA Del. to UN; Rafidain Decoration, Class III (Iraq), Great Golden Order for Merit (Austria). *Leisure interests:* reading and music. *Address:* 43 Maidenhead Court Park, Maidenhead, Berks., SL6 8HN, England (Home); Via Civelli Mario 9, 21100 Varese, Italy; and Masbah, Karadah, Baghdad, Iraq. *Telephone:* (0628) 38573 (England); (0332) 22-88-59 (Italy).

HASANI, Sinan; Yugoslavian (b. Albanian) politician; b. 1922, Požaranju, SAP Kosovo; one s. one d.; with Nat. Liberation Struggle 1941, formed partisan unit 1942; Sec. Regional Bd. Nat. Liberation Front for Kosovo and Metohija; fmr. Sec. Dist. Cttee. of League of Communists in Gnjiglane; fmr. mem. Regional Cttee. League of Communists, fmr. Pres. Prov. Cttee. of Socialist Alliance of Working People of Kosovo; fmr. mem. Prov. Exec. Council and fmr. Dir. Rilindija Publishing Co.; mem. Repub. and Fed. Ass.; fmr. Pres. Ass. of Serbia; fmr. Amb. to Denmark; fmr. Vice-Pres. Yugoslavian Ass.; mem. of Presidency of Prov. Cttee. of League of Communists of Kosovo 1981; mem. of Fed. Conf. of Socialist Alliance of Working People of Serbia, Cen. Cttee. League of Communists of Serbia; mem. Cen. Cttee. League of Communists of Yugoslavia at XI Congress; Pres. Prov. Cttee. of League of Communists of Kosovo 1982; mem. for SAP Kosovo of the Presidency of Yugoslavia 1984–89; Pres. of the Presidency of the SFR of Yugoslavia 1986–87; mem. Acad. of Arts and Sciences of Kosovo; numerous publs. and awards. *Address:* c/o Federal Executive Council, Bul. Lenjina 2, 11075 Novi Beograd, Yugoslavia.

HASE, Karl-Günther von; German civil servant and diplomatist; b. 15 Dec. 1917, Wangern (Breslau); s. of Col. Günther von Hase and Ina Hicketier; m. Renate Stumpff 1945; five. d.; mil. service; German Foreign Service, Bonn and Ottawa; Deputy Chief, later Head of Press Dept., Foreign Office, Bonn 1956–61, Head, Western Dept. 1961–62; State Sec., Head, Press and Information Office of the Fed. Govt. 1962–68; State Sec. Ministry of Defence 1968–69; Amb. to U.K. 1970–77; Dir.-Gen. Second German Television (ZDF) 1977–82; Pres. Anglo-German Asscn. 1982–; Hon. G.C.V.O., K.C.M.G.; Hon. LL.D. (Manchester) 1987. *Leisure interests:* shooting, riding, music. *Address:* Am Stadtwald 60, 5300 Bonn 2, Federal Republic of Germany.

HASEEB, Khair El-Din, M.SC., PH.D.; Iraqi economist and statistician; b. 1 Aug. 1929; m. 1955; one s. two d.; ed. Univ. of Baghdad, London School of Econs. and Univ. of Cambridge; civil servant, Ministry of Interior 1947–54; Head of Research and Statistics Dept., Iraqi Oil Co. 1959–60; Full-time Lecturer, Univ. of Baghdad 1960–61, Part-time 1961–63; Dir.-Gen. Iraqi Fed. of Industries 1960–63; Pres. Gen. Org. for Banks 1964–65; Acting Pres. Econ. Org., Iraq 1964–65; Gov. and Chair. of Bd., Cen. Bank of Iraq 1963–65; Assoc. Prof., Dept. of Econs. Univ. of Baghdad 1965–71, Prof. of Econs. 1971–74; Chief, Programme and Co-ordination Unit, and Natural Resources, Science and Tech. Div. UN Econ. Comm. for Western Asia, then Lebanon and Iraq 1974–76 and 1976–83; Acting Dir.-Gen. Centre for Arab Unity Studies, Lebanon 1978–83, Dir.-Gen. 1983–; mem. Bd. of Dirs. Iraq Nat. Oil Co. 1967–68. *Publications:* The National Income of Iraq 1953–1961, 1964, Workers' Participation in Management in Arab Countries (in Arabic) 1971, Sources of Arab Economic Thought in Iraq 1900–71 (in Arabic) 1972, (Co-Ed.) Arab Monetary Integration 1982, (Ed.) Arabs and Africa 1985; numerous articles. *Address:* Centre for Arab Unity Studies, Sadat Tower Building, 9th Floor, Lyon Street, P.O. Box 113-6001, Beirut, Lebanon. *Telephone:* 801582, 801587, 802234 (Office).

HASEGAWA, Kenko; Japanese business executive; b. 8 June 1916, Fukushima; s. of Mr. and Mrs. K. Hasegawa; m. Eiko Matsui 1944; one s. one d.; ed. Faculty of Naval Architecture, Tokyo Imperial Univ.; joined Kawasaki Heavy Industries Ltd. 1942, Dir. 1971, Man. Dir. 1975, Sr. Man. Dir. 1978, Exec. Vice-Pres. 1980, Pres. 1981–87, Chair. 1987–; Ministry of Transportation Award 1982, Blue Ribbon Award 1983. *Leisure interest:* golf. *Address:* 4-14-14 Takanawa, Minato-ku, Tokyo 108, Japan. *Telephone:* (03) 449-0151.

HASEGAWA, Norishige; Japanese chemical executive; b. 8 Aug. 1907, Kumamoto City; s. of Teiichiro and Sakae (Aochi) Hasegawa; m. Tomiko Ataka 1933; one d.; ed. Tokyo Imperial Univ.; Sumitomo Partnership Co. 1931–34, Sumitomo Chemical Co. 1934–, Dir. 1951–, Man. Dir. 1956, Vice-Pres. 1963–65, Pres. 1965–77, Chair. 1977–85, Dir. and Counsellor 1985–; Chair. Japan-U.S. Business Council; Adviser, Fed. of Econ. Org. (Keidanren); Life Trustee, Japan Cttee. for Econ. Devt.; Exec. Councillor Osaka Chamber of Commerce and Industry; Standing Dir. Kansai Econ. Fed.; Adviser Japan Chem. Industry Asscn.; Chair. Nippon Asahan Aluminium Co. Ltd., Japan-U.S. Southeast Asscn., Japan-U.S. Midwest Asscn.; mem. Comm. on Foreign Exchange and Other Transactions, Ministry of Finance, mem. Visiting Cttee., Center for Int. Studies, M.I.T.; Pres. Japan Greece Soc.; Trustee, Univ. of The Sacred Heart; Commr. for Japan, The Trilateral Comm.; mem. Industrial Problems Research Council; Adviser Japan Petrochemical Industry Asscn.; Dir. numerous other cos. *Leisure interests:* golf, arts, Greek culture. *Address:* Sumitomo Chemical Co. Ltd., 15, 5-chome Kitahama, Higashi-ku, Osaka (Office); 12-7, Aioi-cho, Nishinomiya City, Hyogo Prefecture, Japan (Home). *Telephone:* 06-220-3151 (Office).

HASEGAWA, Takashi; Japanese politician; b. 1 April 1912; ed. Waseda Univ.; Ed. Kyushu daily paper; Private Sec. to Minister of State; mem. House of Reps. 1953–; Deputy Minister of Educ. 1961–62; Vice-Chair. Public Relations Cttee., Liberal Democratic Party (LDP) 1963, Chair. 1966; Minister of Labour 1973–76, of Transport 1982–83, of Justice Dec. 1988; Dir. Japan Athletic Asscn. *Address:* 8-903, Yonban-cho, 9-chome, Chiyoda-ku, Tokyo, Japan (Home).

HASHIM, Jawad M., PH.D.; Iraqi economist and politician; b. 10 Feb. 1938; s. of Mahmoud Hashim and Nasrat Baqer; m. Salwa Al-Rufaiee 1961; two s.; ed. London School of Econs. and Political Science, Univ. of London; Prof. of Statistics, Univ. of Baghdad 1967; Dir.-Gen. Cen. Statistical Org. 1968; Minister of Planning 1968–71; mem. Econ. Office, Revolutionary Command Council 1971–72, 1974–77; Minister of Planning 1972–74; Pres. Arab Monetary Fund (A.M.F.) April 1977–82; Chair. UN Econ. Comm. for Western Asia (ECWA) 1975; mem. Consultative Group on Int. Economic and Monetary Affairs (Rockefeller Foundation), Economists Asscn., Iraq, Study Group on Energy and World Econ.; Fellow, Int. Bankers' Asscn. *Publications:* Capital Formation in Iraq 1957–1970, National Income—Its Methods of Estimation, The Evaluation of Economic Growth in Iraq 1950–1970. Development of Iraq's Foreign Trade Sector 1950–1970, eighteen articles and several papers. *Leisure interests:* sport, driving, reading. *Address:* c/o Arab Monetary Fund, P.O. Box 2818, Abu Dhabi, United Arab Emirates. *Telephone:* 328873 (Office); 828978.

HASHIMOTO, Ryutaro; Japanese politician; b. 1937; previous posts include: Chair. Cttee. on Social and Labour Problems, House of Reps.; Deputy Chair. Liberal Democratic Party (LDP) Policy Research Council; Chair. LDP Research Comm. on Public Admin. and Finances; Minister of Transport 1986–87; Liberal Democratic Party. *Address:* c/o Ministry of Transport, 1-3 Kasumigaseki 2-Chome, Chiyoda-ku, Tokyo, Japan.

HASHMI, Farrukh Siyar, O.B.E., M.B., B.S., D.P.M., F.R.C.PSYCH.; Pakistani consultant psychiatrist; b. 12 Sept. 1927, Gujrat; s. of Dr. Ziaullah Hashmi and Majida Qureshi; m. Shahnaz Nasimullah 1972; one s. two d.; ed. Volkart Foundation, Switzerland; Consultant Psychiatrist, All Saints Hosp. Birmingham 1969–; Visiting Psychiatrist, H.M. Prison, Stafford 1969–; Commr. Comm. for Racial Equality 1980–86; mem. Parole Bd. 1981–85; mem. Swann Cttee. Dept. of Educ. and Science 1982–85; mem. Swann Cttee. Dept. of Educ. and Science 1982–85; mem. Swann Cttee. Dept. of Educ. and Science 1982–85; Advisory Consultant, Church of England Bd. for Social Responsibility 1984–; with Cen. Dist. Health Authority, Birmingham 1982–; mem. Working Party on Ethnic Minorities, West Midlands Regional Health Authority. *Publications:* six books on psychology and racial matters. *Leisure interests:* writing, reading, music. *Address:* 5 Woodbourne Road, Edgbaston, Birmingham, B15 3QJ, England. *Telephone:* (021) 455 0011.

HASIOR, Władysław; Polish sculptor; b. 14 May 1928, Nowy Sącz; s. of Antoni and Waleria Hasior; m. Joanna Narkiewicz; one s.; ed. Acad. of Fine Arts, Warsaw; Teacher of sculpture, Coll. of Art Techniques, Zakopane 1957–70; scenographer State Dramatic Theatre, Wrocław 1964–70, Polish Theatre, Wrocław 1970–71; mem. Polish Fine Arts Asscn. 1958–; numerous one-man exhbns. in Poland, Stockholm, Oslo, Paris, Brussels, Copenhagen, Helsinki, Venice, New York, São Paulo, Montevideo, Göteborg, Malmö, Vienna, Helsinki, London, Coventry, etc.; creator of many monuments commemorating victims of World War II; some works permanently in museums in Stockholm, Göteborg, Oslo, Amsterdam, Bochum, Rome, Milan and Duisberg; prize of Ministry of Culture and Art 1971; Knight's Cross, Order of Polonia Restituta 1974. *Address:* Ul. Jagiellońska 3, "Borek", 34-500 Zakopane, Poland.

HASKELL, Francis, M.A., F.B.A.; British professor of history of art; b. 7 April 1928, London; s. of Arnold Haskell and Vera Saitzoff; m. Larissa Salmina 1965; ed. Eton Coll. and King's Coll. Cambridge; Jr. Library Clerk, House of Commons 1953–54; Fellow of King's Coll. Cambridge 1954–67; Librarian of Fine Arts Faculty, Cambridge Univ. 1962–67; Prof. of History of Art, Oxford Univ. 1967–; Foreign Hon. mem. American Acad. of Arts and Sciences; Corresp. mem. Accad. Pontaniana, Naples; Mitchell Prize 1977, Serena Medal 1985, Prix Vasari. *Publications:* Patrons and Painters 1963 (Italian 1984, Spanish 1985), Rediscoveries in Art 1976 (Italian 1982, French 1986), L'Arte e il Linguaggio della Politica 1977, Taste and the Antique (with Nicholas Penny) 1981, Past and Present in Art and Taste 1987, The Painful Birth of the Art Book 1988. *Leisure interest:* foreign travel. *Address:* Department of History of Art, 35 Beaumont Street, Oxford, OX1 2PG, England.

HASKINS, Caryl Parker, PH.D.; American scientist and educationist; b. 12 Aug. 1908, Schenectady, N.Y.; s. of Caryl Davis and Frances Julia Parker; m. Edna Ferrell 1940; ed. Yale and Harvard Univs.; mem. of research staff Gen. Electric Co., Schenectady 1931–35; Research Assoc. M.I.T. 1935–44; Pres. and Research Dir. Haskins Laboratories, Inc. 1935–55, Dir. 1935–, Chair. 1969–; Research Prof. in Biophysics, Union Coll., Schenectady 1937–55; Liaison Officer 1940–43, Exec. Asst. to the Chair. 1943–44 and Deputy Exec. Officer 1944–45, Nat. Defence Research Cttee.; Scientific Adviser to the Policy Council 1947 and to the Research and Devt. Bd. of the Nat. Mil. Establishment 1948–51; Chair. Advisory Cttee. to the Sec. of Defense on special weapons 1948–49; Consultant to the Sec. of Defense 1948–60, to the Sec. of State 1950–60; mem. President's Science Advisory Cttee. 1955–58, Consultant 1959–70; Pres. Carnegie Inst. of Washington, D.C. 1956–71, Trustee 1949–; Dir. E. I. Du Pont de Nemours & Co. 1971–84; mem. sec. Navy Advisory Cttee. on Naval History 1971–84, Vice-Chair. 1975–84; Dir. Center for Advanced Study in Behavioural Sciences 1960–75, Thomas Jefferson Memorial Foundation 1972–79, Wildlife Preservation Trust Int. Inc. 1976–; Trustee Carnegie Corpn. of New York 1955–79, Hon. Trustee 1979–; Regent Smithsonian Inst. 1956–80, Regent Emer. 1980–; Trustee Nat. Geographic Soc. 1964–84, Nat. Humanities Center 1977–, Council on Library Resources 1965–; Successor Trustee

Yale Univ. 1962–77; numerous hon. degrees; Presidential Certificate of Merit and King's Medal for Service in the Cause of Freedom; Joseph Henry Medal, Smithsonian Inst. *Publications:* Of Ants and Men 1939, The Amazon, The Life History of a Mighty River 1943, Of Societies and Men 1951, Scientific Revolution and World Politics 1964, The Search for Understanding 1967. *Leisure interests:* gardening, walking, travel. *Address:* 545 18th Street, N.W., Washington, D.C. 20036 (Office); Greenacres, 22 Green Acre Lane, Westport, Conn. 06880, U.S.A. (Home). *Telephone:* (202) 332-8700 (Office); (203) 227 2428 (Home).

HASKINS, James George, O.B.E., J.P., M.P.; Botswana politician; b. 24 April 1914, Bulawayo, Zimbabwe (then Rhodesia); s. of George James and Mary Haskins; m. Dorothy Louie Purdue 1939; two s. two d.; ed. Plumtree School, Zimbabwe and J. W. Jagger Business Training Coll.; served South African Service Corps 1939–42; Chair. and Man. Dir. family business, Francistown, Botswana 1945–66; mem. Legis. Council 1961–64; mem. Nat. Ass. and Parl. of Botswana 1965; Minister of Works and Communications 1965–66, 1970–79, of Commerce, Industry and Water Affairs 1966–69, of Finance 1969–70; Speaker, Botswana Nat. Ass. 1979–; Treas. Botswana Democratic Party 1970–79; Chair. Standard Chartered Bank (Botswana) Ltd., Bata Shoe Co. Botswana (Pty.) Ltd., Sedgwick Insurance Brokers (Pty.) Ltd., Botswana Liquor Mfrs. Ltd., J. Haskins & Sons (Pty.) Ltd.; Life mem. Botswana Red Cross Soc.; Chair. Botswana Bowling Asscn. *Leisure interests:* bowls, philately, rugby, cricket. *Address:* Botswana National Assembly, P.O. Box 240, Gaborone; Rosedobrat, corner Khama Street/Lobengula Avenue, Francistown, Botswana (Home). *Telephone:* Gaborone 355681 (Office); 352083 (Home); Francistown: 212301 (Office); 213513 (Home).

HASKINS, Sam (Samuel Joseph); British (b. South African) photographer and designer; b. 11 Nov. 1926, Kroonstad; s. of Benjamin G. Haskins and Anna E. Oelofse; m. Alida Elzabe van Heerden 1952; two s.; ed. Helpmekaar School and Witwatersrand Technical Coll., Johannesburg Bolt Court School of Photography, London; freelance work, Johannesburg 1953–68, London 1968–; one-man exhbns. in Johannesburg 1953, 1960, Tokyo 1970, 1973, 1976, 1979, 1981, 1985, London 1972, 1976, 1978, 1980, Paris 1973, 1981, Amsterdam 1974, 1981, Geneva 1981, Zurich 1981, New York 1981, San Francisco 1982, Toronto 1982, 1986; Fellow, Royal Photographic Soc. 1974, Soc. of Industrial Artists and Designers 1974; Prix Nadar (France) for Cowboy Kate and Other Stories 1964, Israel Museum Award, Int. Art Book Contest Award, Gold Medal Award for Haskins Posters, New York 1974, Kodak Book Prize 1980 (for Photo Graphics). *Publications:* Five Girls 1962, Cowboy Kate and Other Stories 1964, African Image 1966, November Girl 1967, Haskins Posters 1972, Photo Graphics 1980, and portfolios in most major international photographic magazines. *Leisure interests:* vintage car rallying, books, music, horticulture. *Address:* P.O. Box 59, Wimbledon, London, S.W.19, England.

HASLAM, Sir Robert, Kt., B.SC., M.I.MIN.E., F.I.M.E.; British business executive; b. 4 Feb. 1923, Bolton, Lancs. (now Greater Manchester); s. of Percy and Mary Haslam; m. Joyce Quin 1947; two s.; ed. Bolton School and Univ. of Birmingham; joined ICI Nobel Div. 1947, Personnel Dir. Nobel Div. 1960–63, Commercial Dir. ICI Plastics Div. 1963–66, Deputy Chair. Plastics Div. 1966–69, Deputy Chair. ICI Fibres Div. 1969–71, Chair. Fibres Div. 1971–, Dir. ICI Ltd. 1971–, Deputy Chair. 1980–83; Chair. Tate & Lyle 1983–86, British Steel Corpn. 1983–86; mem. British Overseas Trade Bd. 1981–85; mem. Bd. Cable and Wireless 1982–83; mem. Nationalized Industries Chairmen's Group 1983–, Chair. 1985–86; mem. NEDC 1985–; Dir. Bank of England 1984–; fmr. Non-Exec. Deputy Chair. British Coal 1985, Chair. 1986–(90); Advisory Dir. Unilever PLC 1986–; Chair. Manchester Business School; Hon. D.Tech. (Brunel) 1987; Hon. D. Eng. (Birmingham) 1987. *Leisure interests:* golf, travel. *Address:* British Coal, Hobart House, London, SW1X 7AE, England.

HASLER, Arthur Davis, PH.D.; American professor of zoology; b. 5 Jan. 1908, Lehi, Utah; s. of Walter Thalmann Hasler and Ada Broomhead Hasler; m. 1st Hanna Prusse 1932 (deceased); five s. one d.; m. 2nd Hathenay Minton 1971; ed. Brigham Young Univ. and Univ. of Wisconsin; Aquatic biologist, U.S. Fish and Wildlife Service 1935–37; Naturalist, U.S. Nat. Park Services 1937–38; staff, Univ. of Wis. 1937–, Chair. Dept. of Zoology 1953, 1955–57, Prof. of Zoology 1948–79, Prof. Emer. 1979–, Dir. Laboratory of Limnology 1963–79; mem. research Cttee., Wis. Conservation Dept. 1954–66; Chair. Lake Mendota Problems Cttee. 1965–72; Pres. Int. Assen. of Ecology 1974; Dir. Inst. of Ecology 1971–74; mem. Nat. Acad. of Sciences; Foreign mem. Royal Netherlands Acad. of Sciences 1976; Fellow, Philadelphia Acad. of Sciences 1953, American Inst. of Fisheries Research Biology 1958, American Acad. of Arts and Sciences 1972, and numerous other professional and advisory bodies; Hon. D.Sc. (Newfoundland) 1967; Award for Excellence U.S. Fisheries Soc. 1977; Distinguished Service Award, American Inst. of Biological Sciences 1980, Service Award, Wis. Chapter of Soil Conservation Soc. 1980, Nat. Sea Grant Assen. Award 1980, N.A.S. Distinguished Scholar Exchange Program—China 1983; N.A.S.-U.S.S.R. Acad. of Sciences Scholar Exchange Program—U.S.S.R. 1986. *Publications:* Underwater Guideposts 1966, Olfactory Imprinting and Homing in Salmon 1983, and over 200 research publications. *Address:* 1233 Sweet Briar Road, Madison, Wis. 53705 (Home); Centre for Limnology, 680 North Park Street, University of Wisconsin, Madison, Wis. 53706, U.S.A. (Office). *Telephone:* 608 262-1627 (Office).

HASLUCK, Rt. Hon. Sir Paul Meernaa Caedwalla, K.G., G.C.M.G., G.C.V.O., P.C., M.A.; Australian historian, diplomatist and politician; b. 1 April 1905, Fremantle; m. 1932; two s. (one deceased); ed. Perth Modern School, Western Australia Univ.; mem. Editorial staff The West Australian; Hon. Sec. Western Australian Historical Soc. 1930–36; Lecturer in History Western Australia Univ. 1939–40; mem. staff Australian Dept. of External Affairs 1941–47; Sec. Canberra Conf. Jan. 1944; Adviser on Australian del. to Wellington Conf. Nov. 1944; Adviser British Commonwealth meeting London April 1945; Adviser San Francisco Conf. April 1945; Australian del. Exec. Cttee. of United Nations Preparatory Comm. London Aug. 1945; alternate del. Preparatory Comm. Nov. 1945; del. General Assembly Jan. and Sept. 1946; Dir. post-hostilities Div. Australian Dept. of External Affairs April 1945; Counsellor-in-Charge Australian Mission UN H.Q. Mar. 1946; Acting rep. of Australia on Security Council and Atomic Energy Comm. July 1946; Research Reader in History, Univ. of W. Australia 1948; elected to Commonwealth Parl. as Liberal M.P. 1949–69; Minister for Territories, Fed. Cabinet 1951–63; Minister of Defence 1963–64, of External Affairs 1964–69; Gov.-Gen. of Australia 1969–74; Fellow Australian Social Science Acad., Royal Australian Historical Soc., Hon. Australian Humanities Acad., K. St. J.; engaged on official history of Australia in Second World War during 1947, 1948, 1949. *Publications:* Our Southern Half-Castes 1938, Into the Desert 1939, Black Australians 1942, Workshop of Security 1947, The Government and the People, 1939–1945 (Australian Official War History) 1952, 1969, Native Welfare in Australia 1953, Collected Verse 1970, An Open Go 1971, A Time for Building 1976, Mucking About: An Autobiography 1977, Diplomatic Witness 1980, The Office of Governor-General 1980, Sir Robert Menzies 1980, Dark Cottage 1984, Shades of Darkness: Aboriginal Affairs 1925–65, 1988. *Address:* 2 Adams Road, Dalkeith, W.A. 6009, Australia.

HASSAN II, King of Morocco; 17th Sovereign of the Alaouite dynasty; b. 9 July 1929; ed. Bordeaux Univ.; son of Mohammed V; invested as Crown Prince Moulay Hassan 1957; C.-in-C. and Chief of Staff of Royal Moroccan Army 1957; personally directed rescue operations at Agadir earthquake disaster 1960; Minister of Defence 1960–61; Vice-Premier 1960–61; succeeded to throne on death of his father, 26 Feb. 1961; Prime Minister 1961–63, 1965–67; Minister of Defence 1972–73, Commdr.-in-Chief of the Army Aug. 1972–; Chair. OAU Assembly of Heads of State 1972. *Publication:* The Challenge (memoirs) 1979. *Address:* Royal Palace, Rabat, Morocco.

HASSAN IBN TALAL, H.R.H. G.C.V.O., M.A.; Crown Prince of Jordan; b. 20 March 1947, Amman; m. Sarrath Khujista Akhter Banu 1968; one s. three d.; ed. Harrow School, England, Christ Church, Oxford Univ.; brother of H.M. Hussein ibn Talal, King of Jordan (q.v.), and heir to the throne; acts as Regent during absence of King Hussein; Ombudsman for Nat. Devt. 1971–; Founder of Royal Scientific Soc. of Jordan 1970, Royal Acad. for Islamic Civilization Research (Al AlBait) 1980, Arab Thought Forum 1981, Forum Humanum (now Arab Youth Forum) 1982; Co-Chair. Independent Comm. on Int. Humanitarian Issues; Co-Patron Islamic Acad. of Sciences; Pres. Higher Council for Science and Tech.; Hon. Gen. of Jordan Armed Forces; Hon. Ph.D. (Econ.) (Yarmouk) 1980; Hon. D.Sc. (Bogazici, Turkey) 1982; Hon. Dr. Arts and Sciences (Jordan) 1987; Medal of Pres. of Italian Repub. 1982; Kt. of Grand Cross of Order of Merit (Italy) 1983. *Publications:* A Study on Jerusalem 1979, Palestinian Self-Determination 1981, Search for Peace 1984. *Leisure interests:* polo, squash, scuba diving, mountaineering, archaeology, Karate, Taekwondo, helicopter piloting, skiing. *Address:* Office of the Crown Prince, The Royal Palace, Amman, Jordan.

HASSAN, Hon. Sir Joshua (Abraham), G.B.E., K.C.M.G., L.V.O., Q.C., LL.D.; Gibraltar lawyer and politician; b. 1915, Gibraltar; s. of Abraham R. M. Hassan and Lola Hassan (née Serruya); m. 1st Daniela Salazar 1945 (dissolved 1969), two d.; m. 2nd Marcelle Bensimon 1969, two d.; ed. Line Wall Coll., Gibraltar; called to Bar, Middle Temple, London 1939; mem. Exec. Council, Chief mem. Legislative Council, Gibraltar 1950–64; Chief Minister of Gibraltar 1964–69, 1972–87 (retd.); Leader of Opposition, House of Assembly 1969–72; Minister for Information 1976–87; Mayor of Gibraltar 1945–50, 1953–69; Deputy Coroner, Gibraltar 1941–64; Chair. Cttee. of Man. Gibraltar Museum 1952–65; Chair. Cen. Planning Comm. 1947–70, Gibraltar Lottery Cttee. 1955–69; Hon. Bencher, Middle Temple 1983; Pres. Gibraltar Labour Party and Assen. for the Advancement of Civil Rights; Hon. D.Jur. (Hull). *Leisure interest:* reading. *Address:* 11/18 Europa Road, Gibraltar. *Telephone:* 77295.

HASSAN, Moulaye al-; Mauritanian diplomatist; ed. Inst. of Admin. Studies, Faculty of Law, Univ. of Dakar; Chief of Protocol, Ministry of Foreign Affairs 1960–68; Consul-Gen. Mali 1968–70; Amb. to Ivory Coast 1970–71; del. to UN Gen. Assembly 1968; Perm. Rep. to UN 1971–78. *Address:* c/o Ministry of Foreign Affairs, Nouakchott, Mauritania.

HASSAN SHARQ, Mohammad; Afghan politician; b. 1925, Farah, Afghanistan; Deputy Prime Minister, 1974–77; Prime Minister of Afghanistan 1988–. *Address:* Office of the Prime Minister, Kabul, Afghanistan.

HASSEL, Kai-Uwe von, O.B.E.; German politician; b. 21 April 1913; m. 1st Elfriede Fröhlich 1940 (died 1971); one s. (deceased) one d.; m. 2nd Dr. Monika Weichert 1972; one s.; ed. Real Gymnasium, Flensburgh; studied farming and trade in Tanganyika; plantation trader E. Africa 1935–40, deported to Germany 1940; served in Army 1940–45, prisoner 1945; Mayor of Glücksburg 1947–50, mem. of County Council 1948–54; mem. of Schleswig-Holsteinischer Landtag 1950–65; also elected to Bundestag, but resigned on appointment as Minister-Pres. of Schleswig-Holstein 1954–63; Pres. Bundesrat 1955–56; Deputy Chair. CDU 1956–69; Minister of Defence, Fed. Repub. of Germany 1963–66, for Refugees and Expellees 1966–69; mem. of Bundestag 1965–80; Pres. of Bundestag 1969–72, Vice-Pres. 1972–76; Pres. European Union of Christian Democrats 1973–84, Vice-Pres. 1980–84; Pres. Parl. Assembly of WEU 1977–80; mem. European Parl. 1979–84; Comm. of Eminent Statesmen, Council of Europe 1984–; mem. Bd. of Dirs. Konrad-Adenauer Foundation, Bonn 1962–; Pres. Hermann-Ehlers Foundation, Kiel 1968–; Pres. Bd. of Dirs. Inst. for Tropical and Sub-Tropical Agric., Witzenhausen 1957–; Pres. German-Iranian Foundation 1975–; mem. Bd. of Dirs. D.E.G.: German Finance Co. for Investment in Developing Countries 1983–; Grand Cross of Merit (Federal Repub. of Germany) 1956 and 24 other int. awards and honours. *Publications:* Verantwortung für die Freiheit 1966, Waafrika Waleo (Swahili) 1942. *Address:* Lyngsbergstrasse 39b, 5300 Bonn 2, Federal Republic of Germany. *Telephone:* 0228-167493.

HASSELL, Michael Patrick, M.A., PH.D., F.R.S.; British professor of insect ecology; b. 2 Aug. 1942, Tel Aviv; s. of Albert Hassell and Ruth Hassell; m. 1st Glynis M. Everett 1966, 2nd Victoria A. Taylor 1982; three s. one d.; ed. Whitgift School, Croydon, Clare Coll., Cambridge and Oriel Coll., Oxford; Visiting Lecturer, Univ. of Calif., Berkeley 1967–68; NERC Research Fellowship, Hope Dept. of Entomology, Oxford 1968–70; Lecturer, Dept. of Zoology and Applied Entomology, Imperial Coll., London 1970–75, Reader 1975–79, Prof. of Insect Ecology, Dept. of Pure & Applied Biology 1979–, Deputy Head, Dept. of Pure and Applied Biology 1984–, Dir. Imperial Coll., Silwood Park 1988–; Storer Life Sciences Lecturer, Univ. of Calif., Davis 1985; Scientific Medal (Zoological Soc.) 1981. *Publications:* Insect Population Ecology (with G. C. Varley and G. R. Gradwell) 1973, The Dynamics of Competition and Predation 1975, The Dynamics of Arthropod Predator-Prey Systems 1978; numerous publs. on population ecology. *Address:* 2 Oak Lea Cottages, Osborne Lane, Warfield, Berks., RG13 6EB, England. *Telephone:* (0990) 23913 (Office); (0344) 52155 (Home).

HASSETT, Gen. Sir Francis George, A.C., K.B.E., C.B., D.S.O., M.V.O.; Australian army officer; b. 11 April 1918, Sydney; s. of J. F. Hassett; m. Margaret Hallie Spencer 1946; two s. two d.; ed. Canterbury High School, Sydney, Royal Military Coll., Duntroon; mem. of Darwin Mobile Force 1939, Australian Imperial Force 1939–45 (Middle East, S.W. Pacific area); Commdr. 1 RAR and 3 RAR 1951–52 (Korea), 28th Commonwealth Infantry Brigade Group 1960–62 (Malaya); at Imperial Defence Coll. London 1963; Deputy Chief of Gen. Staff 1964–66; Head Australian Joint Services Staff, London 1966–67; Extra Gentleman Usher to H.M. The Queen 1966–68; G.O.C. Northern Command 1968–70; Head Army Reorg. Planning Staff 1970–71; Vice Chief of Gen. Staff 1971–73; Chief of Gen. Staff 1973–75; Chief of Defence Force Staff 1975–77 (retd). *Leisure interests:* boating, reading, fishing, travel. *Address:* 42 Mugga Way, Red Hill, Canberra, A.C.T. 2603, Australia. *Telephone:* Canberra 95-8035.

HASSON, Maurice; French-Venezuelan violinist; b. 6 July 1934, Berck-Plage; m. Jane Hoogesteijn, 1969; one s. three d.; ed. Conservatoire National Supérieure de Musique, Paris, further studies with Henryk Szeryng (q.v.); concert artist in major concert halls throughout world, also in TV and radio performances; First Prize Violin, Prix d'Honneur, and First Prize Chamber Music, Conservatoire National Supérieure de Musique, Paris 1950, Int. Prize Long Thibaut 1951, Int. Prize Youth Festival, Warsaw 1955, Grand Prix Music de Chambre 1957. *Recordings include:* Concerto No. 1 (Paganini), Concerto No. 2 (Prokofiev), Debussy Sonatas, Fauré Sonatas, Concerto No. 1, Scottish Fantasy (Bruch), Concerto for 2 and 4 violins (Vivaldi), Double Concerto (Bach), Concerto (Brahms), Brilliant Showpieces for the Violin, Tzigane (Ravel), Rondo Capriccioso (St. Saens), Poème (Chausson), Gypsy Airs (Sarasate), Violin Concerto (Castellanos-Yumar). *Leisure interests:* painting, sport, cars. *Address:* c/o Anglo-Swiss Artists Management Ltd., 16 Muswell Hill Road, London, N6 5UG; 18 West Heath Court, North End Road, London, N.W.11, England (Home). *Telephone:* 01-444 4123; 01-458 3647 (Home).

HASTINGS, Rev. Adrian Christopher, M.A., TH.D.; British university professor and Catholic priest; b. 23 June 1929, Kuala Lumpur, Malaysia; s. of William George Warren Hastings and Hazel Mary Hastings (née Daunais); m. Elizabeth Ann Spence 1979; ed. Douai Abbey School, Worcester Coll., Oxford, Coll. of Propaganda Fide, Rome, Christ's Coll., Cambridge; ordained Catholic priest 1955; pastoral and educational work, Uganda 1958–66, Tanzania and Zambia 1966–70; Consultant to Anglican archbishops in Africa on marriage problems 1971–72; Research Officer, S.O.A.S., London 1973–76; Lecturer in Religious Studies, Univ. of Aberdeen, Scotland 1976–80, Reader 1980–82; Prof. of Religious Studies, Univ. of Zimbabwe, Harare 1982–85; Prof. of Theology, Univ. of Leeds 1985–; Ed. Journal of Religion in Africa 1985–. *Publications:* Prophet and Witness in Jerusalem 1958, One and Apostolic 1963, Church and Mission in Modern Africa 1967, A Concise Guide to the Documents of the Second Vatican Council (2 vols.) 1968, Christian Marriage in Africa 1973, Wiriyamu 1974, The Faces of God 1975, In Filial Disobedience 1978, A History of African Christianity

1950–1975 1979, In the Hurricane 1986, A History of English Christianity 1920–1985 1986, African Catholicism 1989. *Leisure interests:* walking, visiting ancient buildings, cutting hedges on the Malvern Hills. *Address:* Department of Theology and Religious Studies, The University, Leeds, LS2 9JT (Office); 3 Hollin Hill House, 219 Oakwood Lane, Leeds, LS8 2PE, England (Home). *Telephone:* (0532) 431751 (Office).

HASTINGS, Max Macdonald; British journalist; b. 28 Dec. 1945, London; s. of Macdonald Hastings and Anne Scott-James (Lady Lancaster); m Patricia Edmondson 1972; two s. one d.; ed. Charterhouse and Univ. Coll. Oxford; reporter, London Evening Standard 1965–67, 1968–70; Fellow U.S. World Press Inst. 1967–68; reporter, current affairs, BBC Television 1970–73; freelance journalist, broadcaster and author 1973–86; columnist Evening Standard 1979–85, Daily Express 1981–83, Sunday Times 1985–86 Ed., Daily Telegraph 1986–; Journalist of the Year 1982; Reporter of the Year 1982; Somerset Maugham Prize for Non-fiction 1979. *Publications* America 1968: The Fire, The Time 1968, Ulster 1969 1970, Montrose: The King's Champion 1977, Yoni: Hero of Entebbe 1979, Bomber Commanc 1979, Das Reich 1981, Battle for the Falklands (with Simon Jenkins) 1983 Overlord 1984, Victory in Europe 1985, The Oxford Book of Military Anecdotes (Ed.) 1985, The Korean War 1987. *Leisure interests:* shooting fishing. *Address:* The Daily Telegraph, South Quay Plaza, London, E.14 England. *Telephone:* 01-538 5000.

HASZELDINE, Robert Neville, SC.D., C.CHEM., F.R.S.C., F.R.S.; British pro fessor of chemistry; b. 3 May 1925, Manchester; s. of Walter Haszeldine and Hilda (Webster) Haszeldine; m. Pauline E. Goodwin 1954 (died 1987) two s. two d.; ed. Stockport Grammar School and Univs. of Birmingham and Cambridge; Asst. in Research in Organic Chem. Univ. of Cambridge 1949, Univ. Demonstrator in Organic and Inorganic Chem. 1951, Asst. Dir of Research 1956; Fellow and Dir. of Studies, Queens' Coll. Cambridge 1954–57, Hon. Fellow 1976; Prof. of Chem. Univ. of Manchester Inst. o Science and Tech. (UMIST) 1957–82, Head, Dept. of Chem. 1957–76, Prin 1976–82; mem. various govt. cttees. etc.; Visiting Lecturer at univs. ii U.S.A., Europe, Far East, S. America etc.; Chair. The Langdales Soc. Meldola Medal 1953; Corday-Morgan Medal and Prize 1960. *Publications* scientific papers in professional journals. *Address:* Copt Howe, Chape Stile, Great Langdale, Cumbria, LA22 9JR, England. *Telephone:* (09667 685.

HATANO, Akira; Japanese politician; b. 1911; ed. Nihon Univ.; joine police service; served in prefectural and cen. police depts.; posts include Chief of Nat. Police Agency's Investigation Bureau, Supt.-Gen. Metropoli tan Police Dept., Tokyo; retd. from police service 1971; mem. House o Councillors from Kanagawa Pref.; mem. Liberal-Democratic Party (LDF Foreign Affairs Cttee.; Minister of Justice 1982–83. *Address:* Liberal Democratic Party, 7, 2-chome, Hirakawacho, Chiyoda-ku, Tokyo, Japan.

HATCH, Henry Clifford, Jr.; Canadian business executive; b. 30 Apr 1916, Toronto, Ont.; s. of Harry C. Hatch and Elizabeth Carr; m. Joan Ferriss 1940; two s. two d.; ed. St. Michael's College School, Toronto Salesman, T. G. Bright & Co., Ltd., Niagara Falls 1933–37; Merchandising Staff Hiram Walker Inc., Walkerville, Ont. 1937, Dir. 1938; Dir. Hiram Walker-Gooderham & Worts Ltd. 1946, Vice-Pres. 1955, Exec. Vice-Pres 1961, Pres. 1964–78, Chair. and Chief Exec. Officer 1978–81; Chair. an Dir. Hiram Walker Resources Ltd. 1980–87, C.E.O. 1986–87; Dir. T. G Bright & Co. Ltd., The Toronto-Dominion Bank, Bell Canada, London Life Insurance Co. Ltd., R. Angus Alberta Ltd. *Leisure interests:* sailing curling, swimming, reading, golf. *Address:* 2072 Riverside Drive East Walkerville, Ont., N8Y 4S5 (Office); 7130 Riverside Drive East, Windsor Ont. N8S 1C3, Canada (Home). *Telephone:* (519) 254-5171 (Office); (519 944-1616 (Home).

HATCH, Marshall Davidson, A.M., PH.D., F.A.A., F.R.S.; Australian researc scientist; b. 24 Dec. 1932, Perth; s. of Lloyd D. Hatch and Alice Dalzie m. 2nd Lyndall Langman 1983; two s.; ed. Newington Coll., Sydney Sydney Univ. and Univ. of Calif.; research scientist, CSIRO 1955–59; post doctoral fellow, Univ. of Calif. 1959–61; research scientist, Colonial Suga Refining Co., Ltd. 1961–70; Chief Research Scientist, Div. of Plant Indus try, CSIRO, Canberra 1970–; Clark Medal, Royal Soc. of N.S.W. 1973 Lemberg Medal, Australian Biochem. Soc. 1974, Charles Kettering Awar for Photosynthesis, American Soc. of Plant Physiologists 1980, Ran Award, Rank Foundation 1981. *Publications:* over 130 review articles chapters in books and research papers. *Address:* Division of Plant Industry CSIRO, P.O. Box 1600, Canberra (Office); 34 Dugdale Street, Cook, A.C.T 2614, Australia (Home). *Telephone:* 062-465264 (Office); 062-515159 (Home)

HATCH, Orrin Grant, B.S., J.D.; American lawyer and politician; b. 2 March 1934, Homestead Park Pa.; s. of Jesse Hatch and Helen Kamm Hatch; m. Elaine Hansen 1957; three s. three d.; ed. Brigham Youn; Univ., Univ. of Pittsburgh; journeyman metal lather; Partner, Thomson Rhodes & Grigsby 1962–69; Senior Vice-Pres. and Gen. Counsel, America Minerals Man. and American Minerals Fund Inc., Salt Lake City, Uta 1969–71; Partner, Hatch & Plumb, Salt Lake City 1976; Senator from Utah Jan. 1977–; Chair. Senate Labor and Human Resources Cttee. 1981– Republican. *Publication:* Good Faith under the Uniform Commercial Code articles in legal journals. *Address:* U.S. Senate, Washington, D.C. 20510.

HATEM, Mohammed Abdel Kader, M.SC., PH.D.; Egyptian politician; b. 1917, Alexandria; s. of Abdel Kader Hatem; one s. three d.; ed. Military Acad., Univs. of London and Cairo; mem. Nat. Assembly 1957; Adviser to the Presidency, subsequently Deputy Minister for Presidential Affairs 1957; Minister of State responsible for broadcasting and television 1959; Minister for Culture, Nat. Guidance and Tourism 1962; Deputy Prime Minister for Cultural Affairs and Nat. Guidance 1965; Deputy Prime Minister and Minister for Culture and Information 1971–74; Chair. Al-Ahram 1974; Asst. to Pres. of Repub. and Supervisor-Gen. of Specialized Nat. Councils 1974–; elected mem. of People's Assembly for Abdin Constituency 1979; mem. Gen. Sec. Arab Socialist Union; Head, Egyptian Political Science Soc. 1957–, Egyptian-Japanese Friendship Assćn. 1970–, Egyptian-Spanish Friendship Assćn. 1966–; Prof Al-Azhar 1980–81; hon. doctorates from two French univs. and Dem. People's Repub. of Korea. *Publications:* (in Arabic) Public Opinion, Propaganda (Theories and Experiences), Information and Propaganda, Rommel in Siwa, Iraq Campaign; (in English) Land of the Arabs, The Egyptian Civilization, Life in Ancient Egypt. *Address:* 20 Hassan Assem Zamalek, Cairo, Egypt.

HATFIELD, Mark O.; American politician; b. 12 July 1922, Dallas, Oregon; s. of Mr. and Mrs C. D. Hatfield; m. Antoinette Kuzmanich 1958; two s. two d.; ed. Willamette Univ. and Stanford Univ.; U.S. Navy Second World War; Instructor, Asst. Prof., Assoc. Prof. in Political Science, Willamette Univ. 1949–56, Dean of Students 1950–56; State Rep., Marion County 1951–55, State Senator, Marion County 1955–57; Sec. of State, Oregon 1957–59; Gov. of Oregon 1959–67; U.S. Senator from Oregon 1967–; Chair. Senate Appropriations Cttee. 1981–; mem. Energy and Natural Resources Cttee., and Senate Rules and Admin. Cttee.; numerous awards; Republican. *Publications:* Not Quite So Simple (autobiography), Conflict and Conscience (religious speeches), Between a Rock and a Hard Place 1976, The Causes of World Hunger (co-author) 1982. *Leisure interests:* gardening, reading. *Address:* 711 Hart Senate Office Building, Washington, D.C. 20510, U.S.A. *Telephone:* (202) 224-3753.

HATFIELD, Rt. Hon. Richard Bennett, P.C., B.A., LL.B.; Canadian lawyer and politician; b. 9 April 1931, Woodstock, N.B.; s. of Heber Harold and Dora Fern (Robinson) Hatfield; unmarried; ed. Acadia Univ. and Dalhousie Univ.; admitted to N.S. bar 1956; Exec. Asst., Minister of Trade and Commerce 1957–58; Sales Man. Hatfield Industries Ltd. 1958–65; mem. New Brunswick Legis. Assembly 1961–; Leader, New Brunswick Progressive Conservative Party 1969–; Premier of New Brunswick 1970–87; mem. Queen's Privy Council 1982–; Dir. Canadian Council of Christians and Jews; Hon. Micmac-Maliseet Chieftain 1970; mem. Aboriginal Order of Canada 1985–; Hon. LL.D. (Moncton) 1971, (New Brunswick) 1972, (St. Thomas Univ.) 1973, (Mount Allison Univ.) 1975; Hon. Dr. Pol.Sci. (Univ. Ste. Anne, Nova Scotia) 1983; Canada-Israel Friendship Award 1973. *Address:* P.O. Box 6000, Fredericton, New Brunswick, E3B 5HI, Canada. *Telephone:* (506) 453 2144.

HATOYAMA, Iichiro; Japanese politician; b. 11 Nov. 1918, Tokyo; s. of late Ichiro Hatoyama (Prime Minister of Japan, 1955–56); m. Yasuko Ishibashi 1942; two s. one d.; ed. Faculty of Law, Tokyo Imperial Univ.; joined Ministry of Finance 1941; served Imperial Navy 1941–46; returned to Ministry of Finance 1946, Deputy Dir.-Gen. of Budget Bureau 1964–66; Deputy Vice-Minister for Admin., Econ. Planning Agency 1966; Dir.-Gen. of Financial Bureau of Ministry of Finance 1967, Dir.-Gen. of Budget Bureau 1968–71, Vice-Minister of Finance 1971–72; mem. House of Councillors 1974–; Minister of Foreign Affairs 1976–77. *Leisure interests:* golf, baseball, Noh song. *Address:* 7-1, Otowa 1-chome, Bunkyo-ku, Tokyo, Japan. *Telephone:* 941-2800.

HATSUMURA, Takiichiro; Japanese politician; b. 5 Nov. 1913, Nagasaki Pref.; mem. House of Councillors 1970–, Chair. Standing Cttee. on Agric., Forestry and Fisheries 1973; Vice-Chair. Liberal-Democratic Party Diet Policy Cttee. 1976; Parl. Vice-Minister of Agric., Forestry and Fisheries 1977; Minister of Labour 1981–82. *Address:* c/o Liberal-Democratic Party, 7, 2-chome, Hirakawacho, Chiyoda-ku, Tokyo, Japan.

HATTERSLEY, Rt. Hon. Roy Sydney George, P.C., B.SC.(ECON.), M.P.; British politician; b. 28 Dec. 1932; s. of Frederick Roy and Enid Hattersley (née Brackenbury); m. Edith Mary Loughran 1956; ed. Sheffield City Grammar School, Univ. of Hull; Journalist and Health Service exec. 1956–64; mem. Sheffield City Council 1957–65; M.P. for Sparkbrook Div. of Birmingham 1964–; Parl. Private Sec. to Minister of Pensions and Nat. Insurance 1964–67; Dir. Campaign for European Political Community 1965; Joint Parl. Sec. Dept. of Employment and Productivity 1967–69; Minister of Defence for Admin. 1969–70; Opposition Spokesman for Defence 1970–72, Education 1972–74, for the Environment 1979–80, for Home Affairs 1980–83, on Treasury and Econ. Affairs 1983–87, on Home Affairs 1987–; Deputy Leader of the Labour Party Oct. 1983–; Minister of State for Foreign and Commonwealth Affairs 1974–76; Sec. of State for Prices and Consumer Protection 1976–79; Public Affairs Consultant IBM 1971, 1972; Columnist Punch, The Guardian, The Listener 1979–82; Visiting Fellow, Inst. of Politics, Univ. of Harvard 1972; Hon. LL.D. (Hull) 1985; Labour. *Publications:* Nelson—A Biography 1974, Goodbye to Yorkshire—A Collection of Essays 1976, Politics Apart—A Collection of Essays 1982, Press Gang 1983, A Yorkshire Boyhood 1983, Choose Freedom: The Future for Demo-

cratic Socialism 1987, Economic Priorities for a Labour Government 1987. *Address:* House of Commons, Westminster, London, S.W.1, England.

HATTON, Stephen Paul, B. COMM.; Australian politician; b. 28 Jan. 1948, Sydney; s. of Stanley J. and Pauline (née Taylor) Hatton; m. Deborah J. Humphreys 1969; three s. one d.; ed. Univ. of New South Wales; Personnel Officer, James Hardie & Co. Pty. Ltd. 1965–70; Industrial Officer Nabalco Pty. Ltd. 1970–75; Exec. Dir. N.T. Confed. of Industries and Commerce Inc. 1975–83; elected N.T. Legislative Ass. (Nightcliff) 1983–, Minister for Lands, Conservation, Ports and Fisheries, Primary Production 1983–84, Mines and Energy, Primary Production 1986, Chief Minister for N.T. 1986–88. *Leisure interests:* swimming, bowls, cricket, rugby. *Address:* P.O. Box 40571 Lasvarin, N.T. (Office); 35 Waters Street, Rapid Creek, Darwin, N.T., Australia (Home). *Telephone:* (089) 852533 (Office); (089) 852425 (Home).

HATTORI, Motozo; Japanese shipping executive; b. 1 Jan. 1905; ed. Kyoto Imperial Univ.; Kawasaki Kisen Kaisha Ltd., Kobe 1931–, Rep. New York Branch 1940–41, Sub-Man., Santiago, Chile 1941–42, Man. 1942–43, Sub.Man., later Man. Operating Section, Kobe 1943–46; Gen. Man. Operating and Chartering Dept. 1946, Dir. 1947–49, Exec. Dir. 1949–50, Pres. 1950–70, Chair. 1970–73, Bd. Counsellor 1973–76, Adviser 1976–; official of other firms and business orgs. *Address:* c/o Kawasaki Kisen Kaisha Ltd., 8 Kaigan Dori, Ikutaku, Kobe, Japan.

HAUFF, Volker, DR.RER.POL.; German politician; b. 9 Aug. 1940, Backnang; s. of Richard and Ilse (Dieter) Hauff; m. Ursula Irion 1967; two s.; ed. Free Univ. of Berlin; with IBM Deutschland, Stuttgart 1971–72; Sec. of State to Fed. Minister for Research and Tech. 1972–78; Fed. Minister for Research and Tech. 1978–80, of Transport 1980–82; mem. Bundestag 1969; mem. Social Democratic Party (SPD) 1959, Vice-Pres. of Parl. Group 1983; mem. IG Metall; mem. Advisory Bd. of the Reconstruction Loan Corpn.; Deputy Chair. Volkswagen Bequest. *Publications:* Programmierfibes—Eine verständliche Einführung in das Programmieren digitaler Automaten 1969, Wörterbuch der Datenverarbeitung 1966, Für ein soziales Bodenrecht 1973, Modernisierung der Volkswirtschaft 1975, Politik als Zukunftsgestaltung 1976, Damit der Fortschritt nicht zum Risiko wird 1978, Sprachlose Politik 1979. *Leisure interests:* modern art, cooking. *Address:* Kanalstrasse 29, 7300 Esslingen (Home); Heinemannstrasse 2, Bonn, Federal Republic of Germany (Office). *Telephone:* 357276 (Home).

HAUGE, Jens Chr.; Norwegian lawyer, politician and airline executive; b. 15 May 1915; ed. Oslo Univ.; became mem. Mil. Org. within Home Front Org. from 1941; became Sec. Prime Minister Gerhardsen 1945; Minister of Defence 1945–52; practising lawyer 1952–; temporary Sec. Labour Party 1952; Minister of Justice 1955; Chair. of several Royal Comms.; Chair. of Bd. Royal Norwegian Airlines (now Norske Luftfartselskap A/S) 1962–83 (concurrently S.A.S. Ltd.), Norwegian State Oil Co. 1972–74, Nat. Theatre, Oslo. *Publications:* essays and books on legal and historical subjects. *Address:* c/o Norske Luftfartselskap A/S, Fornebu Airport, Oslo, Norway.

HAUGHEY, Charles James; Irish politician; b. 16 Sept. 1925, Castlebar, Co. Mayo; s. of Commandant John Haughey and Sarah Ann McWilliams; m. Maureen Lemass 1951; three s. one d.; ed. Scoil Mhuire, Marino, Dublin, St. Joseph's Christian Brothers' School, Fairview, Dublin, Univ. Coll. Dublin and King's Inns, Dublin; commissioned Officer Reserve Defence Force 1947–57; Mem. Dublin City Council 1953–55; M.P. 1957– (currently representing Dublin (North Central)); Parl. Sec. to Minister for Justice 1960–61, Minister for Justice 1961–64; Minister of Agric. 1964–66, Minister for Finance 1966–70, for Health and Social Welfare 1977–79; Taoiseach (Prime Minister) Dec. 1979–June 1981, March–Dec. 1982, Feb. 1987–, Minister for the Gaeltacht Feb. 1987–; Leader of the Opposition 1981–82, 1982–87; Chair. Irish Parl. Joint Cttee. on the Secondary Legislation of the European Communities 1973–77; Pres. Fianna Fáil 1979–; mem. Inst. of Chartered Accountants. *Leisure interests:* reading, music, riding, swimming. *Address:* Abbeville, Kinsealy, Co. Dublin, Ireland. *Telephone:* Dublin 450111.

HAUGHTON, Rosemary Elena Konradin; British writer, lecturer, social worker; b. 13 April 1927, London; d. of Peter Luling and Sylvia Luling (née Thompson); m. Algernon Haughton 1948; seven s. three d.; had no formal educ. after age of 15; has lectured internationally; on staff of shelter for homeless families and project for developing low-income housing in Mass., U.S.A 1981–; 5 hon. degrees. *Publications:* 35 books including The Transformation of Man, The Drama of Salvation, Tales from Eternity, Elizabeth's Greeting, The Catholic Thing, The Passionate God, The Re-Creation of Eve. *Leisure interests:* painting, embroidery, gardening, reading. *Address:* 302 Essex Avenue, Gloucester, Mass. 01930, U.S.A.

HAUGLAND, Aage; Danish opera singer; m. Anette Munk-Andersen 1970; one s. one d.; ed. Univ. of Copenhagen; mem. Norwegian Opera 1968–70, Bremer Opera, Fed. Repub. of Germany 1970–73, Royal Danish Opera 1973–; guest appearances with all maj. opera cos. and orchestras, especially in Wagner, Strauss and Russian operas 1974–; recordings, TV and films; Kt. of Dannebrog; Kgl. Kammersanger. *Address:* Skovbrinken 7, 3450 Allerød, Denmark. *Telephone:* (02) 275454 and (03) 419392.

HAUGLAND, Jens, LL.M.; Norwegian lawyer and politician; b. 16 April 1910; ed. Oslo Univ.; with firm of barristers, Stavanger 1937–38; Legal

Adviser City Treas., Stavanger 1938–40; Junior Judge, Ryfylke District 1941; established own practice Kristiansand 1943; fled to Sweden where attached to Norwegian Legation 1944; resumed practice Kristiansand 1945; mem. Storting 1954–; Minister of Justice 1955–63; Minister of Municipal Affairs and Labour 1963–65; Chair. Perm. Cttee. of Justice 1967–, also Country Justice 1968–; mem. Labour Party.

HĂULICĂ, Dan; Romanian art critic; b. 7 Feb. 1932, Iaşi; s. of Neculai Hăulică and Lucreţia Hăulică; m. Cristina Isbăşescu 1971; one d.; ed. Coll. of Philology, Iaşi, N. Grigorescu Fine Arts Inst., Bucharest; Reader Iaşi Coll. of Philology 1954–56; ed. Literary Magazine, Bucharest 1956–58; researcher of the Inst. for Literary History and Theory of the Romanian Acad. 1958–63; Deputy Ed.-in-Chief Secocul 20 journal of synthesis 1963–67, Ed.-in-Chief 1967–; Prof. N. Grigorescu Coll. of Fine Arts, Bucharest 1965–; Chair. Int. Asscn. of Arts Critics 1981–84, Hon. Chair. 1984–; Chair. Conseil audiovisuel mondial de l'édition et la recherche sur l'art (CAMERA) 1986–; UNESCO Consultant; Chair. Int. Confs. on arts, TV and problems of the image 1981–; mem. leading bds. Romanian Writers' Union, Romanian Fine Arts Union; Prize of the Romanian Fine Arts Union 1967, prizes of the Romanian Writers' Union 1974, 1984; Prize of the Romanian Film Studio Al. Sahia, Great Prize of the Romanian Fine Arts Union 1975. *Works include:* Peintres roumains (UNESCO, vol. I 1963, vol. II 1965), Brancusi ou l'anonymat du génie 1967, Critică şi cultură (Criticism and Culture) 1967, Geografii spirituale (Spiritual Geographies) 1973, Nostalgia sintezei (The Nostalgia for Synthesis) 1984. *Address:* Str. Docenţilor 26, Bucharest 71311, (Home); Calea Victoriei 115, Bucharest, Romania (Office).

HAURWITZ, Bernhard, PH.D.; American (naturalized 1946) meteorologist; b. 14 Aug. 1905, Glogau, Germany; s. of Paul Haurwitz and Betty Cohn; m. 1st Eva Schick 1934 (divorced 1946), 2nd Marion B. Wood; one s.; ed. Univs. of Breslau, Göttingen, Leipzig; Privatdozent, Leipzig 1931–32; Research Assoc. Blue Hill Observatory, Harvard 1933–35; Meteorological Service of Canada 1935–41; Assoc. Prof., M.I.T. 1941–47; Prof. and Chair. Dept. of Meteorology and Oceanography, New York Univ. 1947–59; Prof. Univ. of Colo. 1959–64, with Nat. Center for Atmospheric Research, Boulder, Colo. 1964–, Research Assoc. 1964–73, Dir. Advanced Study Program 1967–69; Prof. (Adjoint Emer.), Univ. of Colo. 1968; Prof. Univ. of Alaska 1970–; Prof. of Atmospheric Physics, Colo. State Univ. 1973–80; Gauss Prof. Akad. der Wissenschaften, Göttingen 1971; mem. Nat. Acad. of Sciences 1960, German Leopoldina Acad. 1964; Hon. mem. American Meteorological Soc. 1973; Rossby Award, American Meteorological Soc. 1962, Bowie Medal, American Geophysical Union 1970, Verdienstkreuz 1st class (Fed. Repub. of Germany) 1976. *Publications:* Dynamic Meteorology 1941, Climatology (co-author) 1944, over 100 articles on dynamic meteorology and oceanography. *Leisure interest:* hiking. *Address:* Department of Atmospheric Science, Colorado State University, Fort Collins, Colo. 80523 (Office); 2523 Constitution Avenue, Fort Collins, Colo. 80526, U.S.A.

HAURY, Emil W., A.B., M.A., PH.D.; American university professor and archaeologist; b. 2 May 1904, Newton, Kan.; s. of Gustav and Clara Haury; m. Hulda Penner 1928; two s.; ed. Bethel Coll., Univ. of Ariz. and Harvard Univ.; Instructor, Univ. of Ariz. 1928–29, Research Asst. in Dendrochronology 1929–30; Asst. Dir. of Gila Pueblo, Globe, Ariz. 1930–37; Assoc. Prof. and Head of Dept. of Anthropology, Univ. of Ariz. 1937–38, Prof. and Head of Dept. and Dir. of Ariz. State Museum 1938–64, Prof. of Anthropology and Adviser to Ariz. State Museum 1964–80, Fred A. Riecker Distinguished Prof. of Anthropology 1970–80, Emer. Prof. 1980–; mem. Nat. Acad. of Sciences, American Acad. of Arts and Sciences, American Philosophical Soc.; Hon. LL.D. (Univ. of New Mexico); Viking Fund Medal for Anthropology 1950, Univ. of Ariz. Alumni Achievement Award 1957, Univ. of Ariz. Faculty Achievement Award 1962, Salgo-Noren Foundation Award for Excellence in Teaching 1967, U.S. Dept. of Interior Conservation Service Award 1976, Alfred Vincent Kidder Award 1977, Univ. of Arizona Alumni Asscn. Distinguished Citizen Award 1980, American Soc. for Conservation Archaeology Award 1980, Arizona Historical Soc. Al Merito Award 1981, Southwestern Anthropological Asscn. Distinguished Scholar Award 1982, Soc. for American Archaeology Distinguished Service Award 1985. *Publications include:* The Mogollon Culture of Southwestern New Mexico (Medallion Papers No. 20) 1936, Excavation at Snaketown, Material Culture (with others, in Medallion Papers No. 25) 1937, The Excavation of Los Muertos and Neighboring Ruins in the Salt River Valley, Southern Arizona (Papers of the Peabody Museum of American Archaeology and Ethnology Vol. 24, No. 1) 1945, The Stratigraphy and Archaeology of Ventana Cave, Arizona 1950, Speculations on Prehistoric Settlement Patterns in the Southwest, (Prehistoric Settlement Patterns in the New World, Edited by G. R. Willey) 1956, The Hohokam: Desert Farmers and Craftsmen, Excavations at Snaketown, 1964–65 1976, Mogollon Culture in the Forestdale Valley, East Central Arizona 1985, Emil W. Haury's Prehistory of the American Southwest (ed. by J. Jefferson Reid and David E. Doyel) 1986. *Address:* Department of Anthropology, University of Arizona, Tucson, Ariz. 85721; and P.O. Box 40543, Tucson, Ariz. 85717, U.S.A. *Telephone:* (602) 621-6288.

HAUSER, Erich; German sculptor and professor; b. 15 Dec. 1930, Rietheim, Tübingen; s. of Ludwig and Berta Hauser; m. Gretl Kawaletz 1955; one s. one d.; ed. Volksschule, Rietheim, Oberschule, Spaichingen

and evening classes at Freie Kunstschule, Stuttgart; studied engraving in Tuttlingen and drawing and modelling under Pater Ansgar, Kloster Beuron; independent sculptor, Schramberg 1952; Visiting Lecturer, Hochschule für bildende Künste, Hamburg 1964–65, Visiting Prof. 1984; Visiting Prof., Hochschule der Künste, Berlin 1984–85; has held many one-man exhbns. in galleries throughout Germany and in Austria and Switzerland since 1961; has participated in many group exhbns. in Europe, New Delhi, Cairo and the São Paulo Biennale 1969; has executed sculptures for many public buildings in Germany including Säulenwand for Univ. of Konstanz, a relief for theatre foyer, Bonn and a sculpture for the Düsseldorf Stock Exchange; mem. Akad. der Künste, Berlin; Kunstpreis der Stadt Wolfsburg für Plastik 1965, Burdapreis für Plastik 1966, Premio Itamaraty 1969, Grand Prix, São Paulo Biennale 1969, Verdienstkreuz am Bande des Verdienstordens der Bundesrepublik 1972, Biennale Preis für Kleinplastik, Budapest 1975, Verdienstkreuz, 1st Class 1979, Helmut-Itraft-Stiftung First Prize, etc. *Address:* 7210 Rottweil-Württ., Federal Republic of Germany. *Telephone:* (0741) 21651.

HAUSER, Philip M., PH.D.; American sociologist; b. 27 Sept. 1909, Chicago, Ill.; m. Zelda B. Hauser; one s. one d.; ed. Univ. of Chicago; Deputy Dir., U.S. Bureau of the Census 1938–47, Acting Dir. 1949–50; Asst. to Sec. of Commerce and Dir., Office of Program Planning, U.S. Dept, of Commerce 1945–47; U.S. Rep. to Population Comm., UN 1947–51; Statistical Adviser to Govt. of Union of Burma 1951–52; Statistical Adviser, Thailand 1955–56; Prof. of Sociology, Dir. Population Research Center and Chicago Community Inventory, Univ. of Chicago 1932–37; now Prof Emer.; Chair. Dept. of Sociology, Univ. of Chicago 1956–65; mem. Board, UN Inst. for Research in Social Devt., Geneva 1966–73, Exec. Cttee. Southeast Asia Devt. Advisory Group 1968–71, Statistical Policy Cttee., U.S. Bureau of the Budget, Bd. of Dirs., Nat. Ass. for Social Policy and Devt. 1968–, Advisory Cttee., The Population Council; mem. Council, Nat. Inst. of Child Health and Human Devt. 1965–69; Chair. Technical Advisory Cttee. for Population Statistics, U.S. Bureau of the Census, Census Advisory Cttee., American Statistical Asscn. (Pres. 1962–); Assoc. Leo J. Shapiro and Assoc. Int. 1977–81; Fellow, American Asscn. for the Advancement of Science, American Statistical Asscn.; mem. and fmr. Pres. American Sociological Asscn., Population Asscn. of America, Sociological Research Asscn.; mem. American Philosophical Soc., Int. Statistical Inst. *Publications:* Several books on population, urbanization and other sociological subjects; about 450 articles in professional journals. *Address:* 1440 N. State Parkway, Chicago, Ill. 60610, U.S.A. (Home).

HÄUSER, Rudolf; Austrian politician; b. 19 March 1909, Vienna; m.; four c.; ed. vocational secondary school, Vienna; Instructor, Jugend am Werk; with Milchindustrie A.G. 1937–59; Deputy Chair. Non-Governmental White-Collar Workers Union 1950–60, Exec. Chair. 1962–60, Chair. 1962; Vice-Chair. Austrian Trade Union Fed. 1963; mem. Nationalrat 1962–; Vice-Chancellor and Fed. Minister for Social Welfare 1970–76. *Address:* Nationalrat, Vienna, Austria.

HAUSNER, Gideon; Israeli lawyer; b. 26 Sept. 1915, Lvov, U.S.S.R.; s. of Dr. Bernard and Ema Hausner; m. Yehudit Liphshitz 1944; one s. one d.; ed. Hebrew Coll. Herzliya, Hebrew Univ; Lecturer in Law Hebrew Univ. 1954–60; del. to Zionist Congresses 1954, 1956, 1964; Attorney-Gen. 1960–63; Chief Prosecutor Eichmann Trial 1961–62; mem. Knesset (Parl.) 1965–81; Chair. Independent Liberal Party Parl. Group 1967–74; Minister without Portfolio 1974–77; Chair. Yad Vashem (Commemoration Authority for Martyrs of World War II) 1969–; Legal Adviser, Zionist World Org. 1983–. *Publications:* Justice in Jerusalem 1966, and articles in law journals and general publications 1941–. *Leisure interest:* photography. *Address:* 6 Bartanura Street, Jerusalem, Israel.

HAUSPURG, Arthur, M.S.E.E., F.I.E.E.E.; American business executive; b. 27 Aug. 1925, New York; s. of Otto and Charlotte (Braul) Hauspurg; m. Catherine Dunning Mackay 1947; three s.; ed. Columbia Univ., New York; Asst. Vice-Pres. American Electric Power Corpn. 1968; Vice-Pres. Consolidated Edison Co. of New York Inc. 1969, Sr. Vice-Pres. 1973, Exec. Vice-Pres. 1975, C.O.O. 1975–, Pres. 1975–81, C.E.O. Aug. 1981–, Chair. 1982–; mem. of numerous bodies including Nat. Acad. of Eng. *Publications:* numerous articles and papers on engineering. *Address:* 4 Irving Place, New York, N.Y. 10003 (Office); 5 John Jay Place, Rye, N.Y. 10580, U.S.A. (Home).

HAVASI, Ferenc; Hungarian politician; b. 20 Feb. 1929, Piszke; started as semi-skilled worker in cement factory; became mason's mate; joined Young Workers' Movement after World War II; joined Hungarian Communist Party 1948; Sec. local party org. in factory 1949–50; Head of Dept., Tatabánya Municipal Party Cttee. 1951; Head of Agitation and Propaganda Dept., Komárom Co. Party Cttee. 1952, Second Sec. 1954, First Sec. 1966–75; studied at Political Acad., Moscow 1958–61; mem. Cen. Cttee. Hungarian Socialist Workers' Party (HSWP) 1966–88, Sec. 1978–88, First Sec. Budapest Cttee. 1987–88; M.P. 1980–88; Deputy Prime Minister 1975–78; mem. HSWP Political Cttee. 1980–88; mem. Cen. Leadership of the Miners' Trade Union 1980–; Labour Order of Merit. *Publications:* Uj fejlődési pályán (A New Course of Development) 1982, Gazdaságpolitika, gazdaságirányítás (Econ. Policy, Econ. Direction) 1985; articles on econ. and social policy. *Address:* Budapest Metropolitan Party Cttee., 1430 Budapest, Köztársaság tér 26, PF 18, Hungary. *Telephone:* 134-846.

HAVEL, Richard Joseph, M.D.; American professor of medicine; b. 20 Feb. 1925, Seattle, Wash.; s. of Joseph Havel and Anna Fritz; m. Virginia J. Havel 1947; three s. one d.; ed. Reed Coll., Portland, Ore., Univ. of Ore. Medical School and Cornell Univ. Medical Coll.; Asst. in Biochem. Univ. of Ore. Medical School 1945–49; Asst. Resident in Medicine, New York Hospital 1950–51, Chief Resident in Medicine 1952–53; Instructor Cornell Univ. Medical Coll. 1952–53; Clinical Assoc. Nat. Heart Inst. 1953–54, Research Assoc. 1954–56; Asst. Prof. of Medicine, Univ. of Calif., San Francisco 1956–59, Assoc. Prof. 1959–64, Prof. of Medicine 1964–, Dir. Cardiovascular Research Inst. 1973–; mem. Editorial Bd. Journal of Biological Chemistry 1981–, Journal of Arteriosclerosis 1980–; mem. Food and Nutrition Bd., Nat. Research Council 1983, (Chair. 1987–), Comm. on Life Sciences 1986; mem. N.A.S.; T. Smith Award, A.A.A.S. 1960. *Publications:* 223 scientific articles and book chapters. *Address:* University of California School of Medicine, Moffitt Hospital-1327, San Francisco, Calif. 94143 (Office); P.O. Box 1791, Ross, Calif. 94957, U.S.A. (Home).

HAVEL, Václav; Czechoslovak playwright; b. 5 Oct. 1936, Prague; s. of Václav M. Havel and Božena (Vavrečková) Havel; m. Olga Šplíchalová; ed. Acad. of Arts, Drama Dept., Prague; works freelance; fmr. spokesman for Charter 77 human rights movement, received a sentence of 14 months in 1977, suspended for 3 years, for "subversive" and "antistate" activities, under house arrest 1977–79; Cttee. for the Defence of the Unjustly Persecuted (VONS), convicted and sentenced to 4½ years imprisonment for sedition 1979, released March 1983, arrested Jan. 1989 and sentenced to 9 months imprisonment for incitement and obstruction Feb. 1989; sentence reduced to 8 months, and charge changed to misdemeanour March 1989; Austrian State Prize for European Literature 1969, Jan Palach Prize 1981, Erasmus Prize 1986. *Publications:* Garden Party 1963, The Memorandum 1965, The Increased Difficulty of Concentration 1968, The Conspirators 1971, The Beggar's Opera 1972, The Mountain Resort 1974, Audience 1975, Vernissage 1975 (plays), Protest 1978, Largo Desolato (play) 1985, Václav Havel or Living in Truth 1987, Slum Clearance 1988, Letters to Olga 1989. *Address:* Udejvického rybníčku 4, 16000 Prague 6, Czechoslovakia.

HAVELANGE, Jean Marie Faustin Godefroid (João); Brazilian lawyer; b. 8 May 1916, Rio de Janeiro; m.; practising lawyer 1936–; Head of Importation and Exportation, Cia. Siderúrgica Belgo-Mineira 1937–41; Dir.-Pres. Viação Cometa S.A., EMBRADATA, Orwec Química e Metalúrgica Ltda.; took part in Olympic Games as swimmer, Berlin 1936, as water-polo player, Helsinki 1952, Head of Brazilian Del., Sydney 1956; Pres. Fed. Paulista de Natação, San Paolo 1949–51, Fed. Metropolitana de Natação (GB) 1952–56; mem. Brazilian Olympic Cttee. 1955–73; Vice-Pres. Confed. Brasileira de Desportos 1956–58, Pres. 1958–73; Dir., mem. for South America Cttee. of Int. Cyclists Union 1958; mem. Int. Olympic Cttee. 1963–; Pres. Indoor Football Int. Fed. (FIFUSA) 1971–; Pres. Int. Fed. of Asscn. Football (FIFA) 1974–; Portuguese and Brazilian decorations. *Leisure interest:* swimming and water-polo. *Address:* c/o Fédération Internationale de Football Association, Hitzigweg 11, 8032 Zurich, Switzerland; Praça Pio X No. 79-70, Rio de Janeiro, Brazil.

HAVERS, Baron (Life Peer), cr. 1987, of St. Edmundsbury in the County of Suffolk, **(Robert) Michael (Oldfield) Havers,** Kt., P.C., Q.C., M.P.; British lawyer and politician; b. 10 March 1923; s. of Sir Cecil Havers and late Enid Snelling; m. Carol Elizabeth Lay 1949, two s.; ed. Westminster School, Corpus Christi Coll., Cambridge; Lieut. R.N.V.R. 1941–46; called to the bar, Inner Temple 1948; Master of the Bench 1971; Recorder of Dover 1962–68, of Norwich 1968–71; a Recorder 1972; Chancellor of St. Edmundsbury Diocese and Ipswich Diocese 1965–73, of Ely Diocese 1969–73; Solicitor Gen. 1972–74; M.P. for Wimbledon 1970–74, for Merton, Wimbledon 1974–87; Shadow Attorney-Gen. and Legal Adviser to Shadow Cabt. 1974–79; Attorney-General 1979–87; Lord Chancellor June–Oct. 1987; Dir. RHM Outhwaite 1988–; Hon. Fellow Corpus Christi Coll., Cambridge 1988; Conservative. *Publication:* The Royal Baccarat Scandal (co-author) 1977. *Leisure interests:* reading, photography. *Address:* House of Lords, Westminster, London, S.W.1; 5 King's Bench Walk, Temple, E.C.4; White Shutters, Ousden, Newmarket, England (Home). *Telephone:* 01-353 4713 (Temple).

HAVIARAS, Stratis, M.F.A.; Greek author; b. 28 June 1935, Nea Kios, Argos; s. of Christos Haviaras and Georgia Hadzikyriakos; m. Gail Flynn 1967 (divorced 1973); living with Heather Cole 1977–, one d.; fmr. construction worker; lived in U.S.A. 1959–61; went to U.S.A. following colonels' coup in Greece 1967, obtaining position at Harvard Univ. Library; Curator, Poetry Room, Harvard Univ. Library 1974–. *Publications:* four vols. of Greek verse 1963, 1965, 1967, 1972; Crossing the River Twice (poems in English) 1976; novels: When the Tree Sings 1979, The Heroic Age 1984, Primitive Post-Apocalypse 1989. *Leisure interest:* wood sculpture. *Address:* Poetry Room, Harvard University, Cambridge, Mass. 02138, U.S.A. *Telephone:* (617) 495-2454.

HAVIGHURST, Clark Canfield, J.D.; American professor of law; b. 25 May 1933, Evanston, Ill.; s. of Harold Canfield and Marion Clay (Perryman) Havighurst; m. Karen Waldron 1965; one s. one d.; ed. Princeton and Northwestern Univs.; Research Assoc. Duke Univ. School of Law 1960–61; Private Practice, Debevoise, Plimpton, Lyons & Gates, New York 1958, 1961–64; Assoc. Prof. of Law, Duke Univ. 1964–68, Prof. 1968–86, William

Neal Reynolds Prof. 1986–; Prof. of Community Health Services, Duke Univ. Medical Center 1974–; numerous other professional appts.; mem. Inst. of Medicine, Nat. Acad. of Sciences. *Publications:* Deregulating the Health Care Industry 1982, Health Care Law and Policy 1988; articles on regulation in the health services industry, the role of competition in the financing and delivery of health care and anti-trust issues arising in the health care field. *Address:* Duke University School of Law, Durham, N.C. 27706 (Office); 3610 Dover Road, Durham, N.C. 27707, U.S.A. (Home). *Telephone:* (919) 684-2636 (Office); (919) 489-4970 (Home).

HAVILAND, Denis William Garstin Latimer, M.A., C.B.I.M., F.I.I.M., F.R.S.A., C.B.; British industrialist; b. 15 Aug. 1910, London; s. of late William Alexander Haviland and of Edyth Louise Latimer; ed. Rugby School and St. John's Coll., Cambridge; London Midland and Scottish Railway 1934–39; Army service 1940–46, rising to rank of Col.; Prin., Control Office for Germany and Austria 1946–47; Asst. Sec. Foreign Office, German Section 1947–50; Imperial Defence Coll. 1950; Ministry of Supply 1951–59, Under-Sec. 1953–59, Deputy Sec. 1959; Deputy Sec. Ministry of Aviation 1959–64; Chair. European Launcher Devt. Org. (ELDO) Preparatory Group 1962–64; Deputy Chair. Staveley Industries 1964–65, Chair. and Man. Dir. 1965–69; Dir. Wheelabrator Corpn. of Mishawaka 1967–72, Short Brothers and Harland Ltd. 1964–81, Organized Office Designs Ltd. 1971–; mem. Council British Inst. of Management 1967–83 (Vice-Chair. 1973), Chair. Membership Cttee. 1969–75, Chair. Professional Standards Cttee. 1975–82, mem. Academic Cttee. 1977–82; mem. Business and Man. Bd., Council for Nat. Academic Awards 1977–84, Business and Man. Cttee. 1980, Post-graduate Studies Bd. 1980–84; mem. of court, Cranfield Inst. of Tech. Man. 1970–83; Vice-Pres. Inst. of Industrial Mans. 1979–; Chair. Confed. of Healing Orgs. 1981; Chair. Holistic Council for Cancer 1984–86; Liveryman, Co. of Coachmakers. *Address:* 113 Hampstead Way, London, NW11 7JN, England (Office and Home). *Telephone:* 01-455 2638.

HAWER, Franciszek; Polish farmer and politician; b. 16 Oct. 1911, Gać; runs own farm in Markowa village; active mem. Wici Rural Youth Union 1928–34; co-organizer, Rural Univ., Gać 1932; mem. Peasants' Party (SL) 1934–49; participant in Sept. Campaign 1939, prisoner-of-war 1939–45; then co-organizer Citizens' Militia (rural co-operative movt.), f. and Pres. Village Health Co-operative, Markowa Commune; fmr. Councillor, Commune Nat. Council, Markowa and Dist. Nat. Council, Przeworsk; organizer and Pres. Voivodship Sheep Breeders' Union, Voivodship Union of Growers of Oleaginous Plants, Rzeszów; mem. voivodship authorities of Agricultural Circles Union, Rzeszów; mem. United Peasants' Party (ZSL) 1949–, Pres. ZSL Dist. Cttee., Przeworsk, mem. Presidium ZSL Voivodship Cttee., Rzeszów; mem. Presidium ZSL Chief Cttee. 1980–88, Deputy Chair. 1981–88; mem. Main Revisional Comm. ZSL 1988–; Kt.'s. Cross, Order of Polonia Restituta, and other decorations. *Address:* Naczelny Komitet ZSL, ul. Grzybowska 4, 00-131 Warsaw (Office); 37-120 Markowa nr 1033, woj. rzeszowskie, Poland (Home). *Telephone:* 20-02-51 (Office).

HAWKE, Robert James Lee, A.C., B.A., LL.B., B.LITT.; Australian trade unionist and politician; b. 9 Dec. 1929, Bordertown, S. Australia; s. of A. C. Hawke; m. Hazel Masterson 1956; one s. two d.; ed. Univs. of Western Australia and Oxford; Rhodes scholar 1953; Research Officer, Australian Council of Trade Unions 1958–70, Pres. 1970–80; Senior Vice-Pres. Australian Labor Party 1971–73, Pres. 1973–78, Leader Feb. 1983–; Prime Minister March 1983–, mem. Nat. Exec. 1971–; mem. Bd. Reserve Bank of Australia 1973–83, Governing Body ILO 1972–80; Australian Council for Union Training, Australian Population and Immigration Council; mem. Australian Manufacturing Council 1977, Nat. Labour Consultative Council 1977–, Australian Refugee Advisory Council; M.P. for Wills, Melbourne 1980–; Hon. Fellow, Univ. Coll., Oxford 1984, U.N. Media Peace Prize 1980. *Leisure interests:* tennis, golf, cricket, reading. *Address:* Parliament House, Canberra, A.C.T. 2600 (Office); 57 Waterfield Street, Coburg, Vic. 3058, Australia (Home).

HAWKER, Sir (Frank) Cyril, Kt.; British banker; b. 21 July 1900, London; s. of Frank Charley and Bertha Mary (Bastow) Hawker; m. Marjorie Ann Pearce 1931; three d.; ed. City of London School; Bank of England 1920, Deputy Chief Cashier 1944–48, Chief Accountant 1948–53, Adviser to Governors 1953–54, Exec. Dir. 1954–62; Chair. The Standard Bank Ltd. 1962–74, The Chartered Bank 1973–74, Standard and Chartered Banking Group 1969–74, Standard Bank of W. Africa Ltd. 1965–73; Deputy Chair. Midland and Int. Banks 1969–74; Dir. Head Wrightson & Co. Ltd. 1962–77; Dir. Davy Int. Ltd. 1977–79; Deputy Chair. Nat. Playing Fields Asscn.; Chair. Union Zaïroise de Banques 1971–74; High Sheriff of County of London 1963; Pres. Minor Counties Cricket Asscn., MCC 1970–71; Pres. Overseas Bankers Club 1973–74, Vice-Pres. 1974–; Dir. Davy Int. Ltd. 1977–79; Hon. Vice-Pres. Football Asscn.; Vice-Pres. Amateur Football Alliance. *Leisure interest:* cricket. *Address:* Hadlow Lodge, Burgh Hill, Etchingham, Sussex, TN19 7PE, England (Home). *Telephone:* (058 086) 341.

HAWKES, (Charles Francis) Christopher, M.A., F.B.A., F.S.A.; British archaeologist; b. 5 June 1905, London; s. of late Charles Pascoe and Eleanor Victoria Hawkes (née Cobb); m. 1st Jessie Jacquetta Hopkins (q.v. Jacquetta Hawkes) 1933 (divorced 1953), one s.; m. 2nd Sonia Elizabeth Chadwick 1959; ed. Winchester Coll., and New Coll., Oxford; Asst., Dept. of British and Medieval Antiquities, British Museum 1928, Asst. Keeper, promoted to 1st Class 1938; Ministry of Aircraft Production 1940–45; returned to British Museum 1945, in charge of Prehistoric and Romano-British Antiquities 1946; Prof. of European Archaeology, Oxford Univ. 1946–72, Emeritus Prof. 1972; Fellow Keble Coll., Hon. Fellow 1972; Prof.-in-charge, Inst. of Archaeology 1961–72; elected Nat. Sec. (U.K.) on Council Int. Congress of Prehistoric and Protohistoric Sciences 1931, full mem. 1948, mem. Exec. Cttee. 1950, Cttee. of Honour 1971; excavations on various sites in U.K. and Europe 1925–64; Ed. Archaeological Journal London 1944–50; Pres. Prehistoric Society 1950–54, Council for British Archaeology 1961–64; Ed. Inventaria Archaeologica for Great Britain 1954–76; mem. German Archaeological Inst.; Hon. mem. Royal Irish Acad., Swiss Soc. for Prehistory; Hon. Dr. (Rennes) 1971, Hon. D.Litt. (Nat. Univ., Ireland) 1972; Gold Medal, Soc. of Antiquaries, London 1981. *Publications:* St. Catharine's Hill, Winchester (with J. N. L. Myres and C. G. Stevens) 1931, Archaeology in England and Wales, 1914–31 (with T. D. Kendrick) 1932, Winchester College 1933, The Prehistoric Foundations of Europe 1940, Prehistoric Britain (with Jacquetta Hawkes) 1944, Camulodunum: The Excavations at Colchester, 1930–39 (with M. R. Hull) 1947, Contrib. and Ed. (with Sonia Hawkes) Archaeology into History Vol. I 1973, Contrib. and Ed. (with P. M. Duval) Celtic Art in Ancient Europe 1976, (Ed. and jt. author) Corpus of Brooches in Britain Vol. I (Pre-Roman) 1987. *Address:* Keble College, Oxford, England.

HAWKES, Jacquetta, O.B.E., M.A.; British author and archaeologist; b. 1910, Cambridge; d. of Sir Frederick Gowland Hopkins, O.M. (Nobel prize winner) and Lady Hopkins (née Stephens); m. 1st Prof. (Charles Francis) Christopher Hawkes (q.v.) 1933 (divorced 1953), one s.; m. 2nd J. B. Priestley 1953; ed. Perse School and Newnham Coll., Cambridge; archaeological activities in Great Britain, Eire, France and Palestine 1931–40; Asst. Principal, Post-War Reconstruction Secretariat 1941–43; with Ministry of Education, Sec., U.K. Nat. Comm. for UNESCO 1943–49 (retd.); Vice-Pres. Council for British Archaeology 1949–52; Archaeological Adviser, Festival of Britain 1949–51; Gov. British Film Inst. 1950–55; mem. Culture Advisory Cttee., UNESCO 1966–79; Author Ed. (with Frankfort and Woolley) UNESCO History of Mankind (Vol. I); Archaeological Corresp. Sunday Times; Kemsley Award for A Land 1951, Hon. D.Litt. (Warwick) 1986; Life Trustee Shakespeare Birthplace 1985. *Publications:* Archaeology of Jersey 1939, Prehistoric Britain (with Christopher Hawkes) 1944, Early Britain 1945, Symbols and Speculations (poems) 1948, A Land 1951, Guide to Prehistoric and Roman Monuments in England and Wales 1951, Dragon's Mouth (play), Fables 1953, Man on Earth 1954, Journey Down a Rainbow (with J. B. Priestley) 1955, Providence Island 1959, Man and the Sun 1962, Prehistory and the Beginnings of Civlization (with Sir Leonard Woolley) 1963, The World of the Past 1963, King of the Two Lands 1966, The Pharoes of Egypt 1967, Dawn of the Gods 1968, The First Great Civilizations 1973, Ed. Atlas of Ancient Archaeology 1974, Atlas of Early Man 1976, A Quest of Love 1980, Mortimer Wheeler: Adventurer in Archaeology 1982, The Shell Guide to British Archaeology 1986, Stone Age to Iron Age, in Cambridge Guide to the Arts in Britain 1988. *Leisure interests:* pictures, antiques, gardening, natural history. *Address:* Littlecote, Leysbourne, Chipping Campden, Glos., GL55 6HL, England.

HAWKES, John; American writer; b. 17 Aug. 1925, Stamford, Conn.; m. Sophie Tazewell 1947; three s. one d.; ed. Harvard Coll.; Visiting Lecturer and Instructor, Harvard Univ. 1955–58; Asst. Prof. Brown Univ. 1958–62, Assoc. Prof. 1962–67, Prof. of English 1967–88, Univ. Prof. 1973–88, Prof. Emer. 1988–; mem. American Acad. of Arts and Sciences, American Acad. and Inst. of Arts and Letters; Guggenheim Fellowship; Ford Foundation Fellowship; Rockefeller Foundation Fellowship; Grant in Fiction, Nat. Inst. of Arts and Letters; Prix du Meilleur Livre Étranger. *Publications:* novels: The Cannibal 1949, The Beetle Leg 1951, The Lime Twig 1961, Second Skin 1964, The Blood Oranges 1971, Death, Sleep and the Traveller 1974, Travesty 1976, The Passion Artist 1979, Virginie: Her Two Lives 1982, Adventures in the Alaskan Skin Trade 1985, (Prix Medicis Étranger 1986), Innocence in Extremis 1985, Whistlejacket 1988; plays: The Innocent Party (a collection of 4 short plays) 1966; collected stories and short novels: Lunar Landscapes 1969, Humours of Blood and Skin: A John Hawkes Reader 1984. *Address:* 18 Everett Avenue, Providence, R.I. 02906, U.S.A.

HAWKING, Stephen William, C.B.E., PH.D., F.R.S.; British professor of mathematics; b. 8 Jan. 1942; s. of Dr. F. and Mrs. E. I. Hawking; m. Jane Wilde 1965; two s. one d.; ed. St. Albans School, Univ. Coll., Oxford, Trinity Hall, Cambridge; Research Fellow, Gonville and Caius Coll., Cambridge 1965–69, Fellow for Distinction in Science 1969–; Research Asst., Inst. of Astronomy, Cambridge 1972–73; Research Asst., Dept. of Applied Mathematics and Theoretical Physics, Cambridge Univ. 1973–75, Reader in Gravitational Physics 1975–77, Prof. 1977–79, Lucasian Prof. of Mathematics 1979–; mem. Inst. of Theoretical Astronomy, Cambridge 1968–72; mem. Papal Acad. of Science 1986; Foreign mem. American Acad. Arts and Sciences 1984; several hon. degrees; William Hopkins Prize, Cambridge Philosophical Soc. 1976, Wolf Prize 1988, Maxwell Medal, Inst. of Physics 1976, Hughes Medal, Royal Soc. 1976, Albert Einstein Award 1978, Gold Medal Royal Astronomical Soc. 1985, Sunday Times Special Award for Literature 1989. *Publications:* The Large Scale Structure of Space-Time (with G. F. R. Ellis) 1973, General Relativity: an Einstein centenary survey 1979, Superspace and Supergravity (jt. Ed.) 1981, The Very Early Universe

(jt. Ed.) 1983, 300 Years of Gravitation 1987, A Brief History of Time 1988. *Address:* 5 West Road, Cambridge, England. *Telephone:* (0223) 51905.

HAWKINS, Paula; American politician; b. Salt Lake City, Utah; d. of Paul B. and Leoan (née Staley) Fickes; m. Walter Eugene Hawkins 1947; one s. two d.; ed. Utah State Univ.; mem. Republican Precinct Cttee., Orange Co., Fla. 1965–74, Rep. Nat. Comm. for Fla. 1968–87; Speakers Chair. Fla. Republican Exec. Cttee. 1967–69, mem. Fla. Republican Nat. Convention 1972, S. Regional Rep., Republican Nat., Cttee. 1972–; Republican Senator, Fla. 1981–86; mem. Maitland Civic Cen. 1965–76; Charter mem. Bd. of Dirs. Fla. Americans Constitutional Action Cttee. of 100 1966–68, Sec.-Treas. 1966–68; mem. Gov. of Fla. Comm. on Status of Women 1968–71; Public Service Commr. Fla., Tallahassee 1972–80; fmr. Chair. Legis. Comm. Orange Co. Drug Abuse Council, fmr. co-Chair. Orange Co. March of Dimes; fmr. mem. Cen. Fla. Museum Speakers Bureau; Citation for Service, Fla. Republican Party; Above and Beyond Award (Outstanding Woman in Fla. politics). *Address:* 1214 Park Avenue North, Winter Park, Fla. 32789, U.S.A. (Home).

HAWLEY, Sir Donald Frederick, K.C.M.G., M.B.E., M.A.; British diplomatist (retd.), company chairman and consultant; b. 22 May 1921, Essex; s. of the late F. G. and G. E. C. (née Hills) Hawley; m. Ruth Morwenna Graham 1964; one s. three d.; ed. Radley, New Coll., Oxford; Barrister-at-Law, Inner Temple; served with H.M. Forces 1941–44; Sudan Political Service 1944–47; Sudan Judiciary 1947–55; Foreign Office 1956–58; H.M. Political Agent, Trucial States 1958–61; Head of Chancery British Embassy, Cairo 1962–64; Counsellor, High Commission, Lagos 1965–67; Counsellor (Commercial), Baghdad 1968–71; Amb. to Sultanate of Oman 1971–75; Asst. Under Sec. of State, Foreign and Commonwealth Office 1975–77; High Commr. to Malaysia 1977–81; mem London Advisory Comm. Hongkong and Shanghai Banking Corpn.; Chair. The Centre for British Teachers 1987–; Chair. Ewbank Preece Ltd. 1982–86; Chair. Anglo-Omani Soc. 1975–77, Vice-Pres. 1981; Chair. British-Malaysian Soc. 1983; Pres. of Council Reading Univ. 1987–. *Publications:* Courtesies in the Trucial States 1965, The Trucial States 1970, Oman and its Renaissance 1977, Courtesies in the Gulf Area 1978, Manners and Correct Form in the Middle East 1983. *Leisure interests:* gardening, walking, tennis. *Address:* Little Cheverell House, Devizes, Wilts., SN10 4JS, England (Home). *Telephone:* (038081) 3322.

HAWLEY, Robert, PH.D.; British engineer and business executive; b. 23 July 1936, Wallasey; s. of William Hawley and Eva Hawley; m. Valerie Clarke 1961; one s. one d.; ed. Wallasey Grammar School, Wallasey Tech. Coll., Birkenhead Tech. Coll. and King's Coll., Univ. of Durham; joined C. A. Parsons 1961, Electrical Designer, Generator Dept. 1964, Chief Electrical Eng. 1970, Dir. of Production and Eng. 1973–74; Man. Dir. NEI Parsons 1976; Man. Dir. Power Eng. Group, NEI PLC 1986–88, Man. Dir. Operations 1989–. *Publications:* co-author of Dielectric Solids 1970, Conduction and Breakdown in Mineral Oil 1973, Fundamentals of Electromagnetic Field Theory 1974, Vacuum as an Insulation. *Leisure interests:* philately, gardening. *Address:* Northern Engineering Industries PLC, NEI House, Regent Centre, Gosforth, Newcastle-upon-Tyne, NE3 3SB (Office); Tindal House, Killingworth Village, Tyne and Wear, NE12 0BL, England (Home).

HAWN, Goldie; American actress; b. 21 Nov. 1945, Washington, D.C.; d. of Edward Rutledge Hawn and Laura Hawn; m. 1st Gus Trikonio, 2nd Bill Hudson (divorced); one s. one d.; ed. American Univ., Washington, D.C.; began career as chorus-line dancer, World's Fair, New York 1964. *Stage appearances include:* Romeo and Juliet (Williamsburg), Kiss Me Kate, Guys and Dolls (New York). *TV series include:* Good Morning, World, Rowan and Martin's Laugh-In, Goldie and Kids—Listen to Us. *Films include:* Cactus Flower, There's a Girl in my Soup, Butterflies are Free, The Sugarland Express, $, The Girl from Petrovka, Shampoo, The Duchess and the Dirtwater Fox, Foul Play, Seems Like Old Times, Private Benjamin, Best Friends, Protocol, Swing Shift, Overboard, Bird On A Wire. *Address:* c/o Creative Artists Agency, 1888 Century Park E., Suite 1400, Los Angeles, Calif. 90067, U.S.A.

HAWORTH, Lionel, O.B.E., F.R.S.; British aeronautical engineer; b. 4 Aug. 1912, S. Africa; s. of John B. and Anna S. (née Ackerman) Haworth; m. Joan I. Bradbury 1956; one s. one d.; ed. Rondebosch Boys' High School and Univ. of Cape Town; Graduate apprenticeship with Associated Equipment Co. 1934; Designer Rolls-Royce Ltd., Derby 1936, Asst. Chief Designer 1944; Deputy Chief Designer, Aero Division 1951, Chief Designer (Civil Engines), Aero Div. 1954, Chief Engineer (Propeller Turbines), Aero Div. 1962; Chief Design Consultant, Bristol Siddeley Engines Ltd. 1963, Chief Designer 1964; Dir. of Design, Bristol Siddeley Engines Ltd., Bristol Engine Div. 1965; Dir. of Design, Rolls-Royce Ltd., Bristol Engine Div. 1968, Dir. of Design, Rolls-Royce (1971) Ltd., Bristol Engine Div. 1971–77, Eng. Consultant, Rolls-Royce Ltd., Aero Div., Bristol 1977–81; Eng. Consultant, Lionel Haworth and Assocs. 1977; Founder Fellow, Fellowship of Eng. 1975; Bronze Medal, Royal Aeronautical Soc., British Gold Medal for Aeronautics 1971, Royal Designer for Industry (R.D.I.) 1976. *Leisure interest:* sailing. *Address:* 10 Hazelwood Road, Sneyd Park, Bristol, BS9 1PX, England. *Telephone:* (0272) 683032.

HAWORTH, Robert Downs, D.SC., PH.D., F.R.S.C., F.R.S.; British professor emeritus of chemistry; b. 15 March 1898; s. of J. T. and Emily Haworth;

m. Dorothy Stocks 1930; one d.; ed. Univ. of Manchester; Demonstrator n Organic Chem., Univ. of Oxford 1925–26; Lecturer in Chem., Newcastle upon Tyne 1927–39; Firth Prof. of Chem., Univ. of Sheffield 1939–63, now Prof. Emer.; Visiting Prof. of Organic Chem., Univ. of Madras 1956; Hon. D.Sc. (Sheffield) 1974. *Publications:* papers on organic chemistry in Journal of Chem. Soc. *Address:* 11 Cedar Grove, Bexley, Kent, DA5 3DB, England. *Telephone:* 01-303 9829.

HAWTHORNE, Sir William (Rede), Kt., C.B.E., M.A., SC.D., F.R.S., F.ENG., F.INST.MECH.E.; British professor of applied thermodynamics; b. 22 May 1913, Benton, Newcastle-on-Tyne; s. of William Hawthorne and Elizabeth Curle Hawthorne; m. Barbara Runkle 1939; one s. two d.; ed. Westminster School, London, Trinity Coll., Cambridge, and Mass. Inst. of Tech., U.S.A.; Devt. Eng., Babcock & Wilcox Ltd. 1937–39; Scientific officer, Royal Aircraft Establishment 1940–44, seconded to Sir Frank Whittle 1940–41; British Air Comm., Washington, D.C. 1944–45; Deputy Dir. of Engine Research, Ministry of Supply (U.K.) 1945–46; Assoc. Prof. of Mechanical Eng. M.I.T. 1946–48; George Westinghouse Prof. of Mechanical Eng., M.I.T. 1948–51; Prof. of Applied Thermodynamics Univ. of Cambridge 1951–80, Head of Eng. Dept. 1968–73; Fellow, Trinity Coll., Cambridge 1951–68; Master of Churchill Coll., Cambridge 1968–83; Hunsaker Prof. of Aeronautical Eng., M.I.T. 1955–56; Visiting Inst. Prof., M.I.T. 1962–63; mem. of Corpn. of M.I.T. 1969–73; Chair. Home Office Scientific Advisory Council 1967–76, Advisory Council on Energy Conservation 1974–79; Dir. Cummins Engine Co., Inc. 1974–86, Dracone Developments Ltd. 1957–87; Foreign Assoc. U.S. Nat. Acad. of Sciences, U.S. Nat. Acad. of Eng.; Vice-Pres. Royal Soc. 1969–70, 1979–81; mem. Electricity Supply Research Council 1953–83, Comm. on Energy and the Environment 1978–81; Hon. Fellow, Royal Aeronautical Soc., A.I.A.A.; Fellow of the Fellowship of Eng. 1976; Hon. mem. A.S.M.E. 1982; Hon. Fellow Royal Soc. of Edinburgh 1983, Fellow Imperial Coll. London 1983; Hon. D.Eng. (Sheffield) 1976, (Liverpool) 1982, Hon. D.Sc. (Salford) 1980, (Strathclyde, Bath) 1981, (Oxford) 1982, (Sussex) 1984; Medal of Freedom (U.S.A.) 1957, Royal Medal (Royal Soc.) 1982, Dudley Wright Prize (Harvey Mudd Coll., Calif.) 1985. *Publications:* (Ed.) Aerodynamics of Compressors and Turbines, vol. X, (Co-Ed.) Design and Performance of Gas Turbine Power Plants, vol. XI, High Speed Aerodynamics and Jet Propulsion; numerous papers in scientific and tech. journals. *Address:* Churchill College, Cambridge, CB3 0DS, England; 19 Chauncy Street, Cambridge, Mass. 02138, U.S.A. *Telephone:* (0223) 336219 (England).

HAXEL, Otto Philipp Leonhard, D.RER.NAT; German physicist; b. 2 April 1909, Neu-Ulm; s. of Carl and Emma Haxel; m. Ilse Houtermans-Bartz 1979; two s.; ed. Tübingen, Munich and Berlin Univs.; Lecturer, Berlin Technical High School 1937–45, Max Planck Physics Inst., Göttingen 1945–50; Dir. Second Physical Inst., Heidelberg Univ. 1950–69; Technical-Scientific Dir., Nuclear Research Centre, Karlsruhe 1970–74; Pres. Heidelberger Akad. der Wissenschaften 1978–82; mem. Deutsche Akad. der Naturforscher Leopoldina; Corresp. mem. Oesterreicher Akad. der Wissenschaften; Dr. h.c.; Bundesverdienstkreuz 1971; Otto Hahn Prize 1980. *Address:* Scheffelstrasse Nr. 4, 6900 Heidelberg, Federal Republic of Germany. *Telephone:* 06221/46769.

HAY, Alexandre, L. EN D.; Swiss lawyer; b. 29 Oct. 1919, Berne; m. 1st Hélène Morin Pons 1945 (died 1973), two s. two d.; m. 2nd Verena Vogler 1980; ed. Univ. of Geneva; Fed. Political Dept. (Financial Affairs), Berne 1945–48; Swiss Legation, Paris 1948–53; Head of Div., Swiss Nat. Bank, Zürich 1953–55; Dir. and Asst. to Head of Second Dept., Swiss Nat. Bank, Berne 1955–66, Head of Second Dept. and Vice-Pres. Gen., Management 1966–; mem. Cttee. on European Monetary Agreement 1950–62, Pres. 1962–73; Pres. Int. Cttee. of Red Cross 1976–87, mem. 1987–. *Address:* 18 Chemin du Pommier, 1218 Grand-Saconnex, Switzerland (Home).

HAY, Allan Stuart, PH.D., F.R.S.; Canadian chemist; b. 23 July 1929, Edmonton, Alberta; s. of Stuart L. and Verna E. Hay; m. Janet M. Keck 1956; two s. two d.; ed. Univs. of Alberta and Illinois; Chemist, General Electric Research and Devt. Center 1955–67, Man. Chemical Lab. 1968–80; Research and Devt. Man. Chemical Labs., Gen. Elec. Research and Devt. Center 1980–87; Prof. McGill Univ. 1987–; Int. Gold Medal, Soc. of Plastics Engs.; Industrial Research Inst. Achievement Award. *Publications:* some 50 papers in scientific journals. *Leisure interests:* reading, philately. *Address:* Department of Chemistry, McGill University, 801 Sherbrooke Street W., Montreal, P.Q., H3A 2K6 (Office); 5015 Glencairn Avenue, Montreal, P.Q., H3W 2B3, Canada. *Telephone:* (514) 398-6234 (Office); (514) 483-5469 (Home).

HAY, Andrew Osborne, O.B.E., B.A.; Australian business executive; b. 9 June 1945, Melbourne; s. of Sir David Osborne Hay and Lady Alison Marion Parker Hay; m. Marianne Perrott 1982; two d.; ed. Geelong Grammar School, New York Univ. and Australian Nat. Univ.; Exec. ICI Australia Ltd. 1970–71; Man. Dir. Chapman Hay Ltd 1979–; Chair. Adroyal Ltd. 1987–, Lease Plan Australia Ltd. 1988–, Berklee Ltd. 1988–; Pvt. Sec. to Minister for the Environment 1972, to Deputy Leader of the Opposition 1973–75, Prin. Pvt. Sec. to Treasurer 1975–77, to Minister for Industry and Commerce 1977–78; Pres. Melbourne Chamber of Commerce 1985–87; Chair. Australian Fed. of Employers 1986–87; Pres. Australian Chamber of Commerce 1987–88; Hon. Treas. Royal Humane Soc. of Austra-

lasia 1984–. *Leisure interests:* tennis, golf, sailing, reading. *Address:* 2 Glen Road, Toorak, Vic. 3142, Australia.

HAY, Sir David Osborne, Kt., C.B.E., D.S.O., B.A.; Australian public servant (retd.); b. 1916, Corowa, N.S.W.; s. of late H. A. Hay and Marjory Moule; m. Alison Adams 1944; two s.; ed. Geelong Grammar School, Brasenose Coll., Oxford, and Melbourne Univ.; joined Australian Dept. of External Affairs 1939 and rejoined 1946, after army service 1939–45; Del. to UN 1949 and 1950; served Ottawa 1950–52; attended Imperial Defence Coll., London 1954; Minister of Thailand 1955–56, Amb. 1956–57, concurrently Rep. to SEATO; Asst. Sec. Department of External Affairs 1957–61; High Commr. to Canada 1961–64; Amb. and Perm. Rep. of Australia to the UN 1963–65; Ministry of External Affairs 1965–66, Administrator, Territory of Papua and New Guinea 1967–70; Sec. Dept. of External Territories 1970–73; Defence Force Ombudsman 1974–76; Sec. Dept. of Aboriginal Affairs 1976–80. *Leisure interests:* skiing, sailing, gardening. *Address:* Boomanoomana Homestead, via Mulwala, N.S.W. 2647, Australia.

HAY, David Russell, C.B.E., M.D.(N.Z.), F.R.C.P., F.R.A.C.P.; New Zealand cardiologist; b. 8 Dec. 1927, Chistchurch; s. of Sir James Hay and Lady Davidina Hay; m. Dr. Jocelyn V. Bell 1958; two d.; ed. St. Andrew's Coll., Christchurch and Otago Univ.; Physician, N. Canterbury Hosp. Bd. 1959–64; Cardiologist, Canterbury Hosp. Bd. 1964–, Head, Dept. of Cardiology 1969–78, Chair. of Medical Services and Head of Dept. of Medicine 1978–84; Medical Dir. Nat. Heart Foundation of N.Z. 1977–; Clinical Reader, Christchurch Clinical School of Univ. of Otago 1980–88; mem. WHO Advisory Panel on Smoking and Health 1977–, and other professional appts.; Vice-Pres. R.A.C.P. 1988–(90). *Publications:* 78 publs. in scientific journals. *Leisure interests:* golf, tennis. *Address:* 20 Greers Road, Christchurch 4, New Zealand. *Telephone:* 585-482.

HAY, Raymond A., B.S., M.B.A.; American business executive; b. New York; m. Grace Mattson; two c.; ed. Long Island and St. John's Univs.; fmr. Exec. Vice-Pres., Pres. of U.S. Operations and mem. Bd. of Dirs. and Exec. Cttee. Xerox Corpn.; Pres. and C.O.O. LTV Corpn. 1975, C.E.O. 1982–, Chair. of Bd. 1983–; mem. Bd. of Dirs. Shamrock Corpn., Dallas, Nat. Medical Enterprises, Inc., Los Angeles and MCorp, Dallas; mem. Exec. Cttee. Pres Reagan's Pvt. Sector Survey on Cost Control, Pres.'s Council for Int. Youth Exchange; holder of many other civic offices in Dallas. *Address:* The LTV Corporation, LTV Center, P.O.Box 225003, Dallas, Tex. 75265-5003, U.S.A.

HAYAISHI, Osamu, M.D., PH.D.; Japanese university professor and college president; b. 8 Jan. 1920, Stockton, Calif., U.S.A.; s. of Jitsuzo and Mitsu Hayaishi; m. Takiko Satani 1946; one d.; ed. Osaka High School, Osaka Univ.; Asst. Prof., Dept. of Microbiology, Washington Univ. School of Medicine, St. Louis, Mo., U.S.A., 1952–54; Chief, Toxicology, Nat. Inst. of Arthritis and Metabolic Diseases, Nat. Insts. of Health, Bethesda, Md., U.S.A. 1954–58; Prof., Dept. of Medical Chemistry 1958–83, Prof., Dept. of Molecular Biology, Inst. for Chemical Research, Kyoto Univ. 1959–76; Prof. Dept. of Physiological Chem. and Nutrition, Univ. of Tokyo 1970–74; Prof. Inst. of Scientific and Industrial Research, Osaka Univ. 1975–76; Dean Faculty of Medicine, Kyoto Univ. 1979–81; Prof. Emer. Kyoto Univ. 1983–; Pres. Osaka Medical Coll. 1983–89; Dir. Osaka Bioscience Inst. 1987–; mem. Scientific Council Int. Inst. of Cellular and Molecular Pathology (Belgium) 1979–; Foreign Hon. mem. of American Acad. of Arts and Sciences 1969, Foreign Assoc. of the U.S. Nat. Acad. of Sciences 1972; Dunham Lecture (Harvard) 1980, Pfeizer Lecture, Albert Einstein School of Medicine 1980; mem. Japan Acad. 1974, New York Acad. of Sciences 1975; Hon. mem. American Soc. of Biological Chemists 1974, Int. Soc. on Clinical Entymology 1989, Soc. for Free Radical Research 1988; Hon. D.Sc. (Michigan) 1980; Hon. M.D. (Karolinska Institutet, Sweden) 1985; Dr. h.c. (Padua) 1988; Award of Japan Soc. of Vitaminology 1964, Award of Matsunaga Science Foundation 1964, Asahi Award for Science and Culture 1965, Award of Japan Acad. 1967, Order of Culture 1972, Award of Fujiwara Science Foundation 1975, Médaille de Bronze de la Ville de Paris 1975, CIBA Foundation Gold Medal 1976, Louis and Bert Freedman Foundation Award for Research in Biochemistry 1976, Deutsche Akademie der Naturforscher Leopoldina (G.D.R.) 1978, Jiménez Díaz Memorial Award (Spain) 1979; Hon. Citizen of Kyoto 1984; Wolf Foundation Prize in Medicine, Israel 1986; Jaroslav Heyrovský Gold Medal, Czechoslovak Acad. of Sciences 1988; Special Achievement Award, Miami Biotech. Winter Symposium 1989. *Publications:* Oxygenases 1962, Molecular Mechanisms of Oxygen Activation 1974, Molecular Oxygen in Biology 1974, and 480 scientific reviews and articles. *Leisure interest:* golf. *Address:* Osaka Bioscience Institute, 6-2-4 Furuedai, Suita, Osaka 565 (Office); Royal Court Shimogamo 205, 1–29 Izumigawa-cho, Shimogamo, Sakyo-ku, Kyoto, Japan 606 (Home). *Telephone:* 0726-83-1221 (Office); 075-781-1089 (Home).

HAYAKAWA, Samuel Ichiye, PH.D.; American university professor and politician; b. 18 July 1906, Vancouver, B.C., Canada; s. of Ichiro Hayakawa and Toro Isono; m. Margedant Peters 1937; two s. one d.; ed. schools in Calgary, Vancouver and Winnipeg, and Univ. of Manitoba, McGill Univ., Montreal and Wisconsin Univ.; taught English at Univ. of Wisconsin 1936–39, Ill. Inst. of Tech. 1939–47; Lecturer Univ. of Chicago 1950–55; Prof. of English, San Francisco State Coll. 1955–68, acting Pres. 1968, Pres. 1968–73, Pres. Emer. 1973–; certified psychologist, State of Calif. 1959; U.S. Senator from Calif. 1977–83; Adviser to U.S. Sec. of State on

Asian-Pacific Relations 1983–; fmr. mem. Senate Cttees. for Agric., Nutrition and Forestry, Budget and Human Resources; fmr. mem. U.S. Senate Republican Policy Cttee., Nat. Republican Senatorial Cttee.; Fellow, American Psychological Asscn., A.A.A.S., American Sociological Asscn., Royal Soc. of Arts; Hon. D.F.A. (Calif. Coll. of Arts and Crafts); Hon. D.Litt. (Grinnell Coll., Iowa); Hon. L.H.D. (Pepperdine Univ., Malibu, Calif.); Hon. LL.D. (The Citadel, Charleston, S.C.); Republican. *Publications include:* Oliver Wendell Holmes (selected poetry and prose) 1939, Language in Action 1941, Language in Thought and Action 1949, Language, Meaning and Maturity 1954, Our Language and Our World 1959, The Use and Misuse of Language 1962, Symbol, Status and Personality 1963, Ed. Funk and Wagnalls' Modern Guide to Synonyms 1968, Through the Communication Barrier 1979, and contributions to numerous other vols. *Leisure interests:* collecting African sculpture, Chinese ceramics and old jazz records, tap-dancing, fishing, scuba-diving. *Address:* Mill Valley (Marin County), Calif. 94941, U.S.A. (Home).

HAYASHI, Yoshiro; Japanese politician; b. 16 June 1927, Yamaguchi Pref.; s. of Yoshisuke Hayashi and Tora Hayashi; m. Mariko Hayashi 1960; two s. two d.; fmr. civil servant, Ministry of Int. Trade and Industry and other depts.; with Liberal-Democratic Party (LDP) Accounting Div. for two years; then Dir.-Gen. of Int. Bureau of LDP 1986–; mem. House of Reps. 1969–; Sec.-Gen. Hirakawa Kai (policy study group); Minister of Health and Welfare 1982–83. *Leisure interest:* golf. *Address:* Liberal-Democratic Party, 7, 2-chome, Hirakawacho, Chiyoda-ku, Tokyo, Japan.

HAYASHIDA, Yukio; Japanese politician; b. Nov. 1915, Kyoto Pref.; m.; two s.; ed. Tokyo Imperial Univ.; joined Ministry of Agric. and Forestry 1939, Chief, Fisheries Admin. Dept. Fisheries Agency 1959, Chief Sec. to Minister of Agric. and Forestry 1962; Chief, Kinki Agric. Admin. Bureau 1963; Head, Horticulture Bureau 1964; mem. House of Councillors 1966–78; Parl. Vice-Minister for Int. Trade and Industry 1971; Gov. of Kyoto 1978–86; mem. House of Councillors 1986–; Minister of Justice 1987–88. *Publications:* The Countries of Oceania, Discovering the New History of Kyoto. *Leisure interests:* painting, calligraphy. *Address:* Kojimachi Shuku-sha, 4-7 Kojimachi, Chiyoda-ku, Tokyo, Japan.

HAYCRAFT, Howard; American publisher and author; b. 24 July 1905; ed. Univ. of Minnesota; Univ. of Minn. Press 1928; H. W. Wilson Co., New York 1929–, Vice-Pres. 1940–52, Pres. 1953–67, Chair. Bd. of Dirs. 1967–; army service 1942–46; mem. Pres. Cttee. Employment of Handicapped 1963–74; mem. Mystery Writers of America Club, Pres. 1963; Campbell Medal and Citation (American Library Asscn.) 1966, Centennial Citation 1976. *Publications:* as Author, Ed. or Joint Editor: Authors Today and Yesterday 1933, Junior Book of Authors 1934, Boys' Sherlock Holmes 1936, Boys' Book of Great Detective Stories 1938, American Authors 1600-1900 1938, Boys' Second Book of Great Detective Stores 1940, Murder for Pleasure: The Life and Times of the Detective Story 1941, Crime Club Encore 1942, Twentieth Century Authors 1942, Art of the Mystery Story 1946, Fourteen Great Detective Stories 1949, British Authors before 1800 1952, Treasury of Great Mysteries 1957, Ten Great Mysteries 1959, Five Spy Novels 1962, Books for the Blind: A Postscript and an Appreciation 1965. *Address:* 950 University Avenue, Bronx, N.Y. 10452, U.S.A.

HAYDAR, Mohammad Haydar; Syrian politician; b. 1931; ed. secondary schools, Lattakia, Univ. of Damascus; teacher, Lattakia, Hama 1951–60; with Ministry of Agrarian Reform 1960–63; Dir. Alghab Establishment, Hama 1963; Dir. Agrarian Reform, Damascus, Daraa, Alsuweidaa 1964; Dir. Legal and Admin. Affairs, Ministry of Agric. and Agrarian Reform 1965; Gov. Alhasakeh 1966; teacher, Damascus 1968; mem. Command., Damascus Branch of Baath Arab Socialist Party (BASP) 1968; Temporary Regional Command of BASP 1970; mem. of both Regional and Nat. Commands of BASP, mem. of Cen. Command, Progressive Nat. Front of Syria and Minister of Agric. and Agrarian Reform until 1973; Deputy Premier for Econ. Affairs 1973–76; mem. of Nat. Command of BASP 1980–; mem. of the Nat. Progressive Front 1980–. *Address:* Foreign Relations Bureau, Baath Arab Socialist Party, Damascus, Syria.

HAYDEN, John Michael, M.S.; American politician; b. 16 March 1944, Colby, Kansas; s. of Irven Wesley Hayden and Ruth Kelly; m. Patti Ann Rooney 1968; two d.; ed. Kansas State and Fort Hays State Univs.; Exec. Man. Rawlins Co. Promotional Council, Atwood, Kan. 1973–77; Insurance Agent, E. C. Mellick Agency, Atwood 1977–87; fmr. Speaker Kan. House of Reps.; Gov. of Kan. 1987–; Republican. *Address:* E.C. Mellick Agency, 406 State Street, Atwood, Kan. 67730 (Office); Governor's Mansion, State Capitol, Topeka, Kan. 67730, U.S.A.

HAYDEN, William George, B.ECONS.; Australian politician; b. 23 Jan. 1933, Brisbane, Queensland; m. Dallas Broadfoot; one s. two d.; ed. Brisbane State High School, Univ. of Queensland; Police constable, Queensland 1953–61; mem. Parl. for Oxley 1961–; Parl. Spokesman on Health and Welfare 1969–72; Minister of Social Security 1972–75, of Foreign Affairs 1983–88, of Trade 1987–88; Gov.-Gen. Feb. 1989–; Fed. Treas. June-Nov. 1975; Leader Parl. Labor Party (Opposition) 1977–83. *Leisure interests:* reading, music, squash. *Address:* Parliament House, Canberra, A.C.T. (Office); 16 East Street, Ipswich, Queensland 4305, Australia. (Home).

HAYDON, Sir Robin (Walter Robert), K.C.M.G.; British diplomatist (retd.); b. 29 May 1920, London; s. of Walter Haydon and Evelyn Louise Thom; m. Joan Elizabeth Tewson 1943; one s. two d. (one d. deceased); ed. Dover Grammar School; H.M. Forces 1939–45; served Berne 1946–47, Foreign Office 1947–48, Turin 1948–52; Vice-Consul 1950; Vice Consul, Sofia 1952-53; Second Sec. Bangkok 1953–56; First Sec. and Head of Chancery, Khartoum 1958–61; First Sec. U.K. Mission to UN, New York 1961–65; Counsellor, Washington 1965–67; Head of News Dept., Foreign and Commonwealth Office 1967–71; High Commr. in Malawi 1971–73; Chief Press Sec. to Prime Minister 1973–74; High Commr. in Malta 1974–76; Amb. to Ireland 1976–80; Dir. (Public Affairs) Imperial Group Ltd. 1980–84; Dir. Imperial Tobacco Ltd. 1984–87; Gov. English-Speaking Union 1980–86, 1987–; Gov. Dover Grammar School 1982–; mem. Tobacco Advisory Council 1984–, Reviewing Cttee. Export of Arts 1984–87. *Leisure interests:* walking, swimming, English water-colours. *Address:* c/o Cox's & King's Branch, Lloyds Bank Ltd., 6 Pall Mall, London, S.W.1, England.

HAYE, Colvyn Hugh, C.B.E., B.A.; British colonial civil servant, educator and administrator; b. 7 Dec. 1925, Tundla, U.P., India; s. of Colvyn Hugh Haye and Avis Rose Kelly; m. Gloria Mary Stansbury 1949; two d.; ed. Oak Grove School, Sherwood Coll., Melbourne Teachers' Coll., Univ. of Melbourne, Australia, Christ Church, Oxford; served R.N.V.R. 1944–46; joined Colonial Service (now H.M. Overseas Civil Service), posted Hong Kong as Educ. Officer 1953, Sr. Educ. Officer 1962, Asst. Dir. of Educ. 1969, Deputy Dir. of Educ. 1975, Dir. of Educ. 1980, Sec. Admin. Grade and Commr., London 1984–87. *Leisure interests:* reading, writing, walking and talking. *Address:* Wymering, Sheet Common, Nr. Petersfield, Hants., GU31 5AT, England (Home). *Telephone:* Petersfield 68480 (Home).

HAYEK, Friedrich August (von), C.H., DR.JUR., DR.RER.POL. (Vienna), D.SC. (ECON.) (London), F.B.A.; British (b. Austrian) economist; b. 8 May 1899, Vienna; s. of August von Hayek and Felizitas von Juraschek; m. 1st Helene B. M. von Fritsch, 2nd Helene A. E. Warhanek (née Bitterlich); one s. one d.; ed. Vienna Univ.; Austrian Civil Service 1921–26; Dir. Austrian Inst. for Econ. Research 1927–31; Lecturer in Econs., Vienna Univ. 1929–31; Prof. of Econ. Science and Statistics, London Univ. 1931–50; Prof. of Social and Moral Science, Univ. of Chicago 1950–62; Prof. of Econs., Univ. of Freiburg 1962–70; shared Nobel Prize for Econ. Science 1974; naturalized British 1938; Hon. Fellow L.S.E., Austrian Acad. of Science, Hoover Inst. of War and Peace, Stanford, Ca. and others; Ordre pour le Mérite 1977, Medal of Merit, Baden-Württemberg 1981, Ring of Honour, Vienna 1983, Gold Medal, Paris 1984. *Publications:* Prices and Production 1931, Monetary Theory and the Trade Cycle 1933, Collectivist Economic Planning 1935, Monetary Nationalism and International Stability 1937, Profits, Interest and Investment 1939, The Pure Theory of Capital 1941, The Road to Serfdom 1944, Individualism and Economic Order 1948, J. S. Mill and Harriet Taylor 1950, The Counter-Revolution of Science 1952, The Sensory Order 1952, Capitalism and the Historians 1954, The Political Ideal of the Rule of Law 1955, The Constitution of Liberty 1960, Studies in Philosophy, Politics and Economics 1967, Freiburger Studien 1969, Law, Legislation and Liberty: Rules and Order (Vol. I) 1973, The Mirage of Social Justice (Vol. II) 1976, The Political Order of a Free People (Vol. III) 1979, The Denationalization of Money 1976, New Studies in Philosophy, Politics, Economics and the History of Ideas 1978. *Address:* Urachstrasse 27, D-7800 Freiburg im Breisgau, Federal Republic of Germany. *Telephone:* 0761/77216.

HAYEK, His Beatitude Ignace Antoine II, D.PHIL.; Syrian ecclesiastic; b. 14 Sept. 1910; s. of Naum Hayek and Chafica Sciamsi; ed. Séminaire Patriarcal, Charfé, Lebanon, Pontifical Coll., of Propaganda Fide, Rome, and Oriental Pontifical Inst., Rome; ordained priest 1933, successively or concurrently Dir. of School, Curate and Vicar-Gen., Aleppo; Archbishop of Aleppo 1959–68; Syrian Patriarch of Antioch 1968–. *Address:* Patriarcat Syrien Catholique d'Antioche, B.P. 118879, rue de Damas, Beirut, Lebanon. *Telephone:* 381532.

HAYEK, Nicholas G.; Swiss business executive; b. 1928, Beirut; of American-Lebanese parentage; m.; founded consultancy firm Hayek Eng. 1963; firm acts as adviser to govt.'s and business concerns in Europe and Third World and notably to Swiss watch and high precision industry; Chief Exec. Officer, SMH (high-tech. co.) 1985–.

HAYES, Sir Brian, G.C.B.; British civil servant; b. 5 May 1929, Norwich; s. of Charles Hayes and Flora Hayes; m. Audrey Jenkins 1958; one s. one d.; ed. Norwich School, Corpus Christi Coll., Cambridge; joined Ministry of Agric., Fisheries and Food 1956, Deputy Sec. for Agricultural Commodity Policy 1973–78, Perm. Sec. 1979–83; Jt. Perm. Sec., Dept. of Trade and Industry 1983–85, Perm. Sec. 1985–. *Leisure interests:* reading, watching cricket. *Address:* c/o Department of Trade and Industry, 1 Victoria Street, London, S.W.1, England (Office). *Telephone:* 01-215 4435.

HAYES, Cheryl Davis, M.A.; American research administrator; b. 27 Oct. 1950, Ia.; d. of James G. Hayes and Gloria Westerberg Davis; m. John C. Hayes Jr. 1972; two s. two d.; ed. Skidmore Coll. and Georgetown Univ.; Research Fellow, Smithsonian Inst. 1972–74; Study Dir. Study Project on Children's Service, N.A.S./N.R.C. (Nat. Research Council) 1978–80, Panel for Study of Policy Formation Process, N.A.S./N.R.C. 1978–80, Panel on Work, Family and Community, N.A.S./N.R.C., Panel on Adolescent

Pregnancy and Childbearing, N.A.S./N.R.C. 1984–; Exec. Officer, Cttee. on Child Devt. Research and Public Policy, N.A.S./N.R.C. 1980–; mem. Bd. of Trustees, Nat. Child Research Center. *Publications:* several books on aspects of social policy research. *Address:* Committee on Child Development Research and Public Policy, National Academy of Sciences, 2101 Constitution Avenue, N.W., Washington, D.C. 20418 (Office); 4347 Forest Lane, N.W., Washington, D.C. 20007, U.S.A. (Home). *Telephone:* 202-334-2033 (Office); 202-364-0742 (Home).

HAYES, Helen; American actress; b. 10 Oct. 1900, Washington, D.C.; d. of Francis Van Arnum and Catherine Estelle (Hayes) Brown; m. Charles MacArthur 1928 (died 1956); one s.; ed. Sacred Heart Acad., Washington; first stage appearance at the age of six; fmr. mem. Columbia Players; mem. A.P.A. Phoenix Repertory Co. 1966–; Hon. Pres. American Theatre Wing; Pres. American Nat. Theatre; Hon. L.H.D. (Hamilton, Smith, Elmira); Hon. Litt.D. (Columbia, Denver); Hon. L.H.D. (Princeton); Acad. Award (Oscar) 1932, TV Emmy Award 1954, Antoinette Perry Award (Tony) for best actress 1958, Acad. Award for best supporting actress 1971; American Exemplar Medal, Freedoms Foundation 1978; Kennedy Center Honor Award 1981, Presidential Medal of Honour 1986, Laetrae Medal (Notre Dame), Nat. Medal of Arts 1988. *Stage appearances include:* Old Dutch 1909, Prodigal Husband 1914, Dear Brutus 1918, Clarence 1919, To the Ladies 1922, Caesar and Cleopatra 1925, What Every Woman Knows 1926, Coquette 1927, Mary of Scotland 1933, Victoria Regina 1937–38, Ladies and Gentlemen 1939–40, Twelfth Night 1940–41, Candle in the Wind 1941–42, Harriet 1943, Happy Birthday 1946, The Glass Menagerie 1948, Farewell to Arms, Mrs. McThing 1952, Mainstreet to Broadway 1953, The Skin of our Teeth 1955, Time Remembered 1958, The Front Page 1969, Harvey 1970; *Films include:* The Sin of Madelon Claudet 1932 (Oscar), A Farewell to Arms 1932, My Son John 1951, Anastasia 1956, Airport (Acad. Award) 1970, Herbie Rides Again 1974, One of Our Dinosaurs is Missing 1975, Candleshoe 1978. *Publications:* A Gift of Joy 1965, On Reflection (autobiog. with Sandford Dody) 1969, Twice Over Lightly (with Anita Loos, q.v.) 1971, Our Best Years (with Marion Gladney) 1984, Loving Life (with Marion Glasserow Gladney) 1987. *Address:* Nyack, New York, N.Y. 10960, U.S.A.

HAYES, John Philip, C.B., M.A.; British economist; b. March 1924, Fleet, Hants.; ed. Corpus Christi Coll., Oxford; with political and Econ. Planning, London 1950–53; with OEEC 1953–58; Econ. Dept., IBRD 1958–64; Head, Econ. Devt. Div. OECD 1964–67; Dir. World Economy Div., Econ. Planning Staff, Ministry of Overseas Devt. 1967–69, Deputy Dir.-Gen. of Econ. Planning 1969–71, Overseas Devt. Ministry, then Overseas Devt. Admin.; Dir. Econ. Program and Econ. Analysis and Projections Depts., IBRD 1971–73; Dir. Trade and Finance Div., Commonwealth Secr. 1973–75; Asst. Under-Sec. of State FCO Sept. 1975–84; Sr. Fellow, Trade Policy Research Centre April 1984–. *Publication:* Economic Effects of Sanctions on Southern Africa 1987. *Address:* 51 Enfield Road, Brentford, Middx., TW8 9PA, England (Home).

HAYES, John Trevor, C.B.E., M.A., PH.D., F.S.A.; British art administrator; b. 21 Jan. 1929, London; s. of the late Leslie Thomas Hayes and Gwendoline (née Griffiths) Hayes; ed. Ardingley, Keble Coll., Oxford, Courtauld Inst. of Art, London, Inst. of Fine Arts, N.Y.; Asst. Keeper, London Museum 1954–70, Dir. 1970–74; Dir. The Nat. Portrait Gallery 1974–; Commonwealth Fund Fellow, N.Y. Univ. 1958–59; Visiting Prof. in Hisotry of Art, Yale Univ. 1969; Chair., the Walpole Soc. 1981–; Hon. Fellow, Keble Coll., Oxford. *Publications:* London, A Pictorial History 1969, The Drawings of Thomas Gainsborough 1970, Catalogue of oil paintings in the London Museum, Drawings of Thomas Gainsborough 1970, Gainsborough as Printmaker 1971, Rowlandson, Watercolours and Drawings 1972, Gainsborough, Paintings and Drawings 1975, The Art of Graham Sutherland 1980, Landscape Paintings of Thomas Gainsborough 1982, Gainsborough Drawings (with Lindsay Stainton) 1983. *Leisure interests:* music, walking, gardening, travel. *Address:* National Portrait Gallery, 2 St. Martin's Place, London, WC2H 0HE, England. *Telephone:* 01-930 1552.

HAYES, William, M.B., B.CH., SC.D., B.A., F.R.S., F.R.S.E; Irish/Australian molecular biologist; b. 18 Jan. 1913, Dublin; s. of William Hayes and Miriam Harris; m. Honora Lee 1941; one s.; ed. St. Columba's Coll., Co. Dublin and Trinity Coll., Dublin; medical internships at Victoria Hosp., Blackpool, England and Sir Patrick Dunn's Hosp., Dublin 1937–38; Asst. Dept. of Bacteriology, Trinity Coll., Dublin 1938–41; served R.A.M.C. and Indian Army 1941–46; Lecturer in Bacteriology, Dublin Univ. 1947–50; Sr. Lecturer in Bacteriology, Postgraduate Medical School of London, Univ. of London 1950–57; Research Fellow, Calif. Inst. of Tech. 1953–54; Dir. MRC Microbial Genetics Research Unit 1957–68; Prof. of Molecular Genetics, Edinburgh Univ. 1968–73; Hon. Dir. MRC Molecular Genetics Research Unit 1968–73; Prof. of Genetics, Australian Nat. Univ. 1974–78; Sherman Fairchild Distinguished Scholar, Calif. Inst. of Tech. 1979–80; Visiting Fellow, Dept. of Botany, Australian Nat. Univ. 1980–86, Emer. Prof. 1987–; Pres. Genetical Soc. of G.B. and Ireland 1971–73; Fellow, Australian Acad. of Science; Hon. D.Sc. (Kent, Leicester and Nat. Univ. of Ireland), Hon. LL.D. (Dublin). *Publications:* The Genetics of Bacteria and their Viruses 1964, Experiments in Microbial Genetics (with R. C. Clowes) 1968 and many scientific papers. *Leisure interests:* walking and reading. *Address:* 17 MacPherson Street, O'Connor, A.C.T. 2601, Australia. *Telephone:* (062) 480116.

HAYMAN, Patrick; British artist; b. 20 Dec. 1915, London; m. Barbara Judson 1950; one d.; ed. Malvern Coll., Art Schol, Dunedin, New Zealand and Victoria Univ., Wellington, New Zealand; numerous one-man exhbns. in London, St. Ives, Farnham, and Oxford, England, Edinburgh, Scotland and Canada; numerous group exhbns. in England and Scotland, including exhbn. devoted to arts assoc. with St. Ives, Tate Gallery, London 1985; retrospective exhbns. in Western Canada 1985, London 1986; maj. exhbn. Crane Kalman Gallery, London 1986; Fifty Years of Painting, and illustrated poems, exhbn. at Louise Hallett Gallery, London 1988; works in many public collections, including Tate Gallery and Arts Council of Great Britain, London, Nat. Gallery of Modern Art, Edinburgh, Nat. Art Gallery of New Zealand, Wellington, Art Gallery of Ontario and Univ. of Regina, Canada and Univ. of the South, U.S.A. *Publication:* book of illustrated poems. *Leisure interest:* swimming. *Address:* 15 Byfeld Gardens, Barnes, London, SW13 9HP, England. *Telephone:* 01-748 3256.

HAYMAN, Sir Peter Telford, K.C.M.G., C.V.O., M.B.E.; British diplomatist (retd.); b. 14 June 1914, Deal, Kent; s. of Charles H. T. and Alys H. Hayman; m. Rosemary E. Blomefield 1942; one s. one d.; ed. Stowe School and Worcester Coll., Oxford; Asst. Prin., Home Office 1937–39, Ministry of Home Security 1939–41; Asst. Pvt. Sec. to Home Sec. (Herbert Morrison) 1941–42; army service 1942–45; Prin., Home Office 1945–49; Asst. Sec. Ministry of Defence 1949–52; Counsellor, U.K. Del. at NATO 1952–54; Counsellor, Belgrade 1955–59, Malta 1958–59, Baghdad 1959–61; Dir.-Gen. British Information Services, New York 1961–64; Minister, Berlin 1964–66; Asst. Under-Sec. of State, Foreign Office 1966–69, Deputy Under-Sec. of State 1969–70; High Commr. to Canada 1970–74. *Leisure interests:* travel, fishing, shooting. *Address:* Uxmore House, Checkendon, Oxon., England (Home). *Telephone:* (0491) 680-658.

HAYMAN, Walter Kurt, M.A., SC.D., F.R.S.; British mathematician; b. 6 Jan. 1926, Cologne, Germany; s. of Franz Samuel Haymann and Ruth Therese Hensel; m. Margaret Riley Crann 1947; three d.; ed. Gordonstoun School, Cambridge Univ.; Lecturer, Kings Coll., Newcastle, and Fellow, St. John's Coll., Cambridge 1947; Lecturer 1947–53, and Reader, Univ. of Exeter 1953–56; Visiting Lecturer, Brown Univ., U.S. 1949–50, Stanford Univ. Summer 1950, 1955, American Mathematical Soc. 1961; Prof. of Pure Mathematics, Imperial Coll. of Science and Technology, London 1956–85, Univ. of York 1985–; mem. London Mathematical Soc.; mem. Cambridge Philosophical Soc.; Foreign mem. Finnish Acad. of Science and Letters, Accademia dei Lincei; Corresp. mem. Bavarian Acad. of Science; Hon. D.Sc. (Exeter) 1981, (Birmingham) 1985; first organizer (1964–68) British Mathematical Olympiad; 1st Smiths Prize 1948, shared Adams Prize, Cambridge Univ. 1949, Junior Berwick Prize 1955, Senior Berwick Prize of the London Mathematical Soc. 1964. *Publications:* Multivalent Functions 1958, Meromorphic Functions 1964, Research Problems in Function Theory 1967, Subharmonic Functions 1976, and over 150 articles in various scientific journals. *Leisure interests:* music, travel, television. *Address:* University of York, Heslington, York, YO1 5DD (Office); 24 Fulford Park, Fulford, York, YO1 4QE, England (Home). *Telephone:* (0904) 433076 (Office); (0904) 37713 (Home).

HAYMERLE, Heinrich; Austrian diplomatist; b. 1910; ed. Univ. of Vienna; Diplomatic Service, OEEC, Paris 1948–51; Chief of Protocol, Dept. of Foreign Affairs 1951–53; Austrian Observer at UN 1953–55; Austrian Rep. in Madrid 1955–56; Head, Political Div., Dept. of Foreign Affairs 1956–60; Amb. to U.S.S.R. 1960–64; Head, Political Div., Ministry for Foreign Affairs 1964–68; Deputy Sec.-Gen. 1967–68; Gov. of Austria to the IAEA 1965–67; Vice-Chair. Bd. of Govs. of IAEA 1966–67; Perm. Rep. to UN 1968–70; Chair. of UN-Outer Space Cttee.; Amb. to U.S.S.R., also accred. to Mongolia 1971–74; Sec.-Gen. for Foreign Affairs 1974–. *Address:* c/o Ministry of Foreign Affairs, Vienna, Ballhausplatz, Austria.

HAYNES, Arden Ramon, B.COM.; Canadian business executive; b. 7 Aug. 1927, Saskatchewan; m. Helen Beverly Henderson; two s.; ed. Univ., of Manitoba; joined Imperial Oil Ltd., Winnipeg 1951, various positions in Canada until 1968; with Standard Oil Co. (N.J.), New York (now Exxon Corpn.) 1968–72; rejoined Imperial Oil Ltd. 1972, Dir. and Sr. Vice-Pres. 1974–78, Exec. Vice-Pres. Jan.-Oct. 1982, Pres. and C.O.O. Oct. 1982–, Chair., Pres. and C.E.O. 1985–, Chair. and C.E.O. 1988–; Pres. and C.E.O. Esso Resources Canada Ltd. (subsidiary of Imperial Oil) 1978–81, Chair. 1981–; mem. Fed. Govt.'s Advisory Group on Energy Products and Services; mem. Bd. of Dirs. Royal Bank of Canada, Power Corpn. of Canada, Moore Corpn. Ltd., Alzheimer Soc. of Canada, Centre for Neurodegenerative Diseases, Univ. of Toronto; mem. Policy Cttee., Business Council on Nat. Issues; Gov. Olympic Trust of Canada; Chair. Nat. Advisory Council for the World Energy Congress, Montreal 1989. *Address:* Imperial Oil Limited, 111 St. Clair Avenue West, Toronto, Ont., Canada.

HAYS, Adm. Ronald Jackson, B.S.; American naval officer; b. 19 Aug. 1928, Urania, La.; s. of George H. Hays and Fannie E. (née McCartney) Hays; m. Jane M. Hughes 1951; two s. one d.; ed. Northwestern State Univ., U.S. Naval Acad.; Commdt. ensign U.S. Navy 1950, Destroyer Officer Atlantic Fleet 1950–51, Attack Pilot Pacific Fleet 1953–56; Test Pilot 1956–59, Squadron Leader 1961–63; Air Warfare Officer 7th Fleet Staff 1967–68; Tactical Aircraft Planning Officer, Office Chief Naval Operations 1969–71; C.-in-C. U.S. Naval Force Europe, London 1980–83; Vice-Chief Naval Operations Dept., Washington 1983–85; C.-in-C. U.S. Pacific

Command 1985-88; rank of Adm. 1983; Pres. and C.E.O. The Pacific Int-Center for High Tech. Research; D.S.M. with three gold stars, Silver Star with two gold stars, D.F.C. with gold and silver star; Legion of Merit, and numerous other awards and medals. *Leisure interest:* golf. *Address:* 2875 King Street, 1st Floor, Honolulu, Hawaii 96826, U.S.A.

HAYTER, Sir William Goodenough, K.C.M.G.; British diplomatist and college principal; b. 1 Aug. 1906, Oxford; s. of late Sir William Goodenough Hayter, K.B.E. and Lady Hayter (née Slessor); m. Iris Marie Hoare 1938; one d.; ed. Winchester and New Coll., Oxford; entered Diplomatic Service 1930; served in Foreign Office 1930-31, Vienna 1931, Moscow 1934, Foreign Office 1937, China 1938, Washington 1941, Foreign Office 1944; Asst. Under-Sec. of State 1948; Minister in Paris 1949-53; Amb. to U.S.S.R. 1953-57; Deputy Under-Sec. of State 1957-58; Warden of New Coll., Oxford 1958-76; mem. Council G.B.-U.S.S.R. Assen. 1959-76; Gold Medal for Services to Austria 1967. *Publications:* The Diplomacy of the Great Powers 1960, The Kremlin and the Embassy 1966, Russia and the World 1970, William of Wykeham, Patron of the Arts 1970, A Double Life (autobiog.) 1974, Spooner, a Biography 1977. *Address:* Bassetts House, Stanton St. John, Oxford, England. *Telephone:* Stanton St. John 598.

HAYWARD, Ronald, C.B.E.; British political administrator; b. 27 June 1917, Bloxham, Oxon.; s. of late F. Hayward; m. Phyllis O. Allen 1943; three d.; ed. Bloxham Church of England School and various R.A.F. schools and colls.; Labour Party Agent 1947-50, Asst. Regional Organizer 1950-58, Regional Organizer 1958-69, Nat. Agent 1969-72, Gen. Sec. 1972-82; Vice-Pres. Nat. Union of Labour and Socialist Clubs. *Leisure interests:* oil painting, music. *Address:* Haylens, 1 Sea View Avenue, Birchington, Kent, England.

HAYWARD, Sarel Anton Strydom; South African farmer and politician; b. 5 Aug. 1924, Steytlerville; m. Sally Viljoen 1950; two s. two d.; ed. Outeniqua High School, George and Univ. of Stellenbosch; fmr. mem. and Deputy Mayor Steytlerville Town Council; mem. Cape Provincial Council 1966-69; mem. Exec. Cttee. S.A. Wool Bd. 1968-; mem. Exec., Cape Province Agricultural Union 1968-; Vice-Pres. Nat. Wool Growers' Assen. of S.A. 1971; mem. Gen. Council, S.A. Agricultural Union 1971, mem. Exec. Cttee. 1977-; Pres. Cape Prov. Nat. Wool Growers' Assen. 1978; M.P. 1969-; Deputy Minister of Agric. 1978-82; Minister of Environmental Affairs and Fisheries 1982-84, Agric. and Water Supply 1984-86; Acting Chair. Ministers' Council, House of Ass. 1985-86; mem. numerous dels. around world on behalf of Int. Wool Secr. *Address:* P.O. Box 2, Thornhill, Cape Province, South Africa.

HAYWARD, Admiral Thomas B., M.S.; American naval officer; b. 3 May 1924, Glendale, Calif.; s. of E. Payson Hayward; m. Peggy Keating; two d.; ed. Glendale Junior Coll., Occidental Coll. at Los Angeles, U.S. Naval Acad., George Washington Univ.; Commanding Officer, Fighter Sqn. 103 1964-65; Commdr. Carrier Air Wing 10 1965-66; C.O., USS Grafias (AF-29) 1967-68, Aircraft Carrier USS America (CV-66) 1969-70; Commdr., Hawaiian Sea Frontier and Commdt., 14th Naval Dist. 1970-71; Dir. Office of Program Appraisal, Navy Dept. 1971-73, Dir. of Navy Program Planning 1973-75; Commdr. 7th Fleet 1975-76; C.-in-C. Pacific Fleet 1976-78; Chief of Naval Operations 1978-82; Pres. Thomas B. Hayward Assocs.; Dir. Litton Industries 1983-, Pacific Forum, Bank of Hawaii, Maxwell Labs., Rockford Inst., Hawaii High Tech. Corpn., Ethics Research Center; Assoc. Fellow Center for Strategic and Int. Studies; Defence Distinguished Service Medal with oak leaf cluster, Navy Distinguished Service Medal with two gold stars, Legion of Merit with three gold stars, Distinguished Flying Cross, Air Medal with ten gold stars and Bronze Numeral 3, numerous foreign decorations. *Leisure interests:* golf, tennis. *Address:* 1556 Aulena Place, Honolulu, Hawaii 96821, U.S.A. *Telephone:* 808 373 1213.

HAZELHOFF, Robertus, LL.M.; Netherlands banker; b. 21 Oct. 1930, Delft; s. of Hendricus Hazelhoff and Rinske van Terwisga; m. G. M. van Huet 1960; ed. Univ. of Leiden; Man. Banco Tornquist, Buenos Aires 1965; Man. Algemene Bank Nederland, New York Office 1968, mem. Man. Bd. Algemene Bank Nederland N.V. 1971-, Chair. 1985-. *Leisure interest:* playing golf. *Address:* Algemene Bank Nederland N.V., Vijzelstraat 32, 1017 HL, Amsterdam (Office); Nw. Bussummerweg 208, 1272 CN Huizen, Netherlands (Home).

HÁZI, Vencel, D.ECON.; Hungarian diplomatist and economist; b. 3 Sept. 1925, Budapest; m. Judit Házi 1952; one d.; ed. Technical Univ. and Univ. of Economics, Budapest; entered diplomatic service 1950; Press Attaché, London 1951-53; Counsellor, Stockholm 1957-58; Amb. to Iraq (also accred. to Afghanistan) 1958-61; Amb. to Greece (also accred. to Cyprus) 1962-65; Deputy Minister of Foreign Affairs 1968-70, 1976-83; Head, Hungarian Del. to UN Gen. Assembly 1969; Amb. to U.K. 1970-76, to the U.S.A. 1983-. *Leisure interests:* music, opera, swimming. *Address:* Embassy of the Hungarian People's Republic, 3910 Shoemaker Street, N.W., Washington, D.C. 20008, U.S.A. *Telephone:* 362-6730.

HAZIM, Mgr. Ignace; Syrian ecclesiastic; b. 1921, Mharde; ed. l'Institut Saint-Serge, Paris; Dir. of a secondary Theological Inst., Beirut, Lebanon; Rector of Theological Inst., Antioch, and then elected Bishop of Latakia 1966, took up post 1970; Greek Orthodox Patriarch of Antioch and All the East 1979-; Pres. Middle East Ecumenical Council; mem. Central Cttee. of Ecumenical Council of Geneva. *Publications:* La réssurection et l'homme

d'aujourd'hui and in Arabic: I Believe, The Telling of Your Word Enligh tens, The Church in the Middle East (trans. of the work by Père Corbon God's Design (trans. of the work by Suzanne de Dietrich). *Address:* Bo 9, Damascus, Syria. *Telephone:* 116329-117403.

HAZLITT, Henry; American journalist; b. 28 Nov. 1894, Philadelphia Pa.; s. of Stuart Hazlitt and Bertha Zauner; m. Frances Kanes 1936; ed Coll. of City of New York; mem. staff Wall Street Journal 1913-16 an New York Evening Post 1916-18; Financial Ed. New York Evening Mai 1921-23; editorial writer New York Herald 1923-24; Literary Ed. The Su 1925-29; Literary Ed. The Nation 1930-33; Ed. American Mercury 1934 editorial writer New York Times 1934-46; business columnist Newswee 1946-66; nationally syndicated newspaper columnist 1966-69; Ed. Th Freeman 1950-53; Hon. Litt.D. (Grove City Coll.) 1958, Hon. LL.D (Bethany Coll.) 1961, Hon. S.Sc.D. (Univ. Francisco Marroquin, Guatemala 1976. *Publications:* Thinking as a Science 1916, 1969, The Anatomy o Criticism 1933, A New Constitution Now 1942, 1974, Economics in On Lesson 1946, 1979, Will Dollars Save the World? 1947, The Great Ide 1951, 1964 (British title: Time Will Run Back 1952), The Free Man' Library 1956, The Failure of the "New Economics": An Analysis of th Keynesian Fallacies 1959, 1973, What You Should Know about Inflatio 1960, 1965, The Foundations of Morality 1964, 1972, Man Versus th Welfare State 1970, The Conquest of Poverty 1973, The Inflation Crisi 1978, From Bretton Woods to World Inflation 1984; ed. A Practica Program for America 1932, The Critics of Keynesian Economics 1960 *Address:* The Carolton, 400 Mill Plain Road, Fairfield, Conn. 06430, U.S.A

HAZZARD, Shirley; American author; b. 30 Jan. 1931, Sydney, Australi d. of Reginald Hazzard and Catherine Hazzard; m. Francis Steegmulle 1963; no c.; ed. Queenwood School, Sydney; Combined Services Intell gence, Hong Kong 1947-48; U.K. High Commr.'s Office, Wellington, N.Z 1949-50; UN, New York (Gen. Service Category) 1952-62; novelist an writer of short stories and contrib. to The New Yorker 1962-; Guggenheir Fellow 1974; mem. Nat. Inst. of Arts and Letters; U.S. Nat. Inst. of Art and Letters Award in Literature 1966; First Prize, O. Henry Short Stor Awards 1976; Nat. Critics Circle Award for Fiction 1981; Boyer Lecturer Australia 1984, 1988. *Publications:* short stories: Cliffs of Fall 1963; novels The Evening of the Holiday 1966, People in Glass Houses 1967, The Ba of Noon 1970, The Transit of Venus 1980; History: Defeat of an Ideal: Study of the Self-destruction of the United Nations 1973. *Leisure interest* Parthenophile. *Address:* 200 East 66th Street, New York, N.Y. 10021 U.S.A.

HE BINGLIN, PH.D.; Chinese chemist; b. 24 Aug. 1918, Fanyu Co Guangdon Prov., ed. Southwest Univ., Indiana Univ., U.S.A.; returned t China 1956; Prof. Nankai Univ., Tianjin 1956-; Deputy Dir. Chemistr Dept., Nankai Univ. 1962-; mem. Dept. of Chemistry, Academia Sinic 1980-; Dir. Polymer Chemistry Research Inst., Nankai Univ. 1983-; Pres Qingdao Univ. 1985-. *Address:* 47 Dong Cun, Nankai University, Tianji City, People's Republic of China. *Telephone:* 264253 (Tianjin).

HE DONGCHANG; Chinese politician; b. 1923, Zhejiang; Assoc. Prof. an Chair. Eng. Physics Dept. Qinghua Univ. 1956; Deputy Sec. CCP Cttee and Vice-Pres. Qinghua Univ. 1977; Deputy to 3rd NPC 1964, 5th NPC 1978; mem. Cand. Discipline Inspection Comm., CCP Cen. Cttee. 1978 Minister of Educ. and Sec. of CCP Comm. for Ministry of Educ. 1982-85 Sr. Vice-Chair. State Educ. Comm. and Sec. of CCP Comm. for State Educ. Comm. 1985-; mem. 12th CCP Cen. Cttee. 1982-87, 13th Cen Cttee. 1987-; Vice-Chair. Academic Degrees Cttee. of State Council 1983-*Address:* State Education Commission, Beijing, People's Republic of China

HE GUANGOU; Chinese army officer; Maj.-Gen. Deputy Commdr Guizhou Mil. Dist., People's Liberation Army 1958, Commdr. 1966-80 Vice-Chair. Guizhou Revolutionary Cttee. 1967; Deputy Sec. CCP Guizho 1971; Deputy Commdr. PLA Lanzhou Units 1980-; Dir. Logistics Dept. PLA Lanzhou Mil. Region 1981-. *Address:* People's Republic of China.

HE GUANGYUAN; Chinese state official; b. 1930; Vice-Minister of Mach ine Bldg. Industry 1982-; alt. mem. 12th CCP Cen. Cttee. 1982-87, 13th Cen. Cttee. 1987-. *Address:* Ministry of Machine Building Industry, Beij ing, People's Republic of China. *Telephone:* 867008 (Office).

HE HAI ZIA (YIN); Chinese artist; b. 13 Sept. 1908, Beijing; s. of H Zhe Yuan and He Shu Xiang; m. 1st Yie Yu Zhen 1930 (deceased), 2n Hu Yu Xan 1953 (deceased), 3rd Zhou Shu Yi; two s. two d.; apprentice to Han Gun Dian 1924, to Zhang Da Qian 1934; moved to Xian 1951; with others Changan painting movt.; Vice-Pres. Shaanxi Acad. of Paintin 1980; teacher, Chinese Painting Inst. Acad. 1983. *Publication:* He Ha Xia's Paintings. *Leisure interest:* singing. *Address:* Traditional Chinese Painting Research Studio, Beijing, People's Republic of China. *Telephone* 280514.

HE JINGZHI; Chinese writer and party official; b. 5 Nov. 1924, Zaozhuang Shangdong Prov.; s. of He Dianmo and Wu Jiguo; m. Ke Yan 1953; one s one d.; first poems published in Chengdu 1939; moved to Yan'an Communis Revolutionary base 1940; Stalin Literary and Art Award 1951; council mem Chinese Writers' Assen. 1953; Sec. Playwrights Assen. 1962; disappeare 1967-76; Vice-Minister of Culture 1979-80; Vice-Chair. Chinese Writers Assen. 1980-84; Deputy Dir. Propaganda Dept. under CCP Cen. Cttee

1980-87; Hon. Dir. Chinese Opera Research Inst. 1981; Hon. Chair. Soc. of Chinese Folk Literature 1987-; mem. 12th CCP Cen. Cttee. 1982-. *Publications:* There is No Winter 1942, Night in the Villages 1944, Libretto of The White Haired Girl (with Ding Yi) 1945, The Sunflower Blossom 1949, Singing Loudly 1956, Selected Poems 1979, Theses on Literature and Art 1950-85. *Leisure interest:* travel. *Address:* House 1, Nanshagon, Sanlihe, Beijing, People's Republic of China.

HE JINHENG; Chinese army officer; Commdr. PLA Artillery 1983-; mem. 12th Cen. Cttee. CCP 1982-87. *Address:* People's Liberation Army Headquarters, Beijing, People's Republic of China.

HE KANG; Chinese party and government official; b. 1923, Hebei Prov.; ed. Agric. Coll. of Guangxi Univ.; Chief Div. of Agric. and Forestry under Shanghai Mil. Control Cttee.; Deputy Head Dept. of Agric. and Forestry under E. China Mil. and Political Cttee. 1950-52; Dir. Dept. of Special Forestry of Cen. Ministry of Forestry 1952-54; Dir. Dept. of Tropical Plants, Ministry of Agric. 1954-57; Dir. S. China Tropical Crop Science Research Inst. and Tropical Crop Coll. 1957-72; Deputy Dir. Gen. Bureau of Land Reclamation, Guangdong Prov. 1972-77; Vice-Minister of Agric. and Forestry 1978; Deputy Dir. Nat. Comm. on Agric. and Vice-Minister of Agric. 1979; mem. 12th Cen. Cttee. CCP 1982-87, mem. 13th Cen. Cttee. 1987-; Minister of Agriculture, Animal Husbandry and Fishery 1983-; Deputy Dir. Nat. Planning Comm. 1983-; Deputy to 3rd Nat. People's Congress 1964. *Address:* Ministry of Agriculture, Animal Husbandry and Fishery, He Ping Li, Beijing, People's Republic of China.

HE LUTING; Chinese musician and composer; b. 20 July 1902, Shaoyang Co., Hunan Prov.; organized Chongqing Symphony Orchestra 1938; composed The East is Red; Vice-Chair. Chinese Musicians' Assoc. 1950-66, 1979-85, Hon. Chair. 1985; in political disgrace 1966-76; mem. Presidium CPPCC 6th Nat. Cttee. 1983-; Vice-Chair. China Fed. of Literacy and Art Circles 1979-; Hon. Pres. Shanghai Conservatory 1986-. *Address:* China Federation of Literature and Art, Beijing, People's Republic of China.

HE QIZONG; Chinese army officer; b. 1936, Sichuan Prov.; Deputy Chief of Gen. Staff, PLA 1985-; alt. mem. 13th CCP Cen. Cttee. 1987-. *Address:* People's Liberation Army General Staff Headquarters, Beijing, People's Republic of China.

HE XIAOHUA; Chinese writer; b. 1950, Shanxi; fmrly. a welder; began writing 1972. *Publications:* Structural Beauty, Outside the Marriage Bureau. *Address:* c/o China Federation of Literature and Art, Beijing, People's Republic of China.

HE YIXIANG; Chinese army officer; b. 1911, Xichong Co., Sichuan Prov.; joined Red Army 1930, CCP 1938; took part in capture of Nanjing 1949, mem. Presidium first Nanjing Party Congress 1949; Chief of Staff, Shandong Mil. Dist. 1953; Maj.-Gen. PLA Force in Zhejiang 1963; Acting Dir., Nat. Defence Athletic Assoc. Zhejiang Provincial People's Council 1964; Deputy Commdr. Zhejiang Mil. Dist. 1965; Commdr. Shanghai Garrison Dist. 1978-80; Sec. CCP Cttee. Shanghai Garrison Dist. 1979-80; Deputy Commdr. PLA Nanjing Mil. Region 1979-; Deputy Head Shanghai Group for People's Air Defence 1978-. *Address:* 1899 Huai Hai Zhong Lu, Shanghai, People's Republic of China.

HE YOUFA; Chinese army officer; b. 1920, Jingyang Co., Shaanxi Prov.; joined Red Army 1933, CCP 1938; Deputy Commdr. Jilin Mil. District, People's Liberation Army 1967, Commdr. 1968-84; Vice-Chair. Jilin Revolutionary Cttee. 1968; Sec. CCP Jilin 1971-84; Adviser Shenyang PLA Units 1984. *Address:* Office of the Secretary, Jilin Revolutionary Committee, Jilin, People's Republic of China.

HE YUSHAN; Chinese bodybuilder; b. 1963, Beijing; Men's All-Round Individual Bodybuilding Nat. Champion 1986. *Address:* China Sports Federation, Beijing, People's Republic of China.

HE ZEHUI, ENG.D.; Chinese physician; b. 5 March 1914, Suzhou City, Jiangsu Prov.; m. Qian Sanqiang; three d.; ed. Qinghua Univ., Berlin Univ.; researcher Curie Inst., France 1941-48; researcher Modern Physics Inst., Academia Sinica 1953-; won 3rd prize of Academia Sinica Science Awards for paper Research into the Process of Preparing Nuclear Emulsoid, 1957; Vice-Dir. Inst. of Atomic Energy, Academia Sinica 1964-66; in disgrace during Cultural Revolution 1966-76; rehabilitated 1977; Deputy Dir. Inst. of High Energy Physics, Academia Sinica 1978-; mem., Dept. of Math. and Physics, Academia Sinica 1985-. *Address:* Room 203, Bldg. 14, Zhong Guan Cun, Beijing 100080, People's Republic of China. *Telephone:* 284314 (Beijing).

HE ZHENGWEN; Chinese soldier; Chief of Staff, Third Army Corps 1949; Deputy Commdr. of Chengdu Mil. Region, PLA 1955-74; Deputy Chief of Gen. Staff 1974-; mem. 6th CPPCC Nat. Cttee. 1986-. *Address:* People's Liberation Army Headquarters, Beijing, People's Republic of China.

HE ZHIQIANG; Chinese geologist, party and government official; b. 1934, Lijiang Naxi Autonomous Co. Yunnan Prov.; ed Dept. of Geology, Chongqing Univ.; joined CCP 1956; Deputy Head Production and Tech Sections, Yunnan Prov. Geological Bureau, Deputy Dir. and Leading Party Members Group 1983; Dir. Scientific and Tech. Comm. Yunnan Prov. Party

Group 1983-; Vice-Gov. Yunnan Prov. 1983-85, Gov. 1985-86; Deputy Sec. Yunnan Prov. CCP Cttee. 1985-86; alt. mem. CCP Cen. Cttee. 1987-. *Address:* Yunnan Provincial Geological Bureau, Kunming, People's Republic of China.

HE ZHIYUAN; Chinese soldier; Political Commissar, Shandong Mil. Dist., PLA 1974-. *Address:* People's Republic of China.

HE ZHUKANG; Chinese party and government official; b. 1932; Vice-Gov. of Henan 1980-83, Gov. 1983-87; Acting Gov. Jilin 1987-; alt. mem. 12th Cen. Cttee. CCP 1982; mem. 1985; Deputy Sec. CCP Prov. Cttee., Henan 1984-; mem. Presidium 6th NPC 1986-; Chair. Preparatory Cttee. for First Nat. Jr. Games 1984-. *Address:* Office of the Governor, Jilin Province, People's Republic of China.

HEAD, Alan Kenneth, D.SC., F.A.A., F.R.S.; Australian physicist and mathematician; b. 10 Aug. 1925, Melbourne; s. of Rowland H. J. and Elsie M. (née Burrell) Head; m. Gwenneth N. Barlow 1951; ed. Univ. of Melbourne and Univ. of Bristol; Research Scientist CSIRO Div. of Aeronautics 1947-50, Aeronautical Research Labs. 1953-57, Div. of Tribophysics 1957-81, Div. of Chemical Physics 1981-86, Div. of Materials Science 1987-; Visiting Prof. Brown Univ. 1961-62, Univ. of Fla. 1971; Christensen Fellow, St. Catherine's Coll., Oxford 1986; Syme Research Medal 1965. *Publications:* Computed Electron Micrographs and Defect Identification 1973, numerous scientific papers. *Address:* C.S.I.R.O., Division of Materials Science, Locked Bag 33, Clayton, Vic. 3168 (Office); 6 Duffryn Place, Toorak, Vic. 3142, Australia (Home). *Telephone:* (03) 542 2861 (Office); (03) 241 6149 (Home).

HEAD, Tim David, B.A.; British artist; b. 22 Oct. 1946, London; s. of Percy Head and Muriel Head; m. Vivian Katz 1973; two d.; ed. Dept. of Fine Art, Univ. of Newcastle upon Tyne, St. Martin's School of Art, London; Lecturer, Goldsmith's Coll. School of Art, London 1971-79; Lecturer, Slade School of Fine Art, Univ. Coll. London 1976-; Fellowship at Clare Hall and Kettle's Yard, Cambridge 1977-78; Sculpture Comm., Nat. Museum of Photography, Film and TV, Bradford, Yorks. 1985; solo exhbns. at Museum of Modern Art, Oxford 1972, Gallery House, London 1973, Whitechapel Art Gallery and Garage Gallery, London 1974, Rowan Gallery, London 1975, 1976, 1978, Arnolfini Gallery, Bristol 1975, Anthony Stokes Gallery, London 1977, Kettle's Yard, Cambridge, Henie-Onstad Kunstcenter, Oslo 1978, I.C.A., Brisbane, Paola Betti Gallery, Milan, Serpentine Gallery, London, Third Eye Centre, Glasgow 1979, Gallery Bama, Paris, British Pavilion, Venice Biennale 1980, Locus Solus, Genoa 1981, Prov. Museum, Hasselt 1983, I.C.A., London 1985, Anthony Reynolds Gallery, London 1986; numerous group exhbns. in Milan, Kassel, Paris, Brussels, Sydney, New York, Vienna, London, Pa., Basle, Regensburg, Leeds, Montreal and Swansea; Gulbenkian Foundation Visual Arts Award 1975. *Address:* 17 Belsize Park Gardens, London, NW3 4JG, England.

HEADINGTON, Christopher John Magenis, B.MUS., A.R.A.M., A.R.C.M.; British musician; b. 28 April 1930, London; s. of Kenneth Headington; ed. Taunton School, Royal Acad. of Music; Asst. Music Master Trinity Coll., Glenalmond, Perthshire 1951-54; Deputy Dir. Music, Lancing Coll., Sussex 1954-64; Sr. Asst. Music Presentation, BBC, London 1964-65; Tutor in Music, Dept. for External Studies, Oxford Univ. 1965-72, Part-time Assoc. Tutor 1972-82; freelance composer, pianist, broadcaster, author, etc. 1950-; Piano concert appearances in Europe, Middle and Far East, W. Indies, etc.; Leonard Borwick Prize, Royal Acad. of Music; awarded major Arts Council of Great Britain Bursary for Composers 1978. *Works:* Piano Sonatas 1956, 1974, 1985, String Quartets Nos. 1, 2 and 3 1954, 1974, 1982, Two Piano Sonatas 1956, 1974, Violin Concerto 1959, Song Cycles including Reflections of Summer and A Clouded Starre 1965 and 1975, A Bradfield Mass 1977, Piano Quartet 1978, The Healing Fountain (In Memoriam Benjamin Britten) 1979, Piano Concerto 1982, Sinfonietta 1985. *Publications:* The Bodley Head History of Western Music 1974, The Orchestra and its Instruments 1965, chapters on various composers in A Dictionary of Composers 1977, Illustrated Dictionary of Musical Terms 1980, Britten 1981, The Performing World of the Musician 1981, The Listener's Guide to Chamber Music 1982, The Rape of Lucretia (chapter in the Britten Companion) 1984, Opera: A History (with R. Westbrook and T. Barfoot) 1987. *Leisure interests:* aviation, skiing, travel, cooking, languages. *Address:* 19 Falkland Drive, Kingsteignton, Newton Abbot, Devon, TQ12 3RH, England. *Telephone:* (0626) 51972.

HEALEY, Rt. Hon. Denis Winston, P.C., C.H., M.B.E., M.P.; British politician; b. 30 Aug. 1917, Mottingham; s. of William Healey; m. Edna May (née Edmunds) Healey 1945; one s. two d.; ed. Bradford Grammar School and Balliol Coll., Oxford; Maj., Royal Engineers 1945; Sec. Labour Party Int. Dept. 1945-52; M.P. 1952-; Sec. of State for Defence 1964-70; Chancellor of the Exchequer 1974-79; Opposition Spokesman for Treasury and Econ. Affairs 1979-80, for Foreign and Commonwealth Affairs 1980-87; Chair. Interim Ministerial Cttee. of IMF 1977-79; Deputy Leader of Labour Party 1980-83; Hon. Fellow, Balliol Coll. Oxford 1980; Hon. D. Litt. (Bradford Univ.) 1983, Grand Cross of Order of Merit, Germany 1979. *Publications:* The Curtain Falls 1951, New Fabian Essays 1952, Neutralism 1955, Fabian International Essays 1956, A Neutral Belt in Europe 1958, NATO and American Security 1959, The Race Against the H Bomb 1960, Labour Britain and the World 1963, Healey's Eye (photographs) 1980,

Labour and a World Society 1985, Beyond Nuclear Deterrence 1986. *Address:* House of Commons, London, SW1A OAA, England.

HEANEY, Seamus; Irish author and poet; b. 13 April 1939, Northern Ireland; s. of Patrick and Margaret (née McCann) Heaney; m. Marie Devlin 1965; two s. one d.; ed. St. Columb's Coll., Londonderry, Queen's Univ. of Belfast; Lecturer St. Joseph's Coll. of Educ., Belfast 1963–66, Queen's Univ. of Belfast 1966–72; freelance writer 1972–75, Lecturer, Carysfort Coll. 1975–81, Sr. Visiting Lecturer, Harvard Univ. 1982–84, Boylston Prof. of Rhetoric and Oratory 1985–; W. H. Smith Prize 1975, Bennet Award 1982, Sunday Times Award for Excellence in Writing 1988. *Publications:* (poetry) Death of a Naturalist 1966, Door into the Dark 1969, Wintering Out 1972, North 1975, Field Work 1979, Sweeney Astray 1984, Station Island 1984, The Haw Lantern 1987, The Globe in the Window 1987; (prose) Preoccupations 1980, The Government of the Tongue 1988. *Address:* c/o Faber and Faber, 3 Queen Square, London, WC1N 3AU; c/o Farrar Straus Giroux, 19 Union Square West, New York, N.Y. 10003, U.S.A.

HEAP, Peter William, C.M.G., M.A.; British diplomatist; b. 13 April 1935, Dunchurch, Warwicks.; s. of Roger and Dora Heap; m. 1st Helen Wilmerding; m. 2nd Dorrit Breitenstein, two s. two d.; m. 3rd Ann Johnson, one step. s. one step. d.; ed. Bristol Cathedral School and Merton Coll., Oxford; served Dublin 1959–60, Ottawa 1960–63, Sri Lanka 1963–66; Ministry of Defence 1966–68; FCO 1968–71; Deputy Dir.-Gen. British Information Service, New York 1971–76; Counsellor, Caracas 1976–80; Head, Energy Science and Space Dept., FCO 1980–83; High Commr. in Bahamas 1983–86; Deputy High Commr. Lagos 1986–89; Sr. British Trade Commr. in Hong Kong 1989. *Address:* Foreign and Commonwealth Office, King Charles Street, London, S.W.1; 6 Carlisle Mansions, Carlisle Place, London, S.W.1, England.

HEARNE, Graham James; British solicitor and business executive; b. 27 Nov. 1937, Birmingham; s. of Frank Hearne and Emily (Shakespeare) Hearne; m. Carol Jean Brown 1961; one s. three d.; ed. George Dixon Grammar School, Birmingham; admitted solicitor 1959; with Pinsent & Co. Solicitors 1959–63, Fried, Frank, Harris, Shriver & Jacobson Attorneys, New York 1963–66, Herbert Smith & Co., Solicitors 1966–67, I.R.C. 1967–70, N. M. Rothschild & Sons Ltd. 1970–77; Finance Dir. Courtaulds Ltd. 1977–81; Chief Exec. Tricentrol 1981–83; Group Man. Dir. Carless, Capel & Leonard 1983–84; non-exec. Dir. N. M. Rothschild & Sons Ltd. 1973–; with Northern Foods Ltd. 1976–82; with B.P.B. Industries 1982–; Chief Exec. Enterprise Oil PLC 1984–; part-time mem. BNOC 1975–78; mem. Dover Harbour Bd. 1976–78; Chair. BRINDEX (Asscn. of British Independent Oil Exploration Cos.) 1986–88. *Address:* 1 Hook Lane, Bosham, Chichester, West Sussex, PO18 8EY, England. *Telephone:* 01-794 4987.

HEARNES, Warren Eastman, B.S. A.B., J.D.; American lawyer and politician; b. 24 July 1923, Moline, Ill.; m. Betty Hearnes; three d.; ed. U.S. Mil. Acad., West Point, and Univ. of Missouri; U.S. Army until 1949; mem. Missouri House of Representatives 1951–61, Majority Floor Leader 1957–61; Missouri Sec. of State 1961–65; Gov. of Missouri 1965–73; Chair. Midwest Governors' Conf. 1967–68; mem. Advisory Comm. of Intergovernmental Relations 1969–72, President's Civil Defence Advisory Council 1970–72; Pres. Council of State Govts. 1971; Exec. Dir. Southeast Miss. Legal Services, Inc. 1981–; mem. Missouri Bar, American Bar Asscn.; Democrat. *Address:* 116 North Main Street, Charleston, Mo. 63834 (Office); P.O. Box 349, Route 3, Charleston, Mo. 63834, U.S.A. (Home).

HEARNS, Thomas; American boxer; b. 18 Oct. 1958, Grand Junction, Tenn.; professional boxer 1977–; won WBA World Welterweight Championship 1980, lost it to Sugar Ray Leonard (q.v.) 1981; WBA World Super-Welterweight Champion 1982–86; unsuccessfully challenged Marvelous Marvin Hagler (q.v.) for World Middleweight Championship 1985; won World Light-Heavyweight Championship from Dennis Andries 1987; shares record of winning world titles at three different weights; Golden Gloves Champion 1977. *Address:* c/o Emanuel Steward, 19600 W. McNichol Street, Detroit. Mich. 48219, U.S.A.

HEARST, George Randolph, Jr.; American newspaper executive; b. 13 July 1927, San Francisco; s. of George Randolph Hearst and Blanche Wilbur; m. 1st Mary Thompson 1951 (died 1969), two s. two d.; m. 2nd Patricia Ann Bell 1969; Staff Los Angeles Examiner 1948–50, San Francisco Examiner 1954–56, Los Angeles Evening Herald-Express 1956– (Business Man. 1957–, Publr. 1960–); Publr. Los. Angeles Herald-Examiner 1962–; Vice-Pres. and Dir. The Hearst Corpn. 1977–; Trustee The Hearst Foundation. *Address:* Hearst Corporation, 1150 S. Olive Street, Suite 2620, Los Angeles, Calif. 90015 (Office); 318 North Rockingham Avenue, Los Angeles, Calif. 90049, U.S.A. (Home).

HEARST, Randolph Apperson; American newspaper executive; b. 2 Dec. 1915, New York; s. of William R. Hearst and Millicent V. Willson; brother of William R. Hearst, Jr. (q.v.); m. 1st Catherine Campbell 1938 (divorced 1979), five d.; m. 2nd Maria Scruggs 1982; m. 3rd Veronica de Uribe 1987; ed. Harvard Univ.; Asst. to Ed. Atlanta Georgian 1934–38; Asst. to Publr., San Francisco Call-Bulletin 1938–41, Exec. Editor 1946–, Publr. 1950–53; Ed. and Pres. San Francisco Examiner 1972–; Pres., Dir. and Chief Exec. Hearst Consolidated Publications Inc.; Pres. Hearst Publishing Co. Inc.

1953–64; Chair. Dir. The Hearst Corpn. 1965–; Chair. Exec. Cttee. 1967–72, Chair. Bd. 1973–; Trustee, William Randolph Hearst Foundation; Pres. The Hearst Foundation 1972–. *Address:* 110 Fifth Street, San Francisco, Calif. 94103, U.S.A.

HEARST, William Randolph, Jr.; American newspaper executive; b. 27 Jan. 1908, New York; s. of William R. Hearst and Millicent V. Willson; brother of Randolph A. Hearst (q.v.); m. 3rd Austine McDonnell 1948; two s.; ed. Univ. of California; Reporter, New York 1928; Publr., New York Journal American 1937–56, American Weekly 1945–56; War Corresp. 1943–45; Editor-in-Chief, Hearst Newspapers; Vice-Pres. and Dir. The Hearst Foundation, Inc.; Chair. Exec. Cttee. and Dir. The Hearst Corpn.; Vice-Pres. and Trustee William Randolph Hearst Foundation; Dir. U.P.I.; Hon. LL.D. (Alaska); Pulitzer Prize 1956, Overseas Press Club Award 1958. *Address:* 959 8th Avenue, New York, N.Y. 10019 (Office); 810 Fifth Avenue, New York, N.Y. 10021, U.S.A. (Home).

HEATH, Adrian Lewis Ross; British painter; b. 23 June 1920, Maymyo, Burma; s. of P. C. P. Heath and A. F. Heath (née Ross-Porter); m. Corinne E. Lloyd 1953; one s. one d.; ed. Bryanston School, privately with Stanhope Forbes, R.A. and Slade School of Fine Art, Univ. Coll., London; served R.A.F. (Bomber Command) 1940–45 and P.O.W. Germany from 1942; several one-man exhbns. since 1948, in Carcassonne, London, Newcastle, Dortmund, Bristol, Sheffield, Gothenburg and Stavanger and Bergen, Norway; numerous group exhbns. in London (Whitechapel, Tate and Hayward Galleries and R.A.), Tokyo, Pittsburgh, etc.; works in many collections in U.K. (including British Museum, Victoria & Albert Museum and Tate Gallery), U.S.A., Fed. Repub. of Germany, Sweden, Australia and S.A.; Visiting Lecturer, Bath Acad. of Art 1956–76; part-time Lecturer in Fine Art, Univ. of Reading 1980–85; mem. Art Panel, Arts Council of G.B. 1964–71; mem. Fine Art Bd. and Cttee. of Art and Design, Council of Nat. Acad. Awards 1975–82; Chair. Artists Int. Assoc. 1956–76. *Publication:* Abstract Art, its origins and meaning 1953. *Address:* 28 Charlotte Street, London, W1P 1HJ and Ford Cottage, Freshford, Near Bath, Avon, England. *Telephone:* 01-636 1957 (London).

HEATH, Rt. Hon. Edward Richard George, P.C., M.B.E., M.P.; British politician and conductor; b. 9 July 1916, Thanet; s. of William George Heath and Edith Anne Pantony; ed. Chatham House School, Ramsgate and Balliol Coll., Oxford; fmr. Pres. Oxford Univ. Conservative Assen.; fmr. Chair. Fed. of Univ. Conservative Assens.; fmr. Pres. Oxford Union; served in R.A. during Second World War, rising to rank of Lieut.-Col.; Commdr. 2nd Regt. HAC 1947–51; Master Gunner within Tower of London 1951–54; Civil Service 1946–47; M.P. for Bexley 1950–74, for Bexley, Sidcup 1974–83, for Old Bexley and Sidcup 1983–; Asst. Opposition Whip 1951; Lord Commr. of the Treasury (Sr. Govt. Whip) 1951, Jt. Deputy Chief Whip 1952–53, Deputy Chief Whip 1953–55, Parl. Sec. to Treasury and Govt. Chief Whip 1955–59; Minister of Labour 1959–60; Lord Privy Seal with Foreign Office responsibilities 1960–63, Sec. of State for Industry, Trade and Regional Devt. and Pres. Bd. of Trade 1963–64; Leader British Del., Brussels Conf. for countries seeking entry into Common Market 1961–63; Leader British Del. to first UN Conf. on Trade Aid and Devt. 1964; Leader of Conservative Party 1965–75; Leader of Opposition 1965–70, 1974–75; Prime Minister 1970–74; completed negotiations for Britain's entry into EEC 1971, signed Treaty 1972; mem. Independent Comm. on Int. Devt. Issues (Advisory Cttee. to Brandt Comm.) 1977–80; Chair. IRIS 1981–83; Chair. London Symphony Orchestra (LSO) Trust 1963–70, mem. Trust 1974–, Hon. mem. LSO 1974–, has conducted LSO in London, Cologne, Bonn; has conducted numerous orchestras worldwide, including Liverpool Philharmonic, English Chamber, Berlin Philharmonic, Chicago Symphony, Philadelphia Symphony, Jerusalem Symphony, Shanghai Philharmonic and Beijing Cen. Symphony Orchestras; co-f., Pres. European Community Youth Orchestra 1977–; has conducted on several records; Visiting Chubb Fellow, Yale 1975, Montgomery Fellow, Dartmouth Coll. 1980; Hon. F.R.C.M., Hon. F.R.C.O., Hon. Fellow Balliol Coll., Oxford, Nuffield Coll., Inst. of Devt. Studies, Sussex, Royal Canadian Coll. of Organists; Hon. D.C.L. (Oxford, Kent), Hon. D.Tech. (Bradford), Dr. h.c. (Sorbonne), Hon. LL.D. (Westminster Coll., Salt Lake City), Hon. D.L. (Westminster Coll., Miss.), Hon. D.P.A. (Wesleyan Coll., Ga.); Hon. Bencher, Gray's Inn, Scholar of Gray's Inn 1938; Charlemagne Prize 1963, Freiherr von Stein Foundation Award 1971, Estes J. Kefauver Foundation Award, Stresemann Medal 1971, Gold Medal (City of Paris) 1978, European Peace Cross 1979, World Humanity Award 1980, Gold Medal, European Parl. 1981; Conservative. *Publications:* One Nation: a Tory Approach to Social Problems (co-wrote) 1950, Old World, New Horizons 1970, Sailing—a Course of My Life 1975, Music—a Joy for Life 1976, Travels—People and Places in My Life 1977, Carols—the Joy of Christmas 1977. *Leisure interests:* music, sailing (Capt. British Admiral's Cup Team 1971, 1979, Capt. British Sardinia Cup Team 1980). *Address:* House of Commons, London, SW1A 0AA, England. *Telephone:* 01-219 3561/2.

HEATH-STUBBS, John (Francis Alexander), O.B.E., F.R.S.L.; British poet; b. 9 July 1918; s. of Francis Heath Stubbs and Edith Louise Sara Marr; ed. Bembridge School, Worcester Coll. for the Blind, The Queen's Coll., Oxford; English tutor 1944–45; Editorial Asst., Hutchinson's 1945–46; Gregory Fellow in Poetry, Univ. of Leeds 1952–55; Visiting Prof. of English, Univ. of Alexandria 1955–58, Univ. of Mich. 1960–61; Lecturer in

English Literature, Coll. of St. Mark and St. John, Chelsea 1963-73; Queen's Gold Medal for Poetry 1973, Oscar Williams—Jean Durwood Award 1977. *Publications: Poetry:* Wounded Thammuz, Beauty and the Beast, The Divided Ways, The Swarming of the Bees, A Charm Against the Toothache, The Triumph of the Muse, The Blue Fly in his Head, Selected Poems, Satires and Epigrams, Artorius, A Parliament of Birds, The Watchman's Flute, Birds Reconvened, Buzz Buzz, Naning of the Beast, The Immolation of Adelph, Collected Poems, Cats' Parnassus, A Partridge in a Pear Tree, Time Pieces; *Drama:* Helen in Egypt; *Criticism:* The Darkling Plain, Charles Williams, The Pastoral, The Ode, The Verse Satire; *Translations:* Hafir of Shiraz, The Rubaiyyat of Omar Khayyam (both with Peter Avery), Leopardi: Selected Prose and Poetry (with Iris Origo), The Poems of Anyte (with Carol A. Whiteside); Ed. Selected Poems of Jonathan Swift, of Tennyson, of Alexander Pope, The Forsaken Garden, Faber Book of Twentieth Century Verse (both with David Wright), Images of Tomorrow, Homage to George Barker on his Sixtieth Birthday, Selected Poems of Thomas Gray, Poems of Science (with Philips Salman). *Leisure interest:* taxonomy. *Address:* 35 Sutherland Place, London, W.2, England. *Telephone:* 01-229 6367.

HEBNER, Paul Chester; American businessman; b. 29 Dec. 1919, Warren, Pa.; s. of Henry G. Hebner and Mabel E. Gross; m. Dorothy V. Farrell 1943; one s. five d.; ed. Bliss Coll.; served in U.S.A.F. (rank of Major) 1942-45; Accountant, Admin. Asst. Altman-Coady Co., Columbus, Ohio 1940-41; Accounting Man., Business Man. T & T Oil Co., Los Angeles 1945-56; Sec.-Treas. Occidental Petroleum Corpn. 1958-68, Dir. 1960-, Exec. Vice-Pres. and Sec. 1968-88; Officer-Mem. American Soc. of Corp. Sec.; Dir. West Los Angeles Chamber of Commerce; mem. Los Angeles Beautiful. *Address:* No. 12 Amber Sky Drive, Rancho Palos Verdes, Calif. 90274, U.S.A. *Telephone:* 213-879-1700 (Office).

HECHT, Anthony Evan, M.A.; American poet and professor of English; b. 16 Jan. 1923, New York; s. of Melvyn Hahlo and Dorothea (née Holzman) Hecht; m. 1st Patricia Harris 1954 (divorced 1961), two s.; m. 2nd Helen d'Alessandro 1971, one s.; ed. Bard Coll. and Columbia Univ.; Teacher, Kenyon Coll. 1947-48, State Univ., Iowa 1948-49, New York Univ. 1949-56, Smith Coll. 1956-59; Assoc. Prof. of English, Bard Coll. 1961-67; Faculty mem., Univ. of Rochester 1967, John H. Deane Prof. of Rhetoric and Poetry 1968; Hurst Prof., Washington Univ. 1971; Prof. Graduate School, Georgetown Univ., Washington D.C. 1987-; Visiting Prof., Harvard Univ. 1973, Yale Univ. 1977; Consultant in Poetry, Library of Congress 1982-84; Trustee, American Acad., Rome; mem. Nat. Inst. of Arts and Letters, American Acad. of Arts and Science; Guggenheim Fellow 1954, 1959, Ford Foundation Fellow 1967, Rockefeller Foundation Fellow 1967; Fellow Acad. of American Poets, Chancellor 1971-; Prix de Rome 1950; Brandeis Univ. Creative Arts Award 1965; Bollingen Prize 1983, Eugenio Montale Prize for Poetry 1985. *Publications:* (poetry) A Summoning of Stones 1954, The Seven Deadly Sins 1958, A Bestiary 1960, The Hard Hours (Pulitzer Prize, Miles Poetry Award, Wayne Univ. 1968, Russell Loines Award, Nat. Inst. of Arts and Letters) 1968, Millions of Strange Shadows 1977; Jiggery Pokery (co-author and co-auditor) 1967; Seven Against Thebes (trans. with Helen Bacon) 1973, The Venetian Vespers 1979, Obbligati: Essays in Criticism 1986. *Address:* Graduate School, Georgetown Univ., Washington, D.C. 20057 (Office); 4256 Nebraska Avenue, N.W. Washington, D.C. 20016, U.S.A. (Home).

HECK, Bruno, DR. PHIL.; German teacher and politician; b. 20 Jan. 1917; s. of Josef Heck and Magdalena Ernst; m. Gertrud Mattes 1943; three s. three d.; ed. Tübingen Univ.; fmr. teacher; Ministry of Education, Württemberg 1950-52; Exec. Sec. Christian Democrat Party (CDU) 1952-58; mem. Bundestag 1957-76; Minister of Family and Youth Affairs 1961-68; Sec.-Gen. of CDU 1967-71; Chair. Deutsche Welle 1968-; Pres., Konrad Adenauer Foundation 1968-89, Hon. Pres. 1989-; Chief Ed. Political Opinion magazine. *Publications:* The Catilina Conspiracy, On Solid Ground (articles and essays), Hans Filbinger—The Case and the Facts 1980, The Fatherland—a Federal Republic? 1984, Foundations and Changes 1987, Freedom—Justice—Morals 1988. *Leisure interest:* hiking. *Address:* Heubergstrasse 70, 7209 Gosheim über Spaichingen, Federal Republic of Germany. *Telephone:* 0 7426-7210.

HECKER, François, L. EN D.; French banker; b. 27 Aug. 1919, Paris; m. Geneviève Poves 1945; two s.; ed. Law Faculty, Paris, and Ecole Nat. d'Organisation Economique et Sociale; with Banque Nat. pour le Commerce et l'Industrie (B.N.C.I.) 1945-65, Asst. in Gen. Secr. 1956, Asst. Sec.-Gen. 1963, Sec.-Gen. Banque Nat. de Paris (after merger with Comptoir Nat. d'Escompte de Paris) 1964, Controller-Gen. 1966, Dir. of foreign branches and subsidiaries 1969, Prin. Dir. in charge of int. div. 1973-79, Asst. Dir.-Gen. 1979-83, Hon. Dir. Gen. and Consultant 1983-; Pres. Banque Arabe 1984-86; Officier, Légion d'honneur. *Leisure interests:* golf, cycling. *Address:* 16 blvd. des Italiens, 75009 Paris (Office); 61 boulevard de la Saussaye, 92200 Neuilly-sur-Seine, France (Home).

HECKERT, Richard Edwin, PH.D.; American chemist and business executive; b. 13 Jan. 1924, Oxford, Ohio; s. of John W. Heckert and Winifred E. Yahn; m. Barbara Kennedy 1945; one s. one d.; ed. Miami Univ. of Ohio, Univ. of Illinois; served U.S. Army 1944-46; with Du Pont Co. (now Du Pont Operations) 1949-, Dir., Sr. Vice-Pres. and mem. Exec. Cttee. 1973-81, Pres., C.O.O. and Vice-Chair. Exec. Cttee. 1981, Vice-Chair. Du Pont

1981-85, Deputy Chair. Bd. of Dirs. 1985-86, Chair. and C.E.O. 1986-; Pres. Longwood Gardens Inc., Dean's Assoc. Business Advisory Council, Miami Univ. School of Business Admin., Jt. Council on Econ. Educ.; Chair. Trustees Carnegie Inst. Washington; Dir. Univ., Ill. Foundation, NAM, Provident Mutual Life Insurance Co. of Pa., Seagram Co. Ltd.; Chair. Soc. of Chemical Industry; mem. American Chemical Soc., NACME, A.A.A.S.; fmr. mem. by Presidential appt. Advisory Cttee. for Trade Negotiations. *Address:* 9000 Du Pont Building, 1007 Market Street, Wilmington, Del. 19898, U.S.A.

HECKSCHER, August; American journalist and author; b. 16 Sept. 1913, New York; s. of Gustave Maurice Heckscher and Frances Louise Vanderhoef; m. Claude Chevreux 1941; three s.; ed. St. Paul's School, Concord, Yale and Harvard Univs.; Instructor in Govt., Yale Univ. 1939-41; Army service 1941-45; Ed. Auburn (New York) Citizen-Adviser 1946-48; Chief Editorial Writer New York Herald Tribune 1948-56; Special Consultant, Pres. of U.S.A. on the Arts 1962-63; Parks Commr., New York 1967-74; Dir. Twentieth Century Fund; Gov. Yale Univ. Press, Fellow American Acad. of Arts and Sciences; Chair. Parsons School of Design, New York, Cooper-Hewitt Museum. *Publications:* These Are The Days 1936, A Pattern of Politics 1947, The Politics of Woodrow Wilson 1956, Diversity of Worlds (with Raymond Aron) 1957, The Public Happiness 1963, Alive in the City 1974, Open Spaces—the Life of American Cities 1977, When Laguardia Was Mayor 1978, St. Paul's—The Life of a New England School 1980. *Leisure interest:* fine printing. *Address:* 159 East 94th Street, New York, N.Y. 10028, U.S.A. *Telephone:* 212-289-4094.

HEDBERG, Hollis D., M.S., PH.D.; American petroleum geologist and stratigrapher; b. 29 May 1903, Falun, Kan.; s. of Carl A. Hedberg and Zada Mary Dow; m. Frances Murray 1932; four s. one d.; ed. Kansas, Cornell and Stanford Univs.; Petrographer, Lago Petrol Co. (Venezuela) 1926-28; various posts in geology and exploration for Gulf Oil Corpn. and subsidiaries 1928-; stratigrapher and asst. chief geologist (Venezuela) 1928-46, exploration man., Foreign Production Div. (New York) 1946-52, exploration co-ordinator (Pittsburgh) 1952-57, Vice-Pres. for exploration 1957-64, Exploration Advisor 1964-; Prof. of Geology, Princeton Univ. 1959-71, Prof. Emer. 1971-; American Comm. of Stratigraphic Nomenclature 1946-60, Chair. 1950-52; Pres. Int. Subcomm. on Stratigraphic Classification 1952-76; Vice-Pres. Int. Comm. on Stratigraphy 1968-76; Pres. Geological Soc. of America 1959-60, Pres. American Geological Inst. 1962-63; Chair. U.S. Nat. Cttee. on Geology 1965-66, Nat. Petroleum Council Technical Sub-cttee. 1967-73; mem. U.S. Nat. Cttee. World Petroleum Congresses 1965-83; Vice-Pres. Paleontological Soc. 1952; Assoc. Ed. American Asscn. of Petroleum Geologists 1937-; Dir. Cushman Foram Foundation 1957-63; Chair. JOIDES Safety and Pollution Prevention Panel 1970-77; Ed. International Stratigraphic Guide of Int. Union of Geological Sciences 1975-; mem. U.S. Nat. Cttee. of Int. Geological Correlations Program 1976-79; mem. N.A.S. 1960-; mem. Corpn. Woods Hole Oceanographic Inst. 1972-; Foreign mem. Geological Soc. (London), Royal Danish Acad. of Sciences; Hon. mem. Geological Soc. (Stockholm), Venezuelan Assc. of Minerals and Geology, Medalla Honor Instrucción Pública, Venezuela 1941; Trustee, Geological Soc. of America 1980-83, Hon. Trustee 1983-; Dr. h.c. (Uppsala Univ.) 1977; Sidney Powers Medal of American Assc. of Petroleum Geology 1963, Distinguished Service Award, Univ. of Kansas 1963, Mary Clark Thompson Award, N.A.S. 1973, Human Needs Award, American Assc. Petroleum Geologists 1973, Distinguished Achievement Award, Offshore Tech. Conf. 1975, Wollaston Medal, Geological Soc. of London 1975, Penrose Medal, Geological Soc. of America 1980, Ian Campbell Medal, American Geological Inst. 1983, William B. Heroy, Jr. Award, American Geological Inst. *Publications:* number of principal works by subject: compaction of sediments and sedimentary petrology 3; micropaleontology 4; regional geology of northern South America 10; stratigraphic principles 30; origin and migration of petroleum 8; petroleum geology and geological techniques 6; petroleum developments in Africa 12; petroleum resources 9; geology of the oceans 6; law of the sea 13; history and progress of geology 5. *Leisure interest:* history of geology. *Address:* 118 Library Place, Princeton, N.J. 08540, U.S.A. (Home). *Telephone:* 609-921-7833.

HEDEN, Carl-Göran, M.D.; Swedish scientist; b. 11 Sept. 1920, Stockholm; ed. Karolinska Institutet, Stockholm; Resident Prof. of Bacteriological Bioengineering, (Medical Research Council) 1964-, Head of Dept., Karolinska Institutet 1964-74; mem. Exec. Cttee. Int. Union of Biological Sciences (IUBS), Int. Council of Scientific Unions (ICSU); mem. COSPAR Consultative Group on Potentially Harmful Effects of Space Experiments, WHO Expert Advisory Panel on Immunology; mem. Special Cttee. for Int. Biological Programme; mem. Convenor Panel on Applied Microbiology of Int. Cell Research Org.; Vice-Pres. and Chair. Advisory Council Int. Assc. of Microbiological Socs. (IAMS); Fellow New York Acad. of Sciences, World Acad. of Art and Science (Vice-Pres. 1977); mem. Royal Swedish Acad. of Eng. Sciences and Chair. Div. for Biotechnology. *Address:* Kungliga Karolinska Institutet, Stockholm 60, Sweden.

HEES, George Harris, M.P.; Canadian politician; b. 17 June 1910, Toronto; m. Mabel Dunlop; three c.; ed. Royal Mil. Coll., Univ. of Toronto, Cambridge; Brigade-Maj. overseas with 5th Infantry Brigade; mem. House of Commons 1950-63, 1965-; Minister of Transport 1957-60, of Trade and

Commerce 1960–63, of Veterans Affairs 1984–89, Minister of State (Sr. Citizens) 1987–89; Dir. Montreal World Fair 1963–65; Pres. of Montreal and Canadian Stock Exchanges; Canadian Chair. Canada/U.S.A. Perm. Jt. Bd. on Defence; Progressive Conservative Party. *Leisure interests:* golf, badminton. *Address:* House of Commons, Ottawa, Ont. K1A 0A6, Canada.

HEESCHEN, David Sutphin, PH.D.; American radio astronomer; b. 12 March 1926, Davenport, Iowa; s. of Richard G. and Emily S. Heeschen; m. Eloise St. Clair 1950; two s. one d.; ed. Univ. of Illinois, Harvard Univ.; Lecturer, Wesleyan Univ. 1954–55; Research Assoc. Harvard Univ. 1955–56; Astronomer, Nat. Radio Astronomy Observatory 1956–77, Dir. 1962–78, Sr. Scientist 1977–; mem. Nat. Acad. of Sciences, American Astron. Soc. (Vice-Pres. 1969–71, Pres.-Elect 1979–80, Pres. 1980–82), Int. Astron. Union (Vice-Pres. 1976–82), Int. Scientific Radio Union, American Acad. of Arts and Sciences, American Philosophical Soc., A.A.A.S.; Research Prof. of Astronomy (Univ. of Va.) 1980–; Nat. Science Foundation Distinguished Public Service Award 1980, Alexander von Humboldt Sr. Scientist Award 1985. *Leisure interests:* sailing, scuba clubs. *Address:* National Radio Astronomy Observatory, Edgemont Road, Charlottesville, Va. (Office); 2590 Earlysville Road, Earlysville, Va., U.S.A. (Home). *Telephone:* 804-296-0227 (Office); 804-973-3340 (Home).

HEFNER, Hugh Marston, B.S.; American publisher; b. 9 April 1926, Chicago, Ill.; s. of Glenn L. and Grace (née Swanson) Hefner; m. Mildred Williams 1949 (divorced 1959); one s. one d.; ed. Univ. of Illinois; Ed.-in-Chief Playboy Magazine 1953–, Oui Magazine 1972–81; Chair. Emer. Playboy Enterprises 1988–; Pres. Playboy Club Int. Inc. 1959–86. *Leisure interest:* backgammon. *Address:* Playboy Enterprises Inc., 8560 Sunset Boulevard, Los Angeles, Calif. 90069, U.S.A. *Telephone:* (213) 659-4080.

HEGAZY, Abdel Aziz Muhammad, D.PHIL.; Egyptian politician; b. 3 Jan. 1923; ed. Fuad Univ., Cairo, Birmingham Univ.; Dean, Faculty of Commerce, Ain Shams Univ. 1966–68; mem. Nat. Assembly 1969–75; Minister of the Treasury 1968–73; Deputy Prime Minister, Minister of Finance, Econ. and Foreign Trade 1973–74; First Deputy Prime Minister April–Sept. 1974, Prime Minister 1974–75; Chair. Allied Arab Bank July 1985–; teaching and working as a management consultant and certified accountant in Cairo, Jeddah and Beirut. *Address:* Cairo, Egypt.

HEGDE, Kawdoor Sadanand, M.A., B.L.; Indian lawyer and politician; b. 11 June 1909, Kawdoor, Mysore; s. of late K. Subbaya Hegde; m. Meenakshi S. Hegde 1934; three s. three d.; Advocate 1935; Govt. Pleader and Public Prosecutor 1947–51; mem. Lok Sabha 1952–57, March 1977–, Speaker 1977–79; Judge, High Court of Mysore 1957–66; Chief Justice, Delhi and Himachal Pradesh High Court 1966–67; Judge, Supreme Court of India 1967–73; led parl. del. to Commonwealth parl. conf., Canada 1977; led parl. del. to Japan and Repub. of Korea 1978; Hon. LL.D. (Kyung Hee Univ., Repub. of Korea); mem. Janata Party. *Publications:* Crisis in Judiciary, Directive Principles. *Leisure interest:* gardening. *Address:* 20 Akbar Road, New Delhi; and 244 Palace Upper Orchards, Bangalore 6, India. *Telephone:* 387264 (New Delhi); 32337 (Bangalore).

HEGDE, Rama Krishna; Indian politician; b. 29 Aug. 1927, Doddamane, Siddapur Taluk, Uttara Kannada Dist.; ed. Kashi Vidyapeeta, Benares and Lucknow Univs.; active in Quit India movement, imprisoned twice; organized Ryots' (Tenants') movt., Uttara Kannada Dist.; Pres. Dist. Congress Cttee., Uttara Kannada Dist. 1954–57; entered State Legis. as Deputy Minister for Planning and Devt. 1957; Gen. Sec. Mysore Pradesh Congress 1958–62; Minister in charge of Rural Devt., Panchayatraj and Co-operation, Nijalingappa's Cabinet 1962–65, Minister for Finance, Excise, Prohibition, Information and Publicity 1965–67, for Finance, Excise and Planning 1967–68, for Finance, Planning and Youth Services 1968, 1971; Leader of Opposition 1971–77; imprisoned during Emergency; elected Gen. Sec. All India Janata Party 1977; elected to Rajya Sabha from Karnataka Ass. 1978; Leader, Karnataka Janata Legislature Party 1983; first-ever non-Congress Chief Minister in the State; continued as head of caretaker ministry 1984; following State Legislature by-election, Chief Minister of Karnataka 1985–88. *Address:* Raj Bhavan, Bangalese, Karnataka, India.

HEGEL, Eduard, DR.PHIL., DR.THEOL.; German theologian; b. 28 Feb. 1911, Wüppertal-Barmen; s. of Albert and Maria (née Ommer) Hegel; ed. Univs. Bonn, Münster and Munich; Prof. for Middle and New Church History, Trier 1949, Münster 1953, Bonn 1966–76, Prof. Emer. 1976; mem. Historical Comm. for Westphalia 1958, Rheinisch-Westfälischen Akademie der Wissenschafte 1973–; Apostolic Protonotar, Prelate. *Publications include:* Die Kirchenpolitischen Beziehungen Hannovers 1934, Kirkliche Vergangenheit im Bistüm Essen 1960, Geschichte der Katholisch-Theologischen Fakultät Münster (2 vols.) 1966, 1971, Geschichte des Enzbistüms Köln, Bd. 4–5 1979, 1987, Ecclesiastica Rhenana 1986. *Address:* Gregor-Mendel-Strasse 29, D-5300 Bonn 1, Federal Republic of Germany. *Telephone:* (0228) 23 22 73.

HEI BOLI; Chinese party and government official; alt. mem. 12th Cen. Cttee. CCP 1982–87; Chair. of Ningxia 1983–; Sec. CCP Cttee. Ningxia Autonomous Region 1982–83, Deputy Sec. 1983–86. *Address:* Office of the Governor, Ningxia Hui, People's Republic of China.

HEIDELBERGER, Michael, B.S., A.M., PH.D.; American chemist; b. 29 April 1888, New York; s. of David and Fannie (Campe) Heidelberger; m. 1st Nina Tachau 1916 (died 1946), 2nd Charlotte Rosen Salomonski 1956 (died 1988); one s. (died 1983); ed. public and Ethical Culture schools, Columbia Univ. and Federal Polytechnic Inst., Zürich; Asst. in Chemistry Summer Sessions Columbia Univ. 1909 and 1911; Fellow, Asst., Assoc. and Assoc. mem. of the Rockefeller Inst. for Medical Research 1912–27; Chemist to Mount Sinai Hospital 1927–28; and Presbyterian Hospital of New York 1928–56; Assoc. Prof. of Medicine, Columbia Univ. 1928–29, Assoc. Prof. of Biological Chem. 1929–45, Prof. of Biochemistry 1945–48, Prof. of Immuno-Chem. 1948–56, Emer. 1956–; Visiting Prof. of Immuno-Chem. Rutgers Univ. 1955–64; Adj. Prof. of Pathology (Immunology) New York Univ. 1964–; Chair. of the Research Council, Public Health Research Inst. of New York City 1951–56; Consultant to Sec. of War 1942–46; mem. N.A.S., American Philosophical Soc., American Chemical Soc., American Soc. of Biological Chemists, American Acad. of Microbiology, American Soc. of Microbiologists; Past Pres. Harvey Soc., American Assn. of Immunologists; Foreign mem. Royal Danish Acad. of Sciences 1957–, Accademia Nazionale dei Lincei 1963–, Royal Soc. 1975–; Foreign Assoc. French Nat. Acad. of Medicine 1978–; Hon. mem. French Soc. of Immunologists, German and British Socs. for Immunology, Mexican Soc. for Allergy and Immunology; Hon. Life mem. New York Acad. of Sciences 1976; Hon. mem. American Acad. of Allergy 1978, faculties of several univs.; many honorary doctorates; Ehrlich Silver Medal 1933, Lasker Award 1952, 1978, von Behring Prize 1954, Louis Pasteur Gold Medal (Swedish Medical Soc.) 1960, T. Duckett Jones Memorial Award 1964, Nat. Medal for Science 1967, New York Acad. of Medicine Medal 1968, von Pirquet Gold Medal 1971, Virchow Soc. Gold Medal 1973, shared Louisa Gross Horwitz Prize 1977, Claude Hudson Award 1978, Achievement Medal (Graduate Faculties Assn., Columbia Univ.) 1979, Mayor's Award of Honor for Science and Tech., New York 1987, Dean's Medal for Distinguished Service to Columbia Univ.'s Coll. of Sciences 1987, John Jay Award, Columbia Coll. 1988, Chevalier Légion d'honneur 1949, Officier 1966, Officier, Ordre de Léopold II 1953. *Publications:* Advanced Laboratory Manual of Organic Chemistry 1923, Lectures in Immuno-Chemistry 1956; numerous papers. *Leisure interest:* music. *Address:* c/o Department of Pathology, New York University School of Medicine, 550 First Avenue, New York, N.Y. 10016 (Office); 333 Central Park West, New York, N.Y. 10025, U.S.A. (Home).

HEIDWEILLER, Henricus Augustinus Franciscus; Suriname diplomatist; b. 10 Feb. 1929, Paramaribo; s. of Anton Edwin Louis and Virginia (née Humphrey) Heidweiller; m. Rosario Saenz de Santa María; with Courts of Justice, The Hague and Amsterdam 1953–55; Lecturer in civil law, Suriname Law School 1955–58; mem. Parl. 1958–67; Head of Office for Foreign Relations in Paramaribo 1962–68; del. to Council of Caribbean Org. 1960–64; Minister attached to Netherlands Mission to UN 1968–75; Amb. of Suriname to UN Dec. 1975–81, to Mexico 1976–84, to U.S.A. March 1981–84, to Canada Feb. 1982–84; Vice-Chair. Fourth Cttee. (Trust and Non-Self Governing Territories) of Gen. Assembly 1973, Rapporteur Gen. Summit of Heads of State and Govts. of Non-Aligned Countries Havana 1979; Perm. Rep. of Suriname to OAS 1981–84, to Netherlands 1984–85. *Address:* Ministry of Foreign Affairs, Paramaribo, Suriname.

HEIGERT, Hans A., DR.PHIL.; German journalist; b. 21 March 1925, Mainz; m. Hildegard Straub 1951; three s. two d.; ed. Ludwigburg High School Univs. of Stuttgart, Heidelberg and Oklahoma; served with army 1943–45 before resuming education; worked as a journalist in newspapers, radio and television from 1950, becoming Chief Editor, Süddeutsche Zeitung 1970–85; mem. Presidium Goethe Inst., Munich 1984–; winner of Theodor Heuss Preis 1969; Bayerischer Verdienstorden 1974, Bundesverdienstkreuz 1979. *Publications:* Stätten der Jugend 1958, Sehnsucht nach der Nation 1966, Deutschlands falsche Träume 1968. *Address:* 8034 Germering/Oberbayern, Eichenstr. 12, Federal Republic of Germany.

HEIKAL, Muhammed Hassanein; Egyptian journalist; b. 1923; m.; three s.; Reporter Akher Saa magazine 1944; Ed. Al-Akhbar daily newspaper 1956–57; Editor-in-Chief Al-Ahram daily newspaper 1957–74; mem. Central Cttee. Socialist Union 1968; Chair. Al-Ahram Establishment Bd. 1960–74; ordered to resign Oct. 1975; Minister of Nat. Guidance April–Oct. 1970; arrested Sept. 1981, released Nov. 1981. *Publications:* Nahnou wa America 1967, Nasser: The Cairo Documents 1972, The Road to Ramadan 1975, Sphinx and Commissar 1979, The Return of the Ayatollah 1981, Autumn of Fury 1983, Suez Through Egyptian Eyes 1986. *Address:* c/o André Deutsch Ltd., 105 Great Russell Street, London, W.C.1, England.

HEILBRONER, Robert L., PH.D., LL.D.; American economist; b. 24 March 1919, New York; s. of Louis and Helen (née Weiller) Heilbroner; m. 1st Joan Knapp 1952 (divorced 1975); m. 2nd Shirley Davis 1975; two s.; ed. Harvard Univ., New School for Social Research, New York; Norman Thomas Professor, Dept. of Econs., Graduate Faculty, New School for Social Research 1966–; hon. degrees from La Salle Coll., Philadelphia, Pa., Long Island Univ., and Ripon Coll., Wis. *Publications:* numerous articles and books, including The Worldly Philosophers 1953, The Future as History 1959, An Inquiry into the Human Prospect 1975, Beyond Boom and Crash 1978, Marxism: For and Against 1980, Five Economic Challenges (with Lester Thurrow) 1981, Economics Explained 1982, The Nature and Logic of Capitalism 1985, Behind the Veil of Economics 1988. *Leisure interest:* piano. *Address:* c/o New School for Social Research, 66 West 12th Street, New York, N.Y. 10011, U.S.A.

HEILIGER, Bernhard; German sculptor; b. 11 Nov. 1915, Stettin; ed. Stettin Art School, Berlin Acad. of Fine Arts and in Paris; Prof. of Plastic Arts, High School of Pictorial Arts, Berlin-Charlottenburg 1949–; numerous exhbns. in Europe and elsewhere; works in German and foreign museums and private collections; mem. Berlin Acad. of Arts, Florence Acad. 1978; Berlin Art Prize 1950, Cologne Art Prize 1952, Nat. and Int. Prize, Inst. of Contemporary Arts, London 1953 and Great Art Prize, Nordrhein-Westfalen Louis-Corinth Prize 1975. Notable works include Flamme for Ernst-Reuter-Platz, Berlin, Auftakt for Berlin Philharmonic Orchestra, 15 reliefs in Market Place, Bremen, Kosmos for Reichstag, Berlin 1972. *Address:* Käuzchensteig 8, 1000 Berlin-Dahlem 33, Federal Republic of Germany. *Telephone:* 8312012.

HEIMO, Marcel; Swiss diplomatist; b. 1917, Fribourg; ed. Univs. of Fribourg and Vienna and in U.S.A.; Entered Swiss National Bank, Zurich 1942; Federal Finance Admin. 1945; joined Political Dept. 1947, subsequently posted to London and Brussels; returned to Berne 1952–54; mem. Swiss Del. to OEEC, Paris 1954; transferred to London 1961–66; Personal Adviser to Pres. of Rwanda 1966–68; Amb. to India and Nepal 1968–69; Head Perm. Swiss Del. to OECD 1969–73; del. for Technical Co-operation, Berne 1974; Dir. Devt. Corpn. and Humanitarian Aid 1977–. *Address:* c/o Ministry of Foreign Affairs, 3003 Berne, Switzerland.

HEINDL, Gottfried, PH.D.; Austrian administrator; b. 5 Nov. 1924, Vienna; s. of Edmund Heindl and Eugenie Holzinger; m. Marianne Caliandjiev 1959; two s.; ed. Univ. of Vienna; Ed., Österreichischer Wirtschaftsverlag 1946–50; Neue Wiener Tageszeitung 1950–55; Press Sec. Austrian People's Party 1955–66; Dir. Austrian Inst., New York 1967–70; Gen. Admin. Austrian State Theatres 1970, Dir. for Cultural Affairs 1971–. *Publications:* Geschichten von gestern—Geschichten von heute 1965, Und die Grösse ist gefährlich 1969, Wien—Brevier einer Stadt 1972. *Address:* Vienna 1010, Goethegasse 1, Austria. *Telephone:* 51444/2642.

HEINE, Volker, PH.D., F.R.S.; British professor of theoretical physics; b. 19 Sept. 1930, Germany; m. Daphne Hines 1955; one s. two d.; ed. Wanganui Collegiate School, Otago and Cambridge Univs.; Demonstrator, Lecturer and Reader, Cambridge 1958–76, Prof. in Theoretical Physics 1976–; Visiting Prof. Univ. of Chicago 1965–66; Visiting Scientist Bell Labs., U.S.A. 1970–71; Fellow, Clare Coll., Cambridge 1960–; Maxwell Medal, Inst. of Physics. *Publications:* Group Theory in Quantum Mechanics 1960, Solid State Physics (Vol. 24) 1970, (Vol. 35) 1980; articles in Journal of Physics, Physical Review, etc. *Address:* Cavendish Laboratory, Madingley Road, Cambridge, CB3 0HE, England. *Telephone:* (0223) 337258.

HEINEKEN, Alfred Henry; Netherlands industrialist; b. 4 Nov. 1923, Amsterdam; s. of H. P. Heineken and C. Breitenstein; m. Martha Lucille Cummins 1948; one d.; ed. Kennemer Lyceum; mem. Supervisory Bd. Heineken N.V. (brewing) 1951, del. mem. 1958, mem. Bd. of Man. Dirs. 1964, Vice-Pres. 1969, Pres. 1971–; Pres. Heineken Holding N.V.; mem. Supervisory Bd. Gen. Bank of the Netherlands N.V.; Kt., Order of the Lion of The Netherlands; Chevalier Légion d'Honneur. *Address:* Heineken N.V., 2e Weteringplantsoen 21, 1017 ZD Amsterdam, Netherlands. *Telephone:* (020) 70.91.11.

HEINESEN, Knud; Danish airport administrator and fmr. politician; b. 26 Sept. 1932, Kerteminde; s. of Heine S. Heinesen and Else Rasmussen; m. 1st Aase Windfeld 1955 (died 1980); two s. one d.; m. 2nd Karen Vilhelmsen 1983; Teacher, Roskilde Folk School 1959, Prin. 1962–67; Sec. Econ. Council, Labour Movt. 1960; Gen. Sec. Fed. of Co-operative Socs. 1967–68; Chair. Radio Council 1967; Assoc. Prof. of Political Economy, Copenhagen Graduate School of Econs. and Business Admin. 1968; M.P. 1971–85; Minister for Educ. 1971–73, of the Budget Sept.–Dec. 1973, of Finance 1975–79, 1981–82, of Public Works Oct.–Dec. 1981; Chair. Social Democratic Parl. Group 1979–81; Political Vice-Chair. Social Democratic Party Sept. 1980–85; Dir.-Gen. of Copenhagen Airport 1985–; fmr. mem. numerous educational and radio cttees. etc.; Social Democrat. *Leisure interest:* painting. *Address:* Østerbrogade 95, 2100 Copenhagen Ø, Denmark. *Telephone:* 01-382031 (Office); 01-116600 (Home); 03-469181 (Summer).

HEINESEN, William; Danish (Faeroese) author; b. 15 Jan. 1900, Thorshavn, Faeroe Islands; s. of Zacharias Heinesen and Caroline Restorff; m. Elisa Johansen; three s.; ed. commercial schools, Copenhagen; writes generally about Faeroese subjects; also draws and paints; mem. Danish Literary Acad.; Scandinavian Literature Prize 1965. *Publications:* novels: Noatun 1938, Den sorte gryde 1949, Den fortabte spillemaend 1950, Moder syvstjeme 1952, Det Gode Håb 1964, Tarnet ved Verdens Ende 1976; stories: Det fortryllede lys 1957, Gamaliels besaeltelse 1960, Kur mod onder änder 1967, Don Juan fra Tranhuset 1970; poems: Højbjergning ved Havet 1924, Sange mod Vaardybet 1927, Den dunkle Sol 1936, Digte i udvalg 1959, Hymneog harmsag 1961, Panorama med renbue 1972. *Address:* 3800 Thorshavn, Faeroe Islands. *Telephone:* Thorshavn 1636.

HEINTEL, Erich, DR. PHIL.; Austrian professor of philosophy; b. 29 March 1912, Vienna; s. of Rudolf Heintel and Luise Kästner; m. 1st Margarete Weininger 1939 (died 1982), 2nd Waltraud Sammet 1984; two s. two d.; ed. Univ. of Vienna; Dozent Univ. of Vienna 1940, Prof. of Philosophy 1952–82, Prof. Emer. 1982–; mem. Austrian Acad. of Sciences, Allgemeine Gesellschaft für Philosophie in Deutschland, Humboldt-Gesellschaft, Internationale Hegel-Vereinigung; Hon. Pres. Vienna Philosophical Soc.; Grosses Ehrenzeichen für Verdienste um die Republik Österreich; Ehrenmedaille der Bundeshaupstadt Wien in Gold; Bundesverdienstkreuz (Fed. Republic of Germany); other awards and decorations; D. Theol. h.c. (Hamburg) 1986. *Publications include:* Hegel und die analogia entis 1958, Die beiden Labyrinthe der Philosophie 1968, Einführung in die Sprachphilosophie 1972, Grundriss der Dialektik (2 vols.) 1984, Was kann ich wissen? Was soll ich tun? Was darf ich hoffen? Versuch einer gemeinverständigen Einführung in das Philosophieren 1986, Gesammelte Abhandlungen (2 vols.) 1988, Die Stellung der Philosophie in der "universitas litterarum" 1989, Mündiger Mensch und christlicher Glaube 1989. *Leisure interests:* philosophy, collecting mushrooms, swimming. *Address:* 1190 Vienna, Bauernfeldgasse 7/1/6, Austria. *Telephone:* (222) 36 15 62.

HEINTZE, Gerhard, DR.THEOL.; German ecclesiastic; b. 14 Nov. 1912, Wehre, Kreis Goslar; s. of late Pastor Karl and Cölestine (née Schwerdtmann) Heintze; m. 1st Ilse Hoppe 1941 (died 1977); two s. three d.; m. 2nd Renate Wigand 1979; ed. Humanistisches Gymnasium, Bremen, and theological studies in Tübingen, Göttingen and Manchester; ordained 1938; Pastor of Hollern-Tweilenfleth, Netherlands 1942–46; Insp. of Mission, Hermannsburg 1946–50; Dir. of seminary, Hannover 1950–57; Sr. Minister, Hildesheim 1957–61; Sr. Minister of Lower Saxony, Hildesheim 1961–65; Bishop of Protestant-Lutheran Church, Brunswick 1965–82. *Publication:* Luthers Predigt von Gesetz und Evangelium 1958. *Leisure interest:* music. *Address:* Herdweg 100, 7000 Stuttgart 1, Federal Republic of Germany.

HEINZ, Henry John, III, M.A.; American politician and former company executive; b. 23 Oct. 1938, Pittsburgh, Pa.; s. of Henry John Heinz II and Joan (Diehl) Heinz McCauley; m. Teresa Simoes-Ferreira 1966; three s.; ed. Yale Univ., Harvard Business School; served U.S.A.F. 1963–69; Gen. Production Man. Marketing H. J. Heinz Co. 1965–70; lecturer, Carnegie-Mellon Univ. Graduate School of Industrial Admin. 1970–71; mem. House of Reps. from 18th Dist. of Pa. 1971–76; Senator from Pennsylvania Jan. 1977–; del to Republican Nat. Convention 1968, 1972; Chair. Pa. Republican Platform Cttee. 1970, Chair. Senate Special Cttee. on Aging 1981–, Republican Senatorial Campaign 1985–; Trustee, Howard Heinz Endowment, Children's Hosp., Pittsburgh; Chair. H. J. Heinz II Charitable and Family Trust; mem. Bd. of Overseers, Harvard Business School, mem. American Inst. of Public Service. *Address:* 277 Russell Senate Office Building, Washington, D.C. 20510 (Office); 1950 Squaw Run Road, Pittsburgh, Pa. 15238, U.S.A. (Home).

HEISBOURG, Georges; Luxembourg diplomatist; b. 19 April 1918, Hesperange; s. of Nicolas and Berthe (Ernsterhoff) Heisbourg; m. Hélène Pinet 1945; two s. one d.; ed. Luxembourg and Univs. of Grenoble, Innsbruck and Paris; Chief, Govt. Press and Information Service 1944–45; Attaché and Sec. to Legation, London 1945–51; Sec., Counsellor, Dir. Political Affairs, Ministry of Foreign Affairs 1952–58; Amb. to U.S.A. 1958–64; Perm. Rep. to UN 1958–61; Minister to Canada 1959–60, Amb. 1960–64; Minister to Mexico 1959–60, Amb. 1960–64, to Netherlands 1964–67, to France 1967–70; Perm. Rep. to OECD 1967–70; Sec.-Gen. WEU 1971–74; Amb. to U.S.S.R. 1974–77; head of Luxembourg del. to Conf. on Security and Co-operation in Europe meeting, Belgrade 1977–78; Perm. Rep. to Council of Europe 1978–79; Amb. to Federal Republic of Germany 1979–83; numerous decorations from W. European countries and Mexico. *Leisure interests:* tennis, swimming. *Address:* c/o Ministry of Foreign Affairs, Luxembourg-Ville, Luxembourg.

HEISKELL, Andrew; American press executive; b. 13 Sept. 1915, Naples, Italy; s. of Morgan and Ann (Hubbard) Heiskell; m. 1st Cornelia Scott 1937 (dissolved), 2nd Madeleine Carroll 1950 (dissolved), 3rd Marian Sulzberger Dryfoos 1965; three c.; ed. Germany, Switzerland, Univ. of Paris and Harvard School of Business Administration; Science teacher, Ecole du Montcel; settled in the U.S.A. 1935; Reporter, New York Herald Tribune 1936–37; Editorial staff Life magazine 1937–39, Asst. Gen. Man. 1939–40, Paris office 1940–42, Gen. Man. 1942–46, Publisher 1946–60; Vice-Pres. Time Inc. 1949–50, Chair. of Dirs. 1960–69, C.E.O. 1969–80; Chair. Pres.'s Cttee. on Arts and Humanities 1982–; mem. Bd. of Dirs. Inter-American Press Asscn., Int. Exec. Service Corps., New York Urban Coalition; mem. Bd. of Trustees Bennington Coll., New York Urban Coalition, The New York Public Library (Chair. 1981–); Co-Chair. Nat. Urban Coalition; Fellow, Harvard Coll. *Address:* Time Inc., Time & Life Building, Rockefeller Center, New York, N.Y. 10020, U.S.A. *Telephone:* (212) 841-3495.

HEISLER, Philip Samuel; American journalist; b. 8 Sept. 1915, Dallastown, Pa.; s. of Chauncey Franklin and Anna (Flinchbaugh) Heisler; m. Helen Theresa Surratt 1945; ed. Pennsylvania State Coll.; Reporter McKeesport (Pa.) Daily News 1937–39; Sun-papers War Corresp. 1944–45; Ed. Sunday Sun Magazine, Baltimore 1945–46; Film Dir. Television Station WMAR-TV, Baltimore 1947–49; Reporter Evening Sun, Baltimore 1939–44, Man. Ed. 1949–82; Owner Rabar Racing Stable. *Address:* The Sunpapers, Baltimore, Md. 21201 (Office); 4406 Bedford Place, Baltimore, Md. 21218, U.S.A. (Home).

HEISSENBÜTTEL, Helmut; German writer and broadcasting official (retd.); b. 21 June 1921; s. of Hans and Klara (née Lorenz) Heissenbüttel; m. Ida Warnholtz 1954; one s. three d.; ed. Kaiser-Wilhelms-Gymnasium, Wilhelmshaven, Realgymnasium, Papenburg, Technische Hochschule,

Dresden, and Univs. of Leipzig and Hamburg; Publicity Man. Claassen Verlag, Hamburg 1955-57; Editor, Süddeutscher Rundfunk, Stuttgart, 1957-58, Chief Ed. Radio Essay 1959-81; mem. Akad. der Künste, Berlin, Akad. der Wissenschaften und der Literatur, Mainz; Hugo-Jacobipreis 1960, Georg-Büchner-Preis 1969, Hörspielpreis der Kriegsblinden 1970, Heinrich-Böll-Preis 1984. *Publications:* Kombinationen 1954, Topographien 1956, Textbuch 1-6 1960-65, 8 1985, 9 und 10 1986, 11 1987, Briefwechsel über Literatur (with Heinrich Vormweg) 1971, D'Alemberts Ende (novel) 1971, Zur Tradition der Moderne (essays and notes) 1964-71, 1972; Hörspiele, Gelegenheitsgedichte und Klappentexte 1973; Eichendorffs Untergang 1978, Wenn Adolf Hitler den Krieg nicht gewonnen hätte 1979, Das Ende der Alternative 1980, Ödipus made in Germany 1981, Von fliegenden Fröschen . . .1982, Neue Herbste 1983. *Leisure interests:* photography, detective stories, music, art. *Address:* Dorfstrasse 7, 2209 Borsfleth, Federal Republic of Germany. *Telephone:* (04824) 1891.

HEITSCH, Ernst, D.PHIL.; German professor of classics; b. 17 June 1928, Celle; s. of Ernst Heitsch and Luise Meineke; m. Paula Sötemann 1961; two s. one d.; ed. Univ. Göttingen; Univ. Lecturer in Classical Linguistics Univ. Göttingen 1960-66, Professor 1966-67; Prof. of Classical Linguistics Univ. of Regensburg 1967-; mem. Akad. der Wissenschaften und der Literatur zu Mainz. *Publications:* Die griechischen Dichterfragmente der römischen Kaiserzeit 1963, Epische Kunstsprache und Homer 1968, Parmenides 1974, Parmenides und die Anfänge der Erkenntniskritik und Logik 1979, Xenophanes 1983, Antiphon aus Rhamnus 1984, Willkür und Problembewusstsein in Platons Kratylos 1984, Platon über die rechte Art zu reden und zu schreiben 1987, Überlegungen Platons im Theaetet 1988; numerous articles in periodicals. *Leisure interest:* sailing. *Address:* Mattinger Strasse 1, D-84 Regensburg, Federal Republic of Germany. *Telephone:* (0941) 31944.

HELAISSI, Sheikh Abdulrahman Al-; Saudi Arabian diplomatist; b. 24 July 1922; ed. Univs. of Cairo and London and in Islamic Religious Law; Official at Ministry of Foreign Affairs; Secretary to Embassy London 1947-54; Under-Sec. Ministry of Agriculture 1954-57; Rep. to UN, and at conferences on Health, Agriculture, Wheat, Sugar and Locusts; Head of Del. to FAO 1955-61; Amb. to Sudan 1957-60; Del. to Conf. of Non-Aligned Nations, Belgrade 1961; Amb. to Italy and Austria 1961-66, to U.K. 1966-76, concurrently to Denmark 1966-70. *Publication:* The Rehabilitation of the Bedouins 1959. *Address:* c/o Olaya, Division 3, Riyadh, P.O. Box 8062, Saudi Arabia.

HELD, Al; American artist; b. 12 Oct. 1928, New York; ed. Art Students League, New York, and Acad. de la Grande Chaumière, Paris; Prof. of Art, Yale Univ. 1962-78, Adjunct Prof. of Painting 1978-; one-man shows at André Emmerich Gallery, New York, 1965, 1967, 1968, 1970, 1972, 1973, 1975, 1976, 1978, 1979, 1980, 1982, 1984, Inst. of Contemporary Art, Boston 1978, Robert Miller Gallery, New York 1980, 1982, Richard Gray Gallery, Chicago 1984, Pace Editions, New York 1984 and also in Zürich, Amsterdam, Stuttgart, London etc.; has participated in numerous group shows and work appears in many permanent collections inc. Whitney Museum, Museum of Modern Art, New York, San Francisco Museum of Art, Nat. Gallery Berlin, Hirshhorn Museum and Sculpture Gardens, Washington; co-founder Brata Gallery, New York 1965; Guggenheim Fellow 1966; Logan Medal, Art Inst. of Chicago 1964. *Publications:* articles in professional journals. *Address:* c/o Andre Emmerich Gallery, 41 E. 57th Street, New York, N.Y. 10022, U.S.A.

HELD, Heinz Joachim, DR. THEOL.; German theologian; b. 16 May 1928, Wesseling/Rhein; s. of Heinrich Held and Hildegard Röhrig; m. Anneliese Novak 1959; one s. three d.; ed. Wuppertal, Göttingen, Heidelberg, Bonn and Austin, Tex.; research asst. Wuppertal Theological Seminary 1953-56; clergyman, Friedrichsfeld/Niederrhein 1957-64; Prof. of Theology, Buenos Aires Lutheran Seminary 1964-68; Pres. River Plate Evangelical Church, Buenos Aires 1968-74; mem. Cen. Cttee. World Council of Churches 1968-; Moderator of Cen. Cttee. and Exec. Cttee. 1983-; Pres. Office for Foreign Relations of Evangelical Church in Germany 1975-; Chair. Nat. Council of Churches, Fed. Repub. of Germany 1982-88; Hon. Dr.theol. (Lutheran Theological Acad. Budapest) 1985; Hon. D.D. (Acad. of Ecumenical Indian Theology and Church Admin., Madras) 1988. *Leisure interests:* stamp collecting, amateur music (piano). *Address:* Herrenhäuser Strasse 12, D-3000 Hannover 21, Federal Republic of Germany. *Telephone:* (0511) 71 11 125.

HELD, Martin; German actor; b. 11 Nov. 1908, Berlin; s. of Max and Emma Held; m. Lore Hartling 1967; two s.; ed. schools in Berlin, Staatliche Schauspielschule, Berlin; Apprentice, Siemens 1929; acted in theatre at Tilsit, Elbing, Bremerhaven and Darmstadt 1931-41; Städtische Bühnen, Frankfurt-am-Main 1941-51; mem. Staatstheater, Berlin 1951-; many appearances in films and on television; mem. Acad. der Künste, Berlin, Hamburg Acad. of Dramatic Art; Preis der Deutschen Kritiker 1952, Bundesfilmpreis/Filmband in Gold 1955; Berlin Arts Prize 1958, Ernst-Lubitsch Prize 1967, Gold Kamera Prize 1970, Best Male Actor's Award, Int. Prague Film Festival 1970; Bundesverdienstkreuz (1st class); Staatsschauspieler. *Leisure interests:* general literary interests. *Address:* Albertinenstrasse 15-16, 1000 Berlin 37; Agentur Mackeben, 1 Berlin 33, Douglasstrasse 2, Germany.

HELD, Richard M., M.A., PH.D.; American professor of psychology; b. 10 Oct. 1922, New York; m. Doris Bernays; three c.; ed. Columbia and Harvard Univs. and Swarthmore Coll.; Research Asst. Dept. of Psychology, Swarthmore Coll. 1946-48; Research Asst., Teaching Fellow, and N.I.H. Postdoctoral Fellow, Dept. of Psychology, Harvard Univ. 1949-53; Instructor, Asst. Prof., Assoc. Prof., Prof. and Chair. Dept. of Psychology, Brandeis Univ. 1953-62; mem. Inst. for Advanced Study, Princeton 1955-56; Sr. Research Fellow of Nat. Science Foundation and Visiting Prof. Dept. of Psychology, M.I.T. 1962-63, Prof. of Experimental Psychology, Dept. of Psychology and Brain Sciences, M.I.T. 1963-, Dept. Chair. 1977-86; Fellow, American Acad. of Arts and Sciences; mem. N.A.S. and many other learned socs.; numerous other professional appointments; Glenn A. Fry Award 1979, H. C. Warren Medal 1983, Kenneth Craik Award 1985; Dr. h.c. (Free Univ. of Brussels 1984, New England Coll. of Optometry). *Address:* Department of Brain and Cognitive Sciences, E10-139, Massachusetts Institute of Technology, 79 Amherst Street, Cambridge, Mass. 02139, U.S.A. *Telephone:* 617-253-5745.

HELDERS, Gerardus Philippus, LL.D.; Netherlands civil servant and politician; b. 9 March 1905, Rotterdam; s. of Gerardus Philippus Helders and Jacoba Kleinbloesem; m. Pieternella Margaretha Meijer 1930 (died 1982); one s. four d.; ed. Leiden Univ.; employed in the former Netherlands East Indies, rising to grade of Finance Inspector 1930-40; at Ministry of Finance, The Hague 1946-48; Dir. Nationale Trust Maatschappij, Amsterdam 1948-57; Minister for Overseas Affairs 1957-59; Counsellor of State 1959-75; Pres. Prins Bernhard Foundation 1960-; Hon. mem. Life Int. Fiscal Asscn. 1957; Commdr. Order of Orange Nassau, Kt. Order of the Netherlands Lion, War Cross and other decorations for service in the army (Gen. Staff) and Netherlands East Indies, Grand Cross Order of Homayoun (Iran). *Leisure interests:* music, literature and farming. *Address:* 610 Theo Mann Bouwmeesterlaan, 2597 HM The Hague, Netherlands. *Telephone:* 070-280635.

HELÉN, Nils Gunnar, PH.D.; Swedish politician; b. 5 June 1918, Vingåker; s. of Gustaf Helén and Ingeborg (née Andersson); m. Ingrid Rying 1938; one s. one d.; with Swedish Broadcasting Corpn. 1939-49; Literary Ed. of Stockholms-Tidningen 1949-55; mem. Parl. 1953-66, 1970-76; mem. Nordic Council 1954-64, 1970-76; Asst. Prof. Univ. of Stockholm 1956-; Gov. of Prov. of Kronoberg 1965-70; Chair. Liberal Party of Sweden 1969-75; mem. Bd. of Govs. Swedish Nat. Debt Office 1974-77; Gov. of Stockholm 1977-84; Chair. Swedish Broadcasting Corpn. 1978-83; Chair. Liberal Newspapers K.B. 1976-, Nerikes Allehanda A.B. 1976-, Hjalmar Bergman Soc. 1986-. *Publications:* Birger Sjöberg Kriser och kransar i stilhistorisk belysning 1946, Röst i Radion 1950, Friheten och de två systemen 1954, Skola, yrke, samhälle i USA 1955, 7 år av skolreformer 1957, Rätt till utbildning 1960, Svenska författare 1964, Politik för ett mänskligare samhälle 1970, Frihet i gemenskap 1974, Fröken på Tagel 1977, Bättre Svenska 1984. *Address:* Jakob Dubbesväg, S-13150 Saltsjöduvnäs, Sweden. *Telephone:* 0468-209181 (Office); 0468-7168245 (Home).

HELFET, Arthur (Jacob), M.CH. (ORTH.) M.D., F.R.C.S., F.R.S.M., F.A.C.S.; American orthopaedic surgeon; b. 18 Feb. 1907, Calvinia, Cape Prov., S. Africa; s. of Leon Helfet and Sarah Levin; m. Nathalie Freeman 1939; three s. one d.; ed. Univs. of Cape Town and Liverpool; Robert Gee Fellow in Anatomy 1934; Ridgeway Research Scholar, Univ. of Liverpool 1938; Moynihan Fellow, Asscn. of Surgeons of G.B. and N. Ireland 1938; MRC Grantee 1938; war service 1938-45; Hunterian Prof. Royal Coll. of Surgeons 1941, 1958; Dir. Dept. of Orthopaedic Research, Univ. of Cape Town 1946-55; Sr. Part-time Lecturer in Orthopaedic Surgery, Univ. of Cape Town and Sr. Orthopaedic Surgeon, Groote Schuur Hosp. and Princess Alice Orthopaedic Hosp., Univ. of Cape Town 1946-61; Prof. and Chair. Dept. of Orthopaedic Surgery, Albert Einstein Coll. of Medicine, New York 1961-72, Prof. Emer. 1975-; numerous clinical appts., visiting professorships and other professional appts.; mem. Royal Soc. of S. Africa, American Medical Asscn. and numerous other learned socs. *Publications:* The Management of Internal Derangements of the Knee 1963, Disorders of the Knee 1974, Disorders of the Lumbar Spine (with D. Gruebel-Lee) 1977, Disorders of the Foot (with D. Gruebel-Lee) 1980; book chapters. *Address:* 420 Montebello, Montrose Street, Newlands, Cape Town 7700, South Africa. *Telephone:* 686-8331.

HELGADÓTTIR, Ragnhildur; Icelandic politician; b. 26 May 1930, Reykjavík; m. Þor Vilhjálmsson; four c.; ed. Reykjavík Coll. and Univ. of Iceland; Dist. Court advocate 1965; M.P. 1956-63, 1971-79, 1983-; Speaker, Lower House of the Althing 1961-62, 1974-78; Pres. Nordic Council 1975; mem. Cen. Cttee. Independence Party 1963-71, 1979-; Minister of Educ. 1983-85, of Health, Social Security and Communications 1985-87. *Address:* c/o Ministry of Health, Social Security and Communications, Reykjavík, Iceland.

HELGASON, Hördur, B.A.; Icelandic diplomatist, b. 27 March 1923, Isafjördur; s. of Helgi Gudbjartsson and Sigrún Júlíusdóttir; m. Sarah Ross Boynton 1946; one s. four d.; ed. Duke Univ. N.C.; in govt. service 1947-, Customs and Revenue Dept., Reykjavík 1947-48; Attaché, Paris 1948-49; Deputy Perm. Rep. to NATO Council 1952-60; Head Defence Div., Ministry of Foreign Affairs 1960-66, Counsellor, then Minister-Counsellor, Washington D.C. 1966-73, Deputy Perm. Sec. 1973-76, Amb., Perm. Under-Sec. and Sec. Parl. Foreign Relations Cttee. 1979-82; Perm. Rep. to UN,

1982-86; Amb. to Denmark (also accred. to Italy, Israel and Turkey) 1986-. *Leisure interests:* reading, salmon fishing. *Address:* Icelandic Embassy, Dantes Plads 3, 1556 Copenhagen V, Denmark. *Telephone:* (01) 15-96-04.

HELGASON, Ingi Ragnar; Icelandic lawyer; b. 29 July 1924; s. of Helgi Gudmundsson and Eyrún Helgadóttir; m. 1st Asa Gudmundsdóttir 1951 (died 1962), 2nd Ragna M. Thorsteins 1965; one s. three d.; ed. Univ. of Iceland; mem. City Council of Reykjavík 1950-62; pvt. law practice, Reykjavík 1953-81; mem. Man., Cen. Bank of Iceland 1957-60, Bd. of Dirs. 1960-68, 1973-85, fmr. Chair.; mem. Bd. of Dirs. Icelandic Cement Factory 1960-68; Chair. Bd. of Dirs. Icelandic Industrial Fund 1971-74, 1979-83; Man. Dir. Icelandic Fire Insurance Co. July 1981-. *Leisure interests:* excursions, filming, chess. *Address:* Hagamel 10, Reykjavík (Home); Brunabótafélag Islands, Laugavegur 103, Reykjavík, Iceland (Office). *Telephone:* 18404 (Home); 26055 (Office).

HELGASON, Jón; Icelandic politician; b. 4 Oct. 1931, Seglbúdir, Vestur-Skaftafellssýsla; m. Gudrún Porkelsdóttir; two c.; ed. Reykjavík Coll.; farmer at Seglbúdir 1951-; mem. Althing 1974-, First Vice-Pres. of Upper House 1978-79; Pres. of Althing 1979-83; Minister of Agric. and Minister of Justice and Ecclesiastical Affairs 1983-88; mem. Bd. State Electrical Network 1978-; Chair. of Bd. Jardefnaidnadur 1980-. *Address:* Arnarhváli, Reykjavík, Iceland.

HELINSKI, Donald Raymond, PH.D.; American professor of biology; b. 7 July 1933, Baltimore, Md.; s. of George L. Helinski and Marie M. Helinski; m. Patricia M. Doherty, 1962; one s. one d.; ed. Univ. of Maryland, Western Reserve Univ., Cleveland, Ohio, Stanford Univ.; U.S. Public Health Service Postdoctoral Fellow Stanford Univ. 1960-62; Asst. Prof., Princeton Univ. 1962-65; Assoc. Prof. Dept. of Biology, Univ. of Calif., San Diego 1965-70, Prof. 1970-, Chair. Dept. of Biology 1979-81, Dir. Center for Molecular Genetics 1984-; mem. Nat. Inst. Health Advisory Cttee. on DNA Recombinant Research 1975-78. *Publications:* over 100 publications and 32 review articles in the fields of biochemistry, molecular genetics and microbiology. *Address:* Department of Biology, University of California, San Diego, La Jolla, California, 92093, U.S.A.

HELLER, Joseph, M.A.; American writer; b. 1 May 1923, Brooklyn; m. 1st Shirley Held 1945; one s. one d.; m. 2nd Valerie Humphries 1987; ed. New York Univ., Columbia Univ., New York, Univ. of Oxford; Instructor, Pa. State Univ. 1950-52; advertisement writer, Time magazine 1952-56, Look magazine 1956-58; Promotion Man. McCall's magazine 1958-61; fmr. teacher of writing, Yale Univ., Univ. of Pa., City Univ., New York; Nat. Inst. of Arts and Letters grant for Literature 1963; served in U.S.A.A.F., rank of Lieut., World War II; Prix Médicis Etranger 1985. *Publications:* Catch 22 (novel) 1961, We Bombed in New Haven (play) 1968, Something Happened (novel) 1974, Clevinger's Trial (play) 1974, Good as Gold (novel) 1979, God Knows (novel) 1984, No Laughing Matter (with Speed Vogel) 1985, Poetics (novel) 1987, Picture This (novel) 1988. *Address:* c/o Dell Pub. Co., One Dag Hammarskold Plaza, New York, N.Y. 10017, U.S.A.

HELLESEN, Gunnar; Norwegian politician; b. 23 Feb. 1913, Haugesund; s. of late Captain Gunnar E. Hellesen and Gina Johannessen; m. Marit Landrog 1946; one s. two d.; ed. commercial education; entered insurance business before Second World War; prisoner-of-war 1940-45; mem. Haugesund City Council 1946-, Council Presidency 1952; Mayor of Haugesund 1955, 1958-59; mem. Storting 1961-69, Chair. Finance Cttee. 1965-69; Gov. Province of Rogaland 1969-73; Minister of Defence 1970-71; Bank Man. Norske Creditbank 1974-; Chair. Bd. Norwegian Oil Directorate 1972-78, Norwegian Industrial Fund 1973-76, Bd. Hangesund Mek. Verksted A/S 1980-; Conservative. *Address:* Nedstrandsgt. 8, 5500 Haugesund, Norway.

HELLIWELL, Robert A., PH.D., American professor of radio science; b. 2 Sept. 1920, Red Wing, Minn.; s. of Harold Harlowe and Grace Robson Helliwell; m. Jean Perham 1942; three s. one d.; ed. Stanford Univ.; managed programme of ionospheric measurements and research aimed at improving wartime communications 1942; continued to teach, Stanford Univ., Prof. 1958-, now Dir. Stanford programme of research on whistlers and related ionospheric phenomena, including a world wide network of receiving stations and experiments in the OGO-series satellites; Dir. Center for Space Science and Astrophysics 1983-; mem. N.A.S.; Fellow Inst. of Electrical and Electronic Engineers, American Geophysics Union; mem. various Comms. of U.S. Nat. Cttee. of Int. Scientific Radio Union (URSI); fmr. Chair. Int. Comm. IV of URSI; fmr. Consultant to Environmental Science Services Admin., Boulder Labs., Consultant to Dept. of Defense, Defense Science Board; mem. Improved IME Scientific Advisory Group, NASA; Chair. Panel on Upper Atmosphere Physics, Cttee. of Polar Research, N.A.S. 1970-73; Antarctica Service Medal, N.A.S. 1966, Appleton Prize, Royal Soc. of London 1972. *Publications:* 75 technical and scientific publs.; Whistlers and Related Ionospheric Phenomena (monograph) 1965. *Leisure interests:* hiking, camping, gardening, reading, music, fencing. *Address:* Radioscience Laboratory, Stanford University, Stanford, Calif. 94305, U.S.A. *Telephone:* (415) 723-3582.

HELLMUTH, George Francis, M.ARCH.; American architect; b. 5 Oct. 1907, St. Louis, Mo.; s. of George William and Harriet Fowler Hellmuth; m. Mildred Lee Henning 1941; four s. one d.; ed. Washington Univ., St. Louis, Mo., Ecole des Beaux Arts, Fontainebleau; Gen. practice in father's firm (George W. Hellmuth) 1935-40; Asst. to Pres. Smith, Hinchman &

Grylls, Detroit, Mich. 1940-49; Partner Hellmuth, Yamasaki & Leinweber 1949-55; Chair. Bd. Hellmuth, Obata & Kassabaum, Inc. 1955-78, HOK-International Inc. 1977-86; Vice-Pres. Plannet Corpn. 1986-; f. and Chair. Datacon Techs. Inc. 1987-; principal int. work includes: King Saud Univ.; King Khaled Int. Airport, Riyadh; Nile Tower, Cairo; Univ. of West Indies, Trinidad; American Embassy, El Salvador; Taipei World Trade Center, Taiwan; Air Defence Command H.Q., Saudi Arabia; Burgan Bank, Kuwait; Pres. Bald Eagle Co.; Steedman Travelling Fellowship 1930; First Honor Award, A.I.A. 1956; Coll. of Fellows A.I.A. 1973. *Address:* 100 N. Broadway, St. Louis, Mo. 63102 (Office); 5 Conway Lane, St. Louis, Mo. 63124, U.S.A. (Home). *Telephone:* 314/421-2000 (Office).

HELLWIG, Fritz, DR.PHIL.HABIL.; German economist and European politician; b. 3 Aug. 1912, Saarbrücken; s. of Friedrich H. and Albertine (Christmann) Hellwig; m. Dr. Margarete Werners 1939; two s. one d.; ed. Marburg, Vienna and Berlin Univs.; Staff mem. of the Saarbrücken Chamber of Industry and Commerce 1933-39; Dir. of the Saarwirtschaftsarchiv 1936-39; Man. of the Dist. Orgs. of the Iron and Steel Industry at Düsseldorf and Saarbrücken, 1940-43; war service 1943-47; Econ. Adviser and Dir. of Deutsches Industrieinstitut, Cologne 1951-59; Substitute del., Consultative Assembly of Council of Europe 1953-56; mem. of Bundestag 1953-59; Chair. of the Econ. Affairs Cttee. of the Bundestag 1956-59; mem. of European Parl. 1959; mem. of High Authority of the European Coal and Steel Community, Luxembourg 1959-67; Vice-Pres. of the Comm. of the European Communities, Brussels 1967-70; Exec. mem. Bd. of German Shipowners' Asscn. 1971-73; Grosses Bundesverdienstkreuz mit Stern und Schulterband 1971. *Publications:* Westeuropas Montanwirtschaft, Kohle und Stahl beim Start der Montan-Union 1953, Saar zwischen Ost und West, Die wirtschaftliche Verflechtung 1954, 10 Jahre Schumanplan 1960, Gemeinsamer Markt und Nationale Wirtschaftspolitik 1961, Montanunion zwischen Bewährung und Belastung 1963, Politische Tragweite der europäischen Wirtschaftsintegration 1966, Das schöne Buch und der Computer 1970, Die Forschungs- und Technologiepolitik der Europäischen Gemeinschaften 1970, Verkehr und Gemeinschaftsrecht: Seeschiffahrt und Europäische Wirtschaftgemeinschaft 1971, Die deutsche Seeschiffahrt: Strukturwandel und künftige Aussichten 1973, Zur älteren Kartographie der Saargegend I 1977, II 1981, Alte Pläne von Stadt und Festung Saarlouis 1980, Die Hogenberg-Geschichtsblätter 1983, Landkarten der Pfalz am Rhein (with W. Reiniger and K. Stopp) 1984, Mittelrhein und Moselland im Bild alter Karten 1985, Überwindung der Grenzen. Robert Schuman zum Gedenken 1986, Caspar Dauthendeys Karte des Herzogtums Braunschweig 1987. *Leisure interests:* collecting old maps, views and illustrated books. *Address:* Klosterbergstrasse 117c, 5300 Bonn 2, Federal Republic of Germany. *Telephone:* (0228) 32 20 17.

HELLYER, Hon. Paul Theodore, P.C., B.A.; Canadian fmr. politician; b. 6 Aug. 1923, Waterford, Ont.; s. of Audrey S. Hellyer and Lulla M. Anderson; m. Ellen Jean Ralph; two s. one d.; ed. Waterford High School, Curtiss Wright Tech. Inst., California, and Univ. of Toronto; Fleet Aircraft Manufacturing Co., Fort Erie 1942-44; Royal Canadian Air Force 1944-45; Owner, Mari-Jane Fashions, Toronto 1945-56; Treas. Curran Hall Ltd. 1950, Pres. 1951-62; Pres. Trepil Realty Ltd. 1951-62; Pres. Hendon Estates Ltd. 1959-62; mem. House of Commons 1949-57, 1958-74, Parl. Asst. to Minister of Nat. Defence 1956-57, Assoc. Minister April-June 1957, Minister of Nat. Defence 1963-67, of Transport 1967-69, responsible for Central Mortgage and Housing Corpn. 1968-69; Chair. Task Force on Housing and Urban Devt. 1968; Acting Prime Minister 1968-69; joined Progressive Conservative Party July 1972; re-joined Liberal Party 1982; Opposition spokesman on Industry, Trade and Commerce 1973; Distinguished visitor, Faculty of Environmental Studies, York Univ. 1969-70; Founding Chair. Action Canada 1971; Syndicated Columnist, Toronto Sun 1974-84; Fellow Royal Soc. for Encouragement of the Arts. *Publications:* Agenda: A Plan for Action 1971, Exit Inflation 1981, Jobs For All: Capitalism on Trial 1984. *Leisure interests:* swimming, skin and scuba diving, stamp collecting. *Address:* Suite 506, 65 Harbour Square, Toronto, Ont. M5J 2L4, Canada.

HELMFRID, Staffan, PH.D.; Swedish professor of human geography; b. 13 Dec. 1927, Stockholm; s. of Hartwig E. W. Helmfrid and Greta Helmfrid (née Kristiansson); m. Antje Teichmann 1954; three d.; ed. Stockholm Univ.; Asst., Dept. of Geography, Stockholm Univ. 1951, Asst. Prof. 1955, Assoc. Prof. 1962, Research Fellow 1967, Prof. of Human Geography 1970-, Dean of Faculty of Social Sciences 1970, Pro-Rektor (Vice-Pres.) Stockholm Univ. 1974, Rektor 1978-; Chair. Bank of Sweden Tercentenary Foundation 1980-86, Fulbright Comm. in Sweden 1984-85; Kt., Royal Order of North Star; mem. Royal Acad. of Letters, History and Antiquities, Royal Acad. of Science. *Publications:* Östergötland Västanstång. Studien über die ältere Agrarlandschaft und ihre Genese 1962; books and articles on agrarian and historical geography; textbooks on geography and social science. *Leisure interests:* mountain hiking, folk dance. *Address:* Stockholm University, S-10691 Stockholm; Björkhagsvägen 40, S-18600 Vallentuna, Sweden (Home). *Telephone:* (08) 162271 (Univ.); (0762) 74833 (Home).

HELMREICH, Ernst J.M., M.D.; American professor of physiological chemistry; b. 1 July 1922, Munich, Germany; s. of G. Helmreich and A. Hesselbach; m. Rosemarie Hartmann 1949; two d.; ed. Univs. of Munich and Erlangen and Munich Inst. of Tech.; Fellow, German Research Council,

Dept. of Organic Chem. Munich Inst. of Tech. 1950-53; Instructor-in-charge, Isotope Research Lab. Univ. of Munich School of Medicine; Privat-dozent, Biological Chem., Univ. of Munich School of Medicine 1953-54; N.A.S. Visiting Fellow, Dept. of Biological Chem., Washington Univ. School of Medicine, St. Louis, Mo. 1954-56, Asst. Prof. for Biochem. in Medicine 1956-60, Assoc. Prof. 1961-68; Prof. and Chair. Dept. of Physiological Chem., Univ. of Würzburg School of Medicine 1968-; mem. Bavarian Acad. of Sciences, Deutsche Akad. der Naturforscher, Leopoldina; Pres. Soc. of Biol. Chemists 1973-75; Order of Merit of Fed. Repub. of Germany. *Publications:* numerous articles in international biochemical journals. *Leisure interest:* mountaineering. *Address:* Department of Physiological Chemistry, University of Würzburg Medical School, Koellikerstrasse 2, 8700 Würzburg, Federal Republic of Germany. *Telephone:* 931/31746 (Office); 931/271918 (Home).

HELMS, Jesse; American politician; b. 18 Oct. 1921, Monroe, N.C.; s. of Mr. and Mrs. J. A. Helms; m. Dorothy Jane Coble 1942; one s. two d.; ed. Wingate Coll. and Wake Forest Coll. (now Wake Forest Univ. at Winston-Salem); served U.S. Navy 1942-45; subsequently became city editor, The Raleigh Times and Dir. of news and programmes for Tobacco Radio Network and Radio Station WRAL; Admin. Asst. to Senators Willis Smith and Alton Lennon; Exec. Dir. N.C. Bankers Asscn. and Ed., The Tarheel Banker 1953-60; editorial writer and presenter, WRAL-TV and Tobacco Radio Network 1960; Exec. Vice-Pres., Vice-Chair. of Bd. and Asst. C.E.O. Capitol Broadcasting Co. (which operates WRAL-TV and Tobacco Radio Network) 1960-72; Senator from North Carolina 1973-, Chair. Senate Agric. Cttee. 1981-87, mem. Foreign Relations Cttee. 1981-, Ranking Repub. 1987-; Republican. *Leisure interests:* reading, community service, fishing. *Address:* 409 Dirksen Senate Office Building, Washington, D.C. 20510 (Office); 1513 Caswell Street, Raleigh, N.C. 27608, U.S.A. (Home). *Telephone:* (202) 224-6342 (Office).

HELMS, Richard M.; American government official and international consultant; b. 30 March 1913, St. Davids, Pa.; s. of Herman Helms and Marion McGarrah; m. 1st Julia Bretzman Shields 1939 (divorced 1968), one s.; m. 2nd Cynthia McKelvie 1968; ed. high schools in U.S.A., Switzerland and Germany, and Williams Coll.; worked for United Press and The Indianapolis Times 1935-42; joined U.S. Navy 1942, in Office of Strategic Service, Second World War; Central Intelligence Group 1946-47, Cen. Intelligence Agency 1947-73, Deputy Dir. for Plans 1962, Deputy Dir. 1965, Dir. 1966-73; Amb. to Iran 1973-76; int. consultant 1976-; Pres. Safeer Co., Washington 1977-; Nat. Security Medal 1983. *Address:* Safeer Co., Suite 402, 1627 K Street, Washington, D.C. 20006, U.S.A.

HELØE, Leif Arne; Norwegian dentist and politician; b. 8 Aug. 1932, Harstad; ed. Univ. of Oslo; school and dist. dentist, Harstad region 1957; Prof. of Community Dentistry, Univ. of Oslo 1975; mem. Harstad City Council 1960-69, mem. Municipal Exec. Bd. 1968-69, Mayor of Harstad 1968-69; proxy mem. Storting (Parl.) 1965-73; Minister of Health and Social Affairs 1981-86; Conservative. *Address:* c/o Ministry of Health and Social Affairs, Akersgaten 42, P.O. Box 8011, Oslo, Norway.

HÉLOU, Charles; Lebanese lawyer, journalist and politician; b. 1911; ed. St. Joseph (Jesuit) Univ. and Ecole Française de Droit, Beirut; Barrister, Court of Appeal and Cassation, Beirut 1936; founded newspaper L'Eclair du Nord, Aleppo, Syria 1932; founded Le Jour, Beirut 1934, Political Dir. until 1947; Lebanese Minister to Vatican 1947; Minister of Justice and Health, Lebanon 1954-55, of Educ. Feb.-Sept. 1964; Pres. of Lebanon 1970; Min. of State July-Aug. 1979; Pres. Association des Parlementaires de Langue Française 1973-; fmr. Sec.-Gen. Catholic Action of Lebanon. *Address:* Kaslik, Jounieh, Lebanon.

HEMMING, John Henry, M.A., D.LITT.; Canadian author and publisher; b. 5 Jan. 1935, Vancouver, B.C.; s. of H. Harold Hemming, M.C. and Alice L. Hemming; m. Sukie Babington-Smith 1979; one s. one d.; ed. Eton Coll. and McGill and Oxford Univs.; Dir. and Sec. Royal Geographical Soc. 1975-; Jt. Chair. Municipal Group Ltd., Hemming Publishing Ltd. 1976-; Chair. Brintex Ltd., Newman Books Ltd.; explorations in Peru and Brazil 1960, 1961, 1971, 1972, 1986-88; Pitman Literary Prize 1970; Bolton Prize for Latin American History 1971; Christopher Award (U.S.A.) 1971, Mungo Park Medal, Royal Scottish Geographical Soc. 1988; Orden de Merito (Peru) 1987. *Publications:* The Conquest of the Incas 1970, Tribes of the Amazon Basin in Brazil (with others) 1973, Red Gold: The Conquest of the Brazilian Indians 1978, The Search for El Dorado 1978, Machu Picchu 1982, Monuments of the Incas 1983, Change in the Amazon Basin, 2 vols. (ed.) 1985, Amazon Frontier: The Defeat of the Brazilian Indians 1987, Maracá 1988. *Leisure interests:* exploration, writing. *Address:* Hemming Publishing Ltd., 178-202 Great Portland Street, London, W1N 6NH, England. *Telephone:* 01-637 2400.

HEMMINGS, David Leslie Edward; British actor and feature film director; b. 18 Nov. 1941; m. 1st Genista Ouvry 1960, one d.; m. 2nd Gayle Hunnicutt 1969 (dissolved 1975), one s.; m. 3rd Prudence J. de Casembroot 1976, two s.; ed. Glyn Coll., Epsom; in entertainment industry 1949-, Dir. Int. Home Video FGH Pty. Ltd., Melbourne, Film and General Holdings Inc., California; appeared in The Turn of the Screw (English Opera Group) 1954. *Films include:* Five Clues to Fortune 1957, Saint Joan 1957, The Heart Within 1957, Men of Tomorrow 1958, In The Wake of a Stranger

1958, No Trees in the Street 1959, Some People 1962, Play it Cool 1962, Live it Up 1963, Two Left Feet 1963, The System 1964, Be My Guest 1965, Eye of the Devil 1966, Blow Up 1966, Camelot 1967, Barbarella 1967, Only When I Larf 1968, The Charge of the Light Brigade 1968, The Long Day's Dying 1968, The Best House in London 1968, Alfred the Great 1969, Fragment of Fear 1970, The Walking Stick 1970, Unman, Wittering & Zigo 1971, The Love Machine 1971, Voices 1973, Don't Worry Momma 1973, Juggernaut 1974, Quilp 1974, Profundo Rosso 1975, Islands in the Stream 1975, The Squeeze 1976, Power Play 1978, Harlequin 1980, Beyond Reasonable Doubt 1982; Jeeves (musical), Her Majesty's Theatre, London 1975; Scott Fitzgerald, BBC TV 1975, The Rime of the Ancient Mariner 1978 and Charlie Muffin 1979, ITV; Dir. feature films Running Scared 1972, The 14 1973 (Silver Bear Award, Berlin Film Festival 1973), Just a Gigolo 1978; Produced: Strange Behaviour 1981, Turkey Shoot 1981. *Leisure interest:* painting. *Address:* c/o Michael Whitehall Ltd., 125 Gloucester Road, London, SW7, England.

HEMPEL, Rt. Rev. Johannes, D.THEOL.; German ecclesiastic; b. 23 March 1929, Zittau; s. of Albert Hempel and Gertrud (née Buchwald) Hempel; m. Dorothea Schönbach 1956; two s. one d.; ed. Univs. of Tübingen, Heidelberg, Kirchliche Hochschule, Berlin; Rev. Evangelical Lutheran Church, Saxony 1952-57, Bishop 1972-; Student Pastor and teacher of theology, Leipzig 1957-72; a Pres. of WCC; Hon. D. Theol. *Address:* Tauscherstrasse 44, Dresden 8021, German Democratic Republic. *Telephone:* 35724.

HENDERSON, Denys Hartley, M.A., LL.B., C.B.I.M., F.R.S.A.; British business executive; b. 11 Oct. 1932, Colombo, Sri Lanka; s. of late John Hartley Henderson and Nellie Henderson (née Gordon); m. Doreen Mathewson Glashan 1957; two d.; ed. Aberdeen Grammar School and Univ. of Aberdeen; legal apprentice Messrs. Esslemont and Cameron 1952-55; Staff Capt. R.A.S.C. and Directorate Army Legal Services 1955-57; Commercial Asst. ICI 1957-58, various tasks 1958-74, Gen. Man. (Commercial) 1974-77, Chair. Paints Div. 1977-80, Main Bd. Dir. 1980-, Deputy Chair. 1986-87, Chair. 1987-; Chair. Stock Exchange Listed Cos. Advisory Cttee. 1987-; Dir. (non exec.) Barclays Bank PLC 1983-, Barclays PLC 1985-; mem. Law Soc. of Scotland 1965-; Chair. Court of Govs. of The Man. Coll., Henley 1989-; mem. Advisory Council Prince's Youth Business Trust, Pres.'s Cttee., CBI 1987-, Council, British Malaysian Soc. 1987-, New York Stock Exchange Listed Co. Advisory Cttee. 1988-, The Opportunity Japan Campaign Cttee. 1988-, Appeal Council, Winston Churchill Memorial Trust 1988-, Pres.'s Cttee., The Advertising Asscn. 1988-, Industry & Commerce Group, The Save The Children Fund 1988-; Trustee, British Museum (Natural History) 1989-; Hon. D.Univ. (Brunel) 1987; Hon. LL.D. (Univ. of Aberdeen) 1987. *Leisure interests:* family life, swimming, reading, travel, gardening and "unskilled but enjoyable" golf. *Address:* ICI Group Headquarters, 9 Millbank, London, SW1P 3JF, England (Office). *Telephone:* 01-834 4444.

HENDERSON, Donald Ainslie, M.D., M.P.H.; American professor of health policy and management; b. 7 Sept. 1928, Cleveland, Ohio; s. of David A. Henderson and Grace E. McMillan; m. Nana I. Bragg 1951; two s. one d.; ed. Oberlin Coll., Univ. of Rochester and Johns Hopkins Univ.; Intern, Mary Imogene Bassett Hospital, Cooperstown, New York 1954-55, Resident 1957-59; various posts at Communicable Diseases Center, Dept. of Health, Educ. and Welfare 1955-66, Chief Smallpox Eradication Program 1965-66; Asst. Prof. of Preventive Medicine and Community Health, Emory Univ. School of Medicine 1960-66; Chief Medical Officer, WHO Smallpox Eradication 1966-77; Dean and Prof. of Health Policy and Man., Johns Hopkins Univ. School of Hygiene and Public Health 1977-; mem. numerous professional socs., cttees. and advisory panels, etc. and recipient of numerous scientific awards and recognitions from orgs. in U.S.A., Canada, U.K., Ethiopia, Afghanistan, Germany, India and Pakistan; seven hon. degrees. *Publications:* more than 80 dealing primarily with smallpox eradication, epidemiology and immunization. *Address:* 615 N. Wolfe Street, Baltimore, Md. 21205 (Office); 3802 Greenway, Baltimore, Md. 21218, U.S.A. (Home).

HENDERSON, Eugénie Jane Andrina, B.A., F.B.A.; British professor of phonetics; b. 2 Oct. 1914, Newcastle upon Tyne; d. of William Alexander Cruickshank Henderson and Pansy Viola Schürer; m. George Meier 1941; four s. one d. (deceased); ed. Univ. Coll., London; Asst., British Broadcasting Cttee. on Spoken English 1935-38; Lecturer, Dept. of Phonetics, Univ. Coll., London 1937-39, Lecturer in Phonetics S.O.A.S. 1942-53, Reader 1953-63, Prof. 1963-82, Fellow 1981-, Emer. Prof. 1982-; Ministry of Economic Warfare 1939-41; Visiting Prof., Rangoon Univ. 1954 and Visiting Lecturer at several other univs.; Pres. Philological Soc. 1984-88; Hon. Fellow of S.O.A.S. *Publications:* Tiddim Chin: a descriptive analysis of two texts 1965, The Domain of Phonetics 1965, The Indispensable Foundation: a selection from the works of Henry Sweet 1971; numerous articles in learned journals. *Address:* 9 Briardale Gardens, Hampstead, London NW3 7PN, England. *Telephone:* 01-794 8862.

HENDERSON, Horace Edward; American public affairs consultant; b. 30 July 1917, Henderson, N.C.; s. of Thomas Brantley Henderson M.D. and Ethel Maude Duke; m. Vera Schubert 1966; two d.; ed. Coll. of William and Mary, Williamsburg, Virginia and Yale Univ.; Army Capt., Second World War; Owner, Henderson Real Estate, Williamsburg, Va. 1947-52; Vice-Pres. Jr. Chamber Int. 1951-52; Nat. Pres. U.S. Jr. Chamber of Commerce 1952-53; Asscns. Co-ordinator, Nat. Auto Dealers Asscn., Wash.

1954–55; Dir. Chamber of Commerce of the U.S.A. 1954; Exec. Cttee. U.S. Cttee. for the UN 1954; Trustee, Freedoms Foundation 1955; Vice-Chair. Operation Brotherhood 1954–56; Republican Party cand. for Congress 1956, Lieut.-Gov. of Va. 1957, Independent cand. for Senate 1972; Dir. Office of Special Liaison and Special Asst., Deputy Under-Sec. of State 1958; U.S. Del. to ILO 1959–60, WHO 1959–60, UNESCO 1960, FAO 1959, High Comm. for Refugees 1959, ECOSOC 1959, U.S. Del. to UN 1960; Deputy Asst. Sec. of State for Int. Orgs., Dept. of State, Washington, D.C. 1959–60; Chair. Republican Party of Virginia 1962–64; mem. Republican Nat. Cttee. 1962–64; Chair. of Bd., Henderson Real Estate Agency McLean, Va. 1965–69; Dir.-Gen. World Peace Through Law Center, Geneva 1965–69; Pres. and Chair. Community Methods Inc. 1969–75; Chair. Conv. for Peaceful Settlement of Int. Disputes 1974–75; Pres. Int. Domestic Devt. Corps 1975, Chair. Asscn. for Devt. of Educ. 1977–; Exec. Dir. World Asscn. of Judges 1968; Chair. Congressional Speaker Reform Cttee. 1976; Exec. Vice-Pres. American Lawmakers Asscn. 1977; Real Estate and Man. Consultant 1978–86; Pres. Williamsburg Vacations Inc. 1983–84, Nat. Asscn. for Free Trade 1986; mem. World Affairs Council. *Address:* 1100 Gough Street 15F, San Francisco, Calif. 94109, U.S.A. (Home). *Telephone:* (415) 928-3924 (Home).

HENDERSON, Sir (John) Nicholas, G.C.M.G., M.A.; British diplomatist (retd.); b. 1 April 1919, London; s. of Prof. Sir Hubert Henderson; m. Mary Barber 1951; one d.; ed. Stowe School and Hertford Coll., Oxford; Asst. Private Sec. to British Foreign Sec. 1944–47; served in British Embassies in Washington, Athens, Vienna, Santiago; Prin. Sec. to Foreign Sec. 1963–65; Minister, Madrid 1965–69; Amb. to Poland 1969–72, to Fed. Germany 1972–75, to France 1975–79, to U.S.A. 1979–82; Dir. Hambros PLC 1982–, Foreign and Colonial Investment Trust 1982–, Mercantile and Gen. Reinsurance Co. Ltd. 1982–, Tarmac 1983–, F & C Eurotrust 1984–, Eurotunnel PLC 1986–, Fuel Tech NV 1987–; Lord Warden of the Stanneries and Keeper of the Privy Seal of the Duke of Cornwall 1985–; Chair. Channel Tunnel Group 1985–86; Trustee, Nat. Gallery 1985–; mem. Council Duchy of Cornwall 1985–; Hon. Fellow, Hertford Coll., Oxford Univ.; Hon. D.C.L. (Oxford). *Publications:* Prince Eugen (biography), The Birth of NATO, The Private Office 1984, Channels and Tunnels 1987; various articles and stories in Horizon, New Writing, History Today, Country Life. *Leisure interests:* tennis, gardening. *Address:* 6 Fairholt Street, London, S.W.7, England. *Telephone:* 01-589 4291.

HENDERSON, Julia, M.A., PH.D.; American international official; b. 15 Aug. 1915, Du Quoin, Ill.; d. of Frank and Agnes Youngber Henderson; ed. Univs. of Illinois and Minnesota, and Littauer School of Public Admin., Harvard Univ.; Research Asst., Social Science Research Council; Tech. Adviser to Unemployment Compensation Div., Social Security Board; Lecturer in political science, Wellesley Coll.; worked in London with Preparatory Comm. of UN 1945–46; Chief, Policy Div., UN Bureau of Finance 1945–50; Dir. UN Div. of Social Welfare, Dept. of Econ. and Social Affairs 1950–54, Dir. Bureau of Social Affairs 1955–67; Assoc. Commr. and Dir. of Tech. Co-operation Operations for UN 1967–70; Sec.-Gen. Int. Planned Parenthood Fed. (IPPF) 1971–78; UN Consultant on Population Questions 1978–84; mem. U.S. Nat. Acad. of Public Admin; one of the founders of UN International School, New York 1947, Chair. of Bd. of Trustees 1964–71; Rene Sand Award of the Int. Council of Social Welfare 1962, Margaret Sanger Award (Planned Parenthood Fed. of America), Alumni Distinguished Service Award, Univ. of Ill. 1984, Population Award (Int. Council on Man. of Population Programmes) 1988; Hon. LL.D. (Smith Coll.), Hon. D.Hum.Litt. (Rider Coll.), Hon. D.H. (Silliman Univ., Philippines). *Leisure interests:* theatre, ballet, reading, golf, gardening. *Address:* 1735 Forest Road, Venice, Fla. 34293; 309 Deepwood Road, Chapel Hill, N.C. 27514, U.S.A. (April-Oct.). *Telephone:* (813) 497-4808 (Fla.); (919) 942-2693 (N.C.).

HENDERSON, Sir Nicholas (see Henderson, Sir (John) Nicholas).

HENDERSON, Patrick David, M.A.; British economist and international official; b. 10 April 1927, Sheffield; s. of late David Henderson and Eleanor Rowbotham; m. Marcella Kodicek 1960; one s. one d.; ed. Ellesmere Coll., Shropshire and Corpus Christi Coll., Oxford; Fellow and tutor in econs., Lincoln Coll., Oxford 1948–64; Commonwealth Fund Fellow, Harvard Univ. 1952–53; Econ. Adviser, H.M. Treasury 1957–58; Chief Economist, Ministry of Aviation 1964–66; Adviser, Harvard Devt. Advisory Service (Greece and Malaysia) 1967–68; Visiting Lecturer, Econ. Devt. Inst., World Bank 1968–69; with World Bank (IBRD) 1969–75, Dir. Econs. Dept. 1972–73; Prof. of Political Economy, Univ. Coll., London 1975–83; mem. Nat. Ports Council 1979–81; Special Adviser, Sec. of State for Wales 1978–79; mem. Bd. Commonwealth Devt. Corpn. 1980–83; Head, Dept. of Econs. and Statistics, OECD Jan. 1984–; Reith Lecturer, BBC 1985. *Publications:* Nyasaland: The Economics of Federation (co-author) 1960, Economic Growth in Britain (Ed. and contrib.) 1965, The Energy Sector in India 1975. *Leisure interests:* reading, walking, swimming, looking at buildings. *Address:* c/o Organization for Economic Cooperation and Development, 2 rue André Pascal, 75775 Paris Cedex 16, France. *Telephone:* 524-8710.

HENDERSON, Richard, PH.D., F.R.S.; British molecular biologist; b. 19 July 1945, Edinburgh; s. of John W. and Grace S. (Goldie) Henderson; m. Penelope Fitzgerald 1969; one s. one d.; ed. Hawick High School, Boroughmuir Secondary School, Univs. of Edinburgh and Cambridge; professional interest in structure and function of protein molecules, especially in biological membranes; Helen Hay Whitney Postdoctoral Fellow, Yale Univ., U.S.A. 1970–73; Fellow, Darwin Coll., Cambridge 1982–; mem. research staff, MRC Lab. of Molecular Biology 1973–. *Publications:* many scientific articles in books and journals. *Leisure interests:* canoeing, wine. *Address:* Medical Research Council Laboratory of Molecular Biology, Hills Road, Cambridge, CB2 2QH, England; *Telephone:* (0223) 248011.

HENDERSON, Robert Alistair; British business executive; b. 4 Nov. 1917; s. of Robert E. Henderson and Beatrice J. E. Henderson; m. Bridget E. Lowther 1947; two s. one d.; ed. Eton Coll. and Magdalene Coll. Cambridge; mil. service 1940–45; Jessel Toynbee & Co. Ltd. 1945–48; Borneo Co. Ltd. 1948–51; Robert Benson, Lonsdale & Co. Ltd. 1951, Dir. 1957; Dir. Kleinwort, Benson Ltd. 1961, Vice-Chair. 1970–71, Deputy Chair. 1971–75, Chair. 1975–83; Dir. Equitable Life Assurance Soc. 1958–81; Chair. Kleinwort Devt. Fund PLC (fmrly. Cross Investment Trust, Ltd.) 1969–, Kleinwort, Benson, Lonsdale PLC 1978–, Merchants Trust PLC 1985–, MT Oil & Gas, Ltd. 1985–; Deputy Chair. Cadbury Schweppes PLC 1983–, British Airways 1985–; Dir. Hamilton Bros. Oil & Gas Ltd., Hamilton Oil Great Britain PLC, Hamilton Oil Corpn., Inchcape PLC. *Leisure interests:* gardening, shooting, fishing. *Address:* 7 Royal Avenue, London, SW3 4QE, England.

HENDERSON, Sir William MacGregor, D.SC., F.R.C.V.S., F.R.S.E., F.R.S.; British veterinary surgeon; b. 17 July 1913, Edinburgh, Scotland; s. of the late William Simpson Henderson and Catherine Alice Macus Berry; m. Alys Beryl Goodridge 1941; four s.; ed. George Watson's Boys' Coll., Royal Veterinary Coll., Edinburgh, Univ. of Edinburgh; Research Officer Animal Virus Inst., Pirbright 1939–56, Deputy Dir. 1955–56; Dir. Pan-American Foot-and-Mouth Disease Center, Río de Janeiro, Brazil 1957–65; Dir. Agricultural Research Council Inst. for Research on Animal Diseases, Compton 1967–1972, Sec. to Council 1972–78; Chair. U.K. Genetic Manipulation Advisory Group 1979–82; mem. Bd. Dirs. Celltech Ltd. 1981–84, Wellcome Biotech. Ltd. 1983–, Pacific Aqua Foods Ltd. 1986–; Pres. Zoological Soc. of London 1984–, Royal Asscn. British Dairy Farmers 1985–87; Dalrymple-Champneys Award 1974, Massey-Ferguson Nat. Award 1980, Underwood-Prescott Award 1981; Corresp. mem. Argentinian Acad. Agronomy and Veterinary Science 1980–; Hon. D.M.V. (Edinburgh) 1974, Hon. Dr. Veterinary Science (Liverpool) 1977, Hon. D.Sc. (Bristol) 1985. *Publications:* Quantitative Study of Foot-and-Mouth Disease Virus 1949, Man's Use of Animals 1981, British Agricultural Research and the Agricultural Research Council 1981, A Personal History of Testing Foot-and-Mouth Disease Vaccines in Cattle 1985, numerous papers in scientific journals. *Leisure interests:* fauna and flora. *Address:* Zoological Society of London, Regent's Park, London, NW1 4RY (Office); Yarnton Cottage, High Street, Streatley, Berks., England (Home). *Telephone:* 01-722 3333 (Office); 0491-872612.

HENDRICKS, Barbara, B.SC., B.MUS.; American soprano; b. 20 Nov. 1948, Stephens, Ark.; d. of M. L. and Della Hendricks; m. Martin Engström 1978; one s. one d.; ed. Univ. of Neb. and Juilliard School of Music, New York, studying with Jennie Tourel; operatic début, San Francisco Opera (L'Incoronazione di Poppea) 1976; has appeared with opera companies of Boston, Santa Fe, Glyndebourne, Hamburg, La Scala (Milan), Berlin, Paris, Los Angeles, Florence and Royal Opera, Covent Garden (London), Vienna; recitals in most maj. centres in Europe and America; has toured extensively in U.S.S.R. and Japan; concert performances with all leading European and U.S. orchestras; has appeared at many maj. music festivals including Edin., Osaka, Montreux, Salzburg, Dresden, Prague, Aix-en-Provence, Orange and Vienna; nearly 40 recordings; nominated Goodwill Amb. for Refugees at UN 1987; Commdr. des Arts et des Lettres. *Film appearance:* La Bohème 1988. *Leisure interest:* reading. *Address:* c/o Opéra et Concert, 19 rue Vignon, 75008 Paris, France.

HENDRICKSE, Rev. Helenard Joe (Alan), B.A.; South African politician and religious official; b. 22 Oct. 1927, Uitenhage, Cape; m. Patricia Heber (Terry) 1957; two s. two d.; ed. Univ. of Fort Hare, Rhodes Univ.; ordained Minister of Uitenhage Congregational Church of Southern Africa; f. Blacks School Uitenhage 1951; elected Head United Congregational Church of Southern Africa 1972; teacher 1951–69; elected to Coloured Persons Rep. Council 1969, to Exec., responsible for Educ. 1975; Leader Labour Party of S.A. 1978–; elected to House of Reps. (Coloured Chamber) 1984, Chair. Ministers' Council 1984–86, Minister Without Portfolio and Chair. Ministers' Council, House of Reps. 1986–87. *Address:* Private Bag 9068, Cape Town, South Africa.

HENDRICKSE, Ralph George, M.D., F.R.C.P., F.M.C. (PAED.); British consultant paediatrician; b. 5 Nov. 1926, Cape Town, S. Africa; s. of William G. Hendrickse and Johanna T. (Dennis) Hendrickse; m. Begum Johanahara Abdurahman 1948; one s. four d.; ed. Livingstone High School, Cape and Univ. of Cape Town Medical School; Sr. Medical Officer, McCord Zulu Hosp. Durban 1949–54; Sr. Registrar, Univ. Coll. Hosp. Ibadan, Nigeria 1956–57; Lecturer, Sr. Lecturer, Univ. of Ibadan 1957–62, Prof. and Head, Dept. of Paediatrics 1962–69, Dir. Inst. of Child Health 1964–69; Sr. Lecturer and Dir. Diploma in Tropical Child Health Course, Univ. of Liverpool and Liverpool School of Tropical Medicine 1969–75, Prof. of Tropical Paediatrics 1975–, Dean Liverpool School of Tropical Medicine 1988–, Prof. and Head of newly created Dept. of Tropical Paediatrics and

Int. Child Health, Liverpool Univ. 1988–; Hon. Consultant Paediatrician, Liverpool Health Authority 1969–; founder and Ed.-in-Chief, Annals of Tropical Paediatrics 1981–; Frederick Murgatroyd Memorial Prize, Royal Coll. of Physicians 1970. *Publications:* Tropical Paediatrics: Update and Current Review 1981; over 150 articles in scientific journals (1954–86). *Leisure interests:* swimming, golf, gardening, painting, travel. *Address:* Department of Tropical Paediatrics, School of Tropical Medicine, Pembroke Place, Liverpool, L3 5QA (Office); 25 Riverbank Road, Heswall, Wirral, Merseyside, L60 4SQ, England. *Telephone:* 051 708 9393 (Office); 051 342 5510.

HENDRIKSEN, Hans, DR. PHIL.; Danish professor of oriental philology; b. 6 June 1913, Ulsted; s. of Kai and Gerda Hendriksen; m. Christiane Caspersen 1943; two d.; ed. Univs. of Copenhagen, Leipzig, Paris, and Uppsala; Prof. of Sanskrit and Linguistics, Uppsala Univ. 1947–51; Prof. of Indian Philology, Copenhagen Univ. 1951–83, Prof. Emer. 1983–. *Publications:* Untersuchungen über Bedeutung des Hethitischen für die Laryngaltheorie 1941, Syntax of Infinite Verb-forms of Pali 1944, Himachali Studies: I Vocabulary, II Texts, III Grammar 1976–86. *Leisure interest:* music. *Address:* Søllerød Park, 9-1, 2840 Holte, Denmark. *Telephone:* 02-802167.

HENG SAMRIN; Kampuchean politician; b. 1934; Political Commissar and Commdr. of Khmer Rouge 4th Infantry Div. 1976–78; led abortive coup against Pol Pot and fled to Viet-Nam 1978; Pres. Nat. Front for Nat. Salvation of Kampuchea Dec. 1978–; Pres. People's Revolutionary Council Jan. 1979– (took power after Vietnamese invasion of Kampuchea); Sec.-Gen. People's Revolutionary Party of Kampuchea Dec. 1981–. *Address:* Office of the President, Phnom-Penh, People's Republic of Kampuchea.

HENGSBACH, H.E. Cardinal Franz; German ecclesiastic; b. 10 Sept. 1910, Velmede, Paderborn; ordained 1937, elected to the titular Church of Cantano 1953, consecrated bishop 1953, transferred Essen 1957; cr. Cardinal 1988. *Address:* Bischöfliches Generalvikariat, Zwölfling 16, Postfach 100464, D-4300 Essen 1, Federal Republic of Germany. *Telephone:* (0201) 22; 22041.

HENKEL, Konrad, DR.ING.; German chemist and business executive; b. 20 Oct. 1915, Düsseldorf; s. of Dr. Hugo and Gerda Henkel née Janssen; m. Gabriele Hünermann 1955; four c.; ed. Technische Hochschule, Munich and Brunswick and Freiburg Univs.; Asst. to Prof. Dr. Richard Kuhn, Max-Planck Inst. for Medical Research, Heidelberg 1940–46; Man. Dir. Henkel and Cie. GmbH, Düsseldorf 1956–69, Chair. Supervisory Bd. 1961–; Chair. Bd. of Man. Henkel GmbH 1961–74, Vice-Chair. Supervisory Bd. 1961–74; Pres. and C.E.O. of Man. Bd. Henkel KGaA 1975–80, of Supervisory Bd. 1980–, Vice-Chair. Cttee. of Shareholders 1975–; Vice-Chair. Supervisory Bd. Deutsche Gold- und Silberscheideanstalt, Frankfurt; Chair. Supervisory Bd. Degussa 1982–; Pres. Industry Club e.V., Düsseldorf, Steuben-Schurz Asscn. in Düsseldorf e.V. 1972; mem. Bd. Asscn. of Chem. Industries in Germany 1976–; mem. Admin. Council of Cultural Cttee. of Fed. Asscn. of German Industry 1961–; Dr.rer.nat. h.c. (Düsseldorf). *Leisure interest:* golf. *Address:* Postfach 1100, 4000 Düsseldorf 1, Federal Republic of Germany.

HENLE, Christian Peter; German business executive; b. 9 Nov. 1938, Duisburg; s. of Günter and Anne-Liese (née Küpper) Henle; brother of Jörg Alexander Henle (q.v.); m. Dr. Susanne Beitz 1967; two s.; ed. High School, Duisburg, Institut d'Etudes Politiques, Paris; joined Klöckner Eisenhandel GmbH, Düsseldorf 1963–64; with Klöckner and Co., Duisburg 1964–65, Vice-Pres. Klöckner Inc., New York 1965–67; Pres. Klöckner Industrie-Anlagen GmbH, Duisburg 1967–70; mem. Bd. of Dirs. responsible for depts. for liquid fuels, motor fuels and lubricants, gas, chemicals, industrial plants, Klöckner and Co., Duisburg 1971–, partner 1977–; Chair. Supervisory Bd. Klöckner-Humboldt-Deutz AG (KHD), Cologne, Mietfinanz GmbH, Mülheim/Ruhr; mem. Supervisory Bd. KHD Humboldt Wedag AG, Cologne, Deutsche Babcock AG, Oberhausen, Gerling-Konzern Welt-Versicherungs-Pool AG, Cologne, Gerling-Konzern Globale Rückversicherungs-AG, Cologne, Knipping-Dorn GmbH, Herne; Chair. Advisory Bd. Fisser & v. Doornum, Hamburg, Montan Brennstoffhandel und Schiffahrt GmbH & Co. KG, Munich; mem. Advisory Bd. Dresdner Bank AG, Frankfurt, Arnold Knipping GmbH, Gummersbach; mem. of Bd. Mineralölwirtschaftsverband e.V., Hamburg; mem. Int. Advisory Bd. The American Univ., Washington, D.C., U.S.A.; Pres. Deutsche Gesellschaft für Auswärtige Politik e.V., Bonn; Verdienstkreuz am Bande des Verdienstordens (Fed. Repub. of Germany); Chevalier de l'Ordre du Mérite (Senegal). *Publication:* Auf dem Weg in ein neues Zeitalter (Ed. and Co-Author) 1985. *Leisure interests:* music, sports (tennis, golf), collecting contemporary works of art. *Address:* Klöckner & Co., Klöcknerhaus, 4100 Duisburg 1, Federal Republic of Germany. *Telephone:* 203/18 22 53.

HENLE, Jörg Alexander; German business executive; b. 12 May 1934, Aachen; s. of Dr. Günter and Anne-Liese (née Küpper) Henle; brother of Christian-Peter Henle (q.v.); two s. three d.; ed. Cologne, Munich, Princeton (N.J.), Stanford, Geneva and Berlin Univs.; joined Klöckner-Werke AG 1962; Man. Establecimientos Klöckner S.A., Buenos Aires 1964–65; Deputy mem. directorate of Klöckner Mannstaedt-Werke, Troisdorf 1965–67; mem. directorate, Klöckner-Werke AG, Hütte Bremen 1967–68; mem. Man. Bd. Klöckner-Werke AG 1968–71, Chair. Supervisory Bd. 1979–; Chair.

Supervisory Bd. Klöckner Stahl GmbH; Chair. Bd. of Man. Klöckner & Co. AG; mem. Supervisory Bd. Allianz Lebensversicherungs-AG, Mietfinanz GmbH, AG, Robert Bosch GmbH, Rheinisch-Westfälische Boden-Credit-Bank; mem. Advisory Bd. HERMES Kreditversicherungs-Aktiengesellschaft; Vice-Pres. Niederrheinische Industrie- und Handelskammer Duisburg-Wesel-Kleve zu Duisburg. *Leisure interests:* plastic arts, theatre, music. *Address:* Klöckner & Co. AG, Neudorfer Strasse 3-5, Postfach 10 08 51, 4100 Duisburg 1, Federal Republic of Germany. *Telephone:* 181.

HENLEY, Sir Douglas Owen, K.C.B.; fmr. British civil servant; b. 5 April 1919; m. June Muriel Ibbetson 1942; four d.; ed. London School of Econs.; served army 1939–46 (twice mentioned in despatches); joined H.M. Treasury 1946; Financial Counsellor, Tokyo and Singapore 1956–59; Asst. Under-Sec. of State, Dept. of Econ. Affairs 1964–69, Deputy Under-Sec. of State 1969; Deputy Sec. H.M. Treasury 1969–72, Second Perm. Sec. 1972–76; Comptroller and Auditor-Gen. 1976–81; adviser to Deloitte, Haskins and Sells 1981–; mem. Council, Girls' Public Day School Trust 1981–; Chair. London Small Business Property Trust 1982–; Hon. Fellow, L.S.E. 1974, Hon. LL.D. (Bath) 1981. *Address:* Walwood House, Park Road, Banstead, Surrey, SM7 3ER, England (Home). *Telephone:* (0737) 352626.

HENLEY, Elizabeth Becker, B.F.A., PH.D.; American playwright and actress; b. 8 May 1952, Jackson, Miss.; d. of Charles and Lydy Henley; ed. Univ. of Illinois; Pulitzer Prize for Drama 1981, N.Y. Drama Critics Circle Best Play Award 1981, George Oppenheimer/Newsday Playwriting Award 1980–81. *Publications:* Crimes of the Heart 1981, The Wake of Jamey Foster 1982, Am I Blue 1982, The Miss Firecracker Contest, The Debutante Ball 1985; screenplays: Nobody's Fool 1986, Crimes of the Heart 1986. *Address:* c/o Gilbert Parker, The William Morris Agency, 1350 Avenue of the Americas, New York, N.Y. 10019, U.S.A.

HENLEY, Ernest M(ark), PH.D.; American professor of physics; b. 10 June 1924, Frankfurt, Germany; s. of Fred S. Henley and Josy L. (née Dreyfuss) Henley; m. Elaine D. Dimitman 1948; one s. one d.; ed Coll. of City of New York and Univ. of Calif. (Berkeley); Eng. Airborne Instrument Lab. 1946–48; Physicist, Lawrence Berkeley Lab. 1950–51; Research Assoc. Stanford Univ. 1951–52; Lecturer, Columbia Univ. 1952–54; Asst. Prof., Univ. of Washington 1954–57, Assoc. Prof. 1957–61, Prof. of Physics 1961–, Chair. Dept. of Physics 1973–76, Dean, Coll. of Arts and Sciences 1979–; Chair. Nuclear Science Advisory Cttee. 1986–; mem. Bd. Dirs. Pacific Science Center 1984–, Wash. Tech. Center; mem. N.A.S.; Fellow, American Physical Soc., A.A.A.S.; F. B. Jenett Fellow 1952–53; N.S.F. Sr. Fellow 1958–59; Guggenheim Fellow 1967–68; N.A.T.O. Sr. Fellow 1976–77; Alexander von Humboldt Sr. Award 1984. *Publications:* co-author of Elementary Quantum Field Theory 1962, Subatomic Physics 1974, Nuclear and Particle Physics 1975. *Leisure interests:* skiing, swimming, climbing, tennis, bicycling, photography. *Address:* Department of Physics, FM-15, University of Washington, Seattle, Wash. 98195 (Office); 4408 55th Avenue N.E., Seattle, Wash. 98105, U.S.A.

HENLEY, William Ballentine, A.M., J.D., M.S. (P.A.), LL.D., SC.D., L.H.D.; American lecturer, cattle rancher, educationist and lawyer; b. 19 Sept. 1905, Cincinnati, Ohio; s. of W. H. Ballentine and May Ballentine (née Richards); m. Helen McTaggart 1942; ed. Univ. of Southern California and Yale Univ.; Attorney; Asst. to Co-ordination Officer, Univ. of Southern Calif. 1928–29 and 1930–33; Public Speaking Instructor, American Inst. of Banking 1928–29; Dir. of Religious Education, First Methodist Episcopal Church, New Haven, Conn. 1929–30; Exec. Sec. Women's Civic Conf. Univ. of Southern Calif. 1930–36; Asst. to Dean, School of Govt., Univ. of Southern Calif. 1933–35, Acting Dean and Acting Co-ordinating Officer 1935–37, Dir. Inst. of Govt. 1935–37, Dir. of Co-ordination and Assoc. Prof. of Public Admin. 1937–40; Pres. Calif. Coll. of Medicine 1940–65; Provost, Univ. of Calif., Irvine, Calif. Coll. of Medicine 1965–69; Pres. United Church of Religious Science 1969–, Prof. 1972–; Pres. Rotary Club Los Angeles 1955–56; Gov. District 528 Rotary Int. 1959–60; Chair. Host Club Exec. Cttee. for Rotary Int. Convention 1962; mem. Los Angeles, Calif. and American Bar Asscns., Asscn. of American Medical Schools, Acad. of Political and Social Sciences, Nat. Education Asscn.; Calif. Governor's Medical Advisory Cttee. on Civil Defense 1945–48, American Man. Asscn., American Asscn. for History of Medicine, Western Interstate Comm. for Higher Education; Past Pres. American Asscn. Osteopathic Colls.; Educational Consultant 1956–; owner, Creston Circle Ranch; Gen. Motors Exec. Speakers Panel 1956–73; on Bd. of Los Angeles Community Health Org. and of several charitable orgs.; mem. Defense Orientation Conf. Asscn. 1965–; Vice-Pres. Los Angeles Safety Council 1971–. *Publications:* The History of the University of Southern California, Man's Great Awakening (Beautiful Mud) 1974, and many magazine articles. *Leisure interests:* photography, tree culture. *Address:* Creston Circle Ranch, Paso Robles, Calif. 93446, U.S.A. *Telephone:* (805) 238-0356.

HENN, Walter, DR.ING; German architect; b. 20 Dec. 1912, Reichenberg/Bez. Dresden; s. of Karl Henn and Hedwig Bretschneider; m. Dr. med. Hilde Leistner 1938; two s. three d.; ed. Technische Hochschule Dresden and Akad. der Bildenden Künste, Dresden; Prof. of Bldg. and Industrial Construction, Technische Hochschule, Dresden 1946, Technische Hochschule, Brunswick 1953; founder and dir. of first inst. for industrial construction in Germany 1957; mem. Deutsche Wissenschaftsrat 1969; mem. numerous comms., working parties etc; has undertaken bldgs. in

Germany and elsewhere including industrial, admin. and school bldgs., research centres, electricity and water works etc.; mem. Mainz Acad., Brunswick Scientific Soc.; Dr. techn. h.c. (T.U. Vienna). *Publications:* several books and more than 200 articles in professional journals. *Address:* 3300 Brunswick, Petritorwall 20, Federal Republic of Germany. *Telephone:* 0531/4 54 80.

HENNEBERG, Gerd Michael; German theatre director; b. 14 July 1922, Magdeburg; ed. Acad. of Dramatic Art, Leipzig; Actor, Civic Theatre, Aschaffenburg 1940-44, Producer 1943-44; Artistic Dir. Civic Theatres Ballenstadt/Harz 1945; Asst. Producer Deutsches Theater, Berlin 1946; Producer and Actor, Nat. Theatre, Weimar 1947-50; scenario editor for D.E.F.A. films 1950-; Actor, Berlin 1953-60; Dir. of Friedrich-Wolf Theatre, Neustrelitz 1960-62, 1966-69; Gen. Dir. Staatstheater Dresden 1962-66. *Address:* Staatstheater Dresden, Julien-Grimau Allee 27 Dresden A. 1, German Democratic Republic.

HENNESSY, Edward L., Jr., B.S.; American business executive; b. 22 March 1928, Boston, Mass.; s. of Edward L. Hennessy and Celina Mary Doucette; m. Ruth F. Schilling 1951; one s. one d.; ed. Fairleigh Dickinson Univ., Rutherford, N.J., and New York Univ. Law School; Asst. Controller, Textron 1950-55; Group Controller, Eastern Electronics Group, Lear Siegler Inc. 1956-60; Controller, Int. Electronic Corpn., Int. Telephone & Telegraph Corpn. 1960-61, Controller, Corporate Staff 1961-62, Controller, ITT Europe 1962-64; Dir. of Finance, Europe, Middle East and Africa, Colgate Palmolive Co. 1964-65; Vice-Pres. Finance, Heublein Inc. 1965-68, Sr. Vice-Pres. Admin. and Finance 1969-72; Dir. United Technologies Corpn. 1972-79, Sr. Vice-Pres. Finance and Admin. 1972-77, Exec. Vice-Pres., Group Vice-Pres. Systems & Equipment Group, and Chief Financial Office 1977-79; Chair., C.E.O. and Pres. Allied Corpn. 1979-; Chair. and C.E.O. Allied-Signal Inc. 1985-; Dir. Martin Marietta Corpn., Bank of New York, Coast Guard Foundation; Trustee, Fairleigh Dickinson Univ, Catholic Univ. of America. *Leisure interests:* sailing, tennis, reading. *Address:* P.O. Box 3000 R, Morristown, N.J. 07960, U.S.A.

HENNESSY, Sir James Patrick Ivan, K.B.E., C.M.G.; British diplomatist; b. 23 Sept. 1923; s. of late Richard George Hennessy; m. Patricia Margaret Unwin 1947; one s. (deceased) five d.; ed. Bedford School, Sidney Sussex Coll., Cambridge, L.S.E.; H.M. Forces, Royal Artillery 1942-46; H.M. Overseas Service, Basutoland; District Officer 1948, Judicial Commr. 1953, District Commr. 1954, Sec. of Constitutional Cttee. 1957-59, Sec. to Exec. Council 1960; High Commr's. Office, Cape Town and Pretoria 1961-63; mem. Basutoland Legis. Council 1964; Perm. Sec. for External Affairs, Internal Security and Defence and Perm. Sec. to Prime Minister of Lesotho 1967, retd. 1968; First Sec. U.K. Foreign Office 1968; Embassy in Uruguay 1970, Chargé d'affaires 1971-72; High Commr. in Uganda and Amb. to Rwanda 1973-76; Consul-General, Cape Town 1977-80; Gov. and C.-in-C. Belize 1980-81; H.M. Chief Insp. of Prisons for England and Wales 1982-87. *Address:* c/o Naval & Military Club, Piccadilly, London, S.W.1, England.

HENNESSY, John Basil, D.PHIL., F.S.A., F.A.H.A.; Australian archaeologist; b. 10 Feb. 1925, Horsham Vic.; s. of Thomas B. Hennessy and Nellie M. Poultney; m. Ruth M. R. Shannon 1954; one s. two d.; ed. Villa Maria & St. Patrick's Coll. Ballarat, Univ. of Sydney and Magdalen Coll. Oxford; lecturer, Near Eastern Architecture, Univ. of Sydney 1955-61; Asst. Dir. British School of Archaeology, Jerusalem 1965-66, Dir. 1966-70; Edwin Cuthbert Hall Visiting Prof. of Middle Eastern Archaeology, Univ. of Sydney 1970-72, Edwin Cuthbert Hall Prof. 1973-; Dir. Australian Foundation for Near Eastern Archaeology 1973-; Dir. of Excavations Sphagion, Stephania (Cyprus) 1951, Damascus Gate, Jerusalem 1964-66, Amman 1966, Teleilat Ghassul (Jordan) 1967-77, Samaria 1968, Pella (Jordan) 1978-88. *Publications:* Stephania 1964, The Foreign Relations of Palestine During the Early Bronze Age 1967, World Ceramics, The Ancient Near East 1968, The Arab States in the Modern World 1977-79, Masterpieces of Western Ceramics 1978, Pella in Jordan 1982, Archaeology of Jordan I 1986. *Address:* Department of Archaeology, University of Sydney, N.S.W. 2006; RMB 497, Old Windsor Road, Parklea, N.S.W. 2148, Australia. *Telephone:* 692-3118 (Office).

HENNIKER, 8th Baron (cr. 1800); **John Patrick Edward Chandos Henniker-Major,** K.C.M.G., C.V.O., M.C.; Baron Hartismere; British diplomatist; b. 19 Feb. 1916; s. of late 7th Baron Henniker and Molly (née Burnet); m. 1st Margaret Osla Benning 1946 (died 1974), 2nd Julia Marshall Poland 1976; two s. one d.; three step-d.; ed. Stowe and Trinity Coll., Cambridge; entered Foreign Service 1938; Army Service 1940-45; at Embassy, Belgrade, 1945-46; Asst. Pvt. Sec. to Sec. of State for Foreign Affairs 1946-48; Foreign Office 1948-50; at Embassy, Buenos Aires 1950-52; Counsellor, Foreign Office, Head of Personnel Dept. 1952-60; Amb. to Jordan 1960-62, to Denmark 1962-66; Civil Service Comm. 1966-67; Asst. Under-Sec. for African Affairs at Foreign Office 1967-68; Dir.-Gen. of the British Council 1968-72; Dir. Wates Foundation 1972-78; Trustee, City Parochial Foundation 1973; Gov. London Festival Ballet 1975; Hon. mem. Mental Health Review Tribunal 1976-81; mem. Parole Bd. 1978-82; mem. Council and Finance Bd., Univ. of E. Anglia 1979-86; Deputy Chair. Toynbee Hall 1982-86, mem. Council 1978-87; Hon. D.L. (Suffolk) 1988; Trustee Cripplegate Foundation 1978-; Pres. Rainer Foundation; Chair. Intermediate Treatment Fund 1985-; Pres. Suffolk Community Council 1988-, Suffolk Agricultural Assen. 1989; Hon. (Lay) Canon St.

Edmundsbury Cathedral 1986-. *Address:* Red House, Thornham Magna, Eye, Suffolk, IP23 8HH, England. *Telephone:* 037-983-336.

HENNING, Admiral of the Fleet Geraldo de Azevedo; Brazilian naval officer; b. 1917, Rio de Janeiro; joined Brazilian Navy 1934; Lieut.-Commdr., World War II; fmr. Dir.-Gen. Navy Personnel; Admiral of the Fleet 1973; Minister of the Navy 1974-78. *Address:* c/o Ministério da Marinha, Esplanada dos Ministérios, Bloco 3, Brasília, D.F. Brazil.

HENNINGSEN, Sven, DR. PHIL.; Danish historian; b. 2 Feb. 1910, Stubbekøbing; s. of Andreas and Christine (Jorgensen) Henningsen; m. Eugenie Henningsen 1964; ed. Københavns Universitet; lecturer in Modern History and Political Science, Univ. of Copenhagen 1943; Asst. Prof. Univ. of Gothenburg, Sweden 1944-45; Visiting Prof. Univ. of Minn., U.S.A. 1948-49; Prof. of Contemporary History and Political Science, Univ. of Copenhagen 1953-80, Vice-Chancellor 1967-69; Visiting Rockefeller Prof., Univ. of E. Africa 1962; Chair. Danish Council for UN 1959-65, Council for Danish Nat. UNESCO Cttee. 1961-69, Danish Political Science Assen. 1966-69, Nordic Assen. for Study of Int. Relations 1967-70; mem. Council for Danish Inst. of Foreign Policy, Chair. 1967-79; mem. Council for European Assen. of American Studies. *Publications:* The Polish Corridor and Danzig 1936, The Far East and the Great Powers 1941, Studies in Economic Liberalism 1944, The North Atlantic Treaty 1954, The Foreign Policy of Denmark 1962, The Twentieth Century 1965, Atomic Policy 1939-1945 1971, International Politics 1975, Danish Foreign Policy after 1945 1980. *Leisure interest:* music. *Address:* Dantes Plads 4, Copenhagen V, Denmark. *Telephone:* 126507.

HENRION, Robert; Belgian banker, politician and university professor; b. 23 July 1915, Namur; s. of Edouard Henrion and Marguerite Berthe; m. Marie-Louise Ernst 1939; three s. one d.; Barrister, Brussels 1938-46, Prof. of Political Economy and Financial Affairs, Univ. Libre de Bruxelles; Minister of Finance 1966-68, 1980, of State 1977; Vice-Pres. Senate 1985-86; mem. Conseil Supérieur des Finances, Société Générale de Banque, Chair. Exec. Cttee. 1969-76. *Publications:* La structure juridique de l'entreprise et le rôle de son personnel 1957, Financiers et banquiers 1959, Aspects juridiques et économiques du crédit à court terme 1959 and 1965, L'abus de puissance économique 1960, L'entreprise et le progrès social 1963, Le secret professionel du banquier 1963, Certains aspects récents de droit économique en Belgique 1968, L'expérience des lois de pouvoirs exceptionnels 1968, articles in Institutions et opérations financières, cours donnés à la Faculté de droit de l'U.L.B., 5th edn. 1978-79, Cours sur l'économie nationale et le droit 1979, and many legal and economic journals. *Address:* 196 avenue de Messidor, Bte 23, 1180 Brussels, Belgium. *Telephone:* 02-344 9546.

HENRY, André Armand; French teacher and politician; b. 15 Oct. 1934, Fontenoy-le-Château; s. of Alice Henry; m. Odile Olivier 1956; one s. one d.; Bains-les-Bains, Ecole normale d'instituteurs, Mirecourt; Teacher, Fontenoy-le-Château 1955-56, Thaon-les-Vosges 1956-69; began trade union career with Syndicat Nat. des Instituteurs (S.N.I.), Training Coll. Rep. (Vosges) 1954, mem Exec. Comm. (Vosges) 1955-69, Asst. Sec.-Gen. (Vosges) 1960-63, Sec.-Gen. (Vosges) 1963-69, mem. Nat. Council, S.N.I. 1965-74, Perm. Sec. 1969-74; in charge of youth, then gen. admin. section of S.N.I.; mem. Fed. Council, in charge of culture, youth and leisure sections, Fédération de l'Education Nationale (F.E.N.) 1971, Perm. Sec. and Sec.-Gen. 1974-81; Minister for Free Time 1981-83; Délégué Général à l'économie sociale 1983-; Chair. and Man. Dir. Caisse Nat. de l'Energie 1984-87. *Publications:* Dame l'école 1977, Serviteurs d'idéal (2 vols). *Leisure interests:* football, volleyball, photography, flying light aircraft. *Address:* 1 bis rue de l'Espérance, 94000 Créteil, France (Home).

HENRY, Rev. Dr. Carl F. H., TH.D., PH.D.; American theologian and author; b. 22 Jan. 1913, New York; s. of Karl F. and Johanna (Vaethroeder) Henry; m. Helga I. Bender 1940; one s. one d.; ed. Wheaton Coll., Ill., Northern Baptist Theological Seminary, Boston Univ., New Coll., Edinburgh, and King's Coll., Cambridge; Prof. of Theology, Northern Baptist Theological Seminary, Chicago 1942-47; Prof. of Theology and Christian Philosophy, Fuller Theological Seminary 1947-56; Ed. Christianity Today 1956-68; Visiting Prof. of Theology, Eastern Baptist Theological Seminary 1968-70, Prof.-at-large 1970-74; Lecturer-at-large, World Vision Int. 1974-87; Visiting Prof. of Theology, Calvin Theological Seminary 1986, Trinity Evangelical Divinity School 1987-89; Chair. World Congress on Evangelism, Berlin 1966; Program Chair. Jerusalem Conf. on Biblical Prophecy 1971; Pres. Evangelical Theological Soc. 1969-70, American Theological Soc. 1974-75, Inst. for Advanced Christian Studies 1971-74, 1976-79; Vice-Pres. Inst. for Religion and Democracy 1984-; Sec. the Elmer Bisbee Foundation; Carl F. H. Henry Study and Resource Centre f. at Trinity Evangelical Divinity School 1987; several hon. degrees. *Publications:* author of 35 books, including God, Revelation and Authority (6 vols). *Leisure interests:* writing, browsing in antique shops. *Address:* 3824 N.37th Street, Arlington, Va. 22207, U.S.A. *Telephone:* (703) 528-2401.

HENRY, Joseph Louis, D.D.S., M.S., PH.D., D.H.L., SC.D., F.A.C.D., F.R.S.H., F.I.C.D.; American dentist and professor of oral medicine; b. 2 May 1924, New Orleans; s. of Varice S. Henry and Mabel Mansion Henry; m. 1st Gloria A. Hill 1943, 2nd Dorothy L. Whittle 1954; three s. two d.; ed. Howard and Xavier Univs., Univ. of Illinois and American Coll. of Dentists; Assoc.

Prof. of Oral Medicine, Howard Univ. Coll. of Dentistry 1951–53, Supt. of Clinics 1953–65, Prof. of Oral Medicine 1958–75, Dir. of Clinics 1965–66, Dean 1966–75, Dean Emer. 1981–; Chair. and Prof. of Oral Diagnosis and Oral Radiology, Harvard School of Dental Medicine 1975–, Assoc. Dean for Govt. and Community Affairs 1978–; Trustee and Consultant at several hosps.; Chair. Bd. of Trustees, Ill. Coll. of Optometry; mem. Inst. of Medicine, N.A.S.; over 50 medals, plaques, citations; three hon. degrees. *Publications:* articles in professional journals. *Leisure interests:* bridge, travel, gourmet cooking. *Address:* 342 Dudley Road, Newton Centre, Mass. 02159; Harvard School of Dental Medicine, 188 Longwood Avenue, Boston, Mass. 02115, U.S.A. *Telephone:* 617-732-1457.

HENRY, William Robert, C.B.E.; British business executive; b. 30 April 1915, Glasgow; s. of William Henry and Sarah Lindsay; m. Esther Macfadyen 1947; two s. one d.; ed. Govan High School, Univ. of London; with J. & P. Coats Ltd. (later Coats Patons Ltd.) 1934–, Head of Financial Div. 1955–57, Asst. Accountant 1957–63, Dir. J. & P. Coats Ltd. 1963–66, Coats Patons Ltd. 1966–, Deputy Chair. 1970–75, Chair. 1975–81; Dir. Scottish Amicable Life Assurance Soc. 1977–84, Chair. 1981–84. *Leisure interest:* gardening. *Address:* Hawkstone Lodge, Ascog, Rothesay, Bute, Scotland. *Telephone:* 0700-2729.

HENRY de VILLENEUVE, Xavier, L. EN D.; French banker; b. 8 July 1932, Quintin; s. of Jacques Henry de Villeneuve and Yvonne de la Motte de la Motte Rouge; m. Simone de Vigneral 1963; two s. one d.; ed. Ecole des Frères, Quintin, Coll. des Cordeliers, Dinan, Coll. St. Charles, St. Brieuc and Faculté de Droit, Rennes; joined Banque de Bretagne 1959, Asst. Dir.-Gen. 1971, Dir.-Gen. 1979, Pres. and Man. Dir. 1986–; Pres. and Man. Dir., Banque de la Cité; Pres. Comm. des Affaires Sociales of Asscn. Française des Banques. *Leisure interests:* the arts, reading, old wars, hunting. *Address:* Banque de Bretagne, 283 avenue du Général Patton, 2011X-35040 Rennes Cedex (Office); 21 rue de Paris, 35000 Rennes, France (Home). *Telephone:* 99.28.35.00 (Office); 99.38.85.97 (Home).

HENSEL, Witold, PH.D., SC.D.; Polish archaeologist; b. 29 March 1917, Poznań; s. of Maksymilian Hensel and Maria Formanowicz; m. Maria Chmielewska 1941; three s. one d.; ed. Poznań Univ.; Lecturer and Adjunct, Lublin Univ. 1944–45, Poznań Univ. 1946–50, Prof. 1951–56, Dean History Faculty 1951–53; Prof. Warsaw Univ. 1954–; Dir. Polish Acad. of Sciences Inst. for History of Material Culture 1954–; Ed. and Founder Slavia Antiqua 1948–; Ed. Światowit 1965–; has led excavations at Gniezno, Kłecko, Ostrów Tumski of Poznań and Kruszwica (near Inowrocław), Czersk (near Warsaw), Poland, Styrmen and Odercy, Bulgaria, Debrešte (near Prilep), Yugoslavia, and in St.-Jean-Le-Froid Condorcet and Montaigut, France, Cappacio Vecchia and Venice, Italy and Algiers and Tlemcen, Algeria; mem. Council Int. Congress of Prehistoric Sciences 1956, Istituto Italiano di Preistoria e Protostoria 1961; Pres. Int. Cttee. of Research for Origin of Towns 1962–77, Int. Congress Slavonic Archaeology 1965–67; Vice-Pres. Int. Congress of Slavists 1971–; Corresp. mem. Polish Acad. Sciences 1965, mem. 1973–, Chair. Cttee. for Slavistic Studies; Chair. Nat. Slavists Cttee. 1984–; mem. Presidium Polish Acad. of Sciences 1984–86, Sec. Social Sciences Dept. 1984–; Foreign mem. Acad. of Sciences of G.D.R. 1975–, Macedonian Acad. of Sciences 1977, Saxon Acad of Science, Leipzig 1985, Deutsches Archäologisches Inst. 1978–; mem. Presidium Provisional Nat. Council of Patriotic Movt. for Nat. Rebirth 1982–83; Deputy to Seym 1985–; Dr. h.c. (Poznań); State Prize (2nd Class) 1955, 1966, Copernicus Medal, Polish Acad. of Sciences 1977, Bulgarian Order of Kirill and Methodius (1st Class) 1970, Commdr. Cross of Order of Polonia Restituta 1971, Medal of 30th Anniversary of People's Poland 1974, Commdr. Croce al Merito della Repubblica Italiana 1975, Gold Medal of Czechoslovak Acad. of Sciences 1975, Order of Banner of Labour (1st Class)-1978, Commdr. Cross with Star of Order of Polonia Restituta 1986 and other awards; Hon. citizen of Poznań; Hon. Meritorious Activist of Culture 1979. *Publications:* Studia nad osadnictwem Wielkopolski wczesnohistorycznej (Studies of Settlement in Wielkopolska in the Early Historical Period) Vols. I-VII 1948–80, 1987, Słowiańszczyzna wczesnośredniowieczna—Zarys kultury materialnej (Early Medieval Slav Culture—An outline of Material Culture) 1952, 1956, 1965, 1987, Sztuka społeczeństw paleolitycznych (The Art of Palaeolithic Societies) 1957, Poznań w zaraniu dziejów (Poznań in Protohistoric Times) 1958, Najdawniejsze stolice Polski (Poland's Ancient Capitals) 1960, The Beginnings of the Polish State 1960, Polska przed tysiącem lat (Poland a Thousand Years Ago) 1960, 1964, 1967, Archeologia o początkach miast słowiańskich (Origins of Slavonic Towns in Light of Archaeology) 1963, Die Slawen im Mittelalter 1965, La Naissance de la Pologne 1966, Anfänge der Städte bei den Ost- und Westslawen 1967, Ziemie Polskie w pradziejach (Poland in Prehistoric Times) 1969, Archeologia i Prahistoria (Archaeology and Prehistory) 1971, Polska starożytna (Poland in Ancient Times) 1973, 1980, 1988, Archeologia żywa (Alive Archaeology) 1973, 1983, Ur- und Frühgeschichte Polens 1974; U źródeł Polski średniowiecznej (Sources of Poland in the Middle Ages) 1974, De l'histoire des recherches archéologiques sur les Slaves du Haut Moyen Age 1980, Skąd przyszli Słowianie (Where Slavs Came From) 1984, Le origini della Polonia 1986; more than 500 dissertations, articles and reviews; Ed. Slavia Antiqua, Archaeologia Polona, Archaeologia urbium, Światowit and Polskie Badania Archeologiczne (Polish Archaeological Researches). *Leisure interest:* tennis. *Address:* Al. Świerczewskiego 105, 00-140 Warsaw (Office); Marszałkowska

84/92, m. 109, 00-514 Warsaw, Poland (Home). *Telephone:* 24-01-00 (Office); 21-52-94 (Home).

HENSHAW, Kenneth Ralph, O.B.E., M.A.; British business executive; b. 1 Nov. 1918, Canterbury; s. of Ralph and Elsie Henshaw; m. Patricia Helen Heath 1953; one d.; ed. King's School, Canterbury and Trinity Coll., Oxford; Sr. Vice-Pres. Sinclair and BP Explorations Inc. 1959–63; Regional Man. Exploration Dept. The British Petroleum Co. Ltd. 1963–65; Man. Dir. Kuwait Oil Co. Ltd. 1965–73; Exec. Deputy Chair. Airwork Ltd. 1973–83; Chair. Middle East Navigation Aids Service; Fellow Inst. of Petroleum. *Leisure interests:* golf, tennis, shooting. *Address:* 5 Branksome Cliff, Westminster Road, Poole, Dorset, BH13 6JW, England.

HENTRICH, Helmut; PROF.DR.; German architect; b. 17 June 1905, Krefeld; s. of Dr. Johann Peter Hubert and Helene Emilie (née Bürger) Hentrich; ed. Univ. of Freiburg, Tech. Univs. of Vienna, Berlin; Asst. with Ernö Goldfinger, Paris, Norman Bel Geddes, New York 1930–32; Govt. Master Builder 1933; went into partnership with Hans Heuser 1935, with Hubert Petschnigg 1953, took on new partners to form Hentrich-Petschnigg & Partner Planungsgesellschaft 1969, later became HPP (Hentrich-Petschnigg & Partner) KG 1972; f. HPP Int. Architects and Engineers GmbH 1977; Jan Wellem Ring, Düsseldorf, Grosse Medaille, Düsseldorf, IBI Medal, Liechtenstein, Verdienstkreuz des Bundesordens (1st Class), Grosses Bundesverdienstkreuz, Grosser Ehrenring, Düsseldorf, Schinkel Prize and numerous other awards. *Major works include:* Europa-Center, Berlin, Ruhr Univ., Bochum, Standard Bank Centre, Johannesburg, Diamond Sorting Building, Kimberley, Tonhalle Düsseldorf, Deutsch-Japanisches Center, Düsseldorf, etc. *Publications:* numerous articles in nat. and int. journals. *Leisure interests:* collecting glass and pewter, Haitian art. *Address:* 4000 Düsseldorf-Oberkassel, Düsseldorfer Strasse 65 (Home); 4000 Düsseldorf, Heinrich-Heine-Allee 37, Federal Republic of Germany (Office). *Telephone:* 0211/52485 (Home); 0211/83840 (Office).

HENZE, Hans Werner; German composer and conductor; b. 1 July 1926, Gütersloh; s. of Franz Henze and Margarete Geldmacher; ed. Staatsmusikschule, Brunswick, Kirchenmusikalisches Institut, Heidelberg; Musical Dir. Heinz Hilpert's Deutsches Theater in Constance 1948; Artistic Dir. Ballet of the Hessian State Theatre in Wiesbaden 1950; living in Italy as an independent artist since 1953; Prof. of Composition, Mozarteum, Salzburg 1961; Prof. of Composition, Hochschule für Musik, Cologne 1980–; Artistic Dir. Accad. Filarmonica Romana 1982–; Visiting Prof. Royal Acad. of Music, London 1987; mem. Akademie der Künste, Berlin 1960–68, Bayerische Akademie der Schönen Künste, Munich; Dr. Mus. (Edinburgh) 1971; Robert Schumann Prize 1952, North-Rhine-Westphalia Art Prize 1956, Prix d'Italia 1954, Sibelius Gold Medal, Harriet Cohen Awards, London 1956, Music Critics Prize, Buenos Aires 1958, Kunstpreis, Berlin, Niedersächsischer Kunstpreis 1962, Ludwig-Spohr-Preis 1976. *Composition:* Operas: Das Wundertheater, Boulevard Solitude, König Hirsch, Der Prinz von Homburg, Elegy for Young Lovers 1961, Der Junge Lord 1964, Die Bassariden 1965, The English Cat 1983; Radio Operas: Ein Landarzt, Das Ende einer Welt; Ballets: Jack Pudding, Tancred under Cantylene, Variationen, Labyrinth, The Idiot, Apoll und Hyazirth, Ondine; Oratorio: Novae de Infinito Laudes 1962; Cantatas: Being Beauteous 1963, Ariosi 1963, Cantata della Fiaba Estrema 1963; Choral works: Chorfantasie 1964, Musen Siziliens 1966; Oratorio: Medusa 1968; six Symphonies, Violin and Piano and Violoncello Concertos, Double Concerto for Oboe, Harp and Strings, two String Quartets, Wind Quintet, Kammermusik 1958 (tenor and ensemble), El Cimarron 1969, The Tedious Way to the Place of Natasha Ungeheuer 1970, Heliogabalus Imperator 1971, La Cubana 1972, Voices 1973, Tristan 1974, Ragtime and Habanera 1975, The English Cat 1983; film music for Muriel, etc. *Publication:* Die Englische Katze—Ein Arbeitsbuch 1979–82 1983. *Leisure interests:* poetry, botany. *Address:* B. Schott's Söhne, 6500 Mainz, Weihergarten 1–5, Federal Republic of Germany.

HEPBURN, Audrey; American actress; b. 4 May 1929, Brussels, Belgium; d. of Joseph A. Hepburn and Baroness Ella (van Heemstra) Hepburn; m. 1st Mel Ferrer 1954 (dissolved 1968), one s.; m. 2nd Dr. Andrea Dotti 1969, one s.; ed. Arnhem Conservatoire; studied dancing in Amsterdam and London; ballet appearances in London; stage appearances in Gigi (New York) 1951, Ondine (New York) 1954; Tony award for film acting 1968, Commdr. Ordre des Artes et des Lettres; Special UNICEF Amb. 1988–. *Films include:* Laughter in Paradise 1951, The Lavender Hill Mob 1951, Roman Holiday (Acad. Award) 1953, Sabrina 1954, War and Peace 1956, Funny Face 1957, Love in the Afternoon 1957, The Nun's Story 1959, Green Mansions 1959, The Unforgiven 1960, Breakfast at Tiffany's 1961, The Children's Hour (called The Loudest Whisper in Britain) 1962, Charade 1963, Paris When it Sizzles 1964, My Fair Lady 1964, How to Steal a Million 1966, Two for the Road 1966, Wait Until Dark 1967, Robin and Marian 1976, Bloodline 1978, They All Laughed 1980, Here a Thief (TV film) 1987. *Address:* c/o Kurt Frings, 9440 Santa Monica Boulevard, Beverly Hills, Calif. 90210, U.S.A.

HEPBURN, Davidson Lincoln, M.A., PH.D.; Bahamian diplomatist; b. 7 Dec. 1932, New Bight, Cat Island; m.; one s.; ed. Florida Agric. and Mechanical Univ., Michigan State Univ. and Univ. of Madrid; First Asst. Sec. Ministry of Home Affairs 1969–70; Deputy Perm. Sec. Ministry for External Affairs 1971–73, Under-Sec. 1973; Deputy Perm. Rep. of Bahamas to UN, New York 1973–78, Perm. Rep. 1978–; Del. to all regular sessions of Gen. Ass. 1974–, numerous special Ass. sessions; Chair. First Cttee. (Political and Security) UN 1979–; fmr. Rep. of Bahamas to Third UN Conf. on Law of the Sea; Carnegie Foundation Fellow in Int. Relations and Diplomacy, Geneva 1971–72. *Address:* Permanent Mission of the Bahamas to the United Nations, 767 Third Ave., 9th Floor, New York, N.Y. 10017, U.S.A. *Telephone:* (212) 421-6925.

HEPBURN, Katharine; American actress; b. 9 Nov. 1909, Hartford, Conn.; d. of the late Dr. Thomas N. Hepburn and Katharine Houghton; m. Ludlow Ogden Smith (divorced); ed. Bryn Mawr Coll., Pa.; professional stage actress since 1928; film actress since 1932; also appears on TV; received gold medal for best film actress, Venice 1934, Whistler Soc. award 1957; four Acad. Awards (Oscars). *Stage plays include:* The Lake, The Philadelphia Story, Without Love 1942, As You Like It 1950, The Millionairess 1952, The Taming of the Shrew 1955, The Merchant of Venice 1955, Much Ado About Nothing 1955, Coco (musical) 1970 (on tour 1971), A Matter of Gravity 1976 (on tour 1977), The West Side Waltz 1981. *Films include:* A Bill of Divorcement 1932, Morning Glory 1933 (Acad. Award 1934), Little Women 1933, Alice Adams 1935, Sylvia Scarlett 1935, Mary of Scotland 1936, A Woman Rebels 1936, Quality Street 1937, Stage Doors 1937, Bringing Up Baby 1938, Holiday 1938, The Philadelphia Story (N.Y. Critics' Award) 1940, Woman of the Year 1942, Keeper of the Flame 1942, Undercurrent 1946, Sea of Grass 1947, State of the Union 1948, Adam's Rib 1949, The African Queen 1951, Pat and Mike 1952, Summer Madness 1955, The Rainmaker 1956, Desk Set 1957, Suddenly Last Summer 1959, Long Day's Journey Into Night 1962, Guess Who's Coming to Dinner? 1967 (Acad. Award 1968), The Lion in Winter 1968 (Acad. Award 1969), The Madwoman of Chaillot 1969, The Trojan Women 1971, A Delicate Balance 1973, The Glass Menagerie (TV) 1973, Love Among the Ruins (TV) 1975, Rooster Cogburn 1975, Olly Olly Oxen Free 1976, The Corn is Green (TV) 1979, Christopher Strong 1980, On Golden Pond 1981 (Acad. Award 1982), The Ultimate Solution of Grace Quigley 1984, Mrs. Delafield Wants to Marry (TV) 1986, Laura Lansing Slept Here (TV) 1988. *Publication:* The Making of The African Queen 1987. *Address:* c/o William Morris Agency, 151 El Camino, Beverly Hills, Calif. 90212, U.S.A.

HEPPEL, Leon A., PH.D., M.D.; American biochemist; b. 20 Oct. 1912, Granger, Utah; s. of Leon George Heppel and Rosa Zimmer; m. Adelaide Keller 1944; two s.; ed. Univ. of California at Berkeley and Univ. of Rochester, N.Y.; Officer, U.S. Public Health Service 1942; Stationed at Nat. Insts. of Health, Bethesda, Md. 1942–67; Prof. of Biochemistry, Cornell Univ. 1967–82; Fogarty Scholar 1982–85; mem. N.A.S.; Hillebrand Award, American Chem. Soc. (Washington Section) 1960, 3M Life Sciences Award 1978. *Publications:* 160 scientific papers in biochemistry since 1939. *Leisure interests:* music appreciation, reading. *Address:* c/o Cornell University, Wing Hall, Ithaca, N.Y. 14850, U.S.A.

HEPPLE, Robert Norman, R.A.; British portrait, subject and landscape painter; b. 18 May 1908, London; s. of Robert Watkin Hepple and Ethel Louise Wardale; m. Jillian Pratt 1948; one s. one d.; ed. Goldsmith's College and Royal Acad. Schools, London; Pres. Royal Soc. of Portrait Painters 1979–83. *Address:* 16 Cresswell Place, South Kensington, London, S.W.10 (Studio); 10 Sheen Common Drive, Richmond, Surrey, England (Home). *Telephone:* 01-878 4452 (Studio).

HEPTING, George Henry, PH.D.; American forest pathologist; b. 1 Sept. 1907, Brooklyn N.Y.; s. of George Hepting and Lena Schuler; m. Anna J. Love 1934; two s.; ed. Manual Training High School, Brooklyn, N.Y., Brooklyn Technical High School and Cornell Univ.; Asst. Instructor in Pathology, Cornell Univ. 1929–30; Field Asst., Div. of Forest Pathology, Bureau of Plant Industry, U.S. Dept. of Agriculture (U.S.D.A.), Mass. 1931–32, Louisiana 1932–33, Asst. Pathologist 1933–37, Assoc. Pathologist 1937–40, Pathologist 1940–46, Senior Pathologist 1946–53; Chief, Forest Disease Research, Southeastern Forest Experimental Station, Forest Service 1953–62, Chief Research Scientist 1962–71; Adjunct Prof. of Forestry and Plant Pathology, North Carolina State Univ. 1971–; Fellow, Soc. of American Foresters, American Phytopathological Soc.; mem. N.A.S.; U.S.D.A. Superior Service Award 1954, Barrington Moore Award of Soc. of American Foresters 1963, U.S.D.A. Special Merit Award 1967, Southern Forest Pathological Award 1967, Int. Shade Tree Conf. Citation Award 1972, Weyerhauser Award (for writings on forest history) 1975. *Publications:* Plant-Disease Development and Control 1968, Forest and Shade Tree Diseases of the United States 1971; and 150 scientific articles. *Leisure interests:* mineral collecting, gem-cutting, boating, golf. *Address:* Department of Plant Pathology, North Carolina State University, Raleigh, N.C. 27607 (Office); 11 Maplewood Road, Asheville, N.C. 28804, U.S.A. (Home). *Telephone:* 704-253-5107.

HERB, Raymond George, PH.D.; American emeritus professor of physics; b. 22 Jan. 1908, Navarino, Wis.; s. of Joseph and Annie Herb; m. Anne Williamson 1945; two s. three d.; ed. Univ. of Wisconsin.; Research Assoc. in Physics, Univ. of Wis. 1935–39, Research Assoc. and Asst. Prof. in Physics 1939–40, Assoc. Prof. 1941–45, Prof. 1945–61, Charles Mendenhall Prof. of Physics 1961–72; Pres. and Chair of Bd. Nat. Electrostatics Corp. 1965–; mem. N.A.S.; Distinguished Service Citation for Coll. of Engineers, Univ. of Wis.; Dr. h.c. (Univs. of Basel and São Paulo); Tom W. Bonner Award 1968. *Publication:* Van de Graaf Generators in Handbuch der

Physik XLIV 1959. *Address:* National Electrostatics Corporation, Graber Road, P.O. Box 310, Middleton, Wis. 53562 (Office); P.O. Box 223A, Rural Route 1, Mazomanie Wis. 53560, U.S.A. (Home). *Telephone:* (608) 831-7600 (Office).

HERBERT, (Dennis) Nicholas; 3rd Baron Hemingford, M.A.; British journalist; b. 25 July 1934, Watford, Herts.; s. of Dennis George Ruddock Herbert, 2nd Baron Hemingford and Elizabeth McClare (née Clark); m. Jennifer Mary Toresen Bailey; one s. three d.; ed. Oundle School, Clare Coll., Cambridge; Sports Desk, Reuters 1956–57, Diplomatic Desk 1957–60, Washington Bureau 1960–61; Asst. Washington Corresp., The Times 1961–65, Middle East Corresp. 1966–68, Deputy Features Ed. 1968–70; Ed. Cambridge Evening News 1970–74; Editorial Dir. Westminster Press 1974–; Pres. Guild of British Newspaper Eds. 1980–81, Media Soc. 1982–84; Sec. Asscn. of British Eds. 1985–; mem. British Exec., Int. Press Inst.; mem. E. Anglian Regional Cttee., Nat. Trust 1984–. *Publication:* Jews and Arabs in Conflict 1969. *Leisure interests:* Victorian military history, computers, genealogy, destructive gardening. *Address:* The Old Rectory, Hemingford Abbots, Huntingdon, Cambs., PE18 9AN; Westminster Press Ltd., 8–16 Great New Street, London, EC4P 4ER, England.

HERBERT, Jean Jules M. E.; French surgeon; b. 16 July 1905, St. Médard/Ille; m. Thalia de Almeida Guimaraes 1954; two s. two d.; ed. Lycée de Rennes and Univ. de Paris à la Sorbonne; Head of clinic, Faculty of Medicine, Paris; Surgeon, Hospital Aix-les-Bains 1936–; Chief Surgeon of hospitals Aix-les-Bains 1941–; founder surgical centre for osteoarticular surgery and rheumatology; Pres. Centre de Recherches du Rhumatisme 1948–; founder of the first French bone bank 1948; Ed.-in-Chief Rhumatologie 1950–; Pres. Conseil de l'ordre des médecins de la Savoie 1948–; Pres. French Soc. of Orthopaedic Surgery and Traumatology; mem. Acad. of Surgery, and Int. Soc. of Surgery, numerous socs. including Royal Soc., London, Académie Nationale de Médecine; Officier, Légion d'honneur, Croix de guerre, Officier de la Santé publique. *Publications:* Chirurgie du rhumatisme, Le Froid (with others). *Address:* 11 boulevard de la Roche du Roi, 73100 Aix-les-Bains, France. *Telephone:* (79) 61-22-00.

HERBERT, Walter William (Wally); British explorer; b. 24 Oct. 1934; s. of Capt. W. W. J. Herbert and Helen Manton; m. Marie McGaughey 1969; two d.; trained as surveyor, Royal Engineers 1950–53, Egypt 1953–54; Surveyor with Falklands Islands Dependencies Survey based at Hope Bay, Antarctica 1955–58; travelled in S. and N. America 1958; Expedition to Lapland and Spitsbergen 1960; Surveyor with N.Z. Antarctic Expedition mapping routes of Capt. Scott and Capt. Amundsen 1960–62; Leader Expedition to N.W. Greenland 1967–68; Leader of British Trans-Arctic Expedition 1968–69, which made first surface crossing of Arctic Ocean from Alaska to Spitzbergen via North Pole by dog sledges; Leader Expedition to N.W. Greenland 1971–73, to Lapland 1974, several expeditions to N.W. Greenland 1975–87; second visit to N. Pole April 1987; Polar Medal 1962 and clasp 1969; Livingstone Gold Medal, Royal Scottish Geographical Soc. 1969; Founder's Gold Medal, Royal Geographical Soc. 1970; City of Paris Medal 1983; French Geographical Soc. Medal 1983; Explorer's Medal, Explorer's Club 1985; Finn Ronne Award for Antarctic exploration 1985; Jt. Hon. Pres., World Expeditionary Asscn; Hon. mem. British Schools Exploring Soc. *Publications:* A World of Men 1968, Across the Top of the World 1969, The Last Great Journey on Earth 1971, Polar Deserts 1971, Eskimos 1976, North Pole 1978, Hunters of the Polar North 1982, The Noose of Laurels 1989 and contribs. to several other books. *Leisure interest:* painting. *Address:* c/o Royal Geographical Society, London, S.W.7, England.

HERBERT, William Valentine, LL.M., PH.D.; Saint Christopher and Nevis diplomatist and lawyer; b. 1936, Basseterre, St. Kitts; m.; three c.; ed. London Univ., England; called to Bar (Middle Temple) 1959; founding mem. and first Pres. People's Action Movt.; acted as Constitutional Adviser to Govts. of Turks and Caicos, Anguilla and St. Kitts and Nevis; fmr. Man. Dir. Caribbean Commercial Bank (Anguilla) and Man. Dir. Anguilla Trust Co.; mem. Bar Assn. of St. Kitts-Nevis, Org. of Caribbean Bar Assens., World Peace Through Law and Council of Legal Educ. for the Caribbean; Perm. Rep. to UN 1983–. *Publication:* Natural Justice, the Ammunthodo Case. *Address:* Permanent Mission of Saint Christopher and Nevis to the United Nations, 414 East 75th Street, 5th Floor, New York, N.Y. 10017, U.S.A.

HERBERT, Zbigniew; Polish poet, essayist and playwright; b. 29 Oct. 1924, Lvov; s. of Bolesław Herbert and Maria Kaniak; ed. Cracow, Toruń and Warsaw Univs.; Co-editor Twórczość 1955–65, Poezja 1965–68; mem. Polish Writers' Assen. 1955–83, Gen. Bd. Foreign Cttee.; Prof. of Modern European Literature, Calif. State Coll., Los Angeles 1970; Prize from Polish Inst. of Sciences and Arts in America; Alfred Jurzykowski Foundation Award New York, Lenau Int. Prize for European Literature, Vienna 1965, Knight's Cross of Order Polonia Restituta 1974. *Publications:* Poetry includes: Struna światła (A String of Light) 1956, Hermes, pies i gwiazda (Hermes, A Dog and a Star) 1957, Studium przedmiotu (The Study of an Object) 1961, Napis (The Inscription) 1969, Wiersze Zebrane (Collected Verse) 1971, Pan Cogito (Mr. Cogito) 1974, Selected Poems (in English and German), Wybór wierszy 1983; radio plays and drama include: Dramaty (Dramas) 1970, Inny pokój (The Other Room), Jaskinia filozofów (Cave of Philosophers), Lalek, Rekonstrukcja Poety 1973; essays: Barbarzyńca w ogrodzie (A Barbarian in the Garden) 1962. *Address:* ul. Promenady 21m 4, 00-778 Warsaw, Poland (Home). *Telephone:* 41-26-77.

HERBIG, George Howard, PH.D.; American astronomer; b. 2 Jan. 1920, Wheeling, W. Va.; s. of George A. Herbig and Glenna Howard; m. 1st Delia McMullin 1943, three s. one d.; m. 2nd Hannelore Tillmann 1968; ed. Univ. of California (Los Angeles and Berkeley); Junior Astronomer, Lick Observatory, Mount Hamilton, Calif. 1948-50, Asst. Astronomer 1950-55, Assoc. Astronomer 1955-60, Astronomer 1960-87; Asst. Dir. Lick Observatory 1960-63, Acting Dir. 1970-71; Prof. of Astronomy, Univ. of Calif. (Santa Cruz) 1967-87; Astronomer, Inst. for Astronomy, Univ. of Hawaii 1987-; Visiting Prof. and lecturer Chicago 1959, Mexico 1961, Observatoire de Paris 1965, Max-Planck-Institut für Astronomie, Heidelberg 1969, Stockholm 1973, Hawaii 1976-77; mem. N.A.S. astronomy del. to People's Repub. of China 1977; Henry Norris Russell Lecturer, American Astronomical Soc. 1975; lectured in U.S.S.R. and Poland under exchange agreement, U.S.-U.S.S.R. Acads. of Science 1965, 1987; U.S. Nat. Science Foundation Sr. Postdoctoral Fellow 1965; mem. N.A.S., American Acad. of Arts and Sciences; Corresp. mem. Société scientifique Royale de Liège, Max-Planck-Inst. für Astronomie, Heidelberg; mem. numerous boards, comms., consultancies, etc.; Warner Prize, American Astronomical Soc. 1955; medal from Univ. of Liège 1969; Catherine Wolfe Bruce Gold Medal, Astronomical Soc. of the Pacific 1980. *Publications:* Ed. of and contributor to Non-Stable Stars 1957, Spectroscopic Astrophysics 1970; approximately 220 scientific papers, articles and reviews. *Leisure interests:* none. *Address:* Institute for Astronomy, University of Hawaii, 2680 Woodlawn Drive, Honolulu, Hawaii 96822. *Telephone:* (808) 948-8573.

HERBST, Axel, LL.D.; German diplomatist and fmr. European Econ. Community official; b. 9 Oct. 1918, Mülheim; m. Elfe Bretschneider 1943; two d.; ed. Univs. of Berlin, Cologne and Münster, Acad. of Int. Law, The Hague, and Law Society's School of Law, London; German Foreign Service 1951, German Embassy, Washington; Head, North American Desk, Fed. Ministry of Foreign Affairs 1957-60; Deputy Exec. Sec. Comm. of the European Economic Community (EEC) 1960-63, Dir.-Gen. External Relations 1963-68; Ministerial Dir. and Head of Foreign Trade and Devt. Div. Fed. Ministry of Foreign Affairs 1969-73; Amb., Perm. Rep. to UN, Geneva 1973-76; Amb. to France 1976-83; Consultant for Int. Affairs 1983-. *Address:* Adenaueralle 99-103, 5300 Bonn 1, Federal Republic of Germany. *Telephone:* 34-2747.

HERCUS, Luise Anna, PH.D.; Australian reader in Asian studies; b. 16 Jan. 1926, Munich, Fed. Repub. of Germany; d. of Alfred Schwarzschild and Theodora Schwarzschild; m. Graham Robertson Hercus 1954; one s.; ed. Oxford Univ. and Australian Nat. Univ., Canberra; tutor and lecturer St. Anne's Coll., Oxford 1946-54; Research Fellow Univ. of Adelaide 1965-68; Sr. Lecturer Asian Studies Australian Nat. Univ. 1969-71, Reader 1972-; much work on recording nearly extinct Aboriginal languages 1963-. *Publications:* The Languages of Victoria: A Late Survey 1969, The Bagandji Language 1982, This is What Happened, Historical Narratives by Aborigines (Co-Ed.) 1986, articles on Middle Indo-Aryan and on oral traditions of S. Australian Aborigines. *Leisure interest:* raising orphaned marsupials. *Address:* Kintala via Gundaroo, Dick's Creek Road, N.S.W. 2620, Australia. *Telephone:* 062-368145.

HERCUS, Dame Margaret Ann, D.B.E., B.A., LL.B.; New Zealand politician; b. 24 Feb. 1942, Hamilton; d. of Horace and Mary (née Ryan) Sayers; m. John Hercus; two s.; ed. Victoria, Auckland and Canterbury Univs.; Lawyer and Staff Training Officer, Beath & Co., Christchurch 1969-70; mem. Price Tribunal and Trade Practices Comm. 1973-75; Deputy Chair. Commerce Comm. 1975-78; Chair. Consumer Rights Campaign 1975; M.P. for Lyttelton 1978-; Opposition Spokesperson on Social Welfare, Consumer Affairs and Women's Affairs 1978-84; Minister of Social Welfare, Police and Women's Affairs 1984-87; Labour. *Leisure interests:* collecting original New Zealand prints, theatre, reading.

HERFORTH, Lieselott, DR.ING.; German physicist and politician; b. 13 Sept. 1916, Altenburg; employed in Acad. of Sciences, German Democratic Repub. 1949-60; Prof. of Experimental Physics, Dresden Tech. Univ. 1960-, Rector 1965-68; Prof. Tech. Univ., Leuna-Merseburg 1957-60; mem. Council of State, Volkskammer 1963-81, G.D.R. Acad. of Sciences 1969-; Vaterländischer Verdienstorden in Gold and Silver and other decorations. *Address:* Sektion Physik, Technische Universität, Dresden, German Democratic Republic.

HERINCX, Raimund (Raymond Frederick); British opera and concert singer, voice teacher and therapist; b. 23 Aug. 1927, London; s. of Florent Herincx and Marie Cheal; m. Margaret J. Waugh (known as Astra Blair) 1954; one s. two d.; ed. Thames Valley Grammar School and Univ. of London; Educ. Officer, Household Cavalry 1946-48; studied singing in Antwerp, Brussels, Barcelona and London with Giovanni Valli, Samuel Worthington and Harold Williams 1949-53; mem. Royal Opera House chorus; joined Welsh Nat. Opera 1956; Prin. Baritone, Sadler's Wells Opera 1957-67; début Royal Opera House, Covent Garden 1968; joined Metropolitan Opera House, New York 1976, subsequently appearing in most major U.S. opera houses mainly in works of Wagner and Richard Strauss; Prof. of Voice Royal Acad. of Music 1970-77; Sr. Voice Teacher, North East of Scotland Music School 1979-; lecturer, Univ. Coll., Cardiff

1984-87; Opera Medal, Int. Music Awards 1968; Hon. R.A.M. 1971. *Leisure interests:* United Cancer Concern Foundation, Artists' Assen. Against Aids, vineyard man., plant breeding (begonias and geraniums), wine and its history, wildfowl. *Address:* 54 Regent's Park Road, London, NW1 7SX; Monks' Vineyard, Larkbarrow, East Compton, Pilton, Shepton Mallet, Somerset, BA4 4NR, England. *Telephone:* 01-586 7841; (0749) 4462.

HERING, Gerhard F.; German author and theatrical director; b. 28 Oct. 1908, Rogasen; ed. Humanistisches Gymnasium, Stettin, Univs. of Berlin and Heidelberg; Asst., Preussisches Staatstheater Berlin; joined Magdeburgische Zeitung 1933, theatre critic and literary editor 1934-37; theatre critic Kölnische Zeitung 1937-42; forced to resign for political reasons; editor Vision 1946-48; chief producer Deutsches Theater, Konstanz 1946-50; Dir. Otto-Falckenberg-Schauspielschule der Kammerspiele, Munich 1950-52; chief opera and drama producer, Württembergische Staatstheater, Stuttgart 1952-54; free-lance writer and producer for radio, television and theatre in Munich, Stuttgart, Frankfurt, Göttingen 1954-60; Head of W.D.R.—Studios Kultur, Düsseldorf 1960-61; Dir. Landestheater, Darmstadt 1961-71; Hon. Prof. Theaterwissenschaft, Univ. of Giessen 1967-; productions have included plays of Sophocles, Euripides, Goethe, Schiller, Grillparzer, Lessing, Gerhart Hauptmann, Georg Kaiser, Konrad Wünsche, Sartre, Genet; mem. PEN-Zentrum of Fed. Repub. of Germany, Deutsche Akad. für Sprache und Dichtung; mem. Deutsche Akad. der Darstellenden Künste (Vice-Pres. 1966, Pres. 1970). *Publications include:* Porträts und Deutungen—Von Herder zu Hofmannsthal 1948, Klassische Liebespaare 1948, 1950, Ein Brunnen des Lebens 1950, Gerhart Hauptmann 1955, Der Ruf zur Leidenschaft 1959, Ein grosser Herr: Das Leben des Fürsten Pückler (with Vita Huber) 1969; introductions and contributions to numerous books and texts. *Address:* Park Rosenhöhe, Edschmidweg 25, 6100 Darmstadt, Federal Republic of Germany. *Telephone:* 122005.

HERING, Juergen; German librarian; b. 15 Sept. 1937, Chemnitz; s. of late Karl Hering and of Margot (Schubert) Hering; m. Inge Rich 1961; one s. two d.; ed. Univs. of Stuttgart, Munich and Tübingen; Library Asst. Stuttgart Univ. Library 1968, Library Adviser 1971, Sr. Library Adviser 1972, Librarian 1974, Chief Librarian 1975-; Chair. Verein Deutscher Bibliothekare 1979-83, First Deputy Chair. 1983-85; Dir. Max-Kade-Stiftung Stuttgart 1982-, Wissenschaftliche Beirat Bibliothek für Zeitgeschichte, Stuttgart 1986-; Chair. German Libraries Assen. 1988-. *Leisure interests:* photography, travel. *Address:* Olivenstrasse 1, 7000 Stuttgart 75, Federal Republic of Germany.

HERKE, Horst W., DR.RER.POL.; German business executive; b. 2 Dec. 1931, Mainz; one d.; Man. of financial analyses, Adam Opel AG 1959-74, Asst. to Chair. of Bd. 1976-77, Treasurer 1977-82, Dir. of Purchasing 1982-84, Chair. of Bd. 1986-87; Financial Staff of Gen. Motors overseas org. 1974-76, Gen. Man. Gen. Motors Espana 1984-86.; Vice-Pres. Econ. Affairs, Gen. Motors Europe 1989-. *Leisure interests:* theatre, gardening, cycling. *Address:* Bahnofsplatz 1, 6090 Rüsselsheim, Federal Republic of Germany.

HERMANIUK, Most Rev. Maxim, O.C., D.THEOL.; Ukrainian archbishop; b. 30 Oct. 1911, Nowe Selo; s. of Mykyta and Anna (née Monczak) Hermaniuk; joined Redemptorist Congregation 1933; ed. Univs. of Louvain and Beauplateau, Belgium; ordained 1938; co-founder Ukrainian Relief Comm., Belgium 1942-48; Prof. Moral Theology, Sociology and Hebrew, Beauplateau 1943-45; Organizer Ukrainian Univ. Students Org. (Obnova), Belgium 1946-48, Canada 1953-; Co-founder and Pres. Ukrainian Cultural Soc., Belgium 1947; Maitre Agrege Theology, Univ. of Louvain 1947; Prof. of Moral Theology and Holy Scripture, Redemptionist Seminary, Waterford, Canada 1949-51; Superior, Vice-Prov. of Canada and U.S.A. 1948-51; Auxiliary Bishop, Winnipeg 1956, Archbishop of Winnipeg and Metropolitan of Ukrainian Catholics in Canada 1956; Apostolic Admin. of Exarchate of Man. 1956; mem. Vatican II Council 1962-65; mem. Sec. for promoting Christian Unity, Rome 1963; mem. World Congress of Free Ukrainians 1967; mem. Jt. Working Group Catholic Church and World Council of Churches, Geneva 1969; Counsel to Sec. Synod of Bishops, Rome 1977, mem. council 1983; mem. of Pontifical Comm. for Revision of Kodex of Oriental Canon Law 1983; Hon. mem. Mark Twain Soc. 1972; Officer, Order of Canada 1982. *Address:* 235 Scotia Street, Winnipeg, Man. R3R 0A7, Canada.

HERMANSSON, Steingrímur, M.S.; Icelandic engineer and politician; b. 22 June 1928; s. of Hermann Jonasson and Vigdís Steingrímsdóttir; m. 1st Sara Jane Hermannsson 1951, 2nd Gudlaug Edda Hermannsson 1962; four s. two d.; ed. Illinois and California Insts. of Tech.; electrical engineer, Fertilizer Plant Inc., Iceland 1952-54, S. Calif. Edison Co. 1954-56; Dir. Nat. Research Council, Iceland 1957-78; Minister of Justice, Ecclesiastical Affairs and Agric. 1978-79; Minister of Fisheries and Communications 1980-83; Prime Minister of Iceland 1983-87, Sept. 1988-; Minister of Foreign Affairs and Foreign Trade 1987-88; Chair. Progressive Party 1979-. *Leisure interest:* sport. *Address:* Office of the Prime Minister, Stjórharrádshúsid v/Lkaejartorg, 150 Reykjavík, Iceland.

HERMANS, Christopher, M.A.; Botswana banker; b. 23 Dec. 1936, Cape Town, South Africa; s. of Henry Hodgson Hermans and Marjorie Stanhope Hermans; m. 1st Janet Gallagher 1960 (divorced 1987); one s. two d.; m. 2nd Vonna Deulen 1987; two d.; ed. Diocesan Coll., Rondebosch, Cape

Town, Trinity Coll., Oxford, Howard Univ., Wash., Vanderbilt Univ., Nashville, Tenn.; Asst. Sec. for Devt., Bechuanaland Protectorate Admin. 1961-66; Perm. Sec., Ministry of Devt. Planning, Botswana Govt. 1966-70, Ministry of Finance and Devt. Planning 1970-75; Gov. Bank of Botswana 1975-77, 1987-; Sr. Planning Adviser/Loan Officer, World Bank 1977-82, C.E.O. Thailand and Indonesia Programs Div., 1982-84; C.E.O. of World Bank Regional Mission, Bangkok 1984-87; Presidential Order of Meritorious Service. *Leisure interests:* tennis, wildlife, windsurfing, gardening. *Address:* Bank of Botswana, P.O. Box 712, Gaborone, Botswana.

HERMASZEWSKI, Gen. Mirosław; Polish air force officer and astronaut; b. 15 Sept. 1941, Lipniki; m.; one s. one d.; ed. Gen. Staff Acad., Warsaw; studied at Air Force Officers' School, Dęblin 1961-64; served in Nat. Air Defence 1964-76; 1st class fighter pilot 1966, supersonic MiG-21 pilot 1967, flight leader 1971-72, deputy squadron leader 1972-76, fighter group commdr. 1976; in Cosmonauts' Training Centre, Zvezdnoy Gorodok, nr. Moscow 1976-78; space flight on board Soyuz-30 June–July 1978; service in higher staff of Nat. Air Defence 1978-80; student, Gen. Staff Acad., Moscow 1980-; mem. Space Research Cttee. of Polish Acad. of Sciences 1978-; assoc., Mil. Technological Acad. and Mil. Inst. of Aviation Medicine; mem. Mil. Council of Nat. Salvation 1981-83; Pres. Gen. Bd. Polish Astronautical Soc. 1983-87; Maj.-Gen. 1988; fmr. mem. Polish Youth Union and Socialist Youth Union; mem. Polish United Workers' Party (PZPR) 1963-; Gold Cross of Merit 1976, Cross of Grunwald Order (1st Class) 1978, Gold Star of Hero of U.S.S.R. 1978, Order of Lenin 1978, Mil. Champion Pilot 1978, Cosmonaut of Polish People's Repub. 1978, Merited Mil. Pilot 1978. *Leisure interests:* literature, communion with nature. *Address:* ul. Czeczota 25, 02-607 Warsaw, Poland.

HERMON, Sir John (Charles), Kt., O.B.E.; British police officer; b. 23 Nov. 1928; s. of late William Rowan Hermon and Agnes Hermon; m. Jean Webb 1954; one s. one d.; ed. Larne Grammar School; accountancy training and business 1946-50; joined Royal Ulster Constabulary 1950, Chief Constable 1980-89; C.St.J. 1984. *Leisure interests:* boating, reading and walking. *Address:* Brooklyn, Knock Road, Belfast, BT5 6LE, N. Ireland. *Telephone:* Belfast 652062.

HERNÁNDEZ ACOSTA, Valentín; Venezuelan engineer; b. 1925, San Fernando de Apure; s. of Valentín Hernández and Lola Acosta; m. Isabel Díaz Gorrin 1952; one s. three d.; ed. Univ. Central de Venezuela, London School of Econs.; Amb. to Libya, Tunisia and Morocco, Romania and Austria; Minister of Energy and Mines 1974-79; Pres. OPEC 1975; Chair. Petróleos de Venezuela (PDVSA) Shareholders Assembly. *Leisure interest:* golf. *Address:* Ministerio de Energía y Minas, Terre Norte Piso 25, Centro Simón Bolívar, Caracas, Venezuela.

HERNANDEZ ALCERRO, Jorge Ramon; Honduras diplomatist; b. 29 Aug. 1948; m.; two c.; ed. Inst. Européen de Hautes Etudes Internationales, France, Univ. of Nice and Universidad Nacional Autonoma de Honduras; former attorney and lecturer at Univ. Nacional Autonoma de Honduras; fmr. Judge, Inter-American Court of Human Rights; fmr. Gen. Sec. Innovacion y Unidad Party, Deputy to Nat. Ass. and Deputy to Nat. Congress; fmr. Deputy Foreign Minister; fmr. Amb. on Special Assignment in Latin America, U.S.A. and at UN General Ass.; Perm. Rep. to UN 1987-. *Address:* Permanent Mission of Honduras, United Nations, 866 United Nations Plaza, Suite 509, New York, N.Y. 10017, U.S.A.

HERNÁNDEZ CERVANTES, Héctor; Mexican politician; b. Dec. 1923, Mexico City; ed. Nat. Univ. of Mexico, Colegio de México and Univ. of Melbourne; fmrly. taught econ. theory, Univ. of Mexico and Centre of Latin American Monetary Studies; economist, Banco de México; Asst. Dir. of Financial Studies, Ministry of Finance; Dir.-Gen. of Industry and Commerce, Ministry of Commerce Dir.-Gen. of Financial and Int. Studies, Ministry of Finance; Under-Sec. of Foreign Trade, Ministry of Commerce and Industrial Devt. 1982-83, Sec. of Commerce and Industrial Devt. 1983-88. *Address:* c/o Secretaría de Industria y Comercio, Avenida Cuauhtémoc 80, México, D.F., Mexico.

HERNÁNDEZ COLÓN, Rafael, A.B., LL.B.; Puerto Rican lawyer and politician; b. 24 Oct. 1936, Ponce; s. of Rafael Hernández Matos and Dorinda Colón Clavell; m. Lila Mayoral 1959; three s. one d.; ed. Valley Forge Mil. Acad., Wayne Pa., Johns Hopkins Univ., Univ. of Puerto Rico Law School; private law practice 1959; Assoc. Commr. of Public Service 1960-62; lecturer in Law, Catholic Univ. of Puerto Rico 1961-65; Sec. of Justice 1965-57; Senator at Large, Popular Democratic Party 1968; Pres. of Senate 1967-72; Leader of Popular Democratic Party 1969; Gov. of Puerto Rico 1972-76, Jan. 1985-; Trustee Carnegie Foundation for Int. Peace; mem. Inter American Bar Asscn.; Dr. h.c. (Johns Hopkins Univ., Catholic Univ. of Puerto Rico). *Publications:* Text on Civil Procedure 1968, and many articles on topics of law. *Address:* P.O. Box H1, Caparra Heights Station, San Juan 00922, Puerto Rico.

HERNANDEZ MANCHA, Antonio; Spanish lawyer and politician; state lawyer; mem. Andalusian Parl.; Leader Alianza Popular 1987-89. *Address:* c/o Alianza Popular, Genova 13, Madrid 4, Spain.

HERNÁNDEZ OCHOA, Lic. Rafael; Mexican politician; b. 1915, Vega de la Torre, Ver; ed. Univ. Veracruzana, Univ. de Mexico; fmr. Agent of the Public Ministry and judge in various towns in the province of Veracruz;

subsequently Pres. Nat. Cattle Confed.; Dir. of Population, Ministry of the Interior; Private Sec. to Luis Echeverría; Dir. of Political and Social Investigations; Under-Sec. for the Interior 1964-70; Sec. of Labour and Social Security 1970-72; mem. Chamber of Deputies 1973-; State Gov., Veracruz 1975-80. *Address:* Cámara de Diputados, Ciudad de México, Mexico.

HERNELIUS, (John) Allan, LL.B.; Swedish journalist; b. 19 March 1911, Tidaholm; s. of A. J. and Elsa (Myrsten) Hernelius; m. Jeanette von Heidenstam 1957; ed. Stockholm Univ.; Sec. Swedish Asscn. of Retail Grocers 1939, Man. Dir. 1941; Vice-Man. Dir. Swedish Retail Fed. 1943; Man. Dir. Swedish Newspaper Publishers' Asscn. 1945; Asst. Chief Ed. Svenska Dagbladet 1949, Chief Ed. 1955-70, mem. of Bd. 1956-81; Adviser, UN Conf., Geneva 1948; mem. Psychological Defence Cttee. 1949; Pres. Swedish Cttee., Int. Press Inst. 1955-71; Chair. Stockholm section Conservative Party 1953-55, Parl. Foreign Affairs Cttee. 1976-82; Bd. mem. Royal Defence Coll. 1952-82, Swedish Radio and Television 1953-70, Stockholm Stock Exchange 1959-74; mem. UN Cttee. on Disarmament 1972-76; mem. Swedish del. to UN 1964-66, 1969-70, 1978, Riksdag (Parl.) 1962-82; mem. Bd. Sveriges Riksbanks 1970-83, Vice-Chair. 1974-82. *Address:* Valhallavägen 146 A, 115 24 Stockholm, Sweden (Home). *Telephone:* 62-07-05.

HERNU, Charles; French politician; b. 3 July 1923, Quimper; s. of Eugène Hernu and Laurence Prost; ed. Collège des Minimes, Lyons; Dir. Le jacobin newspaper 1954; Deputy (Seine) to Nat. Assembly 1956-58, Sec. Foreign Affairs Cttee. 1956-58; Sec.-Gen. Colloques juridiques 1960; Gen. Del. Fédération de la gauche démocrate et socialiste 1965-67, fmr. Vice-Pres.; Gen. Del. and Chair. of Presidium, Convention des institutions républicaines until Dec. 1970; Mayor of Villeurbanne 1977; Deputy (Rhône) to Nat. Assembly 1978-81, for Lyons 1986-; Tech. Adviser, Centre nat. du commerce extérieure; fmr. Sec.-Gen. Fédération Nationale des Elus Socialistes et Républicains; fmr. Pres. Conventions pour l'Armée Nouvelle and Dir. Armée Nouvelle periodical; Minister of Defence 1981-85. *Publications:* La colère usurpée 1959, Priorité à gauche 1969, Soldat citoyen 1975, Chroniques d'attente 1976, Nous les grands 1980, Défendre la paix 1985, Lettre ouverte à ceux qui ne veulent pas savoir 1987. *Address:* 107 rue du 4 août, 69100 Villeurbanne, France (Home).

HERON, Patrick, C.B.E.; British painter; b. 30 Jan. 1920, Leeds, Yorks.; s. of late T. M. and Eulalie Heron (née Davies); m. Delia Reiss 1945 (died 1979); two d.; ed. Slade School, London; Art Critic New English Weekly 1945-47, New Statesman and Nation 1947-50; London corresp. Arts, New York 1955, resigned and ceased writing 1958; teacher of painting Cen. School of Arts and Crafts, London 1953-55; John Power Lecturer, Sydney Univ. 1973; Doty Prof., Univ. of Texas at Austin 1978; since 1947 more than 60 one-man exhbns. in London, New York, Paris, Zürich, Edinburgh, Oslo, Rio de Janeiro, Buenos Aires, Santiago, Lima, Caracas, Toronto, Minneapolis, Melbourne, Montreal, Perth, Sydney and Dublin, retrospective exhbns. Wakefield City Art Gallery 1952, Demarco Gallery Edinburgh 1967, Museum of Modern Art, Oxford 1968, Univ. of Texas at Austin Art Museum 1978, Barbican Art Gallery, London 1985; one-man shows at São Paulo Bienal 1954, 1965, Whitechapel Art Gallery, London 1972, Riverside Studios, London 1981 and numerous group exhbns. in Europe and America, many organized by British Council; paintings in numerous public galleries, including Tate Gallery, British Museum, Victoria and Albert Museum, Arts Council, British Council, Nat. Portrait Gallery, Stuyvesant Foundation, C. Gulbenkian Foundation, London; Nat. Museum of Wales, Cardiff; Montreal Museum of Fine Art; Musée d'Art Contemporain, Montreal; Art Gallery of Ont., Toronto; Vancouver Art Gallery; Nat. Gallery of W. Australia, Perth; Power Collection, Sydney; Art Gallery of N.S.W., Sydney; Brooklyn Museum, N.Y.; Boymans-van Beuningen Museum, Rotterdam; Smith Coll. Museum of Art, Northampton, Mass.; Toledo Museum of Art, Ohio; Albright-Knox Art Gallery, Buffalo, N.Y.; Univ. of Michigan Museum of Art, Ann Arbor; Univ. of Texas at Austin Art Museum, Gulbenkian Foundation, Lisbon; Queensland Art Gallery, Brisbane; Art Gallery of S. Australia, Adelaide; Carnegie Museum, Pittsburgh, Pa.; Frederick R. Weisman Foundation, L.A.; Peter Stuyvesant Foundation, Amsterdam, etc.; Trustee, Tate Gallery 1980-87; Main Prize at John Moores Liverpool Exhbn. II 1959, Silver Medal São Paulo Bienal 1965; Hon. D.Litt. (Exeter) 1982, (Kent) 1986; Hon. Dr. (R.C.A.) 1987. *Publications:* Vlaminck Paintings 1900-45 1947, The Changing Forms of Art 1955, Ivon Hitchens 1955, Braque 1958, The Shapes of Colour 1943-78 1978, Paintings by Patrick Heron 1965-77 1978, The Colour of Colour 1979, Patrick Heron (ed. Vivien Knight) 1988 and numerous articles on art. *Leisure interests:* painting, conservation campaigns. *Address:* Eagles Nest, Zennor, near St. Ives, Cornwall; 12 Editha Mansions, Edith Grove, London, S.W.10, England. *Telephone:* (0736) 796921 and 01-352 1787.

HEROUT, Vlastimil, DR. ING., D.SC., F.R.S.C.; Czechoslovak natural products chemist; b. 17 March 1921, Želí; s. of Vojtěch and Marie Herout; m. Hana Freiberková 1946; two. s. two d.; ed. Inst. of Chemical Technology, Prague; Asscn. of Chemical and Metallurgical Production, Pardubice-Rybitví 1941-46; Inst. of Chemical Tech. 1946-50; Inst. of Organic Chem. and Biochem. 1950-; Prof. of Organic Chem., Inst. of Chemical Tech. 1964-85; Consultant, Acad. of Sciences 1985-; Chair. Scientific Collegium of Organic Chem. and Biochem. 1962-75, Scientific Bd. of Organic Chem. and Biochem., C.S.S.R.

675

Acad. of Sciences 1963–; mem. IUPAC Bureau 1969–77; Chair. Czechoslovak Nat. Cttee. of Chem. 1971–; Dir. Inst. of Organic Chem. and Biochem., C.S.S.R. Acad. of Sciences 1970–77; Corresp. mem. Czechoslovak Acad. of Sciences 1960; mem. American Chem. Soc., British Phytochemical Soc., Deutsche Gesellschaft für Arzneipflanzenforschung, American Soc. of Pharmacognosy; State Prize 1951, 1962, several awards of C.S.S.R. Acad. of Sciences. *Publications:* more than 270 scientific publications including original data concerning newly discovered natural compounds from plants and their structures; monographs especially on laboratory techniques and chemical systematics; ten patents in the field of organic chemistry. *Leisure interests:* growing orchids, tourism. *Address:* Flemingovo námestí 2, 166 10 Prague 6, Czechoslovakia. *Telephone:* 311 07 84.

HERR, Dan, B.A.; American publishing executive; b. 11 Feb. 1917, Huron, Ohio; s. of William Patrick Herr and Wilhelmina Margaret (née Slyker) Herr; ed. Fordham Univ., McGill Univ. and Columbia Univ.; served U.S. Army 1941–45; Asst. to Ed. Infantry Journal, Washington 1945–46; freelance writer 1946–48; Pres. Thomas More Asscn., Chicago 1948–82, Chair. Bd. 1985–; publr. The Critic 1948–81, 1985–; Ed. Overview 1967–73; Pres. Nat Catholic Reporter 1968–71; Trustee Rosary Coll., Ill. 1969–73, Chair. Bd. Trustees 1970–72, Hon. LL.D. 1967; Pierre Marquette Award Marquette Univ. 1957; Asscn. of Chicago Priests Award 1978; decorated Purple Heart, Silver Star. *Publications:* Stop Pushing 1961, Start Digging 1987, Co-Ed. of six anthologies. *Address:* 205 W. Monroe Street, Chicago, Ill. 60606, U.S.A. (Office).

HERRERA, Luis Felipe; Chilean lawyer, economist and banker; b. 17 June 1922, Valparaíso; s. of Joaquín Herrera and Inés Lane; m. Inés Olmo 1961; two s.; ed. Colegio Alemán de Santiago, Escuela Militar, Univs. of Chile and London; Legal Dept., Central Bank of Chile 1943–47; Attorney for Central Bank of Chile and private law practice 1947–52; Prof. of Econs., Schools of Law and Sociology, Univ. of Chile 1947–58; Under-Sec. for Economy and Commerce 1952; Minister of Finance April–Oct. 1953; Gen. Man. Central Bank of Chile 1953–58; Gov. Int. Bank for Reconstruction and Development, IMF 1953–58, Exec. Dir. 1958–60; Pres. Inter-American Development Bank 1960–71; Pres. Soc. for Int. Development 1970–71; Co-ordinator-Gen. ECIEL Program (Jt. Studies for Latin American Econ. Integration) 1974–, Perm. Consultant 1981–; Pres. Admin. Council, Int. Fund for Promotion of Culture (UNESCO) 1976–; Chair. Bd. of Trustees, UN Inst. for Training and Research 1976–; Pres. World Soc. of Ekistics, Inst. for Int. Co-operation 1977–80, Corporación Investigaciones para el Desarrollo (CINDE) 1986, Chilean Chapter of S.I.D. 1986; mem. Bd. of Govs. Int. Devt. Research Centre (IDRC) 1980; mem. Bd. of Trustees, Third World Foundation; mem. Hon. Bd., Raul Prebisch Foundation 1986; Perm. Consultant Emer. Int. American Devt. Bank; Great Cross for Distinguished Service, Fed. Repub. of Germany 1958, Kt. Grand Cross, Order of Merit, Italy 1966, Medalla Cívica "Camilo Torres", Colombia 1968, Grand Cross for Educational Merit, Brazil 1969, Bronfman Award, American Public Health Asscn. 1969, Condecoración al Mérito, Minas Gerais State, Brazil 1969, Premio "Diego Portales", Chile 1971, Premio Serfin de Integración Mexico 1987, Premio ONU: Medalla Plata a la Paz, Cepal, Santiago 1988; Gran Cruz de la Orden del Sol, Peru 1971, Gran Cruz Placa de Plata, Dominican Repub. 1971; Gran Cruz Orden Rubén Darío, Nicaragua 1971, Orden Boyacá, Colombia 1971, do Cruzeiro do Sul, Brazil 1971, de la Orden Manuel Amador Guerrero, Panama 1971, Orden Abdón Calderón, Ecuador 1971, al Mérito Nacional, Paraguay 1971, Orden del Aguila Azteca, Mexico 1972, Antonio José de Irisarri, Guatemala 1975; Orden al Mérito Cultural "Andrés Bello", Venezuela 1978; Officier de l'Ordre du Mérite, France 1979; Gran Cruz de Isabel La Católica, Spain 1980; and numerous awards and honorary degrees. *Publications:* El Banco Central de Chile 1945, Política económica 1950, Fundamentos de la Política Fiscal 1951, Manual de Política Económica 1952, Elementos de Economía Monetaria 1955, ¿Desarrollo Económico o Estabilidad Monetaria? 1958, América Latina Integrada 1964, El Desarrollo Latinoamericano y su Financiamiento 1967, Nacionalismo Latinoamericano 1968, Chile en América Latina 1969, Internacionalismo, Regionalismo, Nacionalismo 1970, América Latina: Experiencias y Desafíos 1974, América Latina: Viejas y Nuevas Fronteras 1978, El Escenario Latinoamericano y el Desafío Cultural 1981, Despertar de un Continente: América Latina 1960–1980 1983, Comunidad Latinoamericana de Naciones: presencia de Chile 1983, Visión de América Latina: 1974–1984, 1985, América Latina: Desarollo e Integración 1986. *Address:* CONSULT, Calle Europa 2048, P.O. Box 16.696, Santiago 9 (Office); Calle El Cerro 1991, Santiago 9, Chile (Home). *Telephone:* 223-7008 (Office).

HERRERA-BÁEZ, Lic. Porfiro; Dominican diplomatist and international lawyer; b. 8 Nov. 1915, San Pedro de Macorís; m. Silvia P. de Herrera; ed. Univ. Autónoma de Santo Domingo and Columbia Univ., New York; joined Dominican Foreign Service and served in U.S.A. 1941–45, U.K. 1945–46, Italy 1946–47; Amb. to Brazil 1947–48; Under-Sec. of State for Foreign Affairs 1949; mem. Advisory Comm. on State Affairs 1952; Chief of Div. of UN and OAS Affairs and Int. Confs., Ministry of Foreign Affairs 1953–54; Sec. of State, Office of Pres. 1954–55; Sec. of State for Foreign Affairs 1955–61; Amb. to Vatican 1961–62, to U.K. 1966–75, to Portugal 1972, to Italy (also accred. to Greece and Sweden) 1975–83; del. to UN Gen. Assembly and other int. confs.; decorations include Légion d'honneur (France), Orden de Isabel la Catolica (Spain) and others from Dominican

Repub., Peru, Spain, Panama, China, Mexico, Liberia, Lebanon, Germany, Paraguay and Netherlands. *Publications include:* Pedro Alejandrino Pina, El Consejo Interamericano de Jurisconsultos, Compilación de Tratados y Convenciones de la República Dominicana. *Address:* c/o Ministry of Foreign Affairs, Santo Domingo, Dominican Republic.

HERRERA CACERES, Héctor Roberto; Honduran diplomatist; b. 20 Sept. 1943, Puerto Cortes; s. of Julio Herrera and Graciela Cáceres; m. Sandra Medina; one s. one d.; ed. Honduras Univ., Univ. of Law, Econs. and Political Sciences, Paris; Prof. of Int. Law, Honduras Univ. 1973–77; Amb. to Belgium, Netherlands, Luxembourg and European Communities 1977–83; Amb. and Perm. Rep. to UN 1983–86; Adviser and Amb. in Special Mission to Ministry of Foreign Affairs, Tegucigalpa 1973–77; Legal Adviser Cen. American Common Market 1975–76, Honduran Banana Corpn. 1976–77; Vice-Chair. Legal Cttee. Gen. Ass. of UN, Chair. Cttee. on Good Neighbourliness among States 1985; mem. Perm. Court of Arbitration of The Hague, Netherlands 1977–(90); Legal Adviser to Honduras Navy on Law of the Sea and Maritime Law 1987; Del. to Ass. of IMCO, London 1987; Dir. El ahorro Hondureño bank 1988–(90); Consultant, IDB, UNDP, EEC etc.; mem. Inst. Hispano-Luso-Americano of Int. Law, Société française pour le droit international, Société Belge de droit international. *Publications:* Legal Status of the Bay of Fonseca and the Regime of its Adjacent Zones (French and Spanish) 1974, Honduras and the Problems of the Public International Law of the Sea (Spanish) 1975, The Honduran-Salvadorean Conflict: Its Evolution and Perspectives (Spanish) 1977, The Relations between Central America and the European Community (Spanish) 1980, In Defence of the Common Heritage of Mankind (Spanish) 1982, Diplomacy, Politics and National Development of Honduras, 1983, Honduras in the International Tribune, Honduras and the Salvador frontier controversy before the International Court of Justice (Spanish) 1987. *Address:* Colonia Palmira, 3a calle No. 2115, Tegucigalpa, D.C., Honduras (Home). *Telephone:* 322942.

HERRERA CAMPÍNS, Luis, D.IUR.; Venezuelan politician; b. 4 May 1925, Acarigua, Portuguesa State; mem. Partido Social Cristiano (COPEI) 1946–; represented COPEI at first World Conf. of Christian Democrat Parties 1956; Deputy for Lara State 1958; Pres. COPEI 1961; elected Deputy for Lara 1963, 1968; elected Senator for Portuguesa 1963; Pres. of Venezuela 1979–83. *Address:* c/o Oficina del Presidente, Caracas, Venezuela.

HERRERO RODRIGUEZ DE MIÑON, Miguel; Spanish barrister and politician; b. 18 June 1940; s. of Miguel Herrero Rodriguez de Miñon and Carmen Herrero Rodriguez de Miñon; m. Cristina de Jáuregui; one s. two d.; ed. Univs. of Madrid, Oxford, Luxembourg, Geneva, Paris and Louvain; Lecturer in Int. Law, Univ. of Madrid 1963–65; Sr. Legal Adviser to Spanish Admin. 1966; Lecturer in Constitutional Law, Escuela de Funcionarios Internacionales 1967, Escuela Diplomatica 1972, Int. Univ. Menéndez Pelayo 1976–78; Gen. Sec. Ministry of Justice 1976; mem. Parl. 1977–; Leader, Parl. Group of UCD in Govt. 1980–81; Vice-Leader of Parl. Group of A.P., major opposition Group in Parl. 1982–87; Gran Cruz de Isabel la Católica, Gran Cruz de San Raimundo de Peñafort. *Publications:* El Derecho Constitutional de los nuevos, Estados 1971, El Principio Monàrquíco 1972, Ideas para Moderados 1982, España y la C. E. E.... Un Si para 1986. *Address:* Calle Mayor, 70, bajo, 28013 Madrid (Office); Calle Zorrilla 21, 2°, 28014 Madrid (Parliamentary Office); Calle Mayor 70, 3°, 28013 Madrid, Spain (Home). *Telephone:* (91) 248.5405; (91) 522.8272 (Offices); (91) 247.4830 (Home).

HERRHAUSEN, Alfred, DR.RER.POL.; German banker; b. 30 Jan. 1930; Diplom-Kaufmann; mem. Man. Bd., Deutsche Bank AG (Jt. Spokesman 1985–88, Spokesman 1988–); Chair. Supervisory Bd., Bergmann-Elektrizitäts-Werke AG, Berlin, Continental Gummi-Werke AG, Hanover, Daimler-Benz AG, Stuttgart, Deutsche Texaco AG, Hamburg; Vice-Chair. Supervisory Bd., AKZO N.V., Arnheim, F. M. Hämmerle Textilwerke AG, Dornbirn, Austria; mem. Supervisory Bd., Allianz Lebensversicherungs-AG, Stuttgart, Vereinigte Elektrizitäts-Werke Westfalen AG, Dortmund, F. M. Hämmerle Textilwerke AG, Dornbirn, Austria; mem. Bd. European Banks' Int. Co. S.A. (EBIC), Brussels; mem. Bd. of Dirs. European-American Bancorp, New York, Xerox Corpn., Stamford, Conn., U.S.A. *Address:* Deutsche Bank AG, Taunusanlage 12, 6000 Frankfurt am Main, Federal Republic of Germany.

HERRIDGE, Geoffrey Howard, C.M.G.; British oil executive; b. 22 Feb. 1904, Maisemore; s. of Edward Herridge and Mary Elizabeth Welford; m. Dorothy Elvira Tod 1935; two s. two d.; ed. Crypt School, Gloucester and St. John's Coll., Cambridge; joined Turkish Petroleum Co. Ltd. (later Iraq Petroleum Co. Ltd.) Iraq 1926; served in Iraq, Jordan, Palestine 1926–47; Gen. Man. in Middle East for Iraq, Petroleum Co. and Assoc. Cos. 1947–51, Exec. Dir. 1953–57, Man. Dir. 1957–63, Deputy Chair. 1963–65, Chair. 1965–70; mem. London Cttee., Ottoman Bank 1964–79; Chair. Petroleum Industry Training Bd. 1967–70. *Address:* Flint, Sidlesham Common, Nr. Chichester, Sussex, England. *Telephone:* 0243-56-357.

HERRING, James P.; American retail executive; b. 29 June 1914, Greenville, N.C.; Founder and fmr. Pres. Sav-On Drugs Inc.; Vice-Pres. Drug Div., The Kroger Co. 1960, Corp. Vice-Pres. 1966, Drug Div., The Kroger Co. 1960, Corp. Vice-Pres. 1966, Dir. 1968–, Pres. 1970–75, C.E.O. 1971–75, Chair. 1975–79; Dir. Cen. Trust Co., Cen. Bancorpn. Inc., Cincinnati Gas and Electric Co., Cincinnati Milacron Inc., Anchor Hocker Corpn., Ohio Nat. Life Insurance Co., and mem. various civic orgs., etc. *Address:* 247 River Drive, Tequesta, Fla. 33458, U.S.A.

HERRING, (William) Conyers, PH.D.; American physicist; b. 15 Nov. 1914, Scotia, N.Y.; s. of Dr. W. Conyers Herring and Mary Joy Herring; m. Louise C. Preusch 1946; three s. one d.; ed. Univ. of Kansas and Princeton Univ.; Nat. Research Council Fellow, M.I.T. 1937–39; Instructor in Mathematics, and Research Assoc. in Mathematical Physics, Princeton Univ. 1939–40; Instructor in Physics, Univ. of Missouri 1940–41; mem. Scientific Staff, Columbia Univ. Div. of War Research 1941–45; Prof. of Applied Mathematics, Univ. of Texas 1946; Research Physicist, Bell Telephone Laboratories 1946–78; Prof. of Applied Physics, Stanford Univ. 1978–, Prof. Emer. 1981–; mem. Inst. for Advanced Study, Princeton 1952–53; mem. Nat. Acad. of Sciences; Fellow, American Acad. of Arts and Sciences; Oliver E. Buckley Solid State Physics Prize, American Physical Soc. 1959, Distinguished Service Citation, Univ. of Kansas 1973; James Murray Luck Award for Excellence in Scientific Reviewing, Nat. Acad. of Sciences 1980; Von Hippel Award, Materials Research Soc. 1980; Wolf Prize in Physics 1985. *Publication:* Exchange Interactions among Itinerant Electrons (Vol. 4 of series Magnetism) 1966. *Leisure interests:* church and cultural activities. *Address:* Department of Applied Physics, Stanford University, Stanford, Calif. 94305 (Office); 3945 Nelson Drive, Palo Alto, Calif. 94306, U.S.A. (Home). *Telephone:* 415-723-0686 (Office); 415-856-9649 (Home).

HERRINGTON, John S., J.D.; American politician and lawyer; b. 31 May 1939, Los Angeles; s. of Alan D. Herrington and Jean Stewart; m. Lois Haight 1965; two d.; ed. Stanford Univ., Univ. of California; served U.S. Marine Corps., rank of Lieut.; served at Bar Asst. Attorney, Calif. Dept., Ventura, Calif. 1967–81; Partner Herrington and Herrington 1967–81; f. Quail Hill Ranch Co. 1967–81; Deputy Asst. for Personnel Office of Pres. 1981, Asst. Sec. Dept of Navy 1981, Special Consultant Manpower and Reserve Affairs Office, Chief of Staff 1983–85; Sec. of Energy 1985–89; Trustee Ronald Reagan Presidential Foundation 1985–; Republican. *Address:* c/o Department of Energy, 1000 Independence Avenue, S.W., Washington, D.C. 20585, U.S.A.

HERRIOT, James (James Alfred Wight), O.B.E., F.R.C.V.S.; British writer and practising veterinary surgeon; b. 3 Oct. 1916; s. of James Henry and Hannah Wight; m. Joan Catherine Danbury 1941; one s. one d.; ed. Hillhead High School, Glasgow Veterinary Coll.; started in general veterinary practice, Thirsk, Yorks. 1940; has been there ever since; served with R.A.F., World War II; started writing at age of 50; books on his veterinary experiences have been translated into all European languages and many others including Japanese; Hon. mem. British Veterinary Assen. 1975; Hon. D.Litt. (Heriot-Watt) 1979, Dr. h.c. (Liverpool) 1984. *Publications:* If Only They Could Talk 1970, It Shouldn't Happen to a Vet 1972, All Creatures Great and Small 1972, Let Sleeping Vets Lie 1973, All Things Bright and Beautiful 1973, Vet in Harness 1974, Vets Might Fly 1976, Vet in a Spin 1977, All Things Wise and Wonderful 1977, James Herriot's Yorkshire 1979, The Lord God Made Them All 1981, The Best of James Herriot 1983, Moses the Kitten 1984, Only One Woof 1985, The James Herriot Dog Stories 1986, The Christmas Day Kitten 1986, Dog Stories 1987, Bonny's Big Day 1987. *Leisure interests:* music, dog-walking. *Address:* Mire Beck, Thirlby, Thirsk, Yorkshire, YO7 2DJ, England.

HERRMAN, Frank Joachim; German politician and journalist; b. 15 Nov. 1931, Dresden; worked for newspapers BZ am Abend, Berliner Zeitung, East Berlin 1950–63; mem. Exec. G.D.R. Union of Journalists 1961; Deputy Head of Dept., Cen. Cttee., Socialist Unity Party (SED) 1963–; mem. Agitation Cttee. of Politburo of Cen. Cttee. 1967–; State Sec. and Head of Chancery of Chair. of State Council 1980–; cand. mem. Cen. Cttee. SED 1981–; Patriotic Order of Merit and other decorations. *Address:* c/o Staatsrat, 102 Berlin, German Democratic Republic.

HERRMANN, Joachim; German politician; b. 29 Oct. 1928, Berlin; mem. of the Sozialistische Einheitspartei Deutschlands (SED), E. Germany (now German Democratic Repub.) 1946–; Deputy Ed. Freie Deutsche Jugend (FDJ) newspaper Junge Welt 1949–52, Chief Ed. 1952–60; mem. the FDJ Cen. Council 1952–60; official of SED Cen. Cttee. 1960–62, Cand. mem. 1967–71, mem. 1971–81, Sec. 1976–81; Chief Ed. Berliner Zeitung 1962–65; State Sec. of All-German/West German Affairs 1965–71; mem. Volkskammer 1976–; Chief Ed. Neues Deutschland 1971–78; Cand. mem. SED Politburo 1973–78, mem. 1978–; Sec. for Agitation and Propaganda 1978–; Vaterländischer Verdienstorden in Bronze, Silver and Gold, Orden Banner der Arbeit, Karl-Marx-Orden and other decorations. *Address:* Sozialistische Einheitspartei Deutschlands, 102 Berlin, Am Marx-Engels-Platz 2, German Democratic Republic.

HERRMANN, Siegfried, DR. THEOL., DR. PHIL.; German theologian; b. 15 May 1926, Dresden; s. of Martin Herrmann and Emma Hammer; m. Ruth Herrmann 1957; one s. one d.; ed. Univ. of Leipzig; Asst. in Old Testament Studies, Univ. of Leipzig 1951–59; Dozent, Humboldt Univ. Berlin 1960–66; Prof. of Old Testament, Evangelical Theology Dept., Univ. of Bochum 1966–. *Publications:* Untersuchungen zur Überlieferungsgestalt mittelägyptischer Literaturwerke 1957, Die prophetischen Heilserwartungen 1965, A History of Israel in Old Testament Times 1980, Jeremia 1986,

Ges: Studien zur Geschichte und Theologie des Alten Testaments 1986. *Address:* 4630 Bochum 1, Paracelsusweg 14, Federal Republic of Germany. *Telephone:* 0234/70 17 75.

HERRON, Very Rev. Andrew, M.A., B.D., LL.B.; British (Scottish) clergyman; b. 29 Sept. 1909, Glasgow; s. of John Todd Herron and Mary Skinner Herron (née Hunter); m. Joanna Fraser Neill 1935; four d.; ed. Albert Road Acad., Glasgow Univ., Trinity Coll., Glasgow; Minister (Church of Scotland) of Linwood 1936–40, of Houston and Killellan 1940–59; Clerk to the Presbytery of Paisley 1953–59, of Glasgow 1959–81; Moderator of the Gen. Ass. of the Church of Scotland 1971–72, Convener of the Business Cttee. of the Gen. Ass. 1972–76, Convener Dept. of Publicity and Publ. 1959–69; Special Lecturer in Practical Theology, Univ. of Glasgow 1968–85; Ed. Church of Scotland Year Book 1961–; Baird Lecturer 1985; Hon. D.D. (St. Andrews) 1975; Hon LL.D. (Strathclyde) 1983. *Publications:* Record Apart 1972, Guide to the General Assembly 1976, Guide to Congregational Affairs 1979, Guide to the Presbytery 1982, Guide to the Ministry 1987, Guide to Ministerial Income 1987; Kirk by Divine Right (Baird Lecture) 1985. *Address:* 36 Darnley Road, Glasgow, G41 4NE, Scotland. *Telephone:* (041) 423 6422.

HERSANT, Robert Joseph Emile; French journalist and former public servant; b. 31 Jan. 1920, Vertou; s. of Victor Hersant and Juliette Hugot; ed. high schools at Rouen and Le Havre; editor 1945–; f. and Exec. Pres. Robert Hersant press group 1950–, Ed. Le Figaro, Paris-Normandie, Nord-Eclair, Nord-Matin, Centre-Presse, Le Berry républicain, L'Eclair de l'Ouest, France-Antilles, La Liberté du Morbihan, L'Action républicaine, Le Havre-Presse, La République des Pyrénées, L'Auto-Journal, Yachting, Sport-Auto, Bateaux, Revue de la chasse, La Pêche et les Poissons, Point de vente, Votre tricot, La Bonne Cuisine, Layettes, Market, L'Ami des Jardins, France-Amérique (New York); Pres. Nat. Assen. Gen. or Specialized Periodic Press and French Periodic Press Fed. 1971–, Admin. Council Delaroche SA 1986, Le Progrès 1986; Vice-Pres. French Nat. Press Fed. Assen. of Provincial Dailies 1972–; Pres. Dir.-Gen. Socpresse; Exec. Dir.-Gen. France-Soir 1976–; Mayor of Ravenel 1953–59, of Liancourt 1967–74; Councillor for Saint-Just-en-Chaussée 1954–73; controls "La 5" (TV network) 1987–; mem. Nat. Assembly (Social Democrat) for l'Oise 1956–78, 1986–; mem. European Parl. 1984. *Address:* 12 rue de Presbourg, 75116 Paris, France (Office).

HERSCHBACH, Dudley Robert, B.S., M.S., A.M., PH.D.; American professor of chemistry; b. 18 June 1932, San José, Calif.; s. of Robert Dudley Herschbach and Dorothy Edith Beer; m. Georgene Lee Botyos 1964; two d.; ed. Stanford and Harvard Univs.; Asst. Prof. Univ. of Calif., Berkeley 1959–61, Assoc. Prof. 1961–63; Prof. of Chem., Harvard Univ. 1963–, Frank B. Baird, Jr., Prof. of Science 1976–, Chair. Dept. of Chem. 1977–80, Faculty Council 1980–83, Co-Master of Currier House 1981–86, Fellow, Exxon Faculty 1981–; Assoc. Ed., Journal of Physical Chem. 1980–; Fellow, American Acad. of Arts and Sciences; mem. N.A.S. American Chemical Soc.; Hon. D.Sc. (Toronto) 1977; shared Nobel Prize for Chemistry; Pure Chem. Prize, American Chemical Soc. 1965, Spiers Medal, Faraday Soc. 1976, Pauling Medal, American Chem. Soc. 1978, Polanyi Medal Royal Soc. of Chem. 1982, Langmuir Prize, American Physical Soc. 1983. *Publications:* Research papers in Journal of Chemical Physics, Proceedings of the National Academy, Review of Scientific Instruments, Advances in Chemical Physics, etc. 1955–. *Leisure interests:* viola, running. *Address:* Department of Chemistry, Harvard Univ., 12 Oxford Street, Cambridge, Mass. 02138, U.S.A.

HERSEY, John Richard, B.A.; American writer; b. 17 June 1914, Tientsin, China; s. of Roscoe Monroe Hersey, Sr. and Grace Baird Hersey; m. 1st Frances Ann Cannon 1940 (divorced 1958), 2nd Barbara Day Kaufman, 1958; three s. two d.; ed. Yale Univ. and Clare Coll., Cambridge; Sec. to Sinclair Lewis 1937; Ed. Time 1937–42; War and Foreign Corresp. Time, Life, New Yorker 1942–46; mem. Council, Authors' League of America 1946–70, Vice-Pres. 1948–54, Pres. 1975–80; Fellow, Berkeley Coll., Yale Univ. 1950–65; Master, Pierson Coll., Yale Univ. 1965–70, Fellow 1965–; Writer in Residence, American Acad. in Rome 1970–71; Lecturer, Yale Univ. 1971–76, Visiting Prof. 1976–77, Prof. 1977–84, Adjunct Prof. Emer. 1984–; Visiting Prof. M.I.T. 1975; mem. American Acad. Arts and Letters 1953, Sec. 1961–76, Chancellor 1981–84; mem. Nat. Inst. Arts and Letters 1950, Council, Authors' Guild 1946–, American Acad. of Arts and Sciences 1978–; Hon. Fellow, Clare Coll., Cambridge Univ. 1967; Hon. M.A. (Yale) 1947, LL.D. (Washington, Jefferson Coll.) 1946, D.H.Litt. (Dropsie Coll.) 1950, L.H.D. (New School for Social Research) 1950, D.Litt. (Wesleyan Univ.) 1957, (Clarkson Coll. of Tech.) 1972, (Syracuse) 1983, (Yale) 1984, (William and Mary) 1987, (Albertus Magnus) 1988; Pulitzer Prize for Fiction 1945, Sidney Hillman Foundation Award 1951, Howland Medal (Yale) 1952. *Publications:* Men on Bataan 1942, Into the Valley 1943, A Bell For Adano 1944, Hiroshima 1946, The Wall 1950, The Marmot Drive 1953, A Single Pebble 1956, The War Lover 1959, The Child Buyer 1960, Here to Stay 1962, White Lotus 1965, Too Far to Walk 1966, Under the Eye of the Storm 1967, The Algiers Motel Incident 1968, Letter to the Alumni 1970, The Conspiracy 1972, The Writer's Craft 1974, My Petition for More Space 1974, The President 1975, The Walnut Door 1977, Aspects of the Presidency 1980, The Call 1985, Blues 1987, Life Sketches 1989. *Address:* 719 Windsor Lane, Key West, Fla. 33040 (Oct.–May); RFD 144, Vineyard Haven, Md. 02568, U.S.A. (May–Oct.).

HERSHEY, Alfred Day, PH.D.; American research biologist (retd.); b. 4 Dec. 1908, Owosso, Mich.; s. of Robert D. Hershey and Alma (née Wilbur) Hershey; m. Harriet Davidson Hershey 1946; one s.; ed. Mich. State Univ.; Asst. Bacteriologist, Washington Univ. School of Medicine, St. Louis, Mo. 1934–36, Instructor 1936–38, Asst. Prof. 1938–46, Assoc. Prof. 1942–50; Staff mem. Genetics Research Unit, Carnegie Inst. of Wash., Cold Spring Harbor, N.Y. 1950–62, Dir. 1962–74, (retd.); Fellow, American Acad. of Arts and Sciences; mem. N.A.S.; Hon. D.Sc. (Chicago); Albert Lasker Award of American Public Health Asscn. 1958, Kimber Genetics Award of N.A.S. 1965; Nobel Prize for Medicine (jointly with S. Luria q.v.) 1969. *Publications:* numerous technical articles. *Address:* RD 1640, Moores Hill Road, Syosset, N.Y. 11791, U.S.A.

HERSHEY, Barbara; American actress; b. Hollywood, Los Angeles; unmarried; one s. by David Carradine; ed. Hollywood High School; debut in TV series The Monroes. *Film appearances include:* With Six you get Eggroll, The Last Summer, The Baby Maker, Boxcar Bertha, The Stuntman, The Entity, The Right Stuff, The Liberation of Lord Byron Jones, Love Comes Quietly, The Pursuit of Happiness, Passion Flower, The Natural, Hannah and Her Sisters, Tin Men, Shy People, The Last Temptation of Christ 1988, A World Apart 1988, Beaches 1989. *Address:* c/o Creative Artists Agency, 1888 Century Park East, Los Angeles, Calif. 90067, U.S.A.

HERSI, Dr. Abdurahman Nur, M.A.; Somali economist; b. 1934, Eyl District; m. Saida Hersi; two s. two d.; studied in U.S.A. 1954–60; worked in Planning Office of Council of Ministers 1960–64; worked in UN, New York 1964–68, for UN Econ. Comm. for Africa 1968–70; Gov. Somali Nat. Bank 1970–74; Minister of Finance 1974–78; Econ. Adviser to Pres. 1978. *Leisure interests:* reading, swimming.

HERSOV, Basil Edward, D.M.S., M.A., F.R.S.A.; South African business executive; b. 18 Aug. 1926, Johannesburg; s. of Abraham Sundel Hersov and Gertrude Hersov (née Aronson); m. Antoinette Herbert 1957; two s. two d.; ed. Michaelhouse, Natal and Christ's Coll., Cambridge; pilot in S.A. Air Force 1944–46; joined Anglovaal Ltd. as Learner Official on gold mine 1949, later holding a number of sr. positions with Anglovaal Group: Deputy Chair. 1970, Chair. and Man. Dir. 1973–; Chair. Hartebeestfontein Gold Mining Co. Ltd., Anglovaal Industries Ltd., The Associated Manganese Mines of S.A. Ltd. and S. Atlantic Corpn. Ltd.; mem. bd. of many other cos. within and outside Anglovaal Group; Chair. First Nat. Bank of S.A. Ltd.; Dir. Mutual and Fed. Insurance Co. Ltd., Goodyear Tyre & Rubber Co. (S.A.) Pty Ltd.; Pres. and Fellow Inst. of Dirs. (S.A.); Hon. Pres., mem. Council, S.A. Foundation; Gov. Urban Foundation, Michaelhouse School, Rhodes Univ.; mem. Council, S.A. Chamber of Mines; Fellow, S.A. Inst. of Mining and Metallurgy, S.A. Inst. of Man.; Hon. LL.D. (Rhodes); Hon. Col. 21 Squadron S.A.A.F.; Decoration for Meritorious Service. *Leisure interests:* skiing, horse racing, tennis, flying and sailing. *Address:* Anglovaal Ltd., P.O. Box 62379, Marshalltown 2107 (Office); "Springwaters", Box 65097, Benmore 2010, South Africa (Home). *Telephone:* (011) 634-0223 (Office).

HERTZ, Roy, PH.D., M.D.; American professor of pharmacology and of obstetrics and gynaecology; b. 19 June 1909, Cleveland, Ohio; s. of Aaron D. Hertz and Bertha Lichtman; m. 1st Pearl Ruby Fennell 1934 (died 1962), 2nd Dorothy Oberdorfer 1962; one s. one d.; ed. Univ. of Wisconsin, Johns Hopkins Univ.; U.S. Public Health Service, Div. on Physiology, Nat. Insts. of Health 1941–44; Nat. Cancer Inst. 1944–51; Chair., Endocrinology Section Nat. Cancer Inst. 1946–51; Asst. Clinical Prof. of Medicine, The George Washington Univ. Medical School 1948–66; Nat. Cancer Inst., Nat. Insts. of Health, Bethesda, Md., Chief, Research Medicine, 1951–53, Chief Endocrinology, 1953–65; Scientific Dir., Nat. Inst. of Child Health and Human Devt., Nat. Inst. of Health, Bethesda, Md. 1965–66; Professor of Obstetrics and Gynaecology, The George Washington Univ. School of Medicine, Washington 1966–67; Chief, Reproduction Research, Nat. Inst. of Child Health and Human Devt., Nat. Insts. of Health, Bethesda, Md. 1967–69; Assoc. Dir., the Population Council, The Rockefeller Univ., New York 1969–72, Visiting Scientist 1972–; Prof. of Obstetrics and Gynaecology and of Medicine, Dir. of Clinical Research, New York Medical Coll. Valhalla, N.Y. 1972–73; Research Prof. of Pharmacology and Obstetrics/Gynaecology, George Washington Univ. Medical School 1973–85; Emer. Investigator, N.I.H., Bethesda, Md. 1987–; mem. N.A.S. 1972–; Fellow, American Coll. of Obstetrics and Gynaecology 1970–; mem. numerous other learned societies; Hon. D.Sc. (Wis.) 1986; Lasker Foundation Medical Research Award 1972, Cancer Research Award, Int. Coll. of Surgeons 1969. *Publications:* numerous articles on fertility regulation and cancer research. *Leisure interests:* linguistics, gardening. *Address:* Rt 3, Box 582, Hollywood, Md. 20636, U.S.A. (Home).

HERTZBERGER, Prof. Herman; Dutch architect; b. 6 July 1932, Amsterdam; m. J. C. Van Seters 1959; one s. two d.; ed. Delft Tech. Univ.; pvt. practice, Amsterdam 1958–; Co-Ed. (Dutch) Forum 1959–63; Prof. of Architectural Design, Delft 1970–; architectural award of the town of Amsterdam 1968, Eternit Award 1974, Fritz Schumacher Award 1974, Architecture Award of the City of Amsterdam 1985. *Major works:* office bldg., Centraal Beheer, Apeldoorn 1972, housing for old and disabled people "De Drie Hoven", Amsterdam 1974, music centre, Vredenburg (concert hall), Utrecht 1979; currently designing State Dept. of Soc. Affairs,

The Hague. *Publication:* Homework for More Hospitable Form (Dutch), Forum XXIV 1973. *Leisure interest:* music. *Address:* Vossiusstraat 3, 1071 AB Amsterdam, Netherlands (Office). *Telephone:* 76 58 88.

HERVÉ, Edmond; French politician; b. 3 Dec. 1942, La Bouillie, Côtes du Nord; m.; one c.; Prof. of Constitutional Law, Rennes Univ.; Conseiller général, Ille-et-Vilaine 1973–; Deputy for Ille-et-Vilaine to Nat. Ass. 1986–; Mayor of Rennes 1977–; fmr. Minister of Health; Minister Del. to Minister of Industry for Energy 1981–83; Sec. of State for Health 1983–86; Regional Councillor, Brittany 1986–; fmr. Chair. Bd. of regional hospital centre, Rennes, and study group on reform of social assistance policies; Parti Socialiste. *Address:* Assemblée nationale, 75355 Paris; Mairie, 35000 Rennes, France.

HERVÉ-BAZIN, Jean-Pierre Marie, L. ÈS L. (pseudonym Hervé Bazin); French writer; b. 17 April 1911, Angers; s. of Jacques Hervé-Bazin and Paule Guilloteaux; m. 4th Odile l'Hermitte; one s.; (seven c. by three previous marriages); ed. Faculté des Lettres de Paris; critic for newspaper L'Information; on staff of Editions Grasset, Editions Seuil; critic, Journal du Dimanche 1981–; Pres. Comm. d'Aide à la Création; Vice-Pres. Assen. of Writers; mem. Acad. Goncourt 1958–, Pres. 1973–, PEN Club, Soc. des Gens de Lettres, conseil nat. des Lettres; Officier, Légion d'honneur, Commdr. des Arts et des Lettres, des Palmes académiques, Officier, Ordre nat. du Mérite; numerous prizes. *Publications:* Poetry: Jours 1947, A la poursuite d'Iris 1948, Humeurs 1953; Novels: Vipère au poing 1948, La tête contre les murs 1949, La mort du petit cheval 1950, Le bureau des mariages 1951, Lève-toi et marche 1952, L'huile sur le feu 1954, Qui j'ose aimer 1956, La fin des asiles 1959, Au nom du fils 1960, Chapeau bas 1963, Plumons l'oiseau 1966, Le matrimonie 1967, Les bienheureux de la désolation 1970, Tristan 1972, Cri de la chouette 1972, Madame Ex 1975, Traits 1976, Ce que je crois 1977, Un feu dévore un autre feu 1978, L'eglise verte 1981, Abécédaire 1984, Le Démon de Minuit 1988. *Leisure interest:* gardening. *Address:* 9 rue des Murets, 76130 Mont Saint Aignan, France. *Telephone:* 35.07.49.31.

HERWARTH VON BITTENFELD, Hans; German diplomatist; b. 14 July 1904, Berlin; s. of Hans Richard and Ilse (von Tiedemann) Herwarth von Bittenfeld; m. Elisabeth, Baroness von Redwitz 1935; one d.; ed. Univs. of Berlin, Breslau and Munich; entered Foreign Office 1927; Attaché, Paris 1930; Second Sec. and Personal Sec. to Amb. Moscow 1931–39; mil. service 1939–45; Govt. Counsellor, Dir., Bavarian State Chancellery 1945–49; Ministerialdirigent and Chief of Protocol, Fed. German Govt. 1950; apptd. Minister 1952; Amb. to U.K. 1955–61; State Sec., Chief of Office of Fed. Pres. 1961–65; Amb. to Italy 1965–69; State Sec. Foreign Office, Bonn. March 1969, now retd.; Chair. Comm. for Reform of Foreign Service 1969–71, Supervisory Bd. Deutsche Unilever GmbH 1969–77, Venice Cttee. German UNESCO Comm.; Pres. Goethe-Inst., Munich 1971–77, Int. Advisory Cttee. to Save Venice; Hon. Pres Deutsch—Englische Gesellschaft, Düsseldorf; Grand Cross 2nd Class, Order of Merit (Fed. Germany), G.C.V.O. (U.K.) and other decorations. *Publication:* Against Two Evils 1931–45. *Leisure interests:* antiques, skiing. *Address:* Schloss, 8643 Küps, Federal Republic of Germany.

HERZBERG, Gerhard, C.C., DR.ING., LL.D., D.SC.; Canadian physicist; b. 25 Dec. 1904, Hamburg, Germany; s. of Albin and Ella (Biber) Herzberg; m. 1st Luise Oettinger 1929 (died 1971), one s. one d.; m. 2nd Monika Tenthoff 1972; ed. Darmstadt Inst. of Technology and Univs. of Göttingen and Bristol; Lecturer, Darmstadt Inst. of Technology 1930–35; Research Prof. of Physics, Univ. of Saskatchewan 1935–45; Prof. of Spectroscopy, Yerkes Observatory, Univ. of Chicago 1945–48; Dir. of the Div. of Pure Physics, Nat. Research Council, Ottawa 1949–69, Distinguished Research Scientist, Nat. Research Council 1969–; Bakerian Lecturer, Royal Soc. 1960; George Fisher Baker non-Resident Lecturer in Chemistry, Cornell Univ. 1968; mem. Royal Soc. of Canada, Pres. Section III 1951–52, Pres. 1966–67; Hon. mem. Hungarian Acad. of Sciences 1964, Optical Soc. of America 1968; Hon. Foreign mem. American Acad. of Arts and Sciences 1965; Hon. mem. Japan Acad. 1976, Chem. Soc. of Japan 1978; Foreign Assoc. N.A.S., Washington 1968; Academician Pontifical Acad. of Sciences 1964; Fellow, Royal Soc. of London; Hon. Fellow, Indian Acad. of Sciences, Chemical Soc. of London 1968; Foreign mem. Royal Swedish Acad. of Sciences (Physics) 1981; Univ. of Liège Medal 1950, Henry Marshall Tory Medal (Canadian Royal Soc.) 1953, Joy Kissen Mookerjee Gold Medal (Indian Asscn. for the Cultivation of Science) 1957, Frederic Ives Medal (Optical Soc. of America) 1964, Willard Gibbs Medal (American Chemical Soc.) 1969, Faraday Medal (Chemical Soc. of London) 1970, Royal Medal (Royal Soc. of London) 1971, Linus Pauling Medal (American Chemical Soc.) 1971, Nobel Prize in Chem. 1971, Earle K. Plyler Prize, American Physical Soc. 1985. *Publications:* Atomic Spectra and Atomic Structure 1937, Molecular Spectra and Molecular Structure: I. Spectra of Diatomic Molecules 1939, 1950, II. Infra-red and Raman Spectra of Polyatomic Molecules 1945, III. Electronic Spectra Polyatomic Molecules 1966, IV. Constants of Diatomic Molecules (with K. P. Huber) 1979, The Spectra and Structures of Simple Free Radicals: An Introduction to Molecular Spectroscopy 1971. *Leisure interest:* music. *Address:* National Research Council, Ottawa, Ontario, K1A 0R6 (Office); 190 Lakeway Drive, Ottawa, Ontario, K1L 5B3, Canada (Home).

HERZOG, Gen. Chaim, LL.B.; Israeli lawyer, diplomatist and military expert; b. 17 Sept. 1918, Belfast, N. Ireland; s. of Rabbi Dr. Isaac and Sarah Herzog; m. Aura Ambache 1947; three s. one d.; ed. Wesley Coll. Dublin, Govt. of Palestine Law School, Jerusalem, London and Cambridge Univs., Lincoln's Inn, London; went to Palestine 1935; served in British Army, World War II, rank of Maj.; Dir. Intelligence, Israeli Defence Forces 1948-50; Defence Attaché, Israeli Embassy, Washington, Ottawa 1950-54; Field Commands 1954-59; Dir. Mil. Intelligence 1959-62; Gen. 1961; Man. Dir. G.U.S. Industries 1962-72; Gov. West Bank of the Jordan 1967; Senior Partner, Herzog, Fox and Neeman 1972-83; Perm. Rep. to UN 1975-78; Pres. of Israel May 1983-; mem. Knesset (Labour) 1981-83; fmr. Pres. World ORT Union; Dir. Israel Discount Bank; Hon. Dr. (Yeshiva Univ., N.Y., Jewish Theological Seminary, N.Y., Bar-Ilan Univ., Israel, Georgetown Univ. Washington D.C., Hebrew Univ., Jerusalem, Haifa Univ., Weizmann Inst. of Science, Monrovia Univ., Ben Gurion Univ., Brandeis Univ.); Hon. K.B.E. 1970, Hon. Fellow Univ. Coll. London; Hon. Bencher, Lincolns' Inn 1987; Wingate Book Prize 1983. *Publications:* Israel's Finest Hour (Hebrew and English) 1967, Days of Awe (Hebrew) 1973, Judaism, Law and Ethics 1974, The War of Atonement 1975, Who Stands Accused? 1978, Battles of the Bible (with Mordechai Gichon) 1978, The Arab-Israeli Wars 1982, Heroes of Israel 1988 and numerous articles in foreign and Israeli journals. *Leisure interests:* sailing, golf, writing, broadcasting. *Address:* Beit Hanassi, Jerusalem, Israel. *Telephone:* (02) 707211.

HERZOG, Maurice; French civil servant, businessman and former mountaineer; b. 15 Jan. 1919, Lyons (Rhône); s. of Robert Herzog and Germaine Beaume; m. 1st Comtesse Marie Pierre de Cossé Brissac 1964 (divorced 1976), one s. one d.; m. 2nd Elisabeth Gamper 1976, two s.; ed. Collège Chaptal, Paris, Faculty of Science, Lyon and Faculty of Law, Paris; Leader, French Himalayan Expedition 1950; fmr. Dir. Kléber-Colombes Soc.; High Commr. for Youth and Sport 1958-63, Sec. of State 1963-66; mem. UN Econ. and Social Council 1966-; mem. Int. Olympic Cttee. 1970-, Chief of Protocol 1975; fmr. Deputy, Haute Savoie, Mayor of Chamonix; Pres. Financial Comm. Rhône-Alpes Regional Council; Pres. Triton-France 1984-, Spie-Batignolles Int., Spie-Loisirs; Dir. Jeumont-Industrie 1966-, Mauguière 1966-, Atlas Copco France, Spie-Trindel, Spie-Capag, INEC, Triton-Europe (London), Tractebel-Finance (Geneva), Tractebel (Belgium); Hon. Pres. Société du tunnel du Mont-Blanc 1984-; Commdr., Légion d'honneur; Croix de guerre, and other French and foreign decorations. *Publications:* Annapurna premier 8000, Regards sur L'Annapurna, L'Expédition de l'Annapurna, La Montagne, Les grandes aventures de l'Himalaya. *Leisure interests:* history, literature, science. *Address:* 21 boulevard Richard Wallace, 92200 Neuilly-sur-Seine; La Tournette, 84 chemin de la Tournette, 74400 Chamonix, Haute Savoie, France (Home). *Telephone:* 42.25.16.42 (Office); 47.47.96.11 (Home, Paris).

HERZOG, Raymond Harry, B.A.; American business executive; b. 15 Sept. 1915, Merricourt, N.D.; s. of Harry G. and Mollie Klundt Herzog; m. Jane Cobb 1940; two s. one d.; ed. Lawrence Univ., Appleton, Wis.; Chemist, W. Virginia Coal and Coke Co. 1937-38; Coach and Science Teacher, St. Croix Falls, Wis. 1939-41; joined Minnesota Mining and Manufacturing Co. 1941, Gen. Man. Duplicating Products Div. 1956-59, Div. Vice-Pres. 1959-61, Corporate Vice-Pres. 1961-63, Group Vice-Pres. Graphic Systems Group 1963-70, Pres. 1970-75, Chair. 1975-82, C.E.O. 1975-79; Chair. Business Equipment Mfrs. Assen. 1971; Dir. Nat. Assen. of Mfrs., Gen. Motors Corpn., First Trust Co. of St. Paul, Jim Walter Corpn., First Bank System Inc., Northwest Airlines, United Way of St. Paul, U.S.—U.S.S.R. Trade and Econ. Council, U.S. Steel Corpn., Deluxe Check Printers, West Point Pepperell Inc.; Trustee, Univ. of Minnesota Foundation, Lawrence Univ., Minn. Mutual Life Insurance Co.; mem. Chase Int. Advisory Cttee. *Leisure interests:* golf, fishing, hunting. *Address:* 23 Shady Woods Road, St. Paul, Minn. 55110, U.S.A. (Home). *Telephone:* 426-2691 (Home).

HERZOG, Werner; German film director; b. 1942; *Films directed:* Signs of Life 1967, Even Dwarfs Started Small 1970, Fata Morgana 1971, The Land of Darkness and Silence 1971, Aguirre Wrath of God 1973, The Enigma of Kaspar Hauser 1974, The Great Ecstasy of Woodcutter Steiner 1974, How Much Wood Would Woodchuck Chuck 1976, Heart of Glass 1976, Stroszek 1976-77, Woyzeck 1979, Nosferatu 1979, Le pays du silence et de l'obscurité 1980, Fitzcarraldo 1982, Where the Green Ants Dream 1984, Cobra Verde 1987; *opera directed:* Lohengrin (Bayreuth) 1987.

HESBURGH, Rev. Theodore M., S.T.D.; American university president; b. 25 May 1917; ed. Univ. of Notre Dame, Gregorian Univ., Rome, and Catholic Univ. of America; ordained priest of Congregation of Holy Cross 1943; joined Univ. of Notre Dame 1945, Head of Theology Dept. 1948-49, Exec. Vice-Pres. of Univ. 1949-52, Pres. 1952-87; mem. U.S. Comm. on Civil Rights (Chair. 1969-72), President's Comm. on All-Volunteer Armed Force, Carnegie Comm. on the Future Structure and Financing of Higher Educ., Comm. on the Future of Private and Independent Higher Educ. in New York State, Adlai E. Stevenson Inst. of Int. Affairs; Perm. Rep. of Holy See to Int. Atomic Energy Agency, Vienna 1957; Pres. Int. Fed. of Catholic Univs.; Trustee, Rockefeller Foundation, Chair. Bd. of Trustees 1977-, Carnegie Foundation for Advancement of Teaching (Pres. 1963-64); Chair. Acad. Council, Ecumenical Inst. for Advanced Theological Studies

in Jerusalem; Chair. with rank of Amb. U.S. Del. to UN Conf. on Science and Tech. for Devt. 1977-; fmr. Dir. American Council on Educ.; Dir. Woodrow Wilson Nat. Fellowship Corpn., Nutrition Foundation and other orgs.; Fellow, American Acad. of Arts and Sciences; 89 hon. degrees (June 1982); Distinguished Service Medal, U.S. Navy; Presidential Medal of Freedom 1964, Jefferson Award 1976. *Publications:* God and the World of Man 1950, Patterns for Educational Growth 1958, Thoughts for Our Times 1962, More Thoughts for Our Times 1965, Still More Thoughts for Our Times 1966, Thoughts IV 1968, Thoughts V 1969, The Humane Imperative: A Challenge for the Year 2000 1974, The Hesburgh Papers: Higher Values in Higher Education 1979. *Address:* University of Notre Dame, Notre Dame, Ind. 46556, U.S.A. *Telephone:* 219-283-6383.

HESELTINE, Rt. Hon. Michael Ray Dibdin, P.C., M.P.; British politician; b. 21 March 1933, Swansea, Wales; s. of the late Col. Rupert and of Eileen Ray Heseltine; m. Anne Edna Harding Williams 1962; one s. two d.; ed. Shrewsbury School, Pembroke Coll., Oxford (Hon. Fellow 1986); Pres. Oxford Union 1954; Chair. Haymarket Press 1965-70; M.P. for Tavistock 1966-74, for Henley 1974-; Parl. Sec. Ministry of Transport 1970; Parl. Under-Sec. of State, Dept. of the Environment 1970-72; Minister of Aerospace and Shipping 1972-74; Opposition Spokesman for Industry 1974-76, for the Environment 1976-79; Sec. of State for the Environment 1979-83, for Defence 1983-86; Pres. Assen. of Conservative Clubs 1982-83. *Publications:* Reviving the Inner Cities 1983, Where There's a Will 1987, The Challenge of Europe: Through 1992 and Beyond 1988. *Address:* House of Commons, Westminster, London, S.W.1; Thenford House, nr. Banbury, Oxon., England (Home).

HESLOP-HARRISON, John, D.SC., PH.D., F.L.S., F.INST.BIOL., M.R.I.A., F.R.S.E., F.R.S., F.R.S.A.; British professor of plant physiology; b. 10 Feb. 1920, Middlesbrough; s. of Prof. John W. Heslop-Harrison, F.R.S. and Christian Watson Henderson; m. Yolande Massey 1950; one s.; ed. King's Coll., Durham Univ.; mil. service 1941-46; Lecturer King's Coll., Univ. of Durham 1946; lecturer Queen's Univ., Belfast 1946-50; Lecturer and Reader, Univ. Coll. London 1950-54; Prof. and Head Dept., Queen's Univ., Belfast 1954-60; Mason Prof. and Head Dept., Univ. of Birmingham 1960-67; Editor Annals of Botany 1962-67; Brittingham Visiting Prof., Univ. of Wis. 1965; Visiting Scientist, Forest Genetics Research Station, U.S.D.A. Wis. 1968; Prof. Inst. of Plant Devt., Univ. of Wis., Madison 1967-70; Dir. Royal Botanic Gardens, Kew 1971-76; Visiting Prof. Univ. of Reading, of Massachusetts, Amherst 1976-77, 1978; Pres. Inst. of Biology, London 1974-75; Royal Soc. Research Prof., Univ. Coll. of Wales, Aberystwyth 1977-85; foreign mem. German Acad. of Science 1975, Botanical Soc. of America 1976; Hon. Foreign mem. American Acad. of Arts and Sciences 1982; Corresp. mem. Royal Dutch Botanical Soc.; Foreign Fellow, Indian Nat. Science Acad. 1974; Foreign Assoc. Nat. Acad. Sciences U.S.A. 1983; Samuel Weiner Distinguished Visitor, Univ. of Manitoba, Winnipeg 1976; Croonian Lecturer, Royal Soc. 1974; mem. U.K. Agric. Research Council 1977-82; Hon. D.Sc. (Queen's Univ., Belfast) 1971, (Bath Univ.) 1982, (Edin.) 1984; (Hull) 1986; Trail-Crisp Medal, Linnean Soc. 1967, Medallist, Univ. of Liège 1967, Gunnar Erdtman Int. Medal for Palynology 1971, Cooke Award, American Acad. of Allergy 1974, Darwin Medal, Royal Soc. 1982, Keith Medal, Royal Soc. Edin. 1984. *Publications:* research papers, monographic reviews in international journals. *Leisure interests:* painting, hill walking, field botany. *Address:* Welsh Plant Breeding Station, University College of Wales, Plas Gogerddan, nr. Aberystwyth, SY23 3EB, Wales (Office); The Pleasaunce, 137 Bargates, Leominster, Herefords. HR6 8QS, England (Home). *Telephone:* (0568) 611 566 (Home).

HESS, Benno, M.D.; German medical research director; b. 22 Feb. 1922, Berlin; s. of Ludwig Hess and Herta Hess; m. Ulrike Hess 1955; five c.; ed. Heidelberg Univ.; Dir. and Scientific mem. Max-Planck-Inst. Dortmund 1965-; Prof. Ruhr Univ. Bochum 1970-; Vice-Pres. Max-Planck-Gesellschaft zur Förderung der Wissenschaften, Munich 1980-; mem. European Molecular Biology Org.; Special Adviser, Comm. for Science and Tech. of European Community; mem. Advisory Panel, CIBA Foundation, London; mem. Deutsche Akad. der Naturforscher Leopoldina, Düsseldorf and Heidelberg Acads.; Hon. mem. American Soc. of Biological Chemists; mem. A.A.A.S. and other learned socs. etc. *Publications:* articles in scientific journals. *Leisure interests:* nonlinear dynamics and organization of biology, structure and function of biomembranes, science as a historical process. *Address:* Max-Planck-Institut für Ernährungsphysiologie, Rheinlanddamm 201, D-4600 Dortmund 1, Federal Republic of Germany. *Telephone:* 0231/12061.

HESS, Werner; German broadcasting official; b. 13 Oct. 1914, Frankfurt; s. of Wilhelm Hess; m. Marielies Elbers 1944 (died 1965); studies in evangelical theology, Germanic philology and drama, Univs. of Giessen, Marburg, Jena and Frankfurt/Main; church minister in Frankfurt; military service 1939-45; resumed ministry in Frankfurt-Ginnheim 1945-60; Film Industry Del. of the Evangelical Church of Germany; mem. Broadcasting Council of the Hessian Broadcasting Service 1948-, Chair. 1959-; Founder and mem. of the Soc. for the Voluntary Control of the Film Industry; Chair. Supervisory Bd. of the Matthias Film Distribution Co., Stuttgart; Hessian Broadcasting and Television Service Television Programme Dir. 1960-62, Gen. Dir. 1962-81; Chair. ARD (German Broadcasting Service) 1965, 1966, 1976, 1977; Vice-Pres. European Broadcasting Union 1968-77; Chair. European Broadcasting Union Comm. for Developing Countries.

Address: c/o Hessischer Rundfunk, 6 Frankfurt am Main, Bertramstrasse 8 (Office); 53 Frauenlobstrasse, 6 Frankfurt am Main, Federal Republic of Germany (Home).

HESSE, Gerhard Edmund, DR. PHIL.; German professor of chemistry; b. 21 July 1908, Tübingen; s. of Dr. Richard and Thekla (née Pfleiderer) Hesse; m. Cleo Lotz 1935; three s. one d.; ed. Univs. of Bonn and Munich; lecturer Univ. of Marburg/Lahn 1938; Asst. Prof. of Chem. Univ. of Freiburg 1945; Prof. of Chem., Univ. of Erlangen 1953-75, Emer. 1975-; Pres. Coll. Alexandrinum, Erlangen; mem. Gesellschaft Deutsche Chemiker, Physkalisch-Medizin Soc. Erlangen, Bayerische Akad. der Wissenschaften; Freseniuspreis; 2 Tswett-Medaillien. *Publications:* Adsorptions-methoden im chemische Laboratorien 1943; numerous learned papers. *Leisure interests:* photography, ecological matters, gardening. *Address:* Rathsbergerstrasse 63, App. 2339, 8520 Erlangen, Federal Republic of Germany. *Telephone:* 82 53 39.

HESSEL, Stephane F., M.B.E.; French diplomatist; b. 20 Oct. 1917, Berlin; s. of Franz Hessel and Helen (née Grund) Hessel; m. 1st Vita (née Mirkine-Guetzevitch) Hessel 1939 (died 1986), 2nd Christiane (née Chabry) Hessel 1987; three c.; war service 1941-45; Admin. Dir. Secr. Gen., UN 1946-50; served in Foreign Ministry 1950-54; Asst. to the Pres. 1954-55; Adviser to High Commr., Saigon 1955-57, Foreign Affairs Adviser, Algiers 1964-69; Asst. Admin. UNDP 1970-72; Perm. Rep. to UN Office, Geneva 1977-81; mem. High Authority for Audiovisual Communication 1982-85; Chair. Asscn. France-Algérie 1985-; Commdr., Légion d'Honneur 1982, Grand Officier du Mérite. *Leisure interest:* Greek mythology. *Address:* 5, rue Alexandre Cabanel, 75015 Paris, France. *Telephone:* 45 67 27 37.

HESSELBACH, Walter; German banker and business executive; b. 20 Jan. 1915, Frankfurt am Main; s. of Wilhelm and Elisabeth (née Mayer) Hesselbach; m. Hedwig Huth 1953; three d.; ed. Wöhler Realgymnasium; Foreign Dept., Deutsch-Überseeische Bank, Berlin 1935-37; Merck und Co., Darmstadt 1937-38; Sec. to Georg von Opel 1938-40; mil. service, prisoner of war 1940-47; Bank Deutscher Länder, Frankfurt am Main 1947-52; mem. Bd. Landeszentralbank, Hessen 1952-58; Bank für Gemeinwirtschaft AG, Frankfurt am Main 1958-62, Chair. 1962-77; Chair. of Bd. of Mans. BGAG Beteiligungsgesellschaft für Gemeinwirtschaft AG, Frankfurt am Main 1977-85; Pres. Assen. of Co-operative Businesses 1985-; Chair. of Bd. Allgemeine Hypothekenbank AG, Frankfurt, BSV Bank für Sparanlagen und Vermögensbildung, Frankfurt; Chair. Banking Cttee., Int. Co-operative Alliance, London; Pres. Friedrich Ebert Foundation, Bonn, German Israel Chamber of Commerce, Frankfurt, Fed. Assen. of Socs. of Friends of Hebrew Univ. of Jerusalem in Germany; Hon. Pres. German Israel Friendship League, Bonn, mem. Bd. of Govs. Hebrew Univ., Jerusalem; Hon. mem. Lessing Akademie, Wolfenbüttel; Dr. h.c. (Hebrew Univ., Jerusalem, Univ. of Tel-Aviv); Hon. Senator Johann-Wolfgang-Goethe-Univ., Frankfurt; Golda Meir Prize; Martin Buber Prize; Grosses Bundesverdienstkreuz mit Stern und Schulterband; Wilhelm Leuschner Plakette, Govt. of Hessen, Goethe Plakette, Frankfurt Municipality. *Publication:* The Commonwealth Enterprises 1966. *Leisure interests:* economics, politics, literature. *Address:* Ginnheimer Stadtweg 148, D-6000 Frankfurt am Main 1, Federal Republic of Germany.

HESTER, James McNaughton, D.PHIL.; American university official; b. 19 April 1924, Chester, Pa.; s. of James Montgomery Hester and Margaret (McNaughton) Hester; m. Janet Rodes 1953; three d.; ed. Princeton and Oxford Univs.; Capt., U.S. Marine Corps, Japan 1943-46, 1951-52; Civil Information Officer, Fukuoka Mil. Govt. Team, Japan 1946-47; Rhodes Scholar, Oxford Univ. 1947-50; Asst. to Rhodes Trustees Princeton 1950; Asst. to Pres., Handy Assocs. Inc. (Management Consultants) N.Y. 1953-54; Account Supervisor, Gallup & Robinson Inc. 1954-57; Provost, Brooklyn Center, L.I. Univ. 1957-60, Vice-Pres., Trustee L.I. Univ.; Prof. of History, Exec. Dean Arts and Sciences, Dean Graduate School of Arts and Sciences, N.Y. Univ. 1960-61, Trustee 1962, Pres. 1962-75; Rector, UN Univ., Tokyo 1975-80; Pres. New York Botanical Garden 1980-; Dir. Union Carbide Corpn. 1963-, Lehman Corpn. 1964-, J. Walter Thompson Co. 1974-, Bowery Savings Bank 1974-; Chair. Pres. Nixon's Task Force on Priorities in Higher Educ. 1969; mem. Assen. of American Rhodes Scholars 1962-, Japan Soc. 1962-; Pilgrims, U.S. 1963-, Council on Foreign Relations 1962-, Council for Financial Aid to Educ. 1971-75; Trustee Metropolitan Museum of Art, Inst. of Int. Educ. 1963-75, Phelps-Stokes Fund 1962-75; Hon. LL.D. (Princeton, Moorehouse Coll., Hofstra Univ., Lafayette Coll., Hahnemann Medical Coll., Fordham); Hon. L.H.D. (Hartwick Coll., Pace Univ., Colgate, Pittsburgh, New York); Hon. D.C.L. (Alfred Univ.); Chevalier, Légion d'honneur 1964; First Class Order of the Sacred Treasure 1980. *Address:* New York Botanical Gardens, Bronx, New York, N.Y. 10458 (Office); 37 Washington Square, West, New York, N.Y. 10003, U.S.A. (Home).

HESTON, Charlton; American actor; b. 4 Oct. 1924, Evanston, Ill.; s. of Russell Carter and Lilla Charlton Heston; m. Lydia Clark 1944; one s. one d.; ed. Northwestern Univ., Evanston; first Broadway appearance in Antony and Cleopatra 1948; has starred in more than 50 films, Hollywood 1950-; Pres. Screen Actors Guild 1965-71; mem. Nat. Council of Arts 1967; mem. American Film Inst. 1971-, Chair 1973; Chair. on Arts, Presidential Task Force on Arts and Humanities 1981-; Acad. Award for Best Actor, Ben Hur 1959, Veterans of Foreign Wars Citizenship Medal 1982. Stage

appearances include Macbeth 1954, 1959, 1976 (London), Mister Roberts 1954, Detective Story 1956, A Man for All Seasons 1965, 1987, Caine Mutiny Court Martial (also Dir.), London 1985. Television includes Chiefs (CBS) 1983, Nairobi Affair (CBS) 1984, The Colbys (ABC-TV). *Films include:* Julius Caesar 1950, Dark City 1950, The Greatest Show on Earth 1952, The Savage 1952, Ruby Gentry 1952, The President's Lady 1953, Pony Express 1953, Arrowhead 1953, Bad for Each Other 1953, The Naked Jungle 1954, Secret of the Incas 1954, The Far Horizons 1955, Lucy Gallant 1955, The Private War of Major Benson 1955, Three Violent People 1956, The Ten Commandments 1956, Touch of Evil 1958, The Big Country 1958, The Buccaneer 1958, Ben Hur 1959, The Wreck of the Mary Deare 1959, El Cid 1961, The Pigeon that Took Rome 1962, Diamond Head 1962, 55 Days at Peking 1962, Major Dundee 1964, The Greatest Story Ever Told 1965, The Agony and the Ecstasy 1965, The War Lord 1965, Khartoum 1966, Counterpoint 1967, Will Penny 1967, Planet of the Apes 1967, Beneath the Planet of the Apes 1969, The Hawaiians 1970, Julius Caesar 1970, The Omega Man 1971, Antony and Cleopatra 1972, Skyjacked 1972, The Call of the Wild 1972, Soylent Green 1973, The Three Musketeers 1973, The Four Musketeers 1974, Earthquake 1974, Airport 1975, Midway 1975, Two Minute Warning 1976, The Last Hard Men 1976, The Prince and the Pauper 1976, Gray Lady Down 1978, The Awakening 1980, Mother Lode 1981, Caine Mutiny Court Martial (also Dir.) 1988. *Publication:* The Actor's Life 1979. *Leisure interests:* sketching, tennis. *Address:* c/o Michael Levine Public Relations, 8730 Sunset Boulevard, Sixth Floor, Los Angeles, Calif. 90069, U.S.A.

HETÉNYI, Dr. István; Hungarian economist and politician; b. 3 Aug. 1926, Budapest; s. of Géza Hetényi and Margit Wabrosch; m. Zsuzsa Révész 1950; two c.; joined CP 1951; ed. Budapest Tech. Univ. Dept. of economy; served under Supreme Econ. Council 1949, later under Nat. Planning Office where he became Dept. Head, Chief Head, Vice-Pres. and Sec. of State 1973; Prof. Karl Marx Univ. of Political Economy, Budapest; Vice-Pres. Bd. Soc. of Hungarian Economists; Minister of Finance July 1980-86; Labour Order of Merit, Socialist Labour Medal. *Leisure interest:* old books. *Address:* c/o Ministry of Finance, Budapest V, József nádor tér 2/4, Hungary. *Telephone:* 189-386.

HETHERINGTON, Sir Arthur Ford, Kt., D.S.C., B.A.; British engineer and business executive; b. 12 July 1911; s. of the late Sir Roger Gaskell Hetherington and Lady (Honoria) Hetherington; m. Margaret Lacey 1937; one s. one d.; ed. Highgate School, London, Trinity Coll., Cambridge; Deputy Chair. Southern Gas Bd. 1956-61, Chair. 1961-64; Chair. East Midlands Gas Bd. 1964-66; Deputy Chair. Gas Council 1967-72, Chair. 1972-73; Chair. British Gas Corpn. 1973-76, British Standards Inst. 1976-79; Hon. D.Sc. (London) 1974. *Address:* 32 Connaught Square, London, W.2, England. *Telephone:* 01-723 3128.

HETHERINGTON, (Hector) Alastair, M.A.; British journalist; b. 31 Oct. 1919, Llanishen, Glamorganshire, Wales; s. of late Sir Hector Hetherington and Lady Hetherington; m. 1st Helen Miranda Oliver 1957 (divorced 1978), two s. two d.; m. 2nd Sheila Cameron 1979; ed. Gresham's School, Holt, and Corpus Christi Coll., Oxford; served in Royal Armoured Corps 1940-46; on staff The Glasgow Herald 1946-50; joined (Manchester) Guardian 1950, Foreign Ed. 1953, Ed. 1956-75, Dir. Guardian Newspapers Ltd. 1967-75; with British Broadcasting Corpn. Oct. 1975-80, Controller BBC Scotland 1975-78, Man. BBC Highland 1979-80; Research Prof., Stirling Univ. 1982-87, Emer. Prof. 1987-; Fellow, Nuffield Coll., Oxford 1973-80; mem. Peacock Cttee.; Journalist of the Year, Nat. Press Awards 1970. *Publications:* Guardian Years 1981, News, Newspapers and Television 1985, News in the Regions 1989. *Leisure interest:* hill walking. *Address:* 38 Chalton Road, Bridge of Allan, Stirling, FK9 4EF and Tigh na-Fraoich, High Corrie, Isle of Arran, KA27 8JB, Scotland. *Telephone:* (0786) 832168 and (0770) 81652.

HETTLAGE, Dr. Karl Maria; German university professor; b. 28 Nov. 1902, Essen; s. of Karl Hettlage and Klara Brandenburg; m. Margarete Brenken 1929; two s. two d.; ed. Univs. of Cologne and Münster; Government Official of Prussian Land 1925-30; Financial Adviser, Cologne city admin. 1930-31; Financial Dept., Berlin city admin. 1931-38; sr. bank official 1938-51; Prof. of public Law, Univ. of Mainz 1951-73, Hon. Prof. of Financial Sciences, Univ. of Bonn 1949-; State Sec. Finance Ministry, Fed. German Govt. 1958-62, 1967-69; mem. European Coal and Steel Community (ECSC) High Authority 1962-67, Sciences Council 1965; Pres. IFO Inst. for Econ. Research, Munich. *Leisure interests:* violin, gardening. *Address:* Gumppenbergstrasse 1, 8000 Munich 80, Federal Republic of Germany.

HEUNIS, (Jan) Christiaan, LL.B.; South African politician; b. 20 April 1927, Uniondale; s. of J. C. Heunis and R. C. M. Lamprecht; m. Alida André van Heerden 1951; four s. one d.; ed. Outeniqua High School, George, Univ. of Stellenbosch; Mem. Prov. Council, George 1959, mem. Exec. Cttee. 1965-70; mem. Select Cttee. for Public Funds for Cape Prov. 1960-65, March-May 1962, Chair. April-July 1965; mem. Comm. of Investigation into the Stock Exchange 1970; M.P. for False Bay 1970-74, for Helderburg 1974-; mem. Select Cttee. on Public Funds 1970-72; mem. Parl. Select Cttee. on Certain Orgs. 1972; Deputy Minister of Finance and Econ. Affairs 1972-74; Minister of Indian Affairs and of Tourism 1974-75, of Econ. Affairs 1975-79, of Environmental Planning and Energy 1978-79, of Transport 1979–80, of Internal Affairs 1980–82, of Constitutional Affairs Aug. 1982–, of Planning Sept. 1984–; Acting Pres. Jan. 1989–; mem. and Deputy and Chair. Comm. for Investigation into the Constitution 1979–80, Chair. 1980–, mem. Select Cttee.; Chair. Nat. Party in Cape 1986–; Decoration for Outstanding Service 1980. *Leisure interest:* reading. *Address:* House of Assembly, Cape Town; Halfway, Main Road, Rondebosch, Cape Town, South Africa (Home).

HEUSINGER, Hans-Joachim; German politician; b. 7 April 1925, Leipzig; m.; three c.; ed. Akad. für Staats-und Rechtswissenschaft, Potsdam-Babelsberg; electrician 1945–51; leading positions in Leipzig and Cottbus State Admin. and in Liberal Democratic Party; Dir. Chamber of Commerce, Cottbus; mem., Sec. Central Exec. Cttee., mem. Political Comm., Liberal Democratic Party 1957, Deputy Chair. LDP 1972–; mem. Volkskammer (People's Chamber) 1961–; Deputy Chair. Council of Ministers, Minister of Justice 1972–; mem. Presidium of Nat. Council of Nat. Front 1974–; Vaterländischer Verdienstorden in bronze and silver, and other decorations. *Address:* Clara-Zetkin-Strasse 93, 108 Berlin, German Democratic Republic.

HEWISH, Antony, PH.D., F.R.S., F.R.A.S.; British radio astronomer; b. 11 May 1924, Fowey, Cornwall; s. of Ernest W. Hewish and of the late Grace F. L. Hewish (née Pinch); m. Marjorie E. C. Richards 1950; one s. one d.; ed. King's Coll., Taunton and Gonville and Caius Coll., Cambridge; war service 1943–46; Research Fellow, Gonville and Caius Coll., Cambridge 1951–54, Supernumerary Fellow 1956–61; Univ. Asst. Dir. of Research 1953–61, lecturer 1961–69; Fellow, Churchill Coll. Cambridge 1962–; Reader in Radio Astronomy, Univ. of Cambridge 1969–71, Prof. 1971–; Prof. Royal Inst. 1977; Dir. Mullard Radio Astronomy Observatory, Cambridge 1982–88; Vikram Sarabhai Prof., Ahmedabad 1988; Foreign Hon. mem. American Acad. of Arts and Sciences 1970; Foreign Fellow Indian Nat. Science Acad.; Hon. Sc.D. (Leicester) 1976, (Exeter) 1977, (Manchester) 1989; Hamilton Prize (Cambridge) 1951, Eddington Medal, Royal Astronomical Soc. 1968, Boys Prize, Inst. of Physics 1970, Dellinger Medal, Int. Union of Radio Science, Hopkins Prize, Cambridge Philosophical Soc. 1972, Michelson Medal, Franklin Inst. 1973, Holweck Medal and Prize, Soc. Française de Physique 1974, Nobel Prize for Physics (jointly with Sir Martin Ryle) 1974, Hughes Medal, Royal Soc. 1977. *Publications:* many papers in scientific journals; Editor: Seeing Beyond the Invisible. *Leisure interests:* listening to good music, swimming, sailing. *Address:* Pryor's Cottage, Kingston, Cambridge, England. *Telephone:* (0223) 262657.

HEWITT, Eric John, D.SC., F.R.S.; British plant physiologist (retd.); b. 27 Feb. 1919, London; s. of Harry Edward Hewitt and Blanche née Du Roveray; m. Hannah Eluned Williams 1943; one s.; ed. Whitgift School, Surrey, King's Coll., Univ. of London and Univ. of Bristol; Asst. Chemist, Chemist R.O.F. Pembrey 1940–42; Research Asst., Long Ashton Research Station, Univ. of Bristol 1942–45, Sr. Plant Physiologist (Nutrition and Biochemistry) 1945–84, Head of Biochemistry, and Reader in Plant Physiology, Univ. of Bristol 1967–84; Fellow of Inst. of Biology. *Publications:* Sand and Water Culture Methods used in the Study of Plant Nutrition 1952, Plant Mineral Nutrition (with T. A. Smith) 1975, Nitrogen Metabolism in Plants 1968, Nitrogen Assimilation of Plants (Ed. with C. V. Cutting) 1979, 160 research papers. *Leisure interests:* gardening, fell walking, TV and classical records. *Address:* Langdales, 63 Ridgeway Road, Long Ashton, Bristol, BS18 9EZ, England (Home). *Telephone:* (0272) 392274.

HEWITT, Harry Ronald, B.SC.; British chemical engineer and business executive (retd.); b. 12 April 1920, Leeds; s. of Charles William and Florence (Kelsey) Hewitt; m. Rosemary Olive Hiscock 1954; two s. one d.; ed. City of Leeds High School, Leeds Coll. of Tech., Bradford Coll. of Tech.; Chemist, Joseph Watson and Sons Ltd., Leeds 1936–41; Royal Ordnance Factories 1941–45; Controller, Control Comm. for Germany 1945–47; Production Man. and Works Man. Consolidated Zinc Ltd. and Orrs Zinc White Ltd. 1947–59; with Johnson Matthey and Co. Ltd. 1959– (Gen. Man., Dir., then Chief Exec.), Man. Dir. 1976–83, Chair. 1983–84. *Leisure interests:* golf, tennis, music. *Address:* 6 Loom Lane, Radlett, Herts. WD7 8AD, England. *Telephone:* (09276) 5243.

HEWITT, William Alexander, A.B.; American manufacturing executive and diplomatist; b. 9 Aug. 1914, San Francisco; s. of Edward Thomas Hewitt and Jeanette Brun; m. Patricia Deere Wiman 1948; one s. two d.; ed. Univ of California; Lieut.-Commdr. U.S.N.R. 1942–46; with John Deere Plow Co., San Francisco 1948–54, Vice-Pres. 1950–54; Dir. Deere & Co., Moline Ill. 1951–, Exec. Vice-Pres. 1954–55, Pres. and Chief Exec. Officer 1955–64, Chair. and C.E.O. 1964–82; Dir. Continental Illinois Nat. Bank & Trust Co. of Chicago, Continental Illinois Corpn., American Telephone & Telegraph Co., Conoco Inc. 1965–81; Dir. Nat. Council for U.S.-China Trade 1973–80, Chair. 1975–78; Dir. U.S.-U.S.S.R. Trade and Econ. Council 1973–80; Amb. to Jamaica 1982–85; mem. The Business Council, American Soc. of Agric. Engineers, The Conf. Bd., Int. Council of the Asia Soc. Inc., and many other orgs.; Hon. Trustee, The Wilson Council of the Woodrow Wilson Int. Center for Scholars 1977–, Cttee. for Econ. Devt.; Trustee, U.S. Council Int. Chamber of Commerce; Trustee, Museum of Modern Art (New York City); Laureate, Ill. Business Hall of Fame 1986. *Address:* Rondelay, RD2, Box 50, Chadds Ford, Pa. 19317, U.S.A. (Home). *Telephone:* (215) 388-2518.

HEY, James Stanley, M.B.E., D.SC., F.R.S.; British research scientist (retd.); b. 3 May 1909, Nelson, Lancs.; s. of William R. and Barbara E. Hey; m. Edna Heywood 1934; ed. Rydal School and Univ. of Manchester; scientist, British Army Operational Research Group 1940–52, Head of Establishment 1949–52; scientist, Royal Radar Establishment 1952–69, Chief Scientific Officer 1966–69; Eddington Medal, Royal Astronomical Soc.; Hon. D.Sc. (Birmingham) 1975, (Kent) 1977. *Publications:* The Radio Universe 1971, revised 3rd edn. 1983, The Evolution of Radio Astronomy 1973; research papers in scientific journals. *Address:* 4 Shortlands Close, Eastbourne, East Sussex, BN22 0JE, England.

HEYDE, Christopher Charles, PH.D., F.A.A.; Australian university professor and statistician; b. 20 April 1939, Sydney; s. of G. C. Heyde and A. D. Wessing; m. T. Elizabeth James 1965; two s.; ed. Barker Coll., Hornsby, Sydney Univ. and Australian Nat. Univ.; Asst. Prof. Mich. State Univ. 1964–65; lecturer Univ. of Sheffield, U.K. 1965–67; Special Lecturer Univ. of Manchester, U.K. 1967–68; Reader, Australian Nat. Univ. 1968–75; Prof. and Head Dept. of Statistics, Inst. of Advanced Studies 1986–88, Dean School of Math. Sciences 1989–; Chief Research Scientist CSIRO 1975–83; Prof. and Chair. Dept. of Statistics, Univ. of Melbourne 1983–86; Visiting Prof. Stanford Univ., Calif. 1972–73; Ed. Australian Journal of Statistics 1973–78, Stochastic Processes and Their Applications 1983–88; Fellow Inst. of Mathematical Statistics 1973; Pres. Statistical Soc. of Australia 1979–80, also Hon. Life mem.; mem. Int. Statistical Inst. (Vice-Pres. 1985–87), Australian Acad. of Science (Vice-Pres. 1988–89); Pitman Medallist, Statistical Soc. of Australia 1988. *Publications:* I. J. Bienaymé: Statistical Theory Anticipated (with E. Seneta) 1977, Martingale Limit Theory and Its Application 1980; plus 130 articles on probability theory and mathematical statistics. *Address:* Department of Statistics, Institute of Advanced Studies, Australian National University, G.P.O. Box 4, Canberra, A.C.T. 2601; 22 Nungara Place, Aranda, A.C.T. 2614, Australia (Home). *Telephone:* (062) 493697.

HEYERDAHL, Thor, PH.D.; Norwegian anthropologist and explorer; b. 6 Oct. 1914, Larvik; s. of Thor Heyerdahl and Alison Heyerdahl (née Lyng); m. 1st Liv Coucheron Torp 1936, 2nd Yvonne Dedekam-Simonsen 1948; two s. three d.; ed. Univ. of Oslo; specialized in zoology and geography at univ. but changed to anthropology during field researches among Polynesians in Marquesas Is. 1937–38; research in N.W. Indian territory of Brit. Columbia (ref. theory of two separate American Indian movements into Pacific) 1939–40; served free Norwegian Mil. Forces 1941–45; research in Europe and U.S.A. 1945–47; led Kon-Tiki expedition from Callao, Peru to Raroia, Polynesia (covering 4,300 miles in 101 days and thus proving Peruvian Indians could have settled in Polynesia) 1947; founded (with Knut Haugland) Kon-Tiki Museum, Oslo 1949; research and lectures in Europe and U.S.A. 1948–52; led Norwegian Archaeological Expedition to Galapagos (establishing evidence of pre-European visits by South American Indians), Field Research in Bolivia, Peru and Colombia 1954; led Norwegian Archaeological Expedition to Easter Island and the East Pacific 1955–56; attempted to cross Atlantic in papyrus boat Ra I 1969 (covering 2,800 miles in 56 days); sailed from Safi, Morocco, in papyrus boat Ra II May 1970, in attempt to cross Atlantic and prove that ancient Mediterranean civilization could have sailed a reed boat to America, and arrived in Barbados July 1970; led expedition of Sumerian-type reed boat, Tigris, to test navigational capabilities of such ancient craft from Asia to Africa 1977–78; archaeological excavations, Maldive Islands 1982–83; led archaeological expeditions to Easter Island 1986, 1987; Vice-Pres. World Asscn. of World Federalists 1966–, Worldview Int. Foundation 1982–; Int. Patron United World Colls. 1973–; Int. Trustee, World Wildlife Fund 1979–; mem. Norwegian Acad. of Science 1958; Fellow, New York Acad. of Sciences 1960; Hon. Ph.D. (Oslo) 1961; Commdr. of the Order of St. Olav, Officer Servicio del Mérito Distinguido of Peru 1952, Grande Ufficiale dell' Ordine al Merito della Repubblica Italiana 1965, Order of Merit First Class, Egypt 1971, Grand Officer Royal Alaouites Order, Morocco 1971, and many other awards including Acad. First Award ("Oscar") for Kon-Tiki film 1951; Vega Medal (Swedish Soc. of Anthropology and Geography) 1962, Patron's Gold Medal (Royal Geographical Soc., London) 1964, shared UN Pahlavi Environmental Prize 1978. *Publications:* På Jakt Efter Paradiset 1938, Kon-Tiki Ekspedisjonen (trans. 64 languages) 1948, American Indians in the Pacific: The Theory behind the Kon-Tiki Expedition 1952, Archaeological Evidence of Pre-Spanish Visits to the Galapagos Islands 1956, Aku-Aku: Påskeøoyas Hemmelighet (trans. 32 languages) 1957, Reports of the Norwegian Archaeological Expedition to Easter Island and the East Pacific, (Vol. I Archaeology of Easter Island 1961, Vol. II Miscellaneous Reports 1965) (with E. N. Ferdon), Indianer und Alt-Asiaten im Pazifik 1966, Sea Routes to Polynesia 1968, The Ra Expeditions 1971, Fatuhiva: Back to Nature 1974, Zwischen den Kontinenten 1975, The Art of Easter Island 1975, Early Man and the Ocean 1978, The Tigris Expedition 1980, The Maldive Mystery 1986, and many articles. *Leisure interest:* outdoor life. *Address:* Colla Micheri, 17020 Laigueglia, Italy.

HEYNS, Johan Adam, M.A., B.D., TH.D., D.PHIL.; South African professor of systematic theology and ethics; b. 27 May 1928, Free State; s. of P. S. Heyns and M. J. M. Heyns; m. Renée Spamer 1954; three s.; ed. Univ. of Potchefstroom, Univ. of Pretoria, Free Univ. of Amsterdam and Univ. of Basle, Switzerland; Minister Dutch Reformed Church, Cape Town 1954; Sr. Lecturer Univ. of Stellenbosch 1966; Prof. at Univ. of Pretoria 1971–;

mem. moderature Dutch Reformed Church 1978, Moderator 1986; Chair. S.A. Akademie vir Wetenskap en Kuns 1984; Andrew Murray Prize (twice), Totius Prize, Credo Prize. *Publications:* Systematic Theology 1978, Theology of Revolution 1975, The Church 1977, Theological Ethics 1 1982, Theological Ethics 2/1 1986. *Address:* 18 Plough Avenue, Waterkloof Ridge, Pretoria, South Africa. *Telephone:* 46-4610.

HEYSSEL, Robert Morris, M.D.; American physician; b. 19 June 1928, Jamestown, Mo.; s. of Clarence C. Heyssel and Meta (Reusser) Heyssel; m. Maria McDaniel 1955; five c.; ed. Univ. of Missouri and St. Louis Univ.; postgraduate training, St. Louis Univ. Hosp. 1953-56, Barnes Hosp., St. Louis 1953-56; Haematologist, Acting Dir. Dept. of Medicine, Atomic Bomb Comm., Nagasaki and Hiroshima 1956-58; mem. Faculty, School of Medicine, Vanderbilt Univ. 1959-68, Dir. Div. of Nuclear Medicine 1962-68, Assoc. Prof. of Medicine 1964-68; Assoc. Dean, School of Medicine, Johns Hopkins Univ. 1968-72, Prof. of Medicine 1971-, Prof. Health Care Org. 1972-; Exec. Vice-Pres., Dir. Johns Hopkins Hospital 1972-83, Pres. 1983-87; Pres. Johns Hopkins Health System 1987-; mem. numerous local, state and nat. comms. on health, medicine, medical educ. etc.; mem. Inst. of Medicine, N.A.S.; Fellow American Coll. of Physicians; Hon. D.Sc. (St. Louis) 1985, and other awards. *Publications:* articles in professional journals. *Leisure interests:* hunting, fishing. *Address:* 600 N. Wolfe Street, Baltimore, Md. 21205 (Office); 230 Stoney Run Lane, Baltimore, Md. 21210, U.S.A. (Home).

HIBBERT, Jack, B.SC; British civil servant; b. 14 Feb. 1932, Huddersfield, Yorks.; s. of the late William Collier Hibbert and Ivy Annie Hibbert née Wigglesworth; m. Joan Clarkson 1957; two s. one d.; ed. Leeds Grammar School and London School of Economics; served R.A.F. 1950-52; Exchequer and Audit Dept. 1952-60; Cen. Statistical Office 1960-81, Chief Statistician 1970-77, Under-Sec. 1977-81; Consultant OECD and Eurostat 1981; Under-Sec., Dept. of Trade and Industry 1982-85; Dir. U.K. Cen. Statistical Office and Head of Govt. Statistical Service 1985-. *Publications:* Measuring the Effects of Inflation on Income, Saving and Wealth (for OECD) 1983. *Leisure interests:* bridge, theatre, music, walking. *Address:* Central Statistical Office, Great George Street, London, SW1 3AQ, England. *Telephone:* 01-233 6117.

HIBBERT, Sir Reginald Alfred, G.C.M.G.; British diplomatist (retd.); b. 21 Feb. 1922, London; m. Ann Alun Pugh 1949; two s. one d.; ed. Queen Elizabeth's Grammar School, Barnet, Worcester Coll., Oxford; war service with Special Operations Executive in Albania, and 4th Queen's Own Hussars in Italy; joined Diplomatic Service 1946, served in Romania, Austria, Guatemala, Turkey, Belgium, and in Foreign Office; Chargé d'affaires, Resident Mission to Mongolian People's Repub. 1964-66; Counsellor, Office of the Political Adviser to C.-in-C. Far East, Singapore 1967-69, Political Adviser 1969-71; Minister, Bonn Embassy 1972-75, Asst. Under-Sec. of State, Foreign and Commonwealth Office 1975-76; Deputy Under-Sec. of State for European Affairs and U.K. Political Dir. in Political Cttee. of the Nine 1976-79; Amb. to France 1979-82; Dir. Ditchley Foundation July 1982-87; Visiting Fellow Nuffield Coll., Oxford 1984-88. *Leisure interests:* gardening, reading, music. *Address:* Frondeg, Pennal, Machynlleth, Powys, SY20 9JX, Wales. *Telephone:* 065-475-220.

HICK, Graeme Ashley; Zimbabwean cricketer; b. 23 May 1966, Salisbury (now Harare); s. of John and Eve Hick; ed. Banket Primary School, Prince Edward Boys' High School; right-hand batsman, off-break bowler, slip and gully fielder; county debut for Worcestershire, England 1984, county cap 1986; overseas tours with Zimbabwe XI, World Cup 1983, Zimbabwe v Sri Lanka, Zimbabwe U-23 Triangular Tournament to Zambia, to U.K. 1985. *Leisure interests:* golf, tennis, squash, indoor hockey, cinema, television, listening to music. *Address:* c/o Worcestershire County Cricket Club, New Road, Worcester, England.

HICK, John Harwood, PH.D., D.PHIL., D.LITT.; British university teacher; b. 20 Jan. 1922, Scarborough, Yorks.; s. of Mark Day Hick and Mary Aileen Hirst; m. Joan Hazel Bowers 1953; three s. one d.; ed. Bootham School, York, Edinburgh Univ., Oxford Univ., Westminster Theological Coll., Cambridge; Minister, Belford Presbyterian Church, Northumberland 1953-56; Asst. Prof. of Philosophy, Cornell Univ., U.S.A. 1956-59; Stuart Prof. of Christian Philosophy, Princeton Theological Seminary, U.S.A. 1959-64; Lecturer in Divinity, Cambridge Univ. 1964-67; H. G. Wood Prof. of Theology, Birmingham Univ. 1967-80; Danforth Prof. of Philosophy of Religion, Claremont Graduate Univ., U.S.A. 1980-, Chair., Dept. of Religion, Dir. Blaisdell Programs in World Religions and Cultures; Guggenheim Fellow 1963-64, 1986-87; S.A. Cook Bye-Fellow, Gonville and Caius Coll., Cambridge; Hon Theol. Dr. (Uppsala). *Publications:* Faith and Knowledge, Evil and the God of Love, God and the Universe of Faiths, Death and Eternal Life, Arguments for the Existence of God, Problems of Religious Pluralism, God Has Many Names, Philosophy of Religion, The Second Christianity, An Interpretation of Religion; Ed. The Myth of God Incarnate, The Many-Faced Argument, The Myth of Christian Uniqueness, The Existence of God, Truth and Dialogue, Christianity and Other Religions, Faith and the Philosophers. *Address:* 516 West Ninth Street, Claremont, Calif. 91711, U.S.A. *Telephone:* (714) 626 5005.

HICKEL, Walter Joseph; American business executive; b. 18 Aug. 1919, Claflin, Kansas; s. of Robert A. Hickel and Emma Zecha; m. 1st Janice Cannon 1941 (deceased 1943), 2nd Ermalee Strutz 1945; six s.; ed. High School, Claflin, Kansas; builder, developer, and civic leader 1946-; started building homes, then built, operated and developed rental units, residential areas and hotels; operates inns, hotels and shopping centres in Alaska; Chair. Bd. Hickel Investment Co., Yukon Pacific Corpn.; mem. Republican Nat. Cttee. for State of Alaska 1954-64; Gov. of Alaska 1967-69; Sec. of U.S. Dept. of Interior 1969-70; Chair. Nat. Science Inst., Nat. Science Foundation panel on Geothermal Power; mem. Bd. Int. Regents Gonzaga Univ., World Advisory Council Int. Design Science Inst; Kansas Golden Gloves Welterweight Championship 1938; Hon. LL.D. (St. Mary of the Plains Coll. 1970, St. Martin's Coll. 1971, Maryland 1971, Adelphi Univ. 1971, San Diego 1972, Rensselaer Polytechnic Inst. 1973, Alaska 1976); Hon. D.Eng. (Stevens Inst. of Tech. at Hoboken 1970, Mich. Technological Univ. 1973); Hon. Dr. of Public Admin. (Willamette Univ. 1971); Alaskan of the Year 1969, Horatio Alger Award, New York 1972, Certificate of Award for Best Non-Fiction Book, Who Owns America?, Alaska Press Club 1972; Grand Cordon of Order of Sacred Treasure (Japan) 1988. *Publication:* Who Owns America? *Leisure interests:* reading, boating. *Address:* 1905 Loussac Drive, Anchorage, Alaska 99517, U.S.A. *Telephone:* (907) 276-7400.

HICKEY, H.E. Cardinal James Aloysius; American ecclesiastic; b. 11 Oct. 1920, Midland; ordained 1946, elected to the titular Church of Taraqua 1967, consecrated bishop 1967, transferred to Cleveland 1974, prefect 1980, cr. Cardinal 1988. *Address:* Archdiocesan Pastoral Center, 5001 Eastern Avenue, P.O. Box 29260, Washington, D.C. 20017, U.S.A. *Telephone:* (301) 853-3800.

HICKOX, Richard Sidney, M.A., F.R.C.O., L.R.A.M.; British conductor; b. 5 March 1948, Stokenchurch, Bucks.; s. of Rev. S. E. Hickox and Jean Millar; m. Frances Ina Sheldon-Williams 1976; one s.; ed. Royal Grammar School, High Wycombe, R.A.M., London and Queens' Coll. Cambridge (Organ Scholar); Dir. of Music, High Wycombe Parish Church 1970-71, St. Margaret's, Westminister 1972-82, Barbican Summer Festival 1984-85; Artistic Dir. Wooburn Festival 1967-, Spitalfields Festival 1977-, St. Endellion Festival 1974-, Northern Sinfonia of England 1982-; Dir. London Symphony Chorus 1976-; Music Dir., City of London Sinfonia and Richard Hickox Singers 1971-, Bradford Festival Choral Soc. 1978-; Assoc. Conductor, London Symphony Orchestra 1985-; Music Dir., Opera Stage 1985-; has conducted opera at Covent Garden, English Nat. Opera, Opera N. and Scottish Opera; has recorded Bach Masses, Albinoni Adagio, music by Finzi, Delius and Duruflé, Burgon Requiem, Haydn Nelson Mass (all for Decca, Argo Label); Gluck Armide, Handel Alcina, music by Vaughan Williams, Gilbert and Sullivan, Elgar Miniatures, Delius Miniatures and Berkeley Or Shall We Die? (all for EMI). *Leisure interests:* football, tennis, politics. *Address:* Harrison/Parrott, 12 Penzance Place, London, W.11 (Agent); 35 Ellington Street, London, N.7, England (Home). *Telephone:* 01-229 9166 (Agent); 01-607 8984 (Home).

HICKS, David (Nightingale), F.R.S.A.; British interior decorator and designer; b. 25 March 1929; s. of the late Herbert Hicks; m. Lady Pamela Carmen Louise Mountbatten (d. of the late Earl Mountbatten of Burma) 1960; one s. two d.; ed. Charterhouse and Cen. School of Arts and Crafts, London; Master Salter's Co. 1977-78; interior designs for Helena Rubinstein, QE2, H.R.H. the Prince of Wales (q.v.), Govt. of N.S.W., British Steel Corpn., Aeroflot Offices, Marquess of Londonderry, British Embassy Library, Yachts for H.M. King Fahd (q.v.); Design Council Design Award 1970. *Publications:* David Hicks on Decoration 1966, David Hicks on Living-with taste 1968, David Hicks on Bathrooms 1970, David Hicks on Decoration with fabrics 1971, David Hicks on Decoration-5 1972, David Hicks Book of Flower Arranging 1976, David Hicks Living with Design 1979, David Hicks Garden Design 1982, Style and Design 1987. *Leisure interests:* shooting, riding, gardening, preservation. *Address:* Albany, Piccadilly, London, W.1, England. *Telephone:* 01-627 4400.

HICKS, Henry Davies, C.C., Q.C., M.A., D.C.L.; Canadian barrister, politician and educator; b. 5 March 1915, Bridgetown, N.S.; s. of Henry Brandon Hicks and Annie May Kinney; m. 1st Paulene Agnes Banks (died 1964), two s. one d.; m. 2nd Margaret Gene MacGregor Morison 1965 (died 1988); ed. Mount Allison Univ., Dalhousie, and Exeter Coll., Oxford (Rhodes Scholar); admitted to Nova Scotia Bar 1941; served Royal Canadian Artillery 1941-45; practised law, Bridgetown 1946-50; mem. Nova Scotia Legislature 1945-60; first Minister of Educ. 1949-55, Provincial Sec. 1954-56; Premier of Province of Nova Scotia 1954-56, Leader of Opposition in Nova Scotia Legislature and leader, Nova Scotia Liberal Party 1956-60; Pres. Canadian Nat. Comm. for UNESCO 1963-67; Dean of Arts and Science, Dalhousie Univ. 1960-61, Vice-Pres. 1961-63, Pres. and Vice-Chancellor 1963-80; apptd. to Canadian Senate 1972; Canadian del. to 28th Gen. Assembly of UN 1973; Asscn. of Univs. and Colls. of Canada rep. on Bd. of Govs. Univ. of Guyana; Hon. D.Ed. (St. Anne's), Hon. D.C.L. (Univ. of King's Coll.), Hon. LL.D. (Mount Allison), Hon. D.Litt. (Acadia) 1979, Hon. LL.D. (Dalhousie) 1980, Hon. D.Hum.L. (Mount Saint Vincent) 1981. *Leisure interests:* salmon fishing, philately, bridge. *Address:* 6446 Coburg Road, Halifax, Nova Scotia B3H 2A7, Canada. *Telephone:* 424-2238 (Office); 422-5575 (Home).

HICKS, Sir John Richard, Kt., F.B.A.; British economist; b. 8 April 1904, Warwick; s. of the late Edward Hicks; m. Ursula Kathleen Webb 1935 (died 1985); ed. Clifton Coll. and Balliol Coll., Oxford; Prof. of Political Economy, Univ. of Manchester 1938–46; Fellow of Nuffield Coll. Oxford 1946–52, All Souls Coll. 1952–; Prof. of Political Economy, Univ. of Oxford 1952–65; Research Fellow, All Souls Coll. Oxford 1965–71; Hon. Fellow, L.S.E. 1969; Nobel Memorial Prize for Economics 1972 (with K. Arrow, q.v.); several hon. degrees. *Publications:* Theory of Wages 1932, Value and Capital 1939, The Social Framework 1942, Contribution to the Theory of the Trade Cycle 1950, A Revision of Demand Theory 1956, Essays in World Economics 1959, Capital and Growth 1965, Critical Essays in Monetary Theory 1967, A Theory of Economic History 1969, Capital and Time 1973, The Crises in Keynesian Economics 1974, Economic Perspectives 1977, Causality in Economics 1979, Collected Essays in Economic Theory (3 Vols.) 1981–83. *Address:* All Souls College, Oxford, England.

HIDAYATULLAH, Mohammed, O.B.E., M.A.; Indian judge; b. 17 Dec. 1905, Betul; s. of H. M. Wilayatullah and Mohammadi Begum; m. Pushpa Shah 1948; one s. one d. (deceased); ed. Government High School, Raipur, Morris Coll., Nagpur, Trinity Coll., Cambridge, and Lincoln's Inn, London; Advocate, Nagpur High Court 1930–46; Advocate-Gen. Cen. Prov. and Berar 1943–46; Puisne Judge 1946–54; Dean of Faculty of Law, Nagpur Univ. 1949–53; Chief Justice, Nagpur High Court 1954–56; Chief Justice, Madhya Pradesh High Court 1956–58; Judge, Supreme Court of India 1958–68; Chief Justice of India 1968–70; Acting Pres. of India July–Aug. 1969, 1982; Vice-Pres. of India 1979–84; Chair. Rajya Sabha 1979–84; Chief Scout; Pres. Indian Red Cross Soc.; Hon. Bencher, Lincoln's Inn, London; Mitchell Fellow, State Univ. of N.Y., Buffalo; Hon. LL.D. (Univ. of the Philippines, Ravishankar Univ., Rajasthan Univ. 1975, Benares Hindu, Kashmir, Berhampur, Punjab and Nagpur Agra Univs.); Hon. D.Litt. (Univs. of Bhopal and Kakatiya); Hon. D.C.L. (Delhi Univ.); Silver Elephant Award 1948, Bronze Medal for Gallantry 1969, Order of the Yugoslav Flag with Sash 1971, Knight of Mark Twain. *Publications:* Democracy in India and the Judical Process, The South-West Africa Case, Mulla's Mahomedan Law (editor, 18th edn.), A Judge's Miscellany (I, II, III and IV), U.S.A. and India, My Own Boswell (Memoirs), Right to Property, Taqrir-o-Tabir, Miscellanea 1988. *Leisure interests:* golf, bridge, reading. *Address:* A/10 Rockside, 112 Walkeshwar Road, Bombay 400006, India. *Telephone:* 812-9798.

HIDE, Raymond, PH.D., SC.D., F.R.S.; British research geophysicist; b. 17 May 1929, Doncaster; s. of late Stephen Hide and of Rose Edna Hide (née Cartlidge); m. Phyllis Ann Licence 1958; one s. two d.; ed. Percy Jackson Grammar School, Doncaster, Manchester and Cambridge Univs.; Research Assoc. in Astrophysics, Yerkes Observatory, Univ. of Chicago 1953–54; Sr. Research Fellow, Gen. Physics Div. A.E.R.E., Harwell 1954–57; lecturer in Physics, King's Coll. Univ. of Durham 1957–61; Prof. of Geophysics and Physics at M.I.T. 1961–67; Head of the Geophysical Fluid Dynamics Lab., Chief Scientific Officer (Special Merit), Meteorological Office, Bracknell 1967–; Gresham Prof. of Astronomy, Gresham Coll., City of London 1985–; Visiting Prof. Dept. of Mathematics, Univ. Coll., London 1969–84; Adrian Visiting Fellow, Univ. of Leicester 1981–83; Sr. Research Fellow Jesus Coll., Oxford 1983–; mem. Council, Royal Soc. of London 1988–; mem. American Acad. of Arts and Sciences, Royal Astronomical Soc. (Vice-Pres. 1971–72, 1985–86, Pres. 1983–85), Royal Meteorological Soc. (Pres. 1974–76), European Geophysical Soc. (Pres. 1982–84), Int. Astronomical Union and numerous other socs. and cttees.; Hon. D.Sc. (Leicester) 1985; Chair. British Nat. Cttee. for Geodesy and Geophysics, U.K. Chief Del. to Int. Union of Geodesy and Geophysics 1979–85; Charles Chree Medal and Prize of Inst. of Physics 1975, Holweck Medal and Prize, Societé Francaise de Physique and Inst. of Physics 1982. *Publications:* numerous scientific articles and papers. *Address:* Robert Hooke Institute, Old Observatory, Clarendon Laboratory, Parks Road, Oxford, OX1 3PU, England. *Telephone:* (0865) 272084.

HIEBERT, Erwin Nick, PH.D.; American professor of history of science; b. 27 May 1919, Saskatchewan, Canada; s. of Cornelius N. and Tina Hiebert; m. Elfrieda Franz 1943; one s. two d.; ed. Bethel Coll., N. Newton, Kan., Univs. of Chicago and Wisconsin-Madison; Research Chemist, Standard Oil Co. of Indiana and the Manhattan Project 1943–46; Research Chemist, Inst. for Study of Metals, Univ. of Chicago 1947–50; Asst. Prof. of Chem., San Francisco State Coll. 1952–55; Instr. in History of Science, Harvard 1955–57; Asst. Prof., Assoc. Prof., Prof., History of Science, Univ. of Wis.-Madison 1957–70; Prof. of History of Science, Harvard 1970–, Chair. 1977–84; Pres. Div. of History of Science, Int. Union of History and Philosophy of Science 1982–84; Fellow, American Acad. of Arts and Sciences, Acad. Int. d'Histoire des Sciences. *Publications:* Impact of Atomic Energy 1961, Historical Roots of the Principle of Conservation of Energy 1962, The Conception of Thermodynamics in the Scientific Thought of Mach and Planck 1967, and papers on history and philosophy of physics and chem. since 1800. *Leisure interests:* music, gardening. *Address:* Department of the History of Science, Harvard University, Science Center 235, Cambridge, Mass. 02138, U.S.A. *Telephone:* (617) 495-3741.

HIGAKI, Tokutaro; Japanese politician; b. 1916, Ehime Pref.; ed. High School, Shikoku, Univ. of Tokyo; fmr. Dir.-Gen. Food Agency and Vice-Minister of Agric. and Forestry; mem. House of Councillors from Ehime Pref.; fmr. Chair. Diet Rules and Cabinet Cttees.; Minister of Posts and Telecommunications 1982–83. *Leisure interest:* horse racing. *Address:*

Liberal-Democratic Party, 7, 2-chome, Hirakawacho, Chiyoda-ku, Tokyo, Japan.

HIGGINS, Rev. Mgr. George Gilmary, M.A., PH.D.; American ecclesiastic and teacher; b. 21 Jan. 1916, La Grange, Ill.; s. of Charles Vincent Higgins and Anna Gertrude Rethinger; ed. Quigley Prep. Seminary, Chicago, St. Mary of the Lake Seminary, Mundelin, Ill., Catholic Univ. of America and Inst. for Continuing Theological Educ., Rome; ordained Priest for Catholic Archdiocese of Chicago 1940, Papal Chamberlain 1953, Domestic Prelate 1959; fmr. teacher Dept. of Econs. School of Social Science, Catholic Univ. of America, Adjunct Lecturer 1981–; apptd. to staff Social Action Dept. Nat. Catholic Welfare Conf. May 1944, Asst. Dir. Dept. Jan. 1946, Dir. Nov. 1954; apptd. Sec. for Research U.S. Catholic Conf. June 1972, for Special Concerns Jan. 1979, retd. from Conf. Sept. 1980; Chair. Public Review Bd. United Auto Workers of America AFL-CIO, Bishops' Cttee. for Catholic-Jewish Relations; Adviser to Chair. U.S. Del. to Belgrade Conf. on Human Rights; Consultant Bishops' Cttee. on Farm Labor; mem. Prep. Comm. on Lay Apostolate Vatican Council II and Consultant to Council, Exec. Cttee. Leadership Conf. on Human Rights, Bishops' Cttee. on Catholic Social Teaching and U.S. Econ., Dunlop Comm. on Farm Labor, Advisory Bd. Nat. Council on Foundations, fmr. mem. American Arbitration Assocn.; Hon. degrees from eight univs.; Murray-Green-Meany Award AFL-CIO 1980. *Publications:* syndicated column in The Yardstick and several journal articles. *Leisure interests:* reading, theology, history, politics, swimming, golf. *Address:* 220 Curley Hall, Catholic University of America, Washington, D.C. 20064, U.S.A. *Telephone:* (202) 635-5660.

HIGGINS, George Vincent, M.A., J.D.; American lawyer and author; b. 13 Nov. 1939, Brockton, Mass.; s. of John T. Higgins and Doris (née Montgomery) Higgins; m. 1st Elizabeth Mulkerin 1965 (divorced 1979); one s. one d.; m. 2nd Loretta L. Cubberley 1979; ed. Boston Coll., Stanford Univ., Westfield State Coll.; Barrister 1967; Reporter Providence Journal 1962–63; corresp. A.P. Springfield, Mass. 1963–64, Boston 1964–66; Asst. Attorney Gen., Mass. 1967–70, Asst. U.S. Attorney, Mass. 1970–73; legal practice in Boston 1973–; columnist Boston Herald 1977–79, Boston Globe 1979–85, Wall Street Journal 1984–87; mem. Writers Guild. *Publications:* The Friends of Eddie Coyle 1972, The Digger's Game 1973, Cogan's Trade 1974, A City on a Hill 1975, The Friends of Richard Nixon 1975, The Judgment of Deke Hunter 1976, Dreamland 1977, A Year or So With Edgar 1979, Kennedy for the Defense 1980, The Rat on Fire 1981, The Patriot Game 1982, A Choice of Enemies 1984, Penance for Jerry Kennedy 1985, Impostors 1986, Wonderful Years, Wonderful Years 1988, The Sins of the Fathers 1988. *Address:* 15 Brush Hill Lane, Milton, Mass. 02186, U.S.A.

HIGGINS, Jack (see Patterson, Harry).

HIGGINS, Rosalyn, J.S.D., Q.C.; British professor of international law; b. 2 June 1937; d. of Lewis Cohen and Fay Inberg; m. Rt. Hon. Terence L. Higgins 1961; one s. one d.; ed. Burlington Grammar School, London, Girton Coll. Cambridge and Yale Law School; U.K. Intern, Office of Legal Affairs, UN 1958; Commonwealth Fund Fellow 1959; Visiting Fellow, Brookings Inst. Washington, D.C. 1960; Jr. Fellow in Int. Studies, L.S.E. 1961–63; staff specialist in int. law, Royal Inst. of Int. Affairs 1963–74; Visiting Fellow, L.S.E. 1974–78; Prof. of Int. Law, Univ. of Kent at Canterbury 1978–81; Prof. of Int. Law, L.S.E. 1981–; mem. UN Cttee. on Human Rights 1985–; Visiting Prof. Stanford Univ. 1975, Yale Univ. 1977; Vice-Pres. American Soc. of Int. Law 1972–74; Dr. h.c. (Paris XI). *Publications include:* The Development of International Law through the Political Organs of the United Nations 1963, Conflict of Interests 1965, The Administration of the United Kingdom Foreign Policy through the United Nations 1966, Law in Movement—essays in memory of John McMahon (ed., with James Fawcett) 1974, UN Peacekeeping: documents and commentary: (Vol. I) 1969, (Vol. II) 1971, (Vol. III) 1980, (Vol. IV) 1981; articles in law journals and journals of int. relations. *Leisure interests:* sport, cooking, eating. *Address:* London School of Economics, Houghton Street, London, WC2A 2AE, England.

HIGGINSON, John, M.D., F.R.C.P.; American professor of pathology; b. 16 Oct. 1922, Belfast, N. Ireland; s. of William Higginson and Ellen Margaret Rogers; m. Nan Russell McKee 1949; two d.; ed. Royal Belfast Academical Inst., Belfast, and Univ. of Dublin; Pathologist, S. African Inst. for Medical Research, Baragwanath Hosp., S. Africa 1950–58; Head, Geographical Pathology Unit and Cancer Registry, S. African Inst. for Medical Research 1954–58; Assoc. Prof. of Pathology and Oncology, Univ. of Kansas Medical Center 1958–62; American Cancer Soc. Career Professorship, Univ. of Kansas 1961–66; Prof. of Pathology, Univ. of Kansas Medical Center 1962–66; Dir. Int. Agency for Research on Cancer, Lyons, France 1966–82; Sr. Consultant Scientist, Univs. Associated for Research and Educ. in Pathology Inc. 1982–84; Research Prof. Univ. North Carolina 1982–; Visiting Prof. Univ. Md. 1983–85; Sr. Fellow, Inst. for Health Policy Analysis and Prof. of Community and Family Medicine, Georgetown Univ. Medical Center; Hon. Fellow Royal Acad. of Medicine in Ireland, Fellow, Royal Coll. of Physicians, London, etc. *Publications:* over 200 scientific papers in field of environmental biology and cancer research. *Leisure interests:* golf, sailing, antique maps. *Address:* 2121 Wisconsin Avenue, N.W., Suite 220, Washington, D.C. 20007, U.S.A.

HIGGS, Peter Ware, PH.D., F.R.S.E., F.R.S.; British professor of theoretical physics; b. 29 May 1929; s. of Thomas W. Higgs and Gertrude M. (née Coghill) Higgs; m. Jo Ann Williamson 1963; two s.; ed. Cotham Grammar School, Bristol and King's Coll. London; Sr. Research Fellow, Univ. of Edin. 1955-56; ICI Research Fellow, Univ. Coll. London 1956-57, Imperial Coll. London 1957-58; Lecturer in Math. Univ. Coll., London 1958-60; Lecturer in Mathematical Physics, Univ. of Edin. 1969-70, Reader 1970-80, Prof. of Theoretical Physics 1980-; Hughes Medal, Royal Soc. 1981; Rutherford Medal, Inst. of Physics 1984. *Publications:* papers in scientific journals. *Leisure interests:* walking, swimming, listening to music. *Address:* 2 Darnaway Street, Edin., EH3 6BG, Scotland. *Telephone:* 031-225 7060.

HIGHAM, John, PH.D.; American professor of history; b. 26 Oct. 1920, New York; s. of Lloyd Stuart Higham and Margaret (née Windred) Higham; m. Eileen Moss 1948; two s. two d.; ed. Johns Hopkins Univ. and Univ. of Wisconsin; Instructor in History, Univ. of Calif., Los Angeles 1948-50, Asst. Prof. 1950-54; Assoc. Prof., Rutgers Univ. 1954-58, Prof. 1958-60; Prof. Univ. of Mich., Ann Arbor 1961-67, Moses Coit Tyler Univ. Prof. 1968-71, 1972-73; John Martin Vincent Prof. of History, Johns Hopkins Univ. 1971-72, 1973-; Pres. Immigration History Soc. 1979-82, Org. of American Historians 1973-74; Assoc. Dir. of Studies, Ecole des Hautes Etudes en Sciences Sociales 1981-82; mem. American Acad. of Arts and Sciences; Dunning Prize, American Historical Asscn. 1956; Fulbright-Hays Lecturer, Kyoto American Studies Seminar 1974, Mellon Sr. Fellow, Nat. Humanities Center 1988-89. *Publications:* Strangers in the Land 1955, History: Humanistic Scholarship in America 1965, Writing American History 1970, Send These to Me 1975, The Politics of Ethnicity (with others) 1982. *Address:* Department of History, The Johns Hopkins University, Baltimore, Md. 21218; 309 Tuscany Road, Baltimore, Md. 21210, U.S.A. (Home). *Telephone:* (301) 243-0112 (Home).

HIGHET, Hon. David Allan; New Zealand chartered accountant, business executive and fmr. politician; b. 27 May 1913, Dunedin; s. of David Highet and Elsie M. Bremner; m. 1st Margaret P. Hoyles 1938; one s. one d.; m. 2nd Shona McFarlane 1976; ed. Otago Boys' High School and Otago Univ.; practised as chartered accountant, Wellington 1942-60; Gen. Man. L. J. Fisher & Co. Ltd., Auckland 1960-64; Sr. Partner, Cox, Elliffe, Twomey, Highet & Co. (Chartered Accountants), Auckland 1964-72; Wellington City Councillor 1954-59; M.P. for Remuera 1966-84; Minister of Internal Affairs, of Local Govt., of Civil Defence and Assoc. Minister of Social Welfare Feb.-Nov. 1972, of Internal Affairs, of Local Govt., of Civil Defence, of Recreation and Sport, for the Arts 1975-84; co. Dir. 1984-; Queen's Service Order for Public Service. *Leisure interests:* music, theatre, golf, tennis, bowls, travel. *Address:* 119 Mitchell Street, Brooklyn, Wellington, New Zealand. *Telephone:* 844-356.

HIGHSMITH, Patricia; writer; b. 19 Jan. 1921; d. of Jay Bernard Plangman and Mary Coates (respectively of German and English-Scots descent); name changed to Highsmith by adoption after mother's second marriage; unmarried; ed. Columbia Univ., New York; writing job after univ.; freelance writer until publication of first novel; lived alternately in Europe and U.S.A. 1951-; now living in France. *Publications:* Strangers on a Train 1950, The Blunderer 1955, The Talented Mr. Ripley 1956, Deep Water 1957, A Game for the Living 1958, This Sweet Sickness 1960, The Cry of the Owl 1962, The Two Faces of January 1964, The Glass Cell 1965, A Suspension of Mercy 1965, Plotting and Writing Suspense Fiction 1966, Those Who Walk Away 1967, The Tremor of Forgery 1969, Eleven (short stories) 1970, Ripley Under Ground 1971, A Dog's Ransom 1972, Ripley's Game 1974, The Animal-Lover's Book of Beastly Murder (short stories) 1975, Edith's Diary 1977, Little Tales of Misogyny (short stories) 1977, Slowly, Slowly in the Wind (short stories) 1979, The Boy Who Followed Ripley 1980, The Black House (Short Stories) 1981, People Who Knock on the Door 1983, Mermaids on the Golf Course and Other Stories (Short Stories) 1985, Found in the Street (novel) 1986, Tales of Natural and Unnatural Catastrophes 1987, Those Who Walk Away 1988. *Leisure interests:* drawing, some painting, carpentering, snail-watching.

HIGHTOWER, John B.; American museum director; b. 23 May 1933, Atlanta, Georgia; s. of Edward A. and Margaret K. Hightower; m. 2nd Martha Ruhl 1984; one s. one d (from 1st marriage); ed. Yale Univ.; Gen. Asst. to Pres. and Publisher, American Heritage Publishing Co. 1961-64; Exec. Dir. New York State Council on the Arts 1964-70; Dir. Museum of Modern Art, New York 1970-72; Pres. Assoc. Councils of Arts, New York 1972-74; Pres. South St. Seaport 1977-84; Exec. Dir. Richard Tucker Music Foundation 1977-, The Maritime Center, Norwalk 1984-; adviser to arts councils throughout U.S.A., Cultural Adviser to Presidential Latin American Comm. 1969; Founder and Chair., Advocates for the Arts 1974-77; Instructor, Arts Man., Wharton School 1976-77, New School 1976-77; Chair. Planning Corpn. for the Arts; N.Y. State Award 1970. *Leisure interests:* gardening, cooking, travel. *Address:* 486 Main Street, Ridgefield, Conn. 06877, U.S.A.

HIJIKATA, Takeshi; Japanese business executive; b. 18 March 1915, Ena City, Gifu Prefecture; s. of Kikusaburo and Sue Hijikata; m. Michiko Kumakura; two s. one d.; ed. Tokyo Imperial Univ.; joined Sumitomo Chemical Co. Ltd. 1941, Dir. 1971, Man. Dir. 1973, Exec. Vice-Pres. 1977, Pres. 1977, Chair. 1985-; Chair. Asscn. for the Progress of New Chem.; Dir. Fuji Oil Co. Ltd., Seitetsu Kagaku Co. Ltd., Japan Cttee. for Econ.

Devt.; Dir. and Counsellor Sumitomo Pharmaceuticals Co. Ltd.; Dir. Sumitomo Bakelite Co. Ltd., Inabata and Co. Ltd.; Vice-Chair. Fed. of Econ. Orgs. (Keidanren); Adviser Japan Chem. Industry Asscn.; Standing Dir. Japan Fed. of Employees' Asscn., Kansai Econ. Fed.; mem. Trade Conf., Prime Minister's Office, Atomic Energy Comm., Science and Tech. Agency, Japan Singapore Asscn. *Leisure interests:* golf, reading. *Address:* Sumitomo Chemical Co. Ltd., Kitahama, 4-chome 5-33 Chuo-ku, Osaka 541; 7-9, Nihonbashi 2-chome, Chuo-ku, Tokyo (Offices); 19-11, Midorigaoka 2-chome, Meguro-ku, Tokyo, Japan (Home). *Telephone:* 06 (220) 3272 (Osaka Office); 03 (278) 7227 (Tokyo Office).

HILAL, Ahmed Izzedin, B.SC.; Egyptian engineer and politician; b. 5 Dec. 1924, Alexandria; ed. Univ. of Cairo; Chemical Engineer, Suez Refinery, Anglo-Egyptian Oil Fields Co. 1946-62, Refinery Man. 1962; Operations Man. Egyptian Gen. Petroleum Corpn. (EGPC) 1963, Deputy Gen. Man. EGPC 1964-68, Gen. Man. 1968-71, Chair. and Man. Dir. 1971-73; Minister of Petroleum 1973-84, also of Industry and Mining 1977-78; Deputy Prime Minister for Production 1980-84. *Address:* c/o Ministry of Petroleum, 2 Latin America Street, Garden City, Cairo, Egypt.

HILALY, Agha, M.A., S.PC.; Pakistani diplomatist; b. 20 May 1911, Bangalore; s. of late Agha Abdulla; m. Malek Taj Kazim 1938; three s.; ed. Madras and Cambridge Univs.; entered Civil Service 1936; apptd. Under-Sec. to Finance Ministry, Govt. of Bengal; transferred to pre-partition Govt. of India and served as Under-Sec. in Ministries of Agriculture, Food and Commerce 1941-47; Deputy Sec. Pakistan Foreign Ministry 1947-51, Joint Sec. 1951-54; attended several Int. Confs. as Sec.-Gen. of Pakistan dels.; Amb. to Sweden, Norway, Denmark and Finland 1956-59, to U.S.S.R. (concurrently Minister to Czechoslovakia) 1959-61; High Commr. in India and Amb. to Nepal 1961-63; High Commr. in U.K. and Amb. to Repub. of Ireland 1963-66; Amb. to U.S.A. (concurrently to Mexico, Venezuela and Jamaica) 1966-71; mem. Bd. of Dirs. State Bank of Pakistan 1972-; Chair. Bd. of Govs. Pakistan Inst. of Strategic Studies 1973-; Leader Pakistan del. to Human Rights Comm. 1981-85, UN Working Group on Missing Persons 1983-; Hilal-i-Quaid-i-Azam, Grand Cross of Order of Northern Star (Sweden), Grand Cross of Order of Gurkha (Nepal). *Leisure interests:* photography, hunting. *Address:* 22B Circular Street, Phase 2, Defence Housing Society, Karachi 6, Pakistan. *Telephone:* 540 202 (Home).

HILBE, Alfred J., DR.ECON.; Liechtenstein politician; b. 22 July 1928, Gmunden, Austria; s. of Franz and Elisabeth (née Glatz) Hilbe; m. Virginia Joseph 1951; one d.; ed. classical secondary schools in Vaduz and Zürich, Ecole Nationale des Sciences Politiques, Paris and Univ. of Innsbruck; several posts in private business 1951-54; in foreign service 1954-65; Counsellor, Liechtenstein Embassy, Berne until 1965; Deputy Head of Govt. of Liechtenstein 1965-70, Head of Govt. 1970-74; Financial Consultant 1974-; Grosskreuz of Liechtenstein Order of Merit, Grosses Silbernes Ehrenzeichen am Bande (Austria) 1975, Order of St. Gregory (Vatican); Fatherland Union Party. *Leisure interests:* skiing, tennis, photography. *Address:* FL-9494 Schaan, Garsill 11, Principality of Liechtenstein. *Telephone:* 075-22002 (Home); 28320 (Office).

HILDESHEIMER, Wolfgang; German writer and artist; b. 9 Dec. 1916, Hamburg; s. of Dr. Arnold Hildesheimer and Hanna Hildesheimer (née Goldschmid); m. Silvia Dillmann 1953; ed. Odenwaldschule, Heppenheim, Germany, Frensham Heights School, Surrey, England, and Central School of Arts and Crafts, London; British Information Officer, Palestine 1943-45; Lecturer, British Inst., Tel-Aviv 1945-46; interpreter, War Crimes Trials, Nuremberg 1947-49; now freelance writer and artist; guest lecturer in Poetry at Frankfurt Univ. 1967; mem. Akademie der Künste Berlin; corresp. mem. Deutsche Akademie für Sprache und Dichtung; Dr. h.c. (Giessen); Radio Play Prize in aid of War Blind 1955, Literaturpreis der Freien Hansestadt Bremen 1966, George Büchner Preis der Deutschen Akad. für Sprache und Dichtung, Darmstadt 1966, Grosser Literaturpreis der Bayerischen Akademie der schönen Künste, Munich 1982; Grosses Verdienstkreuz der Bundesrepublik Deutschland. *Publications include:* Short stories: Lieblose Legenden 1952; Plays: Die Verspätung 1962, Nachtstück 1963, Rivalen (adaptation from Sheridan) 1965, Mary Stuart; Novels: Tynset 1965, Masante 1973; Essay: Wer war Mozart?; Biography: Mozart 1977, Marbot 1981. *Address:* 7742 Poschiavo (GR), Switzerland. *Telephone:* (082) 50467.

HILDRETH, Eugene A., B.S., M.D., F.A.C.P.; American physician and university professor; b. 11 March, St. Paul, Minn.; s. of Eugene A. Hildreth and Lila K. Hildreth; m. Dorothy Ann Meyers 1946; four c.; ed. Washington and Jefferson Coll., Univ. of Virginia School of Medicine, Johns Hopkins Hosp., Baltimore, Md., Univ. of Pennsylvania; Research in Dept. of Research Medicine, Univ. of Pa., Philadelphia 1957-60, Markle Scholar in Academic Medicine 1958-63, Assoc. Dean, Univ. of Pa. 1964-67, now Prof. of Clinical Medicine; Dir. Dept. of Medicine, The Reading Hosp. and Medical Center, Reading, Pa.; Chair. Allergy and Immunology Subspeciality Bd. 1966-72, American Bd. of Allergy and Immunology 1971-72, American Bd. of Internal Medicine 1975-82, Federated Council of Internal Medicine 1981-82, American Coll. of Physicians (ACP) Cttee. on Developing Criteria and Standards for Delineation of Clinical Privileges 1986-, Regent ACP 1985-, Chair. Bd. of Regents 1989-, mem. RRC-IM 1989-, Fellow ACP; mem. Fed. of the American Socs. for Experimental Biology, A.A.A.S., ACP Cttee. on Ethics, ACP Cttee. on Int. Medicine, Inst. of Medicine

(I.O.M.), N.A.S., Council of I.O.M., Nominations Cttee. of I.O.M. *Publications:* numerous scientific papers, chapters in books, reviews etc. *Leisure interests:* reading, white water kayaking, backpacking, museums, farming. *Address:* The Reading Hospital and Medical Center, Reading, Pa. 19603, U.S.A. *Telephone:* (215) 378-6133.

HILDREW, Bryan, C.B.E., M.SC., D.I.C.; British engineer; b. 19 March 1920, Sunderland, County Durham (now Tyne and Wear); s. of Alexander William and Sarah Jane Hildrew; m. Megan Kathleen Lewis; two s. one d.; ed. Bede Collegiate School, Sunderland, Sunderland Tech. Coll., City and Guilds Coll., London Univ.; Principal Surveyor Engineering Investigations, Lloyds Register of Shipping 1961-65, Deputy Chief Engineer Surveyor 1965-67, Chief Engineer Surveyor 1967-70, Tech. Dir. 1970-77, Man. Dir. 1977-85; Pres. Inst. Mech. Engs. 1980-81; Chair. Council of Eng. Insts. 1981-82; Pres. Inst. Marine Engs. 1983-85; Chair. Abbeyfield Orpington Soc. 1985-; D.Eng. h.c. (Newcastle upon Tyne) 1987. *Leisure interests:* walking, orienteering. *Address:* 8 Westholme, Orpington, Kent. BR6 0AN, England.

HILGARD, Ernest Ropiequet, PH.D.; American professor of psychology and education; b. 25 July 1904, Belleville, Ill.; s. of Dr. George E. Hilgard and Laura Ropiequet Hilgard; m. Josephine Rohrs 1931; one s. one d.; ed. Univ. of Illinois and Yale Univ.; Instructor in Psychology, Yale Univ. 1928-33; Asst. Prof. to Prof. of Psychology and Educ., Stanford Univ. 1933-69, Exec. Head, Dept. of Psychology 1942-51, Dean of Graduate Div. 1951-55, Emer. Prof. of Psychology and Educ. 1969-; Past Pres. American Psychological Assscn.; mem. Nat. Acad. of Sciences, Nat. Acad. of Educ., American Philosophical Soc., American Acad. of Arts and Sciences; Hon. Fellow, British Psychological Assscn.; Hon. D.Sc. (Kenyon Coll.) 1964, (Colgate) 1987, (Northwestern) 1987; Hon. LL.D. (Centre Coll.) 1974; Warren Medal, Distinguished Scientific Contribution Award, Gold Medal, American Psychological Foundation, Gold Medal, Int. Soc. of Hypnosis. *Publications:* Conditioning and Learning 1940, Theories of Learning 1948, Introduction to Psychology 1953, Hypnotic Susceptibility 1965, Hypnosis in the Relief of Pain 1975, Divided Consciousness 1977, American Psychology in Historical Perspective 1978, Psychology in America: A Historical Survey 1987, Fifty Years of Psychology 1988 and articles in professional journals. *Address:* Department of Psychology, Stanford University, Stanford, Calif. 94305 (Office); 850 Webster, Palo Alto, Calif. 94301, U.S.A. (Home). *Telephone:* (415) 725-2415 (Office).

HILGER, Wolfgang, DR.RER.NAT.; German business executive; b. 16 Nov. 1929, Leverkusen; ed. Univ. of Bonn; joined Hoechst AG 1958, mem. Bd. 1974, Deputy Chair. 1983, Chair. 1985-; Pres. Advisory Bd. Cassella Hoechst Holland, Hoechst CeramTec, Riedel de Haen, Messer Griesheim GmbH; Hon. Prof. Univ. of Frankfurt. *Address:* Hoechst AG, 6230 Frankfurt/Main 80, Federal Republic of Germany. *Telephone:* Frankfurt 305 7239.

HILL, Anthony; British artist and mathematician; b. 23 April 1930, London; s. of Adrian Hill and Dorothy Whitley; m. Yuriko Kaetsu 1978; ed. Bryanston School, St. Martin's School of Art, Cen. School of Arts and Crafts; one-man exhbn. Inst. of Contemporary Arts (ICA), London 1958, exhbn. (with Gillian Wise) 1963; exhbn. Kasmin Gallery, London 1966, 1969, exhbns. (with Redo) 1969, 1980; retrospective exhbn. Hayward Gallery, London 1983; Visiting Lecturer Chelsea School of Art, Visiting Research Assoc., Dept. of Mathematics, Univ. Coll., London; Leverhulme Fellowship 1971-72, Hon. Research Fellow, Univ. Coll. 1971-72. *Publications:* Data: Directions in Art, Theory and Aesthetics (Ed.) 1968, Aimez-vous Duchamp 1989; numerous articles in art and mathematical journals. *Leisure interest:* erotology. *Address:* 24 Charlotte Street, London, W.1, England. *Telephone:* 01-636-5332.

HILL, (Arthur) Derek, F.R.G.S.; British artist and author; b. 6 Dec. 1916, Bassett, Hants.; s. of A. J. L. Hill and Grace L. Mercer; ed. Marlborough Coll.; designer of sets and costumes for Covent Garden and Sadler's Wells; one-man exhbns. Nicholson Gallery, London 1943, Leicester Galleries, London, 1947, 1950, 1953, 1956; retrospective exhbn. Whitechapel Gallery, London 1961, Arts Council of N. Ireland, Belfast 1970, Mun. Gallery, Dublin 1971; work represented in exhbns. in Europe and USA 1957-, and in public collections in U.K., Ireland, Denmark, Liechtenstein, U.S.A. and Canada; organiser of exhbns. at Tate Gallery, Royal Acad. etc. 1934-. *Publications:* Islamic Architecture and Its Decoration (with O. Grabar) 1965, Islamic Architecture in North Africa (with L. Golvin) 1976; articles in magazines and journals. *Leisure interests:* gardening, travel. *Address:* c/o National Art Collections Fund, 20 John Islip Street, London, S.W.1, England.

HILL, Sir Austin Bradford, Kt., C.B.E., PH.D., D.SC., F.R.S.; British university professor; b. 8 July 1897, London; s. of Sir Leonard Hill and Janet Alexander; m. Florence Maud Salmon 1923 (died 1980); two s. one d.; ed. Chigwell School and London Univ.; Research worker for Industrial Health Research Bd. and Medical Research Council 1923-32; London Univ. Reader in Epidemiology and Vital Statistics at the London School of Hygiene and Tropical Medicine 1932-45, Prof. of Medical Statistics 1945-61; Hon. Dir. Statistical Research Unit of Medical Research Council 1945-61; Pres. Royal Statistical Soc. 1950-52; Fellow, Univ. Coll., London 1955; Hon. Fellow, American Public Health Assscn. 1953, Soc. of Occupational Medicine 1957,

Soc. of Social Medicine 1961, Royal Soc. of Medicine 1962, Soc. of Community Medicine 1963, Royal Coll. of Physicians 1963, Faculty of Community Medicine 1973, Faculty of Occupational Medicine 1982-; London School of Hygiene and Tropical Medicine 1976; Hon. mem. Inst. of Actuaries 1956, Faculty of Medicine, Univ. of Chile 1959, Int. Epidemiological Assscn. 1971; Hon. D.Sc. (Oxford) 1963, Hon. M.D. (Edin.) 1968; Gold Medal, Royal Statistical Soc. 1953, Galen Medal, Soc. of Apothecaries 1959, Harben Gold Medal, Royal Inst. of Public Health and Hygiene 1961, Heberden Medal 1965, Jenner Medal of Royal Soc. of Medicine 1965. *Publications:* Statistical Methods in Clinical and Preventive Medicine 1962, A Short Text Book of Medical Statistics (11th edn. of Principles of Medical Statistics) 1985. *Leisure interests:* gardening, walking. *Address:* April Cottage, Lower Hopton, Nesscliffe, Shrewsbury, SY4 1DL, England. *Telephone:* (074381) 231.

HILL, Christopher (see Hill, (John Edward) C.)

HILL, Rev. Canon Christopher John, B.D., M.TH.; British ecclesiastic; b. 10 Oct. 1945; s. of Leonard Hill and Francis Hill; m. Hilary Ann Whitehouse 1976; three s. one d.; ed. Sebright School, Worcs. and King's Coll., London; ordained (Diocese of Wichfield) 1969; Asst. Chaplain to Archbishop of Canterbury for Foreign Relations 1974-81, Sec. for Ecumenical Affairs 1981-; Anglican Sec. Anglican-Roman Catholic Int. Comm. I and II 1974-; Anglican-Lutheran European Comm. 1981-82; Hon. Canon Canterbury Cathedral 1982-; Chaplain to Queen 1987-; Assoc. King's Coll., London. *Publications:* ecumenical articles. *Leisure interests:* music, walking, reading. *Address:* Lambeth Palace, London, SE1 7JU, England. *Telephone:* 01-928 4880/8282.

HILL, David, M.ECON.; Australian broadcasting executive; b. 20 June 1946, Sussex, England; s. of Kathleen Hill; m. Emily Booker 1985; ed. East Sydney Tech. Coll. and Univ. of Sydney; Dir. N.S.W. Govt. Ministerial Advisory Unit 1976-80; mem. Public Transport Comm. 1979; Chief Exec. State Rail Authority 1980-86; mem. Senate, Univ. of Sydney 1983; Commr. Australian Nat. Airlines 1984; Chair. Australian Broadcasting Corpn. 1986, Man. Dir. Dec. 1986-. *Leisure interests:* soccer, reading, chess. *Address:* 150 William Street, Sydney, N.S.W. (Office); Randwick, N.S.W., Australia (Home). *Telephone:* (02) 356 5340 (Office).

HILL, David Keynes, SC.D., F.R.S.; British professor of biophysics (retd.); b. 23 July 1915; s. of Prof. Archibald V. Hill, C.H., and Margaret N. (née Keynes) Hill; m. Stella M. Humphrey 1949; four d.; ed. Highgate School and Trinity Coll. Cambridge; Fellow, Trinity Coll. Cambridge 1940-48; Physiologist, Marine Biological Assscn. Plymouth 1948-49; Sr. Lecturer, Royal Postgraduate Medical School, Univ. of London 1949-62, Reader 1962-75, Prof. of Biophysics 1975-82. *Publications:* papers in Journal of Physiology. *Leisure interests:* woodworking, photography. *Address:* Ivy Cottage, Winksley, Ripon, N. Yorks., HG4 3NR, England. *Telephone:* (076583) 562.

HILL, Dorothy, C.B.E., PH.D., F.A.A., F.R.S.; Australian professor of geology; b. 10 Sept. 1907; d. of R. S. Hill; unmarried; ed. Brisbane Girls' Grammar School, and Univs. of Queensland and Cambridge; Council for Scientific and Industrial Research Fellowship, Univ. of Queensland 1937-42; Second Officer, W.R.A.N.S. 1942-45; Lecturer in Geology, Univ. of Queensland 1946-56, Reader 1956-59, Research Prof. of Geology 1959-72, Prof. Emer. 1972-; Pres. Australian Acad. of Sciences 1970, Geological Soc. of Australia 1973-75; Hon. Fellow, Geological Soc. of America; numerous awards and prizes. *Publications:* articles in learned journals. *Leisure interests:* travel, reading. *Address:* 66 Sisley Street, St. Lucia, Brisbane, Queensland 4067, Australia.

HILL, Geoffrey (William), M.A., F.R.S.L.; British professor of English and poet; b. 18 June 1932; s. of late William George Hill and Hilda Beatrice Hill (née Hands); m. Nancy Whittaker 1956 (marriage dissolved); three s. one d.; ed. County High School, Bromsgrove and Keble Coll., Oxford; mem. acad. staff Univ. of Leeds 1954-80, Prof. of English Literature 1976-80; Univ. Lecturer in English and Fellow of Emmanuel Coll., Cambridge 1981-; Churchill Fellow Dept. of English, Bristol 1980; Clark Lecturer Trinity Coll., Cambridge 1986; Hon. Fellow Keble Coll., Oxford 1981; Whitbread Award 1971, R.S.L. Award (W. H. Heinemann Bequest) 1971, Loines Award, American Acad. and Inst. of Arts and Letters 1983, Ingram Merrill Foundation Award in Literature 1985. *Publications:* poetry: For the Unfallen 1959 (Gregory Award 1961), King Log 1968 (Hawthornden Prize 1969, Geoffrey Faber Memorial Prize 1970), Mercian Hymns 1971 (Alice Hunt Bartlett Award 1971), Somewhere is Such a Kingdom: Poems 1952-71 1975, Tenebrae 1978 (Duff Cooper Memorial Prize 1979), The Mystery of the Charity of Charles Péguy 1983, Collected Poems 1985; poetic drama: Henrik Ibsen, Brand: a version for the English stage 1978 (produced at Nat. Theatre, London 1978); criticism: The Lords of Limit: essays on literature and ideas 1984. *Address:* Emmanuel College, Cambridge, CB2 3AP, England.

HILL, George Roy, B.A.; American film and theatre producer and director; b. 20 Dec. 1921, Minneapolis, Minn.; s. of George Roy and Helen (Owens) Hill; m. Louisa Horton 1951; two s. two d.; ed. Yale Univ. and Trinity Coll., Dublin; Directed first stage production Biography, Gate Theatre, Dublin 1948. *Other productions include:* Look Homeward, Angel 1957, The Gang's All Here 1959, Green-willow, Period of Adjustment 1960, Moon on a Rainbow Shawl 1962, Henry, Sweet Henry 1967; directed first film 1962. *Other films include:* Period of Adjustment 1963, Toys in the Attic 1963, The World of Henry Orient 1964, Hawaii 1966, Thoroughly Modern Millie 1967, Butch Cassidy and the Sundance Kid 1969, Slaughterhouse-Five 1972, The Sting 1973 (Oscar, Best Dir.), The Great Waldo Pepper 1975, Slap Shot 1976, A Little Romance 1979, The World According to Garp 1982, The Little Drummer Girl 1984, Funny Farm 1988; first television production 1954. *Other productions include:* A Night to Remember, Helen Morgan, Child of our Time, Judgement at Nuremberg; Academy Award (The Sting) 1973. *Address:* Pan Arts Productions, 75 Rockefeller Plaza, New York, N.Y. 10019, U.S.A.

HILL, Graham Starforth, M.A., F.R.S.A.; British solicitor and banker; b. 22 June 1927, Oxford, England; s. of late Capt. H. V. J. Hill and late Mrs. H. D. Hill (née Starforth); m. Margaret Elise Ambler 1952 (divorced 1962); one s. one d.; ed. Winchester and St. John's Coll., Oxford; Flying Officer, R.A.F. 1948–50; called to Bar (Gray's Inn) 1951; admitted advocate and solicitor Singapore, W. Malaysia, advocate Brunei, solicitor Hong Kong 1955; admitted solicitor England 1961; Crown Counsel, Colonial Legal Service, Singapore 1953–56; partner (finally sr. partner) Rodyk and Davidson, solicitors, Singapore 1957–76; Pres. Law Soc. of Singapore 1969–73; mem. Council of Int. Bar Asscn. 1970–78; Hon. Legal Adviser, British High Comm., Singapore 1957–76; Dir. Guinness Mahon & Co. Ltd. 1977–83, Chair. 1979–83; Consultant, Frère Cholmeley, Monaco and Rodyk and Davidson, Singapore; Dir. Phelan, Lewis and Peat Ltd. 1984–86; mem. Disciplinary Cttee., Inst. of C.A. 1980–85; Trustee, Southwark Cathedral Devt. Trust 1980–85, Royal Opera House Trust 1982–85; Cavaliere della Stella della Solidarietà; Commendatore al Merito della Repubblica Italiana. *Publication:* Report of the Constitutional Commission of Singapore. *Leisure interests:* music, books, Italy. *Address:* 10 St. Thomas Street, Winchester, Hants., SO23 9HE, England; Casa Claudia, Piccolo Pevero, 07020 Porto Cervo, Sardegna, Italy. *Telephone:* (0962) 54146 (Winchester); (0789) 92317/92157 (Italy).

HILL, John Alexander; American business executive; b. 24 Feb. 1907, Shawnee, Okla.; s. of John E. Hill and Mary B. Cheek; m. Margaret Mikesell 1929; one s. two d.; ed. Univ. of Denver; Aetna Life Insurance Co. 1928–70, Denver 1928–30, Man. Group and Pensions Depts., Detroit 1930–35, Dist. Supervisor 1933–36, Gen. Agent, John A. Hill & Assocs., Toledo 1936–58, Sr. Vice-Pres. 1958–62, Pres. 1962–70, Pres. Hospital Corpn. of America 1970–74, Chair. 1974–; Chair. American Life Insurance Co. of New York 1981–; Dir. of several cos. *Leisure interests:* golf, art. *Address:* Hospital Corporation of America, 1 Park Plaza, Nashville, Tenn. 37202 (Office); Belle Meade Towers Apartments, 105 Leake Avenue, Nashville, Tenn. 37203, U.S.A. (Home).

HILL, (John Edward) Christopher, M.A., D.LITT., F.B.A.; British historian; b. 6 Feb. 1912, York; s. of Edward H. and Janet A. Hill; m. 1st Inez Waugh 1944, 2nd Bridget Irene Sutton 1956; one s. two d. (one deceased); ed. St. Peter's School, York, and Balliol Coll., Oxford; Fellow of All Souls Coll., Oxford 1934–38; Asst. Lecturer, Univ. Coll., Cardiff 1936–38; Fellow and Tutor in Modern History, Balliol Coll., Oxford 1938–65, Master of Balliol Coll. 1965–78; Army and Foreign Office Service 1940–45; Univ. Lecturer in 16th and 17th Century History, Oxford 1959–65; Visiting Prof. Open Univ. 1978–80, Preston Polytechnic 1982–84; mem. Editorial Bd. Past and Present 1952–68, Yale Edition of Milton's Complete Prose; Foreign Hon. mem. American Acad. of Sciences 1973; Hon. D.Litt. (Glasgow, Hull, Norwich, Wales, Exeter, Sheffield), Hon. LL.D. (Bristol), Hon. D.Univ. (York), Hon. Dr. (Sorbonne Nouvelle); shared Heinemann Award for Books 1978; James Holly Hanford Award, Milton Soc. of America 1978. *Publications:* The English Revolution, 1640 1940, Lenin and Russian Revolution 1947, The Good Old Cause (documents, edited jointly with E. Dell) 1949, Economic Problems of the Church 1956, Puritanism and Revolution 1958, The Century of Revolution 1603-1714 1961, Society and Puritanism in Pre-Revolutionary England 1964, Intellectual Origins of the English Revolution 1965, Reformation to Industrial Revolution 1967, God's Englishman 1970, Antichrist in 17th Century England 1971, The World Turned Upside Down 1972, The Law of Freedom and Other Selected Writings of Gerrard Winstanley (editor) 1973, Change and Continuity in 17th Century England 1975, Milton and the English Revolution 1977, Some Intellectual Consequences of the English Revolution 1980, The World of the Muggletonians (co-author) 1983, The Experience of Defeat: Milton and Some Contemporaries 1984, Writing and Revolution in 17th Century England 1985, Religion and Politics in 17th Century England 1986, People and Ideas in 17th Century England 1986, A Turbulent, Seditious and Factious People: John Bunyan and his Church (W. H. Smith Literary Prize) 1988. *Address:* Woodway House, Sibford Ferris, Banbury, Oxon., OX15 5RA, England.

HILL, Sir John McGregor, Kt., F.R.S., F.ENG.; British atomic energy official; b. 21 Feb. 1921; s. of the late John Campbell Hill and of Margaret Elizabeth Park; m. Nora Eileen Hellett 1947; two s. one d.; ed. Richmond County Grammar School, King's Coll., London, and St. John's Coll., Cambridge; Flight Lieut., R.A.F., Second World War; research at Cavendish Laboratory, Cambridge 1946–48; Lecturer, London Univ. 1948–50; U.K. Atomic Energy Authority 1950–81, mem. for Production 1964–67, Chair. 1967–81; Chair. British Nuclear Fuels Ltd. 1971–83, Aurora Holdings PLC 1983–, Rea Bros. 1987–; mem. Energy Comm. Dept. of Energy 1978–79, Nuclear

Power Advisory Bd. 1973–81; Foreign Assoc. mem., Nat. Acad. of Engineering of the U.S.A. 1976; Hon. D.Sc. (Bradford) 1981; Hon. F.I.Chem.E. 1977; Hon. F.I.E.E. 1981. *Address:* Dominic House, Sudbrook Lane, Richmond, Surrey, England (Home).

HILL, Robert, SC.D., F.R.S.; British biochemist; b. 2 April 1899; s. of Joseph A. Hill and Clara M. Jackson; m. Amy P. Worthington 1935; two s. two d.; ed. Bedales School and Emmanuel Coll. Cambridge; served World War I; Sr. Studentship, Emmanuel Coll. Cambridge 1927; Beit Memorial Research Fellow 1929; Sr. Beit Memorial Research Fellow 1935; mem. scientific staff, Agric. Research Council 1943–66; hon. mem. American Assoc. of Biological Chemists, American Acad. of Arts and Sciences etc.; Foreign mem. N.A.S.; Hon. Fellow, Emmanuel Coll. Cambridge. *Publication:* Photosynthesis 1955 (co-author). *Address:* 1 Comberton Road, Barton, Cambridge, CB3 7BA, England.

HILL, Robert Lee, PH.D.; American university professor; b. 8 June 1928, Kansas City, Mo.; s. of William Alfred Hill and Geneva Eunice Sculock Hill; m. 1st Helen Root Hill 1948; m. 2nd Deborah Anderson Hill 1982; one s. three d.; ed. Kansas Univ.; Research Instructor, Univ. of Utah, Salt Lake City 1956–57, Asst. Research Prof. 1957–60, Assoc. Research Prof. 1960–61; Assoc. Prof., Duke Univ., Durham, N.C. 1961–65, Prof. 1965–74, Chair. Dept. of Biochemistry 1969–, James B. Duke Prof. 1974–; Fellow, American Acad. of Arts and Sciences 1974–; mem. N.A.S. 1975–; Pres. American Soc. of Biological Chemists 1976–77; Pres. Assn. of Medical Depts. of Biochemistry 1982–83; Gen. Sec. Int. Union of Biochemistry 1985–. *Publications:* Co-Author: Principles of Biochemistry 1978, Co-Ed. The Proteins (vol.1 1975, vol. V 1982). *Address:* Department of Biochemistry, Duke University Medical Center, Durham, N.C. 27710, U.S.A. *Telephone:* (919) 684-5326.

HILL, Rodney, M.A., PH.D., F.R.S.; British professor of mechanics of solids; b. 11 June 1921; s. of Harold H. Hill; m. Jeanne K. Wickens 1946; one d.; ed. Leeds Grammar School and Pembroke Coll., Cambridge; Armament Research Dept. 1943–46; Cavendish Lab. Cambridge 1946–48; British Iron and Steel Research Assn. 1948–50; Research Fellow, Univ. of Bristol 1950–53, Reader 1953; Prof. of Applied Math. Univ. of Nottingham 1953–62; Professorial Research Fellow 1962–63; Berkeley Bye-Fellow, Gonville and Caius Coll. Cambridge 1963–69, Fellow 1972–88, Life Fellow 1988–; Reader, Univ. of Cambridge 1969–72, Prof. of Mechanics of Solids 1972–79; Hon. D.Sc. (Manchester) 1976, (Bath) 1978; Thrivon Karman Medal, American Soc. of Civil Engineers 1978, Gold Medal and Int. Modesto Panetti Prize, Turin Acad. of Sciences 1988. *Publications:* Mathematical Theory of Plasticity 1950, Principles of Dynamics 1964. *Address:* c/o Department of Applied Mathematics and Theoretical Physics, Silver Street, Cambridge, CB3 9EW, England.

HILL, S. Richardson, Jr., M.D.; American physician and university president; b. 19 May 1923, Greensboro, N.C.; s. of Samuel Richardson Hill and Nona Sink Hill; m. Janet Redman 1950; one s. three d.; ed. Riverside Mil. Acad., Gainesville, Ga., Duke Univ. and Bowman Gray School of Medicine of Wake Forest Univ.; Intern in Medicine, then Asst. Resident, Asst. in Medicine, Peter Bent Brigham Hosp., Boston, Mass. and Teaching Fellow, then Research Fellow in Medicine, Harvard Medical School 1947–50; Chief Resident in Medicine, N.C. Baptist Hosp. and Instructor, Bowman Gray School of Medicine 1950–51; Chief, Medical Service, U.S.A.F. Hosp. Keesler, Miss. 1951–53; Asst. in Medicine, Harvard Medical School and Peter Bent Brigham Hosp. 1953–54; Asst. Prof. of Medicine and Dir. Metabolic and Endocrine Div., Medical Coll. of Ala. (later Univ. of Ala. School of Medicine), Birmingham, Ala. 1954–57, Assoc. Prof. 1957–62, Prof. 1962–, Dean 1962–68, Vice-Pres. for Health Affairs and Dir. of Medical Center, Univ. of Ala. in Birmingham 1968–77, Pres. Univ. of Ala. at Birmingham 1977–87, Distinguished Prof. 1987–; Fellow A.A.A.S., American Coll. of Physicians, Royal Soc. of Medicine, New York Acad. of Sciences; mem. Assn. for Acad. Health Centers (Pres. 1973), N.A.S. Inst. of Medicine. *Leisure interests:* sailing, swimming and reading. *Address:* University of Alabama at Birmingham, University Station, Birmingham, Ala. 35294; 4101 Altamont Road, Birmingham, Ala. 35213, U.S.A. (Home). *Telephone:* (205) 934-3493 (Univ.); (205) 934-0771 (Home).

HILL, Terrell Leslie, PH.D.; American biophysicist and chemist; b. 19 Dec. 1917, Oakland, Calif.; s. of George Leslie and Ollie Moreland Hill; m. Laura Etta Gano 1942; one s. two d.; ed. Univ. of California at Berkeley and Harvard Univ.; Instructor in Chem., Western Reserve Univ. 1942–44; Research Assoc., Radiation Lab., Univ. of Calif. at Berkeley 1944–45; Research Assoc. in Chem., then Asst. Prof. of Chem., Univ. of Rochester 1945–49; Chemist, U.S. Naval Medical Research Inst. 1949–57; Prof. of Chem., Univ. of Oregon 1957–67; Prof. of Chem., Univ. of Calif. at Santa Cruz 1967–71, Vice-Chancellor, Sciences 1968–69, Adjunct Prof. of Chem. 1977–; Sr. Research Chemist, Nat. Insts. of Health 1971–; mem. Nat. Acad. of Sciences, American Chemical Soc., Biophysical Soc., American Civil Liberties Union, Nat. Assn. for Advancement of Coloured People, etc.; Guggenheim Fellow, Yale 1952–53; Sloan Foundation Fellow 1958–62; Arthur S. Flemming Award, U.S. Govt. 1954, Dist. Civilian Service Award, U.S. Navy 1955, Award of Washington Acad. of Sciences 1956, Kendall Award, American Chemical Soc. 1969, Superior Service Award, U.S. Public Health Service 1981, Distinguished Service Award, Univ. of Oregon 1983. *Publications:* Statistical Mechanics 1956, Statistical Thermodynamics 1960,

Thermodynamics of Small Systems Vol. I 1963, Vol. II 1964, Matter and Equilibrium 1965, Thermodynamics for Chemists and Biologists 1968, Free Energy Transduction in Biology 1977, Cooperativity Theory in Biochemistry 1985, Linear Aggregation Theory in Cell Biology 1987; also research papers. *Leisure interests:* tennis, poetry, music. *Address:* National Institutes of Health, Bethesda, Md. 20892 (Office); 9626 Kensington Parkway, Kensington, Md. 20895, U.S.A. (Home). *Telephone:* (301) 496-5436 (Office); (301) 946-7978 (Home).

HILL OF LUTON, Baron (Life Peer), cr. 1963; **Charles Hill,** P.C., M.A., M.D., D.P.H., LL.D.; British doctor and politician; b. 15 Jan. 1904; m. Marion Spencer Wallace 1931; two s. three d.; ed. St. Olave's Grammar School, Trinity Coll., Cambridge, and the London Hospital; Univ. Tutorial Lecturer in Biology 1926-30; Sec. British Medical Asscn. 1944-50; Pres. World Medical Assn. 1949-50; Liberal-Conservative M.P. 1950-63; Parl. Sec., Ministry of Food 1951-55; Postmaster-Gen. 1955-57; Chancellor of the Duchy of Lancaster 1957-61; Minister of Housing and Local Govt. and Minister of Welsh Affairs 1961-62; Dir. Laporte Industries 1962-65, Chair. 1965-70; Dir. Abbey National Building Soc. 1964-78, Chair. 1976-78; Chair. Independent Television Authority 1963-67; Chair. of Govs. BBC 1967-72; Chair. Nat. Joint Council for Local Authorities' Admin., Professional, Technical and Clerical Services 1963-78; Chair. Chest, Heart and Stroke Asscn. 1974-84; Hon. Fellow, American Medical Assn. *Publications:* What is Osteopathy? 1937, Your Health in Wartime 1941, Wartime Food for Growing Children 1942, Wise Eating in Wartime 1943, When Your Baby is Coming 1943, Wednesday Morning Early—by the Radio Doctor 1944, Your Body 1944, Your Aches and Pains 1945, The Way to Better Health 1946, Bringing up Your Child 1950, Dictionary of Health 1951, Both Sides of the Hill 1964, Behind the Screen 1974. *Leisure interests:* golf, walking. *Address:* 9 Borodale, Kirkwick Avenue, Harpenden, Herts., AL5 2QW, England. *Telephone:* (05827) 64288.

HILL SMITH, Marilyn, A.G.S.M.; British soprano opera singer; b. 9 Feb. 1952, Carshalton, Surrey; d. of George and Irene Smith; m. Peter Kemp 1974; ed. Nonsuch High School, Ewell and Guildhall School of Music and Drama; cabaret, pantomime, concerts 1971-74; toured Australia and N.Z. with Gilbert & Sullivan for All 1974, U.S.A. and Canada 1976; Prin. Soprano, English Nat. Opera 1978-84; Covent Garden début in Peter Grimes 1981; has appeared at English Bach Festival, Aldeburgh Festival, with New Sadlers Wells Opera, Canadian Opera Co., Welsh Nat. Opera, Scottish Nat. Opera, etc. and on television and radio and has made several recordings particularly of operetta; Young Musician of the Year 1975 and other prizes. *Leisure interests:* cooking, gardening, sleeping. *Address:* c/o Music International, 13 Ardilaun Road, Highbury, London, N5 2QR, England. *Telephone:* 01-359 5183/4.

HILLABY, John; British writer and naturalist; b. 24 July 1917; s. of late Albert Ewart Hillaby and Mabel Colyer; m. 1st Eleanor Riley 1940 (divorced); two d.; m. 2nd Thelma Gordon 1946 (died 1972); m. 3rd Kathleen Burton 1981; local journalism until 1939; magazine contrib. 1944-; Zoological Corresp., Manchester Guardian 1949; European Science Writer, New York Times 1951-; Biological Consultant, New Scientist 1953-; numerous expeditions on foot all over the world; Woodward Lecturer, Yale Univ. 1973; f. Pres. Backpackers Club; fmr. Dir. Univs. Fed. for Animal Welfare; Radio and TV series include Men of the North, Expedition South, Alpine Venture, Hillaby Walks and Globetrotter. *Publications:* Within The Streams 1949, Nature and Man 1960, Journey to the Jade Sea 1964, Journey through Britain 1968, Journey through Europe 1972, Journey through Love 1976, Journey Home 1983, John Hillaby's London 1987. *Leisure interests:* talking, reading, music, walking alone, observing peculiarities of man, beast, fowl and flora. *Address:* 85 Cholmley Gardens, London, N.W.6.; Rosedale-by-Pickering, North Yorks., England. *Telephone:* 01-435 4626.

HILLARY, Sir Edmund Percival, K.B.E.; New Zealand explorer, bee farmer and diplomatist; b. 20 July 1919, Auckland; s. of Percival Augustus and Gertrude Hillary; m. Louise Mary Rose 1953 (died 1975); one s. two d. (one deceased); ed. Auckland Grammar School and Univ. of Auckland; served R.N.Z.A.F. (on Catalinas in the Pacific) 1944-45; went to Himalayas on N.Z. Garwhal expedition 1951, when he and another were invited to join the British reconnaissance over Everest under Eric Shipton; took part in British expedition to Cho Oyu 1952, and in British Mount Everest Expedition under Sir John Hunt 1953, when he and Tenzing reached the summit on May 29th; Leader N.Z. Alpine Club Expedition to Barun Valley 1954; N.Z. Antarctic Expedition 1956-58, reached South Pole Dec. 1957; Leader Himalayan Expeditions 1961, 1963, 1964; Pres. Volunteer Service Abroad in New Zealand 1963-64; built a hospital for Sherpa tribesmen, Nepal 1966; Leader climbing expedition on Mount Herschel, Antarctica 1967; River Ganges Expedition 1977; High Commr. to India (also accred. to Bangladesh and Nepal) 1984-; Hon. Pres. Explorers Club of New York; Consultant to Sears Roebuck & Co., Chicago; Hubbard Medal 1954, Polar Medal 1958; Gurkha Right Hand (1st Class), Star of Nepal (1st Class), Founders' Gold Medal, Royal Geographical Soc.; James Wattie Book of the Year Award, N.Z. 1975; Hon. LL.D. (Victoria Univ., B.C., Canada, Victoria Univ., New Zealand) and other hon. degrees. *Publications:* High Adventure 1955, The Crossing of Antarctica (with Sir Vivian Fuchs) 1958, No Latitude for Error 1961, High in the Thin Cold Air (with Desmond

Doig) 1963, Schoolhouse in the Clouds 1965, Nothing Venture, Nothing Win (autobiog.) 1975, From the Ocean to the Sky: jet-boating up the Ganges 1979, Two Generations (with Peter Hillary). *Leisure interests:* walking, fishing, camping. *Address:* High Commission of New Zealand, 25 Golf Links, New Delhi, India (Office); 278A Remuera Road, Auckland, SE2, New Zealand (Home).

HILLEBRECHT, Rudolf Friedrich Heinrich, DIPL. ING.; German architect and town planner; b. 26 Feb. 1910, Hanover; s. of Ernst and Bertha (née Arning) Hillebrecht; m. 1st Ruth Frommhold 1937, 2nd Oxana Saweljewa 1967; one d.; ed. Humanistisches Gymnasium, Hanover, and Technische Hochschulen, Hanover and Berlin; worked with Walter Gropius, Berlin 1933-34; Building Inspector, Travemünde, Hamburg and Hanover 1934-37; Office Manager, architectural practice of Konstanty Gutschow, Hamburg 1937-45; worked in Dept. for Replanning of Hamburg 1937-44; Army Service 1944-45; worked with Werner Kallmorgen, Hamburg 1945-46; Deputy Chief, Building Div., British Occupied Zone 1946; Sec. for Building Affairs, German Advisory Council of British Zone 1946-48; Municipal Town Planner and Architect, City of Hanover 1948-75; Pres. Gottfried-Wilhelm-Leibniz-Gesellschaft 1969-85; Pres. German Acad. for Town and Country Planning 1973-79, and other orgs.; Grosses Bundesverdienstkreuz mit Stern und Schulterband, and many other decorations; Hon. Citizen of Hanover 1980. *Leisure interests:* arts, literature, music. *Address:* Gneiststrasse 7, 3 Hanover, Federal Republic of Germany (Home).

HILLEL, Shlomo; Israeli politician; b. 1923, Baghdad, Iraq; m. Tmima Rosner 1952; one s. one d.; ed. Herzliah High School, Tel-Aviv and Hebrew Univ., Jerusalem; mem. Ma'agan Michael Kibbutz 1942-58; Jewish Agency for Palestine—mission to countries in Middle East 1946-48, 1949-51; Israel Defence Forces 1948-49; Prime Minister's Office 1952-53; mem. of Knesset 1953-59, 1974-; Amb. to Guinea 1959-61, to Ivory Coast, Dahomey, Upper Volta and Niger 1961-63; mem. Perm. Mission to UN with rank of Minister 1964-67; Asst. Dir.-Gen. Ministry of Foreign Affairs 1967-69; Minister of Police 1969-77; Co-ordinator of political contacts with Arab leadership in administered territories 1970-77; Minister of the Interior June-Oct. 1974; Chair. Ministerial Cttee. for Social Welfare 1974-77, Cttee. of the Interior and Environment 1977-81, of Foreign Affairs and Defence 1981-84; Perm. Observer to Council of Europe 1977-84; Speaker of the Knesset Sept. 1984-; Chair. Sephardi Fed. 1976-; Commdr. Nat. Order of Repubs. of Ivory Coast, Upper Volta and Dahomey. *Publication:* Operation Babylon 1988. *Address:* The Knesset, Jerusalem, Israel.

HILLEMAN, Maurice Ralph, PH.D.; American virologist; b. 30 Aug. 1919, Miles City, Mont.; s. of Robert A. and Edith M. (Matson) Hilleman; m. 1st Thelma L. Mason 1943 (deceased), 2nd Lorraine Witmer 1963; two d.; ed. Montana State Coll. and Univ. of Chicago; Asst. Bacteriologist, Univ. of Chicago 1942-44; Research Assoc., Virus Laboratories, E.R. Squibb & Sons 1944-47; Chief Virus Dept. 1947-48; Medical Bacteriologist and Asst. Chief, Virus and Rickettsial Diseases, Army Medical Service Graduate School, Walter Reed Army Medical Center 1948-56; Chief, Respiratory Diseases, Walter Reed Army Inst. of Research, Washington 1956-57; Dir. Virus and Cell Biology Research, Merck Inst. for Therapeutic Research, Merck & Co. Inc. 1957-66, Exec. Dir. 1966-70; Dir. Virus and Cell Biology Research, Vice-Pres. Merck Sharp and Dohme Research Laboratories 1970-78, Sr. Vice-Pres. 1978-84; Dir. Merck Inst. for Therapeutic Research 1984-; Visiting lecturer in Bacteriology, Rutgers Univ. 1947; Visiting Investigator, Hospital of Rockefeller Institute for Medical Research 1951; Visiting Prof. Department of Bacteriology, Univ. of Maryland 1953-57; Adjunct Prof. of Virology in Pediatrics, School of Med., Univ. of Pa. 1968-; Consultant, Surgeon-Gen. U.S. Army 1958-63; Children's Hosp. of Philadelphia 1968-; mem. Expert Advisory Panel on Virus Diseases, WHO 1952-, Cttee. on Influenza 1952, Cttee. on Respiratory Diseases 1958, Scientific Group on Measles Vaccine Studies 1963, on Viruses and Cancer 1964, on Human Viral and Rickettsial Vaccines 1965, on Respiratory Diseases 1967; mem. Study Section, Microbiology and Immunology Grants-in-Aid Program 1953-61; mem. Editorial Bd. Int. Soc. of Cancer 1964-71, Inst. for Scientific Information 1968-70, American Journal of Epidemiology 1969-75, Infection and Immunity 1970-76, Excerpta Medica 1971-, Proceedings of the Soc. for Experimental Biology and Medicine 1976, Editorial and Publs. Cttee. 1977-; mem. Council, Tissue Culture Assn. 1977-; mem. Council for Div. of Biological Sciences, Pritzker School of Medicine 1977-; mem. American Type Culture Collection Virology Dept. Review Cttee. 1980; mem. Overseas Medical Research Labs. Cttee., Dept. of Defense 1980; Editorial Bd., Antiviral Research 1980-; mem. Bd. of Dirs., W. Alto Jones Cell Science Center 1980-82, The Joseph Stokes Jr. Research Inst., Univ. of Pa. 1986-, Nat. Foundation for Infectious Diseases; mem. Advisory Bd. Inst. of Biomedical Sciences, Taiwan, 1982-; mem. N.A.S. Cttee. on a Nat. Strategy for AIDS 1986-87, Nat. Vaccine Advisory Cttee. of Nat. Vaccine Program 1988-; mem. Cttee. on New Vaccine Development Nat. Acad. of Sciences 1983-; mem. numerous U.S. and Int. Medical Socs.; John Herr Musser Lecturer, Tulane Univ. School of Med. 1969; 19th Graugnard Lecturer 1978; Fellow, American Acad. of Microbiology, American Acad. of Arts and Sciences; mem. N.A.S.; Hon. D.Sc. (Montana Univ.) 1966, (Maryland Univ.) 1968; Dr. h.c. (Univ. Leuven) 1984; recent awards include Distinguished Civilian Service Award given by Sec. of Defense 1957, Washington Acad. of Sciences Award for Scientific Achievement in the Biological Sciences 1958, Walter Reed Army Medical Center Incentive

Award 1960, Merck Dirs. Scientific Award 1969, 1984, Dean M. McCann Award for Distinguished Service 1970, Procter Award 1971, American Acad. of Achievement, Golden Plate Award 1975, Industrial Research Inst. Achievement Award 1975, Gold Medal for Service to Humanity, Hellenic Red Cross 1982, American Medical Assen. Scientific Achievement Award 1983, Albert Lasker Medical Research Award 1983, Howard Taylor Ricketts Award, Univ. Chicago 1983, Sabin Medal, German Soc. for Social Paediatrics 1988, Nat. Medal of Science, Pres. of U.S.A. 1988. *Publications:* more than 440 original publications on virology, immunology and public health. *Address:* Merck Sharp and Dohme Research Laboratories, Merck Institute for Therapeutic Research, West Point, Pa. 19486, U.S.A. *Telephone:* (215) 661 5532.

HILLENBRAND, Martin Joseph, PH.D.; American diplomatist; b. 1 Aug. 1915, Youngstown, Ohio; s. of Joseph and Maria Hillenbrand; m. Faith Stewart 1941; two s. one d.; ed. Univs. of Dayton and Columbia; Vice-Consul, Zürich 1939, Rangoon 1940, Calcutta 1942, Lourenço Marques 1944, Bremen 1944; Consul, Bremen 1946; Bureau of German Affairs, State Dept. 1950–52; First Sec., Paris 1952–56; U.S. Political Adviser, Berlin 1956–58; Dir. Office of German Affairs, State Dept. 1958–62; Head of "Berlin Task Force" 1962–63; Deputy Chief of Mission, Bonn 1963–67; Chair. Fulbright Comm. for Germany 1963–67; Amb. to Hungary 1967–69; Asst. Sec. of State for European Affairs 1969–72; Amb. to Fed. Repub. of Germany 1972–76; Dir.-Gen. Atlantic Inst. for Int. Affairs, Paris 1977–82; Prof. Univ. of Ga. 1982–; Dir Global Policy Studies 1983–; Grand Order of Merit (Fed. Repub. of Germany) and many other honours. *Publications:* Power and Morals 1948, Zwischen Politik und Ethik (co-author) 1968, The Future of Berlin (co-author and ed.) 1980, Global Insecurity: A Strategy for Energy and Economic Growth (co-ed.) 1982, Germany in an Era of Transition 1983. *Leisure interests:* reading, walking, golf. *Address:* Center for Global Policy Studies, University of Georgia, Athens, Ga. 30602, U.S.A. *Telephone:* (404) 542-2111.

HILLER, Susan, M.A.; American artist; b. 7 March 1940; d. of Paul Hiller and Florence Ehrich; m. David Coxhead 1962; one s.; ed. Smith Coll. and Tulane Univ.; one-woman exhbns. at galleries in London and other British cities, Toronto, Zürich, Warsaw, Adelaide, Sydney, etc. since 1973; has participated in numerous group shows in Britain and abroad; lecturer, Slade School of Art, London 1982–; Artist-in-Residence, Univ. of Sussex 1975; Gulbenkian Foundation Visual Artists Award 1976, 1977. *Address:* c/o Gimpel Fils, 30 Davies Street, London, W.1, England. *Telephone:* 01-493 2488.

HILLER, Dame Wendy, D.B.E.; British actress; b. Stockport; d. of Frank Hiller and Marie Stone; m. Ronald Gow 1937; one s. one d.; ed. Winceby House, Bexhill; trained as an actress Manchester Repertory Theatre; Hon. LL.D (Manchester) 1984; Acad. Award for Best Actress, Separate Tables 1959; numerous stage and film roles. *Plays include:* Love on the Dole (London and New York) 1935, Cradle Song, The First Gentleman 1945, Tess of the d'Urbervilles, The Heiress (London and New York) 1947, Ann Veronica 1949, The Night of the Ball 1955, Waters of the Moon 1955, Moon for the Misbegotten (New York) 1957, Flowering Cherry 1958, Toys in the Attic 1960, Aspern Papers (New York) 1962, The Wings of the Dove 1963, The Sacred Flame 1967, When We Dead Awaken (Edinburgh Festival) 1968, The Battle of Shrivings 1970, Crown Matrimonial 1972, John Gabriel Borkman (London) 1975, Lies 1976, The Aspern Papers 1984, The Importance of being Earnest 1987, Driving Miss Daisy 1988. *Films include:* Pygmalion 1938, Major Barbara 1940, I Know Where I'm Going 1945, Separate Tables 1958, Sons and Lovers 1960, A Man for All Seasons 1966, David Copperfield 1969, Murder on the Orient Express 1975, Voyage of the Damned 1976, Cat and the Canary 1977, The Elephant Man 1979, Making Love 1981, The Kingfisher 1982, The Lonely Passion of Miss Judith Hearne 1987. *Television:* All Passion Spent 1987, A Taste for Death 1988, Ending Up 1989. *Leisure interest:* gardening. *Address:* c/o Laurence Evans, I.C.M., 388/396 Oxford Street, London, W.1, England.

HILLERY, Patrick John, B.SC., M.B., B.CH., B.A.O., D.P.H.; Irish politician and Head of State; b. 2 May 1923, Miltown Malbay, Co. Clare; s. of Dr. Michael Joseph Hillery and Ellen Hillery (née McMahon); m. Mary Beatrice Finnegan 1955; one s.; ed. Miltown Malbay National School, Rockwell Coll., Cashel and Univ. Coll., Dublin; worked in General Children's Tuberculosis and Psychiatric Hospital; mem., Health Council 1955–57; Medical Officer, Miltown Malbay 1957–59; Coroner for West Clare 1958–59; mem. Dáil 1951–73; Minister for Educ. 1959–65, for Industry and Commerce 1965–66, for Labour 1966–69, of Foreign Affairs 1969–72; Vice-Pres. Comm. of European Communities with special responsibility for Social Affairs 1973–76; Pres. of Ireland Dec. 1976–; mem. Royal Irish Acad. 1963; Hon. Fellow Royal Coll. of Surgeons (Ireland), Faculty of Dentistry, Royal Coll. of Surgeons (Ireland), All-India Inst. of Medical Sciences, Royal Coll. of Physicians (Ireland), Royal Coll. of Gen. Practitioners, Pharmaceutical Soc. of Ireland 1984; Hon. LL.D. (Nat. Univ. of Ireland, Trinity Coll., Dublin, Univ. of Melbourne); M.R.I.A. *Address:* Áras an Uachtaráin, Phoenix Park, Dublin 8 (Office); Spanish Point, County Clare, Ireland (Home).

HILLIER, Bevis, F.R.S.A.; British writer and editor; b. 28 March 1940; s. of Jack Ronald Hillier and Mary Louise Palmer; ed. Reigate Grammar School and Magdalen Coll., Oxford; Editorial Staff, The Times 1963–68, Antiques Corresp. 1970–84, Deputy Literary Ed. 1981–84; Ed. British

Museum Soc. Bulletin 1968–70; Guest Curator, Minn. Inst. of Arts 1971; Ed. the Connoisseur 1973–76; Assoc. Ed., Los Angeles Times 1984–. *Publications:* Master Potters of the Industrial Revolution: The Turners of Lane End 1965, Pottery and Porcelain 1700–1914 1968, Art Deco of the 1920s and the 1930s 1968, Posters 1969, Cartoons and Caricatures 1970, The World of Art Deco 1971, 100 Years of Posters 1972, Austerity-Binge 1975, The New Antiques 1977, Greetings from Christmas Past 1982, The Style of the Century 1900–1980 1983, John Betjeman: A Life in Pictures 1984, Young Betjeman 1988; Co-Ed. A Tonic to the Nation: The Festival of Britain 1951 1976. *Leisure interests:* piano, collecting, awarding marks out of ten for suburban front gardens. *Address:* Los Angeles Times, Times Mirror Square, Los Angeles, Calif. 90053, (Office); 527 South Fuller Avenue, Los Angeles, Calif. 90036, U.S.A. (Home).

HILLIER-FRY, William Norman, C.M.G., B.A.; British diplomatist (retd.); b. 12 Aug. 1923, Eltham; s. of William Henry and Emily Hillier-Fry; m. Elizabeth Adèle Misbah 1948; two s. two d.; ed. Colfe's Grammar School, Lewisham, and St. Edmund Hall, Oxford; served in army 1942–45; with Foreign Service 1946–, Iran 1947–52, del. to Council of Europe 1955-56, Turkey 1956–59, Czechoslovakia 1961–63, U.K. del. to Disarmament Conf., Geneva 1968–71, Consul-Gen., Hamburg 1974–79, Amb. to Afghanistan 1979–80, High Commr. in Uganda 1980–83. *Leisure interests:* music, theatre. *Address:* 127 Coombe Lane West, Kingston-upon-Thames, Surrey, KT2 7HF, England.

HILL-NORTON, Baron (Life Peer) cr. 1979, of South Nutfield in the County of Surrey; **Admiral of the Fleet Peter John Hill-Norton,** G.C.B.; British naval officer; b. 8 Feb. 1915, Germiston; s. of Martin J. and Margery B. Norton; m. Margaret E. Linstow 1936; one s. one d.; ed. Royal Naval Coll., Dartmouth and Royal Naval Coll., Greenwich; went to sea 1932; commissioned 1936; served Arctic convoys, N.W. Approaches and Admiralty Naval Staff, Second World War 1939–45; Commdr. 1948; Captain 1952; Naval Attaché, Argentine, Uruguay, Paraguay 1953–55; in command H.M.S. Decoy 1956–57, H.M.S. Ark Royal 1959–61; Asst. Chief of Naval Staff 1962–64; Flag Officer, Second-in-Command Far East Fleet 1964–66; Deputy Chief of the Defence Staff (Personnel and Logistics) 1966; Second Sea Lord and Chief of Naval Personnel Jan.-Aug. 1967; Vice-Chief of Naval Staff 1967–68; Commander-in-Chief, Far East 1969–70; Chief of Naval Staff and First Sea Lord 1970–71; Chief of the Defence Staff 1971–74; Chair. North Atlantic Mil. Cttee. 1974–77, 1980–; Pres. Sea Cadet Assen. 1977–84; Vice-Pres. Royal United Service Inst. 1977; Pres. Friends of Osborne House 1980; Chair. Partridge, Muir & Warren 1982–; Pres. British Maritime League 1982–85; Liveryman, Worshipful Company of Shipwrights 1973; Freeman of the City of London 1974. *Publications:* No Soft Options 1978, Sea Power 1982. *Leisure interests:* golf, shooting. *Address:* Cass Cottage, Hyde, Fordingbridge, Hampshire, England.

HILLS, Carla Anderson, A.B., LL.D.; American lawyer and government official; b. 3 Jan. 1934, Los Angeles; d. of Carl and Edith (Hume) Anderson; m. Roderick Maltman Hills (q.v.) 1958; one s. three d.; ed. Stanford Univ., Calif., St. Hilda's Coll., Oxford, U.K., Yale Law School; Asst. U.S. Attorney, Civil Div., Los Angeles, Calif. 1958–61; Partner, Munger, Tolles, Hills & Rickershauser (law firm) 1962–74; Adjunct Prof., School of Law, Univ. of Calif., Los Angeles 1972; Asst. Attorney-Gen. Civil Div., U.S. Dept. of Justice 1974–75; Sec. of Housing and Urban Devt. 1975–77; Partner, Latham, Watkins & Hills (law firm) 1978–; nominated as Special Trade Rep. Dec. 1988–; Co-Chair. Alliance to Save Energy 1977–; Vice-Chair. Bar of Supreme Court of the U.S., Calif. State and D.C. Bars, Council Section of Anti-trust Law, American Bar Assen. 1974–, American Law Inst. 1974–, Fed. Bar Assen. (Los Angeles Chapter, Pres. 1963), Women Lawyers Assen. (Pres. 1964), Los Angeles County Bar Assen., Chair. of various cttees. including Standing Cttee. on Discipline, Calif. 1970–74; mem. Bd. of Dirs. Int. Business Machines, The Signal Co. Inc., Standard Oil Co. of Calif., American Airlines Inc., Int. Exec. Service Corpns.; mem. Carnegie Comm. on the Future of Public Broadcasting 1977–78, Sloan Comm. on Govt. and Higher Educ. 1977–79, Advisory Cttee. Woodrow Wilson School of Public and Int. Affairs 1977–, Yale Univ. Council 1977–80, Fed. Accounting Standards Advisory Council 1978–, Trilateral Comm. 1977–, American Cttee. on East-West Accord 1977–79, Int. Foundation for Cultural Cooperation and Devt. 1977–, Editorial Bd., National Law Journal 1978–; Contributing Editor, Legal Times 1978–; Fellow, American Bar Foundation 1975–; Trustee, Pomona Coll. 1974–79, Norton Simon Museum of Art 1976–, Brookings Inst. 1977–, Univ. of S. Calif. 1977–; Advisor, Annenberg School of Communications, Univ. of S. Calif. 1977–78; Chair. Urban Inst. 1983–; Hon. degrees from Pepperdine Univ., Calif. 1975, Washington Univ., Mo. 1977, Mills Coll., Calif. 1977, Lake Forest Coll. 1978. *Publications:* Federal Civil Practice (co-author) 1961, Antitrust Adviser (editor and co-author) 1971. *Leisure interest:* tennis. *Address:* Latham, Watkins and Mills, 1001 Pennsylvania Avenue, 1300 Washington, D.C. 20004-2505H (Office); 3125 Chain Bridge Road, N.W., Washington, D.C. 20016, U.S.A. (Home).

HILLS, Roderick Maltman, LL.B.; American lawyer, business executive and government official; b. 9 March 1931, Seattle, Wash.; s. of Kenneth Maltman and Sarah (Love) Hills; m. Carla Anderson (Hills, q.v.) 1958; one s. three d.; ed. Stanford Univ., Calif.; admitted to Calif. Bar 1957, to Supreme Court Bar 1960; Law Clerk to Justice, Supreme Court 1955–57;

Partner, Tolles, Hills and Rickershauser, law firm 1962-71; Chair. of Bd. Repub. Corpn. 1971-75; Counsel to Pres. of U.S.A. 1975; Chair. Securities and Exchange Comm. 1975-83; Chair. Peabody Coal Co. 1977-78; Partner Latham, Watkins and Hills 1978-83; Counsel 1983-86; Dir. Drexel Burnham 1989-; lecturer, Stanford Univ. 1960-69; Visiting Prof. Harvard 1969-70; Distinguished Fellow and Lecturer, Yale School of Finance (Int. Finance); Chair. Research Cttee., American Bar Foundation, Sears World Trade 1983-84; Trustee Comm. for Econ. Devt.; Chair. U.S.-ASEAN Tech. Center; Dir. Anhueser-Busch, Alex & Alex, Fed. Mogul Inc., Oak Industries; Chair. The Manchester Group Ltd.; mem. American Bar Assen., Los Angeles County Bar Assen., Calif. State Bar; Trustee, Claremont Univ. Centre; mem. Editorial Bd., Comment Editor, Stanford Law Review 1953-55. *Leisure interests:* tennis, golf, history. *Address:* 3125 Chain Bridge Road, N.W., Washington, D.C. 20016, U.S.A. (Home). *Telephone:* (202) 966-5065 (Home).

HILSMAN, Roger, PH.D.; American diplomatist and educator; b. 23 Nov. 1919, Waco, Texas; s. of Colonel Roger Hilsman and Emma Prendergast Hilsman; m. Eleanor Hoyt 1946; two s. two d.; ed. West Point and Yale Univ.; U.S. Army 1943-53; Center for Int. Studies, Princeton Univ. 1953-56; Chief Foreign Affairs Div. of Legislative Reference Service, Library of Congress 1956-58, Deputy Dir. (for Research) 1958-61; Dir. Bureau of Intelligence and Research, Dept. of State 1961-63; Asst. Sec. of State for Far Eastern Affairs 1963-64; Prof. of Govt., Columbia Univ. 1964-; Fulbright Distinguished Lecturer to India 1985. *Publications:* Strategic Intelligence and National Decisions 1956, To Move a Nation 1967, The Politics of Policy Making in Defense and Foreign Affairs 1971, The Crouching Future, International Politics and U.S. Foreign Policy, A Forecast 1975, To Govern America 1979, The Politics of Governing America 1985, Conceptual Models and the Politics of Policy Making 1986; co-author: Military Policy and National Security 1956, Foreign Policy in the 60s 1965; contributor to Alliance Policy in the Cold War 1959, NATO and American Security 1959, The Guerrilla—and How to Fight Him 1962, Modern Guerrilla Warfare 1962, A Layman's Guide to Nuclear Military Strategy 1989. *Leisure interest:* designing toys. *Address:* Hamburg Cove, Lyme, Conn., U.S.A. (Home).

HILSUM, Cyril, PH.D., F.ENG., F.INST.P., F.I.E.E., F.I.E.E.E., F.R.S.; British research scientist; b. 17 May 1925, London; s. of Ben and Ada Hilsum; m. Betty Hilsum 1947 (died 1987); two d.; ed. Raines School, London, and Univ. Coll., London; H.Q. Admiralty 1945-47; Admiralty Research Lab., Teddington 1947-50; Services Electronics Research Lab., Baldock 1950-64; Royal Signals and Radar Establishments, Malvern 1964-83; Visiting Prof., Univ. Coll., London 1988-; mem. Science and Eng. Research Council 1984-88; Chief Scientist, Gen. Electric Co. (GEC) Research Labs. 1983-85; mem. Science and Eng. Research Council 1984-; Dir. of Research, GEC PLC 1985-; recipient of several awards. *Publications:* Semiconducting III-V Compounds 1961; over 100 scientific and technical papers. *Leisure interests:* tennis, chess, ballroom dancing. *Address:* GEC Research Laboratories, East Lane, Wembley, Middx., England. *Telephone:* 01-908 9006.

HILTON, Janet; British musician; b. 1 Jan. 1945, Liverpool; d. of H. Hilton and E. Hilton; m. David Richardson 1968; two s. (one deceased) one d.; ed. Belvedere School, Liverpool, Royal Manchester Coll. of Music, Vienna Konservatorium; BBC concerto début 1963; appearances as clarinet soloist with maj. British orchestras including Royal Liverpool Philharmonic, Scottish Nat., Scottish Chamber, City of Birmingham Symphony, Bournemouth Symphony, Bournemouth Sinfonietta, City of London Sinfonia, BBC Scottish and Welsh Symphony, BBC Philharmonic; guest at Edin., Aldeburgh, Bath, Cheltenham, City of London Festivals, Henry Wood Promenade concerts; appearances throughout Europe and N. America; Prin. Clarinet Scottish Chamber Orchestra 1974-80, Kent Opera 1984-; teacher Royal Scottish Acad. of Music and Drama 1974-80, Royal Northern Coll. of Music 1983-87; Visiting Tutor, Exeter Univ.; several recordings; dedicatee of works by Iain Hamilton, John McCabe, Edward Harper, Elizabeth Maconchy, Alun Hoddinott, *Leisure interests:* cookery, reading. *Address:* 27 Cassel Avenue, Branksome Park, Poole, Dorset, England. *Telephone:* (0202) 762232.

HIMLE, Erik; Norwegian economist and politician; b. 10 April 1924; ed. Oslo Univ.; Sec., Ministry of Commerce 1948-49; Int. Bank for Reconstruction and Devt., Washington 1949-51; Ministry of Commerce 1951-52; Chief of Dept., Ministry of Defence 1952-55, Dir. 1956-58, Under-Sec. of State 1958-61, Sec.-Gen. 1961; Under-Sec. of State, Minister of Transport and Communications 1962-63; Minister of Commerce and Shipping 1963-64, of Communications 1964-65; Sec. Labour group in the Storting (Parl.); Sec. financial-political cttee. under Minister of Finance 1966-67; Perm. Sec. of Defence 1967-; Labour. *Address:* Askåsen 15, N-1360 Nesbru, Norway.

HIMMELFARB, Gertrude, PH.D.; American professor of history and author; b. 8 Aug. 1922; d. of Max Himmelfarb and Bertha (Lerner) Himmelfarb; m. Irving Kristol 1942; one s. one d.; ed. Brooklyn Coll. and Univ. of Chicago; Distinguished Prof. of History, Graduate School, City Univ. New York 1965-; Fellow, American Philosophical Soc., American Acad. of Arts and Sciences, Royal Historical Soc., etc.; many public and professional appts.; Rockefeller Foundation Award 1962-63; Guggenheim Fellow 1955-56, 1957-58; Hon. L.H.D. (R.I. Coll.) 1976, (Kenyon Coll) 1985; Hon. Litt.D. (Smith Coll.) 1977, Lafayette Coll. 1978. *Publications:* Lord

Acton: A Study in Conscience and Politics 1952, Darwin and the Darwinian Revolution 1959, Victorian Minds 1968, On Liberty and Liberalism: The Case of John Stuart Mill 1975, The Idea of Poverty 1984, Marriage and Morals Among the Victorians 1986. *Address:* City University of New York, 33 West 42nd Street, New York, N.Y. 10036, U.S.A.

HIMSWORTH, Sir Harold Percival, K.C.B., M.D., F.R.S., F.R.C.P.; British medical research scientist; b. 19 May 1905, Huddersfield, Yorks.; m. Charlotte Gray, M.B. 1932; two s.; ed. Univ. of London; fmrly. Prof. of Medicine Univ. of London and Dir. Medical Unit Univ. Coll. Hospital Medical School, London 1939-49; Sec. Medical Research Council 1949-68; Consulting Physician Univ. Coll. Hospital; Chair. Bd. of Man., London School of Hygiene and Tropical Medicine 1969-76; Prime Warden Goldsmith's Co., London 1974-76; mem. Norwegian Medical Soc., Royal Soc. Arts and Sciences; Hon. mem. Swedish Medical Soc., Belgian Royal Acad. of Medicine, Assen. of American Physicians; Foreign mem. American Philosophical Soc.; Foreign hon. mem. American Acad. of Arts and Sciences; Fellow, Univ. Coll. London, Royal Soc.; Hon. Fellow, Royal Coll. of Radiologists, London School of Hygiene and Tropical Medicine, Royal Soc. of Hygiene and Tropical Medicine; Dr. h.c. (Toulouse), Hon. LL.D. (Glasgow, London, Wales), Hon. D.Sc. (Manchester) 1956, Hon. Sc.D. (Cambridge) 1964, Hon. D.Sc. (Leeds and Univ. of West Indies) 1968; Hon. F.R.C.P. (Edin.) 1960; Hon. F.R.S.M. 1961; Hon. F.R.C.S. 1965; Hon. F.R.C. Path. 1969. *Publications:* The Development and Organisation of Scientific Knowledge 1970, Scientific Knowledge and Philosophical Thought 1986. *Address:* 13 Hamilton Terrace, London, NW8 9RE, England.

HINAULT, Bernard; French cyclist; b. 14 Nov. 1954, Yffiniac, Côtes du Nord; s. of Joseph and Lucie (Guernion) Hinault; m. Martine Lessard 1974; two s.; competitive cycling debut 1971; French junior champion 1972; French Champion 1978; World Champion 1980; winner, Tour de France 1978, 1979, 1981, 1982, 1985, Tour d'Italie 1980, 1982, 1985, Tour d'Espagne 1978, 1983, Grand Prix des Nations 1978, 1982, 1984, Luis Puig Trophy 1986, Coors Classic, U.S.A. 1986 and many other int. racing events; retd. from racing 1986; Chevalier, Ordre Nat. du Mérite. *Publication:* Moi, Berhard Hinault (with others) 1988. *Address:* Les Poteries, Quessoy, 22120 Yffiniac, France.

HINCHCLIFFE, Peter Robert Mossom, C.V.O., M.A.; British diplomatist; b. 9 April 1937, Mahableshwar, India; s. of Peter Hinchcliffe and Jeannie Hinchcliffe; m. Archbold Harriet Hinchcliffe 1965; three d.; ed. Radley Coll., Trinity Coll., Dublin; British Army 1955-57; H.M.O.C. Aden Protectorate 1961-67; Political Officer, FCO 1969-71; mem. U.K. Mission to UN 1971-74; Head of Chancery, British Embassy, Kuwait 1974-76, FCO 1976-78, Deputy High Commr., Dar es Salaam 1978-81, Consul Gen., Dubai 1981-85; Head of Information Dept. FCO 1985-87, Amb. to Kuwait 1987-. *Leisure interests:* golf, tennis, cricket. *Address:* British Embassy, Kuwait (Office); 7 Cranley Gardens, Muswell Hill, London, N10 3AA, England (Home). *Telephone:* Kuwait 249 2046 (Office); 01-444 8565 (Home).

HINCK, Walter, D.PHIL.; German professor of language and literature; b. 8 March 1922, Selsingen; s. of Johann and Anna (née Steffens) Hinck;. m. Sigrid Graupe 1957; one d.; ed. Univ. of Göttingen; Prof. of Modern German Language and Literature, Literary Criticism, Univ. of Cologne 1964-; mem. Rheinisch-Westfälischen Akad. der Wissenschaften 1974-, (Vice-Pres. 1986-87), Sektion Bundesrepublik Deutschland des Internationalen PEN-Clubs 1986-. *Publications:* Die Dramaturgie des späten Brecht 1959, Das deutsche Lustspiel des 17. und 18. Jahrunderts und die italienische Komödie 1965, Die deutsche Ballade von Bürger bis Brecht 1968, Das moderne Drama in Deutschland 1973, Von Heine zu Brecht—Lyrik im Geschichtsprozess 1978, Goethe—Mann des Theaters 1982, Germanistik als Literaturkritik 1983, Heinrich Böll: Ausgewählte Erzählungen 1984, Das Gedicht als Spiegel der Dichter 1985, Theater der Hoffnung, Von der Aufklärung bis zur Gegenwart 1988. *Address:* Am Hammergraben 13/15, D-5064 Rösrath 1, (Hoffnungsthal) bei Cologne, Federal Republic of Germany. *Telephone:* 022205-5147.

HINDE, Robert Aubrey, D.PHIL., SC.D., F.R.S.; British biologist and psychologist; b. 26 Oct. 1923, Norwich; s. of Ernest B. Hinde and Isabella Hinde; m. 1st Hester Cecily Coutts (divorced), two s. two d.; 2nd Joan Stevenson 1971, two d.; ed. Oundle School, St. John's Coll., Cambridge, Balliol Coll., Oxford; pilot, R.A.F. Coastal Command 1940-45; Curator, Ornithological Field Station, Dept. of Zoology, Univ. of Cambridge 1960-64, Fellow of St. John's Coll. 1951-54, 1958-; Royal Soc. Research Prof. 1963-; Hon. Dir. MRC Unit of Devt. and Integration of Behaviour 1970-89; Hitchcock Prof., Univ. of Calif. 1979; Foreign Hon. mem. A.A.A.S. 1974; Hon. Fellow American Ornithologists' Union 1976; Hon. Foreign Assoc. N.A.S. 1978; Leonard Cammer Award, Psychiatric Inst. 1980; Einstein Award in Psychiatry 1987; Osman Hill Medal (Primate Soc. of G.B.) 1988; Hon. Fellow, British Psychological Soc. 1981; Hon. Fellow Balliol Coll. Oxford 1986; Hon. Sc.D. (Univ. Libre, Brussels) 1974, (Nanterre) 1978. *Publications:* Animal Behaviour: A Synthesis of Ethology and Comparative Psychology 1966, Social Behaviour and its Development in Sub-human Primates 1972, Biological Bases of Human Social Behaviour 1974, Towards Understanding Relationships 1979, Ethology 1982, Individuals, Relationships and Culture 1987; Ed. Bird Vocalizations 1969, Primate Social Behaviour 1983; Jt. Ed. Short-term Changes in Neural Activity and Behaviour 1970, Constraints on Learning 1973, Growing Points in Ethology 1976, Social Relationships and Cognitive Development 1985, Relationships Within Families (ed.) Mutual Influences 1988, Aggression and War: Their Biological and Social Bases (ed.) 1988, Education for Peace (ed.); numerous articles in learned journals. *Leisure interests:* ornithology, reading. *Address:* Park Lane, Madingley, Cambridge, England (Home). *Telephone:* 0954-210430 (Home).

HINDE, Thomas (see Chitty, Sir Thomas Wiles).

HINE, Maynard Kiplinger, D.D.S., M.S.; American dentist; b. 25 Aug. 1907, Waterloo, Ind.; s. of Clyde L. and Delia (Kiplinger) Hine; m. Harriett Foulke 1932; two s. one d.; ed. Univ. of Illinois; Instructor at Univ. of Ill. Coll. of Dentistry 1930-32, Assoc. 1936-38, Asst. Prof. 1938-43; Assoc. Prof. and Head of the Div. of Oral Pathology at Indiana Univ. School of Dentistry 1944-45; Prof. and Head of the Dept. of Periodontia and Histopathology, Indiana Univ. School of Dentistry 1945-55; Dean of Indiana Univ. School of Dentistry 1945-68; Chancellor, Indiana Univ.-Purdue Univ. at Indianapolis 1969-73; Exec. assoc. Indiana Univ. 1973-77; Chair. Periodontal Disease Advisory Comm. of Nat. Inst. for Dental Research of Dept. Health Educ. and Welfare 1972-75; Pres. Bd. of Dirs. Cen. Indiana Council on Ageing 1978-80; mem. American Asscn. of Dental Editors, Pres. 1949-50; mem. Nat. Dental Advisory Cttee. of U.S. Public Health Service 1948-50; mem. Int. Asscn. Dental Research, Pres. 1952; mem. Advisory Panel on Medical Sciences, Dept. of Defense; mem. Indiana State Dental Asscn., Pres. 1957-58; Ed. Journal of Periodontology 1950-70; Pres. American Asscn. of Dental Schools 1952, American Acad. of Periodontology 1964, American Dental Asscn. 1966, Féd. Dentaire Int. 1975-77, American Acad. of History of Dentistry 1980; Regent Nat. Library of Medicine 1960-63; mem. Advisory Council of Nat. Inst. for Dental Research; Chair. Section R, American Asscn. for Advancement of Science 1981; Hon. Fellow, Royal Coll. of Surgeons (Ireland) 1974, Royal Coll. of Dentists, Canada 1977, Philippine Coll. of Surgeons 1977; numerous hon. degrees; numerous awards and prizes. *Publication:* Review of Dentistry, Oral Pathology. *Leisure interest:* philately. *Address:* 1121 West Michigan Street, Indianapolis, Ind. 46202, U.S.A. *Telephone:* 274-8717 (Office); 255-2776 (Home).

HINE, Air Chief Marshal Sir Patrick, G.C.B., F.R.AE.S., C.B.I.M.; British air force officer; b. 14 July 1932, Chandlers Ford, Hants.; s. of Eric Graham Hine and Cecile Grace Hine (née Philippe); m. Jill Adèle Gardner 1956; three s.; ed. Sherborne House Preparatory School 1937-41, Peter Symonds School, Winchester 1942-49; fighter pilot and mem. R.A.F. 'Black Arrows' and 'Blue Diamonds' Formation Aerobatic Teams 1957-62; Commdr. No. 92 Squadron 1962-64 and 17 Squadron 1970-71, R.A.F. Germany Harrier Force 1974-75; Dir. R.A.F. Public Relations 1975-77; Asst. Chief of Air Staff for Policy 1979-83; C.-in-C. R.A.F. Germany and Commdr. NATO's 2nd Allied Tactical Air Force 1983-85; Vice-Chief of the Defence Staff 1985-87; Air mem. for Supply and Organisation, Air Force Bd. 1987-88; Air Officer Commanding-in-Chief, Strike Command, C.-in-C. U.K. Air Forces Sept. 1988-. *Leisure interests:* golf, mountain walking, skiing, photography, caravanning, travel. *Address:* c/o Headquarters Strike Command, Royal Air Force High Wycombe, Buckinghamshire, HP14 4UE, England. *Telephone:* (0494) 461461 Ext. 2601.

HINSLEY, Sir (Francis) Harry, Kt., O.B.E., F.B.A.; British university professor; b. 26 Nov. 1918; s. of Thomas Henry Hinsley and Emma Hinsley; m. Hilary Brett 1946; two s. one d.; ed. Queen Mary's Grammar School, Walsall, St. John's Coll., Cambridge; H.M. Foreign Office, war service 1939-46; Research Fellow, St. John's Coll. 1940-50, Tutor 1956-63, Cambridge Univ. Lecturer in History 1949-65, Reader in the History of Int. Relations 1965-69, Prof. 1969-83, Vice-Chancellor 1981-83, Master of St. John's Coll. 1979-89 (Fellow 1944-79, Pres. 1975-79), Chair. Faculty Bd. of History 1970-72; Lee-Knowles Lecturer on Mil. Science, Trinity Coll. 1970-71; U.K. Rep., Provisional Academic Cttee. for European Univ. Inst. 1973-75; Trustee, British Museum 1984-; Hon. Fellow, Trinity Coll. Dublin 1981; Ed. The Historical Journal 1960-71; Hon. D.Litt. (Witwatersrand) 1985. *Publications:* Command of the Sea 1950, Hitler's Strategy 1951, New Cambridge Modern History, Vol. XI (Ed.) 1962, Power and the Pursuit of Peace 1963, Sovereignty 1966, Nationalism and the International System 1973, British Foreign Policy under Sir Edward Grey (Ed.) 1977, British Intelligence in the Second World War (jt. author) Vol. 1. 1979, (Vol. 2) 1981, (Vol. 3, Part 1) 1984, (Vol. 3, Part 2) 1988. *Address:* c/o The Master's Lodge, St. John's College, Cambridge, England. *Telephone:* Cambridge 61621.

HINTEREGGER, Gerald; Austrian United Nations official; joined Austrian diplomatic service 1957; Deputy Chief of Mission, Washington, D.C. 1965-70; Chef de Cabinet, Minister of Foreign Affairs 1970-75; Amb. to Spain 1975-78, to U.S.S.R. 1978-81; Sec.-Gen. for Foreign Affairs and Perm. Rep. to UN, Vienna 1981-87; Exec. Sec. UN Econ. Comm. for Europe (ECE) 1987-. *Address:* United Nations Economic Commission for Europe, Palais des Nations, 1211 Geneva 10, Switzerland.

HINTERSCHEID, Mathias; Luxembourg trade unionist; b. 26 Jan. 1931, Düdelange; m. Marie Morbe; three s.; ed. Ecole Supérieure du Travail; apprentice, then metalworker, Arbed works Düdelange until 1958; mem. Luxembourg Workers' Union (LAV) 1946-, active in youth movement; mem. Exec. of Düdelange Branch, LAV 1955-59; mem. man. cttees. of Health Insurance, Pension and Disability Insurance Funds, Arbed works,

Düdelange 1955-58; full-time Sec. for Youth, Educ. and Propaganda 1958-63; Gen. Sec., Luxembourg Conféd. Gén. du Travail (CGT) 1963-70; Pres of LAV and CGT 1970-76; mem. Exec. Cttee. European Trade Union Confed. (ETUC) 1965-, Gen. Sec. ETUC April 1976-; mem. Presidium o Nat. Trade Union Council 1970-; mem. Luxembourg Socialist Labou Party (LSAP) 1947-, Vice-Pres. 1963-68, mem. Econ. and Social Cttee 1966-76; Gen. Sec. Union Luxembourgeoise des Consommateurs (ULC) consumer org. 1964-70; mem. various state comms. incl. Labour Exchange Price Comm., Index Comm.; fmr. mem. Bd. of Man., Tageblatt co-operativ printing office and newspaper, BfG Luxembourg Bank; fmr. Man. Dir UCL co-operative bank; fmr. Pres. Infraplan planning and building soc *Address:* European Trade Union Confederation, 37-41 rue Montagne au Herbes Potagères, 1000 Brussels, Belgium. *Telephone:* 219-10-90.

HIORT, Esbjörn; Danish architect; b. 2 April 1912, Copenhagen; s. o Ivar Hiort and Emma Hiort (née Lorentzen); m. Bente Andresen 1943 two s. two d.; ed. Det Kongelige Akademi for de Skønne Kunster; practise as Architect 1937-52; Sec. Asscn. of Academic Architects 1945-52; Sec Gen. Nat. Fed. of Danish Architects 1952-59; Gen. Man. Perm. Sale Exhbn. of Danish Arts and Crafts (Den Permanente) 1959-67; Chief Ec Byggedata 1972-82; Chair. School of Arts and Crafts, Copenhagen 1963-82 Soc. of Architectural History 1978-87; Officer Order of Dannebrog, Officie d'Académie (France), Officer, Order of Léopold II (Belgium). *Publications* Contemporary Danish Architecture 1949, Housing in Denmark 1952, Moc ern Danish Silver 1954, Modern Danish Ceramics 1955, Modern Danis Furniture 1956, etc. *Leisure interests:* heraldry and genealogy. *Address* Bel Colles Farm, Parkvej 6, 2960 Rungsted Kyst, Denmark.

HIRAHARA, Tsuyoshi, Japanese diplomatist; b. 25 Oct. 1920, Kagoshima s. of Eisuke Fujita and Shizuko Hirahara; m. Kiyoko Nishi 1946; two d ed. Tokyo Imperial Univ.; mil. service 1943-45; Attaché, Treaty Bureau Ministry of Foreign Affairs 1945-47; Sec. to Foreign Minister 1947-48 Section Chief, Special Procurement Bd. 1948-50; Sec. of Embassy, Belgiur 1950-52; Deputy Dir. Econ. Affairs Bureau, Ministry of Foreign Affair 1952-55, Dir. 1959-61, Counsellor 1961-64, Deputy Dir.-Gen. 1969-70, Dir Gen. 1970-72; Dir. Asian Section, UNESCO, Paris 1955-59; Interprete to H.I.M. the Emperor of Japan 1960-64; Consul-Gen., Milan 1964-6 Minister, Embassy in Belgium and Luxembourg 1966-69; Amb. to Morocc 1972-74, to OECD, Paris 1974-80 (Chair. Exec. Cttee. 1977-80), to th U.K. 1982-85; Commdr., Ordre de la Couronne, Grand Officier, Ordre d Léopold II, Grand Officier, Ouissam Alaouite, Commdr., Légion d'honneu *Leisure interests:* golf, collecting tortoises. *Address:* c/o Ministry of Foreig Affairs, 2-2-1 Kasumigaseki, Chiyoda-ku, Tokyo, Japan.

HIRAI, Takushi; Japanese politician; b. 1931; previous posts include Par Vice-Minister of Int. Trade and Industry and of Justice; Chair. Cttee. o Foreign Affairs, House of Councillors; Dir. Judicial Affairs Div., Libera Democratic Party (LDP) Policy Research Council; Minister of Labou 1986-87. *Address:* 2-2 Kasumigaseki 1-chome, Chiyoda-ku, Tokyo, Japan.

HIRAMATSU, Morihiko, LL.B.; Japanese local official; b. 12 March, 192 Oita; s. of late Oriji Hiramatsu and Kun Hiramatsu; m. 1st Chizuko Ued 1949, 2nd Teruko Mihara 1976; two d.; ed. Kumamoto No. V. High Scho and Tokyo Univ.; employee Ministry of Commerce and Industry 1949-6 Dir. Industrial Pollution Div. Enterprises Bureau, Ministry of Int. Trad and Industry 1964-65, Petroleum Planning Div. Mining Bureau 1965-6 Export Insurance Div. Trade Promotion Bureau 1967-69, Electroni Policy Div. Heavy Industries Bureau 1969-73, Co-ordination Office Bas Industries Bureau 1973-74; Counsellor Secr. Land Agency 1974-75; Vic Gov. of Oita Pref. 1975-79, Gov. 1979-83, 1983-87, 1987-; Gran Cluz d Legiao de Honra Giuseppe Garibaldi (Brazil) 1987. *Publications:* Talks o Software, Exhortations to One Village One Product, Challenging Techn polis, Age of Decentralised Management, Let's Try What's Impossible i Tokyo. *Leisure interests:* reading, golf, early morning walks. *Addres* Governor's Official Residence, 8-20 Niage-machi, Oita City, Oita Prefectu 870, Japan. *Telephone:* 0975-32-2001.

HIRAO, Teruo; Japanese economist and retd. financial official; b. 23 De 1925, Osaka; s. of Katsujiro and Sawa Hirao; m. Kiyoko Hashitani 195 two d.; ed. Kyoto Univ.; joined Ministry of Finance 1951; IMF 1967-7 Dir. Tax Bureau, Ministry of Finance 1970-71, Counsellor Environment Protection Agency 1971-73, Dir. Securities Bureau 1973-75, Dir.-Ge Tohoku District Financial Bureau 1975-76, Deputy Dir.-Gen. Minister Secr. 1976-77, Senior Deputy Dir.-Gen. Int. Finance Bureau 1977-79; Exe Dir. for Japan, IMF 1979-84; Adviser Mitsui Trust Bank 1984-; Cha Mitsui Trust Finanz (Schweiz) AG 1984-; Chair. Mitsui Trust Int. (Londo 1986-. *Leisure interests:* bridge, golf. *Address:* 2-23-5-403 Hatsud Shibuya-ku, Tokyo 151, Japan. *Telephone:* 03-379-1451.

HIRASAWA, Kô, M.D.; Japanese university official; b. 1900, Niigata; s. Heitaro and Chino Hirasawa; m. Matue Naganuma; two s. four d.; e Faculty of Medicine, Kyoto Imperial Univ.; Asst. Prof., Kyoto Imperi Univ. 1925-26; Asst. Prof. Niigata Medical Coll. 1926-30, Prof. 1930-4 Prof. Kyoto Univ. 1946-63, Dean Liberal Arts 1949-51, Dean Medic Dept. 1956-57, Pres. 1957-63; Pres. Kyoto Cancer Asscn. 1962-; mer Japan Soc. of Neurosurgery, Japan Soc. of Neurology and Psychiatr Japan Soc. of Anatomy, Japan Acad. 1967; Acad. Prize for Medical Scien 1951, Takeda Prize 1956. *Publications:* Der Plexus brachialis der Japan

1932, The cortical motor system 1951 and many articles. *Address:* 141 Shinnyo-cho, Jôdoji, Sakyo-ku, Kyoto 606, Japan. *Telephone:* 075-771-0549.

HIRATA, Kusuo; Japanese business executive; b. 7 Sept. 1909, Ooita; s. of Shuzo and Tai Hirata; m. Teruko Koinumaru 1940; two s. one d.; ed. Kwansei Gakuin Univ.; with Daicel Ltd. 1933–34; joined Fuji Photo Film Co., Ltd. 1934, Man. Finance Dept. 1950–62, Dir. 1954–64, Man. Planning Div. 1962–66, Man. Dir. 1964–69, Man. Sales Div. 1966–71, Senior Man. Dir. 1969–71, Pres. 1971–80, Chair. 1980–87, Dir. and Adviser 1987–; Blue Ribbon Medal 1974, Order of the Sacred Treasure 1979. *Leisure interest:* golf. *Address:* Fuji Photo Film Co. Ltd., 26-30 Nishiazabu 2-chome, Minato-ku, Tokyo (Office); 48-12, Utsukushigaoka 2-chome, Midori-ku, Yokohama-shi, Kanagawa, Japan (Home). *Telephone:* 03-406-2111 (Office); 045-901-1771 Home).

HIRATA, Yutaka, M.A.; Japanese banker and business executive; b. 13 May 1925, Tokyo; s. of Minoru and Nobuyo Hirata; m. Teruko Hirata 1973; one d.; ed. Kyoto Univ.; Man Dir. Sanwa Bank 1974–77, Sr. Man. Dir. 1977; Deputy Pres. Unitika Ltd. 1977–82, Chair., Pres. and C.E.O. April 1982–. *Leisure interest:* golf. *Address:* 2-17 Asahigaoka-cho, Ashiya City 659, Japan. *Telephone:* 0797-31-2751.

HIRO, Keitaro; Japanese business executive; b. 7 Dec. 1908, Tsukaguchi, Amagasaki, Hyogo Pref.; s. of Yasukichi and Kimi Hiro; m. Sadano Kubo 1941; two s. two d.; ed. Ohkura Higher Commercial School and Ritsumeikan Univ.; teacher, Ohkura Commercial High School 1938–43; Chief, Accounting Dept., Kubota Ltd. 1946, Man. Financial Dept. 1950, Dir. Financing 1951, Man. Dir. 1953, Senior Man. Dir. 1960, Pres. 1971–82, Chair. 1982–85, Dir. and Adviser 1985–; Dir. Kubota Trane Ltd., Kubota Construction Co; Dir. Japan Productivity Asscn. 1961, Osaka Industrialist Asscn. 1961, Kansai Man. Asscn. 1961. *Leisure interests:* reading, Chinese calligraphy. *Address:* Kubota Ltd., 2-47 Shikitsuhigashi, 1-chome, Naniwa-ku, Osaka; 15-32 Takakuracho Nishinomiya, Hyogo Pref., Japan. *Telephone:* 06-648-2111.

HIROOKA, Tomoo; Japanese newspaper publishing executive; b. 24 Aug. 1907, Hyogo Prefecture; s. of Matomo and Nui Hirooka; m. Mitsu Soga 1934; one s. two d.; ed. Univ. of Tokyo; joined Asahi Shimbun newspaper 1932, Editorial Writer 1942, Econ. Ed. 1948, Man. Ed. 1954, Dir. 1956, Rep. of Seibu Main Office 1960, Rep. Dir., Man. Dir. 1964, Pres. 1967, Chair. of the Bd. 1977–. *Address:* c/o The Asahi Shimbun, 2-6-1 Yuraku-cho, Chiyoda-ku, Tokyo 100, Japan. *Telephone:* 03 (212) 0131.

HIROSE, Shin-ichi, B.LAWS; Japanese business executive; b. 25 Jan. 1913; ed. Tokyo Imperial Univ.; Govt. official 1938–65, Vice-Minister, Ministry of Transport 1964–65, Senior Man. Dir. of Nippon Express Co. Ltd. 1968–72, Exec. Vice Pres. 1972–76, then Pres. 1976–. Cttee. of Overall Nat. Land Devt. Council, 1975–; Dir., Japan Fed. of Employers' Asscns., 1975–, Fed. of Economic Orgs., 1975–. *Address:* 3-12-9, Soto-Kanda, Chiyoda-Ku, Tokyo (Office); 1-29-12, Amanuma, Suginami-ku, Tokyo, Japan Home).

HIRSCH, Etienne; French civil engineer and administrator; b. 24 Jan. 1901, Paris; ed. Ecole des Mines, Paris; joined Etablissements Kuhlmann 1924, attached to research lab. 1924–29, later factory man., Dir. of Research and Devt. and Dir. Société Marles-Kuhlmann, Société Technique pour l'Amélioration des Carburants and Société des Produits Chimiques Ethyl-Kuhlmann; joined Free French Forces 1940; Asst. Dir. of Armaments, Algiers 1943; Pres. French Supply Council, London, French rep. temp. Econ. Cttee. for Europe 1945; Head Technical Div., Commissariat-Général au Plan 1946–49, Deputy Commr.-Gen. 1949–52, Commr.-Gen. 1952–59; participated in negotiations setting up ECSC 1950–52, NATO Cttee. of Wise Men 1951–52; Pres. EURATOM Comm. 1959–62, Inst. Technique de Prévision Economique et Sociale 1962–, Asscn. des Amis de Jean Monnet; Prof. Free Univ. of Brussels 1963–69; Pres. Comité Central du Mouvement Fédéraliste Européen 1964–, Hon. Pres. 1975–; Commdr. Légion d'honneur. *Address:* 10 rue de la Justice, 92310 Sèvres, France. *Telephone:* (1) 45.34.05.49.

HIRSCH, Judd, B.S.; American actor; b. 15 March 1935, New York; s. of Joseph S. Hirsch and Sally Kitzis; ed. City Coll. of New York; Broadway appearances in Barefoot in the Park 1966, Knock Knock 1975 (Drama Desk Award); off-Broadway appearances in Scuba Duba 1967–69, King of the United States 1972, Mystery Play 1972, Hot L Baltimore 1972–73, Prodigal 1973, Chapter Two 1977–78, Talley's Folly 1979 (Obie Award), The Seagull 1983, I'm Not Rappaport 1985–86 (Tony Award); has appeared in numerous television plays, series, films etc; mem. Screen Actors Guild. *Films include:* King of the Gypsies 1978, Ordinary People 1980, Without a Trace 1983, Teachers 1984, The Goodbye People 1986. *Address:* c/o Morton L. Leavy, 11 E. 44th Street, New York, N.Y. 10017, U.S.A.

HIRSCH, Sir Peter Bernhard, Kt., PH.D., F.R.S.; British professor of metallurgy; b. 16 Jan. 1925, Berlin; s. of Ismar Hirsch and Regina Meyer-sohn; m. Mabel A. Kellar (née Stephens) 1959; one step s. one step d.; ed. Univ. of Cambridge; Lecturer in Physics, Univ. of Cambridge 1959–64, Reader 1964–66; Fellow, Christ's Coll., Cambridge 1960–66, Hon. Fellow 1978–; Isaac Wolfson Prof. of Metallurgy, Univ. of Oxford and Fellow, St. Edmund Hall 1966–; Chair. Metallurgy and Materials Cttee., Science Research Council 1968–73; mem. Council, Inst. of Physics 1968–72, Inst. of Metals 1968–73, 1986–, Electricity Supply Research Council 1969–82,

Council for Scientific Policy 1971–72, Metals Soc. Council 1976–82, Council Royal Soc. 1977–79; mem. Bd. UKAEA 1982–, Chair. 1982–84; mem. Tech. Advisory Cttee. Advent 1982–; Dir. Cogent 1985–; mem. Tech. Advisory Cttee. Monsanto Electronic Materials 1985–; Hon. Fellow, St. Catharine's Coll., Cambridge 1982, Royal Microscopical Soc. 1977, Japan Soc. of Electron Microscopy 1979; Rosenhain Medal, Inst. of Metals 1961, Boys' Prize, Inst. of Physics and Physical Soc. 1962, Clamer Medal, Franklin Inst. 1970, Wihuri Int. Prize 1971, Hughes Medal of the Royal Soc. 1973, Platinum Medal of the Metals Soc. 1976, Royal Medal of Royal Soc. 1977, Arthur Von Hippel Award, Materials Research Soc. 1983, Wolf Prize in Physics 1984; Hon. D.Sc. (Newcastle Univ. 1979, City Univ. 1979, Northwestern Univ. 1982, East Anglia Univ. 1983). *Publications:* Electron Microscopy of Thin Crystals (joint author) 1965, The Physics of Metals, 2, Defects (editor) 1975 and numerous articles in learned journals. *Leisure interest:* walking. *Address:* Department of Metallurgy and Science of Materials, University of Oxford, Parks Road, Oxford, OX1 3PH (Office); 104A Lonsdale Road, Oxford, England (Home). *Telephone:* (0865) 273737.

HIRSCH, Robert; French civil servant; b. 20 Nov. 1912, Paris; m. Jacqueline Ogé 1937; two s. three d.; ed. Lycée Janson-de-Sailly, Paris, and Ecole Polytechnique, Paris; Sub-Lieut. French Air Force 1934, Lieut. 1936, Capt. 1940, Commdt. 1944; Dir. Supply, Accommodation and Transport, Sûreté Nationale 1944, Dir.-Gen. 1951–54; Prefect, Charente Maritime 1947, Seine Maritime 1954–59, Nord 1959–63; Admin.-Gen. Atomic Energy Comm. 1963–70; Dir. Electricité de France 1963–70, Centre nationale d'études spatiales 1968–70, Société nationale de pétroles d'Aquitaine 1970–77; Pres. Gaz de France 1970–75, Admin. 1975–; Comité permanent des réformes administratives 1972–77, Pres. Soc. d'Etudes et Réalisations Nucléaires (SODERN), Laboratoires d'Electronique et de Physique appliquée 1978–85; Pres. Télécommunications radio-électriques et téléphoniques (T.R.T.) 1980–86; mem. Bd. of the Order of the Légion d'honneur 1977–83; Grand Officier, Légion d'honneur, Grand Croix, Ordre national du Mérite, Croix de guerre, etc. *Address:* Bureau des préfets, 1 bis place des Saussaies, 75008 Paris, France.

HIRSCH, Robert Paul; French actor; b. 26 July 1925; s. of Joachim Hirsch and Germaine Anne Raybois; mem. Comédie Française 1952–74; numerous appearances include: La belle aventure, Le prince travesti, Monsieur de Pourceaugnac, Les temps difficiles, La double inconstance, Le dindon, Amphitryon, Britannicus, Crime et Châtiment, La faim et la soif, Monsieur Amilcar, L'abîme et la visite, le Piège, Deburau, Chacun sa vérité, Les dégourdis de la 11e 1986. *Films include:* Le dindon, Votre dévoué Blake, En effeuillant la marguerite, Notre-Dame de Paris, Maigret et l'affaire Saint-Fiacre, 125 rue Montmartre, Par question le samedi, Monnaie de singe, Martin soldat, Toutes folles de lui, les Cracks, Appelez-moi Mathilde, Traitement de choc, Chobizenesse, La crime; Officier des Arts et des Lettres. *Address:* 1 place du Palais Bourbon, 75017 Paris, France.

HIRSCHFELDER, Joseph Oakland, B.S., PH.D.; American professor of chemistry; b. 27 May 1911, Baltimore, Md.; s. of Arthur Douglas Hirsch-felder and May Rosalie Straus; m. Elizabeth Stafford Sokolnikoff 1953; ed. Univ. of Minnesota and Yale and Princeton Univs.; Research Assoc., Univ. of Wis. 1937–40, Instructor in Chem. and Physics 1940–41, Asst. Prof. of Chem. 1941–42, Prof. 1946–81, Homer Adkins Prof. and Dir. of Theoretical Chem. Inst. 1962–81, Prof. Emer. 1981–; Adjunct Prof. Univ. of Calif., Santa Barbara 1971–; Consultant, Nat. Defense Research Cttee., Interior Ballistics Guns and Rockets 1942–43; Group Leader, Theoretical Physics and Ordnance, Los Alamos Atomic Bomb Lab.; Head Theoretical Physics Div., Naval Ordnance Test Station, Inyokern and Pasadena 1945–46; Chief Phenomenologist, Bikini Atomic Bomb Test 1946; Fellow, American Physical Soc.; mem. Advisory Bd., Argonne Nat. Lab. 1962–66. Nat. Bureau of Standards 1962–67; mem. Nat. Acad. of Sciences, American Acad. of Arts and Sciences, Int. Acad. of Quantum Molecular Science, A.C.S. (Chair. of Physical Chem. Div. 1959–61), Combustion Inst.; Hon. Fellow A.S.M.E.; Hon. Fellow Royal Soc. of Chemistry (U.K.); Foreign mem. Royal Soc. of Norway; Debye Award of American Chemical Soc. 1966, Sir Alfred Egerton Gold Medal of Combustion Inst. 1966, Nat. Medal of Science 1975. *Publications:* The Effects of Atomic Weapons (Chair. Bd. of Eds.) 1950, Molecular Theory of Gases and Liquids 1954, 1964, Intermolecular Forces 1967, Reminiscences of Los Alamos, 1943–1945 (Ed.) 1979, Lasers, Molecules, Methods (Ed.) Vol. 33 of Advances in Chemical Physics 1988. *Leisure interests:* golf, swimming, jogging. *Address:* (April-Oct.) Department of Chemistry, University of Wisconsin, Madison, Wis. 53706; 1822 Thorstrand Road, Madison, Wis. 53705 (Home); (Oct.–April) Department of Chemistry, University of California, Santa Barbara, Calif. 93106; 5920 Encina Road No. 3, Santa Barbara, Calif., U.S.A. (Home). *Telephone:* (April-Oct.) (608) 262-0258 (Univ.); (608) 233-8433 (Home); (Oct.–April) (805) 961-3049 (Univ.); (805) 967-6921 (Home).

HIRSCHFIELD, Alan J., B.S., M.B.A.; American business executive; ed. Univ. of Okla. and Harvard Univ.; Vice-Pres. Allen and Co. 1959–67; Vice-Pres. (Finance) and Dir. Warner Bros. Seven Arts Inc. 1967–68; Vice-Pres. and Dir. American Diversified Enterprises Inc. 1968–73; Pres. and C.E.O., Columbia Pictures Industries Inc. 1973–79; Consultant, Warner Communications Inc. 1979; Vice-Chair. and C.O.O., 20th Century-Fox Film Corpn. 1979–81, Chair., C.E.O. and C.O.O. 1981–84; Dir. Straight Arrow Publishing

Co., John B. Coleman Co.; Dir. Motion Picture Asscn. of America, New York State Motion Picture and TV Advisory Bd., Film Soc. of Lincoln Cen., Will Rogers Memorial Fund; Trustee, Cancer Research Inst. (Sloan-Kettering). *Address:* c/o 20th Century-Fox Film Corporation, 10201 West Pico Boulevard, Los Angeles, Calif. 90064, U.S.A.

HIRST, John Malcolm, D.S.C., PH.D., F.I.BIOL., F.R.S.; British professor of agricultural and horticultural sciences; b. 20 April 1921; s. of Maurice H. Hirst and Olive M. (Pank) Hirst; m. Barbara M. Stokes 1957; two d.; ed. Solihull School and Univ. of Reading; served R.N. 1941-46; Rothamsted Experimental Station, Harpenden 1950-75, Head, Plant Pathology Dept. 1967-75; Prof. of Agricultural and Horticultural Science, Univ. of Bristol and Dir. Long Ashton Research Station 1975-84, Prof. Emer. 1984-. *Publications:* articles in professional journals. *Address:* The Cottage, Butcombe, Bristol, BS18 6XQ, England. *Telephone:* (027587) 2880.

HIRZEBRUCH, Friedrich Ernst Peter, DR. RER. NAT.; German professor of mathematics; b. 17 Oct. 1927, Hamm, Westf.; s. of Dr. Fritz Hirzebruch and Martha Hirzebruch (née Holtschmit); m. Ingeborg Spitzley 1952; one s. two d.; ed. Westfälische Wilhelms-Univ., Münster, and Technische Hochschule, Zürich; Scientific Asst. Univ. of Erlangen 1950-52; mem. Inst. for Advanced Study, Princeton, N.J., U.S.A. 1952-54; Dozent, Univ. of Münster 1954-55; Asst. Prof., Princeton Univ., N.J. 1955-56; Full Prof., Bonn Univ. 1956-, Dean, Faculty of Mathematics and Natural Sciences 1962-64; Dir. Max-Planck-Inst. für Mathematik, Bonn 1981-; Pres. German Mathematical Soc. 1961-62; mem. Leopoldina, Heidelberg, Mainz, Netherlands and Nordrheinwestf. Acads., N.A.S. (U.S.A.), Bayerische Akad. der Wissenschaften, Finnish Acad. of Sciences, Akad. der Wissenschaften zu Berlin, Akad. der Wissenschaften der D.D.R.; Dr. h.c. (Univs. of Warwick, Göttingen, Wuppertal), Hon. D.Sc. (Oxford) 1984; Silver Medal, Swiss Fed. Inst. of Technology 1950, Wolf prize in Mathematics 1988. *Publications:* Neue topologische Methoden in der algebraischen Geometrie 1956, Collected Papers (2 vols.) 1987. *Address:* Max-Planck-Institut für Mathematik, Gottfried-Claren-Strasse 26, 5300 Bonn 3 (Office); Thüringer Allee 127, D5205 St. Augustin 2, Federal Republic of Germany (Home). *Telephone:* 0228-4021 (Office); 02241-332377 (Home).

HITAM, Dato' Mohd. Yusof, B.A.; Malaysian diplomatist; b. 1 Jan. 1936, Mentakab; m. Datin Michiyo Noor Azian Binti Mustakim 1966; three s.; ed. Univs. of Singapore and Malaya; Amb. to Vietnam 1976-78; High Commr. to New Zealand 1978-80; Dir.-Gen. Ministry of Foreign Affairs, Asscn. of South East Asian Nations Nat. Secr. 1980; Perm. Rep. to UN 1986-88; Sec.-Gen. Ministry of Foreign Affairs 1988-; Pingat Peringatan Malaysia-Gansa 1968, Johan Setia Mahkota 1976, Darjah Indera Mahkota 1986. *Leisure interests:* reading, golf, shooting. *Address:* Ministry of Foreign Affairs, Wisma Putra, 50602 Kuala Lumpur (Office); No. 25, Lorong 2C, Taman Hillview, Ukay Hights, Kuala Lumpur, Malaysia (Home). *Telephone:* 2483690 (Office); 4560918 (Home).

HITAM, Datuk Musa bin, S.P.M.J., S.S.I.J., S.P.M.S., B.S.I., P.I.S.; Malaysian politician; b. 18 April 1934, Johor; ed. English Coll., Johor Baharu Univ. of Malaya and Univ. of Sussex; assoc. sec. Int. Student Conf. Secr. (COSEC), Leiden 1957-59; civil servant 1959-64; political sec. to Minister of Transport 1964; M.P. 1969-; Asst. Minister to Deputy Prime Minister 1969; studied in U.K. 1970, subsequently lectured at Univ. of Malaya; Chair. Fed. Land Devt. Authority 1971; Deputy Minister of Trade and Industry 1972-74; Minister of Primary Industries 1974-78, of Educ. 1978-81; Deputy Prime Minister and Minister of Home Affairs 1981-86; Deputy Pres. UMNO 1981-86, M.P. 1986-. *Address:* No. 12, Selekoh Tunku, Bukit Tunku, 50480, Kuala Lumpur.

HITCH, Brian, C.M.G., C.V.O.; British diplomatist; b. 2 June 1932, Wisbech; s. of the late R. S. Hitch and of G. E. Hitch; m. Margaret Kathleen Wooller 1954; two d.; ed. Wisbech Grammar School and Magdalene Coll., Cambridge; entered Foreign Office 1955, Third, then Second Sec. Tokyo 1955-61, Second then First Sec. Havana 1962-64, First Sec. Athens 1965-68, First Sec. and Head of Chancery Tokyo 1968-72, Asst. Head, Southern European Dept., FCO 1972-73, Deputy Head and Head, Marine and Transport Dept., 1973-75, Counsellor Bonn 1975-77, Algiers 1977-80, Consul-Gen. Munich 1980-84, Minister, Tokyo 1984-87, High Commr. in Malta 1988-. *Leisure interest:* music. *Address:* British High Commission, 7 St. Anne's Street, Floriana, Malta. *Telephone:* 233134-8.

HITCH, Charles Johnston, M.A., LL.D., D.SC; American institution executive; b. 9 Jan. 1910, Boonville, Mo.; s. of Arthur Martin and Bertha Johnston Hitch; m. Nancy W. Squire 1942; one d.; ed. Oxford, Arizona and Harvard Univs.; Fellow, Tutor and Praelector, Queen's Coll. Oxford 1935-48; Staff Economist, U.S. Mission for Econ. Affairs, London 1941-42; Staff Economist, U.S. War Production Bd. 1942-43; Chief of Stabilization Controls Div., U.S. Office of War Mobilization 1945-46; Chief, Econs. Div. and Chair. Research Council Rand Corpn. 1948-60; Asst. Sec. of Defense (Comptroller) U.S. Dept. of Defense 1961-65; Vice-Pres. Business and Finance, Univ. of Calif. 1965-66, Prof. of Econs. 1965-75, Vice-Pres. Admin. 1966-67, Pres. of Univ. 1968-75; Pres. Resources for the Future, Inc. 1975-79; Chair. Gen. Advisory Cttee., Energy Research and Devt. Admin. 1975-78; mem. Assembly of Eng., Nat. Research Council 1975-77; mem. Nat. Petroleum Council 1975-79, Advisory Council, Gas Research Inst. 1976-84, Advisory Council, Electric Power Research Inst. 1978-85; Energy

Research Advisory Bd., Dept. of Energy 1978-85; Hon. Fellow, Queen's Coll. and Worcester Coll., Oxford; Trustee, Asia Foundation, Aerospace Corpn.; Hon. LL.D. (Pittsburgh, Missouri, Arizona, George Washington Univs.), Hon. D.Sc. in Commerce (Drexel Univ.), H.L.D. h.c. (Univ. of Judaism) 1973, Hon. D.Eng. (Colorado School of Mines) 1979, Dr. h.c. of Public Policy (Rand Graduate Inst.) 1985; Distinguished Public Service Award, U.S. Navy; Rhodes Scholar and George Webb Medley Scholar. *Publications:* America's Economic Strength 1941, The Economics of Defense in the Nuclear Age 1960, Decision-Making for Defense 1965, Energy Conservation and Economic Growth 1978. *Address:* Lawrence Berkeley Laboratory, University of California, Berkeley, Calif. 94720 (Office); 1515 Oxford Street, Berkeley, Calif. 94709, U.S.A. (Home). *Telephone:* (415) 486-4110 (Office).

HITCHCOCK, Edward Robert, M.B., CH.B., CH.M., F.R.C.S., F.R.C.S.E.; British neurosurgeon; b. 10 Feb. 1929, Monmouthshire; s. of Edwin Robert Hitchcock and Martha Hitchcock (née Roberts); m. Jillian Trenowath; three s. one d.; ed. Lichfield Grammar School, Univ. of Birmingham; Leader Spitzbergen Expedition 1951; Medical Officer, Scots Guards, B.A.O.R. 1955; registrar appointments in Surgery, Univ. Coll. Hosp. London 1956-66; Fellowship in Neuropathology, MRC, Neurosurgical appointments, Oxford and Manchester 1956-66; Neuro-surgical Fellowship, Univ. of Oxford 1966; Sr. Lecturer in Neurosurgery and Reader in Neurosurgery, Univ. of Edin. 1966-78, Prof. of Neurosurgery, Univ. of Birmingham 1978-; Examiner RCS; Ed. Fellowship Parts I and II, Surgical Neurology; Pres. European Soc. for Stereotactic and Functional Neurosurgery; mem. Council, Soc. of British Neurological Surgeons; Bd. Dir. World Soc. Stereotactic and Functional Neurosurgery; Corresponding mem. American Physiological Soc.; Hon. mem. various int. neurosurgical socs. *Publications:* numerous scientific papers largely on pain, neuro prosthetics, tumours and stereotactic surgery. *Leisure interests:* fishing, history, capology, travel. *Address:* Cubbold House, Ombersley, Nr. Droitwich, England.

HITCHINGS, George Herbert, PH.D.; American biochemist and pharmacologist; b. 18 April 1905, Hoquiam, Wash.; s. of George and Lillian B. (née Matthews) Hitchings; m. Beverly Reimer 1933; one s. one d.; ed. Univ. of Wash. and Harvard Univ.; Teaching Fellow, Univ. of Wash. 1926-28, Harvard Univ. 1928-34; Instructor and Tutor Harvard Univ. 1934-36, Research Fellow 1934-36, Assoc. 1936-39; Sr. Instructor Western Reserve Univ. 1939-42; Biochemist Burroughs Wellcome Co. 1942-46, Chief Biochemist 1946-55, Assoc. Research Dir. 1955-63, Research Dir. (Chemotherapy Div.) 1963-67, Vice-Pres. in charge of Research 1967-75, Dir. 1968-, Scientist Emer. and Consultant 1975-; Prof. of Pharmacology Brown Univ. 1968-80; Adjunct Prof. of Pharmacology and of Experimental Medicine Duke Univ. 1970-; Adjunct Prof. of Pharmacology Univ. of N.C. Chapel Hill 1972-; Visiting Prof. of Clinical Pharmacology Chuang-Ang Univ., Seoul, Repub. of Korea 1974-77; Visiting lecturer, Pakistan and Iran 1976, Japan and India 1980, South Africa 1981; mem. staff, Dept. of Medicine, Roger Williams Gen. Hospital, Brown Univ. 1980; Dir. Burroughs Wellcome Fund 1968-, Pres. 1971-; mem. U.S. Nat. Acad. of Sciences, Chem. Soc., London, American Soc. of Biological Chem., American Soc. of Experimental Biological Medicine, Int. Transplantation Soc., American Asscn. for Cancer Research, and numerous other bodies; Foreign mem. Royal Soc.; Hon. mem. American Soc. of Toxicology; Hon. Fellow, Royal Soc. of Medicine, Royal Soc. of Chem.; fields of activity: chemotherapy anti-metabolites, organic chem. of hetercycles, nucleic acids, anti-tumour anti-malarial, and anti-bacterial drugs; Hon. D.Sc. (Univ. of Michigan) 1971, (Univ. of Strathclyde) 1977, (New York Medical Coll., Valhalla) 1981, (Emory Univ.) 1981, (Duke Univ.) 1982, (Univ. of N.C.) 1982, (Mt. Sinai Univ.) 1983; numerous awards and prizes including Gregor Mendel Medal (Czechoslovak Acad. of Science) 1968, Gairdner Foundation Award (Canada) 1968, Cameron Prize in Practical Therapeutics (Univ. of Edinburgh) 1972, Bertner Foundation Award 1974, Royal Soc. Mullard Award 1976, Nat. Cancer Soc. Annual Award for Scientific Achievement 1978, C. Chester Stock Medal (Sloan Kettering Medal) 1981, Alfred Burger Award, A.C.S. 1984, Alumnus Summa Laude Dignatus Award 1986, Nobel Prize for Medicine (jtly.) 1988. *Publications:* 201 articles in scientific and medical journals, 85 abstracts, letters and reviews, 38 chapters in books. *Address:* 4022 Bristol Road, Durham, N.C. 27707, U.S.A. (Home). *Telephone:* 919-489-1760.

HITE, Shere D., M.A.; American writer; b. St. Joseph, Mo.; m. 1985; ed Univ. of Florida, Columbia Univ.; Dir. feminist sexuality project NOW, New York 1972-78; Dir. Hite Research Int., New York 1978-; instructor in female sexuality, New York Univ. 1977-; lecturer Harvard Univ. McGill Univ., Columbia Univ., also numerous women's groups, int. lecturer 1977-89; mem. Advisory Bd. Foundation of Gender and Genital Medicine Johns Hopkins Univ.; consultant editor Journal of Sex Educ. and Therapy, Journal of Sexuality and Disability; mem. NOW, American Historical Asscn., American Sociological Asscn., A.A.A.S., Acad. of Political Science, Women's History Asscn., Society for Scientific Study of Sex, Women's Health Network. *Publications:* Sexual Honesty: By Women For Women 1974, The Hite Report: A Nationwide Study of Female Sexuality 1976, The Hite Report on Male Sexuality 1981, Hite Report on Women and Love 1987. *Address:* PO Box 5282, Franklin Delano Roosevelt Station, New York, N.Y. 10022, U.S.A.

HITTMAIR, Hans Christoph, PH.D.; Austrian international banking official; b. 17 Dec. 1928, Innsbruck; s. of Prof. Rudolf Hittmair and Margarethe née von Schumacher-Marienfrid; m. Renate Klinger 1960; one s. two d.; ed. Staatsgymnasium Innsbruck, Innsbruck and Vienna Univs. and Bowdoin Coll., Brunswick, Me., U.S.A.; Creditanstalt-Bankverein, Vienna 1953-59; trainee, First Nat. City Bank, New York 1955-56; joined IBRD, Washington 1959, Vice-Pres. and Controller 1983-87, Vice-Pres. and Special Adviser to Sr. Vice-Pres., Operations 1987-88. *Leisure interests:* chamber music, sport. *Address:* Karthäuserstrasse 4, A-1190 Vienna, Austria.

HITTMAIR, Otto, DR.PHIL.; Austrian professor of physics; b. 16 March 1924, Innsbruck; s. of Dr. Rudolf and Margaret (née Schumacher) Hittmair; m. Anna Rauch 1956; one s. three d.; ed. Univ. of Innsbruck, Univ. of Basel, Dublin Inst. for Advanced Studies, M.I.T.; with C.N.R.S., France 1952-54; Fellow, Univ. of Sydney 1954-56; with Comisión Nacional de Energía Atómica, Argentina 1957, Atomic Inst., Vienna 1958-60; Head and Prof., Inst. of Theoretical Physics, Technical Univ. of Vienna 1960-, Dean 1968-69, Rector 1977-79; Vice-Pres. Int. Soc. of Eng. Educ. 1974-; Pres. Austrian Acad. of Sciences; mem. Royal Soc. of Sciences of Uppsala; Dr. Techn. h.c. (Budapest); Jubilee Medal, Univ. of Innsbruck, Erwin Schrödinger Prize, Wilhelm Exner Medal 1980, Science Prize, Vienna 1982. *Publications:* Nuclear Stripping Reactions (with S. T. Butler) 1957, Wärmetheorie (with G. Adam) 1971, Lehrbuch der Quantentheorie 1972, Supraleitung (with H. W. Weber) 1979. *Leisure interests:* mountaineering, chamber music. *Address:* Technical University of Vienna, Karlsplatz 13, A-1040 Vienna, Austria.

HJELM-WALLÉN, Lena; Swedish politician; b. 1943, Sala; teacher in Sala 1966-69; active in Social Democratic Youth League; elected to 2nd Chamber of Parl. 1968; mem. Exec. Cttee. Västmanland branch of Socialdemokratiska Arbetarepartiet (Social Democratic Labour Party—SDLP) 1968, mem. SDLP Parl. Exec. 1976-82, SDLP spokeswoman on schools, mem. Bd. SDLP 1978-87; mem. Bd. Swedish Social Democratic Party 1987-; Minister without Portfolio, with responsibility for schools 1974; Minister of Educ. and Cultural Affairs 1982-85, of Int. Devt. Aid Oct. 1985-. *Address:* Ministry of Foreign Affairs, Stockholm, Sweden.

HJÖRNE, Lars Goran; Swedish newspaper editor and publisher; b. 20 Oct. 1929, Gothenburg; s. of late Harry Hjörne; m. Anne Margaretha Gyllenhammar 1951; one s. one d.; Chief Ed. Göteborgs-Posten 1969-. *Address:* Polhemsplatsen 5, 405 02 Gothenburg (Office); Alfhemsgaten 7, 413 10 Gothenburg, Sweden (Home). *Telephone:* (031) 62-40-00 (Office); (031) 14-05-00 (Home).

HJORTH, Poul Lindegård, DR. PHIL.; Danish philologist; b. 24 July 1927, Holmstrup; s. of Georg L. and Agnes (née Thygesen) Hjorth; m. Karen-Louise Balslöv 1952; one s. one d.; ed. Univ. of Copenhagen; Lecturer in Danish, Univ. of Lund, Sweden 1956-62; Prof. of Danish Language, Royal Danish Acad. of Educational Studies 1965-78; Prof. of Scandinavian Philology, Univ. of Copenhagen 1978-; mem. Royal Danish Acad. of Sciences and Letters 1974-; Chair. Selskab for nordisk Filologi 1963-68, Dansk Sprognævn (Danish Language Bd.) 1966-73, Universitets-Jubilæets danske Samfund 1977-. *Publications:* Nordsamsisk Bøjningslære 1958, Karl Magnus Krønike 1960, Filologiske Studier over Karl Magnus Krønike 1965, Sjælens og Kroppens Trætte 1971, Forvandlingerne, Uddrag af Matthias Moths Oversættelse af Ovids Metamorphoses 1979. *Address:* Anemonevej 25, 2970 Hørsholm, Denmark. *Telephone:* 02 86 26 27.

HJORTH-NIELSEN, Henning; Danish diplomatist; b. 22 July 1913, Copenhagen; m. Ernestine Gottfried 1947; ed. Københavns Universitet; Ministry of Justice 1938; Asst. to Gov. of Faroe Islands 1939; Danish Mil. Mission, London 1944; Ministry for Foreign Affairs 1946-51; mem. Danish Del. to North Atlantic Treaty Org. (NATO) 1951, to OEEC 1954; Commercial Minister, London 1959-63; Amb. to Netherlands 1963-66, to NATO 1966-73, to Belgium and Luxembourg 1967-74, to Canada 1974-75; Perm. Rep. to UN 1975-77; Amb. to Sweden 1977-83; Danish and foreign awards. *Leisure interests:* music, reading. *Address:* St. Kongensgade 116, 1264 Copenhagen K, Denmark.

HLA HAN, Col., M.B., B.S., D.P.H.; Burmese politician; b. 26 Sept. 1918; ed. Rangoon and Liverpool Univs.; served in Burma National Army and Resistance 1942-45; joined Burma Medical Corps 1949; Dir. Medical Services, Ministry of Defence 1955; promoted Col. 1958; mem. Revolutionary Council and Minister for Health and Educ. 1962-74; Minister for Foreign Affairs 1970-72; mem. Council of State 1974-78; Star of Independent Sithu (First Class). *Address:* c/o Council of State, Rangoon, Burma.

HLAWKA, Edmund, DR.PHIL.; Austrian professor of mathematics; b. 5 Nov. 1916, Bruck a.d. Mur; m. Rosa Reiterer; ed. Univ. of Vienna; Asst. Math. Inst., Univ. of Vienna 1938-48, Lecturer 1946, Prof. 1948-81; Prof. Tech. Univ. of Vienna 1981-87, Emer. 1987-; Dannie-Heinemann Prize 1963, Ehrenzeichen für Kunst und Wissenschaften 1964, City of Vienna Prize 1969, Gauss-Medaille 1977, Grosses Goldenes Ehrenzeichen, Repub. of Austria 1987; mem. Austrian Acad. of Sciences, Acad. Leopoldina, Rheinisch-Westfälische Akad., Bayerische Akad. der Wissenschaften, Accad. di Bologna; Dr. h.c. *Publications:* Theory of Uniform Distribution 1974, Zahlentheorie 1979, Grudbegriffe der Mathematik 1979, Zahlentheoretische Methoden in der Numerischen Mathematik 1981, Zahlentheoretische Analysis I 1985, Analysis II 1987, Geometrische und Analytische

Zahlentheorie 1986; more than 140 articles in scientific journals. *Leisure interest:* reading. *Address:* Institut für Analysis, Technische Univeristät Wien, Wiedner Hauptstrasse 8-10, Vienna A-1040 (Office); Margaretenstrasse 27, Vienna 1040, Austria (Home). *Telephone:* (0222) 58801-5364 (Office).

HNATYSHYN, Ramon John, B.A., LL.B. Q.C. M.P.; Canadian politician; b. 16 March 1934, Saskatoon, Saskatchewan; m. Gerda Andreasen; two c.; ed. Univ. of Saskatchewan; fmr. lecturer in Law, Univ. of Saskatchewan; mem. House of Commons 1974-; Pvt. Sec. and Exec. Asst. to Govt. Leader in the Senate; mem. various cttees. in House of Commons; mem. jt. cttees. of Senate and House of Commons; Minister of Energy, Mines and Resources and Minister of State for Science and Tech. 1979; Minister of Justice and Attorney-Gen. 1986-89; Minister of State 1984-85, Govt. House Leader 1984-86, Pres. Queen's Privy Council for Canada 1985-86; past Pres. UNA of Canada (N. Saskatchewan Branch); fmr. Pres. Law Soc. of Saskatchewan, Saskatchewan Gallery and Conservatory Corpn.; mem. Saskatoon and Canadian Bar Asscns.; Progressive Conservative Party. *Address:* House of Commons, Ottawa, Ont. K1A 0A6, Canada.

HO, Guan Lim, M.B., B.S., F.R.C.P.; Singapore medical practitioner and diplomatist; b. 3 April 1925, Kuala Lumpur, Malaysia; s. of the late Ho Sing Ong and Wong Hong Neo; m. Sui Hoi Lee 1952; one s. one d.; ed. Anglo-Chinese School, Malacca and Coll. of Medicine, Univ. of Malaya; Medical Officer, Singapore Govt. Medical Service 1953-61, Medical Admin., retiring as Dir. Medical Services 1961-77; Dir. Social Services 1977-80; Amb. to U.S.S.R. 1981-84; High Commr. in London 1984-87; Silver Medal (Univ. of Malaya) 1951; Public Admin. Gold Medal 1975. *Leisure interests:* reading, sailing. *Address:* c/o Ministry of Foreign Affairs, 2nd Floor, City Hall, St. Andrews Road, Singapore.

HO, Peng-Yoke, PH.D., D.SC., F.INST.P., F.A.H.A.; Australian professor of Chinese; b. 4 April 1926, Malaysia; s. of Tih-Aun Ho (deceased) and Yeen-Kwai Ng; m. Lucy Mei-Yiu Fung 1955; one s. four d.; ed. Raffles Coll., Singapore and Univ. of Malaya, Singapore; Asst. Lecturer in Physics Univ. of Malaya, Singapore 1951-54, lecturer in Physics 1954-60, Reader Dept. of Physics 1960-64; Prof. of Chinese Studies, Univ. of Malaya, Kuala Lumpur 1964-73, Dean of Arts 1967-68; Foundation Prof. Griffith Univ., Queensland 1973-, Foundation Chair. School of Modern Asian Studies 1973-78; Prof. of Chinese, Univ. of Hong Kong 1981-87, Master Robert Black Coll. 1984-87; mem. Acad. Sinica; Dir. (desig.) Needham Research Inst., Cambridge; Hon. Prof. North-West Univ., Xian, China. *Publications:* The Astronomical Chapters of the Chin Shu 1966, Li, Qi and Shu: An Introduction to Chinese Science and Civilization 1985, Science and Civilization in China, Vol. 5, Part 3 1976, Part 4 1980, Part 7 1986. *Leisure interest:* chess. *Address:* 8 Holdway Street, Kenmore, Queensland 4069, Australia. *Telephone:* (07) 378-3246.

HO, Tao, B.A., M.ARCH.; British (b. Chinese) architect; b. 17 July 1936, Shanghai, China; m. 1st Chi-ping Lu 1960, one s. two d.; m. 2nd Irene Lo 1978, one d.; ed. Pui Ching Middle High School, Hong Kong 1950-56, Williams Coll., Williamstown, Mass., and Harvard Univ., U.S.A.; Research Asst., Albright-Knox Art Gallery, Buffalo, N.Y. 1959; Architectural Asst. to Walter Gropius 1963-64; Visiting lecturer, Fine Arts Dept., Chinese Univ., Hong Kong 1965-67; founded own practice, TAOHO Design Architects, Hong Kong 1968-; co-founder, Hong Kong Arts Centre 1969; Visiting Critic, Harvard Univ. Graduate School of Design 1975; External Examiner of Art, Chinese Univ., Hong Kong 1975-79; Visiting Critic, Design Dept., Hong Kong Polytechnic 1979-; Chair. Hong Kong Designers Asscn. 1981; Chair. Visual Arts Cttee., Hong Kong Arts Centre 1972-77; Hon. lecturer, School of Architecture, Hong Kong Univ. 1979-; Hon. Adviser, City Hall Museum, Hong Kong 1981-; mem. Bd. of Architects, Singapore 1981-; Assoc. mem. Chartered Inst. of Arbitrators 1979-; core mem. Asian Planning and Architectural Consultants Ltd. 1975-; mem. Singapore Inst. of Architects 1988; has organized more than 20 exhbns. for Hong Kong Arts Centre 1972-; Arthur Lehman Fellow, Harvard Univ. 1960-63; Hon Fellow American Inst. of Architects 1988; Hon. D.Hum.Litt. (Williams Coll., Mass., U.S.A.) 1979; Design Merit Award (Chinese Manufacturer's Asscn.), Silver Medal (Hong Kong Inst. of Architects). *Prin. works include:* Hong Kong Govt. Pavilion, C.M.A. Exhbn., Hong Kong 1969; Hong Kong Int. Elementary School 1975, Hong Kong Arts Centre 1977, residential devt., Shouson Hill, Hong Kong (with K. C. Lye) 1979, Planning and Urban design of 3 major Chinese cities: Xiamen, Qingdao and Harigzhou 1985-86, 6A Bowen Road Apt 1983 (HKIA Silver Medal), Bayview Residential Devt. 1988, (HKIA Design Award), Hong Kong Baptist Coll. Redevt. 1988-89; designed commemorative stamps for Hong Kong Govt. 1975-. *Publications:* numerous papers on theory and practice of art and architecture. *Leisure interests:* collecting art, writing about art, listening to music, painting, reading in cosmology and philosophy of science. *Address:* 4, Suffolk Road, Kowloon Tong, Kowloon, Hong Kong. *Telephone:* (3) 383848.

HOAGLAND, Edward; A.B.; American author; b. 21 Dec. 1932, New York; s. of Warren Eugene Hoagland and Helen Kelley Morley; m. 1st Amy J. Ferrara 1960 (divorced 1964); m. 2nd Marion Magid 1968; one d.; ed. Harvard Univ.; faculty mem. New School for Social Research, New York 1963-64, Rutgers Univ. 1966, Sarah Lawrence Coll., Bronxville, New York 1967, 1971, City Univ. 1967, 1968, Iowa Univ. 1978, 1982, Columbia Univ. 1980, 1981, Brown Univ., Bennington Coll., Bennington, Vt. 1987, 1988;

Houghton Mifflin Literary Fellow 1954; American Acad. of Arts and Letters Travelling Fellow 1964; Guggenheim Fellow 1964, 1975; mem. American Acad. and Inst. of Arts and Letters; Longview Foundation Award 1961; O. Henry Award 1971; New York State Council on Arts Award 1972; Nat. Endowment Arts Award 1982. *Publications:* Cat Man 1956, The Circle Home 1960, The Peacock's Tail 1965, Notes from the Century Before: A Journal from British Columbia 1969, The Courage of Turtles 1971, Walking the Dead Diamond River 1973, The Moose on the Wall: Field Notes from the Vermont Wilderness 1974, Red Wolves and Black Bears 1976, African Calliope: A Journey to the Sudan 1979, The Edward Hoagland Reader 1979, The Tugman's Passage 1982, City Tales 1986, Seven Rivers West 1986, Heart's Desire 1988; numerous essays and short stories. *Address:* c/o Simon and Schuster, 1230 Avenue of Americas, New York, N.Y. 10020 (Office); P.O. Box 51, Barton, Vt. 05822, U.S.A. (Home).

HOAR, William Stewart, O.C., PH.D., F.R.S.C.; Canadian zoologist; b. 1913, Moncton, N.B.; s. of George W. Hoar and Nina B. Steeves; m. Margaret M. Mackenzie 1941; two s. two d.; ed. Univs. of New Brunswick, Western Ontario and Boston; Demonstrator in Zoology, Univ. of Western Ontario 1934-36; Histology asst., Boston Univ. Medical School 1936-39; Asst. Prof. of Biology, Univ. New Brunswick 1939-42; Physiology Research Assoc., Univ. of Toronto 1942-43; Prof. of Zoology, Univ. of New Brunswick 1943-45; Prof. of Zoology and Fisheries, Univ. of British Columbia 1945-64, Prof. and Head, Zoology Dept. 1964-71, Prof. Zoology 1971-79, Prof. Emer. 1979-; John Simon Guggenheim Fellowship, Oxford 1958-59; Fellow, A.A.A.S. 1981; Hon. D.Sc. and LL.D.; Flavelle Medal Award 1965. *Publications:* Articles on physiology and behaviour of fish; textbook of comparative physiology. *Leisure interest:* gardening, genealogy. *Address:* Department of Zoology, University of British Columbia, Vancouver V6T 2A9, Canada. *Telephone:* 228-4881.

HOARE, Charles Antony Richard, F.R.S.; British professor of computation; b. 11 Jan. 1934, Colombo, Ceylon (now Sri Lanka); s. of Henry S. M. and Marjorie F. (née Villiers) Hoare; m. Jill Pym 1962; one s. one d.; ed. Dragon School, Oxford, King's School, Canterbury, Merton Coll., Oxford, Unit. of Biometry, Oxford, and Moscow State Univ.; with Elliott Bros. (London) Ltd. 1959-68; Prof. of Computing Science, Queen's Univ. of Belfast 1969-77; Dir. of Computing Lab. and Prof. of Computation, Univ. of Oxford 1977-; Fellow Wolfson Coll. 1977-; A.M. Turing Award, Harry Goode Memorial Award, Distinguished Fellow of British Computer Soc.; Hon. D.Sc. (Univ. of S. Calif., Warwick, Pennsylvania, Queens, Belfast 1987); Faraday Medal 1985. *Publications:* Structured Programming (co-author) 1972, Communicating Sequential Processes 1985. *Leisure interests:* walking, music, reading. *Address:* Oxford University Computing Laboratory, Programming Research Group, 8-11 Keble Road, Oxford, OX1 3QD, England. *Telephone:* (0865) 54141 Ext. 286.

HOBAN, Russell Conwell; American author; b. 4 Feb. 1925, Lansdale, Pa.; s. of Abram Hoban and Jenny (née Dimmerman); m. 1st Lillian Aberman 1944 (dissolved 1975), one s. three d.; 2nd Gundula Ahl 1975, three s.; ed. Lansdale High School and Philadelphia Museum School of Industrial Art; served U.S. Infantry, Italy 1943-45; held various jobs including general illustration with Wexton co., New York 1945-51; TV Art Dir BBDO Advertising, N.Y. 1951-56; freelance illustrator 1956-65; copywriter, Doyle Dane Bernbach, New York 1965-67; novelist and author of children's books 1967-; Whitbread Prize for How Tom Beat Captain Najork and His Hired Sportsmen (children's book) 1974; John W. Campbell Memorial Award and Australian Science Fiction Achievement Award for Riddley Walker 1983. *Publications:* novels: The Mouse and His Child 1967, The Lion of Boaz-Jachin and Jachin-Boaz 1973, Kleinzeit 1974, Turtle Diary 1975, Riddley Walker 1980, Pilgermann 1983 and 51 children's picture books and two books of verse for children since 1959; text for The Carrier Frequency (theatre piece, Impact Theatre Co-operative) 1984; stage version of Riddley Walker (Manchester Royal Exchange Theatre Co.) 1986; various essays and pieces for Granta and The Fiction Magazine. *Leisure interests:* stones, short wave listening. *Address:* David Higham Associates Ltd., 5-8 Lower John Street, Golden Square, London, W1R 4HA, England. *Telephone:* 01-437 7888.

HOBBY, Oveta Culp (Mrs. William P.); American newspaper proprietor; b. 19 Jan. 1905, Killeen, Texas; d. of I. W. and Emma (née Hoover) Culp; m. William P. Hobby 1931; one s. one d.; ed. public schools, private tutors and Mary Hardin Baylor Coll.; Parliamentarian, Texas House of Representatives 1926-31 and 1939, 1941; joined Houston Post as Research Ed. 1931, became successively Literary Ed., Asst. Ed., Vice-Pres., Exec. Vice-Pres. and Ed., Ed. and Publisher, resgnd. 1953, returned as Pres. and Ed. 1955-65; Ed. and Chair. of Bd. Houston Post Co. 1965-; Dir. Station KPRC-AM-TV 1945-53, 1955-65, Chair. of Bd. 1970-; Chair. of Bd., Dir. Channel Two TV Co. 1970-; Chair. Bd. H and C Communications Inc. 1978-83, Chair. Exec. Cttee. 1983-; Chief, Women's Interest Section, War Dept. Bureau of Public Relations 1941-42; apptd. Dir. W.A.A.C. 1942; Col. U.S. Army and Dir. W.A.C. 1943-45; Fed. Security Admin. 1953; Sec. Dept. of Health, Educ. and Welfare 1953-55; Charter mem. Acad. of Texas 1969; Hon. LL.D. (Baylor Univ.) 1943, (Sam Houston State Teachers' Coll.) 1943, (Chattanooga) 1943, (Bryant Coll.) 1953, (Ohio Wesleyan Univ.) 1954, (Columbia) 1954, (Smith Coll.) 1954, (Middlebury Coll.) 1954, (Univ. of Pa.)

1955, (Colby Coll.) 1955, (Fairleigh Dickinson) 1956, (Western Coll.) 1956; Hon. L.H.D. (Bard Coll.) 1950; (La Fayette Coll.) 1954; Hon. D.B.A. (Southwestern Business Univ.) 1951; Hon. D.Litt. (Colorado Women's Coll.) 1947; Hon. Dr. of Humanities (Mary Hardin Baylor Coll.) 1956; D.S.M. 1944; Philippine Mil. Merit Medal 1947, Publ. of Year Award 1960, Living History Award, Research Inst. of America 1960, Honor Award, Nat. Jewish Hosp. 1962. *Publications:* Mr. Chairman (parliamentary law textbook) and syndicated column of same title. *Address:* 3050 Post Oak Boulevard, 1330, Houston, Tex. 77056, U.S.A.

HOBDAY, Sir Gordon (Ivan), Kt., PH.D., F.R.S.C.; British business executive (retd.); b. 1 Feb. 1916, Derbyshire; s. of the late Alexander Thomas Hobday and Frances Cassandra (née Meads); m. Margaret Jean Joule 1940; one d.; ed. Long Eaton Grammar School, Univ. Coll., Notts.; joined The Boots Co. Ltd. 1939, Dir. of Research 1952-68, Deputy Man. Dir. 1968-70, Man. Dir. 1970-72, Chair. 1973-81; Dir. The Metal Box Co. Ltd. 1976-81; Dir. Lloyds Bank 1981-86; Deputy Chair. Price Comm. 1977-78; Chair. Cen. Independent Television Co. Ltd. 1981-85; Chancellor Univ. of Nottingham 1979- (Pres. of the Council 1973-82); Lord Lieut. and Keeper of the Rolls for Nottinghamshire 1983-; Hon. LL.D. *Leisure interests:* handicrafts, gardening. *Address:* University of Nottingham, University Park, Nottingham, NG7 2RD, England.

HOBSBAWM, Eric John Ernest, PH.D., F.B.A.; British university professor; b. 9 June 1917, Alexandria; s. of Leopold Percy Hobsbawm and Nelly Gruen; m. Marlene Schwarz 1962; one s. one d.; ed. Cambridge Univ.; Lecturer, Birkbeck Coll. 1947-59, Reader 1959-70, Prof. of Econ. and Social History 1970-82, Prof. Emer. 1982-; Fellow, King's Coll., Cambridge 1949-55; Andrew D. White Prof.-at-Large, Cornell Univ. 1976-82; Prof. Emer. 1982-; Prof., New School for Social Research, New York 1984-; Dr. h.c. (Stockholm) 1970, (Chicago) 1976, (East Anglia) 1982, (New School) 1982, York Univ., Canada 1986, Univ. of Pisa 1987; f. Social Research, Bard Coll.; Hon. Foreign Mem. American Acad. of Arts and Sciences; Foreign Mem. Hungarian Acad. of Sciences. *Publications:* Primitive Rebels 1959, The Age of Revolution 1962, Labouring Men 1964, Industry and Empire 1968, Captain Swing 1969, Bandits 1969, Revolutionaries 1973, The Age of Capital 1975; Ed. Storia del Marxismo (5 vols.) 1978-82, Worlds of Labour 1984, The Age of Empire 1875-1914 1987. *Address:* Birkbeck College, Malet Street, London, W.C.1, England.

HOCH, Orion, PH.D.; American business executive; b. 1928, Canonsburg, Pa.; ed. Carnegie Mellon Univ., Univ. of Calif. Los Angeles and Stanford Univ.; engaged in research and devt. Hughes Aircraft 1952-54; various positions, Electron Devices Div. Litton Industries Inc. 1957-68; Vice-Pres. Litton Components Group 1968-70; Corp. Vice-Pres. Litton Industries Inc. 1970, Sr. Vice-Pres. 1971, Deputy Head, Business Systems and Equipment Group 1973-74; Pres. Advanced Memory Systems (later Intersil Inc.) 1974-81; Pres. Litton Industries Inc. 1982-88, Dir. and C.O.O. 1982-, C.E.O. 1986-, Chair. 1988-. *Address:* Litton Industries Inc., 360 North Crescent Drive, Beverley Hills, Calif. 90210, U.S.A.

HÖCHERL, Hermann; German politician; b. 31 March 1912, Bavaria; m. Theresia Lotter 1936; one s. three d.; ed. Univs. of Berlin, Aix-en-Provence and Munich; Asst. Judge, Regensburg 1938; served Second World War; Public Prosecutor 1950, Sr. Judge 1951, mem. Bundestag 1953-56; Fed. Minister of Internal Affairs 1961-65, Minister for Foods, Agric. and Forestry 1965-69; Chair. Mediation Cttee. between Bundestag and Bundesrat 1969-73; Deputy Chair. Christian Social Union (CSU) and Chief Financial Dept. CDU/CSU in Bundestag 1971-76; many decorations, incl. Hon. O.B.E.; Christian Social Union. *Leisure interests:* literature, plastic arts. *Address:* 8411 Brennberg 124, Regensburg, Federal Republic of Germany. *Telephone:* 09484-271.

HOCHHUTH, Rolf; Swiss playwright; b. 1 April 1931; m.; three s; fmr. publisher's reader; Resident Municipal Playwright, Basel 1963; mem. PEN of Fed. Repub. of Germany. *Publications:* Plays: The Representative 1962, The Employer 1965, The Soldiers 1966, Anatomy of Revolution 1969, The Guerillas 1970, The Midwife 1972, Lysistrata and the NATO 1973, A German Love Story (novel) 1980, Judith 1984. *Address:* P.O. Box 661, 4002 Basel, Switzerland.

HOCHSTRASSER, Robin Main, PH.D.; American academic; b. 1 April 1931, Edinburgh, Scotland; s. of Richard and Margaret Main (née Yzer) Hochstrasser; m. Carol Ann Ostby 1960; two d.; ed. Heriot-Watt and Edinburgh Univs.; Lecturer Univ. of Pa. 1963-81, Donner Prof. of Physical Sciences 1981-; Visiting Prof. Chicago Univ. 1968, Cambridge 1972, Grenoble 1976, 1980, Paris 1977, Calif. Inst. of Tech. 1978, Munich 1981, Oxford 1984; Sloan Fellow 1964, Guggenheim Fellow 1974, Humboldt Prize 1980, N.A.S. Award 1981. *Publications:* over 300 articles in scientific journals and two books 1957 and 1984. *Leisure interest:* tennis. *Address:* Department of Chemistry, University of Pennsylvania, Philadelphia, Pa. 19104, U.S.A. *Telephone:* 215 898 8410, Ext. 8410.

HOCKE, Jean-Pierre; Swiss United Nations official; b. 31 March 1938, Lausanne; two s.; ed. Univ. of Lausanne; joined Int. Cttee. of Red Cross 1968, Head, Operations Dept. 1973, mem. Directorate 1981; UN High Commr. for Refugees 1986-. *Address:* Palais des Nations, 1211 Geneva 10, Switzerland. *Telephone:* 31.02.61.

HOCKETT, Charles F(rancis), PH.D.; American anthropologist, linguist and academic; b. 17 Jan. 1916, Columbus, Ohio; s. of Homer and Amy Hockett; m. Shirley S. Orlinoff 1942; one s. four d.; ed. Ohio State and Yale Univs.; served U.S. army 1942-46; at Cornell Univ. 1946-, Asst. Prof. of Linguistics 1946-49, Assoc. Prof. of Linguistics 1949-53, Prof. of Linguistics 1953-57, Prof. of Linguistics and Anthropology 1957-70, Goldwin-Smith Prof. of Linguistics and Anthropology 1970-82, Prof. Emer. 1982-; Visiting Lecturer Rice Univ. 1984; various positions at Foreign Service Inst., Washington, D.C., Army Language School, Monterey, Calif., Linguistic Insts. at Univs. of Chicago, Ind., Alberta, Mich. and Hawaii, RAND Corpn.; Pres. Linguistic Soc. of America 1964, Linguistic Assen. of Canada and the U.S. 1982; Distinguished Lecturer American Anthropological Assen. 1984; Visiting Prof., Beijing Foreign Studies Univ. 1986; mem. N.A.S., American Acad. of Arts and Sciences. *Publications:* A Manual of Phonology 1955, A Course in Modern Linguistics 1958, Man's Place in Nature 1973, The View From Language: Selected Essays 1948-1974 1977; articles and reviews in journals. *Leisure interest:* composing music (composed opera Doña Rosita). *Address:* 145 North Sunset Drive, Ithaca, N.Y. 14850, U.S.A. *Telephone:* (607) 273-3362.

HOCKIN, Thomas, P.C., M.P., PH.D.; Canadian businessman and politician; b. 5 March 1938, London, Ont.; s. of Thomas Munro Hockin and Margaret Marion McKillop; m. Mary Schaefer 1967; one s. two d.; ed. Medway Secondary School, Univ. of Western Ont., Harvard Univ.; Pres. Markham Imports; Prof. Univ. of Western Ont. School of Business; mem. Ont. Police Comm., Albany Royal Canadian Mil. Inst.; M.P. 1984-; Minister of State for Finance 1986-89, for Small Businesses and Tourism Jan. 1989-; Progressive Conservative. *Leisure interests:* baseball watching, golf, tennis. *Address:* Department of Finance, 140 O'Connor Street, Ottawa, K1A 0G5, Canada.

HOCKNEY, David; British artist; b. 9 July 1937, Bradford; s. of Kenneth and Laura Hockney; ed. Bradford Coll. of Art and Royal Coll. of Art; taught at Maidstone Coll. of Art 1962, Univ. of Iowa 1964, Univ. of Colo. 1965, Univ. of Calif. (Los Angeles) 1966, (Berkeley) 1967; has travelled extensively in Europe and U.S.A.; first one-man exhbn., Kasmin Gallery, London 1963; subsequent one-man exhbns. at Museum of Modern Art, New York 1964, 1968, Laundau-Alan Gallery, New York 1964, 1967, Kasmin Gallery 1965, 1966, 1968, 1969, 1970, 1972, Stedeljik Museum, Amsterdam 1966, Palais des Beaux-Arts, Brussels 1966, Studio Marconi and Galleria dell'Ariete, Milan 1966, Galerie Mikro, Berlin 1968, Whitworth Art Gallery, Manchester 1969, André Emmerich Gallery, New York 1969, 1972, 1979, 1980, 1982, 1983, 1984, 1985, Gallery Springer, Berlin 1970, Kestner-Ges., Hanover 1970, Whitechapel Gallery (retrospective exhbn.), London 1970, Kunsthalle, Bielefeld 1971, Musée des Arts Décoratifs, Louvre, Paris 1974, Galerie Claude Bernard, Paris 1975, Nicholas Wilder, Los Angeles 1976, Galerie Neundorf, Hamburg 1977, Warehouse Gallery 1979, Knoedler Gallery 1979, 1981, 1982, 1983, 1984, 1986, Tate Gallery (retrospective exhbn.) 1980, 1986, 1988, Hayward Gallery (Photographs) 1983, 1985, L.A. County Museum (retrospective) 1988; Assoc. mem. Royal Acad. 1985; has participated in several group exhbns. at Inst. of Contemporary Arts (ICA) and numerous other group exhbns. throughout Europe and U.S.A., and in Japan, Australia, New Zealand and S. America 1960-; group exhbns. include Second and Third Paris Biennales of Young Artists, Musée d'Art Moderne 1961, 1963, Third Inst. Biennale of Prints, Nat. Museum of Art, Tokyo 1962, London Group Jubilee Exhbn. 1914-1964, Tate Gallery 1964, Painting and Sculpture of a Decade, Gulbenkian Foundation, Tate Gallery, London 1964, Op and Pop, Stockholm and London 1965, Fifth Int. Exhbn. of Graphic Art, Ljibljana 1965, First Int. Print Biennale, Cracow 1966, São Paulo Biennale 1967, Venice Biennale 1968, Pop Art Redefined, Hayward Gallery, London 1969; designed sets for Rake's Progress, Glyndebourne 1975, La Scala 1979, The Magic Flute, Glyndebourne 1978, L'Enfant et les sortilèges and Nightingale, Covent Garden 1983; designer of costumes and sets, Metropolitan Opera House, New York 1980, of sets Varii Capricci 1983; appeared in autobiographical documentary film A Bigger Splash 1974; Guinness Award 1961, Graphic Prize, Paris Biennale 1963, First Prize 8th Int. Exhbn. of Drawings and Engravings, Lugano 1964, prize at 6th Int. Exhbn. of Graphic Art, Ljubljana 1965, Cracow 1st Int. Print Biennale 1966; First Prize 6th John Moores Exhbn. 1967, Hamburg Foundation Shakespeare Prize 1983. *Publications:* David Hockney, Travel with Pen, Pencil and Ink 1978 (autobiography), Photographs 1982, China Diary (with Stephen Spender, q.v.) 1982, David Hockney: Cameraworks 1984, Hockney on Photography: Conversations with Paul Joyce 1988. *Address:* 75006 Santa Monica Boulevard, Los Angeles, Calif. 90046, U.S.A.; The Old Bath House, Manor Lane, Shipley, West Yorks., BD18 3EA, England.

HOCQ, Nathalie; French business executive; b. 7 Aug. 1951, Neuilly (Hauts-de-Seine); d. of Robert Hocq and Christiane Arnoult; ed. École Mary Mount, Neuilly, Cours Victor-Hugo, Paris and Univ. of Paris-Dauphine; Publicity Asst., Havas-conseil 1970; in charge of duty-free network, Briquet Cartier 1970; Exec. Cartier S.A. 1974, Gen. Man. 1977, Man. Dir. Devt. 1979-81; Chair. Cartier Int. 1981-. *Leisure interests:* riding, tennis, skiing and swimming. *Address:* Cartier S.A., 13 rue de la Paix, 75002 Paris, France.

HODDINOTT, Alun, D.MUS., C.B.E.; British (Welsh) composer; b. 11 Aug. 1929, Bargoed, S. Wales; s. of Thomas Ivor Hoddinott and Gertrude Jones;

m. Beti Rhiannon Huws 1953; one s.; ed. Gowerton Grammar School and Univ. Coll., Cardiff; Lecturer, Cardiff Coll. of Music and Drama 1951-59; Lecturer Univ. Coll., Cardiff 1959-65, Reader 1965-67, Prof. of Music 1967-87; Artistic Dir. Cardiff Festival of Twentieth Century Music 1966-; Hon. mem. Royal Acad. of Music; Fellow, Royal Northern Coll. of Music 1980; Walford Davies Prize 1954, Bax Medal 1957, Hopkins Medal of the St. David's Soc. of New York 1981; Fellow, University Coll., Cardiff 1981. *Works include:* six symphonies 1955-77; four sinfoniettas, eleven concertos 1951-69, six piano sonatas 1959-72, four violin sonatas 1969-76, sonatas for harp, cello, clarinet, horn, sonata for Cello and Piano 1977, Welsh Dances, Investiture Dances, Black Bart, Dives and Lazarus 1965, Variants 1966, Fioriture 1968, The Tree of Life 1971, Ritornelli 1974, The Beach at Falesa (opera) 1974, The Magician (opera), Ancestor Worship, Five Landscapes (song cycles), A Contemplation upon Flowers (songs for soprano and orchestra), What the Old Man Does is Always Right (opera), Passaggio for orchestra 1977, Dulcia Iuventutis 1977, Sonata for Organ, Voyagers (for baritone solo, male voices and orchestra) sonatina for guitar, sonatina for two pianos, The Rajah's Diamond (opera), scena for string quartet, ritornelli for brass quintet, Hymnus Ante Somnum, nocturnes and cadenza for solo 'cello, The Heaventree of Stars (for violin and orchestra) 1980, The Trumpet Major (opera in three acts) 1981, nocturnes and cadenzas for solo flute, ritornelli for four double basses, Te Deum (for mixed voices and organ), Lanterne des Morts (for orchestra), Six Welsh Folk Songs (soprano and piano), Doubles (for oboe, harpsichord and strings), Five Studies (for orchestra), Four Scenes from the Trumpet Major (for orchestra), Quodlibet for orchestra 1982, Quodlibet for brass quintet 1983, Masks (oboe, bassoon and piano) 1983, Ingravescentem aetatem (chorus and piano duet) 1983, Lady and Unicorn: Cantata for mixed voices and piano, Piano Trio No. 2, Bagatelles for oboe and harp, String Quartet No. 2, Piano Sonata No. 7, Scenes and Interludes: Concertante for trumpet, harpsichord and strings, Symphony No. 6, Hommage à Chopin (orchestra), Bells of Paradise: Cantata for baritone, mixed chorus and orchestra 1984, Welsh Dances, Third Suite (orchestra), Divertimenti for flute, bassoon, double bass and percussion, Scena for string orchestra, Sonata for two pianos, The Silver Hound: Cycle for tenor and piano, Passacaglia and Fugue for organ, Fanfare with Variants for brass band, Green Broom: Ballad for male voices and piano, Sonata for four clarinets, Sing a New Song (anthem for mixed voices and organ) 1985, Flower Songs (women's voices and piano), Concerto for violin, cello and orchestra, Sonata No. 8 for piano, Divisions: Concertante for horn, harpsichord and strings, Concerto for orchestra, Concerto for clarinet and orchestra 1986, Aspiciens A Longe (anthem for mixed voices and organ) 1987, Welsh dances (for brass band) 1987, Cantata: Legend of St. Julian 1987, String Quartet No.3 1988, Dr. Faustus: Scena (for mixed voices and brass) 1988. *Address:* Maesawelon, Mill Road, Lisvane, Cardiff, Wales.

HODEL, Donald Paul, J.D.; American government official; b. 23 May 1935, Portland, Ore.; s. of Philip E. and Theresia R. (Brodt) Hodel; m. Barbara B. Stockman 1956; two s. (one deceased); ed. Harvard Coll. and Univ. of Oregon; admitted to Oregon Bar 1960; attorney, Daview, Biggs, Strayer, Stoel & Boley 1960-63; Georgia Pacific Corpn. 1963-69; Deputy Admin., Bonneville Power Admin. 1969-72, Admin. 1972-77; Pres. Nat. Elec. Reliability Council, Princeton, N.J. 1978-80; Pres. Hodel Assocs. Inc. 1978-81; Under-Sec. Dept. of Interior 1981-83; Sec. of Energy 1982-85, of the Interior 1985-89; Republican. *Address:* Department of the Interior, Washington, D.C. 20240, U.S.A.

HODGKIN, Sir Alan Lloyd, O.M., K.B.E., F.R.S., M.A., SC.D.; British physiologist; b. 5 Feb. 1914, Banbury; s. of G. L. Hodgkin and M. F. Wilson; m. Marion de Kay Rous 1944; one s. three d.; ed. Gresham's School, Holt, and Trinity Coll., Cambridge; Scientific Officer (radar), Air Ministry and Ministry of Aircraft Production 1939-45; Lecturer, later Asst. Dir. of Research, Cambridge 1945-52, John Humphrey Plummer Prof. of Biophysics 1970-81; Master of Trinity Coll., Cambridge 1978-84, Fellow 1984-; Foulerton Research Prof., Royal Soc. 1952-69; Pres. Marine Biological Assen. 1966-76; Pres. of the Royal Soc. 1970-75; Chancellor, Leicester Univ. 1971-84; mem. Medical Research Council 1959-63, Royal Danish Acad. of Sciences, Leopoldina Acad., G.D.R.; Foreign mem. American Acad. of Arts and Sciences; Hon. Fellow, Indian Nat. Science Acad., Royal Soc. of Edinburgh; Hon. mem. Royal Irish Acad., U.S.S.R. Acad. of Sciences 1976; numerous hon. degrees; Royal Medal, Royal Soc. 1958; shared Nobel Prize for Medicine 1963; Copley Medal, Royal Soc. 1965, Lord Crook Medal 1983. *Publications:* papers dealing with the nature of nervous conduction; Conduction of the Nervous Impulse 1963. *Leisure interests:* fishing, travel. *Address:* Physiological Laboratory, Downing Street, Cambridge, England.

HODGKIN, Dorothy Crowfoot, O.M., F.R.S., PH.D.; British crystallographer; b. 1910, Cairo, Egypt; d. of the late John Winter Crowfoot and of Grace Mary Crowfoot (née Hood); m. Thomas Hodgkin 1937 (died 1982); two s. one d.; ed. Sir John Leman School, Beccles, and Somerville Coll., Oxford; Wolfson Research Prof., Royal Soc. 1960-77; Chancellor, Bristol Univ. 1970-; Fellow, Somerville Coll., Oxford 1936-77, Wolfson Coll., Oxford 1977-83; Hon. Fellow Bristol Univ. 1988-; Prof. Emer. Oxford Univ.; Pres. B.A.A.S. 1977-78; Pres. Pugwash Conf. on Science and World Affairs 1975-; Foreign mem. Royal Netherlands Acad. of Science and Letters, American Acad. of Arts and Sciences, Bavarian Acad., Austrian Acad.,

Yugoslav Acad. of Sciences, Ghana Acad. of Sciences, Puerto Rico Acad. of Sciences, Australian Acad. of Sciences, Leopoldina Acad. of Sciences, Norwegian Acad. of Sciences, Indian Acad. of Sciences, Royal Irish Acad. of Sciences, N.A.S., U.S.A.; Hon. mem. U.S.S.R. Acad. of Sciences 1976, Royal Inst. of G.B. 1988-; Hon. D.Sc. (Leeds, Manchester, Cambridge, Sussex, Ghana, Hull, East Anglia, London, Delhi, Harvard, Exeter, Kent, Mount Sinai, Bath, Brown, Chicago, Warwick, Oxford), Hon. LL.D. (Bristol), Hon. D.L. (Dalhousie), Hon. D.Univ. (Zagreb, York, Open), Hon. Dr. Medicine and Surgery (Modena); Royal Medal of Royal Soc. 1957; Nobel Prize for Chem. 1964; Copley Medal of Royal Soc. 1976, Mikhail Lomonosov Gold Medal 1982, Dimitrov Prize 1984, Lenin Peace Prize 1987. *Publications:* Scientific papers on compounds of biological interest including penicillin, vitamin B_{12} and insulin. *Address:* Crab Mill, Ilmington, Shipston-on-Stour, Warwicks., England. *Telephone:* (060 882) 233.

HODGKIN, Howard, C.B.E., D.LITT.; British painter; b. 6 Aug. 1932; m. Julia Lane 1955; two s.; ed. Camberwell School of Art and Bath Acad. of Art; Trustee, Tate Gallery 1970-76, Nat. Gallery 1978-85; first one-man show of paintings Arthur Tooth & Sons, London 1962 since when numerous one-man shows of paintings and prints in U.K., U.S.A., Europe and Australia; has participated in numerous group exhbns. worldwide; British rep., Venice Biennale 1984; works in many public collections including Tate Gallery, London and Museum of Modern Art, New York; Tate Gallery Turner Prize 1985. *Address:* 32 Coptic Street, London, W.C.1, England. *Telephone:* 01-580 7970.

HODGSON, Alfreda Rose, L.R.A.M.; British concert singer; b. 7 June 1940; d. of Alfred Hodgson and Rose Hodgson; m. Paul Blissett 1963; two d.; ed. Northern School of Music; début as concert singer with Royal Liverpool Philharmonic Orchestra 1964; has since toured extensively all over the world; début at Covent Garden in Le Rossignol and in L'Enfant et les Sortilèges 1983-84; Kathleen Ferrier Memorial Scholarship 1964; Hon. Fellow, Northern School of Music 1972; Sir Charles Santley Memorial Gift, Worshipful Co. of Musicians 1985. *Address:* 16 St. Mary's Road, Prestwich, Manchester, M25 5AP, England. *Telephone:* (061) 773 1541.

HODGSON, James Day, A.B.; American government official and diplomatist; b. 3 Dec. 1915, Dawson, Minn.; s. of Fred Arthur Hodgson and Casaraha Day; m. Maria Denend 1943; one s. one d.; ed. Univs. of Minnesota and California (Los Angeles); fmr. consultant to State of Calif. on manpower matters; Community Adviser to Inst. of Industrial Relations, Univ. of Calif.; joined Lockheed Aircraft Corpn. 1941, Corporate Dir. for industrial relations 1962-68, Vice-Pres. 1968-69; Under-Sec. of Labor 1969-70; Sec. of Labor 1970-73; Sr. Vice-Pres. in charge of Corporate Relations, Lockheed Aircraft Corpn. 1973; Amb. to Japan 1974-77; Chair. Uranium Mining Co. 1977-, Pathfinder Mining Co. 1977-; Adjunct Prof. Univ. of Calif, (Los Angeles) 1977-; Dir. Hewlett Packard Co., American Standard Co., ARA Services Inc., United Television Co., Pacific Scientific Co., Calvin Bullock Ltd., Ticor, Calif. Fed. Savings and Loan, Japan Soc. (New York); Adviser Ernst & Whinney, Los Angeles, Mitsui Bank, Los Angeles; Pres. America-Japan Soc., Los Angeles. *Leisure interests:* golf, skiing, reading. *Address:* 550 California Street, Suite 300, San Francisco, Calif. 94104 (Office); 10132 Hillgrove Boulevard, Beverly Hills, Calif. 90210, U.S.A. (Home).

HODGSON, Sir Maurice Arthur Eric, Kt., M.A., B.SC., F.I.CHEM.E., F.ENG., C.CHEM., F.R.S.C.; British company executive; b. 21 Oct. 1919, Bradford; s. of Walter and Amy (née Walker) Hodgson; m. Norma Fawcett 1945; one s. one d.; ed. Bradford Grammar School and Merton Coll., Oxford; joined ICI Ltd., Fertilizer and Synthetic Products Group 1942; Seconded to ICI (New York) Ltd. 1955-58; Head of Technical Dept., ICI Ltd. 1958, Devt. Dir. Heavy Organic Chemicals Div. 1960 (Deputy Chair. 1964), Gen. Man. Co. Planning 1966, Commercial Dir. and Planning Dir. 1970, Deputy Chair. 1972-78, Chair. 1978-82; Dir. Carrington Viyella Ltd. 1970-74, Imperial Chemicals Insurance Ltd. 1970-78 (Chair. 1972-78), Chair. British Home Stores PLC 1982-87; Dir. (non-exec.) Storehouse PLC 1985-; Nominated mem. Council of Lloyd's 1987-; mem. Court of British Shippers' Council 1978-82, Council, CBI 1978-82, Pres.'s Cttee., The Advertising Asscn. 1978-, Int. Council, The Salk Inst. 1978-, Int. Advisory Cttee., Chase Manhattan Bank 1980-83, Int. Advisory Bd. AMAX Inc. 1982-85, European Advisory Council Air Products and Chemicals Inc. 1982-84; Dir. (non exec.) Dunlop Holdings PLC 1982-83, Chair. Jan.-Nov. 1984; Visiting Fellow, School of Business and Organizational Studies, Univ. of Lancaster 1970-; Hon. Fellow, Merton Coll., Oxford 1979; Hon. Fellowship UMIST 1979; Trustee, The Civic Trust 1978-82; mem. of Court, Univ. of Bradford 1979-; Gov., London Graduate School of Business Studies 1978-87; Pres. Merton Soc. 1986-; Chair. Civil Justice Review Advisory Cttee. 1985-; Hon. D.Univ. (Heriot-Watt) 1979, Hon. D.Tech. (Bradford) 1979, Hon. D.Sc. (Loughborough Univ. of Technology) 1981; Messel Medal, Soc. of Chemical Industry 1980, George E. Davis Medal, Inst. of Chemical Eng. 1982. *Leisure interests:* horse-racing, swimming, fishing. *Address:* c/o British Home Stores, Marylebone House, 129-137 Marylebone Road, London, NW1 5QD, England. *Telephone:* 01-262 3288.

HODIN, Dr. Josef Paul, LL.D., PH.D., F.R.S.A.; British author and art historian; b. 17 Aug. 1905, Prague, Czechoslovakia; s. of Eduard David Hodin and Rosa Hodin (née Klug); m. Doris Pamela Simms 1945; one s. one d.; ed. Kleinseitner Realschule, Neustädter Realgymnasium, Prague, Charles Univ., London Univ., Art Academies, Dresden and Berlin; Press Attaché,

Norwegian Govt. in London 1944-45; Dir. of Studies and Librarian, Inst. of Contemporary Arts, London 1949-54; Hon. mem. Editorial Council The Journal of Aesthetics and Art Criticism, Cleveland 1955-; founder mem. British Soc. of Aesthetics; Ed. Prisme des Arts, Paris 1956-59, Quadrum, Brussels 1959-70; Dir. foreign relations, Studio International 1966-76; Pres. British Section, Asscn. Int. des Critiques d'Art; Prof. h.c. (Vienna) 1975; several decorations. *Publications:* Monographs on Sven Erixson 1940, Ernst Josephson 1942, Edvard Munch 1948, Isaac Grünewald 1949, Art and Criticism 1944, J. A. Comenius and Our Time 1944, The Dilemma of Being Modern 1956, Henry Moore 1956, Ben Nicholson 1957, Barbara Hepworth 1961, Lynn Chadwick 1961, Oskar Kokoschka 1963, Walter Kern 1966, Ruszkowski 1967, Bernard Leach 1967, Giacomo Manzú 1970, Emilio Greco 1971, Alfred Manessier 1972, Bernard Stern 1972, Modern Art and the Modern Mind 1972, Ludwig Meidner 1973, Hilde Goldschmidt 1974, Paul Berger-Bergner 1974, John Milne 1977, Kokoschka and Hellas 1978, Else Meidner 1979, Elisabeth Frink, Douglas Portway, Franz Luby 1984, Mary Newcomb 1985, F. K. Gotsch: Leben und Werk 1986, Verlorene Existenzen, Erzählungen 1986, Jan Brazda, Leben und Werk 1989. *Leisure interests:* travelling, reading. *Address:* 12 Eton Avenue, London, NW3 3EH, England. *Telephone:* 01-794 3609.

HODSON, Henry Vincent, M.A.; British editor, author and administrator; b. 12 May 1906, London; s. of the late Prof. Thomas C. Hodson and of Kathleen (née Manly) Hodson; m. Margaret Elizabeth Honey 1933; four s.; ed. Gresham's School, Balliol Coll., Oxford; Fellow All Souls Coll., Oxford 1928-35; Ed. The Round Table 1934-39; Dir. of Empire Div., Ministry of Information 1939-41; Constitutional Adviser to Viceroy of India 1941-42; Principal Asst. Sec., Ministry of Production 1942-45; Asst. Ed. The Sunday Times 1945-50, Ed. 1950-61; Provost of Ditchley Foundation 1961-71; Proprietor Hodson Consultants 1971-; Consultant Ed. The International Foundation Directory 1972-, The Business Who's Who 1973; Ed. Annual Register (of world events) 1973-88, Ed.-in-Chief 1988-. *Publications:* Economics of a Changing World 1933, Slump and Recovery 1928-37 1938, Twentieth Century Empire 1948, The Great Divide: Britain-India-Pakistan 1969, (with Epilogue) 1986, The Diseconomics of Growth 1972. *Leisure interests:* gardening, theatre. *Address:* 18 Northumberland Avenue, London, WC2N 5BJ (Office); 105 Lexham Gardens, London, W8 6JN, England (Home). *Telephone:* 01-930 6046 (Office); 01-373 2859 (Home).

HODŽA, Fadil; Yugoslav (b. Albanian) politician; b. 1916, Djakovica, Kosovo Prov.; ed. Teachers' Coll., Elbasan, Albania and Djuri Djaković Higher Party School, Belgrade; in communist movement, Albania 1936-41; mem. CP (now League of Communists) of Yugoslavia 1941-; Sec. Party org., Djakovica Dist., mem. Bureau of Regional Cttee. CP, Kosovo and Metohija, political commissar, Commdr. Zejnel Hajdini partisan detachment, Commdr. Emin Duraku detachment and GHQ Nat. Liberation Army and Partisan detachments, Kosovo and Metohija, World War II; various positions, Kosovo, Socialist Repub. of Serbia and at federal level; Deputy Anti-Fascist Council of Nat. Liberation of Yugoslavia (AVNOJ), 3rd Session 1945; Deputy in Yugoslav Parl. 1945-69; Deputy Prov. Ass. of Kosovo and Metohija, mem. Bureau, Regional Cttee.; instructor Cen. Cttee. CP of Serbia; Pres. Exec. Council, Kosovo and Metohija; mem. Exec. Council, Serbia, Fed. Exec. Council; Pres. Prov. Assembly, Autonomous Prov. of Kosovo and Metohija; mem. Exec. Bureau Presidency of Cen. Cttee., League of Communists of Yugoslavia (LCY); mem. Cen. Cttee. Congress, League of Communists, Serbia on many occasions; Cen. Cttee. LCY, 7th-13th Congresses LCY; mem. Presidium LCY 1969-83; mem. Collective Presidency Socialist Fed. Repub. of Yugoslavia 1974-84, Vice-Pres. 1978-79; mem. Counsel of Fed. 1984-; Order of People's Hero, Partisan Memorial Badge and other decorations. *Address:* c/o Presidium of SAP of Kosovo, Prishtina, Yugoslavia.

HOELSCHER, Ludwig; German cellist; b. 23 Aug. 1907, Solingen, Rheinland; s. of Heinrich and Elisabeth (née Humberg) Hoelscher; m. 1940; one s. one d.; studied under Lamping, Klengel and Becker; Prof. Hochschule für Musik, Berlin 1936, later at Mozarteum Salzburg; Prof. Staatliche Hochschule für Musik und Darstellende Kunst, Stuttgart 1954-; mem. Jury, Moscow and Florence int. competitions; mem. Elly-Ney-Trio and Strub Quartet 1931-40; mem. trio with Walter Gieseking and Gerhard Taschner after 1945; has appeared as soloist under many of the world's most famous conductors and given first performances of many cello concertos and sonatas by contemporary composers and new works by Hindemith; has undertaken tours throughout Europe, Asia, Africa and N. and S. America; Hon. Prof. Univ. of Tokyo; mem. Bayerische Akad. der schönen Künste; Bayerische Maximilianorden für Wissenschaft und Kunst; Grosses Bundesverdienstkreuz mit Stern; Bayerischer Verdienstorden and several other honours and awards; Mendelssohn Prize 1930. *Address:* 8132 Tutzing bei München, Federal Republic of Germany. *Telephone:* 08158-8742.

HOFF, Lawrence Conrad, A.B.; American pharmaceutical company executive; b. 19 Jan. 1929, Fresno, Calif.; s. of Conrad and Katherine Hoff; m. Jacqueline Goodyear 1950; one s. two d.; ed. Stanford Univ., Calif.; mem. Sales Staff, The Upjohn Co., Kalamazoo, Mich. 1950-66, Dir. Domestic Pharmaceutical Sales 1966-69, Vice-Pres. Domestic Pharmaceutical Marketing 1969-74, Vice-Pres. and Gen. Man. Domestic Pharmaceutical Operations 1974-77, Exec. Vice-Pres. The Upjohn Co. 1974-84, Pres. 1984-87,

Pres. and C.O.O. 1987-. *Leisure interest:* golf. *Address:* The Upjohn Company, 7000 Portage Road, Kalamazoo, Mich. 49001, U.S.A. *Telephone:* (616) 323-6127.

HOFFENBERG, Sir Raymond, K.B.E., M.A., M.D., PH.D., F.R.C.P.(U.K.), F.R.C.P.(E.), F.R.C.P.(I.); British physician; b. 6 March 1923, Port Elizabeth, S. Africa; s. of Benjamin Hoffenberg and Dora Hoffenberg; m. Margaret Rosenberg, 1949; two s.; ed. Grey High School, Port Elizabeth, Univ. of Cape Town Medical School; Sr. Lecturer in Medicine, Groote Schuur Hosp., Cape Town 1955-68; MRC Sr. Scientist and Consultant Physician, Nat. Inst. for Medical Research and Royal Free Hosp., London, England 1968-70, at MRC Clinical Research Centre and Northwick Park Hosp. 1970-72; Prof. of Medicine Univ. of Birmingham 1972-85; Pres. Royal Coll. of Physicians, London 1983-89; Pres. Wolfson Coll. Oxford 1985-; Hon. Fellow, American Coll. of Physicians; Hon. F.R.A.C.P.; Hon. F.R.C.P.; Hon. D.Sc. (Leicester, City Univ., London). *Publications:* numerous chapters and articles on plasma protein metabolism, thyroid function and other aspects of endocrinology. *Leisure interests:* walking, golf. *Address:* Wolfson College, Oxford, OX2 6UD, England. *Telephone:* (0865) 274102.

HOFFMAN, Alan Jerome, A.B., PH.D.; American mathematician and educator; b. 30 May 1924, New York; s. of Jesse and Muriel Hoffman; m. Esther Walker 1947; two d.; ed. George Washington High School, Columbia Univ.; mem. U.S. Army Signal Corps 1943-46; mem. Inst. for Advanced Study 1950-51; Mathematician, Nat. Bureau of Standards 1951-56; Scientific Liaison Officer, Office of Naval Research, London 1956-57; Consultant, Gen. Electric Co. 1957-61; Adjunct Prof. City Univ. of New York 1965-75; Research Staff mem. IBM Research Center 1961-; IBM Fellow 1977-; Visiting Prof., Yale Univ. 1975-80; Consulting Prof., Stanford Univ. 1981-; Fellow, New York Acad. of Sciences, American Acad. of Arts and Sciences; mem. Nat. Acad. of Sciences; Hon. D.Sc. (Technion) 1986. *Publications:* numerous articles in mathematical journals. *Leisure interests:* table tennis, music. *Address:* IBM Research Centre, Box 218, Yorktown Heights, N.Y. 10598, U.S.A. *Telephone:* (914) 945-2270.

HOFFMAN, Dustin Lee; American actor; b. 8 Aug. 1937, Los Angeles, Calif.; s. of Harry Hoffman; m. 1st Anne Byrne 1969 (divorced 1981), two d.; m. 2nd Lisa Gottsegen 1980, two s. one d.; ed. Santa Monica City Coll.; First stage role in Yes is for a Very Young Man (Sarah Lawrence Coll., Bronxville, N.Y.); Broadway debut in A Cook for Mr. General 1961. *Other stage appearances in:* Harry, Noon and Night 1964, Journey of the Fifth Horse (Obie Award) 1966, Star Wagon 1966, Fragments 1966, Eh? (Drama Desk, Theatre World, Vernon Rice Awards) 1967, Jimmy Shine 1968, Death of a Salesman 1984; Asst. Dir. A View from the Bridge; Dir. All Over Town 1974. *Film appearances in:* The Tiger Makes Out 1966, Madigan's Millions 1966, The Graduate 1967, Midnight Cowboy 1969, John and Mary 1969, Little Big Man 1970, Who is Harry Kellerman ...? 1971, Straw Dogs 1971, Alfredo Alfredo, Papillon 1973, Lenny 1974, All the President's Men 1975, Marathon Man 1976, Straight Time 1978, Agatha 1979, Kramer vs. Kramer 1979 (Acad. Award 1980, New York Film Critics Award), Tootsie (New York Film Critics Award, Nat. Soc. of Film Critics Award) 1982, Ishtar 1987, Rain Man (Acad. and Golden Globe Awards) 1988, Family Business 1989. *TV appearance in:* Death of a Salesman 1985. *Leisure interests:* tennis, piano, photography, reading. *Address:* Columbia Pictures, 711 5th Avenue, New York, N.Y. 10022. U.S.A.

HOFFMAN, Grace; American mezzo-soprano singer; b. 14 Jan. 1925, Cleveland, Ohio; d. of Dave and Hermina Hoffman; ed. Western Reserve Univ. and Manhattan School of Music, New York; completed musical studies in Italy (Fulbright Scholarship); appeared at Maggio Musicale, Florence; guest performance as Azucena (Il Trovatore) Zürich Opera and subsequently mem. of this company for two years; debut at La Scala, Milan as Fricka (Die Walküre); with Stuttgart Opera 1955-; given titles Württembergische Kammersängerin 1960, Austrian Kammersängerin 1980; has appeared at Edinburgh and Bayreuth festivals; numerous guest appearances in leading roles at Teatro Colón, Buenos Aires, San Francisco Opera, Chicago Lyric Opera, Covent Garden, Metropolitan Opera, the Vienna Opera, in Berlin, Brussels, etc.; numerous oratorio and concert appearances in the major European music centres; Prof. of Voice, Hochschule für Musik, Stuttgart 1978-; Vercelli Prize, Medal of State of Baden-Württemberg 1978. *Leisure interests:* her house and furnishing it. *Address:* Bergstrasse 19, 7441 Neckartailfingen, Federal Republic of Germany (Home).

HOFFMAN, Michael L., PH.D.; American economist and journalist; b. 13 June 1915, Salisbury, N.C.; s. of Edwin Hoffman and Mary Lindsay; m. Catherine Hughes 1936; one s.; ed. Oberlin Coll., Ohio and Chicago Univ.; Lecturer in monetary theory and international trade at Oberlin Coll. and Trinity Coll., Connecticut; Consultant U.S. Treasury 1941; Acting Dir. wartime Foreign Funds Control; U.S. Treasury Rep. Allied Force HQ, Algiers, London and Paris; European econ. correspondent The New York Times 1945-56; Dir. Econ. Devt. Inst. of the Int. Bank for Reconstruction and Devt. (IBRD) 1956-61, Dir. Devt. Advisory Service 1962-63; Exec. Vice-Pres. and Dir. Lambert Int. Corpn. 1963-65; Assoc. Dir. Devt. Services Dept., IBRD 1965-73, Dir. Int. Relations Dept. 1973-76; Chevalier, Ordre de la Couronne (Belgium). *Address:* RFD, Vineyard Haven, Mass. 02568, U.S.A. (Home).

HOFFMAN, Michael Richard, B.SC.; British engineer, b. 31 Oct. 1939, Letchworth, Herts.; s. of Sydney William Hoffman and Ethel Margaret Hoffman; m. 1st Margaret Edith Tregaskes 1963 (divorced 1979); one d.; m. 2nd Helen Judith Peters 1982; ed. Hitchin Grammar School, Univ. of Bristol; Man. Rolls Royce Ltd. 1961-70; Gen. Man. Cannon and Stokes Ltd. 1970-73; Dir. Turbine Operations AE Ltd. 1973-76; Chair. and Man. Dir. Perkins Engines Ltd. 1976-80; Pres. Farm Machinery, Massey Ferguson Ltd. 1980-83; Man. Dir. Babcock Int. PLC 1983-87; Chief Exec. Airship Industries Ltd. 1987-; mem. Dept. of Trade and Industry, British Overseas Trade Bd. 1986-, Tech. Requirements Bd. 1985-, Monopolies and Mergers Comm.; mem. Council, Brunel Univ. 1984-; Pres. Inst. of Production Engineers 1987-88; Watts Memorial Prize 1961. *Leisure interests:* shooting, real tennis, sailing. *Address:* 43 De Vere Gardens, London, W8 5AW; 29 Millhouse Drive, Leamington Spa, Warwicks., CV32 6AW, England (Homes). *Telephone:* 01-581 4612; 0926 29643.

HOFFMANN, Martin R., LL.B.; American lawyer and government official; b. 20 April 1932, Stockbridge, Mass.; m. Margaret Ann McCabe; three c.; ed. Princeton Univ. and Univ. of Virginia Law School; served U.S. Army 1954-58; Law Clerk in Alexandria, Va.; Asst. U.S. Attorney, D.C. 1962-65; Minority Counsel on House Judiciary Cttee. 1965-66; Legal Counsel to Senator Charles Percy 1967-69; Asst. Gen. Counsel and Asst. Sec. Univ. Computing Co. 1969-71; Gen. Counsel, Atomic Energy Comm. 1971-73; Special Asst. to Sec. and Deputy Sec. of Defense 1973-74, Gen. Counsel of Defense Dept. 1974-75, Sec. of the Army 1975-77; Man. Partner, Gardner, Carton and Douglas (Washington Office) 1977-.

HOFFMANN, Roald, PH.D.; American professor of chemistry; b. 18 July 1937, Złoczow, Poland; s. of Hillel Safran and Clara Rosen, step s. of Paul Hoffmann; m. Eva Börjesson 1960; one s. one d.; ed. Columbia and Harvard Univs.; Jr. Fellow, Soc. of Fellows, Harvard Univ. 1962-65; Assoc. Prof. of Chem., Cornell Univ. 1965-68, Prof. 1968-74, John A. Newman Prof. of Physical Science 1974-; mem. American Acad. of Arts and Sciences, Nat. Acad. of Sciences; Foreign mem. Royal Soc., Indian Nat. Acad. of Sciences, Royal Swedish Acad. of Sciences; Hon. D. Tech. (Royal Inst. of Technology, Stockholm) 1977, Hon. D.Sc. (Yale) 1980, (Columbia) 1982, (Hartford) 1982, (City Univ. of New York) 1983, (Puerto Rico) 1983, (Uruguay) 1984, (La Plata) 1984, (Colgate) 1985, (State Univ. of New York at Binghamton) 1985; American Chem. Soc. Award 1969, Fresenius Award 1969, Harrison Howe Award 1969, Annual Award of Int. Acad. of Quantum Molecular Sciences 1970, Arthur C. Cope Award, A.C.S. 1973, Linus Pauling Award 1974, Nichols Medal 1980, shared Nobel Prize for Chemistry 1981, Inorganic Chemistry Award A.C.S. 1982, Nat. Medal of Science 1984. *Publications:* Conservation of Orbital Symmetry 1969, The Metamict State 1987. *Address:* Department of Chemistry, Cornell University, Ithaca, N.Y. 14850, U.S.A. *Telephone:* 607-255-3419 (Office).

HOFFMEYER, Erik, D.SC.(ECON.); Danish banker; b. 25 Dec. 1924, Rårup; m. Eva Kemp 1949; ed. Copenhagen University; with Danmarks Nationalbank 1951-59, Econ. Counsellor 1959-62, Chair. of Bd. of Govs. 1965-; Rockefeller Fellow, U.S. 1954-55; Lecturer in Econs., Univ. of Copenhagen 1956, Prof. 1959-64; Gen. Man. Bikuben Savings Bank 1962-64; Gov. for Denmark to Int. Monetary Fund (IMF) 1965; mem. Bd. Asscn. of Political Econ. (Pres. 1951-53), Danish Econ. Asscn. 1960-66, Presidency Econ. Council 1962-65, Acad. of Technical Sciences 1963-, Econ. Council 1965-, Danish Science Advisory Council 1965-72, C. L. David Collection 1967- (Chair. 1977-), Nationalbank Anniversary Foundation (Deputy Chair. 1968-77, Chair. 1977-), The Housing Mortgage Fund 1969-72, European Investment Bank 1973-77; Chair. Cttee. of Govs. of Cen. Banks of EEC Countries 1975-76, 1979-81; Deputy Chair. Danish Export Finance Corpn. 1975-; Chair. Trees and Environment Protection Foundation 1979-, Laurits Andersen Foundation 1982-, Group of Thirty 1984-, King Frederik VII Foundation 1987-. *Publications:* Dollar Shortage and the Structure of U.S. Foreign Trade 1958, Stabile priser og fuld beskaeftigelse 1960, Strukturaendringer på penge-og kapitalmarkedet 1960, Velfaerdsteori og velfaerdsstat 1962, Industriel vaekst 1963, Dansk Pengehistorie 1968; contrib. to Nationaløkonomisk Tidsskrift and int. econ. journals. *Address:* Danmarks Nationalbank, Havnegade 5 DK-1093 Copenhagen K; Hegelsvej 22, DK 2920 Charlottenlund, Denmark. *Telephone:* 01-14 14 11 (Office).

HOFLEHNER, Rudolf; Austrian artist and sculptor; b. 8 Aug. 1916, Linz; s. of Johann Hoflehner and Anna Ruf; m. Luise Schaffer 1939; one d.; ed. Akad. der Bildenden Künste, Vienna; teacher, Kunstgewerbeschule, Linz 1945-52; Prof. Akad. de Bildenden Künste, Stuttgart 1952-82; mem. Akad. der Künste Berlin, Akad. der Schönen Künste, Munich; works in many museums in Europe and America; Preis der Stadt Wien 1959; Preis der Stadt Berlin 1967; Grosser Österreichischer Staatspreis 1969. *Leisure interest:* music. *Address:* Ottensteinstrasse 62, 2344 Maria Enzersdorf, Austria. *Telephone:* 02236-814764.

HOFMANN, Klaus, PH.D.; American professor of experimental medicine and biochemistry; b. 21 Feb. 1911, Karlsruhe, Germany; s. of Fritz and Marianne (Bally) Hofmann; m. 1st Paula Blum 1936 (divorced), 2nd Frances M. Finn 1965; one d.; ed. Fed. Inst. of Tech., Zürich; Postdoctoral Fellow, Rockefeller Inst. of Medical Research, New York 1938-40; Cornell Medical Coll., New York 1940-42; Guest worker, Ciba Pharmaceutical Co., Summit, N.J. 1942-44; Asst. Research Prof. Univ. of Pittsburgh 1944-45, Assoc. Prof. 1945-47, Research Prof. 1947-52, Chair. Biochemistry Dept., Medical School 1952-64, Prof. of Experimental Medicine and Biochemistry and Dir. Protein Research Lab. 1964-; mem. N.A.S., American Chem. Soc., American Soc. of Biological Chemists, A.A.A.S., Endocrine Soc., Swiss Chem. Soc.; recipient of Alexander von Humboldt-Stiftung Scientist Award and other honours. *Publications:* Chemistry of Imidazole 1953, Fatty Acid Metabolism in Microorganisms 1963; numerous articles in professional journals. *Address:* University of Pittsburgh, 1276A Scaife Hall, 3550 Terrace Street, Pittsburgh, Pa. 15261 (Office); 1467 Mohican Drive, Pittsburgh, Pa. 15228, U.S.A. (Home). *Telephone:* 412-561-0179 (Home).

HOFMANN, Peter; German tenor; b. 12 Aug. 1944, Marienbad; ed. Hochschule für Musik, Karlsruhe; operatic début as Tamino, Lübeck 1972; mem. Stuttgart Opera 1973–; sang Siegmund, centenary production of The Ring, Bayreuth 1976, Covent Garden London 1976; U.S. début as Siegmund, San Francisco Opera 1977; début Metropolitan New York (Lohengrin) 1980; pop artist 1984–. *Address:* c/o Fritz Höfman, Schlosse Schönreith 8581, Federal Republic of Germany.

HOFMANN, Werner, D.PHIL.; Austrian museum administrator and author; b. 8 Aug. 1928, Vienna; s. of Leopold Hofmann and Anna (née Visvader) Hofmann; m. Jacqueline (née Buron) Hofmann 1950; ed. Univ. of Vienna; Asst. Albertina, Vienna 1950–55; Dir. Museum of the 20th Century, Vienna 1962–69, Hamburger Kunsthalle 1969–; Guest lecturer Barnard Coll., N.Y. 1957; Guest Prof. Berkeley, Calif. 1961, Harvard Univ. 1981, 1982, Columbia Univ. 1984; Gold Ehren-Medaille City of Vienna 1988. *Publications:* Die Plastik des 20. Jahrhunderts 1958, Das irdische Paradies-Kunst im 19. Jahrhundert 1960, Grundlagen der modernen Kunst 1966, Turning Points in 20th Century Art 1969, Gustav Klimt und die Wiener Jahrhundertwende 1970, Nana, Mythos und Wirklichkeit 1973, Kataloge der Ausstellungsreihe "Kunst um 1800" 1974–80, Edouard Manet: Das Frühstück in Atelier 1985, Ausstellungskatalog "Zauber der Medusa" 1987. *Address:* Hamburger Kunsthalle, Glockengiesserwall, 200 Hamburg 1 (Office); Sierichstr. 154, 2000 Hamburg 60, Federal Republic of Germany (Home). *Telephone:* (040) 24825-2607 (Office); 46 47 11 (Home).

HOFMEISTER, Paul Emil Julius; German business executive; b. 28 April 1909, Bremen; s. of Heinrich Hofmeister and Dora Meijer; m. Elisabeth Sommer 1934 (deceased); one d.; ed. commercial school; joined Norddeutsche Affinerie 1927, mem. man. 1947, Pres. 1961–76, Chair. 1976–81, Hon. Chair. 1981–; Chair. Bremer Woll-Kämmerei, Bremen, Otavi Minen AG, Frankfurt; Deputy Chair. Wirtschaftsvereinigung Metalle e.V., Düsseldorf, Fachvereinigung Metallhütten und Umschmelzwerke e.V., Düsseldorf; mem. Bd. H. Maihak AG, Hamburg, Freeport Indonesia Inc., New York; Orden al Mérito Bernardo O'Higgins (Chile). *Leisure interests:* riding, golf. *Address:* Norddeutsche Affinerie, 2000 Hamburg 36, Alsterterrasse 2 (Office); 2000 Hamburg 52, Borchlingweg 11, Federal Republic of Germany (Home). *Telephone:* 44-19-61 (Office); 880-41-34 (Home).

HOFMEKLER, Ori, B.F.A.; Israeli painter and artist; b. 12 March 1952, Israel; s. of Daniel Hofmekler and Rina Kune; m. Ilana Wellisch 1977; one s. one d.; ed. Bezalel Acad., Jerusalem and Jerusalem Univ.; Shtrouk Prize 1976. *Publications:* Hofmekler's People 1983; contribs. to Penthouse Magazine since 1983, and to magazines in France, Fed. Repub. of Germany and U.S.A. *Leisure interests:* reading, sports and travel. *Address:* 35 Hirshfeld Street, Rishon Le-Tzion, Israel. *Telephone:* 03-993891.

HOFMEYR, Murray, M.A.; South African business executive; b. 9 Dec. 1925, Pretoria; s. of William Hendrik and Margarethe Hanna Hofmeyr; m. Johanna Hendrika Verdurmen 1953; two s. two d.; ed. Pretoria High School, Rhodes and Oxford Univs.; joined Anglo American Corpn., Johannesburg 1962, Man. in Zambia 1965–69, Chair. Anglo American Corpn. (Cen. Africa) 1969–72; mem. Bd., Anglo American Corpn. of S.A. Ltd. 1970–72, Exec. Dir. 1972–; Man. Dir. Charter Consolidated Ltd. 1972–79, Chair. 1976–80; Chair. Johannesburg Consolidated Investment Co. Ltd. (JCI) 1987–. *Leisure interest:* tennis. *Address:* P.O. Box 590, Johannesburg 2000, South Africa. *Telephone:* 011-373 3075.

HOFSTADTER, Robert, B.S., M.A., PH.D.; American emeritus university professor; b. 5 Feb. 1915, New York; s. of Louis and Henrietta Hofstadter; m. Nancy Givan 1942; one s. two d.; ed. City Coll. of New York, Princeton Univ.; Instructor, Univ. of Pa., City Coll., New York 1940–42; Physicist, Nat. Bureau of Standards, Washington, D.C. 1942–43; Asst. Chief Physicist, Norden Labs. Corpn., New York 1943–46; Asst. Prof. of Physics, Princeton Univ. 1946–50, Assoc. Prof. Stanford Univ. 1950–53, Prof. 1954–85, Max H. Stein Prof. of Physics 1971–85, Emer. Prof. 1985–; Dir. High Energy Physics Lab., Stanford Univ. 1967–74; Guggenheim Fellowship 1958–59; Assoc. Ed. Physical Review 1951–53, Review of Scientific Instruments 1954–56, Reviews of Modern Physics 1958–61; mem. Nat. Acad. of Sciences 1958–, American Philosophical Soc.; Fellow, American Physical Soc., mem. American Acad. of Arts and Sciences 1970, Ford Foundation Fellow; mem. Bd. of Govs., Weizmann Inst. of Science, Rehovoth, Israel; Sr. mem. Inst. of Medicine 1983; Dr. h.c. 1982 (Wurzburg Univ.) 1983 (Mainz Univ.), (Israel Inst. of Tech.) 1985, and several other hon. degrees; Calif. Scientist of Year 1959; Nobel Prize Winner in Physics (jt.) 1961, Roentgen Medal 1985, Nat. Medal of Science 1986, Prize of Cultural Foundation of Fiuggi (Italy) 1986 and other prizes and awards. *Publications:* Nuclear and Nucleon Structure, Joint author High-Energy Electron Scattering Tables, Electron Scattering and Nucleon Structure 1963, over 300 scientific papers, Co-Ed. Investigations in Physics 1958–65, Nuclear Structure, Assoc. Ed. Reviews in Modern Physics. *Address:*

Department of Physics, Stanford University, Stanford, Calif. 94305 (Office); 639 Mirada Avenue, Stanford, Calif. 94305, U.S.A. (Home). *Telephone:* 415-723-4235.

HOFSTÄTTER, Peter R(obert), DR.PHIL.; Austrian professor emeritus of psychology; b. 20 Oct. 1913, Vienna; s. of Dr. Robert and Josephine (née Heller) Hofstätter; m. 1st Herta Stein 1942 (divorced), 2nd Hertha Rott 1967; four c.; ed. Univ. of Vienna; Lecturer in Psychology, Univ. of Graz 1946–49; Research Assoc. Mass. Inst. of Tech. 1949–50; Assoc. Prof. The Catholic Univ. of America 1950–56; Prof. Hochschule für Sozialwissenschaften 1956–59; Prof. Univ. of Hamburg 1959–79, Prof. Emer. 1979–; Konrad Adenauer Preis 1984. *Publications:* Einführung in die Tiefenpsychologie 1948, Gruppendynamik 1971, Sozialpsychologie 1973, Psychologie zwischen Kenntnis und Kult 1984. *Leisure interest:* archaeology. *Address:* Lehmkuhlenweg 16, 2150 Buxtehude, Federal Republic of Germany. *Telephone:* (04161) 8 22 95.

HOFSTRA, Hendrik Jan; Netherlands lawyer; b. 28 Sept. 1904, Amsterdam; s. of Jan Hofstra and Harmina Fricke; m. Wilhelmina Odilia Petri 1926; one s.; tax inspector prior to 1939, tax consultant 1939–45; mem. Second Chamber of States Gen. 1945–56; Dir. Cen. Life Insurance Bank, The Hague and Cen. Gen. Insurance Co., The Hague prior to 1956; Minister of Finance 1956–58; Gov. European Investment Bank 1956–58; Vice-Pres. Verolme United Shipyards, Rotterdam 1961–66; Prof. Leiden Univ. 1966–75; mem. Labour Party; Kt. of the Netherlands Lion; Commdr. Order of Orange-Nassau. *Publications:* Socialistische Belastingpolitiek 1946, Inleiding Nederlands Belastingrecht 1970 (6th edn. 1986), Inkomstenbelasting 1975, Inflatieneutrale Belastingheffing 1978 and numerous articles on public finance and taxation. *Leisure interests:* gardening, music. *Address:* Adelheidstraat 97, 2595EC, The Hague, Netherlands.

HOGAN, Ben W.; American golfer and businessman; b. 13 Aug. 1912, Dublin, Tex.; m. Valerie Fox 1935; turned professional 1929; U.S. Open Champion 1948, 1950, 1951, 1953 (equalling record number of wins); seriously injured in road accident after winning Open 1948; feared would never play again but adjusted swing to compensate for leg injuries; won U.S. Masters 1951, 1953; British Open Champion 1953 (only time he competed); only player to win three of world's four major titles in one year (1953); failed to win U.S. Professional Golfer's Assen. Championship that year but won 1946, 1948; won team (with Sam Snead) and individual World Cup (then Canada Cup) 1956; voted greatest ever professional golfer by U.S. golf writers 1965; Chair. of Bd. The Ben Hogan Co., Fort Worth; served U.S.A.A.F. 1943–45, rank of Lieut. *Address:* Ben Hogan Company, P.O. Box 11276, Fort Worth, Tex. 76110, U.S.A.

HOGARTH, (Arthur) Paul, R.A., F.R.S.A., F.C.S.D.; British artist; b. 4 Oct. 1917, Kendal, Cumbria; s. of Arthur Hogarth and Janet Bownass Hogarth; m. 1st Doreen Courtman 1940, 2nd Phyllis Pamplin 1953, 3rd Patricia Douthwaite 1961 (divorced 1981); one s.; ed. St. Agnes School, Manchester, Manchester Coll. of Art and St. Martin's School of Art, London; Sr. Tutor, R.C.A. 1964–71; painter in watercolours, draughtsman, illustrator and printmaker; rep. in many perm. collections including: (U.K.) Tate Gallery, Royal Acad. of Arts, Fitzwilliam Museum, Cambridge, Whitworth Art Gallery, Manchester, Carlisle Art Gallery and Victoria and Albert Museum; (U.S.A.) Boston Public Library, Logan Library, Philadelphia and Library of Congress, Washington D.C.; retrospective exhbns. include The World of Paul Hogarth, 1953–69, at R.C.A. 1971, Travels through the Seventies, Kyle Gallery, London 1980, The Other Hogarth: Drawings, Lithographs and Watercolours, 1954–84 (Northern Arts Council), at art galleries in N. England 1984–85; Royal Designer for Industry 1979; Francis Williams Illustration Award 1982. *Publications:* Creative Pencil- Drawing 1964, Artist as Reporter 1967 (revised and enlarged 1986), Creative Ink Drawing 1968, Artists on Horseback 1972, Arthur Boyd Houghton 1983, Graham Greene Country 1986, The Mediterranean Shore 1988. *Leisure interest:* sailing. *Address:* c/o Tessa Sayle, 11 Jubilee Place, London, SW3 3TE, England. *Telephone:* 01-352 4311.

HOGG, Alexander Hubert Arthur, C.B.E., M.A., F.S.A.; British university teacher and archaeologist; b. 2 May 1908; s. of A. F. Hogg; m. Nellie Henderson 1943; one s. one d.; ed. Highgate School and Sidney Sussex Coll., Cambridge; Asst. Eng., Sir Robert McAlpine & Sons 1930–34; Jr. Scientific Officer, Roads Research Lab. 1934–36; Lecturer, Eng. Dept., King's Coll., Newcastle upon Tyne 1936–42; Temporary Experimental Officer, Admiralty Undex Works, Rosyth 1942–45; ICI Fellowship 1945–47; Lecturer, Eng. Lab., Univ. of Cambridge 1947–49; Sec. Royal Comm. on Ancient Monuments in Wales and Monmouthshire 1949–73; Hon. D.Litt. (Wales) 1974. *Publications:* Hill-Forts of Britain 1975, An Index of British Hill-Forts 1979, Surveying for Field Archaeologists 1980, numerous articles in journals. *Address:* Brynfield, Waun Fawr, Aberystwyth, SY23 3PP, Wales. *Telephone:* (0970) 623479.

HOGG, Sir Christopher Anthony, Kt., M.A., M.B.A.; British company director; b. 2 Aug. 1936, London, England; s. of Mr. and Mrs. A. W. Hogg; m. Anne Cathie 1961; two d.; ed. Marlborough, Trinity Coll., Oxford, and Harvard School of Business Administration; taught at Institut pour l'Etude des Méthodes de Direction de l'Entreprise (business school), Lausanne, Switzerland 1962–63; with Philip Hill, Higginson, Erlangers Ltd. (later Hill Samuel & Co. Ltd.) 1963–66; staff mem. Industrial Reorganisation

Corpn. 1966–68; joined Courtaulds Group 1968 as Dir. The Int. Paint Co. Ltd., Overseas Dir. 1969, Man. Dir. 1971; non-exec. Dir. British Celanese Ltd. 1971–72, Exec. Deputy Chair. July–Nov. 1972, Chair. 1972–75; Deputy Chair. the Int. Paint Co. Ltd. 1972–73, Chair. 1973–78; Dir. Courtaulds Ltd. 1973–, a Deputy Chair. 1978–80, Chief Exec. 1979–, Chair. 1980–; Main Bd. Dir. Courtaulds Spun Fabrics etc. 1976–77; Chair. Courtaulds Apparel Ltd. 1977–79; Dir. Novaceta SpA 1973–79, Reuters Holdings PLC 1984– (Chair. 1985–); Chair. Kayser Bondor Ltd. 1977–79; Chair. Courtaulds Hosiery Ltd. 1977–79; Chair. Courtaulds Distributors Ltd. 1977–79; Dir. British Cellophane Ltd. 1978–79, Chair. July–Nov. 1979; mem. Dept. of Industry Industrial Devt. Advisory Bd. 1976–80; Hon. D.Sc. (Cranfield Inst. of Tech.) 1986, (Aston) 1988; Hon. F.C.S.D. 1987. *Publication:* Masers and Lasers 1962. *Leisure interests:* opera, reading, walking. *Address:* Courtaulds PLC, 18 Hanover Square, London, W.1, England (Office). *Telephone:* 01-629 9080 (Office).

HOGG, Sir John Nicholson, Kt., M.A.(OXON.); British banker; b. 4 Oct. 1912, Bombay, India; s. of late Sir Malcolm Hogg and of Lorna Beaman; m. Elizabeth Garmoyle 1948; one s. one d.; ed. Eton Coll. and Balliol Coll., Oxford; joined Glyn Mills and Co. 1934; war service with King's Royal Rifle Corps 1939–45; returned to Glyn Mills and Co. 1945, Man. Dir. 1950, Deputy Chair. 1963–68, Chair. 1968–70; Chair. Abu Dhabi Investment Bd. 1967–75; Chair. Advisory Council of Export Credit Guarantee Dept. 1962–67; Chair. Child Health Research Investment Trust PLC; Deputy Chair. Williams and Glyn's Bank PLC 1970–83; Deputy Chair. Gallaher Ltd. until 1978; Dir. Honeywell Ltd. until 1981, Prudential Corpn. PLC 1964–85, Royal Bank of Scotland Group PLC 1963–82; Fellow Eton Coll. 1951–70; mem. Commonwealth War Graves Comm. 1958–64; Sheriff County of London 1960; Hon. Treas. Inst. of Child Health Ltd. 1974–87 (Hon. Fellow); Hon. T.D. *Leisure interests:* cricket, fishing, gardening. *Address:* The Red House, Shedfield, Southampton, England (Home). *Telephone:* (0329) 832121.

HOGGART, Richard, M.A., D.LITT.; British writer and educator; b. 24 Sept. 1918, Leeds; s. of Tom Longfellow Hoggart and Adeline Emma Hoggart (née Long); m. Mary Holt France 1942; two s. one d.; ed. Leeds Univ.; Royal Artillery 1940–46; Staff Tutor and Sr. Staff Tutor, Univ. Coll. of Hull and Univ. of Hull 1946–59; Sr. Lecturer in English, Univ. of Leicester 1959–62; Visiting Prof. Univ. of Rochester, N.Y. 1956–57; Prof. of English, Birmingham Univ. 1962–73; Pres. British Asscn. of fmr. UN Civil Servants 1978–86; Chair. European Museum of the Year Award Cttee. 1977–, Broadcasting Research Unit 1980–; mem. Albemarle Cttee. on Youth Services 1958–60, Youth Service Devt. Council 1960–62, Pilkington Cttee. on Broadcasting 1960–62; Gov. Birmingham Repertory Theatre 1963–70; Dir. Centre for Contemporary Cultural Studies 1964–73; mem. BBC Gen. Advisory Council 1959–60, 1964–70, Arts Council of G.B. 1976–81, Culture Advisory Cttee. of U.K. Nat. Comm. to UNESCO 1966–70, Communications Advisory Cttee. of U.K. Nat. Comm. to UNESCO 1977–79, Wilton Park Academic Council 1983–; Chair. Arts Council Drama Panel 1977–80, Vice-Chair. Arts Council 1980–81, Chair. Advisory Council for Adult and Continuing Educ. 1977–83, The Statesman and Nation Publishing Co. Ltd. 1978–81; Gov. Royal Shakespeare Theatre 1966–; Asst. Dir.-Gen. for Social Sciences, Humanities and Culture UNESCO 1970–75; Warden of Goldsmiths' Coll. 1976–84; Hon. Visiting Prof., Univ. of E. Anglia 1985–, Univ. of Surrey 1985–; Hon. Fellow Sheffield City Polytechnic 1983, Goldsmiths' Coll. 1987; BBC Reith Lecturer 1971; Hon. D. Univ. (Open Univ.) 1972; Hon. D.-ès-L. (Bordeaux) 1974, (Paris) 1987; Hon. D. Univ. (Surrey) 1981; Hon. LL.D. (CNAA) 1982, (York Univ., Toronto) 1988; Hon. Litt.D.(E. Anglia) 1986, Hon. D. Litt. (Leicester Univ.), (Hull Univ.) 1988. *Publications:* Auden 1951, The Uses of Literacy 1957, W. H. Auden—A Selection 1961, Teaching Literature 1963, The Critical Moment 1964, How and Why Do We Learn 1965, Essays in Literature and Culture 1969, Speaking to Each Other 1970, Only Connect 1972, An Idea and Its Servants 1978, An English Temper 1982, The Future of Broadcasting (ed. with Janet Morgan) 1978, An Idea of Europe (with Douglas Johnson) 1987, A Local Habitation 1988, Liberty as Legislation (Ed.) 1989. *Leisure interest:* family. *Address:* Mortonsfield, Beavers Hill, Farnham, Surrey, GU9 7DF, England. *Telephone:* (0252) 715740.

HOGWOOD, Christopher Jarvis Haley, C.B.E., M.A., F.R.S.A.; British musician; b. 10 Sept. 1941, Nottingham; s. of Haley Evelyn and Marion Constance (née Higgott) Hogwood; ed. Cambridge Univ., Charles Univ., Prague, Czechoslovakia; founder-mem. Early Music Consort of London 1967–76; f. and Dir. Acad. of Ancient Music 1973–; mem. Faculty of Music, Cambridge Univ. 1975–; Dir. Handel and Haydn Soc., Boston, U.S.A. 1986–; Hon. Prof. of Music, Keele Univ. 1986–; Dir. of Music, St. Paul Chamber Orchestra, Minn., U.S.A. 1987–; Walter Wilson Cobbett Medal (Worshipful Co. of Musicians) 1986. *Publications:* Music at Court 1978, The Trio Sonata 1979, Haydn's London Visits 1980, Music in Eighteenth Century England (co-author) 1983, Handel: a documentary biography 1984; many editions of musical scores; contribs. to The New Grove Dictionary of Music and Musicians 1981; numerous recordings. *Address:* 2 Claremont, Hills Road, Cambridge, CB2 1PA, England. *Telephone:* (0223) 63975.

HOHENFELLNER, Peter, D.IUR.; Austrian diplomatist; b. 1939, Vienna; ed. Univ. of Vienna; joined Ministry for Foreign Affairs 1967; served Austrian Legation, Prague 1969–70, Cabinet of Fed. Chancellor 1970, Embassies in Tunis 1972–74, Algiers 1974–75, Budapest 1975–78; Amb. to

Cuba 1978–81, to Lebanon 1982–84; Dir. Dept. for Int. Orgs. 1985–88; Deputy Political Dir. Ministry for Foreign Affairs, Vienna 1986–88; Perm. Rep. to UN Feb. 1988–. *Address:* Permanent Mission of Austria to the United Nations, 809 United Nations Plaza, New York, N.Y. 10017, U.S.A. *Telephone:* (212) 949-1840.

HOHOFF, Curt, DR.PHIL.; German writer; b. 18 March 1913, Emden; s. of Caspar Hohoff and Elisabeth (née Waterman) Hohoff; m. Elfriede Federhen 1949; four s. one d.; ed. Univs. of Münster, Munich, Cambridge and Berlin; journalist Rheinischer Merkur, Koblenz 1948–49, Suddeutsche Zeitung, Munich 1949–50, freelance 1950–; mem. Akad. der Künste Berlin 1956, Bayerische Akademie der Künste Munich 1958. *Publications:* Woina-Woina, Russisches Tagebuch 1951, Geist und Ursprung (essays) 1954, Heinrich von Kleist (biog.) 1957, Schnittpunkte (essays) 1963, Die Märzhasen (novel) 1966, München 1970, Jakob M. R. Lenz (biog.) 1977, Grimmelshausen (biog.) 1978, Unter den Fischen (memoirs) 1982, Die verbotene Stadt (novel) 1986. *Address:* Adalbert-Stifter-Strasse 27, 8000 Munich 81, Federal Republic of Germany. *Telephone:* 982980.

HØJDAHL, Odd; Norwegian trade unionist and politician; b. 5 Jan. 1921, Oslo; m. Gerda Rustbøle 1946; two d.; Vice-Pres. Landsorganisasjonen i Norge (LO) (Norwegian Fed. of Trade Unions) 1969–77; Minister of Social Affairs 1971–72; Dir. Norwegian Developing Aid Directorate, Tiden Norsk Forlag, Arbeiderbladet (daily newspaper), Aktietrykkeriet (printing firm) and the state-run Iron and Steel works; Del. and Adviser, ILO congresses and UN Gen. Assembly; Dir. of Labour and Occupational Health Directorate; Dir. Den norske Creditbank 1978–; Labour. *Address:* Landsorganisasjonen i Norge, Folkets Hus, Youngsgt. 11, Oslo, Norway.

HOLDEN, Roberto; Angolan nationalist leader; b. 1925, São Salvador, Northern Prov.; ed. Belgian Congo (now Zaire); worked in Finance Dept., Belgian Admin., Léopoldville (now Kinshasa), Stanleyville (now Kisangani) and Bukavu; founded União das Populacões de Angola (UPA) 1954; travelled widely in Africa and Europe; attended first and second All African Peoples Confs. Accra 1958, Tunis 1960; elected to the Steering Cttee., Tunis; founded La voix de la nation angolaise, a fortnightly newspaper; assumed leadership of guerrilla liberation operations against the Portuguese in Angola; made several trips to U.S.A. 1961; became leader of Frente Nacional de Libertação de Angola (FNLA) when UPA merged with Partido Democrático Angolano (PDA) March 1962; Premier of Angolan govt. in exile, Governo Revolucionário de Angola no Exílio (GRAE) 1962; leader of defeated FNLA forces in Angolan civil war after Portuguese withdrawal Nov. 1975; exiled to Zaire then Senegal; expelled from Senegal 1979; living in Paris 1980.

HOLDEN-BROWN, Sir Derrick, Kt.; British company director; b. 14 Feb. 1923, Surrey; s. of Harold Walter and Beatrice Florence (née Walker) Holden-Brown; m. Patricia Mary Ross Mackenzie 1950; one s. one d.; ed. Westcliff; served Royal Navy 1941–46; Chartered Accountant 1948; joined Hiram Walker and Sons, (distillers) 1949; Man. Dir., Cairnes Ltd., (brewers) Ireland 1954, Grants of St. James's Ltd. 1960; Dir. Ind Coope Ltd. 1962; Chair. Victoria Wine Co. 1964; Dir. Allied Breweries Ltd. 1967–, Finance Dir. 1972, Vice-Chair. 1975–82, Chair. Beer Div. 1978–86; Chair. Brewers' Soc. 1978–80, Vice-Pres. 1980–; Chair. Allied-Lyons PLC 1982–, C.E.O. 1982–88; Deputy Chair. Sun Alliance and London Insurance PLC 1985–; Dir. Midland Bank PLC March 1984–, FIDC 1984– (Deputy Chair. 1974–76); Pres. Food and Drink Fed. 1984–86; mem. Inst. of Chartered Accountants of Scotland. *Leisure interests:* sailing, offshore cruising. *Address:* Copse House, Milford-on-Sea, Hampshire, England. *Telephone:* (064 62) 2247.

HOLDERNESS, Baron (Life Peer), cr. 1979, of Bishop Wilton in the County of Humberside; **Richard Frederick Wood,** P.C., D.L.; British politician; b. 5 Oct. 1920, London; s. of 1st Earl of Halifax, K.G., O.M., G.C.I.E.; m. Diana Kellett 1947; one s. one d.; ed. Eton and New Coll., Oxford; Attaché, British Embassy, Rome 1940; army 1940–43, wounded; M.P. 1950–79; Parl. Pvt. Sec. to Minister of Pensions 1951–53, to Minister of State, Bd. of Trade 1953–54, to Minister of Agric. and Fisheries 1954–55; Joint Parl. Sec. Ministry of Pensions and Nat. Insurance 1955–58; Parl. Sec. Ministry of Labour 1958–59; Minister of Power 1959–63, of Pensions and Nat. Ins. 1963–64, of Overseas Devt. 1970–74; Dir. Yorks. Conservative Newspapers 1947–55, Hulton Press 1953–55, F. J. C. Lilley and Co. Ltd. 1967–70, Hargreaves Group PLC 1974–86; Gov. Queen Elizabeth's Foundation for the Disabled 1946–, Pres. 1983–; Chair. Disablement Services Authority 1987–; Regional Dir. Yorks. and Humberside Regional Bd., Lloyds Bank Ltd. 1981–; Deputy Lieut. County of Humberside; Hon. Col. 4th Battalion, Royal Green Jackets; Hon. LL.D. (Sheffield, Hull and Leeds Univs.). *Leisure interest:* travel. *Address:* Flat Top House, Bishop Wilton, York, YO4 1RY, England; 65 Les Collines de Guerrevieille, 83120 Ste Maxime, France. *Telephone:* (075 96) 266.

HOLDGATE, Martin Wyatt, C.B., M.A., PH.D.; British biologist; b. 14 Jan. 1931, Horsham; s. of Francis W. Holdgate and Lois M. Bebbington; m. Elizabeth M. Weil (née Dickinson) 1963; two s.; ed. Arnold School, Blackpool and Queens' Coll. Cambridge; Research Fellow, Queens' Coll. Cambridge 1953–56; Jt. leader Gough Island Scientific Survey 1955–56; lecturer in Zoology, Univ. of Manchester 1956–57, Univ. of Durham 1957–60; lecturer, Royal Soc. Expedition to southern Chile 1958–59; Asst. Dir. of Research,

Scott Polar Research Inst. Cambridge 1960-63; Chief Biologist, British Antarctic Survey 1963-66; Deputy Dir. (Research), The Nature Conservancy (U.K.) 1966-70; Dir. Central Unit on Environmental Pollution, Dept. of Environment 1970-74; Dir. Inst. of Terrestrial Ecology 1974-76; Dir.-Gen. of Research, Dept. of Environment 1976-81; Chief Scientist and Deputy Sec. (Environment Protection), Dept. of Environment and Chief Scientific Adviser, Dept. of Transport 1981-88; Dir.-Gen. Int. Union for Conservation of Nature and Natural Resources 1988-; Bruce Medal, Royal Soc. of Edinburgh and Royal Scottish Geog. Soc.; Silver Medal, UNEP. *Publications include:* Mountains in the Sea: The Story of the Gough Island Expedition 1958, A Perspective of Environmental Pollution 1979. *Leisure interests:* natural history, climbing hills. *Address:* c/o IUCN, avenue du Mont Blanc, CH-1196, Gland, Switzerland.

HOLDING, Clyde, LL.B.; Australian politician; b. 27 April 1931, Melbourne; m.; four c.; ed. Melbourne Univ.; solicitor; mem. Victorian Parl. for Richmond 1962-77; Leader State Parl. Labor Party and Leader of Opposition 1967-77; mem. Fed. Parl. for Melbourne Ports 1977-; Minister for Aboriginal Affairs 1983-86, of Employment Services and Youth Affairs, and Minister Assisting the Treasurer 1987-88, for Immigration, Local Govt. and Ethnic Affairs (with Cabinet status) Feb.-Aug. 1988, of Arts and Territories Aug. 1988-, also Minister Assisting the Prime Minister for Multicultural Affairs; Pres. Victorian Labor Party 1977-79. *Address:* Parliament House, Canberra, A.C.T. 2600; 16 Gipps Street, Richmond, Vic. 3121, Australia.

HOLDSWORTH, Sir (George) Trevor, Kt., F.C.A.; British accountant and business executive; b. 29 May 1927, Bradford; m. Patricia June Ridler 1951; three s.; ed. Keighley Grammar School, Bradford; with Rawlinson, Greaves and Mitchell (accountants), Bradford 1944-51; with Bowater Corpn. 1952-63, becoming Dir. and Controller of U.K. paper making subsidiaries; Deputy Chief Accountant, Guest Keen and Nettlefolds Ltd. 1963-64, Group Chief Accountant 1965-67, Chair. 1980-; Gen. Man. Dir., GKN Screws and Fasteners Ltd. 1968-70, Dir. and Group Controller 1970-72, Group Exec. Vice-Chair., Corpn. Controls and Services 1973-74, Deputy Chair. 1974, Man. Dir. and Deputy Chair. 1977, Chair. 1980-(88); Chair. British Satellite Broadcasting 1987-; Dir. Thorn EMI PLC 1977-86, Equity Capital for Industry Ltd. 1976-83, Midland Bank PLC 1979-88, Prudential Corpn. 1986-, Deputy Chair. 1988-; Chair. Allied Colloids Group PLC 1983-; Dir. Opera Now Enterprises Ltd. 1988; mem. Council, British Inst. of Man. 1974-, Vice-Chair. 1978-80, Chair. 1980, Vice-Pres. 1982; mem. Council C.B.I. 1974-, Econ. and Financial Policy Cttee. C.B.I. 1976-80, Pres. C.B.I. 1988-; Council, Inst. of Dirs. 1978-80, Steering Group on Unemployment 1982, Programmes Unit 1982, Bd. of Govs. Ashridge Man. Coll. 1978-; Chair. Tax Reform Working Party 1984- (Deputy Pres. 1987-88); Vice-Pres. Eng. Employers' Fed. 1980; mem. Exec. Cttee. Soc. of Motor Mfrs. and Traders 1980-83; mem. Eng. Industries Council 1980; Trustee, Anglo-German Foundation for the Study of Industrial Soc. 1980-; mem. British North American Cttee. 1981-85, European Advisory Council AMF Inc. 1982-85, Council Royal Inst. Int. Affairs 1983-; Vice-Pres. Ironbridge Gorge Museum Devt. Trust 1981-; Trustee, Royal Opera House Trust 1981-84; mem. Duke of Edinburgh's Award (Business and Commercial Enterprises Group) 1980, Trustee 1988-; Hon. D.Tech. (Loughborough) 1981; Hon. D.Sc. (Aston) 1982, Hon. D.Eng. (Bradford) 1983; Freeman, City of London; Liveryman, Worshipful Co. of Chartered Accountants in England and Wales; Hon. D. Tech. (Loughborough) 1981, Hon. D.Sc. (Aston) 1982, Hon.D. Business Admin. (Inst. Man. Centre from Buckingham) 1986; Hon. D.Sc. Univ. Sussex; British Inst. Man. Gold Medal 1987; Chartered Accountants Founding Societies' Centenary Award 1983. *Leisure interests:* music, theatre. *Address:* British Satellite Broadcasting Limited, 70 Brompton Road, London, SW3 1EY, England. *Telephone:* (01) 581-1166.

HOLIDAY, Harry, Jr., B.S.; American business executive; b. 2 July 1923, Pittsburgh, Pa.; s. of Harry and Charlotte Poe (née Rutherford) Holiday; m. Kathlyn Collins Watson 1947; two s. one d.; ed. Univ. of Michigan; Special Assignment Metallurgical Eng. Admin., Armco Steel Corpn., Middletown, Ohio 1949-55; Asst. to Supt. Blast Furnace, Hamilton, Ohio 1955-57, Supt. 1957-59; Asst. Gen. Supt. Steel Plant, Middletown 1959-64, Gen. Supt. 1964-66; Dir. Raw Materials 1966-67; Vice-Pres. Steel Operations 1967-69; Exec. Vice-Pres. Steel 1969-74, Pres. 1974-79, Chair and C.E.O. 1982-86; Dir. Reserve Mining Co., Nat. Cash Register, Allis-Chalmers Corpn., Asarco Corpn.; mem. American Inst. of Metallurgical Engineers, American and Int. Iron and Steel Insts. (fmr. Vice-Chair.); J. E. Johnson, Jr., Blast Furnace Award, American Inst. of Metallurgical Engineers. *Address:* Armco Inc., 703 Curtis Street, Middletown, Ohio 45042, U.S.A.

HOLKERI, Harri Hermanni, M.POL.SC.; Finnish politician; b. 6 Jan. 1937, Oripää; Sec. Nat. Coalition Party Youth League 1959-60, Information Sec. 1960-62; Information Sec. Nat. Coalition Party 1962-64, Research Sec. 1964-65, Party Sec. 1965-71, Chair. 1971-79; mem. Helsinki City Council 1969-88, Chair. 1981-87; mem. Parl. 1970-78; mem. Bd. of Man. Bank of Finland 1978-; Chair. Admin. Council, Valmet Oy (State-Controlled eng. corpn.) Prime Minister of Finland April 1987-. *Address:* Office of the Prime Minister, Aleksanterinkatu 3D, 00170 Helsinki, Finland. *Telephone:* (90) 1601.

HOLLAI, Imre; Hungarian diplomatist; b. 22 Jan. 1925, Budapest; m. Margit Fejes 1949; one s.; entered Foreign Service 1949; Counsellor Perm. Mission of Hungary to UN 1956-60; Head of Int. Dept., Cen. Cttee., Hungarian Socialist Workers' Party 1960-63; Amb. to Greece, concurrently accred. to Cyprus 1964-70, 1984-; Deputy Minister of Foreign Affairs 1970-74, 1980-84; Perm. Rep. to UN 1974-80; Pres. UN Gen. Assembly 1982. *Leisure interests:* music, hunting. *Address:* Hungarian Embassy, Odos Kalvou 16, Palaio Psychico, Athens, Greece.

HOLLÁN, R. Susan; Hungarian professor of haematology; b. 26 Oct. 1920, Budapest; d. of Dr. Henrik Hollán and Dr. Malvin Hornik; m. Dr. György Révész; one s. one d.; ed. Univ. Medical School, Budapest; Internist, Rokus Hospital, Budapest 1945-50; Research Fellow, Univ. Med. School, Budapest 1950-54; Science Adviser, Inst. for Experimental Medical Research 1954-; Dir. Nat. Inst. of Haematology and Blood Transfusion 1959-85, Dir.-Gen. 1985-; Prof. of Haematology, Postgraduate Med. School 1970-; Corresp. mem. Hungarian Acad. of Sciences 1973, mem. 1982- (mem. of Presidium 1976-84); fmr. Pres. Int. Soc. of Haematology and Vice-Pres. Int. Soc. of Blood Transfusion; Hon. mem. Polish Soc. of Haematology, German Soc. of Haematology (Fed. Repub. of Germany), Purkinje Soc. (Czechoslovakia), Turkish Soc. of Haematology, All-Union Scientific Soc. of Haematology and Blood Transfusion (U.S.S.R.); Foreign Corresp. mem. Soc. de Biologie, Collège de France, Paris; Vice-Pres. Hungarian Soc. of Haematology, Int. Physicians Prevention of Nuclear War 1983-; Hon. Pres. Hungarian Soc. of Human Genetics; mem. WHO Expert Cttee. on Biological Standardization in Haematology; mem. Clinical and Immunological Work Cttee. of Hungarian Acad. of Sciences; mem. Bd. of Special Cttee. for Clinical Sciences; Exec. mem. Hungarian Medical Research Council; Editor-in-Chief Hungarian Medical Encyclopaedia and Haematologia (quarterly); mem. HSWP Cen. Cttee. 1975-; Hungarian Academic Award 1970; State Prize 1974; Socialist Hungary Medal. *Publications:* Basic Problems of Transfusion 1965, Haemoglobins and Haemoglobinopathies 1972, Genetics, Structure and Function of Blood Cells 1980; over 200 papers in Hungarian and international medical journals. *Leisure interest:* fine arts. *Address:* Daróczi ut 24, 1113 Budapest (Office); Palánta u. 10-12, H-1025 Budapest, Hungary (Home). *Telephone:* 666-004 (Office).

HOLLAND, Eric Sidney Fostyn; New Zealand politician and business executive; b. 28 June 1921, Christchurch; s. of the late Sir Sidney Holland (fmr. Prime Minister of New Zealand) and Lady (Florence) Holland; m. 1st 1944, 2nd 1972; one s. two d.; ed. Elmwood School, St. Andrew's Coll. and Canterbury Univ. Coll.; M.P. 1967; Minister of Housing, Minister in Charge of State Advances Corpn. and Assoc. Minister of Labour Feb.-Nov. 1972; Minister of Energy Resources, Electricity and Mines 1975-77, of Housing 1977-78; National Party. *Leisure interests:* golf, contract bridge, lawn bowls.

HOLLAND, Heinrich Dieter, PH.D.; American professor of geology; b. 27 May 1927, Mannheim, Germany; s. of Otto Holland and Jeanette (Liebrecht) Holland; m. Alice Tilghman Pusey 1953; three s. one d.; ed. Princeton and Columbia Univs.; mem. Faculty, Princeton Univ. 1950-72, Prof. of Geology 1966-72; Prof. of Geochemistry, Harvard Univ. 1972-; Visiting Prof., Pa. State Univ. 1985-86; Fellow, Geological Soc. of America, Mineral Soc. of America, Geochemical Soc. (Pres. 1970-71), American Geophysical Union; Nat. Science Foundation Fellow, Oxford Univ. 1956-57; von Humboldt Prize 1980; Guggenheim Fellow 1975-76. *Publications:* Hydrothermal Uranium Deposits 1977, The Chemistry of the Atmosphere and Oceans 1978, The Chemical Evolution of the Atmosphere and Oceans 1984, articles in professional journals. *Address:* Department of Earth and Planetary Sciences, Harvard University, 306 Hoffman Laboratory, 20 Oxford Street, Cambridge, Mass. 02138, U.S.A.

HOLLANDER, John, PH.D.; American poet and professor of English; b. 28 Oct. 1929, New York; s. of Franklin and Muriel (Kornfeld) Hollander; m. 1st Anne Loesser 1953 (divorced 1977); two d.; 2nd Natalie Charkow 1981; ed. Columbia Univ., Harvard Univ., and Indiana Univ.; Lecturer in English, Connecticut Coll. 1957-59; Instructor in English, Yale Univ. 1959-61, Asst. Prof. of English 1961-64, Assoc. Prof. 1964-66, Prof. 1977-85, A. Bartlett Giamatti Prof. 1986-; Prof. of English, Hunter Coll., New York 1966-77; Christian Gauss Seminarian, Princeton Univ. 1962; Visiting Prof., School of Letters and Linguistic Inst., Indiana Univ. 1964; Visiting Prof. Seminar in American Studies, Salzburg, Austria 1965; editorial assoc. for poetry Partisan Review 1959-65; mem. poetry bd. Wesleyan Univ. Press 1959-62; mem. Editorial Bd. 1981-; Fellow, American Acad. of Arts and Sciences; mem. English Inst., Nat. Inst. of Arts and Letters; Fellow Ezra Stiles Coll., Yale Univ. 1961-64; Overseas Fellow Churchill Coll., Univ. of Cambridge 1967-68; Fellow Nat. Endowment for Humanities 1973-, Silliman Coll. 1977-; Hon. D.Litt (Marietta Coll.) 1982; Levinson Prize 1964, Nat. Inst. of Arts and Letters Award 1963, Guggenheim Fellow 1979-80, Chancellor, Acad. of American Poets 1981-, Bollingen Prize 1983. *Publications include:* A Crackling of Thorns 1958, The Untuning of the Sky 1961, Movie-Going and Other Poems 1962, Visions from the Ramble 1965, Types of Shape 1969, The Night Mirror 1971, Town and Country Matters 1972, Selected Poems 1972, The Head of the Bed 1974, Tales Told of the Fathers 1975, Vision and Resonance 1975, Reflections on Espionage 1976, Spectral Emanations 1978, In Place 1978, Blue Wine 1979, The Figure of Echo 1981, Rhyme's Reason 1981, Powers of Thirteen 1983, In

Time and Place 1986, Harp Lake 1988; contributor of numerous poems and articles to journals; editor and contributing editor of numerous books including: Poems of Ben Jonson 1961, The Wind and the Rain 1961, Jiggery-Pokery 1966, Poems of Our Moment 1968, Modern Poetry: Essays in Criticism 1968, American Short Stories since 1945 1968, The Oxford Anthology of English Literature (with Frank Kermode, q.v.) 1973, For I. A. Richards: Essays in his Honor 1973, Literature as Experience (with Irving Howe and David Bromwich) 1979, Some Fugitives Take Cover 1988, Melodious Guile 1988; contributing editor Harper's magazine 1969-71. *Address:* c/o Dept of English, Yale University, New Haven, Conn. 06520, U.S.A.

HOLLENDER, Louis François, DR.MED.; French professor of surgery; b. 15 Feb. 1922, Strasbourg; s. of Emile Hollender and Clotilde Fritsch; m. Nicole Ziegler 1957; two d.; ed. Medical Faculties of Strasbourg and Paris, Harvard Medical School, Boston, U.S.A. and Washington Univ., St. Louis; Resident, Strasbourg Univ. Hosp. 1945-53, Chief Resident 1953-55, Assoc. Prof. of Gen. Surgery 1955-59, Chief Surgeon, Head of Dept. 1959-69, Prof. of Digestive and Gen. Surgery and Head of Dept., Prof. of Digestive and Gen. Surgery 1969-; Dr. h.c. (Athens), (Cordoba), (L'Aquila); mem. Acad. of Surgery; Assoc. mem. Acad. of Medicine; Hon. F.R.C.S. (England); F.A.C.S. *Publications:* numerous scientific papers. *Leisure interests:* skiing, tennis. *Address:* 2 rue Blessig, F 67000 Strasbourg, France (Home). *Telephone:* 88.35.31.84.

HÖLLERER, Walter Friedrich, DR.PHIL.; German writer and critic; b. 19 Dec. 1922, Sulzbach-Rosenberg, Bavaria; s. of Hans and Christine Höllerer, née Pürkner; m. Renate von Mangoldt 1965; two s.; ed. Univs. of Erlangen, Göttingen and Heidelberg; Dozent in German Studies, Frankfurt/Main Univ. 1958, Münster Univ. 1959; Ord. Prof. of Literature, Berlin Technical Univ. 1959-, Dir. Inst. für Sprache im technischen Zeitalter 1961-; Steuben Visiting Prof., Univ. of Wis. 1960; Dir. Literarisches Colloquium, Berlin 1963-; Prof. Univ. of Ill., Urbana 1973; Ed. Akzente: Zeitschrift für Dichtung 1954 (now co-publr.), Sprache im technischen Zeitalter 1961 (now publr.); publr. Literatur als Kunst; mem. German PEN Club, Akad. für Sprache und Dichtung, Berlin Acad. of Arts, Group 1947, Communità Europea degli Scrittori, Schutzverband der Schriftsteller deutscher Sprache; Fontane Prize, Johann Heinrich Merck Prize. *Publications:* Der andere Gast (poems) 1952, 1964, Transit: Lyrikbuch der Jahrhundertmitte (anthology) 1956, Zwischen Klassik und Moderne: Lachen und Weinen in der Dichtung einer Übergangszeit (essays) 1958, Junge amerikanische Lyrik 1961, Spiele in einem Akt 1962, Gedichte 1964, Theorie der modernen Lyrik 1965, Modernes Theater auf kleinen Bühnen 1966, Ein Gedicht und sein Autor (poems and essays) 1967, Ausserhalb der Saison (poems) 1967, Systeme (poems) 1969, Elite und Utopie 1969, Dramaturgisches (correspondence with Max Frisch q.v.) 1969, Die Elephantenuhr (novel) 1973, 1975, Hier wo die Welt anfing 1974, Geschichte, die nicht im Geschichtsbuch steht 1976, Alle Vögel alle (comedy) 1978, Berlin: Übern Damm und durch die Dörfer (essays) 1978, Gedichte 1942-82 1982, Autoren im Haus, Zwanzig Jahre Literatur in Berlin 1982, Die Leute von Serendip erkunden die Giftfabrik, Sprache 1 1986, Walter Höllerers Oberpfälzische Weltei-Erkundungen 1987. *Address:* Heerstrasse 99, 1 Berlin 19, Federal Republic of Germany. *Telephone:* 304-58-79.

HOLLEY, Robert W., PH.D.; American biochemist; b. 28 Jan. 1922, Urbana, Ill.; s. of Charles E. and Viola E. Holley; m. Ann Dworkin 1945; one s.; ed. Univ. of Illinois, Cornell Univ. and State Coll. of Washington; Asst. Prof. and Assoc. Prof. of Organic Chem., Cornell Univ., N.Y., State Agricultural Experiment Station 1948-57; Research-Chemist U.S. Plant, Soil and Nutrition Lab., ARS, USDA 1957-64; at Cornell Univ. Prof. of Biochemistry and Molecular Biology 1964-69, Chair. of Dept. 1965-66; Resident Fellow, Salk Inst. for Biological Studies 1968-; Albert Lasker Award for basic medical research 1965, U.S. Dept of Agric., Distinguished Service Award 1965, U.S. Steel Foundation Award in Molecular Biology, Nat. Acad. of Sciences 1967, Nobel Prize for Medicine (with M. Nirenberg and H. G. Khorana) for work on the genetic code and its function in protein synthesis 1968. *Leisure interests:* hiking, sculpture. *Address:* The Salk Institute for Biological Studies, P.O. Box 85800, San Diego, Calif. 92138, U.S.A. *Telephone:* 619-453-4100.

HOLLIDAY, Robin, PH.D., F.R.S.; British geneticist; b. 6 Nov. 1932, Palestine; s. of Clifford Holliday and Eunice Holliday; m. 1st Diana Collet Parsons 1957 (divorced 1983), one s. three d.; 2nd Lily I. Huschtscha 1986; ed. Hitchin Grammar School and Univ. of Cambridge; mem. scientific staff, Dept. of Genetics, John Innes Inst. Bayfordbury, Herts 1958-65; mem. scientific staff, Div. of Microbiology, Nat. Inst. for Medical Research 1965-70, Head, Div. of Genetics 1970-88; Chief Research Scientist C.S.I.R.O. 1988-. *Publications:* The Science of Human Progress 1981, Genes, Proteins and Cellular Ageing 1986; about 150 research publs. *Leisure interests:* travel, sculpture. *Address:* C.S.I.R.O. Division of Molecular Biology, P.O. Box 184, North Ryde, Sydney, N.S.W. 2113, Australia. *Telephone:* (02) 886 4888.

HOLLIGER, Heinz; Swiss oboist and composer; b. 1939, Langenthal; m. Ursula Holliger; ed. in Berne, Paris and Basel under Emile Cassagnaud (oboe) and Pierre Boulez (composition); Prof. of Oboe, Freiberg Music Acad. 1965-; has appeared at all the major European music festivals and in Japan, U.S.A., Australia, Israel, etc.; recorded over 80 works, mainly

for Philips and Deutsche Grammophon; recipient of several international prizes. *Compositions include:* Der magische Tänzer, Trio, Siebengesang, Wind Quintet, Dona nobis pacem, Pneuma, Psalm, Cardiophonie, Kreis, String Quartet, Atembogen, Die Jahreszeiten, Come and Go, Not I. *Address:* c/o Ingpen & Williams, 14 Kensington Court, London, W.8, England.

HOLLINGS, Ernest F., B.A., LL.B.; American lawyer and politician; b. 1 Jan. 1922; m. 2nd Rita Liddy 1971; two s. two d. (by previous marriage); ed. Charleston Public Schools, The Citadel and Univ. of S. Carolina; served U.S. Army 1942-45; admitted to S. Carolina Bar 1947; mem. S. Carolina House of Reps. 1948-54, Speaker *pro tem.* 1951-53; Lieut.-Gov. of S. Carolina 1955-59, Gov. of S. Carolina 1959-63; law practice, Charleston 1963-66; Senator from S. Carolina 1966-; Chair. Democratic Senatorial Campaign Cttee. 1971-73; mem. Hoover Comm. on Intelligence Activities 1954-55, President's Advisory Comm. on Intergovernmental Relations 1959-63; mem. Senate Cttees. on Appropriations, Commerce, Budget, Chair. Budget Cttee. 1980, Commerce Cttee. 1982; mem. Democratic Policy Cttee., Office of Tech. Assessment, Nat. Ocean Policy Study; Democrat. *Publication:* The Case against Hunger: A Demand for a National Policy 1970. *Address:* Room 125, Russell Senate Office Building, Washington, D.C. 20510, U.S.A. (Office).

HOLLINGS, (George) Leslie, A.M.; British-Australian journalist; b. 25 Feb. 1923, Hull; s. of late John Hollings and Elizabeth (Singleton) Hollings; m. Joan Gwendoline Pratt 1951; two s.; ed. N.E. Tech. School of Art, Colchester, Essex; Sub-Ed. The Daily Telegraph, London 1957-59; Sub-Ed. The Times, London 1959-65; Ed. The Australian 1975-80, Man. Ed. 1980-82, Ed.-in-Chief 1983-88; Dir. News Ltd. 1987-; mem. Policy Cttee., Bureau of Meteorology 1983-87; mem. Council of Australian Nat. Gallery 1985-, Deputy Chair. 1987-. *Leisure interests:* reading, opera, ballet, gardening, walking. *Address:* The Australian, 2 Holt Street, Surry Hills, Sydney, New South Wales 2010, Australia. *Telephone:* (02) 288 3000 (Office).

HOLLINGS, Rev. Michael Richard, M.A., M.C.; British parish priest; b. 30 Dec. 1921; s. of Lieut. Commdr. Richard Eustace Hollings, R.N. and Agnes M. (née Hamilton-Dalrymple) Hollings; ed. Beaumont Coll., St. Catherine's Coll., Oxford; commd. Sandhurst 1941, served as Maj. Coldstream Guards 1942-45; trained for priesthood Beda Coll., Rome 1946-50, ordained Rome 1950; Asst. Priest St. Patrick's, Soho Square, London 1950-54, Chaplain Westminster Cathedral 1954-58, Asst. Chaplain London Univ. 1958-59; Religious Adviser ATV 1958-59, Rediffusion 1959-68, Thames TV 1968; Parish Priest, St. Anselm's, Southall 1970-78, St. Mary of the Angels, Bayswater 1978-; mem. Southall Chamber of Commerce 1971-78, Oxford and Cambridge Catholic Educ. Bd. 1971-, Exec. Council of Christians and Jews 1971-79; Chaplain to Sovereign Mil. Order of Malta 1957, to Roman Catholics at Oxford Univ. 1959-70, to Nat. Council of Lay Apostolate 1970-74, to Catholic Inst. of Int. Relations 1971-. *Publications:* Hey, You! 1955, Purple Times 1957, Chaplaincraft 1963, The One Who Listens 1971, The Pastoral Care of Homosexuals 1971, It's Me, O Lord 1972, Day by Day 1972, The Shade of His Hand 1973, Restoring the Streets 1974, I Will Be There 1975, You Must Be Joking, Lord 1975, The Catholic Prayer Book 1976, Alive to Death 1976, Living Priesthood 1977, His People's Way of Talking 1978, As Was His Custom 1979; contrib. to Tablet, Clergy Review, Life of the Spirit. *Leisure interests:* reading, walking. *Address:* St. Mary of the Angels, Moorhouse Road, Bayswater, London, W2 5DJ, England. *Telephone:* 01-229 0487.

HOLLÓ, Janos; Hungarian chemical engineer; b. 20 Aug. 1919, Szentes; ed. Tech. Univ., Budapest; Tech. Dir. Budapest Breweries 1948; Prof. Agricultural and Chemical Tech., Budapest Tech. Univ. 1952-; Dean Chemical Eng. Faculty 1955-57, 1963-72; Dir. Hungarian Acad. of Sciences Cen. Research Inst. of Chemistry 1972-; mem. Hungarian Acad. of Sciences 1967-; Dr. h.c. (Tech. Univ. of Vienna) 1973, (West Berlin) 1984; foreign mem. Finnish Acad. of Tech. Sciences 1984, Acad. of Sciences G.D.R. 1984; hon. mem. Polish Science Asscn. of Food Industries 1971; Copernicus medal 1974; Vice-Pres. Comm. Int. des Industries Agricoles et Alimentaires (CIIA); science cttee. Chair. Pres., Hon. Pres. 1982-; Chair. Cereals and Pulses Cttee. 1960-, Agricultural and Food Products Cttee. 1971-, Int. Org. for Standardization (ISO); Gen. Sec. Scientific Asscn. of Hungary Food Industry, Co-Chair., Pres. 1981-; Pres. Int. Soc. for Fat Research (ISF) 1964-66, 1982-83, Exec. mem. 1964-, Chief Ed. Acta Alimentaria, Journal of Food Investigations; Order Hungarian People's Repub. 1952, Commandeur Ordre du mérite pour la recherche et l'invention 1962; medal of Comm. Int. des Industries Agriccoles 1963; Chevalier des Palmes académiques 1967; Labour Order of Merit 1971, 1979; Saare medal 1972; Premio d'oro Interpetrol 1973; State Prize 1975; Prix d'Honneur de l'Acad. Int. du Lutèce 1978; Chevreul medal 1986; Normann medal 1986; Hon. mem. Austrian Soc. for Food and Biochemistry 1983; mem. numerous editorial bds. *Address:* 1026 Budapest, Guyon Richárd utca 9, Hungary. *Telephone:* 353-340.

HOLLOM, Sir Jasper (Quintus), K.B.E.; British banker b. 16 Dec. 1917, Bromley, Kent; s. of Arthur Hollom and Kate Louisa Hollom; m. Patricia Elizabeth Mary Ellis 1954; ed. King's School, Bruton; entered Bank of England 1936, Deputy Cashier 1956-62, Chief Cashier 1962-66, Exec. Dir. 1966-70; Deputy Governor 1970-80, Dir. 1980-84; Chair. Panel on Takeovers and Mergers June 1980-87; Dir. Portals Holdings 1980-88, Gen.

Accident, Fire and Life Assurance Corpn. 1980–85; External Dir. BAT Industries 1980–87; Chair. Commonwealth Devt. Finance Co. 1980–86; Pres. Council of Foreign Bondholders 1983–; Chair. Council for the Securities Industry 1985–86; Chair. Eagle Star Holdings PLC 1985–87, Eagle Star Insurance Co. Ltd. 1985–87. *Address:* High Wood, Selborne, Hants., England. *Telephone:* 042 050 317.

HOLLOWAY, Bruce William, PH.D., D.SC., F.A.A.; Australian professor of genetics; b. 9 Jan. 1928, Adelaide; s. of Albert Holloway and Gertrude C. Walkem; m. Brenda D. Gray 1952; one s. one d.; ed. Scotch Coll., Adelaide, Univ. of Adelaide and Calif. Inst. of Tech.; Lecturer in Plant Pathology, Waite Agric. Research Inst. 1949–50; Research Fellow in Microbial Genetics, John Curtin School of Medicine, Australian Nat. Univ. 1953–56; Sr. Lecturer 1956–60, then Reader in Microbial Genetics, Univ. of Melbourne 1956–67; Foundation Prof. of Genetics, Monash Univ. 1968–; Visiting Lecturer in Microbiology and Fellow, M.I.T. 1962–63; Sec. Biological Sciences Acad. of Science 1982–; Visiting Prof. Univ. of Newcastle-upon-Tyne 1977–78; Chair. Nat. Biotechnology Program Research Grants Scheme 1983–86. *Publications:* over 100 papers on genetics and microbiology in scientific journals. *Leisure interests:* music, reading, walking by the sea. *Address:* Department of Genetics, Monash University, Clayton, Vic., 3168 (Office); 22 Reading Avenue, North Balwyn, Vic., 3104, Australia (Home). *Telephone:* 03-541 0811 (Office); 03-857 7171 (Home).

HOLLOWAY, Admiral James Lemuel, III; American naval officer (retd.); b. 23 Feb. 1922, Charleston, S. Carolina; s. of Admiral James L. Holloway and late Jean Hagood; m. Dabney Rawlings 1942; one s. (died 1964) two d.; ed. U.S. Naval Acad., Md; Commissioned Ensign in U.S. Navy 1942, served on destroyers in Atlantic and Pacific Theatres, World War II; Gunnery Officer USS Bennion, took part in Battle of Surigao Straits; Exec. Officer of Fighter Squadron Fifty-two, USS Boxer, Korean War 1952–54; Commdr. Attack Squadron Eighty-three, USS Essex, Sixth Fleet during Lebanon landings 1958; Nat. War Coll. 1961; Nuclear training under Admiral Rickover 1963; Commdg. Officer USS Enterprise (first nuclear-powered carrier) Vietnam War 1965–67; promoted to rank of Rear-Admiral 1967; Dir. Strike Warfare Div., Program Coordinator Nuclear Attack Carrier Program, Office of Chief of Naval Operations; Commdr. Sixth Fleet Carrier Striking Force, directed operations in E. Mediterranean during Jordanian crisis 1970; Deputy C.-in-C. Atlantic and U.S. Atlantic Fleet, Vice-Admiral 1971; Commdr. Seventh Fleet during combat operations in Viet-Nam 1972–73; Vice-Chief of Naval Operations 1973–74; Chief of Naval Operations 1974–78; mem. Jt. Chiefs of Staff 1974–78; Pres. U.S. Naval Historical Foundation 1980–; Chair. Special Operations Review Group, Iranian Hostage Rescue 1981; Special Envoy of Vice-Pres. of U.S.A. to Bahrain 1986; mem. Pres.'s Comm. on Merchant Marine and Defense 1986; Pres. Council of American Flagship Operators 1981–; Chair. of Bd. Assen. of Naval Aviation; Chair. Academic Advisory Bd. to U.S. Naval Acad.; Exec. Dir., Vice-Pres.'s Task Force on Combating Terrorism 1985; Pres.'s Blue Ribbon Comm. on Defense Man. 1985–86; Commr., Comm. on Merchant Marine and Defense 1987, Comm. on Integrated Long-Term Strategy 1987; mem. Bd. of Dirs. UNC Inc. 1987–; Tech. Adviser for film Top Gun 1986; awarded numerous medals for meritorious service including Defence Distinguished Service Medal (twice), Navy Distinguished Service Medal (four times), Legion of Merit, Distinguished Flying Cross, Bronze Star Medal with Combat "V", Air Medal (four times), and many foreign decorations. *Publications:* numerous articles on aviation, sealift and defence organization. *Leisure interest:* sailing. *Address:* 1694 Epping Farms Lane, Annapolis, Md. 21401, U.S.A. *Telephone:* (301) 849-2115.

HOLLOWAY, John, D.LITT., LITT.D., F.R.S.L.; British professor of Modern English (retd.); b. 1 Aug. 1920; s. of George Holloway and Evelyn Astbury; m. 1st Audrey Gooding 1946, one s. one d.; m. 2nd Joan Black 1978; ed. New Coll., Oxford; war service, commissioned in artillery, seconded to Intelligence; temp. lecturer in Philosophy, New Coll. 1945; Fellow of All Souls Coll., Oxford 1946–60; Lecturer in English, Univ. of Aberdeen 1949–54; Lecturer in English, Cambridge Univ. 1954–66, Reader in Modern English 1966, Fellow of Queens' Coll., 1955–, Prof. of Modern English 1972–82; Visiting Prof., Chicago 1965, Johns Hopkins Univ. 1972, Charlottesville, Va. 1979, N.Y. Univ. (Berg Prof.) 1987; Visiting Fellow, Univ. of Wellington 1984, Univ. of Kyoto 1986; various univ. admin. positions. *Publications:* Language and Intelligence 1951, The Victorian Sage 1953, The Charted Mirror (essays) 1960, (ed.) Poems of the Mid-Century 1957, (ed.) Selections from Shelley 1960, Shakespeare's Tragedies 1961, The Colours of Clarity (essays) 1964, The Lion Hunt 1964, Widening Horizons in English Verse 1966, Blake, The Lyric Poetry 1968, The Establishment of English 1972, Later English Broadside Ballads Vol. I 1975, Vol. II 1979 (both vols. with Joan Black), The Proud Knowledge 1977, Narrative and Structure 1979, The Slumber of Apollo 1983, Oxford Book of Local Verses 1987; contribs. to journals; verse: The Minute 1956, The Fugue 1960, The Landfallers 1962, Wood and Windfall 1965, New Poems 1970, Planet of Winds 1977. *Address:* c/o Queens' College, Cambridge, England. *Telephone:* (0223) 335511.

HOLLOWAY, Rt. Rev. Richard Frederick, B.D., S.T.M.; British ecclesiastic; b. 26 Nov. 1933, Glasgow; s. of Arthur Holloway and Mary Holloway; m. Jean Holloway 1963; one s. two d.; ed. Kelham Theological Coll., Edinburgh Theological Coll. and Union Theological Seminary, New York; Curate, St.

Ninian's, Glasgow 1959–63; Priest-in-charge, St. Margaret's and St. Mungo's, Gorbals, Glasgow 1963–68; Rector, Old St. Paul's, Edinburgh 1968–80, Church of the Advent, Boston, Mass. 1980–84; Vicar, St. Mary Magdalen's, Oxford 1984–86; Bishop of Edin. 1986–; Winifred M. Stanford Award for The Killing 1984. *Publications include:* Beyond Belief 1981, The Killing 1984, Paradoxes of Christian Faith and Life 1984, The Sidelong Glance 1985, The Way of the Cross 1986, Seven to Flee, Seven to Follow 1986, Crossfire 1987. *Address:* The Diocesan Centre, Walpole Hall, Chester Street, Edinburgh, EH3 7EN (Office); 30 Kingsburgh Road, Edinburgh, EH12 6DZ, Scotland (Home). *Telephone:* 031-226 3359; 031-337 7010 (Home).

HOLLOWAY, Robin Greville, PH.D., D.MUS.; British composer, writer on music and university teacher; b. 19 Oct. 1943, Leamington Spa; s. of Robert Charles Holloway and Pamela Mary Holloway (née Jacob); ed. St. Paul's Cathedral Choir School, King's Coll. School, Wimbledon, King's Coll., Cambridge and New Coll., Oxford; Lecturer in Music, Univ. of Cambridge 1975–; Fellow of Gonville and Caius Coll., Cambridge 1969–; compositions include Garden Music opus 1 1962, Scenes from Schumann opus 13 1970, Evening with Angels opus 17 1972, Domination of Black opus 23 1973, Clarissa opus 30 1976, Second Concerto for Orchestra opus 40 1979, Brand opus 48 1981, Women in War opus 51 1982, Seascape and Harvest opus 55 1983, Viola Concerto opus 56 1984, Peer Gynt opus 60 1985. *Leisure interest:* cities. *Address:* Gonville and Caius College, Cambridge, CB2 1TA, England. *Telephone:* Cambridge 335424.

HOLM, Elisabeth; Swedish politician; b. 21 Nov. 1917; Karlstad, Sweden; d. of Adolf and Marie-Louise Larsson; m. Nils Holm; three c.; ed. Univ. of Karlstad; State registered nurse; fmr. First Vice-Chair. Moderate Party Women's Assen.; Chair. Swedish Moderate Party, Örebro County; County Councillor for opposition, County of Örebro 1976–; mem. County Admin. Cttee., Health and Medical Services Bd., etc.; mem. Municipal Council and Municipal Admin. Bd., Karlskoga; Opposition Councillor, Karlskoga; Minister for Public Health and Medical Services Oct. 1979–81; Consultant, Inst. for Medical Jurisdiction 1981–. *Address:* Sneddarliden 8, 691 44 Karlskoga, Sweden.

HOLM, Ian; British actor; b. 12 Sept. 1931, Ilford; s. of Dr. James Harvey Cuthbert and Jean Wilson Cuthbert; m. 1st Lynn Mary Shaw 1955 (divorced 1965), one s. three d.; m. 2nd Sophie Baker 1982, one s.; ed. Chigwell Grammar School, Essex, RADA (Royal Acad. of Dramatic Art); joined Shakespeare Memorial Theatre 1954; Worthing Repertory 1956; on tour with Lord Olivier (q.v.) in Titus Andronicus 1957; mem. R.S.C. 1958–67. *Roles include:* Puck, Ariel, Lorenzo, Henry V, Richard III, The Fool (in King Lear), Lennie (in The Homecoming). *Films include:* Young Winston, Oh! What a Lovely War, Alien, All Quiet on the Western Front, Chariots of Fire, The Return of the Soldier, Greystoke 1984, Laughterhouse 1984, Brazil 1985, Wetherby 1985, Dance with a Stranger 1985, Dreamchild 1985, Henry V. *Television appearances include:* The Lost Boys 1979, We, the Accused 1980, The Bell 1981, Strike 1981, Inside the Third Reich 1982, Mr. and Mrs. Edgehill 1985, The Browning Version 1986, Game, Set and Match 1988, The Endless Game 1989. *Leisure interest:* tennis. *Address:* c/o Julian Belfrage Assocs., 60 St. James Street, London, S.W.1, England.

HOLM, Richard H, PH.D.; American professor of chemistry; b. 24 Sept. 1933, Boston, Mass.; m. Florence L. Jacintho 1958; four c.; ed. Univ. of Mass. and M.I.T.; Asst. Prof. of Chem., Harvard Univ. 1960–65; Assoc. Prof. of Chem. Univ. of Wisconsin 1965–67; Prof. of Chem. M.I.T. 1967–75, Stanford Univ. 1975–80; Prof. of Chem. Harvard Univ. 1980–83, Higgins Prof. 1983–, Chair. Dept. of Chem. 1983–86; mem. American Acad. of Arts and Sciences, N.A.S.; several awards for research in inorganic chem.; A.M. (h.c.); D.Sc. (h.c.). *Publications:* numerous research papers in professional journals in the fields of inorganic chemistry and biochemistry. *Address:* Department of Chemistry, Harvard University, Cambridge, Mass. 02138 (Office); 40 Temple Street, Belmont, Mass. 02178, U.S.A. (Home).

HOLM, Tryggve O. A.; Swedish business executive; b. 5 Feb. 1905, Kristinehamn; s. of Hans Th. Holm and Augusta Mathiesen; m. Gunvor Bruu 1929; two d.; ed. Royal Inst. of Technology, Stockholm, and Carnegie Inst. of Technology, Pittsburgh, U.S.A.; Engineer, AB Bofors Sweden 1929–30, Hess Bright Mfg. Co., Philadelphia 1930–31; Engineer, Steel Works, AB Bofors 1932–36, Chief Engineer and Man. 1936–39; Pres. AB Svenska Järnvägsverkstäderna, Linköping 1940–50, Saab Aktiebolag Linköping 1950–67; Chair. Swedish Metal Trades Employers' Assen. 1955–67, Swedish Employers' Confederation 1967–76, Gusums Bruk AB 1964–77, Hexagon AB 1965–77; Chair. of Bd. Skandinaviska Träimport AB 1967–84, of Bd. Vegete Insurance Co. 1968–75, Alfa-Laval AB 1969–80, AB Bofors 1973–78; mem. Bd. AB Svenska Järnvägsverkstäderna 1940–76, Saab-Scania AB 1947–80, AB Bofors 1968–78, SILA 1950–84, Holmens Bruk AB 1955–79, Nat. Pension Insurance Fund 1959–78, ABA 1957–84, Skandinaviska Enskilda Banken 1969–75; mem. Assembly of Reps. Scandinavian Airlines System 1962–84 (mem. Bd. 1957–62); Danish Consul 1949–84; Dr. of Tech. h.c. 1986; several decorations. *Leisure interest:* hunting. *Address:* Nygaten 54, Linköping (Office); Vasavägen 15, Linköping, Sweden (Home). *Telephone:* 013-10-08-20 (Office); 013-12-58-16 (Home).

HOLMAN, Ralph Theodore, PH.D.; American professor of biochemistry; b. 4 March 1918, Minneapolis, Minn.; s. of Alfred Theodore Holman and

May Carlia Anna Nilson; m. Karla Calais 1943; one s.; ed. Univ. of Minnesota and Rutgers Univ., New Brunswick, New Jersey; Instructor, Physiological Chem., Univ. of Minn. 1944–46; Medical Nobel Inst., Stockholm, Sweden 1946–47; American-Scandinavian Foundation Fellow, Univ. of Uppsala, Sweden 1947; Assoc. Prof. of Biochemistry and Nutrition, Texas A. & M. Univ. 1948–51; Assoc. Prof. of Biochemistry, Hormel Inst., Univ. of Minn. 1951–56, Prof. 1956–, Exec. Dir. Hormel Inst. 1975–85, Emer. Exec. Dir. 1985–; Prof. of Biochemistry, Univ. of Minn. Medical School; Prof. of Biochemistry, Mayo Medical School; Pres. American Oil Chem. Soc. 1974–75; Fellow American Inst. of Nutrition; mem. N.A.S., Hormel Foundation; Pres. and Organizer, Golden Jubilee Int. Congress, Essential Fatty Acids Prostaglandins 1980; Borden Award 1966; Bailey Award, American Oil Chem. Soc.; Award in Lipid Chem., American Oil Chem. Soc. and other prizes; research interests: essential polyunsaturated fatty acids, their quantified requirements, role in liver function and abnormalities in disease. *Publications:* 370 publs. on lipid biochemistry and nutrition; Ed. Lipids 1974–85, Progress in Lipid Research 1951–. *Leisure interests:* writing, history, orchids, orchid research, gardening and construction. *Address:* The Hormel Institute, University of Minnesota, 801 16th Avenue N.E., Austin, Minn. 55912; 1403 2nd Avenue S.W., Austin, Minn. 55912, U.S.A. (Home). *Telephone:* (507) 433-8804 (Univ.); (507) 437-3504 (Home).

HOLMBERG, Bo; Swedish politician; b. 17 Nov. 1942, Kramfors; two s. one d.; ed. Univ. Coll. of Social Work and Public Admin. Stockholm; schools asst., planning sec. and political sec. Västernorrland Co. Council 1968–76; Co. Council Commr. 1976–82; Chair. Co. Council Exec. Cttee. 1979; Chair. Dist. Br. Social Democratic Party (SDP) 1977– mem. Bd. 1978–; Deputy mem. Bd. Asscn. of Swedish County Councils 1980; Minister of Public Admin. 1982–88. *Address:* c/o Ministry of Public Administration, Tegelbacken 2, 103 33 Stockholm, Sweden.

HOLMBOE, Vagn; Danish composer; b. 20 Dec. 1909, Horsens, Jutland; s. of Jens Christian Gylding Holmboe and Marie Dreyer; m. Meta Josefa Elisaveta Graf 1933; one s. one d.; ed. Royal Danish Music Conservatory; Teacher at Royal Inst. for Blind 1940–49; music critic Politiken 1947–55; Prof. of Composition and Orchestration, Royal Danish Music Conservatory 1955–66; mem. Bd. of Danish Composers' Asscn.; mem. Royal Swedish Acad. of Music; various prizes; Kt. of Dannebrog Medal. *Compositions:* 12 symphonies, 3 chamber symphonies, 4 symphonic metamorphoses, 16 concertos, 20 quartets, oratorios, chamber and orchestral music, choral works, etc. *Publications:* Mellemspil (Interlude) 1961, Det uforklarlige (The inexplicable) 1981. *Leisure interests:* philosophy, history, planting. *Address:* Holmboevej 6, Ramløse, 3200 Helsinge, Denmark. *Telephone:* 02-112045.

HOLMES, Dyer Brainerd; American engineer and business executive; b. 24 May 1921, New York; s. of Marcellus B. and Theodora (née Pomeroy) Holmes; m. Roberta M. Holmes; two d. by previous marriage; ed. Newark Acad., Carteret Acad., Cornell Univ., Bowdoin Coll., and Massachusetts Inst. of Technology; service in U.S. Naval Reserve; Bell Telephone Labs. and Western Electric Co. 1945–53; Radio Corpn. of America 1953–61, engaged as Project Man. of Talos (ground-to-air missile); Program Man. Ballistic Missile Early Warning System (B.M.E.W.S.), Gen. Man. Defense Systems Div. 1961; First Dir. Manned Space Flight, NASA 1961–63; Sr. Vice-Pres. Raytheon Co. 1963–69, Dir. 1969–, Exec. Vice-Pres. 1969–75, Pres. 1975–, mem. Bd. of Dirs.; Chair. Bd. of Govs. Aerospace Industries Asscn.; Chair. of Bd. Beech Aircraft Corpn. (subs. of Raytheon); Dir. Wyman-Gordon Co., Mass., First Nat. Boston Co., First Nat. Bank of Boston, Kaman Corpn., American Defense Preparedness Asscn.; Fellow, Inst. of Electronic and Electrical Engineers, American Inst. of Aeronautics and Astronautics; mem. Corpn. of Northeastern Univ., Nat. Acad. of Eng., Bd. of Trustees, Nat. Security Industrial Asscn.; Hon. D.Sc. (Univ. of New Mexico) 1963, Hon. D.Eng. (Worcester (Mass.) Polytechnic Inst.); NASA Medal for Outstanding Leadership, Arnold Air Soc.'s Paul T. John's Award 1969. *Address:* Raytheon Company, 141 Spring Street, Lexington, Mass. 02173, U.S.A. (Office).

HOLMES, Admiral Ephraim Paul; American naval officer (retd.); b. 14 May 1908, Downsville, N.Y.; s. of Dr. Edward A. and Dolly M. Hathaway Holmes; m. Nancy Sellers 1933; one s. one d.; ed. Downsville High School and U.S. Naval Acad., Annapolis; commissioned 1930, Capt. 1948; commanded destroyer U.S.S. Stockham 1944; Commdg. Officer U.S.S. Northampton 1955–57; Special Asst. to Deputy Chief of Naval Operations (Plans and Policy), Dept. of Navy 1957–58; Commdr. Cruiser Div. Four 1958–60; Asst. Chief of Naval Operations (Gen. Planning) and Dir. Gen. Planning Group, Dept of Navy 1960–63; Vice-Admiral, Commdr. Amphibious Force, Pacific 1963–64; Commdr. First Fleet 1964; Dir. Navy Program Office, Chief of Naval Operations 1964–67; Supreme Allied Commdr., Atlantic (NATO) 1967–70; C.-in-C. U.S. Atlantic Fleet 1967–70; Exec. Dir., Va. Port Authority 1971–75; numerous medals and decorations. *Leisure interests:* tennis, squash, golf, fishing, boating. *Address:* 3004 Larkspur Run, Williamsburg, Va. 23185, U.S.A.

HOLMES, Geoffrey Shorter, D.LITT., F.B.A., F.R.HIST.S.; British historian and writer; b. 17 July 1928, Sheffield; s. of Horace Holmes and Daisy Lavinia Holmes (née Shorter); m. Ella Jean Waddell Scott 1955; one s. one d.; ed. Woodhouse Grammar School, Sheffield and Pembroke Coll., Oxford; served in army (Royal Army Service Corps) 1948–50, Mil. Adviser's staff,

U.K. High Comm., New Delhi 1949–50; Personnel Dept., Hadfield's Ltd., Sheffield 1951–52; Asst., Lecturer then Sr. Lecturer in Modern History, Univ. of Glasgow 1952–69; Reader in History, Univ. of Lancaster 1969–72, Prof. 1973–83, Emer. Prof. 1983–; Visiting Fellow, All Souls Coll., Oxford 1977–78; Raleigh Lecturer, British Acad. 1979; James Ford Special Lecturer, Oxford Univ. 1981; Vice-Pres. Royal Historical Soc. 1985–. *Publications:* British Politics in the Age of Anne 1967 (revised edn. 1987), The Divided Society (with W. A. Speck) 1967, Britain after the Glorious Revolution (Ed. and Co-Author) 1969, The Trial of Doctor Sacheverell 1973, The Electorate and the National Will in the First Age of Party 1976, Augustan England: Professions, State and Society 1680–1730 1982, The London Diaries of William Nicolson, Bishop of Carlisle 1702–1718 (Ed. with Clyve Jones) 1985, Politics, Religion and Society in England 1679–1742 1986, Stuart England (co-author) 1986. *Leisure interests:* music, gardening, cricket. *Address:* Tatham House, Burton-in-Lonsdale, via Carnforth, Lancs., LA6 3LF, England. *Telephone:* (0468) 61730.

HOLMES, George Arthur, PH.D., F.B.A.; British historian and academic; b. 22 April 1927, Aberystwyth, Wales; s. of the late John Holmes and Margaret Holmes; m. Evelyn Anne Klein 1953; two s. (one deceased), two d.; ed. Ardwyn County School, Aberystwyth, Univ. Coll. Aberystwyth and St. John's Coll. Cambridge; Fellow, St. John's Coll. Cambridge 1951–54; Tutor, St. Catherine's Coll. Oxford 1954–62, Fellow and Tutor 1962–; mem. Inst. for Advanced Study, Princeton, N.J., U.S.A. 1967–68; Vice-Master St. Catherine's Coll. 1969–71; Chair. Victoria County History Cttee., Inst. of Historical Research 1979–; Jt. Ed. English Historical Review 1974–81; Del., Oxford Univ. Press 1982–. *Publications:* The Estates of the Higher Nobility in Fourteenth-Century England 1957, The Later Middle Ages 1962, The Florentine Enlightenment 1400–1450 1969, Europe: Hierarchy and Revolt 1320–1450 1975, The Good Parliament 1975, Dante 1980, Florence, Rome and the Origins of the Renaissance 1986, The Oxford Illustrated History of Medieval Europe (ed.) 1988. *Address:* Highmoor House, Bampton, Oxon., England. *Telephone:* Bampton Castle 850408.

HOLMES, Kenneth Charles, M.A., PH.D., F.R.S.; British research biophysicist; b. 19 Nov. 1934, London; s. of Sidney C. and Irene M. (née Penfold) Holmes; m. Mary Lesceline Scruby 1957; one s. three d.; ed. Chiswick County School, St. John's Coll., Cambridge, and Birbeck Coll., London; Research Asst., Birkbeck Coll. 1955–59; Research Assoc., Children's Hosp., Boston 1960–62; scientific staff, MRC Lab. of Molecular Biology, Cambridge 1962–68; Dir. Dept. of Biophysics, Max-Planck-Inst. für medizinische Forschung, Heidelberg 1968–; Prof. of Biophysics, Heidelberg Univ. 1972–. *Publications:* articles in scientific books and journals. *Leisure interests:* rowing, singing. *Address:* Max-Planck-Institut für medizinische Forschung, Abt. Biophysik, Jahnstrasse 29, 6900 Heidelberg (Office); Mühltalstrasse 117b, 6900 Heidelberg, Federal Republic of Germany (Home). *Telephone:* 06621/486270 (Office); 06221/471313 (Home).

HOLMES, Larry; American boxer; b. 3 Nov. 1949, Cuthbert, Georgia; s. of John and Flossie Holmes; m. Diana Holmes; one s. four d.; ed. Easton, Pa.; amateur boxer 1970–73; 22 amateur fights, 19 wins; lost by disqualification to Duane Bobick in finals of American Olympic trials 1972; won World Boxing Council version of world heavyweight title from Ken Norton June 1978; has made nine defences, all won inside scheduled distance (breaking previous record held by Joe Louis); became first man to stop Muhammad Ali Oct. 1980; stripped of World Boxing Council version 1983; lost Int. Boxing Fed. version to Michael Spinks 1985, beaten again by Spinks 1986; 47 professional fights, 45 wins. *Leisure interests:* food, sport and self-education. *Address:* Larry Holmes Enterprises, U.S. Highway 22, Phillipsburg, N.J. 08865, U.S.A.

HOLMES, Sir Peter F., Kt., M.C., M.A.; British petroleum executive; b. 27 Sept. 1932, Athens, Greece; s. of Gerald Holmes and Caroline Morris Holmes; m. Judith M. Walker 1955; three d.; ed. Malvern Coll., Trinity Coll., Cambridge; with the Shell Group of Cos. 1956–, C.E.O. Shell Markets (Middle East) Ltd. 1965–68, C.E.O. Shell Cos. in Libya 1970–73; Man. Dir. and C.E.O. Shell Petroleum Devt. Co. of Nigeria Ltd. 1977–81, Pres. Shell Int. Trading Co. 1981–83, Man. Dir. Shell Transport and Trading 1982–, Chair. 1985–; Man. Dir. Royal Dutch/Shell Group 1982– (Vice-Chair. Cttee.). *Publications:* Mountains and a Monastery 1958, Nigeria, Giant of Africa 1985, Turkey, A Timeless Bridge 1988. *Leisure interests:* mountaineering, travel in remote areas, 19th century travel literature. *Address:* Shell Centre, London, S.E.1, England.

HOLMES à COURT, (Michael) Robert (Hamilton), LL.B.; Australian business executive; b. 27 July 1937; s. of Peter Worsley Holmes à Court and Ethnee Celia Holmes à Court; m. Janet Lee Ranford 1965; three s. one d.; ed. Michaelhouse, Natal, S. Africa, Univ. of W. Australia; Barrister and Solicitor Supreme Court of W. Australia 1965; Chair. Assoc. Communications Corpn. PLC 1982–, Weeks Petroleum 1984–, The Bell Group Ltd. Australia 1970–88, The Bell Group Int. Ltd. 1982–88; Jt. Deputy Chair. Standard Chartered (now Standard Chartered Group PLC) 1987– (Dir. 1986–). *Leisure interests:* breeding thoroughbred horses, racing. *Address:* 22 The Esplanade, Peppermint Grove, W. Australia 6011. *Telephone:* Perth 384 3894.

HOLOUBEK, Gustaw; Polish actor and theatre director; b. 21 April 1923, Cracow; s. of Gustaw and Eugenia Holoubek; m. 1st Danuta Kwiatkowska,

2nd Maria Wachowiak, 3rd Magdalena Zawadzka; two d.; ed. State Higher Dramatic School, Cracow; actor in Cracow theatres 1947–49, Wyspiański Theatre, Katowice, Artistic Man. 1954–56, Polish Theatre, Warsaw 1958–59; actor Dramatic Theatre, Warsaw 1959–82, Dir. and Artistic Man. 1972–82; Assoc. Prof. State Higher Theatrical School; Vice-Chair. SPATIF (Asscn. of Polish Theatre and Film Actors) 1963–70, Chair. 1970–81; Hon. Pres. of ZASP (Union of Polish Stage Artists) 1981; Deputy to Seym 1976–82; now appears in various Warsaw theatres in leading roles. *Roles include:* Judge Caust in Leprosy at the Palace of Justice, Baron Goetze in Le diable et le bon Dieu (Sartre), Gustaw-Konrad in Dziady (A. Mickiewicz), Violinist in Rzeźnia (S. Mrożek), Beggar in Electra (J. Giraudoux), Hick in The Iceman Cometh (O'Neill), King Lear, Oedipus, Hamlet, Richard II and Hadrian VII (Peter Luke), Gen. Wincenty Krasiński in November Night (Wyspiański), Count Szarma in Operetka (Gombrowicz); also appears in films and television plays; Dir. Mazepa (film) 1976; numerous decorations including State Prize 1953, 1966, 1978 (1st Class), Order of Banner of Labour 2nd Class, Knight's Cross of Polonia Restituta, Award Meritorius Activist of Culture 1972, Warsaw City Prize 1975, Cttee. for Polish Radio and TV Award 1980. *Leisure interest:* sports. *Address:* Ul. Dragonów 4 m. 49 Warsaw, Poland.

HOLROYD, Michael, C.B.E.; British author; b. 27 Aug. 1935, London; s. of Basil and Ulla (née Hall) Holroyd; m. Margaret Drabble (q.v.) 1982; ed. Eton Coll.; Chair. Soc. of Authors 1973–74, Nat. Book League 1976–78; Vice-Chair. Arts Council Literature Panel 1982–83; Pres. English Centre of PEN 1985–88. *Publications:* Hugh Kingsmill 1964, Lytton Strachey 1967–68, Unreceived Opinions 1973, Augustus John 1974–75, Bernard Shaw: Vol. 1: The Search for Love 1988. *Leisure interests:* music, stories. *Address:* c/o A. P. Watt Ltd., 20 John Street, London, WC1N 2DL, England. *Telephone:* 01-405 6774.

HOLSHOUSER, James E., Jr.; American politician; b. 8 Oct. 1934, Watauga Co.; s. of J. E. and Virginia Holshouser; m. Pat Hollingsworth; one d.; ed. Davidson Coll., Univ. of North Carolina School of Law; mem. State House of Reps. 1962, re-elected 1964, 1968, 1970; served as Republican Joint Caucus Sec. 1963, House Minority Leader 1965, Republican Joint Caucus Leader 1969, 1971, Vice-Chair. House Judiciary Cttee. 1965, Vice-Chair. House Rules Cttee. 1969, 1971, served on various legislative study comms.; Republican State Chair. 1966, re-elected 1968, 1970; Gov. of North Carolina 1973–77; mem. Bd. of Dirs., Davidson Coll. and Univ. of N.C. Law Alumni Assens. *Leisure interests:* golf, tennis. *Address:* P.O. Box 116, Southern Pines, N.C. 28387, U.S.A.

HOLST, Johan Jørgen; Norweigan politician; b. 29 Nov. 1937, Oslo; ed. Columbia Univ., Univ. of Oslo; Head Research, Norwegian Inst. Int. Affairs 1969–76, Dir. 1981–86; State Sec. Ministry of Defence 1976–79; State Sec. Ministry of Foreign Affairs 1979–81; Minister of Defence 1986–. *Address:* Ministry of Defence, P.O. Box 8126, Dep., Oslo 1, Norway. *Telephone:* (2) 498001.

HOLSTENER-JØRGENSEN, Helge, M.SC., DR. AGRON.; Danish scientist; b. 10 Dec. 1924, Tingsted; s. of Edgon and Eva Holstener-Jørgensen; m. Agnete Buemann 1949; one s. one d.; ed. Royal Veterinary and Agricultural Univ., Copenhagen; Scientist, The Danish Forest Experiment Station 1950–62, Head 1962–; Sr. Research Fellow, Forestry Research Inst., N.Z. 1967–68; Prof. of Silviculture, Royal Veterinary and Agricultural Univ., Copenhagen 1973–74; Council Chair. The Royal Agricultural Soc. of Denmark 1982–; Fellow, The Royal Danish Acad. of Sciences and Letters 1980–; Foreign Fellow, Royal Swedish Acad. of Agric. and Forestry 1983–; Knight of Dannebrog. *Publications:* numerous publs. on soil science, tree nutrition, irrigation and decoration greenery. *Leisure interests:* literature, gardening. *Address:* The Danish Forest Experiment Station, Skovbrynet 16, DK-2800 Lyngby (Office); Solbjerget 44, DK-3460 Birkerød, Denmark (Home). *Telephone:* 02 93 12 00 (Office); 02 81 20 51 (Home).

HOLT, James Clarke, D.PHIL., F.B.A.; British historian and university professor; b. 26 April 1922, Bradford, Yorks.; s. of the late Herbert Holt and Eunice Holt; m. Alice Catherine Elizabeth Suley 1950; one s.; ed. Bradford Grammar School and Queen's Coll. Oxford; served in army 1942–45; Harmsworth Sr. Scholar, Merton Coll. Oxford 1947–49; Lecturer, Univ. of Nottingham 1949–62, Prof. of Medieval History 1962–66; Prof. of History, Univ. of Reading 1966–78, Dean of Faculty of Letters and Social Sciences 1972–76; Professorial Fellow, Emmanuel Coll. Cambridge 1978–81, Prof of Medieval History, Cambridge Univ. 1978–88, Master of Fitzwilliam Coll. Cambridge 1981–88; Visiting Prof., Univ. of Calif., Santa Barbara, U.S.A. 1977; Visiting Hinkley Prof., Johns Hopkins Univ., U.S.A. 1983; Raleigh Lecturer, British Acad. 1975; Visiting Prof. Japan 1986; mem. Advisory Council on Public Records 1974–81; Pres. Royal Historical Soc. 1980–84; Vice-Pres. British Acad. 1986–88; Corresp. Fellow Medieval Acad. of America; Hon. D.Litt. (Reading) 1984; Hon. Fellow, Emmanuel Coll. 1985–, Ecamienda de la Orden del Merito Gril 1988. *Publications:* The Northerners: A Study in the Reign of King John 1961, Praestitia Rolls 14–18 John 1964, Magna Carta 1965, The Making of Magna Carta 1966, Magna Carta and the Idea of Liberty 1972, The University of Reading: The First Fifty Years 1977, Robin Hood 1982, War and Government in the Middle Ages (Ed. with John Gillingham), Magna Carta and Medieval Government 1985; Hand-list of Acta Henry II and Richard I surviving in British Repositories (with Richard Mortimer) 1986, Domesday Studies

(Ed.) 1987; papers in English Historical Review, Past and Present, Economic History Review, trans. Royal Historical Soc. *Leisure interests:* music, mountaineering, cricket, fly-fishing. *Address:* Fitzwilliam College, Cambridge, CB3 0DG, England. *Telephone:* (0223) 332041.

HOLT, John Riley, PH.D., F.R.S.; British professor of experimental physics; b. 15 Feb. 1918; s. of Frederick and Annie (Riley) Holt; m. Joan S. Thomas 1949; two s.; ed. Runcorn Secondary School and Univ. of Liverpool; British Atomic Energy Project, Liverpool and Cambridge 1940–45; Lecturer, Univ. of Liverpool 1945–53, Sr. Lecturer 1953–56, Reader 1956–66, Prof. of Experimental Physics 1966–83. *Publications:* papers in scientific journals. *Address:* Rydalmere, Stanley Avenue, Higher Bebington, Wirral, L63 5QE, England. *Telephone:* 051-608 2041.

HOLT, Peter Malcolm, D.LITT., F.B.A., F.S.A., F.R.HIST.S.; British professor of history; b. 28 Nov. 1918, Leigh, Lancs.; s. of Rev. Peter Holt and Elizabeth Holt; m. Nancy Bury (née Mawle) 1953; one s. one d.; ed. Univ. Coll., Oxford; Sudan Civil Service, Ministry of Educ. 1941–53, Govt. Archivist 1954–55; joined S.O.A.S. 1955, Prof. of Arab History 1964–75, Prof. of the History of the Near and Middle East 1975–82, Prof. Emer. 1982–, Hon. Fellow 1985. *Publications:* The Mahdist State in the Sudan 1958, 1970, Studies in the History of the Near East 1973, The Memoirs of a Syrian Prince 1983, The Age of the Crusades 1986; Co-Ed. The Cambridge History of Islam 1970. *Leisure interest:* walking. *Address:* Dryden Spinney, Kirtlington, Oxford, OX5 3HG, England.

HOLTE, Johan B.; Norwegian industrialist; b. 19 Feb. 1915, Notodden; s. of Peder O. Holte and Lorentze Indorff; m. Eva Bull; ed. Technical Univ. of Norway, Trondheim; joined Norsk Hydro 1948, Dir. Research Div. 1957–66, Vice-Pres. 1964–66, Pres. 1967–77, Chair. 1977–85; mem. Bd. of Dirs. Norske Fina A/S, Qatar Fertiliser Co., Qatar, The Appalachian Co., Ohio, U.S.A.; Chair. Bd. of Dirs. Soer-Norge Aluminium A/S, Husnes, Standard Telefon og Kabelfabrik A/S, Oslo, Kvaerner Industrier A/S, Oslo; mem. many other industrial and social orgs. *Leisure interests:* fishing, mountain walking. *Address:* Helmerveien 5, 1310 Blommenholm, Norway (Home). *Telephone:* 54-08-29 (Home).

HOLTER, Heinz, DR. PHIL.; Danish biologist and professor; b. 5 June 1904, Leonding, Austria; s. of late M. D. A. Holter and late A. Holter (née Fischer); m. Karen Teisen 1942; one s. one d.; ed. Univ. of Vienna; Asst. Chemical Inst., Univ. of Vienna 1928–30; Dept. of Chem. Carlsberg Lab., Copenhagen 1932–42, Chief of Dept. of Cytochemistry 1942–56, Chief of Dept. of Physiology 1956–71; mem. of Danish Acad. of Sciences 1942, Royal Soc. of Sciences, Uppsala 1960, Royal Physiographical Soc. of Lund 1962, American Acad. of Arts and Sciences 1971. *Publications:* Various scientific papers in the fields of organic chemistry, enzyme chemistry, cytochemistry and cell physiology. *Address:* 37 Farendløse Enghave, DK-4100 Ringsted, Denmark. *Telephone:* (03) 640185.

HOLTFRETER, Johannes F. C., PH.D.; American emeritus professor of zoology; b. 9 Jan. 1901, Richtenberg, Germany; s. of Johannes and Sabine (Peters) Holtfreter; m. Hiroko Ban 1959; ed. Univs. of Rostock, Leipzig, Freiburg and Greifswald; Asst., Dept. of Embryology Kaiser-Wilhelm Inst. of Biology, Berlin-Dahlem 1928–33; Lecturer and Assoc. Prof., Zoological Inst., Univ. of Munich 1933–38; mem. Research Staff Zoology Inst., Univ. of Cambridge, England 1939–40; mem. Zoology Dept., McGill Univ., Montreal, Canada 1942–46; Prof., Dept. of Biology, Univ. of Rochester, New York 1946–66, Tracy H. Harris Prof. of Zoology 1966–69, Prof. Emer. 1969; Jesup Lecturer, Columbia Univ. 1957; numerous lectureships abroad; research in vertebrate devt. and cytology; mem. Editorial Bd. Journal of Embryology and Experimental Morphology, London, Bd. of Advisers Experimental Cell Research, Stockholm, Int. Bd. of Control Hubrecht Lab., Utrecht, Fulbright Fellowships Panel, Guggenheim Fellowships Evaluation Panel, Nat. Acad. of Sciences, American Assen. of Anatomists and many foreign socs. and acads. including Akad. der Naturforscher Leopoldina and Royal Swedish Soc. of Sciences; Rockefeller Fellow 1936–37, Rockefeller and Guggenheim Fellow, McGill Univ., Montreal 1942–46, Fulbright Fellow, Paris 1958; Fellow, American Acad. of Arts and Sciences, A.A.A.S., John Simon Guggenheim Memorial Foundation; Hon. Fellow, Zoological Soc. of India; Dr. h.c. rer. nat. (Freiburg) 1975. *Leisure interests:* painting, gardening, travelling in exotic countries. *Address:* 29 Knolltop Drive, Rochester, N.Y. 14610, U.S.A.

HOLTHUSEN, Hans Egon, D.PHIL.; German writer; b. 15 April 1913, Rendsburg, Schleswig-Holstein; s. of Johannes Holthausen and Alma Holthausen née Hagelstein; m. 1st Lori Holthusen 1950, 2nd Inge Holthusen 1952; one s. one step d.; ed. Tübingen, Berlin and Munich Univs.; served in the army 1939–45; writer 1945–; Dir. Goethe House, New York 1961–64; Del. Biennale Int. de Poésie, Knokke (Belgium) 1951–52; Perm. Prof. German Literature, Northwestern Univ. Evanston, Ill. 1968–81; Pres. Bavarian Acad. of Fine Arts 1968–74; Kiel Kulturpreis 1956, Bavarian Order of Merit 1973, Bayerisches Literaturpreis (Jean Paul Preis) 1983, Bayerische Maximiliansorden 1984, Kunstpreis des Landes Schleswig-Holstein 1984, Grosses Bundesverdienstkreuz 1987. *Publications:* essays: Rilkes Sonette an Orpheus—Versuch einer Interpretation 1937, Der späte Rilke 1949, Der unbehauste Mensch 1951 and 1955, Ja and Nein 1954, Das Schöne und das Wahre 1958, Kritisches Verstehen 1961, Avantgardismus 1964, Plädoyer für den Einzelnen 1967, Kreiselkompass 1976, Amerikaner und Deutsche, Dialog zweier Kulturen 1977, Opus 19 Reden und Widerreden aus 25 Jahren 1983; poems: Hier in der Zeit, Labyrintische Jahre 1952; novel: Das Schiff 1956; biographies: R. M. Rilke in Selbstzeugnissen und Bilddokumenten 1958, Eduard Mörike in Selbstzeugnissen und Bilddokumenten 1971, Sartre in Stammheim 1982, Opus 19: Reden und Widerreden aus 25 Jahren 1983, Gottfried Benn: Leben, Werk, Widerspruch 1986; also: Indiana Campus: ein amerikanisches Tagebuch 1969, Chicago: Metropolis am Michigansee 1981. *Leisure interests:* hiking, swimming, music. *Address:* Agnesstrasse 48, 8 Munich 40, Federal Republic of Germany. *Telephone:* Munich 271 2161.

HOLTON, A. Linwood, Jr., B.A., LL.B.; American lawyer; b. 21 Sept. 1923, Big Stone Gap, Va.; s. of Abner Linwood and Edith (Van Gorder) Holton; m. Virginia Harrison Rogers; two s. two d.; ed. public schools in Big Stone Gap, Washington and Lee Univ., and Harvard Law School; Partner, Eggleston, Holton, Butler and Glenn (law firm); served submarine force during Second World War; fmr. Chair. Roanoke City Republican Cttee.; Vice-Chair. Virginia Republican State Cen. Cttee. 1960-69; del. to Republican Nat. Convention 1960, 1968, 1972; mem. Nat. Nixon for Pres. Cttee. March 1967; Regional Co-ordinator for Nixon for Pres. Cttee.; Gov. of Virginia 1970-74; Asst. Sec. of State for Congressional Relations, Dept. of State 1974-75; partner in law firm of Hogan and Hartson 1975-78; Vice-Pres., Gen. Counsel American Council Insurance, Washington 1978-; Chair. Burket Miller Center for Public Affairs, Univ. of Va. 1979-; Pres. Supreme Court Historical Soc. 1980-; Republican. *Address:* 6010 Claiborne Drive, McLean, Va. 22101, U.S.A. (Home).

HOLTON, Gerald, PH.D.; American physicist and historian of science; b. 23 May 1922, Berlin, Germany; s. of Dr. Emanuel and Regina (Rossman) Holton; m. Nina Rossfort 1947; two s.; ed. Wesleyan Univ., Middletown, Conn., Harvard Univ.; Harvard Univ. staff, officers' radar course and lab. for Research on Sound Control 1943-45, various faculty posts 1945-, Mallinckrodt Prof. of Physics and Prof. of History of Science 1975-; Visiting Prof., MIT 1976-; Nat. Science Foundation Faculty Fellow, Paris 1960-61; Exchange Prof., Leningrad Univ. 1962; founder and Ed.-in-Chief, Daedalus 1958-61; mem. Council, History of Science Soc. 1959-61, Pres. 1982-84; Fellow, American Physical Soc., American Acad. of Arts and Sciences, Académie Internationale d'Histoire des Sciences, (Vice-Pres. 1982-), Deutsche Akademie der Naturforscher Leopoldina; mem. Inst. for Advanced Study, Princeton 1964, 1967; mem. Nat. Acad. of Science Cttee. on Communication with Scholars in the People's Repub. of China, U.S. Nat. Comm. on IUHPS; mem. Bd. of Govs., American Inst. of Physics 1969-74; Fellow, Center for Advanced Study in Behavioral Sciences, Stanford, Calif. 1975-76; mem. U.S. Nat. Comm. on UNESCO 1975-80, Library of Congress Council of Scholars 1979-, U.S. Nat. Comm. on Excellence in Educ. 1981-83; Herbert Spencer Lecturer, Oxford 1979, Jefferson Lecturer 1981; Robert A. Millikan Medal 1967, Oersted Medal 1980, Guggenheim Fellowship 1980-81, Presidential Citation for Service to Educ. 1984. *Publications:* Introduction to Concepts and Theories in Physical Science 1952, Thematic Origins of Scientific Thought 1973, Scientific Imagination 1978, Limits of Scientific Inquiry (Ed.) 1979, Albert Einstein, Historical and Cultural Perspectives (Ed.) 1982, The Advancement of Science, and its Burdens 1986; mem. Editorial Bd., Collected Papers of Albert Einstein. *Leisure interests:* music, kayaking. *Address:* Jefferson Physical Laboratory, Harvard University, Cambridge, Mass. 02138 (Office); 14 Trotting Horse Drive, Lexington, Mass. 02173, U.S.A. (Home). *Telephone:* (617) 495-4474 (Office).

HOLTZMAN, Wayne H(arold), M.S., PH.D.; American psychologist; b. 16 Jan. 1923, Chicago, Ill.; s. of Harold H. Holtzman and Lillian Manny; m. Joan King 1947; four s.; ed. Northwestern and Stanford Univs.; Asst. Prof. Univ. of Texas at Austin 1949-53, Assoc. Prof. 1954-59, Prof. of Psychology 1959-, Dean Coll. of Educ. 1964-70, Hogg Prof. of Psychology and Educ. 1965-; Assoc. Dir. Hogg Foundation for Mental Health 1955-64, Pres. 1970-; Dir. Science Research Assocs. 1975-, Population Resource Center 1980-; Pres. Int. Union of Psychological Science 1984-88; other professional affiliations; Faculty Research Fellow, Social Science Research Council 1953-54, Center for Advanced Study in Behavioral Sciences 1962-63; Hon. L.H.D. (Southwestern) 1980. *Publications:* Tomorrow's Parents (with B. Moore) 1964, Computer Assisted Instruction, Testing and Guidance 1971, Personality Development in Two Cultures (with others) 1975, Introduction to Psychology 1978. *Leisure interests:* travel, photography, gardening. *Address:* Hogg Foundation for Mental Health, The University of Texas, P.O. Box 7998, Austin, Tex. 78713-7998 (Office); 3300 Foothill Drive, Austin, Tex. 78731, U.S.A. (Home). *Telephone:* (512) 471-5041 (Office); (512) 452-8296 (Home).

HOLUB, Miroslav, MU.DR., C.SC.; Czechoslovak writer and poet; b. 13 Sept. 1923, Pilsen; s. of Josef Holub and Františka Dvořáková; m. 1st Věra Koktová 1948, 2nd Marta Svikruhová, 3rd Jitka Langrová 1969; two s. one d.; ed. Charles Univ., Prague; scientific worker, Microbiological Inst., Czechoslovak Acad. of Sciences 1953-71, Public Health Research Inst., New York 1965-67, Max-Planck Inst. of Immunobiology, Freiburg 1968-69, Inst. for Clinical and Experimental Medicine 1972-; mem. Cen. Cttee. Union of Czechoslovak Writers 1963-69, Cen. Cttee. Union of Czech Scientific Workers 1969-71; Ed., Vesmir 1952-65. *Publications:* Poetry: Denní služba (Day Shift) 1958, Achiles a želva (Achilles and the Tortoise)

1960, Slabikář (The Primer) 1961, Jdi a otevři dveře (Go and Open the Door) 1962, Zcela nesoustavná zoologie (Entirely Unsystematic Zoology) 1963, Kam teče krev (Where Blood Flows) 1963, Tak zvané srdce (So-called Heart) 1963, Anamnesa (Selected Poems 1958-63) 1964, Selected Poems (English) 1967, Obwohl (German) 1969, Ačkoli (Although) 1969, Beton (Concrete) 1970, Model člověka (Model of a Man, Polish) 1969, Although (English) 1971, Aktschlüsse/Halbgedichte (German) 1974, Een Machine Van Woorden (Dutch) 1975, Vantunun Mool (The Heart of the Matter—Gujarati) 1976, Notes of a Clay Pigeon (English) 1977, Epiloge apo to ergo tou (Greek) 1979, Sagittal Section (American) 1980, Naopak (On the Contrary) 1982, Interferon (or On the Theater) (American) 1982, On the Contrary (English) 1984, Interferon 1986, The Fly and Other Poems (English) 1987; Prose: Anděl na kolečkách (Angel on Wheels—report of trip through U.S.A.) 1963, Tři kroky po zemi (Three Steps on the Ground) 1965, Die explodierende Metropole (German) 1967, Žít v New Yorku (To Live in New York) 1969, Poe or the Valley of Unrest 1971, K principu volničky (Principle of a jingle bell) 1987; Scientific works: Experimental Morphology of Antibody Formation 1958, Mechanisms of Antibody Formation 1960 (editor), The Lymphocyte and The Immune Response 1967, Cellular Basis of Antibody Formation (German) 1978, Structure of the Immune System (Czech) 1979, Immunology of Nude Mice 1988. *Leisure interests:* tennis, table-tennis, fencing. *Address:* Institute for Clinical and Experimental Medicine, CS 146 22 Prague 4; CS 14900 Prague 4, Chodov, Czechoslovakia (Home). *Telephone:* 4701-3602 (Office).

HOLZACH, Robert, DR.IUR.; Swiss banker; b. 28 Sept. 1922, Zürich; ed. Univs. of Zürich and Geneva; admitted to the bar, Thurgau 1951; Trainee, Union Bank of Switzerland, Geneva and London 1951-53, mem. Secr. Commercial Div. Head Office 1953-56, Asst. Man. Commercial Div. 1956-62, Man. Commercial Div. 1962-66, Deputy Gen. Man. responsible for credit operations in German-speaking Switzerland 1966-67, Gen. Man. 1968-80, Head, Admin. Div. 1971-76, responsible for Gen. Management Staff Depts. 1976-80, Chair. Bd. of Dirs. 1980-88, Hon. Chair. April 1988-; Rep. of Union Bank of Switzerland on Bd. of Dirs. and Advisory Bds., major firms in Switzerland and Fed. Repub. of Germany; Col. in Swiss Army, in command of Infantry Reg. 31 1966-69. *Address:* Union Bank of Switzerland, Bahnhofstrasse 45, 8001 Zürich, Switzerland.

HOLZER, Jenny, M.F.A.; American artist; b. 29 July 1950, Gallipolis, Ohio; d. of Richard Vornholt Holzer and Virginia Beasley Holzer; m. Michael Andrew Glier 1983; ed. Ohio Univ., Rhode Island School of Design, Whitney Museum of American Art Ind. Study Program; became working artist in New York 1977; exhbns. include Westkunst, Cologne, Fed. Repub. of Germany 1981, Documenta 7, Kassel, Fed. Repub. of Germany 1982, Biennial—Whitney Museum of American Art, New York, ICA, London, Pa. 1983, Kunsthalle Basel, Switzerland, Biennale of Sydney, Australia, "Content", Hirschorn Museum, Washington 1984, XIII Biennale de Paris, France, Biennial, Whitney Museum of American Art, Carnegie Int., Pittsburgh 1985, Barbara Gladstone Gallery, New York 1986, La Mode, La Morah, La Passion, Centre Georges Pompidou, Paris, Sculpture Project, Münster, Fed. Repub. of Germany, Brennale of Sydney, Australia, Documents 8, Kassel, Fed. Repub. of Germany 1987; Gallery Artist, Barbara Gladstone Gallery 1982-; Blair Prize, Art Inst. of Chicago. *Publications:* A Little Knowledge 1979, Black Book 1980, Eating Through Living 1981, Truisms and Essays 1983. *Leisure interests:* reading, construction, riding, agriculture. *Address:* 245 Eldridge Street, New York, N.Y. 10002, U.S.A. *Telephone:* (212) 431-3334 (Gallery).

HOMANN, Heinrich, DR.PHIL.; German university professor and politician; b. 6 March 1911, Bremerhaven; ed. Gymnasium and law studies; professional army officer 1934-45, captured at Stalingrad 1943; Co-Founder, Free Germany Nat. Cttee. 1943; mem. Nat. Democratic Party (NDPD) 1948-, Political Man. 1949-52, Deputy Chair. 1952-67, Acting Chair. 1967-72, Chair. 1972-; mem. Volkskammer 1949-, Vice-Chair. 1954-63; Deputy Chair. State Council of German Democratic Repub. 1960; mem. Presidium of the Nat. Council of the Nat. Front of G.D.R. 1957-; mem. Presidium of G.D.R. Peace Council 1955-; Hero of Labour, Vaterländischer Verdienstorden in Gold (twice), Karl-Marx-Orden and other decorations. *Address:* National-Demokratische Partei Deutschlands, Friedrichstrasse 65, 1086 Berlin, German Democratic Republic. *Telephone:* 20 00 441.

HOMANS, George Caspar, M.A.; American sociologist; b. 11 Aug. 1910, Boston, Mass.; s. of Robert and Abigail (Adams) Homans; m. Nancy Parshall Cooper 1941; one s. two d.; ed. St. Paul's School, Concord, N.H. and Harvard Coll.; Jr. Fellow, Harvard Univ. 1934-39, Faculty Instructor 1939-41, Assoc. Prof. 1946-53, Prof. of Sociology 1953-79, Chair. Dept. of Sociology 1970-75, Prof. Emer. 1981-; U.S. Navy 1941-46; mem. Nat. Acad. of Sciences, American Philosophical Soc., American Acad. of Arts and Sciences. *Publications:* Massachusetts on the Sea 1930, An Introduction to Pareto 1934, Fatigue of Workers 1941, English Villagers of the Thirteenth Century 1941, The Human Group 1950, Marriage, Authority and Final Causes 1955, Social Behaviour 1961, 1974, Sentiments and Activities 1962, The Nature of Social Science 1967, Coming to my Senses 1984, Certainties and Doubts 1987, The Witch Hazel (poems) 1988. *Leisure interests:* sailing, forestry. *Address:* 480 William James Hall, Harvard University, Cambridge, Mass. 02138; 11 Francis Avenue, Cambridge, Mass. 02138, U.S.A. (Home). *Telephone:* (617) 495-3820 (Office); (617) 547-4737 (Home).

HOME OF THE HIRSEL, Baron (Life Peer), cr. 1974, of Coldstream in the County of Berwick; **Alexander Frederick Douglas-Home,** K.T., P.C.; British politician; b. 2 July 1903, London; s. of late 13th Earl of Home and Lady Lilian Lambton; m. Elizabeth Alington 1936; one s. three d.; ed. Eton Coll., and Christ Church, Oxford; mem. House of Commons 1931–45, 1950–51, 1963–74, House of Lords 1951–63; Parl. Private Sec. to Sec. of State for Scotland 1931–35, to Chancellor of Exchequer 1935–38, to Prime Minister 1938–39; Joint Parl. Under-Sec. to Foreign Office 1945; Minister of State, Scottish Office 1951–55; Sec. of State for Commonwealth Relations 1955–60, for Foreign Affairs 1960–63; Lord Pres. of the Council 1957, 1959–60; Prime Minister 1963–64; Leader of Conservative Party 1963–65; Leader of Opposition 1964–65; Sec. of State for Foreign and Commonwealth Affairs 1970–74; renounced title of 14th Earl of Home Oct. 1963; Chancellor, Order of the Thistle 1973–; Chancellor Heriot-Watt Univ., Edinburgh 1966–76; Pres. Royal Inst. of Int. Affairs 1977–; Pres. Salmon and Trout Assen. 1985–; Chair. Bilderberg meetings 1977, 1978, 1979, 1980; Hon. D.C.L. (Oxford), Hon. LL.D. (Harvard, Edinburgh, Aberdeen and Liverpool); Conservative. *Publications:* The Way the Wind Blows (autobiography) 1976, Border Reflections 1979, Letters to a Grandson 1983. *Leisure interests:* shooting, fishing, gardening. *Address:* The Hirsel, Coldstream, Berwickshire, Scotland; Castlemains, Douglas, Lanarkshire, Scotland. *Telephone:* (0890) 2345; (0555) 855241.

HOMMEL, Nicolas; Luxembourg diplomatist; b. 8 Oct. 1915, Wolwelange; m. Denise Ruffié 1959; called to the Bar 1939; Foreign Service 1946–; mem. Luxembourg Mil. Mission, Berlin 1946–48; Perm. Rep. to OEEC 1949–58, to NATO 1953–58, Amb. to Belgium 1958–62, to France 1962–67; Sec.-Gen. Ministry of Foreign Affairs 1967–68; Amb. to Fed. Rep. of Germany 1968–73; Sec.-Gen. Council of Ministers, EEC 1973–80; Chair. Cttee. Atlantique du Luxembourg 1983; several Luxembourg and foreign decorations. *Leisure interests:* painting, golf. *Address:* 100 Route d'Arlon, 1150 Luxembourg City, Luxembourg.

HONDA, Soichiro; Japanese business executive; b. 17 Nov. 1906, Iwata Gun; s. of Gihei and Mika Honda; m. Sachi Isobe 1935; two s. (one deceased) two d.; garage apprentice 1922, opened own garage 1928; owner and Head, Piston Ring Production Factory 1934; started producing motor cycles 1948, Pres. Honda Motor Co. until 1973, Dir. and Supreme Adviser 1973–83, Supreme Adviser 1983–; founded Honda Foundation 1977; Vice-Pres. Japan Automobile Manufacturers' Assen. 1967–80; Dir. Japan Automobile Fed. 1972–74; Chair. Europalia Japan Cttee. 1988; Hon. D. Eng. (Sophia Univ., Tokyo) 1973, (Mich. Technological Univ.) 1974, Hon. D.H. (Ohio State Univ.) 1979, Hon. D.S. (Cranfield Inst. of Tech.); Blue Ribbon Medal 1952, Japan Soc. of Mechanical Engineers Award 1959, Mercurio d'Oro 1971, Holly Medal, A.S.M.E. 1980; Hon. Life mem. American Soc. of Metals 1972, mem. Acad. of Distinguished Entrepreneurs, Babson Coll. 1978; Grande Ufficiale dell'Ordine al Merito (Italy) 1978, Grand Officier, Ordre de la Couronne, (Belgium) 1985, Kt. Commdr. Royal Order of the Polar Star (Sweden) 1980, Officier, Ordre des Arts et des Lettres (France) 1980, Order of the Sacred Treasure (First Class, Japan) 1981, Officier, Légion d'Honneur (France) 1984. *Address:* Honda Motor Co. Ltd., 2-6-20, Yaesu, Chuo-ku, Tokyo 104, Japan.

HONE, Major-Gen. Sir (Herbert) Ralph, K.C.M.G., K.B.E., M.C., T.D., G.C.ST.J., Q.C., LL.B.; British lawyer and colonial administrator; b. 3 May 1896, Hove, Sussex; s. of late Herbert Hone and Miriam Grace Hone (née Dracott); m. 1st Elizabeth Daisy Matthews 1918, one s. one d.; m. 2nd Sybil Mary Simond 1945, one s.; ed. Varndean Grammar School, Brighton and London Univ.; joined London Irish Rifles 1915, Lieut. 1916, Capt. 1918, served with B.E.F. France 1916, 1917–18; Staff Capt. Ministry of Munitions 1918–20; called to Bar, Middle Temple, practised S.E. Circuit 1923–24; Registrar Zanzibar High Court 1925, Resident Magistrate 1927; Crown Counsel Tanganyika 1930; Attorney-Gen. Gibraltar 1933–36; Attorney-Gen. Uganda 1937–40; Commdt. Uganda Defence Force 1940; Chief Legal Adviser Political Branch G.H.Q. Middle East 1941, Chief Political Officer 1942–43; attached Gen. Staff War Office 1943–44; Maj.-Gen. serving in E. Africa, Middle East, War Office, India, Ceylon and Malaya 1943–45; Chief Civil Affairs Officer, SEAC 1945–46; Sec.-Gen. to Gov.-Gen. of Malaya 1946–48; Deputy Commr.-Gen. S.E. Asia 1948–49; Gov. and C.-in-C. North Borneo 1949–54; Head Legal Division, Commonwealth Relations Office 1954–61; resumed private practice 1961; Draftsman, S. Rhodesia Constitution 1961, Bahamas Constitution 1963; Constitutional Adviser, Kenya 1962, South Arabia 1965, Bermuda 1966. *Publications:* Index to Gibraltar Laws 1933, Laws of Gibraltar (revised edition) 1935, Laws of the Bahamas (revised edition) 1965, etc. *Leisure interests:* tennis, badminton, philately. *Address:* 1 Paper Buildings, Temple, London, E.C.4. (Office); 56 Kenilworth Court, Lower Richmond Road, London, S.W.15, England (Home). *Telephone:* 01-788 3367 (Home).

HONECKER, Erich; German politician; b. 25 Aug. 1912, Neunkirchen, Saarland; s. of Wilhelm Honecker; m. 1st Edith Baumann 1947 (divorced), 2nd Margot Feist (q.v. Margot Honecker) 1953; two d.; mem. (Kommunistische Partei Deutschlands—KPD) 1929–46; imprisoned for anti-fascist activity 1935–45; Youth Sec., Cen. Cttee. of KPD 1945; mem. Cen. Cttee., KPD 1946; mem. Man. Cttee., Socialist Unity Party of Germany (SED) 1946; Chair. Freie Deutsche Jugend (FDJ) 1946–55; mem. Volkskammer, G.D.R. 1949–; mem. SED Cen. Cttee. 1946–, Cand. mem. Politburo 1950–58,

mem. 1958–, Sec. Cen. Cttee. 1958–71, First Sec. 1971–76, Gen. Sec. 1976–; Sec. Nat. Defence Council 1960–71, Chair. 1971–; mem. Council of State 1971–, Chair. (Head of State) Oct. 1976–; Vaterländischer Verdienstorden in Gold (twice), Held der DDR, Karl-Marx-Orden, Order of Lenin, Hero of Soviet Union with Gold Star (U.S.S.R.), Augusto César Sandino (Nicaragua) 1986, and numerous other decorations. *Publication:* From My Life 1981. *Address:* Sozialistische Einheitspartei Deutschlands, Am Marx-Engels-Platz 2, Berlin 102, German Democratic Republic.

HONECKER, Margot; German politician; b. (as Margot Feist) 17 April 1927, Halle; m. Erich Honecker (q.v.) 1953; one d.; Co-Founder Anti-Fascist Youth Cttee., Halle 1945; mem. CP 1945; Sec., Freie Deutsche Jugend (FDJ) Cttee., Sachsen-Anhalt; Chair. Young Pioneers and Sec., Cen. Council, FDJ 1949–53; mem. Volkskammer 1949–53, 1967–; mem. Cen. Cttee. Socialist Unity Party (SED) 1963–; univ. training in U.S.S.R. 1953–54; Head Teacher Training Dept., Ministry of Educ. 1955–58, Deputy Minister of Educ. 1958–63, Minister of Educ. 1963–; mem. Acad. of Pedagogical Sciences; Dr. h.c.; Karl-Marx-Orden, Vaterländischer Verdienstorden in Gold, Held der Arbeit, and other decorations. *Publication:* On Educational Policy and Pedagogics in the German Democratic Republic 1986. *Address:* Ministerium für Volksbildung, 1086 Berlin, Unter den Linden 69/73, German Democratic Republic.

HONEGGER, Dr. Fritz; Swiss politician; b. 25 July 1917, Bischofszell; m. Lucienne Jacot 1944; two s.; ed. Univ. of Zürich; Cantonal Councillor, Zürich 1957–75, Pres. Cantonal Parl., Zürich 1965–66; Deputy from Canton of Zürich to Council of States 1967–78; Chair. Radical Democratic Party of Switzerland 1974–78; elected Fed. Councillor Dec. 1977; Head Fed. Dept. of Public Economy 1978–82; Vice-Pres. of Switzerland Jan.–Dec. 1981, Pres. Jan.–Dec. 1982; Chair. Swiss Life 1985–90. *Leisure interests:* reading and travelling. *Address:* Schloss-Strasse 29, 8803 Rüschlikon, Switzerland (Home).

HONEYCOMBE, Robert William Kerr, PH.D., D.SC., F.ENG., F.R.S.; Australian professor of metallurgy; b. 2 May 1921, Melbourne; s. of William Honeycombe and Rachael (Kerr) Honeycombe; m. June Collins 1947; two d.; ed. Geelong Coll. and Univ. of Melbourne; research officer CSIRO (Australia) 1942–47; ICI Research Fellow, Cavendish Lab., Cambridge 1948–49; Royal Soc. Armourers and Brasiers' Research Fellow, Cavendish Lab. 1949–51; Sr. Lecturer in Physical Metallurgy, Univ. of Sheffield 1951–55, Prof. 1955–66; Goldsmith's Prof. of Metallurgy, Univ. of Cambridge 1966–84, Prof. Emer. 1984–; Fellow, Trinity Hall, Cambridge 1966–73, Hon. Fellow 1975–; Pres. Clare Hall, Cambridge 1973–80; Pres. Inst. of Metallurgists 1977, Metals Soc. 1980–81; Treasurer and Vice-Pres. Royal Soc. 1986–; recipient of several medals and hon degrees. *Publications:* The Plastic Deformation of Metals 1968, Steels: Microstructure and Properties 1981. *Leisure interests:* walking, gardening, music, photography. *Address:* Department of Materials Science and Metallurgy, University of Cambridge, Pembroke Street, Cambridge, CB2 9QZ; 46 Main Street, Hardwick, Cambridge, CB3 7QS, England. (Home) *Telephone:* (0223) 334356; (0954) 210501 (Home).

HONG XUEZHI, Gen.; Chinese army officer; b. 1913, Jinzhai Co., Anhui Prov.; joined CCP 1929; Deputy Commdr., army corps, 4th Field Army 1949; Commdr. Guangdong Mil. Region 1949–50; mem. Guangzhou Mil. Control Comm. 1949–50; Political Commissar, 16th Corps 1950; Dir. Logistics Dept. Chinese People's Volunteers in Korea 1952; mem. Nat. Defence Council 1954–59; Deputy Dir. PLA Logistics Dept. 1954–56, Dir. 1956–59; alt.-mem. 8th Cen. Cttee. of CCP 1956; mem. Standing Cttee., 5th NPC 1978–; Dir., Gen. Office for Nat. Defence Industry 1978–79; Dir. 2nd Office of Nat. Defence 1979–80; Vice-Chair. Cttee. to Examine Proposals, 2nd Session, 5th NPC 1979; mem. 11th Cen. Cttee. of CCP 1979; mem. 12th Cen. Cttee. CCP 1982–85; Dir. PLA Gen. Logistics Dept. 1980–; mem. and Deputy Sec.-Gen. Cen. Mil. Comm. 1982–; mem. Cen. Party Consolidation Guidance Comm. 1983–; Vice-Chair. Cen. Patriotic Public Health Campaign Cttee. 1983–; Head Leading Group of All-Army Financial and Econ. Discipline Inspection, CCP Cen. Mil. Comm. 1986–; Chair. PLA Greening Cttee. 1984–; Vice-Chair. Cen. Greening Cttee. 1983–; Hon. Vice-Pres. Beijing Social Welfare Foundation 1984–. *Address:* Office of the Director, People's Liberation Army General Logistics Department, Beijing, People's Republic of China.

HONGLADAROM, Sunthorn, M.A.; Thai politician and diplomatist; b. 23 Aug. 1912, Nakorn Sawan; m. Khunying Lamchiag Hongladarom 1937; five s. one d.; ed. Thepsirin School, Bangkok, Weymouth Coll., England and Cambridge Univ.; Chief of Foreign Div. Dept. of Information 1943–46; Asst. Sec.-Gen. of Council of Ministers 1948–50; Sec.-Gen. of Nat. Econ. Council 1950–57; Amb. to Fed. of Malaya 1957–59; Minister of Econ. Affairs 1959; Minister of Finance 1959–65; Deputy Minister of Nat. Devt. 1963; Minister of Econ. Affairs 1965–68; Amb. to the U.K. 1968–69, to the U.S.A. 1969–72; Sec.-Gen. SEATO 1972–77; Hon. Asst. Sec.-Gen. Thai Red Cross Soc. 1977–; Rector of Chiang Mai Univ. 1966; Fellow of Econ. Devt. Inst., Int. Bank of Reconstruction and Devt.; LL.D. h.c.; Knight Grand Commdr. Order of White Elephant, Order of Chula Chom Klao. *Leisure interests:* travel, golf, bowling. *Address:* Thai Red Cross Society, Chulalongkorn Memorial Hospital, Bangkok, Thailand.

HONIG, Edwin, M.A.; American professor of comparative literature and poet; b. 3 Sept. 1919, New York; s. of Abraham David Honig and Jane

Freundlich; m. 1st Charlotte Gilchrist 1940 (died 1963); m. 2nd Margot S. Dennes 1963 (divorced 1978); two s.; ed. Univ. of Wis. and Brown Univ.; Instructor in English Purdue Univ. 1942–43, New York Univ. and Ill. Inst. Tech. 1946–47, Univ. of N.M. 1947–48, Claremont Coll. 1949, Harvard Univ. 1949–52, Briggs-Copeland Asst. Prof. of English, Harvard 1952–57; mem. Faculty Brown Univ. 1957–, Prof. of English 1960–82, of Comparative Literature 1962–82, Chair. Dept. of English 1967, Prof. Emer. 1983–; Visiting Prof. Univ. of Calif., Davis 1964–65; Mellon Prof. Boston Univ. 1977; Dir. Copper Beech Press; Guggenheim Fellow 1948, 1962; Amy Lowell Travelling Poetry Fellow 1968; Golden Rose Award New England Poetry Club 1961; Poetry Prize, Saturday Review 1956; NEA Award (in poetry) 1980, (in transl.) 1983; Columbia Univ. Translation Center Nat. Award 1985. *Publications include: poems:* The Moral Circus 1955, The Gazabos 1960, Survivals 1964, Spring Journal 1968, Four Springs 1972, Shake a Spear With Me, John Berryman 1974, At Sixes 1974, The Affinities of Orpheus 1976, Selected Poems (1955–1976) 1979, Interrupted Praise 1983, Gifts of Light; *plays:* The Widow 1953, The Phantom Lady 1964, Life is a Dream, Calisto and Melibea (play/libretto) 1972, Ends of the World and Other Plays 1983; *criticism:* García Lorca 1944, Dark Conceit: The Making of Allegory 1959, Calderón and the Seizures of Honor 1972, The Poet's Other Voice 1985; *stories:* Foibles and Fables of an Abstract Man 1979; *anthologies* (with Oscar Williams): The Mentor Book of Major American Poets 1961, The Major Metaphysical Poets 1968, Spenser 1968; also translations of works by García Lorca, Calderón de la Barca, Fernando Pessoa and Lope de Vega; produced opera Calisto and Melibea 1979. *Address:* Brown University, Box 1852, Providence, R.I. 02912, U.S.A. (Office).

HOOD, Leroy Edward, M.D., PH.D.; American biologist; b. 10 Oct. 1938, Missoula, Mon.; m. Valerie A. Hood 1963; one s. one d.; ed. Calif. Inst. of Tech. and Johns Hopkins School of Medicine; NIH Predoctoral Fellowship, Calif. Inst. of Tech. 1963–64, NIH Postdoctoral Fellowship 1964–67; Sr. Investigator, Immunology Branch, GL&C, Nat Chemical Industries, Nat. Insts. of Health, Bethesda, Md. 1967–70; Asst. Prof. of Biology Calif. Inst. of Tech. 1970–73, Assoc. Prof. 1973–75, Prof. 1975–77, Bowles Prof. of Biology 1977–, Chair. Div. of Biology 1980–, Dir. Cancer Center 1981–; mem. N.A.S., American Acad. of Arts and Sciences; numerous awards and honours. *Publications:* co-author of five books on immunology and biochemistry. *Leisure interests:* mountaineering, climbing, running, photography, science fiction. *Address:* Division of Biology 156-59, California Institute of Technology, Pasadena, Calif. 91125, U.S.A. *Telephone:* (818) 356-4951.

HOOD, William Clarence, PH.D., F.R.S.C.; Canadian economist; b. 13 Sept. 1921, Yarmouth, N.S.; s. of Percy Alexander Hood and Vida Barr (née Webster) Hood; m. Alville Mary Lennox 1948; one s. one d.; ed. Mount Allison Univ., Sackville, N.B., Univ. of Toronto; Economist, Wartime Prices and Trade Bd., Ottawa 1941; Govt. Meteorologist 1943–44; Instructor in Econs., Univ. of Saskatchewan 1944–46; Asst., Assoc. and Full Prof. of Econs., Univ. of Toronto 1946–64; Adviser to Bank of Canada, Ottawa 1964–69; Asst. Deputy Minister of Finance with responsibility for Econ. Analysis, Fiscal Policy and Int. Finance 1970–74, Assoc. Deputy Minister of Finance 1975–79, Deputy Minister of Finance 1979; Econ. Counsellor and Dir. of Research Dept., IMF, Washington, D.C. 1980–86; Econ. Consultant, Washington, D.C. 1986–; Pres. Canadian Econs. Assen. 1969–70; Fellow of Royal Soc. of Canada 1963–, of Econometric Soc. 1975–; Hon. LL.D. (Mount Allison Univ.) 1970, (McMaster Univ., Hamilton, Ont.) 1980. *Publications:* Studies in Econometric Method (with T. C. Koopmans, q.v.) 1953, Output, Labour and Capital in the Canadian Economy (with A. D. Scott) 1958, Financing of Economic Activity in Canada 1959 and various articles in journals. *Leisure interests:* flying, cycling, skiing. *Address:* 9513 Liberty Tree Lane, Vienna, Va. 22180, U.S.A.

't HOOFT, Gerardus; Netherlands professor of theoretical physics; b. 5 July 1946, Den Helder; s. of H. 't Hooft and M.A. van Kampen; m. Albertha A. Schik 1972; two d.; ed. Dalton Lyceum Gymnasium, The Hague, Rijks Universiteit, Utrecht; Fellow C.E.R.N. (Theoretical Physics Div.), Geneva 1972–74; Asst. Prof., Univ. of Utrecht 1974–77, Prof. 1977–; mem. Koninklijke Acad. von Wetenschappen, Letteren en Schone Kunsten v. België, Koninklijke Nederlandse Acad. von Wetenschappen; Foreign Assoc. N.A.S. (U.S.A.); Foreign Hon. mem. American Acad. of Arts and Sciences; Hon. Dr. (Chicago) 1981; W. Prins Prize 1974, Akzo Prize 1977, Dannie Heineman Prize 1979, Wolf Prize 1982, Pius XI Medal 1983, Lorentz Medal 1986. *Publications:* numerous scientific publs., including papers on Renormalization of Yang-Mills Fields, Magnetic monopoles, Instantons, Gauge theories, quark confinement and quantum gravity. *Leisure interests:* piano, painting. *Address:* University of Utrecht, Institute for Theoretical Physics, P.O. Box 80.006, NL 3508 TA Utrecht, The Netherlands. *Telephone:* 030-532284.

HOOGLANDT, Jan Daniel, D.SC.; Netherlands steel manufacturing executive; b. 15 Feb. 1926, Tangier, Morocco; m.; four c.; ed. Hilversum Gymnasium, Municipal Univ. of Amsterdam; joined Koninklijke Nederlandsche Hoogovens en Staalfabrieken NV 1954 as Asst. in Econ. Dept. 1954; retd. May 1988 as Chair. Bd. Hoogovens Groep BV; mem. Supervisory Bd. Algemene Bank Nederland NV, Koninklijke Nederlandsche Hoogovens en Staalfabrieken NV, NV Koninklijke Nederlandse Petroleum Maatschappij;

Heineken NV, Nederlandse Participatie Maatschappij NV; Order of the Netherlands Lion 1976; Commdr. Order Oranje Nassau 1988. *Address:* Hoogovens Groep BV, Postbus 10,000, 1970 CA Ijmuiden, Netherlands. *Telephone:* (02510) 91820.

HOOK, Sidney, PH.D.; American philosopher and author; b. 20 Dec. 1902, New York; s. of Isaac Hook and Jennie Halpern; m. 1st C. Katz 1924, 2nd Ann Ethel Zinken 1935; two s. one d.; ed. Coll. of City of New York and Columbia Univ.; Instructor of Philosophy, New York Univ. 1927–32, Asst. Prof. of Philosophy 1932–34, Assoc. Prof. and Chair. of Dept. 1934–39, Prof. 1939–70, Head All-Univ. Dept. of Philosophy 1950–69, Emer. Prof. 1970–; Regents Prof. Univ. of Calif.; Dir. New York Univ. Inst. of Philosophy and Ed. of its Proceedings; Sr. Research Fellow Hoover Inst. on War, Revolution and Peace; Thomas Jefferson Lecturer 1984; Fellow, American Acad. of Arts and Sciences, American Acad. of Educ.; Council mem. National Endowment for the Humanities 1973–79; Treas. John Dewey Foundation; D.Hum.Litt. (Maine) 1960, (Utah) 1970, LL.D. (Calif.) 1966, (Rockford Coll.) 1970, (Florida) 1971, (Hebrew Union Coll.) 1976, D.H.L. (Vermont) 1979; Int. Freedom Prize, Valley Forge, Pa.; Presidential Medal of Freedom 1985. *Publications:* The Metaphysics of Pragmatism 1927, Towards the Understanding of Karl Marx 1933, From Hegel to Marx 1936, John Dewey: An Intellectual Portrait 1939, Reason, Social Myth and Democracy 1940, The Hero in History: A Study in Limitation and Possibility 1945, Education for Modern Man 1947, Heresy Yes, Conspiracy No 1953, Common Sense and the Fifth Amendment 1958, Political Power and Personal Freedom 1959, The Ambiguous Legacy: Marx and the Marxists 1960, The Quest of Being 1961, The Paradoxes of Freedom 1962, The Fail-Safe Fallacy 1963, Religion in a Free Society 1967, Academic Freedom and Academic Anarchy 1970, Education and the Taming of Power 1973, Pragmatism and the Tragic Sense of Life 1974, Revolution, Reform and Social Justice 1976, Philosophy and Public Policy 1980, Marxism and Beyond 1983, Out of Step: An Unquiet Life in the XXth Century 1987; Ed. and contributor: The Idea of a Modern University 1975, The Philosophy of the Curriculum 1976, The Ethics of Teaching and Scientific Research 1977, The University and the State 1978, and many others. *Leisure interests:* gardening, reading. *Address:* c/o Hoover Institution, Stanford, Calif. 94305; South Wardsboro, Vt. 05355, U.S.A. *Telephone:* (415) 497-1501; (802) 896-6434.

HOOKER, Charlie (Charles Raymond); British artist; b. 1 June. 1953, London; s. of Raymond C. and Daphne Hooker; m. Stephanie J. Burden 1980; one s.; ed. Purley Grammar School, Croydon Coll. of Art and Brighton Polytechnic; founder mem. The Artistics (music ensemble) 1972–75, 2B Butlers Wharf (art space) 1974–75; Visiting lecturer, Chelsea, Croydon, Winchester, Trent, Cardiff, Central, Brighton, Newport, Newcastle, Camberwell Schools of Art/Polytechnics 1977–; Artist in Residence at Amherst Jr. and Hatcham Wood Secondary Schools 1985; several one-man and group shows of maquettes and drawings and numerous installations and performances in U.K., Europe, America and Australia 1975–; published discussions in Performance and in Aspects 1980, 1984, 1986; audio recordings Restricted Movement 1982, Transitions 1984, Charlie Hooker and Performers 1987, for Audio Arts. *Leisure interests:* snooker, carpentry, gardening. *Address:* 14 Queen Mary Road, London, S.E.19, England. *Telephone:* 01-761 3297.

HOOKWAY, Sir Harry Thurston, Kt., PH.D.; British administrator and librarian; b. 23 July 1921, London; s. of William and Bertha Hookway; m. Barbara Butler 1956; one s. one d.; ed. Trinity School of John Whitgift and London Univ.; Asst. Dir. Nat. Chem. Lab. 1959; Dir. U.K. Scientific Mission (N. America), Scientific Attaché, Embassy, Washington, Scientific Adviser, High Comm., Ottawa 1960–64; Head, Information Div. Dept. of Scientific and Industrial Research 1964–65; Chief Scientific Officer, Dept. of Educ. and Science 1966–69, Asst. Under-Sec. of State 1969–73; Deputy Chair. and Chief Exec. British Library Bd. 1973–84; Pro-Chancellor Loughborough Univ. of Tech. 1987–; mem. Royal Comm. on Historical Monuments (England) 1981–88; Chair. Publrs. Data Bases Ltd. 1984–87, L.A. Publishing Ltd. 1986–89; Pres. The Library Asscn. 1985–; Hon. LL.D., Hon D. Litt., Hon. F.L.A.; Hon. F.I.Inf. Scientists; Gold Medal Int. Asscn. of Library Asscns. 1985. *Publications:* papers in learned and professional journals. *Leisure interests:* music, travel. *Address:* 35 Goldstone Crescent, Hove, East Sussex, BN3 6LR, England.

HOOLEY, Christopher, PH.D., F.R.S.; British university professor; b. 7 Aug. 1928, Edinburgh; s. of Leonard Joseph Hooley and Barbara Hooley; m. Birgitta Kniep 1954; two s.; ed. Abbotsholme School and Corpus Christi Coll. Cambridge; Capt., Royal Army Educational Corps 1948–49; Fellow, Corpus Christi Coll. 1955–58; Lecturer in Math., Univ. of Bristol 1958–65; Prof. of Pure Math., Univ. of Durham 1965–67; Prof. of Pure Math. and Head of Dept. of Pure Math., Univ. Coll. Cardiff 1967–, Dean of Faculty of Science 1973–76, Deputy Prin. Univ. Coll. Cardiff 1979–81; Visiting mem., Inst. for Advanced Study, Princeton, U.S.A. on several oc̅ since 1970, Institut des Hautes Etudes Scientifiques Paris 19̅ Prize, Cambridge 1973; Sr. Berwick Prize, Lor̅ cations: Applications of Sieve Method̅ Recent Progress in Analytic ʌ̅ 1981. *Leisure interes̅ Grange, Bac̅

HOONTRAKUL, Sommai, M.ECON.; Thai politician; b. 15 May 1918; ed. Assumption Coll. and Keio Univ., Japan; joined Bank of Thailand 1943, later Asst. to Gov. of Bank; Gen. Man. Industrial Finance Corpn. of Thailand (IFCT); Gen. Man. Siam Commercial Bank; fmr. Minister of Finance; Minister of Finance 1983–86. *Address:* c/o Ministry of Finance, Na Pralan Road, Bangkok 2, Thailand.

HOOPER, Anthony Sidney Colchester, B.SC.,M.S.; South African librarian; b. 16 Sept. 1943, Pretoria; s. of Winifred Hooper and Henry John Colchester Hooper; m. Adriana Holleman 1969; one s. one d.; ed. Ellis Robins High School, Harare, Univ. of Cape Town and Catholic Univ. of America; Research Asst., Univ. Coll. of Rhodesia 1965; Head, Reference and Translations Service, Council for Scientific and Industrial Research, Pretoria 1969–74; Chief Librarian, Natal Soc. Library, Pietermaritzburg 1974–80; Univ. Librarian, Dir. of Libraries, Univ. of Cape Town 1980–; Pres. S. African Inst. for Librarianship and Information Science 1984–86; mem. Bd. S. African Bibliographic and Information Network (Sabinet) 1984–; Fellow, S. African Inst. for Librarianship and Information Science. *Publications:* numerous professional publs. on libraries and librarianship. *Leisure interests:* reading, carpentry, running and cooking. *Address:* University of Cape Town Libraries, Rondebosch, Cape Town 7700, South Africa. *Telephone:* 6503096.

HOOPMAN, Harold DeWaine, B.S.; American oil executive; b. 22 July 1920, Lucas, Kan.; s. of Ira William Hoopman and Mary Dorman; m. Eleanor Gessner 1946; two s. one d.; ed. Wyoming and Harvard Univs.; Experimental Test Engineer, Wright Aeronautical Co. 1942–43; joined Marathon Oil Co. 1946, Resident Man., Guatemala 1957–62, Vice-Pres. Int. 1962–67, Asst. to Pres. 1967–68, Vice-Pres. Production, U.S. and Canada 1968–69, Vice-Pres. Marketing, U.S. 1969–72, Dir. 1972–, Pres. 1972–85, Chief Exec. Officer 1975–85; Vice-Chair. Oil Gas and Related Resources, U.S. Steel Corpn. 1983–; Dir. American Petroleum Inst., United States Steel Corpn. 1982– (merged with Marathon Oil 1982), Pittsburgh Nat. Corpn., First Nat. Bank of Findlay, PNC Financial Corpn.; Hon. LL.D (Marietta Coll.) 1979, Hon. L.H.D. (Eastern Illinois Univ.) 1982; mem. Soc. of Petroleum Engineers of AIME. *Leisure interests:* antique autos., hunting, fishing. *Address:* Marathon Oil Company, 539 South Main Street, Findlay, Ohio 45840, U.S.A. *Telephone:* (419) 422-2121.

HOÓS János; Hungarian economist and politician; b. 1938, Budapest; ed. Karl Marx Univ. of Economy, Budapest; joined HSWP 1960; univ. asst. lecturer and pursued studies in theoretical research of econ. planning; on staff of HSWP Cent. Cttee. as deputy dept. head and dept. leader 1968–80; mem. Cen. Cttee. 1980–; Sec. of State for Nat. Planning Office 1980–87; Pres. (rank of Minister) for Nat. Planning Office 1988–. *Address:* Budapest V., Roosevelt tér 7/8, Hungary. *Telephone:* 123-480.

HOOVER, Herbert William Jr., A.B.; American business executive; b. 23 April 1918, North Canton, Ohio; s. of Herbert William Hoover and Grace Steele; m. Carla Good 1941; one s. one d.; ed. Rollins Coll.; 2nd Lieut. U.S. Army 1943–45; Exec. Sales, The Hoover Co. 1941–43; Dir. of Public Relations 1945–48, Asst. Vice-Pres. 1948–52, Sales Vice-Pres. 1952–53, Exec. Vice-Pres. 1953–54, Pres. 1954–56, Chair. 1959–66; Dir. Hoover Co., Canada 1952–66, Pres. 1954–66; Dir. Hoover (Great Britain) Ltd. 1954–66, Chair. 1956–66; Dir. and Pres. Hoover (America Latina) S.A., Panama 1955–66, Hoover Mexicana, Mexico 1955–66, Hoover Inc., Panama, Hoover Industrial y Comercial S.A., Colombia 1960–67; Pres. and Chair. Hoover Worldwide Corpn. 1960–66; Pres. Dir.-Gen. S.A. Hoover, France 1965; fmr. Regional Vice-Chair. U.S. Cttee. for UN; Dir. The Harter Bank and Trust Co. Canton, Ohio; Chair. Hoover Foundation; mem. Council on Foreign Relations, New York; Trustee, Univ. of Miami, Florida; Dir. of the Miami Heart Inst.; Hon. LL.D. (Mount Union Coll.); Chevalier de la Légion d'honneur. *Address:* 70 Park Drive, 4 Bal Harbour, Florida 33154, U.S.A. *Telephone:* 305-864-8865.

HOOYKAAS, Reijer, D.SC.; Netherlands university professor; b. 1 Aug. 1906, Schoonhoven; m. Ilona Van Asselt 1936; one s. four d.; ed. Utrecht Univ.; chem. teacher, Amsterdam 1930, Zeist 1932; Extraordinary Prof. of History of Science, Free Univ. of Amsterdam 1945–48, Prof. 1948–66, and of Mineralogy 1948–60, Prof. of History of Science, Univ. of Utrecht 1967–76; Visiting Prof. Open Univ. (U.K.) 1973–74; fmr. Pres. Int. Comm. History Geological Sciences; mem. Royal Netherlands Acad. of Sciences and Letters, Int. Acad. of History of Science, Hollandsche Maatschappij der Wetenschappen; Assoc. mem. Comité belge d'Histoire des Sciences; Foreign mem. Royal Belgian Acad. of Sciences and Acad. da Cultura Portuguesa; Corresp. mem. Inst. de Coimbra; Hon. D.Sc. (Coimbra), Dr. h.c. (Open Univ.); Knight Order of Nederlandse Leeuw, Commdr. Order of Polonia Restituta, Grande-Oficial Order of Infante D. Henrique. *Publications:* The Concept of Element, Its Historical-Philosophical Development 1933, Robert Boyle: A Study in Science and Christianity 1943, The Chemical Revolution: A. L. Lavoisier 1952, Humanisme, science et réforme, Pierre de la Ramée 1958, The Principle of Uniformity in Geology, Biology and Theology 1959, Physik und Mechanik in historischer Hinsicht 1963, Introdução a História das Ciências 1965, Nature and History 1966, Catastrophism in Geology 1970, History of Science, from Babel to Bohr 1971, Religion and the Rise of Modern Science 1972, Humanism and 16th Century Portuguese Science and Letters 1979, Science in Manueline Style: The Historical Context of D. João de Castro's Scientific Works 1980, Selected

Studies in History of Science 1983, G. J. Rheticus' Treatise on Holy Scripture and the Motion of the Earth 1984, Sciences in the Service of the Common Weal 1987; numerous articles in international historical and scientific journals. *Address:* Krullelaan 35, 3701TB Zeist, Netherlands. *Telephone:* 03404-22488.

HOPE, Alec Derwent; Australian poet; b. 21 July 1907, Cooma, N.S.W.; s. of Rev. Percival Hope and Florence Ellen Scotford; m. Penelope Robinson 1938; two s. one d. (deceased); ed. Sydney and Oxford Univs.; fmr. Lecturer Sydney Teachers' Coll. and Sr. Lecturer Melbourne Univ.; Prof. of English, School of Gen. Studies, Australian Nat. Univ. 1951–68; Library Fellow, Australian Nat. Univ. 1969–72; retd. 1973; Visiting Fellow, Clare Hall, Cambridge 1986; Hon. Fellow, Univ. Coll., Oxford 1986; Fellow, Australian Acad. of the Humanities; Hon. D.Litt. (Australian Nat. Univ.) 1972, (New England) 1973, (Monash) 1976, (Melbourne) 1976; Arts Council Prize 1965, Britannica-Australia Award 1966, Levinson Prize for Poetry (Chicago) 1969, Ingram Merrill Award for Literature 1969, Robert Frost Award for Poetry 1976. *Publications:* The Wandering Islands 1955, Poems 1960, The Cave and the Spring 1965, Collected Poems 1966, New Poems 1965–69, Dunciad Minor 1970, A Midsummer Eve's Dream 1970, Collected Poems 1930–1970 1972, Selected Poems 1973, Native Companions 1974, A Late Picking 1975, A Book of Answers 1978, The New Cratylus 1979, The Pack of Autolycus 1979, The Drifting Continent 1979, Antechinus 1981, Doctor Faustus 1982, Tre Volti dell'Amore 1982, The Age of Reason 1985, Selected Poems 1986, Ladies from the Sea 1987, The Shorter Lyrics of Catullus (trans.) 1989, The Lyrics of Luis Vas de Camoens, A Selection (with Isabel Martinho, trans.) 1989, verse and criticism in numerous magazines, including Meanjin, Southerly, M.U.M., Hermes, Quadrant, Westerly, Overland and The Southern Review. *Leisure interests:* camping, travel, reading, music. *Address:* 66 Arthur Circle, Canberra, A.C.T., Australia 2603. *Telephone:* 95-1525.

HOPE, Bob; American (b. British) comedian; b. 29 May 1903, Eltham, England; m. Dolores Reade 1934; two s. two adopted d.; first film 1938; since then has appeared in numerous films and radio and television productions; numerous hon. degrees and awards including American Congressional Medal of Honor 1963, Award of Entertainment Hall of Fame 1975, four special Academy Awards, American Hope Award 1988, Medal of Liberty, Hon. C.B.E. and 44 hon. doctorates (1982). *Films include:* College Swing, Big Broadcast, Give Me A Sailor, Thanks for the Memory 1938, Never Say Die, Some Like it Hot, Cat and the Canary 1939, Road to Singapore 1940, Nothing But the Truth, Road To Zanzibar, Louisiana Purchase, Caught in the Draft 1941, My Favourite Blonde, Star Spangled Rhythm, Road to Morocco 1942, They've Got Me Covered, Let's Face It 1943, Princess and the Pirate 1944, Road to Utopia 1945, Monsieur Beaucaire 1946, My Favourite Brunette 1947, Road To Rio, The Paleface 1948, Sorrowful Jones, The Great Lover 1949, Fancy Pants 1950, My Favourite Spy, Lemon Drop Kid 1951, Son of Paleface 1952, Off Limits, Here Come the Girls 1951, Road to Bali 1953, Casanova's Big Night 1954, Seven Little Foys 1955, Iron Petticoat, That Certain Feeling 1956, Beau James 1957, Paris Holiday 1958, Alias Jesse James 1959, The Facts of Life 1960, Bachelor in Paradise 1961, Road to Hong Kong 1962, Call Me Bwana 1963, A Global Affair 1964, I'll Take Sweden 1965, Boy, Did I Get a Wrong Number! 1966, Eight on the Lam 1967, Private Life of Sgt O'Farrell 1968, How to Commit Marriage 1969, The Road to Ruin 1972, Cancel My Reservation. *Publications:* They've Got Me Covered 1941, I Never Left Home 1944, So This Is Peace 1946, Have Tux, Will Travel 1954, I Owe Russia $1200 1963, Five Women I Love 1966, The Last Christmas Show 1974, Road to Hollywood 1977, Confessions of a Hooker 1985. *Address:* Hope Enterprises Inc., 3808 Riverside Drive, Burbank, Calif. 91505, U.S.A. (Office).

HOPE, Sir Charles Peter, K.C.M.G., B.SC., T.D.; British diplomatist (retd.); b. 22 May 1912, Dartmouth; s. of G. L. N. Hope and H. M. V. Riddell; m. Hazel Mary Turner 1936; three s.; ed. Oratory School and Imperial Coll., London; joined War Office 1938; service with Royal Artillery 1939–46; entered Foreign Service 1946, served Paris 1946–50; Asst. Head, UN Dept., Foreign Office 1950–53; served as Counsellor, High Comm. Germany, later at Embassy 1953–56; Head of News Dept., Foreign Office 1956–59; Minister, Madrid 1959–62; Consul-Gen., Houston, U.S.A. 1963–64; Alternate Rep., UN 1964–68; Amb. to Mexico 1968–72; mem. Acad. of Int. Law; Grand Cross of the Aztec Eagle, Grand Officer Merito Melitense, K. St. J., Kt. of Malta. *Leisure interests:* shooting and fishing. *Address:* North End House, Heyshott, Midhurst, Sussex, England.

HOPE, Maurice; British boxer; b. 6 Dec. 1951, Antigua, West Indies; s. of Norris and Sarah Andrew Hope; m. Patricia Hope; one s. two d.; came to Britain 1961; ed. Hackney Secondary Modern School, London; rep. England and Great Britain as amateur boxer with Repton Amateur Boxing Club; quarter-finalist at Olympic Games, Munich 1972; professional boxer June 1973–; won British light-middleweight title from Larry Paul Nov. 1974, retained it v. Paul (Sept. 1975) and Tony Poole (April 1976); won Lonsdale Belt outright and became Commonwealth champion by beating Poole; lost to Bunny Sterling for vacant British middleweight title, June 1975; won European light-middleweight title from Vito Antuofermo, Rome Oct. 1976; drew with Eckhard Dagge for World Boxing Council (WBC) version of world light-middleweight title, Berlin March 1977; retained

European title v. Frank Wissenbach, Hamburg (May 1977) and Joel Bonnetaz, Wembley (Nov. 1977); relinquished European title Sept. 1978; won WBC version of world light-middleweight title from Rocky Mattioli, San Remo March 1979; retained it v. Mike Baker (Sept. 1979), Mattioli (July 1980) and Carlos Herrera (Nov. 1980), lost it to Wilfredo Benitez (May 1981); 34 fights, 30 wins, one draw; now a trainer. *Leisure interests:* table tennis, snooker, pool. *Address:* c/o British Boxing Board of Control, 2 Ramilles Buildings, Hills Place, London W.1, England.

HOPKIN, Sir (William Aylsham) Bryan, Kt., C.B.E.; British economist; b. 7 Dec. 1914, nr. Cardiff; s. of William Hopkin and Lilian Blanche Cottelle; m. Renée Henriette France Ricour 1938; two s.; ed. St. John's Coll., Cambridge, and Manchester Univ.; Ministry of Health 1938–41; Prime Minister's Statistical Branch 1941–45; Royal Comm. on Population 1945–48; Cabinet Office (Econ. Section, Cen. Statistical Office) 1948–52; Nat. Inst. of Econ. and Social Research 1952–57; Council on Prices, Productivity and Incomes 1957–58; Treasury (Econ. Section) 1958–65; Econ. Planning Unit, Mauritius 1965; Econ. Planning Staff, Ministry of Overseas Devt. 1965–68, Dir.-Gen. of Econ. Planning 1967–68; Dir.-Gen. Dept. of Econ. Affairs 1969; Deputy Chief Econ. Adviser to H.M. Treasury 1969–72, Chief Econ. Adviser 1974–77; Prof. of Econs., Cardiff Univ. 1972–74, 1976–82; Hon. Professional Fellow (Univ. Coll., Swansea) 1988–. *Publications:* articles on economic matters. *Leisure interests:* reading, music. *Address:* Aberthin House, Aberthin, Near Cowbridge, South Glamorgan CF7 7HB, Wales. *Telephone:* (044 63) 2303.

HOPKINS, Anthony, C.B.E.; British actor; b. 31 Dec. 1937, Port Talbot, Wales; s. of Richard Hopkins and Muriel Hopkins; m. 1st Petronella Barker 1967 (divorced 1972), one d.; m. 2nd Jennifer Lynton 1973; ed. Cowbridge Grammar School, S. Wales, Welsh Coll. of Music and Drama, Cardiff, Royal Acad. of Dramatic Art; mil. training and service: clerk Royal Artillery Unit, Bulford 1958–60; joined Manchester Library Theatre, Asst. Stage Man. 1960; then at Nottingham Repertory Co.; joined Phoenix Theatre, Leicester 1963; then Liverpool Playhouse, then Hornchurch Repertory Co.; joined Nat. Theatre Co. 1967; Film Debut The Lion in Winter 1967; film, TV, stage actor in U.K. and U.S.A. 1967–, in U.S.A. 1974–84. *Performances include: stage:* title role in Macbeth, Nat. Theatre 1972, Dr. Dysart in Equus, Plymouth Theatre, New York 1974, 1975, Huntington Hartford Theatre, Los Angeles (also Dir.) 1977, Prospero in The Tempest, Los Angeles 1979, Old Times, New York 1983, The Lonely Road, Old Vic Theatre, London 1985, Pravda, Nat. Theatre 1985, King Lear (title role), Nat. Theatre 1986, Antony and Cleopatra (title role), Nat. Theatre 1987, M. Butterfly 1989; *films:* The Looking Glass War 1967, Claudius in Hamlet 1969, When Eight Bells Toll 1969, Torvald in A Doll's House 1972, The Girl from Petrovka 1973, Juggernaut 1974, A Bridge Too Far 1976, Audrey Rose 1976, International Velvet 1977, Magic 1978, The Elephant Man 1979, A Change of Seasons 1980, Capt. Bligh in The Bounty 1983, The Good Father 1985, 84 Charing Cross Road 1987, The Old Jest 1987, A Chorus of Disapproval 1988, The Tenth Man 1988, The Dawning 1988; *TV:* A Heritage and its History, A Company of Five 1968, The Three Sisters, The Peasants Revolt 1969, title roles in Dickens, Danton, Astrov in Uncle Vanya, Hearts and Flowers 1970, Pierre in War and Peace 1971–72, title role in Lloyd George 1972, QB VII 1973, A Childhood Friend, Possessions, All Creatures Great and Small, The Arcata Promise 1974, Dark Victory, The Lindbergh Kidnapping Case (Emmy Award) 1975, Victory at Entebbe 1976, title role in Kean 1978, The Voyage of the Mayflower 1979, The Bunker (Emmy Award), Peter and Paul 1980, title role in Othello, Little Eyolf, The Hunchback of Notre Dame 1981, A Married Man 1982, Strangers and Brothers 1983, Old Times, The Arch of Triumph, Mussolini and I, Hollywood Wives, Guilty Conscience 1984, Blunt (role of Guy Burgess) 1987, Heartland 1989; B.A.F.T.A. TV Actor Award 1972, Emmy Awards 1976, 1981, Variety Club Film Actor of the Year (The Bounty) 1984, Stage Actor of the Year (Pravda) 1985, S.W.E.T. The Observer Award for Pravda 1985, Best Actor, Moscow Film Festival, for 84 Charing Cross Road 1987. *Leisure interests:* music, playing the piano, reading philosophy and European history. *Address:* c/o Peggy Thompson Business Management, 7 High Park Road, Kew, Richmond, Surrey, TW9 4BL, England.

HOPKINS, Antony, C.B.E., F.R.C.M.; British musician, author and broadcaster; b. 21 March 1921, London; s. of the late Hugh and Marjorie Reynolds; m. Alison Purves 1947; ed. Berkhamsted School and Royal Coll. of Music; composed incidental music for theatre (Old Vic, Stratford-upon-Avon), radio and cinema; composed music for winning entries, Italia Prize 1952 and 1957; radio broadcaster in series Talking about Music; Hon. Fellow R.A.M., Robinson Coll. (Cambridge) 1980; Hon. D.Univ. (Stirling) 1980; City of Tokyo Medal 1973, Grand Prix, Besançon Film Festival for John and the Magic Music Man, Chappell Gold Medal, Cobbett Prize, Royal Coll. of Music. *Compositions:* Five studies for voices, Psalm 42, songs, recorder pieces, two ballets, Magnificat and Nunc Dimittis (for girls' choir), A Time for Growing, Three's Company, Dr. Musikus, Partita (for solo violin), John and the Magic Music Man (for narrator and orchestra; filmed 1976), three piano sonatas and others. *Publications:* Talking about Symphonies 1961, Talking about Concertos 1964, Talking about Sonatas 1971, Music Face to Face, Downbeat 1977, Understanding Music 1979, The Nine Symphonies of Beethoven 1980, Songs for Swinging Golfers 1981, Sounds of Music 1982, Beating Time (autobiog.) 1982, Pathway to Music 1983, The Concertgoer's Companion Vol. I 1984, Vol. II 1986.

Leisure interests: golf, motoring. *Address:* Woodyard Cottage, Ashridge, Berkhamsted, Herts., England. *Telephone:* (044 284) 2257.

HOPKINS, Harold Horace, PH.D., D.SC., F.INST.P., F.R.S.; British professor of applied optics; b. 6 Dec. 1918; s. of William E. Hopkins and Teresa E. Hopkins; m. Christine D. Ridsdale 1950; three s. one d.; ed. Gateway School, Leicester and Univs. of Leicester and London; Physicist, Taylor, Taylor & Hobson 1939–42; Royal Engineers 1942; Physicist, Minister of Aircraft Production 1942–45; W. Watson & Sons 1945–47; Research Fellow, later Reader in Optics, Imperial Coll. London 1947–67; Prof. of Applied Optics, Univ. of Reading 1967–84, Head, Dept. of Physics 1977–80, Prof. Emer. 1984–; numerous awards and honours. *Publications:* Wave Theory of Aberrations 1951, Handbook of Urological Endoscopy (with J. G. Gow) 1978; papers in learned journals. *Leisure interests:* keyboard music, sailing, languages, woodwork. *Address:* 26 Cintra Avenue, Reading, Berks., England. *Telephone:* (0734) 871913.

HOPKINSON, Sir (Henry) Thomas, Kt., C.B.E., M.A.; British journalist and author; b. 19 April 1905, Manchester; s. of the Ven. J. H. Hopkinson and Evelyn Mary Fountaine; m. Dorothy Vernon (widow) 1953; three d.; ed. St. Edward's School and Pembroke Coll., Oxford; Asst. Ed. Weekly Illustrated 1934–38; Ed. Picture Post 1940–50, Lilliput 1941–46; Features Ed. News Chronicle 1954–56; Ed. Drum 1958–61; Dir. for Africa, Int. Press Inst. 1963–66; Sr. Fellow in Press Studies Univ. of Sussex 1967–69; Visiting Prof. of Journalism Univ. of Minnesota 1968–69; Dir. Centre for Journalism Studies, Univ. Coll., Cardiff 1970–75; contributor to The Sunday Times, The Observer, and British and American magazines; Hon. F.R.P.S. *Publications:* A Wise Man Foolish 1930, A Strong Hand at the Helm 1933, The Man Below 1939, Mist in the Tagus 1946, The Transitory Venus 1948, Down the Long Slide 1949, Love's Apprentice, George Orwell 1953, The Lady and the Cut-Throat 1958, In the Fiery Continent 1962, South Africa 1964, Picture Post 1938–50 (Ed.) 1970, Much Silence, The Life and Work of Meher Baba (with Dorothy Hopkinson) 1974, Treasures of the Royal Photographic Society 1980, Of This Our Time (autobiography vol. I) 1982, Under the Tropic (vol. II) 1984, Shady City 1987. *Address:* 26 Boulter Street, St. Clement's, Oxford, OX4 1AX, England. *Telephone:* (0865) 240466.

HOPPE, Iver; Danish shipping executive; b. 25 July 1920, Aarhus; s. of Arthur Hans Knudsen Hoppe and Gerda Raun Byberg; m. Ingeborg Lassen 1943; one d.; ed. Univ. of Copenhagen; Act. Lecturer, Copenhagen Univ. 1946, Jurisprudential Lecturer 1952–58; Advocate to the High Court and Court of Appeal 1948–; joined A. P. Møller Concern, Copenhagen 1955, Asst. Dir. 1960–64, Man. Dir. Odense Steet Shipyard Ltd., Odense and Lindø 1964–71; Chair. A/S Svendborg Skibvaerft 1968–71; Chair. Harland Ocean Transport Co. Ltd. 1971; Man. Dir. and Chief Exec., Harland and Wolff Ltd. 1971–74; mem. Bd. Dansk Boreselskab A/S and other cos. until 1971, Den Danske Landmandsbank A/S 1970–72, Danish Ship Credit Fund 1965–71; mem. Council, Danish Nat. Bank 1967–71; mem. Assen. of Danish Shipyards 1964–71, Assen. of Employers of Iron and Metal Industry in Denmark 1967–71, Assen. of Danish Industries 1965–72, West of England Steam Ship Owners Protection and Indemnity Assen. Ltd. 1960–66, Danish Acad. of Technical Sciences, Shipbuilders and Repairers Nat. Assen. Exec. Council and Man. Bd., Northern Ireland Finance Corpn., British Iron and Steel Consumers' Council, Lloyd's Register of Shipping, General Cttee., Det Norske Veritas (British Cttee.), American Bureau of Shipping and other Danish and foreign orgs.; Knight of Dannebrog, Knight of Icelandic Falcon. *Leisure interests:* swimming, reading, mountain walking, farming. *Address:* Malmmosegård, Dyreborgvej 7, 5600 Fåborg, Denmark.

HOPPER, Dennis; American actor, author, photographer and film director; b. 17 May 1936, Dodge City, Kan.; ed. public schools in San Diego; numerous TV appearances include Loretta Young Show. *Film appearances include:* Rebel without a Cause 1955, I Died a Thousand Times 1955, Giant 1956, Story of Mankind, Gunfight at the O.K. Corral 1957, Night Tide, Key Witness, From Hell to Texas 1958, Glory Stompers 1959, The Trip 1961, The Sons of Katie Elder 1962, Hang 'Em High 1966, Cool Hand Luke 1967, True Grit 1968, The American Dreamer 1971, Kid Blue 1973, The Sky is Falling 1975, James Dean—The First American Teenager 1976, Mad Dog Morgan 1976, Tracks 1979, American Friend 1978, Apocalypse Now 1979, Wild Times 1980, King of the Mountain 1981, Human Highway 1981, Rumble Fish 1983, The Osterman Weekend 1984, Black Widow 1986, Blue Velvet 1986, River's Edge 1987, Chattahoochee 1989; actor, writer, dir. Easy Rider 1969, The Last Movie 1971; actor, dir. Out of the Blue 1980; dir. Colors 1988; has held several public exhbns. of photographs; named Best New Dir., Cannes 1969; Best Film awards at Venice 1971, Cannes 1980. *Address:* c/o The Artists Agency, Michael Menchel, 1888 Century Park East, Suite 1400, Los Angeles, Calif. 90067, U.S.A.

HOPPER, W. David, PH.D.; Canadian agricultural economist; b. 22 Feb. 1927, Ottawa; s. of late Wilbert C. Hopper and Eva Hill; m. 1st Jessie Dodds Hebron 1951 (divorced), 2nd Ruth Kramer 1974; one s. one d.; ed. McGill and Cornell Univs.; Asst. Prof. of Econs. and Anthropology, Univ. of Chicago 1959–62; agricultural economist and dir. of evaluation, Intensive Agric. Dist. Program, Ford Foundation, New Delhi 1962–65; agricultural economist and Assoc. Field Dir. Indian Agric. Program, Rockefeller Foundation, New Delhi and Visiting Prof. of Agric. Econs., Indian Agric.

Research Inst., New Delhi 1965–70; Pres. Int. Devt. Research Centre, Ottawa 1970–77; Vice-Pres. S. Asia Region, IBRD, Washington, D.C. 1978–87, Sr. Vice-Pres. Policy, Planning and Research and Chair. Consultative Group on Int. Agric. Research 1987–; Hon. mem. World Acad. of Arts and Sciences, American Acad. of Arts and Sciences, Royal Agric. Soc. of England; numerous consultancies, visiting professorships etc.; Hon. D.Sc. (McGill) 1976, (Orissa) 1980; Hon. LL.D. (Carleton, Ottawa) 1986. *Leisure interests:* sailing, computer graphics. *Address:* International Bank for Reconstruction and Development, 1818 H Street, N.W., Washington, D.C. 20433, U.S.A. *Telephone:* 202-477-5678/5679/5680.

HOPPER, Wilbert Hill (Bill), O.C., B.SC., M.B.A.; Canadian business executive; b. 14 March 1933, Ottawa, Ont.; s. of Wilbert C. and Eva (Hill) Hopper; m. Patricia M. Walker 1957; two s.; ed. Rockcliffe Park School, American Univ. and Univ. of Western Ontario; Petroleum Geologist, Imperial Oil 1955–57; Petroleum Economist, Foster Assocs. 1959–61; Sr. Energy Economist, Nat. Energy Bd. 1961–64; Sr. Petroleum Consultant, Arthur D. Little, Cambridge, Mass. 1964–73; Sr. Adviser, Energy Policy, Dept. of Energy, Mines and Resources 1973–74; Asst. Deputy Minister 1974–75; Pres., C.E.O. and Dir. Petro-Canada 1976–79, Chair., C.E.O. and Dir. 1979–; Chair. and Dir. Westcoast Transmission Co. Ltd.; Vice-Chair. and Dir. Panartic Oils Ltd.; Vice-Chair. Canadian Petroleum Assen., mem. Bd. of Govs. (Exec. Cttee.); Dir. Syncrude Canada Ltd, Canada-China Trade Council, Petro-Canada Int. Assistance Corpn., Foothills Pipe Lines (Yukon) Ltd.; mem. Bd. of Govs. Acadia Univ., N.S., Schooner Bluenose Foundation, Bd. of Regents, Memorial Univ., Newfoundland, Advisory Cttee. School of Business Admin., Univ. of Western Ont., Canadian Inst. for Advanced Research. *Address:* P.O. Box 2844, Calgary, Alberta, T2P 3E3, Canada (Office).

HOPWOOD, Prof. David Alan, F.R.S.; British professor of genetics; b. 19 Aug. 1933, Kinver, Staffs.; s. of Herbert Hopwood and Dora Grant; m. 1962 Joyce Lilian Bloom; two s. one d.; ed. Purbrook Park County High School, Hants., Lymm Grammar School, Cheshire, St. John's Coll., Cambridge; John Stothert Bye-Fellow, Magdalene Coll., Univ. of Cambridge 1956–58, Research Fellow, St. John's Coll. 1958–61, Univ. Demonstrator 1957–61; Lecturer in Genetics, Univ. of Glasgow 1961–68; John Innes Prof. of Genetics, Univ. of E. Anglia, and Head, Genetics Dept., John Innes Inst. 1968–; Hon. Prof., Chinese Acad. of Medical Science, Inst. of Microbiology and Plant Physiology, Chinese Acad. of Sciences; fmr. Pres. Genetical Soc. of G.B.; Fellow, Inst. of Biology; Foreign Fellow, Indian Nat. Science Acad. *Publications:* Genetics of Bacterial Diversity 1989 (Ed. D.A. Mapwood and K.F. Chater); numerous articles and chapters in scientific journals and books. *Leisure interests:* gardening and coarse fishing. *Address:* John Innes Institute, Colney Lane, Norwich, NR4 7UH (Office); 244 Unthank Road, Norwich, NR2 2AH, England (Home). *Telephone:* (0603) 52571.

HORDERN, Sir Michael Murray, Kt., C.B.E.; British actor; b. 3 Oct. 1911, Berkhamstead; s. of Capt. Edward Joseph Calverly Hordern and Margaret Emily Murray; m. Grace Eveline Mortimer 1943; one d.; ed. Brighton Coll.; fmrly. with The Educational Supply Assen.; amateur actor at St. Pancras People's Theatre; first professional appearance as Lodovico in Othello, People'e Palace 1937; two repertory seasons, Little Theatre, Bristol 1937–39; Royal Navy 1940–46; Hon. Fellow Queen Mary's Coll. 1987; Hon. D.Litt. (Exeter) 1985, Hon. D.Litt. (Warwick) 1987. *Stage roles include:* Mr. Toad (Toad of Toad Hall), Stratford 1948, 1949; Ivanov (Ivanov), Arts Theatre 1950; Jacques, Menenius, Caliban, Stratford season 1952; Polonius, King John, Malvolio, Prospero, Old Vic 1953–54; "BB" (The Doctor's Dilemma), Saville 1956; Cassius, Macbeth, Old Vic 1958–59; Ulysses (Troilus and Cressida), Edinburgh Festival 1962; Herbert George Butler (The Physicists), Aldwych 1969; King Lear, Nottingham Playhouse 1969; Flint, Criterion 1970; appeared in Jumpers 1972 and 1976, Richard II 1972, The Cherry Orchard 1973, all for Nat. Theatre; The Ordeal of Gilbert Pinfold, Manchester 1977, Round House 1979; Prospero (The Tempest) and Armado (Love's Labour's Lost) for R.S.C. 1978, The Rivals (Nat. Theatre) 1983, You Never Can Tell (Haymarket) 1987–88, Diamond Skulls; many roles in films, radio and television. *Leisure interest:* fishing. *Address:* Flat Y, Rectory Chambers, Old Church Street, London, SW3 5DA, England.

HORECKER, Bernard L., B.S., PH.D.; American biochemist; b. 31 Oct. 1914, Chicago, Ill.; s. of Paul Horecker and Bessie Horecker; m. Frances Goldstein 1936; three d.; ed. Univ. of Chicago; Research Assoc., Dept. of Chem., Univ. of Chicago 1939–40; Examiner U.S. Civil Service Comm., Washington, D.C. 1940–41; Biochemist U.S. Public Health Service (U.S.P.H.S.) Nat. Insts. of Health (N.I.H.) Industrial Hygiene Research Lab. 1941–47, Nat. Inst. of Arthritis and Metabolic Diseases 1947–53, Chief, Section on Enzymes and Cellular Biochemistry, N.I.H. Nat. Inst. of Arthritis and Metabolic Diseases 1953–56; Head Lab. of Biochemistry and Metabolism 1956–59; Prof. and Chair. Dept. of Microbiology, New York Univ. School of Medicine 1959–63, Dept. of Molecular Biology Albert Einstein Coll. of Medicine 1962–71, Dir. Div. of Biol. Sciences 1970–72, Assoc. Dean for Scientific Affairs 1971–72; Vice-Chair. Div. of Biological Chem., A.C.S. 1975–76, Chair. 1976–77; mem. Roche Inst. of Molecular Biology 1972–84, Head Lab. of Molecular Enzymology 1977–84; professorial lecturer on Enzymes, George Washington Univ. 1950–57; Visiting Prof.,

Univ. of Calif. 1954, Univ. of Ill. 1957, Univ. of Paraná, Brazil, 1960, 1963, Cornell Univ. 1964, Univ. of Rotterdam 1970; Visiting Investigator, Pasteur Inst. 1957–58, Indian Inst. of Science, Bangalore 1971; Ciba Lecturer, Rutgers Univ. 1962; Phillips Lecturer, Haverford Coll. 1965; Reilly Lecturer, Notre Dame Univ. 1969; Visiting Prof., Albert Einstein Coll. of Medicine 1972–; Adjunct Prof., Cornell Univ. Medical Coll. 1972–84, Prof. of Biochemistry and Dean Graduate School of Medical Sciences 1984–; Ed. Biochemical and Biophysical Research Communications 1959–; Chair. Editorial Cttee. Archives of Biochemistry and Biophysics 1968–84; Ed. Current Topics in Cellular Regulation 1969–; mem. Scientific Advisory Bd., Roche Inst. of Molecular Biology 1967–70, Chair. 1970–72; Dir. Academic Press 1968–73; mem. Comm. on Personnel, American Cancer Soc. 1969–73; Medical Scientist Training Program Study Section N.I.H. 1970–72; mem. Scientific Advisory Comm. for Biochem. and Chemical Carcinogenesis, American Cancer Soc. 1974–78, Council for Research and Clinical Investigation Awards, American Cancer Soc. 1984–; Pres. American Soc. of Biological Sciences 1968–69, Harvey Soc. of New York 1970–71; Vice-Chair. Pan American Assen. of Biochemical Socs. 1971, Chair. 1972; mem. Nat. Acad. of Sciences; Hon. mem. of Swiss, Japanese, Spanish Socs., Hellenic Biochemical and Biophysical Soc., Greece, Brazilian Acad. Sciences; Fellow, American Acad. of Arts and Sciences; mem. Indian Nat. Acad. of Science; Corresp. mem. Argentine Acad. of Science; Prof. h.c. (Univ.of Paraná, Brazil) 1982; Hon. D.Sc. (Univ. of Urbino, Italy); Paul Lewis Labs. Award in Enzyme Chem. 1952, Fed. Security Agency's Superior Accomplishment Award 1952, Hillebrand Prize, A.C.S. 1954, Washington Acad. of Sciences Award in Biological Sciences 1954, Rockefeller Public Service Award 1957, Fulbright Travel Award 1963, Commonwealth Fund Fellow 1967, Merck Award (American Soc. of Biological Chemists) 1981, Carl Neuberg Medal (Virchow-Pirquet Med. Soc.) 1981. *Leisure interests:* gardening, ornithology. *Address:* Cornell University, Graduate School of Medical Sciences—F104, 1300 York Avenue, New York, N.Y. 10021, U.S.A. *Telephone:* 212 746-6023.

HOŘENÍ, Zdeněk, RSDR.; Czechoslovak journalist and politician; b. 9 February 1930, Frýdštejn; ed. Party Coll. CPSU Cen. Cttee, Moscow; Ed., Rudé Právo 1952–68, Deputy Chief Ed. 1969–83, Ed.-in-Chief. 1983–; Ed. Tribuna, 1969; Chair., Czechoslovak Union of Journalists 1972–83; mem. Exec. Cttee. Int. Org. of Journalists 1972–83; Deputy to Czech Nat. Council 1976–; cand. mem. Cen. Cttee., CP of Czechoslovakia 1976–83, mem. 1984, mem. Secr. 1984–; Chair. Union of Czechoslovakia-Soviet Friendships 1987–; extensive publicist activity; several Czechoslovak Awards. *Address:* Rude Pravo, Na Porici 30, 112 86 Prague 1, Czechoslovakia.

HORGAN Paul; American author; b. 1 Aug. 1903, Buffalo, N.Y.; s. of Edward D. Horgan and Rose Marie (Rohr) Horgan; ed. pvt. schools; Dir. Center for Advanced Studies, Wesleyan Univ., 1962–67, Prof. Emer. and Author-in-Residence 1967–; recipient, Pulitzer Prize (history) twice, Bancroft Prize (history), Harper Prize (novel); Hon. Litt.D. (Yale, Wesleyan, Notre Dame and 17 others). *Publications:* history: Great River, The Rio Grande in North American History 1954, Lamy of Santa Fe 1975; fiction: No Quarter Given 1935, Far From Cibola 1937, A Distant Trumpet 1960, The Richard Trilogy 1964, Mexico Bay 1982 and 33 other works (1988). *Leisure interests:* music, painting. *Address:* 77 Pearl Street, Middletown, Conn. 06457, U.S.A.

HORGOS, Dr. Gyula; Hungarian mechanical engineer and politician; b. 23 July 1920, Nagyvárad (now Oradea in Romania); s. of Pál Horgos; two s. one d.; ed. Budapest Technical Univ.; engineer, Csepel Machine Tool Plant 1943–49; post-graduate studies 1949–53; Chief Engineer, Csepel Metal Works 1954, later Vice-Pres. Nat. Planning Office, later Technical Dir.; Deputy Minister of Metallurgy and Machine Industry 1960–63, Minister 1963–75; mem. CP 1945–, Cen. Cttee. 1970–75; Man. Pres. Fed. of Tech. and Scientific Socs. 1978–; Prof. Tech. Univ. 1978–; Labour Order of Merit Gold Medal 1969. *Leisure interests:* mathematics and chess. *Address:* c/o Müszaki és Természettudományi Egyesületek Szövetsége, 1055 Budapest, Kossuth Lajos tér 6/8, Hungary. *Telephone:* 329-571.

HORIKOSHI, Teizo, LL.B.; Japanese business executive; b. 13 Dec. 1898; ed. Tokyo Imperial Univ.; entered Bank of Japan 1924, Dir. 1947–; Deputy Dir. Econ. Stabilization Agency 1947; Sec.-Gen. Japanese Nat. Cttee. of Int. Chamber of Commerce 1950; Exec. Dir. and Sec.-Gen. Japan Fed. of Econ. Orgs. (Keidanren) 1954–; Auditor, Toho Mutual Life Insurance Co. 1959–; Pres. Securities and Exchange Council, Ministry of Finance 1961–; Pres. Nippon Usiminas Co. Ltd. 1965–76, Chair. 1976–; Hon. C.B.E. (U.K.) 1966. *Address:* Kyodo 2-23-5, Setagaya-ku, Tokyo, Japan.

HORIUCHI, Toshio; Japanese politician; b. Feb. 1918, Nara Pref.; four s.; ed. Nara Normal School; Mayor of Tenri City 1966; mem. Nara Prefectural Ass.; mem. House of Councillors 1976–; Parl. Vice-Minister of Econ. Planning 1979; Deputy Sec.-Gen. Liberal-Democratic Party (LDP); Minister of State, Dir.-Gen. Environment Agency 1987–88. *Leisure interests:* golf, floriculture. *Address:* Kojimachi Shukusha, 4-7 Kojimachi, Chiyoda-ku, Tokyo, 102, Japan.

HORLOCK, John Harold, SC.D., F.ENG., F.R.S.; British engineer and university administrator; b. 19 April 1928, Edmonton; s. of Harold E. and Olive M. Horlock; m. Sheila J. Stutely 1953; one s. two d.; ed. Latymer School,

Edmonton, and St. John's Coll., Cambridge; design engineer, Rolls-Royce Ltd. 1949–51; Demonstrator, Lecturer in Eng., Univ. of Cambridge 1952–58; Harrison Prof. of Mech. Eng., Univ. of Liverpool 1958–67; Prof. of Eng., Univ. of Cambridge 1967–74; Vice-Chancellor, Univ. of Salford 1974–80, Open Univ. 1981–; Hawksley Gold Medal (Inst. of Mech. Eng.). *Publications:* Axial Flow Compressors 1958, Axial Flow Turbines 1967, Actuator Disc Theory 1978, Thermodynamics and Gas Dynamics of I.C. Engines (Ed.) Vol. I 1982, Vol. II 1986, Cogeneration: Combined Heat and Power 1987. *Leisure interests:* music, sport. *Address:* Open University, Walton Hall, Milton Keynes, MK7 6AA (Office); Wednesden, Aspley Guise, Milton Keynes, MK17 8DQ, England (Home). *Telephone:* (0908) 653214 (Office); (0908) 582130 (Home).

HORN, Francis H., M.A., PH.D.; American academic; b. 18 Nov. 1908, Toledo, Ohio; s. of Henry Frederick Horn and Orpha Ford (Bennett) Horn; m. Xenia Beliavsky 1935; one s. two d.; ed. public schools, Toledo, Dartmouth Coll., Univ. of Va., Yale Univ.; Instructor in English and History, American Univ., Cairo 1930–33; served U.S. Army 1942–45 (Lieut.-Col.); Asst. Dean, Biarritz American Univ. 1945–46; Dean, Evening Coll., Dir. Summer Session and Assoc. Prof. of Educ. Johns Hopkins Univ., Baltimore, Md. 1947–51; Exec. Sec. American Asscn. for Higher Educ., Washington, D.C. 1951–53; Pres. Pratt Inst., New York 1953–57, Pres. Emer. 1984; Distinguished Visiting Prof. of Higher Educ. Southern Ill. Univ. 1957–58; Pres. and Prof. of Higher Educ. Univ. of R.I. 1958–67, Pres. Emer. 1979–; Pres. Comm. on Independent Colls. and Univs., New York State 1967–71; Pres. Albertus Magnus Coll., New Haven, Conn. 1971–74, Pres. Emer. 1974; Exec. Vice-Pres. Wagner Coll., Staten Island, New York 1974–76; Pres. American Coll. of Switzerland 1977–79; Vice-Pres. British Campus and Dir. New England Coll., Arundel, Sussex, England 1980–81; Adviser to Pres., Tunghai Univ., Taiwan 1982–85; Dir. Near East Foundation 1955, mem. Exec. Cttee. 1967–84; mem. and trustee, etc. numerous insts., 28 hon. degrees; U.S. Army Legion of Merit 1945, U.S. Navy Medal for Distinguished Public Service 1967, U.S. Army Outstanding Civilian Service Award 1967 and several other awards. *Publications:* Challenge and Perspective in Higher Education 1971, ed. of several books and over 100 articles and chapters in books; many reviews. *Leisure interests:* gardening, travel, stamp collecting. *Address:* 42 Upper College Road, Kingston, R.I. 02881, U.S.A. *Telephone:* 401-789 0353.

HORN, Gabriel, M.A., M.D., SC.D., F.I.BIOL., F.R.S.; British professor of zoology; b. 9 Dec. 1927; s. of late A. Horn; m. 1st Ann L. D. Soper 1952 (divorced 1979), two s. two d.; m. 2nd Edith P. Barrett 1980; ed. Univ. of Birmingham; house appts. in Birmingham hosps. 1955–56; demonstrator in Anatomy, Univ. of Cambridge 1956–62, Lecturer 1962–72, Reader in Neurobiology 1972–74, Fellow, King's Coll. 1962–74, 1978–; Prof. Univ. of Bristol 1974–77; Prof. of Zoology, Univ. of Cambridge 1978–, Head of Dept. 1980–; numerous other professional appts.; Kenneth Craik Award 1962. *Publications:* Memory, Imprinting and the Brain 1985; papers in scientific journals. *Leisure interests:* walking, cycling, riding, music. *Address:* King's College, Cambridge, England. *Telephone:* (0223) 350411.

HORN, Heinz, DR.RER.POL.; German company executive; b. 17 Sept. 1930, Duisberg; s. of Heinrich and Elisabeth (née Eckernkamp) Horn; m.; two s. two d.; ed. Univ. of Frankfurt, Univ. of Munster; fmrly. with Mannesmann for 6 years; Financial Dir., Erschweiler Bergweks-Verein 1965–68, mem. Bd. and later Pres. 1974–83; mem. Bd., Krupp 1968–72; Deputy Chair. of the Bd., Ruhrkohle AG, Essen 1983–85, Chair. Man. Bd. 1985–; Chair. Supervisory Bd. Rütgerswerke AG. *Address:* Ruhrkohle AG, Rellinghauser Strasse 1, 4300 Essen 1, Federal Republic of Germany. *Telephone:* (0201) 1771.

HORNE, Colin James, A.M., M.A., M.LITT., DIP.ED., F.A.H.A.; Australian professor of English; b. 31 Oct. 1912, Bendigo, Vic.; s. of Thomas J. Horne and Nellie Horne; m. 1st Margaret E. Parsons 1939 (deceased 1962); four s.; m. 2nd Cynthia N. Werfel 1968; ed. Melbourne Univ. and Balliol Coll., Oxford; Asst. and Lecturer in English, Queen's Univ., Belfast 1939–48; Lecturer in English, Univ. of Leicester 1948–57; Jury Prof. of English Language and Literature, Univ. of Adelaide 1957–77, Dean, Faculty of Arts 1969–70, Emer. Prof. 1977–; Chair. Writers Week; Vice-Pres. Australian Acad. of the Humanities 1977–78; Pres. Australasian Pacific Soc. for Eighteenth Century Studies 1976–80, Adelaide Festival of Arts 1969–74, Cttee. 1960–80. *Publications:* Swift on His Age 1953, Studies in the Eighteenth Century 1968, The Dunstan Decade 1981, The Classical Temper in Western Europe 1983. *Leisure interests:* walking, travelling, golf, book-collecting. *Address:* Department of English, University of Adelaide, Box 498, G.P.O., Adelaide, South Australia 5001; Woodstock, 12 Bracken Road, Stirling, South Australia 5152, Australia (Home). *Telephone:* 228-5130 (Office); 339-2303 (Home).

HORNE, Donald Richmond, A.O.; Australian author and lecturer; b. 26 Dec. 1921, Sydney; s. of David Horne and Florence Carpenter; m. Myfanwy Gollan 1960; one s. one d.; ed. Univ. of Sydney, Univ. Coll., Canberra; Ed. The Observer 1958–61, The Bulletin 1961–62, 1967–72; Co-Ed. Quadrant 1963–66; Contributing Ed. Newsweek Int. 1973–77; Advisory Bd. The Australian Encyclopedia 1973–, Chair. 1987–; served Advisory Council for N.S.W. Cultural Affairs 1976–80; Council, Soc. of Authors 1982–, Pres. 1984–85; Chair. Copyright Agency Ltd. 1983–84; Chair. The Australia Council 1985–; Research Fellow, Univ. of N.S.W. 1973–74, Sr. Lecturer

1975–79, Assoc. Prof. 1980–84, Prof. 1984–, Chair. Arts Faculty 1982–86, Council 1983–86; Hon. D.Litt. (Univ. of N.S.W.) 1986. *Publications:* The Lucky Country 1964, The Permit 1965, The Education of Young Donald 1967, God is an Englishman 1969, The Next Australia 1970, But What If There Are No Pelicans? 1971, The Australian People 1972, Death of the Lucky Country 1976, Money Made Us 1976, His Excellency's Pleasure 1977, Right Way, Don't Go Back 1978, In Search of Billy Hughes 1979, Time of Hope 1980, Winner Take All 1981, The Great Museum 1984, Confessions of a New Boy 1985, The Public Culture 1986, The Lucky Country Revisited 1987, Portrait of an Optimist 1988. *Leisure interest:* writing. *Address:* 53 Grosvenor Street, Woollahra, Sydney, Australia (Home). *Telephone:* 389 4212 (Home).

HORNE, Marilyn; American mezzo-soprano; b. 16 Jan. 1934, Bradford, Pa.; d. of Bentz and Berneice Horne; m. Henry Lewis (divorced); one d.; ed. Univ. of Southern California (under William Vennard); performed in several German opera cos. in Europe 1956; debut, San Francisco Opera 1960; has since appeared at Covent Garden, London, the Chicago Lyric Opera, La Scala, Milan, Metropolitan Opera, New York; repertoire includes Eboli (Don Carlo), Marie (Wozzeck), Adalgisa (Norma), Jane Seymour (Anna Bolena), Amneris (Aida), Carmen, Rosina (Barbiere di Siviglia), Fides (Le Prophète), Mignon, Isabella (L'Italiana in Algeri), Romeo (I Capuletti ed i Montecchi), Tancredi (Tancredi), Orland (Orlando Furioso); many recordings; five hon. doctorates. *Leisure interests:* needlepoint, swimming, reading, sightseeing. *Address:* c/o Colombia Artists Management Inc., 165 West 57th Street, New York, N.Y. 10019, U.S.A.

HORNE, Michael Rex, O.B.E., M.A., SC.D., F.R.S., F.ENG.; British consulting, structural and civil engineer; b. 29 Dec. 1921, Leicester; s. of Rev. Ernest and Katie Horne; m. Dorcas Mary Hewett 1947; two s. two d.; ed. Boston Grammar School, Lincs., Leeds Grammar School, St. John's Coll., Cambridge; Asst. Engineer, Great Ouse Catchment Bd. 1941–45; Research Officer, British Inst. of Welding 1945–51; Asst. Dir. of Research and Lecturer, Eng. Dept., Univ. of Cambridge 1951–60; Prof. of Eng., subsequently Beyer Prof. and Head, Dept. of Eng., Univ. of Manchester 1960–83; Chair. U.K. Govt. Review of Public Utilities Streetworks Act 1985; Pres. Inst. of Structural Engineers 1980–81; Fellow, St. John's Coll., Cambridge 1957–60; Baker Gold Medal (Inst. of Civil Engineers) 1977, Gold Medal, Inst. of Structural Engineers 1986. *Publications:* The Steel Skeleton (jt. author) 1956, The Stability of Frames (jt. author) 1965, Plastic Theory of Structures 1971, Plastic Design of Low Rise Frames (jt. author) 1981; over 100 papers (mainly on steel frame and box girder theory) in learned journals. *Leisure interests:* wine-making, photography, walking. *Address:* 19 Park Road, Hale, Altrincham, Cheshire, WA15 9NW, England. *Telephone:* 061-941 2223.

HORNER, Hon. John Henry (Jack), P.C.; Canadian politician; b. Blaine Lake, Sask.; s. of late Senator R. B. Horner and of Mae Horner (née Macarthur); m. Leola Margaret Funnell 1950; three s.; ed. Olds School of Agric. and Univ. of Alberta; mem. House of Commons 1958–79; Minister without Portfolio April-Sept. 1977, of Industry, Trade and Commerce 1977–79; mem. Canadian Privy Council; Admin. Prairie Grain Agency 1984–; Liberal Party. *Publication:* My Own Brand (autobiog.) 1980. *Leisure interests:* horse riding, golf, curling, skating, baseball. *Address:* Pollockville, Alberta J0J 2L0, Canada.

HORNER, Richard Elmer, B.S., M.S.E.; American business executive; b. 24 Oct. 1917, Wrenshall, Minn.; s. of Marion Chester and Maude Eckert Horner; m. Jean Margaret Hodgson 1941; one s. one d.; ed. Univ. of Minnesota and Princeton Univ.; U.S.A.F. 1940–49; civilian aeronautical devt. engineer, Air Force Flight Test Center, Edwards Air Force Base, Calif. 1949–53, Technical Dir. 1953–55; Deputy for Requirements to Asst. Sec. of Air Force for Research and Devt. 1955–57; Asst. Sec. to A.F. for Research and Devt. 1957–59; Assoc. Administrator, Nat. Aeronautics and Space Admin. 1959–60; Sr. Vice-Pres. (Technical) Northrop Corpn. 1960–70; Pres. and C.E.O., E. F. Johnson Co. 1970–82, Chair., Pres. and C.E.O. 1980–82, Chair. and C.E.O. 1982–84; Pres. and C.E.O. Western Union Personal Communications Inc. 1984–86; Dir. Western Union Corpn., Northrop Corpn., Medtronic Inc., ConferTech Int.; Fellow, American Inst. of Aeronautics and Astronautics; mem. Bd. of Govs. Electronic Industries Asscn.; Trustee, Fuller Theological Seminary, Univ. of Min. Foundation; Silver Star, Air Medal with 4 clusters, Presidential Unit Citation. *Leisure interests:* skiing, sailing. *Address:* 1581 Via Entrada del Lago, Lake San Marcos, Calif. 90269, U.S.A.

HORNIG, Donald Frederick; American chemist and university administrator; b. 17 March 1920, Milwaukee, Wis.; s. of Chester Arthur and Emma (Knuth) Hornig; m. Lilli Schwenk 1943; one s. three d.; ed. Harvard Univ.; Research Assoc. Woods Hole (Mass.) Oceanographic Inst. 1943–44; Scientist, Los Alamos Lab., New Mexico 1944–46; Pres. Radiation Instruments Co. 1945–47; Asst. Prof. of Chemistry Brown Univ. 1946–49, Assoc. Prof. 1949–51, Prof. 1951–57, Dir. Metcalf Research Lab. 1949–57; Assoc. and Acting Dean, Graduate School, Brown Univ. 1952–53, Pres. Brown Univ. 1970–76; Prof. of Chemistry Princeton Univ. 1957–63, Chair. Dept. 1958–63, Donner Prof. of Science 1959–63; Dir. W. A. Benjamin Inc. 1962–64; Dir. Office of Science and Technology, Exec. Office of Pres. of U.S.A. 1964–69; Vice-Pres. and Dir. Eastman Kodak Co. 1969–70; Hon. Research Assoc. in Applied Physics, Harvard Univ. 1976–77, Prof. of

Chemistry in Public Health, Dir. Interdisciplinary Programs in Health 1977–81, Alfred North Whitehead Prof. of Chem. 1981–; Dir. Chemical Industry Inst. of Toxicology 1985–; Chair. Bd. on Environmental Studies and Toxicology (N.A.S.); Dir. Upjohn Co. 1971–, Westinghouse Electric Co. 1972–; mem. Bd. of Trustees, Manpower Inst. 1970–77, Overseas Devt. Council 1969–77; mem. American Chemical Soc., American Physical Soc., etc.; Hon. mem. Nat. Acad. of Sciences (U.S.A.), American Acad. of Arts and Sciences, etc.; numerous awards and hon. degrees. *Address:* Harvard School of Public Health, 665 Huntington Avenue, Boston, Mass. 02115 (Office); 16 Longfellow Park, Cambridge, Mass. 02138, U.S.A. (Home). *Telephone:* 617-732-1258 (Office); 617-492-0327 (Home).

HOROVITZ, Joseph, M.A., B.MUS., F.R.C.M.; British composer-conductor; b. 26 May 1926, Vienna; ed. New Coll., Oxford Univ. and Royal Coll. of Music, London, and studied with Nadia Boulanger, Paris; resident in U.K. 1938–; Mus. Dir. Bristol Old Vic 1949–51; Conductor Festival Gardens Orchestra and open-air ballet, London 1951; Co-conductor Ballet Russes, English season 1952; Assoc. Dir. Intimate Opera Co. 1952–63; Assoc. Conductor Glyndebourne Opera 1956; Prof. of Composition, Royal Coll. of Music 1961–; mem. Council, Composers' Guild 1970–, Exec. Council, Performing Right Soc. 1971–; Pres. Int. Council of Composers and Lyricists of Int. Fed. of Socs. of Authors and Composers 1982–; Commonwealth Medal Composition 1959; Leverhulme Music Research Award 1961. *Compositions:* 16 ballets including Alice in Wonderland, Les Femmes d'Alger, Miss Carter Wore Pink, Concerto for Dancers; The Dumb Wife, Gentlemen's Island (one-act operas); concertos for violin, trumpet, jazz harpsichord, clarinet, bassoon, percussion; other orchestral works include Horizon Overture, Jubilee Serenade, Sinfonietta for Light Orchestra, Fantasia on a Theme of Couperin, Toy Symphony; brass band music includes a euphonium concerto, Sinfonietta, Ballet for Band, Concertino Classico, The Dong with a Luminous Nose; music for wind band includes a divertimento, Bacchus on Blue Ridge, and a transcription of Bach's Fantasia and Fugue in G minor; choral music includes Samson, Captain Noah and his Floating Zoo (Ivor Novello Award for best British music for children 1976), Summer Sunday, Endymion, Sing unto the Lord a New Song, 3 choral songs from As You Like It; vocal music includes Lady Macbeth (mezzo-soprano and piano) and works for the King's Singers (e.g. Romance); chamber music includes 5 string quartets, oboe sonatina, oboe quartet and clarinet sonatina; contribs. to Hoffnung Concerts: Metamorphoses on a Bed-Time Theme and Horrortorio for chorus, orchestra and soloists; numerous scores for theatre productions, films and TV series; productions of Son et Lumière include St. Paul's Cathedral, Canterbury Cathedral, Brighton Pavilion, English Harbour Antigua, Bodiam Castle. *Address:* 7 Dawson Place, London, W2 4TD, England. *Telephone:* 01-229 5333.

HOROWITZ, Norman Harold, PH.D.; American biologist; b. 19 March 1915, Pittsburgh, Pa.; s. of Joseph Horowitz and Jeanette Miller; m. Pearl Shykin 1939 (died 1985); one s. one d.; ed. Univ. of Pittsburgh and Calif. Inst. of Technology; National Research Council Fellow 1939–40; Research Fellow, Calif. Inst. of Technology, Pasadena 1940–42; Research Assoc. Stanford Univ. 1942–46; Assoc. Prof. of Biology, Calif. Inst. of Technology 1947–53, Prof. 1953–, Prof. Emer. 1982–, Chair., Division of Biology 1977–80; Chief, Bioscience Section, Jet Propulsion Lab., Pasadena 1965–70; Fulbright and Guggenheim Fellow, Univ. of Paris 1954–55; mem. Nat. Acad. of Sciences; Fellow, American Acad. of Arts and Sciences. *Publications:* To Utopia and Back: The Search for Life in the Solar System 1986, numerous technical articles on genetics, biochemistry and space exploration. *Leisure interests:* gardening, music. *Address:* Biology Division, California Institute of Technology, Pasadena, Calif. 91125, U.S.A. *Telephone:* 818-356-4926.

HOROWITZ, Vladimir; American pianist; b. 1 Oct. 1904, Kiev, Russia; s. of Samuel and Sophie (née Bodik) Horowitz; m. Wanda Toscanini 1933; one d. (deceased); studied under Felix Blumenfeld and Sergei Tarnowsky; first appearance 1917; U.S. debut with New York Philharmonic Orchestra 1928; most recent European tour including concerts in London and Paris 1982; recitals in U.S.S.R. 1986; soloist New York Symphony Orchestra, Philadelphia Orchestra, NBC Symphony Orchestra, Cleveland, Boston, Chicago, Detroit and St. Louis and other orchestras; Royal Philharmonic Soc. Gold Medal 1972, Prix du Disque 1970, 1971 and winner of 23 Grammy awards for best classical performance; shared Wolf Foundation Prize 1983; Kt. Grand Cross, Order of Merit 1985. *Leisure interest:* collecting antique American furniture and Americana. *Address:* c/o Columbia Artists Management Inc., 165 West 57th Street, New York, N.Y. 10019, U.S.A.

HORRIDGE, G. Adrian, M.A., PH.D., F.A.A., F.R.S.; Australian professor of biology; b. 12 Dec. 1927, England; m. Audrey A. Lightburne 1953; one s. three d.; ed. St John's Coll., Cambridge; worked in Dept. of Structures (New Materials), Royal Aircraft Establishment, Farnborough 1953–56; Lecturer, then Reader, Dept. of Zoology, Univ. of St. Andrews 1956–69; Dir. Gatty Marine Lab., St. Andrews 1959–69; Prof., Dept. of Neurobiology, Research School of Biological Sciences, Australian Nat. Univ. 1969–; fmr. Prof. Yale Univ.; Fellow, St. John's Coll., Cambridge; Visiting Fellow, Balliol Coll., Oxford, Churchill Coll., Cambridge, Centre for Advanced Studies in Behavioral Science, Stanford Univ., Calif. *Publications:* Structure and Function of the Nervous Systems of the Invertebrates (with T. H. Bullock) 1965, Interneurons 1968, The Compound Eye 1973, The Prahu,

Traditional Sailing Boat of Indonesia 1981, Sailing Craft of Indonesia 1986, The Outrigger Canoes of Bali and Madura 1987, and numerous articles on neurobiology, nerve cell functions and traditional boats of south-east Asia. *Leisure interests:* science, arts, travel, boats and people of Indonesian fishing villages, sailing, writing. *Address:* Research School of Biological Sciences, Australian National University, P.O. Box 475, Canberra, A.C.T. 2601, Australia. *Telephone:* (062) 494532.

HORROCKS, Raymond, C.B.E., C.B.I.M., F.I.M.I., F.R.S.A.; British business executive; b. 9 Jan. 1930, Bolton, Lancs. (now Greater Manchester); s. of Cecil and Elsie Horrocks; m. Pamela F. Russell 1953; three d.; ed. Bolton Grammar School, Wigan Tech. Coll., Univ. of Liverpool; man. trainee, textile industry, Bolton and Manchester 1944–48, 1950–51; Army Intelligence Corps 1948–50; sales rep. Proctor and Gamble 1951–52; merchandiser, Marks and Spencer 1953–58; Buying Controller, Littlewoods Mail Order Stores 1958–63; Man. Replacement Parts, Ford Motor Co. 1963, Man. Warranty and Customer Relations 1964, Man. Car Supply 1965, Divisional Man. Engine and Special Equipment Operations 1966, Marketing Man. Cars 1967, Man. Advanced Vehicle Operations 1968–72; Regional Dir. (Europe and Middle East), Materials Handling Group, Eaton Corpn. 1972–77; Deputy Man. Dir. Leyland Cars, British Leyland Ltd./BL PLC 1977–78, Chair. and Man. Dir. Austin Morris Ltd. 1978–80, Man. Dir. BL Cars Ltd. 1980–81, Dir. BL Ltd. 1981–86; Chair. and Chief. Exec. BL Cars Ltd. 1981–82, ARG Holdings Ltd. 1981–86; Chair. Unipart Group Ltd. 1981–86; Group Chief Exec. Cars, BL PLC 1982–86; Chair. Jaguar Cars Holdings Ltd. 1982–84, Exide Europe 1986–88, Owenbell Ltd. 1986–, Chloride Group PLC 1988–, SMAC Group PLC 1988–; Dir. (non-Exec.) Kay Consultancy Group Ltd. 1988–; Dir. Nuffield Services Ltd. 1982–86; Dir. (non-exec.) Electrocomponents 1986–, Lookers 1986–, The Caravan Club 1983–87, Jaguar PLC 1984–85, Image Interiors (Wessex) Ltd. 1985–86, Chloride Group PLC 1986–88; mem. CBI Council 1981–86, CBI Europe Cttee. 1985–86; Trustee, British Motor Industry Heritage Trust 1983–86. *Leisure interests:* fishing, caravanning, steam engines. *Address:* Far End, Riverview Road, Pangbourne, Reading, Berks., RG8 7AU, England. *Telephone:* 073-57-4623; 073-57-5124.

HORSFALL, James Gordon, B.SC., PH.D.; American plant pathologist and science administrator; b. 9 Jan. 1905, Mountain Grove, Mo.; s. of Frank Horsfall and Margaret Vaulx Horsfall; m. Sue Belle Overton 1927; two d.; ed. Univ. of Arkansas and Cornell Univ.; Instructor, Cornell Univ. 1928–29, Asst. Prof. to Prof. 1929–39; Chief of Dept. of Plant Pathology, Conn. Agricultural Experiment Station 1939–48, Dir. 1948–71, S. W. Johnson Distinguished Scientist, Dir. Emer. 1972–; Ed. Annual Review of Phytopathology 1962–71; Lecturer in Microbiology, Yale Univ. 1950–63; Fellow and Pres. American Phytopathological Soc. 1951; Pres. Soc. of Industrial Microbiology 1954; Consultant, Pres. Science Advisory Cttee. 1960–69, NASA 1972–78, Environmental Protection Agency 1975–78; Pres. IXth Int. Congress of Plant protection 1979; mem. Advisory Cttee. on Biology and Medicine U.S. Atomic Energy Comm. 1957–64, Nat. Advisory Comm. on Food and Fiber 1965–67, Latin America Science Bd., Nat. Acad. of Sciences 1965–66; Chair. Agricultural Bd., Nat. Acad. of Sciences 1971–73, Governor's Cttee. on Environmental Policy 1970; mem. American Acad. of Arts and Sciences, Nat. Acad. of Sciences, American Phytopathological Soc.; Charter mem. Conn. Acad. Science and Eng. 1970, Power Facility Evaluation Council of Conn. 1972–88; Hon. mem. Società Italiana de Fitoiatria, Pavia, Italy; mem. Accad. Nazionale di Agricoltura (Italy); Hon. Fellow, Indian Phytopathological Soc.; Hon. D.Sc. (Vermont), D.Agr. (Turin), LL.D. (Ark.); Award of Distinction, Phytopathological Soc. 1972, American Inst. of Biological Science 1974, Mérite Agricole Medal (France), Gold Medal, 10th Int. Congress of Plant Protection 1981, New England Fellowship of Agricultural Adventurers 1978. *Publications:* Fungicides and Their Action 1945, Principles of Fungicidal Action 1956, Plant Pathology—An Advanced Treatise (3 vols.) 1959–60, Plant Disease—An Advanced Treatise (ed.) (5 vols.) 1977–80; numerous station bulletins and articles in scientific journals. *Leisure interests:* woodworking, gardening. *Address:* Connecticut Agricultural Experiment Station, 123 Huntington Street, P.O. Box 1106, New Haven, Conn. 06504; Apt. 522, 200 Leeder Hill Drive, Hamden, Conn. 06517, U.S.A. (Home).

HÖRSTADIUS, Sven (Otto); Swedish zoologist; b. 18 Feb. 1898, Stockholm; s. of Wilhelm Hörstadius and Svea Hård; m. Greta Kjellström 1928 (died 1987); one s. one d.; ed. Univ. of Stockholm; Reader in Zoology, Univ. of Stockholm 1928–32, Assoc. Prof. 1932–42; Head of Dept. of Developmental Physiology and Genetics, Wennergren Inst. of Experimental Biology 1938–42; Prof. of Zoology, Uppsala Univ. 1942–64; research work at several marine biological stations all over the world; Pres. Int. Union of Biological Sciences 1953–58, Sveriges Ornitologiska Forening 1947–68, Int. Council Scientific Unions 1962–63; Chair. European Section of Int. Council for Bird Preservation 1960–72; Fellow, Royal Swedish Acad. of Science, Royal Soc. of Science, Uppsala, Royal Danish Acad. of Science, Acad. Pontificia, Rome; foreign mem. Royal Soc., London, Accad. Naz. dei Lincei, Rome, Finnish Soc. of Science, Zoological Soc., London; hon. mem. Belgian Royal Zoological Soc., Soc. Zoologique de France, British Ornithologists Union, Soc. Philomatique, Paris, Royal Inst. of Gt. Britain, etc.; Gen. Sec. Congress of Ornithology, Uppsala 1950; Dr. h.c. (Univs. of Paris, Bristol and Cambridge); Prix Albert Brachet of Belgian Royal Acad. of Science 1938. *Publications:* The Neural Crest 1950, Expermental Embryology of Echinoderms 1973. *Leisure interests:* bird photography, ornithology, tourism. *Address:* Froostavägen 5E, 75263 Uppsala, Sweden. *Telephone:* 018-460858.

HORTON, Alexander Romeo; Liberian banker; b. 20 Aug. 1923, Monrovia; s. of Rev. Dr. Daniel R. Horton and Ora Milner Horton; m. Mary E. C. Horton 1956; one s. two d.; ed. B.W.I. Inst. Coll. of West Africa, Morehouse Coll., Atlanta, U.S.A. and Wharton School of Finance and Commerce, Pennsylvania Univ.; Founder and Pres., Bank of Liberia 1954-76; Asst. Econ. Adviser to Liberian Govt. 1954-63; Chair. Steering Cttee. of Conf. of African Businessmen 1960; Chair. ECA Cttee. of Nine African Countries on African Devt. Bank 1962; Sec. of Commerce and Industry, Liberia 1964-68; Man. Dir. Fund for Co-operation, Compensation and Devt., of the Econ. Community of West African States (ECOWAS) 1977-79; fmr. Pres. Liberia Bankers Assen.; fmr. Dean, Coll. of Business and Public Admin., Univ. of Liberia; Chair. Liberia Insurance Agency; has attended numerous int. confs.; Hon. LL.D. (Atlanta); decorations include Knight Commdr. Order of Ivory Coast, Grand Commdr. Order of Star of Africa, Grand Band Order of Star of Africa, Grand Cross Order of Orange-Nassau. *Leisure interest:* reading. *Address:* c/o Ministry of Foreign Affairs, Monrovia, Liberia.

HORTON, Jack King, LL.B.; American businessman; b. 27 June 1916, Stanton, Neb.; s. of Virgil L. and Edna L. (King) Horton; m. Betty Lou Magee 1937; one s. two d.; ed. Stanford Univ. and Oakland Coll. Law School; admitted to Calif. Bar 1941; Treasury Dept. Shell Oil Co. 1937-42; private law practice 1942-43; Attorney, Standard Oil Co. 1943-44; Sec., Legal Counsel, Coast Counties Gas & Electric Co. 1944-51, Pres. 1951-54; Vice-Pres. Pacific Gas & Electric Co., San Francisco 1954-59; Pres. S. Calif. Edison Co. 1959-68, Chief Exec. Officer 1965-, Chair of Bd. 1968-80, Chair. Exec. Cttee. 1980-; Dir. First Interstate Bank of Calif., First Interstate Bancorp., Pacific Mutual Life Insurance, Lockheed Aircraft Corpn. *Address:* 2244 Walnut Grove Avenue, Rosemead, Calif. 91770, U.S.A. (Office).

HORTON, Robert Baynes, S.M., C.B.I.M.; British petroleum executive; b. 8 Aug. 1939, Bushey; s. of William H. Horton and D. Joan Baynes; m. Sally Doreen Wells 1962; one s. one d.; ed. King's School, Canterbury, St. Andrews Univ., Massachusetts Inst. of Technology; with British Petroleum Ltd. (Now BP PLC) 1960-86, Gen. Man. BP Tankers 1975-76, Gen. Man. Corporate Planning 1976-79, Man. Dir. BP Chemicals Int. 1980-83, Man. Dir. BP PLC 1983-86, 1988-; Chair. C.E.O. Standard Oil Co. 1986-88, Dir. 1983-; Vice-Chair., C.E.O. BP America Inc. 1987-88, Chair. 1988-; Pres. Chemical Industries Assen. 1982-84; Dir. ICL PLC 1982-84, SOHIO 1983-84; mem. Univs. Funding Council 1989-; Gov. King's School, Canterbury 1984-; Corporate Leadership Award, MIT 1987. *Leisure interests:* opera, shooting, political biography. *Address:* BP America Inc., 200 Public Square, Cleveland, Ohio 44114-2375, U.S.A.

HORVAT, Branko, DIPL. in ECON., PH.D., D.SC.; Yugoslav university professor and economist; b. 1928, Petrinja; s. of Artur and Dolores (Stöhr) Horvat; m. Ranka Peašinović 1952; two d.; ed. Zagreb Univ., Victoria Univ. of Manchester, Harvard Univ., M.I.T.; partisan 1944-45; Researcher, Inst. of Petroleum, Inst. of Econ., Zagreb 1952-55; Research Dir. Fed. Planning Bureau, Belgrade 1958-62; Visiting Research Fellow, Inst. of Int. Econs. Stockholm 1973-74; f. and Dir. Inst. of Econ. Sciences, Belgrade 1963-70; mem. Fed. Econ. Council, Fed. Cttee. for Market and Prices 1963-71; Econ. Adviser, govts. of Yugoslavia, Peru and Turkey 1970-74, 1979-80; Visiting Prof. in Econ. Theory, Planning or Comparative Social Systems, Univs. of Belgrade, Ljubljana, Mich., Fla., Stockholm, Paris, Dar es Salaam, American Univ., Univ. Católica de Chile, Univ. of Notre Dame, Yale Univ.; Prof. of Econs., Univ. of Zagreb 1975-; Visiting Prof., Univ. of Cambridge, England 1986; f. Pres. Int. Assen. for the Econ. of Self-Man.; f. Ed. Econ. Analysis and Workers' Man.; mem. Yugoslav govt. Cttls. on planning to UN, Poland, U.S.S.R., Int. Foundation for Devt. Alternatives, Centre International de Coordination des Recherches sur l'Autogestion; councils of various int. asscns. and ed. bds.; lecturer at over 50 int. educational establishments; Medal of Merit, May Festival Prizes, Zagreb 1948, 1949, 1950, Manchester Statistical Soc. Prize. *Publications include:* Economics of the Petroleum Industry (4 vols.) 1954-65, Towards a Theory of Planned Economy 1961, Interindustry Analysis 1962, Economic Models 1962, Economic Science and National Economy 1968, An Essay of Yugoslav Society 1969, Business Cycles in Yugoslavia 1969, Economic Analysis 1972, Economic Policy of Stabilization 1976, Self-Governing Socialism (co-author) 1976, Political Economy of Socialism 1982, Yugoslav Economy 1967-83, 2 vols. 1984, Social Crisis 1985, The Labour Theory of Prices and Other Unsolved Problems of Economic Theory 1986, The Kosovo Question 1988, Foundations of Yugoslav Socialism 1989 and 200 articles in prof. journals. *Leisure interest:* manual labour. *Address:* 32 Gornji Lukšić, Zagreb, Yugoslavia.

HORVÁTH, Dr. István; Hungarian politician; b. 1935, Paks; ed. Eötvös Loránd Univ., Budapest; joined youth movement and functioned as Pres. Science Assen. of Law Students; joined HSWP 1956; various positions in law admin. Bács-Kiskun County; Presiding Judge, dist. court 1958; worked political staff of County Party Cttee. 1959, later dept. leader; Sec. Bács-Kiskun County Party Cttee. 1968; First Sec. Communist Youth League Hun. Cttee. 1970-73; mem. HSWP Cen. Cttee. 1970-; First Sec. Bács-

Kiskun County Party Cttee 1973; mem. Presidential Council of Hungarian People's Republic 1971-75; mem. Nat. Assembly for Borsod County 1971-75; Minister of Home Affairs 1980-85, 1987-; Deputy Prime Minister June-Dec. 1987; Sec. HSWP Cen. Cttee. 1985-87; Labour Order of Merit. *Address:* Ministry of Home Affairs, 1903 Budapest, József Attila utca 2-4, Hungary. *Telephone:* 121-710.

HORWOOD, Owen Pieter Faure, B.COM.; South African economist and politician; b. 6 Dec. 1916, Somerset West; s. of late Stanley Ebden Horwood and Anna Johanna Horwood; m. Helen Mary Watt 1946; one s. one d.; ed. Boys' High School, Paarl, Univ. of Cape Town; Assoc. Prof. of Commerce, Univ. of Cape Town 1954-56; Prof. of Econs., Univ. Coll. of Rhodesia and Nyasaland 1956-57; Prof. of Econs., Univ. of Natal 1957-65, Prin. Vice-Chancellor 1966-70; Visiting Prof. of Econ., Duke Univ., U.S.A. 1961-62; Senator 1970-80; Dir. of Cos. 1970-; Minister of Indian Affairs and Tourism 1972-74, of Econ. Affairs 1974-75, of Finance 1975-84; Leader of the Senate 1978-80; mem. House of Ass. 1981-84; Chair. Nedbank Ltd., Nedbank Group Ltd.; Pres. Council of Govs., Devt. Bank of Southern Africa; Dir. S.A. Mutual Life Assurance Soc., S.A. Permanent Building Soc.; Pres. Econ. Soc. of South Africa 1964, 1965; Chair., mem. several govt. comms. including Sugar Industry Comm. 1967-69, Universities Comm. 1968-72; Chancellor, Univ. of Durban-Westville; Gen. Ed., Natal Regional Survey Publs. 1958-69; Hon. D.Com., Hon. D.Econ.; Decoration for Meritorious Service (S.A.). *Publications:* Economic Systems of the Commonwealth (Co-author) 1962, and numerous articles on economics and finance in professional journals. *Leisure interests:* sport, gardening, book collecting. *Address:* 18 Chesterfield Road, Bryanston 2021; P.O. Box 1144, Johannesburg 2000, South Africa.

HOSKINS, Bob (Robert William); British actor; b. 26 Oct. 1942; s. of Robert Hoskins and Elsie Lillian Hoskins; m. 1st Jane Livesey 1970, one s. one d.; m. 2nd Linda Banwell 1984, one s. one d.; ed. Stroud Green School; several stage roles at Nat. Theatre. *Films include:* National Health 1974, Royal Flash 1975, Zulu Dawn 1980, The Long Good Friday 1981, The Wall 1982, The Honorary Consul 1984, Lassiter 1984, The Cotton Club 1985, Brazil 1985, The Woman Who Married Clark Gable 1985, Sweet Liberty 1986, Mona Lisa 1986 (Best Actor Award, Cannes Festival), A Prayer for the Dying 1987, The Lonely Passion of Judith Hearne 1988, Who Framed Roger Rabbit? 1988, The Raggedy Rawney (dir. and wrote) 1988. *TV appearances include:* Softly, Softly 1973, Thick as Thieves 1973, On The Move 1976, Van der Valk 1979, Pennies From Heaven 1979, The Dunera Boys 1985; Evening Standard Award 1988. *Leisure interests:* photography, gardening, playgoing. *Address:* c/o Anne Hutton, 200 Fulham Road, London, S.W.10, England.

HOSKINS, William George, C.B.E., F.B.A.; British fmr. university professor and author; b. 22 May 1908, Exeter, Devon; s. of William Hoskins and Alice Dymond; m. Frances Jackson 1933; one s. (deceased) one d.; ed. in Exeter, then self-ed.; mem. Cen. Regulations Cttee. for Price Control 1941-45; Reader in Econ. History, Oxford Univ. 1951-65; Prof. of English Local History, Univ. of Leicester 1965-68; mem. Royal Comm. on Common Land 1955-58; BBC TV programmes 1976-78; Hon. M.A. (Oxon), D.Litt. (various univs.); Hon. F.R.I.B.A.; Murchison Prize (Royal Geographical Soc.) 1976. *Publications:* The Making of the English Landscape 1955, Local History in England 1959, The Age of Plunder 1976, One Man's England 1978. *Leisure interests:* remembering, reading. *Address:* 20 Sanson Close, Stoke Canon, Exeter, England. *Telephone:* (0392) 841865.

HOSKYNS, Sir John Austin Hungerford Leigh, Kt.; British business executive; b. 23 Aug. 1927, Farnborough, Hants.; s. of late Lieut.-Col. Chandos Hoskyns and Joyce Hoskyns; m. Miranda Jane Marie Mott 1956; two s. one d.; ed. Winchester Coll.; Capt. British Army 1945-57; with IBM U.K. Ltd. 1957-64; Chair. and Man. Dir. Hoskyns Group Ltd. 1964-75; Part-time Policy Adviser to Opposition 1975-77, Full-time Adviser to Rt. Hon. Margaret Thatcher (q.v.) and Shadow Cabinet 1977-79, Head Prime Minister's Policy Unit 1979-82; Dir.-Gen. Inst. of Dirs. 1984-89; Dir. of the following cos.: ICL PLC 1982-84, AGB Research PLC 1983-, Clerical Medical and Gen. Life Assurance Soc. 1983-, McKechnie Brothers PLC 1983-, Ferranti PLC 1986-; Hon. D.Sc. (Salford) 1986; Dr. h.c. (Essex) 1987. *Leisure interests:* opera, shooting. *Address:* 83 Clapham Common West Side, London, S.W.4; Windrush, Great Waldingfield, Nr. Sudbury, Suffolk, England (Homes). *Telephone:* 01-228 9505, 0787 210419.

HOSODA, Kichizo; Japanese politician; b. 2 May 1912; ed. Tokyo Univ.; joined Ministry of Transport 1936, Chief Sec. 1958; mem. House of Reps. 1960-; Parl. Vice-Minister for Home Affairs 1967-68; Chair. Standing Cttee. on Transport, House of Reps. 1972; Dir.-Gen. Admin. Management Agency 1974; Chair. Steering Cttee., House of Reps. 1977-79; Dir.-Gen. Defence Agency Feb.-July 1980; Minister of Transport 1983-84; Liberal-Democratic Party. *Publications:* Kamotsu Yuso, Yardman Hikkei, Kotsu to Kanko 1960. *Address:* House of Representatives, Tokyo, Japan.

HOSS, Dr. Selim al-; Lebanese politician and professor of economics; b. 1930; Chair. Banking Control Comm. 1967-73; Chair. Nat. Bank for Industrial and Tourist Devt. 1973-76; Prime Minister 1976-80, remaining as Prime Minister in caretaker capacity July-Oct. 1980, Minister of the Econ. and Trade and Information 1976-79, of Industry and Petroleum 1976-77, of Labour, Fine Arts and Educ. 1984-85 (resgnd), 1985; Acting Prime

Minister June 1987-, also Minister of Foreign and Expatriate Affairs; Chair. Compagnie Arabe et Internationale d'Investissement 1981-; Dir. Banque Arabe et Int. d'Investissement 1983-. *Publications:* The Development of Lebanon's Financial Markets 1974, Nafiza Ala Al Mustakbal (Window on the Future) 1981. *Address:* B.A.I.I. Centre Géfinor, Bloc B, Apartment 1401, 14th Floor, P.O. Box 11-9692, Beirut and Doha, Na'meh, Beirut, Lebanon.

HOSSAIN, Anwar, M.S.; Bangladesh politician; b. 1944, Barisal; s. of the late Tofazzal Hossain; m.; four c.; ed. Georgetown Univ., Washington; Journalist 1969, Ed. Dainik Ittefaq 1972-85; Pres. Nat. Press Club 1980; Chair. Eds. Council of Bangladesh; has represented Bangladesh at numerous int. confs.; Minister of Energy and Mineral Resources 1985-88. *Address:* Ministry of Energy and Mineral Resources, Bangladesh Secretariat, Bhaban 6, New Bldg., 2nd Floor, Dhaka, Bangladesh.

HOSSAIN, Kemaluddin, LL.B.; Bangladeshi judge; b. 31 March 1923, Calcutta, India; ed. Ballygunge Govt. High School, Calcutta, St. Xavier's Coll. and Calcutta Univ. Law Coll.; Advocate, High Court, Dacca 1950-69; Sr. Advocate Supreme Court, Pakistan 1966-69; Deputy Attorney-Gen., Pakistan 1968-69; Judge, High Court, Dacca 1969-72; Judge, High Court, Bangladesh 1972-75, Appellate Div. 1975-78; Chief Justice, Bangladesh 1978-82; Negotiator, Indus Water Treaty 1960; part-time law lecturer, City Law Coll., Dacca 1956-68; Chair. Law Cttee. 1978; attended several int. law confs. incl. Commonwealth Chief Justices Conf., Canberra May 1980. *Address:* c/o Chief Justice's House, 19 Hare Road, Dhaka, Bangladesh. *Telephone:* 243585 (Office); 404849 (Home).

HOSSAIN, Shah Moazzem, M.A.; Bangladesh politician; b. 10 Jan. 1939, Munsigonj Dist.; m.; one s. one d.; ed. Dhaka Univ.; Gen. Sec. East Pakistan Students League 1959-60, Pres. 1960-63; Chair. the All-Party Action Cttee. 1962; political prisoner for many years between 1953 and 1978; Chief Whip, Bangladesh Parliament 1972-73; co-f. Democratic League 1976, Gen. Sec. 1977-83; Minister of Land Admin. and Land Revenue 1973-75, in charge of Ministry of Labour and Manpower 1984-85, of Information 1985-86, of Local Govt., Rural Devt. and Co-operatives 1986-88, of Labour and Manpower 1988-, Deputy Prime Minister 1987-. *Publications:* Nitta Keragarey 1976. *Address:* Bangladesh Secretariat, 6th Floor, 1st 9-Storey Building, Bhaban 7, Dhaka, Bangladesh.

HOSSEIN, Robert; French actor and director; b. 30 Dec. 1927, Paris; s. of Amin Hossein and Anna Mincovschi; m. 1st Marina de Poliakoff 1955 (divorced), two s.; m. 2nd Caroline Eliacheff 1962 (divorced), one s.; stage actor, dir. and playwright, film dir. and producer, scriptwriter and actor; Chair. and Man. Dir. Sinfonia Films 1963-; Founder and Dir. Théâtre populaire de Reims and of Théâtre-Ecole de Reims 1971-; Artistic Dir. Théâtre de Paris-Théâtre moderne 1975-; *plays include:* La neige était sale, Haute surveillance, Les voyous (writer), La p . . . respectueuse, Huis-Clos, Vous qui nous jugez (writer), Les six hommes en question (co-writer with Frédéric Dard and producer), La moitié du plaisir (producer), Crime et châtiment, Les bas-fonds, Roméo et Juliette, Pour qui sonne le glas, La maison des otages, Hernani (produced for the Comédie Française) 1974, La maison de Bernada (produced at the Odéon) 1975, Le cuirassé Potemkine (dir. at Palais des Sports) 1975, Des souris et des hommes, Shéhérazade (ballet) 1975, Procès de Jeanne d'Arc (producer) 1976, Pas d'orchidées pour Miss Blandish (producer and actor) 1977, Notre-Dame de Paris (producer) 1978, Le cauchemar de Bella Manningham (producer) 1978, Danton et Robespierre (producer) 1979, Lorna et Ted 1981, Un grand avocat 1983, Les brumes de Manchester 1986, Liberty or Death and the Heritage of the French Revolution (Dominique Prize for Best Dir.) 1988; *films include:* Quai des blondes, Du rififi chez les hommes, Crime et châtiment, Toi le venin (script-writer and producer), Le jeu de la vérité (writer), Le goût de la violence (script-writer and producer), Le repos du guerrier, Le vice et la vertu, Les yeux cernés, Angélique marquise des anges, Banco à Bangkok, Le vampire de Düsseldorf, Le tonnerre de Dieu, La seconde vérité, J'ai tué Raspoutine (writer and producer), Indomptable Angélique, Don Juan 1973, Prêtres interdits, Le protecteur, Le faux cul 1975, Les uns et les autres, Le professionnel 1981, Les Misérables (producer) 1982, Un homme nommé Jésus (director) 1983, Jules César 1985, Les brumes de Manchester 1986; prix Orange 1963; Officier, Ordre nat. du Mérite. *Leisure interest:* skiing. *Publications:* La sentinelle aveugle 1978, Nomade sans tribu 1981. *Address:* c/o Mlle Dewing Guislaine, 10 rue du Docteur Roux, 75015 Paris, France.

HOTCHKISS, Rollin Douglas, B.S., PH.D; American bacterial physiologist; b. 8 Sept. 1911, S. Britain, Conn.; s. of Charles Leverett Hotchkiss and Eva Judith Platt; m. 1st Shirley Dawson 1933, 2nd Magda Gabor 1967; one s. one d.; ed. Yale Univ; Fellow, Rockefeller Inst. (later Rockefeller Univ.) 1935, Asst., Assoc., Assoc. Prof., then Prof. 1955-82, Prof. Emer. 1982-; Research Prof. of Biology, State Univ. of New York, Albany 1982-; Rockefeller Foundation Fellow, Copenhagen, Carlsberg Lab. 1937-38; Visiting Prof. of Biology, M.I.T. 1958, Univ. of Utah 1972, 1973; Visiting Prof. of Genetics, Univ. of Calif. at Berkeley 1968; Visiting Scientist, Hungarian Acad. of Sciences, Inst. of Genetics, Szeged 1972, 1974, 1975; Visiting Prof. of Microbiology, Univ. of Paris, Orsay 1975; Fogarty Scholar-in-Residence, Nat. Insts. of Health, Bethesda 1971-72; Jesup Lecturer, Columbia Univ. 1954, Dyer Lecturer, Nat. Insts. of Health 1961; mem. N.A.S. American Asscn. Biol. Chemists, American Soc. Cell Biol., Harvey

Soc. (Pres. 1958), Genet Soc. of America (Pres. 1972); Hon. mem. Hungaria﬈ Acad. of Science 1976; Hon. D.Sc. (Yale Univ.) 1962; Fellow-Commone﬈ Corpus Christi Coll., Cambridge 1970; Award in Antibiotics Research, Soc﬈ of American Bacteriologists 1953. *Publications:* About 100 scientific article﬈ and monographs including: Gramicidin, tyrocidin and tyrothricin 194﬈ Bacterial action of surface active agents 1946, Microchemical reaction f﬈ polysaccharides 1948, Chemical studies on transforming agent 1949, Tran﬈ fer of penicillin resistance by DNA 1951, Double Marker transformatio﬈ as evidence of linked factors in DNA 1954, Criteria for quantitative genet﬈ transformation 1957, Analysis of the sulfonamide resistance locus 195﬈ Fate of transforming DNA 1960, Selective heat inactivation of DNA 196﬈ Regulation of transformability 1964, Genetic engineering 1965, Mutationa﬈ modified specific exonucleases 1971, 1972, Mechanism of Recombinati﬈ 1971, 1973, 1974. *Leisure interests:* mineralogy, charcoal-drawing, bo﬈ construction, stained glass construction. *Address:* State University of Ne﬈ York, Department of Biology, Albany, New York 12222 (Office); Rolli﬈ Hills Condominium, 2-4 Lenox, Mass. 02140, U.S.A. (Home).

HOTSON, Leslie, A.B., A.M., PH.D., M.A., LITT.D. (Cantab.), F.R.S.L.; Americ﬈ literary scholar; b. 16 Aug. 1897, Delhi, Ont.; s. of John Hastie Hots﬈ and Lillie Swayze; m. Mary May Peabody 1919; ed. Harvard Univ﬈ travelling Scholar and Fellow 1922-25 and Instructor, Harvard Uni﬈ 1924-25; Sr. Research Fellow, Yale Univ. 1926-27, Research Assoc. 195﬈ 66; Assoc. Prof. of English, New York Univ. 1927-31; Prof. of Englis﬈ Haverford Coll. 1931-42; Capt. U.S. Army Signal Corps 1943-46; Fulbrig﬈ Sr. Research Fellow, England 1949-50; Fellow, King's Coll., Cambrid﬈ 1954-60. *Publications:* The Death of Christopher Marlowe 1925, T﬈ Commonwealth and Restoration Stage 1928, Shelley's Lost Letters ﬈ Harriet 1930, Shakespeare versus Shallow 1931, I, William Shakespea﬈ 1937, Shakespeare's Sonnets Dated 1949, Shakespeare's Motley 195﬈ Queen Elizabeth's Entertainment at Mitcham 1953, The First Night ﬈ Twelfth Night 1954, Shakespeare's Wooden O 1959, Mr. W. H. 196﬈ Shakespeare by Hilliard 1977. *Address:* White Hollow Road, Northfor﬈ Conn., U.S.A. *Telephone:* 203-484-0323.

HOTTEL, Hoyt Clarke, A.B., S.M.; American professor of chemical engine﬈ ing and engineering consultant; b. 15 Jan. 1903, Salem, Ind.; s. of Lou﬈ Weaver and Myrtle Clarke Hottel; m. Nellie Louise Rich 1929; one ﬈ three d.; ed. Indiana Univ. and Massachusetts Inst. of Technology (M.I.T﬈ Asst. Prof., Prof. M.I.T. 1927-41, Prof. of Fuel Eng. 1941-66, Carb﬈ Dubbs Prof. of Chemical Eng. 1966-68, Prof. Emer. 1968-; Dir. Fue﬈ Research Lab. 1934-68; Section Chief on Fire Warfare, Nat. Defen﬈ Cttee. 1942-45; Chair. Nat. Acad./Nat. Research Council Cttee. on Fi﬈ Research 1955-67, American Flame Research Cttee. 1952-73; Hon. Cha﬈ 1973-; Vice-Pres. Combustion Inst. 1952-64; mem. Advisory Panel ﬈ Fire Research 1985-88; Lecture series on radiative tranfer and furnace﬈ Budapest, Naples, Beijing, Xian 1985-86; mem. numerous other scienti﬈ cttees. and comms.; mem. Nat. Acad. of Sciences, Nat. Acad. of En﬈ American Acad. of Arts and Sciences, A.C.S., A.I.Ch.E.; Fellow, Americ﬈ Inst. of Chemical Engineers; numerous medals and awards including U﬈ Medal for Merit, Egerton Gold Medal, King's Medal for Service in ﬈ Cause of Freedom (U.K.), Jakob Award, A.S.M.E./A.I.Ch.E., Dani﬈ Award, Int. Solar Energy Soc., Melchett Medal, Inst. of Energy (U.K﬈ Gold Medal, Royal Soc., Founders Award, Nat. Acad. of Eng. 19﬈ *Publications:* Thermodynamic Charts for Combustion Processes (w﬈ others) 1949, Radiative Transfer (with A. F. Sarofim) 1967, New Ener﬈ Technology—Some Facts and Assessments (with J. B. Howard) 19﬈ Reaction Kinetics of Carbon Dioxide with Electrode Carbon Particles, ﬈ Fuel 1988; sections in handbooks and about 150 papers on combusti﬈ thermodynamics, jet and flame structure, radiative transfer, solar ener﬈ utilization, energy conversion, industrial furnace Design. *Leisure intere﬈* gardening, books, grandchildren. *Address:* Room 66-458, Departme﬈ Chemical Engineering, Massachusetts Institute of Technology, Cambrid﬈ Mass. 02139 (Office); 27 Cambridge Street, Winchester, Mass. 01890, U.S﬈ (Home). *Telephone:* (617) 253-4578 (Office); (617) 729-3873 (Home).

HOTTER, Hans; German singer; b. 19 Jan. 1909, Offenbach; m. He﬈ Fischer 1936; one s. one d.; ed. Munich; concert debut 1929, opera de﬈ 1930; mem. Vienna, Hamburg and Munich Opera cos.; has appeared﬈ concerts and operas in major cities in Europe, Australia and the U.S﬈ and in Festivals at Salzburg, Bayreuth and Edinburgh; renowned﬈ Wagnerian roles; retd. 1972. *Address:* c/o Bayerische Staatsoper, 8﬈ Munich, Federal Republic of Germany.

HOU GUANGJIONG; Chinese soil scientist; b. May 1905, Jinshan Cou﬈ Shanghai; m. Jingxian Huang 1931; one s. four d.; Prof. S.W. Agricultu﬈ Univ. 1988-. *Publications:* six books on soil science. *Address:* Departm﬈ of Soil Science, Southwest Agricultural University, Beibei, Chongqi﬈ 630716, People's Republic of China.

HOU JIE; Chinese party and state official; Vice-Chair. Revolution﬈ Cttee., Heilongjiang Prov. 1977-78; Vice-Gov., Heilongjiang 1979-85, G﬈ Feb. 1985-; Sec. CCP Cttee., Heilongjiang 1982-83, Deputy Sec. 198﬈ mem. 12th CCP Cen. Cttee. 1985, 13th Cen. Cttee. 1987. *Address:* H﬈ longjiang Provincial Chinese Communist Party, Harbin, Heilongjia﬈ People's Republic of China.

HOU RUNYU; Chinese orchestral conductor; b. 6 Jan. 1945, Kunming﬈ of Hou Zhu and Zhu Bangying; m. Su Jia 1971; one s. one d.;﬈

Music Middle School of Shanghai Conservatory, Shanghai Conservatory (conducting); studied at Musikhochschule, Cologne, Fed. Repub. of Germany, and Mozarteum, Salzburg, Austria 1981–85; started playing piano aged 7, debut, Kunming 1954; Vice-Music Dir. Shanghai Symphony Orchestra. *Leisure interest:* sport. *Address:* 105 Hunan Road, Shanghai, People's Republic of China. *Telephone:* 311468.

HOUGHTON, Amory, Jr., M.B.A.; American business executive; b. 7 Aug. 1926; s. of the late Amory Houghton and of Laura DeKay Richardson; m. Ruth Frances West 1950; two s. two d.; ed. Harvard Univ. Business School; served in U.S. Marine Corps 1945–46; joined Corning Glass Works 1951, Dir. 1955, Staff Vice-Pres. 1957, Pres. 1961–64, Chair. and Chief Exec. Officer 1964–83, Chair. Exec. Cttee. 1983–; Chair. of Bd. and Dir. Corning Glass Works of Canada Ltd.; Dir., Dow Corning Corpn., Pittsburgh Corning Corpn., B.F. Goodrich Co., Corhart Refractories Co., New York Telephone Co., Corning Fibre Box Corpn.; Trustee Corning Glass Works Foundation, The Corning Museum of Glass, Episcopal Theological School (Cambridge, Mass.), Nat. Security Industrial Asscn.; mem. Bd. Nat. Industrial Conf. *Address:* Corning Glass Works, Corning, N.Y. 14830 (Office); 33 East 3rd Street, Corning, N.Y. 14830, U.S.A. (Home).

HOUGHTON, Arthur Amory, Jr.; American executive; b. 12 Dec. 1906, Corning, N.Y.; s. of Arthur Amory and Mabel Hollister Houghton; m. Nina Rodale 1973; one s. three d. (by previous marriage); ed. St. Paul's School, Concord (N.H.) and Harvard Univ.; Corning Glass Works, Mfg. Dept. 1929, Treas. Dept. 1929–30, Asst. to Pres. 1930–32, Vice-Pres. 1935–42; Pres. Steuben Glass 1933–72, Chair. 1973–; Dir. Corning Glass Works; fmr. Dir. U.S. Steel Corpn., Past Dir. Nat. Book Cttee. Inc.; Vice-Pres. Corning Museum of Glass; Curator of Rare Books, Library of Congress 1940–42; Hon. Consultant in English Bibliography; Trustee and Chair. Emer. Cooper Union New York; Chair. Wye Inst. Inc.; Past Chair. and Hon. Trustee, Parsons School of Design, New York, Philharmonic Symphony Soc. of New York, Inst. of Int. Educ.; fmr Vice-Chair. Lincoln Center for the Performing Arts, New York; Trustee Emer. Pierpont Morgan Library, Metropolitan Museum of Art, fmr. Pres. and Chair.; Hon. Trustee, New York Public Library; fmr. Trustee, Rockefeller Foundation, U.S. Trust Co; fmr. Dir. New York Life Insurance Co.; fmr. Pres. U.S. English-Speaking Union; mem. Council on Foreign Relations; service in U.S. Air Force (Lieut.-Col.) 1942–45; Sr. Fellow Royal Coll. of Art; Fellow Royal Soc. of Arts; Friedsam Industrial Art Medal 1953, Officier, Légion l'honneur, Commdr. de l'Ordre des Arts et des Lettres; Knight Most Venerable Order of the Hospital of St. John of Jerusalem, Skowhegan School-Gertrude Vanderbilt Whitney Award; hon. degrees from 20 colls. and univs. *Address:* Wye Plantation, Queenstown, Md. 21658, U.S.A. (Home). *Telephone:* (301) 827-7163.

HOUGHTON, James Richardson, A.B., M.B.A.; American business executive; b. 6 April 1936, Corning, New York; s. of the late Amory Houghton and Laura Richardson Houghton; m. May Kinnicutt 1962; one s. one d.; ed. St. Paul's School, Concord, N.H., Harvard Coll. and Harvard Univ. Business School; worked in investment banking, Goldman, Sachs and Co., New York 1959–61; in Production and Finance, Corning Glass Works, Danville, Ky. and Corning, New York 1962–64; Vice-Pres. and Area Man., Corning Glass Int., Zurich and Brussels 1964–68; Vice-Pres. and Gen. Man. Consumer Products Div., Corning Glass Works, Corning, New York 1968–71, Vice-Chair. of Bd. 1971–83, Chair. of Bd. and C.E.O. 1983–; Dir. 'BS Inc., Dow Corning Corpn., Metropolitan Life Insurance Co., J. P. Morgan Co. Inc., U.S./U.S.S.R. Trade and Econ. Council; Trustee Corning Glass Works Foundation, Corning Museum of Glass, Metropolitan Museum of Art, Pierpont Morgan Library, U.S. Council of ICC; mem. Business Cttee. for the Arts Inc., Council on Foreign Relations, The Business Roundtable, The Business Council. *Address:* c/o Corning Glass Works, Houghton Park, Corning, N.Y. 14831; 36 Spencer Hill Road, Corning, N.Y. 14830 U.S.A. (Home).

HOUGHTON, John Theodore, C.B.E., M.A., D.PHIL., F.R.S.; British physicist; b. 30 Dec. 1931, Dyserth, Clwyd; s. of Sidney and Miriam (née Yarwood) Houghton; m. 1st Margaret E. Broughton 1962 (died 1986), one s. one d.; m. 2nd Sheila Thompson 1988; ed. Rhyl Grammar School and Jesus Coll., Oxford ; Research Fellow, Royal Aircraft Establishment. Farnborough 1954–57; Lecturer in Atmospheric Physics, Univ. of Oxford 1958–62, Reader 1962–76, Prof. 1976–83, Fellow. Jesus Coll. 1960–83, Hon. Fellow 1983–; Dir. Appleton, Science and Eng. Research Council 1979–83; Chair. Earth Observation Advisory Cttee. European Space Agency 1980–; Chair. Jt. Scientific Cttee., World Climate Research Prog. 1981–83; Dir.-Gen. Meteorological Office 1983–; mem. Exec. Cttee. WMO 1983–, Vice-Pres. 1987–; Pres. Royal Meteorological Soc. 1976–78; Charles Chree Medal and Prize (Inst. of Physics) 1979. *Publications:* Infra Red Physics (with S. D. Smith) 1966, The Physics of Atmospheres 1977, 1986, Remote Sounding of Atmospheres (with F. W. Taylor and C. D. Rodgers) 1984, Does God Play Dice? 1988. *Address:* Meteorological Office, London Road, Bracknell, Berks., England. *Telephone:* 0344-420242.

HOUGHTON OF SOWERBY, Baron (Life Peer), cr. 1974, of Sowerby, West Yorkshire; **(Arthur Leslie Noel) Douglas Houghton,** C.H., P.C.; British trade unionist and politician; b. 11 Aug. 1898; s. of John and Martha Houghton; m. Vera Travis 1939; ed. Derbyshire County Secondary School; Civil Service Rifles 1916–19; Gen. Sec. Inland Revenue Staff Fed. 1922–60;

mem. Gen. Council, TUC 1952–60; mem. Civil Service, Staff Whitley Council 1923–58, Chair. 1954–56; Alderman, London County Council 1947–49; M.P. 1949–74, Chair. Public Accounts Cttee. House of Commons 1963–64; Chancellor, Duchy of Lancaster 1964–66; Minister without Portfolio 1966–67; Chair. Parl. Labour Party 1967–74; Chair. Party Funds Cttee. 1975; Chair. Cttee. on Security of Cabinet Papers 1976; Vice-Pres. RSPCA 1978–82; mem. Cttee. for Reform of Animal Experimentation 1977–; Labour. *Publication:* Paying for the Social Services 1968. *Address:* 110 Marsham Court, London, S.W.1, England (Home). *Telephone:* 01-834 0602 (Home).

HOUGRON, Jean (Marcel), L. EN D.; French writer; b. 1 July 1923, Caen; s. of Jean Hougron and Denise Grude; m. 1st Noëlle Desgouille (divorced), two s. two d.; m. 2nd Victoria Sanchez, one d.; ed. Faculty of Law, Univ. of Paris; schoolmaster 1943–46; commercial employment in export-import firm, Saigon 1946–47; lorry driver 1947–49; translator in American Consulate 1950; news ed. Radio France Asie 1951; returned to France to write 1952; bookseller in Nice 1953–54; lived in Spain 1958–60; Grand Prix du Roman, Acad. Française 1953, Prix Populiste 1965; Grand Prix de la Science-Fiction for Le Naguen 1982; Chevalier des Arts et des Lettres. *Publications:* Tu récolteras la tempête 1950, Rage blanche 1951, Soleil au ventre 1952, Mort en fraude (film) 1953, La nuit indochinoise 1953, Les portes de l'aventure 1954, Les Asiates 1954, Je reviendrai à Kandara (film) 1955, La terre du barbare 1958, Par qui le scandale 1960, Le signe du chien 1961, Histoire de Georges Guersant 1964, Les humiliés 1965, La gueule pleine de dents 1970, L'homme de proie 1974, L'anti-jeu 1977, Le Naguen 1979, La chambre (novel) 1982, Coup de soleil 1984. *Address:* Hachette Littérature, 79 boulevard Saint-Germain, 75006 Paris (Office); 1 rue des Guillemites, 75004 Paris, France (Home).

HOUMANN, Borge Kruuse; Danish journalist; b. 26 March 1902, Fredericia; ed. Denmark and Derby Grammar School, England; sailor 1920; started writing poems and short stories 1923; econ. dir. of Riddersalen Theatre 1933; Man. Dir. of publishing firm Arbejderforlaget 1935; mem. of Danish Freedom Council (underground) 1943–45; mem. Danish Parl. 1945–46; mem. Danish Radioraadet (Danish Broadcasting Council) 1946–50; Chief Ed. of Communist daily Land og Folk 1945–54; Dir. publishing firm of Sirius 1957; D. Phil. h.c. (Copenhagen, Greifswald Univs.). *Publications:* Huset ved Havet 1923, translation of Whitman's Leaves of Grass 1927, Lystgas (a novel) 1932, Forlis (poems) 1934, Martin Andersen Nexø, Selected Speeches and Articles, Vols. 1-3 (Editor) 1954, Martin Andersen Nexø Bibliography (with notes) Vols. I-II, 1961, 1967, Martin Andersen Nexø: Letters (Ed. and annotator) Vol. I 1969, Vol. II 1971, Vol. III 1972, Martin Andersen Nexø and his Time: I 1869–1919, II 1919–33, III 1933–54, Otto Gelsted: Tilbageblik på fremtiden Vols. I-II (Ed.), Otto Gelsted Bibliography 1978, and a number of books on Martin Andersen Nexø and many translations from English and German. *Address:* Aage Bergsvej 19, DK 8240 Risskov, Denmark. *Telephone:* (06) 179549.

HOUNSFIELD, Sir Godfrey Newbold, Kt., C.B.E., F.R.S.; British research scientist; b. 28 Aug. 1919; s. of Thomas Hounsfield; unmarried; ed. Magnus Grammar School, Newark, City and Guilds Coll., London, and Faraday House Electrical Eng. Coll.; served R.A.F. 1939–46; with EMI Ltd. 1951–, Head of Medical Systems section 1972–76, Chief Staff Scientist 1976–77, Senior Staff Scientist, Central Research Labs. of EMI (now THORN EMI Central Research Labs.) 1977–86, Consultant to Labs. 1986–; inventor EMI-scanner computerized transverse axial tomography system for X-ray examination; Professorial Fellow in imaging sciences, Univ. of Manchester 1978–; MacRobert Award 1972; Wilhelm-Exner Medal, Austrian Industrial Asscn. 1974; Ziedses des Plantes Medal, Physikalisch-Medizinische Gesellschaft, Würzburg 1974; Prince Philip Medal Award, City and Guilds of London Inst. 1975; ANS Radiation Award, Georgia Inst. of Tech. 1975; Lasker Award 1975; Duddell Bronze Medal, Inst. of Physics 1976; Golden Plate, American Acad. of Achievement 1976; Churchill Gold Medal 1976; Gairdner Foundation Award 1976; shared Nobel Prize in Medicine and Physiology 1979 with Prof. A. M. Cormack (q.v.) for development of computer-assisted tomography; Dr.Med. h.c. (Basel) 1975; Hon. D.Sc. (City Univ., London) 1976, (London) 1976; Hon. D. Tech. (Loughborough) 1976; Hon. F.R.C.P., Hon. Fellow Royal Coll. of Radiologists and other awards and prizes. *Publications:* articles in professional journals. *Leisure interests:* mountain walks and country rambles, music, playing piano. *Address:* THORN EMI Central Research Laboratories, Dawley Road, Hayes, Middx., UB3 1HH (Office); 15 Crane Park Road, Whitton, Twickenham, Middx., England (Home). *Telephone:* 01-848 6404 (Office); 01-984 1746 (Home).

HOUPHOUËT-BOIGNY, Félix; Côte d'Ivoire politician; b. 18 Oct. 1905, Yamoussoukro; ed. School of Medicine, Dakar, Senegal; Doctor, Medical Assistance Service 1925–40; Canton Chief 1940; Pres. Syndicat Agricole Africain 1944; mem. French Constituent Assembly 1945–46; mem. French Nat. Ass. 1946–59; successively Territorial Councillor for Korhogo, Pres. Territorial Ass., Ivory Coast, Grand Conseiller for French West Africa; Minister attached to the Prime Minister's Office (France) 1956–57; Minister of Health (France) 1957–58; Minister of State (Pflimlin Cabinet) May 1958, (de Gaulle Cabinet) 1958–59, (Debré Cabinet) Jan.-May 1959; Pres. Ass., Ivory Coast Repub. 1958–59, Pres. Council 1959–60; Pres. of the Republic Nov, 1960–, concurrently Minister of Foreign Affairs 1961, of Interior,

Educ. and Agric. 1963; Pres. of Council of Ministers; Minister of Defence 1963–74; Minister-Counsellor to French Govt. 1959–60; Hon. Pres. Parti Démocratique de la Côte d'Ivoire; Dr. h.c. (Univs. of Aix-Marseille and René-Descartes) 1978. *Address:* Présidence de la République, Abidjan, Côte d'Ivoire.

HOUSE, Lieut-Gen. Sir David George, G.C.B., K.C.V.O., C.B.E., M.C.; British army officer; b. 8 Aug. 1922; s. of A. G. House; m. Sheila Betty Darwin 1947; two d.; ed. Regent's Park School, London; war service in Italy and then various regimental appointments with the King's Royal Rifle Corps, 1st Bn. The Royal Green Jackets and staff appointments; Commanded 51st Gurkha Brigade in Borneo 1965–67; Chief, BRIXMS 1967–69; Deputy Mil. Sec. 1969–71; Chief of Staff, HQ British Army of the Rhine 1971–73; Dir. of Infantry 1973–75; Gen. Officer Commdg. Northern Ireland 1975–77; Col. Commdt. The Light Div.; Col. Commdt. Small Arms School Corps 1974–77; Gentleman Usher of the Black Rod, House of Lords 1978–85. *Leisure interests:* music, gardening. *Address:* Dormer Lodge, Aldborough, North Yorks., England.

HOUSHIARY, Shirazeh, B.A.; British sculptor; b. 15 Jan. 1955, Iran; ed. Tehran Univ., Chelsea School of Art and Cardiff Coll. of Art; sculptor at the Lisson Gallery, London. *Address:* 15 Star and Garter Mansions, Lower Richmond Road, Putney, London, SW15 1JW, England. *Telephone:* 01-788 6320.

HOUSIAUX, Albert, D.RER.POL.; Belgian journalist; b. 1914; ed. Athénée Royal, Ixelles, Brussels Free Univ.; joined staff of Le Peuple 1937; news bulletin editor I.N.R.; Editorial Sec. Socialisme; served in the army and captured during the Second World War; Inspector-Gen. Ministry of Imports 1945; Dir.-Gen. Le Peuple 1948–54, Political Dir. (later Ed.) 1954–69; mem. Bureau Belgian Socialist Party (with vote); Chevalier Ordre de Léopold, Ordre de la Couronne, Officer of the Order of Merit (Italy). *Address:* 201 Avenue Rommelaere, Jette-St.-Pierre, Brussels 9, Belgium.

HOUSLAY, Miles Douglas, PH.D., F.R.S.E., F.R.S.A.; British professor of biochemistry; b. 25 June 1950, Wolverhampton; s. of Edwin Douglas Houslay and Georgina Marie Houslay (née Jeffs); m. Rhian Mair Gee 1972; two s. one d.; ed. The Grammar School, Brewood, Staffs., Univ. Coll., Cardiff, King's Coll., Cambridge; ICI Postdoctoral Research Fellow, Univ. of Cambridge 1974–76, Research Fellow, Queen's Coll. 1975–76; Lecturer in Biochemistry, UMIST 1976–82, Reader 1982–84; Gardiner Prof. of Biochemistry, Univ. of Glasgow 1984–; Hon. Sr. Research Fellow, Calif. Metabolic Research Foundation, La Jolla, U.S.A. 1980–; Deputy Chair. Editorial Bd. Biochemical Journal; Ed.-in-C., Cellular Signalling; mem. Cttee., Biochemical Soc. 1982–86; Colworth Medal, Biochemical Soc. *Publications:* Dynamics of Biological Membranes, and various scientific articles. *Leisure interests:* walking, gardening, music, boating. *Address:* Department of Biochemistry, University of Glasgow, Glasgow, G12 8QQ, Scotland. *Telephone:* (041) 339 8855 Ext. 5903.

HOUŠTECKÝ, Miroslav, RS.DR.; Czechoslovak diplomatist; b. 10 June 1926; s. of Josef Houštecký and Blazena Houštecká; m. Marie Sedláková 1953; one s. two d.; ed. School of Political and Economic Sciences, Prague; Lecturer and Reader, Charles Univ., and School of Political and Econ. Sciences, Prague, 1950–64; Cand., Historical Sciences 1958; Corresp. of Rudé Právo and Czechoslovak News Agency, India 1964–69, Ed. and Deputy Dir. Gen., Prague, 1969–77; Sr. Official, Cen. Cttee. of Czechoslovak C.P. 1977–83; Amb. to U.K. 1983–86, to U.S.A. 1986–. *Publications:* (Co-Author) History of Czechoslovak Foreign Policy 1958, Survey of Modern World History vols I–II 1963. *Address:* Czechoslovak Embassy, 3900 Linnean Avenue, N.W. Washington, D.C. 20008, U.S.A. *Telephone:* (202) 363-6315.

HOUTHAKKER, Hendrik Samuel; American economist; b. 31 Dec. 1924, Amsterdam, Netherlands; s. of Bernard and Marion (née Lichtenstein) Houthakker; m. Anna-Teresa Tymieniecka 1955; two s. one d.; ed. Univ. of Amsterdam; Research Staff mem., Dept. of Applied Econs., Univ. of Cambridge 1949–51; on Research Staff, Cowles Comm. for Research in Econs., Univ. of Chicago 1952–53; Prof. of Econs., Stanford Univ. 1954–60, Harvard Univ. 1960–, Chair. 1987–88; Sr. Staff Economist, Council of Econ. Advisers 1967–68, mem. 1969–71; Vice-Pres. American Econ. Asscn. 1972; Dir. New York Futures Exchange 1979–; Fellow, Econometric Soc. (Past Pres. and Council mem.); mem. Nat Acad. of Sciences; Corresp. mem. Royal Netherlands Acad. of Sciences; Dr. h.c. (Amsterdam) 1972, (Fribourg) 1974; John Bates Clark Medal of American Econ. Asscn. 1963. *Publications:* The Analysis of Family Budgets (with S. J. Prais) 1955, Consumer Demand in the United States (with L. D. Taylor) 1966, Economic Policy for the Farm Sector 1967, The World Price of Oil, 1976; also articles. *Address:* 348 Payson Road, Belmont, Mass. 02178 (Home); Littauer Center, Harvard University, Cambridge, Mass. 02138, U.S.A. (Office). *Telephone:* 617-495-2111 (Office).

HOUTTE, Baron Jean van, D. EN D.; Belgian emeritus university professor and politician; b. 17 March 1907, Ghent; s. of Hubert van Houtte; m. Cécile de Stella 1932; one s. three d.; ed. Univ. of Ghent; Prof. Univ. of Liège 1931, Univ. of Ghent 1937; Head of Secretariat, Ministry of the Interior 1944–45; co-opted Senator 1949–68; Minister of Finance 1950–52; Prime Minister 1952–54; Minister of Finance 1958–61; Minister of State 1966; Hon. Pres. Sabena Airlines; various Belgian and foreign decorations.

Publications: Traité des sociétés de personnes à responsabilité limitée 1935, 1950, 1962, La responsabilité civile dans les transports aériens 1940, La réparation des dommages de guerre aux biens privés 1948, Formulierboek voor notarissen 1947, Principes du droit fiscal belge 1958, 1966, 1979. *Address:* 54 Boulevard St. Michel, Brussels, Belgium. *Telephone:* 733-62-94.

HOVEYDA, Fereydoun, LL.D.; Iranian diplomatist; b. 21 Sept. 1924, Damascus; ed. Univ. of Paris; various positions, Imperial Iranian Embassy, Paris 1946–51; Programme Specialist, Mass Communications Dept. UNESCO 1952–64; Under-Sec. of State for Int. and Econ. Affairs, Ministry of Foreign Affairs 1965–71; Perm. Rep. to UN 1971–79; del to various int confs. including UN Gen. Assembly 1948, 1951, 1965, UNESCO Confs. 1966, 1968, 1970 and ECOSOC sessions 1966–69; Léopold Sédar Senghor Literary Prize 1973. *Publications:* studies: Le plan septennal iranien 1948, La nationalisation du pétrole en Iran 1951, Histoire du roman policier 1968, The Fall of the Shah 1979; novels: Les quarantaines 1962, L'aérogare 1965, Dans une terre étrange 1968, Le losange 1969, Les neiges du Sinaï 1973.

HOVHANISSIAN, Hratchia; Soviet (Armenian) literary figure and poet; b. 1919, Shahab (now Mayakovsky), Armenia; ed. Yerevan secondary school and State Univ.; served in Soviet army 1941–45; worked in broadcasting –1948; ed. literary weekly Grakan Tert; began publishing in 1948.

HOVING, Thomas, PH.D.; American editor and cultural administrator; b. 15 Jan. 1931; s. of Walter Hoving and Mary Osgood Field; m. Nancy Bell 1953; one d.; ed. The Buckley School, New York, Eaglebrook School, Deerfield, Mass., Exeter Acad., Exeter N.H., The Hotchkiss School, Lakeville, Conn., and Princeton Univ.; Curatorial Asst. of Medieval Art and The Cloisters, Metropolitan Museum of Art 1959–60, Asst. Curator 1960–63, Assoc. Curator 1963–65, Curator of Medieval Art and The Cloisters 1965; Commr. of Parks, New York 1966; Admin. of Recreation and Cultural Affairs, New York 1967; Dir., The Metropolitan Museum of Art, 1966–77; Ed.-in.-Chief Connoisseur Magazine 1981–; Arts and Entertainment Corresp. ABC News 1978–84; Pres. Hoving Assn. cultural affairs consulting; Pres. Hoving Assn. Inc.; Bd. of Dirs. IBM World Trade Corpn., Americas/Far East, Manhattan Industries Inc.; Fellowship, Nat. Council of Humanities 1955, Kienbusch and Haring Fellowship 1957; Hon. LL.D. (Pratt Inst.) 1967, Hon. D.F.A. (New York) 1968, Hon. D. Hum. (Princeton) 1968, Hon. D. Litt. (Middlebury Coll.) 1968; Distinguished Citizen's Award, Citizen's Budget Cttee. 1967, Creative Leadership in Educ. Award, New York Univ. 1975, Woodrow Wilson award, Princeton 1975. *Publications:* Guide to the Cloisters 1962, Tutankhamun, The Untold Story 1978, Two Worlds of Andrew Wyeth 1978, King of the Confessors 1981, Masterpiece 1986. *Leisure interests:* sailing, skiing, bicycling, flying. *Address:* Hoving Associates Inc., 150 East 73rd Street, New York, N.Y. 10021, U.S.A.

HOWARD, Alan Mackenzie; British actor; b. 5 Aug. 1937, London; s. of Arthur John and Jean (Compton Mackenzie) Howard; m. 1st Stephanie Hinchcliffe Davies 1965; m. 2nd Sally Beauman 1976; one s.; ed. Ardingly Coll.; National Service with R.A.F. in Germany 1956–58; Stage Hand, Asst. Stage Man., Actor, Belgrade Theatre Coventry 1958–60; London West End debut, Duke of York's Theatre in Roots 1959; played in London at Royal Court, Arts, Mermaid, Strand, Phoenix theatres, also outside London 1960–65; with Royal Shakespeare Co. 1966–, Assoc. Artist 1967–; Plays and Players London Theatre Critics most promising Actor Award 1969, Best Actor Award 1977; Soc. of West End Theatre Managers Best Actor in a Revival Award 1976, 1978; Evening Standard Drama Award for Best Actor 1978, 1981; Variety Club of Great Britain Best Actor Award 1980. Appeared in RSC productions: Twelfth Night, Revenger's Tragedy, As You Like It, The Relapse, King Lear, Troilus and Cressida, Much Ado About Nothing, Bartholomew Fair, Dr. Faustus, Hamlet, Midsummer Night's Dream, Enemies, Man of Mode, The Balcony, The Bewitched, Henry IV parts 1 and 2, Henry V, Wild Oats, Henry VI parts 1, 2 and 3, Coriolanus, Anthony and Cleopatra, Children of the Sun, Richard II, Richard III, The Forest, Good 1981, 1982–83, Breaking the Silence 1985; also films and TV. *Leisure interests:* reading, music. *Address:* c/o Julian Belfrage Associates, 60 St. James's Street, London, S.W.1, England. *Telephone:* 01-491 4400.

HOWARD, Ann; British mezzo-soprano opera singer; b. 22 July 1936, Norwood, London; d. of William A. Howard and Gladys W. Swadling; m. Keith Giles 1954; one d.; ed. with Topliss Green and Rodolfa Lhombino, London, and Dominic Modesti, Paris; repertoire includes Carmen, Dalila (Samson et Dalila), Dulcinée (Don Quichote), Hélène (La Belle Hélène), Eboli (Don Carlos), Azucena (Il Trovatore), Amneris (Aida), Isabella (Italiana in Algeri), Proserpina (Orfeo), Ortrud (Lohengrin), Brangaene (Tristan und Isolde), Baba the Turk (The Rake's Progress) and numerous other roles in the international operatic repertoire; performed in world première of Mines of Sulphur (Bennett) 1970, Rebecca (Josephs) 1982, The Tempest (Eaton, U.S.A.) 1985, and in U.K. première of Le Grand Macabre 1982; has appeared in U.K., France, Canada, U.S.A., Mexico, Chile and Italy, and on BBC radio and TV. *Leisure interests:* gardening, cooking. *Address:* 5 Catherine Road, Surbiton, Surrey, KT6 4HA, England.

HOWARD, Anthony Michell, M.A.; British journalist; b. 12 Feb. 1934, London; s. of the late Canon W. G. Howard and Janet (née Rymer

Howard; m. Carol Anne Gaynor 1965; ed. Westminster School and Christ Church, Oxford; on editorial staff Manchester Guardian 1959-61; Political Corresp. New Statesman 1961-64; Whitehall Corresp. Sunday Times 1965; Washington Corresp. Observer 1966-69; Asst. Ed. New Statesman 1970-72, Ed. 1972-78; Ed. The Listener 1979-81; Deputy Ed. The Observer 1981-88; Presenter Face the Press, Channel Four 1982-85; Presenter, reporter BBC TV 1989-; Harkness Fellow, U.S.A. 1960. *Publications:* The Making of the Prime Minister (with Richard West) 1965, ed. The Crossman Diaries 1964-70, 1979, Rab: The Life of R. A. Butler 1987. *Address:* 17 Addison Avenue, London, W11 4QS, England. *Telephone:* 01-603 3749.

HOWARD, Elizabeth Jane; British novelist; b. 26 March 1923; d. of David Liddon and Katharine M. Howard; m. 1st Peter M. Scott 1942; one d.; m. 2nd James Douglas-Henry 1959; m. 3rd Kingsley Amis (q.v.) 1965 (divorced 1983); ed. London Mask Theatre School; BBC TV modelling 1939-46; Sec. Inland Waterways Asscn. 1947; then professional writer including plays for TV; John Llewellyn Rhys Memorial Prize 1950; Hon. Artistic Dir. Cheltenham Literary Festival 1962; Artistic Co-Dir. Salisbury Festival of Arts 1973. *Publications:* The Beautiful Visit 1950, The Long View 1956, The Sea Change 1959, After Julius 1965, Something in Disguise 1969 (TV series 1982), Odd Girl Out 1972, Mr. Wrong 1975; Ed. A Companion for Lovers 1978; Getting it Right 1982 (Yorkshire Post Prize) (film script 1985), Alone Together (film script) 1986, Howard and Maschler on Food: cooking for occasions (jtly.) 1987. *Leisure interests:* music, gardening, enjoying all the arts, travelling, natural history. *Address:* c/o Jonathan Clowes, 22 Prince Albert Road, London, NW1 7ST, England.

HOWARD, Harry Nicholas, PH.D.; American historian; b. 19 Feb. 1902, Excelsior Springs, Mo.; s. of Alpheus and Lois A. (Foster) Howard; m. Virginia Faye Brubaker 1932; two s.; ed. William Jewell Coll., Univs. of Missouri and California; Gregory Fellow in History, Univ. of Mo. 1926-27; Research Asst. in Modern European History, Univ. of Calif. 1928-29; Asst. Prof. History, Univ. of Okla. 1929-30, Miami Univ. 1930-37, Assoc. Prof. 1937-40, Prof. 1940-42; Lecturer Contemporary Problems, Univ. of Cincinnati 1937-42; Head, East European Unit Div. of Territorial Studies, Dept. of State 1942-44; mem. Div. Int. Org. Aff. 1944-46; Tech. Expert, U.S. Del., UNCIO 1945; Adviser, Special Interrogation Comm., Germany 1945; Chief Near East Branch, Div. of Research for Near East and Africa 1946-47; Adviser, Div. of Greek, Turkish, and Iranian Affairs 1947-49; Adviser U.S. Del., UN Gen. Assembly 1947-50; UN Adviser, Dept. of State, Bureau of Near East, S. Asian and African Affairs 1949-56; Acting U.S. Rep. Advisory Comm. UNRWA, Beirut 1956-62; Special Asst. to Dir. of UNRWA 1962-63; Adviser U.S. Del. UN Balkan Comm. 1947-50; Prof. of Middle East Studies, School of Int. Service, American Univ., Washington, D.C. 1963-68, Adjunct Prof. 1968-; Lecturer U.S. Army War Coll. 1970-72; Chair. Middle East Program, Foreign Service Inst., Dept. of State 1966, 1971-73; Faculty Adviser Foreign Service Inst. 1967-68; Reserve Consultant, Dept. of State 1967-; Book Review Adviser Middle East Journal 1963-; Chief Consultant Middle East and North Africa, Cincinnati World Affairs Council 1968-69; mem. Middle East Inst., Bd. of Govs. 1963-79, Emer. 1979-; mem. American Historical Asscn. Dacor; Citation of Achievement Recipient (William Jewell Coll.) 1947; Commdr. Royal Order of the Phoenix (Greece). *Publications:* The Partition of Turkey, A Diplomatic History 1913-1923 1931, Military Government in the Panama Canal Zone 1931 (with Prof. R. J. Kerner), The Balkan Conferences and the Balkan Entente 1930-35, A Study in the Recent History of the Balkan and Near Eastern People 1936, The Problem of the Turkish Straits 1947, The United Nations and the Problem of Greece 1947, The General Assembly and the Problem of Greece 1948, Yugoslavia (co-author) 1949, Soviet Power and Policy (co-author) 1955, The King-Crane Commission 1963, Turkey, the Straits and U.S. Policy 1974. *Leisure interests:* swimming, walking, reading. *Address:* 6508 Greentree Road, Bradley Hills Grove, Bethesda, Md. 20817, U.S.A. (Home). *Telephone:* 301-365-3693 (Home).

HOWARD, Jack Rohe; American newspaper and broadcasting executive; b. 31 Aug. 1910, New York; s. of Roy Wilson and Margaret (Rohe) Howard; m. 1st Barbara Balfe 1934 (died 1962); one s. one d.; m. 2nd Eleanor Sallee Harris 1964; ed. Yale Univ; journalist, Tokyo, Shanghai, Indianapolis, Washington 1932-35; with radio cos., Knoxville, Washington and New York (now Scripps-Howard Broadcasting Co.) 1936-39; Asst. Exec. Ed. Scripps-Howard Newspapers 1939-42, 1945-48, Gen. Ed. Man. 1948-75, subsequently Chair.; U.S. Navy 1942-45; Pres. E. W. Scripps Co. 1953-75, Chair. Exec. Cttee. 1976-85; Pres., Dir. and Chair. Exec. Cttee. Scripps-Howard Broadcasting Co. 1937-42, 1945-74, Chair. Bd. and mem. Exec. Cttee. 1974-; Dir. Trans-World Airlines 1965-81. *Address:* 200 Park Avenue, New York, N.Y. 10166, U.S.A.

HOWARD, Hon. John Winston, LL.B.; Australian politician; b. 26 July 1939, Sydney; s. of Lyall Falconer and Mona Jane Howard; m. Alison Janette Parker 1971; two s. one d.; ed. Univ. of Sydney; solicitor to Supreme Court, N.S.W. 1962; partner, Sydney solicitors' firm 1968-74; Liberal M.P. for Bennelong, N.S.W., Fed. Parl. 1974-; Minister for Business and Consumer Affairs 1975-77, Minister Assisting Prime Minister 1977, Fed. Treas. 1977-83; Deputy Leader of Opposition 1983-85, Leader 1985-; Leader Liberal Party Sept. 1985-; mem. State Exec., N.S.W. Liberal Party 1963-74; Vice-Pres., N.S.W. Div., Liberal Party 1972-74.

Leisure interests: reading, cricket, tennis. *Address:* 19 Milner Crescent, Wollstonecraft, N.S.W., Australia. *Telephone:* 02 439 4360.

HOWARD, Sir Michael Eliot, Kt., C.B.E., M.C., D.LITT., F.B.A.; British historian; b. 29 Nov. 1922, London, England; s. of the late Geoffrey Eliot Howard and of Edith Howard (née Edinger); ed. Wellington Coll., Christ Church, Oxford; served in army 1942-45; Asst. lecturer, lecturer in History, King's Coll., London 1947-53; lecturer, Reader in War Studies, Univ. of London 1953-63; Prof. of War Studies, Univ. of London 1963-68; Fellow in Higher Defence Studies, All Souls Coll., Oxford 1968-77; Chichele Prof. of the History of War, Univ. of Oxford 1977-80; Regius Prof. of Modern History, Univ. of Oxford 1980-89; Robert E. Lovett Prof. of Mil. and Naval History, Yale Univ. 1989-; Pres. Int. Inst. for Strategic Studies; Foreign mem. American Acad. of Arts and Sciences; Hon. Litt.D. (Leeds) 1979; Hon. D. Litt. (London) 1988; Duff Cooper Memorial Prize 1961, Wolfson Literary Award 1972; Chesney Memorial Gold Medal, R.U.S.I. *Publications:* The Franco-German War 1961, Grand Strategy, Vol. IV (in UK History of Second World War) 1972, The Continental Commitment 1973, War in European History 1976, trans. (with Peter Paret) Clausewitz on War 1976, War and the Liberal Conscience 1978, Restraints on War 1979, The Causes of Wars 1983, Clausewitz 1983. *Leisure interests:* music, gardening. *Address:* Department of History, Yale University, Newhaven, Connecticut, U.S.A.

HOWARTH, Elgar, B.MUS.; British musician; b. 4 Nov. 1935, Cannock, Staffs.; s. of Oliver Howarth and Emma Wall; m. Mary Bridget Neary 1958; one s. two d.; ed. Eccles Grammar School and Manchester Univ.-Royal Manchester Coll. of Music (jt. course); orchestral player 1958-70; Chair. Royal Philharmonic Orchestra 1968-70; Prin. Guest Conductor Opera North 1985-88; freelance orchestral conductor 1970-; compositions: Trumpet Concerto 1968, Trombone Concerto 1962, Music for Spielberg 1984; Fellow, Royal Manchester Coll. of Music; Eddison Award 1977. *Leisure interest:* hypochondria. *Address:* 27 Cromwell Avenue, London, N.6, England.

HOWARTH, Leslie, O.B.E., PH.D., F.R.AE.S., F.R.S.; British professor of mathematics; b. 23 May 1911; s. of late Fred Howarth and Elizabeth E. Howarth; m. Eva Priestley 1934; two s.; ed. Accrington Grammar School, Manchester Univ. and Gonville and Caius Coll. Cambridge; Berry-Ramsey Research Fellow, King's Coll. Cambridge 1936-45; Lecturer in Math. Univ. of Cambridge 1936-49, Fellow, St. John's Coll. 1945-49; Prof. of Applied Math. Univ. of Bristol 1949-64, Henry Overton Wills Prof. of Math. 1964-76, now Prof. Emer.; Smith Prize 1935, Adams Prize 1951. *Publications:* papers on aerodynamics. *Address:* 10 The Crescent, Henleaze, Bristol, BS9 4RW, England. *Telephone:* Bristol 629621.

HOWARTH, Thomas, PH.D., F.R.I.B.A., F.R.A.I.C.; British (Canadian citizen) architect, planning consultant and university professor; b. 1 May 1914, Wesham, Lancs.; s. of Lawrence Howarth and Agnes Cornall; m. Edna Marland 1940 (separated 1971); one s. one d.; ed. Kirkham Grammar School, Univs. of Manchester and Glasgow; Lecturer in Architecture, Glasgow School of Arch. and Glasgow School of Art 1939-46; Lecturer, then Sr. Lecturer in Arch., Manchester Univ. 1946-58; Dir. School of Architecture, Univ. of Toronto 1958-83, Dean. Faculty of Arch., Urban and Regional Planning and Landscape Architecture 1967-74, Prof. Emer. 1983-; Master Planner, Glendon Coll. Campus and Adviser to Bd. of Govs., York Univ., Ont. 1960-87; Master Planner, Laurentian Univ., Ont. 1962-; served on Advisory Design and Planning Cttees. of Nat. Capital Comm. 1964-80; has contributed to educ. and professional affairs in various parts of world especially N. America, Europe, Asia and the Caribbean; Vice-Pres. Commonwealth Asscn. of Architects and Regional Rep. for the Americas 1981-87; Founder mem. and Past Pres. Canadian Soc. of the Decorative Arts 1981-; Hon. Fellow, American Inst. of Architects; R.I.B.A. Alfred Bossom Research Fellow 1952; U.S. Soc. of Architectural Historians Book Award 1953; Killam Sr. Research Scholar, Univ. of Calgary 1977; Dr h.c., (Stirling) 1981. *Publication:* Charles Rennie Mackintosh and the Modern Movement 1952, 1977. *Leisure interests:* travel, collecting art nouveau, lecturing, photography. *Address:* University of Toronto, Department of Architecture, 230 College Street, Toronto, Ont. (Office); 131 Bloor Street West, Apt. 817, Toronto, Ont. M5S 1S3, Canada (Home). *Telephone:* (416) 978 6763; (Office); (416) 920 5171 (Home).

HOWE, Brian Leslie, B.A.; Australian politician; b. 28 Jan. 1936, Melbourne; m. Renate Howe; one s. two d.; ed. Melbourne Univ., McCormick Theological Seminary, Chicago; worked as Uniting Church Minister, Melbourne and Morwell, Victoria; fmr. Sr. Lecturer in Sociology and Chair. Dept. of Social and Political Studies, Swinburne Inst. of Tech., Melbourne; joined Australian Labor Party 1961; M.P. for Batman, House of Reps. Dec. 1977-; Minister for Defence Support 1983-84, for Social Security Dec. 1984-; fmr. Chair. Caucus Econs. Cttee.; fmr. mem. Caucus Resources Cttee., Urban and Regional Affairs Cttee., House of Reps. Standing Cttee. on the Environment, Jt. House Cttee. on Publs. *Address:* Department of Social Security, Julianna House, Bowes Street, Phillip, A.C.T. 2617, Australia.

HOWE, Harold, II; American educator; b. 1918, Hartford, Conn.; s. of Margaret Armstrong and Arthur Howe; m. Priscilla Foster Lamb 1940; one s. two d.; ed. Yale and Columbia Univs., Univ. of Cincinnati, and

Harvard Univ; history teacher, Darrow School, New Lebanon, New York 1940–42; Lt. U.S. Naval Reserve 1942–45; history teacher, Phillips Acad., Andover, Mass. 1947–50; Prin., Andover High School and Junior High School 1950–53; Prin., Walnut Hills High School, Cincinnati, Ohio 1953–57; Prin., Newton High School, Newton, Mass. 1957–60; Supt. of Schools, Scarsdale, N.Y. 1960–64; Exec. Dir. Learning Inst. of N. Carolina, Chapel Hill, N. C. 1964–65; U.S. Commr. of Educ. 1965–68; Adviser on Educ., Ford Foundation, India 1968–70; Vice-Pres. for Educ., Ford Foundation 1971–79, for Educ. and Public Policy 1979–81; Sr. Lecturer, Harvard Graduate School of Educ. 1981–; fmr. Trustee, Vassar Coll., Yale Univ.; Trustee Teachers' Coll. Columbia Univ. 1982, Educational Testing Service 1985–; Trustee and Vice-Chair. Coll. Entrance Examination Bd. 1963–65; Visiting Cttee. of Harvard Graduate School of Educ. 1980; Chair. William T. Grant Foundation Comm. on Work, Family and Citizenship 1986–88; Hon. LL.D. (Univ. of Notre Dame, Shaw Univ., N. Carolina, Princeton Univ., Adelphi Univ., N.Y., St. Louis Univ., Missouri, Hunter Coll. of City Univ. of New York, Univ. of Hartford); James Bryant Conant Award, Educ. Comm. of the States, for contribs. to American Educ. 1986. *Publication:* Picking up the Options 1968. *Leisure interest:* fishing. *Address:* Harvard Graduate School of Education, Cambridge, Mass. 02138; 55 Alcott Road, Concord, Mass. 01742, U.S.A. (Home). *Telephone:* 617-495-3577 (Office); 617-369-8265 (Home).

HOWE, Rt. Hon. Sir (Richard Edward) Geoffrey, Kt., P.C., Q.C., M.P.; British lawyer and politician; b. 20 Dec. 1926, Port Talbot, Glam.; s. of late B. Edward and of Mrs. E. F. Howe, J.P.; m. Elspeth R. M. Shand 1953; one s. two d.; ed. Winchester Coll. and Trinity Hall, Cambridge; called to the Bar, Middle Temple 1952, Bencher 1969; Deputy Chair. Glamorgan Quarter Sessions 1966–70; M.P. for Bebington 1964–66, for Reigate 1970–74, for East Surrey 1974–; Solicitor-Gen. 1970–72; Minister for Trade and Consumer Affairs 1972–74; Opposition Spokesman for Social Services 1974–75, for Treasury and Econ. Affairs 1975–79; Chancellor of the Exchequer 1979–83; Sec. of State for Foreign and Commonwealth Affairs 1983–; a Gov. IMF 1979–83; Chair. Int. Cttee. 1983; fmr. Pres. British Overseas Trade Bd.; Dir. Sun Alliance and London Insurance Group 1974–79; fmr. Dir. EMI Ltd., AGB Research Ltd.; Conservative. *Leisure interests:* photography, gardening. *Address:* 1 Carlton Gardens, London, S.W.1, England.

HOWE, Richard J., M.M.E., PH.D., M.S.; American business executive; b. 15 Oct. 1928, Minneapolis; s. of Chauncey E. Howe and Mildred Rall; m. Charlotte Relf 1951; three s.; ed. Univ. of Minnesota and M.I.T.; Engineer, Shell Oil Co., Houston 1953–59; Gen. Man. Production Research, Exxon Co. U.S.A., Houston 1959–78; Pres. and C.O.O. Pennzoil Co., Houston 1978–; Dir. Battle Mountain Gold Co., Houston; mem. Soc. of Petroleum Engineers, Distinguished Lecturer 1969. *Address:* Pennzoil Co., P.O. Box 2967, Houston, Tex. 77252, U.S.A.

HOWE YOON CHONG, B.A., D.S.O.; Singapore politician and banker; b. 1923, China; m.; three c.; ed. St. Francis' Inst. Malacca, Raffles Coll. and Univ. of Malaya in Singapore; fmr. civil servant; Sec. to Public Service Comm.; C.E.O. Housing and Devt. Bd. 1960; Perm. Sec. Ministries of Finance and Nat. Devt.; Deputy Chair. Econ. Devt. Bd.; Chair. and Pres. Devt. Bank of Singapore, concurrently Chair. and Gen. Man. Port of Singapore Authority; Perm. Sec. Prime Minister's Office and Head of Civil Service; mem. Parl. 1979–84; Minister of Defence 1979–82, of Health 1982–84; Chair. and Chief Exec. Devt. Bank of Singapore 1985–; Malaysia Medal, Meritorious Service Medal; Hon. D. Litt. (Singapore). *Address:* c/o Development Bank of Singapore, 6 Shenton Way, Singapore 0106.

HOWELL, Rt. Hon. David Arthur Russell, P.C., B.A., M.P.; British journalist and politician; b. 18 Jan. 1936; s. of the late Col. Arthur Howell and of Beryl Howell; m. Davina Wallace 1967; one s. two d.; ed. Eton Coll., King's Coll., Cambridge; Lieut. Coldstream Guards 1954–56; Econ. Section, H.M. Treasury 1959, resgnd. 1960; Leader-writer The Daily Telegraph 1960; Chair. Bow Group 1961–62; fmr. ed. Crossbow; M.P. for Guildford 1966–; a Lord Commr. of Treasury 1970–71; with Civil Service Dept. 1970–72; Parl. Under-Sec. Dept. of Employment 1971–72; Minister of State, Northern Ireland Office 1972–74, Dept. of Energy Jan.-Feb. 1974; Sec. of State for Energy 1979–81, for Transport 1981–83; Chair. House of Commons Foreign Affairs Cttee. 1987–, One Nation Group of Conservative M.Ps 1987–; Joint Hon. Sec. U.K. Council of European Movt. 1968–70; Dir. of Conservative Political Centre 1964–66; Dir. Savory Milln Ltd. *Publications:* Principle in Practice (co-author) 1960, The Conservative Opportunity 1965, Freedom and Capital 1981, Blind Victory 1986. *Leisure interests:* family life, writing. *Address:* House of Commons, Westminster, London, S.W.1, England. *Telephone:* 01-219 4094.

HOWELL, Francis Clark, PH.D.; American professor of anthropology; b. 27 Nov. 1925, Kansas City, Mo.; s. of E. Ray and Myrtle M. Howell; m. Betty Ann Tomsen 1955; one s. one d.; ed. Univ. of Chicago; Instructor in Anatomy, Washington Univ. 1953–55; Asst. Prof. of Anthropology, Univ. of Chicago 1955–59, Assoc. Prof. of Anthropology 1959–62, Prof. of Anthropology 1962–70; Prof. of Anthropology, Univ. of Calif., Berkeley 1970–; mem. N.A.S., American Philosophical Soc.; Fellow American Acad. of Arts and Sciences; Trustee, Fellow and fmr. Pres., Calif. Acad. of Science. *Publications:* African Ecology and Early Man (ed.) 1963, Early Man 1965, Earliest man and environments in the Rudolf Basin (ed.) 1975; numerous

papers on anthropology in professional journals. *Address:* Department of Anthropology, University of California, Berkeley, Calif. 94720; 1994 San Antonio, Berkeley, Calif. 94707, U.S.A. (Home). *Telephone:* 415-642-1393 (Office); 415-524-6243 (Home).

HOWELL, Margaret, DIP.A.D.; British couturier; b. 5 Sept. 1946, Tadworth; d. of E. H. Howell; m. Paul Renshaw 1974 (divorced 1987); one s. one d.; ed. Tadworth Primary School, Deburgh Co-Educational, Goldsmith's Coll., London; 1st Margaret Howell Collection 1972; opened Margaret Howell Ltd., London 1977; 8 Branches in Japan and more int. expansion planned; Co. Dir. Margaret Howell Ltd. 1985–; Designer of the Year. *Leisure interests:* films, art exhbns., visiting country houses and gardens, walking, the countryside. *Address:* Margaret Howell 87' Ltd., 5 Garden House, 8 Battersea Park Road, London, SW8; Margaret Howell Shop, 29 Beauchamp Place, Knightsbridge, London, SW1. *Telephone:* 01-627 5587.

HOWELL, Michael Edward, O.B.E.; British diplomatist; b. 2 May 1933; s. of Edward Howell and Fanny Howell; m. Joan Little 1958; one s. one d.; ed. Newport High School; Colonial Office 1953; Commonwealth Relations Office 1958; served Karachi 1959, Bombay 1962, UK Del. to Disarmament Cttee. Geneva 1966; First Sec. FCO 1969; Consul, New York 1973; FCO 1976; Head of Chancery and Consul, Kabul 1978; Consul-Gen. Berlin 1981, Frankfurt 1983; High Commr. in Papua New Guinea 1986–. *Leisure interest:* tennis. *Address:* c/o Foreign & Commonwealth Office, London, SW1A 2AH, England.

HOWELL, Wilson Nathaniel, PH.D.; American diplomatist; b. 14 Sept. 1939, Portsmouth, Va.; s. of Wilson N. Howell and Josephine Edwards Howell; m. Margie Ann Saunders 1961; two s.; ed. Univ. of Virginia, Charlottesville, Foreign Service Inst., Beirut, Nat. War Coll., Fort McNair, Washington, D.C.; Instructor in Govt. and Foreign Affairs, Univ. of Va. 1964–65; Exec. Asst. to Amb. to Egypt 1965–67; Political Officer, U.S. Mission to NATO, Paris and Brussels 1967–68; Egyptian Analyst, Bureau of Intelligence and Research (INR) 1968–70; Deputy Prin. Officer, U.A.E. 1972–74; Political Officer, Beirut 1974–76; served in Dept. of State successively as Country Officer for Lebanon, Deputy Dir. Office of N. Arabian Affairs (NEA/ARN) and Special Asst. to Asst. Sec. of State for Near East and S. Asian Affairs 1976–80; Dir. NEA/ARN 1980–82; Deputy Chief of Mission, Embassy in Algiers 1983–85; Political Adviser to C.-in-C. U.S. Cen. Command 1986–87; Amb. to Kuwait 1987–; Dept. of State Superior Honor Award 1967, Meritorious Honor Award 1976, Award for Valor 1977, Sec. of Defense Medal for Meritorious Civilian Service 1988. *Leisure interests:* music, reading, amateur athletics. *Address:* American Embassy, P.O. Box 77, Safat, Kuwait; Kuwait, Department of State, Washington, D.C. 20520, U.S.A. *Telephone:* (965) 242-4151 (U.S.A.).

HOWELLS, Anne Elizabeth; British opera and concert singer; b. 12 Jan. 1941, Southport, Lancs.; d. of Trevor and Mona Howells; m. 1st Ryland Davies (q.v.) 1966 (divorced 1981); m. 2nd Stafford Dean 1981, one s. one d.; ed. Sale County Grammar School, Royal Manchester Coll. of Music; three seasons in Chorus with Glyndebourne Festival Opera 1964–66, took leading role at short notice in L'Ormindo (Cavalli) 1967, subsequent roles include Dorabella in Così fan tutte, Cathleen in world premiere Rising of the Moon (Nicholas Maw), Composer in Ariadne, Diana in Calisto; with Royal Opera House, Covent Garden 1969–71, appearing as Lena in world premiere of Victory (Richard Rodney Bennett), Rosina in The Barber of Seville, Cherubino in The Marriage of Figaro; Guest Artist with Royal Opera House 1973–; has also appeared with Welsh Nat. Opera, Scottish Opera, English Nat. Opera, Chicago Opera, Geneva Opera, Metropolitan Opera, New York, Lyons Opera, Marseilles Opera, Nantes Opera, Netherlands Opera, and in Naples, San Francisco and in Belgium and at La Scala, and Salzburg Festival 1976 and 1980 (Tales of Hoffmann and film version of Clemenza di Tito), and in Hamburg and Berlin; Fellow Royal Manchester Coll. of Music. *Leisure interests:* cinema, reading. *Address:* c/o Harrison Parrott Ltd., 12 Penzance Place, London, W11 4PA, England.

HOWELLS, Gwyn, C.B., M.B., B.S., M.D., F.R.C.P., F.R.A.C.P.; Australian company director and medical practitioner (retd.); b. 13 May 1918, Birmingham, England.; s. of Albert H. Howells and Ruth W. (Horton) Howells; m. Simone Maufe 1942; two s. two d.; ed. Univ. Coll. School, London and St. Bartholomew's Hosp., London Univ.; Captain, R.A.M.C. and Indian Army Medical Corps 1942–46; Sr. Medical Registrar, West Cornwall 1950–53; Chest Physician, Derby Clinical Area 1953–57; Consultant Chest Physician, Toowoomba, Queensland 1957–66; First Asst. Dir. of Gen. Fed. Dept. of Health 1966–73; Dir. Gen. of Health 1973–83; Chair. Nat. Health and Medical Research Council 1973–83; Dir. of Quarantine, Australia 1973–83; Chair. Health Insurance Comm. 1974–76; Dir. Nucleus (Australia) Ltd. and Chair. Cochlear Ltd. 1984–. *Leisure interests:* gardening, squash, tennis. *Address:* 23 Beauchamp Street, Deakin, A.C.T. 2600, Australia. *Telephone:* (062) 812575.

HOWELLS, William White, D.SC., PH.D., F.S.A.; American anthropologist; b. 27 Nov. 1908, New York; s. of John Mead Howells and Abby MacDougall White; m. Muriel Gurdon Seabury 1929; one s. one d.; ed. St. Paul's School, Concord, N.H. and Harvard Univ.; Asst. Prof. to Prof., Univ. of Wis. 1939–54; Ed. American Journal of Physical Anthropology 1949–54; Prof. of Anthropology, Harvard Univ. 1954–74, Emer. 1974–; Curator of Somatology, Peabody Museum 1955–75, Honorary Curator 1975–; Pres. American Anthropological Assen. 1951; F.S.A.; mem. N.A.S., American Acad. of Arts and Sciences; Corresp. mem. Royal Soc. of S.A., Austrian Acad. of Sciences, Anthropological Socs. of Paris and Vienna, Soc. of Antiquaries of London, Geographical Soc. of Lisbon, Spanish Soc. for Biological Anthropology; Hon. Foreign Fellow, Indian Anthropological Assen.; Viking Fund Medal in Physical Anthropology 1955, Hon. D.Sc. (Beloit College) 1975, (Witwatersrand Univ.) 1985; Hon. Fellow, School of American Research 1975; Distinguished Service Award, American Anthropological Assen. 1978; Broca Prix du Centenaire, Anthropological Soc. of Paris 1980. *Publications:* Mankind So Far 1944, The Heathens 1948, Back of History (British edn. Man in the Beginning) 1954, Mankind in the Making 1959, Ideas on Human Revolution (ed.) 1962, The Pacific Islanders 1973, Cranial Variation in Man 1973, Evolution of the Genus Homo 1973, Multivariate Statistical Methods in Physical Anthropology 1984. *Leisure interests:* travel, stamp collecting. *Address:* Peabody Museum, Harvard, Cambridge, Mass. 02138; Kittery Point, Maine 03905, U.S.A. *Telephone:* 617-495-2244 (Mass.); 207-439-1302 (Maine).

HOWIE, Archibald, PH.D., F.R.S.; British university professor and research physicist; b. 8 March 1934, Kirkcaldy, Scotland; s. of Robert Howie and Margaret Marshall McDonald; m. Melva Jean Scott 1964; one s. (deceased), one d.; ed. Kirkcaldy High School, Univ. of Edinburgh, California Inst. of Tech., U.S.A., Univ. of Cambridge; ICI Research Fellow (Cavendish Lab.) and Research Fellow (Churchill Coll.) 1960–61; Demonstrator in Physics (Cavendish Lab.) 1961–65; Teaching Fellow and Dir. of Studies in Physics (Churchill Coll.) 1961–, Lecturer 1965–79, Reader 1979–86, Prof. 1986–; part-time Consultant Union Carbide Corpn. 1977–78, World Bank China Univ. Devt. Programme 1984, Norwegian Research Council 1986; Pres. Royal Microscopical Soc. 1984–86; C. V. Boys Prize (jtly), Inst. of Physics; Hon. Fellow, Royal Microscopical Soc. *Publications:* Electron Microscopy of Thin Crystals (Jt. author) 1965 and numerous articles on electron microscopy and related subjects in scientific journals. *Leisure interest:* making wine. *Address:* Cavendish Laboratory, Madingley Road, Cambridge, CB3 0HE (Office); 194 Huntingdon Road, Cambridge, CB3 0LB, England (Home). *Telephone:* (0223) 337334 (Office); (0223) 276131 (Home).

HOWIE, J. Robert, B.A., B.C.L.; Canadian politician; b. 29 Oct. 1929, Fredericton, New Brunswick, Canada; s. of James R. Howie and Mary L. Pond; m. Nancy Gowlding 1955; one s. three d.; ed. University of New Brunswick; solicitor, Oromocto 1962–72; Clerk of the New Brunswick Legislature 1970–72; mem. House of Commons 1972, 1974; Minister of State (Transport) 1979–80; Progressive Conservative. *Leisure interests:* curling, hockey, theatre, swimming. *Address:* 678 Churchill Row, Fredericton, New Brunswick, Canada.

HOWLAND, The Hon. William G. C., C.ST.J., LL.B.; Canadian judge; b. 7 March 1915, Toronto, Ont.; s. of Goldwin W. Howland and Margaret Christian Howland; m. Margaret Patricia Greene; ed. Upper Canada Coll., Toronto, Univ. of Toronto, Osgoode Hall Law School; Called to Bar of Ont. 1939; practised with Reid Wright & McMillan (subsequently McMillan Binch) 1936–42, 1945–75 (Partner 1939–75); war service 1942–45; Hon. Lecturer, Osgoode Hall Law School 1950–67; Q.C. 1955; mem. Council Canadian Bar Assen. 1959–62, 1973–74; elected Bencher, Law Soc. of Upper Canada 1961, 1966, Treasurer 1968–70, Life Bencher; Pres. Fed. of Law Socs. of Canada 1973–74; apptd. Justice of Appeal, Supreme Court of Ont. 1975, Chief Justice of Ont. 1977–; mem. Bd. of Govs. Upper Canada Coll. 1968–70, 1977–, Advisory Council The Toronto Symphony, Univ. Coll. Cttee. Toronto Univ.; Trustee Wycliffe Coll., Toronto; Chair. Advisory Council of Order of Ont. 1986–; Hon. LL.D. (Queen's) 1972, (Toronto) 1981, (York) 1984, (Law Soc. of Upper Canada) 1985; Hon. Dr. Sacred Letters (Wycliffe Coll.) 1985. *Address:* Osgoode Hall, Toronto, Ontario, M5H 2N5, Canada. *Telephone:* 363-4101.

HOWMAN, John Hartley; Zimbabwean lawyer and politician (retd.); b. 11 Aug. 1918, Selukwe; m. Moira W. Maidman 1946; three d.; ed. Plumtree School, Bulawayo; fmr. Partner, Coghlan, Welsh & Guest (law firm); M.P. 1962–74; Minister of Internal Affairs, Local Govt. and African Educ. 1962–64, of Information, Immigration and Tourism 1965–68, of Foreign Affairs, Defence and Public Service 1968–74; Grand Officer of the Legion of Merit; Independence Decoration. *Address:* 18 Cecil Rhodes Drive, Highlands, Harare, Zimbabwe. *Telephone:* Harare 732426.

HØYEM, Tom, M.PHIL.; Danish university teacher, journalist and politician; b. 10 Oct. 1941, Nykøbing, Falster; s. of Ove Charles Høyem; m. 1969; one s. one d.; ed. Univ. of Copenhagen; Asst. Prof. of Danish Language and Literature, Univ. of Stockholm; Danish corresp. for the Berlingske Tidende in Sweden; Chair. of Centre Democrat Party; fmr. Headmaster of Høng Upper Secondary School; Minister for Greenland 1982–; Headmaster, European School, Abingdon, U.K. 1987–; cand. for European Parl. 1989. *Publications:* Avisens spiseseddel-arisens ansigt 1975, Lægæst 1985, Mulighedernes Samfund 1985, Dagens Grønland 1986, Gud, konge, fædreland 1987, Nordisk: Europa 1988. *Leisure interests:* politics, literature. *Address:* European School, Culham, Abingdon, Oxon., OX14 3DZ (Office); Larkhill House, 6, Godwyn Close, Abingdon, Oxford, 14 1BU, England. *Telephone:* 0235-22621 (Office); (0235) 553894 (Home).

HOYLAND, John, A.R.A.; British artist; b. 12 Oct. 1934, Sheffield; s. of John Kenneth and Kathleen Hoyland; m. Airi Karkkainen 1957 (m. dissolved 1968); one s.; ed. Sheffield Coll. of Art and Crafts and Royal Acad.

Schools; taught Hornsey School of Art 1960–61; Chelsea School of Art 1962–69, Prin. Lecturer 1965–69; St. Martin's School of Art 1974–77; Slade School of Fine Art 1974–77, 1979–85; Charles A. Dana Prof., Colgate Univ., New York, U.S.A. 1972; Artist in Residence, Studio School, New York 1978, Melbourne Univ., Australia 1979; has exhibited all over the world; Selector, Hayward Annual and Silver Jubilee R.A. Exhbns. 1979; Faculty mem. and Visitor, British School at Rome 1984; Curator, Hans Hofman Exhbn., Tate Gallery, London 1988; Young Artist Int. Award, Tokyo 1963; Gulbenkian Foundation Award 1964; Peter Stuyvesant Travel Award 1964; John Moores Exhbn. Prize 1965; First Prize Edin. Open 100 1969; Chichester Nat. Art Award 1975; Arts Council of G.B. Purchase Award 1979; First Prize John Moores Exhbn. 1983; Order of the Southern Cross (Brazil) 1986; First Prize Athena Award, Barbican Gallery, London 1987. *Address:* c/o Waddington Galleries, 2 Cork Street, London, W1X 1PA, England.

HOYLE, Sir Fred, Kt., M.A., F.R.S.; British astronomer, mathematician and author; b. 24 June 1915, Gilstead, Bingley, Yorks.; s. of Ben and Mabel (née Pickard) Hoyle; m. Barbara Clark 1939; one s. one d.; ed. Bingley Grammar School and Emmanuel Coll. and St. John's Coll., Cambridge; Fellow, St. John's Coll. 1939–72, Hon. Fellow 1973–; Univ. lecturer in Mathematics, Cambridge 1945–58; Staff mem. Mount Wilson and Palomar Observatories, Calif., U.S.A. 1956–62; Plumian Prof. of Astronomy and Experimental Philosophy, Cambridge Univ. 1958–72, Dir. Inst. of Theoretical Astronomy 1966–72; Visiting Prof. of Astrophysics at Calif. Inst. of Technology 1963–; Hon. Prof. of Physics and Astronomy, Manchester Univ. 1973–; Visiting Prof. at Large, Cornell Univ. 1973–79; Hon. research Prof. Cardiff Univ. 1975–; Prof. of Astronomy Royal Institution 1969–72; Hon. mem. American Acad. of Arts and Sciences 1964, Royal Irish Acad. 1977, Mark Twain Soc. 1978; Foreign Assoc. Nat. Acad. of Sciences 1969; Vice-Pres. Royal Soc. 1970–71; Pres. Royal Astronomical Soc. 1971–73; Foreign Mem. American Philosophical Soc. 1980; Hon. Fellow, Emmanuel Coll., Cambridge 1983; Hon. Sc.D. (East Anglia) 1967, Hon. D.Sc. (Leeds) 1969, (Bradford) 1975, (Newcastle) 1976; Mayhew Prizeman 1936, Smith's Prizeman 1938, Goldsmith Exhibitioner 1938, Sr. Exhibitioner Royal Comm. of 1851 1938, Kalinga Prize 1968, Gold Medal, Royal Astronomical Soc. 1968, Bruce Medal, Astronomical Soc. of the Pacific 1970, Royal Medal, Royal Soc. 1974, Dag Hammarskjöld Gold Medal, Academie Diplomatique de la Paix. *Publications:* Recent Research in Solar Physics 1949, Nature of the Universe 1950, Decade of Decision 1953, Frontiers of Astronomy 1955, The Black Cloud (novel) 1957, Ossian's Ride 1958, A for Andromeda (television series with John Elliot) 1962, Astronomy 1962, Fifth Planet (with Geoffrey Hoyle) 1963, Of Men and Galaxies 1964, Galaxies, Nuclei and Quasars 1965, October First is too late 1966, Man in the Universe 1966, Rockets in Ursa Major (with Geoffrey Hoyle) 1969, Seven Steps to the Sun (with Geoffrey Hoyle) 1970, The Molecule Men (with Geoffrey Hoyle) 1971, From Stonehenge to Modern Cosmology 1972, The Inferno (with Geoffrey Hoyle) 1972, Nicolaus Copernicus 1973, Into Deepest Space (with Geoffrey Hoyle) 1974, Action at a Distance in Physics and Cosmology 1974, Highlights in Astronomy (U.S.)/Astronomy Today (U.K.) 1975, Astronomy and Cosmology 1975, Ten Faces of the Universe 1977, On Stonehenge 1977, The Incandescent Ones (with Geoffrey Hoyle) 1977, Energy or Extinction: the case for Nuclear Energy 1977, Lifecloud (with N. C. Wickramasinghe) 1978, The Westminster Disaster (novel, with Geoffrey Hoyle) 1978, Diseases from Space (with N. C. Wickramasinghe) 1979, Physics-Astronomy Frontier (with J. V. Narlikar) 1980, Common Sense in Nuclear Energy (with Geoffrey Hoyle) 1980, Space Travellers, the Origins of Life (with N. C. Wickramasinghe) 1980, Evolution from Space (with N. C. Wickeramasinghe), Ice: The Ultimate Human Catastrophe 1981, The Giants of Universal Park, The Frozen Planet of Azuron, The Energy Pirate, The Planet of Death (children's stories) 1982, The Intelligent Universe 1983, Comet Halley 1985, The Small World of Fred Hoyle 1986. *Leisure interests:* music, mountaineering. *Address:* c/o The Royal Society, 6 Carlton House Terrace, London, SW1Y 5AG, England.

HOYTE, Hugh Desmond, S.C., B.A., LL.B.; Guyanese politician; b. 9 March 1929, Georgetown; s. of George Alphonso Hoyte and Gladys Marietta Hoyte; m. Joyce Noreen (née De Freitas) Hoyte; ed. Progressive High School, Univ. of London and Middle Temple, London; master at Grenada Boys' Secondary School 1955–57; mem. Legal Practitioners' Cttee. 1964–68; Sec. Guyana Bar Assen. 1962–66, Vice-Pres. 1967–68; Chair. Customs Tariff Tribunal 1966–69; Chair. Timber Grants Wages Council 1967–68; mem. Elections Comm. 1967–68; elected M.P. 1968; Minister of Home Affairs 1969–70, of Finance 1970–72, of Works and Communications 1972–74, of Econ. Devt. 1974; then mem. Admin. Cttee., Cen. Exec. Cttee. and Gen. Council of the People's Nat. Congress, Vice-Pres., responsible for Econ. Planning and Finance and subsequently Production, Leader 1985–; First Vice-Pres. and Prime Minister 1984; Pres. Co-operative Repub. of Guyana Aug. 1985–, also responsible for Production, Ministry of Public Service and Gold and Diamond Industries. *Leisure interests:* literature and historical research. *Address:* Office of the President, New Garden Street, Georgetown; 14 North Road, Bourda, Georgetown, Guyana (Home).

HRABAL, Bohumil; Czechoslovak writer; b. 28 March 1914, Brno; ed. Charles Univ., Prague; lawyer's clerk, railway worker, insurance agent, travelling salesman, foundry worker, paper salvage worker, stage hand and stage extra 1939–62; professional writer 1962–; Klement Gottwald

State Prize 1968. *Publications:* short stories: Perlička na dně (Pearl at the Bottom, some stories filmed) 1963, Pábitelé 1964, Inzerát na dům, ve kterém už nechci bydlet (An Ad. for a House in Which I Don't Want to Live Any More) 1965, Automat svět (selected stories, some filmed) 1966; short novels: Taneční hodiny pro starší a pokročilé (Dancing Lessons for Adults and Advanced) 1964, Ostře sledované vlaky (Closely Observed Trains, film 1966) 1965, Morytáty a legendy (These Premises are in the Joint Care of Citizens) 1968, Postřižiny 1976, Slavnosti sněženek 1978, Kluby poezie 1981, Harlekýnovy milióny 1981, Domácí úkoly z pilnosti 1982, Autobiog. (3 vols.) 1985, Proluky 1987, I Served the King of England 1989. *Address:* Na Hrázi 24, Prague 8-Liben, Czechoslovakia.

HRIVNAK, Pavel; Czechoslovak politician; b. 9 Oct. 1931, Malý Čepčin; ed. Faculty of Chemical Eng. Slovak Tech. Univ. Bratislava; mem. CP of Czechoslovakia 1956–; Slovak Deputy Minister of Industry 1974–82, Minister 1982–84; Slovak Deputy Premier and Chair. Slovak Planning Comm. 1984–86; mem. Presidium, CP of Slovakia 1986–; Federal Deputy Premier of Czechoslovakia 1986–88, Minister in Charge of Fed. Price Office April-Sept. 1988; First Deputy Premier of Czechoslovakia, Chair. State Comm. for Science, Tech. and Investments Oct. 1988–. *Address:* State Commission for Science, Technology and Investments, Slezská 9, 120 29 Prague 2, Czechoslovakia.

HROUDA, Barthel, DR.PHIL.; German academic; b. 28 June 1929, Berlin; s. of Fritz Hrouda and Frieda Hrouda; m. 1957; two s. one d.; ed. Gymnasium Graues Kloster Berlin and Freie Universität Berlin; Lecturer, Univ. of Saarbrücken 1963; Prof. Univ. of Munich 1963–64, 1969–, Univ. of Berlin 1964–69; mem. German Inst. of Archaeology, Munich and Brussels Acads. *Publications:* Kulturgeschichte assyrischen Flachbildes 1965, Handbuch der Archaeologie, Vorderasien 1971, Isin-Išān Bahrīyāt I-III 1977, 1981, 1987. *Leisure interest:* travel. *Address:* D-8034 Germering, Sternstrasse 4B, Federal Republic of Germany. *Telephone:* (089) 84 55 49.

HRUŠKOVIČ, Miloslav, ING.; Czechoslovak engineer and politician; b. 25 Jan. 1925, Pukanec; ed. Faculty of Electrical Engineering, Slovak Tech. Univ., Bratislava; Deputy Dir. "Slovak Nat. Rising" Works, Žiar nad Hronom 1953–62; Dir. Research Inst. of Welding, Bratislava 1962–68; Minister of Tech. 1968; Minister, Chair. of Cttee. for Technological and Investment Devt., Fed. Govt. of C.S.S.R. 1969–70; Deputy Prime Minister 1969–70; mem. Cen. Cttee. of CP of Slovakia 1955–58, 1962–68, 1969–71, 1972–; Alt. mem. Cen. Cttee. CP of Czechoslovakia 1958–62; Alt. mem. Presidium, Cen. Cttee. of CP of Slovakia 1962–68; Deputy, Slovak Nat. Council 1964–71; mem. Presidium of Cen. Cttee., CP of Slovakia 1968, 1972–, Sec., mem. Secr. 1972–, Chair. Econ. Comm. of Cen. Cttee. 1972–; mem. Econ. Council 1968–70; mem. Cen. Cttee. CP of Czechoslovakia 1970–, Sec., mem. Secr. 1970–72, Chair. Econ. Comm. 1970–71, Alt. mem. Presidium 1971–, Chair. Scientific Technical Devt. Comm. 1971–76; Deputy to House of Nations, Fed. Assembly 1970–71, Deputy to House of the People 1971–; mem. Technical Cttee., Int. Inst. of Welding 1964–70; Order of Victorious February 1973, Order of the Repub. 1975, and several other awards. *Publications include:* Method of Automatic Regulation of the Working Stress of Aluminium Electrolysers 1959 (patented 1959). *Address:* Central Committee of the Communist Party of Czechoslovakia, nábř. Ludvíka Svobody 12, Prague, Czechoslovakia.

HSIUNG SHIH-I; Chinese author; b. 14 Oct. 1902, Nanchang; s. of Yung Yu Hsiung and Ti-ping Chou; m. Dymia Tsai 1923; three s. four d.; Assoc.-Man. Chen Kwang Theatre, Peking 1922; Prof. Agricultural Coll., Nanchang 1923; Ed. Commercial Press, Shanghai 1926, Special Ed. 1928; Prof. Chung Shan Univ., Nanchang 1927; Man.-Dir. Pantheon Theatres Ltd., Shanghai 1929; Prof. Min Kuo Univ., Peiping 1930; Sec. China Soc., London 1933, Hon. Sec. 1935–; Chinese Del. to Int. PEN Congress 1934, 1935, 1938, 1939, 1940, 1947, Hong Kong Del. 1971, 1973, Guest of Honour 1976; del. to Int. Theatre Inst. Congress 1948; lecturer, Cambridge Univ. 1950–53; Dean, Coll. of Arts, Nanyang Univ. 1954–55; Managing Dir. Pacific Films Co. Ltd., Hong Kong 1955–; Dir. Konin Co. Ltd., Hong Kong 1956–; Chair. Bd. of Dirs. Standard Publishers Ltd, Hong Kong 1961–; Founder and First Pres. Tsing Hua Coll., Hong Kong 1963–; Hon. Ph.D. *Publications:* in English: Lady Precious Stream 1934, The Romance of Western Chamber 1935, Professor from Peking 1939, The Bridge of Heaven 1943, Life of Chiang Kai-Shek 1948, The Gate of Peace 1949, The Story of Lady Precious Stream 1950, Book of Chinese Proverbs 1953, Memoirs (Vols. I and II), 1978; translations into Chinese of B. Franklin's Autobiography 1923, of Barrie's and Shaw's plays, and Hardy's novels 1926–33. *Leisure interests:* calligraphy, painting. *Address:* Tsing Hua College, Kowloon; 170 Boundary Street, Kowloon, Hong Kong.

HSU CHING-CHUNG, D.AGRIC.; Chinese politician; b. 19 July 1907, Taipei; s. of Teh An Hsu and Shyh Iuan Hung; m. Hwang Chen; two s. one d.; ed. Taipei Acad., Taipei Imperial Univ; Prof., Nat. Taiwan Univ. 1945–47; Dir. Agricultural and Forestry Admin., Taiwan Provincial Govt. 1947–49; Commr. Dept. of Agric. and Forestry, Taiwan Provincial Govt. 1949–54; Commr. 1954–57; mem. Cen. Planning and Evaluation Cttee., China Nationalist Party 1955–61, Deputy Sec.-Gen. Cen. Cttee. 1961–66; Minister of the Interior 1966–72; Vice-Premier of Exec. Yuan 1972–81; mem. Standing Cttee., Taiwan Land Bank 1946–67, China Farmers' Bank 1967–72; Medal of Clouds and Banner. *Publications:* several studies on agricultural

problems in Taiwan. *Leisure interests:* horticulture, reading, painting, golf. *Address:* 180 Yenping S. Road, Taipei, Taiwan.

HSU SHUI-TEH, M.A.; Chinese politician; b. 1 Aug. 1931, Kaohsiung City; m.; two s.; ed. Nat. Taiwan Normal Univ., Nat. Chengchi Univ. and Japan Univ. of Educ.; official, Pingtung County Govt. 1968–70, Kaohsiung City Govt. 1970–75; Commr. Dept. of Social Affairs, Taiwan Provincial Govt. 1975–79; Dir. Dept. of Social Affairs, Cen. Cttee., Kuomintang 1979; Sec.-Gen. Kaohsiung City Govt. 1979–82; Mayor of Kaohsiung 1982–85, of Taipei 1985–; Hon. LL.D. (Lincoln Univ.) 1985. *Publication:* The Childhood Education of Emile. *Address:* Taipei City Council, Taipei, Taiwan.

HSU TZU-CHIU, D.MED.; Chinese government official; b. 5 Feb. 1920, Tainan City; m.; two s. one d.; ed. Medical Coll., Kyoto Imperial Univ., and Univ. of Pittsburgh; Dir. Provincial Inst. of Public Health, Taiwan Provincial Govt. 1959–62; Commr. Dept. of Health, Taiwan Provincial Govt. 1962–70; Visiting Prof. of Public Health, Nat. Taiwan Univ., Kaohsiung Medical Coll. and Nat. Taiwan Normal Univ. 1953–70; Regional Adviser, WHO 1970–79; Acting Dir. Manpower Devt. and Family Health, West Pacific Region Office, WHO 1979–80; Acting Dir., Health Protection and Promotion, West Pacific Region Office, WHO 1980–81; Dir.-Gen. Dept. of Health, Exec. Yuan 1981. *Address:* Office of the Director-General, Department of Health, Executive Yuan, Taipei, Taiwan.

HU BINGYUN, Maj.-Gen.; Chinese army officer; b. 1911, Nanchong Co., Sichuan Prov., joined Red Army 1932, CCP 1933; Cadre, 6th Company, Red 4th Regiment, 8th Route Army 1935; took part in Long March 1935; Maj. Gen., PLA Units in Lanzhou 1959; Vice-Commdr. PLA Lanzhou Mil. Region 1960; Commdr. PLA Shaanxi Mil. Dist. 1964; Vice-Chair. Shaanxi Prov. People's Congress 1979–81; Sec. Shaanxi CCP Cttee. *Address:* Provincial People's Congress, Xian, Shaanxi, People's Republic of China.

HU HAN; Chinese academic; Dir. Inst. of Genetics 1977–. *Address:* Chinese Academy of Sciences, Beijing, People's Republic of China.

HU HONG; Chinese party and government official; Vice-Chair. Prov. Revolutionary Cttee., Jiangsu 1975–79; Sec. CCP Cttee., Jiangsu 1977–82; Deputy for Jiangsu, 5th NPC 1978; Permanent Sec., CCP Cttee., Fujian; mem. 12th Cen. Cttee. CCP 1982–87; Chair. Prov. People's Congress, Fujian 1983–85; Chair. Advisory Cttee., CCP Cttee., Fujian 1985–. *Address:* c/o Provincial People's Congress, Fujian, People's Republic of China.

HU JINTAO; Chinese party and state official; b. 1943; ed. Qinghua Univ.; alt. mem. 12th CCP Cen. Cttee. 1982, mem. 1985; Dir. Construction Comm., Gansu Prov. Govt. 1982; Sec. Gansu Prov. Branch Communist Youth League 1982; Sec. Communist Youth League 1982; mem. Standing Cttee., 6th NPC, mem. Presidium and mem. Standing Cttee., CPPCC 6th Nat. Cttee. 1983–; Pres. Soc. of Young Pioneers Work 1984–; Vice-Pres. China Int. Cultural Exchange Centre 1984–; Chair. Nat. Organizational Cttee. for Int. Youth Year 1984–; Sec. CCP Cttee., Guizhou 1985–88, Tibet Dec. 1988–; mem. 13th CCP Cen. Cttee. 1987–. *Address:* Construction Commission, Gansu Provincial Government, Lanzhou, Gansu, People's Republic of China.

HU JIWEI; Chinese journalist; Deputy Dir. Information Bureau, North-West China Mil. and Admin. Council 1950; Ed.-in-Chief and Deputy Dir. The Masses Daily, Xian 1950; Ed.-in-Chief N.W. Branch Xinhua News Agency and N.W. People's Broadcasting Station 1950; Deputy Ed.-in-Chief People's Daily 1953–66, Ed.-in-Chief 1977–82, Dir. 1982–83; Pres. Beijing Journalism Studies Soc. 1980–; mem. Standing Cttee. 6th NPC 1983–; Vice-Chair. Educ., Science, Culture and Public Health Cttee., NPC 1983–; Pres. Chinese Confed. of Societies of Journalism 1984–. *Address:* Renmin Ribao, Jin Tai Xi Lu, Beijing, People's Republic of China.

HU JUEWEN: Chinese politician; b. 1894, Jiangsu; Dir. Standing Cttee. China Democratic Nat. Construction Asscn. (CDNCA) 1945; mem. Nat. Cttee. 1st CPPCC 1949; mem. Financial and Econ. Cttee., GAC 1949–54; mem. East China Mil. and Admin. Cttee. 1949–53; mem. Cen. Standing Cttee. CDNCA 1952; mem. East China Admin. Cttee. 1953; mem. Credentials Cttee. 1st Nat. People's Congress (NPC) 1954; Vice-Chair. CDNCA 1955; mem. Credentials Cttee. and Standing Cttee. 2nd NPC 1959; Vice-Chair. 2nd Cen. Cttee. CDNCA 1960–79; Vice-Mayor, Shanghai 1962–67; mem. Credentials Cttee., Standing Cttee. 3rd NPC 1964; Vice-Chair. Standing Cttee. 4th NPC 1975–78; mem. Standing Cttee. 5th CPPCC 1978, 1980; Vice-Chair. Standing Cttee. 5th NPC 1978–83, 1983–86; Exec. Chair. Presidium, 6th NPC 1986–; Chair. Cen. Cttee. CDNCA 1979–; Vice-Chair. Cttee. for Revision of CPPCC Constitution; Pres. China Vocational Educ. Service 1983–. *Address:* Standing Committee, National People's Congress, People's Republic of China.

HU KANG; Chinese woodcut artist; b. 21 July 1941, Hong Kong; s. of Hu Slu Chun and Shing Kinchoi; m. Le Ten Pen 1969; one s.; ed. Fine Art Acad.; Art Ed. Hunan Cultural Life 1984–; mem. Artists' Union of China; counsellor Union of wood-cutting; Dir. Woodcutting Cttee., Hunan Province; attended All-China Fine Art exhbn.; one-man shows in America, France, Japan, Sweden, Hong Kong, Taiwan, etc. *Leisure interest:* piano. *Address:* Hunan Cultural Life Magazine, Changsha, People's Republic of China.; 7/F29, Mody Road, Kowloon, Hong Kong. *Telephone:* (3) 7232444.

HU LIJIAO; Chinese party official; b. 1914, Jiangxi; m. Gu Ming; one s.; joined CCP 1930; took part in Long March as mem. Little Devils 1934; Deputy Dir. Org. Dept. E. China Bureau 1950; Vice-Chair. People's Control Cttee., E. China Mil. and Admin. Council (ECMAC) 1951, Dir. Personnel Dept. ECMAC 1951, Vice-Chair. Labour Employment Cttee. ECMAC 1952; Vice-Minister of Finance 1954–58; Sec. CCP Cttee. Ministry of Finance 1954–58; Prin. Cadres School, Ministry of Finance 1957–58; 1st Sec. Secr., Songjiang Dist., Heilongjiang CP 1958; Deputy Dir. People's Bank of China 1961–66, Acting Pres. 1966; disappeared during Cultural Revolution; Deputy Sec. CCP Cttee., Henan 1975–77, 2nd Sec. 1977–; Vice-Chair. Prov. Revolutionary Cttee., Henan 1977–79; mem. 11th CCP Cen. Cttee. 1977; Chair. Standing Cttee. People's Congress, Henan 1979; 2nd Sec. CCP Cttee., Shanghai 1981–85; Chair. Municipal People's Congress, Shanghai 1981–; mem. 12th CCP Cen. Cttee. 1982–85; Deputy to 3rd, 5th and 6th NPC; mem. Presidium 6th NPC 1986–; mem. Cen. Advisory Comm. CCP 1987–. *Leisure interests:* tennis, swimming, chess. *Address:* 200 The People's Square, Shanghai, People's Republic of China. *Telephone:* 289977.

HU PING; Chinese government official; b. 1930, Jiaxing Co., Zhejiang Prov.; Vice-Gov. of Fujian 1981–83; Sec. CCP Prov. Cttee. Fujian 1982–; Deputy Sec. CCP Prov. Cttee., Fujian 1982–; Dir. Fujian Cttee. for Econ. Reconstruction 1983–; alt. mem. 12th Cen. Cttee. CCP 1982, mem. 1985, 13th Cen. Cttee. 1987–; Sec. CCP Prov. Cttee. 1982–83; Acting Gov. of Fujian 1983, Gov. 1983–87 (removed from post); Vice-Minister, State Planning Comm. 1987–; Chair. Bd. of Regents, Overseas Chinese Univ. 1986–. *Address:* Office of the Governor, Fuzhou, Fujian, People's Republic of China.

HU QIAOMU; Chinese party official; b. 1912, Yancheng, Jiangsu Prov.; m. Gu Yu; two s. one d.; joined CCP 1932; Sec. to Mao Zedong 1940–66; Sec. of Political Bureau of Party Cen. Cttee. after 1941; Dir. Xinhua News Agency June–Nov. 1949; Dir. Information Admin. 1949–52; Deputy Head Propaganda Dept. CCP Cen. Cttee. 1950–54; Deputy Sec.-Gen. CCP Cen. Cttee. 1954–56; Alt. Sec. Secretariat, Party Cen. Cttee. 1956–66; helped draft Constitution of the People's Republic of China and compile The Selected Works of Mao Zedong 1954; mem. Del. of CCP to the Soviet Union 1956, 1957, 1960; Pres. Chinese Acad. of Social Sciences 1978–82, Hon. Pres. 1982–; Deputy Sec.-Gen. CCP Cen. Cttee. 1978–80; Sec. Secr. of CP Cen. Cttee. 1980–82; mem. 8th, 11th and 12th Central Cttees. of CCP; mem. Politburo CCP 1982–87; mem. Standing Cttee. of Cen. Advisory Comm. 1987–; Vice-Chair. Cttee. of Legis. Affairs, NPC 1979–83; Vice-Chair. Bills Cttee. 1979–83; Sec.-Gen. Cttee. for Revision of PRC Constitution 1980–82; Chair. Academic Degrees Cttee., State Council 1983–; Adviser Cen. Party Consolidation Guidance Comm. 1983–; Hon. Chair. Shakespeare Research Soc. 1984–, Wu Yuzhang Award Fund Cttee. 1986–; Hon. Pres. China Wildlife Conservation Asscn. 1983–. *Publication:* The 30 Years of the Communist Party of China 1951, Act According to Economic Laws and Speed up the Realization of Four Modernizations 1978, Some Questions in Current Ideological Trends 1981, On Humanism and Alienation 1984. *Address:* General Office, Central Committee of the Chinese Communist Party, Beijing, People's Republic of China.

HU QILI; Chinese politician; b. 1929, Yulin Co., Shaaxi Prov.; Sec. Communist Youth League (CYL) Cttee., Beijing Univ. 1954; Vice-Chair. Students' Fed. 1954; mem. Standing Cttee., Youth Fed. 1958; Sec. CYL 1964, 1978; Vice-Chair. Youth Fed. 1965; purged 1967; Vice-Pres. Qinghua Univ., Beijing 1978; Sec. CYL 1978; Chair. Youth Fed. 1979–; mem. Standing Cttee., 5th CPPCC 1979–; Mayor, Tianjin 1979–82; Sec. CCP Cttee., Tianjin 1981–82; Dir. Gen. Office Cen. Cttee. CCP 1982; mem. 12th Cen. Cttee. CCP 1982, elected to Politburo 1985, mem. Politburo Standing Cttee. 1987–; Sec. Secr. CCP 1982; Vice-Chair. Cen. Party Consolidation Comm. 1983–. *Leisure interests:* tennis, cycling. *Address:* Chinese Communist Party Committee, Tianjin, People's Republic of China.

HU SHENG; Chinese party official and historian; b. 1911, Suzhou City, Jiangsu Prov.; Sec.-Gen. Propaganda Dept., CCP 1951; in political disgrace 1966–77; Dir. CCP History Research Centre 1982–; Pres. Soc. of Research into the History of the CCP 1983–; Deputy Sec.-Gen., Constitution Revision Cttee. 1982–; mem. 12th Cen. Cttee., CCP 1982–87; Pres. Sun Yat-sen Soc. 1984–; Vice-Chair. Cttee. for Drafting Basic Law of Hongkong Special Admin. Region 1985–; Pres. Chinese Acad. of Social Sciences 1985–; Deputy Dir. Comm. for Commemorating 40th Anniversary of UN 1985; Pres. Postgraduate Inst. 1987–. *Publications:* Systems of Thought and Study 1946, Imperialism and Chinese Politics 1948.

HU TSU TAU, Richard, PH.D.; Singapore politician; b. 30 Oct. 1926; m. Irene Tan Dee Leng; one s. one d.; ed. Anglo-Chinese School, Univ. of California (Berkeley), U.S.A., Univ. of Birmingham, U.K.; Lecturer in Chemical Eng., Univ. of Manchester, U.K. 1958–60; joined Shell (Singapore and Malaysia) 1960, Dir. Marketing and Gen. Man. Shell (KL) 1970, with Shell Int. Petroleum Co., Netherlands 1973, Chief Exec. Shell Cos. (Malaysia) 1974, Chair. and Chief Exec. Shell Cos. (Singapore) 1977, Chair. 1982; Man. Dir. The Monetary Authority of Singapore and Man. Dir. Govt. of Singapore Investment Corpn. Pte. Ltd. 1983–84; elected M.P. (People's Action Party) 1984; Chair. The Monetary Authority of Singapore, Chair. Bd. of Commrs. of Currency 1985–; Minister for Trade and Industry Jan.–May 1985, for Health 1985–87, for Finance 1985–. *Leisure interests:*

golf, swimming. *Address:* Ministry of Finance, 43rd, 44th and 50th Storeys, Treasury Building, Singapore 0106. *Telephone:* 2259911.

HU YAOBANG; Chinese government official; b. 1915, Liuyang City, Hunan Province; m. Li Zhao; three s. one d.; Head Communist Youth League's Org. Dept. 1935; mem. Cen. Cttee. Communist Youth League 1936; Head Political Dept., 2nd Field Army 1948; Vice-Chair., Taiyuan Mil. Control Comm. 1949; mem. Cen. Cttee. Communist Youth League 1949, First Sec. 1957; mem. Exec. Bd. Sino-Soviet Friendship Asscn. 1949–54; Head Political Dept. 18th Corps, 2nd Field Army 1949; Dir., and Head Finance and Econs. Cttee., N. Sichuan People's Admin. Office 1950; Political Commissar N. Sichuan Mil. Dist. 1950; mem. S.W. Mil. and Admin. Cttee. 1950–52; Head, New Democratic Youth League 1952; Sec. New Democratic Youth League 1953; mem. Nat. Cttee. of the All-China Fed. of Democratic Youth 1953–58; Vice-Chair. World Fed. of Democratic Youth 1953–59; mem. Standing Cttee INPC 1954–59 (re-elected 2nd NPC 1959, 3rd NPC 1964); mem. Exec. Cttee. All-China Fed. of Trades Unions 1953–57; mem. Cen. Work Cttee for the Popularisation of Standard Spoken Chinese 1956; Vice-Chair. Nat. Association for the Elimination of Illiteracy 1956; mem. 8th Cen. Cttee. CCP 1956–67; Acting First Sec. Shaanxi CCP Cttee. 1965; mem. 11th Cen. Cttee. CCP 1977, 12th 1982; mem. Politburo CCP Cen Cttee 1978–, Standing Cttee. 1980–87; Sec.-Gen. CCP Cen. Cttee. 1978–80, Gen. Sec. CCP 1980–87; Third Sec. Cen. Cttee. for Inspecting Discipline 1978–87; Dir. Propaganda Dept. CCP Cen. Cttee. 1978–80; Sec.-Gen. Secr., Cen Cttee. 1980; Chair. 11th Cen. Cttee. 1981–82; Deputy, Beijing Municipality to 6th NCP 1983; mem. 12th Cen. Cttee. CCP 1985–87, 13th Cen. Cttee. 1987; mem. Politburo 1987; Chair. Cen. Party Consolidation Guidance Cttee. 1983–87; mem. Presidium 6th NPC 1986. *Leisure interest:* reading sports news.
[*Died 15 April 1989.*]

HU YONGKAI; Chinese artist; b. 25 June 1945, Beijing; s. of Hu Shi Qin and Su Hui Yuan; m. He Ji Su 1974; one s.; specialist in decorative painting. *Leisure interests:* travelling, photography, stamp collecting. *Address:* No. 30 Kaixuan Road, The College of Fine Arts, Shanghai University, Shanghai (Office); Room 402, No. 11 35 Branch, The 63rd Lane, Street Wan Chun, Shanghai (Home). *Telephone:* 523190X41 (Office); 582750 (neighbourhood telephone).

HUA GUOFENG; Chinese politician; b. 1920, native of Shanxi; m. Han Chih-chun; Vice-Gov. Hunan 1958–67; Sec. CCP Hunan 1959; Vice-Chair. Hunan Revolutionary Cttee. 1968, Chair. 1970; mem. 9th Cen. Cttee. of CCP 1969; First Sec. CCP Hunan 1970–77; Political Commissar Guangzhou Mil. Region, People's Liberation Army 1972; First Political Commissar Hunan Mil. District, PLA 1973; mem. Politburo, 10th Cen. Cttee. of CCP 1973; Deputy Premier and Minister of Public Security 1975–76, Acting Premier Feb.–April 1976, Premier 1976–81, Deputy Premier 1981–; First Vice-Chair. Cen. Cttee. of CCP April–Oct. 1976, Chair. 1976–81; Chair. CCP Military Affairs Comm. 1976–81; Chair. and mem. Politburo, 11th Cen. Cttee. CCP 1977–81, Vice-Chair. 1981–82; mem. Cen. Cttee. CCP 1982–. *Address:* Central Committee, Zhongguo Gongchan Dang, Beijing, People's Republic of China.

HUANG, Rayson Lisung, C.B.E., D.SC., D.PHIL., F.R.C.P. (EDIN.); Hong Kong retd. professor of chemistry and university vice-chancellor; b. 1 Sept. 1920, Swatow, China; s. of Rufus and Roseland Huang; m. Grace Wei Li 1949; two s.; ed. Munsang Coll., Hong Kong, Univs of Hong Kong and Oxford; Demonstrator in Chemistry, Nat. Kwangsi Univ., Kweilin, China 1943; Post-Doctoral Fellow and Research Assoc., Univ. of Chicago 1947–50; lecturer in Chem. Univ. of Malaya, Singapore 1951–54, Reader in Chem. 1955–59; Prof. of Chem. Univ. of Malaya, Kuala Lumpur 1959–69, Dean of Science 1962–65; Vice-Chancellor, Nanyang Univ., Singapore 1969–72, Univ. of Hong Kong 1972–86; Pres. Asscn. of Southeast Asian Insts. of Higher Learning 1970–72, 1981–83; Chair. Council, Asscn. of Commonwealth Univs. 1980–81; unofficial mem. Legis. Council of Hong Kong 1977–83; Vice-Chair. of Council, Shantou Univ., China 1987–; mem. Drafting Cttee. and Vice-Chair. Consultative Cttee. for Basic Law of the Hong Kong Special Admin. Region of the People's Repub. of China 1985–; Life mem. of Court, Univ. of Hong Kong; Hon. D.Sc. (Hong Kong); Hon. LL.D. (E. Asia); J.P. *Publications:* Organic Chemistry of Free Radicals 1974; about 50 research papers on chemistry of free radicals, molecular rearrangements and synthetic oestrogens. *Leisure interests:* music, violin-playing. *Address:* 41 Stubbs Road, Hong Kong. *Telephone:* 5-738854.

HUANG AN-LUN; M.M., F.T.C.L.; Chinese composer; b. 15 March 1949, Guang Zhou, Canton; s. of Huang Fei-Li and Zhao Fang-Xing; m. Ouyang Rui-Li 1974; one s.; ed. Central Conservatory of Music, Beijing, Univ. of Toronto, Canada, Trinity Coll. of Music, London and Yale Univ., U.S.A.; started piano aged 5; studied with Shaw Yuan-Xin and Chen Zi; works have been widely performed in China, Hong Kong, Philippines, northern Africa, Australia, Europe, U.S.A. and Canada; Resident Composer, Cen. Opera House of China 1976–; Fellowship in Composition, Trinity Coll. of Music, London 1983; Yale Alumni Asscn. Prize, Yale Univ. 1986; *compositions:* operas: Flower Guardian op. 26 1979, Yeu Fei op. 37 1986 and 6 others; symphonic, chamber, vocal, choral and film music, including: Symphonic Concert op. 25, Symphonic Overture, The Consecration of the Spring in 1976 op. 25a 1977, Piano Concerto in G op. 25b 1982, Symphony in C op. 25c 1984, The Sword (symphonic poem) op. 33 1982, Easter

Cantata (text by Semuel Tang) op. 38 1986; Psalm 22-A Cantata in Baroque Style op. 43c. 1988 Piano Concerto in G; ballets: The Little Match Girl op. 24 1978, A Dream of Dun Huang op. 29 1980, and 7 other records. *Leisure interests:* reading, sport. *Address:* The Central Opera House of China, Zuojia Zhuang, Out of Dongzhimen Gate, Beijing, People's Republic of China. *Telephone:* (416) 423-6396.

HUANG ANREN; Chinese artist; b. 8 Oct. 1924, Yangjiang County, Guandong; s. of Huang Ting Jin and Lin Fen; m. Tan Su 1941; two s. two d.; fmr. Vice-Sec.-Gen. Guangdong Branch, Chinese Artists' Asscn.; Chair. Guangzhou Hairi Research Inst. of Painting and Calligraphy; Adviser, Guangdong Writers' Asscn. of Popular Science. *Publications:* Selected Paintings of Huang Anren, Album of Sketches by Huang Anren, On Arts: Collection of Commentaries by Huang Anren. *Leisure interests:* literature, music. *Address:* Chinese Artists' Association, Guangdong Branch, 69, Wende Road, Guangzhou, People's Republic of China. *Telephone:* 662409.

HUANG BINGWEI; Chinese academic; b. 1 Feb. 1913, Guangzhou; s. of Y. L. Huang and P. Y. Deng; m. Ai Yung Wang 1940; one s. two d.; ed. Sun Yatsen Univ. 1931–34; Rockefeller Foundation Fellow (research on Geomorphology in Geological Survey, China) 1934–35; preparation of monograph Geography of China 1935–38; lecturer, Zhekiang Univ., Assoc. Prof. 1939–43; mem. Nat. Resources Comm. 1942–49; Deputy Dir. Inst. of Industrial Econ., East China, Bureau of Capital Construction, East China 1949–53; mem. Chinese Acad. of Sciences 1955–; Acting Dir. Inst. of Geography, Chinese Acad. of Sciences 1953–57; Vice-Pres. Geographical Soc. 1956, Pres. 1980–; Dir. Inst. of Geography 1957–83, Hon. Dir. 1983–; mem. Presidium 6th NPC 1983–88; mem. China-Italy Friendship Group 1985–. *Publications:* Geography of China 1939, Physical Geography 1941, Natural Resources of China 1948, Physico-Geographic Regions of China 1959; various articles on soil conservation, physical factors of agriculture of China, energy and water balances at the Earth's surface, perspectives of physical geography, etc. *Address:* Institute of Geography, Chinese Academy of Sciences, Building 917, Bei Sha Tang, Beijing, People's Republic of China. *Telephone:* 4021541 (Office); 283853 (Home).

HUANG DEMAO; Chinese army officer; Deputy for PLA to 5th NPC 1978; Deputy Commdr., Kunming Mil. Region 1978– (now Chengdu Mil. Region); alt. mem. 12th CCP Cen. Cttee. 1982–87. *Address:* c/o Chengdu Military Region Headquarters, Chengdu, Sichuan, People's Republic of China.

HUANG DUFENG; Chinese artist; b. 1913, Jieyang Co., Guangdong; taught by Gao Jianfu; studied in Japan; taught fine arts in China; Prof. Guangxi Inst. of Fine Arts; Deputy Dir. Guangxi Branch, Chinese Artists' Asscn. Vice-Chair. Autonomous Regional CPPCC Cttee., Guangxi 1979–. *Address:* People's Republic of China.

HUANG, Fan-Zhang; Chinese economist; b. 8 Feb. 1931, Nanchang; s. of Qi-Kun Huang and Yun-Lin Hua; m. Yue-Fen Xue 1959; two s.; ed. Peking Univ., Researcher, Inst. of Econs. Chinese Acad. of Social Science (CASS) 1954–; Sr. Researcher and Prof. 1979–, Deputy Dir. 1982–85; Visiting Scholar, Harvard Univ. 1980–82, Stockholm Univ. 1982; Exec. Dir. for China, IMF 1985–86; Visiting Research Assoc. Center for Chinese Studies, Univ. of Mich. 1986–87; Consultant to World Bank 1987–88; Dir. Dept. of Int. Econ. Studies, State Planning Comm. of PRC Sept. 1988–; CASS Prize 1985. *Publications:* Modern Economics in Western Countries (with others) 1963, The Evolution of Socialist Theories of Income Distribution 1979, Swedish Welfare State in Practice and its Theories 1987, The Economic Journal for Chinese Economic Planners, No. 53 1988, The Reform in Banking System and The Role of Monetary Policy in China 1989. *Leisure interest:* classical music. *Address:* Apt. 6, Entrance 3, Building 5, Apt. Buildings of Chinese Academy of Social Sciences, Zao-Jun-Miao, South College Road, Beijing, People's Republic of China. *Telephone:* 89-8536, ext. 38 (Home).

HUANG GANYING; Chinese women's federation administrator and representative; Dir. Int. Liaison Dept., Chinese Women's Fed. 1961; Sec. Chinese Women's Fed. 1961; Deputy for Guangdong Prov. to 3rd NPC 1964; disappeared during Cultural Revolution 1967–78; Vice-Pres. and Sec. Chinese Women's Fed. 1978; alt. mem. 12th CCP Cen. Cttee. 1982–87; Vice-Chair. Nat. Cttee. for Defence of Children 1983; Head of many women's Dels. from China to other nations. *Address:* Chinese Women's Federation, Beijing, People's Republic of China.

HUANG HOU; Chinese army officer; Commdr. Nei Monggol Autonomous Region Mil. District 1981. *Address:* People's Liberation Army Headquarters, Hohhot, Nei Monggol Autonomous Region, People's Republic of China.

HUANG HUA; Chinese diplomatist; b. 1913, Hebei; m. He Liliang; two s. one d.; ed. Yanqing Univ., Beijing; fmr. Dir., Foreign Affairs Bureau of Tianjin, Nanking and Shanghai; later Dir., West European Dept., Ministry of Foreign Affairs; Chief. Chinese del. at Panmunjom (Korean War political negotiations) 1953; Political adviser to Premier Zhou En-lai, spokesman of Chinese del. to Geneva Conf. on Indo-China and Korea 1954, First Afro-Asian Conf., Bandung 1955; Adviser, Sino-American negotiations, Warsaw 1958; Amb. to Ghana 1960–66, to Egypt 1966–69, to Canada July-Nov. 1971; Perm. Rep. to UN 1971–76; Minister of Foreign Affairs 1976–83;

mem. 10th Cen. Cttee. CCP 1974, 11th 1978, 12th 1983–87; a Vice-Premier, State Council 1980–82; State Councillor 1982–83; Vice-Chair. Standing Cttee., 6th NPC 1983–; Exec. Chair. Presidium 6th NPC 1986–; mem. Standing Cttee. of Cen. Advisory Comm. 1987–; Pres. Exec. Cttee., China Welfare Inst. 1988–; Hon. Pres. Yenching Alumnae Assoc.; Pres. Smedley, Strong, Snow Soc. of China; mem. Policy Board Interaction Council; Hon. D.Hum.Litt. (Missouri). *Leisure interests:* fishing, jogging. *Address:* Standing Committee, National People's Congress, Beijing, People's Republic of China.

HUANG HUANG; Chinese party official; b. 1933; Leading Sec. CCP Cttee., Anhui Prov. 1983–; mem. 12th CCP Cen. Cttee. 1985–87; mem. Presidium 6th NPC 1986–; Deputy Gov. Jianxi Prov. 1987–. *Address:* Chinese Communist Party Headquarters, Hefei, Anhui Province, Peoples Republic of China.

HUANG JINGBO; Chinese government official; b. 1919; Vice-Minister of Food Industry 1958; Vice-Chair. Prov. Revolutionary Cttee., Guangdong 1978–79; Vice-Gov. Guangdong Prov. 1979–83; Gov. of Qinghai Prov. 1983–85; mem. CPCC Nat. Comm. 1986–. *Address:* Office of the Governor, Xining, Qinghai Province, People's Republic of China.

HUANG JINGKUN; Chinese army officer; Commdr. Jiangsu Mil. District 1980–. *Address:* People's Liberation Army Headquarters, Nanjing, Jiangsu Military District, People's Republic of China.

HUANG JU; Chinese party and government official; b. 1939; mem. Standing Cttee. of Shanghai Municipal CCP Cttee. 1983–, Deputy Sec. 1985–86; Vice-Mayor Shanghai 1986–; alt. mem. CCP Cen. Cttee. 1987–. *Address:* Central Committee of the Chinese Communist Party, Zhongnanhai, Beijing, People's Republic of China.

HUANG KEWEI, B.SC., M.D.; Chinese neuropathologist; b. 1907, Zhanjiang, Jiangsu Prov.; m. Bai-Xi Wang 1935; two s. two d.; ed. Yencheng Univ., Peiping, Peking Union Medical Coll., Harvard Medical School, London Univ. Medical School; Prof. of Medicine at Nat. Cen. Univ., Chengdu, Sichuan Prov. 1940–62; Beijing PLA Gen. Hosp. 1962–. *Leisure interests:* music, English novels. *Address:* PLA General Hospital, Beijing, People's Republic of China.

HUANG KUN; Chinese university professor and politician; b. 1919, Zhejiang Prov.; Prof. of Physics, Beijing Univ. 1959; Deputy to NPC 1964; Dir. Inst. of Semi-Conductors of the Chinese Acad. of Sciences 1977; mem. Standing Cttee. of 5th CPPCC 1978; Pres. Chinese Soc. of Physics 1987–. *Address:* Chinese Society of Physics, Beijing, People's Republic of China.

HUANG LUOBIN; Chinese soldier, party and government official; commdr. PLA div. 1949; Council mem. Ningxia Prov. People's Govt. 1949–; mem. Financial and Econ. Comm. Ningxia 1953–; mem. Gansu Prov. CCP Cttee. 1958–, Chair. 1983–; Vice-Gov. Gansu Prov. 1958–64; Sec. Xinjiang Autonomous Region CCP Cttee.; mem. Cen. Advisory Cttee. of CCP Cen. Cttee. 1987–. *Address:* Central Advisory Committee of the Central Committee of the Chinese Communist Party, Zhongnanhai, Beijing, People's Republic of China.

HUANG MINGDA; Chinese diplomatist; Counsellor, Embassy, Burma 1965–66, Chargé d'Affaires, 1970–71; Amb. to Sri Lanka and Maldive Islands 1973–77, to Afghanistan 1977–82, to Burma 1982.

HUANG RONG; Chinese party official; Zhuang nationality; served in Nationalist Govt. as mil. officer, later joined Communists; Deputy for Guangxi, 1st NPC 1954, 2nd NPC 1958, 3rd NPC 1964, 5th NPC 1978; mem. Minorities Cttee. NPC 1958; Vice-Chair. CPPCC, Guangxi 1964; disappeared during Cultural Revolution; Vice-Chair. Autonomous Regional Revolutionary Cttee., Guangxi 1977–79; mem. Cen. Comm. for Inspecting Discipline, CCP Cen. Cttee. 1978; mem. State Nationalities Affairs Comm., State Council 1979; Chair. Autonomous Regional People's Congress, Guangxi 1979–85; Sec. CCP Cttee., Guangxi 1980. *Address:* c/o Office of the Chairman, People's Congress, Guangxi Autonomous Region, People's Republic of China.

HUANG SHAO-KU; Chinese politician; b. 9 June 1901; ed. National Peking Normal Univ.; Sec.-Gen. of Exec. Yuan 1949–54; Vice-Premier, Exec. Yuan 1954–58, 1966–69; Minister of Foreign Affairs 1958–60; Amb. to Spain 1960–62; Sec.-Gen. Nat. Security Council 1967–79; Pres. of Judicial Yuan 1979–87; Sr. Adviser to Pres. 1976–. *Address:* 4th Floor, 650 Tunhua South Road, Taipei, Taiwan.

HUANG SHU; Chinese party official; alt. mem. 12th CCP Cen. Cttee. 1982–87; Deputy Dir. Science and Tech. Cttee. 1988–. *Address:* c/o Chinese Communist Party Central Committee, Beijing, People's Republic of China.

HUANG XINTING, Lieut.-Gen.; Chinese soldier; b. 1913, Honghu Co., Hubei Prov.; joined Red Army 1931, CCP 1932; Regimental Commdr., Second Front Army 1935; Deputy Commdr. of Chengdu Mil. Region, PLA 1955–66; criticized and removed from office during Cultural Revolution 1967; Commdr. PLA Armoured Corps 1975–; mem. 12th Cen. Cttee. CCP 1982–85; mem. Cen. Advisory Comm. 1985–87. *Address:* People's Republic of China.

HUANG YENGU; Chinese woodcut artist; b. 1924, Fenghuang County., Hunan (Tujia nationality); ed. Secondary Fine Arts School; Assoc. Prof.

Cen. Acad. of Fine Arts. *Address:* Central Academy of Fine Arts, Beijing, People's Republic of China.

HUANG YONGYU; Chinese (Miao nationality) artist and poet; b. 1924, Fenghuang Co., Hunan Prov.; best known for his satirical picture of an owl with its left eye closed, produced during the 'Gang of Four' era; Vice-Chair. Chinese Artists' Asscn. 1985-. *Address:* Central Academy of Fine Arts, Beijing, People's Republic of China.

HUANG ZHEN; Chinese diplomatist; b. Dec. 1910, Tong Chen Country, Anhui; ed. Shanghai Art Coll.; numerous posts in Red Army, took part in Long March, Pol. Commissar, Shanxi-Hebei-Shandong-Henan border region 1927-49; Amb. to Hungary 1950-54, to Indonesia 1954-61; rep. at the Afro-Asian Conf. 1955; Vice-Minister of Foreign Affairs 1961-64; Amb. to France 1964-73, Yemen 1986-; Head of Mission, U.S.A. 1973-77; Minister of Culture 1977-81; First Deputy Dir., CCP Propaganda Dept. 1977-82; mem. 9th, 10th, 11th Cen. Cttees. CCP; Rep. for Literature and Art Circle, 5th CPPCC 1978; mem. Presidium and Standing Cttee., 5th CPPCC 1978-; mem. Standing Cttee., Cen. Advisory Comm. 1985-; Pres. China-U.S. People's Friendship Asscn. 1986-; Hon. Chair. China Asscn. for Advancement of Int. Friendship 1985-; Adviser to Foreign Affairs Cttee. of NPC 1983-. *Leisure interests:* painting, calligraphy. *Address:* 145 Andalus Gardens, Khormaksar, Aden, People's Democratic Republic of Yemen.

HUANG ZHIZHEN; Chinese party official; b. 1909, Jiangxi; joined CCP 1930; guerrilla activities CCP N. Fujian Special Cttee. 1934; Dir. United Front Work Dept. CCP, Jiangxi Prov. 1954; Vice-Chair. CPPCC, Jiangxi Prov., and mem. People's Govt. Council, Jiangxi 1955; Sec.-Gen. CCP Cttee., Jiangxi 1957, mem. Standing Cttee. 1958, alt. mem. CCP Cttee. 1962; Deputy for Jiangxi, 3rd NPC 1964; disappeared during Cultural Revolution; mem. Standing Cttee. CP, Jiangxi 1973, Sec. CCP Cttee. 1973-78; alt. mem. CCP Cen. Cttee., 10th Party Congress 1973; Vice-Chair. Prov. Revolutionary Cttee., Jiangxi 1977-78; mem. CCP Cen. Cttee. 11th Party Congress 1977; mem. Birth Planning Leading Group, State Council 1978; Sec. CCP Cttee., Hubei 1979, Deputy Sec. 1983-; Vice-Chair. Prov. Revolutionary Cttee. Hubei 1979; Vice-Gov. Hubei 1980, Acting Gov. 1982-83, Gov. 1983-; Chair. Standing Cttee., Hubei Prov. People's Congress 1986-; mem. CCP Cen. Cttee., 12th Party Congress 1982-87. *Address:* Office of the Secretary, Communist Party Central Committee, Hubei, People's Republic of China.

HUANG ZHOU; Chinese painter; b. 1925, Zixian Co., Hebei Prov.; trained in shuimo (ink-wash) painting; joined PLA 1947, resident artist 1950s-; bulk of 10,000 sketches destroyed during Cultural Revolution; Vice-Pres. Research Inst. of Traditional Chinese Painting; retrospective exhbn., China Art Asscn. Aug. 1982. *Works include:* 100 Donkeys 1979, Sing Along. *Address:* Research Institute of Traditional Chinese Painting, Beijing, People's Republic of China.

HUANG ZONGYING; Chinese writer; b. 1925, Beijing; m. Zhao Dan 1949; joined CCP 1956; wrote film script of The Common Cause 1956; imprisoned 1966-76; Special Science Policy Research Fellow, State Scientific and Technological Commission 1981. *Publications:* Beautiful Eyes, The Flight of the Wild Geese. *Address:* Chinese Federation of Literature and Art, Beijing, People's Republic of China.

HUANT, Ernest Albin Camille; French doctor, writer, philosopher, sociologist and historian; b. 29 Oct. 1909, Vouziers, Ardennes; s. of Alphonse Huant and Hélène Potier; m. Odette Mazoyer 1942; one s. one d.; ed. Lycée de Charleville, Louis le Grand, Faculté des Sciences, Faculté de Médecine, Paris; medical radiologist, Paris hospitals 1943; Pres. Centre d'Etudes des Problèmes de l'Homme 1960; mem. Soc. d'Economie Politique, Paris 1958-; Scientific Adviser to Labs. 1957-; mem. Int. Cttee. and French Del. to Int. Soc. for Cybernetic Medicine 1965; Lauréat de l'Institut de France 1964-65; Pres. de la Société d'études philosophiques des Sciences de la nature 1967; Pres. du Centre Int. de Cyto-Cybernétique 1967, Pres. and Founder of Centre Int. Humanae Vitae 1968; Sorbonne Thesis Prize 1933; Prix de l'Acad. de Médecine pour Les traitements mitotiques du cancer 1958, and Les maladies de société 1961; Prix de l'Acad. des Sciences Morales et Politiques for Florence et Rome and Prix Littré (Union Int. des Ecrivains Médecins) 1965; Chevalier, Légion d'honneur; Carnegie Foundation Medal (U.S.A.), Kt. St. George 1984. *Publications:* Les radiations et la vie 1942, Déterminisme et finalités 1946, Connaissance du temps 1951, Biologie et cybernétiques 1954, Credo de Jean Rostand 1957, L'anti-masse 1957, Du biologique au social 1957, Milieu et adaptation 1959, Les maladies de société 1961, Le péché contre la chair 1961, Naître ou ne pas naître 1963, A.D.N. Recherches expérimentales et cliniques 1964, Florence et Rome 1964, Economie et cybernétique 1965, Voyage en Assuro-Socyalie 1965, Masses-Morale-Machines 1967, Le troisième triumvirat 1967, Les pressions du nouveau temporel 1968, Les structures intelligibles du réel 1968, L'unité romaine de l'an 1000: Othon III 1971, Non à l'avortement 1972, Temporalité, Finalité, Survie, Analyse psycho-cybernétique 1975, La nouvelle face de Méduse 1976, Mort, mémoire et rêves 1978, Cybernétique des 3 "E": économie, environnement, écologie 1980, Information, Temps, Mémoire 1980, Dialogues avec Craonne 1983, La Pensée cybernétique dans l'oeuvre de P. Valéry 1984, Antinous II 1984, Le principe de complémentarité en histoire 1984, Le Christ à Prague 1985, Parfait … trop parfait!

1985, Les étranges courses du Colonel d'Hourdoff 1986, Base Minos 1986, Réfléchissons Porphyre! 1986, Dresde ou l'Horreur Expantielle 1987, Robespierre ou la Dictature de l'Idée 1987. *Leisure interests:* Roman history, Florentine art. *Address:* 9 avenue Niel, 75017 Paris, France. *Telephone:* 4572 28 62.

HUAYTA NÚÑEZ, Wilfredo; Peruvian politician and mining engineer; b. Ayacucho; ed. Universidad Nacional de Ingeniería; various exec. positions in pvt. mining cos. 1948-63; fmr. Dir. of Mining Concessions at Ministry of Energy and Mines; Prof., Faculty of Geology, Mining and Metallurgy, Universidad Nacional de Ingeniería; Minister of Energy and Mines 1985-87; expert on problems of environmental pollution caused by refineries; mem. Instituto Nacional de Derecho de Minería y Petróleo, Instituto de Ingenieros de Minas del Perú, Sociedad Progreso de la Pequeña Minería, Colegio de Ingenieros del Perú; Del. and Founder, Andean Eng. Council. *Publications:* numerous studies on hydroelectric and irrigation projects in Ayacucho. *Address:* c/o Ministry of Energy and Mines, Avenida Las Artes s/n, San Borja, Lima, Peru. *Telephone:* 410065.

HUBA, Mikuláš; Czechoslovak actor; b. 19 October 1919, Spišská Nová Ves; ed. Comenius Univ. Bratislava, Acad. of Dramatic Art, Bratislava; mem. drama ensemble, Slovak Nat. Theatre, Bratislava 1938-; teacher, Coll. of Performing Arts, Bratislava 1951-; head of drama co. Slovak Nat. Theatre, Bratislava 1953-63, 1972-76; cand. mem. Cen. Cttee. CP of Slovakia 1968-76, mem. 1976-; Deputy Chair. Union of Slovak Dramatic and Radio Artists 1969-70, Chair. 1970-72; mem. Presidium, Union of Slovak Dramatic Artists 1972-, Chair. 1982-; mem. Presidium, Union of Czechoslovak Dramatic Artists (SČSDU) 1978-, Deputy Chair., 1982-; roles in theatre, television and radio plays, gramophone recordings, recitation; numerous Czechoslovak awards.

HUBBARD, John, B.A.; American painter; b. 26 Feb. 1931, Ridgefield, Conn.; s. of G. Evans Hubbard and Dorothea Denys Hubbard; m. Caryl Whineray 1961; one s. one d.; ed. Milton Acad., Harvard Univ. and Art Students' League; served U.S. army in Counter-Intelligence 1953-56; exhbns. include nine at New Art Centre, London 1961-75, three at Fischer Fine Art, London 1979-85, Ten Americans, Rome 1959, British Painting in the Sixties, European Tour 1963, British Painting 1974, Hayward Gallery, London 1974, Jubilee Exhbn., R.A., London 1977, Yale Center for British Art 1986, and others in London, Oxford and elsewhere; designed décor and costumes for Le Baiser de la Fée, Dutch Nat. Ballet 1968, Midsummer, Royal Ballet, London 1983 and Sylvia Pas de Deux, Royal Ballet, London 1985. *Publication:* Second Nature 1984. *Leisure interests:* walking and gardening. *Address:* Chilcombe House, Chilcombe, nr. Bridport, Dorset, England. *Telephone:* 03083-234.

HUBBARD, John Ingram, PH.D., F.R.A.C.P., F.R.S.N.Z.; New Zealand physiologist; b. 1 Dec. 1930, Wellington; s. of John Hubbard and Anne A. (née Ingram) Hubbard; m. 1st Patricia M. Sargent 1954; two s. three d.; m. 2nd Carolyn W. Burns 1981; ed. Otago Univ., Oxford Univ., Australian Nat. Univ.; Research Fellow Medical School, Australian Nat. Univ. 1961-62, Fellow 1962-64, Sr. Fellow 1964-67; Prof. Biological Sciences and Eng. Sciences, Northwestern Univ., Ill. 1967-72; Prof. Neurophysiology Otago Univ. 1972-, Pro Vice-Chancellor 1981-83, Chair. Dept. of Physiology 1973, 1975-79, 1987-. *Publications:* Electrophysiological Analysis of Synoptic Transmission 1969, The Peripheral Nervous System 1974, The Biological Bases of Mental Activity 1975, over 100 learned papers and reviews. *Leisure interests:* tennis, gardening. *Address:* Department of Physiology, Otago University, Otago (Office); 10 Haddon Place, Dunedin, New Zealand (Home). *Telephone:* 770-590 (Home).

HUBBERT, Marion King, PH.D.; American geologist and geophysicist; b. 5 Oct. 1903, San Saba, Tex.; s. of William Bee Hubbert and Cora Virginia Lee; m. Miriam Graddy Berry 1938; ed. Weatherford Coll., Tex. and Univ. of Chicago; Asst. Geologist, Amerada Petroleum Corpn. 1927-28; Teaching Asst. Univ. of Chicago 1928-30; Instructor in Geophysics, Columbia Univ. 1931-40; Geophysicist, Ill. State, and U.S. Geological Surveys 1931-37; Sr. Analyst, U.S. Bd. of Econ. Warfare, Washington 1942-43; Research Geophysicist, Shell Oil Co., Houston 1943-45, Assoc. Dir. of Research 1945-51, Chief Consultant (Gen. Geology), Shell Oil Co. and Shell Devt. Co., Houston 1951-64; Visiting Prof., Geology and Geophysics Stanford Univ. 1962-63, Prof. 1963-68; Research Geophysicist, U.S. Geological Survey 1964-76, Emer. Prof. 1969-; Regents' Prof., Univ. of Calif., Berkeley 1973; mem. Cttee. on Natural Resources, Adviser to Pres. John F. Kennedy 1961-62; author of report, Energy Resources; mem. Cttee. on Geoscience and Man, Int. Union of Geological Sciences 1973-76; mem. Nat. Acad. of Sciences, American Acad. of Arts and Sciences and others; Hon. mem. Soc. of Exploration Geophysicists 1960, Hon. mem. American Asscn. of Petroleum Geologists 1974, Canadian Soc. of Petroleum Geologists 1974, American Inst. of Mining, Metallurgical and Petroleum Engineers 1978; D.Sc. h.c. (Syracuse Univ.) 1972, (Indiana State) 1980; Arthur L. Day Medal of Geological Soc. of America 1954, Anthony F. Lucas Gold Medal Award, American Inst. of Mining, Metallurgical and Petroleum Engineers 1971; Penrose Medal Geological Soc. of America 1973; Rockefeller Public Service Award 1977; William Smith Medal, Geological Soc. of London 1978, Elliott Cresson Medal, Franklin Inst. 1981, Vetlesen Prize, Columbia Univ. 1981. *Publications:* six books and numerous articles in various scientific journals. *Leisure interests:* reading, conversation, music, experimentation.

Address: 5208 Westwood Drive, Bethesda, Md. 20816, U.S.A. *Telephone:* (301) 229-7798.

HUBEL, David Hunter, M.D.; American professor of neurobiology; b. 27 Feb. 1926, Windsor, Ont., Canada; s. of Jesse H. Hubel and Elsie M. Hunter; m. S. Ruth Izzard 1953; three s.; ed. McGill Univ; Prof. of Neurophysiology, Harvard Medical School 1965–67, George Packer Berry Prof. of Physiology and Chair. Dept. of Physiology 1967–68, George Packer Berry Prof. of Neurobiology 1968–82; John Franklin Enders Univ. Prof. 1982–; mem. N.A.S., Leopoldina Acad., Bd. of Syndics, Harvard Univ. Press 1979–83; Foreign mem. Royal Soc., London; Sr. Fellow, Harvard Soc. of Fellows 1971–; Fellow American Acad. of Arts and Sciences; Hon. A.M. (Harvard) 1962, Hon. D.Sc. (McGill) 1978, (Manitoba) 1983; Lewis S. Rosenstiel Award for Basic Medical Research (Brandeis Univ.) 1972, Friedenwald Award (Asscn. for Research in Vision and Ophthalmology) 1975, Karl Spencer Lashley Prize (American Philosophical Soc.) 1977, Louisa Gross Horwitz Prize, (Columbia Univ.) 1978, Dickson Prize in Medicine, Univ. of Pittsburgh 1979, Soc. of Scholars, John Hopkins Univ. 1980, Ledlie Prize (Harvard Univ.) 1980, Nobel Prize in Medicine or Physiology 1981, New England Ophthalmological Soc. Award 1983. *Publications:* Eye, Brain and Vision 1987; articles in scientific journals. *Leisure interests:* music, photography, astronomy, Japanese. *Address:* Department of Neurobiology-B, Harvard Medical School, 25 Shattuck Street, Boston, Mass. 02115; 98 Collins Road, Waban, Mass. 02168, U.S.A. (Home). *Telephone:* (617) 732-1655 (Office); (617) 527-8774 (Home).

HUBER, Antje Charlotte; German politician; b. 23 May 1924, Stettin (now Szczecin, Poland); d. of Bruno and Charlotte Hedwig Luise Pust; m. Karl Huber 1950; ed. Sozialakademie, Dortmund; Tutor, Sozialakademie 1962–69; mem. Sozialdemokratische Partei Deutschlands (SPD) 1948–; mem. Essen Municipal Council; mem. various local, state and fed. bodies of SPD 1948–69; mem. Bundestag (Lower House of Parl.) 1969–87, later SPD spokesman on Finance and Taxation, Vice-Chair. Finance Cttee. of Bundestag; Fed. Minister for Youth, Family Affairs and Health 1976–82; mem. SPD Presidium 1977–84; Grosses Bundesverdienstkreuz 1984. *Address:* Am Vogelherd 12, 4300 Essen-Werden, Federal Republic of Germany. *Telephone:* (0228) 167383.

HUBER, Karl, PH.D.; Swiss government official; b. 18 Oct. 1915, Häggenschwil; s. of Carl Huber and Mathilde Haessig; m. Elizabeth Fink 1945; one s. two d.; ed. high school, St. Gall, and Univ. of Berne; entered Fed. Admin. 1941, mem. staff of Gen. Secr. of Ministry of Political Econ.; Sec.-Gen. Ministry of Political Econ. 1954; Fed. Chancellor of Swiss Confederation 1967–81. *Leisure interests:* history, swimming, walking. *Address:* Steingrubenweg 23, 3028 Spiegel, Switzerland.

HUBER, Robert, DR. RER. NAT.; German biochemist; b. 20 Feb. 1937; fmr. Prof. Tech. Univ. Munich; now Prof. and Dir. of Dept. Max-Planck-Inst. für Biochimie; mem. Bavarian Acad. of Sciences; E.K. Frey Prize (German Surgical Soc.) 1972; Otto Warburg Medal (Soc. for Biological Chemistry) 1977; Emil von Behring Prize (Univ. of Marburg) 1982; Keilin Medal (Biochem. Soc. London); Richard Kuhn Medal (Soc. of German Chemists) 1987; Dr. h.c. (Louvain) 1987. *Address:* Max Planck Institut für Biochemie, 8033 Martinsried/Obb., Federal Republic of Germany.

HUCK, John Lloyd, B.S.; American business executive; b. 17 July 1922, Brooklyn, New York; s. of Adrienne Byron Warner and John Lloyd Huck; m. Dorothy B. Foehr 1943; one s. two d.; ed. Nutley High School, N.J. and Pennsylvania State Univ.; on staff of Hoffmann-LaRoche, Nutley, N.J. 1946–58; Dir. of Marketing, Merck Sharp & Dohme Div., Merck & Co. Inc. 1958–66, Vice-Pres., Marketing Planning 1966–68, Vice-Pres., Sales and Marketing 1968–69, Exec. Vice-Pres. 1969–72, Exec. Vice-Pres. and Gen. Man. 1972–73, Pres. 1973–75; Sr. Vice-Pres., Merck & Co. Inc. 1975–77, Exec. Vice-Pres. 1977–78, mem. Bd. of Dirs. 1977–86, Pres. and C.O.O. 1978–85, Chair. 1985–86; Chair., C.E.O. Nova Pharm Corp., Morristown, N.J. 1986–88, Chair. Bd. 1988–. *Leisure interests:* tennis, golf. *Address:* Village Road, P.O. Box 474, New Vernon, N.J. 07976, U.S.A. (Home). *Telephone:* (201) 898-4774 (Office).

HUCKSTEP, Ronald Lawrie, C.M.G., F.T.S., M.A., M.D., F.R.C.S., F.R.C.S.E., F.R.A.C.S.; British-Australian consultant orthopaedic surgeon and university professor; b. 22 July 1926, Chefoo, China; s. of Herbert George Huckstep and Agnes Huckstep (née Lawrie-Smith); m. Ann Macbeth 1960; two s. one d.; ed. Cathedral School, Shanghai, Queens' Coll., Cambridge, Middlesex, Royal Nat. Orthopaedic and St. Bartholomew's Hosps., London; Registrar and Chief Asst., Orthopaedic Dept., St. Bartholomew's Hosp. and various surgical appts., Middx. and Royal Nat. Orthopaedic Hosps. 1952–60; Hunterian Prof., Royal Coll. of Surgeons 1959–60; Lecturer, Sr. Lecturer and Reader in Orthopaedic Surgery, Makerere Univ., Kampala, Uganda 1960–67, Prof. 1967–72; Hon. Consultant Orthopaedic Surgeon, Mulago and Mengo Hosps. and Round Table Polio Clinic, Kampala 1960–72; Hon. Consultant Orthopaedic Surgeon, Mulago and Mengo Hosps. and Round Table Polio Clinic, Kampala 1960–72; Hon. Orthopaedic Surgeon to all Govt. and Mission hosps. in Uganda and Adviser on Orthopaedic Surgery to Ministry of Health, Uganda 1960–72; Prof. and Head, Dept. of Traumatic and Orthopaedic Surgery and Rotating Chair., School of Surgery, Univ. of N.S.W. 1972–; Chair. Dept. of Traumatic and Orthopaedic Surgery and Dir. of Accident Services, Prince of Wales/Prince Henry

Hosps., Consultant Orthopaedic Surgeon, Royal S. Sydney and Sutherland Hosps., Sydney 1972–; Hon. Adviser, Rotary Int., The Commonwealth Foundation, WHO and UN on starting services for the disabled in developing countries 1970–; Sr. Medical Disaster Commdr., Dept. of Health, N.S.W. and Chair. and mem. of various disaster and emergency cttees. in Australia 1972–; Corresp. Ed. British and American Journals of Bone and Joint Surgery 1965–72, Injury, British Journal of Accident Surgery 1972; mem. Traffic Authority of N.S.W. 1982–; Consultant to Archives of Orthopaedic Surgery 1984–; Founder World Orthopaedic Concern 1973, Hon. Fellow 1978; Patron Medical Soc. of Univ. of N.S.W. 1976; Hon. Dir. Orthopaedic Overseas, U.S.A. 1978; Vice-Pres. Australian Orthopaedic Asscn. 1982; Pres. Coast Medical Asscn., Sydney 1985–86; Hon. Fellow Western Pacific Orthopaedic Asscn.; Chair. or mem of numerous other bodies; Hon. M.D. (Univ. of N.S.W.) 1987; Irving Geist Award, Int. Soc. for Rehabilitation of the Disabled 1969, Melsome Memorial Prize, Cambridge 1948, Raymond Horton Smith Prize, Cambridge 1957, Betts Memorial Medal, Australian Orthopaedic Asscn. 1983, James Cook Medal, Royal Soc. of N.S.W. 1984, K. L. Sutherland Medal, Australian Acad. of Tech. Sciences 1986, Paul Harris Fellow and Medal, Rotary Int. and Rotary Foundation 1987; numerous orthopaedic inventions including Huckstep nail, hip, femur, knee, shoulder, humerus, staple, circlip, plate, bone screw, caliper, wheelchairs and skelecasts. *Publications:* Typhoid Fever and other Salmonella Infections 1962, A Simple Guide to Trauma 1970, Poliomyelitis: A Guide for Developing Countries, including appliances and rehabilitation 1975; numerous chapters in books and papers. *Leisure interests:* photography, designing orthopaedic appliances and implants, swimming and travel. *Address:* Department of Traumatic and Orthopaedic Surgery, The Prince of Wales Hospital, Randwick, Sydney, N.S.W. 2031; 108 Sugarloaf Crescent, Castlecrag, Sydney, N.S.W. 2068, Australia (Home).

HUDA, Dr. Mirza Nurul, PH.D.; Bangladesh politician and professor of economics; b. 1 Aug. 1919, Tangail; s. of Lak Mouli Mirzq Abdul Karim and Ayesha Begum Huda; m. Umme Kulsum Siddiqua Banu; one s. two d.; ed. Dacca Univ., Cornell Univ., U.S.A.; Reader in Econs., Dacca Univ. 1949, later Prof. of Econs., Chair. Dept. of Econs., Chair. Bureau of Econ. Research, Dean, Faculty of Social Sciences; Minister for Finance and Planning, East Pakistan 1965, Gov. of East Pakistan 1969; mem. Council of Advisers to Pres. of Bangladesh 1975–78 and in charge of Ministry of Planning; Minister of Planning 1978–79, of Finance 1979–80; Vice-Pres. of Bangladesh 1981–82; Pres. Bangladesh Econ. Asscn. 1965; Chair. Social Science Research Council, Soc. for Int. Devt. *Publications:* 18 research works and books on economics. *Leisure interests:* walking, writing, watching television. *Address:* 57 Dhanmondi Road, 6a Dhaka 9, Bangladesh.

HUDDLESTON, Most Rev. (Ernest Urban) Trevor, M.A.; British ecclesiastic; b. 15 June 1913, Bedford; s. of Ernest and Elsie Huddleston; ed. Christ Church, Oxford; ordained Deacon 1936, Priest 1937; Curate, St. Mark's, Swindon 1936–39; professed Community of the Resurrection, Mirfield 1941; Prior and Priest-in-Charge, Sophiatown, Orlando, and Pimville, Johannesburg 1943; Provincial of the Community of the Resurrection, South Africa 1949–56; Novice-Master, Community of the Resurrection, England 1956–58; Prior, London Community of the Resurrection 1958–60; Bishop of Masasi, Tanzania 1960–68; Suffragan Bishop of Stepney 1968–78 (resgnd.); Bishop of Mauritius 1978–83, also Archbishop of the Anglican Prov. of the Indian Ocean 1978–83; Chair. Int. Defence and Aid Fund for Southern Africa 1983–; Provost, Selly Oak Colls. 1983–; Vice-Pres. Anti-Apartheid Movement 1969–81, Pres. 1981–; Pres. Nat. Peace Council 1983–, Int. Voluntary Service 1984–; Trustee, Runnymede Trust 1972–; Hon. D.D. (Aberdeen Univ.), Hon. D.Litt. (Lancaster Univ.), (Warwick Univ.) 1988; Order of the Grand Companion of Freedom (Zambia) 1984. *Publications:* Naught for Your Comfort 1956, The True and Living God 1964, God's World 1966, I Believe: Reflections on the Apostle's Creed 1986, Trevor Huddleston: Essays on His Life and Work 1988. *Address:* House of the Resurrection, Mirfield, W. Yorks., WF14 0BN, England.

HUDDLESTON, Walter D., B.A.; American politician; b. 15 April 1926, Cumberland County, Kentucky; s. of W. F. and Lottie (Russell) Huddleston; m. Martha Jean Pearce 1947; two s.; ed. Jeffersontown High School, Ky. and Univ. of Kentucky; State Senator, Kentucky 1965, 1971; Chair. Democratic Caucus, Ky. Gen. Assembly, twice Majority Leader of Ky. Senate; U.S. Senator from Kentucky 1972–85, mem. Agric. and Forestry, Appropriations, Intelligence Cttees., 93rd Congress; Sr. Consultant Hecht Spencer and Assocs., Wash., D.C.; Democrat. *Leisure interests:* tennis, golf. *Address:* Hecht, Spencer and Assocs., 499 South Capital Street, S.W. Washington, D.C. 20003, U.S.A.

HUDEČEK, Václav; Czechoslovak violinist; b. 7 June 1952, Rožmitál pod Třemšínem, Příbram Dist.; m. Eva Trejtnarova 1977; ed Faculty of Music, Acad. of Musical Arts, Prague 1968–73; worked with David Oistrakh, Moscow 1970–74; worked as musician 1974–; mem., Union of the Czech Composers and Concert Artists 1977–; individual concerts, 1967–; soloist with Czech Philharmonic Orchestra 1984–; concert tours to Austria, G.D.R., Norway, Hungary, U.S.S.R., Switzerland, Turkey, U.S.A., Yugoslavia, Japan, Italy, Iceland, Finland; also gramophone recordings; Concertino Praga int. radio competition 1967, Award for Outstanding Labour 1978, Artist of Merit 1981. *Address:* 120 00 Praha 2, Londynska 25, Czechoslovakia. *Telephone:* (02) 255172.

HUDON, L. Denis, M.A.; Canadian financial executive; b. 21 Dec. 1924; ed. Laval Univ., Quebec, and Toronto Univ.; Econ. Policy Div., Dept. of Finance, Ottawa 1948-51; Sec. (Financial), Perm. Canadian Mission to NATO 1952-54; Int. and Econ. Div. (Int. Programmes and Contributions), Dept. of Finance, Ottawa 1954-60; Dir. Policy and Planning Coordination, External Aid Office 1960-61; Alt. Dir. IMF, IBRD, IDA 1961-64, Exec. Dir. for Canada, Ireland and Jamaica 1965-68; Deputy Dir.-Gen. External Aid Office 1967-68; Vice-Pres. (Planning) Canadian Int. Devt. Agency (fmrly. External Aid Office) 1968-71; Asst. Sec. to Cabinet (Econ. Policy) Privy Council Office Feb.-Dec. 1971; Deputy Sec. to Cabinet (Operations) Privy Council Office 1971; Financial Counsellor, Canadian Embassy, Washington 1961-64; Dir. Int. Programmes Div., Dept. of Finance, Ottawa 1964-66.

HUDSON, Sir Havelock Henry Trevor, Kt.; British underwriter; b. 4 Jan. 1919, Hong Kong; s. of Savile E. and Dorothy (née Cheetham) Hudson; m. 1st Elizabeth Home 1944 (dissolved 1956), two s.; m. 2nd Cathleen Blanch Lily 1957, one s. one d.; ed. Rugby School; merchant service 1937-38; joined Lloyd's 1938; war service 1939-45, Royal Hampshire Regt. (Maj.) 1939-42, 9th Parachute Bn. 1942-44; mem. Cttee. Lloyd's Underwriters' Assen. 1963, mem. Cttee. Lloyd's 1965-68, 1970-73, 1975-78, Deputy Chair. 1968, 1971, 1973, Chair. 1975-77; mem. Exec. Bd. Lloyd's Register of Shipping 1967-78; mem. Working Party under Lord Cromer on Conditions of Underwriting Membership of Lloyd's 1968; Chair. Arvon Foundation 1973-86; Vice-Pres. Chartered Insurance Inst. 1973-77; Chair. Oxford Artificial Kidney and Transplant Trust 1977-; mem. Bd. of Govs. Pangbourne Coll. 1976-88, Bradfield Coll. 1977-88; Pres. City of London Outward Bound Assen. 1979; Dir. Ellerman Lines 1979-83; Freeman of the City of London; Lloyds Gold Medal 1977. *Leisure interest:* shooting. *Address:* The Old Rectory, Stanford Dingley, Near Reading, Berkshire, RG7 6LX, England. *Telephone:* (0734) 744346 (Home).

HUDSON, Hugh; British film director. *Films include:* Chariots of Fire 1983, Greystoke: The Story of Tarzan 1984, Revolution 1986, Lost Angels 1989. *Address:* 11 Queen's Gate Place Mews, London S.W.7, England.

HUDSON, Robert Francis, PH.D., F.R.S.; British professor of organic chemistry; b. 15 Dec. 1922; s. of late John F. Hudson and Ethel Hudson; m. Monica A. Stray 1945; one s. two d.; ed. Brigg Grammar School and Imperial Coll., London; Asst. Lecturer, Imperial Coll. 1945-47; Consultant, Wolsey Ltd. Leicester 1945-50; Lecturer, Queen Mary Coll. London 1947-59; Research Fellow, Purdue Univ. 1954; Group Dir. Cyanamid European Research Inst. Geneva 1960-66; Prof. of Organic Chem. Univ. of Kent at Canterbury 1967-85, Prof. Emer. 1985-; Consultant British Petroleum 1983-; Visiting Prof. at univs. in U.S.A., Canada, France, Germany etc. *Publications:* Wool—Its Physics and Chemistry (with P. Alexander) 1954, Structure and Mechanism in Organophosphorus Chemistry 1965; papers in scientific journals. *Address:* 37 Puckle Lane, Canterbury, Kent, CT1 3LA, England. *Telephone:* (0227) 61340.

HUDSON, Thomas Charles, C.B.E., C.A.; British business executive; b. 23 Jan. 1915, Sidcup, Kent; s. of Charles B. and Elsie E. (née Harris) Hudson; m. 1st Lois A. Johnson 1944 (divorced 1973), two s. one d.; m. 2nd Susan Gillian Gibbs 1986; ed. Middle High School, Nova Scotia; articled to Nightingale Hayman, Nova Scotia 1935-40; Lieut. Royal Canadian Volunteer Reserve 1942-46; joined IBM 1946, Man. Dir. IBM (U.K.) Ltd. 1954-65; Dir. of Finance and Corporate Planning, The Plessey Co. 1966-68; mem. GLC 1970-73; Chair. International Computers (Holdings) Ltd. 1972-80, Infa Communications Ltd. 1985-. *Leisure interests:* tennis, gardening, skiing. *Address:* Hele Farm, North Bovey, Devon, TQ13 8RW, England (Home). *Telephone:* (0647) 40249 (Home).

HUEBNER, Robert Joseph; American virologist (retd.); b. 23 Feb. 1914, Cincinnati (Cheviot), Ohio; s. of Joseph and Philomena (Brickner) Huebner; m. 1st Grace Berdine Hoffman 1939, three s. six d.; m. 2nd Harriet Lee Streicher 1975; ed. Xavier Univ., Univ. of Cincinnati and St. Louis Univ. School of Medicine; Intern U.S. Public Health Service (U.S.P.H.S.) Hosp., (U.S. Coast Guard) 1942-43; Medical Officer, Coast Guard, Alaska Command 1943-44; Commissioned Officer, U.S.P.H.S. Lab. of Infectious Diseases, Nat. Microbiological Inst. 1944-49, Chief Section on Virus and Rickettsial Diseases 1949-56; Chief Lab. of Viral Diseases, Nat. Inst. of Allergy and Infectious Diseases 1956-68; Chief, Lab. of RNA Tumor Viruses, Nat. Cancer Inst. 1968-82; mem. N.A.S.; Scientist Emer. Nat. Insts. of Health 1982; Hon. LL.D. (Cincinnati) 1965; D.Sc. h.c. (Edgecliff Coll., Cincinnati) 1970; Hon. D.Sc. (Parma) 1970; Dr. h.c. (Leuven) 1973; Pasteur Medal 1965; Distinguished Service Medal, Public Health Service 1966; Howard Taylor Ricketts Award 1968; Nat. Medal of Science 1969; Kimble Methodology Award 1970; Rockefeller Public Service Award 1970; Guido Lenghi Award, Accad. Naz. dei Lincei, Rome 1971; Founders Award in Cancer Immunology, Cancer Research Inst., New York 1975. *Publications:* 425 articles in professional journals. *Address:* c/o National Cancer Institute, Bethesda, Md. 20205; 12100 Whippoorwill Lane, Rockville, Md. 20852, U.S.A. (Home). *Telephone:* 301-496-3301 (Office); 301-770-2565 (Home).

HUERTA DÍAZ, Vice-Admiral Ismael; Chilean naval officer and diplomatist; b. 13 Oct. 1916; s. of Rear-Adm. Ismael Huerta Lira and Lucrecia Díaz Vargas; m. Guillermina Wallace Dunsmore Aird 1942; two s. two

d.; ed. Sacred Heart School, Valparaíso, Naval Acad., Ecole Supérieure d'Electricité, Paris, Naval Polytechnic Acad., Chile; successive posts in Chilean Navy include Dir. of Armaments, Dir. of Instruction, Dir. of Scientific Investigation, Dir. of Naval Polytechnic Acad., Dir. of Shipyards, Dir.-Gen. of Army Services; Prof. of Electronics, Univ. de Concepción 1954, 1955, 1956; Prof. of Radionavigation, Univ. Católica de Valparaíso 1962-67; mem. Org. Cttee., Pacific Conf., Viña del Mar 1970, Pres. Centre of Pacific Studies 1970-72; Dir. Compañía de Acero del Pacífico (CAP) 1970, 1971, 1972; Pres. Nat. Transport Cttee. 1972; Minister of Public Works 1973, of Foreign Affairs 1973-74; Perm. Rep. to UN 1974-77; Rector Univ. Técnica Federico Santa María 1977-85; Chair. Bd. Empresa Marítima del Estado 1978-; mem. Coll. of Chilean Engineers. Inst. of Mechanical Engineers of Chile; Decoration of Pres. of the Repub. (Chile), Grand Officer Order of Léopold II (Belgium), Gran Cruz de la Orden del Libertador San Martín (Argentina), Gran Cruz Extraordinaria de la Orden Nacional al Mérito (Paraguay), Medall Kim-Kank (Repub. of Viet-Nam). *Publications:* The Role of the Armed Forces in Today's World 1968, Volveria a ser Marino (memoirs) 1988, and various technical articles. *Address:* c/o Universidad Técnica Federico Santa María, Casilla 110V, Valparaíso, Chile.

HUET, Philippe Emile Jean, D. en D. ET SC. POL.; French economist and civil servant; b. 17 March 1920, Paris; s. of Paul Huet and Marcelle Weill; m. Antoinette Ripert 1950; two s. three d.; ed. Ecole Saint-Louis de Gonzague, Sorbonne and Law Faculty, Paris, Ecole des Sciences Politiques, Paris; studied at Inspectorate-Gen. of Finance 1946; Adviser to Office of the Pres. of Council 1947-48, to Office of the Minister of Defence 1949, to Office of the Minister of Finance 1950-51; Head of Finance and Defence Budgets Div., NATO 1951-56; Dir. of Cabinet of Minister of Econ. and Financial Affairs 1956-57; Financial Counsellor to French Embassy, London 1957-62; Dir.-Gen. for Internal Trade and Prices, Ministry of Econ. and Finance 1962-68; Auditor Bank of France 1962-71; Dir.-Gen., Head of Mission for the rationalization of budget choices 1968-71; Insp.-Gen. of Finance 1971-; Consultant OECD Council 1972-; Pres. Man. Bd. SEITA 1974-80; Pres. Conseil de Surveillance CCCE (Caisse centrale de Coopération économique) 1981-84; Chair. Charbonnages de France 1983-85, Pres. Conseil d'Administration; Commdr., Légion d'honneur, Commdr. ordre nat. du Mérite; Commdr. du Mérite commercial et industriel, de l'Economie nationale; Chevalier du Mérite agricole, etc. *Publications:* La politique économique de la Grande-Bretagne depuis 1945 1969, L'expérience française de rationalisation des choix budgétaires 1973. *Leisure interests:* gardening, pottering about. *Address:* 10 avenue d'Eylau, 75116 Paris, France (Home). *Telephone:* 4553-29-84.

HUET, Pierre, D. en D.; French civil servant; b. 12 Nov. 1920, Paris; m. Catherine Viénot 1944; one s. two d.; ed. Paris Law Faculty and Ecole des Sciences Politiques; Special Asst., French Govt. Refugee Del. 1940, Asst. to Sec. of State, Ministry of Food 1944; Jr. mem. Conseil d'Etat, mem. Legal Cttee. of French Union 1946; Asst. to Sec.-Gen., Cttee. for European Econ. Co-operation 1947; Legal Adviser, OEEC 1948; Gen. Counsel, OEEC 1956; Dir.-Gen. European Nuclear Energy Agency 1958-64; Sec.-Gen. Council of State 1966-70; Councillor of State 1970; Chair. Bd., Assen. Technique pour l'Energie Nucléaire 1965-75; Pres. Centre d'Informatique Juridique 1971-75; Vice-Chair. European Atomic Forum (FORATOM) 1973-75; Chair. Comm. Interministérielle des radioéléments artificiels, Comm. Nationale des Sondages, Comm. Nationale des Réseaux Cablés, Comm. de la télématique, Comm. Consultative des services télématiques; mem. Comm. Nat. de la Communication et des Libertés (CNCL); Commdr., Ordre de Léopold (Belgium); Grosses Goldenes Ehrenzeichen für Verdienste (Austria), Officier, Légion d'honneur, Commdr., Ordre nat. du Mérite. *Address:* 56 rue Jacob, 75006 Paris, France.

HUG, Michel, PH.D.; French civil engineer; b. 30 May 1930, Courson; s. of René and Marcelle (née Quenee) Hug; m. Danielle Michaud; one s. two d.; ed. Ecole Polytechnique, Ecole Nationale des Ponts et Chaussées, State Univ. of Iowa; joined Electricité de France 1956, various positions at the Chatou Research and Test Centre 1956-66, Regional Man. (Southern Alps) 1967-68, Research and Devt. Man. 1969-72, Planning and Construction Man. 1972-82; Gen. Man. Charbonnages de France (French Coal Bd.) 1982-85, Dir. Gen. 1985-86; Prof. of Fluid Mechanics, Ecole Nationale des Ponts et Chaussées 1963-80; mem. Bd. Ecole Nationale Supérieure de l'Electronique et de ses applications 1975-; Chair. Bd. Ecole Nationale Supérieure d'Electrotechnique, d'Electronique, d'Informatique et d'Hydraulique de Toulouse 1980-; Chair. Bd. CdF Chimie 1985-; hon. mem. Int. Assoc. of Hydraulics Research; foreign mem. U.S. Nat. Acad. of Eng. 1979-; Lauréat de l'Institut (Prix des Laboratoires) 1964; Commdr. Ordre nat. du Merite 1980; Chevalier, Légion d'Honneur 1977; Palmes Académiques (Ministry of Educ.) 1979; Chevalier des Arts et Lettres 1981. *Publications:* Mecanique des fluides appliquée aux problèmes d'aménagement et d'énergétique 1975, Organiser le changement dans l'entreprise—une expérience à E.D.F. 1975. *Leisure interests:* tennis, shooting, swimming, flying.

HUGEL, Charles E., A.B.; American business executive; b. 9 Aug. 1928, Plainfield, N.J.; s. of Charles E. Hugel and Alice Durr; m. Cornelia Fischer 1953; two s.; ed. Lafayette Coll.; with N.J. Bell Telephone Co. 1952-66, 1970-73; Gen. Man. N.E. Region, Western Electric Co. Newark 1966-70;

Vice-Pres. Operations, New England Telephone Co., Boston 1974–75; Pres. Ohio Bell Telephone Co., Cleveland 1975–78; Exec. Vice-Pres. AT&T, Basking Ridge, N.J. 1978–82; Pres., C.O.O., Dir. Combustion Eng. Inc., Stamford, Conn. 1982–84, Pres., C.E.O. and Dir. 1984–; Chair. Bd. RJR Nabisco, Inc.; Dir. Primerica Corpn., Eaton Corpn., RJR Nabisco Inc., Pitney Bowes Inc. *Address:* Combustion Engineering Inc., 900 Long Ridge Road, P.O. Box 9308, Stamford, Conn. 06904, U.S.A.

HUGGINS, Charles B., M.D.; American professor of surgery and cancerologist; b. 22 Sept. 1901, Halifax, Canada; s. of Charles Edward and Bessie (Spencer) Huggins; m. Margaret Wellman 1927; one s. one d.; ed. Acadia and Harvard Univs.; houseman in surgery, Univ. of Mich. 1924–26, Instructor 1926–27; Instructor in Surgery, Univ. of Chicago 1927–29, Asst. Prof. 1929–33, Assoc. Prof. 1933–36, Prof. 1936–, William B. Ogden Distinguished Service Prof. 1962–; Dir. Ben May Laboratory for Cancer Research 1951–69; Chancellor, Acadia Univ. 1972–79; mem. N.A.S., American Philosophical Soc.; Hon. mem. Royal Soc. of Medicine 1956; Hon. Fellow, Royal Coll. of Surgeons, Edinburgh 1958, London 1959, American Coll. of Surgeons 1963, Royal Coll. Surgeons, Canada 1973; Orden Pour le Mérite (Federal Republic of Germany), Orden El Sol del Perú; numerous gold medals and prizes; Charles L. Mayer Award, Nat. Acad. of Sciences 1944, Francis Amory Prize 1948, Ferdinand Valentine Award 1962; Gold Medal Soc. Int. d'Urologie 1947, Walker Prize, Royal Coll. of Surgeons, England 1961, Albert Lasker Award for Clinical Research 1963, Gold Medal in Therapeutics, Worshipful Soc. of Apothecaries of London 1966, Gairdner Award, Toronto 1966, Nobel Prize for Medicine 1966, Bigelow Medal, Boston Surgical Soc. 1967, Distinguished Service Award, American Soc. of Abdominal Surgery 1972, Sesquicentennial Commemorative Award, Nat. Library of Medicine 1986. *Address:* Ben May Institute, University of Chicago, 5841 S. Maryland, Chicago, Illinois 60637, U.S.A.

HUGHES, Anthony Vernon, M.A.; Solomon Islands banking executive and civil servant; b. 29 Dec. 1936, England; s. of Henry Norman Hughes and Marjorie Hughes; m. 1st Carole Frances Robson 1961 (divorced 1970), one s.; m. 2nd Kuria Vaze Paia 1971, one s. one d. two adopted d.; ed. Queen Mary's Grammar School, Walsall, England, Pembroke Coll., Oxford and Bradford Univ.; Commr. of Lands, Registrar of Titles, Solomon Islands 1969–70, Head of Planning 1974–76, Perm. Sec. Ministry of Finance 1976–81, Gov. Cen. Bank 1982–; Devt. Sec., Gilbert and Ellice Islands 1971–73; Cross of Solomon Islands 1981. *Publications:* numerous articles on land tenure, econ. planning, devt. admin., foreign investment, expecially jt. ventures, with special emphasis on small countries. *Leisure interests:* working outside, squash, cricket, sailing. *Address:* P.O. Box 634, Honiara (Office); P.O. Box 486, Honiara, Solomon Islands (Home).

HUGHES, Rt. Hon. Cledwyn (see Cledwyn of Penrhos, Baron).

HUGHES, Sir Edward Stuart Reginald, Kt., C.B.E., F.R.A.C.S., F.R.C.S., F.A.C.S.; Australian professor of surgery; b. 4 July 1919, Victoria; s. of R. H. Hughes and A. Langford; m. Alison Clare Lelean 1944; two s. two d.; ed. Melbourne and Oxford Univs.; Sr. Consultant Surgeon, Royal Melbourne Hosp. 1963–83; Prof. of Surgery, Alfred Hosp., Monash Univ. 1972–84, Prof. Emer. 1984–; Dr. h.c. (Monash) 1986; mem. of Council, R.A.C.S. 1967–78, Pres. 1975–78; Chair. Menzies Foundation 1979–. *Publications:* several books on surgery and over 300 scientific articles. *Leisure interests:* writing, travelling. *Address:* 24 Somers Avenue, Malvern, Victoria 3144, Australia. *Telephone:* 20.7688.

HUGHES, H. Richard; British architect; b. 4 July 1926, London; s. of Major Henry and Olive (née Curtis) Hughes; m. Anne Hill 1951; one s. two d.; ed. Kenton Coll., Nairobi, Kenya, Hilton Coll., Natal, S.A., Architectural Assocn. School of Architecture, London; Corporal, Kenya Regt., attached to Royal Engineers 1944–46; Asst. Architect Kenya and Uganda 1950–51; Architect, Hartford, Conn., U.S.A. 1953–55, Nairobi, Kenya 1955–57; Prin. Richard Hughes and Partners 1957–87; Chair. Kenya Branch, Capricorn Africa Soc. 1958–61, Environment Liaison Cen. 1976–78, Lamu Soc. 1977–79; UN Environment Programme (UNEP) Consultant on Human Settlements Tech. 1978; UN Cen. for Human Settlements Consultant on building materials, Construction tech. in developing countries 1979; Ed., Fireball Int. 1986; mem. Exec. Cttee., Friends of the Elderly, London 1987; trustee, Zebra Trust, London 1988; Voluntary Guide, The Tate Gallery, London 1988. *Publications:* joint author (with Graham Searle) Habitat Handbook 1982 and many contribs. to books on architecture and articles in New Commonwealth, Architectural Review and Architects Journal. *Leisure interests:* collecting modern art, dinghy sailing. *Address:* 47 Chiswick Quay, London, W4 3UR, England. *Telephone:* 01-995-3109.

HUGHES, James Ernest, PH.D., A.R.S.M., D.I.C., F.I.M.M., F.ENG., F.I.M., F.R.S.A.; British metallurgist and business executive; b. 3 Nov. 1927, London; m. Hazel Longuet-Layton; three d.; ed. Spring Grove School, Imperial Coll., London and Harvard Business School; research scientist, London Univ. 1949–52; Chief Metallurgist, Siemens, Edison, Swan 1962; Dir. Johnson Matthey PLC 1973, Man. Dir. and Chief Exec. 1983–85; Visiting Prof. Univ. of Surrey 1974–80; Pres. Inst. of Metals 1972–73, Metals Soc. 1981–82, Inst. of Metallurgists 1982–83; Bessemer Medal, Imperial Coll.; Glorney Award; Matthey Prize. *Publications:* numerous papers on metallurgy. *Leisure interests:* antiques, music, clocks, recuperating. *Address:* Lower Farm, Rimpton, near Yeovil, Somerset, England.

HUGHES, John Lawrence, B.A.; American publisher; b. 13 March 1925, New York; s. of John C. Hughes and Margaret Kelly; m. Rose M. Pitman 1947; three s. one d.; ed. Yale Univ.; reporter, Nassau Review Star, Rockville Centre, Long Island, N.Y. 1949; Asst. Sr. Ed., Pocket Books, Inc. New York 1949–59; Vice-Pres. Washington Square Press 1958; Sr. Ed., Vice-Pres., Dir. William Morrow & Co. 1960–65, Pres. and C.E.O. 1965–85; Pres. The Hearst Trade Book Group 1985–87, Chair. of Bd. 1988–; Trustee, Yale Univ. Press, Pierpont Morgan Library; mem. Bd. Assocn. of American Publishers; Chair. 1987 Nat. Book Awards. *Leisure interest:* golf. *Address:* 105 Madison Avenue, New York, N.Y. 10016 (Office); P.O. Box 430, Southport, Conn. 06490, U.S.A. (Home). *Telephone:* 212-889-3050 (Office); 203-259-8957 (Home).

HUGHES, Leslie Ernest, M.D., B.S., D.S., F.R.C.S., F.R.A.C.S.; Australian professor of surgery; b. 12 Aug. 1932, Parramatta; s. of Charles J. Hughes and Vera D. (Laines) Hughes; m. Marian Castle 1955; two s. two d.; ed. Parramatta High School and Univ. of Sydney; surgical trainee, Sydney 1955–59; Registrar, Derby and London, U.K. 1959–61; British Empire Cancer Research Campaign Research Fellow, King's College Hospital, London 1962–63; Reader in Surgery, Univ. of Queensland 1964–71; Eleanor Roosevelt Int. Scholar, Roswell Park Memorial Inst., Buffalo, New York 1969–71; Prof. of Surgery, Univ. of Wales Coll. of Medicine, Cardiff 1971–; Visiting Prof. Univs. of Queensland, Allahabad, Sydney, Witwatersrand, Cairo, Melbourne, Lund, Albany, New York and N.S.W. *Publications:* Benign Disorders and Diseases of the Breast 1989; more than 100 papers and book chapters dealing mainly with tumour immunology, disease of the breast, inflammatory bowel disease, surgical oncology, surgical pathology and wound healing. *Address:* Department of Surgery, University Hospital of Wales, Heath Park, Cardiff, CF4 4XN, Wales. *Telephone:* (0222) 755944 (Ext. 2749).

HUGHES, Sean Patrick Francis, M.S., F.R.C.S., F.R.C.S.(E.), F.R.C.S.I.; British orthopaedic surgeon; b. 2 Dec. 1941, Farnham, Surrey; s. of Patrick J. Hughes and Kathleen E. Hughes; m. Felicity M. Anderson 1971; one s. two d.; ed. Downside School and St. Mary's Hosp. Medical School, Univ. of London; Asst. Lecturer in Anatomy, St. Mary's Hosp. Medical School 1969; Research Fellow, Mayo Clinic, U.S.A. 1975; Sr. Registrar in Orthopaedics, Middlesex Hosp. London 1977; Sr. Lecturer in Orthopaedics, Royal Postgraduate Medical School, London 1979; Prof. of Orthopaedic Surgery, Univ. of Edinburgh 1979–. *Publications:* several books and papers on orthopaedics. *Leisure interests:* sailing, golf, lying in the sun. *Address:* Princess Margaret Rose Orthopaedic Hospital, Fairmilehead, Edinburgh, EH10 7ED, Scotland. *Telephone:* 031-445 4123.

HUGHES, Ted, O.B.E.; British poet; b. 17 Aug. 1930, Mytholmroyd, W. Yorkshire; s. of William Henry and Edith Farrar Hughes; m. 1st Sylvia Plath (died 1963), one s. one d.; m. 2nd Carole Orchard 1970; ed. Cambridge Univ.; Guinness Poetry Award 1958, John Simon Guggenheim Fellow 1959, Somerset Maugham Award 1960, Int. Poetry Prize, City of Florence 1969, Premio Internazionale Taormina 1973, Queen's Medal for Poetry 1974, Signal Award 1978, Heinemann Award (shared) 1980; Poet Laureate 1984–; Hon. Fellow Pembroke Coll., Cambridge 1986; Dr. h.c. (Exeter) 1982, (Open Univ.) 1983, (Bradford) 1984; Hon. D.Litt. (Cambridge) 1986; Guardian Children's Fiction Award 1985. *Publications:* The Hawk in the Rain 1957, Lupercal 1960, Meet My Folks 1961, Selected Poems: Thom Gunn and Ted Hughes 1962, How the Whale Became 1963, The Earth Owl and Other Moon People 1963, Nessie the Mannerless Monster, Selected Poems of Keigh Douglas (Ed.) 1964, Wodwo 1967, Poetry in the Making 1967, The Iron Man 1968, Crow 1970, A Few Crows 1970, Crow Wakes 1970, Shakespeare's Poem 1971, Eat Crow 1971, Prometheus on His Crag 1973, Spring, Summer, Autumn, Winter 1974, Cave Birds 1976, Season Songs 1976, Earth-Moon 1976, Gaudete 1977, Orts 1978, Moortown Elegies 1978, Remains of Elmet 1978, Cave Birds 1978, Moon-Bells and other poems 1978, Adam and the Sacred Nine 1979, Moortown 1979, 12 poems in Michael Morpurgo's All Around the Year 1979, Henry Williamson—A Tribute 1979, Sylvia Plath: Collected Poems (Ed.) 1981, Selected Poems 1957–81 1982, Under the North Star 1981, The Rattle Bag (Ed. with Seamus Heaney) 1983, River 1983, What is the Truth? 1984, Ffangs the Vampire Bat and the Kiss of Truth 1986, Flowers and Insects 1987, Tales of the Early World 1988. *Address:* c/o Faber & Faber, 3 Queen Square, London, W.C.1, England.

HUI YUYU; Chinese politician; b. 1906, Shanxi Prov.; Dir. N. Jiangsu Admin. Office –1952; Vice-Chair. Cttee. for Harnessing the Huai River 1950; mem. People's Council, Jiangsu 1952; Mayor, Nanjing 1954–55; Sec. Municipal CCP Cttee., Nanjing 1954–55; Gov. Jiangsu Prov. 1955–Cultural Revolution; Sec. CCP Cttee., Jiangsu 1955–Cultural Revolution; Vice-Chair. Prov. Revolutionary Cttee. Jiangsu 1977–79; mem. Standing Cttee., CCP Cttee. 1978–79, Sec. 1979–; Chair. Prov. CPPCC Cttee., Jiangsu 1979; mem. Cttee. to Examine Proposals, 2nd Session, 5th NPC 1979; Gov. Jiangsu 1979–82; mem. Cen. Advisory Comm. 1982–. *Address:* Office of the Governor, Jiangsu, People's Republic of China.

HUIZENGA, John R., PH.D.; American nuclear chemist and educator; b. 21 April 1921, Fulton, Ill.; s. of Harry M. and Josie B. (Brands) Huizenga; m. Dorothy J. Koeze 1946; two d. two s.; ed. Calvin Coll., Grand Rapids, Mich. and Univ. of Illinois, Urbana, Ill.; Lab. Supervisor, Manhattan Wartime Project, Oak Ridge 1944–46; Assoc. Scientist, Argonne Nat. Lab.,

Chicago 1949-57, Sr. Scientist 1958-67; Prof of Chem. and Physics Univ. of Rochester, New York 1967-78, Tracy H. Harris Prof. of Chem. and Physics 1978-, Chair. Dept. of Chem. 1983-88; Fulbright Fellow, Netherlands 1954-55; Guggenheim Fellow, Paris 1964-65, Berkeley, Munich and Copenhagen 1973-74; E. O. Lawrence Award, Atomic Energy Comm. 1966, Award for Nuclear Application in Chem., A.C.S. 1975; mem. N.A.S., A.C.S.; Fellow American Physical Soc., A.A.A.S. *Publications:* Nuclear Fission (with R. Vandenbosch) 1973, Damped Nuclear Reactions (with W. U. Schröder), Treatise on Heavy-Ion Science, Vol. 2 1984; 250 articles in professional journals. *Leisure interests:* tennis, golf. *Address:* Department of Chemistry, University of Rochester, N.Y. 14627, U.S.A. *Telephone:* (716) 275-4231.

HUJIO, Masayuki; Japanese politician; b. 1 Jan. 1917, Tokyo; ed. Sophia Univ., Tokyo; with newspaper Yomiuri Shimbun 1941; mem. House of Reps. 1963-; Parl. Vice-Minister of Int. Trade and Industry 1968-69, of Construction 1971-72; Chair. House of Reps. Standing Cttee. on Cabinet 1975-76, on Educ. 1976-77; Vice-Chair. Liberal-Democratic Party (LDP) Policy Affairs Research Council 1979; Minister of Labour July 1980-81. *Address:* 7, 2-chome, Hirakawacho, Chiyoda-ku, Tokyo, Japan.

HULCE, Jerry Ted (Josh), B.A., J.D.; American business executive; b. 2 April 1942, Chelsea, Mich.; s. of Elwin Leigh Hulce and Thelma U. Hulce; m. Carol Ann Jones 1964; one d.; ed. Northwestern Univ. and Univ. of Michigan Law School; lawyer with Pepper, Hamilton and Scheetz, Philadelphia 1967-72; lawyer, Manville Corpn. 1972-76, Manufacturing Industrial Engineer 1976, Asst. to Chair. and Sr. Dir. Strategic Planning 1976-78, Vice-Pres. Purchasing 1978-80, Gen. Man. Industrial Specification 1980-82, Sr. Vice-Pres. 1982-84, Pres. 1984-86; Chair. Freshfields Capital Ltd. 1986-. *Address:* Freshfields Capital Ltd., Republic Plaza, Suite 3400, Denver, Colo. 80202, U.S.A. *Telephone:* (303) 573-2888.

HULCE, Tom; American actor; b. White Water, Wis.; ed. N. Carolina School of Arts. *Films:* September 30th 1955, National Lampoon's Animal House, Those Lips Those Eyes, Amadeus 1985, Echo Park 1985, Slam Dance 1987, Nicky and Gino, The Black Rainbow 1989, Parenthood 1989. *TV includes:* Emily Emily, St. Elsewhere.

HULL, John Folliott Charles, M.A.; British banker; b. 21 Oct. 1925, London; s. of Sir Hubert and Lady Hull; m. Rosemarie Waring 1951; one s. three d.; ed. Downside, Jesus Coll., Cambridge; Cap. Royal Artillery 1944-48, serving with Royal Indian Artillery; called to Bar, Inner Temple 1952; Dir. Schroders PLC 1969-72, 1974-85, Deputy Chair. 1977-85; J. Henry Schroder Wagg & Co. Ltd. 1957-72, 1974-85, Dir. 1961-72, Deputy Chair. 1974-77, Chair. 1977-83, Dir. 1984-85; Dir.-Gen. City Panel on Take-overs and Mergers 1972-74, Deputy Chair. 1987-; Deputy Chair. Land Securities PLC 1976-; Dir. Lucas Industries PLC 1975-, Legal & Gen. Group PLC 1976-; Chair. Bank of England's City Co. Law Cttee. 1976-78; mem. Council Manchester Business School 1974-86, Lay mem. of the Council of the Stock Exchange 1983-84. *Leisure interests:* reading political history and 19th-century novelists. *Address:* J. Henry Schroder Wagg & Co. Ltd., 120 Cheapside, London, EC2V 6DS (Office); 33 Edwardes Square, London, W8 6HH, England (Home). *Telephone:* 01-382 6000 (Office); 01-603 0715 (Home).

HULL, Field Marshal Sir Richard Amyatt, K.G., G.C.B., D.S.O., LL.D.; British army officer; b. 7 May 1907, Cosham, Hants; s. of late Major-Gen. Sir Amyatt Hull, K.C.B.; m. Antoinette de Rougemont 1934; one s. two d.; ed. Charterhouse and Trinity Coll., Cambridge; joined 17th/21st Lancers 1928; commanded 17th/21st Lancers 1941, 12th Infantry Brigade 1943, 26th Armoured Brigade 1943, 1st Armoured Div. 1944, 5th Infantry Div. 1945; Commdt. Staff Coll., Camberley 1946-48; Dir. of Staff Duties, War Office 1948-50; Chief Army Instructor, Imperial Defence Coll. 1950-52; Chief of Staff, GHQ, Middle East Land Forces 1952-54; GOC British Troops in Egypt 1954-56; Deputy Chief of Imperial Gen. Staff (C.I.G.S.) 1956-58; C.-in-C. Far East Land Forces 1958-61; C.I.G.S. 1961-65; ADC (Gen.) to the Queen, 1961-64; Chief of Defence Staff 1965-67; Col. Commdt. R.A.C. 1968-71; Pres. Army Benevolent Fund 1968-71; Constable H.M. Tower of London 1970-75; Deputy Lieut., Devon 1973, Lord Lieut. 1978-82; Hon. LL.D. (Exeter) 1965. *Leisure interest:* fishing. *Address:* Beacon Downe, Pinhoe, Nr. Exeter, Devon, England.

HULME, Keri; New Zealand novelist; b. 1947, Christchurch; worked as tobacco picker, fish and chip cook, TV dir. and woollen mill worker and studied law, before becoming full-time writer 1972. *Publications:* The Bone People 1984, The Windeater 1987; awarded Booker McConnell Prize for Fiction, U.K. 1985. *Address:* c/o Hodder & Stoughton Ltd., 47 Bedford Square, London, W.C.1, England.

HULSE, Frederick Seymour, PH.D.; American professor of anthropology; b. 11 Feb. 1906, New York; s. of Hiram R. Hulse and Frances B. Seymour; m. Leonie R. Mills 1934 (died 1982); two s.; ed. Harvard Coll. and Univ.; Instructor in Anthropology, Washington Univ. 1936-37, Asst. Prof. 1948-49, Assoc. Prof. 1949-58; WPA Supervisor in Georgia 1938-42; Officer of Strategic Services 1942-45; Asst. Prof. of Anthropology, Colgate Univ. 1946-48; Prof. Arizona Univ. 1958-76, Prof. Emer. 1976-; Pres. American Assocn. of Physical Anthropologists 1967-69; mem. N.A.S. 1974; D. Hum. Litt. (Univ. of Arizona) 1988. *Publications:* The Human Species 1963, 1971; Ed. Man and Nature 1975. *Leisure interests:* reading, travel, photography.

Address: 4067 Crest Road, Pebble Beach, Calif. 93953, U.S.A. *Telephone:* (408) 625-6327.

HULST, Hendrik Christoffel van de, PH.D.; Netherlands astronomer; b. 19 Nov. 1918, Utrecht; m. Wilhelmina Mengerink 1946; two s. two d.; ed. Utrecht Univ.; Post-Doctoral Fellow Chicago Univ. 1946-48; lecturer in Astronomy, Leiden Univ. 1948-52, Prof. of Astronomy 1952-84; Pres. Comm. 1934 (Interstellar Matter) Int. Astronomical Union 1952-58, Nederland Astronomen Club 1953-56, Cttee. on Space Research (COSPAR) 1958-62; Chair. Netherlands Comm. for Geophysical and Space Research 1960-83; Vice-Chair. European Space Research Org. (ESRO) 1960-65, Chair. 1968-70; mem. Royal Neths. Acad. of Sciences; Eddington Medal, Royal Astronomical Soc. (U.K.) 1955, Draper Medal, Nat. Acad. of Sciences (U.S.A.) 1956, Rumford Medal, Royal Soc. (U.K.) 1964, Bruce Medal of the Astronomical Soc. of the Pacific 1978. *Publications:* A Course of Radio Astronomy 1951, Phaenomenologie en Natuurwetenschap (with C. A. van Peursen) 1953, Light Scattering by Small Particles 1957, Multiple Light Scattering 1980; numerous articles and papers, particularly on interstellar matter. *Address:* Sterrewacht Leiden, Huygens Laboratorium, P.O. Box 9513, 2300 RA Leiden; Sterrewacht 8, Leiden, Netherlands. *Telephone:* 071-131192 (Home).

HULTERSTRÖM, Sven Åke; Swedish politician; b. 14 May 1938, Mölndal; s. of Anna and Rickard Hulterström; m. Birgitta Reidun 1958; three s.; ed. secondary school; Ombudsman in Gothenburg Dist. SSU (Social Democratic Youth of Sweden) 1958-61; Sec. for Educ. and Sec. of Nat. Asscn. of SSU 1961-64; Ombudsman in local Labour Community, Gothenburg 1964-70; Municipal Commr., Gothenburg 1971-85, Chair. City Exec. Bd. 1976-79, 1982-85, mem. Municipal Council 1967-85; Minister of Transport and Communications 1985-; Chair. Gothenburg Labour Community 1975-; mem. Exec. Cttee. Swedish Social-Democratic Party 1975-. *Address:* Ministry of Transport and Communications, S 103 33 Stockholm, Sweden. *Telephone:* (00946-8) 763 3601.

HULTIN, Sven Olof, SC.D.; Finnish business executive; b. 16 June 1920, Kittilä; s. of Erik and Agnes Hultin; m. Agnes C. Ekerodde 1946; one s. one d.; ed. Åbo Univ.; Instructor and Lecturer, Åbo Univ. 1948-51; Project Eng., EKONO Oy 1951-53, Head of Dept. 1954-59, Exec. Vice-Pres. 1960-63, Pres. 1964-84, Chair. and C.E.O. EKONO Inc., U.S.A. 1974-85; Vice-Chair. Gruneko AG, Basle, Switzerland 1974-; Partner Nestor-Partners Oy 1985-; Foreign mem. Royal Swedish Acad. of Eng. Sciences 1971-; Chair. Int. Exec. Council, World Energy Conf. 1980-86; Hon. Chair. 1986-; Trustee Åbo Foundation 1970-; Commdr., Finnish Order of Lion; Finnish Liberty Cross; Merit Cross of Finnish Sports in Gold; war medals. *Publications:* about 90 publications in technical journals covering subjects of wood pulping, chemicals recovery and effluent treatment, hydroelectric, steam-electric and nuclear power economy. *Leisure interests:* yachting, slalom. *Address:* Tegelbacken 29, 00330 Helsinki 33, Finland. *Telephone:* 482 760.

HUMAIDAN, Ali; United Arab Emirates diplomatist; b. 20 Sept. 1931, Bahrain; ed. univs. of Baghdad and Paris; Deputy Rep. of Kuwait to UNESCO 1967-69; Prof. of Political Science, Univ. of Kuwait 1969-70; Legal Adviser to the Abu Dhabi Govt. 1971-72; Perm. Rep. of the United Arab Emirates to UN 1972-81; Chargé d'affaires a.i., Oman 1981. *Address:* c/o Ministry of Foreign Affairs, United Arab Emirates.

HUMAN, Cornelis J. F.; South African businessman; b. 6 Oct. 1922, Reitz, O.F.S.; s. of Petrus Gerhardus and Anna Susanna van Deventer Human; m. Elsie Francina Stiglingh 1949; two s. one d.; ed. Reitz High School and Stellenbosch Univ.; joined Federale Volksbeleggings Beperk (The Federale Group) 1947, Gen. Man. 1959-66, Vice-Chair. and Man. Dir. 1966-82; Chair. 1982-; Dir. Federale Electronics Ltd., SATV Manufacturing Co. Ltd., Siemens Ltd., Bankorp, Sentrachem, Fedfood Ltd., Fedlec Ltd.; mem. Atomic Energy Comm.; Chair. Nat. Botanic Gardens; Trustee South Africa Nature Foundation, South African Foundation and Urban Foundation; Councillor, Univ. of Stellenbosch; Hon. D.Comm. (Univ. of O.F.S.) 1979. *Leisure interests:* gardening, golf. *Address:* Central Avenue 81, Illovo, Johannesburg, South Africa (Home).

HUMBLET, Antoine; Belgian politician; b. 28 Dec. 1922, Serinchamps; m.; nine c.; ed. Bagstogne, Namur and Catholic Univ. of Louvain; founder of forestry and timber enterprise, Haversin; Founder Union des Exploitants Forestiers et Scieurs du Sud-Est de la Belgique, Centre Belge du Bois; Local Councillor, Alderman, Serinchamps 1952-58; Councillor, Namur 1961-68; Founder Econ. Office of Namur Prov. 1961; mem. CERW, Vice-Pres. 1971; mem. Chamber of Reps. 1968-71, Senate 1971-; Sec. of State for Budget 1973-74; Minister of Nat. Educ., French Sector 1974-77, of Agric. and the Middle Classes 1977-79, of Walloon Affairs 1979; Christian Social Party. *Address:* c/o Ministry of Walloon Affairs, Brussels, Belgium.

HUME, H.E. Cardinal (George) Basil, M.A. (Oxon.), S.T.L. (Fribourg); British ecclesiastic; b. 2 March 1923, Newcastle upon Tyne; s. of the late Sir William and Lady Hume; ed. Ampleforth Coll., York, St. Benet's Coll., Oxford, and Fribourg Univ., Switzerland; ordained as a Catholic priest 1950; Sr. Master in Modern Languages, Ampleforth Coll., York 1952-63; Housemaster of St. Bede's 1955-63; Prof. of Dogmatic Theology at Ampleforth Abbey 1955-63; Magister Scholarum, English Benedictine Congregation 1957-63; Abbot of Ampleforth 1963-76; Archbishop of Westminster

March 1976-; cr. Cardinal May 1976; Secr. for Christian Unity, Sacred Congregation for Religious; Pres. Bishops' Conf. of England and Wales 1979-, Council of European Bishops' Confs. 1979-87; mem. Council of Secr. of Int. Synod of Bishops 1978-; mem. Jt. Comm. of Roman Catholic and Orthodox Churches 1980-; Hon. D.D. (Newcastle) 1979, (Cambridge) 1979, (London) 1980, (Oxford) 1981, (York) 1982, (Kent) 1983, (Hull) 1989; Dr. h.c. (Durham) 1987, (San Anselmo, Rome) 1987; Hon. Freeman of City of Newcastle 1980, City of London 1981. *Publications:* Searching for God 1977, In Praise of Benedict 1981, To be a Pilgrim 1984, Towards A Civilization of Love 1988. *Leisure interest:* angling. *Address:* Archbishop's House, Westminster, London, S.W.1, England. *Telephone:* 01-834 4717.

HUME, John, M.A.; Irish politician and fmr. teacher; b. 18 Jan. 1937, Londonderry, N. Ireland; s. of Samuel and Anne (née Doherty) Hume; m. Patricia Hone 1960; two s. three d.; ed. St. Colomb's Coll., Londonderry, St. Patrick's Coll., Maynooth, Nat. Univ. of Ireland; Research Fellow, Trinity Coll., Assoc. Fellow, Centre for Int. Affairs, Harvard; Founder mem. Credit Union in N. Ireland, Pres. 1964-68; Non-violent Civil Rights leader 1968-69; rep. Londonderry in Northern Ireland Parl. 1969-72, in N. Ireland Assembly 1972-73; Minister of Commerce, Powersharing Exec. 1974; rep. Londonderry in N. Ireland Convention 1975-76; elected to European Parl. June 1979-; Leader, Social Democratic and Labour Party (SDLP) Dec. 1979-; mem. N. Ireland Ass. 1982-; M.P. for Foyle 1983-; mem. SDLP New Ireland Forum 1983-84, Irish Transport and General Workers Union, Bureau of European Parliament Socialist 1979-, Regional Policy and Regional Planning Cttee., EEC, A.C.P.-EEC Joint Ass., Socialist Co.-Chair. Intergroup on Ministry of Cultures and Languages; Dr. h.c. (Massachusetts) 1985; Sponsor, Irish Anti-Apartheid Movement; Dr. h.c. (Catholic Univ. of America) 1986, (St. Joseph's Univ., Phila.) 1986; Hon. Dr. (Univ. of Mass., Catholic Univ. of America, Wash. D.C., St. Joseph's Univ., Phila., Tusculum Coll., Tenn.). *Address:* 6 West End Park, Derry, BT48 9JF, (Home); 5 Bayview Terrace, Derry, BT48 7EE, Northern Ireland (Office). *Telephone:* 0504-265340 (Office); 363423 (Home).

HUMMEL, Arthur William, Jr., M.A.; American diplomatist; b. 1 June 1920, Fenzhou (Fenchow), China; s. of Arthur William Hummel and Ruth Emily Bookwalter; m. Betty L. Fristenberger 1951; two s.; ed. Antioch Coll., Coll. of Chinese Studies, Beijing, Univ. of Chicago: English teacher Fu Jen Middle School, Beijing 1941; interned by Japanese 1941-44, escaped 1944; mem. Chinese guerrilla unit 1944-45; Liaison Officer UNRRA, Tianjin, China 1945-46; Staff Lecturer, United Service to China, New York 1946-47; Intelligence Analyst Officer, Naval Intelligence 1950; Foreign Affairs Officer, Dept. of State 1950-52; Consul, Deputy Public Affairs Officer, Hong Kong 1952, Public Affairs Officer 1953-55; Attaché, Deputy Public Affairs Officer, U.S. Embassy, Tokyo 1955-57; Attaché, Public Affairs Officer, Rangoon, Burma 1957-60; Nat. War Coll. 1960-61; Deputy Dir. Voice of America 1961-63; Deputy Asst. Sec. of State for Cultural and Educational Affairs 1963-65; Deputy Chief of Mission, Taipei, Taiwan 1965-68; Amb. to Burma 1968-71; Deputy Asst. Sec. of State for Far Eastern and Pacific Affairs 1971-75; Amb. to Ethiopia 1975-76; Asst. Sec. of State for Far Eastern and Pacific Affairs 1976-77; Amb. to Pakistan 1977-81, to People's Repub. of China 1981-85; Arthur S. Fleming Award 1959, Sec. of State's Distinguished Honor Award 1985; mem. Far Eastern Assen. *Address:* 4923 Essex Avenue, Chevy Chase, Md. 20815, U.S.A.

HUMO, Avdo; Yugoslav politician; b. 1914; ed. Mostar and Belgrade Univ.; mem. Fed. Exec. Council and fmr. Chair. Cttee. Nat. Devt. Plan of Fed. Exec. Council; Chair. Cttee. for Econ. Relations with Foreign Countries of Fed. Exec. Council 1962-; mem. Parl., Cen. Cttee. Yugoslav League of Communists, Fed. Cttee. for Nuclear Energy 1960-; Maj.-Gen. of Reserve; Chair. of Fed. Council for Co-ordination of Scientific Activities 1963-67; mem. of Presidency Yugoslav League of Communists 1967-69; mem. of Council of Fed. Commission of Presidency Yugoslav League of Communists for Culture 1969-; mem. of Council of Fed. Commission of Presidency Yugoslav League of Communists for Culture 1969-; mem. of Conference Yugoslav League of Communists 1969-; 1941 Partisan Commemoration Medal, Orders of Nat. Hero, Nat. Liberation, Meritorious Service to the People, 1st Class, Bravery. *Address:* Council of Federation, Bulevar Lenjina 2, Novi Beograd, Yugoslavia. *Telephone:* 332-590.

HUMPHREY, Gordon John; American politician; b. 9 Oct. 1940, Bristol, Conn.; s. of Gordon and Regina Humphrey; m. Patricia Green 1978; one s.; ed. George Washington Univ. and Univ. of Md.; served, U.S.A.F. 1958-62; ferry pilot 1964-65; with Universal Air Transport Co. Detroit 1966-67; pilot, Allegheny Airlines 1967-78; Senator from New Hampshire 1979-; Republican. *Address:* U.S. Senate, 531 Hart Senate Building, Washington, D.C. 20510, U.S.A.

HUMPHREY, John Peters, O.C., PH.D.; Canadian international official and university professor; b. 30 April 1905, Hampton, New Brunswick; s. of Frank M. Humphrey and Nellie Peters; m. 1st Jeanne Godreau 1929, 2nd Margaret Kunstler 1981; ed. Rothesay Coll., Mount Allison Univ., McGill Univ. and Univ. de Paris; called to Montreal Bar 1929, practised law with Wainwright, Elder & McDougall 1930-36; lecturer in Roman Law, McGill Univ. 1936, Sec. of Law Faculty 1937-46, Gale Prof. of Roman Law and Dean of Law Faculty 1946, Prof. of Law and Political Science 1966-71; Visiting Prof., Law Faculty, Univ. of Toronto 1971-72, Univ. of Western Ont. 1981-82; Inaugural Lecturer John Humphrey Lectureship on Human

Rights, McGill Univ. 1988; Carnegie Fellow in Int. Law, Paris 1936-37; Dir. Div. of Human Rights, UN Secr. 1946-66; Exec. Sec. UN Conf. on Freedom of Information 1948, Refugees 1951, Status of Stateless Persons 1954, Slavery Conf. 1956; Prin. Sec. UN Fact-Finding Mission to S. Viet-Nam 1963; Nat. Pres. UN Assen. in Canada 1968-70, Hon. Vice-Pres. 1967-68, Hon. Pres. Montreal Branch 1966-68, Pres. 1945-46; mem. UN Sub-Comm. on Prevention of Discrimination and Protection of Minorities 1966, Chair. 1970; Rapporteur, Cttee. on Human Rights, Int. Law Assen. 1966-78; Pres. Canadian Comm., Int. Year for Human Rights 1968; mem. and past Vice-Pres. Int. Comm. of Jurists; mem. Royal Comm. on Status of Women in Canada, Canadian Council of Int. Law, Int. Law Assen., Canadian Inst. of Int. Affairs; mem. Bd. of Dirs. Int. League for Human Rights; Pres. Emer. Canadian Foundation for Human Rights, Amnesty Int. (Canada) 1973-76; mem. Conseil d'Admin. Soc. Québecoise de Droit Int.; Vice-Pres. UNESCO Conf. on Human Rights Teaching, Malta 1987; mem. Bd. of Trustees, Atwater Inst.; mem. Int. Comm. of Inquiry into the 1932-33 Famine in Ukraine; Rapporteur, Conf. on Human Rights and the Protection of Refugees under Int. Law, Montreal 1987; Hon. LL.D. (Carleton) 1968, Hon. Dr. Soc. Sciences (Ottawa) 1966, Hon. LL.D. (St. Thomas) 1971, (Dalhousie) 1975, (McGill) 1976, Dr. h.c. (Univ. of Algiers) 1944, Hon. D.C.L. (Mount Allison) 1977, (Saint Mary's) 1984, Hon. D.Litt. (Acadia) 1980; Officer, Nat. Order of Quebec 1985; World Jewish Congress Citation 1966, World Legal Scholar Award, World Peace Through Law Center 1973, John Read Medal, Canadian Council of Int. Law 1973, World Federalists of Canada Peace Award 1981, Nova Scotia Human Rights Award 1982, Saul Hayes Human Rights Award 1983, UN Award for outstanding achievements in the field of Human Rights 1988. *Publications:* The Inter-American System: A Canadian View 1942, Human Rights and the United Nations: A Great Adventure 1983 and articles in American, British and Canadian periodicals on international, political and legal subjects. *Address:* Law Faculty, McGill Univ., 3644 Peel Street, Montreal H3A 1W9; 30 Thurlow Road, Hampstead, P.Q., H3X 3G6, Canada. *Telephone:* (514) 398-6611 (Office); 484-0131 (Home).

HUMPHREYS, David Colin, C.M.G., M.A. (CANTAB.); British civil servant (retd.); b. 23 April 1925, Sunningdale, Berks.; s. of Charles Roland L. and Joan Bethia (née Bowie) Humphreys; m. Jill Allison Cranmer 1952; two s. one d.; ed. Eton Coll. (King's Scholar), King's Coll., Cambridge; British Army 1943-46; joined Air Ministry 1949; Private Sec. to Sec. of State for Air 1958; Counsellor U.K. Del., NATO 1960; Asst. Sec. Air Force Dept., London 1963; Imperial Defence Coll. 1970; Civilian Dir. Defence Policy Staff 1971; Asst. Sec.-Gen. Defence Planning and Policy, NATO 1972-76; Asst. Under-Sec. (Naval Staff) Ministry of Defence 1977-78; Deputy Under-Sec. of State (Air) 1979-84; Dir. of Devt. Royal Inst. of Int. Affairs 1985-86. *Address:* Rivendell, North Drive, Virginia Water, Surrey, GU25 4NQ, England. *Telephone:* Wentworth 2130.

HUMPHREYS, James Charles, B.COM., M.SC.; Australian diplomatist; b. 6 Oct. 1934, Melbourne; s. of James Thomas and Mary Charlotte Humphreys; m. Diane May Dummett 1962; two d.; ed. Scotch Coll., Melbourne, Univs. of Melbourne and London; with Dept. of Trade and Customs 1951-62; Dept. of Treasury 1963-71; Counsellor (Financial), Tokyo 1972-74; Dept. of Foreign Affairs, Canberra 1974-78; Amb. to Denmark 1978-80, to OECD Paris 1980-83; First Asst. Sec. (Econ.) Dept. of Foreign Affairs, Canberra 1984-86; First Asst. Sec., Dept. of Foreign Affairs and Trade, Canberra 1987-. *Leisure interests:* sailing, tennis, reading, music. *Address:* Department of Foreign Affairs and Trade, Canberra 2600, A.C.T., Australia.

HUMPHREYS, Sir Olliver William, Kt., C.B.E., B.SC., F.INST.P., C.ENG., F.I.E.E., F.R.AE.S.; British physicist; b. 4 Sept. 1902, London; s. of late Rev. J. Willis Humphreys; m. Muriel Mary Hawkins 1933 (died March 1985); ed. Caterham School, Univ. Coll., London Univ.; joined scientific staff of the G.E.C. Research Labs. 1925; Dir. G.E.C. Research Labs. 1949-61; Dir. G.E.C. 1953-69, Vice-Chair. 1962-68; Chair. G.E.C. (Research) 1962-68; mem. Bd. Assoc. Semiconductor Mfrs. Ltd. 1962-69; mem. Bd. of Trade Cttee. on the Org. and Constitution of the British Standards Inst. 1949-50; mem. Bd. of Inst. of Physics 1951-59 and Pres. 1956-58; mem. Council Inst. Electrical Engineers 1952-55, Vice-Pres. 1959-64, Pres. 1964-65; mem. British Standards Inst. Gen. Council 1953-56, and mem. of Exec. Cttee. 1953-60; Chair. Int. Special Cttee. on Radio Interference 1953-61, Dept. of Scientific and Industrial Research, Radio Research Bd. 1957-62; mem. British Nat. Cttee. of the Int. Electrotechnical Comm.; mem. of Bd. of British Nuclear Energy Conf. 1955-58; Chair. Council of British Electrical and Allied Industries Research Assen. 1958-61; Pres. Electrical Eng. Assen. 1962-64; Chair. Conf. of Electronics Industry 1963-68; mem. Nat. Electronics Research Council 1963-68; Fellow of Univ. Coll., London 1963. *Publications:* include lectures and papers on scientific and engineering subjects. *Leisure interests:* reading, walking. *Address:* The Victoria Hotel, Sidmouth, Devon, EX10 8RY, England. *Telephone:* (03955) 2651.

HUMPHRIES, (John) Barry, A.O.; Australian entertainer and author; b. 17 Feb. 1934; s. of J. A. E. Humphries and L. A. Brown; m. 1st Rosalind Tong 1959, two d.; m. 2nd Diane Millstead, two s.; ed. Melbourne Grammar and Univ. of Melbourne; repertory seasons Union Theatre, Melbourne 1953-54, Phillip Street Revue Theatre, Sydney 1956, Demon Barber Lyric, Hammersmith 1959, Oliver, New Theatre 1960; one-man shows (author and performer): A Nice Night's Entertainment 1962, Excuse I 1965, Just a Show 1968, A Load of Olde Stuffe 1971, At Least You Can Say That You've Seen It 1974, Housewife Superstar 1976, Isn't It Pathetic at His Age 1979, A Night with Dame Edna 1979, An Evening's Intercourse with Barry Humphries 1981-82, Tears Before Bedtime 1986, Back with a Vengeance, London 1987-88; numerous plays, films and broadcasts; best-known for his comic characterisations of Dame Edna Everage and Sir Les Patterson. *Publications:* Bizarre 1964, Innocent Austral Verse 1968, The Wonderful World of Barry McKenzie (with Nicholas Garland) 1970, Bazza Holds His Own (with Nicholas Garland) 1972, Dame Edna's Coffee Table Book 1976, Les Patterson's Australia 1979, Treasury of Australian Kitsch 1980, A Nice Night's Entertainment 1981, Dame Edna's Bedside Companion 1982, The Traveller's Tool 1985, The Complete Barry McKenzie 1988. *Leisure interests:* reading secondhand booksellers' catalogues in bed, inventing Australia. *Address:* c/o Allen, Allen and Hemsley, P.O. Box 50, Sydney, N.S.W. 2001, Australia.

HUN SEN; Kampuchean politician; b. 1950, Kompang-Cham Prov.; ed. Phnom Penh; joined Khmers Rouges 1970, rising to Commdt.; in Viet-Nam with pro-Vietnamese Kampucheans 1978, returned to Kampuchea after Vietnamese-backed take-over; Minister for Foreign Affairs 1979-85; Chair. Council of Ministers Jan. 1985-. *Address:* Council of Ministers, Phnom Penh, Kampuchea.

HUND, Friedrich, DR. PHIL; German physicist; b. 4 Feb. 1896, Karlsruhe; m. Dr. Ingeborg Seynsche 1931; five c.; Asst. Prof., Göttingen Univ. 1925; Extraordinary Prof., Rostock Univ. 1927 and Prof. 1928; Prof. of Mathematical Physics, Leipzig Univ. 1929-46; Prof. of Theoretical Physics, Jena Univ. 1946-51; Prof. of Theoretical Physics, Frankfurt (Main) Univ. 1951-56; Prof. of Theoretical Physics, Göttingen Univ. 1956-64, Emer. 1964-; mem. Acad. of Sciences, Göttingen; Dr. phil. nat. h.c., Dr.phil. h.c. (Uppsala), Dr. rer. nat. h.c. *Publications:* on quantum theory of atoms, molecules and solids: Linienspektren 1927, Einführung in die theoretische Physik (5 vols.) 1945-50, Materie als Feld 1954, Theoretische Physik (3 vols.) 1956-57, Theorie des Aufbaues der Materie 1961, Geschichte der Quanten-Theorie 1967, 1975, 1984, Grundbegriffe der Physik 1969, 1979, Geschichte der physikalischen Begriffe 1972, 1978. *Leisure interest:* history of physics. *Address:* Charlottenburgerstrasse 19, D3400 Göttingen, Federal Republic of Germany. *Telephone:* (0551) 799-2009.

HUNDERTWASSER, Friedensreich (Friedrich Stowasser); Austrian artist; b. 15 Dec. 1928, Vienna; s. of the late Ernst and Elsa Stowasser; m. 1st 1958 (dissolved 1960), 2nd Yuko Ikewada 1962 (dissolved 1966); first one-man exhbn. at Art Club, Vienna 1952; evolved theory of "Transautomatism" and developed it into a "Grammar of Vision"; exhbns. at Studio Paul Facchetti, Paris 1954, Galleria del Naviglio, Milan 1955, Galerie H. Kamer, Paris 1957-60, Aberbach Fine Art, New York 1973, Vienna 1974, at galleries in Milan, Tokyo, at Venice Biennale, etc.; travelling exhbns. Austria Presents Hundertwasser to the Continents 1964- (shown in 32 museums in 4 continents by 1981) Albertina 1974-, Hundertwasser is Painting 1979-; Guest Lecturer Kunsthochschule, Hamburg 1959; has travelled extensively round the world; nude demonstration against sterile architecture, Munich and Vienna 1968; has designed postage stamps for numerous countries; Prix du Syndicat d'Initiative, Bordeaux, 1957, Sanbra Prize, São Paulo Biennale 1959, Mainichi Prize, Sixth Int. Art Exhbn., Tokyo 1961, Austrian State Prize (from Kunstsenat) 1980, Austrian Environment Award 1981. *Publications:* issued manifestos: Mouldiness Manifesto: Against Rationalism in Architecture 1958, Les Orties 1960, Individual Building Alteration Law and Architecture Boycott Manifesto 1968, Los von Loos 1968, Good Morning City—Bleeding Town 1969-71, Your Right to Windows—Your Duty to the Trees 1972, Nana Hiaku Mizu 1973, The Colour in Town Architecture 1981, Construction of Apartment House for the City of Vienna 1983-85; Hundertwasser's Rainy Day (film) 1972. *Address:* P.O.B. 28, 1182 Vienna, Austria. *Telephone:* 344673.

HUNGER, Herbert, DR.PHIL.; Austrian professor of Byzantine studies; b. 9 Dec. 1914, Vienna; s. of Dr. Hermann and Johanna (née Kölbl) Hunger; m. Ruth Friedrich 1941; two s. one d.; ed. Humanistisches Gymnasium and Univ. of Vienna; Librarian Austrian Nat. Library 1948-56, Dir. Papyrus Collection 1956-62; Prof. of Byzantine Studies, Univ. of Vienna 1962-85; Pres. Austrian Acad. of Sciences 1973-82; hon. or corresp. mem. of 18 foreign Acads.; Österreichisches Ehrenzeichen für Wissenschaft und Kunst and many other awards and prizes; Dr. h.c. (Chicago, Thessalonika, Helsinki, Athens). *Publications:* Lexikon der griechischen und römischen Mythologie 1953, 1988, Byzantinische Geisteswelt 1958, Katalog der griechischen Handschriften der Österreichischen Nationalbibliothek (4 vols.) 1961-84, Prooimion 1964, Reich der Neuen Mitte 1965, Johannes Chortasmenos 1969, Byzantinistische Grundlagenforschung 1973, Die hochsprachliche profane Literatur der Byzantiner (2 vols.) 1978, Anonyme Metaphrase zu Anna Komnene, Alexias XI-XIII 1981, Des Nikephoros Blemmydes "Basilikos Andrias" und dessen Metaphrase (with I. Ševčenko) 1986, Schreiben Und Lesen in Byzanz 1989. *Leisure interest:* chamber music. *Address:* A 1030 Vienna, Weissgerberlände 40, Austria.

HÜNIG, Siegfried Helmut, DR.ING.; German professor of organic chemistry; b. 3 April 1921, Dresden; s. of Oswald and Gertrud (née Bellmann) Hünig; m. Annemarie Haussig 1944; five s. one d.; ed. Technische Universität Dresden; lecturer Univ. of Marburg 1950, Asst. Prof. 1950-60; Assoc. Prof. Univ. of Munich 1960-61; Full Prof., Head of Inst., Univ. of Würzburg

1961-87, Prof. Emer. 1987-; Max Lüthi Medal 1985; mem. Bayerische Akademie der Wissenschaften 1971-, Deutsche Akademie der Naturforscher 1981-. *Publications:* numerous scientific papers covering research in organic chemistry. *Address:* Institute of Organic Chemistry, Am Hubland, D-8700 Würzburg (Office); Mittl. Neubergweg 16, 8700 Würzburg, Federal Republic of Germany (Home). *Telephone:* 0931-888326 (Office).

HUNLÉDÉ, Ayi Houénou, L. en D.; Togolese politician; b. 2 Feb. 1925, Anécho; ed. Univ. of Montpellier, France; Asst. Insp. of schools, Northern Togo, then teacher at Ecole Normale d'Atakpamé 1953-56; worked for French Overseas Territories Admin. 1958; Asst. Admin. Mayor, Lomé; Chief, admin. subdivision of Tabligbo; Admin. Mayor of Tsévié 1958-60; Amb. to France, U.K., EEC 1960-65; High Commr. for Planning 1965-67; Minister of Foreign Affairs 1967-76; ordained pastor in Togolese Evangelical Church Aug. 1977; Commdr., Légion d'honneur, Great Cross of Merit (Fed. Repub. of Germany), Commdr., Order of Liberia. *Address:* c/o Togolese Evangelical Church, Lomé, Togo.

HUNN, John Murray, B.COMM., A.C.A.; New Zealand business executive; b. 5 Nov. 1937, Auckland; s. of Sir Jack Hunn and Dorothy Hunn (née Murray); m. Margaret Rhodes 1960; two s. one d.; ed. Victoria Univ.; various positions with William Cable Ltd. 1956-61; Sec. of N.Z. subsidiary Cos., Hawker Siddeley Int. (N.Z.) Ltd. 1961-67; Controller, IBM N.Z. 1967-70; Gen. Man. Devt. Finance Corpn. N.Z. Ltd. 1973-86, Chief Exec. 1975-86; Group Man. Dir. Crown Corpn. Ltd. 1986-. *Leisure interests:* golf, tennis. *Address:* 15 Woodmancote Road, Khandallah, Wellington 4, New Zealand. *Telephone:* 795-615.

HUNT, Caroline Rose, PH.D.; American business executive; b. 8 Jan. 1923, El Dorado; d. of H. L. Hunt and Lyda Bunker; divorced; four s. one d.; ed. Mary Baldwin Coll., Univs. of Texas and Charleston; beneficiary of Caroline Hunt Trust Estate which includes Corpn., Rosewood Properties, Rosewood Resources with interests in oil and gas properties, luxury hotels, office devts. in maj. cities; owner Lady Primrose's Shopping English Countryside; Hon. Chair. and Chair. numerous socs. and cttees.; Award for Excellence in Community Service in the Field of Business, Dallas Historic Soc. 1984, Les Femmes du Monde Award 1988. *Publication:* The Compleat Pumpkin Eater. *Leisure interest:* writing. *Address:* 100 Crescent Court, Ste. 1700, Dallas, Tex. 75201, U.S.A.

HUNT, Baron (Life Peer), cr. 1966, of Llanfair Waterdine; **John Hunt,** K.G., Kt., C.B.E., D.S.O.; British army officer, mountaineer and administrator; b. 22 June 1910; s. of Capt. C. E. Hunt, M.C. and Ethel Helen (née Crookshank); brother of Hugh Hunt (q.v.); m. Joy Mowbray-Green 1936; four d.; ed. Marlborough Coll. and Royal Mil. Coll., Sandhurst; took part in expeditions to Karakoram 1935 and to S.E. Himalayas 1937 and 1940; led British Expedition to Mount Everest, when Hillary and Tenzing reached the summit on May 29th 1953; British Expedition to Caucasus 1958, to N.E. Greenland 1960; British-Soviet Expedition to the Pamirs 1962; Canadian Centennial Expedition in St. Elias Mountains 1967; Asst. Commdt. Staff College, Camberley 1953-55; Pres. The Alpine Club 1956-58; Chair. Mount Everest Foundation 1956-57; Pres. British Mountaineering Council 1965-68, Nat. Ski Fed. of G.B. 1969-72; Dir. The Duke of Edinburgh's Award Scheme 1956-66; Rector, Aberdeen Univ. 1963-66; Chair. Parole Bd. 1968-74, Young Immigrants (1966-67), Advisory Cttee. on Police forces in Northern Ireland (1969); Personal Rep. of British Prime Minister in Nigeria 1968, 1970; Pres. Council for Volunteers Overseas 1968-74, Nat. Asscn. of Probation Officers 1974-80, Pres. Rainer Foundation 1965-85, The Royal Geographical Soc. 1977-80 (Hon. F.R.G.S. and Hon. mem.), Council for Nat. Parks 1980-86; Nat. Asscn. of Youth Clubs 1954-69, Britain-Nepal Soc. 1960-75, Intermediate Treatment Fund 1980-86; mem. Royal Comm. on the Press 1974-77; Hon. D.C.L. (Durham, Leeds, City Univ.), Hon. LL.D. (Aberdeen and London); Indian Police Medal; Indian Everest Medal; Founder's Medal of Royal Geographical Soc.; Hubbard Medal; Lawrence Memorial Medal; Order (1st Class) of Gurkha Right Hand of Nepal. *Publications:* The Ascent of Everest 1953, Our Everest Adventure 1954, The Red Snows (with Christopher Brasher) 1960, Life is Meeting 1978, My Favourite Mountaineering Stories (Ed.) 1978. *Leisure interests:* languages, mountaineering, skiing. *Address:* Highway Cottage, Aston, Henley-on-Thames, Oxon, RG9 3DE, England.

HUNT, Sir David Wathen Stather, K.C.M.G., O.B.E.; British diplomatist; b. 25 Sept. 1913, Durham; s. of Canon B. P. W. Stather Hunt and Elizabeth Milner; m. 1st Pamela Medawar 1948, 2nd Iro Myrianthousi 1968; two s.; ed. St. Lawrence Coll., Ramsgate and Wadham Coll., Oxford; served in the Middle East, Greece, N. Africa and Italy during the Second World War; Commonwealth Relations Office 1947, service in S. Africa, Pakistan, Nigeria 1947-50, 1952-62; Deputy High Commr., Lagos, Nigeria 1960-62; Private Sec., Office of the British Prime Minister 1950-52, 1960; British High Commr. in Kampala, Uganda 1962-65, in Nicosia, Cyprus 1965-66, in Lagos, Nigeria 1967-69; Amb. to Brazil 1969-73; Chair. Bd. of Govs. Commonwealth Inst. 1974-84; Dir. Observer Newspapers Ltd. 1982-; mem. Appointments Comm. of Press Council 1977-82; Ed. The Times Yearbook of World Affairs 1978-80; Montague Burton Visiting Prof. of Int. Relations, Univ. of Edinburgh 1980; Pres. Soc. for Promotion of Hellenic Studies 1986-; Hon. Citizen of Limassol, Cyprus 1980. *Publications:* A Don at War 1966, On the Spot 1975, Footprints in Cyprus 1982, Gothic Art and the Renaissance in Cyprus 1987, Caterina Cornaro, Queen of Cyprus 1989.

Leisure interests: reading, writing, gardening. *Address:* Old Place, Lindfield, West Sussex, RH16 2HU, England.

HUNT, Gilbert Adams, C.B.E., C.ENG., M.I.BRIT.F., F.I.PROD.E., C.I.MECH.E.; British engineer and motor executive; b. 29 Dec. 1914, Wolverhampton; s. of Harold W. Hunt; m. Diane R. Cook 1975; ed. Old Hall School, Wellington and Malvern Coll.; Dir. Gen. Man. High Duty Alloys 1954-60; Man. Dir. Massey-Ferguson (U.K.) Ltd. 1960-67; Chair. Massey-Ferguson (Farm Services) Ltd. 1960-67; Chair. and Man. Dir. Massey-Ferguson (Eire) Ltd., Joint Man. Dir. Massey-Ferguson Perkins Ltd.; Man. Dir. and Chief Exec. Officer, Chrysler United Kingdom Ltd. 1967-73, Chair. 1973-79, Pres. 1979; fmr. Dir. Chrysler Int. S.A., Chrysler Scotland Ltd., Chrysler Ireland Ltd., Chrysler France S.A. and Chrysler España S.A.; Dir. Reed Group Ltd. 1968-75, Tech. Transfer Assocs. Ltd. 1981-, Equity & General PLC (fmrly. Emray PLC) 1982-; fmr. Chair. Emerald Offshore Services Ltd.; Chair. Gov. Cttee. for Industrial Technologies 1972-78, Thurgar-Bardex 1978-, (Deputy Chair. 1985-), Hedin Ltd. 1979-85; Pres. Soc. of Motor Mfrs. and Traders 1972-73; Hon. D.Sc. (Cranfield). *Leisure interests:* golf, sailing. *Address:* The Dutch House, Sheepstreet Lane, Etchingham, East Sussex, TN19 7AZ, England. *Telephone:* 058 081 414.

HUNT, Hugh Sydney, C.B.E., M.A.; British theatrical director; b. 25 Sept. 1911, Camberley; s. of Capt. C. E. Hunt, M.C. and Ethel Helen (née Crookshank); brother of Lord Hunt (q.v.); m. Janet Mary Gordon 1940; one s. one d.; ed. Marlborough Coll., Sorbonne, Heidelberg Univ. and Magdalen Coll., Oxford; Producer, Maddermarket Theatre, Norwich 1934, Croydon Repertory Theatre 1934, Abbey Theatre, Dublin 1935-38; served Second World War 1939-45; directed Bristol Old Vic Co. 1945-49; Dir. Old Vic Co. 1949-53; Dir. Elizabethan Theatre Trust, Sydney, Australia 1955-60; Prof. of Drama, Univ. of Manchester 1961-73, now Emer.; Artistic Dir., Abbey Theatre, Dublin 1969-71; Vice-Pres. Int. Fed. for Theatre Research 1969-74; Chair. Welsh Arts Council Drama Cttee. 1982-85. *Publications:* Old Vic Prefaces, The Director in the Theatre 1934, The Making of Australian Theatre 1960, The Living Theatre 1961, The Revel's History of Drama in English, vol. vii, 1880 to the Present Day, The Abbey, Ireland's National Theatre 1904-1979, Sean O'Casey 1980. *Plays:* The Invincibles, Moses' Rock (both with Frank O'Connor). *Leisure interest:* travel. *Address:* Cae Terfyn, Criccieth, Gwnedd LL52 0SA, Wales. *Telephone:* Criccieth 522528.

HUNT, James Simon Wallis; British racing driver; b. 29 Aug. 1947, Surrey; s. of Wallis and Susan (née Davis) Hunt; m. 1st Susan Miller 1974 (divorced); m. 2nd Sarah Lomax 1983; two s.; ed. Wellington Coll., Crowthorne, Berks.; joined Lord Hesketh's Formula One Grand Prix team 1973; raced in Monaco Grand Prix 1973; winner of Netherlands Grand Prix 1975; joined McLaren team for 1976 season; World Champion Driver 1976 (retd. 1979); Golden Shield (Royal Swedish Automobile Club) 1978. *Leisure interests:* golf, tennis, backgammon, squash, music, budgerigars. *Address:* c/o Peter Hunt & Co., 2 Seagrave Road, London, SW6 1RR, England.

HUNT, Jonathan Lucas, M.A.; New Zealand politician; b. 2 Dec. 1938, Lower Hutt; s. of H. Lucas and A. Z. Hunt; ed. Auckland Grammar School, Auckland Univ.; teacher Kelston Boys' High School 1961-66; tutor Univ. of Auckland 1964-66; mem. for New Lynn 1966-; Jr. Govt. Whip 1972, Chair. of Cttees. and Deputy Speaker of House of Reps. 1974-75, Acting Speaker 1975; Labour Opposition Spokesman on Health 1976-79, Constitution and Parl. Affairs 1978-81; Sr. Opposition Whip 1980-84; Shadow Minister of Broadcasting 1982; Minister of Broadcasting and Postmaster-Gen. 1984-87, Minister of State and Leader of the House Aug. 1987-, Minister for Tourism 1988-89. *Leisure interests:* music, international affairs, cricket, literature. *Address:* Parliament House, Wellington I (Office); Lone Kauri Road, Kare Kare, R.D.I., New Lynn, Auckland, New Zealand (Home). *Telephone:* 749-187 (Office); PIHA 864 (Home).

HUNT, Adm. Sir Nicholas Streynsham, G.C.B.; British naval officer; b. 7 Nov. 1930, Hawarden, N. Wales; s. of J. M. Hunt; m. Meriel Eve Givan 1966; two s. one d.; ed. Britannia Royal Naval Coll. (BRNC), Dartmouth; C.O. H.M.S. Burnaston, H.M.S. Palliser, H.M.S. Troubridge, H.M.S. Intrepid and BRNC Dartmouth; Asst. Pvt. Sec. to late Princess Marina, Duchess of Kent; Exec. Officer H.M.S. Ark Royal 1969-71; at Royal Coll. of Defence Studies 1974; Dir. of Naval Plans 1976-78; Flag Officer Second Flotilla 1980-81; Dir. Gen. Naval Manpower and Training 1981-83; Flag Officer Scotland and Northern Ireland, Port Adm.; Rosyth and NATO Commdr. Northern Area Eastern Atlantic and Northern Area Allied Command Channel 1983-85; C.-in-C. Fleet, and Allied Commdr. in Chief Channel and Eastern Atlantic 1985-87; Deputy Man. Dir. (Org. and Devt.), Eurotunnel 1987-89. *Leisure interest:* family. *Address:* Eurotunnel, Victoria Plaza, 111 Buckingham Palace Road, London, SW1W 0ST, England. *Telephone:* 01-326 7013.

HUNT, Pierre; French diplomatist; b. 3 Sept. 1925, Paris; ed. Lycée Janson-de-Sailly, Faculté de Droit de Paris and Ecole nat. de la France d'outre-mer; Deputy Dir. Services de Presse et d'Information 1965; Sec.-Gen. Comité interministeriel pour l'Information 1969; Admin. SOFIRAD and Radio Monte Carlo 1970; Amb. to Congo 1972-76, to Madagascar 1976-78, to Tunisia 1980-83, to Egypt 1985-; Spokesman for the Pres. 1978-80; Officier Légion d'honneur, Ordre national du Mérite. *Leisure interests:* tennis, golf, swimming, painting, photography. *Address:* c/o Mini-stry of Foreign Affairs, 37 quai d'Orsay, 75700 Paris (Office); 12 rue de la Comète, 75007 Paris, France (Home).

HUNT, Sir Rex Masterman, Kt., C.M.G., B.A.; British diplomatist (retd.); b. 29 June 1926; s. of the late H. W. Hunt and of Ivy Masterman; m. Mavis Buckland 1951; one s. one d.; ed. Coatham School, St. Peter's Coll., Oxford; service with R.A.F. 1944-48; with Overseas Civil Service 1951; Dist. Commr., Uganda 1962; in Commonwealth Relations Office 1963-64; First Sec., Kuching, Malaysia 1964-65, Jesselton (now Kota Kinabalu), Malaysia 1965-67, Brunei 1967; First Sec., (Econ.), Embassy, Turkey 1968-70; First Sec. and Head of Chancery, Embassy, Indonesia 1970-72; Asst., Middle East Dept., FCO 1972-74; Counsellor, Embassy, S. Viet-Nam 1974-75, Deputy High Commr., Malaysia 1976-79; Gov. and C.-in-C. Falkland Islands and Dependencies 1980-82, expelled after Argentine seizure of Falkland Islands April 1982, returned as Civil Commr. June, after UK recapture of Islands; Civil Commr. Falkland Islands 1982-Sept. 1985, Gov. Oct. 1985, High Comm. British Antarctic Territory 1980-85. *Leisure interests:* gardening, golf. *Address:* Old Woodside, Broomfield Park, Sunningdale, Berks., SL5 0JS, England. *Telephone:* Ascot 25563.

HUNT OF TANWORTH, Baron (Life Peer), cr. 1980, of Stratford-on-Avon in the County of Warwickshire; **John Joseph Benedict Hunt,** G.C.B.; British fmr. civil servant and company director; b. 23 Oct. 1919, Minehead; s. of Major and Mrs. A. L. Hunt; m. 1st Magdalen Mary Lister Robinson 1941 (died 1971), 2nd Madeleine Frances Charles 1973; two s. one d.; ed. Downside School and Magdalene Coll., Cambridge; served in R.N.V.R. 1940-46; joined Home Civil Service (Dominions Office) 1946; Private Sec. to Parl. Under-Sec. 1947; Second Sec., Colombo 1948-50; Directing Staff, Imperial Defence Coll. 1951-52; First Sec., Ottawa 1953-56; Private Sec. to Sec. of Cabinet and Head of Civil Service 1956-58; Asst. Sec. Commonwealth Relations Office 1958-60; Cabinet Office 1960-62; H.M. Treasury 1962-67, Under-Sec. 1965; First Civil Service Commr. 1968-71; Third Sec. Treasury 1971-72; Second Permanent Sec., Cabinet Office 1972-73; Sec. of the Cabinet 1973-79; Chair. Banque Nat. de Paris (U.K.) April 1980-, Disasters Emergency Cttee. 1981-, Inquiry into Cable Expansion and Broadcasting Policy 1982; Dir. Unilever March 1980-, IBM United Kingdom Holdings, IBM United Kingdom Ltd., Prudential Corpn. PLC 1980-82, Prudential Pensions Ltd. 1981-, Deputy Chair. Prudential Corpn. PLC and Assurance Co. Ltd. 1982-85, Chair. 1985-(90); Chair. Ditchley Foundation 1983-; Chair. Tablet Publishing Co. Ltd. 1984-. *Leisure interest:* gardening. *Address:* 8 Wool Road, London, SW20 0HW, England.

HUNTEN, Donald Mount, PH.D.; American astronomer and physicist; b. 1 March 1925, Montreal, Canada; s. of Kenneth William Hunten and Winnifred Binnmore Mount; m. Isobel Ann Rubenstein 1949; two s.; ed. Univ. of Western Ontario, McGill Univ.; Research Assoc. to Prof. Univ. of Sask., Saskatoon 1950-63; Physicist Kitt Peak Nat. Observatory 1963-78; Consultant to NASA 1965-, Science Adviser to NASA Assoc. Admin. for Space Science 1977-78; Prof. of Planetary Science Univ. of Ariz., Tucson 1978-; mem. N.A.S. (1977, 1985). *Publications:* Introduction to Electronics 1964, Theory of Planetary Atmospheres (with J. W. Chamberlain) 1987, several NASA publs., numerous papers in scientific journals. *Leisure interest:* music. *Address:* 10 Calle Corta, Tucson, Ariz. 85716, U.S.A. *Telephone:* (602) 621-4002.

HUNTER, Evan, B.A.; American author; b. 15 Oct. 1926, New York; s. of Charles and Marie Lombino; m. 1st Anita Melnick 1949, three s.; m. 2nd Mary Vann Finley 1973, one step d.; ed. Cooper Union and Hunter Coll.; *Publications:* The Blackboard Jungle 1954, Second Ending 1956, Strangers When We Meet 1958 (screenplay 1959), A Matter of Conviction 1959, Mothers and Daughters 1961, The Birds (screenplay) 1962, Happy New Year, Herbie 1963, Buddwing 1964, The Easter Man (play) 1964, The Paper Dragon 1966, A Horse's Head 1967, Last Summer 1968, Sons 1969, The Conjurer (play) 1969, Nobody Knew They Were There 1971, Every Little Crook and Nanny 1972, The Easter Man 1972, Come Winter 1973, Streets of Gold 1974, The Chisholms 1976, Me and Mr. Stenner 1976, Love, Dad 1981, 87th Precinct Mysteries, Far From the Sea 1983, Lizzie 1984; under pseudonym Ed McBain: Cop Hater 1956, The Mugger 1956, The Pusher 1956, The Con Man 1957, Killer's Choice 1957, Killer's Payoff 1958, Lady Killer 1958, Killer's Wedge 1959, 'Til Death 1959, King's Ransom 1959, Give the Boys a Great Big Hand 1960, The Heckler 1960, See Them Die 1960, Lady, Lady, I Did It 1961, Like Love 1962, The Empty Hours (three novelettes) 1962, Ten·plus One 1963, Ax 1964, He Who Hesitates 1965, Doll 1965, The Sentries 1965, Eighty Million Eyes 1966, Fuzz 1968 (screenplay 1972), Shotgun 1969, Jigsaw 1970, Hail, Hail, The Gang's All Here 1971, Sadie When She Died 1972, Let's Hear It for the Deaf Man 1972, Hail to the Chief 1973, Bread 1974, Where There's Smoke 1975, Blood Relatives 1975, So Long as You Both Shall Live 1976, Long Time No See 1977, Goldilocks 1977, Calypso 1979, Ghosts 1980, Rumpelstiltskin 1981, Heat 1981, Ice 1983, Beauty and the Beast 1983, Jack and the Beanstalk 1984, Lightning 1984, Snow White and Rose Red 1985, Eight Black Horses 1985, Cinderella 1986, Another Part of the City 1986, Poison 1987, Puss in Boots 1987, Tricks 1987, McBain's Ladies 1988, The House that Jack Built 1988. *Leisure interests:* skiing and snorkeling. *Address:* c/o John Farquharson Ltd., 250 West 57th Street, New York, N.Y. 10019, U.S.A.

HUNTER, Robert John, PH.D., F.A.A., F.R.A.C.I., C.CHEM.; Australian research chemist; b. 26 June 1933, Abermain, N.S.W.; s. of Ronald J. Hunter and Elizabeth Dixon; m. Barbara Robson 1954; one s. one d.; ed. Cessnock High School, N.S.W., New England Univ. Coll. and Univ. of Sydney; secondary school teacher 1953–54; Tech. Officer, CSIRO 1954–57; postgraduate student, Univ. of Sydney 1957–60; Research Officer, CSIRO 1960–64; lecturer, Univ. of Sydney 1964, Assoc. Prof. of Physical Chemistry 1972–, Head, School of Chem. 1987–; Alexander Memorial Lecturer 1987, Liversidge Lecturer of Royal Soc. of N.S.W. 1988; Archibald Olle Prize 1982. *Publications:* Chemical Science 1976, Zeta Potential in Colloid Science 1981, Foundations of Colloid Science, (Vol. I) 1987. *Leisure interests:* music, drama, reading. *Address:* School of Chemistry, The University of Sydney, N.S.W. 2006 (Office); 68 Gordon Crescent, Lane Cove, N.S.W. 2066, Australia (Home). *Telephone:* 61-2-692-2176 (Office); 61-2-427-6261 (Home).

HUNTER, Tony (Anthony Rex), M.A., PH.D. F.R.S.; British molecular biologist and virologist; b. 23 Aug. 1943, Ashford; s. of Ranulph Rex Hunter and Nellie Ruby Elsie Hitchcock; m. Philippa Charlotte Marrack 1969 (divorced 1974); ed. Felsted School, Essex and Gonville and Caius Coll., Cambridge; Research Fellow Christ's Coll., Cambridge 1968–71, 1973–75; Research Assoc. Salk Inst., San Diego, Calif. 1971–73, Asst. Prof. 1975–78, Assoc. Prof. 1978–82, Prof. 1982–; Adjunct Assoc. Prof. Dept. of Biology Univ. of California, San Diego 1979–82, Adjunct Prof. 1982–; American Business Foundation for Cancer Research Award 1988; Fellow Royal Soc. for Encouragement of Arts, Manufactures and Commerce (RSA) 1989. *Publications:* c. 180 papers and journal articles. *Leisure interests:* white water rafting, desert camping. *Address:* Molecular Biology and Virology Laboratory, The Salk Institute, P.O. Box 85800, San Diego, Calif. 92138 (Office); 4578 Vista de la Patria, Del Mar, Calif. 92014, U.S.A. (Home). *Telephone:* 619-453-4100 (Ext. 385) (Office); 619-792-1492 (Home).

HUNTER OF NEWINGTON, Baron (Life Peer), of Newington in the District of the City of Edinburgh; **Robert Brockie Hunter,** LL.D., D.SC., F.R.C.P., F.A.C.P.; British clinical professor; b. 14 July 1915, Edin.; s. of the late Robert Marshall Hunter; m. Kathleen Margaret Hunter 1940; three s. one d.; ed. George Watson's Coll., Edin.; Personal Physician to Field-Marshal Montgomery, N.W. Europe 1944–45; Prof. of Materia Medica, Pharmacology and Therapeutics, Univ. of St. Andrews 1948–67, Dean of Faculty of Medicine 1958–62; mem. Clinical Research Bd., M.R.C. 1960–64; Ministry of Health Cttee. on Safety of Drugs 1963–68; Prof. of Materia Medica, Pharmacology and Therapeutics, Dundee Univ. 1967–68; Vice-Chancellor and Prin., Birmingham Univ. 1968–81; mem., West Midlands Regional Health Authority 1974–80, House of Lords Select Cttee. on Science and Tech. 1980–87. *Leisure interest:* fishing. *Address:* 3 Oakdene Drive, Fiery Hill Road, Barnt Green, Birmingham, B45 8LQ, England.

HUO SHILIAN; Chinese politician; b. 1911, Shaanxi; joined CCP 1932; Deputy Gov. Zhejiang 1954–68; Sec. CCP, Zhejiang 1957–66; First Sec. CCP, Shaanxi 1966–68; Sec. North-West Bureau CCP 1966; criticized and removed from office during Cultural Revolution 1968; Sec. CCP, Shaanxi 1973; First Sec. CCP, Ningxia 1977–80; Chair. Ningxia Hui Revolutionary Cttee. 1977–79; mem. 11th Cen. Cttee. CCP 1977; First Political Commissar, Ningxia Mil. District, PLA 1978–80; Minister of Agric. 1979–81; First Sec., Shanxi CCP 1980–83; 1st Political Commr., Shanxi Mil. Dist. 1981–83; mem. Cen. Advisory Comm. 1982–. *Address:* Office of the First Secretary, Shanxi, People's Republic of China.

HUONG, Tran Van (see Tran Van Huong).

HUPAŁOWSKI, Gen. Tadeusz; Polish army officer and politician; b. 25 June 1922, Złoczów; ed. Infantry Coll., Acad. of Political Sciences, Warsaw, Mil. Acad., Czechoslovakia and Higher Acad. of Gen. Staff, U.S.S.R.; Maj.-Gen. 1963; Chief, Operation Bd. of Polish Army Gen. Staff 1965, Chief, Territorial Defence Inspectorate 1965–68, Chief of Staff of Silesian Mil. Dist. 1968–72, Lieut.-Gen. 1972, Deputy Chief of Gen. Staff for Organization and Mobilization 1972–73, First Deputy Chief of Polish Army Gen. Staff 1973–81; Minister of Admin., Local Economy and Environmental Protection 1981–83; Chair. Supreme Chamber of Control March 1983–; mem. Mil. Council of Nat. Salvation 1981–83; Chair. Bd. Polish-Libyan Friendship Soc. 1982–; mem. Polish United Workers' Party (PZPR) 1951–, mem. Cen. Party Control Comm. of PZPR 1975–81; Deputy Chair. Cen. Control and Revisional Comm. of PZPR 1986–; Chair. Polish-Libyan Friendship Soc. 1982–; Commdr.'s Cross with Star of Order of Polonia Restituta, Order of Banner of Labour (1st and 2nd Class) and other decorations. *Address:* Najwyższa Izba Kontroli, ul. Filtrowa 57, 00-950 Warsaw, P.O. Box P-14, Poland. *Telephone:* 25-44-81.

HUPPERT, Herbert Eric, M.A., PH.D., SC.D., F.R.S.; Australian scientist; b. 26 Nov. 1943, Sydney; s. of Leo Huppert and Alice (née Neumann) Huppert; m. Felicia Ferster 1966; two s.; ed. Sydney Boys High School, Univ. of Sydney, Australian Nat. Univ. and Univ. of California, San Diego; ICI Research Fellow Cambridge Univ. 1968–69, Asst. Dir. Research Dept. Applied Math. and Theoretical Physics 1970–81, Univ. Lecturer 1981–88, Reader Geophysical Dynamics 1988–, BP Venture Unit Sr. Research Fellow 1983–89; Fellow King's Coll., Cambridge 1970–; fmr. Visiting Research Scientist Univs. of Calif., Canterbury, New South Wales and Australian Nat. Univ., M.I.T., Woods Hole Oceanographic Inst. and California Inst. of Tech.; Vice-Chair. Scientists for the Release of Soviet Refu-

seniks 1985–88, Co-Chair. 1988–; Ed. Journal of Soviet Jewry 1986–; Assoc. Ed. Journal of Fluid Mechanics 1971–. *Publications:* c. 80 papers on fluid motions associated with the atmosphere, oceans and volcanoes. *Leisure interests:* my children, squash, mountaineering and learning the viola. *Address:* Department of Applied Mathematics and Theoretical Physics, University of Cambridge, Silver Street, Cambridge, CB3 9EW (Office); 46 De Freville Avenue, Cambridge, CB4 1HT, England (Home). *Telephone:* (0223) 356071 (Office); (0223) 337853 (Home).

HUPPERT, Isabelle Anne; French actress; b. 16 March 1953, Paris; d. of Raymond Huppert and Annick Beau; one d.; ed. Lycée de Saint-Cloud, Ecole nat. des langues orientales vivantes; Prix Susanne Blanchetti 1976, Prix Bistingo 1976, Prix César 1978, Gold Palm, Cannes 1978, Prix d'interpretation, Cannes 1978. *Films include:* Le bar de la Fourche, César et Rosalie, Les valseuses, Aloïse, Dupont la joie, Rosebud, Docteur Françoise Gailland, Le juge et l'assassin, Le petit Marcel 1976, Les indiens sont encore loin 1977, La dentellière, Violette Nozière 1978, Les soeurs Brontë 1978, Loulou 1980, Sauve qui peut (la vie), Les Héritières 1980, Heaven's Gate 1980, Coup de Torchon 1981, Dame aux Camelias 1981, Les Ailes de la Colombe 1981, Eaux Profondes 1981, Passion, travail et amour, La Truite 1982, Entre Nous 1984, My Best Friend's Girl 1984, La Garce 1984, Signé Charlotte, Sac de noeuds 1985, Cactus 1986, Sincerely Charlotte 1986, The Bedroom Window 1986, The Possessed 1988. *Address:* c/o Art Media, 10 avenue George V, 75008 Paris, France.

HUQ, Muhammad Shamsul, M.A.; Bangladeshi politician, educationist and economist; b. 2 Dec. 1910, Comilla; s. of the late M. Karimul Huq and Mahmuda Khatoon; m. Tayyeba Huq 1938; two s.; ed. Univs. of Calcutta, Dhaka and London; Chair. Cttee. on Int. Co-operation apptd. by Commonwealth Educ. Conf., New Delhi 1962; Vice-Chancellor Rajshahi Univ. 1965–69; Minister for Educ., Scientific and Technological Development of fmr. Pakistan 1969–70; led Del. 25th Anniversary of ESOSOC, Geneva and Del. Gen. Conf. of ESOSOC, Paris 1970; mem. UNESCO Int. Experts Cttee. on formulation of policy of training abroad, Paris 1970; Fellow, Woodrow Wilson Int. Center for Scholars, Smithsonian Inst., Washington, D.C. 1971–73; Vice-Chancellor Dhaka Univ. 1975–76; Chair. Planning Cttee. Social Science Research Council 1977–; mem. Pres.'s Council of Advisers in charge of Ministry of Foreign Affairs 1977–78; Foreign Minister 1978–82; Trustee Bangladesh Nat. Museum, Dhaka 1983–; Gov. Bangladesh Inst. of Int. and Strategic Studies 1982–; Pres. Foundation for Research on Educational Planning and Devt.; Chair. Nat. Foundation for Research on Human Resource Devt.; Minister of Information 1983, of Social Welfare and Women's Affairs 1987–; led Del. to UN 1977, 1978, 1979, 1980, 1981; active in negotiation of Ganges Water Agreement with India 1977, repatriation of two hundred thousand Burmese refugees 1978, election of Bangladesh to Security Council, UN 1979–80, Commonwealth Conf. initiative on Zimbabwe, Lusaka 1978–79, the Middle East issue (mem. Ministerial Cttee. on Jerusalem) and preparations for Cancun Summit March 1981 (attended Summit Oct. 1981); B.B. Gold Medal, Univ. of Calcutta 1933; Scholar-in-Residence Advanced Projects, East-West Centre, Honolulu 1963–64. *Publications:* Changing Education in England 1948, Compulsory Education in Pakistan 1954, Education and Development Strategy in South and South East Asia 1965, Education, Manpower and Development in South and South East Asia 1975, Higher Education and Employment in Bangladesh (jointly) 1983, The Patterns of Education in South and South East Asia (in Encyclopaedia Britannica and German encyclopaedia Lexikon der Pedagogik), Tragedy in Lebanon, Geo-political Implications, Cancún and after: from Hope to Despair. *Leisure interests:* reading, gardening. *Address:* 10 Eskaton Garden Road, Dhaka 2, Bangladesh. *Telephone:* 405050 and 407339.

HUQ, Maj.-Gen. Shamsul; Bangladeshi army officer and politician; b. 1 Sept. 1931, Shugandhi, Comilla Dist.; m.; two s. two d.; ed. Sengarchar High School, Dhaka Coll.; commissioned Army Medical Corps 1955, served Army and Air Force Medical Services, then joined War of Liberation, organised Medical Services, achieved rank of Lieut.-Col. 1971, then Dir.-Gen. Medical Services, rank of Col., then Brig. 1983, rank of Maj.-Gen. 1979; Minister of Health and Population Control 1982–86, of Relief and Rehabilitation 1986–87. *Leisure interest:* gardening. *Address:* c/o Ministry of Relief and Rehabilitation, Bangladesh Secretariat, Dhaka, Bangladesh.

HURD, Rt. Hon. Douglas Richard, C.B.E., P.C., M.P.; British diplomatist and politician; b. 8 March 1930, Marlborough; s. of the late Baron Hurd and Stephanie Corner; m. 1st Tatiana Elizabeth Michelle Eyre 1960 (dissolved 1982), three s.; m. 2nd Judy Smart 1982, one s. one d.; ed. Eton Coll., Trinity Coll., Cambridge; joined diplomatic service 1952; served in Beijing 1954–56, U.K. Mission to UN 1956–60, Private Sec. to Perm. Under-Sec. of State, Foreign Office 1960–63, in British Embassy, Rome 1963–66; joined Conservative Research Dept. 1966, Head of Foreign Affairs Section 1968; Private Sec. to Leader of the Opposition 1968–70, Political Sec. to the Prime Minister 1970–74; M.P. for Mid-Oxon 1974–83, for Witney 1983–; Opposition Spokesman on European Affairs 1976–79, Minister of State, FCO 1979–83, Home Office 1983–84; Sec. of State for N. Ireland 1984–85; Home Sec. 1985–. *Publications:* The Arrow War 1967, Send Him Victorious (with Andrew Osmond) 1968, The Smile on the Face of the Tiger 1969, Scotch on the Rocks 1971, Truth Game 1972, Vote to Kill 1975, An End to Promises 1979, War Without Frontiers (with Andrew Osmond)

1982, Palace of Enchantments (with Stephen Lamport) 1985. *Leisure interest:* writing thrillers. *Address:* House of Commons, London, SW1A 0AA, England.

HURFORD, Christopher John, B.ECONS., A.C.I.S.; Australian politician; b. 30 July 1931; m. Lorna Seedsman 1960; two s. three d.; ed. L.S.E.; served Royal Australian Navy Reserve 1951-52; M.P. for Adelaide, House of Reps. 1969-; Minister for Housing and Construction and Minister Assisting the Minister for Industry and Commerce 1983-84, Minister Assisting, the Treas. 1983-87, Minister for Immigration and Ethnic Affairs 1984-87; Minister for Community Services Feb.-July 1987; Consul-Gen. of Australia, New York 1988-; Treas. Aboriginal Educ. Foundation 1965-67, S. Australian Council of Civil Liberties 1967-68; Appeal Chair. Austcare 1968-70; Fellow, Inst. of Chartered Accountants in Australia; Australian Labor Party. *Leisure interests:* golf, cinema, reading. *Address:* 102 Finniss Street, North Adelaide, 5006 South Australia.

HURFORD, Peter John, O.B.E., M.A., MUS.B., F.R.C.O., F.R.C.M.; British organist; b. 22 Nov. 1930, Minehead, Somerset; s. of Hubert John Hurford and Gladys Winifred James; m. Patricia Mary Matthews 1955; two s. one d.; ed. Blundell's School, Royal Coll. of Music (Open Foundation Scholar), Jesus Coll. Cambridge (organ scholar) and private studies with André Marchal, Paris; served Royal Signals 1954-56; Organist and Choirmaster Holy Trinity Church, Leamington Spa 1956-57; Dir. of Music, Bablake School, Coventry 1956-57; Master of the Music, Cathedral and Abbey Church of St. Alban 1958-78; freelance concert and recording organist 1978-; Visiting Prof., Coll. Conservatory of Music, Cincinnati, U.S.A. 1967-68, Univ. of Western Ont., Canada 1976-77; Visiting Artist-in-Residence, Sydney Opera House 1980-82; Decca exclusive recording artist 1977-: 60 records, including complete organ works of J. S. Bach, Handel, F. Couperin, P. Hindemith and music of Franck, Mendelssohn, etc.; concerts in U.S.A., Canada, Australia, N.Z., Japan, Far East, E. and W. Europe 1960-; f. Int. Organ Festival 1963, Artistic Dir. 1963-79, Pres. 1981-; Council mem. Royal Coll. of Organists 1964-, Pres. 1980-82; Fellow Royal School of Church Music; Hon. mem. R.A.M.; Hon. D.Mus. (Baldwin-Wallace Coll., Ohio, U.S.A.) 1981; Gramophone Award 1979; compositions include (organ music) Suite—Laudate Dominum, Chorale Preludes, (choral music) The Communion Service, Series III, The Holy Eucharist, Rite 2 (for American Episcopal Church). *Publications:* Making Music On The Organ 1988, Sundry forewords, contribs. to journals. *Leisure interests:* walking and wine. *Address:* Broom House, St. Bernard's Road, St. Albans, Herts., AL3 5RA, England and c/o Karen McFarlane Artists, 3269 West 30th Street, Cleveland, Ohio 44109, U.S.A. *Telephone:* (216) 398 3990 (U.S.A.).

HURLEY, Denis Eugene, PH.L., S.T.L.; South African ecclesiastic; b. 9 Nov. 1915, Cape Town; s. of Denis Hurley and Theresa May (née O'Sullivan) Hurley; ed. St. Charles' Coll., Pietermaritzburg, St. Thomas' Univ., Rome, Gregorian Univ., Rome; ordained priest 1939; Curate, Emmanuel Cathedral, Durban 1940-43; Superior of St. Joseph's Scholasticate Prestbury (now Cedera) 1944-46; Vicar Apostolic of Natal with rank of Bishop March 1947; promoted Archbishop of Durban Jan. 1951; Pres. S.A. Catholic Bishops' Conf. 1952-60, 1981-87; attended Second Vatican Council 1962-65; Pres. S.A. Inst. of Race Relations 1965-66; Chair. Int. Comm. on English in the Liturgy 1975-; founded ecumenical agency for social concern known as Diakonia in Durban 1976; charged with offence against S. African law for making 'false statement' concerning atrocities by para-military police unit in Namibia Oct. 1984, acquitted Feb. 1985; Hon. Dr. Iur. (Notre Dame) 1978, (De Paul Univ.) 1986; Hon. D. Litt. (Natal) 1978; Hon. D.Hum. Litt. (Univ. of America) 1982; (Georgetown Univ.) 1987; Hon. D.S.T. (Univ. of Santa Clara) 1986; Hon. Dr. (Univ. of Louvain) 1988; Hon. D.Sc. (Univ. of Cape Town) 1988; civic honours, City of Durban 1972, Chevalier of the Legion of Honour (France) 1975. *Leisure interests:* reading, following cricket and rugby on radio and TV. *Address:* Archbishop's House, 154, Gordon Road, Durban 40001; P.O. Box 47489, Gregville, South Africa. *Telephone:* (031) 3031417.

HURLEY, Rev. Michael Anthony, S.J., S.T.D.; Irish ecumenical theologian and ecclesiastic; b. 10 May 1923, Ardmore, Co. Waterford; s. of Johanna Foley and Martin Hurley; ed. Mount Melleray Seminary, Cappoquin, Univ. Coll., Dublin, Jesuit Theological Faculty, Louvain, Pontifical Gregorian Univ., Rome; entered Soc. of Jesus 1940; ordained priest 1954; lecturer in Dogmatic Theology, Jesuit Theological Faculty, Dublin 1958-70; Dir. Irish School of Ecumenics, Dublin 1970-80; Leader, Columbanus Community of Reconciliation, Belfast 1983-. *Publications:* Church and Eucharist (Ed.) 1966, Ecumenical Studies: Baptism and Marriage (Ed.) 1968, Theology of Ecumenism 1969, John Wesley's Letter to a Roman Catholic (Ed.) 1968, Irish Anglicanism (Ed.) 1970, Beyond Tolerance: The Challenge of Mixed Marriage (Ed.) 1975; articles in various periodicals. *Leisure interest:* reading. *Address:* 683 Antrim Road, Belfast, BT15 4EG, Northern Ireland. *Telephone:* 778009.

HURLEY, Dame Rosalinde, D.B.E.; British professor of microbiology; b. 30 Dec. 1929, London; d. of William Hurley and of the late Rose Hurley; m. Peter Gortuai 1963; ed. Acad. of the Assumption, Wellesley Hills, Mass., Queen's Coll., London, Univ. Coll., London, Inns of Court; Consultant Microbiologist 1962-75; Prof. of Microbiology, Royal Postgraduate Medical School's Inst. of Obstetrics and Gynaecology 1975-, Queen Charlotte's and Chelsea Hosp., London; Vice-Chair. Cttee. on Dental and Surgical

Materials 1975-78, Chair. 1979-81; Chair. Medicines Comm. 1982-. *Publications:* Candida Albicans 1964; numerous papers on candidosis, and infections in pregnant women and the newborn. *Leisure interests:* reading, gardening. *Address:* Queen Charlotte's and Chelsea Hospital, 8, Goldhawk Road, London W6 0X9, England. *Telephone:* (01) 740-3923.

HÜRLIMANN, Hans, LL.D.; Swiss lawyer and politician; b. 6 April 1918, Walchwil, Zug; m. Marie Theres Duft 1947; two s. one d.; ed. Univs. of Fribourg and Berne; Barrister, Zug 1946; Legal Adviser, Zug 1946, Town Clerk 1949; mem. Legis. Chamber, Zug Canton 1946, mem. Cantonal Govt. as Head of Dept. of Justice, Police and Mil. Affairs 1954-62, of Educ., Cultural and Mil. Affairs 1962-73; mem. Council of States 1966-73; mem. Fed. Council as Head of Dept. of Home Affairs (the Interior) 1974-82, Vice-Pres. Jan.-Dec. 1978, Pres. Jan.-Dec. 1979; Chair. Conf. of Heads of Cantonal Mil. Depts. 1960-68, Conf. of Heads of Cantonal Educ. Depts. 1968-73; mem. Council of Swiss Fed. Insts. of Tech. 1970-73; fmr. mem. Exec. Bd., Christian-Democratic People's Party. *Publications:* Das Recht der Stadtgemeinde Zug, and many publications on juridical, educational and military topics. *Leisure interests:* music, books, theatre, skiing, hiking. *Address:* Schönbühl 3, 6300 Zug, Switzerland.

HURNÍK, Ilja; Czechoslovak pianist and composer; b. 25 Nov. 1922, Ostrava-Poruba; m. Jana Hurníková 1966; one s.; ed. Conservatoire, Prague; composition: Acad. of Music and Dramatic Arts, Prague 1948-52; self-employed artist 1942-; one-man concerts since 1942, Poland, Switzerland, Fed. Repub. of Germany, Cuba; Czech Musical Fund Prize 1967, Supraphon Prize 1971; *Works:* piano compositions: The First Melodies 1931, Concert for Oboe and Strings 59, Preludes for piano 1943, Studies for four hands 1975; chamber compositions: Sonata for viola and piano, Four Seasons of the Year for 12 instruments 1952, Sonata da camera, Moments musicaux for 11 wind instruments 1955, Esercizii for wind quartet 1963; vocal works: cantata Maryka 1948, Children's Tercets 1956, oratorio Noah 1959, Choirs about Mothers for mixed choir 1962, cantata Aesop, songs for alto and orchestra Sulamit 1965; ballet: Ondráš 1950, Faux pas de quatre 1979; opera: The Lady and Robbers 1966, (opera): Diogenes 73, Brass quintet 87, Fishermen in the Net 1981. *Address:* Národní Třída 35, 11000, Prague 1, Czechoslovakia. *Telephone:* 227079.

HURST, (Charles) Angas, PH.D., F.A.A.; Australian professor of mathematical physics; b. 22 Sept. 1923, Adelaide; s. of W. W. and A. C. A. (Morris) Hurst; m. Barbara L. Stevens 1945; one s. two d.; ed. Scotch Coll., Melbourne, and Univs. of Melbourne and Cambridge; served in R.A.A.F. 1942-45; Sr. Lecturer, Dept. of Math., Univ. of Melbourne 1952-56; Sr. Lecturer, Mathematical Physics Dept., Univ. of Adelaide 1957-60, Reader 1960-64, Prof. 1964-; Chair. Nat. Cttee. for Physics 1979-; Pro-Vice-Chancellor, Univ. of Adelaide 1986-. *Publications:* Order—Disorder Phenomena (with H. S. Green); articles in scientific journals. *Leisure interest:* walking, cycling. *Address:* Mathematical Physics Department, University of Adelaide, Adelaide, South Australia 5001 (Office); 99 Fifth Avenue, Joslin, South Australia 5070, Australia. (Home).

HURT, John; British actor; b. 22 Jan. 1940, Chesterfield; s. of Rev. Arnould Herbert and Phyllis (née Massey) Hurt; m. Donna Peacock 1984; ed. The Lincoln School, Lincoln and Royal Acad. of Dramatic Art; began as painter; stage debut, Arts Theatre, London 1962; Dir. United British Artists 1983-. *Stage appearances include:* Chips With Everything, Vaudeville Theatre 1962, The Dwarfs, Arts 1963, Hamp (title role), Edinburgh Festival 1964, Inadmissible Evidence, Wyndhams 1965, Little Malcolm and his Struggle against the Eunuchs, Garrick 1966, Belcher's Luck, (RSC), Aldwych 1966, Man and Superman, Gaiety, Dublin 1969, The Caretaker, Mermaid 1972, The Only Street, Dublin Festival and Islington 1973, Travesties (RSC), Aldwych and The Arrest, Bristol Old Vic 1974, The Shadow of a Gunman, Nottingham Playhouse 1978. *Films include:* The Wild and the Willing 1962, A Man for All Seasons 1966, Sinful Davey 1968, Before Winter Comes 1969, In Search of Gregory 1970, Mr. Forbush and the Penguins 1971, 10 Rillington Place, The Ghoul 1974, Little Malcolm 1974, East of Elephant Rock 1977, The Disappearance, The Shout, Spectre, Alien, Midnight Express 1978, Heaven's Gate 1980, The Elephant Man 1980, Champions 1983, The Hit 1983, 1984 1984, Jake Speed 1985, Rocinante 1986, Aria 1987, White Mischief 1987, Scandal 1988. *TV appearances include:* The Waste Places 1968, The Naked Civil Servant (Emmy Award 1976) 1975, Caligula in I, Claudius 1976, Treats 1977, Raskolnikov in Crime and Punishment 1979, Poison Candy 1988, Deadline 1988. *Address:* c/o Leading Artists Ltd., 60 St. James's Street, London, S.W.1, England.

HURT, William; American actor; b. 20 March, 1950, Wash.; m. 2nd Heidi Henderson 1989; ed. Tufts Univ., Juilliard School; appeared with Ore. Shakespeare Festival production of A Long Day's Journey Into Night, N.Y.; *stage appearances include:* Henry V 1976, Mary Stuart, My Life, Ulysses in Traction, Lulu, Fifth of July, Childe Byron, The Runner Stumbles, Hamlet, Hurlyburly, others; *films include:* Altered States, Eyewitness, Body Heat (Theatre World Award 1978), The Big Chill, Gorky Park, Kiss of the Spider Woman (Best Actor Award Cannes Film Festival 1985, Acad. Award for Best Actor 1985), Children of a Lesser God, Broadcast News 1987, A Time of Destiny 1988, The Accidental Tourist 1989; mem. Circle Repertory Co., N.Y.; recipient 1st Spencer Tracy Award 1988, for outstanding screen performances and professional achievement.

Address: c/o Triad Artists Inc., 1100 Santa Monica Boulevard, Los Angeles, California 90067, U.S.A.

HURTADO LARREA, Oswaldo, B.RER.POL., D.IUR.; Ecuadorian politician; b. 1940; founded Ecuadorian Christian Democratic Party 1964; Pres. of Congress 1966; Prof. of Political Sociology, Catholic Univ., Quito; Dir. Instituto Ecuatoriano de Desarrollo Social (INEDES) 1966; Under-Sec. of Labour 1969; Sub-Dean, Faculty of Econs. and Dir. Inst. of Econ. Research, Catholic Univ., Quito 1973; invited to form part of World Political Council of Christian Democracy 1975; joined with other political groups to form Popular Democracy 1978; Vice-Pres. of Ecuador and Pres. Consejo Nacional de Desarrollo (Nat. Devt. Council) 1979–81; Pres. of Ecuador 1981–84. *Publications include:* El orden político en Ecuador 1977. *Address:* Quito, Ecuador.

HURVICH, Leo M., PH.D.; American sensory psychologist; b. 11 Sept. 1910, Malden, Mass.; s. of Julius S. Hurvich and Celia Chikinsky; m. Dorothea Jameson 1948; ed. Harvard Coll. and Harvard Univ.; Asst., Dept. of Psychology, Harvard Univ. 1936–37, Instructor and Tutor 1936–40, Research Asst., Div. of Research, Graduate School of Business Admin. 1941–47; Research Psychologist, Color Tech. Div., Eastman Kodak Co. 1947–57; Prof. of Psychology, New York Univ. 1957–62; Prof. of Psychology, Dept. of Psychology and Inst. of Neurological Sciences, Univ. of Pa. 1962–79, Prof. Emer., mem. Inst. of Neurological Sciences, Dir. Vision Training Program 1979–; Fellow, Center for Advanced Study in the Behavioral Sciences, Stanford 1981–82; Fellow American Acad. of Arts and Sciences, American Psychological Assen., Soc. of Experimental Psychologists; mem. N.A.S., Int. Brain Research Org.; Guggenheim Fellow 1964–65; several awards including Howard Crosby Warren Medal for Outstanding Research, Soc. of Experimental Psychologists 1971, Distinguished Scientific Contrib. Award, American Psychological Assen. 1972, Deane B. Judd-AIC Award, Assen. Internationale de la Couleur 1985, Helmholtz Prize 1987 (Cognitive Neuroscience Institute). *Publications:* The Perception of Brightness and Darkness (with D. Jameson) 1966, Outlines of a Theory of the Light Sense (trans., with D. Jameson) 1964, Handbook of Sensory Physiology (Ed., with D. Jameson) 1972, Color Vision 1981. *Address:* Department of Psychology, 3815 Walnut Street, Philadelphia, Pa. 19104, U.S.A. *Telephone:* 215-898-7313.

HURWITZ, Emanuel, C.B.E., F.R.A.M.; British violinist; b. 7 May 1919, London; s. of Isaac Hurwitz and Sarah Gabrilovitch; m. Kathleen Grove 1948; one s. one d.; ed. Royal Acad. of Music, London; Leader, Hurwitz String Quartet 1946–53, Melos Ensemble 1956–74; mem. Goldsborough Orchestra 1947–57, English Chamber Orch. 1957–69, Aeolian String Quartet 1970–81; Prof. Royal Acad. of Music 1968–; recorded complete Haydn Quartets with Aeolian Quartet 1972–76; Gold Medal, Worshipful Company of Musicians 1965. *Leisure interests:* collecting books and antique violin bows, listening to Beethoven piano works, Mozart operas and Schubert songs. *Address:* 25 Dollis Avenue, London, N3 1DA, England. *Telephone:* 01-346 3936.

HURWITZ, Jerard, PH.D.; American research scientist; b. 20 Nov. 1928, New York; ed. Coll. of City of New York, Indiana Univ. and Western Reserve Univ., Cleveland, Ohio; Research Asst., Dept. of Biochemistry, Western Reserve Univ. 1949–50; Instructor in Microbiology, Washington Univ., St. Louis 1956–58; Asst. Prof. in Microbiology, New York Univ. School of Medicine 1958–60, Assoc. Prof. of Microbiology 1960–63; Prof. of Molecular Biology, Albert Einstein Coll. of Medicine, New York 1963–65, Prof. Developmental Biology and Cancer 1965–; Brown-Hazen Lectureship 1972; mem. Biochemical Soc. of England, American Soc. of Biological Chemists, N.A.S. 1974; Fellow, New York Acad. of Sciences 1977; American Cancer Soc. Research Prof.; Fogarty Scholar 1980; Eli Lilly Award in Biochemistry 1962, Charles Mickle Fellowship Award of Canada 1967, Guggenheim Fellowship Award 1968. *Address:* Department of Developmental Biology and Cancer, Albert Einstein College of Medicine, Yeshiva University, 1300 Morris Park Avenue, Bronx, New York, N.Y. 10461, U.S.A. *Telephone:* (212) 430-3127.

HUSAIN, Maqbool Fida; Indian painter; b. 17 Sept. 1915, Sholapur, Maharashtra State; s. of Fida and Zainub Husain; m. Fazila Abbasi 1943; four s. two d.; joined Progressive Artists Group, Bombay 1948; first one-man exhbn., Bombay 1950, later at Rome, Frankfurt, London, Zürich, Prague, Tokyo, New York, New Delhi, Calcutta, Kabul and Baghdad; mem. Lalit Kala Akademi, New Delhi 1954, Gen. Council Nat. Akademi of Art, New Delhi 1955; mem. Rajya Sabha 1986–; First Nat. Award for Painting 1955; Int. Award, Biennale Tokyo 1959. *Major works:* Murals for Air India Int. at Hong Kong, Bangkok, Zürich and Prague 1957, and WHO Building, New Delhi 1963; Mural in Mosaic for Lever Bros. and Aligarh Univ. 1964; High Ceramic Mural for Indian Govt. Building, New Delhi; Exhibitor "Art now in India" exhbn., London 1967; world's largest painting on canvas (240 ft. × 12 ft.) 1985; India through the Lens of a Painter (photographic show), U.S.S.R. 1988. *Publications:* Husain's Letters 1962, Husain 1971, Poetry to be seen 1972, Triangles 1976, Tata's book Husain 1988. *Film:* Through the Eyes of the Painter 1967 (Golden Bear Award, Berlin 1967). *Address:* 11 Jolly Maker Apts. No. 3, 119 Cuffe Prade, Bombay 400 005, India.

HUSÁK, Gustáv, JU.DR., C.SC.; Czechoslovak politician; b. 10 Jan. 1913, Bratislava; m. Viera Husák (died 1977); ed. Law Faculty, Comenius Univ.,

Bratislava; Jr. lawyer, Bratislava 1938–42; office worker 1943–44; took part in Slovak Nat. Rising; Commr. of Interior 1944–45; Commr. for Transport and Technology 1945–46; Chair. of Bd. of Commrs. 1946–50, concurrently Commr. for Agric. 1948; Dept. Head at Cen. Cttee. of CP of Slovakia 1950–51; political imprisonment 1951–60; Building Works, Bratislava 1960–63; Scientific Worker, Inst. of Law, Slovak Acad. of Sciences 1963–68; Deputy Premier 1968; mem. 5th illegal Cen. Cttee. of CP of Slovakia; mem. Cen. Cttee. CP of Slovakia 1943–44, 1945–50, 1968–71, of Presidium 1943–44, 1945–50, 1968–69, of Secr. 1968–69, First Sec. 1968–69; mem. Presidium of Slovak Nat. Council 1943–46, 1968–69, Deputy of Slovak Nat. Council 1945–50, 1968–71; mem. Cen. Cttee. CP of Czechoslovakia 1945, 1949–51, 1968–, of Presidium 1945–50, 1968–, Exec. Cttee. of Presidium 1968–69, mem. Secr. 1969–, First Sec. 1969–71, Gen. Sec. 1971–87; mem. Nat. Assembly 1945–51; Deputy to House of Nations, Fed. Assembly 1968–71, Deputy to House of the People 1971–73, mem. Presidium of Fed. Assembly 1969–75; mem. Presidium, Cen. Cttee. Nat. Front of C.S.S.R. Jan. 1971–, Chair. Cen. Cttee 1971–; C.-in-C. People's Militia of C.S.S.R. April 1969, of Armed Forces 1975–; Pres. of Repub. of Czechoslovakia 1975–; Klement Gottwald Order 1968, 1973, 1983, Order of Lenin 1969, 1973, 1983, 1988, Hero of C.S.S.R. 1969, 1973, 1983, Order of Victorious February 1973, Pahlavi Order 1st Class (Iran), Order of Republic 1978, Order of October Revolution (U.S.S.R.) 1978, Karl Marx Gold Medal (U.S.S.R. Acad. of Sciences) 1981, and numerous other foreign decorations. *Publications:* On the Agricultural Problem in Slovakia 1948, The Struggle for Tomorrow 1948, Evidence on Slovak National Rising 1964. *Address:* c/o Secretariat of the Communist Party of Czechoslovakia, Prague 1, nábř. Ludvíka Svobody 12; Prague-Hrad, Czechoslovakia.

HUSÉN, Torsten, PH.D.; Swedish educationist; b. 1 March 1916, Lund; s. of Johan and Betty (née Prawitz) Husén; m. Ingrid Joensson 1940; two s. one d.; ed. Univ. of Lund; Research Asst., Inst. of Psychology, Univ. of Lund 1938–43; Sr. Psychologist, Swedish Armed Forces 1944–51; Reader in Educational Psychology, Univ. of Stockholm 1947–52, Prof. 1953–56; Prof. of Educ. and Dir. Inst. of Educ. Research, Univ. of Stockholm 1956–71, Prof. of Int. Educ. 1971–82; Chair. Int. Assen. for the Evaluation of Educ. Achievement 1962–78; Fellow, Center for Advanced Study in the Behavioural Sciences, Stanford, Calif. 1965–66, 1973–74, Wissenschaftskolleg, Berlin 1984; mem. Panel of Scientific Advisers to Swedish Govt. 1962–69; Expert in Royal Comms. on Swedish School Reform 1957–65; Consultant to OECD and the World Bank 1968–, United Nations Univ.; Co-Ed. in Chief, Int. Encyclopedia of Educ.; Chair. Governing Bd., Int. Inst. Educ. Planning, Paris 1970–81; mem. Governing Bd. Max Planck Inst., Berlin 1964–82, Int. Council for Educ. Devt. 1971–; Chair. Int. Acad. of Educ. 1986–; Visiting Prof., Univs. of Chicago 1959, Hawaii 1968, Ontario Inst. for Studies in Educ. 1971, Stanford Univ. 1981, California 1984; mem. Swedish Royal Acad. of Sciences 1972–, U.S. Nat. Acad. of Educ. 1967–, American Acad. of Arts and Sciences 1982; LL.D. h.c. (Chicago) 1967, (Glasgow) 1974, D.Tech. (Brunel Univ.) 1974; L.H.D. (Rhode Island Univ.) 1975; D.Ed. (Joensuu) 1979, (Amsterdam) 1982, (Ohio State Univ.) 1985; Hon. Prof. (East China Normal Univ.) 1984; Medal for Distinguished Service in Int. Educ., Teachers Coll., Columbia Univ. 1970. *Publications:* Psychological Twin Research 1959, Problems of Differentiation in Swedish Compulsory Schooling 1962, International Study of Achievement in Mathematics I-II 1967, Educational Research and Educational Change 1968, Talent, Opportunity and Career 1969, Talent, Equality and Meritocracy 1974, Social Influences on Educational Attainment 1975, The School in Question 1979, An Incurable Academic (autobiog.) 1983, Educational Research and Policy 1984, Becoming Adult in a Changing Society (with James Coleman) 1985, The Learning Society Revisited 1986, Higher Education and Social Stratification 1987, Educational Research and School Reforms 1988. *Leisure interest:* book collecting (old books). *Address:* Institute for International Education, S-10691 Stockholm; Armfeltsgatan 10, S-11534 Stockholm, Sweden (Home). *Telephone:* 08-16-20-62 (Office); 08-664-19-76 (Home).

HUSH, Noel Sydney, D.SC., F.A.A., F.R.S.; Australian theoretical chemist; b. 15 Dec. 1924, Sydney; s. of Sidney E. Hush and Adrienne Cooper; m. Thea L. Warman 1949 (deceased); one s. one d.; ed. Univ. of Sydney; Research Fellow, Univ. of Sydney 1946–49; lecturer in Physical Chem., Univ. of Manchester 1950–54; lecturer and Reader in Chem., Univ. of Bristol 1955–71; Foundation Prof. of Theoretical Chem. and Head Dept. of Theoretical Chem., Univ. of Sydney 1971–. *Publications:* ed. Reactions of Molecules at Electrodes 1971, articles in professional journals. *Leisure interests:* literature, music, travel. *Address:* Department of Theoretical Chemistry, University of Sydney, Sydney, N.S.W. (Office); 170 Windsor Street, Paddington, Sydney, N.S.W. 2021, Australia (Home). *Telephone:* 02-692-3330 (Office); 02-328-1685 (Home).

HUSIMI, Kodi, DR.SC.; Japanese physicist; b. 29 June 1909, Nagoya; s. of Manziro and Kané Husimi; m. Mitsue Matsumura 1939; two s. two d.; ed. Imperial Univ. of Tokyo; Prof. of Physics, Imperial Univ. in Osaka (later Osaka Univ.) 1940–61; Prof. and Dir. Inst. of Plasma Physics, Nagoya Univ. 1961–73, now Prof. Emer. of both univs.; mem. Science Council of Japan 1949-57, 1966-85, Pres. 1978-82; mem. Int. Fusian Research Council, Int. Atomic Energy Agency 1971-82, House of Councillors 1983–; Foreign mem. U.S.S.R. Acad. of Sciences 1982, Norwegian Acad. of Arts and Sciences; Medal with Purple Ribbon 1973; Fujiwhara Prize 1980. *Publi-*

cations: Treatise on Probability and Statistics 1942, Quantum Statistical Mechanics 1948, Origami and Geometry 1979. *Leisure interests:* symmetric patterns, Japanese art of paper folding. *Address:* 2-803 Okurayama Heim, 941 Futocho, Kohoku-ku, Yokohama-shi, 222, Japan. *Telephone:* 045-543-2462.

HUSSAIN, Mohammed Mustafa; Maldivan civil servant and diplomatist; b. 1948; m.; two d.; ed. Armidale Coll. of Advanced Education, Australia; taught Majeedliyya School, Malé, Maldive Islands 1974; Dir. Radio Maldives 1974; Under-Sec. Dept. of Educ. 1975; Under-Sec. Dept. of Home Affairs in charge of Atolls Div. 1976; Under-Sec. in charge of Foreign Investments, Div. of Dept. of External Affairs 1976; Counsellor to Maldives Mission to UN 1976; Deputy Perm. Rep. and Deputy to Head of the Dept. of External Affairs of the Maldives 1977; Perm. Rep. of Maldives to the UN 1978-80, 1984-88. *Address:* c/o Ministry of Foreign Affairs, Marine Drive (North) Malé 20-05, The Maldives.

HUSSEIN, Abdirizak Haji; Somali politician and diplomatist; b. 1924, Galkayo District; joined Somali Youth Club which became Somali Youth League 1944, Pres. 1956-58; Pres. of Univ. Inst., Mogadishu 1956-59, mem. Nat. Assembly 1959-69, later formed Popular Movt. for Democratic Action; Minister of Interior, later of Works and Communications 1960-64; Prime Minister 1964-67; detained following coup 1969, released April 1973; Perm. Rep. to UN 1974-80. *Address:* c/o Ministry of Foreign Affairs, Mogadishu, Somalia.

HUSSEIN, Abdul-Aziz; Kuwaiti diplomatist and politician; b. 1921, Kuwait; m. 1948; two s. one d.; ed. Teachers Higher Inst., Cairo and Univ. of London; fmr. Dir. "House of Kuwait", Cairo, Dir.-Gen. Dept. of Educ., Kuwait; Amb. to the U.A.R. 1961-62; Perm. Rep. to Arab League Council; State Minister in Charge of Cabinet Affairs 1963-64; Minister of State for Cabinet Affairs Feb. 1971-85; Counsellor for H.M. the Amir of Kuwait 1985-. *Publication:* Lectures on Arab Society in Kuwait 1960. *Address:* Amari Diwan, Seif Palace, Kuwait City, Kuwait.

HUSSEIN, Hamzah Abbas, B.A.(ECONS.); Kuwaiti central banker; b. 1 Oct. 1934, Kuwait; m. Laila Ahmad Al-Jasem 1964; three d.; ed. American Univ. of Beirut; Govt. official 1959; Admin. Asst., Civil Service Comm. 1959-60; attended several courses on money and banking 1961-62; Sec. and Currency Officer, Kuwait Currency Bd. 1963-68; Deputy Gov. Cen. Bank of Kuwait 1968-73, Gov. 1973-83; Chair. of Bd., Banking Studies Centre of Kuwait 1970-83. *Leisure interest:* swimming. *Address:* c/o Central Bank of Kuwait, Abdulla Al-Salem Street, P.O. Box 526, Kuwait City, Kuwait.

HUSSEIN, Mansour, B.SC.; Egyptian politician; b. 1923; fmr. school teacher and headmaster in El-Fayoum; Ministry of Planning 1962-67; First Under-Sec., then Deputy Minister of Educ. 1977-84; mem. Shoura (Advisory) Council 1981; Pres. Egyptian Teachers' Union; Minister of Educ. 1985-86. *Publications:* many books and studies in the field of educ. *Address:* c/o Ministry of Education, Sharia El Falaky, Cairo, Egypt. *Telephone:* 27363.

HUSSEIN, Saddam, LL.B; Iraqi politician; b. 1937, Tikrit, nr. Baghdad; m. Sajida Khairalla 1963; two s. two d.; ed. al-Karkh Secondary School, Baghdad, al-Qasr al-Aini Secondary School, Cairo, Cairo Univ. and al-Mustanseriya Univ., Baghdad; joined Arab Baath Socialist Party 1957; sentenced to death for attempted execution of Gen. Abdul Karim Qassim 1959; joined leadership of Cairo branch of Baath Party 1962; returned to Iraq following revolution 1963; mem. 4th Regional Congress and 6th Nat. Congress of Baath Party 1963; mem. Regional Leadership of Baath Party in Iraq following overthrow of Party rule 1963; mem. 7th Nat. Congress, Syria 1964; arrested for plotting overthrow of Abdul Salam Aref 1964; elected mem. leadership by 8th Nat. Congress while still in prison 1965; Deputy Sec. Regional Leadership of Baath Party 1966-79, Sec. 1979-; played prominent role in July 1968 revolution; Act. Deputy Chair. Revolutionary Command Council 1968-69; Deputy Chair. Revolutionary Command Council 1969-79, Chair. 1979-; Pres. of Iraq July 1979- also Prime Minister; Deputy Sec. Regional Leadership in 7th Regional Congress 1968; mem. Nat. Leadership of Party in 10th National Congress 1970; rank of Gen. 1976; Order of Rafidain, 1st Class 1976. *Publication:* One Trench or Two. *Address:* Revolutionary Command Council, Baghdad, Iraq.

HUSSEIN BIN ONN, Datuk, S.P.M.J.; Malaysian barrister and politician (retd.); b. 12 Feb. 1922; s. of the late Dato Onn bin Ja'afar (founder-president of UMNO); ed. Cambridge School, Indian Mil. Acad., Dehra Dun, Lincoln's Inn, England; commissioned in Indian Army 1942, served in Middle East and India; Mil. Gen. H.Q., New Delhi; with British Liberation Forces, Malaya 1945; served Malay Admin. Service, Kuala Selangor and Klang 1946-47; Nat. Youth Leader and Sec.-Gen. United Malays Nat. Org. (UMNO) 1947; mem. Fed. Legislative Council, Jahore Council of State and State Exec. Council 1948-57; called to the Bar, London 1960; rejoined UMNO 1968, Pres. 1976-81; M.P. 1970; Minister of Educ. 1970-73; Deputy Prime Minister 1973-76, Minister of Finance and Co-ordinator of Public Corpns. 1974-76; Prime Minister 1976-81, also Minister of Defence 1976-78, 1980-81, of the Fed. Territory 1978-80; Seri Paduka Mahkota Johor, Seri Maharaja Mangku Negara 1981. *Address:* 3 Jalan Kenny, Kuala Lumpur, Malaysia (Home).

HUSSEIN IBN TALAL, King of Jordan; b. 14 Nov. 1935; ed. Victoria Coll., Alexandria, Harrow School, and Royal Mil. Acad., Sandhurst, England; succeeded his father 11 Aug. 1952; came to power 2 May 1953; married 1955, Princess Dina, d. of Abdel-Hamid Aoun of Hijaz (marriage dissolved); daughter Princess Alia b. 1956; married 1961, Antoinette Gardiner (assumed name of Muna el Hussein, divorced 1972); sons, Prince Abdullah b. 1962, Prince Feisal b. 1963, twin daughters, Princess Zein and Princess Ayesha, b. April 1968; married 1972, Alia Baha Eddin Toukan (died 1977), daughter of Baha ud-Din Toukan (q.v.); daughter Princess Haya b. 1974, son Prince Ali b. 1975; married 1978 Lisa Halaby (now Queen Noor); sons Prince Hamzeh b. 1980, Prince Hashem b. 1981, daughters Princess Iman b. 1983, Princess Rayah b. 1986; Order of Al-Nahda, of Al-Kawkab, of Al-Istiqlal; many other decorations. *Publications:* Uneasy Lies the Head 1962, My War with Israel 1967. *Leisure interests:* water sports, karate, flying, driving, fencing, photography, ham radio. *Address:* Royal Palace, Amman, Jordan.

HUSSEY, Gemma, B.A.; Irish politician; b. 1938, Bray, Co. Wicklow; m. Dermot R. Hussey; one s. two d.; ed. Loreto Convent, Bray, Convent of the Sacred Heart, Mount Anville, Dublin and Univ. Coll., Dublin; Chair. Women's Political Assen. 1973-75, Vice-Chair. 1975-77; mem. Council for the Status of Women 1973-75; mem. Seanad Eireann 1977-82, Govt. Leader of Seanad 1981-82; mem. Dail Eireann 1982-; Minister for Educ. 1982-86, for Social Welfare 1986-87; Fine Gael. *Address:* c/o Department of Social Welfare, Arus Mhic Dhiarmada, Store Street, Dublin 1, Ireland. *Telephone:* 786444.

HUSSEY, Marmaduke James, M.A.; British business executive; b. 29 Aug. 1923; s. of late E. R. J. Hussey, C.M.G. and Christine Hussey; m. Lady Susan K. Waldegrave 1959; one s. one d.; ed. Rugby School and Trinity Coll., Oxford; served with Grenadier Guards, Italy 1939-45; joined Associated Newspapers 1949, Dir. 1964; Man. Dir. Harmsworth Publs. 1967-70; mem. Thomson Org. Exec. Bd. 1971; Chief. Exec. and Man. Dir. Times Newspapers Ltd. 1971-80, Dir. 1982-86; Chair. Bd. of Govs. BBC Nov. 1986-; Chair. Royal Marsden Hosp. 1985-; a Rhodes Trustee 1972-; mem. Bd. British Council 1983-; Trustee Royal Acad. Trust 1988-; Vice-Chair. Appeals Cttee. B.L.E.S.M.A.; Dir. Colonial Mutual Group PLC, Wm. Collins PLC 1985-89; Jt. Chair. Great Western Radio 1985-86; mem. Govt. Working Party on Artificial Limb and Appliance Centres in England 1984-86, Man. Cttee. and Educ. Cttee. King Edward's Hosp. Fund for London 1987-89. *Address:* BBC, Portland Place, London, W.1.; Flat 15, 45147 Courtfield Road, London, SW7 4DB, England (Home).

HUSZÁR, István; Hungarian economist; b. 1927, Hernádkak; s. of István Huszár and Mária Kovács; m. Mária Forgó 1953; one c.; ed. Karl Marx Univ. of Econs., Budapest; joined CP 1948; Asst. Lecturer, Dept. of Statistics, Karl Marx Univ. of Econs. 1951-53; worked in party HQ 1953-63, Deputy Head Dept. of State Econs. 1961-63; mem. Cen. Cttee. Hungarian Socialist Workers' Party 1970-, Political Cttee. 1975-80; First Deputy Pres., then Pres. Cen. Statistics Office 1963-73; First Deputy Pres. Nat. Planning Office 1973; Deputy Prime Minister 1973-80; mem. Cttee. of Econ. Policy attached to HSWP Cen. Cttee. 1975-80; MP 1980-85; Pres. Nat. Planning Office 1975-80; Dir.-Gen. HSWP Inst. for Social Sciences 1980-85; Dir. HSWP Inst. for Party History 1985-88; mem. Cttee. for Agitation and Propaganda attached to HSWP Cen. Cttee. 1980-, Nat. Council Patriotic People's Front 1985-; Sec.-Gen. Hungarian Patriotic People's Front; Titular Univ. Prof. *Address:* 1360 Budapest, Hungary.

HUTASINGH, Prakob, D.JUR.; Thai judge; b. 5 Feb. 1912; s. of Praya Sapakit Kasertakarn and Lady Sawong Sapakit Kasertakarn; m. Lady Chuanchuen 1942; three s. one d.; ed. Vajiravuth Coll., Univ. of Jena and Thammasat Univ., Bangkok; joined the judiciary 1937; Asst. Judge Court of Appeal 1941; Sec. Supreme Court 1948; Asst. Judge Supreme Court 1950; Judge, Appeal Court 1953; Judge, Supreme Court 1960; Pres. Supreme Court 1967-72; Minister of Justice 1973-74; Deputy Prime Minister 1974-75; Pres. Thai Bar and Inst. of Legal Educ., Thai Bar; mem. Thai Privy Council 1975-; Hon. D.C.L. *Publications:* various legal textbooks. *Address:* 71 Soi Senanikom 1, Phaholyotin Road, Bangkhen, Bangkok, Thailand. *Telephone:* 579-5445 or 579-5446.

HUTCHINSON, G(eorge) Evelyn, M.A.; American (b. British) professor emeritus of zoology; b. 30 Jan. 1903, Cambridge, England; s. of Arthur Hutchinson and Evaline Demezy Shipley; m. 1st G. Margaret Seal 1933 (died 1983), m. 2nd Anne Washington 1985; ed. St Faith's School, Cambridge, Gresham's School, Holt, and Emmanuel Coll., Cambridge; Int. Educ. Fellow, Rockefeller Foundation, Stazione Zoological, Naples, Italy 1925-26; Sr. Lecturer in Zoology, Univ. of the Witwatersrand, S. Africa 1926-28; Instr., rising to Sterling Prof. of Zoology, Yale Univ. 1928-72, Prof. Emer. and Sr. Research Biologist 1972-; Foreign mem. Royal Soc.; Tyler Award; Franklin Medal; Kyoto Prize (Inamori Foundation) 1986. *Publications:* The Clear Mirror, A Pattern of Life in Goa and Indian Tibet 1936, The Itinerant Ivory Tower 1953, Treatise on Limnology Vol. I 1957, Vol II 1967, Vol. III 1975, The Enchanted Voyage 1962, The Ecological Theatre and the Evolutionary Play 1965, Introduction to Population Ecology 1978, The Kindly Fruits of the Earth 1979; about 180 scientific papers. *Leisure interests:* art history, writings of Dame Rebecca West. *Address:* Department of Biology, OML 231, Yale University, Box 6666, New Haven,

Conn. 06511 (Office); 269 Canner Street, New Haven, Conn. 06511, U.S.A. (Home). *Telephone:* (203) 432-3866 (Office); (203) 865-6837 (Home).

HUTCHINSON, Maxwell, F.R.S.A.; British architect; b. 3 Dec. 1948; s. of late Frank M. Hutchinson and Elizabeth R. M. Wright; ed. Oundle, Scott Sutherland School of Architecture, Aberdeen and Architectural Asscn. School of Architecture; founder, Hutchinson & Partners (Chartered Architects) 1972, Chair. Hutchinson & Partners Architects Ltd. 1987–; Chair. Permarock Products, Ltd., Loughborough 1985–; mem. Council, Royal Inst. of British Architects (RIBA) 1978–, Sr. Vice-Pres. 1988–89, Pres. 1989–(91); Vice-Pres. Industrial Bldg. Bureau 1988–; Chair. Property Discussion Group, City Branch Cttee., B.I.M., London Branch Elgar Soc., Freeman of London; occasional broadcaster on radio and TV. *Publications:* contributions to tech. and nat. press on architectural subjects. *Leisure interests:* composing, recording, playing the guitar loudly, music of Edward Elgar, opera, ballet, theatre, riding, running, Rutland. *Address:* Hutchinson & Partners, 33 Upper Street, London, N1 0PN, England. *Telephone:* 01-226 9708.

HUTCHISON, Clyde A., Jr., PH.D.; American university professor; b. 5 May 1913, Alliance, Ohio; s. of Clyde A. and Bessie G. Hutchison; m. Sarah Jane West 1937; two s. one d.; ed. Ohio State Univ.; Nat. Research Council Fellow, Columbia Univ. 1937–38; Asst. Prof. of Chem., Univ. of Buffalo 1939–45; Research Assoc., Univ. of Va. 1942–43, Manhattan District Project 1943–45; Asst. Prof. Enrico Fermi Inst., Univ. of Chicago 1945–50, Dept. of Chem. 1948–50; Assoc. Prof. Enrico Fermi Inst. and Dept. of Chem. 1950–54, Prof. 1954–63, Carl William Eisendrath Prof. 1963–69, Carl. W. Eisendrath Distinguished Service Prof. of Chem. 1969–83, Emer. 1984–, Chair. Dept. of Chem. 1959–62; Consultant Argonne Nat. Lab. 1946–; Ed., Journal of Chemical Physics, American Inst. of Physics 1953–59; mem. Nat. Acad. of Sciences, A.C.S.; Visiting Prof. sponsored by Japan Soc. for the Promotion of Science 1975; Eastman Prof., Oxford Univ. 1981–82; Visiting Lecturer, Chinese Acad. of Sciences 1986; Fellow, American Acad. of Arts and Sciences, American Physical Soc. (mem. Council 1967–71); Guggenheim Fellow, Oxford Univ. 1955–56, 1972–73; Hon. D.Sc. (Cedarville); Ohio State Univ. Centennial Achievement Award 1970; Peter Debye Award, A.C.S. 1972. *Publications:* 103 scientific papers, documents and contribs. to books. *Address:* Department of Chemistry, University of Chicago, Chicago, Ill. 60637, U.S.A. *Telephone:* (312) 702-7069.

HUTCHISON, Sir W(illiam) Kenneth, Kt., C.B.E., F.R.S.; British engineer; b. 30 Oct. 1903; s. of the late William Hutchison; m. Dorothea Bluett 1929; one d.; ed. Edinburgh Acad. and Corpus Christi Coll. Oxford; Research Chemist, Gas, Light & Coke Co. 1926; Asst. Dir. of Hydrogen Production, Air Ministry 1940, Dir. 1942; Dir. of Compressed Gases 1943; Controller of By-Products, Gas, Light & Coke Co. 1945, Man. Dir. 1947; Chair. South Eastern Gas Bd. 1948–59; Deputy Chair. Gas Council 1960–66; Chair. Int. Man. and Eng. Group 1967–69; Dir. Newton Chambers & Co. Ltd. 1967–73; Pres. Inst. of Gas Engs. 1955–56, British Road Tar Assen. 1953–55, Inst. of Chem. Engs. 1959–61, Soc. of British Gas Industries 1967–68, Nat. Soc. for Clean Air 1969–71. *Publications:* High Speed Gas (autobiog.) 1987, papers in learned journals. *Leisure interests:* garden, golf. *Address:* 2 Arlington Road, Twickenham, Middx., TW1 2BG, England. *Telephone:* 01-892 1685.

HUTT, Peter Barton, B.A., LL.M.; American lawyer; b. 16 Nov. 1934, Buffalo, N.Y.; s. of Lester Ralph Hutt and Louise Rich Fraser; m. Eleanor Jane Zurn 1959; two s. two d; ed. Phillips Exeter Acad., Yale and Harvard Univs.; Assoc., Covington and Burling (law firm) 1960–68, Partner 1968–71, 1975–; Chief Counsel, U.S. Food and Drug Admin. 1971–75; Underwood-Prescott Award, M.I.T. 1977. *Publications:* Dealing with Drug Abuse (with Patricia M. Wald) 1972, Food and Drug Law: Cases and Materials (with Richard A. Merrill) 1980. *Leisure interests:* research on the history of govt. regulation of food and drugs. *Address:* Covington & Burling, 1201 Pennsylvania Avenue, N.W., Washington, D.C. 20004, U.S.A. *Telephone:* (202) 662-5522.

HUTTEROVA, Marie; Czechoslovak politician; b. 1940, Sachtice; mem. CP of Czechoslovakia (CPCZ) 1940–; active in Nat. Front, youth movt., Co-operative Farmers' Union and Czechoslovakia-Soviet Friendship Cttee.; mem. CPCZ Cen. Control and Audit Comm.; mem. Presidium, Breclav Party District Cttee.; mem. Secr. CPCZ Cen. Cttee. Oct. 1988–. *Address:* Central Committee of the Communist Party of Czechoslovakia, Prague, Czechoslovakia.

HUTTON, Sir Leonard, Kt.; British cricketer and company director; b. 23 June 1916, Pudsey, Yorkshire; s. of Henry Hutton; m. Dorothy Mary Dennis 1939; two s.; ed. Littlemoor School, Pudsey; right-hand batsman; first played for Yorkshire 1934; first played for England 1937; captained England v India 1952, v Australia 1953, v Pakistan 1954, v Australia 1954; captained M.C.C. v West Indies 1953–54; made record Test score, 364 runs v Australia at the Oval, London 1938; made 1,294 runs in single month, June 1949; more than 100 hundreds in first-class cricket; retd. from cricket 1956, from Business 1984; a selector, M.C.C. 1975–77; served in Royal Artillery and Army Physical Training Corps, Second World War; Dir. Fenner Int. (Power Transmission); 1970–84; writes on cricket for The Observer; Hon. mem. M.C.C. 1955. *Publications:* Cricket is My Life 1950, Just My Story 1956, Fifty Years in Cricket 1984. *Leisure interests:* golf,

interior decorating, family. *Address:* Ebor House, 1 Coombe Neville, Warren Road, Kingston-upon-Thames, Surrey, KT2 7HW, England. *Telephone:* 01-942 0604.

HUVELIN, Paul; French engineer; b. 22 July 1902, Chorey-les-Beaune, Côte d'Or; s. of Henri and Louise Ricaud; m. Madeleine Giros 1928; six s. two d.; ed. Lycée Carnot, Dijon, and Ecole Polytechnique, Paris; Engineer in charge of production, Société Métallurgique de Normandie 1924–27; Chief Engineer, Sec. and Man. l'Electrique Lille-Roubaix-Tourcoing and Chemin de fer de l'Est de Lyon 1928–36; Man. Soc. Industrielle de Gérance et d'Exploitation, later Man. Soc. Gén. d'Exploitations Industrielles (SOGEI) 1936–47, Chair. of Bd. and Pres. 1947–; Chair. and Pres. Energie Electrique du Nord de la France 1940–46, Cie. Electrique de la Loire et du Centre 1945–46; Chair. and Pres. Société Kleber-Colombes 1959–70, Hon. Pres. 1970–; Pres. Centre Français de Promotion Industrielle en Afrique 1972–; Vice-Pres. and Dir. Thomson-Brandt 1972–76; Dir. Soc. Générale d'Entreprises (SGE), Sogelerg from 1978, CGE until 1982; Pres. Conseil Nat. du Patronat Français from 1966 and Hon. Pres. 1973–; Pres. l'Union des Industries de la Communauté Européenne (UNICE) 1972–76. *Leisure interests:* music, golf, tennis. *Address:* 37 rue de Sèvres, 75006 Paris, France (Home). *Telephone:* 42.22.47.40 (Home).

HUXLEY, Sir Andrew Fielding, Kt., O.M., SC.D., F.R.S.; British physiologist; b. 22 Nov. 1917, London; s. of Leonard and Rosalind (née Bruce) Huxley; m. Jocelyn Richenda Gammell Pease 1947; one s. five d.; ed. Univ. Coll. School, Westminster School and Trinity Coll., Cambridge; Operational Research, Anti-Aircraft Command 1940–42, Admiralty 1942–45; Fellow of Trinity Coll., Cambridge 1941–60, Dir. of Studies 1952–60, Hon. Fellow 1967; Master of Trinity College 1984–; Demonstrator, Dept. of Physiology, Cambridge Univ. 1946–50, Asst. Dir. of Research 1951–59, Reader in Experimental Biophysics 1959–60; Jodrell Prof. of Physiology, Univ. Coll., London 1960–69; Royal Soc. Research Prof. 1969–83, Prof. Emer. of Physiology, Univ. of London 1983–; Pres. British Assen. for the Advancement of Science 1976–77; Chair. Medical Research Cttee. of the Muscular Dystrophy Group 1974–80, Vice-Pres. Muscular Dystrophy Group 1980–; mem. Govt.'s Scientific Authority for Animals 1976–77, Agric. Research Council 1977–81, Council of the Royal Soc. 1960–62, 1977–79, 1980–85, Council of the Int. Union of Physiological Sciences (IUPS) 1983–; Chair. Agric. Research Council's Research Grants Cttee.—Animals 1978–81, British Nat. Cttee. for Physiological Sciences 1979–80; Pres. Royal Soc. 1980–85, Int. Union of Physiological Sciences 1986–; Trustee, British Museum (Natural History) 1981–, Science Museum 1983–88; First Florey Lecturer, Australia 1982; Romanes Lecturer, Oxford 1982–83, Fenn Lecturer, Sydney 1983; Nobel Prize for Physiology or Medicine 1963; Copley Medal (Royal Soc.) 1973; Fellow, Imp. Coll. of Science and Tech. 1980–; Hon. Fellow, Univ. Coll., London 1980–, Inst. of Biology 1981–, Darwin Coll., Cambridge 1981–, Royal Soc. of Edinburgh 1983–, Fellowship of Eng. 1986; Hon. Fellow, Queen Mary Coll. 1987; Hon. mem. Royal Irish Acad. 1986, Japan Acad. 1988; Hon. Research Fellow, Dept. of Physiology, Univ. Coll.; London 1983; Foreign Fellow Indian Natural Sciences Acad. 1985; mem. Home Office Animal Procedures Cttee. 1987; hon. mem. American Soc. Zoologists 1985; Trustee Nature Conservancy Council 1985–87; Assoc. mem. Royal Acad. of Sciences, Letters and Fine Arts, Belgium 1978; Hon. Foreign mem. American Acad. of Arts and Sciences 1961, Royal Acad. of Medicine, Belgium 1978; Hon. M.D. (Saar) 1964, Hon. D.Sc. (Sheffield) 1964, (Leicester) 1967, (London) 1973, (St. Andrews) 1974, (Aston) 1977, (Oxford) 1983, (Keele) 1985, (Md.) 1987, (Brunel) 1988, Hon. Sc.D. (Cambridge) 1978, Hon. LL.D. (Birmingham) 1979; Dr. h.c. (Marseilles) 1979, (York) 1981, (W. Australia) 1982, (Harvard Univ.) 1984, (Humboldt Univ.) 1985, Hon. Sc.D. (East Anglia) 1985. *Publications:* papers chiefly in Journal of Physiology, Reflections on Muscle (Sherrington Lectures, Liverpool Univ.). *Leisure interests:* walking, design of scientific instruments. *Address:* The Master's Lodge, Trinity College, Cambridge, CB2 1TQ, England. *Telephone:* (0223) 338412.

HUXLEY, Elspeth Josceline, C.B.E., J.P.; British author; b. 23 July 1907, London; d. of the late Josceline Grant and of Eleanor Grant; m. Gervas Huxley 1931 (died 1971); one s.; ed. Reading and Cornell Univs.; Asst. Press Officer, Empire Marketing Bd. 1929–32; extensive travels in America, Africa and elsewhere with her husband Gervas Huxley; mem. Monckton Comm. on Cen. Africa 1960. *Publications:* White Man's Country, Lord Delamere and the Making of Kenya (2 vols.) 1933, Red Strangers (novel) 1939, The Walled City (novel), The Sorcerer's Apprentice (travel) 1948, Four Guineas (travel) 1952, A Thing to Love (novel) 1954, The Red Rock Wilderness (novel) 1957, The Flame Trees of Thika (autobiog.) 1959, A New Earth 1960, The Mottled Lizard 1962, The Merry Hippo 1963, A Man from Nowhere 1963, Forks and Hope 1964, Back Street New Worlds 1964, Brave New Victuals 1965, Their Shining Eldorado (travel) 1967, Love Among the Daughters (3rd Vol. of autobiog.) 1968, The Challenge of Africa 1971, Livingstone and his African Journeys 1974, Florence Nightingale 1975, Gallipot Eyes: A Wiltshire Diary 1976, Scott of the Antarctic 1977, Nellie: Letters from Africa 1980, Whipsnade: Captive Breeding for Survival 1981, The Prince Buys the Manor (novel) 1982, Last Days in Eden 1984, Out in the Midday Sun: My Kenya 1985; detective novels: Murder at Government House 1937, Murder on Safari 1938, Death of an Aryan 1939 (reprinted as African Poison Murders 1985). *Leisure interests:* reading, walking and country pursuits. *Address:* Green End, Oaksey, nr. Malmesbury, Wilts., England. *Telephone:* 06667 252.

HUXLEY, Hugh Esmor, M.B.E., F.R.S., PH.D., SC.D.; British scientist; b. 25 Feb. 1924, Birkenhead, Cheshire; s. of Thomas Hugh Huxley and Olwen Roberts; m. Frances Fripp 1966; one d.; two step s., one step d.; ed. Park High School, Birkenhead and Christ's Coll., Cambridge; Radar Officer, R.A.F. Bomber Command and Telecommunications Research Establishment, Malvern 1943–47; Research Student, Medical Research Council Unit for Molecular Biology, Cavendish Lab., Cambridge 1948–52; Commonwealth Fund Fellow, Biology Dept., M.I.T. 1952–54; Research Fellow, Christ's Coll., Cambridge 1953–56; mem. of External Staff of Medical Research Council and Hon. Research Assoc., Biophysics Dept., Univ. Coll. London 1956–61; mem. of Scientific Staff, Medical Research Council Lab. of Molecular Biology, Cambridge 1962–87, Jt. Head, Structural Studies Div. 1976–87, Deputy Dir. 1977–87; Prof. of Biology and Dir., Rosenstiel Basic Medical Sciences Research Centre, Brandeis Univ., Boston, Mass. 1988–; Fellow, King's Coll., Cambridge 1961–67, Churchill Coll., Cambridge 1967–87; Harvey Soc. Lecturer, New York 1964–65; Sr. Visiting Lecturer, Physiology Course, Woods Hole, Mass. 1966–71; Wilson Lecturer, Univ. of Tex. 1968; Dunham Lecturer, Harvard Medical School 1969; Croonian Lecturer, Royal Soc. of London 1970; Ziskind Visiting Prof. of Biology, Brandeis Univ. 1971; Penn Lecturer, Univ. of Pa. 1971; Mayer Lecturer, M.I.T. 1971; Miller Lecturer, State Univ. of N.Y. 1973; Carter-Wallace Lecturer, Princeton Univ. 1973; Pauling Lecturer, Stanford Univ. 1980; Jesse Beams Lecturer, Univ. of Va. 1980; Ida Beam Lecturer, Univ. of Ia. 1981; mem. Advisory Bd. of Rosentiel Basic Medical Sciences Center, Brandeis Univ. 1971–77; mem. Council of Royal Soc. of London 1973–75, 1984–86; mem. Scientific Advisory Cttee., European Molecular Biology Lab. 1975–81; mem. Bd. of Trustees, Associated Univs. Inc. 1987–; mem. German Acad. of Science, Leopoldina 1964; Foreign Hon. mem. American Acad. of Arts and Sciences 1965, Danish Acad. of Sciences 1971, American Soc. of Biological Chemists 1976, Foreign Assoc. N.A.S. 1978, American Assscn. of Anatomists 1981, American Physiological Soc. 1981, American Soc. of Zoologists 1986; Hon. Fellow, Christ's Coll., Cambridge 1981; Hon. D.Sc. (Harvard) 1969, (Univ. of Chicago) 1974, (Univ. of Pa.) 1976, (Leicester) 1988; Feldberg Award for Experimental Medical Research 1963, William Bate Hardy Prize of the Cambridge Philosophical Soc. 1965, Louisa Gross Horwitz Prize 1971, Int. Feltrinelli Prize for Medicine 1974, Int. Award, Gairdner Foundation 1975, Baly Medal, Royal Coll. of Physicians 1975, Royal Medal, Royal Soc. of London 1977, E. B. Wilson Medal, American Soc. for Cell Biology 1983, Albert Einstein World Award of Science 1987. *Publications:* articles in scientific journals. *Leisure interests:* skiing, sailing. *Address:* Rosenstiel Basic Medical Sciences Research Center, Brandeis University, Waltham, Mass. 02254, U.S.A.

HUXTABLE, Ada Louise, A.B.; American writer and critic; b. New York; d. of Michael Louis and Leah (Rosenthal) Landman; m. L. Garth Huxtable 1942; ed. Hunter Coll., and Inst. of Fine Arts, New York Univ.; Asst. curator of architecture and design, Museum of Modern Art, New York 1946–50; Fulbright Scholarship to study contemporary Italian architecture and design 1950, 1952; contributing ed. Progressive Architecture, Art in America, freelance writer on architecture and design 1952–63; architecture critic, New York Times 1963–82; mem. Times Editorial Bd. 1973–82; mem. Corpn. Visiting Cttees. on Architecture, Harvard Univ. and the M.I.T., Rockefeller Univ. Council, Smithsonian Council, Advisory Bd. of the Centre for the Study of American Architecture, Columbia Univ.; professional socs.: Soc. of Architectural Historians; mem. American Acad. and Inst. of Arts and Letters; Hon. mem. American Inst. of Architects; Hon. Fellow Royal Inst. of British Architects; Fellow of American Acad. of Arts and Sciences; Fellow New York Inst. for the Humanities; Guggenheim fellowship for studies in American architecture 1958; numerous hon. degrees; numerous prizes and awards including: Frank Jewett Mather Award of Coll. Art Asscn. for art criticism 1967, Pulitzer Prize for Distinguished Criticism 1970, Architectural Criticism Medal of American Inst. of Architects 1969, Special Award of Nat. Trust for Historic Preservation 1970, Nat. Arts Club Medal for Literature 1971, Diamond Jubilee Medallion of the City of New York 1973, U.S. Sec. of Interiors' Conservation Award 1976, Thomas Jefferson Medal for Architecture 1977, Jean Tschumi Prize for Architectural Criticism, Int. Union of Architects 1987, Medal for Architectural Criticism (Acad. d'Architecture Française) 1988, MacArthur Prize Fellowship 1981–86. *Publications:* Pier Luigi Nervi 1960, Classical New York 1964, Will They Ever Finish Bruckner Boulevard? 1970, Kicked a Building Lately? 1976, The Tall Building Artistically Reconsidered: The Search for a Skyscraper Style 1985, Architecture, Anyone? 1986, Goodbye History, Hello Hamburger 1986. *Address:* 969 Park Avenue, New York, N.Y. 10028, U.S.A.

HUYDECOPER, Jonkheer (Jan Louis) Reinier, LL.M.; Netherlands diplomatist; b. 23 Feb. 1922, Utrecht; s. of Jonkheer Louis Huydecoper and Jonkvrouwe Laurence B. W. Ram; m. Baroness Constance C. van Wassenaer 1944; one s. two d.; ed. Univ. of Utrecht; banking 1942–44; Legal Dept., Ministry of Finance 1945–46; entered Ministry of Foreign Affairs 1946; served UN, New York 1946, Ottawa 1947–48, Military Mission, Berlin 1949–50, Bonn 1950–52, London 1952–56, Djakarta 1956–59, Washington 1959–62, Rome 1962–66, Ministry of Foreign Affairs 1966–70, London 1970–73; Amb. and Head. of Del. to European Security Conf., Helsinki

and Geneva 1973–74; Amb. to U.S.S.R. 1974–77, to Portugal 1978–80; Inspector of Foreign Service 1981–82; Amb. to U.K. (also accred. to Iceland) 1982–86; Chevalier, Order of Netherlands Lion, Commdr. Order of Orange Nassau; Hon. G.C.V.O. and other foreign decorations. *Address:* Wassenaarseweg 132, The Hague, Netherlands.

HUYGENS, Robert Burchard Constantijn, PH.D.; Netherlands professor of Medieval Latin; b. 10 Dec. 1931, The Hague; m. Caroline Sprey 1962; one s. two d.; ed. Leiden Univ.; army service 1952–54; lecturer in Medieval Latin, Univ. of Leiden 1964, Prof. 1968–; Fellow, Dumbarton Oaks, Washington, D.C. 1982, Inst. for Advanced Study, Jerusalem 1983–84, Inst. for Advanced Study, Princeton, N.J. 1986–87, Herzog August Bibliothek, Wolfenbüttel 1987; mem. Royal Netherlands Acad., Soc. des Antiquaires de France, Monumenta Germaniae Historica. *Publications include:* Jacques de Vitry 1960, Accessus ad Auctores 1970, Vézelay 1976, William of Tyre 1986, Berengar of Tours 1988. *Address:* Witte Singel 28, 2311 BH Leiden, Netherlands. *Telephone:* 071-143798/272746.

HUYGHE, René; French art critic and historian; b. 3 May 1906, Arras, Pas de Calais; s. of Louis Huyghe and Marie Delvoye; m. Lydie Bouthet 1950; one s. one d.; ed. Ecole du Louvre and Faculty of Letters, Paris; on staff of Musée du Louvre 1927; Asst. Keeper 1930; Keeper of Paintings 1937; Head Keeper of Paintings and Drawings 1945; Prof. Ecole du Louvre; Prof. of Psychology of Plastic Arts, Coll. de France 1950–76; mem. French Museum Council 1952, Vice-Pres. 1964, Pres. 1974–88; Res. Prof. Nat. Gallery of Art Washington 1968; fmr. Pres. UNESCO Int. Cttee. of experts to save Venice; Dir. Musée Jacquemart André 1974–; Dir. of art review L'Amour de l'Art 1930–; founder and dir. of review Quadrige 1945–; Vice-Pres. Acad. Européenne; has collaborated or organized numerous exhbns., including French Art, London 1931, Van Gogh and Masterpieces of French Art, Paris 1937, Modern Painting, Rio de Janeiro 1945, etc.; has made art films, including Rubens and His Age (Venice Festival Prize); mem. and fmr. Pres. Académie Septentrionale; Grand Officier Légion d'honneur, Grand Croix Ordre du Mérite, Commdr. Ordre de Léopold, Commdr. Order of Merit (Italy), Commdr. and Mérite Culturel (Monaco), Commdr. Couronne de chêne (Luxembourg); mem. Acad. Française 1960–; Erasmus Prize 1966. *Publications:* Histoire de l'art contemporain 1934, Cézanne 1936, La peinture française: le portrait (2 vols.) 1937, Les dessins de Van Gogh 1937, Les contemporains 1939, La peinture actuelle 1945, La poétique de Vermeer 1948, Le dessin français au XIXe siècle 1949, Univers de Watteau 1950, Gauguin et Noa-Noa 1951, Le carnet de Gauguin 1952, La peinture d'occident 1952, Dialogue avec le visible 1955, L'art et l'homme, Vol. I 1957, Vol. II 1958, Vol. III 1961, Van Gogh 1958, Gauguin 1959, L'art et l'âme 1960, Peinture française aux XVIIe et XVIIIe siècles 1962, Delacroix ou le combat solitaire 1963, Les puissances de l'image 1965, Sens et destin de l'art 1967, L'art et le monde moderne 2 vols. 1970, Formes et forces 1971, La relève du réel 1974, La relève de l'imaginaire 1976, Ce que je crois 1976, De l'art à la philosophie 1980, La nuit appelle l'aurore 1980, Les signes du temps et l'art moderne 1985. *Address:* 3 rue Corneille, 75006 Paris, France (Home).

HUYGHUES-des-ETAGES, Jacques, D. EN MED.; French doctor and politician; b. 15 Nov. 1923, Paris; m. Simone Lebois 1953; one s. one d.; resistance fighter Jan. 1941–46; Doctor, Alligny-Cosne 1953–69, Cosne 1969–88; Town Councillor 1965–; Regional Councillor 1971–82, Deputy 1973–86, 1988–; Mayor of Cosne 1977–; Perm. Rep. Council of Europe 1986–88; Chevalier Légion d'honneur. *Leisure interests:* hunting, fishing, photography, trips abroad. *Address:* 14 rue Waldeck-Rousseau, 58200 Cosne-Cours sur Loire, France. *Telephone:* 86 28 10 84.

HUYNH TAN PHAT; Vietnamese politician; b. 1913; mem. Vanguard Youth 1945; Ed. Thanh-nien during anti-French struggle; remained in S. Viet-Nam after Geneva Agreement 1954; Sec.-Gen. Democratic Party; mem. Cen. Cttee. Nat. Liberation Front (NLF) 1964–; Pres. Provisional Revolutionary Govt. of Repub. of S. Viet-Nam 1969–76 (in Saigon 1975–76); Vice-Premier Council of Ministers, Socialist Repub. of Viet-Nam 1976–82, also Chair. for State Comm. for Capital Construction 1982–83; Vice-Pres. Council of State June 1982–; Pres. Viet-Nam Fatherland Front. *Address:* Council of Ministers, Hanoi, Viet-Nam.

HVEDING, Vidkunn; Norwegian engineer, economist and politician; b. 27 March 1921, Orkdal; s. of Johan and Ida Marie (née Songlid) Hveding; m. 1st Ellen Palmstrom 1948 (divorced 1963), 2nd Tone Barth 1963 (died 1980); one s. three d.; ed. Norwegian Inst. of Tech. (N.T.H.), Univ. of Trondheim; eng. (design and supervision), various hydro-power projects 1946–54; Assoc. Prof. of Hydroelectric Eng., N.T.H. 1954–56; Adviser, Ethiopian Electric Light and Power Authority 1956–57; Man. Project Dept., Noreno Brasil SA, São Paulo 1957–58; Prof. of Hydroelectric Eng., N.T.H. 1958–61; Asst. Dir.-Gen. Norwegian Water Resources and Elec. Bd. 1961–63; Adviser, Kuwait Fund for Arab Econ. Devt. 1963–65; Sec.-Gen. Norwegian Ministry of Industry 1967–68; Chair. and Chief Exec., Norwegian Water Resources and Electricity Bd. 1968–75; Planning Man. Industrial Bank of Kuwait 1975–77; dir. of various cos. in banking industry, shipping, consulting 1977–81; Minister of Petroleum and Energy 1981–83; Commdr., Royal Order of St. Olav. *Publications:* Comprehensive Energy Analysis 1969, and numerous articles on hydroelectric power tech., energy econs., resource conservation and political philosophy. *Leisure interests:*

skiing, sailing, woodwork. *Address:* Rödkleivfaret 6, Oslo 3, Norway (Home). *Telephone:* 14 34 84 (Home).

HYDE-WHITE, Wilfred; British actor; b. 12 May 1903, Bourton-on-the-Water, Glos.; s. of William Edward White and Ethel Adelaide Drought; m. 1st Blanche Hope Aitken 1927, one s.; m. 2nd Ethel Korenman 1957, one s. one d.; ed. Marlborough; first appeared in London in Beggar on Horseback, Queen's Theatre 1925. *Stage appearances include:* Rise Above It, Comedy Theatre, It Depends What You Mean, Westminster, Britannus in Caesar and Cleopatra, St. James's, London, and Ziegfeld, New York, Affairs of State, Cambridge, Hippo Dancing, Lyric, The Reluctant Debutante, Cambridge, and Henry Miller's Theatre, New York, Not in the Book, Criterion, Miss Pell is Missing, Criterion, The Doctor's Dilemma, Haymarket, Lady Windermere's Fan, Phoenix, Meeting at Night, Duke of York's, The Jockey Club Stakes, Duke of York's, and Cort Theatre, New York, The Pleasure of His Company, Phoenix, Rolls Hyphen Royce, Shaftesbury. *Films include:* The Third Man, The Browning Version, Golden Salamander, The Million Pound Note, Libel, Two Way Stretch, North West Frontier, Let's Make Love, His and Hers, On the Double, Ada, The Castaways, Crooks Anonymous, On the Fiddle, Aliki, My Fair Lady, Ten Little Indians, The Liquidator, The Toy 1981, The Associates (TV) 1982, Fanny Hill 1982, In God We Trust. *Leisure interests:* golf, horse racing, fine dining. *Address:* 67157 Santa Barbara Drive, Palm Springs, Calif. 92262, U.S.A.; c/o Chatto and Linnit Ltd., Prince of Wales Theatre, Coventry Street, London, W1V 7FE, England. *Telephone:* (619) 327-3276.

HYLAND, William G., M.A.; American intelligence officer; b. 18 Jan. 1929; ed. Univs. of Washington and Missouri; mem. staff, Nat. Security Council, White House 1969–73; Dir. Intelligence, U.S. State Dept. 1973–75; Deputy Asst. to Pres. (Nat. Security) 1975–77; Georgetown Univ. 1977–81; Sr. Assoc. Carnegie Endowment, Washinton, D.C. 1981–84; Ed. Foreign Affairs 1984–. *Publication:* Mortal Rivals: Superpower Relations from Nixon to Reagan 1987. *Address:* c/o Council on Foreign Relations, 58 East 68th Street, New York, N.Y. 10021, U.S.A.

HYMAN, Joe, F.R.S.A.; British textile executive; b. 14 Oct. 1921; m. 1st Corrine I. Abrahams 1950 (marriage dissolved), one s. one d.; m. 2nd Simone Duke 1963, one s. one d.; ed. North Manchester Grammar School; entered father's General Textile Merchanting Co. 1937; founder Portland Woollen Co. 1946; owner Melso Fabrics Ltd., now Gainsborough Cornard Ltd. (Cornard Knitting Mills Ltd., Fine Jersey Ltd., and Cooper Bros.) 1957; Gainsborough Cornard and William Hollins Ltd. merged to form Viyella Int. Ltd. 1961, Chair. 1962–69, Dir. 1961–70; Chair. John Crowther and Sons (Milnsbridge) Ltd. 1971–81; mem. Lloyds; Trustee, Pestalozzi Children's Village 1967–; mem. Textile Council 1968; Gov. Bedales School 1966, L.S.E. 1968; British Inst. of Man.; Companion of Textile Inst.; Pres. Textile Benevolent Asscn. *Leisure interests:* music, golf, gardening. *Address:* 24 Kingston House North, Prince's Gate, London, S.W.7; Lukyns, Ewhurst, Surrey, England.

HYMAN, Timothy; British painter and writer on art; b. 17 April 1946, Brighton; s. of Alan Hyman and Noreen Gypson; m. Judith Ravenscroft 1982; ed. Charterhouse and Slade School of Fine Art; publ. numerous articles on contemporary figurative painting in London Magazine and Artscribe 1975–; mounted Narrative Paintings at Arnolfini and ICA Galleries, etc. 1979–80; started to exhibit at Blond 1980, one-man exhbns. 1981, 1983 and 1985; group exhbns. at Royal Acad., Hayward Gallery, Whitechapel Art Gallery, Nat. Portrait Gallery; public collections include Arts Council, Bristol City Art Gallery, A. Anderson and Co.; Visiting Prof. at Baroda, two British Council lecture tours 1981–83; Artist in Residence at Lincoln Cathedral 1983–84; Purchaser for Arts Council Collection 1985; prizewinner, South Bank Show 1988. *Publications:* Hodgkin 1975, Kitaj 1977, Beckmann 1978, Balthus 1980, Narrative Paintings 1979, Inquisitioning Our Realisms 1981, English Romanesque 1984, In Their Circumstances 1985, Kiff 1986, Domenico Tiepolo 1987. *Leisure interests:* the novels of John Cowper Powys, reading, travel, cinema. *Address:* 62 Myddelton Square, London, E.C.1, England. *Telephone:* 01-837 1933.

HYUGA, Hosai; Japanese metals executive; b. 24 Feb. 1906, Yamanashi Pref.; m. 1933; one s. one d.; ed. Univ. of Tokyo; Head Office, Sumitomo Group 1931–41; Govt. Service 1941; Sumitomo Group 1941–, Dir. Sumitomo Metal Industries Ltd. 1949–, Man. Dir. 1952–58, Sr. Man. Dir. 1958–60, Exec. Vice-Pres. 1960–62, Pres. 1962–74, Chair. 1974–86, Hon. Chair. 1986–; Chair. Kansai Econ. Fed. 1977–; Hon. Chair. Kansai Econ. Fed. 1987–. *Leisure interests:* short poem writing. *Address:* 22-13 Higashiyama-cho, Ashiya-shi, Hyogo-ken, 659 Japan. *Telephone:* 0797-22-3249.

I

IACOCCA, Lee A.; American automobile executive; b. 15 Oct. 1924, Allentown, Pa.; s. of Nicola Iacocca and Antoinette Perrotto; m. 1st Mary McCleary 1956 (died 1983); two d.; m. 2nd Peggy Johnson 1986; ed. Lehigh and Princeton Univs.; with Ford Motor Co. 1946; District Sales Man., Washington 1956; Ford Div. Truck Marketing Man. 1956; Car Marketing Man. 1957; Vice-Pres. and Gen. Man., Ford Div. 1960–65; Vice-Pres. Car and Truck Group 1965; Exec. Vice-Pres., North American Automotive Operations 1967; Exec. Vice-Pres., Ford Motor Co. and Pres. Ford North American Automotive Operations 1969–70, Pres. Ford Motor Co. 1970–78; Pres., C.O.O., Chrysler Corpn. 1978–79, Chair. and C.E.O. Sept. 1979–; mem. Soc. Automotives Engineers, Hon. doctorates, Muhlenberg Coll. and Babson Inst.; Chair. of Presidential Comm. to restore Statue of Liberty 1982–86; Detroit's Man of the Year 1982; Jefferson Award 1985. *Publication:* Iacocca, An Autobiography (with William Novak) 1984, Talking Straight 1988. *Address:* 12000 Chrysler Drive, Highland Park, Mich. 48288 (Office); 571 Edgemere Court, Bloomfield Hills, Mich., U.S.A. (Home).

IACOVOU, Georgios, M.A., M.SC.; Cypriot diplomatist and politician; b. 19 July 1938; s. of Kyriacos Iacovou and Maria Michalopoulou; m. Jennifer Bradley 1963; one s. three d.; ed. Greek Gymnasium for Boys, Famagusta, and Univ. of London; Eng., Cyprus Building and Road Construction Corpn. Ltd 1960–61; Man. Electron Ltd., Nicosia 1961–63; with Operations Research and Finance Depts., British Railways Bd., London 1964–68; Sr. Consultant (Management), Price Waterhouse Assocs., London 1968–72; Dir. Cyprus Productivity Centre, Nicosia 1972–76; Dir. Special Service for Care and Rehabilitation of Displaced Persons 1974–76; Chief, E. African Region, UNHCR, Geneva 1976–79; Amb. to Fed. Repub. of Germany (also accred. to Austria and Switzerland) 1979–83; Dir.-Gen. Ministry of Foreign Affairs Jan.-Sept. 1983; Minister of Foreign Affairs 1983–89; Pres. Cttee. of Ministers, Council of Europe Nov. 1983; participated in Commonwealth Heads of State and Govt. Confs. in Delhi 1983, Bahamas 1985, Vancouver 1987 and non-Aligned Summit, Harare 1986; Grosses Verdienstkreuz mit Stern und Schulterband (Fed. Repub. of Germany), Grosses Goldenes Ehrenzeichen (Austria), Grand Cross, Order of Phoenix (Greece), Grand Cross of the Order of Isabella the Catholic (Spain), Grand Cross of the Order of Honour (Greece). *Address:* c/o Ministry of Foreign Affairs, Nicosia, Cyprus. *Telephone:* 40:2101.

IAKOVOS, Archbishop; American ecclesiastic; b. 29 July 1911, Island of Imbros, Turkey; s. of Maria and Athanasios Coucouzis; baptismal name Demetrios; ed. Theological School of Halki, Istanbul; Deacon 1934; ordained priest in Lowell, Mass., U.S.A. 1940; Dean Cathedral of the Annunciation, Boston 1942–54; Bishop of Malta 1954; Rep. of Patriarch of Constantinople to World Council of Churches, Geneva 1955; Archbishop, Greek Orthodox Church in North and South America 1959–; Exarch, Ecumenical Patriarchate of Constantinople; Pres. World Council of Churches 1959–68; fmr. Dean Holy Cross Orthodox Theological School, Mass., now Pres.; Presidential Medal of Freedom 1980, Inaugural Award New York Univ. 1981, Great Cross of the Holy Sepulchre, Patriarchate of Jerusalem 1982, Gold Medal of Acad. of Athens 1985, numerous hon. degrees. *Address:* Greek Orthodox Archdiocese, 8–10 East 79th Street, New York, N.Y. 10021, U.S.A.

IANNELLA, Egidio, C.P.N.; Argentine banker and consultant; b. 16 May 1921, Buenos Aires; s. of Antonio and Carmen Bárbaro; m. Isobel Rodriguez; one s. one d.; ed. Escuela Nacional de Comercio, Buenos Aires, Univ. Nacional de Buenos Aires and Centro de Estudios Monetarios Latinoamericanos, Mexico; various positions in Banco Central de la República Argentina 1939–56, Gen. Man. 1967–69, Pres. 1969–70 and 1981–82, Dir. 1978–81; Gen. Man. Banco Argentino de Comercio 1956–66; Exec. Vice-Pres. Banco Federal Argentino 1971–77; Pres. Banco Nacional de Desarrollo 1978–81; Pres. Asociación Latinoamericana de Instituciones de Desarrollo (ALIDE), Lima 1979–81; Prof., Pontificia Univ. Católica Argentina 1966–; Pres. VISA Argentina S.A. 1983–. *Address:* Calle Tucumán 540, 6°A (1049), Buenos Aires, Argentina. *Telephone:* 325-1403; 325-3091.

IAREZZA, Juan Carlos, B.PHIL.; Argentine economist and international official; b. 16 April 1942, Buenos Aires; s. of José A. Iarezza and Dora N. Beya; m. María Celia Iarezza; ed. Univs. of Buenos Aires and Oxford, England; with Econ. Research Dept., Banco Cen. de la República Argentina 1964–68; Deputy Dir. Dept. of Fiscal Analysis, Treasury 1968–70, 1974; post-graduate studies, Univ. of Oxford 1971–73; Dir. Dept. of Int. Orgs., Ministry of Economy 1975; Lecturer, Fiscal Theory and Policy, Univ. Católica, Buenos Aires, Macroecons., Univ. Nacional de la Plata, Buenos Aires 1975; Adviser to Govt. of Uruguay, OAS Technical Assistance Programme 1976; Deputy Financial Rep. of Argentina, U.S.A. and Canada 1977–78, Financial Rep. 1979–; Exec. Dir. of IMF for Argentina, Bolivia, Chile, Paraguay, Peru and Uruguay, Washington, D.C. 1980–82. *Address:* Ministerio de Relaciones Exteriores y Culto, Arenales no. 761, Buenos Aires, Argentina.

IBARRURI GÓMEZ, Dolores; Spanish politician and journalist; b. 9 Dec. 1895, Gallarta, Vizcaya; d. of Antonio Ibarruri and Juliana Gómez; m.

Julián Ruiz (deceased) 1916; one s. five d.; Joined Partido Socialista 1917; journalist for workers' press under pseudonym "La Pasionaria"; participated in formation of first communist groups in Spain; joined Partido Comunista de España (PCE) 1920, mem. Cen. Cttee. PCE 1930; leader of Vizcaya Communist Party, del. to 1st Congress of PCE; mem. Cortes 1936–39, 1977–79; mem. Political Bureau of PCE 1932; worked on organ of PCE, El Mundo Obrero; a founder of Agrupación de Mujeres Antifacistas (Anti-fascist Women's Group) 1934; mem. PCE del. to 7th Congress of Communist Int. 1935, deputy mem. Exec. Cttee. 1940–43; Vice-Pres. Cortes 1937; emigrated to France 1939, then to the U.S.S.R.; Sec.-Gen. PCE 1942–60, Pres. 1960–; returned to Spain 1977; Vice-Pres. Consejo Mundial de la Paz (World Council for Peace); Hon. Vice-Pres. Fed. Democrática Int. de Mujeres (Int. Democratic Fed. of Women); Dr. h.c. (Moscow); many awards incl. Order of Lenin, Order of the October Revolution, Lenin Peace Prize. *Publications:* El Unico Camino 1967, De febrero a octubre 1917–1967, En la Lucha 1968, España estado multinacional 1970; co-editor Historia del PCE 1960, Guerra y Revolución en España 1960–77, Memorias de Pasionaria 1939–77, Memorias de Dolores Ibarruri: Pasionaria La Lucha y la Vida 1985, Pasionaria: Memoria Grafica 1985; numerous articles on Spanish and int. problems. *Leisure interest:* reading. *Address:* Santísima Trinidad 5, Madrid 10, Spain. *Telephone:* 4461100.

IBBS, Sir (John) Robin, Kt., K.B.E., M.A., C.B.I.M.; British industrialist; b. 21 April 1926, Birmingham; s. of late T. L. Ibbs and of Marjorie Bell; m. Iris Barbara Hall 1952; one d.; ed. Gresham's School, Upper Canada Coll., Toronto, Univ. of Toronto, Trinity Coll., Cambridge, and Lincoln's Inn; Instructor Lieut., R.N. 1947–49; C. A. Parsons & Co. Ltd. 1949–51; joined ICI 1952, held various eng., tech., production, commercial and gen. man. appointments at Head Office, Gen. Chemicals Div. and Metals Div.; Man. Planning Dept., Imperial Metal Industries Ltd. 1969–74, Exec. Dir. 1972–74, Non-Exec. Dir. 1974–76; Gen. Man. Planning, ICI 1974–76, Exec. Dir. 1976–80, 1982–88; Dir. ICI Americas Inc. 1976–80; Dir. Lloyds Bank PLC 1985–88, Deputy Chair. 1988–; Deputy Chair. (desig.) Oct. 1988–; mem. Industrial Devt. Advisory Bd., Dept. of Industry 1978–80, Head Central Policy Review Staff, Cabinet Office 1980–82; mem. Council, Chemical Industries Asscn. 1976–80, 1982–88, Vice-Pres. 1983–87, Hon. mem. 1987; mem. Governing Body and Council, British Nat. Cttee., ICC 1976–80, Chair. Finance and Gen. Purposes Cttee. 1976–80; mem. Top Salaries Review Body 1983–88; mem. Council, Royal Inst. of Int. Affairs, Chatham House 1983–; mem. Court, Cranfield Inst. of Tech. 1983–; Adviser to the Prime Minister on Efficiency and Effectiveness in Govt. 1983–88; Hon. D.Sc. (Bradford) 1986. *Leisure interests:* walking, natural history, gardening, social history, music and arts. *Address:* c/o Lloyds Bank PLC, 71 Lombard Street, London, EC3P 3BS, England.

IBE, Kyonosuke; Japanese banker; b. 28 July 1908, Tokyo; s. of Naomitsu Ibe; m. Kimi Yokoyama 1934; two s. one d.; ed. Tokyo Imperial Univ. (now Tokyo Univ.); joined Sumitomo Bank 1933, Dir. 1957–60, Man. Dir. 1960–64, Sr. Man. Dir. 1964–71, Deputy Pres. 1971–73, Pres. 1973–77, Chair. 1977–83, Dir., Adviser and Sr. Counsellor 1983–; Chair. Bd. of Trustees, Kansai Cttee. for Econ. Devt. 1967–69, Trustee 1969–; Trustee, Japan Cttee. for Econ. Devt. 1971–72, 1973–; Vice-Chair. Fed. of Bankers' Asscns. 1973–74; Chair. Osaka Bankers' Asscn. 1973–74, Vice-Chair. 1974–77; Chair. Kyoto Int. Conf. Hall 1984–; Exec. Dir. Fed. of Econ. Orgs. 1973–; Dir. Kubota Ltd. 1978–83 (Adviser 1983–), Matsushita Electric Industrial Co. Ltd. 1979–, Nippon Electric Co. 1979–, Sumitomo Realty and Devt. Co. Ltd. 1979–, Mitsui O.S.K. Lines Ltd. 1980–, Sumitomo Cement Co. Ltd. 1980–; Pres. Bd. of Trustees, Osaka Philharmonic Soc. 1977; Order of the Sacred Treasure (First Class) 1981. *Leisure interests:* opera, classical music, reading, painting. *Address:* The Sumitomo Bank, 5-22 Kitahama, Higashi-ku, Osaka; (Home); 20-41 Higashiashiya-cho, Ashiya city, Hyogo, Japan. *Telephone:* 06-227-2000 (Office); 0797-22-4153 (Home).

IBEKWE, Hon. Dan Onwura, Q.C.; Nigerian barrister-at-law; b. 23 June 1919, Onitsha, Anambra State; s. of Chief Akukalia Omedike Ibekwe and Amaliwu Nwabunie Ibekwe; m. Cecilia Nkemdilim Ibekwe 1953; two s. six d.; ed. Saint Mary's School, Onitsha, Christ the King Coll., Onitsha, Council on Legal Educ. Law School, London; called to the English and Nigerian Bars 1951; law practice with J. I. C. Taylor 1951–54; at Aba, Nigeria 1954–56; Legal Adviser to the Premier, Eastern Region 1956–58; Solicitor-Gen., Eastern Region 1958–64; Senator and Fed. Minister in charge of Commonwealth Relations, Ministry of External Affairs 1965–66; Solicitor, firm of Messrs. Irving and Bonnar 1966; detained in Biafra 1967–70; Commr. for Works, Housing and Transport, East Cen. State 1970–72; Justice of the Supreme Court 1972–76; Attorney-Gen. and Commr. for Justice 1975–76; Pres. Fed. Court of Appeal 1976; Chair. Nigerian Inst. of Int. Affairs 1976. *Publications:* Justice in Blunderland. *Leisure interests:* gardening, music, table tennis, reading. *Address:* c/o Federal Court of Appeal, Parliament Buildings, Lagos, Nigeria.

IBIAM, Sir Francis Akanu; Nigerian medical missionary and politician; Eze Ogo Isiala I: Unwana and the Osuji of Uburu; b. 29 Nov. 1906; ed.

Hope Waddell Training Inst., Calabar, King's Coll., Lagos and Univ. of St. Andrews (Scotland); Medical Missionary, Church of Scotland Mission, Calabar, Nigeria 1936-, built Abiriba Hospital 1936-45, Medical Supt. C.S.M. Hospital, Itu 1945-48, Uburu 1952-57; mem. Bd. of Govs. Hope Waddell Training Inst. 1945-57 (Prin. 1957-60), Queen Elizabeth Hosp. Umuahia-Ibeku; mem. Admin. Cttee., Int. Missionary Council 1957-61; mem. Legislative Council, Nigeria 1947-52, Exec. Council 1949-52, Privy Council E. Region of Nigeria 1954-59; Gov. E. Nigeria 1960-66; Adviser to Mil. Gov. of Eastern Provinces, Nigeria 1966; Pres. Christian Council of Nigeria 1955-58; Chair. Provisional Cttee. of All-Africa Church Council 1958-62, Council of Univ. Coll., Ibadan 1958-61; one of six Pres. World Council of Churches 1961; Chair. Council, United Bible Socs. 1966-72, Vice-Pres. 1972-; Founder and Pres. Bible Soc. of Nigeria 1963-74, Patron 1974; Chair. Imo State Council of Traditional Rulers; Elder, Presbyterian Church; appointed O.B.E. 1949, K.B.E. 1951, K.C.M.G. 1962 and renounced these honours in 1967 in protest against British policy regarding Biafra; Hon. D.Sc. (Univ. of Ife) 1966, Hon. LL.D. (Univ. of Ibadan). Order of Russian Orthodox Church, Grand Cross Order of the Niger and other decorations. *Address:* Ganymede, Unwana, P.O. Box 240, Afikpo, Imo State, Nigeria.

IBRAHIM, Maj. Abu al-Qassim Mohammed; Sudanese army officer and politician; b. 1937, Omdurman; ed. Khartoum Secondary School and Military Coll.; commissioned 1961; mem. Revolutionary Council 1969; Minister of Local Govt. 1969-70; Asst. Prime Minister for Services 1970; Minister of Interior 1970-71, of Health and Social Welfare 1971-73, of Agric., Food and Natural Resources 1974-76; mem. Political Bureau of Sudanese Socialist Union 1971-79, Deputy Sec.-Gen. 1975-76, Sec.-Gen. 1976-79; Commr. for Khartoum Prov. 1976-79; First Vice-Pres. of Sudan 1977-79; reportedly left Sudan for Saudi Arabia Aug. 1979.

IBRAHIM, Encik Anwar bin, B.A.; Malaysian politician; b. 10 Aug. 1947; ed. Univ. of Malaya; Pres. UMNO Youth Movt. 1982-; Vice-Pres. UMNO 1982-; Head UMNO Permatang Pauh Div. 1982-; Deputy Minister, Prime Minister's Dept. 1982; Minister of Sport, Youth and Culture 1983, of Agric. 1984-86, of Educ. May 1986-. *Address:* Ministry of Education, Bangunan Bank Pertanian, Leboh Pasar Besar, 50604 Kuala Lumpur, Malaysia.

IBRAHIM, Hassan Hamdi. M.D.; Egyptian medical doctor and university president; b. 27 Aug. 1925, Cairo; s. of Mohamed Ibrahim and Zenab Kamel; ed. Cairo Univ.; Demonstrator, Cairo Univ. 1951-59, Lecturer 1959-64, Assoc. Prof. of Physiology 1964-70, Prof. and Chair. Dept. of Physiology 1970-72, Dean, Faculty of Medicine 1974-77, Vice-Pres. Cairo Univ. 1977-79; Pres. Assiut Univ. 1979-80, Cairo Univ. 1980; decoration from Sudan. *Publications:* more than 60 publications on physiology in int. journals. *Leisure interests:* sports and youth activities. *Address:* c/o Cairo University, Orman, Giza, Cairo, Egypt. *Telephone:* 988869 (Home).

IBRAHIM, Izzat; Iraqi politician; b. 1942, al-Dour Shire; ed. secondary schools; Ed. Voice of the Peasant 1968, Head Supreme Cttee., for People's Work 1968-70; Minister of Agrarian Reform 1970-74; Vice-Pres. Supreme Agric. Council 1970-71, Head 1971-79; Minister of Agriculture 1973-74; Minister of Interior 1974-79; mem. Revolutionary Command Council, Vice-Chair. 1979-; Asst. Sec. Regional Command of Arab Baath Socialist Party July 1979-; mem. Nat. Command Arab Baath Socialist Party. *Address:* Vice-Chairman Revolutionary Command Council, Baghdad; Karkh, Baghdad, Iraq (Home).

IBRAHIM, Sir Kashim, K.C.M.G., C.B.E.; Nigerian politician; b. 10 June 1910; s. of Mallam Ibrahim Lakkani; m. 1st Halima Ibrahim 1943; m. 2nd Khadija Ibrahim 1944; m. 3rd Zainaba Ibrahim 1957; four s. three d.; ed. Bornu Provincial School, Katsina Teachers' Training Coll.; Teacher 1929-32; Visiting Teacher 1933-49; Educ. Officer 1949-52; Cen. Minister of Social Services 1952-55; Northern Regional Minister of Social Devt. and Surveys 1955-56; Waziri of Bornu 1956-62; Gov. of Northern Nigeria 1962-66; Chair. Nigerian Coll. of Arts, Science and Technology 1958-62, Provincial Council of Ahmadu Bello Univ. 1961-62; Adviser to Mil. Gov. of Northern Nigeria 1966; Chancellor Ibadan Univ. 1967-77, Univ. of Lagos 1977-84; Hon. LL.D. (Ahmadu Bello Univ., Univs. of Nsukka and Lagos) Grand Cross Order of the Niger. *Publications:* Kanuri Reader Elementary I-IV, Kanuri Arithmetic Books I-IV for Elementary Schools and Teachers' Guide. *Leisure interests:* walking, riding, polo playing. *Address:* P.O. Box 285, Maiduguri, Bornu State, Nigeria.

IBRAHIM, Sid Moulay Abdullah; Moroccan politician; b. 1918; ed. Ben Youssef Univ., Marrakesh and the Sorbonne, Paris; mem. Istiqlal (Independence) Party 1944-59; mem. Editorial Cttee. Al Alam (Istiqlal organ) 1950-52; imprisoned for political reasons 1952-54; Sec. of State for Information and Tourism, First Moroccan Nat. Govt. 1955-56; Minister of Labour and Social Affairs 1956-57; Prime Minister and Minister of Foreign Affairs 1958-60; leader Union Nationale des Forces Populaires 1959-72. *Address:* c/o Union Nationale des Forces Populaires, B.P. 747, Casablanca, Morocco.

IBRAHIMOV, Mirza Azhdar oglu; Soviet politician and writer; b. 15 Oct. 1911, Eva village, Sarab Machal, Iran; s. of Azhdar oglu Ibrahimi and Zohra Mamedbagir gyzy Ibrahimi; m. Zarahanum Ibrahimova 1938; one s. three d.; ed. Inst. of Oriental History, U.S.S.R. Acad. of Sciences; mem. CPSU 1930-; Ed. Azerbaijani newspaper, Minister for the Arts, Azerbaijan

1938-42; Minister of Educ., Azerbaijan 1942-47; Vice-Chair. Azerbaijan S.S.R. Council of Ministers 1947-50; Chair. of Azerbaijan S.S.R. Union of Writers 1948-57, First Sec. 1965-75; Chair. of the Supreme Soviet of the Azerbaijan S.S.R. 1954-58; Chair. Soviet Cttee. of Solidarity with Countries of Africa and Asia 1977-88; mem. Acad. of Sciences of Azerbaijan; State prizewinner 1951; Red Banner of Labour; Order of Lenin (three times); Order of October Revolution 1971. *Publications:* plays: Khaiat 1935, Madrid 1938, Mahabbeth 1942, Kendchi Kyzy 1962, Yakshy Adam 1965, Kezaran ochzhaglar 1967, Human Comedy of Don Juan 1977; novels: The Day Will Come 1948, Beyuk Dayag 1967, Parvane 1971; short stories: Fyrtyna Gushu 1966, On the Slopes of the Murovdag 1967; scholarly works: Beyuk democrat 1939, Hayat ve edebijath 1947, Halcilik ve realizm jabhesinden 1962, On the Laws of Beauty 1964, Realism in Ashug poetry 1966, Sketches on Literature 1971, Azerbaijani Prose: an Anthology 1977. *Leisure interests:* reading, music. *Address:* Writers' Union, 25 Khagany Baku, Azerbaijan S.S.R.; 19/13, Flat 23, Khagany Baku, Azerbaijan S.S.R., 370000 U.S.S.R. (Home).

IBUKA, Masaru; Japanese industrialist; b. 11 April 1908; ed. Waseda Senior High School and Waseda Univ.; Research Engineer, Photo-Chemical Lab. 1933-37; Man. Radio Telegraphy Dept., Japan Audio Optical Industrial Corpn. 1937-40; Man. Dir. Japan Measuring Apparatus Co. Ltd. 1940-45; Organizer, Tokyo Telecommunications Eng. Corpn. 1945- (Sony Corpn. since 1958), Pres., Man. Dir. 1950-71, Chair. 1971-76, Hon. Chair. and Dir. 1976-; Chair. Railway Tech. Research Inst. 1987-; Chair. Japan Cttee. for Econ. Devt.; mem. Econ. Council; Dir. several industrial assccns.; Blue Ribbon Medal 1960; Founders Medal, IEEE 1972; Hon. D.Sc. (Plano Univ.) 1974, (Waseda Univ.) 1979; Hon. D.Eng. (Sophia Univ., Tokyo) 1976; Hon. D.H. (Mindanao State Univ.) 1982; Order of Sacred Treasure (First Class) 1978, Humanism and Technology Award (Aspen Inst. for Humanistic Studies) 1981. *Publication:* Kindergarten is too late 1977. *Address:* Sony Corporation, 7-35 Kitashinagawa 6-chome, Shinagawuku, Tokyo; 7-1-701 Mita 2-chome, Minatoku, Tokyo, Japan.

ICAHN, Carl C.; American business executive; b. 1936, Queens; m. Liba Icahn; two c.; ed. Princeton Univ. and New York Univ. School of Medicine; apprentice broker, Dreyfus Corpn., New York 1960-63; Options Man. Tessel, Patrick & Co., New York 1963-64, Gruntal & Co. 1964-68; Chair. and Pres. Icahn & Co., New York 1968-; Chair. and C.E.O. ACF Industries Inc., Earth City, Mo. 1984-; Chair. Trans World Airlines Inc. 1986-. *Address:* Icahn & Co., 1370 Avenue of the Americas, New York, N.Y. 10019; ACF Industries, Inc., 3301 Rider Trail S, Earth City, Mo. 63045, U.S.A.

ICHIKAWA, Kon; Japanese film director; b. 1915; ed. Ichioka Commercial School, Osaka. *Films include:* Poo-San 1953, A Billionaire 1954, The Heart 1954, Punishment Room 1955, The Burmese Harp 1956, The Men of Tohoku 1956, Conflagration 1958, Fires on the Plain 1959, The Key 1959, Bonchi 1960, Her Brother 1960, The Sin 1961, Being Two Isn't Easy 1962, The Revenge of Yuki-No-Jo 1963, Alone on the Pacific 1963, Tokyo Olympiad 1964, Seishun 1970, To Love Again 1971, The Wanderers 1973, Visions of Eight (co-dir.) 1973, Wagahai wa Neko de Aru 1975, The Ingunami's 1976, Gokumon-to 1977, Joobachi 1978, Byoin-zaka no Kubikukuri no le 1979, Ancient City 1980, The Makioka Sisters 1983, Actress 1987.

IDELER TONELLI, Santiago, D.IUR.; Argentinian professor of law and politician; b. 18 Dec. 1924, Bragado; m. Carmen María Garganta; three c.; ed. Univ. Católica de la Plata; Pres. Fed. Univ., La Plata 1946-48; Deputy for Prov. of Buenos Aires 1958-62; Pres. Unión Cívica Radical Intransigente (UCRI), La Plata 1958-62; Prof. and Dean, Faculty of Law, Univ. Católica de la Plata 1967-71; lectured in Madrid on Legal System and the Spanish World; Adviser to Minister of Defence 1971-73; Rep. for UCRI and Adviser to Minister of the Economy in Civil Assembly 1973; Judge, Nat. Chamber of Appeals 1973-85, Pres. 1983; held other posts in the field of Social Econs.; Sec. of Justice to the Nation 1986; Minister of Labour 1987-. *Address:* Ministerio de Trabajo, Buenos Aires, Argentina.

IDEMITSU, Keisuke; Japanese business executive; b. 1900; ed. Tokyo Commercial Coll.; Man. Dir. Idemitsu Kosan Co., Ltd. 1947, Sr. Man. Dir. 1950, Pres. 1966, Chair. 1972-77, 1978-, Exec. Adviser April 1977-. *Address:* Idemitsu Kosan Co. Ltd., 1-1, 3-chome, Marunouchi, Chiyoda-ku, Tokyo, Japan.

IDHAM CHALID, Dr. Kyai Haji; Indonesian politician; b. 27 Aug. 1922, Amuntai, Kalimantan; ed. Islamic Teachers' Coll., Ponorogo, E. Java; Teacher 1943-47; M.P. of Repub. of United States of Indonesia 1948; mem. House of Reps. 1950; mem. Constituent Ass. 1956; Second Deputy Prime Minister 1956-59; mem. Supreme Advisory Council 1959-; mem. Exec. Bd. of Nat. Front 1960, Deputy Chair. 1961; mem. and Deputy Chair. Provisional People's Consultative Ass. (MPRS) 1960-65; First Minister of Peoples' Welfare 1967-71; Chair. People's Consultative Ass. 1973-77; mem. Exec. Bd. Nahdlatul-'Ulama (Moslem Scholars' Party); Pres. Partai Persatuan Pembangunan (Devt. Unity Party) 1973-85; Star of Yugoslav Flag, Medal of Honour (Egypt), Groot Kruis (Netherlands), Star of Belgium, Star of Gwan Hwa (Repub. of Korea). *Address:* 15 Mangunsarkoro, Jakarta, Indonesia.

IENG SARY; Kampuchean politician; m. Khieu Thirith; ed. Paris; fmr. teacher; active in left-wing movts. and forced to flee Phnom-Penh 1963;

prominent in Khmer Rouge insurgent movement 1963-75; Khmer Rouge liaison officer to Royal Govt. of Nat. Union of Cambodia (GRUNC) in exile 1971-75; mem. Politburo Nat. United Front of Cambodia (FUNC) 1970-79; Second Deputy Prime Minister of Democratic Kampuchea with special responsibility for Foreign Affairs, GRUNC 1975-79; charged with genocide by Heng Samrin regime and sentenced to death *in absentia* Aug. 1979; Deputy Prime Minister in charge of Foreign Affairs of Democratic Kampuchean Govt. in exile (Khmer Rouge) fighting Vietnamese forces 1979-82; rep. for Finance and Econ. Affairs (in coalition in exile) 1982-.

IEVLEV, Aleksandr Ivanovich, CAND.ECON.SC.; Soviet politician; b. 1926; ed. Voronezh Agric. Inst.; Voronezh Higher Party School; accountant on collective farm in Voronezh Dist. 1941-45; served in Soviet Army 1943-50; Komsomol work 1950-52; Section Head, Sec. of Talovo Regional Cttee. of CPSU 1951-60; Second, First Sec. Vorobyovo Regional Cttee. of CPSU 1960-62; Sec. Party Cttee. Buturlinovo State Collective Farm 1962-65, First Sec. 1965-71; Sec. Voronezh Dist. Cttee. of CPSU 1971-77; U.S.S.R. Deputy Minister of Agric. 1977-85; First Deputy Pres. of U.S.S.R. State Agroprom, U.S.S.R. Ministry 1985-; cand. mem. of CPSU Cen. Cttee. 1986. *Address:* Gosagroprom, Orlikovsky per. 1/11, Moscow, U.S.S.R.

IGGO, Ainsley, PH.D., D.SC., F.R.C.P.(E.), F.R.S.E., F.R.S.; British professor of veterinary physiology; b. 2 Aug. 1924; s. of the late Lancelot G. Iggo and Catherine J. Fraser; m. Betty J. McCurdy 1952; three s.; ed. Gladstone School, New Zealand, Southland Tech. High School, N.Z., Lincoln Coll., N.Z. and Univs. of Otago and Aberdeen; Asst. Lecturer in Physiology, Otago Univ. Medical School 1948-50; N.Z. McMillan Brown Travelling Fellow, Rowett Inst. 1950-51; Lecturer in Physiology, Univ. of Edin. Medical School 1952-60; Nuffield Royal Soc. Commonwealth Fellow, Australian Nat. Univ. 1959; Royal Soc. Locke Research Fellow 1960-62; Prof. of Veterinary Physiology, Univ. of Edin. 1962-, Dean, Faculty of Veterinary Medicine 1974-77, Dean Veterinary Medicine 1986-; Visiting Prof. Univ. of Ibadan 1968, Univ. of Kyoto 1970, Univ. of Heidelberg 1972. *Publications:* articles in scientific journals. *Leisure interests:* bee-keeping, gardening. *Address:* 5 Relugas Road, Edin. EH9 2NE, Scotland. *Telephone:* 031-667 4879.

IGLER, Hans, D.ECON.; Austrian business administrator; b. 29 July 1920, Vienna; s. of Robert and Maria (née Seidel) Igler; m. Dorothea Monti 1948; one s. three d.; ed. Hochschule für Welthandel, Vienna; Mil. service until 1945, Marshall Plan consultant in Fed. Ministry of Property Control and Econ. Planning 1946-50; Head ERP Office, Fed. Chancellery 1950-55; Chair. Bd. Man. Dirs. Österreichische Industrie-u. Bergbauverwaltungsges. m.b.H. (holding for nationalized industries) 1956-59; Consultant to Govt. of Chile for UN and FAO econ. programme 1959; Partner, Bankhaus Schoeller & Co. and Gebr. Schoeller, Vienna 1960-; Pres. Fed. of Austrian Industrialists 1972-; Chair. Austro-Olivetti Büro-maschinen AG, Elin-Union AG für elektrische Industrie, Kabel & Drahtwerke AG, Vienna; Dir. Österr. Mineralölverwaltung AG, Vienna, Gebrüder Böhler & Co. AG, Vienna, Wertheim AG, Vienna, Österr. Stickoffwerke AG, Linz, Wiener Starkstromwerke GmbH, Vienna, Leipnik-Lundenburger Zuckerfabriken AG, Vienna, Kosmos AG, Vienna; mem. Österr. Inst. für Wirtschaftsforschung, Vienna. *Address:* 1010 Wien I, Renngasse 3, Austria.

IGLESIAS, Enrique V.; Uruguayan international official; b. 26 July 1931, Astwias, Spain; s. of Isabel García de Iglesias; ed. Univ. de la República, Montevideo; held several positions including Prof. Agregado, Faculty of Political Economy, Prof. of Econ. Policy and Dir. Inst. of Econs., Univ. de la República, Montevideo 1952-67; Sec.-Gen. Sugar Comm. of Uruguay 1959-60; Technical Dir. Nat. Planning Office of Uruguay 1961-65; Pres. (Gov.), Banco Central del Uruguay 1967-69; Pres. Gov. Council, Latin American Inst. for Econ. and Social Planning (ILPES), UN 1967-71; Adviser, Inter-American Devt. Bank 1968-70; Rapporteur, FAO World Food Conf. 1970; Head, Advisory Mission on Planning, Govt. of Venezuela 1970-71; Adviser UN Conf. on Human Environment 1971-72; Exec. Sec. Econ. Comm. for Latin America (ECLA) 1972-85; Minister of External Affairs 1985-88; Pres. Inter-American Devt. Bank (IADB) Feb. 1988-; Acting Dir.-Gen. Latin American Inst. for Econ. and Social Planning 1973-78; Pres, Third World Forum 1973-76; mem. Steering Cttee., Soc. for Int. Devt. 1973-, Selection Cttee., Third World Prize 1979-82; Sec.-Gen. UN Conf. on New and Renewable Sources of Energy Feb.-Aug. 1981; Hon. LL.D. (Liverpool) 1987. *Leisure interests:* music, art. *Address:* Inter-American Development Bank, 1300 New York Avenue, N.W., Washington, D.C. 20577, U.S.A.

IGNATIEFF, George, C.C., M.A., LL.D., D.C.L., D.LITT.S.; Canadian diplomatist; b. 16 Dec. 1913, St. Petersburg, Russia; s. of Count Paul Ignatieff and Princess Natalie Mestchersky; m. Alison Grant 1945; two s.; ed. Jarvis Coll. Inst., Toronto, Univs. of Toronto and Oxford; Dept. of External Affairs, Ottawa 1940-, 1944-45; Third Sec., London 1940-44; Adviser, Canadian Del., UN Atomic Energy Comm. 1946, UN Ass. 1946-47; Alt. Rep. UN Security Council 1945-49; Chair. Admin. and Budgetary Cttee., UN Gen. Ass. 1949; Counsellor, Washington 1949-53; attended Imperial Defence Coll., London 1953-54; Head of Defence Liaison (First Div.) Dept. of External Affairs, Ottawa 1955; Amb. to Yugoslavia 1956-58; Deputy High Commr., London 1959-60; Asst. Under-Sec. Dept. of External Affairs, Ottawa 1960-62; Perm. Rep. and Amb. to NATO 1962-66; Perm. Rep. to UN 1966-68, Rep. of Canada to 18 Nation Disarmament Cttee., Geneva

1968-72; Provost, Trinity Coll., Toronto 1972-79 (Hon. Pres. 1979); Chancellor, Univ. of Toronto 1980-; Adviser to Govt. on Disarmament 1984-; Hon. Fellow, St. John's Coll., Winnipeg, Trinity Coll., Toronto 1986; Chair. Bd. of Trustees, Nat. Museums of Canada 1973-79; mem. Governing Council, Univ. of Toronto 1974-75; Brockington lecturer, Queen's Univ. 1986-; Pres. Science for Peace in Canada; hon. degrees from several Canadian and foreign univs.; Centenary Medal, Jubilee Medal 1977, Pearson Peace Medal 1984. *Publication:* The Making of a Peacemonger (autobiog.) 1985. *Leisure interest:* gardening. *Address:* 18 Palmerston Gardens, Toronto, Ont., M6G 1V9; University of Toronto, Toronto, Ont. M5S 1A1, Canada.

IGNATIUS, Paul Robert; American business executive (retd.); b. 11 Nov. 1920, Los Angeles; s. of H. B. Ignatius and Elisa Jamgochian; m. Nancy Sharpless Weiser 1947; two s. two d.; ed. Univ. of Southern California and Harvard Business School; Instructor in Business Admin., Harvard Business School 1947-50; Vice-Pres., Dir. Harbridge House Inc. (man. consultants), Boston 1950-61; Asst. Sec. of Army for Installations and Logistics 1961-63; Under-Sec. of Army 1964; Asst. Sec. of Defence 1964-67; Sec. of Navy 1967-69; Pres. The Washington Post 1969-71; Exec. Vice-Pres. Air Transport Asscn. of America 1972, Pres. and Chief Exec. Officer 1972-84; Chair. and C.E.O. 1984-85; Chair. Bd. of Trustees Logistics Man. Inst. 1987-; Bd. of Dirs. Nat. Symphony Orchestra 1972-; U.S. Naval Reserve 1943-46. *Leisure interests:* tennis, swimming. *Address:* 3650 Fordham Road, Washington, D.C. 20016, U.S.A. (Home).

IGNATIUS ZAKKA I IWAS, His Holiness Patriarch; Iraqi ecclesiastic; b. 21 April 1933, Mosul, Iraq; ed. St. Aphrem Syrian Orthodox Theol. Seminary, Mosul, Gen. Theol. Seminary, New York and New York Univ.; ordained 1957; consecrated Metropolitan for Archdiocese of Mosul 1963, transferred to Archdiocese of Baghdad 1969; Patriarch of Antioch and All the East (Supreme Head of Universal Syrian Orthodox Church) 1980-; mem. Iraq Acad. of Science; hon. mem. Arabic Acad. of Jordan; fmr. mem. Cen. Cttee. WCC; Fellow, Faculty of Syriac Studies, Lutheran School of Theol., Chicago 1981; hon. doctorates, Swedish Inst. of Oriental Studies Cen. School of Religion, and Gen. Theol. Seminary, N.Y., *Publications:* several books and articles. *Address:* Syrian Orthodox Patriarchate, Bab Toma, PB 22260, Damascus, Syria. *Telephone:* Damascus 432401.

IGNATOV, Vadim Nikolaevich; Soviet politician; b. 8 Sept. 1931; s. of late N.G. Ignatov; ed. Leningrad Agric. Inst.; agronomist at Leningrad Agric. Inst. 1952-61; chief agronomist of Leningrad Dist. State Farms 1952-61; mem. CPSU 1953-; Deputy Head 1961-62, Head, Dept. of Agric., Leningrad Dist. Cttee. CPSU 1962-68; Sec. (responsible for agric.) 1968-73, Second Sec. 1973-75; Deputy to R.S.F.S.R. Supreme Soviet 1971-75; Deputy to Council of the Union, U.S.S.R. Supreme Soviet 1974-; First Sec., Voronezh Dist. Cttee. CPSU and mem. Mil. Council, Moscow Mil. Dist. 1975-; mem. Cen. Cttee. CPSU 1976-; Deputy Pres. U.S.S.R. State Agroindustries 1976-; Deputy to U.S.S.R. Supreme Soviet; Order of Lenin; Order of October Revolution 1977, other medals. *Address:* Central Committee of the Communist Party of the Soviet Union, Staraya pl. 4, Moscow, U.S.S.R.

IHAMUOTILA, Jaakko, M.S.ENG.; Finnish business executive; b. 15 Nov. 1939, Helsinki; s. of Veikki Artturi Ihamuotila and Anna-Liisa (née Kouki) Ihamuotila; m. Tuula Elina Turja 1965; two s. one d.; ed. Univ. of Tech., Helsinki; Asst. in Reactor Technics 1963-66, Acting Asst. to Prof. of Physics 1964-66; with Canadian Gen. Electric Co. Ltd., Toronto 1966; Imatran Voima Oy 1966-68; Valmet Oy 1968-70, Asst. Dir. 1970-72, Dir. of Planning 1972-73, Man. Dir. 1973-79, mem. Bd. 1980-82; mem. Bd. Neste Oy. 1979-, Chair. and Chief Exec. 1980-; Vice-Chair. Finnish Cultural Foundation 1978-, Kansallis-Osake-Pankki 1980-, Pohjola Insurance Co. 1979-; mem. Bd. UNISYS 1977-(88), (Chair. 1984-), Fed. of Finnish Chemical Industry 1980-, Kemira Oy 1980-82, Confed. of Finnish Industries 1980-; mem. Man. Study Group 1974-, State Tech. Research Inst. 1977-, Finnish-American Chamber of Commerce 1979-, Finnish-British Trade Asscn., Nat. Bd. of Econ. Defence 1980-, Council of the Univ. of Tech., Bd. Finnish Employers' Co. 1981-, Bd. Finnish Employers' Gen. Group 1977-, ICC, Comm. on Energy 1981-, Cttee. Finnish-Soviet Comm. for Econ. Co-operation 1985-, Bd. EFFOA-Finland Steamship Co. Ltd., Nat. Energy Policy Council 1982-, Finnish Section, World Wildlife Fund 1979-, Bd. Wärtsilä Ab. 1983-. *Address:* Neste Oy, 02150 Espoo, Finland (Office). *Telephone:* 4501.

IHSANOĞLU, Ekmeleddin, PH.D.; Turkish professor of history of science; b. 1943; m.; three c.; instructor and researcher Ain Shams Univ. and Al-Azhar Univ., Cairo 1966-70, Exeter Univ., England 1975-77; Assoc. Prof. Univ. of Ankara 1979; now Prof. and Head Dept. of History of Science Univ. of Istanbul; Dir. Gen. Research Centre for Islamic History, Art and Culture, Org. of the Islamic Conf., also Sec. Int. Comm. for Preservation of Islamic Cultural Heritage; mem. numerous orgs. concerned with study of Islamic issues, including Middle E. Studies Asscn. of N. America, Royal Acad. of Islamic Civilisation Research, Jordan, Nat. Council for Translation of Studies and Research, Tunisia, Inst. of Islamic Research, Istanbul etc. *Publications:* has written, edited and translated several books on Islamic culture and science; over 70 articles and papers. *Address:* Research Centre for Islamic History, Art and Culture, Yıldız Sarayı, Seyir Köşku, Barbaros Bulvarı, 80700 Beşiktaş, Istanbul, Turkey.

IDA, Keizo; Japanese retail executive; b. 13 April 1900, Osaka City; m. Miyoko 1931; one s.; ed. Keio Univ.; Osaka Branch, Takashimaya Dept. Store 1926, Man. 1941, Dir. Takashimaya 1942-, Man. Dir. 1943-52, Pres. 1952-60, now Chair. *Leisure interest:* painting. *Address:* 1-2-18, Hibari-gaoka, Takarazuka City, Hyogo Pref., Japan.

IDA, Yotaro; Japanese business executive; b. 25 Feb. 1920; ed. Univ. of Tokyo; joined Mitsubishi Heavy Industries Ltd. 1943, Gen. Man. Utility Power Systems 1973-76, Gen. Man. Utility and Industrial Power Systems 1976-77, Gen. Man. Utility Power Systems 1977, Dir. and Deputy Gen. Man. of Power Systems 1977-81, Man. Dir. and Gen. Man. of Power Systems 1981-83, Exec. Vice-Pres. and Gen. Man. of Power Systems 1983-85, Pres. 1985-86, 1988-; Chair. Soc. of Japanese Aerospace Cos. Inc. *Address:* No. 32-4, Shimouma 6-chome, Setagaya-ku, Tokyo, Japan (Home).

IKEDA, Daisaku; Japanese religious leader; b. 2 Jan. 1928, Tokyo; s. of Nenokichi and Ichi Ikeda; m. Kaneko Shiraki 1952; two s.; ed. Fuji Junior Coll.; Pres. Soka Gakkai 1960-79, Hon. Pres. 1979-, Pres. Soka Gakkai Int. 1975-; Founder of Tokyo and Osaka Soka Junior and Senior High Schools, of Soka Univ., Min-on Concert Asscn., Inst. of Oriental Philosophy, Tokyo and Shizuoka Fuji Art Museum, Tokyo, Sapporo Soka Kindergarten, Tokyo and Osaka Soka Primary Schools; Hon. Pres. Seikyo Press 1987-; Dr. h.c. (Moscow State Univ.) 1975, (Sofia) 1981, (Soka) 1983; Hon. Prof. Nat. Univ. of San Marcos 1981, Beijing Univ. 1984, Fudan Univ. 1984; UN Peace Award 1983, Order of the Sun of Peru with Grand Cross 1984, Kenya Oral Literature Award 1986, Chinese Peace and Friendship Trophy 1986. *Publications:* The Human Revolution Vols. I-V 1972-84, Buddhism: The Living Philosophy 1974, The Living Buddha 1976, Choose Life 1976, Buddhism: The First Millennium 1977, Songs from my Heart 1978, Glass Children and Other Essays 1979, On the Japanese Classics 1979, Letters of Four Seasons 1980, La Nuit Appelle L'Aurore 1980, A Lasting Peace 1981, Life: An Enigma, a Precious Jewel 1982, Human Values in a Changing World 1984, Before It Is Too Late 1984, The Flower of Chinese Buddhism 1986, Buddhism and Cosmos 1986, Daisaku: Unlocking the Mysteries of Birth and Death 1988 and other writings on Buddhism, civilization, life and peace. *Leisure interests:* music, art, table tennis, calligraphy. *Address:* 32 Shinano-machi, Shinjuku-ku, Tokyo 160, Japan.

IKEURA, Kisaburo, B.L.; Japanese banker; b. 21 April 1916, Wakayama Prefecture; s. of Kunitaro and Sae Ikeura; m. Sumi Ueda 1944; one s. one d.; ed. Tokyo Univ.; joined Industrial Bank of Japan Ltd. 1939, Dir. 1964, Man. Dir. 1965, Deputy Pres. 1973, Pres. 1975-84, Chair. March 1984-. *Address:* 3-3 Marunouchi 1-chome, Chiyoda-ku, Tokyo 100; 22-12, 4-chome Numabukuro, Nakano-ku, Tokyo 165, Japan (Home). *Telephone:* 214-1111 (Office); 386-1443 (Home).

IKLÉ, Fred Charles, PH.D.; American social scientist and government official; b. 21 Aug. 1924, Samaden, Switzerland; m. Doris Eisemann 1959; two d.; ed. Univ. of Chicago; research scholar, Bureau of Applied Social Research, Columbia Univ. 1950-54; Consultant to Nat. Research Council 1950-54; mem. Social Science Dept., Rand Corpn. 1955-61; Research Assoc. in Int. Relations, Centre for Int. Affairs, Harvard Univ. 1962-63; Assoc. Prof., then Prof. of Political Science, M.I.T. 1963-67; Head of Social Science Dept., Rand Corpn. 1968-73; Dir. U.S. Arms Control and Disarmament Agency 1973-77; Under-Sec. of Defense for Policy 1981-88; Distinguished Scholar, Centre for Strategic Int. Studies 1988-; Co-Chair. U.S. Comm. on Integrated Long Term Strategy 1987-88; mem. Bd. Int. Peace Acad. (1977-81); Chair. Council on Nat. Security of Republican Nat. Cttee. 1977-79; Chair. Conservation Man. Corpn.; Dir. Zürich-American Insurance; Consultant, Dept. of State 1966-68, Los Alamos Science Laboratory 1977-81; Rockefeller Fellowship 1953, 1962; U.S. Defense Dept. Distinguished Public Service Awards 1975, 1987, 1988. *Publications:* The Social Impact of Bomb Destruction 1958, After Detection...What? 1961, How Nations Negotiate 1964, Every War Must End 1971, Can Social Predictions be Evaluated? 1967, Can Nuclear Deterrence Last Out The Century? 1973, and many articles on int. affairs and negotiations. *Address:* CSIS, 1800 K Street, N.W., Washington D.C. 20006, U.S.A. *Telephone:* (202) 775-3155.

ILANGARATNE, Tikiri Bandara; Sri Lankan politician, writer, playwright, novelist; b. 27 Feb. 1913, Hatarliyadda; s. of Mr. and Mrs. T. A. Ilangaratne; m. Tamara Kumari Aludeniya 1944; two s. two d.; ed. St. Anthony's Coll., Kandy; clerical posts until 1947; M.P. for Kandy 1948, for Galaha 1952; Gen. Sec. Sri Lanka Freedom Party 1954; M.P. for Hewaheta 1956; Minister for Social Services and Housing 1956-59, of Home Affairs 1959, of Trade, Commerce, Food and Shipping 1961-63, of Finance 1963-64, of Trade and Supplies 1964-65; Vice-Pres. Sri Lanka Freedom Party 1966, 1981-; M.P. for Kolonnawa 1967; responsible for nationalizing foreign oil companies in Sri Lanka; Minister of Foreign and Internal Trade 1970-77, Public Admin. and Home Affairs Sept. 1975-77; Pres. Sri. Lanka Mahajana (People's) Party 1984-86. *Publications:* (in Sinhalese): novels: Wilambeeta, Denuwara, Kathava, Thilaka, La Sanda, Thilaka and Thilaka, Nedeyo, Piyadaraya, Dayadaya, Okkoma Rajawaru, Himi Gamanak Gosin; Plays: Häramitiya, Manthri Hamuduruwo, Jataka Natyaya, Rangamandala, Handahana, Ambaryaluwo, Malsarawa, Mangala, Delova Sihina, Nivena Ginna; short stories: Onchillawa; Journey of an Era (autobiog.). *Address:* 302 High Level Road, Colombo 6, Sri Lanka. *Telephone:* 553509.

ILEO SONGOAMBA; Zairian politician; b. (as Joseph Ileo) 15 Sept. 1921, Léopoldville (now Kinshasa); m. Elisabeth Bongo; five s. five d.; studied philosphy and sociology in Europe; held post in African Territories Div. of Belgian Gov.-Gen's Office; active in movement for independence, signatory of the "Memorandum of the Sixteen" 1958; formed Congolese Nat. Movement Party with Patrice Lumumba; joined Abako Party 1959; fmr. Ed. The African Conscience; Head of Congolese Senate July-Sept. 1960; Premier 1960-61; Minister of Information and Cultural Affairs 1961-62; Minister without Portfolio in charge Katangese Affairs 1963-64; now mem. Political Bureau, Mouvement populaire de la révolution, mem. Perm. Cttee. 1975-; Pres. Office Nat. de la Recherche et du Développement. *Address:* B.P. 3474, Kinshasa, Zaire. *Telephone:* 2452.

ILETO, Rafael M.; Philippine politician; b. 24 Oct. 1920, Neuva Ecija; three s. four d.; ed. Univ. of the Philippines, Philippine and U.S. Mil. Acads.; served U.S. Army World War II; Officer in Philippine Army 1950, f. and Head Scout Rangers 1950-55; Mil. Attaché in Laos and S. Vietnam 1955-59; Operations Chief, Nat. Intelligence Co-ordinating Agency 1959; fmr. Commanding Gen. of Philippine Army and Deputy Chief of Staff; rank of Lieut.-Gen.; Amb. to Iran 1975, later Amb. to Thailand; Deputy Defence Minister Feb.-Nov. 1986, Defence Minister 1986-88; Pres. Adviser on Nat. Security Affairs Feb. 1989-. *Address:* National Security Council; V. Luna Road, cor. East. Avenue, Diliman, Quezon City, Metro Manila, The Philippines.

ILIESCU, Ion; Romanian politician ; b. 3 March 1930, Oltenita, Ilfov District; m. Elena Iliescu; ed. Bucharest Polytechnic Inst., and Moscow; Member of Union of Communist Youth (U.C.Y.) 1944; mem. Romanian CP 1953-; mem. Cen. Cttee. of U.C.Y. 1949-60, Sec. 1956-60; Pres. of Union of Student Asscns. 1957-60; Propaganda Dept. Cen. Cttee. of R.C.P., Alt. mem. Cen. Cttee. of RCP 1965-68, mem. 1968-84; First Sec. Cen. Cttee. of U.C.Y. and Minister of Youth Problems 1967-71; First Sec. CP Cttee., Jassy County 1974-79; Dir. of tech. publishing house 1984-; Chair. Nat. Council for Water Resources 1979-84; Alt. mem. of Exec. Pol. Cttee. of Cen. Cttee. of RCP 1969-79; mem. Bureau of Nat. Council of Socialist Unity Front 1968-72; Sec. CP Cttee., Timiş County 1971-74; mem. Nat. Ass. 1957-; mem. Acad. of Social and Political Sciences 1970-. *Address:* R.71341, Piata, Scînteii 1, Bucharest, Romania. *Telephone:* 176010.

ILLICH, Ivan PH.D.; American educator and writer; b. 4 Sept. 1926, Vienna, Austria; ed. Gregorian Univ., Rome, Univ. of Salzburg; went to U.S.A. 1951; Asst. Pastor in New York; Vice-Rector Catholic Univ. of Puerto Rico 1956-60; Co-Founder Center for Intercultural Documentation (CIDOC), Cuernavaca, Mexico 1961-76; Lecturer, Dept. of Pol. Science, Fordham Univ. (Pres. 1963-68, mem. 1968-, researcher 1973-); Guest Prof. of Medieval History, Univ. of Kassel, 1979-81, Univ. of Calif. in Berkeley 1982, Univ. of Marburg 1983-; Prof. of the Humanities and Sciences, Pennsylvania State Univ. 1986-; mem. Berlin Inst. of Advanced Studies 1981-82. *Publications:* Celebration of Awareness 1969, Deschooling Society 1971, Tools for Conviviality 1973, Energy and Equity 1973, Medical Nemesis 1975, The Right to Useful Unemployment 1979, Toward a History of Needs 1979, Shadow-Work 1981, Gender 1982, H²O and the Waters of Forgetfulness 1985; contributed to Esprit, Temps Modernes, Kursbuch, New York Review of Books, New York Times, Le Monde. *Address:* Apdo. 479, 62000 Cuernavaca, Mexico.

ILLUECA, Jorge E., LL.D.; Panamanian diplomatist and politician; b. 17 Dec. 1918, Panama City; m.; four c.; ed. Univ. de Panamá, Harvard Law School, Univ. of Chicago; Prof., Univ. de Panamá 1962-63, 1966-68; Pres. Nat. Bar Asscn. 1963-64, 1966-68; Dir. El Panamá América (newspaper) 1963-64, 1967-68; Special Amb. to U.S.A. to begin negotiations for new Panama Canal Treaty 1964, Special Envoy for negotiations on the treaty 1972; mem. del. to UN Gen. Assembly 1957, 1961, 1975, also to 3rd Special Emergency Session; Head of del. to 1st Session of 3rd UN Conf. on Law of the Sea 1974, mem. del to 4th Session 1976; Deputy Perm. Rep. to UN 1957, Perm. Rep. 1960, 1976-81, Pres. 38th Session of UN Gen. Ass. Sept.-Dec. 1983; mem. Perm. Court of Arbitration, The Hague, Netherlands 1974-76; fmr. Foreign Minister; Vice-Pres. of Panama 1982-83, Pres. Feb.-Oct. 1984; U Thant Award 1983.

ILYICHEV, Leonid Fyodorovich; Soviet journalist and politician; b. 15 March 1906, Krasnodar; ed. North Caucasian Communist Univ. and Inst. of Red Profs., Moscow; worker at a factory, Krasnodar 1918-24; Young Communist League work 1924-27; student and asst. teacher, North Caucasian Communist Univ. 1930-31; party work 1931-34; Sec. Bolshevik Journal 1938-40; mem. staff Pravda 1940-44, Deputy Ed.-in-Chief, later Ed.-in-Chief 1949-52; Ed.-in-Chief Izvestia 1944-48; on staff CPSU Cen. Cttee. 1948-49; Dir. Press Dept., Ministry of Foreign Affairs 1953-58; Dir. CP Agitation and Propaganda Service 1958-61; Sec. Cen. Cttee. of CPSU 1961-65, mem. 1961-66, Cand. mem. March 1981-; Deputy Foreign Minister of U.S.S.R. 1965-; mem. U.S.S.R. Acad. of Sciences 1962-; Lenin Prize 1960, Order of Lenin, Order of October Revolution and other decorations. *Publications:* On the Role of the Individual in History 1941, Progress of Science and Technology on International Relations 1958, Scientific Foundation of the Management of the Development of Society. *Address:* 32-34 Smolenskaya-Sennaya ploshchad, Moscow, U.S.S.R.

IMADY, Dr. Mohammed; Syrian economist and planner; b. 1 Dec. 1930, Damascus; s. of Omar Imady and Yosra Hawasly; m. Mildred Elaine Rippey 1958; one s. two d.; ed. Damascus Secondary School, Damascus

Univ. and New York Univ.; Deputy Minister of Planning 1968–72, Minister 1972; Minister of Economy and Foreign Trade 1972–79; Pres. Arab Econ. Soc. 1974–75, Syrian Econ. Soc. 1976; Chair. Bd. of Govs. IMF, IBRD 1975–76; Dir.-Gen. and Chair. Arab Fund for Econ. and Social Devt. 1979–85; Minister of Economy and Foreign Trade April 1985–; Founders Day Award (New York Univ.). *Publication:* Economic Development and Planning (textbook in Arabic for Damascus Univ.) 1968. *Address:* Ministry of Economy and Foreign Trade, Damascus, Syria.

IMAI, Nobuko; Japanese viola soloist; b. 18 March 1943, Tokyo; m. Aart von Bochove 1981; one s. one d.; ed. Toho School of Music, Tokyo, Juilliard School of Music, Yale Univ.; mem. Vermeer Quartet 1974–79; soloist with London Symphony Orchestra, Royal Philharmonic, Chicago Symphony, Concertgebouw, Montreal Symphony, Boston Symphony, Vienna Symphony, Stockholm Philharmonic; festival performances include Marlborough, Casals, South Bank, Bath, Cheltenham, Aldeburgh, London Proms, Int. Viola Congress (Houston), Lockenhaus; Prof. High School of Music, Detmold 1985–; recordings include Tippett Triple Concerto and Berlioz Harold in Italy; awarded First Prize Geneva and Munich Int. Viola Competitions. *Address:* c/o Terry Harrison Artists Management, 9a Penzance Place, London W11 4PE, England.

IMAI, Tadashi; Japanese film director; b. 1912, Tokyo; joined Toho production company with first film Numazu Naval Academy 1939; films concerned with plight of the poor, e.g. Rice 1975, A Story from Echigo 1964, and oppressed minorities, e.g. Kiku and Isamu 1959 and two-part The River Without a Bridge 1969–70; Grand Prix, Berlin Int. Film Festival for Bushido 1963; Gold Prize, Int. Film Festival of India for Brother and Sister (1976) 1977. *Other films include:* Minshu no Teki 1946, Blue Mountain 1949, Till We Meet Again 1950, And Yet We Live 1951, School of Echo 1952, Lily Corps, Nigorie 1953, Here is a Fountain 1955, Darkness at Noon 1956, Tale of Pure Love 1957, The Adulteress 1958, A Woman Named Oen 1971, My Voiceless Friends, Eternal Cause 1972, Kobayashi Takiji 1974, Rika 1978, Yuki 1980, Lily Corps 1982. *Address:* 1-40, Yazaki, Fuchu-shi, Tokyo 183, Japan.

IMAM, Zafar; Bangladesh politician; b. 1940, Feni; ed. Punjab Univ.; joined Pakistan Army 1966, C.O. 10th Bengal Regt. 1971, Lieut.-Col. 1975; mem. Bangladesh Nationalist Party Exec. Cttee. 1978; M.P. 1979; Deputy Minister of Relief and Rehabilitation 1980, Minister 1985–86, Minister of Jute 1986–88, of Textiles March 1988–; Bir Birkram Award. *Address:* Ministry of Textiles, Dhaka, Bangladesh.

IMANAGA, Fumio; Japanese business executive; b. 22 Feb. 1928; s. of Fumihiko Imanaga; m. 1953; two c.; ed. Moji Middle School and First Imperial Fisheries Inst.; joined Nippon Suisan Kaisha Ltd. 1948, mem. Bd. of Dirs. 1977, Man. Dir. 1980, Sr. Man. Dir. 1983, Exec. Vice-Pres. 1985, Pres. 1986–. *Leisure interests:* golf, reading. *Address:* 2-chome, Kamada, Setagaya Ward, Tokyo, Japan.

IMBERT, Bertrand Sainclair Maire; French hydrographic engineer and naval officer; b. 23 Oct. 1924; s. of Jean Imbert and Marie-Hélène Gérard; m. 2nd Mira Pavelic 1974; five c. by first marriage; ed. Collège Saint-Martin de France and Collège Sainte Geneviève; entered Free French Navy, Ecole Navale 1943; served in Indo-China Campaign 1945–47; Antarctic expeditions 1951, 1956 and 1957; Principal Marine Nationale; Chief of French Antarctic Expeditions of the Int. Geophysical Year 1956–59; mem. Atomic Energy Comm. 1959–69; Asst. Man. Dir. Control-Data France 1969, Man. Dir. 1970–75, Vice-Pres. 1975–; Croix de guerre, Chevalier, Légion d'honneur. *Leisure interest:* sailing.

IMBERT, Jean Raoul Léon, DIP.; French university professor; b. 23 June 1919, Calais; s. of Léon Imbert and Maria (née Decobert) Imbert; m. Thérèse Chombart 1945; two s. one d.; ed. Faculté de Droit de Paris (Sorbonne); mem. Faculty of Law, Nancy 1947–58; Prof. of Law, Paris 1958, Tech. Adviser to the Ministry of Health 1958; Dean of the Faculty of Law, Phnom-Penh, Cambodia 1959–61; Rector of the Univ. of Yaoundé, Cameroon 1971–73; Rector of the Acad. of Versailles 1973–75; Dir. of Higher Studies, Ministry of Univs. 1976–79; Dir. Centre Nat. des Oeuvres Universitaires et Scolaires 1979–82; Pres. of the Univ. of Law, Econs. and Social Sciences, Paris; Lauréat de l'Acad. des Inscriptions et Belles Lettres 1948, Lauréat de l'Acad. Française 1983; mem. Acad. des Sciences morales et politiques 1982; Foreign mem. Acad. of Science and Letters, Milan 1983–; Commdr. Légion d'Honneur 1989; Silver Medal Int. Asscn. of Univ. Presidents 1972. *Publications:* Histoire du droit privé 1950 (trans. into Japanese), Le droit hospitalier de la Révolution et de l'Empire 1954, Le droit antique 1960 (trans. into Greek and Portuguese), Histoire des institutions khmères 1961, Histoire économique des origines à 1789 1965 (trans. into Spanish), La peine de mort 1967, La France et les droits de l'homme 1968, Le pouvoir, les juges et les bourreaux 1972, Le Cameroun 1973, Le procès de Jésus 1980, Histoire des hôpitaux de France 1982. *Leisure interest:* flying. *Address:* 16 rue du Maréchal Lyautey, 95620 Parmain, France. *Telephone:* 34 73 00 48.

IMBERT, Sir Peter Michael, Kt.; British police officer; b. 27 April 1933, Kent; s. of the late William Henry Imbert and of Frances May Hodge; m. Iris Rosina Dove 1956; one s. two d.; ed. Harvey Grammar School and Holborn Coll. of Law; Metropolitan Police 1953–, Asst. Chief Constable, Surrey Constabulary 1976–77, Deputy Chief Constable 1977–79, Chief Constable, Thames Valley Police 1979–85, Deputy Commr. Metropolitan Police 1985–87, Commr. Aug. 1987–; Metropolitan Police Anti-Terrorist Squad 1973–75; Police negotiator in Balcombe Street (London) IRA Siege Dec. 1975; Sec. Nat. Crime Cttee., ACPO Council 1980–83, Chair. 1983–85; mem. Gen. Advisory Council, BBC 1980–. *Leisure interests:* golf, gardening. *Address:* New Scotland Yard, Broadway, London, SW1H 0BG, England. *Telephone:* 01-230 1212.

IMDAHL, Max, D.PHIL.; German professor of the history of art; b. 6 Sept. 1925, Aachen; s. of Joseph and Emilie (née Krabbel) Imdahl; m. Ebba Freiin von Klot-Trautvetter; five c.; ed. Kaiser Karl Gymnasium, Aachen Münster Univ.; lecturer in History of Art, Univ. of Münster 1961–65 Guest Prof. Hamburg Acad. 1963; Prof. History of Art, Ruhr Univ. Bochum 1965–; Dean, Dept. of History 1970–71; Dir. Univ. Museum Bochum 1975–; Bevin Davis Prize for Young German Art 1950. *Publications:* books and articles on medieval art (Ottonian art, Giotto) and especially contemporary art (Marées, Cézanne, Picasso, Braque, Newman, Stella, Delauney). *Address:* Askulapweg Nr. 3, 4630, Bochum-Querenburg Federal Republic of Germany. *Telephone:* 701156.

IMRAN TUANKU JAAFAR, Tunku; Malaysian business executive; ed The King's School, Canterbury and Univ. of Nottingham; formerly worked for nat. oil co.; with father opened own co. in partnership with Jardine Matheson Holdings 1977; founder and Man. Dir. Antah Holdings (with holdings in Arab-Malaysian Bank, Pepsi-Cola Bottling, joint venture rural water supply, leasing cos., insurance cos., security, tech. products and real estate) 1983–. *Address:* Antah Holdings, Berhad, Complex Bejabat Damansaia, Kuala Lumpur, Malaysia.

IMRAY, Colin Henry, M.A., C.M.G.; British diplomatist; b. 21 Sept. 1933, Newport; s. of Henry Gibbon Imray and Frances Olive Badman; m. Shirley Margaret Matthews 1957; one s. three d.; ed. Highgate School, London Hotchkiss School, Conn., U.S.A. and Balliol Coll., Oxford; Second Lieut. Seaforth Highlanders, Royal W. African Frontier Force 1952–54; Asst. Prin. Commonwealth Relations Office 1957–58, 1961–63; Third then Second Sec. British High Comm., Canberra 1958–61; First Sec., Nairobi 1963–66; Asst. Head Personnel Dept. FCO 1966–70; British Trade Commr., Montreal 1970–73; Counsellor, Consul Gen. and Head of Chancery, Islamabad 1973–77; Royal Coll. of Defence Studies 1977; Commercial Counsellor British Embassy, Tel Aviv 1977–80; Deputy High Commr., Bombay 1980–84; Asst. Under-Sec. of State (Chief Inspector and Deputy Chief Clerk) 1984–85; High Commr. in Tanzania 1986–. *Leisure interests:* travel, walking. *Address:* c/o Heads of Mission Section, Foreign and Commonwealth Office, London, SW1A 2AH, England.

IMRU HAILE SELASSIE, Lij Mikhail; Ethiopian politician; b. 1930; ed. Oxford Univ., England; fmr. Dir.-Gen. Ministry of Defence and mem. Planning Bd., Ministry of Agriculture; fmr. Amb. to U.S., then to U.S.S.R.; Head Ethiopian mission to UN Office, Geneva until 1974; Minister of Commerce and Industry March 1974; Minister in the Prime Minister's Office in charge of Econ. and Social Affairs April-July 1974, Prime Minister July-Sept. 1974; Minister of Information 1974–75; Chief Pol. Adviser to Head of State 1975–76.

IMSHENETSKY, Aleksandr Aleksandrovich; Soviet microbiologist; b. 8 Jan. 1905, Kiev; ed. Voronezh State Univ.; Teacher of Microbiology, Leningrad Chemico-Tech. Inst. 1932–34; Sr. Scientific Worker, Inst. of Microbiology, U.S.S.R. Acad. of Sciences 1932–41, Head of Dept. 1941–; Deputy Dir. 1945–49, Dir. 1949–; Prof. of Microbiology, Piscicultural Faculty, Timiryazev Agricultural Acad. 1935–37; corresp. mem. U.S.S.R. Acad. of Sciences 1946–62, mem. 1962–; First Pres. (and Founder) U.S.S.R. Microbiological Soc. 1960; Ed. Microbiology; Order of Lenin (twice), Order of Red Banner of Labour (twice), Hero of Socialist Labour; Pasteur Medal and other decorations. *Publications:* The Structure of Bacteria 1940 Microbiological Processes at High Temperatures 1944, Microbiology of Celluloses 1953, Morphology of Bacteria 1962, Perspectives for the Development of Exobiology 1963, On the Multiplication of Xerophilic Micro organisms under Simulated Martian Conditions 1973, Detection of Extra Terrestrial Life by Radiometric Techniques 1974, Microbiological Research in Space Biology 1974, On Micro-organisms of the Stratosphere 1975, Biological Effects of Extreme Environmental Conditions 1975. *Address:* Institute of Microbiology of the U.S.S.R. Academy of Sciences, Profsoyuz naya ul. 7, Moscow, U.S.S.R.

INABA, Osamu; Japanese politician; b. 1910; ed. Chuo Univ.; Prof. of Law, Chuo Univ.; mem. House of Reps. for Niigata Pref. 1947–; fmr. Parl. Vice-Minister of Educ.; Vice-Chair. Policy Affairs Research Council of Liberal Democratic Party; Minister of Educ. July-Dec. 1972, of Justice 1974–76. *Address:* c/o Ministry of Justice, Tokyo, Japan.

INAI, Yoshihiro; Japanese business executive; b. 8 July 1911, Hyogo, Japan; m. Masayo Mori; two s. one d.; ed. Dairoku Higher School, Kyoto Teikoku Univ.; entered Mitsubishi Mining Co. (later Mitsubishi Metal Mining Corporation) 1938; Gen. Man. Metal Fabricating Dept. 1962; Dir. 1963; Man. Dir. 1965; Senior Man. Dir. 1971; Vice-Pres. Mitsubishi Metal Mining 1972; Pres. Mitsubishi Metal (fmrly. Mitsubishi Metal Mining) Corpn. 1973–. *Leisure interests:* golf, reading. *Address:* 4-chome 14-30 Hujigaya, Kugenuma, Hujisawa-shi, Tokyo, Japan. *Telephone:* (0466) 22-5572.

INAMURA, Sakonshiro; Japanese politician; worked as newspaper boy, longshoreman, labourer, foreman; mem. House of Reps. 1963-; fmr. Deputy Minister for Int. Trade and Industry; Minister of State, Dir.-Gen. Prime Minister's Office and Okinawa Devt. Agency 1977-78; Dir. Gen. Nat. Land Agency 1983-85; Liberal-Democratic Party. *Address:* c/o Office of the Prime Minister, 6-1 Nagatacho 1-chome, Chiyoda-ku, Tokyo, Japan.

INAMURA, Toshiyuki; Japanese politician; b. 1935; previous posts include: Pvt. Sec. to the Labour Minister; Parl. Vice-Minister of Posts and Telecommunications and of Finance; Chair. Cttees. on Construction and on Social and Labour Affairs, House of Reps.; Deputy Sec.-Gen. Liberal Democratic Party (LDP), Chair. LDP Nat. Org. Cttee.; Minister of State (Dir.-Gen. Environment Agency) 1986-87; Liberal Democratic Party. *Address:* c/o House of Representatives, Tokyo, Japan.

INBAL, Eliahu; British/Israeli conductor; b. 16 Feb. 1936, Jerusalem; s. of Jehuda Joseph and Leah Museri Inbal; m. Helga Fritzsche 1968; three s.; ed. Acad. of Music, Jerusalem, Conservatoire National Supérieur, Paris; from 1963 guest conductor with numerous orchestras including Milan, Rome, Berlin, Munich, Hamburg, Stockholm, Copenhagen, Vienna, Budapest, Amsterdam, London, Paris, Tel-Aviv, New York, Chicago, Toronto and Tokyo; Chief Conductor, Radio Symphony Orchestra, Frankfurt 1974-; has made numerous recordings, particularly of Mahler and Bruckner. *Leisure interests:* music, photography. *Address:* Hessischer Rundfunk, Bertramstrasse 8, 6000 Frankfurt, Federal Republic of Germany. *Telephone:* 0611/ 1552371.

INCE, Basil André, PH.D.; Trinidadian politician; b. 1 May 1933, Trinidad; s. of Arthur Johnson and Leonora (née Williams) Brown; m. Laurel Barnwell 1961; two s.; ed. Tufts Univ. Mass., New York Univ.; Second Sec. UN 1963-66; Asst. Prof. City Univ. N.Y. 1966-68; Assoc. Prof., Univ. of Puerto Rico 1968-70; Assoc. Prof., State Univ. of New York 1970-73; Sr. Lecturer Inst. of Int. Relations, Trinidad 1973-78, Dir. 1978-81; Minister of External Affairs, Trinidad and Tobago 1981-85, of Sport, Culture and Youth Affairs 1985-86; High Commr. in U.K. 1986-87. *Publications:* Decolonization and Conflict in the United Nations: Guyana's Struggle for Independence 1972, Essays on Race, Economics and Politics in the Caribbean (ed.) 1972, Contemporary International Relations of the Caribbean (ed.) 1979, Issues in Caribbean International Relations (ed.) 1983, many articles in periodicals. *Leisure interests:* reading, tennis, track athletics and boxing. *Address:* c/o Ministry of Foreign Affairs, Knowsley Building, Queen's Park West, Port of Spain, Trinidad and Tobago.

INCHCAPE, 3rd Earl of; Kenneth James William Mackay, M.A.; British company executive; b. 27 Dec. 1917, Uckfield, Sussex; s. of 2nd Earl of Inchcape and Joan Moriarty; m. 1st Mrs. Aline Thorn Hannay 1941 (dissolved 1954), two s. one d.; m. 2nd. Caroline Cholmeley-Harrison 1965, two s.; one adopted s.; ed. Eton, Trinity Coll., Cambridge; Chair. Inchcape PLC 1958-82, C.E.O. 1981-82; Chair. P. & O. Steam Navigation Co. 1973-83, Chief Exec. 1973-81, Pres. 1984-; Dir. Standard Chartered Bank Ltd., Banque Arabe et Int. d'Investissement 1983-; Pres. and Dir. Inchcape PLC 1984-; Pres. Gen. Council of British Shipping 1976-77, of Royal Soc. for India, Pakistan and Ceylon 1970-76, of Commonwealth Soc. for the Deaf; Prime Warden Shipwrights Co. 1967-68, Fishmongers Co. 1977-78. *Leisure interests:* field sports, farming. *Address:* Addington Manor, Addington, Buckingham, MK18 2JR, England (Home); Forneth House, Blairgowrie, Perthshire, Scotland (Home).

INCHYRA, 1st Baron (cr. 1962), of St. Madoes in the County of Perth; **Frederick Robert Hoyer Millar,** G.C.M.G., C.V.O.; British diplomatist; b. 6 June 1900, Montrose, Scotland; s. of the late R. Hoyer Millar; m. Elizabeth de Marees van Swinderen 1931; two s. two d.; ed. Wellington Coll. and New Coll., Oxford; Hon. Attaché Brussels 1922; entered Diplomatic Service 1923; served as Third Sec. Berlin and Paris, Second Sec. Cairo; Asst. Private Sec. to Sec. of State for Foreign Affairs 1934-38; First Sec. Washington 1939, Counsellor 1941-42; Sec. British Civil Secr., Washington 1943; Counsellor, Foreign Office 1944, Asst. Under-Sec. 1947; Minister, British Embassy, Washington 1948; Deputy NATO 1950-52; Perm. Rep. North Atlantic Council 1952-53, High Commr. in Germany 1953-55, Amb. to Fed. Repub. of Germany 1955-57; Perm. Under-Sec. of State 1957-61; retd. 1962. *Leisure interest:* shooting. *Address:* Inchyra House, Glencarse, Perthshire, Scotland. *Telephone:* Glencarse 210.

INDIANA, Robert, B.F.A.; American artist; b. 13 Sept. 1928, New Castle Ind.; ed. John Herron School of Art, Indianapolis, Munson-Williams-Proctor Inst., Utica, New York, Art Inst. of Chicago, Skowhegan School of Painting and Sculpture, Univ. of Edinburgh and Edinburgh Coll. of Art; served U.S.A.A.F. 1946-49; lived and worked in New York 1954-; Artist-in-Residence, Center of Contemporary Art, Aspen, Colo. 1968; Hon. D.F.A. (Franklin and Marshall Coll., Lancaster, Pa.) 1970. One-man exhbns.: Stable Gallery, New York 1962, 1964, 1966, Walker Art Center, Minneapolis 1963, Inst. of Contemporary Art, Boston 1963, Rolf Nelson Gallery, Los Angeles 1965, Dayton's Gallery 1912, Minneapolis 1966, Galerie Alfred Schmela, Düsseldorf 1966, Stedelijk van Abbemuseum, Eindhoven 1966, Museum Hans Lange, Krefeld (Fed. Repub. of Germany) 1966, Württembergischer Kunstverein, Stuttgart 1966, Inst. of Contemporary Art, Univ. of Pennsylvania 1968, Marion Koogler McNay Art Inst., San Antonio, Tex. 1968, Herron Museum of Art, Indianapolis 1968, Toledo Museum of Art, Ohio

1968, Hunter Gallery, Aspen, Colo. 1968, Creighton Univ., Omaha 1969, St. Mary's Coll., Notre Dame, Ind. 1969, Colby Coll. Art Museum, Waterville, Maine 1969-70, Currier Gallery of Art, Manchester, N.H. 1970, Hopkins Center, Dartmouth Coll. Hanover, N.H. 1970, Bowdoin Coll. Museum of Art, Brunswick, Maine 1970, Brandeis Univ., Waltham, Mass. 1970, Heron Art Museum, Indianapolis 1977, Univ. of Texas 1977, Osuna Gallery, Washington 1981, Tex. Art Centre 1982, William A. Farnsworth Library and Art Museum, Maine 1982. *Major group exhbns. include:* Painting and Sculpture of a Decade, Tate Gallery, London 1964, Twenty-ninth Biennial Exhbn. of American Painting, Corcoran Gallery of Art, Washington, D.C. 1965, Pop Art and the American Tradition, Milwaukee 1965, White House Festival of the Arts, Washington 1965, American Painting Now, Expo 67, Montreal 1967, Annual Exhbns. of American Painting, Documenta IV, Kassel 1968, Art in the Sixties, Cologne 1969. *Address:* c/o Star of Hope, Vinalhaven, Maine, U.S.A. (Summer Residence).

INDRA, Alois; Czechoslovak politician; b. 17 March 1921, Medzev; fmr. Head of Planning, Finance and Foreign Trade Dept., Cen. Cttee. of Czechoslovak CP; Minister-Chair. State Planning Comm. 1962-63, mem. 1965-68; Minister of Transport 1963-68; mem. Secr. of Cen. Cttee. and Sec. of Cen. Cttee. of CP 1968-71; mem. Cen. Cttee. of CP 1962- (Econ. Comm. 1963-66); Deputy to Nat. Assembly 1964-69; Deputy to Czech Nat. Council 1968-71; Deputy to House of the People, Fed. Assembly 1969-; mem. Presidium of Fed. Assembly 1969-, Chair. 1971-; Alt. mem. Presidium of Cen. Cttee., CP of Czechoslovakia 1970-71, mem. 1971-; Presidium mem. of Cen. Cttee. of Nat. Front 1971-; Chair. CPCZ Legal Comm. 1988-; Medal of Govt. of Czech Socialist Repub.; Order of the Repub. 1971, Order of Victorious February 1973, Hero of Socialist Labour 1981, Klement Gottwald Order 1981, Order of October Revolution (U.S.S.R.) 1981. *Address:* Federal Assembly of the Czechoslovak Socialist Republic, Vinohradská I, Prague I, Czechoslovakia.

INGALLS, Daniel Henry Holmes, A.B., M.A.; American orientalist; b. 4 May 1916, New York; s. of late Fay Ingalls and Rachel Holmes Ingalls; m. Phyllis Sarah Day 1936; one s. two d.; ed. Harvard Univ.; Jr. Fellow, Harvard Univ. 1939-42 and 1946-49; Office of Strategic Services 1942-44, U.S. Army 1944-46; Asst. Prof. Harvard Univ. 1949-54, Assoc. Prof. 1954-58, Wales Prof. of Sanskrit 1956-83; Ed. Harvard Oriental Series 1949-83; Pres. American Oriental Soc. 1959-60; Dir. Virginia Hot Springs, Inc. 1946-57, Pres. 1957-63, Chair. of Bd. 1963-. *Publications:* Materials for the Study of Navya-nyaya Logic 1950, An Anthology of Sanskrit Court Poetry 1964. *Leisure interests:* reading, music. *Address:* The Yard, Hot Springs, Va. 24445, U.S.A.

INGAMELLS, John, B.A.; British museum director and art historian; b. 12 Nov. 1934, Northampton; s. of the late George H. Ingamells and Gladys L. (Rollett) Ingamells; m. Hazel Wilson 1964; two d.; ed. Hastings and Eastbourne Grammar Schools and Fitzwilliam House, Cambridge; Art Asst. York Art Gallery 1959-62; Asst. Keeper of Art, Nat. Museum of Wales 1963-67; Curator, York Art Gallery 1967-77; Asst. to Dir. Wallace Collection 1977-78, Dir. 1978-. *Publications;* The Davies Collection of French Art 1967, The English Episcopal Portrait 1981, Wallace Collection, Catalogue of Pictures (Vol. I) 1985, (Vol. II) 1986, (Vol. III) 1989; numerous museum catalogues, exhibition catalogues and articles in learned journals. *Address:* The Wallace Collection, Hertford House, Manchester Square, London, W1M 6BN, England. *Telephone:* 01-935 0687.

INGELMAN-SUNDBERG, Axel, M.D., F.R.C.O.G.; Swedish gynaecologist and university professor; b. 22 Dec. 1910, Uppsala; s. of Isidor Sundberg and Maria Ingelman; m. 1st Anna Brandberg 1937; m. 2nd Mirjam Furuhjelm 1965; three s. one d.; ed. Uppsala Univ. and Royal Caroline Inst., Stockholm; Asst. in Gen. Chemistry, Uppsala Univ. 1929, in Histology 1930-31, in Pathology 1937; Asst. Prof. of Obstetrics and Gynaecology, Royal Caroline Inst. 1947-49, Assoc. Prof. 1949-58, Royal Prof. 1958-77; Chair. Univ. Dept. of Obstetrics and Gynaecology, Sabbatsberg Hosp. 1958-79; Scientific Consultant, Swedish Defence Forces 1969-79; Swedish Nat. Bd. of Health and Welfare 1960-79; Consultant, Sophiahemmet Hosp. 1979-, Ersta Hosp. 1983-; Hon. Prof., Univ. of Montevideo and Visiting Prof. at numerous univs.; Pres. Int. Fertility Asscn. 1968-74; Pres. Swedish Gynaecological Soc. 1961-69; Pres. Scandinavian Asscn. of Obstetricians and Gynaecologists 1966-68; Pres. 5th World Congress on Fertility and Sterility 1966; The Hwasser Prize 1934. *Publications:* The Childbearing Years 1951; Co-author: A Child Is Born 1965-82; Chief Ed. Acta Obstetricia et Gynaecologica Scandinavica 1970-77, Assoc. Ed. Int. Journal of Fertility 1972-77, Int. Journal of Gynaecology and Obstetrics 1974-86; 198 scientific papers. *Leisure interest:* salmon fishing. *Address:* Fjalarstigen 1A, S-182 64, Djursholm, Sweden. *Telephone:* 08/755 44 18.

INGHAM, Bernard: British civil servant; b. 21 June 1932, Halifax, Yorkshire; s. of Garnet Ingham and Alice Ingham; m. Nancy Hilda Hoyle 1956; one s.; ed. Hebden Bridge Grammar School; reporter Hebden Bridge Times 1948-52, The Yorkshire Post and Yorkshire Evening Post, Halifax 1952-59; with The Yorkshire Post, Leeds 1959-61, Northern Industrial Corresp. 1961; with The Guardian 1962-67, Labour Staff, London 1965-67; Press and Public Relations Adviser Nat. Bd. for Prices and Incomes 1967-68; Chief Information Officer, Dept. of Employment and Productivity 1968-72; Dir. of Information Dept. of Employment 1973; with Dept. of Energy 1974-79, Dir. of Information 1974-77, Under-Sec. and Head of

Energy Conservation Div. 1978-79; Chief Press Sec. to the Prime Minister 1979-. *Leisure interests:* walking, reading, gardening, visiting Yorkshire. *Address:* 9 Monahan Avenue, Purley, Surrey, CR2 3BB, England. *Telephone:* 01-660 8970.

INGHRAM, Mark Gordon, PH.D.; American professor and physicist; b. 13 Nov. 1919, Livingstone, Mont.; s. of Mark G. and Luella McNay Inghram; m. Evelyn M. Dyckman 1946; one s. one d.; ed. Olivet Coll. and Univ. of Chicago; Physicist, Univ. of Minn. 1942, Manhattan Project, Columbia Univ. 1943-45; Sr. Physicist Argonne Nat. Lab. 1945-49; Instructor in Physics, Univ. of Chicago 1947-49, Asst. Prof. 1949-51, Assoc. Prof. 1951-57, Prof. of Physics 1957-69, Samuel K. Allison Distinguished Service Prof. of Physics 1969-84; Chair. Dept. of Physics 1959-70, Assoc. Dean Div. of Physical Sciences 1964-71, 1981-84, Assoc. Dean, The College 1981-84, Master, Physical Sciences Collegiate Div. 1981-84, Samuel K. Allison Distinguished Service Prof. Emer. 1985-; mem. N.A.S.; Lawrence Smith Medal of N.A.S. 1957. *Publications:* Over 150 research papers in scientific journals. *Address:* 3077 Lakeshore Avenue, Holland, Mich. 49423, U.S.A. *Telephone:* (616) 399-8638.

INGLÉS, José D., D.C.L.; Philippine lawyer, professor and diplomatist; b. 24 Aug. 1910, Mauban, Tayabas; m. Josefina M. Feliciano 1942; two s. two d.; ed. Univ. of the Philippines, Santo Tomás Univ., Manila, and Columbia Univ., New York; Attorney 1932-36; Private Sec. Assoc. Justice of Supreme Court; Legal Asst., Pres. of the Philippines 1936-39; Asst. Solicitor-Gen. 1940; Judge First Instance 1941-43; Asst. Exec. Sec. to Pres. of the Philippines 1944; Counsel, Senate of Philippines 1945-47; Prof. Philippine Law School 1945-46; Vice-Chair. Trusteeship Cttee., Paris 1951, Special Political Cttee. 1963 and 1965; Chair. Credentials Cttee. 1974; mem. Philippine Del. to UN 1946-56, 1962-69, Vice-Chair. of Del. 1986; Vice-Pres. UN Gen. Assembly 1974, mem. numerous UN Cttees.; Minister to Fed. Republic of Germany 1956-58, Amb. 1958-62; Amb. to Thailand 1962-66; Rep. South East Asia Treaty Org. (SEATO) 1962-66; mem. Standing Cttee. Asscn. of South East Asia (ASA) 1963-66; Under-Sec. of Foreign Affairs 1966-78; Deputy Minister of Foreign Affairs 1978-81; Acting Foreign Minister at various times 1978-81; Jose P. Laurel Chair. in Int. Relations, Claro M. Recto Acad. of Advanced Studies; Dean Coll. of Foreign Service, Lyceum of Philippines 1981-; Chair. UN Cttee. on Elimination of Racial Discrimination 1982-84; Sec.-Gen. Nat. Secr. (ASEAN) 1967-69; mem. Civil Aeronautics Bd. 1969-70, 1986-; Chair. Philippine Air Services Negotiating Panel 1969-81, 1986-; Chair. Philippine Del., SEATO Council of Ministers, Wellington 1968, UNESCO Gen. Conf., Paris 1970, ASEAN and ASPAC Standing Cttees., Manila 1970-81, Fifth ASEAN Ministerial Conf., Singapore 1972; Special ASEAN Ministerial Meetings, Bangkok Jan. 1979, Kuala Lumpur Dec. 1979, ASEAN-EEC Ministerial Meeting, Jakarta Oct. 1986; Acting Perm. Rep. to the UN 1974; First Deputy Minister for Foreign Affairs March 1986-; Grosskreuz des Verdienstordens der Bundesrepublik Deutschland, Most Noble Order of the Crown of Thailand, Most Exalted Order of the White Elephant, Gran Cruz del Orden de Mayo, Grand-Croix de l'Ordre de Léopold II, Nat. Order of Viet-Nam, Grand Cross of Sovereign Military Order of Malta, Datu of the Order of Sikatuna. *Publications:* Philippine Foreign Policy 1982 and numerous papers on economics and int. affairs. *Leisure interest:* orchid culture. *Address:* 1 Vinzons Street, Heroes' Hill, Quezon City, Philippines. *Telephone:* 99-3808.

INGLIS, Kenneth Stanley, M.A., D.PHIL.; Australian professor and university administrator; b. 7 Oct. 1929, Melbourne; s. of Stanley W. Inglis and Irene (née Winning) Inglis; m. 1st Judy Betheras 1952 (deceased 1962); one s. two d.; m. 2nd Amirah Gust 1965; ed. Univs. of Melbourne and Oxford; Sr. Lecturer Univ. of Adelaide 1956-60, Reader 1960-62; Reader Australian Nat. Univ. 1963-65, Prof. 1965-66; Prof. Univ. of Papua New Guinea 1967-72, Vice-Chancellor 1972-75; Professorial Fellow Australian Nat. Univ. 1975-76, Prof. of History, Research School of Social Sciences 1977-; Ernest Scott Prize for History 1983-84. *Publications:* Churches and the Working Classes in Victorian England 1963, The Australian Colonists 1974, This is the ABC: The Australian Broadcasting Comm. 1932-1983, 1983, The Rehearsal 1985, Australians. A Historical Library, 11 vols. (Gen. Ed.) 1987-88. *Address:* Australian National University, Box 4, G.P.O., Canberra 2601, Australia. *Telephone:* 062 492 534.

INGOLD, Keith Usherwood, PH.D., F.R.S., F.R.S.C.; Canadian research chemist; b. 31 May 1929, Leeds, England; s. of Sir Christopher Kelk Ingold and Lady Edith Hilda Usherwood; m. Carmen Cairine Hodgkin 1956; two s. one d.; ed. Univ. Coll., Univ. of London, Oxford Univ.; Postdoctoral Fellow Nat. Research Council of Canada 1951-53, Research Officer Div. of Chem. 1955-, Head Hydrocarbon Chem. Section 1965-, Assoc. Dir. 1977-; Postdoctoral Fellow Univ. of B.C. 1953-55; visiting scientist to numerous univs. internationally, numerous lectureships in U.S.A.; Sr. Carnegie Fellowship Univ. of St. Andrews (Scotland) 1977; Fellow Univ. Coll. London 1987; Adjunct Prof. Dept. of Chem. and Biochem. Univ. of Guelph, Ont. 1985-; Fellow Chem. Inst. of Canada; mem. Royal Soc. of Chem. (U.K.), American Chem. Soc.; Vice-Pres. Canadian Soc. for Chem. 1985-87, Pres. 1987-; Hon. D.Sc. (Guelph, Ontario) 1985; Hon. LL.D. (Mount Allison) 1987; American Chem. Soc. Award in Petroleum Chem. 1968; The Queen's Silver Jubilee Medal (U.K.) 1978; U.K. Chem. Soc. Award in Kinetics and Mechanism 1979; Chem. Inst. of Canada Medal

1981, Syntex Award in Physical Organic Chem. 1983; Royal Soc. of Canada Centennial Medal 1982; Henry Marshall Tory Medal, Royal Soc. of Canada 1985. *Publications:* Free-Radical Substitution Reactions (with B. P. Roberts) 1971, over 300 publications in the open scientific literature. *Address:* Division of Chemistry, National Research Council of Canada, Ottawa, Ont., K1A 0R6, Canada. *Telephone:* (613) 990-0938.

INGRAM, Alvin John, M.D., M.S.; American orthopaedic surgeon; b. 31 March 1914, Tennessee; s. of Alvin W. Ingram and Margaret Gallagher; m. Catherine Davis 1943; three d.; ed. Jackson High School, Union Univ., Univs. of Tenn. and Mich.; Resident, Orthopaedic Surgery, Campbell Clinic, Tenn. 1941-42, 1946-47; U.S. Army Medical Corps 1942-46; mem. staff, Campbell Clinic 1947-83, Chief of Staff 1969-77, Emer. 1978-; Univ. of Tenn. Coll. of Medicine, Dept. of Orthopaedic Surgery 1947-83, Prof. and Chair. 1969-78, Prof. Emer. 1979-; Orthopaedic Consultant, Richards Medical Co., Memphis 1984-; mem. numerous medical orgs., asscns., etc.; recipient of several distinguished service awards. *Leisure interests:* golf, swimming, U.S. coins. *Address:* Richards Medical Company, 1450 Brooks Road E., Memphis, Tenn. 38116 (Office); 190 Belle Meade Lane, Memphis, Tenn. 38117, U.S.A. (Home). *Telephone:* 901-396-2121 (Office); 901-683-9571 (Home).

INGRAM, James Charles, A.O., B.A.(ECON.); Australian diplomatist and international civil servant; b. 27 Feb. 1928, Warragul; m. Odette d.M. Koven 1950; one s. two d.; ed. De la Salle Coll., Melbourne Univ.; joined Dept. of External Affairs 1946; Third Sec., Tel-Aviv 1950; First Sec., Washington 1956; Chargé d'Affaires, Brussels 1959; Counsellor, Djakarta 1962, Australian Mission to UN 1964; Asst. Sec. External Affairs, Canberra 1967; Amb. to Philippines 1970-73; High Commr. to Canada, Jamaica, Barbados, Guyana, Trinidad and Tobago 1973-74; First Asst. Sec. Australian Devt. Assistance Agency 1975-76; Dir. Australian Devt. Assistance Bureau, Dept. of External Affairs 1977-82; Exec. Dir. World Food Programme 1982-. *Leisure interests:* sailing, music. *Address:* World Food Programme, Via Cristoforo Colombo 426, 00145 Rome, Italy. *Telephone:* Rome 57973030.

INGRAM, Vernon M., F.R.S., F.A.A.A.S., PH.D., D.SC.; British professor of biochemistry; b. 19 May 1924, Breslau, Germany; s. of Kurt and Johanna Immerwahr; m. 1st Margaret Young 1950; one s. one d.; m. 2nd Beth Hendee 1983; ed. Birkbeck Coll., Univ. of London; Research Chemist, Thos. Morson and Son 1941-45; Lecture Demonstrator, Birkbeck Coll., London 1945-47, Asst. Lecturer 1947-50; Rockefeller Foundation Fellow, New York 1950-51; Coxe Fellow, Yale Univ. 1951-52; mem. staff, Molecular Biology Unit, Cavendish Lab., Cambridge 1952-58; Visiting Assoc. Prof. M.I.T. 1958-59; Assoc. Prof. M.I.T. 1959-61, Prof. of Biochem. 1961-; Guggenheim Fellow, Univ. of London 1967-68; Fellow American Acad. of Arts and Sciences. *Publications:* Haemoglobin and its Abnormalities 1961, The Haemoglobins in Genetics and Evolution 1963, The Biosynthesis of Macromolecules 1965, 1972. *Leisure interest:* music. *Address:* Department of Biology, Massachusetts Institute of Technology, 77 Massachusetts Avenue, Cambridge, Mass. 02139, U.S.A. *Telephone:* 617-253-3706.

INGRAMS, Richard Reid; British journalist; b. 19 Aug. 1937, London; s. of Leonard St. Clair and Victoria (née Reid) Ingrams; m. 1962; two s. (one deceased) one d.; ed. Shrewsbury School, Univ. Coll., Oxford; joined Private Eye 1962; Ed. 1963-86, Chair. 1974-; TV critic The Spectator 1976-84; columnist, The Observer 1988-. *Publications:* Private Eye on London (with Christopher Booker and William Rushton) 1962, Private Eye's Romantic England 1963, Mrs. Wilson's Diary (with John Wells) 1965, Mrs. Wilson's Second Diary 1966, The Tale of Driver Grope 1968, The Bible for Motorists (with Barry Fantoni) 1970, The Life and Times of Private Eye (Ed.) 1971, Harris in Wonderland (as Philip Reid with Andrew Osmond) 1973, Cobbett's Country Book (Ed.) 1974, Beachcomber; the works of J. B. Morton (Ed.) 1974, The Best of Private Eye 1974, God's Apology 1977, Goldenballs 1979, Romney Marsh (with Fay Godwin) 1980, Dear Bill: the collected letters of Denis Thatcher (with John Wells) 1980, The Other Half 1981, Piper's Places (with John Piper) 1983, Dr. Johnson by Mrs. Thrale (Ed.) 1984, Down the Hatch (with John Wells) 1985, Just the One (with John Wells) 1986, John Stewart Collis: a memoir 1986, The Best of Dear Bill (with John Wells) 1986, Mud in Your Eye (with John Wells) 1987, The Eye Spy Look-alike Book (ed.) 1988, The Ridgeway 1988, You Might as Well Be Dead 1988, England: An Anthology 1989. *Leisure interests:* music, book selling. *Address:* c/o Private Eye, 6 Carlisle Street, London, W.1, England. *Telephone:* 01-437 4017.

INGRAND, Henry, M.D.; French doctor, civil servant and diplomatist; b. 18 Aug. 1908, Echire, Deux-Sèvres; ed. Univ. of Paris; Head of a Surgical Clinic, Paris until 1939; active in French Resistance Movement during 1939-45 war; Commr. for Auvergne Region 1944; High Commr. for Tourism 1946; Chair. Tourism Cttee. OEEC 1949-52; Pres. Union Internationale des Organismes officiels de Tourisme 1951-52; entered Ministry of Foreign Affairs 1952; Del. to UNRWA Beirut 1952-55; Amb. to Colombia, 1955-59; Sec.-Gen. for Algerian Affairs Jan.-Dec. 1959; Amb. to Venezuela 1961-63; Ministry of Foreign Affairs 1963; Pres. Admin. Council of Houillères, Provence 1964-69; Adviser on Int. Affairs, Groupe des Charbonnages de France 1967-73; Adviser on Int. Affairs, Soc. Chimique des Charbonnages 1973; Commdr., Légion d'honneur, Compagnon de la Libération, Croix de guerre, Hon. C.B.E. (U.K.) *Address:* Les Fenouillères, 13122 Ventabren, France.

INGRAO, Pietro; Italian journalist and politician; b. 30 March 1915, Lenola, Latina; m. Laura Lombardo Radice 1944; one s. four d.; ed. Univ. of Rome; began career as a journalist; active in anti-fascist student groups at Univ. of Rome 1939; joined Italian Communist Party (PCI) 1940; joined editorial staff of l'Unità (PCI newspaper) 1943; took part in resistance movement in Rome and Milan 1943–45; Ed. l'Unità 1947–57; mem. Nat. Exec. and Secretariat of PCI 1956–; mem. Chamber of Deputies (lower house of Parl.) for Rome, Latino, Frosinore, Viterbo 1948–58, for Perugia, Terni, Rieti 1958–63, 1968–, for Ancona and Perugia 1963–68; Pres. of PCI Parl. Group 1972–76; Pres. of Chamber of Deputies 1976–79; Pres. of Centre of Studies and Activities for the Reform of the State 1979. *Publications:* essays on political and social subjects in periodicals, incl. Rinascita, Critica Marxista 1945–, Masse e Potere 1977, Crisi e Terzavia 1978, Tradizione e Progetto 1982, Il Dubbio dei Vincitori (poetry) 1987. *Address:* Centro Studie Iniziative per la Riforma dello Stato, via Della Vite, 13- Rome, Italy. *Telephone:* 6784101.

INGSTAD, Helge Marcus; Norwegian author and explorer; b. 30 Dec. 1899, Meråker; s. of Olav and Olga Marie (née Qvam) Ingstad; m. Anne Stine Moe 1941; one d.; Barrister, Levanger, Norway 1922–25; lived as trapper N.E. of Great Slave Lake, Arctic Canada 1926–30; Norwegian Gov., N.E. Greenland 1932–33; Norwegian Gov. of Svalbard (Spitsbergen) 1933–35; studied Apache Indians, Arizona, and made expedition to Sierra Madre Mountains, Mexico, in search of some primitive Apache Indians 1936–38; studied Eskimo group Nunamiut, Brooks Range, N. Alaska 1949–50; made expedition with wife to W. Greenland to study old Norse settlements 1953; made eight archaeological expeditions to N. America, where at N. tip of Newfoundland (L'Anse aux Meadows) a Norse pre-Columbian site was discovered and excavated 1960–68; made expedition to Eastern Coast of Baffin Island and located Helluland, mentioned in Vinland Saga 1970; Hon D.Sc. (St. Olaf Coll., Minn.) 1965, (Memorial Univ. St. John's Newfoundland) 1969, (McGill Univ., Montreal) 1975, (Oslo) 1976, (Calgary) 1977; numerous awards including Franklin L. Burr Award (Nat. Geographic Soc., Washington) 1964, The Wahlberg Award 1968, The Gunnerus Award, Commdr., Order of St. Olav (Norway) 1970, Fridtjof Nansen Award 1977. *Publications:* Pelsjegerliv blant Nord-Kanadas Indianere (Land of Feast and Famine) 1931, Øst for Den Store Bre (East of the Great Glacier) 1935, Apache–Indianerne. Jakten pa den tapte stamme 1939, Klondyke Bill 1945, Siste Båt (play) 1946, Landet med De Kalde Kyster 1948, Nunamiut. Blant Alaskas Innlands-eskimoer (Nunamiut-Among Alaska's Inland Eskimos) 1951, Landet under Leidarstjernen (Land under the Pole Star) 1959, Vesterveg til Vinland (Westwards to Vinland) 1965, The Norse Discovery of America (vol. II) 1985, Nunamiut Stories 1987. *Leisure interest:* chess. *Address:* Vettalivei 24, 0389 Oslo 3, Norway. *Telephone:* 14-21-35.

INGVARSSON, Ingvi S.; Icelandic diplomatist; b. 12 Dec. 1924; m.; one d.; ed. Akureyri Coll., Glasgow Univ. and London School of Econs.; entered diplomatic service 1956; First Sec., Moscow 1958–62, Washington, D.C. 1962–66; Deputy Perm. Rep. to NATO 1966–71, concurrently Counsellor, Paris and Brussels; Deputy Sec.-Gen. Ministry of Foreign Affairs 1971–72; Perm. Rep. to UN 1973–77; Amb. to Sweden, concurrently to Finland and Yugoslavia 1977–82, to Albania 1978–82, to Saudi Arabia 1981–82; Perm. Under-Sec. Ministry of Foreign Affairs, Reykjavík, Iceland 1982–86; Amb. to U.S.A. 1986– (also accred. to Canada, Argentina, Chile, Brazil and Mexico. *Address:* 2443 Kalorama Road, N.W., Washington, D.C. 20008, U.S.A. *Telephone:* (202) 332-3040.

INK, Claude; French business executive; b. 17 March 1928, Hussigny; s. of Gilbert Ink and Paule Rollin; m. Annie Beaurain-Verdollin 1952; two s. one d.; ed. Ecole Polytechnique; engineer, Sollac 1952, Asst. Dir.-Gen. 1966, Vice-Pres., Dir.-Gen. Sollac 1978; Dir.-Gen. SCAC 1969; Pres. of Bd. of Dirs., Solmer 1980, Dir. Gen. 1985; Pres, and Dir.-Gen. Solnetal, Vice-Pres. Sollac; Dir.-Gen. Sacilor; Pres. Chambre syndicale Fer blanc 1986; Del. Gen. Fondation Ecole Polytechnique 1987; Pres. Asscn. Professionnelle Producteurs Européens Acier pour Emballage (A.P.E.A.L.) 1988; Chevalier, Légion d'honneur. *Address:* 5 rue Paul Cézanne, 75008 Paris (Office); 65 bis avenue du Belloy, 78110 Le Vesinet, France. *Telephone:* (1) 45.63.17.10 (Office); (3) 9524503 (Home).

INKELES, Alex, PH.D.; American professor of sociology; b. 20 April 1920, Brooklyn, New York; s. of Meyer Inkeles and Ray Gewer Inkeles; m. Bernadette Mary Kane 1942; one d.; ed. Cornell and Columbia Univs., Washington School of Psychiatry; Social Science Research Analyst, Dept. of State 1942–46, Int. Broadcasting Div. 1949–51; Instructor in Social Relations, Harvard Univ. 1948–49, Lecturer in Sociology 1948–57, Prof. 1957–71, Dir. Russian Research Center Studies in Social Relations 1963–71, Dir. Center of Int. Affairs Studies on Social Aspects of Econ. Devt. 1963–71; Margaret Jacks Prof. of Educ., Stanford Univ. 1971–78, Prof. of Sociology and, by Courtesy, Educ. 1978–, Sr. Fellow, Hoover Inst. on War, Revolution and Peace 1978–; numerous fellowships including Inst. for Advanced Study, Princeton, Guggenheim, Fulbright, Rockefeller Foundation, Bellagio, Italy, N.A.S. Exchange Program with People's Repub. of China, Nankai Univ. 1983; mem. American Acad. of Arts and Sciences, N.A.S., A.A.A.S., American Philosophical Soc., American Psychology Assen.; numerous awards. *Publications:* Public Opinion in Soviet Russia 1950, How the Soviet System Works 1956, The Soviet Citizen: Daily Life in a Totalitarian Society 1959, What is Sociology? 1964, Social Change in Soviet Russia 1968, Becoming Modern: Individual Change in Six Developing Countries 1974, Exploring Individual Modernity 1983. *Leisure interests:* travel, East Asian art collection, biking, swimming. *Address:* Hoover Institution, HHMB-112, Stanford University, Stanford, Calif. 94305; 1001 Hamilton Avenue, Palo Alto, Calif. 94301, U.S.A. (Home). *Telephone:* (415) 723-4856 or 723-0310 (Office); (415) 327-4197 (Home).

INNES, Hammond (see Hammond Innes, Ralph).

INNES OF EDINGIGHT, Malcolm Rognvald, C.V.O.; Baron of Yeochrie; b. 25 May 1938; s. of the late Sir Thomas Innes of Learney and of Lady Lucy Buchan; m. Joan Hay 1963; three s.; ed. Edinburgh Acad., Univ. of Edinburgh; Falkland Pursuivant Extraordinary 1957; Carrick Pursuivant 1958; Lyon Clerk and Keeper of the Records 1966; Marchmont Herald 1971, Lord Lyon King of Arms 1981–; Secretary to Order of the Thistle 1981–; mem. Queen's Body Guard for Scotland (Royal Company of Archers) 1971; Pres. Heraldry Soc. of Scotland; Grand Officer of Merit, Sovereign Mil. Order, Malta. *Leisure interests:* archery, fishing, shooting, visiting places of historic interest. *Address:* 35 Inverleith Row, Edinburgh, EH3 5QH; Edingight House, Banffshire, Scotland. *Telephone:* 031-552 4924; Knock 270.

INNIS, Roy Emile Alfredo; American chemist and human rights organization executive; b. 6 June 1934, St. Croix, Virgin Islands; s. of Alexander and Georgianna Innis; m. Doris Funnye 1965; six c.; ed. City Coll., New York; joined U.S. Army 1950, Sergeant 1951, discharged 1952; pharmaceutical research work, Vick Chemical Co., then medical research Montefiore Hosp. until 1967; active in Harlem chapter of Congress of Racial Equality (CORE) 1963, Chair. Harlem Educ. Cttee. 1964, Chair. Harlem CORE 1965–67, Second Nat. Vice-Chair. 1967–68, Assoc. Nat. Dir. CORE Jan.-Sept. 1968, Nat. Dir. Sept. 1968–; Founder Harlem Commonwealth Council, First Exec. Dir. 1967–68, now mem. of Bd.; Res. Fellow, Metropolitan Applied Research Center 1967–; Co-Publisher The Manhattan Tribune (weekly); mem. Bd. and Steering Cttee. Nat. Urban Coalition; mem. of Bd. New York Coalition, Haryou Inc., Bd. of Dirs. New Era Health Educ. and Welfare, Bd. of Advisers Pan-African Journal; mem. Editorial Staff Social Policy Magazine; Publr. The Correspondent; Co-Chair. Econ. Devt. Task Force, New York Urban Coalition; founder CORE Community School, South Bronx 1977. *Publications:* The Little Black Book 1971; chapters in: The Endless Crisis, Black Economic Development 1970, Integrating America's Heritage: A Congressional Hearing to Establish A National Commission on Negro History and Culture 1970; articles and editorials in Manhattan Tribune, CORE Magazine, Business Weekly, etc. *Leisure interests:* reading, sports, music. *Address:* 1457 Flatbush Avenue, Brooklyn, N.Y. 11210 (Office); 800 Riverside Drive, Apartment 6E, New York, N.Y. 10032, U.S.A. (Home). *Telephone:* (718) 434-3580 (Office).

INNOCENTI, H.E. Cardinal Antonio; Italian ecclesiastic; b. 23 Aug. 1915, Poppi, Fiesole, Tuscany; ordained 1938; consecrated Bishop, Titular See of Aeclanum 1968, then Archbishop; fmr. Apostolic Nuncio in Spain; cr. Cardinal 1985; Prefect of Congregation for the Clergy. *Address:* Città del Vaticano, Rome, Italy. *Telephone:* 698-4151.

INNOCENTI, Luigi; Italian industrialist; b. 19 Dec. 1923; ed. Massimo Coll., Rome and School of Engineering, Rome; Manager, Innocenti 1948–51, Gen. Vice-Dir. 1951–58, Vice-Chair. 1958–66, Chair 1966–. *Address:* Via Senato 19, Milan, Italy.

INOSE, Hiroshi, DR.ENG.; Japanese professor of electronic engineering; b. 5 Jan. 1927, Tokyo; s. of Yoshikazu and Kyo Inose; m. Mariko Inose 1960; no c.; ed. Univ. of Tokyo; Assoc. Prof., Univ. of Tokyo 1956–61, Prof. of Electronic Eng. 1961–; Dir. of Educ. Computer Center, Univ. of Tokyo 1974–78, Dir. of Computer Center (for nationwide service) 1977–81, Dean, Faculty of Eng. 1986–87; Science Adviser to Minister of Educ., Science and Culture 1978–82; Special Adviser to Minister for Science and Tech. 1979–; Special Asst. to Minister for Foreign Affairs 1983–; Dir. Centre for Bibliographic Information 1983–86; Dir.-Gen. Nat. Centre for Science Information System 1987–; Chair. Cttee. for Scientific and Technological Policy, OECD, 1984–87; Chair. Cttee. for Information, Computer and Communications Policy, OECD 1987–; Foreign Assoc., Nat. Acad. of Sciences (U.S.A.), Nat. Acad. of Eng. (U.S.A.); Foreign mem. American Philosophical Soc., Royal Swedish Acad. of Eng. and Sciences; Fellow, I.E.E.E.; Marconi Int. Fellowship; Japan Acad. Prize; I.E.E.E. Award in Int. Communication. *Publications:* Road Traffic Control 1977, An Introduction to Digital Communications Systems 1979, Information, Technology and Civilisation (with J. R. Pierce) 1984. *Leisure interests:* reading Japanese classics, gardening, travelling. *Address:* 3-29-1 Orsuka, Bunkyo-ku, Tokyo, 112 Japan (Office); 39-9, Jingumae 5-chome, Shibuya-ku, Tokyo, 150 Japan (Home). *Telephone:* 942-2351 (Office); 03-486-1051 (Home).

INOUE, Yoshimi, LL.B.; Japanese business executive; b. 26 March 1908, Hiroshima Pref.; s. of Yonetaro and Risu Inoue; m. Motoko Nakano 1933; one s. two d.; ed. Tokyo Univ.; Man. Printing Bureau, Ministry of Finance 1954–56; Dir. Kobe Steel Ltd. 1958–65, Dir. and Exec. Officer 1965–69, Dir. and Sr. Exec. Officer 1969–71. Dir. and Vice-Pres. 1971–72, Dir. and Pres. 1972–74, Chair. Bd. of Dirs. 1974–77, Adviser and Dir. 1977–. *Leisure* *interests:* golf, kouta, igo. *Address:* 4-20-14, Miyamae, Suginami-ku, Tokyo, Japan. *Telephone:* Tokyo 333-6751.

INOUYE, Daniel Ken, A.B., J.D.; American lawyer and politician; b. 7 Sept. 1924, Honolulu, Hawaii; s. of Hyotaro and Kame Imanaga Inouye; m. Margaret Shinobu Awamura 1949; one s.; ed. Univ. of Hawaii and George Washington Univ. Law School.; U.S. Army 1943–47; Majority Leader, Territorial House of Reps. 1954–58, mem. Territorial Senate 1958–59; mem. U.S. Congress 1959–62; U.S. Senator from Hawaii 1963–; Democrat; mem. Senate Cttee. on Appropriations, Commerce Cttee., Asst. Majority Whip 1964–76; mem. Dem. Senatorial Campaign Cttee., Senate Select Cttee. on Indian Affairs; Chair. Senate Appropriations Subcttee. on Foreign Operations; Chair. Senate Commerce Subcttee. on Merchant Marine and Tourism; Chair. Senate Select Cttee. on Intelligence 1976–77; Chair. Senate Sub-Cttee. on Budget Authorizations 1979–84, Head Special Cttee. on Iran Affair 1986; Temp. Chair. and Keynoter 1968 Dem. Nat. Convention; Sec. Dem. Conf. 1977–; Horatio Alger Award 1989. *Address:* 722 Hart Senate Office Building, Washington, D.C. 20510; 469 Ena Road, Honolulu, Hawaii 96814, U.S.A. *Telephone:* 202-224-3934; (808) 546-7550 (Hawaii).

INOUYE, Kaoru; Japanese banker; b. 13 May 1906, Chiba Pref.; s. of Jiro and Masa Inouye; m. Mitsuko Shibuya 1932; three c.; ed. Tokyo Univ.; joined the Dai-Ichi Bank, Ltd. 1929, Dir. 1954, Deputy Pres. 1961, Pres. 1962–66, 1969–71, Chair. 1966–69; Chair. The Dai-Ichi Kangyo Bank 1971–76, Dir., Hon. Chair. 1976–82, Hon. Chair. 1982–; Dir. Asahi Mutual Life Insurance Co., Taisei Fire and Marine Insurance Co., K. Hattori and Co.; Adviser, Furukawa Electric Co. Ltd. until 1984. *Address:* The Dai-Ichi Kangyo Bank, Uchisaiwaicho 1, Chiyoda-ku, Tokyo 100, Japan.

INOUYE, Minoru, B.L.; Japanese banker; b. 10 Jan. 1924, Tokyo; m. Kazuko Nakase; one s.; ed. Univ. of Tokyo; joined Bank of Tokyo 1947, Deputy Agent, New York 1964–66, Deputy Gen. Man. Int. Funds and Foreign Exchange Div. 1966–67, Deputy Gen. Man. Planning and Co-ordination Div. 1967–70, Gen. Man. 1970–72, Dir. and Gen. Man. London Office 1972–75, Resident Man. Dir. for Europe 1975, Man. Dir. 1975–79, Sr. Man. Dir. 1979–80, Deputy Pres. 1980–85, Pres. Sept. 1985–; Dir. Bank of Tokyo Australia Ltd.; Représentant Perm., Banque Européenne de Tokyo S.A. *Leisure interests:* golf, travel. *Address:* The Bank of Tokyo, Ltd., 3-2 Nihombashi Hongokucho 1-chome, Chuo-ku, Tokyo 103 (Office); 11-7, Kohinata 1-chome, Bunkyo-ku, Tokyo 112, Japan (Home). *Telephone:* (03) 245-9021.

INSANALLY, Samuel Rudolph, B.A.; Guyanese diplomatist; b. 23 Jan. 1936; unmarried; ed. Univs. of London and Paris; teacher of modern languages Kingston Coll., Jamaica, Queen's Coll., Guyana and Univ. of Guyana 1959–66; Counsellor at Guyanese Embassy, Washington D.C. 1966–69; Chargé d'affaires at Embassy, Venezuela 1970, Amb. 1972–78; Deputy Perm. Rep. of Guyana to UN, New York 1970–72, Perm. Rep. 1987–; Perm. Rep. to EEC 1978–81; Amb. to Belgium (also accred to Sweden, Norway and Austria) 1978–81, to Colombia 1982–86; Head of Political Div. I Ministry of Foreign Affairs of Guyana 1982–86; High Commr. to Barbados, Trinidad and Tobago and the Eastern Caribbean 1982–86; mem. Bd. of Governors Inst. of Int. Relations, Trinidad and Tobago 1982–86. *Address:* Permanent Mission of Guyana to United Nations, 622 Third Ave., 35th Floor, New York, N.Y. 10017, U.S.A. *Telephone:* (212) 953-0930.

INTZES, Vassilios; Greek politician; b. 1929, Strymochori, Serres; ed. studies in electrical and mechanical eng.; Centre Union Party Deputy to Parl., Pref. of Serres 1963–64; Pasok Deputy 1974, 1977; five times Sec. to Presidency of Greek Parl.; mem. Cen. Cttee. of Pasok; Minister for Northern Greece 1982–85. *Address:* 48 El. Venizelou Street, Thessalonika, Greece. *Telephone:* (031) 26.0659.

IOANNIDES, George X.; Cypriot politician; b. 1924, Ktima Paphos; m.; ed. Greek Gymnasium, Paphos, Middle Temple, London; called to bar, London 1947; law practice, Paphos 1948–70; mem. House of Reps. (Patriotic Front Group) for Paphos 1960–70; Minister of Justice 1970–72, of the Interior and Defence 1972–74, of Justice and Health 1976–78, Minister to the Presidency 1978–80; mem. of Cyprus del. to many int. meetings. *Address:* c/o Office of the President, Nicosia, Cyprus.

IOANNISIANI, Bagrat Konstantinovich; Soviet designer; b. 1921; Chief Designer of the Vavilov State Inst. of Optics; awarded Lenin Prize for designing new astronomical instruments 1957. *Principal works:* ASI-4 astro-photo-camera, meniscus telescope with 70 cm. aperture and 98 cm. mirror (Abastumani Observatory, Georgia), 50-metre nebular spectrograph (Crimean Observatory); BTA-6 (with 600 metre mirror). *Address:* State Institute of Optics, Leningrad, U.S.S.R.

IOFAN, Boris Mikhailovich; Soviet architect; b. 28 April 1891, Odessa; ed. Odessa School of Art, Architectural Dept. of the Rome Higher Inst. of Fine Arts; State Prize winner 1939, 1941; awarded Order of Red Star, Order of the Red Banner of Labour (twice); mem. CPSU 1926–; People's Architect of U.S.S.R. 1970–. *Designs include:* first draft of the Palace of Soviets in Moscow; the U.S.S.R. Pavilions at the World Fairs in Paris 1937, New York 1939; the Baumann underground station in Moscow; design of reconstruction of city of Novorossiysk; regional plan and supervision of redevt. of Pervomaysky Borough, Moscow, also Sverdlovsky Borough,

Moscow; design and construction of Inst. of Physical Culture, Moscow; Oil Scientific Research Inst., Lenin Ave., Moscow; sixteen-storey blocks of flats, Moscow; experimental block of flats with extensive use of plastics. *Address:* U.S.S.R. Union of Architects, 3 Ulitsa Shchuseva, Moscow, U.S.S.R.

IONESCO, Eugène; Romanian-born French playwright; b. 13 Nov. 1912, Slatina; s. of Eugène Ionesco and Thérèse Icard; m. Rodica Burileano 1936; one d.; ed. Bucharest and Paris; lecturer and critic in Bucharest before finally settling in Paris 1938; Chevalier, Légion d'honneur, Officier, Ordre nat. du Mérite, Commdr., ordre des Arts et des Lettres; mem. Acad. Française 1970–; Dr. h.c. (New York, Louvain, Warwick, Tel-Aviv); Grand Prix littéraire, Monaco 1969; Austrian Prize for European Literature 1971; Jerusalem Prize 1973; Int. Writers' Fellowship, Welsh Arts Council 1973, Ingersoll Prize 1985. *Publications:* Plays: The Bald Prima Donna (first produced Paris 1950, London 1957), Jacques, The Lesson (Paris 1951, London 1955, New York 1958), The Chairs (Paris 1952, London 1957, New York 1958), Amédée (Paris 1954, London 1957), Victims of Duty (Cambridge 1957), The New Tenant (London 1956, Paris 1957), Rhinocéros (Düsseldorf 1959, Paris 1960, London 1960), The Killer, L'Impromptu de l'Alma, The Picture, Le piéton de l'air (Paris 1962), Chemises de nuit 1962, Le roi se meurt 1963, La soif et la faim 1964, Peste 1967, Jeux de massacre 1970, Ce formidable bordel 1973, L'homme aux valises 1975, Contes et exercices de conversation et de diction pour étudiants américains 1979, Noir et Blanc 1980, Journeys Among the Dead 1986; radio play: Le salon de l'automobile; short stories: Oriflamme (adapted as the play Amédée), La Photo du Colonel 1962 (adapted as the play The Killer); ballet: Jeune homme à marier (with Flemming Flindt) 1965; essays: Notes et contre notes, Entretiens avec Claude Bonnefoy, Journal en miettes (autobiog. journal) 1967, Présent passé, passé présent (autobiog.), Le solitaire (novel) 1973; film: La vase 1973, and numerous articles, essays and stories. *Address:* c/o Editions Gallimard, 5 rue Sébastien-Bottin, 75007 Paris; 96 boulevard du Montparnasse, 75014 Paris, France (Home).

IORDANOGLOU, Ippocrates; Greek lawyer and politician; b. 1909; m.; two s.; ed. Univ. of Athens; admitted to Thessaloniki Bar 1932; Chair. Thessaloniki School Bldg. Fund; M.P. for Thessaloniki 1963; Minister of Commerce April. 1967; Minister of Agriculture 1974–77. *Address:* c/o Ministry of Agriculture, Athens, Greece.

IOSIFESCU, Marius Vicenţiu Viorel, PH.D., D.SC.; Romanian mathematician; b. 12 Aug. 1936, Piteşti; s. of Victor and Ecaterina Iosifescu; m. Ştefania Eugenia Zamfirescu 1973; one s.; ed. Bucharest Univ.; consultant Cen. Statistical Bd. 1959–62; Asst. Prof. Bucharest Polytech. Inst. 1961–63; Research Mathematician Inst. of Math. and Centre of Math. Statistics, Bucharest 1963–76, head Centre of Math. Statistics 1976–; Visiting Prof. Univs. of Paris 1974, Mainz 1977–78, Frankfurt am Main 1979–80, Bonn 1981–82; Overseas Fellow Churchill Coll., Cambridge Univ. 1971; mem. Int. Statistical Inst.; mem. Bernoulli Soc. for Mathematical Statistics and Probability (mem. council 1975–79); mem. Biometric Soc. (mem. council 1976–79); Prize of Romanian Acad. 1965, 1972; Bronze Medal Helsinki Univ. 1975; mem. editorial bds. Probability Theory and Related Fields (continuation of Zeitschrift für Wahrscheinlichkeitstheorie und verwandte Gebiete), Journal of Multivariate Analysis; Deputy Chief Ed. Revue Roumaine de Mathématiques Pures et Appliquées. *Publications:* Random Processes and Learning (with R. Theodorescu) 1969, Stochastic Processes and Applications in Biology and Medicine, Vol. I Theory, Vol. II Models (with P. Tăutu) 1973, Finite Markov Processes and Their Applications 1980, ed. Proceedings of Braşov Conference on Probability Theory 1971, 1974, 1979, 1982, Dependence with Complete Connections and its Applications (with Ş. Grigorescu) 1982, ed. Studies in Probability and Related Topics 1983, Elements of Stochastic Modelling (with Ş. Grigorescu, G. Opriṣan and G. Popescu) 1984, From Real Analysis to Probability: Autobiographical Notes 1986. *Leisure interests:* music, playing violin. *Address:* Str. Ştirbei Vodă 174, 77104 Bucharest (Office); Str. Dr. N. Manolescu 9-11, 76222 Bucharest 35, Romania (Home). *Telephone:* 313623 (Home).

IRAN, fmr. Empress of (see Pahlavi, Farah Diba).

IRANI, Jamshed Jiji, PH.D.; Indian business executive; b. 2 June 1936, Nagpur; s. of Jiji D. Irani and Khorshed Irani; m. Daisy Irani 1971; one s. two d.; ed. Sheffield Univ.; worked for British Iron and Steel Research Asscn. 1963–67; Tata Iron and Steel Co. Ltd. 1968–, Gen. Man. 1979–81, Deputy Man. Dir. 1981–83, Vice-Pres. (Operations) 1983–85, Pres. 1985–, Jt. Man. Dir. 1988–; Dir. of numerous cos.; Nat. Metallurgist Award 1974, Platinum medal of 11m 1988. *Publications:* numerous tech. papers. *Leisure interests:* philately, photography. *Address:* 3 C Road, Northern Town, Jamshedpur, 831001 Bihar, India. *Telephone:* 23400 (Office); 24049 (Home).

IREDALE, Randle W., F.R.A.I.C., B.ARCH.; Canadian architect; b. 1 June 1929, Calgary, Alberta; s. of William E. Iredale and Isobel M. Fielden; m. Kathryn Margaret Bahr 1953; two s. one d.; ed. Univ. of British Columbia; Registered Architect, British Columbia 1957; established practice 1958; formed Rhone & Iredale, Architects 1960; Chair. of Bd. and Dir. of Research, Fabtec Structures 1969–72; established Canadian Environmental Services 1968; Dir. Cancon-Canadian Eng. Services 1969–74; Guest lecturer on architectural practice and design methods (for American Inst. of Architects), Seattle 1969, Sun Valley 1971, Chicago 1972; Guest Lecturer, Pa.

State Univ. 1971, Univ. of Wis. 1972; Adjunct Assoc. Prof., Univ. of British Columbia School of Architecture 1980-; mem. Council, Architectural Inst. of British Columbia 1973-80; mem. Vancouver City Design Panel 1963-65; Dir. Canadian Construction Information Corpn. 1972-74; f. The Iredale Partnership for urban design and planning; Fellow, Royal Canadian Architectural Inst. 1977; Canadian Housing Design Council Awards 1966, 1975; American Public Power Assen. Awards 1971, 1973; American Iron & Steel Inst. Citation 1971; Canadian Architect Award of Excellence 1970; Royal Architectural Inst. of Canada Award 1974. *Publications:* articles in specialized journals. *Leisure interests:* skiing, gardening, carpentry. *Address:* 1151 West 8th Avenue, Vancouver, B.C., V6H 1C5 (Office); 1537 Westbrook Crescent, Vancouver, B.C., Canada (Home). *Telephone:* (604) 736 5581 (Office); (604) 224-7003 (Home).

IRELAND, Norman Charles, C.A., F.C.M.A.; British business executive; b. 1927, Aden; s. of Charles Ireland and Winifred A. Ireland; m. Gillian M. Harrison 1953; one s. one d.; ed. in U.K., U.S.A. and India; Finance Dir. BTR PLC 1967-87; Chair. London & Metropolitan 1986-, Bowater Industries PLC 1987-, Bricom Ltd.; non exec. Dir. BTR PLC. *Leisure interests:* music, gardening. *Address:* Bowater Industries PLC, Bowater House, Knightsbridge, London, SW1X 7NN; Hunter's Wood, 13 Prince Consort Drive, Ascot, Berks., SL5 8AW, England. *Telephone:* 01-584 7070.

IRIANI, Abdul Karim al-, PH.D. ECONS.; Yemeni economist and politician; b. Djibla, Southern Province, Yemen Arab Republic; ed. univ. in U.S.A.; Dir. Yemen Bank of Reconstruction and Devt. July 1973-; Minister of State for Socio-Economic Devt. March-June 1974; Cen. Planning Office; Minister of Devt. 1976-77, of Educ. and Rector Sana'a Univ. 1977-78; Chief Planner, Devt. Office 1977-79; Chair. Cen. Planning Office 1979-80; Minister of Agric. March-July 1979; Prime Minister 1980-83; Deputy Prime Minister and Minister of Foreign Affairs Nov. 1984-; Chair. Council for the Reconstruction of Earthquake Areas 1983-84. *Address:* P.O. Box 38, Sana'a, Yemen Arab Republic.

IRIBARRÉN BORGES, Ignacio; Venezuelan lawyer and diplomatist; b. 1912, Valencia, Venezuela; s. of late Ignacio Iribarrén and Mary Borges; m. Carolina Terrero 1938; two s. one d.; ed. Don Bosco Coll., Valencia and Univ. Central de Venezula; District Attorney, Valencia 1936; Judge, Primary Court of Claims, Valencia 1936-39; Prof. of Roman Law, Miguel José Sanz School of Law, Valencia 1938-39; Asst. Prof. of Civil Law, Univ. Central de Venezuela 1940-44; Counsellor Cen. Univ. City Inst. 1945-47; mem. Univ. Council 1946-47; later Pres. Compañía Conahotu Ltda; Sec. Governing Junta (under Presidency of Dr. Edgard Sanabria) 1958-59; Amb. to U.K. 1959-64, to U.S.A. 1976-79; Minister of Foreign Affairs 1964-69, of Information and Tourism (acting) 1984-85, Minister of State and Minister of Culture 1984-87; Grand Cordon, Order of the Liberator and numerous other decorations. *Leisure interests:* literature, history. *Publications:* La Poesía de Vicente Gerbasi 1972, A Literary Revolution: Yeats, Joyce, Pound, Eliot 1980, On Theatre, Poetry, and Novel 1980. *Address:* c/o Ministry of Culture, Palacio de Miraflores, Caracas; Cerro Quintero, Urbanización Las Mercedes 3, Quinta Pandora, Caracas, Venezuela.

IRIGOIN, Jean, D.ÈS.L.; French professor; b. 8 Nov. 1920, Aix-en-Provence; s. of Paul Irigoin and Isabelle Gassier; m. Janine Garaud 1954; two s. two d.; ed. Collège St.-Louis-de-Gonzague, Paris, Sorbonne and Ecole pratique des Hautes Etudes, Paris; Prof. Univ. of Poitiers 1953-65, Univ. of Paris X 1965-72, Univ. of Paris IV 1972-85; Collège de France (chaire de Tradition et critique des textes grecs) 1985-; mem. Institut de France 1981. *Publications:* Histoire du texte de Pindare 1952, Règles et recommandations pour les éditions critiques 1972. *Address:* 11 Place Marcelin-Berthelot, F-75231 Paris Cedex 05, France. *Telephone:* (1) 43 29 12 11/22 40.

IRIMESCU, Ion; Romanian sculptor; b. 27 Feb. 1903, Preuțesti, Suceava County; s. of Petru and Maria Iremescu; m. Eugenia Melidon 1932; ed. School of Fine Arts, Bucharest and Académie Grande Chaumière, Paris; Prof. Fine Arts Inst. N. Grigorescu, Bucharest 1966-; Vice-Chair. Romanian Artists' Union 1963-68; Chair. Romanian Artists' Union 1978-; exhbns. in Bucharest, Cluj-Napoca, Iasi, Athens, Oslo, Moscow, Anvers-Middleheim, Paris, Barcelona, Zürich, Sofia, Budapest, Berlin, Ankara, Cairo, Belgrade; perm. sculptures in Modern Art Museum, Tel Aviv, Pushkin Art Museum, Moscow, and numerous works (sculptures and drawings) in Romanian museums, including 450 works at the Ion Irimescu Museum at Fălticeni, Suceava County; State Prize 1954, 1955; Prize of Romanian Acad. 1943; People's Artist 1964. *Major works* include mostly portraits (Mircea the Old, Brâncusi, Vasile Pârvan, George Enescu, Nicolae Iorga, Nicolae Titulescu) and monographs (M. Mihalache, E. Schileru, M. Deac, A. Cebuc); Retrospective Exhbn., Fine Arts Museum, Bucharest 1983. *Leisure interest:* classical music. *Address:* Uniunea Artistilor Plastici, Str. Nicolae Iorga 42, Bucharest; Zambaccian St. 12, Sector 1, Bucharest, Romania. *Telephone:* 332751.

IRMAK, Sadi; Turkish professor and politician; b. 15 May 1904, Seydișehir, Konya; s. of Sarbri and Saliha Irmak; m. Semiha Irmak 1934; one s. one d.; ed. Konya, Univs. of Istanbul and Berlin; Teacher, Gazi Educ. Inst.; Chief Medical Officer, Ankara; Lecturer in Physiology, Istanbul Univ. 1932, Prof. 1940; mem. Nat. Assembly for Konya 1943-50; Minister of Labour 1945-47; Faculty of Medicine, Munich Univ. 1950-52; Senator

1974-80; Prime Minister Nov. 1974-March 1975; Pres. Constituent Ass. 1981-83; Pres. Istanbul Univ. Inst. of Research on Atatürk's Reforms; Republican People's Party. *Address:* Yesilyurt-Basak 50, Istanbul, Turkey. *Telephone:* 5738651.

IROBE, Yoshiaki; Japanese banker; b. 18 July 1911, Tokyo; s. of Tsuneo and Tsuneko (Hirohata) Irobe; m. Kiyoko Kodama 1939; three s. one d.; ed. Tokyo Imperial Univ.; Man., Matsuyama Branch, The Bank of Japan 1954, Deputy Chief, Personnel Dept. 1956, Chief Sec. and Chief, Foreign Relations Dept. 1959, Chief, Personnel Dept. 1962, Man. Nagoya Branch 1963; Sr. Man. Dir., The Kyowa Bank Ltd. 1966, Deputy Pres. 1968, Pres. 1971-80; Chair. 1980-86, Adviser 1986-, Hon. Chair. 1986-. *Leisure interests:* 'Go', travel, reading. *Address:* 26-6, Saginomiya 6-chome, Nakano-ku, Tokyo, Japan (Home). *Telephone:* 999-0321 (Home).

IROK, Datuk Leo Moggie Anak, M.A., M.B.A.; Malaysian politician; b. 1 Oct. 1941, Kanowit, Sarawak; m.; five c.; ed. Univ. of Otago and Pennsylvania State Univ.; Dist. Officer, Kapit, Sarawak 1966-68; Dir. Borneo Literature Bureau, Kuching, Sarawak 1968-69; attached to Office of Chief Minister, Kuching, Sarawak 1969-72; Deputy Gen. Man. Borneo Devt. Corpn., Kuching 1973-74; elected to Sarawak State Legis. Ass. and Parl. 1974; Minister for Welfare Services, State Govt. of Sarawak 1976-77, of Local Govt. 1977-78; Fed. Minister of Energy, Telecommunications and Posts July 1978-; Sec.-Gen. SNAP 1976; Panglima Negara Bintang Sarawak. *Address:* Ministry of Energy, Telecommunications and Posts, Ground Floor, Wisma Damansara, Jalan Semantan, Kuala Lumpur, Malaysia.

IRONS, Jeremy; British actor; b. 19 Sept. 1948, Isle of Wight; m. Sinead Cusack; two s.; TV debut 1968. *TV appearances include:* Notorious Woman, Love for Lydia, Langrishe Go Down, Voysey Inheritance, Brideshead Revisited, The Captain's Doll; *Films:* Nijinsky 1980, The French Lieutenant's Woman 1980, Moonlighting 1981, Betrayal 1982, The Wild Duck 1983, Swann in Love 1983, The Mission 1986, A Chorus of Disapproval 1988, Dead Ringers (New York Critics Best Actor Award 1988) 1988, Australia 1989. *Stage appearances:* The Real Thing, Broadway 1984, Rover 1986, The Winter's Tale 1986, Richard II, Stratford 1986. *Address:* c/o Hutton Management, 200 Fulham Road, London, SW10 9PN, England. *Telephone:* 01-352 4825.

IRVINE, Sir Robin Orlando Hamilton, Kt., M.D., F.R.A.C.P., F.R.C.P., F.R.S.A., F.N.Z.I.M.; New Zealand university administrator; b. 15 Sept. 1929, Dunedin; s. of Claude Turner Irvine and Benita Florence Gertrude Irvine; m. Elizabeth Mary Corbett 1957; one s. two d.; ed. Wanganui Collegiate School and Univ. of Otago Medical School; House Physician, Registrar, Research Asst. at N.Z. hosps. 1954-57; postgraduate work at Middx. Hosp. and Postgraduate Medical School, London 1958-60; Physician and Research Fellow, Auckland Hosp. 1961-63; Lecturer, Sr. Lecturer, Assoc. Prof., Prof., Dept. of Medicine, Univ. of Otago Medical School 1963-73, Clinical Dean 1969-73, Vice-Chancellor, Otago Univ. 1973-; Girdler's Co. Sr. Visiting Research Fellowship, Green Coll., Univ. of Oxford 1986-87; Chair. McMillan Trust; mem. Pharmacology and Therapeutics Advisory Cttee. to Minister of Health 1967-73; mem. Minister of Educ.'s Cttee. on Nursing 1972; Chair. Otago Medical Research Foundation 1975-81; Trustee, NZ Red Cross Foundation, the Motor Industries Road Safety Trust; Nuffield Dominion Travelling Fellowship in Medicine 1957; Leverhulme Research Scholarship, Middx. Hosp., London 1958; Dr. h.c. (Edinburgh); Queen's Jubilee Medal 1977. *Publications:* several scientific papers. *Leisure interests:* reading, music, tramping. *Address:* University Lodge, St. Leonard's, Dunedin, New Zealand. *Telephone:* 710-541.

IRVING, Edward, SC.D., F.R.S.C., F.R.A.S., F.R.S.; research scientist; b. 27 May 1927; s. of George E. Irving and Nellie Irving; m. Sheila A. Irwin 1957; two s. two d.; ed. Colne Grammar School and Univ. of Cambridge; army service 1945-48; Research Fellow, Fellow and Sr. Fellow, Australian Nat. Univ. 1954-64; Dominion Observatory, Canada 1964-66; Prof. of Geophysics, Univ. of Leeds 1966-67; Research Scientist, Dominion Observatory, later Earth Physics Br. Dept. of Energy, Mines and Resources, Ottawa 1967-81; Research Scientist, Pacific Geoscience Centre, Sidney, B.C. 1981-; Adjunct Prof. Carleton Univ. Ottawa 1975-81, Univ. of Vic. 1985-; Fellow, American Geophysical Union, Geological Soc. of America; several awards and medals. *Publications:* Palaeomagnetism 1964; contributions to learned journals. *Leisure interests:* gardening, carpenty, choral singing. *Address:* Pacific Geoscience Centre, 9860 West Saanich Road, Box 6000, Sidney, B.C., V8L 4B2; 9363 Carnousti Crescent, Sidney, B.C., V8L 3S1, Canada (Home). *Telephone:* (604) 656-8208 (Office); (604) 656-9645 (Home).

IRVING, Robert Augustine, D.F.C., B.A., B.MUS.; British conductor, pianist and composer; b. 28 Aug. 1913, Winchester, Hants.; s. of Robert L. G. Irving and Oriane Sophy Tyndale; ed. Winchester Coll., New Coll., Oxford, and Royal Coll. of Music; navigator, R.A.F. (coastal command) 1942-46; Assoc. Conductor, BBC Scottish Orchestra 1946-49; Musical Dir. then adviser, Royal Ballet 1949-58; Musical Dir. and Prin. Conductor, New York City Ballet 1958-; has made numerous recordings and appearances as guest conductor; Capezio Dance Award 1975; Dance Magazine Award 1984; works include music for feature film Floodtide 1949, and orchestration of a number of ballet scores. *Leisure interests:* racing, bridge, mountaineering, travel. *Address:* 160 West End Avenue (Apt. 27T), New York, N.Y.

10023; c/o New York City Ballet, Lincoln Center, New York, N.Y. 10023, U.S.A. *Telephone:* (212) 877-4700 (New York City Ballet).

IRWIN, John Nichol, II; American government official and lawyer; b. 31 Dec. 1913, Keokuk, Iowa; s. of John R. and Florence V. (Johnstone) Irwin; m. 1st Jane Watson 1949 (died 1970), one s. one d.; m. 2nd Jane German Reimers 1976; ed. Princeton, Oxford and Fordham Univs.; served U.S. Army, Second World War; with law firm Patterson, Belknap and Webb, New York 1950–57, 1961–70, 1974–77, of Counsel 1977–; Deputy Asst. Sec. and Asst. Sec. of Defense for Int. Security Affairs 1957–61; Special Envoy of Pres. of U.S. to Peru in dispute over Peru's seizure of U.S.-owned oil properties; U.S. Rep. in negotiations for new draft Panama Canal Treaty 1965–67; Under-Sec. of State 1970–73; Amb. to France 1973–74; mem. Bar Asscn. of New York, American Fed. of New York, State Bar Asscns., Council on Foreign Relations, Morningside Community Center Inc.; fmr. Chair. Bd. of Dirs. Union Theological Seminary; Trustee numerous orgs.; Chair. French-American-Foundation, New York 1984. *Address:* 848 Weed Street, New Canaan, Conn. 06840, U.S.A. (Home).

IRWIN, William Arthur, O.C., B.A.; Canadian journalist and diplomatist; b. 27 May 1898, Ayr, Ont.; s. of Alexander J. and Amelia (Hassard) Irwin; m. 1st Jean Olive Smith 1921 (died 1948); m. 2nd Patricia Kathleen Page 1950; one s. two d.; ed. Univs. of Manitoba and Toronto; fmr. rodman, Canadian Northern Railway Construction; served in France during First World War; later Reporter, Toronto Mail and Empire, and subsequently Reporter, Corresp. (Parl. Press Gallery, Ottawa) and Editorial Writer Toronto Globe; Assoc. Ed. Maclean's Magazine 1925–42, Man. Ed. 1943–45, Ed. 1945–50; Chair. Nat. Film Bd. 1950–53; High Commr. in Australia 1953–56; Amb. to Brazil 1957–59, to Mexico 1960–64; Publisher Victoria Daily Times; Vice-Pres. Victoria Press Ltd. 1964–71; LL.D. (Victoria Univ.) 1977. *Publications:* The Wheat Pool 1929, Motor Vehicle Transportation Briefs (Royal Comm. on Railways and Transportation 1932, Royal Comm. on Transportation in Ontario 1937), The Machine 1938. *Address:* 3260 Exeter Road, Victoria, B.C., V8R 6H6, Canada. *Telephone:* (604) 592-1880.

IRYANI, Sheikh Qadi Abdul Rahman; Yemeni religious and political leader; b. 18 July 1917; took part in abortive revolution against Imam of the Yemen 1948; imprisoned 1948–54; took part in uprising 1955; mem. Revolutionary Council, Yemen Arab Repub. 1962–74; Minister of Justice 1962–63; Vice-Pres. Exec. Council 1963–64; mem. Political Bureau 1964–74; Chair. Peace Cttee. set up after Khamer Peace Talks May 1965; Head of State 1967–69; Chair. Presidential Council 1969–74 (deposed by mil. coup); in exile 1974–81; leader of Zaidi Community of Shi'a Muslims. *Address:* c/o Military Command Council, Sana'a, Yemen Arab Republic.

ISA BIN SULMAN AL-KHALIFA, H.H. Shaikh (see Khalifa, H.H. Shaikh Isa bin Sulman al-).

ISAACS, Jeremy Israel, M.A.; British opera house director; b. 28 Sept. 1932; s. of Isidore Isaacs and Sara Jacobs; m. 1st Tamara (née Weinrich) 1958 (deceased 1986); m. 2nd Gillian Widdicombe 1988; one s. one d.; ed. Glasgow Acad., Merton Coll., Oxford; TV Producer, Granada TV (What the Papers Say, All Our Yesterdays) 1958, Associated Rediffusion (This Week) 1963, B.B.C. TV (Panorama) 1965; Controller of Features, Associated Rediffusion 1967; with Thames TV 1968–78, Producer, The World at War 1974, Dir. of Programmes 1974–78; special independent consultant TV series Hollywood, ITV, A Sense of Freedom, ITV, Ireland, a Television Documentary, B.B.C., Battle for Crete, N.Z. TV; C.E.O., Channel Four TV Co. 1981–88; Gen. Dir. Royal Opera House 1988– (Dir. 1985–); Gov. British Film Inst. 1979–; Chair., British Film Inst. Production Bd. 1979–81; James MacTaggart Memorial Lecturer, Edinburgh TV Festival 1979; Fellow, Royal Television Soc. 1978, B.A.F.T.A. 1985, B.F.I. 1986; Hon. D.Litt. (Strathclyde) 1983, (Liverpool) 1988; Dr. h.c. (Council for Nat. Academic Awards) 1987, (R.C.A.) 1988; Desmond Davis Award for outstanding creative contrib. to TV 1972; George Polk Memorial Award 1973; Cyril Bennett Award 1982; Lord Willis Award for Distinguished Service to TV 1985. *Leisure interests:* books, walks, sleep. *Address:* Royal Opera House, Covent Garden, London, W.C.2, England.

ISAKOV, Victor Fyodorovich, PH.D.; Soviet diplomatist; b. 12 Dec. 1932, Leningrad; m. Natalia Isakov; two s. one d.; mem. diplomatic service 1956–; attached to Soviet Embassy, Washington 1956–60; U.S.S.R. Ministry for Foreign Affairs 1960–63; Embassy, Washington 1963–67; U.S.S.R. Ministry for Foreign Affairs 1967–71; Counsellor, Embassy, Washington 1971–77; Deputy Dir., U.S.A. Dept., U.S.S.R. Ministry for Foreign Affairs 1977–83; Minister-Counsellor, Embassy, Washington 1983–86; Amb. to Brazil 1986–. *Address:* Embassy of the U.S.S.R, SES, Av. das Nações, Lote A, 70. 476, Brasília, D.F., Brazil. *Telephone:* (061) 223-30-94.

ISARANGKUN NA AYUTHAYA, Charunphan; Thai politician; b. 14 March 1914; ed. Chulalongkorn and Thammasat Univs., Bangkok, Nat. Defence Coll.; served in Ministry of Interior 1934–43; joined Ministry of Foreign Affairs 1943; posted to Berne 1947–51, London 1956–60; Deputy Under-Sec. of State for Foreign Affairs 1960; Amb. to Laos 1961–65, to Spain, concurrently to Tunisia 1965–70, to Austria, concurrently to Turkey 1970–71; Under-Sec. of State for Foreign Affairs 1971–73; Minister of Foreign Affairs 1973–75. *Address:* c/o Ministry of Foreign Affairs, Bangkok, Thailand.

ISARANGKUN NA AYUTHAYA, Chirayu; Thai economist and politician; b. 12 Nov. 1942, Bangkok; m.; two s.; ed. St. Gabriel's School, Bangkok, King's Coll. School, Wimbledon, England, Univ. of London and Australian Nat. Univ.; joined Dept. of Tech. and Econ. Co-operation 1964; transferred to Nat. Inst. of Devt. Admin. (NIDA) 1967, Assoc. Dean School of Devt. Cons. 1974–76, Dean 1976–80, Acting Vice-Rector 1981–; Adviser to Prime Minister in third govt. of Gen. Kriangsak Chomanan and first govt. of Gen. Prem Tinsulanonda; Deputy Minister of Industry in second, third and fourth Prem govts.; Minister in the Prime Minister's Office 1986–87. *Address:* c/o Office of the Prime Minister, Nakhon Pathom Road, Bangkok 10300, Thailand.

ISARD, Walter, PH.D.; American regional scientist; b. 19 April 1919, Philadelphia, Pa.; s. of Lazar and Anna (Podolin) Isard; m. Caroline Berliner 1943; four s. four d.; ed. Temple, Harvard and Chicago Univs.; Instructor Wesleyan Univ. 1945, M.I.T. 1947; Visiting Lecturer Tufts Coll. 1947; Assoc. Prof. of Econs., Assoc. Dir. of Teaching, Inst. of Econs., American Univ. 1948–49; Research Fellow and Lecturer, Harvard Univ. 1949–53; Assoc. Prof. of Regional Econs., Dir. Urban and Regional Studies, M.I.T. 1953–56; Prof. of Econs., Chair. Dept. of Regional Science, Univ. of Pa. 1956–75, Head Dept. of Peace Science 1975–77; Visiting Prof. of Regional Science, Yale Univ. 1960–61, of Landscape Architecture and Regional Science, Harvard Univ. 1966–71; Chair. Graduate Group in Peace Research and Peace Science Unit 1970–78; Sr. Research Assoc., Visiting Prof. of Econs., Regional Science and Policy Planning, Cornell Univ. 1971–79, Prof. 1979–; Distinguished Visiting Prof., Inst. für Regionalwissenschaft, Karlsruhe 1972; Consultant, Tenn. Valley Authority 1951–52, Resources for the Future Inc. 1954–58, Ford Foundation 1955–56; Founder Regional Science Assn. 1954, Editor, Co-Ed. Papers 1954–58, Pres. 1959, Hon. Chair. 1960–; Ford Foundation Fellow in Econs. and Business Admin. 1959–60; Editor, Co-Editor, Journal of Regional Science 1960–; Chair. OEEC Econ. Productivity Agency Conf. on Regional Econs. and Planning, Bellagio, Italy 1960; Founder Peace Science Soc. (Int.) 1963, Co-Ed. Papers 1963–, Exec. Sec. 1964–, Pres. 1968; Pres. World Acad. of Art and Science 1977–81; Assoc. Ed. Quarterly Journal of Economics 1968–71; mem. Editorial Bd. Journal of Conflict Resolution 1972–; mem. N.A.S. 1985; Fellow, American Acad. of Art and Sciences 1980; Dr. h.c. (Poznan Acad. of Econ.) 1976, (Erasmus Univ.) 1978, (Karlsruhe) 1979, (UMEA) 1980, (Univ. of Ill.) 1982. *Publications:* Atomic Power: An Economic and Social Analysis 1952, Location Factors in the Petrochemical Industry 1955, Location and Space Economy 1956, Municipal Costs and Revenues resulting from Community Growth 1957, Industrial Complex Analysis and Regional Development 1959, Methods of Regional Analysis 1960, Regional Economic Development 1961, General Theory: Social, Political, Economic and Regional 1969, Regional Input-Output Study 1971, Ecologic-Economic Analysis for Regional Planning 1971, Spatial Dynamics and Optimal Space-Time Development 1979, Conflict Analysis and Practical Conflict Management Procedures 1982, Arms Races, Arms Control and Conflict Analysis 1988. *Leisure interest:* music. *Address:* Department of Economics, 476 Uris Hall, Cornell University, Ithaca, N.Y. 14853 (Office); 3218 Garrett Road, Drexel Hill, Pa. 19026, U.S.A. (Home). *Telephone:* (607) 255-3306 (Office).

ISAYEV, Vasiliy Yakovlevich; Soviet engineer and politician; b. 1917; ed. Leningrad Eng. Construction Inst.; admin. work in construction orgs. 1937–55; mem. CPSU 1939–; Chief Bd. of Housing, Civil and Industrial Construction in Leningrad 1955–61; Deputy Chair., then Chair. Exec. Cttee. Leningrad City Council of Working People's Deputies (Mayor of Leningrad) 1962–64; Deputy of Supreme Soviet U.S.S.R. 1962–; mem. Comm. for Youth Affairs, Soviet Union; Deputy Chair. of Gosplan U.S.S.R. 1965–; Cand. mem. Cen. Cttee. CPSU 1966–81, mem. 1981–. *Address:* U.S.S.R. Gosplan, 12 Prospekt Marxa, Moscow, U.S.S.R.

ISBĂȘESCU, Mihai, PH.D.; Romanian philologist and translator; b. 14 Jan. 1915, Bucharest; s. of Dumitru G. Isbășescu and Filofteia Isbășescu (née Stâlpeanu); m. Maria Golea 1940; one d.; ed. Bucharest Univ. and Tübingen Univ.; Prof., Head of Chair. Bucharest Univ. 1946, Coll. of Construction 1967, Coll. of Germanic Languages 1970, Consulting Prof. 1984–; mem. Romanian Writers' Union 1955 (mem. Bd. 1972–81, mem. Bureau of Translation and World Literature Dept. 1972–), mem. curator Faust-Gesellschaft Stuttgart-Knittlingen 1970, Int. Fed. of Modern Languages and Literature, Deutschlehrerverband, Societas Linguistica Europea, Féd. Int. des Traducteurs, Int. Assn. for Germanic Studies, Assn. Int. de Linguistique Appliquée, corresp. mem. Inst. fur deutsche Sprache, Mannheim 1970–; Prize of Writers' Assn. of Bucharest 1975, Romanian Writers' Union 1978, Goethe Gold Medal, Goethe-Institut, Munich 1970, Humboldt Medal 1985; Bundesverdienstkreuz, Fed. Repub. of Germany 1971. *Publications:* numerous translations (Schiller, Goethe, Kafka, Mann, Wickert, Schlegel, Hofmannstahl etc.), studies in early, classical and contemporary German literature, comparative studies of German and Romanian literature and linguistics, and bilingual dictionaries. *Address:* Str. Docentilor No. 26, 71311 Bucharest, Romania.

ISBISTER, Claude Malcolm, PH.D.; Canadian international finance official; b. 15 Jan. 1914, Winnipeg, Manitoba; s. of Claude and Margaret (McKechnie) Isbister; m. Ruth Cunningham 1938; three c.; ed. Univs. of Manitoba and Toronto and Harvard Univ.; Instructor, Econs. Dept., Harvard Univ. 1942–45; entered govt. service 1945, served in Bureau of Statistics 1945–47,

Dept. of Reconstruction and Supply 1947-49, Dept. of Trade and Commerce 1949-58; Asst. Deputy Minister, Dept. of Finance 1958-63; Dir. Canadian Nat. (West Indies) Steamships Ltd. 1959-62; Deputy Minister, Dept. of Citizenship and Immigration 1963-65, Dept. of Mines and Tech. Surveys 1965-66, Dept. of Energy, Mines and Resources 1966-70; Chair. Dominion Coal Bd. 1969-70; Exec. Dir. IBRD, IFC and IDA 1970-76; Consulting Partner Currie, Coopers & Lybrand 1976-78; Consultant 1978-; Consultant African Devt. Bank, Caribbean Devt. Bank, IBRD, IMF, Canadian Govt., etc. *Address:* 260 Heath Street West, Suite 1703, Toronto, M5P 3L6, Canada (Home and Office). *Telephone:* (416) 481-4159.

ISHAY, Ram Raymond, M.D.; Israeli physician; b. 17 May 1931, Tunisia; s. of Joseph Ishay and Mary Ishay; m. Rachel Ishay 1960; three c.; ed. Univ. of Montpellier; physician of kibbutzim in the Negev and head of plot project in integrative medicine in new settlements area in the South 1956-86; Chair. Kupat-Holim Doctors' Org. 1969-80; Maj. Israeli Defence Armed Forces; Chair. Confed. of Intellectual Workers Asscn., Israel 1987; mem. Exec. Nat. Council of Health 1974-, Helsinki Cttee. for Medical Experimentation 1982-, Exec. Council, World Medical Asscn. 1983-; Pres. Israeli Medical Asscn. 1971-, Pres. elect World Medical Asscn. 1988. *Publication:* Anatomy of Struggle 1986. *Leisure interests:* painting, classical music. *Address:* 39 Shaul Hamelech Boulevard, Tel Aviv, Israel. *Telephone:* (03) 266968.

ISHIBA, Jiro; Japanese politician; b. 29 July 1908, Tottori Prefecture; ed. Tokyo Univ.; entered Home Affairs Ministry 1932; Dir. City Bureau, Construction Ministry 1952; Vice-Minister of Construction 1955-58; Gov. Tottori Pref. 1958-74; Minister of Home Affairs July-Dec. 1980; fmr. Dir.-Gen. Nat. Public Safety Comm.; mem. House of Councillors 1974- (fmr. Chair. Foreign Affairs Cttee.). *Address:* c/o Liberal-Democratic Party, 7, 2-chome, Hirakawacho, Chiyoda-ku, Tokyo, Japan.

ISHIBASHI, Kanichiro; Japanese business executive; b. 1 March 1920, Kurume-shi, Fukuoka-ken; s. of Shojiro and Masako Ishibashi; m. Saeko Ishibashi 1944; one s. two d.; ed. Faculty of Law, Univ. of Tokyo; naval service 1943-45; joined Bridgestone Tire Co. Ltd. (now called Bridgestone Corpn.) 1945, Dir. 1949-, Vice-Pres. 1950-63, Pres. 1963-73, Chair. 1973-85, Hon. Chair. Feb. 1985-; Exec. Dir. Fed. of Econ. Orgs., Japan Fed. of Employers' Asscns.; Pres. Japan Rubber Mfrs. Asscn. *Leisure interests:* pictures, photography, music, golf. *Address:* 10-1, Kyobashi 1-chome, Chuo-ku, Tokyo (Office); 1 Nagasaka-cho, Azabu, Minato-ku, Tokyo, Japan (Home). *Telephone:* 03-567-0111 (Office); 03-583-0150 (Home).

ISHIDA, Hirohide; Japanese politician; b. 1914, Akita Prefecture; ed. Waseda Univ.; mem. House of Reps. 1938-; fmr. Chair. Steering Cttee. of House of Reps.; fmr. Chair. Russo-Japanese Parliamentarians League; Dir. of Cabinet Secr. 1956-57; Minister of Labour 1957-58, 1960-61, 1964-65, 1976-77; Minister of Transport Sept.-Dec. 1976; assoc. of Takeo Miki (q.v.); fmr. Acting Sec.-Gen. of Liberal-Democratic Party (LDP). *Publications:* Wasurerareta Kodomotachi (Forgotten Children), Ijoji-To Sono Sakuhim (Abnormal Children and Their Works). *Address:* c/o House of Representatives, Tokyo, Japan.

ISHIHARA, Shintaro; Japanese politician; b. Sept. 1932, Kobe; m.; four s.; ed. Hitotsubashi Univ.; mem. House of Councillors 1972; mem. House of Reps. 1972; Minister of State, Dir.-Gen. Environment Agency 1976; Minister of Transport 1987-88; Akutagawa Prize for Literature; Liberal-Democratic Party. *Publications include:* The Season of the Sun, The Tree of the Young Man, The Forest of Fossils etc. *Leisure interests:* yachting, skiing. *Address:* Ministry of Transport, 2-1, Kasumigaseki, Chiyoda-ku, Tokyo, Japan.

ISHIHARA, Takashi; Japanese motor industry executive; b. 3 March 1912, Tokyo; s. of Ichija Ishihara; m. Shizuko Nakajo 1943; one s.; ed. Tohoku Univ.; entered Nissan Motor Co. Ltd. 1937, Dir. Finance and Accounting 1954; Pres. Nissan Motor Corpn. in U.S.A. 1960-65; Man. Dir. Nissan Motor Co. Ltd. 1963, Domestic Sales Dir. 1965, Exec. Man. Dir. 1969, Exec. Vice-Pres. 1973, Pres. 1977-85, Chair. 1985-; Adviser Nikkeiren (Japan Fed. of Employers' Asscns.), Keidanren (Fed. of Econ. Orgs.); Pres. Japan Automobile Mfrs. Asscn. 1980-; Chair. Keizai Doyukai (Japan Asscn. of Corp. Execs.); Dr. h.c. (Durham) 1988; Blue Ribbon Medal 1974, Order of the Sacred Treasure (1st class), Grand Cross (Spain). *Leisure interests:* reading, golf, ocean cruising. *Address:* 17-1, Ginza 6-chome, Chuo-ku, Tokyo, Japan. *Telephone:* 03-543-5523.

ISHIKAWA, Shigeru, D.ECON.; Japanese economist; b. 7 April 1918; ed. Tokyo Univ. of Commerce (now Hitotsubashi Univ.); attached to Jiji Press News Agency 1945-56, Hong Kong Corresp. 1951-53; Asst. Prof., Inst. of Econ. Research, Hitotsubashi Univ. 1956-63, Prof. 1963-82, Dir. 1972-74, Prof. Emer. 1982-; Visiting Prof. School of Oriental and African Studies, Univ. of London 1980; Prof. School of Int. Politics, Econs. and Business, Aoyama Gakuin Univ. 1982. *Publications:* National Income and Capital Formation in Mainland China 1965, Economic Development in Asian Perspective 1967, Agricultural Development Strategies of Asia 1970, Labor Absorption in Asian Agriculture 1978, Essays on Technology, Employment and Institutions in Economic Development: Comparative Asian Experience 1981. *Address:* 19-9, 4 chome Kugayama, Suginami-ku, Tokyo 168, Japan. *Telephone:* 332-8376.

ISHIMOTO, Shigeru; Japanese politician; b. 6 Sept. 1913; ed. Japanese Red Cross Nurses Training Centre; mil. nurse, Chief Nurse Nat. Cancer Centre; mem. House of Councillors 1965-; Parl. Vice-Minister for Health and Welfare 1976-77; Chair. Japan Nurses Asscn. 1980-; Minister of State, Dir.-Gen. Environment Agency 1984-85; Liberal Democratic Party. *Publications:* Nursing Management, Guide to Home Nursing. *Leisure interest:* reading. *Address:* c/o Environment Agency, 3-1, Kasumigaseki, Chiyoda-ku, Tokyo 100, Japan. *Telephone:* 3-581-3351.

ISHINO, Shinichi; Japanese banker; b. 13 March, Hyogo-Ken; s. of Takuji and Yoshio Ishino; m. Kazu Ujiie 1936; ed. Tokyo Imperial Univ.; Dir.-Gen. Banking Bureau, Ministry of Finance 1959-61, Budget Bureau 1961-63; Vice-Minister of Finance 1963-65; Pres. Bank of Kobe Ltd. 1967-73, Taiyo Kobe Bank Ltd. 1973-78; Chair. Taiyo Kobe Bank 1978-83, Dir. and Advisor 1983-, Pres. Kobe Chamber of Commerce and Industry 1984-. *Leisure interests:* Haiku, Go, golf. *Address:* Kobe CIT Center Building, 1-14 Hamabe-dori 5-chome, Chuo-ku, Kobe 651; 5-31 Rokuban-cho, Kurakuen, Nishinomiya-shi, Hyogo-Ken, Japan. *Telephone:* 0798 73 1020.

ISHIZUKA, Yoshiaki; Japanese professor; b. 14 March 1907, Tokyo; s. of Hide Ishizuka and Kiichiro Ishizuka; m. Kinu Yamashita 1941; two s.; ed. Hokkaido Univ.; Professor of Soil Science, Hokkaido Univ. 1945-70, Prof. Emer. 1970-; Dean Faculty of Agriculture, Hokkaido Univ. 1966-69; Dir. Food and Fertilizer Tech. Center, Asia 1973-75; Chair. Cttee. Int. Soil Science Soc. 1964-68, Hon. mem. 1978-; Purple Ribbon Medal 1970, Japan Acad. Prize 1975, Order of the Second Treasure (Second Class) 1976. *Publications:* Physiology of the Rice Plant 1971, Nutrient Deficiency of Crops 1971, Rice Growing in a cool Environment 1975, numerous Japanese books. *Leisure interest:* photography. *Address:* 3-Jo, 4-chome, Kotoni, Sapporo 063, Japan. *Telephone:* (011) 611-7944.

ISHLINSKY, Aleksandr Yulevich; Soviet applied mathematician; b. 6 Aug. 1913, Moscow; s. of Yuliy Eduardovich Ishlinsky and Sofia Ivanovna Kirillova; m. Natalia Vladimirovna Zaporozhets 1943; ed. Moscow Univ.; Prof., Moscow Univ. 1944-48; mem. CPSU 1940, Ukrainian Acad. of Sciences 1948; Prof. Kiev Univ. 1949-55; Prof. and Head of Dept., Moscow Univ. 1955; Dir. Inst. for Problems in Mechanics U.S.S.R. Acad. of Sciences 1964-88, Hon. Dir. 1989-; mem. U.S.S.R. Acad. of Sciences 1960-; Chair. U.S.S.R. Union of Scientific and Eng. Socs.; Regional mem. Int. Fed. Scientific Workers; Deputy to Supreme Soviet U.S.S.R.; Pres. World Fed. of Eng. Orgs. 1987; Hero of Socialist Labour, Order of Lenin (three times), Order of the October Revolution, Order of the Red Banner of Labour (three times), Order of the Badge of Honour, Lenin Prize 1960, and other decorations. *Publications:* The Dynamics of Ground Masses 1954, The Theory of the Horizon Compass 1956, On the Equation of Problems Determining the Position of Moving Objects by Using a Gyroscope and Measuring Acceleration 1957, The Mechanics of Gyroscopic Systems 1963, Inertial Guidance of Ballistic Rockets 1968, Orientation, Gyroscopes and Inertial Navigation 1976, Applied Problems in Mechanics 1986, Classical Mechanics and Inertia Forces 1987. *Leisure interests:* radiotechnique, chess. *Address:* Institute for Problems in Mechanics, U.S.S.R. Academy of Sciences, prospekt Vernadskogo 101, Moscow 117526, U.S.S.R. *Telephone:* 434 3465

IŞIK, Hasan Esat; Turkish diplomatist and politician; b. 21 Oct. 1916; ed. Ankara Univ.; Ministry of Foreign Affairs 1940-; Consulate-Gen., Paris 1945-49; Head of Section, Dept. of Commerce and Econ. Affairs, and Dept. of Int. Econ. Relations 1949-52; mem. Perm. Turkish Del. to European Office of UN, Geneva 1952-54; Dir.-Gen. of Dept. of Commerce and Commercial Agreements, Ministry of Foreign Affairs 1954-57; Asst. for Econ. Affairs to Sec.-Gen. of Ministry of Foreign Affairs 1957-62; Amb. to Belgium 1962-64, to U.S.S.R. 1964-65, 1966-68; Minister of Foreign Affairs Feb.-Oct. 1965; Amb. to France 1968-73; Minister of Defence Jan.-Nov. 1974, June-July 1977, 1978-79. *Address:* c/o Ministry of Foreign Affairs, Ankara, Turkey.

ISKANDER, Fazil Abdulovich, Soviet author; b. 6 March 1929, Sukhumi, Georgian SSR; ed. Maxim Gorky Inst. of Literature, Moscow. *Publications include:* Green Rain 1960, Youth of the Sea 1964; Forbidden Fruit 1966 (trans. Eng. 1972), Summer Forest 1969, Time of Lucky Finds 1970, Tree of Childhood & Other Stories 1970, Sandro from Chegem 1978, Metropol (co-ed.) 1979, Small Giant of the Big Sex 1979. *Address:* USSR Union of Writers, Ulitsa Vorovskogo 52, Moscow, U.S.S.R.

ISLAM, A.K.M. Nurul; Bangladeshi judge and politician; b. 1925, Khajilpur, Dhaka Dist. m. Jahanara Arjoo; two s. two d.; ed. in Calcutta; Advocate, Dhaka High Court 1951, Supreme Court 1956; Additional Judge, Dhaka High Court 1968, Judge 1970; Chief Election Commr. of Bangladesh 1977, 1982; founder and Sr. Prof. City Law Coll. Dhaka; active in independence movt. 1971; Vice-Pres. of Bangladesh 1986-88, 1989-, also Minister of Law and Justice 1986-. *Address:* Office of the Vice President, Dhaka, Bangladesh.

ISLAM, Nurul, PH.D.; Bangladesh economist; b. 1 April 1929, Chittagong; s. of Abdur Rahman and Mohsena Begum; m. Rowshan Ara 1957; one s. one d. ed. Univ. of Dhaka and Harvard Univ.; Reader in Economics, Dhaka Univ. 1955-60, Prof. 1960-64; Dir. Pakistan Inst. of Devt. Econs., Karachi 1964-72; Visiting Prof. Econ. Devt. Inst., World Bank 1967-68; Professorial Research Assoc., Yale Econ. Growth Cen. 1968 and 1971; Deputy Chair.

Bangladesh Planning Comm. (with ministerial status) 1972–75; Chair. Bangladesh Inst. of Devt. Studies, Dhaka 1975–77; mem. Bd. of Trustees Int. Rice Research Inst., Manila 1973–77, Exec. Cttee. Third World Forum 1974–, Bd. of Govs. Int. Food Policy Research Inst. 1975–, UN Cttee. on Devt. Planning 1975–77; Asst. Dir.-Gen. Econ. and Social Policy Dept., Food and Agric. Org. of UN 1977–; mem. Editorial Bd. The World Economy, London, Research Advisory Cttee., World Bank 1980, Advisory Group, Asian Devt. Bank, Manila 1981–82, Advisory Cttee., Inst. of Int. Econ., Washington, D.C.; Consultant with various UN Cttees, ESCAP, UNESCO, UNCTAD etc.; Nuffield Foundation Fellow at Univs. of London and Cambridge 1958–59; Rockefeller Fellow, Netherlands School of Economics 1959. *Publications:* A Short-Term Model of Pakistan's Economy: An Econometric Analysis 1964, Studies in Foreign Capital and Economic Development 1960, Studies in Consumer Demand 1965, Studies in Commercial Policy and Economic Growth 1970, Development Planning in Bangladesh—A Study in Political Economy 1977, Development Strategy of Bangladesh 1978, Interdependence of Developed and Developing Countries 1978, Foreign Trade and Economic Controls in Development: The Case of United Pakistan 1980, Aid and Influence: The Case of Bangladesh (co-author) 1981; Co-Author: Agriculture Towards 2000 1981, The Fifth World Food Survey 1985, Agriculture Price Policies 1985. *Leisure interests:* reading political and historical books, movies. *Address:* Viale Piramide Cestia 1.C., Apt. 19, 00153 Rome (Home); FAO, 00153 Rome, Italy (Office). *Telephone:* 577.9962 (Home); 5797.3001 (Office).

ISLAM, Sheikh Shahidul, M.SC., LL.B.; Bangladesh politician; b. 2 Jan. 1948, Tungipara; m. Yasmin Islam 1975; two s. one d.; ed. G.T. High School, Dhaka Coll., Dhaka Univ.; led Dist. Liberation Force, Faridpur 1971; Pres. Bangladesh Students' League 1972; Social Welfare Sec. of Bangladesh Awami League Central Comm. 1974–75; Chief Ed. Nayabarta 1979–83; Organizing Sec. Janadal (People's Party) 1983; Pres. Nat. Youth Solidarity Org. 1985; Deputy Minister of Youth and Sports 1985; mem. Parl. 1986–; Minister of State for Youth and Sports 1986, for Works 1987–88, of Educ. 1988–; Pres. Nat. Anti-Drug. Comm. 1987. *Leisure interests:* gardening, games, writing, reading. *Address:* 25 Baily Road, Minister's Bungalow, Ramna, Dhaka, Bangladesh (Home). *Telephone:* 416130 (Home).

ISMAEL, Dr. Julius Emanuel: Indonesian economist and banker; b. 16 July 1927, Jakarta; m. Hermien S. Hardjodiwirjo 1957; two s. one d.; ed. Univ. of Indonesia, Cornell Univ., Univ. of Pittsburgh; Ass. to the Chair. Nat. Planning Agency 1968–70; Pres. Bank Ekspor-Impor Indonesia 1970–73; Man. Dir. Bank of Indonesia 1973–83; Prof. of Financial Man. Univ. of Indonesia 1974–; Exec. Dir. IMF 1983–. *Address:* c/o International Monetary Fund, 700 19th Street, N.W., Washington, D.C. 20431, U.S.A. *Telephone:* (202) 477-2908.

ISMAIL, Abdul Malek; Yemeni diplomatist; b. 23 Nov. 1937, Aden; m.; four c.; ed. Tawahi and Crater, Aden, Tech. School, Maalla, Khediwi High School, Cairo and Cairo Univ. Faculty of Commerce; mem. Nat. Lib. Front; Ed. Al-Nour and Hakikah (newspapers) 1961–63; Vice-Chair. Gen. Union of Petroleum Workers 1961–62, Chair. 1962–64; Vice-Pres. Arab Fed. of Petroleum Workers 1962–65; leading mem. Arab Nationalist Movement 1956–63; leading mem. Nat. Front for Liberation of Occupied S. Yemen (FLOSY) 1963–65; Dir. Nat. Front Office, Cairo 1965–66; mem. Gen. Command of Nat. Liberation Front 1966–68; Minister of Labour and Social Affairs 1967–68, of Econs., Commerce and Planning April 1968; Perm. Rep. to UN 1970–73; Vice-Pres. UN Gen. Ass. 26th Session; Amb. to Egypt 1973–75; Head of Nairobi Mission of Arab League States Org. March 1983–. *Address:* c/o Ministry of Foreign Affairs, Aden, People's Democratic Republic of Yemen.

ISMAIL, Ahmed Sultan, B.SC.; Egyptian mechanical engineer; b. 14 April 1923, Port Said; s. of Ismail Ahmed and Fatma Sultan; m. Rawhia Riad 1957; ed. Cairo Univ., Nat. Defence Coll.; worked as shift engineer, maintenance engineer at various power stations 1945–64; Dir. and mem. Electrical Corpn. 1964–68; Gov. Menufia Prov. 1968–71; Minister of Power 1971–76, Deputy Premier for Production and Minister for Electric Power and Energy 1976–78; Consulting Engineer Oct. 1978–; Order of Repub. (First Class). *Leisure interests:* reading, travel. *Address:* 43 Ahmed Abdel Aziz Street, Dokki, Cairo, Egypt (Home). *Telephone:* Cairo 3474422, 3468700, 3486374, 3487754.

ISMAIL, Mohamed Ali, M.A.; Malaysian investment banker; b. 16 Sept. 1918, Port Kelang, Selangor; s. of Haji Mohamed Ali bin Taib and Hajjah Khadijah binti Haji Ahmad; m. Maimunah binti Abdul Latiff 1949; two s.; ed. Univ. of Cambridge and Middle Temple, London; joined Malayan Civil Service 1946; Asst. State Sec., Selangor State 1948–50; Asst. Sec. Econ. Div. of Fed. Treasury 1950–53; Econ. Officer, Penang 1954–55; Controller, Trade Div., Ministry of Commerce and Industry 1955–57; Minister Malaysian Embassy, Washington 1957–58, Econ. Minister 1958–60; Exec. Dir. IBRD, Int. Finance Corpn., Int. Devt. Assen. 1958–60; Deputy Gov. Cen. Bank of Malaysia 1960–62, Gov. 1962–80; Chair. Capital Issues Cttee. 1968–80, Malaysian Industrial Devt. Finance Ltd. 1969–; Pres. Malaysian Inst. of Man. 1966–68; Chair. Nat. Equity Corpn. 1978–; Chair. of Council, Malaysia Inst. of Bankers 1978–80; mem. Nat. Devt. Planning Cttee. 1962–80, Council of Univ. of Malaya 1962–72; Adviser, Nat. Corpn. (PERNAS) 1971–80; mem. Foreign Investment Cttee 1974–80; mem. Bd. of

Govs., Asian Inst. of Man., Manila 1971–; Dir. Sime, Darby Berhad 1980–; Chair. Guthrie Corpn. Ltd. April 1982–, Harrisons Malaysian Plantations Berhad 1982–; Malaysian Nat. Reinsurance Berhad 1985, Commodities Trading Comm. 1981–, Panglima Mangku Negara 1964, Order of Panglima Negara Bintang Sarawak 1976; Hon. LL.D. (Univ. of Malaya) 1973, (Univ. of Singapore) 1982; Hon. D.Econ. (Univ. Kebangsaan Malaysia) 1982; Seri Paduka Mahkota Selangor award 1977; Seri Paduka Mahkota Johor Award 1979; Tun Abdul Razak Foundation Award 1980. *Leisure interests:* golf, swimming. *Address:* National Equity Corporation, P.O.B. 745, Kuala Lumpur (Office); 23 Jalan Natesa, off Cangkat Tunku, Kuala Lumpur, Malaysia (Home). *Telephone:* 03-2613313 (Office); 03-2425597 (Home).

ISMAIL AMAT; Chinese politician; b. 1934, Xinjiang; active in People's Commune Movt. –1960; Deputy Sec. CCP Cttee., a country admin., Xinjiang 1960; Deputy Dir. Dept. of Political Work in Culture and Educ. Xinjiang 1960; mem. 10th Cen. Cttee., CCP 1973–77; Sec. CCP Cttee., Xinjiang 1974–79; Vice-Chair. Aubnavan Regional Revolutionary Cttee., Xinjiang 1974–; Political Commissar, Xinjiang Mil. Region 1976–; First Deputy Dir. Party School, Xinjiang 1977–85; Chair People's Govt., Xinjiang 1979–85; mem. 12th Cen. Cttee. CCP 1982–; Minister of State Nationalities Affairs Comm. 1986–. *Address:* People's Government, Xinjiang, People's Republic of China.

ISODA, Ichiro, LL.B.; Japanese banker; b. 12 Jan. 1913, Kumamoto Prefecture; s. of Toshisuke and Chikatsuru Isoda; m. Umeko Kawamura 1941; one s. one d.; ed. Kyoto Univ.; joined Sumitomo Bank Ltd. 1935, Gen. Man. Koraibashi Br. 1953–60, Dir. 1960–, Man. Dir. 1963–68, Sr. Man. Dir. 1968–73, Deputy Pres. 1973–77, Pres. 1977–83, Chair. Bd. Nov. 1983–; Medal of Honour with Blue Ribbon 1978, Commdr., Ordre de la Couronne (Belgium) 1983, Order of the Sacred Treasure (First Class) 1984. *Leisure interests:* literature, Japanese music, pottery, sport. *Address:* 12-18 Minamiazabu 5-chome, Minato-ku, Tokyo; 18-46 Uenohigashi 3-Chome, Toyonaka, Osaka, Japan (Homes). *Telephone:* (03) 440-1465 (Tokyo).

ISONG, Clement Nyong, PH.D.; Nigerian economist and banker; b. 20 April 1920, Ikot Osong, Akwa Ibom State; s. of Nathaniel Udo Isong and Maggie Udo; m. Nne B. Akpaete 1958; two s. four d.; ed. Univ. Coll. Ibadan, Iowa Wesleyan Coll. and Harvard Graduate School of Arts and Sciences; Asst. economist, Fed. Reserve Bank of New York 1957; Lecturer in Econs., Money and Banking, Univ. Coll. Ibadan 1957–59; Sec., Cen. Bank of Nigeria 1959–61, Dir. of Research 1961–62; Adviser to African Dept. of IMF 1962–67; Gov. of Cen. Bank of Nigeria 1967–75, Chair. Bd. of Dirs.; Alt. Gov. for Nigeria, IMF; Chair. Bankers' Cttee., Assen. of African Cen. Banks 1973–75, Man. Dir., Chair. of Bd. FIBA Consultants Ltd. 1976–79, 1986–; Gov., Cross River State 1979–83. *Leisure interest:* local civic duties. *Address:* Plot No. 7, Prince O.U. Utuk Street, P.O. Box 2311, Uyo, Nigeria.

ISOZAKI, Arata; Japanese architect; b. 23 July 1931, Oita City; m. Aiko Miyawaki 1974; ed. Univ. of Tokyo; with Kenzo Tange's team 1954–63; established Arata Isozaki and Assocs. 1963; juror, Pritzker Architecture Prize 1979–84, Concours Int. de Parc de la Villette 1982, The Peak Int. Architectural Competition 1983, R. S. Reynolds Memorial Award 1985, The Architectural Competition for the New Nat. Theatre of Japan; visiting prof. at numerous univs. including Harvard, Yale and Columbia; Architectural Inst. of Japan annual prize 1967, 1975, Special Prize of Expo '70 1970; *works include:* Expo '70, Osaka 1966–70, Oita Medical Hall 1959–69, Annex 1970–72, Oita Prefectural Library 1962–66, head office of Fukuoka Mutual Bank 1968–71, Gunma Prefectural Museum of Fine Arts 1971–74, Kitakyushu City Museum of Art 1972–74, Kitakyushu Cen. Library 1972–75, Shuko-sha Bldg. 1974–75, Kamioka Town Hall 1975–78, Gymnasium and Dining Hall, NEG Co. 1978–80, Los Angeles Museum of Contemporary Art 1981–86, Tsukuba Centre Building 1978–83, Palladium, New York 1983, Sports Hall, Barcelona 1984; Hon. Fellow Acad. Tiberina, A.I.A.; Hon. mem. B.D.A.; Mainichi Art Award 1983; R.I.B.A.'s Gold Medal for Architecture 1986; Chevalier Ordre des Arts et des Lettres. *Publications:* Kukan-e 1971, Kenchiku no Kaitai 1975, Shūho ga 1979, Kenchiku no Shūji 1979. *Address:* Arata Isozaki and Associates, 6-14, Akasaka 9-chome, Minato-ku, Tokyo 107, Japan. *Telephone:* (03) 405-1526.

ISRAELACHVILI, Jacob Nissim, PH.D., F.A.A., F.R.S.; Australian/Israeli university professor; b. 19 Aug. 1944, Tel Aviv; s. of Haim Israelachvili and Hela Israelachvili; m. Karin Haglund 1971; two d.; ed. Univ. of Cambridge; Postdoctoral Research Fellow, Cavendish Lab. Cambridge 1971–72; European Molecular Biology Org. (EMBO) Research Fellow, Univ. of Stockholm 1972–74; Professorial Fellow, Inst. of Advanced Studies, Australian Nat. Univ., Canberra 1974–86; Professor of Chemical Eng. and Materials Science, Univ. of Calif. Santa Barbara 1986–; Debye Lecturer, Cornell Univ. 1987; Pawsey Medal, Australian Acad. of Science 1977. *Publications:* Intermolecular and Surface Forces 1985; numerous scientific publs. on surface forces in liquids and biological membrane structure and interactions. *Leisure interests:* history, backgammon. *Address:* Department of Chemical and Nuclear Engineering, University of California, Santa Barbara, Calif. 93105 (Office); 2233 Foothill Lane, Santa Barbara, Calif. 93106, U.S.A. (Home). *Telephone:* 805-961-8407 (Office); 805-963-9545 (Home).

ISSELBACHER, Kurt Julius, M.D.; American professor of medicine; b. 12 Sept. 1925, Wirges, Germany; s. of Albert and Flori Isselbacher; m.

Rhoda Solin 1950; one s. three d.; ed. Harvard Univ. and Harvard Medical School; Chief. Gastrointestinal Unit, Mass. Gen. Hosp. 1957-88, Chair. Research Cttee. 1967, Dir. Cancer Centre 1987-; Mallinckrodt Prof. of Medicine, Harvard Medical School 1966-, Chair. Exec. Cttee. Medicine Depts. 1968-, Chair. Univ. Cancer Cttee. 1972-87; mem. governing bd. Nat. Research Council 1987-; mem. N.A.S. (Chair. Food and Nutrition Bd. 1983-, Exec. Cttee. and Council 1987-); Distinguished Achievement Award, American Gastroenterological Asscn. (AGA) 1983; Friedenwald Medal, AGA 1985, John Phillips Memorial Award, American Coll. of Physicians 1989. *Leisure interest:* tennis. *Address:* Massachusetts General Hospital Cancer Centre, Building 149, 7th Floor, Charlestown, Mass. 02129 (Office); 20 Nobscot Road, Newton Center, Mass., 02159, U.S.A. (Home). *Telephone:* (617) 726-5610 (Office).

ISTOMIN, Eugène George; American pianist; b. 26 Nov. 1925, New York; s. of George T. Istomin and Assia Chavin; m. Marta Montanez Casals 1975; ed. Curtis Inst., Philadelphia; studied under Kyriena Silote, Rudolf Serkin; Concert pianist 1943-; toured with Adolf Busch Chamber Players 1944-45; first European appearance 1950; charter mem. Casals Prades and Puerto Rico festivals 1950-; several world tours; founded Trio with Isaac Stern and Leonard Rose 1961; numerous recordings of solo, orchestral and chamber works; Leventritt Award 1943. *Leisure interests:* archaeology, history, painting, baseball. *Address:* c/o ICM Concerts, 40 West 57th Street, New York, N.Y. 10019, U.S.A. (Office).

ITALIAANDER, Rolf Bruno Maximilian; German writer, ethnologist and explorer; b. 20 Feb. 1913, Leipzig, Germany (Dutch citizen); s. of Kurt and Charlotte Italiaander; Explorer in Africa for over forty years; Visiting Prof. Inst. for European Studies, Univ. of Vienna 1959, Univ. of Michigan 1961, Hope Coll., Michigan 1961, Kalamazoo Coll., Michigan 1961, American Negro Univ. 1962, Univ. de Bahia and Inst. Joaquim Nabuco, Recife, Brazil 1967; Co-Founder and Hon. Sec. Free Acad. of Art, Hamburg 1948-69; Founder Museum Rade am Schloss Reinbek; Founder German Translators' Union 1954, Hon. Pres. 1960-; Co-founder Fed. Int. de Traducteurs, Paris; mem. American Acads.; Order of Merit of Fed. Repub. of Germany (First Class), Order of Merit (Austria), Officer Order of Merit (Senegal), Hans Henny Jahnn Award and other decorations. *Publications:* Der ruhelose Kontinent 1958, The New Leaders of Africa 1960, Schwarze Haut im roten Griff 1962, Die neuen Männer Asiens 1964, Immer wenn ich unterwegs bin 1963, König Leopolds Kongo 1964, Dappers Afrika 1668 1964, The Challenge of Islam 1964, Im Namen des Herrn im Kongo 1965, Die Friedensmacher 1965, In der Palmweinschenke 1966, Rassenkonflikte in der Welt 1966, Frieden in der Welt 1967, Lebensentscheidung für Israel 1967, Heinrich Barth 1967, Aufstieg und Sturz des Oscar Wilde 1967, Terra Dolorosa (Indoamerika) 1969, Weder Krankheit noch Verbrechen 1969, Junge Kunst aus Afrika: Kongo-Bilder und Verse 1969, Heinrich Barth: Er schloss uns einen Weltteil auf 1969, Akzente eines Lebens 1970, Kultur ohne Wirtschaftswunder 1970, Albanien: Chinas Vorposten in Europa 1970, Naive Kunst aus aller Welt 1970, Ade, Madam Muh! 1970, Profile und Perspektiven 1971, Argumente kritischer Christen 1971, Die neuen Herren der alten Welt 1972, Moral—wozu? 1972, Partisanen und Profeten 1972, Heisses Land (New Guinea) 1972, 12 Grafiken europäischer Naiver 1972, Verantwortliche Gesellschaft (Indonesien) 1974, Spass an der Freud (Naive Maler) 1974, Diktaturen im Nacken 1974, Congo-Grafik 1975, Always when I am Travelling 1976, Herausforderung in der Südsee 1977, Afrika hat viele Gesichter 1979, Hugo Eckener, ein moderner Columbus 1979, Berlin Stunde Null 1979, Graf Zeppelin 1980, Xocolatl 1980, Ich bin ein Berliner 1980, Jenseits der deutsch-deutschen Grenze 1981, Die grosse Zeit der deutschen Hanse 1981, Mein afrikanisches Fotoalbum 1981, Ein Deutscher namens Eckener 1981, Wir erlebten das Ende der Weimarer Republik 1982, Ein Mann kämpft für den Frieden (N. Niwano) 1982, Europa ist doch wunderschön 1982, Schwarze Magie 1982, Durchschrittene Räume 1983, Lichter im Norden 1983, Geh hin zu den Menschen 1983, Von Lust und Leid des Schriftstellers 1983, Fremde Raus? 1983, Anfang mit Zuversicht 1984, Besinnung auf Werte 1984, Kunstsammler, glückliche Menschen 1985, Mut, Fantasie und Hoffnung 1985, Vielvölkerstadt: Hamburg und seine Nationalitäten 1986, Hans Hasso von Veltheim-Ostrau-Privatgelehrter und Weltbürger 1987, Die Herausforderung des Islam 1987, Gedanken-Austausch-Erlebte Kulturgeschichte in Zeugnissen aus 6 Jahrzehnten 1988, Loki - die ungewöhnliche Geschichte einer deutschen Lehrerin 1988, and numerous others; Biography: Unterwegs mit Rolf Italiaander 1963, Diaboado Lompo: Schwarz-weisser Dialog. Rolf Italiaander und sein Afrika-Bild 1989. *Leisure interests:* meditation, singing, gardening. *Address:* St. Benedictstrasse 29, 2000 Hamburg 13, Federal Republic of Germany. *Telephone:* 473435.

ITO, Masayoshi; Japanese politician; b. 15 Dec. 1913, Fukushima Pref.; m. Teruko Ito; ed. Urawa Higher School, Tokyo Univ.; mem. House of Reps. 1963-; served in Agric. and Forestry Ministry 1936-56; Dir.-Gen. Comprehensive Devt. Bureau, Econ. Planning Agency 1957-58, Agric. Land Bureau, Ministry of Agric. and Forestry 1958-61, Fisheries Agency 1961-62; Vice-Minister of Agric. and Forestry 1962-63; Minister of State and Chief Cabinet Sec. 1979-80; Acting Prime Minister June-July 1980; Minister of Foreign Affairs 1980-81; Chair. Finance Cttee., Liberal-Democratic Party (LDP) 1978, Exec. Cttee. 1987-; Vice-Chair. LDP Policy Affairs Research Council 1977-86, Chair. 1986-. *Leisure interests:* theatre, reading. *Address:* 1-28-3 Chitose-dai, Setagaya-ku, Tokyo 157, Japan.

ITO, Soichiro; Japanese politician; b. March 1924, Miyagi Pref.; m.; ed. Tohoku Univ.; mem. House of Reps. (elected 9 times); fmr. Parl. Vice-Minister of Agric., Forestry and Fisheries; Parl. Vice-Minister for Science and Tech.; Dir.-Gen. Defence Agency; Minister of State, Dir.-Gen. Science and Tech. Agency 1987-88. *Publications:* Danshi no Honkai 363-nichi, Wa no Naka no Ketsudan. *Leisure interest:* reading.

ITOH, Junji; Japanese business executive; b. 10 July 1922, Qingdao, China; s. of Hideo and Fudechiyo Itoh; m. Mizuko Takeoka 1953; two s.; ed. Keio Univ.; with Kanegafuchi Spinning Co. Ltd. (now Kanebo Ltd.) 1948-; Dir. Kanebo Ltd. 1961, Man. Dir. 1964, Exec. Dir. 1966, Vice-Pres. 1968, Pres. and Rep. Dir. 1968-84, Chair. of Bd. and Rep. Dir. 1984; Pres. Kanebo Cosmetics Inc. 1969-81, Kanebo Pharmaceuticals Ltd. 1972-84, Chair. of Bd. and Rep. Dir. 1984-86, Kanebo Fibres Ltd. 1979-84, Chair. of Bd. and Rep. Dir. 1984-87, Kanebo Synthetic Textiles Ltd. 1983-84, Chair. of Bd. and Rep. Dir. 1984-, Kanebo Foods Ltd. 1981-84, Chair. of Bd. and Rep. Dir. 1984-86, Kanebo Fabrics Ltd. 1982-83; Vice-Chair. Japan Airlines 1985-86, Chair. 1986-87; Rep. Dir. Nippon Ester Co. Ltd. 1968-83; Exec. Dir. Japan Fed. of Econ. Orgs. 1968-, Japan Fed. of Employers' Assen. (NIKKEIREN) 1968-; Dir. Japan Cttee. for Econ. Devt. 1970-; Trustee, Keio Univ. 1970-78, 1982-; Grão Cruz Orden Academico São Francisco (Brazil) 1972, Orden do Cruzeiro do Sul (Brazil) 1976. *Address:* Kanebo Ltd., 5-90, Tomobuchi-cho 1-chome, Miyakojima-ku, Osaka 534 (Office), 6-29 Omiya 5-chome, Asahi-ku, Osaka 535, Japan (Home). *Telephone:* (06) 922-8002 (Office); (06) 953-1187 (Home).

ITOH, Kyoichi; Japanese textile executive; b. 27 May 1914, Kobe; s. of Chubei and Chiyo (Nagata) Itoh; m. Chikako Hongo 1941; one s. two d.; ed. Kobe Univ.; Dir. Kureha Spinning Co. Ltd. 1956, Man. Dir. 1956-63, Exec. Dir. 1963-, Pres. 1963-66; Exec. Vice-Pres. Toyobo Co. Ltd. 1966-73, Chair. 1973-74, Counsellor 1974-; Chair. Nippei Industrial Co. 1969-84; Dir. Toyo Pulp Co. 1965-74, Chair. 1975-81; Dir. Rotary Int. 1985-87; Hon. Consul-Gen. of Salvador, Osaka 1958-73, Hon. Consul-Gen. 1973-; Pres. Japan-El Salvador Soc. 1967-, Japan-America Soc. of Osaka 1979-80, Chair. 1980-81; Pres. and Chair. Osaka-San Francisco Sister City Assen. 1980-81; Pres. Japan Men's Fashion Unity 1979-83, Chair. 1978-85, Hon. Chair. 1986-. *Leisure interest:* golf. *Address:* Toyobo Co. Ltd., 2-8, Dojima Hama 2-chome, Kita-ku, Osaka 530 (Office); LOT H. 8-30 Sumiyoshi-Yamate 4 chome, Higashinada-ku, Kobe 658, Japan (Home). *Telephone:* 06-348-3248 (Office); 078-851-5211 (Home).

ITOKAWA, Hideo; Japanese aeronautic engineer; b. 20 July 1912; ed. Tokyo Univ.; Engineer, Nakajima Aircraft Co. 1935-41; Asst. Prof. of Eng. at Tokyo Univ. 1941-48, Prof. 1948-67; Exec.-Dir. Space Eng. Dept., Inst. of Industrial Science 1955-; Pres. Japanese Rocket Soc. 1956-58; Convenor Nat. Cttee. on Space Research, Japan Science Council 1956-; mem. Nat. Space Council 1960-; Deputy Dir. Inst. of Space and Aeronautical Science 1964-67; Dir. of Systems Research Inst. 1967. *Address:* 34-15, 4-chome, Matsubara, Setagaya-ku, Tokyo, Japan.

IVANOV, Anatoliy Stepanovich; Soviet author; b. 1928, Shemonaikha, Kazakhstan; ed. Univ. of Kazakhstan; mem. CPSU 1952-; first works published 1948. *Publications include:* Alka's Songs 1956, Shadows Disappear at Noon 1963, The Eternal Call, Enmity, Collected Works 1979. *Address:* U.S.S.R. Union of Writers, Ul. Vorovskogo 52, Moscow, U.S.S.R.

IVANOV, Vladimir; Bulgarian physician; b. 6 June 1923, Simeonovgrad; s. of Boris Ivanov and Maria Ivanova; m. Liliana Kirova 1948; one s.; ed. Univ. of Sofia, Acad. of Medical Sciences, Moscow and Univ. of London; Deputy Dir. Scientific Psychoneurological Inst. Sofia 1956-63; Asst. Prof. and Head Dept. of Psychiatry and Medical Psychology, Varna 1963-67, Prof. 1967-85; Deputy Rector, Higher Medical Inst. Varna, 1964-66, Rector 1966-72; Dir. Scientific Inst. of Neurology, Psychiatry and Neurosurgery, Medical Acad. Sofia and Head, First Psychiatric Clinic 1985-88; Ed.-in-Chief Neurology, Psychiatry and Neurosurgery; Adviser to Ministry of Public Health, Bulgarian Medical Acad. 1989-; several awards and medals. *Publications:* some 13 monographs. *Leisure interests:* philosophy, poetry. *Address:* Bulgarian Medical Academy, 1 Psychiatric Clinic, Sofia 1431 (Office); Praga 26, Sofia 1606, Bulgaria (Home). *Telephone:* 52-03-33 (Office); 52-46-68 (Home).

IVANOV, Yuriy Aleksandrovich; Soviet banking official (retd.); b. 1928, Moscow; ed. Moscow State Inst. of Int. Relations; Legal adviser Bd. of U.S.S.R. State bank (Gosbank) 1951-54, Deputy Man., Export Dept. 1954-60, First Deputy Chair. 1976-; mem. Bd. of External Trade Bank of U.S.S.R. 1961-, First Deputy Chair. 1964-69, Chair. 1969-87. *Address:* External Trade Bank of U.S.S.R., Kopyevsky per. 3/5, Moscow, U.S.S.R.

IVANOVA, Tatyana Georgiyevna; Soviet politician; b. 1940; mem. CPSU 1968-; ed. Moscow Univ.; Jr. Ed. 'Molodaya gvardiya'; Sr. Ed. 'Novy mir', Ed. Nauka Publ. House 1960-72; party work 1972-; Second Sec. 1977-79, First Sec. of Kalinin Regional Cttee. of CPSU (Moscow) 1979-85; Deputy Pres. Praesidium of RSFSR Supreme Soviet 1985-; cand. mem. CPSU Cen. Cttee. 1981-. *Address:* The Kremlin, Moscow, U.S.S.R.

IVANOVSKY, Gen. Yevgeniy Filippovich; Soviet army officer and military official; b. 7 March 1918, Byelorussia; m. Raisa Fyodorovna Ivanovsky 1938; two s.; ed. Mil. Acad. for Mechanization of the Soviet Army and Acad. of Gen. Staff; served in Soviet Army 1936-; mem. CPSU 1941-;

Chief of Staff, Head of a Reconnaissance Tank Corps, Commdr. of a Tank Regt. on W., Stalingrad, S.W., 1st and 2nd Byelorussian Fronts 1941–45; Chief of Staff, Commdr. of Div., First Deputy Chief of Staff of a mil. dist., First Deputy Commdr. of Moscow Mil. Dist. 1968–72; Deputy to U.S.S.R. Supreme Soviet 1970–; mem. Cen. Cttee. CPSU 1971–; C.-in-C. of Soviet Forces in G.D.R. 1973–80; Commd. Byelorussian Mil. Dist. 1980–84; C.-in-C. of Infantry 1985–89; U.S.S.R. Deputy Minister of Defence 1985–89; mem. Cen. Cttee. Byelorussian CP 1981–. *Address:* c/o Byelorussian Communist Party, Minsk, Byelorussian S.S.R.

IVANTSOV, Anatoliy Ivanovich; Soviet diplomatist; b. 11 Feb. 1922, Moscow; ed. Moscow Inst. of Railway Transport and High Diplomatic School, Ministry of Foreign Affairs, U.S.S.R.; joined Diplomatic Service 1944; First Sec., Soviet Embassy, Canada 1961–66; ranking official, Ministry of Foreign Affairs, U.S.S.R. 1966–69, 1974–79; Minister to N.Z. 1969–73, Amb. 1973–74; Amb. to Ghana 1979–84. *Address:* c/o Ministry of Foreign Affairs, Smolenskaya-Sennaya pl. 32/34, Moscow, U.S.S.R.

IVÁNYI, Pál; Hungarian politician; b. 1942, Budapest; ed. Budapest Tech. Univ.; unskilled worker, later Tech. Inspector Csepel Motorcar Works; Research engineer, Deputy Dept. Head Csepel Works 1967–76; Sec. MALÉV Hung. Airlines Party Cttee. 1976–80; Dept. Head Budapest Party Cttee. 1981–84; Dept. Head Party Cen. Cttee. Dept. of Economy 1984–86; Pres. Budapest Metropolitan Council, Mayor of Budapest 1986–88; mem. HSWP Cen. Cttee. 1987, mem. Political Cttee. 1988–, Sec. 1988–. *Address:* Central Committee of the Hungarian Socialist Workers Party, 1358 Budapest, Széchenyi rakpart 19. *Telephone:* 111-400.

IVASHUTIN, Gen. Pyotr Ivanovich; Soviet army officer; b. 18 Sept. 1909, Brest-Litovsk; mem. CPSU 1930–; in Soviet army 1931–; fought in Finno-Soviet War 1939–40, on Transcaucasian, Caucasian, Crimean, N. Caucasian, S.W. and 3rd Ukrainian Fronts 1941–45; employed in cen. apparatus, Ministry of Defence 1945–; Deputy Chief of Gen. Staff March 1963–; Chief of Main Intelligence Directorate March 1963–; rank of Gen. 1971; mem. Supreme Soviet 1950–54, 1966–; Order of Lenin, Order of October Revolution, Order of the Red Flag (four times) and other decorations. *Address:* c/o Ministry of Defence, Moscow, U.S.S.R.

IVEAGH, 3rd Earl of; Arthur Francis Benjamin Guinness; Irish brewing executive; b. 20 May 1937; m. Miranda Smiley 1963; two s. two d.; ed. Eton Coll., Trinity Coll., Cambridge and Univ. of Grenoble; Dir. Arthur Guinness Son & Co. Ltd. (now Guinness PLC) 1958, Chair. 1962–75, 1978–86, Jt. Chair. 1975–78, Pres. 1986–; Dir. Bank of Nova Scotia and several other Canadian cos.; mem. Senate 1973–77. *Leisure interest:* Irish books and bookbindings. *Address:* c/o Guinness PLC, St. James's Gate, Dublin 8, Ireland.

IVEROTH, C. Axel; Swedish business executive; b. 4 Aug. 1914, Ekerö; m. Inger Dorthea Iveroth; two s. two d.; ed. Stockholm School of Econ.; Producer, Swedish Broadcasting Corpn. 1937–41; Sec. Industrial Inst. for Econ. and Social Research 1939–44; Industrial Counsellor, Swedish Embassy, Washington 1944–45; Man. Dir. Cementa 1945–52; Chair. and Man. Dir. Cembureau (Cement Statistical and Tech. Asscn.) 1949–57; Dir.-Gen. Fed. of Swedish Industries 1957–77, Vice-Chair. 1977; Chair. Int. Council of Swedish Industry 1977–81; Ed.-in-Chief Industria 1946, Swedish-American News Exchange 1952–66; Chair. and Founder Industrial Council for Social and Econ. Studies 1948–60; Chair. Advisory Bd. European Productivity Agency, Paris 1954–56; Chair. Swedish Productivity Council 1957–; Bd. mem. Gen. Export Asscn. of Sweden 1961, Chair. and Exec. Bd. mem. 1971–81; Chair. Sweden-America Foundation 1970–88; Chair. Integration Cttee. of European Industrial Feds. 1958–; Sec.-Gen. Business and Industry Advisory Cttee. to OECD (BIAC) 1962–63, Vice-Chair. 1974–82; Chair. Swedish Nat. Cttee. of the European League for EEC Co-operation 1965–; Vice-Chair. Union des Industries de la Communauté européenne, Brussels 1977–79; mem. Bd. Royal Swedish Acad. of Eng. Sciences 1957–; Chair. Securitas Int. AB 1950–83, Banque nat. de Paris, Sweden 1986–88, AIM AB 1985, Sweden-Japan Foundation 1979–87, Chair. Asscn. of Swedish Chambers of Commerce Abroad 1979–; Int. Adviser Swedish Builders Group, Japan 1987–; Knight Commdr. of the Royal Order of Vasa (Sweden), Hon. C.B.E., Officier Ordre de la Couronne (Belgium), Officier, Légion d'honneur, Commdr. Ordine al Merito della Repubblica Italiana, Order of the White Rose of Finland. *Publications:* Handicraft and Small Industries in Sweden 1943, The Good Society 1980; numerous articles on politics and economics in press and professional journals. *Leisure interests:* angling, farming. *Address:* Gräsmarö, 610 42 Gryt, Sweden.

IVERSEN, Leslie Lars, PH.D., F.R.S.; British scientist; b. 31 Oct. 1937; s. of Svend and Anna Caia Iversen; m. Susan Diana (née Kibble) 1961; one s. one d. (one s. deceased); ed. Cambridge, Harkness Fellow, U.S.A.; with Nat. Inst. of Mental Health and Dept. of Neurobiology, Harvard Medical School 1964–66; Locke Research Fellow of Royal Soc., Dept. of Pharmacology, Cambridge 1967–71, Dir. MRC Neurochemical Pharmacology Unit 1971–82; Exec. Dir. Merck, Sharp and Dohme Neuroscience Research Centre 1982–; Fellow Trinity Coll., Cambridge 1964; Foreign Assoc. N.A.S. 1986. *Publications:* The Uptake and Storage of Noradrenaline in Sympathetic Nerves (with S. D. Iversen) 1967, Behavioural Pharmacology 1975. *Leisure interests:* reading, gardening. *Address:* Merck, Sharp and Dohme Research Laboratories, Neuroscience Research Centre, Terlings Park,

Eastwick Road, Harlow, Essex, CM20 2QR, England. *Telephone:* (0279) 440160.

IVES, Burl Icle Ivanhoe; American actor and singer; b. 14 June 1909, Hunt City, Ill.; m. 1st Helen Ives 1946, 2nd Dorothy Koster 1971; one s.; began stage career 1938; has appeared in the musicals: The Boys from Syracuse, I Married An Angel, Heavenly Express, This is the Army, Sing Out Sweet Land, Knickerbocker Holiday, Paint Your Wagon, Show Boat; the stage plays: The Man Who Came to Dinner, She Stoops to Conquer, Cat on a Hot Tin Roof, Joshua Beene and God; the films: Smokey, Green Grass of Wyoming, Station West, So Dear to my Heart, Sierra, East of Eden, The Power and the Prize, Desire Under the Elms, The Big Country, The Everglades, Cat on a Hot Tin Roof, The Day of the Outlaw, Our Man in Havana, The Spiral Road, Summer Magic, The Brass Bottle, Mediterranean Holiday, Ensign Pulver, Pt. Barnum's Rocket to the Moon; American Motion Picture Award for best supporting actor (The Big Country) 1959 and many other awards; resumed concert career at Colo. Springs 1974; since then has toured U.S.A., U.K., Israel, Australia and N.Z.; numerous recordings; Hon. LL.D. (Fairleigh Dickinson Coll., Teaneck, N.J.) and many other hon. degrees. *Publications:* The Wayfaring Stranger, The Wayfaring Stranger's Notebook, Sailing on a Very Fine Day, Burl Ives' Tales of America; ed. The Burl Ives Song Book, The Burl Ives Book of Sea Songs, The Burl Ives Book of Irish Songs, America's Musical Heritage (six records with sing-along book), Song in America—A New Song Book, Albad the Oaf. *Leisure interests:* sailing, camping. *Address:* Beakel and Jennings, 427 North Canon Drive, Suite 205, Beverley Hills, Calif. 90210, U.S.A.

IVORY, James Francis, M.F.A.; American film director; b. 7 June 1928, Berkeley, Calif.; s. of the late Edward Patrick Ivory and Hallie Millicent De Loney; ed. Univs. of Oregon and Southern California; began to work independently as a film maker 1956; dir., writer and cameraman in first films; Partner (with Indian producer Ismail Merchant (q.v.)) Merchant Ivory Productions 1962–; has collaborated on screenplay of numerous films with author Ruth Prawer Jhabvala (q.v.); Guggenheim Fellow 1974. *Films:* documentaries: Venice, Theme and Variations 1957, The Sword and the Flute 1959, The Delhi Way 1964; feature films: The Householder 1963, Shakespeare Wallah 1965, The Guru 1969, Bombay Talkie 1970, Savages 1972, The Wild Party 1975, Roseland 1977, The Europeans 1979, Quartet 1981, Heat and Dust 1983, The Bostonians 1984, A Room with a View 1986, Maurice 1987, Mr and Mrs Bridge 1989, Slaves of New York 1989; TV films: Adventures of a Brown Man in Search of Civilisation 1971, Autobiography of a Princess 1975 (also published as a book 1975), Hullabaloo over Georgie and Bonnie's Pictures 1978, The Five Forty Eight 1979, Jane Austen in Manhattan 1980. *Leisure interest:* looking at pictures. *Address:* Merchant Ivory Productions, 250 W. 57th Street, New York, N.Y. 10019; Patroon Street, Claveack, New York 12513, U.S.A. *Telephone:* (212) 759-3694, (518) 851-7808 (Home).

IWAI, Akira; Japanese railwayman and trade unionist; b. 1922; ed. Matsumoto High Elementary School, Nagano Prefecture; Kamisuwa Engine Section, Nat. Railway 1937–42; Mil. Service 1942–46; Engine Driver, Kamisuwa Engine Section, Nat. Railway 1946; Chief Joint Struggle Dept., Nat. Railway Workers' Union 1950–51, Chief of Planning Dept. 1951–55; Sec.-Gen., Gen. Council of Trade Unions of Japan (SOHYO) 1955; Lenin Prize 1970. *Publications:* We, Born in Taisho Era, The Workers, Diary of a General Secretary. *Address:* Sohyo Kaikan, 8-2 Shiba Park, Minato-ku, Tokyo, Japan.

IWAMURA, Eiro; Japanese engineer; b. 13 Sept. 1915; m.; three s.; ed. Imperial Univ., Tokyo; joined Kawasaki Dockyard Co. Ltd. (now Kawasaki Steel Corpn. 1983–), Dir. Bd. and Asst. Gen. Supt. Mizushima Works 1966–69, Man. Dir. Tech. Dept., Tech. Devt. Dept., Overseas Tech. Assistance Dept. and Order Center 1969–73, Sr. Man. Dir. Tech. Dept., Subcontract Planning Dept. 1973–75; Exec. Vice-Pres., Gen. Supt. Chiba Works and Welding Rod and Iron Powder Plant 1975–77; Pres. Kawasaki Steel Corpn. 1977–82, Chair. 1982–, Chair. Cttee. on Environment and Safety, Fed. of Econ. Orgs. 1982–, Vice-Chair. Kansai Econ. Fed. 1982–. *Leisure interests:* classical music, golf and "Go" game. *Address:* Kawasaki Steel Corporation, Hibiya Kokusai Building, 2-3 Uchisaiwaicho 2-chome, Chiyoda-ku, Tokyo 100, Japan.

IWAN, Dafydd, B.ARCH.; Welsh politician, singer-composer and record company manager; b. 24 Aug. 1943, Brynaman, Wales; s. of Rev. Gerallt and Elizabeth J. Jones; m. Marion Thomas 1968; two s. one d.; ed. Aman Valley Grammar School, Ysgol Ty Tan Domen, Y Bala, Univ. Coll. of Wales, Aberystwyth and Welsh School of Arch., Cardiff; f. Sain (Recordiau) Cyf (now Wales' leading record co.) 1969; Man. Dir. 1983–; f. Tai Gwynedd Housing Asscn. 1971; founder-trustee, Nant Gwrtheyrn Language Centre 1975; mem. Nat. Eisteddfod of Wales Council; Chair. Welsh Language Soc. 1968–71; parl. cand. 1974, 1983, 1984; Chair. Plaid Cymru (Nationalist Party of Wales) 1982–84, Vice-Pres. 1984–; Gold Disc for services to Welsh music; hon. mem. Gorsedd of Bards for services to Welsh language. *Publications:* Dafydd Iwan (autobiog.) 1982, 100 O Ganeuon (collection of songs) 1983. *Leisure interests:* composing songs, sketching, reading. *Address:* SAIN, Llandwrog, Caernarfon, Gwynedd, LL54 5TG (Office). *Telephone:* (0286) 831-111 (Office).

IYANAGA, Shokichi; Japanese professor of mathematics; b. 2 April 1906; s. of Katsumi Iyanaga and Kiyono (née Shidachi) Iyanaga; m. Sumiko Kikuchi 1936; three s. one d.; ed. First High School, Univ. of Tokyo and Athénée Français, Tokyo; Assoc. Prof., Univ. of Tokyo 1935–42, Prof. 1942–67, Prof. Emer. 1967–; Visiting Prof., Chicago Univ. 1960–61; Dean Faculty of Science, Univ. of Tokyo 1965–67; Prof., Gakushuin Univ. 1967–77; Assoc. Prof., Univ. of Nancy 1967–68; Pres. Math. Soc. of Japan, Int. Comm. on Math. Instruction 1975–78, Vice-Pres. Council of Admin. Maison franco-japonaise 1978–; mem. Science Council of Japan 1948–58, Exec. Cttee. Int. Math. Union 1952–55, Japan Acad. 1978–; Chevalier, Ordre Palmes Académiques, Officier Légion d'honneur, Order of Rising Sun (2nd Class) 1976. *Publications:* Introduction to Geometry 1968, Theory of Numbers 1969, Encyclopaedic Dictionary of Mathematics (editor in chief) 1954. *Leisure interests:* literature and western music. *Address:* 12-4 Otsuka 6-chome, Bunkyo-ku, Tokyo 112, Japan. *Telephone:* (03) 945-5977.

IZMEROV, Nikolay Fedotovich, M.D.; Soviet doctor; b. 19 Dec. 1927, Frunze, Kirghizia; ed. Tashkent Medical School and Moscow Cen. Inst. for Advanced Medical Training; worked as doctor in Khavast rural areas, Tashkent Dist.; Postgraduate training, Moscow 1952–53; Sr. Insp. U.S.S.R. Ministry of Health 1953–55; Postgraduate training (Municipal Hygiene) 1955–58; doctor in Moscow City Sanitary Epidemiological Station 1956–59; Deputy Dir. (Int. Health), Dept. of External Relations, U.S.S.R. Ministry of Health 1960–62; Vice-Minister of Health of R.S.F.S.R., Moscow and Chief Sanitary Insp. 1962–64; Asst. Dir.-Gen. WHO 1964–71; Dir. Inst. of Industrial Hygiene and Occupational Diseases of the U.S.S.R. Acad. of Medical Sciences 1971–. *Address:* Institute of Industrial Hygiene and Occupational Diseases of the U.S.S.R. Academy of Medical Sciences, 31 Budionovsky proezd, Moscow 105275, U.S.S.R.

IZRAEL, Yuri Antonovich, DR. PHYS.-MATH. SC.; Soviet geophysicist and state official; b. 1930; ed. Central Asian State Univ.; engineer, sr. engineer, research assoc., Geophysics Inst. of U.S.S.R., U.S.S.R. Acad. of Sciences 1953–63; mem. CPSU 1955–; Deputy Dir., Dir. of Inst. of Applied Physics of Main Admin. of Hydrometeorological Service and Environmental Control Service of U.S.S.R. Council of Ministers 1963–70; First Deputy Chief of Control Service 1970–74, Chief 1974–78; Prof. 1973; Corresp. mem. U.S.S.R. Acad. of Sciences 1974–; Chair. of U.S.S.R. State Cttee. for Environmental Control 1978–; Deputy to Supreme Soviet 1979–; mem. of Cen. Auditing Comm. 1981–; State prizes. *Address:* The Kremlin, Moscow, U.S.S.R.

IZZIDDIN, Ibrahim, B.A.; Jordanian government official and diplomatist; b. 3 Dec. 1934, Beirut, Lebanon; s. of Yousef Izziddin and Rushdiah Fakhuri; m. Nour Janbek 1973; ed. American Univ. of Beirut; served in Ministry of Communications, Prime Minister's Office, and Press Section of Ministry of Foreign Affairs 1955–58; Deputy Dir. Book Publishers, Beirut 1958–65; Dir. of Foreign Press, Ministry of Information 1965–68, Under-Sec. 1971–75; Press Sec. to H.M. King Hussein (q.v.) 1968–70; Dir. Public Relations for Alia (Royal Jordanian Airlines) 1970–71; Amb. to Switzerland 1975–77, to Fed. Repub. of Germany 1977–78, to U.K. 1978–83, to U.S.A. 1983–85; Head Civil Service Comm. 1985–; Order of Istiqlal (Second Class), Cedar of Lebanon. *Address:* c/o Ministry of Foreign Affairs, Amman, Jordan.

IZZO, Lucio; Italian economist and financial executive; b. 5 April 1932, Rome; m. Marga Berg; two d.; ed. Univ. of Oxford and M.I.T.; Econ. Research Dept., Bank of Italy 1958–60, 1962–63; Rockefeller Fellow, Dept. of Econs., M.I.T. 1960–62; Asst. Prof. of Econs., Univ. of Rome 1963–66; Assoc. Prof., then Prof. of Econs., Univ. of Siena 1966–74; Visiting Prof. of Econs., L.S.E. 1971–72; Prof. of Econs., Univ. of Rome 1975–; Econ. Adviser to Minister of the Budget 1974–78, to Minister of the Treasury 1980–82; Vice-Pres. and Vice-Chair. Bd. of Dirs. European Investment Bank (EIB) 1982–; Italian Rep. OECD Working Party 3, Econ. Policy Cttee. 1976–81; mem. American Econ. Assen., American Finance Assen., Econometric Soc.; Pres. of Italy's Gold Medal for studies in field of public finance 1978. *Address:* European Investment Bank, 100 boulevard Konrad Adenauer, L-2950 Luxembourg. *Telephone:* 43 79-1.

J

JABŁOŃSKI, Henryk, PH.D.; Polish historian and politician; b. 27 Dec. 1909, Waliszew; s. of Władysław Jabłoński and Pelagia Jabłońska; m. Jadwiga Wierzbicka 1946; one s. one d.; ed. Univ. of Warsaw; Prof. Acad. of Political Sciences, Warsaw 1946-50, Warsaw Univ. 1950-; mem. Nat. Council 1945-47, Seym 1947-; Deputy Minister of Educ. 1947-53; Sec. Polish Socialist Party 1946-48; mem. Cen. Cttee. Polish United Workers' Party 1948-81, 1986-, Deputy mem. Political Bureau 1970-71, mem. 1971-81; Minister of Higher Educ. 1965-66; Minister of Educ. and Higher Educ. 1966-72; Pres. Council of State (Head of State) 1972-85, Chair. Seym Nat. Defence Comm. 1985-; Maj.-Gen. 1988; corresp. mem. Polish Acad. of Sciences 1952-56, mem. 1956-, Gen. Sec. 1955-65, Vice-Pres. 1966-71; mem. Presidium of All-Polish Cttee. of Nat. Unity Front 1972-76, Chair. 1976-83; Chair. of the Supreme Council of the Asscn. of Fighters for Freedom and Democracy 1983-; mem. Acad. of Romanian Socialist Repub. 1965-; mem. Czechoslovak. Acad. of Sciences 1965-; Foreign mem. U.S.S.R. Acad. of Sciences 1966-; mem. Mongolian Acad. of Sciences 1975-; corresp. mem. Mexican Acad. of History 1979-; Hon. L.H.D. (Moscow), Dr. h.c. (Higher School of Econs., Wrocław) 1972, (Roland Eotvos Univ.) 1973, (Łódź) 1975, (Wrocław) 1975, (Jagellonian Univ., Cracow) 1980, (Higher School of Pedagogics, Cracow) 1985; State Prize (2nd class) 1955, (1st class) 1964, Special State Prize 1979, Grand Cross, Order of Polonia Restituta 1974, Order of Banner of Labour (First Class) 1959, Order of the Builders of People's Poland 1964, Order of Friendship of Nations, Grand Croix Légion d'honneur, Great Ribbon, Order of Leopold (Belgium) and numerous other orders and decorations. *Publications:* The Military Criminal Court in 1794 1935, Aleksander Waszkowski—Warsaw's Last Military Chief in the Insurrection of 1863-64 1937, Public Opinion, Parliament and the Press, At the Origins of the Present Day 1947, Polish National Autonomy in the Ukraine in 1917-18, 1948, The Policy of the Polish Socialist Party during the First World War 1958, The Birth of the Second Republic 1918-19 1962, School, Teacher, Education 1972, Independence and National Traditions 1978, International Importance of Polish Fights for National Independence in XVIII and XIX Centuries 1978, Selected Works Vols. I-III 1986, Vols. IV-VI 1987. *Leisure interests:* reading, walking. *Address:* ul. Klonowa 4, 00-591 Warsaw, Poland. *Telephone:* 29-71-70.

JACHACZ, Bogdan, M.A.; Polish journalist and politician; b. 14 Dec. 1941, Zemborzyce; s. of Jan Jachacz and Wanda Jachacz; m. Barbara Jachacz 1969; one s.; ed. Nicolaus Copernicus Univ., Toruń; active mem. youth orgs.: Polish Youth Union 1955-56, Socialist Youth Union 1959-64, Polish Students' Asscn. 1959-73; Head of Section students' weekly ITD, Warsaw 1965-69, sub-ed. 1969-72, Ed.-in-Chief 1972-75; sub-ed. daily Express Wieczorny, Warsaw 1976-80, First Sub-ed. 1980-81; Deputy Govt. Press Spokesman and Head, Press Office of Council of Ministers 1981-82; Head of Press, Radio and TV Dept., Cen. Cttee. of Polish United Workers' Party (PZPR) 1982-86, Head of Propaganda Dept. 1986; Pres. and Ed.-in-Chief Polish Press Agency PAP (Polska Agencja Prasowa) 1986-; Deputy Chair. Council of Workers' Publishing Co-operative Prasa-Książka-Ruch 1982-86; mem. PZPR 1962-; mem. Press Council attached to Chair. of Council of Ministers; Gold Cross of Merit 1973, Officer's Cross, Order of Polonia Restituta 1985 and other decorations. *Leisure interests:* films, music, literature, horsemanship. *Address:* Polish Press Agency PAP, Al. Jerozolimskie 7, 00-950 Warsaw (Office); ul. Pięciolinii 10/20, Warsaw, Poland (Home). *Telephone:* 213439 (Office).

JACK, Kenneth Henderson, F.R.S.; British professor of applied crystal chemistry; b. 12 Oct. 1918, North Shields, Northumberland (now Tyne and Wear); s. of late John Henderson Jack, and Emily (née Cozens); m. Alfreda Hughes 1942 (died 1974); two s.; ed. Tynemouth Municipal High School, King's Coll., Univ. of Durham, Fitzwilliam Coll., Univ. of Cambridge; Experimental Officer Ministry of Supply 1940-41; Lecturer in Chem., Univ. of Durham 1941-45, 1949-52, 1953-57; Sr. Scientific Officer British Iron and Steel Research Asscn. 1945-49; Research at Cavendish Lab., Cambridge 1947-49; Research Engineer Westinghouse Electrical Corpn., Pittsburgh, Pa., U.S.A. 1952-53; Research Dir. Thermal Syndicate Ltd., Wallsend 1957-64; Prof. of Applied Crystal Chem. Univ. of Newcastle-upon-Tyne 1964-84, Prof. Emer. 1984-; Consultant Cookson Group PLC 1986-; Dir. Wolfson Research Group for High-Strength Materials 1970-84; Fellow American Ceramic Soc. 1984; hon. mem. Soc. Française de Métallurgie 1984; numerous awards and prizes including Prince of Wales Award for Industrial Innovation and Production 1984, Royal Soc. Armourers and Brasiers Award 1988. *Publications:* papers on solid state chem., crystallography, metallurgy, ceramic science and glass tech. in scientific journals and conference proceedings. *Leisure interests:* grandchildren, walking. *Address:* Cookson House, Willington Quay, Wallsend, Tyne and Wear, NE28 6UQ (Office); 147 Broadway, Cullercoats, North Shields, Tyne and Wear, NE30 3TA, England. *Telephone:* (091) 2622211 (Office); 091-2573664 (Home).

JACKLIN, Tony, O.B.E.; British golfer; b. 7 July 1944, Scunthorpe; s. of Arthur David Jacklin; m. Vivien Jacklin 1966 (died 1988); three c.; Lincolnshire Open champion 1961; professional 1962-; won British Asst. Profes-

sionals' title 1965; won Dunlop Masters 1967, 1973; first British player to win British Open since 1951 1969; U.S. Open Champion 1970; first British player to win U.S. Open since 1920 and first since 1900 to hold U.S. and British Open titles simultaneously; Greater Greensboro Open champion, U.S.A. 1968, 1972; won Italian Open 1973, German Open 1979, Venezuelan Open 1979, Jersey Open 1981, British P.G.A. champion 1982 and 15 major tournaments in various parts of the world; played in eight Ryder Cup matches and four times for England in World Cup; Capt. of 1983 G.B. and Europe Ryder Cup Team; Capt. of victorious European Ryder Cup Team 1985 (first win for Europe since 1957), 1987; BBC TV golf commentator; moved to Sotogrande, Spain from Jersey Oct. 1983, Commr. of Golf, Las Aves Club, Sotogrande 1983-; Hon. Life Pres. British Professional Golfers' Asscn. *Publications:* Golf With Tony Jacklin 1969, The Price of Success 1979, Jacklin's Golfing Secrets (with Peter Dobereiner), The First Forty Years (with Renton Laidlaw) 1985. *Address:* c/o International Management Group, The Pier House, Strand on the Green, Chiswick, London, W4 3NN, England; Las Aves Club, Sotogrande, Costa del Sol, Spain. *Telephone:* 01-486 7171.

JACKSON, Betty, M.B.E.; British couturier; b. 24 June 1949, Lancashire; d. of Arthur Jackson and Phyllis Gertrude Jackson; m. David Cotton 1985; one s. one d.; ed. Bacup and Rawtenstall Grammar School and Birmingham Coll. of Art and Design; Chief Designer Querum 1975-81; f. Betty Jackson Ltd. 1981, Dir. 1981-; Designer of the Year 1985, Royal Designer for Industry (Royal Soc. of Arts) 1988. *Leisure interests:* reading, listening to music. *Address:* 33 Tottenham Street, London, W1 (Office); 30 Ashchurch Park Villas, London, W12, England (Home). *Telephone:* 01-631-1010 (Office); 01-743 6864 (Home).

JACKSON, Daryl Sanders, DIP.ARCH., B.ARCH., F.R.A.I.A., A.R.I.B.A.; Australian architect; b. 7 Feb. 1937, Clunes, Victoria; s. of Cecil John and Doreen May Jackson; m. Kay Jackson 1960; one s. three d.; ed. Wesley Coll., Melbourne, Royal Melbourne Inst. of Tech., Univ. of Melbourne; Asst., Edwards, Madigan and Torzillo, Sydney 1959, Don Henry Fulton, Melbourne 1960, Chamberlin, Powell and Bon, London 1961-63, Paul Rudolph, New Haven, Conn. 1963-64, Skidmore, Owings and Merrill, San Francisco 1964; Partner, Daryl Jackson, Evan Walker Architects, Melbourne 1965-79; Dir. Daryl Jackson Pty. Ltd. Architects 1979-, Dir. Daryl Jackson Basil Carter Pty. Ltd., Sydney 1982-; ; Dir. RAIA Victorian Chapter Housing Service 1966-69; mem. RAIA Victorian Chapter Council 1967-77, Public Service Cttee. 1969-72, Monash Univ. Council 1973-77, Victorian Tapestry Workshop Cttee. 1975-, Architectural Asscn., London 1960-75; Trustee, Nat. Gallery of Victoria 1982-; numerous architectural and design awards. *Publications:* numerous articles and papers. *Major works:* Y.W.C.A. Community Resource Centre, Suva, Fiji 1973, Princes Hill High School, Melbourne 1973, Methodist Ladies' Coll., Library Resource Centre, Melbourne 1973, City Edge Housing Devt., Melbourne 1976, School of Music, Canberra 1976, Asscn. for Modern Educ. School, Canberra 1977, Emu Ridge Govt. Housing Devt., Canberra 1978, School of Art, Canberra 1980, McLachlan Offices, Canberra 1980, Army Apprentices Training School, Mess and Recreation Centre, Bonegilla 1981, The Walter and Eliza Hall Inst. of Medical Research, Melbourne 1982, Nat. Sports Centre, Swimming Training Hall, Bruce, A.C.T. 1982, Australian Film and TV School, Sydney 1983, State Insurance Office, Melbourne 1984. *Address:* 35 Little Bourke Street, Melbourne, Vic. 3000, Australia.

JACKSON, Edwin Sydney, F.S.A., F.C.I.A., B.COM.; Canadian financial executive; b. 17 May 1922, Regina, Sask.; s. of late Edwin and Dorothy Hazel (née Bell) Jackson; m. Nancy Joyce (née Stovel) 1948; three d.; ed. Univ. of Manitoba; joined Mfrs. Life Insurance Co. 1948, Pres. and CEO 1972-, Chair. 1985-; Pres. Canadian Inst. of Actuaries 1966-67; Chair. Life Office Man. Asscn. 1982-83; Chair. Canadian Life and Health Insurance Asscn. 1977-78; Dir. American Coll. of Life Insurance; Dir. Manufacturers Life Capital Corpn. Inc.; mem. Soc. of Actuaries; Past Pres. Ont. Div. Canadian Arthritis and Rheumatism Soc.; Dir. Canadian Centre for Philanthropy. *Leisure interests:* skiing, curling, golf. *Address:* Manufacturers Life Insurance Co., 200 Bloor Street East, Toronto, Ont. M4W 1E5; 101 Stratford Crescent, Toronto, Ont. M4N 1C7, Canada. *Telephone:* (416) 926-0100 (Office).

JACKSON, Eric Stead, C.B., M.A.; British civil servant; b. 22 Aug. 1909, Bradford; s. of E. S. Jackson; m. Yvonne Renée Doria de Bretigny 1938; one s. one d.; ed. Corpus Christi Coll., Oxford; on Air Ministry Staff 1932-40; Private Sec. to Minister of Aircraft Production 1942, to Minister Resident in Washington 1943; Dir.-Gen. Aircraft Branch, Control Comm., Germany 1945; Deputy Pres. Econ. Sub-Comm., Berlin 1947; British Head of Del. from Western Zone of Germany to OEEC, Paris 1948; Under-Sec. Ministry of Supply 1950; Dir.-Gen. Atomic Weapons, Ministry of Supply 1956-59; Under-Sec. Ministry of Aviation 1959-67, Ministry of Tech. 1967-70, Dept. of Trade and Industry 1970-71; mem. British Film Fund Agency 1971-88. *Address:* 10 Ditchley Road, Charlbury, Oxon., England. *Telephone:* 810682.

JACKSON, Francis Alan, D.MUS., F.R.C.O.; British organist and composer; b. 2 Oct. 1917, Malton, Yorks.; s. of William Altham Jackson and Eveline May (née Suddaby); m. Priscilla Procter 1950; two s. one d.; ed. York Minster Choir School and with Sir Edward Bairstow; Organist Malton Parish Church 1933–40; war service with 9th Lancers in N. Africa and Italy 1940–46; Asst. Organist York Minster 1946, Master of the Music 1946–82; Conductor York Musical Soc. 1947–82, York Symphony Orchestra 1947–80; now freelance organist and composer; published works include Symphony in D minor 1957, Organ Concerto 1985, Eclogue for piano and organ 1987, organ music including 4 sonatas, church music, songs and monodramas; Hon. D. Univ. (York) 1983; Hon. Fellow Royal School of Church Music, Westminster Choir Coll., Princeton, N.J., U.S.A., Royal Northern Coll. of Music; Order of St. William of York 1983. *Leisure interests:* gardening, art and architecture. *Address:* Nether Garth, Acklam, Malton, North Yorkshire, YO17 9RG and 3/20 St. Andrewgate, York, YO1 2BR, England. *Telephone:* (065 385) 395 Burythorpe; (0904) 20632 (York).

JACKSON, Glenda, C.B.E.; British actress; b. 9 May 1936, Birkenhead, Cheshire; d. of Harry and Joan Jackson; m. Roy Hodges 1958 (divorced 1976); one s.; ed. Royal Acad. of Dramatic Art; fmr. mem. Royal Shakespeare Co. where roles included Ophelia in Hamlet and Charlotte Corday in Marat/Sade (in London and New York); played Queen Elizabeth I in television series Elizabeth R; Pres., Play Matters (fmrly Toy Libraries Asscn.) 1976–; Dir. United British Artists 1983–; Hon. D.Litt (Liverpool) 1978; Hon. Fellow, Liverpool Polytechnic 1987; Acad. Award ("Oscar") for Women in Love 1971, for A Touch of Class 1974. *Plays include:* Marat/Sade, New York and Paris 1965, The Investigation 1965, Hamlet 1965, US 1966, Three Sisters 1967, Collaborators 1973, The Maids 1974, Hedda Gabler 1975, The White Devil 1976, Antony and Cleopatra 1978, Rose 1980, Strange Interlude 1984, Phaedra 1984, 1985, Across from the Garden of Allah 1986, Strange Interlude 1986, The House of Bernarda Alba 1986, Macbeth 1988. *Films include:* Marat/Sade 1966, Negatives 1968, Women in Love 1969, The Music Lovers 1970, Sunday, Bloody Sunday 1971, The Boy Friend 1971, Mary, Queen of Scots 1971, The Triple Echo 1972, Bequest to the Nation 1972, A Touch of Class 1973, The Romantic Englishwoman 1975, The Tempter 1975, The Incredible Sarah 1976, The Abbess of Crewe 1976, Stevie 1977, Hedda 1977, House Calls 1978, The Class of Miss McMichael 1978, Lost and Found 1979, Hopscotch 1980, The Return of the Soldier 1982, Giro City 1982, Summit Conference 1982, Great and Small 1983, And Nothing But the Truth 1984, Turtle Diary 1985, Beyond Therapy 1985, Business as Usual 1986, Salome's Last Dance 1988, The Rainbow 1989. *Television appearances include:* Sakharov 1984. *Leisure interests:* gardening, reading, listening to music. *Address:* c/o Crouch Associates, 59 Frith Street, London, W.1, England.

JACKSON, Gordon Cameron, O.B.E.; British actor; b. 19 Dec. 1923, Glasgow, Scotland; s. of Thomas Jackson and Margaret Fletcher; m. Rona Anderson 1951; two s.; ed. Hillhead High School, Glasgow; film debut in Foreman Went to France 1941. *Films include:* Tunes of Glory 1960, Mutiny on the Bounty 1961, The Great Escape 1962, The Ipcress File 1964, The Prime of Miss Jean Brodie 1968, Hamlet 1969, Scrooge 1970, Kidnapped 1971, Golden Rendezvous 1976, The Medusa Touch 1977, The Shooting Party 1984, Gunpowder 1985, The Whistle Blower 1985, Dangerous Love 1988. *Theatre includes:* Moby Dick 1955, Macbeth 1966, Hedda Gabler 1970, Veterans 1972, Twelfth Night 1976, Death Trap 1981, Cards on the Table 1982, Mass Appeal 1982. *Television appearances include:* Upstairs, Downstairs (Variety Club Award 1975, Emmy Award, U.S.A. 1976) 1970–75, The Professionals 1977–81, A Town Like Alice 1980 (Australian Logie Award 1981), Masks of Death 1984, My Brother Tom (Australia) 1986, Noble House 1987, Look to the Lady 1988, Winslow Boy 1988. *Leisure interest:* listening to Mozart. *Address:* c/o ICM Ltd., 388 Oxford Street, London, W1N 9HE, England. *Telephone:* 01-629 8080.

JACKSON, Rev. Jesse Louis; American clergyman and civic leader; b. 8 Oct. 1941, Greenville, N. Carolina; s. of Charles Henry and Helen Jackson; m. Jacqueline Lavinia Brown 1964; three s. two d.; ed. Univ. of Illinois, Illinois Agricultural and Tech. Coll., Chicago Theological Seminary; ordained to Ministry Baptist Church 1968; active Black Coalition for United Community Action 1969; Co-Founder Operation Breadbasket S. Christian Leadership Conf.; Co-ordinating Council Community Orgs., Chicago 1966, Nat. Dir. 1966–77; Founder and Exec. Dir. Operation PUSH (People United to Save Humanity), Chicago 1971–; unsuccessful cand. for Democratic nomination for U.S. Presidency 1983–84, 1987–88; Pres. Award Nat. Medical Asscn. 1969; Humanitarian Father of the Year Award Nat. Father's Day Cttee. 1971. *Address:* 930 E. 50th Street, Chicago, Ill. 60615, U.S.A.

JACKSON, Laura (Riding) (see Riding, Laura (Jackson)).

JACKSON, Michael Joseph; American singer; b. 29 Aug. 1958, Gary, Ind.; s. of Joseph W. and Katherine E. (Scruse) Jackson; ed. privately; lead singer, Jackson-Five (group now called Jacksons) 1969; records for Epic Records; recordings include Off The Wall 1979, Thriller (listed in Guinness Book of Records as the most successful LP in record history) 1982; appeared in film The Wiz 1978, Moonwalker 1988 and has made numerous television appearances; performed at Silver Jubilee of H.M. Queen Elizabeth II 1977; leader of Jackson's US Tour; recipient of gold and platinum record awards. *Publication:* Moonwalk (autobiog.) 1988.

Address: c/o Ziffren, Brittenham and Gullen, 2049 Century Park E., Suite 2350, Los Angeles, Calif. 90067, U.S.A.

JACKSON, Rashleigh Esmond; Guyanese diplomatist; b. 12 Jan. 1929, New Amsterdam, Berbice; m.; two s. two d.; ed. Queen's Coll., Georgetown, Univ. Coll., Leicester, England, Columbia Univ., New York.; entered public service 1948; Master, Queen's Coll. 1957; Principal Asst. Sec., Ministry of Foreign Affairs 1965, Perm. Sec. 1969–73; Perm. Rep. to UN 1973–78; Minister for Foreign Affairs 1978–; Pres. UN Council for Namibia 1974. *Address:* Ministry of Foreign Affairs, Georgetown, Guyana.

JACKSON, Commdr. Sir Robert Gillman Allen, A.C., K.C.V.O., Kt., C.M.G., O.B.E.(MIL.); Australian international administrator and consultant; b. 8 Nov. 1911, Melbourne, Australia; m. Barbara Ward, Baroness of Lodsworth (died 1981); one s.; Royal Australian Navy 1929–37; Royal Navy 1937–41; Dir.-Gen. Middle East Supply Centre and Prin. Adviser to War Cabinet Minister 1942–45; H.M. Treasury 1945–; Sr. Deputy Dir. UNRRA 1945–47; Asst. Sec.-Gen. for Co-ordination in UN 1948; Perm. Sec. Ministry of Nat. Devt., Australia 1950–52; Adviser to Govts. of India and Pakistan on Devt. Plans 1952–62; Chair. Preparatory Comm. for Volta River Project, Gold Coast 1953–56; Chair. Devt. Comm., Ghana 1957–63; Adviser to Pres. of Liberia 1961–75; Sr. Consultant UN Special Fund 1962–65, UN Devt. Programme 1966–68; mem. of and Consultant to Volta River Authority, Ghana 1962–; mem. Comm. on Mekong Project 1961–77; Adviser to Planning Comm., Govt. of India 1963; Commr. in charge, Survey of UN Devt. Org. 1968–71; Consultant to McKinsey and Co. 1970–; Under Sec.-Gen. UN Relief Operation in Bangladesh 1972–75; Under Sec.-Gen. in charge of UN Humanitarian Operations on Sub-Continent 1973–77; UN Co-ordinator for Assistance to Zambia 1973–77, to Indo-China 1975–77, to Cape Verde 1975–77, to São Tomé and Príncipe 1977; Special Adviser to Admin. of UNDP 1978–79; Counsellor to Interim Mekong Cttee. 1978–; Survey of UNIDO country representation 1979; Special Rep. of the Sec.-Gen. and Under-Sec.-Gen. in charge of UN system Humanitarian Operations arising out of developments in Kampuchea 1979–84; Under Sec.-Gen. and Sr. Adviser to the UN 1984–87; Chair. Global Broadcasting Foundation, Washington, D.C. 1987–; mem. IUCN Comm. on Govt. Policy, Law and Admin.; mem. Cttee. Fédération Mondiale des Villes Jumelées-Cités Unies; mem. Dag Hammarskjold Foundation; services recognized by various govts. in Europe, Asia and Africa; Trustee Inter-Action (UK) 1986–; Chisholm Memorial Lecture, WHO 1986, Brunel Memorial Lecture MIT 1987; Hon. LL.D. (Syracuse). *Publications:* An International Development Authority 1955, Report on the Volta River Project 1957, The Capacity of the United Nations Development System 1969, Survey of the United Nations System and Investment 1980. *Leisure interests:* deep sea fishing, preservation of tigers. *Address:* c/o United Nations, New York, N.Y. 10017, U.S.A.; Palais des Nations, Geneva, Switzerland.

JACKSON, Ronald Gordon, A.K., B.COM., F.A.S.A., F.A.I.M.; Australian business executive; b. 5 May 1924, Brisbane; s. of Rupert Vaughan Jackson and Mary O'Rourke; m. Margaret Alison Pratley 1948; one s. one d.; ed. Brisbane Grammar School and Univ. of Queensland; joined CSR Ltd. 1941; mil. service 1942–46; Head, Sugar Marketing Div., CSR Ltd. 1958, Sr. Exec. Officer 1964, Gen. Man. 1972–82, Dir. 1972–85, Deputy Chair. 1983–85; Chair. Australian Industry Devt. Corpn.; Dir. Rothmans Holdings Ltd., Rockwell Int. Pty. Ltd. 1985–88; mem. Bd. Reserve Bank of Australia, Pacific Advisory Council United Technologies Corpn.; Foundation Pres. German-Australian Chamber of Industry and Commerce 1977–80, Chair. until 1985; Chair. Cttee. to Advise on Policies for Mfg. Industry 1974–75, Consultative Cttee. on Relations with Japan 1978–81, Cttee. to Review Australia's Overseas Aid Programme 1983–84, Bd. of Govts. Arthur Phillip German Australian Foundation 1984–88; Pres. Salvation Army Red Shield Appeal, Sydney 1986–, Chair. 1981–85; Chair. Order of Australia Asscn. 1980–83, Pres. 1983–86; Foundation Chair. Bd. of Man. Australian Graduate School of Man. 1976–81; Pro-Chancellor Australian Nat. Univ., Chancellor 1987–; Vice-Pres. Australia-Japan Business Co-operation Cttee.; Gov. Asian Inst. of Man., Manila 1979–; Councillor N.S.W. Branch, Inst. of Dirs. in Australia 1982–88; Trustee Mitsui Educational Foundation; mem. Advisory Bd. Salvation Army, Cttee. for Devt. of Youth Employment 1983–88, Bd. of Trustees Sydney Hospital Foundation for Research, Advisory Cttee. Centre for Resource and Environmental Studies, Pres.'s Council National Parks and Wildlife Foundation (N.S.W.), Police Bd. N.S.W. 1983–88, Chair. 1988–; Hon. D.Sc. (Univ. of New South Wales); James N. Kirby Memorial Medal 1976, John Storey Medal 1978; Commdr.'s Cross Order of Merit (Fed. Repub. of Germany) 1980; Prime Minister of Japan's Trade Award 1987; Grand Cordon (First Class), Order of the Sacred Treasure, of Japan. *Leisure interests:* sailing, fishing, photography. *Address:* 24th Floor, Qantas International Centre, 18–30 Jamison Street, Sydney, N.S.W. 2000, Australia. *Telephone:* (02) 232-6522.

JACKSON, Gen. Sir William Godfrey Fothergill, G.B.E., K.C.B., M.C., M.A.; British army officer; b. 28 Aug. 1917, Lancashire; s. of late Col. A Jackson and of Mrs. E. M. (née Fothergill) Jackson; m. Joan Mary Buesden 1946; one s. one d.; ed. Shrewsbury School, Royal Mil. Acad., Woolwich, King's Coll., Cambridge; commissioned into Royal Engineers 1937; served in Norway, N. Africa, Italy, Far East 1939–45; G.S.O.1 Allied Land Forces, S.E. Asia 1945–48; Instructor Staff Coll., Camberley 1948–50, Royal Mil. Acad., Sandhurst 1950–52; Staff and Regimental Service 1952–58; Commdr.

Gurkha Engineers 1958-60; Col. Gen. Staff, Minley Div. of Staff Coll., Camberley 1960-62; Deputy Dir. Staff Duties, War Office 1962-65; Imperial Defence Coll. 1965-66; Dir. Chief of Defence Staff Exercise Unison 1966-67; Asst. Chief of Gen. Staff, Ministry of Defence 1968-70; G.O.C.-in-C. Northern Command 1970-72; Quartermaster-Gen. 1973-77; Cabinet Office, Historical Section 1977-78 and 1982-; Gov. and C.-in-C., Gibraltar 1978-82; Col. Commdt. of Royal Engineers, and of Gurkha Engineers 1971-; Royal Army Ordnance Corps 1973-; Eng. and Railway Staff Corps. 1977-; ADC (Gen.) to the Queen 1974-76; Kt. of Justice, Order of St. John; King's Medal, Royal Mil. Acad., Woolwich. *Publications:* Attack in the West 1952, Seven Roads to Moscow 1956, Battle for Italy 1967, Battle for Rome 1970, Alexander of Tunis 1972, North African Campaigns 1975, Overlord 1978, British Official History of Second World War, The Mediterranean and Middle East, Part I 1984, Part II 1987, The Rock of the Gibraltarians 1985, The Alternative Third World War 1985-2035 1987. *Leisure interests:* writing, salmon fishing.

JACOB, Lieut.-Gen. Sir Edward Ian Claud, G.B.E., C.B., B.A.; British soldier and broadcasting administrator; b. 27 Sept. 1899, Quetta, India; s. of Field-Marshal Sir Claud Jacob, G.C.B., G.C.S.I., K.C.M.G.; m. Cecil Bisset Treherne 1924; two s.; ed. Wellington Coll., Royal Mil. Acad. Woolwich, and King's Coll., Cambridge; 2nd Lieut. Royal Engineers 1918; Capt. 1929; Maj. 1938; Col. 1943; T/Maj.-Gen. 1944; Mil. Asst. Sec. to Cttee. of Imperial Defence 1938 and to War Cabinet 1939-46; attended Confs. at Atlantic Meeting, Washington, Casablanca, Quebec, Moscow, Yalta, Potsdam; retd. July 1946; Controller European Services of of BBC 1946-47; Dir. Overseas Services BBC 1947-52, Dir.-Gen. BBC 1952-59; Pres. European Broadcasting Union 1950-52 and 1954-60; mem. Co. Council East Suffolk 1960-74, Co. Council Suffolk 1974-76; Chair. Covent Garden Market Authority 1960-66; Dir. E.M.I. 1960-73, Dir. Fisons 1960-70; Trustee Imperial War Museum 1966-73; Chair. Matthews Holdings Ltd. 1969-76. *Address:* The Red House, Woodbridge, Suffolk, England. *Telephone:* Woodbridge 2001.

JACOB, François, M.D., D.SC.; French professor of genetics; b. 17 June 1920, Nancy; m. Lise Bloch 1947 (died 1984); three s. one d.; ed. Lycée Carnot and Univ. de Paris à la Sorbonne; Officer Free French Forces 1940-45; with Inst. Pasteur 1950-, Asst. 1950-56, Head of Laboratory 1956-60, Head of Cellular Genetics Unit 1960-, Pres. 1982-; Prof. of Cellular Genetics Coll. de France 1964-; mem. Acad. des Sciences 1977; Foreign mem. Royal Danish Acad. of Sciences and Letters 1962, American Acad. of Arts and Sciences 1964; Foreign Assoc. Nat. Acad. of Sciences (U.S.A.) 1969; Foreign mem. Royal Soc., London 1973, Acad. Royale Médicale Belgique 1973, Acad. of Sciences of Hungary 1986, Royal Acad. of Sciences of Madrid 1987; Prix Charles Léopold Mayer, Acad. des Sciences 1962, Nobel Prize for Medicine (jointly with A. Lwoff and J. Monod) 1965; Croix de la Libération, Grand Croix Légion d'honneur. *Publications:* La logique du vivant 1970, Le jeu des possibles 1981, La statue intérieure 1987, and over 200 scientific papers. *Address:* Institut Pasteur, 28 rue du Dr. Roux, 75015 Paris, France.

JACOBI, Derek George, C.B.E., M.A.; British actor; b. 22 Oct. 1938, London; s. of Alfred George Jacobi and Daisy Gertrude Masters; ed. Leyton County High School and St. John's Coll., Cambridge; Birmingham Repertory Theatre 1960-63 (first appeared in One Way Pendulum 1961); National Theatre 1963-71; Prospect Theatre Co. 1972, 1974, 1976-78, Artistic Assoc. 1976-; Old Vic Co. 1978-79; joined R.S.C. April 1982; Vice-Pres., Nat. Youth Theatre 1982-; Hon. Fellow St. John's Coll., Cambridge; Variety Club Award 1976, British Acad. Award 1976, Press Guild Award 1976, Royal Television Soc. Award 1976. *TV appearances include:* She Stoops to Conquer, Man of Straw, The Pallisers, I Claudius, Philby, Burgess and Maclean, Tales of the Unexpected, A Stranger in Town, Mr. Pye. *Films:* Odessa File, Day of the Jackal, The Medusa Touch, Othello, Three Sisters, Interlude, The Human Factor, Charlotte 1981, The Man who went up in Smoke 1981, The Hunchback of Notre Dame 1981, Inside the Third Reich 1982, Little Dorrit 1986, The Tenth Man 1988, Henry V. *Plays Include:* The Lunatic, Lover and the Poet 1980, The Suicide 1980, Much Ado about Nothing, Peer Gynt, The Tempest 1982, Cyrano de Bergerac 1983, Breaking the Code 1986, Richard II 1988, Richard III 1989; dir. Hamlet 1988. *Leisure interests:* gardening, reading, looking for the next job. *Address:* c/o Duncan Heath Assocs., Paramount House, 162-170 Wardour Street, London, W1, England.

JACOBS, Francis Geoffrey, D.PHIL.; British barrister; b. 8 June 1939, Cliftonville; s. of the late Cecil Sigismund Jacobs and of Louise (née Fischhof) Jacobs; m. 1st Ruth (née Freeman) Jacobs 1964, 2nd Susan Felicity Gordon (née Cox) Jacobs 1975; two s. three d.; ed. City of London School, Christ Church, Oxford and Nuffield Coll., Oxford; lecturer in Jurisprudence, Univ. of Glasgow 1963-65; lecturer in Law, L.S.E. 1965-69; Prof. of European Law, King's Coll., London 1974-88; Secr. European Comm. of Human Rights and Legal Directorate, Council of Europe 1969-72; Legal Sec. Court of Justice of the EEC 1972-74, Advocate Gen. 1988-; Barrister, Middle Temple 1964, Q.C. 1984; Commdr., Ordre de Mérite 1983. *Publications include:* several books on European law and Yearbook of European Law (founding Ed.) 1981-88. *Address:* Court of Justice of the European Communities, 2920, Luxembourg. *Telephone:* 43031.

JACOBS, Lloydstone Leonard Fitzmorgan, B.A., M.ED.; Antiguan diplomatist and politician; b. 1937, Antigua; ed. Inter-American Univ., Puerto Rico, and Columbia Univ. Teachers' Coll., New York; teacher, Antigua, Puerto Rico and New York 1953-75; Minister without Portfolio 1976-77; mem. Senate 1976-77; Dir. Trade and Investment Promotion Activities of Antigua 1977-81; Perm. Rep. of Antigua and Barbuda to the UN 1981-; co-founder, Harlem Trailblazers Community Service 1966. *Address:* Permanent Mission of Antigua and Barbuda to the United Nations, 610 Fifth Avenue, Suite 311, New York, N.Y. 10017, U.S.A.

JACOBS, Patrick William McCarthy, PH.D., D.SC.; Canadian professor of chemistry; b. 15 Sept. 1923, Durban, S. Africa; s. of Lewis Masterman and Florence Edith (née McCarthy) Jacobs; m. 1st Elizabeth Menzies 1950 (divorced 1980), two s. one d.; m. 2nd Rita Anne Kirkwood Charter 1981; ed. Natal Univ. Coll. and Imperial Coll., London Univ.; Asst. Lecturer in Physical Chem., Imperial Coll., London 1950-52, Lecturer 1952-62, Sr. Lecturer 1962-64, Reader 1964-65; Prof. of Chem., Univ. of W. Ontario 1965-; Overseas Fellow, Churchill Coll., Cambridge 1973-74; Visiting Fellow, Wolfson Coll., Oxford 1982. *Publications:* approximately 240 papers in scientific journals. *Leisure interest:* skiing. *Address:* Department of Chemistry, University of Western Ontario, London, Ont. N6A 5B7 (Office); 457, Grangeover Avenue, London, Ont. N6G 4K7, Canada (Home). *Telephone:* (519) 679-2111, Ext. 6329 (Office).

JACOBS, Peter Alan, B.SC.; British business executive; b. 22 Feb. 1943, Ayrshire; m. Eileen Dorothy Jacobs; two s. one d.; ed. Glasgow and Aston Univs.; Production Man. Pedigree Petfoods 1981-83; Sales Dir. Mars Confectionary 1983-86; Man. Dir. British Sugar PLC 1986-; Dir. S. and W. Berisford PLC 1986-. *Leisure interests:* tennis, squash, music, theatre, fund-raising. *Address:* British Sugar PLC, P.O. Box 26, Oundle Road, Peterborough, PE2 9QU, England. *Telephone:* (0733) 63171.

JACOBS, Piers; British administrator; b. 27 May 1933, London; s. of Selwyn Jacobs and Dorothy Jacobs; m. 1964; one d.; joined Hong Kong civil service, Registrar Gen.'s Office 1962; Registrar Gen. 1976; Sec. for Econ. Services 1982-86; Financial Sec. 1986-. *Leisure interests:* walking, reading. *Address:* c/o Central Government Offices, Main Wing, 5th Floor, Lower Albert Road, Hong Kong. *Telephone:* 5-8102589.

JACOBS, Robert Allan, A.B.; American architect; b. 16 Sept. 1905; s. of Harry Allan and Elsie (Wolf) Jacobs; m. 1st Frances Cullman 1934 (divorced 1956), one s. one d.; m. 2nd Margot Helland Koehler 1966; ed. Amherst, Columbia Architectural School; worked with Le Corbusier 1934-35, with Harrison and Fouilhoux 1935-38; in partnership with E. J. Kahn under the name of Kahn and Jacobs 1940-73; Pres. Kahn & Jacobs/Hellmuth, Obata & Kassabaum 1973-76; Chair. Advisory Bd., Hellmuth, Obata & Kassabaum 1976-; designed bldgs. for World's Fair, New York 1964; Fellow American Inst. of Architects, Associated Architects on U.S. Mission to the UN; mem. Beaux Arts Inst., Architectural League of New York and New York Bldg. Congress; Hon. Master of Fine Arts (Amherst Coll.) 1957. *Address:* 1270 Avenue of the Americas, New York, N.Y. 10020 (Office); 1065 Lexington Avenue, New York, N.Y. 10021, U.S.A. (Home).

JACOBS, Sir Wilfred Ebenezer, G.C.M.G., G.C.V.O., O.B.E., Q.C.; Antiguan lawyer and administrator; b. 19 Oct. 1919; m. Carmen Sylva Knight 1947; one s. two d.; ed. Grenada Boys Secondary School, Gray's Inn, London; called to the Bar, Registrar and Additional Magistrate, St. Vincent; apptd. Magistrate, Dominica 1947, St. Kitts 1952; Attorney-Gen. for the Leeward Is. 1957-59, for Antigua 1960; Acting Admin. for various periods Dominica, St. Kitts, Antigua; apptd. Legal Draughtsman and Acting Solicitor-Gen., Trinidad and Tobago 1960, Solicitor-Gen. and Acting Attorney-Gen., Barbados 1961-63; mem. Legis. Council 1962-63; Dir. of Public Prosecutions 1964; Judge of Supreme Court of Judicature 1967; Gov. Antigua 1967-81; Gov.-Gen. Antigua and Barbuda 1981-. *Leisure interests:* gardening, swimming. *Address:* Office of the Governor-General, St. John's, Antigua, West Indies.

JACOBSON, (Alfred) Thurl, M.A.; American petroleum geologist and executive; b. 12 Nov. 1919, Utah; s. of Joseph Alfred Jacobson and Ella Adelia Robison; m. Virginia Lorraine LaCom 1942; one s. two d.; ed. Univ. of Utah; Field Artillery Officer, later Maj. 1941-46; with Amerada Petroleum Corpn., Geologist 1946-47, Man. of Exploration, Calgary, Canada 1948-49, Man. Canadian Div. 1949-56, Man. Int. Operations, Tulsa, Okla. 1956-61, Vice-Pres. 1961-62, Sr. Vice-Pres. 1962-63, Dir. 1963-69, Exec. Vice-Pres. 1963-67, Pres. Dir. and C.E.O. 1967-69; Pres. and Dir. Amerada Hess Corpn. 1969-72; Petroleum Industry Consultant 1972-76; Worldwide Exploration Admin., Amerada Hess Corpn. 1976-79; Group Vice-Pres. Exploration and Production Group 1980-86; Ind. Operator 1987-; Croix de guerre (France). *Leisure interests:* tennis, fishing, golf, reading, opera. *Address:* 1734 North Oak Crest Drive, Orem, Utah 84057, U.S.A. *Telephone:* (801) 225-1750.

JACOBSON, Dan, B.A.; British (b. South African) writer; b. 7 March 1929, Johannesburg; s. of Hyman Michael and Liebe (Melamed) Jacobson; m. Margaret Pye 1954; two s. one d.; ed. Boys' High School, Kimberly, Univ. of Witwatersrand, S. Africa; worked in business and journalism in S. Africa, settled in England 1955; Fellow in Creative Writing, Stanford Univ., Calif. 1956-57; Prof. of English, Syracuse Univ., New York 1965-66; Visiting Fellow, State Univ. of N.Y. 1971; Lecturer Univ. Coll., London 1975-79; Reader in English, Univ. of London 1979-; Prof. of English, Univ. Coll., London 1988-; Fellow Royal Soc. of Literature, London 1975; John

Llewelyn Rhys Award 1958, W. Somerset Maugham Award 1961, Jewish Chronicle Award 1971, H. H. Wingate Award 1978, J. R. Ackerley Award for Autobiography 1986. *Publications:* novels: The Trap 1955, A Dance in the Sun 1956, The Price of Diamonds 1957, The Evidence of Love 1960, The Beginners 1965, The Rape of Tamar 1970, The Wonder-Worker 1973, The Confessions of Josef Baisz 1977, Her Story 1987; short stories: Inklings 1973; criticism: The Story of the Stories 1982; Adult Pleasures 1988; (autobiography) Time and Time Again 1985. *Address:* c/o A. M. Heath & Co., 79 St. Martin's Lane, London, W.C.2, England. *Telephone:* 01-836 4271.

JACOBSON, Leon Orris, M.D.; American professor of medicine; b. 16 Dec. 1911, Sims, N.D.; s. of John and Rachael Johnson Jacobson; m. Elizabeth Louise Benton 1938 (deceased); one s. one d.; ed. North Dakota State Univ. and Univ. of Chicago; at Univ. of Chicago 1939-, Health Officer, Metallurgical Lab., where first self-sustaining pile built and operated 1942, Assoc. Dir. of Biology and Medicine 1945, Dir. 1945-46, Prof. of Medicine and Head of Haematology Sec. 1951-61, Prof. and Chair. Dept. of Medicine 1961-65, Joseph Regenstein Prof. of Biological and Medical Sciences 1965-81, Emer. 1981-; Dean Div. of Biological Sciences and Pritzker School of Medicine 1966-75; mem. Advisory Cttee. on Isotope Distribution, U.S. Atomic Energy Comm. 1952-56, Cttee. for Radiation Studies, U.S. Public Health Service 1951-55; mem. Expert Advisory Panel on Radiation, WHO 1959; U.S. Rep. to Confs. on Peaceful Uses of Atomic Energy, Geneva 1955, 1958; mem. Bd. of Scientific Counsellors, Nat. Cancer Inst. 1963-67; mem. Nat. Advisory Cancer Council, Nat. Insts. of Health 1968-72; mem. Space Biology Advisory Sub-cttee., Space Science and Applications Steering Cttee., NASA 1968-; mem. many other cttees., advisory councils, etc.; Lecturer Int. Congress of Radiology 1950, 1959, Fifth Int. Cancer Congress, Paris 1950, Congresses of Int. Soc. of Haematology 1952-64; Dir. Argonne Cancer Research Hosp. 1951-67, Franklin McLean Memorial Research Inst., Univ. Chicago 1974-77; Janeway Lecture, American Radium Soc. 1953, Jacobaeus Memorial Lecture, Helsinki 1962, Malthe Foundation Lecture, Oslo 1962 and many other guest and hon. lectureships; mem. N.A.S., American Acad. of Arts and Sciences, A.A.A.S., American Asscn. for Cancer Research, American Coll. of Physicians, American Medical Asscn., American Nuclear Soc., Asscn. of American Physicians, etc.; mem. Academia Nacional de Medicina de Buenos Aires; Hon. D.Sc. (N. Dakota) 1966, Hon. D.Sc. (Acadia Canada) 1972; Janeway Medal, American Radium Soc. 1953, Robert Roesler de Villiers Award, Leukemia Soc. 1956, Modern Medicine Award 1963, American Nuclear Soc. Award 1963, Johns Phillips Memorial Award 1975, Theodore Roosevelt Rough Riders Award, State of N.D. 1977, and other awards. *Leisure interests:* making jams and jellies from wild fruit, chemically curing hardwood, sculpting various hardwoods. *Address:* University of Chicago, Box 420, 5841 South Maryland, Chicago, Ill. 60637 (Office); 5801 Dorchester Avenue, Chicago, Ill. 60637, U.S.A. (Home). *Telephone:* (312) 702-6739 (Office): (312) 324-8232 (Home).

JACOBSON, Nathan, PH.D.; American professor of mathematics; b. 8 Sept. 1910, Warsaw, Poland; s. of Charles Jacobson and Pauline Ida Rosenberg; m. Florence Dorfman 1942; one s. one d.; ed. Univ. of Alabama, Princeton Univ.; Asst. Inst. for Advanced Study, Princeton 1933-34, Lecturer Bryn Mawr Coll. 1935-36; Nat. Research Council Postdoctoral Fellow, Chicago 1936-37; Instructor Univ. of North Carolina 1937-38, Asst. Prof. 1938-40, Assoc. Prof. 1940-43; Assoc. Ground School Instructor, Navy Preflight School 1942-43; Assoc. Prof. Johns Hopkins Univ. 1943-47; Assoc. Prof. Yale Univ. 1947-49, Prof. 1949-, Henry Ford II Prof. of Maths 1964-; Visiting Prof. Univ. of Calif. at Berkeley and at Los Angeles, Univ. of Chicago, Tata Inst., Bombay, ETH Zürich; Hon. Prof. Univ. of Alabama 1981; Guggenheim Fellow 1951-52, Fulbright Fellow 1951-52; Visiting Lecturer Japan, Italy, Israel, Australia, Taiwan, People's Repub. of China; Pres. American Mathematical Soc. 1971-73; Vice-Pres. Int. Mathematical Union 1972-74; hon. mem. London Mathematical Soc.; mem. Nat. Acad. of Sciences, American Acad. of Arts and Sciences; Hon. D.Sc. (Chicago) 1972. *Publications:* Theory of Rings 1943, Lectures in Abstract Algebra (3 vols.) 1953-64, Structure of Rings 1956, Lie Algebras 1962, Structure and Representations of Jordan Algebras 1968, On Quadratic Jordan Algebras 1969, Exceptional Lie Algebras 1971, Basic Algebra I 1974, PI—Algebras 1975, Basic Algebra II 1980, Structure Theory of Jordan Algebras 1981, and numerous articles. *Leisure interests:* travel, tennis, gardening. *Address:* Department of Mathematics, Yale University, New Haven, Conn. 06520 (Office); 2 Prospect Court, Hamden, Conn., U.S.A. (Home). *Telephone:* (203) 432-4194 (Office).

JACOMB, Sir Martin Wakefield, Kt., M.A.; British banker; b. 11 Nov. 1929, Chiddingfold, Surrey; s. of Felise Jacomb and Hilary W. Jacomb; m. Evelyn Heathcoat Amory 1960; two s. one d.; ed. Eton Coll. and Worcester Coll. Oxford; practised at the Bar 1955-68; Kleinwort, Benson Ltd. 1968-85, Vice-Chair. 1976-85; Chair. The Merchants Trust PLC 1974-85, Transatlantic Fund Inc. 1978-85; Dir. Christian Salvesen PLC 1974-88, Hudson's Bay Co., Canada 1971-86; Deputy Chair. Barclays Bank PLC 1985-; Chair. Barclays de Zoete Wedd 1986-; Deputy Chair. Securities and Investments Bd. Ltd. 1985-87; Dir. Hudson's Bay Co., Canada 1971-86, British Gas PLC 1981-88, Daily Telegraph 1986-, Bank of England 1986-; Hon. Master Bench of the Middle Temple 1987; External mem., Finance Cttee., Oxford Univ. Press 1971-; Dir. Commercial Union Assurance Co. PLC 1984-88,

Deputy Chair. 1988-, Royal Opera House Covent Garden Ltd. 1987-, Fed. Reserve Bank Int. Capital Markets Advisory Cttee. 1987-, RTZ Corp. PLC 1988-; Trustee, Nat. Heritage Memorial Fund 1982-. *Leisure interests:* theatre, family bridge, tennis. *Address:* 54 Lombard Street, London, EC3P 3AH; Barclays de Zoete Wedd, Ebbgate House, 2 Swan Lane, London, EC4R 3TS, England. *Telephone:* 01-626 1567; 01-623 2323.

JACQUEMARD, Simonne; French novelist, journalist and traveller; b. 6 May 1924, Paris; d. of André and Andrée (Raimondi) Jacquemard; m. Jacques Brosse 1955; ed. Inst. Saint-Pierre, Univ. of Paris; Teacher of music, Latin and French; collaborator, Laffont-Bompiani Dictionaries; contributor to Figaro littéraire, La table ronde; travelled in U.S.S.R., Egypt, Greece, Italy, N. Africa and Spain; Prix Renaudot 1962, Grand prix Thyde-Monnier 1984; Chevalier, Ordre des Arts et des Lettres. *Publications:* Les fascinés 1951, Sable 1952, La leçon des ténèbres 1954, Judith Albarès 1957, Planant sur les airs 1960, Compagnons insolites 1961, Le veilleur de nuit 1962, L'oiseau 1963, L'orangerie 1963, Les derniers rapaces 1965, Dérive au zénith 1965, Exploration d'un corps 1965, Navigation vers les îles 1967, A l'état sauvage 1967, L'eruption du Krakatoa 1969, La thessalienne 1973, Des roses pour mes chevreuils 1974, Le mariage berbère 1975, Danse de l'orée 1979, Le funambule 1981, Lalla Zahra 1983, La tête en éclats 1985; studies on music (with Lucette Descave), and on bird life and observation of wild animals.

JACQUES, Yves Henri, M.A.; French diplomatist; b. 31 Aug. 1929, Marseille; s. of Ivan Jacques and Fernande (née Fabrega) Jacques; m. Monique Serre 1956; two s.; ed. Ecole Nat. d'Admin.; French Embassy, Bonn 1960-63, Washington 1966-70, Rabat 1970-72; Foreign Office 1972-74, 1977-83; Ministry of Industry and Research 1974-77; OECD 1983-86; Defence Studies Inst. 1987-; Chair. Asscn. Pour le Devt. d'Echanges Int. de Produits et de Tech. Agro-Alimentaires 1988-; Légion d'honneur, Ordre du Mérite, Bundesverdienst, Germany. *Publications:* Poèmes des Années 50 1963, L'Eternel Septembre 1976. *Leisure interests:* sport (jogging, skiing, surfing), music. *Address:* 8, Rue de Villersexel, 75007 Paris, France. *Telephone:* (45) 44-46-11.

JACQUINOT, Louis, D.IUR.; French lawyer and politician; b. 16 Sept. 1898; s. of Camille and Julie (Claudin) Jacquinot; m. Simone Petsche (née Lazard) 1953; ed. Coll. de Bar-le-Duc; served French army 1914-19; called to Paris Bar; Deputy, Nat. Assembly 1932-40, 1945-73; Under-Sec. for Interior 1939-40; served French Army 1940; escaped and joined Gen. de Gaulle; Commr. for Navy 1943; Minister of War 1944-45; Pres. Gen. Council of the Meuse 1945-73; Minister of State 1945, for Navy 1945, 1947, for War Veterans 1949, for Overseas Territories 1951, 1953-54; Presidential cand. 1954; Minister of State 1958-61; Minister for Overseas Territories 1961-66; Pres. Nat. Comm. for Admin. of Territories 1967-70; Grand Officier Légion d'honneur, Croix de guerre (1914-18, 1939-45), Rosette de la Résistance, and other medals. *Address:* 3 avenue du Maréchal Maunoury, 75016 Paris, France (Home).

JACQUINOT, Pierre, D.ÈS.SC.; French academic; b. 18 Jan. 1910, Frouard; s. of Georges Auguste Jacquinot and Eugénie Louise Vicq; m. Françoise Touchot 1937; three s. one d.; ed. Univ. of Nancy; Researcher C.N.R.S. 1933-42, Dir.-Gen. 1962-69; Prof. Univ. of Clermont Ferrand 1942-46; Prof. Univ. of Paris 1946-79, Emer. Prof. 1979-; mem. Acad. des Sciences 1966-, Pres. 1980-82; Commdr. Légion d'Honneur; Holweck Prize (London-Paris) 1950; Golden Medal C.N.R.S. 1978. *Publications:* more than 150 articles on optics and atomic physics in scientific journals. *Address:* Laboratoire Aime Cotton-C.N.R.S. II, Bât. 505-Campus d'Orsay, 91405 Orsay Cedex, France (Office). *Telephone:* 69-82-40-53 (Office).

JAEGER, Richard, DR.IUR.; German politician; b. 16 Feb. 1913, Berlin-Schoneberg; s. of late Dr. Heinz and Elsbeth Jaeger; m. Rose Littner 1939; one s. five d.; ed. Maximilian Gymnasium, Munich, Ludwig-Maximilians Universität, Munich, Humboldt-Univ. zu Berlin and Rheinische Friedrich-Wilhelms-Universität, Bonn; Military Service, Second World War 1939-45; Govt. Counsel, Bavarian Ministry of Educ., Munich 1947-48; Lord Mayor Eichstätt, Bavaria 1949; mem. Bundestag 1949-80, Vice-Pres. Bundestag and Chair. Defence Cttee. 1953-65; Fed. Minister of Justice 1965-66; Vice-Pres. Bundestag 1967-76; Pres. German Atlantic Asscn. 1957-; Vice-Pres. Atlantic Treaty Asscn. 1958-66; Rep. of the Fed. Repub. of Germany, UN Comm. on Human Rights 1984-; Christian Social Union (CSU); Grosskreuz des Bundesverdienstordens and other decorations. *Publications:* Soldat und Bürger—Armee und Staat 1956, Sicherheit und Rüstung 1962, Richard Jaeger-Bundestagsreden. *Address:* Bergmillerstrasse 4, 8918 Diessen/Ammersee, Federal Republic of Germany (Home); Bundeshaus, 5300 Bonn 1, Federal Republic of Germany (Office).

JAENICKE, Joachim; German diplomatist (retd.); b. 2 Aug. 1915, Breslau (now Wrocław, Poland); s. of Wolfgang Jaenicke; m. Jane Nicholl Jaenicke 1942; two s. one d.; ed. Univ. of Geneva, Graduate Inst. of Int. Studies, Geneva, Haverford Coll., and Fletcher School of Law and Diplomacy, U.S.A.; Teacher of Modern Languages and History, Westtown School, Pa. 1941-46; Asst. Prof. of History and German, Earlham Coll., Richmond, Ind. 1946-48; returned to Germany 1948; German Foreign Service 1950-80; Vice-Consul, New York 1951; Second Sec., Washington 1951-55; Chief, American Section, Fed. Press Office, Bonn 1955-56; Chief of Press Section and Spokesman of German Foreign Office, Bonn 1956-58; Counsellor,

Ottawa 1959–62; Far East Desk, Foreign Office 1962–63; Dir. in Div. of Political Affairs, North Atlantic Treaty Org. (NATO), Paris 1963–65, Asst. Sec.-Gen. for Political Affairs, NATO, Brussels 1966–69; Amb. to Yugoslavia 1969–75; Deputy Asst. Sec. and Amb.-at-Large, Foreign Office, Bonn 1975–77; Amb. to Argentina 1977–80. *Leisure interests:* swimming, tennis, windsurfing. *Address:* 8172 Lenggries/Obb., Ludwig Thoma Weg 23, Federal Republic of Germany.

JAENICKE, Lothar, DR.PHIL., DIPL.CHEM.; German biochemist; b. 14 Sept. 1923, Berlin; s. of Johannes Jaenicke and Erna (née Buttermilch) Jaenicke; m. Doris Heinzel 1949; two s. two d.; ed. Univ. of Marburg; taught Univ. of Marburg 1946–57, Munich 1957–62, Cologne 1962–, apptd. Prof. Cologne Univ. 1963, also Dir. Inst. of Biochem.; Visiting Scientist All India Inst. of Medicine, New Delhi 1961, Univ. of Texas, Austin 1977; Visiting Prof. American Univ. of Beirut 1971, Ain Shams Univ., Cairo 1974, Indian Inst. of Science, Bangalore 1980; Paul Ehrlich/Ludwig-Darmstaedter-Preis 1963, Otto Warburg Medal 1979, Richard Kuhn Medal 1984. *Publications:* c. 200 original papers in scientific journals. *Address:* Institut für Biochemie, Universität zu Köln, An der Bottmühle 2, D-5000 Cologne 1, Federal Republic of Germany. *Telephone:* 0221-311331.

JAFFAR, Khalid Mohammad; Kuwaiti diplomatist; b. 12 Aug. 1922; s. of Muhammad Jaffar and Aminah Abdulla; m. Mariam Al-Askar 1942; four s. three d.; ed. Mubarakia School, Kuwait; Schoolteacher 1940–43; Chief Cashier, Kuwait Municipality 1943–45; Kuwait Oil Co. 1945–61; mem. of Goodwill Mission to Latin American Countries 1961; Lord Chamberlain to Amir of Kuwait 1961–62; Head of Cultural and Press Dept., Foreign Office, Kuwait 1962; mem. del. to UN; deputized for Under-Sec. of State, Ministry of Foreign Affairs 1962–63; Amb. to U.K. 1963–65, to Lebanon 1965–70, concurrently to France 1965–67, and to Turkey 1968–73, concurrently to Bulgaria, Greece 1971–73, to U.S.A. (also accred. to Canada and Venezuela) 1975–80; Dir. Political Dept., Ministry of Foreign Affairs Jan. 1982–; Chair. Kuwait Investment Bd. in London 1964–65; several foreign decorations. *Leisure interests:* swimming, fishing, travelling, reading. *Address:* P.O. Box 5418, Safat, Kuwait. *Telephone:* 2513104.

JAFFÉ, Andrew Michael, C.B.E., LITT.D., F.R.S.A.; British art historian; b. 3 June 1923, London; s. of Arthur Daniel Jaffé and Marie Marguerite (née Strauss) Jaffé; m. Patricia Ann Milne-Henderson 1964; two s. two d.; ed. Eton Coll., King's Coll., Cambridge, Courtauld Inst. of Art; Lieut-Commdr., Royal Naval Volunteer Reserve; Commonwealth Fund Fellow, Harvard and N.Y. Univs. 1951–53; Fellow, King's Coll., Cambridge 1952–; Asst. lecturer in Fine Arts, Cambridge 1956; Prof. of Renaissance Art, Wash. Univ., St. Louis 1960–61; Reader in History of Western Art, Cambridge 1968, Head of Dept., History of Art 1970–73, Prof. of History of Western Art 1973–; Syndic, Fitzwilliam Museum, Cambridge 1971–73, Dir. 1973–; mem. Advisory Council, Vic. and Albert Museum 1971–76; Organiser (for Nat. Gallery of Canada) of Jordaens Exhbn., Ottawa 1968–69; Visiting Prof. Harvard Univ. 1968–69; Officier, Ordre de Léopold (Belgium) 1980. *Publications:* Van Dyck's Antwerp Sketchbook 1966, Rubens 1967, Jordaens 1968, Rubens and Italy 1977; art historical articles and reviews in European and N. American journals. *Leisure interest:* viticulture. *Address:* Grove Lodge, Trumpington Street, Cambridge.

JAGAN, Cheddi, D.D.S.; Guyanese politician; b. 22 March 1918, Plantation Port Mourant, Berbice; m. Janet Jagan (q.v.) 1943; one s. one d.; ed. Queen's Coll., Guyana, Howard Univ., Washington, YMCA (now Roosevelt) Coll., Chicago and Northwestern Univ. Dental School, Chicago; mem. Legis. Council 1947–53; Leader of People's Progressive Party (PPP), formed 1950; Minister of Agric., Lands and Mines and Leader of House of Assembly April-Oct. 1953; six months' political imprisonment 1954; Minister of Trade and Industry 1957–61; Leader and Chief Minister of the PPP Majority Party 1957–61; First Premier British Guiana (now Guyana), Minister of Devt. and Planning 1961–64; Leader of Opposition 1964–73, 1976–; Gen. Sec. PPP 1970–; Pres. Guyana Peace Council; mem. Presidential Cttee. of World Peace Council; Hon. Pres. Guyana Agricultural Workers' Union. *Publications:* Forbidden Freedom 1954, Anatomy of Poverty in British Guiana 1964, The West on Trial (autobiog.) 1966, West Indian State Pro-Imperialist or Anti-Imperialist 1972, The Struggle for a Socialist Guyana 1976, Trade Unions and National Liberation 1977, The Caribbean Revolution 1979, The Caribbean, Whose Backyard? 1985. *Leisure interest:* tennis. *Address:* 65 Pln. Bel Air, East Coast Demerara, Guyana. *Telephone:* 72096 (Office); 62899 (Home).

JAGAN, Janet; Guyanese politician; b. 20 Oct. 1920, Chicago, Ill., U.S.A.; d. of Charles and Kathryn Rosenberg; m. Cheddi Jagan (q.v.) 1943; one s. one d.; Gen. Sec. People's Progressive Party (PPP) 1950–70; Ed. Thunder 1950–56; Deputy Speaker House of Assembly 1953; six months' political imprisonment 1954; Minister of Labour, Health and Housing 1957–61; Minister of Home Affairs 1963–64; Ed. Mirror 1969–72, 1973–; Int. Sec. PPP 1970–84, Exec. Sec. 1984–; mem. Nat. Assembly 1976–; Pres. Women's Progressive Org., Union of Guyanese Journalists; mem. Exec. Council, Int. Org. of Journalists; Bureau mem., Women's Int. Dem. Fed. *Publications:* History of the People's Progressive Party 1971, Army Intervention in the 1973 Elections in Guyana 1973, An Examination of National Service 1976. *Leisure interest:* swimming. *Address:* 65 Pln. Bel Air, East Coast Demerara, Guyana.

JAGANNATHAN, S., B.SC.(HONS.); Indian civil servant and international banking official; b. 18 May 1914, Srirangam, S. India; m.; two s.; ed. Univs. of Madras and London, and Imperial Defence Coll., London; recruited in London to Indian Civil Service 1935; Sub-div. Officer and later Under Sec. to Govt., Prov. of Bihar 1936–42; in Defence, Supply and Civil Divs. of Ministry of Finance, Govt. of India 1942–46; Deputy Sec., Cabinet Secr. of Govt. of India and also of Partition Secr. for the Partition of India into the Dominions of Pakistan and India 1946–47; Deputy Sec. Ministry of Commerce 1948; Chief Controller of Imports 1949; Dir.-Gen. of Shipping 1950–53; Jt. Sec. Ministry of Production 1953–56; Additional Sec. (in charge of External Finance) Ministry of Finance 1958–60; Financial Commr. Indian Railways 1960–66; mem. Atomic Energy Comm. of India 1962–68; Perm. Sec. Ministry of Finance (Dept. of Econ. Affairs) and Alt. Gov. for India in Int. Bank for Reconstruction and Devt. (IBRD) and affiliates 1966–68, Amb. (Econ.), Embassy of India, Wash. D.C., Exec. Dir. for India of IBRD and its affiliates 1968–70; Gov. Reserve Bank of India 1970–75; Exec. Dir. IMF 1975–76; Chair. Madras Refineries 1978–80; Chair. and Dir. various cos.. *Address:* E.54 19th Cross Street, Besantnagar, Madras 90, India. *Telephone:* 413199.

JAGENDORF, André Tridon, PH.D.; American professor of plant physiology; b. 21 Oct. 1926, New York; s. of Moritz A. and Sophie S. Jagendorf; m. Jean Whitenack 1952; three c.; ed. Cornell and Yale Univs.; Postdoctoral Fellow, Univ. of Calif., Los Angeles 1951–53; Asst. Prof., Johns Hopkins Univ. 1953–58, Assoc. Prof. 1958–65, Prof. of Biology 1966; Prof. of Plant Physiology, Cornell Univ. 1966–; Liberty Hyde Bailey Prof. 1981–; mem. N.A.S. 1980; Pres. American Soc. of Plant Physiologists; Merck Fellow in Natural Sciences 1951–53; Weizmann Fellow 1962; A.A.A.S. Fellow 1964; Fellow American Acad. of Arts and Sciences 1972; Outstanding Young Scientist Award, Md. Acad. of Sciences 1961, Kettering Research Award 1963, C. F. Kettering Award in Photosynthesis, American Soc. of Plant Physiologists 1978. *Publications:* 142 papers in scientific journals. *Address:* Plant Biology Section, Plant Sciences Building, Cornell University, Ithaca, N.Y. 14853 (Office); 309 Brookfield Road, Ithaca, N.Y. 14850, U.S.A. (Home). *Telephone:* (607) 256-8423 (Office).

JAGGER, Mick; British vocalist, song writer and actor; b. 26 July 1943, Dartford, Kent; m. Bianca Pérez Morena de Macías 1971 (divorced 1979); one s. three d.; ed. London School of Econs., London Univ.; began singing career with Little Boy Blue and the Blue Boys while at L.S.E.; appeared with Blues Inc. at Ealing Blues Club, Singer with Blues Inc. at London Marquee Club 1962; formed Rolling Stones 1962; wrote songs with Keith Richard under pseudonyms Nanker, Phelge until 1965, without pseudonyms 1965–; first own composition to reach no. 1 in U.K. charts The Last Time 1965; first major U.K. tour 1964; major U.S. tours 1964, 1966, 1969, 1972, 1973, 1975, 1981; toured Europe 1973, 1982, the Americas 1975; title role in film Ned Kelly 1969, appeared in Performance 1969, Gimme Shelter 1972; lived in France for some years. Records: singles include: Come On 1963, I Wanna Be Your Man 1963, It's All Over Now 1964, Little Red Rooster 1964, Satisfaction 1965, Jumping Jack Flash 1968, Honky Tonk Women 1969, Brown Sugar 1971, Miss You 1978, Emotional Rescue 1980, Beast of Burden, She's So Cold, Dancing in the Street (with David Bowie for Live Aid Appeal) 1985; albums include: The Rolling Stones 1964, The Rolling Stones No. 2 1965, Out of Our Heads 1965, Aftermath 1966, Between the Buttons 1967, Their Satanic Majesties Request 1967, Beggar's Banquet 1968, Let it Bleed 1969, Get Yer Ya-Ya's Out 1969, Sticky Fingers 1971, Exile on Main Street 1972, Goat's Head Soup 1973, It's Only Rock'n'Roll 1974, Black and Blue 1976, Some Girls 1978, Emotional Rescue 1980, Still Life 1982, She's the Boss (solo) 1985, Primitive Cool 1987. *Address:* Cheyne Walk, Chelsea, London, S.W.3, England; Château Fourchette, Loire Valley, France.

JAHN, Gerhard; German lawyer and politician; b. 10 Sept. 1927, Kassel; s. of Ernst and Lilly (née Schlüchterer) Jahn; m. 1st Anna Waas 1950, one s. two d.; m. 2nd Ursula Müller 1986; ed. Humanistisches Friedrichs Gymnasium, Kassel and Univ. Marburg; qualified as lawyer 1956; mem. Parl. Sozial-Demokratische Partei (SPD) 1957; mem. Bundestag 1957–; Parl. State Sec. to Minister of Foreign Affairs 1967; Minister of Justice 1969–74; Pres. Deutscher Mieterbund 1979; Freeman of Marburg 1977; Grosses Bundesverdienstkreuz mit Stern und Schulterband 1984. *Leisure interest:* photography. *Address:* Bundeshaus, 5300 Bonn 1; Ernst-Lemmer-strasse 10, Postfach 1560, 3550 Marburg 6, Federal Republic of Germany.

JAICKS, Frederick Gillies; American business executive (retd.); b. 26 July 1918, Chicago; m. Mignon Dake 1954; two s. one d.; ed. Hinsdale High School, Cornell Univ.; joined Inland Steel Co. as open hearth trainee 1940; served in U.S. Navy during Second World War; served in various positions in steelmaking operations at Inland Steel Co.'s Indiana Harbor Works, E. Chicago 1945–54; Asst. Gen. Man. of Primary Production 1956–59; Gen. Man. Indiana Harbor Works 1959–61; Vice-Pres. Steel Mfg.1961–62; Vice-Pres. Mfg. and Research 1962–63; Dir. Inland Steel Co. 1963–, Pres. 1966–71, Chair. and CEO 1971–83; Dir. R.R. Donnelley & Son 1973–; Dir. Champion Int. 1980–; Dir. Standard Oil Co. (Ind.), Zenith Electronics Corpn.; mem. American Iron and Steel Inst.; Dir. Int. Iron and Steel Inst. 1971–83, Chair. 1981–83; Hon. LL.D. (St. Joseph's Coll.) 1968, (DePaul Univ.) 1978, (Valparaiso Univ.) 1980, (Illinois Inst. of Tech.) 1985. *Address:* Inland Steel Co., 30 West Monroe Street, Chicago, Ill. 60603 (Office); 155 North Harbor Drive, Chicago, Ill. 60601, U.S.A. (Home).

JAIDAH, Ali Mohammed, M.SC.; Qatari petroleum company executive; b. 1941, Doha; ed. London Univ.; Head of Econs. Div. in Dept. of Petroleum Affairs, Ministry of Finance and Petroleum 1966–71, Dir. of Petroleum Affairs 1971–76; mem. Exec. Office of OAPEC; Gov. for Qatar, OPEC until Dec. 1976; Sec.-Gen. OPEC 1977–78; Dir., Man. Dir., Qatar Gen. Petroleum Corpn. 1979–85; Head of dels. to OPEC, OAPEC and other petroleum confs; Silver Medallion (Austria). *Publications:* articles on petroleum economics in numerous publications. *Address:* c/o Qatar General Petroleum Corporation, P.O. Box 3212, Doha, Qatar.

JAIN, Girilal, B.A.; Indian journalist; b. 21 Sept. 1923, Pipli Khere, Haryana; s. of late Shahzad Rai and Bhagwani Devi; m. Sudarshan Jain 1951; one s. three d.; ed. Delhi Univ.; went into journalism 1945, Sub-Ed. Times of India, Delhi 1950, reporter 1951, Chief Reporter 1958, Foreign Corresp. Pakistan 1961, London 1962, Asst. Ed., Delhi 1964, Resident Ed. 1970, an Ed. 1976, Ed.-in-Chief April 1978–. *Publications:* What Mao Really Means 1957, India Meets China in Nepal 1959, Panchshila and After 1960. *Leisure interests:* reading, listening to music. *Address:* The Times of India, The Times of India Building, Dadabhai Naoroji Road, Bombay 1 (Office); 22 Ashoka Apartment, Napean Sea Road, Bombay 6, India (Home). *Telephone:* 262493 (Office); 816242 (Home).

JAIN, Surendra Kumar, M.A., LL.M.; Indian international official (retd.); b. 22 Dec. 1922, Multan; s. of Padam Sain Jain; m. Chakresh Kumari 1941; one s. twò d.; ed. High School, New Delhi, Punjab Univ. and Lucknow Univ.; Lecturer, Delhi School of Law, Delhi Univ. 1946–47; joined Int. Labour Office, Geneva 1947, Chef de Cabinet to Dir.-Gen. 1957–59, Dir. Office for Near and Middle East, Istanbul 1959–62, Field Office for Asia, Colombo 1962–65, Regional Dir. for Asia, Bangkok 1966–75, Deputy Dir.-Gen. in charge of Tech. Programmes 1975–87; Gold Medal (Lucknow Univ.). *Publications:* articles on labour and social problems in International Labour Review and other journals; papers including Management Education to the End of the Century: The Asian Scene, Human Resources Development–Some Operational Issues, The Impact of Present Adjustment Policies on Employment, Adjustment, Employment and Basic Needs, Technology, Work and Leisure, etc. *Leisure interests:* photography, swimming, badminton, music. *Address:* c/o ILO Area Office, 7 Sardar Patel Marg, Chanakyapuri, New Delhi 110021 (Office); D414 Defence Colony, New Delhi 110024, India (Home). *Telephone:* 3012101 (Office); 622884 (Home).

JAISINGH, Hari, M.A.; Indian newspaper editor; b. 29 March, 1941, Karachi, Pakistan; ed. Calcutta; with Hindustan Standard, Calcutta 1963–67, Ed.-in-charge overseas edn.; columnist Indian Scene; Asst. Ed. The Tribune, Chandigarh 1967–79; Resident Ed. Indian Express 1979–80; Ed. National Herald 1980–83; corresp. for Morning Telegraph India; lectured Punjab Univ., Chandigarh, Punjabi Univ., Patiala. *Address:* C-146, Defence Colony, New Delhi, India (Home). *Telephone:* 622838 (Home).

JAKEŠ, Miloš; Czechoslovak politician; b. 12 Aug. 1922, České Chalupy, Český Krumlov Dist.; ed. Industrial School of Electrical Eng., Gottwaldov, and Coll. of Party Educ. of CPSU, Moscow; apprenticed in electrical eng. and design, Zlín and Gottwaldov 1937–50; various functions at district and regional level, CP of Czechoslovakia, and active in Czechoslovak Union of Youth 1945–55; mem. Council, World Fed. of Democratic Youth 1953–55; Head, Nat. Cttees. Div., Cen. Cttee. CP of Czechoslovakia 1958–61, Head, Cen. Office for Nat. Cttees. Affairs 1961–63; First Deputy Chair., Cen. Admin. for Devt. of Communal Economy 1963–66; Deputy Minister of Interior 1966–68; mem. Cen. Control and Auditing Comm., CP of Czechoslovakia 1966–77, Chair. 1968–77; Deputy, House of People, Fed. Assembly 1971–; mem. Cen. Cttee. CP of Czechoslovakia 1977–, cand. mem. Presidium 1977–, Sec. and mem. Secr. 1977–81; Chair. Comm. of Cen. Cttee. of CP for Agric. and Food 1977–81; Chair. Nat. Econ. Comm. of Cen. Cttee. of CP of Czechoslovakia 1981–88; Gen. Sec. CP of Czechoslovakia Dec. 1987–; mem. Presidium of Cen. Cttee. CP of Czechoslovakia 1981–; mem. Presidium of Fed. Assembly 1981–; Order of 25 February 1948, Order of Labour, Order of the Republic, Order of Victorious February, Hero of Socialist Labour 1982, Klement Gottwald Order 1982, Order of October Revolution (U.S.S.R.) 1982. *Address:* Ústřední výbor KSČ, Prague 1, nábřeží Ludvíka Svobody 12, Czechoslovakia.

JAKHAR, Bal Ram; Indian politician; b. 23 Aug. 1923, Panjkosi, Ferozepur Dist., Punjab; s. of Chaudhri Raja Ram Jakhar; m.; three s. two d.; elected to Punjab Ass. 1972, Deputy Minister of Co-operatives and Irrigation 1972–77, Leader of Opposition 1977–79; Speaker, Lok Sabha (House of the People) 1980–; Pres. Indian Parl. Group, Indian Group of IPU, Indian Branch, CPA 1979–; Chair. Bharat Krishak Samaj 1979–; led numerous Indian parl. dels. overseas 1980–. *Publication:* People, Parliament and Administration. *Address:* Lok Sabha, New Delhi 110001; Village and P.O. Panjkosi, Tehl Fazilka, Dist. Ferozepur, Punjab, India (Home). *Telephone:* 3017795, 3017914 (Office); 3018264 (Home).

JAKI, Stanley L., S.T.D., PH.D.; American university professor and ecclesiastic; b. 17 Aug. 1925, Györ, Hungary; s. of Imre Jaki and Etelka Szabo; ed. Pontifical Atheneum San Anselmo, Rome and Fordham Univ., New York; mem. of staff Seton Hall Univ., S. Orange, N.J. 1965–72, Prof. of Physics 1972–75, Distinguished Univ. Prof. 1975–; R.C. Priest of Benedictine Order; Gifford Lecturer Univ. of Edinburgh 1974–76; Fremantle Lecturer Oxford Univ. 1977; Lecomte du Nouy Prize 1970; Templeton Prize 1987. *Publications:* The Relevance of Physics 1966, Brain, Mind and Computers 1969, The Milky Way: An Elusive Road for Science 1972, Science and Creation 1974, The Road of Science and the Ways to God 1978, Planets and Planetarians: A History of Theories of the Origin of Planetary Systems 1978, The Origin of Science and the Science of its Origin 1978, Cosmos and Creator 1980, Uneasy Genius: The Life and Work of Pierre Duhem 1984, Chance or Reality and Other Essays 1986, The Keys of the Kingdom: A Tool's Witness to Truth 1986, The Absolute Beneath the Relative and Other Essays 1988, The Savior of Science 1988. *Address:* P.O. Box 167, Princeton, N.J. 08542, U.S.A. *Telephone:* 609 896 3979.

JAKOBOVITS, Baron (Life Peer), cr. 1987, of Regents Park in Greater London, **Immanuel Jakobovits,** Kt., PH.D.; British Rabbi; b. 8 Feb. 1921, Königsberg, Germany (now Kaliningrad, U.S.S.R.); s. of Rabbi Dr. Julius Jakobovits and Paula Wreschner; m. Amélie Munk 1948; two s. four d.; ed. Jews' Coll. London, Yeshivah Etz Chaim, London, Univ. of London; Minister of Brondesbury Synagogue, London 1941–44, of S.E. London Synagogue 1944–47, of Great Synagogue, London 1947–49; Chief Rabbi of Ireland 1949–58; Rabbi of Fifth Avenue Synagogue, New York 1958–67; Chief Rabbi of the United Hebrew Congregations of the British Commonwealth of Nations, London 1967–; Fellow, Univ. Coll., London 1984; Hon. D.D. (Lambeth) 1987, Hon. D.Litt. (City Univ., London) 1986, Hon Fellow Queen Mary Coll., 1987. *Publications:* Jewish Medical Ethics 1959, Journal of a Rabbi 1966, Jewish Law Faces Modern Problems 1966, The Timely and the Timeless 1977, If Only My People . . . Zionism is My Life (autobiog.) 1985. *Address:* Office of the Chief Rabbi, Alder House, Tavistock Square, London, W.C.1, England.

JAKOBSEN, Frode, M.A.; Danish politician and author; b. 21 Dec. 1906, Mors; s. of Ole Jakobsen and Ane Mette Lorentsen; m. 1st Ruth Goldstein 1937 (died 1974), one s. one d.; m. 2nd Agnes Malé 1977; ed. Univ. of Copenhagen; agricultural worker until 1925; Lecturer in Phil. and Literature until 1940; Leader, Resistance Movement 1941–45; founder-mem. Danish Freedom Council (illegal govt. during occupation) 1943–45; Chief of all armed underground forces 1943–45; mem. Cabinet May-Nov. 1945; M.P. 1945–73; Civil Chief of Home Guard 1948–72; mem. Consultative Assembly, Council of Europe 1949–64, Vice-Pres. 1953–54; mem. Govt. Cttee. for Foreign Affairs; Pres. European Movement in Denmark 1949–64; Social Dem. Party; mem. Danish Defence Cttee., Govt. Cttee. on Disarmament Questions 1966–; Danish Del. to UN 1956–57, 1961, 1973, Head of Del. 1962–65; Int. Council, Congress for Cultural Freedom 1960–66. *Publications:* Nietzsches Kamp med den kristelige Moral 1940, The European Movement and the Council of Europe 1950, Europe—and Denmark 1953, Standpunkter 1966, Nej, Der Skal Ikke Ties 1972, I Danmarks Frihedsraad 1975, Da Leret Tog Form 1976, Alt hvad der jager min sjael 1977, Jeg vil vaere en fugl før jeg dør 1979, Nazismen blev min Skaebne 1982, Til sidst kommer man hjem 1984, Mod et mål man aldrig skal nå 1987. *Leisure interest:* ornithology. *Address:* Hedetoften 5, 2680 Solröd Strand, Denmark. *Telephone:* 0314 1968.

JAKOBSEN, Mimi Stilling; Danish politician; b. 19 Nov. 1948, Copenhagen; d. of Erhard Jakobsen; Lecturer in German Philology and Phonetics, Univ. of Copenhagen; M.P. 1977–, Minister for Cultural Affairs. 1982–86; Centre Democrat. *Address:* c/o Ministry of Cultural Affairs, Nybrogade 2, 1203 Copenhagen, Denmark.

JAKOBSON, Max; Finnish journalist and diplomatist; b. 1923, Viipuri: s. of Jonas and Helmi (née Virtanen) Jakobson, m. Marilyn S. Medney 1954; two s. one d.; Journalist until 1953; Press Attaché, Finnish Embassy, Washington 1953–59; Chief of Press Dept., Ministry of Foreign Affairs 1959–62; Asst. Dir. for Political Affairs, Ministry of Foreign Affairs 1959–62, Dir. 1962–65; Perm. Rep. of Finland to UN 1965–72; Amb. to Sweden 1972–75; Man. Dir. Council of Econ. Orgs. in Finland 1975–84, independent consultant 1985–. *Publications include:* The Diplomacy of the Winter War, Finnish Neutrality, Finland: Myth and Reality. *Address:* Rahapajankatu 3B 17, 00160, Helsinki 16, Finland. *Telephone:* 651884.

JAKUBOWSKI, Janusz Lech; Polish scientist; b. 9 Dec. 1905, Warsaw; s. of Władysław and Wiktoria (Handzelewicz) Jakubowski; m. 1st Hanna Wiszniewska 1931; m. 2nd Zofia Wysocka-Bernadzikiewicz 1948; one d.; ed. Warsaw Polytechnic; Asst. Prof. of High Voltage Tech., Warsaw Polytechnic 1938–46, Dean Electrical Faculty 1945–52, Extraordinary Prof. 1946–54, Ordinary Prof. 1954–76, Prof. Emer. 1976–; Founder and Chief Dir. State Electrotech. Research Inst. 1945–56; mem. Polish Acad. of Sciences, mem. Presidium 1952–69; Dir. Centre Polish Acad. of Sciences in Paris 1959–61; Hon. mem. Polish Asscn. of Electrical Engineers; corresp. mem. Acad. des Sciences, Inscriptions et Belles Lettres de Toulouse 1962; UNESCO Project Man., Ecole Nat. Polytechnique, Algiers 1967–71; Chair. Cttee. of Electrotechnics, Polish Acad. of Sciences 1952–65 and 1975–; Hon. Pres. Polish Cttee. of Lightning Protection; Hon. mem. Nicolaus Copernicus Polish Naturalists Soc. 1980; Dr. h.c. (Łódź Polytechnic) 1984, (Warsaw Polytechnic) 1986; State Prize 2nd class 1950, 1st class 1988; Officer's, Commdr.'s and Commdr.'s Cross with Star, Order of Polonia Restituta 1951, 1954, 1985, Order of Banner of Labour 2nd Class 1966, 1st Class 1977, Silver Medal Société d'Encouragement pour la Recherche et Invention (France) 1968 and various other awards and prizes. *Publications:* New method of High Voltage Measurement 1935, Measurement of Distorted High Voltages 1937, Actual Problems of High Voltage Engineering 1939, High Voltage Engineering 1951, Travelling Waves in High Voltage

Systems 1962, Over Voltages in High Voltage Systems 1968, and numerous articles. *Leisure interest:* ecology of coral reefs. *Address:* Ul. Igańska 9 m. 2, 04-087 Warsaw, Poland. *Telephone:* Warsaw 10-11-71.

JALAL, Mahsoun B., PH.D.(ECON.); Saudi Arabian businessman; b. 26 June 1936; m. Michele Marie Garein Jalal 1967; three s. one d.; ed. Univ. of Cairo, Egypt, Rutgers Univ., New Brunswick, N.J., U.S.A., Univ. of California, U.S.A.; Prof., Chair. Dept. of Econs., Riyadh Univ. 1967-75; Consultant to various Govt. agencies 1967-75; formed the Consulting Centre (Pres. 1981-); Vice-Chair. and Man. Dir. Saudi Fund for Devt. 1975-79; mem. Civil Service Council 1977-78; Dir. Saudi Int. Bank, London 1975-; Chair. Saudi Int. Bank, Nassau, Bahamas 1979-81; Chair. Saudi Investment Banking Corpn. 1977-82, OPEC Special Fund (now OPEC Fund) 1979-82; Dir. Saudi Basic Industries Corpn. 1975-86; Exec. Dir. IMF 1978-81; Chair. Saudi United Commercial Bank 1983-85; Chair. Eastern Petrochemical Co. 1981-86; Chair. Tunisian-Saudi Devt. Investment Co. 1981-; Chair. and CEO Nat. Industrialization Co. 1984-; Chair. various investment cos.; Golden Star, First Class (Taiwan) 1973, Tanda Mahputera (Indonesia) 1978, Chevalier Ordre National (Mali) 1978, Order of the Repub., First Class (Tunisia) 1985. *Publications:* Principles of Economics, other books and articles on econ. devt. and econ. theory. *Leisure interests:* travel, sports. *Address:* P.O. Box 26707, Riyadh 11496, Saudi Arabia (Office). *Telephone:* 476-7166 (Office).

JALAN-AAJAV, Sampilyn; Mongolian politician; b. 18 June 1923; ed. Cen. School for Party and State Cadres, and Higher Party School of Mongolian People's Revolutionary Party (MPRP) Cen. Cttee., Ulan Bator, and law studies in U.S.S.R.; lecturer and Vice-Rector, Higher Party School 1943-51, lecturer and Dean 1956-58; Head of Propaganda and Culture Dept. of MPRP Cen. Cttee. 1958-59; Procurator of the Mongolian People's Repub. 1959-60; Chair. Legal Cttee. of Council of Ministers 1960-64; Chair. State Cttee. for Information, Broadcasting and TV 1964-71; Deputy to People's Great Hural (Assembly) 1966-; Deputy Chair. Parl. Group 1971-77; Deputy Chair. Presidium, People's Great Hural 1977-83; Sec. Cen. Cttee. MPRP 1971-83; cand. mem. MPRP Cen. Cttee. 1961-71, mem. Cen. Cttee. 1971-83; cand. mem. Political Bureau, MPRP Cen. Cttee. 1971-73, mem. Political Bureau 1973-83; Order of the Red Banner of Labour 1983. *Address:* c/o Central Committee of the Mongolian People's Revolutionary Party, Ulan Bator, Mongolia.

JALLOUD, Major Abdul Salam Ahmed; Libyan army officer and politician; b. 15 Dec. 1944; ed. Secondary School, Sebha, Mil. Acad., Benghazi.; mem. of Revolutionary Command Council 1969-77, Gen. Secr. of Gen. People's Congress 1977-79; Minister of Industry and the Econ., Acting Minister of the Treas. 1970-72; Prime Minister 1972-77. *Address:* c/o General Secretariat of the General People's Congress, Tripoli, Libya.

JAMAL, Amir Habib, B.COMM.(ECON.); Tanzanian politician; b. 26 Jan. 1922, Dar es Salaam; s. of Habib Jamal and Kulsum Thawer; m. 1st Zainy Kheraj, 2nd Shahsultan Cassam 1967; three s. one d.; ed. primary school, Mwanza, secondary school, Dar es Salaam, and Univ. of Calcutta, India; elected mem. Tanganyika Legis. Council 1958; Minister of Urban Local Govt. and Works 1959, of Communication, Power and Works 1960; Minister of State, President's Office, Directorate of Devt. 1964; re-elected M.P. 1965; Minister of Finance 1965-72; Minister for Commerce and Industries 1972-75, of Finance and Econ. Planning 1975-77, of Communications and Transport 1977-79, of Finance 1979-83, without Portfolio 1983-84, Minister of State for Cabinet Affairs, Pres.'s Office 1984-85; Head, Perm. Mission to the UN, Geneva Nov. 1985-; Chair. Interpress Service, Third World, Rome; Chair. Governing Council Sokoine Univ. of Agric., Morogoro; mem. Nat. Exec. CCM Party; Dr. h.c. (Uppsala) 1973, (Dar es Salaam) 1980; mem. Brandt Comm. 1977-80, Trustee Dag Hammarskjold Foundation; mem. Advisory Panel, World Inst. for Devt. Economics Research. *Leisure interests:* gardening, reading, bridge, swimming. *Address:* 47 avenue Blanc, 1202 Geneva, Switzerland.

JAMAL, Jasim Yousif; Qatar diplomatist; b. 17 Sept. 1940; m.; three c.; ed. Northeast Missouri State Univ., New York Univ.; Ministry of Education, Dir. Admin. Affairs 1958-63, Cultural Adviser, U.S. 1963-68, Dir. of Cultural Affairs 1968-72; Perm. Rep. to UN 1972-84, concurrently accred. as Amb. to Canada, Brazil and Argentina. *Address:* Ministry of Foreign Affairs, Doha, Qatar.

JÁMBOR, Ági; American pianist; b. 4 Feb. 1909, Budapest, Hungary; d. of Vilmos Jámbor and Olga Riesz; ed. Budapest Acad. of Music under Kodály and Weiner, and Musikhochschule, Berlin; regular concert tours throughout U.S.A.; Full Prof., Dept. of Music and Anthropology/Ethno-Musicology, Bryn Mawr Coll., Pa. 1958-77, Prof. Emer. 1977-; Curator of Music Instruments, Univ. Museum, Pa.; Brahms Prize, Deutsche Akad., Berlin 1928, Int. Chopin Prize, Warsaw 1937. *Address:* Bryn Mawr College, Bryn Mawr, Pa. 19010 (Office); 103 Pine Tree Road, Radnor, Pa. 19087, U.S.A. (Home). *Telephone:* (215) 688-8683 (Home).

JAMES, Anthony Trafford, C.B.E., PH.D., F.R.S.; British research manager; b. 6 March 1922, Cardiff; s. of J. M. and Ivy James; m. 1st Olga I. Clayton 1945 (died 1980), 2nd Linda Beare 1982; three s. one d.; ed. Univ. Coll. School, Northern Polytechnic, Univ. Coll. London and Harvard Business School; MCR Jr. Fellowship, Bedford Coll. London 1945-47; jr. staff mem. Lister Inst. for Preventive Medicine, London 1947-50; mem. scientific staff, Nat. Inst for Medical Research, London 1950-62; Div. Man. and

Head, Biosynthesis Unit, Unilever Research Lab. 1962-67, Head, Div. of Plant Products and Biochem. 1967-69, Group Man. Biosciences Group 1969-72, mem. Exec. Cttee. and Head, Div. of Biosciences 1972-85; mem. Exec. Cttee., Unilever Research, Colworth Lab. 1972-85; Industrial Prof. of Chem. Loughborough Univ. of Tech. 1966-71; various other professional appointments; non-exec. Dir. The Wellcome Foundation 1985-; Dr.h.c. (Dijon) 1981, (Cranfield) 1985 and other awards. *Publications:* Lipid Biochemistry: an Introduction 1972 (co-author) articles in professional journals. *Leisure interests:* glass engraving, antique collecting, fishing, gardening. *Address:* 9 High Street, Harrold, Beds., MK43 7DG, England.

JAMES, Sir Cynlais (Kenneth) Morgan, K.C.M.G., M.A. (HONS.); British diplomatist; b. 29 April 1926; s. of Thomas Ellis James and Lydia Ann (Morgan) James; m. Teresa Girouard 1953; two d.; ed. St. Marylebone Grammar School, Durham Univ., Trinity Coll., Cambridge; in R.A.F. 1944-47; Sr. Branch of Foreign Service 1951-, in Tokyo 1953, Brazil 1956, Cultural Attaché, Moscow 1959, Foreign Office 1962, Paris 1965, Saigon 1969; FCO, Head of Western European Dept. 1971-75; NATO Defence Coll. 1975-76; Minister, Paris 1976-81; Amb. to Poland 1981-83; Asst. Under-Sec. of State 1983-; Amb. to Mexico 1983-; Non-Exec. Dir. Thomas Cook Group 1986-; Dir.-Gen. Canning House; Consultant British Rail Eng. Ltd. (BREL), Darwin Instruments; Chair. British Inst., Paris; mem. Franco-British Council; Order of the Aztec Eagle; Dr. h.c. Mexican Acad. of Int. Law. *Leisure interests:* history, music, tennis, cricket. *Address:* 20 Greville Road, Flat 2, London, N.W.6, England.

JAMES, Forrest Hood, Jr., B.S.; American business executive and politician; b. 15 Sept. 1934, Lanett, Ala.; s. of Forrest Hood James Sr. and Rebecca Ellington James; m. Bobbie Mooney James 1955; three s.; ed. Auburn Univ., Ala.; Founder, Pres., Chair. Bd. Diversified Products Corpn., Opelika, Ala. 1962-78; Gov. of Alabama 1979-83; Democrat. *Leisure interests:* duck hunting, reading, history. *Address:* c/o The Governor's Office, State Capitol, Montgomery, Ala. 36130, U.S.A.

JAMES, Harold L., PH.D.; American geologist; b. 11 June 1912, Nanaimo, B.C., Canada; of Welsh parentage; m. Ruth Graybeal 1936; four s.; ed. Washington State Univ. and Princeton Univ.; Geologist, U.S. Geological Survey 1941-, Chief Geologist 1965-71, Research Geologist 1971-; Visiting Lecturer, Northwestern Univ. 1953, 1954; Prof., Univ. of Minnesota 1961-65; mem. Nat. Acad. of Sciences; Pres. Soc. of Econ. Geologists 1970. *Publications:* About 70 papers in professional journals and in U.S. Geological Survey. *Leisure interests:* reading, fishing, writing. *Address:* 1617 Washington Street, Port Townsend, Washington 98368, U.S.A. *Telephone:* (206) 385-0878 (Home).

JAMES, Ioan Mackenzie, M.A., D.PHIL., F.R.S.; British professor of geometry; b. 23 May 1928; s. of Reginald D. James and Jessie A. James; m. Rosemary G. Stewart 1961; no c.; ed. St. Paul's School and Queen's Coll. Oxford; Commonwealth Fund Fellow, Princeton, Univ. of Calif. Berkeley and Inst. for Advanced Study 1954-55; Tapp Research Fellow, Gonville & Caius Coll. Cambridge 1956; Reader in Pure Math. Univ. of Oxford 1957-69, Sr. Research Fellow, St. John's Coll. 1959-69, Savilian Prof. of Geometry 1970-, Fellow, New Coll. 1970-; Ed. Topology 1962-; Whitehead Prize and Lecturer 1978. *Publications:* The Mathematical Works of J.H.C. Whitehead 1963, The Topology of Stiefel Manifolds 1976, Topological Topics 1983, General Topology and Homotopy Theory 1984, Aspects of Topology 1984, Topological and Uniform Spaces 1987, Fibrewise Topology 1988; papers in mathematical journals. *Address:* Mathematical Institute, 24-29 St. Giles, Oxford, England. *Telephone:* (0865) 273541.

JAMES, Sir (John) Morrice Cairns (See Saint Brides, Baron).

JAMES, Michael Leonard, M.A., F.R.S.A.; British government official; b. 7 Feb. 1941; s. of Leonard James and Marjorie James; m. Jill Elizabeth Tarján 1975; two d.; ed. Christ's Coll., Cambridge; entered govt. service (GCHQ) 1963; Pvt. Sec. to Rt. Hon. Jennie Lee, Minister for the Arts 1966-68; Prin. D.E.S. 1968-71; Planning Unit of Rt. Hon. Margaret Thatcher, Sec. of State for Educ. and Science 1971-73, Asst. Sec. 1973; Deputy Chief Scientific Officer 1974; Adviser to OECD, Paris, and U.K. Gov., Int. Inst. for Man. of Tech., Milan 1973-75; Int. negotiations on nonproliferation of nuclear weapons 1975-78; Dir., IAEA Vienna 1978-83; Adviser Int. Relations and Nuclear Energy, Comm. of the European Communities, Brussels 1983-; a Chair. Civil Service Comm. Selection Bds. 1983-; Chair. The Hartland Press Ltd. 1985-; Hon. Fellow Univ. of Exeter 1985-; Gov. East Devon Coll. of Further Educ., Tiverton 1985-, Colyton Grammar School 1985-, Sidmouth Community Coll. 1988-; Chair. Bd. of Man. Axe Vale Further Educ. Unit, Seaton 1987-, (mem. 1985-); mem. Exeter Social Security Appeal Tribunal 1986-, Exeter and Taunton VAT Appeal Tribunal 1987-; South West Arts Literary Award 1984. *Publications:* Co-Author: Internationalization to Prevent the Spread of Nuclear Weapons 1980; four novels under a pseudonym; articles on int. relations and nuclear energy. *Address:* Cotte Barton, Branscombe, Devon, EX12 3BH, England.

JAMES OF RUSHOLME, Baron (Life Peer), cr. 1959, Kt. (cr. 1956); **Eric John Francis James,** D.PHIL. (Oxon.); British educationist; b. 13 April 1909, Derby; s. of Francis and Lilian James; m. Cordelia Wintour 1939; one s.; ed. Taunton's School, Southampton and Queen's Coll., Oxford; Asst. Master Winchester Coll. 1933-45; High Master The Manchester Grammar School

1945-62; Vice-Chancellor, Univ. of York 1962-73; mem. Univ. Grants Cttee. 1948-58; Chair. Headmasters Conf. 1953 and 1954; mem. Cen. Advisory Council for Educ. 1957; Fellow, Winchester Coll. 1963; mem. Press Council 1963-67, Social Science Research Council 1965-69; Chair. Cttee. on Training and Educ. of Teachers 1970-71; Chair. Personal Social Services Council 1973-76; mem. Royal Fine Arts Comm. 1973-79, Chair. 1976-79; Hon. F.R.I.B.A.; Hon. Fellow Queen's Coll., Oxford 1960; Hon. LL.D. (McGill, York, Toronto), Hon. D.Litt. (New Brunswick), D. Univ. (York). *Publications:* Elements of Physical Chemistry (in part) 1938, Science and Education (in part) 1942, An Essay on the Content of Education 1949, Education and Leadership 1951. *Address:* Penhill Cottage, West Witton, Leyburn, Yorkshire, England.

JAMES, Phyllis Dorothy, (Mrs C. B. White) O.B.E., J.P.; British authoress; b. 3 Aug. 1920; d. of Sidney Victor James and Dorothy Amelia Hone; m. Connor Bantry White (deceased) 1941; two d.; ed. Cambridge Girl's High School; Admin., Nat. Health Service 1949-68; Prin., Home Office 1968; Police Dept. 1968-72; Criminal Policy Dept. 1972-79; J.P., Willesden 1979-82, Inner London 1984; Chair. Soc. of Authors 1984-86; Gov. of BBC 1988-; Assoc. Fellow Downing Coll., Cambridge 1986; mem. Crime Writers' Assocn. *Publications:* Cover Her Face 1962, A Mind to Murder 1963, Unnatural Causes 1967, Shroud for a Nightingale 1971, The Maul and the Pear Tree (with T. A. Critchley) 1971, An Unsuitable Job for a Woman 1972, The Black Tower 1975, Death of an Expert Witness 1977, Innocent Blood 1980, The Skull beneath the Skin 1982, A Taste for Death 1986. *Leisure interests:* exploring churches, walking by the sea. *Address:* c/o Elaine Greene Ltd, 31 Newington Green, London, N16 9PU, England.

JAMES, Thomas Garnet Henry, C.B.E., M.A., F.B.A.; British museum curator (retd.); b. 8 May 1923, Neath, Wales; s. of Thomas Garnet James and Edith James (née Griffiths); m. Diana Margaret Vavasseur-Durell 1956; one s.; ed. Neath Grammar School and Exeter Coll. Oxford; served in army (R.A.) 1942-45; Asst. Keeper, British Museum 1951-74; Laycock Student, Worcester Coll. Oxford 1954-60; Keeper of Egyptian Antiquities, British Museum 1974-88; Chair. Egypt Exploration Soc. 1983-, Advisory Cttee., Freud Museum 1987-; Wilbour Fellow, The Brooklyn Museum 1964; Visiting Prof., College de France 1983; mem. German Archaeological Inst. *Publications:* The Mastaba of Khentika 1953, The Hekanakhte Papers 1962, Hieroglyphic Texts in the British Museum, I (revised) 1961, 9 1970, Archaeology of Ancient Egypt 1972, Corpus of Hieroglyphic Inscriptions in The Brooklyn Museum, 1 1974, Pharaoh's People 1984, Egyptian Painting 1985, Ancient Egypt: The Land and Its Legacy 1988. *Leisure interests:* music, cooking. *Address:* 14 Turner Close, London, NW11 6TU, England (Home). *Telephone:* 01-455 9221 (Home).

JAMIESON, John Kenneth, B.S.; American (b. Canadian) oil executive; b. 28 Aug. 1910, Medicine Hat, Alta.; s. of John L. and Kate Alberta Herron Jamieson; m. Ethel May Burns Jamieson 1937; one s. one d.; ed. Univ. of Alta. and M.I.T.; British American Oil Co., Canada 1934-48; Vice-Pres. Imperial Oil Co. Ltd., Toronto 1948-58; Pres. Int. Petroleum Co. Ltd., Florida 1959-61; Vice-Pres. Exxon Co., U.S.A., Houston, Texas 1961-62, Exec. Vice-Pres. 1962-63, Pres. 1963-64; Dir. Exxon Corpn. 1964-81, Exec. Vice-Pres. 1964-65; Pres. and Dir. 1965-69, Chair. of Bd. 1969-75; Dir. Chase Manhattan Bank 1965-76, Equitable Life Assurance Soc. of the U.S. 1971-82, Raychem Corpn. 1977-. *Leisure interests:* golf, fishing. *Address:* 1100 Milam Building, Suite 4601, Houston, Tex. 77002, U.S.A. *Telephone:* (713) 656-6694.

JAMIR, S. C., B.A., LL.B.; Indian politician; b. 17 Oct. 1931; s. of Shri Senayangba; m. 1959; ed. Univ. of Allahabad; mem. Interim Body of Nagaland, then Jt. Sec. Naga People's Convention; Vice-Chair. Mokokchung Town Cttee. 1959-60; M.P. 1961-70; Parl. Sec., Ministry of External Affairs, Govt. of India 1961-67; Union Deputy Minister of Railways, of Labour and Rehabilitation, of Community Devt. and Co-operation, Food and Agric. 1968-70; re-elected mem. from Aonglenden Consituency 1974; subsequently apptd. Minister of Finance, Revenue and Border Affairs; re-elected 1977 and apptd. Deputy Chief Minister in UDF Ministry; Chief Minister of ULP Ministry April 1980; resgnd. when NNDP Ministry came to power June 1980; Leader of Opposition Congress (I) in State Legis. Ass. 1980-82; elected from 26 Aonglenden Constituency, Gen. Elections 1982; unanimously elected Leader Congress (I) Legislature Party, Chief Minister Nagaland 1982-86. *Address:* c/o Raj Bhavan, Kohima, Nagaland.

JAMISON, Robin Ralph, PH.D., F.R.AE.S., F.ENG., F.R.S., C.CHEM., M.R.C.S.; British engineer (retd.); b. 12 July 1912, Horsham; s. of Reginald Jamison and Eanswyth Elstreth Heyworth; m. Hilda Watney Wilson 1937; two s. two d.; ed. Univ. of Cape Town; Fitter and Tester Rolls Royce Ltd. 1937-40, Tech. Engineer 1940-50; Head of Ramjet Dept., Bristol Aeroplane Co., later Bristol Siddeley and Rolls Royce (Bristol) 1950-55, Asst. Chief Engineer 1950-60, Head of Research and Chief Engineer 1960-72, Chief Tech. Exec. (Research) 1972-75; Silver Medal Royal Aeronautical Soc., Enoch Thulin Medal Swedish Aeronautical Soc. *Publications:* articles in aeronautical journals. *Leisure interests:* photography, gardening, sailing. *Address:* 2, The Crescent, Henleaze, Bristol, BS9 4RN, England. *Telephone:* 0272 620328.

JANABIL; Chinese party official; b. April 1934, Khaba Co., Xinjiang; s. of Simagul Janabil and Ajikhan Janabil; m. Zubila Janabil 1955; two s. two

d.; alt. mem. 10th CCP Cen. Cttee. 1973; Vice-Chair. Revolutionary Cttee., Xinjiang Autonomous Region 1975-79; Chair. Revolutionary Cttee., and First Sec. CCP Cttee., Ili Autonomous Kazakh Pref. 1975-80; Deputy Sec. CCP Cttee., Xinjiang 1977-83, Sec. 1983-; Vice-Chair. Xinjiang 1979-83; Pres. Xinjiang Br. Futurology Soc. 1980; alt. mem. 12th CCP Cen. Cttee. 1982, 13th Cen. Cttee. 1987. *Address:* Xinjiang Autonomous Regional Chinese Communist Party, Urumqi, Xinjiang, People's Republic of China. *Telephone:* 22961.

JANAK, Ignac; Czechoslovak politician; b. 4 Oct. 1930, Velke Zaluzice, E. Slovakia; ed. teacher training and CPSU Acad. of Social Sciences; fmr. secondary school headmaster; mem. Cen. Cttee. of CP of Slovakia (CPSL) 1961, Head of Section, CPSL Educ. Dept. 1967; Sec. W. Slovak Regional Cttee. of CPSL 1973; mem. CPSL Presidium 1977; Sec. Cen. Cttee. 1987; mem. Cen. Cttee. CP of Czechoslovakia (CPCZ) 1973, cand. mem. Presidium 1986, mem. Presidium 1988-; Deputy to House of the People. *Address:* Central Committee of Communist Party of Czechoslovakia, nábř Ludvíka Svobody 12, 125 11 Prague 1, Czechoslovakia.

JANCSÓ, Miklós; Hungarian film director; b. 27 Sept. 1921, Vác; s. of Sándor Jancsó and Angela Poparad; m. 1st Márta Mészáros 1958; two s. one d.; m. 2nd Csákány Zsuzsa 1981, one s.; studied legal sciences and ethnography at Kolozsvár (now Cluj), Romania, and Budapest Coll. of Cinematographic Art; worked at newsreel studio 1953-58; Documentary film studio 1962; Chief Producer, Hunnia Film Studio 1963-; Grand Prix of San Francisco 1961, Prize of Fédération Internationale de la Presse Cinématographique (FIPRESCI), Béla Balázs prize 1965, Merited artist 1970, Eminent Artist of the Hungarian People's Repub. 1980, Best Dir. Award, Cannes Festival 1972, Kossuth Prize (2nd Degree) 1973. *Films:* A harangok Rómába mentek (The Bells have gone to Rome) 1959, Oldás és Kötés (Cantata) 1963, Szegény Legények (The Round-Up) 1966, Igy Jöttem (My Way Home) 1965, Csillagosok—Katonák (The Red and the White) 1967, Csend és Kiáltás (Silence and Cry) 1968, Fényes Szelek (The Confrontation) 1969, Sirókkó (Winter Wind) 1969, La Pacifista 1970, Agnus Dei 1971, Red Psalm 1972, Elektreia (Electra) 1975, Private Vices, Public Virtues 1976, Hungarian Rhapsody 1978, Allegro Barbaro 1978, The Tyrant's Heart or Boccaccio in Hungary 1981, Omega 1984, Season of Monsters 1987; For Italian TV: Il Tecnico e il Rito, Roma rivuole Cesare, La Pacifista; Stage production: Othello 1974; *Opera directed:* Otello 1980. *Address:* MAFILM Studio, Lumumba utca 174, Budapest XIV (Office); Sólyom Làszló utca 17, H-1022 Budapest II, Hungary (Home). *Telephone:* 831-750 (Office); 353-761 (Home).

JANDL, Ernst, D.PHIL.; Austrian poet and dramatist; b., 1 Aug. 1925, Vienna; s. of Viktor and Luise (née Rappel) Jandl; ed. Univ. of Vienna; teacher at grammar schools 1946-79; writer 1952-; Visiting Prof., Univ. of Texas, Austin 1971; Lecturer in Poetics, Johann Wolfgang Goethe Univ., Frankfurt am Main, winter term 1984; Georg-Trakl-Prize for Poetry 1974; Great Austrian State Prize 1984; Georg-Büchner-Prize 1984. *Publications:* poetry: Andere Augen 1956, Laut und Luise 1966, Sprechblasen 1968, Der künstliche Baum 1970, Dingfest 1973, Die Bearbeitung der Mütze 1978, Der gelbe Hund 1980, Selbstporträt des Schachspielers als trinkende Uhr 1983; play: Aus der Fremde 1980; lectures and essays: Die schöne Kunst des Schreibens 1976, Das Öffnen und Schliessen des Mundes 1985; Collected Works (3 vols.) 1985. *Leisure interests:* jazz, chess. *Address:* P.O. Box 227, A-1041 Vienna, Austria. *Telephone:* 33-22-18, 65-09-500.

JANE, Col. Alexander Lesole; Lesotho police officer and politician; b. 23 Jan. 1945, Berea; ed. Immaculate Conception Elementary School, Liphookoaneng and Police Mobile Unit Private School; joined Lesotho Mobile Unit (PMU) 1967; Minister of Water, Energy and Mining 1986-; Meritorious Medal. *Address:* The Military Council, Maseru, Lesotho.

JANEWAY, Eliot, B.A.; American economist, author and lecturer; b. 1913, New York; s. of Meyer J. and Fanny (Siff) Janeway; m. Elizabeth Hall (Elizabeth Janeway, q.v.) 1938; two s.; ed. Cornell Univ. and London School of Econs.; Business Ed. and Adviser to Editor-in-Chief, Time, and Business Trends Consultant, Newsweek 1932-50; now Pres. Janeway Publishing & Research Corpn.; Chair. Classic Rarities Inc.; Treas. American PEN Center; Syndicated columnist, Chicago-Tribune New York News Service; econ. adviser to numerous industries, govt. officials and private companies. *Publications:* The Struggle for Survival 1952, The Economics of Crisis 1968, What Shall I Do With My Money? 1970, You and Your Money 1972, Musings on Money 1976, Prescriptions for Posterity 1983. *Leisure interest:* reading political history. *Address:* 15 East 80th Street, New York, N.Y. 10021, U.S.A. *Telephone:* (212) 249-8833.

JANEWAY, Elizabeth Hall, A.B.; American author; b. 7 Oct. 1913, Brooklyn, New York; d. of Charles H. and Jeannette F. (Searle) Hall; m. Eliot Janeway (q.v.) 1938; two s.; ed. Barnard Coll.; Assoc. Fellow Yale Univ.; educator's award Delta Kappa Gamma, 1972; mem. Council, Authors Guild, Council Authors League America, PEN; Chair. N.Y. State Council for the Humanities; Hon. Ph.D. (Simpson Coll., Cedarcrest Coll., Villa Maria Coll., Russell Sage Coll. 1981), Medal of Distinction, Barnard Coll. 1981, Fellow A.A.A.S. *Publications:* The Walsh Girls 1943, Daisy Kenyon 1945, The Question of Gregory 1949, The Vikings 1951, Leaving Home 1953, Early Days of the Automobile 1956, The Third Choice 1959, Angry Kate 1963, Accident 1964, Ivanov Seven 1967, Man's World, Women's Place 1971,

Between Myth and Morning: Women Awakening 1974, Harvard Guide to Contemporary American Writing 1979, Powers of the Weak 1980, contributions to Comprehensive Textbook of Psychology 1974, 1980, Cross Sections from a Decade of Change 1982, Improper Behaviour 1987. *Address:* 15 East 80th St., New York, N.Y. 10021, U.S.A. *Telephone:* (212) 249 8833.

JANEWAY, Richard, A.B., M.D.; American physician and medical school administrator; b. 12 Feb. 1933, Los Angeles, Calif.; s. of VanZandt and Grace Eleanor Bell Janeway; m. Katherine Esmond Pillsbury 1955; one s. two d.; ed. Colgate Univ., Univ. of Pennsylvania School of Medicine; Instructor in Neurology, Bowman Gray School of Medicine of Wake Forest Univ. 1966-67, Asst. Prof. 1967-70, Assoc. Prof. 1970-71, Prof. 1971-, Dean 1971-85, Vice-Pres. for Health Affairs 1983-, Exec. Dean 1985-; John and Mary R. Markle Scholar in Acad. Medicine; mem. Inst. of Medicine of N.A.S., American Medical Asscn., A.A.A.S., American Heart Asscn., American Neurological Asscn., Soc. for Neuroscience, Soc. of Medical Admins.; Fellow American Acad. of Neurology; Life Fellow American Coll. of Physicians; Chair. Asscn. of American Medical Colls. 1984-85, Bd. Dirs., S. Nat. Corpn. 1989-. *Leisure interests:* tennis, golf, photography. *Address:* The Bowman Gray School of Medicine of Wake Forest University, 300 S. Hawthorne Road, Winston-Salem, N.C. 27103; 2815 Country Club Road, Winston-Salem, N.C. 27104, U.S.A. (Home). *Telephone:* (919) 748-4424 (Office); (919) 768-7545 (Home).

JANISZEWSKI, Gen. Michał, D.MIL.SCI.; Polish politician; b. 15 June 1926, Poznań; ed. Gdańsk Tech. Univ., Mil. Acad. of Communications, Gen. Staff Acad. of Polish Army; prisoner of Gestapo during German occupation 1940, forced labour in Germany, electrician 1943; active service in Polish Army 1950-; tech. posts, organizing and planning in Corps of Signals 1951-63, operational and staff posts 1963-71, Chief of Office of Minister of Nat. Defence 1972-81; rank of Col. 1966, Maj.-Gen. 1976, Lieut.-Gen. 1983; Chief, Office of Council of Ministers 1981-; mem. Mil. Council of Nat. Salvation 1981-83; mem. Presidium of Govt., Minister, Chief of Office of Council of Ministers, supervising activity of state admin. 1985-; participant works of Econ. Cttee., Council of Ministers, WERM 1988-; mem. PZPR 1950-; Minister of Nat. Defence Prize 1965; Order of Banner of Labour (1st Class), Commdr.'s and Kt.'s Cross Order of Polonia Restituta, Gold Cross of Merit, Soviet Order of Friendship Among Nations, many other Polish and foreign distinctions. *Address:* Urząd Rady Ministrów, Al. Ujazdowskie 1/3, 00-583 Warsaw, Poland.

JANIUREK, Włodzimierz; Polish politician and journalist; b. 21 Sept. 1924, Chorzów; s. of Stefan and Helena (née Sroka) Janiurek; m. Janina Goliasz 1946 (died 1984); three d.; ed. Higher School of Pedagogy, Katowice; engaged as manual worker during occupation, then as a journalist with Trybuna Robotnicza, Katowice; in Press Dept. of Cen. Cttee., Polish United Workers' Party (PZPR) 1951-54; Editor-in-Chief Trybuna Robotnicza, Katowice 1954-66; Amb. to Czechoslovakia 1966-71; Under-Sec. of State for Information to Council of Ministers, Govt. Press Spokesman 1971-80; Amb. to Mexico 1980-81; Deputy to Seym (Parl.) 1957-69; mem. Cttee. on Foreign Affairs; Chair. Sub-Cttee. for Poles Living Abroad; Sec. Polish-British Group of Interparliamentary Union 1957-69; Deputy mem. Cen. Cttee. PZPR 1975-80; mem. Cen. Revisional Comm. 1980-81; Gold Cross of Merit 1954, Kt.'s Cross, Order of Polonia Restituta 1955, Order of Banner of Labour (Second class) 1960, (First Class) 1974, Commdr.'s Cross of Order of Polonia Restituta 1970, Medal of Thirty Years of the Polish People's Repub. 1974, Medal of Forty Years of the Polish People's Repub. 1984 and several foreign decorations. *Publications:* The Bitter Taste of Transitoriness 1986, Mexico, Mexico 1986, Trybuna Robotnicza 1945-66 (Workers' Tribune) (essay) 1987; books on politics and economics, collections of newspaper articles. *Leisure interests:* literature, sport, stamp collecting, gardening. *Address:* Ul. Kormoranów 10, 40-521 Katowice, Poland. *Telephone:* 515-915.

JANKLOW, William John, B.S., J.D.; American lawyer and politician; b. 13 Sept. 1939, Chicago, Ill.; s. of Arthur and LouElla Janklow; m. Mary Dean Thom 1960; one s. two d.; ed. Flandreau High School, South Dakota, Univ. of South Dakota; Staff Attorney and Chief Officer, S. Dakota Legal Services 1966-67; Directing Attorney and Chief Officer, S. Dakota Legal Services 1967-72; Chief Trial Attorney, S. Dakota Attorney Gen.'s Office 1973-74; Attorney Gen. of S. Dakota 1975-79; Gov. of S. Dakota 1979-87; apptd. Bd. of Dir. of Nat. Legal Services Corpn.; Nat. award for legal excellence and skill; various awards; mem. Exec. Cttee. of the Nat. Governors' Asscn.; Republican. *Leisure interests:* waterskiing, collecting 1950s music.

JANKOVIC, Tomislav; Yugoslav diplomatist; b. 1933, Arandjelovac; m.; two d.; ed. Univ. of Belgrade; joined Foreign Service 1961; Third Sec. Prague 1963-66; with Fed. Secr. for Foreign Affairs; Second Sec. London 1969-74; Deputy Head, Mission to European Communities, Brussels 1978-82; Minister Plenipotentiary, Ministry of Foreign Affairs 1982; Head, Perm. Del. of Yugoslavia to OECD 1986-. *Address:* Delegation of Yugoslavia, Organization for Economic Cooperation and Development, 2 rue André Pascal, 75775 Paris Cedex 16, France.

JANKOWITSCH, Peter, D.D.L.; Austrian diplomatist; b. 10 July 1933, Vienna; s. of Karl and Gertrude (née Ladstaetter) Jankowitsch; m. Odette

Prevor 1962; one s.; ed. Vienna Univ. and The Hague Acad. of Int. Law; fmr. lawyer; joined foreign service 1957, worked in Int. Law Dept.; Private Sec., Cabinet of Minister of Foreign Affairs 1959-62; posted to London 1962-64; Chargé d'affaires, Dakar, Senegal 1964-66; Head of Office of Bruno Kreisky, Chair. Austrian Socialist Party 1967; Chief of Cabinet of Fed. Chancellor (Kreisky) 1970-72; Perm. Rep. to UN 1972-78; Perm. Rep. to OECD 1978-82; Deputy Perm. Under-Sec., Chief of Cabinet, Fed. Ministry of Foreign Affairs 1982-83; Fed. Minister for Foreign Affairs 1986-87; mem. Austrian Nat. Ass. (Nationalrat) 1983; Chair. UN Cttee. on Peaceful Uses of Outer Space 1972-; Vice-Chair. of Bd., Int. Energy Agency 1979-83; Rep. for Austria to UN Security Council 1973-75, Pres. Security Council Nov. 1973, Vice-Pres. 29th Gen. Assembly; Vice-Pres. 7th Special Session of Gen. Assembly Sept. 1975; mem. UN Security Council Mission to Zambia 1973; mem. of Bd., Vienna Inst. for Devt. 1973-, Acting Vice-Pres. 1984; Sec.-Gen. Franco-Austrian Inst. of East-West Encounters 1982-; Int. Sec. Socialist Party of Austria 1983; Chair. Foreign Relations Cttee. mem. Austrian Nat. Ass. 1987, Human Rights Cttee. Socialist Int. 1987; mem. Bd. Austrian Foreign Policy Soc. and Austrian UN League. *Publications:* Kreisky's Era in Austrian Foreign Policy (Ed. with E. Bielka and H. Thalberg) 1982, Red Markings—International (Ed. with H. Fischer) 1984 and papers and articles on Austria and on econ. and political devt. of the Third World; contrib. to Wörterbuch des Völkerrechts 1960. *Leisure interests:* history and baroque music. *Address:* Parliament, Dr. Karl Renner Ring 3, 1017 Vienna, Austria.

JANNE, Henri, D.PHIL. ET LETTRES; Belgian university professor and sociologist; b. 20 Feb. 1908, Brussels; s. of Emile and Anne (née Matthys) Janne; m. Elisabeth Houtman 1936; one s.; ed. Athénée Royal d'Ixelles, Univ. of Brussels; Directed a number of govt. econ. and social services, including Dir. Office Nat. des Vacances Ouvrières 1936, Dir.-Gen. Rééquipement Nat. 1947, Dir.-Gen. Coordination Economique (Prime Minister's Office) 1949; Chef du Cabinet, Ministries of Econ. Affairs, Supplies, and Econ. Co-ordination 1945-49; Pres. Defence Production Bd. NATO 1949-51; Pres. Belgian del. to UN Econ. and Social Council 1954 session; Prof. of Sociology, Univ. of Brussels 1951-; Dir. Inst. de Sociologie Solvay 1953-56; Pres. Conseil Nat. du Travail 1958-61; Prof. Coll. of Europe, Bruges 1952-; mem. Senate 1961; Minister of Nat. Educ. and Culture 1963-65; Vice-Pres. Nat. Council for Scientific Policy; mem. Int. Cttee. for Social Sciences Documentation, Int. Cttee. of UNESCO for Social Science Terminology 1954, Libre Acad. de Belgique; Pres. Acad. Royale de Belgique des Sciences et des Lettres 1973, Coll. Scientifique de l'Inst. de Sociologie; Rector Brussels Univ. 1956-59; Pres. d'honneur de l'Asscn. Int. des Sociologues de Langue française; Pres. Scientific Cttee. of Plan 2000 Educ., European Cultural Foundation 1968; mem. Bd. Int. Council on the Future of the Univ. 1973; mem. of Gov. Bd. of Centre for Educ. Research and Innovation, OECD 1969-70; mem. of Bd. of Trustees of Int. Council for Educ. Devt. (ICED); Chair. Adult Educ. Experts Cttee., Council of Europe 1974-, mem. Evaluation Group of Postgraduate Studies 1982; mem. Governing Bd., European Cultural Foundation, Amsterdam; mem. Exec. Cttee. Société Européenne de Culture (Venice); Corresp. mem. Inst. de France 1974; mem. European Acad. of Arts, Sciences and Humanities (Paris) 1981; Hon. Pres. European Inst. for Educ. and Social Policy, Paris; Dr. h.c. (Sorbonne, Univ. René Descartes, Paris) 1982; Croix de guerre avec palme, Officier Légion d'honneur, Grand Officier Ordre de Léopold, Medal of the Council of Europe 1981. *Publications:* L'antialcibiade 1946, Sociologie et politique sociale dans les pays occidentaux 1962, Technique, développement économique et technocratie 1963, Le système social, essai de théorie générale 1968, Le temps du changement 1970, Educational Needs of the Age Group 16-19 1973, For a Community Policy on Education 1973, Foundations of Lifelong Education 1976, Le développement européen de l'éducation permanente (with Bertrand Schwartz) 1977, Education and Youth Employment in Belgium 1979, Egalité et Education (European Inst. of Educ., Paris) 1981, Les finalités culturelles du développement (Council of Europe) 1981. *Leisure interest:* travelling. *Address:* Avenue Jeanne 44, 1050 Brussels (Office); 244 avenue Louise, Bôite 13, 1050 Brussels, Belgium (Home). *Telephone:* (02) 647 1312.

JANOT, Raymond Marcel Louis, L. EN D., L. ÈS L.; French civil servant; b. 9 March 1917, Paris; s. of Gaston Janot and Madeleine Paumier; m. Catherine de Brunel de Serbonnes; two s. two d.; ed. Coll. Stanislas, Lycée Henry-IV, Paris Univ. and Ecole Libre des Sciences Politiques; Auditeur, Conseil d'Etat 1946, Maître des Requêtes 1948; Legal Counsellor, Présidence de la République 1947-51; Econ. Counsellor French High Comm. in Indo-China 1951-52; Dir. du Cabinet, Minister for Relations with Associated States 1952-53; Sec.-Gen. Conseil d'Etat 1956-59; Mayor of Serbonnes, Conseiller général of canton of Sergines 1959-; Tech. Counsellor, Gen. de Gaulle 1958-59; Sec.-Gen. French Community 1959-60; Dir.-Gen. Radiodiffusion-Télévision française 1960-62; mem. Conseil d'Etat 1962-; Pres. Devt. Cttee. of Yonne 1964-; mem. Econ. and Social Cttee. Bourgogne 1974-; Pres. Admin. Council of the commune and dept. of Paris 1983-; Vice-Pres. Syndicat Nat. de l'Industrie Pharmaceutique 1975-; Conseil régional de Bourgogne 1985-; Officier Légion d'honneur, Croix de guerre, Médaille des Evadés, Commdr. Ordre nationale du Mérite. *Address:* 11 avenue d'Eylau, 75116 Paris, France. *Telephone:* 727-72-89.

JANOWITZ, Gundula; Austrian opera singer; b. 2 Aug. 1937, Berlin, Germany; d. of Theodor and Else (née Neumann) Janowitz; m.; one d.; ed.

Acad. of Music and Performing Arts, Graz; Début with Vienna State Opera; has sung with Deutsche Oper, Berlin 1966, Metropolitan Opera, New York 1967, Teatro Colón, Buenos Aires 1970, Munich State Opera 1971, Grand Opera, Paris 73, Covent Garden Opera 1976, La Scala 1978; concerts in major cities throughout the world, appearances at Bayreuth, Aix-en-Provence, Glyndebourne, Spoleto, Salzburg, Munich Festivals; mem. Vienna State Opera, Deutsche Oper, Berlin; recordings with Deutsche Grammophon, EMI, Decca. *Leisure interest:* modern literature. *Address:* c/o Wiener Staatsoper, 1010 Vienna, Opernring 2, Austria.

JANOWSKI, Jan, D.SC.; Polish professor of metallurgy and politician; b. 20 June 1928, Kielce; m. Maria Janowski; one s. one d.; Projects Office of Industry and Cement, Cracow 1951-54; Head, Sub-Dept. of Pig Iron Metallurgy, Univ. of Mining and Metallurgy, Cracow 1954-69, Asst. Prof. 1969-72, Extraordinary Prof. 1972-78, Prof. 1978-, Dean Metallurgical Faculty 1972-78, Dir. Inst. of Metallurgy 1974-78, Vice-Rector 1978-81, now Head, Blast Furnace Dept., Inst. of Metallurgy, Rector 1987; mem. Inst. of Metals (U.K.) and other scientific bodies; mem. Presidium, Cen. Cttee. of Democratic Party of Poland 1976-81, 1985-; Deputy to Seym (Parl.) Vice-Pres. Foreign Affairs Cttee., Polish Group of Interparl. Union 1976-; State prize (1st class) 1972; Commdr.'s and Officer's Cross, Order of Polonia Restituta; Gold Cross of Merit and other decorations.. *Address:* 30-047 Cracow, ul. Szymanowskiego 1m. 10a, Poland. *Telephone:* 33-58-35 (Home); 33-26-13 (Office).

JANSON, Teunis Nicolaas Hendrik, B.A., B.D.; South African politician; b. 27 May 1919, Lydenburg, Eastern Transvaal; m. Corrie Rossouw; six c.; ed. Univ. of Pretoria; minister of religion 1952-66; fmr. mem. Witbank Town Council; fmr. Mayor Witbank; Chair. Transvaal Municipal Bd.; mem. exec. S.A. Municipal Asscn.; mem. Parl. 1966-; Deputy Minister of Bantu Admin. and Bantu Educ. 1972-78; Minister of Educ. and Training 1978-80; mem. Pres.'s Council (Chair. Community Relations Cttee.) 1980-. *Address:* c/o President's Council, P.O. Box 3601, Cape Town 8000, South Africa.

JANSONS, Maris Arvidovich; Soviet conductor; b. 14 Jan. 1943, Riga: s. of Arvid Jansons and Erahida Jansons; m. Irina Jansons 1967; one d.; ed. by father (also conductor), then Leningrad Conservatory (under N. Rabinovich), Vienna Conservatory (with Hans Swarovsky) and Salzburg (under von Karajan); second conductor of Leningrad Philharmonic Orchestra, Chief Conductor of Oslo Philharmonic 1978-; Guest Conductor of Welsh Symphony Orchestra 1985-; has appeared in 22 countries, prin. recordings include Tchaikovsky's symphonies, Grieg, Sibelius, Rachmaninov, Shostakovich and Prokofiev; worldwide concert tours with Leningrad and Oslo Philharmonic; R.S.F.S.R. People's Artist 1986. *Leisure interests:* arts, theatre, films, sports. *Address:* Leningrad Philharmonia, Polshchad Iskusstv, Leningrad, U.S.S.R.; Oslo Philharmonic Orchestra, P.O. Box 1607, 0119 Oslo, Norway.

JANSSEN, Baron Daniel, ING., LIC., M.B.A.; Belgian business executive; b. 15 April 1936, Brussels; s. of Baron Charles-E. Janssen and Marie-Anne (née Boël) Janssen; m. Thérèse Bracht 1970; three s.; ed. Univ. of Brussels, Harvard Univ.; Asst. Sec. Euratom Comm., Brussels 1959-60; Prof. Brussels Univ. 1965-71; mem. Club of Rome 1968-87; Bd. of Dirs. Brussels Univ. 1969-70; mem. of Bd. Inst. pour l'Encouragement de la Recherche Scientifique dans l'Industrie et l'Agriculture (IRSIA) 1971-77, Vice-Chair. 1974-77; mem. of Bd. Belgian Fed. of Chemical Industries 1972-76, Chair. 1976-79; mem. European Cttee. for R & D, EEC 1974-79; Chair. Exec. Cttee. UCB 1975-84, Fed. of Belgian Enterprises 1981-84, Solvay & Cie. S.A. 1986; holds non-exec. functions on numerous enterprises; recipient of Alumni Achievement Award, Harvard Business School. *Leisure interests:* tennis, skiing, shooting. *Address:* Solvay & Cie S.A., 33 rue du Prince Albert, 1050 Brussels (Office); La Roncière, 108 avenue Ernest Solvay, 1310 La Hulpe, Belgium (Home).

JANSSON, Jan-Magnus, PH.D.; Finnish publisher; b. 24 Jan. 1922, Helsinki; s. of Carl Gösta and Anna-Lisa Jansson (née Kuhlefelt); m. 1st Kerstin Edgren 1948 (divorced 1970), 2nd Marita Hausen 1970 (divorced 1975), 3rd Siv Dahlin 1976; two d.; ed. Helsinki Univ.; Prof. of Political Science, Helsinki Univ. 1954-74; Minister of Trade and Industry 1973-74; Ed.-in-Chief Hufvudstadsbladet 1974-87; Chair. Bd. Finnish Inst. of Foreign Affairs 1959-85; Chair. Paasikivi Soc. 1964-66, 1975-85, Swedish People's Party in Finland 1966-73, Parl. Defence Comms. 1970-71, 1975-76, 1980-81; mem. Bd. Int. Political Science Assoc. 1966-73; Chancellor Åbo Akad. (Swedish Univ. of Finland) 1985-; Commdr. Order of the White Rose of Finland, Commdr. Grand Cross of the Order of the Lion of Finland. *Publications:* Hans Kelsens statsteori 1950, Frihet och jämlikhet 1952, Politikens teori 1969, Idé och verklighet i politiken 1972, Ledare 1981 and two collections of poetry. *Leisure interest:* literature. *Address:* Åbo Akademi, Domkyrkotorget 3, 20500 Åbo (Office); Linnankoskigatan 15 B 16, 00250 Helsinki 25, Finland (Home). *Telephone:* 493424 (Home).

JANSZ, Hendrik Simon; Netherlands professor of biochemistry; b. 30 April 1927, Wonosobo; m. Julie Lamberti 1954; four s. three d.; ed. Univ. of Leiden; Prof. of Biochemistry, Univ. of Utrecht 1967-; mem. European Molecular Biol. Org. 1983, Royal Netherlands Acad. of Arts and Sciences; Saal van Zwanenburg Award 1968. *Address:* Laboratorium voor Fysiologische Chemie, Vondellaan 24 A, 3521 GG Utrecht, The Netherlands.

JANZA, Vladimír, ING.; Czechoslovak politician; b. 10 March 1929, Zilina; ed. Comenius Univ. of Bratislava, State Inst. for Econ., Moscow; State Planning Office 1953-63, Sec. State Price Cttee. 1963-65; Deputy Minister-Chair. State Comm. on Finance, Prices and Wages 1965-68; Deputy Minister, Fed. Price Office 1968-71; Deputy Chair. State Planning Comm. 1971-73, Minister, Vice-Chair. 1973-88; Rep. for Czechoslovakia, CMEA Cttee. for Material Technological Supplies 1977-87; Distinction for Merit in Construction, Order of Labour 1979. *Address:* c/o State Planning Commission, Prague 7, nábř. kpt. Jaroše 1000, Czechoslovakia.

JANZEN, Daniel Hunt, PH.D.; American professor of biology; b. 18 Jan. 1939, Millwaukee, Wis.; s. of Daniel Hugo Janzen and Floyd Foster Janzen; twice m., twice divorced; one s. one d. from 1st marriage; ed. Univ. of Minnesota and Univ. of California, Berkeley; Asst. and Assoc. Prof., Univ. of Kansas 1965-68; Assoc. Prof., Univ. of Chicago 1969-72; Assoc. Prof. and Prof. of Ecology and Evolutionary Biology, Univ. of Mich. 1972-76; Prof. of Biology, Univ. of Pa., Philadelphia 1976-; teaching responsibility with Org. for Tropical Studies in Costa Rica 1965-; field research in tropical ecology, supported mainly by grants from Nat. Science Foundation, U.S.A. 1963-; Gleason Award, American Botanical Soc. 1975; Crafoord Prize, Coevolutionary Ecology, Swedish Royal Acad. of Sciences 1984. *Publications:* Herbivores (Ed., with G. A. Rosenthal) 1979, Costa Rican Natural History (Ed.) 1983 and 250 papers in scientific journals. *Leisure interest:* tropical ecology. *Address:* Department of Biology, University of Pennsylvania, Philadelphia, Pa. 19104, U.S.A. and Parque Nacional Santa Rosa, Apdo. 169, Liberia, Guanacaste Province, Costa Rica. *Telephone:* (215) 898-5636 (U.S.A.); 69-55-98 (Costa Rica).

JAPAN, Emperor of (see Akihito).

JARAY, Tess, D.F.A.; Britsh artist, b. 31 Dec. 1937, Vienna; d. of Dr Francis F. and Pauline Jaray; m. 1960 (divorced 1983); two d.; ed. Alice Ottley School, Worcester, St. Martin's School of Art and Slade School of Fine Art; French Govt. scholarship 1961; commissioned to paint mural for British Pavilion, Expo '67, Montreal; individual exhbns. Grabowski Gallery, London 1963, Hamilton Galleries, London 1965, 1967, Axiom Gallery, London 1969, Whitechapel Gallery, London 1973, Adelaide Festival Centre 1980, Whitworth Art Gallery, Manchester, and Ashmolean Museum, Oxford 1984; lecturer, Slade School of Fine Art. *Address:* 29 Camden Square, London, N.W.1, England. *Telephone:* 01-485 5057.

JARMAN, Derek; British director and designer; b. 31 Jan. 1942; s. of Lance Jarman and Elizabeth Evelyn Puttock; ed. King's Coll. Univ. of London, Slade School; exhbns. include: Edward Totah Gallery, Lission Gallery, Int. Contemporary Art Fair, I.C.A.; designed Jazz Calendar, Royal Ballet 1968, Don Giovanni, ENO 1968, The Devils 1971, Savage Messiah 1972 (both for Ken Russell), Rake's Progress, Maggio Musicale, Florence 1973. *Films directed:* Sebastiane 1975, Jubilee 1977, The Tempest 1979, The Angelic Conversation 1985, Caravaggio 1986, The Last of England 1987, Aria (segment) 1987, War Requiem 1989; Dir. L'ispirazione (opera) 1988. *Publication:* Dancing Ledge 1984. *Address:* c/o British Film Institute, 29 Rathbone Place, London, W.C.2, England.

JARMAN, Franklin Maxey; American business executive; b. 10 Nov. 1931, Nashville, Tenn.; s. of late Walton Maxey Jarman and of Sarah (Anderson) Jarman; m. Nancy M. Smith 1970; ed. Montgomery Bell Acad. and M.I.T.; joined GENESCO 1957, mem. Bd. of Govs. 1960, Advisory Bd. 1960, Bd. of Dirs. 1961, Treas. 1962, Financial Vice-Pres. 1964, Exec. Vice-Pres. mem. Finance and Exec. Cttees. 1966, Pres 1969-77, Chair. GENESCO May 1969-, C.E.O. 1973-77. *Leisure interests:* water sports, flying. *Address:* GENESCO, 111 Seventh Avenue, Nashville, Tenn. (Office); 601 Bowling Avenue, Nashville, Tenn. 37215, U.S.A. (Home).

JAROCKI, Jerzy; Polish theatre director; b. 11 May 1929, Warsaw; s. of Bohdan and Leokadia Jarocki; m. 1st 1962, one d.; m. 2nd Danuta Maksymowicz 1980; ed. State Higher School of Drama, studies in drama production in Cracow and in U.S.S.R.; directs plays mainly by Polish writers S. Witkiewicz, W. Gombrowicz, T. Różewicz and S. Mrożek, also by Shakespeare and Chekov; productions abroad; with Old Theatre, Cracow 1962-; teacher, State Higher School of Drama, Cracow 1963-, Asst. Prof. 1965-85, Extraordinary Prof. 1985-; has directed over 90 plays including: Ślub (The Wedding) 1960, 1973, 1974, Cymbeline 1967, Moja Córeczka (My Little Daughter) 1968, Stara Kobieta Wysiaduje (Old Woman Brooding) 1969, Three Sisters 1969, 1974, Pater Noster 1971, Szewcy (The Shoemakers) 1972, On All Fours 1972, Matka (The Mother) 1966, 1974, The Trial 1973, The Cherry Orchard 1975, Rzeźnia (The Slaughterhouse) 1975, Bal Manekinów (Mannequins Ball) 1976, King Lear 1977, White Glove 1978, Twilight 1979, The Dream of the Sinless 1979, The Inspector General 1980, Murder in the Cathedral 1982, Pieszo (On Foot) 1981, La Vida es Sueno 1983, Sceny z Jaffy (Scenes from Jaffa) 1984, Samobójca (The Suicide) 1987, Portret (Portrait) 1988; Gold Cross of Merit, Kt.'s Cross, Order of Polonia Restituta, Gold Award of City of Cracow, Minister of Culture and Arts Prize (1st class) 1971, State Prize (2nd Class) 1976 and others. *Address:* ul. Moniuszki 33, 31-523 Kraków, Poland.

JAROSZEK, Henryk, M.A.; Polish diplomatist; b. 1 Oct. 1926, Kajetanów, Kielce district; s. of Jan and Aniela Jaroszek; m. Anna Holendzka 1950;

one s.; ed. Acad. of Political Sciences, Warsaw; Ministry of Foreign Affairs, Warsaw 1947–51; Attaché and Second Sec. at Embassy, London 1951–54, First Sec., New Delhi 1954–55; Counsellor, Washington, D.C. 1955–58; Amb. to Iraq 1959–62; Dir. of Asian and Middle Eastern Affairs, Ministry of Foreign Affairs 1962–65; Amb. and Perm. Rep. to UN Office and Specialized Agencies, Geneva 1965–69; Dir. Dept. of Int. Orgs., Ministry of Foreign Affairs 1969–75; Amb., Perm. Rep. to UN 1975–80; Under-Sec. of State, Ministry of Foreign Affairs 1982–; Chair. First Cttee. (Political and Security) of Gen. Assembly 1976; Sec.-Gen. Political Consultative Cttee. of Warsaw Treaty Org. 1987–88; mem. Polish United Workers' Party (PZPR); Commdr.'s and Kt.'s Cross, Order of Polonia Restituta, Partisan Cross and other state distinctions. *Leisure interests:* walking, angling. *Address:* Ministerstwo Spraw Zagranicznych, Al. I Armii Wojska Polskiego 23, 00-580 Warsaw, Poland.

JAROUDI, Saeb, M.A.; Lebanese international official; b. 25 Nov. 1929, Beirut; m. Leila Salam 1963; one s. one d.; ed. Int. Coll. Beirut, Univ. of California at Berkeley, Columbia Univ.; Instructor in Econs. and Research Economist, American Univ. of Beirut 1953–56; Econ. Officer UN Secr., New York 1956–65, detailed from UN as Econ. Adviser to Govt. of Kuwait 1962–64; Chief Economist, Kuwait Fund for Econ. and Social Devt. 1966–69; Minister of Nat. Econ., Lebanon 1970–72; Pres. Arab Fund for Econ. and Social Devt. 1972–79; Chair. Saudi Finance Group 1980–. *Leisure interest:* numismatics. *Address:* c/o Arab Fund for Economic and Social Development, P.O. Box 21923, Kuwait.

JAROWINSKY, Werner; German economist and politician; b. 25 April 1927, Leningrad, U.S.S.R.; m.; one c.; ed. Berlin and Halle Univs.; joined Socialist Unity Party (SED) 1946, mem. Cen. Cttee. 1963, Sec. Cen. Cttee. 1963–, Cand. mem. Politburo 1963–84, mem. 1984–; Section head, Ministry of Trade 1956–59, Deputy Minister 1959–61, State Sec. and First Deputy Minister of 1961–63; mem. Volkskammer 1963–; Chair. Cttee. on Trade 1971–; Vaterländischer Verdienstorden in Silver, Banner der Arbeit. *Address:* Am Marx-Engels-Platz 2, 102 Berlin, German Democratic Republic.

JARRATT, Sir Alexander Anthony, Kt., C.B.; British company executive; b. 19 Jan. 1924, London; s. of Alexander and Mary Jarratt; m. (Mary) Philomena Keogh 1946; one s. two d.; ed. Royal Liberty Grammar School, Essex, and Birmingham Univ.; mil. service in Fleet Air Arm; Asst. Prin. Ministry of Power 1950–53, Prin. 1953–54; Treasury 1954–55; Prin. Private Sec. to Minister of Fuel and Power 1955–59; Asst. Sec. in Oil Div. of Ministry 1959–63, Under-Sec. in Gas Div. 1963–64; Cabinet Office 1964–65; First Sec., Nat. Bd. for Prices and Incomes 1965–68; Deputy Under-Sec. of State, Dept. of Employment and Productivity 1968; Deputy Sec. Ministry of Agric. 1970; mem. Bds. of IPC and Reed Int. Ltd. 1970–; Man. Dir. IPC 1970–74, Chair. 1974–86, also of IPC Newspapers 1974; Chair. and C.E.O. Reed Int. Ltd. 1974–85; mem. Supervisory Bd., Thyssen-Bornemisza 1972; non-exec. Dir. ICI Ltd. 1975–, Smith's Industries 1984–, Chair. (non-exec.) 1985–; Dir. and Deputy Chair. Midland Bank 1980–; Deputy Chair. Prudential Corpn. 1987– (Dir. 1985–); Chair. Admin. Staff Coll., Henley; Pres. Advertising Asscn. 1979–83; Chair. C.B.I. Employment Policy Cttee. 1982–86; Pres. Periodical Publishers Asscn. 1983–85; Vice-Pres. Inst. of Marketing 1982–; Chancellor Birmingham Univ. Sept. 1983–; Gov. Ashridge Man. Coll.; mem. Council Confed. of British Industries; Hon. D.Sc. (Cranfield), Hon. Doc. Univ. (Brunel), Hon. Doc.L.I. (Birmingham). *Leisure interests:* countryside pursuits, reading. *Address:* 765, Finchley Road, Childs Hill, London, NW11 8DS, England.

JARRE, Jean-Michel André, L. ès L.; French composer; b. 24 August 1948, Lyon; s. of Maurice Jarre and Pejot (née France) Jarre; m. 2nd Charlotte Rampling (q.v.) 1978; two s. one d.; ed. Lycée Michelet, Conservatoire de musique de Paris; composer of electronic music 1968–; int. concerts include shows in China and U.S.A.; shows incorporate laser tech. illumination; Composer for ballet Aor, Paris 1971. *Albums include:* Oxygène 1976, Equinoxe 1978, Champs magnétiques 1980, les Concerts en Chine 1982, Musique pour supermarchés 1983, Zoolook 1984, Rendez-vous 1986 (Best Instrumental Album, Victoire de la Musique 1986); Chevalier des Arts et Lettres; Soc. des auteurs, compositeurs et éditeurs de musique Gold Medal 1980. *Address:* c/o Francis Dreyfus Music, 26 avenue Kléber, 75016 Paris, France.

JARRETT, Keith; American pianist and composer; b. 8 May 1945, Allentown, Pa.; gave first solo concert aged 7, followed by professional appearances; 2 hour solo concert of own compositions 1962; led own trio in Boston; worked with Roland Kirk, Tony Scott and others in New York; joined Art Blakely 1965; toured Europe with Charles Lloyd 1966; with Miles Davis 1970–71; soloist and leader of own groups 1969–. *Address:* Vincent Ryan, 135 West 16th Street, New York, N.Y. 10011, U.S.A.

JARRETT, Sylvester; Liberian diplomatist; b. 26 Sept. 1926, Timbo, River Cess Co.; m.; two c.; ed. Grammar School, Freetown, Pace Univ., New York and London Univ. Inst. of Int. Affairs; Sec. Liberian Consulate, Sierra Leone 1952–55, Finance Officer, Consulate Gen., New York 1955–60, Consul Gen. 1973–75, Second Sec. and Consul, Embassy in London 1960–69, First Sec. and Consul, Tokyo 1969–73; Deputy Minister of Foreign Affairs for Admin., then Asst. Minister, Acting Chief of Protocol 1979–81, Sr. Amb.-at-Large 1981–85, Perm. Rep. of Liberia to UN 1985–. *Address:*

Permanent Mission of Liberia to the United Nations, 820 Second Avenue, 4th Floor, New York, N.Y. 10017, U.S.A. *Telephone:* 687-1033.

JARRETT, William Fleming Hoggan, PH.D., M.R.C.V.S., F.R.C.PATH., F.R.S.E., F.R.S.; British professor of veterinary pathology; b. 2 Jan. 1928; s. of James Jarrett and Jessie Jarrett; m. Anna F. Sharp 1952; two d.; ed. Lenzie Acad., Glasgow Veterinary Coll. and Univ. of Glasgow; A.R.C. Research Student 1949–52; Lecturer, Dept. of Veterinary Pathology, Univ. of Glasgow Veterinary School 1952–53; Head of Hosp. Pathology Dept. of Veterinary Hosp., Univ. of Glasgow 1953–61; Reader in Pathology, Univ. of Glasgow 1962–65, Prof. of Veterinary Pathology 1968–; seconded to Univ. of E. Africa 1963–64; Feldberg Prize 1987. *Publications:* articles in scientific journals. *Leisure interests:* skiing, sailing, mountaineering, music. *Address:* 60 Netherblane, High Pines, Blanefield, Glasgow, G63 9JP, Scotland. *Telephone:* (0360) 70332.

JARRING, Gunnar, PH.D.; Swedish diplomatist; b. 12 Oct. 1907, Brunnby; m. Agnes Charlier 1932; one d.; ed. Lund Univ.; Assoc. Prof. Turkic Languages Lund Univ. 1933–40; Attaché Ankara 1940–41; Chief Section B Teheran 1941; Chargé d'affaires a.i. Teheran and Baghdad 1945, Addis Ababa 1946–48; Minister to India 1948–51, concurrently to Ceylon 1950–51, to Iran, Iraq and Pakistan 1951–52; Dir. Political Div. Ministry of Foreign Affairs 1953–56; Perm. Rep. to UN 1956–58; rep. on Security Council 1957–58; Amb. to U.S.A. 1958–64, to U.S.S.R. 1964–73, and to Mongolia 1965–73; Special Envoy of UN Sec.-Gen. on Middle East situation Nov. 1967–; Grand Cross Order of the North Star. *Publications:* Studien zu einer osttürkischen Lautlehre 1933, The Contest of the Fruits—An Eastern Turki Allegory 1936, The Uzbek Dialect of Qilich, Russian Turkestan 1937, Uzbek Texts from Afghan Turkestan 1938, The Distribution of Turki Tribes in Afghanistan 1939, Materials for the Knowledge of Eastern Turkestan (Vols.I-IV) 1947–51, An Eastern Turki-English Dialect Dictionary 1964, Literary Texts from Kashghar 1980, Return to Kashghar 1986. *Address:* Karlavaegen 85, 11459 Stockholm, Sweden.

JARUZELSKI, Gen. Wojciech; Polish army officer and politician; b. 6 July 1923, Kurów, Lublin Voivodship; m. Barbara Jaruzelska; one d.; ed. Infantry Officers' School and Karol Świerczewski Gen. Staff Acad., Warsaw; served with Polish Armed Forces in U.S.S.R. and Poland 1943–45; various Sr. Army posts 1945–65; Chief of Cen. Political Bd. of the Armed Forces 1960–65; Deputy Minister of Nat. Defence 1962–68, Minister 1968–83; Chair. Council of Ministers 1981–85; First Sec. Cen. Cttee. Polish United Workers Party (PZPR) Oct. 1981–; Chief of Gen. Staff 1965–68; Brig.-Gen. 1956, Divisional-Gen. 1960, Gen. of Arms 1968, Gen. of Army 1973; mem. Polish United Workers' Party Cen. Cttee. 1964–, mem. Political Bureau Dec. 1971–; Deputy to Seym (Parl.) 1961–; Vice-Pres. Chief Council of Union of Fighters for Freedom and Democracy 1972–; Chair. Comm. for Econ. Reform 1981–86; Chair. Mil. Council for Nat. Salvation 1981–83; mem. Presidium All-Poland Cttee. of Nat. Unity Front 1981–83, Provisional Nat. Council of Patriotic Movt. for Nat. Rebirth (PRON) 1982–83, mem. Nat. Council PRON 1983–; Chair. Country Defence Cttee. 1983–, Supreme Commdr. of the Armed Forces of Polish People's Repub. for Wartime 1983–; Pres. Council of State (Head of State) Nov. 1985–; decorations include Order of Builders of People's Poland, Order of Banner of Labour (First Class), Kt.'s Cross of Order of Polonia Restituta, Silver Cross of Virtuti Militari and Cross of Valour, Medals of 30th and 40th Anniversary of People's Poland, Hon. Miner of People's Repub., Order of Lenin 1968, 1983, Commdr.'s Cross Order of the Crown (Belgium) 1967, Order of the October Revolution (U.S.S.R.) 1973, Scharnhorst Order (G.D.R.) 1975, Grand Cross Order of Henry the Navigator (Portugal) 1975, Order of State Banner (Dem. People's Repub. of Korea) 1977, Order of Suche Bator (Mongolia) 1977, Order of the Red Banner (Hungary) 1977, Order of the Red Banner (U.S.S.R.) 1978, Order of the White Lion (Czechoslovakia) 1979, Order of Klement Gottwald (Czechoslovakia) 1983, Karl Marx Order (G.D.R.) 1983, Order of the Star of the Socialist Repub. (First class with Riband) (Romania) 1983, Order of the Golden Star (Vietnam) 1983, Order of Georgi Dimitrov (Bulgaria) 1983, Order of the Red Battle Banner (Mongolia) 1983, Order of the Banner (First Class with Diamonds) (Hungary) 1983, Order of José Martí (Cuba) 1983, Grand Cross of Order of the Holy Saviour (Greece) 1987. *Leisure interests:* literature, history, skiing, horse-riding and walking. *Address:* Komitet Centralny Polskiej Zjednoczonej Partii Robotniczej, Novy Świat 6/12, 00-920 Warsaw; Rada Państwa Polskiej Rzeczypospolitej Ludowej, Wiejska 4/8, 00-902 Warsaw, Poland.

JÄRVI, Neeme; Soviet (Estonian) symphony and opera conductor; b. 7 June 1937, Tallinn, Estonia; s. of Elss and August Järvi; m. Liilia Järvi 1961; two s. one d.; ed. Tallinn Music School, Leningrad Conservatorium and Leningrad Post-Graduate Studium; Conductor Estonian Radio Symphony Orchestra 1960–63, Chief Conductor 1963–76; Chief Conductor Estonian State Opera House 1963–76; Chief Conductor Estonian State Symphony Orchestra 1976–80; emigrated to U.S.A. 1980; Principal Guest Conductor City of Birmingham Symphony Orchestra, England 1980–83; Chief Conductor Gothenburg Symphony Orchestra, Sweden 1981–; Prin. Conductor and Musical Dir. Scottish Nat. Orchestra 1984–; Guest Conductor of many int. symphony orchestras including New York Philharmonic, Boston, Chicago, Concertgebouw, Philharmonia, London Symphony, London Philharmonic; conducted Eugene Onegin 1979, 1984, Samson and Delilah 1982 and Khovanshchina 1985 at Metropolitan Opera House, New

York; many recordings including all Prokoviev, Franz Berwald, Sibelius and Stenhammar symphonies; First Prize, Accademia Nazionale di Santa Cecilia Conductors' Competition 1971. *Address:* c/o Van Walsum Management, 40 St. Peter's Road, London, W6 9BH, England. *Telephone:* (201) 741-59-05 (Sweden).

JÄRVI, Osmo Henrik, M.D.; Finnish pathologist; b. 1 Jan. 1911, Helsinki; s. of Prof. Toivo Henrik Järvi and Helfrid Helena (née Soderman-Siutila); m. Dr. Enne-Maija Kinnunen 1937; one s. three d.; ed. Helsinki and Utrecht Univs. and Karolinska Inst., Stockholm; Asst. Anatomy Dept., Helsinki Univ. 1932-38; Asst., Dept. of Pathological Anatomy 1938-44; Lecturer, Microscopical Anatomy, 1940-45, Prof. of Pathological Anatomy, Turku Univ. 1944-77; Dean, Faculty of Medicine 1945-54, Rector 1954-60; Chair. Finnish Medical Research Council 1961-67; mem. Finnish Acad. of Science and Letters 1960 (Chair. 1980), Finnish Medical Soc. "Duodecim", Hon. mem. Finnish Medical Soc. "Läkaresällskapet" 1960, Finnish Soc. of Gastroenterology 1986, Finnish Soc. of Cytology 1987; mem. Swedish Medical Soc., Finnish Asscn. of Pathologists (Chair. 1956-62), Swedish Asscn. of Pathologists, Scandinavian Asscn. of Pathologists (Chair. 1958-61), Pathological Soc. of G.B. and Ireland, American Soc. of Clinical Pathologists, Int. Acad. of Pathology, New York Acad. of Sciences, Cancer Asscn. of Finland (Chair. of Del. 1967-69 and 1978-80, Chair. of Bd. 1969-75), Cancer Foundation of Finland (Chair. 1960-66), Fellow, Int. Acad. of Cytology, etc.; Hon. mem. Finnish Cultural Foundation 1978; Hon. Ph.D. (Åbo Acad., Finland) 1968, Hon. M.D. (Turku Univ.) 1980, (Oulu Univ.) 1983; Pohjola Medical Award 1983, Finnish Acad. of Science and Letters Award 1986. *Publications:* works on secretion process and Golgi apparatus, morbid pathology of respiratory and intestinal tract, especially neoplasms, etc., exfoliated cytology; Pohdintaa (Meditations) 1967. *Leisure interest:* the fine arts. *Address:* Yliopistonkatu 2K, 20110 Turku, Finland. *Telephone:* 317390.

JARVIK, Robert Koffler, M.D.; American physician; b. 11 May 1946, Midland, Mich.; s. of Norman Eugene and Edythe (née Koffler) Jarvik; one s. one d.; ed. Syracuse Univ., New York, Univ. of Bologna, New York Univ., Univ. of Utah; research asst., Div. of Artificial Organs, Univ. of Utah 1971-77; Acting Dir. Old St. Mark's Hosp., Div. of Artificial Organs 1977-78, Asst. Dir. 1978-82; Pres. Symbian Inc., Salt Lake City 1982-87; Asst. Research Prof. of Surgery, Univ. of Utah 1982-; awards include Inventor of the Year 1983, Outstanding Young Men of America 1983, Gold Heart Award 1983, Par Excellence Award (Univ. of Utah); Hon. D.Sc. (Syracuse) 1983, (Hahnemann Univ.) 1985; mem. American Soc. for Artificial Internal Organs, Int. Soc. for Artificial Organs. *Publication:* Ed. (U.S. Section) The International Journal of Artificial Organs. *Address:* Department of Surgery, College of Medicine, University of Utah, Salt Lake City, Utah, U.S.A.

JARVIS, William Herbert, P.C., LL.B., B.A.; Canadian lawyer and politician; b. 15 Aug. 1930, Hamilton, Ont.; s. of Garfield L. Jarvis and Nina M. McBean; ed. Univ. of W. Ontario; with Marketing Div. Burroughs Corpn., Toronto 1953-59; lawyer, Riddell, Mountain, Jarvis, Mitchell, Hill & Monteith 1963-72; mem. of Parl. for Perth-Wilmot 1972, 1974, for Perth 1979-84; Minister of State for Fed.-Prov. Relations 1979-80; Lawyer, Clarkson, Tetrault 1984-; Pres. Progressive Conservative Party of Canada 1986-. *Address:* 161 Laurier Avenue West, Suite 200, Ottawa, Ont. K1P 5J2, Canada.

JARZĘBSKI, Stefan; Polish environment engineer and politician; b. 16 Sept. 1917, Będzin; m.; two s.; ed. Mining Acad., Cracow; Extraordinary Prof. 1972, Ordinary Prof. 1977; posts in secondary and higher schools 1940-52; posts in industry 1946-51, 1958-61; Polish Acad. of Sciences 1961-, Dir. Inst. of Environmental Eng., Polish Acad. of Sciences, Zabrze 1975-83; Prof. in Botanical Gardens, Warsaw, Polish Acad. of Sciences 1987-; Prof. Inst. of Environmental Eng., Polish Acad. of Sciences, Zabne 1989-; Minister-Head of Office for Environmental Protection and Water Economy 1983-85, Minister of Environmental Protection and Natural Resources 1985-87; mem. State Council for Environmental Protection 1983-87, Vice-Pres. Asscn. "Responsibility and Action" 1987; mem. Cttee. for Science and Tech. Progress attached to Council of Ministers 1986-; Commdr.'s and Officer's Cross Order of Polonia Restituta; Gold Cross of Merit; achievements include over 60 research studies applied in practice. *Publications:* over 12 monographs, over 100 papers and dissertations. *Address:* Ul. Wiktorii Wiedenskiej 1m. 2, 02-954 Warsaw, Poland. *Telephone:* 42-33-17 (Home).

JASKIERNIA, Jerzy, D.JUR.; Polish politician and diplomatist; b. 21 March 1950, Kudowa Zdrój; s. of Zofia Jaskiernia and Mieczysław Jaskiernia; m. Alicia Stowińska 1980; one d.; ed. Jagellonian Univ., Cracow; asst. Law and Admin. Faculty of Jagellonian Univ., Cracow 1972-75, Sr. Asst. 1975-77, Adjunct 1977-81; mem. Main Bd. of Socialist Youth Union 1973-76; mem. Polish Socialist Youth Union (ZSMP) 1976-85; mem. Main Arbitration Bd. 1976-80, Chair. 1980-81, Chair. ZSMP Gen. Bd. 1981-84; mem. Polish United Workers' Party (PZPR) 1970-, deputy mem. PZPR Cen. Cttee. 1982-86, Vice-Chair., Youth Comm. of PZPR Cen. Cttee. 1981-86; mem. Inter-party Problems Comm. of PZPR Cen. Cttee. 1986-; mem. Nat. Council of Patriotic Movement for Nat. Rebirth (PRON) 1983-, Sec.-Gen. 1984-87; Deputy to Seym (Parl.) 1985-; Adviser to Minister of Foreign Affairs 1987-88; Counsellor, Embassy in Washington Feb. 1988-; mem.

Scientific Bd., Research Inst. of Youth Problems (Warsaw) 1984-. *Publications:* Pozycja stanów w systemie federalnym USA 1979, Dylematy młodych 1984, Dialog naszą szansą 1985, (co-author) System polityczny PRL w procesie przemian 1988. *Address:* Embassy of Poland, 2640 16th Street, N.W., Washington, D.C. 20009, U.S.A. *Telephone:* (202) 234-38-00.

JASRAI, Puntsagiin; Mongolian politician; b. 26 Nov. 1933; ed. Moscow Inst.; teacher then headmaster of primary school, Gobi-Altai Aimag (Prov.) 1950-54; Insp. of the Exec. Bd. People's deputies of Gobi-Altai Aimag 1954-56; lecturer at the Inst. of Econs. 1961-65; Deputy Chief of Cen. Statistical Bd. of the MPR 1966-70; Chair. of the State Prices Cttee. 1970-75, of the State Prices and Standard 1975-76; Head of the Dept. of the Cen. Cttee. of the MPRP 1976-78; First Deputy Chair. of the State Planning Comm. MPRP 1978-84; Deputy Chair. Council of Ministers, Chair. of the State Planning Comm. 1984-; Deputy Chair. Council of Ministers, Chair. of the State Planning and Economy Cttee. 1988-; mem. of the Cen. Cttee. of the MPRP, Deputy to the People's Great Hural. *Address:* Government Palace, Ulan Bator, Mongolia.

JASTROW, Robert; American physicist and writer; b. 7 Sept. 1925, New York; s. of Abraham Jastrow and Marie Jastrow; Asst. Prof., Yale Univ. 1953-54, Consultant nuclear physics, U.S. Naval Research Lab. 1958-62; Head Theoretical Div., Goddard Space Flight Centre, NASA 1958-61, Chair. Lunar Exploration Comm. 1959-60, Dir. Goddard Inst. Space Studies 1961-81; Adjunct Prof. of Astronomy, Columbia Univ., New York 1961-77, of Earth Sciences, Dartmouth Coll., Hanover, N.H. 1973-, of Geology and Astronomy, Columbia Univ. 1977-81; Pres. G. C. Marshall Inst. 1985-; Hon. D.Sc.(Manhattan Coll.) 1980; Arthur S. Flemming Award 1965; NASA Medal for exceptional scientific achievement 1968. *Publications:* Red Giants and White Dwarfs, The Origin of the Solar System 1963, The Evolution of Stars, Planets and Life 1967, Astronomy: Fundamentals and Frontiers 1972, The Venus Atmosphere 1969, Until the Sun Dies 1977, God and the Astronomers 1978, The Enchanted Loom 1981, How to Make Nuclear Weapons Obsolete 1985. *Address:* Dartmouth College, Earth Sciences Department, Hanover, N.H. 03755 (Office); Box 90, Hanover, N.H. 03755, U.S.A. (Home).

JASTRZĘBSKI, Dominik, M.ENG.; Polish forestry engineer and politician; b. 21 June 1942, Tabędz, Łomża Voivodship; m. Grażyna Makowska; one d. one s.; ed. Forestry Faculty of Main School of Farming, Warsaw 1966, Postgraduate Study of Faculty of Foreign Trade, Cen. School of Planning and Statistics, Warsaw 1971; active mem. Polish Students' Asscn. (ZSP) and Rural Youth Union (ZMW) 1960-67; employed with Forest Inspectorate, Spała 1967-68; Inspector, then Deputy Dir. Dept. of Production, Ministry of Forestry and Timber Industry 1968-76; Deputy Dir. Paper and Cellulose Office, PAGED Foreign Trade Enterprise Ltd., Warsaw 1976-77; Gen. Dir. Polish-British Company "Polish Timber Products", London 1977-83; Dir. Sawn Timber Office, PAGED Foreign Trade Enterprise Ltd., Warsaw 1983-86, Dir. Gen. 1986-88; Minister for Foreign Econ. Co-operation 1988-; mem. Econ. Cttee. Council of Ministers 1988-; mem. Polish United Workers' Party (PZPR) 1967-; Knight's Cross of Polonia Restituta Order, Silver Cross of Merit and other decorations. *Leisure interests:* reading, yachting, hunting, angling. *Address:* Ministerstwo Współpracy Gospodarczej z Zagranicą, ul. Wiejska 10, 00-489 Warsaw, Poland. *Telephone:* 21 03 31 (Office).

JATTI, Basappa Danappa, B.A., LL.B.; Indian politician; b. 10 Sept. 1912, Savalgi, Bijapur District; ed. Bijapur Govt. High School, Rajaram Coll., Sykes Law Coll., Kolhapur; practised law at Jamkhandi; State Minister, Jamkhandi, later Chief Minister; mem. Legis. Assembly, Bombay, later Mysore; Deputy Minister of Health and Labour, Bombay 1952; Chair. Land Reforms Cttee., Chief Minister, Mysore 1958-62; Minister of Finance, Mysore 1962-65, of Food, Mysore 1965-67; Lieut.-Gov. of Pondicherry 1968; Gov. of Orissa 1972-74; Vice-Pres. of India 1974-79, Acting Pres. Feb.-July 1977; Chair. Rajya Sabha 1974-79; LL.D. h.c. (Karnatak Univ., Guru Nanak Dev Univ.). *Address:* c/o Office of the Vice-President of India, 6 Maulana Azad Road, New Delhi, India.

JAUDEL, Jean Emmanuel; French publisher; b. 6 Jan. 1910, Strasbourg; s. of Armand Jaudel and Lucie Jaudel; m. Nicole Weill 1946; one s. one d.; ed. Faculty of Law of Paris Univ., Ecole libre des sciences politiques, Ecole des hautes etudes internationales, Geneva; Man. Dir. Atlantique française 1945-; Chair. La Revue des Deux Mondes, publrs. of La Revue des Deux Mondes (monthly review) 1969-; Pres. Asscn. Presse-Enseignement 1981-; Officier Légion d'honneur, Ordre nationale du Mérite, Médaille militaire, Croix de guerre, other French and foreign awards. *Leisure interest:* riding. *Address:* La Revue des Deux Mondes, 51 avenue Franklin-Roosevelt, 75008 Paris, France (Office). *Telephone:* 359-68-36 (Home).

JAUHO, Pekka Antti Olavi; Finnish scientist; b. 27 April 1923, Oulu; s. of Antti Arvid Jauho and Sylvi (née Pajari) Jauho; m. Kyllikki Hakala 1948; one s.; ed. Univ. of Helsinki; Chief Mathematician, Insurance Co. Kansa 1951-54; Assoc. Prof., Tech. Univ. of Helsinki 1955-57 (now Helsinki Univ. of Tech.), Prof. in Tech. Physics 1957-70; Dir.-Gen. The State Inst. for Tech. Research (Tech. Research Centre of Finland since 1972) 1970-; mem. American Nuclear Soc., European Physical Soc., RILEM, Gen. Council, Acad. of Tech. Sciences, Finnish Acad. of Sciences, Nordisk

Institut för Teoretisk Atomfysik (NORDITA) and several Finnish socs.; Hon. Prize of YDIN Power Asscn. *Publications:* about 100 articles. *Leisure interest:* music. *Address:* Vuorimiehentie 5, 02150 Espoo 15 (Office); Menninkäisentie 6L, Tapiola, Finland (Home). *Telephone:* 4564100 (Office); 461437 (Home).

JAUMOTTE, André; Belgian mechanical engineer and university official; b. 8 Dec. 1919, Jambes; s. of Jules Jaumotte and Marie Braibant; m. Valentine Demoulin 1946; one d.; ed. Free Univ. of Brussels; Head Depts. of Applied Mechanics and Aerodynamics, Free Univ. of Brussels 1958–86; Pres. Free Univ. of Brussels 1974–81; mem. Bd. UN Univ., Tokyo 1980–86; Hon. Pres. Asscn. des Universités partiellement ou entièrement de langue française (AUPELF) 1981–84; mem. Royal Acad., Belgium, Royal Acad. of Overseas Science, European Acad. of Sciences, Letters and Arts, Int. Acad. of Astronautics; Foreign mem. Czechoslovak Acad. of Science; mem. Nat. Acad. of Air and Space, France; Hon. D.H.C. Free University, Brussels and Laval Univ., Quebec; Commdr. Légion d'honneur 1971, Grand Officier Ordine al Merito della Repubblica Italiana 1973, Commdr. Ordre du Mérite (Gabon), Grand Officier Ordre de la Couronne (Belgium) 1983, Grand Officier Ordre de Léopold 1988 and various other awards. *Publications:* Rocket Propulsion 1967, Choc et Ondes de Choc 1971, 1973 and 300 articles on internal aerodynamics and thermodynamics of turbomachines. *Leisure interests:* painting and sculpture. *Address:* Université Libre de Bruxelles, avenue Franklin Roosevelt 50, B1050 Brussels; 33 avenue Jeanne Bte. 17, B1050 Brussels, Belgium (Home). *Telephone:* 642-3271 (Office); 647-5413 (Home).

JAUNARENA, José Horacio, D.JUR.; Argentinian politician; b. 29 Nov. 1942, Pergamino; m. Ana O'Ana; one d.; ed. Univ. Nacional de Buenos Aires, also law studies in Madrid; practised law in Buenos Aires and Pergamino; lecturer-in-charge Democratic Educ., Inst. Superior del Prof. Joaquín V. González, Pergamino 1976; Dir. Sunday Supplement, La Opinión de Pergamino; mem. Unión Cívica Radical, Pergamino 1973–76; Under-Sec. of Defence, Ministry of Defence 1983–84, Sec. 1984–86, Minister of Defence 1986–. *Address:* Ministerio de Defensa, Buenos Aires, Argentina.

JAVIERRE ORTAS, H.E. Cardinal Antonio María, S.D.B.; Vatican ecclesiastic; b. 21 Feb. 1921, Siétamo, Huesca; ordained 1949, elected 1976, consecrated bishop 1976, then Archbishop of Meta; Sec. of the Congregation for Catholic Educ.; cr. Cardinal 1988. *Address:* Città del Vaticano, Rome, Italy.

JAWARA, Hon. Alhaji Sir Dawda (Kairaba), Kt., M.R.C.V.S., D.T.V.M.; Gambian politician; b. 16 May 1924, Barajally; s. of Almamy and the late Mama Jawara; ed. Achimota Coll., Glasgow Univ.; Principal Veterinary Officer, Gambian Civil Service 1957–60; entered politics 1960; Minister of Educ. 1960–61; Premier 1962–65; Prime Minister 1965–70; Pres. of Repub. of The Gambia April 1970–; Vice-Pres. of Confed. of Senegambia Feb. 1982–; Minister of Defence 1985–; Pres. Comité Inter-Etats de Lutte contre la Sécheresse du Sahel; mem. Board, Peutinger Coll. (Fed. Repub. of Germany); Hon. G.C.M.G. 1974; decorations from Senegal, Mauritania, Lebanon, Grand Master Nat. Order of the Repub. of Gambia 1972, Peutinger Gold Medal 1979; numerous other decorations. *Leisure interests:* golf, gardening, sailing. *Address:* Office of the President, Banjul, The Gambia.

JAY, Baron (Life Peer), cr. 1987, of Battersea in Greater London; **Douglas Patrick Thomas Jay,** P.C.; British politician, economist and author; b. 23 March 1907, Woolwich; s. of Edward Aubrey Hastings Jay and Isobel Violet Jay; m. 1st Margaret Christian Garnett 1933 (divorced 1972), two s. (Peter Jay, q.v.) two d.; m. 2nd Mary Lavinia Thomas 1972; ed. Winchester Coll. and New Coll. Oxford; mem. staff The Times 1929–33, Economist 1933–37; City Ed. Daily Herald 1937–41; Fellow All Souls Coll. Oxford 1930–37, 1968–; Ministry of Supply 1941–43; Prin. Asst. Sec. Bd. of Trade 1943; Personal Asst. to Prime Minister 1945–46; M.P. for Battersea North 1946–74, Wandsworth, Battersea North 1974–83; Econ. Sec. to Treasury 1947–50; Financial Sec. to the Treasury 1950–51; Pres. of Bd. of Trade 1964–67; Dir. Courtaulds 1967–70, Trades Union Unit Trust 1967–80, Consultant 1980–; Chair. London Motorway Action Group 1968–81; Chair. Common Market Safeguards Campaign 1970–75; Fellow of All Souls Coll., Oxford; Labour. *Publications:* The Socialist Case 1937, Who is to Pay for the War and the Peace? 1941, Socialism in the New Society 1962, After the Common Market 1968, Change and Fortune: A Political Record (autobiog.) 1980, Sterling: a Plea for Moderation 1985. *Address:* Causeway Cottage, Minster Lovell, Oxford, OX9A 5RN, England. *Telephone:* Witney 775235.

JAY, Peter, M.A.; British economic journalist and fmr. diplomatist; b. 7 Feb. 1937; s. of Lord Jay (q.v.); m. 1st Margaret Ann, d. of Lord Callaghan (q.v.), 1961 (divorced 1985); two s. two d.; m. 2nd Emma Thornton 1986; one s.; ed. Winchester Coll. and Christ Church, Oxford; Midshipman and Sub-Lieut., R.N.V.R. 1956–57; Asst. Prin., H.M. Treasury 1961–64, Private Sec. to Jt. Perm. Sec. 1964, Prin. 1964–67; Econs. Ed. The Times 1967–77, Assoc. Ed. Times Business News 1969–77; Presenter, Weekend World, ITV 1972–77, The Jay Interview 1975–77; Amb. to U.S.A. 1977–79; Consultant, Economist Group 1979–; Dir. The Economist Intelligence Unit (EIU) 1979–83; Corresp. The Times 1980; Dir. New Nat. Theatre, Washington, D.C. 1979–81; Chair. TV-AM 1980–83, TV-AM News 1982–83, Pres. TV-AM 1983–; Presenter, A Week in Politics, Channel 4 1980–86; Dir. Landen

Press Ltd. 1982–; Sr. Ed. Consultant, Man. Dir. Banking World BPCC, Editor Banking World 1983–86, Supervising Ed. 1986–; Chair. United Way of G.B. 1982–83, Feasibility Study 1982–83; Chair. Nat. Council for Voluntary Orgs. 1981–86; Chief of Staff to Robert Maxwell 1986–; Dir. Mirror Holdings Ltd. 1986–, Pergamon Holdings Ltd. 1986–; mem. Bd. BPCC (now Maxwell Corpn. PLC) 1986–; Visiting Scholar, Brookings Inst., Washington, D.C. 1979–80; Copland Memorial Lecturer, Australia 1980; Gov. Ditchley Foundation 1982–; Hon. D.H. (Ohio State Univ.) 1978; Political Broadcaster of Year 1973, Royal TV Soc.'s Male Personality of Year (Pye Award) 1974, Shell Int. TV Award 1974, Wincott Memorial Lecturer 1975. *Publications:* The Budget 1972, Foreign Affairs, America and the World 1979 (Contrib.) 1980, The Crisis for Western Political Economy and other essays 1984, Apocalypse 2000 (with Michael Stewart) 1987; numerous newspaper and magazine articles. *Leisure interest:* sailing. *Address:* 39 Castlebar Road, London, W5 2DJ, England; and Elm Bank, Glandore, Co. Cork, Ireland. *Telephone:* 01-998 3570 (London); (0860) 335584.

JAYAKUMAR, Shunmugam, LL.M.; Singapore diplomatist; b. 12 Aug. 1939, Singapore; m. Dr. Lalitha Rajahram 1969; two s. one d.; ed. Univ. of Singapore and Yale Univ.; Dean, Law Faculty, Univ. of Singapore 1974–80, Prof. of Law; Perm. Rep. of Singapore to UN 1971–74, High Commr. to Canada 1971–74; M.P. 1980–; Minister of State for Law and Home Affairs 1981–83; Minister of Labour 1983–85, of Home Affairs Jan. 1985–, of Law Sept. 1988–; Second Minister of Law 1985–88; mem. Singapore del. to UN Gen. Assemblies 1970, 1971, 1972, to Human Environment Conf., Stockholm 1972, to 3rd UN Law of Sea Conf. *Publications:* Constitutional Law Cases from Malaysia and Singapore 1971, Public International Law Cases from Malaysia and Singapore 1974, Constitutional Law (with documentary material) 1976, and articles in journals. *Address:* Ministry of Home Affairs, Singapore.

JAYAWARDENE, Junius Richard; Sri Lankan lawyer and politician; b. 17 Sept. 1906, Colombo; s. of Justice E. W. and A. H. (Wijewardene) Jayawardene; m. Elina B. Rupesinghe 1935; one s.; ed. Royal Coll., Univ. Coll., and Law Coll., Colombo; mem. Colombo Muncipal Council 1941, State Council 1943, House of Reps. 1947–; Minister of Finance 1947–53; Hon. Sec. Ceylon Nat. Congress 1940–47; Hon. Treas. United Nat. Party 1947–48 and Vice-Pres. 1953; Leader of the House of Reps. and Minister of Agric. and Food 1953–56; Minister of Finance, Information, Broadcasting, Local Govt. and Housing March–July 1960; Deputy Leader of Opposition July 1960–65; Minister of State, and Parl. Sec. to Minister of Defence, External Affairs and Planning 1965–70; Leader of Opposition 1970–77; Prime Minister, Minister of Defence, Planning and Econ. Affairs and of Plan Implementation 1977–78, Pres. of the Dem. Socialist Repub. of Sri Lanka 1978–89, Minister of Defence 1978–84 and of Plan Implementation 1978–89, also of Aviation 1978, of Higher Educ., Janatha (People's) Estate Devt. and State Plantations 1981–88, of Power and Energy 1982–88, of State Plantations 1982–88, also fmrly. of Civil Security; Chair. of Janatha (People's) Estates Devt. Bd.; Sec. United Nat. Party 1972, Leader 1973–June 1975, July 1975–; del. to numerous confs. *Publications:* Some Sermons of the Buddha, Buddhist Essays, In Council (speeches), Buddhism and Marxism, Selected Speeches. *Address:* President's House, Colombo; 66 Ward Place, Colombo 7, Sri Lanka (Home). *Telephone:* Colombo 95028 and 92332.

JAYEWARDENE, Hector Wilfred, Q.C.; Sri Lankan lawyer; b. 3 Nov. 1916, Colombo; s. of E. W. Jayewardene, K.C. and Agnes H. Wijewardene; m. Claribel E. Fernando 1946; one s. four d.; ed. Royal Coll. Colombo and Sri Lanka Law Coll.; called to Bar of Sri Lanka 1941; First Pres. Bar Asscn. of Sri Lanka; Chair. Bd. of Dirs. and Dir. of several industrial commercial orgs.; Chair. Bd. of Man., Sri Lanka Foundation, Human Rights Centre, Sri Lanka Television Training Inst.; Pres. Law Asscn. for Asia and Western Pacific 1979–81; Pres. Org. of Professional Asscns. of Sri Lanka 1980–82; Leader, Sri Lanka Del. to UN Human Rights Comm., Geneva 1985–88; special envoy of Pres. of Sri Lanka to meet Heads of State in India and E. Asian and S.E. Asian countries; mem. various UN and Commonwealth comms. and working parties; Deshamanya award (Pres. of Sri Lanka); Hon. LL.D. (Colombo). *Leisure interest:* reading. *Address:* Sri Lanka Foundation, 27 Independence Avenue, Colombo 7 (Office); 218 Bullers Road, Colombo 7, Sri Lanka (Home). *Telephone:* 598377 (Office); 581670 (Home).

JAYSTON, Michael; British actor; b. 29 Oct. 1935, Nottingham; s. of Aubrey Jayston and Edna Myfanwy Llewelyn; m. 1st Lynn Farleigh 1965 (divorced 1970); m. 2nd Heather Mary Sneddon (divorced 1977); m. 3rd Elizabeth Ann Smithson 1978; three s. one d.; with the Nat. Theatre 1976–79. *Films include:* Cromwell 1970, Nicholas and Alexandra 1971, Follow Me 1972, Bequest to the Nation 1972, Tales That Witness Madness 1973, Craze 1973, The Internecine Project 1974. *TV appearances include:* Power Game, Charles Dickens, Beethoven, Solo—Wilfred Owen, Quiller 1975, Tinker, Tailor, Soldier, Spy 1979, Dr. Who 1986. *Theatre appearances include:* Private Lives 1980, Sound of Music 1981, Way of the World 1984–85. *Leisure interests:* cricket, darts, chess. *Address:* c/o Michael Whitehall Ltd., 125 Gloucester Road, London, S.W.7, England.

JAZAIRY, Idriss; Algerian diplomatist and international administrator; b 29 May 1936, Neuilly-sur-Seine, France; four c.; Chief Econ. and Social

Dept. Algiers 1963–71; Dir. Int. Co-operation, Ministry of Foreign Affairs 1963–71; Adviser to Pres. of Repub. 1971–77; Under-Sec.-Gen. Ministry of Foreign Affairs 1977–79; Amb. to Belgium, Luxembourg and EEC 1979–82; Amb.-at-large specializing in int. econ. affairs, Ministry of Foreign Affairs 1982–84; Pres. Bd. of Govs. African Devt. Bank 1971–72; Chair. UN Gen. Ass. Cttee. on North-South Dialogue 1978–79; Pres. Int. Fund for Agricultural Devt. (IFAD) 1984–. *Address:* Office of the President, IFAD, Via del Serafico 107, 00142-Rome, Italy.

JEAN BENOÎT GUILLAUME MARIE ROBERT LOUIS ANTOINE ADOLPHE MARC D'AVIANO, H.R.H. Grand Duke of Luxembourg, Duke of Nassau, Prince of Bourbon-Parma; b. 5 Jan. 1921, Colmar Berg; m. Princess Josephine-Charlotte of Belgium April 1953; three s. two d.; Lieut.-Rep. of Grand Duchess 1961–64; became Grand Duke of Luxembourg on abdication of Grand Duchess Charlotte Nov. 1964. *Leisure interests:* photography and natural history. *Address:* Grand Ducal Palace, Luxembourg.

JEANCOURT-GALIGNANI, Antoine; French banking executive; b. 12 Jan. 1937, Paris; s. of Paul and Germaine (née Verley) Jeancourt-Galignani; m. 1st Brigitte Auzouy; m. 2nd. Hannelore Wagner; five c.; ed. Univ. of Paris; Teacher, École nat. d'admin. 1963–64; Insp. des Finances 1965–; special assignments, office of the Minister of Finance 1968–70, Treasury Dept., Ministry of Finance 1970–71; Sr. Exec. Vice-Pres., Crédit Agricole 1973–79; Man. Dir., Banque Indosuez 1979–81, Chair. and C.E.O. 1981–82, Dir.-Gen. and Pres. 1982–86, Vice-Pres.-Dir.-Gen. 1986–; Chair., Indosuez Asia Holding; Chair., Supervisory Bd., Bankhaus Marcard and Co., Hamburg; Dir. Banque Líbano-Française S.A.L., Beirut, Al Bank Al Saudi Al Fransi, Jeddah, Alsthom-Atlantique, Paris, Imetal, Paris, SCAC, Paris, Compagnie Financière du Groupe Victoire, Paris, Degremont, Paris; mem., Int. Advisory Council, Morgan Grenfell Holdings, London; mem., Supervisory Bd., Caisse Cen. de Cooperation Econ., Paris; Croix de la Valeur militaire, Chevalier Ordre nationale du Mérite, Chevalier du Mérite agricole. *Address:* Banque Indosuez, 96 boulevard Haussmann, 75008 Paris (Office); 3 avenue Bosquet, 75007 Paris, France (Home). *Telephone:* (1) 561 20 20 (Office).

JEANMAIRE, Renée Marcelle (Zizi); French actress, dancer and singer; b. 29 April 1924; m. Roland Petit (q.v.) 1954; one c.; student, Paris Opera Ballet 1933–40, Dancer 1940–44; with Ballets de Monte-Carlo, Ballets Colonel de Basil, Ballets Roland Petit; Dir. (with Roland Petit) Casino de Paris 1969–; Chevalier Légion d'honneur, Chevalier des Arts et des Lettres, Officier, Ordre nat. du Mérite; leading roles in Aubade, Piccoli, Carmen, La Croqueuse de Diamants, Rose des Vents, Cyrano de Bergerac, La Dame dans la Lune, La Symphonie Fantastique 1975, Le loup, La chauve-souris 1979, Hollywood Paradise Show 1985. *Films:* Hans Christian Andersen, Anything Goes, Folies Bergères, Charmants Garçons, Black Tights, la Revue, Zizi je t'aime; musical: The Girl in Pink Tights (Broadway); music hall appearances. *Address:* 22 rue de la Paix, 75002 Paris, France.

JEANNENEY, Jean-Marcel, L. ès L., D. EN D.; French economist and politician; b. 13 Nov. 1910, Paris; s. of Jules Jeanneney (fmr. Pres. of the Senate and Minister); m. Marie-Laure Monod 1936; seven c.; ed. Ecole Libre des Sciences Politiques, Paris; Prof. of Political Economy, Grenoble Univ. 1937–51, Dean of Law Faculty 1947–51; Prof. of Social Econs. Paris Univ. 1951–56, of Financial Econs. 1957–59, of Political Econs. 1970–80; Dir. du Cabinet of his father, Jules Jeanneney, Minister of State, de Gaulle Prov. Govt. 1944–45; mem. Admin. Council, Ecole nat. d'admin. 1945–58; Dir. Econ. Activity Study Service, Fondation Nat. des Sciences politiques 1952–58; Consultant to OEEC 1953; mem. Rueff Cttee. 1958; Rapporteur and del. to numerous confs.; Minister of Industry, (Debré Cabinet) 1959–62; Amb. to Repub. of Algeria 1962–63; Chair. French Cttee. on Co-operation with Developing Countries 1963; mem. and French Rep. to UN Econ. and Social Council 1964–66; Minister of Social Affairs 1966–May 1968; Deputy June 1968; Minister of State 1968–69; Pres. L'Observatoire français des Conjonctures économiques 1981. *Publications:* Essai sur les mouvements des prix en France depuis la stabilisation monétaire (1927–1935) 1936, Economie et droit de l'électricité (with C. A. Colliard) 1950, Les commerces de détail en Europe occidentale 1954, Forces et faiblesses de l'économie française 1945–1956, Textes de droit économique et social français 1789-1957 (with Perrot), Documents économiques (2 Vols.) 1958, Economie politique 1959, Essai de comptabilité interrégionale française pour 1954, 1969, Régions et sénat 1969, A mes amis gaullistes 1973, Pour un nouveau protectionnisme 1978, Les economies occidentales du XIXème siècle à nos jours 1985. *Address:* 102 rue d'Assas, 75006 Paris and Rioz 70190, France (Homes). *Telephone:* 43-26-39-46 (Paris) and 84-91-82-52 (Rioz).

JEANNENEY, Jean-Noel, D. ès L.; French professor; b. 2 April 1942, Grenoble; s. of Jean-Marcel Jeanneney and Marie-Laure (née Monod) Jeanneney; m. 2nd Annie-Lou Cot 1985; two s.; ed. Lycées Champollion and Louis-le-Grand, Ecole normale supérieure, Inst. d'études politiques de Paris; Asst. lecturer in Contemporary History, Univ. de Paris X 1969–77, lecturer 1968, Univ. lecturer 1977; Univ. Prof. Inst. d'études politiques de Paris 1979–; Pres., Dir.-Gen. Radio-France Int. 1983–86; Pres. Bicentenary of the French Revolution 1988–; mem. Bd. of Dirs. France-Presse 1982–84, Télédiffusion de France 1982–86, Saint-Simon Foundation 1986–, Seuil Publs. 1987–. *Publications:* le Riz et le Rouge, cinq mois en Extrême-

Orient 1969, le Journal politique de Jules Jeanneney 1939–42 1972, François de Wendel en République, l'Argent et le Pouvoir 1976, Leçon d'histoire pour une gauche en pouvoir, la Faillite de Cartel 1924–26 1977, le Monde de Beuve-Méry ou le métier d'Alceste (with others) 1979, l'Argent caché, milieux d'affaires et pouvoirs politiques dans la France du XXe Siècle 1981, Télévision nouvelle mémoire, les magazines de grand reportage 1959–68 (with others) 1982, Echec à Panurge, l'audiovisuel public au service de la différence 1986, Concordances des temps, chroniques sur l'actualité du passé 1987. *Address:* 7 avenue Franco-Russe, 75007 Paris (Office); 48 rue Galande, 75005 Paris, France (Home).

JEBSEN, Atle, M.A.; Norwegian shipowner; b. 10 Nov. 1935, Bergen; s. of Kristian S. Jebsen and Sigfrid Kjerland; m. 2nd Arnhild Høivik 1984; two s. one d.; ed. Univ. of Cambridge; chartering broker, A/S Kristian Jebsens Rederi 1962, mem. of Bd. 1965, Pres. and Man. Dir. 1967–, Chair. and C.E.O.; Pres. Norwegian Shipowners Asscn. 1982–83; Chair. Den Norske Krigsforsikring; Chair. Norges Skibshypotekbank A/S 1978–85, Skibsfartens Arbeidsgiverforening, Oslo 1982–83, Felleskontoret 1982–83, Jebsen Group; Pres. Bimco 1985–86; Company of the Year Prize 1977, Farmandprize 1979. *Leisure interests:* jogging, skiing, fishing. *Address:* A/S Kristian Jebsens Rederi, Sandbrugt. 5, P.O. Box 4145, 5015 Dreggen/Bergen, Norway.

JEDYNAK, Andrzej, M.ENG.; Polish politician; b. 4 July 1932, Rzeszów; ed Rzeszów Tech. Univ.; worked in Transport Equipment Factory, Rzeszów 1952–59; Tech. Dir. Voivodship Union of Local Industry, Rzeszów 1959–61; Dir. Motor-Bus Factory, Sanok 1961–63; Tech. Dir. Union of Motorized Industry (Polmo) 1963–70, Dir.-Gen. 1974–76; Dir. Union of Aviation and Motor Industry (PZL) 1970–74; Under-Sec. of State, Ministry of Eng. Industry 1976–78; Amb. to Austria 1978–80; Minister of Heavy and Agric. Machine Industries 1980–81; Vice-Chair. Council of Ministers 1981–82; Amb. to Czechoslovakia 1982–88; mem. PZPR 1953–; Order of Banner of Labour (1st and 2nd class), Officer's and Kt.'s Cross, Order of Polonia Restituta, Order of the White Lion, 2nd Class, Czechoslovakia. *Address:* Ministerstwo Spraw Zagranicznyoh, Al. I. Armii Wojska Polskiego 23, 00-580, Warsaw, Poland.

JEELOF, Gerrit; Netherlands business exective; b. 13 May 1927, Leeuwarden; m. Jantje Aleida Plinsinga 1951; two d.; ed. Dutch Training Inst. for Foreign Trade, Nijenrode; Philips Industries, Eindhoven, Netherlands 1950–53, Spain and S. America 1953–65, Eindhoven 1965–70, Varese, Italy 1970–76, Chair. and Man. Dir. U.K. 1976–80; mem. Man. Bd., Philips' Gloeilampenfabrieken 1981–88, Chair. and C.E.O. U.S. 1988–; Commdr. del Ordine al Merito della Repubblica Italiana 1974, Hon. C.B.E. 1981, Officer Orde van Oranje Nassau 1985. *Leisure interests:* sailing, golf. *Address:* N.V. Philips' Gloeilampenfabrieken, Groenewoudseweg 1, 5621 BA Eindhoven, The Netherlands. *Telephone:* 040-757735.

JEFFARES, Alexander Norman, M.A., PH.D., D.PHIL.; British professor of English; b. 11 Aug. 1920, Dublin; s. of Cecil N. Jeffares and Agnes Fraser; m. Jeanne A. Calembert 1947; one d.; ed. The High School, Dublin, Trinity Coll., Dublin and Oriel Coll., Oxford; Lecturer in Classics, Trinity Coll., Dublin 1943–45; lector in English, Groningen Univ., Netherlands 1946–48; lecturer in English Literature, Univ. of Edinburgh 1949–51; Prof. of English Language and Literature, Univ. of Adelaide 1951–57; Prof. of English Literature, Univ. of Leeds 1957–74; Prof. of English, Univ. of Stirling 1974–86, Hon. Prof. 1986–; Man. Dir. Academic Advisory Services Ltd. 1974–; Chair. Book Trust, Scotland 1986–; Pres. Scottish PEN 1986–; mem. Arts Council of G.B. 1980–84; mem. Council, Royal Soc. of Edinburgh 1986–, Vice-Pres. 1988–; Dir. Edinburgh Book Festival 1982–; Hon. Fellow, Trinity Coll. Dublin; Hon. D. de l'Univ. (Lille). *Publications:* W. B. Yeats: man and poet 1949, Seven Centuries of Poetry 1955, The Circus Animals 1970, Restoration Drama (4 vols.) 1974, A History of Anglo-Irish Literature 1982, Poems of W. B. Yeats: a new selection 1984, A New Commentary on the Poems of W. B. Yeats 1984, Brought up in Dublin (poems) 1987, Brought up to Leave (poems) 1987, An Irish Childhood (with A. Kamm) 1987, A Jewish Childhood (with A.Kamm), W.B. Yeats: A New Biography 1989. *Leisure interests:* drawing, restoring old houses, travel. *Address:* Craighead Cottage, Fife Ness, Crail, Fife, Scotland. *Telephone:* 0333 50898.

JEFFERSON, Sir George Rowland, Kt., C.B.E., F.ENG., F.I.E.E., F.R.AE.S., F.R.S.A., C.B.I.M., F.C.G.I.; British business executive; b. 26 March 1921; s. of Harold Jefferson and Eva Elizabeth Ellen; m. Irene Watson-Browne 1943; three s.; ed. Dartford Grammar School, Kent; eng. apprentice, Royal Ordnance Factory, Woolwich 1937–42; with R.A.O.C. and R.E.M.E. 1942; Anti-Aircraft Command and Armament Design Dept., Fort Halstead 1942–45; Ministry of Supply, Fort Halstead 1945–52; joined Guided Weapons Div., English Electric Co. Ltd. 1952, Chief Research Engineer 1953, Deputy Chief Engineer 1958; Dir. English Electric Aviation Ltd. 1961; with British Aircraft Corpn. (BAC), Dir. and C.E.O., BAC (Guided Weapons) Ltd. 1963, Deputy Man. Dir. 1964, mem. Bd. 1965–77; Dir. British Aerospace, Chair. and C.E.O. its Dynamics Group 1977–80; Chair. BAC (Anti-Tank) 1968–78; Deputy Chair. Post Office 1980–87; Chair. British Telecommunications 1981–87, C.E.O. -1986; Dir. Babcock Int. 1980–, Lloyds Bank 1986–; Chair. Matthew Hall PLC 1987–88; Dir. AMEC PLC Dec. 1988–; mem. Nat. Enterprise Bd. 1979–80, Governing Council Business in the Community Ltd. 1984–; Freeman of the City of London; Hon.

F.I.Mech.E., Hon. D.Sc. (Bristol), Hon. D.Univ. (Essex). *Address:* AMEC PLC, 14, South Audley Street, London W17 5DP, England.

JEFFORDS, James Merrill, B.S., LL.B.; American politician; b. 11 May 1934, Rutland, Vt.; s. of Ilin M. Jeffords and Marion Hausman; m. Elizabeth Daley; one s. one d.; ed. Yale and Harvard Univs.; admitted to Vermont Bar 1962; law clerk, Judge Ernest Gibson, Vt. District 1962; Partner, Bishop, Crowley & Jeffords 1963–66, Kinney, Carbine & Jeffords 1967–68; mem. Vt. Senate 1967–68; Attorney-Gen. State of Vt. 1969–73; Partner, George E. Rice, Jr. and James M. Jeffords 1973–74; mem. 94th-100th Congresses from Vt.; Senator from Vermont 1989–; Republican. *Address:* United States Senate, Washington, D.C., U.S.A.

JEFFRIES, Carson Dunning, PH.D.; American professor of physics; b. 20 March 1922, Lake Charles, La.; s. of Charles W. Jeffries and Yancey D. Jeffries; m. Elizabeth Dyer 1945 (divorced 1976); one s. one d.; ed. Louisiana State Univ., Baton Rouge, Stanford Univ.; Research Assoc. Radio Research Lab., Harvard Univ. 1943–45; Research Asst., Stanford Univ. 1946–50; Instructor, Physikalishes Institut der Universität, Zurich 1951; Instructor, Dept. of Physics, Univ. of Calif., Berkeley 1952, Asst. Prof. 1953–57, Assoc. Prof. 1958–62, Prof. 1963–; Faculty Sr. Scientist, Lawrence Berkeley Lab. 1977–; mem. N.A.S., Fellow, American Acad. of Arts and Sciences, American Physical Soc. *Publications:* Dynamic Nuclear Orientation 1963, Electron Hole Droplets in Semiconductors (Ed.) 1983. *Leisure interests:* sculpture, painting. *Address:* Physics Department, Le Conte Hall, Univ. of California (Berkeley), Calif. 94720, U.S.A. *Telephone:* 415-642 3382.

JEFFRIES, Lionel; British actor and director; began career in film industry 1942; writer and dir. The Railway Children, The Amazing Mr Blunden, Wombling Free; dir. Baxter, The Water Babies; London stage appearances include Hello Dolly 1983–84 and, with Theatre of Comedy, See How They Run, Two into One 1984–85. *Films include:* Bhowani Junction, The Nun's Story, Law and Disorder, Life is a Circus, Idle on Parade, Jazzboat, Please Turn Over, Two-Way Stretch, Trials of Oscar Wilde, Fanny, The Hellions, Operation Snatch, Mrs Gibbon's Boys, Wrong Arm of the Law, Call Me Bwana, The Long Ships, First Men in the Moon, Secret of my Success, Murder Ahoy, You Must be Joking, Journey to the Moon, Camelot, Chitty Chitty Bang Bang, Ménage à trois, Ending Up (TV) 1989. *Address:* c/o John Redway, 16 Berners Street, London, W.1, England.

JEFFRIES, William Patrick, LL.B.; New Zealand politician; b. 1945, Wellington; m.; five c.; ed. St. Patrick's Coll. and Victoria Univ., Wellington; established own law firm in Wellington; mem. Parl.; fmr. Parl. Under-Sec. to Minister of Transport and to Minister of Works and Devt.; Minister of Transport and Minister of Civil Aviation 1987–; Labour Party. *Leisure interests:* reading (int. affairs). *Address:* Parliament House, Wellington, New Zealand.

JEK, Yeun-Thong; Singapore politician and diplomatist; b. 29 July 1930, Singapore; s. of Keng-Hing Jek and Hup-Yee Kwok; m. Kek-Chee Huang 1958; two s.; ed. Singapore Chinese High School; M.P. 1963; Minister of Labour 1963–68, of Culture 1968–72, 1972–77; High Commr. in U.K. 1977–83. *Leisure interests:* swimming, walking, reading. *Address:* c/o Ministry of Foreign Affairs, 1st Floor, Government Offices, St. Andrew's Road, Singapore 1, Republic of Singapore.

JEKER, Robert A.; Swiss banker; b. 26 Aug. 1935, Basle; m. Verena Blumer 1965; one s. two d.; bank training at Credit Suisse, Basle 1951–54, then professional training in Italy, France, U.S.A., Argentina, Sr. Vice-Pres., Basle Branch, Credit Suisse 1972, Exec. Vice-Pres. Credit Suisse 1975, Assoc. mem. of Exec. Bd. 1976, mem. 1977, Pres. Exec. Bd. 1983–; Dir. Soc. Int. Pirelli S.A., Basle 1979–, George Fischer Ltd., Schaffhausen 1980–, Bayer AG, Leverkusen 1985–, BBC Brown Boveri Ltd., Baden 1986–; Vice-Chair. Asscn. Suisse des banquiers, Basle 1988–. *Leisure interests:* sport, travelling. *Address:* Credit Suisse, Paradeplatz 8, CH-8021 Zurich, Switzerland (Office). *Telephone:* (01) 215 11 11 (Office).

JELINEK, Hon. Otto John; Canadian politician; b. 1940, Prague, Czechoslovakia; m. Leata Mary Bennett 1974; two s.; ed. Oakville, Ont., Swiss Alpine Business Coll., Davos, Switzerland; business exec.; first elected M.P. 1972, fmr. Party spokesperson on Fitness and Amateur Sport, then on Corporate Affairs and on Small Businesses and Tourism; apptd. Parl. Sec. to Minister of Transport 1979; fmr. mem. Caucus Cttee. on Trade, Finance, Econ. Affairs, fmr. mem. Standing Cttee. on Transport and Communications, on External Affairs; fmr. mem. Parl. Cttee. on Miscellaneous Estimates, Minister of State (Fitness and Amateur Sport) 1984–88, for Multiculturalism 1985–86, of Supply and Services 1988–; Acting Minister of Public Works 1988–89, Minister of Nat. Revenue Jan. 1989–; Chair. Canada-Taiwan Friendship Cttee.; mem. Big Brothers' Asscn. of Canada, Olympic Club of Canada, Canadian Sports Hall of Fame; Fed. Progressive Conservative Party. *Address:* House of Commons, Ottawa, Ont., K1A 0A6, Canada.

JELJASZEWICZ, Janusz, M.D.; Polish microbiologist ; b. 8 Aug. 1930, Wilno; s. of Aleksander and Helena Jeljaszewicz; m. (divorced); one d.; ed. Medical Acad., Poznań; Asst., Microbiology Research Centre of Medical Acad., Poznań 1952–60; Lecturer, Microbiology Research Centre of Medical Acad., Warsaw 1960–63; with Nat. Inst. of Hygiene, Warsaw 1963–; Head, Bacteriology Research Centre 1963–, Asst. Prof. 1965, Extraordinary Prof. 1973, Ordinary Prof. 1978–; mem. comms. and cttees. of Polish Acad. of Sciences, Chair. Scientific Council attached to Minister of Health and Social Welfare 1979–; Chair. and mem. many int. cttees., scientific councils and editorial bds. in Poland and abroad; in charge of Polish-American scientific project "Pathogenesis of Staphylococcal and Streptococcal Infections" 1963–80; mem. numerous medical socs.; Kt.'s Cross of Order of Polonia Restituta, Gold Cross of Merit; State Award for Achievements in Science 1976. *Publications:* Bacterial Toxins and Cell Membranes 1978, Bacteria and Cancer 1983, Staphylococci and Staphylococcal Infections (5 vols.) 1965–85, Medical Microbiology (5 vols.) 1983–85, Chemotherapy and Immunity 1985, Bacterial Protein Toxins 1984– (3 vols.), about 300 research works in Polish and foreign professional journals. *Leisure interests:* collecting bibliophile editions, history, symphonic music, Polish painting. *Address:* Department of Bacteriology, National Institute of Hygiene, ul. Chocimska 24, 00-791 Warsaw, Poland (Office). *Telephone:* 49-77-81.

JELLICOE, 2nd Earl, (cr. 1925); **George Patrick John Rushworth Jellicoe,** K.B.E., P.C., D.S.O., M.C.; British diplomatist, politician and businessman; b. 4 April 1918, Hatfield; s. of 1st Earl Jellicoe (Admiral of the Fleet); m. 1st Patricia O'Kane 1944; m. 2nd Philippa Ann Bridge 1966; three s. four d.; ed. Winchester and Trinity Coll., Cambridge; Mil. Service 1939–45; joined Foreign Office 1947; First Sec. Washington, Brussels, Baghdad; Deputy Sec.-Gen. Baghdad Pact; Lord-in-Waiting 1961; Jt. Parl. Sec., Ministry of Housing and Local Govt. 1961–62; Minister of State, Home Office 1962–63; First Lord of Admiralty 1963–64; Minister of Defence for the Royal Navy 1964; Deputy Leader of the Opposition, House of Lords 1967–70; Lord Privy Seal and Leader of House of Lords 1970–73; mem. Bd. S. G. Warburg 1966–70, 1973–; Dir. Smiths Industries, Tate & Lyle 1974– (Chair. 1978–83), Morgan Crucible 1974–; Sotheby's (Holdings) 1973–, Davy Corpn. 1985–; Pres. London Chamber of Commerce and Industry 1979–82; Parl. and Scientific Cttee. 1980–83; Chancellor Univ. of Southampton 1984–; Chair. Council of King's Coll., Univ. of London 1977–86, Medical Research Council 1982–, British Overseas Trade Bd. 1983–86; fmr. Dir. Kennet and Avon Canal Trust; Croix de guerre, Légion d'honneur, Greek Mil. Cross. *Leisure interests:* skiing and travel. *Address:* Tidcombe Manor, Tidcombe, Nr. Marlborough, Wilts., and 97 Onslow Square, London, S.W.7, England. *Telephone:* 01-584 1551 (London).

JELLICOE, Sir Geoffrey (Alan), Kt., C.B.E., F.R.I.B.A.; British architect; b. 8 Oct. 1900, London; s. of George Edward Jellicoe; m. Ursula Pares 1936 (died 1986); ed. Cheltenham Coll., Architectural Assocn., and British School, Rome; fmrly. Sr. Partner, Jellicoe and Coleridge, Architects; Gardens for: Sandringham, Royal Lodge (Windsor), Ditchley Park, Royal Horticultural Soc. cen. area, Wisley, Chequers, Chevening (Kent), Horsted Place (Sussex), Hartwell House (Aylesbury), Shute House (Wilts.), Delta Works (W. Bromwich), Hilton Hotel (Stratford-upon-Avon), Dewlish House (Dorchester), The Grange (Winchester), Sutton Place, Public Park (Modena, Italy); Town Plans for: Guildford, Wellington (Salop), Hemel Hempstead New Town; Architectural Consultant to N. Rhodesian Govt. 1947–52; Housing for: Basildon, Scunthorpe, London Co. Council; Plymouth Civic Centre; Chertsey Civic Centre; Cheltenham Sports Centre; GLC Comprehensive School, Dalston; Durley Park, Keynsham; Grantham Crematorium and Swimming Pool; comprehensive plans for cen. area, Gloucester, and for Tollcross, Edin.; Kennedy Memorial, Runnymede; Plans for Sark, Isles of Scilly, and Bridgefoot, Stratford-upon-Avon, The Moody Gardens, Galveston, Texas; Visiting Fellow, Thames Polytechnic School of Landscape 1979; Pres. Inst. of Landscape Architects 1939–49; Hon. Pres. Int. Fed. of Landscape Architects; mem. Royal Fine Art Comm. 1954–68; fmr. Trustee, Tate Gallery, London; Hon. Corresp. mem. American and Venezuelan Socs. of Landscape Architects; American Soc. of Landscape Architects Medal 1981. *Publications:* Italian Gardens of the Renaissance 1925, Gardens and Design (with J. C. Shepherd) 1927, Baroque Gardens of Austria 1931, Studies in Landscape Design (3 vols.) 1959, 1966, 1970, Motopia 1961, Water (with Susan Jellicoe) 1971, The Landscape of Man 1975, The Guelph Lectures on Landscape Design 1983, Oxford Companion to Gardens 1987; Gold Medal, Sofia 1987. *Address:* 14 Highpoint, North Hill, Highgate, London, N6 4BA, England. *Telephone:* 01-348 0123.

JENCKS, William Platt, M.D.; American biochemist; b. 15 Aug. 1927, Bar Harbor, Me.; s. of Gardner Jencks and Elinor Melcher Cheetham; m. Miriam Ehrlich Jencks 1950; one s. one d.; ed. Harvard Coll. and Harvard Medical School; Intern, Peter Bent Brigham Hosp., Boston, Mass. 1951–52; mem. staff, Dept. of Pharmacology, Army Medical Service Graduate School 1953–54, Chief, Dept. of Pharmacology 1954–55; Life Insurance Medical Research Fund Postdoctoral Fellow, Mass. Gen. Hosp. 1955–56; U.S. Public Health Service Postdoctoral Fellow, Dept. of Chem., Harvard 1956–57; Asst. Prof. of Biochem., Brandeis Univ. 1957–60, Assoc. Prof. of Biochem. 1960–63, Prof. of Biochem. 1963–, of Biochem. and Molecular Pharmacodynamics 1977–; Fellow A.A.A.S., American Acad. of Arts and Sciences; Guggenheim Memorial Foundation Fellow 1973–74; mem. Nat. Acad. of Sciences, American Soc. of Biological Chemists; American Chem. Soc. Award in Biological Chem. 1962. *Publications:* Catalysis in Chemistry and Enzymology 1969 and over 250 articles in journals. *Leisure interest:* music. *Address:* Brandeis University, Graduate Department of Biochemistry,

Waltham, Mass. 02254 (Office); 11 Revere Street, Lexington, Mass. 02173, U.S.A. (Home).

JENKIN OF RODING, Baron (Life Peer), cr. 1987, of Wanstead and Woodford in Greater London; **(Charles) Patrick Fleeming Jenkin,** P.C., M.A., F.R.S.A.; British politician; b. 7 Sept. 1926, Edinburgh; s. of late C. O. F. Jenkin and Margaret E. Jenkin (née Sillar); m. Alison Monica Graham 1952; two s. two d.; ed. Clifton Coll., Bristol, Jesus Coll., Cambridge; called to the Bar, Middle Temple 1952; Adviser Distillers Co. Ltd. 1957-70; Hornsey Borough Council 1960-63; M.P. for Wanstead and Woodford 1964-74, Redbridge, Wanstead and Woodford 1974-87; Opposition Spokesman on Finance, Econs. and Trade 1965-66, 1967-70; Financial Sec. to Treasury 1970-72, Chief Sec. 1972-74; Minister for Energy Jan.-March 1974; mem. Shadow Cabinet 1974-79; Opposition Spokesman on Energy 1974-76, on Social Services 1976-79; Sec. of State for Social Services 1979-81, for Industry 1981-83, for the Environment 1983-85; Non-Exec. Dir. Tilbury Contracting Group Ltd. 1974-79, Royal Worcs. Co. Ltd. 1975-79; Dir. Continental and Industrial Trust Ltd. 1975-79; Chair. Lamco Paper Sales Ltd. 1987, U.K.-Japan 2000 Group 1986-, Taverner Concerts Trust 1987-, Friends Provident Life Office 1988-, Crystalate Holdings PLC 1988-; Vice-Pres. Assen. of Metropolitan Authorities 1987-, Nat. Assen. of Local Councils 1987-, Greater London Area Conservatives 1987-; Dir. U.K. Advisory Bd. Nat. Econ. Research Assocs. Inc. 1985-, U.K. Council for Econ. and Environmental Devt. Ltd. 1986-; Council mem. Guide Dogs for the Blind Assen. 1987-; Conservative. *Leisure interests:* music, gardening, sailing. *Address:* 15 Old Bailey, London, EC4M 7AP (Office); 703 Howard House, Dolphin Square, London, SW1 V3LX, England (Home). *Telephone:* 01-329 4454 (Office); 01-798 8724 (Home).

JENKINS, David, M.R.C.V.S., M.A., D.PHIL., D.SC., F.R.S.E.; British biologist and ecologist (retd.); b. 1 March 1926, Birmingham; s. of Alfred Thomas Jenkins and Doris Cecilia Jenkins; m. Margaret Wellwood Johnston 1961; one s. one d.; ed. Marlborough Coll., Royal Veterinary Coll., Emmanuel Coll., Cambridge, Univ. Coll., Oxford; Head Unit of Grouse and Moorland Ecology, Nature Conservancy/Natural Environmental Research Council 1956-66; Asst. Dir. (Research) Nature Conservancy 1966-72; Sr. Officer Banchory Research Station, Inst. of Terrestrial Ecology 1973-86; Prof. Zoology Dept., Aberdeen Univ. 1986-; Chair. Steering Cttee., Aberdeen Centre for Land Use, Scientific Advisory Cttee., World Pheasant Assen. *Publications:* articles in scientific journals. *Leisure interests:* natural history, walking, gardening. *Address:* Aberdeen University, Department of Zoology, Tillydrone Avenue, Aberdeen, AB9 2TN; Whitewalls, Barclay Park, Aboyne, Aberdeenshire, AB3 5JB, Scotland (Home). *Telephone:* (0224) 272858 (Office); (0339) 2526 (Home).

JENKINS, (David) Clive; British trade unionist; b. 2 May 1926, Port Talbot; s. of David Samuel and Miriam Harris (née Hughes) Jenkins; m. Moira McGregor Hilley 1963; one s. one d.; ed. Port Talbot Central Boys' School, Port Talbot County School and Swansea Tech. Coll.; employed in metallurgical test house 1940; mem. Port Talbot Co-operative Soc. Educ. Cttee. 1945; Branch Sec. and Area Treas., Assen. of Scientific Workers 1946; Asst. Midlands Div. Officer, Assen. of Supervisory Staffs, Execs. and Technicians (ASSET) 1947, Transport Industrial Officer 1949, Nat. Officer 1954, Gen. Sec. ASSET 1961-68; Jt. Gen. Sec. Assen. of Scientific, Tech. and Man. Staffs 1968-70, 1988-, Gen. Sec. 1970-88; Metropolitan Borough Councillor 1954-60; Chair. Nat. Jt. Council for Civil Air Transport 1967-68, London Enterprise Devts. 1984-; Ed. Trade Union Affairs 1961-63; mem. Gen. Council of Trades Union Congress 1974-; Dir. Unity Trust 1984-; mem. Nat. Research Devt. Corpn. 1974-80; mem. British Overseas Trade Bd.; mem. Cttee. of Enquiry on Industrial Democracy 1976; mem. Cttee. to Review the Functioning of Financial Insts. 1977; mem. TUC Econ. Cttee. 1978-, TUC Gen. Purposes and Finance Cttee. 1979-, TUC-Labour Party Liaison Cttee. 1979-, Comm. of Inquiry into Labour Party 1979; mem. Int. Cttee., Social Insurance and Ind. Welfare Cttee., Employ and Org. Cttee.; mem. NEDC 1983; mem. Bd. BNOC 1979-82; mem. Advisory, Conciliation and Arbitration Service (ACAS) 1986-; Trustee, Nat. Heritage Memorial Fund 1980-88; Gov. Royal Sadlers Wells Foundation 1985-88; Chair. Roosevelt Memorial Trust, Educ. Trust, Friends of the Earth Trust 1984-86; Gov. Commonwealth Inst. *Publications:* Power at the Top 1959, Power Behind the Screen 1961, British Trade Unions Today (with J. E. Mortimer) 1965, The Kind of Laws the Unions Ought to Want (with J. E. Mortimer) 1968, Computers and the Unions (with Barrie Sherman) 1977, Collective Bargaining (with Barrie Sherman) 1977, The Collapse of Work (with Barrie Sherman) 1979, White Collar Unionism: The Rebellious Salariat (with Barrie Sherman) 1979, The Leisure Shock (with Barrie Sherman) 1981; pamphlets and essays. *Address:* 79 Camden Road, Camden Town, London, NW1 9ES (Office); 16 St. Marks Crescent, London, N.W.1, England (Home). *Telephone:* 01-267 4422 (Office); 01-485 4509 (Home).

JENKINS, Most Rev. David Edward, M.A. (OXON.); British ecclesiastic; b. 26 Jan. 1925, London; s. of Lionel C. Jenkins and Dora K. (née Page) Jenkins; m. Stella M. Peet 1949; two s. two d.; ed. St. Dunstan's Coll., Catford, Queen's Coll., Oxford, Lincoln Theological Coll.; Capt. R.A. 1943-47; priest 1954; Succentor Birmingham Cathedral 1953-54; Fellow and Chaplain/Praelector in Theology, Queen's Coll., Oxford 1954-69; Dir. Humanum Studies, WCC, Geneva 1969-73; Dir. William Temple Foun-

dation, Manchester 1979-; Prof. of Theology Leeds Univ. 1979-84; Bishop of Durham 1984-; Dir. SCM Press; Hon. D.D. (Durham). *Publications:* The Glory of Man 1967, Living With Questions 1969, What is Man? 1970, The Contradiction of Christianity 1979, God, Miracles and the Church of England 1987, God, Politics and the Future 1988, God, Jesus and Life in the Spirit 1988, contrib. to Man, Fallen and Free 1969. *Leisure interests:* music (opera and church music), walking, birdwatching, nature and conservation, travel and books. *Address:* Auckland Castle, Bishop Auckland, Co. Durham, DL14 7NR, England. *Telephone:* (0388) 602576.

JENKINS, David Graham, PH.D., D.SC., F.R.S.N.Z., F.G.S.; British micropaleontologist; b. 27 July 1933, Burry Port, Wales; s. of Joseph Jenkins and Marged Jenkins; m. Judith Mary Beynon 1959; one s. one d.; ed. Llanelli Grammar School and Univ. Coll. of Wales; geologist, Bureau of Mineral Resources, Canberra 1956-57; paleontologist British Petroleum 1959-62; Micropaleontologist N.Z. Geological Survey 1962-66; Sr. Lecturer in Geology Univ. of Canterbury, Christchurch, N.Z. 1966-70, Reader 1970-77; Consultant to Open Univ., Milton Keynes 1977-78, Lecturer in Earth Sciences 1978-; Pres. Geological Soc. of N.Z. 1975-76; mem. Int. Union of Geological Sciences Subcomm. on Paleogene Stratigraphy 1973-, Sec. 1985-; Micropaleontologist on Deep Sea Drilling Project 'Glomar Challenger' 1969-70, 1973, 1982-83; mem. JOIDES Stratigraphic Correlations Panel 1980-83, UK-IPOD Co-ordinating Cttee. 1980-, Subcomm. on Neogene Stratigraphy 1980-; McKay Hammer Award, N.Z. Geological Soc. 1972. *Publications:* over 100 publs. in professional journals etc. *Leisure interests:* walking and beachcombing in Wales, writing short stories. *Address:* Department of Earth Sciences, Open University, Milton Keynes, England; The Old Chapel, Rhossili, Swansea, Wales (Home).

JENKINS, Elizabeth, O.B.E.; British writer; ed. Newnham Coll. Cambridge. *Publications:* The Winters 1931, Lady Caroline Lamb: a Biography 1932, Portrait of an Actor 1933, Harriet (Femina Vie Heureuse Prize) 1934, The Phoenix Nest 1936, Jane Austen—a Biography 1938, Robert and Helen 1944, Young Enthusiasts 1946, Henry Fielding, English Novelists Series 1947, Six Criminal Women 1949, The Tortoise and the Hare 1954, Ten Fascinating Women 1955, Elizabeth the Great 1958, Elizabeth and Leicester 1961, Brightness 1963, Honey 1968, Dr. Gully 1972, The Mystery of King Arthur 1975, The Princes in the Tower 1978, The Shadow and the Light 1983. *Address:* 8 Downshire Hill, Hampstead, London, N.W.3, England. *Telephone:* 01-435 4642.

JENKINS, Harold, M.A., D.LITT.; British university professor (retd.); b. 19 July 1909, Shenley, Bucks.; s. of Henry Jenkins and Mildred (Carter) Jenkins; m. Gladys Puddifoot 1939 (died 1984); no c.; ed. Wolverton Grammar School and Univ. Coll. London; Quain Student, Univ. Coll. London 1930-35; William Noble Fellow, Univ. of Liverpool 1935-36; Jr. Lecturer in English, Univ. of the Witwatersrand 1936-38, Lecturer 1939-44, Sr. Lecturer 1945; Lecturer in English, Univ. Coll. London 1945-46, Reader 1946-54; Prof. of English, Westfield Coll, Univ. of London 1954-67; Regius Prof. of Rhetoric and English Literature Univ. of Edin. 1967-71, Prof. Emer. 1971-; Visiting Prof. Duke Univ. 1957-58, Univ. of Oslo 1974; Gen. Ed. Arden Shakespeare 1958-82; Shakespeare Prize, FVS Foundation, Hamburg 1986; Hon. D. Litt. (Iona Coll., U.S.A.) 1983. *Publications:* Henry Chettle 1934, Edward Benlowes: Biography of a Minor Poet 1952, Hamlet (Arden Shakespeare) 1982. *Address:* 22 North Crescent, Finchley, London, N3 3LL, England.

JENKINS, Dame (Mary) Jennifer, D.B.E.; British administrator; b. 18 Jan. 1921; d. of the late Sir Parker Morris; m. Roy Jenkins (q.v.) 1945; two s. one d.; ed. St. Mary's School, Calne, Girton Coll., Cambridge; with Hoover Ltd. 1942-43; Ministry of Labour 1943-46; Political and Econ. Planning 1946-48; part-time extra-mural lecturer 1949-61; part-time teacher Kingsway Day Coll. 1961-67; Chair. Consumers Assen. 1965-76; mem. Exec. Bd. British Standards Inst. 1970-73, Design Council 1971-74, Cttee. of Man. Courtauld Inst. 1981-84, Exec. Cttee., Nat. Trust 1984 (Chair. March 1986-), Ancient Monuments Bd. 1982-84, Historic Bldgs. Advisory Cttee. 1984-85, Historic Bldgs. and Monuments Comm. 1984-85; Chair. Historic Bldgs. Council for England 1975-84; Pres. Ancient Monuments Soc. 1985- (Sec. 1972-75); Chair. N. Kensington Amenity Trust 1974-77; Trustee Wallace Collection 1977-83; Dir. J. Sainsbury Ltd. 1981-84, Abbey Nat. Bldg. Soc. 1984-; J.P. London Juvenile Courts 1964-74; Hon. F.R.I.B.A., Hon. R.I.C.S.; Hon. LL.D. (Univ. of London) 1988. *Address:* 2 Kensington Park Gardens, London, W.11; St. Amand's House, East Hendred, Oxon.; 12 Kirklee Terrace, Glasgow, G12 0TH, Scotland.

JENKINS, Michael Romilly Heald, C.M.G., B.A.; British diplomatist; b. 9 Jan. 1936, Cambridge; s. of Prof. Romilly Jenkins and Celine J. (née Haeglar) Jenkins; m. Maxine L. Hodson 1968; one s. one d.; ed. King's Coll., Cambridge; entered Foreign (subsequently Diplomatic) Service 1959; served in Paris, Moscow and Bonn; Deputy Chef de Cabinet 1973-75, Chef de Cabinet to George Thomson, EEC 1975-76; Principal Adviser to Roy Jenkins (now Lord Jenkins q.v.) Jan.-Aug. 1977; Head, European Integration Dept. (External), FCO 1977-79; Head, Cen. Advisory Group, EEC 1979-81; Deputy Sec.-Gen., Comm. of the European Communities 1981-83; Asst. Under-Sec. of State (Europe), FCO 1983-85; Minister, British Embassy, Washington 1985-87; Amb. to the Netherlands 1988-. *Publications:* Arakcheev, Grand Vizier of the Russian Empire 1969, contrib.

to History Today. *Leisure interest:* tennis. *Address:* c/o Foreign and Commonwealth Office, King Charles Street, London, S.W.1., England.

JENKINS OF HILLHEAD, Baron (Life Peer), cr. 1987, of Pontypool in the County of Gwent; **Roy Harris Jenkins,** P.C.; British politician and writer and former President of the European Commission; b. 11 Nov. 1920; s. of Arthur Jenkins, M.P.; m. Jennifer Morris (q.v.); two s. one d.; ed. Abersychan Grammar School and Balliol Coll., Oxford; Royal Artillery 1942–46; mem. Staff of Industrial and Commercial Finance Corpn. 1946–48; M.P. (Labour) for Cen. Southwark, London 1948–50, for Stechford, Birmingham 1950–77; M.P. (S.D.P.) for Glasgow Hillhead 1982–87; Parl. Private Sec. to Sec. of State for Commonwealth Relations 1949–50; Gov. British Film Inst. 1955–58; mem. Cttee. of Man., Soc. of Authors 1956–60; Chair. Fabian Soc. 1957–58; mem. Council, Britain in Europe; Chair. Britain in Europe Campaign for referendum of 1975; Dir. of Financial Operations, John Lewis Partnership Ltd. 1962–64; Minister of Aviation 1964–65; Sec. of State for Home Dept. 1965–67, 1974–76; Chancellor of the Exchequer 1967–70; Deputy Leader of Labour Party 1970–72; Pres. Comm. of the European Communities 1977–81; mem. Council for Social Democracy Jan.-March 1981; co-founder Social Democratic Party (SDP) March 1981, Leader 1982–83; Leader Social and Liberal Democratic Party Peers House of Lords 1988–; Pres. R.S.L. April 1988–; Chancellor, Oxford Univ. March 1987–; Adviser (part-time) Morgan Grenfell 1981–82, Dir. Morgan Grenfell Holdings Ltd. 1981–82; Hon. Foreign mem. American Acad. of Arts and Sciences 1973; Hon. Fellow, Berkeley Coll., Yale, Balliol Coll., Oxford, Loughborough, University Coll., Cardiff; Hon. LL.D. (Leeds) 1971, (Harvard) 1972, (Pennsylvania) 1973, (Dundee) 1973, (Bath) 1978, (Michigan) 1978, (Essex) 1978, (Wales) 1978, (Reading) 1979, (Bristol) 1980, Hon. D.Litt. (Glasgow) 1972, (City University, London) 1976, Hon. D.C.L. (Oxford) 1973, Hon. D.Sc. (Warwick) 1978, (Univ. of Aston in Birmingham) 1977, Hon. Doctor of Univ. of Keele 1977; Dr. h.c. (Open Univ.) 1979, (Louvain) 1979, (Urbino) 1979; Charlemagne Prize 1972, Robert Schumann Prize 1972. *Publications:* Purpose and Policy (Editor) 1947, Mr. Attlee: An Interim Biography 1948, New Fabian Essays (contributor) 1952, Pursuit of Progress 1953, Mr. Balfour's Poodle 1954, Sir Charles Dilke: A Victorian Tragedy 1958, The Labour Case 1959, Asquith 1964, Essays and Speeches 1967, Afternoon on the Potomac? 1972, What Matters Now 1973, Nine Men of Power 1974, Partnership of Principle 1985, Truman 1986, Baldwin 1987, Gallery of Twentieth Century Portraits 1988, European Diary 1977–81, 1989. *Address:* 2 Kensington Park Gardens, London, W.11; St. Amand's House, East Hendred, Oxon., England.

JENKINS, Simon David, B.A.; British journalist; b. 10 June 1943, Birmingham; s. of Daniel Jenkins; m. Gayle Hunnicutt 1978; one s. one step-d.; ed. Mill Hill School, St. John's Coll., Oxford; worked for Country Life Magazine 1965; News Ed. Times Educ. Supplement 1966–68; Leader-Writer, Columnist, Features Ed. Evening Standard 1968–74; Insight Editor, Sunday Times 1974–76; Ed. Evening Standard 1977–78; Political Ed. The Economist 1979–86; columnist Sunday Times 1986–; Dir. Faber and Faber (Publrs.) Ltd. 1981–; mem. Bd., Old Vic Co. 1979–81; Part-time mem. British Rail Bd. 1979–, London Regional Transport Bd. 1984–86; Gov. Museum of London 1984–87; Dir. The Municipal Journal 1980–; mem. Historic Bldgs. and Monuments Comm. 1985–, South Bank Bd. 1985–. *Publications:* A City at Risk 1971, Landlords to London 1974, Newspapers: The Power and the Money 1979, The Companion Guide to Outer London 1981, Images of Hampstead 1982, The Battle for the Falklands 1983, With Respect, Ambassador 1985, The Market for Glory 1986. *Leisure interests:* architecture, history of London. *Address:* 174 Regents Park Road, London, N.W.1, England.

JENKINS OF PUTNEY, Baron (Life Peer), cr. 1981, of Wandsworth in Greater London; **Hugh Gater Jenkins;** British politician; b. 27 July 1908, Enfield; s. of Joseph and Florence Jenkins; m. Marie Crosbie 1936; ed. Enfield Grammar School; Prudential Assurance Co. 1930–40; wartime service in Royal Observer Corps and R.A.F.; Dir. English Programmes, Rangoon Radio; Greater London Organizer, Nat. Union of Bank Employees, later research and publicity officer, Ed. The Bank Officer; Asst. Sec. British Actors' Equity Assocn. 1950, Asst. Gen. Sec. 1957–64; M.P. (Labour) for Putney 1964–79; Opposition Spokesman on the Arts 1973–74; Parl. Under-Sec. of State, Dept. of Educ. and Science, Minister responsible for the Arts 1974–76; fmr. Chair. Standing Advisory Cttee. on Local Authorities and the Theatre; mem. Arts Council 1968–71, Drama Panel 1972–74, mem. Bd. Nat. Theatre 1977–80; Vice-Pres. Theatres Advisory Council 1985–, Pres. Battersea Arts Centre; Vice-Pres. Campaign for Nuclear Disarmament 1981; Consultant, Theatres Trust. *Publications:* The Culture Gap 1979, Rank and File 1980; articles and broadcasts on politics, the arts, disarmament, government and socialism; Radio Plays: Solo Boy, When You and I were Seventeen, A Day in September, In Time of War, Lost Tune, View to a Death, A Swing In The Sixties. *Leisure interests:* reading, writing, talking, viewing, listening and occasionally thinking. *Address:* House of Lords, London, S.W.1, England. *Telephone:* (01) 219 6706; 788 0371.

JENKS, Downing Bland; American railroad executive; b. 16 Aug. 1915, Portland, Ore.; s. of Charles and Della Downing Jenks; m. Louise Sweeney 1940; one s. one d.; ed. St. Paul Acad. and Yale Univ.; Asst. on Engineer Corps., Pennsylvania Railroad 1937–38; Trainmaster, Div. Engineer,

Roadmaster, Great Northern Railway 1938–47; Div. Supt. 1947; Vice-Pres. and Gen. Man., Chicago & Eastern Ill. Railroad 1948; Asst. Vice-Pres. Rock Island Lines 1950, Vice-Pres. operation 1951, Exec. Vice-Pres. 1953, Pres. 1956–60; Pres. Missouri Pacific Railroad Co. 1961–72, Chair. C.E.O. 1972–74, Chair. of Bd. 1974–83; C.E.O., Missouri Pacific Corpn. 1971–83, Pres. 1971–74, Chair. 1974–83; Dir. Union Pacific Corpn. 1983–, Union Pacific Railroad 1983–; Dir. Centerre Bank in St. Louis, Centerre Bancorp, Bankers Life Co., Mississippi River Transmission Corpn.; U.S. Army service, N. Africa, Italy, France, Germany, Lieut.-Col. Mil. Railway Service 1942–45; Bronze Star Medal. *Leisure interests:* hunting and fishing. *Address:* 9900 Clayton Road, St. Louis, Mo. 63124 (Office); 8 Greenbriar, St. Louis, Mo. 63124, U.S.A. (Home).

JENNINGS, Elizabeth, M.A.; British poet and critic; b. 18 July 1926, Boston, Lincs.; d. of Dr. H. C. Jennings; ed. Oxford High School, St. Anne's Coll., Oxford; Asst. at Oxford City Library 1950–58; Reader for Chatto & Windus Ltd. 1958–60; freelance writer 1960–; Arts Council Prize for Poems, 1953, Somerset Maugham Award for A Way of Looking 1956, Richard Hillary Prize for The Mind has Mountains 1966, Arts Council Award 1981. *Publications:* Poetry: Poems 1953, A Way of Looking 1955, A Sense of the World 1958, a translation of Michelangelo's Sonnets 1961, Song for a Birth or Death 1961, Recoveries 1963, The Mind has Mountains 1966, The Secret Brother (for children) 1966, Collected Poems 1967, The Animals' Arrival 1969, Lucidities 1971, Relationships 1972, Growing Points 1975, Consequently I Rejoice 1977, After the Ark (for children) 1978, Moments of Grace 1979, Celebrations and Elegies 1982, Extending the Territory 1985, Collected Poems 1953–86 1986 (W.H. Smith Award 1987); Criticism: Every Changing Shape 1961, Seven Men of Vision 1976; ed. Batsford Book of Religious Verse 1982, In Praise of Our Lady 1982; writings also include contributions to New Yorker, Southern Review, Poetry (Chicago), Botteghe Oscure, Daily Telegraph, Encounter, New Statesman, Observer, Scotsman, Country Life, Listener and others. *Leisure interests:* theatre, music, looking at pictures, conversation. *Address:* c/o David Higham Assocs. Ltd., 5-8 Lower John Street, London, W1R 4HA, England.

JENNINGS, Jesse David, PH.D, D.S.; American anthropologist; b. 7 July 1909, Oklahoma City; m. Jane Noyes Chase 1935; two c.; ed. Estancia, Montezuma Coll., New Mexico, Univ. of Chicago; short-term archaeological posts 1930–36; Lieut. U.S.N.R. 1942–45; Ranger with Nat. Park Service, Camp Verde, Ariz. 1937–38, Acting Supt., Macon, Georgia 1938–39, Archaeologist Natchez Trace Parkway 1938–42, Tupelo, Miss. 1945–46, Regional Archaeologist, Omaha, Nebraska 1947–48; Prof. Dept. of Anthropology, Univ. of Utah 1948–86, Prof. Emer. 1986–, Dist. Prof. 1975–86; Dir. Utah Museum of Nat. History, Salt Lake City 1963–73; Adjunct Prof. Univ. of Oregon 1980–; Viking Medalist in Archaeology 1958, Distinguished Service Award, Soc. for American Archaeology 1982, mem. Nat. Acad. of Sciences 1977. *Publications:* Prehistory of North America 1968, Readings in Anthropology 1972, Prehistory of Polynesia 1979, Ancient North Americans 1983 and numerous articles and papers. *Leisure interest:* gardening. *Address:* 21801 Siletz Highway, Siletz, Ore. 97380, U.S.A. *Telephone:* 503-444-2843.

JENNINGS, Keith Lynden, B.A., M.ED.; Australian administrative official; b. 6 Feb. 1932, Sydney, N.S.W.; s. of Herbert Ernest Jennings; m. Moira Hodgekiss 1953; one s. one d.; ed. Balmain Teachers' Coll. and Univ. of Sydney; teacher, N.S.W 1950–58; short service comm., educ. branch, R.A.A.F. 1958–61; housemaster, The King's School, Parramatta, N.S.W. 1962–64; Educ. Officer, Commonwealth Office of Educ. 1964–67; posts in Commonwealth Educ. Dept. 1967–73; Sec. Universities Comm. 1973; First Asst. Sec. Dept. of Special Minister of State 1974; mem. Gov. Bd. OECD Centre for Educ., Research and Innovation 1973, 1974; post at Univ. of Sydney 1975; Registrar, Univ. of N.S.W. 1976, also Asst. Prin. 1979; Asst. Gen. Man. Australian Broadcasting Comm. (ABC) 1980–82, Gen. Man. 1982–83; Registrar, Univ. of Sydney 1983–85, Registrar and Deputy Prin. 1986–. *Leisure interests:* golf, sailing. *Address:* University of Sydney, Sydney, N.S.W. 2006, Australia. *Telephone:* (02) 6923003.

JENNINGS, Sir Robert Yewdall, M.A., LL.B.; British judge of the International Court of Justice; b. 19 Oct. 1913, Idle, Yorks; s. of Arthur Jennings and Edith Schofield Jennings; m. Christine Dorothy Bennett 1955; one s. two d.; ed. Belle Vue Grammar School, Bradford, Downing Coll., Cambridge, Harvard Univ.; war service 1940–46; Asst. Lecturer in Law, L.S.E. 1938–39, Lecturer 1946–55; called to the Bar, Lincoln's Inn 1943, Hon. Bencher 1970–; Q.C. 1969; Whewell Prof. of Int. Law, Cambridge Univ. 1955–81; Reader in Int. Law, Council of Legal Educ. 1959–70; Ed. Int. and Comparative Law Quarterly 1957–59, British Yearbook of Int. Law 1959–81, Sr. Ed. 1974–81; Assoc. Inst. of Int. Law 1957, mem. 1967, Vice-Pres. 1979–81, Pres. 1981–83, Hon. mem. 1985–; Judge, Int. Court of Justice, The Hague Feb. 1982–; mem. Perm. Court of Arbitration; fmr. legal consultant to numerous govts.; Counsel in several int. arbitrations; Fellow Jesus Coll., Cambridge 1939–, Sr. Tutor 1949–55, fmr. Pres., Hon. Fellow 1982–; Hon. Fellow Downing Coll. 1982–; Hon. LL.D. (Hull) 1987, Hon. Dr. Juris (Scotland). *Publications:* The Acquisition of Territory 1963, General Course on International Law 1967 and numerous articles and monographs. *Leisure interests:* music, walking in Lake District. *Address:* International Court of Justice, Peace Palace, 2517 KJ The Hague, Netherlands. *Telephone:* 45-76-13; 92 44 41.

JENRETTE, Richard Hampton, M.B.A.; American insurance executive; b. 5 May 1929, Raleigh, N.C.; s. of Joseph M. Jenrette and Emma Love; ed. Univ. of N. Carolina and Harvard Grad. School of Business Admin.; New England Life Insurance Co. 1951-53; Brown Bros. Harriman & Co. 1957-59; now Chair. of Bd. Donaldson, Lufkin & Jenrette, New York and of Equitable Life Assurance Soc., New York; Dir. Advanced Micro Devices, Sunnyvale, Calif.; Trustee, The Rockefeller Foundation, many other public affiliations and appts.; Hon. D.Litt. (Univ. of S.C.) and other awards. *Address:* Donaldson, Lufkin & Jenrette, 140 Broadway, New York, N.Y. 10005; Equitable Life Assurance Society, 1285 Avenue of the Americas, New York, N.Y. 10019 (Offices); 67 East 93rd Street, New York, N.Y. 10128, U.S.A. (Home).

JENS, Walter, D.PHIL.; German philologist, critic and novelist; b. 8 March 1923, Hamburg; s. of Walter and Anna (Martens) Jens; m. Inge Puttfarcken 1951; two s.; ed. Hamburg and Freiburg im Breisgau Univs.; Asst. Hamburg and Tübingen Univs. 1946-50; Dozent, Tübingen Univ. 1950-56, Prof. of Classical Philology and Rhetoric 1956-67; mem. German PEN (Pres. 1976-82), Berliner Akad. der Künste, Deutsche Akad. für Sprache und Dichtung; D.Phil., h.c.; Lessingpreis der Hansestadt Hamburg 1968, TV Prize, Trade Union of German Employees 1976, Heinrich Heine Prize 1981, Hamburger Medaille für Kunst und Wissenschaft 1984. *Publications:* Nein—Die Welt der Angeklagten (novel) 1950, Der Blinde (novel) 1951, Vergessene Gesichter (novel) 1952, Der Mann, der nicht alt werden wollte (novel) 1955, Die Stichomythie in der frühen griechischen Tragödie 1955, Hofmannsthal und die Griechen 1955, Das Testament des Odysseus (novel) 1957, Statt einer Literaturgeschichte (Essays on Modern Literature) 1957, Moderne Literatur—moderne Wirklichkeit (essay) 1958, Die Götter sind sterblich (Diary of a Journey to Greece) 1959, Deutsche Literatur der Gegenwart 1961, Zueignungen 1962, Herr Meister (Dialogue on a Novel) 1963, Euripides-Büchner 1964, Von deutscher Rede 1969, Die Verschwörung (TV play) 1970, Am Anfang der Stall, am Ende der Galgen 1973, Fernsehen-Themen und Tabus 1973, Der tödliche Schlag (TV play) 1974, Der Prozess Judas (novel) 1975, Der Ausbruch (libretto) 1975, Republikanische Reden 1976, Eine deutsche Universität, 500 Jahre Tübinger Gelehrtenrepublik 1977, Zur Antike 1979, Die Orestie des Aischylos 1979, Warum ich Christ bin (Ed.) 1979, Ort der Handlung ist Deutschland (essays) 1979, Die kleine grosse Stadt Tübingen 1981, Der Untergang (drama) 1982, In letzter Stunde (Ed.) 1982, Aufruf zum Frieden 1983, Der Untergang 1983, In Sachen Lessing 1983, Kanzel und Katheder 1984, Momos am Bildschirm 1984, Dichtung und Religion (with H. Küng) 1985, Roccos Erzählung 1985, Die Friedensfrau 1986. *Address:* Sonnenstrasse 5, 7400 Tübingen, Federal Republic of Germany. *Telephone:* 07071 292114.

JENSEN, Arthur Robert, PH.D.; American educational psychologist; b. 24 Aug. 1923, San Diego; s. of Arthur Alfred Jensen and Linda Schachtmayer; m. Barbara Jane Delarme 1960; one d.; ed. Calif. (Berkeley), Columbia and London Univs.; Asst. in Medical Psychology, Univ. of Maryland 1955-56; Research Fellow, Inst. of Psychiatry, London Univ. 1956-58; Asst. Prof. to Prof. of Educational Psychology, Univ. of Calif., Berkeley 1958-; Research Psychologist, Inst. of Human Learning 1962-; Guggenheim Fellow 1964-65; Fellow, Center for Advanced Study in the Behavioral Sciences 1966-67; Visiting Lecturer, Melbourne, La Trobe, Adelaide and Sydney Univs. 1977, various univs. in India 1980. *Publications:* Genetics and Education 1972, Educability and Group Differences 1973, Educational Differences 1973, Bias in Mental Testing 1980, Straight Talk About Mental Tests 1981. *Address:* School of Education, University of California, Berkeley, Calif. 94720 (Office); 30 Canyon View Drive, Orinda, Calif. 94563, U.S.A. (Home). *Telephone:* (415) 642-7978 (Office).

JENSEN, Elwood V., PH.D.; American academic and director of research; b. 13 Jan. 1920, Fargo, N.D.; s. of Eli A. and Vera Morris Jensen; m. 1st Mary Collette 1941 (died 1982), one s. one d.; m. 2nd Hiltrud Herborg 1983; ed. Wittenberg Coll. and Univ. of Chicago; Guggenheim Fellowship E.T.H. Zurich 1946-47; at Univ. of Chicago 1946-47, Asst. Prof. Dept. of Surgery 1947-51, Asst. Prof. Ben May Lab. for Cancer Research and Dept. of Biochemistry 1951-54, Assoc. Prof. 1954-60, Prof. Ben May Lab. for Cancer Research 1960-63, American Cancer Soc. Research Prof. Ben May Lab. and Dept. of Physiology 1963-69, Prof. Dept. of Physiology 1969-73, Dept. of Biophysics and Theoretical Biology 1973-84, Dept. of Physiological and Pharmacological Sciences 1977-84, Dept. of Biochemistry 1980-84, Dir. Ben May Lab. for Cancer Research 1969-82, Charles B. Huggins Distinguished Service Prof. Univ. of Chicago 1981-; Research Dir. Ludwig Inst. for Cancer Research, Zürich 1983-87; mem. N.A.S. (mem. Council 1981-84), American Acad. of Arts and Sciences; Hon. D.Sc. (Wittenberg Univ.) 1963, (Acadia Univ.) 1976; numerous awards and prizes. *Publications:* 209 articles and reviews since 1945. *Leisure interests:* tennis, squash, riding. *Address:* Ben May Institute, University of Chicago, 5841 Maryland Avenue, Chicago, Ill. 60637 (Office); 5803 Anniston Road, Bethesda, Md. 20817 (Home). *Telephone:* (312) 702-6994 (Office); (301) 530-1729 (Home).

JENSEN, Erling, LL.B.; Danish politician; b. 1 Nov. 1919, Frederiksberg; s. of Franciskus and Mary Jensen; m. Ria Jorgensen 1951; two s.; Clerk, later Man. Clerk, Credit Asscn. of Estate Owners 1946-57; Sec.-Gen. Union of Urban Co-operative Socs. 1957-60; Dir. of Labour, Folk High Schools 1960-71; Minister of Trade 1971-73, 1975-76; mem. Folketing (Parl.) 1973-

87; Minister of Labour 1976-77, of Justice 1977-78, of Social Affairs 1978-79, of Industry 1979-82; Social Democrat. *Address:* Nørrevej 11, DK 3070 Snekkersten, Denmark. *Telephone:* 02-221655.

JENSEN, Kai Arne, DR. PHIL.; Danish chemist; b. 27 March 1908, Copenhagen; m. Ida Reichardt 1932; three d.; ed. Københavns Univs.; Chemical Laboratory, Univ. of Copenhagen 1933-; Assoc. Prof. of Chem. 1943-50, Prof. 1950-78, Head of Chemical Laboratory II 1950-78; Chair. Comm. on Nomenclature of Inorganic Chem. of Int. Union of Pure and Applied Chem. (IUPAC) 1959-72; mem. Royal Danish Acad. of Sciences and Letters, Danish Acad. of Tech. Sciences, Royal Physiographical Soc. (Lund, Sweden); Kt. Order of Dannebrog; Julius Thomsen Gold Medal, H. C. Ørsted Gold Medal. *Publications:* textbooks on organic and general chemistry and over 200 research papers. *Address:* Bøgehøj 64, 2900 Hellerup, Denmark (Home). *Telephone:* (01) 67-93-75.

JENSEN, Ole Vig; Danish politician; b. 17 May 1936, Frederikssund; fmr. teacher; mem. Folketing (Parl.) 1971-73, 1978-, mem. Presidium 1984-; mem. Gen. Council, Radical Liberal Party 1968-, Exec. Council 1974-, Deputy Chair. Parl. Group 1979-; mem. Cen. Land Bd. 1983-; Chair. Parl. Cttee. for Agric. and Fisheries 1979-84; Deputy Chair. Parl. Educ. Cttee. 1979-82; Minister of Cultural Affairs 1988-. *Address:* Ministry of Cultural Affairs, Nybrogade 2, 1203 Copenhagen K, Denmark. *Telephone:* (01) 92-33-70.

JENTSCHKE, Willibald Karl, PH.D.; Austrian physicist; b. 6 Dec. 1911, Vienna; m. Ingeborg Fielitz 1953; three c.; ed. Univ. of Vienna; Dozent, Univ. of Vienna 1942; Research Asst. Prof., Univ. of Illinois 1948, Assoc. Prof. 1955, Prof. 1956; Prof. Univ. of Hamburg 1970-, 1976; mem. Arbeitskreis Physik (Advisory Cttee. to German Nuclear Energy Comm.) 1957; Dir. DESY Lab., Hamburg 1959-70; del. of Fed. Repub. of Germany to CERN Council and mem. Scientific Policy Cttee. 1964-67; Dir.-Gen. CERN 1971-75; mem. Akad. der Wissenschaft und der Literatur, Mainz, Österreichische Akad. der Wissenschaft, Deutsche Physikalische Gesellschaft, Soc. Italiana di Fisica; Fellow, American Physical Soc., European Physical Soc. *Address:* Kiefernweg 18, 2080 Pinneberg, Federal Republic of Germany.

JEPSEN, Roger W., M.A.; American politician; b. 23 Dec. 1928, Cedar Falls, Ia.; s. of Ernest E. and Esther Jepsen; m. Dee Ann Delaney; three s. three d.; ed. Arizona State Univ.; Iowa State Senator 1966-68, Lieut.-Gov. 1969-73, Chair. Nat. Lieut.-Governors' Conf. 1970-72, U.S. Senator from Iowa 1979-85; Chair. Armed Services Manpower-Personnel Subcttee., Agric. Soil Conservation Sub-cttee.; Vice-Chair. Jt. Econ. Cttee.; Chair. Nat. Credit Union Admin. 1985-; del. to Republican Nat. Conventions 1972, 1980.

JERE, Ndinda Stanley, LL.B., M.SC., PH.D.; Malawian judge; b. 8 Aug. 1938, Embangweni; m. Molly Chamahiya (née Ngwira) Jere 1967; three s. two d.; ed. Nkhata Bay and Zomba Catholic Secondary Schools, Council of Legal Educ. School of Law, Gray's Inn, London, Columbia Pacific Univ., U.S.A.; Agric. Instructor, Dept. of Agric. 1957-61; Legal Aid Advocate 1966-67; State Advocate and Traditional Courts Commr. 1968-71; apptd. Resident Magistrate 1969, Registrar of High Court 1975; apptd. to High Court Bench 1976; acting Chief Justice 1978-79; Founder mem. Malawi Road Safety Cttee. (now Nat. Road Safety Council) 1972. *Publications:* Identification of Accused Person, Motor Vehicle Law and Society, Malawi Government and International Institutions. *Leisure interests:* fishing, gardening. *Address:* High Court of Malawi, Private Bag 15, Lilongwe, Malawi. *Telephone:* 720 666, Ext. 1; 722 876; 732 649 (Home).

JEREZ GARCÍA, Cesar A., S.J., M.A., PH.D.; Guatemalan university president; b. 7 Aug. 1936, Guatemala; ed. Univ. of Ecuador, Sankt Georgen, Frankfurt-am-Main and Univ. of Chicago; teacher in Panama 1960-63; ordained priest, Loyola, Spain 1966; Dir. Center of Social Research and Social Action for Cen. America, Guatemala 1972-76; Provincial Soc. of Jesus in Cen. America 1976-82, External Consultor to Gen. 1979-82; Dir. of Research, Cen. American Univ. Managua 1983, Pres. and Prof. 1985-; Hon. D.H.L. (Canisius, Buffalo, N.Y.) 1977; Hon. D.Theol. (Holy Cross, Worcester, Mass.) 1978. *Publications:* El Salvador, Año Político 1973, Decisiones Politicas e Integración Centroamericana 1974, Christians and Development 1982, The Church and the Nicaraguan Revolution 1984. *Leisure interests:* theology, political sciences, reading, writing research, teaching. *Address:* Universidad Centro-americana, Rectoria, Apartado 69, Managua, Nicaragua. *Telephone:* 7.28.85 (Office); 7.40.42 (Home).

JERNE, Niels Kaj, M.D.; Danish scientist; b. 23 Dec. 1911, London; s. of Hans Jessen and Else Marie (née Lindberg) Jerne; m. Ursula Alexandra Kohl 1964; two s.; ed. Univ. of Leiden, Univ. of Copenhagen; research worker, Danish State Serum Inst., Copenhagen 1943-55; Chief Medical Officer WHO, Geneva 1956-62; Prof. of Biophysics, Univ. of Geneva 1960-62; Chair. Dept. of Microbiology, Univ. of Pittsburgh 1962-66; Prof. of Experimental Therapy, J. W. Goethe Univ., Frankfurt 1966-69; Dir. Basel Inst. for Immunology 1969-80; Prof., Inst. Pasteur, Paris 1981-82; mem. American Acad. of Arts and Sciences 1967, Royal Danish Acad of Sciences 1969, U.S.A. Nat. Acad. of Sciences 1975, Royal Soc. (London) 1980, American Philosophical Soc. 1979, Acad. des Sciences de l'Inst. de France 1981, Yugoslav Acad. of Sciences 1985 and various other socs.; Marcel Benoist Prize, Berne 1979, Paul Ehrlich Prize, Frankfurt 1982;

Nobel Prize for Medicine 1984; Hon. degrees from Univs. of Chicago, Copenhagen, Basel, Rotterdam and Columbia, N.Y., Weizmann Inst. of Science, Israel. *Publications:* articles on theoretical and experimental aspects of immunology in scientific journals. *Leisure interest:* language. *Address:* Château de Bellevue, Castillon-du-Gard, 30210, France. *Telephone:* 66 370075.

JEROME, Rt. Hon. James Alexander, P.C., B.A.; Canadian politician and judge; b. 4 March 1933, Kingston, Ont.; s. of Joseph Leonard Jerome and Phyllis Devlin; m. Barry Karen Hodgins 1958; three s. two d.; ed. St. Michael's Coll., Univ. of Toronto and Osgoode Hall; Lawyer; Alderman, Sudbury 1966-67; M.P. 1968-80; Parl. Sec. to Pres. of Privy Council; Speaker House of Commons 1974-80; Assoc. Chief Justice, Fed. Court of Canada 1980-; Liberal. *Address:* Supreme Court of Canada Building, Ottawa, Ont.; 12 Claret Court, Ottawa, Ont., Canada (Home).

JERUSALEM, Siegfried; German tenor; b. 17 April 1940, Oberhausen; m.; studied violin and piano at Folkwang Hochschule, Essen; played bassoon in German orchestras, including Stuttgart Radio Symphony Orchestra; studied voice and started singing career in Zigeunerbaron 1975; début Metropolitan New York 1980, La Scala 1981, Vienna State Opera 1979. *Leisure interests:* tennis, photography. *Address:* Postfach 120 208, 8500 Nuremberg 12, Federal Republic of Germany.

JESIH, Boris; Yugoslavian artist; b. 8 Aug. 1943, Škofja Loka; s. of Svetoslav and Kristina Jesih; m. Bojana Žokalj 1970 (divorced 1981); one s. one d.; ed. Acad. of Fine Arts, Ljubljana, Berlin; works appear in numerous collections; major exhbns. include: 37th Biennale, Venice 1978, Premio le Arti 1971, 11-15th Biennale of Graphic Arts, Ljubljana 1975-83, 6-10th Biennale of Graphic Art, Cracow 1976-84, Premio Biella 1976, British Print Biennale, Bradford 1980, 1982, 1984, Die Kunst vom Stein, Vienna 1985; 10 nat. and 10 int. Awards. *Leisure interests:* basketball, fishing. *Address:* Valjavčeva 17, 61000 Ljubljana, Yugoslavia. *Telephone:* 061-332008.

JESSEN, Borge, DR. PHIL.; Danish mathematician; b. 19 June 1907, Copenhagen; m. Ellen Pedersen 1931 (died 1979); ed. Univ. of Copenhagen; Docent, Royal Veterinary and Agricultural Coll., Copenhagen 1930-35; Prof. Tech. Univ. of Denmark, Copenhagen 1935-42; Prof. Univ. of Copenhagen 1942-77; mem. Royal Danish Acad. of Sciences and of Acad. of Tech. Sciences; Dir. Carlsberg Foundation 1950-63, Pres. 1955-63. *Address:* Dantes Plads 3, 1556 Copenhagen V, Denmark. *Telephone:* 01-145844.

JEWISON, Norman Frederick, O.C., B.A.; Canadian film director; b. 21 July 1926, Toronto; s. of Percy Joseph and Dorothy Irene (née Weaver) Jewison; m. Margaret Dixon 1953; two s. one d; ed. Malvern Collegiate High School, Toronto, Victoria Coll., Univ. of Toronto; stage actor, Toronto; TV actor 1950-52; TV dir. for CBC 1953-58, CBS 1958-61; film dir. 1961-; Faculty mem. Inst. for American Studies, Salzburg, Austria 1969; Pres. D'Avoriaz Film Festival 1981-; Dir. Centre for Advanced Film Studies 1987-; mem. Electoral Bd., Dirs. Guild of America; mem. Canadian Arts Council; Emmy Award 1960; Golden Globe Award 1966; Best Dir., Berlin Film Festival for Moonstruck 1988; Hon. LL.D. (Univ. of Western Ont.) 1974. *Films Include:* Forty Pounds of Trouble, The Thrill of It All 1963, Send Me No Flowers 1964 (all for Universal Studios), Art of Love, The Cincinnati Kid 1965, The Russians are Coming (also producer) 1966, In the Heat of the Night (Acad. Award 1967), The Thomas Crown Affair (also producer) 1967, Gaily, Gaily 1968, The Landlord (producer) 1969, Fiddler on the Roof (also producer) 1970, Jesus Christ Superstar (also producer) 1972, Billy Two Bats (producer) 1972, Rollerball 1974, F.I.S.T. (also producer) 1977, And Justice for All 1979, Best Friends 1982, A Soldier's Story 1984, Agnes of God 1985, Moonstruck 1987; dir. TV shows for Harry Belafonte, Andy Williams, Judy Garland and Danny Kaye. *Leisure interests:* skiing, yachting, tennis. *Address:* Yorktown Productions Ltd., 18 Gloucester Street, Toronto, Ont. M4Y 1L5; Putney Heath Farm, Caledon East, Ont. L0N 1E0, Canada (Home).

JEWKES, Gordon Wesley, C.M.G.; British diplomatist; b. 18 Nov. 1931; s. of the late Jesse Jewkes; m. Joyce Lyons 1954; two s.; ed. Barrow Grammar School, Magnus Grammar School, Newark-on-Trent; joined Colonial Office 1948; with army 1950-52; with Gen. Register Office 1950-63, 1965-68; mem. Civil Service Pay Research Unit 1963-65; joined FCO 1968; Commercial Consul, Chicago 1969-72, Consul-Gen. 1982-85; Deputy High Commr. Port of Spain 1972-75; Head of Finance Dept., FCO and Finance Officer of Diplomatic Service 1975-79; Consul-Gen. Cleveland 1979-82; Gov. Falkland Islands, Commr. South Georgia and South Sandwich Islands, High Commr. British Antarctic Territory 1985-88; Consul-Gen., N.Y. and Dir.-Gen. Trade and Investment, U.S.A. Jan. 1989-. *Leisure interests:* music, travel, walking, boating. *Address:* c/o Foreign and Commonwealth Office, London, SW1A 2AL, England.

JEYARETNAM, J. B., LL.B.; Singapore lawyer and politician; b. 5 Jan. 1926, Ceylon; ed. Muar, Johore, Malaysia, St. Andrew's School, Singapore, Univ. Coll. London; joined Singapore legal service 1952; First District Judge until 1963; legal practice 1963-87 (disbarred 1987); Sec.-Gen. Workers' Party 1971-; M.P. for Anson 1981-87; fined and jailed for one month on charge of fraud; first opposition M.P. for 15 years. *Address:* Workers' Party, Suite 602, Colombo Court, Singapore 0617, Singapore.

JHABVALA, Ruth Prawer, M.A.; British writer; b. 7 May 1927, Cologne, Germany; d. of Marcus Prawer and Eleonora Cohn; sister of Siegbert Salomon Prawer (q.v.); m. C. S. H. Jhabvala 1951; three d.; ed. Hendon Co. School and London Univ.; born in Germany of Polish parentage; refugee to England 1939; lived in India 1951-75, in U.S.A. 1975-; Neill Gunn. Int. Fellowship 1979; Booker Award for best novel 1975; MacArthur Foundation Award 1984. *Publications:* novels: To Whom She Will 1955, Nature of Passion 1956, Esmond in India 1958, The Householder 1960, Get Ready for Battle 1962, A Backward Place 1962, A New Dominion 1971, Heat and Dust 1975, In Search of Love and Beauty 1983, The Nature of Passion 1986; short story collections: A Stronger Climate 1968, An Experience of India 1970, How I Became a Holy Mother 1976, Out of India: Selected Stories 1986, Three Continents 1987; film scripts (for James Ivory q.v.): Shakespeare Wallah 1965, The Guru 1969, Bombay Talkie 1971, Autobiography of a Princess 1975, Roseland 1977, Hullabaloo over Georgie and Bonnie's Pictures 1978, Jane Austen in Manhattan 1980, Quartet 1981, Room with a View 1986, Mr and Mrs Bridge 1989. *Address:* c/o Harper and Row, 10 East 53rd Street, New York, N.Y. 10022, U.S.A.

JI PENGFEI; Chinese politician; b. 1910, Yongji, Shaanxi; m. Xu Hanbing; three s. three d.; ed. Mil. Medical Coll.; joined Communist Party 1931; on Long March in Medical Dept., Red Army 1935; Deputy Political Commissar, Army Corps, 3rd Field Army 1950; Amb. to German Dem. Repub. 1950-55; Vice-Minister of Foreign Affairs 1955-72; Acting Minister of Foreign Affairs 1968-72, Minister 1972-74; Sec.-Gen. Standing Cttee., Nat. People's Congress 1975-79; Vice-Premier, State Council 1979-82, Sec.-Gen. 1980-81; State Councillor 1982-; Head of CP Liaison Office 1981-82; mem. Political and Legal Affairs Group, Cen. Cttee., CCP 1978-; mem. 10th Cen. Cttee., CCP 1973, 11th Cen. Cttee. 1977; in charge Hong Kong and Macao Affairs June 1983-, Chair. Cttee. for Drafting Basic Law of Hong Kong Special Admin. Region 1985-; mem. Standing Cttee. of Cen. Advisory Comm. 1987-. *Address:* Beijing, People's Republic of China.

JI XIANLIN; Chinese university professor; b. 6 Aug. 1911, Shandong Prov.; one s. one d.; ed. Qinghua Univ., Beijing, Univ. of Göttingen, Fed. Repub. of Germany; Prof., Dir. Dept. of Oriental Languages, Beijing Univ. 1946; disappeared during Cultural Revolution; Vice-Pres. Beijing Univ. and Prof. of Indian Classical Lit. 1978, Pres. Beijing Univ. 1978-84; Head, Eastern Languages Dept., Beijing Univ., South Asian Inst., Chinese Acad. of Social Sciences 1978-; Pres. Foreign Languages Research Soc. 1981; Pres. Soc. of Linguistics 1986-. *Publications include:* Collected Papers on the History of Cultural Relations Between China and India 1982, Studying the Ramayana 1981, Selected Papers on the Languages of Ancient India 1982, and trans. of various Indian classics including 7 vols. of Valmiki's Ramayana 1980, Problems of the Language of Primitive Buddhism 1985. *Address:* c/o Beijing University, Beijing, People's Republic of China.

JIA CHUNWANG; Chinese state official; b. 1938; Vice-Chair. Tibet Autonomous Regional People's Govt. 1984-85; Minister of State Security 1985-; mem. 12th CCP Cen. Cttee. 1985, 13th Cen. Cttee. 1987. *Address:* Tibet Autonomous Regional People's Government, Lhasa, Tibet, People's Republic of China.

JIA GUOZHONG; Chinese artist; b. 1940, Wuhan; specialises in depiction of national minority life. *Address:* Yunnan Art Academy, Kunming, People's Republic of China.

JIA LANPO; Chinese archaeologist and palaeontologist; b. 25 Nov. 1908, Yutian Co., Hebei Prov.; ed. Huiwen High School; joined Peking Man excavation work at Zhoukoudian 1931-37; researcher, Inst. of Vertebrate Palaeontology and Palaeoanthropology, Academia Sinica 1949-; Vice-Pres., Society for Pacific Region History 1984-; mem. Dept. of Earth Sciences, Academia Sinica 1985-. *Publications:* The Land of Peking Man 1950, Prehistoric Residents on China's Mainland 1978, China's Old Stone Age 1984. *Address:* Room 5, Gate 1, 2 Sanlihe Road, Beijing, People's Republic of China.

JIA ZHIJIE; Chinese party and government official; b. 1936; ed. Soviet Union; Dir. Lanzhou Petrochemical Machinery Plant; Deputy Sec. Plant CCP Cttee.; Deputy Sec. Gansu Prov. CCP Cttee. 1983-; Gov. Gansu Prov. 1986-; alt. mem. CCP Cen. Cttee. 1987-. *Address:* Central Committee of the Chinese Communist Party, Zhongnanhai, Beijing, People's Republic of China.

JIAGGE, Annie Ruth, LL.D.; Ghanaian judge and voluntary worker; b. 7 Oct. 1918, Lomé, Togo; d. of the late Rev. R. D. Baëta and Henrietta L. Baëta; m. F. K. A. Jiagge 1953; ed. Achimota Training Coll., London School of Econs., Lincoln's Inn; Headmistress of Keta Presbyterian Sr. Girls' School for 5 years; admitted to bar, Ghana 1950, practised law 1950-55; Dist. Magistrate 1955-57, Sr. Magistrate 1957-59; Judge, Circuit Court 1959-61, High Court 1961-69, Court of Appeal 1969-86 (Pres. 1980-83); Pres. Cttee. of Churches' Participation in Devt. 1985-; Ghanaian Rep. on UN Comm. on the Status of Women 1962-72, Chair. 1968; Chair. Comm. on Investigation of Assets 1966, Ghana Council on Women and Devt. 1975-; Moderator WCC Programme to Combat Racism 1984-; mem. Court, Univ. of Legon 1968-; fmr. Pres. Y.W.C.A. of Ghana, mem. Exec. Cttee. for 12 years and fmr. Vice-Pres. of World Y.W.C.A.; mem. Presidium World Council of Churches 1975-; Hon LL.D. (Legon) 1974; Gimbles' Int. Award for Humanitarian Work 1969, Ghana Grand Medal 1969. *Leisure* *interests:* music, gardening, crafts. *Address:* CCPD, P.O. Box 8301, 37 Dadeban Road, Industrial Area, Accra North, Ghana. *Telephone:* 228066 (Ext. 16).

JIANG BAOLIN; Chinese artist; b. 20 Jan. 1942, Penglai Cty., Shandong; s. of the late Jiang Chunfu and Dai Shuzhi; m. Ling Yunhua 1970; one s. one d.; ed. Dept. of Traditional Chinese Painting, Inst. of Fine Arts, Zhejiang; postgraduate Cen. Acad. of Fine Arts 1979; works in Zhejiang branch of Chinese Artists' Assen.; Dir. Zhejiang Artists' Gallery 1982-84; Vice-Pres. Zhejiang Landscape Painting Research Assen. 1982-; mem. Comm. of Zhejiang Painters' Assen. 1984-. *Paintings include:* Spring in Remote Valley 1972, Pear Blossoms in Spring Rain 1981, He Lan Mountain 1983, Cottages in Si Ming 1983, Autumn Jubilation in She Village, Mountains and Rocks in Home Village, Rainy Season, Autumn Flavour 1984, Grapes 1986, Moonlight, Hurricane, Bumper Harvest 1987. *Publication:* Collections of Jiang Baolin's Paintings 1984. *Leisure interests:* literature, Peking opera, music and gardening. *Address:* No. 53, Building 27, Taoyuan Xinchuen, Shuguang Road, Hangzhou, People's Republic of China.

JIANG CHUNYUN; Chinese party official; Deputy Sec. Shandong Prov. CCP Cttee. 1983-86; mem. CCP Cen. Cttee. 1987-. *Address:* Central Committee of the Chinese Communist Party, Zhongnanhai, Beijing, People's Republic of China.

JIANG HONGQUAN; Chinese soldier and party official; Commdr. Autonomous Region Mil. Dist., Tibet 1984-; alt. mem. 12th CCP Cen. Cttee. 1985; mem. CCP Cen. Cttee. 1987-. *Address:* Central Committee of the Chinese Communist Party, Zhongnanhai, Beijing, People's Republic of China.

JIANG HUA; Chinese party official; b. 1907, Hunan; guerrilla activist with new 4th Army, CCP 1940; Mayor of Hangzhou 1949-51; Deputy Sec. CCP Zhejiang 1951-54, Sec. 1954, First Sec. 1956; Alt. mem. 8th Cen. Cttee. of CCP 1956; Sec., Secr. E. China Bureau 1961; criticized and removed from office during Cultural Revolution 1968; Alt. mem. 10th Cen. Cttee. of CCP 1973; mem. 11th Cen. Cttee. of CCP 1977; Pres. Supreme People's Court 1975-83; mem. and Standing mem. Cen. Advisory Cttee. CCP 1982-. *Address:* c/o Supreme People's Court, Beijing, People's Republic of China.

JIANG JIALIANG; Chinese table tennis player; b. 1964; Men's Singles World Champion 1986. *Address:* China Sports Federation, Beijing, People's Republic of China.

JIANG MING; Chinese government official; Head Trade Admin. Bureau in North China People's Govt. 1949; Chief of Trade Planning Office, Planning Dept. of Financial and Econ. Cttee. of the Govt. Admin. Council 1950-52; Deputy Dir. Foreign Trade Dept. 1952-54; Vice-Minister Foreign Trade 1955-66; Vice-Minister Scientific and Tech. Comm. 1978; Dir. State Tobacco Monopoly Comm. and Man. of China Nat. Tobacco Corpn. 1987-. *Address:* China National Tobacco Corporation, Beijing, People's Republic of China.

JIANG MINKUAN; Chinese party and state official; b. 1930; ed. Shanghai Polytechnic School; fmr. technician, workshop dir., factory dir. and chief engineer; Deputy Sec. CCP Cttee., Sichuan Prov. 1983-88; Vice-Gov., Sichuan 1983-85, Gov. 1985; Vice-Minister State Science and Tech. Comm. Jan. 1988-; Dir. State Patent Bureau May 1988-; mem. 12th CCP Cen. Cttee. 1985, 13th Cen. Cttee. 1987. *Address:* Office of the Governor, Chengdu, Sichuan, People's Republic of China.

JIANG QING; Chinese fmr. party official; b. 1914, Zhucheng, Shandong; m. Mao Zedong (Mao Tse-tung) 1939 (died 1976); ed. Shandong Experimental Drama Acad., Qingdao; Librarian, Qingdao Univ. 1933; Film Actress 1934-38; joined CCP 1937; Instructor Lu Xun Art Acad., Yenan 1939; Head of Cen. Film Admin. Bureau, Propaganda Dept., CCP 1949; with Ministry of Culture 1950-54; Organizer of Reforms in Beijing Opera 1963; First Deputy Head of Cen. Cultural Revolution Group 1966; leading pro-Maoist activist in propaganda work during Cultural Revolution 1965-69; mem. Politburo, 9th Cen. Cttee. of CCP 1969, Politburo, 10th Cen. Cttee. 1973; arrested as mem. "gang of four" 1976; expelled from CCP July 1977; in detention; on trial Nov. 1980-Jan. 1981; sentenced to death, suspended for two years Jan. 1981, commuted to life imprisonment Jan. 1983. *Address:* People's Republic of China.

JIANG QINGXIANG; Chinese economist; b. 1918; m.; three s. four d.; Prof., Econs. Dept., Law School, Sun Yat-sen Univ. 1944-45; Prof. Chongqing Univ., Researcher Sichuan Prov. Bank 1945-46; Prof. Nat. Coll. of Commerce 1947-49; Dir. and Prof. Great China Univ. 1949-52; Prof. Fu Tan Univ. 1952-57; Prof. and Research Fellow, Inst. of Econs., Shanghai Acad. of Social Sciences 1957-; mem. Nat. Cttee. People's Political Consultative Conf. *Publications:* China's Wartime Economy (co-author), An Investigative Report on the Silk Industry in Sichuan Province, Principles of National Economy Planning, Glimpses of Urban Economy in Bianjing. *Address:* Academy of Social Sciences, Shanghai, People's Republic of China.

JIANG WEIQING; Chinese party official; b. 1907, Yangzhou City, Jiangsu Prov.; m. Xu Ming (died); one d.; one s. by previous marriage; Deputy Political Commissar, People's Liberation Army, Nanjing 1949; Second Sec. CCP Jiangsu 1953-55, First Sec. 1956-68; Alt. mem. 8th Cen. Cttee. of

CCP 1956; First Political Commissar Jiangsu Mil. Dist., PLA 1960-68; Sec. E. China Bureau, CCP 1966; criticized and removed from office during Cultural Revolution 1968; Alt. mem. 10th Cen. Cttee. of CCP 1973; First Sec. CCP Jiangxi Prov. Cttee. 1975-79; Chair. Jiangxi Revolutionary Cttee. 1975-79; mem. 11th Cen. Cttee. of CCP 1977; Political Commissar, Fujian PLA Mil. Region 1976-86; Political Commissar Fozhou PLA Mil. Region, First Political Commissar Jiangxi PLA Mil. Dist. 1978; mem. CCP Cen. Advisory Comm. 1987-. *Address:* c/o People's Liberation Army, Jiangxi Military District, People's Republic of China.

JIANG WEN; Chinese official; ed. School of Telephone Communications, Ruijin 1933; Field Communications Officer, Red Army 1937-49; Head PLA Field Communications 1958-79; Deputy Procurator-Gen. 1981-. *Address:* Supreme People's Procuratorate, Beijing, People's Republic of China.

JIANG WENZHEN; Chinese traditional painter; b. 1940, Shandong. *Address:* Xian Academy of Fine Arts, Xian, People's Republic of China.

JIANG XIESHENG; Chinese engineer and business executive; alt. mem. 12th CCP Cen. Cttee. 1982, 13th Cen. Cttee. 1987; Chief Engineer and Man. Machine Building Factory, Xindu, Sichuan 1982; Vice-Minister of Aviation Industry 1984-88, of Aeronautics and Astronautics Industry May 1988-. *Address:* Machine Building Factory, Xindu, Sichuan, People's Republic of China.

JIANG XINXIONG; Chinese party and government official; b. 6 July 1931; Vice-Minister of Nuclear Industry 1982-83, Minister 1983-; Chair. Bd. of Dirs., China Isotopes Co. 1983-; alt. mem. 12th Cen. Cttee. CCP 1982, mem. 13th Cen. Cttee. 1985-. *Address:* China Isotopes Co., Sanlihe Road, Beijing, People's Republic of China. *Telephone:* 868381.

JIANG YIWEI; Chinese economist; b. 14 Feb. 1920, Fu Jian; m. Cheng Xi; three s. one d.; Dir. Industrial Econs. Inst. 1984-; Vice-Pres. Industrial Econs. Soc. 1984-. *Address:* Chinese Academy of Social Sciences, Beijing, People's Republic of China. *Telephone:* 89-2552, 87-4655.

JIANG YIZHEN; Chinese party and government official; Vice-Chair. Land Reform Cttee. Fujian Prov. People's Govt. 1951-; Dir. Agric. and Forestry Dept. and Council mem. Fujian Prov. People's Govt 1952-; Vice-Gov. Fujian Prov. 1955-56; Pres. Fujian Agricultural Coll. 1955-57; Chair. Fujian CPPCC Prov. Cttee. 1956-; Chair. Planning Comm. Fujian Prov. CCP Cttee. 1956-, Fujian Congress of Model Workers in Agric., Forestry and Fishery Feb. 1958; Deputy for Fujian Prov. to 2nd NPC Feb. 1959; Deputy Head Fujian 10,000 Man Work Team to Inspect People's Communes 1959; Gov. Fujian Prov. 1959-62; Vice-Minister of State Farms and Land Reclamation 1962-64; mem. 3rd NPC Sept. 1964; Vice-Minister of Agric. 1964-67; branded a deviationist and paraded through the streets of Beijing Jan. 1967; Acting Minister of Agric. Dec. 1967; Minister of Public Health 1977-79; mem. 5th NPC March 1978; mem. Standing Cttee. CPPCC 1978; Chair. Hebei Prov. CCP Cttee. 1980-82; mem. Cen. Advisory Cttee. of CCP Cen. Cttee. 1987-. *Address:* Central Advisory Committee of the Central Committee of the Chinese Communist Party, Zhongnanhai, Beijing, People's Republic of China.

JIANG YONGHUI; Chinese army officer; b. 1916, Ruijin Co., Jiangxi Prov.; guerrilla fighter before 1945; Shenyang Mil. Region 1958-69; mem. 11th Cen. Cttee. CCP 1977 and 1982-87; Commdr. Fuzhou Mil. Region 1983; mem. Cen. Advisory Comm. 1987-. *Address:* Fuzhou People's Liberation Army Units, Fujian, People's Republic of China.

JIANG ZEMIN; Chinese party and government official; b. 1926, Yangzhou City, Jiangsu Prov.; Commercial counsellor, Embassy, U.S.S.R. 1950-56; Asst. to Minister, 1st Ministry of Machine Building 1956-59; Vice-Minister Import and Export Comm., State Council 1980-82; Vice-Chair. Foreign Investment Control Comm., State Council 1980-82; Vice-Minister of Electronics Industry 1982-83, Minister 1983-85; Hon. Chair. Software Industry Assen. 1984-; Mayor of Shanghai 1985-; Deputy for Shanghai to 6th NPC 1986-; mem. 12th Cen. Cttee. CCP 1982-, Politburo 1987-. *Address:* Mayor's Residence, Shanghai, People's Republic of China.

JIANG ZILONG; Chinese writer; b. 2 June 1941, Cang Xian, Hebei; s. of Jiang Junsan and Wei Huanzhang; m. Zhang Qinglian 1968; one s. one d.; worker Tianjin Heavy Machinery Plant 1958; navy conscript 1960-65; Nat. Short Story Prize 1979. *Publications:* A New Station Master 1965, One Day for the Chief of the Bureau of Electromechanics 1976, Manager Qiao Assumes Office 1979, Developer 1980, Diary of a Plant Secretary 1980, All the Colours of the Rainbow 1983, Yan-Zhao Dirge 1985, Serpent Deity 1986. *Address:* Tianjin Writers' Association, Tianjin, People's Republic of China. *Telephone:* 334980 (Office); 398250 (Home).

JIAO LINYI; Chinese party official; b. 1920, Hebei Prov.; m. 1935; four c.; Deputy Mayor, Guangzhou 1955; Deputy for Guangdong Prov. to 2nd NPC 1958; Sec. CCP Cttee., Guangzhou Municipality 1958, Second Sec. 1965-73, Acting First Sec. 1966, First Sec. 1973-79, Vice-Chair. Revolutionary Cttee. 1969-73, Chair. 1973-78; alt. mem. CCP Cen. Cttee. 1969; Vice-Chair. Revolutionary Cttee. Guangdong Prov. 1973-79; mem. 10th CCP Cen. Cttee. 1973; Sec. CCP Cttee. Guangdong 1975-79; Deputy for Guangdong to 5th NPC 1978; Sec. CCP Cttee. Hunan Prov. 1979-85, Deputy Sec. 1985-. *Leisure interest:* calligraphy. *Address:* Hunan Provincial Chinese Communist Party, Changsha, Hunan, People's Republic of China.

JIAO RUOYU; Chinese politician; b. 1916 Yexian Co., Henan Prov.; Mayor, Shenyang 1954; Amb. to Democratic People's Repub. of Korea 1965-67, to Peru 1972-77, to Iran 1977-79; Minister of the Eighth Ministry of Machine Building 1979-81; Mayor of Beijing 1981-83; Second Sec. CCP Cttee., Beijing 1981-84; mem. Municipal CCP Comm., 12th CCP Nat. Congress 1982; Pres. Beijing Social Welfare Foundation 1984-; mem. Cen. Advisory Comm. 1987-. *Address:* c/o Office of the Mayor, Beijing, People's Republic of China.

JIMÉNEZ DE ARÉCHAGA, Eduardo, DR.JUR.; Uruguayan international lawyer; b. 8 June 1918, Montevideo; s. of E. Jiménez de Aréchaga and Ester Sienra; m. Marta Ferreira 1943; three s. two d.; ed. School of Law, Univ. de la República; Prof. of Int. Law, Montevideo Law School 1949-69; Under-Sec., Foreign Relations 1950-52; Sec. Council of Govt. of Uruguay 1952-55; mem. Int. Law Comm. of UN 1961-69, Pres. 1963; Rapporteur Cttee., Vienna Conf. on Law of Treaties 1968-69; Minister of Interior 1968; Judge, Int. Court of Justice 1970-79, Pres. 1976-79; Pres. Admin. Tribunal, IBRD 1981-; Head Court of Arbitration on Rainbow Warrior Dispute 1988-; Book award, Inter-American Bar Asscn. 1961. *Publications:* Reconocimiento de Gobiernos 1946, Voting and Handling of Disputes in the Security Council 1951, Treaty Stipulations in Favour of Third States 1956, Derecho Constitucional de las Naciones Unidas 1958, Curso de Derecho Internacional Público (2 vols.) 1959-61, El Derecho Internacional Contemporáneo 1980. *Address:* Cerrito 461, esc. 310, P.O. Box 539, Montevideo, Uruguay.

JIN BAOSHENG; Chinese party official; b. Oct. 1927, Jinxiu, Guangxi; m. Wu Jianzhen 1954; one s. one d.; Deputy for Guangxi Prov. to 1st NPC 1954, 2nd NPC 1958, 3rd NPC 1964; Deputy for Guangxi Autonomous Region to 5th NPC 1978; mem. State Nationalities Affairs Comm. 1979-83; Vice-Chair., Guangxi 1979-83; alt. mem. 12th CCP Cen. Cttee. 1982-87; Deputy Sec. CCP Cttee. Guangxi 1983-. *Publication:* My Beloved Yao Mountains. *Address:* Guangxi Autonomous Regional Chinese Communist Party, Nanning, Guangxi, People's Republic of China.

JIN HONGJUN; Chinese painter; b. 1937, Beijing; s. of Jin Ru Yang and Wu Zhuang Sheng; m. Peng Hongying; one s. one d.; ed. Cen. Acad. of Arts 1962; Lecturer, Cen. Acad. of Arts. *Publications:* numerous books about his work, including many examples of his art. *Leisure interest:* Beijing opera. *Address:* Central Academy of Arts, Beijing, People's Republic of China. *Telephone:* 55-4731.

JIN JIAN; Chinese party official; Deputy Sec. Beijing Municipal CCP Cttee. 1984-86; alt. mem. CCP Cen. Cttee. 1985-. *Address:* Central Committee of Chinese Communist Party, Zhongnanhai, Beijing, People's Republic of China.

JIN MING; Chinese government official; b. 1908, Shandong Prov.; mem. Hunan Prov. People's Govt. 1950, Chair. Land Reform Cttee. 1950; Deputy Political Commissar PLA Hunan Mil. Dist. 1950; Vice-Chair. of Hunan 1952-55; Deputy Sec. CCP Hunan Prov. Cttee. 1952; mem. Cen.-S. Mil. and Admin. Cttee. 1952; mem. Admin. Cttee. 1953-54; Sec. CCP Hunan Prov. Cttee. 1953-55; Vice-Minister of Finance 1953-61; Alt. Sec. Secr. of Cen.-S. Bureau CCP 1961; Sec. 1964-68; criticized and removed from office during Cultural Revolution 1968; First Sec. CCP Hebei Prov. Cttee. 1980-82; mem. Cen. Advisory Cttee. 1982. *Address:* Zhongguo Gongchan Dang, Tianjin, Hebei Province, People's Republic of China.

JIN SHANBAO; Chinese agricultural scientist; b. 1910, Zhuji Co., Zhejiang Prov.; Prof., Agric. Coll., Nanjing Univ. 1949, Dean 1952-58; mem. E. China Civil and Mil. Cttee., Deputy Minister, Ministry of Agric. and Forestry 1950-54; Deputy Mayor, Nanjing 1950-57; joined CCP 1956; Vice-Chair. Chinese Acad. of Agric. Sciences 1957-65, Chair. 1965-82, Hon. Chair. 1982-; Deputy from Zhejiang Prov., 1st-5th NPC 1954-; mem. Biology Dept., Chinese Acad. of Sciences 1958; Vice-Pres. Chinese Soc. of Agric.; Vice-Chair. Chinese Scientific and Tech. Asscn. 1978-; Vice-Pres. Jiusan Soc. 1979-. *Address:* The Chinese Academy of Agricultural Sciences, Beijing, People's Republic of China.

JIN SHANGYI; Chinese artist; b. 1934 Jiaozuo City, Henan Prov.; ed. Cen. Fine Arts Acad., Beijing; known as the forerunner of classicism in Chinese Art; Pres. Cen. Fine Arts Acad. *Works include:* Mao Zedong Leads the Red Army on the Long March 1964, A Maiden 1981, A Tajik Girl 1983. *Address:* Central Fine Arts Academy, Beijing, People's Republic of China.

JIN SHUI; Chinese writer (b. Shi Tiesheng); b. 1951, Beijing; graduated from middle school 1967; paralysed while working in countryside. *Publications:* The Professor of Law and His Wife, Half Hour Lunch Break, Brothers. *Address:* China Federation of Art and Literature, Beijing, People's Republic of China.

JIRA, Jiri; Czechoslovak politician; b. 1929; officer, Czechoslovak People's Army 1950-71; mem. CP of Czechoslovakia 1951-, now mem. Econ. Comm. of Cen. Cttee.; Deputy Minister of Posts and Communications 1972; Minister of Posts and Telecommunications 1986-88. *Address:* c/o Ministry of Posts and Communications, Prague, Czechoslovakia.

JIROUDEK, František; Czechoslovak painter; b. 17 Feb. 1914, Lhota, Semily district; ed. School of Arts and Crafts, Prague, Coll. of Tech.,

Prague, Acad. of Fina Arts, Prague; mem. of Asscn. of Visual Artists, Mánes 1941-; Prof., Acad. of Fine Arts 1961-, Pres. 1970-76; mem. Visual Arts Council of Czech Ministry of Culture 1970-; mem. Preparatory Cttee. of Union of Czech Visual Artists (SČVU) 1970-72, Presidium of SČVU 1972-; Co-founder, group of Seven in October; mem. Presidium of Union of Czechoslovak Visual Artists (SČSVU) 1978-, Vice-Chair. 1983-; Corresp. mem., Acad. of Arts of the German Democratic Repub.; Klement Gottwald State Prize 1963, 1978, Artist of Merit 1964, First Prize in Competition for Anniversary of October Revolution 1967, Prize at Int. Exhbn. of Committed Painting, Sofia 1973, Nat. Artist 1976, Order of Victorious Feb. 1984; One-man exhbns.: 19 in Prague, Brno, Ostrava, W. Berlin, Warsaw, Vienna, Cairo, Olomouc, Pardubice, Bratislava, New Delhi. *Paintings include:* Trója Château 1937, From the Dressing Room, Actresses 1943, People in the Shelter, Wandering Musicians, Landscapes from Polabí 1944, Seine Embankment 1946, Prague 1948, Autumn in Liběchov, Vineyards in Autumn 1955, Summer in the Vineyard 1956, Landscape at Lopud, Dubrovnik 1957, Florence, Landscape near Litoměřice 1958, Czech Landscape, The Vintage Season, Child with Pigeons, Child's Song 1961-62, Czech Landscape 1964, By the well 1966, Against War (cycle) 1964-67, Autumn Landscape, In the Theatre Dressing Room 1967, Tree, River, Reclining Woman 1970. *Address:* Akademie vytvarnych uměni, Ul. Akademie 172, Prague 7, Czechoslovakia.

JOBERT, Michel; French politician; b. 11 Sept. 1921, Meknès, Morocco; s. of Jules and Yvonne (Babule) Jobert; m. Muriel Frances Green; one s.; ed. Meknès Lycée, Ecole Libre des Sciences Politiques, Paris, and Nat. School of Admin., Paris; Auditor Court of Accounts 1949, Counsel 1953, Conseiller-Maître 1971, Conseiller honoraire Cour des Comptes 1986; attached to Departmental Staff of Sec. of State for Finance 1952; Tech. Adviser, Ministry of Labour and Social Security 1952-54; attached to the Office of Pierre Mendès-France 1954-55 and Feb.-May 1956; Dir. of Cabinet to the High Commr. for French W. Africa 1956-58, to M. Lecourt, Minister of State 1959-61; Deputy Dir. of Cabinet to Prime Minister Georges Pompidou 1963-66, Prin. Private Sec. 1966-68; Sec.-Gen. of the Presidency 1969-73; Minister of Foreign Affairs 1973-74, of Foreign Trade 1981-83; founder and leader Mouvement des Démocrates June 1974-; fmr. mem. Bd. of SOFIRAD (Radio Monte-Carlo), Havas Agency and French Radio and Television Org.; Chair. Bd. of Dirs. Nat. Forestry Office 1966-73; Publr. of monthly newsletter La Lettre de Michel Jobert 1974-84; Officier Légion d'honneur, Croix de guerre. *Publications:* Mémoires d'avenir 1974, L'autre regard 1976, Lettre ouverte aux femmes politiques 1976, Parler aux français 1977, La vie d'Hella Schuster 1977, Maroc, extrême Maghreb du soleil couchant 1978, Chroniques du Midi Libre, La Rivière aux grenades 1982, Par Trente-six chemins 1984, Maghreb, à l'ombre de ses mains 1985, Les Américains 1987, Journal immédiat 1987. *Address:* 108 Quai Louis Blériot, 75016 Paris (Office); 21 quai Alphonse-Le Gallo, 92100 Boulogne-Billancourt, France (Home).

JOBS, Steven Paul; American business executive; b. 1955; adopted s. of Paul J. and Clara J. Jobs; ed. Reed Coll.; with Hewlett-Packard, Palo Alto, Calif.; designer, video games, Atari Inc. 1974; Chair. of Bd. Apple Computer Inc., Cupertino, Calif. 1975-85; Pres. NeXT Inc., Calif. 1985-; co-designer (with Stephan Wozniak), Apple I Computer 1976. *Address:* NeXT Inc., 3475 Deer Creek Rd, Palo Alto, Calif. 94304, U.S.A.

JOCELYN, Henry David, PH.D., F.B.A.; Australian university teacher; b. 22 Aug. 1933, Bega, N.S.W.; s. of John Daniel Jocelyn and Phyllis Irene Burton; m. Margaret Jill Morton 1958; two s.; ed. Canterbury Boys' High School, Univ. of Sydney and St. John's Coll., Cambridge, U.K.; mem. teaching staff, Univ. of Sydney 1960-73, Prof. of Latin 1970-73; Hulme Prof. of Latin, Univ. of Manchester 1973-; Visiting Prof. Yale Univ., U.S.A. 1967, Australian Nat. Univ. 1979, Univ. of Cape Town 1985. *Publications:* The Tragedies of Ennius 1967, Regnier de Graaf on the Human Reproductive Organs 1972; contribs. on Greek and Latin philology to periodicals 1964-. *Address:* 4 Clayton Avenue, Manchester, M20 0BN, England. *Telephone:* (061) 434 1526.

JOFFE, Roland I. V.; British film director; b. 17 Nov. 1945, London; m. Jane Lapotaire (divorced); one s.; ed. Carmel Coll., Berks. and Univ. of Manchester. *Films:* The Killing Fields 1984, The Mission 1986, Fat Man and Little Boy. *Television Films:* The Spongers 1978, No Mama No 1980, United Kingdom 1981, Tis Pity She's a Whore 1982; Prix Italia 1978, Prix de la Presse, Prague 1978, Premio San Fidele 1985. *Address:* c/o Judy Daish Associates, 83 Eastbourne Mews, London, W2 6CQ, England. *Telephone:* 01-262 1101.

JOHANES, Jaromir; Czechoslovak diplomatist and politician; b. 21 Aug. 1933, Dobra nad Sazavou, E. Bohemia; ed. Moscow Inst. of Int. Relations; joined Ministry of Foreign Affairs 1958; served London; later Consul-Gen. Australia; Amb. to U.S.A. and Canada; Deputy Foreign Minister 1982, First Deputy Foreign Minister 1987; Minister of Foreign Affairs Oct. 1988-. *Address:* Ministry of Foreign Affairs, Prague, Czechoslovakia.

JOHANNES, Herman; Indonesian engineer, professor and politician; b. 28 May 1913, Roti; s. of D. A. Johannes and A. Dirk; m. Annie M. G. Johannes-Amalo 1955; two s. two d.; ed. Tech. Hochschule, Bandung, Faculty of Tech. Yogyakarta; High School teacher 1940; Lecturer, Medical Faculty, Jakarta Univ. 1943-45, Faculty of Tech., Yogyakarta and Medical

Faculty, Klaten 1946–48; Prof. of Physics Faculty of Tech and Gadjah Mada Univ., Yogyakarta 1948, Rector 1961–66; Minister of Public Works and Power, Repub. of Indonesia 1950–51; Co-ordinator of Higher Educ., Cen. Java 1966–78; Chair. Regional Scientific and Devt. Centre 1969–; mem. Exec. Bd. UNESCO 1954–56; mem. Supreme Advisory Council 1968–78, Nat. Research Council, Repub. of Indonesia 1984–; Dr. h.c. 1975 and many other awards. *Publications:* Flexure-factors Method for Analyzing Structures 1953, Squeeze Technique in Bridge 1972, Colloid and Surface Chemistry 1975, Mathematics in Economics 1975, Electricity and Magnetism 1978, Dictionary of Scientific and Technological Terms 1981, Dictionary of Physics 1984, and numerous scientific articles. *Leisure interest:* bridge. *Address:* Pandega Duta III/17, Yogyakarta 55581, Indonesia. *Telephone:* (0274) 2341.

JÓHANNSON, Kjartan, C.E., PH.D.; Icelandic politician; b. 19 Dec. 1939, Reykjavík; s. of Jóhann and Astrid Dahl Thorsteinsson; m. Irma Karlsdottir 1964; one d.; ed. Reykjavík Coll., Tech. Univ. of Stockholm, Sweden, Univ. of Stockholm, Illinois Inst. of Tech., Chicago; Consulting Eng. in Reykjavík 1966–78; Teacher in Faculty of Eng. and Science, later in Faculty for Econs. and Business Admin., Univ. of Iceland 1966–78, 1980–; Chair. Org. for Support of the Elderly, Hafnarfjörður; mem. Bd. of Dir. Icelandic Aluminium Co. Ltd. 1970–75; Chair. Fisheries Bd. of Municipal Trawler Co., Hafnarfjörður 1970–74; mem. Municipal Council, Hafnarfjörður 1974–78; mem. Party Council and Exec. Council, Social Democratic Party 1972–, Vice-Chair. of Social Democratic Party 1974–80, Chair. 1980–84; mem. Althing (Parl.) 1978–, Speaker of the Lower House 1988–; Minister of Fisheries 1978–80, also Minister of Commerce 1979–80. *Address:* Jófríðarstaðvegi 11, Hafnarfirdi, Iceland. *Telephone:* 91-52597.

JOHANSEN, Hans Christian, DR.OEC.; Danish professor of economic history; b. 27 June 1935, Aarhus; s. of Vilhelm Johansen and Clara Andersen; m. Kirstine Madsen 1967; one s. one d.; ed. Univ. of Aarhus; Danish Foreign Service 1963–64; Sr. Lecturer, Univ. of Aarhus 1964–70; Prof. of Econ. History, Univ. of Odense 1970–. *Publications:* books and articles on Danish and int. econ. and social history in the eighteenth, nineteenth and twentieth centuries. *Address:* Anne Maries Alle 4A, 5250 Odense SV, Denmark. *Telephone:* 09-172105.

JOHANSEN, Holger Friis, D.PHIL.; Danish professor of classical philology; b. 29 April 1927, Copenhagen; s. of Prof. K. Friis Johansen and C. Brøndsted; m. Bente Harkjer-Simonsen 1952; one d.; ed. Metropolitanskolen and Copenhagen Univ.; Asst. Ed. Lexicon Mediae Latinitatis Danicae 1952–60; Archivist Nat. Archives, Copenhagen 1954–61; Prof. of Classical Philology, Aarhus Univ. 1961–, Pro-Rector 1973–74; mem. Royal Danish Acad. of Sciences and Letters 1977–. *Publications:* General Reflection in Tragic Rhesis 1959, Sophocles 1939–59 1969, Aeschylus: The Suppliants 1970, Fri Mands Tale 1984. *Address:* 38 Fortebakken, 8240 Risskov, Denmark. *Telephone:* 06175110.

JOHANSEN, John MacLane, M.ARCH.; American architect; b. 29 June 1916, New York; s. of John C. and Jean MacLane Johansen; m. 1st Mary Lee Longcope 1945, 2nd Beate Forberg 1981; one s. one d.; ed. Harvard Coll. and Harvard Grad. School of Design; self-employed architect 1947, est. office in New York 1950, est. firm of Johansen-Bhavnani 1973; Pres. Architectural League 1968–70; Prof. Pratt Inst.; Prof. of Architecture at Yale Univ. at various times and has taught for short periods at M.I.T., Columbia and Harvard Univs., and Univ. of Pa.; Architect in Residence, American Acad. in Rome 1975; mem. Nat. Inst. of Arts and Letters; Brunner Award 1968; Gold Medal, New York Chapter, American Inst. of Architects 1976; Hon. D.F.A. (Maryland Inst. and Clark Univ.). *Publication:* An Architecture for the Electronic Age, The Three Imperatives of Architecture, Observations and Deductions. *Leisure interests:* painting, writing, music, building construction, sport, travel. *Address:* 650 First Avenue, New York, N.Y. 10016, U.S.A. *Telephone:* (212) 889-2560.

JOHANSEN, Peter, PH.D.; Danish professor of computer science; b. 29 Jan. 1938, Copenhagen; s. of Paul Johansen and Grethe (née Smith) Johansen; m. Jytte (née Jepsen) Johansen 1963; one s. two d.; ed. Univ. of Copenhagen; Asst. Prof. Tech. Univ. 1964–67; mem. Research Staff M.I.T. 1967–69; Asst. Prof. of Computer Science, Univ. of Copenhagen 1969–74, Prof. 1974–, Dean of Faculty 1988–; Visiting Prof. Univ. of Manoa, Hawaii 1977–78; mem. Danish Natural Science Research Council 1981–84, Royal Danish Acad. of Sciences 1984–. *Publications:* An Algebraic Normal Form for Regular Events 1972, The Generating Function of the Number of Subpatterns 1979, Representing Signals by their Toppoints in Scale Space 1986, Inductive Inference of Ultimately Periodic Sequences 1988. *Address:* Ornebakken 72, 2840 Holte, Denmark. *Telephone:* (02) 805302.

JOHANSON, Donald Carl, PH.D.; American physical anthropologist; b. 28 June 1943, Chicago; s. of Carl Torsten and Sally Eugenia Johanson; m. 1st Susan Whelan Johanson 1981 (divorced); one s. one d.; m. 2nd Lenora Carey Johanson 1988; ed. Univ. of Illinois, Univ. of Chicago; mem. Dept. of Physical Anthropology, Cleveland Museum of Natural History 1972–81, Curator 1974–81; Dir. Inst. of Human Origins 1981–; Adjunct Prof. Case Western Reserve Univ. 1982; Prof. of Anthropology, Stanford Univ. 1983–; host, Narrator Series, Public Broadcasting Service 1982; Dir. Inst. for Study of Human Origins, Berkeley 1981–82; Fellow California Acad. of Sciences; D.Sc. (Hon.) (John Carroll) 1979, (The College of Wooster) 1985;

Fregene Prize 1987. *Films Produced:* The First Family, Lucy in Disguise; American Book Award 1982, Distinguished Service Award, American Humanist Asscn. 1983, Golden Plate American Acad. of Achievement 1976, Professional Achievement Award 1980, Outstanding Achievement Award 1979, Golden Mercury Int. Award 1982. *Publications:* The Fossil Hominids and an Introduction of Their Context 1980, Lucy: The Beginnings of Human Kind (with M. A. Edey) 1981 (American Book Award), Dating of South Africa Hominids Sites 1982, Blueprints: Solving the Mystery of Evolution (with M. A. Edey) 1989; contributed a large number of scientific articles, papers, reviews and other features. *Address:* 2453 Ridge Road, Berkeley, Calif. 94709, U.S.A. *Telephone:* 415-845 0333.

JOHANSSON, Bengt K. Å., M.A.; Swedish politician; b. 4 Jan. 1937, Sandared, Borås; m. Sonja Johansson; one s. one d.; ed. Univ. of Gothenburg; teacher 1961–63; Personal Asst. to Prime Minister Erlander 1963–66; Budget Sec. Ministry of Finance 1966–70; with Ministry for Home Affairs 1970–74; Head, Dept. for Working Environment, Ministry of Labour 1974–76; Sec. Parl. Standing Cttee. on Finance 1977–82; Under-Sec. of State, Ministry of Finance 1982; Minister for Wages in Public Admin. 1982–88, of Public Admin. Oct. 1988–. *Address:* Ministry of Public Administration, Tegelbacken 2, 103 33 Stockholm, Sweden.

JOHANSSON, (Erik) Lennart Valdemar; Swedish industrialist; b. 3 Oct. 1921, Gothenburg; s. of Waldemar and Alma Johansson (née Nordh); m. Inger Hedberg 1944; two s. one d.; ed. Tech. Coll.; Production Engineer AB SKF 1943, Man. of Mfg. 1961, Gen. Man. 1966, Deputy Man. Dir. 1969, Pres. and Group C.E.O. 1971–, Chair. 1985–; Dir. ESAB AB 1968–, AB Volvo 1972, Swedish Eng. Employers' Asscn. 1963, Swedish Employers' Confed. 1971; Dir. Skandinaviska Enskilda Banken 1977, Fed. of Swedish Industries 1981–; Dir. Skanska AB 1982, ASEA AB 1983, Svenska BP AB 1984, STORA 1985, Atlas Copco AB 1985, AB Investor 1985; mem. Royal Swedish Acad. of Eng. Sciences 1971; D. Tech. h.c. (Chalmers Univ. of Tech., Gothenburg) 1979; Hon. D.Tech. (Sarajevo) 1983; King of Sweden's Medal; Commdr. Merito della Repub. Italiana, Commdr. Royal Order of Vasa, Yugoslav Star Medal with Golden Garland, Das grosse Bundesverdienstkreutz, Kt. Commdr.'s Cross (1st Class), Finnish Order of the Lion, John Ericsson Medal 1986. *Leisure interests:* sailing, swimming. *Address:* Chairman's Office, AB SKF, S-405 04 Gothenburg (Office); Götabergsgatan 22, 411 34 Gothenburg, Sweden (Home). *Telephone:* 031/622350 (Office); 031/812518 (Home).

JOHN, David Dilwyn, C.B.E., T.D., D.SC., LL.D.; British museum director; b. 20 Nov. 1901, Llangan, Glam., Wales; s. of Thomas and Julia John; m. Marjorie Emily Page 1929; one s. one d.; ed. Univ. Coll. of Wales; Zoologist, engaged in oceanographical research in Antarctic seas 1925; Asst. Keeper, British Museum (Natural History) 1935, Deputy Keeper 1948; Dir. Nat. Museum of Wales, Cardiff 1948–68; Hon. LL.D. (Univ. of Wales) 1969; Polar Medal. *Leisure interest:* preservation of the countryside. *Address:* 7 Cyncoed Avenue, Cardiff, CF2 6ST, Wales. *Telephone:* 752499.

JOHN, Elton Hercules; British musician; b. (as Reginald Kenneth Dwight) 25 March 1947, Pinner, Middx.; s. of Stanley Dwight and Sheila Farebrother; m. Renata Blauel 1984 (separated 1988); ed. Pinner Co. Grammar School; began piano lessons 1951; played piano in Northwood Hills Hotel bar 1964; joined local group Bluesology 1965; began writing songs with Bernie Taupin 1967; recording contract with DJM Records 1967; first single I've Been Loving You 1968, first LP Empty Sky 1969; concerts in Los Angeles 1970; engaged Man. John Reid 1971–; formed Rocket Record Co. with Bernie Taupin 1973; frequent tours in U.K., U.S.A., Japan, Australia 1971–76; first int. star to perform concerts in U.S.S.R. 1979; first album released by Rocket Record Co. 1976; produced records with Clive Franks for Kiki Dee, Blue, Davey Johnstone's China 1976–77; Chair. Watford Football Club 1976–; visited China with Watford Football Club 1983; Ivor Novello Awards 1976, 1977, and silver and gold discs in various countries for singles and albums. *Records:* singles: Lady Samantha, It's Me That You Need, Border Song, Rock and Roll Madonna, Your Song, Friends, Rocket Man, Honky Cat, Crocodile Rock, Daniel, Saturday Night's Alright (for fighting), Goodbye Yellow Brick Road, Step into Christmas, Candle in the Wind, Don't Let the Sun Go Down on Me, The Bitch is Back, Lucy in the Sky with Diamonds, Philadelphia Freedom, Someone Saved My Life Tonight, Island Girl, Grow Some Funk of Your Own, Pinball Wizard, Don't Go Breaking My Heart (with Kiki Dee), Sorry Seems to be the Hardest Word, Crazy Water, Bite Your Lip, Ego, Part Time Love, Song for Guy, Are You Ready for Love, Victim of Love, Johnny B. Goode, Little Jeanie, Sartorial Eloquence, Nobody Wins, Just like Belgium, Blue Eyes, Empty Garden, Princess, All Quiet on the Western Front, I Guess that's Why They Call It the Blues, Sad Songs (Say So Much); albums: Empty Sky, Elton John, Tumbelweed Connection, Friends (film soundtrack), 17-11-70, Madman Across the Water, Honky Chateau, Don't Shoot Me I'm Only the Piano Player, Goodbye Yellow Brick Road (double), Caribou, Elton John's Greatest Hits (2 vols.), Captain Fantastic and the Brown Dirt Cowboy, Rock of the Westies, Here and There, Blue Moves (double), A Single Man, Victim of Love, Lady Samantha, 21 at 33, The Fox, Jump Up, Love Songs, Too Low for Zero, Breaking Hearts. *Films:* Goodbye to Norma Jean 1973, To Russia with Elton 1980, The Rainbow 1989; played Pinball Wizard in Tommy 1973. *Leisure interests:* football, collecting records, tennis, all sports. *Address:* c/o John Reid

Enterprises Ltd., 125 Kensington High Street, London, W8 5SN, England. *Telephone:* 01-938 1741.

JOHN, Fritz, PH.D., F.R.S.; American mathematician; b. 14 June, 1910, Berlin, Germany; s. of Herman Jacobsohn and Hedwig (Bürgel) Jacobsohn-John; m. Charlotte Woellmer John 1933; two s.; ed. Göttingen and Cambridge Univs.; Asst. and Assoc. Prof., Univ. of Kentucky 1935–42; Mathematician, Aberdeen Proving Ground, Maryland 1943–45; Assoc. Prof., New York Univ. 1946–51, Prof. of Math., Courant Inst. of Mathematical Sciences, New York Univ. 1951–, Richard Courant Prof., New York Univ. 1976–79; Sherman Fairchild Distinguished Prof. California Inst. of Tech. 1979; Dir. of Research, Inst. of Numerical Analysis 1950–51; mem. N.A.S., Deutsche Akad. Naturforscher Leopoldina; Benjamin Franklin Fellow, Royal Soc. of Arts, London, MacArthur Fellow 1984; Birkhoff Prize in Applied Math. 1973; Sr. U.S. Scientist Humboldt Award 1980, Steele Prize of the American Mathematical Soc. 1982; Hon. Dr. (Rome, Bath, Heidelberg). *Publications:* Plane Waves and Spherical Means 1955, Lecture on partial differential equations (Co-Author) 1964, Calculus and Analysis 1 (Co-Author) 1965, Lectures on Advanced numerical analysis 1967, Partial Differential Equations 1971. *Leisure interests:* hiking, astronomy. *Address:* Courant Institute of Mathematical Sciences, 251 Mercer Street, New York, N.Y. 10012, U.S.A.

JOHN, Patrick; Dominica politician; b. 7 Jan. 1937; fmr. mem. Parl.; Leader Dominica Labour Party 1974–83, Deputy Leader 1983–84; Minister of Communications and Works 1970–73, Deputy Premier and Minister of Finance 1974, Premier of Dominica 1974–78, Prime Minister 1978–79, Minister for Housing, Security and Devt. 1978–79; Gen. Sec. Labour Party of Dominica 1985; M.P. July–Nov. 1985; arrested 1981, tried and acquitted May 1982, re-tried Oct. 1985; sentenced to 12 years imprisonment for conspiracy to overthrow govt. *Address:* H.M. Prison, Stock Farm, Goodwill, Dominica.

JOHN PAUL II, His Holiness Pope (Karol Wojtyła); b. 18 May 1920, Wadowice; s. of Karol Wojtyła and Emilia Kaczorowska; ed. Jagiellonian Univ., Cracow, Angelicum, Rome; ordained Priest 1946; Prof. of Moral Theology at Univs. of Cracow and Lublin 1953–58; Chair. Dept. of Ethics, Catholic Univ., Lublin; Titular Bishop of Ombi and Vicar-Gen. of Archdiocese 1958, Scholastic of Metropolitan Chapter and Vicar of Archdiocese 1960–63; Archbishop of Cracow 1963–78; cr. Cardinal by Pope Paul VI 1967; elected Pope Oct. 1978, Hon. Freeman of Dublin 1979; Dr. h.c. (Mainz) 1977, (Coimbra) 1982, (Salamanca) 1982, (Cracow) 1983, (Lublin) 1983. *Publications:* (as Karol Wojtyła) Love and Responsibility 1960, The Jeweller's Shop (play) 1960, The Acting Person 1969, Sources of Renewal-The Implementation of the Second Vatican Council 1972, Sign of Contradiction 1976, Brother of Our Lord (play) 1979, Collected Poems 1982; (as John Paul II) The Redeemer of Man 1979, On the Mercy of God 1980, On Human Work 1981, The Role of the Christian Family in the Modern World 1981, Be Not Afraid 1982, On Reconciliation and Penance 1984, Christian Meaning of Human Suffering 1984, The Apostles of the Slavs 1985, The Lord, the Giver of Life 1986. *Leisure interests:* skiing, rowing, sport. *Address:* Apostolic Palace, Vatican City.

JOHNS, Anthony Hearle, PH.D.; Australian professor of Islamic studies; b. 28 Aug. 1928, Wimbledon, U.K.; s. of late Frank Charles Johns and of Ivy Doris Kathleen Johns (née Hearle); m. Yohanni Bey 1956; four s. one d.; ed. St. Boniface's Coll., Plymouth, U.K. and School of Oriental and African Studies, Univ. of London; lecturer Ford Foundation-sponsored Training Project, Indonesia 1954–58; Sr. Lecturer in Indonesian Languages and Literatures, Australian Nat. Univ. 1958–63, Chair. and Head. Dept. 1963–83, Dean Faculty of Asian Studies 1963–64, 1965–67, 1975–79, 1988–91, Prof. and Head Southeast Asia Centre 1983–; Visiting Prof., Univ. of Toronto (Dept. of Religious Studies and Dept. of Middle East and Islamic Studies); Fellow Inst. for Advanced Studies, Hebrew Univ. of Jerusalem 1984–85; Fellow Australian Acad. of Humanities 1972; Univ. of London Sr. Studentship 1953–54, Rhuvon Guest Prize in Islamic Studies, S.O.A.S. 1953–54. *Publications:* The Gift Addressed to the Spirit of the Prophet 1965, A Road with No End (trans. and Ed.) 1968, Cultural Options and the Role of Tradition 1981, Islam in Asia II Southeast and East Asia (Ed. and contrib. with R. Israeli) 1984. *Leisure interests:* music, literature. *Address:* 70 Duffy Street, Ainslie, Canberra, A.C.T. 2602, Australia. *Telephone:* 062-496574.

JOHNS, Jasper; American painter; b. 15 May 1930, Augusta; s. of Jasper Johns Sr. and Jean Riley; ed. Univ. of South Carolina; works in following collections: Tate Gallery, London, Museum of Modern Art, New York, Albright-Knox Art Gallery, Buffalo, N.Y., Museum Ludwig, Cologne, Hirshhorn Museum and Sculpture Garden, Washington, D.C., Whitney Museum of American Art, Stedelijk Museum, Amsterdam, Moderna Museet, Stockholm, Dallas Museum of Fine Arts; one-man exhibitions: Leo Castelli, New York 1958, 1960, 1961, 1963, 1966, 1968, 1976, 1981, 1984, Galerie Rive Droite, Paris 1959, 1961, Galleria d'Arte del Naviglio, Milan 1959, Columbia Museum of Art, Columbia, S. Carolina 1960, Ileana Sonnabend, Paris 1962, Jewish Museum, New York 1964, Whitechapel Gallery, London 1964, Pasadena Museum, Calif. 1965, Smithsonian Inst. 1966, Arts Council of G.B. 1974–75, Philadelphia Museum of Art 1970, Museum of Modern Art, New York 1970, Whitney Museum of American Art 1977, Kunsthalle, Cologne, 1978, Centre Georges Pompidou, Paris 1978, Hayward

Gallery, London 1978, Seibu Museum, Tokyo 1978, San Francisco Museum of Modern Art 1978, Kunstmuseum, Basel 1979, Des Moines Art Center 1983, Museum of Modern Art 1986, Kunsthalle 1986; mem. American Acad. of Arts and Letters; Prize, Pittsburgh Int. 1958, Wolf Foundation Prize 1986, Gold Medal (American Acad. and Inst. of Arts and Letters) 1986, Int. Prize, Venice Biennale 1988. *Address:* c/o Leo Castelli Gallery, 420 W. Broadway, New York, N.Y. 10012, U.S.A.

JOHNSON, Barry Edward, PH.D., F.R.S.; British mathematician; b. 1 Aug. 1937, Woolwich, London; s. of Edward and Evelyn May (née Bailey) Johnson; m. 1961 (dissolved 1979); two s. one d.; ed. Epsom County Grammar School, Hobart State High School, Univs. of Tasmania and Cambridge; Instructor Univ. of Calif. 1961–62, Visiting Lecturer Yale Univ. 1962–63, Visiting Prof. 1970–71, Lecturer Exeter Univ. 1963–65, Univ. of Newcastle upon Tyne 1965–68, Reader 1968–69, Head of Dept. of Pure Mathematics 1976–84, Prof. of Pure Mathematics 1969–, Head of School of Mathematics 1983–86, Dean Faculty of Science Aug. 1986–(89); mem. London Mathematical Soc. Council 1974–78, Pres. 1981–82. *Publications:* Cohomology of Banach algebras 1972 and numerous scientific papers. Leisure interests: reading, travel. *Address:* 12 Roseworth Crescent, Gosforth, Newcastle upon Tyne, NE3 1NR, England. *Telephone:* Tyneside 2845363.

JOHNSON, Ben; Canadian (b. Jamaican) athlete; b. 30 Dec. 1961, Falmouth, Jamaica; emigrated with family to Canada 1976; began athletics career coached by Charlie Francis 1977; finished last, Commonwealth Games 100 metres trial, Canada 1978; won Canadian jr. title, became Canadian citizen 1979; selected for Olympic Games, Moscow, but Canada boycotted Games 1980; came sixth in 100 metres, Pan-American Jr. Games 1980, second, Commonwealth Games 1982; semi-finalist, World Championships 1983; bronze medallist, Olympic Games, L.A., U.S.A.; won World Cup 1985, Commonwealth title 1986, indoor 60 metres in record time 1987; gold medallist, World Championships, with time of 9.83 seconds, Rome 1987; came first in final, Olympic Games, in world record 9.79 seconds, Seoul 1988; medal withdrawn after allegations concerning drug-taking.

JOHNSON, David Gale; American economist; b. 10 July 1916, Vinton, Iowa; s. of Albert D. Johnson and Myra Jane Reed; m. Helen Virginia Wallace 1938; one s. one d.; ed. Iowa State Coll., Univs. of Wisconsin and Chicago; Research Assoc. Iowa State Coll. 1941–42, Asst. Prof. of Econs. 1942–44; Dept. of Econs., Univ. of Chicago 1944–, Asst. Prof. 1944–54, Prof. 1954–, Assoc. Dean Div. of Social Sciences 1957–60, Dean 1960–70, Chair. Dept. of Econs. 1971–75, 1980–84, Dir. Office of Econ. Analysis 1975–80, Vice-Pres. and Dean of Faculties 1975–76, Provost 1976–80; Economist, Office of Price Admin. 1942, Dept. of State 1946, Dept. of Army 1948; Office of the President's Special Rep. for Trade Negotiations 1963–64; Agency for Int. Devt. 1961–62; Tenn. Valley Authority 1950–55; RAND Corpn. 1953–71; Dir. Social Science Research Council 1954–57; Pres. American Farm Econ. Asscn. 1964–65, Nat. Opinion Research Center 1962–75, 1979–, Southeast Chicago Comm. 1980– (Pres. 1980–); Treas. American Asscn. for the Advancement of Slavic Studies (AAASS) 1980–82; mem. President's Nat. Advisory Comm. on Food and Fibre 1965–67; Adviser, Policy Planning Council, U.S. Dept. of State 1966–69; mem. Nat. Research Council, mem. Exec. Cttee. Div. of Behavioural Sciences, Nat. Research Council 1969–73, Asscn. for Comparative Econ. Studies (ACES) 1982–; mem. Bd. of Dirs., William Benton Foundation 1981–; mem. Nat. Comm. on Population Growth and the American Future 1970; Acting Dir. Univ. of Chicago Library 1971–72; mem. Council on Int. Econ. Policy 1972–75; mem. Steering Cttee., Nat. Acad. of Sciences World Food and Nutrition Study 1975–77; Co-Chair. Cttee. on Population and Econ. Growth, Nat. Research Council 1984–86; Fellow, American Acad. of Arts and Sciences 1976–. *Publications:* Forward Prices for Agriculture 1947, Trade and Agriculture 1950, Grain Yields and the American Food Supply 1963, World Agriculture in Disarray 1973, World Food Problems and Prospects 1975, Prospects for Economic Reform in the People's Republic of China 1982. *Leisure interests:* reading, travel. *Address:* Department of Economics, The University of Chicago, 1126 E. 59th Street, Chicago, Ill. 60637 (Office); 5617 S. Kenwood Avenue, Chicago, Ill. 60637, U.S.A. (Home). *Telephone:* (312) 702-8251 (Office); (312) 493-4015 (Home).

JOHNSON, Frederick Ross, B.COMM., M.B.A.; Canadian business executive; b. 13 Dec. 1931, Winnipeg, Man.; s. of Frederick H. Johnson and Caroline Green; m. Laurie A. Graumann 1979; two s.; ed. Univs. of Manitoba and Toronto; Vice-Pres. Merchandising, T. Eaton Co. (Canada) 1965–66; Exec. Vice-Pres. and C.O.O., GSW Ltd. 1966–71; Pres. and C.E.O., Standard Brands Ltd., Canada 1971–74; Dir. Standard Brands Inc. 1974–, Sr. Vice-Pres. 1974–75, Pres. 1975–76, Chair. and C.E.O. 1977–81; Pres. and C.O.O. Nabisco Brands Inc. 1981–83, Vice-Pres. and C.E.O. 1984–85, Chief Exec. R.J.R. Nabisco 1987–89 (after take over of Nabisco by Reynolds), Pres. and C.O.O. R. J. Reynolds Industries 1985–87, Pres. and C.E.O. 1987–89; Dir. Wosk's Ltd., Vancouver, Bank of Nova Scotia, Toronto; mem. Advisory Council, Columbia Univ., New York; Trustee, Econ. Club of New York; Chair. Multiple Sclerosis Soc., New York branch; Hon. Dr. (St. Francis Xavier Univ., Antigonish, N.S.) 1978, (Univ. of Newfoundland) 1980. *Leisure interests:* golf, skiing, tennis. *Address:* c/o R. J. Reynolds Industries Inc., R.J.R. World Headquarters Building, Winston-Salem, N.C. 27102; 625 Madison Avenue, New York, N.Y. 10022, U.S.A. *Telephone:* (212) 227-7546.

JOHNSON, Gabriel Ampah, D.D.'ÉTAT; Togolese professor of biology and administrator; b. 13 Oct. 1930, Aneho; s. of William K. K. Johnson and Rebecca A. Ekue-Hettah; m. Louise Chipan 1960; three s. three d.; ed. Univ. of Poitiers, France; Teaching Asst., Univ. of Poitiers until 1956; Research Fellow, C.N.R.S., France 1958-60; Deputy Dir. of Educ., Togo 1959-60; Asst. Prof. Nat. Univ. of Ivory Coast, Abidjan 1961-64, Assoc. Prof. 1965-66, Prof., Chair. of Biology 1966-; Asst. Dean, Faculty of Science 1963-68, Founding Dir. Nat. Centre for Social Services 1964-68; Founding Rector, Univ. du Bénin, Lomé, Togo 1970-; Dir. of Higher Educ., Togo 1970-75; Pres. Nat. Planning Comm. of Togo 1973; Pres. Assćn. of African Univs. 1977-80; mem. Bd. of Admin., Asscn. of Partially or Fully French-Speaking Univs. 1975-, Pan African Inst. for Devt. 1977-; mem. Cen. Cttee. Togo People's Rally (ruling party) 1976-; Founding Pres. Africa Club for an Integrated Devt. 1980-; mem. Zoological Soc. of France 1956, Biological Soc. of France 1962, Endocrinological Soc. of France 1966; Medal of Honour, Univ. of São Paulo, Brazil 1980; Hon. Vice-Pres. Gold Mercury Int. 1983; Hon. Dr. Sherbrooke, Canada) 1979, (Lille) 1983, (Bordeaux) 1986; Gold Mercury Int. Award 1982, Chevalier Ordre nationale de la Côte d'Ivoire 1966; Officier Ordre du Mono (Togo), Officier Légion d'honneur 1971, Commdr. Order of Cruzeiro do Sul (Brazil) 1976, Commdr. Order of Merit (France) 1983, Commdr. of Academic Palms (France) 1986. *Publications:* several articles in scientific journals. *Leisure interests;* reading, classical and modern music, swimming, farming (cattle breeding). *Address:* Université du Bénin, B.P. 1515, Lomé, Togo (Office); B.P. 7098, Lomé, Togo. *Telephone:* 21-52-41, 21-30-27, 21-35-00 (Office); 21-53-65 (Home).

JOHNSON, Howard Wesley, M.A.; American educator; b. 2 July 1922, Chicago, Ill.; s. of Albert and Laura (Hansen) Johnson; m. Elizabeth J. Weed 1950; two s. one d.; ed. Central Coll., Univ. of Chicago and Glasgow Univ.; U.S. Army 1943-46; Assoc. Prof. and Dir. of Man. Research, Univ. of Chicago 1948-55; Assoc. Prof., Assoc. Dean, Alfred P. Sloan School of Man., M.I.T., 1955-59, Prof., Dean 1959-66; Exec. Vice-Pres., Federated Dept. Stores 1966, mem. Bd. of Dirs. 1966-; Dir. Hitchiner Mfg. Co. 1961-71, Putnam Funds 1961-71 Morgan Guaranty Trust Co. 1971-; mem. Council on Foreign Relations, President's Advisory Cttee. on Labor-Man. Policy 1966-68; Pres. M.I.T. 1966-71, Chair. of Corpn. 1971-83, Hon. Chair. 1983-; Dir. Fed. Reserve Bank of Boston 1967-68, Chair. 1968-69; Dir. John Hancock Mutual Life Insurance Co. 1968-, Reader's Digest Assćn. Inc. 1982-83; mem. at Large, Boy Scouts of America 1968-; Trustee Cttee. for Econ. Devt. 1968-71; Trustee, Inst. for Defense Analyses 1971-79; Overseer Boston Symphony Orchestra 1968-72; mem. Scientific Advisory Cttee., Mass. Gen. Hosp. 1968-70, Corpn. Museum of Science (Boston) 1966-, NASA ad hoc Science Advisory Cttee. 1966-71, Nat. Manpower Advisory Cttee. 1967-69, Nat. Comm. on Productivity 1970-72; Dir. Champion Int. Corpn. 1970-, E. I. Du Pont de Nemours and Co. 1972-; Vice-Chair. Federated Dept. Stores 1971-73; Trustee, Radcliffe Coll. 1973-79, Aspen Inst. for Humanistic Studies 1973-, Wellesley Coll. 1968-86, Trustee Emer. 1986-; Pres. Boston Museum of Fine Arts 1975-80, Chair. Bd. of Overseers 1980-83; Trustee Alfred P. Sloan Foundation 1982-; Fellow, American Acad. of Arts and Sciences, A.A.A.S., mem. American Philosophical Soc. *Leisure interests:* antique clocks, fly fishing, trap shooting. *Address:* Massachusetts Institute of Technology, Cambridge, Massachusetts 02139, U.S.A. *Telephone:* (617) 253-0636.

JOHNSON, Hugh Eric Allan, M.A.; British author and editor; b. 10 March, 1939, London; s. of Guy F. Johnson and Grace Kittel; m. Judith Eve Grinling 1965; one s. two d.; ed. Rugby School, King's Coll., Cambridge; feature writer Condé Nast Magazines 1960-63, Ed. Wine and Food Magazine 1963-65, wine corresp. Sunday Times 1965-67, Travel Ed. 1967, Ed. Queen Magazine 1968-70, Wine Ed. Cuisine Magazine (New York) 1983-84, Pres. Sunday Times Wine Club 1973-, Editorial Dir. The Garden (Royal Horticultural Soc. Journal) 1975-, Chair. Winestar Productions Ltd, The Hugh Johnson Collection Ltd. Consultant, Jardines Wines and Spirits International Ltd.; British Airways (Consultant); Hon. Chair. 'Wine Japan' 89 1989; Sec. Wine and Food Soc. 1963-65; TV series Wine-A Users Guide 1986; Vintage-A History of Wine 1989; Gardening Corresp. New York Times 1986-87; André Simon Prize 1967, 1984, Glenfiddich Award 1972, 1984, Marques de Caceres Award 1984, Wines and Vines Trophy 1982 etc. *Publications:* Wine 1966, The World Atlas of Wine 1971, The International Book of Trees 1973, The California Wine Book (with Bob Thompson) 1975, Hugh Johnson's Pocket Wine Book (annually since 1977), The Principles of Gardening 1979, Hugh Johnson's Wine Companion 1983, How to Handle a Wine (video) 1984; Hugh Johnson's Cellar Book 1986, The Atlas of German Wines 1986, How to Enjoy Your Wine 1985, Understanding Wine (A Sainsbury Guide) 1986, The Wine Atlas of France (with Hubrecht Duijker) 1987. *Leisure interests:* travel, gardening, music. *Address:* 73 St. James's Street, London, S.W.1; Saling Hall, Great Saling, Braintree, Essex, England.

JOHNSON, Joe; British snooker player; fmr. motor mechanic and gas board employee; became professional snooker player 1979; winner, Embassy world snooker championship title (beating Steve Davis) 1986; runner-up 1987.

JOHNSON, John H.; American publisher; b. 19 Jan. 1918, Arkansas; m. Eunice Johnson; one s. (deceased), one d.; ed. DuSable High School and Chicago and Northwestern Univs.; Asst. Ed. 1936, later Man. Ed. of employees' publication, Supreme Life Insurance Co. of America; founded Ebony 1945, Jet 1951, Black Stars, Black World, Ebony Jr.; first Black businessman to be selected as one of the "ten outstanding young men of the year" by U.S. Jr. Chamber of Commerce 1951; accompanied Vice-Pres. Nixon at Ghana Independence celebrations 1957, appointed Special Amb. representing the U.S. at Ivory Coast Independence celebrations 1961, and Kenya Independence ceremony 1963; founder and Pres. Johnson Publishing Co. Inc.; Dir. and Chair. of Bd. Supreme Life Insurance Co.; Dir. Marina City Bank of Chicago, Service Fed. Savings and Loan Asscn., Chicago, Greyhound Corpn., Zenith, Bell & Howell, Arthur D. Little Corpn., 20th Century-Fox Corpn., United Negro Coll. Fund, etc.; Trustee, Inst. of Int. Educ., Tuskegee Inst., Howard and Fisk Univs.; Dir. Chicago Asscn. of Commerce; Hon. LL.D. of several univs. and colls.; Horatio Alger Award 1966, named Publr. of the Year by Magazine Publrs.' Asscn. 1972, and numerous other awards. *Address:* 3600 Wilshire Boulevard, Los Angeles, Calif. 90005; 820 South Michigan Avenue, Chicago, Ill. 60605, U.S.A. (Office). *Telephone:* (312) 786-7600.

JOHNSON, Sir John Rodney, K.C.M.G., M.A.; British diplomatist; b. 6 Sept. 1930, India; s. of late Edwin Done and Florence Mary (née Clough) Johnson; m. Jean Mary Lewis 1956; three s. one d.; ed. Manchester Grammar School, Oxford Univ.; Colonial Service, finally Dist. Comm., Thika, Kenya 1954-64; Admin., Cttee. of Vice-Chancellors of U.K. Univs. 1964-65; First Sec. Foreign and Commonwealth Office (FCO) 1966-69; Head of Chancery, British Embassy, Algiers 1969-72; Deputy High Commr. Barbados 1972-74; Political Counsellor, High Comm. in Nigeria 1975-78; Head, West African Dept., FCO, and Amb. (non-resident) to Chad 1978-80; High Commr. in Zambia 1980-84, in Kenya 1986-; Asst. Under-Sec. of State (Africa), FCO 1984-86. *Leisure interests:* African history, mountains. *Address:* c/o Foreign and Commonwealth Office, King Charles Street, London, SW1A 2AP, England.

JOHNSON, III, Joseph Eggleston, M.D.; American professor of medicine and administrator; b. 17 Sept. 1930, Elberton, Ga.; s. of Joseph Eggleston Johnson and Marie (Williams) Johnson; m. Judith H. Kemp 1956; one s. two d.; ed. Vanderbilt Univ., Nashville, Tenn., Johns Hopkins Univ.; Instructor in Medicine, Johns Hopkins Univ. School of Medicine 1961-62, Physician, Johns Hopkins Hosp 1961-66, Asst. Prof. of Medicine 1962-66, Asst. Dean for Student Affairs 1963-66; Assoc. Prof. of Medicine, Univ. of Fla. Coll. of Medicine 1966-68, Chief, Div. of Infectious Disease 1966-72, Prof. of Medicine 1968-72, Assoc. Dean 1970-72; Prof. and Chair. Dept. of Medicine, Bowman Gray School of Medicine 1972-85; Chief of Medicine, N.C. Baptist Hosp. 1972-85; Dean, Univ. of Mich. Medical School and Prof. of Internal Medicine 1985-; Markle Scholar, Royal Soc. of Medicine; mem. Johns Hopkins Soc. of Scholars. *Publications:* 100 articles and book chapters on infectious disease, immunology and internal medicine. *Address:* 1301 Catherine Road, M7324 Medical Sciences I, Ann Arbor, Mich. 48109-0624 (Office); 3880 Waldenwood, Ann Arbor, Mich. 48105, U.S.A. (Home). *Telephone:* (313) 764-8175 (Office).

JOHNSON, Keith; Jamaican civil servant and diplomatist; b. 29 July 1921, Spanish Town, St. Catherine; s. of Septimus A. and Emily A. Johnson; m. Dr. Pamela E. B. Rodgers 1973; two d.; ed. Columbia Univ., New York and Univ. of London; Jamaican Civil Service 1940-48; Research Asst., Bureau of Applied Social Research, Columbia Univ. 1948; Population Div., Dept. of Econ. and Social Affairs, UN Secr. 1949-62; Consul-Gen. of Jamaica in New York 1962-67; Perm. Rep. of Jamaica to UN 1967-73; Chair. Preparatory Cttee. for UN Conf. on Human Environment; Chair. Fourth Cttee. of UN Gen. Assembly Session 1971; Amb. (non-resident) to Argentina 1969-73; Amb. to Fed. Repub. of Germany, also accred. to Netherlands and Luxembourg 1973-81, (also accred. to Israel 1975-81, to Vatican City 1980-85), to the U.S.A. 1981-; Rep. to O.A.S. 1981-; Kt. Grand Commdr. of Humane Order of African Redemption (Liberia) 1969, Grand Cross of the Order of Merit (Fed. Repub. of Germany) 1981, Grand Cross of Luxembourg 1981, and numerous other awards. *Leisure interests:* listening to music, walking. *Address:* Embassy of Jamaica, Suite 355, 1850 K Street, N.W., Washington, D.C. 20006, U.S.A. *Telephone:* (202) 452-0660.

JOHNSON, Kenneth Langstreth, PH.D., F.R.S., F.ENG.; British engineer and university professor; b. 19 March 1925, Barrow-in-Furness, Lancs.; s. of F. H. Johnson and E. H. Langstreth; m. Dorothy Rosemary Watkins 1954: one s. two d.; ed. Barrow-in-Furness Grammar School for Boys, Univ. of Manchester; Tech. Asst. Messrs. Rotol Ltd., Gloucester 1945-49; Asst. Lecturer Mechanical Eng., Manchester Coll. of Tech. 1949-54; Lecturer, then Reader in Eng., Univ. of Cambridge 1954-77, Prof. 1977-; Fellow Jesus Coll. 1957-; Fellow Inst. Mechanical Engs. 1948; prize papers, Inst. Mechanical Engs. 1961, 1969, 1975, 1986, 1987; Gold Medal, Inst. Mechanical Eng. 1985. *Publications:* One Hundred Years of Hertz Contact 1982, Contact Mechanics 1985; over 60 papers in scientific and eng. journals. *Leisure interests:* music, swimming, mountain walking. *Address:* University Engineering Department, Trumpington Street, Cambridge, CB2 1PZ (Office); 13 Park Terrace, Cambridge, CB1 1JH, England (Home). *Telephone:* 0223-332709 (Office); 0223-355287 (Home).

JOHNSON, Leslie Royston; Australian politician; b. 22 Nov. 1924, Sydney; s. of W.C. Johnson and M. H. English; m. Gladys Jones 1949; one s. two d.; mem. House of Reps. for Hughes, N.S.W. 1955, 1958, 1961, 1963, 1969,

1972, 1974, 1975, 1977, 1980, 1983; Minister of Housing 1972–73, for Housing and Construction 1973–75, of Aboriginal Affairs June–Nov. 1975; Opposition Whip 1977–83; Deputy Speaker and Chair. of Cttees. 1983; High Commr. in New Zealand 1984–87; Parl. Adviser to Australian Del. to UN 1981. *Leisure interests:* swimming, photography. *Address:* 25/1 Koorooma Place, Sylvania, N.S.W., Australia (Home).

JOHNSON, Manuel H., Jr.; American economist; b. 10 Feb. 1949, Troy, Alabama; s. of Manuel Holman Johnson Sr. and Ethel Lorraine Jordan; m. Mary Lois Wilkerson 1972; two s.; ed. Troy State Univ., Florida State Univ., George Mason Univ., Fairfax, Va.; currently Asst. Sec. of Treasury for Econ. policy; mem. Fed. Reserve Bd. Oct. 1985–, Vice-Chair. 1986–. *Publications: Co-author:* Political Economy of Federal Government Growth 1980, Better Government at Half Price 1981, Deregulating Labor Relations 1981. *Address:* Federal Reserve System, 20th and C Streets, N.W., Washington, D.C. 20551, U.S.A.

JOHNSON, Paul (Bede), B.A.; British historian, journalist and broadcaster; b. 2 Nov. 1928, Barton; s. of William Aloysius and Anne Johnson; m. Marigold Hunt 1957; three s. one d.; ed. Stonyhurst and Magdalen Coll., Oxford; Asst. Exec. Ed. Réalités, Paris 1952–55; Asst. Ed. New Statesman 1955–60, Deputy Ed. 1960–64, Ed. 1965–70, Dir. 1965; DeWitt Wallace Prof. of Communications, American Enterprise Inst., Washington, D.C. 1980; mem. Royal Comm. on the Press 1974–77, Cable Authority 1984–; free-lance writer; Book of the Year Prize, Yorkshire Post 1975, Francis Boyer Award for Services to Public Policy 1979; King Award for Excellence (Literature) 1980. *Publications:* The Offshore Islanders 1972, Elizabeth I: a Study in Power and Intellect 1974, Pope John XXIII 1975, A History of Christianity 1976, Enemies of Society 1977, The National Trust Book of British Castles 1978, The Civilization of Ancient Egypt 1978, Civilizations of the Holy Land 1979, British Cathedrals 1980, Ireland: Land of Troubles 1980, The Recovery of Freedom 1980, Pope John Paul II and the Catholic Restoration 1982, History of the Modern World: From 1917 to the 1980s 1984, The Pick of Paul Johnson 1985, Saving and Spending: The working-class economy in Britain 1870–1939 1986, The Oxford Book of Political Anecdotes (ed.) 1986, The History of the Jews 1987, Intellectuals 1988. *Leisure interests:* painting, mountaineering. *Address:* Copthall, Iver, Bucks., England. *Telephone:* (0753) 653-350.

JOHNSON, Philip Cortelyou, A.B.; American architect; b. 8 July 1906; ed. Harvard Univ; Dir. Dept. of Architecture and Design, Museum of Modern Art 1932–54, Trustee 1958–; works include the Annexe and Sculpture Court, Museum of Modern Art, and the Glass House, New Canaan, Conn., Lincoln Center Theater; assoc. with the late Mies van der Rohe in design of Seagram Building, New York; mem. Acad. of Arts and Letters; Bronze Medallion (City of New York) 1980; Pritzker Prize 1979, Fellows Award R.I. School of Design 1983. *Publications:* The International Style, Architecture since 1922 (with H. R. Hitchcock, Jr.) 1932, Machine Art 1934, Mies van der Rohe 1947, Architecture 1949–1965 1966. *Address:* 885 Third Avenue, New York, N.Y. 10022 (Office); Ponus Street, New Canaan, Conn. 06840, U.S.A. (Home).

JOHNSON, Pierre Marc, M.N.A., B.A., LL.L., M.D.; Canadian politician; b. 5 July 1946, Montreal; s. of late Daniel Johnson and Reine (Gagné) Johnson; m. Marie-Louise Parent 1973; one s. one d.; ed. Coll. Jean-Brébeuf, Montreal, Univ. de Montréal and Univ. de Sherbrooke; called to Quebec Bar 1971; admitted Quebec Coll. of Physicians and Surgeons 1976; elected to Quebec Nat. Ass. 1976; mem. Nat. Exec. Council, Parti Québécois 1977–79, Pres. Parti Québécois 1985–87; Minister of Labour and Manpower, Quebec 1977–80, of Consumer Affairs, Cooperatives and Financial Insts. 1980–81, of Social Affairs 1981–84, of Justice, Attorney-Gen. and Minister Responsible for Canadian Intergovernmental Affairs 1984–85; Premier of Quebec Oct.–Dec. 1985; Leader of Opposition, Quebec Nat. Ass. 1985–87; Visiting Prof. Osgoode Law School, York Univ., Toronto 1987–. *Leisure interests:* skiing, swimming, music. *Address:* 800 Place Victoria, Tour de la Bourse, CP 204, Montreal, P.Q., H4Z 1E3, Canada.

JOHNSON, Richard Keith; British actor; b. 30 July 1927, Upminster, Essex; s. of Keith Holcombe and Frances Louisa Olive (Tweed) Johnson; m. 1st Sheila Ann Sweet 1957 (divorced); m. 2nd Marilyn Kim Novak 1965 (divorced); m. 3rd Marie-Louise Nordlund 1982; two s. two d.; ed. Parkfield School, Felsted School, Royal Acad. of Dramatic Art; Nat. Theatre Player, Assoc. Artist R.S.C.; first stage appearance in Hamlet, Opera House, Manchester 1944; major parts include Marius Tertius (The First Victoria) 1950, Pierre (The Madwoman of Chaillot) 1951, Demetrius (A Midsummer Night's Dream) 1951, George Phillips (After My Fashion) 1952, Beauchamp, Earl of Warwick (The Lark) 1955, Laertes (Hamlet) 1955, Jack Absolute (The Rivals) 1956, Lord Plynlimmon (Plaintiff in a Pretty Hat) 1956, Orlando (As You Like It), Mark Antony (Julius Caesar), Leonatus (Cymbeline), Ferdinand (The Tempest), Romeo (Romeo and Juliet), Sir Andrew Aguecheek (Twelfth Night), title-role in Pericles, Don Juan (Much Ado About Nothing) 1957–58, Ferdinand (The Tempest) 1957, Romeo (Romeo and Juliet), Sir Andrew Aguecheek (Twelfth Night), Moscow and Leningrad; Charles (Blithe Spirit), Pinchwife (The Country Wife), Pilate (The Passion), title-role in The Guardsman all at Nat. Theatre 1975–78; U.K. tour, Death Trap 1982; first film appearance in Captain Horatio Hornblower 1950; films include Never so Few 1959, The Haunting 1963, The Pumpkin Eater 1964, Operation Crossbow 1965, Khartoum 1966, Deadlier Than the

Male 1966, Hennessy 1975; first appeared on TV 1949; TV films include: Man for All Seasons 1988, Voice of the Heart 1988; leading roles in productions including Rembrandt, Antony and Cleopatra, Hamlet (Claudius), The Member for Chelsea (Sir Charles Dilke), Cymbeline; founder, Chair. and C.E.O. United British Artists 1982–, Dir. 1983–; mem. Council British Acad. Film and Television Arts 1976–78; recent productions include: The Biko Inquest, Serjeant Musgrave's Dance, The Playboy of the Western World, Old Times, Turtle Diary, Castaway, The Lonely Passion of Judith Hearne. *Publication:* Hennessy 1974. *Leisure interests:* gardening, music, travel. *Address:* 2 Stokenchurch Street, London, SW6 3TR, England. *Telephone:* 01-736 5920.

JOHNSON, Thomas S., A.B., M.B.A.; American bank executive; b. 1940; m.; ed. Trinity Coll., Harvard; Head Graduate Business Program, Instructor Finance and Control Ateneo de Manila Univ. 1964–66; Special Asst. to Controller, Dept. of Defense 1966–69; with Chemical Bank and Chemical Banking Corpn. 1969–, Exec. Vice-Pres. 1979, Sr. Exec. Vice-Pres. 1981, Pres. 1983–; Chair. Bd. of Dirs. Union Theological Seminary, Harvard Business School Club of Greater New York; Bank Capital Market Asscn's Cttee. for Competitive Securities Market; Dir. Bond Club of New York Inc.; Vice-Pres. and Bd. mem. Cancer Research Inst. of America; Bd. mem. Texas Commerce Bancshares Inc., Pan Atlantic Re, Inc., Phelps Stokes Fund, Montclair Art Museum; mem. Council on Foreign Relations, Inc., Financial Execs. Inst. Asscn. of Reserve City Bankers, The Group of Thirty. Trustee Trinity Coll.; mem. Business Cttee., Museum of Modern Art, Consultative Group on Int. Econ. and Monetary Affairs. *Address:* Chemical Banking Corporation, 277 Park Avenue, New York, N.Y. 10172, U.S.A.

JOHNSON, U. Alexis; American diplomatist; b. 17 Oct. 1908, Falun, Kansas; s. of Carl Theodore and Ellen Forsse Johnson; m. Patricia Ann Tillman 1932 (died 1981); two s. two d.; ed. Occidental Coll., Los Angeles, and Georgetown Univ., Washington D.C.; entered foreign service 1935; served Tokyo 1935, Seoul 1937, Tianjin, China 1939, Seoul 1939, Manchuria 1940, Rio de Janeiro 1942; U.S. Army Civil Affairs Training Schools 1944, Manila 1945; Staff Political Adviser to SCAP, Japan 1946; Consul, Yokohama 1946; Deputy Dir. Office N.E. Asian Affairs, Dept. of State 1949–51, Dir. 1951; Deputy Asst. Sec. of State for Far Eastern Affairs 1951–53; Amb. to Czechoslovakia 1953–58; U.S. Rep. Geneva Conf. June–July 1954, and in subsequent talks with People's Repub. of China 1955–57; Amb. to Thailand 1958–61; Deputy Under-Sec. of State for Political Affairs 1961–64; Deputy Amb. to Repub. of Viet-Nam 1964–65; Deputy Under-Sec. of State for Political Affairs 1965–66; Amb. to Japan 1966–69; Under-Sec. of State for Political Affairs 1969–73; U.S. Envoy to SALT 1973–77; Vice-Chair. Atlantic Council of U.S.; Pres. Washington Inst. of Foreign Affairs; President's Award for Distinguished Fed. Civilian Service; Dept. of Defence Medal for Distinguished Public Service, Dept. of State Distinguished Honor Award, Medal of Freedom, Career Service Award of Nat. Civil Service League, Rockefeller Public Service Award. *Publications:* The Common Security Interests of Japan, The United States and NATO (Ed.) 1981, China Policy for the Next Decade (Ed.) 1984, The Right Hand of Power 1984. *Leisure interest:* golf. *Address:* 3133 Connecticut Avenue, N.W., Washington, D.C. 20008, U.S.A. *Telephone:* (202) 234-3549.

JOHNSON, William, F.R.S., D.SC., F.ENG., F.I.MECH.E.; British professor of mechanical engineering; b. 20 April 1922, Manchester; s. of James Johnson and Elizabeth Riley; m. Heather M. Thornber 1946; three s. two d.; ed. Univ. of Manchester; Prof. of Mech. Eng. U.M.I.S.T. 1960–75; Prof. of Mechanics, Eng. Dept. Univ. of Cambridge 1975–82 (retd.); Visiting Prof., Industrial Eng. Dept., Purdue Univ., Ind., U.S.A. 1984–85, United Technologies Distinguished Prof. of Eng. 1987–; Foreign Fellow Acad. of Athens 1982; Fellow of Univ. Coll. London 1981; Hon. D. Tech. (Bradford) 1976, Hon. D.Eng. (Sheffield) 1986; T. Bernard Hall Prize 1965, 1966, James Clayton Fund Prize 1972, 1977, Safety in Mech. Eng. Prize 1980, Silver Medal Inst. Sheet Metal 1987. *Publications:* Plasticity for Mechanical Engineers 1962, Mechanics of Metal Extrusion 1962, Bibliography of Slip Line Fields 1968, Impact Strength of Materials 1972, Engineering Plasticity 1973, Engineering Plasticity: Metal Forming Processes 1976, Crashworthiness of Vehicles 1978, Theory of Slip Line Fields 1982. *Leisure interests:* walking, gardening. *Address:* Ridge Hall, Chapel-en-le-Frith, Via Stockport, Derbyshire, SK12 6UD, England.

JOHNSON, William Summer, PH.D.; American professor of chemistry; b. 24 Feb. 1913, New Rochelle, N.Y.; s. of Roy Wilder Johnson and Josephine (Summer) Johnson; m. Barbara Allen 1940; ed. Amherst Coll. and Harvard Univ.; Research Chemist, Eastman Kodak Co. summers of 1936–39; Instructor Amherst Coll. 1936–37; Instructor, Univ. of Wisconsin 1940–42, Asst. Prof. 1942–44, Assoc. Prof. 1944–46, Prof. 1946–54, Homer Adkins Prof. of Chem. 1954–60; Visiting Prof. Harvard Univ. 1954–55; Prof. and Exec. Head of Dept. of Chem., Stanford Univ. 1960–69, Prof. of Chem. 1969–78, J. G. Jackson-C. J. Wood Prof. of Chem. 1975–78, Jackson-Wood Prof. Emer. 1978–; mem. Nat. Acad. of Sciences, American Acad. of Arts and Sciences, American Chemical Soc., Swiss Chemical Soc.; Fellow, London Chemical Soc.; American Chemical Soc. Award for Creative Work in Synthetic Organic Chem. 1958, Synthetic Organic Chemical Mfg. Award for Creative Research in Organic Chem. 1963, New York Section of American Chemical Soc. Nichols Medal 1968, Roussel Prize 1970, Roger

Adams Award 1977. *Publications:* Scientific articles on synthesis and constitution of natural products, particularly steroids and related compounds. *Address:* Department of Chemistry, Stanford University, Stanford, Calif. 94305 (Office); 191 Meadowood Drive, Portola Valley, Calif. 94025, U.S.A. (Home). *Telephone:* (415) 723-2784 (Office); (415) 851-7886 (Home).

JOHNSON-LAIRD, Philip Nicholas, PH.D., F.B.A.; British psychologist; b. 12 Oct. 1936, Leeds, Yorks.; s. of Eric Johnson-Laird and Dorothy Johnson-Laird (née Blackett); m. Maureen Mary Sullivan 1959; one s. one d.; ed. Culford School, Univ. Coll., London; left school at age 15 and worked as quantity surveyor and in other jobs before univ.; Asst. Lecturer, Dept. of Psychology, Univ. Coll., London 1966, Lecturer 1967-73; Visiting mem. Inst. for Advanced Study, Princeton, U.S.A. 1971-72; Reader in Experimental Psychology, Univ. of Sussex 1973, Prof. 1978-82; Asst. Dir., MRC Applied Psychology Unit, Cambridge 1982-; Visiting Fellow, Cognitive Science, Stanford Univ., U.S.A. 1980, Visiting Prof. of Psychology 1985, Visiting Prof. of Psychology, Princeton Univ., U.S.A. 1986; Dr. h.c. (Gothenburg) 1983; Rosa Morison Memorial Medal, Univ. Coll. London, James Sully Scholarship; Spearman Medal, British Psychological Soc. 1974, Pres.'s Award 1985. *Publications:* Thinking and Reasoning (Ed. with P. C. Wason) 1968, Psychology of Reasoning (with P. C. Wason) 1972, Language and Perception (with G. A. Miller) 1976, Thinking (Ed. with P. C. Wason) 1977, Mental Models 1983; numerous articles in psychological journals; reviews. *Leisure interests:* arts and music, talking and arguing. *Address:* Medical Research Council Applied Psychology Unit, 15 Chaucer Road, Cambridge, CB2 2EF, England.

JOHNSON-SIRLEAF, Ellen; Liberian politician; b. 1939; ed. Harvard Univ.; fmr. employee, Ministry of Finance; later Minister of Finance; also held posts with IBRD and as Vice-Pres. for Africa, Citibank, Nairobi; helped organize Liberian Action Party to oppose General Doe in elections of Oct. 1985; led campaign alleging ballot-rigging following election; arrested following abortive coup against regime of Pres. Doe Nov. 1985; detained until June 1986, thereafter under house arrest; fled to U.S.A. Sept 1986.

JOHNSTON, Allen Howard, C.M.G., L.TH., LL.D.; New Zealand ecclesiastic; b. 2 Sept. 1912, Auckland; s. of Joseph Howard Johnston and Clara Johnston; m. Joyce Rhoda Grantley 1937; four d.; ed. Univ. of Auckland, St. John's Coll., Auckland; Asst. Curate in Anglican Church, St. Mark's, Remuera 1935; Vicar of Northern Wairoa 1937, of Otahuhu 1944, of Whangarei 1949; Archdeacon of Waimate 1949; Bishop of Dunedin 1953-69, Waikato 1969-80; Primate and Archbishop of New Zealand 1972-80; Chaplain and Sub-Prelate, Order of St. John of Jerusalem 1974-; Chair. N.Z. Church Pension Bd. 1973-88; mem. Royal Comm. of Inquiry into Arthur Allan Thomas Case 1979; Fellow of St. John's Coll., Auckland; Hon. LL.D. (Otago). *Leisure interest:* gardening. *Address:* 3 Wymer Terrace, Hamilton, New Zealand. *Telephone:* 553-238 (Home).

JOHNSTON, Don, M.A.; American advertising executive; b. 9 March 1927; s. of George D. Johnston and Isabella Mann Johnston; m. Sarita Behar Villegas 1954; three s.; ed. Michigan State and Johns Hopkins Univs; with J. Walter Thompson Co. 1951-, Trainee 1951, Asst. Account Rep., New York 1952, Rep. Bogotá 1953, Account Rep., Account Supervisor, New York 1956, Man. Dir. Amsterdam 1961, Tokyo 1964, Vice-Pres. Europe, Frankfurt 1966, Vice-Pres. Europe, London 1967, Sr. Vice-Pres. Europe, London 1969, Sr. Vice-Pres. Latin America and Sr. Vice-Pres. Admin. and Planning, New York 1971, Exec. Vice-Pres. Int. 1972, Dir. 1972-, Pres. and C.E.O. Aug. 1974-87, Chair., C.E.O. 1978-87; C.E.O. JWT Group Inc. 1978-87, also Chair. Euro-Advertisement, B.V. 1980-; Dir. Continental Group Inc. 1981-. *Leisure interests:* tennis, guitar. *Address:* c/o JWT Group Inc., 466 Lexington Avenue, New York, N.Y. 10017, U.S.A..

JOHNSTON, Harold S., PH.D.; American professor of chemistry; b. 11 Oct. 1920, Woodstock, Ga.; s. of Smith L. Johnston and Florine Dial; m. Mary Ella Stay 1948; one s. three d.; ed. Emory Univ., Ga. and California Inst. of Tech.; Instructor, Stanford Univ. 1947-49, Asst. Prof. 1949-53, Assoc. Prof. 1953-56; Assoc. Prof. Calif. Inst. of Tech. 1956-57; Visiting Asst. Prof., Univ. of Calif. at Berkeley 1953, Prof. of Chem. 1957-, Dean Coll. of Chem. 1966-70; mem. N.A.S., American Acad. of Arts and Sciences, American Chemical Soc., American Physical Soc.; Hon. D.Sc. (Emory Univ); Gold Medal, Calif. Section of American Chemical Soc., Pollution Control Award of American Chemical Soc. 1974, John and Alice Tyler Ecology-Energy Prize 1983, California Inst. of Tech. Alumni Award 1985. *Publications:* Gas Phase Reaction Rate Theory 1966, Gas Phase Kinetics of Neutral Oxygen Species 1968, Catalytic Reduction of Stratospheric Ozone by Nitrogen Oxide Catalysts from Supersonic Transport Exhaust 1971. *Leisure interests:* gardening, astronomy. *Address:* Department of Chemistry, University of California, Berkeley, Calif. 94720 (Office); 132 Highland Boulevard, Berkeley, Calif. 94708, U.S.A. (Home). *Telephone:* (415) 642-3674 (Office).

JOHNSTON, Sir John (Baines), G.C.M.G., K.C.V.O.; British diplomatist (retd.); b. 13 May 1918; m. Elizabeth Mary Crace 1969; one s.; ed. Banbury Grammar School and Queen's Coll., Oxford; Army service 1940-46; Asst. Prin. Colonial Office 1947, Prin. 1948; Asst. Sec. W. African Council, Accra 1950-51; U.K. Liaison Officer, Comm. for Tech. Co-operation in Africa South of the Sahara 1952; Prin. Private Sec. to Sec. of State for Colonies 1953, Asst. Sec. 1956, Head of Far Eastern Dept., Colonial Office 1956;

transferred to Commonwealth Relations Office 1957, Deputy High Commr. in S. Africa 1959-61; High Commr. in Sierra Leone 1961-63, in Fed. of Rhodesia and Nyasaland 1963, in Rhodesia 1964-65; Asst. Under-Sec. of State, Commonwealth Office 1966-68, Deputy Under-Sec. of State, Foreign and Commonwealth Office 1968-71; High Commr. in Malaysia 1971-74, in Canada 1974-78; Gov. of BBC 1978-85; Chair. ARELS Examinations Trust; mem. Disasters Emergency Cttee. *Address:* 5 Victoria Road, Oxford OX2 7QF, England. *Telephone:* 0865-56927.

JOHNSTON, J(ohn) Bennett, Jr.; American politician; b. 10 June 1932, Shreveport, La.; s. of J. Bennett Johnston; m. Mary Gunn; two s. two d.; ed. Byrd High School, Washington and Lee Univ., U.S. Mil. Acad. and Louisiana State Univ. Law School; School of Law; Mil. service in Judge Advocate Gen. Corps La.; State Senator 1968-72; Senator from Louisiana 1972-; Chair. Democratic Senatorial Campaign Cttee. 1975-76; mem. Senate Cttee. on Energy and Natural Resources, on Appropriations, Senate Budget Cttee., mem. Senate Bldg. Cttee.; Democrat. *Leisure interest:* tennis. *Address:* 136 Hart Senate Office Building, Washington, D.C. 20510, U.S.A. *Telephone:* (202) 224-5824.

JOHNSTON, Robert Alan, A.C., B. COMM.; Australian banker; b. 19 July 1924, Melbourne; m. Verna Mullin 1948; two s. two d.; ed. Essendon High School, Univ. of Melbourne; Commonwealth Bank of Australia 1940-60; R.A.A.F. 1943-46; with Reserve Bank of Australia 1960-, Deputy Man. then Man., Investment Dept. 1964-70, Chief Man. Int. Dept. 1970-76, Adviser to the Gov. 1973, Chief Rep., London 1976-77, Sec. 1980-82, Gov. and Chair. Bd. 1982-; Exec. Dir. World Bank Group, Washington, D.C. 1977-79. *Address:* Reserve Bank of Australia, 65 Martin Place, Sydney, N.S.W. 20001, Australia. *Telephone:* Sydney 234 9333.

JOHNSTON, Very Rev. William Bryce, M.A., B.D., D.D., D.LITT.; British ecclesiastic; b. 16 Sept. 1921, Edinburgh; s. of William B. Johnston and Isabel W. Highley; m. Ruth M. Cowley 1947; one s. two d.; ed. George Watson's Coll. Edinburgh and Univ. of Edinburgh; Chaplain to H.M. Forces 1945-49; Minister, St. Andrew's Bo'ness 1949-55, St. George's Greenock 1955-64, Colinton Parish Church, Edinburgh 1964-; Chaplain to H.M. The Queen in Scotland 1981-; Moderator of Gen. Ass. of Church of Scotland 1980-81, Chair. Judicial Comm. 1987-; Visiting Lecturer in Social Ethics, Heriot-Watt Univ. 1966-87; Cunningham Lecturer, New Coll. Edinburgh 1968-71. *Leisure interests:* organ-playing, bowls. *Address:* The Manse of Colinton, Edinburgh, EH13 0JR, Scotland. *Telephone:* 031 441 2315.

JOHNSTONE, John W., Jr., B.A.; American business executive; b. 19 Nov. 1932, Brooklyn, New York; s. of John W. Johnstone Sr. and Sarah J. (Singleton) Johnstone; m. Claire Lundberg 1956; three s.; ed. Hartwick Coll., Oneonta, New York and Harvard Univ.; Hooker Chemical Corpn. 1954-75, Group Vice-Pres., Niagara Falls, New York 1973-75; Pres. Airco Alloys, Div. of Airco Inc., Niagara Falls, New York 1976-79; Vice-Pres. and Gen. Man., Industrial Products, Olin Corpn., Stamford, Conn. 1979-80, Sr. Vice-Pres., Chemicals Group 1980, Pres. and Vice-Pres. Olin Corpn. 1980, Exec. Vice-Pres. 1983, Dir. 1984, Pres. Olin Corpn. 1985-, C.O.O. 1986-87, C.E.O. 1987-; Chair., Pres. and C.E.O. Olin Corpn. 1988-; Dir. H.L. Financial Group 1986-, Research Corpn. 1987-. *Leisure interests:* golf and shooting—Trap/skeet. *Address:* Olin Corporation, P.O. Box 1355, 120 Long Ridge Road, Stamford, Conn. 06904-1355; 467 Carter Street, New Canaan, Conn. 06840, U.S.A. (Home). *Telephone:* (203) 356-2060 (Office); (203) 966-7976 (Home).

JOHORE, H.H. Sultan of, Sultan Mahmood Iskandar ibni Al-Marhum Sultan Ismail; Malaysian Ruler; b. 8 April 1932, Johore Bahru, Johore; s. of Sultan Tengku Ismail of Johore; m. 1st Josephine Trevorrow 1956; m. 2nd Tengku Zanariah Ahmad Zanariah Ahmad 1961; ed. Sultan Abu Bakar English Coll., Johore Bahru, Trinity Grammar School, Sydney, Australia, Devon Tech. Coll., Torquay, U.K.; Tengku Makota (Crown Prince) 1959-61, 1981; Raja Muda (second-in-line to the throne) 1966-81; fifth Sultan of Johore 1981-; Col.-in-Chief, Johore Mil. Forces 1981-; Yang di-Pertuan Agung (Supreme Head of State) 1984-89; f. Mado's Enterprises and Mados-Citoh-Daiken (timber cos.). *Leisure interests:* hunting, tennis, golf, flying, water sports.

JOKIPII, Liisa, M.D.; Finnish medical doctor and university teacher; b. 26 March 1943, Helsinki; m. Anssi Jokipii 1968; two s. two d.; ed. Univ. of Helsinki; Asst., Dept. of Serology and Bacteriology, Univ. of Helsinki 1973, Dozent in Clinical Microbiology and Immunology 1977-; Prof. of Clinical Microbiology and Immunology, Univ. of Oulu 1977; Prof. of Bacteriology and Serology, Univ. of Turku 1978. *Publications:* scientific articles on cell-mediated immunity, bacteriology and parasitology; textbook chapters on parasitology. *Leisure interests:* classical music (opera), old Finnish handicrafts and design. *Address:* Vanhaväylä 37, 00830 Helsinki, Finland (Home). *Telephone:* 358-0-783 827 (Home).

JOKLIK, Wolfgang Karl, D.PHIL.; American professor of microbiology and immunology; b. 16 Nov. 1926, Vienna, Austria; s. of Karl F. Joklik and Helene (née Giessl) Joklik; m. 1st Judith V. Nicholas 1955 (died 1975), one s. one d.; m. 2nd Patricia H. Downey 1977; ed. Sydney and Oxford Univs.; Research Fellow, Australian Nat. Univ. 1954-56, Fellow 1957-62; Assoc. Prof. of Cell Biology, Albert Einstein Coll. of Medicine, New York 1962-65, Siegfried Ullman Prof. 1966-68; Prof. and Chair. Dept. of Microbiology and Immunology Duke Univ. 1968–; Pres. Virology Div. American Soc. for Microbiology 1966–69; Chair. Virology Study Section Nat. Insts. of Health 1973–75; Pres. American Medical School Microbiology Chairs.' Assen. 1979; Pres. American Soc. for Virology 1982–83; Ed.-in-Chief Virology 1975–; Assoc. Ed. Journal of Biological Chem. 1978–; mem. N.A.S., mem. N.A.S. Inst. of Medicine. *Publications:* Contrib. to and Sr. Ed. specialist books, including Zinsser Microbiology, Principles of Animal Virology, The Reoviridae, more than 200 articles in specialist journals. *Leisure interests:* travel, photography, music, tennis and squash. *Address:* Department of Microbiology and Immunology, P.O. Box 3020, Duke University Medical Center, Durham, N.C. 27710, U.S.A. *Telephone:* (919) 684-5138.

JOLIET, René, D.END., LL.M., S.J.D.; Belgian lawyer; b. 17 Jan. 1938, Jupille-sur-Meuse; s. of Jean Joliet and Josephine Pirnay; ed. Univ. of Liège, Northwestern Univ., Chicago, U.S.A.; Research and Teaching Assoc., Law Faculty, Univ. of Liège 1960–70 (leave of absence 1965–68), Assoc. Prof. of Law 1970–74, Prof. 1974–; Visiting Prof. Univ. of Nancy 1971–78, Europa Inst., Univ. of Amsterdam 1976–85, Northwestern Univ., Chicago 1974, 1983, Univ. of Louvain-La-Neuve 1980–82; Belgian Chair at Univ. of London (King's Coll.) 1977; Prof. of EEC Competition Law, Coll. of Europe, Bruges 1979–84; mem. Kuratorium Max Planck Inst. for Foreign and Int. Patent, Copyright and Competition Law, Munich 1983, of Fachbeirat 1984; Judge at Court of Justice of European Communities 1984–; U.S. Educational Foundation Fellow 1965–67; Gen. Electric Fellow 1965–67. *Publications:* The Rule of Reason in Antitrust Law 1967, Monopolization and Abuse of Dominant Position 1970, Droit institutionnel des Communautés européenes, 2 vols. 1981, 1983; numerous articles on competition law and intellectual property. *Leisure interests:* literature, photography, cinema, hiking, travel. *Address:* European Communities Court of Justice, Plateau de Kirchberg, Luxembourg (Office); 25 rue de l'Arbois, B-4501 Neupré, Belgium (Home). *Telephone:* 352-4303229 (Office); 041-80.33.67 (Home).

JOLLES, Paul Rodolphe, PH.D.; Swiss diplomatist, government official and business executive; b. 25 Dec. 1919, Berne; s. of Leo Jolles and Ida Hegnauer; m. Erna Ryffel 1956; two s. one d.; ed. Berne and Lausanne Univs. and Harvard Univ., U.S.A.; diplomat, Embassy, Washington, D.C. 1943–49; Civil Servant, Foreign Office/Ministry of Econs., Berne 1949–56; Exec. Sec./Deputy Dir.-Gen. IAEA, UN, New York, then Vienna 1957–61; Govt. Del. (Amb.) for trade negotiations, Berne 1961–66; State Sec., Fed. Office of Foreign Econ. Affairs, Berne 1966–84; Chair. Bd. UNCTAD, Geneva 1967; Chair. Exec. Cttee. in Special Session of OECD, Paris 1973–80; Head Swiss Del. to Conf. on Int. Econ. Co-operation (N.-S. Dialogue, Paris) and to UNCTAD Confs., Nairobi and Manila 1979; Chair. Bd., Nestlé S.A., Vevey; Hon. Prof. of Int. Econs., Univ. of Berne; Hon. D.Econ. (Berne); John Harvard Fellowship; Prize of Freedom, Max Schmidheiny Foundation. *Publications:* Von der Handelspolitik zur Aussenwirtschaftspolitik 1983 and numerous articles on Swiss foreign trade policy, Swiss position regarding European integration, North-South relations, oil and int. energy issues, devts. in world econ. etc. *Leisure interest:* contemporary art. *Address:* Nestlé S.A., Avenue Nestlé, 1800 Vevey (Office); Herrengasse 23, 3011 Berne, Switzerland (Home). *Telephone:* (021) 924 21 11 (Office).

JOLY, Alain; French business executive; b. 18 April 1938, Nantes; s. of Albert Joly and Yvonne Poyet Rolin; m. Marie-Helène Capbern-Gasqueton 1966; two s. one d.; ed. Lycée Louis Le Grand, Paris and Ecole Polytechnique Paris; Engineer, L'Air Liquide 1962–67; Dir. of Operations, Canadian Liquid Air 1967–73; Dir. Corp. Planning, Société L'Air Liquide 1973–76, Regional Man. 1976–78, Gen. Sec. 1978–81, Vice-Pres. 1981, Dir. 1982, Man. Dir. 1985–; Croix de la Valeur Militaire. *Leisure interests:* tennis, sailing. *Address:* Société L'Air Liquide, 75 Quai d'Orsay, 75007 Paris, France (Office).

JONAS, Peter, B.A., L.R.A.M.; British arts administrator; b. 14 Oct. 1946, London; s. of Walter Adolf and Hilda May Jonas; ed. Worth School, Univ. of Sussex, Northern Coll. of Music, Manchester, Royal Coll. of Music, London, Eastman School of Music, Univ. of Rochester, U.S.A.; Asst. to Music Dir., Chicago Symphony Orchestra 1974–76, Artistic Admin. 1976–85; Dir. of Artistic Admin., The Orchestral Assen., Chicago 1977–85; Man. Dir. English Nat. Opera 1985–; Bd. of Man. Nat. Opera Studio 1985–; mem. Council Royal Coll. of Music 1988–. *Leisure interests:* 20th Century architecture, cinema, theatre, skiing. *Address:* c/o English National Opera, London Coliseum, St. Martin's Lane, London, WC2N 4ES, England. *Telephone:* 01-836 0111.

JONCKHEER, Efrain; Netherlands (Antilles) politician; b. 1917; ed. in Netherlands Antilles; Dir. of several cos. in Curaçao; first Pres. Dem. Party 1944; mem. of all Round Table Confs. leading to full autonomous status of Netherlands Antilles 1947–54; mem. Staten (Legis. Ass.) 1945–; Leader Dem. Party Group in Staten 1945–54; mem. Island Council of Curaçao 1951–53; Prime Minister of Netherlands Antilles and Minister of Gen. Affairs 1954–67; Minister of Transport and Communications 1954–56; Minister of Social Affairs 1956–57; Minister Plenipotentiary for the Netherlands Antilles at The Hague 1968–70; Netherlands Amb. to Venezuela 1971–76, also fmrly to Costa Rica, also accred. to Nicaragua and Panama 1976; Commdr. Order of Lion of Netherlands, Commdr. Order of House of Orange; Grand Cross Order of Liberator of Venezuela; Grand Officer

Order of Vasco Núñez de Balboa (Panama); Commdr. Order of Merit for Commerce and Industry (France). *Address:* Ministry of Foreign Affairs, Plein 23, P.O. Box 20081, 2500 EA, The Hague, Netherlands.

JONES, Mrs. Abeodu Bowen, PH.D.; Liberian diplomatist; b. Robertsport; ed. Cuttington Coll., Liberia, and Northwestern Univ., Ill.; Deputy Dir. Bureau of African and Asian Affairs, Ministry of Foreign Affairs 1962–68; Dir. Social Studies Div., Ministry of Educ. 1968–72; Dir. of Regional Devt. Planning, Ministry of Planning and Econ. Affairs 1972; Ministry of Postal Affairs 1976–77, of Health and Social Welfare 1977–78; Dir. UNESCO-Liberian Oral Tradition Research, Niamey, Niger 1970–72; mem. UNESCO Int. Cttee. for Drafting a Gen. History of Africa 1971–; Rural Devt. Consultant, FAO, Nairobi, Kenya 1976; UN/Govt. of Liberia Consultant, Rural Devt. Task Force 1979; Perm. Rep. of Liberia to UN 1981–85; Vice-Pres. UN Gen. Ass. 1983; consultant for an African Social Studies Programme, Nairobi, Kenya 1970–72; Special Consultant, Phelps Stokes Fund Int. Educ. Curriculum 1978; Fulbright Consultant in Int. Educ. Curriculum for U.S. Govt. 1979–80; Dip., Comprehensive Rural Regional Devt. Planning, Settlement Study Center (Israel) 1974; mem. Constitution Comm. of Liberia 1981. *Publications:* A History of Grand Cape Mount County, Liberia 1964, numerous articles about Liberia; Ed. Papers of late Pres. William Tubman 1968. *Address:* c/o Ministry of Foreign Affairs, P.O. Box 9002, Monrovia, Liberia.

JONES, Alan Stanley, O.B.E.; Australian racing driver; b. 2 Nov. 1946, Melbourne; s. of Stan Jones (fmr. Australian champion racing driver); m. Beverly Jones 1971; one adopted s.; ed. Xavier Coll., Melbourne; began racing in 1964 in Australia, raced in Britain from 1970; World Champion 1980, runner-up 1979; CanAm Champion 1978. *Grand Prix wins:* 1977 Austrian (Shadow-Ford), 1979 German (Williams-Ford), 1979 Austrian (Williams-Ford), 1979 Dutch (Williams-Ford), 1979 Canadian (Williams-Ford); 1980 Argentine (Williams-Ford), 1980 French (Williams-Ford), 1980 British (Williams-Ford), 1980 Canadian (Williams-Ford), 1980 U.S. (Williams-Ford), 1981 U.S. (Williams-Ford); announced retirement in 1981. *Leisure interests:* collecting interesting cars, farming in Australia. *Address:* c/o Williams Grand Prix Engineering Ltd., Unit 10, Station Road Industrial Estate, Didcot, Oxon., England. *Telephone:* Didcot 813678.

JONES, Allen, R.A.; British artist; b. 1 Sept. 1937, Southampton; s. of William and Madeline Jones; m. Janet Bowen (divorced 1978); two d.; ed. Hornsey School of Art, Royal Coll. of Art; Sec., Young Contemporaries, London 1961; lived in New York 1964–65; Tamarind Lithography Fellowship, Los Angeles 1966; Guest Prof. Dept. of Painting, Univ. of S. Florida 1969; Hochschule für Bildende Künste, Hamburg 1968–70, Hochschule der Künste, Berlin 1982–83; Guest Lecturer Univ. of Calif. 1977; first one-man exhbn., London 1963, one-man exhbns. in U.K., U.S.A., Switzerland, Fed. Repub. of Germany, Italy, Australia, Japan, Netherlands, Belgium, Austria, Scandinavia 1963–; many group exhbns. of paintings and graphic work; tours in Mexico, Canada 1975; first travelling retrospective, Europe 1979–80; Commercial Mural Project, Basel 1979; designs for TV and stage in Fed. Repub. of Germany and U.K.; Prix des Jeunes Artistes, Paris Biennale 1963. *Publications:* Allen Jones Figures 1969, Allen Jones Projects 1971, Waitress 1972, Ways and Means 1977, Sheer Magic (Paintings 1959–79) 1979, U.K. 1980. *Address:* c/o Waddington Galleries, 2 Cork Street, London, W.1, England.

JONES, Rt. Hon. Aubrey, B.SC.; British economist and industrialist; b. 20 Nov. 1911, Merthyr Tydfil; s. of Evan and Margaret Aubrey Jones; m. Joan Godfrey-Isaacs 1948; two s.; ed. London School of Econs.; on foreign and editorial staff The Times 1937–39 and 1947–48; served with Army Intelligence Staff, War Office and Mediterranean 1940–46; joined British Iron and Steel Fed. as Special Asst. to Chair. 1949, Econ. Dir. 1954 and Gen. Dir. 1955; M.P. for Birmingham (Hall Green) 1950–65; Minister of Fuel and Power 1955–57, of Supply 1957–59; mem. Council of Assen. with European Coal and Steel Community 1955–57; fmr. Dir. Guest, Keen & Nettlefolds Steel Co. Ltd., fmr. Chair. Staveley Industries Ltd., fmr. Dir. Courtaulds Ltd.; Chair. Nat. Bd. for Prices and Incomes 1965–70; Chair. Laporte Industries (Holdings) Ltd. 1970–72; Dir. Thomas Tilling Ltd. 1970–82, Incubon Int. Ltd. 1975–79, Black and Decker Ltd. 1977–81; Dir. Cornhill Insurance Co. Ltd. 1971–82, Chair. 1971–73; Hon. Fellow, London School of Econs. 1959, mem. Court of Govs. 1964; Hon. Fellow Commoner, Churchill Coll., Cambridge 1972–73, 1982–86; Regent Lecturer, Univ. of Calif., Berkeley 1968; Visiting Fellow, New Coll. Oxford 1978, Science Policy Research Unit, Univ. of Sussex 1986–; Sr. Research Assoc., St. Antony's Coll., Oxford 1979–81; Gov. Nat. Inst. Econ. and Social Research 1967; Hon. Vice-Pres. Consumers' Assen. 1967–72; Adviser to Public Service Review Comm. of Nigerian Govt. 1973–74; mem. Council Int. Inst. for Strategic Studies 1962–74, Int. Council for Settlement of Investment Disputes, Washington D.C. 1974–81; Leading Adviser to Iranian Govt. on Agricultural Devt. Plan 1974–75; UN Adviser to Iranian Govt. on Public Sector Problems 1975–79, on Productivity, Prices and Incomes 1976–79; Hon. Pres. Oxford Energy Policy Club 1977–88; fmr. Conservative, joined Liberal Party 1980, Pres., Fulham Democrats 1988. *Publications:* The Pendulum of Politics 1946, Right and Left 1944, Industrial Order 1950, The New Inflation—The Politics of Prices and Incomes 1973, Oil: The Missed Opportunity 1981, Britain's Economy: The Roots of Stagnation 1985. *Leisure interests:* sailing, skiing. *Address:* "Arnen", 120 Limmer

Lane, Felpham, Bognor Regis, W. Sussex, PO22 7LP, England. *Telephone:* 01-937 4247.

JONES, Barry Owen, M.A., LL.B., F.R.S.A.; Australian politician, fmr. public servant, teacher, univ. lecturer and lawyer; b. 11 Oct. 1932, Geelong, Vic.; s. of Claud Edward Jones and Ruth Marion (née Black) Jones; m. Rosemary Hanbury 1961; M.P. Victorian Parl. 1972–77, House of Reps. 1977–; Minister for Science March 1983–, Minister for Technology 1983–84, Minister Assisting the Minister for Industry, Tech. and Commerce 1984–87, Minister for Science, Customs and Small Business Jan. 1988–; Chair. Australian Film and TV School 1973–75, Australian Film Inst. 1974–80; Deputy Chair. Australian Council for the Arts 1969–73; mem. Australian Film Devt. Corpn. 1970–75; Raymond Longford Award (Australian Film Inst.) 1986; Australian Labor Party. *Publications include:* Macmillan Dictionary of Biography 1981, Sleepers, Wake!: Technology and the Future of Work 1982, Managing Our Opportunities 1984, Living by Our Wits 1986. *Leisure interests:* films, music, travel, collecting autographed documents, antique terracottas and paintings, reading. *Address:* Parliament House, Canberra, A.C.T. 2600, Australia. *Telephone:* (062) 777280.

JONES, Ben Joseph, LL.B.; Grenada lawyer and politician; b. 5 Aug. 1924, St. Andrews; unmarried; ed. Belair Presbyterian School, Chiswick Polytechnic, London, Gray's Inn, London and Univ. of London; attached to firm of solicitors, London 1962–64; private practice, Grenada 1964–65; magistrate, St. George's, Grenada 1965–66; Sr. Asst. Sec. Ministry of External Affairs 1966–67; Opposition Senator 1967–79; Minister of External Affairs and Legal Affairs 1984–87, of Legal Affairs, External Affairs, Tourism, Agric., Land and Forestry, Attorney Gen. 1987–88, of External Affairs, Agric., Lands, Forestry and Tourism March 1988–; *Leisure interests:* tennis, gardening, reading. *Address:* Ministry of External Affairs, St. George's, Grenada.

JONES, Daniel Jenkyn, O.B.E., M.A., D.MUS., D.LITT., F.R.A.M.; British composer and conductor; b. 7 Dec. 1912, Pembroke, Wales; s. of Jenkyn D. Jones and Margaret F. (née Bonnyman) Jones; m. twice; three d. by first m., one s. one d. by second m.; ed. Swansea Grammar School, Swansea Univ. Coll. and Royal Acad. of Music; devised system of Complex Metres 1936; Capt. Intelligence Corps 1940–45. *Works include:* 12 symphonies, 2 operas (The Knife 1961, Orestes 1967), 5 cantatas, oratorio St. Peter 1962, 3 concerti for violin, oboe and 'cello respectively, Capriccio for flute, harp, orchestra, Sinfonietta 1972, Dance Fantasy 1976, 4 overtures, Symphonic Prologue, Suite Dobra Niva, Salute to Dylan Thomas (orchestral suite), Tone Poems, Miscellany for small orchestra (20 pieces), Investiture Processional Music 1969, 7 string quartets, 6 string trios, 'cello sonata, wind septet, kettledrum sonata, Sonata (4 trombones), Divertimento (Strings and percussion), sonatas and 24 bagatelles for piano, chamber works, piano and organ pieces and incidental music for plays, radio, etc. Oliveira Prescott Prize 1936, Royal Philharmonic Prize 1950, Italia Prize 1954. *Leisure interests:* philosophy, languages, world literature, natural history. *Address:* 53 Southward Lane, Newton, Mumbles, Swansea, SA3 4QD, Wales. *Telephone:* 0792-368656.

JONES, Gen. David Charles, D.F.C.; American air force officer (retd.); b. 9 July 1921, Aberdeen, S. Dak.; s. of Maurice Jones and Helen Meade; m. Lois M. Tarbell 1942; one s. two d.; ed. Univ. of North Dakota and Minot State Coll., N. Dak., U.S.A.F. Flying School, Nat. War Coll.; Commdr. 22nd Air Refueling Squadron 1953–54, 33rd Bomb Squadron 1954; Operations Planner, Bomber Mission Branch, HQ Strategic Air Command Sept.–Dec. 1954, Aide to C.-in-C., SAC 1955–57; Dir. of Material, later Deputy Commdr. for Maintenance, 93rd Bomb Wing 1957–59; Chief, Manned Systems Branch, Deputy Chief and later Chief, Strategic Div., DCS/Operations, HQ U.S.A.F. 1960–64; Commdr. 33rd Tactical Fighter Wing March-Oct. 1965; Insp.-Gen. HQ United States Air Forces in Europe 1965–67, Chief of Staff Jan.-June 1967, Deputy Chief of Staff, Plans and Operations 1967–69; Deputy Chief of Staff, Operations, HQ 7th Air Force, Repub. of Viet-Nam 1969, Vice-Commdr. 7th Air Force, Tan Son Nhut Airfield, Repub. of Viet-Nam 1969; Commdr. 2nd Air Force 1969–71; Vice-C.-in-C. U.S.A.F.E., later C.-in-C. U.S.A.F.E. and Commdr. 4th Allied Tactical Air Forces, Ramstein Air Base, Fed. Repub. of Germany 1971–74; Chief of Staff, U.S. Air Force 1974–78, Chair. Jt. Chiefs of Staff 1978–82; Dir. USAir, Radio Corpn. of America, Nat. Broadcasting Co., Kemper Group 1982–, US Steel, Nat. Educ. Corpn.; Hon. D. Hum. Litt. (Nebraska) 1974; Hon. D. Laws (Louisiana Tech. Univ.) 1975; Distinguished Service Medal with Oak Leaf Cluster, Legion of Merit, Distinguished Flying Cross, Bronze Star Medal, Air Medal W/I OLC, and many other decorations. *Leisure interests:* jogging, skiing, racquetball, flying, historical novels.

JONES, Douglas Samuel, M.B.E., F.R.S., F.R.S.E.; British professor of mathematics; b. 10 Jan. 1922, Corby, Northants.; s. of Jesse Dewis Jones and Bessie Streather; m. Ivy Styles 1950; one s. one d.; ed. Wolverhampton Grammar School, Corpus Christi Coll., Univ. of Oxford; Flight Lieut., R.A.F. Volunteer Reserve 1941–45; Commonwealth Fellow, Mass. Inst. of Tech. 1947–48; Asst. Lecturer, then Lecturer, Univ. of Manchester 1948–54, Sr. Lecturer 1955–57; Visiting Prof., New York Univ. 1955, 1962–63; Prof. of Math., Univ. of Keele 1957–64; Ivory Prof. of Math., Univ. of Dundee 1965–; mem. Univ. Grants Cttee. 1976–86, Chair. Math. Sciences sub-cttee. 1976–86; mem. Computer Bd. 1976–82; mem. Open Univ. Visiting Cttee. 1982–87; mem. Council, Inst. of Math. and its applications 1982–

(Pres. 1988–); Van Der Pol Gold Medal, Int. Scientific Radio Union; Keith Prize, R.S.E., Naylor Prize of London Math, Soc.; Hon. Fellow, Corpus Christi Coll., Univ. of Oxford; Hon. D.Sc. (Strathclyde). *Publications include:* Electrical and Mechanical Oscillations 1961, The Theory of Electromagnetism 1964, Introductory Analysis (vol.1) 1969, (vol.2) 1970, Methods in Electromagnetic Wave Propagation 1979, Elementary Information Theory 1979, The Theory of Generalised Functions 1982, Differential Equations and Mathematical Biology 1983, Acoustic and Electromagnetic Waves 1986, Assembly Programming and the 8086 Microprocessor 1988. *Address:* Department of Mathematical Sciences, The University, Dundee, DD1 4HN (Office); 1 The Nurseries, St. Madoes, Glencarse, Perth, PH2 7NX, Scotland (Home). *Telephone:* 0382 23181 (Office); Glencarse 544 (Home).

JONES, E. Bradley, B.A.; American business executive; b. 8 Nov. 1927, Cleveland, Ohio; s. of Eben Hoyt Jones and Alfreda Sarah (Bradley) Jones; m. Ann Louise Jones 1954; one s. three d.; ed. Yale Univ. and Harvard Univ.; joined Republic Steel Corpn. (name changed to LTV Steel 1984) 1954–84; Asst. Dist. Sales Man. 1965–67, Asst. Man. Sales Flat Rolled Div. 1965–67, Man. Sales 1967–71, Vice-Pres. Marketing 1971–74; Vice-Pres. Commercial 1974–76, Exec. Vice-Pres. 1976–79, Dir. 1978, Pres. 1979–82, Chair. and C.E.O. 1982–84; Dir. Nat. City Bank (Cleveland), TRW Inc., Nat. City Corpn. (Cleveland), Cleveland Cliffs Inc., NACCO Industries, Consolidated Rail Corpn., Birmingham Steel Corpn.; Trustee First Union Real Estate Investments. *Leisure interests:* golf, tennis, paddle tennis. *Address:* 3401 Enterprise Parkway, Cleveland, Ohio 44122 (Office); 2775 Lander Road, Pepper Pike, Ohio 44124, U.S.A. (Home). *Telephone:* (216) 831-4955 (Office).

JONES, (Everett) Le Roi (Imamu Baraka); American poet and dramatist; b. 7 Oct. 1934, Newark, N.J.; s. of Coyette L. Jones and Anna Lois (Russ) Jones; ed. Howard Univ., New School and Columbia Univ.; served with U.S.A.F.; taught poetry at New School Social Research, drama at Columbia Univ., literature at Univ. of Buffalo; Visiting Prof., San Francisco State; began publishing 1958; founded Black Arts Repertory Theater School, Harlem 1964, Spirit House, Newark 1966; Whitney Fellowship 1963, Guggenheim Fellowship 1965; Fellow, Yoruba Acad. 1965; Visiting Lecturer, Afro-American Studies, Yale Univ. 1977–; mem. Int. Co-ordinating Cttee. of Congress of African Peoples; mem. Black Acad. of Arts and Letters. *Publications:* Preface to a Twenty Volume Suicide Note 1961, Dante 1962, Blues People 1963, The Dead Lecturer 1963, Dutchman 1964, The Moderns 1964, The System of Dante's Hell 1965, Home 1965, Jello 1965, Experimental Death Unit 1965, The Baptism—The Toilet 1966, Black Mass 1966, Mad Heart 1967, Slave Ship 1967, Black Music 1967, Tales 1968, Great Goodness of Life 1968, Black Magic, Four Black Revolutionary Plays 1969, Black Art 1969, In Our Terribleness 1970, Junkies are Full of Shhh ..., Bloodrites 1970, Raise 1971, It's Nation Time 1971, Kawaida Studies 1972, Spirit Reach 1972, African Revolution 1973; ed. Hard Facts 1976. *Address:* c/o William Morrow Co., 105 Madison Avenue, New York, N.Y. 10017, U.S.A.

JONES, Sir Ewart Ray Herbert, Kt., F.R.S., F.R.S.C., D.SC., PH.D.; British professor of chemistry (retd.); b. 16 March 1911, Wrexham, Denbighs.; m. Frances Mary Copp 1937; one s. two d.; ed. Grove Park School, Univ. Coll. of North Wales, Univ. of Manchester; Fellow, Univ. of Wales 1935–37; Lecturer, Imperial Coll. of Science and Tech. 1938; Reader in Organic Chem. and Asst. Prof., Univ. of London 1945; Sir Samuel Hall Prof. of Chem., Manchester Univ. 1947–55; Arthur D. Little Visiting Prof. of Chem., M.I.T. 1952; Waynflete Prof. of Chem., Oxford Univ. 1955–78; Prof. Emer. Oxford Univ. 1978–; Chair. Anchor and Guardian Housing Assns. 1979–85; Karl Folkers Lecturer, Univs. of Illinois and Wisconsin 1957; Pedler Lecturer 1959; mem. Council for Scientific and Industrial Res. and Chair. Research Grants Cttee. 1961–65; mem. Science Research Council and Chair. Univ. Science and Tech. Bd. 1965–69; Pres. Chemical Soc. 1964–66; Fellow, Imperial Coll. 1967; Pres. Royal Inst. of Chem. 1970–72, Royal Soc. of Chem. 1980–82; mem. Council of Royal Soc. 1969–71; Foreign mem. American Acad. of Arts and Sciences; Hon. D.Sc. (Birmingham, Nottingham, New South Wales, Sussex, Salford, East Anglia, Ulster); Hon. LL.D. (Manchester); Meldola Medal, Royal Inst. of Chem. 1940, Fritzsche Award, American Chemical Soc. 1962. *Publications:* scientific papers in Journal of The Chemical Society. *Address:* 6 Sandy Lane, Yarnton, Oxford, England (Home). *Telephone:* Kidlington 2581.

JONES, Geraint Iwan; British conductor, organist and harpsichordist; b. 16 May 1917, Porth, Glamorgan; s. of Evan Jones and Caroline Davies; m. 1st M. A. Kemp 1940; m. 2nd Winifred Roberts 1949; one d.; ed. Caterham School and Royal Acad. of Music; concert organist, Nat. Gallery Concerts 1940–44; Conductor, Purcell's Dido and Aeneas, Mermaid Theatre 1950–53; Founder, Geraint Jones Singers and Orchestra 1951; Musical Dir. Lake District Festival 1960–78, Kirckman Concert Soc. 1963–; Artistic Dir. Salisbury Festival of the Arts 1972–77, Manchester Int. Organ Festival 1977–; Prof., Royal Acad. of Music; Grand Prix du Disque 1959 and 1966; frequent harpsichord recitals with violinist wife Winifred Roberts; frequent tours of Europe and America 1948–; complete organ works of Bach in London 1945–46 and 1955; has recorded on most historic organs in Europe. *Leisure interests:* photography, antiques, architecture, motoring. *Address:* The Long House, Arkley Lane, Barnet Road, Arkley, Herts., England.

JONES, Dame Gwyneth, D.B.E., F.R.C.M.; British soprano; b. 7 Nov. 1936, Pontnewynydd, Mon., Wales; d. of Edward George Jones and Violet

Webster; m. Till Haberfeld; one d.; ed. Royal Coll. of Music, London, Accad. Chigiana, Siena, Zürich Int. Opera Centre; with Zürich Opera House 1962–63; with Royal Opera House, Covent Garden 1963–; Vienna State Opera House 1966–, Bavarian State Opera 1967–; Shakespeare Prize 1986; guest performances in numerous opera houses throughout the world including La Scala, Milan, Rome Opera, Berlin State Opera, Munich State Opera, Hamburg, Paris, Metropolitan Opera, New York, San Francisco, Los Angeles, Zürich, Geneva, Dallas, Chicago, Teatro Colón, Buenos Aires, Tokyo, Bayreuth Festival, Salzburg Festival, Arena di Verona, Edinburgh Festival and Welsh Nat. Opera; Kammersängerin in Austria and Bavaria; known for many opera roles including Leonara, Il Trovatore, Desdemona, Otello, Aida, Aida (Verdi), Leonore, Fidelio (Beethoven), Senta, The Flying Dutchman (Wagner), Medea, Medea (Cherubini), Sieglinde, Die Walküre (Wagner), Lady Macbeth, Macbeth (Verdi), Elizabeth, Don Carlos (Verdi), Madame Butterfly (Puccini), Tosca (Puccini), Donna Anna, Don Giovanni (Mozart), Salome (R. Strauss), Kundry, Parsifal and Isolde, Tristan und Isolde (Wagner), Helena, Aegyptische Helena (R. Strauss), Färberin, Frau ohne Schatten, Elektra, Elektra (R. Strauss), Elizabeth/Venus, Tannhäuser (Wagner), Marschallin, Der Rosenkavalier (R. Strauss), Brünnhilde, Der Ring des Nibelungen (Wagner); TV films: Fidelio, Aida, Flying Dutchman, Beethoven 9th Symphony, Tannhäuser, Poppea (Monteverdi), Rosenkavalier (R. Strauss), Die Walküre, Siegfried, Götterdämmerung, Die lustige Witwe; recordings for Decca, DGG, EMI, CBS. *Address:* P.O. Box 556, CH-8037 Zürich, Switzerland.

JONES, Horace C.; American business executive; b. 1916, Philadelphia, Pa.; m. Helen Allen; seven c.; ed. Hill School, Pottstown, Pa., Princeton Univ.; served with U.S.A.A.F. Second World War, with rank of Lieut.-Col.; Asst. Treas., Lees Carpets 1938, Pres. 1960–70 (became division of Burlington Industries Inc. 1960); Dir. Burlington Industries Inc. 1960, Exec. Vice-Pres. 1967, Vice-Chair. 1972, Pres. 1973–75, C.E.O. 1973–76, Chair. April 1975–76, Chair. Exec. Finance Cttee. Sept. 1976–. *Address:* Burlington Industries Inc., Greenboro, N.C. 27420, U.S.A.

JONES, James Larkin (Jack), C.H., M.B.E.; British trade unionist; b. 29 March 1913, Liverpool; s. of George and Anne Sophie Jones; m. Evelyn Mary Taylor 1938; two s.; ed. Liverpool; worked in eng. and dock industries 1927–39; served in Spanish Civil War; Midlands Official, Transport and Gen. Workers' Union 1939–63, Exec. Officer 1963–69, Gen. Sec. 1969–78; Dist. Sec. Confed. of Shipbuilding and Eng. Unions 1939–63; mem. Labour Party Nat. Exec. Cttee. 1964–67; Deputy Chair. Nat. Ports Council 1967–78; mem. Council, Trades Union Congress 1968–78; Chair. Int. Cttee., TUC 1972–78; mem. Exec. Bd. Int. Confed. of Free Trade Unions, European Trade Union Confed., Pres. EFTA Trade Union Council 1973–; British Overseas Trade Bd. 1975–78, Advisory, Conciliation and Arbitration Service (ACAS) 1975–78; mem. Royal Comm. on Criminal Procedure 1978–; mem. NEDC 1969–78; mem. Econ. and Social Cttee., EEC 1975–78; Pres. Retd. Mems. Assocns., TGWU 1978–; Vice-Pres. Int. Transport Workers Fed. 1974–80; Vice-Pres. Age Concern (England), Anti-Apartheid Movement; Hon. D. Litt. (Warwick); Fellow, Nuffield Coll., Oxford 1970–78, Chartered Inst. of Transport 1971; Assoc. Fellow L.S.E. 1978; Hon. Fellow, Liverpool Polytechnic 1988; City of Coventry Medal of Merit; Freeman City of London; Dimbleby Lecture, BBC-TV 1977. *Publications:* Incompatibles 1968, A to Z of Trade Unionism and Industrial Relations 1982, A Union Man (autobiog.) 1986. *Leisure interests:* walking, painting. *Address:* 74 Ruskin Park House, Champion Hill, London, SE5 8TH, England (Home). *Telephone:* 01-274 7067.

JONES, Le Roi (see Jones, (Everett) Le Roi).

JONES, Lyle Vincent, PH.D.; American professor of psychology and university administrator; b. 11 March 1924, Grandview, Wash.; s. of Vincent F. Jones and Matilda M. (née Abraham) Jones; m. Patricia Edison Powers 1949 (divorced 1979); three c.; ed. Reed Coll., Univ. of Washington, Stanford Univ.; Nat. Research Fellow 1950–51; Asst. Prof. of Psychology, Univ. of Chicago 1951–57; Visiting Assoc. Prof., Univ. of Texas 1956–57; Assoc. Prof., Univ. of N. Carolina 1957–60, Prof. 1960–69, Vice-Chancellor, Dean of Graduate School 1969–79; Alumni Distinguished Prof. 1969–; Dir. Univ. of N. Carolina L. L. Thurstone Psychometric Lab. 1957–74, 1979–; Fellow Center of Advanced Studies in Behavioral Sciences 1964–65, 1981–82; mem. Inst. of Medicine, N.A.S. 1984–; Fellow American Acad. of Arts and Sciences. *Publications:* (with others) Studies in Aphasia: An Approach to Testing 1961, The Measurement and Prediction of Judgment and Choice 1968, An Assessment of Research Doctorate Programs in the United States (5 vols.) 1982. *Address:* L. L. Thurstone Psychometric Laboratory, University of North Carolina at Chapel Hill, Davie Hall 013-A, Chapel Hill, N.C. 27514; Route 1, Pittsboro, N.C. 27312, U.S.A. (Home). *Telephone:* 919-962 2325 (Office).

JONES, Mary Ellen, PH.D.; American professor of biochemistry; b. 25 Dec. 1922, La Grange, Ill.; d. of Elmer Enold Jones and Laura Anna Klein Jones; one s. one d.; ed. Univ. of Chicago, Yale Univ.; Bacteriologist and Chemist, Armour and Co., Springfield, Mo. and Chicago 1942–48; Atomic Energy Comm. Postdoctoral Fellow, Biochemical Research Lab., Mass. Gen. Hosp., Boston 1951–53, Fellow, American Cancer Soc. 1953–55, Assoc. Biochemist 1955–57; Asst. Prof., Graduate Dept. of Biochemistry, Brandeis Univ., Waltham, Mass. 1957–60, Assoc. Prof. 1960–66; Assoc. Prof., Dept. of Biochemistry, School of Medicine, Univ. of N.C., Chapel Hill 1966–68,

Prof. 1969–71; Prof., Dept. of Biochemistry, School of Medicine, Univ. of Southern Calif., Los Angeles 1971–78; Chair. and Prof., Dept. of Biochemistry and Nutrition, School of Medicine, Univ. of N.C., Chapel Hill 1978–, Kenan Prof. 1980–; mem. Editorial Bd. Journal of Biological Chem. 1975–80, 1982–87, Cancer Research 1981–86; Fellow A.A.A.S.; mem. N.A.S., Inst. of Medicine of N.A.S., American Soc. of Biological Chemists (Pres. 1985), Biochemistry Div. of American Chemical Soc., New York Acad. of Science. *Address:* Department of Biochemistry, University of North Carolina at Chapel Hill, Chapel Hill, N.C. 27514, U.S.A. *Telephone:* (919) 962-8326 (Office); (919) 942-5598 (Home).

JONES, Norman William, C.B.E., T.D., F.I.B., F.R.S.A.; British banker; b. 5 Nov. 1923, Chorlton-cum-Hardy; s. of late James William and of Mabel Jones; m. Evelyn June Hall 1950; two s.; ed. Gravesend Grammar School, Harvard A.M.P.; Commissioned, Beds. and Herts. Regt. 1943; with Airborne Forces 1944–47; joined Lloyds Bank 1940; held various man. positions, becoming Gen. Man. (Group Co-ordination) 1973; Asst. Chief Gen. Man. 1975; Deputy Group C.E.O. 1976; Dir. of Main Bd., Lloyds Bank Ltd. 1976–, Group C.E.O. 1978–83, Deputy Chair. 1984–; Dir. Nat. Bank of N.Z. 1978–; Dir. Lloyds Merchant Bank Holdings 1985–; Chair. Lloyds Bank Stockbrokers Ltd. 1986–. *Leisure interests:* sailing, photography, gardening, "do-it-yourself". *Address:* Rowans, 21 College Avenue, Grays, Essex, England. *Telephone:* Grays Thurrock 373101.

JONES, Philip James, D.PHIL., F.B.A.; British historian and academic; b. 19 Nov. 1921, London; s. of John David Jones and Caroline Susan Jones née Davies; m. Carla Susini 1954; one s. one d.; ed. St. Dunstan's Coll., London and Wadham Coll., Oxford; Asst. Lecturer in Modern History, Glasgow Univ. 1949–50; Lecturer in Medieval History, Leeds Univ. 1950–61, Reader 1961–63; Fellow and Tutor in Modern History, Brasenose Coll., Oxford 1963–, Librarian 1965–; Eileen Power Memorial Studentship 1956–57; Corresp. mem. Deputazione Toscana di Storia Patria 1975–; Serena Medal for Italian Studies 1988. *Publications:* The Malatesta of Rimini 1974, Economia e Societá nell'Italia medioevale 1980; contribs. to Cambridge Economic History I 1966, Storia d'Italia, II 1974, Storia d'Italia, Annali, I 1978, articles. *Address:* 167 Woodstock Road, Oxford, OX2 7NA, England; Piazza Pitti 3, Florence, Italy. *Telephone:* Oxford 57953; Florence 282924.

JONES, Philip Mark, C.B.E., F.R.N.C.M., F.R.C.M., F.G.S.M., F.R.S.A.; British musician; b. 12 March 1928, Bath; s. of John and Mabel Jones; m. Ursula Strebi 1956; ed. Battersea Grammar School, London, Royal Coll. of Music; Prin. Trumpet, all major London orchestras 1949–72; f. and Dir. Philip Jones Brass Ensemble 1951–86; Head of School of wind and percussion, Royal Northern School of Music, Manchester 1975–77; Head, Wind and Percussion Dept., Guildhall School of Music and Drama, London 1983–88; Prin. Trinity Coll. of Music, London 1988–; Ed. 'Just Brass' music series, Chester Music, London 1973–; mem. Arts Council of G.B. 1984–; Grand Prix du Disque 1977, Composers Guild Award 1979, Cobbett Medal of the Worshipful Company of Musicians 1986. *Publications:* over 50 gramophone records with Philip Jones Brass Ensemble. *Leisure interests:* history, mountain walking, skiing. *Address:* 14 Hamilton Terrace, London, NW8 9UG, England. *Telephone:* 01-286 9155.

JONES, Reginald Victor, C.B., C.B.E., M.A., D.PHIL., F.R.S.; British physicist; b. 29 Sept. 1911, London; s. of Harold V. and Alice M. Jones; m. Vera M. Cain 1940; one s. two d.; ed. Alleyn's School, Dulwich, Wadham and Balliol Colls., Oxford; Scientific Officer, Royal Aircraft Establishment and Admiralty Research Lab. 1936–39; Head Scientific Intelligence, Air. Staff 1939–46, Dir. 1946; Dir. Scientific Intelligence, Ministry of Defence 1952–54; Chair. Research Advisory Cttee., British Transport Comm. 1956–57, Safety in Mines Research Advisory Bd. 1956–60, Electronic Research Council, Ministry of Aviation/Tech. 1964–70, Paul Instrument Fund, Royal Soc. 1960–; Pres. Crabtree Foundation 1958, Section A British Asscn. 1971; Prof. of Natural Philosophy, Aberdeen Univ. 1946–81, Prof. Emer. 1981–; Visiting Prof. Univ. of Colorado 1982; Chair. British Nat. Cttee. for History of Science 1970–79; Visitor Royal Mil. Coll. of Science 1983; Hon. Fellow, Wadham Coll. Oxford 1968; Vice-Pres. Royal Soc. 1972; Commonwealth Prestige Fellow, N.Z. 1973; Hon. Fellow, Coll. of Preceptors 1978, Balliol Coll., Oxford 1981, Inst. of Electronic and Radio Engineers 1982, Inst. of Measurement and Control 1984, British Horological Inst. 1985; Hon. Freeman Clockmakers Co. of London 1984; Companion, Operational Research Soc. 1983; Hon. Mayor San Antonio, Texas 1983; Hon. D.Sc. (Strathclyde) 1969, (Kent) 1980, D.Univ. (York) 1976, (Open) 1978, (Surrey) 1979, LL.D. (Bristol) 1979; B.O.I.M.A. Prize, Inst. of Physics 1934, Medal of Freedom with Silver Palm 1946, Medal for Merit (U.S.A.) 1947, Duddell Medal, Physical Soc. 1960, Parsons Medal 1967, Hartley Medal 1972, Mitchell Medal 1979. *Publications:* Most Secret War 1978, Future Conflict and New Technology 1981, Some Thoughts on 'Star Wars' 1985, Instruments and Experiences 1988; various scientific, biographical and philosophical articles in journals; Ed. Notes and Records of the Royal Society. *Address:* 8 Queen's Terrace, Aberdeen, AB1 1XL, Scotland (Home). *Telephone:* (0224) 648184 (Home).

JONES, Richard M.; American business executive; b. 26 Nov. 1926, Eldon, Mo.; m. Sylvia A. Richardson 1950; three c.; ed. Olivet Nazarene Coll. and Harvard Univ. Graduate Advanced Management Program; joined Sears Roebuck & Co. 1950, Store Man. 1963–68, Gen. Man. Washington &

Baltimore 1974, Exec. Vice-Pres.-East 1974–80, Corp. Vice-Pres. 1980, Vice-Chair. and Chief Financial Officer 1980–85, Pres. and Chief Financial Officer 1986–; Dir. Sears Roebuck Foundation; various public appts. Hon. LL.D. (Olivet Nazarene Coll.) 1983. *Address:* Sears Roebuck & Co., Sears Tower, Chicago, Ill. 60684, U.S.A.

JONES, Robert Thomas; American scientist and engineer; b. 28 May 1910, Macon, Mo.; s. of Edward S. Jones and Harriet E. Johnson; m. 1st Hazel St. Clair; m. 2nd Doris Cohen; m. 3rd Barbara Spagnioli; four s. two d.; ed. Univ. of Missouri and Max M. Munk Catholic Univ. of America; Asst. Aero Engineer Nicholas-Beasley Aircraft Co., Marshall, Mo. 1929–30; Scientific Aide to U.S. Nat. Advisory Comm. for Aeronautics, Langley Field, Va. 1934–46; Sr. Staff Scientist, NACA-NASA 1946–63; Prin. Research Scientist Avco Everett Research Lab., Everett, Mass. 1963–70; Sr. Staff Scientist NASA-Ames. Research Center, Moffett Field, Calif. 1970–81, research assoc. 1981–; Consulting Prof. Stanford Univ. 1981; mem. Nat. Acad. of Sciences, Nat. Acad. of Eng., American Acad. of Arts and Sciences; Hon. Fellow American Inst. of Aeronautics and Astronautics 1979; S. A. Reed Award (American Inst. of the Aero Sciences) 1946, Prandtl Ring Award (Deutsche Gesellschaft für Luft und Raumfahrt 1978, Pres.'s Medal 1981, Langley Medal (Smithsonian Inst.) 1981, Excalibur Award, U.S. Congress 1981. *Publications:* High Speed Wing Theory (with Doris Cohen) 1960, Collected Works of Robert T. Jones 1976; numerous scientific papers and reports. *Leisure interests:* violin-making, acoustics, optics, flying. *Address:* 25005 La Loma Drive, Los Altos Hills, Calif., U.S.A. *Telephone:* (415) 948-4817.

JONES, Roger Warren, M.A., LL.D.; American government official (retd.); b. 3 Feb. 1908, New Hartford, Conn.; s. of H. Roger Jones and Eleanor Drake; m. Dorothy Heyl 1930; two s. one d.; ed. Cornell and Columbia Univs; Instructor, Coral Gables, Mil. Acad. 1928–29; in commerce 1929–31; Asst. Exec. Officer, Cen. Statistical Bd., Washington 1933–39; Admin. Officer, Budget Bureau, 1939–42; Col. in U.S. armed forces 1942–45; Budget Examiner, and subsequently Asst. Dir. for Legis. Reference and Deputy Dir. Bureau of the Budget 1945–59; Chair., Civil Service Comm. 1959–61; Deputy Under-Sec. of State for Admin. 1961–62; Sr. Consultant, Budget Bureau (renamed Office of Man. and Budget Jan. 1970) 1962–69, Asst. Dir. 1969–71; mem. Comm. on Political Activity of Govt. Personnel 1967–68; mem. Bd. of Higher Educ., Dist. of Columbia 1968–73; Sr. Fellow in Public and Int. Affairs, Woodrow Wilson School, Princeton Univ. 1977–88, Emer. 1988–; Hon. D.P.S. (George Washington Univ.) 1969, Hon. LL.D. (Princeton Univ. and Otterbein Coll.) 1962, Hon. O.B.E.; Legion of Merit (U.S.A.). *Leisure interests:* gardening, walking, military history. *Address:* Brookside, New Hartford, Conn. 06057, U.S.A. *Telephone:* (203) 379-4996.

JONES, Sir Thomas Philip, Kt., C.B.; British business executive; b. 13 July 1931, Erith; s. of Mary Elizabeth Jones and William Ernest Jones; m. Mary Phillips 1955; two s.; ed. Cowbridge Grammar School, Jesus Coll., Oxford; Asst. Prin., Ministry of Supply 1955; Prin., Ministry of Aviation 1959; on loan to H.M. Treasury 1964–66; Prin. Private Sec. to Minister of Aviation 1966–67; Asst. Sec., Ministry of Tech., then to Ministry of Aviation Supply 1967–71; Under-Sec., Dept. of Trade and Industry 1971, Under Sec., Dept. of Energy 1974, Deputy Sec. 1976–83; mem. BNOC 1980–82; Chair. Electricity Council 1983–. *Leisure interests:* walking, watching rugby, football, reading. *Address:* Electricity Council, 30 Millbank, London, SW1P 4RD, England. *Telephone:* 01-834 2333.

JONES, Thomas Victor; American aircraft executive; b. 21 July 1920, Pomona, Calif.; m. Ruth Nagel 1946; one s. one d.; ed. Pomona Jr. Coll. and Stanford Univ; Engineer, El Segundo Div., Douglas Aircraft Co. 1941–47; Tech. Adviser, Brazilian Air Ministry 1947–51; Prof., Head of Dept., Brazilian Inst. of Tech. 1947–51; Rand Corpn. 1951–53; Asst. to Chief Engineer, Northrop Aircraft Inc. 1953, Deputy Chief Engineer 1954–56, Dir. Devt. Planning 1956–57, Corporate Vice-Pres. 1957, Sr. Vice-Pres. 1958–59, Pres. 1959–76, C.E.O. 1960–, Chair. of Bd. 1963–. *Publications:* Capabilities and Operating Costs of Possible Future Transport Airplanes 1953. *Address:* Northrop Corporation, 1800 Century Park East, Los Angeles, Calif. 90067 (Office); 1050 Moraga Drive, Los Angeles, Calif. 90049, U.S.A. (Home). *Telephone:* (213) 553-6262 (Office).

JONES, Tom; Welsh singer; b. (as Thomas Jones Woodward) 7 June 1940, Treforest, Glamorgan; m. Malinda Trenchard 1956; one s.; made first hit record It's Not Unusual 1965; other records include Once Upon A Time, Green Green Grass of Home, I'll Never Fall in Love Again, I'm Coming Home, Delilah, Help Yourself, I Who Have Nothing, Close Up, Body and Soul; appeared in TV shows Beat Room, Top Gear, Thank Your Lucky Stars, Sunday Night at the London Palladium; toured U.S.A. 1965; appeared in Ed Sullivan Show at Copacabana, New York, and in variety show This Is Tom Jones in U.K. and U.S.A. 1969; made 26 singles with Decca, 16 albums; Britain's Most Popular Male Singer in Melody Maker Poll 1967, 1968; Film: Yockowald 1976. *Address:* c/o MAM Ltd., 24-25 New Bond Street, London, W.1, England.

JONES, Wilfred; British diplomatist; b. 29 Nov. 1926; joined Foreign Office (FO) 1949; served in Tamsui, Taiwan 1950, Jedda 1952; FO 1952, 1957, 1963; Vice-Consul, Brussels 1954; Second Sec. (Admin.), Athens 1959; First Sec. (Admin.), Canberra 1966; Foreign and Commonwealth Office

(FCO) 1968; Copenhagen 1971–74; First Sec. and Head of Chancery, Blantyre, Malawi 1974–75; Deputy High Commr. and Head of Chancery, Lilongwe, Malawi 1975–77; First Sec. FCO 1977–79, Head of Nationality and Treaty Dept. 1979–81; High Commr. in Botswana 1981–86. *Address:* Conifers, 16 The Hummicks, Dock Lane, Beaulieu, Hants., SO4 7YJ, England.

JONG, Erica Mann, M.A.; American author and poet; b. 26 March 1942, New York; d. of Seymour Mann and Eda (Mirsky) Mann; m. 1st Allan Jong (divorced 1975), 2nd Jonathan Fast 1977 (divorced 1983); one d.; ed. Barnard Coll. and Columbia Univ., New York; mem. Faculty, English Dept. City Univ. of New York 1964–65, 1969–70; Overseas Div. Univ. of Md. 1967–69; mem. Literature Panel, N.Y. State Council on Arts 1972–74; Bess Hokin Prize, Poetry magazine 1971, Alice Faye di Castagnola Award, Poetry Soc. of America 1972; Nat. Endowment Arts grantee 1973. *Publications:* poems: Fruits & Vegetables 1971, Half-Lives 1973, At the Edge of the Body 1979, Ordinary Miracles 1983; novels: Fear of Flying 1973, How to Save Your Own Life 1977, Fanny 1980, Parachutes and Kisses 1984, Serenissima 1987; poetry and non-fiction: Loveroot 1975, Witches 1981; Megan's Book of Divorce (for children) 1984. *Address:* c/o Morton L. Janklow Assocs., 598 Madison Avenue, New York, N.Y. 10022, U.S.A.

JONG, Petrus J. S. de, D.S.C.; Netherlands naval officer and politician; b. 3 April 1915, Apeldoorn; m. Anna Geertriida Jacoba Henriette Bartels; three c.; ed. Royal Naval Coll.; entered Netherlands Royal Navy 1931, commissioned 1934; submarine commdr. during Second World War; Adjutant to Minister for Navy 1948; Capt. of frigate De Zeeuw 1951; Staff Officer on staff Allied Commdr.-in-Chief, Channel, Portsmouth 1953; Adjutant to Queen of Netherlands 1955; Capt. of destroyer Gelderland 1958; State Sec. for Defence 1959–63; Minister of Defence 1963–67; Prime Minister and Minister of Gen. Affairs 1967–71; mem. First Chamber (Parl.) 1971–74; Catholic Party. *Address:* c/o Christian Democratic Appel, The Hague, Netherlands.

JONKISZ, Władysław, D.SC.TECH.; Polish politician; b. 7 June 1939, Stara Wieś, Bielsko-Biała Voivodship; ed. Częstochowa Tech. Univ.; former active leader of Socialist Youth Union (ZMS) including First Sec. ZMS Univ. Cttee. at Częstochowa Tech. Univ., Econ. Sec. of ZMS Voivodship Cttee., Katowice; Asst., then Lecturer of Częstochowa Tech. Univ. 1960–80; mem. Polish United Workers' Party (PZPR) 1960–; First Sec. PZPR Univ. Cttee. at Częstochowa Tech. Univ. until 1977; First Sec. PZPR Voivodship Cttee., Częstochowa 1980–85; alt. mem. PZPR Cen. Cttee. 1981–82, mem. PZPR Cen. Cttee. 1982–; Deputy to Seym (Parl.) 1976–; mem. Council of State Nov. 1985–; Officer's Cross, Order of Polonia Restituta, Gold and Bronze Cross of Merit and other decorations. *Publications:* some 30 papers, numerous research works, co-author of 8 patents. *Address:* Kancelaria Rady Państwa, ul. Wiejska 4/6, 00-902 Warsaw, Poland (Office).

JONSEN, Albert R., M.A., PH.D., S.T.M.; American professor of ethics in medicine; b. 4 April 1931, San Francisco; s. of Albert R. Jonsen and Helen C. Sweigert; m. Mary E. Carolan 1976; ed. Gonzaga Univ., Spokane, Wash., Santa Clara Univ., Calif. and Yale Univ.; Instructor in Philosophy, Loyola Univ. of Los Angeles 1956–59; Instructor in Divinity, Yale Univ. 1966–67; Asst., Assoc. Prof. in Philosophy and Theology, Univ. of San Francisco 1968–73, Pres. 1969–72; Prof. of Ethics in Medicine and Chief, Div. of Medical Ethics, Univ. of Calif., San Francisco 1973–87; Prof. of Ethics in Medicine, Chair. Dept. of Medical History and Ethics, Univ. of Wash., Seattle 1987–; Commr. US Nat. Comm. for Protection of Human Subjects of Biomedical and Behavioral Research 1974–78; Commr. President's Comm. for Study of Ethical Problems in Medicine and in Biomedical and Behavioral Research 1979–82; mem. Nat. Bd. of Medical Examiners 1985–; Consultant American Bd. of Internal Medicine 1978–; mem. N.A.S. Inst. of Medicine; Pres. Soc. for Health and Human Values 1986. *Publications:* Responsibility in Modern Religious Ethics 1968, Ethics of Newborn Intensive Care 1976, Clinical Ethics (with H. Siegler and W. Winslade) 1982, The Abuse of Casuistry (with S. Toulmin) 1986. *Leisure interests:* sketching, swimming, walking, music. *Address:* University of Washington, Seattle, Wash. 98195, U.S.A.

JÓNSSON, Eysteinn; Icelandic politician; b. Djupivogur; s. of Jón Finnson and Sigridur Hansdóttir Beck; m. Sólveig Eyjólfsdóttir 1932; four s. two d.; ed. Co-operative Commercial Coll.; Dir. of Taxes Reykjavík 1930–34; mem. Althing (Parl.) 1933–74; mem. Exec. Bd. Progressive Party 1934–83; Minister of Finance 1934–39, of Commerce 1939–42; Dir. Printwork Edda 1943–47; Chair. Progressive Party Althing Group 1943–69; Minister of Educ. 1947–49, of Finance 1950–58; Leader, Progressive Party 1962–68; mem. Council of Europe 1967–69; mem. Nordic Council 1969–71, Chair. Cultural Cttee. 1969–71; Speaker United Althing 1971–74; Vice-Chair. Fed. of Iceland Co-operative Socs. 1946–74, Chair. 1974–78; Chair. Iceland Nature Conservation Council 1972–78. *Publications:* Selection of Speeches and Articles 1977. *Leisure interests:* skiing, hiking, books. *Address:* Miðleiti 7, Reykjavík, Iceland. *Telephone:* 37127.

JOPE, Edward Martyn, M.A., D.SC., F.S.A., F.B.A.; British professor of archaeology (retd.); b. 28 Dec. 1915, Carshalton, Surrey; s. of Edward M. Jope and Frances M. (née Chapman) Jope; m. Henrietta M. Halliday 1941; no c.; ed. Whitgift Grammar School, Croydon, Kingswood School, Bath and Oriel Coll., Oxford; Investigator, Royal Comm. for Ancient Monuments,

Wales 1938–39; Research Biochemist, Medical Research Council 1939–49; Lecturer, Reader, Prof. of Archaeology, Queen's Univ. Belfast 1949–53, 1963–81; Visiting Prof. in Archaeological Sciences, Bradford Univ. 1973–81, Hon. Visiting Prof. 1982–; Rhys Fellow, Jesus Coll., Oxford 1977–78; Commr. Royal Comm. on Ancient Monuments, Wales 1963–86; other professional appointments. *Publications:* Early Celtic Art in the British Isles (with P. F. Jacobsthal) 1986; ed. of other vols. and articles in professional journals. *Leisure interests:* music, watercolours, travel. *Address:* 1 Chalfont Road, Oxford, England. *Telephone:* (0865) 59024.

JOPLIN, Graham Frank, M.B., CH.B., F.R.C.P., PH.D.; British professor of clinical endocrinology; b. 11 May 1927, Wellington, N.Z.; s. of the late Frank Joplin and Mary Joplin; m. Helen Logan 1959; two s.; ed. Wellington Boys' Coll., Victoria Univ., Wellington and Otago Univ. Medical School, Dunedin; rotating internship Wellington Hosp. 1952–53; Pathology Registrar, Palmerston North Hosp. 1954; House Physician Hammersmith, Cen. Middx., and Brompton Hosps. London 1955–56; Registrar, Sr. Registrar, Hammersmith Hosp. 1957–63, Hon. Consultant Physician 1963–, Sr. Lecturer, Reader, Prof. of Clinical Endocrinology; Wellcome Clinical Research Fellowship 1963–67. *Publications:* approx. 300 research papers on mostly endocrine topics, published in medical journals. *Leisure interests:* gardening, travel. *Address:* Royal Postgraduate Medical School, Hammersmith Hospital, Du Cane Road, London, W12 0HS (Office); Woodview, Warren Road, Kingston, Surrey, KT2 7HN, England (Home). *Telephone:* 01-740 3024 (Office); 01-942 8435 (Home).

JOPLING, Rt. Hon. (Thomas) Michael, P.C., B.SC., M.P.; British politician and farmer; b. 10 Dec. 1930, Ripon, Yorks.; s. of Mark Bellerby Jopling; m. Gail Dickinson 1958; two s.; ed. Cheltenham Coll. and King's Coll., Newcastle upon Tyne; mem. Thirsk Rural Dist. Council 1958–64; Conservative M.P. for Westmorland 1964–83, Westmorland and Lonsdale 1983–; Jt. Sec. Conservative Parl. Agric. Cttee. 1966–70; Parl. Pvt. Sec. to Minister of Agric. 1970–71; an Asst. Govt. Whip 1971–73; Lord Commr. of the Treasury 1973–74; an Opposition Spokesman on Agric. 1974–75, 1976–79; Shadow Minister of Agric. 1975–76; Parl. Sec. to H.M. Treasury and Chief Whip 1979–83; Minister of Agric., Fisheries and Food 1983–87; mem. Nat. Council, Nat. Farmers' Union 1962–64, U.K. Exec., Commonwealth Parl. Asscn. 1974–79, 1987–, Vice-Chair. 1977–79, Int. Exec. 1988–; Hon. Sec. British American Parl. Group 1987–. *Address:* Ainderby Hall, Thirsk, North Yorks.; Clyder Howe Cottage, Windermere, Cumbria, England. *Telephone:* (0845) 567224; (096 62) 2590.

JORDAN, Hamilton (see Jordan, W. H. M.).

JORDAN, (William) Hamilton (McWhorter), B.A.; American politician; b. 21 Sept. 1944, Charlotte, N.C.; s. of Richard and Adelaide Jordan; m. 1st Nancy Jordan (divorced); m. 2nd Dorothy A. Henry 1981; one s.; served in S. Viet-Nam with Int. Voluntary Services 1967–68; Youth Co-ordinator in Jimmy Carter's campaign for Governorship of Ga. 1966, Man. 1970; Campaign Dir. for Nat. Democratic Party Campaign Cttee. 1973–74, for Carter's Pres. Campaign 1975–76, for Carter's re-election campaign 1980; an Asst. to Pres. 1977–81; White House Chief of Staff 1979–81; Distinguished Visiting Fellow, Emory Univ. 1981–82; political commentator Cable News Network 1981–; consultant in Corp. and int. communications 1984–. *Publication:* Crisis: The Last Year of the Carter Presidency 1982. *Address:* Cable News Network Inc., 1050 Techwood Drive, N.W., Atlanta, Ga. 30318, U.S.A.

JORDENS, Joseph Teresa Florent, F.A.H.A., L.PH.; Australian professor; b. 28 June 1925, Belgium; s. of Hubert Constant Jordens and Elisabeth Mertens; m. Ann-Mari Williams 1962; two s. two d.; ed. St. Jozef's Coll. and Univ. of Louvain; Teacher of French and German, Melbourne Church of England Grammar School 1959–61; lecturer, later Sr. lecturer, Dept. of Indian Studies, Univ. of Melbourne 1961–69; Sr. lecturer, Reader in Asian History, A.N.U. 1970–, Head Dept. of Asian History and Civilizations 1980–83, Dean Faculty of Asian Studies 1983–88; Visiting Prof. of Indian Religions, Univ. of Wisconsin at Madison 1968–69; Meyer Foundation Asian Fellow 1967–68, A.N.U. Leverhulme Asian Fellow 1972–. *Publications:* The Generational Gap and Australian-Asian Relations (Ed.) 1969, Dayananda Sarasvati, His Life and Ideas 1978, Swami Shraddhananda, His Life and Causes 1981, numerous articles on ancient and modern Hinduism. *Address:* 155 La Perouse Street, Redhill, A.C.T. 2603, Australia. *Telephone:* 49 33 77 (Univ.); 95 97 68 (Home).

JØRGENSEN, Anker; Danish trade unionist and politician; b. 13 July 1922, Copenhagen; s. of Johannes Jørgensen; m. Ingrid Jørgensen 1948; four c.; ed. School for Orphans and evening classes; messenger, shipyard worker, warehouse worker 1936–50; Vice-Pres. Warehouse Workers' Union 1950, Pres. 1958–62; Group Sec. Transport and Gen. Workers' Union 1962–68, Pres. 1968–72; mem. Folketing (Parl.) 1964–; mem. Social Dem. Union 1966; mem. Bd. of Dirs., Workers' Bank of Denmark 1969–; Prime Minister 1972–73; Parl. Leader, Social Democratic Group 1973–75; Prime Minister 1975–82; Chair. Social Democratic Party, Social Democratic Parl. Group 1982–87. *Address:* Borgbjergvej 1, 2450 S.V. Copenhagen, Denmark.

JØRGENSEN, Bo Barker, PH.D.; Danish biologist; b. 22 Sept. 1946, Copenhagen; s. of Carl C. B. Jørgensen and Vibeke Balslev Smidt; m. Inga M. Vestergaard 1971; two s. one d.; ed. Univs. of Copenhagen and Aarhus; lecturer, Dept. of Ecology and Genetics, Univ. of Aarhus 1973–77, Sr.

lecturer 1977–87, Prof. 1987–; research, Marine Biology Lab., Eilat, Israel 1974, 1978, NASA–ARC, Moffett Field, Calif. 1984–85. *Publications:* about 70 scientific publs. in int. journals in the field of ecology, microbiology and geochemistry. *Leisure interests:* photography, music. *Address:* Tranebaerkaeret 3, 8220 Braband, Denmark. *Telephone:* 6-263123.

JORGENSEN, Erling; Danish banker; b. 1931; Prin. Asst. Statistical Dept., Ministry of Econs. 1953–63; Head of Research., Inst. of Applied Social Research 1963–69; Head of Section, Head of Dept., Central Statistical Office 1969–75; Perm. Sec., Ministry of Finance 1975–88; Pres. Bd. Dirs., Kongeriget Danmarks Hypotekbank og Finansforvaltning 1975–78; teacher, examiner of Macroeconomics, Univ. of Copenhagen 1957–88; Dir. School of Public Admin. Studies 1983–86; mem. Bd. Dirs. Dansk Olie og Naturgas A/S 1983–88, OECD's Econ. Policy Cttee. 1975–78; mem. Bd. Dirs., European Investment Bank 1986–88, Vice-Pres. 1988–. *Address:* c/o European Investment Bank, 100 blvd. Konrad Adenauer, 2950 Luxembourg.

JØRGENSEN, Sven-Aage, M.A.; Danish professor of German philology; b. 22 July 1929, Herstedvester; s. of Aage Julius Jørgensen and Emma Lydia (née Eriksen) Jørgensen; m. Elli Andresen 1957 (divorced 1985); two s. one d.; ed. Birkerød Statsskole, Univ. of Copenhagen, Univ. of Würzburg and Warburg Inst., London; lecturer Univ. of Copenhagen 1961, Prof. of German Philology 1968–; Research Prof. Univ. of Bielefeld 1980–81; Visiting Prof. Heidelberg 1973, Regensburg 1985, Kiel 1986; Visiting Fellow A.N.U. 1975; mem. Royal Danish Acad. of Sciences and Letters 1986; Univ. Gold Medal 1957. *Publications:* J. G. Hamann's Fünf Hirtenbriefe 1962, J. G. Hamann's Sokratische Denkwurdigeiten und AESTHETICA IN NUCE 1962, J. G. Hamann 1976, numerous articles. *Leisure interests:* jogging, swimming. *Address:* Institut for germansk filologi, Københavns universitet, Njalsgade 80, Tr. 16, 2300 Copenhagen S., Denmark. *Telephone:* 01 54 22 11.

JORGENSON, Dale W., PH.D.; American economist; b. 7 May 1933, Bozeman, Mont.; s. of Emmett B. Jorgenson and Jewell T. Jorgenson; m. Linda Ann Mabus 1971; one s. one d.; ed. Reed Coll. and Harvard Univ.; Asst. Prof. of Econs. Univ. of Calif., Berkeley 1959–61, Assoc. Prof. 1961–63, Prof. 1963–69; Prof. of Econs. Harvard Univ. 1969–80, Frederic Eaton Abbe Prof. of Econs. 1980–; Dir. Program on Tech. and Econ. Policy, Kennedy School of Govt., Harvard Univ. 1984–; Visiting Prof. of Econs. Hebrew Univ., Jerusalem 1967, Stanford Univ. 1973; Visiting Prof. of Statistics Oxford Univ. 1968; Consulting Ed., North-Holland Publishing Co., Amsterdam, Netherlands 1970–; Fellow, A.A.A.S., American Acad. of Arts and Sciences, American Statistical Asscn., Econometric Soc. (Pres. 1987); mem. N.A.S., American Econ. Asscn., Royal Econ. Soc., Econ. Study Soc., Conf. on Research in Income and Wealth, Int. Assn. for Research in Income and Wealth; several fellowships including Nat. Science Foundation Snr. Postdoctoral Fellowship, Netherlands School of Econs., Rotterdam 1967–68; lectures include Shinzo Koizumi, Keio Univ., Tokyo, Japan 1972, Fisher-Schultz, 3rd World Congress, Econometric Soc. 1975, Frank Paish, Assn. of Univ. Teachers of Econs. Conf., U.K. 1980; prizes include John Bates Clark Medal, American Econ. Assn. 1971. *Publications:* Technology and Economic Policy (with R. Landau) 1986, over 150 papers and contribs. to learned journals and collections of essays. *Address:* Dept. of Economics, Harvard University, Cambridge, Mass. 02138 (Office); 1010 Memorial Drive, 14C Cambridge, Mass. 02138, U.S.A. (Home). *Telephone:* (617) 495-0833 (Office); (617) 491-4069 (Home).

JORTNER, Joshua, PH.D.; Israeli professor of physical chemistry; b. 14 March 1933, Poland; s. of Arthur Jortner and Regina Jortner; m. Ruth (née Sanger) Jortner 1960; one s. one d.; ed. Hebrew Univ. of Jerusalem; Instructor Dept. of Physical Chemistry, Hebrew Univ. of Jerusalem 1961–62, Sr. lecturer 1963–65; Research Assoc. Univ. of Chicago 1962–64; Assoc. Prof. of Physical Chem., Tel-Aviv Univ. 1965–66, Prof. 1966–, Head Inst. of Chem. 1966–72, Deputy Rector 1966, Vice-Pres. 1970–72, Heinemann Prof. of Chem. 1973–; Visiting Prof. H.C. Orsted Inst., Univ. of Copenhagen 1974, Visiting Prof. of Chem. 1978; Visiting Prof. UCLA-Berkeley 1975; Vice-Pres. Israeli Acad. of Sciences and Humanities 1980–86, Pres. 1986–; Int. Acad. of Quantum Science Award 1972, Weizmann Prize 1973, Rothschild Prize 1976, Kolthof Prize 1976, Israel Prize in Chem. 1982, Wolf Prize 1988. *Publications:* Intramolecular Radiationless Transitions (with M. Bixon) 1968, Molecular Crystals (with M. Bixon) 1969, Electronic Relaxation in Large Molecules (with M. Bixon) 1969, Long Radiative Lifetimes of Small Molecules (with M. Bixon) 1969, The Jerusalem Symposia on Quantum Chemistry and Biochemistry (Ed. with Bernard Pullman) Vols. 15-21 1982–87. *Leisure interests:* reading, writing. *Address:* Israel Academy of Sciences and Humanities, P.O. Box 4040, Jerusalem 91 040, Israel. *Telephone:* (02) 636 211.

JORY, Edward John, PH.D.; British/Australian professor of classics; b. 20 June 1936, England; s. of E. Jory; m. Marie McGee 1965; three s.; ed. Humphry Davy Grammar School, Penzance and Univ. Coll., London; lecturer Dept. of Classics and Ancient History Univ. of Western Australia 1959–65, Sr. Lecturer 1966–73, Assoc. Prof. 1974–78, Dean of Faculty of Arts 1976–79, Prof. and Head of Dept. 1979–84, 1988–; Fellow Australian Acad. of Humanities. *Publications:* contrib. to Corpus Inscriptionum Latinarum 1974. *Leisure interests:* cricket, skin diving, golf. *Address:* 36 Marita Road, Nedlands, 6009 W. Australia. *Telephone:* 386-2714.

JOSEPH, Cedric Luckie, M.A.; Guyanese diplomatist; b. 14 May 1933, Georgetown; s. of Frederick McConnell Joseph (deceased) and Cassie Edith Joseph, née Austin; m. Dona Avril Barrett 1973; two s. (adopted); ed. L.S.E., Univ. Coll. of Wales, Aberystwyth; taught history at a London Comprehensive School 1962-66; Lecturer in History, Univ. of the W. Indies, Kingston, Jamaica 1966-71; Prin. Asst. Sec., Ministry of Foreign Affairs, Guyana 1971-74; Deputy High Commr. for Guyana in Jamaica 1974-76, Counsellor, Embassy of Guyana, Washington, D.C. 1976, Deputy Perm. Rep., Perm. Mission of Guyana to the UN 1976-77; High Commr. for Guyana in Zambia (also accred. to Angola, Botswana, Mozambique, Tanzania and Zimbabwe) 1977-82, in the U.K. (also accred. as Ambassador to France, the Netherlands, Yugoslavia and UNESCO) 1982-86; Chair. Commonwealth Cttee. on Southern Africa 1983-86, Head of the Presidential Secretariat 1986-, Sec. to the Cabinet 1987-; Cacique's Crown of Honour 1983. *Publications:* three articles in Caribbean journals. *Leisure interests:* tennis, walking. *Address:* Office of the President, Vlissengen Road, Georgetown, Guyana. *Telephone:* 02-57051.

JOSEPH, Baron (Life Peer), cr. 1987, of Portsoken in the City of London; **Keith Sinjohn,** Bt., P.C., M.P.; British politician; b. 17 Jan. 1918, London; s. of the late Sir Samuel George Joseph and the late Edna Cicely Phillips; m. Hellen Louise Guggenheimer 1951 (separated 1978); one s. three d.; ed. Harrow School and Magdalen Coll., Oxford; mil. service 1939-46; Barrister, Middle Temple 1946; Councilman, City of London 1946, Alderman 1946-49; fmr. Underwriter, Lloyd's; Dir. Bovis Holdings Ltd. 1951-59, Chair. Bovis Ltd. 1958-59, Deputy Chair. 1964-70, Consultant 1986-; M.P. for Leeds North-East 1956-87; Parl. Private Sec. to Parl. Under-Sec. of State, Commonwealth Relations Office 1957-59; Parl. Sec. Ministry of Housing and Local Govt. 1959-61; Minister of State, Bd. of Trade 1961-62; Minister of Housing and Local Govt. and Minister for Welsh Affairs 1962-64; Sec. of State for Social Services 1970-74; Shadow Spokesman for Industry 1977-79; Sec. of State for Industry 1979-81, of Educ. and Science 1981-86; Founder and Chair. Man. Cttee. of Centre for Policy Studies Ltd. 1974-79; part-time consultant Bovis Ltd. 1986-, Cable and Wireless PLC 1986-, Trusthouse Forte PLC 1986-; Fellow, All Souls' Coll., Oxford 1946-60, 1971-; Conservative. *Publication:* Equality 1979. *Address:* 63 Limerston Street, Chelsea, London, SW10 0BL, England.

JOSEPHS, Wilfred, B.D.S.; British composer; b. 24 July 1927; s. of Philip Josephs and Rachel (née Block) Josephs; m. Valerie Wisbey 1956; two d.; ed. Rutherford Coll. Boys' School, Newcastle upon Tyne, Univ. of Durham at Newcastle, Guildhall School of Music and studied composition in Paris with Max Deutsch as Leverhulme Scholar; army service 1951-53; abandoned dentistry to become full-time composer; works include ten symphonies, many film and TV scores and themes including music for I, Claudius, Cider with Rosie, All Creatures Great and Small, Swallows and Amazons, The Brontë Series, The Somerset Maugham Series, Horizon, The Norman Conquests, The Hunchback of Notre Dame, The Voyage of Charles Darwin, People Like Us, Churchill and the Generals, Pride and Prejudice, A Walk in the Dark, The Moles, The Making of Britain, A Married Man, The Gay Lord Quex, The Return of the Antelope, Redbrick, Drummonds, Evil, Art of the Western World; feature films include: Swallows and Amazons, All Creatures Great and Small, The Uncanny, This is Callan, Martin's Day, Mata Hari, Pope John Paul II; also a TV opera, The Appointment, a stage opera Rebecca, children's operas and children's musical, King of the Coast (Guardian/Arts Council Prize 1969) and numerous other works; Hon. D.Mus. (Newcastle) 1978; Harriet Cohen Commonwealth Medal (for 1st quartet); First Prize, La Scala, Milan for Requiem 1963; mem. Inc. Soc. of Musicians, Composers' Guild of G.B. and other orgs; Music Consultant London Int. Film School. *Leisure interests:* writing music, swimming, reading, opera, theatre and films. *Address:* 15 Douglas Court, Quex Road, London, NW6 4PT, England. *Telephone:* 01-625 8917.

JOSEPHSON, Brian David, PH.D., F.INST.P., F.R.S.; British physicist; b. 4 Jan. 1940, Cardiff; s. of Abraham and Mimi Josephson; m. Carol Anne Olivier 1976; one d.; ed. Cardiff High School, Cambridge Univ.; Fellow, Trinity Coll., Cambridge 1962-; Research Asst. Prof. Univ. of Illinois 1965-66; Asst. Dir. of Research, Cambridge Univ. 1967-72, Reader in Physics 1972-74, Prof. of Physics 1974-; faculty mem. Maharishi European Research Univ. 1975; Hon. mem. Inst. of Electrical and Electronic Engineers; Foreign Hon. mem. American Acad. of Arts and Sciences; New Scientist Award 1969, Research Corpn. Award 1969, Fritz London Award 1970, Hughes Medal Royal Soc. 1972, shared Nobel Prize for Physics 1973. *Publications:* Co-ed. Consciousness and the Physical World 1980; research papers on superconductivity, critical phenomena, theory of intelligence, science and mysticism. *Leisure interests:* walking, ice skating, photography, astronomy. *Address:* Cavendish Laboratory, Madingley Road, Cambridge, CB3 0HE, England. *Telephone:* (0223) 66477.

JOSEPHSON, Erland; Swedish actor and theatre director; b. 15 June 1923; at Municipal Theatre, Helsingborg 1945-49, Gothenburg 1949-56, Royal Dramatic Theatre, Stockholm 1956-; Dir. of Royal Dramatic Theatre, Stockholm 1966-75. *Film appearances include:* Montenegro 1981, Fanny and Alexander 1983, After the Rehearsal 1984, The Unbearable Lightness of Being 1988, Hanussen 1989. *Publications include:* Cirkel 1946, Spegeln

och en portvakt 1946, Spel med bedrövade artister 1947, Ensam och fri 1948, Lyssnarpost 1949, De vuxna barnen 1952, Utflykt 1954, Sällskapslek 1955, En berättelse om herr Silberstein 1957, Kungen ur leken 1959, Doktor Meyers sista dagar 1964, Kandidat Nilssons första natt 1964, Lejon i Övergångsåldern (pjas Dromaten) 1981. *Address:* c/o Royal Dramatic Theatre, Nybroplan, Box 5037, 102 41 Stockholm, Sweden.

JOSHI, Damayanti, B.A.; Indian classical dancer; b. 5 Dec. 1932, Bombay; d. of Ramchandra Joshi and Mrs. Vatsala Joshi; ed. numerous Schools of Classical Dancing; leading exponent of Kathak Dance; has choreographed numerous productions, holding dance seminars throughout India and touring extensively in Asia, Africa and Europe; acts as examiner in music and dance for numerous Indian univs.; holds numerous public service posts connected with the dance; Chair. Dancers' Guild, Bombay; Life mem. numerous dance socs.; Visiting Prof. IndiraKala Sangeet Vishwavidyalaya, Khairagarh, also conducts teachers' workshops; has performed before Heads of State of Nepal, Afghanistan, U.S.S.R., Laos, Yugoslavia, Indonesia, Philippines, Mexico; TV appearances and film Damayanti Joshi on Kathak Dance; lecture demonstrations in G.B., Germany, China and India. *Publications:* Madame Menaka (monograph), articles for art magazines, weeklies, dailies. *Leisure interests:* reading, writing, sitar. *Address:* D-1, Jeshtharam Baug, Ground Floor, Dadar, Bombay 400014, India. *Telephone:* 4306589.

JOSHI, Harideo; Indian politician; b. 17 Dec. 1921, Khandu, Banswara Dist., Rajasthan; s. of Pannalal Joshi and Kamala Devi; m. Subhadra Joshi; two s. one d.; active in political movts. 1942-46; Pres. Rajasthan PCC 1952; mem. Ass.1952-77, 1980-; Chief Whip, Congress Party 1957-63; Minister for Mines, Industries, State Enterprises and Irrigation 1965-72, for Medicine and Health, Public Works, Power and Transport 1972-73; Chief Minister 1973-77; Chief Minister of Rajasthan 1985-87; fmr. Ed. Navyug, Jaipur. *Address:* Raj Bhavan Jaipur, Rajasthan, India.

JOSIC, Alexis; French architect; b. 24 May 1921, Stari Becej, Yugoslavia; s. of Mladen Josic and Asia Petrova; m. Douchanka Ivanovic 1961; two s.; ed. Nat. Fine Art School, Josic Fine Art School, Grate Tech. School, Belgrade; architect, Ministry of Construction, Belgrade 1945-47; Prof. of Painting, Josic Fine Art School, Belgrade 1946-47; scenographer, Nat. Movie Industry, Belgrade 1948-50; architect, Atelier des Bâtisseurs (ATBAT), Paris 1953-54; partner in architectural practice, Atelier Candilis, Josic, Woods, Paris 1955-63, in private practive, Sèvres 1963-; Prof. of Architecture, Fine Art School of Paris 1961-64, Faculty of Architecture, Unité Pédagogique 5, Paris 1971-74; French Govt. First Prize in town planning 1959, 1st Prize, Toulouse le Mirail new town competition 1960, Gold Medal for Architecture, Soc. for the Encouragement of Arts and Industry, France 1974. *Leisure interests:* talking with friends. *Address:* 5 rue Carle Vernet, 92310 Sèvres, France. *Telephone:* 45 34 80 00.

JOSPIN, Lionel Robert; French politician; b. 12 July 1937, Meudon, Hauts-de-Seine; s. of Robert Jospin and Mireille Dandieu; m. Elisabeth Dannenmüller, 1973; one s. one d.; ed. École nat. d'administration; Sec. Ministry of Foreign Affairs 1965-70; Prof. Econ. Inst. universitaire de tech. de Paris-Sceaux, also attached to Univ. de Paris XL 1970-81; Nat. Sec. Socialist Party, mem. steering cttee. 1973-75, spokesman on Third World Affairs 1975-79, Int. Relations 1979-81, First Sec. 1981-; Councillor for Paris (18e arrondissement) 1977-86; Socialist Deputy to Nat. Ass. for Paris (27e circ.) 1981-86, for Haute-Garonne 1986-88; Minister of Nat. Educ., Research and Sport May 1988-. *Leisure interest:* basketball. *Address:* Assemblée Nationale, 75355 Paris; Parti socialiste, 10 rue de Solférino, 75007 Paris, France (Offices).

JOUKHDAR, Mohammed Saleh, M.A.; Saudi Arabian economist; b. 1932, Jeddah; m. Malik Intabi 1957; one s. two d.; ed. Univs. of California and Southern California; Econ. Adviser to Directorate-Gen. of Petroleum and Minerals, Saudi Arabia 1958; Dir.-Gen. Ministry of Petroleum and Mineral Resources 1961; Dir. Arabian Oil Co. 1961-66; Sec.-Gen. of OPEC 1967-68; Deputy Minister of Petroleum and Mineral Resources 1969; Dir. PETROMIN 1970-73; Amb. in Charge of Petroleum and Econ. Desk, Ministry of Foreign Affairs 1973-74; on leave of absence as petroleum consultant 1974-; mem. American Soc. of Economists; Trustee, Coll. of Petroleum and Minerals. *Address:* c/o Ministry of Petroleum and Mineral Resources, P.O. Box 247, Riyadh, Saudi Arabia.

JOUVEN, Pierre Jean Antoine; French industrialist; b. 29 March 1908, Paris; s. of Alphonse Jouven and Jeanne Bouhey; m. Madeleine Huguet 1931; three s. three d.; ed. Ecole Polytech. and Ecole des Mines, Paris; Engineer, Corps des Mines 1931-42; with Compagnie Pechiney, Paris 1943-72, Chair. of Bd. 1968-72; Chair. Pechiney Ugine Kuhlmann 1972-75, Hon. Pres. 1975-; Chair. Int. Primary Aluminium Inst. 1972-74; Pres. Fondation Franco-Americaine 1976-81, now Hon. Pres.; Commdr. Légion d'honneur, Grand Officier, Ordre nat. du Mérite. *Address:* 34 rue Guynemer, 75006 Paris, France (Home). *Telephone:* 45-48-01-98.

JOVA, Joseph John, A.B.; American international official; b. 7 Nov. 1916, Newburgh, N.Y.; s. of Joseph Luis and Maria Josefa (Gonzalez-Cavada) Jova; m. Pamela Johnson 1949; two s. one d.; ed. Dartmouth Coll.; with Guatemala Div. United Fruit Co. 1938-41; mil. service U.S. Navy 1942-47; foreign service officer, Dept. of State 1947-77; Vice-Consul, Basra 1947-49; Second Sec. and Vice-Consul, Tangier 1949-52; Consul, Oporto 1952-54;

First Sec., Lisbon 1954–57; Officer-in-Charge French-Iberian Affairs 1957–58; Asst. Chief Personnel Operations Div. 1959–60, Chief 1960–61; Deputy Chief of Mission, Santiago 1961–65; Amb. to Honduras 1965–69; Amb. to OAS, Washington 1969–74; Amb. to Mexico 1974–77; Chair. Dept. of State Man. Reform Task Force; Chair. U.S. dels to Inter-American Council on Educ., Science and Culture, Panama 1972, Mar del Plata 1973, UN Econ. Comm. for Latin America, Santiago 1971, UN Econ. Comm. for Latin American Population Conf., Mexico 1974; Chair. Int. America Cttee. on Culture 1983–; Vice-Chair. U.S. del. to Gen. Assembly OAS 1970, 1971, 1972, 1973; Pres. Meridian House Int. 1977–; Dir. First American Bank of Washington; Chair. Hispanic Council on Foreign Affairs; mem. Mexican Acad. of Int. Law and several other American and foreign academic insts.; LL.D. (Dowling Coll.) 1973; Grand Cross Order Morazán (Honduras), Constantinian Order St. George, Order of the Aztec Eagle (Mexico), Grand Cross Order of Isobel la Catolica, Commdr. Oranje-Nassau (Netherlands), Knight of Malta. *Publications:* Private Investment in Latin America—Renegotiating the Bargain, Hispanic Americans and U.S. Independence, Art as a Tool of Diplomacy, Galvez and the Hispanic Contribution to U.S. Independence and various other works. *Address:* Meridian House International, 1630 Crescent Place N.W., Washington, D.C. 20009; 1336 31st Street N.W., Washington, D.C. 20007, U.S.A. (Home). *Telephone:* (202) 667-6800.

JOVANOVICH, William Iliya; American publisher; b. 6 Feb. 1920, Louisville, Colo.; s. of Iliya M. and Hedviga (Garbatz) Jovanovich; m. Martha Evelyn Davis 1943; ed. Univ. of Colorado and Harvard and Columbia Univs.; Harcourt Brace Jovanovich, Inc., New York 1947–, Assoc. Ed. 1947–53, Vice-Pres. 1953–54, Pres. 1955–70, Chair. and C.E.O. 1970–, Dir. 1953–; Chair. Longmans Canada Ltd. 1961; Regent, State of N.Y. 1974–77; D.Litt. (Colo. Coll., Adelphi Univ., Alaska Univ.) *Publications:* Now, Barabbas 1964, Madmen Must 1978. *Address:* 757 Third Avenue, New York, N.Y. 10017, U.S.A. (Office).

JOXE, Louis, L. ÈS L.; French diplomatist and politician; b. 16 Sept. 1901; m. Françoise-Hélène Halévy 1926; three s. one d.; ed. Lycée Lakanal and Faculty of Arts, Paris; mem. French del. League of Nations 1932, 1933, 1939; Deputy Chief of Secr. to Minister for Air and mem. French del. to Conf. for Reduction of Armaments 1933–34; attached to Information Service, League of Nations 1933–39; Sec.-Gen. Centre d'Etudes de Politique Etrangère, Paris Univ.; Insp. of Foreign Services, Agence d'Information 1935–39; Sec.-Gen. of Cttee. for Nat. Liberation 1943–44; Sec.-Gen. of Govt. 1944–46, Councillor of State 1944; in charge of cultural relations Ministry of Foreign Affairs, Paris 1946–52; Amb. to U.S.S.R. 1952–55, to Germany 1955–56; Sec.-Gen. Ministry of Foreign Affairs 1956–59; Sec. of State, Prime Minister's Office 1959–60; Minister of Nat. Educ. Jan.-Nov. 1960; Minister of State in charge of Algerian Affairs 1960–62, for French Admin. Reform 1962–67; Minister of Justice 1967–68; elected Deputy for Rhône, Nat. Assembly 1967, 1968, 1973; mem. French del. to UNESCO Conf. 1946, 1947, 1949, 1950, 1951; mem. Conseil Constitutionnel 1977–; Ambassadeur de France; Commdr. Légion d'honneur, Médaille de la Résistance. *Publication:* Victoires sur la nuit (mémoires) 1981. *Address:* 39 quai de l'Horloge, 75001 Paris, France.

JOXE, Pierre Daniel, L. EN D.; French politician; b. 28 Nov. 1934, Paris; s. of Louis Joxe (q.v.) and Françoise-Hélène Halevy; m. Valérie Cayeux 1981; two s. two d. from previous marriage; ed. Lycée Henri IV, Faculté de droit and Ecole Nat. d'Admin.; Mil. Service 1958–60; Auditor, later Counsellor Cour des Comptes; mem. Exec. Bureau and Exec. Cttee., Socialist Party 1971–; Deputy for Saône and Loire 1973, 1978, 1981, 1986, 1988; Minister of Industry and Admin. May–June 1981, of the Interior, Decentralization and Admin. July 1984 and March 1986, of the Interior May 1988–; mem. European Parl. 1977–79; Pres. Regional Council, Burgundy 1979–82, Socialist Parl. Group 1981–84, 1986–88. *Address:* Ministry of the Interior, Place Beauvau, 75800 Paris, France. *Telephone:* (1) 45 22 90 90.

JOYCE, Eileen, C.M.G.; Australian concert pianist; b. Zeehan, Tasmania; d. of Joseph and Alice Joyce; ed. Loreto Convent, Perth, Leipzig Conservatoire, studied in Germany under Teichmuller and Schnabel; concert début, London, at Promenade Concerts under Sir Henry Wood; numerous concert tours, radio performances and gramophone recordings; during Second World War played in asscn. with London Philharmonic Orchestra; concerts with all prin. orchestras in U.K., Berlin Philharmonic Orchestra, Conservatoire and Nat. Orchestras, France, Concertgebouw Orchestra, Netherlands, La Scala Orchestra, Italy, Philadelphia Orchestra, Carnegie Hall, New York and Royal Philharmonic Soc.; concert tours, Australia 1948, S. Africa 1950, Scandinavia and Netherlands 1951, S. America, Scandinavia and Finland 1952, Yugoslavia 1953, N.Z. 1958, U.S.S.R. 1961, India 1962; contributed to sound tracks of films, including The Seventh Veil and Brief Encounter; appeared in films, including Wherever She Goes (autobiographical); gramophone recordings include first recording of John Ireland's Pianoforte Concerto; Hon. D.Mus. (Cambridge) 1971, (Univ. of Western Australia) 1979, (Melbourne) 1982. *Address:* White Hart Lodge, High Street, Limpsfield, Oxted, Surrey, RH8 0DT, England.

JÓŹWIAK, Jerzy, M.A.; Polish politician; b. 28 Jan. 1937, Tarnowskie Góry, Katowice Voivodship; s. of Stanisław Jóźwiak and Maria Jóźwiak; ed. Jagellonian Univ., Cracow; Legal Adviser of Food Industry Plants, Ruda Śląska 1960–61; mem. Democratic Party (SD) 1960–, Sec. SD Town Cttee.,

Chorzów 1962–69; Deputy Chair. Presidium of Municipal Nat. Council, Chorzów 1969–73; Chair. SD Town Cttee., Chorzów and Deputy Chair. SD Voivodship Cttee., Katowice 1973–76; Deputy Mayor of Chorzów 1973–75, of Katowice 1975–76; Sec. SD Voivodship Cttee., Katowice 1976–78; Deputy Voivode of Katowice Voivodship 1978–80; mem. Presidium SD Cen. Cttee. 1976–81, Chair. SD Voivodship Cttee., Katowice 1980–85, mem. Presidium SD Cen. Cttee. 1985–, and Sec. SD Cen. Cttee. 1985–86; Minister of Home Trade and Services 1985–87, Minister of Home Market 1987–88; Deputy to Seym (Parl.) 1976–85, fmr. Chair. Seym Comm. of Home Trade, Small Industries and Services; Commdr.'s Cross of Order of Polonia Restituta and other decorations. *Address:* c/o Ministerstwo Rynku, Pl. Wewnętrznego, Powstańców Warszawy 1, 00-030 Warsaw, Poland (Office).

JUAN, H.R.H. Prince, Count of Barcelona; b. 20 June 1913; m. H.R.H. Doña María de las Mercedes de Borbón y Orleans 1935; father of Juan Carlos (q.v.), King of Spain; went into exile with his father King Alfonso April 1931; recognized as King of Spain by his father 1941, renounced right to Spanish throne 1977. *Address:* Guisando 25, Ciudad Puerta de Hierro, Madrid 28035, Spain. *Telephone:* 209-1744.

JUAN CARLOS I, King of Spain; b. 5 Jan. 1938, Rome; s. of H.R.H. Don Juan de Borbón y Battenberg, Count of Barcelona (q.v.), and H.R.H. Doña María de las Mercedes de Borbón y Orleans, and grandson of King Alfonso XIII and Queen Victoria Eugenia of Spain; m. Princess Sophia, d. of the late King Paul of the Hellenes and of Queen Frederica, 1962; heir, Crown Prince Felipe, b. Dec. 1968; daughters Princess Elena, Princess Cristina; ed. privately in Fribourg (Switzerland), Madrid, San Sebastián, Inst. of San Isidro, Madrid, Colegio del Carmen, Gen. Mil. Acad., Zaragoza and Univ. of Madrid; spent childhood in Rome, Lausanne, Estoril and Madrid; commissioned into the three armed forces and undertook training in each of them 1957–59; has studied the organization and activities of various govt. ministries; named by Gen. Franco as future King of Spain 1969, inaugurated as King of Spain 22 Nov. 1975, named as 'Capt.-Gen. of the Armed Forces Nov. 1975; Foreign mem. Académie des sciences morales et politiques, Assoc. mem. 1988; Charlemagne Prize 1982, Bolivar Prize (UNESCO) 1983; Nansen Medal 1987; Dr. h.c. (Strasbourg Univ.) 1979, (Univ. of Madrid), (Harvard Univ.) 1984, (Sorbonne) 1985, (Oxford) 1986, (Trinity, Dublin) 1986, (Bologna) 1988. *Address:* Palacio de la Zarzuela, Madrid, Spain.

JUBANY ARNÁU, H.E. Cardinal Narciso, D.C.N.L.; Spanish ecclesiastic; b. 12 Aug. 1916, Sta. Coloma, Gerona; ordained 1939; Auxiliary Bishop of Barcelona 1955; Bishop of Gerona 1964–71; Archbishop of Barcelona 1971–; cr. Cardinal 1973; Pres. Episcopal Comm. on Liturgy; mem. Sacred Congregation for Divine Worship. *Address:* Calle Obispo Irurita 5, Barcelona 2, Spain. *Telephone:* 218-37-34.

JUCKER, Hans, D.SC.; Swiss business executive; b. 1927, Riehen, Basle; ed. Fed. Polytechnic, Zürich and Univ. of London; chemical research, Ciba Co., Basle; later head of research at two Swiss precision instrument cos.; Head of Research Alusuisse 1969; Chief Exec. Lonza (subsidiary of Alusuisse), Basle 1974; Chief Exec. Alusuisse 1986–. *Address:* Alusuisse, Feldegstrasse 4, 8034 Zürich, Switzerland.

JUDD, Donald Clarence, B.S., M.F.A.; American artist; b. 3 June 1928, Excelsior Springs, Missouri; s. of Roy and Effie Judd; m. (divorced); one s. one d.; ed. Coll. of William and Mary, Williamsburg, Columbia Univ., Art Students League, New York; Critic for Arts Magazine 1959–65; numerous one-man exhbns. including Panoras Gallery 1957, Whitechapel Art Gallery 1970, Kunsthalle Bern 1976, Leo Castelli Gallery, New York 1981, Blum Helman Gallery, New York 1983, Paula Cooper Gallery 1985, 1986; numerous group exhbns. *Address:* P.O. Box 218, Marfa, Tex. 79843, U.S.A.

JUDGE, Thomas Lee; American state governor; b. 12 Oct. 1934, Helena, Mont.; s. of Thomas P. Judge and Blanche Gulliot; m. Carol Anderson 1966; two s.; ed. Univs. of Notre Dame and Louisville; Second Lieut. U.S. Army 1958; Advertising Exec. Louisville Courier Journal 1959–60; Pres. Judge Advertising 1960–73; State Rep. Lewis and Clark County 1960–66, State Senator 1967–68; Lieut.-Gov. of Montana 1968–72, Gov. 1973–81; Man. Partner Mountain States Man. Co. 1981–; Democrat. *Leisure interests:* skiing, hunting, fishing, reading. *Address:* Box 503, Helena, Mont. U.S.A. *Telephone:* (051) 327-3221.

JUGNAUTH, Rt. Hon. Aneerood, P.C., Q.C.; Mauritian lawyer and politician; b. 29 March 1930, Palma; m. Sarojini Devi Ballah; one s. one d.; ed. Church of England School, Palma, Regent Coll., Lincoln's Inn, London; called to Bar 1954; won seat on Legis. Ass., Mauritius 1963; Minister of State and Devt. 1965–67, of Labour 1967; Dist. Magistrate 1967; Crown Counsel and Sr. Crown Counsel 1971; co-founder and Pres. Mouvement Militant Mauricien with Paul Bérenger (q.v.) Dec. 1971–; Leader of Opposition 1976; Prime Minister of Mauritius June 1982–, also Minister of Finance 1983–84, also of Defence and Internal Security, Interior, Information, External Relations and Institutional Reform; Q.C. 1980. *Leisure interests:* football, swimming. *Address:* Government House, Port Louis; La Caverne No. 1, Vacoas, Mauritius. *Telephone:* 011001 (Office).

JUHÁR, Dr. Zoltán; Hungarian politician; b. 19 Jan. 1930, Hernádnémeti; ed. Karl Marx Univ. of Political Economy, Budapest; held positions at Budapest Tech. Univ.; worked in dept. of Marxism-Leninism, Ministry of Educ. and Bldg. Industry Mechanization Trust 1952-56; secondary school teacher 1957; joined Ministry of Internal Trade and worked consecutively as sr. exec., head of dept. and leader of the chief dept. for Int. Co-operation and Goods Exchange; Deputy Minister of Internal Trade 1969, Sec. of State 1976, Minister 1982-87; mem. nat. bd. Hungarian–Soviet Friendship Soc.; Pres. Nat. Council of Tourism; Amb. to Australia 1988-. *Address:* Hungarian Embassy, 79 Hopetoun Circuit, Yarralumla, A.C.T. 2600, Australia.

JULESZ, Bela, PH.D.; American experimental psychologist and business executive; b. 19 Feb. 1928, Budapest, Hungary; s. of Jeno Julesz and Klementin Fleiner; m. Margit Fasy 1953; ed. Tech. Univ. Budapest and Hungarian Acad. of Sciences; Asst. Prof. Dept. of Communication, Tech. Univ. Budapest 1950-51; mem. tech. staff, Telecommunication Research Inst. Budapest 1951-56; mem. tech. staff, Bell Labs, Murray Hill, N.J. 1956-64, head, sensory and perceptual processes 1964-83; research head, visual perception research, AT & T Bell Labs. Murray Hill, N.J. 1984-; Visiting Prof. Dept. of Biology Calif. Inst. of Tech. 1985-; Fellow, American Acad. of Arts and Sciences, A.A.A.S.; mem. N.A.S.; corresp. mem. Göttingen Acad.; hon. mem. Hungarian Acad.; H.P. Heineken prize, Royal Netherlands Acad. of Arts and Sciences 1985. *Publications:* Foundations of Cyclopean Perception; 140 scientific papers on visual perception. *Address:* AT & T Bell Laboratories, 600 Mountain Avenue, Murray Hill, N.J. 07974-2070, U.S.A. *Telephone:* 201-582-3000.

JULIANA Louise Emma Marie Wilhelmina, H.R.H., former Queen of the Netherlands; Princess of the Netherlands, Princess of Orange-Nassau, Duchess of Mecklenburg, Princess of Lippe-Biesterfeld; b. 30 April 1909; daughter of Queen Wilhelmina and Prince Henry of Mecklenburg-Schwerin; married Prince Bernhard of Lippe-Biesterfeld 1937; daughters Princess Beatrix Wilhelmina Armgard (now Queen Beatrix, q.v.), b. Jan. 1938, Princess Irene Emma Elisabeth, b. Aug. 1939, Princess Margriet Francisca, b. Jan. 1943, Princess Maria Christina, b. Feb. 1947; went to Canada after German occupation 1940; in England 1944; returned to Netherlands 1945; Princess Regent Oct.-Dec. 1947, May-Aug. 1948; Queen of Netherlands 1948-80 (abdicated 30 April 1980). *Address:* c/o Palace of Soestdijk, Amsterdamsestraatweg 1, 3744 AA Baarn, Netherlands.

JULIEN, A. M., (pseudonym of Aman Maistre); French theatrical director and administrator; b. 24 July 1903; m. 1st Suzanne Saint-Denis 1923, two s. two d.; m. 2nd Nicole Obey (Dominique Vincent) 1950, one d.; m. 3rd Denise Pelletier 1962; m. 4th Nicole Obey; ed. Inst. St. Joseph, Toulon; Founder, Compagnie des Quinze; Asst. to Cavalcanti; Artistic Dir., Radio-Cité, Ed. Vedettes 1942-44; Producer, Théâtre Sarah-Bernhardt 1944, Dir. 1947-59, 1962-67; Dir.-Gen. Paris Drama Festival 1954-; Dir.-Gen. Théâtre des Nations 1958-65; Admin. Paris Opéra and Opéra Comique 1959-62; Pres. Syndicat des Dirs. de Théâtre; staged 444 plays 1958-65; Officier Légion d'honneur; Commdr. des Arts et des Lettres; Hon. C.B.E. *Leisure interest:* helping others. *Address:* Le Presbytère, Comprégnac, 12100 Millau, France.

JULIEN, Claude Norbert; French journalist; b. 17 May 1925, Saint-Rome de Cernon; s. of Henry Julien and Léontine (née Gau); m. Jacqueline Tannery 1949; two s. two d.; ed. Ecole primaire de Labruguière, Univ. of Notre Dame, Ind., U.S.A.; Ed.-in-Chief Vie catholique illustrée 1949-50, Dépêche Marocaine à Tanger 1950-51; Foreign Ed. Le Monde 1951, Asst. Head Foreign Service 1960-69, Head 1969-73, Ed.-in-Chief Le Monde diplomatique 1973-82, Dir. 1982- (Man. Le Monde 1981-82); Admin. l'Institut français de recherche scientifique pour le développement en co-opération, la Maison de l'Amérique latine, Malesherbes Publications; Pres. du Cercle Condorcet, Paris; Prix Aujourd'hui for book L'Empire américain. *Publications:* L'Amérique en révolution (with J. Julien) 1956, Le Nouveau Nouveau Monde 1960, La Révolution cubaine 1962, God's Trombones 1960, Le Canada—dernière chance de l'Europe 1968, L'Empire américain 1968, Le suicide des démocraties 1972, Le Rêve et l'histoire—deux siècles d'Amérique 1976, Le devoir d'irrespect 1979. *Address:* Le Monde, 7 rue des Italiens, Paris 75009 (Office); 37 rue Henri Barbusse, 75005 Paris, France (Home).

JULIS, Karel; Czechoslovak politician; b. 10 Nov. 1929; ed. Tech. Univ. of Prague; mem. CP of Czechoslovakia (CPCZ) 1965-, cand. mem. Cen. Cttee. 1986-, mem. Econ. Comm. 1986-; worked in Bechovice State Research Inst. for Construction of Machinery 1953-82, Dir. 1971-82; concurrently Head, Dept. of Mechanics and Dean, Faculty of Civil Eng., Tech. Univ. of Prague; Academician, Czechoslovak Acad. of Sciences 1984-, Deputy Chair. 1986-87; Dir. Inst. of Theoretical and Applied Mechanics, Czechoslovak Acad. of Sciences 1987-88; Deputy Premier and Minister of Metallurgy, Machine Building and Electrical Eng. Oct. 1988-. *Address:* Ministry of Metallurgy, Machine Building and Electrical Engineering, Prague, Czechoslovakia.

JULLIEN, Mgr. Jacques; French ecclesiastic; b. 7 May 1929, Brest; s. of Pierre Jullien and Jeanne Maudon; eleven c.; ed. Grand-Séminaire de Quimper, Univ. Catholique d'Angers, Univ. Catholique de Paris et Hautes-Etudes, Paris; ordained priest 1954; Vicar, Locmaria-Quimper; Prof. of Moral Theology, Grand-Séminaire de Quimper 1957-69; Curé, Saint-Louis de Brest 1969-78; Bishop of Beauvais 1978-84; Coadjutor Bishop to Cardinal Gouyon 1984; Archbishop of Rennes, Dol and Saint-Malo 1985-; Chair. Episcopal Comm. for the Family; Chevalier, Légion d'honneur. *Publications:* Le Chrétien et la politique 1963, Les Chrétiens et l'état (Co-author) 1967, La régulation des naissances, Humanae Vitae 1968, Pour vous, qui est Jésus-Christ? (Co-author) 1968, Faire vivre, livre blanc sur l'avortement (Co-author) 1969, Les prêtres dans le combat politique 1972, L'homme debout 1980, En paroles et en actes 1983. *Address:* Archevêché, 45 rue de Brest, 35042 Rennes Cedex, France. *Telephone:* 99.54.06.06.

JULY, Serge; French television executive and journalist; b. 27 Dec. 1942, Paris; one s.; journalist Clarté 1961-63; Vice-Pres. Nat. Union of Students 1965-66; French teacher Coll. Sainte-Barbe, Paris 1966-68; Asst. Leader Gauche prolétarienne 1969-72 (disbanded by the Govt.); f. with Jean-Paul Sartre, Jean-Claude Vernier and Philippe Gavi Libération Feb. 1973, Chief Ed. 1973-, Publ. Dir. 1974-75, Jt. Dir. Nov. 1981, Man. Dir. Jan. 1987-; Reporter Europe 1 April 1983; Dir. Télélibération March 1984-; mem. Club de la presse Europe 1 Oct. 1976-. *Publications:* Vers la guerre civile (with Alain Geismar and Erlyne Morane) 1969, Dis maman, c'est quoi l'avant-guerre? 1980, Les Années Mitterrand 1986, La Bataille de Bouvines, La Drôle d'Année 1987. *Address:* Libération, 11 rue Beranger, 75003 Paris, France (Office). *Telephone:* 42 76 19 78 (Home).

JUMBE, (Mwinyi) Aboud; Tanzanian politician (retd.); b. 14 June 1920, Zanzibar; s. of Jumbe Mwinyi and Sanga Mussa; m. Khadija Ibrahim 1947, Zeyena Rashid 1976, Fatma Muhammed 1980; fourteen s. four d.; ed. secondary school, Zanzibar and Makerere Univ. Coll., Uganda; Teacher 1946-60; fmr. mem. Zanzibar Township Council; mem. Afro-Shirazi Party (ASP) 1960-77, later Organizing Sec., Head 1972-77; Vice-Chair. Chama Cha Mapinduzi (formed by merger of TANU and ASP) 1977-84; mem. Nat. Assembly of Zanzibar (ASP) 1961-84; Opposition Whip 1962-64; Minister of Home Affairs, Zanzibar Jan.-April 1964; Minister of State, First Vice-President's Office, Tanzania 1964-72, concurrently responsible for Ministry of Health and Social Services 1964-67; First Vice-Pres. of Tanzania 1972-77, Vice-Pres. 1977-84; Chair. Zanzibar Revolutionary Council 1972-84; fmr. Vice-Chair. Revolutionary Party of Tanzania; has resgd. all govt. and party positions and now resides as a villager; engaged in small-scale fishing, animal husbandry and land cultivation. *Leisure interests:* reading and writing Islamic materials. *Address:* Mjimwema, P.O. Box 19875, Dar es Salaam, Tanzania. *Telephone:* 33969; 31359.

JUMINER, Bertène Gaëtan, LIC.MED.; French professor of medicine; b. 6 Aug. 1927, Cayenne, French Guiana; s. of Félix Juminer and Marie-Léone Placide; m. Bernadette Stephenson 1977; three s. five d.; Head Lab. of Exotic Pathology, Faculty of Medicine, Montpellier 1956-58; Head of Lab. Inst. Pasteur, Tunis 1958-66; Maître de Conf. Agrégé and Hosp. Biologist, Faculty of Medicine, Meched, Iran 1966-67; Prof. and Hosp. Biologist, Faculty of Medicine, Dakar, Senegal 1967-73; Prof. and Hosp. Biologist Faculty of Medicine, Amiens, Univ. of Picardie 1972-81; Rector of Acad. des Antilles et de la Guyane and Chancellor of Univ. Jan. 1982-; Chevalier, Légion d'honneur; Officier de l'Ordre national du Mérite; Prix des Caraïbes 1981. *Publications:* Les Bâtards 1961, Au seuil d'un nouveau cri 1963, La revanche de Bozambo 1968, Les héritiers de la presqu'île 1979; about 120 articles on parasitology, epidemiology, medical mycology and medical entomology. *Leisure interests:* music, jazz. *Address:* Rectorat de Antilles et de la Guyane, B.P. 681, 97208 Fort-de-France Cedex (Office); Villa "Les Roches", Anse Gouraud, 97233 Schoelcher, French Guiana (Home).

JUNEAU, Pierre, O.C., LL.D.; Canadian public servant; b. 17 Oct. 1922, Verdun, Que.; s. of Laurent Edmond and Marguerite (Angrignon) Juneau; m. Fernande Martin 1947; two s. one d.; ed. Coll. Ste-Marie, Montreal and Inst. Catholique, Paris; joined Nat. Film Bd. 1949, Head of European Office 1952, Sec. 1954, Senior Asst. to Commr. and Dir. of French Language Productions 1964, Vice-Chair. Bd. of Govs. 1966; Chair. Canadian Radio-TV Comm. 1968; Pres. Montreal Int. Film Festival 1959-68; Ministry of Communications 1975; special policy adviser, Office of Prime Minister 1975; Chair. Nat. Capital Comm. 1976; Under-Sec. of State 1978; Deputy Minister of Communications 1980; Pres. Canadian Broadcasting Corpn. Aug. 1982-; mem. Bd. of Dirs. Nat. Arts Centre; mem. Bd. of Govs. of the Univ. of Ottawa; mem. Royal Soc. of Canada, Club of Rome. *Leisure interests:* tennis, music, reading. *Address:* 1500 Bronson Avenue, P.O. Box 8478, Ottawa, Ont. K1G 3J5, Canada (Office). *Telephone:* (613) 724-1200.

JUNEJO, Muhammad Khan; Pakistan politician; b. 18 Aug. 1932, Sindhri, District Sanghar; s. of Din Mohammad Junejo; m.; ed. St. Patrick's School, Karachi and Hastings Agricultural Inst., Sussex; mem. West Pakistan Provincial Ass. 1962, Minister 1965-69; Minister for Railways, Fed. Cabinet 1978-79; Prime Minister of Pakistan 1985-88; Pres. Pakistan Muslim League 1986-. *Leisure interests:* farming, reading. *Address:* PO Sindhri via Mirpurkhas, Pakistan (Home). *Telephone:* Mirpurkhas 2756 (Home).

JUNG, Hans-Gernot; German ecclesiastic; b. 10 Feb. 1930, Marburg/Lahn; s. of late Dr. Wilhelm Jung and of Annemarie (née Schweitzer) Jung; m. Nina Schwerdtfeger 1961; two s. one d.; ed. Univs. of Marburg and Heidelberg, Presbyterian Seminary of Univ. of Dubuque, Iowa; Minister, Kreuzkirche, Kassel 1958-62; Student Chaplain, Marburg 1962-65; Dir. Evangelische Akad. Hofgeismar 1965-74; Adviser, diocesan office of Evangelical Church in Kurhessen-Waldeck, Kassel 1974–78; Bishop of Kurhessen-Waldeck 1978–. *Publications:* Befreiende Herrschaft, Die politische Verkündigung der Herrschaft Christi 1965, Gemeinden im Bildungsprozess 1977. *Address:* Burgfeldstrasse 14, 3500 Kassel-Wilh., Federal Republic of Germany.

JUNG, Nawab Mir Nawaz (M. Mir Khan), B.A., LL.B., M.SC.; Pakistan financier and diplomatist; b. 4 Jan. 1904, Hyderabad; s. of Nawab and Begum Ameer Nawaz Jung; one c.; ed. Nizam's Coll., Hyderabad and Univs. of London, Paris and Geneva; in service of Hyderabad State, holding posts of Cabinet Sec., Sec. Railways and Civil Aviation, Sec. Finance, Official Dir. State Bank, Deccan Airways, Coal Mines Co., etc.; prior to partition was Hyderabad's Envoy in London; Minister of Pakistan to Sweden, Norway, Denmark and Finland 1951–53; Amb. to the UN 1954–57, Pres. Econ. and Social Council of the UN 1957–58; Amb. to France and to the Vatican 1957–59; Amb.-at-Large to African States 1960; Regional Rep. to UN to N.W. Africa, Dakar 1961–65; UN Rep., Tunis 1965–68; Sr. Consultant to UN Devt. Programme (UNDP); Grand Officier Légion d'honneur, Ordre nationale (Senegal, Mauritania), Grand Cordon Ordre nationale (Tunisia). *Publications:* Federal Finance 1936, Central Banking 1945, Five Year Appraisals (1960–64) of UN and Agencies (co-author). *Leisure interest:* history. *Address:* 137 rue de Lausanne, Geneva, Switzerland. *Telephone:* 317082 (Home).

JUNGALWALLA, Nowshir K., O.B.E., M.B.B.S., M.R.C.S., F.R.C.P., M.P.H.; Indian public health official; b. 1 Dec. 1912, Rangoon, Burma; s. of Dr. K. T. Jungalwalla and Freny Anklesaria; m. Piloo Nanavutty 1950; one s.; ed. Univ. of Rangoon and Johns Hopkins Univ., U.S.A.; Indian Medical Service 1939–46; Deputy Public Health Commr., Ministry of Health 1946–50; Regional Adviser, Regional Office for S.E. Asia, World Health Org. (WHO) 1950–52, Rep. in Indonesia 1952–55, Dir. Public Health Services, Geneva 1967–72; Deputy Dir.-Gen. of Health Services, India 1955–57, 1960–65, Additional Dir.-Gen. 1965–67; Dir. All-India Inst. of Hygiene and Public Health 1957–60, Nat. Inst. Health Admin. and Educ. 1964–65; Dir. Health Services, Regional Office for S.E. Asia, New Delhi 1972–74; Vice-Pres. Nat. Bd. of Examinations; mem. Panel WHO Expert Cttee. on Educ. and Training; Hon. Fellow American Public Health Asscn.; Fellow, Nat. Acad. of Medical Sciences (India). *Address:* A2/2 Safdarjang Enclave, New Delhi 110029, India (Home). *Telephone:* 608391 (Home).

JÜNGER, Ernst; German writer; b. 29 March 1895, Heidelberg; s. of Dr. Ernst Jünger and Lily Lampl; m. 1st Gretha v. Jeinsen 1925 (died 1960); m. 2nd Dr. Liselotte Lohrer 1962; two s. (one deceased); ed. Hanover, Leipzig and Naples; served in German Army in both World Wars; awarded Pour le Mérite in First War; involved in July 20th 1944 plot while on Staff of Gen. Stülpnagel in Paris; Ehrenbürger von Wilflingen 1960, Stadt Rehburg 1965, Montpellier 1983; Hon. Chief of Tallah, Liberia 1976; Literary Award of City of Bremen 1956, Goslar 1956, Grand Cross of Merit 1959, Culture Award, Fed. of German Industries 1960, Immermann Award of Düsseldorf 1965, Freiherr vom Stein Gold Medal 1970, Schiller Gedächtnispreis 1974, Star of the Grand Cross of Merit (Fed. Repub. of Germany) 1977 and Sash 1985, Golden Eagle (City of Nice) 1977, Médaille de la Paix, Verdun 1979, Verdienstorden des Landes Baden-Württemberg 1980, Goldene Medaille der Humboldt-Gesellschaft 1981, Prix Europa-Littérature (Int. Foundation for Propagation of Arts and Literature) 1981, Prix Mondial Cino-del-Duca 1981, Goethe-Preis der Stadt Frankfurt 1982, Diplôme d'Honneur et Médaille, Montpellier 1983, Premio Capo Circeo 1983, Hon. Pres. Deutsch-Togolesische Gesellschaft 1985, Premio Mediterraneo des Centro di Cultura, Palermo, Bayerischer Maximiliansorden für Wissenschaft und Kunst 1986, Prix Int. Dante Alighieri dell'Accad. Casentinese 1987. *Publications:* In Stahlgewittern 1920, Der Kampf als inneres Erlebnis 1922, Das Wäldchen 125 1925, Feuer und Blut 1925, Das abenteuerliche Herz 1929, Die Totale Mobilmachung 1931, Der Arbeiter 1932, Blätter und Steine 1934, Afrikanische Spiele 1936, Das Abenteuerliche Herz 1938, Auf den Marmorklippen 1939, Gärten und Strassen 1942, Myrdun 1943, Der Friede 1945, Atlantische Fahrt 1947, Sprache und Körperbau 1948, Ein Inselfrühling 1948, Heliopolis 1949, Strahlungen 1949, Über die Linie 1950, Der Waldgang 1951, Das Haus der Briefe 1951, Am Kieselstrand 1951, Besuch auf Godenholm 1952, Der Gordische Knoten 1953, Das Sanduhrbuch 1954, Am Sarazenenturm 1955, Rivarol 1956, Gläserne Bienen 1957, Serpentara 1957, San Pietro 1957, Mantrana 1958, Jahre der Okkupation 1958, An der Zeitmauer 1959, Der Weltstaat 1960, Ein Vormittag in Antibes 1960, Sgraffiti 1960, Werke (collected works, 10 vols.) 1960–65, Das spanische Mondhorn 1962, Typus, Name, Gestalt 1963, Sturm 1963, Dezember 1964, Grenzgänge 1965, Im Granit 1967, Subtile Jagden 1967, Zwei Inseln (Formosa, Ceylon) 1968, Federbälle 1969, Lettern und Ideogramme (Japan), Ad Hoc 1970, Annäherungen, Drogen und Rausch 1970, Träume 1970, Sinn u. Bedeutung, ein Figurenspiel 1971, Philemon u. Baucis 1972, Die Zwille 1973, Zahlen und Götter 1974, Ernst Jünger-Alfred Kubin, eine Begegnung 1975, Myrdun (illustrated by A. Kubin, 2nd edn.) 1975, Eumeswil 1977, Collected Works (18 vols.) 1978–83, Siebzig verweht (2 vols.) 1980–81, Aladin's Problem 1983, Autor und Autorschaft 1984, Eine gefährliche Begegnung 1985, Zwei Mal Halley 1987. *Leisure interest:* entomology. *Address:* D7945, Langenenslingen/Wilflingen 60, Federal Republic of Germany.

JUNGERS, Francis; American oil executive; b. 12 July 1926; s. of Frank Jungers and Elizabeth Becker; m. Alison F. Morris 1947; two s.; ed. Willamette Univ. and Univ. of Washington; joined Arabian American Oil Co. 1947, various eng. and operating positions 1947–62, Gen. Man. U.S. Offices 1964–65, Vice-Pres. Concession Affairs 1969, Dir. 1970, Sr. Vice-Pres. Finance & Relations 1970, Pres. 1971, Chair. of Bd. and C.E.O. 1973–78; Dir. GaPacific Corpn., Donaldson Lufkin and Jenrette, Hyster Co., Orbanco Financial, Thermo Electron, Dual Drilling Co., Welltech, Star Technologies, Applied Energies Service; mem. Visiting Cttee., Coll. of Eng., Univ. of Washington; Consultant, Bechtel Group; Trustee, American Univ. of Cairo 1975–. *Leisure interests:* golf, swimming. *Address:* P.O. Box 16386, Portland, Ore. 97216, U.S.A. (Office).

JUNID, Datuk Seri Sanusi bin, A.I.B.; Malaysian politician; b. 10 July 1943, Jerlun Langkawi, Kedah; m. Nila Inangda Manjam Keumala; three c.; ed. City of London Coll., Univ. of London and Berlitz School of Languages, Hamburg; fmr. bank manager for seven years; Deputy Minister of Home Affairs 1978–81; Minister of Rural and Nat. Devt. 1981–86, of Agric. 1986–; mem. UMNO Supreme Council 1981–83. *Address:* Ministry of Agriculture, Wisma Tani, Jalan Mahameru, 50624 Kuala Lumpur, Malaysia.

JUNKER, Wolfgang; German building engineer and politician; b. 23 Feb. 1929, Quedlinburg; mem. Sozialistische Einheitspartei Deutschlands (SED), German Dem. Repub. 1951–; various posts in building industry 1951–61; Deputy Minister of Construction 1961–63, Minister 1963–; Cand. mem. Cen. Cttee. SED 1967–71, mem. 1971–; Vaterländischer Verdienstorden in Gold and Silver and other decorations. *Address:* Ministerium für die Bauindustrie, Berlin, German Democratic Republic.

JUNOR, Sir John Donald Brown, Kt., M.A.; British journalist; b. 15 Jan. 1919, Glasgow; s. of Alexander Junor; m. Pamela Welsh 1942; one s. one d.; ed. Glasgow Univ.; served Fleet Air Arm 1940–45; political columnist Sunday Express 1948–50; Asst. Ed. Daily Express 1951–53; Deputy Ed. Evening Standard 1953–54; Ed. Sunday Express 1954–86, Dir. 1956–86, Chair. 1968–86; Dir. Express Newspapers 1960–86, Fleet Holdings PLC 1982–85; Hon. Dr. of Law (New Brunswick) 1973. *Publications:* Proletariat of Westminster 1949, Equal Shares 1950, The Best of J.J. 1981. *Leisure interests:* golf, tennis, sailing. *Address:* c/o United Newspapers PLC, 23–27 Tudor Street, London, EC4 0HR, England.

JUPPÉ, Alain Marie; French government finance official and politician; b. 15 Aug. 1945, Mont-de-Marsan, Landes; s. of Robert Juppé and Marie (Darroze) Juppé; m. Christine Leblond 1965; one s. one d.; ed. Lycée Louis-le-Grand, Paris, Ecole normale supérieure, Inst. d'études politiques, Paris and Ecole Nat. d'Amin.; Insp. of Finance 1972; Office of Prime Minister Jacques Chirac (q.v.) June-Aug. 1976; Technical adviser, Office of Minister of Cooperation 1976–78; Nat. del. of R.P.R. 1976–78; Tech. Adviser, Office of Jacques Chirac (q.v.), Mayor of Paris 1978; Dir.-Gen. with responsibility for finance and econ. affairs, Commune de Paris 1980; Councillor, 18th arrondissement, Paris 1983–; Second Asst. to Mayor of Paris in charge of budget and financial affairs 1983–; Nat. Sec. of R.P.R. with responsibility for econ. and social recovery 1984–88, Sec.-Gen. June 1988–; Rep. to European Parl. 1984–86; Deputy to Minister of Economy, Finance and Privatization with responsibility for budget 1986–88. *Address:* c/o Rassemblement pour la République, 123 rue de Lille, 75707 Paris, France.

JURGENSEN, Jean-Daniel; French diplomatist; b. 4 July 1917, Paris; s. of Philippe Jurgensen and Annette Boyenval; m. Marie-Rose Treffot 1939; two s. one d.; ed. Ecole Normale Supérieure, Paris; Deputy to Nat. Assembly 1944–46; mem. French del. to UN 1947–51; Ministry of Foreign Affairs 1951–59; Deputy Rep. of France to NATO 1959–64; Dir. of American Affairs, Ministry of Foreign Affairs 1964–69, Deputy Dir. of Political Affairs 1969–72; Amb. to India 1972–76, to Netherlands 1980–82; Chair. and French Rep. Preparatory Cttee. of the European Foundation 1982–; mem. Bd., Télédiffusion de France 1977–80; Pres. Maison de l'Amérique latine, Paris 1982–83; Ambassadeur de France, Croix de guerre, Commdr., Légion d'honneur. *Publications:* Chrétien ou Marxiste? 1949, Orwell, ou la route de 1984, 1983 and articles in journals. *Leisure interests:* music, linguistics. *Address:* 22 rue Emériau, 75015 Paris, France.

JURINAC, Sena; Yugoslav-born Austrian singer; b. 24 Oct. 1921; m. Dr. Josef Lederle; studied under Milka Kostrencíc; first appearance as Mimi, Zagreb 1942; mem. Vienna State Opera Co. 1944–82; now works as a voice teacher; has sung at Salzburg, Glyndebourne Festivals, etc.; sang in Der Rosenkavalier 1966 and 1971, Tosca 1968, Iphigénie en Tauride 1973, Covent Garden; Austrian State Kammersängerin 1951; numerous tours and recordings; Ehrenkreuz für Wissenschaft und Kunst 1961; Grosses Ehrenzeichen für Verdienste um die Republik Österreich 1967; Ehrenring der Wiener Staatsoper 1968; Ehrenmitglied der Wiener Staatsoper 1971. *Address:* c/o State Opera House, Vienna 1, Austria.

JUSUF, Lieut.-Gen. Andi Mohamad; Indonesian army officer and politician; b. 23 June 1929, Sulawesi; ed. Dutch Secondary School, and Higher Secondary School; fmr. Chief of Staff of Hasanuddin and Commdr. S.E. Mil. Dist.; Minister of Light and Basic Industry 1966, of Basic Industry and Power 1966, of Trade and Commerce 1967, of Industry 1968–78, of Defence and Security, also C.-in-C. of the Armed Forces 1978–82. *Address:* c/o Ministry of Defence, Jakarta, Indonesia.

JUTIKKALA, Eino Kaarlo Ilmari, PH.D.; Finnish historian; b. 24 Oct. 1907, Sääksmäki; s. of Kaarle Fredrik Rinne and Hilma Maria Hagelberg; ed. Helsinki Univ.; Docent, Helsinki Univ. 1933, Prof. of Finnish History 1947-50, 1954-74, Prof. of Econ. History 1950-54, Dean of Faculty of Arts 1966-69; Chair. State Comm. for the Humanities 1967-70; mem. Culture Foundation for Finland and Sweden 1960-71; Academician, Finnish Acad. 1972; Ph.D. h.c. (Stockholm), Pol.D. h.c. (Helsinki), D. h.c. (Helsinki Commercial Univ.), D. h.c. (Tampere). *Publications include:* Suomen talonpojan historia 1942, Atlas of Finnish History 1949, Turun kaupungin historia 1856-1917 1957, A History of Finland 1962, Pohjoismaisen yhteiskunnan historialliset juuret 1965, Bonden adelsmannen kronan i Norden 1550-1750 1979, Tampereen kaupungin historia 1905-45 1979, Desertion in the Nordic Countries 1300-1600 (with others) 1982, Kuolemalla on aina Syyn Sä 1987; studies dealing with demographic, agrarian and parliamentary history, the history of communications, etc.; editor of several historical works and learned journals (Historiallinen Aikakauskirja 1970-82). *Address:* Merikatu 3B, Helsinki 14, Finland. *Telephone:* 90-62-65-08.

JYRÄNKI, Antero, D.IUR.; Finnish professor of constitutional law; b. 9 Aug. 1933, Hamina; m. Leena Koistinen 1980; two s. one d.; ed. Univ. of Helsinki; Assoc. Prof. of Public Law, Univ. of Tampere 1966-70; Gen. Sec. to the Pres. of the Repub. 1970-73; Sr. Research Fellow, Acad. of Finland 1974-77; Vice-Chair., Comm. on the Revision of the Constitution 1970-74; Assoc. Prof. of Public Law, Univ. of Tampere 1977-79; Prof. of Constitutional Law, Univ. of Turku 1980-, Dean, Law Faculty 1981-83; Research Prof., Acad. of Finland 1983-87; Pres. Finnish Asscn. of Constitutional Law 1982-88; mem. Council of the Int. Asscn. of Constitutional Law 1983-, Admin. Bd. Finnish Broadcasting Corpn. 1983-, Finnish Acad. of Science 1987-; Perm. Expert for the Constitutional Comm. of Parl. 1982-. *Publications:* Sotavoiman ylin päällikkyys (The Command-in-Chief of the Armed Forces) 1967, Yleisradio ja sananvapaus (The Freedom of Expression and Broadcasting) 1969, Perustuslaki ja yhteiskunnan muutos (The Constitution and the Change of Society) 1973, Presidentti (The President of the Republic) 1978. *Leisure interests:* languages, literature, problems of mass communication. *Address:* Calonia 311, Vänrikink. 2, 20500 Turku, Finland. *Telephone:* 21-645522.

K

KAARSTED, Tage, DR.PHIL.; Danish historian; b. 27 May 1928, Silkeborg; s. of Itta Kaarsted and Jacob Kaarsted; m. Soes Roenlev 1955; two s. one d.; ed. Aarhus Univ.; master at Grammar School, H.M. Inspector (social sciences) and Extra-mural Univ. lecturer, Aarhus 1955–68; Prof. of Contemporary History, Odense Univ. 1968–; Historiographer to H.M. Queen Margrethe II 1976–; mem. Bd. of Dirs. Albani Breweries, Funen Newspaper syndicate, Odense Theatre etc.; mem. Royal Danish Acad.; Soeren Gyldendal Prize; Radio Denmark Prize. *Publications:* several books about Danish politics and foreign policy. *Address:* Odense University, 5230 Odense M; Amalienborg Palace, 1257 Copenhagen K, Denmark.

KABACHNIK, Martin Izrailevich; Soviet organic chemist; b. 9 Sept. 1908, Yekaterinburg (now Sverdlovsk); ed. Moscow Higher Chemicotechnical School; Assoc. of Inst. of Organic Chem. 1939–54; Assoc. of Inst. of Elemental-Organic Compounds, U.S.S.R. Acad. of Sciences 1954–; mem. CPSU 1957; Corresp. mem. U.S.S.R. Acad. of Sciences 1953–58, mem. 1958–; State Prize 1946, 1985, Lenin Prize 1974, Order of Lenin and other decorations. *Publications:* Investigation in the Field of Organo-Phosphorus Compounds 1946–, Some Problems of Tautomerism 1956, Dual Reaction Capacity and Tautomerism 1960, Conjugation in Non-Coplanar Systems 1962, The Tautomerism of Free Radicals, Wandering Valence 1981, Phosphorus-Carbon Prototropic Tautomerism 1983, Reaction of Phosphorus Monothio, Monoseleno and Selenothio Acids with Aliphatic Diazo Compounds 1984, New Organophosphorus Cyclopendant Complexones 1986, Sterical Aspects of Co-ordination Polyphosphoryl Ligands and Selectivity of Complex Formation 1988. *Address:* Institute of Elemental-Organic Compounds, U.S.S.R. Academy of Sciences, 28 Ulitsa Vavilova, Moscow B-334, U.S.S.R.

KABANDA, Célestin; Rwandese diplomatist; b. 1936, Rusagara; ed. Petit Séminaire de Kabgayi, Grand Séminaire de Nyakibanda, Univ. of Lovanium (now campus of Kinshasa, Zaire); Pvt. Sec. to Pres. of Rwanda 1961; served in Legislation Bureau, Office of the Pres. and as Sec. of the Council of Ministers 1962–64; Amb. to U.S.A. 1964–69; Amb. to Canada and Perm. Rep. to UN 1966–69; Amb. to France, Italy and Spain and Perm. Rep. to UNESCO, Paris 1969–72; Dir. of Telecommunications, Ministry of Posts, Telecommunications and Transport 1973; Préfet, Ruhengeri 1973–74; Préfet, Gikongoro 1975–77; Amb. to Libya 1977–79, to Ethiopia and to OAU, Addis Ababa 1979–84; Perm. Rep. to UN 1984–. *Address:* Permanent Mission of Rwanda to the United Nations, 124 East 39th Street, New York, N.Y. 10016, U.S.A.

KABANOV, Viktor Aleksandrovich; Soviet chemical scientist; b. 15 Jan. 1934, Moscow; ed. Moscow Univ.; Prof. of High Molecular Compounds, Moscow Univ. 1970–; corresp. mem. of U.S.S.R. Acad. of Sciences 1968–. *Address:* U.S.S.R. Academy of Sciences, Leninsky Prospekt 14, Moscow V-71, U.S.S.R.

KABASIN, Gennadiy Sergeyevich, CAND.ECON.SC.; Soviet politician; b. 1937; ed. Voronezh Veterinary Inst.; work on collective farm 1953–60; mem. CPSU 1960–; Sec. of Party Cttee. on collective farm in Voronezh Dist. 1960–63; Deputy Sec. of another collective farm 1963–65; Second, First Sec. of Panin Regional Cttee. 1965–78; work on CPSU Cen. Cttee. 1978–79; Sec., Second Sec. of Bryansk Dist. Cttee. of CPSU 1979–85; work on CPSU Cen. Cttee. 1985–86; Deputy Head of Section of CPSU Cen. Ctte. 1986–; mem. of CPSU Cen. Inspection Cttee. 1986–; First Sec. CPSU Voronezh Dist. Cttee; elected to Congress of People's Deputies of the U.S.S.R. 1989. *Address:* Communist Party of Soviet Union District Committee, Voronezh, U.S.S.R.

KABAT, Elvin Abraham, B.S., A.M. PH.D.; American biochemist, immunochemist and professor of microbiology and genetics and development; b. 1 Sept. 1914, New York; s. of Harris Kabat and Doreen Otesky; m. Sally Lennick 1942; three s.; ed. Coll. of City of New York and Columbia Univ.; Lab. Asst. in Immunochemistry, Presbyterian Hosp., New York 1933–37; Rockefeller Foundation Fellow at Inst. of Physical Chem., Uppsala, Sweden 1937–38; Instructor in Pathology, Cornell Medical Coll. 1938–41; mem. of Faculty, Columbia Univ. 1941, Asst. Prof. of Bacteriology 1946–48, Assoc. Prof. of Bacteriology 1948–52, Prof. of Microbiology 1952–, Prof. of Human Genetics and Devt. 1969–; Higgins Prof. of Microbiology 1983–85, Emer. 1985–; Arthur A. Hirata Memorial Lecturer, Univ. of Kansas 1988; Microbiologist, Medical Service, Presbyterian Hosp., Neurological Inst. 1956–; Expert Nat. Cancer Inst. 1975–82, Nat. Insts. of Allergy and Infectious Diseases 1982–, Nat. Inst. of Health 1988–; Pres. American Asscn. of Immunologists 1965–66; Pres. Harvey Soc. 1976–77; mem. World Health Org. (WHO) Advisory Panel on Immunology 1965–80, Editorial Bd. Journal of Immunology 1961–76, Editorial Bd. Immunochemistry, Carbohydrate Research; consultant, Nat. Cancer Inst. 1975–79; mem. N.A.S.; Fellow, American Acad. of Arts and Sciences, Fogarty Scholar, Nat. Inst. of Health 1974–75; Third Alexander S. Wiener Lecture, New York Blood Center 1979; Hon. Doctor of Laws (Glasgow) 1976, Hon. Ph.D. (Weizmann Inst. of Science, Israel) 1982, Hon. Dr. (Univ. d'Orleans) 1982; Eli Lilly Award in Bacteriology and Immunology 1949, Golden Hope Chest

Award Nat. Multiple Sclerosis Soc. 1962, Karl Landsteiner Memorial Award, American Asscn. of Blood Banks 1966, Claude Bernard Medal, Univ. of Montreal 1968, City of Hope Annual Research Award 1974, Award of Fifth Int. Convocation on Immunology 1976, Louisa Gross Horwitz Prize 1977, R. E. Dyer Lecture Award, Nat. Insts. of Health 1979, Townsend Harris Medal, City Coll., New York, Graduate Faculties Alumni Award for Excellence (Pure Sciences) Columbia Univ. 1982, Philip Levine Award, American Soc. of Clinical Pathologists 1982, Dickson Prize in Medicine, Univ. of Pittsburgh 1986, 1st Pierre Grabar Lecturer Société Française d'Immunologie and German Soc. of Immunology, Distinguished Service Award, Columbia Univ. 1988. *Publications:* Experimental Immunochemistry (with M. Mayer) 1948, Blood Group Substances, Their Chemistry and Immunochemistry 1956, Structural Concepts in Immunology and Immunochemistry 1968, Variable Regions of Immunoglobulin Chains, Tabulations and Analyses of Amino Acid Sequences 1976, Sequences of Immunoglobulin Chains, Tabulation and Analysis of Amino Acid Sequences of Precursors, V-regions, C-regions, J-Chain and β2-Microglobulins 1979; and numerous scientific papers. *Address:* Columbia University, College of Physicians and Surgeons, Department of Microbiology, 701 West 168th Street, New York, N.Y. 10032 (Office); 70 Haven Avenue, New York, N.Y. 10032, U.S.A. (Home). *Telephone:* 212-694-3519 (Office); 212-WA-7-6807 (Home).

KABEYA WA MUKEBA; Zaire lawyer and diplomatist; b. 28 Dec. 1935, Tshilomba, Zaire; m.; eight c.; magistrate, Léopoldville (now Kinshasa) 1963–65; Prosecutor, Chief Prosecutor –1968; Counsellor, Supreme Court of Zaire 1968–73; mem. Zaire del. 1964 session of Gen. Assembly UN; Amb. to Ethiopia and OAU 1975–77, to Cen. African Repub. 1973–76; Perm. Rep. of Zaire to UN 1977–80; Amb. to U.S.S.R. 1980–87.

KABRHELOVÁ, Marie; Czechoslovak politician; b. 4 May 1925, Opatov, Jihlava district; ed. Political Coll. of Cen. Cttee. of Czechoslovak Communist Party; mem. of Jihlava Regional Cttee. of Czechoslovak Communist Party (CCP) 1946–48; official of Cen. Council of Trade Unions 1948–61, mem. Plenum 1949–52, of Presidium 1950–52; Deputy Chair. of Cen. Cttee. of Union of Consumer Goods Industry Workers 1966–68; Chair. Fed. Cttee. of Union of Textile, Clothing and Leather Processing Workers 1969; Deputy Minister of Labour and Social Affairs, Czech Socialist Repub. 1969–70; mem. Presidium of Cen. Cttee. of Czech Union of Women 1969–74; mem. Czechoslovak Women's Council 1969–74; Gen. Sec. of Trade Union Int. of Textile, Clothing, Leather and Fur Workers 1970–71; mem. Bureau of WFTU 1970–72, Chair. WFTU working group on issues of working women 1969–74; Sec. of Cen. Council of Czechoslovak Revolutionary Trade Union Movement 1971–72, of Cen. Council of Trade Unions 1972–74, Sec. Gen. Cen. Cttee. 1983–; Chair. Cen. Cttee., Czechoslovak Union of Women 1974–; mem. Bureau and Council, Int. Fed. of Dem. Women 1974–; mem. World Peace Council 1974–; mem. Presidium of Cen. Cttee. of Czechoslovak Nat. Front 1974–; mem. Cen. Cttee. of CCP April 1976–, mem. Secr. of Cen. Cttee. 1986–, Presidium Fed. Assembly 1976–; Deputy, House of Nations, Fed. Assembly 1976–; Order of Labour 1973, Gold Medal of Revolutionary Trade Union Movement 1974, Order of Victorious February 1975, Medal of Eugénic Cotton 1983. *Address:* Central Committee of the Communist Party of Czechoslovakia, Nábř. Ludvíka Svobody 12, 125 11 Prague 1, Czechoslovakia.

KACHALOVSKY, Yevgeniy Viktorovich; Soviet politician; b. 20 March 1926, Dnepropetrovsk, Ukrainian S.S.R.; ed. Dnepropetrovsk Inst. of Railway Transport Engineers; m.; one d.; Dir. Dnepropetrovsk Electric Locomotive-building Factory 1962–67; Chair. Dnepropetrovsk City Exec. Council 1967; mem. Cen. Cttee. Ukrainian CP 1971–; Deputy to Supreme Soviet of Ukrainian S.S.R. 1971–, Deputy Chair. 1975–; First Sec. of Dnepropetrovsk City Cttee. of Ukrainian CP 1971–74; Second Sec. of Dnepropetrovsk Dist. Cttee. of Ukrainian CP 1974–76; First Sec. 1976–79; cand. mem. of Politburo of Ukrainian S.S.R. 1979–80, mem. 1980–; Deputy to U.S.S.R. Supreme Soviet 1979–; mem. Cen. Cttee. CPSU 1981–; First Deputy Pres. of Ukrainian Council of Ministers 1983–; elected to Congress of People's Deputies of the U.S.S.R. 1989. *Leisure interests:* technology, electrical engineering. *Address:* Politburo of Communist Party of Ukrainian S.S.R., Kiev Ukrainian S.S.R., U.S.S.R.

KACHIN, Dmitri Ivanovich; Soviet politician and diplomatist; b. 1929; ed. Moscow Tech. Inst. of Agric. and Fisheries, and Cen. Cttee. Party Higher School; service on Baikalgosryb Trust fishing vessels 1947–54; mem. CPSU 1953–; trawler capt., engineer, head of section with man. of Kamchatrybprom 1954–59; party work 1961–63; Second, First Sec. of Petropavlovsk-Kamchatsky CPSU City Cttee. 1963–68; Sec. of Kamchatka Dist. Cttee. 1968–69; Pres. of Kamchatka Dist. Exec. Cttee. 1969–71, First Sec. 1971–86; Amb. to Vietnam 1986–; mem. of CPSU Cen. Cttee. 1981–; Deputy to U.S.S.R. Supreme Soviet. *Address:* U.S.S.R. Embassy, Hanoi, People's Democratic Republic of Vietnam.

KACHURA, Boris Vasilievich; Soviet politician; b. 1930; ed. Khartov Polytechnic; mem. CPSU 1954–; worked in factories in Donetsk Dist. 1954–63; Second Sec., First Sec. Zhdanov City Cttee. (Ukraine) 1963–68,

1968–74; Second Sec. of Donetsk Dist. Cttee., Ukrainian CP 1974–76, First Sec. 1976–80; cand. mem. Cen. Cttee. of Ukrainian CP 1971–76, mem. 1976–, cand. mem. Politburo 1976–80, mem. 1980–, Sec. Cen. Cttee. Oct. 1982–; mem. Cen. Cttee. of CPSU 1976–. *Address:* Politburo of Communist Party of Ukrainian S.S.R., Kiev, Ukrainian S.S.R., U.S.S.R.

KACZMAREK, Jan, DR.T.SC.; Polish scientist and politician; b. 2 Feb. 1920, Pabianice; s. of Władysław and Zofia Kaczmarek; m. Olga Steranka 1946; one s. one d.; ed. Cracow Tech. Univ. and Acad. of Mining and Metallurgy, Cracow; Acad. of Mining and Metallurgy, Cracow 1947–58; Head, Dept. of Metal Working, Cracow Tech. Univ. 1955–63, Asst. Prof. 1958–62, Prof. 1962–, Pro-Rector for Scientific Affairs and Rector 1966–68; Pres. Cttee. for Science and Tech. 1968–71; Chair. Gen. Council Polish Fed. of Eng. Assens. 1972–75, Vice-Chair. 1976–80, Vice-Pres. 1982–84, Pres. 1984–; Deputy Chair. Comm. of Nat. Prizes 1971–83; mem. Govt. Praesidium 1972–74; mem. Presidium Polish Acad. of Sciences 1972–80, 1984–, Scientific Sec. Polish Acad. of Sciences 1972–80; Minister of Science, Higher Educ. and Technics 1972–74; Vice-Pres. and Deputy to Seym 1972–75, 1985–; mem. of State Cttee. for Science and Tech. Progress 1985–; Head Dept. of Mechanical Systems, Inst. of Fundamental Technological Research 1978–; Pres. Coll. Int. pour l'Etude Scientifique des Techniques de Production Mécanique 1972–74; Foreign mem. Bulgarian Acad. of Sciences, American Acad. of Eng. Sciences 1977–, Royal Acad. of Sciences, Literature and Arts, Belgium 1978–, and mem. numerous other foreign scientific socs.; mem. Cen. Cttee. PZPR 1971–75, mem. Cen. Revisional Cttee. 1976–80; Dr. h.c. Tech. Univ., Karl-Marx-Stadt (German Democratic Repub.) 1973, Bauman Polytechnic, Moscow 1974; Kt.'s Cross of Polonia Restituta; Order Banner of Labour (2nd Class); Commdr. Cross of Order of Polonia Restituta 1974, Grand Officier Légion d'Honneur 1972; Gold Order of Palmes Acadé-miques 1971. *Publications:* Author of numerous publs. on production engineering and theory of machining by cutting, incl. Principles of Cutting Metals 1956, Theory of Machining by Cutting, Abrasion and Erosion 1970, Principles of Machining 1976. *Leisure interest:* gardening. *Address:* Al. 1 Armii Wojska Polskiego 16 m. 46, 00-582 Warsaw, Poland. *Telephone:* 26-98-06 (Office).

KACZMAREK, Zdzisław; Polish scientist; b. 7 Aug. 1928, Poznań; s. of Edward and Klara Kaczmarek; m. Imelda Kaczmarek 1950; two s. one d.; ed. Polytech. Univ., Warsaw; scientific worker in Polytech. Univ., Warsaw 1947–78, Doctor of Tech. Sciences 1958, Assoc. Prof. 1961–67, Extraordi-nary Prof. 1967–72, Ordinary Prof. 1972–, fmr. Dir. of Inst. of Environmen-tal Eng. in Dept. of Water and Sanitary Eng.; Chief of Div. in the State Hydro-Meteorological Inst. (PIH-M), Warsaw 1957–60, Vice-Dir. 1960–63, Gen. Dir. of Hydro-Meteorological Inst. 1963–66; Dir. of Inst. for Meteor-ology and Water Economy, Warsaw 1976–80; Chair. of Cttee. of Water Economy, Polish Acad. of Sciences; mem. Polish United Workers' Party (PZPR); Deputy mem. of Warsaw Cttee. of PZPR 1955–57, worked in Dept. of Science and Educ. of Central Cttee of PZPR, Senior Instructor 1960–63, Deputy Chief of Dept. 1966–71; member of Comm. of Science in Cen. Cttee. of PZPR, mem. of Cen. Cttee. 1986–; former mem. of Gen. Bd. of Polish Teachers' Assen. (ZNP); First Deputy Minister of Science, Higher Educ. and Tech. 1972–74; Project Leader, Int. Inst. of Applied Systems Analysis, Austria 1974–75, 1989–; Deputy Chair. of Cen. Qualify-ing Comm. for Scientific Personnel, attached to Chair. of Council of Ministers; Corresp. mem. Polish Acad. of Sciences 1969–80, mem. 1980–, Deputy Scientific Sec. Polish Acad. of Sciences 1971–72, Sec. of VII Dept. of Polish Acad. of Sciences 1978–80, Sec.-Gen. Polish Acad. of Sciences 1981–88; Foreign mem. Acad. of Sciences of German Democratic Repub.; Chair. State Council for Environmental Protection 1981–; Poland 2000 Cttee. for Prognosis on Country Devt. 1984–, Nat. Cttee. of Int. Council of Scientific Unions, Cttee. on Water Resources; mem. Cttee. for Research on World Socialist System's Countries, Cttee. for Peaceful Research; Silver and Gold Cross of Merit, Kt.'s and Officer's Cross of Order of Polonia Restituta, Order of Banner of Labour (1st Class), Order of Friendship of Nations (U.S.S.R.), Silver Star of Order of Friendship (G.D.R.), and other decorations. *Publications:* numerous works on hydrology and water resources, on organization of scientific research and on co-operation of science and national economy. *Leisure interest:* sightseeing. *Address:* Al. I Armii Wojska Polskiego 16 m.51, 00-582 Warsaw, Poland. *Telephone:* 291057.

KADANOFF, Leo Philip, PH.D.; American physicist; b. 14 Jan. 1937, New York; s. of Abraham Kadanoff and Celia (Kibrick) Kadanoff; m. Ruth Ditzian 1979; three d.; ed. Harvard Univ.; postdoctoral research at Bohr Inst. for Theoretical Studies, Copenhagen 1960–62; Asst. Prof. of Physics, Univ. of Ill. 1962–63, Assoc. Prof. 1963, Prof. 1965–69; Visiting Prof., Cambridge Univ., England 1965; Univ. Prof. of Physics, Brown Univ. 1969–78, Prof. of Eng. 1971–78; Prof. of Physics, Univ. of Chicago 1978–82, John D. MacArthur Distinguished Service Prof. of Physics 1982–; Alfred P. Sloan Foundation Fellow 1962–67; Fellow American Acad. of Arts and Sciences, American Physical Soc., mem. N.A.S., Buckley Prize, American Physical Soc. 1977; Wolf Foundation Award 1980. *Publications:* Quantum Statistical Mechanics (with G. Baym) 1962, Scaling Laws for Ising Models near Tc, in Physics *2* 263 1966. *Address:* James Franck Institute, Univer-sity of Chicago, Chicago, Ill. 60637 (Office); 5424 S. Eastview Park, Chicago, Ill. 60615, U.S.A. (Home).

KÁDÁR, János; Hungarian politician; b. 26 May 1912, Fiume (now Rijeka, Yugoslavia); original profession mechanic; mem. Young Communist Wor-kers Fed. 1931, illegal Communist Party 1931; helped to organize resistance movement Second World War; Deputy Police Chief 1945; mem. Greater Budapest Party Cttee. 1945–48; Asst. Gen. Sec. Communist Party 1946–48, re-elected on merger of Communist and Social Democratic Parties to become Hungarian Working People's Party 1948–51; mem. Nat. Ass. 1945–51, 1958–; Minister of Internal Affairs 1948–50; imprisoned during Rákosi régime 1951–54; Party Sec. for Budapest Dist., later for Co. of Pest 1954–56; First Sec. Cen. Cttee. Hungarian Socialist Workers' Party 1956–85, Gen. Sec. 1985–88, mem. Political Cttee. 1956–88; Pres. HSWP 1988–; Chair. Council of Ministers 1956–58, 1961–65; mem. Presidential Council 1965–; Minister of State 1958–61; Hero of Socialist Labour, Hero of the Soviet Union; Order of Lenin, Gold Star Order 1964, 1972, 1982; Joliot Curie Gold Medal Award, World Peace Council 1974, Int. Lenin Peace Award 1977. *Publications:* Szilárd népi hatalom—független Magyarország (Firm People's Power—Independent Hungary) 1959, A szocializmus teljes gyözelméért (For the Complete Victory of Socialism) 1962, Tovább a lenini uton (Further Ahead on Lenin's Road) 1964, Hazafiság és internacional-izmus (Patriotism and Internationalism) 1968, A szocialista Magyarország-ért (For a Socialist Hungary) 1972, Válogatott beszédek és cikkek (Selected Speeches and Articles) 1974, A fejlett szocialista társadalom építésének utján (On the Road to the Construction of the Developed Socialist Society) 1975, Internacionalizmus, szolidaritás, szocialista hazafiság (International-ism, Solidarity, Socialist Patriotism) 1977, A szocializmusért—a békéért (For Socialism—for Peace) 1978, Párt, szakszervezet, szocializmus (Party, Trade Union, Socialism) 1982, Socialism and Democracy in Hungary (in six languages) 1985, Békéért, népünk boldogulásáért (For Peace, for our People's Prosperity) 1985, A szocializmus megujulása Magyarországon (The Renewal of Socialism in Hungary) 1986, Kádár János müvei I. kötet 1956–58 (Works by J. Kádár) 1987. *Leisure interests:* hunting, chess. *Address:* Hungarian Socialist Workers Party Central Committee, Széch-enyi rakpart 19, H-1387 Budapest, Hungary. *Telephone:* 111-400.

KADDORI, Fakhri Yassin, DR.RER.POL.; Iraqi economist; b. 28 Aug. 1932, Baghdad; s. of Yasin Kaddori Kaddori and Rafiqa (née Abdul Kadar Kalamchi); m. Marie-Louise Classen 1965; one s. two d.; ed. Adhamiya Intermediate School and Central Secondary School, Baghdad, Coll. of Commerce and Econs. (Univ. of Baghdad), State Univ. of Iowa, Cologne Univ., Int. Marketing Inst. (Harvard Univ.); Dir. of Internal Trade, Minis-try of the Economy 1964–68; Minister of the Economy 1968–71; mem. Planning Bd. 1968–; mem. Econ. Affairs Bureau, Revolutionary Command Council 1971–73; Chair. 1973–76, Acting Chair. 1976; Gov., Cen. Bank of Iraq 1976–78; Chair. Iraqi Economist Assen. 1972–74, 1977–; Sec.-Gen. Arab Econ. Unity Council, Cairo 1978–82; Pres. Exec. Cttee. for Professional and Popular Orgs. in Iraq 1975–77. *Publications:* several articles on economic topics in professional journals. *Leisure interests:* reading, music, swimming, travelling. *Address:* c/o Arab Economic Unity Council, Cairo (Office); 20 Aisha El-Taymouria Street, Garden City, Cairo, Egypt (Home). *Telephone:* 24293/32143 (Office); 982100 (Home).

KADHAFI, Col. (see Gaddafi, Col. Mu'ammar Muhammed al-).

KADIJEVIC, Col.-Gen. Veljko; Yugoslav army officer and politician; Fed. Sec. for Nat. Defence May 1988–. *Address:* Federal Secretariat for National Defence, 11000 Belgrade, Kneza Miloša 29, Yugoslavia. *Telephone:* (011) 656122.

KADOMTSEV, Boris Borisovich; Soviet physicist; b. 9 Nov. 1928, Penza; ed. Moscow State Univ.; Scientist, Physics-Energetics Inst. 1952–56; Sr. Research Scientist, Kurchatov Inst. of Atomic Energy, U.S.S.R. Acad. of Sciences 1956–73; Dir. Plasma Physics Div., Kurchatov Inst. of Atomic Energy 1973–; Corresp. mem. U.S.S.R. Acad. of Sciences 1962–70, Acade-mician 1970–; Foreign mem. Royal Swedish Acad. of Sciences; State Prize 1970; Lenin Prize 1984. *Address:* U.S.S.R. Academy of Sciences, 14 Leninsky Prospekt, Moscow, U.S.S.R.

KADOORIE, Baron (Life Peer), cr. 1981, of Kowloon in Hong Kong and of the City of Westminster; **Lawrence Kadoorie,** Kt., C.B.E., LL.D., J.P., K.ST.J.(A); Hong Kong business executive; b. 2 June 1899, Hong Kong; s. of late Sir Elly Kadoorie and Lady Kadoorie; brother of Horace Kadoorie (q.v.); m. Muriel Gubbay 1938; one s. one d.; ed. Cathedral School, Shanghai, Ascham St. Vincents, Eastbourne, Clifton Coll., Bristol and Lincoln's Inn, London; Partner, Sir Elly Kadoorie and Sons, Hong Kong; Chair. Sir Elly Kadoorie Successors Ltd.,China Light and Power Co. Ltd., Hong Kong Engineering and Construction Co. Ltd., Hong Kong Carpet Manufacturers Ltd., Major Contractors Ltd., Nanyang Cotton Mills Ltd., Schroders and Chartered Ltd. (now Schroders Asia Ltd.); Dir. numerous other public cos.; mem. and official numerous Hong Kong civic orgs.; Hon. LL.D. (Univ. of Hong Kong) 1961; Solomon Schechter Award 1959; Commdr., Légion d'honneur 1982, Ordre de la Couronne 1983; Officier, l'Ordre de Léopold 1966; Ramon Magsaysay Award 1962. *Leisure interests:* travel, sports cars, photography and Chinese works of art. *Address:* Sir Elly Kadoorie and Sons, St. George's Building, 24th Floor, 2 Ice House Street, Hong Kong. *Telephone:* 5-249221.

KADOORIE, Horace, C.B.E., J.P.; Hong Kong business executive; b. 28 Sept. 1902, London, England; s. of late Sir Elly Kadoorie and Lady

Kadoorie; brother of Baron Kadoorie (q.v.); unmarried; ed. Cathedral School, Shanghai, Ascham St. Vincents, Eastbourne, and Clifton Coll., Bristol; Partner, Sir Elly Kadoorie and Sons, Hong Kong; Hon. Life Pres. Hong Kong & Shanghai Hotels Ltd.; Dir. numerous public companies incl. China Light and Power Co. Ltd., Hutchison Whampoa Ltd., Hong Kong Carpet Manufacturers Ltd.; mem. and official numerous Hong Kong civic orgs.; Chevalier, Légion d'honneur; Solomon Schechter Award 1959, Ramon Magsaysay Award 1962, Order of Leopold 1966. *Publication:* The Art of Ivory Sculpture in Cathay (3 vols.). *Leisure interests:* agriculture and gardening. *Address:* Sir Elly Kadoorie and Sons, St. George's Building, 24th Floor, Hong Kong. *Telephone:* 5-249221.

KADRA, Nourredine; Algerian politician; b. 20 March 1943, Sougueur; m.; four c.; agricultural engineer 1966–75; Dir.-Gen. Inst. des Grandes Cultures 1975; Dir.-Gen. Vegetable Production, Ministry of Agric. 1980–84, Sec.-Gen. Ministry of Agric. 1984–88; Sec.-Gen. Ministry of Public Health; Minister of Agric. 1988–. *Address:* 12 blvd Col Amirouche, Algiers, Algeria. *Telephone:* (2) 63-89-50.

KADUMA, Ibrahim Mohamed, B.SC.(ECON.). B.PHIL.; Tanzanian economist and politician; b. 1937, Mtwango Njombe, Iringa Region; s. of the late Mohamed Maleva Kaduma and of Mwanaidza Kaduma; m. Happiness Y. Mgonja 1969; three s. one d.; ed. Makerere Univ. Coll. Uganda, and Univ. of York, England; Accounts Clerk, the Treasury 1959–61, Accounts Asst. 1961, Asst. Accountant 1962–65, Economist 1965–66, Dir. of External Finance and Technical Co-operation 1967–69, Deputy Sec. Treasury 1969–70; Principal Sec. Ministry of Communications, Transport and Labour, 1970–72, Treasury 1972–73; Dir. Inst. of Devt. Studies, Univ. of Dar es Salaam 1973–75, Centre on Integrated Rural Devt. for Africa 1982–; Minister for Foreign Affairs 1975–77, of Trade 1980–81, of Communications and Transport 1981–82; Vice-Chancellor Univ. of Dar es Salaam 1977–80; Arts Research Prize, Makerere Univ., Uganda 1964–65. *Leisure interests:* tennis, squash, gardening. *Address:* P.O. Box 6115, Arusha, Tanzania.

KADYROV, Gairat Khamidullaevich; Soviet politician; b. 1939, Uzbekistan; ed. Tashkent Polytechnic Inst.; mem. CPSU 1965–; engineer and leader of a group of construction workers in plant in Uzbekistan 1962–67; political work in plant at Chirchik 1968–70; sr. post in Cen. Cttee. of Uzbek CP 1970–73; attended Higher Party School of Cen. Cttee. CPSU 1973; First Sec. of Chirchik City Cttee. of Uzbek CP 1975–79; Sec. of Cen. Cttee. of Uzbek CP 1984; mem. of Politburo of Cen. Cttee. of Uzbek CP, Deputy to U.S.S.R. Supreme Soviet, Chair. of Council of Ministers of Uzbek S.S.R. 1984–; elected to Congress of People's Deputies of the U.S.S.R. 1989. *Address:* Council of Ministers, Tashkent, Uzbek, S.S.R., U.S.S.R.

KAEL, Pauline; American author and film critic; b. 19 June 1919, Sonoma County, Calif.; d. of Isaac P. Kael and Judith (née Friedman) Kael; one d.; ed. Univ. of California, Berkeley; film critic on The New Yorker 1968–; Guggenheim Fellow 1964, George Polk Memorial Award for Criticism 1970, Nat. Book Award (Arts and Letters) 1974 for Deeper into Movies, Best Magazine Column Award 1974, Distinguished Journalism Award 1983; Hon. D.LL. (Georgetown) 1972, D. Arts & Lit. (Columbia Coll.) 1972, D. Lit. (Smith Coll.) 1973, D. Hum. Litt. (Kalamazoo Coll.) 1973, (Reed Coll.) 1975, (Haverford Coll.) 1975, D. Lit. (Allegheny Coll.) 1979, D. Fine Arts (New York School of Visual Arts) 1980. *Publications:* I Lost it at the Movies 1965, Kiss Kiss Bang Bang 1968, Going Steady 1970, Raising Kane (in The Citizen Kane Book) 1971, Deeper into Movies 1973, Reeling 1976, When the Lights Go Down 1980, 5001 Nights at the Movies 1982, Taking It All In 1984, State of the Art 1985, Hooked 1989; contrib. to Partisan Review, Vogue, The New Republic, McCall's, The Atlantic, Harpers, etc. *Address:* c/o The New Yorker, 25 West 43rd Street, New York, N.Y. 10036, U.S.A.

KAESTLE, Carl F., PH.D.; American historian of American Education; b. 27 March 1940, Schenectady, New York; s. of Francis L. Kaestle and Regina Perreault Kaestle; m. Elizabeth K. Mackenzie 1964; two d.; ed. Scotia-Glenville High School, Yale and Harvard Univs.; Prin. American School of Warsaw, Poland 1964–66; Teaching Fellow, History Dept., Harvard Univ. 1969–70; Asst. Prof. of Educational Policy Studies and History, Univ. of Wis.-Madison 1970–73, Assoc. Prof. 1973–78, Prof. 1978–; Vilas Prof. 1988–; Visiting Lecturer in American Studies, Flinders Univ., Adelaide, Australia 1981; John Simon Guggenheim Fellowship 1977–78; Pres. History of Ed. Soc. 1980–81; Vice-Pres. American Educational Research Asscn. 1985–87; Dir. Wis. Center for Educ. Research 1986–88; mem. Nat. Acad. of Educ., Vice-Pres. 1987–89. *Publications:* The Evolution of an Urban School System: New York City, 1750–1850 1973, Joseph Lancaster and the Monitorial School Movement 1973, Education and Social Change in 19th Century Massachusetts (with Maris Vinovskis) 1981, Pillars of the Republic: Common Schools and American Society 1983; many articles on history of American educ. and history of literacy, in Journal of Interdisciplinary History, The Harvard Educational Review and other journals. *Leisure interests:* vocal and piano music. *Address:* Department of Educational Policy Studies, 221 Education Building, University of Wisconsin, Madison, Wis. 53706; Department of History, 3211 Humanities Building, University of Wisconsin, Madison, Wis. 53706; 2006 Van Hise Avenue, Madison, Wis. 53705, U.S.A. (Home). *Telephone:* (608) 262-1760 and (608) 263-1800 (Offices); (608) 238-5910 (Home).

KAFANDO, Michel; Burkinabê diplomatist; b. 1942, Ouagadougou; one c.; Univs. of Dakar and Bordeaux, Sorbonne, Inst. of Political Science, Paris, and Inst. for Int. Studies, Geneva; Ed.-in-Chief, Broadcast News, Voltavision (nat. TV) 1972–74; Dir. of Int. Co-operation, Ministry of Foreign Affairs 1976–78, Tech. Adviser for Legal Questions and Int. Co-operation 1979–81; rep. at Conf. on Desertification, UN 1977, UNCTAD 1979; Chief of del., 3rd UN Conf. on Sanctions against South Africa 1981; Perm. Rep. of Upper Volta to the UN 1981–83. *Address:* c/o Ministry of Foreign Affairs, Ouagadougou, Burkina Faso.

KAFAOĞLU, Adnan Başer, B.A.; Turkish politician; b. 1926, Yozgat; s. of Mehmet Edip Bey Kafaoğlu and Meryem Hanim Erzurumluoğlu; m. Seyhan Kuyumcu 1953; one s. one d.; ed. Yozgat High School, Ankara Univ.; studied tax admin., U.S.A. 1953–54; Inspector of Finance 1946–66; Sec. and Chair. Nat. Unity Cttee. Econ. Comm. 1960–61; mem. Constitutional Ass. 1961; training programme in int. taxation, Harvard Law School 1963–64; Gen. Dir. of Revenues, Ministry of Finance 1966; Deputy Rep. Perm. Del. of Turkey to UN, Geneva 1972; mem. Senate 1978; Adviser to Pres. Repub. of Turkey 1980; Minister of Finance 1982–84. *Leisure interests:* reading, tennis, soccer, skiing. *Address:* Tepegöz Sokak 25/A, Göztepe-Istanbul, Turkey. *Telephone:* 355 40 26.

KAFAROV, Viktor Vyacheslavovich; Soviet chemist; b. 18 June 1914, Shyaulyay, Lithuania; ed. Kirov Chemical Tech. Inst., Kazan; Engineer at designing org. in aniline industry 1938–40; Postgraduate, Research Assoc. Colloid-Electrochemical Inst. U.S.S.R. Acad. of Sciences 1940–44; Asst. Prof. 1945–52, Prof. 1953–, Head of Chair 1960–, Mendeleyev Inst. of Chemical Technology; mem. CPSU 1952–; mem. U.S.S.R. Acad. of Sciences 1979–; Order of Lenin, Order of the Red Banner of Labour (twice) and other decorations. *Publications:* Works on chemical technology, mathematical modelling of chemical technology processes. *Address:* Mendeleyev Institute of Chemical Technology, Miusskaya pl. 9, 125820 Moscow A-47, U.S.S.R. *Telephone:* 258-92-65.

KAFKA, Alexandre; Brazilian professor of economics; b. 25 Jan. 1917; s. of late Bruno and Jana Kafka (née Bondy de Bondrop); m. Rita Petschek 1947; two d.; Prof. of Econs., Univ. de São Paulo 1941–46; Adviser to Brazilian Del. to Preparatory Cttee. and Conf. of Int. Trade Org. 1946–48; Asst. Div. Chief, Int. Monetary Fund (IMF) 1949–51, Exec. Dir. 1966–, Vice-Chair. Deputies of Cttee. on Reform of Int. Monetary System and Related Matters 1972–74; Adviser, Superintendency of Money and Credit (now Banco Central do Brasil); Dir. of Research, Brazilian Inst. of Econs. 1951–56, Dir. 1961–63; Chief Financial Inst. and Policies Section, UN 1956–59; Prof. of Econs., Univ. of Va., U.S. 1959–60, 1963–75, Lecturer Law School 1977–87; lecturer, George Washington Univ., Elliott School of Int. Studies 1989–; Visiting Prof. of Econs., Boston Univ. 1975–79; Adviser to Minister of Finance 1964; Ordem do Rio Branco, Comendador 1973, and other decorations. *Address:* International Monetary Fund, 700-19th Street, N.W., Room 13-210, Washington, D.C. 20431; 4201 Cathedral Avenue, N.W., Washington, D.C. 20016 (Apt. 805-E), U.S.A. *Telephone:* (202) 623 7880 (Office); (202) 362 1737 (Home).

KAFRAWY, Hasaballah El-; Egyptian politician; b. Nov. 1930; ed. Alexandria Univ.; Dir. southern region of High Dam electricity lines until 1966; Chair. Canal Gen. Contracting Co.; Vice-Pres. of exec. organ for reconstruction of Suez Canal region 1974, Pres. 1975; Gov. of Damietta 1976; Deputy Minister for Reconstruction; supervised planning of satellite cities of Sadat, Ramadan 10 and El-Ameriya (west of Alexandria); Minister of Reconstruction and Minister of State for Housing and Land Reclamation Oct. 1978–86, of Devt., New Communities, Housing and Public Utilities 1986–. *Address:* Ministry of Housing and Reconstruction, 1 Sharia Ismail Abaza, Cairo, Egypt.

KAGAMI, Hideo; Japanese diplomatist; b. 1923, Yamanashi Pref.; m.; two s.; ed. Tokyo Univ.; joined Ministry of Foreign Affairs 1948; Dir.-Gen. Public Information and Cultural Affairs Bureau, Middle Eastern and African Affairs Bureau, Research and Planning Dept., European and Oceanic Affairs Bureau; Counsellor Perm. Mission to UN 1969–71; Embassy Counsellor, Cambodia 1971–74; Amb. to Iraq 1979–82, to the EEC 1982–88; Perm. Rep. to UN Feb. 1988–. *Address:* Permanent Mission of Japan to the United Nations, 866 United Nations Plaza, 2nd Floor, New York, N.Y. 10017, U.S.A. *Telephone:* (212) 223-4300.

KÄHLER, Erich Ernst, DR.PHIL.; German mathematician; b. 16 Jan. 1906, Leipzig; s. of Ernst and Elsa Kähler (née Götsch); m. 1st Luise Günther 1938 (died 1970), two s. (one deceased) one d. (deceased); m. 2nd Charlotte Schulze 1972; ed. Leipzig Univ.; Lecturer Hamburg 1930; Prof. Univ. Königsberg 1936; Prof. (with Chair) Univ. Leipzig 1948; Prof. Tech. Univ. Berlin 1958; Prof. Univ. Hamburg; Hon. Prof. Tech. Univ. Berlin 1964, Emer. 1974–; mem. Akademie der Wissenschaften der D.D.R., Sächsische Akad. der Wissenschaften and Deutsche Akad. der Naturforscher Leopoldina; Foreign mem. Accad. Nazionale dei Lincei 1961–, Istituto Lombardo 1987. *Publications:* Einführung in die Theorie der Systeme von Differentialgleichungen 1934, Geometria Aritmetica 1958, Der innere Differentialkalkul 1963, Wesen und Erscheinung als mathematische Prinzipen der Philosophie 1965, Saggio di una dinamica della vita 1973, Monadologie (Vol. I) 1975, (Vol. II) 1978, (Vol. III) 1983, Also sprach Ariadne 1984, Die Poincaré-Gruppe 1985. *Leisure interests:* philosophy, theology. *Address:*

Mozartstrasse 42, 2 Wedel, Holstein, Federal Republic of Germany. *Telephone:* (04103) 86535.

KAHN, Baron (Life Peer), cr. 1965, of Hampstead; **Richard Ferdinand Kahn,** C.B.E., M.A., F.B.A.; British economist; b. 10 Aug. 1905, London; s. of the late Augustus and Rosa Kahn; ed. St. Paul's School and King's Coll., Cambridge; employed in various govt. depts. 1939–46; Prof. of Econs., Cambridge Univ. 1951–72; on leave of absence to work in UN Econ. Comm. for Europe 1955; Fellow of King's Coll., Cambridge. *Publications:* numerous articles, Selected Essays on Employment and Growth 1973, The Making of Keynes' General Theory 1984. *Leisure interests:* walking, visiting Italian cities. *Address:* King's College, Cambridge CB2 1ST, England. *Telephone:* (0223) 350411.

KAHN, Alfred E., PH.D.; American economist and government official; b. 17 Oct. 1917, Paterson, N.J.; s. of the late Jacob M. and Bertha Orlean Kahn; m. Mary Simmons 1943; one s. two d.; ed. New York Univ. and Graduate School, Univ. of Missouri, Brookings Inst., Yale Univ.; Research Staff of Brookings Inst. 1940, 1951–52; joined U.S. Govt. Service with Antitrust Div., Dept. of Justice, Dept. of Commerce, War Production Bd. 1941–43; Research Staff, 20th Century Fund 1944–45; Asst. Prof. Dept. of Econs., Ripon Coll., Wis. 1945–47; joined Dept. of Econs., Cornell Univ., Ithaca, N.Y., as Asst. Prof. 1947, Chair. Econs. Dept. 1958–63, Robert Julius Thorne Prof. of Econs. 1966–, mem. Bd. of Trustees 1964–69, Dean Coll. of Arts and Sciences 1969–74; Chair. New York Public Service Comm. 1974–77, Civil Aeronautics Bd. 1977–78; Adviser to the Pres. on Inflation and Chair. Council on Wage and Price Stability 1978–80; Special Consultant, Nat. Econ. Research Associates 1980–; Vice-Pres. American Econ. Assen. 1981–82; mem. American Acad. of Arts and Sciences; Hon. LL.D. (Colby Univ., Ripon Coll., Univ. of Mass., Northwestern Univ., Colgate Univ.), Hon. D.H.L. (State Univ. of New York) 1985. *Publications:* Great Britain in the World Economy 1946, (co-author) Fair Competition, the Law and Economics of Antitrust Policy 1954, (co-author) Integration and Competition in the Petroleum Industry 1959, The Economics of Regulation (two vols.) 1970, 1971. *Leisure interests:* sports, dramatics, music. *Address:* c/o Department of Economics, Cornell University, Ithaca, N.Y. 14853 (Office); R.D.3, Trumansburg, N.Y. 14886, U.S.A. (Home). *Telephone:* (607) 277-3007 (Office); (607) 387-5773 (Home).

KAHN-ACKERMANN, Georg; German journalist, broadcaster and politician; b. 4 Jan. 1918, Berlin-Charlottenburg; s. of Lucian Kahn-Ackermann and Maria Gretor; m. Rosemarie Müller-Diefenbach 1945; one s. two d.; ed. Starnberg Grammar School; mem. Social Democratic Party (Sozialdemokratische Partei Deutschlands—SPD) 1946–; mem. Bundestag 1953–57, 1962–69, 1970–74; Vice-Pres. Admin. Council Deutschlandfunk; Pres. Political Comm., Western European Union; Vice-Pres. Assembly, Council of Europe 1973–74: Sec.-Gen. Council of Europe 1974–79; Pres. V. G. Wort 1979–; Vice-Pres. Deutsche Welthungerhilfe 1968–89. *Leisure interests:* archaeology, horse riding. *Address:* c/o D-8 Munich, 22 Postfach 221234; Sterzenweg 3, 8193 Ammerland, Upper Bavaria, Federal Republic of Germany. *Telephone:* 08177 206.

KAIFU, Toshiki; Japanese politician; b. 1932; elected to House of Reps. six times; Parl. Vice-Minister of Labour; Chair. Steering Cttee. of House of Reps.; various posts in admin. of the late Takeo Miki 1974–76, incl. Deputy Chief Cabinet Sec., Chair. of Diet Policy Cttee. of Liberal Democratic Party (LDP); Minister of Educ. 1976–77, 1985–86. *Address:* House of Representatives, Tokyo, Japan.

KAIM, Franciszek, M.ENG.; Polish politician; b. 13 Feb. 1919, Wola Drwińska; m.; three s.; ed. Acad. of Mining and Metallurgy, Cracow; labourer, then accountant, in agriculture and forestry 1939–45; worked at "Bobrek" foundry, later Chief Man. at "Małapanew" foundry 1951–53; Under-Sec. of State, Ministry of Metallurgy 1953–57, Ministry of Heavy Industry 1957–64; Deputy Minister of Heavy Industry and Metallurgy 1964–67, Minister of Heavy Industry 1967–70, of Metallurgy March 1976–80; Vice-Pres. Council of Ministers 1970–79; mem. Polish United Workers' Party 1951–81, Deputy mem. Cen. Cttee. PUWP 1968–71, mem. Cen. Cttee. 1971–81; Deputy to Seym 1972–80; Perm. Rep. to CMEA 1978–80, mem. Exec. Cttee. 1978–79; sentenced to a year's imprisonment on corruption charges March 1982; Dr. h.c. Acad. of Mining and Metallurgy, Cracow 1979; Order of Banner of Labour (1st Class).

KAIN, Karen; Canadian ballet dancer; b. 28 March 1951, Hamilton, Ont.; d. of Charles A. Kain and Winifred Mary Kelly; m. Ross Petty 1983; ed. Nat. Ballet School; joined Nat. Ballet 1969, Prin. 1970–; has danced most of major roles in repertoire; appeared as Giselle with Bolshoi Ballet on U.S.S.R. tour, Aurora in the Sleeping Beauty with London Festival Ballet in U.K. and Australia, in Swan Lake with Vienna State Opera Ballet; toured Japan and Korea with Ballet national de Marseille 1981; created roles of Chosen Maiden in The Rite of Spring for Nat. Ballet 1979, Giuletta in Tales of Hoffman for Ballet national de Marseille 1982, the Bride in The Seven Daggers/Los Siete Punales etc.; appeared in CBC-TV productions of Giselle and La Fille Mal Gardée; Silver Medal, Second Int. Ballet Competition, Moscow 1973. *Address:* c/o The National Ballet of Canada, 157 King Street E., Toronto, Ont., M5C 1G9, Canada.

KAISER, Philip M., A.B., M.A.; American diplomatist, publisher and banker; b. 12 July 1913, New York; s. of Morris and Temma Kaiser; m. Hannah

Greeley 1939; three s.; ed. Univ. of Wisconsin and Balliol Coll., Oxford (Rhodes Scholar); Fed. Reserve System 1939–42, Bd. of Econ. Warfare 1942–46; joined Research Planning Div. Dept. of State 1946; Exec. Asst. to Asst. Sec. of Labor (Int. Labor Affairs) 1946–47; Dir. Office of Int. Labor Affairs, Dept. of Labor 1947–49; Asst. Sec. of Labor 1949–53; U.S. Govt. mem., Governing Body, Int. Labor Org. 1949–53; Labor Adviser, Comm. for Free Europe 1953–54; Special Asst. to Gov. of New York 1955–58; Prof. of Int. Labor Relations, American Univ. 1958–61; Amb. to Senegal and Mauritania 1961–64; Minister, American Embassy in London 1964–69; Amb. to Hungary 1977–80, to Austria 1980–81; Professorial Lecturer Johns Hopkins School for Advanced Int. Studies 1981–83; Chair. and Man. Dir. Encyclopaedia Britannica Int. Ltd., London 1969–75; Sr. Consultant SRI Int. 1981–; mem. Board, Guinness Mahon Holdings Ltd. 1975–77, Weidenfeld and Nicolson 1969–77, Bradford Insurance Co. 1983–, American Ditchley Foundation 1981–, Soros Foundation 1983–, Council of American Ambs. 1984–, Assen. of Diplomatic Studies 1987–. *Leisure interests:* tennis, swimming, music, ballet, theatre. *Address:* 2101 Connecticut Avenue, N.W., Washington, D.C. 20008, U.S.A. *Telephone:* (202) 667-6095.

KAJANTIE, Keijo Olavi, PH.D.; Finnish professor of physics; b. 31 Jan. 1940, Hämeenlinna; m. Riitta Erkiö 1963; one s. one d.; ed. Univ. of Helsinki; Visiting Scientist C.E.R.N., Geneva 1966–67, 1969–70; Assoc. Prof. of Physics, Univ. of Helsinki 1970–72, Prof. 1973–; Visiting Prof., Univ. of Wis., Madison 1975; Research Prof. Acad. of Finland 1985–(90). *Publications:* approx. 100 publs. in the field of elementary particle physics. *Address:* Department of Theoretical Physics, Siltavorenpenger 20C, 00170 Helsinki (Univ.); Liisankatu 12D 26, 00170 Helsinki, Finland (Home). *Telephone:* (358-0) 650 211 (Univ.); (358-0) 1352232 (Home).

KAJIKI, Matazo; Japanese politician; b. 1919, Arima, Hyogo Pref.; ed. Kyoto Univ.; joined Ministry of Agric. and Forestry; mem. House of Councillors, mem. Budget, Steering, Agric. and Forestry, and other cttees.; various party and govt. posts, including Parl. Vice-Minister of Finance; Chair. Liberal-Democratic Party (LDP) Diet Rules Cttee., House of Councillors; Minister of State and Dir.-Gen. Environment Agency 1982–83. *Address:* Liberal-Democratic Party, 7, 2-chome, Hirakawacho, Chiyoda-ku, Tokyo, Japan.

KAJIYAMA, Seiroku; Japanese politician; b. March 1926, Ibaragi Pref.; m.; one s.; ed. Nihon Univ.; mem. House of Reps. 1969–; Deputy Chief Cabinet Sec. 1974; Parl. Vice-Minister for Construction 1976, for Int. Trade and Industry 1979; Chair. House of Reps. Standing Cttee. on Commerce and Industry 1983; Chair. Exec. Council of Liberal Democratic Party (LDP) 1986; Minister of Home Affairs 1987–88. *Leisure interests:* golf, shogi (4th dan), reading. *Address:* Kudun Shukusha, 2-14-3 Fujimi, Chiyoda-ku, Tokyo 102, Japan.

KAKHIDZE, Dzhansug Ivanovich; Soviet-Georgian conductor; b. 1936, Georgia; graduated from Tbilisi Conservatory 1958; postgraduate work 1958–64; Chief Conductor Georgian State Chapel Choir 1955–62; Conductor Paliashvili Opera and Ballet Theatre, Tbilisi 1962–71, Chief Conductor 1982–; Chief Conductor of Georgian Symphony Orchestra 1973–; Rustaveli Georgian S.S.R. State Prize 1977. *Address:* Paliashvili Opera Theatre, Tbilisi, Georgian S.S.R., U.S.S.R.

KAKLAMINIS, Apostolos; Greek lawyer and politician; b. 1936, Levkas; m.; two c.; Gen. Sec. Ministry of Welfare 1964–67; political prisoner during colonels' dictatorship; founding mem. Pasok and mem. Cen. Cttee.; M.P. 1974–; Minister of Labour 1981–82, of Educ. and Religious Affairs 1982–86, of Justice 1986–87, Minister in charge of the Prime Minister's Office 1987–88, Minister of Health, Welfare and Social Services 1988–. *Address:* Ministry of Health, Odos Zalokosta 10, Athens, Greece.

KĄKOL, Kazimierz, D.ECON.; Polish politician and journalist; b. 22 Nov. 1920, Warsaw; s. of Bronisław and Zofia Kąkol; m. Irena Janasik 1953; one s. two d.; ed. Univ. of Łódź; teacher in resistance during German occupation; mem. Home Army (AK) taking part in Warsaw uprising 1944; worked in science faculty of Łódź Univ., then in Inst. of Legal Sciences of Polish Acad. of Sciences (PAN) 1945–68; Asst. Prof., Inst. of Journalism, Warsaw Univ. 1968–75, Dir. 1973–74, Extraordinary Prof. 1975–; Ed.-in-Chief, Prawo i Zycie (Law and Life) weekly 1957–74; mem. Congress of Int. Fed. of Resistance Movements (FIR); mem. Cen. Council of Int. Assen. of Democratic Lawyers; Minister, Head of Bureau for Denominational Affairs 1974–80; Chief Ed. Związkowiec 1984–85; Deputy mem. Cen. Cttee. of Polish United Workers' Party (PZPR) 1971–80, mem. Cen. Revisional Cttee. 1980–81; Dir. Main Comm. for Investigation of Nazi Crimes in Poland, Inst. of Nat. Memory 1985–; numerous decorations including Kt.'s, Officer's and Commdr.'s Cross of Order Polonia Restituta, Banner of Labour (1st Class). *Publications:* Books include: Cardinal Wyszynski as I Know Him, Evolution of Socio-Political Doctrine of Polish Roman Catholic Church, Controversies About Warsaw Uprising, Główna Komisja Badania Zbrodni Hitlerowskich w Polsce-Instytut Pamięci Narodowej; about 300 essays and articles on social problems, Polish-German relations and Nazi crimes. *Leisure interests:* swimming, football, sports. *Address:* Główna Komisja Badania Zbrodni Hitlerowskich w Polsce-Instytut Pamieci Narodowej, Al. Ujazdowskie 11, 00-950 Warsaw, Poland.

KAKOURIS, Constantine; Greek judge; b. 16 March 1919, Pyrgos, s. of Nicolas and Helen Kakouris; m. Zöe Gaki 1981; ed. Univs. of Athens and

Paris; called to Bar, Athens 1942; Auxiliary Judge, Supreme Admin. Court 1951–62, Asst. Judge 1962–70, Judge 1970–83; Judge, Court of Justice of EEC 1983–; several times mem. or Pres. High Council of the Judiciary and High Council of Diplomatic Corps, Chief Assessor for Admin. Tribunals; Pres. or mem. several cttees. *Publications:* A study of General Theory of Law on Judiciary Power and the Mission of the Courts; articles and reviews in legal and philosophical journals. *Leisure interest:* philosophy. *Address:* 41 allée Scheffer, L-2520, Luxembourg; 12 Bizaniou Street, Filothei, Athens, Greece. *Telephone:* (352) 21.777 (Luxembourg); 6715245, 6719094 (Athens).

KAŁASA, Tadeusz Marian; Polish craftsman and politician; b. 17 Sept. 1917, Warsaw; s. of Aleksander Kałasa and Janina Leszowska; m. Janina Brandt 1944; two s. one d.; trained in baker's trade 1936–39, worked as baker, Warsaw 1939–, owner of bakery 1957–; mem. Democratic Party (SD) 1948–, mem. SD District Cttee., Warsaw-Wola 1965–68, mem. Capital Cttee. and Presidium 1968–81, Deputy Chair. SD Cen. Cttee. 1976–81; founder and fmr. Chair. SD Circle attached to Bakers' Guild, Warsaw; mem. Presidium of Capital Cttee. Nat. Unity Front (FJN) 1972–76; Pres. Council Warsaw Craft Chamber 1973–81; mem. Co. Craft Council 1981–; Deputy to Seym 1980–85; numerous hon. professional awards, Commdr. and Kt.'s Cross of Order of Polonia Restituta, Gold Cross of Merit. *Leisure interest:* stamp collecting. *Address:* Polna 18/20, 00-625 Warsaw, Poland. *Telephone:* 25-46-53 (Office).

KALASHNIKOV, Vladimir Ilich; Soviet politician; b. 1929; ed. Stavropol Agric. Inst.; party work, Stavropol Dist. 1950–71; mem. CPSU 1954–; Head of Admin. of Land Reclamation, Stavropol 1971–73; Head of Dept. of Agric., Stavropol Dist. Cttee. CPSU 1973–75; Sec. (responsible for agric.), Stavropol Dist. Cttee. CPSU 1975–82; R.S.F.S.R. Minister for Land Reclamation and Water Resources 1982–84; First Sec., Volgograd Dist. Cttee. CPSU and mem. Mil. Council, North Caucasian Mil. Dist. 1984–; Deputy to Council of the Union, U.S.S.R. Supreme Soviet 1984–; mem. Cen. Cttee. CPSU 1986–; elected to Congress of People's Deputies of the U.S.S.R. 1989. *Publications include* articles on agro-industrial development, agricultural improvements and innovations.

KALCKAR, Herman Moritz; Danish biochemist; b. 26 March 1908, Copenhagen, Denmark; s. of Ludvig Kalckar and Bertha Melchior; one s. two d.; ed. Univ. of Copenhagen; Assoc. Prof. Inst. of Medical Physiology, Univ. of Copenhagen 1938–43, Research Prof. of Cytophysiology 1949; Research Fellow, Rockefeller Foundation 1939–41; staff mem. Public Health Research Inst., New York 1943–46; Visiting Scientist, Nat. Inst. of Health 1953; Prof. of Biology, Johns Hopkins Univ. 1958; Prof. of Biological Chem., Harvard Medical School, and Chief, Biochemical Research, Mass. Gen. Hospital 1961–; Prof. Emer., Harvard Univ. 1974–; Research Prof. of Biochemistry, Boston Univ.; mem. Nat. Acad. of Sciences, American Acad. of Arts and Sciences; Foreign mem. Royal Danish Acad.; mem. Harvey Soc. and Harvey Lecturer 1949–50; First Weigle Memorial Lecturer, Calif. Inst. of Tech. 1970; Hon. mem., Japanese Biochemical Soc. 1988; Hon. D.Sc. (Washington, St. Louis, Chicago, Copenhagen, Boston). *Publications:* Biological Phosphorylations Development of Concepts 1969, The Role of Nucleotides for the Function and Conformation of Enzymes 1969; scientific papers on Cell Physiology, Cell(ular) Physio(logy) (Assoc. Ed.) 1976–86. *Leisure interest:* classical music. *Address:* 16 Channing Street, Cambridge, Mass. 02138, U.S.A. (Residence). *Telephone:* 617 354-4222.

KALEMLİ, Mustafa; Turkish politician; b. 1943, Tavşanli; m.; two c.; ed. Eskişehir High School and Ankara Medical School; Tunçbilek Clinic 1967–68; Urology Dept. Ankar School of Medicine 1968; Deputy Dir. 1974; mem. staff, Univ. of Hamburg 1978, later Assoc. Prof.; Head, Urology Dept. Ankara Medical School; Dir. Social Insurance Tavşanli Hosp.; Chief, Urology Clinic, Izmir Hosp.; fmr. Minister of Labour and Social Security; Minister of Health and Social Welfare 1986–87, of Interior Dec. 1987–. *Address:* Ministry of the Interior, Icisleri Bakanlığı, Bakanlıklar, Ankara, Turkey.

KALILOMBE, Rt. Rev. Patrick-Augustine, S.T.L., S.S.L., PH.D.; Malawi ecclesiastic and lecturer; b. 28 Aug. 1933, Dedza; s. of Pierre Kalilombe and Helena Mzifei; ed. Kasina Seminary, Kachebere Theological Coll., Gregorian Univ., Rome, Graduate Theological Union, Berkeley, U.S.A.; trained as White Father, Algeria and Tunisia 1954–58; ordained priest 1958; teacher and Rector, Kachebere Major Seminary 1964–72; Bishop of Lilongwe 1972–78; Fellow and Lecturer in Third World Theologies, Selly Oak, Birmingham, U.K. 1982–86, Dir. Centre for Black and White Christ, Selly Oak 1985–87, Sr. Lecturer, Third World Theologies 1982–87; Vice-Pres. East African Episcopal Confs. 1974–76, Ecumenical Assen. of Third World Theologians 1976–78, Ecumenical Assen. of African Theologians 1985–; Cttee. mem. Symposium of Episcopal Confs. of Africa and Madagascar 1974–76; mem. Council, Malawi Univ. 1974–76. *Publications:* Christ's Church in Lilongwe 1973, From Outstations to Small Xtian Communities 1983. *Address:* Selly Oak Colleges, Bristol Road, Birmingham, B29 61Q (Office); Flat 10, Elizabeth Court, 107 Metchley Lane, Harborne B17 0JH, England (Home). *Telephone:* (021) 472-4231; 472-7952; (021) 426-1738 (Home).

KALIN, Ivan Petrovich; Soviet party worker and politician; mem. CPSU 1955–; ed. Kishinev Agric. Inst. and Cen. Cttee. Party Higher School; agronomist, Deputy Pres., of a kolkhoz and Sec. of party org. on Viața

Nouă kolkhoz in Moldavian S.S.R. 1960–63; First Sec. of Kalarash (Calaraş) Regional Cttee. of Moldavian CP 1965–67, 1969–71; head of a section of Cen. Cttee. of Moldavian CP 1971–76, 1976–80; Sec. of Cen. Cttee. of Moldavian CP 1976–80; Pres. of Presidium of Supreme Soviet of Moldavian S.S.R. 1980–; Deputy Pres. of Presidium of Supreme Soviet of U.S.S.R. 1980–; Pres. Moldavian Council of Ministers 1985–; cand. mem. CPSU Cen. Cttee. 1986–; mem. of Politburo of Cen. Cttee. of Moldavia and Deputy to U.S.S.R. Supreme Soviet; elected to Congress of People's Deputies of the U.S.S.R. 1989. *Address:* Central Committee of Moldavian CP, Kishinev, U.S.S.R.

KALINOWSKY, Lothar Bruno, M.D.; American neuropsychiatrist; b. 28 Dec. 1899, Berlin, Germany; s. of Alfred Kalinowsky and Anna Schott; m. Hilda Pohl 1925; two d.; ed. Berlin, Heidelberg and Munich Univs.; Asst. in Neuropsychiatry at hospitals in Berlin, Hamburg, Breslau, Vienna 1922–32, Rome 1933–39; Clinical Prof. of Psychiatry, New York Medical Coll.; Consultant Psychiatrist, St. Vincent's Hospital, New York 1957–; Hon. Prof. of Psychiatry, Free Univ., Berlin; Hon. mem. German Soc. for Neurology and Psychiatry; Corresp. Fellow, Royal Coll. of Psychiatry; Gold Medal, American Soc. of Biological Psychiatry 1979, Distinguished Service Award, New York Acad. of Medicine. *Publications:* Somatic Treatments in Psychiatry (with Paul H. Hoch and Brenda Grant) 1961; Pharmacological, convulsive and other somatic treatments in psychiatry (with Hans Hippius) 1969, Biological Treatment in Psychiatry (with Hans Hippius and H. E. Klein) 1982. *Leisure interest:* travelling. *Address:* 155 East 76th Street, New York, N.Y. 10021, U.S.A. *Telephone:* 73 7-0800.

KAŁKUS, Stanisław, Polish politician; b. 9 Sept. 1932, Poznań; worker, later foreman in quality control, Aggregate and Traction Engines Factory of H. Cegielski Metal Industry Works, Poznań 1949–; mem. Polish Youth Union 1949–53; mem. Polish United Workers' Party (PZPR) 1953–, mem. PZPR Cen. Cttee. 1981, mem. Political Bureau of PZPR Cen. Cttee. 1982–86; Medal of 30th Anniversary of People's Poland and other decorations. *Address:* Komitet Centralny PZPR, ul. Nowy Świat 6, 00-497 Warsaw, Poland.

KÁLLAI, Gyula; Hungarian journalist and politician; b. 1 June 1910, Berettyóujfalu; s. of Sándor Kállai and Eszter Kiss; m. Gabriella Alnoch 1957; two d.; joined Hungarian Communist Party 1931; as a student active in left-wing univ. movements in Budapest and Debrecen; helped to organize prewar March Front Movement; one of leaders and organizers Hungarian Historical Memorial Cttee; mem. Editorial Bd. of Népszava, organ of Social Democratic Party 1939–44; Rep. Communist Party, Hungarian Front Exec. Cttee.; co-signatory to the agreement for amalgamation of Hungarian Communist Party and Social Democratic Party; Leader Dept. of Agitation and Propaganda, H.C.P. 1945–; Ed. Szabadság; mem. Parl. 1945–; Sec. of State Prime Minister's Office 1945; Head Party Intellectual Dept. 1947–49; Minister for Foreign Affairs 1949–51; mem. Cen. Cttee., Hungarian Socialist Workers' Party 1956–, mem. Politburo 1956–75; Pres. of the Nat. Council of the Patriotic People's Front 1957–; Deputy Minister of Culture 1955–56; Minister of Culture 1957–58; Minister of State 1958–60; First Deputy Chair. Council of Ministers 1960–65, Chair. 1965–67; Speaker of Nat. Assembly 1967–70; mem. Presidential Council; Pres. Hungarian Nat. Cttee. for European Peace and Co-operation; Dr. h.c. Kossuth Univ., Debrecen 1975; Socialist Hungary Medal of Distinction. *Publications:* For Socialist Culture 1958, Socialism and Culture 1962, The Hungarian Movement for Independence 1939–45 1965, Socialism—People's Front—Democracy 1971, The Birth of our Freedom 1973, About the Past to the Present 1976, Four Decades of the Hungarian People's Front 1977, Our Place in the World 1977, Életem törvénye (The Law of My Life) 1980, On the Border of Two Worlds 1984, Megkésett börtönnapló (Belated Prison Diary) 1987. *Leisure interests:* fine arts, literature, theatre. *Address:* The National Council of Patriotic People's Front, Budapest 5, Belgrád rakpart 24, Hungary. *Telephone:* 182-855.

KALLIO, Heikki Olavi; Finnish administrator; b. 9 June 1937, Turku; m. Liisa Anita Toivonen 1961; three s. one d.; ed. Helsinki Univ.; Chief Admin. Officer Univ. of Turku 1963–71; Admin. Dir. Acad. of Finland 1971–72, Sec.-Gen. Cen. Bd. and Admin. Dir. 1973–; Admin. Dir. State Tech. Research Centre 1973. *Leisure interest:* sailing. *Address:* Hameentie 68 B, 00550 Helsinki, Finland. *Telephone:* (358-0) 775 8230.

KALLÓS, Ödön; Hungarian commercial official; b. 6 Feb. 1917, Győr; s. of Ernő Kallós and Olga László; m. Hedvig Gárdonyi 1952; one d.; Commercial Attaché, Egypt 1948, later Trade Counsellor until 1955; Deputy Dir. MOGURT Hungarian Trading Co. for Motor Vehicles 1955–56; Commercial Counsellor and Head of Hungarian Trade Comm. to India 1956–59; Pres. Hungarian Chamber of Commerce 1959–81, Co-Pres. 1981–; Co-Chair. East-West Cttee., Int. Chamber of Commerce, Paris 1975; fmr. Pres., mem. of the Presidium 1987; Chair. of Bd. Hungaroswiss Ltd., Budapest and Zurich; Chair. Manager's Forum, Patriotic People's Front 1987–; Labour Order of Merit, golden degree 1958, 1969, and other decorations. *Leisure interests:* rowing, tourism. *Address:* Hungarian Chamber of Economy, Kossuth Lajos tér 6-8, H-1389 Budapest V, Hungary. *Telephone:* 533-853.

KALULE, Ayub; Ugandan boxer; b. 16 July 1953, Kampala; m.; three d.; amateur boxer 1967–76; lightweight gold medal, Commonwealth Games 1974; inaugural winner of world amateur light-welterweight championship

1974; professional boxer April 1976–; won Commonwealth middleweight title May 1978 (first Ugandan to win a Commonwealth championship); defended it Sept. 1978; won World Boxing Assen. version of world light-middleweight title from Masashi Kudo, Akita, Japan Oct. 1979; retained title v. Steve Gregory Dec. 1979, Emiliano Villa April 1980, Marijan Benes June 1980 and Bushy Bester Sept. 1980; first Ugandan to win a world title; won all 35 fights before losing to Sugar Ray Leonard (q.v.) 1981. *Leisure interest:* table tennis. *Address:* c/o Palle, Skjulet, Bagsvaert 12, Copenhagen 2880, Denmark.

KAMALIDENOV, Sakash; Soviet party official; b. 1938, Kazakhstan; ed. Gubkin Petroleum Inst., Moscow; First Sec. and mem. Politburo of Cen. Cttee. of Kazakh Komsomol 1970–83; mem. Cen. Cttee. of Kazakh CP 1971–; , mem. Politburo March 1980–; mem. Politburo of Cen. Cttee. of U.S.S.R. Komsomol 1974–; Chair. of Cttee. on State Security, Council of Ministers Kazakh S.S.R. 1983–87; a Sec. Cen. Cttee. of Kazakhstan CP 1985–; cand. mem. CPSU Cen. Cttee. 1986–; Pres. Presidium of Supreme Soviet of Kazakh SSR 1987–88; Vice-Chair. Supreme Soviet of U.S.S.R. 1987–88. *Address:* Council of Ministers, Alma Ata, Kazakhstan, U.S.S.R.

KAMANA, Dunstan Weston; Zambian diplomatist; b. 19 April 1937, Choma; m.; four c.; ed. St. Mark's Coll., Mapanza; joined N. Rhodesian Govt. Service 1959; Information Officer, Zambia Information Service 1964; First Press Sec. at High Comm. in U.K. 1964, to Pres. of Zambia 1965; Asst. Sec. Ministry of Defence 1965–66; Dir. of Zambia Information Services 1966–68, of Zambia Information and Broadcasting Services 1968–72; Editor-in-Chief, Times of Zambia 1968–72; Gen. Man. Dairy Produce Bd. 1972; Amb. to U.S.S.R. 1972–74; High Commr. in Canada 1974–75; Perm. Rep. to UN 1975–77. *Address:* c/o Ministry of Foreign Affairs, Lusaka, Zambia.

KAMANDA WA KAMANDA, L. EN D.; Zairian lawyer and administrator; b. 10 Dec. 1940, Kikwit; s. of Raphaël Kamanda and Germaine Kukikidika; two s. one d.; ed. Coll. St. Ignace de Kiniati, Coll. Notre Dame de Mbansa Boma, Univ. Lovanium, Kinshasa; Lawyer, Court of Appeal 1964–; Legal Adviser, Féd. congolaise des travailleurs 1964–65; Prof. Inst. Nat. d'Etudes Politiques 1965–66; Legal Adviser to Presidency of Repub. 1965–66, Sec.-Gen. 1966–67; Principal Adviser with responsibility for legal, administrative, political and diplomatic affairs to Presidency of Repub.; Dir. de Cabinet to Sec.-Gen. of Org. of African Unity 1967–72, Asst. Sec.-Gen. 1972–78; Perm. Rep. to UN 1979–82; State Commr. for Foreign Affairs and Int. Co-operation 1982–83, for Justice 1983–84; Deputy Sec.-Gen. MPR Dec. 1987–; Assoc. mem. Office Nat. de la Recherche Scientifique et du Développement; Vice-Pres. Zairian section, Soc. Africaine de la Culture; del. to several int. confs. *Publications:* Essai-critique du système de la criminalité d'emprunt 1964, Négritude face au devenir de l'Afrique 1967, L'université aujourd'hui en Afrique 1969, L'intégration juridique et le développement harmonieux des nations africaines 1969, L'incidence de la culture audio-visuelle sur le phénomène du pouvoir 1970, Les organisations africaines Vol. I: L'OUA ou la croisade de l'unité africaine 1970, Vol. II: 1970, Le défi africaine—une puissance économique qui s'ignore 1976, L'enracinement- culture et progrès 1976. *Address:* c/o Ministry of Justice, Kinshasa, Zaire.

KAMANGA, Reuben Chitandika; Zambian politician; b. 26 Aug. 1929, Chitandika Village, Chipata District, Eastern Prov. of Zambia; m. Edna Mwansa 1963; three s. three d.; ed. Munali; imprisoned several times for political reasons 1952–60; lived in Cairo 1960–62; Deputy Pres. United Nat. Ind. Party; fmr. Minister of Labour and Mines; Minister of Transport and Communications 1964; Vice-Pres. 1964–67; Leader of House, National Assembly 1964–67; Minister of Foreign Affairs 1967–69, of Rural Devt. 1969–73; mem. Cen. Cttee. United Nat. Independence Party (UNIP), Chair. Rural Devt. Sub-Cttee. 1973–76, Cttee. on Politicial, Constitutional, Legal and Foreign Affairs 1975–. *Leisure interests:* football, dancing (traditional), music, gardening, hunting. *Address:* UNIP, Freedom House, P.O. Box 302, Lusaka, Zambia. *Telephone:* 74321.

KAMARA, János; Hungarian politician, b. 1 May 1927, Budapest; engine fitter; ed. Budapest Univ. of Sciences; with Home Ministry 1945–; Brig.-Gen. of Police; Sec. of State for Home Ministry 1974–85; Lieut.-Gen. of Police 1979; Minister of Home Affairs 1985–87; mem. HSWP Cen. Cttee. 1980–88; Order of Merit for Socialist Hungary 1977; Red Banner Order of Labour 1985. *Address:* Ministry of Home Affairs, 1903 Budapest. József Attila utca 2–4, Hungary. *Telephone:* 121-710.

KAMARCK, Andrew Martin, B.S., M.A., PH.D.; American international bank official; b. 10 Nov. 1914, Newton Falls, New York; s. of Martin Kamarck and Frances Earl; m. Margaret Goldenweiser Burgess 1941; one s. two d.; ed. Harvard Univ.; International Section, Fed. Reserve Bd. 1939–40; U.S. Treasury 1940–42; U.S. Army 1942–44; Allied Control Comm., Italy 1943–44; Allied Control Council, Germany 1945; Office of Int. Finance, U.S. Treasury, Chief of Nat. Advisory Council on Int. Monetary and Financial Problems (N.A.C.) Div., Financial Policy Cttee. preparing Marshall Plan 1945–48; U.S. Treasury Rep., Rome 1948–50; Chief of Africa section, Econ. Dept., World Bank 1950–52; Econ. Adviser, Dept. of Operations, Europe, Africa and Australasia, World Bank, Chief of Econ. Missions to 14 countries, 1952–64; Dir. Econ. Dept., World Bank 1965–71; Dir. Econ. Devt. Inst. 1972–77, Sr. Fellow 1977–78; mem. American Econ.

Assen., Council on Foreign Relations; Dir. African Studies Assen. 1961–64; Visiting Fellow, Harvard Inst. Int. Devt. 1977–86; Regents Prof., Univ. of Calif. 1964–65; Council, Soc. for Int. Devt. 1967–70, 1973–76; Pres. Housing Assistance Corpn. of Cape Cod 1980–83. *Publications:* The Economic Development of Uganda (co-author) 1961, The Economics of African Development 1967, The Tropics and Economic Development 1976, La Politica Finanziaria Degli Alleati in Italia 1977, Economics and the Real World 1983. *Leisure interests:* sailing, skiing. *Address:* 118 Pine Ridge Road, Rural Route 1, Brewster, Mass. 02631, U.S.A. (Home). *Telephone:* 385-8221 (Home).

KAMAU, John Cauri; Kenyan physiotherapist, businessman and administrative official; b. 19 Nov. 1923, Githunguri; s. of Cauri Wa Kamau and Njeri Cauri; m. V. Wanjiru Kamau 1950; three s. four d.; ed. medical school, Nairobi; medical physiotherapist 1945–46; teacher, Kenya Teachers' Coll. Githunguri 1946–52; detained for political activities with Mau Mau; Gen. Sec. Nat. Council of Churches of Kenya 1958–87; Dir. of five pvt. cos.; Long Service Presidential Award for Service to Youth. *Leisure interests:* farming, reading, Christian Church activities. *Address:* P.O. Box 72766, Nairobi, Kenya. *Telephone:* 330142.

KAMBA, Walter Joseph, B.A., LL.B., LL.M.; Zimbabwean administrator and professor; b. 6 Sept. 1931, Marondera; s. of Joseph Mafara and Hilda Kamba; m. Angeline Saziso Dube 1960; three s.; ed. Univ. of Cape Town, Yale Law School; Attorney High Court of Rhodesia (now Zimbabwe) 1963–66; Research Fellow Inst. of Advanced Legal Studies, London Univ. 1967–68; Lecturer then Sr. Lecturer in Comparative Law and Jurisprudence, Univ. of Dundee 1969–80, Dean Faculty of Law 1977–80; Legal Adviser ZANU (PF) 1977–80; Professor of Law, Univ. of Zimbabwe 1980–, Vice-Prin. 1980–81, Vice-Chancellor 1981–; Vice-Chair. Zimbabwe Broadcasting Corpn. 1980–87, Chair. 1987–; Trustee Zimbabwe Mass Media Trust 1981–, Conservation Trust of Zimbabwe 1981–87, Zimbabwe Cambridge Trust 1987–; mem. Council, Exec. Cttee. and Budget Review Cttee. Assen. of Commonwealth Univs. 1981–83; mem. Council UN Univ. for Peace, Costa Rica 1982–, Univ. of Zambia 1982–, Commonwealth Standing Cttee. on Student Affairs 1982–, UN Univ., Tokyo 1983–, Bd. of Govs. Zimbabwe Inst. of Devt. Studies 1982–, Chair. 1986–, Exec. Bd. Assen. African Univs.; Chair. Electoral Supervisory Comm. 1984–, Kingston's (Booksellers and Distributors) 1984–, Assen. of Eastern and Southern African Univs. 1984–87; Chair. Council UN Univ., Tokyo 1985–87; Vice-Pres. Int. Assen. of Univs. 1985–; Trustee, African-American Inst. (New York) 1985–; mem. Int. Bd., United World Colls. 1985–87, Bd. of Govs., Int. Devt. Research Centre, Canada 1986–, Swaziland Univ. Planning Comm. 1986, Bd., Commonwealth of Learning 1988, Int. Cttee. for Study of Educ. Exchange 1988–; Hon. LL.D. (Dundee) 1982; Officer, Ordre des palmes académiques. *Publications:* articles in law journals. *Address:* University of Zimbabwe, P.O. Box MP 167, Mount Pleasant, Harare, Zimbabwe. *Telephone:* 303211.

KAMEI, Masao; Japanese business executive; b. 20 April 1916, Kobe City, Hyogo Pref.; s. of Einosuke Kamei and Sei Kamei; m. Hanae Kamei; two s. one d.; ed. Tokyo Univ.; Director Sumitomo Electric Industries Ltd. 1964–66, Man. Dir. 1966–69, Senior Man. Dir. 1969–71, Exec. Vice-Pres. 1971–73, Pres. 1973–82, Chair. June 1982–; Exec. Dir. Fed. of Econ. Orgs. (Keidanren) 1973–, Kansai Econs. Fed. 1974–; Vice-Pres. Japan Fed. of Employers' Assens. (Nikkeiren) May 1977–; Commr. Local Govt. System Investigation Council 1977–88; Chair. Japanese Nat. Railways Reform Comm. 1983–87; Commr. Employment Council 1986–; Vice-Chair. Japan Productivity Center 1987–; Chair. Kansai Int. Airport Co. Ltd., Osaka, Japan 1988–; Chair. Housing and Bldg. Land Council 1988–; Blue Ribbon Medal 1976, Order of the Sacred Treasure (First Class) 1986. *Leisure interests:* paintings, golf. *Address:* 34-11, Kyodo 1-chome, Setagaya-ku, Tokyo 156, Japan.

KAMEN, Martin D., B.S., PH.D.; American professor of chemistry; b. 27 Aug. 1913, Toronto, Canada; s. of Harry Kamen and Goldie Achber; m. 1st Beka Doherty (died 1963), 2nd Dr. V. L. Swanson 1967 (deceased 1987), one s.; ed. elementary and secondary schools, Chicago, and Univ. of Chicago; Research Chemist (Assoc.), Radiation Lab., Univ. of Calif. (Berkeley) 1937–44; Assoc. Prof. of Biochemistry and Research Assoc., Inst. of Radiology, Washington Univ. Medical School, St. Louis 1945–57; Prof. of Biochemistry, Brandeis Univ., Waltham, Mass. 1957–61, Univ. of Calif., La Jolla 1961, Univ. of Southern Calif., Los Angeles 1975–78, Prof. Emer. 1978–; Prof. Emer. Univ. of Calif. (San Diego Campus), La Jolla 1978–; Dir. Laboratoire de Photosynthèse C.N.R.S., France 1967–69; mem. N.A.S., American Acad. of Science and Letters, American Philosophical Soc.; Fellow, American Inst. of Chemists; Sr. Fellow Humboldt Foundation; American Chemical Soc. Award for Applications of Nuclear Science to Chem. 1963; American Soc. of Plant Physiologists, Kettering Award 1968, American Soc. of Biological Chem., Merck Award 1981; Dr. h.c. (Sorbonne, Paris) 1969, Hon. D.Sc. (Chicago) 1969, (Washington Univ., St. Louis, Illinois (Circle Campus) 1977, (Freiburg) 1979, (Weizmann Inst., Rehovoth, Israel) 1987, (Brandeis Univ., Waltham, Mass.) 1988; Alumni Medal, Univ. of Chicago 1973; Sr. Scientist Award, von Humboldt Foundation, Univ. of Freiburg 1974; Patten Prof., Indiana Univ. 1975. *Publications:* Isotopic Tracers in Biology 1961, Primary Processes in Photosynthesis 1963, A Tracer Experiment 1964; and over 200 papers on chemical microbiology, photosynthesis and nuclear chemistry. *Leisure interest:* music. *Address:*

1390 Plaza Pacifica, Montecito, Calif. 93108, U.S.A. *Telephone:* (805) 969-5102.

KAMENKA, Eugene, B.A., PH.D.; Australian professor of the history of ideas; b. 4 March 1928, Cologne, W. Germany; s. of Sergei Kamenka and Nadia Litvin; m. Alice Erh-Soon Tay 1964; ed. Sydney Tech. High School, Univ. of Sydney and Australian Nat. Univ.; Cable Sub-Ed. The Jerusalem Post 1950–51; journalist and Cable Sub-Ed. The Sydney Morning Herald 1952–54; Research Scholar Dept. of Philosophy Australian Nat. Univ. 1955–57, Research Fellow in Philosophy 1961–62, Research Fellow, Fellow, Sr. Fellow and Professorial Fellow in History of Ideas 1962–74; Prof. of History of Ideas and Head of Unit Inst. of Advanced Studies 1974–; Lecturer in Philosophy Univ. of Malaya, Singapore 1957–58; Fellow Australian Acad. of Humanities, Acad of Social Sciences. *Publications:* The Ethical Foundations of Marxism 1962, Marxism and Ethics 1970, The Philosophy of Ludwig Feuerbach 1970; (ed. with A. E.-S. Tay) Law and Society 1978, Human Rights 1978, Justice 1979, Lawmaking in Australia 1980, Law and Social Control 1980; Bureaucracy (ed. with M. Krygier) 1979, Intellectuals and Revolution (ed. with F. B. Smith) 1979, Justice (with A. E.-S. Tay) 1979, Community as a Social Ideal 1982, The Portable Karl Marx 1983, Utopias 1987, Bureaucracy 1989. *Address:* History of Ideas Unit, Australian National University, P.O. Box 4, Canberra, A.C.T. 2601, Australia. *Telephone:* 49 2343 (062).

KAMENTSEV, Vladimir Mikhailovich; Soviet politician; b. 1928; ed. Moscow Tech. Fisheries Inst.; worker on Moscow River navigation 1942–44; on man. Bd. of Murmanryba trawler fleet 1950–57; mem. CPSU 1954–; Sr. engineer, Deputy Pres. of Murmanryba 1957–62; Deputy, First Deputy Pres. of U.S.S.R. State Cttee. on Fisheries 1962–65; First Deputy U.S.S.R. Minister of Fisheries 1965–79, Minister 1979–86; Deputy Pres. of U.S.S.R. Council of Ministers 1986–; mem. of CPSU Cen. Cttee. 1986–; Deputy to U.S.S.R. Supreme Soviet. *Address:* The Kremlin, Moscow, U.S.S.R.

KAMIL, Abdullah; Indonesian diplomatist; b. 27 Dec. 1919, Binjai; s. of H. Mohamad Noor Ismail; m. Acharawarn Kamil; one s. three d.; Information Officer, Indonesian Office, then Second Sec. Indonesian Embassy, Bangkok 1948–52; Deputy Chief, Information Directorate, Ministry of Foreign Affairs 1952–56; First Sec. Indonesian Embassy, The Hague 1955–56; Indonesian Consul in Kuala Lumpur 1956–57; Counsellor, Indonesian Mission to UN 1957–60, acting Head of Mission 1966, Indonesian Embassy, Tunis 1965–66; Ministry of Foreign Affairs 1960–65, Head Int. Org. Directorate 1971–75; Amb. to Yugoslavia 1968–71, to Austria 1975–79; Perm. Rep. to UN 1979–82; Dir.-Gen. for Political Affairs, Dept. of Foreign Affairs 1983; Sr. Adviser to Ministry of Foreign Affairs 1984–. *Leisure interest:* reading. *Address:* c/o Ministry of Foreign Affairs, Jakarta, (Office); Jalan Terogong Kecil 45, Kel. Pondok Pinong, Jakarta Selatan, Indonesia (Home).

KAMIŃSKI, Jan, M.ENG.; Polish agricultural administrator and politician; b. 1 Jan. 1922, Jarosław; s. of Władysław and Aniela Kamiński; m. Jadwiga Kamiński; one s. one d.; ed. Higher School of Agriculture, Łódź; Army service 1944–45; worked at Central Bd. of Agric. Co-operatives (CRS), Samopomoc Chłopska, Warsaw 1948–51; Deputy Dir., then Dir. of Cen. Bd. of Polish Grain Org. 1951–56; Head of Dept. in Ministry of Purchases 1956–57; Dir.-Gen. of Cen. Bd. of Grain Milling Industry 1957–65; Deputy Chair. Cen. Bd. of Agric. Co-operatives (CRS), Samopomoc Chłopska 1965–69, Chair. 1971–76; Chair. Cen. Union of Agric. Co-operatives (CZSR), Samopomoc Chłopska 1976–88; Deputy Minister of Food, Industry and Purchases 1969–71, of Internal Trade and Services Jan.-March 1976; Minister without Portfolio 1976–80; Chair. Supreme Co-operative Council (NRS) June 1976–; Deputy to Seym 1972–85; mem. Cen. Cttee. of Polish United Workers' Party (PZPR) 1975–81, 1986–, Cen. and Exec. Cttees. ICA 1980–; Order of Banner of Labour (1st Class), Kt.'s Cross and Officer's Cross, Order Polonia Restituta and other decorations. *Address:* Naczelna Rada Spółclziekza, 00-013 Warsaw, ul. Jazna 1, Poland. *Telephone:* 27-13-16.

KAMIŃSKI, Janusz, M.ENG.; Polish electrical engineer and politician; b. 13 Nov. 1933, Siedlce; ed. Warsaw Tech. Univ.; since 1955 in transport insts.; sr. mechanic, in charge of rolling-stock and traction maintenance, Polish State Railways Electric Locomotive Shed, Warsaw 1955–61, Deputy Head of Div., Warsaw-Ochota 1959–61, instructor, Sr. Comptroller, Head of Traction Bd. State Railways Regional Admin., Warsaw 1970–73; Under-Sec. of State for Railway Operation at Ministry of Transport 1973–81; Minister of Transport 1981–87, Transport, Shipping and Communication 1987–; mem. Econ. Cttee., Council of Ministers KERM 1988–; mem. Polish United Workers' Party (PZPR) 1960–; Kt. Commdr.'s Cross of Polonia Restituta Order and other decorations. *Address:* Ministerstwo Transportu, Żeglugi i Łączności, ul. Chałubińskiego 4, 00-928 Warsaw, Poland.

KAMIŃSKI, Gen. Józef; Polish army officer and politician; b. 3 March 1919, Brzeżany, Tarnopol Dist.; s. of Antoni and Tekla (née Szpakowska) Kamiński; m. Krystyna Kamiński (née Podlaszewska); one s. one d.; ed. Infantry Training Centre, Rembertów; during Second World War in U.S.S.R., served in Red Army unit in the Far East 1940–43 in Polish Army 1943–, soldier of Tadeusz Kościuszko First Infantry Div. Platoon Commdr., subsequently Co. and Battalion Commdr.; Deputy C.-in-C., 34th Infantry Regt., 8th Infantry Div.; took part in fighting against armed underground Ukrainian org. in Bieszczady Mountains 1946; Commdr. of

Regt. then of Infantry Div. and Armoured Div.; Brig.-Gen. 1954; Armoured Corps Commdr. 1954–64; Commdr., Pomeranian Mil. Dist. 1964–71, Silesian Mil. Dist. 1971–76; rank of Gen. 1974; Deputy Chief of Staff of United Armed Forces of Warsaw Treaty, then Commdt. of Karol Świerczewski Gen. Staff Acad. of Polish Army, Warsaw; mem. Union of Fighters for Freedom and Democracy (ZBoWiD), fmr. mem. ZBoWiD Voivodship Bd, Bydgoszcz, mem. ZBoWiD Chief Council, Pres. ZBoWiD Gen. Bd. 1983–; mem. Polish United Workers' Party (PZPR); mem. PZPR Cen. Revisional Comm. 1972–75; Order of Banner of Labour (1st and 2nd Class), Grunwald Cross (3rd Class), Order Polonia Restituta (4th and 5th Class), Order of Lenin, Order of Friendship among the Nations, Virtuti Militari Cross (5th Class). *Leisure interest:* military history. *Address:* Zarząd Główny ZBoWiD, Aleje Ujazdowskie 6a, 00-461 Warsaw, Poland. *Telephone:* 29-30-33 (Office).

KAMINSKY, Horst, M.A.; German central banker; b. 1927; Sec. of State, Ministry of Finance 1963–74; Pres. Staatsbank der Deutschen Demokratischen Republik 1974–; Vaterländischer Verdienstorden in Gold and Silver, Orden Banner der Arbeit (twice) and other high state decorations. *Address:* Staatsbank der Deutschen Demokratischen Republik, 1086 Berlin, Charlottenstrasse 33, German Democratic Republic.

KAMMERER, Hans, F.R.I.B.A.; German architect; b. 25 Feb. 1922, Frankfurt; ed. Univ. of Stuttgart; Asst. Prof. Univ. of Stuttgart 1951–52; Visiting Prof. Kingston School of Art 1952–53; teaching, professional practice etc. 1953–63; Prof. of Design, Dept. of Architecture, Stuttgart 1973–86; Guest Prof. Univ. of Calif. Berkeley 1978; teaching, Univ. of Arizona, Phoenix 1983, 1986; mem. Akad. der Künste Berlin; numerous nat. and int. awards and prizes. *Address:* Hartstrasse 39, 7055 Stetten, Wurtemberg, Federal Republic of Germany.

KAMOUGUE, Lt.-Col. Wadal Abdelkader; Chad army officer and politician; Minister of Foreign Affairs and Co-operation, mem. of Supreme Mil. Council in Govt. of Brig.-Gen. Félix Malloum 1975–78; Commdr. of Gendarmerie 1978–79; mem. Provisional State Council following Kano peace agreement March–May 1979, in charge of Agric. and Animal Resources; Leader of Front Uni du Sud (later Forces Armées Tchadiennes) 1979–; Vice-Pres. of Transitional Gov. of Nat. Unity (GUNT) Nov. 1979–82; now Vice-Pres. in exile; Leader Mouvement révolutionnaire du peuple; Pres. of State Council June–Sept. 1982; fled to Cameroon, then Gabon Sept.–Oct. 1982, after defeat by forces of FAN; returned to Ndjamena Feb. 1987. *Address:* c/o GUNT, Bardai, Chad.

KAMP, Norbert, DR. PHIL.; German university administrator; b. 24 Aug. 1927, Niese; s. of Otto Kamp and Valerie (née Steier) Kamp; m. Rosemarie Füllner 1958; two s. one d.; ed. Univs. of Göttingen and Münster; Research Asst. Universität Göttingen 1957; mem. Istituto Storico Germanico Rome 1957–61; Research Asst. Univ. of Münster 1961–69; Asst. Prof. History of Middle Ages, Tech. Univ. of Berlin 1969–70; Ordinary Prof. History of Middle Ages, Tech. Univ. of Brunswick 1970–, Rector 1976–78; Pres. Georg-August-Univ., Göttingen 1979–; mem. Akad. der Wissenschaften Göttingen 1986, Accademia Pontaniana Napoli 1986. *Publications:* Moneta Regis 1957, Kirche und Monarchie im staufischen Königreich Sizilien I, 1-4 1973–82. *Address:* Georg-August-Universität, Göttingen; Leipziger Strasse 236B, 33 Brunswick, Federal Republic of Germany (Home).

KAMPELMAN, Max M., J.D., PH.D.; American diplomatist; b. 7 Nov. 1920, New York; s. of Joseph Kampelmacher and Eva Gottlieb; m. Marjorie Buetow 1948; two s. three d.; ed. New York and Minnesota Univs.; Partner, Fried, Frank Harris, Shriver and Kampelman, Washington 1956–85; Visiting Prof. Political Science, Claremont Coll., Calif. 1963; Sr. Advisor, U.S. Del. to the U.N. 1966–67; Chair. Emer., Greater Washington Telecommunications Asscn. (WETA-TV); Co-Chair., U.S. Del. to observe the Elections in El Salvador 1984; Bd. of Dirs., U.S. Inst. of Peace 1985–86; Amb., Head of U.S. Del. to the Negotiations on Nuclear and Space Arms 1985–; Counselor Dept. of State 1987–; Amb. and Chair. U.S. Del. to the Conf. on Security and Co-operation in Europe, Madrid 1980–83; Legis. Counsel to Sen. H. H. Humphrey 1949–55; Bd. of Trustees Woodrow Wilson Int. Center for Scholars 1979– (Chair. 1979–81); Chair. Freedom House 1983–85; Dr. h.c. (Hebrew Univ. of Jerusalem) 1982, (Hebrew Union Coll.) 1984, (Georgetown Univ.) 1984, (Bates Coll.) 1986, (Minn.) 1987, (Bar Ilan) 1987; D.lur. h.c. (Jewish Theological Seminary of N.Y.) 1988, (N.Y. Univ.) 1988; The Anatoly Scharansky Award 1981; Vanderbilt Gold Medal, New York Univ. Law Center 1982; Human Rights Award, American Fed. of Teachers 1983; Masaryk Award, Czechoslovak Nat. Council of America 1983; Golden Plate Award, American Acad. of Achievement 1984; Kt. Commdr's Cross of the Order of Merit (Fed. Repub. of Germany) 1984; Henry M. Jackson Award (JINSA) 1987; Sec. of State's Distinguished Service Award 1988; Trainar Award for Distinction In The Conduct of Diplomacy, Georgetown Univ. 1988. *Publications:* The Communist Party vs. the C.I.O.: A Study in Power Politics 1957, Three Years at the East-West Divide 1983; Co-Author: The Strategy of Deception 1963; contrib. to Congress Against the President 1976. *Address:* Department of State, 2201 C Street, N.W., Washington, D.C. 20520, U.S.A. *Telephone:* (202) 647-6240.

KAN, Yuet Wai, M.D., D.SC., F.R.C.P., F.R.S.; American physician and investigator; b. 11 June 1936, Hong Kong; s. of Tong Po Kan and Lai Wai Li; m. Alvera Lorraine Limauro 1964; two d.; ed. Wah Yan Coll., Hong Kong and Univ. of Hong Kong Medical School; Asst. Prof. of Pediatrics, Harvard

Medical School, U.S.A. 1970-72; Assoc. Prof., Dept. of Medicine, Univ. of Calif., San Francisco 1972-77, Prof., Depts. of Medicine, Lab. Medicine 1977-, Prof., Dept. of Biochemistry and Biophysics 1979-, Head, Div. of Genetics and Molecular Hematology 1983-, Louis K. Diamond Prof. of Hematology 1983-, Investigator, Howard Hughes Medical Inst. 1976-; mem. N.A.S.; mem. N.I.H. Blood Diseases and Resources Advisory Cttee. 1985-; Assoc. Fellow, Third World Acad. of Sciences; Damashek Award, American Soc. of Hematology 1979; Stratton Lecture Award, Int. Soc. of Hematology 1980; George Thorn Award, Howard Hughes Medical Inst. 1980; Gairdner Foundation Int. Award 1984; Allan Award, American Soc. of Human Genetics 1984; Lita Annenberg Hazen Award for Excellence in Clinical Research 1984. *Publications:* more than 147 articles and chapters in many scientific journals and books. *Leisure interests:* tennis and skiing. *Address:* Room U-426, University of California, San Francisco, Calif. 94143-0724, U.S.A. *Telephone:* (415) 476-5841.

KAN YUESAI; Chinese TV personality; b. 1949, Guilin; ed. Brigham Young Univ., Hawaii; Presenter of One World on Chinese TV; Producer and Presenter of Looking East on TV U.S.A.; created Caijin Import-Export Business. *Address:* Caijin Import-Export Company, Beijing Offices, Beijing, People's Republic of China.

KANAAN, Taher Hamdi, PH.D.; Jordanian economist, politician and civil servant; b. 1 March 1935, Nablus, Palestine; s. of Hamdi and Najiah (née Quttainah) Kanaan; m. Ilham Kahwaji 1960; three s.; ed. American Univ. of Beirut, Trinity Coll., Cambridge; Econ. Adviser, Ministry of Planning, Iraq 1964-65; Dir. of Programmes at Arab Fund for Econ. and Social Devt., Kuwait 1973-76; Consultant in Industrial Devt., Ministry of Planning, Morocco 1977-78; Chief External Financing and Devt., UNCTAD, Geneva 1979-83; Dir. and Econ. Adviser Arab Fund 1983-85; Minister of Occupied Territories Affairs 1985, of Planning 1986-; mem. Bd. of Trustees, Centre for Arab Unity Studies; mem. Arab Thought Forum. *Publications:* Input-Output and Social Accounts of Iraq 1960-63, Direction of and Contribution to Arab Fund, Basic Programme for Agricultural Development in the Sudan 1976-85; contributions to: UNCTAD Capital Needs of Developing Countries 1967, UNESOB Selected Studies on Economic and Social Development, Series 1968, 1969, 1970, 1971, 1972, UNCTAD Trade and Development Report 1981, 1982, 1983. *Leisure interests:* swimming, music, history and philosophy. *Address:* Ministry of Planning, P.O. Box 555, Amman, Jordan. *Telephone:* 644381, 644466, 644385.

KANAGARATNAM, Kandiah, M.B.; Singapore international medical officer; b. 16 Oct. 1922, Ceylon; m. Manoranjitham Arunasalam 1954; two d.; ed. Raffles Inst., Singapore, Univ. of Malaya and London School of Hygiene and Tropical Medicine; various posts in Ministry of Health, Singapore 1953-69, including Deputy Dir. of Medical Services 1964, and Chair. of Singapore Family Planning and Population Bd. 1966; Consultant, World Health Org. (WHO), Philippines 1968, Int. Bank for Reconstruction and Devt. (IBRD)—World Bank, Jamaica and Mauritius; Dir. of Population Projects Dept., World Bank 1969-79; Sr. Adviser Health, Population and Nutrition Dept. 1979-; Adjunct Prof., Dept. of Health Admin. Univ. of N. Carolina 1980-; Chair. Second Overall Assessment of Human Reproduction Programme (WHO) 1982; Family Planning Pioneer Award, Population Inst., Washington 1984. *Publications:* Numerous papers on public health, population and family planning. *Leisure interest:* tennis. *Address:* International Bank for Reconstruction and Development, 1818 H Street, Washington, D.C. 20433, U.S.A. *Telephone:* (202) 477-6065.

KANAKARATNE, Neville, M.A., LL.B.; Sri Lankan diplomatist; b. 19 July 1923, Colombo; s. of Mudaliar Kanakaratne and Mildrid de Silva; unmarried; ed. Royal Coll., Colombo, Univs. of Ceylon and Cambridge and Middle Temple, London; Crown Counsel, Dept. of Attorney-Gen. 1951-57; First Sec. and Legal Adviser, Perm. Mission of Ceylon at UN 1957-61; Legal Adviser to Special Rep. of UN Sec.-Gen. in the Congo 1961-62; Legal and Political Adviser to Commdr., UN Emergency Force, Gaza 1962-64; Legal Adviser to Commdr. UN Peace Keeping Force, Cyprus and to Special Rep. of UN Sec.-Gen. 1964-65; Sr. Fellow, Centre for Int. Studies, New York Univ. 1965-66; Minister for Econ. Affairs, Ceylon High Comm., London 1967-70; Amb. to U.S.A. 1970-78, to U.S.S.R. 1982-88; del. to numerous int. confs. and several sessions of UN Gen. Assembly; U.N. Survey Mission to Namibia Aug. 1978, Deputy Special Rep. to Namibia Office of Sec.-Gen. Sept. 1978-81; Hon. LL.D. (George Washington Univ.). *Leisure interests:* theatre, music, reading. *Address:* c/o Ministry of Foreign Affairs, Republic Bldg., Colombo 1, Sri Lanka.

KANAMORI, Masao; Japanese business executive; b. 18 Dec. 1911, Ehime Pref., Japan; m. Keiko Akamatsu 1939; two s. two d.; ed. Kyushu Imperial Univ.; Mitsubishi Heavy Industries Ltd. 1935-50; W. Japan Heavy Industries Ltd. 1950-52; Mitsubishi Shipbuilding & Eng. Co. Ltd. 1952-64; Mitsubishi Heavy Industries Ltd. 1964-, Dir. 1969-71, Man. Dir. 1971-75, Exec. Vice-Pres. 1975-77, Pres. 1977-81, Chair. 1981-82, Pres. 1982-; Purple Ribbon Medal 1968, Order of the Sacred Treasure (First Class) 1984. *Leisure interest:* reading. *Address:* 5-1, 2-chome, Marunouchi, Chiyoda-ku, Tokyo (Office); 6-22, Mitakedai, Midori-ku, Yokohama City, Japan (Home). *Telephone:* 03-212-3111 (Office); 045-973-4282 (Home).

KANANIN, Roman Grigorevich; Soviet architect; b. 1935, Moscow; ed. Moscow Architectural Inst. *Works include:* Patrice Lumumba Univ.,

Moscow (with others) 1969-73, Kazakhstan Cinema, Moscow and 16 twenty-five-storey residential blocks on Lenin Prospekt, Moscow 1965-70, Novyye Cheremushki complex 1973-84, various monuments in Moscow and Magnitogorsk, Head of section No. 3. of 'Mosproyekt-1' 1972-; Lenin Prize 1984.

KANAO, Minoru, B.A.; Japanese business executive; b. 30 July 1914, Toyama Prefecture; s. of Muneyoshi and Kiyoko Kanao; m. Yaeko Yamada 1957; two d.; ed. School of Commerce, Waseda Univ.; joined N.K.K. Corpn. 1938, Gen. Man. Personnel Dept. 1965-70, mem. Bd. of Dirs. 1967-, Man. Dir. 1971-74, Sr. Man. Dir. 1974-78, Exec. Vice-Pres. 1978-80, Pres. 1980-85, Chair. 1985-; Chair. Japan-Canada Econ. Cttee., Fed. of Econ. Orgs. (Keidanren); Officier, Ordre de la Couronne, Belgium; Commdr., Order of Merit, Norway; Order of the Sacred Treasure (1st class). *Leisure interests:* golf, reading. *Address:* N.K.K. Corporation, 1-1-2 Marunouchi, Chiyoda-ku, Tokyo 100 (Office); 5-12-5 Fukazawa, Setagaya-ku, Tokyo 158, Japan (Home). *Telephone:* (03) 704-0126 (Home).

KANAZAWA, Shuzo, B.ECONS.; Japanese business executive; b. 10 Nov. 1910; ed. Kyoto Univ.; one s.; joined Mitsubishi Bank 1933, mem. Bd. Dirs. 1962-, Man. Dir. 1965; Exec. Vice-Pres. Mitsubishi Rayon 1967-73, Pres. 1973-83, Chair. 1983-88; Ranju-houshou Prize. *Leisure interests:* Go, art.

KANDIL, Abdel Hadi; Egyptian politician; b. 1935; Damietta; m.; two c.; ed. Ain Shams Univ. and Petroleum Inst. of Milan; held various posts with General Petroleum Corpn., then Pres.; mem. Acad. of Scientific Research and Tech., Faculty of Science, Ain Shams Univ. Council; mem. Bd. Arab Oil Transporting Co., Nat. Devt. Bank; Minister of Petroleum and Mineral Resources 1985-. *Address:* Ministry of Petroleum, 2 Sharia Latin America, Cairo (Garden City), Egypt. *Telephone:* 25022.

KANE, Edward R., PH.D.; American business executive; b. 13 Sept. 1918, Schenectady, N.Y.; s. of Edward and Elva Kane; m. Doris Peterson 1948; two d.; ed. Union Coll., M.I.T.; joined E. I. du Pont de Nemours & Co. 1943; Textile Fibres 1943-66; Asst. Gen. Man. Industrial and Biochemicals Dept. 1966, Gen. Man. 1967, Dir. 1969-; Vice-Pres., Dir., mem. Exec. Cttee. E. I. du Pont de Nemours & Co. 1969-73, mem. Finance Cttee. and Vice-Chair. Exec. Cttee. 1971-79, Pres. and C.O.O. 1973-79; Dir. J. P. Morgan & Co. Inc., Morgan Guaranty Trust Co., Inco Ltd.; Gen. Dir. Texas Instruments Inc.; mem. Corpn. M.I.T.; mem. Nat. Acad. of Eng. (Treas., Council mem. 1986-), American Chemical Soc., American Inst. of Chemical Engineers, Soc. Chemical Industry (Chair. American Section 1973-74, Pres. London Soc. 1980-81); Int. Palladium Medal (American Section) Soc. de Chimie Industrielle 1979. *Address:* c/o E. I. du Pont de Nemours & Co., Wilmington, Del. 19898, U.S.A.

KANE, Falilou; Senegalese diplomatist and politician; b. 14 July 1938, Joal; s. of Moustapha Kane and Yacine Niang; m. Rabia Ben Zekry 1963; five s.; ed. Coll. Blanchot, Saint-Louis, Lycée Van Vollenhoven, Dakar, and Faculty of Law and Econs., Univ. of Dakar; entered Ministry of Foreign Affairs, Senegal 1960, successively Head of Div. of UN Affairs, Int. Orgs. and Gen. Affairs, Div. of Political Affairs, concurrently Tech. Adviser to Minister of Foreign Affairs; Tech. Adviser in Ministry of Justice Nov.-Dec. 1962; Dir. of Political, Cultural and Social Affairs, Ministry of Foreign Affairs; Minister at Perm. Mission of Senegal to UN 1966; Minister, Embassy of Senegal, Washington until Dec. 1967; Sec.-Gen. Org. Commune Africaine et Malgache (OCAM) 1968-74; Amb. to Canada 1975-79; Perm. Rep. to UN 1979-80; Minister of Commerce Jan. 1981-83; has taken part in numerous int. confs.; decorations from Morocco, Upper Volta, Cameroon, Chad and Repub. of Zaire. *Leisure interests:* sport, reading. *Address:* c/o Ministère de Commerce, Dakar, Senegal.

KANEKO, Ippei, LL.B.; Japanese politician (retd.); b. 12 Feb. 1913, Kokufu-machi, Gifu; s. of Denjiro and Sano Kaneko; m. Shibata Yasuko 1938; one s. three d.; ed. Imperial Univ. of Tokyo; joined Ministry of Finance 1937, Dir.-Gen. Hokkaido Regional Financial Bureau 1954-55, Dir. of Direct Tax Dept. in Nat. Tax Admin. Agency 1956-59, Dir.-Gen. Osaka Regional Tax Admin. Bureau 1959-60; mem. House of Reps. 1960-; Parl. Vice-Minister of Econ. Planning Agency 1966-67; Chair. House of Reps. Standing Cttee. on Finance 1972, Liberal-Democratic Party Research Comm. on Tax System 1976-78; Minister of Finance 1978-79, of Econ. Planning Agency 1984-85; Pres. Nat. Asscn. of Alcoholic Distillate Producers 1986-. *Publications:* Sozeiho Gairon (Outline of Tax Laws) 1950, Sozeiho Riron (Theory of Tax Laws) 1953 and others. *Leisure interests:* golf, photography, travelling. *Address:* 3-14 Shoan-machi 20-chome, Suginami-ku, Tokyo, Japan (Home). *Telephone:* 334-8888 (Home).

KANEKO, Iwazo; Japanese politician; b. 1907, Nagasaki Pref.; m.; elected to House of Reps. nine times; fmr. Vice-Minister of Home Affairs and Transport; Chair. Diet Cttees. on Telecommunications and Agric., Forestry and Fisheries; Dir.-Gen. Science and Tech. Agency 1978-79; Minister of Agric., Forestry and Fisheries 1982-83; Chair. Nat. Round Haul Net Fishery Asscn. *Address:* Liberal-Democratic Party, 7, 2-chome, Hiraka-wacho, Chiyoda-ku, Tokyo, Japan.

KANEMARU, Shin; Japanese politician; b. 1915; mem. House of Reps., re-elected six times; fmr. Chair. Liberal Dem. Party (LDP) Diet Policy Cttee.; Minister of Construction 1972-73; Dir. Nat. Land Agency, then of Defence Agency until 1978; Sec.-Gen. LDP 1984-86; Deputy Prime Minister

(State Minister in charge of Special Assignments) 1986–87; Liberal Democratic Party. *Address:* House of Representatives, Tokyo, Japan.

KANERVA, Ilkka Armas Mikael, M.POL.SC.; Finnish politician; b. 28 Jan. 1948, Lokalahti; Chair. Nat. Coalition Party Youth League 1972–76; mem. Party Man. Nat. Coalition Party 1972–, mem. Exec. Cttee. 1975–; mem. Turku City Council 1972–; mem. Parl. 1975–; Minister without Portfolio, attached to Office of the Council of State 1987–. *Address:* Valtioneuvosto, Helsinki, Finland.

KANG, Young Hoon, M.A., PH.D.; Korean diplomatist and politician; b. 30 May 1922; m. Hyo-Soo Kim 1947; two s. one d.; ed. Univs. of Manchuria and Southern California; Mil. Attaché to Embassy, Washington, D.C. 1952–53; Div. Commdr. 1953, Corps Commdr. 1959–60; retd. rank of Lieut.-Gen. 1961; Asst. Minister of Defence 1955–56; Staff mem. Research Inst. on Communist Strategy and Propaganda, Univ. of S. California 1968–69; Dir. Research Inst. on Korean Affairs, Silver Spring, Md. 1970–76; Dean Graduate School, Hankuk Univ. of Foreign Studies 1977–78; Chancellor Inst. of Foreign Affairs and Nat. Security, Ministry for Foreign Affairs 1978–80; Amb. to U.K. 1981–84, to the Holy See 1985–88; Prime Minister of the Repub. of Korea Dec. 1988–; numerous mil. medals. *Address:* Office of the Prime Minister, Chong Wa Dae (The Blue House), 1 Sejong-no, Chongno-ku, Seoul, Republic of Korea.

KANG KEQING; Chinese politician; b. 1912 Wan'an, Jiangxi; m. Marshal Zhu De (died 1976); ed. Jinggangshan Red Army Coll. 1933, Anti-Japan Mil. and Political Acad. 1936–37; joined the Communist Youth League 1927; engaged in organizational and propaganda work during Long March 1934–35; Dir. Political Dept. 8th Route Army 1937; mem. Standing Cttee. Democratic Women's Fed. 1949–75; mem. Council. Sino-Soviet Friendship Asscn. 1949–54; mem. Standing Cttee. Athletics Fed. 1952–56; Deputy for Henan to 1st NPC 1954, 2nd NPC 1958; Sec. Democratic Women's Fed. 1955–57; Vice-Chair. Women's Fed. 1957–58, Chair 1978–88, Hon. Chair. Sept. 1988–; Deputy for Jiangxi Prov. to 4th NPC 1975, 5th NPC 1978; mem. 11th CCP Cen. Cttee. 1977–82, 12th Cen. Cttee. 1982–87; Vice Chair. Credentials Cttee. 5th NPC 1979; Vice Chair. Nat. Cttee. for the Defence of Children 1980, Chair. 1983–; mem. Presidium 5th NPC 1980, 6th NPC 1986–; mem. Constitution Revision Cttee. 1980; Chair. Children's Foundation 1981–; Chair. Soong Ching Ling Foundation 1982–. *Address:* Chinese Women's Federation, Beijing, People's Republic of China.

KANG KYUNG-SHIK; Korean politician; b. 10 May 1936; ed. Coll. of Law, Seoul Nat. Univ., Graduate School of Public Admin., Syracuse Univ., U.S.A.; Head Budget Man. Div., Econ. Planning Bd. (EPB) 1969; Dir. Price Policy Bureau, EPB 1973, Econ. Planning Bureau 1974, Budget Bureau 1976; Asst. Minister for Planning, EPB 1977; Asst. Minister EPB 1981; Vice-Minister of Finance 1982, Minister of Finance 1982–83; mem. Exec. Cttee. Seoul Olympics Organizing Cttee. 1982–88.

KANG MAOZHAO; Chinese diplomatist; Political Commissar, PLA –1949; Cultural Attaché, Embassy, India 1950; Attaché, Embassy, Nepal 1955, Embassy, Afghanistan 1956; Counsellor, Kabul Embassy, Afghanistan 1957–59; Deputy Dir. Information Dept., Ministry of Foreign Affairs 1959–64; Chargé d'affaires (a.i.), Yugoslavia 1964–66; Amb. to Cambodia 1969–74, to Mauritania 1975–78, to EEC 1978–81 and concurrently to Belgium and Luxembourg 1978–81. *Address:* c/o Ministry of Foreign Affairs, 225 Chaoyangmennei Street, Dongsi, Beijing, People's Republic of China.

KANG SHI'EN; Chinese government official; b. 1915, Huyang Co., Hebei Prov.; Asst. Minister of Petroleum Industry 1955–56; Vice-Minister of Petroleum Industry 1956; criticized and removed from office during the Cultural Revolution 1967; Minister of Petroleum and Chemical Industries 1975, of State Econ. Comm. 1978–81, of Petroleum Industry 1981–82; mem. 11th Cen. Cttee. CCP 1977, 12th Cen. Cttee. CCP 1982–87, Vice-Premier, State Council 1978–82, State Councillor May 1982–; mem. Standing Cttee. Cen. Advisory Comm. 1987–; Hon. Chair. Asscn. for Devt. and Man. of Coastal Zones 1985–. *Address:* c/o State Council, Beijing, People's Republic of China.

KANIA, Stanisław; Polish politician; b. 8 March 1927, Wrocanka, Jasło district; ed. Higher School of Social Sciences of Central Cttee. of Polish United Workers' Party, Warsaw; mem. Polish Workers' Party 1945–48, Polish United Workers' Party (PZPR) 1948–; Head, Agricultural Dept., Warsaw Voivodship Cttee., PZPR, then Sec. Warsaw Voivodship Cttee. 1958–68; Deputy mem. Cen. Cttee., PZPR 1964–68, mem. 1968–86, Sec. 1971–81, Deputy mem. Politburo 1971–75, mem. 1975–81; First Sec. PZPR Cen. Cttee. Sept. 1980–Oct. 1981; Head, Admin. Dept., Cen. Cttee., PZPR 1968–71; mem. Council of State 1982–85; Deputy to Seym (Parl.) 1972–; Chair. Seym Comm. for Self-Govt. 1985–; Order of Banner of Labour (1st and 2nd Class); Knight's Cross and Officer's Cross, Order of Polonia Restituta; Order of Builders of People's Poland 1977. *Address:* Kancelaria Sejmu, ul. Wiejska 2/6, 00-902, Warsaw, Poland.

KANIN, Garson; American writer and director; b. 24 Nov. 1912, Rochester, New York; s. of David and Sadie (née Levine) Kanin; m. Ruth Gordon 1942 (died 1985); ed. James Madison High School, New York, American Acad. of Dramatic Arts, New York; initially actor on Broadway stage 1933–36; began directing films (asst.) 1935; mem. production staff Samuel

Goldwyn, Hollywood, Calif. 1937; dir. films for R.K.O. including A Man to Remember 1938, My Favorite Wife 1940, Tom, Dick and Harry 1941; dir. play Rugged Path with Spencer Tracy 1945; writer, dir. of play Born Yesterday 1946; dir. plays including Years Ago 1946, The Leading Lady 1948, The Diary of Anne Frank 1955, A Hole in the Head 1957; writer, dir.: The Rat Race 1949, The Live Wire 1950, The Good Soup 1960, Do Re Mi 1961, Come on Strong 1962, Peccadillo 1985, Happy Ending 1988; dir.: Sunday in New York 1961, Funny Girl 1964, I Was Dancing 1964, A Very Rich Woman 1965, We Have Always Lived in the Castle 1965, Idiot's Delight 1970; adapted and dir. The Amazing Adele 1950, A Gift of Time 1962, Remembering Mr. Maugham 1967, Dreyfus in Rehearsal 1974; dir. Ho! Ho! Ho! 1976; *screen plays for films* co-author (with Ruth Gordon): A Double Life 1948, Adam's Rib 1949, Pat and Mike 1952, The Marrying Kind 1952, author: It Should Happen to You 1953, The Girl Can't Help It 1957, The Rat Race 1959, High Time 1960; *co-author:* Woman of the Year 1942, The More the Merrier 1943, From This Day Forward 1946; writer and dir. Some Kind of a Nut 1969; wrote libretto and dir. Die Fledermaus, Metropolitan Opera, New York 1950, 1966; co-dir. (with Carol Reed) The True Glory, Gen. Eisenhower's film report (Acad. Award) 1945; citation New York Film Critic's Circle (for The True Glory); American Acad. of Dramatic Arts Alumni Award; Sidney Howard Memorial Award, Donaldson Award for Best First Play of Season and Best Dir. 1945–46 (all for Born Yesterday); Gold Medal, Holland Soc. 1980. *Publications:* Do Re Mi 1955, Blow Up a Storm 1959, The Rat Race 1960, Remembering Mr. Maugham 1966, Cast of Characters 1969, Tracy and Hepburn: An Intimate Memoir 1971, A Thousand Summers 1973, Hollywood 1974, One Hell of an Actor 1977, It Takes a Long Time to Become Young 1978, Moviola 1979, Smash 1980, Together Again 1981, Cordelia? 1982 and articles and stories in numerous collections and anthologies. *Address:* 200 West 57th Street, Suite 1203, New York, N.Y. 10019, U.S.A. (Office).

KANKAANPÄÄ, Matti, M.SC.; Finnish business executive; b. 6 Nov. 1927, Jyväskylä; s. of Emil Kankaanpää and Aino Häkkinen; m. Iris Veriö 1952; two s. one d.; ed. Helsinki Univ. of Technology; Design Eng. Wärtsilä yhtymä Oy Kone ja Silta, Helsinki 1950–53, Chief Eng. 1953–56; Chief Eng. Tekno-Invest Oy., Helsinki 1956; Research Eng. Beloit Corpn., Beloit, Wis., U.S.A. 1957–58, Staff Eng. 1958–63; Project Man. Jaakko Pöyry & Co. (consulting engs.) 1963–67, Vice-Pres. 1968–71; Asst. Dir., Dir. of Pulp, Paper and Woodworking Machinery Group, Valmet Corpn. 1971–73, Vice-Pres. Pulp, Paper and Woodworking Machinery Group 1974–79, mem. Bd. of Dirs. 1978–82, Pres. and C.O.O. 1980–82, Chair., Pres. and C.E.O. Valmet Corpn. 1982–; Chair. Fed. of Finnish Metal and Eng. Industries 1985. *Address:* Valmet Corporation, Punanotkonkatu 2, 00130 Helsinki, Finland. *Telephone:* 358 0 13291.

KANTARAT, Air Chief Marshal Panieng; Thai air force officer and politician; b. 1 April 1922, Samut Prakan; m. Khunying Suranooch; three s. one d.; ed. Wat Thep Sirin School, Bangkok, Royal Thai Army Tech. School, Flying Training School, Air Command and Staff Coll., Thailand Air Command. and Staff Coll., U.S.A., Army War Coll., Bangkok, Nat. Defence Coll.; attended courses R.A.F. Teachers' Flying Training School, U.K., Fighters' Flying School, U.S.A.; started air force career as Pilot Officer, Lop Buri; Air Attaché, Thai Embassy, London 1958; Deputy Chief of Staff, Thai Army Command 1962; Dir., Directorate of Operations 1963; Deputy Chief of Air Staff for Operations 1971; Vice-Chief of Air Staff 1974, Chief 1975; Deputy Minister of Defence 1976–86, Minister 1986–88; C.-in-C. Royal Thai Air Force 1977–81. *Address:* c/o Ministry of Defence, Sanamchai Road, Bangkok 10200, Thailand.

KANTE, Mamadou Boubacar; Mali diplomatist; b. Sept. 1926, Hombori; m.; two c.; entered govt. service, Chief of Office Staff, Ministry of Labour 1961–62, of Interior, Information and Tourism 1962–64, of Interior 1964–66; tech. adviser to Office of Pres. of Mali 1966–67; Perm. Rep. to UN and Amb. to Cuba 1967–69; Dir.-Gen. of Political, Admin., Legal and Financial Affairs in Ministry of Foreign Affairs and Co-operation 1969–71, Sec.-Gen. of Ministry 1971–75; Amb. to U.S.A. 1975–77; Perm. Rep. to UN 1975–79; Deputy Head of del. to UN Gen. Assembly 1967, 1968, 1971–74. *Address:* c/o Ministry of Foreign Affairs, Bamako, Mali.

KANTER, Rosabeth Moss, M.A., PH.D.; American professor of management, consultant and writer; b. 15 March 1943, Cleveland; d. of Nelson Nathan Moss and Helen (née Smolen) Moss; m. 1st Stuart Alan Kanter 1963 (died 1969); m. 2nd Barry Alan Stein 1972; one s.; ed. Bryn Mawr Coll., Univ. of Michigan and Harvard Univ. Law School; Assoc. then Asst. Prof. Brandeis Univ. 1967–77; Prof. Yale Univ. 1977–86; Class of 1960 Prof. of Man. Harvard Univ. Business School 1986–; Visiting Prof. M.I.T. 1973–74, Harvard 1979–80; Chair. Bd. Goodmeasure Inc., Cambridge, Mass. 1980–; consultant to BellSouth, Apple Computer, Proctor and Gamble, IBM, Int. Harvester Co., Honeywell Corpn. and numerous other cos.; mem. Bd. Nat. Org. Women Legal Defence and Educ. Fund, New York 1979–86; mem. American Sociological Asscn. (Exec. Council 1982–85), Eastern Sociological Soc. (Exec. Council 1975–78, Gellman Award 1978), Acad. of Man., Cttee. of 200 (also f.); Incorporator Babson Coll. 1984–, Boston Children's Museum 1984–; Trustee Coll. Retirement Equities Fund, New York 1985–; Guggenheim Fellow; numerous hon. degrees; Woman of the Year, New England Women's Business Owners 1981, Int. Asscn. Personnel Women

1981, MS Magazine 1985, Working Woman AT & T Hall of Fame 1986; Athena Award, Intercollegiate Asscn. of Women Students 1980. *Publications:* Work and Family in the U.S. 1977, Men and Women of the Corporation 1977 (C. Wright Mills Award), The Change Masters 1983, and five other books; also over 100 articles in professional journals, magazines, books etc. *Leisure interests:* tennis, swimming. *Address:* Goodmeasure Inc., 330 Broadway, P.O.B. 3004, Cambridge, Mass. 02139 (Office); Harvard School of Business, Boston, Mass. 02163, U.S.A. (Office).

KANTOR, Tadeusz; Polish painter and theatre organizer; b. 6 April 1915, Wielopole, near Cracow; s. of Marian and Helena Kantor; m. Maria Stangret-Kantor 1960; ed. Cracow Acad. of Fine Arts; organized underground theatre, Cracow, during occupation; Prof. Cracow Acad. of Fine Arts 1948, 1969; mem. Asscn. of Polish Plastic Artists; founded Cricot 2 Theatre, Cracow 1955, participated with theatre in festivals: Premio Roma 1969, 1974, Mondial du Théâtre, Nancy 1971–77, Edinburgh Festival 1972, 1973, 1976, 1980 (First Prize for Dead Class, 30th Festival 1976), 8th Arts Festival, Shiraz 1974–77, Festival d'Automne, Paris 1977; dir. of numerous plays including Cuttle Fish 1956, In a Little Manor House 1961, Madman and Nun 1963, Happening-Cricotage 1965, Water-hen 1967, Dead Class 1975, Où sont les neiges d'antan 1978, Wielopole-Wielopole 1980; Tutaj nie powróce juz nigdy, Krótka lekcja; exhibited paintings at: 30th Biennale of Art, Venice 1960, L'Art Théâtre exhbn., Baden-Baden 1965, São Paulo Biennale 1967, Happening and Fluxus exhbn., Cologne and Stuttgart 1970, Whitechapel Gallery, London 1976, Documenta 6, Kassel 1977, ROSC 1977 Dublin, also at Moderna Museet, Stockholm, Museum of Modern Art, New York and Solomon R. Guggenheim Museum, New York; exhibits in Foksal Gallery, Warsaw: Linia Podziału (The Line of Division) 1965, List (A Letter) 1967, Lekcja anatomii wg. Rembrandta (Rembrandt's Anatomy Lesson) 1968, Panoramiczny happening morski (Panoramic Sea Happening) 1967, 1977; Multipart 1970, Cambriolage 1971, Tout ne tient qu'à un fil 1973; exhbn. in Modern Art Gallery, Warsaw: Zapiecek 1976, Palazzo del esposizione, Rome 1978, Palazo Reale, Milan 1979; Premio Marzotto, Rome 1968, Prize for Painting, São Paulo 1967, Prix Rembrandt, J. W. Goethe-Stiftung Basel 1978, Grand Prix "Le Théatre des Nations", Caracas 1978, OBIE Prize, New York 1979, 1982, Minister of Culture and Art (1st Prize) 1981, Commdr.'s Cross, Order of Polonia Restituta 1982, Diploma of Minister of Foreign Affairs 1982, Chevalier, Ordre de la Légion d'Honneur (France) 1986. *Publications:* Emballages 1976, Teatr Śmierci (Theatre of Death) 1976, La Classe Morta, Milano 1981, Wielopole-Wielopole, Milano 1981. *Address:* Ul. Elbląska 6 m. 11, 30-054 Cracow, Poland.

KANTROWITZ, Adrian, M.D.; American heart surgeon; b. 4 Oct. 1918, New York City; s. of Bernard Abraham and Rose Esserman Kantrowitz; m. Jean Rosensaft 1947; one s. two d.; ed. New York Univ. and Long Island Coll. of Medicine; Cleveland Teaching Fellow in Physiology, Western Reserve Univ. School of Medicine 1951–52; Instructor in Surgery, New York Medical Coll. 1952–55; Asst. Prof. of Surgery, New York Downstate Medical Center 1955–57, Assoc. Prof. of Surgery 1957–64, Prof. of Surgery 1964–70; Adjunct Surgeon, Montefiore Hospital, Bronx, New York 1951–55; Dir. (full-time) Cardiovascular Surgery, Maimonides Hospital 1955–64; Attending Surgeon, Maimonides Medical Center 1955–64; Dir. Surgical Services (full-time), Maimonides Medical Center and Coney Island Hospital, Brooklyn 1964–70; Chair. Dept. of Surgery, Sinai Hospital, Detroit 1970–73, Chair. Dept. of Cardiovascular-Thoracic Surgery 1973; Prof. Surgery, Wayne State Univ. School of Medicine 1970; Pres. Brooklyn Thoracic Soc. 1967–68; Pres. American Soc. of Artificial Internal Organs 1968–69; mem. Editorial Bd. Journal of Biomedical Materials Research 1966–, mem. Scientific Review Bd. Medical Research Engineering 1966–; Henry L. Moses Research Prize 1949–; New York State Medical Soc., First Prize, Scientific Exhibit 1952, First Prize Maimonides Hospital Research Soc. for work in Bladder Stimulation 1963, Gold Plate Award, American Acad. of Achievement 1966, Max Berg Award for Outstanding Achievement in Prolonging Human Life 1966, Brooklyn Hall of Fame Man of Year Award for Science 1966, Theodor and Susan B. Cummings Humanitarian Award, American Coll. of Cardiology 1967; performed first human implantation of a partial mechanical heart 1966; performed first U.S. human heart transplantation 1967 and first human intra-aortic balloon pump 1968. *Publications:* numerous articles and films on heart surgery. *Leisure interests:* flying, skiing, sailing, music. *Address:* 70 Gallogly Road, Pontiac, Mich. 48055, U.S.A. *Telephone:* 313-338-4167.

KANTROWITZ, Arthur Robert, PH.D.; American physicist and university professor; b. 20 Oct. 1913, New York; s. of Bernard A. Kantrowitz and Rose (née Esserman) Kantrowitz; m. 1st Rosalind Joseph 1943 (divorced 1974), three d.; m. 2nd Lee Stuart 1980; ed. Columbia Univ.; Physicist and Chief of Gas Dynamics Section Nat. Advisory Cttee. for Aeronautics 1935–46; Prof. Aero Eng. and Eng. Physics Cornell Univ. 1946–56; Fulbright and Guggenheim Fellow Cambridge and Manchester Univs. (U.K.) 1953–54; Founder and C.E.O. Avco Everett Research Lab. Inc., Everett, Mass. 1955–78, Sr. Vice-Pres. and Dir. Avco Corpn. 1956–78; Prof. of Eng. Thayer School of Eng., Dartmouth Coll. 1978–; mem. N.A.S., Nat. Acad. of Eng., American Inst. of Physics, American Acad. of Arts and Sciences, American Physical Soc., American Inst. of Aeronautics and Astronautics, Int. Acad. of Astronautics; mem. Presidential Advisory Group on Anticipated Advances in Science and Tech., "Science Court" Task Force Chair. 1975–76; Hon. Prof. Huazhong Inst. of Tech., Wuhan, People's Repub. of

China 1980; Theodore Roosevelt Medal of Science 1967; Hon. Life mem. Bd. of Govs., The Technion; M. H. D. Faraday Medal, UNESCO 1983. *Publications:* co-author Fundamentals of Gas Dynamics 1958, author or co-author of more than 175 scientific and professional articles. *Leisure interests:* sailing, tennis. *Address:* Dartmouth College, H.B. 8000, Hanover, N.H. 03755 (Office); 4 Downing Road, Hanover, N.H. 03755, U.S.A. (Home). *Telephone:* (603) 646-2611 (Office); (603) 643-3639 (Home).

KAO, Henry Yu-shu; Chinese politician; b. 3 Sept. 1913, Taipei; m.; three s.; ed. Waseda Univ., Tokyo; Mayor of Taipei 1954–57, 1964–67, 1967–72; Minister of Communications 1972–76, of State 1976–. *Address:* The Executive Yuan, Taipei, Taiwan.

KAPEK, Antonín, ING.; Czechoslovak politician; b. 6 June 1922, Roudnice nad Labem; ed. Czech Technical Univ., Prague; Chief Technologist, Chief Engineer, later Dir., ČKD-Sokolovo Engineering Works, Prague 1953–58; Dir. ČKD-Praha Eng. Works 1958–65, Gen. Dir. 1965–68; mem. Cen. Cttee. CP of Czechoslovakia 1958–88, alt. mem. Presidium of Cen. Cttee. 1962–68, mem. Presidium (Politburo) 1970–88; mem. Nat. Ass. 1964–69; Deputy to House of People, Fed. Ass. 1969–88; mem. Bureau of Cen. Cttee., CP of Czechoslovakia, for directing party work in the Czech lands 1969–70; Chief Sec. and mem. Presidium of Prague City Cttee., CP of Czechoslovakia 1969–88; Chair. Prague City Cttee. of the Nat. Front 1975–77; Order for Merits in Construction, Distinction of Outstanding Work 1965, Order of Red Banner of Labour (U.S.S.R.) 1966, 1982, Order of the Repub. 1972, Order of Victorious February 1973, Hero of Socialist Labour 1982, Klement Gottwald Order 1982. *Address:* Central Committee of the Communist Party of Czechoslovakia, nabřeží Ludvíka Svobody 12, Prague 1, Czechoslovakia.

KAPITAN, Bolesław, M.A.; Polish politician; b. 21 Sept. 1932, Ostrów Lubelski, Lublin Voivodship; ed. M. V. Lomonosov Univ., Moscow; teacher in secondary and higher educ., Łódź 1958–65; simultaneously political activity until 1973, including Propaganda Sec. of Polish United Workers' Party (PZPR) Dist. Cttee., Łódź-Polesie, then Head of Propaganda Dept. of PZPR Łódź Cttee. and Organizational Sec. of PZPR Łódź Cttee.; Chair. Chief Cttee. for Physical Culture and Tourism 1973–78; Pres. Polish Olympic Cttee. 1973–78; First Sec. PZPR Voivodship Cttee., Toruń 1978–80; Deputy to Seym (Parl.) 1980–83; Dir. Centre for Personnel Training and Improvement of Workers' Publishing Co-operative "Prasa-Książka-Ruch", Warsaw 1984–85; Chair. Chief Cttee. for Physical Culture and Tourism 1985–87; numerous decorations. *Address:* Polski Komitet Olimpijski, ul. Frascati 2/4, 00-483 Warsaw, Poland (Office). *Telephone:* 28-50-38.

KAPITANETS, Ivan Matveyivich, Adm.; Soviet politician; b. 1928; ed. Caspian Higher Mil. Naval School, Mil. Naval Acad., Acad. of GHQ; served in Soviet Navy 1946–; mem. CPSU 1952–; series of posts particularly in Pacific Ocean Div.; First Deputy Commdr. 1978–81; Commdr. of several fleets 1981–; rank of Adm. 1982; cand. mem. of CPSU Cen. Cttee. 1986–; Deputy to U.S.S.R. Supreme Soviet. *Address:* The Kremlin, Moscow, U.S.S.R.

KAPITONOV, Ivan Vasiliyevich; Soviet politician; b. 23 Feb. 1915, Ryazan Oblast'; ed. Moscow Municipal Engineering Inst.; Managerial, Party and Govt. work 1938–54; mem. CPSU 1939–; mem. Cen. Cttee. CPSU 1952–, mem. Secretariat 1965–; mem. Pres. of U.S.S.R. Supreme Soviet 1954–62; First Sec. Moscow Regional Party Cttee. 1954–59, Ivanovo Regional Party Cttee. 1959–64; Head of Dept. of Party Organs Cen. Cttee. of CPSU for R.S.F.S.R. 1964–65, mem. Bureau, Cen. Cttee. 1964–66, Head Dept. Organizational Party Work and Sec. Cen. Cttee. 1965–; Chair. Cen. Auditing Comm. March 1986–; mem. Budget Comm. 1962–66; Deputy to U.S.S.R. Supreme Soviet 1950–, fmr. Chair. Legis. Proposals Comm.; Pres. CPSU Cen. Auditing Comm. 1986–; Order of Lenin (three times) and other decorations. *Address:* Central Committee of CPSU, Staraya ploshchad 4, Moscow, U.S.S.R.

KAPITSA, Mikhail Stepanovich; Soviet diplomatist and politician; b. 1921; ed. Moscow Oriental Inst., Dr. of Historical Science; Diplomatic Service 1943–; Consultant to Far East Dept. of U.S.S.R. Ministry of Foreign Affairs 1954–56, Deputy Head 1956–60; Amb. to Pakistan 1960–61; sr. posts in Ministry of Foreign Affairs 1961–66; Head of South-East Asia Dept. of Ministry 1966–70, Head of First Far East Dept. 1970–82; mem. Bd. Ministry of Foreign Affairs 1970–; U.S.S.R. Deputy Foreign Minister 1982–. *Address:* Ministry of Foreign Affairs, Smolenskaya Square, Moscow, U.S.S.R.

KAPLAN, Rabbi Jacob, L. EN PHIL.; French rabbi; b. 7 Nov. 1895, Paris; s. of Benjamin Kaplan and Eidel Klein; m. Fanny Dichter 1925; three s. two d.; ed. Séminaire Israélite de France; Rabbi of Mulhouse 1922; Rabbi in Paris 1929; Auxiliary Rabbi to Chief Rabbi of France 1939; Chief Rabbi of Paris 1950; Chief Rabbi of France 1955–81, of the Cen. Consistory 1981–; mem. Acad. des Sciences Morales et Politiques, Paris 1967–; Grand Croix, Légion d'honneur, Croix de guerre (twice), Grande Plaque de la Ville de Paris, Grand Croix, Ordre Nat. du Mérite; Dr. h.c. (Theological Seminary of New York); citation by Mayor of New York for distinguished service, Grand-Croix 1988. *Publications:* Le judaïsme et la justice sociale 1937, Racisme et judaïsme 1940, French Jewry under the Occupation (American Jewish Year Book) 1945–46, Le judaïsme dans la société française contemporaine 1948, Témoignages sur Israël 1949, Les temps d'épreuve

1952, Judaïsme français et sionisme 1976, Le vrai visage du judaïsme 1976, Justice pour la Foi juive 1977, Un Enseignement de l'Estime 1982, N'oublie pas 1984. *Address:* 1 rue Andrieux, 75008 Paris, France. *Telephone:* 4522-33-97.

KAPLAN, Joseph, A.M., PH.D.; American physicist; b. 8 Sept. 1902, Tapolcza, Hungary; s. of Heinrich and Rosa (Löwy) Kaplan; m. 1st Katherine E. Feraud 1933 (died 1966); m. 2nd Frances Baum-Kaplan 1984; ed. Johns Hopkins Univ.; Instructor in Physics Johns Hopkins Univ. 1926; Nat. Research Fellow in Physics Princeton Univ. 1927-28; Asst. Prof. Univ. of California 1928-35, Assoc. Prof. 1935, Prof. 1940-70, Prof. Emer. 1970-, and Chair. Dept. of Physics 1938-44, Dept. of Meteorology 1940-44; Acting Dir. Inst. of Geophysics, Univ. of Calif., Dir. 1946-47; mem. Comm. Int. Astronomical Union 1922; Chief Operations Analysis Section 2nd Air Force 1943-45, Air Forces Weather Service Jan.-Sept. 1945; fmr. mem. Bd. of Dir. Microdot Inc., New World Fund Inc.; Adviser, Axe Science Corpn.; Fellow, Physical Soc. and fmr. Local Sec. for Pacific Coast; mem. Exec. Cttee. Int. Assen. of Terrestrial Magnetism and Electricity; Chair. Mixed Cttee. on Upper Atmosphere TMS and (IAIAM) and U.S. Cttee. for the Int. Geophysical year; Fellow, The Meteoritical Soc. (Councillor 1946-50); Pres. Int. Assen. of Geomagnetism and Aeronomy, Int. Union of Geodesy and Geophysics; Chair. U.S. Nat. Cttee. for the Int. Geophysical Year; mem. N.A.S.; Fellow, Inst. of Aeronautics and Astronautics; mem. Astronomical Soc., Astronomical Soc. of the Pacific, Optical Soc. of America; Fellow, American Geophysical Union; mem. Bd. of Govs. Hebrew Univ. of Jerusalem, Weizmann Inst. of Science at Rehovoth; Hon. mem. and Fellow, American Meterological Soc.; Hon. D.Sc. (Univ. of Notre Dame, Carleton Coll.), Hon. L.H.D. (Yeshiva Univ., Jewish Theological Seminary and Hebrew Union Coll.). *Publications:* Across the Space Frontier 1950, Physics and Medicine of the Upper Atmosphere 1952, Great Men of Physics 1969. *Leisure interests:* walking, golf, writing. *Address:* 1565 Kelton Avenue, Los Angeles, Calif. 90024, U.S.A. *Telephone:* 213-4738839.

KAPLANSKY, Irving, B.A., M.A., PH.D.; American mathematician; b. 22 March 1917, Toronto, Canada; s. of Samuel Kaplansky and Anna Zuckerman; m. Rachelle Brenner 1951; two s. one d.; ed. Univ. of Toronto and Harvard Univ.; Instructor, Harvard Univ. 1941-44; Research Mathematician, Columbia Univ. 1945; Instructor, Univ. of Chicago 1945-47, Asst. Prof. 1947-52, Assoc. Prof. 1952-56, Prof. 1956-, Chair. Dept. of Maths. 1962-67; Pres. American Math. Soc. 1984; Dir. Berkeley Math. Sciences Research Inst. 1984; mem. N.A.S. 1966; apptd. to George Herbert Mead distinguished service Professorship 1969; Hon. Dr. of Maths. (Waterloo) 1968, Hon. LL.D. (Queen's) 1969. *Publications:* numerous research papers and books on mathematics. *Leisure interests:* music, swimming. *Address:* Mathematical Sciences Research Institute, 1000 Centennial Drive, Berkeley, Calif. 94720, U.S.A. *Telephone:* 642-0143.

KAPNICK, Harvey Edward, Jr., B.S., C.P.A.; American accountant; b. 16 June 1925, Palmyra, Mich.; s. of Harvey E. and Beatrice Bancroft Kapnick; m. 1st Jean Bradshaw 1947 (died 1962), 2nd Mary Redus Johnson 1963; three s.; ed. Cleary Coll. and Univ. of Michigan; joined Arthur Andersen & Co. (Accountants) 1948, Partner 1956, Man. Partner, Cleveland Office 1962, mem. Bd. of Dirs. 1966-, Chair. and Chief Exec. 1970-79, Deputy Chair. and C.O.O., First Chicago Corpn., First Nat. Bank, Chicago 1979-80; Pres. Kapnick Investment Co. 1980-84; Chair., Pres. and C.E.O. Chicago Pacific Corpn. 1984-; Dir. Dearborn Park Corpn., Chicago Council on Foreign Relations, Lyric Opera of Chicago, United Way of Metropolitan Chicago; Chair. U.S. Treasury Advisory Cttee. on Fed. Consolidated Financial Statements; mem. Iran-U.S. Business Council (Chair. U.S. Section), U.S. Advisory Cttee. for Trade Negotiations, U.S. Advisory Cttee. on Transnational Enterprises; mem. American Inst. of Certified Public Accountants; mem. U.S. del. to Ad Hoc Working Group on Accounting Standard, OECD Cttee. on Int. Investment and Multinational Enterprises; mem. Bd. of Trustees Menninger Foundation, Orchestral Assen., Logistics Man. Inst., Museum of Science and Industry Northwestern Univ.; Hon. D.Sc. (Cleary Coll.) 1971, Hon. D.H.L. (DePauw Univ.) 1979. *Address:* 200 S. Michigan, Chicago, Ill. 60604 (Office); 4000 Run Row, Naples, Fla. 33940, U.S.A. (Home).

KAPOLYI, Dr. László; Hungarian engineer and politician; b. 1932, Budapest; ed. Budapest Technical Univ., Univ. of Heavy Industry, Miskolc and Karl Marx Univ. of Political Economy, Budapest; worked as engineer at Coal Mines of Tatabánya 1953-76; Deputy Minister of Heavy Industry 1976-81, Sec. of State 1981-83; Minister of Industry 1983-87; Govt. Commr. for coal mining 1988-; Corresp. mem. Hungarian Acad. of Sciences 1979-85, mem. 1985-; Titular Prof. Eötvös Loránd Univ., Budapest; mem. Hungarian Socialist Workers Party 1967-; Pres. Scientific Soc. of Energetics 1984-; State Prize 1983. *Address:* Ministry of Industry, Mártirok utja 85, Budapest II, Hungary. *Telephone:* 751-682.

KAPOOR, Anish, M.A.; Indian artist; b. 12 March 1954, Bombay; s. of Rear-Adm. and Mrs. D. C. Kapoor; m. 1953; ed. Hornsey Coll. of Art, Chelsea Coll. of Art, London; teacher, Wolverhampton Polytechnic 1979; Artist-in-Residence, Walker Art Gallery, Liverpool 1982; one-man exhbns. in Paris 1980, London 1981, 1982, 1983, 1985, Liverpool 1982, 1983, Rotterdam, Lyon 1983, New York, Cologne 1984, Chicago, Basel 1985, Oslo, New York, Buffalo 1986 and has participated in group exhbns. since 1974

throughout Britain and in Europe, Australia and New York. *Address:* 33 Coleherne Road, London, S.W.10, England.

KAPPEL, Frederick R., B.S.E.; American businessman; b. 14 Jan. 1902, Minnesota; s. of Fred Albert and Gertrude May Kappel (née Towle); m. 1st Ruth Carolyn Ihm 1927 (deceased 1974), two d.; m. 2nd Alice McWh. Harris 1978; ed. Univ. of Minnesota; joined Bell System as groundman Northwestern Bell Telephone Co. 1924, Asst. Vice-Pres. (Operations) 1939, Vice-Pres. (Operations) and Dir. 1942; Asst. Vice-Pres. (Operation and Eng.) American Telephone and Telegraph Co. 1949, Vice-Pres. (Long Lines) 1949, (Operation and Eng.) 1949, Pres. Western Electric Co. 1954, Pres. American Telephone and Telegraph Co. 1956-67, Chair. 1961-67, Chair. Exec. Cttee. 1967-69; Chair. Bd. Int. Paper Co. 1969-70, Chair. Exec. Cttee. 1971-; responsible for Telstar communications satellite July 1962; Dir. Chase Manhatten Bank 1956-72, Metropolitan Life Insurance Co., Gen. Foods Corpn. 1961-73, Acad. of Political Sciences; Trustee, New York Presbyterian Hospital, Cttee. for Econ. Devt., Boys' Clubs of America 1956-74; mem. of Advisory Bd. Salvation Army 1949-67; mem. The Business Council, Chair. 1963-64; Trustee, Columbia Univ. 1962-69, Minn. Univ., Inst. of Electrical and Electronics Engineers; Chair. President's Comm. on Postal Org. 1967-68; Chair. Bd. of Govs., U.S. Postal Service 1970-74; numerous hon. degrees and awards, including Outstanding Achievement Award (Minnesota) 1954. *Publications:* Vitality in a Business Enterprise 1960, Business Purpose and Performance 1964. *Leisure interests:* golf, fishing, hunting, family. *Address:* 435 South Gulf Stream Avenue, Sarasota, Florida 33577, U.S.A. (Home).

KAPRIO, Leo, M.D., M.P.H., DR.P.H., F.A.P.H.A. ; Finnish and international public health officer; b. 28 June 1918, Tuusula, Finland; s. of Dr. Arthur J. T. M. and Mrs. K. Molander; m. Aini Korhonen, M.PH.ED. 1943; two s. one d.; ed. Helsinki, Johns Hopkins and Harvard Univs.; Finnish Army Medical Corps during Second World War; Chief Medical Adviser to Finnish Population Assen. (Vaestoliitto) 1944-49; Chief Medical Adviser, Finnish Red Cross 1951-56; Chair. of State Cttee. to reorganize Finnish Health Services 1953-54; mem. of WHO Advisory Panel on Public Health Admin. 1951-56, 1985-; Chief, Div. of Public Health, Nat. Health Service 1952-56; Regional Officer, E. Mediterranean and Europe, WHO 1956-63; Finnish del. to WHO 1953-54; Bd. mem. WHO of UN R.I.S.D. (Geneva) 1964-67; WHO rep. at World Population Conf. 1965; Dir. Div. of Public Health Services 1963-67; Regional Dir. for Europe 1967-85; Special Adviser to Dir.-Gen. WHO 1985-88; Chair. of Global Advisory Group of WHO Expanded Programme of Immunization 1986-; Hon. mem. Schools Public Health Assen. for the European Region 1978, Int. Epidemiological Assen. 1987; Foreign Corresp. mem. Div. des Sciences, Acad. des Sciences, Inscriptions et Belles Lettres de Toulouse 1977; Dr. h.c. (Leuven), Dr. Med. h.c. (Uppsala), Prof. h.c. (Govt. of Finland). Dr. h.c. (Cracow Medical Acad.) 1976, LL.D. h.c. (Leeds) 1982, Hon. F.F.C.M. (U.K.); J. E. Purkyne Medal (Czechoslovakia), Johan Peter Frank Medal (Fed. Repub. of Germany), Commdr. of the Order of the Finnish White Rose 1982, Commdr.'s Cross of the Icelandic Order of the Falcon 1982, Commdr.'s Cross of the Swedish Royal Order of North Star 1984, and numerous other awards and medals. *Publications:* Primary Health Care in Europe 1979 (trans. into 7 languages), over 100 health policy documents, articles and scientific publs. in Finnish, Swedish, English and German. *Leisure interest:* history. *Address:* P. Hesperiamkatv 7, 00260 Helsinki, Finland (Home). *Telephone:* 406752 (Home).

KAPTO, Aleksandr Semenovich, CAND. PHIL. SC.; Soviet party official; b. 1933; ed. Dnepropetrovsk State Univ.; mem. CPSU 1955-; Komsomol party work 1957-66; Second Sec. of Cen. Cttee. of Ukrainian Komsomol 1966-68, First Sec. 1968-72; mem. Cen. Cttee. of Ukrainian CP 1971-; Sec. of Kiev City, then Kiev Dist. Cttee. of Ukrainian CP 1972-78; Head of Cultural Dept. of Cen. Cttee. of Ukrainian CP and mem. of Politburo of Cen. Cttee. of UCP 1979-86; Head Cen. Cttee. Ideology Dept. 1988-; cand. mem. of Cen. Cttee. of CPSU 1981-; Amb. to Repub. of Cuba 1986-88; elected to Congress of People's Deputies of the U.S.S.R. 1989.

KAPUŚCIŃSKI, Ryszard, M.A.; Polish journalist; b. 4 March 1932, Pińsk; s. of Józef and Maria Bobka Kapuścińska; m. Alicja Mielczarek; one d.; ed. Faculty of History, Warsaw Univ.; began career with Sztandar Młodych 1951, with Polityka 1957-61; later Corresp. Polish Press Agency (PAP) in Africa and Latin America 1962-72; Kultura 1974-81; Deputy Chair. Poland 2000 Cttee., Polish Acad. of Sciences 1981-85; mem. Polish Journalists Assen. -1982; Sr. Assoc. mem. St. Antony's Coll., Oxford 1985; Visiting Scholar Bangalore Univ. 1973, Univ. of Caracas 1978, Columbia Univ. 1983, Temple Univ., Phila. 1988; Gold Cross of Merit, Kt.'s Cross, Order of Polonia Restituta 1974, B. Prus Prize 1975, Julian Brun Prize, Int. Prize of Int. Journalists Org. five times, State Prize (Second Class) 1976. *Publications:* Busz po polsku 1962, Czarne gwiazdy 1963, Kirgiz schodzi z konia 1968, Gdyby cała Afryka... 1969, Dlaczego zginął Karl von Spreti 1970, Chrystus z karabinem na ramieniu 1975, Jeszcze dzień życia 1976, Cesarz 1978, Wojna futbolowa 1978, Szachinszach 1982, Notes (poems) 1986. *Leisure interest:* photography. *Address:* ul. Prokuratorska 11m. 2, 02-074 Warsaw, Poland. *Telephone:* 252223.

KARABASOV, Yuriy Sergeyevich, DR.TECH.SC.; Soviet politician; b. 1939; ed. Moscow Steel and Alloy Inst.; jr., sr. asst., lecturer, Sec. of Party Cttee. at inst. 1961-72; Head of Section, Sec. of Oktyabrsky Regional

Cttee. of Moscow CPSU 1972–77; Head of Section of Moscow City Cttee. 1977–80; First Deputy Pres. of man. of All-Union Soc. Znanie 1980–81; Pro-rector of Acad. of Nat. Econ. with U.S.S.R. Council of Ministers 1981–83; mem. CPSU 1986–; First Sec. of Gagarino Regional Cttee., Moscow 1983–86; Sec. of Moscow City Cttee. 1986–; cand. mem. of CPSU Cen. Cttee. 1986. *Address:* Moscow City Committee of Communist Party of the Soviet Union, Moscow, U.S.S.R.

KARAEVLİ, Ahmet; Turkish politician; b. 1949, Tekirdağ; m.; two c.; ed. Middle East Tech. Univ.; fmr. metallurgical engineer and projects specialist; Deputy for Tekirdağ; mem. Motherland Party; Minister of State 1986–88. *Address:* Parliament Building, Ankara, Turkey.

KARAGEORGHIS, Vassos, PH.D., F.S.A., F.R.S.A.; Cypriot archaeologist; b. 29 April 1929, Trikomo; s. of George and Panagiota Karageorghis; m. Jacqueline Girard 1953; one s. one d.; ed. Pancyprian Gymnasium, Nicosia, Univ. Coll., and Inst. of Archaeology, London Univ.; Asst. Curator, Cyprus Museum 1952–60, Curator 1960–63, Acting Dir., Dept. of Antiquities, Cyprus 1963–64, Dir. 1964–, Dir. d'Etudes, Ecole Pratique des Hautes Etudes, Sorbonne, Paris 1983–84; Adjunct Prof. of Classical Archaeology, State Univ. of New York, Albany; fmrly. Geddes-Harrower Prof. of Classical Art and Archaeology, Univ. of Aberdeen; mem. Governing Body, Cyprus Research Centre; mem. Royal Swedish Acad.; Ordinary mem. German Archaeological Inst., Berlin; Corresp. mem. Archaeological Soc., Athens, Acad. of Athens, Acad. des Inscriptions et Belles Lettres, Paris, Austrian Acad. Sciences, Vienna; Foreign mem. Accademia Nazionale Dei Lincei; Hon. mem. Council of Greek Archaeological Soc., Athens; Fellow, Univ. Coll., London, Soc. of Antiquaries, London, Royal Soc. of Humanistic Studies, Lund; Corresp. Fellow, British Acad.; Visiting Research Fellow, Merton Coll., Oxford 1979; Sr. Research Fellow, Merton Coll., Oxford 1980; Visiting Fellow, All Souls Coll., Oxford 1982, Merton Coll., Oxford 1988; R. B. Bennett Commonwealth Prize 1978; Dr. h.c. (Lyon, Göteborg, Athens, Birmingham, Toulouse, Brock); Chevalier, Légion d'honneur 1971, Order of Merit (1st class), Fed. Repub. of Germany. *Publications:* Treasures in the Cyprus Museum 1962, Nouveaux documents pour l'étude du bronze récent à Chypre 1964, Corpus Vasorum Antiquorum 1964, 1965, Sculptures from Salamis, Vol. I 1964, Vol. II 1966, Excavations in the Necropolis of Salamis, Vol. I 1967, Vol. II 1970, Vol. III 1974, Vol. IV 1978, Mycenaean Art from Cyprus 1968, Cyprus (Archaeologia Mundi) 1968, Salamis in Cyprus 1969, Altägäis und Altkypros (with H. G. Buchholz) 1971, Cypriot Antiquities in the Pierides Collection, Larnaca, Cyprus 1972, Fouilles de Kition I 1974, Kition, Mycenaean and Phoenician discoveries in Cyprus 1976, The Civilization of Prehistoric Cyprus 1976, La céramique chypriote de style figuré I-III (with Jean des Gagniers) 1974–79, Vases et figurines de l'Âge du Bronze (with Jean des Gagniers) 1976, Fouilles de Kition II (with J. Leclant and others) 1976, Hala Sultan Tekké I (with P. Åström, D. M. Baily) 1976, Fouilles de Kition III (with M. G. Guzzo Amadasi) 1977, Two Cypriot sanctuaries of the end of the Cypro-Archaic period 1977, The Goddess with Uplifted Arms in Cyprus 1977, Cypriot Antiquities in the Medelhavsmuseet, Stockholm (with C. G. Styrenius and M.-L. Winbladh) 1977, Mycenaean Vases of the Pictorial Style (with Emily Vermeule) 1981, Excavations at Kition IV (with J. N. Coldstream and others) 1981, Cyprus from the Stone Age to the Romans 1982, Palaepaphos-Skales—An Iron Age Cemetery in Cyprus 1983, Pyla-Kokkinokrenos—A late 13th Century B.C. fortified settlement in Cyprus (with M. Demas) 1984, Cyprus at the close of the Late Bronze Age (with J. D. Muhly, eds.) 1984, Ancient Cypriot Art in the Pierides Foundation Museum (with others) 1985, Archaeology in Cyprus 1960–85 (ed.) 1985, Excavations at Kition V (with M. Demas) 1985, La Nécropole d'Amathonte III: Les Terres Cuites 1987, Excavations at MAA—Palaiokastro 1979–86, 1988 (with M. Demas), Blacks in Ancient Cypriot Art 1988 and articles in German, American, English and French Journals. *Leisure interest:* gardening. *Address:* c/o Department of Antiquities, Nicosia (Office); 12 Kastorias Street, Nicosia, Cyprus (Home). *Telephone:* 402191 (Office); 465249 (Home).

KARAJAN, Herbert von; Austrian conductor; b. 5 April 1908; ed. Salzburg Gymnasium and Mozarteum, Vienna Univ. and Conservatoire; successively Musical Dir. Ulm, Opera and Gen. Musical Dir. Aachen, Kapellmeister, Berlin State Opera, Conductor, Berlin Philharmonic Orch., Lifetime Dir. 1954–89; Dir. Berlin Staatskapelle 1941–45; concert tours in Europe, U.S.A. and Far East 1945–; Artistic Dir. Berlin Philharmonic Orchestra 1955–56, Vienna State Opera 1956–64 (Dir. 1976–); mem. Bd. of Dirs., Salzburg Festival 1965–88; Life Dir. Gesellschaft der Musikfreunde, Vienna; conducted at Salzburg and Lucerne Festivals; Mozart Ring 1957; Hon. D. Mus. (Oxford) 1978; Prix France-Allemagne 1970, UNESCO Music Prize 1983; Hon. Citizen of Berlin 1973; Gold Medal, Royal Philharmonic Soc. 1984. *Leisure interests:* skiing, mountaineering, flying, yachting, motoring, theatre, acoustical research. *Address:* c/o Festspielhaus, Salzburg, Austria.

KARAMANLIS, Konstantinos G.; Greek lawyer and politician; b. 8 March 1907, Prote; m. Amalia Kanelopoulos (divorced); ed. Univ. of Athens; practising lawyer since 1932; M.P. 1935–67, 1974–80; Minister of Labour 1946, of Transport 1947, of Social Welfare 1948–50, of Nat. Defence 1950–52, of Public Works 1952–54, of Communications and Public Works 1954–55; f. Nat. Radical Union 1956; Prime Minister 1955–58, 1958–61, 1961–63; self-imposed exile in France 1963–74; Founder and party leader New Democracy Party 1974, Leader 1974–80; Prime Minister of Greece 1974–80; Pres.

1980–85; Gold Medal (Onassis Foundation) 1981. *Address:* c/o Office of the President, Athens, Greece.

KARANJA, Josphat Njuguna, PH.D.; Kenyan diplomatist and university official; b. 5 Feb. 1931; ed. Alliance High School, Kikuyu, Makerere Coll., Univ. of Delhi and Princeton Univ.; lecturer in African Studies, Fairleigh Dickinson Univ., New Jersey, U.S.A. 1961–62; Lecturer in African and Modern European History, Univ. of E. Africa 1962–63; High Commr. for Kenya in U.K. 1963–70, also accred. to Holy See 1966–70; Vice-Chancellor, Univ. of Nairobi 1970–79; mem. Parl. 1986–; Vice-Pres. of Kenya March 1988–; Minister of Home Affairs and Nat. Heritage 1988–; mem. Bd. of UNITAR; Chair., Gen. Accident Insurance Co. (Kenya) Ltd. 1980–. *Address:* General Accident Insurance Co. (Kenya) Ltd., Icea Building, Kenyatta Avenue, P.O. Box 42166, Nairobi, Kenya.

KARAOSMANOGLU, Attila, PH.D.; Turkish economist; b. 20 Sept. 1932, Manisa; s. of Ibrahim Ethem Karaosmanoglu and Fatma Eda Karaosmanoglu; m. Sukriye Ozyet 1960; one s.; ed. Univs. of Ankara and Istanbul, Harvard and New York Univs., U.S.A.; faculty mem. Middle East Tech. Univ. and Ankara Univ. 1954–63; Head Econ. Planning Dept., State Planning Org. of Turkey 1960–62; Adviser, Fed. of Turkish Trade Unions, Consultant, Turkish Scientific and Tech. Research Council 1963–65; Consultant, Directorate for Scientific Affairs, OECD 1965–66; Economist, then Sr. Economist, World Bank 1966–71; Deputy Prime Minister in Charge of Econ. Affairs and Chair. of the High Planning Council, Turkish Govt. 1971; mem. Exec. Bd., Is Bank, Turkey 1972; Chief Economist, World Bank 1973–75, Dir. of Devt. Policy 1975–79, Dir. of Europe, Middle East and N. Africa Region Country Programmes 1979–82, Vice-Pres. E. Asia and Pacific Region 1983–87, Asia Region 1987–. *Publication:* Towards Full Employment and Price Stability (OECD publ., with others) 1977. *Address:* World Bank, 1818 H Street N.W., Washington, D.C. 20433 (Office); 7408 Helmsdale Road, Bethesda, Md. 20817, U.S.A. (Home). *Telephone:* (202) 676-9001 (Office); (301) 229-4584 (Home).

KARASAWA, Shunjiro; Japanese politician; b. 1930; previous posts include: Parl. Vice-Minister of Finance and of Educ.; Deputy Chief Cabinet Sec.; Chair. Cttee. on Social and Labour Affairs, House of Reps.; Deputy Chair. Liberal Democratic Party (LDP) Policy Research Council; Minister of Posts and Telecommunications 1986–87. *Address:* c/o Ministry of Posts and Telecommunications, 3-2 Kasumigaseki 1-chome, Chiyoda-ku, Tokyo, Japan.

KARASZ, Arthur, LL.D.; American international finance official; b. 13 Dec. 1907, Kolozsvar, Hungary; s. of Ernest Karasz and Helen Fleischer; m. Eva Waldhauser 1939; one s. two d.; ed. high school in Budapest, Univ. of Budapest and the Sorbonne, Paris; mem. Nat. Bank of Hungary 1932–45, Pres. 1945–46; Prof. in Cen. Banking Econ., Univ. of Budapest 1946–48; Chair. Swedish Match Co., Hungary; Lecturer, New School for Social Research, New York 1948–49; Prof. in Monetary Policy, De Paul Univ., Chicago 1949–52; UN Adviser on Monetary Matters to Bolivia 1952–56; joined IBRD (World Bank) 1956, Dir. European Office 1968–72; Adviser to Akbank, Istanbul 1973–75; Vice-Pres. Siemens S.A., St. Denis, France 1974–75, Pres. 1976–79, Dir. 1979–83; mem. Bd. The Royal Bank of Canada, France 1974–83. *Publications:* L'école des totalitaires 1948, Inflación, Estabilización 1955, Bolivia—An Experiment in Development 1957, Reforming the World Economy 1976; numerous articles in economic publications. *Leisure interest:* farming. *Address:* 192 rue Lecourbe, 75015 Paris, France. *Telephone:* 4250 3031.

KARAVAYEV, Georgiy Arkadiyevich; Soviet banker and statesman; b. 3 April 1913; ed. Leningrad Water Transport Eng. Inst.; mem. CPSU 1940–; worker in building enterprises and ministries 1935–57; Deputy Chair. Sverdlovsk Nat. Econ. Council for Construction 1957–59; First Deputy Chair. State Cttee. for Construction 1959–61; Chair. Stroibank (All-Union Capital Investment Bank) 1962–63; First Deputy Chair. U.S.S.R. State Cttee. for Construction 1963–67; Minister of Construction 1967–86; Cand. mem. Cen. Cttee. 1971–76, mem. 1976–; Deputy, U.S.S.R. Supreme Soviet 1966–; State Prize 1950, Order of Lenin (twice), and other decorations. *Address:* c/o Ministry of Construction, 8 ulitsa Stroitelei, Moscow, U.S.S.R.

KAREFA-SMART, John Musselman, B.A., B.SC., M.D., C.M., D.T.M., M.P.H., F.R.S.H., F.A.P.H.A., F.R.S.A.; Sierra Leonean politician and physician; b. 17 June 1915, Rotifunk; s. of Rev. James Karefa-Smart and May Karefa-Smart (née Caulker); m. Rena Joyce Weller 1948; one s. two d.; ed. Fourah Bay and Otterbein Colls., McGill and Harvard Univs.; lecturer, Union Coll., Bunumbu 1936–38; ordained Elder of Evangelical United Brethren Church 1938; Medical Officer, R.C.A.M.C. 1943–45; Sierra Leone Missions Hospitals 1946–48; Lecturer, Ibadan Univ. Coll. (Nigeria) 1949–52; Health Officer, WHO 1952–55, Leader del. to WHO 1956 and 1959; mem. House of Reps. 1957–64; Minister of Lands and Survey 1957–59; Africa Consultant, World Council of Churches 1955–56; Minister for External Affairs 1960–64; Asst. Prof. Columbia Univ. 1964–65; Asst. Dir.-Gen. WHO, Geneva 1965–70; Visiting Prof. of Int. Health, Harvard Univ. 1971–73; lecturer Harvard Medical School 1973–; Medical Dir. Roxbury Health Centre 1973–78, Health and Devt. Consultant 1978–; Clinical Prof. Boston Univ. 1976–; Visiting Prof. Harvard Univ. 1977–; Hon. LL.D. (Otterbein, McGill, Boston); Commdr. Order of Star of Africa (Liberia), Kt. Grand Band, Order of African

Redemption (Liberia), Grand Cordon, Order of the Cedar (Lebanon). *Publications:* The Halting Kingdom 1959, Evaluating Health Program Impact 1974. *Leisure interests:* private flying, photography, stamps. *Address:* Department of Medicine, Harvard University, Cambridge, Mass. 02138, U.S.A.

KARELSKAYA, Rimma Klavdiyevna; Soviet ballet dancer; b. 1927; ed. Moscow Ballet School of Bolshoi Theatre; joined Bolshoi Ballet 1946; has toured with Bolshoi Ballet in U.K., Australia, Belgium, China, Netherlands, New Zealand, Egypt, Poland, Federal Republic of Germany, France, Czechoslovakia and Japan; Honoured Artist of R.S.F.S.R. 1962. *Main roles include:* Raymonda (Raymonda by Glazunov), Laurencia (Laurencia by Krein), Lilac Fairy (Sleeping Beauty by Tchaikovsky), Sovereign of the Dryads and Street Dancer (Don Quixote by Minkus), Mirta (Giselle by Adan), Odette-Odille (Swan Lake by Tchaikovsky), Zaremba (Fountains of Bakhchisarai by Asafyev), Firebird (Firebird by Stravinsky), the Servant Girl (Thunder Road by Kara Karayev), Tsar Devitsa (Humpbacked Horse by Pugni), the Swan (Dying Swan by Saint-Saëns). *Address:* State Academic Bolshoi Theatre of U.S.S.R., Ploshchad Sverdlova 1, Moscow, U.S.S.R.

KARETNIKOV, Nikolai Nikolayevich; Soviet composer; b. 28 June 1930, Moscow; m. Olga Karetnikova 1969; two s.; ed. Moscow Conservatory. *Compositions include:* concert plays for pianoforte 1946, 1961, 1970, 1978, four symphonies 1952, 1956, 1958, 1963, Vanina Vannini (ballet) 1962, string quartet 1962, sonata for piano and pianoforte 1962, concerto for wind instruments 1964, chamber symphony 1967, Klein Zack gennant Zinnober (ballet) 1968, five spiritual songs 1970, Kleinenachtmusik 1971, Til Uhlenshpigel (opera) 1983, Iz Sholom-Aleikhoma (suite) 1984, The Mystery of the Apostle Paul (opera) 1985; also music for theatre, cinema, radio etc. *Leisure interest:* reading. *Address:* Sadovo-Triumfalnaya 12-14, kvartira 37, 103006 Moscow, U.S.S.R. *Telephone:* (095) 209-51 11.

KARGBO, Tom Obakeh, B.A., DIP.ED., M.SC., PH.D.; Sierra Leone diplomatist; b. 17 July 1945, Mabonto; s. of Pa Yamba Kargbo and Leah Susannah Kargbo; m. Mary Kargbo 1980; one s. two d.; ed. Fourah Bay Coll., Univ. of Sierra Leone and Univ. of Salford, Manchester, England; Lecturer St. Augustine's Teachers' Coll., Makeni 1969-72; Sr. teacher Muslim Brotherhood Secondary School, Freetown 1973-75; Lecturer Dept. of Environmental Studies and Geography, Njala Univ. Coll., Univ. of Sierra Leone 1984-87; Perm. Rep. of Sierra Leone to UN, New York 1987-. *Publications:* numerous papers including two for UNICEF (on disability) and one for FAO (on rural issues). *Leisure interests:* reading, games (outdoor). *Address:* Permanent Mission of Sierra Leone to the United Nations, 57 East 64th Street, New York, N.Y. 10021, U.S.A. *Telephone:* (212) 570-0030.

KARHILO, Aarno, LL.M.; Finnish diplomatist; b. 22 Nov. 1927, Helsinki; m.; two c.; ed. Univ. of Helsinki; entered diplomatic service 1952, served in Helsinki, Washington and Rio de Janeiro; First Sec., Rome 1961; Counsellor and Deputy Chief of Mission, UN 1963-65, Moscow 1966-68; Adviser to del. at UN Gen. Ass. 1959-60, 1963-65, 1969-71, Vice-Chair. 1972-76; Amb. to Japan 1971-72; Perm. Rep. to UN 1972-77; Perm. Rep. to UNESCO and Amb. to France 1977-82, to U.S.S.R. 1983-88; Under-Sec. of State for Political Affairs, Ministry for Foreign Affairs, Helsinki 1988-; Vice-Pres. ECOSOC 1973, Pres. 1974; Chair. Finnish del. for ECOSOC Sessions 1972-74. *Publications:* Articles on foreign policy and cultural policy. *Address:* P.O. Box 176, Helsinki, Finland.

KARIEVA, Bernara Rakhimovna; Soviet ballerina; b. 28 Jan. 1936, Tashkent, Uzbekistan; ed. Tashkent Choreography School (under N. A. Dovgelli and L. A. Zass) 1947-51, and Moscow School of Choreography (under M. A. Kozhukhova); Prin. ballerina with Navoi Theatre, Tashkent 1955-; mem. CPSU 1967-; dances frequently with the Bolshoi and has given many performances abroad. *Roles include:* Odile-Odette (Giselle), Francesca (da Rimini), the Young Lady (Young Lady and Hooligan by Shostakovich), Anna (Karenina), Donna Anna (Don Juan), Zarrina (Love and the Sword by Ashrafi); awards include Uzbek State Prize 1970, People's Artist of U.S.S.R. 1973, U.S.S.R. State Prize 1982.

KARIM, Amin Abdul; Iraqi politician; b. 1921, Baghdad; ed. Coll. of Law; entered Govt. service March 1943; has held various govt. posts including Dir.-Gen. of Finance and Revenues, and Pres. State Org. of Banks (until 1968); Minister of Finance 1968-75. *Address:* c/o Ministry of Finance, Baghdad, Iraq.

KARIM, Mustai (pseudonym of Mustafa Safich Karimov); Soviet writer and poet; b. 1919, Kliashevo, Bashkir ASSR; ed. Bashkir Pedagogical Inst. 1940; mem. CPSU 1944-, Soviet Army 1941-45; Chair. Bashkir Writers' Union 1962-; first publ. 1935; Order of Lenin, State Prize (U.S.S.R.) 1972, Hero of Socialist Labour 1979, five other orders and medals. *Publications include:* The Detachment Moves Off 1938, Spring Voices 1941, December Song 1942, The Girls from Our Kolkhoz 1948, Sabantui 1953, Europe-Asia 1951-54, Poems on Viet-Nam 1956-57, The Wedding Feast Goes On 1947, Lonely Birch 1950, Viet-Nam Is Not Far 1958, Abduction of a Girl 1959, A Song Unsung 1961, On the Night of the Lunar Eclipse 1964, Selected Works (2 vols.) 1969, Year by Year 1971, Salavat 1973. *Address:* U.S.S.R. Union of Writers, ul. Vorovskogo 52, Moscow, U.S.S.R.

KARIM-LAMRANI, Mohammed; Moroccan politician and government official; b. 1 May 1919, Fez; economic adviser to H.M. King Hassan II; Dir.-Gen. Office Chérifien des Phosphates 1967-; Chair. Crédit du Maroc; Minister of Finance April-Aug. 1971; Prime Minister 1971-72, 1983-84, 1984-86; now Pres. Crédit du Maroc, Phosphates de Boucraa, Société Marocaine de Distillation et Rectification; Econ. Adviser to King Hassan II of Morocco (q.v.); f. and Pres. Soc. Nat. d'Investissements 1966-. *Address:* Direction Générale O.C.P., Angle Route d'El Jadida, Boulevard de la Ceinture, Casablanca 02, Morocco.

KARINA, Anna (Hanne Karin Bayer); Danish-born, French film actress; b. 22 Sept. 1940, Fredriksburg, Solbjerg; m. 1st Jean-Luc Godard (q.v.) (divorced); m. 2nd Pierre-Antoine Fabre 1968 (divorced); m. 3rd Daniel Georges Duval 1978; Prix Orange. *Films include:* She'll Have To Go 1961, Une femme est une femme 1961, Vivre sa vie 1962, Le petit soldat 1963, Bande à part 1964, Alphaville 1965, Made in the USA 1966, La religieuse 1968, The Magus 1968, Before Winter Comes 1968, Laughter in the Dark 1969, Justine 1969, The Salzburg Connection 1972, Living Together 1974, L'assassin musicien 1975, Les oeufs brouillés 1976, Boulette chinoise 1977, L'ami de Vincent 1983, Ave Maria 1984; has also appeared on television and in theatre. *Publication:* Golden City 1983. *Address:* 78 boulevard Malesherbes, 75008 Paris, France (Office); 8733 Loak Out Montain Road, Los Angeles, Calif. 90046, U.S.A.

KARINTHY, Ferenc, PH.D.; Hungarian writer; b. 2 June 1921, Budapest; s. of Frigyes Karinthy and Aranka Böhm; m. Ágnes Boros; one s. one d.; ed. Budapest Univ. of Arts and Sciences; lecturer in History of Literature and Theatre M.I.T., Columbia Univ. New York, Univ. of Calif. at Los Angeles and Chicago State Univ.; Drama adviser Nat. Theatre of Budapest 1949-50, Madách Theatre 1952-53, Hungarian TV 1965-70. Baumgarten Prize for Literature 1948, József Attila Prize three times, Kossuth Prize 1955. Bd. mem. Hungarian PEN and Int. Theatre Inst. *Publications:* novels: Don Juan éjszakája 1943, Szellemidézés 1946, Kentaur 1947, Budapesti tavasz (Spring Comes to Budapest) 1953, Epepe 1970, Ősbemutató 1972, Alvilági napló 1979, Budapesti Ősz (Fall Comes to Budapest) 1982, Uncle Joe 1987. *Short stories:* Irodalmi történetek 1956, Ferencvárosi sziv 1960, Kék-zöld Florida 1962, Hátország 1965, Viz fölött, viz alatt 1966, Végtelen szőnyeg 1974, Harminchárom (Thirty three) 1977, Marich Géza utolsó kalandja 1979, Mi van a Dunában? 1980, Zenebona 1986. *Plays:* Ezer év 1956, Bösendorfer (Steinway Grand) 1966, and Gőz (Hot Air) 1967, Dunakanyar (Cheese and Eggs) 1967, Hét játék 1969, Gellérthegyi álmok (Dreams on the Hill) 1972, Pesten és Budán 1972, Korallzátony 1976. *Sketches:* Hazai tudósitások 1964, Téli fürdő 1964, Leányfalu és vidéke 1973, Leánykereskedo 1988, Vége a világnak 1988. *Studies:* Olasz jövevény szavaink 1947, Nyelvelés 1964, Dialógus 1978, Óvilág és Ujvilág 1985. *Address:* 1118 Budapest, Ménesi ut 71, Hungary.

KARJALAINEN, Ahti, PH.D.; Finnish economist and politician; b. 10 Feb. 1923, Hirvensalmi; s. of Anshelm Karjalainen and Anna Viherlehto; m. Päivi Helinä Koskinen 1947; three s. one d.; ed. Helsinki Univ.; Prime Minister's Sec. 1950-56; Minister of Finance 1957-58, of Trade and Industry 1959-61, of Foreign Affairs 1961-62, 1964-70, 1972-75; Prime Minister 1962-63, 1970-71; Minister for Economy and Minister to the Cabinet Office, Deputy to the Prime Minister 1976-77; mem. Bd. of Govs., Bank of Finland 1958-83, Deputy Gov. 1979, Acting Gov. 1979-81, Gov. 1982; mem. Parl. 1966-79; Chair. Perm. Intergovernmental Comm. for Econ. Co-operation between Finland and U.S.S.R. 1968-83; Centre Party, mem. Party Cttee. and Exec. Cttee.; presidential elector 1962, 1968, 1978; Grand Cross of the Order of the White Rose of Finland, Commdr. of the Order of the Lion of Finland, Medal of Liberty (Second Class) and other decorations. *Publications:* A National Economy on Wood (in French and German) 1953, The Relation of Central Banking to Fiscal Policy in Finland 1911-1953 1959, From My Point of View 1970, My Years in Finnish Politics 1976, My Homeland is Finland 1981. *Leisure interests:* literature and fishing. *Address:* Perustie 13, 00330 Helsinki, Finland (Home). *Telephone:* 48-45-48 (Home).

KARK, Austen Steven, C.B.E., M.A.; British writer and broadcaster; b. 20 Oct. 1926, London; s. of Maj. Norman Kark and late Ethel Kark; m. 1st Margaret Solomon 1949 (dissolved 1954); m. 2nd Nina Bawden (q.v.) 1954; two step-s. (one deceased) three d.; ed. Upper Canada Coll., Toronto, Nautical Coll., Pangbourne, Royal Naval Coll. and Magdalen Coll., Oxford; dir. first production in U.K. of Sartre's The Flies, Oxford 1948; trained as journalist with Belfast Telegraph and L'Illustré, Switzerland; freelance Journalist and Broadcaster, London and New York 1952-54; joined BBC as Scriptwriter European Productions 1954; Head S. European Services 1964, E. European Services 1972, Controller English Services and Ed. World Service 1974, Deputy Man. Dir. External Broadcasting 1981-85, Man. Dir. 1985-86; Chair. CPC Guidebooks 1987; Adviser to Lord Soames on broadcasting during Independence Elections, Rhodesia 1980, later returned to Zimbabwe to advise Prime Minister on radio and television in Zimbabwe 1980. *Leisure interests:* real tennis, mosaics, croquet. *Address:* 22 Noel Road, London, N1 8HA, England (Home).

KARKOSZKA, Alojzy; Polish politician; b. 15 June 1929, Roczyny, Cracow Voivodship; ed. Tech. Univ., Warsaw; mem. Fighting Youth Union 1945-49, Polish Youth Union 1949-51; mem. Polish United Workers' Party (PUWP) 1951-, Deputy mem. Cen. Cttee. 1964-71, mem. Cen. Cttee. Dec. 1971-81,

Sec. Cen. Cttee. 1976–80; Sec. Warsaw Cttee., PUWP 1960–70; First Sec. PUWP Voivodship Cttee., Gdańsk 1970–71, Warsaw 1976–80; Minister of Construction and Construction Materials Industry 1971–75; mem. Presidium of Govt. 1974–75, Deputy Chair. Council of Ministers 1975–76; Chair. Capital Nat. Council, Warsaw 1977–80; mem. Political Bureau Feb.–Dec. 1980; Deputy to Seym (Parl.) 1976–85; Order of Banner of Labour (1st and 2nd Class); Kt.'s Cross, Order of Polonia Restituta, Order of Builders of People's Poland 1979 and other decorations. *Address:* Polska Zjednoczona Partia Robotnicza, Nowy Świat 6, 00-497 Warsaw, Poland.

KARL, Elfriede; Austrian politician; b. 14 Sept. 1933, Salzburg; ed. Acad. for Social Studies; completed commercial apprenticeship 1950; saleswoman 1950–53; shorthand typist, Building and Timber Workers Union, Salzburg office 1953–60; joined Salzburg Chamber of Labour 1961, Sec. to Econs. Dept. 1968; State Sec. for Family Affairs Policy, Kreisky Govt. 1971–79; State Sec., Fed. Ministry of Finance 1979–83; Fed. Minister for Family Affairs 1983–84; mem. Austrian Socialist Party (SPÖ). *Address:* c/o Federal Ministry for Family Affairs, Vienna, Austria.

KARLE, Isabella, PH.D.; American chemist; b. 2 Dec. 1921, Detroit, Mich.; d. of Zygmunt A. and Elizabeth (Graczyk) Lugoski; m. Jerome Karle (q.v.) 1942; three d.; ed. Univ. of Michigan; Assoc. Chemist, Univ. of Chicago 1944; Instructor in Chem., Univ. of Mich. 1944–46; Physicist, Naval Research Lab., Washington, D.C. 1946–; mem. N.A.S., American Crystallographic Assen. American Chem. Soc., American Inst. of Chemists, American Physical Soc., American Biophysical Soc.; Hon. D.Sc. (Mich.) 1976, (Wayne State) 1979, (Md.) 1986; Hon. D. Hum. Lett. (Georgetown) 1984, Lifetime Achievement Award (Women in Science and Eng.) 1986, Gregori Aminoff Prize (Swedish Royal Acad. of Sciences) 1988 and other awards and honours. *Leisure interests:* swimming, ice skating, needlework. *Publications:* over 200 scientific articles, chapters and reviews. *Address:* Naval Research Laboratory, Code 6030, Washington, D.C. 20375 (Office); 6304 Lakeview Drive, Falls Church, Va. 22041, U.S.A. (Home). *Telephone:* 202-767-2624 (Office).

KARLE, Jerome, PH.D.; American government scientist; b. 18 June 1918, Brooklyn, New York; s. of Louis Karfunkle and Sadie Helen Kun; m. Isabella (née Lugoski) Karle (q.v.) 1942; three d.; ed. Abraham Lincoln High School, City Coll. of New York, Harvard Univ. and Univ. of Mich.; Head, Electron Diffraction Section, Naval Research Lab. 1946–58, Head, Diffraction Branch 1958–68, Chief Scientist, Lab. for the Structure of Matter 1968–; Prof. (part-time), Univ. of Maryland 1951–70; Pres. American Crystallographic Assen. 1972; Chair. U.S. Nat. Cttee. for Crystallography of N.A.S. and Nat. Research Council 1973–75; Pres. Int. Union of Crystallography 1981–84; Charter mem. Sr. Exec. Service 1979–; Fellow, American Physical Soc.; mem. N.A.S.; jt. recipient of Nobel Prize for Chemistry 1985, for development of methods to determine the structures of crystals, and several other awards. *Publications:* one book and about 200 research and review articles on theoretical and experimental topics associated with the study of the structures of materials by diffraction methods. *Leisure interests:* stereo-photography, swimming, ice-skating. *Address:* Laboratory for the Structure of Matter, Code 6030, Naval Research Laboratory, Washington, D.C. 20375, U.S.A. *Telephone:* (202) 767-2665.

KARLIN, Dr. Samuel, PH.D.; American mathematician; b. 8 June 1924, Poland; m.; three c.; ed. Illinois Inst. of Technology and Princeton Univ.; Calif. Inst. of Tech., Bateman Research Fellow 1947–48, Asst. Prof. 1949–51, Assoc. Prof. 1951–55, Prof. 1955–56; Visiting Asst. Prof. Princeton Univ. 1950; Prof. Stanford Univ. 1956–70, 1973–; Guggenheim Fellow to Israel and France 1960–61; Guest Mathematical Soc. of Japan 1964; Head, Dept. of Pure Mathematics, Weizmann Inst. of Science, Rehovot, Israel 1970–73, Dean, Faculty of Mathematics 1973; Consultant Rand Corpn., Santa Monica; Chief Ed. Theoretical Population Biology; Ed. or Assoc. Ed. Journal of Mathematical Analysis, Logistics Journal, Journal of Applied Probability, Journal d'analyse, Journal of Mathematics and Mechanics, Journal of Mathematical Biosciences, Journal of Approximation Theory and Advances in Mathematics; Fellow, Inst. of Mathematical Statistics 1956, American Acad. of Arts and Sciences 1981; fmr. mem. Int. Statistics Inst., American Acad. of Arts and Sciences and Council of American Mathematical Soc.; mem. of American Mathematical Soc., Applied Mathematics, panel Nat. Research Council, N.A.S.; Pres.-elect. Inst. of Mathematical Statistics 1977, Pres. 1978–79; Procter Fellow, Princeton Univ. 1946; Wald Memorial Lecturer 1957; Henry and Bertha Benson Chair of Mathematics 1971; Andrew D. White Prof.-at-Large, Cornell Univ. 1975–81; Wilks Lecturer at Princeton 1977; Seymour Sherman Memorial Lecturer 1978; Commonwealth Lecturer, Univ. of Mass. 1980; Gibbs Lectures, American Mathematical Soc. 1983; Mahalanobis Memorial Lectures, Indian Statistical Inst. 1983; Fisher Memorial Lectures 1983; Robert Grimmitt Chair, Stanford 1978. *Publications:* Sex Ratio Evolution (with Sabin Lessard) 1986, Evolutionary Processes and Theory (Ed. with E. Nevo) 1986, over 300 articles in various journals on topics of pure and applied probability theory, game theory, decision theory and statistical methodology, mathematical analysis and mathematical biology. *Address:* Department of Mathematics, Stanford University, Stanford, Calif. 94305, U.S.A. *Telephone:* (415) 723-2204.

KARLOV, Vladimir Alekseyevich; Soviet party official; b. 1914, Voronezh, R.S.F.S.R.; ed. Voronezh Zootech. Inst., CPSU Cen. Cttee.

Party High School; mem. CPSU 1940–; veterinary technician head of stock-raising dept. of dist. agricultural bd.; sec. of a regional Komsomol cttee. 1933–41; party work Volgograd Dist. CP 1941–46, All-Union Cen. Cttee. 1948–49; Sec. Volgograd Dist. Cttee. CPSU 1949–53; party work Cen. Cttee. CPSU 1954–59; Deputy to and Chair. of Agricultural Comm. of R.S.F.S.R. Supreme Soviet 1959–63; cand. mem. Cen. Cttee. CPSU 1960–, mem. 1962–; Chair. of Agricultural Comm. at Council of Nationalities of U.S.S.R. Supreme Soviet 1966–; mem. and Second Sec. of Politburo of Cen. Cttee. of Uzbek CP 1962–65; mem. R.S.F.S.R. Politburo of Cen. Cttee. CPSU 1965–66; First Deputy Head of Agricultural Dept. Cen. Cttee. CPSU 1966–83, Head 1983–86; First Sec. Gagavino Regional Cttee. (Moscow) 1983–86; Sec. Moscow City Cttee. 1986–; Order of Lenin, Order of Red Banner of Labour (twice). *Address:* The Kremlin, Moscow, U.S.S.R.

KARLSSON, Erik Lennart, B.A.; Swedish banker; b. 25 Nov. 1918, Stenbrohult; s. of Karl Karlsson and Jenny Karlsson; m. Maj-Lis Wannefors 1953; five s.; ed. School of Social Work, Stockholm and Univ. of Stockholm; employed in agric., manufacture and construction 1930s; Swedish State Railways 1939–52; research work Govt. Comm. on Econ. Policy and Price Stability 1952–56; employed at Nat. Debt Office 1956–58; Inst. for Econ. Research 1958–60; Cen. Bank of Sweden 1960–67, Exec. Dir. 1971–85; Tech. Asst. IMF, Washington D.C. 1967–68; Exec. Dir. IBRD 1968–71; Gov. of Cen. Bank of Lesotho 1985–. *Leisure interests:* badminton and chess. *Address:* Central Bank of Lesotho, P.O. Box 1184, Maseru, Lesotho. *Telephone:* 312118.

KARMAL, Babrak; Afghan politician and diplomatist; b. c. 1929; ed. Kabul Univ.; detained for 5 years for political activities in 1950s; in Ministry of Planning 1957–65; mem. of Parl 1965–73; f. Khalq political party 1965, Leader breakaway Parcham party 1967–77; after merger in 1977 of Khalq and Parcham parties (now known as People's Democratic Party of Afghanistan (PDPA)) Deputy Leader 1977–78; ed. underground newspaper Parcham; Deputy Prime Minister and Vice-Pres. of Revolutionary Council April–July 1978; Amb. to Czechoslovakia (also accred. to Hungary) 1978–79; returned to Afghanistan after Soviet invasion Dec. 1979; apptd. Prime Minister of Afghanistan 1979–81; Pres. of the Revolutionary Council 1979–86, Gen. Sec. of PDPA Cen. Cttee. and mem. Politburo, then Gen. Sec. 1979–86; C.-in-C. of the Armed Forces 1979–81; reconstituted PDPA as Nat. Fatherland Front June 1981. *Address:* c/o Office of the President, Revolutionary Council, Da Khalkoo Koor, Kabul, Afghanistan.

KARMEL, Peter Henry, A.C., C.B.E., B.A., PH.D.; Australian academic administrator; b. 9 May 1922, Melbourne; s. of Simon and Ethel Karmel; m. Lena Garrett 1946; one s. five d.; ed. Univ. of Melbourne, Trinity Coll., Cambridge; Research Officer, Commonwealth Bureau of Census and Statistics 1943–45; Lecturer in Econs., Univ. of Melbourne 1946, Sr. Lecturer 1948–49; George Gollin Prof. of Econs. and Dean of Faculty of Econs., Univ. of Adelaide 1950–62, Prin. (desig.), Univ. of Adelaide at Bedford Park (later Flinders Univ. of S. Australia) 1961–66, Vice-Chancellor 1966–71; Visiting Prof., Queen's University, Belfast 1957–58; Chair., Interim Council, Univ. of Papua New Guinea 1965–69, Chancellor 1969–70; Chair., Australian Univs. Comm. 1971–77, Australia Council 1974–77, Commonwealth Tertiary Educ. Comm. 1977–82; Pres., Australian Council for Educational Research 1979–; Vice-Chancellor, Australian Nat. Univ. 1982–87; Chair., Commonwealth Govt. Quality of Educ. Review Cttee. 1984–85, Australian Inst. of Health 1987–; Pres. Acad. of Social Sciences in Australia 1987–; Exec. Chair., Canberra Inst. of the Arts 1988–; Chair., Australian Nat. Council on AIDS 1988–; Mackie Medal 1975, Australian Coll. of Educ. Medal 1981. *Address:* 4/127 Hopetoun Circuit, Yarralumla, A.C.T. 2600, Australia. *Telephone:* (062) 852414.

KARNAD, Girish, M.A.; Indian playwright, film-maker and actor; b. 19 May 1938, Matheran; s. of Raghunath Karnad and Krishnabai Karnad; m. Saraswarthy Ganapathy 1980; one s. one d.; ed. Karnatak Coll., Dharwad and Univ. of Oxford; Pres. Oxford Union Soc. 1963; Asst. Man. Oxford Univ. Press, Madras 1963–69, Man. 1969–70; Homi Bhabha Fellow 1970–72; Dir. Film & TV Inst. of India, Pune 1974, 1975; Padma Shri; several awards for film work. *Plays:* Yayati 1961, Tughlaq 1964, Hayavadana 1971, Anjumallige 1976, Hittina Munja 1980. *Films:* Vamsha Vriksha 1971, Kaadu 1973, Tabbaliyu Neenade Magane 1977, Ondanondu Kaaladalli 1978, Utsav 1984. *Address:* 301 Silver Cascade, Mount Mary Road, Bombay 400 050; 18 Saraswatpur, Dharwad 580002, India. *Telephone:* 642 0988; 80224.

KAROLI, Hermann, DR. RER. POL.; German chartered accountant; b. 27 March 1906, Hahnbach; s. of Rudolf and Emma (née Fleischer) Karoli; m. Susanne Seeberg 1943; one s. one d.; ed. Univs. of Leipzig and Innsbruck; mem. of Man. Bd., Deutsche Revisionsund Treuhand A.G., Berlin 1938–45; independent accountant 1948–; Sr. Partner Karoli-Wirtschaftsprüfung GmbH, Essen and Berlin; mem. various advisory bds. and cttees. *Leisure interests:* music, golf. *Address:* 4300 Essen-Bredeney, Am Ruhrstein 37, Federal Republic of Germany (Home).

KARP, David, B.S.S.; American writer; b. 5 May 1922, New York; s. of Abraham Karp and Rebecca Levin; m. Lillian Klass 1944 (died 1987); two s.; ed. City Coll. of the City of New York; Continuity Dir. Station W.N.Y.C., New York 1948–49; free-lance writer 1949–; Guggenheim Fellowship for creative writing 1956–57; mem. editorial board Television Quarterly 1965–71, 1972–; mem. Council, Writers' Guild of America, West,

Inc. 1967-74; Pres. Leda Productions, Inc. 1968-; film and television producer (20th Century Fox, Metro-Goldwyn-Mayer, Paramount Pictures) 1970-; Emmy Award by Acad. of Television, Arts and Sciences 1964-65; mem. PEN Club; mem. Acad. of Motion Picture Arts and Sciences; Pres. Television-Radio Branch, Writers' Guild of America, West 1969-71; Trustee, Producer-Writers' Guild Pension Fund 1970-, Vice-Chair. 1976, Sec. 1977, Chair. 1978-79, Chair. Finance Cttee. 1975; Trustee, Writers' Guild Health Fund 1974-; Chair. Benefits Comm. Health Fund 1978; Sec. Health Fund 1979, Chair. 1980-; Co-Chair. Building Cttee. Pension Plan 1980-. *Publications:* One 1953, The Day of the Monkey 1955, All Honorable Men 1956, Leave Me Alone 1957, The Sleepwalkers 1960, Vice-President in Charge of Revolution (with M. D. Lincoln) 1960, The Last Believers 1964, Café Univers (play) 1967; also contributed many articles and reviews to magazines and has written for radio, cinema and television. *Leisure interests:* reading, photography. *Address:* 300 East 56th Street, 3C, New York, N.Y. 10022, U.S.A.

KÁRPÁTI, Ferenc; Hungarian army officer; b. 1926, Putnok, County Borsod; ed. mil. acad; joined CP 1946; joined the army and has served throughout as political officer, rising from co. through bn. to brigade. First Sec. People's Army Cttee. of HSWP 1958-70; Head of Army Political Dept. and Deputy Minister of Defence 1970, Minister of Defence 1986-; M.P. 1971-; mem. HSWP Cen. Supervisory Cttee. 1975-85; mem. Cen. Cttee. Holder of Medal of Merit for Socialist Hungary. *Address:* Honvédelmi Minisztérium, 1055 Budapest, Pálffy György utca 7/11, Hungary. *Telephone:* 322-500.

KARPLUS, Martin, PH.D.; American professor of chemistry; b. 15 March 1930, Vienna, Austria; m. Marci Hazard 1981; one s. two d.; ed. Harvard Univ. and Calif. Inst. of Technology; Nat. Science Foundation Postdoctoral Fellow, Mathematical Inst., Oxford; Asst. Prof., Dept. of Chem., Univ. of Illinois 1955-59; Assoc. Prof. 1960; Prof. of Chem., Columbia Univ. 1960-66, Harvard Univ. 1966-, Theodore William Richards Prof. of Chem., Harvard Univ. 1979-; Visiting Prof. Univ. of Paris 1972-73, 1980-81, 1987-88 (Prof. 1974-75), Collège de France 1980-81; mem. European Acad. of Arts, Sciences and Humanities, N.A.S., American Acad. of Arts and Sciences, Int. Acad. of Quantum Molecular Science; Fellow, American Physical Soc.; Harrison Howe Award, American Chem. Soc. (Rochester Section), Phi Lambda Upsilon Frensenius Award, Distinguished Alumnus Award (Calif. Inst. of Tech.), Irving Langmuir Award (American Physical Soc.). *Publications:* Atoms and Molecules (with R. N. Porter) 1970, A Theoretical Perspective of Dynamics, Structure and Thermodynamics (with C. L. Brooks III and B. M. Pettitt) 1988; over 350 articles in the field of theoretical chemistry. *Address:* Department of Chemistry, Harvard University, 12 Oxford Street, Cambridge, Mass. 02138, U.S.A.

KARPOV, Anatoliy Yevgenievich; Soviet chess player; b. 23 May 1951, Zlatoust; s. of Yevgeniy Stepanovich Karpov and Nina Karpov; m. Irina Karpov; one s.; ed. Leningrad Univ.; U.S.S.R. Candidate Master 1962, Master 1966; European Jr. Champion 1967, 1968, World Jr. Champion 1969; Int. Master 1969, Int. Grandmaster 1970; U.S.S.R. Champion 1976, 1983; World Champion 1975-85; became World Champion when the holder Bobby Fischer (q.v.) refused to defend the title and he retained his title against Viktor Korchnoi in 1978 and in 1982; defended against Garry Kasparov (q.v.) in Moscow Sept. 1984, the match later adjourned due to the illness of both players; lost to the same player in 1985; unsuccessfully challenged Kasparov 1986, 1987; 16 tournament wins between 1973 and 1981, 29 in all. *Publications:* Chess is My Life 1980, Karpov Teaches Chess 1987. *Address:* c/o U.S.S.R. Chess Federation, Luzhnetskaya 8, Moscow 119270, U.S.S.R.

KARPOV, Viktor; Soviet scientist and diplomatist; b. 9 Oct. 1928; m.; one d.; ed. Moscow State Inst. for Int. Relations; scientific work 1951-55; joined U.S.S.R. Ministry of Foreign Affairs 1955, with Soviet Embassy, Washington 1962-66; participated in Soviet-U.S. Strategic Arms Limitation Talks SALT-1 and SALT-2 (headed Soviet Del. at SALT-2 1978), Head, Soviet Del., Soviet-U.S. Arms Talks 1982-83, Geneva 1985-87. *Address:* c/o Ministry of Foreign Affairs, Moscow, U.S.S.R.

KARPOV, Vladimir Vasilyevich; Soviet author and editor; b. 22 June 1922; m.; ed. Military Acad., Moscow; arrested 1941, sent to camp, released to join a penal battalion, subsequently distinguishing himself in reconnaissance work; Guards Col., Hero of Soviet Union; ed. Gorky Literary Inst.; started publishing (novels, stories, essays) 1948-; Deputy Ed. of Oktyabr 1974-77; Sec. of Presidium of U.S.S.R. Union of Writers 1981-86, First Sec. 1986-; Chief Ed. of Novy mir 1981-86; Hero of Soviet Union 1944; State Prize 1986; Deputy to U.S.S.R. Supreme Soviet. *Publications:* The Marshal's Baton 1970, Take Them Alive 1975, The Regimental Commander 1982-84, The Eternal Struggle 1987; elected to Congress of People's Deputies of the U.S.S.R. 1989. *Address:* U.S.S.R. Union of Writers, ulitsa Vorovskogo 52, Moscow, U.S.S.R.

KARPOVA, Yevdokiya Fyodorovna; Soviet politician; b. 1923; ed. Moscow Textile Inst.; head of factory combine 1949-54; mem. CPSU 1952-; Second, First Sec. of Yegorovo (Moscow Dist.) City Cttee. 1956-61; worked with Moscow Dist. Cttee. of CPSU 1961-63; worked on CPSU Cen. Cttee. 1963-65; U.S.S.R. Deputy Minister of Light Industry 1965-66; deputy pres. of R.S.F.S.R. Council of Ministers 1966-; cand. mem. of CPSU

Cen. Cttee. 1966-76, mem. 1976-, reconfirmed 1986; Deputy to U.S.S.R. Supreme Soviet. *Address:* R.S.F.S.R. Council of Ministers, Moscow, U.S.S.R.

KARRYEV, Chary Soyunovich; Soviet politician; b. 17 Oct. 1932, Turkmen S.S.R.; ed. Gubkin Moscow Petroleum Inst.; worked at Krasnovodsk Oil Refinery Plant 1955-57; postgrad. studies at Inst. of Chemistry, Acad. of Sciences of Turkmen S.S.R. 1957-60; mem. CPSU 1958-; Dir. of Krasnovodsk Plant, Deputy Dir. of Mining and Chemical Industries of Sovnarkhoz of Turkmen S.S.R. 1960-65; Dir. of Dept. of Oil and Chemical Industries for Cen. Cttee. of Turkmen CP 1965-; mem. of Auditing Comm. of Cen. Cttee. of Turkmen CP 1971-76; First Sec. of Ashkhabad Dist. Cttee. 1974-76; cand. mem. of Cen. Cttee. 1971-76, and mem. of Politburo of Turkmen CP 1976-, Sec. of Cen. Cttee. 1976-; Chair. of Council of Ministers of Turkmen S.S.R. 1978-86; Deputy to Supreme Soviet of Turkmen S.S.R. and to Supreme Soviet of U.S.S.R. 1978-. *Address:* Central Committee of the Communist Party of the Turkmen S.S.R., Ashkhabad, Turkmen S.S.R., U.S.S.R.

KARSH, Yousuf; Canadian photographer; b. 23 Dec. 1908, Mardin, Armenia-in-Turkey; s. of Bahia and Amsih Karsh; m. 1st Solange Gauthier 1939 (died 1961), 2nd Estrellita Nachbar 1962; ed. Sherbrooke, Quebec and School of Art and Design, Boston, Mass.; Photo apprenticeship to John Garo of Boston; arrived in Canada from Armenia-in-Turkey 1925; specialized in portrait photography; Canadian citizen 1946; Visiting Prof. of Photography, Ohio Univ. 1967-69; Photographic Adviser to Expo 1970, Osaka, Japan 1969; Visiting Prof. of Fine arts, Emerson Coll., Boston 1972-73; numerous one-man exhbns., North America 1967-; touring exhbn. Men Who Make Our World Japan 1970, U.S.A. 1971-68, France, Germany, Netherlands 1971-73, Belgium, Arles 1974-75, Athens 1978 (now in perm. collection Museum of Contemporary Art, Tokyo, Nat. Gallery of Australia and Province of Alberta, Canada), Bradford, England 1983, Int. Center of Photography, New York 1983, Nat. Portrait Gallery, London 1984, Nat. Gallery Edinburgh, Scotland 1984, Nat. Portrait Gallery, Helsinki 1985, Beijing, China 1985, Muscarelle Museum of Art, Coll. of William and Mary 1986, 80th Birthday Celebration, Barbican Centre, London 1988, subsequently on tour; fmr. Nat. Vice-Pres. now corp. mem. Muscular Dystrophy Assens. of America 1970-; mem. Royal Acad. Arts and Sciences, Canada 1975; Trustee, Photographic Arts and Sciences Foundation 1970-; Hon. LL.D. (Queen's Univ., Kingston, Ont., Carleton Univ. and Savannah Coll. of Art and Design), Hon. D.H.L. (Dartmouth Coll. at Hanover, New Hampshire, Emerson Coll., Boston, Mass., Mount Allison Univs.), Hon. D.C.L. (Bishop's Univ., Quebec), LL.D. h.c. (Brooke Inst.) 1973, (Univ. of Mass.) 1978, (Hartford Univ.) 1980, (Tufts Univ.) 1982, D.F.A. (Syracuse Univ.) 1986; Canada Council Medal 1965, Centennial Medal 1967, Order of Canada 1968, Univ. of Detroit President's Cabinet Annual Award 1979, Encyclopaedia Britannica Achievement in Life Award 1979, Silver Shingle Award, Boston Univ. Law School 1982. *Publications:* Faces of Destiny 1946, This is the Mass (English and French editions), This is Rome 1959, Portraits of Greatness 1959, This is the Holy Land 1961, In Search of Greatness (autobiog.) 1962, These are the Sacraments (co-author) 1963, The Warren Court 1964 (co-author), Karsh Portfolio 1967, Faces of our Time 1971, Karsh Portraits 1976, Karsh Canadians 1978, Karsh: A Fifty-Year Retrospective 1983, Karsh: The Searching Eye (film) 1986. *Leisure interests:* tennis, reading, archaeology, music. *Address:* Chateau Laurier Hotel, Suite 660, Ottawa, Ont., Canada (Office).

KARSKI, Ryszard, DR.ECON.SC.; Polish politician; b. 16 May 1926, Borek, Krosno Voivodship; m.; one s.; ed. Acad. of Commerce, Cracow, Higher School of Socio-Economic Studies, Katowice, Warsaw Tech. Univ.; managerial posts in chemical industry establishments 1949-57; Asst., Warsaw Tech. Univ. 1954-56; managerial posts in foreign trade 1960-, fmr. Dir. Centre of Foreign Trade (CIECH), Deputy Chief of Polish Commercial Agency, Frankfurt am Main (Fed. Repub. of Germany), then Dir. of Dept., Ministry of Foreign Trade until 1969; Under-Sec. of State, Ministry of Foreign Trade 1969-73; Amb. to Austria 1973-78; Under-Sec. of State and First Deputy Minister of Foreign Trade and Maritime Economy 1978-79, Head of Ministry Jan.-Feb. 1980, Minister of Foreign Trade and Maritime Economy July-Oct. 1981; Pres. Polish Chamber of Foreign Trade 1982-87; Amb. to Fed. Repub. of Germany 1987-; mem. PZPR, deputy mem. PZPR Cen. Cttee. 1980-81; Commdr.'s and Kt.'s Cross Order of Polonia Restituta, Order of Banner of Labour (Second Class) and other decorations. *Address:* Botschaft der Volksrepublik Polen, Lindenallee 7, 5000 Cologne 51-Marienburg, Federal Republic of Germany.

KARTASHOV, Nikolay Semenovich, PH.D.; Soviet library administrator; b. 14 March 1928, Kursk; ed. Moscow Library Inst. (now Moscow State Inst. of Culture); Head and Chair. of Librarianship, East Siberia Inst. of Culture 1961-65; Dir. State Public Library of Science and Tech., Siberian Br. U.S.S.R. Acad. of Sciences 1965-79; Dir. V. I. Lenin State Library of the U.S.S.R. 1979-. *Publications:* The Relationship between the Research Libraries in the Russian Soviet Federative Socialist Republic (1917-1967) 1975, Formirovaniye bibliotechno-territorialnykh kompleksov 1978, over 100 articles in library journals. *Address:* The V.I. Lenin State Library of the U.S.S.R., 3 Prospekt Kalinina, 101000 Moscow, U.S.S.R. *Telephone:* 202-40-56.

KARTOMI, Margaret Joy, DR. PHIL., F.A.H.A.; Australian musicologist; b. 24 Nov. 1940, Adelaide; d. of George and Edna Hutchesson; m. Hidris Kartomi 1960; one d.; ed. Univ. of Adelaide; Chair. Monash Univ. Music Dept. 1969-70, lecturer and Sr. Lecturer 1971-73, Reader 1974-; Dir. Symposium of Int. Musicological Soc., Melbourne 1988; Alexander Clarke Prize for Pianoforte Performance 1960, Dr. Ruby Davy Prize for Musical Composition 1961, West German Record Critics' Prize 1983. *Publications:* some 50 books and papers on the music of Indonesia and musicological theory, including Javanese Vocal Music 1973, Indonesian Musical Instruments 1985. *Leisure interests:* tennis, badminton, concerts, theatre. *Address:* Department of Music, Monash University, Wellington Rd. Clayton, Vic. 3168 (Office); 174 Lum Road, Glen Waverley, Vic., Australia (Home). *Telephone:* 03-560 3966 (Home).

KARTTE, Wolfgang; German government official; b. 7 June 1927, Berlin; s. of Vinzenz and Gertrud (née Vogelsang) Kartte; m. Gerda Kartte; three s. two d.; ed. legal studies; adviser, Bundeskartellamt 1959-61; Federal Ministry for the Economy 1961-76; Pres. Bundeskartellamt 1976-; Hon. Prof. Univ. of Bonn; Dr. iur. h.c.; Advisory mem. Alexander Rüstow Foundation. *Publication:* Ein neues Leitbild für die Wettbewerbspolitik 1969. *Leisure interests:* cooking, fishing. *Address:* Bundeskartellamt, Mehringdamm 129, 1000 Berlin 61, Federal Republic of Germany. *Telephone:* 030/69 01-200.

KARTVELISHVILI, Dmitriy Levanovich; Soviet official; b. 1927, Georgian S.S.R.; ed. Georgian Polytechnic Inst., Tbilisi; worked as engineer, chief engineer, head of lab., head of Kutaisi motor works 1951-71; mem. CPSU 1956-; First Deputy Pres. of Gosplan of Georgian S.S.R. 1976-78; work for Cen. Cttee. of Georgian CP 1978-79; Deputy Pres. of Council of Ministers of Georgian S.S.R. 1979-82, Chair. 1982-86; mem. of Politburo of Cen. Cttee. of Georgian CP; Deputy to Supreme Soviet of U.S.S.R. 1982-. *Address:* Central Committee of Georgian Communist Party, Tbilisi, Georgian S.S.R., U.S.S.R.

KARTZEV, Vladimir Petrovich, PH.D.; Soviet publisher; b. 14 Sept. 1938, Samarkand; s. of Pyotr Kartzev and Sofia Kartzeva; m. 1st Galina Petrova 1961; one d.; m. 2nd Tania Bloshchitzina 1977; ed. Leningrad Polytechnic Inst.; Scientist 1961-73; Ed.-in-Chief Voprosy istorii estestvoznania i techniki (Problems in the History of Nat. Sciences and Tech.) 1973-82; Dir., Gen. Man. Mir Publishing House 1982-; Golden Pen, Moscow Union of Journalists 1984. *Publications:* Treatise on Attraction 1969, Maxwell 1974, Krzhizhanovsky 1980, Social Psychology of Science 1984, Newton 1987. *Leisure interests:* music, painting. *Address:* 2 Perviy Rizhsky pereulok, Moscow 129820, U.S.S.R. *Telephone:* 286 17 83.

KARUNAKARAN, Shri K.; Indian politician; b. July 1918; s. of K. Rammuny Marar; m. Kalliani Amma; one s. one d.; active in Freedom Movt. while a student and imprisoned many times; founder mem. of INTUC, Kerala, fmr. Pres. INTUC, Kerala; fmr. Vice-Chair. Rubber Bd.; mem. Trichur Municipality 1945-47, Cochin Legis. Ass. 1948-49; elected to Kerala Legis. Ass. 1965-; Chief Whip, Congress Legislature Party 1952-53, 1954-56; Leader Congress Legislature Group 1967-70; Chair. Cttee. on Public Accounts 1968-69, 1969-70; Minister for Home Affairs 1971-77; Chief Minister of Kerala March 1977, resgnd. April 1977; Leader of Opposition 1978, 1980-81; Chief Minister of Kerala 1981-87; mem. AICC Working Cttee., Parl. Bd.; Leader Congress Legislature Party 1967-; Leader Opposition, Kerala Legis. Ass. *Address:* Muralimandiram, Trichur-2, India.

KARUNANDHI, Muthuvel; Indian politician and playwright; b. 3 June 1924, Thirukkuvalai, Thanjavur; Editor-in-Charge Kudiarasu; journalist and stage and screen playwright in Tamil, acting in his own plays staged to collect party funds; has written over 35 film-plays including the screen version of the Tamil classic Silappadhikaram, stage plays and short stories; started first student wing of the Dravidian movement called Tamilnadu Tamil Manavar Mandram; one of the founder mems. of Dravida Munnetra Kazhagam Legislative Party (D.M.K.) 1949, Treas. 1961, Deputy Leader 1968, Leader 1969-; founder-editor of the Tamil daily organ of the D.M.K. Murasoli; represented Kulittalai in State Assembly 1957-62, Thanjavur 1962-67, Saidapet 1968; led the Kallakkudi Agitation and was imprisoned for six months; fmr. Minister of Public Works; Chief Minister of Tamil Nadu (Madras) 1969-76 (presidential rule imposed), Jan. 1989-; Thamizha Vell (Patron of Tamil), Asscn. of Research Scholars in Tamil 1971; Hon. D.Litt. (Annamalai Univ., Tamil Nadu) 1971. *Address:* Dravida Munnetra Kazhagam, Arivagam, Royapuram, Madras 13, Tamil Nadu, India.

KARUNARATNE, Hon. Nuwarapaksa Hewayalage Asoka Mahaname; Ceylonese politician; b. 26 Jan. 1918; s. of Abileenu Mudalali and Siri Nuvasa; m. 1951; four s. five d.; ed. St. Anthony's Coll., Kandy and Nalanda Vidyalaya, Colombo; M.P. 1958-; Parl. Sec. to Minister of Justice 1960; Junior Minister of Justice 1963, removed from office because of critical attitude to Govt.; helped to form Sri Lanka Freedom Socialist Party 1964; Minister of Social Services 1967-70, 1977-88; United Nat. Party. *Leisure interest:* reading. *Address:* c/o Ministry of Social Services, 14 Barnes Place, Colombo 7, Sri Lanka.

KASAHARA, Yukio, B.ENG.; Japanese business executive; b. 27 Jan. 1925, Tokyo; m. Yuri Tsumura 1983; no c.; ed. Tokyo Univ.; joined Nippon Mining Co. 1949, mem. Bd. of Dirs. 1974, Man. Dir. and Gen. Man.

Petroleum Group 1976, Sr. Man. Dir. and Gen. Man. Petroleum Group 1979, Exec. Vice-Pres. and Gen. Man. of Planning and Devt. Group and Petroleum Group 1981, Pres. and Rep. Dir. 1983-. *Leisure interests:* reading, model railroading. *Address:* Nippon Mining Co. Ltd., 10-1, Toranomon 2-chome, Minato-ku, Tokyo, 107 (Office); 3-6-1201, Okubo 2-chome, Shinjuku-ku, Tokyo 160, Japan (Home). *Telephone:* (03) 505-8111 (Office); (03) 202-3119 (Home).

KASATKINA, Natalya Dmitriyevna; Soviet ballet dancer and choreographer; b. 7 June 1934, Moscow; d. of Dmitriy A. Kasatkin and Anna A. Kardasheva; m. Vladimir Vasilyev 1956; one s.; ed. Bolshoi Theatre Ballet School; joined Bolshoi Theatre Ballet Company 1954, main roles including Frigia (Spartacus), Fate (Carmen), The Possessed (Rites of Sacred Spring); Choreographer (with V. Vasilyev) of Vanini Vanini 1962, Geologist 1964, Rites of Sacred Spring 1965, Tristan and Isolde 1967, Preludes and Fugues 1968, Our Yard 1970, The Creation of the World 1971, Romeo and Juliet 1972, Prozrienie 1974, Gayane 1977, The Magic Cloak 1982, The Mischiefs of Terpishore 1984, Pushkin 1986, The Faces of Love 1987, Petersburg's Twilights 1987; TV Film: Choreographic Novels; Head (with V. Vasilyev) choreography co.; Moscow State Ballet Theatre of U.S.S.R. 1977-; wrote libretto and produced opera Peter I 1975, Così fan Tutte (with V. Vasilyev) 1978; State Prize of U.S.S.R., People's Actress of RSFSR 1984. *Address:* Moscow State Ballet Theatre of U.S.S.R., Pushechnaya 2/6, Moscow 103012; St. Karietny Riad, h.5/10, B 37, Moscow, 103006, U.S.S.R. (Home). *Telephone:* 924 55 24 (Office); 299 95 24 (Home).

KASATONOV, Admiral Vladimir Afanasiyevich; Soviet naval officer; b. 21 July 1910, Novy Peterhof, Leningrad Region; ed. Naval Acad.; Naval service 1927; Commanding and Staff posts 1931-; with Gen. Staff 1945-55; Commdr. Black Sea Fleet 1955-62, N. Fleet 1962-64; First Deputy C.-in-C. Soviet Navy 1964-74; Deputy to U.S.S.R. Supreme Soviet 1958-; mem. Comm. for Transport and Communications, Soviet of Nationalities; Hero of Soviet Union 1966, medal Gold Star, Orders of Lenin (three times), Red Banner of Labour, etc. *Address:* Ministry of Defence, Naberezhnaya M. Thoreza 34, Moscow, U.S.S.R.

KASDAN, Lawrence Edward, B.A., M.A.; American film director and screenwriter; b. 14 Jan. 1949, Miami Beach, Florida; s. of Clarence Norman Kasdan and Sylvia Sarah (née Landau) Kasdan; m. Meg Goldman 1971; two s.; ed. Univ. of Mich.; copywriter W.B. Doner and Co. (Advertising), Detroit 1972-75, Doyle, Dane Berbach, L.A. 1975-77; Freelance Screenwriter 1977-80; Motion Picture Dir., Screenwriter, L.A. 1980-; Co-Screenwriter, The Empire Strikes Back 1980; Screenwriter, Continental Divide 1981, Raiders of the Lost Ark 1981; Writer, Dir., Body Heat 1981; Co-screenwriter, Return of the Jedi 1982; Co-screenwriter, Dir., Exec. Producer, The Big Chill 1983, Silverado 1985, An Accidental Tourist 1989; Producer, Cross My Heart 1987; recipient Clio awards for Advertising, Writers Guild Award for The Big Chill 1983; mem. Writers Guild, W. America, Dirs. Guild, W. America. *Address:* c/o Peter Benedek, 9255 Sunset Boulevard, Suite 710, Los Angeles, California 90069, U.S.A.

KÄSER, Helmut Alfred; Swiss lawyer and sports administrator; b. 14 Nov. 1912; m. Silvia Löpfe 1946; ed. Commercial High School, Neuchâtel, and Univs. of Berne and Zürich; Lawyer, Zürich court; fmr. lawyer, Ministry of Economics; Gen. Sec. Swiss Football Asscn. 1942-60; Sec.-Gen. Fédération Internationale de Football Asscn. (FIFA) 1961-83. *Publications:* Untersuchungen über den Begriff des Ersatzwertes in der Versicherung 1937. *Leisure interests:* colour photography, shooting, skiing, mountaineering. *Address:* Hitzigweg 11, 8032 Zürich, Switzerland.

KASER, Michael Charles, M.A.; British economist; b. 2 May 1926, London; s. of Joseph Kaser and Mabel Blunden; m. Elizabeth Anne Mary Piggford 1954; four s. one d.; ed. King's Coll., Cambridge; with Econs. Section Ministry of Works, London 1946-47; H.M. Foreign Service 1947-51, Second Sec., Moscow 1949; UN Econ. Comm. for Europe, Geneva 1951-63; lecturer in Soviet Econs., Univ. of Oxford 1963-72, Chair. Faculty Bd. 1974-76, mem. Gen. Bd. of Faculties 1972-78, Chair. Advisory Council of Adult Educ. 1972-78, Univ. Latin preacher 1982; Gov. Plater Coll., Oxford 1968-; Visiting Prof. of Econs., Univ. of Mich., U.S.A. 1966; Visiting lecturer, European Inst. of Business Admin., Fontainebleau 1959-, Univ. of Cambridge 1967-68, 1977-78, 1978-79; Reader in Econs. and Professorial Fellow, St. Antony's Coll., Oxford 1972-, Sub-Warden 1986-87; Dir., Inst. of Russian, Soviet and E. European Studies, Univ. of Oxford 1988-; Assoc. Fellow Templeton Coll., Oxford 1983-; Assoc. Fellow Henley Man. Coll. 1987-; Vice-Chair. Social Science Research Council Int. Activities Cttee. 1980-84; Special Adviser House of Commons Foreign Affairs Cttee. 1985; Chair. Co-ordinating Council, Area Studies Asscns. 1986-88, Wilton Park Academic Council (FCO); Pres. British Asscn. of Soviet, Slavic and E. European Studies 1988-; mem. Int. Social Science Council (UNESCO), Council Royal Inst. of Int. Affairs, Cttee. Nat. Asscn. for Soviet and East European Studies 1965-88, Steering Cttee. Königswinter Anglo-German Confs., also various editorial bds. and Anglo-Soviet, British-Mongolian, Anglo-Polish and British-Romanian Round Tables. *Publications:* Comecon: Integration Problems of the Planned Economies 1965, Planning in East Europe (with J. Zielinski) 1970, Soviet Economics 1970, Health Care in the Soviet Union and Eastern Europe 1976, ed. Economic Development for Eastern Europe 1968, Planning and Market Relations 1971, The New Economic Systems of Eastern Europe 1975, The Soviet Union since the

Fall of Khrushchev 1975, Soviet Policy for the 1980s 1982, Economic History of Eastern Europe, Vols. I-III 1985-86; articles in econ. and Slavic journals. *Address:* St. Antony's College, Oxford, OX2 6JF (Office); 7 Chadlington Road, Oxford, OX2 6SY, England (Home). *Telephone:* (0865) 59651 (Office); (0865) 515581 (Home).

KASHIWAGI, Yusuke, LL.B.; Japanese banker; b. 17 Oct. 1917, Dalian; s. of Hideshige and Kiyo Kashiwagi; m. Kazuko Sohma 1946; two s. two d.; ed. Tokyo Imperial Univ.; entered Ministry of Finance 1941; Foreign Exchange Bureau 1941, Minister's Secr. 1945, Budget Bureau 1948, Sr. Budget Examiner 1951, Dir. Research Section of Foreign Exchange Bureau 1954, Dir. Planning Section 1956; Financial Sec. Embassy in Washington, D.C. 1958; Financial Counsellor, Ministry of Finance 1961; Financial Commr. 1965; Dir.-Gen. Int. Finance Bureau 1966; Vice-Minister of Finance for Int. Affairs 1968; resgnd. from Ministry of Finance 1971; Special Adviser to Minister of Finance 1971-72; Deputy Pres. Bank of Tokyo Ltd. 1973-77, Pres. 1977-82, Chair. Bd. of Dirs. 1982-; Dir. Sony Corpn. 1976-; mem. Exec. Cttee. Trilateral Comm. 1973-; Adviser, Int. Finance Corpn., Washington, D.C. 1979-; mem Int. Monetary Conf. 1977-; Dir. Meiji Seika Kaisha, Tokyo 1983-; Chair. BIAC Japan 1985-, BIAC OECD 1988-; Adviser Robeco Group, Rotterdam 1985-. *Leisure interests:* golf, travelling. *Address:* The Bank of Tokyo Ltd., 3-2 Nihombashi Hongokucho 1-chome Chuo-ku, Tokyo 103 (Office); 11-16 Nishi-Azabu 1-chome, Minato-ku, Tokyo 106, Japan (Home). *Telephone:* (03) 245-9021 (Office); 03-405-7897 (Home).

KAŠLÍK, Václav; Czechoslovak composer and conductor; b. 28 Sept. 1917, Poličná; s. of Hynek and Paula Kašlíková; m. Růžena Stučesová 1942; three s.; ed. Faculty of Philosophy, Charles Univ., Prague, Prague Conservatoire and Conductors' Master School, Prague; Conductor, E. F. Burian Theatre, Prague 1940-41; Asst. Dir. Nat. Theatre, Prague 1941-43; Chief of Opera Ensemble, Opera of May 5th 1945-48; Conductor, Smetana Theatre, Prague 1952-62; Chief Opera Dir., Nat. Theatre, Prague 1961-65, Opera Dir. 1966-; tours include New York, Leningrad, Moscow, Vienna, Munich; Klement Gottwald State Prize 1956; Honoured Artist 1958. *Works:* Operas: Robbers' Ballad 1944, 2nd version 1970, Calvary 1950, Krakatit 1960, La Strada 1980, Der Ratten-fänger 1982; ballets: Don Juan 1939, Jánošík 1951, Prague Carnival 1952; Dir. of operas: The Water Nymph (Dvořák), Vienna 1965, Julietta (Martinů), Hanover 1966, Albergo dei Poveri (Testi), Milan 1966, Die Soldaten (Zimmermann), Munich 1969, Pelléas (Debussy), Covent Garden 1969, Don Giovanni (Mozart), Prague 1969, Cardillac (Hindemith), La Scala 1969, Idomeneo (Mozart), Vienna 1971, The Greek Passion (Martinů), Spain 1972, The Queen of Spades (Tchaikowsky), Stockholm 1973, Katya Kabanová (Janáček), Geneva 1975, Queen of Spades (Tchaikovsky) Ottawa 1977, Ariadne auf Naxos (Strauss) Ottawa 1979, Idomeneo (Mozart) Ottawa 1980, Queen of Spades (Tchaikovsky) Huston 1980, Macbeth (Verdi) Montreal 1981, Salomé (Strauss) Montreal 1985; over 30 productions for TV, including: Hoffman's Tales 1962; Katya Kabanová (Janáček), TV production, Copenhagen 1970, Boris Godunov (Mussorgsky), Verona 1976, Rusalka (Dvořák), Haag 1976, Karlsruhe 1977, Ariadne auf Naxos (Strauss), Prague 1977, Carmen (Bizet), Geneva 1977. *Address:* Kašlík Vaclav Prahai Össr, Soukenická 11, Czechoslovakia. *Telephone:* 2317514.

KASPAROV, Garri Kimovich; Soviet chess player; b. (as Harry Weinstein) 13 April 1963, Baku; Azerbaidzhan Champion 1975; U.S.S.R. Jr. Champion 1975; Int. Master 1979, Int. Grandmaster 1980; World Jr. Champion 1980; won U.S.S.R. Championship 1981, subsequently replacing Anatoliy Karpov (q.v.) at top of world ranking list; challenged Karpov for World Title in Moscow, Sept. 1984, the match being adjourned due to the illness of both players; won rescheduled match to become the youngest ever World Champion in 1985; successfully defended his title against Karpov 1986, 1987; series of promotional matches in London Feb. 1987. *Publication:* Child of Change (with Donald Trelford) 1987. *Address:* c/o U.S.S.R. Chess Federation, Luzhnetskaya 8, Moscow 119270, U.S.S.R.

KASPER, Walter Josef, DR.THEOL.; German theologian; b. 5 March 1933, Heidenheim/Brenz; s. of Josef Kasper and Theresia Bacher; ed. Univs. of Tübingen and Munich; ordained Priest 1957; Prof. of Dogmatism, Univ. of Münster 1964-70, Univ. of Tübingen 1970-; mem. Comm. of Faith and Order of WCC, Int. Theological Comm. Rome; Adviser, German Conf. of Bishops; Special Sec. Synod of Bishops in Rome 1985; mem. Heidelberg Akad. der Wissenschaften; Bundesverdienstkreuz. *Publications:* Die Tradition in der Römischen Schule 1962, Das Absolute in der Geschichte 1965, Glaube und Geschichte 1970, Einführung in den Glauben 1972, Jesus der Christus 1974, Der Gott Jesu Christi 1982, Theologie und Kirche 1987. *Leisure interest:* climbing. *Address:* 7400 Tübingen 1, Schwabstrasse 65, Federal Republic of Germany. *Telephone:* 07071/52997.

KASRASHVILI, Makvala; Soviet soprano and opera singer; b. 1946, Georgia; ed. Tbilisi and Moscow Conservatory; soloist with Bolshoi Theatre, Moscow 1969-; has performed internationally, including Royal Opera House, Covent Garden; Georgian State Prize 1983; People's Artist of U.S.S.R. 1986. *Roles include:* Liza, Violetta, Tatiana, Iolanthe. *Address:* Bolshoi Theatre, Sverdlov Square, Moscow, U.S.S.R.

KASSEBAUM, Nancy Landon, M.A.; American politician; b. 29 July 1932, Topeka; d. of Alfred M. Kassebaum and Theo Landon; three s. one d.; ed. Univs. of Kansas and Mich.; mem. Washington staff of Senator James B.

Pearson of Kansas 1975-76; Senator from Kansas 1979-; Republican. *Address:* United States Senate, 302 Russell Senate Building, Washington, D.C. 20510, U.S.A.

KASSEM, Dr. Abdul-Rauf al-, D.ARCH.; Syrian politician; b. 1932, Damascus; ed. Damascus Univ. School of Arts, Istanbul and Geneva Univs.; teacher of architecture, School of Fine Arts Damascus, Dean 1964-70, Head, Architecture Dept., School of Civil Engineering Damascus Univ. 1970-77, Rector 1977-79; concurrently engineer 1964-77; Gov. of Damascus 1979-80; elected mem. Baath party Regional Command Dec. 1979, Cen. Command of Progressive Nat. Front April 1980; Prime Minister 1980-87; mem. Higher Council for Town Planning 1968-; mem. Nat. Union of Architects' Perm. Comm. on Town Planning 1975-; Hon. Prof. Geneva Univ. 1975-. *Address:* c/o Office of the Prime Minister, Damascus, Syria.

KASTEN, Robert W., Jr., B.A.; American politician; b. 19 June 1942, Milwaukee, Wis.; s. of Robert W. and Mary (Ogden) Kasten; m. Eva E. Nimmons 1986; one d.; ed. Univ. of Arizona and Columbia Univ., New York; with Genesco, Nashville, Tenn. 1966-68; Dir. and Vice-Pres. Gilbert Shoe Co., Thiensville, Wis. 1968-75; mem. Wis. Senate 1972-75; Joint Finance Cttee. 1973-75, Chair. Joint Survey Cttee. on Tax Exemptions 1973-80; Designee Eagleton Inst. of Politics 1973; mem. House of Reps. 1975-79 from 9th Dist., Wis., mem. Govt. Operations Cttee., Small Businesses Cttee.; alt. del. Republican Nat. Convention 1972, del. 1976; Senator from Wisconsin 1981-; serves on Appropriations, Budget, Commerce, Science and Transportation Cttee., and Small Business Cttee. *Address:* U.S. Senate, Washington, D.C. 20510, U.S.A.

KASTL, Jörg; German diplomatist; b. 21 June 1922, Berlin; s. of Dr. Ludwig Kastl and Gertrud Otto; m. Eva M. L. von Essen; two d.; ed. Neubeuern, Bavaria, and law studies in Lausanne and Munich; served in armed forces 1941-45; German Foreign Service School 1950-51; Vice-Consul, Paris 1951-52; Second Sec. Buenos Aires 1953-55, Asunción, Paraguay 1955-57; First Sec. Foreign Office, Bonn 1957-59, Moscow 1959-61; Fellow, Center for Int. Studies, Harvard Univ. 1961-62; First Sec., Washington 1962-63; Counsellor, Spokesman of German Foreign Office 1963-66; Head of East European Desk, Foreign Office, Bonn 1967-69; Asst. Sec.-Gen. for Political Affairs, NATO 1969-75; Amb. to Argentina 1975-77, to Brazil 1977-80, to U.S.S.R. 1980-83, 1984-88; Head German Del. to CSCE Conf., Madrid. *Address:* Römerstrasse 4, 8000 München 40, Federal Republic of Germany.

KASTNER, Elliott; American film producer; b. 7 Jan. 1933, New York; in partnership with Jerry Gershwin produced films Harper (The Moving Target), Kaleidoscope 1965, The Bobo 1967, Where Eagles Dare, Night of the Following Day 1968, The Walking Stick 1969, A Severed Head, Tam Lin, When Eight Bells Toll 1970, Villain, Zee and Co., The Nightcomers 1971, Big Truck and Poor Clare 1972, The Long Goodbye, Cops and Robbers, Eleven Harrowhouse 1972-73; since 1974 has produced films: Jeremy, Russian Roulette, Rancho Deluxe, 92 in the Shade, Farewell My Lovely, The Missouri Breaks, The Swashbuckler, A Little Night Music, Equus, Black Joy, The Stick Up, The Medusa Touch, The Big Sleep, Golden Girl, The First Deadly Sin, North Sea Hijack, Death Valley, Man, Woman and Child, Oxford Blues, Garbo Talks, Nomads, White of the Eye, Heat, Angel Heart etc. *Address:* Winkast Programming Ltd., Pinewood Studios, Iver Heath, Bucks., England.

KASUYA, Shigeru; Japanese politician; b. Feb. 1926, Tokyo; m.; ed. Nihon Univ.; mem. House of Reps. 1972-; Parl. Vice-Minister for Admin. Man. Agency 1978; Deputy Sec.-Gen. Liberal-Democratic Party (LDP) 1982, 1986, Chair. Exec. Council 1986; mem. Tokyo Metropolitan Ass.; Minister of State, Dir.-Gen. Hokkaido Devt. Agency, Dir.-Gen. Okinawa Devt. Agency 1987-88; Chair. House of Reps. Standing Cttee. on Commerce and Industry 1988-. *Leisure interests:* go (5th dan), reading, golf, judo. *Address:* Kasuya Shigeru Jimusho, 3-1-6 Sasazaka, Shibuya-ku, Tokyo 151, Japan.

KATES, Robert William, PH.D.; American professor of geography; b. 31 Jan. 1929, Brooklyn, New York; s. of Simon J. Kates and Helen G. Brener; m. Eleanor C. Hackman 1948; one s. two d.; ed. Univ. of Chicago; Asst. Prof. Graduate School of Geography, Clark Univ. 1962-65, Assoc. Prof. 1965-67, Prof. 1968-, Univ. Prof. 1974-80, Research Prof., Center for Tech., Environment and Devt. 1981-; Univ. Prof. and Dir. Alan Shawn Feinstein World Hunger Program 1986-; Dir. Bureau of Resource Assessment and Land Use Planning, Univ. Coll., Dar es Salaam 1967-68; Hon. Research Prof. Univ. of Dar es Salaam 1970-71; Fellow, Woodrow Wilson Int. Center for Scholars 1979; many other professional appointments; mem. N.A.S., A.A.A.S., American Acad. of Arts and Sciences etc.; several awards. *Publications:* books, monographs and articles on environmental topics. *Address:* Brown University, Box 1831, 130 Hope Street, Providence, R.I. 02912, U.S.A.

KATIN, Peter, F.R.A.M.; British pianist; b. 14 Nov. 1930, London; s. of Jerrold and Gertrude Katin; m. Eva Zweig 1954; two s.; ed. Henry Thornton School, Royal Acad. of Music; London debut, Wigmore Hall 1948; extensive concert tours in U.K., Europe, Africa, Canada, U.S.A. and Far East; special interest in Chopin; recordings for Decca, EMI, Unicorn, Everest, Philips, CFP, Lyrita and Pickwick Int., Claudio, Olympia, Virgin Classics; Prof., Univ. of Western Ont. 1978-84; Chopin Arts Award (New York) 1977; Assoc. Royal Coll. of Music. *Leisure interests:* writing, tape-recording, fishing, theatre, reading, photography. *Address:* John Wright, 5 Kintbury Mill, Kintbury, Berks., RG15 0UN, England; Steorra Enterprises, Suite 907, 243 West End Avenue, New York, N.Y. 10023, U.S.A. *Telephone:* 0488-58963 (England); (212) 799-5783 (U.S.A.).

KATO, Ichiro, LL.D.; Japanese lawyer, professor and university administrator; b. 28 Sept. 1922, Tokyo; s. of Shuichi and Tomi Kato; m. Teruko Aoki 1947; one s. two d.; ed. Faculty of Law, Univ. of Tokyo; Assoc. Prof. of Law, Univ. of Tokyo 1948–57, Prof. of Law 1957–68, 1974–83; Dean of Law and Acting Pres., Univ. of Tokyo 1968–69, Pres. 1969–73; Vice-Rector UN Univ. 1975–76, Sr. Adviser to the Rector 1976–79; Chancellor of Seijo Gakuen 1983–; Attorney at Law 1983–; mem. Admin. Bd. Int. Asscn. of Univs. 1970–80; Pres. Nat. Univ. Asscn. (Japan) 1969–73; Matsunaga Foundation Prize 1966. *Publications:* several books and numerous articles on civil law (especially law of torts, family law and environmental law). *Leisure interests:* golf, "Go". *Address:* Seijo Gakuen, 6-1-20 Seijo Setagaya-ku, Tokyo (Univ.); Kato Law Office, 360 Marunouchi Building, 2-4-1 Marunouchi, Chiyoda-ku, Tokyo (Office); 3-10-30, Seijo, Setagaya-ku, Tokyo, Japan (Home). *Telephone:* 03-482-1181 (Univ.); 03-201-1301 (Law Office).

KATO, Koichi; Japanese politician; b. 17 June 1939, Tsuruoka, Yamagata Pref.; m. Aiko Sugiura 1967; one s. three d.; ed. Univ. of Tokyo, Harvard Univ.; entered Ministry of Foreign Affairs 1964, Vice-Consul, Japanese Consulate Gen., Hong Kong 1967–69, Deputy Dir., Chinese Div., Asian Affairs Bureau 1969–71; M.P. for 2nd Dist., Yamagata Pref., House of Reps. 1972–, Deputy Chief Cabinet Sec. 1978–80, Minister of State for Defence 1984–86; Dir. House Cttee. on Rules and Admin. 1980–81, on Agric., Forestry and Fisheries 1981–83; Vice-Chair., Diet Policy Cttee. of the Liberal Democratic Party (LDP) 1980–81; Dir., Agric. and Forestry Div., LDP Policy Affairs Research Council 1981–83; Dir.-Gen., LDP Gen. Affairs Bureau 1983–84; Chief Deputy Chair. of Political Research Council LDP 1986–87. *Address:* Room 711, House Office Building No. 2, 2-1-2 Nagato-cho, Chiyoda-ku, Tokyo 100, Japan. *Telephone:* 03-508-7461.

KATO, Mutsuki; Japanese politician; b. 1926; elected to House of Reps. from Okayama Pref. six times; fmr. Parl. Vice-Minister for Transport; fmr. Vice-Chair. Liberal-Democratic Party Policy Affairs Research Council; Minister of State and Dir.-Gen. Nat. Land Agency 1982–83, of Agric., Forestry and Fisheries 1986–87. *Address:* c/o Ministry of Agriculture, Forestry and Fisheries, 1-2, Kasumigaseki, Chiyoda-ku, Tokyo, Japan.

KATO, Shuichi; Japanese author and lecturer; b. 1919, Tokyo; ed. Univ. of Tokyo Faculty of Medicine; haematologist, Tokyo Univ. Clinic 1950–59; medical research, Univ. of Paris and Inst. Pasteur 1951–54; full-time author and lecturer in Japanese Culture 1960–; Lecturer in Humanities, Univ. of Tokyo 1960; Lecturer, Dept. of Asian Studies, Univ. of British Columbia 1960–69; later taught at Freie Universität Berlin, Univ. of Munich, Yale and Brown Univs., Univ. of Cambridge School of Oriental Studies, Univs. of Geneva and Venice; Prof. Dept. of Comparative Culture, Sophia Univ. Tokyo 1976–85; monthly columnist, Asahi Shimbun 1976–; Jiro Osagari Prize for History of Japanese Literature 1980. *Publications include:* History of Japanese Literature (3 vols.), Collected Works (15 vols.) 1978–80, Hitsuji no Uta (autobiography), Six Lives/Six Deaths: Portraits of Modern Japan (with R.J. Lifton and M. Reich), The Japan-China Phenomenon, Form, Style, Tradition: Reflections on Japanese Art and Society. *Address:* c/o Asahi Shimbun, 3-2, Tsukiji 5-chome, Chuo-ku, Tokyo 104, Japan.

KATO, Susumu, PH.D.; Japanese professor of atmospheric physics; b. 27 Aug. 1928, Saitama; s. of Nimpei Kato (deceased) and Minoru Kato; m. Kyoko Kojo; no c.; ed. Kyoto Univ.; lecturer, Faculty of Eng., Kyoto Univ. 1955–61, Asst. Prof. Ionosphere Research Lab. 1961–62, Assoc. Prof. 1964–67, Prof. 1967–81, Dir. and Prof. Radio Atmospheric Science Center 1981–; Research Officer, Upper Atmosphere Section, CSIRO, N.S.W., Australia 1962–64; Visiting Scientist, High Altitude Observatory, NCAR, Colo. 1967–68, 1973–74; Visiting Prof., Dept. of Meteorology, UCLA, Los Angeles 1973–74; Tanakadate Prize 1959, Yamaji Science Prize 1974, Appleton Prize 1987, Hasegawa Prize 1987. *Publications:* Dynamics of the Upper Atmosphere 1980; over 100 scientific papers on atmospheric tidal theory, observation of atmospheric waves by MST radar. *Leisure interests:* reading, music, jogging, Japanese calligraphy. *Address:* Radio Atmospheric Science Center, Kyoto University, Kyoto (Office); 22-15 Fujimidai, Otsu, Shiga Prefecture 520, Japan (Home). *Telephone:* 0775-34-1177 (Home).

KATO, Tadao; Japanese diplomatist; b. 13 May 1916, Tokyo; s. of Shizuo and Kae Kato; m. Yoko Kato 1946; two s.; ed. Tokyo Univ. and Univ. of Cambridge, England; Chief of Overseas Market Section, Int. Trade Bureau, Ministry of Int. Trade and Industry 1947–51; rejoined Ministry Foreign Affairs, Consul, Singapore 1952; First Sec., London 1953; Counsellor, Econ. Affairs Bureau, Foreign Office 1956–59; Counsellor, Washington, D.C. 1960–63; Deputy Dir. of Econ. Affairs Bureau 1963–66, Dir. 1966–67; Amb. to Org. for Econ. Co-operation and Devt. (OECD) 1967–70, to Mexico 1970–74, to U.K. 1975–79; Counsellor, John Swire and Sons Dec. 1979–; Adviser, Imperial Chemicals (Japan), Sumitomo Metal Industries, Suntory and Long-Term Credit Bank Jan. 1980–; mem. Bd. Advisory Council Texas Instruments 1981–, Econ. Council (Econ. Planning Agency), Export and Import Transaction Council, Ministry of Int. Trade and Industry, Overseas Information and Cultural Council, Ministry of Foreign Affairs 1982–; Head

Japanese del. to Int. Sugar Conf., UN, New York 1958, to Food Aid Conf., Rome 1974, to Gen. Assembly, UNIDO 1975; Chair. Japan-British Soc. 1982–88; Advisor Hotel Okura 1982; Vice-Chair. Research Council for Internationalization of Service Industries 1983–; Counsellor of Cabinet, Admin. Reform Council, Japanese Chair. U.K.–Japan 2,000 Group 1984–88; Pres. Cambridge English School 1984–; Adviser Nitto Kogyo Enterprise 1984–; Visiting Fellow Center for Int. Affairs, Harvard Univ. 1959–60; Pres. Hamano Golf Club, Green Acad. Country Club, Mito Golf Club; K.B.E.; Order of the Sacred Treasure (First Class) 1988. *Publication:* Three Times In Britain 1988. *Leisure interests:* golf, bridge, "Go". *Address:* 3-10-22 Shimo-Ochiai, Shinjuku-ku, Tokyo, Japan. *Telephone:* 954-3043.

KATONA, Imre; Hungarian politician; b. 1921, Turkeve; ed. Eötvös Lóránd Univ., Budapest; factory worker until 1945; joined Communist Party (now HSWP) 1946; Youth Movement Sec. in Óbuda 1948; Leading Official, Hungarian-Soviet Soc.; various positions as Party functionary, later as Party Dept. Leader in Budapest; First Sec. District 6 Party Cttee. 1963–65; Sec. Metropolitan Party Cttee. 1965–74, First Sec. 1974–78; mem. Party Cen. Cttee. 1966–; mem. Nat. Ass. 1975–; mem. Presidential Council, Hungarian People's Republic 1975–78, Sec. 1978–; mem. Bd. Nat. Peace Council 1978–. *Address:* Magyar Népköztársaság Elnöki Tanácsa, Budapest V. Kossuth Lajos tér 1, Hungary. *Telephone:* 120-600.

KATRITZKY, Alan Roy, M.A., D.PHIL., PH.D., SC.D., F.R.S.; British professor of chemistry, researcher and consultant; b. 18 Aug. 1928, London; s. of Frederick C. and Emily C. (Lane) Katritzky; m. Agnes née Kilian 1952; one s. three d.; ed. Oxford and Cambridge Univs.; Univ. Lecturer, Cambridge 1958–63; Fellow Churchill Coll., Cambridge 1959–63; Prof. of Chem., Univ. of East Anglia 1963–80, Dean, School of Sciences 1963–70, 1976–80; Kenan Prof. Univ. of Fla. 1980–; Hon. Fellow, Italian Chem. Soc., Polish Chem. Soc.; Hon. D.Sc. (Madrid); Tilden Lecturer, Chem. Soc.; Heterocyclic Award, Royal Soc. of Chem.; Cavaliere ufficiale (Italy). *Publications:* three books and 700 papers in heterocyclic chemistry; Ed. Advances in Heterocyclic Chemistry (40 vols.) and Comprehensive Heterocyclic Chemistry (8 vols.). *Leisure interests:* walking, wind surfing. *Address:* Department of Chemistry, University of Florida, Gainesville, Fla. 32611 (Office); 1221 SW 21st Avenue, Gainesville, Fla. 32601, U.S.A. (Home). *Telephone:* (904) 392-0554 (Office); (904) 378-1221 (Home).

KATSAMBAS, Christakis Joannou; Cypriot journalist; b. 15 Aug. 1925, Nicosia; s. of Ioannis and Panayiota Katsambas; m. 1951 (separated 1981); two s.; ed secondary school, Cyprus; active in left-wing youth movement 1943, Sec-Gen. of the youth org. 1943–53; detained by British colonial Govt., Cyprus 1955–57; journalist Fileleftheros (daily newspaper) 1957–, Ed.-in-Chief 1967–; Vice-Chair. Union of Cyprus Journalists 1980–. *Leisure interests:* classical music, gardening. *Address:* P.O. Box 1098, Nicosia; Flat 405, Prespas 2, Ayii Omologitae, Nicosia, Cyprus. *Telephone:* 477031; 473277.

KATSIFARAS, Georgios; Greek politician; b. 1935, Kallensi, Peloponnese; ed. Univ. of Athens; Deputy Minister of Co-ordination 1964; arrested and deported to remote areas 1968–71; in Canada with Andreas Papandreou (q.v.) 1971–74; mem. Cen. Cttee. Panhellenic Socialist Movement (PASOK) 1974–, mem. Econ. Cttee. 1977–; Minister for Merchant Marine July 1982–85, of Commerce 1986–87. *Address:* c/o Ministry of Merchant Marine 150 Odos Vassilissis Sophias, Piraeus, Greece. *Telephone:* 412.1211.

KATTAN, Naim, O.C., F.R.S.C.; Canadian writer; b. 28 Nov. 1928, Baghdad, Iraq; s. of Nessim and Hela Kattan; m. Gaetane Laniel 1961; one s.; ed. Univ. of Baghdad and Sorbonne, Paris; newspaper corresp. in Near East and Europe, broadcaster throughout Europe; emigrated to Canada 1954; Int. Politics Ed. for Nouveau Journal 1961–62; fmr. teacher at Laval Univ.; fmr. Sec. Cercle Juif de langue française de Montréal; freelance journalist and broadcaster; mem. Académie Canadienne-Française; Pres. Royal Soc. of Canada. *Publications: novels:* Babylone 1975, Les Fruits arrachés 1981, La Fiancée promise 1983, La Fortune du passage 1989; *essays:* Le réel et le théâtral 1970 (trans. into English), Ecrivains des Amériques, Tomes I-III, Le Repos et l'Oubli 1987, also numerous short stories and criticisms. *Address:* 4803 Mira Street, Montreal, Quebec, H3W 2B5, Canada. *Telephone:* 514-733-1460.

KATUSHEV, Konstantin Fyodorovich; Soviet politician and diplomatist; b. 1 Dec. 1927; ed. Zhdanov Polytechnical Inst., Gor'kiy; mem. CPSU 1952–; Designer, senior engineer, deputy chief engineer at Gor'kiy automobile works 1951–57; Official of Gor'kiy Region Cttee. CPSU 1957–63, First Sec. 1965–68; First Sec. Gor'kiy city cttee. CPSU 1963–65; mem. Cen. Cttee. CPSU 1966–, Sec. Cen. Cttee. CPSU 1968–; Deputy to U.S.S.R. Supreme Soviet 1966–, mem. 1966–67, Chair. Comm. for Construction and Building Materials Industry, Soviet of the Union 1966–70; Chair. Exec. Cttee. COMECON 1978–79; mem. and Vice-Chair. U.S.S.R. Council of Ministers 1979–82; Amb. to Cuba 1982–86; Pres. U.S.S.R. State Cttee. on External Econ. Relations 1985–; Order of Lenin and other decorations. *Address:* c/o Ministry of Foreign Affairs, 32-34 Smolenskaya-Sennaya Ploschad, Moscow, U.S.S.R.

KATZ, Abraham, M.I.A., PH.D.; American diplomatist (retd.); b. 4 Dec. 1926, Brooklyn; s. of Alexander and Zina (née Rabinowitz) Katz; one s. two d.; ed. Brooklyn Coll., Columbia Univ., Harvard Univ.; Foreign Service Officer, Dept. of State 1951; Vice-Consul, Prin. Officer, American Consulate, Merida, Yucatan, Mexico 1951–53; Second Sec., Vice-Consul, Embassy, Mexico 1953–56; Bureau of Intelligence and Research and Office of Under-Sec. Dept. of State 1957–59; First Sec. to NATO and OECD 1959–64, Sec. of Del. to OECD 1959–64; Counsellor, Econ. Affairs, Moscow Embassy 1964–66; Dir. Office of OECD, European Communities and Atlantic Political Econ. Affairs 1967–74; Deputy Chief Mission to OECD 1974–78; Deputy Asst. Sec. for Int. Econ. Policy and Research, Dept. of Commerce 1978–80, Asst. Sec. 1980–81; Rep. and Amb. to OECD 1981–84; Pres. U.S. Council for Int. Business, New York June 1984–; mem. Bd. of Govs., Atlantic Inst., Paris 1985–; Dept. of State Commendable Service Award 1953, Meritorious Service Award 1962, Grand Officier Ordre Nat. du Mérite. *Publications:* The Atlantic Community Reappraised-A Washington Perspective (Proceedings of Acad. of Political Science) 1958, The Politics of Economic Reform in the Soviet Union 1972. *Leisure interests:* tennis, jogging. *Address:* United States Council for International Business, 1212 Avenue of the Americas, 21st Floor, New York, N.Y. 10036, U.S.A.

KATZ, Sir Bernard, M.D., D.SC., F.R.C.P., F.R.S.; British professor of biophysics; b. 26 March 1911, Leipzig, Germany; s. of Max Katz; m. Marguerite Penly 1945; two s.; ed. Univs. of Leipzig and London; Biophysical Research, Univ. Coll. London 1935–39, Beit Memorial Fellow 1938–39; Carnegie Research Fellow, Sydney Hospital, Sydney, N.S.W. 1939–42; Royal Australian Air Force 1942–45; Asst. Dir. of Research in Biophysics and Henry Head Research Fellow, Royal Soc. 1946–50; Reader in Physiology, Univ. Coll. London 1950–51; Prof. of Biophysics and Head of Dept., Univ. Coll. London 1952–78, Prof. Emer. 1978–; mem. Royal Soc., Sec. 1968, and Vice-Pres. 1970–76; mem. Agricultural Research Council 1967–77; Herter Lecturer, Johns Hopkins Univ. 1958; Dunham Lecturer, Harvard Univ. 1961; Croonian Lecturer, Royal Soc. 1961; Foreign mem. Accademia Nazionale Dei Lincei, Royal Danish Acad. of Sciences 1968, American Acad. Arts and Sciences 1969, U.S. Nat. Acad. Sciences 1976; Hon. D.Sc. (Southampton, Melbourne Univs.) 1971, (Cambridge Univ.) 1980, Hon. Ph.D. (Weizmann Inst. Science) 1979; Baly Medal, Royal Coll. of Physicians 1967, Copley Medal, Royal Soc. 1967, Nobel Prize (jtly.) for Physiology or Medicine 1970; Foreign mem. Orden pour le mérite für Wissenschaften und Künste 1982. *Publications:* Electric Excitation of Nerve 1939, Nerve, Muscle and Synapse 1966, The Release of Neural Transmitter Substances 1969. *Address:* c/o Department of Physiology, University College, Gower Street, London, W.C.1, England. *Telephone:* 01-387 7050.

KATZ, Katriel; Israeli diplomatist; b. 16 Oct. 1908, Warsaw, Poland; s. of Asher and Haya Katz; m. Ova Grunhut 1932; one s. two d.; ed. Herzliya Gymnasium and Warsaw Univ.; went to Palestine 1924; Head, Dept. of Propaganda and Education, Haganah 1942–43; spokesman of the Haganah 1948; spokesman, Public Relations Office, Israel Defence Army 1949; on staff of Ministry of Foreign Affairs 1949–; former Head, Div. of Political Research; Chargé d'affaires, Budapest 1953–56; Minister to Poland 1956–58; Sec. to the Govt. 1958–62; Consul-Gen., New York 1962–65; Amb. to U.S.S.R. 1965–67; Chair. Yad-Vashem Memorial Authority, Jerusalem 1967–72; Amb. to Finland 1972–73; Deputy Chair. Israeli Council of Int. Relations 1974–; mem. Bd. of Governors, Hebrew Univ. 1975–, mem. Editorial Bd., Magnes Pres Publishers, Hebrew Univ. 1976–. *Publications:* Five Years of Israel's Foreign Policy 1948–53, A Diplomat in Lands of Estrangement (Hebrew) 1976. *Address:* 4 Hamaapilim Street, Jerusalem, Israel.

KATZ, Michael, A.B.; American pediatrician and educator; b. 13 Feb. 1928, Lwow, Poland; s. of Edward Katz and Rita Gluzman; ed. Univ. of Pennsylvania, State Univ. of New York, Brooklyn, Columbia Univ. School of Public Health; Intern, Univ. of California, Los Angeles, Medical Center 1956–57; Resident, Presbyterian Hosp. New York 1960–62, Dir. Pediatric Service 1977–; Hon. lecturer in Pediatrics, Makerere Univ. Coll., Kampala, Uganda 1963–64; Instructor in Pediatrics, Columbia Univ. 1964–65, Prof. in Tropical Medicine, School of Public Health 1971–, Prof. in Pediatrics, Coll. of Physicians and Surgeons 1972–77, Reuben S. Carpentier Prof. and Chair. Dept. of Pediatrics 1977–; Assoc. mem. Wistar Inst., Philadelphia 1965–71; Asst. Prof. of Pediatrics, Univ. of Pa. 1966–71; Consultant, WHO regional offices, Guatemala, Venezuela, Egypt, Yemen; mem. U.S. Del. to 32nd World Health Ass., Geneva 1979; Consultant, UNICEF, New York and Tokyo; Jurzykowski Foundation Award in Medicine 1983; mem. numerous medical socs. including Inst. of Medicine, N.A.S. *Publications:* contributions to numerous journals and medical works. *Address:* 930 Fifth Avenue, New York, N.Y. 10021 (Home); College of Physicians and Surgeons, Columbia University, 630 West 168th Street, New York, N.Y. 10032, U.S.A. (Office).

KATZ, Milton, A.B., J.D., LL.D.; American professor of law and public official; b. 29 Nov. 1907, New York; s. of Morris and Clara (Schiffman) Katz; m. Vivian Greenberg 1933; three s.; ed. Harvard Univ.; mem. anthropological expedition to Central Africa 1927–28; various official posts U.S. Govt. 1932–39; Lecturer on Law Harvard Univ. 1939–40, Prof. of Law 1940–50; Solicitor War Production Bd. 1941–43; U.S. Exec. Officer, Combined Production and Resources Bd. 1942–43; Office of Strategic Services 1943–44; Lieut.-Commdr. U.S.N.R. on active duty 1944–46; Ambassador of the U.S. and U.S. Special Rep. in Europe 1950–51; U.S. mem. Defence, Financial and Economic Cttee. under North Atlantic Treaty 1950–51; U.S. Rep. Economic Comm. for Europe (UN) 1950–51; Assoc. Dir. Ford Foundation

1951–54; Dir. Int. Legal Studies and Henry L. Stimson Prof. of Law, Harvard Univ. 1954–78 (Emer.); Chair. Cttee. on Manpower, White House Conf. on Int. Co-operation 1965; Consultant and Chair. Energy Advisory Bd., U.S. Office of Tech. Assessment 1972–82; mem. Advisory Bd., Energy Lab., M.I.T. 1974–85; Distinguished Prof. of Law, Suffolk Univ. 1978–; Pres. American Acad. of Arts and Sciences 1979–82; Dir. Int. Friendship League; mem. Corpn. Boston Museum of Science; Chair. Comm. on Life Sciences and Social Policy, N.A.S.—Nat. Research Council 1968–75; mem. panel on Technology Assessment, N.A.S. 1968–69; mem. Visiting Comm., Dept. of Humanities, M.I.T. 1970–73; Sherman Fairchild Distinguished Scholar, Calif. Inst. of Tech. 1974; Consultant Programme on Social Man. of Tech., Univ. of Washington 1974; Co. Chair. A.B.A./A.A.A.S. Cttee. on Science and Law 1978–81, mem. Nat. Acad. Eng. Cttee. on Tech. and Int. Economy and Trade Issues; mem. advisory Bd. Consortium on Competitiveness and Co-operation, Univ. of Calif. 1986–; Trustee Carnegie Endowment for Int. Peace (Chair. of Bd. 1970–78), World Peace Foundation (Exec. Cttee.), Citizens Research Foundation (Pres. 1969–78), Brandeis Univ., Int. Legal Center (Chair. of Bd. 1971–78), Case Western Reserve Univ.; Legion of Merit; Commdr.'s Cross, Order of Merit (Fed. Repub. of Germany). *Publications:* Cases and Materials on Administrative Law 1947, Government under Law and the Individual (with others) 1956, The Law of International Transactions and Relations: Cases and Materials (with Kingman Brewster, Jr.) 1960, The Things that are Caesar's 1966, The Relevance of International Ajudication 1968, The Modern Foundation: Its Dual Nature, Public and Private 1968, Man's Impact on the Global Environment (with others) 1970, Assessing Biomedical Technologies (with others) 1975, Technology, Trade, and the U.S. Economy (with others) 1978, Strengthening Conventional Deterrence in Europe: Proposals for the 1980's (with others) 1983, contrib. The Positive Sum Strategy: Harnessing Technology for Economic Growth 1986. *Address:* Harvard Law School, Cambridge, Mass. (Office); 6 Berkeley Street, Cambridge, Mass., U.S.A. (Home). *Telephone:* 495-3115 (Office); Kirkland 7-0057 (Home).

KATZ, Samuel Lawrence, M.D.; American professor of pediatrics; b. 29 May 1927, Manchester, N.H.; m. 1st Betsy Jane Cohan 1950, four s. three d. (divorced 1971); m. 2nd Catherine Minock Wilfert 1971; ed. Dartmouth Coll. and Harvard Coll.; hosp. appts., Boston, Mass. 1952–56; Exchange Registrar, Pediatric Unit, St. Mary's Hosp. Medical School, London, England 1956; Research Fellow in Pediatrics, Harvard Medical School at Research Div. of Infectious Diseases, Children's Hosp. Medical Center, Boston 1956–58, Research Assoc. 1958–68; Pediatrician-in-Chief, Beth Israel Hosp., Boston 1958–61, Visiting Pediatrician 1961–68; Assoc. Physician, Children's Hosp. Medical Center, Boston 1958–63, Sr. Assoc. in Medicine 1963–68, Chief, Newborn Div. 1961–67; Instructor in Pediatrics, Harvard Medical School, Boston 1958–59, Assoc. 1959–63, Tutor in Medical Sciences 1961–63, Asst. Prof. of Pediatrics 1963–68; Co-Dir. Combined Beth Israel Hosp.-Children's Hosp. Medical Center, Infectious Disease Career Training Programe 1967–68; Prof. and Chair. Dept. of Pediatrics, Duke Univ. School of Medicine, Durham, N.C. 1968–, Wilburt C. Davison Prof. of Pediatrics 1972–; mem. Bd. of Dirs. Nat. Foundation for Infectious Diseases 1980–; Consultant, Nat. Insts. of Health, AIDS Exec. Cttee. 1986–; mem. Editorial Bd. Annual Review in Medicine, Postgraduate Medicine, Reviews of Infectious Diseases, Current Problems in Pediatrics, Ped Sat (TV Educ.); Fellow American Acad. of Pediatrics, Infectious Diseases Soc. of America; mem. A.A.A.S., Soc. for Pediatric Research, American Soc. for Microbiology, American Assen. of Immunologists, American Public Health Assen., American Soc. for Clinical Investigation, American Pediatric Soc., American Epidemiological Soc., American Soc. for Virology, American Fed. for Clinical Research. *Publications:* numerous articles in scientific journals. *Address:* Department of Pediatrics, Duke University School of Medicine, Durham, N.C. 27706, U.S.A.

KATZAV, Moshe; Israeli politician and economist; b. 1945, Iran; m.; five c.; ed. Hebrew Univ., Jerusalem; mil. service Israeli Defence Forces; mem. 9th Knesset (Parl.), mem. Labour and Social Affairs Cttee., Educ. and Culture Cttee. 1971, mem. Tenth Knesset; Deputy Minister of Construction and Housing; mem. Educ. and Culture Cttee. –1984; Minister of Labour and Social Affairs 1984–88, of Transport Dec. 1988–; fmr. Chair. Kiryat Malachi Council. *Address:* Ministry of Transport, Klal Bldg., 97 Jaffa Road, Jerusalem, Israel.

KATZENBACH, Nicholas deBelleville; American lawyer and government official; b. 17 Jan. 1922, Philadelphia; s. of Edward and Marie Katzenbach; m. Lydia King Phelps Stokes 1946; two s. two d.; ed. Philips Exeter Acad., Princeton and Yale Univs. and Balliol Coll., Oxford; U.S. Army Air Force 1941–45; admitted to N.J. Bar 1950, Conn. Bar 1955, New York Bar 1972; with firm Katzenbach Gildea and Rudner, Trenton, N.J. 1950; Attorney-Adviser, Office of Gen. Counsel, Air Force 1950–52, part-time Consultant 1952–56; Assoc. Prof. of Law, Yale Univ. 1952–56; Prof. of Law, Univ. of Chicago 1956–60; Asst. Attorney-Gen., U.S. Dept. of Justice 1961–62, Deputy Attorney-Gen. 1962–64, Attorney-Gen. 1965–66; Under-Sec. of State 1966–69; Sr. Vice-Pres. and Gen. Counsel, IBM Corpn. 1969–86; Partner Riker, Danzig, Scherer, Hyland and Perretti 1986–; mem. American Bar Assen., American Judicature Soc., American Law Inst.; hon. degrees from Rutgers Univ., Univ. of Bridgeport (Conn.), Tufts Univ., Georgetown Univ., Princeton, Northeastern Univ., Brandeis Univ.; Democrat. *Publications:* The Political Foundations of International Law (with

Morton A. Kaplan) 1961, Legal Literature of Space (with Prof. Leon Lipson) 1961. *Address:* Riker, Danzig, Scherer, Hyland & Perretti, Headquarters Plaza, One Speedwell Avenue, Morristown, N.J. 07960 (Office); 906 The Great Road, Princeton N.J. 08540, U.S.A. (Home). *Telephone:* (201) 538-0800, Ext. 358 (Office).

KATZER, Hans; German politician; b. 31 Jan. 1919, Cologne; s. of Karl Katzer and Rosa Franke; m. Elisabeth Kaiser 1949; one d.; ed. Volksschule, Realgymnasium and Höhere Fachschule für Textil; Nat. and Mil. Service 1939–45; employed in Labour Office, Cologne 1945–49; Man. Dir.Social Cttee. of Christian Dem. Employees Asscn. of Germany 1950–63, Chair. 1963–77, publr. of political monthly Soziale Ordnung; Man. Chair. of Jakob Kaiser Foundation 1963–65; mem. Union of Transport Workers; mem. Christian Democratic Union (CDU) 1945–; mem. Cologne City Council 1950–57; mem. Bundestag 1957–; mem. European Parl. 1979–; Chair. Parl. Cttee. for Fed. Econ. Assets 1961–65; Fed. Minister of Labour and Social Welfare 1965–69; Grosses Bundesverdienstkreuz mit Stern 1969, mit Schulterband 1973. *Publications:* Aspekte moderner Sozialpolitik 1969, Bundestagsreden 1972. *Leisure interests:* reading, walking, table tennis. *Address:* 5000 Köln-Marienburg, Kastanienallee 7, Federal Republic of Germany.

KATZIR, Ephraim, M.SC., PH.D.; Israeli scientist, teacher and administrator; b. (as Ephraim Katchalski) 16 May 1916, Kiev, Russia; s. of Yehuda and Tsila Katchalski; m. Nina Gotlieb 1938 (deceased); one s. one d.; ed. Hebrew Univ., Jerusalem; Prof. and Head, Dept. of Biophysics, Weizmann Inst. of Sciences 1951–73; Chief Scientist, Ministry of Defence 1966–68; Pres. of Israel 1973–78; Prof. Weizmann Inst. of Science 1978–, Prof. Tel Aviv Univ. 1978–; first incumbent Herman F. Mark Chair in Polymer Science, Polytechnic Inst. of New York 1979; Pres. World ORT Union (Org. for Rehabilitation Through Training) 1987; mem. Israel Acad. of Sciences and Humanities, Biochemical Soc. of Israel, Israel Chemical Soc., N.A.S., U.S.A., Leopoldina Acad. of Science, German Democratic Repub., American Soc. of Biological Chemists (Hon.), The Royal Soc. of London (Foreign mem.), American Acad. of Arts and Sciénces (Foreign Hon. mem.), Int. Union of Biochemistry and many other orgs.; Hon. Prof. Polytechnic Inst., New York; Hon. Ph.D. (Brandeis, Michigan, Harvard, Northwestern, Jerusalem Hebrew, McGill, Thomas Jefferson, Oxford, Miami Univs., Weizmann Inst., Israel Technion and Hebrew Union Coll., Jerusalem, Eidgenossische Technische Hochschule, Univ. of Buenos Aires); Tchernikhovski Prize 1948; Weizmann Prize 1950; Israel Prize Natural Sciences 1959; Rothschild Prize Natural Sciences 1961; Linderstrøm-Lang Gold Medal 1969; Hans Krebs Medal 1972; Underwood Prescott Award, M.I.T. 1982; first recipient of Japan Prize, Science.and Tech. Foundation of Japan 1985; Enzyme Eng. Award 1987. *Publications:* numerous papers and articles on proteins and polyamino acids, polymers structure and function of living cells and enzyme engineering. *Leisure interest:* swimming. *Address:* Weizmann Institute of Science, Rehovot 76100, Israel.

KAUFMAN, Rt. Hon. Gerald Bernard, P.C., M.A., M.P., F.R.S.A.; British politician; b. 21 June 1930; s. of Louis and Jane Kaufman; ed. Leeds Grammar School and Queen's Coll., Oxford; Asst. Gen. Sec. Fabian Soc. 1954–55; political staff, Daily Mirror 1955–64; political corresp. New Statesman 1964–65; Parl. Press Liaison, Labour Party 1965–70; M.P. for Manchester, Ardwick 1970–83; for Manchester, Gorton 1983–; Under-Sec. of State for the Environment 1974–75, for Industry 1975; Minister of State, Dept. of Industry 1975–79; mem. Parl. Cttee. of Labour Party 1980–; Opposition Spokesman for Home Affairs 1983–87; Shadow Foreign Sec. 1987–. *Publications:* How to Live under Labour (co-author) 1964, To Build the Promised Land 1973, How to be a Minister 1980, Renewal: Labour's Britain in the 1980's 1983, My Life in the Silver Screen 1985, Inside the Promised Land 1986. *Leisure interests:* cinema, opera, records, theatre, concerts, travel. *Address:* House of Commons, London, S.W.1; 87 Charlbert Court, Eamont Street, London, N.W.8, England. *Telephone:* 01-722 6264.

KAUFMAN, Henry, B.A., M.S., PH.D.; American banker; b. 20 Oct. 1927, Wenings, Germany; s. of Gustav and Hilda (née Rosenthal) Kaufman; m. Elaine Reinheimer 1957; three s.; ed. New York and Columbia Univs.; went to U.S.A. 1937; Asst. Chief Economist, Research Dept., Fed. Reserve Bank of New York 1957–61; with Salomon Bros., New York 1962–, Gen. Partner 1967–, mem. Exec. Cttee. 1972–, Man. Dir. 1981–, also Chief Economist, in charge Bond Market Research, Industry and Stock Research, and Bond Portfolio Analysis Research Depts.; Pres. Money Marketeers, New York Univ. 1964–65; Trustee, Hudson Inst.; mem. Bd. of Govs., Tel-Aviv Univ.; mem. American Econ. Asscn., American Finance Asscn., Conf. of Business Economists, Econ. Club, New York (also Dir.), UN Asscn. (also Dir), Council on Foreign Relations. *Publication:* Interest Rates, the Markets and the New Financial World 1986. *Address:* Salomon Bros., 1 New York Plaza, New York, N.Y. 10004, U.S.A.

KAUFMANN, Arthur, DR.IUR.; German university professor; b. 10 May 1923, Singen; s. of Edmund Kaufmann and Elisabeth (née Gsell) Kaufmann; m. Dorothea Helffrich 1949; one s. three d.; ed. Univs. of Frankfurt and Heidelberg; judge at Landgericht Karlsruhe 1951–57; Docent Univ. of Heidelberg 1957–60; Ordinary Prof. Univ. of Saarbrücken 1960–69, Univ. of Munich 1969–, Dir. Inst. for Legal Philosophy and Legal Information, Univ. of Munich 1969–; Ordinary mem. Bayerische Akademie der Wissenschaften 1980–; mem. many other academies and orgs.; Hon. Pres. German

Section Int. Asscn. for Philosophy of Law and Social Philosophy 1982–; Dr. h.c.; Hon. mem. Inst. for Advanced Studies in Jurisprudence, Univ. of Sydney. *Publications:* Naturrecht und Geschichtlichkeit 1957, Das Schuldprinzip 1976, Rechtsphilosophie im Wandel 1984, Schuld und Strafe 1983, Strafrecht zwischen Gestern und Morgen 1983, Beiträge zur Juristischen Hermeneutik 1984, Analogie und 'Natur der Sache' 1982, Einführung in Rechtsphilosophie und Rechtstheorie der Gegenwart 1988, Gerechtigkeit, der vergessene Weg zum Frieden 1986, Gustav Radbruch 1987, etc.; 250 articles and trans. into 13 languages. *Leisure interests:* literature, music, travel. *Address:* Longinusstrasse 3, D-8000 Munich 60, Federal Republic of Germany. *Telephone:* 089/8111723.

KAUFMANN, Johan, PH.D.; Netherlands fmr. diplomatist; b. 20 April 1918, Amsterdam; m.; one d.; entered Civil Service 1945; Commercial Sec. Netherlands Embassy, Washington, later Mexico; Counsellor, Perm. Mission to UN 1956–61; Minister Plenipotentiary, Office of UN and Int. Orgs., Geneva; Amb. Extraordinary and Plenipotentiary 1967–83; Head Perm. del. to OECD 1969–73; Perm. Rep. to UN 1974–78; Pres. UNDP 1977; Amb. to Japan 1978–83; Cleveringa Chair. Prof. Leyden Univ. 1983–84; Visiting Prof. Int. Univ. of Japan 1985; Trustee UN Inst. for Training and Research 1977–85. *Publications:* How UN Decisions are Made 1958, Conference Diplomacy 1968, United Nations Decision Making 1980. *Address:* Alexander Gogelweg 1, 2517 JD 's-Gravenhage, Netherlands.

KAUL, Pratap Kishen, M.A.; Indian diplomatist; b. 3 July 1929, Calcutta; s. of late K. K. Kaul; m. Usha Kaul 1932; three d.; ed. Allahabad and Harvard Univs.; Deputy Sec., Ministries of Home Affairs and Finance 1965–66, Joint Sec. Ministry of Finance 1967–73, Finance Sec. and Sec. Economic Affairs 1983–85; Joint Sec. Ministry of Steel and Mines 1975–76; Chief Controller, Imports and Exports, Ministry of Commerce Jan.–July 1976, Additional Sec. 1976–80, Sec. (Export Devt.) Feb.–May. 1980, Sec. (Textiles) July–Sept. 1980, Sec. 1980–81; Chair. State Trading Corpn. 1980–81; Defence Sec. Ministry of Defence 1981–83; Cabinet Sec. 1985–86; Amb. to the U.S.A. 1986–. *Leisure interests:* reading, sports. *Address:* Indian Embassy, 2107 Massachusetts Avenue, N.W., Washington, D.C. 20008; 2700 Macomb Street, N.W., Washington D.C. 20008, U.S.A. *Telephone:* (202) 939 9800.

KAUL, Prince Mohan, M.B., B.S., D.P.H., F.R.C.P., F.I.A.M.S., F.P.H.A.; Indian physician and health official; b. 1 March 1906, Hindaon; s. of late S. M. Kaul and late Mrs. R. R. Kaul; m. Krishna Razdon 1935; one s. four d.; ed. Punjab Univ. and Guy's Hospital, London; Teacher, Infectious Diseases, and Medical Officer, Campbell Medical School, Calcutta 1933–34; commissioned Indian Medical Service 1934; army service, rose to Acting Col. 1934–45; Deputy, Public Comm. Govt. of India 1946; Deputy Dir.-Gen. Health Services, Ministry of Health; Dir. WHO Epidemiological Intelligence Station, Singapore 1947–49; Dir. WHO Liaison Office to UN, New York 1950–52; Dir. Div. External Relations and Tech. Assistance 1953–56; Asst. Dir.-Gen. WHO 1956–67; Special Consultant to Dir.-Gen. WHO 1968–69; Consultant to WHO 1970–72, short-term Consultant 1973–75. *Leisure interest:* philately. *Address:* 17-G Maharani Bagh, New Delhi, India. *Telephone:* 631481.

KAUL, Triloki Nath; Indian diplomatist; b. 18 Feb. 1913, Baramulla, Kashmir; s. of T. Kaul Jalali and Gunwanti Kaul; m. Sati Kaul 1931; one s. one d.; ed. Univs. of Punjab, Allahabad, London; joined Indian Civil Service 1936; served in United Provinces as Joint Magistrate and Collector 1937–47; Sec. Indian Council of Agricultural Research, New Delhi 1947; First Sec. Indian Embassy, Moscow 1947–49, Washington 1949–50, Counsellor 1950–52, and Minister 1952–53, Beijing; Joint Sec. Ministry of External Affairs, New Delhi 1953–57; Chair. Int. Comm. for Supervision and Control, Viet-Nam 1957–58; Amb. to Iran 1958–60; Deputy High Commr. U.K. 1960–61, Acting High Commr. 1961–62; Amb. to U.S.S.R. and Mongolia 1962–66; Sec. to Govt. of India, Ministry of External Affairs, New Delhi 1966–68; Sec.-Gen. Ministry of External Affairs 1968–73; Amb. to U.S.A. 1973–76; Pres. Indian Council for Cultural Relations 1977 (resigned April 1977); mem. Exec. Bd. UNESCO 1980–85; Amb. to U.S.S.R. May 1986–; Hon. Fellow, King's Coll., London 1962; Hon. Prof. Kashmir Univ. 1978; Hon. LL.D. (Aradh Univ.) 1977. *Publications:* Diplomacy in Peace and War: Recollections and Reflections 1978, India, China and Indochina 1979, The Kissinger Years—Indo-U.S. Relations 1980. *Leisure interests:* reading, writing, teaching, travel, farming, photography. *Address:* 1037, Sector 21B, Chandigarh; Moscow, ul. Obukha 6-8, U.S.S.R. *Telephone:* 23136.

KAULA, Prithvi Nath, M.A., M.LIBR.SC.; Indian professor of library science; b. 13 March 1924, Srinagar; s. of Damodar Kaula; m. Asha Kaula 1941; two s. three d.; ed. S.P. Coll., Srinagar, Punjab Univ., Delhi Univ., Banaras Hindu Univ.; mem. Council, Indian Library Asscn. 1949–53, 1956–62; Man. Ed. Annals, Bulletin and Granthalays of Indian Library Asscn. 1949–53; Sec. Ranganathan Endowment for Library Science 1951–61; Gen. Sec. Delhi Library Asscn. 1953–55, 1958–60, Vice-Pres. 1956–58; Visiting lecturer in Library Science, Aligarh Muslim Univ. 1951–58; Reader Dept. of Library Science, Univ. of Delhi 1958–60; Vice-Pres. Govt. of Indian Libraries Asscn. 1958–61; mem. Review Cttee. on Library Science, Univ. Grants Comm. 1961–63, mem. Panel on Library and Information Science 1978–80, 1982–; Visiting lecturer Documentation, Research and Training Centre, Bangalore 1962, 1965; Ed. Library Herald 1958–61, Herald of Library Science 1962–;

Chair. Fed. of Indian Library Asscns. 1966, Pres. 1974–; mem. Governing Council, Nat. Library of India 1966–69; UNESCO Expert, UNESCO Regional Centre in the Western Hemisphere, Havana 1967–68; Gen. Sec. Indian Asscn. of Teachers of Library Science 1969, Pres. 1973–85; Ed. Granthalaya Vijnana 1970–; Librarian, Banaras Hindu Univ., and Prof. of Library Science 1971–78, Dean Faculty of Arts 1980–82; Prof. Emer. Kaslin Vidyapith 1983–, UGC Prof. Emer. Lucknow Univ. 1985–; Ed. Research Journal of the Banaras Hindu Univ. 1980–, Ed. Progress in Library and Information Science 1980–; Ed.-in-Chief International Information, Communication and Education 1982–; Chair. Council of Literacy and Adult Educ. 1971–; Bureau for Promotion of Urdu Library Science 1980–84; mem. State Library Cttee., Uttar Pradesh 1981–85; Raja Rammohun Roy Library Foundation 1981–84, Bd. of Studies in Library and Information Science of 11 univs.; Expert mem. UNESCO Advisory Group on Comparability of Higher Degrees in Library Science 1973–; Visiting Prof. 35 Indian Univs., 7 American Univs., Univ. of Havana, Hebrew Univ., Jerusalem, and Univs. in France, Cuba, the G.D.R., Hungary, Mexico, Spain, Thailand, the U.S.S.R. and the U.K.; Consultant and Adviser on Library Science to several int. orgs. and nat. asscns.; Organizing Sec. and Pres. of numerous confs.; honoured by Int. Festschrift Cttee. 1974; Indian Library Movement Award 1974; Pro Mundi Beneficio Medal 1975; Deutsche Bucherei Medal 1981, and numerous other awards. *Publications:* 48 books and monographs and numerous other publs. including over 700 technical papers and book reviews on library science, labour problems and student unrest. *Leisure interests:* reading, writing, the study of library and information science. *Address:* C-239 Indira Nagar, Lucknow 226016, India.

KAUNDA, Dr. Kenneth David: Zambian politician; b. 28 April 1924, Lubwa; ed. Lubwa Training School and Munali Secondary School; Schoolteacher at Lubwa Training School 1943, Headmaster 1944–47; Sec. Chinsali Young Men's Farming Asscn. 1947; welfare officer, Chingola Copper Mine 1948; school teaching 1948–49; Founder-Sec. Lubwa branch, African Nat. Congress 1950, district organizer 1951, prov. organizer 1952, Sec.-Gen. for N. Rhodesia 1953; broke away to form Zambia African Nat. Congress 1958; Pres. United Nat. Independence Party 1960–; Minister of Local Govt. and Social Welfare, N. Rhodesia 1962–64; Prime Minister of N. Rhodesia Jan.-Oct. 1964; Pres. Pan-African Freedom Movement for East, Central and South Africa (PAFMECSA) 1963; First Pres. of Zambia Oct. 1964–, and Minister of Defence 1964–70, 1973–78; Head of Sub-Cttee. for Defence and Security 1978–; Minister of Foreign Affairs 1969–70, also of Trade, Industry, Mines and State Participation 1969–73; Chancellor, Univ. of Zambia 1966–; Chair. Mining and Industrial Devt. Corpn. of Zambia April 1970–; Chair. Org. of African Unity (OAU) 1970–71, 1987–88, Non-Aligned Nations Conf. 1970–73, Chair. ZIMCO Jan. 1983–; Hon. Dr. of Laws (Fordham, Dublin, Windsor (Canada), Wales, Sussex, York and Chile Univs.), Dr. h.c. (Humboldt State Univ., Calif.) 1980; Order of the Collar of the Nile, Kt. of the Collar of the Order of Pius XII, Order of the Queen of Sheba, Jawaharlal Nehru Award for Int. Understanding, Quaide Azam Human Rights Inst. Prize (Pakistan) 1976. *Publications:* Black Government 1961, Zambia Shall Be Free 1962, A Humanist in Africa (with Colin Morris) 1966, Humanism in Zambia and its Implementation 1967, Letter to my Children 1977, Kaunda On Violence 1980. *Address:* State House, P.O. Box 135, Lusaka, Zambia. *Telephone:* 50122 (Lusaka).

KAUR, Prabhjot (see Prabhjot Kaur).

KAUSHAL, Jagan Nath, B.A., LL.B.; Indian lawyer and politician; b. Patiala; s. of Shri Tara Chand; m. Kanta Kausha 1933; three s. six d.; ed. Mohindra Coll., Patiala, and Punjab Univ., Lahore; dist. and sessions judge, Patiala, later Patiala and E. Punjab States Union 1947–49; Advocate-Gen., Punjab 1964–66, Haryana 1969–76; additional judge, Punjab High Court 1966–67; now Sr. Advocate, Supreme Court; mem. Rajya Sabha 1952–64; Gov. of Bihar 1976–79; Minister of Law, Justice and Company Affairs 1982–85; Congress (I). *Leisure interests:* reading, billiards. *Address:* c/o Ministry of Law, Justice and Company Affairs, Shastri Bhavan, Dr. Rajendra Prasad Road, New Delhi 110001, India.

KAUSHIK, Purushottam Lal, LL.B.; Indian politician; b. 24 Sept. 1930, Mahasamund; s. of Dhalu Ram and Ramkunwar Kaushik; m. Amrit Kaushik 1945; three s.; ed. Raipur, Sagar, Nagpur Univ.; joined Socialist Party 1952; engaged in political org. of Adivasi peasants and agricultural workers in Chattisgarh; organized hunger marches 1965, 1974; helped to form Kisan Khetihar Mazdoor Sangh (co-operative org.) in Chattisgarh; mem. Vidhan Sabha (legislature) of Madhya Pradesh for Mahasamund 1972–75; mem. Exec., Madhya Pradesh Unit of Socialist Party, also mem. Nat. Cttee.; Chair. Madhya Pradesh Socialist Party 1975–77; detained during emergency 1975–77; mem. Janata Party 1977–; mem. Lok Sabha from Raipur March 1977–; Minister for Tourism and Civil Aviation 1977–79, of Information and Broadcasting 1979–80. *Leisure interests:* farming, music. *Address:* Raipur Co-operative Housing Soc., Rajendra Nagar, Raipur, Madhya Pradesh, India.

KAUZMANN, Walter Joseph, PH.D.; American professor of chemistry; b. 18 Aug. 1916, Mount Vernon, New York; s. of Albert Kauzmann and Julia Kahle; m. Elizabeth Flagler 1951; two s. one d.; ed. Cornell, Princeton Univs.; Research Fellow, Westinghouse Co.; with Nat. Defense Council Explosives Research Lab.; worked on Atomic Bomb project, Los Alamos Labs., New Mexico 1944–46; Asst. Prof. Princeton Univ. 1946–51, Assoc.

Prof. 1951–60, Prof. 1960–83, David B. Jones Prof. of Chem. 1963–83, Chair. Dept. of Chemistry 1963–68, Dept. of Biochemical Sciences 1980–82; Visiting Scientist, Nat. Resources Council of Canada, Halifax 1983; mem. N.A.S., American Acad. of Arts and Sciences, American Chem. Soc., American Physical Soc., A.A.A.S., Fed. of American Scientists, American Soc. of Biochemists, American Geophysical Union, American Ornithologists' Union; Guggenheim Fellow 1957, 1974–75; Visiting Lecturer Kyoto Univ. 1974, Ibadan Univ. 1975; first recipient Kaj Ulrik Linderstrøm-Lang Medal 1966. *Publications:* Introd. to Quantum Chemistry 1957, Thermal Properties of Matter (2 vols.) 1966, 1967, Structure and Properties of Water 1969. *Address:* c/o Department of Chemistry, Princeton University, Princeton, N.J. 08544, U.S.A.

KAWAHARA, Masato; Japanese broadcasting executive; b. 18 Oct. 1921; ed. Tokyo Univ.; joined Nippon Hoso Kyokai (NHK) News Dept. 1946; Head of Social Educ. Div., Educational Dept. 1960, Deputy Dir. Educational Dept. 1965, Dir. Staff Admin. Dept. 1967, Deputy Dir.-Gen. of Broadcasting in charge of News Dept. 1971; Man. Dir., Dir.-Gen. of Audience Service 1973; Gen. Man. Dir. 1976, retd. from NHK 1979, Exec. Man. Dir. NHK Arts Center (stage setting co.) 1980, Pres. NHK July 1982–. *Address:* Nippon Hoso Kyokai, 2-2-1, Jinnan, Shibuya-ku, Tokyo (Office); 5-11-7, Mejiro, Toshima-ku, Tokyo, Japan (Home).

KAWAI, Ryoichi; Japanese business executive; b. 18 Jan. 1917; s. of Yoshinari Kawai and Chieko Kawai; m. 1st Kiyoko Kawai 1942 (died 1973), 3 s.; m. 2nd Junko Kawai 1976; ed. Tokyo Univ.; fmr. Pres. Komatsu Ltd., Chair. Sept. 1982–. *Leisure interest:* golf. *Address:* Komatsu Building, 3-6, Akasaka 2-chome, Minato-ku, Tokyo, Japan.

KAWAKAMI, Hiroshi, B.S.; Japanese business executive; b. 5 Jan. 1942; m. Toshiko Nagai 1966; two s.; ed. Hamamatsu-Kita High School and Nippon Univ.; Tape Recorder Div. Sony Inc. 1965–71; Stereo Hi-Fi Div. Nippon Gakki Co., Ltd. (Yamaha) 1971–72; Gen. Man. Stereo Hi-Fi Div. Yamaha 1972–76, Gen. Man. Production Admin. Div. 1976–77, Dir. 1977–79, Man. Dir. 1979–81, Vice-Pres. 1981–83, Pres. 1983–; Dir. Teac Corpn.; Trustee, Yamaha Music Foundation; Chair. Nat. Musical Instrument Cos. Asscn. *Leisure interests:* music, reading, golf, skiing, archery. *Address:* 10-1 Nakazawa-Cho, Hamamatsu, Shizuoka 430, Japan. *Telephone:* 0534-60-2030.

KAWAKUBO, Rei; Japanese couturier; b. 1943; ed. Keio Univ., Tokyo; joined Asahikasei 1964; Freelance Designer 1966; launched Comme des Garçons Label 1969; f. and Pres. Comme des Garçons Co. Ltd. 1973; Japan Comme des Garçons Collection presented twice a year, Tokyo; 254 outlets in Japan, 8 Comme des Garçons Shops and 87 outlets outside Japan; currently has 8 lines of clothing and 1 line of furniture; opened 1st overseas Comme des Garçons Boutique in Paris 1982; joined Fed. Française de la Couture 1982; Mainichi Newspaper Fashion Award 1983. *Address:* c/o Comme des Garçons Co. Ltd., 5-11-5 Minamiaoyama, Minatoku, Tokyo, Japan.

KAWAMOTO, Nobuhiko; Japanese business executive; b. 24 March 1917, Hyogo; m.; two s.; ed. Kyoto Univ.; joined Mitsubishi Bank Co., Ltd. 1939, Branch Man. 1960–68; joined Konishiroku Photo Ind. Co., Ltd. 1968, Dir. 1968–70, Man. Dir. and Sr. Man. Marketing Div. 1970–73, Sr. Man. Dir. 1973–78, Exec. Vice-Pres. 1978–79, Pres. 1979–83, Chair. 1983–. *Leisure interest:* reading. *Address:* 2-4-7 Minamisawa, Higashi-kurume-shi, Tokyo, Japan.

KAWARA, Tsutomu; Japanese politician; b. April 1937, Ishikawa Pref.; m.; three d.; ed. Chuo Univ.; mem. House of Reps. (elected 6 times); Chair. Liberal-Democratic Party (LDP) Nat. Org. Cttee.; Deputy Chief Cabinet Sec.; Parl. Vice-Minister of Labour; Minister of State, Dir.-Gen. Defence Agency 1987–88; Deputy Chair. LDP Diet Affairs Cttee. *Leisure interests:* reading, sport, judo (3rd dan). *Address:* Kudan Shukusha, 2-14-1 Fujimi, Chiyoda-ku, Tokyo 102, Japan.

KAWARI, Hamad Abdelaziz al-, B.A.; Qatari diplomatist; b. 1948, Doha, Qatar; s. of Abdelaziz Al-Kawari; m. Zeinab Al-Badrawi 1973; two s. one d.; ed. Coll. of Dar Al-Ulum, Cairo Univ. and Jesuit Univ., Beirut; Chargé d'Affaires, Beirut 1972–74; Amb. to Syria 1974–79, to France, also accred. to Spain, Switzerland, Italy and Greece and Perm. Rep. to UNESCO 1979–84; Perm. Rep. to UN 1984–; Légion d'Honneur, and honours from govts. of Syria, France, Spain and Italy. *Leisure interests:* sport, reading. *Address:* Permanent Mission of Qatar to the United Nations, 22nd Floor, 747 Third Avenue, New York, N.Y. 10017, U.S.A.

KAWASAKI, Seiichi; Japanese banker; b. 13 Nov. 1922, Tokyo; s. of Hachiroemon Kawasaki and Mine Kawasaki; m. Ruriko Yamaguchi 1957; three d.; ed. Tokyo Univ.; joined Mitsui Trust 1946; Dir. and Gen. Man. Marunouchi branch 1974, Osaka branch 1975; Man. Dir. 1977, Sr. Man. Dir. 1979, Deputy Pres. 1980, Pres. 1982, Chair. Mitsui Trust 1983–. *Publication:* Knowledge of Trusts 1957. *Leisure interests:* walking, reading. *Address:* 5-18 Minami Aoyama 4-chome, Minato-ku, Tokyo, Japan. *Telephone:* (03) 401-4095.

KAWASAKI, Teruo, B.ECONS.; Japanese business executive; b. 11 June 1918; m. Miyoko Kawasaki 1951; one s.; ed. Keio Univ.; joined Nihon Kasei 1943; mem. Bd Dirs. Mitsubishi Rayon 1971–, Man. Dir. 1975–79, Exec.

Man. Dir. 1979-82, Exec. Vice-Pres. 1982-83, Pres. 1983-88, Chair. 1988-. *Address:* 18-37 Higashiashiya-cho, Ashiya City, Hyogo Prefecture, Japan.

KAWAWA, Rashidi Mfaume; Tanzanian politician; b. 1929, Songea; ed. Tabora Secondary School; fmr. Pres. of the Tanganyikan Fed. of Labour; Minister of Local Govt. and Housing 1960-61; Minister without Portfolio 1961-62; Prime Minister Jan.-Dec. 1962, Vice-Pres. 1962-64; Second Vice-Pres., United Republic of Tanzania 1964-77, also Prime Minister 1972-77; Minister of Defence and Nat. Service 1977-80, Minister without Portfolio 1980-; fmr. Vice-Pres. of TANU (Tanganyika African Nat. Union); Sec.-Gen. Chama Cha Mapinduzi Nov. 1982-. *Address:* c/o Office of the Prime Minister, Dar es Salaam, Tanzania.

KAWUSU CONTEH, Sheku Bockari; Sierra Leonean politician; b. 1928; m.; c.; ed. Koyeima Govt. Secondary School; Sec. Koinadugu District Council 1956-59; Town Clerk, Bo Municipality 1962, 65-68; Exec. Officer, Cen. Govt. 1964-65; M.P. 1967-; Deputy Minister, Prime Minister's Office 1968-69; Minister of Housing and Country Planning 1969-70; Resident Minister for the Southern Province 1970-71; Acting Prime Minister Sept. 1970; Minister of Interior May-Nov. 1971, of Lands and Mines 1971-73, 1976-77, of Mines 1973-76, of Internal Affairs 1985-86; Philip Murray-William Green Humanitarian Award 1978. *Address:* c/o Ministry of Internal Affairs, Freetown, Sierra Leone.

KAYLA, Ziya; Turkish economist; b. 1912, Istanbul; s. of Col. Sevki Kayla and Zehra Vefkioglu; m. Sevinc Cenk 1967; ed. School of Political Sciences, Istanbul; Ministry of Finance 1934-63, Asst. Inspector, Inspector and Chief Inspector of Finance 1934-60, Deputy Minister of Finance 1960-63; Chair. Bd. of Dirs. and Dir.-Gen. Central Bank of Turkey 1963-66; Alternate Gov. for Turkey of Int. Bank for Reconstruction and Devt. 1961-65; Pres. Banks' Asscn. of Turkey 1963-66; Sec.-Gen. Comm. of Regulation of Bank Credits 1963-66; Head of Foreign Investment Encouragements Cttee. 1963-66; mem. Bd. of Controllers of the Prime Ministry 1966-70; Chair.Türkiye Vakiflar Bankasi 1971-76; mem. Bd. Central Bank of Turkey 1978-80; mem. Higher Educ. Council 1981-82; Auditor Türkiye İş Bankasi 1983-88. *Publications:* Emission Movements in Turkey 1967, Treasury and Central Banks Relations 1970, Knowledge of Economic Situation by Central Bank's Bulletin of Statistics 1978, Central Bank's Operations 1981. *Leisure interest:* writing articles on economics for newspapers. *Address:* Mesnevi Sokak 8/8 Çankaya, Ankara, Turkey. *Telephone:* 138-71-09.

KAYSEN, Carl, A.B., M.A., PH.D.; American economist; b. 5 March 1920, Philadelphia; s. of Samuel and Elizabeth Resnick; m. Annette Neutra 1940; two d.; ed. Overbrook High School, Philadelphia, Univ. of Pennsylvania and Harvard Univ.; Nat. Bureau of Econ. Research 1940-42; Office of Strategic Services, Washington, D.C. 1942-43; U.S. Army (Intelligence) 1943-45; Teaching Fellow in Econs., Harvard Univ. 1947, Jr. Fellow, Soc. of Fellows 1947-70, Asst. Prof. in Econs. 1950-55, Assoc. Prof. 1955-57, Prof. 1957-66, Assoc. Dean, Graduate School of Public Admin. 1960-66, Lucius N. Littauer Prof. of Political Economy 1964-66; Dir., Inst. of Advanced Study, Princeton 1966-76, Prof. of Social Science 1976-77, Dir. Emer. 1976-; David W. Skinner Prof. Political Econ., M.I.T. 1976-; Dir. Program in Science, Tech. and Soc. 1981-86; Vice-Chair. and Dir. Research, Sloan Comm. on Govt. and Higher Educ. 1977-79; Sr. Fulbright Research Scholar, London School of Econs. 1955-56; Econ. Consultant to Judge Wyzanski, Fed. District Court of Mass. 1950-52; Deputy Special Asst. to Pres. for Nat. Security Affairs 1961-63. *Publications:* United States v. United Shoe Machinery Corporation, an Economic Analysis of an Anti-Trust Case 1956, The American Business Creed (with others) 1956, Anti-Trust Policy (with D.F. Turner) 1959, The Demand for Electricity in the United States (with Franklin M. Fisher) 1962, The Higher Learning, the Universities and the Public 1969, Nuclear Power, Issues and Choice, Nuclear Energy Policy Study Group Report (with others) 1977, A Program for Renewed Partnership, Report of the Sloan Commission on Government and Higher Education (with others) 1980. *Address:* Massachussets Institute of Technology, E51-110D, Cambridge, Mass. 02139 (Office); 1 Hilliard Place, Cambridge, Mass. 02138, U.S.A. (Home). *Telephone:* (617)253-4054 (Office); (617) 661-0004 (Home).

KAZAKOV, Vasiliy Aleksandrovich: Soviet politician; b. 1916; mem. CPSU 1941-; mechanic, engineer; worked in aviation industry 1935-65; Deputy Minister of Aviation Industry of U.S.S.R. 1965-74, First Deputy Minister 1974-77, Minister 1977-81. *Address:* c/o Ministry of the Aviation Industry, Moscow, U.S.S.R.

KAZAKOV, Yuriy Pavlovich; Soviet short-story writer; b. 8 Aug. 1927, Moscow; began publishing 1952. *Publications:* collections of short stories: Manka 1958, The Small Station 1959, On the Road 1961, Blue and Green 1963, The Smell of Bread 1965, Arcturus, The Hunting Dog 1958, Two in December 1966, Autumn in the Oakwoods 1969, A Northern Diary 1973; English trans.: Selected Short Stories (New York) 1963, The Smell of Bread and Other Stories (London) 1965, Autumn in the Oakwoods (Moscow) 1970.

KAZAN, Elia (Elia Kazanjoglous), A.B., M.F.A.; American (of Greek extraction) stage and film director; b. 7 Sept. 1909, Istanbul, Turkey; s. of George and Athena (Sismanoglou) Kazan; m. 1st Molly Day Thacher 1932 (died 1963), two s. two d.; m. 2nd Barbara Loden 1967 (died 1980); one s.; m. 3rd Frances Rudge 1982; ed. Williams Coll. and Yale Dramatic School;

Apprentice and Stage Man. with Group Theatre; acted on stage 1935-41 in Waiting for Lefty, Golden Boy, Gentle People, Fire-Alarm Waltz, Liliom and in two films City for Conquest and Blues in the Night 1941; stage dir. Skin of Our Teeth (Drama Critics Award), One Touch of Venus, Harriet, Jacobowsky and the Colonel (Drama Critics Award), Streetcar Named Desire, Death of a Salesman (Drama Critics Award), Tea and Sympathy, Cat on a Hot Tin Roof (Drama Critics Award), The Dark at the Top of the Stairs, J. B., Sweet Bird of Youth, for Lincoln Center Repertory Theatre After the Fall, But for Whom Charlie, The Changeling; *directed films:* A Tree Grows in Brooklyn 1945, Gentlemen's Agreement (Academy Award) 1947, Boomerang 1947, Pinky 1949, Panic in the Streets 1950, Streetcar Named Desire 1951, Viva Zapata 1952, Man on a Tightrope 1953, On the Waterfront (Acad. Award) 1954, East of Eden 1955, Baby Doll 1956, A Face in the Crowd 1957, Wild River 1960, Splendor in the Grass 1961, America, America 1963, The Arrangement 1969, The Visitors 1972, The Last Tycoon 1976, Beyond The Aegean 1989. Best Picture of Year Award, New York Film Critics 1948, 1952, 1955; D. W. Griffith Award, Dirs. Guild of America 1987; fmr. Dir. of Actors Studio. *Publications:* America, America 1962, The Arrangement 1967, The Assassins 1972, The Understudy 1974, Acts of Love 1978, The Anatolian 1982, A Life (autobiog.) 1988. *Address:* New York, N.Y. 10023, U.S.A.

KAZANETS, Ivan Pavlovich; Soviet politician; b. 12 Dec. 1918; ed. Siberian Metallurgical Inst.; Electrician, Head of Workshop, Kuznetsk Metallurgical Factory 1937-44; mem. CPSU 1944-; Shift Foreman, Trainee Electricians Factory, Yenakievo, Rep. Sec. Factory Cttee. 1944-52; First Sec. Yenakievo City Cttee. CP Ukraine, later First Sec. Makeyev City Cttee. CP Ukraine 1952-53; First Sec. District Cttee., Donetsk 1953-60; Sec. and mem. Central Cttee., CP of Ukraine 1960-63, Chair. Council of Ministers of Ukraine 1963-65; Minister of Iron and Steel Industry, U.S.S.R. 1965-85; Cand. mem. Cen. Cttee. CPSU 1956-61, mem. 1961-; Deputy to U.S.S.R. Supreme Soviet 1954-; Order of Lenin (five times), Order of October Revolution and other decorations. *Address:* c/o Ministry of Iron and Steel Industry, 2/5 Ploshchad Nogina, Moscow, U.S.S.R.

KAZANKINA, Tatyana; Soviet athlete; b. 17 Dec. 1951, Petrovsk, Saratov Region; m.; one d.; int. athlete since 1972; competed Olympic Games Montreal 1976, winning Gold Medals at 800 m. and 1500 m., Moscow 1980, won Gold Medal at 1500 m.; European Indoor Silver Medallist 1975; held World records at 800 m. and 1500 m.; suspended for life by IAAF 1984, reinstated July 1985; economist, Leningrad; Master of Sport. *Address:* c/o Light Athletic Federation, Skatertnyi per 4, Moscow G.69, U.S.S.R.

KAZI, Hyder Ali, D.P.M., F.R.C.PSYCH.; Pakistani psychiatrist; b. 31 Jan. 1934, Sukkur Sind; s. of late Ghulam Mustafa Kazi and Sikandar Both Kazi; m. Nasra Naqvi 1960; two d.; ed. Sind and Karachi Univs.; Medical Officer, Jinnah Postgraduate Medical Centre, Karachi 1959-61, Registrar 1965-67; Postgraduate Student, Inst. of Psychiatry, London 1961-65; Medical Superintendent, Inst. of Psychiatry, Hyderabad 1967-; Asst. Prof. of Psychiatry, Liaquat Medical Coll., Jamshoro Univ., Sind 1967-77, Prof. 1977-; Medical Dir. Drug Abuse Control Centre, Hyderabad 1977-; Dean, Faculty of Medicine, Univ. of Sind; Pres. Pakistan Medical Asscn., Hyderabad Branch 1975, 1984, 1985 and 1986; Vice-Pres. Pakistan Psychiatric Soc. 1969-82, Pres. 1985-86; Fellow of the Royal Coll. of Psychiatrists 1986, Fellow Coll. of Physicians and Surgeons, Pakistan 1987. *Publications:* several booklets on social issues. *Leisure interests:* social work, reading, travelling. *Address:* Sir Cowasjee Jehangir Institute of Psychiatry, P.O. Box 366, Hyderabad, Sind, Pakistan. *Telephone:* 83256 (Office); 83890, 81178 (Home).

KAZIM, Parvez, M.A.; Pakistani publisher and author; b. 21 April, Rangoon; s. of Ali Khan Kazim and Begum (née Shaheda) Kazim; ed. Univs. of Punjab and Karachi; Exec. mem. S.W.O. 1975-76; Formed S.W.P.S. Islamabad 1975-76, C.A.O. 1980-83; Consultant P.O.F. Islamabad 1982-83; Exec. Dir. Teenage Publishers, Karachi 1981-82; Patron-in-Chief Gen. Knowledge Acad., Karachi 1981-82; Man. Dir. Pixy Publishers 1986-87; Dir. (Admin.) Parvez Acad. 1985-86; Chair. Fantasia Group of Publication F.G.P., Karachi 1987-; Aria and I.P.A. Excellence Awards. *Publications:* Pakistan, a Land of Many Faces, Safina-e-Maloomat, Islam, the Greatest Religion in the World, Jazira-e-Maloomat, Karachi, A City of Lights, Jeeway Pakistan, Archaeological Sites of Pakistan, Ganjina-e-Maloomat, Mohammed, the Messenger of God, Uks-e-Quran, Treasure of Knowledge; Compiler and Ed. Who is Who in Pakistan, Who is Who in the Muslim World, 200 Great Scientists, Ocean of Knowledge and Universal Encyclopaedia; numerous articles for newspapers and magazines. *Leisure interests:* collecting rare antiques, postcards and coins, cricket, badminton, draughts. *Address:* B-3, Commercial Area, Nazimabad No. 2, Karachi-18; III/F/8/14-A, Nazimabad, Karachi-18, Pakistan. *Telephone:* 610046, 612567, 625956.

KAZIMIROV, Vladimir Nikolayevich; Soviet diplomatist; Amb. to Costa Rica 1971-75, to Venezuela 1975-80; Head of First Dept. of Latin American Countries, Ministry of Foreign Affairs 1980-. *Address:* Ministry of Foreign Affairs, Moscow, U.S.S.R.

KAZIN, Alfred, M.A.; American writer; b. 5 June 1915; s. of Charles and Gita (Fagelman) Kazin; m. 1st Caroline Bookman 1947 (divorced), one s. one d.; m. 2nd Ann Birstein 1952 (divorced), one d.; m. 3rd Judith Dunford 1983; ed. New York City Coll. and Columbia Univ.; began his career as free-lance literary reviewer 1934; Instructor in English Literature successively at New York City Coll., Queen's Coll., New School 1937-41; Literary Ed. New Republic 1942, Assoc. Ed. Fortune; War Corresp. in Great Britain 1945; Prof. of American Studies, Amherst Coll. 1955-58; Berg Prof. of Literature, New York Univ. 1957; Distinguished Prof. of English, State Univ. of N.Y., Stony Brook 1963-73, Hunter Coll., City Univ., New York 1973-78, 1979-85; Writer-in-residence, American Acad. in Rome 1975; mem. Nat. Inst. of Arts and Letters, American Acad. of Arts and Sciences; Sr. Fellow, Nat. Endowment Humanities, Center for Advanced Study of Behavioral Sciences, Stanford 1977-78; Brandeis Univ. Medal 1973, Creative Award in Literature 1973, Hubbell Memorial Prize (Modern Language Asscn.) 1982. *Publications:* On Native Grounds: An Interpretation of Modern American Literature 1942, A Walker in the City 1951, The Inmost Leaf 1955, Contemporaries 1962, Starting Out in the Thirties 1965, Bright Book of Life 1973, New York Jew 1978, An American Procession 1984; edited: The Portable Blake 1946, F. Scott Fitzgerald: The Man and His Work 1951, The Stature of Theodore Dreiser 1955, Melville's Moby Dick 1956, Ralph Waldo Emerson: A Modern Anthology 1958, The Open Form: Essays for Our Times 1961, The Short Stories of Nathaniel Hawthorne 1966, The Ambassadors 1969, A Writer's America 1988, Our New York (with David Finn) 1988. *Address:* English Department, City University, Graduate Center, 33 West 42nd Street, New York, N.Y. 10036, U.S.A.

KAZNIN, Georgiy Vladimirovich; Soviet lawyer; b. 2 March 1922, Boy-arnshchiuo, Yaroslavl Region; ed. U.S.S.R. Correspondence Inst. of Law; Chair. of Regional Court, Pskov, N.W. R.S.F.S.R. until 1961; mem. Collegium of Ministry of Justice of R.S.F.S.R. 1961-63; on staff of Cen. Cttee. of CPSU 1962-63; mem. U.S.S.R. Supreme Court 1965-; Order of Badge of Honour and other decorations. *Address:* U.S.S.R. Supreme Court, 15 Ulitsa Vorovskogo, Moscow, U.S.S.R.

KE HUA; Chinese diplomatist; b. 19 Dec. 1915, Guandong Province; m. Chang Ming 1944; three s. three d.; fmr. Head of Protocol Dept., Head of West Asia and Africa Dept., Ministry of Foreign Affairs; fmr. Amb. to Guinea, Ghana and the Philippines; Amb. to U.K. 1978-83; Vice-Chair. China Int. Cultural Exchange Centre 1984-, China Nat. Funding Office 1989-; mem. Standing Cttee. CPPCC 1988-. *Leisure interests:* hunting, swimming, travelling. *Address:* c/o Hong Kong and Macao Office, State Council, Beijing, People's Republic of China.

KEAN, Thomas H., M.A.; American politician; b. 21 April 1935, New York; m. Deborah Bye; two s. one d.; fmr. teacher of history and govt.; mem. N.J. Ass. 1967-77, Speaker 1972, Minority Leader 1974; Acting Gov. of N.J. 1973, Gov. 1981-89; mem. White House Conf. on Youth 1970-71. *Address:* c/o Carl Golden, 112 State House, Trenton, N.J. 08625, U.S.A.

KEANY, John William, B.EC.; Australian civil servant and banking official; b. 25 May 1923, Brisbane; s. of William Christian Keany and Kathleen Mary (née Clark) Keany; m. Lorna McGovern 1949; two s. three d.; ed. Univ. of Adelaide, Australian Nat. Univ., and Econ. Devt. Inst., Washington, D.C.; served R.A.A.F. 1942-46; Australian Taxation Office 1949-56; Australian Treasury 1956-72; Exec. Dir. Asian Devt. Bank 1972-76; Australian Treasury 1976-79; Exec. Dir. Int. Bank for Reconstruction and Devt., Int. Finance Corpn. and Int. Devt. Asscn. (representing Australia, Repub. of Korea, New Zealand, Papua New Guinea, Solomon Islands and W. Samoa) 1979-81; Minister (Economic) Australian Embassy, Washington, D.C. 1982-. *Leisure interests;* music, reading, golf. *Address:* 5330 Chamberlin Avenue, Chevy Chase, Md. 20815, U.S.A.

KEAR, David, C.M.G., B.SC.ENG., PH.D., A.R.S.M., F.R.S.NZ.; British and New Zealand geologist, administrator and consultant; b. 29 Oct. 1923, London; s. of Harold and Constance May (née Betteridge) Kear; m. Joan Kathleen Bridges 1948; two s. one d.; ed. Sevenoaks School, Imperial Coll., London; served in Royal Navy 1944-47; Prospecting Officer, Ministry of Fuel and Power, U.K. 1947; Geologist, N.Z. Geological Survey 1948, Dist. Geologist, Ngaruawahia 1949-58, Auckland 1958-65, Chief Econ. Geologist 1963-67, Dir. N.Z. Geological Survey 1967-74; Asst. Dir.-Gen. Dept. of Scientific and Industrial Research, N.Z. 1974-80, Dir.-Gen. 1980-83; with FAO, W. Samoa 1969-74; with Ministry of Energy, N.Z. 1978; Pres. Geological Soc. of N.Z. 1959-60; Vice-Pres. Royal Soc. of N.Z. 1975-79 (Fellow 1973); Pres. N.Z. Exec. Man. Club 1978-79; mem. N.Z. Liquid Fuels Trust Bd. 1978-83; Dir. Circum-Pacific Council for Energy and Mineral Resources 1983-, Cluff Oil (N.Z.) N.L. 1984-; Consultant Geothermal Energy N.Z. Ltd. for Kenya, Indonesia and N.Z. 1985-; mem. UN Advisory Cttee. on Science and Tech. for Devt. 1988-; Warrington-Smyth Prize 1949; Frecheville Prize 1952. *Publications:* approx. 125 bulletins, scientific papers and maps on New Zealand geology, volcanology, mineral resources and energy prospects, also on Western Samoa geology, volcanology and water supply. *Leisure interests:* golf, theatre, New Zealand and Pacific science. *Address:* 34 West End, Ohope, New Zealand (Home). *Telephone:* (Whakatane) 24635.

KEARNEY, Richard D., LL.B.; American lawyer; b. 3 Jan. 1914, Dayton, Ky.; s. of David Richard Kearney and Mary Estelle Manouge; m. Margaret Helen Murray 1944; ed. Xavier High School and Univ., Cincinnati and Univ. of Cincinnati; practising lawyer, Cincinnati 1938-41; Special Attorney, Anti-Trust Div., Dept. of Justice 1941-42; U.S. Army 1942-46; Legal Div., Mil. Govt. Headquarters, Berlin 1946-48; Chief, Legal Group, Bipartite Control

Office, Frankfurt 1948-49; Asst. Gen. Counsel, Office of U.S. High Commr. for Germany 1949; German Bureau, Dept. of State 1950; Gen. Counsel, Tripartite Comm. on German External Depts. 1951-53; Deputy U.S. mem., Validation Bd. for German Dollar Bonds 1953-56; Asst. Legal Adviser for Far Eastern Affairs, Dept. of State 1956-57, for European Affairs 1957-62; Deputy Legal Adviser 1962-67; mem. UN Int. Law Comm. (with ambassadorial rank) 1967-77, Pres. 1972-73; Chair. Sec. of State's Advisory Cttee. on Private Int. Law 1964-78, Hon. mem. 1979-; mem. Gov. Council, Int. Inst. for Unification of Private Law 1966-78, Hon. mem 1979-; Sr. Adviser American Soc. of Int. Law (Vice-Pres. 1978-81), American Acad. of Political and Social Science, American Law Inst; Sr. Consultant World Bank 1982; Chair. or mem. U.S. Dels. to several int. confs. on legal matters; Dept. of State Award for Outstanding Service 1979, A.B.A. Medal for Contributions to pvt. int. law 1984. *Publications:* articles on codification and unification of law in several professional journals. *Address:* 167 Friar Tuck Hill, Sherwood Forest, Md. 21405, U.S.A. (Home).

KEARNS, David Todd, B.S.; American business executive; b. 11 Aug. 1930, Rochester, N.Y.; s. of Wilfrid M. and Margaret May (née Todd) Kearns; m. Shirley Virginia Cox 1954. two s. four d.; ed. Univ. of Rochester; served with U.S.N.R. 1952-54; with IBM Corpn. 1954-71, Vice-Pres. Marketing Operations, Data Processing Div. until 1971; joined Xerox Corpn., Stamford, Conn. 1971, Group Vice-Pres. for Information Systems 1972-75, Group Vice-Pres. in charge of Rank Xerox and Fuji Xerox 1975-77, Exec. Vice-Pres. Int. Operations 1977, Pres. and C.E.O. 1977-85, Chair. and C.E.O. May 1985-, also Dir.; Dir. Rank Xerox Ltd. (non-exec. Chair. 1986-), Time Inc., Fuji Xerox, Chase Manhattan Corpn., Dayton Hudson Corpn.; mem. Bd. of Trustees, Univ. of Rochester; Chair. Pres.'s Comm. on Exec. Exchange; mem. Nat. Urban League. *Address:* Xerox Corporation, P.O. Box 1600, Stamford, Conn. 06904, U.S.A. (Office).

KEARTON, Baron (Life Peer), cr. 1970, of Whitchurch; **Christopher Frank Kearton,** Kt., O.B.E., F.R.S., C.B.I.M.; British scientist and industrialist; b. 17 Feb. 1911; ed. Hanley High School and St. John's Coll., Oxford; Imperial Chemical Industries Billingham Div. 1933-40; Atomic Energy Project, U.K. and U.S.A. 1940-45; Courtaulds Ltd. 1946-, in charge Chemical Eng. 1946, Dir. 1952-, Deputy Chair. 1961, Chair. 1964-75; part-time mem. U.K. Atomic Energy Authority 1955-81; mem. Electricity Supply Research Council 1954, Chair. 1960-77; mem. Govt. Advisory Council on Tech. 1964-70, Nat. Econ. Devt. Council 1965-71; Chair. Industrial Reorganization Corpn. 1966-68, BPC Ltd. 1981; Chancellor, Univ., of Bath 1980-; mem. Cen. Advisory Council for Science and Technology 1969-70; Dir. Hill Samuel 1970-81; Pres. Royal Soc. for the Prevention of Accidents (ROSPA) 1973-80, Soc. of Chemical Industry 1972-73; Part-time mem. Cen. Electricity Generating Bd. 1974-80; Chair. East European Trade Council 1975-77; Chair. and Chief Exec. BNOC 1976-79; Pres. A.S.L.I.B. 1980-82; Pres. Market Research Soc. 1983-87; mem. U.K. Energy Comm. 1976-79; mem. Offshore Energy Tech. Bd. 1976-79; Pres. British Asscn. for Advancement of Science 1978-79; Companion, Textile Inst.; Hon. Fellow, Inst. of Chemical Engineers, Soc. of Dyers and Colourists; Hon. Fellow, St. John's Coll., Oxford 1965, Manchester Coll. of Science and Tech. 1966, Imperial Coll. of Science, London 1976; Hon. LL.D. (Leeds, Strathclyde) 1981, (Bristol) 1988, Hon. D.Sc. (Bath, Aston in Birmingham, Reading, Keele Univs., New Univ. of Ulster), Hon. D.C.L. (Oxford), Hon. D.Univ. (Heriot-Watt), Grande Ufficiale, Order of Merit (Italy) 1977. *Address:* The Old House, Whitchurch, nr. Aylesbury, Bucks., HP22 4JS, England. *Telephone:* Whitchurch 232.

KEATING, Justin; Irish politician and veterinary surgeon; b. 1931; s. of Sean Keating; m.; three c.; ed. Veterinary Coll., Univ. Coll., Dublin and London Univ.; lecturer in Anatomy, Veterinary Coll., Ballsbridge 1955-60; Sr. lecturer, Dept. of Preclinical Studies, Trinity Coll., Dublin 1960-65, 1967-; Head Agricultural Programmes, Radio Telefís Éireann 1965-67; mem. Dáil for North Co. Dublin 1969-81; Labour Party Rep. to European Parl.; Minister for Industry and Commerce 1973-77; mem. Trilateral Comm. 1980-. *Address:* Bishopland, Ballymore Eustace, Co. Kildare, Ireland.

KEATING, Hon. Paul John; Australian politician; b. 18 Jan. 1944, Sydney; s. of Matthew Keating and Minnie Keating; m. Anita van Iersel 1975; one s. three d.; ed. De la Salle Coll., Bankstown; elected to the House of Reps. for the Fed. Seat of Blaxland 1969, Minister for N. Australia Oct.-Nov. 1975; Opposition Spokesman on Agric. Jan.-March 1976; on Minerals and Energy 1976-83, on Treasury Matters Jan.-March 1983; Fed. Treas. March 1983-; Pres. of N.S.W. Branch Labor Party 1979-83. *Address:* Parliament House, Canberra, A.C.T. 2600, Australia.

KEATING, Stephen Flaherty, B.S., J.D.; American business executive; b. 6 May 1918, Graceville, Minn.; s. of Luke J. and Blanche F. Keating; m. Mary Davis 1945; two s. two d.; ed. Univ. of Minnesota; admitted to Minn. Bar 1942; Special Agent, F.B.I., Norfolk, Va., Detroit 1942-43; U.S. Naval Reserve 1943-46; Assoc. Otis, Faricy & Burger, St. Paul 1946-48; Man. Mil. Contracts, Aero Div., Honeywell Inc. 1948-54, Div. Vice-Pres. 1954-56, Vice-Pres. 1956-62, Dir. 1960-, Exec. Vice-Pres. 1961-65, Pres. 1965-74, Chair. of Bd. 1974-78, Vice-Chair of Bd. 1978-80; Chair. Exec. Comm. Toro Co.; Dir. The Toro Co., PPG Industries Corpn., Donaldson Co., Ecolab, St. Paul, Minn., Inco Ltd., Toronto, Ont., Canada. *Leisure interests:*

golf, hunting. *Address:* 340 Peavey Road, Wayzata, Minn. 55402, U.S.A. (Home).

KEATINGE, William Richard, M.A., M.B., B.CHIR., PH.D., M.R.C.P.; British professor of physiology; b. 18 May 1931, London; s. of Edgar Mayne Keatinge and Katherine Lucille Keatinge; m. Margaret Ellen Annette Hegarty 1955; one s. two d.; ed. Univ. of Cambridge, St. Thomas's Hosp. Medical School; Dir. of Studies in Medicine, Pembroke Coll., Cambridge 1956–60; Fellow of Cardiovascular Research Inst., San Francisco 1960–61; Dept. of Regius Prof. of Medicine, Oxford, M.R.C. appt. 1961–68; Fellow and Tutor in Physiology, Pembroke Coll., Oxford 1956–68; Reader in Physiology, London Hosp. Medical Coll. 1968–71, Prof. 1971–; Oliver-Sharpey Lecturer, Royal Coll. of Physicians 1986. *Publications:* Survival in Cold Water: The Physiology and Treatment of Immersion Hypothermia and Drowning 1970, Local Mechanisms Controlling Blood Vessels (with C. Harman) 1980, numerous articles and papers. *Leisure interests:* archaeology, sailing. *Address:* Department of Physiology, London Hospital Medical College, Turner Street, London, E1 2AD, England.

KEATON, Diane; American actress; b. Calif.; student Neighbourhood Playhouse, New York; New York stage appearances in Hair 1968, Play It Again Sam 1971, The Primary English Class 1976; *films include:* Lovers and Other Strangers 1970, Play It Again Sam 1972, The Godfather 1972, Sleeper 1973, The Godfather Part 2 1974, Love and Death 1975, I Will-I Will-For Now 1975, Harry and Walter Go To New York 1976, Annie Hall 1977, (Acad. Award for Best Actress and other awards), Looking for Mr. Goodbar 1977, Interiors 1978, Manhattan 1979, Reds 1981, Shoot the Moon 1982, Mrs Soffel 1985, Crimes of the Heart 1986, Trial and Error 1986, Radio Days 1987, Heaven (Dir.) 1987, Baby Boom 1988, The Good Mother 1988. *Publications:* Reservations, Still Life. *Address:* c/o Stan Kamen, William Morris Agency, 1350 Avenue of the Americas, New York, N.Y. 10019, U.S.A.

KEDAH, H.R.H. The Sultan of; Tuanku Haji Abdul Halim Mu'adzam Shah ibni Al-Marhum Sultan Badishah, D.K., D.K.H., D.K.M., D.M.N., D.U.K., D.K. (KELANTAN), D.K. (PAHANG), D.K. (SELANGOR), D.K. (PERLIS), D.K. (JOHORE), D.K. (TRENGGANU), D.P. (SARAWAK), S.P.M.K., S.S.D.K., D.H.M.S.; Ruler of Kedah, Malaysia; b. 28 Nov. 1927, Alor Setar; m. Tuanku Bahiyah binti Al-marhum, Tuanku Abdul Rahman, d. of 1st Yang di Pertuan Agong of Malaya, 1956; three d.; ed. Sultan Abdul Hamid Coll., Alor Setar and Wadham Coll., Oxford; Raja Muda (Heir to Throne of Kedah) 1949, Regent of Kedah 1957, Sultan 1958–; Timbalan Yang di Pertuan Agong (Deputy Head of State of Malaysia) 1965–70, Yang di Pertuan Agong (Head of State) 1970–75; Col. Commdt. Malaysian Reconnaissance Corps 1966; Col.-in-Chief of Royal Malay Regiment 1975; First Class Order of the Rising Sun (Japan) 1970, Bintang Maha Putera, Klas Satu (Indonesia) 1970, Knight Grand Cross of the Bath (U.K.) 1972, Kt. of the Order of St. John 1974, Most Auspicious Order of the Rajamithrathorn (Thailand) 1973. *Leisure interests:* golf, billiards, photography, tennis. *Address:* Alor Setar, Kedah, Malaysia.

KEDDAFI, Col. Mu'ammar al- (see Gaddafi, Col. Mu'ammar al-).

KEDOURIE, Elie, B.SC., F.B.A.; British professor of politics; b. 25 Jan. 1926, Baghdad, Iraq; s. of A. Kedourie and L. Kedourie; m. Sylvia G. Haim 1950; two s. one d.; ed. London School of Econs. and St. Antony's Coll., Oxford; Lecturer and Reader, L.S.E. 1953–65, Prof. 1965–; Ed. Middle Eastern Studies 1964–; Visiting Fellow Netherlands Inst. for Advanced Study 1980–81, Sackler Inst. for Advanced Studies, Tel-Aviv Univ. 1982–83; Fellow in Residence, Brandeis Univ. 1982, Visiting Prof. 1985–86. *Publications:* England and the Middle East 1956, Nationalism 1960, Afghani and Abduh 1966, The Chatham House Version 1970, Nationalism in Asia and Africa 1971, Arabic Political Memoirs 1974, In the Anglo-Arab Labyrinth 1976, Islam in the Modern World 1980, The Crossman Confessions 1984, Diamonds Into Glass 1988. *Address:* London School of Economics, Houghton Street, London, WC2A 2AE, England.

KĘDZIERSKA, Anna, M.ENG.; Polish politician; b. 30 July 1932, Ostrowiec Świętokrzyski, Kielce Voivodship; ed. Higher Econs. School, Częstochowa; worked in Food Dept., then in Goods Quality Bureau, Ministry of Internal Trade 1954–58; teacher, secondary school, Warsaw 1958–60; sr. designer in Design Bureau of Internal Trade, Warsaw 1960–64; managerial functions in Cttee. for Housekeeping Matters, Polish Women's League, including Head of Section, subsequently Deputy Dir. 1964–73, Dir. of Cttee. 1973–; fmr. women's League rep. to Internal Market Council attached to Minister of Internal Trade and Services; Deputy Pres. Consumers' Fed. 1980–83, Pres. 1983–; Minister of Internal Trade and Services May 1984–85; Deputy Chair. Polish Cttee. for Standardization, Measures and Quality Control 1986–; Govt. Plenipotentiary for Women's Matters in Ministry of Labour, Wages and Social Affairs 1986–; mem. Polish United Workers' Party (PZPR); mem. scientific councils of Inst. of Internal Market and Consumption, Polish Cttee. for Standarization, Measures and Quality Control, Społem Consumers' Co-operatives Cen. Union; Kt's. Cross of Order of Polonia Restituta and other decorations. *Address:* Polski Komitet Normali-zacji, Miar i Jakości, ul. Elektoralna 2, 00-139 Warsaw, Poland. *Telephone:* 20-40-29.

KEE, Robert, M.A.; British journalist, author and broadcaster; b. 5 Oct. 1919, Calcutta, India; s. of late Robert and Dorothy F. Kee; m. 1st Janetta Woolley 1948, 2nd Cynthia Judah 1960; one s. (and one s. deceased) two d.; ed. Rottingdean School, Stowe School and Magdalen Coll., Oxford; journalist, Picture Post 1948–51; picture ed. WHO 1952; foreign corresp. Observer 1956–57, Sunday Times 1957–58; literary ed. Spectator 1957; with BBC 1958–62, 1979–82, Independent Television 1962–79, 1984–; now freelance broadcaster, Presenter 7 Days (Channel 4), TV series include: Ireland: a television history (13 parts), The Writing on the Wall. *Publications:* A Crowd Is Not Company 1947, The Impossible Shore, A Sign of the Times, Broadstrop in Season, Refugee World, The Green Flag 1972, Ireland: A History 1980, The World We Left Behind 1939, 1984, 1945: The World We Fought For 1985, Trial and Error 1986, Munich: The Eleventh Hour 1988. *Leisure interests:* swimming, music. *Address:* c/o Lloyds Bank, 112 Kensington High Street, London, W.8, England.

KEEBLE, Sir (Herbert Ben) Curtis, G.C.M.G.; British diplomatist (retd.); b. 18 Sept. 1922, London; s. of Herbert and Gertrude Keeble; m. Margaret Fraser 1947; three d.; ed. Clacton County High School, London Univ.; served Royal Irish Fusiliers 1942–47; entered Foreign Service 1947; served in Batavia (now Jakarta, Indonesia) 1947–49; Foreign Office 1949–51, 1958–63; Berlin 1951–54; Washington 1954–58; Counsellor and Head of European Econ. Orgs. Dept. 1963–65; Counsellor (Commercial), Berne 1965–68; Minister, Canberra 1968–71; Asst. Under-Sec. of State, FCO 1971–74; Amb. to G.D.R. 1974–76; Deputy Under-Sec. of State, FCO 1976–78; Amb. to U.S.S.R. 1978–82; Chair. G.B.-U.S.S.R. Assen. 1985–; Gov. of BBC 1985–; mem. Council of Royal Inst. of Int. Affairs, Council of the School of Slavonic and East European Studies; Sr. Assoc. St. Antony's Coll., Oxford. *Publication:* The Soviet State: The Domestic Roots of Soviet Foreign Policy 1985. *Leisure interests:* sailing, skiing. *Address:* Dormers, St. Leonards Road, Thames Ditton, Surrey, England. *Telephone:* 01-398 7778.

KEEFE, Bernard, B.A.; British conductor, broadcaster and professor; b. 1 April 1925, London; s. of Joseph Keeffe and Therea Keeffe (née Quinn); m. Denise Walker 1954; one s. one d.; ed. St. Olave's Grammar School and Clare Coll., Cambridge; served in Intelligence Corps 1943–47; mem. Glyndebourne Opera Co. 1951–52; BBC Music Staff 1954–60; Asst. Music Dir., Royal Opera House 1960–62; Conductor BBC Scottish Orchestra 1962–64; Prof., Trinity Coll. of Music 1966–; freelance conductor and broadcaster on radio and TV, concerts with leading orchestras 1966–; mem. int. juries, competitions in Sofia, Liège, Vienna and London; Warden solo performers section, Inc. Soc. of Musicians 1971; mem. Exec. Cttee. Anglo-Austrian Music Soc.; Hon. Fellow Trinity Coll. of Music. *Leisure interest:* photography. *Address:* 153 Honor Oak Road, London, SE23 3RN, England. *Telephone:* 01-669 3672.

KEEL, Alton G., Jr., PH.D.; American civil servant and diplomatist; b. 8 Sept. 1943, Va.; s. of Alton G. Keel and Ella Kennedy; m. Franmarie Kennedy-Keel 1982; one d.; ed. Univ. of Virginia and Univ. of California, Berkeley; Facility Man. Naval Weapons Center 1971–77; Sr. Official Senate Armed Services Cttee., US Senate 1977–81; Asst. Sec. Air Force for Research, Devt. and Logistics, The Pentagon 1981–82; Assoc. Dir. Nat. Security and Int. Affairs 1982–86; Exec. Dir. Pres. Comm. on Space Shuttle Challenger Accident 1986; Acting Asst. to the Pres. for Nat. Security Affairs 1986; Perm. Rep. to NATO 1987–; Nat. Congressional Science Fellow A.I.A.A. 1977; Air Force Decoration Exceptional Civilian Service 1982; NASA Group Achievement Award 1987, Distinguished Alumnus Award (Univ. of Va.) 1987. *Publications:* numerous scientific and tech. articles, foreign policy and nat. security publs. *Leisure interests:* running, golf, sailing, physical fitness. *Address:* USNATO Box 148, APO, New York, U.S.A.; USNATO Box 148, 1110 Brussels, Belgium. *Telephone:* 09667-5028; (32) 2 242-5280 (ext. 3230).

KEELEY, Robert Vossler, A.B.; American diplomatist; b. 4 Sept. 1929, Beirut, Lebanon; s. of James Hugh Keeley and Mathilde Vossler Keeley; m. Louise Schoonmaker 1951; one s. one d.; ed. Princeton Univ.; with U.S. Foreign Service since 1956; with Embassy, Athens 1966–70; Deputy Chief of Mission, Kampala, Uganda 1971–73; Phnom Penh, Cambodia 1974–75; Alt. Dir. E. African Affairs, Washington 1974; Deputy Dir. Interagency Task Force for Indo-China Refugees 1975–76; Amb. to Mauritius 1976–78, to Zimbabwe 1980–84, to Greece 1985–; Deputy Asst. Sec. for African Affairs, Dept. of State 1978–80. *Address:* American Embassy, Leoforos Vasilissis Sofias 112, Athens, Greece.

KEENAN, Patrick John, C.A., B.COMM., A.C.I.S.; Canadian business executive; b. 7 Jan. 1932, Montreal; s. of Thomas P. Keenan and Catherine S. Collins; m. Barbara G. Fraser 1959; one s. three d.; ed. McGill Univ.; Insp. Crawley & McCracken 1957–59; Chief Accountant, then Sec.-Treas. Iroquois Glass Ltd. 1959–63; Accounting Man. Pfizer (Canada) Ltd. 1963–64; Asst. Treas. and Controller Patino Mining Corpn., Toronto 1964, Treas. 1965–66, Vice-Pres. (Finance) and Treas. 1967–70, Treas. and Dir. Patino, N.V., The Hague 1971, Vice-Pres., Treas. and Dir. 1972–74, Pres., Chief Exec. and Dir. 1975–81; Chief Exec. and Dir. Consolidated Tin Smelters Ltd., London 1971–74, Vice-Chair. 1975; Chief Exec. Amalgamated Metal Corpn. Ltd. 1971–75; Chair. and Chief Exec. Keewhit Investments Ltd. 1975–; Chair. Barnes Wines 1981–; Vice-Chair. St. Michael's Hosp., Canada Devt. Corpn.; Dir. London Life Insurance Co., Brascan Ltd., Onitap Resources Inc., Canada Devt. Investment Corpn., Westmin Resources Ltd., The Hume Group Ltd., Belmoral Mines Ltd., Newlands Textiles Inc., The Ireland

Fund of Canada; Patron Grenville Christian Coll. *Leisure interests:* skiing, golf. *Address:* P.O. Box 40, One First Canadian Place, Suite 6050, Toronto, Ont., M5X 1A9 (Office); 16 Whitney Avenue, Toronto, Ont., M4W 2A8, Canada (Home).

KEENLEYSIDE, Hugh Llewellyn, C.C., PH.D.; Canadian diplomatist and administrator; b. 7 July 1898, Toronto; s. of Ellis William and Margaret Louise (Irvine) Keenleyside; m. Katherine Hall Pillsbury 1924; one s. three d.; ed. Univ. of British Columbia, Vancouver and Clark Univ., Worcester, Mass., U.S.A.; served with C.F.A. First World War; Lecturer in History, Univ. of B.C. 1925–27; entered Dept. of External Affairs 1928; opened First Canadian Mission in Japan 1929, promoted to Counsellor 1940; Asst. Under-Sec. of State for External Affairs 1941; Canadian Amb. to Mexico 1944–47; Deputy Minister of Mines and Resources 1947–50; Dir.-Gen. UN Technical Assistance Admin. 1950–59; UN Under-Sec. for Public Admin. 1959; Chair. British Columbia Power Comm. and Adviser to Govt. of British Columbia on Resource Devt. Policies 1959–62; Chair. British Columbia Hydro and Power Authority 1962–69; mem. numerous wartime cttees., including Canada-U.S. Jt. Bd. on Defence 1940–45 and War Technical and Scientific Devt. Cttee. 1941–45; Chancellor, Notre Dame Univ. 1969–77, Chair. Bd. of Govs. 1972–75; Hon. Chair. Canadian Nat. Cttee. on UN Conf. on Human Settlements and Assoc. Commr.-Gen. of Habitat Conf.; mem. numerous govt. comms. of investigation 1972–74; Dir. and one of founders of Arctic Inst. of N. America; Dir. various companies; Officer or mem. numerous welfare, educational and int. orgs.; hon. degrees from numerous Canadian and U.S.A. Univs.; Haldane Medal of Royal Inst. of Public Admin. 1954, Vanier Medal of Inst. of Public Admin. of Canada 1962; Companion of Canada 1969. *Leisure interests:* gourmet cooking, reading, poker. *Publications:* Canada and the United States, History of Japanese Education (with A. F. Thomas), International Aid; Memoirs; Hammer the Golden Day (vol. 1), On the Bridge of Time (vol. 2). *Address:* Office and Home: 3470 Mayfair Drive, Victoria, B.C. V8P 1PG, Canada. *Telephone:* 592-9331.

KEETON, George Williams, M.A., LL.D., F.B.A.; British lawyer and educationist; b. 22 May 1902, Sheffield; s. of John William and Mary Emma Keeton; m. 1st Gladys Edith Calthorpe 1924, 2nd Kathleen Marian Willard 1946; two s.; ed. Gonville and Caius Coll. Cambridge and Gray's Inn, London; Reader in Law and Politics, Hong Kong Univ. 1924–27; Senior Law lecturer, Manchester Univ. 1928–31; Reader in Law, Univ. Coll. London 1931–37, Prof. English Law 1937–69, Dean Law Faculty 1939–54, Vice-Provost 1966–69; Principal London Inst. of World Affairs 1938–52, Pres. 1952–; Dean of Faculty of Laws, London Univ. 1942–46; Prof. of Law, Brunel Univ. 1969–77; Ed. Anglo-American Law Review 1970–76; Distinguished Visiting Prof., Univ. of Miami 1971–73; Leverhulme Research Fellow 1971–73; mem. Bd. of Dirs., American Judicature Soc. 1974–77; Hon. LL.D. (Sheffield) 1966, (Hong Kong) 1972, Hon. D. Univ. (Brunel) 1977. *Publications:* The Development of Extra-territoriality in China 1928, The Law of Trusts 1934, National Sovereignty and International Order 1939, Russia and Her Western Neighbours 1942, China, the Far East and the Future 1943, Making International Law Work (with Dr. Schwarzenberger) 1946, Extra-territoriality in International and Comparative Law 1949, The Passing of Parliament 1952, Social Change in the Law of Trusts 1958, Trial for Treason 1959, Trial by Tribunal 1960, Guilty but Insane 1961, The Modern Law of Charities 1962, Lord Chancellor Jeffreys and the Stuart Cause 1965, The Norman Conquest and the Common Law 1966, Shakespeare's Legal and Political Background 1967, Equity 1969, Government in Action 1970, The Football Revolution 1972, English Law: The Judicial Contribution 1974, Trusts in the Commonwealth 1976, Keeping the Peace 1976, Harvey the Hasty 1978. *Address:* Picts Close, Picts Lane, Princes Risborough, Bucks., England. *Telephone:* Princes Risborough 5094.

KEGEL, Gerhard Theodor Otto, DR.; German professor of law; b. 26 June 1912, Magdeburg; s. of Martin Kegel and Wilhelmine Schönbach; m. Irmgard Vethake 1940; one s. three d.; ed. Joachimsthalsches Gymnasium and Univs. of Erlangen, Göttingen and Berlin; Prof. of Law 1950–78, Prof. Emer. 1978–; Pres. German Council of Private Int. Law 1964–85; Berkeley Citation 1981; Grosses Bundesverdienstkreuz. *Publication:* Internationales Privatrecht. *Leisure interest:* music. *Address:* Gyrhofstrasse 192, 5000 Cologne 41, Federal Republic of Germany. *Telephone:* 0221-416421.

KEILIS-BOROK, Vladimir Isaakovich, PH.D., D.SC.; Soviet geophysicist and applied mathematician; b. 31 July 1921, Moscow; s. of Isaak Moiseyevich and Kseniya Ruvimovna; m. L. N. Malinovskaya 1955; one d.; ed. S. Ordzhonikidze Inst. of Geological Prospecting; Chair. Div. of Methods of Interpretation, O. Schmidt Inst. of Earth Physics, U.S.S.R. Acad. of Sciences 1960, Chair. Dept. of Computational Geophysics 1970–, mem. editorial bd. of several int. journals; mem. U.S.S.R. Acad. of Sciences; Foreign Assoc. U.S. Nat. Acad. of Sciences; Foreign Hon. mem. American Acad. of Arts and Sciences. *Publications:* Computational Seismology series, Vols. 1-21 1966–88. *Leisure interests:* mountaineering, sociology. *Address:* Soviet Geophysical Committee, Molodezhnaya ul. 3, 117296 Moscow; O.Y. Schmidt Institute of Earth Physics, B. Gruzinskaja ul. 10, 123810 Moscow, U.S.S.R. *Telephone:* 254-24-78.

KEITH, Penelope Anne Constance, O.B.E.; British actress; b. 2 April 1940, Sutton, Surrey; d. of Frederick Hatfield and Constance Mary Keith; m.

Rodney Timson 1978; ed. Annecy Convent, Seaford, Sussex, Convent Bayeux, Normandy, Webber Douglas School, London; first professional appearance, Civic Theatre, Chesterfield 1959; repertory, Lincoln, Salisbury, Manchester 1960–63, Cheltenham 1967; R.S.C., Stratford 1963, Aldwych 1965. *Stage appearances include:* Suddenly at Home 1971, The Norman Conquests 1974, Donkey's Years 1976, The Apple Cart 1977, The Millionairess 1978, Moving 1980, Hobson's Choice, Captain Brassbound's Conversion 1982, Hay Fever 1983, The Dragon's Tail 1985, Miranda 1987, The Deep Blue Sea 1988. *Film appearances include:* Rentadick, Take a Girl Like You, Every Home Should Have One, Sherlock Holmes, The Priest of Love; *TV appearances include:* The Good Life (Good Neighbors in U.S.A.) 1974–77, Private Lives 1976, The Norman Conquests 1977, To the Manor Born 1979–81, On Approval 1980, Spider's Web, Sweet Sixteen, Waters of the Moon, Hay Fever, Moving, Executive Stress, Chair. What's My Line, Growing Places; Best Light Entertainment Performance (British Acad. of Film and TV Arts) 1976, Best Actress 1977, Show Business Personality (Variety Club of G.B.) 1976, BBC TV Personality 1979, Comedy Performance of the Year (Soc. of West End Theatre) 1976, Female TV Personality, T.V. Times Awards 1976–78, BBC TV Personality of the Year 1978–79, TV Female Personality (Daily Express) 1979–82. *Leisure interest:* gardening. *Address:* London Management, 235/241 Regent Street, London W1A 2JT, England. *Telephone:* 01-493 1610.

KEITH OF CASTLEACRE, Baron (Life Peer), cr. 1980, of Swaffham in the County of Norfolk; **Kenneth Alexander Keith;** British banker and industrialist; b. 30 Aug. 1916; s. of late Edward Charles Keith; m. 1st Ariel Olivia Winifred Baird 1946 (divorced 1958), one s. one d.; m. 2nd Mrs. Nancy Hayward 1962 (divorced 1972); m. 3rd Mrs. Marie Hanbury 1973; ed. Rugby and Dresden; trained as Chartered Accountant, London 1934–39; Army Service 1939–45; Asst. to Dir.-Gen. Political Intelligence Dept., Foreign Office 1945–46; Asst. to Managing Dir. Philip Hill & Partners, London 1946–48, Dir. 1947; Dir. Philip Hill Investment Trust 1949, Managing Dir. 1951; Managing Dir. Philip Hill, Higginson & Co. Ltd. 1951–59, Philip Hill, Higginson, Erlangers Ltd. 1959–62, Chair. 1962–65; Deputy Chair. and Chief Exec. Hill Samuel & Co. 1965–70, Group Chair. 1970–80; Chair. Rolls-Royce 1972–80, Arlington Securities PLC 1982–; mem. Bd. Standard Telephone and Cables 1977–85, Chair. 1985–89; Dir. Guinness Peat Aviation Group 1983–; Vice-Chair. Beecham Group Ltd. 1970–85, Chair. Nov. 1985–; Dir. Times Newspapers Ltd. 1967–81; mem. Nat. Econ. Devt. Council 1964–71; Chair. Econ. Planning Council for East Anglia 1965–70; Gov. Nat. Inst. of Econ. and Social Research; Council mem. Manchester Business School. *Leisure interests:* shooting, farming. *Address:* 9 Eaton Square, London, S.W.1; The Wicken House, Castle Acre, Norfolk, England. *Telephone:* (076 05) 225.

KEKWICK, Ralph Ambrose, D.SC., F.R.S.; British professor of biophysics; b. 11 Nov. 1908; s. of Oliver Kekwick and Mary Kekwick; m. 1st Barbara Stone 1933 (died 1973), one d.; m. 2nd Dr Margaret Mackay 1974 (died 1982); ed. Leyton Co. High School and Univ. Coll. London; Bayliss-Starling Scholar, Univ. Coll. London 1930–31; Commonwealth Fund Fellow, New York and Princeton Univs. 1931–33; Lecturer in Biochem. Univ. Coll., London 1933–37; Rockefeller Fellow, Univ. of Uppsala 1935; MRC Fellow, Lister Inst. 1937–40; mem. staff, Lister Inst. 1940–71, Head, Div. of Biophysics 1943–71; Reader in Chemical Biophysics, Univ. of London 1954–66, Prof. of Biophysics 1966–71, now Prof. Emer. *Publications:* papers in scientific journals. *Address:* 31 Woodside Road, Woodford Wells, Essex, IG8 0TW, England. *Telephone:* 01-504 4264.

KELANI, Haissam; Syrian diplomatist; b. 6 Aug. 1926, Hamah; s. of Amine Kelani and Saba Azem; m. Daad Tayeh 1951; one s. one d.; ed. Military Coll., Air Gen. Staff Coll., Paris and High Military Air Acad., Paris; General Pilot 1961–62; Syrian Amb. to Algeria 1962–63 and Morocco 1965–67; Sec.-Gen. Ministry of Foreign Affairs 1967–69; Amb. to the German Democratic Repub. 1969–72; Perm. Rep. to UN 1972–76; Dir. Int. Orgs., Ministry Foreign Affairs 1976; mem. Expert, Human Rights Cttee. 1977–80; Chief Ed. Arab Affairs (review of League of Arab States) 1983–; Hon. PH.D. (Leipzig) 1973; 12 medals. *Publications:* 16 books; many articles in Arab reviews. *Address:* League of Arab States, 37 Avenue Kheriddine Pacha, Tunis, Tunisia.

KELBERER, John Jacob, B.S.; American oil industry executive; b. 14 Aug. 1926, Rochester, Minn.; s. of William James Kelberer and Agnes Catherine McElrone; m. Arlyne Mardell Enenson 1949; one s. six d.; ed. Univ. of Minnesota, Harvard Univ.; Supt., Communications Tapline 1956–59; Asst. Chief Engineer 1959–62, Chief Engineer 1962–64, Man., Operations 1964–69, Vice-Pres., Operations and Engineering Tapline 1969–71; acting Gen. Man. Govt. Relations, Arabian American Oil Company (Aramco) 1971–72; acting Gen. Man. Oil Processing & Movement 1972–73, Gen. Man. Oil & Materials Supply 1973–74, Dir. 1974–, Vice-Pres. 1974–77, Senior Vice-Pres. 1975, Sr. Vice-Pres. Operations 1975–77, Chair. of Bd. and C.E.O., Aramco 1978–; Trustee, American Univ., Cairo 1978–. *Leisure interest:* golf. *Address:* c/o Arabian American Company, Box 5000, Dhahran, Saudi Arabia (Office).

KELER, Hans von; German ecclesiastic; b. 12 Nov. 1925, Bielitz; s. of Erwin and Maria von Keler; m. Brigitte Holland 1951; one s. two d.; ed. Univ. of Tübingen; Asst. Minister, Haigstkirche, Stuttgart 1951–53; Parish Minister, Wildenstein/Hohenlohe 1953–57; Dir. of YWCA work, Württemberg 1957-64; Parish Minister, Neuenstein/Hohenlohe 1964-69; Exec. Dir. Herrenberger Diakonieschwesternschaft 1969-76; Gen. Supt. Ulm Dist., Evangelical-Lutheran Church 1976-79; Presiding Bishop, Evangelical-Lutheran Church of Württemberg 1979-; Dr. theol. h.c. *Publications:* more than 50 articles in the field of youth work, pastoral counselling, etc. *Leisure interest:* studies in history. *Address:* D-7000 Stuttgart 1, Gaensheidestrasse 2-4, Federal Republic of Germany.

KELLAS, Arthur Roy Handasyde, C.M.G., M.A.; British diplomatist (retd.); b. 6 May 1915, Aberdeen; s. of Henry Kellas and Mary Brown; m. Katharine B. Le Rougetel 1952; two s. one d.; ed. Aberdeen Grammar School, Aberdeen Univ., Balliol Coll., Oxford and Ecole des Sciences Politiques, Paris; joined diplomatic service 1939; served in army 1939-44; Third Sec., Teheran 1944-47; First Sec., Helsinki 1949-51, Cairo 1952-53, Baghdad 1954-58; Counsellor, Teheran 1958-62; Imperial Defence Coll. 1963; Counsellor and Consul-Gen., Tel-Aviv 1964-66; Amb. to Nepal 1966-70, to People's Democratic Repub. of Yemen (Aden) 1970-72; High Commr. to Tanzania 1972-75; Pres. Britain-Nepal Soc. 1975-79. *Leisure interests:* walking, reading. *Address:* Inverockle, Achateny, Ardnamurchan, Argyll, PH36 4LG, Scotland. *Telephone:* Kilchoan 265.

KELLBERG, Love, B.L.; Swedish diplomatist; b. 6 Nov. 1922, Stockholm; m. 1st 1947; m. 2nd Gunvor Perman 1976; one s. two d.; entered Swedish Foreign Service 1946; Attaché, legation at Warsaw, Poland 1947-49; Attaché, legation at New Delhi, India 1950-51; Trade Commr. at Bombay 1952; Second Sec. Min. of Foreign Affairs, Stockholm 1953; Chargé d'Affaires at Karachi, Pakistan 1954-56; First Sec./Head of Div. Ministry of Foreign Affairs, Stockholm 1957-60; Amb. to Nigeria 1961-62; Consul-Gen., New York 1963; Dir.-Gen. for Legal Affairs, Ministry of Foreign Affairs, Stockholm 1964-75; Under-Sec. of State for Admin. Affairs, Stockholm 1976-78; Amb. to Norway 1978-88; inter alia mem. European Comm. of Human Rights 1969-82; mem. Perm. Court of Arbitration, The Hague 1979-; decorations from Sweden, Denmark, Finland, Iceland, Norway, Italy, Fed. Repub. of Germany and others. *Publications:* articles on human rights and international public law in Swedish law journals. *Leisure interests:* international law, literature, outdoor life. *Address:* Mistelragen 8, 181 60 Lidingo, Sweden (Home).

KELLEHER, James Francis, B.A.; Canadian politician and lawyer; b. 2 Oct. 1930, Sault Ste. Marie, Ont.; m. Helen Kelleher; two d.; ed. Queen's Univ, Osgoode Hall; Dir. Ont. Housing Corpn., Great Lakes Power Ltd.; Pres. Plummer Memorial Public Hospital; Minister for Int. Trade 1984-86, Solicitor Gen. of Canada 1986-89; mem. Sault Ste. Marie Int. Bridge Authority; fmr. Chair. United Way Campaign; fmr. Pres. Kiwanis Club of Sault Ste. Marie, Sault and Dist. Law Asscn., Nat. Retriever Club of Canada; fmr. Dir. Art Gallery of Algoma, Sault Ste. Marie Chamber of Commerce; fmr. mem. Council of Asscn. of Professional Engineers of Ont., Council, Township of Tarentorus; Progressive Conservative Party. *Address:* House of Commons, Parliament Buildings, Ottawa, Ont. K1A 0A6, Canada.

KELLENBENZ, Hermann, DR.PHIL.; German professor of economic and social history; b. 28 Aug. 1913, Suessen, Württemberg; m. Maria Duerhofer 1940; one d.; ed. Univs. of Tübingen, Munich, Kiel and Stockholm; Fellow Rockefeller Foundation 1952-53, Ecole Practique des Hautes Etudes, Paris VI 1953-54; Prof. of Econ. and Social History, Univ. of Würzburg 1957, Nuremberg 1957, Cologne 1960, Erlangen-Nuremberg 1970-83, Prof. Emer. 1983-; Dir. Fugger Archives 1970-; mem. Historical Comm., Munich; mem. Acads. of Göttingen, Copenhagen, Brussels, London (British Acad.) and Madrid; Bayerische Verdienstorden; Lappenberg Medal, Hamburg. *Publications include:* Deutsche Wirtschaftsgeschichte (vols. I, II) 1978, 1981, Skizzen von unterwegs 1983, Schleswig in der Gottorfer Zeit 1985, Anton Fugger (with G. Freiherr von Pölnitz) 1986, Handbuch der europäischen Wirtschafts-und Sozialgeschichte, Vol. III (Ed.) 1986, Die Fugger in Spanien und Portugal 1988. *Leisure interests:* drawing, painting. *Address:* 8151 Warngau, Federal Republic of Germany.

KELLER, Andrew, PH.D., F.INST.P., F.R.S.; British research scientist; b. 22 Aug. 1925; s. of Imre Keller and Margit Klein; m. Eva Bulhack 1951; one s. one d.; ed. Univs. of Budapest and Bristol; Technical Officer, ICI Ltd. Manchester 1948-55; Ministry of Supply research appt. Univ. of Bristol 1955-57, Research Asst. 1957-63, Lecturer 1963-65, Reader 1965-69, Research Prof. in Polymer Science 1969-; High Polymer Prize, American Physics Soc. 1964; Swinburne Award, Plastics Inst. 1974; Max Born Medal, Inst. of Physics and Deutsche Physik Gesellschaft 1983. *Publications:* numerous papers in scientific journals. *Leisure interests:* outdoor sports, mountain walking, concerts. *Address:* 41 Westbury Road, Bristol, BS9 3AU, England. *Telephone:* Bristol 629767.

KELLER, George M., B.S.; American chemical engineer and business executive; b. 3 Dec. 1923, Kansas City, Mo.; s. of George Matthew and Edna Louise (Mathews) Keller; m. Adelaide McCague 1946; three s.; ed. M.I.T.; served U.S. Air Force, World War II; joined Engineering Dept., Standard Oil Co. of Calif. (now Chevron Corpn.) 1948, Asst. Vice-Pres. of Foreign Operations 1967, Asst. to Pres. 1968, Vice-Pres. 1969-74, Dir. 1970-, Vice-Chair. 1974-81, Chair., C.E.O. 1981-88. *Address:* Chevron Corpn., 225 Bush Street, San Francisco, Calif. 94104 (Office); San Mateo, Calif., U.S.A. (Home).

KELLER, Hans Gustav, PH.D., LL.D.; Swiss librarian and historian; b. 12 Nov. 1902, Thun; s. of late Gustav Keller and Lina Keller-Kehr; m. Margaretha Meyer 1937; two s. one d.; ed. Berne, Vienna, Clermont-Ferrand, Heidelberg, Berlin and Basel Univs.; Librarian Zürich Municipal Museum of Applied Art 1934-37, Swiss Nat. Library, Berne 1937-44; Dir. Cen. Fed. Library, Berne 1944-67; lecturer in Modern History, Univ. of Berne 1948-63, Prof. 1963. *Publications:* Die politischen Verlagsanstalten und Druckereien in der Schweiz 1840-1848 1935, Das "Junge Europa" 1834-1836 1938, Das historische Museum im Schloss Thun 1887-1937 1938, Der Brudermord im Hause Kiburg 1939, Das Leben und Leiden Jesu Christi 1940, "La Chartreuse" 1941, Minister Stapfer und die Künstlergesellschaft in Bern 1945, Einigen 1946, Vom Staatsgedanken und von der Sendung der Schweiz 1947, Thun 1949, Legislative und Exekutive in den Vereinigten Staaten von Amerika 1951, Hutten und Zwingli 1952, Chr. von Graffenried und die Gründung von Neu-Bern in Nord-Carolina 1953, Die Wurzeln der amerikanischen Demokratie 1958, Die Quellen der amerikanischen Verfassung 1958, Unitarismus und Föderalismus im Werke der amerikanischen Verfassunggebenden Versammlung 1958, Der "Virginia-Plan" 1960, Die Idee der Unabhängigkeit 1962, Pitt's "Provisional Act" 1962, Die Metaphysik Montesquieus 1965, Montesquieu's "Esprit des lois" 1969, Die amerikanische Verfassunggebende Versammlung 1971. *Leisure interests:* walking, travelling. *Address:* Zumbachstrasse 30, 3028 Spiegel b. Bern, Switzerland. *Telephone:* 031-53-45-03.

KELLER, Joseph Bishop, PH.D.; American professor of mathematics and mechanical engineering; b. 31 July 1923, Paterson, N.J.; s. of Isaac Keller and Sally Bishop; m. Evelyn Fox 1963 (divorced 1976); one s. one d.; ed New York Univ.; Prof. of Math. Courant Inst. of Math. Sciences, New York Univ. 1948-79, Chair. Dept. of Math., Univ. Coll. of Arts and Sciences and Graduate School of Eng. and Sciences 1967-73; Prof. of Math. and Mechanical Eng. Stanford Univ. 1979-; Hon. D.Tech. (Tech. Univ. of Denmark) 1979; Hon. D.Sc. (North Western Univ.) 1988; mem. N.A.S., Foreign mem. Royal Soc.; Nat. Medal of Sciences 1988, numerous awards and lectureships. *Publications:* about 300 articles in professional journals. *Leisure interests:* hiking, skiing. *Address:* Department of Mathematics, Stanford University, Stanford, Calif. 94305 (Office); 820 Sonoma Terrace, Stanford, Calif. 94305, U.S.A. (Home). *Telephone:* (415) 497-0851 (Office).

KELLETT, Sir Brian Smith, Kt., M.A.; British industrialist; b. 8 May 1922, Romiley, Cheshire; s. of late Harold Lamb Kellett and of Amy Elizabeth (née Smith); m. Janet Lesly Street 1947; three d.; ed. Manchester Grammar School and Trinity Coll., Cambridge; Experimental Officer, Admiralty 1942-46; Asst. Prin., Ministry of Transport 1946-48; with Sir Robert Watson-Watt and Partners 1948-49; with Pilkington Brothers Ltd. 1949-55; with Tube Investments Ltd. (now TI Group) 1955-; Dir. 1966-, Man. Dir. 1968-82, Chair. 1976-84; Chair. British Aluminium Co. 1972-79, Port of London Authority 1985-; Dir. Unigate 1974-, Nat. Westminster Bank 1981-, Lombard North Cen. 1985-, Investment Man. Regulatory Org. 1987-; Vice-Pres. Eng. Employers' Fed. 1976-84; Gov. London Business School 1976-84, Imperial Coll. 1979-. *Address:* The Old Malt House, Deddington, Oxford, OX5 4TG, England.

KELLEY, Clarence M., B.A., LL.B., J.D.; American fmr. government official; b. 24 Oct. 1911, Kansas City, Mo.; s. of Clarence Bond Kelley and Minnie (Brown) Kelley; m. 1st Ruby D. Pickett 1937 (deceased), one s. one d.; m. 2nd Shirley Ann Dyckes 1976; ed. Univs. of Kansas and Missouri; admitted to Mo. Bar 1940; with Fed. Bureau of Investigation 1940-61; Special Agent in Charge, FBI Birmingham Office 1957-60, FBI Memphis Office 1960-61; Chief of Police, Kansas City, Mo. 1961-73; Dir. FBI 1973-78; mem. Presidential Advisory Cttee. 1971, Nat. Advisory Comm. on Criminal Justice, Standards and Goals, FBI Nat. Acad. Review Cttee. 1972-73, Nat. Advisory Council, Nat Advisory Bd. Salvation Army; mem. U.S. Supreme Court Practice 1977-; mem. Exec. Cttee. Int. Asscn. of Chiefs of Police; Chair. Clarence M. Kelley & Assocs.; Hon. LL.D. (Baker Univ., Kansas, Culver-Stockton Coll., Mo., Southeastern Univ., Washington, D.C.); Hon. Dr.rer.-Pol. (Westminster Coll., Fulton Mo.); J. Edgar Hoover Gold Medal for Outstanding Job Service 1970, CIA Distinguished Service Award 1979. *Address:* 221 W. 48th Street, Apt. 1601, Kansas City, Mo. 64112, U.S.A.

KELLEY, Harold H., PH.D.; American professor of psychology; b. 16 Feb. 1921, Boise Idaho; s of Harry H. Kelley and Maud M. Little; m. Dorothy Drumm 1942; one s. two d; ed. Univ. of Calif., Berkeley and M.I.T.; Study Dir. and lecturer, Dept. of Psychology, Univ. of Mich. 1948-50; Asst. Prof., Dept. of Psychology, Yale Univ. 1950-55; Assoc Prof., then Prof., Dept. of Psychology, Univ. of Minn. 1955-61; Prof. Dept. of Psychology, Univ. of Calif., Los Angeles 1961-; Fellow N.A.S., American Acad. of Arts and Sciences; Distinguished Sr. Scientist Soc. for Experimental Social Psychology; Distinguished Scientific Contribution Award, American Psychological Asscn. *Publications:* The Social Psychology of Groups (with J. W. Thibaut) 1959, Attribution (co-author) 1972, Interpersonal Relations (with J. W. Thibaut) 1978, Personal Relationships 1979, Close Relationships (co-author) 1983. *Leisure interests:* music, backpacking. *Address:* Department of Psychology, Franz Hall, University of California, Los Angeles, Calif. 90024, U.S.A. *Telephone:* (213) 825-2289.

KELLOU, Mohamed; Algerian lawyer and diplomatist; b. 27 March 1931, Mansoura; s. of Arezki Kellou and Zehoua Kellou; m. Annyssa Abdelkader 1965; three d.; ed. Univs. of Algiers and Montpellier; Lawyer, Algiers;

fmr. Vice-Pres. Union Générale des Etudiants Musulmans Algériens (U.G.E.M.A.) (in charge of Foreign Affairs); Front de Libération Nationale (F.L.N.) Rep. in U.K. 1957-61; Chief of Provisional Govt. of Algeria Diplomatic Mission to Pakistan 1961-62; Dir. of African, Asian and S. American Affairs, Ministry of Foreign Affairs, Repub. of Algeria 1962-63; Amb. to U.K. 1963-64, to Czechoslovakia 1964-70, to Argentina 1970-75, to People's Repub. of China 1975-77, to Fed. Repub. of Germany 1979-82, to Zimbabwe 1982-84; Minister Plenipotentiary, Ministry of Foreign Affairs, Algiers Sept. 1984-; mem. People's Nat. Ass. and Chair. Foreign Affairs Cttee. 1977-79. *Leisure interests:* reading, tennis. *Address:* 40 boulevard des Martyrs, Algiers, Algeria (Home).

KELLY, Anthony, PH.D., F.ENG., F.R.S.; British university vice-chancellor; b. 9 Jan. 1929, Hillingdon, Middx.; s. of Group Capt. V. G. Kelly and Violet E. M. Kelly; m. Christina M. Dunleavie 1956; three s. one d.; ed. Presentation Coll., Reading, Univ. of Reading and Trinity Coll., Cambridge; Research Assoc. Univ. of Ill. 1953-55; Univ. of Birmingham 1955; Founding Fellow, Churchill Coll., Cambridge and Lecturer in Metallurgy 1958-67; Supt. of Div., later Deputy Dir. Nat. Physical Lab. 1967-75; Vice-Chancellor, Univ. of Surrey 1975-; Chair. Eng. Materials Requirements Board, Dept. of Industry 1976-80; Dir. Johnson Wax UK 1981-, Teddington Devts. 1981-, QUOTEC 1984-; Chair. Surrey Satellite Tech. 1985-; Foreign Assoc. U.S. Acad. of Eng.; Fellow Churchill Coll., Cambridge; awards include William Hopkins Prize 1967, Beilby Medal 1967, A. A. Griffith Medal (Univ. of Del.) 1974. *Publications:* Strong Solids 1966, Crystallography and Crystal Defects (with G. W. Groves) 1970; many papers in journals of physical sciences. *Leisure interests:* science of materials, sailing. *Address:* University of Surrey, Guildford, Surrey, GU2 5XH (Office); Yardfield, Church Lane, Worplesdon, Guildford, Surrey, GU3 3RU, England (Home). *Telephone:* (0483) 509249 (Office); (0483) 234116 (Home).

KELLY, Donald P.; American business executive; b. 24 Feb. 1922, Chicago; m. Byrd M. Sullivan; two s. one d.; ed. De Paul, Loyola and Harvard Univs.; Man. Data Processing, Swift & Co. 1953, Asst. Controller 1965, Controller 1967, Vice-Pres. Corp. Devt. 1968, Financial Vice-Pres. and Dir. 1970-; Financial Vice-Pres. and Dir. Esmark April-Oct. 1973, Pres., C.O.O. 1973-77, Pres. and C.E.O. 1977-82, Chair., Pres. and C.E.O. 1982-84; Chair., C.E.O. BCI Holdings Corpn. 1986-87; Pres. Kelly Briggs & Assocs., Inc. 1984-86; Chair. and C.E.O. EII Holdings Inc. 1987-; Dir. Gen. Dynamics Corpn., Inland Steel Co. *Address:* 2 N. La Salle, 26th Floor, Chicago, Ill. 60602, U.S.A.

KELLY, Gene Curran, A.B.; American dancer and actor; b. 23 Aug. 1912, Pittsburgh; s. of James Patrick Joseph and Harriet (Curran) Kelly; m. 1st Betsy Blair 1941 (divorced 1957), one d.; m. 2nd Jeanne Coyne 1960, one s. one d.; ed. Univ. of Pittsburgh; Recipient, Kennedy Center Honours 1982, American Film Inst. Life Achievement Award 1984; has appeared in Leave It to Me 1938, Time of Your Life 1940, One for the Money 1939, Pal Joey 1941; staged: Billy Rose's Diamond Horseshoe 1940, Best Foot Forward 1941; Dir. of dances for films: Anchors Aweigh 1944, The Pirate 1948, Living in a Big Way 1947; appeared in films: Me and My Girl 1942, The Pirate 1948, The Three Musketeers 1950, An American in Paris 1950, The Devil Makes Three 1952, Invitation to the Dance 1953, Brigadoon 1954, Les Girls 1957, Inherit the Wind 1960, Gigi 1961, The Young Girls of Rochefort 1967, 1940, Carats 1973, Xanadu 1980; Co-Dir. On the Town 1949, Singin' in the Rain 1951, It's Always Fair Weather 1955; Dir. Invitation to the Dance 1953, What a Way to Go 1964, A Guide for the Married Man 1966, Hello Dolly! 1968, The Cheyenne Social Club 1970; Producer, Dir. The Happy Road (France) 1956, Flower Drum Song 1958; Dir. and appeared in That's Entertainment Part II 1976. *Publication:* Take Me Out to the Ball Game 1948. *Address:* 725 N. Rodeo Drive, Beverly Hills, Calif., U.S.A.

KELLY, Gregory Maxwell, PH.D., F.A.A.; Australian professor of pure mathematics; b. 5 June 1930, Sydney; s. of Owen S. Kelly and Rita M. (née McCauley) Kelly; m. 1960; three s. one d.; ed. Univs. of Sydney and Cambridge, England; Lecturer in Pure Math. Univ. of Sydney 1957-60, Sr. Lecturer 1961-65, Reader 1965-66; Prof. of Pure Math. Univ. of N.S.W. 1967-72, Univ. of Sydney 1973-. *Publications:* An Introduction to Algebra and Vector Geometry 1972, Basic Concepts of Enriched Category Theory 1981, over 60 learned papers. *Leisure interests:* bridge, music, tennis, swimming. *Address:* University of Sydney, Department of Pure Mathematics, Sydney, N.S.W. 2006 (Office); 319 Mona Vale Road, St. Ives, N.S.W. 2075, Australia (Home). *Telephone:* 692-3796 (Office); 440-8178 (Home).

KELLY, John Hubert, B.A.; American diplomatist; b. 20 July 1939, Fond du Lac, Wis.; ed. Emory Univ., Atlanta; Second Sec. U.S. Embassy, Ankara 1966-67; American Consul, Songkhala, Thailand 1969-71; First Sec. U.S. Embassy, Paris 1976-80; Deputy Exec. Sec., Dept. of State, Washington D.C. 1980-81, Sr. Deputy Asst. Sec. of State for Public Affairs 1982-83, Prin. Deputy Asst. Sec. of State for European Affairs 1983-85; Amb. to Lebanon 1986-89; Asst. Sec. for Near Eastern and S.E. Asian Affairs Feb. 1989-. *Address:* c/o Dept. of State, Washington, D.C. 20521, U.S.A.

KELLY, Rev. Canon John Norman Davidson, M.A., D.D.; British scholar, lecturer and university official; b. 13 April 1909, Bridge of Allan, Scotland;

s. of John Davidson and Ann (Barnes) Kelly; ed. Univs. of Glasgow and Oxford; Chaplain and Tutor, St. Edmund Hall, Oxford 1935-37, Vice-Prin., Fellow and Trustee 1937-51, Prin. 1951-79; Oxford Univ. Lecturer in Patristic Studies 1948-76, Pro-Vice-Chancellor 1964-66, 1972-79; Dean of Degrees St. Edmund's Hall 1982-; Birkbeck Lecturer, Cambridge 1973; Hensley Henson Lecturer, Oxford 1980; during World War II did part-time work for Chatham House; Canon of Chichester Cathedral 1948; Hon. Fellow Queen's Coll., Oxford 1963, St. Edmund Hall, Oxford 1979; F.B.A. 1965; Hon. D.D. (Glasgow) 1958, (Wales) 1971. *Publications:* Early Christian Creeds 1950, Rufinus: A Commentary on the Apostles' Creed 1955, Early Christian Doctrines 1958, The Pastoral Epistles 1963, The Athanasian Creed 1964, The Epistles of Peter and Jude 1969, Aspects of the Passion 1970, Jerome 1975, The Oxford Dictionary of Popes 1986. *Leisure interests:* gardening, travel, sightseeing. *Address:* 7 Crick Road, Oxford OX2 6QJ, England. *Telephone:* (0865) 512907.

KELLY, Patrick Altham, S.T.L., PH.L.; British ecclesiastic; b. 23 Nov. 1938, Morecambe; s. of John Kelly and Mary (née Altham) Kelly; ed. Preston Catholic Coll., Venerable English Coll., Rome; Asst. Priest, Lancaster Cathedral 1964-66; Prof. of Dogmatic Theology, Oscott Coll., Birmingham 1966-79, Rector 1979-84; Bishop of Salford 1984-. *Address:* Wardley Hall, Worsley, Manchester, M28 5ND, England. *Telephone:* 061-794 2825.

KELLY, Petra K.; German politician; b. 29 Nov. 1947, Günzburg, Bavaria; step-d. of Lieut.-Col. John E. Kelly, d. of Marianne Kelly; ed. Roman Catholic Convent, Bavaria, High School, Newport News, Va., U.S.A., School of Int. Service, American Univ., Washington, D.C., Univ. of Amsterdam, Europe Inst., Netherlands; family moved to Columbus, Ga., U.S.A. when she was a teenager; student volunteer on presidential campaigns of Robert F. Kennedy and Hubert H. Humphrey; joined Sozialdemokratische Partei Deutschlands (SPD), left after seven years; joined EEC, Brussels 1972, later became full-time civil servant at the Econ. and Social Cttee., responsible for social policy affairs; founded Die Grünen (Green Party), Fed. Repub. of Germany 1972, Speaker 1980-82, mem. Bundestag (parl.) 1983-; fmr. Leader (mem. Exec.) Die Grünen; founder and Chair. Grace P. Kelly Asscn. for Cancer Research for Children; joint recipient Right Livelihood Award 1982, Peace Woman of the Year (USA) 1982. *Publications:* Fighting for Hope 1984, Hiroshima 1985, A Nuclear Ireland, Viel Liebe gegen Schmezen. *Leisure interests:* photography, painting, reading, travel. *Address:* Die Grünen, Bundeshaus, HT 718, 5300 Bonn 1, Federal Republic of Germany. *Telephone:* 0228-167918.

KELLY, Sir Theo (William Theodore), Kt., O.B.E., J.P., F.R.S.A., F.A.I.M.; Australian business executive (retd.); b. 27 June 1907, Sydney, N.S.W.; s. of William Thomas Kelly and Lily Elizabeth Kelly (née Neely); m. Nancy Margaret Williams 1944; two s. two d.; ed. Sydney; served World War II, Wing Commdr. R.A.A.F. 1942-44; Chair. Canteen Services Bd. 1946-59; Man. Dir. Woolworths Ltd. Australia 1945-70, Chair. 1963-80; Chair. Woolworths Properties Ltd. 1963-79; mem. Bd. Reserve Bank of Australia 1961-75; fmr. Deputy Chair., Dir. Australian Mutual Life Assurance Soc.; Chair. Computer Sciences of Australia Ltd.; Dir. A.M.P. Soc. 1967-79, A.N.T.A. 1959-; mem. Royal Soc. of Arts; Trustee, Nat. Parks and Wild Life Asscn. 1969-; Life Gov., Royal Life Saving Soc. *Leisure interests:* boating, golf. *Address:* c/o Key Travel Service, 432-436 Elizabeth Street, Surrey Hills, N.S.W. 2010 (Office); 8/73 Yarranabbe Road, Darling Point, N.S.W. 2027, Australia (Home).

KELMAN, Arthur, PH.D.; American plant pathologist and university professor; b. 11 Dec. 1918, Providence, R.I.; s. of Philip Kelman and Minnie Kollin; m. Helen Moore Parker 1949; one s.; ed. Univ. of Rhode Island and North Carolina State Univ.; served U.S. Signal Corps 1942-45; Asst. Prof., N.C. State Univ. 1949-53, Assoc. Prof. 1954-57, Prof. 1957-62, W.N. Reynolds Distinguished Prof. of Plant Pathology and Forestry 1962-65; Visiting Scientist, Rockefeller Inst. for Medical Research, New York 1953-54; Chair. and Prof., Dept. of Plant Pathology, Univ. of Wis. at Madison 1965-75, L.R. Jones Prof. 1975-, Warf Sr. Distinguished Prof. of Plant Pathology and Bacteriology 1984-; Sr. Postdoctoral Fellowship, Cambridge Univ., England 1971-72; Pres. American Phytopathological Soc. 1967, Int. Soc. for Plant Pathology 1973-78; Chair. Div. of Biological Sciences, Comm. on Life Sciences, Nat. Research Council 1979-82, Bd. on Basic Biology 1984-85; mem. Council, N.A.S. 1986-89, Cttee. on Science Eng. and Public Policy, Nat. Acad. 1986-89; Fellow American Phytopathological Soc., Award of Distinction; mem. N.A.S., American Acad. of Arts and Sciences; Dr. h.c. (Rhode Island) 1977. *Publication:* The Bacterial Wilt caused by Pseudomonas Solanacearum 1953. *Leisure interests:* gardening, wood carving. *Address:* Department of Plant Pathology, University of Wisconsin-Madison, Madison, Wis. 53706; 234 Carillon Drive, Madison, Wis. 53705, U.S.A. (Home).

KELMAN, Bryan Nivison, A.O., C.B.E., B.E.; Australian business executive (retd.); b. 8 Dec. 1925, Sydney; s. of the late W. Kelman; m. Winsome Shand 1952; two s.; ed. Knox Grammar School, Sydney Univ.; Gen. Man. and Dir. Ready Mixed Concrete (WA) Pty. Ltd., Perth 1952-55, Ready Mixed Concrete (U.K.) Ltd. 1955-62, Man. Dir. 1962-64, Chair. and Man. Dir. 1964-66; Sr. Exec. Officer CSR Ltd. 1966-72, Deputy Gen. Man. 1972-82, Dir. 1972-87, C.E.O. 1982-87; Dir. Macquarie Bank Ltd.; Chair. Trade Devt. Council 1978-81, Australian Commercial Disputes Centre Ltd. 1986-, Australian Meat and Livestock Industry Policy Council 1987-; Dir.

Jennings Industries Ltd. 1987-, Prudential Assurance Co. Ltd. 1987-, Fletcher Challenge Ltd. 1987-, Homestake Gold of Australia Ltd. 1987-; mem. Exec. Cttee. Australian Mining Industry Council 1980-; mem. Econ. Planning Advisory Council; mem. Australian Wool Corpn. 1978-. *Leisure interests:* golf, trout fishing. *Address:* O'Connell Street Associates, 16 O'Connell Street, Sydney 2000 (Office); 15 Bangalla Street, Turramurra, N.S.W. 2074, Australia (Home). *Telephone:* (02) 225 3244 (Office); (02) 487 2321 (Home).

KELMAN, Charles, B.S., M.D.; American ophthalmologist; b. 23 May 1930, Brooklyn, New York; s. of Eva Kelman and David Kelman; m. (divorced); one s. two d.; ed. Tuft's Univ., Univ. of Geneva Medical School, Switzerland and Bellevue Hosp., New York; Residency in Ophthalmology, Wills Eye Hosp., Pa. 1956-60; Attending Surgeon, Manhattan Eye, Ear and Throat Hosp., New York 1967-, New York Eye and Ear Infirmary 1983-; Attending Ophthalmologist, Riverside Gen. Hosp., Secaucus, N.J. 1979-; Clinical Prof., New York Medical Coll., Valhalla, New York 1980-; developed new techniques for cataract removal and lens implantation and invented surgical instruments for these operations 1962-67; has taught method to over 3,000 ophthalmologists from hospitals throughout world; Physician's Recognition Award, American Medical Asscn., American Acad. of Achievement Gold Plate Award, and numerous other awards. *Publications:* Phacoemulsification and Aspiration: The Kelman Technique of Cataract Removal 1975, Cataracts—What You Must Know About Them 1982, Through My Eyes (autobiography) 1985 and numerous articles. *Leisure interests:* writing, golf, helicopter flying, music, comedy. *Address:* 350 Fifth Avenue, 21st Floor: Empire State Building, New York, N.Y. 10118, U.S.A. *Telephone:* (212) 736-9696.

KEMAL, Yashar; Turkish writer and journalist; b. 1923, Adana; m. Thilda Serrero 1952; one s.; self-educated; Commdr., Légion d'honneur 1984; Prix Mondial Cino del Duca 1982. *Publications:* (in English) Memed, My Hawk 1961, The Wind from the Plain 1963, Anatolian Tales 1968, They Burn the Thistles 1973, Iron Earth, Copper Sky 1974, The Legend of Ararat 1975, The Legend of the Thousand Bulls 1976, The Undying Grass 1977, The Lords of Akchasaz (Part I), Murder in the Ironsmiths' Market 1979, The Saga of a Seagull 1981, The Sea-Crossed Fisherman 1985, The Birds Have Also Gone 1987, novels, short stories, plays and essays in Turkish. *Leisure interest:* folklore. *Address:* P.K. 14, Basinköy, Istanbul, Turkey. *Telephone:* 5790887.

KEMBALL, Charles, M.A., SC.D., M.R.I.A., F.R.S.E., F.R.S.; British professor emeritus of chemistry; b. 27 March 1923, Edinburgh; s. of Charles H. and Janet (née White) Kemball; m. Kathleen P. Lynd 1956; one s. two d.; ed. Edinburgh Acad. and Trinity Coll., Cambridge; Fellow, Trinity Coll., Cambridge 1946-54, Junior Bursar 1949-51, Asst. Lecturer 1951-54, Univ. Demonstrator 1951-54; Prof. of Physical Chem., Queen's Univ. of Belfast 1954-66, Dean, Faculty of Science 1957-60, Vice-Pres. 1962-65; Prof. of Chem. Univ. of Edinburgh 1966-83, Dean, Faculty of Science 1975-78; Pres. Royal Soc. of Edin. 1988-; Gunning Victoria Jubilee Prize 1981; Award for Service to Chemical Soc. 1985. *Publications:* numerous articles on adsorption and catalysis in various scientific journals. *Leisure interests:* hill-walking, making and drinking wine. *Address:* Department of Chemistry, University of Edinburgh, King's Buildings, West Mains Road, Edinburgh, EH9 3JJ (Office); 5 Hermitage Drive, Edinburgh, EH10 6DE, Scotland (Home). *Telephone:* (031) 667 1081 Ext. 3402 (Office); (031) 447 2315 (Home).

KEMENY, John G., PH.D.; American mathematician, philosopher and teacher; b. 31 May 1926, Budapest, Hungary; s. of Tibor and Lucy (Fried) Kemeny; m. Jean Alexander 1950; one s. one d.; ed. George Washington High School, New York, and Princeton Univ.; arrived in U.S.A. 1940; U.S. Army Service in theoretical div. of Manhattan Project, Los Alamos, N.M. 1945; Research Asst. to Prof. Einstein 1948; Fine Instructor in Mathematics, Princeton 1949-51, Asst. Prof. Dept. of Philosophy 1951-52; Prof. of Mathematics and Philosophy, Dartmouth Coll. 1953-70, 1981-, Chair of Dept. 1954-66, Albert Bradley Third Century Prof. to encourage innovation in teaching 1969-72, Adjunct Prof. of Maths. 1972-81, Prof. of Maths. and Computer Science 1981-; Pres. of Dartmouth Coll. 1970-81; Chair. U.S. Comm. on Mathematical Instruction 1957-60, True BASIC, Inc., Hanover, N.H. 1983-; mem. Bd. of Govs. Mathematical Assn. of America 1960-63; co-inventor of computer language BASIC and co-designer of Dartmouth Time-Sharing System; Vice-Chair. Nat. Science Foundation Advisory Cttee. on Computing 1968-69; Consultant to Research Council of Greater Cleveland 1959-70; Assoc. Ed. of Journal of Mathematical Analysis and Applications 1959-70; mem. Nat. Research Council 1963-66; mem. Nat. Comm. on Libraries and Information Science 1971-73; Chair. Pres.'s Comm. on the accident at Three Mile Island April-Dec. 1979; Chair. Consortium on Financing Higher Education 1978-80; Fellow, American Acad. of Arts and Sciences; mem. American Mathematical Soc., American Philosophical Asscn.; 18 hon. degrees; American Fed. of Information Processing Socs. Educ. Award 1983, New York Acad. of Science Award 1984. *Publications:* thirteen books ranging from mathematics and computing to philosophy of science and educ., including Man and The Computer 1972. *Address:* Dartmouth College, Hanover, N.H. 03755 (Office); P.O. Box 195, Etna, N.H. 03750, U.S.A. *Telephone:* (603) 646-3864 (Office).

KEMMER, Nicholas, D.PHIL., M.A., F.R.S.E., F.R.S.; British theoretical physicist; b. 7 Dec. 1911, St. Petersburg (Leningrad), Russia; s. of late Nikolai Pavlovich Kemmer and Barbara née Stutzer; m. Margaret Wragg 1947; two s. one d.; ed. Bismarckschule, Hanover, Univs. of Göttingen and Zürich; Beit Scientific Research Fellow, Imperial Coll., London 1936-38, Demonstrator 1939; war work for U.K. Atomic Energy, Cambridge 1940-44, Montreal 1944-46; Lecturer and Fellow, Trinity Coll., Cambridge 1946-53; Tait Prof. of Mathematical Physics, Edinburgh 1953-79, Prof. Emer. 1979-; Hon. Fellow, Imperial Coll., London; Hughes Medal, Royal Soc. 1966, Oppenheimer Prize and medal 1975, Max-Planck Medal 1983. *Publications:* articles in professional journals. *Leisure interests:* music, gardening, crosswords, stamp-collecting. *Address:* 35 Salisbury Road, Edinburgh, EH16 5AA, Scotland. *Telephone:* 031-667 2893.

KEMOULARIA, Claude de; French international administrator and diplomatist; b. 30 March 1922, Paris; m. Chantal Julia de Kemoularia 1951; one d.; ed. Coll. Carnot, Fontainebleau, Faculté de Droit, Univ. de Paris and Ecole Libre des Sciences Politiques; early career with Ministry of Interior 1945, Office of Gov.-Gen. French Zone of Occupied Germany 1946-47, Ministry of Finance 1948; Parly. Sec. to Paul Reynaud 1948-56; Personal Asst. to Sec.-Gen. of UN, Dag Hammarskjöld 1957-61, in charge of World Refugee Year 1959-60; Dir. European Information Services of UN 1961; entered private business 1962; Dir. Forges de Chatillon-Commentry 1962-79, Paribas North America 1979-82, S. G. Warburg 1980-82; Sr. Consultant to Administrator, UN Devt. Programme 1964-82; Private Adviser to Prince Rainier of Monaco 1965-67; financial adviser for int. operations (Banque de Paris et des Pays-Bas) 1968-; Chair. Soc. Néo-Calédonienne de Dévt. et Participations, Soc. Gabonaise de Participations, Soc. Camerounaise de Participations 1980-82; Amb. to Netherlands 1982-84; Perm. Rep. to UN 1984-87; Admin. S. G. Warburg 1987-; mem. Exec. Cttee. European Movement; Pres. French UN Assn. *Address:* 41 Boulevard du Commandant-Charcot, 92200 Neuilly-sur-Seine, France.

KEMP, Rt. Rev. Eric Waldram, M.A., D.D., D.LITT., F.R.HIST.S.; British ecclesiastic; b. 27 April 1915, Grimsby; s. of Tom Kemp and Florence L. Waldram; m. Leslie Patricia Kirk 1953; one s. four d.; ed. Brigg Grammar School, Lincs., Exeter Coll., Oxford and St. Stephen's House; ordained Deacon 1939; Priest 1940; Curate St. Luke's, Southampton 1939-41; Librarian Pusey House, Oxford 1941-46; Chaplain Christ Church, Oxford 1941-46; Acting Chaplain St. John's Coll., Oxford 1943-45; Fellow, Chaplain, Tutor and Lecturer in Theology and Medieval History Exeter Coll. 1946-69; Dean of Worcester 1969-74; Lord Bishop of Chichester 1974-; Canon and Prebendary of Caistor in Lincoln Cathedral 1952; Hon. Provincial Canon of Cape Town 1960; Bampton Lecturer 1959-60; Chaplain to the Queen 1967-69. *Publications:* Canonization in the Western Church 1948, 25 Papal Decretals Relating to the Diocese of Lincoln 1954, An Introduction to Canon Law in the Church of England 1957, Life and Letters of K. E. Kirk 1959, Counsel and Consent 1961, Man: Fallen and Free 1969, Square Words in a Round World 1980. *Leisure interests:* music and travel. *Address:* The Palace, Chichester, W. Sussex, PO19 1PY, England. *Telephone:* Chichester 782161.

KEMP, Jack F., B.A.; American politician; b. 13 July 1935, L.A.; m. Joanne Main; two s. two d.; ed. Occidental Coll., Long Beach State Univ., Calif., Western Univ.; special Asst. to Gov. of Calif. 1967, to Chair. Republican Nat. Cttee. 1969; mem. 92nd-100th congresses from 31st N.Y. Dist. 1971-; professional football player for thirteen years; Public Relations officer Marine Midland Bank, Buffalo; Cand. for Republican Pres. nomination 1987-88; nominated Sec. of Housing and Urban Devt. Dec. 1988; mem. Pres. Council on Physical Fitness and Sports, Exec. Cttee. Player Pension Bd., Nat. Football League, Nat. Assn. Broadcasters, Engineers and Technicians, Buffalo Area Chamber of Commerce, Sierra Club, American Football League Players Assn. (co-founder, Pres. 1965-70). *Address:* Office of the Secretary of Housing and Urban Development, 451 7th Street, S.W., Washington, D.C. 20410; 2252, Rayburn House Office Building, Washington, D.C. 20515, U.S.A.

KEMPARA, Eugenia, M.JUR.; Polish lawyer and politician; b. 29 Sept. 1928, Księżyno, Białystok voivodship; m.; one c.; ed. Warsaw Univ.; served in army legal service, later Col. 1946-75; Co-ordinator and fmr. Chair. Org. of Soldiers' Families; Chair. Gen. Council, Women's League 1975-81; Deputy Chair. Nat. Council of Polish Women until 1976, Chair. 1977-83; mem. Gen. Council, Polish Lawyers' Assn.; fmr. mem. World Council of Democratic Women's Feds., Council of Int. Feds. of Women of Legal Professions; Deputy mem. Cen. Cttee. Polish United Workers' Party (PZPR) 1975-80, mem. Cen. Cttee. 1980-81; Deputy to Seym 1976-85; mem. State Council Dec. 1976-85; mem. Presidium of All-Poland Cttee. of Nat. Unity Front 1977-83, World Peace Council 1980-83; Kt.'s Cross of Order of Polonia Restituta, Order of Banner of Labour (Second Class) 1978, (First Class) 1984 and other decorations. *Leisure interest:* lecturing. *Address:* ul. Bonifraterska 6m. 23, 00-123 Warsaw, Poland (Home).

KEMPNÝ, Josef, PROF. ING., C.SC.; Czechoslovak politician; b. 19 July 1920, Lazy-Orlová; s. of Karel and Anežka Kempný; m.; one s.; ed. Technical Univ.; worker, foreman building technician in different firms 1939-48; Regional Man. Assn. of Building Works, Ostrava 1948-51; various managerial posts in building enterprises 1951-64; Chair. Municipal Nat. Cttee., Ostrava 1964-68; Sec. Cen. Cttee. CP Czechoslovakia 1968-69, 1970-;

Deputy Prime Minister of Č.S.S.R. 1969-70; Prime Minister of the Czech Socialist Republic 1969-70; Chair. Bureau of Cen. Cttee., CP of Czechoslovakia for Directing Party Work in the Czech Lands 1970-71; Sec. of Cen. Cttee., CP of Czechoslovakia 1968-69, 1970-81, mem. Presidium 1969-88; mem. Cen. Cttee. of CP of Czechoslovakia 1969-; mem. of Czech. Nat Council 1968-76, mem. Presidium 1971-76, Chair. 1981-; Deputy and mem. Presidium Czech Nat. Council 1981-; Deputy to House of Nations, Fed. Assembly 1969-; mem. Presidium of Fed. Assembly 1970-; Deputy Chair. Cen. Cttee. Front of Č.S.S.R. 1971-88; Chair. Cen. Cttee. of Nat. Front of Czech Socialist Repub. 1971-88; Sec. of Cen. Cttee. CP of Czechoslovakia; Chair. Nat. Econ. Comm. Cen. Cttee. CP of Czechoslovakia 1971-81; mem. Cttee. of Party Work 1988; Order of the Repub. 1970; Order of Bulgarian People's Republic (1st Class) 1971; Order of Victorious February 1973; Hero of Socialist Labour 1980, Klement Gottwald Order 1980. *Address:* Czech National Council, Sněmovni, Mala Strana, Prague 1, Czechoslovakia (Office). *Telephone:* 2105.

KENDAL, Felicity; British actress; b. 25 Sept. 1946; d. of Geoffrey and Laura Kendal; m. 1st (divorced), one s.; m. 2nd Michael Rudman 1983; one s.; ed. six convents in India; first appeared on stage 1947, at age nine months in A Midsummer Night's Dream; grew up touring India and Far East with parents' theatre co., playing pageboys at age eight and Puck at age nine, graduating to roles such as Viola in Twelfth Night, Jessica in The Merchant of Venice and Ophelia in Hamlet; returned to England 1965; London debut as Carla in Minor Murder, Savoy Theatre 1967. *Other stage roles include:* Katherine in Henry V, Lika in The Promise, Leicester 1968, Amaryllis in Back to Methuselah, Nat. Theatre, Hermia in A Midsummer Night's Dream, Hero in Much Ado About Nothing, Regent's Park, London 1970, Anne Danby in Kean, Oxford 1970, London 1971; Romeo and Juliet, 'Tis Pity She's a Whore and The Three Arrows 1972; The Norman Conquests, London 1974, Viktosha in Once Upon a Time, Bristol 1976, Arms and The Man, Greenwich 1978, Mara in Clouds, London 1978; Constanza Mozart in Amadeus, Desdemona in Othello; On the Razzle 1981, The Second Mrs. Tanqueray, The Real Thing 1982, Jumpers 1985, Made in Bangkok 1986, Hapgood 1988, Ivanov 1989. *TV appearances include:* four series of The Good Life; Solo; The Mistress; Viola in Twelfth Night 1979, plays and serials. *Films:* Shakespeare Wallah 1965, Valentino 1976; Variety Club Most Promising Newcomer 1974, Best Actress 1979, Clarence Derwent Award 1980. *Leisure interest:* golf. *Address:* c/o Chatto and Linnit, Prince of Wales, Theatre, Coventry Street, London, W.1, England.

KENDALL, David George, D.SC., F.R.S.; British mathematician; b. 15 Jan. 1918, Ripon, Yorkshire; s. of Fritz Ernest Kendall and Emma Taylor; m. Diana Louise Fletcher 1952; two s., four d.; ed. Ripon Grammar School, The Queen's Coll., Oxford; Experimental Officer, Ministry of Supply 1940-45, Fellow, Magdalen Coll., Oxford 1946-62, Prof. of Mathematical Statistics, Univ. of Cambridge 1962-85, Emer. Prof. 1985-, Fellow of Churchill Coll. 1962-; Pres. London Mathematical Soc. 1972-74, Bernoulli Soc. 1975, Sections for Mathematics and Physics, British Asscn. 1982; mem. of Council, Royal Soc. 1967-69, 1982-83; Milne Lecturer (Oxford) 1983; Hotelling Lecturer (N. Carolina) 1985; Hon. Fellow Queen's Coll., Oxford 1985-; Hon. D.Sc. (Bath) 1986; Royal Statistical Soc. Silver Medal 1955, Gold Medal 1981, Weldon Prize and Medal, Oxford Univ. 1974, Royal Soc. Sylvester Medal 1976, London Mathematical Soc. Whitehead Prize 1980. *Publications:* Jt. Editor: Mathematics in the Archaeological and Historical Sciences 1971, Stochastic Analysis 1973, Stochastic Geometry 1974, Analytic and Geometric Stochastics 1986. *Leisure interests:* archaeology, genealogy, geology and local history. *Address:* Statistical Laboratory, 16 Mill Lane, Cambridge, CB2 1SB (Office); 37 Barrow Road, Cambridge, CB2 2AR, England (Home). *Telephone:* 0223-337948 (Office); 0223-353991 (Home).

KENDALL, Donald M.; American business executive; b. 16 March 1921, Sequim, Wash.; s. of Carroll C. and Charlotte (McIntosh) Kendall; m. 1st Anne McDonnell Linkins 1945, 2nd Sigrid Ruedt von Collenberg 1965; four c.; ed. Western Kentucky State Coll.; Air Corps, U.S. Naval Reserve 1942-47; Vice-Pres. Pepsi-Cola Co. 1952-57; Pres. Pepsi-Cola Int. 1957-63, Pepsi-Cola Co. 1963-65; Pres. and C.E.O., PepsiCo Inc. 1965-71, Chair. and Chief Exec. Officer 1971-86 and Chair. Exec. Cttee. 1980-86, 1988-; Dir. Pan American Airways, Atlantic Richfield, Investors Diversified Services Mutual Fund Group; Chair. Exec. Cttee. U.S.-U.S.S.R. Trade and Econ. Council; mem., fmr. Chair., Nat. Center for Resource Recovery and Emergency Cttee. for American Trade; mem. Bd., Chamber of Commerce of the United States. *Leisure interests:* tennis, golf, jogging, skiing, salmon fishing. *Address:* PepsiCo Inc., Anderson Hill Road, Purchase, N.Y. 10577 (Office); Porchuck Road, Greenwich, Conn. 06830, U.S.A. (Home).

KENDELL, Robert Evan, M.A., M.D., F.R.C.P., F.R.C.P. (E), F.R.C.PSYCH.; British university teacher and psychiatrist; b. 28 March 1935, Rotherham, Yorks.; s. of Robert Owen Kendell and Joan Evans; m. Ann Whitfield 1961; two s. two d.; ed. Mill Hill School, Peterhouse, Cambridge, King's Coll. Hosp. Medical School, London; psychiatric training, Maudsley Hosp., London 1962-66; Visiting Prof., Univ. of Vermont Coll. of Medicine, U.S.A 1969-70; Reader in Psychiatry, Inst. of Psychiatry, Univ. of London 1970-74; Prof. of Psychiatry, Univ. of Edin. 1974-, Dean of Faculty of Medicine 1986-; mem. WHO Expert Advisory Panel on Mental Health 1979-; Chair. WHO

Expert Cttee. on Problems related to Alcohol Consumption 1979; mem. MRC 1984-88; H.B. Williams Travelling Prof. of Royal Australian and N.Z. Coll. of Psychiatrists 1981; Gaskell Gold Medal, Royal Coll. of Physicians 1967; Paul Hoch Medal of the American Psychopathological Asscn. 1988. *Publications:* The Classification of Depressive Illnesses 1968, Psychiatric Diagnosis in New York and London 1972, The Role of Diagnosis in Psychiatry 1975, Companion to Psychiatric Studies (Ed.) 1983, 1988. *Leisure interests:* over-eating, walking up hills. *Address:* University Department of Psychiatry, Royal Edinburgh Hospital, Edinburgh, EH10 5HF; 3 West Castle Road, Edinburgh, EH10 5AT, Scotland (Home). *Telephone:* (031) 447 2011; (031) 229 4966 (Home).

KENDREW, Sir John Cowdery, Kt., C.B.E., SC.D., F.R.S.; British molecular biophysicist; b. 24 March 1917, Oxford; s. of late W. G. Kendrew and of Evelyn May Graham Sandberg; ed. Dragon School, Oxford, Clifton Coll. and Trinity Coll., Cambridge; Ministry of Aircraft Production 1940-45; Fellow of Peterhouse, Cambridge 1947-75; Medical Research Council 1947-74, Deputy Chair. Medical Research Council Laboratory of Molecular Biology, Cambridge 1953-74; Reader, Davy-Faraday Lab., Royal Inst. 1954-68; Mem. Council for Scientific Policy 1965-72, Deputy Chair. 1970-72; Sec.-Gen. European Molecular Biology Conf. 1970-74; Editor-in-Chief Journal of Molecular Biology 1959-87; Dir.-Gen. European Molecular Biology Lab., Heidelberg 1975-82; Pres. British Asscn. for the Advancement of Science 1974; Sec.-Gen. Int. Council of Scientific Unions 1974-80, Vice-Pres. 1982, Pres. 1983-88, Pres. Emer. 1988-; mem. Council UN Univ. 1980-86, Chair. Council 1982-84; Pres. St. John's Coll., Oxford 1981-87; Chair. Bd. of Govs., Jt. Research Centre, EEC 1985-; Trustee, British Museum 1974-79; Foreign Assoc. U.S. Nat. Acad. of Sciences 1972; Hon. mem. American Acad. of Arts and Sciences 1964, Leopoldina Acad. 1965, Max-Planck-Gesellschaft 1969, Heidelberg Acad. of Sciences 1978, Bulgarian Acad. of Sciences 1979, Royal Irish Acad. 1981; Hon. Fellow, Trinity Coll., Cambridge 1972, Peterhouse, Cambridge 1975; Hon. Prof. Univ. of Heidelberg 1982; Hon. D.Sc. (Keele, Reading, Exeter and Buckingham); D.Univ. (Stirling) 1974; Dr. h.c. (Pécs, Hungary); Nobel Prize for Chem. 1962; Royal Medal, Royal Soc. 1965; Order of the Madara Horsemen (Bulgaria) 1980. *Publication:* The Thread of Life 1966. *Address:* The President's Lodgings, St. John's College, Oxford, OX1 3JP; 4 Church Lane, Linton, Cambridge, CB1 6JX, England.

KENEALLY, Thomas Michael, A.O., F.R.S.L.; Australian author; b. 7 Oct. 1935, Sydney; s. of Edmund Thomas and Elsie Margaret Keneally; m. Judith Mary Martin 1965; two d.; Lecturer in Drama, Univ. of New England, Armidale, N.S.W. 1968-70; Pres. Nat. Book Council of Australia; mem. Australia-China Council; Royal Soc. of Literature Prize, Booker Prize 1982 (for Schindler's Ark), Los Angeles Times Fiction Prize 1983. *Publications:* Bring Larks and Heroes 1967, Three Cheers for the Paraclete 1968, The Survivor 1969, A Dutiful Daughter 1970, The Chant of Jimmie Blacksmith 1972, Blood Red, Sister Rose 1974; Gossip from the Forest 1975, Season in Purgatory 1976, A Victim of the Aurora 1977, Passenger 1978, Confederates 1979, Schindler's Ark 1982, Outback 1983, The Cut-Rate Kingdom 1984, A Family Madness 1985, Australia: Beyond the Dreamtime (contrib.) 1987, The Playmaker 1987, Asmara, Asmara 1989. *Leisure interests:* swimming, hiking. *Address:* Tessa Sayle Agency, 11 Jubilee Place, London, SW3 3TE, England.

KENGO WA DONDO, LL.D.; Zaire lawyer, diplomatist and politician; b. 1935; fmr. Procurator-Gen. and Pres. of Judicial Council of Zaire; Minister of Justice 1979-80; Amb. to Belgium 1980-82; First State Commr. 1982-86, Nov. 1988-; State Comm. for Foreign Affairs 1986-87. *Address:* c/o Office of First State Commissioner, Kinshasa, Zaire.

KENILOREA, Rt. Hon. Sir Peter, DIP. ED.; Solomon Islands politician; b. 23 May 1943, Takataka, Malaita; m. Margaret Kwanairara 1971; two s. two d.; ed. Teachers' Coll. in New Zealand; Schoolmaster, King George VI Secondary School 1968-70; Asst. Sec. Finance 1971; Admin. Officer, district admin. 1971-73; Lands Officer 1973-74; Deputy Sec. to Cabinet and to Chief Minister 1974-75; District Commr., Eastern Solomons 1975-76; mem. Legis. Assembly 1976-78; M.P. for East Are Are 1976-; Chief Minister of the Solomon Islands 1976-78; Prime Minister of Solomon Islands 1978-81, 1985-86; Deputy Prime Minister 1986-89, Minister of Foreign Affairs 1988-89; mem. Nat. Parl. 1976-; Queen's Silver Jubilee Medal 1977. *Publications:* numerous articles for political and scientific publications. *Leisure interests:* reading, sports. *Address:* c/o Office of the Deputy Prime Minister, Honiara, Guadalcanal, Solomon Islands.

KENNAN, George Frost, A.B.; American diplomatist and scholar; b. 16 Feb. 1904, Milwaukee, Wis.; m. Annelise Sørensen 1931; one s. three d.; ed. Princeton Univ.; Vice-Consul Hamburg 1927, Tallin 1928; Third Sec. Riga, Kovno and Tallin 1929; Language Officer, Berlin 1929; Third Sec. Riga 1931, Moscow 1934; Consul Vienna 1935, Second Sec. 1935; Second Sec. Moscow 1935; Dept. of State 1937; Second Sec. Prague 1938, Consul 1939; Second Sec. Berlin 1939, First Sec. 1940; Counsellor, Lisbon 1942; Counsellor to U.S. del. European Advisory Comm. London 1944; Minister-Counsellor Moscow 1945; Deputy for Foreign Affairs, Nat. War Coll. Washington 1946; Policy Planning Staff, Dept. of State 1947; Chief, Policy Planning Staff, Dept. of State 1949-50; on leave, at Inst. for Advanced Study, Princeton, N.J. 1950-51, Prof. 1956; Amb. to U.S.S.R. 1952-53; retd. from Foreign Service 1953; Charles R. Walgreen Foundation Lecturer, Univ. of Chicago 1951; Stafford Little Lecturer, Princeton 1954; George Eastman Visiting Prof. Oxford Univ. 1957–58; Reith Lecturer on Russia, The Atom and the West 1957; Visiting Lecturer, History, Harvard Univ. 1960, Yale Univ. 1960; Amb. to Yugoslavia 1961–63; Prof. Inst. for Advanced Study, Princeton 1963–74, Prof. Emer. 1974–; Prof. Princeton Univ. 1964–66; mem. Nat. Inst. of Arts and Letters (Pres 1965–68); American Acad. of Arts and Letters (Pres 1967–71); Univ. Fellow in History and Slavic Civilizations; Harvard Univ. 1966–70; Fellow, All Souls Coll., Oxford 1969; Fellow, Woodrow Wilson Int. Center for Scholars, Smithsonian Inst. 1974–75; Nat. Book Award, Bancroft Prize, Pulitzer Prize history 1956, biography 1968, Francis Parkman Prize; LL.D. h.c. (Yale, Dartmouth, Colgate, Notre Dame, Kenyon, Princeton, Michigan, Northwestern, Brandeis, Denison, Harvard, Rutgers, Wisconsin Univs., Lake Forest, Clark, Oberlin, Brown, William & Mary Coll., Columbia, New York), Hon. D.C.L. (Oxford) 1969; Hon. degrees (Univ. of Helsinki) 1986, (Ricler Coll.) 1988; Benjamin Franklin Fellow of the Royal Soc. of Arts, London 1968; Albert Einstein Peace Prize 1981; Grenville Clarke Prize 1981; Peace Prize of the W. German Book Trade 1982, Union Medal, Union Theological Seminary 1982, American Acad. and Inst. of Arts and Letters Gold Medal for History 1984, Freedom from Fear Medal, Franklin D. Roosevelt Foundation, Physicians for Social Responsibility Annual Award 1988, Toynbee Award 1988. *Publications:* American Diplomacy 1900–1950 1952, Das Amerikanisch-Russische Verhältnis 1954, Realities of American Foreign Policy 1954, Soviet-American Relations 1917–1920, Vol. I, Russia Leaves the War 1956, Vol. II, The Decision to Intervene 1958, Russia, The Atom and the West (Reith Lectures) 1958, Soviet Foreign Policy 1917–45 1960, Russia and the West under Lenin and Stalin 1961, On Dealing with the Communist World 1963, Memoirs 1925–1950 1967, Democracy and the Student Left 1968, From Prague After Munich: Diplomatic Papers 1938–1940 1968, The Marquis de Custine and his "Russia in 1839" 1971, Memoirs 1950–1963 1972, The Cloud of Danger 1977, The Decline of Bismarck's European Order: Franco-Russian Relations 1875–1890 1979, The Nuclear Delusion: Soviet-American Relations in the Atomic Age 1982, The Fateful Alliance 1984, Sketches from a Life's Journey 1988. *Address:* The Institute for Advanced Study, Princeton, N.J. 08540, U.S.A.

KENNARD, Olga, SC.D., F.R.S., O.B.E.; British research scientist; b. 23 March 1924, Budapest, Hungary; d. of Joir Weisz and Catherina Weisz; m. David Kennard 1948 (divorced 1961); two d.; ed. schools in Hungary, Prince Henry VIII Grammar School, Evesham and Newnham Coll. Cambridge; Research Asst. Cavendish Lab. Cambridge 1944–48; MRC Scientific Staff, London 1948–61; MRC External Scientific Staff, Univ. of Cambridge 1961–; Dir. Cambridge Crystallographic Data Centre 1965–; Head, Crystallographic Chemistry, Univ. Chemical Lab., Cambridge; MRC Special Appt. 1969–; Royal Soc. Chem. Prize for Structural Chem. 1980. *Publications:* about 200 papers in scientific journals and books on X-ray crystallography, molecular biology, information technology; 20 scientific reference books. *Leisure interests:* swimming, music, modern architecture and design. *Address:* University Chemical Laboratory, Lensfield Road, Cambridge, CB2 1EW, England. *Telephone:* (0223) 336408.

KENNEDY, Anthony M., LL.B.; American judge; b. 23 July 1936, Sacramento; s. of Anthony J. Kennedy and Gladys Kennedy; m. Mary Davis; three s.; ed. Stanford and Harvard Univs. and London School of Econs. and Political Science; mem. Calif. Bar 1962, U.S. Tax Court Bar 1971; Assoc. Thelen Marvin John & Bridges, San Francisco 1962–67; partner, Evans, Jackson & Kennedy (law firm) 1967–75; Prof. of Constitutional Law, McGeorge School of Law, Univ. of Pacific 1965–; Judge, U.S. Court of Appeals, 9th Circuit, Sacramento 1976–88; Judge Supreme Court of U.S.A. Jan. 1988–. *Address:* Supreme Court Building, 1 First Street, N.E., Washington, D.C. 20543, U.S.A.

KENNEDY, David Matthew, A.B., M.A., LL.B.; American banker; b. 21 July 1905, Randolf, Utah; s. of George Kennedy and Katherine Johnson; m. Lenora Bingham 1925; four d.; ed. Weber Coll., George Washington Univ., and Stonier Graduate School of Banking, Rutgers Univ.; Special Asst. to Chair. Bd., Fed. Reserve System 1930–46; Vice-Pres. in charge Bond Dept. Continental Ill. Nat. Bank and Trust Co. of Chicago 1946–53, Pres. 1956–59, Chair. of Bd. and C.E.O. 1959–69; Asst. to Sec. of Treasury, Washington 1953–55; Sec. of U.S. Treasury 1969–71; Amb.-at-Large dealing with int. finance 1970–71; Amb. to NATO 1971–73; U.S. Gov. IBRD, IMF, Inter-American Bank, Asian Devt. Bank 1969–71; Special Rep. of First Pres., The Church of Jesus Christ of Latter-day Saints; Chair. Pres.'s Comm. on Budgetary Concepts, Joint Comm. on the Coinage, Nat. Advisory Council for Int. Monetary and Fiscal Policies, Exec. Bd. Comm. for Econ. and Cultural Devt. of Chicago; fmr. Dir. Abbott Laboratories, Int. Harvester Co., Commonwealth Edison Co., Pullman Co., Swift and Co., Radio New York Worldwide Communications Satellite Corpn., United States Gypsum Co.; mem. Fed. Advisory Comm. on Econ. Assets, Nat. Public Advisory Comm. for Regional Econ. Devt.; Fed. Advisory Council, Fed. Reserve Bd.; Trustee, Univ. of Chicago, Presbyterian-St. Luke's Hosp., Equitable of Iowa, Brookings Inst., George Washington Univ.; Republican. *Leisure interests:* riding, hunting, fishing. *Address:* 3793 Parkview Drive, Salt Lake City, Utah 84124, U.S.A.

KENNEDY, Donald, M.A., PH.D.; American academic; b. 18 Aug. 1931, New York; s. of William D. and Barbara Kennedy; m. Barbara J. Dewey 1953;

two d.; ed. Harvard Univ.; Asst. Prof. Syracuse Univ. 1956–59, Assoc. Prof. 1959–60; Asst. Prof. Stanford Univ. 1960–62, Assoc. Prof. 1962–65, Prof. 1965–77, Chair. Dept. of Biological Sciences 1965–72, Benjamin Crocker Prof. of Human Biology 1974–77, Vice-Pres. and Provost 1979–80, Pres. 1980–; Sr. Consultant, Office of Science and Tech. Policy, Exec. Office of the Pres. 1976–77; Commr. of Food and Drug Admin. 1977–79; Fellow, American Acad. of Arts and Sciences; mem. N.A.S.; Dinkelspiel Award 1976; Hon. D.Sc. (Columbia Univ., Williams Coll., Michigan, Rochester, Ariz.). *Publications:* The Biology of Organisms (with W. M. Telfer) 1965; over 60 articles in scientific journals. *Leisure interests:* skiing, fly fishing. natural history. *Address:* Stanford University, Stanford, Calif. 94305, U.S.A.

KENNEDY, Eamon, M.A., PH.D.; Irish diplomatist; b. 13 Dec. 1921, Dublin; s. of Luke W. and Ellen (née Stafford) Kennedy; m. Barbara J. Black 1960; one s. one d.; ed. O'Connell School, Dublin, Univ. Coll. Nat. Univ. of Ireland, Dublin and the Sorbonne, Paris; Third Sec., Dept. of Foreign Affairs, Dublin 1943; Consul, New York 1947; Second Sec., Canada 1947–49; First Sec., Washington 1949–50, Paris 1950–54; First Sec. and Acting Chief of Protocol, Dept. of Foreign Affairs 1954–56; Counsellor, Irish Mission to UN 1956–61; Irish del. to UN Gen. Assembly 1956–60; Amb. to Nigeria 1961–64, to Fed. Repub. of Germany 1964–70, to France 1970–74; Perm. Rep. to OECD, Perm. del. to UNESCO 1970–74; Perm. Rep. to UN 1974–78; Amb. to U.K. 1978–83, to Italy (also accred. to Turkey and Libya) 1983–86; Special Adviser, with rank of Amb., Perm. Mission of Ireland to the UN 1987–; Grosses Bundesverdienstkreuz mit Stern, Grand Croix de Mérite de la Répub. Française. *Leisure interests:* golf, languages, theatre, music. *Address:* The Rivergate, 401 East 34th Street, Apartment 533A, New York, N.Y. 10016, U.S.A.

KENNEDY, Edward Moore, A.B., LL.B.; American lawyer and politician; b. 22 Feb. 1932, Boston, Mass.; s. of late Joseph Kennedy and of Rose Kennedy; brother of late Pres. John F. Kennedy; m. Virginia Joan Bennett 1958; two s. one d.; ed. Milton Acad., Harvard Coll. and Univ. of Virginia Law School; U.S. Army, Infantry, Private 1st Class 1951–53; Reporter, Int. News Service, N. Africa 1956; Man. Western States, John F. Kennedy Presidential Campaign 1960; fmr. Asst. District Attorney, Mass.; U.S. Senator from Massachusetts 1963–; Asst. Majority Leader, U.S. Senate 1969–71; Chair. Senate Judiciary Comm. 1979–81, ranking Democrat Labour and Human Resources Cttee. 1981–86; Pres. Joseph P. Kennedy Jr. Foundation 1961–; Trustee, Boston Univ., Boston Symphony, John F. Kennedy Library, Lahey Clinic, Boston, John F. Kennedy Center for the Performing Arts, Robert F. Kennedy Memorial Foundation; Bd. mem. Fletcher School of Law and Diplomacy, Mass. Gen. Hospital; mem. Bd. Advisers, Dunbarton Oaks Research Library and Collections; numerous hon. degrees; Order of the Phoenix (Greece) 1976; Harvard Univ. John F. Kennedy School of Govt. Medal 1986; Democrat. *Publications:* Decisions for a Decade 1968, In Critical Condition 1972, Our Day and Generation 1979, Freeze: how you can help prevent nuclear war (with Senator Mark Hatfield, q.v.) 1982. *Address:* Senate Office Building, Washington, D.C. 20510, U.S.A.

KENNEDY, Eugene Patrick, B.SC., PH.D.; American professor of biological chemistry; b. 4 Sept. 1919, Chicago; s. of Michael and Catherine Frawley Kennedy; m. Adelaide Majewski 1943; three d.; ed. De Paul Univ. and Univ. of Chicago; Asst. Prof., Ben May Lab., Univ. of Chicago 1952–55, Assoc. Prof. 1955–56, Prof. of Biological Chem. 1956–60; Prof. and Head, Dept. of Biological Chem., Harvard Medical School 1960–65, Hamilton Kuhn Prof. of Biological Chem., Harvard Medical School 1960–; Assoc. Ed. Journal of Biological Chemistry 1969; Pres. American Soc. of Biol. Chemists 1970–71; mem. N.A.S., American Acad. of Arts and Sciences; Hon. D.Sc. (Chicago) 1977; Glycerine Research Award 1956; Paul-Lewis Award, American Chem. Soc. 1959; Lipid Chem. Award of the American Oil Chemists Soc. 1970, Josiah Macy, Jr. Foundation Faculty Scholar Award 1974, Gairdner Foundation Award 1976, George Ledlie Prize (Harvard) 1976, Sr. U.S. Scientist Award, Alexander von Humboldt Foundation 1983, Passano Award 1986, Heinrich Wieland Prize 1986. *Address:* Harvard Medical School, 25 Shattuck Street, Boston, Mass. 02115, U.S.A.

KENNEDY, George Danner, B.A.; American business executive; b. 30 May 1926, Pittsburgh, Pa.; s. of Thomas Reed and Lois (Smith) Kennedy; m. Valerie Putis 1972; three s. two d.; ed. Williams Coll.; Scott Paper Co. 1947–52; Champion Paper Co. 1952–65; Pres. Brown Co. 1965–71; Exec. Vice-Pres., Int. Minerals & Chemical Corpn. 1971–78, Dir. 1975–, Pres. 1978–86, C.E.O. 1983–, Chair. of Bd. 1986–; Dir. SCM Corpn. 1978–82; Dir. Brunswick Corpn. 1979–; Dir., Exec. Cttee., Kemper Group and Foundation 1982–; Dir. Ill. Tool Works 1988–; Bd. Chair. Children's Memorial Hosp., Chicago; Vice-Pres., Dir. N.E. Ill. Boy Scout Council; Trustee Nat. Comm. Against Drunk Driving. *Address:* 2315 Sanders Road, Northbrook, Ill. 60062, U.S.A. (Office).

KENNEDY, Jacqueline Lee Bouvier (see Onassis, Mrs. Jacqueline).

KENNEDY, John Stodart, D.SC., F.R.S.; British research entomologist; b. 19 May 1912, Pa., U.S.A.; s. of James J. S. and Edith R. (née Lammers) Kennedy; m. 1st Dorothy V. Bartholomew 1936 (divorced 1946), 2nd Claude J. Bloch (née Raphael) 1950; two s. one d.; one step s.; ed. Westminster School and Univ. Coll., London; locust investigator, Imperial Inst. of

Entomology, Univ. of Birmingham and Anglo-Egyptian Sudan 1934-37; Research Fellow, Rockefeller Foundation, Tirana, Albania 1938-39; Research Officer, Wellcome Foundation, Esher 1939-42; Research Officer, Middle East Anti-Locust Unit (Colonial Office), Iran, India, Arabia, E. Africa 1942-44; Chemical Defence Experimental Station, Porton 1944-45; mem. Agric. Research Council Unit. of Insect Physiology, Univ. of Cambridge 1946-67; Deputy Chief Scientific Officer, Agric. Research Council and Prof. of Animal Behaviour, Imperial Coll., London 1967-77, Prof. Emer. 1977-; Pres. Royal Entomological Soc. 1967-69; Sr. Research Fellow, Imperial Coll. 1977-83; Research Assoc. Dept. of Zoology, Univ. of Oxford 1983-; Fellow, Univ. Coll. London 1965, Univ. Coll., Cambridge 1965, Imperial Coll., London 1982; Gold Medal, Linnean Soc. 1984, Wigglesworth Medal, Royal Entomological Soc. 1985. *Publications:* numerous research papers, reviews and essays on locusts, moths, mosquitos, aphids and behavioural theory. *Leisure interests:* interior design. *Address:* Department of Zoology, South Parks Road, Oxford, OX1 3PS (Office); 17 Winchester Road, Oxford, OX2 6NA, England. *Telephone:* (0865) 54484 (Home).

KENNEDY, Ludovic Henry Coverley, M.A.; British writer and broadcaster; b. 3 Nov. 1919, Edinburgh; s. of late Capt. E. C. Kennedy, R.N., and of Rosalind Kennedy; m. Moira Shearer King 1950; one s. three d.; ed. Eton Coll., Christ Church, Oxford; served in Navy 1939-46 (attained rank of Lieut.); Private Sec. and A.D.C. to Gov. of Newfoundland 1943-44; Librarian, Ashridge (Adult Educ.) Coll. 1949; Editor, feature, First Reading (BBC Third Programme) 1953-54; Lecturer for British Council, Sweden, Finland, Denmark 1955, Belgium, Luxembourg 1956; Contested Rochdale by-election 1958, gen. election 1959 as Liberal candidate; Pres. Nat. League of Young Liberals 1959-61, mem. Liberal Party Council 1965-67; TV and radio: Introduced Profile, ATV 1955-56; Newscaster, ITV 1956-58; Introducer On Stage, Associated Rediffusion 1957, This Week, Associated Rediffusion 1958-59; Chair. BBC features: Your Verdict 1962, Your Witness 1967-70; commentator BBC's Panorama 1960-63, Television Reports Int. (also producer) 1963-64; Introducer BBC's Time Out 1964-65, World at One 1965-66; Presenter Liberal Party's Gen. Election TV Broadcasts 1966, The Middle Years, ABC 1967, The Nature of Prejudice, ATV 1968, Face The Press, Tyne-Tees 1968-69, 1970-72, Against the Tide, Yorkshire TV 1969, Living and Growing, Grampian TV 1969-70, 24 Hours, BBC 1969-72, Ad Lib, BBC 1970-72, Midweek, BBC 1973-75, Newsday, BBC 1975-76, interviewer Tonight, BBC 1976-80, A Life with Crime BBC 1979, presenter Lord Mountbatten Remembers 1980, Change of Direction 1980, Did You See BBC 1980-, Great Railway Journeys of the World BBC 1980, Chair. Indelible Evidence BBC 1987; mem. Council Navy Records Soc. 1957-70; Pres. Sir Walter Scott Club, Edinburgh 1968-69; Chair. Royal Lyceum Theatre Co. of Edinburgh 1977-84; F.R.S.A. 1974-76; Voltaire Memorial Lecturer 1985; Hon. D.L. (Strathclyde) 1985; Cross First Class, Order of Merit (Fed. Repub. of Germany); Richard Dimbleby Award (BAFTA) 1989. *Films include:* The Sleeping Ballerina, The Singers and the Songs, Scapa Flow, Battleship Bismarck, Life and Death of the Scharnhorst, U-Boat War, Target Tirpitz, The Rise of the Red Navy, Lord Haw-Haw, Who Killed the Lindbergh Baby?, Elizabeth: The First Thirty Years. *Publications:* Sub-Lieutenant 1942, Nelson's Band of Brothers 1951, One Man's Meat 1953, Murder Story 1956, Ten Rillington Place 1961, The Trial of Stephen Ward 1964, Very Lovely People 1969, Pursuit: the Chase and Sinking of the Bismarck 1974, A Presumption of Innocence: the Amazing Case of Patrick Meehan 1975, The Portland Spy Case 1978, Wicked Beyond Belief: The Luton Post Office Murder Case 1980, A Book of Railway Journeys 1980, A Book of Sea Journeys 1981, A Book of Air Journeys 1982; Gen. Ed. The British at War 1973-, Menace; The Life and Death of the Tirpitz 1979, The Airman and the Carpenter; The Lindberg Case and the Framing of Richard Hauptmann 1985, On My Way to the Club (autobiog.) 1989. *Address:* c/o Royal Bank of Scotland, 8 Burlington Gardens, London, W1, England.

KENNEDY, Michael, O.B.E., M.A., F.R.N.C.M.; British journalist and critic; b. 19 Feb. 1926, Manchester; s. of Hew G. and Marian F. Kennedy; m. Eslyn Durdle 1947; no c.; ed. Berkhamsted School; staff music critic, The Daily Telegraph 1950-, Northern Ed. 1960-86, Assoc., Northern Ed. 1986-. *Publications:* The Hallé Tradition 1960, The Works of Ralph Vaughan Williams 1964, Portrait of Elgar 1968, History of Royal Manchester College of Music 1971, Barbirolli 1971, Portrait of Manchester 1971, Mahler 1974, Strauss 1976, Britten 1980, Concise Oxford Dictionary of Music (Ed.) 1980, Oxford Dictionary of Music 1985, Adrian Boult 1987, Portrait of Walton 1989. *Leisure interest:* cricket. *Address:* 3 Moorwood Drive, Sale, Cheshire, England. *Telephone:* 061-973-7225.

KENNEDY, Nigel; British violinist; b. 28 Dec. 1956; s. of John Kennedy and Scylla Stoner; ed. Yehudi Menuhin School, Juillard School of Performing Arts; chosen by the BBC as the subject of a five-year documentary on the devt. of a soloist following his début with the Philharmonia Orchestra 1977; has since appeared with all the maj. British orchestras; has made appearances at all the leading U.K. festivals and in Europe at Stresa, Lucerne, Gstaad, Berlin and Lockenhaus; début at the Tanglewood Festival with the Boston Symphony under André Previn 1985, at Minn. with Sir Neville Marriner, at Montreal with Charles Dutoit; has given concerts in the field of jazz with Stephane Grappelli at Carnegie Hall and Edin. and runs his own jazz group; recordings include the Elgar Sonata with Peter Pettinger (Chandos Records) and the Elgar Concerto with the London

Philharmonic Orchestra (EMI/Eminence); for his recording of the Elgar Concerto he received the Record of the Year nomination by Gramophone Magazine Feb. 1985 and received the Best Classical Disc of the Year award, London 1985. *Address:* c/o Terry Harrison Artists Management, 9A Penzance Place, London, W11 4PE, England. *Telephone:* 01-229 9166.

KENNEDY, Paul Michael, M.A., D.PHIL., F.R.HIST.S.; British historian; b. 1 June 1945, Wallsend; s. of John Patrick Kennedy and Margaret (née Hennessy) Kennedy; m. Catherine Urwin 1967; three s.; ed. St. Cuthbert's Grammar School, Newcastle upon Tyne, Univ. of Newcastle and Oxford Univ.; Research Asst. to Sir Basil Liddell Hart 1966-70; lecturer, Reader and Prof., Univ. of E. Anglia 1970-83; J. Richardson Dilworth Prof. of History, Yale Univ. 1983-; Visiting Fellow, Inst. for Advanced Study, Princeton 1978-79; Fellow, Alexander von Humboldt Foundation. *Publications:* The Samoan Triangle 1974, The Rise and Fall of British Naval Mastery 1976, The Rise of the Anglo-German Antagonism 1980, The Realities Behind Diplomacy 1981, Strategy and Diplomacy 1983, The Rise and Fall of the Great Powers 1988. *Leisure interests:* jogging, soccer, hill walking, old churches. *Address:* Department of History, Yale Univ., P.O. Box 1504 A, Yale Station, New Haven, Connecticut 06520, U.S.A.; 26 Underhill Road, Hamden, Conn. 06517. *Telephone:* (203) 432 1366 (Office).

KENNEDY, William Joseph, B.A.; American author and professor of English; b. 16 Jan. 1928, Albany, New York; s. of William J. Kennedy and Mary E. McDonald; m. Ana Segarra 1957; one s. two d.; ed. Siena Coll. Asst. Sports Ed., columnist, Glens Falls Post Star, New York 1949-50, reporter, Albany Times-Union, New York 1952-56, special writer 1963-70, Asst. Man. Ed., columnist, P.R. World Journal, San Juan 1956; reporter, Miami Herald 1957; corresp. Time-Life Publs., Puerto Rico 1957-59, reporter, Knight Newspapers 1957-59; Founding Man. Ed. San Juan Star 1959-61; lecturer, State Univ. of New York, Albany 1974-82, Prof. of English 1983-; Visiting Prof. Cornell Univ. 1982-83; founder, N.Y. State Writers' Inst. 1983; Nat. Endowment for Arts Fellow 1981, MacArthur Foundation Fellow 1983, Gov. of New York Arts Award 1984, Creative Arts Award, Brandeis Univ. 1986; Pulitzer Prize and Nat. Book Critics Circle Award 1984 for Ironweed; several hon. degrees. *Publications include:* The Ink Truck 1969, Legs 1975, Billy Phelan's Greatest Game 1978, Ironweed 1983, Quinn's Book 1988; film scripts, The Cotton Club 1984, Ironweed 1987; also short stories, articles in professional journals. *Address:* State University of New York, Department of English, State University Plaza, Albany, N.Y. 12246, U.S.A.

KENNET, (2nd Baron) cr. 1935, of the Dene; **Wayland Young,** F.R.I.B.A.; British writer and politician; b. 2 Aug. 1923, London; s. of Edward Hilton Young (Lord Kennet) and Kathleen Bruce; m. Elizabeth Ann Adams 1948; one s. five d.; ed. Stowe School, Trinity Coll., Cambridge; Royal Navy 1942-45; Foreign Office 1946-47, 1949-51; mem. Parl. Assembly Council of Europe and Western European Union 1962-65; Chair. British Cttee for International Co-operation Year 1965; Parl. Sec. Ministry of Housing and Local Govt. 1966-70; Chair. Int. Parl. Confs. on the Environment 1971-78; Chair. Advisory Cttee. on Oil Pollution of the Sea 1970-74, Chair. Council for the Protection of Rural England 1971-72; Opposition Spokesman on Foreign Affairs, House of Lords 1971-74; Dir. Europe Plus Thirty Project 1974-75; mem. European Parl. 1978-79; Chief Whip S.D.P., House of Lords 1981-83, Spokesman on Foreign Affairs and Defence 1981-. *Publications:* The Italian Left 1949, The Deadweight 1952, Now or Never 1953, Old London Churches (with Elizabeth Young) 1956, The Montesi Scandal 1957, Still Alive Tomorrow 1958, Strategy for Survival 1959, The Profumo Affair 1963, Eros Denied 1965, Preservation 1972, The Futures of Europe 1976, The Rebirth of Britain 1982, London's Churches (with Elizabeth Young); Ed. Disarmament and Arms Control 1963-65. *Leisure interests:* sailing, swimming, music. *Address:* House of Lords, London S.W.1, England.

KENNEY, Edward John, M.A., F.B.A.; British professor of Latin; b. 29 Feb. 1924, London; s. of George Kenney and Carlina Elfrida Schwenke; m. Gwyneth Anne Harris; ed. Christ's Hosp. and Trinity Coll. Cambridge; served in Royal Signals, U.K. and India 1943-46; Asst. Lecturer, Univ. of Leeds 1951-52; Research Fellow, Trinity Coll., Cambridge Univ. 1952-53, Fellow of Peterhouse 1953-, Asst. Lecturer in Classics, Cambridge Univ. 1955-60, Lecturer 1960-70, Reader in Latin Literature and Textual Criticism 1970-74, Kennedy Prof. of Latin 1974-82, Emer. Prof. 1982-; Pres. Jt. Asscn. of Classical Teachers 1977-79, Classical Asscn. 1982-83; Treas. and Chair. Council of Almoners, Christ's Hosp. 1984-86; Foreign mem. Royal Netherlands Acad. of Arts and Sciences. *Publications:* P. Ouidi Nasonis Amores, etc. 1961, Lucretius, De Rerum Natura III 1971, The Classical Text 1974, The Cambridge History of Classical Literature, Vol. II, Latin Literature (Ed. and Contrib.) 1982, The Ploughman's Lunch (Moretum) 1984, Ovid's Metamorphoses—Introduction and Notes 1986. *Leisure interests:* cats, books. *Address:* Peterhouse, Cambridge, CB2 1RD, England. *Telephone:* Cambridge 338246.

KENNY, Anthony John Patrick, D.PHIL., F.B.A.; British philosopher and university teacher; b. 16 March 1931, Liverpool; s. of John and Margaret (Jones) Kenny; m. Nancy Caroline Gayley 1966; two s.; ed. Gregorian Univ., Rome, St. Benet's Hall, Oxford; ordained Catholic priest, Rome 1955; Curate, Liverpool 1959-63; returned to lay state 1963; Asst. Lecturer, Univ. of Liverpool 1961-63; Lecturer in Philosophy, Exeter and Trinity

Colls., Oxford 1963–64; Tutor in Philosophy, Balliol Coll, Oxford 1964, Sr. Tutor 1971–72, 1976–77, Master 1978–(89); Warden (desig.) Rhodes House 1989–; Wilde Lecturer in Natural and Comparative Religion, Oxford 1969–72; Joint Gifford Lecturer, Univ. of Edinburgh 1972–73; Stanton Lecturer, Univ. of Cambridge 1980–83; Speaker's Lecturer in Biblical Studies, Oxford Univ. 1980–83; Visiting Prof. Stanford and Rockefeller Univs., Univs. of Chicago, Washington, Michigan, Cornell; Vice-Pres. British Acad. 1986–88; Edited The Oxford Magazine 1972–73; Fellow of Balliol Coll. 1964–78; Hon. D.Litt. (Bristol) 1982, (Denison Univ.) 1986, (Liverpool) 1988; Hon. D.C.L. (Oxford) 1987. *Publications:* Action, Emotion and Will 1963, Responsa Alumnorum of English College, Rome (2 vols.) 1963, Descartes 1968, The Five Ways 1969, Wittgenstein 1973, The Anatomy of the Soul 1974, Will, Freedom and Power 1975, Aristotelian Ethics 1978, Freewill and Responsibility 1978, The God of the Philosophers 1979, Aristotle's Theory of the Will 1979, Aquinas 1980, The Computation of Style 1982, Faith and Reason 1983, Thomas More 1983, The Legacy of Wittgenstein 1984, A Path from Rome 1985, The Logic of Deterrence 1985, The Ivory Tower 1985, Wyclif—Past Master 1985, Wyclif's De Universalibus 1985, Rationalism, Empiricism and Idealism 1986, Wyclif in His Times 1986, The Road to Hillsborough 1986, Reason and Religion (essays) 1987, The Heritage of Wisdom 1987, God and Two Poets 1988. *Address:* Balliol College, Oxford, OX1 3BJ, England. *Telephone:* (0865) 249601.

KENNY, General Sir (Brian) Leslie Graham, K.C.B., C.B.E.; British army officer; b. 18 June 1934; s. of late Brig. James W. Kenny, C.B.E. and Aileen A. G. Swan; m. Diana C. J. Mathew 1958; two s.; ed. Canford School; commissioned into 4th Hussars (later Queen's Royal Irish Hussars) 1954; served British Army of the Rhine (BAOR), Aden, Malaya, Borneo and Cyprus; pilot's course 1961; Ministry of Defence 1966–68; Instructor Staff Coll. 1971–73; C.O. Queen's Royal Irish Hussars, BAOR and UN, Cyprus 1974–76; Col. G.S. 4 Armoured Div. 1977–78; Command, 12 Armoured Brigade (Task Force D) 1979–80; Royal Coll. of Defence Studies 1981; Commdr. 1st Armoured Div. 1982–83; Dir. Army Staff Duties, Ministry of Defence 1983–85; Col. Commandant RAVC Aug. 1983; Col. QRIH July 1985; Command, 1st British Corps 1985–87; C.-in-C. BAOR and Commdr. NATO's Northern Army Group 1987–89; Deputy Supreme Commdr. Europe 1989–. *Leisure interests:* skiing, cricket, tennis, golf, shooting, racing, moving house. *Address:* c/o Lloyds Bank PLC, Camberley, Surrey, England.

KENNY, Douglas T., PH.D.; Canadian professor of psychology and fmr. university administrator; b. 20 Oct. 1923, Victoria, B.C.; s. of late John Ernest Kenny and Margaret (née Collins) Kenny; m. Margaret Lindsay; one s. one d.; ed. Victoria Coll., B.C., Univ. of British Columbia, Univ. of Washington, Seattle, Wash., U.S.A.; mem. now Prof., Dept. of Psychology, Univ. of British Columbia 1950–, Head of Dept. 1965–69, Acting Dean of Faculty of Arts 1969–70, Dean 1970–75, Pres. and Vice-Chancellor of Univ. July 1975–83; Teacher of Psychology, Univ. of Washington 1947–50, Washington State Univ. 1953, Harvard Univ. 1963–65; mem. Bd. of Trustees Vancouver Gen. Hosp. 1976–78, Canada Council 1975–78, Social Sciences and Research Council 1978–83, Monterey Inst. of Int. Studies, Monterey, Calif. 1980–83, The Discovery Foundation (B.C.) 1979–83; Founding mem., Bd. of Govs., Arts, Sciences and Tech. Centre, Vancouver 1980; Past mem. of Commonwealth Asscn. of Univs., Int. Asscn. of Univ. Pres.; Hon. Patron The Int. Foundation of Learning 1983–; mem. American Psychological Asscn. 1950–; LL.D. h.c. (Univ. of B.C.) 1983; Queen's Silver Jubilee Medal 1977, Park O. Davidson Memorial Award for Outstanding Contribution to Devt. of Psychology 1984. *Publications:* numerous articles and chapters on psychology and educ. in Canada, U.S., and Japan. *Leisure interests:* collecting Chinese and Japanese art, painting. *Address:* University of British Columbia, Vancouver, B.C. V6T 2B3 (Office); 4180 Crown Crescent, Vancouver, B.C. V6R 2A9, Canada (Home). *Telephone:* (604) 228 8762 (Home).

KENNY, Michael, R.A.; British sculptor; b. 10 June 1941, Liverpool; s. of James and Ellen (née Gordon) Kenny; m. 1st Rosemary Flood; m. 2nd Angela Smith 1978; one s. two d.; ed. St. Francis Xavier's Coll., Liverpool, Liverpool Coll. of Art and Slade School of Fine Art, London; Dir. of Fine Art Studies, Goldsmith's Coll., Univ. of London 1983–88; one-man exhbns. in Oxford 1964, Southampton 1965, London 1966, 1969, 1977, 1978, 1979, 1981, 1984, in Manchester 1977, Liverpool, Birmingham, Portsmouth, Glasgow, Newcastle-upon-Tyne 1981, Aberdeen, Brighton 1982, Tokyo 1983, 1985, Duisburg (retrospective), Paris, Harrogate 1984, Frankfurt 1985, Royal Acad. 1986, Hong Kong, Galleria dell' Naviglio, Milan 1987; has participated in numerous group exhbns. in England, Europe, America, Australia and Japan, including Royal Acad. Summer Exhbn. *Leisure interests:* ornithology, cosmology, physics. *Address:* c/o Annely Juda Fine Art, 11 Tottenham Mews, London, W1P 9PJ; 71 Stepney Green, London, E1 9LE, England (Studio). *Telephone:* 01-790 3409 (Studio).

KENT, H.R.H. the Duke of; Prince Edward George Nicholas Paul Patrick, K.G., G.C.M.G., G.C.V.O., A.D.C.; the Earl of St. Andrews and the Baron Downpatrick; b. 9 Oct. 1935; s. of the late Duke of Kent (fourth s. of King George V) and Princess Marina (d. of late Prince Nicholas of Greece); m. Katherine Worsley 1961; two s. (George, Earl of St. Andrews, and Lord Nicholas Windsor) one d. (Lady Helen Windsor); ed. Eton Coll. and Le Rosey, Switzerland; Second Lieut., Royal Scots Greys 1955; attended Army Staff Course 1966, later on staff, G.O.C. Eastern Command,

Hounslow, Major 1967; Lieut.-Col. Royal Scots Dragoon Guards 1972, Maj. Gen. 1983; Ministry of Defence 1972–76; Vice-Chair. British Overseas Trade Bd. 1976–; Pres. Royal Inst. of Great Britain 1976–; Chancellor Univ. of Surrey 1977–; Patron Inst. of Export 1977–; Kent Opera 1978–; Dir. BICC 1980–, Vickers; Pres. Business and Technicians Educ. Council 1984–; as Queen's Special Rep. has visited Sierra Leone 1961, Uganda 1962, The Gambia 1965, Guyana and Barbados 1966, Tonga 1967; A.D.C. to H.M. The Queen 1967; Grand Master of the United Grand Lodge of England June 1967–; Pres. All-England Lawn Tennis Club 1969–; Col.-in-Chief Royal Regt. of Fusiliers 1969–, Devonshire and Dorset Regt. 1978–, Lorne Scots Regt. 1978–; Col. Scots Guards 1974; decorations from Greece, Nepal, Liberia and Jordan; Hon. D.C.L. (Durham), Hon. LL.D. (Leeds), D.Univ. (York). *Leisure interests:* skiing, shooting, photography, opera. *Address:* York House, St. James's Palace, London, S.W.1; Anmer Hall, Norfolk, England.

KENT, Bruce, LL.B.; British campaigner for nuclear disarmament; b. 22 June 1929; s. of Kenneth Kent and Rosemary Kent (née Marion); m. Valerie Flessati 1988; ed. Lower Canada Coll., Montreal, Univ. of Oxford; ordained at Westminster 1958, Curate, Kensington North and South 1958–63; Sec., Archbishop's House, Westminster 1963–64; Chair. Diocesan Schools Comm. 1964–66; Catholic Chaplain to Univ. of London 1966–74; Chaplain, Pax Christi 1974–77; Parish Priest, Somers Town, London 1977–80; resigned from active Ministry 1987; Gen. Sec. Campaign for Nuclear Disarmament (CND) 1980–85, Vice-Chair. 1985–87, Chair. 1987–; Pres. Int. Peace Bureau 1985–; Hon. LL.D. (Manchester) 1987. *Publications:* numerous articles on disarmament, Christianity and peace. *Address:* c/o Campaign for Nuclear Disarmament, 22-24 Underwood Street, London, N1 7JG, England.

KENT, Francis William, PH.D., DIP.ED., F.A.H.A.; Australian university teacher; b. 30 March 1942, Melbourne; m. 1st Dale V. Kent 1964 (divorced 1984); one d.; m. 2nd Carolyn James 1987; ed. Univ. of Melbourne and Univ. of London; lecturer, Sr. Lecturer and Reader in History, Monash Univ. 1971–; Fellow Harvard Univ. at Centre for Italian Renaissance Studies, Florence 1977–78, Visiting Scholar 1982, Visiting Prof. 1986–87; Foundation Co-Ed. I Tatti Studies: Essays in the Renaissance 1982; mem. Nat. Cttee. for an Australian Study Centre in Italy; Socio Straniero Deputazione di Storia Patria per la Toscana. *Publications:* Household and Lineage in Renaissance Florence 1977, A Florentine Patrician and His Palace (with others) 1981, Neighbours and Neighbourhood in Renaissance Florence (with D. V. Kent) 1982, Patronage, Art and Society in Renaissance Italy (ed. with P. Simons) 1987; numerous articles. *Leisure interests:* reading, gardening, travel. *Address:* 42 Broughton Road, Surrey Hills, Vic. 3127, Australia. *Telephone:* 890 6662.

KENT, Geoffrey Charles, C.B.I.M., F.INST.M.; British business executive; b. 2 Feb. 1922, Clevelys; s. of late Percival Whitehead and Madge Kent; m. Brenda G. Conisbee 1955; ed. Blackpool Grammar School; Flight Lieut. in R.A.F. 1939–46; advertising and marketing appts., Colman, Prentis & Varley, Mentor, Johnson & Johnson 1947–58; Advertising Man. John Player & Son 1958, Marketing Dir. 1964, Asst. Man. Dir. 1969, Chair. and Man. Dir. and Dir. Imperial Group 1975; Chair. and Chief Exec. Imperial Group PLC 1981–86; Deputy Chair. and Dir. Corah PLC 1986–; Dir. Team Lotus Int. Ltd. 1974–83; Chair. and Chief Exec. Courage Ltd. 1978–81; Dir. Brewers' Soc. 1978–86, Lloyds Bank PLC 1981–, Lloyds Bank Int. 1983–85, Lloyds Merchant Bank Holdings 1985–87, John Howitt Group Ltd. 1986–; mem. Lloyd's of London 1985–, Dir. and Deputy Chair. Mansfield Brewery PLC 1988, Chair. 1989–. *Leisure interests:* flying, skiing. *Address:* Hill House, Gonalston, Nottingham, NG14 7JA, England (Home). *Telephone:* (0602) 663303 (Home).

KENT, John Philip Cozens, PH.D., F.B.A., F.S.A.; British numismatist; b. 28 Sept. 1928, London; s. of John Cozens Kent, D.C.M. and late Lucy Ella (née Binns) Kent; m. Patricia Eleanor Bunford 1961; one s. one d.; ed. Minchenden County Grammar School and Univ. Coll., London; Asst. Keeper Dept. of Coins and Medals, British Museum 1953–74, Deputy Keeper 1974–83, Keeper 1983–; Pres. British Asscn. of Numismatic Socs. 1974–78, Royal Numismatic Soc. 1984–89, London and Middx. Archaeological Soc. 1985–88; Reginald Taylor Prize, British Archaeological Asscn. 1948; Lhotka Memorial Prize, Royal Numismatic Soc. 1977; mem., Inst. de Sintra 1986. *Publications:* Late Roman Bronze Coinage (with R. A. G. Carson and P. V. Hill) 1960, Wealth of the Roman World (with K. S. Painter) 1977, Roman Coins 1978, 2000 Years of British Coins and Medals 1978, Roman Imperial Coinage Vol. VIII: The Family of Constantine I (337–364) 1981, A Selection of Byzantine Coins in the Barber Inst. of Fine Arts 1985, A Catalogue of Celtic Coins in the British Museum Vol. I (ed. with M. R. Mays) 1987. *Leisure interests:* local history and archaeology, medieval music, railway history. *Address:* 16 Newmans Way, Hadley Wood, Barnet, Herts., EN4 0LR, England.

KENT, Leslie Errol, PH.D., F.R.S.S.A.; South African geologist; b. 7 Aug. 1915, Pietermaritzburg; s. of Samuel James Kent and Rosalie (née Hyde) Kent; m. Maryna Ferreira 1957 (divorced 1969); one s.; ed. Maritzburg Coll., Natal Univ. Coll. (now Univ. of Natal), Rhodes Univ. Coll. (now Rhodes Univ.), Univ. of California and U.S. Bureau of Reclamation; Apptd. Geological Survey of South Africa 1936; S.A. Rep. Int. Union of Geodesy and Geophysics, Oslo 1948, Brussels 1951; mem. Council, Geological Society of S.A. 1955–74, Pres. 1965; Chair. Cttee. of S.A. Antarctic Asscn. 1970;

mem. S.A. Cttee. for Stratigraphy 1971–77, Chair. 1974–77; Pres. Jt. Council, Scientific Socs. of S.A. 1974; mem. summer expeditions to Marion Island 1980, Gough Island 1983, for volcanological and geomorphological research; Hon. mem. Geological Soc. of S.A. 1985–; Schwarz Prize 1934, James Moir Memorial Prize 1935–36. *Publications:* Diatomaceous deposits in the Union of South Africa (with A. W. Rogers) 1947, Geological investigations in Western Dronning Maud Land, Antartica—a synthesis (with L. G. Wolmarans) 1982, Compiled Lithostratigraphy of the Republic of South Africa, South West Africa/Namibia and the Republics of Bophuthatswana, Transkei and Venda (also prin. contrib.) 1980, 60 papers in scientific journals. *Leisure interests:* archaeology, ice skating, mountain climbing, photography, reading, spelaeology, theosophy, travel. *Address:* 44 Toledo, 150 Troye Street, Sunnyside, Pretoria, South Africa. *Telephone:* 44 7895.

KENT, Thomas Worrall, O.C., M.A.; Canadian editor and consultant; b. 3 April 1922, Stafford, England; s. of John T. and Frances (Worrall) Kent; m. Phyllida A. Cross 1944; three s.; ed. Wolstanton Grammar School, Newcastle-under-Lyme and Corpus Christi Coll., Oxford; editorial writer, Manchester Guardian 1946–50; Asst. Ed., The Economist 1950–54; Ed., Winnipeg Free Press 1954–59; Vice-Pres. Chemcell Ltd., Montreal 1959–61; Special Consultant to Leader of Opposition, Ottawa 1961–63; Co-ordinator of Programming, Policy Sec. to Prime Minister and Dir. of Special Planning Secr., Privy Council Office 1963–65; Deputy Minister of Manpower and Immigration 1966–68, of Regional Econ. Expansion 1968–71; Pres. and Chief Exec. Cape Breton Devt. Corpn. 1971–77, Sydney Steel Corpn. 1977–79; Dean, Faculty of Admin. Studies, Dalhousie Univ. 1980–83; Prof. of Public Admin. 1983–; Bd. mem. Pearson Inst. for Int. Devt. 1985–; Chair. Royal Comm. on Newspapers 1980–81; Fellow Inst. for Research on Public Policy, Ed. Policy Options 1980–. *Publications:* Social Policy for Canada 1962, Management for Development 1985, A Public Purpose 1988, Getting Ready for 1999: A Canadian Agenda 1989; numerous articles, papers and speeches on econ. and political subjects. *Leisure interest:* gardening. *Address:* Box 115, Mabou, Nova Scotia, B0E 1X0, Canada. *Telephone:* (902) 945-2181.

KENTRIDGE, Sydney, Q.C., M.A.; British lawyer; b. 5 Nov. 1922, Johannesburg; s. of Morris Kentridge and May Kentridge; m. Felicia Geffen 1952; two s. two d.; ed. King Edward VII School, Johannesburg, Univ. of the Witwatersrand and Exeter Coll., Oxford; war service with S. African forces 1942–46; Advocate, S. Africa 1949; Sr. Counsel 1965; called to Bar, Lincoln's Inn, London 1977; Queen's Counsel, England 1985; Judge, Court of Appeal, Jersey and Guernsey 1988–; Roberts Lecturer, Univ. of Pa. 1979; Hon. LL.D. (Leicester) 1985, (Cape Town) 1987; Hon. Fellow Exeter Coll., Oxford 1986; Granville Clark Prize, U.S.A. 1978. *Leisure interest:* opera. *Address:* 1 Brick Court, Temple, London, E.C.4, England. *Telephone:* 01-583 0777.

KENYON, John Philipps, LITT.D., PH.D., F.B.A.; British professor of modern history; b. 18 June 1927, Sheffield; s. of William Houston Kenyon and Edna Grace (née Philipps) Kenyon; m. Angela Jane Ewert Venables 1962; one s. two d.; ed. King Edward VII School, Sheffield, Univ. of Sheffield, Univ. of Cambridge; Univ. Lecturer, Fellow of Christ's Coll., Cambridge 1955–62; G. F. Grant Prof. of History, Univ. of Hull 1962–81; Prof. of Modern History, Univ. of St. Andrews 1981–87; Joyce and Elizabeth Hall Distinguished Prof. in Early Modern British History, Univ. of Kansas 1987–. *Publications:* Robert Spencer Earl of Sutherland 1958, The Stuart Constitution 1966, Stuart England 1977, The Popish Plot 1972, The History Men 1983. *Leisure interest:* bridge. *Address:* Department of History, University of Kansas, 3001 Wescoe Hall, Laurence, Kansas 66045-2130, U.S.A. *Telephone:* (913) 864-3569.

KEOGH, James; American journalist and government official; b. 29 Oct. 1916, Nebraska; joined Omaha Herald 1938, rising to Ed. 1948–51; contrib. to Time 1951, Ed. 1956–68; chief of research, Presidential election campaign 1968; special asst. to Pres. Nixon 1969–70; Dir. U.S. Information Agency 1973–76; Exec. Dir., Business Roundtable 1976–86. *Publications:* This is Nixon 1956, President Nixon and the Press 1972. *Address:* 200 Park Avenue, New York, N.Y. 10166, U.S.A. (Office).

KEPPEL, Francis, A.B.; American educational administrator; b. 16 April 1916, New York; s. of Frederick and Helen T. Keppel; m. Edith Moulton Sawin 1941; two d.; ed. Harvard Coll., American Acad., Rome; Sec. Joint Army and Navy Cttee. on Welfare and Recreation, Washington 1941–44; U.S. Army 1944–46; Asst. to Provost, Harvard 1946–48, Dean, Harvard Graduate School of Education 1948–62; U.S. Commr. of Educ., U.S. Dept. of Health, Educ. and Welfare 1962–65, Asst. Sec. (for Educ.) 1965–66; Chair. of Bd. Gen. Learning Corpn. 1966–74, Appropriate Tech. Int., Washington 1981–86; Vice-Chair. Lincoln Center Bd. of Dirs. 1983–86; Sr. Fellow, Aspen Inst. for Humanistic Studies 1981–84; Vice-Chair. Bd. of Higher Educ., City Univ. of New York 1967–70; mem. Bd. of Overseers, Harvard Univ. 1967–73; Sr. Lecturer in Educ., Harvard Univ. 1977–; mem. Bd. of Govs., Int. Devt. Research Centre, Ottawa 1980–; Fellow, American Acad. of Arts and Sciences; Trustee Carnegie Corpn. 1970–80; Pres. American Trust for the British Library 1981–. *Publication:* The Necessary Revolution in American Education 1966. *Address:* 984 Memorial Drive, Cambridge, Mass. 02138, U.S.A. *Telephone:* 617-492-1121 (Home).

KÉRÉKOU, Brig.-Gen. Mathieu (Ahmed); Benin army officer and politician; b. 2 Sept. 1933, Natitingou; ed. Saint-Raphael Mil. School, France;

served French Army until 1961; joined Dahomey Army 1961; Aide-de camp to Pres. Maga 1961–63; took part in mil. coup d'état which removed Pres. Christophe Soglo 1967; Chair. Mil. Revolutionary Council 1967–68 continued studies at French mil. schools 1968–70; Commdr. Ouidah Para troop Unit and Deputy Chief of Staff 1970–72; leader of the military coup d'état which ousted Pres. Ahomadegbe Oct. 1972; Pres. and Head of Mil Revolutionary Govt., Minister of Nat. Defence 1972–, fmr. Minister of Planning, of Co-ordination of Foreign Aid, Information and Nat. Orientation; Chair. Cen. Cttee. Parti de la Révolution Populaire du Bénin. *Address:* Présidence de la République, Cotonou, Benin.

KERESZTURY, Dezső, PH.D.; Hungarian literary historian and writer; b. 6 Sept. 1904, Zalaegerszeg; s. of József Keresztury and Etelka Eőry; m. Mária Seiber 1934; ed. Budapest, Vienna and Berlin; Lecturer and librarian in Hungarian Inst. of Berlin Univ. 1928–36; lecturer in Hungarian Literature, Eötvös Coll., Budapest 1935–45, Dir. of Coll. 1945–48; Minister of Educ. 1945–47; Chief Librarian of Hungarian Acad. 1948–51; Head of Historical Collections in Nat. Széchényi Library until 1971; Vice-Pres. World Fed. of Hungarians, and Int. Lenau Soc.; mem. Hungarian Acad. of Sciences; edited selected speeches of Mihály Babits, Géza Laczkó, Károly Pap, the complete works of János Batsányi and János Arany; Banner Order of Hungarian People's Repub. 1974; Grillparzer Ring, Vienna 1974, Herder Prize 1976, State Prize 1978, Ady Prize 1978. *Publications:* Arany János, Ungarn, A német irodalom kincseskháza, Balaton, Helyünk a világban, A magyar irodalom képeskönyve, A magyar zenetörténet képeskönyve, Magyar Opera és Balett Szcenika, A német elbeszélés mesterei, A német lira kincseskháza, Dunántuli hexameterek, Lassul a szél, Emberi Nyelven, Festbeleuchtung auf dem Holzmarkt, S mi vagyok én, Üzenet, Örökség, A Szépség haszna, Egry breviarium, Árnyak Nyomában, Égő türelem; revised and adapted two plays by Imre Madách: Mózes and Csák végnapjai and Grillparzer's Medea; Tragedy: Nehéz méltóság, Poems: Igy éltem, Pásztor. *Leisure interests:* music, walking, water-colour painting. *Address:* Semmelweis utca 4, 1052 Budapest V, Hungary. *Telephone:* 185045.

KERIN, John Charles, B.ECONS.; Australian politician; b. 21 Nov. 1937, Bowral, N.S.W.; s. of late Joseph Sydney and Mary Louise (née Fuller) Kerin; m. 1st Barbara Elizabeth Large 1971, 2nd Dr.J. R. Verrier; one s. three d.; ed. Univ. of New England, Australian Nat. Univ.; Econs. Research Officer in wool marketing, Bureau of Agricultural Econs. 1971, 1975–78; M.P. for Macarthur, House of Reps. 1972–75, for Werriwa Sept. 1978–; Minister for Primary Industry 1983–86, for Primary Industries and Energy July 1987–; Leader, Labor Party Del. to E. Timor 1975; mem. Australian Devt. Assistance Agency Bd. 1975, Commonwealth Scientific and Industrial Research Org. Advisory Council 1980, Industry and Econ. Policy Cttees. of Cabinet and Caucus 1983; Leader Australian Del. to U.S.A. 1986; Australian Labor Party. *Leisure interests:* opera, ballet, bush-walking, tennis, classical music. *Address:* Parliament House, Canberra, A.C.T. 2600 (Office); 18/207 Lagonda Drive, Ingleburn, N.S.W., Australia (Home).

KÉRINEC, Roger, D. EN D.; French retailer and administrator (retd.); b. 10 June 1921, Telgruc-sur-Mer, Finistère; s. of Michel Kérinec and Marie Jolais; m. Gilberte Riou 1946; two s.; ed. Lycée du Havre, Univ. de Paris; Chief-Ed., then Dir. Coopérateur de France periodical 1947–85; apptd. Gen. Sec. Fed. Nat. des coopératives consommateurs 1965–69, Vice-Pres., Gen. Del. 1969–73, Pres. 1973–85; Vice-Pres. Int. Co-operative Alliance 1972–75, Pres. 1975–85; mem. Econ. and Social Council 1969, 1974, 1979; Hon. mem. Conseil Econ. et Social 1984, mem. Comm. de la Concurrence 1977–85; Admin. Banque Nat. de Paris 1981–85; Admin. and Pres. FNAC store 1983–85; Chevalier, Légion d'honneur, Commdr., ordre nat. du Mérite. *Leisure interests:* skiing, sailing, swimming. *Address:* 35 ter, avenue de l'Île de France, 92160 Antony, France (Home).

KERMODE, (John) Frank, M.A., F.B.A., F.R.S.L.; British university professor; b. 29 Nov. 1919, Douglas, Isle of Man; s. of John Pritchard Kermode and Doris Kennedy; m. 1st Maureen Eccles 1947 (divorced), one s. one d.; m. 2nd Anita Van Vactor 1976; ed. Liverpool Univ.; John Edward Taylor Prof., Manchester Univ. 1958–65; Winterstoke Prof., Bristol Univ. 1965–67; Lord Northcliffe Prof., Univ. Coll., London 1967–74; King Edward VII Prof., Cambridge Univ. 1974–82; Julian Clarence Levi Prof., Humanities Dept., Univ. of Columbia New York 1982 and 1984; Charles Eliot Norton Prof. of Poetry, Harvard Univ. 1977–78; Foreign mem. American Acad. Arts and Sciences; Hon. D.H.L. (Chicago); Hon. D.Litt. (Liverpool) 1981, (Amsterdam) 1989; Officier de l'Ordre des Arts et des Sciences. *Publications:* Romantic Image 1957, The Sense of an Ending 1967, Lawrence 1973, The Classic 1975, The Genesis of Secrecy 1979, The Art of Telling 1983, Forms of Attention 1985, History and Value 1988, The Literary Bible (ed. with Robert Alter) 1989. *Leisure interests:* squash, music. *Address:* King's College, Cambridge (Office); 27 Luard Road, Cambridge, CB2 2PJ, England (Home). *Telephone:* (0223) 247398 (Home).

KERN, Karl-Heinz, DIPL.JUR.; German diplomatist; b. 18 Feb. 1930, Dresden; s. of Fritz and Elfriede Kern; m. Ursula Bennmann 1952; one s.; ed. Technical Coll., Dresden and Academy for Political Science and Law; positions in various regional authorities in German Democratic Repub. until 1959; Ministry of Foreign Affairs 1959–, Deputy Head G.D.R. Mission in Ghana 1962–63, Head 1963–66, Head African Dept. 1966–71, Minister and Chargé d'affaires, Trade Mission in U.K. 1971-73; Amb. to U.K. 1973-80; Vaterländischer Verdienstorden in Bronze. *Publications:* various publs. on foreign affairs. *Leisure interests:* sports, reading, music. *Address:* c/o Bundesministerium für Auswärtigen, Berlin, German Democratic Republic.

KERR, Chester Brooks, B.A.; American publisher; b. 5 Aug. 1913, Norwalk, Conn.; s. of Chester M. Kerr and Mary Seymour; m. 2nd Joan Paterson Mills 1964; four s. by previous marriage; ed. La Villa, Lausanne (Switzerland), Univ. School, Cleveland (Ohio) and Yale Univ.; Ed. Harcourt, Brace & Co. 1936-40; Dir. Atlantic Monthly Press 1940-42; Chief Book Div., Office of War Information and Dept. of State 1942-46; Vice-Pres. Reynal & Hitchcock 1946-47; Sec. Yale Univ. Press 1949-59, Dir. 1959-79; Pres. Ticknor and Fields 1979-84; Sec.-Treas. Asscn. of American Univ. Presses 1957-59, Pres. 1965-67; Consultant to Dept. of State 1951, to Ford Foundation 1957-65, to Library of Congress 1976-77; Dir. New Haven Public Library 1954-70; Dir. American Book Publishers' Council 1966-69; Exec. Comm. Nat. Book Cttee. 1968-75; Dir. Franklin Book Program 1971-74; mem. Admin. Bd. Papers of Benjamin Franklin 1954-77; Dir. Assoc. of American Publrs. 1974-78; Dir. Nat. Enquiry 1975-78; Chair. Nat. Cttee. Book-Across-The-Sea, English-Speaking Union. *Publications:* A Report on American University Presses 1949, American University Publishing 1955. *Leisure interest:* skiing. *Address:* Ticknor and Fields, 52 Vanderbilt Avenue, New York, N.Y. 10017 (Office); 421 Humphrey Street, New Haven, Conn. 06520, U.S.A. (Home).

KERR, Clark, PH.D.; American educator; b. 17 May 1911, Reading, Pa.; s. of Samuel W. and Caroline Clark Kerr; m. Catherine Spaulding 1934; two s. one d.; ed. Swarthmore Coll., Stanford Univ., and Univ. of California (Berkeley); Asst. later Assoc. Prof. of Industrial Relations, Univ. of Washington 1940; Assoc. Prof., later Prof. of Industrial Relations, Univ. of Calif. (Berkeley) 1945, Chancellor 1952; Pres. Univ. of Calif. 1958-67, Pres. Emer. 1974; Chair. of Carnegie Comm. on Higher Educ. 1967-73, Chair. Carnegie Council Studies in Higher Educ. 1973-79; Program Director, Strengthening Presidential Leadership Project, Asscn. of Governing Bds. of Univ. and Colls., 1982-85; Godkin Lecturer, Harvard 1963, Marshall Lecturer, Cambridge 1967-68; has held various public posts, mainly in the field of labour relations; mem. American Econ. Asscn., Industrial Relations Research Asscn., Nat. Acad. of Educ., American Acad. of Arts and Sciences; many hon. degrees. *Publications:* Unions, Management, and the Public (with E. W. Bakke) 1948, revised 1960, 1967, Industrialism and Industrial Man (with Dunlop, Harbison and Myers) 1960, The Uses of University 1964, with new Postscripts 1972, 1982, Labour and Management in Industrial Society 1964, Marshall, Marx and Modern Times 1969, Labor Markets and Wage Determination 1977, Education and National Development 1979, The Future of Industrial Societies 1983, The Many Lives of Academic Presidents (with M. L. Gade) 1986, Industrial Relations in a New Age (Co-Ed. with P. D. Staudohar) 1986, Economics of Labor in Industrial Society (Co-Ed. with P. D. Staudohar) 1986. *Leisure interest:* gardening. *Address:* Institute of Industrial Relations, Univ. of California, Berkeley, Calif. 94720 (Office); 8300 Buckingham Drive, El Cerrito, Calif. 94530, U.S.A. (Home). *Telephone:* (415) 642-8106 (Office).

KERR, David Wylie, B.SC., C.A.; Canadian business executive; b. 14 Oct. 1943, Montreal; s. of Dudley Holden and Cecelia K. McGuire; m. Sheryl Drysdale 1969; one s. one d.; ed. Town of Mount-Royal High School and McGill Univ.; Touche Ross & Co. (chartered accountants) 1965-72; Vice-Pres. and Chief Financial Officer, Edper Investments Ltd. 1972-78; C.O.O. Hees Int. Corpn. 1978-85; Exec. Vice-Pres. Brascan Ltd. 1985-87; Pres. Noranda Inc. 1987-. *Leisure interests:* squash, hockey, tennis, golf, skiing. *Address:* P.O. Box 45, Suite 4500, Commerce Court West, Toronto, Ont., M5L 1B6, Canada. *Telephone:* 416-982-7111.

KERR, Deborah Jane; British actress; b. 30 Sept. 1921, Helensburgh, Dunbarton, Scotland; d. of Arthur Kerr Trimmer and Colleen Smale; m. 1st Anthony Bartley 1945 (divorced 1960), two d.; m. 2nd Peter Viertel 1960, one step-d.; ed. Rossholme Prep., Weston-super-Mare, Northumberland House, Bristol; began acting career at Open Air Theatre, Regent's Park 1939; first film Contraband, first major role as Jenny Hill in film Major Barbara; went to Hollywood 1946; film awards include four New York Drama Critics' Awards, 1947 (two), 1957, 1960; Hollywood Foreign Press Asscn. Awards 1956 (for The King and I), 1958; Variety Club of G.B. Award 1961; six Acad. Award Nominations; awards for plays include Donaldson and Sarah Siddons Awards for Tea and Sympathy. *Films include:* Major Barbara 1940, Love on the Dole 1940, Penn of Pennsylvania 1940, Hatter's Castle 1941, The Day Will Dawn 1941, The Life and Death of Colonel Blimp 1942, Perfect Strangers 1944, Black Narcissus 1945, I See a Dark Stranger 1945, The Hucksters 1946, If Winter Comes 1947, Edward My Son 1948, The Prisoner of Zenda 1948, Young Bess 1949, King Solomon's Mines 1950, Quo Vadis 1950, Rage of The Vulture 1951, Dream Wife 1952, From Here to Eternity 1953, The End of the Affair 1954, The Proud and the Profane 1955, The King and I 1956, Heaven Knows Mr. Allison 1957, An Affair to Remember 1957, Separate Tables 1957/58, The Journey 1958, The Blessing 1958, Beloved Infidel 1960, The Sundowners 1960, The Innocents 1961, The Chalk Garden 1963, The Night of the Iguana 1963, Marriage on the Rocks 1965, Gypsy Moths 1968, The Arrangement 1968/69, The Assam Garden 1984, Reunion at Fairborough 1984.

Plays: Heartbreak House 1943, Tea and Sympathy 1953 (U.S. tour 1954/55), The Day After the Fair (U.S. tour 1973/74), Seascape 1974/75, Souvenir 1975, Long Day's Journey Into Night (U.S.) 1977, Candida (London) 1977, The Last of Mrs. Cheyney (U.S. tour 1978), The Day After the Fair (Australian tour 1979), Overheard (London and U.K. tour 1981), The Corn is Green (London) 1985. *Television:* A Song at Twilight 1981, Witness for the Prosecution (TV film) 1982, Ann & Debbie, 1984, A Woman of Substance 1984, Hold the Dream 1986. *Leisure interests:* painting, gardening. *Address:* Wyhergut, 7250 Klosters, Grisons, Switzerland.

KERR, Jean; American writer; b. July 1923, Scranton; d. of Thomas J. Collins and Kitty O'Neill; m. Walter Kerr (q.v.) 1943; five s. one d.; ed. Catholic Univ. of America; mem. Nat. Inst. of Arts and Sciences; Hon. L.H.D. (Northwestern Univ.) 1962, (Fordham Univ.) 1965; Campion Award 1971, Laetare Medal 1971. *Publications:* Jenny Kissed Me (play) 1949, Touch and Go (play) 1950, King of Hearts (with Eleanor Brooke) 1954, Please Don't Eat the Daisies 1957, The Snake Has All the Lines 1960, Mary, Mary (play) 1962, Poor Richard (play) 1963, Penny Candy 1970, Finishing Touches (play) 1973, How I Got to Be Perfect 1978, Lunch Hour (play) 1980. *Address:* 1 Beach Avenue, Larchmont, Manor, New York, N.Y. 10538, U.S.A.

KERR, Rt. Hon. Sir John Robert, A.K., G.C.M.G., G.C.V.O., P.C., LL.B., Q.C.; Australian lawyer and fmr. Governor-General; b. 24 Sept. 1914, Sydney; s. of late H. Kerr; m. 1st Alison Worstead 1938 (died 1974), one s. two d.; m. 2nd Anne Robson 1975; ed. Fort St. Boys' High School, Sydney Univ.; admitted to N.S.W. Bar 1938; war service 1939-46, Col. 1945-46; First Prin., Australian School of Pacific Admin. 1946; Organizing Sec. South Pacific Comm. 1946-47, Acting Sec.-Gen. 1948; returned to Bar 1948; Queen's Counsel (N.S.W.) 1953; mem. N.S.W. Bar Council 1960-64; Vice-Pres. N.S.W. Bar Asscn. 1962-63, Pres. 1964; Vice-Pres. Law Council of Australia 1962-64, Pres. 1964-66; Pres. N.S.W. Marriage Guidance Council 1961-62, Industrial Relations Soc. 1960-63, Industrial Relations Soc. of Australia during formation (pro tem) 1964-66, Law Asscn. for Asia and Western Pacific 1966-70; Deputy Pres. Trades Practices Tribunal 1966-72, Copyright Tribunal 1969-72; presided at Third Commonwealth and Empire Law Conf., Sydney, 1965; mem. Medical Bd. of N.S.W. 1963-66, Bd. of the Council on New Guinea Affairs 1964-71; Judge of Commonwealth Industrial Court and Judge of Supreme Court of A.C.T. 1966-72, Judge of Courts of Marine Inquiry 1967-72; Chief Justice, Supreme Court, N.S.W. 1972-74; Lieut.-Gov. N.S.W. 1973-74; Gov.-Gen. of Australia 1974-77; Hon. Life mem. Law Soc. of England and Wales 1965; Hon. mem. American Bar Asscn. 1967; World Lawyer Award of the World Peace Through Law Conf. in the Philippines 1977; K.St.J. 1974. *Publications:* Matters For Judgment: An Autobiography 1979, papers and articles on industrial relations, New Guinea affairs, organization of legal profession, etc. *Address:* Suite 2404, 56 Pitt Street, Sydney, N.S.W., Australia, 2000.

KERR, Walter, M.A., B.S.; American drama critic; b. 8 July 1913, Evanston, Ill.; s. of Walter Sylvester Kerr and Esther Daugherty; m. Jean Collins (Jean Kerr, q.v.) 1943; five s. one d.; ed. Northwestern Univ.; Assoc. Prof. Catholic Univ. of America 1939-49; Drama Critic The Commonweal 1949-51, New York Herald Tribune 1951-66, New York Times 1966-83; mem. New York Critics Circle (Pres. 1955-57); Hon. LL.D. (St. Mary's, Notre Dame), Hon. D.Litt. (La Salle Univ., Fordham Univ., Notre Dame, Mich. Univ.); Campion Award 1971, Laetare Medal 1971, Award of Nat. Inst. of Arts and Letters 1972, Pulitzer Prize for Criticism 1978, elected to Theater Hall of Fame 1982. *Publications:* Plays: Sing Out Sweet Land 1945, Touch and Go (with Jean Kerr) 1950, Goldilocks (with Jean Kerr) 1958; also How Not To Write A Play 1955, Criticism and Censorship, Pieces at Eight (essays) 1957, The Decline of Pleasure 1962, The Theatre in Spite of Itself 1963, Tragedy and Comedy 1967, Thirty Plays Hath November 1969, God on the Gymnasium Floor 1971, The Silent Clowns 1975, Journey to the Center of the Theatre 1979. *Address:* 1 Beach Avenue, Larchmont Manor, New York, N.Y. 10538, U.S.A. (Home).

KERREY, Bob (J. Robert), B.S.; American politician; b. 27 Aug. 1943, Lincoln, Neb.; s. of James Kerrey and Elinor Kerrey; two c.; ed. Univ. of Nebraska; owner, founder, developer, outlets in Omaha and Lincoln, Grandmother's Skillet Restaurant 1972-75; owner, founder fitness enterprises, including Sun Valley Bowl and Wall-Bankers Racquetball Club and Fitness Center, Lincoln, Neb.; Gov. of Nebraska 1983-87; Partner, Printon, Kane & Co., Lincoln 1987; Senator from Nebraska 1989-; Medal of Honor; Bronze Star; Purple Heart; Democrat. *Address:* United States Senate, Washington, D.C. 20510, U.S.A.

KERRUISH, Sir (Henry) Charles, Kt., O.B.E.; Manx farmer and politician; b. 23 July 1917; Isle of Man; s. of Henry Howard Kerruish and Clara May Kewin; m. 1st Margaret Gell 1944, one s. three d.; m. 2nd Kay Warriner 1975, three step-d.; ed. Ramsey Grammar School; mem. House of Keys, Isle of Man 1946-, Speaker 1962-; fmr. Chair. Health Services Bd., Tynwald, and mem. Gov.'s Exec. Council; Regional Councillor Commonwealth Parl. Asscn. 1975-77, Pres. 1983-84; mem. Court, Liverpool Univ. 1974-; Pres. Manx Loaghtan Sheep Breed Soc.; Capt. Parish of Maughold. *Leisure interests:* horse breeding, motor cycling, reading. *Address:* Ballafayle, Maughold, Isle of Man. *Telephone:* Isle of Man 812293.

KERRY, John Forbes, J.D.; American politician; b. 11 Dec. 1943, Denver; s. of Richard J. and Rosemary (Forbes) Kerry; m. Julia S. Thorne 1970;

two d.; ed. Yale Univ. and Boston Coll.; called to Bar, Mass. 1976; Nat. co-ordinator, Vietnam Veterans Against The War 1969–71; Asst. Dist. Attorney, Middx. County, Mass. 1976–79; Partner, Kerry & Sragow, Boston 1979–82; Lieut Gov. State of Mass. 1983; Senator from Massachussetts 1985–; Democrat. *Publication:* The New Soldier 1971. *Address:* c/o United States Senate, Washington, D.C. 20510, U.S.A.

KERST, Donald William, PH.D., D.SC.; American professor of physics; b. 1 Nov. 1911, Galena, Ill.; s. of Herman Samuel and Lilian (Wetz) Kerst; m. Dorothy Birkett 1940; one s. one d.; ed. Univ. of Wisconsin; Instructor in Physics, Univ. of Ill. 1938, Asst. Prof. 1940, Assoc. Prof. 1942, Prof. 1943; War Work, Los Alamos 1943–45; Tech. Dir. Midwestern Univs. Research Assen. 1953–57; with John Jay Hopkins Lab. for Pure and Applied Science, Atomic Div., Gen. Dynamics Corpn. 1957–62; E. M. Terry Prof. of Physics, Univ. of Wis. 1962–80, Prof. Emer. 1980–; mem. N.A.S., American Physical Soc. (Chair. Plasma Physics Div. 1972); Dr. h.c. (Univ. São Paulo, Brazil), Hon. Dr.Sc. (Lawrence Coll.) 1942, (Univ. Wis.) 1964, (Ill.) 1987; Comstock Prize, N.A.S., for devt. of betatron 1945; John Scott Award 1946; John Price Wetherill Medal, Franklin Inst., for devt. of betatron 1950; James Clerk Maxwell Prize for Plasma Physics, American Physical Soc. 1984, R. R. Wilson Prize American Physical Soc. 1988. *Major works:* devt. of betatron, devt. of spiral sector accelerator, thermonuclear-plasma physics. *Leisure interests:* sailing, skiing, canoeing, swimming. *Address:* Department of Physics, University of Wisconsin, Physics-Astronomy Building, 1150 University Avenue, Madison, Wis. 53706 (Office); 1506 Wood Lane, Madison, Wis. 53705, U.S.A. (Home). *Telephone:* 238-8142.

KERWIN, Larkin, C.C., D.SC., LL.D., F.R.S.C.; Canadian physicist; b. 22 June 1924, Quebec City; s. of Timothy and Catherine (née Lonergan) Kerwin; m. Maria G. Turcot 1950; five s. three d.; ed. St. Francis Xavier Univ., Massachusetts Inst. of Tech., Laval Univ.; Asst. Prof. of Physics, Laval Univ.; 1948–51, Assoc. Prof. 1951–56, Prof. 1956, Chair. Physics Dept. 1961–67, Vice-Dean, Faculty of Sciences 1967–69, Vice-Rector 1969–72, Rector 1972–77; Vice-Pres. Natural Sciences and Eng. Research Council, Canada 1978–80; Pres. Nat. Research Council of Canada 1980–89; Pres. Canadian Space Agency March 1989–; research physicist, Geotech. Corpn., Cambridge 1945–46; Pres. Canadian Assen. of Physicists 1954–55, Int. Scientific and Tech. Affiliations Cttee. of Nat. Research Council 1972–80, Acad. of Science, Royal Soc. of Canada 1973–74, Assen. of Univs. and Colls. of Canada –1975, Royal Soc. of Canada 1976; Sec.-Gen. Int. Union of Pure and Applied Physics 1972–84, First Vice-Pres. 1984–; mem. Bd. of Dirs., Canada-France-Hawaii Telescope Corpn. 1973–78; Hon. LL.D. (St. Francis Xavier) 1970, (Toronto) 1973, (Concordia) 1976, (Alberta) 1983; Hon. D.Sc. (British Columbia) 1973, (McGill) 1974, (Memorial, Newfoundland) 1978, (Ottawa) 1981, (Royal Mil. Coll.) 1982, (Winnipeg) 1983, (Windsor) 1984, (Moncton) 1985; Hon. D.C.L. (Bishop's) 1978; Hon. LL.D. (Dalhousie) 1983, Prix David 1951; Médaille Pariseau, A.C.F.A.S. 1965, Centennial Medal 1967, Medal of Canadian Assen. of Physicists 1969, Jubilee Medal 1977; Laval Alumni Medal (Gloire de l'Escolle) 1978, Canadian Council of Professional Engineers Gold Medal 1982, Médaille Rousseau de l'ACFAS 1983; developed an ion optics theory; invented inflection mass spectrometer; developed electron selector; discovered P8 and numerous excited states in various atoms and molecules; research into determination of isotopic abundance ratios. *Publications:* Atomic Physics: An Introduction 1963, and 50 scientific articles. *Address:* National Research Council of Canada, Ottawa, Ont. K1A OR6 (Office); 2166 Parc Bourbonnière, Sillery, Quebec G1T 1B4, Canada (Home).

KESHISHEV, Konstantin Odisseyevich, DR.PHYS.-MATH.SC.; Soviet physicist; b. 1945; ed. Moscow Inst. of Physics; researcher 1969–71; postgraduate, jr., sr. scientific asst. 1971–86; sr. scientific researcher Inst. for the Study of Physics, U.S.S.R. Acad. of Sciences 1986–; Lenin Prize 1986. *Address:* U.S.S.R. Academy of Sciences, Institute for Study of Physics, Moscow, U.S.S.R.

KESSELLY, Edward Binyah, PH.D.; Liberian politician; b. Lofa County; m. Linnie Kesselly; ed. Xavier Univ., Cincinnati, Ohio, U.S.A., Univ. of Chicago, U.S.A., Geneva Inst. of Int. Studies, Switzerland and Univ. of Manchester, England; Minister of Information and Cultural Affairs, then of Posts and Telecommunications, then of Local Govt. and Rural Devt. in Govt. of Pres. Tolbert; Chair. Anglophone W. African countries, FESTAC '77, African Group, 18th Congress UPU, Rio de Janeiro; Chair. Constitution Advisory Ass. for reviewing and revising new draft constitution of Second Repub., adopted 1984; Head of Unity Party 1984–; cand. in Presidential elections.

KESTEN, Hermann; American (b. German) writer; b. 28 Jan. 1900, Nuremberg; s. of Isaak Kesten and Ida Tisch; m. Toni (née Warowitz) Kesten 1928; ed. Erlangen, Frankfurt and Rome Univs.; Chief Ed. Gustav Kiepenheuer Verlag, Berlin 1927–33, Allert de Lange Verlag, Amsterdam 1933–40; mem. PEN Club of Fed. Repub. of Germany (Pres. 1972); Corresp. mem. Akad. der Wissenschaft und der Literatur, Mainz, Deutsche Akad. für Sprache und Dichtung; Dr. h.c. (Univ. Erlangen-Nurnberg, The Free Univ. of Berlin); Kleist Prize 1928, Nuremberg Prize 1954, Premio di Calabria 1969, Büchner Prize 1974, Nelly Sachs Prize 1977, Hon. Citizen of the City of Nuremberg 1980, of Berlin 1982. *Publications:* Josef Breaks Free 1927, Happy Man 1931, Ferdinand and Isabella 1936, I The King, Philip II 1938, The Children of Guernica 1939, The Twins of Nuremberg

1946 (novels), Copernicus and His World 1945, Casanova 1952 (biography), Die fremden Götter 1949, Ein Sohn des Glücks 1956, Abenteuer eines Moralisten 1961, Die Zeit der Narren 1966, Ein Mann von sechzig Jahren 1972, (novels); Dichter im Café 1959, Meine Freunde die Poeten 1960, Filialen des Parnass 1961 (essays), Die 30 Erzählungen 1962, Deutsche Literatur im Exil 1964, Der Gerechte 1967, Die Lust am Leben (essays) 1968, Ein Optimist (essays) 1970, Revolutionäre mit Geduld (essays) 1973, Ich bin der ich bin (poems) 1974, collected works (20 vols.) 1980–84. *Leisure interests:* travelling, reading, writing. *Address:* Ullstein-Verlag, Lindenstrasse 76, 1000 Berlin 61, Federal Republic of Germany.

KESWICK, Henry Neville Lindley, B.A.; British businessman; b. 29 Sept. 1938, Shanghai, China; s. of Sir William Keswick and Lady Keswick; brother of Simon Keswick (q.v.); m. Lady Tessa Reay 1985; ed. Eton and Trinity Coll., Cambridge; commissioned in Scots Guards; joined Jardine, Matheson & Co. Ltd. in Hong Kong 1961, Dir. 1967–75, Sr. Man. Dir. and Chair. 1972–75; mem. Bd. 1975–; Chair. Hong Kong Land Co. Ltd., Jardine Fleming & Co. Ltd., Textile Alliance Ltd., City Hotels Ltd. (all Hong Kong) until 1975; Chair. Matheson & Co. Ltd. (London) and subsidiaries July 1975–; Chair. Jardine Matheson Insurance Brokers Management Ltd. 1977–; Proprietor, The Spectator 1975–81; Dir. Sun Alliance Insurance Group 1975–, Robert Fleming Holdings Ltd. (London); United Racecourses Ltd.; Trustee, Nat. Portrait Gallery 1982–. *Leisure interest:* country pursuits. *Address:* Matheson & Co. Ltd., 3 Lombard Street, London, EC3V 9AQ (Office); 10 Egerton Place, London, SW3 2EF, England (Home). *Telephone:* 01-528 4000 (Office).

KESWICK, Simon Lindley; British business executive; b. 20 May 1942; s. of Sir William and Lady Keswick; brother of Henry N. L. Keswick (q.v.); m. Emma Chetwode 1971; two s. two d.; ed. Eton Coll. and Trinity Coll., Cambridge; Dir. Fleetways Holdings Ltd., Australia 1970–72, Greenfriar Investment Co. 1979–82, Matheson & Co. Ltd. 1978–82; Chair. Jardine Matheson Insurance Brokers 1978–82; Dir. Jardine Matheson & Co. Ltd., Hong Kong 1972–, Man. Dir. 1982, Chair. 1983–; Chair. Hongkong Land Co. 1983–, Hongkong & Shanghai Banking Corpn. 1983–, Jardine Matheson Holdings Ltd. 1984–, Mandarin Oriental Int. Ltd. 1984–, Jardine Strategic Holdings Ltd. 1987–. *Leisure interests:* country pursuits, Tottenham Hotspurs. *Address:* 35 Mount Kellett Road, Hong Kong.

KETELAAR, Jan Arnold Albert, PH.D.; Netherlands university professor; b. 21 April 1908, Amsterdam; s. of Albert Jans Ketelaar and L. C. M. Struycken; m. Sytske Bessem 1949; three s.; ed. Univ. of Amsterdam and California Inst. of Technology, Pasadena; Priv. Doz. Chemical Crystallography, Univ. of Leiden 1936–40, Lecturer in Physical Chemistry 1940–41; Prof. of Physical Chemistry and Chemical Thermodynamics, Univ. of Amsterdam 1941–60; Visiting Prof. of Chemistry, Brown Univ., Providence, R.I. 1958–59; Prof. of Electrochemistry, Univ. of Amsterdam 1960–78; mem. Nat. Bd. of Educ. 1960–78; mem. Royal Netherlands Acad. of Sciences. *Publications:* Monomorphe overgangen in de kristalstructuren van zilverkwikjodide, natriumnitraat en aluminium fluoride 1933, De Chemische Binding 1947, 1952, 1966, Physische Scheikunde 1950, Chemical Constitution 1953, 1958, Liaisons et propriétés chimiques 1960, Chemische Konstitution 1964. *Address:* Park de Eschhorst 6, 7461 BN Rÿssen, Netherlands. *Telephone:* 05480-12841.

KETELSEN, James Lee, B.S., C.P.A.; American business executive; b. 14 Nov. 1930, Davenport, Ia.; s. of Ernest Henry Ketelsen and Helen Schumann Ketelsen; m. Joan Velde 1953; one s. one d.; ed. Northwestern Univ., Evanston, Ill.; Accountant with Price Waterhouse & Co., Chicago 1955–59; Treasurer, Vice-Pres. Finance, J.I. Case Co., Racine, Ill. 1962–68, Pres. 1968–72; Exec. Vice-Pres Tenneco Inc., Houston 1972–; Pres. Tenneco Inc. 1977–78, Chair. and C.E.O. 1977–; Dir. Morgan Guaranty Trust Co., Sara Lee Corpn., GTE Corpn. *Leisure interest:* golf. *Address:* 1010 Milam Street, Houston, Tex. 77002, U.S.A.

KETTERL, Werner; German professor of dentistry; b. 14 Jan. 1925, Munich; s. of A. L. Ketterl; m. Susanne Vogel 1953; two d.; ed. studies in medicine and dentistry; Prof. of Conservative Dentistry and Paradontology, Univ. of Mainz 1964–, Dean, Faculty of Medicine 1971–72, 1983–85, Pres. Deutsche Gesellschaft für Parodontologie 1972–76, Deutsche Gesellschaft für Zahn-, Mund- und Kieferheilkunde 1977–81; Ed. Praxis der Zahnheilkunde, Deutsche Zahnarztekalender. *Address:* Poliklinik für Zahnerhaltung und Paradontologie, Johannes Gutenberg Universität, Augustusplatz 2, 6500 Mainz; An der Steige 18, 6500 Mainz-Finthen, Federal Republic of Germany (Home). *Telephone:* 06131/17-2246 (Office); 06131/472658 (Home).

KETY, Seymour S., M.D.; American professor of neuroscience; b. 25 Aug. 1915, Philadelphia; s. of Louis and Ethel Kety; m. Josephine Gross 1940; one s. one d.; ed. Univ. of Pennsylvania, post-doctoral Harvard Medical School and Massachusetts General Hospital; Instructor, Asst. Prof., Univ. of Pa. Medical School 1943–48; Prof. of Clinical Physiology, Univ. of Pa. 1948–51; Scientific Dir., Nat. Insts. of Mental Health and Neurological Diseases 1951–56, Chief, Lab. of Clinical Sciences 1956–61, 1962–67; Henry Phipps Prof. of Psychiatry, Johns Hopkins School of Medicine 1961–62; Prof. of Psychiatry, Harvard Medical School 1967–83, Prof. Emer. of Neuroscience in Psychiatry 1983–; Dir. Psychiatric Research Lab., Mass. Gen. Hospital 1967–77; Dir. Labs. for Psychiatric Research, Mailman

Research Center, McLean Hosp., Belmont, Mass. 1977–83; Sr. Scientist Nat. Inst. Mental Health 1983–; Dir. McKnight Endowment for Neuroscience; Ed.-in-Chief Journal of Psychiatric Research 1961–82; past Pres. Asscn. for Research in Nervous and Mental Disease, American Psychopathological Asscn.; mem. N.A.S., American Philosophical Soc., American Soc. of Pharmacology and Experimental Therapeutics, American Acad. Arts and Sciences; Hon. Fellow, Royal Coll. of Psychiatrists, London; Distinguished Fellow, American Psychiatric Asscn.; Hon. M.A., Sc.D., M.D.; many awards including Theobold Smith Award, A.A.A.S. 1949, Distinguished Service Award, Dept. of Health Educ. and Welfare 1958, McAlpin Medal, Nat. Asscn. for Mental Health 1972, Kovalenko Award, Nat. Acad. of Sciences 1973, William Menninger Award, American Coll. of Physicians 1976, Passano Award, Baltimore, Mihara Award, Tokyo, Emil Kraepelin Award, Max Planck Inst., Munich 1984, Ralph Gerard Award, Soc. for Neuroscience, N.A.S. Neuroscience Award 1988, de Hevesy Pioneer Award, Soc. of Nuclear Medicine 1988. *Publications:* Measurement of human cerebral blood flow and metabolism 1948, Theory of exchange of diffusible substances between capillaries and tissues 1951, Biochemical studies in schizophrenia 1959, The heuristic aspect of psychiatry 1961, Genetic-environmental interactions in the transmission of schizophrenia 1968, The biogenic amines in arousal, emotion and learning 1969, The Harvey Lecture: Biological Roots of Mental Illness 1975, The 52nd Henry Maudsley Lecture: The Syndrome of Schizophrenia 1979. *Leisure interests:* music, art. *Address:* Clinical Center, National Institutes of Mental Health, Bethesda, Md. 20892, U.S.A. *Telephone:* (301) 496-4737.

KEUTCHA, Jean; Cameroonian civil servant, politician and diplomatist; b. June 1923, Bangangté; m.; three c.; ed. Ecole Supérieure d'Agriculture de Yaoundé; Chef de Cabinet, Minister of State with Special Responsibilities 1957, subsequently Chef de Cabinet, Sec. of State with responsibility for Information, Posts and Telecommunications; Asst. to Chief of Bamiléké Region 1959; Sub-Prefect, Bafoussam 1960; Prefect of Mifi, subsequently of Menoua 1962–64; Sec. of State for Public Works 1964, subsequently Sec. of State for Rural Devt. and Sec. of State for Educ.; Minister of Foreign Affairs 1971–72, 1975–80, of Agriculture 1972–75; Amb. to EEC 1984–85, to People's Repub. of China 1985–88; Commdr. Order Camerounais de la Valeur, Grand Officier, Légion d'honneur, Grand Officier de l'Ordre National Gabonais, etc. *Publication:* Le guide pratique pour la taille du Caféier Arabica. *Address:* c/o Ministry of External Relations, Yaoundé, Cameroon.

KÉVÉS, György; Hungarian architect; b. 20 March 1935, Osi; s. of Kandor Kévés and Ványi Piroska; m. Éva Földvári 1966; ed. Tech. Univ., Budapest; designer for firms, Agroterv and Eliti, Budapest 1959–61, Iparterv, Budapest 1961–69, Studio 'R' 1983–; private practice with Éva Földvári 1966–; teacher, Faculty of Architecture, Tech. Univ., Budapest 1966–73; Sr. Architect and Prof., Architectural Masterschool, Budapest 1974–; organizes confs. and exhbns. Masterschool, including exhbns. of post-modern architecture and Mario Bottá's works 1980–; organized lectures by Rob Krier and Mario Bottá, Hungary 1980; Visiting Lecturer, Washington Univ., St. Louis, U.S.A. 1981; exhbns.: Budapest, Milano Triennale 1973, Stuttgart 1977, Canada 1978, Washington Univ. St. Louis 1983; Ybl Prize; Hungarian State Prize; several first prizes in architecture competitions. *Publications include:* Architecture of the 70s, Architecture of the 20th century; and numerous articles in architectural magazines. *Leisure interest:* all kinds of art.

KEYFITZ, Nathan, PH.D., F.R.S.C., F.R.S.S.; American statistician; b. 29 June 1913, Montreal, Canada; s. of Arthur Keyfitz and Anna (née Gepstein) Keyfitz; m. Beatrice Orkin 1939; one s. one d.; ed. McGill Univ. and Univ. of Chicago, U.S.A.; Statistician, then Sr. Research Statistician, Dominion Bureau of Statistics, Ottawa 1936–56; Lecturer in Sociology, McGill Univ. 1948–51; Adviser to Indonesian Planning Bureau, Jakarta 1952–53; Prof. of Sociology, Univ. of Montreal 1962–63, Univ. of Toronto 1959–63, Univ. of Chicago 1963–68, Chair. Dept. of Sociology 1965–67; Prof. of Demography, Univ. of Calif., Berkeley 1968–72; Andelot Prof. of Sociology and Demography, Harvard Univ. 1972–73, Prof. Emer. 1983–, Chair. Dept. of Sociology 1978–80; Lazarus Prof. of Social Demography, Ohio State Univ. 1981–83, Prof. Emer. 1983–; Visiting Fellow Statistics Canada 1983–; Leader Population Programme, Int. Inst. for Applied Systems Analysis, Laxenburg, Austria 1984–; Consultant, Dept. of Finance, Jakarta, Indonesia 1984–; Fellow American Statistical Asscn. mem. Int. Statistical Inst.; Pres. Population Asscn. of America 1970; Life Trustee, Nat. Opinion Research Center; mem. N.A.S.; Hon. M.A. (Harvard), Hon. LL.D. (Western Ont., Montreal, McGill and Alberta, Edmonton); Hon. mem. Canadian Statistical Soc. 1980–. *Publications:* Applied Mathematical Demography 1985, Introduction to the Mathematics of Population 1977. *Leisure interests:* computers, foreign languages. *Address:* International Institute for Applied Systems Analysis, Schlossplatz 1, A-2361 Laxenburg (Office); 11ASA, Schlossplatz 1, A-2361 Laxenburg, Austria (Home). *Telephone:* 02236-71521/297.

KEYNES, Richard Darwin, C.B.E., M.A., PH.D., SC.D., F.R.S.; British scientist; b. 14 Aug. 1919, London; s. of the late Sir Geoffrey Keynes and the late Margaret Elizabeth Darwin; m. Anne Pinsent Adrian; four s.; ed. Oundle School and Trinity Coll., Cambridge; Temporary Experimental Officer, Anti-Submarine Establishment and Admiralty Signals Establishment

1940–45; Demonstrator, later Lecturer in Physiology Univ. of Cambridge 1949–60; Research Fellow, Trinity Coll., Cambridge 1948–52; Fellow of Peterhouse, Cambridge, and Dir. of Studies in Medicine 1952–60; Head of Physiology Dept., Babraham 1960–65, Dir. of Inst. 1965–73; Prof. of Physiology, Univ. of Cambridge 1973–86; Sec.-Gen. of Int. Union for Pure and Applied Biophysics 1972–78, Vice-Pres. 1978–81, Pres. 1981–84; Fellow of Churchill Coll., Cambridge 1961–, Fellow of Eton 1963–78; Ed. The Beagle Record 1979. *Publications:* Nerve and Muscle (with D. J. Aidley) 1981, Charles Darwin's Beagle Diary 1988. *Leisure interest:* sailing. *Address:* 4 Herschel Road, Cambridge, England. *Telephone:* (0223) 353107.

KEYWORTH, George Albert, II, PH.D.; American scientist and government official; b. 30 Nov. 1939, Boston; s. of Robert Allen and Leontine Briggs Keyworth; m. Polly Lauterbach 1962; one s. one d.; ed. Deerfield Acad., Yale Univ., Duke Univ., Research Asst. Duke Univ. 1963–68, Research Assoc. 1968; Staff mem. Physics, Los Alamos Nat. Lab. 1968–73; Asst. Group Leader, Neutron Physics, Los Alamos 1973–74, Group Leader 1974–77, Deputy Physics Div. Leader 1978, Div. Leader 1978–81, Acting Laser Fusion Div. Leader 1980–81; Science Adviser to Pres. of U.S.A., Dir. Office of Science and Tech. Policy, Washington, D.C. 1981–85, Consultant 1985–86; Chair. The Keyworth Co. 1986–; Dir. of Research, Hudson Inst. 1988–; mem. American Physical Soc., A.A.A.S.; Hon. Prof. (Fudan Univ.) 1984; Hon. D.Sc. (Rennselaer Polytechnic Inst.) 1982, (Univ. of Alabama) 1985; Hon. D.Eng. (Mich. Tech. Univ.) 1984. *Publications:* numerous publs. on science and tech., nat. defence, and nuclear physics. *Leisure interests:* skiing, backpacking. *Address:* Hudson Institute, 5395 Emerson Way, Indianapolis, Indiana, 46226, U.S.A.

KGAREBE, Aloysius William, B.A.; Botswana educationalist; b. 17 Aug. 1923, Mafeking (now Mafikeng), South Africa; s. of Daniel Oabile Kgarebe and Elizabeth Dibolelo Kgarebe; m.; two s. three d.; ed. St. Joseph's Coll., Roma, Lesotho, Univ. of South Africa, Univ. of Leeds, England; taught St. Joseph's Coll., Orlando, Johannesburg; Mamelodi, Pretoria, 1946–61; Vice-Prin. Teachers Coll., Lobatse 1962–65, Prin. 1966–68; Senior Educ. Officer, Ministry of Educ. 1968–70; Chief Educ. Officer, Ministry of Educ. 1970–75; High Commr. in Zambia 1976–78, in U.K. 1978–81. *Leisure interests:* reading, tennis, gardening. *Address:* c/o Ministry of Foreign Affairs, Gaborone, Botswana.

KHACHATUROV, Tigran Sergeyevich; Soviet economist; b. 6 Oct. 1906, Moscow; s. of Sergey Ivanovich Khachaturov and Domna Ivanovna Khachaturova; m. 1st Vera Sheremeteva (divorced 1962), two d.; m. 2nd Alexandra Aksenova Demianovich 1962; ed. Moscow State Univ.; scientific researcher, Cen. Statistic Bd. 1926–30, Scientific Research Inst. of Transportation Economy 1930–33; Lecturer and Prof. Moscow Electro-Mechanical Inst. of Transportation Engineers 1931–41; Chief of Dept. later Deputy Dir. and Dir. All Union Scientific Research Inst. of Railway Transport 1941–49; Ed.-in-Chief, Railway Technology (monthly journal) 1943–49; Prof. Moscow Inst. of Railway Engineers 1949–63; Dir. Inst. of Complex Transportation Problems 1955–59; mem. Editorial Bd. (Ed.-in-Chief 1966–81), Problems of Economics (monthly journal); Chief of Dept. Inst. of Econs. 1959–67; Chair. Scientific Council of Effectiveness of Investments 1957–; mem. State Expert Comm. 1958; Academic Sec. (and mem. Presidium of Acad.) Econ. Dept., Acad. of Sciences 1967–71; mem. Exec. Cttee. Int. Econ. Asscn. 1968–74, Adviser 1974–89, Hon. Pres. 1989–; Chair. Presidium, Asscn. of Soviet Econ. Scientific Insts. 1969–; Prof. Acad. of Socialist Sciences 1964–; Deputy Chair. Comm. of Natural Resources 1971–80; Prof. Chief of Dept. of Econs. of Natural Resources, Moscow Univ. 1971–; Chair. Scientific Econ. Soc.; mem. Acad. of Sciences; Foreign mem. Polish Acad. of Sciences; Hon. mem. Hungarian Acad. of Sciences; Hon. Dr. (Econ. Acad., Vroclaw); Order of October Revolution, Order of the Red Banner of Labour (four times), Order of the Red Star, Order for Services (Poland); various medals including Nicolas Copernicus Medal (Poland). *Publications:* Allocation of Transports 1939, Transport Development Ways 1941, Principles of Economics of Railway Transportation 1946, Railway Transport of U.S.S.R. 1952, Economics of Transportation 1959, Economic Effectiveness of Capital Investments 1964, Soviet Economy Today 1975, Intensification and Effectiveness in Developed Socialism 1978, Effectiveness of Capital Investments 1979, Economics of Natural Resources, numerous articles on Soviet Economy. *Leisure interests:* music (piano), paintings, stamps. *Address:* 3 Ulitsa Academica Petrovskogo, app. 30, Moscow 117419, U.S.S.R. *Telephone:* (237)-07-47 (Home); (939)-33-65 (Office).

KHADDAM, Abdel Halim; Syrian politician; Minister of the Economy and Foreign Trade 1969–70; Deputy Prime Minister and Minister of Foreign Affairs 1970–84; Vice-Pres. for Political and Foreign Affairs 1984–; mem. Regional Command, Baath Party 1971–84. *Address:* c/o Office of the President, Damascus, Syria.

KHADDURI, Majid, B.A., L.H.D., PH.D.; Iraqi educationist and writer; b. 27 Sept. 1908, Mosul, Iraq; m. Majdia Khadduri 1942 (died 1972); one s. one d.; ed. American Univ. of Beirut and Univ. of Chicago; Sec.-Treas. Baghdad PEN Club; mem. American Soc. of Int. Law; Iraqi del. to the 14th Conf. of the PEN Clubs in Buenos Aires 1936; mem. the Iraq del. at the San Francisco Conf. 1945; Visiting Lecturer in Near Eastern Politics at Indiana Univ. 1947–48; fmr. Prof. Modern Middle-Eastern History at the Higher Teachers' Coll., Baghdad, Iraq 1938–49; taught Middle East politics at

Chicago and Harvard Univs. 1949-50; Prof. Middle East Studies, Johns Hopkins Univ. 1950-80, Emer. 1980-; Dir. of Research and Education, Middle East Inst. 1950-; Visiting Middle East Prof., Columbia Univ.; mem. American Political Science Assen. and Pres. Shaybani Soc. of Int. Law (Washington); Order of Rafidain (Iraq), Order of Merit, 1st Class (Egypt). *Publications:* The Liberation of Iraq from the Mandate (in Arabic) 1935, The Law of War and Peace in Islam 1941, The Government of Iraq 1944, The System of Government in Iraq (in Arabic) 1946, Independent Iraq 1951, War and Peace in the Law of Islam 1955, Islamic Jurisprudence 1961, Modern Libya 1963, The Islamic Law of Nations 1966, Republican Iraq 1969, Political Trends in the Arab World 1970, Arab Contemporaries 1973, Socialist Iraq 1978, Arab Personalities in Politics 1981, The Islamic Conception of Justice 1983, The Gulf War 1988. *Leisure interest:* long distance walking. *Address:* 4454 Tindall Street, N.W., Washington 16, D.C., U.S.A. *Telephone:* 244-4454.

KHAIN, Viktor Yefimovich, D.SC.; Soviet professor of geology; b. 26 Feb. 1914, Baku; s. of Sophia and Yefim Khain; m. Valentina Kuzmina 1949; two s.; ed. Azerbaidzhan Industrial Inst.; Geologist at oil fields, Azerbaidzhan 1935-39; Assoc. Azerbaidzhan Oil Research Inst. 1939-41; army service 1941-45; mem. CPSU 1943-; Senior Assoc., Inst. of Geology, Acad. of Sciences, Azerbaidzhan S.S.R. 1945-54; Prof. Azerbaidzhan Industrial Inst. 1949-54; Head of Dept. Museum of Earth Sciences, Moscow Univ. 1954-60; Senior Assoc., Vernadsky Inst. of Geochemistry and Analytical Chem., U.S.S.R. Acad. of Sciences 1957-71; Prof. Geology Dept., Moscow Univ. 1961-; Sec.-Gen. Subcomm. for the Tectonic Map of the World, Int. Geological Congress 1972-87, Pres. 1988-; Senior Assoc., Geological Inst., U.S.S.R. Acad. of Sciences 1972-; Corresp. mem. U.S.S.R. Acad. of Sciences 1966-87, mem. 1987-; mem. Moscow Soc. of Naturalists; Foreign mem. Soc. Géologique de France; Hon. mem. Bulgarian Geological Soc.; Order of Red Banner of Labour, Order of People's Friendship 1987; Hon. D.Sc. (Univ. P. et M. Curie, Paris) 1975. *Publications include:* Geotectonic Principles of Oil Prospecting 1954, The Geology of Caucasus (with E. E. Milanovsky) 1963, General Geotectonics 1964, Regional Geotectonics, Vol. I 1971, Vol. II 1977, Vol. III 1979, Vol. IV 1984, Vol. V 1985, Geology of U.S.S.R. 1985, Historical Geotectonics (Vol. 1) 1988. *Address:* Department of Geology, Moscow State University, Moscow 119899, U.S.S.R. *Telephone:* 939-11-09; 203-65-12.

KHAITAN, Krishan, B.COM.; Indian business executive; b. 15 Dec. 1939, Jhunjhunu, Rajasthan; s. of Chiranjilal Khaitan and Durgadevi Khaitan; m. Rampati Khaitan 1956; one s. three d.; ed. Univ. of Calcutta; started business specializing in production of electric fans 1960; now Chair. Khaitan India Ltd., Khaitan Tibrewala Electricals Ltd., Khaitan Electricals Ltd., Khaitan Fans (India) Ltd., Khaitan Industrial Complex Ltd. *Address:* Khaitan (India) Ltd., 46-C, J. L. Nehru Road, Calcutta 700 071 (Office); 7 Keyatala Lane, Calcutta 700 029, India (Home). *Telephone:* 44-0581 (Office); 46-6187 (Home).

KHAKETLA, Benett Makalo, B.A.; Lesotho writer and politician; b. 1914, Qacha's Nek; ed. Bantu High School, Heilbron O.F.S., Univ. of South Africa; teacher, apptd. Prin. Charterson High School, Nigel; co-founder Sesotho newspaper Mohlabani; Deputy Leader Basutoland Congress Party (B.C.P.) 1959-60; f. Basutoland Freedom Party 1961; Pres. Marematlou Freedom Party; mem. Legis. Council 1960-65; Minister of Justice and Prisons 1986-. *Address:* c/o The Military Council, Maseru, Lesotho.

KHALDEYEV, Mikhail Ivanovich; Soviet journalist; b. 1921, Moscow; ed. Party High School of Cen. Cttee. CPSU; served in Soviet Army 1939-45; mem. CPSU 1942-; Komsomol work 1945-50; Moscow City Sec. 1950-51; Moscow Dist. Sec. 1951-52; First Moscow Sec. of U.S.S.R. Komsomol 1952-53, First Moscow Dist. Sec. 1953-57; Chief Ed. of Journal Molodoi Kommunist 1957-59; First Sec. of Timiryazev Regional Cttee. of CPSU in Moscow 1959-63; Head of Ideology for R.S.F.S.R. 1963-66; Chief Ed. of journal Partiinaya zhizn (Party Life) 1966-; mem. Cen. Auditing Cttee. of CPSU 1966-, Deputy Chair. 1976-; Cand. mem. Cen. Cttee. CPSU 1986; Deputy Chair. Cen. Revision Comm. of CPSU 1987; Order of October Revolution 1981. *Address:* Central Auditing Commission of Communist Party of the Soviet Union, Staraya pl. 4, Moscow, U.S.S.R.

KHALID, Mansour, LL.D.; Sudanese diplomatist and lawyer; b. 13 Dec. 1931, Omdurman; s. of Khalid Mohammed and Sara Sawi; ed. Univs. of Khartoum, Pennsylvania and Paris; began his career as an attorney, Khartoum 1957-59; Legal officer, UN, New York 1962-63; Deputy UN resident rep., Algeria 1964-65; Bureau of Relations with Member States, UNESCO, Paris 1965-69; Visiting Prof. of Int. Law, Univ. of Colo. 1968, Univ. of Khartoum 1982; Minister of Youth and Social Affairs, Sudan 1969-71; Chair. of del. of Sudan to UN Gen. Assembly, Special Consultant and Personal Rep. of UNESCO Dir.-Gen. for UNWRA fund-raising mission 1970; Perm. Rep. of Sudan to UN 1971; Pres. UN Security Council; Minister of Foreign Affairs 1971-75, of Educ. 1975-77, of Foreign Affairs Feb.-Sept. 1977; Asst. to Pres. for Co-ordination and Foreign Affairs 1976, Asst. to Pres. for Co-ordination 1977; fmr. mem. Political Bureau and Asst. Sec.-Gen., Sudan Socialist Union 1978; resgnd. from all political posts July 1978 but remained mem. of Gen. Congress of the Sudan Socialist Union; Chair. Bureau of Trilateral Co-operation, Khartoum 1978-80; Personal Rep. for Exec. Dir. of UNEP Anti-desertification Programme 1981-82; UN Special Consultant on Co-ordination of UN Information System 1982;

Chair. Univ. Devt. Cttee., Univ. of Khartoum 1982; Fellow, Woodrow Wilson Center, Smithsonian Inst. 1978-80, Financial and Investment Consultant 1980-; Loyal Son of Sudan and numerous foreign decorations. *Publications:* Private Law in Sudan 1970, The Nile Basin, Present and Future 1971, Solution of the Southern Problem and its African Implications 1972, The Decision-Making Process in Foreign Policy 1973, Sudan Experiment with Unity 1973, A Dialogue with the Sudanese Intellectuals, Nimeiri and the Revolution of Dis-May 1985, 1985. *Leisure interests:* music, gardening. *Address:* P.O. Box 2930, Khartoum, Sudan (Home); 9 Jubilee Palace, London, S.W.3, England.

KHALIFA BIN HAMAD AL-THANI, Sheikh (see Thani, Sheikh Khalifa bin Hamad al-).

KHALIFA, Sheikh Hamed bin Isa al-; Crown Prince of the State of Bahrain; Heir Apparent to His Highness the Amir of Bahrain; b. 28 Jan. 1950, Bahrain; m. Sheikha Sabeeka bint Ibrahim Al-Khalifa 1968; three s.; ed. Secondary School, Manama, Bahrain, Leys School, Cambridge, Mons Officer Cadet School, Aldershot, England, and U.S. Army Command and Gen. Staff Coll., Fort Leavenworth, Kansas, U.S.A.; founder and Gen. Commdr. Bahrain Defence Force 1968, Head Defence Dept. 1968-, raised Defence Air Wing 1978; mem. State Admin. Council 1970-71; Minister of Defence 1971-88; Deputy Pres. Family Council of Al-Khalifa 1974-, created Historical Documents Centre 1976; founder-mem. and Pres. Bahrain High Council for Youth and Sports 1975-; initiated Al-Areen Wildlife Parks Reserve 1976; f. Sulman Falcon Centre 1977; f. Bahrain Equestrian and Horse Racing Assen., Pres. 1977-; f. Amiri Stud of Bahrain 1977; Orders of the Star of Jordan (1st Class) 1967, Arafa Dain of Iraq (1st Class) 1969, National Defence of Kuwait (1st Class), Al-Muhammedi of Morocco (1st Class) 1970, An-Nahatha of Jordan (1st Class) 1972, Giladat Gumhooreeya of Egypt (1st Class), The Taj of Iran (1st Class) 1973, King Abdul-Aziz of Saudi Arabia (1st Class) 1976, Repub. of Indonesia (1st Class) 1977, Repub. of Mauritania (1st Class), Hon. K.C.M.G. (U.K.), El-Fateh Al-Adheem of Libya (1st Class) 1979, Ordre nationale du Mérite de la République Française (1st Class) 1980, Grand Cross of Isabel la Católica of Spain (1st Class) 1981; Freedom of the City of Kansas 1971, U.S. Army Certificate of Honour 1972; Hon. mem. Helicopter Club of G.B. *Leisure interests:* study of ancient history and prehistory of Bahrain, water skiing, swimming, fishing, horse riding, falconry, shooting, football, golf, tennis. *Address:* Office of the Crown Prince, Court of His Highness the Amir of Bahrain, Rifa'a Palace, Manama, Bahrain. *Telephone:* 661681.

KHALIFA, H.H. Sheikh Isa bin Sulman al-; Ruler of the State of Bahrain; b. 3 July 1933; appointed heir-apparent by his father, H.H. Sheikh Sulman bin Hamad al-Khalifah 1958, succeeded as Ruler on the death of his father Nov. 1961; took title of Amir Aug. 1971; Hon. K.C.M.G. *Address:* Rifa'a Palace, Manama, Bahrain.

KHALIFA, Sheikh Khalifa bin Sulman al-; Bahrain politician; b. 1935; son of the late Sheikh Sulman and brother of the ruler, Sheikh Isa (q.v.); Dir. of Finance and Pres. of Electricity Bd. 1961; Pres. Council of Admin. 1966-70; Pres. State Council 1970-73, Prime Minister 1973-; Chair. Bahrain Monetary Agency. *Address:* Office of the Prime Minister, Manama, Bahrain.

KHALIL, Mustafa, M.SC., D.PHIL.; Egyptian engineer, politician and banker; b. 18 Nov. 1920, El Kalyoubieh; ed. Univ. of Cairo, Illinois Univ., U.S.A.; served in Egyptian State Railways 1941-47, 1951-52; training with Chicago-Milwaukee Railways (U.S.A.) 1947; lecturer in Railways and Highway Engineering, Ain Shams Univ., Cairo 1952; Tech. Consultant to Transport Cttee., Perm. Council for Nat. Production 1955; Minister of Communications and Transport 1956-64, of Industry, Mineral Resources and Electricity 1965-66; Deputy Prime Minister 1964-65; resigned from Cabinet 1966; Head of Broadcasting Corpn. 1970; Prime Minister 1978-80, also Minister of Foreign Affairs 1979-80; Deputy Chair. Nat. Democratic Party May 1980-; Chair. Arab Int. Bank, Cairo 1980-. *Leisure interest:* music. *Address:* Arab International Bank, 35 Abdel Khalek Sarwat Street, Cairo (Office); 9A El Maahad El Swisry Street, Zamalek, Cairo, Egypt (Home). *Telephone:* 3416111 (Home).

KHALILOV, Kurban Ali; Soviet politician; b. 1906, Azerbaijan; ed. Azerbaijan Industrial Inst.; mem. CPSU 1926-; lathe-turner, student 1923-33; engineer, dept. head 1933-37 and dir. of various plants 1937-42; Sec. of Baku City Cttee. of Azerbaijan CP 1942-45; econ. and state posts 1945-54; Deputy Minister of Building Materials and Industry for Azerbaijan S.S.R., Minister of Local Industry 1954-58; Deputy to Supreme Soviet of Azerbaijan 1954-58, 1959-; Minister of Finance for Azerbaijan S.S.R. 1958-69; mem. of Cen. Cttee. of Azerbaijan CP 1960-, mem. of Politburo of Cen. Cttee. 1969-; Chair. of the Presidium of the Supreme Soviet of the Azerbaijan S.S.R. 1969-; Deputy to and Deputy Chair. of Presidium of Supreme Soviet of U.S.S.R. 1970-; mem. of Cen. Auditing Comm. of CPSU 1971-; Order of Lenin 1976. *Address:* Presidium of the Supreme Soviet of the Azerbaijan S.S.R., Baku, Azerbaijan S.S.R., U.S.S.R.

KHAMENEI, Hojatoleslam Ali; Iranian religious leader and politician; b. 1940, Meshed, Khorassan; m. 1964; four s. one d.; ed. Qom; studied under Ayatollah Khomeini (q.v.); returned to Meshed 1964; imprisoned six times 1964-78, once exiled in 1978; fmr, personal rep. of Ayatollah Khomeini, Supreme Defence Council; Friday Prayer Leader, Teheran 1980-; Sec.-

Gen. (and Pres. Cen. Cttee.) Islamic Republican Party 1980–87; Pres. of Iran Oct. 1981–; mem. Revolutionary Council until its dissolution Nov. 1979; survived assassination attempt June 1981, Commdr. Revolutionary Guards 1980; Rep. of Revolutionary, Ministry of Defence. *Leisure interests:* traditional Persian athletics. *Address:* Office of the President, Teheran, Iran.

KHAN, Ali Akbar; Indian musician; b. 14 April 1922, Shivpur (now in Bangladesh); s. of late Allauddin Khan; debut Allahabad 1936; world tours since 1955; Founder Ali Akbar Coll. of Music, Calcutta 1956, and Ali Akbar Coll., San Rafael, Calif. 1968; Musical Dir. of many films including award-winning Hungry Stones; numerous appearances at concerts and major festivals, world-wide; musical collaboration with Yehudi Menuhin, Ravi Shankar (qq.v.), the late Duke Ellington and others; Lecture recitals at major univs., incl. Montreal, McGill, Washington, San Diego and Tennessee; composer of concerti, orchestra pieces and several ragas, notably Chandran-andan, Gauri Manjari, Alamgiri, Medhavi; Hon. D.Litt. (Rabindra Bharati Univ., Calcutta) 1974; Pres. of India Award 1963, 1966; Padmabhushan Award; Grand Prix du Disque 1968. *Address:* 159/1A Rashbehari Avenue, Calcutta 70029, India.

KHAN, Amjad Ali; Indian musician; b. 9 Oct. 1945, Gwalior; s. of the late Hafiz Ali Khan and of Rahat Jahan Begum; m. Subhalakshmi Khan 1976; two s.; sarod player; numerous concert performances including Pakistan 1981, China 1981, Hong Kong Arts Festival 1982, Festival of India (London) 1982; composed music for Kathak ballet Shan-E-Mughal; awards include UNESCO Award, Int. Music Forum 1970; Padma Shree 1975; Special Honour, Sahitya Kala Parishad, Delhi 1977; Musician of Musicians, Bhartiya Vidhya Bhavan, Nagpur 1983. *Leisure interests:* writing my autobiography, teaching students, reading newspapers and magazines. *Address:* 3 Sadhana Enclave, Panch Shila Park, New Delhi 110 017, India. *Telephone:* 6442749, 6449062.

KHAN, Ghulam Ishaq; Pakistani civil servant; b. 1915; m. 1950; one s. five d.; ed. Islamia Coll., Peshawar, and Punjab Univ.; North-West Frontier Province (N.W.F.P.) Civil Service (India) 1940–47, Sub-Divisional Officer, Treasury Officer and Magistrate First Class 1940–44; Bursar and Sec. to Council of Management of Islamia Coll., Peshawar; Sec. to Chief Minister, N.W.F.P. 1947; Home Sec. Food and Dir. Civil Supplies to Govt. N.W.F.P. 1948; Devt. and Admin. Sec. for Agriculture, Animal Husbandry, Forests, Industries, Co-operatives and Village Aid 1949–52; Devt. Commr. and Sec. to Devt. Dept., N.W.F.P. 1953–56; Sec. for Devt. and Irrigation, Govt. of W. Pakistan 1956–58; mem. W. Pakistan Water and Power Devt. Authority 1958–61, Chair. 1961–66; mem. Land Reforms Comm. 1958–59, Chair. 1978–; Sec. Finance, Govt. of Pakistan 1966–70; Cabinet Sec. Govt. of Pakistan 1970; Gov. State Bank of Pakistan 1971–75; Sec.-Gen. Ministry of Defence 1975–77; Sec.-Gen.-in-Chief (status of Fed. Minister), Adviser for Planning and Co-ordination 1977–78; Adviser to Chief Martial Law Administrator 1978–; Minister for Finance and Co-ordination 1978–79, for Finance, Commerce and Co-ordination 1979–85; Chair. Econ. Co-ordination Cttee. of the Cabinet 1978–85; Chair. Exec. Cttee. Nat. Econ. Council 1978; Deputy Chair. of Planning Comm. 1979–82, Chair. 1982; Chair. of Senate 1985–88; Acting Pres. Aug.–Nov. 1988, Pres. Dec. 1988–; Chair. of Jt. Ministerial Cttee. of Bd. of Govs. of World Bank and IMF 1982–; Tamgha-i-Pakistan 1959, Sitara-i-Pakistan 1962, Halal-i-Quaid-i-Azam 1968. *Address:* 2, 52nd Street, Shalimar 6/4, Islamabad, Pakistan.

KHAN, Humayun, M.A., D.P.A.; Pakistani diplomatist; b. 31 Aug. 1932, Abbottabad; s. of M. Safdar Khan and Mumtaz Begum; m. Munawar Sultana 1961; three d.; ed. Bishop Cotton School, Simla, Trinity Coll., Cambridge, Lincoln's Inn, London and Univ. of S. Calif.; Deputy Commr. Bannu 1961–62; Political Agent, North Waziristan 1965–66, Malakand 1968–69; Home Sec. North-West Frontier Province 1972–73; Minister, Embassy, Moscow 1974–77; Deputy Perm. Rep. to UN, Geneva 1977–78; Amb. to Bangladesh 1979–82, to India 1984–88; Additional Foreign Sec. 1982–84. *Leisure interests:* golf, tennis, shooting, fishing. *Address:* c/o Ministry of Foreign Affairs, Islamabad, Pakistan. *Telephone:* 827041.

KHAN, Imran (see Khan, Niazi Imran).

KHAN, Inamullah; Pakistani religious leader; b. 17 Sept. 1914, Rangoon, Burma; s. of Karim Khan; m. Khadoja Khalik 1939; one s. five d.; ed. Rangoon Univ.; Ed.-in-Chief Burma Muslim Daily –1942; in India 1942–46; Pakistani citizen 1948–; f. Modern World Muslim Congress; Hon. Pres. World Conf. on Religion and Peace. *Address:* D-26, Block 8, Gulshan-e-Iqbal, Karachi 75300, Pakistan. *Telephone:* (021) 468737.

KHAN, Muhammad Ishtiaq, M.A., F.R.A.S., F.S.A.; Pakistani museum director and archaeologist; b. 1 May 1934, Jhajjar, Rohtak Dist., India; s. of late Haji Muhammad Ishaq Khan and Amna Khatoon; m. Perveen Ishtiaq 1964; one s. four d.; ed. Punjab and Harvard Univs.; went to Pakistan 1947; Univ. Research Scholar, Lahore 1956–57, Archaeological Scholar 1957–58; Custodian, Archaeological Museum, Moenjodaro 1959–61, Taxila 1961–65, Harappa 1965; Asst. Supt. of Archaeology, Directorate of Archaeology 1965–66; Asst. Supt. of Archaeology, Nat. Museum of Pakistan, Karachi 1966–70; Supt. of Archaeology, W. Pakistan Circle, Lahore 1970–73; Dir. of Archaeology and Museums, Govt. of Pakistan 1973–83, Dir.-Gen. 1983–; Chair. Pakistan ICOM Nat. Cttee.; Gold Medal, Mongol Acad., Lahore. *Publications:* Lahore Fort 1974, Archaeology of Sind 1975, Shalamar 1977;

articles in various journals. *Leisure interest:* reading. *Address:* Department of Archaeology and Museums, 27-A, Al-Asif Building, Commercial Area, Shaheed-e-Millat Road, Karachi, Pakistan. *Telephone:* 430638.

KHAN, Niazi Imran: Pakistani cricketer; b. 25 Nov. 1952; ed. Aitchison Coll. and Cathedral School, Lahore, Worcester Royal Grammar School, England, Keble Coll., Oxford; Test début 1971; Capt. Oxford Univ. 1974; played County Cricket for Worcs. 1975–77, Sussex 1978–; Capt. of Pakistan 1982–83, 1985–87, 1988–; over 325 wickets in test matches; became second player to score a century and take 10 wickets in a Test Jan. 1983; only the third player to score over 3,000 test runs and take 300 wickets; Special Rep. for Sports, UNICEF March 1989–. *Publications:* Imran 1983, All-Round View (autobiog.) 1988. *Address:* c/o Sussex County Cricket Club, County Ground, Eaton Road, Hove, Sussex, England.

KHAN, Lieut.-Gen. Sahabzada Yaqub; Pakistani politician, diplomatist and retd. army officer; b. 1920; served Second World War, Middle East; joined Pakistan Army, Commdr. armoured regt. 1947; attended Army Staff Coll., Quetta 1949, Ecole Supérieure de Guerre, Paris 1953–54, later Imperial Defence Coll., London; Vice-Chief Gen. Staff, Pakistan Army 1958; Commdr. armoured div.; Commandant Army Staff Coll., Quetta; Chief Gen. Staff; Corps Commdr. and Commdr., Eastern Command until 1970; Amb. to France (also accred. to Ireland and Jamaica) 1972, to U.S.A. 1973–79, to U.S.S.R. 1979–80, to France 1980–82; Minister of Foreign Affairs 1982–87, June 1988–. *Address:* c/o Ministry of Foreign Affairs, Islamabad, Pakistan.

KHAN, Sirajul Hossain, M.A.; Bangladesh politician; b. 17 July 1926, Baniachang, Habiganj; m.; two s. two d.; ed. Dhaka Univ.; Sub-Ed. Bangladesh Observer, then News Ed. 1949–51; Press Reporter, East Bengal Govt., then Asst. Dir. of Publicity 1951–61; fmr. Dhaka Corresp. and East Pakistan Bureau Chief, Pakistan Times; Chief, Corresp. Unit, East Pakistan Union of Journalists 1962–63, Gen. Sec. 1963–64; Gen. Sec. East Pakistan Workers' Council 1964–66, Gen. Sec. Workers' Fed. 1966–70; Gen. Sec. Bangladesh Worker's Fed. 1971–73, Pres. 1981–; Exec. Pres. Jatiya Workers' Fed. 1974–80; f. Sec.-Gen. People's Nat. Liberation Union 1974; Chair. Ganatantrik Party; f. Ed. Eastern News Agency 1970; Minister for Information 1985–86, for Fisheries and Livestock 1985–87, of Land Admin. and Land Reform 1987–88, of Relief and Rehabilitation Dec. 1988–. *Address:* c/o Jatiya Sangsad, Dhaka, Bangladesh.

KHAN, Sultan Mohammad, B.A.; Pakistani diplomatist; b. 1919; ed. Ewing Christian Coll. and Allahabad Univ.; commissioned Indian Army 1942; Indian Political Service 1946; Pakistan Diplomatic Service 1947–; Pakistan High Comm., New Delhi 1947, Cairo and Rome 1948–50; Ministry of External Affairs, Karachi 1950–53; Embassy, Beijing and Ankara 1953–57; Deputy High Comm. London 1957–59; Ministry of External Affairs, Karachi 1959–61; High Commr. in Canada 1961–66, concurrently accred. as High Commr. in Jamaica 1963–66, Trinidad and Tobago 1963–66; Amb. to Cuba 1964.–66, to People's Repub. of China 1966–68; Asst. Sec., then Under-Sec. for Foreign Affairs 1969–79; Amb. to U.S.A. 1972–73, 1979–80, concurrently accred. to Jamaica and Venezuela 1972–73, to Mexico 1973; Amb. to Japan 1974–76; Adviser and Chief Rep. in China for the Int. Bank of Credit and Commerce, Beijing 1982–. *Address:* 9 Chongwenmen Xi Dajie, Building No. 3, Beijing, People's Republic of China.

KHAN, Air Chief Marshal Zulfiqar Ali; Pakistani air force officer and government official; b. 10 Dec. 1930, Lahore; s. of Agha Shujaat Ali Khan and Anjum Shujaat Ali Khan; m. Sajidah Haq Nawaz Khan; two s. one d.; ed. Pakistan Air Force (P.A.F.) Acad., Risalpur and P.A.F. Staff Coll., Karachi; Air Attaché Pakistan Embassy, India 1964–68; Base Commdr. P.A.F. Base, Dhaka 1968–71, Badaber 1971–72, Sargodha 1972–73; Commandant P.A.F. Acad., Risalpur 1973–74; Dir. Operations and Plans and Chief of Air Staff (Operations) –1974, Chief of Air Staff 1974–78; mem. Mil. Council (mil. govt. under Gen. Mohammad Zia ul-Haq q.v.) 1977–78; Amb. to Switzerland 1979–81; Chair. Comm., Review of Security and Intelligence Agencies 1989–. *Publications:* Pakistan's Security: The Challenge and the Response 1988; numerous articles on foreign affairs and geopolitics. *Leisure interests:* golf, hunting. *Address:* Bungalow No. 19, Street 89, G-6/3, Islamabad, Pakistan. *Telephone:* 812728.

KHANDKER, Air Vice-Marshal (retd.), A.K.; Bangladesh politician; two s. one d.; joined Pakistan Air Force (PAF) 1951, fighter squadron 1952–55, Flying Instructor and Flight Commdr. 1958–60, Squadron Commdr. 1960–62, Squadron Commdr., Jet Fighter Conversion School 1962–65, Wing Commdr. 1965, Officer Commanding, Flying Training Wing 1966–67, Pres. Planning Bd. 1967–69, Officer Commanding, Admin. Wing 1969, Group Capt. 1970; Deputy Chief of Staff, Bangladesh Liberation Forces and officially accepted surrender of Pakistani Forces 1971; Air Cdre. Bangladesh Air Force 1973, Air Vice-Marshal 1973–; Chair. Bangladesh Air Lines 1973; joined Ministry of Foreign Affairs 1975, High Commr. in Australia 1976–82, in India 1982–86; Adviser to Pres. for Ministry of Planning 1986, Minister of Planning Nov. 1986–. *Address:* c/o Jatiya Sangsad, Dhaka, Bangladesh.

KHANE, Abd-El Rahman, M.D.; Algerian politician, administrator, and physician; b. 6 March 1931, Collo; m. 1955; three s. one d.; ed. Univ. of Algiers; served as officer in Nat. Liberation Army until Algerian independence 1962; Sec. of State, provisional govt. (GPRA) 1958–60; Gen. Controller Nat. Liberation Front 1960–61; Head of Finance Dept., GPRA 1961–62; Pres. Algerian-French tech. org. for exploiting wealth of Sahara sub-soil 1962–65; Pres. Electricité et Gaz d'Algérie July-Oct. 1964; mem. Bd. Dirs. Nat. Petroleum Research and Exploitation Co. 1965–66; Minister of Public Works and Pres. Algerian-French Industrial Co-operation Org. 1966–70; Physician, Cardiology Dept., Univ. Hosp. of Algiers 1970–73; Sec.-Gen. OPEC 1973–74; Exec. Dir. UNIDO 1975–85. *Address:* 42 Chemin B. Brahimi, El Biar, Algiers, Algeria.

KHANI, Abdallah Fikri El-; Syrian politician, diplomatist and judge; b. 1925, Damascus; two d.; ed. Syrian Univ., Damascus, St. Joseph, Beirut, and American Univ., Beirut; lawyer 1947–49; various functions including Sec.-Gen. in Presidency of Repub. 1949–59; lecturer, School of Law, Syrian Univ. 1954–58; Minister Counsellor then Minister Plenipotentiary, Madrid, Brussels, Ankara, London and Paris 1959–69; Perm. Rep. to UNESCO 1966–69; Head del. to UN Gen. Assembly and Security Council 1970; Chair. Syro-Lebanese Perm. Comm. 1969–72; Minister for Tourism 1972–76; Sec.-Gen. of Ministry of Foreign Affairs 1969–72, Minister of Foreign Affairs (acting) 1973–74, Deputy Minister 1976–77; Amb. to India (also accred. to Bangladesh, Burma, Nepal and Sri Lanka) 1978–81; mem. and Vice-Chair. UN Sub.-Comm. on Prevention of Discrimination and Protection of Minorities 1978–81; mem. Int. Court of Justice, The Hague 1981–85; mem. The American Soc. of Int. Law; Order of Merit (Syria, Egypt, Jordan, Indonesia), Order of the Egyptian Repub., Grand Cross of the Argentine Order of May, His Holiness Pope Paul VI Bronze Medal. *Address:* c/o Ministry of Foreign Affairs, Baghdad, Syria.

KHARCHEV, Konstantin Mikhailovich; Soviet politician; b. 1 May 1934, Gorky; m. Ludmilla Ivanovna Kharcheva 1959; one s.; ed. Vladivostok Higher Navigation, Acad. of Social Sciences and Foreign Ministry Acad.; fmr. Amb. Extraordinary to Guyana; Chair. U.S.S.R. Council of Ministers' Council for Matters of Religion 1985–. *Leisure interest:* literature. *Address:* Council for Matters of Religion, U.S.S.R. Council of Ministers, 11/2 Smolensky Boulevard, Moscow, U.S.S.R.

KHARLAMOV, Aleksandr Pavlovich; Soviet journalist; b. 1929; ed. Leningrad State Univ. and Acad. of Social Sciences of Cen. Cttee. of CPSU; party work with Orenburg Dist. Cttee. of CPSU 1954–70; Ed. of dist. newspaper Yuzhny Ural (The South Urals) in Orenburg 1959–64; mem. of the Apparat Cen. Cttee. of CPSU 1967–70; First Deputy Chief Ed. of newspaper Sovetskaya Rossia (Soviet Russia) 1970–76; Chief Ed. newspaper Selskaya Zhizn (Country Life) 1976–; mem. Cen. Auditing Comm. of CPSU. 1976–; mem. CPSU Cen. Cttee. 1986–. *Address:* Selskaya Zhizn, Ul. Pravdy 24, Moscow, U.S.S.R.

KHARLAMOV, Mikhail Averkyevich; Soviet diplomatist; b. 1913; ed. Inst. of History, Philosophy and Literature, Moscow, Party High School of Cen. Cttee. of CPSU; machine fitter 1929–31; Sec. of Radio Cttee. of Council of People's Commissars of Byelorussian S.S.R. 1931–35; mem. Apparat of Cen. Cttee. CPSU 1942–48; ed. of various newspapers and journals 1948–53; mem. Ministry of Foreign Affairs 1953–58; Chief of Press Dept. and mem. of Collegium of U.S.S.R. Foreign Ministry 1961–62; Chair. of State Radio Cttee. of U.S.S.R. Council of Ministers 1962–64; Deputy to U.S.S.R. Supreme Soviet 1962–66; Sec. of Union of U.S.S.R. Journalists; Deputy Chief Ed. of 'Politizdat' 1966–68; Chief of Diplomatic Admin. of U.S.S.R. Foreign Ministry 1968–70; Ministerial Counsellor to Embassy U.S.A. 1970–78; Deputy Chair. U.S.S.R. State Cttee. for Publishing, Polygraphy and the Book Trade Oct. 1980–; Lenin Prize; Order of Lenin. *Address:* c/o Ministry of Foreign Affairs, Moscow, U.S.S.R.

KHASHOGGI, Adnan M.; Saudi Arabian business entrepreneur; b. 1935, Mecca; s. of Mohammad Khashoggi; m. 1st Soraya Khashoggi (divorced 1980); four s. one d.; m. 2nd Laura Khashoggi (née Laura Biancolini) 1978; one s.; ed. Victoria Coll., Egypt and Calif. State Univ.; businessman in Seattle 1953–56; contract to sell trucks to Saudi Arabian Army 1956; Sales Agent in Saudi Arabia for Chrysler, Fiat, Westland Helicopters Ltd. and Rolls-Royce 1962, for Lockheed, Northrop and Raytheon 1964; came to prominence with oil-boom in mid-1970s, founding his own co. Triad, based in the U.S.A.; owns houses in Marbella, Paris, Cannes, Madrid, Rome, Beirut, Riyadh, Jeddah, Monte Carlo and the Canary Islands; arrested in Berne over illegal property deals April 1989. *Address:* La Baraka, Marbella, Spain.

KHATIB, Ahmed al-; Syrian politician; b. 1933, Al Suwaydaa; s. of Hassan al Khatib and Hindiya al Farra; m. Souraya al Khatib 1959; two s. one d.; fmrly. Head, Syrian Teachers Asscn.; mem. Presidential Council 1965–66; Pres. of Syria 1970–71; Chair. People's Council Feb.-Dec. 1971; Pres. Fed. Ministerial Council Fed. of Arab Repubs. 1972–75; mem. Ba'ath Party, elected to Leadership Cttee. May 1971. *Leisure interest:* shooting. *Address:* c/o Syrian Ba'ath Party, Damascus, Syria.

KHATIB, Mohammad al-, B.A.; Jordanian journalist and politician; b. 1930, Ramtha; ed. Cairo Univ.; Dir. of Middle East News Agency, Cairo until 1964; Founder of Jordanian News Agency, Petra; fmr. Dir. of Press and Publs., Dir. Radio Jordan, Plenipotentiary Minister at Ministry of Foreign Affairs and Gov. of Ma'an, Karak and Balqa Govts.; Minister of Information and Minister of Culture, Tourism and Antiquities 1985–88. *Address:* c/o Ministry of Information, POB 1854, Amman; Ministry of

Culture, Tourism and Antiquities, POB 224, Amman, Jordan. *Telephone:* 21523; 42311.

KHATIB, Mohammed Fathalla El-, B.COMM., PH.D.; Egyptian politician; b. 1 Jan. 1927, Gharbiyah; m. Amira Mohamed Khadr 1960; three d.; ed. Univs. of Cairo and Edinburgh; Dir. of Research and UN sections, Arab States Delegations Office, New York 1958–61; Lecturer in Political Science 1954–58, Reader 1961–67, Prof. of Comparative Govt., Univ. of Cairo 1967–71, Dean of Faculty of Econs. and Political Science 1968–71, Prof. of Political Science 1977–85, Dean of Faculty of Political Science 1984–85; Minister of Social Affairs May-Sept. 1971; Adviser to the Pres. on Home, Econ. and Social Affairs. 1971–72; Sec.-Gen. Arab Socialist Union Governorate of Cairo 1971–72; Minister of State, Chair. Council of Foreign Affairs, U.A.R. Dec. 1971; mem. Exec. Bd. UNESCO 1985–. *Publications:* include Power Politics in the UN 1962, Local Government in U.A.R. 1964, Studies in the Government of China 1965, Studies in Comparative Government 1967, Introduction to Political Science 1969, Evaluation of the Local Government System in Egypt 1985, Political Institutions of Egypt 1952–80 1985, (jt. author) The Poor Man's Model of Development 1985. *Leisure interests:* reading, music. *Address:* 11 Sharia Ibn Zinki-Zamalek, Cairo, Egypt. *Telephone:* 3407240.

KHAVIN, Vladimir Vosifovich; Soviet architect; b. 1931; ed. Moscow Architectural Inst.; Head of Workshop no. 12 of Mosproekt-1; mem. C.P.S.U. 1967; Lenin Prize 1984. *Works include:* Circus Bldg. on Vernadsky St., Moscow 1963–71, October Square 1972, Intourist Hotel Complex by Kakhovskaya Metro Station 1980, Monument to Frunze, Frunze 1965, The Rear to the Front Monument, Magnitogorsk 1972–79, memorial complex To the Heroes of the Civil War and the Great Patriotic War, Novosibirsk 1982.

KHAYATA, Abdul Wahab Ismail, PH.D.(ECONS.); Syrian economist; b. 24 Feb. 1924, Aleppo; s. of Ismail Khayata and Fatma Othman Hammami; m. 1st Fathia Dabbas 1955; two s. two d.; m. 2nd Lamya Zakri 1983; ed. Ecole Française de Droit, Beirut, L.S.E., Univ. of Louvain, Belgium; Lecturer, then Prof. of Econs. and Financial Analysis, Univ. of Damascus 1956–68; with Cen. Bank of Syria, rising to Deputy Gov. 1953–63; Under-Sec. Ministry of Planning 1963–68, Minister for Planning 1965; Deputy Dir. for Europe and the Middle East, UNDP, New York 1971–73; Financial Adviser, UN, Beirut 1969–71, 1973–74; Gen. Man. FRAB Bank Int. Paris. 1974–78; Pres. and Deputy Chair. Cen. Bank of Oman 1978–; Order of Oman Award (Third Class) 1984. *Publications:* papers on finance in the Middle East and international economic co-operation, three books on economics. *Leisure interests:* tennis, swimming, chess. *Address:* Central Bank of Oman, P.O. Box 4161, Ruwi, Muscat, Sultanate of Oman. *Telephone:* 704341.

KHEDIRI, El-Hadi; Algerian politician; b. 16 Dec. 1934, Tebessa; m.; two c.; Prin. Pvt. Sec. Ministry of Foreign Affairs; Dir.-Gen. Nat. Security; Minister of the Interior, of Transport 1988–; mem. Cen. Cttee. Nat. Liberation Front 1979–. *Address:* chemin Abd al-Kader Gadouche, Hydra, Algiers, Algeria. *Telephone:* (2) 60-60-33.

KHELIL, Ismail, L. EN D.; Tunisian fmr. diplomatist and international official; b. 11 July 1932, Gafsa; s. of Khelil Khelil and Mahbouba Lejri; m. Mary Finn 1964; one d.; ed. Sadiki Coll., Tunis, Univ. of Grenoble, France; U.S. Div., Secr. of State for Foreign Affairs 1957; Sec. Embassy, Rome and Rep. to FAO 1957–60; Counsellor, later Minister Plenipotentiary, Embassy, Washington D.C. 1960–64; Alt. Exec. Dir. Tunisia, IBRD 1962–64; Amb. Dir. Int. Co-operation, Ministry of Foreign Affairs 1964–69; Sec.-Gen. Ministry of Foreign Affairs 1967–69; Amb. to U.K. 1969–72, to Belgium and Luxembourg and Rep. to European Communities 1972–78; Dir.-Gen. Int. Co-operation, Ministry of Foreign Affairs 1978–79; Pres., Dir.-Gen. Tunis Air 1979–80; Exec. Dir. IBRD 1981–84; Minister of Planning and Finance 1986–87; Gov. Cen. Bank 1987–; Gov. IMF Oct. 1987–; Commdr. Ordre de la République; Officier, Ordre de l'Indépendance de Tunisie and decorations from eleven other countries. *Address:* Banque Centrale de Tunisie, rue de la Monnaie, B.P. 369, Tunis, Tunisia.

KHEYFITS (Heifitz), Yosif Yefimovich; Soviet film director and scriptwriter; b. 5 Dec. 1905; ed. Leningrad Tech. School of Cinema and Inst. of Art History; has worked for Leningrad film-studios 'Sovkino' (Lenfilm) since 1928; First Sec. of Leningrad Br. of U.S.S.R. Soviet Cinema Org. 1970–71, Sec.-Gen. 1971–; mem. CPSU 1945–; People's Artist of U.S.S.R. 1964, Hero of Socialist Labour 1975. *Films include:* The Moon on the Left 1929, Wind in Your Face 1930, Noonday 1931, The Deputy from the Baltic 1937 (First Prize, Paris Exbn.; U.S.S.R. State Prize 1941), Member of Government 1940, The Fall of Japan 1945 (U.S.S.R. State Prize 1946), A Big Family 1954, The Rumyantsev Affair 1956, The Lady and the Lapdog 1960 (Cannes Prize), In the Town of S. 1967, A Bad Good Man 1973, Asya 1978, The Duel 1983, Married for the First Time (First Prize, Karlovy Vary), Prisoner at the Bar, Whose are you Old Chaps? *Address:* U.S.S.R. Soviet Cinema Organization, Leningrad, U.S.S.R.

KHIEM, Gen. Tran Thien (see Tran Thien Khiem, Gen.).

KHIEU, Samphan; Kampuchean politican; b. 1932, Svay Rieng Prov.; m. Khieu Ponnary; ed. Paris Univ.; founded French-language journal, Observer, Cambodia; Deputy, Nat. Assembly in Prince Sihanouk's party,

Sangkum Reastr Nyum (Popular Socialist Community); served as Sec. of State for Commerce; left Phnom-Penh to join Khmer Rouge 1967; Minister of Defence in Royal Govt. of Nat. Union of Cambodia (GRUNC) 1970-76, Deputy Prime Minister 1970-76 (in exile 1970-75, in Phnom-Penh 1975-76); mem. Politburo Nat. United Front of Cambodia (FUNC) 1970-79; C.-in-C. Khmer Rouge High Command 1973-79; Pres. of State Presidium (Head of State) 1976-79; Prime Minister of the Khmer Rouge opposition Govt. fighting Vietnamese forces Dec. 1979-; Vice-Pres. of Govt. of Democratic Kampuchea (in exile) June 1982- (responsibility for Foreign Affairs); Pres. Khmer Rouge 1985-.

KHITROV, Stepan Dmitriyevich; Soviet politician; b. 27 Dec. 1910, Verkhny Karachan; ed. All-Union Polytechnic Inst.; mem. CPSU 1932-; Soviet Army service 1933-35; Deputy Chief Engineer of state farm, later construction technician, then Ed. of newspaper on construction, Voronezh 1935-38; Party work 1938-47; Sec., then Second Sec. Voronezh Regional Cttee. of CP 1943-59 then Chair. Exec. Cttee. of Voronezh Oblast Soviet of Working People's Deputies 1959-60; Official, Cen. Cttee. CPSU 1959-60; First Sec. Voronezh Oblast Cttee. of CP 1960-67; First Sec. Voronezh Oblast Agricultural Cttee. 1963-64; Minister of Agricultural Construction of U.S.S.R., later named Minister for Construction of Agricultural Enterprises 1967-82; Cand. mem. Cen. Cttee. CPSU 1961-66, mem. 1966-; Deputy to U.S.S.R. Supreme Soviet 1962-; Order of Lenin (twice) and other decorations. *Address:* c/o U.S.S.R. Ministry for Construction of Agricultural Enterprises, 4 Building 1, Prospekt Marksa, Moscow, U.S.S.R.

KHITRUN, Leonid Ivanovich, Soviet politician; b. 1930; ed. Byelorussian Agricultural Acad.; mem. CPSU 1955-; tractor and truck driver 1946-48; chief engineer of machinery and tractor station, then chief engineer, then head of regional agricultural admin. 1953-60; Chair. of Grodno Regional Assen. Selkhozteknnika 1961-62; Chair. of Byelorussian S.S.R. Assen. Selkhozteknnika 1962-71; Vice-Chair. of Council of Ministers of Byelorussian S.S.R. 1971-72, 1976-79; First Deputy Minister of Agric. of U.S.S.R. 1972-76; Deputy Dept. Head CPSU Cen. Cttee. 1979-80; Chair. of U.S.S.R. State Cttee. for Production and Tech. Servicing of Agric. Oct. 1980-; mem. of Cen. Auditing Comm. CPSU 1981-86; U.S.S.R. Minister for Machine Construction for Livestock and Fodder Industries 1986-87; First Sec. Ryazan Cen. Cttee. July 1987-. *Address:* Orlikovsky per. 5, The Kremlin, Moscow, U.S.S.R.

KHLEFAWI, Gen. Abdel Rahman; Syrian army officer; b. 1927, Damascus; m.; four c.; ed. schools in Damascus; entered Mil. Coll. 1949, graduated as Lieut. 1950; promoted to Maj.-Gen. 1971; attended courses abroad, especially in France and the U.S.S.R.; served in Syrian Arab Army; Gov. Deraa, Chair. of Municipality and Chief of its Police; later Gov. of Hama; Rep. of Syria, Joint Arab Command, Cairo 1965-67; Chief of Martial Court; Chief, Dept. of Officers' Affairs 1968-70; Minister of the Interior, Deputy Martial Judge 1970-71; mem. House of People 1971; Prime Minister 1971-72, 1976-78; mem. Progressive Nat. Front; elected as mem. in Regional Leadership of Socialist Arab Ba'ath Party and Chief of Econ. and Financial Bureau.

KHODYREV, Vladimir Yakovlevich, CAND.TECH.SC.; Soviet politician; b. 1930; ed. Makarov Higher Arctic Maritime School; mem. CPSU 1954-; jr. researcher, deputy head of section of Cen. Inst. of Maritime Fleet 1957-61; instructor with Leningrad Dist. Cttee. 1961-66; Head of Section, Sec. of Party Cttee., Leningrad Inst. of Water Transport 1966-72; Dir. of Cen. Inst. of Maritime Fleet 1972-74; Second Sec. Leningrad Dist. Cttee. 1974-79, 1982-83, Pres. 1983-; Sec., Second Sec. of Leningrad City Cttee. 1979-82; mem. of CPSU Cen. Cttee. 1986-; Deputy to U.S.S.R. Supreme Soviet. *Address:* Leningrad District Committee of Communist Party of Soviet Union, Leningrad, U.S.S.R.

KHOKHLOV, Boris Ivanovich; Soviet ballet dancer; b. 22 Feb. 1932; ed. Bolshoi Theatre Ballet School; joined Bolshoi Theatre Ballet Company 1951; Order of Lenin 1980; Honoured Artist of R.S.F.S.R. *Chief roles include:* Prince Desire (Sleeping Beauty), Siegfried (Swan Lake), the Prince (Cinderella), the Poet (Chopiniana), Basil (Don Quixote), Albert (Giselle). Vatshar (Bakhchisarai Fountain). *Address:* State Academic Bolshoi Theatre of U.S.S.R., 1 Ploshchad Sverdlova, Moscow, U.S.S.R.

KHOKHLOV, Vitaly Sergeyevich; Sovet banker; b. 1938; ed. Moscow Inst. of Nat. Econ., All-Union Acad. of Foreign Trade; Sr. Adviser, Bank for Foreign Trade, U.S.S.R. 1964-71; Sr. Economist, Eurobank, Paris 1971-74; Vice-Pres., East-West United Bank, Luxembourg 1974-77; Adviser, CP Cen. Cttee. Econs. Dept. 1977-87; Deputy Chair. Bd., Bank for Foreign Econ. Affairs, U.S.S.R. 1987-88; Chair. Bd., Int. Bank for Econ. Co-operation Nov. 1988-. *Address:* International Bank for Economic Co-operation, 15, Kuznetski Most, Moscow 103031, U.S.S.R.

KHOMEINI, Ayatollah Ruhollah; Iranian religious leader; b. 17 May 1900, Khomein; m. Khanom Batool Saghati; two s. (one deceased), three d.; ed. in Khomein and at theological school, Qom; religious teacher in theological school, Qom; arrested in Qom after riots over Shah's land reforms June-Aug. 1963; in exile, Turkey 1964-65, Najaf, Iraq 1965-78, Neauphlé-le-Château, France Oct. 1978-Feb. 1979; while in exile aimed to create an Islamic Republic and from France was the most powerful influence on the revolution which toppled Shah Mohammad Reza Pahlavi;

returned to Iran Feb. 1979; appointed Government of Mehdi Bazargan (q.v.) after collapse of the Bakhtiar Government; returned to theological seminary, Qom, but continued as leader of Islamic movement March 1979-; under new constitution, became Velayat Faghih (religious leader) 1980-. *Publications:* The Government of Theologians (lectures whilst in exile) and numerous religious and political books and tracts. *Address:* Madresseh Faizieh, Qom; 61 Kuche Yakhchal Ghazi, Qom, Iran (Home).

KHOMYAKOV, Aleksandr Aleksandrovich; Soviet politician; b. 25 Aug. 1932; ed. Polytech. Inst., Novocherkassk (Rostov Dist.); factory work 1955-58; mem. CPSU 1958-; party work in Krasnodar Dist. 1958-65; Second Sec., Krasnodar City Cttee. CPSU 1965-69, 1971-78, Sec. (for industry) 1969-71; Deputy to R.S.F.S.R. Supreme Soviet 1971-80; First Sec., Tambov Dist. Cttee. CPSU and mem. Mil. Council, Moscow Mil. Dist. 1978-85; Deputy, Council of the Union, U.S.S.R. Supreme Soviet 1979; mem. Cen. Cttee. CPSU 1981-; First Sec. Saratov Dist. Cttee. CPSU and mem. Mil. Council, Volga Mil. Dist. 1985-; elected to Congress of People's Deputies of the U.S.S.R. 1989; Order of Lenin 1982, other medals. *Address:* The Kremlin, Moscow, U.S.S.R.

KHORAICHE, H.E. Cardinal Antoine Pierre; Lebanese ecclesiastic; b. 20 Sept. 1907, Ain Ebel; ordained priest 1930; Church of Tarsus of Maronites 1950-57; Saida of Maronites 1957-75; Maronite Patriarch of Antioch 1975; cr. Cardinal 1983; mem. of Pontifical Comm. for the revision of the Code of Oriental Canon Law. *Address:* Patriarcat Maronite, Bkerké, Lebanon (winter); Patriarcat Maronite Dimane, Lebanon (summer). *Telephone:* 930011 (winter); 675107 (summer).

KHORANA, Har Gobind, PH.D., M.SC.; Indian-born scientist; b. 9 Jan. 1922, Raipur; m. Esther Elizabeth Sibler 1952; one s. two d.; ed. Punjab Univ.; began career as organic chemist; worked with Sir Alexander Todd on building nucleotides, Cambridge 1950-52; later worked with Nat. Research Inst., Canada, until 1960; Prof. and Co-Dir. Inst. of Enzyme Chem., Univ. of Wis. 1960-64, Conrad A. Elvehjem Prof. in Life Sciences 1964-70; Alfred P. Sloan Prof. M.I.T. Sept. 1970-; mem. N.A.S.; Foreign Academician U.S.S.R. Acad. of Sciences 1971-; Foreign mem. Royal Soc. London 1978; Pontifical Acad. of Sciences 1978; Hon. D.Sc. (Chicago, Liverpool, Delhi), Hon. LL.D. (Simon Fraser Univ.) 1969; Nobel Prize for Medicine and Physiology (with Holley and Nirenberg) for interpretation of genetic code and its function in protein synthesis 1968, Louisa Gross Horwitz Prize for Biochem. 1968, American Chem. Soc. Award for creative work in Synthetic Chem. 1968, Lasker Foundation Award 1968, American Acad. of Achievement Award 1971, Willard Gibbs Medal 1974. *Publications:* Some Recent Developments in the Chemistry of Phosphate Esters of Biological Interest 1961; articles on Biochemistry in various journals. *Leisure interests:* music, hiking. *Address:* Departments of Biology and Chemistry, Massachusetts Institute of Technology, Cambridge, Mass. 02139. U.S.A.

KHOSLA, Sheelkumar Lalchand, M.A.; Indian business executive; b. 27 Sept. 1934, Amritsar; m. Snehlata Khosla 1959; two s. one d.; ed. Bombay Univ.; Indian Admin. Service 1958-86; Financial Adviser and Jt. Sec., Ministry of Petroleum 1976-81; Adviser (Energy), Planning Comm. of India 1983-86; Chair. Indian Oil Corpn. Ltd. 1986-; Dir. Nat. Thermal Power Corpn., Oil India Ltd., Rural Electric Corpn. *Publications:* many papers on energy-related subjects. *Leisure interest:* reading. *Address:* Indian Oil Bhavan, Janpath, New Delhi 110 001 (Office); K-99 Hauz Khas Enclave, New Delhi 110 016, India (Home). *Telephone:* 350833/312767 (Office); 667406 (Home).

KHOURI, Issam; Lebanese lawyer and politician; b. 4 Sept. 1934, Beirut; s. of Fonad El Khouri and Wajiha (née Ballane) Khouri; m. Marcelle Aoun 1964; Dean, Beirut Bar Assen. 1981-82; Dean, Lebanese Lawyers; Minister of Defence, Educ. and Arts 1982-84. *Publications:* numerous articles on political, legal and intellectual subjects. *Leisure interests:* tennis, swimming, jogging, walking, social activities. *Address:* c/o Conseil des Ministres, Place de l'Etoile, Beirut, Lebanon.

KHOURI, Pierre; Lebanese architect and politician; b. 1929, Metn; nephew of Lebanon's first Pres., Bishara Khouri; Sr. Partner, architectural practice; Minister of Public Works, Transport and Agric. 1982-84. *Address:* c/o Conseil des Ministres, Place de l'Etoile, Beirut, Lebanon.

KHOVRIN, Nikolai Ivanovich; Soviet naval officer; b. 1922; ed. Pacific Ocean Naval Coll., Naval Acad.; served in Soviet Navy, rank of Adm. 1941-45; mem. CPSU 1943-; Commdr. of various units in Pacific 1945-70; First Deputy Commdr. of Northern Fleet 1970-74; Commdr. of Black Sea Fleet 1974-; mem. Cen. Cttee. of Ukrainian CP 1976-; Deputy to U.S.S.R. Supreme Soviet 1979-. *Address:* The Kremlin, Moscow, U.S.S.R.

KHRENNIKOV, Tikhon Nikolayevich; Soviet composer; b. 10 June 1913, Elets, Lipetsk region; s. of Nikolay Khrennikov and Varvara Kharlamova; m. Klara Arnoldovna Vax (Khrennikova) 1936; one d.; ed. Moscow Conservatoire, attended Music Tech. Coll., Moscow, 1929-32; Dir. of Music Central Theatre of Soviet Army 1941-54; Gen. Sec. Soviet Composers' Union 1948-57, First Sec. 1957-; Deputy to U.S.S.R. Supreme Soviet 1962-; mem. Cttee. U.S.S.R. Parl. Group; mem. Cen. Auditing Comm., CPSU 1961-76; mem. CPSU 1947-, cand. mem. Cen. Cttee. 1976-; mem. Santa Cecilia 1983; State Prize 1942, 1946, 1951, 1967, 1979, People's Artist of the R.S.F.S.R. 1955, of the U.S.S.R. 1963; Order of Lenin 1963, Red

Banner of Labour 1967, Lenin Prize 1973, Gorky Prize 1979. *Principal compositions:* Two Piano Concertos 1933, 1971, Five Pieces for Piano 1933, First Symphony 1935, Three Pieces for Piano 1935, Suite for Orchestra from Music for Much Ado About Nothing, In the Storm (Opera) 1939, Second Symphony 1941, incidental music for play Long Ago 1942, Frol Skobeyev (Opera) 1950, Mother (Opera) 1956, Concerto for Violin and Orchestra 1959, A Hundred Devils and One Girl (Operetta) 1961, Two Concertos for Violin 1964, 1976, White Nights (Operetta) 1967, Boy Giant (opera for children) 1969, Our Courtyard (ballet for children) 1970, Much Ado About Hearts (chamber opera) 1974, Third Symphony 1975, Love for Love (ballet) 1975, Concerto No. 2 for violin and orchestra 1976, The Hussars' Ballad (Ballet) 1980. *Address:* Composers' Union of the U.S.S.R., Ulitsa Nezhdanovoi 8/10, Moscow, U.S.S.R.

KHRISTORADNOV, Yuriy Nikolayevich; Soviet politician and economic planning specialist; b. 11 Nov. 1929; worked in automobile plant in Gorky; ed. Moscow All-Union Finance and Economics Inst.; mem. CPSU 1951-; party work at plant 1960-62; Sec., then First Sec. of a regional cttee. in Gorky Dist. 1962-66; Second Sec. 1966-68; First Sec., Gorky City Cttee. CPSU 1968-74; Deputy to R.S.F.S.R. Supreme Soviet 1971-75; First Sec., Gorky Dist. Cttee. CPSU and mem. of Mil. Council, Moscow Mil. Dist. 1974-; Deputy to Council of the Union, U.S.S.R. Supreme Soviet 1974-; Chair. (speaker) Soviet of the Union of U.S.S.R. Supreme Soviet May 1988-; mem. Cen. Cttee. CPSU 1976-; Order of Lenin (twice). *Address:* Central Committee of the Communist Party of the Soviet Union, Staraya pl. 4, Moscow, U.S.S.R.

KHRZHANOVSKY, Andrei Yurevich; Soviet maker of animated films; b. 30 Nov. 1939; ed. VGIK; worked with 'Soyuzmultfilm' since 1962. *Films include:* Once upon a time there lived a man by the name of Kozyavin 1966, The Glass Harmonica 1968, The Cupboard 1971, The Butterfly 1972, In the World of Fables 1973, A Wonderful Day 1975, The House that Jack Built 1976, I Fly to You in Memory (trilogy of films based on Pushkin's doodles) 1977, 1981, 1982 (Prize at Venice Film Festival).

KHUDAIBERDYEV, Narmankhonmadi Dzhurayevich; Soviet politician; b. 1928, Uzbekistan; ed. Uzbek Agric. Inst.; mem. CPSU 1948-; dept. head, sec. of a Regional Uzbek Komsomol Cttee.; lecturer and Assistant Prof. at Agric. Inst., Samarkand 1943-54; leading CPSU and state posts 1954-; Sec. of Bukhara Dist. Cttee. of Uzbek CP, Head of Agric. Dept. of Cen. Cttee. of Uzbek CP; Second Sec. of Bukhara Dist. Cttee. 1956-60; Deputy to Supreme Soviet of Uzbek S.S.R. 1959-63, 1967-; mem. of Cen. Cttee. of Uzbek CP 1960-; Deputy Chair. of Council of Ministers of Uzbek S.S.R. 1960-61; First Sec. of Surkhan-Darya Dist. Cttee. of Uzbek CP 1961-62; cand. mem. of Cen. Cttee. of CPSU 1961-66, mem. 1971-; mem. of Foreign Affairs Comm. of Soviet of the Union, U.S.S.R. Supreme Soviet 1962-66; Sec. and mem. of the Presidium of the Cen. Cttee. of the Uzbek CP 1962-65, Chair. of Agric. Bureau 1962-64; Chair. of Council of Ministers of Uzbek S.S.R. 1971-84; mem. of Politburo of Cen. Cttee. of Uzbek CP 1971-84; Order of Red Banner of Labour. *Address:* c/o Council of Ministers of the Uzbek S.S.R., Tashkent, Uzbek S.S.R., U.S.S.R.

KHURANA, Shri Sundar Lal, M.A.; Indian politician; b. 28 Feb. 1919, Jhang (now in Pakistan); ed. Govt. Coll., Lahore; m. 1955; two s.; joined Defence Forces as Civilian Officer in 1943, subsequently obtaining regular comm.; joined Indian Admin. Service 1949; various posts in Rajasthan 1950-55; Deputy Sec., Ministry of Community Devt., Govt. of India and mem. Exec. Cttee. on Social Welfare Bd. 1955-59; Sr. UN Adviser to Govt. of Afghanistan 1959-62; Collector and Dist. Magistrate, Commr. for Border Dists., Rajasthan 1963-66; Chair. Rajasthan State Electricity Bd. 1966-70; Commr. for Home Affairs, Sec. for Jails, Transport and Information and Public Relations Depts., Rajasthan 1970-71; Chief. Sec. to Govt. and Sec. various Depts., Rajasthan 1971-75; Sec., Ministry of Home Affairs and Sec. Justice Dept., Govt. of India 1975-77; Exec. Pres. Hindustan Times Group of Publs. 1979-80 and 1980-81; Adviser to Gov. of Rajasthan March-June 1980; Lieut.-Gov. of Delhi 1981-82; Gov. of Tamil Nadu 1982-88; Past Nat. Pres. All India Inst. of Marketing Man.; Vice-Pres. All India Inst. of Public Admin. *Address:* Raj Bhavan, Madras, Tamil Nadu, India.

KHUSSAIBY, Salim Bin Mohammed Bin Salim al-; Omani diplomatist; b. 11 March 1939; m.; three c.; ed. Teachers Coll., Zanzibar and Police Officers Coll., Kenya; teacher Secondary School, Dubai 1964-70; joined Royal Omani Police 1970, apptd. Deputy Inspector Gen. of Police and Customs; Minister Plenipotentiary Ministry of Foreign Affairs 1976, later Chargé d'Affaires Omani Embassy, Nairobi; Consul Gen. Bombay 1979; Amb. to Kuwait 1980, to Pakistan, (also accred. to Nepal, Bangladesh, Brunei, Darussalem, Indonesia and Malaysia) 1982-87; Perm. Rep. to the UN Sept. 1987-. *Address:* Permanent Mission of Oman to the United Nations, 866 United Nations Plaza, Suite 540, New York, N.Y. 10017, U.S.A. *Telephone:* 355-3505.

KIANO, Julius Gikonyo, M.A., PH.D.; Kenyan economist and politician; b. 1 June 1926, Weithaga, Kenya; s. of Jonathan Kiano and Damari Wanjiru Kiano; m. Jane Mumbi Kiano 1966; two s. three d.; ed. Alliance High School, Kikuyu, Makerere Univ. Coll., Uganda, Antioch Coll. Ohio, Stanford Univ. and Univ. of California at Berkeley, U.S.A.; lecturer in Econs. and Constitutional Law at Royal Tech. Coll., Kenya (now Univ. of Nairobi)

1956-58; elected mem. Kenya Legis. Council 1958-63; mem. Indian Govt. Cultural Scholarships Cttee. and U.S. Scholarship Cttee. 1959-62; mem. Kenya Advisory Council on Tech. Educ. and Vocational Training 1960-62; mem. Kenya Parl. 1963-79; Minister of Commerce and Industry 1963-66, Minister of Labour 1966-67, Minister of Educ. 1968-70, Minister of Local Govt. 1970-73, Minister of Commerce and Industry 1973-76, Minister of Water Devt. 1976-79; Chair. African Ministers of Educ. Conf. 1968, African Ministers of Industry Conf. 1975; mem. Common Market and Econ. Consultative Council of the East African Community 1973-76; Pres. UN Conf. on Desertification Aug.-Sept. 1977; Man. Dir. Industrial Devt. Bank of Kenya 1980-83; mem. Freedom from Hunger Council 1976-; mem. Governing Council UNEP 1977-79; mem. Exec. Cttee. Kenya African Nat. Union (KANU) 1978-79, Sec. KANU Parl. Group 1978-79; mem. exec. Cttee. Assoc. of African Devt. Finance Insts. 1981-83; Chair. Nat. Oil Corpn. of Kenya 1983-. *Leisure interest:* social welfare. *Address:* P.O. Box 30582, Nairobi, Kenya.

KIBAKI, Mwai, B.A., B.SC.(ECON.); Kenyan politician; b. 1931, Othaya, Kenya; ed. Makerere Univ. Coll.; lecturer in Econs. at Makerere Univ. Coll. 1959-60; Nat. Exec. Officer Kenya African Nat. Union 1960-62; elected by Legis. Council as one of Kenya's nine reps. in Central Legis. Assembly of East African Common Services Org. 1962; mem. House of Reps. for Nairobi Doonholm 1963-; Parl. Sec. to Treasury 1963; Asst. Minister of Econ. Planning and Devt. 1964-66; Minister for Commerce and Industry 1966-69; Minister of Finance 1969-70; Minister of Finance and Econ. Planning 1970-78, of Finance 1978-82, of Home Affairs 1978-79, 1982-88, of Health March 1988-; Vice-Pres. of Kenya 1978-88; Vice-Pres. of Kenya African Nat. Union (KANU) 1978-. *Address:* Ministry of Health, Nairobi, Kenya.

KIBANDA, Simon-Pierre; Central African Republic diplomatist; b. 8 March 1927, Kouanga; mem. Central African Repub. Dels. to UN 1960-64; First Sec. Embassy in Paris 1961-62; Amb. to Israel 1962-63, to Chad 1964-65, to Fed. Repub. of Germany 1965-70; Sec. Gen. Ministry of Foreign Affairs 1970-71, 1977-78, concurrently Dir. of State Protocol 1970-71; Chair. State Cttee. in charge of Financial Affairs 1972-73; Perm. Rep. to UN 1978-83. *Address:* c/o Ministry of Foreign Affairs, Bangui, Central African Republic.

KIBBLE, Thomas Walter Bannerman, M.A., PH.D., F.R.S.; British professor of physics; b. 23 Dec. 1932, Madras, India; s. of Walter F. Kibble and Janet C. W. (née Bannerman) Kibble; m. Anne R. Allan 1957; one s. two d.; ed. Melville Coll., Edinburgh and Univ. of Edinburgh; Commonwealth Fund Fellow, Calif. Inst. of Tech. 1958-59; NATO Fellow, Imperial Coll., London 1959-60, Lecturer in Physics 1961-65, Sr. Lecturer 1965-66, Reader in Theoretical Physics 1966-70, Prof. of Theoretical Physics 1970-, Head, Dept. of Physics 1983-; Sr. Visiting Research Assoc. Univ. of Rochester, N.Y. 1967-68; Chair. Scientists Against Nuclear Arms 1985-; Hughes Medal 1981, Rutherford Medal 1984. *Publication:* Classical Mechanics 1966. *Address:* Blackett Laboratory, Imperial College, Prince Consort Road, London, SW7 2BZ, England. *Telephone:* 01-589 5111 Ext. 6601.

KIBE, Yoshiaki; Japanese politician; b. 7 June 1926; ed. Chuo Univ.; Private Sec. to Minister of Agric.; mem. House of Reps. 1963-; Parl. Vice-Minister for Econ. Agency; Chair. Liberal Democratic Party (LDP) Transport Cttee.; Minister of Construction 1984-85. *Leisure interest:* sport. *Address:* 2-1, Kasumigaseki, Chiyoda-ku, Tokyo 100, Japan.

KIBEDI, Wanume, LL.B.; Ugandan lawyer and politician; b. 3 Aug. 1941, Busesa; s. of Mr. and Mrs. E.M. Kibedi; m. Elizabeth Kibedi (née Amin) 1970; one d.; ed. Busoga Coll. and Univ. of London; articled with Waterhouse and Co., London 1961-66, admitted solicitor 1966; worked in office of Attorney-Gen., Uganda 1968; Partner, Binaisa and Co. (advocates) 1969-70; Minister of Foreign Affairs Feb. 1971-73. (resigned); del. to UN Gen. Ass. 1971; Perm. Rep. to the UN 1986-. *Leisure interests:* chess, tennis, reading. *Address:* Permanent Mission of Uganda to the United Nations, 336 East 45th Street, New York, N.Y. 10017, U.S.A. *Telephone:* 949-0110, 949-0111.

KIBEDI VARGA, Aron, PH.D.; Netherlands professor of French literature and poet; b. 4. Feb. 1930, Szeged, Hungary; m. 1st T. Spreij 1954, 2nd K. Agh 1964; four s. one d.; ed. Univs. of Amsterdam, Leiden, Sorbonne; lecturer in French Literature, Free Univ. of Amsterdam 1954-66, Prof. 1971-; Prof. of French Literature, Univ. of Amsterdam 1966-71; Visiting Prof. Iowa Univ. 1971, Yale Univ. 1975, Princeton Univ. 1980, Rabat Univ. 1985; mem. Cttee. Int. Soc. for the History of Rhetoric 1979-83; Pres. Int. Asscn. Word and Image Studies 1987-90. *Publications:* Criticisms: Les Constantes du Poème 1963, Rhetorique et Littérature 1970, Théorie de la Littérature (Ed.) 1981; Poetry (in Hungarian): Keint es Bent 1963, Teged 1975. *Address:* Department of French, Vrije Universiteit, Amsterdam, The Netherlands. *Telephone:* 5483766.

KIBRIA, Shah A. M. S., M.A.; Bangladesh United Nations official; b. 1 May 1931, Sylhet; m.; one s. one d.; ed. Univ. of Dacca, Fletcher School of Law and Diplomacy, Boston, Mass., U.S.A.; joined diplomatic service of Pakistan 1954; served various embassies until 1971; declared allegiance to Bangladesh and joined Bangladesh mission, Washington, D.C. Aug. 1971; Dir.-Gen. Political Affairs Dept., Ministry of Foreign Affairs March 1972; Sec. Ministry of Foreign Affairs 1972-73; High Commr. in Australia (also accred. to New Zealand and Fiji) 1973-76; Perm. Rep. to UN Offices, Geneva 1976-78; Chair. Preparatory Cttee., Group of 77 for UNCTAD V, Geneva 1978; Foreign Sec., Ministry of Foreign Affairs 1978-81; Exec. Sec. UN Econ. and Social Comm. for Asia and the Pacific (ESCAP) May 1981-; Special Rep. of UN Sec.-Gen. for Co-ordination of Kampuchean Humanitarian Assistance Programmes 1987-. *Address:* Economic and Social Commission for Asia and the Pacific, UN Building, Rajdamnern Avenue, Bangkok 10200, Thailand.

KIBRICK, Anne, ED.D.; American professor of nursing; b. 1 June 1919, Palmer, Mass.; d. of Martin Karlon and Christine Grigas Karlon; m. Sidney Kibrick 1949; one s. one d.; ed. Boston Univ., Columbia Univ., Harvard Univ.; Head Nurse, Worcs. Hahnemann Hosp. 1941-43; Staff Nurse, Children's Hosp. Medical Center, Boston 1943-45; Educ. Dir., Charles V. Chapin Hosp., Providence, R.I. 1945-47; Asst. Educ. Dir., Veterans Admin. Hosp. 1948-49; Asst. Prof. Simmons Coll., Boston 1949-55; Dir. Graduate Programmes in Nursing, Boston Univ. 1958-63, Prof. and Dean 1963-70; Dir. Graduate Programs in Nursing, Boston Coll. 1970-74; Chair. School of Nursing Boston State Coll. 1974-82; Dean School of Nursing Univ. of Mass., Boston 1982-; Consultant Nat. Student Nurses Assen. 1985-; D.H.L. (St. Joseph's Coll.), Mary Adelaide Nutting Award and Distinguished Service Award, Nat. League for Nursing, Service Award, Nat Hadassah Org.; Consultant, Cumberland Coll. of Health Sciences, N.S.W., Australia. *Publications:* (with H. Wechsler) Explorations in Nursing Research 1979, numerous professional articles. *Leisure interests:* reading, knitting, travel. *Address:* Univ. of Massachusetts, Harbor Campus, Boston, Mass. 02125 (Office); 381 Clinton Road, Brookline, Mass. 02146, U.S.A. (Home). *Telephone:* 617-929 8501 (Office); 617-734 4751 (Home).

KIDU, Hon. Sir Buri (William), Kt; Papua New Guinea judge; b. 8 Aug. 1945; s. of Kidu Gaudi and Dobi Vagi; m. Carol Anne Kidu 1969; three s. two d.; ed. Univ. of Queensland; Barrister-at-law, Supreme Courts of Queensland and Papua New Guinea; Legal Officer, Dept. of Law 1971; Crown Prosecutor 1972; Deputy Crown Solicitor 1973-74; Crown Solicitor 1974-77; Sec. for Justice 1977-79; Sec. Prime Minister's Dept. 1979-80; Chief Justice of Papua New Guinea 1980-; Chancellor, Univ. of Papua New Guinea 1981-. *Leisure interests:* reading, swimming. *Address:* Supreme Court, P.O. Box 7018, Boroko, Port Moresby, Papua New Guinea. *Telephone:* 25 7099.

KIDWAI, Mohsina; Indian politician; b. 1 Jan. 1932, Banda Dist.; d. of Qutubuddin Ahmed; m. Khalilur Rahman Kidwai 1953; three d.; ed. Women's Coll., Aligarh; mem. U.P. Legis. Council 1960-74, Legis. Ass. 1974-77, Lok Sabha 1978-79, 1980-84; Minister of State for Food and Civil Supplies, Govt. of U.P. 1973-74, Minister of Harijan and Social Welfare 1974-75, of Small-Scale Industries 1975-77; Union Minister of State for Labour and Rehabilitation 1982-83, for Health and Family Welfare 1983-84, for Rural Devt. Aug.-Oct. and Nov.-Dec. 1984; Minister of Health and Family Welfare 1984-88, of Urban Devt. 1988-; Pres. U.P. Congress Cttee. (I) 1982-; Founder Patron Nat. Girls' Higher Secondary School, Bara Banki and other insts. helping women, children and destitutes, including Harijans. *Leisure interests:* reading biographies and other literary works, music, badminton. *Address:* Civil Lines, Bara Banki, Uttar Pradesh, India.

KIEBER, Walter, D.JUR.; Liechtenstein lawyer and politician; b. 20 Feb. 1931, Feldkirch, Austria; s. of Alfons and Elisabeth Kieber; m. Selma Ritter 1959; one s. one d.; ed. Grammar School in Bregenz, Austria, Univ. of Innsbruck; lawyer in Vaduz 1955-59, 1981-; entered civil service as Head of the Govt. Legal Office 1959; Chief of Presidential Office 1965-; Sec.-Gen. of Govt. 1969, Deputy Head of Govt. 1970-74, Head of Govt. 1974-78, Deputy Head of Govt. 1978-80; partner in Law Office, Vaduz 1981-; Grand Cross, Liechtenstein Order of Merit, Grosses Goldenes Ehrenzeichen am Bande für Verdienste um die Republik Österreich (Austria); Progressive Citizens' Party. *Address:* Landstrasse 22, FL-9494 Schaan, Liechtenstein (Home); Heiligkreuz 6, FL-9490 Vaduz, Liechtenstein (Office). *Telephone:* 2-25-29 (Home); 5-81-00 (Office).

KIELMANSEGG, Gen. Johann Adolf, Graf von; German army officer (retd.); b. 30 Dec. 1906, Hofgeismar; s. of the late Adolf Graf von Kielmansegg and the late Eva Graefin von Kielmansegg (née von Werner); m. Mechthild Freiin von Dincklage 1933; two s. two d.; ed. Monastic School, Rossleben; Army Service 1926, Officer 1930; War Acad., Berlin 1937-39; Gen. Staff, 1st and 6th Panzer Div. 1939-42; OKH (High Command of the Army) 1942-44, C.O. Armed Infantry Regiment 111 1944-45; journalistic activities 1945-50; Office of the Fed. Chancellor 1950-55; Mil. Rep. of Fed. Repub. of Germany to SHAPE, Paris 1955-58; Second-in-Command, 5th Panzer Div. 1959-60, C.O. 10th Panzer Div. 1960-63; Defence Ministry, Bonn until 1963, promoted to rank of Gen. 1963; C.-in-C. Allied Land Forces, Cen. Europe 1963-66; C.-in-C. Allied Forces, Cen. Europe 1966-68; now writer on politico-military matters; mem. Int. Inst. for Strategic Studies (London), and German Assen. for Foreign Affairs; mem. U.S. Strategic Inst. Washington, D.C., Inst. for Foreign Policy Analysis, Cambridge, Mass. Chair. Advisory Bd. Inst. for Research into Military History; Grand Cross of the Fed. Repub. with Ribbon and Star, Commdr. Légion d'honneur, Commdr. Legion of Merit. *Leisure interests:* history, political science. *Address:* Batzenbergstr. 7, 7812 Bad Krozingen, Federal Republic of Germany. *Telephone:* 07633-3352.

KIENIEWICZ, Stefan, PH.D.; Polish historian; b. 20 Sept. 1907, Dereszewicze, U.S.S.R.; m.; three c.; ed. Poznań Univ.; Docent 1946-49, Assoc. Prof. 1949-58; Prof. Warsaw Univ. 1949-77; Prof. Emer. 1977-; Corresp. mem. Polish Acad. of Sciences (PAN) 1965-70, mem. 1970-, Chair. Cttee. of Historical Sciences 1969-71, 1972-83, mem. 1971-75, mem. Scientific Council of PAN History Inst. 1969-84; Head of Contemporary Polish History Group, Warsaw Univ.; Ed. Przegląd Historyczny 1952-; mem. Polish Historical Soc., Hon. mem. 1974-; Foreign mem. Hungarian Acad. of Science 1975-; Dr. h.c. (The Maria Curie-Skłodowska Univ., Lublin) 1975; Knight's Cross, Order of Polonia Restituta 1954, Officer's Cross 1958, Commdr.'s Cross 1973, State Prize 1955, 1964, Minister of Nat. Defence Prize 1972, State Prize (1st Class) 1978, Order of Banner of Labour (1st Class) 1980. *Publications:* Społeczeństwo polskie w powstaniu poznańskim 1848 1935, Ruch chłopski w Galicji 1846 1951, Sprawa włościańska w Powstaniu Styczniowym, 1953, Między ugodą a rewolucją, 1962, Andrzej Zamoyski w latach 1861-1862, Historia Polski 1795-1918 1968, Powstanie Styczniowe 1972, Historia Polski 1976, Dzieje Warszawy 1795-1914 1976, Dzieje Uniwersytetu Warszawskiego 1981. *Address:* Ul. Wiktorska 83/87 m. 32, 02-582 Warsaw, Poland. *Telephone:* 44-23-47.

KIEP, Walther Leisler: German business executive and politician; b. 5 Jan. 1926, Hamburg; s. of late Louis Leisler Kiep and of Eugenie vom Rath; m. Charlotte ter Meer 1950; three s. (one deceased), two d.; ed. Hamburg, Istanbul, Frankfurt; with Ford Motor Co., then Insurance Co. of North America 1948-55, joined Gradmann and Holler 1955-, man. partner 1968-; mem. bds. of Volkswagenwerk AG, Deutsche ICI, Imperial Chemical PLC, London, Bank of Montreal, Canada; Advisory Council of Deutsche Bank; mem. CDU 1961-, mem. Bundestag 1965-80, 1980-81; fmr. Chair. Parliamentary Cttee. on Foreign Aid, Treasurer, mem. Exec. Cttee. 1971-; Lower Saxony Minister for Econs. and Finance 1976-80, concurrently Special Envoy for Turkish aid; Deputy to Leader of Opposition 1980-81; Chair. Atlantik-Brücke, Hamburg 1984-; mem. Supervisory Bd. Volkswagen AG, Wolfsburg 1983; rep. to John J. McCloy Fund, New York; Bundesverdienstkreutz mit Stern. *Publications:* Goodbye Amerika-Was Dann? 1972, A New Challenge for Western Europe 1974. *Leisure interests:* reading, sport. *Address:* Lyonerstrasse 26, 6000 Frankfurt a.M., Federal Republic of Germany.

KIERANS, Eric William; Canadian economist and politician; b. 2 Feb. 1914, Montreal; s. of Hugh Kierans and Lena (née Schmidt); m. Teresa Catherine Whelan 1938; one s. one d.; ed. Loyola Coll., Montreal, and McGill Univ., Montreal; Prof. of Commerce and Finance 1953-60; Dir. McGill School of Commerce 1953-60; Pres. Montreal and Canadian Stock Exchanges 1960-63; Minister of Revenue, Quebec 1963-65; Minister of Health, Quebec 1965-66; Pres. Quebec Liberal Fed. 1966-68; Postmaster-Gen. and Minister responsible for Dept. of Communications 1968-69; Minister of Communications 1969-71; Consultant to Manitoba Govt. on Resources Policy 1972; Dir. Savings and Trust Corpn. of B.C. 1975, Sidbec-Dosco Ltée 1978; Prof. of Econs., McGill Univ. 1972-80; Chair. Canadian Adhesives Ltd. 1980; Prof. of Econs., Dalhousie Univ., Halifax 1983-84; Hon. LL.D (McGill Univ.) 1980; Liberal. *Publications:* Challenge of Confidence: Kierans on Canada 1967, Natural Resources Policy in Manitoba 1973. *Leisure interest:* sports. *Address:* 1000 Winwick Road, Halifax, N.S. B3H 4LS, Canada.

KIESCHNICK, William F., B.S.; American industrialist and civic leader; b. 5 Jan. 1923, Dallas, Texas; s. of William F. Kieschnick and Effie Meador; m. 1st Betty Camp 1948 (deceased); m. 2nd Keith Ann Chapman 1979; one s. one d.; ed. Rice Univ. Houston, Univ. of California Los Angeles, Scripps Oceanographic Inst. La Jolla, Calif.; joined Atlantic Richfield Co. as engineer 1947, rose to Vice-Pres. Crude and Mineral Operations 1966-69, Vice-Pres. Chemical Operations 1969-70, Vice-Pres. Corporate Planning 1970-72, Exec. Vice-Pres. Corporate Planning 1970-72, Exec. Vice-Pres. Downstream Operations 1972-79, Vice-Chair. and C.O.O. 1979-81, Pres. and C.O.O. 1981-85, mem. Bd. of Dirs. 1972-; Dir. First Interstate Bancorp, American Petroleum Inst., Pres. and C.E.O. 1982-; mem. Bd. of Govs. Rice Univ., Bd. of S. Calif. Region of Nat. Conf. of Christians and Jews, Bd. of Trustees of Museum of Contemporary Art, Calif. Inst. of Tech., Exec. Council on Foreign Diplomats, American Fed. for Aging Research, L.A. World Affairs Council, Performing Arts Council, L.A. Music Centre, Leadership Council of Elderhostel, Exec. Cttee. of United Way; Trustee, Aspen Inst. for Humanistic Studies; Vice-Chair. Corporate Fund for John F. Kennedy Center of Performing Arts; mem. A.I.Ch.E., American Assen. Petroleum Geologists, American Inst. of Mining and Petroleum Engineers, Soc. of Petroleum Engineers; Distinguished Alumni Award, Rice Univ. 1981. *Leisure interests:* photography, cross-country skiing, oceanography and meteorology, the arts. *Address:* c/o Atlantic Richfield Company, 515 S. Flower Street, Los Angeles, Calif. 90071, U.S.A.

KIILU, Raphael Muli, B.SC.; Kenyan diplomatist; b. 1938; ed. Xavier Univ., Cincinnati, Ohio; Chargé d'Affaires, Embassy, Washington D.C. 1964-67; First Sec., Kenya High Comm., London 1967-68; First Sec., Kenya Embassy, Cairo 1968-70; Under-Sec. Gen. and Head of UN and Americas Div., Ministry of Foreign Affairs 1970-74; High Commr. to Nigeria 1974-77; Amb. to Egypt 1977-84; Perm. Rep. to UN, New York 1984-. *Address:* Permanent Mission of Kenya to the United Nations, Room 486, 866 United Nations Plaza, New York, N.Y. 10017, U.S.A.

KIJIMA, Torazo, B.ECONS.; Japanese business executive; b. 18 Dec. 1901; ed. Tokyo Imperial Univ. (now Univ. of Tokyo). Dir. Japanese Nat. Railways 1950–52; mem. House of Councillors 1953–59; Pres. Hinomaru Ceramic Industry Co. Ltd. 1953, Aito Vehicles Industries Co. Ltd.; Chair. Bd. of Dirs. Nippon Express Co. Ltd. 1968–; Second Grand Order of Sacred Treasure (Japan) 1972, Commdr., Grand Order (Madagascar) 1973. *Address:* 3-12-9, Soto-Kanda, Chiyoda-ku, Tokyo (Office); 3-42-17, Wakamiya, Nakano-ku, Tokyo, Japan (Home).

KIKABIDZE, Vakhtang Konstantinovich; Soviet actor; b. 20 March 1938; soloist and leader of Georgian pop-group Orero 1966–; film debut in 1967 with Meeting in the Hills; dir. and acted in TV film 'Hi! Friend . . .' 1981; U.S.S.R. State Prize, People's Artist of Georgian S.S.R. 1980. *Film roles include:* Pavel in The Melodies of Veriysky Block 1973, the Count in Completely Gone to Seed 1973, Valiko in Mimino 1978.

KIKHIA, Mansur Rashid; Libyan lawyer and diplomatist; b. 1 Dec. 1931, Benghazi; ed. Cairo and Paris Univs.; joined Diplomatic Service 1957; Asst. in Nationality and Consular Affairs Section, Ministry of Foreign Affairs 1957, Head, Treaties and Int. Confs. Section 1958–60, 1962–65; Second Sec. for Consular and Cultural Affairs, Paris 1960–62; Chargé d'affaires, Paris 1962, Algiers 1963; Consul-Gen., Geneva 1965–67; mem. Perm. Mission to UN 1967–69; Under-Sec. Ministry of Unity and Foreign Affairs 1969–72; Perm. Rep. to UN Jan.–July 1972, 1975–81; Minister of Foreign Affairs 1972–73; private law practice in Tripoli 1973–75; mem. dels. to UN Gen. Assembly 1961, 1966–70, Chair. of del. 1970, 1972, 1975, 1976, Vice-Chair. 1977, 1978, Rep. Libyan del. UN Security Council 1976, 1977, Pres. Security Council Sept. 1976, Nov. 1977, Chair. Libyan del. Third UN Conf. Law of the Sea 1977, 1978, ad hoc comm. on drafting of int. convention against taking of hostages 1977, Chair. UN Security Council Sanctions Comm. 1977, Chair. Libyan del. to preparatory comm. for special session devoted to disarmament. 1977–78. *Address:* 72 Baghdad Street, Tripoli, Libya.

KIKI, Sir Albert Maori, K.B.E.; Papua New Guinea politician; b. 21 Sept. 1931, Orokolo, Gulf Province; s. of Erevu Kiki and Eau Ulamare; m. Elizabeth Arivu Miro 1958; two s. three d.; ed. Fiji School of Medicine; Papua New Guinea Admin. Coll. Public Health Officer, Welfare Officer, Patrol Officer 1954–64; founded first trade union in Papua New Guinea 1962; Pres. Council of Trade Unions 1962–; land claims work with Koiari people; founder mem. Pangu Pati 1965–, Gen. Sec. 1965–72; mem. City Council, Port Moresby 1971–73; mem. for Port Moresby Inland, House of Ass. 1972–; Minister for Lands and Environment 1972–73, for Defence, Foreign Affairs, Trade, Migration and Customs 1974–77; Deputy Prime Minister 1975–77; Chair. Constitutional Comm. 1976–; Chair. of Dirs. Kwila Insurance Corpn. Ltd., Maho Investments Corpn. Ltd., Maruka Pty. Ltd., Or i Pty. Ltd., Ovameveo Devts. Pty. Ltd., New Guinea Motors Pty. Ltd., Credit Corpn. PNG Ltd., Nat. Shipping Corpn.; Hon. LL.D. (Kyung Hee Univ., Repub. of Korea) 1976. *Publications:* Ten Thousand Years in a Lifetime (autobiography) 1970; co-author Ho Hao (arts and culture of the Orokolo people) 1972. *Leisure interests:* reading, writing, hunting, gardening. *Address:* P.O. Box 1739, Boroko; Granville Farm, 8 Mile, Port Moresby, Papua New Guinea (Home). *Telephone:* 258801/258811. Guinea (Home).

KIKUCHI, Kiyoaki, B.L.; Japanese diplomatist; b. 1 Dec. 1922, Sendai City; s. of Yaemon and Shuku (née Arima) Kikuchi; m. Fusako Sato 1952; two d.; ed. Imperial Univ., Tokyo, Johns Hopkins Univ., U.S.A.; Lieut. in navy 1943–46; entered Foreign Service 1946; First Sec., Embassy in U.S.A. 1958; Private Sec. to Foreign Minister (Masayoshi Ohira) 1962; Dir. U.S.A. and Canada Section, Econ. Affairs Div., Ministry of Foreign Affairs 1964; Counsellor at Embassy in Fed. Repub. of Germany 1966; Deputy Dir.-Gen. (1971) and Dir.-Gen. Econ. Co-operation Bureau, Ministry of Foreign Affairs 1975; Amb. to Singapore 1978; Deputy Minister of Foreign Affairs (Personal Rep. of Prime Minister, Annual Summit Meetings of Industrialized Countries) 1980; Amb. to Mexico 1981–84, to Canada 1984–86; Perm. Rep. to UN 1986–88; Grossdienstkrenz (Fed. Repub. of Germany), Cruz del Sur (Brazil), Al-Kawab (Jordan). *Publications:* Political Parties of the United States 1946, Foreign Economic Cooperation of Japan 1977. *Leisure interests:* music, golf. *Address:* c/o Ministry of Foreign Affairs, 2-2, Kasumigaseki, Chiyoda-ku, Tokyo, Japan.

KIKUTAKE, Kiyonori, B.A., F.A.I.A.; Japanese architect; b. 1 April 1928, Kurume; s. of Kiyoshi and Masue Kikutake; m. Norie Sasaki 1953; one s. two d.; ed. Waseda Univ.; est. Kiyonori Kikutake & Assocs. (Architects) 1953, now Rep. Dir.; Prof. Dept. of Architecture, Waseda Univ. 1959; Vice-Pres. Japan Fed. of Professional Architects Asscns., Tokyo Professional Architects' Asscn., Japan Architects' Asscn. 1982–; mem. Bd. Architectural Inst. of Japan 1962–; Visiting Prof. Univ. of Hawaii 1971; del. ↓ UNESCO Int. Conf., Zürich 1970; Hon. Fellow, American Inst. of Architects 1971. *Major works include:* Shimane Prefectural Museum 1958, Sky House 1958, Admin. Building for Izumo Shrine, Tatebayashi City Hall 1963, Hotel Tokoen, Yonago-City, Miyakonojo City Hall, Pacific Hotel, Chigasaki 1966, Iwate Prefectural Library 1967, Shimane Prefectural Library, Hagi Civic Centre 1968, Kurume Civic Centre 1969, Expo Tower for Expo 70, Osaka 1970, Pasadena Heights (tiered mass housing) 1974, Aquapolis (floating module for ocean), Ocean Expo 75 1975, Hagi City Hall 1975, Redevelopment of Yamaga city centre 1975, Tsukuba Academic New Town, Ped-

estrian Deck Network and the Symbol Tower 1976, Otsu Shopping Centre 1976, branches of Kyoto Community Bank 1971–, Tanabe Museum, Matsue City 1979, Darumaya-Seibu Dept. Store 1980, Treasury of Izumo Shrine 1981, Seibu-Yaow Shopping Centre 1981, Karuizawa Art Museum 1981, Kuamoto Pref. Arts and Crafts Centre 1982, Fukuoka City Hall (Assembly Hall) 1982; now Exec. Dir. Tokyo YMCA Inst. of Design; several awards including Ministry of Educ. Arts Award 1964, Architectural Inst. of Japan Award 1964, Pan Pacific Architectural Citation of the Hawaii Chapter, AIA 1964, Cultural Merits of Kurume City 1975, Auguste Perret Award UIA 1978, XXI Mainichi Art Awards 1979. *Publications:* Metabolism 1960 1960, Taisha Kenchiku-ron (Metabolic Architecture) 1968, Ningen-no-Kenchiku (Human Architecture) 1970, Ningen-no-Toshi (A Human City) 1970, Essence of Architecture 1973, Floating City 1973, Kiyonori Kikutake—Works and Methods 1956–70 1973, Community and Civilization 1978, Kiyonori Kikutake-Concepts and Planning 1978, Ningen-no-Kankyo (Human Environment) 1978, Community and City 1978, Tight Spaces, Macro-Engineering 1982. *Leisure interests:* swimming, photography, reading, travel. *Address:* 1-11-15 Ohtsuka, Bunkyo-ku, Tokyo, Japan. *Telephone:* 03-941-9184; 03-941-0830.

KILBRANDON, Baron (Life Peer), cr. 1971, of Kilbrandon, Argyll; **Charles James Dalrymple Shaw,** P.C., LL.D., D.SC.; British judge; b. 15 Aug. 1906, Ayrshire; s. of James E. and Gladys E. Shaw; m. Ruth C. Grant 1937; two s. three d.; ed. Charterhouse School, Balliol Coll., Oxford and Univ. of Edinburgh; Scottish Bar 1932; K.C. 1949; Sheriff of Ayr and Bute 1954, of Perth and Angus 1957; Dean of Faculty of Advocates 1957; Senator, Coll. of Justice 1959–71; Chair. Scottish Law Comm. 1965–71; Lord of Appeal in Ordinary 1971–76; Chair. Royal Comm. on Constitution 1972–73; Head of Inquiry to consider report of New Ireland Forum 1984–; Hon. Fellow, Balliol Coll., Oxford, and Visitor of the Coll. 1974–86; Hon. Bencher, Gray's Inn; Hon. LL.D. (Aberdeen) 1965; Hon. D.Sc. (Edinburgh) 1970. *Publication:* Other People's Law (Hamlyn Lectures) 1966. *Address:* Kilbrandon House, Balvicar, by Oban, Argyll, Scotland. *Telephone:* (085 23) 239.

KILBURN, Tom, C.B.E., PH.D., F.I.E.E., F.ENG., F.R.S.; British professor of computer science; b. 11 Aug. 1921; s. of John W. Kilburn and Ivy Kilburn; m. Irene Marsden 1943; one s. one d.; ed. Wheelwright Grammar School, Dewsbury and Sidney Sussex Coll. Cambridge and Manchester Univ.; Telecommunications Research Establishment, Malvern 1942–46; Lecturer, Univ. of Manchester 1949, Sr. Lecturer 1951, Reader in Electronics 1955, Prof. of Computer Eng. 1960, Prof. of Computer Science 1964–81, now Prof. Emer.; Hon. Fellow, UMIST 1984; Foreign Assoc. Nat. Acad. of Eng. of U.S.A.; Royal Medal, Royal Soc. 1978; Fellow, British Computer Soc.; four hon. degrees and other awards and prizes. *Publications:* papers in professional journals. *Address:* 11 Carlton Crescent, Urmston, Lancs., England. *Telephone:* Urmston 3846.

KILLANIN, 3rd Baron, cr. 1900; **Rt. Hon. Michael Morris,** M.B.E., T.D., M.A., M.R.I.A.; film producer, author and company director; b. 30 July 1914, London; s. of Lieut.-Col. Hon. George H. Morris and Dora Maryan Wesley Hall; m. Sheila M. C. Dunlop, M.B.E. 1945; three s. one d.; ed. Eton Coll., Sorbonne, Paris and Magdalene Coll., Cambridge; mem. of staff, Daily Express then Daily Mail, London 1935–39, War Corresp., Daily Mail, Sino-Japanese War 1937–38, subsequently Asst. Political and Diplomatic Corresp.; served in Second World War 1939–45; Chair. Chubb Ireland Ltd. 1975–88, Ulster Investment Bank, Lombard & Ulster Banking Ltd. 1967–86; Dir. of Irish Shell Ltd. 1947–80, Ulster Bank; Dir. and Chair. Gallahers (Dublin) Ltd. 1978–88, Northern Telecom (Ireland) Ltd.; Chair. Hibernian Life Assen. 1983–86; Syntex Ireland Ltd., Irish Govt. Inquiry into Thoroughbred Industry; Pres. Dublin Theatre Festival 1960–70; Pres. Olympic Council of Ireland 1950–73, Hon. Pres. 1981–; Vice-Pres. Int. Olympic Cttee. 1968–72, Pres. 1972–80, Hon. Life Pres. 1980–; Pres. Irish Nat. Heritage Council 1988; mem. Cultural Relations Cttee. 1947–72, Irish Red Cross Soc. 1947–72, Irish Turf Club, Steward 1973–75, 1981–83; Hon. LL.D. (Nat. Univ. of Ireland) 1975, Hon. D.Litt. (New Univ. of Ulster) 1977; decorations from France, Japan, Germany, Finland, Italy, Monaco, Spain, etc. *Films include:* The Rising of the Moon, Playboy of the Western World, Gideon's Day, etc. *Publications:* Shell Guide to Ireland (with Professor Michael Duignan), Sir Godfrey Kneller, Four Days, The Olympic Games (with John Rodda), The Olympic Games, Moscow and Lake Placid (with John Rodda), My Olympic Years 1983, My Ireland: An Impression 1987; contributions to British, European and American press. *Address:* 9 Lower Mount Pleasant Avenue, Dublin 6; St. Annins, Spiddal, Co. Galway, Ireland. *Telephone:* Dublin 972114; Galway 83103.

KILLEN, Sir (Denis) James, K.C.M.G., LL.B.; Australian barrister and politician (retd.); b. 23 Nov. 1925, Dalby, Queensland; s. of James Walker Killen and Mabel E. Sheridan; m. Joyce Claire Buley 1949; two d.; ed. Brisbane Grammar School, Queensland Tech. Coll. and Univ. of Queensland; mem. House of Reps. 1955–83; Minister of the Navy 1969–71, of Defence 1975–82; Vice-Pres. of Exec. Council and Leader of the House of Reps. 1982–83. *Leisure interests:* horse-racing, golf, reading. *Address:* 253 Chapel Hill Road, Chapel Hill, Queensland 4069, Australia.

KILLICK, Sir John Edward, G.C.M.G.; British diplomatist; b. 18 Nov. 1919, Isleworth; s. of late Edward W. J. Killick and Doris M. Stokes; m. 1st Lynette de Preez 1949 (died 1984); no c.; m. 2nd Irene M. H. Easton, O.B.E.

1985; ed. Latymer Upper School, Univ. Coll., London and Univ. of Bonn; Mil. Service 1939–46; Control Comm. for Germany 1946; entered diplomatic service 1946; Foreign Office 1946–48, Berlin, Frankfurt and Bonn 1948–51; Foreign Office 1951–53; British Embassy, Addis Ababa 1953–57; Nat. Defence Coll. of Canada 1957–58; Foreign Office 1958–61; Imperial Defence Coll. 1962; British Embassy, Washington 1963–68; Asst. Under-Sec. of State, FCO 1968–71; Amb. to U.S.S.R. 1971–73; Deputy Under-Sec. of State, FCO 1973–75; Perm. Rep. to NATO 1975–79; Dir. Dunlop S. Africa 1980–85; Pres. British Atlantic Cttee.; Chair. S.A. Club. *Address:* Challoner's Cottage, 2 Birchwood Avenue, Southborough, Kent, TN4 0UE, England. *Telephone:* (0892) 45702.

KILPATRICK, Robert, B.A.; American insurance company executive; b. 5 Feb. 1924, Fairbanks, La.; s. of Thomas D. and Lula Crowell Kilpatrick; m. Faye Hines 1948; two s. three d.; ed. Univ. of Richmond and Harvard Univ.; Graduate School of Business Admin.; held underwriting positions, Conn. Gen. Life Insurance Co. 1954–58, Asst. Sec. Policyholder and Field Services Dept. 1961–66, Dir. Org. and Systems 1966–68, Sr. Vice-Pres. in charge of group insurance operations 1973–76, Pres. and Chief Exec. Officer 1976–81; Pres., Chair. Exec. Cttee. Connecticut Gen. and INA Corpn. (CIGNA) 1981–85, Chair. 1984– and C.E.O. 1983–88, Chair. Bd. of Dirs. 1988–; Vice-Pres. and Chief Admin. Officer, Aetna Insurance Co. (property and casualty affiliate of Conn. Gen.) 1968–73; Dir. Conn. Business and Industry Asscn., Greater Hartford Chamber of Commerce; mem. Bd. of Dirs. Fed. Reserve Bank of Boston, Scoville Mfg. Co., American Council of Life Insurance, Health Insurance Asscn. of America; Trustee, Conn. Public Expenditure Council Inc., Univ. of Richmond, S. S. Huebner Foundation for Insurance Educ. of the Wharton School (Univ. of Pa.); Corporator Hartford Hosp., Inst. of Living, Hartford. *Address:* Connecticut General and INA Corporation, Hartford, Conn. 06152, U.S.A. (Office).

KIM, Jung Won; Korean business executive; b. 3 March 1948; ed. Kyungnam Sr. High School, Guilford Coll., New York; joined Hanil Synthetic Fiber Ind. Co. Ltd. 1972, Exec. Man. Dir. 1974, Vice-Pres. 1975, Pres. 1979–; Pres. Hanhyo Co. Ltd. 1977, Chair. 1984–; Pres. Hanhyo Devt. Co. Ltd. 1978, Chair. 1984–; Pres. Kyungnam Woollen Textile Co. Ltd. 1979; First Chair. Hanhyo Acad. 1982; Pres. Korean Amateur Volleyball Asscn. 1983, Vice-Pres. Asian Volleyball Asscn. 1983; awarded Saemaul Decoration 1974; First Hon. Consul Kingdom of the Netherlands 1985. *Address:* Kukje-ICC Corpn., C.P.O. Box 747, Seoul, Republic of Korea.

KIM, Nelli; Soviet gymnast (retd.); b. 29 July 1957, Shurab, Tazhikistan; m.; many times nat. title and Soviet Cup winner; mem. European and World Champion teams 1974, individual champion vault, floor exercises 1978, overall World Champion 1979; team, vault and floor exercises Gold Medal, overall Silver Medal, Olympic Games, Montreal 1976; team championship Gold Medal, shared Floor Exercises Gold Medal, Olympic Games, Moscow 1980. *Address:* c/o Soviet Sports Council, Sports Committee of the U.S.S.R., Skaternyi per 4, Per eu lok, Moscow, U.S.S.R.

KIM, H.E. Cardinal Stephen Sou-hwan; Korean ecclesiastic; b. 8 May 1922, Taegu; ed. Sophia Univ., Tokyo, Major Seminary, Seoul, and Sociology Dept., Univ. of Munster, Germany; ordained priest 1951; Pastor of Andong, Archdiocese of Taegu 1951–53; Sec. to Archbishop of Taegu 1953–55; Pastor of Kimchon (Taegu) 1955–56; Dir. Sung-Eui Schools, Kimchon 1955–56; sociology studies, Univ. of Munster, Germany 1956–64; Editor-in-Chief Catholic Shibo (weekly) 1964–66; Bishop of Masan 1966–68; Archbishop of Seoul 1968–; cr. Cardinal 1969; Pres. Bishops' Conf. of Korea until 1987, Pres. Follow-up Cttee. for Fed. of Asian Bishops' Conf. 1971–74; Dr. h.c. (Sogang Univ. Seoul) 1974, (Notre Dame Univ., U.S.A.) 1977. *Leisure interests:* music, literature. *Address:* Archbishop's House, 2-Ga 1, Myong-dong, Chung-ku, Seoul, Republic of Korea. *Telephone:* (02) 771-76.

KIM DAE JUNG; Korean politician; b. 1924, Mokpo; m. Lee Hee Ho; imprisoned by Communist troops during Korean war; mem. Finance Cttee. Nat. Assembly 1960; presidential cand., Korean Democratic Party 1971; kidnapped, Tokyo, and held for three days Aug. 1973; served part of five-year prison sentence for anti-government activities 1976–78; arrested May 1980 and sentenced to death for plotting to overthrow the Govt. Sept. 1980; sentence commuted to life and then to 20 years' imprisonment; released Dec. 1982; went to U.S.A. for medical treatment; returned to Seoul 1985; Presidential Cand. 1987 Elections; Pres. Peace and Democracy Party 1987–88. *Address:* c/o Party for Peace and Democracy, Dae-Ha Bldg., 14–11 Yoedo-dong, Yungdungpo-Ku, Seoul, Republic of Korea.

KIM DONG-JO; Korean diplomatist; b. 14 Aug. 1918, Pusan; s. of the late Byung Woo Kim and Won Tong Cho; m. Duman Song 1944; two s. four d.; ed. Seoul Coll. of Commerce, Kyushu Imperial Univ. Law School, Japan; Chief Sec. to Minister of Communications 1949–51, Dir.-Gen. Admin. and Inspection Bureau, Ministry of Communications 1951; Dir. Bureau of Political Affairs, Ministry of Foreign Affairs 1951–52, 1954–57; Counsellor, Korean Embassy, Taiwan 1952–54; Deputy Minister of Foreign Affairs 1957–59; Special Envoy to Repub. of China, Malaysia, Philippines, Thailand and Repub. of Viet-Nam 1959; private law practice 1960–63; Head del. to Asian People's Anti-Communist League, Viet-Nam 1963; Chair. Foreign Relations and Defence Cttee. 1963; Pres. Korea Trade Promotion Corpn. 1964; Amb. to Japan 1964–67, to U.S.A. 1967–73; Minister for Foreign Affairs 1973–75; Special Asst. to The Pres. for Foreign Affairs 1976–79;

Pres. Korea Petroleum Devt. Corpn. 1979–80; Partner Han Bok Law Firm and Adviser to Hyundai Heavy Industries 1981–; Hon. LL.D. (Illinois Coll.) 1969, Hon. PH.D. (de la Salle Coll., Philippines) 1975. *Publications:* Reminiscence of Three Decades of Korea-Japan Diplomatic Relations 1986. *Leisure interest:* golf. *Address:* 345-59 Pyung Chang Dong, Chong Ro Ka, Seoul, Republic of Korea.

KIM IL SUNG, Marshal; Korean politician; b. (as Kim Song Ju) 15 April 1912, Mangyongdae, Pyongyang; s. of late Kim Hyong Jik and Kang Ban Sok; m. 1st Kim Jung Sook, 2nd Kim Song Ae; f. Down-With-Imperialism Union (T.D.) 1926; f. Young Communist League 1927, imprisoned 1929–30; f. Korean Revolutionary Army 1930; organized and led Korean People's Revolutionary Army to victory in struggle against the Japanese 1932–45; f. Fatherland Restoration Assen., elected Chair. 1936; liberated Korea Aug. 1945; f. Workers' Party of Korea, elected Chair. 1945; Supreme Commdr. Korean People's Army during Korean War 1950–53; proclaimed the Democratic People's Repub. of Korea 1948; Premier 1948–72, Pres. (Head of State) Dec. 1972–; organized struggle for complete cooperativization of rural economy 1953–58; organized struggle for transformation of pvt. trade and industry for complete socialization 1957–70; Gen. Sec. Cen. Cttee. Workers' Party of Korea 1966–; Marshal, Hero of Labour, and Hero of the Democratic People's Repub. of Korea (three times), Order of Nat. Flag (1st Class) (six times), Order of Freedom and Independence (1st Class) (twice), Order Commemoration of Democratic People's Repub. of Korea (twice), numerous foreign hon. titles and decorations including Order of the Yugoslav Great Star 1977, Order of Lenin 1972 (twice), Karl Marx Order (G.D.R.) 1982 (twice), National Necklace Order of Merit (Central African Repub.), Gold Star of Nahouri (Burkina Faso) 1985, November 17 Medal (Int. Union of Students) 1986 and numerous other leading decorations. *Publications:* Collections of Works of Kim Il Sung (35 vols.), Selected Works of Kim Il Sung (9 vols.), Selections of Works of Kim Il Sung (6 vols.) and many other works. *Address:* Office of the President, Pyongyang, Democratic People's Republic of Korea.

KIM JONG IL; Korean politician; b. 16 Feb. 1942, secret camp on Mt. Paekdu; s. of Kim Il Sung (q.v.) and Kim Jung Sook; m.; one c.; ed. Kim Il Sung Univ., Pyongyang; Vice-Dir., then Dir. Dept. of Cen. Cttee. Workers' Party of Korea 1964–73; Sec. Cen. Cttee. Workers' Party of Korea 1973; mem. Political Cttee. Cen. Cttee. 1974; mem. Presidium of Political Bureau, Sec. Cen. Cttee., mem. Mil. Comm. Cen. Cttee. at Sixth Congress 1980; Deputy to Supreme People's Assembly 1982–; Hon. Dr. (Checlaeo Univ., Peru) 1986; Hon. Prof. Inka Garsilaso, Dega Univ., Peru 1986; Hero of Democratic People's Repub. of Korea (twice), Kim Il Sung Order (twice), Grand Croix de l'Ordre Nat. des Mille Collines, Rwanda, Rorima Order, Guyana and many other foreign and domestic awards and honours. *Publications:* On the Juche Idea, On Some Problems of Education in the Juche Idea, Let Us Advance Under the Banner of Marxism-Leninism and the Juche Idea, etc. *Address:* Central Committee of the Workers' Party of Korea, Pyongyang, Democratic People's Republic of Korea.

KIM JONG PIL, Brig.-Gen.; Korean politician; b. 7 Jan. 1926, Puyo; m. Park Young Ok (niece of the late Pres. Park Chung Hee); one s. one d.; ed. High School, Kongju, Seoul Nat. Univ. and Korean Military Acad.; served in Korean war; Dir. Korean Central Intelligence Agency 1961–63; mem. Nat. Assembly 1963–68, 1971–80; Chair. Democratic Republican Party 1963–68; Senior Adviser to Pres. 1970; Vice-Pres. Democratic Republican Party 1971, Pres. 1979–80 (banned from political activity 1980); Pres. New Democratic Republican Party 1987–; Prime Minister 1971–75; mem. Spanish Nat. Acad., Korean Acad.; numerous awards from Korean and foreign govts.; Hon. LL.D. (Long Island Univ., N.Y.) 1964, (Chungang Univ., Seoul) 1966, (Fairleigh Dickinson Univ.) 1968; Hon. D.Hum.Litt. (Westminster Coll., Fulton, Mo.) 1966; Hon. Ph.D. (Hongik Univ.) 1974. *Leisure interests:* painting, music. *Address:* New Democratic Republican Party, 58-18 Shimmuno 1 ka, Seoul; 340-38, Sindang 4-dong, Sungdong-ku, Seoul, Republic of Korea.

KIM JOON-SUNG; Korean banker and politician; ed. Seoul Commercial High School; Branch Dir. Nat. Agric. Co-operatives Fed., Pusan 1958; Chair. Knitted Wear Makers Assen., Kvongsang Pukto 1963; Vice-Chair. Korea Chamber of Commerce and Industry, Taegu Chapter 1967; Pres. Taegu Bank 1967, then Pres. Korea First, Korea Exchange Bank, Korea Devt. Bank –1980; Gov. Bank of Korea 1980–82; Deputy Prime Minister and Minister of Econ. Planning 1982–83. *Address:* c/o Office of the Deputy Prime Minister, Seoul, Republic of Korea.

KIM MAHN-JE, D.ECON.; Korean economist and politician; b. 3 Dec. 1934, Sonsan; ed. Univs. of Denver and Missouri, U.S.A.; Assoc. Prof., Sogang Univ., Seoul 1965–70, Prof. 1982–; mem. Legis. Ass. 1980–; Minister of Finance 1983–86; Deputy Prime Minister and Minister of Econ. Planning 1986–88; Pres. Korean Devt. Inst. 1971–82, Korean Int. Econ. Inst. (KIEI) 1981–, Koram Bank 1983–84; Sr. Policy Researcher, Policy Research Inst. of Democratic Justice Party (DJP) 1982–; mem. Monetary Bd. 1975–, Econ. Planning Bd. Advisory Cttee. 1982–. *Address:* Ministry of Finance, 108-4 Susong-dong, Chongno-ku, Seoul, Republic of Korea.

KIM SANG-HYUP; Korean politician; b. 20 April 1920; ed. Tokyo Univ.; Prof. Korea Univ. 1946–62; mem. Nat. Acad. of Sciences 1960–; Minister of Educ. 1962; Pres. Korea Univ. 1970–75, 1977–82; Vice-Chair. Constant

Revision Deliberation Cttee., Govt. of Repub. of Korea 1980; mem. Legis. Assembly 1980; mem. Advisory Cttee., Ministry of Foreign Affairs 1982; Prime Minister of Repub. of Korea 1982-83. *Address:* c/o Prime Minister's Residence, 106 Samchongdong Chongnoku, Seoul, Republic of Korea.

KIM WOUN-GIE; Korean politician and banker; b. 3 Dec. 1924, Dangjin, Chungchong Namdo; ed. Korea Univ.; Dir. Finance Management Bureau, Ministry of Finance 1961; Vice-Minister of Construction 1969-70; Vice-Minister of Finance 1970-72; Standing mem. Korean Olympic Cttee. 1971-, Vice-Chair. 1974-; Pres. Korean Devt. Bank 1972-78; Vice-Chair. Seoul Bank Asscn. 1975-; Minister of Finance 1978-80; Deputy Prime Minister and Minister of Economic Planning June-Sept. 1980; Pres. Korean Traders Asscn. Nov. 1980. *Address:* 201-17, Tonggyo-dong, Mapogu, Seoul, Republic of Korea.

KIM YONG SHIK; Korean diplomatist; b. 11 Nov. 1913, Choongmu; s. of Kim Chai Ho and Chung Ok; m. Park Kyung Hee; ed. Chu-ou Univ., Tokyo; Consul, Hong Kong 1949; Consul-Gen., Honolulu 1949; Minister, Korean Mission, Japan 1951; Minister, Korean Legation, France 1957; Minister, Korean Mission, Geneva 1959; Perm. Vice-Minister, Ministry of Foreign Affairs 1960; Amb. to U.K. (also accred. to Sweden, Denmark, and Norway) 1961; Amb. to the Philippines 1962; Minister of Foreign Affairs March 1963; Minister without Portfolio Dec. 1963; Perm. Observer of Republic of Korea at UN, concurrently accred. as Amb. to Canada 1964-70; Special Asst. to Pres. for Foreign Affairs Dec. 1970; Minister of Foreign Affairs 1971-73, of the Bd. of Nat. Unification 1973-74; Amb. to U.K. 1974-77, to U.S.A. 1977-81; Chair. Advisory Cttee. for Nat. Unification Policy 1984-; Pres. Korean Nat. Red Cross 1981-82, Seoul Olympic Organizing Cttee. for 1988 Olympics, 1982-; D.Jur. (Missouri Valley Coll.). *Leisure interests:* reading, swimming. *Address:* c/o Ministry of Foreign Affairs, Seoul, Republic of Korea.

KIM YOUNG SAM, B.A.; Korean politician; b. 20 Dec. 1927, Geoje Dist., South Kyongsang Prov.; s. of Hong-Jo Kim; m. Myoung-Soon Sohn; two s. three d.; ed. Kyungnam High School and Seoul Nat. Univ.; mem. Nat. Ass. 1954-79; re-elected Pres. New Democratic Party 1974, 1979; expelled from Nat. Ass. for opposition to regime of Pres. Park. 1979; arrested under martial law 1980-81; banned from political activity Nov. 1980; organized Democratic Mountain Club 1981; again under house arrest 1982-83; staged 23-day hunger strike demanding democracy May-June 1983; Co-Chair. Council for Promotion of Democracy 1984; played leading role in org. of New Korea Democratic Party (absorbing Democratic Korea Party) which won large number of seats in 1985 election; under house arrest several times; political ban lifted May 1985; Presidential Cand. 1987 Elections; Pres. Reunification Democracy Party 1987-88; made frequent visits to U.S.A., Europe, Middle East and S.E. Asia until 1979; Dr. h.c. (Towson State Univ., Baltimore) 1974. *Publications:* There is No Hill We Can Depend On, Politics is Long and Political Power is Short, Standard-Bearer in his Forties, My Truth and My Country's Truth. *Leisure interests:* calligraphy, mountain climbing, jogging, swimming. *Address:* Sangdo-dong 7-6, Tongjak-ku, Seoul, Republic of Korea.

KIMBER, Derek Barton, O.B.E., M.SC., D.I.C., F.C.G.I.; British shipbuilder and business executive; b. 2 May 1917, Stockport; s. of George and Marion Kimber (née Barton); m. Gwendoline Margaret Maude Brotherton 1943; two s. two d.; ed. Bedford School, Imperial Coll., London Univ., Royal Naval Coll., Greenwich; with Royal Corps of Naval Constructors 1939-49; Consultant, Urwick Orr and Partners Ltd. 1950-54; Man. Fairfield Shipbuilding and Eng. Co. Ltd. 1954, Dir. 1961, Deputy Man. Dir. 1963-65; Dir. Harland and Wolff Ltd. 1966-69; Dir.-Gen. Chemical Industries Asscn. 1970-73; Dir. British Ship Research Asscn. (Trustees) Ltd. 1973-81; Chair. Austin and Pickersgill Ltd. 1973-83, Smiths Dock Co. Ltd. 1980-83, Sunderland Shipbuilders Ltd. 1980-83, Govan Shipbuilders Ltd. 1980-83; Dir. A. and P. Appledore Int. Ltd. 1974-77; Dir. Equity Capital for Industry Ltd. 1977-86, Eggar Forrester 1983-; numerous official posts including: Dir. Glasgow Chamber of Commerce 1962-65; Pres. Clyde Shipbuilders Asscn. 1964-65; Vice-Pres. Shipbuilders and Repairers Nat. Asscn. 1976-77; mem. Shipbuilding Industry Training Bd. 1964-69, Econ. Devt. Cttee., Chemical Industry 1970-72, Council, Royal Inst. of Naval Architects 1961- (Chair. 1973-75, Pres. 1977-81), Council N.E. Inst. Engineers and Shipbuilders 1974-, Vice-Pres. 1978-; Gen. Cttee. Lloyds Register of Shipping 1973-, Tech. Cttee. 1976-80, Exec. Bd. 1978-84; CBI Cen. Council 1970-72, 1975-84, Northern Region Council 1973-80 (Chair. 1975-77); British Tech. Cttee., American Bureau of Shipping 1976-; Liveryman, Worshipful Co. of Shipwrights 1967 (Asst. to Court 1974-, Warden 1982-); Dir. London and Overseas Freighters PLC 1979-, Chair. 1984-; Dir. Wilks Shipping Co. Ltd. 1986-; Deputy Chair. AMARC 1986-; Gov. Imperial Coll., London Univ. 1967-87; mem. Bd. Council of Eng. Insts. 1977-81; Founder Fellow, Fellowship of Eng., CEI; Hon. F.R.I.N.A. 1981; R.I.N.A. Gold Medal 1977. *Publications:* numerous papers on shipbuilding. *Leisure interests:* shipbuilding, golf, rough gardening. *Address:* Broughton, Monks Road, Virginia Water, Surrey, England. *Telephone:* 099-04-4274.

KIMURA, Motoo, PH.D., D.SC.; Japanese geneticist; b. 13 Nov. 1924, Okazaki; s. of Issaku Kimura and Kana Kaneiwa; m. Hiroko Mino 1957; one s.; ed. Kyoto Univ., Univ. of Wisconsin; Asst., Kyoto Univ. 1947-49; Researcher Nat. Inst. of Genetics 1949-57, Lab. Head 1957-64, Head of Dept. of Population Genetics 1964-, Prof. 1984-; Visiting Prof. Univ. of

Pavia 1963, 1965, Univ. of Wis. 1966, Princeton Univ. 1969, Stanford Univ. 1973; Foreign Assoc. Nat. Acad. of Sciences, U.S.A. 1973; Foreign Hon. mem. American Acad. Arts and Sciences 1978; mem. Japan Acad. 1982; Hon. D.Sc. (Chicago) 1978, (Wis.) 1986; Japanese Genetics Soc. Prize, Weldon Memorial Prize, Japan Acad. Prize, Japan Soc. of Human Genetics Prize, Order of Culture from Japanese Govt. 1976; Hon. Citizen of Okazaki 1977; Chevalier Ordre Nat. du Mérite 1986; Asahi Prize, Asahi Shimbun 1986, John J. Carty Award for the Advancement of Science, N.A.S. 1987; Hon. mem. Genetical Soc. of G.B. 1987. *Publications:* Outline of Population Genetics (Japanese) 1960, Diffusion Models in Population Genetics 1964, An Introduction to Population Genetics Theory (with J. F. Crow) 1970, Theoretical Aspect of Population Genetics (with T. Ohta) 1971, Future of Man from the Standpoint of Genetics (Editor, Japanese) 1974, The Neutral Theory of Molecular Evolution 1983. *Leisure interest:* raising and hybridizing Lady's Slipper orchids. *Address:* National Institute of Genetics, Yata 1, 111, Mishima 411 (Office); 7-24 Kiyozumi-cho, Mishima 411, Japan (Home). *Telephone:* 0559-75-0771 (Office); 0559-75-8635 (Home).

KINAST, Jan, M.A.; Polish diplomatist and lawyer; b. 26 Jan. 1928, Warsaw; ed. Warsaw Univ.; mem. Grey Ranks of Polish Pathfinders' Union during Nazi Occupation 1942-44; subsequently prisoner in Nazi concentration camps Auschwitz, Flossenburg and Dachau; journalist, managerial posts in youth journals 1954-58; Dir. Horyzonty Publishing House, Warsaw 1958-62; Deputy C.-in-C. of Polish Pathfinders' Union 1959-62; with Ministry of Foreign Affairs 1962-; Second, then First Sec. of Polish Embassy in U.S.A., Washington D.C. 1964-68; Dir. of Dept., Ministry of Foreign Affairs 1973-77; Amb. to Brazil 1977-81, to U.S.A. 1987-; Dir. of Dept., Ministry of Foreign Affairs 1981-84, Under-Sec. of State 1984-87; mem. Polish United Workers' Party (PZPR). *Address:* Embassy of the Polish People's Republic, 2640 16th Street, N.W., Washington, D.C. 20009, U.S.A.

KINCL, Frantisek; Czechoslovak politician; b. 2 Feb. 1941, Ricany, Brno; ed. Tech. Univ. Brno; mem. Regional CP Cttee. Ostrava; Deputy, Czech Nat. Council; mem. Nat. Security Corps 1965-, Head, Ostrava Regional Admin. 1979-88; Deputy Minister of Interior 1988; Minister of Interior Oct. 1988-. *Address:* Ministry of the Interior, Prague, Czechoslovakia.

KIND, Dieter Hans, DR. ING.; German electrical engineer; b. 5 Oct. 1929, Reichenberg, Bohemia; s. of Hans Kind and Gerta Kind; ed. Technical Univ., Munich; Prof. and Dir. High-Voltage Inst., Technical Univ., Brunswick 1962; Pres. Physikalisch-Technische Bundesanstalt, Brunswick and Berlin 1975-, Comité Int. des Poids et Mésures, Sèvres/Paris 1984-; Fellow, I.E.E.E.; Bundesverdienstkreuz. *Publications:* High-Voltage Experimental Technique 1978, High-Voltage Insulation Technology 1985; about 50 scientific articles. *Leisure interests:* sport, literature. *Address:* Bundesallee 100, 3300 Brunswick, Federal Republic of Germany. *Telephone:* (0531) 592 1000.

KIND, Friedrich; German politician; b. 20 Dec. 1928, Leipzig; Chair., Potsdam District Cttee., Christlich-Demokratische Union (CDU), German Democratic Republic 1952-; mem. Presidium, Cen. Cttee. CDU 1960-74; mem. Volkskammer 1952-54, 1958-; mem. Cttee. for Nat. Defence, Volkskammer 1969-71; mem. State Council of German Democratic Repub. 1960-; Vaterländischer Verdienstorden in Bronze and Silver, Verdienstmedaille and other decorations. *Address:* Staatsrat, Marx-Engels-Platz, 1020 Berlin, German Democratic Republic.

KING, Billie Jean; American tennis player; b. 22 Nov. 1943, Long Beach, Calif.; d. of Willard J. Moffitt; m. Larry King 1965; ed. Los Angeles State Univ.; Amateur player 1958-67, professional 1967-; Australian Champion 1968; Italian Champion 1970; French Champion 1972; Wimbledon Champion 1966, 1967, 1968, 1972, 1973, 1975; U.S.A. Champion 1967, 1971, 1972, 1974; Fed. Repub. of Germany Champion 1971; South African Champion 1966, 1967, 1969; has won record 20 Wimbledon titles (6 singles, 10 doubles, 4 mixed) and played more than 100 matches; had won 1,046 singles victories by 1984; Top Woman Athlete of Year 1973; sports commentator, ABC-TV 1975-78; Publisher, Women Sports 1973-; Commr., U.S. Tennis Team 1981-. *Publications:* Tennis to Win 1970, Billie Jean (with Kim Chapin) 1974. *Address:* c/o Future Inc., 1801 Century Park East, Suite 1400, Los Angeles, Calif. 90067, U.S.A.

KING, Bruce; American politician; b. 6 April 1924, Stanley, N.M.; s. of William and Molly (Schooler) King; m. Alice M. Martin 1947; two s.; ed. Stanley High School and Univ. of New Mexico; County Commr., Santa Fé County 1955-58, Chair. 1957-58; mem. New Mexico House of Reps. 1959-68, Speaker 1963-64, 1965-66, 1967-68; legis. mem. State Bd. of Finance 1961-62; Chair. Legis. Council 1964, 1966, 1968; Democratic State Chair. 1966; Pres. of State Constitutional Convention 1969; Gov. of New Mexico 1971-73, 1979-82; Dir. of various business concerns and mem. numerous civic orgs. *Address:* c/o Office of the Governor, State Capitol, Santa Fé, New Mexico, U.S.A.

KING, Coretta Scott, A.B., MUS.B.; American singer and civil rights campaigner; b. 27 April 1927, Marion, Ala.; d. of Obidiah Scott and Bernice McMurray; m. Martin Luther King, Jr. 1953 (murdered 1968); two s. two d.; ed. Antioch Coll., New England Conservatory of Music; concert debut as singer, Springfield, Ohio 1948; numerous concerts throughout U.S.A.; performed in India 1959, and at Freedom Concert, U.S.A.; Voice Instructor, Morris Brown Coll., Atlanta, Ga. 1962; Del. to White House Conf. on

Children and Youth 1960; sponsor, Cttee. for Sane Nuclear Policy, Cttee. on Responsibility, Mobilization to End War in Viet-Nam 1966–67; mem. Southern Rural Action Project, Inc.; Pres. Martin Luther King Jr. Foundation; Chair. Comm. on Econ. Justice for Women; mem. Exec. Cttee., Nat. Cttee. of Inquiry; Co-Chair. Clergy and Laymen Concerned about Viet-Nam, Nat. Comm. for Full Employment 1974; Pres. Martin Luther King Jr. Center for Social Change; Co-Chairperson Nat. Cttee. for Full Employment; mem. Exec. Bd. Nat. Health Insurance Cttee.; mem. Bd. Southern Christian Leadership Conf., Martin Luther King Jr. Foundation, U.K.; Trustee, Robert F. Kennedy Memorial Foundation, Ebenezer Baptist Church; sponsor, Margaret Sanger Memorial Foundation; Commentator, Cable News Network, Atlanta 1980–; lecturer and writer; numerous awards including Universal Love Award, Premio San Valentine Cttee. 1968, Wateler Peace Prize 1968, Dag Hammarskjöld Award 1969, Pacem in Terris Award, Int. Overseas Service Foundation 1969, Leadership for Freedom Award, Roosevelt Univ. 1971, Martin Luther King Memorial Medal 1971, Int. Viareggio Award 1971; Hon. L.H.D. (Boston Univ.) 1969, (Marymount-Manhattan Coll., New York) 1969, (Morehouse Coll., Atlanta) 1970; Hon. H.H.D. (Brandeis Univ., Waltham, Mass.) 1969, (Wilberforce Univ., Ohio) 1970, (Bethune-Cookman Coll., Daytona Beach, Fla.) 1970, (Princeton Univ.) 1970; Hon. LL.D. (Bates Coll., Lewiston, Me.) 1971; Hon. Mus.D. (New England Conservatory of Music, Boston) 1971. *Publications:* My Life With Martin Luther King, Jr. 1969; articles in magazines. *Address:* Martin Luther King Jr. Center for Nonviolent Social Change, 449 Auburn Avenue, N.E., Atlanta, Ga. 30312; 671 Beckwith Street, S.W., Atlanta, Ga. 30314, U.S.A.

KING, Francis Henry, C.B.E., O.B.E., M.A., F.R.S.L.; British writer; b. 4 March 1923, Adelboden, Switzerland; s. of Eustace Arthur Cecil King and Faith Mina Read; ed. Shrewsbury School and Balliol Coll., Oxford; served in British Council 1948–62, Regional Dir., Kyoto, Japan 1958–62; theatre critic Sunday Telegraph 1978–88; Pres. English PEN 1978–86, Int. PEN 1986–89; Somerset Maugham Prize 1952, Katherine Mansfield Short Story Prize 1965, Yorkshire Post Prize 1984. *Publications:* novels To the Dark Tower 1946, Never Again 1947, The Dividing Stream 1951, The Widow 1957, The Man on the Rock 1957, The Custom House 1961, The Last of the Pleasure Gardens 1965, The Waves Behind the Boat 1967, A Domestic Animal 1970, Flights 1973, A Game of Patience 1974, The Needle 1975, Danny Hill 1977, The Action 1978, Act of Darkness 1983, Voices in an Empty Room 1984, Frozen Music (novella) 1987, The Woman Who Was God 1988, Punishments 1989; short stories: So Hurt and Humiliated 1959, The Japanese Umbrella 1964, The Brighton Belle 1968, Hard Feelings 1976, Indirect Method 1980, One is a Wanderer 1985; biography: E. M. Forster and His World 1978, My Sister and Myself: The Diaries of J. R. Ackerley 1982; travel: Florence 1982. *Leisure interests:* pictures and music. *Address:* 19 Gordon Place, London, W8 4JE, England. *Telephone:* 01-937 5715.

KING, Gen. Sir Frank Douglas, G.C.B., M.B.E.; British army officer (retd.); b. 9 March 1919, Brightwell, Berkshire; s. of Arthur King and Kate Eliza Sheard; m. Joy Emily Ellen Taylor-Lane 1947; one s. two d.; ed. Wallingford County Grammar School; served with 21st Royal Fusiliers 1940–42, Airborne Forces 1943–45; Royal Mil. Coll. of Science 1946; Staff Coll. 1950; Command, Second Bn. Parachute Regt. 1960–62, 11th Infantry Brigade Group, British Army of the Rhine (B.A.O.R.) 1962–64; Dir. Land-Air Warfare, Ministry of Defence 1967–68; Commdt. Royal Mil. Coll. of Science 1969–70; G.O.C.-in-C. Strategic Command 1971–72; G.O.C.-in-C. Dir. of Operations, N. Ireland 1973–75; Commdr., Northern Army Group and C.-in-C., B.A.O.R. 1976–78; Dir. John Taylor (Mansfield), Springthorpe, Kilton Property Cos., Control Risks Ltd. 1979, Airborne Forces Charitable Devt. Trust 1988–; Sr. Mil. Adviser, Short Brothers 1979–84; Deputy Chair. Control Risks Ltd. 1980–86; Chair., John Taylor Trust 1978–; Chair. Asset Protection Int. Ltd. 1981–86; mem. Council Air League; Trustee Airborne Forces Security Trust. *Leisure interests:* golf, gardening. *Address:* c/o Royal Bank of Scotland, 69 Aldwych, London, W.C.2, England.

KING, Ivan R(obert), PH.D.; American astronomer; b. 25 June 1927, New York; s. of Myram King and Anne (Franzblau) King; m. Alice Greene 1952 (divorced 1982); two s. two d.; ed. Woodmere Acad., Hamilton Coll., Harvard Univ.; served U.S.N.R. 1952–54; Methods Analyst, U.S. Dept. of Defence 1952–56; Asst. Prof., then Assoc. Prof., Univ. of Ill. 1956–64; Assoc. Prof., then Prof. of Astronomy Univ. of Calif. at Berkeley 1964–, Chair. Astronomy Dept. 1967–70; Pres. American Astronomical Soc. 1978–80; mem. A.A.A.S., Chair. Astronomy Section 1973; mem. N.A.S., American Acad. of Arts and Sciences. *Publications:* The Universe Unfolding 1976; 90 articles in scientific journals. *Address:* Astronomy Department, University of California, Berkeley, Calif. 94720, U.S.A. *Telephone:* (415) 642-2206.

KING, Kurleigh Dennis, PH.D.; Barbadian economist; b. 10 Dec. 1933; s. of Burleigh St.C. and Germaine (née Rice) King; m. 1st Herma Graham 1957 (divorced 1977), one d.; m. 2nd Berenice Johnson 1978; ed. London Univ. and Graduate School of Business, Columbia Univ., New York; Asst. Dean, Graduate School of Business, Columbia Univ. 1967–68; Gen. Man. Barbados Ind. Devt. Corpn. 1968–74; Exec. Trustee, Barbados Inst. of Man. and Productivity 1971–74; Vice-Pres. Int. Bureau for Professional Devt. 1973–76; Dir. Industry Div., Caribbean Devt. Bank 1974–78, 1984–87; Gov. Cen. Bank of Barbados 1987–; Vice-Pres. Int. Council for Adult Educ.

1979–; Sec.-Gen. Caribbean Community (CARICOM) 1978–84; Trustee, Maharishi Int. Univ., Ia., U.S.A. 1979–. *Publications:* various articles on development and administration. *Leisure interest:* classical music. *Address:* Central Bank of Barbados, P.O. Box 1016, Church Village, Bridgetown, Barbados.

KING, Leonard James, LL.B.; Australian judge; b. 1 May 1925, Norwood, S. Australia; s. of Michael and Mary King; m. Sheila T. Keane 1953; two s. three d.; ed. Marist Brothers' School, Norwood and Univ. of Adelaide; admitted to bar 1950, Q.C. 1967; mem. House of Ass. 1970; Attorney-Gen. 1970–75; Minister of Social Welfare and Aboriginal Affairs 1970–72, of Community Welfare 1972–75, of Prices and Consumer Affairs 1973–75; Judge, Supreme Court of South Australia 1975-78, Chief Justice 1978–. *Leisure interests:* reading, tennis. *Address:* c/o Chief Justice's Chambers, Supreme Court House, Victoria Square, Adelaide, Australia. *Telephone:* 2186211.

KING, Maurice Athelstan, LL.B.; Barbados lawyer and politician; b. 1 Jan. 1936; s. of James Cliviston King and Caroline Constance King; m. Patricia A. Williams; one s. one d.; ed. Harrison Coll., Barbados, Univ. of Manchester and Gray's Inn, London; lawyer in pvt. practice 1960–; Chair. Natural Gas Corpn. 1964–76; mem. Barbados Senate 1967–75; Gen. Sec. Democratic Labour Party 1968–69; Amb. to U.S.A. and Perm. Rep. to O.A.S. Jan.–Sept. 1976; mem. Parl. 1981–; Attorney-Gen. and Minister of Legal Affairs 1986–. *Leisure interests:* music, tennis, reading, swimming. *Address:* Office of the Attorney-General, Marine House, Hastings, Christ Church, Barbados.

KING, Phillip, C.B.E., M.A. (CANTAB); British sculptor; b. 1 May 1934, Tunis, Tunisia; s. of Thomas J. King and Gabrielle Liautard; m. Lilian Odelle 1957 (divorced 1986); one s. (deceased); ed. Mill Hill School, Christ's Coll., Cambridge, St. Martin's School of Art, London; Asst. to Henry Moore (q.v.) 1957–59; taught at St. Martin's School of Art 1959–74; one-man exhbn., Whitechapel Gallery 1968, British Pavilion at Venice Biennale with Bridget Riley (q.v.) 1968, British Council touring exhbn., Kroller Muller (Netherlands), Düsseldorf, Bern, Paris and Belfast 1974–75, Arts Council Exhbn., Hayward Gallery 1981; Prof. of Sculpture, Royal Coll. of Art 1980–; Trustee, Tate Gallery 1967–69; mem. Art Panel, Arts Council 1977–79; Assoc. Royal Acad. 1977; 1st Prize Int. Sculpture Exhbn., Piestany (Czechoslovakia) 1968. *Leisure interest:* holidays in Corsica close to both land and sea. *Address:* Major Rowan Gallery, London W1X 7AB, England. *Telephone:* (01) 499-3011.

KING, Stephen Edwin, B.S.; American author; b. 21 Sept. 1947, Portland, Me.; s. of Donald King and Nellie R. (Pillsbury) King; m. Tabitha J. Spruce 1971; two s. one d.; ed. Univ. of Maine; teacher of English, Hampden Acad., Me. 1971–73; writer-in-residence, Univ. of Maine at Orono 1978–79; mem. Authors' Guild of America, Screen Artists' Guild, Screen Writers of America, Writers' Guild. *Publications:* novels include Carrie 1974, Salem's Lot 1975, The Shining 1976, The Stand 1978, Firestarter 1980, Danse Macabre 1981, Cujo 1981, Different Seasons 1982, The Dark Tower: The Gunslinger 1982, Christine 1983, Pet Sematary 1983, Cycle of the Werewolf 1985, Skeleton Crew 1986, It 1987, Misery 1988, Horror: 100 Best Books (Jt. Ed.) 1988; Night Shift (short story collection) 1978 and numerous other short stories. *Address:* c/o Press Relations, Viking Press, 625 Madison Avenue, New York, N.Y. 10022, U.S.A.

KING, Thea, O.B.E., F.R.C.M., A.R.C.M.; British clarinettist; b. 26 Dec. 1925, Hitchin, Herts.; m. Frederick J. Thurston 1953; no. c.; ed. Bedford High School and Royal Coll. of Music; Sadler's Wells Orchestra 1950–52; Portia Wind Ensemble 1955–68; London Mozart Players 1956–84; Prof. Royal Coll. of Music 1961–87, Guildhall School of Music 1988–; now mem. English Chamber Orchestra, Melos Ensemble of London, Robles Ensemble; frequent soloist, broadcaster and recitalist; recordings include works by Mozart, Spohr, Mendelssohn, Bruch, Finzi, Stanford and 20th Century British music; Prof. Royal Coll. of Music 1961–. *Publications:* Clarinet Solos (Chester Woodwind Series) 1977, Arrangement of J. S. Bach: Duets for Two Clarinets 1979. *Leisure interests:* cows, pillow-lace. *Address:* 16 Milverton Road, London, NW6 7AS, England. *Telephone:* 01-459 3453.

KING, Rt. Hon. Thomas (Tom) Jeremy, M.A., M.P.; British politician; b. 13 June 1933, Glasgow; s. of John H. King and Mollie King; m. Elizabeth J. Tilney 1961; one s. one d.; ed. Rugby School and Emmanuel Coll., Cambridge; in packaging and printing industry 1958–70; M.P. for Bridgwater 1970–; Parl. Private Sec. to Rt. Hon. Christopher Chataway 1970–74; Shadow Spokesman for Energy 1976–79; Minister for Local Govt. 1979–83; Sec. of State for the Environment Jan.–June 1983 for Transport June–Oct. 1983, for Employment 1983-85, for Northern Ireland Sept. 1985–; Conservative. *Leisure interests:* cricket, skiing. *Address:* House of Commons, Westminster, London, SW1A 0AA, England. *Telephone:* 01-219 3000.

KING OF WARTNABY, Baron (Life Peer), cr. 1983, in the County of Leicestershire; **John Leonard King,** F.B.I.M.; British business executive; b. 29 Aug. 1918; s. of Albert John and Kathleen King; m. 1st Lorna Kathleen Sykes 1941 (died 1969), three s. one d.; m. 2nd Isabel Monckton 1970; f. Whitehouse Industries Ltd. 1945, and Ferrybridge Industries Ltd. (subsequently Pollard Ball & Roller Bearing Co.), Man. Dir. 1945, Chair. 1961–69; Chair. Dennis Motor Holdings Ltd. 1970–72, Babcock Int. PLC (fmrly. Babcock & Wilcox Ltd.) 1972–, British Airways 1981–, Babcock Int. Inc., British Nuclear Assocs. Ltd., SKF (U.K.) Ltd. 1976–, R. J. Dick

Inc. (U.S.A.), Dick Corpn. (U.S.A.), Dick Precismeca Inc. (U.S.A.); Dir. First Union Corpn. (U.S.A.), Nat. Nuclear Corpn., Royal Ordnance Factories; mem. NEDC Cttee. on Finance for Investment 1976-78, Review Bd. for Govt. Contracts 1975-78; Chair., British Olympic Appeals Cttee. 1975-78; Vice-Pres. Nat. Soc. for Cancer Relief; Hon. Fellow The Coke Oven Man. Assoc.; Fellow Inst. of Chartered Transport; Commdr. Royal Order of the Polar Star (1983); Hon. Dr.Hum. (Gardner-Webb Coll., U.S.A.) 1980. *Leisure interests:* hunting, field sports, racing. *Address:* Cleveland House, St. James's Square, London, SW1Y 4LN, England. *Telephone:* 01-930 9766.

KING-HELE, Desmond George, M.A., F.R.S.; British scientist and author; b. 3 Nov. 1927, Seaford, Sussex; s. of late S. G. King-Hele and Mrs. B. King-Hele; m. Marie Newman 1954; two d.; ed. Epsom Coll. and Trinity Coll., Cambridge; Royal Aircraft Establishment, Farnborough 1948-88 (research on earth's gravity field and upper atmosphere by analysis of satellite orbits), Deputy Chief Scientific Officer, Space Dept. 1968-88; mem. Int. Acad. of Astronautics; Eddington Medal, Royal Astronomical Soc. 1971, Chree Medal, Inst. of Physics 1971, Chair. British Nat. Cttee. for the History of Science, Medicine and Tech. 1985-; Ed. Notes and Records of the Royal Soc. 1989-. *Publications:* Shelley: His Thought and Work 1960, Satellites and Scientific Research 1960, Erasmus Darwin 1963, Theory of Satellite Orbits in an Atmosphere 1964, Observing Earth Satellites 1966, Essential Writings of Erasmus Darwin 1968, The End of the Twentieth Century? 1970, Poems and Trixies 1972, Doctor of Revolution 1977, Letters of Erasmus Darwin 1981, The R.A.E. Table of Earth Satellites 1957-1986, 1987, Animal Spirits 1983, Erasmus Darwin and the Romantic Poets 1986, Satellite Orbits in an Atmosphere 1987, and more than 200 scientific or literary papers in various learned journals. *Leisure interests:* playing tennis, savouring the beauties of nature, growing flowers. *Address:* 3 Tor Road, Farnham, Surrey, GU9 7BX, England (Home). *Telephone:* 0252-714755.

KINGMAN, Sir John Frank Charles, Kt., SC.D., F.R.S.; British mathematician and university Vice-Chancellor; b. 28 Aug. 1939, Beckenham; s. of Frank E. T. and Maud Elsie (née Harley) Kingman; m. Valerie Cromwell 1964; one s. one d.; ed. Christ's Coll., Finchley, London, Pembroke Coll., Cambridge; Asst. Lecturer in Mathematics, Univ. of Cambridge 1962-64, Lecturer 1964-65; Reader in Mathematics and Statistics, Univ. of Sussex 1965-66, Prof. 1966-69; Prof. of Mathematics, Univ. of Oxford 1969-85; Chair. Science and Eng. Research Council 1981-85; Vice-Chancellor Univ. of Bristol 1985-; Hon. Fellow, St. Anne's Coll., Oxford, Pembroke Coll., Cambridge; Hon. D.Sc. (Sussex) 1983, (Southampton) 1985, (Bristol) 1989. *Publications:* Introduction to Measure and Probability (with S. J. Taylor) 1966, The Algebra of Queues 1966, Regenerative Phenomena 1972, Mathematics of Genetic Diversity 1980. *Address:* Senate House, Tyndall Avenue, Bristol, BS8 1TH, England. *Telephone:* (0272) 303960.

KINGON, Alfred Hugh, B.S.; American government official; b. 11 May 1931, New York; s. of Nathan N. Kingon and Grace J. (née Linde) Kingon; m. Jacqueline J. Goldwyn 1962; one s.; ed. Union Coll., New York Univ.; Assoc. Investment Advisory Dept., Burnham & Co. 1963-67; Vice-Pres., Research Dir. Scheinman, Hochstin & Trotta 1967-70; Vice-Pres. Portfolio Man. The Business Man's Fund 1970-71; Exec. Vice-Pres. Macro Communications 1971-82; Asst. Sec. of Commerce for Int. Econ. Policy, Dept. of Commerce, Washington 1983; Asst. Sec. for Policy Planning and Communications Dept. of Treasury, Washington 1984; Asst. to Pres., Sec. to Cabinet 1985-87; Perm. Rep. to EEC 1987-89; mem. Pres.'s Nat. Productivity Advisory Cttee. Pres.'s Private Sector Survey on Cost Control 1982. *Publication:* The New Deal, The Fair Deal, The Coming Ordeal 1971. *Address:* 700 New Hampshire Avenue, N.W., Washington, D.C. 20037, U.S.A. (Home).

KINGS NORTON, Baron (Life Peer), cr. 1965, of Wotton Underwood; **Harold Roxbee Cox,** Kt., PH.D., D.I.C., B.SC.(ENG.), F.I.MECH.E., HON. F.R.AE.S.; British engineer and scientist; b. 1902, Birmingham; s. of William John Roxbee Cox and Amelia (née Stern); m. 1st Marjorie Withers 1927 (died 1980); two s.; m. 2nd Joan Pascoe 1982; ed. Kings Norton Grammar School, Imperial Coll. of Science and Technology; Engineer on construction of airship R.101 1924-29; Chief Technical Officer, Royal Airship Works 1931; Royal Aircraft Establishment investigations in wing-flutter and stability of structures 1931-35; Principal Scientific Officer, Aerodynamics Dept., R.A.E. 1935-36; Head of Air Defence Dept. R.A.E. 1936-38; Chief Technical Officer, Air Registration Bd. 1938-39; Supt. of Scientific Research, R.A.E. 1939-40; Deputy Dir. Scientific Research, Ministry of Aircraft Production 1940-43; Dir. of Special Projects, M.A.P. 1943-44; Chair. and Man. Dir. of Power Jets (Research and Devt.) Ltd. 1944-46; Dir. Nat. Gas Turbine Establishment 1946-48; Chair. Gas Turbine Collaboration Cttee. 1941-44, 1946-48; Chief Scientist, Ministry of Fuel and Power 1948-54; Chair. Civil Aircraft Research Cttee. 1953-58; Dir. Wilmot Breeden Ltd. 1954-60; Chair. Naval Educ. Advisory Cttee. 1956-60; Chancellor, Cranfield Inst. of Technology 1969-; Chair. Air Registration Bd. 1959-66, Chair. 1966-72; Deputy Chair. The Metal Box Co. 1959-61, Chair. 1961-67; Dir. Boulton Paul Aircraft Co. Ltd. 1958-68, Ricardo and Co. Engineers (1927) Ltd. 1965-77, Steel Co. of Wales Ltd. 1965-67, Dir. Dowty Rotol Ltd. 1968-75, British Printing Corpn. Ltd. 1968-77, Hoechst, U.K. 1970-75; Chair. Berger Jenson and Nicholson Ltd. 1967-75, Applied Photophysics Ltd. 1972-81, Landspeed Ltd. 1975-, Withers Estates Ltd. 1977-81, Submarine Products Ltd. 1978-82; Chair. of Nat. Council for Technological

Awards 1960-64; Chair. of Council for Scientific and Industrial Research 1961-65; Chair. Council for Nat. Academic Awards 1964-71; Chair. Cotswold Research Ltd. 1978-; Pres. Royal Aeronautical Soc. 1947-49, Campden Food Preservation Research Assoc. 1961-, Royal Inst. of Great Britain 1969-76; Fellow of Imperial Coll., Thames Polytechnic, Newcastle Polytechnic; Hon. D.Sc. (Birmingham Univ., Cranfield, Warwick Univ.), Hon. D.Tech. (Brunel Univ.), Hon. LL.D. (Council for Nat. Academic Awards); Medal of Freedom (U.S.A.) with Silver Palm, Bronze Medal (Univ. Louvain) 1946, Freeman, City of London; Liveryman, Guild of Air Pilots and Air Navigators. *Leisure interest:* collecting aeronautical antiques. *Address:* Westcote House, Chipping Campden, Glos., England. *Telephone:* (0386) 840440.

KINGSBURY-SMITH, Joseph; American journalist; b. 20 Feb. 1908, New York; s. of William Barstow Kingsbury-Smith and Maria Jordan; m. Ruth Eileen King 1940; two d.; ed. Friends' School, Poughkeepsie, and London Univ.; International News Service 1924-26; United Press 1926-27; I.N.S. London 1927-31, Washington 1931-36; Man. London Bureau 1936-38, Washington 1940-44; European Gen. Dir. 1944-55; Pres. and Gen. Man. I.N.S. 1955-57; Vice-Pres., Assoc. Gen. Man. United Press Int. 1958-59; Trustee Hearst Estate and Fordham Univ.; Publr. N.Y. Journal-American 1959-66; Vice-Pres. and European Dir. Hearst Corpn. 1966-75; Vice-Pres. and Dir. Hearst Corpn.; Sr. Washington rep. and Nat. Ed. The Hearst Newspapers 1976-; Trustee and Dir. The Hearst Foundations 1976-; Chief Foreign Writer, the Hearst Newspapers and King Features Syndicate; various journalistic awards, and Officier, Légion d'honneur, mostly in recognition of an exchange of correspondence with Stalin (1949) during the blockade of Berlin; Pulitzer Prize 1956 for Int. Reporting, U.S. Govt. Distinguished Service Award 1961. *Address:* 1701 Pennsylvania Avenue, N.W., Washington, D.C. 20006, U.S.A. (Office).

KINGSLEY, Ben; British actor; b. 31 Dec. 1943; s. of Rahimtulla Harji Bhanji and Anna Leina Mary Bhanji; m. Gillian Alison Macaulay Sutcliffe 1978; one s.; ed. Manchester Grammar School; with R.S.C. 1970-80; Nat. Theatre 1977-78; Assoc. Artist, R.S.C. *Stage appearances include:* A Midsummer Night's Dream, Occupations, The Tempest, Hamlet, The Merry Wives of Windsor, Baal, Nicholas Nickleby, Volponë, The Cherry Orchard, The Country Wife, Judgement, Statements After An Arrest, Othello (title role), Caracol in Melons. *Television appearances include:* The Love School 1974, Kean, Silas Marner, The Train 1987, Murderous Amongst Us 1988, several plays. *Films:* Gandhi (two Hollywood Golden Globe Awards 1982, New York Film Critics' Award, two BAFTA Awards, Acad. Award, Los Angeles Film Critics' Award 1983), Betrayal 1982, Harem 1985, Turtle Diary 1985, Lenin the Train 1987, Without A Clue 1988, Testimony 1988, Pascali's Island 1988, Slipstream 1989; Hon. M.A. (Salford Univ.); awarded Padma Shri (Govt. of India); London Standard Best Film Actor 1983. *Leisure interests:* music, gardening. *Address:* c/o ICM Ltd., 388/396 Oxford Street, London, W.1, England.

KINNEAR, James Wesley, III; American business executive; b. 21 March 1928, Pittsburgh, Pa.; s. of James Wesley and Susan (Jenkins) Kinnear; m. Mary Tullis 1950; two s. two d.; ed. St. Paul's School, Concord, N.H., U.S. Naval Acad.; service in Korean war; joined marketing org. of Texaco Inc. 1954, subsequently held sales positions in Puerto Rico, Jamaica and Hawaii, Div. Sales Man., Los Angeles 1963, Asst. to Vice-Chair., New York 1964, Asst. to Chair. and Gen. Man., Marine Dept. 1965, Vice-Pres. Texaco Inc. 1966, Sr. Vice-Pres. 1970-78, mem. Bd. of Dirs. 1977-, Exec. Vice-Pres. and mem. Exec. Cttee. 1978-83, Pres. and C.E.O. Jan. 1987-, Pres. Texaco U.S.A., Houston 1982-85, Vice-Chair. of Bd. 1985-, Pres. 1987-; Dir. Corning Glass Works, American Petroleum Inst.; fmr. Dir. Caltex Petroleum Corpn. *Address:* Texaco Inc., 2000 Westchester Avenue, White Plains, N.Y. 10650; 149 Taconic Road, Greenwich, Conn. 06830, U.S.A. (Home).

KINNELL, Galway, M.A.; American writer; b. 1 Feb. 1927, Providence, R.I.; s. of James S. Kinnell and Elizabeth Mills; m. Inès Delgado de Torres 1965; one s. one d.; ed. Princeton Univ.; mem. Nat. Inst., Acad. of Arts and Letters; Guggenheim Fellow 1963-64, 1974-75, MacArthur Fellow 1984-; Award of Nat. Inst. of Arts and Letters 1962, Cecil Hemley Poetry Prize 1969, Medal of Merit 1975, Pulitzer Prize 1983, American Book Award 1983. *Publications:* poetry: What a Kingdom it Was 1960, Flower Herding on Mount Monadnock 1963, Body Rags 1966, The Book of Nightmares 1971, The Avenue Bearing the Initial of Christ into the New World 1974, Mortal Acts, Mortal Words 1980, Selected Poems 1982, The Past 1985; novel: Black Light 1966; children's story: How the Alligator Missed Breakfast 1982; trans.: The Poems of François Villon 1965, On the Motion and Immobility of Douve 1968, The Lackawanna Elegy 1970; interviews: Walking Down the Stairs 1977. *Address:* 432 Hudson Street, New York, N.Y. 10014, U.S.A.

KINNEY, E. Robert, A.B.; American business executive; b. 12 April 1917, Burnham, Me.; s. of Harry E. and Ethel (née Vose) Kinney; m. Margaret Velie Thatcher 1977; one s. two d.; ed. Bates Coll., Harvard Graduate School; joined Gorton Corpn. 1954, Pres. 1958-68; Vice-Pres. General Mills Inc. (following merger with Gorton Corpn.) 1968, Dir. 1969-, Exec. Vice-Pres. 1969-70, Chief Financial Officer 1970-73, Pres., C.O.O. 1973-77, Chair. and C.E.O. 1977-81; Pres. and C.E.O. IDS Mutual Fund Group 1982-; Dir. Sun Co., Nashua Corpn., Jackson Lab., Hannaford Bros. Co.,

Union Mutual Insurance Co., Deluxe Check Printers Inc.; Sr. mem. The Conf. Bd. Trustee, Bates Coll. *Address:* IDS Mutual Fund Group, 1000 Roanoke Building, Minneapolis, Minn. 55402, U.S.A. *Telephone:* 612-372 3719.

KINNOCK, Rt. Hon. Neil Gordon, P.C., B.A., M.P.; British politician; b. 28 March 1942; s. of Gordon Kinnock and Mary Howells; m. Glenys Elizabeth Parry 1967; one s. one d.; ed. Lewis School, Pengam, Univ. Coll., Cardiff; Pres. Univ. Coll., Cardiff Students' Union 1965-66; Tutor Organizer in Industrial and Trade Union Studies, Workers' Educational Assen. 1966-70; M.P. for Bedwellty 1970-83, for Islwyn 1983-; mem. Welsh Hosp. Bd. 1969-71; Parl. Pvt. Sec. to Sec. of State for Employment 1974-75; mem. Nat. Exec. Cttee., Labour Party 1978-; Leader of Labour Party Oct. 1983-; Leader of the Opposition 1983-; Dir. Tribune Publs. 1974-82, Fair Play for Children 1979-, 7:84 Theatre Co. Ltd. 1979-; mem. Editorial Bd., Labour Research Dept. 1974-77; mem. Socialist Educational Assen. 1975-; Pres. Assen. of Liberal Educ. 1980-82; Labour. *Publications:* Wales and the Common Market 1971, Making Our Way 1986; contribs. in newspapers and periodicals. *Leisure interests:* male voice choral music, reading, children, rugby union and soccer. *Address:* House of Commons, London, S.W.1, England.

KINOSHITA, Keisuke; Japanese film director; b. 1912; ed. Hamamatsu Industrial Coll.; began career in Shochiku Studio, Kamata; directed first film Hanasaku Minato 1943; Henrietta Award for Nijushi no Hitomi 1955, Golden Globe Award of Hollywood Foreign Press for Taiyo to Bara 1957. *Films include:* Hanasaku Minato (Port of Flowers) 1943, Yabure Daiko (Torn Drum), Carmen kokyo ni Kaeru (Carmen Comes Home) 1949, Nippon no Higeki (The Tragedy of Japan) 1953, Nijushi no Hitomi (Twenty-Four Eyes) 1954, Nogiku no Gotoki Kimi Nariki (My First Love Affair) 1955, Yuyakegumo (Farewell to Dreams), Taiyo to Bara (The Rose of his Arm) 1956, Yorokobi-mo Kanashimimo Ikutoshitsuki (The Lighthouse), Fuzen no Tomoshibi (Danger Stalks Near) 1957, Narayama-bushi Ko (Ballad of the Narayama), Kono ten no Niji (The Eternal Rainbow) 1958, Kazahana 1959, Sekishuncho, The River Fuefuki 1961, Eien no Hito (Bitter Spirit) 1962. *Address:* 1366 Tsujido, Fujisawa, Japan.

KINSELLA, Thomas; Irish poet and teacher; b. 4 May 1928, Dublin; s. of John Paul and Agnes Casserly Kinsella; m. Eleanor Walsh 1955; one s. two d.; Irish Civil Service 1946-65, resgnd. as Asst. Prin. Officer, Dept. of Finance 1965; Artist-in-Residence, Southern Ill. Univ. 1965-67, Prof. of English 1967-70; Prof. of English, Temple Univ., Philadelphia 1970-; Dir. Dolmen Press Ltd., Cuala Press Ltd., Dublin; founded Peppercanister (private publishing enterprise), Dublin 1972; mem. Irish Acad. of Letters 1965-; Guggenheim Fellowship 1968-69, 1971-72; Guinness Poetry Award 1958; Irish Arts Council Triennial Book Award 1960; Denis Devlin Memorial Award 1966, 1969, Hon. D.Litt. (Nat. Univ. of Ireland) 1985. *Publications:* Poems 1956, Another September 1958, Downstream 1962, Nightwalker and Other Poems 1966, Notes from the Land of the Dead 1972, New Poems 1973, Selected Poems 1956-1968 1973, Song of the Night and Other Poems 1978, The Messenger 1978, Fifteen Dead 1979, One and Other Poems 1979, Poems 1956-1973, Peppercanister Poems 1972-1978 1979, One Fond Embrace 1982; The Táin (trans.) 1968; ed. Selected Poems of Austin Clarke 1976; co-ed. Poems of the Dispossessed 1600-1900 (with 100 translations from the Irish) 1981, Ireland's Musical Heritage: Sean O'Riada's Radio Talks on Irish Traditional Music 1981, Songs of the Psyche (poems) 1985, Her Vertical Smile (poem) 1985, Ed. The New Oxford Book of Irish Verse (new trans. from the Irish) 1986, St. Catherine's Clock 1987, Out of Ireland 1987, The Complete Fond Embrace 1988, Blood and Family (collected poems from 1978) 1988. *Leisure interests:* history, publishing. *Address:* Killalane, Laragh, County Wicklow, Ireland.

KINSKI, Klaus; German actor; b. (as Claus Günther Nakszynski) 1926, Sopot, Danzig (now Poland); early stage experience in Berlin followed by numerous film roles in German and int. films. *Films include:* Morituri 1948, Ludwig II 1955, Kinder Mütter und ein General 1955, Sarajevo 1955, Waldwinter 1956, Der Rächer 1960, Dead Eyes of London 1961, The Devil's Daffodil 1961, The Counterfeit Traitor 1962, Scotland Yard jagt Dr Mabuse 1963, Winnetou II 1964, Last of the Renegades 1964, The Pleasure Girls 1965, Doctor Zhivago 1965, For a Few Dollars More 1966, Our Man in Marrakesh 1966, Jules Verne's Rocket to the Moon 1967, Sumuru 1967, Circus of Fear 1967, A Bullet for the General 1967, Grand Slam 1967, Ognuno per sè 1968, Venus in Furs 1969, Count Dracula 1971, L'Occhio del Ragno 1971, Aguirre the Wrath of God 1973, L'important c'est d'aimer 1975, Der Netz 1976, Nuit d'or 1976, Operation Thunderbolt 1977, Madame Claude 1977, Mort d'un pourri 1977, Nosferatu 1979, Fitzcarraldo 1982, Cobra Verde 1987.

KINSKI, Nastassja (b. Nastassja Nakszynski); actress (b. German); b. 24 Jan. 1961, W. Berlin; d. of Klaus Kinski (q.v.) and Ruth Brigitte Kinski; m. Ibrahim Moussa 1984; one s.; film début in Falsche Bewegung 1975; Bundespreis 1983. *Films include:* Stay As You Are 1978, Tess 1978, One From The Heart 1982, Cat People 1982, Moon In The Gutter 1983, Spring Symphony 1983, Unfaithfully Yours 1984, The Hotel New Hampshire 1984, Maria's Lovers 1984, Paris, Texas 1984, Revolution 1985, Torrents of Spring, Crystal or Ash, Fire or Wind, as long as It's Love 1989. *Address:* 888 Seventh Avenue, New York, N.Y. 10106, U.S.A.

KINTANAR, Roman, M.A., PH.D.; Philippine scientist, government official and university professor; b. 13 June 1929, Cebu City; s. of Augustin Y. Kintanar and Pureza Lucero; m. Generosa Perez-Kintanar 1959; two s. one d.; ed. Univ. of the Philippines, Univ. of Texas; Prof. of Physics, Univ. of the Philippines 1955-56, Feati Univ. 1958-65; Professorial lecturer, Ateneo de Manila Univ. 1966-68; Chief Geophysicist, Philippine Weather Bureau 1953-58, Dir. 1958-72; Admin. Philippine Atmospheric, Geophysical and Astronomical Services Admin. (PAGASA) 1972-77, Dir.-Gen. 1977-; del. or invited participant to 57 Regional or Int. Scientific Confs. 1959-79; Chair. or Vice-Chair. sessions WMO/ESCAP Typhoon Cttee. 1967-79; Perm. Rep. to WMO 1958-; Vice-Pres. Regional Assen. V for S.-W. Pacific (WMO-RA V) 1966-74; Pres. 1974-78; Vice-Pres. WMO 1978-79, Pres. 1979-; mem. Philippine Assen. for the Advancement of Science, Nat. Research Council of the Philippines, Philippine Meteorological Soc., Int. Assen. of Seismology and Physics of the Earth's Interior, UNESCO/UNDRO Int. Advisory Cttee. on Earthquake Damage and Mitigation, and many other scientific socs.; Fulbright Smidthmundt Scholarship (U.S. Educational Foundation), Office of the Pres. Ecology Award, Budiras Award for Outstanding Performance (Bureau Dirs. Assen.), Parangal ng PAGASA Award, Lingkod Bayan Award 1982, Padre Faura Astronomy Medal 1982. *Publications:* A Study of Typhoon Microseisms 1958 and many articles in scientific journals. *Leisure interests;* playing golf, chess. *Address;* World Meteorological Organization, Case postale 5, CH-1211 Geneva 20, Switzerland; 100 Don Primitivo cor. Don Vicente Street, Don Antonio Heights, Quezon City, Philippines.

KINTNER, William R., B.S., M.A., PH.D.; American professor and writer; b. 21 April 1915, Lock Haven, Pa.; s. of late S. S. Kintner and F. Kendig Kintner; m. Xandree Hyatt 1940; one s. three d.; ed. U.S. Mil. Acad., N.Y., Georgetown Univ., Washington, D.C.; Colonel in U.S. Army 1940-61, European Theatre World War II, Korea 1950-52; Prof. Emer. of Political Science, Univ. of Pennsylvania 1961-85; Deputy Dir. Foreign Policy Research Inst. 1961-69, Dir. 1969-73, Pres. 1976; Amb. to Thailand 1973-75; mem. Bd. of Freedom House, New York; mem. Bd. U.S. Peace Inst. 1986-; Ed. Orbis 1969-73, 1976-. *Publications:* Atomic Weapons in Land Combat (with George C. Reinhardt) 1953, Protracted Conflict (co-author) 1959, The Haphazard Years (with George C. Reinhardt) 1960, A Forward Strategy for Tomorrow (co-author) 1961, Building the Atlantic World (co-author) 1963, Peace and the Strategy Conflict 1967, The Nuclear Revolution in Soviet Military Affairs (with Harriet Fist Scott) 1968, Safeguard: Why the ABM Makes Sense (Ed., Contrib.) 1969, Eastern Europe and European Security 1971, SALT: Implications for Arms Control in the 1970s (with Robert L. Pfaltzgraff) 1973, National Strategy in a Decade of Change (with Richard B. Foster) 1973, A Matter of Two Chinas (with J. Copper) 1979, Arms Control: The American Dilemma 1987, Soviet Global Strategy (Ed., Contrib.) 1987, The Crucial Struggle over Central America (Ed., Contrib.) 1987. *Leisure interests:* tennis, gardening. *Address:* University of Pennsylvania, Philadelphia, Pa. 19104 (Office); 2259 Pennypack Lane, Bryn Athyn, Pa. 19009, U.S.A. (Home). *Telephone:* (215) 382-0685. (Office).

KIPPENHAHN, Rudolf; German astronomer; b. 24 May 1926, Bärringen; s. of Rudolf Kippenhahn and Alma Belz; m. Johanna Rasper 1955; three d.; ed. Graslitz and St. Joachimsthal Schools, Univs. of Halle and Erlangen; Scientific Asst. Bamberg Observatory 1951-57; staff mem. Max-Planck-Inst. für Physik und Astrophysik, Inst. für Astrophysik 1957-65, mem. of directorate 1963, Dir. 1975-; Visiting Prof. Caltech, Pasadena and Princeton Univs. 1961-62; Prof. Univ. Observatory, Göttingen 1965-75; Visiting Prof. Univ. of Calif., L.A. 1968, Ohio State Univ. 1979, Univ. Observatory, Hamburg 1986-87; Hon. Prof. Univ. of Munich 1975-; Carus-Medal (Leopoldina, Halle); Carus Prize (City of Schweinfurt); Verdienstkreuz (1st Class) (Fed. Repub. Germany); Lorenz-Oken-Medal (Gesellschaft Deutscher Naturforscher und Ärzte). *Publications:* One Hundred Billion Suns: The Birth, Life and Death of the Stars 1983, Light from the Depth of Time 1987, Unheimliche Welten 1987, and numerous articles in astronomical and astrophysical journals. *Address:* Max-Planck-Institut für Physik und Astrophysik, Institut für Astrophysik, Karl-Schwarzschild-Strasse 1, 8046 Garching (Office); Rheinlandstrasse 10b, 8000 München 40, Federal Republic of Germany (Home). *Telephone:* 089-3299 0 (Office); 089-3231872 (Home).

KIRBY, Anthony John, PH.D. (CANTAB.), F.R.S.; British university teacher and research scientist; b. 18 Aug. 1935, Welwyn Garden City, Herts.; s. of Samuel A. Kirby and Gladys R. (née Welch) Kirby; m. Sara Nieweg 1962; one s. two d.; ed. Eton Coll., Gonville & Caius Coll., Cambridge; NATO Research Fellow, Brandeis Univ., Mass. 1963-64; demonstrator, then lecturer Organic Chem., Univ. of Cambridge 1968-85; Fellow, Tutor 1967-75 and Dir. of Studies in Natural Sciences, Gonville & Caius Coll., Cambridge 1962-; Royal Soc. of Chemistry Award in Organic Reaction Mechanisms 1983, Telden Lecturer of Royal Soc. of Chem. 1987. *Publications:* The Organic Chemistry of Phosphorus (with S. G. Warren) 1967, Stereoelectronic Effects of Oxygen 1983; over 150 articles on mechanistic bioorganic chemistry. *Address:* University Chemical Laboratory, Cambridge, CB2 1EW (Office); 14 Tenison Avenue, Cambridge, CB1 2DY, England (Home). *Telephone:* (0223) 336370 (Office); (0223) 359343 (Home).

KIRBY, Louis Albert Francis; British journalist; b. 30 Nov. 1928, Liverpool; s. of late William J. Kirby and Anne Kirby; m. 1st Marcia Teresa Lloyd 1952 (divorced 1976); two s. three d.; m. 2nd Heather Veronica

Nicholson 1976; one s. one d.; m. 3rd Heather Margaret McGlone 1983; one d.; ed. Our Lady Immaculate, Liverpool, Coalbrookdale High School; gen. reporter, then Court Corresp., Daily Mail 1953-60, Political Corresp. 1960-62; Chief Reporter, then Leader Writer and Political Ed., Daily Sketch 1962-64, Asst. Ed. 1964-67, Exec. Ed., then Acting Ed. 1967-71; Deputy Ed. Daily Mail 1971-76; Ed. Evening News 1976-80; Dir. Associated Newspapers Group Ltd. and Vice-Chair. Evening News 1976-80; Ed. The New Standard 1980-81, The Standard 1981-86; Dir. Evening Standard Co. Ltd. 1980-86; Dir. Mail Newspapers PLC 1986-88; Ed. Dir. Associated Newspapers 1986-88; Political Consultant, Daily Mail 1988-. *Leisure interests:* theatre, reading. *Address:* Northcliffe House, London, E.C.4, England.

KIRBY, Michael Donald, C.M.G., LL.M., B.A., B.ECONS.; Australian judge; b. 18 March 1939, Sydney; s. of Donald and Jean (née Knowles) Kirby; ed. Fort Street Boys' High School and Univ. of Sydney; Fellow, Senate, Univ. of Sydney 1964-69; mem. N.S.W. Bar Council 1974; Deputy Pres., Australian Conciliation & Arbitration Comm. 1975-83; Chair. Australian Law Reform Comm. 1975-84; mem. Admin. Review Council of Australia 1976-84; mem. Council, Univ. of Newcastle, N.S.W. 1977-83, Deputy Chancellor 1978-83; mem. Australian Nat. Comm. for UNESCO 1980-84, Australian Inst. of Multicultural Affairs 1979-83; Judge Fed. Court of Australia 1983-84; mem. Exec. Commonwealth Scientific and Industrial Org. 1983-86; Chancellor, Macquarie Univ., Sydney 1984-; Pres. Court of Appeal, Supreme Court, Sydney 1984-; Acting Chief Justice of N.S.W. 1988; Commr. WHO Global Comm. on Aids 1988-; mem. Int. Comm. of Jurists, Geneva 1985-, Council of the Australian Opera; Loewenthal Medal, Sydney Univ. *Publications:* Industrial Index to Australian Labour Law 1978, 1984, Reform the Law 1983, The Judges 1984, Jt. Ed. A Touch of Healing 1986. *Leisure interest:* work. *Address:* Court of Appeal, Supreme Court, Sydney, N.S.W., 2000 (Office); 4A Dumaresq Road, Rose Bay, N.S.W., 2029, Australia. *Telephone:* 02-230-8202 (Office); 02-371-8818 (Home).

KIRBY, Robert E., B.S., M.B.A.; American business executive; b. 8 Nov. 1918, Ames, Ia.; s. of Robert Stearns and Ora (Walker) Kirby; m. Barbara McClintock 1942; two d. (one deceased); ed. Pennsylvania State Univ.; Radar Officer, U.S. Navy, World War II; joined Westinghouse Electric Corpn. 1946, Man. Industrial Electronics Eng. 1952, Man. Ordnance Dept., Gen. Man. Electronics Div. 1958, Vice-Pres. Eng. 1963, Industrial Group Vice-Pres. 1963, Exec. Vice-Pres., Dir. 1966, Dir. Industry and Defence Co. 1969, fmr. Vice-Chair. Operations, Chair., C.E.O. 1975-83; Vice-Chair. Bd. of Trustees, Univ. of Pittsburgh; Chair. Fed. Reserve Bank of Cleveland; Dir. Pittsburgh Symphony Soc., Mellon Nat. Corpn. and Mellon Bank, N.A., Allegheny Int. Inc.; mem. American Soc. of Naval Architects and Engs., American Ordnance Asscn., Inst. of Electrical and Electronic Engs., Nat. Advisory Cttee. on Professional Golfers' Asscn. of America; Hon. H.H.D. (Thiel Coll.) 1976. *Leisure interests:* golf, athletics, music. *Address:* 250 Tech. Road, Pittsburgh, Pa. 15205, U.S.A. (Home).

KIRCA, Ali Coşkun, LL.D.; Turkish diplomatist; b. 1927, Istanbul; ed. Galatasaray Lycée, Istanbul, Law School, Istanbul Univ.; with Ministry of Foreign Affairs, Third Sec., then Second Sec., NATO 1950-56; lecturer in Political Science, Ankara Univ. 1956-61; mem. Constituent Assembly 1961; mem. for Istanbul, Nat. Assembly 1961-69; Minister, Ministry of Foreign Affairs 1969; UN Office, Geneva 1970; Perm. Rep. of Turkey to NATO 1976-78, to UN 1980-85; Amb. to Canada 1985-86; Sr. Adviser, Ministry of Foreign Affairs 1978-80. *Address:* c/o Ministry of Foreign Affairs, Disisleri Bakanlığı, Istanbul, Turkey.

KIRCHSCHLÄGER, Rudolf, DR.JUR.; Austrian politician; b. 20 March 1915, Niederkappel, Upper Austria; s. of Johann and Anna Kirchschläger; m. Herma Sorger 1940; one s. one d.; ed. Univ. of Vienna; Judge until 1954; joined Ministry of Foreign Affairs 1954, Head of Dept. of Int. Law 1956, Deputy Sec.-Gen. for Foreign Affairs 1962-67; Principal Private Sec. to the Minister of Foreign Affairs 1963-67; Minister to Czechoslovakia until 1970; Minister of Foreign Affairs 1970-74; Fed. Pres. of Austria 1974-86; has attended numerous int. confs. and been mem. of Austrian del. to UN Gen. Assembly. *Leisure interests:* music, walking. *Address:* Anderg. 9, A-1170, Vienna, Austria. *Telephone:* 45-11-45.

KIRICHENKO, Yuriy Alekseyevich; Soviet diplomatist; b. 13 Jan. 1936, Zernograd, Rostov region; s. of Aleksey and Yevdokiya Kirichenko; m. Tatyana Grechko; ed. Kiev Univ.; Diplomatic Service 1958-; Counsellor, Egypt 1964-70; on staff of Ministry of Foreign Affairs 1970-72; Minister Counsellor, Turkey 1972-73; Amb. to Iceland 1973-75, to Norway 1975-82; Head of Cultural Relations Dept. of Foreign Ministry Jan. 1982-. *Address:* c/o Ministry of Foreign Affairs, Moscow, U.S.S.R.

KIRILLIN, Vladimir Alekseyevich; Soviet thermophysicist and politician; b. 20 Jan. 1913, Moscow; ed. Power Engineering Inst., Moscow; Lecturer 1938-41, 1943-52; Prof. Moscow Power Engineering Inst. 1952-53; Corresp. mem. U.S.S.R. Acad. of Sciences 1953-62, mem. 1962-, Vice-Pres. 1963; U.S.S.R. Deputy Minister of Higher Education 1954-55; Head, Dept. of Science, Higher Education Inst. and School, Cen. Cttee. of CPSU 1955-63; mem. Central Auditing Comm. CPSU 1956-61; Cand. mem. CPSU Cen. Cttee. 1961-66, mem. 1966-81; Deputy to U.S.S.R. Supreme Soviet 1962-; fmr. Chair. State Cttee. for Science and Engineering 1965, fmr. Chair. State Cttee. for Science and Tech.; Vice-Chair. U.S.S.R. Council of Minis-

ters 1965-80; State Prize 1951, 1959, Order of Lenin (four times), and other decorations. *Publications:* Cycles of Turbines of Internal Combustion 1949, Fundamentals of Experimental Thermodynamics 1950, Steam in Power 1953, Thermodynamics of Solutions 1956, Thermodynamic Properties of Gases 1953, Investigation of Thermodynamic Properties of Substances 1963, Technical Thermodynamics 1968. *Address:* c/o Council of Ministers, The Kremlin, Moscow, U.S.S.R.

KIRK, Geoffrey Stephen, LITT.D., F.B.A., D.S.C.; British professor of Greek; b. 3 Dec. 1921, Nottingham; s. of Frederic T. Kirk and Enid H. Pentecost; m. Kirsten Jensen Ricks 1975; one d. (from previous marriage); ed. Rossall School and Clare Coll., Cambridge; Fellow, Trinity Hall, Cambridge 1946-70, Trinity Coll. 1974-82; Commonwealth Fund Fellow, Harvard 1949; Lecturer, then Reader in Classics, Univ. of Cambridge 1950-64, Regius Prof. of Greek 1974-82, Prof. Emer. 1982-; Prof. of Classics, Yale Univ. 1964-70; Bristol Univ. 1971-73; Sather Prof. in Classical Literature, Berkeley, Calif. 1969; Mellon Prof., Tulane Univ. 1979; Blegen Prof. Vassar Coll. 1986; Visiting Prof. Yale Univ. 1988. *Publications:* Heraclitus, the Cosmic Fragments 1954, The Presocratic Philosophers (with J. E. Raven) 1957, The Songs of Homer 1962, Myth, its Meaning and Functions 1970, The Nature of Greek Myths 1974, Homer and the Oral Tradition 1977, The Iliad: a Commentary (Vol. I) 1985, Vol. II 1989. *Leisure interests:* sailing, 18th century architecture, living in S.W. France. *Address:* 10 Sion Hill, Bath, BA1 2UH, Avon, England.

KIRK, Grayson, PH.D.; American former university president; b. 12 Oct. 1903, Jeffersonville, Ohio; s. of Traine C. and Nora Eichelberger Kirk; m. Marion Sands 1925; one s.; ed. Miami Univ., Clark Univ., Ecole Libre des Sciences Politiques, Paris, Univ. of Wisconsin, London School of Economics; Instructor in Political Science, Univ. of Wisconsin 1929-30, Asst. Prof. 1930-36, Assoc. Prof. 1936-38, Prof. of Political Science 1938-40; Assoc. Prof. of Govt., Columbia Univ. 1940-43; Research Assoc., Yale Inst. of International Studies 1943-44; Prof. of Govt., Columbia Univ. 1943-47, Prof. of Int. Relations 1947-49, Provost 1949-50, Vice-Pres. and Provost 1950-53, Acting Pres. 1951, Pres. and Trustee 1953-68, Pres. Emer. and Trustee Emer. 1968-; Bryce Prof. Emer. of the History of Int. Relations, Columbia Univ.; Head of Security Section, Div. of Political Studies, State Dept. 1942-43; mem. U.S. Del. Dumbarton Oaks 1944; Exec. Officer, Third Comm. (Security Council), San Francisco Conf. 1945; mem. Bd. of Dirs. France-America Soc.; Dir. and Vice-Pres. The Tinker Foundation; Vice-Pres. Acad. of Political Science; Hon. LL.D. (Miami, Waynesburg, Brown, Union, Princeton, Wisconsin, Syracuse, Williams, Pennsylvania, Harvard, Tennessee, Washington, New York, Clark, Puerto Rico, Johns Hopkins, Columbia, Amherst, Dartmouth Coll., Northwestern, Jewish Theol. Seminary, St. Lawrence, Denver, Notre Dame, Bates Coll., Univ. of Mich., Waseda (Japan), Sussex, Venezuelan Univs. and Univs. in India and Thailand), Hon. PH.D. (Bologna), D.C.L. (Univ. of King's Coll., Halifax, Nova Scotia), Hon. L.H.D. (N. Dakota); Commdr. Order of Orange Nassau (Netherlands), Hon. K.B.E., Grand Officier Légion d'honneur, K.St.J., Officer, Order of Grand Cross of George I (Greece), Order of the Sacred Treasure, 1st Class (Japan), and Italian and Iranian decorations, Commdr. de l'Ordre des Palmes académiques (France). *Publications:* Philippine Independence 1936, Contemporary International Politics (with W. R. Sharp) 1940, War and National Policy, Syllabus (with R. P. Stebbins) 1941, The Study of International Relations in American Colleges and Universities 1947. *Address:* 28 Sunnybrook Road, Bronxville, N.Y. 10708, U.S.A. (Home). *Telephone:* (914) 793-0808.

KIRK, Kent Sand; Danish fishing captain; b. 29 Aug. 1948, Esbjerg; s. of Sand and Brynhild Kirk; m. Ruth Henriksen 1971; three s.; Master's certificate; capt. of fishing boat 1971-; Gen. Man. K. and K. Kirk Ltd. 1973-; Chair. Bd. Fishermen's Asscn., Esbjerg 1975-; mem. Bd. Danish Deep Sea Fishing Fed., Danish Fishermen's Producers' Org., Esbjerg Harbour Council 1976-; mem. European Parl. 1979-; mem. Bd. Danish Conservative Party 1980-; Vice-Pres. European Democratic Group 1981-83; Partner, Esvagt Ltd. (Stand-by vessels) 1981-; Chair. Bd. Int. School, Esbjerg 1982-. *Leisure interests:* skiing, reading. *Address:* Bellisvaenget 33 Hjerting, DK 6700 Esbjerg (winter); Dalen 10, DK 6720 Fanø, Denmark (summer). *Telephone:* 05 116 031 (winter); 05 163 562 (summer).

KIRK, Paul Grattan, Jr., A.B., LL.B.; American lawyer and political official; b. 18 Jan. 1938, Newton, Mass.; m. Gail Loudermilk; ed. Harvard Univ.; partner, Sullivan & Worcester, Boston and Washington 1977-; Special Asst. to Senator Edward Kennedy (q.v.); Nat. Political Dir. Kennedy for Pres. Cttee. 1980; Treas. Democratic Nat. Cttee. 1983-85, Chair. 1985-89; Visiting Lecturer, Mass. Continuing Legal Educ. Program, New England Law Inst., J. F. Kennedy Inst. of Politics, Harvard Univ.; mem. Bd. of Dirs. J. F. Kennedy Library Foundation, Nat. Democratic Inst. for Int. Affairs, mem. Bd of Trustees, Stonehill Coll.; Co-Chair. Comm. on Pres. Debates; etc. *Address:* Sullivan and Worcester, 1025 Connecticut Avenue, N.W., Washington, D.C. 20036, U.S.A.

KIRKBY, Emma, M.A.; British singer; b. 26 Feb. 1949, Camberley, Surrey; d. of Capt. Geoffrey Kirkby and Beatrice Daphne Kirkby; ed. Sherborne School for Girls and Somerville Coll., Oxford and pvt. singing lessons with Jessica Cash; specialist singer of renaissance, baroque and classical repertoire; started full-time professional singing 1975; since mid-1970s involved in revival of performances with period instruments and the attempt to recreate the sounds the composers would have heard; works as freelance, particularly with Consort of Musicke (dir. Anthony Rooley), Taverner Players (dir. Andrew Parrott) and Acad. of Ancient Music (dir. Christopher Hogwood); Hon. D.Litt. (Salford) 1985. *Recordings include:* Complete songs of John Dowland 1976-77, Messiah (Handel), Gloria (Vivaldi), English Madrigals by Wilbye, Morley, John Ward and Italian Madrigals by Monteverdi, d'India and Scarlatti, Vespers (Monteverdi) 1983, Exsultate Jubilate (Mozart) 1984, Mass in B minor (Bach) 1984, Italian Arias (Handel) 1985, Monteverdi duets (with Evelyn Tubb), Arne songs, Vivaldi and Handel 1987. *Address:* c/o Ibbs & Tillett, 18b Pindock Mews, Little Venice, London, W9 2PY, England. *Telephone:* 01-286 7526.

KIRKINEN, Heikki, PH.D.; Finnish university professor; b. 22 Sept. 1927, Liperi; s. of Sulo A. Kirkinen and Anna Hirvonen; m. Maire Mirjam Rehvonen 1953; one s.; ed. Joensuu Lycée, Univ. of Helsinki; lecturer in History and Finnish, Orthodox Seminary of Finland 1953-59; lecturer in History, Univ. of Jyvaskyla 1960-62; Researcher, Acad. of Finland 1962-66; Assoc. Prof. Sorbonne, Paris 1966-70; Prof. of History, Univ. of Joensuu 1970-, Rector 1971-81, Prof. and Dir. Inst. of History 1981-; Assoc. Prof., Sorbonne Nouvelle 1984-85; Assoc. Dir. of Studies, Ecole Pratique des Hautes Etudes, Paris 1988-89; mem. History Soc., Kalevala Soc., Finnish Literature Soc., Acad. of Sciences of Finland; Corresp. mem. Acad. Européenne des Sciences, des Arts et des Lettres; Commdr., Order of the White Rose; Officier, Ordre des Palmes Académiques, Ordre Nat. du Mérite (France). *Publications:* Karelia between East and West, I. Russian Karelia in the Renaissance (1478-1617) 1970, Karelia on the Battlefield. Karelia between East and West, II 1976, Problems of Rural Development in Finland and in France (Ed.) 1982, Europas födelse. Bonniers varldshistoria 7 1984, The Kalevala, an Epic of Finland and all Mankind (with H. Sihvo) 1985, History of Russia and the Soviet Union (Ed.-in-Chief) 1986, Le monde kalévaléen en France et en Finlande avec un regard sur la tradition populaire et l'épopée brétonnes (Ed. with Jean Perrot) 1987, Byzantine Tradition and Finland 1987, Structures and Forces in History 1987. *Leisure interests:* music, fishing. *Address:* University of Joensuu, B.P. 111, 80101 Joensuu, Finland.

KIRKLAND, Gelsey; American ballerina; b. 1953, Bethlehem, Pa.; m. Greg Lawrence; ed. School of American Ballet; youngest mem. of New York Ballet at 15 in 1968, Soloist 1969-72, Prin. Dancer 1972-74; American Ballet Theater 1974-81, 1982-84; Guest Dancer, Royal Ballet, London 1980, 1986, Stuttgart Ballet 1980; performed in numerous ballets including: Firebird, The Goldberg Variations, Scherzo fantastique, An Evening's Waltzes, The Leaves are Fading, Hamlet, The Tiller in the Field, Four Bagatelles, Stravinsky Symphony in C, Song of the Nightingale Connotations, Romeo and Juliet and others; appeared in TV show The Nutcracker 1977. *Publication:* Dancing on My Grave (autobiog.) 1987. *Address:* c/o Dubé Zakin Management Inc., 1841 Broadway, New York, N.Y. 10023, U.S.A.

KIRKLAND, (Joseph) Lane, B.S.; American trade unionist; b. 12 March 1922, Camden, S.C.; s. of Randolph Withers Kirkland and Louise Richardson; m. 1st Edith Hollyday 1944; m. 2nd Irena Neumann 1973; ed. U.S. Merchant Marine Acad. and School of Foreign Service, Georgetown Univ.; Deck Officer, U.S. Merchant Marine 1941-46; Nautical Scientist, Hydrographic Office, Navy Dept. 1947-48; mem. of research staff, AFL 1948-53; Asst. Dir. Social Security Dept., AFL and AFL-CIO 1953-58; Dir. Research and Educ., Int. Union of Operating Engineers 1958-60; Exec. Asst. to Pres. AFL-CIO 1961-69, Sec.-Treas. 1969-79, Pres. 1979-; mem. Nat. Bipartisan Comm. on Cen. America 1983-84; Hon. LL.D. (Duke Univ. and Princeton Univ.). *Leisure interests;* reading, gardening, archaeology. *Address:* AFL-CIO, 815 16th Street, N.W., Washington, D.C. 20006, U.S.A. *Telephone:* (202) 637-5231.

KIRKPATRICK, Clayton, A.B.; American newspaper editor; b. 8 Jan. 1915, Waterman, Ill.; s. of Clayton Matteson Kirkpatrick and Mable Rose Swift; m. Thelma Marie De Mott 1943; three s. two d.; ed. Univ. of Ill.; Reporter, City News Bureau, Chicago 1938; mem. staff Chicago Tribune 1938-, Day City Ed. 1958-61, City Ed. 1961-63, Asst. Man. Ed. 1963-65, Man. Ed. 1965-67, Exec. Ed. 1967-69, Ed. 1969-79; Vice-Pres. Chicago Tribune Co. 1967-77, Exec. Vice-Pres. 1977-79, Pres. 1979-81, Chair. 1981; Del. to 19th Gen. Conf., UNESCO, Nairobi 1976; Bronze Star Medal for service in World War II; Elijah Parish Lovejoy Award, Colby Coll. 1978; William Allen White Award, Univ. of Kansas 1977; Fourth Estate Award, Nat. Press Club 1979. *Address:* 435 North Michigan Avenue, Chicago, Ill. 60611 (Office); 156 Sunset Avenue, Glen Ellyn, Ill. 60137, U.S.A. (Home).

KIRKPATRICK, Jeane Duane Jordan, M.A., PH.D.; American diplomatist and professor of political science; b. 19 Nov. 1926, Duncan, Okla.; d. of Welcher F. and Leona (Kile) Jordan; m. Evron M. Kirkpatrick 1955; three s.; ed. Stephens Coll., Columbia, Mo., Barnard Coll., Columbia Univ., New York, and Inst. de Science Politique, Univ. of Paris; Research Analyst, Dept. of State 1951-53; Research Assoc., George Washington Univ., Washington, D.C. 1954-56; Fund for the Republic 1956-58; Asst. Prof. of Political Science, Trinity Coll., Washington, D.C. 1962-68; Assoc. Prof. of Govt., Georgetown Univ., Washington, D.C. 1967-78, Prof. 1978-80; Leavey Prof. in Foundations of American Freedom 1978-; Sr. Fellow American Enterprise Inst. for Public Policy Research 1977-; Perm. Rep. to UN 1981-85; fmr. mem. Democratic Nat. Comm.; Vice-Chair. Comm. on Vice-

Presidential Selection 1972-74, mem. Nat. Comm. on Party Structure and Presidential Nomination 1975; mem. Int. Research Council Cen. for Strategic and Int. Studies, Georgetown Univ.; Earhart Fellow 1956-57; Hon. L.H.D. (Georgetown Univ., Univ. of Pittsburgh, Charleston Coll., Univ. of West Fla.; St. Anselm's Univ., Mt. Vernon Coll.) 1978; Distinguished Alumna Award, Stephens Coll. 1978, Distinguished Alumna Medal, Barnard Coll. 1983, B'nai B'nith Award 1982; Pres. Medal of Freedom 1985; fmr. Democrat; joined Republican Party 1985. *Publications:* Foreign Students in the United States: A National Survey 1966, Mass Behavior in Battle and Captivity 1968, Leader and Vanguard in Mass Society: The Peronist Movement in Argentina 1972, Political Woman 1974, The New Presidential Elite 1976, Dismantling the Parties: Reflections on Party Reform and Party Decomposition 1978, Dictatorships and Double Standards 1982, The Reagan Phenomenon 1983; ed. and contributor to several others; also articles in political journals. *Leisure interests:* contemporary fiction, Bach, gourmet cooking. *Address:* American Enterprise Institute, 1150 17th Street, N.W., Washington, D.C. 20036, U.S.A.

KIRKUP, James, B.A., F.R.S.L.; British writer; b. 23 April 1918, South Shields; s. of James Harold Kirkup and Mary Johnson; ed. Durham Univ.; Gregory Fellow in Poetry, Leeds Univ. 1950-52; Visiting Poet, Bath Acad. of Art 1953-56; travelling lectureship from Swedish Ministry of Education 1956-57; Prof. of English Language and Literature, Salamanca (Spain) 1957-58; Prof. of English Literature, Tohoku Univ. 1959-61; Visiting Prof. of English Literature, Japan Women's Univ., Tokyo 1964-69; Visiting Prof. and Poet in Residence, Amherst Coll. Mass. 1968-69; Prof. of English Literature, Univ. of Nagoya, Japan 1969-72; Morton Visiting Prof. in Int. Literature, Ohio Univ. 1975-76; Playwright in Residence, Sherman Theatre, Univ. Coll., Cardiff 1976-77; Prof. of English Literature, Kyoto Univ. of Foreign Studies 1977-; Tutor, Arvon Foundation 1979; Literary Ed. Orient-West Magazine, Tokyo 1963-65; Atlantic Award in Literature (Rockefeller Foundation) 1959, F.R.S.L. 1962, First Prize, Japan PEN literary contest 1965, Mildred Batchelder Award, A.L.A. 1968, Crowned Ollave of the Order of Bards, Ovates and Druids 1974; Hon. Fellow (Inst. of Psychophysical Research, Oxford) 1970; Fellow in Creative Writing (Sheffield Univ.) 1974-75. *Publications:* The Cosmic Shape 1947, The Drowned Sailor 1948, The Creation 1950, The Submerged Village 1951, A Correct Compassion 1952, A Spring Journey 1954, Upon This Rock, The Dark Child, The Triumph of Harmony 1955, The True Mystery of the Nativity, Ancestral Voices, The Radiance of the King 1956, The Descent into the Cave, The Only Child (autobiography) 1957, The Peach Garden, Two Pigeons Flying High (TV plays), Sorrows, Passions and Alarms (autobiography) 1960, The True Mystery of the Passion, The Prodigal Son (poems) 1956-60, These Horned Islands (travel) 1962, The Love of Others (novel) 1962, Tropic Temper (travel) 1963, Refusal to Conform, Last and First Poems 1963, The Heavenly Mandate 1964, Japan Industrial, Vols. I and II 1964-65, Tokyo (travel) 1966, Bangkok (travel) 1967, Paper Windows: Poems from Japan 1967, Michael Kohlhaas 1967, Filipinescas (travel) 1968, One Man's Russia (travel) 1968, Streets of Asia (travel) 1969, Hong Kong (travel) 1969, White Shadows, Black Shadows: Poems of Peace and War 1969, The Body Servant: Poems of Exile 1971, Japan Behind the Fan 1970, Streets of Asia 1969, Insect Summer (novel) 1971, (children's novel) 1977, A Bewick Bestiary 1971, Transmental Vibrations 1972, Brand (Ibsen) 1972, The Magic Drum (play for children) 1972, (story for children) 1973, Peer Gynt 1973, The Winter Moon, Selected Poems of Takagi Kyozo, Cyrano de Bergerac 1974, Play Strindberg 1974, The Conformer 1975, Don Carlos 1975, Heaven, Hell and Hara-Kiri: The Rise and Fall of the Japanese Superstate 1975, Background to English Literature 1975, An English Traveller in Japan 1975, Frank the Fifth, Portrait of a Planet 1976, Scenes from Sesshu 1977, Modern Japanese Poetry (anthology) 1978, Dengoban Messages: One-line Poems, Zen Contemplations, Enlightenment 1979, Cold Mountain Poems, The Guardian of the Word, Aspects of Europe, Countries and Customs, British Traditions and Superstitions 1980, James Kirkup's Tales from Shakespeare 1969-84, Scenes from Sutcliffe 1981, The British Lady and Gentleman, I am Count Dracula 1981, Ecce Homo: My Pasolini 1981, To The Unknown God 1982, The Bush Toads 1982, Folktales Japanesque 1982, To the Ancestral North (poems for autobiog.) 1983, The Glory that was Greece 1984, The Sense of the Visit: New Poems 1984, Hearn in my Heart 1984; operas: An Actor's Revenge 1979, Friends in Arms, Shunkinsho 1980, No More Hiroshimas 1982, The Damask Drum 1984, Trends and Traditions 1985, Dictionary of Body Language 1985, English with a Smile 1986, Fellow Feelings (poems) 1986, Portraits and Souvenirs 1987, The Mystery and Magic of Symbols 1987, The Cry of the Owl: Native American Folktales and Legends 1987, I of All People: An Autobiography of Youth, Scenes from American Life, I Remember America, Everyday English Superstitions 1988, The Best of Britain 1989, Everyday English Proverbs 1989, and others; numerous poems, plays and essays and trans. from French, German, Japanese, Italian and Norwegian. *Leisure interests:* macrobiotic diet, Zen Buddhist meditation, listening to good jazz (leading fan of Anita O'Day, Blossom Dearie, Lee Wylie, etc.). *Address:* c/o British Monomarks, BM-Box 2780, London, WC1N 3XX, England; Department of English Literature, Kyoto University of Foreign Studies, Sai'in, Ukyo-ku, Kyoto-fu 615, Japan. *Telephone:* 01-405 0463.

KIRLOSKAR, Shantanu Laxman, B.SC.; Indian industrialist; b. 28 May 1903, Sholapur, Maharashtra State; m. Yamutai R. Phatak 1927; two s.

one d.; ed. Massachusetts Inst. of Technology, U.S.A.; Kirloskar Brothers 1926-; Chair. Kirloskar Oil Engines Ltd., Poona; Chair. Bd. of Dirs. Kirloskar Pneumatic Co. Ltd., Poona, Kirloskar Consultants Ltd., Poona, Padamjee Pulp and Paper Mills Ltd., Poona, Poona Industrial Hotels Ltd., Kirloskar Brothers Ltd.; Dir. numerous other companies; fmr. Chair. Indian Inst. of Management; mem. Maharatta Chamber of Commerce and Industries, Poona; Pres. Fed. of Indian Chambers of Commerce and Industry, New Delhi 1965-66; First Pres. Indo-American Chamber of Commerce; Padma Bhushan 1965; Chair. Cttee. for Econ. Devt. in India; Dir. Reserve Bank of India, Industrial Devt. Bank of India; mem. Exec. Cttee. Int. Chamber of Commerce 1976-; Life mem. Inst. of Engineers (India) 1970; Sir Walter Puckey Prize 1968, Karma Virottama, Eng. Asscn. of India 1972, Vanijya Ratna 1976. *Publications:* Jet Yugateel Marathi Manus (A Man from Maharashtra in the Jet Age), Cactus and Roses (autobiog.). *Leisure interests:* Western classical music, painting. *Address:* Kirloskar Oil Engines Ltd., Corporate Office, 11 Koregaon Road, Poona 411001 (Office); "Lakaki", Shivajinagar, Poona 411016, India (Home). *Telephone:* 60018 (Office); 56471 (Home).

KIRPAL, Prem Nath, M.A., LL.B.; Indian educationist; b. 30 April 1909, Moga, Punjab; s. of Raibahadur Ishwardas and Bibi Kesari; ed. Punjab Univ. and Balliol Coll., Oxford; Lecturer, then Prof. of History and Political Science 1934-45; Educ. Adviser, Indian High Comm., London 1945-48; Deputy Sec. Ministry of Educ. and Sec.-Gen. Indian Nat. Comm. for UNESCO 1948-52; Deputy Dir. then Dir. UNESCO Dept. of Cultural Activities 1952-57; Joint Sec. Ministry of Educ. and Joint Educ. Adviser to Govt. of India 1957-60; Sec. Ministry of Educ. 1960-69; Sr. Specialist, East-West Centre, Honolulu Hawaii 1969; Dir. Int. Study of Private Philanthropy 1969-; Pres. Exec. Board, UNESCO 1970-72; Founder, Pres., Inst. of Cultural Relations and Devt. Studies, New Delhi 1971-; Pres. Indian Council of Peace Research 1972-; Pres. Int. Educational Consortium, New Delhi 1979-81; Consultant, World Bank, Washington, D.C.; mem. Exec. Council, Delhi Univ.; Chair. Delhi Public Library, Delhi School of Social Work; Pres. Forum of Educ., India; Hon. LL.D. (Temple Univ.), Hon. D.Sc. (Leningrad), Hon. D.Litt. (Punjab Univ.); UNESCO Gold Medal 1972; Orders of Repub. of Egypt and of U.A.R. 1972; 30th Anniversary Award, UNESCO 1976, and other awards. *Publications:* East India Company and Persia 1800-1810: A Study in Diplomatic Relations, Memoirs of Wollebrant de Jong 1624, Life of Dyal Singh Majithia, Main Trends in Cultural Development of India, A Decade of Indian Education 1958-68, Indian Education—Twenty-five Years of Independence, Youth Values and Established Culture, Education and Development, In Quest of Humanity, The Cosmic Sea and other Poems 1980, Songs of Psyche, Spirit's Musings, Songs of Eternity (philosophical poems), Voices from the Deep 1986, From Near and Far (poems) 1988, and over 20 articles on education, culture and international co-operation. *Leisure interests:* hiking, painting, poetry and meditation. *Address:* Executive Bd. UNESCO, Place de Fontenoy, 75700 Paris, France; 63F Sujan Singh Park, New Delhi 3, India (Home). *Telephone:* 566-57-57 (UNESCO); 693-258 (New Delhi).

KIRSCHSTEIN, Ruth L., A.B., M.D.; American physician and administrator; b. 12 Oct. 1926, Brooklyn, New York; d. of Julius and Elizabeth (Berm) Kirschstein; m. Alan S. Rabson 1950; one s.; ed. Long Island Univ., New York and Tulane Univ., New Orleans, La.; Hosp. intern and resident 1951-54; Instructor in Pathology, Tulane Univ. 1954-55; Medical Officer, Resident in Pathology, then Pathologist, Lab. of Viral Products, Nat. Insts. of Health 1956-60, Chief, Section of Pathology, Lab. of Viral Immunology 1960-62, Asst. Chief, Lab. of Viral Immunology 1962-64, Acting Chief, Lab. of Pathology 1964-65, Chief 1965-72; Asst. Dir. Div. of Biologics Standards, Nat. Insts. of Health 1971-72, Acting Deputy Dir., Bureau of Biologics 1972-73, Deputy Assoc. Commr. for Science 1973-74, Dir. Nat. Inst. of Gen. Medical Sciences, Nat. Insts. of Health 1974-; mem. Inst. of Medicine of N.A.S.; Hon. LL.D. (Atlanta) 1985; D.Sc. h.c. (Mount Sinai School of Medicine) 1984, (Medical Coll. of Ohio) 1986; Presidential Meritorious Exec. Rank Award 1980, Distinguished Exec. Service Award Sr. Exec. Asscn. 1985, Presidential Distinguished Exec. Rank Award 1985. *Publications:* numerous scientific papers. *Address:* National Institute of General Medical Sciences, Building 31, Room 4A52, Bethesda, Md. 20892, U.S.A. *Telephone:* (301) 496-5231.

KIRSOP, Arthur Michael Benjamin, B.A.JURIS., F.B.I.M.; British business executive; b. 28 Jan. 1931, Manchester; s. of Arthur and Sarah Cauthery Kirsop; m. Patricia Cooper 1957; two s.; ed. Glasgow Acad. and Oxford Univ.; Dir., English Sewing Cotton Co. Ltd. 1967; Dir., English Calico Ltd. (now Tootal Ltd.) 1968, Joint Man. Dir. 1973, Deputy Chair. 1974, Chair. Feb. 1975-76; Chair. Forth Thyme Ltd. 1976-; Hon. Consul for the Netherlands 1971-79; Chair. and Man. Dir. Ollerenshaw Threads Ltd. 1981-85. *Leisure interests:* gardening, sport. *Address:* 237 Ashley Road, Hale, Cheshire WA15 9NE, England. *Telephone:* 061-941 5173.

KIRST, Michael, M.P.A., PH.D.; American professor of education; b. 1 Aug. 1939, West Reading, Pa.; m. Wendy Burdsall 1975; one s. one d.; ed. Dartmouth Coll., and Harvard Univ.; Assoc. Dir. President's Comm. on White House Fellows, Nat. Advisory Council on Educ. of Disadvantaged Children 1966; Dir. Program Planning and Evaluation, Bureau of Elementary and Secondary Educ., U.S. Office of Educ. 1967; Staff Dir. U.S. Senate Sub-Cttee. on Manpower, Employment and Poverty 1968; Prof. of Educ. and Business Admin. Stanford Univ. 1968-; mem. numerous educ. bds., cttees., etc. *Publications include:* Schools in Conflict: Political Turbulence in American Education (with F. Wirt) 1982, Contemporary Issues in Education: Perspectives from Australia and U.S.A. (with G. Hancock and D. Grossman) 1983, Who Controls Our Schools: American Values in Conflict 1984. *Address:* School of Education, Stanford University, Stanford, Calif. 94305, U.S.A. *Telephone:* 415-497-4412.

KIRSTEIN, Lincoln; American ballet promoter; b. 4 May 1907, Rochester, N.Y.; s. of Louis and Rose Kirstein; m. Fidelma Cadmus 1941; ed. Harvard Univ.; Ed. Hound and Horn (literary periodical) 1927-34; Ed. The Dance Index 1941-47; established School of American Ballet, New York City, and Dir.; Dir. New York City Ballet Co.; Dir.-Gen. American Ballet; Benjamin Franklin Medal (R.S.A.) 1981, Medal of Freedom 1984, Heart of New York Award 1984, Lincoln Nat. Medal of Arts 1985, Notable Achievement Award (Branders Univ.) 1986. *Publications:* A Short History of Theatrical Dancing 1935, Blast at Ballet 1938, Low Ceiling (poems) 1935, Ballet Alphabet 1939, Rhymes of a P.F.C. (Private First Class) (poems) 1964, Rhymes and more Rhymes of a P.F.C. 1966, The Hampton Album 1966, Three Pamphlets Collected 1967, Movement and Metaphor: Four Centuries of Ballet 1969, The New York City Ballet 1973, Elie Nadelman 1973, Lay this Laurel 1974, Nijinsky, Dancing 1974, Ballet: Bias and Belief 1983, A. Hyatt Mayor: collected writings (Ed.) 1983, Quarry: a collection in lieu of memoirs 1986, The Poems of Lincoln Kirstein 1987. *Address:* School of American Ballet, 144 West 66th Street, New York, N.Y. 10023, U.S.A.

KIRSZENSTEIN-SZEWIŃSKA, Irena, M.ECON.; Polish athlete; b. 24 May 1946, Leningrad, U.S.S.R.; m.; one s.; ed. Warsaw Univ.; took part in Olympic Games, Tokyo 1964 (silver medals for long jump and 200 m., gold medal for 4 × 100 m. relay), Mexico City 1968 (bronze medal for 100 m., gold medal for 200 m.), Munich 1972 (bronze medal for 200 m.), Montreal 1976 (gold medal for 400 m.); seven times world record holder, especially for 200 m. and 400 m.; mem. Provisional Nat. Council of Patriotic Movt. for Nat. Rebirth (PRON) 1982-83, mem. Nat. Council PRON 1983-; Gold Cross of Merit 1964, Officer's Cross, Order of Polonia Restituta 1968, Commdr.'s Cross 1972. *Address:* Ul. Bagno 5 m. 80, 00-112 Warsaw, Poland. *Telephone:* 20-63-73.

KIRYAK, Nellia Pavlovna; Soviet official; b. 1935, Moldavia; mem. CPSU 1961-; ed. Moscow Tech. Inst. of Light Industry, Cen. Cttee. Party Higher School of CPSU; head of enterprise, Kishinev 1958-63; Deputy Chief of Dept. for Industry and Transport, Cen. Cttee. of Moldavian CP 1964-69; First Deputy Minister of Local Industry of Moldavian S.S.R. 1969-72; Head of Finance and Planning , Dept. of Cen. Cttee. of Moldavian CP 1974-76; Deputy to U.S.S.R. Supreme Soviet 1975-; Chief of Dept. for Light Industry, Trade, Cen. Cttee. of Moldavian CP 1976-78; mem. Cen. Cttee. of Moldavian CP 1976-; Deputy Chair. of Council of Ministers of Moldavian S.S.R. 1980-. *Address:* Council of Ministers of Moldavian S.S.R., Kishinev, Moldavian S.S.R., U.S.S.R.

KISEKKA, Samson; Ugandan medical practitioner and politician; Chief Spokesman for Nat. Resistance Army; Adviser to Yoweri Museveni (q.v.); Prime Minister of Uganda Jan. 1986-. *Address:* Office of the Prime Minister, Kampala, Uganda.

KISELEV, Gennadiy Nikolayevich, CAND.ECON.SC.; Soviet politician; ed. Tomsk Polytechnic Inst., and CPSU Cen. Cttee. Higher Party School; chief Section Foreman Ust-Magadan fishing combine 1959-60; mem. CPSU 1961-; Second Sec. of Magadan City Komsomol Cttee. 1960-61; Second, First Sec. of Magadan Dist. Komsomol Cttee.; head of section of Cen. Cttee. of Komsomol 1969-72; First Sec. of Chukotsky Dist. Cttee. of CPSU (Magadan Dist.) 1972-75; Sec. of Magadan Dist. Cttee. 1975-78, 1980-; work for CPSU Cen. Cttee. 1985-; Second Sec. of Cen. Cttee. of CP of Kirghizia Dec. 1985-; cand. mem. of CPSU Cen. Cttee. 1986-; Deputy to U.S.S.R. Supreme Soviet. *Address:* Central Committee of Communist Party Kirghizia, Frunze, Kirghiz S.S.R., U.S.S.R.

KISHIMOTO, Yasunobu; Japanese business executive; b. 23 July 1919, Okayama Pref.; s. of Ichiji and Harue Kishimoto; m. Yoko Kobayashi 1946; two s.; ed. Tokyo Univ.; joined Showa Denko K.K. 1942, Works Man. Yokohama Works (Alumina) 1963, Works Man. Kawasaki Works (Chemicals) 1965, Dir. Feb. 1967, Man. Dir. Aug. 1967, Sr. Man. Dir. 1973, Exec. Vice-Pres. 1976, Pres. 1981-87, Chair. March 1987-; Chair. Abrasive Industry Asscn. 1981-87, The Japan Petrochemical Industry Asscn. 1984-86, Japan Carbon Asscn. 1985-87; Vice-Pres. Japan Chemical Industry Asscn. 1984-86; Pres. 1986-88; Pres. Soc. of Chemical Engineers 1988-; Vice-Chair. Asscn. for Progress in Chem. *Leisure interests:* golf, maps. *Address:* 13-9, Shiba Daimon 1-chome, Tokyo 105, Japan.

KISHTMAND, Sultan Ali; Afghan politician; b. 1935; ed. univ.; mem. of Hazara ethnic minority; a founder mem. People's Democratic Party of Afghanistan (PDPA) and mem. Cen. Cttee. 1965; with Parcham faction when PDPA split 1967; Minister of Planning April-Aug. 1978; tried on charges of conspiracy and sentenced to death 1978; sentence commuted by Pres. Amin. Oct. 1978; fmr. Vice-Pres. of Revolutionary Council; Deputy Prime Minister and Minister of Planning after Soviet intervention Dec. 1979-81; Prime Minister of Afghanistan and Chair. Council of Ministers

1981–88; Pres. State Planning Cttee.; mem. Politburo, Cen. Cttee. PDPA. *Address:* c/o Office of the Prime Minister, Kabul, Afghanistan.

KISIEL, Henryk, M.ECON.; Polish banker and politician; b. 1 July 1921, Łódź; ed. Faculty of Law and Econs., Łódź Univ.; manual worker during occupation; joined Nat. Bank of Poland as trainee, Łódź 1945, Dir. of Head Office 1961–64; Dir. Bank Handlowy SA w Warszawie 1964–66, Pres. 1966–68; Under-Sec. of State, Ministry of Finance 1968–71, Ministry of Foreign Trade 1971; Vice-Chair. Planning Comm. attached to Council of Ministers 1971–74; First Deputy Minister of Foreign Trade and Maritime Econ. 1974; Minister of Finance 1974–80; Minister of Finance and Chair. of Planning Comm. 1980–81; mem. Polish United Workers' Party (PZPR), Deputy mem. Cen. Cttee. PZPR 1975–80, mem. 1980–81; Gold Cross of Merit 1954, Order of Banner of Labour, 2nd Class 1964, Knight's Cross, Order of Polonia Restituta 1959, Officer's Cross 1969, Commdr.'s Cross 1974. *Leisure interests:* literature, history, sport.

KISIM, Marwan al-, PH.D.; Jordanian politician; b. 12 May 1938, Amman; ed. Eastern Michigan, Columbia and Georgetown Univs., U.S.A.; joined Ministry of Foreign Affairs 1962; Consul-Gen., New York 1964–65; Deputy Dir. of Protocol 1966; Political Officer, Jordanian Embassy, Beirut 1967–68, U.S.A. 1968–72; Sec. to Crown Prince Hassan (q.v.) 1972–75; Dir.-Gen. Royal Hashemite Court 1975–76, Chief 1988; Minister of State 1976; Minister of Supply 1977–79; Minister of State for Foreign Affairs 1979–80, Minister of Foreign Affairs 1980–83; Deputy Prime Minister and Minister of Foreign Affairs Dec. 1988–; Jordanian, Syrian, Mexican, Lebanese, Chinese and Italian decorations. *Address:* Ministry of Foreign Affairs, Amman, Jordan.

KISSIN, Baron (Life Peer), cr. 1974, of Camden in Greater London; **Harry Kissin**, LL.D., F.R.S.A.; British company executive; b. 23 Aug. 1912; s. of Israel Kissin and Reusi (née Model); m. Ruth Deborah Samuel 1935; one s. one d.; ed. Danzig and Switzerland; Vice-Chairman, Lewis & Peat Ltd. 1955–61, Chair. 1961–73; Chair. Guinness Peat Group Ltd. (now GPG PLC) 1973–79, Pres. 1979–; Pres. Guinness Mahon Holdings PLC 1988–; Chair. Lewis & Peat Holdings Ltd. 1982–87, Life Pres. 1987–; Chair./Dir. Fenchurch Insurance Holdings Ltd. 1962–82; Chair. Esperanza Ltd. 1970–82; Chair. Linfood Holdings Ltd. 1974–81; Dir. Transcontinental Services Group N.V. 1982–86; Chair. Inst. of Contemporary Arts 1968–76; Dir. Royal Opera House, Covent Garden 1973–84; Chair. Royal Opera House Trust 1974–80, ex-officio mem. 1980–87; Gov. Bezalel Acad. Arts & Design 1975–, Haifa Univ. 1976–81, Hebrew Univ. of Jerusalem 1980–; Freeman of the City of London 1975, Commdr. Ordem Nacional do Cruzeiro do Sul (Brazil) 1977; Chevalier, Légion d'honneur 1981, '1300 Years Bulgaria' Medal 1982. *Address:* c/o House of Lords, London, SW1 0AA, England.

KISSINGER, Henry Alfred, M.A., PH.D.; American (German-born) government official, university professor and consultant; b. 27 May 1923, Fuerth, Germany; m. 1st Anne Fleisher 1949 (divorced 1964), one s. one d.; m. 2nd Nancy Maginnes 1974; ed. George Washington High School, Harvard Coll., Harvard Univ.; went to U.S.A. 1938; naturalized U.S. Citizen 1943; U.S. Army 1943–46; Dir. Study Group on Nuclear Weapons and Foreign Policy, Council of Foreign Relations 1955–56; Dir. Special Studies Project, Rockefeller Brothers Fund 1956–58; Consultant, Weapons System Evaluation Group, Joint Chiefs of Staff 1956–60, Nat. Security Council 1961–63, U.S. Arms Control and Disarmament Agency 1961–68, Dept. of State 1965–68, and to various other bodies; Faculty mem. Harvard Univ. 1954–71; Dept. of Govt. and Center for Int. Affairs (on leave of absence 1969–71); Assoc. Dir. Harvard Univ. Center for Int. Affairs 1957–60; Dir. Harvard Int. Seminar 1951–71, Harvard Defense Studies Program 1958–71, Special Asst. to Pres. of U.S.A. for Nat. Security Affairs 1969–75; Sec. of State 1973–77; prominent in American negotiations for the Viet-Nam settlement of Jan. 1973, and in the negotiations for a Middle East ceasefire 1973, 1974; Univ. Prof. of Diplomacy, Georgetown School of Foreign Service and Counsellor, Center for Strategic and Int. Studies 1977–; Chair. Kissinger Associates, Inc. 1982–; mem. Pres.'s Foreign Intelligence Advisory Bd. 1984–; Chair. Nat. Bipartisan Comm. on Cen. America 1983–84; Counsellor to Chase Manhattan Bank and mem. of its Int. Advisory Cttee.; Hon. Gov. Foreign Policy Assen.; Trustee Rockefeller Brothers Fund; Sr. Fellow, Aspen Inst., syndicated columnist L.A. Times; mem. Bd. of Dirs. American Express, Union Pacific Corpn., R. H. Macy & Co.; Guggenheim Fellowship 1965–66, Woodrow Wilson Book Prize 1958, American Inst. for Public Service Award 1973, Nobel Peace Prize 1973, American Legion Distinguished Service Medal 1974, Wateler Peace Prize 1974, Presidential Medal of Freedom 1977, Medal of Liberty 1986, and many other awards and prizes. *Publications:* Nuclear Weapons and Foreign Policy 1956, A World Restored: Castlereagh, Metternich and the Restoration of Peace 1812-22 1957, The Necessity for Choice: Prospects of American Foreign Policy 1961, The Troubled Partnership: A Reappraisal of the Atlantic Alliance 1965, American Foreign Policy (3 essays) 1969, White House Years 1979, For the Record 1981, Years of Upheaval 1982, Observations: Selected Speeches and Essays 1982-84 1985 and numerous articles on U.S. foreign policy, international affairs and diplomatic history. *Address:* 350 Park Avenue, New York, N.Y. 10022 and Suite 400, 1800 K Street, N.W., Washington, D.C. 20006, U.S.A.

KISZCZAK, Gen. Czesław; Polish army officer and politician; b. 19 Oct. 1925, Roczyny; s. of Jan and Rozalia Kiszczak; m. Maria Teresa Korzonkiewicz 1958; one s. one d.; ed. Acad. of Gen. Staff, Warsaw; in resistance movement during Nazi occupation; with Polish People's Army 1945–; for many years served in mil. counter-intelligence, Chief of Mil. Intelligence, Deputy Chief of Gen. Staff 1972–79, Maj.-Gen. 1973, Lieut.-Gen. 1979, Gen. 1983–; Chief, Mil. Police of Ministry of Nat. Defence 1979–81; Under-Sec. of State, Head of Ministry of Internal Affairs July 1981; Minister of Internal Affairs Aug. 1981–; mem. Mil. Council of Nat. Salvation Dec. 1981–83; mem. Polish Workers' Party 1945-48, Polish United Workers' Party (PZPR) 1948–, deputy mem. PZPR Cen. Cttee. 1980–81, mem. 1981–, alt. mem. Political Bureau of PZPR Cen. Cttee. 1982–86, mem. Political Bureau 1986–; Deputy to Seym (Parl.) 1985–; Order of the Banner of Labour (1st Class), Order of Cross of Grunwald (3rd Class), Order of the Builders of People's Poland 1984, other nat., foreign and mil. decorations. *Leisure interests:* hunting, tourism. *Address:* Ministerstwo Spraw Wewnętrznych, ul. Rakowiecka 2b, 00-904 Warsaw, Poland. *Telephone:* 45-18-20.

KITAGAWA, Takeshi; Japanese business executive; b. 27 June 1916, Kumamoto, Kyushu; s. of Otsuhei and Chie Kitagawa; m. Masako Tsukada 1947; one s. one d.; ed. Tokyo Univ.; entered Industrial Bank of Japan 1939, Dir. 1964–67, Man. Dir. 1966–67; Vice-Pres. Tekkosha Co. Ltd. 1967, Pres. 1968; Vice-Pres. Toyosohda Kogyo Co. Ltd. 1975; Pres. Japan Line Ltd. June 1978–. *Leisure interests:* golf, baseball, mah-jong. *Address:* 3-21-38, Kohyama, Nerima-ku, Tokyo, Japan. *Telephone:* 999-0269.

KITAJ, R. B.; American artist; b. 1932, Ohio; m.; three c.; ed. New York, Vienna and Royal Coll. of Arts, London; has lived in London since 1960; Guest Prof. Univ. of Calif., Berkeley 1967–68, Univ. of Calif., Los Angeles 1970–71; one-man exhbns. in Marlborough New London Gallery 1963, 1970, Marlborough Gerson Gallery, New York, Los Angeles County Museum of Art 1965, Stedelijk Museum, Amsterdam, Museum of Art, Cleveland and Univ. of Calif., Berkeley 1967, Galerie Mikro, Berlin and tour of Fed. Germany 1969–70, Kestner Gesellschaft, Hanover, Boymans-van-Beuningen Museum, Rotterdam 1970, Cincinnati Art Museum, Ohio (with James Dine, q.v.) 1973, Marlborough, New York 1974, 1978, Marlborough, Zürich 1977, Marlborough, London 1977, 1980, 1985; retrospective tour Hirshorn Museum, Washington, Cleveland Museum and Kunsthalle, Dusseldorf 1981–; public collections in museums in Australia, Denmark, Fed. Repub. of Germany, Netherlands, Norway, Sweden, Switzerland, U.K. and U.S.A.; mem. American Inst. of Arts and Letters 1982; Assoc. mem. Royal Acad. 1984; Hon. L.H.D. (Univ. of London) 1982. *Publication:* David Hockney: A Retrospective (with others) 1988. *Address:* c/o Marlborough Fine Art Ltd., 6 Albemarle Street, London, W.1, England.

KITBUNCHU, H.E. Cardinal Michael Michai; Thai ecclesiastic; b. 25 January 1929, Samphran, Nakhon Pathom; ordained priest 1959; Archbishop of Bangkok 1973–; cr. Cardinal 1983. *Address:* Assumption Cathedral, 51 Oriental Avenue, Bangkok 10500, Thailand. *Telephone:* 2338712.

KITCHEN, Lawrence Oscar; American business executive; b. 8 June 1923, Fort Mill, S.C.; s. of Samuel Sumpter Kitchen and Ruby Azalee Grigg; m. 2nd Brenda Lenhart 1978; one s. two d. by 1st marriage; ed. Foothill Coll.; aeronautical engineer, U.S. Navy Bureau of Aeronautics, Washington 1946–58, Staff Asst. to Asst. Chief of Bureau 1958; with Lockheed Missiles and Space Co., Sunnyvale, Calif. 1958–70, Man. Product Support Logistics 1964–68, Dir. Financial Controls 1968–70; Vice-Pres. Finance Lockheed-Ga. Co., Marietta 1970–71, Pres. 1971–75; Pres. Lockheed Corpn., Burbank, Calif. 1975–85, C.O.O. 1976–85, Chair., C.E.O. 1986–88, Chair. Exec. Cttee. Bd. of Dirs. Jan. 1989–; mem. Int. Bd. Security Pacific Nat. Bank 1976–; mem. Bd. of Visitors, Emory Inst., Founders Bd. Hollywood Presbyterian Hospital; mem. Nominating Cttee. Aviation Hall of Fame; mem. Nat. Assen. of Accountants, American Inst. of Aeronautics Astronautics, etc. *Address:* Lockheed Corporation, 4500 Park Granada Boulevard, Calabasas, Calif. 91399, U.S.A. (Office).

KITCHING, John Alwyne, O.B.E., M.A., PH.D., F.R.S.; British professor emeritus of biology; b. 24 Oct. 1908, York; s. of John and Alice Kitching; m. Evelyn M. Oliver 1934; one s. three d.; ed. Cheltenham Coll. and Trinity Coll., Cambridge; Lecturer in Zoology, Birbeck Coll., London 1931–36; Lecturer in Experimental Zoology, Univ. of Edinburgh 1936, Univ. of Bristol 1937; Rockefeller Fellow, Princeton Univ. 1938; Assoc. in Aviation Medical Research (Nat. Research Council of Canada), Banting Inst., Toronto 1939–45; Lecturer in Zoology, later Reader, Univ. of Bristol 1945–62; Prof. of Biology Univ. of East Anglia 1962–74, Prof. Emer. 1974–; Hon. D.Sc. (Nat. Univ. of Ireland) 1983. *Publications:* many research papers in scientific journals. *Leisure interests:* travel, gardening. *Address:* School of Biological Sciences, University of East Anglia, Norwich, NR4 7TJ (Office); 29 Newfound Drive, Cringleford, Norwich, NR4 7RY, England (Home).

KITSON, Linda Frances, M.A.; British artist and teacher; b. 17 Feb. 1945 London; d. of Capt. James B. Kitson and Hon. Margaret Palmer (née Howard); ed. West Preston Manor School, Rustington, Tortington Park, Arundel, Ecole des Beaux Arts, Lyons, St. Martin's School of Art and Royal Coll. of Art; visiting tutor, Royal Coll. of Art, St. Martin's School of Art 1972–78, Chelsea School of Art, Camberwell School of Art and Crafts, City & Guilds of London Art School 1972–82; Lecturer, Royal Coll, of Art 1979–82, visiting tutor 1984–; Official War Artist, Falkland Islands Task Force 1982; several one-man exhbns. and contrib. to Royal Acad. Summer Exbn. since 1971; Pres. Army Arts and Crafts Soc. 1983; South Atlantic Medal (with rosette) 1983. *Publication:* The Falklands War: A Visual Diary 1982. *Leisure interests:* dancing, music. *Address:* Royal College of Art, Exhibition Road, London, S.W.7; 1 Argyll Mansions, Kings Road, London, SW3 5ER, England. *Telephone:* 01-584 5020, Ext. 238; 01-352 9043.

KITTANI, Ismat; Iraqi diplomatist; b. 1930, Emadieh, Mesopotamia (now part of Iraq); m.; one s.; ed. Know Coll., Galesburg, Ill., U.S.A.; taught English, high school, Iraq; with Ministry of Foreign Affairs, Baghdad; Embassy, Cairo 1952; Perm. Mission of Iraq to UN (Perm. Rep. 1961–64) 1957–64; joined UN Secr. 1964; mem. Social and Econ. Cttee., Geneva; Asst. Sec.-Gen. UN 1973–75; Deputy Minister of Foreign Affairs, Head Dept. of Int. Orgs. and Confs. 1975–80; Pres. 36th Gen. Assembly of UN 1981–82; Perm. Rep. to UN 1985–. *Address:* Permanent Mission of Iraq to United Nations, 14 East 79th Street, New York, N.Y. 10021, U.S.A. *Telephone:* 737-4433.

KITTEL, Charles, PH.D.; American professor of physics and author; b. 18 July 1916, New York; s. of George Paul Kittel and Helen Lemler Kittel; m. Muriel Agnes Lister 1938; two s. one d.; ed. Massachusetts Institute of Technology and Univs. of Cambridge and Wisconsin; Prof. of Physics, Univ. of Calif. at Berkeley 1951–78, Prof. Emer. 1978–; mem. N.A.S., American Acad. of Arts and Sciences; Buckley Prize for Solid State Physics, Berkeley Distinguished Teaching Award, Oersted Medal, American Asscn. of Physics Teachers. *Publications:* Introduction to Solid State Physics 1953, Quantum Theory of Solids 1963, Thermal Physics 1980. *Leisure interests:* friends, wine. *Address:* Department of Physics, University of California, Berkeley, Calif. 94720, U.S.A.

KITTIKACHORN, Field-Marshal Thanom; Thai army officer and politician; b. 11 Aug. 1911, Tak; ed. Wat Kokplu School (Tak) and Military Acad. Bangkok; entered Mil. Survey Dept. as student officer 1931, assigned to Planning Section 1934; Lieut. in Mil. Educ. Dept. 1935, Instructor 1936–38, 1939–41, 1944–46; Capt. 1938, student officer in Infantry School, active service in Shan State 1941; Major 1943, Lieut.-Col. 1944; Instructor Mil. Acad. technical branch 1946–47; Commdr. 21st Infantry Regt. 1947; Colonel, Commdr. 11th Infantry Regt. 1948; Deputy Commdr. 1st Infantry Div. 1949, Commdr. 1950; Major-Gen., Deputy Commdr. 1st Army 1951; Commdr. 1st Army 1954; Lieut.-Gen., mem. Defence Coll. 1955; Deputy Minister of Co-operatives 1955; Asst. C.-in-C. of Army 1957; Deputy Minister of Defence April 1957, Minister Sept. 1957; Prime Minister, Minister of Defence, General 1958; Deputy Prime Minister and Minister of Defence 1959–63; Prime Minister 1963–71, 1972–73; Minister of Defence and Foreign Affairs 1973; Chair. Nat. Exec. Council Dec. 1971–72; Special A.D.C. to King; Chair. United People's Party 1968–73; in U.S.A. 1973–74; detained upon return to Bangkok Dec. 1974; exile in Singapore 1976; returned to Bangkok Sept. 1976; served as monk Sept. 1976–Feb. 1977.

KITZINGER, Uwe, C.B.E., M.LITT., M.A.; British author and specialist in European affairs; b. 12 April 1928, Nuremberg, Germany; s. of late Dr. G. and Lucy Kitzinger; m. Sheila Helena Elizabeth Webster 1952; five d.; ed. Watford Grammar School, Balliol and New Coll., Oxford; Foundation Scholar, New Coll., Oxford; Pres. of Oxford Union 1950; Econ. Section, Council of Europe 1951–58; Research Fellow, Nuffield Coll., Oxford 1956–62, Official Fellow and Investment Bursar 1962–76, Emer. Fellow 1976–; Dean, European Inst. of Business Admin. (INSEAD), Fontainebleau 1976–80; Dir. Oxford Centre for Management Studies Sept. 1980–84; Pres. Templeton Coll., Oxford 1984–; Founding Editor, Journal of Common Market Studies 1962–; Visiting Prof. Univ. of West Indies 1964–65; Visiting Prof. and Assoc., Centre for Int. Affairs, Harvard 1969–70; Visiting Prof. Univ. of Paris VIII 1970–73; Adviser to the late Baron Soames (Vice-Pres. Comm. of the European Communities) 1973–75; Founding Chair. Major Projects Asscn. 1981–86; Pres. Int. Asscn. of Macro-Eng. Socs. 1987–; Council mem. Royal Inst. of Int. Affairs 1976–85; Chair. Oxfordshire Radio Ltd. 1988; mem. British Univs. Cttee., Encyclopaedia Britannica, Beirat Wissenschaftszentrum Berlin and Advisory Council, Pace Univ. New York; Hon. LL.D. *Publications:* German Electoral Politics 1960, The Challenge of the Common Market 1961, Britain, Europe and Beyond 1964, The Second Try 1968, Diplomacy and Persuasion 1973, Europe's Wider Horizons 1975, The 1975 Referendum (with David Butler) 1976. *Leisure interest:* sailing. *Address:* Templeton College, Kennington, Oxford (Office); Standlake Manor, near Witney, Oxon., England and La Rivière, 11100 Bages, France (Home). *Telephone:* (0865) 735422 (Office); (086731) 266 (England) and 68.41.29.60 (France).

KIVENGERE, Rt. Rev. Festo, M. DIV.; Ugandan ecclesiastic; b. 1920; m. Mera Kivengere 1942; four d.; ed. Univ. of London, Pittsburgh Theological Seminary; teacher and evangelist, Tanzania 1946–59; School Supervisor, Kizegi Dist., Uganda 1960–62; full-time evangelist 1962–66, ordained Deacon 1966, Priest 1967, consecrated Bishop 1972, Bishop of Kigezi Diocese, Church of Uganda 1972–; Team Leader African Evangelistic Enterprise 1971–; Int. Freedom Prize, Oslo 1977, Distinguished Public Service Award of Messiah Coll., Penn. 1977, Lindsborg Medal of Honor, Kan. 1980, Edward W. Browning Achievement Award, World Council of Churches 1980, St. Augustine's Cross 1981; Hon. Dr. Div. (Univ. of the

South, Sewanee). *Publications:* When God Moves in Revival 1973, Love Unlimited 1975, I Love Idi Amin 1977, The Spirit is Moving 1979, Hope for Uganda and the World 1980, Revolutionary Love 1981. *Address:* P.O. Box 3, Kabale, Uganda; P.O. Box 53012, Nairobi, Kenya.

KJELLEN, Bo, M.POL.SC.; Swedish diplomatist; b. 8 Feb. 1933, Stockholm; s. of John Kjellen and Elsa Kjellen; m. 1st Margareta Lindblom 1959 (deceased 1978), 2nd Gia Boyd 1980; four c.; ed. Univ. of Stockholm; entered Foreign Service 1957, posted to Rio de Janeiro, Brussels, Stockholm 1959–69; Prin. Pvt. Sec. to Sec.-Gen., OECD 1969–72; Deputy Head of Mission Del. to EEC, Brussels 1972–74; Amb. to Viet-Nam 1974–77; Head Multilateral Dept. for Devt. Co-operation, Ministry of Foreign Affairs 1977–81; Under-Sec. Admin. and Personnel 1981–85; Amb. to OECD and UNESCO 1985–. *Address:* 39 Boulevard du Commandant Charcot, 92200 Neuilly, France. *Telephone:* 1- 46 24 53 84.

KLAFKOWSKI, Alfons, D.JUR.; Polish international lawyer and politician; b. 2 Aug. 1912, Poznań; s. of Jan and Władysława Klafkowski; m. Alicja Klafkowska 1946; two s.; ed. Poznań Univ.; teacher, Faculty of Law, Poznań Univ. (now Adam Mickiewicz Univ.) 1945–, Head Int. Public Law Dept. 1950–, Pro-Dean 1950–52, Dean, Faculty of Law 1952–55, Rector 1956–62, Extraordinary Prof. 1956–62, Ordinary Prof. 1962–, Dir. Inst. of Legal System Sciences 1968–; Deputy to Seym 1980–85; mem. Council of State 1982–85; mem. Presidium, Provisional Nat. Council of Patriotic Movement for Nat. Rebirth (PRON) 1982–83; mem. Nat. Council PRON 1983–; Pres. of Constitutional Tribunal 1985–; Dr. h.c. (Nicolaus Copernicus Univ., Toruń) 1973; State Prize (1st Class) 1976, Commdr.'s Cross, Order of Polonia Restituta 1964, Order of Banner of Labour (1st Class) 1968. *Publications:* Okupacja niemiecka w Polsce w świetle prawa narodów 1946, Podstawy prawne granicy Odra-Nysa Łużycka 1947, Umowa poczdamska z dnia 2 VIII 1945. Podstawy prawne likwidacji skutków wojny polsko-niemieckiej z lat 1939–1945 1960, Obozy koncentracyjne hitlerowskie jako zagadnienie prawa międzynarodowego 1968, Ściganie zbrodniarzy wojennych w NRF w świetle prawa międzynarodowego 1968, The Legal Effects of the Second World War and the German Problem 1968, The Treaty of 7 December 1970 between Poland and the Federal Republic of Germany: Bases of an Interpretation in the Light of International Law 1973, and many others. *Leisure interests:* ornithology, collecting medals and coins. *Address:* ul. Marszałkowska 30, 60-327 Poznań, Poland. *Telephone:* 679244.

KLANICZAY, Tibor; Hungarian literary historian; b. 5 July 1923, Budapest; s. of Dr. Gyula Klaniczay and Gizella Heyszl; m. Mária Bessenyei 1949; two s. one d.; Lecturer, Eötvös Loránd Univ., Budapest 1949–57; Deputy Dir. Inst. for Literary Studies Hungarian Acad. of Sciences 1956–; Ed. periodical Irodalomtörténeti Közlemények 1958–80; mem., Advisory Bd., Revue de Littérature Comparé, Paris and Canadian Review of Comparative Literature; Visiting Prof., Sorbonne, Paris 1967–68, Univ. of Rome 1975–79; Dir. Gen. for Renaissance Research, Budapest 1970–; Dir. Inst. for Literary Studies, Hungarian Acad. of Sciences 1984–; Corresp. mem. Acad. of Sciences 1965–78, mem. 1979–; Corresp. Fellow, Mediaeval Acad. of America; Bd. mem. Int. Asscn. for Comparative Literature, Fédération des Sociétés et des Institutes pour l'Étude de la Renaissance, Fédération Internationale des Langues et Littératures Modernes (FILLM), Paris; mem. consiglio direttivo Associazione Internazionale per gli Studi di Lingua e Letteratura Italiana; Gen. Secr. Int. Asscn. for Hungarian Studies, Budapest; Dr. h.c., Univ. of Tours, France; Kossuth Prize 1955; Labour Order of Merit, Order of Merit for Socialist Hungary, Officier de l'Ordre des Palmes Académiques, Cavaliere dell'Ordine al Merito della Republica Italiana. *Publications:* Zrinyi Miklós 1954, 1964; Reneszánsz és Barokk 1961; co-author: History of Hungarian Literature 1964; Marxizmus és Irodalomtudomány 1964; Ed. and co-author: A magyar irodalom története I-II 1964; A mult nagy korszakai 1973; La crisi del Rinascimento e il Manierismo 1973; A Manierizmus 1975; Hagyományok ébresztése 1976; Renaissance und Manierismus 1977, Pallas magyar ivadékai 1985, Renesans, Manieryzm, Barok 1986. *Address:* Magyar Tudományos Akadémia, Irodalomtudományi Intézet, 1118 Budapest, Ménesi ut. 11/13, Hungary. *Telephone:* 451-156.

KLARE, Hermann, DR.PHIL.; German scientist; b. 12 May 1909, Hameln, Weser; m. Hildegard Hoeder 1936; one s. three d.; ed. Heidelberg and Kiel Univs.; industrial chemist in Bitterfeld, Berlin, Landsberg; employed in the U.S.S.R. 1947–49; Dir. of the Wilhelm Pieck Kunstfaserwerk, Schwarza 1949–53, Section Head 1953–61; Dir. Institut für Faserstoff-Forschung of G.D.R. Acad. of Sciences, Teltow-Seehof 1961–69, Vice-Pres. 1963–68, Pres. 1968–79, Vice-Pres. 1979–84, mem. Presidency, G.D.R. Acad. of Sciences 1984–88; mem. Research Council 1966–; mem. Akademie der Naturforscher, Polish Acad. of Sciences, Mongolian Acad. of Sciences, U.S.S.R. Acad. of Sciences, Č.S.S.R. Acad. of Sciences, Bulgaria Acad. of Sciences; Dr.rer.nat. h.c. (Tech. Hochschule, Leuna-Merseburg), Dr.rer.nat. h.c. (Tech. Univ., Dresden), Dr.rer.nat. h.c. (Univ. of Sofia, Bulgaria); Nat. Prize (Second and Third Class), Vaterländischer Verdienstorden (gold), Lomonossov Medal (gold) of Acad. of Sciences U.S.S.R. and other decorations. *Publications:* Synthetische Fasern aus Polyamiden: Chemie und Technologie 1963, Geschichte der Chemie Faserforschung 1985, numerous publs. on fibre research. *Address:* Akademie der Wissenschaften der D.D.R., Otto-Nuschke-Str. 22/23, 1080 Berlin, German Democratic Republic. *Telephone:* 2070242.

KLASEN, Karl Ferdinand, D.IUR.; German banker; b. 23 April 1909, Hamburg; s. of Heinrich and Marianne Treckan Klasen; m. Ilse Jacob 1937; one s. two d.; ed. law studies in Freiburg, Berlin and Hamburg; with Deutsche Bank, Hamburg 1935–, Dir. 1948; Pres. Landeszentralbank (Hamburg) 1948–52; mem. Management Bd. Norddeutsche Bank 1952–83, Deutsche Bank 1957–; Pres. Deutsche Bundesbank 1970–77; fmr. Chair. Supervisory Board, VIAG; mem. Bd. of Dirs. Kreditanstalt für Wiederaufbau 1970–; Hon. Pres. Atlantike-Brücke, Hamburg –1984; fmr. Gov. for Germany, Int. Monetary Fund, Washington, D.C.; Bundesverdienstkreuz mit Stern und Schulterband 1974, Grosskreuz Verdienstorden 1977. *Leisure interests:* books, modern art, growing orchids. *Address:* Brabandstr. 34, 2000 Hamburg 60, Federal Republic of Germany.

KLAUS, Josef, LL.D.; Austrian lawyer and politician; b. 15 Aug. 1910, Mauthen, Carinthia; m. Erna Seywald 1936; five c.; ed. Univs. of Vienna, Marburg/Lahn; Sec., Vienna Chamber of Labour 1934–38 (Deputy-Chair. of Political Economy Dept.); with timber trade firm, Vienna 1938–39; war service 1939–45 (prisoner of war); lawyer, Hallein, Salzburg 1945–49; Gov. of Salzburg 1949–61; Fed. Minister of Finance 1961–63; Fed. Chancellor 1964–70; fmr. Chair. Austrian People's Party. *Address:* Österreichische Volkspartei, 1 Kärntnerstrasse 51, Vienna, Austria.

KLAUSON, Valter Ivanovich; Soviet politician; b. 1914, Estonia; labourer, asst. engine-driver 1928–33; tech. dir. of construction of bridges, railways and roads 1933–41; served in Soviet Army 1941–44; mem. of CPSU 1943–; Chief Mechanic, Head of Roads Comm. at Ministry of Motor Transport and Highways, Estonian S.S.R. 1944–54; First Deputy Chair. Council of Ministers of Estonian S.S.R. 1954–61, Chair. 1961–83; mem. Supreme Soviet of Estonian S.S.R. 1955–59, 1963–; cand. mem., later mem. Politburo of Cen. Cttee. of Estonian CP 1956–; mem. Supreme Soviet of U.S.S.R. 1958–; cand. mem. Cen. Cttee. of CPSU 1961–80, mem. 1980; awards include Order of Lenin (three times), Order of Patriotic War, Order of Red Banner, Order of Red Star. *Address:* c/o Council of Ministers of Estonian S.S.R., Tallinn, Estonia, U.S.S.R.

KLEBE, Giselher; German composer; b. 28 June 1925, Mannheim; s. of Franz Klebe and Gertrud Michaelis Klebe; m. Lore Schiller 1946; two d.; ed. Berlin Conservatoire and with Boris Blacher; Composer in Berlin until 1957; Prof. of Composition and Theory of Music, Nordwestdeutsche Musik-Akademie, Detmold 1957–; mem. Acad. of Arts, Berlin and Hamburg, Bavarian Acad. of Fine Arts 1978; Bundesverdienstkreuz (1st Class) 1975; several prizes for composition. *Principal works:* Operas: Die Räuber (Schiller) 1957, Die tödlichen Wünsche (Balzac) 1959, Die Ermordung Cäsars (Shakespeare) 1959, Alkmene (Kleist) 1961, Figaro lässt sich scheiden (Ödön von Horvath) 1963, Jakobowsky und der Oberst (Werfel) 1965, Das Märchen von der Schönen Lilie (nach Goethe) 1969, Ein wahrer Held (Synge/Böll) 1975, Das Mädchen aus Domremy (Schiller) 1976, Rendezvous (Sostschenkow) 1977, Der jüngste Tag (Ödön von Horwath) 1980, Die Fastnachtsbeichte (nach Zuckmayer) 1983; Ballets: Signale 1955, Menagerie 1958, Das Testament (nach F. Villon) 1970; Orchestral Works: Zwitschermaschine 1950, Deux Nocturnes 1952, 5 Sinfonien 1952, 1953, 1967, 1971, 1977, Adagio und Fuge (with theme from Wagner's Walküre) 1962, Herzschläge (for Beatband and Symphony Orchestra), Konzert für Cembalo mit elektrischen Klangveränderungen und kleines Orchester 1972, Orpheus (Dramatic scenes for orchestra) 1976, Salutations 1981, Boogie Agitato 1981, Konzert für Clarinette und Orchester op. 92; Songs: Fünf Lieder 1962, Vier Vocalisen für Frauenchor 1963, La Tomba di Igor Strawinsky (for oboe and chamber orch.) 1979, Konzert for organ and orch. 1980; Church music: Missa (Miserere Nobis) 1964, Stabat Mater 1964, Messe (Gebet einer armen Seele) 1966, Beuge dich, du Menschenseele (after S. Lagerlöf) for Baritone and Organ, Choral und Te deum for Solo Soprano, Choir and Orchestra 1978; Chamber Music: 3 String Quartets 1949, 1963, 1981, 2 Solo Violin Sonatas 1952 and 1955, 2 Sonatas for Violin and Piano 1953 and 1974, "Römische Elegien" 1953, Piano Trio Elegia Appassionata 1955, Introitus, Aria et Alleluja for Organ 1964, Quintet for Piano and Strings quasi una fantasia 1967, Fantasie und Lobpreisung (for organ) 1970, Variationen über ein Thema von Hector Berlioz (for organ and three drummers) 1970, Sonate für Kontrabass und Klavier 1974, "Nenia" for solo violin cello 1975, Der Dunkle Gedanke for Clarinets and Piano 1980, Klavierstücke für Sonya (piano) 1980, Feuersturz für Klavier (op. 91) 1983. *Leisure interest:* photography. *Address:* c/o Academy of Arts, Hanseatenweg 10, 1000 Berlin 21; Bruchstrasse 16, 4930 Detmold 1, Federal Republic of Germany (Home). *Telephone:* 030-391 10 31 (Office); (05231) 2 34 14 (Home).

KLECATSKY, Dr. Hans Richard, D.IUR.; Austrian lawyer and politician; b. 6 Nov. 1920, Vienna; s. of Josef and Maria Klecatsky; m. Friederike Wallmann 1947; two d.; in Air Force, Second World War; Clerk in Admin. Courts 1948; Constitutional Dept. of Chancellery 1951; rose to rank of Hofrat in Admin. Courts 1959; Lecturer in Constitutional and Admin. Law and Politics, Innsbruck Univ. 1964, Prof. of Public Law, Faculty of Jurisprudence and Political Science 1965; Deputy mem. Court of Constitutional Law 1965; Minister of Justice 1966–70. *Publications:* Österreichisches Staatskirchenrecht (with H. Weiler) 1958, Das österr. Zollrecht (with A. Kobzina) 1966, Der Rechtsstaat zwischen heute und morgen 1967, Staat und Verkehr 1968, Das Österreichisches Bundesverfassungsrecht 1977–82, and many other publs. especially about transnational cooperation in the

European Alps 1971–79. *Leisure interests:* mountaineering, lyric poetry. *Address:* Innsbruck, Reithmannstrasse 20, Austria.

KLEENE, Stephen Cole, PH.D.; American mathematician and educator; b. 5 Jan. 1909, Hartford, Conn.; s. of Gustav Adolph and Alice Cole Kleene; m. 1st Nancy Elliott 1942 (died 1970); three s. one d.; m. 2nd Jeanne Steinmetz 1978; ed. Hartford Public High School, Amherst Coll. and Princeton Univ.; Instructor, Univ. of Wisconsin 1935–37, Asst. Prof. 1937–41, Assoc. Prof. 1946–48, Prof. 1948–64, Chair. Dept. of Mathematics 1957–58, 1960–62, Chair. Dept. of Numerical Analysis 1962–63, Cyrus C. MacDuffee Prof. of Mathematics 1964–74, of Mathematics and Computer Sciences 1974–79, Dean of the Coll. of Letters and Science 1969–74; Emer. Dean and Emer. Prof. of Math. and Computer Science 1979–; Assoc. Prof. Amherst Coll. 1941–42; U.S.N.R. 1942–46; mem. Inst. for Advanced Study 1939–40, 1965–66; Ed. Journal for Symbolic Logic 1950–62; Pres. Asscn. for Symbolic Logic 1956–58, Int. Union of the History and Philosophy of Science 1961; Chair.-Designate Div. of Mathematical Sciences, Nat. Research Council 1969–72; Guggenheim Fellow, Univ. of Amsterdam 1950, Visiting Prof., Princeton Univ. 1956–57; Nat. Science Foundation Grantee, Univ. of Marburg 1958–59; mem. N.A.S., American Acad. of Arts and Sciences. *Publications:* Introduction to Metamathematics 1952, The Foundations of Intuitionistic Mathematics (with Richard E. Vesley) 1965, Mathematical Logic 1967; and articles on mathematics and mathematical logic in various journals and collections. *Leisure interests:* natural history, conservation. *Address:* University of Wisconsin, Madison, Wis. 53706, U.S.A. *Telephone:* (608) 263-7901 (Office); 231-2118 (Home).

KLEIBER, Carlos; German conductor; b. 3 July 1930, Berlin; s. of Erich Kleiber; Conductor, Theater am Gärtnerplatz, Munich 1953, in Potsdam 1954; Conductor, Deutsche Oper am Rhein, Düsseldorf 1956–64, Zürich Opera 1964–66, Württemberg State Theater, Stuttgart 1966–68, Bavarian State Opera, Munich 1968–73, Vienna State Opera 1973; guest appearances include Bayreuth Festival 1974, Covent Garden and with Berlin and Vienna Philharmonic Orchestras; American début with San Francisco Opera, conducting Verdi's Otello 1977. *Address:* Max-Joseph-Platz 2, 8000 München, Federal Republic of Germany.

KLEIBER, Günther; German politician and electrician; b. 16 Sept. 1931, Eula; m.; two c.; ed. Rostock and Dresden Univs.; joined Sozialistische Einheitspartei Deutschlands (SED) 1949, mem. Cen. Cttee. 1967–, Cand. mem. Politburo 1967–84, mem. 1984–; Deputy Minister of Electronics 1966; State Sec. for introduction of data processing 1966–71; Deputy Chair. Council of Ministers 1971–88, First Deputy Chair. Nov. 1988–; mem. Presidium, Council of Ministers, Minister for Machine and Transport Manufactures 1973–80, for Mechanical Eng., Farm Machinery and Vehicle Construction 1980–86; Perm. Rep. to CMEA 1986–88; mem. Volkskammer 1967–; Order Banner der Arbeit and other decorations. *Address:* Am Marx-Engels-Platz 2, 102 Berlin, German Democratic Republic.

KLEIN, Calvin Richard; American fashion designer; b. 19 Nov. 1942, New York; s. of Leo Klein and Flore Klein (née Stern); m. 1st Jayne Centre 1964 (divorced 1974); one d.; m. 2nd Kelly Rector 1986; ed. Fashion Inst. of Tech., New York, and High School of Art and Design; started own fashion business 1968; Pres./Designer Calvin Klein Ltd. 1968–; Dir. Fashion Inst. of Tech. 1975–; Coty Award 1973, 1974, 1975; Coty Hall of Fame. *Leisure interests:* yoga, gymnastics. *Address:* Calvin Klein Industries Inc., 205 West 39th Street, New York, N.Y. 10018, U.S.A.

KLEIN, David, A.B., A.M., M.B.A.; American diplomatist (retd.); b. 2 Sept. 1919, New York; s. of Samuel and Fannie H. Klein; m. Anne L. Cochran 1953; four s. two d.; ed. Brooklyn Coll., New York, Columbia Univ. and Harvard School of Business Admin.; served in U.S. Army 1941–46; entered foreign service 1947; served in Mozambique and Burma 1947–50, U.S. Embassy, Moscow 1952–54, U.S. Mission, Berlin 1955–58, U.S. Embassy, Bonn 1958–60; Soviet Desk, Dept. of State 1960–62; Asst. for European Affairs to McGeorge Bundy, White House 1962–65; Nat. War Coll. 1965–66; Counsellor, Moscow 1966–68; U.S. Mission, Berlin 1968–74; Asst. Dir. ACDA, Washington 1974–75; Exec. Dir. American Council on Germany 1975– (Dir. 1978–), John McCloy Fund 1975–, U.S. Minister in Berlin 1971–74; Consultant U.S. Arms Control and Disarmament 1976–; Pres. German American Partnership Program 1977–85; Special Asst. for Foreign Affairs Fairleigh Dickinson Univ., N.J. 1986–; Chair. Bd. of Dirs. Zeiss Avionics (Calif.); Vice-Chair. Bd. of Trustees Merzer County Community Coll., N.J.; mem. Council on Foreign Relations, New York; Special Asst. for Foreign Affairs to the Pres., Fairleigh Dickinson Univ., Rutherford, N.J.; Superior Honor Award, Dept. of State 1964; Legion of Merit. *Publication:* Basmachi: Study in Soviet Treatment of Minority Peoples 1952. *Leisure interests:* tennis, golf, music. *Address:* 16 East 60th Street, New York, N.Y. 10022 (Office); 6 Greenhouse Drive, Princeton, N.J., U.S.A. (Home).

KLEIN, George, M.D., D.SC.; Swedish (b. Hungarian) tumour biologist; b. 28 July 1925, Budapest, Hungary; s. of Henrik Klein and Ilona Engel; m. Eva Fischer 1947; one s. two d.; ed. medical schools at Pécs, Szeged and Budapest, Hungary, and Stockholm, Sweden; Instructor Histology, Budapest Univ. 1945, Pathology 1946; Research Fellow, Karolinska Inst. 1947–49, Asst. Prof. of Cell Research 1950–57; Prof. of Tumour Biology and Head of the Inst. for Tumour Biology, Karolinska Inst. Med. School,

Stockholm; Guest Investigator, Inst. for Cancer Research, Philadelphia, Pa. 1950; Visiting Prof., Stanford Univ. 1961; Fogarty Scholar, NIH 1972; Dunham Lecturer, Harvard Med. School 1966; Visiting Prof., Hebrew Univ., Jerusalem 1973-83; Harvey Lecturer 1973; mem. Scientific Advisory Council of Swedish Med. Bd., Royal Swedish Acad. of Sciences; Corresp. mem. American Asscn. of Cancer Research; Foreign Assoc. N.A.S. of United States; hon. mem. American Asscn. of Immunologists, French Soc. of Immunology, Hungarian Acad. of Sciences, American Acad. of Arts and Sciences; Fellow, New York Acad. of Science; Ed. Advances in Cancer Research; Bertha Goldblatt Teplitz Award (jointly) 1960; Rabbi Shai Shacknai Prize in Tumour Immunology 1972; Bertner Award 1973; Award of American Cancer Soc. 1973; Prize of Danish Pathological Soc.; Harvey Prize 1975; Prize of Cancer Research Inst. 1975; Gairdner Prize 1976; Behring Prize 1977; Annual Award Virus Cancer Program 1977, Gen. Motors Sloan Prize for Cancer Research, Björlien Award of Uppsala Univ. 1979, Award of the Santa Chiara Acad., Italy, 1979, Erik Fernström Prize (with Eva Klein) 1983, Anniversary Prize of the Swedish Med. Asscn. 1983. *Publications:* 700 papers in fields of experimental cell research and cancer research. *Address:* Institutet für Tumörbiologi, Karolinska Institutet, 04 01 Stockholm 60; Kottlavagen 10, 181 61 Lidingö, Sweden.

KLEIN, Helmut, PROF.DR.; German academic; b. 2 March 1930, Berlin; s. of Robert and Charlotte Klein; m. Ingetraud Horschke 1951; one s.; ed. Humboldt Univ., Berlin; teacher in various schools; Assoc. Prof. Humboldt Univ. 1959, Prof. of Educ. 1961, Dir. Educ. Section 1969-76, Rector 1976-; mem. Volkskammer (G.D.R. Parl.) 1976-; mem. Acad. of Pedagogical Science 1979, Corresp. mem. of G.D.R. Acad. of Science 1979; Hon. D. Phil. (Helsinki Univ.) 1977; Hon. D. Psych. and Ped. (Ghent). *Publications:* Didaktische Prinzipien und Regeln 1958, Polytechnische Bildung und Erziehung in der DDR 1962, Bildung in der DDR 1974, Didaktik 1956, Schulpadagogik (with K. Tomaschewsky) 1965, Zu Bildungsstrategien kapitalistischer Lander 1982. *Leisure interests:* sports, literature and music. *Address:* Unter den Linden 6, 1086 Berlin, German Democratic Republic. *Telephone:* 20930.

KLEIN, Herbert George; American journalist and government official; b. 1 April 1918, Los Angeles; s. of George J. and Amy Cordes Klein; m. Marjorie Galbraith 1941; two d.; ed. Univ. of Southern Calif; Journalist 1940-42; U.S. Naval Reserve 1942-46; Political Reporter and News Ed., Post Advocate 1946; Feature Writer, San Diego Evening Tribune 1950, Editorial Writer 1951; Chief Editorial Writer, San Diego Union 1951, Ed. 1959; mem. office staff of Vice-Pres. Nixon 1959-60; Dir. of Communications for the Exec. Branch 1969-73; publicist and press sec. for many of Richard Nixon's election campaigns; Vice-Pres. Corporate Relations Metromedia Inc. 1973-77; Pres. H. G. Klein Media Consultants 1977-80; Ed.-in-Chief, Vice-Pres. Copley Newspapers, San Diego 1980-; Trustee, Univ. S. Calif., Los Angeles. *Address:* 5100 Saddlery Square, P.O. Box 8935, Rancho, Santa Fé, Calif. 92067, U.S.A.

KLEIN, Lawrence Robert, PH.D.; American economist and lecturer; b. 14 Sept. 1920, Omaha, Neb.; s. of Leo Byron Klein and Blanche Monheit; m. Sonia Adelson 1947; one s. three d.; ed. Univ. of Calif. at Berkeley, M.I.T., Lincoln Coll., Oxford; joined Faculty, Univ. of Chicago 1944-47; Research Assoc., Nat. Bureau of Econ. Research, Cambridge, Mass. 1948-50; with Univ. Michigan 1949-54; Research Assoc., Survey Research Center 1949-54; Oxford Inst. Statistics 1954-58; faculty, Univ. of Philadelphia 1958-; Prof. 1958-, Univ. Prof. 1964-; Benjamin Franklin Prof. 1968-; Visiting Prof., Osaka Univ. 1960, Univ. of Colorado 1962, City Univ., New York 1962-63, Hebrew Univ. of Jerusalem 1964, Princeton Univ. 1966, Stanford Univ. 1968, Univ. of Copenhagen 1974; Ford Visiting Prof. Univ. of Calif. at Berkeley 1968; Inst. for Advanced Studies, Vienna 1970-74; Econ. Consultant to Canadian Govt. 1947, UNCTAD 1966, 1967, 1975, McMillan Co. 1965-74, E. I. du Pont de Nemours 1966-68, State of N.Y. 1969, American Telephone and Telegraph Co. 1969, Fed. Reserve Bd. 1973, UNIDO 1973-75, Congressional Budget Office 1977-, Council of Econ. Advisers 1977-; Chair. Bd. of Trustees, Wharton Econometrics Forecasting Assoc. Inc. 1969-80, Chair. Professional Bd. 1980-; Dir. Uni-Coll Corpn.; Trustee, Maurice Falk Inst. for Econ. Research, Israel, 1969-75; mem. Advisory Council, Inst. for Advanced Studies, Vienna 1977-; Chair. Econ. Advisory Cttee. Gov. of Pa. 1976-78; mem. Cttee. on Prices, Fed. Reserve Bd. 1968-70; Principal Investigator, Econometric Model Project of Brookings Inst., Washington, D.C. 1963-72, Project LINK 1968-, Sr. Adviser Brookings Panel on Econ. Activity 1970-; co-ordinator Jimmy Carter's Econ. Task Force 1976; mem. Advisory Bd., Strategic Studies Center, Stanford Research Inst. 1974-76; Ed. International Economic Review 1959-65, Assoc. Ed. 1965-; mem. Editorial Bd. Empirical Economics 1976-; Fellow, Econometrics Soc., American Acad. of Arts and Sciences, N.A.S., Social Sciences Research Council, American Economists' Asscn., Eastern Econ. Asscn., American Asscn. of Univ. Profs.; Hon. LL.D. (Mich.) 1977; Hon. Sc.D. (Widener Coll.) 1977; Dr. h.c. (Univ. of Vienna) 1977; Hon. Dr. Ed. (Villanova) 1978; Dr. h.c. (Bonn Univ., Free Univ. of Brussels and Univ. of Paris) 1979, (Univ. of Madrid) 1980; William F. Butler Award, New York Asscn. of Business Economists 1975; Golden Slipper Club Award 1977; Nobel Prize in Econ. Science for work on econometric models 1980. *Publications:* The Keynesian Revolution 1947, Textbook of Econometrics 1953, An Econometric Model of the United States 1929-1952 1955, Wharton Econometric Forecasting Model 1967, Essay on the Theory

of Economic Prediction 1968, Brookings Quarterly Econometric Model of U.S. Econometric Model Performance (author-ed.) 1976, The Economics of Supply and Demand 1983. *Address:* Department of Economics, University of Philadelphia, Philadelphia, Pa. 19104 (Office); 1317 Medford Road, Wynnewood, Philadelphia, Pa. 19096, U.S.A. (Home).

KLEIN, Peter Wolfgang, PH.D.; Netherlands professor of history; b. 10 Dec. 1931, Vienna, Austria; ed. Netherlands School of Econs., Rotterdam; Asst. Prof. of Econ. History 1959-65; Reader in Social History 1965-67; Prof. of Econ. and Social History, Erasmus Univ., Rotterdam 1969-85, Part-time Prof. of Econ. History 1969-74, Vice-Chancellor 1974-75, Dean Faculty of Econs. 1977-78, Head History Dept. 1979-81; Prof. of Early Modern History, State Univ. Leiden 1985-, Head History Dept. 1986-88; Pres. Dutch Historical Soc. 1987-; mem. State Cttee. for Nat. History 1981-, Bd. State Inst. for History Second World War 1972-, Scientific Cttee. Inst. of Econ. History Francesco Dartini 1986-, Cttee. Int. Asscn. of Econ. History 1985-, Royal Netherlands Acad. of Arts and Sciences 1979; Founding mem. Academica Europaea. *Publication:* Dr. Triffen in de 17e. eeuw 1965. *Address:* Vakgroep Geschiedenis, Doelensteeg 16, 2311VL Leiden (Office); Oltmausdreef 4, 2353 Leidendorp, Netherlands (Home). *Telephone:* 071-272759 (Office); 071-894998 (Home).

KLEINDIENST, Richard Gordon, LL.B.; American lawyer; b. 5 Aug. 1923, Winslow, Ariz.; s. of Alfred R. Kleindienst and the late Gladys Love; m. Margaret Dunbar 1948; two s. two d.; ed. Winslow High School, Univ. of Ariz., Harvard Coll. and Harvard Law School; Law Clerk, Ropes, Gray, Best, Coolidge and Rugg, Boston 1949-50; Partner, Jennings, Strouss, Salmon and Trask, Phoenix, Ariz. 1950-57; mem. Ariz. House of Reps. 1953-54; Partner, Shimmel, Hill, Kleindienst and Bishop, Phoenix 1958-68; Chair. Ariz. State Republican Cttee. 1956; mem. Republican Nat. Cttee. 1956-60, 1960-63; Nat. Dir. of Field Operations, Goldwater for Pres. 1964, Nixon for Pres. 1968; Deputy Attorney-Gen. of U.S.A. 1969-72, Attorney-Gen. June 1972-April 1973; Pres. Fed. Bar Asscn. 1974-. *Leisure interests:* golf, chess, classical music, art. *Publication:* Justice (memoirs) 1985. *Address:* 3773 E. Broadway, Tucson, Arizona 85716. *Telephone:* (602) 795-4800.

KLEINMAN, Arthur, M.D., M.A.; American professor of anthropology and psychiatry; b. 11 March 1941, New York; m. Joan A. Ryman 1965; one s. one d.; ed. Stanford and Harvard Univs.; Assoc. Prof., Prof. Dept. of Psychiatry and Behavioural Sciences, Univ. of Washington 1976-82; Prof. of Medical Anthropology and Psychiatry, Dept. of Anthropology, Harvard Univ. and Dept. of Social Medicine, Harvard Medical School 1982-; mem. Inst. of Medicine, N.A.S.; Wellcome Prize, Royal Anthropological Inst. 1980. *Publications:* Patients and Healers in the Context of Culture 1980, Culture and Depression (Co-ed.) 1985, Social Origins of Distress and Disease: Depression and Neurasthenia in China 1986, The Illness Narratives. *Address:* Department of Anthropology, 330 William James Hall, Harvard University, Cambridge, Mass. 02138, U.S.A. *Telephone:* (617) 495 3846.

KLEMPERER, William, PH.D.; American professor of chemistry; b. 6 Oct. 1927, New York; s. of Paul Klemperer and Margit (Freund) Klemperer; m. Elizabeth Cole 1949; one s. two d.; ed. Harvard Univ. and Univ. of California, Berkeley; Instructor, Berkeley 1954; Instructor, Harvard Univ. 1954-57, Asst. Prof. 1957-61, Assoc. Prof. 1961-65, Prof. 1965-; Asst. Dir. Nat. Science Foundation (for math. and physical sciences) 1979-81; mem. American Physical Soc., N.A.S., American Acad. of Arts and Sciences, American Chemical Soc.; Wetherill Medal, Franklin Inst.; Irving Langmuir Prize, American Chemical Soc.; Earle Plyler Award, American Physical Soc.; Distinguished Service Medal, Nat. Science Foundation. *Address:* Department of Chemistry, Harvard University, 12 Oxford Street, Cambridge, Mass. 02138 (Office); 53 Shattuck Road, Watertown, Mass. 02172, U.S.A. (Home). *Telephone:* (617) 495-4094 (Office).

KLEPPE, Johan; Norwegian veterinarian and politician; b. 29 Sept. 1928, Bjørnskinn, Andøya; s. of Jon Kleppe and Alvhild Caroliussen Kleppe; m. Inger Johansen 1961; one s. one d.; ed. Veterinary Coll. of Norway; Veterinarian 1954-63, Dist. Veterinarian, Andøy 1963-76, Supervisory Veterinarian 1966-76; Regional Veterinary Officer of North Norway 1976-; mem. Bjørnskinn Municipal Council 1956-64; Deputy Mayor of Andøy 1964-66, Mayor 1966-68, 1975-78, mem. Exec. Cttee. Andøy municipality 1964-78; Deputy mem. of Parl. 1967; Parl. Under-Sec. of State, Ministry of Agriculture 1968-69; Liberal mem. of Parl. for Nordland 1969-73, mem. Bd. of Liberal Parl. faction 1969-73, mem. Liberal Party's Cttee. on Oil Policy and EC Cttee., mem. Prin. Planning Cttee.; Minister of Defence 1972-73; mem. Liberal Nat. Exec. 1966-72; Leader, Norwegian del., FAO confs., Rome and Malta 1969; Norwegian Del., UN Gen. Ass., New York 1971; fmr. Bd. mem. Nordland Co. Liberal Asscn.; fmr. Chair. Students Liberal Asscn., Oslo and Bjørnskinn and Andøy Liberal Asscn.; Chair. of Board, Directorate of State Forests 1969-77, Chair. Nat. Council on Sheepbreeding 1969-82; Chair. of Bd. Nordlandsbanken A/S, 8480 Andenes 1974-, State Veterinary Laboratory for Northern Norway 1976-, Vesteraalen Intermunicipal Planning Office 1978-88; Vice-Chair. Cttee. Norwegian Veterinary Asscn. 1981-84, Chair. 1984-; Chair. of Bd. Andøyposten a/s 1981-, Troms Population Acad. Asscn. 1987-. *Address:* 8484 Risøyhamn, Norway. *Telephone:* 08261123 (Office); 08847630 (Home).

KLEPPE, Per; Norwegian politician and economist; b. 13 April 1923, Oslo; s. of Knut Sigurd and Nathalie Kleppe; m. Margaretha (née Ström)

1951; two d. one step-s. one step-d.; Sec., Ministry of Finance 1952-53; with Cen. Bureau of Statistics 1953-54; mem. Research Councils Joint Cttee. 1954-57; Asst. Sec. of State, Ministry of Finance 1957-62, Chair. and Sec. Finance Policy Cttee. 1962-63; Head, Econ. section, EFTA Secr., Geneva 1963-67; Dir. Labour Party Research Office 1967-71; Minister of Commerce and Shipping 1971-72, of Finance 1973-79, of Long-term Planning and Coordination 1980-81; Sec.-Gen. EFTA, Geneva 1981-88. *Publications:* EFTA-EEC-NORDEK 1970, Bank og Kredittvesen 1974, 1979, numerous econ. and political articles. *Leisure interests:* skiing, gardening. *Address:* Björnveien 52, N-0387, Oslo 3, Norway. *Telephone:* (02) 491259.

KLEPPE, Thomas S.; American politician; b. 1 July 1919, Kintyre, N.D.; m. 2nd Glendora Loew 1958; one s. three d.; ed. Valley City Teachers' Coll; served in U.S. Army, Warrant Officer 1942-46; joined Gold Seal Co. 1946; Treas. 1948-58, Pres. and Treas. 1958-64; Vice-Pres. J. M. Dain and Co. 1964-66; Mayor of Bismarck, N.D. 1950-54; mem. House of Reps. for Second Congressional District, N.D. 1967-71, House Cttee. on Agriculture, House Republican Policy Cttee.; Administrator, Small Business Admin. 1971-75; Sec. of the Interior 1975-77; consultant with Alexander Proudfoot Co., Chicago, Ill. 1978-; Lecturer 1977-. *Address:* 7100 Darby Road, Bethesda, Md. 20817, U.S.A.

KLESTIL, Thomas, D.ECON.; Austrian diplomatist; b. 4 Nov. 1932; m.; two s. one d.; ed. Economic Univ., Vienna; Office for Econ. Co-ordination in Fed. Chancellery, Vienna 1957-59; mem. of Austrian Del. to OECD, Paris 1959-62; Embassy, Washington D.C. 1962-66; Sec. to Fed. Chancellor 1966-69; Consul Gen. of Austria in Los Angeles, Calif. 1969-74; Perm. Rep. of Austria to UN 1978-80; Amb. to U.S.A. 1981-88. *Address:* c/o Ministry of Foreign Affairs, 1014 Vienna, Ballhausplatz 2, Austria.

KLIBI, Chedli, B.A.; Tunisian politician and international official; b. 6 Sept. 1925, Tunis; s. of Hassouna Klibi and Habiba Bannani; m. Kalthoum Lasram 1956; one s. two d.; ed. Sadiki Coll., Tunis, Sorbonne, Paris; successively high school teacher, lecturer, Univ. of Tunis and journalist 1951-57; Dir.-Gen. Tunisian Radio and TV 1958-61; Minister of Information and Cultural Affairs 1961-64, 1969-73, of Cultural Affairs 1976-78, of Information Sept. 1978; Minister, Dir. Cabinet of Pres. 1974-76; Sec.-Gen. League of Arab States 1978-; Mayor of Carthage 1963-; mem. Political Bureau and Cen. Cttee., Neo Destour (Parti Socialiste Destourien) June 1979-; mem. Cairo Arabic Language Acad.; Grand Cordon, Order of Independence and Order of Repub. (Tunisia) and several foreign decorations. *Publications include:* The Arabs and the Palestinian Question, Islam and Modernity, Culture is a Civilisational Challenge. *Leisure interest:* reading. *Address:* c/o Ministry of Foreign Affairs, Place du Gouvernement le Kasbah, Tunis, Tunisia.

KLIEN, Walter; Austrian concert pianist; b. 27 Nov. 1928, Graz; m. Chizuko Kojima, 16 June 1981; ed. Music Acad. Vienna; appears with leading orchestras and conductors; world-wide tours; soloist at musical festivals of Salzburg, Berlin, Vienna, Lucerne, Edinburgh, Israel, Prague, Bonn; Wiener Flötenuhr Award for best Mozart record of year 1969 and 1983, Joseph-Marx-Musikpreis (Graz) 1987. *Recordings:* numerous albums incl. complete solo piano music of Mozart and Brahms, complete Schubert sonatas and Mozart Piano Quartets with Amadeus Quartet, complete Mozart sonatas with Arthur Grumiaux. *Address:* Singerstrasse 27, 1010 Vienna, Austria.

KLIKS, Rudolf Rigoldovich; Soviet architect; b. 25 June 1910, Moscow; ed. Kharkov Inst. of Constructional Engineers; Asst. Chief Architect for U.S.S.R. Agricultural Exhbn. 1945-56; Chief Architect and Chief Artist U.S.S.R. Econ. Achievements Exhbn. 1956-60; Chief Architect for U.S.S.R. Chamber of Commerce 1960-. *Principal works include:* stadium to seat 10,000 in Orjonikidze 1937; general plan for the reconstruction of the U.S.S.R. Agricultural Exhbn. 1950-54; designs, displays and interiors of pavilions for about 40 exhbns. in the U.S.S.R. and other countries including: Czechoslovakia 1948, Yugoslavia 1955, Leipzig, G.D.R. 1956, Science section of the Soviet Pavilion, Brussels World Exhbn. 1958, Helsinki, Finland 1959, New Delhi Int. Agricultural Exhbn. 1960, Damascus Int. Fair 1961, Pavilion at Trade and Industry Exhbn. in London 1961, Rio de Janeiro 1963, Nehru Commemorative Exhbn., Moscow 1963, Izmir Int. Fair 1964, Pavilion at Montreal Expo 1967. *Publications:* Architecture of the U.S.S.R. Agricultural Exhibition 1954. *Address:* U.S.S.R. Chamber of Commerce, Ulitsa Kuibysheva 6, Moscow, U.S.S.R.

KLIMASZEWSKI, Mieczysław, PH.D.; Polish scientist and politician (retd.); b. 26 July 1908, Stanisławów; m. Janina Klimaszewski 1947; one s.; ed. Jagiellonian Univ., Cracow; Scientific Research Work 1931-; Population and Social Welfare Office, Cracow 1939-45; Prof. Extraordinary, Wrocław Univ. 1946-49; Prof. Jagiellonian Univ., Cracow 1949-78, fmr. Dir. Inst. of Geography, Head, Dept. of Geomorphology; Rector of Jagiellonian Univ., Cracow 1964-72; Deputy to Seym 1965-72; mem. Council of State 1965, Vice-Chair. 1965-72; Chair. Cttee. for Research on Problems of Polish Emigrants, Polish Acad. of Sciences 1971-73; Chair. Polish Social Cttee. for Security and Co-operation in Europe 1971-73; Chair. Polonia Assen. 1967-72; Chair. Scientific Council of Tatra Nat. Park 1974-; Chair. Scientific Council, Inst. of Geography, Polish Acad. of Sciences, Chair. Cttee. of Geographical Sciences; mem. Polish Acad. of Sciences, Finnish Acad. Sciences, Leopoldina Acad. (German Democratic Repub.), Sächsische Akad.

der Wissenschaften, Leipzig, Yugoslav Acad. Sciences and Arts, Netherlands Geographical Soc., Soviet Geographical Soc., Finnish Geographical Soc., Hungarian Geographical Soc., Belgian Geological Soc.; Foreign mem. Royal Swedish Acad. of Sciences; Dr. h.c. (Jena) 1964, (Kiev T. G. Shevchenko State Univ.) 1966, (Komensky Univ., Bratislava) 1970, (Alliance Coll., Cambridge) 1972, (St. Andrews) 1973, (Uppsala) 1977, (Silesian Univ. of Katowice) 1977; Commdr. Cross with Star and Officer's Cross of Order Polonia Restituta; Grand Officier de l'Ordre du Mérite 1967; Order of Banner of Labour 1st Class 1972, 1985, and numerous other decorations; A. Humboldt Medal, M. K. Sapper Medal, Patron's Medal, Royal Geographical Soc. 1978, M. Bela Medal, Slovak Acad. of Sciences 1986. *Publications:* Geomorphological Development of W. Carpathians 1934, 1948, 1965, 1966, Problems of Geomorphological Mapping 1956, 1960, 1963, Detailed Hydrographical Map of Poland 1956, Geomorphological Studies of Spitsbergen 1960, Geomorfologia Ogólna 1961, The Effect of Solifluction Processes on the Development of Mountain Slopes in the Beskidy 1971, Geomorfologia Polski (editor) 1972, Geomorfologia 1978, Geomorphological Evolution of the Tatra Mountains 1987. *Leisure interests:* trips, travels, reading. *Address:* Ul. Wyspiańskiego 3, 30-035 Cracow, Poland.

KLIMENKO, Ivan Yefimovich; CAND. OF ECON. SC.; Soviet politician; b. 1921; ed. Rostov Inst. of Railway Transport Engineers, Party Higher School of Cen. Cttee. of CPSU, Acad. of Social Sciences of Cen. Cttee. of CPSU; mem. CPSU 1945; Asst. engine-driver, engineer, teacher, head of teaching dept. of an engine-drivers' school, Deputy Head of Cadre Admin. with Northern Railway 1942-49; CPSU and state posts 1949-52; Second Sec. of Yaroslavl City Cttee. of CPSU 1952-53; Chair. of Yaroslavl Dist. Cttee. Council of Workers' Deputies 1953-54, 1962-64; admin. of Yaroslavl Dist. Cttee. of CPSU 1960-61; Second Sec. 1961-62, Sec. 1964-65; Second Sec. of Smolensk Dist. Cttee. of CPSU 1965-69, First Sec. 1969-87; Deputy to R.S.F.S.R. Supreme Soviet 1967-; Deputy to U.S.S.R. Supreme Soviet 1970-; cand. mem. of Cen. Cttee. of CPSU 1971-76, mem. 1976-; Chair. of U.S.S.R. Comm. on Building and Industrial Building Materials 1979, Transport and Communications Comm. *Address:* Commission of Building and Industrial Building Materials, Moscow, U.S.S.R.

KLIMOV, Elem; Soviet film director; b. 1935; m. Larisa Shepit'ko (died 1981); ed. Aviation Inst., All-Union State Cinematography Inst. (VGIK), Moscow; Gen. Sec. U.S.S.R. Union of Film Makers 1986-88; Chair. Union of Cinematographers May 1986-. *Films include:* The Fiancée, Careful—Banality!, Look, the Sky! (shorts) 1962-64; Welcome 1964, Adventures of a Dentist 1967, Sport, Sport, Sport 1971, Agony (on Rasputin) 1981 (with Alexei Petzenko), Come and See 1985.

KLINE, Kevin Delaney, B.A.; American actor; b. 24 Oct. 1947, St. Louis; s. of Robert J. Kline and Peggy Kirk; m. Phoebe Cates 1989; ed. Indiana Univ. and Julliard School Drama Div. New York; founding mem. The Acting Co. New York 1972-76; Broadway appearances in On the Twentieth Century 1978 (Tony Award 1978), Loose Ends 1979, Pirates of Penzance 1980 (Tony Award 1980, Obie Award 1980), Arms and the Man 1985; off-Broadway appearances in Richard III 1983, Henry V 1984, Hamlet 1986. *Films include:* Sophie's Choice, Pirates of Penzance, The Big Chill 1983, Silverado 1985, Violets are Blue 1985, Cry Freedom 1987, A Fish Called Wanda (Acad. Award for Best Supporting Actor 1989) 1988. *Address:* 1888 Century Park E., Suite 1400, Los Angeles, Calif. 90067, U.S.A.

KLINGENBERG, Wilhelm; German professor of mathematics; b. 28 Jan. 1924, Rostock; s. of Paul Klingenberg and Henny Klingenberg; m. Christine Kob 1953; two s. one d.; ed. Kiel Univ.; Asst. Hamburg Univ. 1952-55; Asst. Prof., Assoc. Prof. Göttingen Univ. 1955-63; Prof. Univ. of Mainz 1963-66; Prof. of Math. Univ. of Bonn 1966-; mem. Acad. of Science and Literature, Mainz. *Publications:* A Course in Differential Geometry 1978, Lectures on Closed Geodesics 1978, Riemannian Geometry 1982. *Leisure interests:* piano, horseback riding, Chinese art. *Address:* Am Alten Forsthaus 42, 5300 Bonn I, Federal Republic of Germany.

KLOCHEK, Vasiliy Ivanovich; Soviet foreign trade official; b. 1912; ed. Moscow Economic Inst. and Acad of Foreign Trade; mem. CPSU 1940-; Chief of Section Ministry of Foreign Trade 1946-47; Deputy Commercial Rep. in Hungary 1947-50; Deputy Chief of Dept., Ministry of Foreign Trade 1950-53; Commercial Rep. in Austria 1953-58; Chief of Dept., Ministry of Foreign Trade 1958-63; Commercial Rep. in G.D.R. 1963-69; Dir. Main Bd., U.S.S.R. Ministry of Foreign Trade 1969-; Order of Lenin, Badge of Honour and other decorations. *Address:* U.S.S.R. Ministry of Foreign Trade, Smolenskaya-Sennaya ploshchad 32-34, Moscow, U.S.S.R.

KŁONICA, Leon, AGR. ENG.; Polish politician; b. 10 Nov. 1929, Kraszków, Kielce Voivodship; ed. Higher Agric. School, Olsztyn; Agronomist, State Centre of Agricultural Machines, Pionki 1953-56; Head of Dept. Agric. and Forestry, Presidium of District Nat. Council, Mrągowo 1956-63, Deputy Head, then Head of Dept. Agric. and Forestry, Presidium of Voivodship Nat. Council, Olsztyn 1964-67; mem. Polish United Workers' Party (PZPR) 1955-, Sec. PZPR Dist. Cttee., Mrągowo 1962-63, Agric. Sec. PZPR Voivodship Cttee., Olsztyn 1971-75, First Sec. of PZPR Voivodship Cttee., Olsztyn 1975-77, mem. PZPR Cen. Cttee. 1975-81; Deputy to Seym (Parliament) 1976-80; Chair. Gen. Council Cen. Union of Agric. Co-operatives (CZKR) 1977-; Minister of Agric. 1977-81; decorations include

Commdr.'s Cross of Order Polonia Restituta. *Address:* c/o Ministerstwo Rolnictwa, ul. Wspólna 30, 00-930 Warsaw, Poland.

KLOS, Elmar; Czechoslovak fmr. film director; b. 26 Jan. 1910, Brno; s. of Rudolf and Marie Klos; m. Anne Vopalka 1935; one s. one d.; ed. Faculty of Law, Charles Univ., Prague; Dir., Short Film Studios 1946–47; Head of Creative Art Staff, and Scriptwriter, Barrandov Feature Film Studio 1948–74; Prof. of Film and TV Faculty, Prague Univ. 1956–70; Pres. Czechoslovak Union of Film Artists 1963–66; Awards include State Prize 2nd Class 1960, Gold Prize, Moscow Int. Film Festival 1963, State Prize 1964, Grand Prix, Karlovy Vary Int. Film Festival 1964, U.S. Acad. Award Oscar 1965, New York Film Critics Award 1967, Selznik Prize, U.S. 1966; Honoured Artist 1965, Nat. Artist 1968; Co-Dir. with Ján Kadár (q.v.): Únos (Kidnapped) 1952, Smrt si říká Engelchen (Death is Called Engelchen) 1963, Obžalovaný (The Accused) 1964, Obchod na korze (The Shop on the High Street) 1965 (all award-winning films), Touha zvaná Anada (Desire called Anada), Co-Dir. with J. Kadár 1969. *Address:* Strahovská 203, Hradčany, Prague 1, Czechoslovakia. *Telephone:* 536297.

KLOSE, Wolfgang Dietrich E. A., DR.RER.NAT.; German solid state research scientist; b. 1 Jan. 1930, Berlin; s. of Albert and Hedwig Klose; m. Christine Kümmel 1953; one s. one d.; ed. Humboldt Univ., Berlin and Univ. of Erlangen; Deutsche Akad. der Wissenschaften, Berlin 1956–61; Siemens Research Lab., Erlangen 1961–67; Prof. Univ. of Saarbrücken 1967–74; Exec. Dir. Nuclear Research Centre, Karlsruhe 1974–; mem. Low Temperature Comm., Bavarian Acad. of Sciences 1974–81; Chair. Fed. Govt. Research Council for Forest Decline 1983–; mem. German Scientific Council 1978–84. *Publications:* textbook on solid state physics 1973, Alba Amicorum of the XVIth century 1988, and articles in int. journals of physics. *Address:* Kernforschungszentrum GmbH, Weberstrasse 5, Postfach 3640, D-7500 Karlsruhe 1, Federal Republic of Germany.

KŁOSKOWSKA, Antonina, PH.D.; Polish sociologist; b. 7 Nov. 1919, Piotrków Trybunalski; d. of Wincenty and Cecylia Kłoskowski; ed. Łódź Univ; Doctor 1950–54, Docent 1954–66, Assoc. Prof. 1966–73, Prof. 1973–; Expert, UNESCO 1967–; Head, Sociology of Culture Dept., Sociology Inst., Warsaw Univ. –1983; Ed.-in-Chief "Kultura: Społeczenstwo" 1981–; Chair. Cttee. of Sociological Sciences, Polish Acad. of Sciences (PAN) 1973–81; corresp. mem. PAN 1974–83, ordinary mem. 1983–; mem. Nat. Cttee. of Int. Sociological Assen. attached to Social Sciences Dept. of Polish Acad. of Sciences 1984; Chair. Scientific Council of Inst. of Culture, Warsaw; mem. Bd., Cttee. of Communication, Culture and Science, Int. Sociological Assen.; Medal of 10th and 30th Anniversaries of People's Poland; Gold Cross of Merit, Kt.'s Cross, Order of Polonia Restituta; Scientific Prize, City of Łódź; Meritorious Teacher of People's Poland 1978. *Publications:* Kultura masowa, Krytyka i obrona 1964, Z historii i socjologii kultury 1969, Społeczne ramy kultury 1973, Machiavelli jako humanista na tle włoskiego Odrodzenia 1954, Education in a Changing Society 1977 (co-ed.), Socjologia kultury (Sociology of Culture) 1981, Ed. of quarterly journal of Cttee. of Sociology PAN. *Leisure interests:* Literature, theatre, music, cinema. *Address:* Dzika 6 m. 270, 00-172 Warsaw, Poland. *Telephone:* 268599 (Office).

KLOSSOWSKI de ROLA, Comte Balthasar (pseudonym Balthus); French artist; b. 29 Feb. 1908, Paris; s. of Victor Klossowski de Rola and Dorothé Spiro; m. 1st Antoinette von Wattenwyl 1937, two c.; 2nd Setsuko Ideta; exhibited Galerie Pierre, Paris 1934, Pierre Matisse Gallery, New York City 1938, 1939, 1949, 1956, Moos Gallery, Geneva 1943, Wildenstein Galleries, Paris 1946, 1956, Dunn Int. Exhbn., London 1963; Retrospective Exhbn. at Tate Gallery, London 1968, at Georges Pompidou Centre, Paris 1983; Dir. Accademia di Francia, Villa Medici, Rome 1961–77; Grand Prix Nat. des Arts. *Works include:* Frescoes, Church of Beatenberg, Switzerland 1928; costumes and sets for Artaud's The Cenci 1935, for Così Fan Tutte, Aixen-Provence 1950; numerous paintings. *Address:* Grand Chalet Rossinière, Canton de Vaux, Switzerland.

KLOSTER, Einar, B.A.; Norwegian business executive; b. 22 Sept. 1937, Oslo; s. of Knut Utstein Kloster and Ingeborg (née Ihlen) Kloster; m. Elizabeth (née Hajan) Blake 1961; two d.; ed. Dartmouth Coll. and Harvard Univ.; Marketing Man. Philips Norway Jan. 1961–68, Philips Head Office, Holland 1968–70; Marketing Dir. Philips Japan 1970–74; C.E.O. Philips East Africa 1974–77, Philips Norway 1978–82, Philips Brazil 1982–85; Exec. Vice-Pres. North American Philips Corpn. 1985–86, Pres. Jan. 1989–; Chair. and C.E.O. Kloster Cruise Ltd. 1986–88, Chair. Jan. 1989–. *Leisure interests:* golf, tennis, skiing. *Address:* 100 E. 42nd Street, New York, N.Y. 10017 (Office); 102 Zaccheus Head Lane, Greenwich, Conn. 06831, U.S.A. (Home).

KLOTZ, Irving Myron, PH.D; American professor of chemistry and biochemistry; b. 22 Jan. 1916, Chicago, Ill.; s. of Frank and Mollie Nasatir Klotz; m. Mary S. Hanlon 1966; two s. one d.; ed. Univ. of Chicago; Research Assoc., Northwestern Univ. 1940–42, Instructor in Chem. 1942–46, Asst. Prof. of Chem. 1946–47, Assoc. Prof. of Chem. 1947–50; Prof. of Chem. and Biochemistry 1950–, Morrison Prof. 1963–; Fellow, American Acad. of Arts and Sciences; mem. N.A.S.; Eli Lilly Award 1949 and Midwest Award 1970 (A.C.S.). *Publications:* Chemical Thermodynamics 1950, 1964, 1972, 1986, Energy Changes in Biochemical Reactions 1957, 1967, Introduction to Biomolecular Energetics 1986, Diamond Dealers,

Feather Merchants: Tales from the Sciences 1986; over 200 research papers. *Address:* c/o Department of Chemistry, Northwestern University, Evanston, Ill. 60201 (Office); 2515 Pioneer Road, Evanston, Ill. 60201, U.S.A. (Home).

KLOTZBACH, Günter, DR.ING.; German engineer and metals executive; b. 16 Feb. 1912, Essen; s. of Dr. Arthur Klotzbach and Elisabeth Koerwer; m. Grete Holtermann 1940; three s.; ed. Goethe Gymnasium, Essen, Univ. de Lausanne and Technische Hochschule, Aachen; with Fried. Krupp Gussstahlfabrik, Essen 1937–46; Asst. to Tech. Direction Friedrich-Alfred-Hütte, then Hüttenwerk Rheinhausen AG, Rheinhausen 1946–59, Tech. Man. 1959–62; mem. Directorate, Fried. Krupp, Essen 1963–65; Chair. Man. Bd. Fried. Krupp Hüttenwerke AG 1966–73, Verein Deutscher Eisenhüttenleute, Düsseldorf 1973–78. *Address:* 433 Mülheim-Speldorf, Tannenstrasse 27, Federal Republic of Germany (Home). *Telephone:* Mülheim 50813 (Home).

KLUG, Sir Aaron, Kt., PH.D., F.R.S.; British biochemist; b. 11 Aug. 1926; s. of Lazar Klug and Bella Silin; m. Liebe Bobrow 1948; two s.; ed. Durban High School and Univs. of the Witwatersrand and Cape Town; Jr. Lecturer 1947–48; Research Student, Cavendish Lab., Cambridge 1949–52; Rouse-Ball Research Studentship, Trinity Coll., Cambridge 1949–52; Colloid Science Dept., Cambridge 1953; Nuffield Research Fellow, Birkbeck Coll., London 1954–57; Dir. Virus Structure Research Group, Birkbeck Coll. 1958–61; mem. staff, MRC Lab. of Molecular Biology, Cambridge 1962–; Jt. Head, Div. of Structural Studies 1978–86, Dir. 1986–; Fellow of Peterhouse 1962–; Foreign Assoc. N.A.S.; Foreign mem. Max Planck Gesellschaft 1984; Foreign Hon. mem. American Acad. of Arts and Sciences; Hon. Fellow, Trinity Coll., Cambridge, Royal Coll. of Physicians 1987; Hon. D.Sc. (Chicago) 1978, (Columbia) 1978, (Hull) 1986, (St. Andrews) 1987; Dr. h.c. (Strasbourg) 1978; Hon. Dr. Fil. (Stockholm) 1980; Heineken Prize, Royal Netherlands Acad. of Science 1979; Louisa Gross Horwitz Prize (Columbia Univ.) 1981; Nobel Prize for Chemistry 1982, Copley Medal, Royal Soc. 1985, Harden Medal, Biochemical Soc. 1985, Baly Medal, Royal Coll. of Physicians 1987. *Publications:* articles in scientific journals. *Leisure interests:* reading, gardening. *Address:* MRC Laboratory of Molecular Biology, Cambridge, CB2 2QH, England. *Telephone:* 248011.

KLUGT, Cornelius J. van der; Netherlands business executive; b. 30 March 1925, Haarlem; joined Philips 1950, Man. Philips Uruguay 1963–67, Commercial Man. Philips Brazil 1968–70, Gen. Man. 1971–77, mem. Bd. of Man., N.V. Philips Gloeilampenfabrieken, Vice-Pres. and Vice-Chair. 1982–86, Pres. and Chair. Man. Bd. April 1986–, Group Man. Cttee. 1987–; Chair. Assen. for Monetary Union of Europe, European Foundation for Quality Man.; mem. European Round Table of Industrialists. *Awards include:* Kt. of Order of the Dutch Lion, Commdr. of the Crown Order of Belgium, Grand Officer Order of Merit (Italy). *Address:* N.V. Philips, 5621 BA Eindhoven, The Netherlands. *Telephone:* (31) 40 791111.

KLUSÁK, Milan, LL.D., CSC.; Czechoslovak jurist and politician; b. 8 June 1923, Staŕeč; ed. Brno Univ. imprisoned by Gestapo 1942–45; official Foreign Affairs Ministry 1948–73; official in the secr. of the Ministry of Foreign Affairs 1948–50 First Sec. Embassy, Moscow 1950–53, Perm. Rep. to UN, Geneva 1960–63; Head of a Foreign Ministry Dept. 1963–65, 1968–69; Amb. and Head of Mission to UN, New York 1965–68; Chair. UN Econ. and Social Council 1967–68; Dep. Minister of Foreign Affairs 1969–73; Head, Chair. of Int. Law and Politics, Faculty of Law, Charles Univ. Prague 1971–83; Minister of Culture of the Czech Socialist Republic 1973–88; cand. mem., CP Cen. Cttee. 1976–81, mem. 1981–; Deputy, Czech Nat. Council 1976–; numerous decorations. *Address:* c/o Ministry of Culture of the Czech Socialist Republic, Prague, Czechoslovakia.

KLUXEN, Wolfgang, DR.PHIL.; German professor of philosophy; b. 31 Oct. 1922, Bensberg; m. Rosemarie Schmitz 1961; one s. two d.; ed. Univs. of Cologne, Bonn and Louvain; Asst. Univ. of Cologne 1953–60; Visiting Prof. Villanova Univ. 1960–61; Prof. Pädagogische Hochschule Neuss 1962–64; Prof. Ruhr Univ. Bochum 1964–69, Univ. of Bonn 1969–88, Prof. Emer. 1988–; Pres. Int. Soc. for Study of Medieval Philosophy 1973–83, Allgemeine Gesellschaft für Philosophie in Deutschland 1978–84; mem. Rhineland-Westphalian Acad. of Sciences; Grosses Bundesverdienstkreuz, Order of St. Gregory (Vatican). *Publications:* Philosophische Ethik bei Thomas von Aquin 1964, Joh. Duns Scotus Tractatus de primo principio 1974, Ethik des Ethos 1974; numerous articles. *Address:* 5300 Bonn 1, Humboldtstrasse 9, Federal Republic of Germany. *Telephone:* 0228-636714.

KLUYVER, Jan Cornelis, PH.D.; Netherlands physicist; b. 3 Feb. 1920, The Hague; s. of Albert J. Kluyver and Helena J. van Lutsenburg Maas; m. Cornelia J. Hoeneveld 1957; three d.; ed. Univ. of Utrecht; Fellow and Research Assoc. Fundamental Research of Matter, Utrecht 1948–56; Fellow of C.E.R.N., Nuclear Physics Research Lab. Liverpool 1956–57; staff mem. C.E.R.N. Geneva 1957–60; Prof. of Experimental Physics, Univ. of Amsterdam 1960–86, Prof. Emer. 1986–; Dir. Zeeman Lab. 1960–71, Dean, Faculty of Physics and Astronomy 1972–76; del. of Netherlands to C.E.R.N. Council 1980–87, Vice-Pres. 1985–87; Kt., Order of Netherlands Lion. *Publications:* 80 papers on infra-red isotope analysis, nuclear physics, elementary particle physics. *Leisure interests:* field hockey, reading. *Address:* Cannenburg 24, 1081 GZ Amsterdam; NIKHEF-H, P.O. Box

41882, 1009 DB Amsterdam, Netherlands. *Telephone:* 020-423760; 020-5925020.

KŁYSZEWSKI, Wacław; Polish architect (retd.); b. 7 Sept. 1910, Warsaw; s. of Antoni and Stanisława Kłyszewski; m. Marta Suchanek 1951; ed. Warsaw Polytechnic; Mem., Polish Asscn. of Architects (SARP) 1936-; Studio with J. Mokrzyński (q.v.) and E. Wierzbicki (q.v.) 1936-39; Designer, Office of Rebuilding of the Capital (with Mokrzyński and Wierzbicki) 1945-47; Senior Asst., Warsaw Polytechnic 1945-49; now Collective Judge, SARP; Chief Designer, Warsaw Design Office of Gen. Architecture until 1976, Emer. 1977; First Prizes (with Mokrzyński and Wierzbicki) for: Polish Savings Bank in Warsaw, Polish United Workers' Party Building in Warsaw. Architect's House in Zakopane, Railway Station in Katowice, Seamen's House, Szczecin 1972, Tatry Park Museum 1980, Museum of Modern Art in Skopje, Yugoslavia; Gold Cross of Merit 1955, Gold Award for Rebuilding Warsaw 1958, Officer's Cross, Order of Polonia Restituta 1964, Order of Banner of Labour, 2nd Class 1969, State Prize 3rd Class 1951, 2nd Class 1955, 1st Class 1974; Hon. Prize, SARP 1968, Prize of Katowice Branch of SARP 1972; Prize of Minister of Construction, 1st Class 1973. *Address:* Ul. Górnośląska 16 m. 15a, 00-432 Warsaw, Poland. *Telephone:* 21-98-49.

KLYUYEV, Vladimir Grigorovich; Soviet official; b. 1924, Ivanovo Dist.; ed. Ivanovo Textile Inst.; mem. CPSU 1949-; foreman, Dir. of a cotton combine 1949-61; Head of a Dept. of Ivanovo Dist. CPSU Cttee. 1961-64; First Sec. of Ivanovo City Cttee. of CPSU 1964-66; Second Sec. of Ivanovo Dist. Cttee. CPSU 1966-72, First Sec. 1972-85; Deputy to U.S.S.R. Supreme Soviet 1970-; mem. Cen. Cttee. of CPSU 1976-; Minister for Light Industry 1985-. *Address:* Ministry of Light Industry, Verkhnyaya Krasnoselskaya 15, Moscow, U.S.S.R.

KNACKSTEDT, Günter Wilhelm Karl, PH.D.; German diplomatist; b. 29 July 1929, Berlin; s. of Willi and Anni Knackstedt; m. (divorced); two s.; m. 2nd Marianne Fischbach 1984; ed. Univs. of Frankfurt, Paris, Cincinnati and Harvard; Ed. at Cincinnati Enquirer 1958-59; Chief Ed. You and Europe, Wiesbaden 1959-61; joined diplomatic service 1961; Press Attache, Havana 1963, Caracas 1963-66; Ministry of Foreign Affairs 1966-74, Sec. for Parl. Affairs 1976-79; Political Counsellor, Madrid 1974-76; Amb. to Luxembourg 1979-84, to Council of Europe, Strasbourg 1985-88, to Chile 1988-. *Publications:* Compendium of World History 1954, Living with Venezuelans 1968. *Leisure interests:* skiing, tennis, collecting old clocks. *Address:* 785 Agustinas, Santiago, Chile. *Telephone:* 335031.

KNAPP, J. Burke; American banker; b. 25 Jan. 1913, Portland, Ore.; s. of Mr. and Mrs. J. B. Knapp; m. 1st F. A. Hilary Eaves 1939 (divorced 1976), two s. two d.; m. 2nd Iris Hay-Edie Johannessen 1976; ed. Stanford Univ. and Oxford Univ; joined Brown Harriman and Co., Ltd. 1936-40; economist of the Fed. Reserve Bd., Washington 1940-44; economic adviser to the American Mil. Govt. in Germany 1944-45; Special Asst. on Int. matters to the Chair. of the Bd. 1945-48; Dir. of Office of Financial and Devt. Policy, Dept. of State 1948-49; Asst. Economic Dir. of the World Bank 1949-50; econ. adviser to the U.S. NATO del. in London 1950-51; U.S. Chair. of the Joint Brazil-U.S. Economic Development Comm., Rio de Janeiro 1951-52; Dir. of the World Bank's operations in Latin America 1952-56; Vice-Pres. of the Int. Bank for Reconstruction and Devt. 1956-72, Sr. Vice-Pres. Operations 1972-78; int. consultant 1978-. *Leisure interests:* theatre, swimming. *Address:* 4144 River Street N., Arlington, Va. 22207, U.S.A. (Home).

KNAPP, Stefan; British (born Polish) artist; b. 11 July 1921, Bilgoraj; ed. Lwów High School, Cen. School of Art, London, Slade School of Art, London Univ; imprisoned in Siberia 1939-42; fighter pilot in R.A.F. 1942-45; student 1945-50. *Exhibitions:* 14 one-man Shows in London between 1947 and 1986, also in Paris 1955, New York 1957, Caracas 1958, 1960, 1973, Warsaw 1962, 1974, Buenos Aires 1961, Lima 1962, Linz 1963, Munich 1963, 1968, Dusseldorf 1964, Manchester 1965, Detroit 1966, Amsterdam 1968, 1973, 1979, Bordeaux 1984, London 1986; inventor of technique of large-scale painting on copper and steel for architectural use; murals include those at Hallfield School, Esso Bldg., Heathrow Airport (London), St. Anne's Coll. (Oxford), C.I.N. Bldg. (Paris), Synagogue (Ontario), N.G.C. Omaha (Nebraska), Park East Hospital, Seagram Bldg., Queens Coll. (New York), Alexanders Store, Alexanders Valley Stream (New Jersey), Colombia Univ., City Hospital (Düsseldorf), Unilever Bldg. (Hamburg), Univ. of Brunswick (Fed. Repub. of Germany), Univ. of Freiburg, Copernicus Univ. (Warsaw), Torun Planetarium (Olsztyn), Lod Airport (Israel), Safa Park (Dubai), McCann Erikson (London), Hotel 83, La Fossette (St.-Tropez), Grabowski Gallery 2 (London); museum collections in Museo Nacional de Bellas Artes and Museo de Arte Moderno, Buenos Aires; National Museum of Finland; Museo de Bellas Artes, Caracas; Museum of Fine Arts, Dallas; Contemporary Arts Soc. and Victoria and Albert Museum, London; Stedelijk Museum, Amsterdam; Breda Museum, Netherlands; Museum of Modern Art, New York; Neue Gallerie de Stad, Linz; National Museum, Warsaw; Katowice Museum; Royal Palace, Rabat; Vatican Museum; Art Center, Milwaukee; Lissone Prize, Milan 1957, Churchill Fellowship 1975, Kt.'s Cross of the Order of Polonia Restituta 1975. *Publication:* The Square Sun (autobiography) 1956. *Address:* The Studio, Sandhills, Godalming, Surrey, England. *Telephone:* (042 879) 2430.

KNEALE, (Robert) Bryan (Charles), R.A.; British sculptor; b. 19 June 1930; m. Doreen Lister 1956; one s. one d.; ed. Douglas High School, Douglas School of Art, Isle of Man, Royal Acad. Schools; Tutor, R.C.A. Sculpture School 1964-, Sr. Tutor 1980-85, Head Dept. of Sculpture 1985-; Head of Sculpture School, Hornsey 1967; Assoc. Lecturer, Chelsea School of Art 1970; Fellow R.C.A. 1972, Sr. Tutor 1980-; Master of Sculpture R.A. 1982-85, Prof. 1985-; mem. Fine Art Panels, Nat. Council for Art Design 1964-71, Arts Council 1971-73, CNAA 1974-82; Chair. Air and Space 1972-73; organized Sculpture '72, R.A. 1972, Battersea Park Silver Jubilee Sculpture 1977, Sade Exhbn., Cork 1982; exhbns. at Redfern Gallery, John Moores, Sixth Congress of Int. Union of Architects, Art Aujourd'hui, Paris, Battersea Park Sculpture, Tate Gallery, Whitechapel Gallery, Hayward Gallery, Serpentine Gallery, Compass Gallery, Glasgow, 51 Gallery, Edin., Arts Council Tours 1966-71 etc.; Collections Arts Council of G.B., Contemporary Art Soc., Manx Museum, Nat. Galleries of Victoria, S. Australia and N.Z., City Art Galleries York, Nottingham, Manchester, Bradford, Leicester, Tate Gallery, Beaverbrook Foundation, Fredericton, Museum of Modern Art, Sao Paulo, Brazil, Bahia Museum, Brazil, Oriel Coll., Oxford, Museum of Modern Art, New York, Fitzwilliam Museum, Cambridge, etc. *Address:* c/o Royal Academy, Piccadilly, London, W.1, England.

KNEALE, William Calvert, M.A., F.B.A.; British professor of philosophy; b. 22 June 1906, Liverpool; m. Martha Hurst 1938; one s. one d.; ed. Liverpool Inst. High School, Brasenose Coll. Oxford, Freiburg and Paris; Asst. in Mental Philosophy, Univ. of Aberdeen 1929-31; Asst. Lecturer in Philosophy, Armstrong Coll., Newcastle upon Tyne 1931-32; Lecturer in Philosophy and Fellow, Exeter Coll. Oxford 1932-60; (temporary Civil Servant, Ministry of War Transport 1940-45); White's Prof. of Moral Philosophy and Fellow of Corpus Christi Coll. Oxford 1960-66; Hon. Fellow Brasenose and Corpus Christi Colls. Oxford; Dr. h.c. (Aberdeen, Durham and St. Andrews). *Publications:* Probability and Induction 1949, The Development of Logic (with Martha Kneale) 1962. *Address:* 4 Bridge End, Grassington, via Skipton, North Yorks., BD23 5NH, England. *Telephone:* (0756) 752710.

KNEF, Hildegard; British (b. German) actress, singer and authoress; b. 28 Dec. 1925, Ulm, Germany; d. of Hans Theodor and Frieda Auguste (née Groehn) Knef; m. 2nd David Cameron, one d.; m. 3rd Paul Rudolph Schell 1977; ed. art studio, Ufa Babelsberg; acted in Schlossparktheater, Berlin 1945, 1960, Imperial Theatre, New York 1955-56, Berliner Schaubühne 1961, 1964-65; Edison Prize 1972, Bundesverdienstkreuz (First Class) 1975, award for best female role, Karlsbad film festival 1976, Bundesfilmpreis 1959, 1977, Golden Tulip, Amsterdam 1981 and other film awards. *Films include:* Die Mörder sind unter uns 1946, Film ohne Titel 1948, Die Sünderin 1950, Entscheidung vor Morgengrauen 1951, Schnee am Kilimandscharo 1952, Alraune 1952, Illusion in Moll 1952, The Man Between 1953, Svengali 1954, La Fille de Hambourg 1958, Der Mann der sich verkaufte 1958, Lulu 1962, Landru 1962, Dreigroschenoper 1962, Das Grosse Liebesspiel 1963, Wartezimmer zum Jenseits 1964, The Lost Continent 1967, Jeder Stirbt für sich allein 1975, Fedora 1977; numerous recordings and numerous TV appearances. *Publications:* Der Geschenkte Gaul 1970, Ich brauche Tapetenwechsel 1972, Das Urteil 1975, (Mark Twain Prize 1980), Heimwehblues 1978, Nicht als Neugier 1978, So nicht 1982, Romy 1983. *Leisure interests:* reading, art, philosophy, painting, literature. *Address:* c/o Agentur Jovanovic, Perfallstr. 6, 8000 Munich 80, Federal Republic of Germany.

KNELLER, Eckart Friedrich, DR. RER. NAT., DIPL. PHYS.; German professor of materials science; b. 1 Jan. 1928, Magdeburg; s. of Friedrich Kneller and Anna M. (née Mathiszig) Kneller; m. Brigitte Quasz 1968; one s. one d.; ed. Technische Hochschule Stuttgart; scientific staff mem. Max-Planck-Inst. Metallforschung, Stuttgart 1953-59, 1963-67; Guest Lecturer Tech. Hochschule Vienna and Univ. of Göttingen 1958-59; Consultant IBM Research Center, Yorktown Heights, N.Y. 1960-62; Lecturer in Physical Metallurgy, Tech. Hochschule Stuttgart 1962-66, Prof. 1966-67; Prof. of Materials Science, Ruhr Univ. Bochum 1967-, Dean Faculty of Electrical Eng. 1968-69, 1987; Sec. Nordrhein-Westfälische Acad. of Sciences, Düsseldorf; DGM Masing Gedächtnis Preis 1962. *Publications:* Ferromagnetismus 1962, Magnetism and Metallurgy (Co-Ed. A.E. Berkowitz) 1969; numerous articles on magnetism, magnetic materials and metallurgy. *Leisure interests:* painting, graphic arts, history, mountaineering. *Address:* Institut Werkstoffe der Elektrotechnik, Ruhr Universität, Postfach 102148, D-4630 Bochum 1 (Office); Vossegge 23, D-5810 Witten 3, Federal Republic of Germany. *Telephone:* 0234-7002300 (Office); 02302-73851 (Home).

KNEŽEVIĆ, Stojan, D. EN MED., D. ÈS SC.; Yugoslav professor of medicine; b. 6 Dec. 1923, Split; m. Jelena Konstantinović 1947; one s. one d.; ed. Univ. of Zagreb, intern Hosp. St. Antoine, Paris; Zagreb Hosp. 1951-52; country doctor DZ-Sisak 1952-54; Specialist in Internal Medicine 1954-57; Asst. Clinic for Internal Medicine, Zagreb 1957-63; Asst. Prof., then Prof. of Medicine, Univ. of Zagreb-Croatia 1963-; Head of Gastroenterology Inst., Univ. of Zagreb; Pres. Medical Acad. of Croatia; Hon. mem. Czecho-Slovak Medical Asscn. *Publications:* Klinička medicina 1959, Interna medicina 1970, Etika i medicina 1976, San je java snena 1977 (literary), Medicinske razglednice 1985 (poetry). *Leisure interests:* writing, poetry. *Address:* Smičiklasolva 19, Zagreb, Yugoslavia.

KNIGHT, Andrew Stephen Bower, F.R.S.A.; British journalist and newspaper executive; b. 1 Nov. 1939; s. of M. W. B. Knight and S. E. F. Knight; m. 1st Victoria Catherine Brittain (marriage dissolved) 1966, one s.; m. 2nd Begum Sabiha Rumani Malik 1975, two d.; Ed. The Economist 1974–86; Chief Exec. Daily Telegraph 1985–, Ed.-in-Chief 1987–; Chair. Ballet Rambert 1984–87, Dir. 1987–; Dir. Tandem Computers Inc. 1984–, Reuters Holdings PLC 1988–; mem. Advisory Bd. Center for Econ. Policy Research, Stanford Univ., U.S.A. 1981–, Council, Royal Inst. of Int. Affairs 1976–, Council, Templeton Coll. Oxford 1984–; Gov. mem. Council of Man. Ditchley Foundation 1982–; Gov. Atlantic Inst. 1985–; mem. Council Friends of Covent Garden 1981–. *Address:* Daily Telegraph PLC, 181 Marsh Wall, London, E14 9SR, England.

KNIGHT, Douglas Maitland, PH.D.; American educational and corporate administrator; b. 8 June 1921, Cambridge, Mass.; s. of Claude Rupert and Fanny Sarah Douglas Brown Knight; m. Grace Wallace Nichols 1942; four s.; ed. Yale Univ; Instructor of English, Yale 1946–47; Asst. Prof. of English Literature, Yale 1947–53; Morse Research Fellow 1951–52; Pres., Lawrence Coll., Appleton, Wisconsin 1954–63; Pres. Duke Univ., Durham, N. Carolina 1963–69; Chair. Woodrow Wilson Nat. Fellowship Foundation; Chair. Nat. Library Comm. 1966–67; Div. Vice-Pres. Educational Devt., RCA, New York 1969–71, Div. Vice-Pres. Educ. Services 1971–72, Staff Vice-Pres. Educ. and Community Relations 1972–73, Consultant 1973–; Pres. RCA, Iran 1971–72, Dir. 1971–73; Pres. Social Econ. and Educ. Devt. Inc. 1973–, Questar Corpn. 1976–; Dir. Near East Foundation 1975–; Co-Founder and Trustee, Questar Library of Science and Art 1981–; mem. Nat. Comm. on Higher Educ. Issues 1981–84; Trustee, Solebury School, American Asscn. for the Advancement of the Humanities; numerous hon. degrees. *Publications:* Alexander Pope and the Heroic Tradition 1951, The Dark Gate (poems) 1971; Ed. and contrib.: Medical Ventures and the University 1967; Ed. The Federal Government and Higher Education 1960; Joint Ed. Twickenham edn. of Iliad and Odyssey (trans. by Alexander Pope) 1965, Libraries at Large 1968, Street of Dreams: The Nature and Legacy of the 1960s 1989. *Leisure interests:* farming, sailing. *Address:* c/o Questar Corporation, New Hope, Pa. 18938 (Office); R3, Box 539, Stockton, N.J. 08559, U.S.A. *Telephone:* (215) 862-5277 (Office); (201) 996-2054 (Home).

KNIGHT, Sir Harold Murray, Kt., K.B.E., D.S.C., M.COMM.; Australian banker; b. 13 Aug. 1919, Melbourne; s. of W. H. P. Knight; m. Gwenyth Catherine Pennington 1951; four s. one d.; ed. Scotch Coll., Melbourne, and Melbourne Univ; Commonwealth Bank of Australia 1936–40, 1946–55; served Australian Imperial Forces and Royal Australian Navy 1940–45 (awarded D.S.C.); Statistics Div., Research and Statistics Dept. of IMF 1955–59, Asst. Chief 1957–59; Research Economist, Reserve Bank of Australia 1960, Asst. Man. Investment Dept. 1962–64, Man. Investment Dept. 1964–68, Deputy Gov. Reserve Bank of Australia and Deputy Chair. of Bank's Bd. 1968–75, Gov. and Chair. of Bd. 1975–82; Dir. Western Mining Corpn. 1982–, Mercantile Mutual Group 1983–, Chair. 1985–; Chair. I.B.J. Australia Bank Ltd. 1985–; Dir. Angus and Coote Holdings Ltd. 1986–; Pres. Scripture Union, N.S.W. 1983–; Hon. Visiting Fellow, Macquarie Univ. 1983–86, Councillor 1984–87. *Publication:* Introducción al Análisis Monetario 1959. *Address:* 146 Springdale Rd, Killara, N.S.W. 2071, Australia.

KNIGHT, Reo Lindsay, B.COMM., A.C.A.; New Zealand economist and central banker; b. 22 April 1931, Wellington; s. of Alfred R. Knight and Jessie E. Mason; m. 1st Zena Julian 1955 (divorced 1980), one s. one d.; m. 2nd Margot E. Hankin 1982; ed. Rongotai Coll., Wellington, Victoria Univ. of Wellington and IMF Inst., Washington, D.C.; joined Reserve Bank of N.Z. 1948, Deputy Chief Economist 1965–67, Chief Cashier 1973–77, Asst. Gov. 1977–86, Deputy Gov. 1986–; Exec. Dir. for Australia and N.Z., I.B.R.D. 1970–73; Deputy Gov. Bank of Papua New Guinea (under IMF Tech. Assistance Programme) 1979–81. *Leisure interests:* golf, bridge, public speaking and debating. *Address:* Reserve Bank of New Zealand, P.O. Box 2498, Wellington (Office); 33a Roseneath Terrace, Wellington, New Zealand (Home). *Telephone:* 722-029 (Office); 847-137 (Home).

KNILL, John Lawrence, D.SC., F.I.C.E., F.I.GEOL.; British engineering geologist; b. 22 Nov. 1934, Wolverhampton; s. of William C. Knill and Mary Dempsey; m. Diane C. Judge 1957; one s. one d.; ed. Whitgift School, Croydon and Imperial Coll. London; Asst. Lecturer, Imperial Coll. 1957–59, Lecturer 1959–65, Reader 1965–73, Prof. of Eng. Geology 1973–, Head, Dept. of Geology 1979–88; Dean, Royal School of Mines 1980–83; mem. Nature Conservancy Council 1985–; Chair. Radioactive Waste Man. Advisory Cttee. 1985–, Natural Environment Research Council 1988–; British Geotechnical Soc. Prize 1966; Whitaker Medal (INEM) 1969. *Publication:* Industrial Geology 1977. *Leisure interest:* viticulture. *Address:* Natural Environment Research Council, Polaris House, North Star Avenue, Swindon, Wilts., SN2 1EU (Office); Highwood Farm, Shaw-cum-Donnington, Newbury, Berks., RG16 9LB, England (Home). *Telephone:* 0793-40101 (Office).

KNIPLING, Edward Fred, B.S., M.S., PH.D.; American agricultural research administrator and entomologist; b. 20 March 1909, Port Lavaca, Tex.; s. of Henry J. and Hulda Rasch Knipling; m. Phoebe Hall Knipling 1934; three s. two d.; ed. Texas A. and M. Univ. and Iowa State Univ; Entomologist, U.S. Dept. of Agriculture (U.S.D.A.) 1931–73, various research positions in veterinary and medical problems 1931–42, Dir. Research programme for devt. of control measures for diseases among

U.S. and Allied Mil. Forces 1942, Prin. Entomologist in charge of Research on Insects Affecting Men and Animals 1946, Dir. of Entomology Research Div. of Agricultural Research Services, U.S.D.A. 1953–71, Science Adviser, Agricultural Research Services, U.S.D.A. 1971–73; mem. N.A.S.; awards include President's Medal for Merit, U.S. Army Typhus Comm. Medal, U.S. Dept. of Agriculture's Distinguished Service Medal, Rockefeller Public Service Award, Nat. Medal of Science, King's Medal for Services in the Cause of Freedom (U.K.). *Publications:* about 200 scientific articles, principally on entomology including The Basic Principles of Insect Population Suppression and Management 1979. *Leisure interests:* hunting with bow and arrow, fishing, watching sporting events. *Address:* 2623 Military Road, Arlington, Va. 22207, U.S.A. (Home). *Telephone:* 527-5668 (Home).

KNIPPING VICTORIA, Eladio, LL.B.; Dominican diplomatist; b. 23 June 1933, Santiago de los Caballeros; s. of Elpidio Knipping and Luz Victoria; m. Soledad Knipping 1963; one s. one d.; ed. Autonomous University of Santo Domingo, Diplomatic School of Spain, School of Int. Affairs, Madrid; Asst. to Madrid Consulate 1963–65, Econ. Attaché, Netherlands 1966–68; Sec. Consultative Comm. Ministry of Foreign Affairs; Minister-Counsellor and Deputy Chief of Div. of UN Affairs, OAS and Int. Orgs. 1966–68, 1969–74; Minister-Counsellor Perm. Mission to UN, New York 1968–69, Amb. to Honduras 1974–78; Perm. Rep. to OAS 1981; Pres. Comm. Juridical and Political Affairs OAS Perm. Council 1981–82; Perm. Rep. to UN, New York 1983–87; Dominican mem. Int. Court of Arbitration, The Hague; Del. UN III Conf. of Law of the Sea; Lecturer in Int. Law Pedro Henriquez Ureña Univ. 1969; f. Inst. Comparative Law; mem. Spanish-Portuguese-American and Philippine Inst. of Int. Law; UN Adlai Stevenson Fellow. *Leisure interests:* reading, listening to music. *Address:* c/o Ministry of Foreign Affairs, Avda Independencia, Santo Domingo, Dominican Republic.

KNOLL, Jacob Egmont (Monty), B.A., LL.B.; South African lawyer; b. 20 March 1919, Cape Town; m. Valerie Phyllis Trow 1944; one s. two d.; ed. South African Coll. School, Cape Town, Univ. of Cape Town; practised with law firm 1946–88, sr. partner 14 years; Advocate Supreme Court of South Africa, later Attorney; mem. of Council Transvaal Law Soc. 1966–87, Pres. 1971–73; Pres. Asscn. of Law Socs. of S.A. 1982; mem. Council Int. Bar Asscn. 1980–86, Section on Gen. Practice 1978–86, Hon. Life mem. 1987–, Chair. Cttee. on Constitutional Drafting 1984–; mem. S.A. Patents Examination Bd., Lawyers for Human Rights (S.A.), Law Faculty Bd. Univ. of S.A., S.A. Law Comm. 1973–; Vice-Chair. Bd. of Govs. St. Alban's Coll., Pretoria 1962–; has served on numerous other professional cttees.; Order for Meritorious Service (S.A.); Meritorious Service Award Asscn. of Law Socs. (S.A.). *Leisure interests:* travel, history, music, nature conservation, outdoor life. *Address:* P.O. Box 276, Pretoria 0001 (Office); 432 Marais Street, Brooklyn, Pretoria 0181, South Africa (Home). *Telephone:* 012-286770 (Office); 012-464478 (Home).

KNOLL, József; Hungarian pharmacologist; b. 30 May 1925; s. of Jakab Knoll and Blanka Deutscher; m. Berta Knoll; one d.; ed. Medical Univ., Budapest; asst. lecturer Univ. Pharmacological Inst.; lecturer Medical Univ. 1958, Prof. and Head 1962–, Vice-Rector 1964–70; corresp. mem. Hungarian Acad. of Sciences 1970, mem. 1979–; Gen. Sec. Hungarian Pharmacological Soc. 1962–67, Pres. 1967–83; Chair. Nat. Drug Admin. Cttee. and Drug Research Cttee. of the Acad. of Sciences; Vice-Pres. Medical Sciences Section, Hungarian Acad. of Sciences 1967–76; mem. Leopoldina Deutsche Akad. der Naturwissenschaften, Halle 1974–; councillor Int. Union of Pharmacological Sciences 1981–84, First Vice-Pres. 1984–87; hon. dr. Medizinische Akad., Magdeburg 1984–; hon. mem. Pharmacological Socs. of Czechoslovakia, Bulgaria, Poland and of Italy; mem. editorial bd. of numerous int. pharmacological periodicals; Nat. Prize of Hungary 1984. *Leisure interest:* visual arts. *Publications:* Theory of Active Reflexes 1969, Handbook of Pharmacology, six editions since 1965; over 300 papers in int. trade journals. *Address:* Semmelweis University of Medicine, Department of Pharmacology, Budapest 1445, Nagyvárad tér 4, Hungary. *Telephone:* 137-015 (Office); 533-125 (Home).

KNOPF, Alfred, Jr., A.B.; American publisher; b. 17 June 1918, New York; s. of Alfred A. Knopf and Blanche Wolf; m. Alice Laine 1952; one s. two d.; ed. Union Coll.; Chair. Atheneum Publishers 1959–88. *Address:* Bayberry Ridge, Westport, Conn. 06880, U.S.A.

KNOPOFF, Leon, M.S., PH.D.; American professor of physics and geophysics; b. 1 July 1925, Los Angeles, Calif.; s. of Max Knopoff and Ray Singer; m. Joanne Van Cleef 1961; one s. two d.; ed. Calif. Inst. of Tech.; Asst. Prof., Assoc. Prof. of Physics, Miami Univ. 1948–50; mem. staff Univ. of Calif. (Los Angeles) 1950–, Prof. of Geophysics 1959–, of Physics 1961–, Research Musicologist 1963–, Assoc. Dir. Inst. of Geophysics and Planetary Physics 1972–86; Prof. of Geophysics, Calif. Inst. of Tech. 1962–63; Visiting Prof. Technische Hochschule, Karlsruhe (Germany) 1966; Chair. U.S. Upper Mantle Cttee. 1963–71, Sec.-Gen. Int. Upper Mantle Cttee. 1963–71; Nat. Science Foundation Sr. Postdoctoral Fellow 1960–61; Guggenheim Foundation Fellowship (Cambridge) 1976–77; Visiting Prof., Harvard Univ. 1972, Univ. of Chile, Santiago 1973; Chair. Int. Cttee. on Mathematical Geophysics 1971–75; H. Jeffreys Lecturer, Royal Astronomical Soc. 1976; mem. N.A.S., American Physical Soc., American Geophysical Soc., Royal Astronomical Soc.; Fellow, American Acad. of Arts and Sciences; Int. Co-operation Year Medal (Canada) 1965, Wiechert Medal, German Geophysical

Soc. 1978, Gold Medal of the Royal Astronomical Soc. 1979. *Publications:* The Crust and Upper Mantle of the Pacific Area (co-ed.) 1968, The World Rift System (co-ed.); chapters in Physics and Chemistry of High Pressures (ed. R. L. Bradley) 1963, Physical Acoustics (ed. W. P. Mason) 1965, The Earth's Mantle (ed. T. Gaskell) 1967, The Megatectonics of Oceans and Continents (ed. H. Johnson and B. L. Smith); papers in professional journals. *Leisure interests:* mountaineering, gardening, playing piano and harpsichord. *Address:* Institute of Geophysics and Planetary Physics, University of California, Los Angeles, Calif. 90024, U.S.A. *Telephone:* 213 825-1580.

KNORRE, Dmitri Georgievich; Soviet chemist and biochemist; b. 28 July 1926, Leningrad; s. of Georgy F. Knorre and Elena A. Knorre; m. Valeria L. Knorre 1959; one d.; ed. Moscow Chemical-Technological Inst.; worked in U.S.S.R. Acad. of Sciences Inst. of Chemical Physics 1947–61, then in all grades to Head Dept. of Biochemistry at Acad. of Sciences, Inst. of Organic Chemistry 1961–84, Dir. at Acad. of Sciences Inst. of Bio-organic Chem., Novosibirsk 1984–; also Prof. of Univ. of Novosibirsk 1961–; Hon. Dr. of Chemical Science 1967; Corresp. mem. of Acad. 1968–81, mem. 1981–. *Leisure interest:* hiking. *Address:* Institute of Bio-organic Chemistry, Prospekt Lavrenteva 8, 630090, Novosibirsk, U.S.S.R. *Telephone:* 35-64-41.

KNOTEK, Ivan; Czechoslovak politician; b. 1936, Trinec; ed. High School of Agric., Nitra; mem. CP of Czechoslovakia (CPCZ) 1954–; Sec. CP of Slovakia (CPSL) District Cttee. Galanta 1969; Sec. for Party works, CPSL District Cttee. Galanta 1980; Head of Dept. CPCZ Cen. Cttee. 1986; Deputy, Slovak Nat. Council 1986–; Leading Sec. W. Slovak CPSL Regional Cttee. 1987; Sec. and mem. Presidium, CPSL Cen. Cttee. 1988; mem. CPCZ Cen. Cttee. 1988–, mem. Presidium Oct. 1988–; Deputy Prime Minister Fed. Govt. and Prime Minister of Slovak Govt. Oct. 1988–; mem. Nat. Front Cen. Cttee.; Order of Labour and other state awards. *Address:* Central Committee of the Communist Party, Prague, Czechoslovakia.

KNOWLES, Jeremy Randall, M.A., D.PHIL., F.R.S.; British professor of chemistry and biochemistry; b. 28 April 1935; s. of Kenneth G. J. C. Knowles and Dorothy H. Swingler; m. Jane S. Davis 1960; three s.; ed. Magdalen Coll. School, Balliol Coll., Merton Coll. and Christ Church Oxford; Research Assoc. Calif. Inst. of Tech. 1961–62; Fellow, Wadham Coll. Oxford 1962–74; Univ. Lecturer, Univ. of Oxford 1966–74; Amory Houghton Prof. of Chem. and Biochem. (fmrly of Chem.), Harvard Univ. 1974–; Fellow, American Acad. of Arts and Sciences; Charmian Medal, Royal Soc. of Chem. 1980. *Publications:* research papers and reviews in learned journals. *Address:* 44 Coolidge Avenue, Cambridge, Mass. 02138, U.S.A. *Telephone:* 617-876-8469.

KNOWLES, Stanley Howard, P.C., O.C., LL.D.; Canadian (b. American) politician; b. 18 June 1908, Los Angeles, Calif.; s. of Stanley E. Knowles and Margaret B. Murdock; m. Vida C. Cruikshank 1936 (died 1978); one s. one d.; ed. Brandon and Winnipeg Univs.; Minister, United Church of Canada 1933–40; Mem. Parl. 1942–58, 1962–84; Hon. Officer, Canadian House of Commons March 1984–; New Democratic Party. *Publication:* The New Party 1961. *Address:* 17 Apache Crescent, Ottawa, Ont. K2E 6H8; 343 Cordova Street, Winnipeg, Man. R3N 1A5, Canada.

KNOWLTON, Richard L., B.A.; American business executive; b. 1932; m.; ed. Univ. of Colorado; joined George A. Hormel & Co. (food and meat packing co.) 1948, Asst. Man. Austin Plant 1969, Gen. Man. 1974, Vice-Pres. Operations 1974, Group Vice-Pres. Operations 1975–79, Pres. and C.O.O. 1979, Chair., Pres. and C.E.O. 1981–; Dir. Nat. Livestock and Meat Bd., Hormel Foundation Bd., First Nat. Bank of Austin, First Bank of Minn., Canada Packers; Chair. American Meat Inst.; Dir. Minn. Business Partnership. *Address:* George A. Hormel & Co., 501 16th Avenue, N.E., Austin, Minn. 55912, U.S.A.

KNUDSEN, Conrad Calvert, J.D.; American company executive; b. 3 Oct. 1923, Tacoma, Wash.; s. of Conrad D. and Annabelle Callison Knudsen, m. Julia Lee Roderick 1950; three s. one d.; ed. Washington Univ. and Law School, Seattle, and Columbia Univ., New York, N.Y.; Partner, Bogle, Bogle & Gates law firm, Seattle 1951–60; Exec. Vice-Pres. and Dir. Aberdeen Plywood and Veneer Inc. 1961–63; Pres. and Dir. Evans Products Co. 1963–68; Sr. Vice-Pres. Weyerhaeuser Co. 1969–76; Dir. Rainier Nat. Bank, Rainier Bancorporation, Castle & Cooke Inc., Cascade Corpn., West Fraser Timber Co. Ltd., Safeco Corpn., Koninklijke Nederlandse Papierfabrieken N.V. 1969–80; Pres. and C.E.O. MacMillan Bloedel Ltd. Sept. 1976–80, Chair. and C.E.O. 1980–83, Vice-Chair. Aug. 1983–; mem. U.S. and Washington State Bar Asscns. *Address:* MacMillan Bloedel Ltd., 1075 West Georgia Street, Vancouver, B.C., Canada V6E 3R9 (Office); 1853 41st Avenue E., Seattle, Wash. 98112, U.S.A. (Home). *Telephone:* 206-322 1158.

KNUDSEN, Semon Emil; American automobile executive; b. 2 Oct. 1912, Buffalo, N.Y.; s. of William S. and Clara Euler Knudsen; m. Florence Anne McConnell 1938; one s. three d.; ed. Dartmouth Coll. and M.I.T.; with Gen. Motors Corpn. 1939–68, Vice-Pres. and Gen. Man. Pontiac Motor Div. 1956–61, Chevrolet Div. 1961–65, Group Vice-Pres. in charge of Overseas and Canadian Group 1965–68, also responsible for domestic non-automotive divs. 1966–68, Exec. Vice-Pres. (Int. Operations) 1967–68; Pres. Ford Motor Co. 1968–69; Founder, Chair. Rectrans Inc. 1970–71; Pres.

and C.E.O. White Motor Corpn. 1975–79, Chair. and C.E.O. 1979–80; dir. several cos.; mem. Motor Vehicles Mfrs. Asscn. (Chair. 1977–78). *Address:* 34500 Grand River Avenue, Farmington Hills, Mich. 48024 (Office); 1700 Woodward Avenue, Suite E., Bloomfield Hills, Mich. 48013, U.S.A. (Home).

KNUSSEN, (Stuart) Oliver; British composer and conductor; b. 12 June 1952, Glasgow; s. of Stuart Knussen and Ethelyn Jane Alexander; m. Susan Freedman 1972; one d.; ed. Watford Field School, Watford Boys Grammar School, Purcell School; pvt. composition study with John Lambert 1963–68; conducted first performance of his First Symphony with London Symphony Orchestra 1968; Fellowships to Berks. Music Center, Tanglewood, U.S.A. 1970, 1971, 1973; Caird Travelling Scholarship 1971; Composer-in-residence, Aspen Festival, U.S.A. 1976, Arnolfini Gallery, U.S.A. 1978; Instructor in Composition, Royal Coll. of Music 1977–82; Guest Teacher, Tanglewood 1981; Composer-in-residence, Philharmonia Orchestra 1984–; guest conductor, London Sinfonietta, Philharmonia Orchestra and many other ensembles U.K. and abroad 1981–; mem. Exec. Cttee., Soc. for Promotion of New Music 1978–85; mem. Leopold Stokowski Soc., Int. Alban Berg Soc., New York; Countess of Munster Awards 1964, 1965, 1967; Peter Stuyvesant Foundation Award 1965; Watney-Sargent Award for Young Conductors 1969; Margaret Grant Composition Prize (for Symphony No. 2), Tanglewood 1971; Koussevitzky Centennial Comm. 1974; BBC commission for Promenade Concerts 1979 (Symphony No. 3); Arts Council Bursaries 1979, 1981; winner, first Park Lane Group Composer Award (suite from Where the Wild Things Are) 1982; BBC commission for Glyndebourne Opera 1983. *Compositions include:* operas: Where the Wild Things Are 1979–81, Higglety Pigglety Pop! 1983–84; symphonies: No. 1 1966–67, No. 2 (soprano and small orchestra) 1970–71, No. 3 1973–79; other works: Concerto for Orchestra 1968–70, Ophelia Dances, Book I 1975; other works for chamber ensemble and for voice and ensemble, for orchestra and for piano. *Leisure interests:* cinema, foreign literature, record collecting, record producing. *Address:* Flat 3, 167 West End Lane, London, NW6 2LG, England.

KNUTH, Donald Ervin, M.S., PH.D.; American professor of computer science; b. 10 Jan. 1938, Milwaukee, Wis.; s. of Ervin Henry Knuth and Louise Marie (née Bohning) Knuth; m. Nancy Jill Carter 1961; one s. one d.; ed. Case Inst. of Tech., California Inst. of Tech.; Asst. Prof. Math. Calif. Inst. of Tech. 1963–66, Assoc. Prof. 1966–68; Prof. of Computer Science, Stanford Univ. 1968–77, Fletcher Jones Prof. of Computer Science 1977–; mem. N.A.S., Nat. Acad. of Eng.; numerous hon. degrees, including (Paris) 1986, (Oxford) 1988; Nat. Medal of Science 1979; Steele Prize, American Math. Soc. 1986; Franklin Medal, Franklin Inst. of Philadelphia 1988. *Publications:* The Art of Computer Programming, (Vol. 1) 1968, (Vol. 2) 1969, (Vol. 3) 1973, Surreal Numbers 1974, Mariages Stables 1976, Computers and Typesetting (5 vols.) 1986, Concrete Mathematics 1986. *Leisure interests:* piano and organ playing, browsing in libraries. *Address:* Computer Science Department, Stanford University, Stanford, Calif. 94305-2149, U.S.A. *Telephone:* 415-723-4367.

KNUTH-WINTERFELDT, Count Kield Gustav, LL.D.; Danish diplomatist; b. 17 Feb. 1908, Copenhagen; s. of Count Viggo Christian Knuth-Winterfeldt and Countess Clara Knuth-Winterfeldt (née Grüner); m. Gertrud Lina Baumann 1938 (died 1978); two s. one d.; ed. Univ. of Copenhagen; Danish Foreign Service 1931, Vice-Consul Hamburg 1935; Sec. of Legation, Tokyo 1938; Sec. Ministry for Foreign Affairs 1939–45, Deputy Chief of Section 1945, Chief 1950; Envoy to Argentina, Uruguay, Paraguay, Bolivia and Chile 1950; Chief, Commercial Information Dept., Ministry of Foreign Affairs 1954, Deputy Dir. Economic Division 1956; Ambassador to U.S.A. 1958–65, to France 1965–66, to Fed. Repub. of Germany 1966–72; Lord Chamberlain at the Royal Danish Court 1972–76; Grand Cross (Diamonds), Order of Dannebrog; Grand Cross, Order of Merit, (Fed. Rep. of Germany); Officer, Order of George I (Greece), Grand Cross, Order of North Star (Sweden), Grand Officer, Order of Merit (Argentina), Grand Officer, Order of Merit (Chile), Grand Cross, Order of Falcon (Iceland), Hon. G.C.V.O. Grand Cross, Order of St. Olav (Norway), Order of the Yugoslav Flag with Ribbon, Grand Cross, Order of the House of Orange (Netherlands). *Leisure interest:* farming. *Address:* Rosendal, 4640 Fakse, Denmark. *Telephone:* (03) 71-30-34.

KNYAZYUK, Mikhail Aleksandrovich; Soviet politician; ed. Minsk Polytechnic, Byelorussian Polytechnic Inst., and CPSU Cen. Cttee.; Higher Party School; served in Soviet Army 1959–62; mem. CPSU 1963–; construction engineer, Lenin Factory, Minsk 1962–67; party work 1967–68; Deputy Head of Section Minsk City Cttee. 1968–70; work for Cen. Cttee. of Byelorussian CP 1970–73; First Sec. of Leninsky Regional Cttee. (Minsk) 1973–75; Second Sec. of Minsk City Cttee. 1975–77, Sec. 1983–; Second Sec. of Minsk Dist. Cttee. of Byelorussian CP 1983–84; work for CPSU Cen. Cttee. 1984–85; First Sec. of Ivanovsk Dist. Cttee. 1985–; mem. of CPSU Cen. Cttee. 1986–. *Address:* The Kremlin, Moscow, U.S.S.R.

KOBAYASHI, Koji, D.ENG.; Japanese business executive; b. 17 Feb. 1907, Yamanashi Prefecture; s. of Tsuneo and Den Kobayashi; m. Kazuko Noda 1935; three d.; ed. Tokyo Imperial Univ.; Sr. Vice-Pres. and Dir. NEC Corpn. 1956–61, Exec. Vice-Pres. and Dir. 1961–62, Sr. Exec. Vice-Pres. and Dir. 1962–64, Pres. 1964–76, Chair. Bd. and C.E.O. 1976–88, Chair. Emer. 1988–; dir. of numerous cos.; Exec. Dir. Fed. of Econ. Orgs. 1966; Governing Dir. Japan Fed. of Employers Asscns. 1966; Chair. Space Devt.

Promotion Council, Fed. of Econ. Orgs. 1970; Pres. Japan Techno-Econs. Soc.; Pres. Optoelectronic Industry and Tech. Devt. Assoc.; Foreign Associate of the Nat. Acad. of Engineering; Prime Minister's Prize for Export Promotion 1964; Blue Ribbon Medal 1964; Grand Cross (Peru) 1970; Medal of Honour (Paraguay) 1971; Jordan Star with Order 3rd Class 1972, First Class Order of the Sacred Treasure (Japan) 1978, Commdr., Orden Nacional del Merito (Paraguay) 1978, Order of Merit (First Grade) (Egypt) 1979, Commdr. Nat. Order of Southern Cross (Brazil) 1979, Commdr.'s Cross of Order of Merit (Poland) 1980, Commdr. (Third Class), Order of the White Elephant (Thailand) 1981; IEEE Frederik Philips Award 1977, Chevalier du Mérite de Madagascar 1981, The Order of San Carlos (Colombia) 1985, Grand Cordon Order of the Rising Sun 1987. *Publications:* Carrier Transmission System 1937, Challenge to the Computer Age 1968, The Problem of Management in the 1970s 1971, Quality-Oriented Management 1976, C & C (Computer and Communications) is Japan's Wisdom 1981, C & C (Computer and Communications): The Software Challenge—A Human Perspective 1982, C & C: Modern Communications—Development of Global Information Media 1985, Computers and Communications: A Vision of C & C 1986, My Personal History 1988. *Leisure interests:* golf, gardening. *Address:* NEC Corporation, 33-1 Shiba 5-chome, Minato-ku, Tokyo 108; and 15-10 Denenchofu 5-chome, Ohta-ku, Tokyo 145, Japan. *Telephone:* 03-721-8581.

KOBAYASHI, Taiyu; Japanese company executive; b. 13 June 1912, Hyogo Prefecture; m. Nagae Sano 1938; two s.; ed. Kyoto Univ.; joined Fuji Electric Co. 1935; joined Fujitsu Ltd. 1935, Dir. 1964, Man. Dir. Nov. 1969, Exec. Dir. 1972, Exec. Vice-Pres. 1975, Pres. 1976-81, Chair 1981-; Pres. Communications Industries Assen. of Japan 1976-78; Pres. Japan Electronic Industry Devt. Assen. 1979-; Chair. Eng. Research Assen. of Opto-Electronics Applied System 1981-; Purple Ribbon Award with Medal of Honour, Blue Ribbon Award with Medal of Honour. *Leisure interests:* gardening, golf. *Address:* 674 Nitta Kannami-cho, Tagata-gun, Shizuoka, Japan. (Home).

KÖBBEN, André J. F., PH.D.; Netherlands professor of cultural anthropology and administrator; b. 3 April 1925, 's-Hertogenbosch; m. Agatha M. van Vessem 1953; one s. two d.; ed. Municipal Gymnasium and Univ. of Amsterdam; Prof. of Cultural Anthropology, Univ. of Amsterdam 1955-76; Visiting Prof. Univ. of Pittsburgh 1972; Cleveringa Prof. Univ. of Leiden 1980-81; Prof. Erasmus Univ. 1981-; Dir. Centre for the Study of Social Conflicts 1976-; Curl Bequest Prize, Royal Anthropological Inst. 1952; mem. Royal Netherlands Acad. of Science 1975, Hon. mem. Anthropological Soc. 1986. *Publications:* Le planteur noir 1956, Van primitieven tot medeburgers 1964, Why exceptions? The logic of cross-cultural analysis 1967, Interests, partiality and the scholar 1987, Oud en machteloos? 1988. *Address:* Libellenveld 2, 2318 VG Leiden; C.O.M.T., Hooigracht 15, 2312 KM Leiden, The Netherlands. *Telephone:* (071) 215369; (071) 273845.

KOBZAREV, Yuriy Borisovich, D.SC.; Soviet radiophysicist; b. 8 Dec. 1905, Voronezh; ed. Kharkov Inst. of Educ.; Sr. Research Assoc., Physical-Tech. Inst., U.S.S.R. Acad. of Sciences 1926-43; Chair., Prof., Moscow Energy Inst. 1944-55; Research Assoc., Inst. of Radiotechnics and Electrotechnics 1955-, Chair. of Dept. 1968-; Corresp. mem. U.S.S.R. Acad. of Sciences 1953-70, mem. 1970-; State Prize 1941, 1949; Order of Lenin (twice) and other decorations. *Address:* U.S.S.R. Academy of Sciences, 14 Leninsky Prospekt, Moscow, U.S.S.R.

KOÇ, Vehbi: Turkish businessman; b. 1901; opened first grocery shop in Ankara 1917; formed Koç Trading Corpn. 1937, Gen. Elektrik Türk 1949, and many other cos.; assoc. with numerous major firms in U.S.A. and Europe; Chair. Koç Holding Corpn. 1964-84, Hon. Chair. 1984-; manufactured Turkey's first passenger car (Anadol) 1966, second (Murat, under licence from Fiat) 1971; Founded Vehbi Koç Foundation 1969, Turkish Educ. Foundation 1969; Order of Merit (Fed. Repub. of Germany) 1974. *Publications:* My Life Story (in Turkish) 1973, My Reminiscences, My Views and My Advices 1987. *Address:* Koç Holding Corporation, Findikli, Ankara, Turkey.

KOCH, Edward I., LL.B.; American lawyer, politician and local government official; b. 12 Dec. 1924, New York; s. of Louis Koch and Joyce Silpe; ed. City Coll. of New York and New York Univ. Law School; served Second World War in U.S. Army; admitted to New York bar 1949; sole practice law, New York 1949-64; Sr. partner Koch, Lankenau, Schwartz & Kovner 1965-69; mem. Council, New York 1967-68, Mayor 1978-; mem. U.S. House of Reps. from New York, 17th Dist. 1969-72, 18th District 1973-77; mem. House Appropriations Cttee.; Sec. New York Congressional Del.; Democratic District Leader, Greenwich Village 1963-65, mem. Village Ind. Democrats; appears in film segment Oedipus Wrecks 1989. *Publications:* Mayor (autobiog.) 1984, Politics 1985, His Eminence and Hizzoner (with Cardinal J. O'Connor, q.v.) 1989. *Address:* Office of the Mayor, City Hall, New York, N.Y. 10007 (Office); 14 Washington Place, New York, N.Y. 10023, U.S.A. (Home).

KOCH, Marita; German athlete (retd.); b. 1957; career total of 11 individual world records over 200 m. and 400 m. and 5 relay world records as part of East German team; also (at end of 1986) holder of third fastest time over 100 m.; lost 400 m. world record to Jarmila Kratochvilova (q.v.) 1983, Helsinki, regained it 1985, Canberra; individual gold medals include

Moscow Olympics 1980, World Cup 400 m., Canberra, 1985, European Championship 400 m., Stuttgart, 1986; retd. from competitive athletics March 1987.

KOCH, Werner; German professor and author; b. 4 Aug. 1926, Cologne; s. of Robert Koch and Martha Kammern; mem. editorial staff, Rheinische Zeitung, Cologne 1946-52; Producer and Dir. Städtische Bühnen, Cologne 1953-61; Cultural Ed., Westdeutscher Rundfunk 1961-; mem. Int. PEN Club, German PEN Centre; mem. Akad. der Wissenschaften und Literatur. *Publications include:* novels: Sondern Erlöse Uns von den Ubel 1955, Pilatus Errinerungen 1959, See-Leben I 1971, Wechseljahre oder See-Leben II 1975, Jenseits des Sees 1979, Diesseits von Golgotha 1986; short stories, essays etc. *Leisure interest:* dreaming. *Address:* Am Wingert 28, 5000 Cologne 50, Federal Republic of Germany. *Telephone:* 02236-6 36 88.

KOCHERGA, Anatoly Ivanovich; Soviet opera singer (baritone); b.1947, Kiev; ed. Kiev Conservatoire; mem. CPSU 1977-; studied at La Scala, Milan; soloist with Shevchenko Opera and Ballet, Kiev since 1972; Glinka Prize 1971, Tchaikovsky Prize 1974; *major roles include:* Boris Godunov, Galitsky (Borodin's Prince Igor), Don Basilio (Barber of Seville), Mephistopheles (Gounod's Faust). *Address:* c/o Shevchenko Opera and Ballet Co., Kiev, U.S.S.R.

KOCHERGIN, Edvard Stepanovich; Soviet theatrical designer; b. 22 Sept. 1937, Leningrad; m. Ina Gabai 1969; one s.; ed. workshops of Leningrad Maly Theatre (pupil of N. Akimov and T. Bruni); worked in Pskov, Krasnoyarsk, Riga, Tbilisi, Moscow; chief designer in a series of Leningrad theatres 1972-; chief designer for Gorky Theatre under direction of Tovstonogov 1972-; much work also for Bolshoi, Moscow; teacher course in theatre design, Leningrad Inst. of Theatre, Music and Cinema; State Prize 1972, 1978; R.S.F.S.R. Award of Merit. *Address:* Gorky Theatre, Fontanka 65, Leningrad, U.S.S.R.

KOCHETKOV, Prof. Nikolay Konstantinovich: Soviet chemist; b. 18 May 1915, Moscow; s. of Konstantin Kochetkov and Marie Kochetkova; m. Dr. Vera Volodina 1945; one s. one d.; ed. M. V. Lomonosov Inst. of Light Chem. Tech.; Asst., Chemistry Dept. of Moscow Univ. 1945-52, Dozent 1952-56, Prof. 1956-60; Head of Dept. of Organic Synthesis, Inst. of Pharmacology 1953-60; Deputy Dir., Head of nucleic acids and carbohydrates laboratory, Inst. of Natural Products 1960-66; Dir., Head of carbohydrates laboratory, Zelinsky Inst. of organic chem. 1966-; Corresp. mem. U.S.S.R. Acad. of Medical Sciences 1957-; Corresp. mem. U.S.S.R. Acad. of Sciences 1960-79, mem. 1979-; mem. Soc. de Chimie 1972-; Order of Lenin, Hero of Socialist Labour and other decorations. *Publications:* Chemistry of Natural Products 1961, Chemistry of Carbohydrates 1967, Organic Chemistry of Nucleic Acids 1970. *Address:* Zelinsky Institute of Organic Chemistry, Leninsky Prospekt 47, Moscow B-334, U.S.S.R. *Telephone:* 137-29-44.

KOCHETKOV, Yuriy Petrovich; Soviet politician; b. 1932; ed. Saratov Polytechnic; technician in Saratov Aviation Factory 1951-55; mem. CPSU 1956-; First Sec. of Zavodsk Regional Komsomol Cttee. 1955-57; Second Sec., First Sec. of Saratov City Komsomol Cttee. 1957-60; Second Sec., First Sec. of Saratov Dist. Komsomol Cttee. 1960-67; Sec. of Party Cttee. of Saratov Aviation Works 1967-70; First Sec. of Zavodsk Regional Cttee. of CPSU 1970-74; First Sec. of Saratov CPSU City Cttee. 1974-84; work for CPSU Cen. Cttee. 1984-85; Second Sec. of Cen. Cttee. of Armenian CP 1985-; cand. mem. of CPSU Cen. Cttee. 1986-; Deputy to U.S.S.R. Supreme Soviet. *Address:* Central Cttee. of Armenian CP, Yerevan, Armenian S.S.R., U.S.S.R.

KOCHI, Jay K., PH.D.; American professor of chemistry; b. 17 May 1927, Los Angeles; s. of Tsuruzo Kochi; m. Marion K. Kiyono 1961; one s. two d.; ed. Cornell and Iowa State Univs.; Instructor Harvard Univ. 1952-55; Nat. Inst. of Health Special Fellow, Univ. of Cambridge (U.K.) 1955-56; Shell Devt. Co. Emeryville, Calif. 1956-62; Case Western Univ., Cleveland, Ohio 1962-69; with Ind. Univ. 1969-84; Robert A. Welch Distinguished Prof. of Chem. Univ. of Houston, Tex. 1984-; chemical consultant; mem. N.A.S.; J. F. Norris Award, American Chem. Soc. 1981; A. C. Cope Scholar Award, American Chem. Soc. *Publications:* three books and more than 300 research papers. *Address:* Department of Chemistry, University of Houston, University Park, Houston, Tex. 77204-5641; 4372 Faculty Lane, Houston, Tex. 77004, U.S.A. (Home). *Telephone:* 713-741-2113 (Home).

KOCIOŁEK, Stanisław, M.A.; Polish politician; b. 3 May 1933, Warsaw; m.; two c.; ed. Faculty of Philosophy, Univ. of Warsaw; fmr. primary school master and dir.; local functions in Polish Youth Union (ZMP), Warsaw 1954-56, Socialist Youth Union (ZMS) 1958-60, Sec. ZMS Cen. Cttee. 1960-63; mem. Exec. Warsaw Cttee., Polish United Workers' Party (PZPR) 1963-64, First Sec. 1964-67; First Sec., PZPR Voivodship Cttee., Gdańsk 1967-70; Deputy Chair. Council of Ministers July-Dec. 1970; Amb. to Belgium and Luxembourg 1971-78, to Tunisia June-Nov. 1980; Chair. Bd., Cen. Union of Co-operative Labour Movt. 1978-80; mem. Cen. Cttee. PZPR 1964-71, Sec. 1970-71, mem. Political Bureau 1968-71; Deputy to Seym 1965-72; First Sec. Warsaw Cttee. of PZPR 1980-82; Amb. to U.S.S.R. 1982-85; Ed.-in-Chief Polish Perspectives Perspectives Polonaises (monthly) 1986-; numerous decorations including Order of Banner of Labour (1st Class). *Address:* Redakcja Perspektywy Polskie, ul. Warecka 1a, 00-034 Warsaw, Poland. *Telephone:* 27-70-99.

KOCK, Nils G., M.D., PH.D.; Finnish professor of surgery; b. 29 Jan. 1924, Jakobstad; s. of Emil Kock and Aili Lönnmark; m. Birgit Breitenstein 1950; two d.; ed. Univs. of Helsinki and Göteborg; Asst. Prof., Assoc. Prof. Dept. of Surgery, Univ. of Göteborg 1958-73, Prof. of Surgery 1974-; Research Assoc. Prof. State Univ. of N.Y. Buffalo 1968-69; Visiting Prof. Univ. of Zürich 1973-74; numerous awards for surgery. *Publications:* some 300 publications in the field of surgery, physiology, gastroenterology and urology. *Leisure interests:* boating, fishing. *Address:* Department of Surgery II, Sahlgrenska sjukhuset, University of Göteborg, 413 45 Göteborg (Office); Apotekaregatan 3, S-413 19 Göteborg, Sweden (Home). *Telephone:* 33-82 62 99.

KOCK-PETERSEN, Elsebeth, B.LL.; Danish politician; b. 15 Jan. 1949, Copenhagen; d. of Rev. Ejnar Larsen; Sec. in Nat. Asscn. of Local Authorities, subsequently Ministry of Foreign Affairs; organizer in Liberal Party, mem. of Exec. Cttee. 1979-; M.P. 1975-77, 1984-; Minister for Ecclesiastical Affairs 1982-84, for Social Affairs 1984-86, for Health 1988-; Liberal. *Address:* c/o Ministry of Health, Herluf Trolles Gade 11, 1052 Copenhagen K, Denmark.

KOÇMAN, Ali, M.SC.; Turkish business executive; b. 1943, Turkey; ed. lycée and Acad. of Econ. and Commercial Sciences, Istanbul; spent two years in the shipping industry in U.K. and U.S.A.; Gen. Man. Koç shipping, automotive, food, import and export cos.; Pres. CONTURCON Int. Shipping Conf. 1977-; Turkish del. to numerous int. confs. and Head economic dels. to U.S.A., U.K. and Japan 1980-; Pres. Turkish Businessmen's and Industrialists' Asscn. (TUSIAD) 1980; mem. Bd. of Dirs. Turkish Employee Confed. *Address:* Koç Holding Corporation, Fındıklı, Ankara, Turkey.

KOCSIS, Zoltán; Hungarian pianist and composer; b. 30 May 1952, Budapest; s. of Ottó Kocsis and Mária Mátyás; ed. Budapest Music Acad. (under Pál Kadosa); has appeared with Dresden Philharmonic Orchestra in G.D.R., and performed in Fed. Repub. of Germany, U.S.S.R., Austria and Czechoslovakia 1971; toured U.S.A. together with Dezső Ranki (q.v.) and Budapest Symphony Orchestra (under George Lehel, q.v.) 1971; recitals in Netherlands, Paris, London and Ireland 1972; concerts in Norway, with Svyatoslav Richter (q.v.) in France and Austria, with Claudio Abbado (q.v.) and London Symphony Orchestra and at Promenade Concerts in London, and Festival Estival, Paris 1977, Edinburgh Festival 1978; Asst. Prof. Music Acad. Budapest 1976-79, Prof. 1979-; Producer of Archive Section of Hungaroton (record co.); First Prize, Beethoven Piano Competition, Hungarian Radio and Television 1970, Liszt Prize 2nd Degree 1973, Kossuth Prize; Merited Artist's title 1984. *Publications:* Miscellaneous publs., Arrangements for Piano and 2 Pianos, etc. *Leisure interest:* photography. *Address:* H-1126 Budapest, Nárcisz u. 29; Interconcert Agency, 1051 Budapest V, Vörösmarty tér I, Hungary. *Telephone:* 176-222 (Agency).

KODAMANOĞLU, Nuri, M.SC.; Turkish politician; b. 16 Aug. 1923, Ulukışla-Niğde; s. of Fazil and Hatice Kodamanoğlu; m. Ayten Unal Kodamanoğlu 1951; ed. Istanbul Univ.; fmr. civil servant, Ministry of Educ.; later Under-Sec. Ministry of Educ.; Deputy to Grand Nat. Assembly; Minister of Energy and Natural Resources 1972; mem. Business Admin. Inst., Faculty of Political Science, Univ. of Ankara; mem. Bd. of Dirs. Turkish Petroleum Corpn.; Consultant, Asscn. of Turkish Chambers of Commerce, Chambers of Ind. and Exchange. *Publications:* Principles of New Education 1954, Education in Turkey 1963; various articles and reports. *Leisure interests:* handicrafts, gardening. *Address:* Bükreş Sokak No. 6 Daire 8, Çankaya, Ankara, Turkey. *Telephone:* 127-15-15.

KODEŠ, Jan; Czechoslovak tennis player; b. 1 March 1946, Prague; s. of Jan Kodeš and Vlasta Richterová-Kodešová; m. Lenka Rösslerová-Kodešová 1967; one s. one d.; ed. Coll. of Econs., Prague; Wimbledon Champion 1973, French Champion 1970 and 1971, runner-up U.S. Championships 1971, 1973, Italian Championships 1970, 1971, 1972; mem. Czechoslovak Davis Cup Team 1964-80, incl. 1975 (runners-up), 1980 (winners), non-playing Capt. 1982-87; Czechoslovak No. 1 player 1966-77; Dir. Czechoslovak Tennis Center 1986-; Bd. mem. Czechoslovak Tennis Asscn. (CTA), rep. for Czechoslovakia on int. bodies including ITF and ETA 1982-; Tournament Dir. Nabisco Grand Prix event Czechoslovak Čedok Open, Prague 1987-; Meritorious Master of Sports 1971, State Decoration for Outstanding Work 1973. *Leisure interests:* football, other sports, stamp collecting, films. *Address:* Na Beránce 18, Prague 6, 160.00 Czechoslovakia. *Telephone:* 42-2-231 12 70 (Office); 42-2-360485 (Home).

KODJO, Edem; Togolese politician and administrator; b. 23 May 1938, Sokodé; ed. Coll. Saint Joseph, Univ. of Rennes, Ecole Nat. d'Administration, Paris; worked as administrator for Office de Radiodiffusion-Télévision Française (ORTF) 1964-67; returned to Togo 1967; Sec.-Gen., Ministry of Finance, Economy and Planning 1967-72; Dir.-Gen. Société Nat. d'Investissement 1972-73; Administrator, Banque Centrale des Etats de l'Afrique de l'Ouest 1967-76, Pres of Admin. Council 1973-76; Minister of Finance and Economy 1973-76, of Foreign Affairs 1976-77, of Foreign Affairs and Co-operation 1977-78; Sec.-Gen. of the OAU 1978-84; mem. Rassemblement du Peuple Togolaise (RPT), RPT Political Bureau (Sec.-Gen. 1967-71); Gov. for IMF 1973-76; fmr. Chair. OAU Council of Ministers, Afro-Arab Perm. Comm. on Co-operation, OAU Cttee. of Ten; Officier, Légion d'honneur; decorations from many African countries. *Address:* General Secretariat of the Organization of African Unity, P.O. Box 3243,

Addis Ababa, Ethiopia; c/o Ministère des Affaires Etrangères et de la Coopération, Lomé, Togo.

KOECHLIN, Dr. Samuel; Swiss business executive; b. 29 March 1925, Basel; ed. Univs. of Basel and Paris and London School of Econs.; fmrly. with New York Agency of Swiss Credit Bank; joined Geigy Co. Inc., New York 1952, J. R. Geigy, S.A., Basel 1954, Chair. Man. Cttee. 1965-68, CIBA-Geigy Ltd. 1970-83, Chair. Man. Cttee. 1970-72, Chair. Exec. Cttee. 1972-82, Dir. 1983-. *Address:* CIBA-Geigy Ltd., Basel, Switzerland.

KOELLE, George Brampton, PH.D., M.D.; American pharmacologist; b. 8 Oct. 1918, Philadelphia, Pa.; s. of Frederick C. Koelle and Emily M. Brampton; m. Winifred J. Angenent 1954; three s.; ed. Univ. of Pennsylvania and Johns Hopkins Univ.; Bio-Assayist, LaWall and Harrisson Labs. 1939-42; Laboratory Instructor in Biological Assaying and Pharmacology, Philadelphia Coll. of Pharmacy and Science 1939-42; Chalfont Fellow in Ophthalmology, Wilmer Inst., Johns Hopkins Univ. and Hospital 1946-50; Asst. Prof. of Pharmacology, Coll. of Physicians and Surgeons, Columbia Univ. 1950-52; Prof. of Pharmacology, Graduate School of Medicine, Univ. of Pa. 1952-65, Chair. Dept. of Pharmacology, Medical School, 1959-81, Distinguished Prof. 1981-; Visiting Prof. and Guggenheim Fellow, Univ. of Lausanne 1963-64; Visiting Prof. and Acting Chair. Dept. of Pharmacology and Assoc. Dir. of Penn Team, Pahlavi Univ., Iran 1969-70; Visiting Prof. Mahidol Univ., Bangkok 1978; Visiting Lecturer, Polish Acad. of Science 1979; Sr. Int. Fellow, C.N.R.S., Paris 1986-87; mem. Editorial Advisory Bd. Int. Journal of Neurosciences 1970-; mem. Nat. Acad. of Sciences, A.A.A.S. (Vice-Pres. 1971), American Soc. of Pharmacology (Pres. 1965, Plenary Lecturer 1981), Int. Union of Pharmacology (Vice-Pres. 1969-72); Hon. D.Sc. (Philadelphia Coll. of Pharmacy and Science), Hon. D.Med. (Univ. of Zürich); Borden Award 1950, Abel Prize 1950, Univ. of Turku Memorial Medal 1972, and other awards and prizes. *Publications:* more than 180 papers on pharmacology, histochemistry, neurotropic factors and electron microscopy. *Leisure interests:* Sherlock Holmes, ornithology. *Address:* University of Pennsylvania School of Medicine, Department of Pharmacology, Philadelphia, Pa. 19104 (Office); 205 College Avenue, Swarthmore, Pa. 19081, U.S.A. (Home). *Telephone:* 215 898-8418 (Office); 215 544-4566 (Home).

KOFOD-SVENDSEN, Flemming, B.D.; Danish politician; b. 21 March 1944, Åkirkeby, Bornholm; s. of Poul Anker Svendsen and Helga Kofod Svendsen; m. Inger Margrethe Kofod-Svendsen 1971; three s. one d.; Chair. Christian People's Party 1979-; M.P. 1984-; Minister of Housing and Bldg. 1987-88. *Address:* c/o Ministry of Housing, Slotsholmsgade 12, DK-1216 Copenhagen K, Denmark.

KOFOED, Niels Anker; Danish farmer and politician; b. Feb. 1929, Bodilsker; m. Rita Mortensen 1957; one s. two d.; ed. Holley Royde Coll., Manchester Univ. and Tune Agric. School; farmer 1957-, also running machine station municipal politics 1958-73; mem. Folketinget (Venstre-Liberal Party) 1968-73, 1975-; mem. European Parl. 1975-, mem. Cttee. for Agric. 1978-; Minister of Agric. and Fisheries 1973-75, of Agric. 1978-79, 1982-86. *Address:* Knarregård, 3730 Nekso, Denmark. *Telephone:* 03 99 21 04.

KOFOED-HANSEN, Otto Mogens, DR.PHIL.; Danish architect; b. 25 April 1921, Frederiksberg; s. of Olaf M. Kofoed-Hansen and Anna Hansen; m. Anne B. Skovgaard 1946; one s. one d.; ed. Univ. of Copenhagen; Research Assoc. Niels Bohr Inst. 1946-54, Columbia Univ. New York 1954-55; Assoc. Prof. Columbia Univ. 1955; lecturer, Univ. of Copenhagen 1955-56; Head of Physics, Danish A.E.C. Risø 1956-68; Prof. Danish Tech. High School 1960-68; Sr. Physicist, CERN, Geneva 1968-76; Group Leader at Niels Bohr Inst. for Danish SPS-group to CERN, UA2 1976-87; now Prof. Risø Nat. Lab.; mem. Royal Danish Soc., Danish Acad. of Tech. Sciences; Gold Medal, Univ. of Copenhagen 1948; Helsinki Univ. Medal 1982. *Leisure interests:* stamp collecting, cooking. *Publications:* The Negotiators 1963, Råstoffer, mætning og velfærdseksplosion 1966; textbooks on radioactivity, energy production etc.; contribs. to scientific literature. *Address:* Risø National Laboratory, P.O. Box 49, 4000 Roskilde (Office); Forelvej 12, 3450 Allerød, Denmark (Home). *Telephone:* 45 2 37 12 12 (Office); 45 2 27 52 40 (Home).

KOH, Tommy Thong Bee, LL.M.; Singapore law teacher and diplomatist; b. 12 Nov. 1937, Singapore; s. of Koh Han Kok and Tsai Ying; m. Siew Aing 1967; two s.; ed. Univ. of Singapore, and Harvard and Cambridge Univs.; Asst. lecturer, Univ. of Singapore 1962-64, lecturer 1964-; Sub-Dean, Faculty of Law, Univ. of Singapore 1965-67, Vice-Dean 1967-68; Visiting lecturer, State Univ. of New York at Buffalo 1967; fmr. Legal Adviser to trade unions in Singapore and fmr. Sec. Inst. of Int. Affairs, Singapore; Amb. and Perm. Rep. of Singapore to UN 1968-71, concurrently High Commr. to Canada 1969-71; Assoc. Prof. of Law and Dean, Faculty of Law, Singapore Univ. 1971-74, 1978- (now no longer Dean); Amb. and Perm. Rep. to UN, High Commr. to Canada 1974-84; Amb. to U.S.A. 1984-; Pres. Third UN Law of the Sea Conf. (Chair. Singapore Del. to Conf.) 1981-82; Hon. LL.D. (Yale); Adrian Clarke Memorial Medal, Leow Chia Heng Prize, Public Service Star, Meritorious Service Medal, Wolfgang Friedman Prize, Jackson H. Ralston Prize, Annual Award of the Asia Soc., New York, 1985, Int. Service Award by Fletcher School of Law and Diplomacy, Tufts Univ., U.S.A. 1987, Jit Trainor Award for Distinction in the Conduct of Diplomacy, Georgetown Univ., U.S.A. 1987. *Publications:* law articles in Malaya Law Review and Malayan Law Journal. *Leisure interests:* sport, reading, music. *Address:* Singapore Embassy, 1824 R Street N.W., Washington, D.C. 20009, U.S.A.

KOHL, Helmut, DR.PHIL.; German politician; b. 3 April 1930, Ludwigshafen; s. of Hans and Cecilie Kohl; m. Hannelore Renner 1960; two s.; ed. Univs. of Frankfurt and Heidelberg; Mem. of man. of an industrial union 1959; Chair. Christian Democrat Party (CDU), Rhineland-Palatinate 1966–73, Deputy Chair. CDU Deutschlands 1969–73, Chair. 1973–; Minister-Pres. Rhineland-Palatinate 1969–76; Leader of the Opposition in the Bundestag 1976–82; Fed. Chancellor, Fed. Repub. of Germany Oct. 1982–; Grosses Bundesverdienstkreuz 1970, Grosskreuz Verdientstorden 1979. *Address:* 6700 Ludwigshafen/Rhein, Marbacher Strasse 11, Federal Republic of Germany.

KOHLER, Foy D., B.S.; American diplomatist; b. 15 Feb. 1908, Oakwood, Ohio; s. of Leander David and Myrtle McClure Kohler; m. Phyllis Penn 1935; ed. Toledo and Ohio State Univs.; joined Foreign Service 1931; Vice-Consul, Windsor (Canada) 1932, Bucharest 1933–35, Belgrade 1935; Legation Sec. and Vice-Consul Bucharest 1935–36, Athens 1936–41, Cairo 1941; Specialist Dept. of State 1941–44, Asst. Chief Div. of Near Eastern Affairs 1944–45; London Embassy and Adviser to U.S. Del. UNRRA Council 1944; Political and Liaison Officer to U.S. Del. San Francisco Conf. 1945; Sec.-Gen. U.S. Greek Elections Mission 1945–46; studies at Cornell Univ. and Nat. War Coll. 1946; 1st Sec. Moscow 1947, Counsellor 1948, Minister 1948; Chief Int. Broadcasting Div. Dept. of State 1949; Dir. Voice of America 1949–52; Counsellor Ankara 1953–56; seconded to Int. Co-operation Admin. (ICA) 1956–58; Deputy Asst. Sec. of State 1958–59, Asst. Sec. of State (European Affairs) 1959–62; Amb to U.S.S.R. 1962–66; Deputy Under Sec. of State 1966–68; Prof., Univ. of Miami 1968–78; mem. Bd. Int. Broadcasting 1974–78; Consultant 1978–82; Sr. Assoc. Advanced Int. Studies Inst., Washington, D.C. 1978–85; Consultant, Dept. of State 1968–82; D.Hum. (Ohio State), LL.D. (Univ. of Toledo, Ohio). *Publications:* Understanding the Russians—A Citizen's Primer 1970, Co-author Science and Technology as an Instrument of Soviet Policy 1972, Convergence of Communism and Capitalism 1973, Soviet Strategy for the 1970s: From Cold War to Peaceful Coexistence 1973, The Role of Nuclear Forces in Current Soviet Strategy 1974, The Soviet Union—Yesterday, Today, Tomorrow 1975, Custine's Eternal Russia 1976, War Survival in Soviet Strategy—U.S.S.R. Civil Defence (foreword) 1976, SALT II: How Not to Negotiate with the Russians 1979, Co-Ed. Soviet World Outlook (monthly) 1976–85. *Leisure interests:* golf, swimming. *Address:* Waterford Tower Apt. 1102, 605 South U.S. Highway 1, Juno Beach, Fla. 33408, U.S.A. *Telephone:* (407) 627-2344.

KOHLMEY, Gunther, DR.RER.POL.; German professor of economics; b. 27 July 1913, Berlin; m. Gerda Dörfel 1951; one d.; ed. Berlin and Freiburg im Breisgau; library asst., Univ. of Berlin 1937–39, Prof. of Econs. 1947; Dean of Econ. Faculty, Acad. of Admin. 1947–53; Dir. of Econ. Inst., Acad. of Sciences, G.D.R. 1953–58, Head of Staff Int. Econs. Dept. 1958–73, Chair. Nat. Cttee. of Econ. Sciences 1979–81; mem. Acad. of Sciences 1964; Hon. mem. Hungarian Acad. of Sciences 1979; Dr. h.c. 1978; Nat. Prize 1955; Golden State Awards 1978, 1983. *Publications include:* several papers for Int. Econ. Asscn. and workshops of East-West Steering Cttee.; (in German) The Democratic World Market 1954, The Monetary System of G.D.R. 1958, Karl Marx's Theory of International Values 1962, National Productivity, Dynamic Productions, International Division of Labour 1965, Planning as Regulation and Control 1968, Socialization and Integration 1973, Ed. and co-translator Production of Commodities by Means of Commodities (P. Sraffa) 1968. *Leisure interests:* literature, fine arts. *Address:* Akademie der Wissenschaften DDR, Prenzlauer Promenade 149, 1100 Berlin (Office); Kl. Homeyerstrasse 2a, DDR 1110, German Democratic Republic (Home).

KOHN, Walter, PH.D.; American professor of physics; b. 9 March 1923, Vienna, Austria; s. of Solomon Kohn and Gusti Rappaport; m. 1st Lois Mary Adams 1948 (divorced), three d.; 2nd Mara Schiff 1978; ed. Toronto and Harvard Univs.; served with Canadian Infantry 1944–45; Instructor Harvard Univ. 1948–50; Asst. Prof., Assoc. Prof., then Prof., Carnegie Inst. of Tech. 1950–59; Prof. Univ. of Calif. at San Diego 1960–79, Chair. Dept. of Physics 1961–63, Dir. Inst. for Theoretical Physics July 1979–84; Prof. of Physics, Univ. of Calif. at Santa Barbara 1984–; Visiting Prof., Univs. of Mich. and Pa. 1957–58, Imperial Coll. of Science and Tech. London 1960; Nat. Research Council Fellow, Inst. of Theoretical Physics, Copenhagen 1951–52; Guggenheim Fellow and Visiting Prof. Ecole Normale Supérieure Paris 1963–64; Nat. Science Foundation Sr. Postdoctoral Fellow Univ. of Paris 1967; Councillor-at-Large, American Physical Soc. 1968–72; Visiting Prof. Hebrew Univ., Jerusalem 1970; Fellow American Acad. of Arts and Sciences; mem. N.A.S.; Hon. LL.D. (Toronto); Hon. D.Sc. (Univ. of Paris) 1980, (Queen's Univ., Canada) 1986, Hon. D.Phil. (Brandeis Univ.) 1981; (Hebrew Univ. of Jerusalem) 1981; Oliver E. Buckley Prize in Solid State Physics 1960; Davisson-Germer Prize in Surface Physics 1977. *Publications:* 140 scientific articles 1945–85. *Leisure interests:* flute, reading, sports. *Address:* Dept. of Physics, University of California, Santa Barbara, Calif. 93105, U.S.A. *Telephone:* (805) 961-2280.

KOHONEN, Teuvo Kalevi, DR.ENG.; Finnish physicist; b. 11 July 1934, Lauritsala; s. of Väinö Kohonen and Tyyne E. Koivunen; m. Elvi Anneli Trast 1959; two s. two d.; ed. Helsinki Univ. of Tech.; Teaching Asst. in Physics, Helsinki Univ. of Tech. 1957–59; Research Assoc. Finnish Atomic Energy Comm. 1959–62; Asst. Prof. in Physics, Helsinki Univ. of Tech. 1963–65, Prof. of Tech. Physics 1965–; on leave as Visiting Prof. Univ. of Washington, Seattle 1968–69; Research Prof. Acad. of Finland 1975–78, 1980–; Commdr. Order of Lion of Finland; Kt., Order of White Rose of Finland; Eemil Aaltonen Prize 1983; Cultural Prize, Finnish Commercial TV (MTV) 1984. *Publications:* Digital Circuits and Devices 1972, Associative Memory: A System Theoretical Approach 1977, Content-Addressable Memories 1982, Self-Organization and Associative Memory 1984. *Leisure interests:* philosophy of music, literature. *Address:* Helsinki University of Technology, Laboratory of Computer and Information Science, Rakentajanaukio 2 C, 02150 Espoo, Finland. *Telephone:* 358-0-4513268.

KOIRALA, Matrika Prasad; Nepalese politician and diplomatist; b. 1 Jan. 1912; ed. Banares and Patna, India; fmr. Pres. Nepali Congress Party; Prime Minister and Minister of Gen. Admin. and Foreign Affairs 1951–52, 1953–55; nominated to Upper House of Parl.; Amb. to U.S. 1962–64; Perm. Rep. to UN 1962–64; now in exile in India.

KOITER, Warner Tjardus; Netherlands professor of engineering; b. 16 June 1914, Amsterdam; s. of Klaas Koiter and Jacoba U.M. Greidanus; m. Louise Clara Spits 1939; two s. two d.; ed. Univ. of Tech., Delft; with Nat. Aeronautical Research Inst., Amsterdam 1936–38; Govt. Patent office 1938–39; Dept. of Civil Aviation 1939–49; Prof. of Eng. Mechanics, Delft Univ. of Tech. 1949–79, Prof. Emer. 1979–; Pres. Int. Union of Theoretical and Applied Mechanics 1968–72; mem. Royal Netherlands Acad. of Sciences 1959, Deutsche Akad. der Naturforscher Leopoldina 1976; Foreign hon. mem. American Acad. Arts and Sciences 1974; Foreign Assoc., Nat. Acad. of Engineering, Washington 1977; Hon. mem. American Soc. of Mechanical Engineers 1980; Foreign Assoc. Acad. des Sciences, Paris 1981; Foreign mem. Istituto Lombardo, Accad. di Scienze e lettere, Milan 1981, Acad. dei Lincei, Rome 1988; Foreign mem. Royal Soc. London 1982; Hon. D.Sc. (Univ. of Leicester) 1969, (Univ. of Glasgow) 1978, (Ruhr Univ., Bochum) 1978, (Univ. of Ghent) 1979, (Univ. of Liège) 1986; Von Kármán Medal ASCE 1965; Timoshenko Medal ASME 1968; Modesto Panetti Prize 1971, Fairchild Distinguished Scholar, Calif. Inst. of Tech. 1973–74. *Publications:* On the Stability of Elastic Equilibrium 1945, many papers on elasticity, plasticity, elastic stability and theory of thin shells. *Leisure interests:* travel, hiking, reading. *Address:* Laboratory of Engineering Mechanics, Mekelweg 2, Delft (Office); Charlotte de Bourbon Straat 14, Delft, Netherlands. (Home). *Telephone:* 781523 (Office); 570427 (Home).

KOIVISTO, Mauno Henrik, PH.D.; Finnish politician; b. 25 Nov. 1923, Turku; s. of Juho and Hymni Sofia (née Eskola) Koivisto; m. Taimi Tellervo Kankaanranta 1952; one d.; ed. Turku University; Man. Dir. Helsinki Workers' Savings Bank 1959–67; Gov. Bank of Finland 1968–82; Minister of Finance 1966–67; Prime Minister 1968–70, 1979–82; Minister of Finance and Deputy Prime Minister Feb.-Sept. 1972; Pres. of Finland Jan. 1982–; Chair. Bd. of Postipankki 1970–82, Mortgage Bank of Finland Oy 1971–82, Bd. of Admin. of Co-operative Soc. ELANTO 1966–82; mem. Bd. of Admin. of Co-operative Union KK 1964–82; Gov. for Finland in the Int. Bank for Reconstruction and Devt. 1966–69; Gov. for Finland IMF 1970–79; Order of Lenin 1983, Hon. K.C.M.G. 1984 and numerous other decorations. *Publications:* three books on econs. and social politics, Landmarks—Finland in the World 1985. *Address:* Presidential Palace, Helsinki, Finland.

KOJIMA, Kiyoshi, PH.D.; Japanese economist; b. 22 May 1920, Nagoya; m. Keiko Kojima 1947; ed. Tokyo Univ. of Commerce and Econs., Leeds Univ. (U.K.) and Princeton Univ. (U.S.A.); Asst. Prof. of Int. Econs., Hitotsubashi Univ. 1945–60, Prof. 1960–84; Secr. (Dir.) for UN Conf. on Trade and Devt. 1963; Prof. Int. Christian Univ. 1984–; mem. Science Council of Japan 1985–; British Council Scholarship 1952–53, Rockefeller Foundation Fellowship 1953–55. *Publications:* (in Japanese): Theory of Foreign Trade 1950, Japan's Economic Development and Trade 1958, Japan in Trade Expansion for Developing Countries 1964 (in English), Japan and a Pacific Free Trade Area 1971, Japan and a New World Economic Order 1977, Direct Foreign Investment 1978, Japanese and American Direct Investment in Asia 1985; Ed. Papers and Proceedings of a Conference on Pacific Trade and Development 1968, 1969, 1973; also articles in English on int. trade. *Leisure interests:* golf, Noh (Utai). *Address:* 3-24-10 Maehara-cho, Koganei-shi, Tokyo, Japan. *Telephone:* 0423-81-1041.

KOK, Wim; Netherlands politician; b. 1938; ed. Netherlands School of Int. Business; Advisor to Bldg. Workers Union 1961–67, Sec. 1967–69; mem. Exec. Bd. of Netherlands Fed. of Trade Unions 1969–73, Chair. (later renamed Confed. Netherlands Trade Unions Movt.) 1973–85; Chair., European Trade Union Confed. 1979–82; mem. Parl. 1986–, Chair. Labour Party Parl. 1986–. *Address:* Partij van de Arbeid, Nicolaas Witsen Kade 30, 1017 ZT Amsterdam, Netherlands.

KOL, Moshe; Israeli educator and politician; b. 28 May 1911, Pinsk, Poland; s. of Mordechai and Judith Kolodny; m. Keta Muskat 1939; three d.; ed. Hebrew Secondary School, Pinsk and Hebrew Univ. Jerusalem; Co-Founder Hanoar Hazioni (Zionist Youth) movement in Poland and its Rep. on Cen. Cttee. of Zionist Org. in Poland; came to Israel and joined

Hamefales pioneer group in Kfar Saba 1932; Del. to all Zionist Congresses 1933-; mem. Histadrut Exec. 1941-46; mem. Jewish Agency Exec. and Head of its Youth Aliya Dept. 1946-66; mem. Provisional State Council 1948, and Chair. of its Foreign Affairs Cttee.; mem. Knesset (Parl.) 1949-66; Min. of Devt. and of Tourism 1966-69, of Tourism 1969-77; Co-Founder (in Israel), Oved Hazioni (Zionist Workers') Movement, World Confed. of Gen. Zionists; Vice-Pres. Int. Fed. of Children's Communities, Liberal Int.; Chair. Ind. Liberal Party, Liberal Youth Villages of Yesodoth, Masuah Inst. for Teaching the Holocaust Period, Dr. Foerder Liberal Inst. in Kibbutz Tel Izchak, Int. Cultural Cen. for Youth in Jerusalem; D. Hum. Litt. h.c. (The Jewish Theological Seminary of America); Hon. Treas. Israel Archeological Soc.; mem. Bd. of Govs. Hebrew Univ., Jerusalem, and Tel Aviv Univ., World Council of United Synagogues/Conservative World Movt.; Fellow Hebrew Union Coll. in Cincinnati; Hon. Citizen of Safed, Netanya, Daliat El Carmiel, Fasuta. *Publications:* Arichim (in Hebrew), Youth Aliya (in English and Hebrew), Paths in Education and Rehabilitation (in Hebrew), Teachers and Friends (in Hebrew), Directions in Zionism and Liberalism (in Hebrew), Mentors and Friends (in English), Holocaust and Revival (in Hebrew), Liberalism and Zionism (in Spanish), War in Lebanon (in Hebrew). *Address:* 10 Jabotinsky Street, Jerusalem, Israel. *Telephone:* 02-669788.

KOLAJA, Jiri, M.A., PH.D.; American sociologist; b. Oct. 1919, Czechoslovakia; m. Beata Kolaja; two c.; ed. Charles Univ. Prague, Masaryk Univ. Brno, Univ. of Chicago and Cornell Univ.; Instructor in Visual Communication, Ill. Inst. of Tech. 1950-51; Coder and research asst. Russian Research Center, Harvard Univ. 1951-52; Graduate Asst. N.Y. State School of Industrial and Labour Relations, Cornell Univ. 1952-53; Asst. Prof. to Prof. of Sociology, Talladega Coll. Ala. 1954-58; Asst. Prof. Univ. of Ky. 1958-66; Prof. of Sociology, McMaster Univ., Hamilton, Ont. 1966; mem. Dept. of Sociology, West Va. Univ. 1970-. *Publications include:* A Polish Factory: A Case Study of Workers' Participation in Decision Making 1960, Workers' Council: The Yugoslav Experience 1965, Social System and Time and Space 1969, Socialism in Eastern Europe (ed. with M. S. Das) 1984. *Address:* 109 Deahl Hall, Department of Sociology and Anthropology, West Virginia University, Morgantown, West Va. 26505; 674 Manor Place, Morgantown, West Va. 26505, U.S.A. *Telephone:* 304-599-5789 (Home).

KOŁAKOWSKI, Leszek, DR. PHIL., F.B.A.; Polish professor of philosophy; b. 23 Oct. 1927, Radom; s. of Jerzy and Lucyna (née Pietrusiewicz) Kołakowski; m. Tamara Dynenson 1949; one d.; ed. Univs. of Łódź and Warsaw; Asst. (logic), Łódź Univ. 1947-49; Asst. Warsaw Univ. 1950-54, Chair. Section of History of Philosophy 1959-68 (expelled by Govt. for political reasons); Visiting Prof. McGill Univ., Montreal 1968-69; Prof. Univ. of Calif., Berkeley 1969-70; Sr. Research Fellow, All Souls Coll., Oxford 1970-; Prof. Yale Univ. 1975, Univ. of Chicago 1981-; several prizes including Erasmus Prize and McArthur Foundation Prize 1983. *Publications:* Chrétiens sans église 1968, Positivist Philosophy 1970, Die Gegenwärtigkeit des Mythos 1973, Husserl and the Search for Certitude 1975, Leben trotz Geschichte 1977, Main Currents of Marxism 1978, Religion 1982, Metaphysical Horror 1988; three vols. of short stories in Polish and three plays. *Address:* 77 Hamilton Road, Oxford, OX2 7QA, England.

KOLAR, Jiri; French (fmrly. Czech) writer; b. 24 Sept. 1914, Protivin, Czechoslovakia; s. of Frantisek Kolar and Anna (née Simakova) Kolar; m. Bela Helclova 1949; first exhbn. of collages, Prague 1937; founding mem. SKUPINA (Group) 42 with fellow writers and artists; arrested and imprisoned 1953; weekly diary in collages, Tydenik 1967-70; exhbns. Kassel 1968, Brasilia 1969, Osaka 1970, New York 1975, 1985, Paris 1981; French nationality 1984; Collages 1952-82 at Albermarle Gallery, London 1987; Gottfried von Herder Award 1971. *Publications:* Krestny List (poems) 1941, Limb a Jine Basne (poems) 1945, Sedm Kantat (poems) 1945, Dny v Roce (poems) 1947, Mistr Sun o Basnickem Umeni 1956, Novy Epiktet 1957, Mor v Athenach 1958, Basne Ticha (poems) 1961, Navod k Upotrebeni (poems) 1967, Slovnik Metod 1983, Odpovedi 1984, Prometheova Jatra 1985, etc.; many titles also published in French. *Address:* 61 rue Olivier-Métra, 75020 Paris, France. *Telephone:* 43.66.01.55.

KOLB, Hans Werner; German industrialist; b. 23 Aug. 1920, Mainz; ed. Univs. of Frankfurt and Giessen; Chair. Supervisory Bd. Buderus Aktiengesellschaft, Wetzlar; Chair. of Bd., Krauss-Maffei AG, München-Allach. *Leisure interests:* literature, sport. *Address:* Buderus Aktiengesellschaft, 6330 Wetzlar, Federal Republic of Germany. *Telephone:* 06441-4031.

KOLBIN, Genadiy Vasilevich; Soviet party official; b. 1927; ed. Urals Polytechnic; mem. CPSU 1954-; technician, engineer 1942-59; Second Sec., First Sec. Regional Cttee., Second Sec., First Sec. of Nizhetalgisk City Cttee. 1959-70; Second Sec. of Sverdlovsk Dist. Cttee. CPSU 1971-75; mem. Second Sec. of Politburo of Cen. Cttee., Georgian CP 1975-; Deputy to Supreme Soviet of Georgian S.S.R. 1975-; mem. Cen. Cttee. Georgian CP 1976-; cand. mem. Cen. Cttee. CPSU, mem. 1976-; First Sec. Kazakh CP 1986-; Deputy to U.S.S.R. Supreme Soviet; Order of Lenin 1977. *Address:* Central Committee of the Georgian Communist Party, Tbilisi, Georgian S.S.R., U.S.S.R.

KOLDUNOV, Chief Marshal Aleksandr Ivanovich; Soviet air force officer; b. 20 Sept. 1923, Moshchinovo, Smolensk Oblast; joined CPSU 1944; served in Soviet army 1941-; graduated Kachinsky Mil. Aviation Acad. 1943, Mil. Aviation Acad. 1952, Mil. Acad. of Gen. Staff 1960; fought on S.W. and Third Ukrainian Fronts 1943-45; flew 358 missions, involved in 96 air battles and personally shot down 46 enemy aircraft; Commdr. of Air Regt., then Deputy Commdr. of Aviation, then Commdr., Baku Dist.; First Deputy Commdr., then Commdr. of air defence forces, Baku Dist. 1945-70; Chief of Air Defence Forces, Moscow Dist. 1970-75; First Deputy C.-in-C. U.S.S.R. Air Defence Forces 1975-78, C.-in-C. 1978-87; rank of Chief Marshal of Aviation 1984; Cand. mem. Cen. Cttee. CPSU 1971-81, mem. 1981-; Deputy to Supreme Soviet 1974-; Deputy Minister of Defence 1978-87; Gen. Inspector, U.S.S.R. Ministry of Defence Inspectorate 1987-; Order of Lenin, Order of the Red Banner (six times), Aleksandr Nevsky Order, Hero of the Soviet Union (twice) and other decorations. *Address:* c/o Ministry of Defence, Moscow, U.S.S.R.

KOLESNIKOV, Vladislav Grigoryevich, CAND.TECH.SC.; Soviet politician; b. 1925; ed. Voronezh Polytechnic; work in arms factory 1941-48; engineer, Head of Lab. in radio parts factory, Voronezh 1948-52; mem. CPSU 1961-; chief tech. engineer 1954-67, Factory Dir. 1967-69; Gen. Dir. Elektronika factory-chain 1969-71; U.S.S.R. First Deputy Minister of Electronics Industry 1971-85, Minister 1985-; corresp. mem. U.S.S.R. Acad. of Sciences 1984-; Deputy to U.S.S.R. Supreme Soviet; Lenin Prize 1966, U.S.S.R. State Prize 1984; Hero of Socialist Labour 1975. *Address:* The Kremlin, Moscow, U.S.S.R.

KOLFF, Willem Johan, M.D., PH.D.; American professor of surgery; b. 14 Feb. 1911, Leiden, Netherlands; s. of Jacob and Adriana Pieternella Kolff; m. Janke Cornelia Huidekoper 1937; four s. one d.; ed. Univs. of Leiden and Groningen; Asst. Pathological Anatomy, Univ. of Leiden 1934-36; Asst. Medical Dept. Univ. of Groningen 1938-41; Head, Medical Dept., Municipal Hosp., Kampen 1941-50; Privaat Docent, Univ. of Leiden Medical School 1949-51; mem. of staff, Research Div., Cleveland Clinic Foundation 1950-63; Asst. Prof., later Prof. of Clinical Investigation, Educ. Foundation of Cleveland Clinic Foundation 1950-67; mem. staff, Surgical Div., Cleveland Clinic Foundation 1958-67, Head, Dept. of Artificial Organs 1958-67, Scientific Dir. Artificial Organs Program 1966-67; Prof. of Surgery, Head of Div. of Artificial Organs, Univ. of Utah Coll. of Medicine 1967-86, Distinguished Prof. of Medicine and Surgery 1982-, also Research Prof. of Eng., Prof. of Internal Medicine Oct. 1981-; Hon. mem. Peruvian Urological Soc., Greek Soc. of Cardiology, Sociedad Médica de Santiago, Austrian Soc. for Nephrology, Fundacion Favaloro, Buenos Aires, Argentina 1981-; developed artificial kidney for clinical use; Foreign mem. Hollandsch Maatschappij der Wetenschappen; Hon. D.Sc. (Allegheny Coll.) 1960, (Tulane Univ.) 1975, (City Univ. New York) 1982, (Temple, Univ. Philadelphia) 1983, (Univ. of Utah) 1983; Hon. M.D. (Rostock) 1975, (Univ. of L'Aquila, Italy) 1981, (Univ. of Bologna) 1983; Commdr. Order of Orange-Nassau, Orden de Mayo al Mérito en el Grado de Gran Oficial (Argentina) 1974; numerous medals, awards and prizes from several countries including Francis Amory Award (American Acad. of Arts and Sciences) 1948, Cameron Prize (Univ. Edinburgh) 1964, Gairdner Prize (Gairdner Foundation, Toronto) 1966, Gold Medal (Netherlands Surgical Soc.) 1970, Benjamin Franklin Fellow (Royal Soc. of Arts, London) 1972, Leo Harvey Prize (Technion Inst. of Israel) 1972, Ray C. Fish Award and Medal Tex. Heart Inst. 1975, Senior U.S. Scientist Award, Alexander von Humboldt Foundation 1978, Gewerbevereins Wilhelm-Exner Award (Austria) 1980, American Medical Assen.'s Scientific Achievement Award for Outstanding Work 1982, Japan Prize, Science and Tech. Foundation of Japan 1986, ANNA Hon. mem. 1987, First Jean Hamburger Award in Clinical Nephrology, Int. Soc. of Nephrology 1987. *Publications:* De Kunstmatige Nier 1946, New Ways of Treating Uraemia 1947; over 600 articles in learned journals and chapters in books. *Leisure interests:* bird-watching, hiking, camping. *Address:* Division of Artificial Organs, Building 535, University of Utah, Salt Lake City, Utah 84112 (Office); 2894 Crestview Drive, Salt Lake City, Utah 84108, U.S.A. (Home). *Telephone:* (801) 581-6296 (Office); (801) 582-3056 (Home).

KOLINGBA, Gen. André; Central African Republic army officer and politician; fmr. Chief of Staff; overthrew Pres. David Dacko (q.v.) in coup Sept. 1981; Pres. Mil. Cttee. for Nat. Recovery 1981-85; Pres. of Cen. African Repub. Sept. 1981-, Minister of Defence and of War Veterans 1981-83, 1984-85, Prime Minister and Minister of Defence and War Veterans Oct. 1985-, of War Veterans Jan. 1987-. *Address:* Présidence de la République, Bangui, Central African Republic.

KOLIŠEVSKI, Lazar; Yugoslav politician; b. 12 Feb. 1914; fmr. metal worker; mem. Yugoslav Communist Party (now League of Communists) 1935-; partisan, Sec. Prov. Cttee. of CP of Macedonia, and leader of Prov. Mil. Staff 1941; imprisoned 1941-44; Pres. Govt. of Macedonia 1945; Sec. Cen. Cttee. of League of Communists of Macedonia until 1963; mem. Exec. Cttee. Cen. Cttee. of League of Communists of Yugoslavia 1952-; fmr. Pres. Macedonian Ass. and Chair. Socialist Alliance of Working People of Macedonia; Chair. Cen. Bd. of Socialist Alliance of Working People of Yugoslavia 1963-67; mem. Council of Federation 1967-72, 1984-; mem. Collective Presidency of Yugoslavia 1972-84, Vice-Pres. 1979-80, Pres. 4-16 May 1980. *Address:* Sobranie na SRM 320 no. 1, Skopje, Yugoslavia.

KOLLE GRØNDAHL, Kirsti; Norwegian politician; b. 1 Sept. 1943, Oslo; m.; fmr. schoolteacher; mem. Røyken Municipal Council and Municipal

Exec. Bd. 1972-77; elected to Storting 1977, mem. Standing Cttee. on Foreign Affairs and the Constitution 1985-86; Minister of Church and Educ. 1986-88, of Devt. Co-operation 1988-. *Address:* Ministry of Development Co-operation, 8142 Dep., 0033 Oslo 1, Norway. *Telephone:* (2) 31-40-55.

KOLLEK, Theodore (Teddy); Israeli public administrator; b. 27 May 1911, Vienna; s. of S. Alfred and Margaret Fleischer Kollek; m. Tamar Schwartz 1937; one s. one d.; ed. secondary school, Vienna; founder mem. Kibbutz Ein Gev 1937; Political Dept. Jewish Agency for Palestine 1940; established Jewish Agency office, Istanbul, for contact with Jewish underground in Europe 1942; Mission to U.S.A. for Haganah 1947-48; Head of U.S. Div., Israel Foreign Ministry 1950; Minister, Washington 1951-52; Dir.-Gen. of Prime Minister's Office, Jerusalem 1952-65; Chair. Israel Govt. Tourist Corpn. 1955-65; Chair. Israel Govt. Water Desalination Joint Project with U.S. Govt. 1964-66; Chair. Bd. of Govs. Israel Museum, Jerusalem 1964-, Africa-Israel Investment Co. Ltd. 1964-65; Mayor of Jerusalem 1965-; Hon. Doctorate (Hebrew Univ., Jerusalem) 1977, (Univ. of Notre Dame) 1981, (Brown Univ.) 1983, (Jewish Theological Seminary, Harvard Univ.) 1984, (Ben Gurion Univ.) 1985; Rothschild Medal for Public Service 1975, Bublick Prize of the Hebrew Univ. 1975, Romano Guardini Prize 1976, Peace Prize of the German Book Publishers Asscn. *Publications:* Jerusalem: A History of Forty Centuries (Co-Author), Pilgrims to the Holy Land 1970 (Co-Author), For Jerusalem (autobiography) 1978. *Leisure interests:* archaeology, reading, collecting ancient maps and books on Holy Land. *Address:* 6 Rashba Street, Rechavia, Jerusalem, Israel (Home). *Telephone:* 232251 (Office); 633147 (Home).

KOLLER, Arnold; Swiss politician; fmr. univ. prof.; mem. Bundesrat (Fed. Council) Dec. 1986-, Head of Fed. Mil. (Defence) Dept. 1986-89, Vice-Pres. and Head Fed. Dept. of Justice and Police Feb. 1989-; Christian Democratic Party. *Address:* Federal Department of Justice and Police, Bundeshaus-West, 3003 Berne, Switzerland.

KOLLER, Herbert Josef, IUR.D.; Austrian business executive; b. 1911, Wösendorf; m. Dr. Eva Koller 1940; one s.; ed. elementary and secondary schools, Melk, and Univ. of Vienna; law practice and business appointments 1935-44; Mil. Service and P.O.W. 1944-47; Vereinigte Österreichische Eisen- und Stahlwerke (Vöest) 1948-77; Works Man., Hütte Krems 1955-61; Gen. Man. and Chair. of Bd. of Dirs., Vöest 1961-77; First Vice-Pres. of the Austrian Nationalbank, Vienna 1981-. *Address:* P.O. Box 61, A-1011 Vienna, Austria. *Telephone:* (0222) 43-60-901.

KOLLIAS, Konstantinos V.; Greek politician; b. 1901; ed. Athens Univ.; Prosecutor, Court of Appeal 1945-46; Vice-Prosecutor, Supreme Court 1946-62; Prosecutor, Supreme Court, Athens 1962-68; Prime Minister April-Dec. 1967. *Address:* 124 Vassil. Sophias Street, Ampelokipi, Athens, Greece.

KOLLO, René; German opera singer; b. 20 Nov. 1937, Berlin; s. of Willi and Marie-Louise Kollodzieyski; m. 1st Dorthe Larsen 1967; m. 2nd Beatrice Bouquet 1982; one d.; began career with Staatstheater, Brunswick 1965; First Tenor, Deutsche Oper am Rhein 1967-71; guest appearances with numerous leading opera cos. and at annual Bayreuth Wagner festival; Bundesverdienstkreuz. *Performances include:* The Flying Dutchman 1969, 1970, Lohengrin 1971, Die Meistersinger von Nürnberg 1973, 1974, Parsifal 1975, Siegfried 1976, 1977, Tristan (Zürich) 1980, (Bayreuth) 1981. *Publication:* Imre Fabian im Gespräch mit René Kollo 1982. *Leisure interests:* sailing, tennis, flying. *Address:* Wilhelmstrasse 4, 8000 Munich 40, Federal Republic of Germany. *Telephone:* (089) 39 54 50.

KOLMOGOROV, Georgiy Dmitriyevich; Soviet politician; b. 1929; mem. C.P.S.U. 1952-; started career as tractor driver; rose from foreman to dir. in no. of plants; Dr. Tech.; First Deputy Minister of Manufacture of Means of Communication 1975-; Chair. USSR State Cttee. for Standards Jan. 1984-; Deputy to U.S.S.R. Supreme Soviet; cand. mem. CPSU Cen. Cttee. 1986-; State Prize. *Address:* The Kremlin, Moscow, U.S.S.R.

KOŁODZIEJ, Emil, LL.M.; Polish politician; b. 2 Jan. 1917, Futoma, Rzeszów Voivodship; s. of Józef and Zofia Kołodziej; m. Lidia Prokopiak 1948; two d.; ed. Univs. of Lwów and Warsaw; activist of Peasant Party 1936-39; soldier in the Peasant Battalions during the occupation; held exec. positions, Cen. Bd. of Agricultural Co-operatives, Warsaw 1945-57; mem. Cen. Cttee. United Peasant Party (ZSL) 1959-84, mem. Presidium 1969-81, Sec. 1969-71; Deputy to Seym 1969-; Sec. ZSL Deputies' Club; Deputy Minister of Home Trade 1957-69; Minister of Food Industry and Purchases 1971-80; mem. Council of State 1980-85; Order of Banner of Labour (1st and 2nd Class), Commdr. and Knight's Cross, Order of Polonia Restituta, Gold Cross of Merit. *Address:* Kancelaria Sejmu PRL, ul. Wiejska 4/6, 00-489 Warsaw, Poland.

KOLOMIETS, Yuriy Afanasiyevich; Soviet politician; b. 1925; ed. Umansk Agric. Inst.; served in Soviet Army 1944-48; mem. CPSU 1953-; collective-farm agronomist 1954-59; party work, Cherkassk Dist. 1959-63; Head Agric. Section of Cherkassk Dist. Cttee. of Ukrainian CP 1963-65, Sec. 1965-70; Deputy Minister, First Deputy Minister of Agric. for Ukrainian S.S.R. 1970-77, Minister of State Farms 1977-79; First Deputy Pres. of Gosplan 1979-80; First Deputy Pres. Council of Ukrainian S.S.R. 1980-

86, 1986-; Pres. of Gosagroprom of Ukrainian S.S.R. 1986-; cand. mem. of CPSU Cen. Cttee. 1981-; Deputy to U.S.S.R. Supreme Soviet. *Address:* Gosagroprom of Ukrainian S.S.R., Kiev, Ukraine, U.S.S.R.

KOLOSOV, Mikhail Nikolayevich; Soviet chemist; b. 11 May 1927, Kursk; ed. Lomonosov Inst. of Fine Chemical Tech.; Postgraduate Lomonosov Inst. of Fine Chemical Tech. 1948-51; Research Assoc. Inst. of Biological and Medical Chem., U.S.S.R. Acad. of Medical Sciences 1951-59; Inst. of Chem. of Natural Compounds, U.S.S.R. Acad. of Sciences 1959-; Corresp. mem. U.S.S.R. Acad. of Sciences 1966-, now mem.; mem. CPSU 1963-. *Publications:* Works on chemistry of biopolymers and other natural compounds including The Chemistry of Antibiotics (co-author) 1961. [*Deceased.*]

KOLOTYRKIN, Yakov Mikhailovich; Soviet physical chemist; b. 14 Nov. 1910, Zanino Yartsevsky District, Smolensk region; s. of Mikhail and Galina Sysoevna Kolotyrkin; m. Galina Elena Konstantinovna Goun 1947; two s. two d.; ed. Moscow Univ.; Research Assoc., Karpov Physico-Chemical Inst. 1938-, Dir. 1957-; mem. CPSU 1940-; Dr. Sc. (Chem.) Prof. 1954; Corresp. mem. U.S.S.R. Acad. of Sciences 1966-70, Academician 1970-; Hon D.Sc. (Eötvös Univ., Budapest) 1985; hon. mem., Saxony Acad. of Sciences; Corresp. mem., Yugoslav Acad. of Sciences; Badge of Honour 1953, Order of Lenin (three times), Order of the Red Banner of Labour 1970, Hero of Socialist Labour and numerous medals. *Address:* Karpov Institute of Physical Chemistry, ul. Obukha 10, 107120, Moscow B-120, U.S.S.R. *Telephone:* 297-32-57.

KOLOZSVÁRI-GRANDPIERRE, Emil, D.PHIL.; Hungarian novelist; b. 15 Jan. 1907, Kolozsvár; s. of the late Emil Grandpierre and Janka Krassowsky; m. Magda Szegö 1946 (died 1981); one d.; ed. secondary school in Transylvania, Pécs Univ.; Publisher's reader 1941-44; Dir. of literature dept. of Hungarian Radio 1946-49; József Attila Literary Prize 1964, 1975, Labour Order of Merit (gold) 1976, Kossuth Prize 1980. *Publications:* A Rosta, Dr. Csibráky szerelmei, A Nagy Ember, Alvajárók, A sárgavirágos leány, Tegnap, Szabadság, Lófö és kora, Az értelem dicsérete, Lelkifinomságok, Mérlegen, A Csodafurulya, A Csillagszemü, A Törökfejes kopja, Elmés mulatságok, A büvös kaptafa, A tisztesség keresztje, Foltonfolt Királyfi, A boldogtalanság müvészete, Legendák nyomában, Csinnadári, Gyalogtündér, Egy szereplö visszatér, Párbeszéd a Sorssal, A lóvátett sárkány, Csendes rév a háztetön, A Burok, Aquincumi Vénusz, Változatok hegedüre, Arcok napfényben, Utazás a valóság körül, Dráma félvállról, Nök apróban, Szellemi Galeri, Keresztben az uton, Az utolsó hullám, Harmatcseppek, Táguló mult, A szerencse mostohafia, Hullámtörők, Béklyok és barátok, Árnyak az alagutban, A szeplös Veronika, Egy házasság elötörténete, Eretnek Esszék 1986, Összefüggések Emberi környezet 1986, A rosta 1987, Elmés multságok 1987, A beton virágau 1989. *Leisure interests:* women, jokes, walking, swimming. *Address:* Berkenye-u 19, 1025 Budapest, Hungary. *Telephone:* 363-935.

KOLPAKOV, Serafim Vasilyevich; Soviet politician; b. 1933; ed. Moscow Steel and Alloys Inst.; foundry worker, Asha metallurgical works; Dir. Novolipetsk metallurgical combine; mem. CPSU 1956-; served in Soviet Army 1954-57; worked for tractor factory 1957-63; Dir. Metallurgical Combine 1970-78; fmr. Deputy Minister of Ferrous Metallurgy and head, All-Union Industrial Asscn. of Metallurgical Enterprises; First Deputy Minister of Ferrous Metallurgy 1982-85; Minister of Ferrous Metallurgy 1985-; mem. CPSU Cen. Cttee. 1986; Deputy to U.S.S.R. Supreme Soviet; recipient of U.S.S.R. State Prizes. *Address:* Ministry of Ferrous Metallurgy, Moscow, U.S.S.R.

KOLPAKOVA, Irina Aleksandrovna; Soviet ballerina; b. 22 May 1933; ed. Leningrad Choreographic School. Prima Ballerina, Kirov Theatre of Opera and Ballet, Leningrad; People's Artist of the R.S.F.S.R. and the U.S.S.R., Grand Prix de Ballet, Paris 1966; Principal Roles; Aurora (Sleeping Beauty), Juliet (Romeo and Juliet), Desdemona (Othello), Tao Khao (The Red Poppy), Maria (Fountain of Bakhchisarai), Giselle, Zolushka, Raymonda; first performer of part of Katerina (The Stone Flower) and Shirin (Legends of Love); Order of the Red Banner, Hero of Socialist Labour, Order of Lenin 1983, and other decorations. *Address:* c/o Kirov Theatre of Opera and Ballet, 1 ploshchad Iskusstv, Leningrad, U.S.S.R.

KOLSTAD, Eva; Norwegian chartered accountant and politician; b. 6 May 1918, Halden; d. of Chr. Hartvig and Otlu Lundegaard; m. Ragnar Kolstad 1942; teacher of book-keeping and other commercial subjects 1938-40; Asst. Accountant 1940-44; independent chartered accountant 1945-; mem. Board, Int. Alliance of Women 1949-58, 1961-68, 1973, Hon. mem. 1979; Pres. Norwegian Asscn. for Rights of Women 1956-68; mem. Oslo City Council 1960-75; mem. UN Comm. on Status of Women 1969-75; deputy mem. Parl. 1958-61, 1966-69; Minister of Consumer Affairs 1972-73; Pres. Liberal Party 1974-76; Co-ordinator Int. Women's Year 1975; Leader, Govt. Council, Equal Status of Men and Women 1977-78, Ombud for Equal Status between Men and Women 1979-88; Commdr. of Royal Norwegian Order of St. Olav 1983. *Publications:* numerous articles in newspapers, periodicals and encyclopedias. *Address:* Schivesgt. 6 B III, Oslo 2, Norway. *Telephone:* 02-448794.

KOLTAI, Ralph, C.B.E.; British stage designer; b. 31 July 1924, Berlin, Germany; s. of Alfred Koltai and Charlotte née Weinstein; m. Annena

Stubbs 1954 (divorced 1976); ed. Cen. School of Art and Design, London; Head of Theatre Design Dept., Cen. School of Art and Design 1965–72; Assoc. Artist R.S.C. 1964–66, 1976–; Opera Dir. The Flying Dutchman, Hong Kong Arts Festival 1987; Designer, musical Metropolis 1989 (London); over 150 productions of opera, drama and dance throughout Europe, the U.S.A., Canada and Australia. *Leisure interest:* wildlife photography. *Address:* 46 Leverton Street, London, N.W.5, England. *Telephone:* 01-482 6195.

KOŁTEK, Andrzej, M.A.; Polish politician; b. 1942, Malec; ed. Higher School of Econs., Wrocław; activist in youth orgs.; mem. Polish Students' Asscn. (ZSP) 1960–67, Chair. ZSP School Council in Higher School of Econs., Wrocław 1960–65, Chair. ZSP Regional Council, Wrocław 1965–67; mem. Socialist Youth Union (ZMS) 1960–76, Chair. ZMS Voivodship Bd., Wrocław 1967–72, Sec. ZMS Gen. Bd. 1972–76; mem. Union of Polish Socialist Youth (ZSMP) 1976–, mem. ZSMP Gen. Bd. 1976, Sec. ZSMP Gen. Bd. 1976–77, Chair. ZSMP Gen. Bd. 1980–81; Chair. Chief Council of Fed. of Socialist Unions of Polish Youth (FSZMP) 1980–81; mem. PZPR, Sec. Voivodship Cttee. PZPR, Krosno 1977–80, Deputy mem. PZPR Cen. Cttee. 1980–81. *Address:* Akademia Nauk Społecznych Polskiej Zyednoczonej Partii Robotniczej, ul. Bagatela 2, 00-585 Warsaw, Poland.

KOLVENBACH, Peter-Hans, S.J.; Netherlands ecclesiastic; b. 30 Nov. 1928, Druten (Gelderland); s. of Gerard A. J. Kolvenbach and Jacqueline J. P. Domensino; ed. Canisius Coll., Nijmegen, language studies in Netherlands and in Beirut, Inst. of Oriental Languages, Paris, Schools of Ancient Oriental Languages, Sorbonne; theological studies in Beirut, spiritual theology in Pomfret, Conn.; entered Soc. of Jesus 1948, ordained as a priest 1961; Prof. of General Linguistics and Armenian, Inst. of Oriental Languages and Faculty of Humanities, St Joseph's Univ., Beirut 1968–81; Prof. of Gen. Linguistics, then, Dir. Inst. of Philosophical Studies and Prof. of Hermeneutics, St. Joseph's Univ. 1968–74; del. to 32nd Gen. Congregation of Society of Jesus 1974; Provincial, Jesuit Vice-Province of the Near East 1974–81; Rector, Pontifical Oriental Inst., Rome 1981–83; Superior Gen. of the Society of Jesus Sept. 1983–. *Publications:* In Cammino verso la Pasqua; various articles and reviews primarily in the field of linguistics and spiritual theology. *Address:* Borgo Santo Spirito 5, 00193 Rome, Italy. *Telephone:* 686.9841.

KOLVENBACH, Walter; German solicitor; b. 28 Jan. 1922, Düsseldorf; s. of Jean Kolvenbach and Henriette Kolvenbach; m. Irmgard Schmidt 1954; two s.; ed. Univs of Cologne and Frankfurt/Main; Gen. Counsel Henkel & Cie Gmbh 1972–85; Chair. Legal Cttee. Verband der Chemischen Industrie e.v. 1977–85; Pres. European Co. Lawyers Assen. 1984–87; partner Law offices of Heuking, Kuhn, Düsseldorf 1987; Chair. Legal Cttee. Industrie und Handelskammer 1987, Int. Bar Assen. 1988; Verdienstkreuz (1st Class) 1981, Grosses Verdienstkreuz der Verdienstordens 1987. *Publications include:* Workers' Participation in Europe 1977, Employee Councils in European Companies 1978, Privatrechtlicher Schutz für Auslands-vermögen 1985, Kolvenbach-Hanau, Handbook on European Employee Co-Management 1987, Protection of Foreign Investments 1988. *Address:* Peter-Roos-Strasse 6, 4000 Düsseldorf 11, Federal Republic of Germany. *Telephone:* 0211/588774.

KOMAR, Vitaliy; Soviet dissident artist; b. 1943, Moscow; initial artistic training at Moscow Art School; originator with Aleksander Melamid (q.v.) of 'Sots-art'; mem. of U.S.S.R. Union of Artists, expelled for "distortion of Soviet reality and non-conformity with the principles of Socialist realism" 1972; emigrated to U.S.A. 1979. *Principal works include:* Young Marx 1976, Colour Writing 1972, Quotation 1972, Post Art 1973, Factory for Producing Blue Smoke 1975, Poster Series 1980; some work shown at Ronald Feldman Gallery, New York 1976; two-man exhbn. with Alek at same gallery 1985. *Address:* Ronald Feldman Gallery, New York, U.S.A.

KOMAROV, Igor Sergeyevich; Soviet geologist; b. 1917; ed. Moscow Geological Prospecting School; prospecting work 1938–43; served in Soviet Army 1943–47; on staff of Moscow Geological Prospecting School Asst. Prof., Dean, then Prof. 1948–; Lenin Prize for work on Eng. Geology of the U.S.S.R., 8 vols., published 1976–80. *Address:* Moscow Geological-Prospecting School, Moscow, U.S.S.R.

KOMATINA, Miljan; Yugoslav diplomatist; b. 22 Aug. 1922; m.; two c.; ed. Univ. of Paris; entered Diplomatic Service 1948, served in Norway, Hungary, Tunisia, Algeria and Austria; Del. to UN Gen. Assembly 1970–, participated in Fifth Conf. of Heads of State or Govt. of Non-Aligned Countries in Colombo, the Ministerial Conf. of Non-Aligned Countries in Lima, and the ministerial meetings of the Co-ordinating Bureau of Non-Aligned Countries in Algiers, New Delhi and Havana; Deputy Perm. Rep. to UN and Dir. of Dept. of Int. Orgs.; Asst. Fed. Sec. for Foreign Affairs; Perm. Rep. of Yugoslavia to UN 1978–83. *Address:* c/o Ministry of Foreign Affairs, Belgrade, Yugoslavia.

KOMATSU, Koh, B.ECONS.; Japanese banker; b. 14 March 1921, Kobe City; s. of Masanori and Sumi Komatsu; m. Setsuko Itoh 1948; one s. two d.; ed. Tokyo Univ.; joined Sumitomo Bank Ltd. 1946, Dir. 1971–, Man. Dir. 1973–77, Sr. Man. Dir. 1977–81, Deputy Pres. 1981–83, Pres. 1983–87, Deputy Chair. 1987–; Dir. Fed. of Bankers Asscns. of Japan 1983–; Standing Dir. Kansai Econ. Fed. 1984–. *Leisure interest:* literature. *Address:* Sumitomo Bank, 3-2 Marunouchi 1-chome, Chiyoda-ku, Tokyo 100 (Office); 301

Higashimatsubara Terrace, 24-15, Daita 4-chome, Setagaya-ku, Tokyo, Japan (Home). *Telephone:* (03) 282-5111 (Office); (03) 323-3154 (Home).

KOMENDER, Janusz, M.D.; Polish politician and physician; b. 24 March 1931, Piastów; m.; one d.; ed. Medical Acad., Warsaw; Asst. Prof. 1969, Extraordinary Prof. 1980; scientific worker, Histology and Embryology Research Centre of Medical Acad., Warsaw 1952–70, head, Transplantology Research Centre 1970–, Pro-Dean 1st Medical Faculty, 1975–81, Dean 1981–84; Pro-Rector of Medical Acad., Warsaw; Researcher, Histology Research Centre Univ. of Liverpool 1962–63, Enzymology Research Centre Univ. of Buffalo, N.Y. 1967–68; mem. Immunology Cttee. of Polish Acad. of Sciences 1975–; Deputy Scientific Sec., Medical Sciences Dept. of Polish Acad. of Sciences 1984–; Minister of Health and Social Welfare 1987–88; non-party; Kt.'s Cross of Polonia Restituta Order, Gold Cross of Merit, Nat. Education Comm. Medal and other decorations. *Publications:* over 70 works, including Przeszczepy biostatyczne (co-author) Part I 1977, Part II 1981. *Leisure interests:* sightseeing, reading. *Address:* c/o Ministerstwo Zdrowia i Opieki Społecznej, ul. Miodowa 15, 00-923 Warsaw, Poland.

KOMENDER, Zenon, M.ENG.; Polish politician; b. 21 Oct. 1923, Częstochowa; ed. Wrocław Tech. Univ.; in resistance movt. during Nazi occupation, mem. Grey Ranks of Polish Pathfinders Union, subsequently in Nat. Mil. Org. and Home Army; employed in building enterprises, Gdańsk Sea-Coast 1953–56; active mem. PAX Assen. (Roman Catholic Org.) 1956–; fmr. Head of PAX Voivodship Bds. in Katowice and Gdańsk, mem. Presidium PAX Assen. 1965–, Vice-Chair., subsequently Chair. 1982–; managerial posts in United Econ. Co-operatives of PAX Assen. 1962–82; Minister of Internal Trade and Services 1981–82; Vice-Chair. Presidium of Council of Ministers July 1982–85; Chair. Council for Family Matters July 1982–; mem. Presidium, Provisional Nat. Council of Patriotic Movt. for Nat. Rebirth (PRON) 1982–83, mem. Presidium Nat. Council of PRON 1983–; non-party; Deputy to Seym 1969–, Chair. Seym Deputies' Circle PAX; Deputy Chair. of Council of State 1985–; Włodzimierz Pietrzak Prize 1968, 1977; Officer's Cross of Order of Polonia Restituta, Order of Banner of Labour (2nd Class), Gold Cross of Merit, Gold Star of Friendship of Nations (G.D.R.), other decorations. *Publications:* O program rozwoju społeczno-ekonomicznego 1970, Pracą pokoleń 1977, others. *Address:* Kancelaria Rady Panstwa, ul. Wiejska 4-6, 00-902 Warsaw, Poland.

KOMER, Robert William, S.B., M.B.A.; American diplomatist and social scientist; b. 23 Feb. 1922, Chicago, Ill.; s. of Nathan A. Komer and Stella D. Komer; m. Geraldine M. Peplin 1961; two s. one d.; ed. Harvard Coll., Harvard Graduate School of Business Admin. and Nat. War Coll.; U.S. Army 1943–46; Lieut.-Col. in U.S. Army Reserves 1946–81; Foreign Affairs Analyst, Central Intelligence Agency 1948–60; Senior Staff Asst., White House 1961–65; Deputy Special Asst. to Pres. for Nat. Security Affairs 1965–66; Special Asst. to Pres. 1966–67; Deputy to COMUSMACV for Civil Operations and Revolutionary Devt. with rank of Amb. (pacification in Viet-Nam) 1967–68; Amb. to Turkey 1968–69; Senior Social Science Researcher, Rand Corpn. 1970–76; Adviser to Sec. of Defense for NATO Affairs 1977–79; Under-Sec. of Defense 1979–81; Consultant Rand Corpn. 1982–; Presidential Medal of Freedom, Sec. of State's Distinguished Honor Award, Dept. of Defense Medal for Distinguished Public Service, U.S. Bronze Star, Vietnamese Orders, Grosses Bundesverdienstkreuz (Fed. Repub. of Germany) 1984. *Publications:* Civil Affairs and Military Government in the Mediterranean Theater (2 vols.) 1949, Establishment of ACC in Italy 1950, Treating NATO's Self-Inflicted Wound 1973, Origins of NATO Long Term Defense Program 1978, Maritime Strategy v. Coalition Defense 1984, Strategy-Making in the Pentagon (in Reorganizing America's Defense) 1985, Bureaucracy at War: U.S. Performance in the Vietnam Conflict 1986, and many articles. *Leisure interests:* tennis, swimming, military history. *Address:* Rand Corporation, 2100 M Street, N.W., Washington D.C. 20037 (Office); 214 Franklin Street, Alexandria, Va. 22314, U.S.A. (Home).

KOMIYAMA, Jushiro; Japanese politician; b. 1928; ed. Waseda Univ.; Reporter, Yomiuri Shimbun; Private Sec. to the late Eisaku Sato (Prime Minister of Japan 1964–72); elected five times to House of Reps. from constituency in Saitama Prefecture; fmr. Parl. Vice-Minister of Int. Trade and Industry; fmr. Deputy Dir.-Gen. of Admin. Affairs in Office of P.M.; fmr. Chair. Judicial Affairs Cttee. House of Reps.; fmr. Deputy Sec.-Gen. of Liberal Democratic Party (LDP); Minister of Posts and Telecommunications, 1976–77. *Address:* c/o Ministry of Telecommunications, Tokyo, Japan.

KOMLEVA, Gabriela Trofimovna; Soviet ballerina; b. 27 Dec. 1938, Leningrad; d. of Trofim Ivanovich Komlev and Lucia Petrovna Komlev; m. Arkady Andreevich Sokolov-Kaminsky 1971; ed. Leningrad Ballet School (teacher Kostrovitskaya) and Leningrad Conservatoire; with Kirov Ballet Sept. 1957–, teacher Sept. 1978–; teacher Leningrad Conservatoire Sept. 1987–; Presenter Terpsichore's Finest Points, Leningrad TV 1985–; numerous awards including People's Artist of U.S.S.R. 1983. *Major roles:* Odette-Odile in Swan Lake, Aurore in Sleeping Beauty, Nikiya in Bayadere, Raimonda, Giselle, Kitry in Don Quixote, Cinderella, Sylphide, Sylphides, Fire-Bird, Paquita, Pas de Quatre, and many modern ballets; *films:* Don Quixote, La Bayadère, The Sleeping Beauty, Paquita, Pas de Quatre, Cinderella, Moor's Pavana. The Firebird, Leningrad Symphony, Furious

Isadora. *Leisure interests:* painting, music. *Address:* The Kirov Theatre, Teatralnaya Ploshschad 1, Leningrad 198000, U.S.S.R.

KOMLÓS, Péter; Hungarian violinist; b. 25 Oct. 1935, Budapest; s. of László Komlós and Franciska Graf; m. 1st Edit Fehér 1960, two s.; m. 2nd Zsuzsa Árki 1984; ed. Budapest Music Acad.; Founded Komlós String Quartet 1957; First Violinist, Budapest Opera Orchestra 1960; Leader Bartók String Quartet 1963; extensive concert tours to U.S.S.R., Scandinavia, Italy, Austria, German Democratic Repub. Czechoslovakia 1958-64, U.S.A., Canada, New Zealand and Australia 1970, including Day of Human Rights concert, UN H.Q. New York, Japan, Spain and Portugal 1971, Far East, U.S.A. and Europe 1973; performed at music festivals of Ascona, Edinburgh, Adelaide, Spoleto, Menton, Schwetzingen, Lucerne, Aix-en-Provence; recordings of Beethoven's string quartets for Hungaroton, Budapest and of Bartók's string quartets for Erato, Paris; First Prize, Int. String Quartet Competition, Liège 1964, Liszt Prize 1965, Gramophone Record Prize of Germany 1969, Kossuth Prize 1970, Eminent Artist Title 1980, UNESCO Music Council Plaque 1981. *Leisure interests:* ship model building, watching sports. *Address:* 1025 Budapest, Törökvész ut 94, Hungary. *Telephone:* 873-335.

KOMMANDEUR, Jan, PH.D.; Netherlands professor of physical chemistry; b. 29 Nov. 1929, Amsterdam; s. of Jan Kommandeur and Rika Jorna; m. Elizabeth Eickholz 1951; two s.; ed. Univ. of Amsterdam; Postdoctoral Fellow, Research Council, Ottawa 1955-57; research scientist, Union Carbide Corpn., Cleveland, Ohio 1958-61; Prof. of Physical Chem. Univ. of Groningen 1961-; mem. Royal Netherlands Acad. of Science. *Publications:* Photoconductivity in Aromatic Hydrocarbons 1958, Electric Conductivity in Organic Complexes 1961, Ions in Iodine 1966, Natural Gas in Europe: How much, for how long? 1977, Radiationless Transitions 1988. *Leisure interests:* literature, theatre, popularizing science. *Address:* Laboratory for Physical Chemistry, 9747 AG, Groningen (Office); Lekstraat 18, 9725 KM, Groningen, Netherlands (Home). *Telephone:* 050-634322.

KOMOTO, Toshio; Japanese politician; b. 22 June 1911, Aioi City, Hyogo Prefecture; ed. Nihon Univ.; mem. House of Reps. 1949-; Parl. Vice-Minister for Econ. Planning Agency 1958-; fmr. Chair. of Justice Cttee., House of Reps.; Chair. Cabinet Cttee., House of Reps. 1965; Minister of Posts and Telecommunications 1968-70, of Int. Trade and Industry 1974-76, 1977-78; Chair. Policy Research Council, Liberal Democratic Party 1974-75, 1978-79; Minister of State; Dir.-Gen. of Econ. Planning Agency 1980-82, 1983-84, Dir-Gen Keizai Kikaku Devt. Agency 1984-85; fmr. Pres. Sanko Steamship Co.; Liberal Democrat. *Leisure interests:* go, golf, reading. *Publication:* Nihon no Shinro (Future Direction of Japan) 1948. *Address:* c/o Liberal Democratic Party, 7, 2-chome, Hirakawacho, Chiyoda-ku, Tokyo, Japan.

KOMPLEKTOV, Viktor Georgiyevich; Soviet politician and diplomatist; b. 1932; ed. Moscow Inst. of Int. Relations; diplomatic corps 1955-; work in central directorate of U.S.S.R. Ministry of Foreign Affairs 1955-56, 1959-63; mem. CPSU 1962-; counsellor, Embassy, U.S.A. 1956-59, 1963-68; counsellor, Deputy Head 1968-78, Head of Section; corresp. mem. U.S.S.R. Ministry of Foreign Affairs 1978-82; U.S.S.R. Deputy Minister of Foreign Affairs 1982-; mem. of CPSU Cen. Auditing Cttee. 1986-. *Address:* U.S.S.R. Ministry of Foreign Affairs, Moscow, U.S.S.R.

KONAREV, Nikolai Semyonovich; Soviet politician; b. 1927; ed. Kharkov Eng. Transport Inst.; mem. CPSU 1952-; employed over 30 years as engineer, head of railway section, Chief of Southern Railway; U.S.S.R. Deputy Minister of Railways 1976-77, First Deputy Minister 1977-82; Minister of Transport 1982-; mem. CPSU Cen. Cttee. 1986-; Deputy to U.S.S.R. Supreme Soviet. *Address:* U.S.S.R. Ministry of Railways, Novobasmannaya ul. 2, Moscow, U.S.S.R.

KONDAKOV, Mikhail Ivanovich; Soviet pedagogist; b. 1 July 1920, Tula Province; m. Galina Gurieva 1958; one s.; ed. Moscow State Pedagogical Inst.; school teacher 1941, school prin. 1941-43; Head, Kiselevsk city public educ. dept. 1943-48; research student, Inst. of Hist. and Theory of Pedagogics 1948-51, Assoc. 1951-53, Head of Research Dept. 1953-60, Deputy Dir. of Research 1960-65, Dir. of Inst. 1965-67; Deputy Minister of Educ. of U.S.S.R. 1967-77; Vice-Pres. Soviet Acad. of Pedagogical Sciences 1977-81, Pres. 1981-; several orders and decorations. *Publications:* Administrative Functions of Department of Public Education 1955, Schools in the Republic of India 1958, Lenin Principles of Organization of Public Education 1970, School: to date and to be 1979, Theoretical Foundations of School Administration 1982. *Leisure interests:* collection of belles-lettres. *Address:* Pogodinskaya 8, 119905 Moscow, U.S.S.R. *Telephone:* 248 57 62.

KONDO, Tetsuo; Japanese politician; b. 1929; previous posts include: Parl. Vice-Minister of Admin. Man. Agency, of Educ. and of Agric., Forestry and Fisheries; Chair. Cttee. on Science and Tech., House of Reps.; Deputy Chair. Liberal Democratic Party (LDP) Policy Research Council; Minister of State (Dir.-Gen. Econ. Planning Agency) 1986-87. *Address:* c/o House of Representatives, Tokyo, Japan.

KONDRATIYEVA, Maria Viktorovna; Soviet ballet dancer; b. 1934; ed. Bolshoi Theatre Ballet School; joined Bolshoi Ballet Co. 1953; People's Artist of R.S.F.S.R.; Main roles include: Cinderella (Cinderella), Maria

(Fountain of Bakchisarai), Aurora (Sleeping Beauty), Juliet (Romeo and Juliet), Katerina (Stone Flower), Giselle (Giselle), Gayane (Gayane), Odette-Odile (Swan Lake), Shirin (Legend of Love). *Address:* c/o State Academic Bolshoi Theatre of U.S.S.R., 1 Ploshchad Sverdlova, Moscow, U.S.S.R.

KONG FEI; Chinese party official; b. 20 Nov. 1911, Inner Mongolia; m. Yunqing 1941; three s. three d.; ed. Law Coll., Northeastern Univ., Yanan Mil. and Political Univ.; joined CCP 1936, Red Army 1938; Column and Div. Commdr., Zhuoshuotu Pref. Inner Mongolia 1946, Div. Commdr. 10th and 3rd Cavalry Div., Inner Mongolia 1948, Xinan Pref., Inner Mongolia 1950, Deputy Chief of Staff Regional Mil. HQ and Dir. Eastern Mil. Command 1952; at Nanjing Mil. Coll. 1953-55; Deputy Commdr. and Staff Chief, Inner Mongolia 1955; suffered political persecution during Cultural Revolution 1966; Vice-Chair. Inner Mongolia Political Consultative Cttee. 1977, Chair. Autonomous Region (Inner Mongolia) 1978; mem. Standing Cttee. Chinese People's Political Consultative Cttee. 1983-; awarded Liberation Medal 1955. *Leisure interest:* reading. *Address:* 1 Victory Road, Hohhot City, Inner Mongolia, People's Republic of China.

KONG SHIQUAN, Lieut.-Gen.; Chinese soldier and party official; b. 1909, Liuyong Co., Hunan Prov.; joined Red Army and CCP 1930; Deputy Commdr. 15th Corps, 4th Field Army 1949; Deputy Dir. Political Dept. Guangdong Mil. Dist. 1949-; mem. Land Reform Cttee. Guangdong Prov. Peoples Govt. 1950; PLA Political Acad. 1958; Lieut.-Gen. PLA 1961-; Control Cttee. of CCP Cen. Cttee. 1962-; Political Cttee. Guangxi Mil. Dist. 1966; criticized for involvement in armed conflict between rival "rebel groups" in Canton Aug. 1967; First Vice-Chair. Revolutionary Cttee. Guangdong 1968-74; mem. CCP Cen Cttee. 1969-82; Sec. Guangdong Prov. CCP Cttee. 1971-73; mem. Political Cttee. Guangdong Mil. Region 1971-74, Chengdu Mil. Region 1977-78; mem. Cen. Advisory Cttee. of CCP Cen. Cttee. 1982-; Order of Liberation (1st Class). *Address:* Central Advisory Committee of the Central Committee of the Chinese Communist Party, Zhongnanhai, Beijing, People's Republic of China.

KONIE, Gwendoline C.; Zambian diplomatist; b. 9 Oct. 1938, Lusaka; d. of William Bernard Chinyimba and Hilda Kalulu Konie; ed. Swansea Univ. Coll., U.K., and American Univ., Washington, D.C., U.S.A.; Asst. Social Welfare Officer, Ministry of Local Govt. and Social Welfare 1961, Social Welfare Officer 1962; mem. Legislative Council 1963, Asst. Sec. Ministry of Foreign Affairs 1964; Deputy Commr.-Gen. Zambian Pavilion at Expo 70, Japan 1970; Under-Sec. Personnel Div., Office of the Pres. 1972; Amb. to Sweden, Denmark, Norway and Finland 1974-77, to UN 1977-79; Perm. Sec. in Civil Service 1979-; fmr. Pres. UN Council for Namibia; twice Pres. Lusaka Branch of YWCA, twice Pres. of nat. YWCA; mem. or fmr. mem. Bd. of Govs. Northern Rhodesia Broadcasting Corpn., Interim Cttee. on Establishment of Univ. of Zambia, Hotels Bd. of Zambia, YWCA Exec. Board, Adult Educ. Assocn. of Zambia, Family Planning Assocn. of Zambia; currently mem. Univ. of Zambia Council; Chair. Univ. of Zambia Bldgs. Cttee. of the Council; Commr. Comm. of Churches on Int. Affairs of World Council of Churches; Trustee, UN Inst. for Training and Research; Publr. Woman's Exclusive. *Leisure interests:* music, reading, drama, writing, golf. *Address:* P.O. Box 1646, Lusaka, Zambia.

KÖNIG, Barbara, B.A.; German author; b. 9 Oct. 1925, Reichenberg, Bohemia; d. of Dr. Arthur König and Hedwig Glauz; m. 1st Dr. Wolfgang Metzner 1955 (divorced 1961), 2nd Hans Mayer 1969; one d.; ed. School of Journalism, Univ. of Wisconsin; journalist, DENA (Deutsche Nachrichten-agentur) and Die Neue Zeitung 1947-51; Editor, Kontakt magazine 1952-53; freelance author 1958-; Visiting Lecturer, Univ. of Texas 1975; mem. PEN; mem. Acad. of Sciences and Literature, Mainz and Bavarian Acad.; Hon. Guest Lecturer Villa Massimo, Rome 1989; several literary awards. *Publications:* Das Kind und sein Schatten (novelette) 1958, Kies (novel) 1961, Die Personenperson (novel) 1965, Spielerei bei Tage (stories) 1969, Schöner Tag, dieser 13. (novel) 1973, Der Beschenkte (novel) 1980, Ich bin ganz Ohr (radio plays) 1985; essays, contribs. to anthologies etc. *Address:* Brunnenstrasse 14, 8918 Diessen; Schellingstrasse 88/II, 8000 Munich, Federal Republic of Germany. *Telephone:* 08807-332; 089-5233363.

KÖNIG, H.E. Cardinal Franz; Austrian ecclesiastic; b. 3 Aug. 1905, Rabenstein, Pielach; ed. Univs. of Rome, Vienna and Lille; ordained 1933; Dozent, Vienna Univ. 1946; Prof., Faculty of Theology, Salzburg 1948; Titular Bishop of Livias 1952; Archbishop of Vienna 1956-85; cr. Cardinal by Pope John XXIII 1958; fmr. Pres. Secr. for Non-Believers, Rome. *Publications include:* Christus und die Religionen der Erde, Religionswissenschaftliches Wörterbuch, Zarathustras Jenseitsvorstellungen und das Alte Testament 1964, Die Stunde der Welt 1971, Aufbruch zum Geist 1972, Das Zeichen Gottes 1973, Der Mensch ist für die Zukunft angelegt 1975, Kirche und Welt 1978, Glaube ist Freiheit 1981, Der Glaube der Menschen (Herausgeber) 1985, Der Weg der Kirche 1986, Lexikon der Religionen 1987. *Address:* Wollzeile 2, 1010 Vienna, Austria.

KÖNIG, Gerd; German diplomatist; b. 24 June 1930, Klettwitz; ed. Akad. für Staats- und Rechtswissenschaften 1952-53, and at Inst. for Int. Relations, Moscow, U.S.S.R.; on staff of G.D.R. Ministry of Foreign Affairs, Cultural Attaché at Belgrade Embassy 1959-62; leading functionary in Int. Relations Section of Cen. Cttee., Sozialistische Einheitspartei Deutschlands (SED) 1962-73; Cand. mem. SED Cen. Cttee. 1976-; Amb. to Czechoslovakia 1973-80; Vaterländischer Verdienstorden in Bronze and other decorations. *Address:* c/o Ministry of Foreign Affairs, Berlin, German Democratic Republic.

KÖNIG, Herbert, DR.RER.POL.; German lawyer, professor, political and financial scientist and international consultant; b. 25 July 1925, Frankfurt; m. Brygida König 1978; ed. Univs. of Frankfurt and Graz.; entered local govt. service, Frankfurt 1945, Fed. Govt. Service 1956; Fed. Acad. of Finance 1957; Asst. to Pres. Fed. Audit Bd. 1958; Budget Officer, Fed. Ministry for Econ. Affairs 1962, Counsellor for Mining Affairs 1966, Deputy Dir.-Gen. Cen. Dept. 1968; Deputy mem. Comm. for Reform of Foreign Service 1969; Asst. Sec.-Gen. OECD 1970–72; Consultant to Council of Europe and other orgs.; mem. Fed. Govt.'s Project Group on the Reform of Govt. and Admin. 1973–75; Fed. States and Local Govt. Adviser 1976–; part-time Prof. Univ. of Cologne; Chairholder for Admin. Sciences, Univ. of the Bundeswehr, Hamburg 1978–; Dir. Inst. for Innovative Devt., Bonn 1988. *Publications:* books and studies on governmental and admin. man., controlling and auditing. *Leisure interests:* photography, numismatics. *Address:* 5309 Meckenheim-Merl, Auf der Lehmwiese 11, Federal Republic of Germany (Home). *Telephone:* (02225) 6847 (Home); (0228) 223083 (Bonn Office).

KÖNIG, René, PH.D.; German sociologist; b. 5 July 1906, Magdeburg; s. of Gustav König and Marguerite Godefroy-Leboeuf; m. Irmgard Tillmanns 1947; two s.; ed. Univs. of Vienna, Berlin and Paris; mem., Faculty Zürich Univ. 1938; apptd. to Chair of Sociology, Cologne Univ. 1949–74; Sec. First World Congress of Sociology, Zürich 1950; Ed. Kölner Zeitschrift für Soziologie und Sozialpsychologie 1955–85; Pres. Int. Sociological Assen. 1962–66; Guest Prof. Univs. of Mich. 1957, 1974, Calif. 1957, 1959–60, 1964–65, Columbia Univ. 1959, Colo. 1962, Arizona 1968–69, 1975, Vienna 1980–81; Rockefeller Fellow 1952; mem. Royal Netherlands Acad. of Sciences 1970; Hon. mem. German Sociological Assen. 1975; D.Hum.Lett. (Univ. of Ill.) 1980, Dr.rer.pol. h.c. 1980, Dr.rer.soc. et oec. 1984; Commendatore del Ordine al Merito della Repubblica Italiana; Gold Medal, German Criminological Assen., Gold Medal German Assen. of Engineers, Premio Verga 1967, Medal for Education (Afghanistan) 1975, Grosses Bundesverdienstkreuz 1986. *Publications:* Naturalistische Ästhetik in Frankreich 1931, Niccolo Macchiavelli 1941, Materialien zur Soziologie der Familie 1946, Soziologie heute 1949, Soziologie 1957, 1967, Grundformen der Gesellschaft: Soziologie der Gemeinde 1958 (English trans. The Community 1967), Das Buch der Mode 1958, Handbuch der empirischen Sozialforschung 1962, 1968, 1973, 1979, Soziologische Orientierungen 1972, Macht und Reiz der Mode (English trans. The Restless Image) 1971, Soziologische Studien 1971, Indianer wohin? Alternativen in Arizona 1973, Kritik der historischexistenzialistischen Soziologie 1975, Durkheim zur Diskussion 1978, Leben im Widerspruch 1980, Navajo Report 1970–80, 1983, Ethnologie als Sozialwissenschaft 1983, Menschheit auf dem Laufsteg 1985, Soziologie in Deutschland 1987. *Address:* Marienstrasse 9, 5 Cologne 40, Federal Republic of Germany. *Telephone:* Cologne 50-86-13 (Home).

KONOPHAGHOS, Constantine; Greek professor and politician; b. 1912; m.; one s. one d.; ed. Ecole Centrale, Paris; with Soc. Française du Laurion; with Soc. Anonyme de Produits Chimiques et d'Engrais; Prof. at Polytechnic 1963, Rector 1973; mem. Parl. for Preveza 1974–77; Minister of Industry 1974–77; Gold Cross of George I, Commdr. Order of the Phoenix, Légion d'honneur, Médaille de la Ville de Gand (Belgium). *Publications:* many scientific and literary works. *Address:* c/o Ministry of Industry, Athens, Greece.

KONOTOP, Vasiliy Ivanovich; Soviet politician; b. 1916, Ukrainian S.S.R.; ed. Kharkov Machine-Bldg. Inst.; mem. CPSU 1944–; worked Kolomna Eng. Works 1942–52; party work, Moscow Dist. 1952–59; Chair. Exec. Cttee. Moscow Dist. Council for Deputies of Labour 1959–63; First Sec. Moscow Dist. Cttee. CPSU 1963–; Cand. mem. Cen. Cttee. of CPSU 1961–64, mem. 1964–84; mem. Presidium of Supreme Soviet 1966; Deputy to U.S.S.R. Supreme Soviet 1954; mem. Cttee. U.S.S.R. Parl. Group. *Address:* Moscow Regional Committee of CPSU, 6 Staraya ploshchad, Moscow, U.S.S.R.

KONOVALOV, Vasiliy Nikolayevich, CAND.ECON.SC.; Soviet politician; ed. Higher Professional Promotion School, Moscow; mem. CPSU 1947–; mechanic, Sec. of Komsomol 1943–49; Sec. Zhalomov Regional Komsomol Cttee. 1949–50; Pres. Trade Union Cttee. of Iskozh Combine, Kirov 1950–54; Head of Section, Sec. Mikhnevsky Regional Cttee. of CPSU 1954–57; Deputy Head of Section Moscow Dist. Cttee. of CPSU 1957–67; work for CPSU Cen. Cttee. 1967–83; Second Sec. of Cen. Cttee. of Azerbaijan CP 1983–; cand. mem. of CPSU Cen. Cttee. 1986–; Deputy to U.S.S.R. Supreme Soviet. *Address:* Central Committee of Azerbaijan Communist Party, Baku, Azerbaijan S.S.R., U.S.S.R.

KONSALIK, Heinz G.; German author; b. 28 May 1921 (as Heinz Günther), Cologne; s. of Heinz Arno Max Günther and Wanda Günther (née Konsalik); m. Elsbeth Langenbach 1948; two d.; ed. Univ. of Munich; worked as war corresp. 1939–45; Chief Ed. Liberator publishing co., Cologne 1946–48; Ed. Lustige magazine 1950. *Publications:* 131 novels including Der Arzt von Stalingrad, Strafbataillon 999, Russische Sinfonie, Die Rollbahn, Schicksal aus zweiter Hand, Rostende Ruhm, Der letzte Gefangene, Manöver im Herbst, Liebe am Don, Palmen I, II, Ein Sommer mit Danica, Heiss wie der Steppenwind, Die weisse Front, Liebe ist stärker als der Tod,

Promenadendeck 1985, Sibirisches Roulette 1986. *Leisure interests:* Asian art, opera, travel, animals. *Address:* Elizabethenhof, 5340 Aegidienberg bei Bad Honnef am Rhein, Federal Republic of Germany.

KONSTANTINOV, Marshal Anatoliy Ustinovich; Soviet politician; b. 1923; ed. GHQ Mil. Acad.; active service in Soviet Army 1940–45; mem. CPSU 1943–; after Second World War command posts in aviation 1945–73; Commdr. of air forces in Baku 1973–80, Moscow Dists. 1980–87; counsellor to U.S.S.R. Minister of Defence 1987–; mem. of CPSU Cen. Auditing Cttee. 1981–86; cand. mem. of CPSU Cen. Cttee. 1986–; Deputy to U.S.S.R. Supreme Soviet; Hero of Soviet Union 1946, Marshal of Aviation 1984. *Address:* U.S.S.R. Ministry of Defence, Moscow, U.S.S.R.

KONSTANTINOV, Fyodor Vasiliyevich; Soviet philosopher; b. 21 Feb. 1901, Novoselki, Gorky region; ed. Inst. of Red Professors; teacher and party worker 1932–41; Soviet Army 1942–45; Assoc. Inst. of Philosophy, U.S.S.R. Acad. of Sciences 1945–62, then Dir.; Rector, Acad. of Social Sciences of Cen. Cttee. of CPSU 1954–55; Head, Dept. of Propaganda and Agitation, Cen. Cttee. of CPSU 1955–58; Cand. mem. Cen. Cttee. of CPSU 1956–61; Corresp. mem. U.S.S.R. Acad. of Sciences 1953–66, mem. 1966–; Academic Sec. Philosophy and Law Branch, U.S.S.R. Acad. of Sciences; Chief Ed. Encyclopaedia of Philosophy; Pres. Philosophy Soc. of U.S.S.R. 1971–; Order of Lenin, Order of October Revolution and other decorations. *Publications:* For a Revolution on the Philosophy Front 1931, What is Marxist-Leninist Philosophy? 1941, Historical Materialism as a Science 1949, V. I. Lenin—a Biography 1972, Socialist Internationalism 1977, Marxist-Leninist Theory of Historical Process 1982. *Address:* c/o Institute of Philosophy of U.S.S.R. Academy of Sciences, 14 Ulitsa Volkhonka, Moscow, U.S.S.R.

KONTOGEORGIS, Georgios; Greek politician and public servant; b. 21 Nov. 1912; m.; Prin. Admin., Ministry of Economy and of Trade 1941–52; Dir.-Gen. Ministry of Trade until 1967; Sec. of State for Econ. Co-ordination and Planning 1974–77; mem. Parl. (New Democracy Party) 1977; Minister for Relations with the EEC 1977 (led negotiations for Greece's entry); Commr. for Transport, Fisheries and Co-ordination of Tourism, Comm. of European Communities 1981–85. *Publication:* The Association of Greece with the European Community 1961. *Address:* c/o Commission of the European Communities, 200 rue de la Loi, 1049 Brussels, Belgium.

KONTOS, Constantine William; American government official; b. 10 Aug. 1922, Chicago, Ill.; s. of William C. and Irene Thomas Kontos; m. Joan Fultz 1948; two s.; ed. Univ. of Chicago and L.S.E.; Special Asst. to Dir. of Econ. Co-operation Admin., Mission to Greece 1949–53; Programme Budget Officer, Foreign Operations Admin., Washington, D.C. 1953–55; Sr. Man. Officer Int. Co-operation Admin., Washington, D.C. 1955–57; Exec. Officer, Bureau of Africa and Europe 1957–59; Deputy Dir. U.S. AID Mission, Ceylon 1959–61; Deputy Dir. U.S. AID Mission, Nigeria 1961–64; attended Nat. War Coll. 1964–65; Dir. Personnel Agency for Int. Devt. 1965–67; Dir. U.S. AID Mission, Pakistan 1967–69; Dir. Office of Programme Evaluation, AID 1969–72; Deputy Commr.-Gen. UN Relief and Works Agency (UNRWA) 1972–74; mem. policy planning staff, State Dept., Washington 1974–76; special rep. of Pres., Dir. Sinai support mission, Washington 1976–80; Amb. to Sudan 1980–83; Sec. Policy Planning Council, Dept. of State 1983–86, Exec. Dir. of Advisory Cttee. to Sec. of State on South Africa 1986–87, Policy Planning Staff 1987; Dept. of State Meritorious Honour Award 1971. *Address:* c/o Room 7315, The Department of State, 2201 C Street, N.W., Washington, D.C. 20520, U.S.A.

KONUK, Nejat; Turkish Cypriot lawyer, politician and writer; b. 1928, Nicosia; unmarried; ed. Turkish Lycée, Cyprus, and Law Faculty of Ankara Univ., Turkey; Legal Adviser in Turkish Civil Service, Turkey; Sec.-Gen. and Acting Dir.-Gen. of Turkish Communal Chamber, Cyprus; Under-Sec. to Rauf Denktaş (q.v.) 1968–69; Minister of Justice and Internal Affairs, Turkish Cypriot Admin. 1969–75; mem. for Nicosia, Turkish Communal Chamber, Constituent Assembly, Turkish Cypriot Legislative Assembly 1970–; founder mem. Nat. Unity Party 1975, Leader 1976–78; Prime Minister "Turkish Federated State of Cyprus" 1976–78; Leader of the Democratic People's Party 1979–82 (resgnd.); Pres. Legis. Assembly "Turkish Federated State of Cyprus" July–Dec. 1981, 1982–83; Prime Minister "Turkish Repub. of N. Cyprus" 1983–85. *Publications:* essays on literature, various papers on Cyprus, political articles 1953–77. *Leisure interests:* reading, swimming. *Address:* Kumsal, Lefkoşa, Mersin 10, Turkey.

KONWICKI, Tadeusz; Polish writer and film director; b. 22 June 1926, Nowa Wilejka, U.S.S.R.; m. Danuta Lenica; ed. Jagellonian Univ., Cracow, Warsaw Univ.; Partisan, Home Army detachment 1944–45; mem. Polish Writers' Assen. 1949–, Editorial Staff of Nowa Kultura (weekly) 1950–57. *Films directed:* Ostatni dzień lata (Last Day of Summer) 1958, Zaduszki 1962, Salto 1965, Jak daleko stąd, jak blisko 1972, Dolina Issy 1982; State Prize, 3rd Class 1950, 1954, 1st Class 1966, Knight's Cross, Order of Polonia Restituta 1954, Officer's Cross 1964, Medal of 10th Anniversary of People's Poland 1955, Mondello Prize for Literature 1981. *Publications:* novels: Władza 1954, Z oblężonego miasta 1954, Godzina smutku 1954, Rojsty 1956, Dziura w niebie 1959, Sennik współczesny (A Dreambook of Our Time) 1963 (French version 1984), Ostatni dzień lata, Scenariusze filmowe 1966, Wniebowstąpienie 1967, Zwierzoczłekoupiór 1969, Nic albo nic 1971, Kronika wypadków miłosnych 1974, Kalendarz i klepsydra (The

Calendar and the Sand-Glass) 1976, Kompleks polski 1977, Mała Apokalipsa 1979, Wschody i zachody Księżyca 1982, Nowy Świat i Okolice 1986; film scripts: Zimowy zmierzch (Winter Twilight), Matka Joanna od Aniołów, Faraon, Jowita, Austeria. *Address:* Ul. Górskiego 1 m. 68, 00-033 Warsaw, Poland.

KONZETT, Heribert, M.D.; Austrian pharmacologist; b. 21 June 1912, Bludenz; s. of Dr. Andreas Konzett and Maria Theresia (née Stocker) Konsett; m. Imma Haid 1944; two s. one d.; ed. Univs. of Innsbruck and Vienna; Staff mem. Pharmacology Dept., Univ. of Vienna 1936–46; joined Sandoz-Pharmaceuticals Basle 1949–58; Prof. of Pharmacology and Head of Dept., Univ. of Innsbruck 1958–80, Prof. Emer. 1980–; Dean of Faculty of Medicine, Univ. of Innsbruck 1965–66; Visiting Prof. of Pharmacology, Medical Coll. of Va. 1969–70; Pres. German Pharmacology Soc. 1967–68, Hon. mem. 1981; mem. Austrian Acad. of Sciences. *Publications:* numerous papers in scientific journals on pharmacology and physiology. *Leisure interests:* music, literature. *Address:* Department of Pharmacology, Peter Mayr Strasse 1, 6020 Innsbruck; Reithmannstrasse 18, 6020 Innsbruck, Austria.

KOOP, C. Everett, A.B., M.D., SC.D.; American surgeon; b. 14 Oct. 1916, New York; s. of J. Everett Koop and Helen Apel; m. Elizabeth Flanagan 1938; three s. one d.; ed. Dartmouth Coll., Cornell Medical School and Graduate School of Medicine, Univ. of Pennsylvania; Surgeon-in-Chief, Children's Hospital of Philadelphia 1948–; Prof. of Pediatric Surgery, Univ. of Pa. 1959–; Prof. of Pediatrics 1976–; U.S. Surgeon Gen. 1985–; Deputy Asst. Sec. for Health and Dir. Office of Int. Health, U.S. Public Health Service (U.S.P.H.S.) 1982–; Consultant, U.S.N. 1964–; Ed. of various medical journals 1961–; mem. Asscn. Mil. Surgeons (Pres. 1982, 1987); nine hon. degrees; Hon. F.R.C.S.; Denis Browne Gold Medal (British Asscn. of Pediatric Surgeons) 1971, Duarte, Sanchez and Mella Award of the Dominican Repub., Drexel Univ. Eng. and Science Day Award 1975, Chevalier, Legion d'honneur 1980, U.S.P.H.S. Distinguished Service Medal 1983, Department of Health and New Human Services, Secretary's Recognition Award 1986, and other U.S.P.H.S. awards. *Publications:* over 175 papers and monographs, five books. *Leisure interest:* lapidary art. *Address:* Department of Health and Human Services, 716G Humphrey Building, 200 Independence Avenue, S.W., Washington, D.C. 20201; 4 West Drive, Bethesda, Md. 20814, U.S.A. (Home). *Telephone:* (202) 245 6467 (Office).

KOOPMAN, Antonius (Ton) Gerhardus Michael; Netherlands professor of harpsichord; b. 2 Oct. 1944, Zwolle; m. Christine H. H. Mathot 1975; three d.; ed. Amsterdam Conservatory and Univ. of Amsterdam; Prof. of Harpsichord, Sweelinck Conservatory, Amsterdam and Royal Acad. of Music, London; founded Amsterdam Baroque Orchestra 1979; appears on concert platforms around the world and on radio and TV; has made over 150 recordings of harpsichord and organ works by Bach, Handel etc. for Philips, Deutsche Grammophon and Erato; winner of several prizes. *Publications:* Interpretation of Baroque Music 1985 and a small book about J. S. Bach 1985. *Leisure interests:* art and culture of the renaissance and baroque period. *Address:* Meerweg 23, 1405 BC Bussum, The Netherlands. *Telephone:* (0)2159-13676.

KOORNHOF, Pieter Gerhardus Jacobus, B.A. (STELL.), D.PHIL. (OXON.); South African politician; b. 2 Aug. 1925, Leeudoringstad; s. of Gerhardus Willem and Elizabeth Sarellina Koornhof; m. J. L. Steyn 1951; two s.; ed. Cen. High School, Bloemfontein, Paul Roos Gymnasium, Stellenbosch, Stellenbosch Univ. and Oxford Univ.; Research Officer Dept. of Bantu Admin. and Devt. 1953–58; Under-Sec. Nat. Party of Transvaal 1958–62; Dir. Cultural Information, FAK 1958–64; Council mem. Johannesburg Gen. Hosp. Bd. and Staff Officer Pongola Regt., Citizens Force 1962–63; mem. S. African First Aid League, Nat. Youth Bd. and Vice-Chair. Man. Bd., Inst. for Youth Leaders 1963–64; mem. Parl. for Primrose (fmrly. Edenvale) 1964–84; Public Relations Officer for Immigrants 1964–65; Chair. S. African Cultural Acad. and Dir. Soc. for European Immigrants 1965–66; Man. Dir. Nat. Veldtrust of S. Africa 1966; mem. Council for Rand Afrikaans Univ.; Deputy Minister of Bantu Admin. and Devt., Bantu Educ. and Immigration 1968–72; Minister of Mines, of Immigration and of Sport and Recreation 1972–76, of Nat. Educ. and of Sport and Recreation 1976–78, of Plural Relations and Devt. 1978–84; Chair. Pres.'s Council 1984–86; Amb. to U.S.A. 1987–; Freedom of Soweto 1980; Grand Officer's Cross of Merit, Order of the Kt. of Malta 1973, Decoration for Meritorious Service 1980. *Leisure interests:* reading, golf. *Address:* South African Embassy, 3051 Massachusetts Avenue, N.W., Washington, D.C. 20008, U.S.A.

KOPEĆ, Aleksander, M.SC.(ENG.), PH.D.; Polish politician; b. 12 Oct. 1932, Wąsowiczówka, U.S.S.R.; s. of Władysław and Aniela Kopeć; m. Adela Sudoł 1958; one d.; ed. Wrocław Tech. Univ.; Man. posts, Industrial Eng. Factory, Świdnica 1957–62; Chief Engineer, Dir., Van Factory, Świdnica 1962–67; Dir. Dolmel Works, Wrocław 1967–70; Deputy Minister, Ministry of the Machine (Engineering) Industry Feb.-Dec. 1970, First Deputy Minister 1970–75, Minister 1975–80, Deputy Prime Minister Sept. 1980–81; Deputy mem. Cen. Cttee., Polish United Workers' Party (PZPR) 1975–80, mem. 1980–81; Chair. Main Board, Chief Tech. Org. 1976–84; Pres. Main Bd. Polish Sec. Mechanical Engineers and Technicians (SIMP) 1987–; Vice-Chair. Fed. of Scientific-Technological Orgs. of Socialist Countries 1982–; Order of Banner of Labour (1st and 2nd Class), Officer's Cross of Order of

Polonia Restituta and other decorations. *Address:* c/o Naczelna Organizacja Techniczna, ul. Czackiego 3/5, 00-043 Warsaw, Poland.

KÖPECZI, Béla; Hungarian literary historian and politician; b. 16 Sept. 1921, Nagyenyed (Aiud in Romania); s. of Árpád Köpeczi and Anna Tomai; m. Edit Bölcskei 1951; ed. Budapest and Paris Univs.; Publr. 1949–53; Vice-Pres., Hungarian Council of Publishing 1953–55; Chair. Hungarian Bd. of Publishing 1955; Head, Cultural Dept. Hungarian Socialist Workers' Party 1964–66; Prof. Univ. of Budapest 1964, Vice-Rector 1967; mem. Hungarian Acad. of Sciences, Deputy Gen. Sec. 1970–72, Gen. Sec. 1972–75, Deputy Sec.-Gen. 1975–82; Minister of Culture and Educ. 1982–88; Dr. h.c. (Paris) 1979, (Rome); State Prize 1980; Commdr. Palmes académiques (France). *Publications:* La France et la Hongrie au début du XVIIIe siècle 1971, Révolté ou révolutionnaire 1973, L'autobiographie d'un prince rebelle 1977, Kulturrevolution in Ungarn 1978, Staatsräson und christliche Solidarität 1983, Hongrois et Français de Louis XIV á la Révolution française 1983, A francia felvilágosodás (The Age of French Enlightenment) 1986. *Leisure interests:* literature, music, travelling. *Address:* Il Tulipán-u. 5, 1022 Budapest, Hungary (Home).

KOPKIN, Aleksandr Gavrilovich; Soviet politician; b. 1927; ed. Magnitogorsk Mining Inst.; foreman of works on construction of the Karaganda Hydro-Electric Station 1949–51; mem. of CPSU 1949–; Head of Section, First Sec. Temirtau City Cttee., Sec. of party cttee. Kazmetallurgstroy trust 1951–61, Man. of trust 1961–72; Minister in Charge of Heavy Industrial Enterprises, Kazakh S.S.R. 1972–75; Sec., Second Sec. of Cen. Cttee. of Karaganda Dist. Cttee., of Kazakh CP 1979–86; U.S.S.R. First Deputy Minister of Coal Industry 1986–; cand. mem. of CPSU Cen. Cttee. 1981–; Deputy to U.S.S.R. Supreme Soviet. *Address:* The Kremlin, Moscow, U.S.S.R.

KOPPER, Hilmar; German banker; b. 13 March 1935; Acting mem. Man. Bd., Deutsche Bank AG; Chair. of Supervisory Bd. AKA Ausfuhrkredit-Gesellschaft mbH, Frankfurt, Flachglas AG, Fürth, Bavaria, H. Albert de Bary & Co. N.V., Amsterdam, Kali-Chemie AG, Hanover; Deputy-Chair. of Supervisory Bd. Industriebank von Japan (Deutschland) AG, Frankfurt, Banco Comercial Transatlántico, Barcelona, Deutsche Bank Compagnie Finanière, Luxembourg; mem. of Supervisory Bd. Schering AG, Berlin, Herberts GmbH, Wuppertal, Honsel Werke AG, Meschede, PHB Weserhütte Ak AG, Cologne, Rheinisch-Westfälische Kalkwerke AG, Wuppertal-Dornap, Enka AG, Wuppertal, Deutsche Bank (Asia) AG, Hamburg; Chair. Advisory Bd. Wilhelm Berg GmbH & Co. KG, Lüenscheid; mem. of Advisory Bd. R. & G. Schmöle Metallwerke GmbH & Co. KG, Menden; mem. of Admin. Council Pilkington Brothers PLC, St. Helens, England, Solvay & Cie., Brussels, Banca d'America e d'Italia, Milan. *Address:* Taunusanlage 12, 6000 Frankfurt/Main, Federal Republic of Germany.

KOPTYUNG, Valentin Afanasiyevich, DR.CHEM.SC.; Soviet chemist; b. 1931; ed. Moscow Inst. of Chemistry; engineer, jr., sr. scientific asst. 1957–59; mem. CPSU 1961–; sr. scientific asst., head of lab. Novosibirsk Inst. of Organic Chemistry 1959–78; Prof. 1968; corresp. mem. Acad. of Sciences 1968–; Rector Novosibirsk Univ. 1978–80; Vice-Pres. of Siberian Br., U.S.S.R. Acad. of Sciences 1980–; mem. of CPSU Cen. Auditing Cttee. 1981–86; cand. mem. of CPSU Cen. Cttee. 1986–; Deputy to U.S.S.R. Supreme Soviet; Hero of Socialist Labour 1986. *Address:* U.S.S.R. Academy of Sciences, 14 Leninsky Prospekt, Moscow, U.S.S.R.

KORČÁK, Josef; Czechoslovak politician (retd.); b. 17 Dec. 1921, Holštejn; s. of Jaroslav and Marie Korčák; m. Růžena Ježková 1943; two d.; ed. School of Political Studies of Cen. Cttee. of CP of Czechoslovakia; Turner, Zbrojovka Brno 1937–48; posts in regional cttees. of CP 1948–60; mem. Cen. Cttee. CP of Czechoslovakia 1958–, mem. Presidium of Cen. Cttee. 1970–87; mem. Bureau of Cen. Cttee., CP of Czechoslovakia for directing Party work in the Czech lands 1969–87; Minister of Construction 1962–63; Minister in charge of Cen. Admin. of Power Supply 1963–68; Chair. Cen. Cttee. of Czech Nat. Front 1969–71; Prime Minister of Czech S.R. and Deputy Prime Minister of Č.S.S.R. 1970–; Deputy to Nat. Assembly 1962–69, to House of People, Fed. Assembly 1969–; Deputy to Czech Nat. Council 1971–87; Chair., Govt. Cttee. for Physical Fitness and Sports 1978–81; Award for Merits in Construction 1958, Order of the Repub. 1971, Order of Victorious February 1973, Hero of Socialist Labour 1981, Klement Gottwald Order for the Construction of Socialist Homeland 1981. *Address:* Nábřeží Karla Marxe 8, Podolí, Prague 4, Czechoslovakia. *Telephone:* 43.76.17.

KORDA, Michael Vincent, B.A.; American publishing executive; b. 8 Oct. 1933, London, England; s. of Vincent Korda and Gertrude (née Musgrove) Korda; m. Carolyn Keese 1958; one s.; ed. Magdalen Coll., Oxford; served R.A.F. 1952–54; joined Simon and Schuster, New York 1958–, firstly as Ed., then Sr. Ed., Man. Ed., Exec. Ed., now Sr. Vice-Pres. and Ed.-in-Chief; mem. Nat. Soc. of Film Critics, American Horse Shows Asscn. *Publications:* Male Chauvinism: How It Works 1973, Power: How to Get It, How to Use It 1975, Success! 1977, Charmed Lives 1979, Worldly Goods 1982, The Fortune 1989. *Address:* Simon and Schuster, 1230 Avenue of Americas, New York, N.Y. 10020, U.S.A.

KOREN, Petter Mørch; Norwegian lawyer and politician; b. 22 Jan. 1910, Edinburgh, Scotland; s. of Dean Laurentius Stub Koren and Thordis Andrea Mørch Koren; m. Aase Dahl 1938; two s. three d.; ed. Univ. of

Oslo; Solicitor 1934; Clerk 1935–36; Deputy Judge, District Judge of Larvik 1936–38; Sec. Ministry of Commerce 1938, Ministry of Shipping 1940; Head of Div. Ministry of Shipping 1942, Norwegian Govt. Savings and Contribution Office 1945, Ministry of Commerce 1948; Judge, City Court of Oslo 1956–65; Gov. of Oslo and Akershus 1966–79; Minister of Justice 1963, 1972–73; Commdr. of St. Olav's Order. *Address:* Østhornveien 3, Oslo, Norway (Home). *Telephone:* 02 23 20 15.

KORF, Willy Wilhelm; German industrialist; b. 13 Aug. 1929, Hamm, Sieg; s. of Arthur Korf and Margarete Giershausen; m. Brigitte Kaiser 1962; two. d.; ed. High School, Business High School; began industrial career in parents' trading co. for buildings supplies and steel products; f. Korf (first venture, steel-processing plant), Kehl/Rhine 1955, from which developed first 'mini-steel mill', then est. corporate HQ in Baden-Baden for worldwide operations (including steel processing plants, rolling mills and eng. cos. in Fed. Repub. of Germany, France, U.S.A., Brazil); following financial collapse of old group est. new co. Korf KG, Gen. Partner 1982–, Pres. Korf-Transport GmbH.; Chair. Conn. Steel Corpn., Ocean State Steel Corpn., Korf Lurgi Stahl Eng. GmbH, Frankfurt; two hon. degrees in eng. *Leisure interests:* hunting, flying. *Address:* Winterhalterstrasse 4, D-7570 Baden-Baden, Federal Republic of Germany. *Telephone:* (7221) 3-30-94.

KORHONEN, Gunnar Aleksander, B.SC. (ECON.); Finnish aviation executive; b. 22 April 1918, Finland; m. 1st Elli Tamminen 1943 (divorced), 2nd Seija Vapaa (née Niemi) 1969; one s.; employed by Bank of Savo-Karjala 1937–38; Office Man. and Head of Dept. of Ministry of Supply 1944–47; Sec. State Price and Wage Council 1947; Vice-Pres. Oy Masalin & Co. 1947–50; Pres. Hoyryvarustin Oy 1950–51; Head of Price Dept. Ministry of Social Affairs 1951–53; Dir.-in-Chief, Trade and Supply Section of Ministry of Commerce and Industry 1953–60; Chair. Bd. of Dirs. and Pres. of Finnair 1960–; Chair. Econ. Council 1957–58; Del. to the Scandinavian Council 1956–59; Chair. of the Finnish Group of the Collaboration Comm. on Scandinavian Econs. 1957–59; Del. at ECOSOC; mem. Bd. of Dirs. Area Travel Agency Ltd. 1960–, Chair. 1985–; Chair. of Bd. of Dirs. of Kar-Air Oy 1968–; Chair. Bd. of Dirs. Interhotel Oy 1968–82, Oy Finnmatkat-Finntours Ab 1973–, Nordic-Hotel Oy 1975–, Finnaviation Oy 1979–, Matka-toimisto Matkayhtymä Oy-United Travel Ltd. 1979–, Oy Aurinkomatkat-Suntours Ltd. Ab 1985–, Finncatering Oy 1985– and Suomen Matkatoimisto Oy-Finland Travel Bureau Ltd. 1985–; Minister of Social Affairs and Public Health 1970, of Commerce and Trade 1971–72; mem. of various Bds. of Admin. and Dirs. *Leisure interests:* reading, boating, skiing. *Address:* Finnair, Töölönkatu 4, 00100 Helsinki (Office); Vanrikki Stoolinkatu 3 A 7, Helsinki 10, Finland (Home).

KORHONEN, Keijo Tero, PH.D.; Finnish diplomatist; b. 23 Feb. 1934, Paltamo; s. of Hannes Korhonen and Anna née Laari; m. Anneli née Torkkila 1958; three s.; ed. Turku Univ.; Deputy Dir. for Political Affairs, Ministry of Foreign Affairs 1971–74; Prof. of Political History, Univ. of Helsinki 1974–77; Minister of Foreign Affairs 1976–77; Under-Sec. of State for Political Affairs, Ministry of Foreign Affairs 1977–83; Perm. Rep. to UN 1983–. *Publications:* four books about Finnish-Soviet and Finnish-Russian relations since 1808; Finland in the Russian Political Thought of the 19th century 1966, An Ambassador's Journal, Urho Kekkonen, the Leader and the Man. *Leisure interests:* reading, jogging. *Address:* Permanent Mission of Finland to the United Nations, 866 UN Plaza, New York, N.Y. 10017, U.S.A. *Telephone:* 355-2100.

KORLE, Sinan A., M.A.; Turkish diplomatist; b. 4 April 1914, Istanbul; m.; ed. Robert Coll., Istanbul, Univ. of Istanbul and Iowa State Univ.; fmr. journalist; Information Officer, Office of Public Information, UN Sec. HQ 1951, Acting Dir., UN Information Office in Athens 1954, Dir. 1955–57; Observer with a Trusteeship Council Mission to French Togoland 1958; Dir., Information Centre in Teheran 1959–61; Information Officer, UN Operation in Congo 1960; Special Asst. to Pres. of 16th session of Gen. Assembly 1961; Information Officer in Ruanda-Urundi 1962; Deputy Chief of Protocol, UN 1962–68, UN Chief of Protocol 1968. *Address:* Office of the Chief of Protocol, United Nations, First Avenue, New York, N.Y. 10017, U.S.A.

KORLÉN, Gustav, DR.; Swedish professor of German language and literature; b. 27 Jan. 1915, Falun; s. of Artur Korlén and Ingeburg Hansen; m. Majken Andersson 1941; one s. one d.; ed. Univs. of Lund, Kiel and Paris and King Alfred's Coll. Winchester, U.K.; Docent Lund Univ. 1945–52; Prof. of German Language and Literature, Univ. of Stockholm 1952–80, Prof. Emer. 1980–; mem. various professional socs. etc.; Konrad-Duden-Pres, Mannheim 1967; Preis der Deutschen Akad. 1972; Swedish Acad. Prize 1983; Hon. Senator, Univ. of Münster. *Publications:* Die mittelniederdeutschen Texte des 13. Jahrhunderts 1945, Norddeutsche Stadtrechte 1951–52; articles in journals. *Leisure interest:* tennis. *Address:* Storängens strandväg 2B, S-131 41 Nacka, Sweden.

KORNAI, János, DR.SC.; Hungarian economist; b. 21 Jan. 1928, Budapest; m. Zsuzsa Dániel 1971; two s. one d.; ed. Univ. of Budapest; Econ. Ed. 1947–55; Research Assoc. Inst. of Econs., Hungarian Acad. of Sciences 1955–58, Inst. of Textile Industry 1958–63; Sr. Research Assoc., Computer Centre, Hungarian Acad. of Sciences 1963–67; Prof. of Econs. and Head of Dept., Inst. of Econs., Hungarian Acad. of Sciences 1967– and Prof. of

Econs., Harvard Univ. 1986– (a jt. appointment with the Hungarian Acad. of Sciences); Visiting Prof., L.S.E. 1964, Univ. of Sussex 1966, Stanford Univ. 1968, Yale 1970, Princeton and Stanford 1972–73, Stockholm 1976–77, Geneva 1981, Munich 1983, Princeton 1983–84, Harvard 1984–85; mem. Hungarian Acad. of Sciences; Corresp. mem. British Acad.; Foreign mem. Royal Swedish Acad., Finnish Acad.; Hon. mem. American Acad. of Arts and Sciences, American Econ. Asscn.; Hon. Dr. (Paris) 1978, (Poznań) 1978; Seidman Award 1982, Hungarian State Prize 1983, Humboldt Prize 1983. *Publications:* Overcentralization of Economic Administration 1959, Mathematical Planning of Structural Decisions 1967, Anti-Equilibrium 1971, Rush versus Harmonic Growth 1972, Economics of Shortage 1980, Non-Price Control 1981, Growth, Shortage and Efficiency 1982, Contradictions and Dilemmas 1985. *Address:* Dobsinai utca 13, 1124 Budapest; Institute of Economics, Hungarian Academy of Sciences, Budaörsi ut 45, 1112 Budapest, Hungary.

KORNBERG, Arthur, M.D., D.SC., LL.D., L.H.D.; American biochemist; b. 3 March 1918, New York; s. of Joseph and Lena Katz Kornberg; m. Sylvy R. Levy 1943; three s.; ed. City Coll. of New York and Univ. of Rochester; commissioned Officer, U.S. Public Health Service 1941–42; Nat. Insts. of Health, Bethesda, Md. 1942–52; Prof. and Chair. Dept. of Microbiology, Washington Univ. School of Medicine 1953–59; Prof., Dept. of Biochemistry, Stanford Univ. School of Medicine 1959–, Head 1959–69; mem. N.A.S., American Philosophical Soc., American Acad. of Arts and Sciences, Foreign mem. Royal Soc. 1970; Hon. LL.D., City Coll. of New York 1960, D.Sc. (Notre Dame, Washington, Rochester and Pennsylvania), L.H.D. (Yeshiva Univ.) 1962, D.Sc. (Princeton) 1970, D.Sc. (Colby Coll.) 1970, M.D. (Univ. of Barcelona) 1970; Nobel Prize in Medicine and Physiology (with Prof. Ochoa) 1959 and many other awards. *Publications:* numerous original research papers and reviews on subjects in biochemistry, particularly enzymatic mechanisms of biosynthetic reactions. *Address:* c/o Department of Biochemistry, Stanford University School of Medicine, Stanford, Calif. 94305 (Office); 365 Golden Oak Drive, Portola Valley, Calif. 94025, U.S.A. (Home). *Telephone:* (415) 851-0287.

KORNBERG, Sir Hans (Leo), Kt., M.A., D.SC., SC.D., PH.D., F.R.S., F.R.S.A.; British professor of biochemistry; b. 14 Jan. 1928, Herford, Germany; s. of Max and Margarete (née Silberbach) Kornberg; m. Monica M. King 1956; twin s. two d.; ed. Queen Elizabeth Grammar School, Wakefield and Univ. of Sheffield; John Stokes Research Fellow, Univ. of Sheffield 1952–53; mem. Medical Research Council Cell Metabolism Research Unit, Univ. of Oxford 1955–61; Lecturer in Biochem., Worcester Coll., Oxford 1958–61; Prof. of Biochem., Univ. of Leicester 1961–75; Sir William Dunn Prof. of Biochem., Univ. Cambridge 1975–; Fellow Christ's Coll., Cambridge 1975–, Master 1982–; Chair. Science Bd., S.R.C. 1969–72, mem. 1967–72; Chair. Royal Comm. on Environmental Pollution 1976–81; mem. Agric. Research Council 1980–84; mem. Priorities Bd. for Research and Devt. in Agric. 1984–; Chair. Advisory Cttee. Genetic Manipulations 1986–, Jt. Policy Group Agric. and Environment 1986–; mem. of Bd. NIREX 1986–; Pres. Elect Int. Union of Biochem. 1988–91; mem. Advisory Council for Applied Research and Devt. 1982–85; CIBA Lecturer, Rutgers N.J. 1968; Life Sciences Lecturer, Univ. of Calif. (Davis) 1971; Visiting Lecturer, Australian Biochemical Soc. 1973; Distinguished Visiting Prof., Univ. of Cincinnati 1974; Visiting Prof., Univ. of Miami, Medical School 1970–74; Weizmann Memorial Lecturer 1975; FEBS-Springer Lecturer 1975; Griffith Memorial Lecturer 1976; Leverhulme Memorial Lecturer 1977; Barton-Wright Memorial Lecturer 1977; Sir Henry Tizard Lecturer 1979; Redfearn Memorial Lecturer 1981; Commonwealth Fund Fellow (Yale and N.Y. Univs.) 1953–55; Hon. mem. Soc. Biological Chem. (U.S.A.) 1972, Japanese Biochem. Soc. 1981; mem. German Acad. of Sciences Leopoldina 1982; Foreign Assoc. N.A.S. 1986; Foreign Hon. mem. American Acad. of Arts and Sciences 1987; mem. Acad. Europaea 1988; Fellow, Inst. of Biology 1966, Vice-Pres. 1969–72; Vice-Chair. European Molecular Biological Org. 1978–81; Pres. British Assocn. for the Advancement of Science 1984–85; Leeuwenhoek Lecturer, Royal Soc. 1972; Man. Trustee, Nuffield Foundation 1973–; Hon. Sc.D. (Cincinnati) 1974, Hon. D.Sc. (Warwick) 1975, (Leicester) 1979, (Sheffield) 1979, (Bath) 1980, (Strathclyde) 1985; Hon. D.Univ. (Essex) 1979, Hon. M.D. (Leipzig) 1984; Colworth Medal (Biochemical Soc.) 1965, Warburg Medal (Gesellschaft für biologische Chemie der Bundesrepublik, Fed. Repub. of Germany) 1973. *Publications:* numerous articles in scientific journals. *Leisure interests:* conversation, cooking. *Address:* Department of Biochemistry, Tennis Court Road, Cambridge, CB2 1QW (Office); Master's Lodge, Christ's College, Cambridge, CB2 3BU, England (Home). *Telephone:* 0223-333628 (Office); 0223-334940 (Home).

KÖRNER, Stephan, JUR.DR., PH.D., F.B.A.; British philosopher; b. 26 Sept. 1913, Ostrava, Czechoslovakia; s. of Emil Körner and Erna Maier Körner; m. Edith Laner 1944; one s. one d.; ed. Classical Gymnasium, Charles Univ., Prague, and Trinity Hall, Cambridge; Army Service 1936–39, 1943–46; Lecturer in Philosophy, Univ. of Bristol 1946–52, Prof. 1952–79, Dean, Faculty of Arts 1965–66; Pro-Vice-Chancellor, Univ. of Bristol 1968–71; Prof. Yale Univ. 1970–83; Visiting Prof. of Philosophy, Brown Univ. 1957, Yale Univ. 1960, Texas Univ. 1964, Indiana Univ. 1967, Graz Univ. 1980–84; Ed. Ratio 1961–80; Pres. British Soc. for Philosophy of Science 1965, Aristotelian Soc. 1967, Int. Union of History and Philosophy of Science (Div. of Logic, Methodology and Phil. of Science) 1969–71, Mind Asscn. 1973; Fellow of British Acad. 1967; mem. Int. Inst. of Philosophy 1971;

Hon. D.Litt. (Queen's Univ.) Belfast 1983, Dr. h.c. (Graz Univ.) 1984, Hon. Fellow, Bristol Univ. 1986. *Publications:* Kant 1955, Conceptual Thinking 1955, The Philosophy of Mathematics 1960, Experience and Theory 1966, Kant's Conception of Freedom (British Acad. Lecture) 1967, What is Philosophy? 1969, Categorial Frameworks 1970, Abstraction in Science and Morals 1971, Experience and Conduct 1976; Ed. Observation and Interpretation 1957, Ed. Philosophy of Logic 1976, Metaphysics: Its Structure and Function 1984; contributor to philosophical periodicals. *Leisure interest:* walking. *Address:* 10 Belgrave Road, Bristol, BS8 2AB, England. *Telephone:* (0272) 733036.

KORNIENKO, Georgiy Markovich; Soviet diplomatist; b. 1925, Ukraine; ed. Moscow Law Inst.; mem. CPSU 1947–; entered diplomatic service 1949; Chief of Dept., U.S.S.R. Ministry of Foreign Affairs 1959–60; Counsellor, Embassy, U.S.A. 1960–63, Counsellor-Envoy 1963–65; Deputy Chief, Chief of American Dept., U.S.S.R. Ministry of Foreign Affairs 1965–78; U.S.S.R. Deputy Minister of Foreign Affairs 1975–77; First Deputy Minister 1977–86; First Deputy Head of Section CPSU Cen. Cttee. 1986–; Deputy to U.S.S.R. Supreme Soviet 1979–; mem. Cen. Cttee. CPSU 1981–; Hero of Socialist Labour 1985. *Address:* Central Committee of CPSU, Moscow, U.S.S.R.

KORNILOV, Vladimir Nikolaevich; Soviet author and poet; b. 1928, Dnepropetrovsk; ed. Gorky Inst. of Literature; first works published 1953. *Publications include:* The Drive (Pages from Tarusa) 1961, The Chauffeur 1961, The Harbour 1964, The Age (lyrics) 1967, Without Arms, Without Legs 1975. *Address:* c/o U.S.S.R. Union of Writers, ulitsa Vorovskogo 52, Moscow, U.S.S.R.

KOROLEV, Mikhail Antonovich, DR.ECON.SC.; Soviet statistician; b. 1931; ed. Moscow Plekhanov Inst. of Nat. Econ.; Asst. Dean, Dept. Head, Moscow Inst. of Econ. Statistics 1954–66, Rector 1966–72, Prof. 1967–; Deputy, First Deputy Dir. Cen. Statistics Board of U.S.S.R. 1972–85, Dir. 1985–87; Pres. U.S.S.R. State Cttee. on Statistics Aug. 1987–; cand. mem. of CPSU Cen. Cttee. 1986; Deputy to U.S.S.R. Supreme Soviet. *Address:* U.S.S.R. State Committee on Statistics, The Kremlin, Moscow, U.S.S.R.

KOROLEV, Yuri Konstantinovich; Soviet monumentalist sculptor; b. 1929; ed. Leningrad Mukhina Higher Art School; mem. CPSU 1964–; Dir. of Tretyakov Gallery, Moscow 1980–86, of All-union Museum Foundation of Tretyakov Gallery 1986–; corresp. mem. of U.S.S.R. Acad. of Arts 1983; head of a studio for monumental art at Surikov Inst., Moscow, Prof. 1985–; People's Artist of U.S.S.R. 1985. *Works include:* murals, mosaics and stained glass for theatres in Murmansk 1963–64 and Petrozavodsk 1957; stained glass for Soviet Pavilion at Montreal Exhbn. 1966–67, mosaic for Museum of Armed Forces, Moscow 1961–65. *Address:* All-Union Museum Foundation of Tretyakov Gallery, Moscow, U.S.S.R.

KOROM, Mihály, LL.D.; Hungarian lawyer and politician; b. 9 Oct. 1927, Mindszent; ed. Budapest Univ., Hungarian Socialist Workers Party Univ.; farmhand until 1945; joined Communist Party 1946; army and police service 1945–51; mem. Party Cen. Cttee. 1951–55; later Dept. Head, Ministry of Interior; Maj.-Gen. and Nat. Commdr. Frontier Guard Force 1960–63; Sec. Cen. Cttee. Hungarian Socialist Workers' Party 1963–66, 1978–85; Minister of Justice 1966–78; mem. HSWP Political Cttee. 1980–85, M.P. 1980–; Labour Order of Merit. *Address:* c/o Hungarian Socialist Workers' Party, H-1387 Budapest, Széchenyi rakpart 19, Hungary. *Telephone:* 111-400.

KOROMA, Abdul G.; Sierra Leonean diplomatist and lawyer; ed. King's Coll., Univ. of London, Kiev State Univ.; barrister and legal practitioner, High Court of Sierra Leone; joined Sierra Leone govt. service 1964, Int. Div., Ministry of External Affairs 1969; del., UN Gen. Assembly; mem. Int. Law Comm.; mem. of dels. to 3rd UN Conf. on the Law of the Sea, UN Conf. on Succession of States in Respect of Treaties, UN Comm. on Int. Trade Law, Special Cttee. on the Review of the Charter and on the Strengthening of the Role of the Org. Cttee. on the Peaceful Uses of Outer Space; Vice-Chair. UN Charter Cttee. 1978–; Deputy Perm. Rep. of Sierra Leone to the UN 1978–82, Perm. Rep. 1982; fmr. Amb. to EEC and Perm. Del. to UNESCO; Chair., UN 6th Cttee. (Legal). *Address:* c/o Sierra Leone Embassy, 410 Avenue de Tervueren, 1150 Brussels, Belgium. *Telephone:* (02) 771 00 52/53.

KOROMA, Sorie Ibrahim; Sierra Leonean politician; b. 30 Jan. 1930, Port Loko; m.; c.; ed. Govt. Model School, Freetown, Bo Govt. School and Co-operative Coll., Ibadan, Nigeria; worked in Co-operative Dept. 1951–58; in pvt. business 1958–62; First Sec.-Gen. Sierra Leone Motor Transport Union 1958; M.P. 1962–65, 1967; Councillor and Deputy Mayor of Freetown 1964; Minister of Trade and Industry 1968–69, of Agric. and Nat. Resources 1969–71; Vice-Pres. of Sierra Leone 1971–79, First Vice-Pres. 1981–86; Prime Minister 1971–75, Minister of the Interior 1971–73, 1981–82, of Finance 1975–78, of Devt. and Econ. Planning 1977–78, of State Enterprises 1978–79; Vice-Chair. FAO Conf., Rome 1971; Rep. of Sierra Leone to OAU Summit Conf., Addis Ababa 1971, Morocco 1972; Commdr. of the Republic of Sierra Leone; decorations from Lebanon, People's Repub. of China, Ethiopia, Liberia. *Leisure interests:* reading, football, sport. *Address:* c/o Office of the First Vice-President, Tower Hill, Freetown, Sierra Leone. *Telephone:* 2757.

KOROTYCH, Vitaliy Alekseyevich; Soviet (Ukrainian) writer and poet; b. 26 May 1936, Kiev; s. of Alexy Korotych and Zoa Korotych; m. Linaida Korotych 1958; two s.; ed. Kiev Medical Inst.; physician 1959–66; ed. of Ukrainian literary journal Ranok 1966–; Ed.-in-Chief Jesuit magazine 1978–86; Ed.-in-Chief Ogoniok weekly magazine 1986–; Sec. of Ukrainian Writers' Union 1966–69; two State Prizes, U.S.S.R. *Publications include:* Golden Hands 1961, The Smell of Heaven 1962, Cornflower Street 1963, O Canada! 1966, Poetry 1967, Memory, Bread and Love 1986, many translations from English into Ukrainian and other Slavonic languages. *Address:* Ukrainian Writers' Union, Kiev, U.S.S.R.

KORRY, Edward M.; American journalist and diplomatist; b. 7 Jan. 1922, New York; m. Patricia McCarthy 1950; one s. three d.; ed. Washington and Lee Univ. and Harvard Graduate School of Business Management; Nat. Broadcasting Co. 1942; United Press, New York 1943–47, London 1947, Chief Corresp. for U.N. 1948, for Eastern Europe (Belgrade) 1948–50, Man. for Germany 1951, for France 1952, Chief European Corresp. 1954; European Ed., Look magazine 1955–60; Asst. to Gardner Cowles, Pres. Cowles Magazine and Broadcasting Inc. 1960–63; Amb. to Ethiopia 1963–67, to Chile 1967–71; Consultant to Pres. of Overseas Pvt. Investment Corpn. 1972; Pres. Asscn. of American Publrs. 1972–73, UN Assscn., U.S.A. 1973–74; Visiting Prof. of Govt. (Conn. Coll.) 1979–; Visiting Scholar, Center for Int. Affairs, Harvard Univ. 1981–; Superior Honor Award, Dept. of State; Hon. LL.D. (Washington and Lee Univ.). *Address:* Center for International Affairs, Harvard University, 1737 Cambridge Street, Cambridge, Mass. 02138, U.S.A. *Telephone:* (617) 495-5388 (Office).

KORS, Michael; American couturier; b. 9 Aug. 1959, New York; s. of Bill Kors and Joan L. Kors; ed. Fashion Inst. of Tech.; f. own. Kors Co. 1981, Pres. 1981–; Dumonts American Original Prize. *Publications:* articles in Vogue, The New York Times and other newspapers and magazines. *Leisure interests:* theatre, film, travel. *Address:* 140 Charles Street, New York, N.Y. 10019, U.S.A. *Telephone:* (212) 620-4677.

KORSBÆK, Vagn Aage, M.A. (ECON.); Danish diplomatist; b. 22 Oct. 1923, Høve; s. of late Johs. Korsbæk and Marie Kirkegaard; m. Karen Nielsen 1951; one s. two d.; ed. Univs. of Wisconsin and Aarhus; Dept. of Foreign Affairs 1951; First Sec. Washington, D.C. 1955; Dept. of Foreign Affairs 1960; Econ. Counsellor, Bonn 1964; Minister Counsellor 1966; Dept. of Foreign Affairs 1969; Head, Perm. Del. of Denmark at OECD, Paris 1973; Amb. to Canada 1977–85, to Ireland 1985–. *Address:* Royal Danish Embassy, 121 St. Stephen's Green, Dublin 2, Ireland. *Telephone:* 1-75 64 04.

KORSHAK, Vasily Vladimirovich; Soviet chemical scientist; b. 9 Jan. 1909, Vysokoye, Chernigov; s. of Vladimir F. Korry and Tatyana Y. Korshak; m. Zoya A. Mirolyubova 1932; two s. one d.; ed. Mendeleyev Chemical Technological Inst. Moscow; mem. CPSU 1940–; Prof. Mendeleyev Chemical Technological Inst. 1942; Corresp. mem. of U.S.S.R. Acad. of Sciences, mem. 1953–; worked at U.S.S.R. Acad. of Sciences Inst. of Organo-Elemental Compounds 1954–; main research has been into the chemistry of higher molecular compounds, the process of polycondensation (for which he worked out a theory) and the mechanics of the Friedel-Crafts reaction; numerous publs.; chief ed. of journal 'High-Molecular Compounds'; Foreign mem. Finland and G.D.R. Acads. of Science; U.S.S.R. State Prize 1949, 1951, Lenin Prize 1986, 4 Orders, several medals. *Address:* Institute of Organo-Elemental Compounds, Vavilov Street 28, 117813 Moscow (Office); Gubkin Street 4, Apt. 81, 117333, Moscow, U.S.S.R.; (Home): *Telephone:* D7 19 30.

KORTELAINEN, Karl Efremovich; Soviet politician; Chair. of Cttee. of State Security for Estonian S.S.R. 1982–. *Address:* Committee for State Security, Tallinn, Estonian S.S.R., U.S.S.R.

KORTH, Fred, A.B., LL.B.; American banker, lawyer and government official; b. 9 Sept. 1909, Yorktown, Texas; s. of Fritz R. J. and Eleanor Marie Stark Korth; m. 1st Vera Connell 1934 (divorced 1964), one s. two d.; m. 2nd Charlotte Brooks Williams 1980; ed. Texas and George Washington Univs.; admitted to Bar 1935; law practice Fort Worth 1935–62; Deputy Counsellor, Dept. of the Army 1951–52, Asst. Sec. of Army 1952–53; Consultant to Sec. of Army 1953–60; Exec. Vice-Pres. Continental Nat. Bank, Fort Worth 1953–59, Pres. 1959–62; Sec. of the Navy 1962–64; pvt. law practice 1964–; Co-Executor and Co-Trustee, Marjorie Merriweather Post Estate; fmr. Dir. Bell Aerospace Corpn., T. & P. Railway, Panama Canal Co.; mem. American Bar Assscn., American Law Inst., Nat. Council Salk Inst.; recipient of Exceptional Civilian Service Award, Army Dept. 1953; fmr. Dir. Fischbach and Moore, American Air Filter Co., OKC Corpn.; Dir. Fischbach Corpn.; Hon. LL.D. *Leisure interests:* hunting and fishing. *Address:* 1700 K Street, N.W., Suite 501, Washington, D.C. 20006-2689; 1054 Torrey Pines, El Paso, Tex. 79912; El Retiro, P.O. Box 13, Ecleto, Tex. 78111, U.S.A. (Summer Home). *Telephone:* (202) 223-3630; 915-584-7060 (El Paso); 512-789-4455 (Summer).

KORTHALS, Hendrik Albertus; Netherlands politician; b. 3 July 1911, Dordrecht; s. of A. H. Korthals; m. Marie Cécile Hamming 1940; two s. two d.; ed. Rotterdam Econ. High School; Ed. Nieuwe Rotterdamse Courant 1936–40; official, Ministry for Trade, Shipping and Industry 1940–45; mem. of Parl. 1945–59; mem. Cons. Assembly of Council of Europe 1949–59; Parl. Coal and Steel Community and European Parl. 1952–59;

Deputy Premier and Minister of Transport and Waterways 1959–63; mem. Council of State; Pres. Press Council; Adviser Bd. Netherlands Org. for Int. Devt. Co-operation; Vice-Pres. World Broadcasting; Liberal. *Leisure interest:* history. *Address:* 63 Witte Singel, Leiden, Netherlands. *Telephone:* 133790.

KORTHALS, Robert W., B.SC., M.B.A.; Canadian banker; b. 7 June 1933, Maracaibo, Venezuela; ed. Univ. of Toronto, Harvard Business School; with Electric Reduction Co. of Canada Ltd. 1955–59; with Nesbitt, Thomson and Co. Ltd. 1961–67; with Toronto-Dominion Bank 1967–, Supt. Term Financing, Int. Div. 1967–68, Supt. Nat. Accounts Div. 1968–69, Asst. Gen. Man. 1969–72, then Gen. Man. Nat. Accounts Div. 1972, Vice-Pres. Admin. 1972–76, Sr. Vice-Pres. 1976–78, Exec. Vice-Pres. and Chief Gen. Man. 1978–81, Pres. June 1981–; Dir. many other cos. including TD Mortgage Corpn., Hayes-Dana Inc., Toronto Dominion Bank, Jannock Ltd. and Consolidated Talcorp Ltd.; Gov. Cen. Hospital, Toronto; mem. Ont. Econ. Council. *Leisure interests:* sailing, tennis, skiing. *Address:* The Toronto Dominion Bank, Head Office, P.O. Box 1, Toronto Dominion Centre, Toronto, Ont. M5K 1A2, Canada.

KORTLANDT, Frederik H. H., PH.D.; Netherlands professor of linguistics; b. 19 June 1946, Utrecht; ed. Univ. of Amsterdam; Asst. Prof. of Slavic Linguistics, Univ. of Amsterdam 1969–72; Assoc. Prof. of Balto-Slavic Languages, Univ. of Leiden 1972–74, Prof. 1974–; Prof. of Descriptive and Comparative Linguistics 1985–; mem. Royal Netherlands Acad. 1986–. *Publications:* Modelling the phoneme 1972, Slavic accentuation 1975, numerous articles on linguistics and Slavic, Germanic, Celtic, Armenian and other languages. *Address:* Faculty of Letters, P.O. Box 9515, 2300 RA Leiden (Office); Cobestraat 24, 2313 KC Leiden, Netherlands (Home).

KORVALD, Lars; Norwegian politician; b. 29 April 1916, Nedre Eiker; s. of Engebret Korvald and Karen Wigen; m. Ruth Borgersen 1943; one s. four d.; ed. Coll. of Agriculture; Teacher, Tomb School of Agric. 1943–48; Chief Adviser, League of Norwegian Agricultural Clubs 1948–52; Headmaster, Tomb School of Agric. 1952–77; mem. Storting 1961–81; del. to UN Gen. Assembly 1963, 1968; mem. Advisory Assembly, Council of Europe 1965–70; mem. Nordic Council 1966–81, Vice-Pres. 1979–81; Chair. Christian Dem. Party 1967–75, 1977–79; Pres. Lagting (Upper House of Storting) 1969–72; Prime Minister 1972–73; Gov. Østfold Dist. 1981–86; Commdr. St. Olav's Order (Norway) 1986. *Publication:* Politics and Christianity (memoirs, with Per Øyvind Heradstveit) 1982. *Leisure interests:* skiing, literature. *Address:* Vinkelgt. 6, 3050 Mjondalen, Norway.

KORZENIEWSKI, Bohdan, DR.PHIL.; Polish theatre and film director (retd.); b. 12 April 1905, Siedlce; s. of Józef and Stanisława Korzeniewski; 1st m. Ewa Rostkowska (died 1983); one s. one d.; m. 2nd Anna Kuligowska 1984; ed. Faculty of Humanities, Warsaw Univ.; worked at Nat. Library, Warsaw 1932; studied eighteenth-century theatre in Paris 1933–34; theatre critic 1934–; Lecturer in History of Theatre, State Inst. of Theatrical Art, Warsaw 1934–39; active in resistance movt. during World War II; Literary Dir. Theatre of Polish Army, Łódź 1945–47; lecturer, State Higher School of Theatrical Art, Łódź 1946–48, Warsaw 1949–75, Prof. and Dean, Dept. of Staging 1956–75; Prof. Emer. 1975–; co-ed. Teatr 1948–51; Dir. Teatr Polski 1949–52, Artistic Man., Narodowy 1952–54; Ed.-in-Chief Pamiętnik teatralny 1956–; has produced plays by Shakespeare, Molière, Mayakovsky, Mickiewicz, Krasiński and Fredro in the G.D.R., France, the U.K., Czechoslovakia and the U.S.S.R.; mem. Polish Cultural Council and Science Council of State Inst. of Art; State Prize 1951, 1954, Alfred Jurzykowski Foundation Award 1972; Officer's Cross, Order of Polonia Restituta 1954, Order of Banner of Labour (2nd class) 1959, Home Army Cross 1971, Nat. Educ. Comm. Medal, Officier de l'Ordre des Arts et des Lettres (France) 1964. *Publications:* Drama in Warsaw National Theatre, a book on early 19th century melodrama, Discussions About Theatre (theatrical reviews), I Want Freedom for Thunder ... in the Theatre (essays), and numerous translations of English, French and Russian plays. *Leisure interests:* gardening, car, walking. *Address:* Ul. Miączyńska 11, 02-637 Warsaw, Poland. *Telephone:* 44-1831.

KORZHAVIN, Naum (pseudonym of Naum Moiseyevich Mandel); Soviet author and poet; b. 1925, Kiev; ed. Karaganda Mining Inst. and Gorky Inst. of Literature, Moscow 1959; first publication 1941; exiled to West 1974. *Publications include:* The Years 1963, Where Are You? 1964, Bread, Children in Auschwitz, Autumn in Karaganda; contributor to émigré dissident journal Kontinent.

KORZHEV-CHUVELYOV, Gely Mikhailovich; Soviet artist; b. 7 July 1925, Moscow; ed. Surikov State Inst. of Arts, Moscow; professional artist 1950–; has participated in many Soviet and foreign exhbns. 1950–; Prof. Moscow Higher Artist-Tech. Inst. 1966–; mem. U.S.S.R. Acad. of Arts 1970–; Chair. of Bd. of Artists' Union of R.S.F.S.R. 1968–; Sec. Bd. of Dirs. of Artists' Union of U.S.S.R.; Merited Worker of Arts of the R.S.F.S.R.; Repin State Prize of U.S.S.R.; People's Artist of the R.S.F.S.R. 1972. *Address:* c/o Artists' Union of the U.S.S.R., Gogolevsky boulevard 10, Moscow, U.S.S.R.

KOSAKA, Tokusaburo; Japanese politician; b. 20 Jan. 1916, Nagano Pref.; s. of Jyunzo and Hanako Kosaka; m. Asako Mitsui, 1942; three d.; ed. Tokyo Univ.; joined Asahi Newspaper Co.; Man. Shinetsu Chemical Industry Co. 1949, Vice-Pres. 1951, later Pres.; lecturer, Dept. of Econs., Univ. of Tokyo

1959–62, Dept. of Commercial Sciences, Keio Univ. 1960–62, Dir. Japan Chemical Industry Asscn., Coal Industry Asscn., Shinano Mainichi Newspaper Co., Shinano Broadcasting Co.; mem. House of Reps. 1969–; Dir.-Gen. Prime Minister's Office 1973–74; Chair. Public Relations Cttee., Liberal-Democratic Party (LDP) 1976–77, Econ. and Price Policy Bd., LDP 1977–78; Minister of State for Econ. Planning 1978–79; Minister of Transport 1981–82. *Publications:* The New Industrialists' Manifesto 1967, People First 1969. *Leisure interests:* tennis, skiing, swimming. *Address:* 21-28, Fukazawa-cho, 7-chome, Setagaya-ku, Tokyo 158, Japan. *Telephone:* 03-701-1400 (Home).

KOSCHNICK, Hans Karl-Heinrich; German politician; b. 2 April 1929, Bremen; s. of Dreher Koschnick; m. Christel Risse; ed. Mittelschule; Local Govt. Official, Bremen 1945–51, 1954–63; Trade Union Sec. of the Union of Public Employees, Transport and Communications (ÖTV) 1951–54; mem. Social Democratic Party (SPD) 1950–, Fed. Exec. Council 1970–, Party Bd. 1975–, Deputy Chair. SPD 1975–79; mem. Provincial Diet of Land Bremen (Landtag) and City Admin. 1955–63; Senator for the Interior 1963–67; Mayor of Bremen 1967–85; Pres. of the Senate, Bremen 1967–85; mem. Fed. Council (Bundesrat) 1965–, Pres. 1970–71, 1981–82; Nat. Vice-Chair. SPD 1975–79; Chair., German Union of Local Authorities (Deutscher Städtetag) 1971–77; mem. Bd. Städtetag (Assoc. of German Municipalities) 1970–, Pres. 1971–77; mem. Exec. Cttee. Int. Union of Local Authorities (IULA) 1972–77, 1980–85, Pres. 1981–85; M.P. 1987–. *Address:* 2800 Bremen, Rudolstädter Weg 9, Federal Republic of Germany. *Telephone:* 4673733.

KOSCIUSKO-MORIZET, Jacques; French diplomatist; b. 31 Jan. 1913, Paris; s. of Charles and Diane Milliaud Kosciusko; m. Marianne Morizet 1939; two s. two d.; ed. Lycée Rollin and Lycée Henri IV, Paris, and Ecole Normale Supérieure; Teacher Lycée de Grenoble, Teacher Lycée Marcelin-Berthelot 1941–42, Lycée Buffon, Paris 1943–44; Asst. Prof. of French Literature, Faculty of Letters, Paris 1944–46; Prof. Columbia Univ., U.S.A. 1946; Asst. Chief of Civil Staff of Pres. of Nat. Assembly Jan.-Dec. 1946, of Pres. of Provisional French Govt. 1946–47; Chief of Civil Staff of Pres. of France 1946–53, Chief of Civil Staff of Félix Houphouët-Boigny 1956–57; French Del. to UN Trusteeship Council 1957–63; Amb. to Congo (Kinshasa) 1963–68; Dir. of Tech. and Cultural Affairs at Secr. of State for Foreign Affairs Feb.-Dec. 1968; French Perm. Rep. to North Atlantic Council, Brussels 1969–70; Perm. Rep. to UN 1970–72; Amb. to U.S.A. 1972–77; Mayor of St. Nom la Breteche 1977; Pres. CEAC (Confederation of European Veterans) 1981–; Trustee, Christian Dior 1981–; Nat. Sec. for Foreign Affairs, R.P.R. (Gaullist Movt.) 1983–; Grande Officier, Légion d'honneur, Croix de guerre, Rosette de la Résistance; Hon. K.C.V.O.; Ambassadeur de France. *Publications:* Diderot et Hagedorn 1935, Propos sur le Ministère des Jeunes 1955, Pari sur la Communauté franco-africaine 1957. *Leisure interests:* piano, tennis, skiing, golf. *Address:* 20 rue de Tournon, 75006 Paris, France. *Telephone:* 354-11-70 (Paris); 550-32-19 (Office).

KOSHIRO, Matsumoto, IX (b. Teruaki Fujima); Japanese actor; b. 1942; s. of the late Koshiro VIII; m.; one s.; debut in Kabuki (Japanese traditional theatre) when child; as child acted under name Kintaro, as young man Somegoro Ichikawa; became Koshiro IX 1980. *Plays acted in include:* Kanjincho (and many other Kabuki plays), Man of La Mancha (included 10-week run on Broadway), The Passion of Dracula, The King and I, Half a Sixpence, Sweeney Todd, Fiddler on the Roof, Amadeus (Salieri). *Address:* c/o Kabukiza Theatre, No. 12-15 Ginza 4 chome, Chuo-ku, Tokyo 104, Japan.

KOSHKIN, Lev Nikolaevich, D.TECH.; Soviet specialist on automation; b. 1912; ed. Moscow Bauman Tech. Inst.; cement-worker 1929–30; chief lathe-operator 1930–36; construction worker 1936–37; chief construction worker in Ulyanovsk machine plant 1940–43; mem. CPSU 1941–; Dir. of Cen. Cttee. for Cement Production in U.S.S.R. 1943–66; Prof. 1964; mem. U.S.S.R. Acad. of Sciences 1984–. Lenin Prize 1962; State Prize 1943, 1980, Hero of Socialist Labour 1982. *Address:* c/o U.S.S.R. Academy of Sciences, Moscow V-71, Leninsky Pr. 14, U.S.S.R.

KOSHLAND, Daniel E., Jr., B.S., PH.D.; American professor of biochemistry; b. 30 March 1920, New York; s. of Daniel E. and Eleanor Haas Koshland; m. Marian Elizabeth Elliott 1945; two s. three d.; ed. Univs. of California and Chicago; Analytical Chemist, Shell Chemical Co. 1941–42; Research Assoc. and Group Leader, Manhattan District, Univ. of Chicago and Oak Ridge Nat. Lab. 1941–46; Post-doctoral Fellow, Harvard Univ. 1949–51; Assoc. Biochemist, Biochemist, Sr. Biochemist, Brookhaven Nat. Lab. 1951–65; Affiliate, Rockefeller Univ. 1958–65; Prof. of Biochem., Univ. of Calif., Berkeley 1965–, Chair. Dept. Biochem. 1973–77; Visiting Prof. Cornell Univ. 1957–58; Pres. American Soc. of Biological Chemists 1973–74; Ed.-in-Chief, Science Magazine 1985–; mem. N.A.S., American Acad. of Arts and Sciences; Hon. mem. Japanese Biochem. Soc., Royal Swedish Acad. of Science; Guggenheim Fellow 1972, Visiting Fellow, All Souls' Coll., Oxford 1971–72; Fellow, American Asscn. for Advancement of Science; Hon. Ph.D. (Weizmann Inst.) 1984; Hon. Sc.D. (Carnegie Mellon Univ.) 1985, Hon. LL.D. (Simon Fraser Univ.) 1986; J. Duckett Jones Award 1977, Pauling Award, American Chemical Soc. 1979, Edgar Fahs Smith Award, American Chemical Soc. 1979, Rosenstiel Award 1984, Waterford Prize 1984. *Publications:* articles on enzymes in scientific journals; Bacterial Chemotaxis as a Model Behavioural System 1980. *Leisure interests:* tennis, golf, sailing. *Address:* c/o Department of Biochemistry, University of California, Berkeley, Calif. 94720, U.S.A. *Telephone:* (415) 642-0416.

KOSHOEV, Tamirbeka Khudaybergenovich; Soviet politician; b. 1931; ed. Kirghiz Agric. Inst.; forester on state forest-farm in Kirghizia 1950–52; mem. CPSU 1952–; party work on state farm 1957–60; Pres. Karasuisky regional Exec. Cttee. 1960–62; First Sec. Suzak (Kirghizia) Regional Cttee. 1962–63; Pres. Osh Dist. Cttee. of Kirghiz CP 1966–78, First Sec. 1978–81; Pres. of Presidium of Supreme Soviet of Kirghizia 1981–; Deputy Pres. of Presidium of U.S.S.R. Supreme Soviet; mem. of CPSU Cen. Auditing Cttee. 1981–86; cand. mem. of CPSU Cen. Cttee. 1986–. *Address:* Presidium of Supreme Soviet of Kirghizia, Frunze, Kirghiz S.S.R., U.S.S.R.

KOSICKI, Stanisław, M.ECON.; Polish politician and journalist; b. 5 Feb. 1924, Łódź; ed. Higher School of Econs., Łódź; managerial posts in editorial offices of local party newspapers, Łódź, Białystok and Opole 1945–62; Sec. of Propaganda, Voivodship Cttee., Polish United Workers' Party (PZPR), Opole 1961–67; Deputy Head, Dept. of Propaganda and Agitation PZPR Cen. Cttee. 1967–71, First Deputy Head, Dept. of Propaganda, Press and Editions, PZPR Cen. Cttee. 1971–72; Pres. Cen. Office for Press, Publications and Entertainments Control Jan. 1972–81, Cen. Office for Publs. and Entertainments Control 1981–; mem. PZPR Cen. Comm. of Party Control 1975–81. *Address:* Główny Urząd Kontroli Publikacji i Widowisk, ul. Mysia 5, 00-496 Warsaw, Poland.

KOŠLER, Zdeněk, Czechoslovak conductor; b. 25 March 1928, Prague; s. of Malvina and Václav Košler; m. Jana Svobodova 1954; ed. Acad. of Music and Dramatic Arts, Prague; in concentration camp during Second World War; Guest Conductor, Prague Nat. Theatre 1951–; Artistic Dir. Olomouc Opera 1958–62; Chief, Ostrava Opera 1962–66; Asst. Conductor, New York Philharmonic Orchestra 1963–64; F.O.K. Orchestra, Prague 1965–67; Chief Conductor Berlin Komische Oper 1966–68, Opera of the Slovak Nat. Theatre, Bratislava 1971–76; Conductor of Czech Philharmonic Orchestra, Prague 1971–80; Chief Conductor of Prague Nat. Theatre Opera 1980–; concert tours of Japan since 1968, Great Britain 1975, 1977, Austria, France, Italy and Switzerland 1976, Canada; Award for Outstanding Work 1958, First Prize in young conductors' competition, Besançon 1956, First Prize and Gold Medal, D. Mitropoulos Int. Competition, New York 1963, Artist of Merit 1974, Nat. Artist 1984. *Address:* Prague 4, M. Pujmanové 882; and Česká filharmonie, Dům umělců, Prague 1, Czechoslovakia. *Telephone:* Prague 435-80-32.

KOSOLAPOV, Richard Ivanovich; Soviet official and news editor; b. 1930; ed. Moscow Univ. Komsomol work 1955–58; mem. CPSU 1957–; teaching and research at Moscow Univ. and Acad. of Sciences 1958–66; party work for Cen. Cttee. CPSU 1966–74; First Deputy Ed. Pravda 1974–76; Ed.-in-Chief of Kommunist 1976; cand. mem. Cen. Cttee. CPSU 1976-81, mem. 1981–86; Deputy to U.S.S.R. Supreme Soviet. *Address:* The Kremlin, Moscow, U.S.S.R.

KOSSACK, Georg, F.B.A.; German professor of pre- and early history; b. 25 June 1923, Neuruppin; s. of Fritz Kossack and Franziska (née Unruge) Kossack; m. Ruth Kossack 1947; one s. one d.; Prof. Univ. of Kiel 1959–75, Univ. of Munich 1975–; mem. German Archaeological Inst., Bayerischer Akademie der Wissenschaften. *Publications:* Studien zum Symbolgut Urnenfelder und Hallstallzeit 1954, Sübayern während Hallstallzeit 1959, Graberfelder Hallstallzeit 1979, Archsum auf Sylt I 1980, II 1987, Ed. Siedlungen im deutschen Küstengebiet 1984. *Leisure interest:* reading nineteenth century history. *Address:* Pietzenkirchen 56A, 8201 Riedering, Federal Republic of Germany. *Telephone:* 08036-7342.

KOSSMANN, Ernst Heinrich, D.LITT.; Netherlands professor of modern history; b. 31 Jan. 1922, Leiden; s. of F.K.H. Kossmann and D. Touw; m. Johanna A. Putto 1950; two s. one d.; ed. Gymnasium Erasmianum, Rotterdam, Univ. of Leiden; Asst. lecturer, then lecturer in Modern History, Univ. of Leiden 1950–57; Reader, then Prof. of Dutch History, Univ. Coll. London 1957–66; Prof. of Modern History, Groningen Univ. 1966–87, Emer. Prof. 1987–; mem. Royal Netherlands Acad. of Sciences; Foreign mem. Royal Belgian Acad. of Sciences. *Publications:* La Fronde 1954, Politieke theorie in het zeventiende-eeuwse Nederland 1960, Texts concerning the Revolt of the Netherlands (with A. F. Mellink) 1974, The Low Countries 1780–1940, 1978, De Lage Landen 1780–1980, (2 vols.) 1986, Politieke theorie en geschiedenis 1987. *Address:* Thorbeckelaan 180, 9722 NJ Groningen, The Netherlands. *Telephone:* 050-252617.

KOSTER, Henri Johan de; Netherlands industrialist and politician; b. 5 Nov. 1914, Leiden; s. of Arie de Koster and Johanna Adriana Sythoff; m. Goverdina Burgersdyk 1958; one s. three d.; ed. Amsterdam Univ. and in London, Dublin and New York; with Meelfabriek De Sleutels 1937–, Man. Dir. 1939–67; Netherlands Commr. in New York, Food Purchasing Bureau 1945; Pres. Federation of Netherlands' Employers 1960–67, Union des Industries de la Communauté Européenne (UNICE) 1962–67; Sec. of State for Foreign Affairs 1967–71; Minister of Defence 1971–73; mem. Parl. 1971–77; Senator 1977–81; Pres. Parl. Council of Europe 1977–81; mem. Council of State 1980–85; Pres. Europa Nostra Montreux 1984–; Knight, Order of Netherlands Lion, Grand Officer Order of Orange Nassau, and other decorations. *Leisure interests:* reading, swimming, golf, art. *Address:*

1816 Chailly sur Montreux, Switzerland. *Telephone:* The Hague 649395 (Office).

KOSTERLITZ, Hans Walter, D.SC., F.R.S., F.R.S.E.; British pharmacologist; b. 27 April 1903, Berlin, Germany; s. of Bernhard and Selma Kosterlitz; m. Johanna Maria Katherina Gresshöner 1937; one s.; ed. Univs. of Heidelberg, Freiburg, Berlin, Aberdeen; Asst. 1st Medical Dept., Univ. of Berlin 1928–33; Research Worker in Physiology, Univ. of Aberdeen 1934–35, Asst. and Carnegie Teaching Fellow 1936–39, Lecturer in Physiology 1939–45, Sr. Lecturer 1945–55, Reader 1955–68, Prof. of Pharmacology and Chair. of Dept. 1968–73, Dir. of Unit for Research on Addictive Drugs 1973–; Foreign Assoc. N.A.S.; Dr. h.c. (Liège) 1978, LL.D. h.c. (Aberdeen) 1979, D.Sc. h.c. (St. Andrews) 1982, L.L.D. h.c. (Dundee) 1988. *Publications:* Agonist and Antagonist Actions of Narcotic Analgesic Drugs 1972, Opiates and Endogenous Opioid Peptides 1976, Pain and Society 1980, Neuroactive Peptides 1980. *Address:* Unit for Research on Addictive Drugs, University of Aberdeen, Marischal College, Aberdeen, AB9 1AS (Office); 16 Glendee Terrace, Cults, Aberdeen, AB1 9HX, Scotland (Home). *Telephone:* 0224-273000 (Office); 0224-867366 (Home).

KOSTRZEWSKI, Jan Karol, M.D., M.P.H.; Polish scientist and politician; b. 2 Dec. 1915, Cracow, Poland; s. of Jan Kostrzewski and Maria Sulikowska; m. Ewa Sobolewska 1948; one s. three d.; ed. Jagiellonian Univ., Cracow and Harvard School of Public Health, Boston; Health Service Doctor 1939–51; Head of Epidemiology Dept., State Hygiene Inst., Warsaw 1951–78; Prof. of Epidemiology Warsaw Medical Acad. 1954–60; Under-Sec. of State, Ministry of Health and Social Welfare and Chief Sanitary Inspector 1961–68; Minister of Health and Social Welfare 1968–72; Scientist State Hygiene Inst. 1973–78; fmr. Head of Epidemiology Dept.; Corresp. mem. Polish Acad. of Sciences 1967–76, mem. 1976–, mem. Presidium 1971–, Sec. Dept. of Medical Sciences 1972–80, Vice-Pres. 1981–83, Pres. 1984–; Chair. Cttee. Nat. Health Protection Fund 1981–; Chair. Research Strengthening Group UNDP/World Bank/WHO Special Programme on Tropical Diseases Research; Vice-Chair. Nat. Council of Patriotic Movt. for Nat. Rebirth 1983–; Deputy to Seym (Parl.) 1985–; Chair. Presidium of Ecological Social Movt. 1986–; mem. Consultative Council attached to Chair. of Council of State; mem. Exec. Bd. WHO 1973, Chair. 1975; mem. Council Int. Epidemiological Asscn. 1974, Pres. 1977–81; Hon. mem. Mechnikov Soc. Microbiologists and Epidemiologists 1956–, later Pres.; Sec. Int. Comm. for Assessment of Smallpox Eradication in India, Nepal, Ethiopia, Horn of Africa and Bhutan 1977–79; Corresp. mem. Acad. Nationale de Médecine 1979, Global Advisory Comm. for Medical Research 1980, Foreign mem. Acad. of Medical Sciences, U.S.S.R. 1986, Foreign Fellow Indian Nat. Science Acad. 1986; Heath Clark Lecturer Univ. of London; Dr. h.c. (WAM, Łódź) 1979, (AM, Lublin) 1985; Order of Banner of Labour 1st and 2nd Class, Commdr. and Knight's Cross, Order of Polonia Restituta, Cross of Valour, Gold Cross of Merit, Warsaw Insurgent Cross and others. *Publications:* numerous works on epidemiology. *Leisure interests:* sport, photography, skiing, fishing. *Address:* Aleja Róż 10 m. 6, 00-556 Warsaw, Poland. (Home). *Telephone:* 497702.

KOSYGIN, Yuriy Aleksandrovich; Soviet geologist; b. 22 Jan. 1911, St. Petersburg (now Leningrad); s. of Aleksandr Ivanovich Kosygin and Zoya Aleksandrovna Kosygina; m. Mariya Iosiphovna Kosygina 1945; two s.; ed. Moscow Oil Inst.; Sr. Scientific Assoc., Geological Inst., U.S.S.R. Acad. of Sciences 1945–58, Inst. of Geology and Geophysics, Siberian Br. 1958–70, and Dir. Inst. of Tectonics and Geophysics, Soviet Far East Science Centre (Deputy Pres. 1970–), Khabarovsk 1971–; Pres. Scientific Council on Siberia and Far East Tectonics 1959–; corresp. mem. U.S.S.R. Acad. of Sciences 1958–70, Academician 1970–; Hero of Socialist Labour 1981, Order of Lenin (twice) and other decorations. *Publications:* Oil deposits in Turkmenia 1933, Tectonics of Oil-Producing Regions 1958, Tectonics 1969, The Principles of Tectonics 1974, Tectronics 1983. *Leisure interests:* arts and philosophy. *Address:* c/o Institute of Tectonics and Geophysics, 65 Kim Yu Chen Street, 680063 Khabarovsk, U.S.S,R. *Telephone:* 33-06-35.

KOSZAROWSKI, Tadeusz Tomasz; Polish surgeon and oncologist; b. 16 Sept. 1915, Bicas (Brazil); s. of Walery and Stanisława Koszarowski; m. Alina Węgrowicz Koszarowski 1941; ed. Warsaw Univ.; Asst., Prof. 1954, Extraordinary Prof. 1961, Ordinary Prof. 1973; with Inst. of Tuberculosis, Wola Hospital, Warsaw: surgeon 1939–52, Head Oncological Surgery Ward 1948–52, Maria Skłodowska-Curie Radium Inst. (later Oncological Inst.) Warsaw, Chief Surgeon, Vice-Dir. 1952–72, Dir. 1972–86; Dir. Nat. Cancer Programme 1975–85; Pres. Polish Medical Soc. 1962–70, Pres. Main Council Asscn. of Polish Medical Socs. 1966–70; Deputy to Seym (Parl.) 1980–85, mem. Consultative Council Presidium of Seym 1986; mem. of Consulting Bd. to the Pres. of the State Supreme Council 1986; Chair. Social Health Council attached to Ministry of Health and Social Welfare 1982–86; mem. Science Council of Minister of Health and Social Welfare 1962–83; mem. New York Acad. of Science 1984–; Alfred Jurzykowski Foundation Award, New York 1969; numerous Polish decorations including Order of Builders of People's Poland, Order of Banner of Labour (First Class) 1984. *Publications:* over 200 scientific works in Polish and foreign journals on oncological surgery, combating cancer and epidemiology of cancer; major works: Onkologia praktyczna w klinice chirurgicznej 1965, Chirurgia onkologiczna 1972, Cancer in Poland, City of Warsaw and Selected Rural Areas 1977, Oncological Surgery 1980, Cancer Surgery 1982, Onkologia kliniczna 1984,

Epidemiology of Cancer in Poland 1952–82 1985. *Leisure interests:* literature, art. *Address:* ul. Orłowicza 6 m. 22, 00-414 Warsaw, Poland. *Telephone:* 43-44-00 (Office).

KOTAITE, Assad, LL.D.; Lebanese lawyer and international aviation official; b. 6 Nov. 1924, Hasbaya; s. of Adib Kotaite and Kamle Abousamra; m. Monique Ayoub 1983; ed. French Univ., Beirut, Univ. of Paris and Acad. of Int. Law, The Hague; Head of Legal and Int. Affairs, Directorate of Civil Aviation, Lebanon 1953–56; Rep. of Lebanon, Council of ICAO 1956–70; Sec.-Gen. ICAO, 1970–76, Pres. Council 1976–. *Address:* c/o International Civil Aviation Organisation, 1000 Sherbrooke Street West, Montreal, Quebec (Office); 5955 Wilderton Avenue, Apt. O4A, Montreal H3S 2V1, Canada. (Home). *Telephone:* 285-8011 (Office).

KOTCHEFF, Ted; Canadian film and stage director; b. 7 April 1931, Toronto; joined CBC Television; went to England 1957; plays include Play With A Tiger, Maggie May. *Films include:* Life At The Top 1965, Two Gentlemen Sharing 1968, Wake In Fright 1971, The Apprenticeship of Duddy Kravitz (in Canada) 1973–74, Fun with Dick and Jane 1977, Who is Killing the Great Chefs of Europe? 1978, First Blood, Split Image, 1982–83, Uncommon Valour 1984, Joshua, Then and Now 1985; *TV plays include:* The Human Voice 1966, Of Mice And Men 1968, Edna The Inebriate Woman 1971. *Address:* 10 Martha Eaton Way, Toronto, Ont., M6M 5B3, Canada.

KOTELNIKOV, Vladimir Aleksandrovich; Soviet radio and electronics engineer; b. Sept. 1908, Kazan; ed. Power Eng. Inst., Moscow; Prof. and Dean, Radio Eng. Faculty, Moscow Power Eng. Inst. 1931–47, Head, Chair. of Radio Eng. Principles, Moscow Power Eng. Inst. 1947–; Deputy Dir. Inst. of Radio Eng. and Electronics, U.S.S.R. Acad. of Sciences 1953–54, Dir. 1954–; mem. U.S.S.R. Acad. of Sciences 1953–, Vice-Pres. 1970–88, Acting Pres. May-Nov. 1975; Deputy and Chair. Supreme Soviet of R.S.F.S.R.; Fellow, American Inst. of Electrical and Electronics Engineers; Foreign mem. G.D.R. Acad. of Sciences, Polish Acad. of Sciences, Czechoslovak Acad. of Sciences, Mongolian Acad. of Sciences; Ed.-in-Chief Radio Eng. and Electronics; State Prize 1943, 1946, Lenin Prize 1964, Hero of Socialist Labour (twice), Order of Lenin (five times), Hammer and Sickle Gold Medal and other decorations. *Address:* c/o Institute of Radio Engineering and Electronics, U.S.S.R. Academy of Sciences, 18 Prospekt K. Marxa, Moscow, U.S.S.R.

KOTOŃSKI, Włodzimierz; Polish composer; b. 23 Aug. 1925, Warsaw; s. of Stanislaw Kotoński and Marianna Krysiak; m. Jadwiga Chlebowska 1951; one s.; ed. Warsaw State Higher School of Music; interested in folk music, especially of the Podhale region 1950–56; worked with Experimental Music Studio of Polish Radio and Electronic Music Studio of Westdeutscher Rundfunk, Cologne 1966–67; with Groupe de Recherches Musicales ORTF, Paris 1970; Assoc. Prof. of Composition and Head of Electronic Music Studio, State Higher School of Music (F. Chopin Music Acad. since 1972), Warsaw 1967–83, Head Composition Dept. 1981–, Extraordinary Prof. 1983–; Lecturer Acad. of Music, Stockholm 1971, State Univ. of N.Y. 1978; Chief Music Dir. of Polish Radio and TV 1974–76; Music Adviser of Chair. Cttee. for Radio and TV 1977–79; Deputy Chair. Polish Composers' Union 1965–71; DAAD Fellowship in W. Berlin 1970–71; mem. Presidential Council of Int. Soc. of Contemporary Music (ISCM) 1975–77, Pres. Polish Section 1983–; lectures and seminars on composition in U.S.A. 1978; compositions include orchestral and chamber music, some with percussion; also electronic and tape music, and instrumental theatre; Minister of Culture and Art Prize (2nd Class) 1973, Prize of Pres. Polish Radio and TV Cttee. (1st Class) 1979, Gold Cross of Merit, Officer's Cross of Order Polonia Restituta. *Publications:* Instrumenty perkusyjne we współczesnej orkiestrze (Percussion Instruments in the Modern Orchestra) 1965, Muzyka elektroniczna 1988. *Leisure interest:* tourism. *Address:* ul. Okolska 3 m. 6, 02 509 Warsaw, Poland. *Telephone:* 44-72-32.

KOTSOKOANE, Joseph Riffat Larry; Lesotho politician; b. 19 Oct. 1922, Johannesburg, South Africa; s. of Daniel Kotsokoane and Dolly Kotsokoane; m. Elizabeth Molise 1947; two s. three d.; ed. South Africa, Fort Hare Univ. Coll., Univ. of the Witwatersrand; teacher 1945–50; Agricultural Officer, Dept. of Agriculture, Basutoland, later Prin. of Agricultural Training School 1951–64, Prin. Agricultural Officer 1964–66; with British Embassy, Bonn 1966–67; High Commr. in the U.K. 1967–69; Perm. Sec., Ministry of Foreign Affairs 1969–70, Ministry of Educ., Health and Social Welfare 1970–72; High Commr. to Kenya, also accred. to Uganda and Tanzania 1972–74; Minister of Foreign Affairs 1974–75, of Educ. 1975–76, of Agric. 1976–78, of Educ., Sports and Culture 1984–85, to Prime Minister 1985–86; Perm. Rep. to the UN 1978, Cabinet Sec. 1978–84; Consultant in Human and Natural Resources 1986–. *Leisure interests:* photography, mountaineering, amateur dramatics, travel. *Address:* P.O. Box 1015, Maseru 100, Lesotho.

KOTSONIS, Archbishop Ieronymos; Greek ecclesiastic; b. Ysternia, Tinos; s. of Ieronymos and Angelica Kotsonis; fmr. Prof. of Canon Law, Univ. of Salonica; Chaplain to Greek Royal Family 1949–67; Archbishop of Athens and Primate of Greece 1967–73; Pres. of the Int. of Love. *Publications:* 110 works including (in Greek) Steering the Church 1975, On the Financial Problems of the Church of Greece 1975, The Drama of an Archbishop 1975, Agapism, the Only Way for Peace (in Greek) 1980,

Love is Not a Utopia (To avoid the Nuclear War) (in Greek) 1981, Am I a Christian? 1983. *Leisure interests:* fishing, swimming. *Address:* Ysternia, Tinos 84201, *or* Hatzichristou 8, Athens 10679, Greece. *Telephone:* 0283-31397 (Tinos); 9218-580 (Athens).

KOTT, Jan, PH.D.; American (b. Polish, naturalized 1978) literary critic and university professor; b. 27 Oct. 1914, Warsaw; s. of Maurycy Kott and Kazimiera Wertenstein; m. Lidia Steinhaus 1939; one s. one d.; served with Polish Army 1939, Polish Resistance Movt. 1942–45; Prof. of History of Polish Literature, Univ. of Warsaw; Visiting Prof. at Univ. of Calif. 1967–68, at Yale 1978–79; Prof. of Comparative Drama, State Univ. N.Y. at Stony Brook 1969–74, of English and Comparative Literature 1974–82, Prof. Emer. 1983–; Visiting Prof. of English at Istituto Universitario Orientale, Naples 1983; Guggenheim Fellow 1972–73; Getty Scholar 1985–86; Herder Award, Vienna 1964, Alfred Jurzykowski Award, New York 1976, George G. Nathan Award, Best Dramatic Criticism 1985; Hon. mem. Modern Language Asscn. *Publications:* Mitologia i realizm (Mythology and Realism) 1946, Szkoła klasyków (The School of the Classics) 1949, Jak wam się podoba (As You Like It) 1955, Postęp i głupstwo (Progress and Folly) 1956, Szkice o Szekspirze (Essays on Shakespeare) 1961, Shakespeare, notre contemporain (French trans.) 1962, Miarka za miarkę (Measure for Measure) 1962, Shakespeare, Our Contemporary (English trans.) 1964, Szekspir Współczesny 1965, Aloes 1966, Theatre Notebook 1947–67 1968, The Eating of the Gods: An Interpretation of Greek Tragedy 1973, Arcadia amara 1978, The Publications of Jan Kott 1979, Kamienny Potok (essays) 1981, The Theater of the Essence 1984, Gledaliski Ejeji 1985, Zjadanie Bogow 1986, Pozorište Esencije i Drugi Esei (essays) 1986, Kamienny Potok (essays) 1986, Marlowe and Shakespeare and the Carnival Tradition 1987. *Leisure interest:* collecting kitsch postcards. *Address:* 29 Quaker Path, Stony Brook, N.Y. 11790, U.S.A. *Telephone:* (516) 751-7614.

KOTZEE, Flores Petrus, M.B.A.; South African business executive; b. 27 May 1926, Reddersburg, O.F.S.; s. of Floris Petrus and Maria Alida; m. Naomi Botha 1949; four s.; ed. Hendrik Potgieter High School, Reddersburg, Stellenbosch and Pretoria Univs.; Gen. Works Man., Pretoria, ISCOR (S. African Independent Iron and Steel Corpn.) Ltd. 1974–76, Newcastle 1976–78, Divsional Gen. Man. (Steel Operations) 1978–80, Gen. Man. and Chief Exec. 1980–82, Man. Dir. 1982–83, Chair. 1984–87; Chair. Dorbyl Ltd., Union Steel Corpn. Ltd. *Leisure interest:* golf. *Address:* 1408 Breyer Avenue, Waverley, Pretoria, South Africa. *Telephone:* 73-8816.

KOUANDÉTÉ, Lieut.-Col. Maurice; Benin army officer and politician; b. 1939; ed. Ecole de Guerre, Paris; Dir. of Cabinet of Head of State 1967–69; Head of State and Head Provisional Govt. Dec. 1967; Chief of Staff of Dahomey (now Benin) Army 1969–70; leader of coup which overthrew Pres. Zinsou Dec. 1969; mem. of Directory (three man body ruling Dahomey), Minister of the Economy, Finance and Co-operation 1969–70; arrested 1970; Deputy Sec. for Defence 1970–72; arrested Feb. 1972, sentenced to death May 1972, granted amnesty and released Dec. 1972.

KOUASSI, Kwam, DR.RER.POL.; Togolese diplomatist; ed. Caen Univ. and the Sorbonne, Paris; Asst. in Public Law, Univ. of Benin 1975, then Lecturer at Ecole Supérieure d'Administration et des Carrières Juridiques, later Asst. Dir. of Univ. and Chair. of Univ.'s Comité de Lectures des Annales; served as Togo's Amb. to Cuba and to Costa Rica; Vice-Pres. UN's Conf. for the Announcement of Contributions to the Int. Year of Peace and Pres. of same to the World Disarmament Campaign, Perm. Rep. of Togo to UN 1985–88, Vice-Chair. UN Special Political Cttee. 1985, Chair. 1986–88. *Address:* c/o Ministry of Foreign Affairs and Co-operation, place du Monument aux Morts, Lomé, Togo.

KOULOUMBIS, Evangelos; Greek engineer and politician; b. 1929, Athens; s. of Athanasios Kouloumbis and Anastasia Kouloumbis; m. Dimitra Lambrou; one s. one d.; ed. Athens Polytechnic Univ.; founder mem. Civil Eng. Asscn., mem. Gov. Council 1965–67, Pres. 1974–75; Pres. of Tech. Chamber and Minister of Public Works in caretaker Govt. 1974; Pres. Greek Cttee. for Balkan Agreement and Co-operation 1975–; Chair. Council of Energy Ministers of EEC 1983 and many Greek and int. conventions, Perm. Conf. of Engs. of S.E. Europe (COPISEE) 1978–80; hon. mem. League of Cypriot Engs. and Architects; mem. Greek Cttee. UNESCO 1982–83; Minister without Portfolio 1981–82, for Energy and Nat. Resources 1982–84, of Physical Planning, Housing and Environment 1984, for Physical Planning, Housing, Public Works, Transport 1985–88, for the Environment, Physical Planning and Public Works 1985–88. *Publications:* articles on economic, social and political matters. *Address:* c/o Ministry for the Environment and Town Planning, Odos Amaliados 17, Athens, Greece.

KOULOURIANOS, Dimitri, PH.D.; Greek economist; b. 4 Dec. 1930, Koroni; m.; one s. one d.; ed. School of Econ. and Commercial Sciences, Athens and Univ. of Calif., Berkeley; Econ. Research Dept. Bank of Greece 1957–67; World Bank (IBRD) 1968–81, during which time he participated in many missions to Africa, Asia and Latin America and was seconded as econ. adviser to Govt. of Ethiopia; mem. European Parl. 1981; Gov. Hellenic Industrial Devt. Bank; Minister of Finance 1982–83; fmr. consultant to UNESCO; Perm. Rep. of Greece to OECD 1986–. *Address:* Permanent Delegation of Greece to OECD, 15 Villa Said, 75116 Paris, France.

KOURGANOFF, Vladimir, D.SC.; French astronomer; b. 1912, Moscow, Russia; m. Ruth Moj 1935; one s. one d.; ed. Lycée Saint-Louis, Sorbonne, Astrophysical Insts. of Paris and Oslo; C.N.R.S. 1938–52; Exchange Prof. Oslo Univ. 1946–48; Dir. Astronomical Laboratory, Lille Univ. 1952–61; Visiting Prof. Berkeley Univ. 1959; Prof. Univ. of Paris XI (Orsay) 1961–77. *Publications include:* L'ion H⁻ dans le soleil, Basic Methods in Transfer Problems, La recherche scientifique (with J. C. Kourganoff), Astronomie fondamentale élémentaire 1961, Initiation à la théorie de la relativité 1964, Introduction à la théorie générale du transfert des particules 1967, Exercices d'initiation rapide au Russe scientifique (with Ruth Kourganoff) 1969, Introduction à la physique des intérieurs stellaires 1969, La face cachée de l'université 1972, Introduction to Advanced Astrophysics 1980, Quelle école? Pour un enseignement véritable 1984. *Leisure interests:* piano, general problems of research and of education. *Address:* 20 avenue Paul Appell, 75014 Paris, France. *Telephone:* (1) 45-40-50-53, 92-45-83-58.

KOUROS, Andreas Kyriakou, M.A., PH.D.; Cypriot educationist; b. 6 Nov. 1918, Vasilia; s. of Kyriacos Kouros and Eleni Sava; m. Sonia Koskarian 1946; two d.; ed. London and Oxford Univs., Int. Inst. of Educ. Planning, Paris; Teacher 1944–53; Inspector of Schools, Ministry of Educ. 1953–59, Sr. Inspector 1959–61; Head Dept. of Primary Educ. 1961–68; Head of Educ. Planning 1968–70; Dir. of Educ. 1970–72, Minister 1972–74; Educ. Specialist, Int. Bank for Reconstruction and Devt. (World Bank) 1975–80; Educ. Consultant 1981–. *Publications:* The Construction and Validation of a Group Test of Intelligence for Greek Cypriot Children 1956, Education in Cyprus under the British Administration 1959, Electra 1968. *Leisure interests:* swimming, walking. *Address:* The Kenwood, 5101 River Road, Apartment 610, Bethesda, Md. 20816, U.S.A. *Telephone:* (301) 652-2894.

KOUTSOGIORGAS, Agamemnon; Greek politician; b. Rodini, Achaia; ed. Athens Univ. and Paris Univ. Law School; during World War II joined a resistance org., arrested by Italians and spent 18 months in prison camps; active in Centre Union in 1960's; during mil. dictatorship arrested and imprisoned for anti-regime activities 1967, imprisoned again, then hospitalized as result of maltreatment 1970; M.P. (PASOK) with particular interest in educ., public admin., justice and environmental issues; Minister of Interior 1986–87; Second Deputy Prime Minister 1987–88, Minister of Justice 1987–88, Minister to the Prime Minister Nov. 1988–. *Address:* Leoforos Vassilissis Sophias 15, 10674 Athens, Greece.

KOUTSOHERAS, Ioannis (see Coutsoheras, John).

KOUYOUMZELIS, Theodore, M.CHEM., D.SC.; Greek physicist; b. 1 Dec. 1906, Kydoniai, Ayvalik; s. of George Kouyoumzelis and Polyxeni Petridou; m. Stella Grigoriou 1940; one d.; ed. Univs. of Athens, Munich, Manchester and Heidelberg; Asst. Prof. Physics, Athens Univ. 1937–49, Prof. Extraordinary 1949–58; Prof. Physics, Athens Nat. Tech. Univ. 1958–72, Emer. 1972, Dean Faculty of Chemical Eng. 1961–69; Prof. War Naval Acad., Piraeus 1947–77; Sec.-Gen. Greek Atomic Energy Comm. 1954–60, Vice-Pres. 1972–74; Perm. Rep. of Greece to CERN 1955–82, Vice-Pres. 1973–75; Commdr. Orders of Phoenix and of George I. *Publications:* Alternating Currents 1948, 1958, Nuclear Physics 1947, Theoretical Electricity 1948, 1957, 1969, Wave Theory 1948, 1963, 1969, Elements of Nuclear Physics 1960, Elements of Physics (4 vols. with S. Peristerakis) 1960–73; articles in learned journals on research into Raman effect and structure of ions, glass and water molecular vibrations, gamma rays and their inter-action with matter, counting and electronic devices, fallout measurement. *Leisure interests:* hi-fi, classical music. *Address:* Nuclear Research Centre Democritos, Aghia Paraskevi, Athens (Office); 23 Pindou St., Filothei, 15237 Athens, Greece (Home). *Telephone:* 65-13-111 (Office); 6814-993 (Home).

KOVÁCS, András; Hungarian film director and script writer; b. 20 June 1925, Kide (now in Romania); ed. Győrffy Coll. and Acad. of Dramatic and Cinematic Arts; Drama reader, Hungarian Film Studio 1950, Drama Dept. Head 1951–57, Film Dir. 1960–; Pres. Fed. of Hungarian Film and TV Artists 1981–; Balázs B. Prize, Kossuth Prize 1970; named Eminent Artist. *Author:* Egy film forrásvidéke. (The Riverhead of a film) 1972; *TV films:* Menekülés Magyarországra (Flight to Hungary) 1980, György Lukács Portray 1986. *Screenplays:* Zápor (Summer Rain) 1960, Pesti háztetők (On the Roofs of Budapest) 1961, Isten őszi csillaga (Autumn Star) 1962, Nehéz emberek (Difficult People) 1964, Hideg napok (Cold Days) 1966, Falak (Walls) 1968, Ecstasy from 7 to 10 1969, Staféta (Relay Race) 1970, A magyar ugaron (Fallow Land) 1973, Bekötött szemmel (Blindfold) 1975, Labirintus (Labyrinth) 1976, A ménesgazda (The Stud Farm) 1978, Októberi vasárnap (A Sunday in October) 1979, Szeretők (An Afternoon Affair) 1983, A vörös grófnö (The Red Countess) 1985, Két választás Magyarországon (Two Elections in Hungary) 1987, Rearguard Struggle 1987. *Leisure interest:* gardening. *Address:* 1122 Budapest, Magyar akobinusok tere 2/3, Hungary. *Telephone:* 567-129.

KOVÁCS, Dénes; Hungarian violinist; b. 18 April 1930, Vác; s. of József Kovács and Margit Juhász; m.; one s. one d.; ed. Budapest Acad. of Music under Ede Zathureczky; First Violinist, Budapest State Opera 1951–60; leading Violin Prof. at Budapest Music Acad. 1957–, Dir. of Budapest Music Acad. 1967–; Rector Ferenc Liszt Acad. of Music 1971–80, Dean of String Dept. 1980–; concert tours all over Europe, in U.S.A., U.S.S.R., Iran, India, China and Japan; mem. jury in int. competitions: Tchaikovsky, Moscow; Long-Thibaud, Paris; Jean Sibelius, Helsinki; Joseph Joachim,

Vienna; Wieniawski, Warsaw; Tokyo; Kossuth Prize 1963, awarded Eminent Artist title 1970, Golden Medal of Labour 1974. *Address:* Music Academy, 1061 Budapest VI, Liszt Ferenc tér 8 (Office); Irányi utca 12, Budapest V, Hungary (Home). *Telephone:* 414-788 (Office).

KOVALEV, Anatoliy Gavrilovich; Soviet diplomatist; b. 1923; entered diplomatic service 1948; mem. Apparat U.S.S.R. Foreign Ministry 1957–65; Head of First European Dept. at Foreign Ministry 1965–71; U.S.S.R. Deputy Minister of Foreign Affairs and Head of Admin. for Foreign Planning 1971–. *Address:* The Kremlin, Moscow, U.S.S.R.

KOVALEV, Mikhail Vasilevich; Soviet Party official; b. 1925; ed. Leningrad Mining Inst. mem. of CPSU 1962–; Red Army 1941–45; worker, then dir. of a construction works trust in Siligorsk 1954–66; Deputy Minister of Construction Industry for Byelorussian S.S.R. 1966–67; Pres. of Minsk Soviet of Popular Deputies 1967–77; First Deputy Pres. of Byelorussian S.S.R. Gosplan 1977–78; Deputy, First Deputy of Pres. of Council of Ministers for Byelorussian S.S.R. 1978–86, Pres. 1986–; mem. of Cen Cttee; elected to Congress of People's Deputies of the U.S.S.R. 1989–. *Address:* Council of Ministers, Minsk, Byelorussian S.S.R., U.S.S.R.

KOVANOV, Vladimir Vasiliyevich; Soviet surgeon; b. 13 March 1909, St. Petersburg (now Leningrad); m. K. Andreyevna 1928; two s. one d.; ed. Moscow Univ.; Postgraduate Asst., First Moscow Medical Inst. 1931–41; mem. CPSU 1939–; Soviet Army Medical Officer 1941–45; Instructor, Head of Section, Deputy Head of Dept., CPSU Cen. Cttee. 1945–50; Head of Dept., First Moscow Medical Inst. 1946–; Pro-rector, First Moscow Medical Inst. 1950–56, Rector 1956–66; Corresp. mem. U.S.S.R. Acad. of Medical Sciences 1960–63, mem. 1963–; Vice-Pres., U.S.S.R. Acad. of Medical Sciences 1966; mem. Presidium Soviet Peace Cttee.; Order of Lenin (twice), Red Banner (twice), Red Star 1942, Patriotic War, First Class 1944, Patriotic War, Second Class 1944, Honoured Scientist of R.S.F.S.R. 1965, Spasokukotsky Prize, Shevkunenko Prize. *Publications:* over 250 works, including 40 monographs, on treatment of thoracic cage wounds, traumatic shock, surgical anatomy of extremities, cardiac surgery, and transplantation of organs. *Leisure interests:* journalism, writing. *Address:* c/o U.S.S.R. Academy of Medical Sciences, 14 Ulitsa Solyanka, Moscow, U.S.S.R.

KOWALCZYK, Edward, D.ING.; Polish politician and engineer; b. 25 May 1924, Warsaw; m. Maria Krystyna Toniakiewicz; two s.; ed. Technical Univ. of Warsaw, and Warsaw Univ.; took part in Resistance in Warsaw during Second World War and imprisoned in Germany; mem. Democratic Party 1967–, mem. Cen. Cttee. 1973–76, Presidium Cen. Cttee. 1976–, Chair. Cen. Cttee. 1981–85; Deputy to Seym 1969–72, 1985–; Minister of Posts and Telecommunications 1969–80; Vice-Chair. Supreme Chamber of Control 1981, Council of Ministers 1981–85; mem. Presidium, Provisional Nat. Council of Patriotic Movt. for Nat. Rebirth (PRON) 1982–83, mem. Presidium Nat. Council of PRON 1983–87; Chair. Polish Cybernetic Asscn. 1970–81; fmr. mem. Council of Science and Technics; Vice-Chair. Scientific Society of Płock; fmr. Head of Płock Branch of Warsaw Tech. Univ.; Extraordinary Prof., then Ordinary Prof. Inst. of Telecommunications, Warsaw; mem. Union of Fighters for Freedom and Democracy (ZBoWiD); awards include Cross of Gold for Merit, Kt.'s and Commdr.'s Crosses of Polonia Restituta, Order of Banner of Labour 1st Class, Warsaw Insurgent Cross. *Publications:* several books on electronics and telecommunications. *Leisure interests:* scientific and political activities. *Address:* Centralny Komitet SD, ul. Rutkowskiego 9, P.O. Box 381, 00-950, Warsaw, Poland.

KOWALCZYK, Gen. Stanisław; Polish politician; b. 12 Dec. 1924, Pabianice; ed. Acad. of Mining and Metallurgy, Cracow; mem. Polish Socialist Party 1947–48, Polish United Workers' Party (PZPR) 1948–, successively Head of Econ. Dept. of Voivodship Cttee., Katowice, Sec. Voivodship Cttee., Katowice, Head of Dept. of Heavy Industry and Transport, Cen. Cttee. PZPR 1968–71, Deputy mem. Cen. Cttee. PZPR 1964–68, mem. Cen. Cttee. 1968–81, Sec. Cen. Cttee. 1971–73, Deputy mem., Political Bureau of Cen. Cttee. 1973–75, mem. Political Bureau 1975–80; Deputy to Seym (Parl.) 1969; Chair. Seym Comm. for Econ. Planning, Budget and Finance 1972–73; Minister of Internal Affairs 1973–80; Deputy Chair. Council of Ministers 1980–81; Brig.-Gen. 1974–77, Divisional Gen. 1977; Order of Banner of Labour (1st and 2nd Class), Kt.'s Cross, Officer's Cross Order of Polonia Restituta, Order of Builders of People's Poland 1974, Medal of 30th Anniversary of People's Poland 1974, and other decorations.

KOYAMA, Goro; Japanese banker; b. 25 March 1909, Gunma Prefecture; s. of Toichi Oshimà and Han Oshima; m. Atsu Koyama 1934; two s. one d.; ed. Tokyo Univ.; Man. Dir. The Mitsui Bank Ltd. 1963–65, Deputy Pres. 1965–68, Pres. 1968–72, Chair. 1974–82. *Leisure interests:* painting, golf. *Address:* c/o The Mitsui Bank Ltd., 1-2 Yurakucho 1-chome, Chiyoda-ku, Tokyo (Office); 3-15-10 Takaido-Higashi, Suginamiku, Tokyo, Japan (Home). *Telephone:* 501-1111(Office); 333-0843 (Home).

KOYAMBA, Alphonse; Central African Republic politician; Sec. of State for Finance, Industry and Commerce July–Oct 1972; Minister of Finance 1972–73; Minister of State charged with Finance 1974–75; with Org. of the Public Treasury 1975–76; Third Deputy Prime Minister charged with org. of the Public Treasury Sept.-Dec. 1976; First Deputy Prime Minister charged with the Public Treasury 1976–78, with Co-ordination of Econ.

and Financial Questions 1978-79, responsible for Economy and Finance, Posts and Telecommunications, and Control of State Enterprises 1979-80; Gov. of IMF 1979-80, C.A.R. Dir. Banque des Etats de l'Afrique Centrale 1982-. *Address:* B.P. 151, Bangui, Central African Republic.

KOZÁK, Jan, RSDR.; Czechoslovak writer; b. 25 March 1921, Roudnice nad Labem; ed. Commercial Coll., České Budějovice, Cen. Political Coll., office worker, Meva firm, Roudnice nad Labem 1940-45; with SPOFA enterprise, Roudnice nad Labem, 1945-49; official of the Cen. Cttee. of the CP of Czechoslovakia, 1949-50, mem. Cen. Cttee. 1971-; scientific worker, external worker, dept. of the History of Czechoslovakia and the History of the CP of Czechoslovakia, Political Coll. of the Cen. Cttee. of the CP of Czechoslovakia, Prague, 1952-75, Assoc. Prof. 1965; Deputy Chair. Preparatory Cttee. of the Union of Czech Writers 1970-72; Chair. of the Union of Czech Writers 1972-77; Chair. Czechoslovak Cttee. of the Union of Writers 1973-77; Chair. Union of Czechoslovak Writers 1977-89; Presidium mem. 1977-. *Work:* novels, short stories: Views through Windows 1941, Hot Breath 1961, Mariana Radvaková 1962, ... Strong Arm 1966, Trap 1968, Hunting in Bambuika 1970, Saint Michael 1971, Hunter in the Taiga 1974, The White Stallion 1975, The Stork Nest 1976, Autumn in the Land of Tigers 1979, Wellsprings of Creation 1981; Order of Labour 1971, State Prize of Klement Gottwald 1972, 1977, National Artist 1980, Order of Victorious February 1981, Order of Friendship of Nations, U.S.S.R. 1981, Nat. Prize of Czech Socialist Repub. 1983. *Address:* Central Committee of the Communist Party of Czechoslovakia, Nábr Ludvíka Svobody 12, 125 11 Prague 1, Czechoslovakia.

KOZIOŁ, Józef, D. ECON. SC.; Polish economist and politician; b. 26 Feb. 1939, Szalowa, Nowy Sącz Voivodship; m.; two c.; ed. Main School of Planning and Statistics, Warsaw; former mem. youth orgs. Polish Youth Union 1953-56, Polish Students' Asscn. 1957-62; mem. United Peasant Party (ZSL) 1959-, Pres. ZSL Circle of Main School of Planning and Statistics, Warsaw 1960-61; Inspector of Agric. Bank, Grodzisk Mazowiecki 1962-63; Sr. Inspector of Agric. Bank Head Office, Warsaw 1963-66; Lecturer of Inst. of Finance, Warsaw 1966-74; Ed. of monthly Wieś Współczesna, Warsaw 1972-74; Deputy Gen. Dir. Agric. Bank Head Office, Warsaw 1974-75; Vice-Pres. Head Office, Food Economy Bank, Warsaw 1975-80; Vice-Pres. 1980, Pres. 1980-81; mem. Presidum ZSL Chief Cttee. 1980-81, Sec. 1981-83, Deputy Pres. 1984-; First Deputy Minister of Agric. and Food Econs. 1982-83; Deputy Chair. Planning Comm. attached to Council of Ministers 1983-85; Deputy to Seym (Parl.) 1985-; Deputy Chair. Council of Ministers 1985-88; Minister of Environmental Protection and Natural Resources 1988-; mem. Econ. Cttee. of Council of Ministers 1988-; Officer's Cross of Order of Polonia Restituta, Silver Cross of Merit and other decorations. *Publications:* numerous works on economy, mainly on agric. and food economy. *Leisure interests:* gardening, history. *Address:* Ministerstwo Ochrony Środowiska i Zasobow Naturalnych, ul. Wawelska 52/54, 00-922 Warszawa, Poland.

KOZLOV, Nikolay Timofeyevich; Soviet politician; b. 1925; ed. Moscow Timiryazev Acad. of Agriculture; mem. CPSU 1946; Soviet Army service 1943-47; Official, Moscow Regional Cttee. of CPSU 1952-58, 1959-60; Head of Statistics Dept., Moscow Region 1958-59; First Vice-Chair. Moscow Regional Soviet of Working People's Deputies 1960; Sec. Moscow Regional Cttee., CPSU 1960-63; Chair. Moscow Regional Soviet of Working People's Deputies 1963-; Minister of Fruit and Vegetable Production 1980-86; Cand. mem. CPSU Cen. Cttee. 1966-71; mem. 1971-; Deputy to U.S.S.R. Supreme Soviet 1966-; Sec. Comm. for Legislative Proposals; mem. Cttee., U.S.S.R. Parl. Group. *Address:* Skatertny per. 4, Moscow, U.S.S.R.

KOZLOVSKY, Yevgeniy Aleksandrovich; Soviet engineer and politician; b. 1929; mem. CPSU 1955; graduated from Moscow Geology Inst. 1953; worked in Amur Oblast and Khabarovsk Territory as chief engineer and head of expedition 1953-65. Head of admin. of U.S.S.R. Ministry of Geology 1965-73, Director of scientific research institution 1973-74, U.S.S.R. Deputy Minister of Geology 1974-75, Minister of Geology Dec. 1975-; Cand. mem. of the CC, CPSU 1976-; Order of Lenin, Lenin Prize and other decorations. *Address:* U.S.S.R. Ministry of Geology, Bolshaya Gruzinskaya ul. 4/6, Moscow, U.S.S.R.

KOZŁOWSKI, Waldemar; Polish politician; b. 3 March 1927, Gościniec; ed. Main School of Agric., Warsaw; farm and forest labourer during Nazi occupation, mem. Peasant Battalions 1943-44; worked in PAGED Foreign Trade Enterprise, Warsaw 1950-51, in enterprises for railway works and at Cen. Bd. of Railway Works Enterprises 1952-55; employee, Ministry of Timber and Paper Industry, later of Forestry and Timber Industry 1955-, Sr. inspector 1955-61, Counsellor to Minister in Planning Dept. 1961-64, Deputy Dir. Timber Industry Dept. 1969-72, Dir. 1972-73, Dir. Production, Co-operation and Sales Dept. 1974-81, Minister of Forestry and Timber Industry 1981-85; mem. United Peasant Party (ZSL) 1959-, Sec. ZSL Dist. Cttee. Warsaw-Ochota 1965-69, ZSL Warsaw Cttee. 1971-73, 1980-; Kt.'s Cross of Polonia Restituta Order and other decorations.

KOŹNIEWSKA, Halina, M.D.; Polish neurosurgeon and politician; b. 28 May 1920, Tomczyn, near Kutno; ed. Warsaw Univ.; Doctor 1949-57, Docent 1957-68, Extraordinary Prof. 1968-75, Ordinary Prof. 1975-; Head of Neurosurgery Dept., Clinic of Nervous Diseases, Medical Acad., Lublin 1957-64; Dir. Neurosurgery Clinic 1964-73; Dir. Neurosurgery Clinic and

Inst. of Nervous Diseases, Medical Acad. of Lublin 1973-84, Dir. Neurosurgery Dept. and Clinic 1984-; Deputy Dean of Medical Faculty 1966-69; Deputy to Seym (Parl.) 1969-85; mem. Council of State 1972-80; Sec. Polish Neurosurgical Soc. until 1970, mem. Cen. Bd. and Chair. Science Comm. 1970-; mem. Scandinavian and Yugoslav Neurosurgical Socs.; Award of Minister of Health and Social Welfare (1st Class) 1984; Order of Banner of Labour (Second Class), Commdr's., Officer's and Kt's. Cross of Order of Polonia Restituta, Gold and Silver Cross of Merit, Meritorious Teacher of Polish People's Repub. *Publications:* about 85 works on pathophysiology, neuro-oncology and neuro-traumatology. *Address:* ul. Gliniana 12m. 38, 20-616 Lublin, Poland (Home). *Telephone:* 22713 (Office).

KOZOL, Jonathan, B.A.; American author; b. 5 Sept. 1936, Boston; s. of Dr. Harry L. Kozol and Ruth Massell Kozol; ed. Harvard Coll. and Magdalen Coll., Oxford; teacher in Boston area 1964-72; lecturer at numerous univs. 1973-85; Guggenheim Fellow 1972, 1984, 1985; Field Foundation Fellow 1973, 1974; Rockefeller Fellow 1978, Sr. Fellow 1983; Rhodes Scholar 1954; Nat. Book Award 1968. *Publications:* Death At An Early Age 1967, Free Schools 1972, The Night Is Dark 1975, Children of the Revolution 1978, On Being a Teacher 1979, Prisoners of Silence 1980, Illiterate America 1985, Rachel and Her Children: Homeless Families in America 1988. *Leisure interests:* reading history and religion. *Address:* P.O. Box 145, Byfield, Mass. 01922, U.S.A. *Telephone:* 508-465-9325.

KRACKOW, Jürgen, DR.; German business executive; b. 30 May 1923; s. of late Hanns Krackow and Ursula Gebauer; Apprentice, Commerz-Bank; Asst. Trinkhaus-Bank; Boswall and Knauer (construction co.); Man. Sidol-Werke Siegel 1957; joined man. of Berliner Handelsgesellschaft (BHG) 1962, Berliner Maschinenbau AG 1963; mem. Man. Bd., Holding AG für Industrie und Verkehrswesen 1967; mem. Man. Bd. AG "Weser" (member of Krupp group) 1969, subsequently Chair.; Chair. Man. Bd. Fried. Krupp GmbH Oct.-Dec. 1972, Man. Dir. May 1972; Chair. Man. Bd. Stahlwerke Röchling-Burbach 1975-85; mem. Supervisory Bd., Berliner Maschinenbau AG; Chair. Council EEC Builders of Large Ships; Dir. Arbed Saarstahl GmbH, Völklingen 1985-. *Address:* Schumannstrasse 100, 4000 Düsseldorf, Federal Republic of Germany.

KRAFT, Christopher Columbus, Jr., B.S.; American space administrator; b. 28 Feb. 1924, Phoebus, Va.; s. of Christopher Columbus and Vanda Olivia (Suddreth) Kraft; m. Elizabeth Anne Turnbull 1950; one s. one d.; ed. Virginia Polytechnic Inst.; mem., Langley Aeronautical Lab., Nat. Advisory Cttee. for Aeronautics 1945; selected to join Space Task Group on Project Mercury 1958; Flight Dir. all Mercury Missions: Dir. of Flight Operations, Manned Spacecraft Center 1963-69; Deputy Dir. Johnson Space Center 1970-72; Dir. NASA Johnson Space Center 1972-82; Fellow, American Inst. of Aeronautics and Astronautics 1966; Fellow, American Astronautical Soc; Hon. D.Eng. (Indiana Inst. of Tech.) 1966, (St. Louis Univ., Ill.) 1967, (Villanova) 1979; Arthur S. Fleming Award 1963, NASA Outstanding Leadership Award 1963, Spirit of St. Louis Medal, American Soc. of Mechanical Engineers 1967, NASA Distinguished Service Medal (twice) 1969, Chevalier, Légion d'honneur 1976, Nat. Civil Service League Career Service Award 1976, W. Randolph Lovelace Award (American Astronautical Soc.) 1977, Daniel and Florence Guggenheim Award (Int. Astronautics Fed.) 1978, AAIA von Karman Lectureship Award 1979, Goddard Memorial Trophy 1979, Roger W. Jones Award 1979, inducted into Virginia Aviation Hall of Fame 1979. *Address:* Rockwell International, 1840 NASA Boulevard, Houston, Tex. 77058, U.S.A.

KRAFT, Robert Paul, PH.D.; American professor of astronomy and astrophysics; b. 16 June 1927, Seattle, Wash.; s. of Victor P. Kraft and Viola E. Ellis; m. Rosalie A. Reichmuth 1949; two s.; ed. Univ. of Washington and Univ. of California at Berkeley; Instructor in mathematics and astronomy, Whittier Coll. 1949-51; Asst. Prof. of Astronomy, Indiana Univ. 1956-58; Asst. Prof. of Astronomy, Univ. of Chicago 1958-59; mem. staff, Mt. Wilson and Palomar Observatories 1960-67; Astronomer and Prof., Lick Observatory 1967-; Acting Dir. Lick Observatory 1968-70, 1971-73, Dir. 1981-; Dir. Univ. of California Observatories 1988-; Visiting Fellow, Joint Inst. of Laboratory Astrophysics, Univ. of Colo. 1970; Pres. American Astronomical Soc. 1974-76; Vice-Pres. Int. Astronomical Union 1982-88; mem. N.A.S., American Acad. of Arts and Sciences; Nat. Science Foundation Fellow 1953-55, Fairchild Scholar, California Inst. of Tech. 1980; Warner Prize, American Astronomical Soc. 1962. *Publications:* articles in professional journals. *Leisure interests:* music (classical and rock), oenology, duplicate bridge. *Address:* Lick Observatory, University of California, Santa Cruz, Calif. 95064, U.S.A. *Telephone:* 408 429-2991.

KRAIGHER, Sergej; Yugoslav (Slovene) politician; b. 30 May 1914, Postojna, Slovenia; s. of Anton Kraigher and Marija Joške; m. Lidija Sentjurc 1939; two d.; ed. Zagreb Univ.; mem. CP Cttee., Ljubljana Univ.; imprisoned 1934-36; Sec. Regional Cttee. CP of Slovenia, Ljubljana, Instructor of Cen. Cttee. Trbovje, active in war 1941-45 as Sec. of provincial cttee. and Liberation Front for Styria; various regional posts after war; Pres. Planning Comm. of Slovenia 1946-50; Vice-Pres. of Govt. of Slovenia 1951; Gov. Nat. Bank 1951-53; Dir. Fed. Office for Econ. Planning 1953-58; Sec. for Industry 1958-59; Pres. Foreign Trade Cttee., Sec. of State for Foreign Trade 1959-63; Vice-Pres. Fed. Chamber, Pres. Comm. for Socio-Econ. Relations and for Econ. System of Fed. Assembly 1963-67; Pres. Assembly Socialist Repub. of Slovenia 1967-74; mem. Presidency of S.F.R. of Yugoslavia 1979-84; Pres. of Presidency of Slovenia 1974-79; mem. Cen. Cttee., League of Communists of Slovenia 1952-, of Yugoslavia 1969-73; mem. Collective Presidency of Yugoslavia 1979-84, Vice-Pres. 1980-81, Pres. 1981-82; Hon. Dr. Edvard Kardelj Univ., Maribor 1979; national decorations including partisan Memorial Badge and foreign decorations. *Publications:* numerous articles on socio-political and economic issues. *Leisure interests:* literature, fine arts, theatre, mountaineering, swimming. *Address:* c/o Presidency of the Socialist Federal Republic of Yugoslavia, Bulevar Lenjina 2, Belgrade, Yugoslavia.

KRAIJENHOFF, Jonkheer Gualtherus; Netherlands business executive; b. 1922; ed. Switzerland; Royal Air Force (U.K.) pilot 1943-47; joined N.V. Organon, Oss 1947, Man. Dir. 1957; mem. Bd. of Man. N.V. Kon. Zwanenberg-Organon 1959, Pres. 1963; mem. Bd. of Man., Kon. Zout-Organon N.V. 1967, Pres. 1969; Vice-Pres. AKZO N.V., Arnhem 1969, Pres. 1971-78, mem. Supervisory Council May 1978- (Chair. 1980-); Dir. S. G. Warburg and Co. 1978-; Dir. APV Holdings 1983-; Pres. Netherlands. Red Cross 1966; Kt., Netherlands Lion, Order of St. John. *Address:* Zomerland, Louiseweg 15, Nijmegen, Netherlands (Home).

KRAIVICHIEN, Thanin, LL.B.; Thai jurist and politician; b. 5 April 1927; m. Karen Andersen; five c.; ed. Suan Kularp School, Thammasat Univ., Univ. of London, Gray's Inn; Sr. Judge, Civil Court 1969; Sr. Judge, Court of Appeal 1972; Judge, Supreme Court 1972-76, Sr. Judge 1976; mem. Nat. Assembly 1973-76; Prime Minister 1976-77 (deposed in coup); Chair. Investment Bd. of Thailand 1976-77. *Publications:* Democracy, Communist Ideology and Tactics, The Language of the Thai Law, The Use of Anti-Communist Law, Constitutional Monarchy, The Reform of the Legal and Judicial Systems during the Reign of King Chulalongkorn. *Address:* c/o Office of the Prime Minister, Government House, Bangkok, Thailand.

KRAJINA, Borislav; Yugoslav politician; b. 1930, Doboj, Bosnia and Herzegovina; ed. Sarajevo Univ.; fmr. Judge Dist. and Regional Courts, Doboj, Supreme Court of Bosnia and Herzegovina, and Pres. Municipal Assembly Doboj; Chair. Supreme Court Bosnia and Herzegovina 1974-; mem. and Sec. Republican Conf., Socialist Alliance of Working People of Bosnia and Herzegovina and Deputy Organizational Political Council, Fed. Assembly; Chair. Conf. Section for Realization of Self-Man. Rights and Duties of Working People and Citizens; Minister for Justice and Org. of Fed. Admin., Fed. Exec. Council 1982-85. *Address:* c/o Federal Executive Council, Bul. Lenjina 2, 11075 Novi Beograd, Yugoslavia.

KRAMER, Dame Leonie Judith, D.B.E., D.PHIL., F.A.H.A., F.A.C.E.; Australian professor of literature; b. 1 Oct. 1924; d. of the late A. L. Kramer and G. Gibson; m. Harold Kramer 1952; two d.; ed. Presbyterian Ladies Coll., Melbourne and Univs. of Melbourne and Oxford; Tutor, St. Hugh's Coll., Oxford 1949-52; Assoc. Prof. Univ. of N.S.W. 1963-68; Prof. of Australian Literature, Univ. of Sydney, 1968-, Fellow of Senate 1969-74; Vice-Pres. Australian Assen. for Teaching of English 1967-70; Vice-Pres. Australian Soc. of Authors 1969-71; mem. Nat. Literature Bd. of Review 1970-73; mem. Council, Nat. Library of Australia 1975-81; Pres., then Vice-Pres. Australian Council for Educ. Standards 1973-; mem. Univs. Council 1974-85; Commr. Australian Broadcasting Comm. (ABC) 1977-81, Chair. 1982-83, Dir. Australia and N.Z. Banking Group 1983-, Western Mining Corpn. 1984-, Australian Fixed Trusts Group 1986-, Quadrant Magazine Co. Ltd. 1987-; mem. Council Nat. Roads and Motorists' Assen.; Nat. Pres. Australia—British Soc.; mem. Council Australian Nat. Univ. 1984-87; Chair. Bd. of Dirs. Nat. Inst. of Dramatic Art (NIDA) 1987-; Sr. Fellow Inst. of Public Affairs (IPA) 1988-; Hon. D.Litt. (Tasmania), Hon. LL.D. (Melbourne), (Australian Nat. Univ.). *Publications include:* Henry Handel Richardson and Some of Her Sources 1954, Australian Poetry (ed.) 1961, Companion to Australia Felix 1962, Myself When Laura 1966, A. D. Hope 1979, The Oxford History of Australian Literature (ed.) 1981, The Oxford Anthology of Australian Literature (Ed. with Adrian Mitchell) 1985, My Country: Australian Poetry and Short Stories—Two Hundred Years (2 vols.) 1985. *Leisure interests:* gardening, music. *Address:* 12 Vaucluse Road, Vaucluse, N.S.W., 2030 Australia.

KRAMER, Paul Jackson, A.B., PH.D., D.SC.; American plant physiologist; b. 8 May 1904, Brookville, Ind.; s. of LeRoy Kramer and Minnie Jackson; m. Edith Sarah Vance 1931; one s. one d.; ed. Miami Univ., Ohio and Ohio State Univ.; Instructor in Botany, Duke Univ. 1931, Prof. 1945, James B. Duke Prof. of Botany 1954-74, Emer. 1974-; Dir. Sarah P. Duke Gardens 1945-74, Consultant 1974-78; Program Dir. Nat. Science Foundation 1960-61; Visiting Prof. Univ. of Tex., Austin Sept. 1976; Walker-Ames Visiting Prof. Univ. of Wash., Seattle Feb. 1977-; Chair. Section G., A.A.A.S. 1956; Pres. American Soc. of Plant Physiologists 1945, N. Carolina Acad. of Sciences 1962, American Inst. of Biological Sciences, and Botanical Soc. of America 1964; Barnes Life mem. American Soc. of Plant Physiologists; mem. Nat. Acad. of Sciences, American Acad. of Arts and Sciences and American Philosophical Soc.; Certificate of Merit, Botanic Soc. of America, Outstanding Achievement Award, Soc. of American Foresters. *Publications:* Plant and Soil Water Relationships 1949, 2nd edn. 1969, Physiology of Trees (with T. T. Kozlowski) 1960, Physiology of Woody Plants (with T. T. Kozlowski) 1979, Adaptation of Plants to Water and High Temperature Stress (Ed. with N. C. Turner) 1980, Crop Reactions to Water and Temperature Stresses in Humid, Temperate Climates (Ed. with C. D. Raper) 1983, A Collection of Lectures in Tree Physiology (in Chinese)

1982, Water Relations of Plants 1983; over 150 research papers in plant science journals and chapters in several books. *Leisure interests:* gardening, photography, bird-watching. *Address:* Department of Botany, Duke University, Durham, N.C. (Office); Carolina Meadows, 1-301 Chapel Hill, N.C. 27514, U.S.A. (Home). *Telephone:* (919) 684-2359 (Office), (919) 942-4480 (Home).

KRAMER, Stanley, B.SC.; American film producer, director; b. 29 Sept. 1913, New York; m. 1st Ann Pearce 1950; two s.; m. 2nd Karen Sharpe 1966; two d.; ed. New York Univ.; M.G.M. Research Dept.; film cutter for three years and film ed.; film and radio writer; served U.S. Signal Corps; formed own film production co. to produce This Side of Innocence; founder and Pres. Kramer Pictures 1949-. *Films include:* (assoc. producer) So Ends Our Night 1941, The Moon and Sixpence 1942; (producer) So This is New York 1948, Home of the Brave 1949, The Men 1950, Cyrano de Bergerac 1950, Death of a Salesman 1951, High Noon 1952, The Happy Time 1952, Eight Iron Men 1952, The Caine Mutiny; (producer-dir.) Not As a Stranger 1955, The Pride and the Passion 1957, The Defiant Ones 1958, On The Beach 1959, Inherit the Wind 1960, Judgment at Nuremberg 1961, It's a Mad, Mad, Mad, Mad World 1963, Ship of Fools 1965, Guess Who's Coming to Dinner 1967, The Secret of Santa Vittoria 1969, R.P.M. 1971, Bless the Beasts and Children 1971, Oklahoma Crude 1973, The Domino Principle 1977, The Runner Stumbles 1979. *Address:* Stanley Kramer Productions, P.O. Box 158, Bellevue, Wash. 90889, U.S.A. (Office).

KRÄMER, Werner, DR.PHIL.; German archaeologist; b. 8 March 1917, Wiesbaden; s. of Max and Martha Krämer; ed. Univs. of Munich, Frankfurt, Kiel, Marburg; Curator and Departmental Dir. Bavarian State Office for Preservation of Monuments 1947-56; First Dir. and Prof. Roman-German Comm. of German Archaeological Inst. Frankfurt 1956-72; Pres. German Archaeological Inst. 1972-79; mem. Royal Irish Acad., Soc. of Antiquaries, London, Istituto Italiano di Preistoria e Prostoria, British Acad., etc. *Address:* Klopstockstrasse 5, 6200 Wiesbaden, Federal Republic of Germany. *Telephone:* (06 121) 84 22 20.

KRANIDIOTIS, Nicos; Cypriot scholar, journalist and diplomatist; b. 25 Nov. 1911, Kyrenia; s. of John N. Kranidiotis and Polyxeni J. Kranidiotis; m. Chryssoula Vizakas 1946; one s. one d.; ed. Pan Cyprian Gymnasium, Cyprus, Athens Univ. and Harvard Univ. Center for Int. Affairs; worked as schoolmaster in Cyprus; Dir. of Hellenic Cyprus (official political organ of Cyprus Ethnarchy) 1949; Gen. Sec. Cyprus Ethnarchy 1953-57, Councillor 1957-60; Amb. to Greece 1960-79, concurrently Amb. to Yugoslavia 1963-79, to Italy 1964-79, to Bulgaria 1970-79, to Romania 1970-79; Sec. of 2nd and 3rd Cyprus Nat. Assemblies 1954, 1955; Founder, Dir. (with others) of Kypriaka Grammata (Cyprus Literature), a literary magazine 1934, Ed. 1946-56. *Publications:* Chronicles (short stories) 1945, The Neohellenic Theatre (Essay) 1950, Studies (poems) 1951, Forms of Myth (short stories) 1954, The Poet G. Seferis (essay) 1955, The National Character of Cyprus Literature 1958, Cyprus in her Struggle for Freedom (history) 1958, Introduction to the Poetry of G. Seferis (essay) 1965, Cyprus-Greece (essay) 1966, Cypriot Poetry (essay) 1969, Kypriaka Grammata (essay) 1970, Epistrophi (poems) 1974, Poesie (poems) 1974, The Cyprus Problem (history) 1975. *Leisure interests:* reading, writing. *Address:* Dimokratias 44, P. Psychico, Athens, Greece; 16 Prometheus Street, Nicosia, Cyprus (Home). *Telephone:* 6712744 (Athens); 2907.

KRANTZ, Judith; American author; b. 9 Jan. 1928, New York City; contrib. to Good Housekeeping 1948-54, McCalls 1954-59, Ladies Home Journal 1959-71; contributing ed. Cosmopolitan 1971-79. *Publications:* Scruples 1978, Princess Daisy 1980, Mistral's Daughter 1982, I'll Take Manhattan 1986. *Address:* Krantz Productions, 9601 Wilshire Boulevard, Suite 343, Beverly Hills, Calif. 90210, U.S.A.

KRASIL'NIKOV, Dmitriy Danilovich; Soviet physicist; b. 1920; ed. Yakutsk Pedagogical Inst.; teacher 1940-; served in Soviet Army 1943-44; mem. of staff of Yakutsk Inst. for Research into Space Physics, U.S.S.R. Acad. of Sciences 1948-, head of lab. 1964-; mem. CPSU 1953; Lenin Prize 1982. *Publications* include numerous works on space research 1947-80. *Address:* U.S.S.R. Academy of Sciences, Leninsky Pr.14, Moscow V-71, U.S.S.R.

KRASIŃSKI, Zdzisław, D.ECON.SC.; Polish economist and politician; b. 17 Nov. 1930, Poznan; m.; two c.; ed. Higher School of Econs., Poznań; teacher Higher School of Econs. (now Econs. Acad.), Poznań 1961-, Asst. Prof. 1972, Extraordinary Prof. 1978, Dean, Faculty of Production and Turnover Econs. 1975-81; mem. Council of Ministers 1981-85, Chair. State Prices Comm. 1981-82, Minister for Prices Matters 1982-85; Econ. Counsellor to Minister Plenipotentiary of Polish Embassy in U.S.A., Washington, D.C. 1986-; non-party; Gold Cross of Merit, Kt.'s Cross of Order of Polonia Restituta and other awards. *Publications:* Prices and Market 1985; numerous works on econs. of internal trade and consumption. *Address:* Embassy of the Polish People's Republic, 2640 16th Street, N.W., Washington, D.C., U.S.A. (Office); Osiedle Jagiellońskie 80m. 6, 61-217 Poznań, Poland (Home).

KRASOVSKAYA, Vera Mikhailovna; Soviet ballet historian and critic; b. 11 Sept. 1915; d. of Mikhail Krasovskiy and Maria Krasovskaya; m. David Zolotnitskiy 1949; one s.; ed. Choreographical School, Leningrad and Inst. of Theatre, Music and Cinematography, Leningrad; Ballet Dancer, Kirov Ballet 1933-41; Sr. Scientific Worker Inst. of Theatre, Music and Cinematography 1953–, Prof. 1975; mem. Union of Soviet Writers 1966; Dr. of Arts 1965. *Publications:* Vachtang Chabukiani 1956, 1960, Russian Ballet Theatre from the Beginning to the middle of the XIX Century 1958, Leningrad's Ballet 1961, Russian Ballet Theatre of the Second Half of the XIX Century 1963, Anna Pavlova 1964, 1965, Russian Ballet Theatre at the beginning of the XX Century, vol. I Choreographers 1971, vol. II Dancers 1972, Nijinsky 1974, The Ballet of Western Europe: Vol. I From the Beginning to the Middle of the 18th Century 1979, Vol. II The Era of Noverre 1981, Vol. III The Pre-Romantic Ballet 1983, Nikita Dolgushin 1985, Ivanovna 1989. *Leisure interest:* reading. *Address:* c/o Institute of Theatre, Music and Cinematography, Leningrad; Leningrad 191011, Sadovaya 14, ap. 14, U.S.S.R. (Home). *Telephone:* 311-72-50 (Home).

KRASOVSKIY, Nikolay Nikolayevich, DR. PHYS. AND MATH. SC.; Soviet mathematician and mechanician; b. 7 Sept. 1924, Sverdlovsk; ed. Ural Polytechnic Inst.; teaching and scientific work, Ural Polytechnic Inst. 1949–55, 1957–59; mem. CPSU 1954–; Research workers, Inst. of Mechanics, U.S.S.R. Acad. of Sciences 1955–57, Prof. Ural Univ. 1959–; scientific and admin. work, Inst. of Math. and Mechanics of Ural Scientific Centre, U.S.S.R. Acad. of Sciences 1970–; Corresp. mem. U.S.S.R. Acad. of Sciences 1964–68, Academician 1968–; Order of Lenin, Order of the Red Banner and other decorations. *Publications:* works in field of stability of motion theory and theory of control. *Address:* c/o Institute of Mathematics and Mechanics, Sverdlovsk, U.S.S.R.

KRASUCKI, Henri: French (b. Polish) machine-fitter and trade union official; b. 2 Sept. 1924, Wolomin, Poland; s. of Isaac Krasucki and Léa Krasucki; one s. one d.; ed. Lycée Voltaire, Paris; Sec. Seine Dept. CGT 1949, mem. confederal bureau 1961, Gen. Sec. 1982–; mem. Cen. Cttee. CP 1956, Politbureau 1964; mem. Admin. Council la Vie Ouvrière. *Publications:* Syndicats et luttes de classes 1969, Syndicats et socialisme 1972, Syndicats et unité 1980, Un Syndicat moderne? Oui! 1987. *Address:* Confédération générale du travail, 263 rue de Paris, 93516 Montreuil, France.

KRATOCHVÍL, Miloš Václav, PH.DR.; Czechoslovak writer; b. 6 January 1904, Vienna; ed. Philosophical Faculty, Charles Univ., Prague 1923–28; office worker, City of Prague Archives, 1929–44; dramaturgist, Nat. Film, Prague, 1944–45; official, Ministry of Finance, Prague 1945–47; dramaturgist, Czechoslovak Film, Prague 1947–51; Prof., Film and Television Faculty, Acad. of Music and Dramatic Arts, Prague 1951–72; Dean, Film Faculty, Acad. of Music and Dramatic Arts, Prague 1952–54, 1960–62; retd. 1972; mem. Cen. Cttee. of the Union of Czech Writers; Cttee. Chair. Czechoslovak Foreign Inst. 1980–; *Novels:* Lonely Fighter 1942, The King Puts on a Blouse 1945, The Torch 1950, Remarkable Stories and Adventures of Jan Kornel 1954, Napoleon from the Black Island 1966; *Short stories:* Stories of Love and Death 1943; *Historical books:* The Czech Past 1961, Discoverers and Conquerors 1962, The Time of Stars and Mandragoras 1972, Royal Loves 1974, Europe Danced a Waltz 1974, The Life of Jan Amos 1976, Europe in Trenches 1977, Jan Amos Commenius 1983, The Nation to Itself 1983. For Merit in Construction 1964, Artist of Merit 1970, Nat. Artist 1974, Nat. Prize 1977, Order of Labour 1979, Order of Victorious February 1984.

KRATOCHVÍLOVÁ, Jarmila; Czechoslovak athlete; b. 26 Jan. 1951, Golčův Jeníkov; ed. gymnasium, Čáslav 1966–70; accountant, Triola, Golčův Jeníkov 1970–71, mem. of the centre of top-level performance sports, Vysoké školy, Prague 1971–87 (retd.); now coach; *world records:* 400-metre track event, Helsinki, 1983, 800-metre track event, Munich 1983; *international competitions include:* Gold Medal, 400-metre track event, World Cup, Rome 1981; Silver Medal, Olympic Games, Moscow 1980; Silver Medal, 400-metre track event, European Championships, Athens 1982; Gold Medal, 400- and 800-metre track events, World Championships, Helsinki 1983; Order of Labour 1983.

KRAUCH, Carl Heinrich, DR.RER.NAT.; German chemist and business executive; b. 14 Sept. 1931, Heidelberg; s. of Carl Krauch and Maria (Lüders) Krauch; m. Ursula Kneller 1958; three s. one d.; ed. Ruprecht-Karl Univ., Heidelberg, Georg-August Univ., Göttingen; Head of research group, radiochemical dept., Max-Planck Inst. für Kohlenforschung, Mülheim/Ruhr 1958–67; Lecturer, Univ. of Cologne 1965; Head of research group testing plastic materials, BASF, Ludwigshafen 1967; Prof. Johannes Gutenberg Univ., Mainz 1971–; Head of Research and Devt., mem. Bd., Henkel & Cie. GmbH., Düsseldorf 1971–80, Head, Chemical Products Div. 1975–80; mem. Bd., Hüls AG, Marl Jan. 1980–, Chair. June 1980–; mem. Bd., VEBA AG, Düsseldorf July 1980–. *Publications:* over 40 in field of chemistry. *Leisure interests:* hunting and farming. *Address:* Vorsitzender des Vorstandes, Hüls AG, Postfach 1320, D-4370 Marl, Federal Republic of Germany. *Telephone:* 02365/49 52 71.

KRAUPP, Otto, M.D.; Austrian professor of pharmacology; b. 20 Oct. 1920, Krems; s. of Josef Kraupp and Josefine Kraupp; m. Adele Pachinger 1945; one s. four d.; ed. Univ. of Vienna; Asst. and Assoc. Prof., Inst. of Pharmacology, Univ. of Vienna 1947–67; Head Inst. of Pharmacology 1972–; Head Inst. of Pharmacology and Toxicology, Ruhr Univ. 1967–72; Dean of Medical Faculty, Univ. of Vienna 1975–79, 1984–86, 1988–; Ed. Wiener Klinische Wochenschrift 1972–; Dir. Physiological Dept., Paracelsus Inst. 1972–; Pro-Meritis-Medaille 1969, Wilhelm Exner-Medaille 1973, Österreicher Ehrenkreuz für Wissenschaft und Kunst (First Class) 1978,

Universitätspreis der Wiener Wirtschaft 1984, Goldene Ehrenmedaille der Bundeshauptstadt Wien 1986. *Publications:* 205 publs. on muscle- and circulation pharmacology. *Address:* 1090 Vienna, Währinger Str. 13a, Austria. *Telephone:* (0222) 43 15 26 286.

KRAUS, Andreas, D.PHIL.; German historian; b. 5 March 1922, Erding; s. of Karl Kraus and Katharina Mayer; m. Maria Kastner 1947; one d.; ed. Univ of Munich; teacher 1949–61; Extraordinary Prof. of History, Philosophy and Theology Hochschüle, Regensburg 1961–67; Prof. Univ. of Regensburg 1967–77; Prof. of Bavarian History Univ. of Munich 1977–; mem. Bayerischen Akad. der Wissenschaften 1971; Bayerischer Verdienstorden 1983. *Publications:* Die historische Forschung an der bayerischen Akademie der Wissenschaften 1959, Vernunft und Geschichte 1963, Das päpstliche Staatssekretariat 1964, Civitas Regia 1972, Regensburg 1979, Die naturwissenschaftliche Forschung an der bayerischen Akademie der Wissenschaften 1979, Geschichte Bayerns 1983. *Address:* Nederlingstrasse 30a, München 19 (Home); Institut für Bayerische Geschichte, Ludwigstrasse 14, München 22, Federal Republic of Germany (Office). *Telephone:* 089-1575354 (Home); 089-2798507 (Office).

KRAUSHAAR, William L., PH.D.; American professor of physics; b. 1 April 1920, Newark, N.J.; s. of Lester A. Kraushaar and Helen Ousterhoudt; m. 1st Margaret Freidinger 1943 (divorced 1978), two s. one d.; m. 2nd Elizabeth Demoss 1980; ed. Lafayette Coll. and Cornell Univ.; with Nat. Bureau of Standards 1942–45; Pres. White Fellow Cornell Univ. 1946–49; Asst. Prof., Assoc. Prof. then Prof. of Physics M.I.T. 1949–65; Max Mason Prof. of Physics Univ. of Wis. 1965–; Fulbright Fellow, Japan 1953–54, Guggenheim Fellow, Harvard and Calif. Inst. of Tech. 1963, mem. Bd. of Trustees Coll. of the Atlantic 1970–74, Univs. Research Asscn. 1983–; mem. N.A.S., American Acad. of Arts and Sciences; Sr. Scientist Prize, Humboldt Foundation 1983. *Publications:* Introduction to Mechanics, Matter and Waves (with Uno Ingard) 1960; numerous publications on cosmic ray, x-ray and gamma ray astronomy. *Address:* Department of Physics, Chamberlin Hall, University of Wisconsin, Madison, Wis. 53711 (Office); 462 Togstad Glen, Madison, Wis. 53711, U.S.A. (Home). *Telephone:* 262-5916 (Office); 238-5945 (Home).

KRAUSKOPF, Konrad Bates, PH.D.; American geologist; b. 30 Nov. 1910, Madison, Wis.; s. of Francis C. and Maude Bates Krauskopf; m. Kathryn Isabel McCune 1936; one s. three d.; ed. Univ. of Wisconsin, Univ. of Calif. and Stanford Univ.; Instructor in Chem., Univ. of Calif. 1934–35; Asst. Prof. of Geology, Stanford Univ. 1939–42, Assoc. Prof. 1942–50, Prof. of Geochem. 1950–76, Assoc. Dean, School of Earth Sciences, Stanford Univ. 1963–76, Prof. Emer. 1976–; Chief, Geographical Section, G.2, U.S. Army, Far East Command 1947–48; Geologist, U.S. Geological Survey, various times 1942–; Pres. American Geological Inst. 1964, Geological Soc. of America 1967, Geochemical Soc. 1970; mem. Nat. Acad. of Sciences; Hon. D.Sc. (Wisconsin) 1971, Day Medal, Geological Soc. of America 1961, Goldschmidt Medal, Geochemical Soc. 1982, Ian Campbell Medal, American Geological Inst. 1984. *Publications:* Fundamentals of Physical Science 1941, Introduction to Geochemistry 1967, The Third Planet 1974, The Physical Universe (with Arthur Beiser) 1986, Radioactive Waste Disposal and Geology 1988; articles in tech. scientific journals. *Address:* Geology Department, Stanford University, Calif. 94305 (Office); 806 La Mesa Drive, Menlo Park, Calif. 94025, U.S.A. (Home). *Telephone:* 415 723-3325 (Office); (415) 854-4506 (Home).

KRAVETS, Vladimir A., PH.D.; Soviet diplomatist and university professor; b. 3 May 1930; m.; one s.; ed. Faculty of Int. Affairs, Kiev State Univ.; worked as a professor in various Univs. and Higher Educ. Insts., Ukraine 1956–67; Counsellor of Perm. Mission of Ukraine to UN 1967–71; Deputy Minister for Foreign Affairs of the Ukraine 1971–79; Chair. Ukrainian Comm. for UNESCO 1971–79; Ukrainian Perm. Rep. to UN 1979–85. *Publications:* articles and publications on history and int. affairs. *Address:* Ministry of Foreign Affairs, Kiev, Ukrainian S.S.R., U.S.S.R.

KRAVTSOV, Boris Vasilevich; Soviet lawyer and politician; b. 28 Dec. 1922, Moscow; worked in legal system; ed. Inst. of Juridical Sciences, Moscow; position in U.S.S.R. Ministry of Justice 1950–56; Instructor in Dept. of Admin., Trade and Finance Organs of Cen. Cttee. CPSU 1956–60; First Deputy R.S.F.S.R. Procurator 1960–71; R.S.F.S.R. Procurator, State Counsellor of Justice 1971–84; Deputy to R.S.F.S.R. Supreme Soviet 1971–85; U.S.S.R. Minister of Justice and mem. U.S.S.R. Council of Ministers 1984–; Deputy to U.S.S.R. Supreme Soviet 1985–; cand. mem. Cen. Cttee. CPSU 1986–. Hero of Soviet Union 1944, Order of Lenin, Order of October Revolution, 1982, Order of Red Banner (twice), other medals. *Publications:* on legal questions related to Soviet society. *Address:* Council of Ministers, The Kremlin, Moscow, U.S.S.R.

KRAWCZUK, Aleksander, H.H.D.; Polish historian, writer and politician; b. 7 June 1922, Kraków; m.; two s.; ed. Jagiellonian Univ., Kraków; served with Home Army during Nazi occupation; scientific worker of Jagiellonian Univ., Kraków, Asst., subsequently Sr. Asst. and lecturer 1949–64, Asst. Prof. 1964–74, Extraordinary Prof. 1974–85, Ordinary Prof. 1985–, Head Ancient History Research Centre, History Inst.; Minister of Culture and Art 1986–; mem. Polish Writers' Union 1971–83, newly created Polish Writers' Union (ZLP) 1983–, Pres. ZLP Kraków Br. 1986–87; mem. Nat. Culture Council 1986–; mem. Seym Advisers' Team; mem. Civic Cttee. for

Rescue of Kraków Monuments; Pres. Gen. Bd. Soc. of Popular Knowledge, Soc. of Polish-Italian Friendship; Commdr.'s Cross of Polonia Restituta Order and other Polish awards and decorations. *Publications:* Kolonizacja Sullańska 1960, Gajusz Juliusz Cezar 1962, Virtutis ergo, nadania obywatelstwa rzymskiego przez wodzów republiki 1963, Cesarz August 1964, Herod król Judei 1965, Neron 1965, Perykles i Aspazja 1967, Siedmiu przeciw Tebom 1968, Sprawa Alkibiadesa 1968, Wojna trojańska 1969, Kleopatra 1969, Pan i jego filozof 1970, Konstantyn Wielki 1970, Ród Konstantyna 1972, Sennik Artemidora 1972, Tytus i Berenika 1972, Groby Cheronei 1972, Rzym i Jerozolima 1974, Julian Apostata 1974, Maraton 1976, Ostatnia Olimpiada 1976, Upadek Rzymu 1978, Mitologia starożytnej Italii 1982, Ród Argeadów 1982, Stąd do starożytności 1985, Poczet cesarzy rzymskich 1986. *Leisure interest:* hiking. *Address:* Ministerstwo Kultury i Sztuki, ul. Krakowskie Przedmieście 15/17, 00-071 Warsaw (Office); ul. Radockiego 5 m. 1, 30-540 Kraków, Poland (Home). *Telephone:* 66 09 94 (Home).

KRAYEVSKIY, Nikolay Aleksandrovich; Soviet pathologist; b. 17 Sept. 1905, Pashkovo, Smolensk Region; ed. Moscow Univ.; Asst. Moscow Univ. 1928-30; Asst., Inst. of Occupational Diseases 1930-32; Asst., Lecturer, Prof., Second Moscow Medical Inst. 1931-54; Head of Laboratory, Cen. Inst. of Hematology and Blood Transfusion 1939-51; Head of Dept., Cen. Inst. for Postgraduate Medical Training 1954-60; Corresp. mem. U.S.S.R. Acad. of Medical Sciences 1953-60, mem. 1960-; Academician-Sec. U.S.S.R. Acad. of Medical Sciences 1960-62; Head of Dept. Inst. of Experimental and Clinical Oncology, U.S.S.R. Acad. of Medical Sciences 1962-; Chair. of Bd. of All-Union Scientific Soc. of Pathologists; mem. WHO Expert Advisory Panel; mem. Editorial Bd. of Archives of Pathology; Order of Red Star 1944, Patriotic War, First Class 1945, Badge of Honour, Lenin Prize 1963. *Publications:* Over 150 works on gastric pathology, morbid anatomy of haemotransfusional complications and radiation complications in oncology. *Address:* c/o Institute of Experimental and Clinical Oncology, Kashirskoye Chaussée 6, Moscow, U.S.S.R.

KREBS, Robert Duncan, M.B.A.; American transport executive; b. 2 May 1942, Sacramento; s. of Ward C. Krebs and Eleanor B. (née Duncan) Krebs; m. Anne Lindstrom 1971; two s. one d.; ed. Stanford Univ., Harvard Univ.; Asst. Gen. Man. S. Pacific Transportation Co., Houston 1974-75, Asst. Regional Operations Man. 1975-76, Asst. Vice-Pres. San Francisco 1967-77, Asst. to Pres. 1977-79, Gen. Man. 1979, Vice-Pres. Transportation 1979-80, Operations 1980-82, Pres. 1982-83; Dir. and Pres. Santa Fe S. Pacific Corpn. 1983-, Chair. and C.E.O. 1988-. *Address:* Santa Fe South Pacific Corporation, 224 S. Michigan Avenue, Chicago, Ill. 60604, U.S.A.

KREDEL, Elmar Maria, DR.THEOL.; German ecclesiastic; b. 24 Feb. 1922, Nuremberg; s. of Georg and Josephine (née Weirather) Kredel; ed. gymnasium in Nuremberg and studies in philosophy and theology in Bamberg and Innsbruck and Papal Inst., Rome; ordained in Bamberg 1950; chaplain, Pegnitz 1952-54; studies in Rome 1954-56; Asst., Exeget Seminar, Univ. of Munich 1958-62; parish admin. and parson, Freienfels and Hollfeld 1962-67; cathedral staff, Bamberg 1967; diocesan adviser in youth work, adult educ., Caritas, Pro-synodal judge, Deputy Vicar-Gen. and Canonicus theologus 1967-77; hon. papal prelate 1975; Archbishop of Bamberg 1977-; Pres. of the Episcopal Comm. for Social and Charitable Questions, Comm. VI of the German Bishop's Conf. 1977-86; Roman Catholic Mil. Bishop, Deutsche Bundeswehr 1978-; Bayerische Verdienstorden; Grosses Bundesverdienstkreuz; Hon. Citizen, Bamberg 1987. *Publications:* various theological articles. *Leisure interest:* classical music. *Address:* Obere Karolinenstrasse 5, D-8600 Bamberg, Federal Republic of Germany. *Telephone:* 0951/502 202.

KREISEL, Georg; F.R.S.; British (b. Austrian) professor of logic; b. 15 Sept. 1923, Graz, Austria; s. of Heinrich Kreisel and Bertha (née Wahrmann) Kreisel; Prof. of Logic and the Foundation of Math., Stanford Univ., Calif. *Address:* Institut für Wissenschaftstheorie Internationales Forschungszentrum Salzburg, Mönchsberg 2, A-5020 Salzburg, Austria. *Telephone:* (0662) 842521.

KREISKY, Bruno, LL.D.; Austrian politician; b. 22 Jan. 1911, Vienna; s. of Max and Irene Felix Kreisky; m. Vera Fuerth 1942 (died 1989); one s. one d.; ed. Univ. of Vienna; Aceste mem. Austrian Social Democratic Party to 1934; arrested and imprisoned 1935 and again 1938, then escaped to Sweden; mem. scientific staff Stockholm Co-operative Society 1939-46; joined Austrian Foreign Service 1946; Austrian Legation, Stockholm 1946-51; Austrian Fed. President's Office 1951-53; State Sec. for Foreign Affairs in Fed. Chancellery 1953; elected to Parl. 1956; Minister of Foreign Affairs 1959-66; Chair. Socialist Party of Austria 1967-83, Hon. Chair. 1983-87; Fed. Chancellor of Austria 1970-83; initiator and Vice-Pres. Theodor Körner Fund for Promotion of Arts and Sciences; Vice-Chair. of Bd., Inst. for Advanced Studies and Scientific Research, Vienna; Pres. Vienna Inst. for Devt.; Gold Grand Cross of Honour, numerous foreign decorations including Freedom Award, 1975, Jawaharlal Nehru Award for Int. Understanding 1985. *Publications:* The Challenge: Politics on the Threshold of the Atomic Age 1963, Aspects of Democratic Socialism 1974, Neutrality and Co-existence 1975, The Times We Live In: Reflections on International Politics 1978, Between the Times: Memoirs from five centuries 1986, In The Stream of Politics: Memoirs 1988 and numerous articles mainly on the international position of Austria and economic subjects. *Leisure interests:*

history, baroque art. *Address:* Armbrustergasse 15, 1190 Vienna, Austria. *Telephone:* 50-200.

KREJČA, Otomar: Czechoslovak actor and director; b. 23 Nov. 1921, Skrýšov; ed. Charles Univ., Prague; Mem. Prague Nat. Theatre 1951-69, Art Chief, Nat. Theatre Drama Section 1956-61; Artistic Dir. of Divadlo za branou (Theatre Beyond the Gate) 1965-71, Dir. 1971-72; Producer Divadlo S. K. Neumanna 1973-; Chair. Union of Czechoslovak Theatre Artists 1965-69; Chair. Union of Czech Theatre and Broadcasting Artists 1969-70; Artistic Dir. l'Atelier Théâtral de Louvain-la-Neuve 1979-(81); Ordre des Arts et des Lettres 1978; State Prize 1951, 1968, Honoured Artist 1958, Kainz Medal (Austria) 1969, Int. Pirandello Prize (Italy) 1978. *Plays directed include:* The Seagull, Ivanov, Three Sisters, Platonov (Chekhov), Romeo and Juliet, Hamlet, Measure for Measure (Shakespeare), Waiting for Godot (Beckett) and other classical and modern dramas; Guest Dir. for productions in Havana, Brussels, Cologne, Salzburg, Vienna, Stockholm and Avignon. *Address:* Prague 8, Kubišova 26, Czechoslovakia; Ferme de Blocry, Place de L'Hocaille, 1348 Louvain-la-Neuve, Belgium. *Telephone:* 843667 (Prague).

KREKELER, Heinz L., DR. PHIL.; German diplomatist; b. 20 July 1906, Bottrop; s. of Heinrich and Helene Lindemann Krekeler; m. 1st Ilse Goebel 1931 (died 1963), 2nd Helga Finke 1965; one s.; ed. Univs. of Freiburg, Munich, Göttingen and Berlin; Chem. engineer with different firms 1930-46; mem. Lippe Diet 1946, Diet of North Rhine-Westphalia 1947-50, Fed. Assembly 1949; partner and fmr. Dir. F. Eilers-Schünemann Verlag (Publishers), Bremen 1948-; Consul-Gen. in N.Y. 1950-51; Chargé d'affaires, Fed. Repub. of Germany, Washington, D.C. 1951-53, Amb. 1953-58; mem. Euratom Comm. 1958-64; Lecturer on Int. Relations and Political Science, Hochschule für Politische Wissenschaften, Munich and Univ. of Münster; mem. Deutsche Gesellschaft für Auswärtige Politik; mem. Max-Planck-Gesellschaft zur Förderung der Wissenschaften; Grand Cross Order of Merit, 2nd Class (Germany); Grande Ufficiale dell'Ordine al Merito 1959; Commendatore con Placca dell'Ordine S. Gregorio il Grande; Grand Officier Ordre de Léopold; Hon. LL.D. (Xavier and South Carolina); Drake-Medaille, Kreis Lippe 1987. *Publications:* Die Diplomatie 1965, Die Aussenpolitik 1967, Wissenschaft und Politik 1975, Gedanken zu Problemen unserer Zeit 1984. *Leisure interests:* shooting (deer stalking), yachting, travelling. *Address:* Gut Lindemannshof, 4902 Bad Salzuflen, Federal Republic of Germany. *Telephone:* 05222-20076.

KRELLE, Wilhelm Ernst, DR.RER.POL.; German professor of economics; b. 24 Dec. 1916, Magdeburg; s. of Dr. Willy and Elisabeth (née Dienemann) Krelle; m. Rose-Alix Scholz 1944; two s. (one deceased) two d.; ed. gymnasium in Magdeburg and Nordhausen and Univs. of Frankfurt, Tübingen and Freiburg; Officer, German Army 1937-45; Rockefeller Fellow, Harvard Univ. 1953-54; Assoc. Prof. Univ. of St. Gall, Switzerland 1956-59; Prof. of Econs. Univ. of Bonn 1959-; mem. Supervisory Bd., Krupp Stahl AG; mem. Bd. of econ. advisers to Minister of Commerce; mem. Gesellschaft für Wirtschafts- und Sozialwissenschaften (Pres. 1974-78), Acad. of Sciences of North Rhine-Westphalia, American Econ. Asscn.; corresp. mem. Bavarian Acad. of Sciences; Fellow, Econometric Soc.; Dr. h.c. (St. Gall, Vienna, Karlsruhe, Münster, Mannheim), Hon. Prof. Univ. of Vienna. *Publications:* Theorie wirtschaftl. Verhaltensweisen 1953, Lohnhöhe und Beschaftig. (with H. Haller) 1955, Beitrag z. Theorie d. Produktion u.d. Einkommensverteil (with K. Brandt and J. H. Müller) 1956, Lineare Programmierung (with H. P. Künzi) 1958, Volksw. Gesamtrechnung inschl. Input-Output-Analyse m. Zahlen f.d. BRD 1959, Preistheorie 1960, Verteilungstheorie 1962, Nichtlineare Programmierung (with Künzi) 1962, Präferenz- u. Entscheidungstheorie 1968, Übertriebliche Ertragsbeteiligung der Arbeitnehmer (with Schunk and Siebke) 1968, Produktionstheorie 1969, Einführung in d. math. Optimierung (with Künzi) 1969, Ein Prognosesystem f.d. wirtschaftl. Entwicklung d. BRD 1969, (with Beckerhoff, Langer and Fuss) 1969, Wachstumstheorie (with Gabisch) 1972, Erfahr. mit einem ökonometrischen Prognosemodell f.d. BRD 1974, Gesamtwirtschaftliche Auswirkungen einer Ausweitung des Bildungssystems (with Fleck and Quinke) 1975, Preistheorie II 1976, Nichtlineare Programmierung (with Künzi and von Randow) 1979, Theorie des Wirtschaftlichen Wachstums 1985, Der "Maschinenbeitrag" (with others) 1985, Gossen und seine Gesetze in unserer Zeit (with Recklenwald) 1987; many articles and contributions to books. *Leisure interests:* music, hiking, mountain climbing. *Address:* Institut für Gesellschafts- und Wirtschaftswissenschaften der Universität Bonn, Adenauerallee 24-42, D-5300 Bonn (Office); Am Domblick 15, D-5300 Bonn 2, Federal Republic of Germany (Home). *Telephone:* 0228/73 79 57 (Office); 0228/32 31 35 (Home).

KREMER, Gidon; Soviet violinist; b. 27 Feb. 1947, Riga, Latvia; ed. Riga School of Music, Moscow Conservatory (with David Oistrakh); prizewinner at Queen Elizabeth Competition, Brussels, Montreal Competition and Fourth Int. Tchaikovsky Competition (First Prize) 1970, Paganini Prize, Genoa; recitalist and orchestral soloist worldwide; has played in most major int. festivals including Berlin, Dubrovnik, Helsinki, London, Moscow, Prague, Salzburg, Tokyo and Zürich; has played with most major int. orchestras including Berlin Philharmonic, Boston Symphony, Concertgebouw, L.A. Philharmonic, New York Philharmonic, Philadelphia, San Francisco Symphony, Vienna Philharmonic, London Philharmonic, Royal Philharmonic, Philharmonia, NHK Symphony of Japan and all main Soviet orchestras; has worked with Bernstein, von Karajan, Giulini, Jochum, Previn, Abbado, Levine, Maazel, Muti, Harnoncourt, Mehta and Marriner; has made more than 45 records and has won Grand Prix du Disque and Deutsche Schallplattenpreis; first performances include Henze, Stockhausen, Schnittke and Part; f. Lockenhaus Chamber Music Festival 1981; plays a stradivarius. *Address:* c/o ICM Artists, 40 West 57th Street, New York, N.Y. 10023, U.S.A.

KREMNEV, Roald Savvovich; Soviet scientist and mechanic; b. 1929; ed. Kazan Aviation Inst.; mem. CPSU 1961–; engineer, leading constructor, deputy chief constructor in aviation industry 1954–85; Dir. Babakin Scientific Experimental Centre 1985–; State Prize 1972; Lenin Prize 1986, for work on research into the surface of planet Venus, and cosmic apparatus for Venus 15 and 16. *Address:* Babakin Scientific Experimental Centre, Novosibirsk, U.S.S.R.

KREMP, Herbert, DR.PHIL.; German journalist; b. 12 Aug. 1928, Munich; s. of Johann and Elisabeth Kremp; m. Brigitte Steffal 1956; two d.; ed. Munich Univ.; Reporter, Frankfurter Neue Presse 1956–57; Political Ed. Rheinische Post 1957–59; Dir. Political Dept., Der Tag, Berlin 1959–61; Bonn Corresp. Rheinische Post 1961–63; Ed.-in-Chief, Rheinische Post 1963–68; Ed.-in-Chief, Die Welt 1969–77, Joint Ed. 1981–, Co-Publr. April 1981–; Chief Corresp. in Peking 1977–81, Editor-in-Chief 1981–85, Joint Ed., Springer Group newspapers 1984–; Konrad Adenauer Prize 1984. *Publications:* Am Ufer der Rubikon: Eine politische Anthropologie, Die Bambusbrücke: Ein asiatisches Tagebuch 1979. *Address:* Die Welt, Godesberger Allee 99, 5300 Bonn 2, Federal Republic of Germany. *Telephone:* 304312.

KRENEK, Ernst; American (b. Austrian) composer; b. 23 Aug. 1900, Vienna, Austria; m. Gladys Nordenstrom 1950; ed. Univ. of Vienna and Acads. of Music in Vienna and Berlin; lived in Switzerland 1923–25; Asst. to Dir. of Staatstheater, Kassel 1925–27; lived in Vienna 1927–37; emigrated to U.S.A. 1937, naturalised 1945; Prof. of Music, Vassar Coll. 1939–42; Prof. of Music and Dean of Fine Arts, Hamline Univ., St. Paul, Minn. 1942–47; Grosses Bundesverdienstkreuz 1965; Hamburg Bach Prize 1966; Order of Merit for Science and Art (Austria) 1975; Hon. Citizen of Vienna 1980. *Compositions include:* Der Sprung über den Schatten 1923, Orpheus und Eurydike 1923, Jonny spielt auf 1925–26, Karl V 1930–33, Dark Waters 1950, Pallas Athene 1952–55, Golden Ram 1962, Sardakai 1967–69 (operas); symphonies: No. 1 1921, No. 2 1922, No. 3 1922, No. 4 1947, No. 5 1949; piano concertos: No. 1 1923, No. 2 1937, No. 3 1946, No. 4 1956; Sestina 1957, Quaestio Temporis 1959, Horizon Circled 1967, Perspectives 1967–68, Kitharaulos 1971, Static and Ecstatic 1972–73, Dream Sequence 1975–76, Arc of Life 1980, Organ Concerto 1982, 8 string quartets, 6 piano sonatas, 4 song cycles, choral works. *Publications:* Music Here and Now 1939, Studies in Counterpoint 1940, Musik im goldenen Westen 1949, Zur Sprache gebracht 1958, Gedanken unterwegs 1959, Horizons Circled 1974, Im Zweifelsfalle 1980. *Address:* c/o BMI, 320 West 57th Street, New York, N.Y. 10019, U.S.A.

KRENZ, Jan; Polish conductor and composer; b. 14 July 1926, Włocławek; s. of Otton and Eleonora Krenz; m. Alina Krenz 1958; one s.; ed. Warsaw and Łódź; Conductor Łódź Philharmonic Orch. 1945; Conductor, Poznań Philharmonic Orchestra 1948–49; Dir. and First Conductor Polish Radio Symphony Orchestra, Katowice 1953–67; Artistic Dir., First Conductor Grand Opera House (Teatr Wielki), Warsaw 1967–73; Gen. Dir. of Music, Bonn Orchestra 1978–; tours in Hungary, Romania, Czechoslovakia, France, U.S.S.R., Germany, Italy, U.K., U.S.A., Japan, Australia etc.; State Prize 1955, 1972; Prize Minister of Culture and Art 1955, 1963; Prize of Union of Polish Composers 1968; Grand Prix du Disque, France 1972; Prize of Polish Artists' and Musicians' Assen. (SPAM) "Orfeusz" 1974; Diploma of Ministry of Foreign Affairs 1980; numerous decorations. *Compositions include:* Symphony, two String Quartets, Nocturnes for Orchestra, Rozmowa dwóch miast (Conversation of Two Towns) (cantata), Rhapsody for Strings, Xylophone, Tam-Tam, Timpani and Celesta 1952, Concertino for Piano and Small Symphony Orchestra 1952; orchestral transcriptions of three fugues from The Art of Fugue (J. S. Bach) entitled: Polyphonic Suite 1950, Classical Serenade 1950; orchestral transcriptions of Microcosm (B. Bartók) 1958, Masses (Szymanowski) 1964. *Leisure interest:* painting. *Address:* Al. 1 Armii Wojska Polskiego 16/38, 00-582 Warsaw, Poland.

KREPS, Juanita Morris, M.A., PH.D.; American economist, teacher and government official; b. 11 Jan. 1921, Lynch, Ky.; d. of the late Elmer and Cenia Blair Morris; m. Dr. Clifton H. Kreps, Jr. 1944; one s. two d.; ed. Berea Coll., Duke Univ.; Instructor in Econs., Denison Univ., Ohio 1945–46, Asst. Prof. 1947–50; Lecturer, Hofstra Univ., N.Y., 1952–54, Queens Coll., N.Y. 1954–55; Visiting Asst. Prof. Duke Univ., N.C., Asst. Prof. 1958–61, Assoc. Prof. 1962–67, Prof. 1967–77, Dean of Women's Coll., Asst. Provost 1969–72, James B. Duke Prof. 1972–77, Vice-Pres. of Univ. 1973–77; U.S. Sec. of Commerce 1977–79; Ford Faculty Research Fellow 1964–65; Dir. New York Stock Exchange 1972–77, AT & T, Armco Inc., Citicorp, UAL Inc., Eastman Kodak Co., J. C. Penney Co., Zurn Industries Inc., Deere & Co., Chrysler Corpn.; Trustee, Coll. Retirement Equities Fund 1972–77, Berea Coll.; Duke Endowment; Chair. Bd. of Trustees, Educational Testing Service 1975–76; Pres. elect American Assen. for Higher Educ.; Trustee of TIAA Stock and mem. of Coll. Retirement Equities Fund 1985–; N.C. Public Service Award 1976, Hoskins Award 1984; fifteen hon. degrees.

Publications: ed.: Employment, Income and Retirement Problems of the Aged 1963, Technology, Manpower and Retirement Policy 1966; ed. and contrib.: Lifetime Allocation of Work and Income 1971, Sex in the Marketplace: American Women at Work 1971; co-author: Principles of Economics (with C. E. Ferguson) 1962, 1965, Contemporary Labor Economics 1974, Sex, Age and Work 1975, Women and the American Economy, a Look to the 1980s 1976; over 60 papers on ageing, retirement and econs. *Leisure interests:* music, art. *Address:* 115 E. Duke Building, Duke University, Durham, N.C. 27708, U.S.A.

KRESA, Kent, M.S.; American business executive; b. 24 March 1938, New York; s. of Helmy Kresa and Marjorie Boutelle; m. Joyce A. McBride 1961; one c.; ed. M.I.T.; sr. scientist Research and Advanced Devt. Div., AVCO, Wilmington, Mass. 1959–61; staff mem. M.I.T. Lincoln Lab. Lexington, Mass. 1961–68; Deputy Dir. Strategic Tech. Office, Defense Advanced Research Projects Agency, Washington 1968–73, Dir. Tactical Tech. Office 1973–75; Vice-Pres. Man. Research and Tech. Center, Northrop Corpn. Hawthorne, Calif. 1975–76, Vice-Pres. Gen. Man. Ventura Div., Newbury Park, Calif. 1976–82, Group Vice-Pres. Aircraft Group, L.A. 1982–86, Sr. Vice-Pres. Tech. Devt. and Planning 1986–87, Pres. and C.O.O. 1987–; mem. Chief of Naval Operations Exec. Panel, U.S.A.F. Science Advisory Bd., etc.; Fellow, A.I.A.A.; Arthur D. Flemming Award 1975, Sec. of Defense Meritorious Civilian Service Medal 1975, U.S.N. Meritorious Public Service Citation 1975, U.S.A.F. Exceptional Civilian Service Award 1987. *Address:* Northrop Corporation, 1840 Century Park E., Los Angeles, Calif. 90067, U.S.A.

KRETZENBACHER, Leopold, DR. PHIL.; Austrian/German academic; b. 13 Nov. 1912, Leibnitz, Steiermark; s. of Michael Kretzenbacher and Franziska Kuder; m. Elfriede Jauker 1940; two s. four d.; ed. Univ. of Graz; Univ. of Zagreb 1943–44; Prof. Univ. of Kiel 1961–66, Univ. of Munich 1966–78; Prof. Emer. Inst. für Deutsche und Vergleichende Volkskunde, Univ. of Munich 1978–; has undertaken extensive travels in Europe for purpose of ethnological research; mem. Acads. of Munich, Uppsala, Vienna; Dr.iur. h.c. (Graz). *Publications:* approximately 20 books. *Leisure interests:* mountain walking, langlauf skiing, swimming, listening to music. *Address:* 8000 Munich 40, Clemensstrasse 36, Federal Republic of Germany; 8403 Lebring, Stangersdorf 20, Austria.

KRIANGSAK CHOMANAN, Gen.; Thai army officer and politician; b. 1917; ed. Thai Royal Mil. Acad. and U.S. Army Staff Coll.; served in Second World War and Korean War; Deputy Chief of Staff, Supreme Command Headquarters to 1974, Chief of Staff 1974–76; Deputy Supreme Commdr. of Royal Thai Armed Forces 1976–77, Supreme Commdr. 1978; participated in mil. coups Oct. 1976 and 1977–78; Gen. Sec. Nat. Admin. Reform Council Oct. 1976; Vice-Chair. Prime Minister's Advisory Council Oct. 1976–Oct. 1977; Sec.-Gen. Revolutionary Council, Nat. Dir. of Peacekeeping Oct.-Nov. 1977; Sec.-Gen. Nat. Policy Council 1977–79; Prime Minister 1977–80, Minister of Finance 1979–80, of the Interior 1977–78, of Defence 1978–79, of Agric. 1979–80; M.P. for Muang Roi Et Aug. 1981; ordained as monk Jan. 1983; Leader, Nat. Democratic Party; arrested Sept. 1985, granted bail Feb. 1986. *Address:* National Assembly, Bangkok, Thailand.

KRIELE, Martin, DR.JUR., LL.M.; German professor of law; b. 19 Jan. 1931, Opladen; s. of late Dr. Rudolf Kriele and Konstanze Henckels; m. Christel Grothues 1960; one s. one d.; ed. Freiburg, Münster, Bonn and Yale Univs.; admitted to the Court 1961; Prof. of Philosophy of Law and Public Law, Univ. of Cologne 1967–; Dir. Inst. for Political Philosophy and Problems of Legislation 1967; Judge, Constitutional Court of North Rhine-Westphalia 1976–; Ed. Zeitschrift für Rechtspolitik 1968–. *Publications:* Kriterien der Gerechtigkeit 1963, Theorie der Rechtsgewinnung 1967, Einführung in die Staatslehre 1975, Legitimitätsprobleme der Bundesrepublik 1977, Die Menschenrechte zwischen Ost und West 1977, Recht und praktische Vernunft 1979, Befreiung und politische Aufklärung 1980, Nicaragua, das blutende Heiz Amerikas 1985, Die Demokratische Weltrevolution 1987. *Leisure interest:* music (piano). *Address:* University of Cologne, Seminar für Staatsphilosophie und Rechtspolitik, Albertus-Magnus-Platz 1, D-5000 Cologne 41; Richard Wagner Strasse 10, D-5090 Leverkusen, Federal Republic of Germany (Home). *Telephone:* (0221) 4702230 (Office); (0214) 51564 (Home).

KRIEPS, Robert, D.EN D.; Luxembourg politician and lawyer; b. 16 Oct. 1922, Dalheim; m. Renée Ketter 1950; three s. one d.; Minister of Justice, Nat. Educ. and Cultural Affairs 1974–79, of Justice, the Environment and Cultural Affairs July 1984–; Prof. Univ. de Nancy, Univ. Libre de Bruxelles; Rep. to Parl. Ass. of Council of Europe; Grand Officier, Ordre de Mérite, Ordre de Couronne de Chêne; Médaille de la Résistance. *Publications:* numerous articles on politics, legal subjects, cultural policy and consumer rights. *Leisure interest:* mountaineering. *Address:* Ministry of Justice, the Environment and Cultural Affairs, 16 boulevard Royal, Luxembourg.

KRINGS, Hermann, DR.PHIL.; German professor of philosophy; b. 25 Sept. 1913, Aachen; s. of Wilhelm Krings and Jenny Dechamps; m. Inge Birkmann 1949; one d.; Prof. of Philosophy, Univ. of Munich 1956–60; Prof. of Philosophy, Univ. of Saarland, Saarbrücken 1960–68, Univ. Rector 1965–67; Prof. of Philosophy, Univ. of Munich 1968- (now Prof. Emer.); mem.

Bayerische Akad. der Wissenschaften. *Publications:* Ordo. Philosophisch-historische Grundlegung einer abendländischen Idee 1941, Fragen und Aufgaben der Ontologie 1954, Meditation des Denkens 1956, Transzendentale Logik 1964, System und Freiheit. Gesammelte Aufsätze 1980. *Address:* Zuccalistrasse 19a, 8000 Munich 19, Federal Republic of Germany. *Telephone:* 089/17 05 36.

KRISHNA RAO, Gen. Kotikalapudi Venkata; Indian army officer; b. 16 July 1923, Lukulam, Andhra Pradesh; s. of K. S. Narayan Rao and K. Lakshmi Rao; m. K. Radha Rao 1953; one s. one d.; ed. Andhra Univ. and Imperial Defence Coll. (now Royal Coll. of Defence Studies); commissioned into army 1942; served in Burma and N.W. Frontier, World War II; participated, Jammu and Kashmir operations 1947–48; Instructor, Nat. Defence Acad. 1949–51, Defence Services Staff Coll., Wellington 1963–65; trained in Europe, U.S.A., Canada and U.S.S.R.; Deputy Dir. Mil. Operations, Army HQ; Commdr. Infantry Div. 1969–70, Mountain Div. 1970–72; Chief of Staff, Western Command 1972–74; Corps Commdr. Jammu 1974–78; Chair. Expert Cttee. on Reorganization and Modernization of Army; Deputy Chief of Army Staff 1978–79; Gen. Officer Commander-in-Chief, Western Command 1979–81; Chief of Army Staff 1981–83, Chair. Chiefs of Staff 1982–83; Gov. of N.E. States of Nagaland, Manipur and Tripur June 1984–; Col. Mahar Regt. 1968; Col.-in-Chief, Nat. Cadet Corps June 1981–; Col. 61st Cavalry June 1981–; Hon. Col. Brigade of Guards and Mechanized Infantry Regt. 1981–; Prin. Hon. Army ADC to the Pres. 1981; Hon. Gen. Royal Nepalese Army; Patron Indian Ex-Services League; Vice-Patron United Services Inst. of India; D.Litt. h.c. (Andhra Univ.); Param Vishisht Seva Medal 1971. *Leisure interests:* welfare activities, gardening, golf, cricket, photography. *Address:* A/2 Sainikpuri, Secunderabad, Andhra Pradesh 500594, India (Home). *Telephone:* 820303 (Home).

KRISHNAN, Natarajan, B.A.ECONS.; Indian diplomatist; b. 6 Oct. 1928, Mayuram, Tamil Nadu; s. of the late V. Natarajan; m. Lalitha Krishnan; one s. two d.; ed. Univ. of Madras; joined Indian Foreign Service 1951; Third Sec., later Second Sec., Bangkok 1955–56; Second Sec., Chargé d'Affaires, Phnom-Penh 1956–57; Under Sec. Ministry of External Affairs 1957–58; First Sec., Chargé d'Affaires, Buenos Aires 1959–62; Deputy Sec., Dir. Ministry of External Affairs 1962–67; Consul-Gen. and Perm. Rep. to UN Offices, Geneva 1967–71; Joint Sec. Ministry of External Affairs 1971–76; Amb. to Yugoslavia 1976–79; Additional Sec. Ministry of External Affairs 1979–81; Amb. and Perm. Rep. to UN 1981–87. *Address:* c/o Ministry of External Affairs, South Block, New Delhi 110011, India.

KRISHNAN, Rappal Sangameswara, D.SC., PH.D., Indian physicist; b. 1911, Rappal, Kerala; s. of R. P. Sangameswara Iyer and C. R. Ammani Ammal; m. Rajammal 1934; two s. three d.; ed. Univ. of Madras, St. Joseph's Coll., Trichy, Indian Inst. of Science, and Trinity Coll., Cambridge; Research Asst. Indian Inst. of Science 1935–38; 1851 Exbn. Overseas Scholar, Univ. of Cambridge 1938–41; lecturer in Physics, Inst. of Science 1942–45, Asst. Prof. 1945–48, Prof. and Head of Dept. of Physics 1948–72, Emer. Prof. 1972–73; Vice-Chancellor Kerala Univ. 1973–77; Prin. Investigator, DST Project, Indian Inst. of Science, Bangalore 1977–82, Emer. Prof. 1983–; Fellow of Inst. of Physics, London, of American Physical Soc., of Indian Acad. of Sciences and of Nat. Inst. of Sciences; Pres. Physics Section, Indian Science Congress 1949; Nat. Science Foundation Sr. Foreign Scientist, Fellow, Dept. of Physics, North Tex. State Univ. Denton, Tex. 1971–72; original contributions to colloid optics (Krishnan Effect), light-scattering, Raman effect, crystal physics, etc. *Publications:* Progress in Crystal Physics, Vol. I 1958, Two Chapters in Raman Effect, Vol. I 1971, Thermal Expansion of Crystals 1979, and contributions to other books. *Leisure interests:* tennis, photography. *Address:* Physics Department, Indian Institute of Science, Bangalore 560012, Karnataka (Office); 232, 18th Cross, Palace, Upper Orchards, Sadasivanagar, Bangalore 560080, Karnataka, India (Home). *Telephone:* 344411 (Office); 340703 (Home).

KRISHNASWAMY, K. S., PH.D.; Indian bank official; b. 1920, Chikkamagalur; m. Madhura Krishnaswamy 1947; one s. one d.; ed. Univ. of Mysore and L.S.E.; lecturer in Econs., Univ. of Bombay 1946–47; Research Officer, Planning Comm., New Delhi; Research Officer, Research Dept., Reserve Bank of India, Bombay 1952–54, Deputy Dir. of Research, Research Dept. 1954–56; Staff mem. Econ. Devt. Inst. (World Bank), Wash., D.C. 1956–59; Deputy Chief, Industrial Finance Dept., Reserve Bank of India 1959–61; Chief, Econ. Policy Section, Planning Comm. 1961–64, Econ. Adviser, Planning Comm. 1964–67; Dir. Econ. Devt. Inst., Int. Bank for Reconstruction and Devt. 1967–71; Prin. Adviser Reserve Bank of India 1972, Exec. Dir. 1973–, Deputy Gov. 1975–; Chair. Oil Prices Cttee., Govt. of India 1974–76; Pres. Indian Econ. Assocn. 1976. *Leisure interests:* music and letters. *Address:* Reserve Bank of India, Central Office, P.O. Box 406, Mint Road, Bombay 400001; 27 Bank House, 156 Backbay Reclamation, Bombay 400020, India. *Telephone:* 267661 (Office); 295754 (Home).

KRISS, Anatoliy Yevseyevich; Soviet microbiologist; b. 16 Sept. 1908, ed. Leningrad Medical Inst.; Scientific worker, Inst. of Microbiology, U.S.S.R. Acad. of Sciences 1935–; Dr. of Biological Sciences 1947; Head of Marine Microbiology Dept., Inst. of Microbiology 1948–; Head of Electron Microscopy Laboratory, U.S.S.R. Acad. of Sciences 1946–; microbiological research, Antarctic 1967–; awarded title of Prof. of Microbiology 1950; Lenin Prize 1960. *Publications:* The Variability of Actinomycetes 1937, Deep-Sea Microbiology 1959 (German edn. 1961, English edn. 1963,

Japanese edn. 1963), Microbial Population of the World Ocean 1964 (English edition 1967), Life Processes and Hydrostatic Pressure 1973, Microbiological Oceanography 1976, Microbiology of Polar Countries 1978, and over 200 scientific papers. *Address:* c/o U.S.S.R. Academy of Sciences, Institute of Microbiology, 7a Profsojuznaja Street, Moscow, U.S.S.R.

KRISTENSEN, Finn; Norweigan politician; b. 24 July 1936, Brevik, Telemark; s. of Bjarne Kristensen and Jenny Eikefjord; m. Bodil Lia 1957; three c.; ed. Oslo Elementary Tech. School; maritime electrician 1955–56; electrician, Dalen Portland Cement Plant 1958–62; Instructor, Norwegian Workers' Educational Assocn. 1963–66; Dir. T-Invest of Porsgrunn 1985–86; Sec. Telemark Co. Labour Party 1966–; mem. Storting 1969–; Minister of Industry Feb.–Oct. 1981, 1986–; mem. Labour Party Nat. Bd. 1977; Chair. Standing Cttee. on Industry 1979–81. *Address:* Ministry of Industry, P.O. Box 8014, Dep., Oslo 1, Norway. *Telephone:* (2) 11-90-90.

KRISTENSEN, Sven Möller, DR. PHIL.; Danish writer, literary critic and editor; b. 12 Nov. 1909, Darum, Jutland; m. Hanne Hahne 1937; three d.; ed. Copenhagen Univ.; Literary and Theatre Critic, Land og Folk 1945–53; Ed. Athenæum (literary magazine) 1945–49, Dialog 1950–53; Prof. of Scandinavian Literature Aarhus Univ. 1953–64, Copenhagen Univ. 1964–79; mem. Danish Acad. 1960; mem. Norwegian Acad. of Science 1968. *Publications:* Æstetiske studier i dansk fiktionsprosa 1870-1900 1938, Digteren og samfundet I-II 1942, 1945; Amerikansk litteratur 1920–1940 1942, Dansk Litteratur 1918-1950 1950, En musaik af moderne dansk litteratur 1954, Digtningens Teori 1958, Digtning og Livvsyn 1959, Vurderinger 1961, Den dobbelte Eros 1966, Frammede digterei det 20 aarhundrede (editor) 1967–68, Litteratursociologiske (essays) 1970, Den store generation 1974, Georg Brandes 1980. *Leisure interest:* music. *Address:* Copenhagen University, Vingårds allé 53, 2900 Hellerup, Denmark. *Telephone:* 0161-1521.

KRISTENSEN, Thorkil; Danish business economist; b. 9 Oct. 1899; ed. High School, Askov and Univ. of Copenhagen; Teacher at Commercial Acad., Aarhus 1927; Inspector of Savings-Banks 1928–35; Asst. Lecturer, Univ. of Copenhagen 1936–38; Prof. of Business Econs., Univ. of Aarhus 1938; Copenhagen School of Econs. 1948; Minister of Finance 1945–47, 1950–53; mem. of Bd. of Court of Conciliation in Labour questions 1940–45; mem. of Folketing 1945–60; mem. Acad. of Tech. Sciences 1946–; Sec.-Gen. OEEC 1960–61; Chair. Preparatory Cttee. Organisation for Econ. Co-operation and Devt. (OECD) 1960–61, Sec.-Gen. 1961–69; Dir. Inst. for Devt. Research, Copenhagen 1969–72, Inst. for Future Studies, Copenhagen 1970–. *Publications:* Danmarks Driftsregnskab 1930, Undersøgelser af det kommunale Skattespørgsmaal 1935, Faste og variable Omkostninger 1939, Haandbog i Kredit og Hypotekforeningsforhold 1944, The Economic World Balance 1960, The food problem of developing countries 1968, U-lands-planlaegning: Landbrug contra industrie 1968, Development in Rich and Poor Countries 1974 (revised edn. 1982), Inflation and Unemployment in the Modern Society 1981. *Address:* 18 Odinsvej, 3460 Birkerod, Denmark.

KRISTIANSEN, Erling (Engelbrecht); Danish diplomatist and government official; b. 31 Dec. 1912, Terndrup; s. of the late Kristian E. Kristiansen and Andrea née Madsen; m. Annemarie Selinko 1938 (died 1986); ed. Herning Gymnasium, Univs. of Copenhagen and Geneva, Paris and London; Danish Civil Service, Ministry of Labour 1941, with Free Danish Legations Stockholm 1943, Washington 1944, London 1945; Commercial Sec. Danish Legation, London 1945–47; Head, Del. to OEEC 1948–50; Sec., Econ. Cttee. of Cabinet 1950–51; Asst. Under-Sec. of State, Ministry of Foreign Affairs 1951–53, Deputy Under-Sec. 1954–64; Amb. to U.K. 1964–77, (Doyen of the Diplomatic Corps 1973–77); concurrently to Ireland 1964–73; Chair. Danish Dels. to major econ. confs. 1954–63; Chair. Nordic Investment Bank 1978–80, mem. 1980–86; mem. Bd., The East Asiatic Co.; mem. Int. Advisory Bd. S. G. Warburg & Co. (Mercury Int. Group); Dir. several cos.; Knight Grand Cross, Order of Dannebrog, Royal Victorian Order, Order of Falcon of Iceland, Grand Officier Légion d'honneur and other decorations. *Publication:* Folkeforbundet (The League of Nations) 1938. *Leisure interests:* outdoor sports, languages. *Address:* Granhøjen 4, 2900 Hellerup, Denmark. *Telephone:* 01-68-1375.

KRISTIANSEN, Georg; Norwegian diplomatist; b. 4 March 1917; ed. Univ. of Oslo and Norwegian War Coll.; Army Service 1940–45; Sec., Ministry of Foreign Affairs 1946–47; Attaché, Paris 1947–52; Sec. later Counsellor, of Foreign Affairs 1952–57; Instructor Nat. Defence Coll., Oslo 1957–59; Dir. later Dir.-Gen. Political Affairs, Ministry of Foreign Affairs 1959–64; Perm. Rep. to NATO 1964–70, and OECD 1964–67; Dir.-Gen. Civil Defence and Emergency Planning 1970–74; Amb. to OECD 1974–77; Sec.-Gen. Ministry of Foreign Affairs 1977–80; Amb. to France 1980–85. *Address:* Bergesvevn. 94, Lillehammer, Norway.

KRISTOFFERSON, Kris, B.A.; American singer, song writer and actor; b. 22 June 1936, Brownsville, Texas; one s. one d. (by first marriage); m. 2nd Rita Coolidge 1973 (divorced 1980); one s.; m. 3rd Lisa Meyers 1983; ed. Pomona Coll. and Oxford Univ,; Capt. in U.S. Army 1960–65; performed at Newport Folk Festival 1969; recording artist 1970–. *Songs include:* Help Me Make It Through the Night, Me and Bobby McGee, For the Good Times, When I Loved Her; *albums include:* Kristofferson, The Silver-Tongued Devil and I, Border Lord, Jesus Was a Capricorn, Spooky Lady's Sideshow, Songs of Kristofferson, Who's to Bless and Who's to Blame, Easter Island. *Films include:* Cisco Pike 1972, Pat Garrett and

Billy the Kid 1973, Blume in Love 1973, Bring Me the Head of Alfredo Garcia 1974, Alice Doesn't Live Here Anymore 1974, The Sailor Who Fell From Grace With The Sea 1976, A Star is Born 1976, Vigilante Force 1976, Semi-Tough 1977, Convoy 1978, Heaven's Gate 1981, Rollover 1981; TV appearances include: Freedom Road (TV film) 1979, Amerika (series) 1987. *Address:* c/o ICM, 8899 Beverly Boulevard, Los Angeles, Calif. 90048, U.S.A.

KRIVINE, Alain; French journalist; b. 10 July 1941, Paris; m. Michèle Martinet 1960; two d.; ed. Lycée Condorcet and Faculté des Lettres de Paris; mem. Jeunesses communistes 1956, French Communist Party 1958; leader Union of Student Communists, Paris-Sorbonne Univ. 1964–65; f. Revolutionary Communist Youth 1966 (disbanded by the Govt. 1968), Communist League 1969 (dissolved 1973); Cand. Presidential Elections 1969, 1974; Journalist Rouge 1969–. *Publications:* La farce électorale 1969, Questions sur la révolution 1973, Mai si, rebelles et repentis (with Daniel Bensaid) 1988. *Address:* 2 rue Richard-Lenoir, 93100 Montreuil, France. *Telephone:* 48 59 23 00.

KROGH, Desmond Charles, M.A., EC. DRS., D.PHIL.; South African banking and assurance executive; b. 19 July 1931, Windhoek, Namibia (S.W. Africa); s. of P. I. Krogh and B. Theron; m. Surine Groenewald 1956; two s.; ed. Swakopmund High School, Univs. of Cape Town, Amsterdam and Pretoria; lecturer in Econs., Univ. of Orange Free State 1956, Univ. of Pretoria 1957–61; Asst. Econ. Adviser to Prime Minister 1961; Prof. of Econs., Univ. of South Africa 1962–69; Expert Witness to Int. Court of Justice on Econ. Devt. of S.W. Africa 1966; mem. Prime Minister's Econ. Advisory council 1967–73; Full-time Adviser to Fiscal and Monetary Policy Comm. 1968–69; Exec. Dir. of South African Federated Chamber of Industries 1969–73; Adviser to Govt. negotiations with GATT; Adviser to Reserve Bank of Zimbabwe (fmrly. Rhodesia) 1973–74, Deputy Gov. 1974–76, Gov. 1976–83; Alt. Gov. IMF and World Bank 1980–83; Alt. Dir. Devt. Bank of South Africa; Pres. Zimbabwe Inst. of Bankers 1981–82; Exec. Deputy Chair. Lifegro Assurance Ltd. 1983–86; Dir. Devt. Bank of Southern Africa; Special Adviser to Ministry of Finance 1986; mem. Rhodesian Comm. on Import Control 1975; Medal and Prize of S.A. Econ. Soc. 1953, Netherlands-S. African Scholarship 1954–55, Ebden Prize 1957, U.S.A. Carnegie Study Grant 1960, Official Visitor to U.K. 1971; Commdr. Order of Legion of Merit (Rhodesia) 1978. *Publications:* numerous articles on economic structure, development, inflation and finance in Southern Africa. *Leisure interests:* golf, history. *Address:* P.O. Box 475, Cramerview 2060, South Africa.

KROGSGAARD-LARSEN, Povl, PH.D.; Danish professor of pharmacy; b. 17 May 1941, Frøslev Mors; s. of Niels Saaby and Marie Søbye (née Krogsgaard) Larsen; m. Tove Krogsgaard-Larsen 1964; one s. one d.; Asst. Prof. Royal Danish School of Pharmacy 1970–75, Assoc. Prof. 1975–86, Prof. 1986–; mem. Royal Danish Acad. of Science and Letters 1986, Danish Acad. of Natural Sciences 1987, Danish Acad. of Tech. Sciences 1987. *Publications:* 150 scientific articles, 30 scientific reviews, 2 science books (ed.). *Leisure interests:* history, sport. *Address:* Department of Chemistry BC, The Royal Danish School of Pharmacy, 2 Universitetsparken, DK-2100 Copenhagen (Office); Elmevej 25, Blovstrød DK-3450 Allerød, Denmark (Home). *Telephone:* 01370850, Ext. 247 (Office); 02271215 (Home).

KROHN, Peter Leslie, B.M., B.CH., F.R.S.; British professor of endocrinology; b. 8 Jan. 1916; s. of Eric L. Krohn and Doris E. Krohn; m. Joanna M. French 1941; two s.; ed. Sedbergh and Balliol Coll. Oxford; wartime research work for Ministry of Home Security 1940–45; Lecturer, later Reader in Endocrinology, Univ. of Birmingham 1946–53, Nuffield Sr. Gerontological Research Fellow and Hon. Prof. 1953–62, Prof. of Endocrinology 1962–66. *Publications:* contributions to scientific journals. *Leisure interests:* skiing, mountain walking. *Address:* Coburg House, New St. John's Road, St. Helier, Jersey, Channel Islands. *Telephone:* Jersey 74870.

KROL, H.E. Cardinal John Joseph J.C.D.; American ecclesiastic; b. 26 Oct. 1910, Cleveland, Ohio; s. of John and Anna Pietruszka Krol; ed. St. Mary's Seminary, Cleveland and Pontifical Gregorian Univ., Rome, Pontifical Catholic Univ. of America; ordained Priest 1937; Prof. of Canon Law, St. Mary's Seminary 1942; Vice-Chancellor, Diocese of Cleveland 1943–51, Chancellor 1951–53; Titular Bishop of Cadi, Auxiliary Bishop to Bishop of Cleveland, also Vicar-Gen. 1953–61; Archbishop of Philadelphia 1961–87; cr. Cardinal by Pope Paul VI 1967; mem. Pontifical Comm. for Mass Media Communications 1964–69; Vice-Pres. Nat. Conf. of Catholic Bishops and U.S. Catholic Conf. 1966–72, Pres. 1973–75; fmr. mem. Pontifical Comm. for Revision of Code of Canon Law; mem. Sacred Congregation for the Oriental Churches 1967–, Sacred Congregation for the Doctrine of Faith 1973–, of the Clergy, Pref. of Econ. Affairs of the Holy See 1982–; Vice-Chair. Cttee. for the Year of the Bible; Dr. h.c. of sixteen American univs.; numerous decorations. *Address:* 5700 City Avenue, Philadelphia, Pa. 19131, U.S.A. (Home).

KROLIKOWSKI, Herbert, DR.PHIL.; German diplomatist; b. 15 March 1924, Oels, Silesia; brother of Werner Krolikowski (q.v.); war service from 1942, prisoner-of-war in the U.S.S.R. to 1949; on staff of the G.D.R. Embassy in the U.S.S.R. 1955–58; Head of Scandinavian Section of the Ministry of Foreign Affairs 1958–60; Head, First European Dept. (U.S.S.R.), Ministry of Foreign Affairs 1962–63, Deputy Minister for Foreign Affairs 1963–69, First Deputy Minister 1975–; Amb. to Czecho-slovakia 1969–73; mem. Sozialistische Einheitspartei Deutschlands (SED) 1952–; Cand. mem. SED Cen. Cttee. 1971–76, mem. 1976–; Vaterländischer Verdienstorden in Bronze, Verdienstmedaille der DDR. *Address:* c/o Ministerium für Auswärtige Angelegenheiten, Berlin, German Democratic Republic.

KROLIKOWSKI, Werner; German politician; b. 12 March 1928, Oels, Silesia; m.; two c.; brother of Herbert Krolikowski (q.v.); joined Sozialistische Einheitspartei Deutschlands (SED) 1946–; First Sec. of SED dist. party branch Ribnitz-Damgarten 1952, First Sec. SED, Dresden County 1960–73; mem. Cen. Cttee. 1963–; mem. Politburo 1971–; mem. Volkskammer 1963–, of Volkskammer Cttee. of Nat. Defence 1971–; Sec. for Economy in Cen. Cttee. 1973–76; First Deputy Chair. Council of Ministers 1976–88; First Sec. Dresden County Cttee. of SED; Vaterländischer Verdienstorden in gold, Medaille für Waffenbrüderschaft in gold, Karl-Marx-Orden and other decorations. *Address:* 102 Berlin, Klosterstrasse 47, German Democratic Republic.

KROLL, Lucien; Belgian architect and town-planner; b. 17 March 1927, Brussels; two d.; ed. Athénée Royal de Huy, Ecole Nat. Supérieure de la Cambre, Institut Supérieur de la Cambre, Institut Supérieur et International d'Urbanisme Appliqué, Brussels; numerous works in Belgium, France, Italy, Fed. Repub. of Germany and Italy 1953–; founder mem. Inst. d'Esthétique Industrielle 1956; own architectural practice 1952–; works include houses, churches, schools, exhbns., industrial design, monasteries Ottignies and Rwanda; town-planning in Brussels and Kigali, Rwanda, including Eau d'Heure, Brussels (housing, with participation of future inhabitants) 1967, ministries and Pres.'s Palace, Rwanda Medical Faculties Neighbourhood, Brussels, Froidmont Dominican house 1970, housing, Cergy-Pontoise (with participation of future inhabitants) 1977, housing rehabilitation, Alençon 1978, Alma underground station, Brussels 1979, housing, Marne-la-Vallée 1980, Utrecht Acad., computer-aided design and creation of "Landscape" program 1981, Tech. School, Belfort, France 1983, housing, Laroche-Clermault, France, Bordeaux, St-Germain, France 1984; exhbns. of work in Brussels, Hanover, Utrecht, Auvervilliers, Copenhagen, Aarhus, Luxembourg, Boston; organized confs. including Habiter?, Brussels 1972; visiting prof. and lecturer many univs. throughout Europe and U.S.A.; mem. Acad. Française d'Architecture 1985–; Médaille J.-F. Delarue (Acad. Française d'Architecture) 1980. *Publications:* Architecture of Complexity 1986, Works 1986, over 500 articles on industrial and urban architectural design and comparative architecture. *Address:* Atelier d'Urbanisme, d'Architecture et d'Informatique L.Kroll, avenue Louis Berlaimont 20, Boîte 9, B-1160, Brussels, Belgium. *Telephone:* 673 35 39.

KROLOW, Karl; German poet and essayist; b. 11 March 1915; ed. Univs. of Göttingen and Breslau; writer 1942–; mem. Deutsche Akad. für Sprache und Dichtung (Vice-Pres. 1966, 1975, Pres. 1972), Mainzer Akad. der Wissenschaften und der Literatur, Acad. of Fine Arts of Bavaria, PEN Club; Dr. h.c. (Darmstadt) 1976; Georg Büchner Prize 1956, Grosser Niedersächsischer Kunstpreis 1965, Rainer-Maria-Rilke-Preis 1975; Grosses Bundesverdienstkreuz 1975; Hessischer Kulturpreis 1983. *Publications:* Poetry: Die Zeichen der Welt 1952, Wind und Zeit 1954, Tage und Nächte 1956, Fremde Körper 1959, Gedichte 1962, Unsichtbare Hände 1962, Gesammelte Gedichte 1965, Landschaften für mich 1965, Alltägliche Gedichte 1968, Nichts weiter als leben 1970, Zeitvergehen 1972; Essays: Poetisches Tagebuch 1966, Minuten-Aufzeichnungen 1968, Ein Land, das es nicht gibt 1972, Ein Gedicht entsteht—Selbstdeutungen, Interpretationen, Aufsätze 1973; Trans.: Contemporary French Lyric Poetry 1957, Spanish Poems of the 20th Century 1962. *Address:* 61 Darmstadt, Rosenhöhe 5, Federal Republic of Germany.

KRONACKER, Baron Paul Georges, O.B.E., DR.SC.; Belgian Minister of State and industrialist; b. 5 Nov. 1897, Antwerp; s. of Leopold Kronacker and Marie-Laure Brunard; m. Mary Elisabeth Good 1948; two s. one d.; ed. Univ. of Brussels; Lieut.-Col. Reserve; served army 1915–19; Chair. and Dir. various industrial concerns, particularly in sugar industry; led Belgian Econ. Mission in Netherlands 1939; enlisted again 1939; escaped to England 1940; missions abroad for Belgian Govt. (London) 1940–43; Mil. Attaché in London 1943–44; Senator for Louvain 1939–46; mem. House of Reps. 1946–68; successively Minister of Imports, Minister for Supplies 1944–47; Speaker, House of Reps. 1958–61; member Govt. Comm. for Peaceful Atomic Energy Devt.; fmr. Chair. Int. Sugar Council; Pres. of Belgian Del. at Int. Sugar Council; Chair. Nat. Perm. Comm. for Agricultural Industries (Brussels); Hon. Chair. Int. Comm. for Agricultural Industries (Paris); mem. Control Comm. of Ecole Nationale Supérieure d'architecture et des arts visuels; mem. Bd. Les Amis des Musées Royaux des Beaux Arts de Belgique; awards include Grand Croix de l'Ordre de la Couronne, Grand Officier de l'Ordre de Léopold, Croix de Guerre (Belgium) 1914–18 and 1940–45, Officer of the Legion of Merit (Mil.) (U.S.A.), Commdr. de la Légion d'honneur (France), Officer Order of Orange Nassau (Holland), Officer Order of Merit (Hungary), Commdr. Orden Nacional de Mérito Carlos Manuel de Céspedes (Cuba), Gran Cruz, Placa de Plata Orden del Mérito Juan Pablo Duarte (Dominican Repub.), Grand Cross Order of Tadj (Iran), Gran Cruz Orden de San Martin (Argentina), Grand Cordon Order of the Trinity (Ethiopia), Grand Cross Order of the White Elephant (Thailand), Commdr. de l'Ordre national (Senegal), Grand Officier de l'Ordre du Ouissam Alaouite (Morocco), Jean Stas Prize. *Leisure interests:* music, painting, horse-riding, tennis, shooting, yachting. *Address:* 54 St. Katelijnevest, B-2000 Antwerp (Office); Wolvenbosch, B-2080 Kapellen, Belgium (Home). *Telephone:* 233-59-40 (Office); 664-30-62 (Home).

KRÖNMARK, Eric Allan; Swedish politician; b. 2 June 1931, Näfstad; s. of Edvin Krönmark and Erin Johansson; m. Inga Gustavii; two s. two d.; ed. Svalöv School of Agric.; Chair. of Youth League, Swedish Moderate Party 1965-66, Chair. Kalmar Country, Second Vice-Chair., Chair. of Steering Cttee.; mem. Riksdag (Parl.) 1965-; Minister of Defence 1976-78, 1979-81; Gov. Kalmar Admin. Dist. 1981. *Address:* Länstyrelsen, Malmbrogatan 6, 39186 Kalmar, Sweden.

KROÓ, György, PH.D.; Hungarian music historian and music critic; b. 26 Aug. 1926, Budapest; s. of Miklós Kroó and Sári Engländer; m. Ilona Balogh; one s. one d.; ed. Music Acad. of Budapest; Ed. Hungarian Radio Music Dept. 1957, columnist 1958-; lecturer in music history, Music Acad., Budapest 1961-, Prof. of musicology 1975-; Ford Scholarship to research in Bartók Archives of New York 1967-68; represents Hungarian Radio at Rostrum of Composers, UNESCO, Paris; active as music critic for New Music Review (Hungarian Radio), Élet és Irodalom (weekly); specialist in 19th-Century opera, Bartók and contemporary Hungarian music; Erkel prize 1963, TUC award 1970, Labour Order of Merit, Order of the Star with the Golden Laurels 1986. *Publications:* Robert Schumann 1958, Hector Berlioz 1960, 1980; Bartók Béla szinpadi művei (The Stage Works of B.B.) 1962, A "szabaditó" opera (The "Rescue" Opera) 1966, Richard Wagner 1968, Bartók kalauz (A Guide to B.), A magyar zeneszerzés 25 éve (Twenty-five Years of Hungarian Composition) 1971, A magyar zeneszerzés 30 éve (Thirty Years of Hungarian Composition), Aladár Rácz 1979, Heilawâc (four Wagner Studies) 1983, Az Első Zarándokév (The First Année de Péregrinage) 1986. *Address:* Liszt Ferenc Zeneművészeti Főiskola, 1061 Budapest, Liszt Ferenc tér 8, Hungary. *Telephone:* 414-788.

KROOK, Dorothea, M.A., PH.D.(CANTAB.); British/Israeli professor of English literature; b. 11 Feb. 1920, Riga, Latvia; d. of Rachel Bergman (poet); m. 1st Max Krook 1943 (dissolved 1954); m. 2nd Zerubavel Gilead 1968 (deceased 1988); ed. Univ. of Cape Town, Newnham Coll., Cambridge; Jr. Lecturer, Dept. of English, Univ. of Cape Town 1944-46; Research Fellow Newnham Coll., Cambridge 1950-53, 1958-59; Asst. Lecturer, Faculty of English, Cambridge Univ. 1954-59; lecturer, Assoc. Prof., Prof., Hebrew Univ. of Jerusalem 1960-72; Prof. Tel-Aviv Univ. 1973-85, Prof. Emer. 1985-; Israel Prize in Humanities 1973; mem. Israel Nat. Acad. of Sciences and Humanities 1974. *Publications:* Three Traditions of Moral Thought 1959, The Ordeal of Consciousness in Henry James 1962, Elements of Tragedy 1969, Gideon's Spring: A Man and His Kibbutz (with Zerubavel Gilead) 1985. *Leisure interest:* translating poetry of Zerubavel Gilead from Hebrew into English. *Address:* Kibbutz Ein-Harod (Meuchad), 18 965 Israel. *Telephone:* (06) 535471.

KROON, Ciro Dominico; Netherlands Antilles politician; b. 31 Jan. 1916, Curaçao, Netherlands Antilles; s. of Eduard Bernardus Kroon and Catrijn Zimmerman; m. Edna Huis 1936; three s. one d.; ed. Higher Grade School; in business until 1942; Admin., Social and Econ. Dept., Netherlands Antilles 1942-51; mem. Legis. Council of Netherlands Antilles 1949-51; Deputy for Social and Econ. Affairs and mem. Admin. Bd. of island territory of Curaçao 1951-57; on various occasions Acting Gov. of Curaçao; Minister for Social and Econ. Affairs and Public Health, Netherlands Antilles 1957-68; Prime Minister of Netherlands Antilles Feb. 1968-May 1969; mem. Island Council of Curaçao 1971-73; Minister of Econ. Affairs 1973-75; Pres. Banco Mercantil Venezolano N.V. 1976-; Commdr. Order of Orange-Nassau, Knight Order of Netherlands Lion, and Orders from Venezuela, Colombia and France. *Leisure interests:* sailing, fishing. *Address:* Banco Mercantil Venezolano N.V., Abraham de Veerstraat No. 1, P.O. Box 565, Willemstad, Curaçao, Netherlands Antilles.

KROTOV, Viktor Vasil'evich; Soviet politician; mem. of CPSU 1944-; Dir. of a machine construction works in Urals 1958-63; cand. mem. Cen. Cttee. of CPSU 1961-66 and 1976-81, mem. 1981-; Chair. Econ. Council of Cen. Urals 1963-65; Chair. State Planning Cttee. for Heavy Power and Transport Machine Construction 1966-75; U.S.S.R. Minister of Power Machine Construction 1975-83. *Address:* c/o Ministry of Power Machine Construction, Moscow, U.S.S.R.

KRÖYER, Haraldur, M.A.; Icelandic diplomatist; b. 9 Jan. 1921, Akureyri; m.; four c.; ed. Akureyri Coll. and Univ. of California (Berkeley); joined foreign service 1945; Sec. Stockholm 1947-49, Oslo 1949-52, Paris 1952-54; Counsellor, Paris and Perm. Rep. to Council of Europe 1954-56; Sec. to Pres. of Iceland 1956-62; Counsellor, Moscow 1962-66; Deputy Perm. Rep. to UN 1966-69; Amb. to Sweden, Finland and Austria 1970-72; Perm. Rep. to UN 1972-73; Amb. to U.S.A., Canada, Cuba, Mexico and Brazil 1973-76; Perm. Rep. to Int. Orgs., Geneva and Amb. to Egypt, Kenya and Tanzania 1976-80, to U.S.S.R., Bulgaria, G.D.R., Hungary, Mongolia and Romania 1980-85; Amb. to France, Spain, Portugal and Cape Verde and Perm. Rep. to OECD and UNESCO 1985-. *Address:* c/o Ministry of Foreign Affairs, Reykjavík, Iceland.

KRUCHINA, Nikolai Yefimovich; Soviet politician; b. 14 May 1928, Novaya Pokrovka, Altai Dist.; ed. Zernograd Azov-Black Sea Agric. Inst.;

Second Sec. Kamensk Dist. Cttee. CPSU 1954-55, First Sec. 1955-57; First Sec. Smolensk Dist. Cttee. 1957-59; mem. Cen. Cttee. All-Union Komsomol 1958-62; Head of Rural Youth Dept. of Cen. Cttee. All-Union Komsomol 1959-62; mem. of Cen. Cttee. Politburo of All-Union Komsomol 1962-; Sec. Virgin Lands Dist. Cttee. of Kazak CP 1963-65; First Sec. Tselinograd Dist. Cttee. of Kazak CP 1965-78; mem. Cen. Cttee. Kazak CP 1966-76; mem. Cen. Auditing Comm. CPSU 1966-71; mem. Comm. on Budget and Planning 1966-70; mem. Comm. on Youth Affairs 1970-; mem. Council of the Union, U.S.S.R. Supreme Soviet 1966-; cand. mem. Cen. Cttee. CPSU 1971-76, mem. 1976-; First Deputy Head of Dept. of Agric. of Cen. Cttee. CPSU 1978-83; Admin. of Affairs, Cen. Cttee. CPSU 1983-; Hero of Socialist Labour 1973, Order of Lenin 1973, Order of Red Banner, Badge of Honour (twice), other medals. *Publications include:* Contemporary Agricultural Policy of the CPSU 1981. *Address:* Central Committee of the Communist Party of the Soviet Union, Staraya pl. 4, Moscow, U.S.S.R.

KRUCZEK, Władysław; Polish politician and trade unionist; b. 27 April 1910, Rzeszów; s. of Tomasz and Rozalia Kruczek; m. Irena Rusiecka; one s. one d.; ed. Party School of Polish United Workers' Party (PZPR) Cen. Cttee., Warsaw; mem. Communist Union of Polish Youth 1929, subsequently mem. CP of Poland; political imprisonment 1934-37; active in leadership of Int. Workers' Aid Org. 1939-41; army service and P.O.W. 1942-44; Instructor, Polish Workers' Party (PPR) Cttee., Rzeszów; First Sec. PPR Town Cttee. Rzeszów 1947-48; First Sec. Polish United Workers' Party (PZPR) Dist. Cttee. Rzeszów 1948-49; Sec. Voivodship Cttee. Poznań 1951-52; First Sec. Voivodship Cttee. PZPR Bydgoszcz 1952-56, Rzeszów 1956-71; mem. PZPR Cen. Cttee. 1954-80, Politburo PZPR Cen. Cttee. 1968-80; Chair. PZPR Cen. Comm. of Party Control Feb. 1980-81; Deputy to Seym (Parl.) 1961-85; Chair. Cen. Council of Trade Unions (CRZZ) 1971-80; Presidium mem. All-Polish Cttee. of Nat. Unity Front 1971-83; mem. Council of State (Vice-Chair. 1972-80); Chair. Cttee. Nat. Health Protection Fund 1972-80; Order of Builders of People's Poland, Order of Banner of Labour 2nd and 1st Class, Medal of 30th Anniversary of People's Poland, Partisan's Cross Order of October Revolution (U.S.S.R.) and other decorations.

KRUEGER, Anne O., PH.D.; American economist and international official; b. 12 Feb. 1934, Endicott, N.Y.; d. of Leslie A. Osborn and Dora W. Osborn; m. James Henderson 1981; one d.; ed. Oberlin Coll. and Univ. of Wisconsin; Asst. Prof. of Econs., Univ. of Minn. 1959-63, Assoc. Prof. 1963-66, Prof. 1966-82; Research Assoc., Nat. Bureau of Econ. Research 1969-82; Vice-Pres. Econs. and Research, IBRD Sept. 1982-86; Univ. Arts and Sciences Prof. of Econs., Duke Univ. Jan. 1987-; visiting prof. at univs. in U.S.A., Denmark, Australia and Sweden; mem. editorial bds. of several int. econ. journals; Vice-Pres. American Econ. Asscn.; Fellow, American Acad. of Arts and Sciences, Econometric Soc. *Publications:* Foreign Trade Regimes and Economic Development; Turkey 1974, The Benefits and Costs of Import Substitution in India: A Microeconomic Study 1975, Trade and Development in Korea 1975, Growth, Distortions and Patterns of Trade Among Many Countries 1977, Liberalization Attempts and Consequences 1977, The Development Role of the Foreign Sector and Aid: Korea 1979, Trade and Employment in Developing Countries 1981, Exchange Rate Determination 1983. *Address:* Department of Economics, Duke University, N.C. 27706, U.S.A. *Telephone:* (919) 684-2271.

KRÜGER, Hardy; German actor and writer; b. 12 April 1928, Berlin; s. of Max and Auguste (née Meier) Krüger; m. 1st Renate Damrow, one d.; m. 2nd Francesca Marazzi, one s. one d.; m. 3rd Anita Park 1978; German repertory theatre 1945-56, entered films in 1943; several awards and prizes. *Films include:* Der Rest ist Schweigen 1959, Blind Date 1959, Taxi pour Tobrouk 1961, Hatari 1961, Les Dimanches de Ville d'Avray 1962, Les Quatre Verités 1962, Le Gros Coup 1963, Le Chant du Monde 1964, Flight of the Phoenix 1965, The Defector 1966, La Grande Sauterelle 1966, The Battle of Neretva 1968, The Secret of Santa Vittoria 1969, Death of A Stranger 1972, Le Solitaire 1973, Barry Lyndon 1974, Paper Tiger 1974, Potato Fritz (Best Actor Award, Cannes) 1975, A Bridge Too Far 1976, L'Autopsie d'un Monster 1976, The Wild Geese 1978. *Publications:* Ein Farm in Afrika 1970, Sawimbulu 1971, Wer stehend stirbt, lebt länger 1973, Der Schallmauer 1978, Das Frau der Griechen 1980, Junge Unrast 1983, Sibirienfahrt, Tagebuch einer Reise 1985. *Address:* Neuer Wall 61, 2000 Hamburg 36, Federal Republic of Germany.

KRÜGER, Horst; German author; b. 17 Sept. 1919, Magdeburg; s. of Fritz and Margarethe Krüger; m. (divorced); ed. Grunewald Gymnasium, Berlin and philosophical studies in Berlin and Freiburg i. Br.; started as literary critic and essayist, Badische Zeitung, Freiburg im Breisgau after World War II; ed. of night programmes, Südwestfunk, Baden-Baden 1952-67; now freelance author; mem. Deutsche Akad. für Sprache und Dichtung, Darmstadt and German PEN Centre; several prizes inc. Goethe-Plakette (City of Frankfurt/Main) 1980 and Golden Camera for screenplay for film Der Kurfürstendamm 1982. *Publications:* Fremde Vaterländer 1971, Zeitgelächter 1973, Ostwest-Passagen 1975, Das zerbrochene Haus 1976, Poetische Erdkunde 1978, Ludwig lieber Ludwig 1979, Unterwegs 1980, Spötterdämmerung 1981, Der Kurfürstendamm 1982, Tiefer deutscher Traum 1983, Zeit ohne Wiederkehr: gesammelte Feuilletons 1985, Kennst du das Land: Reiseerzählungen 1987. *Address:* D-6000 Frankfurt/Main, Mendelssohnstrasse 49, Federal Republic of Germany. *Telephone:* 069-74 62 65.

KRUIJTBOSCH, Egbert Diederik Jan, DR. ECON.; Netherlands international civil servant; b. 28 Aug. 1925, Wageningen; s. of Dr. D. J. Kruijtbosch and C. G. Everts; m. Johanna Grietje Thomas; one d.; ed. Municipal Univ. of Amsterdam; mil. service, ending with rank of Lieut. 1948-51; Gen. Directorate for Programme of Econ. and Mil. Aid (later Gen. Directorate for European Co-operation) in Dept. of Foreign Affairs 1953-59; studied at Harvard Univ. and M.I.T. 1958; First Sec., later Commercial Counsellor at Netherlands Del. to OEEC (later OECD) 1960-64; Chair. of Alternates of OECD Steering Bd. for Trade, Chair. Working Group of Trade Cttee.; Co-ordinator of Medium-Term Planning at Cen. Planning Bureau (Netherlands) 1965-66; Chair. of a number of Working Cttees. for medium-term planning in several branches of industry; mem. of staff for econ. affairs and transport, Rijnmond (public authority), Rotterdam; travelled as Eisenhower Fellow in U.S.A. 1970; Sec. Scientific Council for Govt. Policy, Prime Minister's Office 1972-75; Sec.-Gen. Benelux Econ. Union, Brussels Sept. 1975-; Hon. mem. Groupement Interuniversitaire Benelux des Economistes des Transports, Netherlands Chamber of Commerce for Belgium and Luxembourg, Belgian Luxembourg Chamber of Commerce for the Netherlands, Royal Netherlands Econ. Soc. *Publications:* co-author C.P.B. report The Netherlands Economy in 1970; paper Economically Feasible Physical Planning 1969; co-author Studies in Long-Term Development of the Port of Dublin 1971, Model of the Economic Structure of the Greater Rotterdam Region 1972, Long-Term Planning in the Netherlands 1974. *Leisure interests:* long distance skating, wild flowers, skiing, piano. *Address:* rue de la Régence 39, 1000 Brussels, Belgium. *Telephone:* 02-519.38.65.

KRUMM, Daniel J., B.A.; American business executive; b. 15 Oct. 1926, Sioux City, Iowa; m. Ann Klingner; two s.; ed. Primghar High School, Univ. of Iowa, Univ. of Mich. Graduate School; served U.S. Navy 1944-46; Salesman, Globe Office Furniture Co., Minneapolis, Minn. 1950-52; Sales Analyst, The Maytag Co., Newton, Iowa 1952-62, Man., Brussels, Belgium and Wuppertal, Fed. Repub. of Germany 1962-67, Admin. Asst. to Pres. 1967-79, Vice-Pres. 1970-71, Exec. Vice-Pres. 1971-72, Pres. and Treasurer 1972-74, Pres. and C.E.O. 1974-86, Chair. and C.E.O. Maytag Corpn. 1986-; Dir. Signode Corpn. 1975-83, Centel Corpn. 1977-, Prin. Mutual Life Insurance Co. 1980-, Snap-on Tools Corpn. 1984-, Nat. Asscn. of Mfrs. 1986-, Des Moines Symphony Asscn. 1978-, Univ. of Iowa Foundation Bd. 1986-; Trustee Iowa Nat. Heritage Foundation 1979-, Cttee. for Econ. Devt., Washington, D.C. 1987-; FINE Educ. Research Foundation 1987-; Chair. Iowa Business Council 1985-; Hon. Ph.D. (Westmar Coll.) 1981, (Luther Coll.) 1982; Gold Kt. of Man. Award, Nat. Man. Asscn. 1978, Outstanding C.E.O., Financial World Magazine 1979-81, Iowa Business Leadership Award 1983. *Leisure interest:* gardening. *Address:* Maytag Corporation, 403 West 4th Street North, Newton, Iowa 50508, U.S.A. *Telephone:* (515) 791-8210.

KRUMNIKL, Antonin; Czechoslovak politician and mining engineer; b. 1941, Plzen; mem. CP of Czechoslovakia 1959-; fmr. mem. Cen. Cttee. and Presidium, Socialist Youth Union; expert in field of deep coal extraction; Minister of Fuel and Power Oct. 1988-. *Address:* Ministry of Fuel and Power, Prague, Czechoslovakia.

KRUPP, Georg; German banker; b. 15 July 1936; Deputy mem. Bd. of Man. Dirs. Deutsche Bank; Chair. Supervisory Bd. Deutsche Bank Saar AG, Saarbrücken, Deutsche Gesellschaft für Fondsverwaltung mbH (DEGEF), Frankfurt, Deputy Chair. of Supervisory Bd.; Deutsche Kreditbank für Baufinanzierung AG, Cologne; mem. Supervisory Bd. ARBED Saarstahl GmbH, Völklingen, Cassella AG, Frankfurt, FRANKONA Rückversicherungs-Aktiengesellschaft, Munich, Konrad Hornschuch AG, Weissbach, IVECO MAGIRUS AG, Ulm, Strabag Bau-AG, Cologne, Deutsche Centralbodenkredit–AG, Berlin, Cologne, Digital Equipment GmbH, Munich, Ludwig Schokolade GmbH, Aachen, Thyssen Edelstahlwerke AG, Düsseldorf, Wurtembergische Metallwarenfabrik AG, Geislingen; mem. Advisory Bd. GESAT, Gesellschaft für die Vermarktung von Fernmeldesatelliten-Systemen mbH, Munich. *Address:* Deutsche Bank, Generalsekretariat, Postfach 10 06,01, 6000 Frankfurt 1; Königsallee 51, 4000 Düsseldorf, Federal Republic of Germany.

KRUSE, Martin, DR.THEOL.; German ecclesiastic; b. 21 April 1929, Lauenberg, Einbeck; s. of late Walter Kruse and of Gertrud (neé Oppermann); m. Marianne Kittel 1959; two s. two d.; ed. Mainz, Heidelberg, Bethel and Göttingen; Bishop of Evangelical Church in Berlin-Brandenburg (Berlin West) 1977-; mem. Council of Evangelical Church in Germany 1979-, Chair. 1985-; mem. Cen. Cttee. Ecumenical Council of Churches 1983-. *Publications:* Die Kritik am Landesherr-lichen Kirchenregiment bei Ph.J. Spener und ihre Vorgeschichte 1971, Verführung zur Güte 1977, Gruppierungen in der Kirche 1982, Hochwürden 10% 1984, Aufmerksamkeiten 1984. *Leisure interests:* walking, playing the piano, reading. *Address:* Bachstrasse 1-2, D-1000 Berlin 21, Germany. *Telephone:* 39 09 10.

KRUSZEWSKI, Krzysztof; Polish educator and politician; b. 30 March 1939, Warsaw; s. of Włodzimierz and Simona Kruszewski; m. Anna Kruszewska 1960; one s.; ed. Pedagogical Faculty of Warsaw Univ.; scientific worker of Warsaw Univ. 1962-, Asst. Prof. 1971, Extraordinary Prof. 1979-, Didactics Dept., Paedagogic Faculty; mem. PZPR 1963-, Sec. PZPR Univ. Cttee., Warsaw 1972-73, worked in Dept. of Ideological and Educational Labour of PZPR Cen. Cttee. 1974-77, Sec. PZPR Warsaw

Cttee. 1977-80; Minister of Educ. 1980-81; mem. of staff of daily newspaper Rzeczpospolita; Vice-Pres. Bull Terrier Club of Poland; Kt.'s Cross, Order of Polonia Restituta, Gold Cross of Merit and other decorations. *Leisure interest:* breeding bull terriers. *Address:* Wydział Pedagogiczny UW, Warsaw University, ulica Szturmowa 1, 02-678, Warsaw, Poland.

KRYUCHKOV, Col.-Gen. Vladimir; Soviet army officer and politician; b. 1924; ed. in law; practised in public procurator service for many years; on staff of Party Cen. Cttee. 1959-67; has held posts in KGB (State Security Service) 1967-, Deputy Chair. 1978-, Chair. Oct. 1988-; Col.-Gen. in Army and mem. Party Cen. Cttee. *Address:* Central Committee of the Communist Party of the Soviet Union, Staraya pl. 4, Moscow, U.S.S.R.

KRZAK, Marian, M.A.; Polish politician and diplomatist; b. 26 June 1931, Krynica; s. of Jan and Agnieszka Stettner Krzak; m. Danuta Brzezińska 1953; one s. one d.; ed. Main School of Planning and Statistics, Warsaw; Asst. at Main School of Planning and Statistics, then scientific worker at Inst. of Social Sciences attached to PZPR Cen. Cttee., Warsaw until 1954; studied for doctorate 1954-58; Deputy Ed. Życie Gospodarcze (weekly) 1959-60; managerial posts in Ministry of Finance 1960-, Minister's Councillor, then Dir. Dept. of Financial Co-ordination and State Budget until 1968, Under-Sec. of State 1969-80, Minister of Finance 1980-82; Amb. to Austria 1983-88; Pres. PKO State Bank 1988-; mem. PZPR; Commdr.'s and Knight's Cross, Order of Polonia Restituta, and other decorations. *Publications:* Financial Policy, Economic Policy of the Polish People's Republic 1962 and publs. on economics and finance in Życie Gospodarcze, Polityka, Finanse and others. *Leisure interests:* skiing, swimming. *Address:* Powszechna Kasa Oszczednósci-Bank Państwowy, ul. Swietokrzyska 11/21, 00-049 Warsaw, Poland. *Telephone:* 263839.

KRZYŻAGÓRSKI, Klemens, M.A.; Polish journalist; b. 1 Oct. 1930, Zduny; m. Barbara Jakubowska 1957; studied Acad. of Political Sciences, Warsaw; Head, Artistic Programmes, Section of TV Wrocław 1965-67; Ed.-in-Chief literary monthly Odra, Wrocław 1967-72 and Kontrasty, Białystok 1974-79; Ed.-in-Chief of monthly Prasa Polska (Polish Press), Warsaw 1981-85; Ed.-in-Chief weekly Kultura 1985-86, monthly Literatura 1986-; mem. Nat. Council of Culture, Press Council attached to Chair. of Council of Ministers 1985-; mem. Polish Journalists' Asscn. 1960-82; Pres. Asscn. of Journalists of Polish People's Repub. 1982-87; Head, Information Comm. of Provisional Nat. Council of Patriotic Movt. for Nat. Rebirth (PRON) 1982-83; mem. Exec. Cttee. of Nat. Council of PRON 1983-; mem. Polish Writers' Asscn., ZAIKS Asscn. of Authors; Julian Brun Prize (1st Class) 1956, Prizes of City of Wrocław 1956, City of Wałbrzych 1964 and City of Białystok 1975, Bolesław Prus Prize (2nd Class) 1981 and other prizes; Kt.'s and Officer's Cross of Polonia Restituta Order. *Publications:* collected journalism Kłopoty z ciałem 1969, co-author and co-editor of five vols. of prose, essays in literary and socio-cultural journals, theatre scenarios Albertus Return 1966 and Long Live the King 1966. *Leisure interest:* reading books. *Address:* ul. Dobra 29m. 10, 00-344 Warsaw, Poland. *Telephone:* 26 09 76.

KUANG YAMING; Chinese philosopher; b. 1903; Vice.-Chair. of Jiangsu 1978-; Hon. Pres. Nanjing Univ. 1982-; Pres. Confucius Foundation 1985-. *Address:* Office of the President, Nanjing University, Nanjing, Jiangsu, People's Republic of China.

KUBADINSKI, Pencho; Bulgarian politician; b. 1918; ed. High School and Higher Party School; Young Communist League 1934-40, CP 1940-; Local leader, later Cen. Cttee., Young Communist League 1945-51; First Sec. Rousse District Party Cttee. 1952-58; Sec. Cen. Cttee. of CP 1958, Cand. mem. Political Bureau 1962, now mem.; Deputy Prime Minister 1962; mem. Nat. Ass.; Pres. Nat. Council, Fatherland Front 1974-; mem. State Council 1975-. *Address:* c/o Central Committee of the Communist Party, Sofia, Bulgaria.

KUBAR, Abd al-Majid (see Coobar, Abdulmegid).

KUBASIEWICZ, Janusz Bogusław, M.A.; Polish politician; b. 26 Dec. 1938, Warsaw; m. Teresa Kubasiewicz 1961; one d.; ed. Cen. School of Komsomol, Moscow and Higher School of Social Sciences attached to (PZPR) Cen. Cttee., Warsaw; active in youth movt., mem. Polish Youth Union 1954-56, Socialist Youth Union (ZMS) 1960-72; Sr. Instructor of Organizational Dept. of ZMS Cen. Cttee. 1962-63, Deputy Chair. of ZMS Capital Bd., Warsaw 1963-66, Sec. of ZMS Gen. Bd. 1968-72; mem. Polish United Workers' Party (PZPR) 1961-; Instructor, Organizational Dept. of PZPR Warsaw Cttee. 1968; Instructor, then Sr. Instructor, Organizational Dept. of PZPR Cen. Cttee. 1972-76, Deputy Head, Organizational Dept. PZPR Cen. Cttee. 1976-80, alt. mem. PZPR Cen. Cttee. 1980-81; First Sec. of PZPR Voivodship Cttee., Skierniewice 1980-84; Head of Social and Legal Dept., PZPR Cen. Cttee. 1984-85, alt. mem. Political Bureau 1986-; First Sec. PZPR Warsaw Cttee. Nov. 1985-; mem. PZPR Cen. Cttee. 1986-; Officer's and Knight's Cross of Order of Polonia Restituta, Gold Cross of Merit and other decorations. *Leisure interests:* socio-political and historical literature, angling. *Address:* Komitet Warszawski PZPR, ul. Chopina 1, 00-559, Warsaw, Poland.

KUBÁT, Milan, ING., D.C.S.; Czechoslovak technician and economist; b. 20 Jan. 1927, Bratislava; s. of Miloslav Kubát and Blazena Kubátová; m. Jitka Kubátová 1956; two s.; ed. Czech Tech. Coll., Prague; worker at Research Inst. of Heavy-Current Electrical Eng., Běchovice, later ČKD Prague

1951–62; Tech. Dir., ČKD Prague 1962–65; various posts in cen. authorities, Prague 1966–72; Deputy Minister for Tech. Devt. and Investments, Prague 1972–79; Prof., Electrical Eng. Faculty, Czech Tech. Coll, Prague 1974–; Fed. Minister of the Electrical Eng. Industry 1979–88; mem. of scientific councils at academic insts. of higher learning and of the Czechoslovak Acad. of Sciences; Klement Gottwald State Prize 1960, 1980, Prize for Merit in Construction 1977, Victorious February Award 1987. *Publications:* Power Semiconductors 1985; five books in Czech; numerous articles. *Leisure interests:* windsurfing, travel. *Address:* Na Babě 2095/38, 1600 00 Prague 6, Czechoslovakia. *Telephone:* 311 2724.

KUBEL, (Gottfried Hermann) Alfred; German politician; b. 25 May 1909, Brunswick; s. of Hermann and Anna Jordan Kubel; two d.; ed. middle school, Brunswick; Minister-Pres. of Brunswick 1946; mem. Diet of Lower Saxony 1946–; Minister of Economy, Lower Saxony 1946, Labour, Bldg. and Health 1948, Finance 1951, Transport and Economy 1957, Food, Agric. and Forestry 1959, Finance 1964; Minister-Pres. of Lower Saxony 1970–76; Chair. Bundesrat 1974–75; Chair. Bd. of Trustees Georg Eckert Inst. 1977–85; Grosses Bundesverdienstkreuz mit Stern und Schulterband 1961, Grosskreuz des Verdienstordens der Bundesrepublik Deutschland 1971; Order of Orange-Nassau (Netherlands); Ernst Reuter Medal; Social Democrat. *Leisure interests:* nature, sport, history. *Address:* Heinrich-Wilhelm-Kopf-Platz 4, 3000 Hannover 1, Federal Republic of Germany.

KUBELIK, Rafael; Czech musician; b. 29 June 1914, Bychory; m. 1st Ludmila Bertlova (died 1961), one s.; m. 2nd Elsie Morison 1963; ed. Prague Conservatorium; Conductor, Czech Philharmonic Society, Prague 1936–39; Head of Opera, Brno 1939–41; Chief Conductor, Czech Philharmonic, Prague 1941–48; Musical Dir. Chicago Symphony Orchestra 1950–53; Musical Dir. Royal Opera House, Covent Garden 1955–58; Chief Conductor Bayerischer Rundfunk, Munich 1961–79; Musical Dir. Metropolitan Opera, N.Y. 1973–74; Guest Conductor, all major orchestras in Europe, North America and Australia. *Compositions include:* 5 operas, 2 symphonies with chorus, Quattro Forme per Archi, Sequences for Orchestra, Orphicon, 6 string quartets, 1 violin concerto, concerto for violoncello, songs, piano, violin music, requiem Pro Memoria Uxoris and cantatas Pro Memoria Patris, Libera Nos, Cantata without words for Chorus and Orchestra, Peripeteia for organ and orchestra, Invocation for tenor solo and boys' choir. *Address:* 6047 Kastanienbaum, Haus im Sand, Switzerland.

KUBERSKI, Jerzy, M.A.; Polish politician and educator; b. 22 March 1930, Paschalin, Warsaw Voivodship; s. of Wacław and Natalia Kuberski; m. Krystyna Kuberski 1951; one d.; ed. Higher School of Pedagogy, Warsaw and Warsaw Univ.; Active mem. youth organizations ZWM (Fighting Youth Union) 1946–48, and ZMP (Polish Youth Union) 1948–56; teacher in tech. and training schools, then Dir. Teachers' Coll.; School Superintendents' Office, Warsaw 1964–70; School Superintendent, Warsaw Dist. 1965–70; Pres. Headquarters AZS (Students' Sports and Athletics Club); Sec. Warsaw Cttee. PZPR (Polish United Workers' Party) July 1970–March 1972; Deputy mem. Cen. Cttee. PZPR 1971–75, mem. Cen. Cttee. 1975–81; Minister of Educ. and Pedagogy 1972–79, of Denominational Affairs 1980–82; Head of Dept. of Civic Orgs., Sport and Tourism, Cen. Cttee. PZPR 1979–80; scientific worker, Teachers' Training School, Warsaw, Extraordinary Prof. 1980–; Counsellor, Minister Plenipotentiary at the Apostolic See, Rome 1982–; Hon. Meritorious Teacher of People's Poland 1979; Order of Banner of Labour 2nd Class, Kt.'s Cross Order of Polonia Restituta, Gold Cross of Merit, Meritorious Teacher of People's Poland, Commdr. des Palmes Académiques (France) and others. *Leisure interest:* aeronautics. *Address:* Borgo Santo Spirito 16/4, Rome 00193, Italy. *Telephone:* 654 2000.

KUBIAK, Hieronim, PH.D.; Polish sociologist and politician; b. 30 Sept. 1934, Łódź; ed. Jagellonian Univ., Cracow; teacher Jagellonian Univ., Cracow 1961–, Asst. Prof. 1972–78, Extraordinary Prof. of Sociology Faculty 1978–, Dir. Polonia Research Inst. 1973–81; Ed.-in-Chief of quarterly Przegląd Polonijny 1976–; Sec. Polonia Research Cttee. of Polish Acad. of Sciences 1975–81; mem. Polish United Workers' Party (PZPR) 1953–, mem. PZPR Cen. Cttee. 1981–, mem. Political Bureau 1981–86, Sec. 1981–82, Chair Culture Comm. 1981–86, Chair. PZPR Cen. Cttee. Comm. for Investigation into Social Conflicts in the History of Polish People's Repub. 1981–83; Chair. All-Poland Peace Cttee. 1986–; Kt.'s Cross of Order of Polonia Restituta and other decorations. *Publications:* Polski Narodowy Kościoł Katolicki w USA 1970, Religijność a środowisko społeczne 1972, Rodowód narodu amerykańskiego 1975, Stan i potrzeby badań nad zbiorowościami polonijnymi 1976, Polonia wobec niepodległości Polski w czasie I wojny światowej 1979, Założenia teorii asymilacji 1980, Poszukiwania 1987. *Address:* Ogólnopolski Komitet Pokoju, ul. Rajców 10, 00-220 Warsaw, Poland.

KUBO, Ryogo; Japanese professor and physicist; b. 15 Feb. 1920, Tokyo; s. of Tokuji Kubo and Sei Terada; m. Chizuko Kamijo 1946, one s. two d.; ed. Tokyo Imperial Univ. and Tokyo Univ.; Asst. Prof., Dept. of Physics, Tokyo Univ. 1948–54, Prof. 1954–80, Dean, Faculty of Science 1968–71; Prof., Research Inst. of Fundamental Physics, Kyoto Univ. 1980–81; Prof. Faculty of Science and Tech., Keio Univ. 1981; mem. American Acad. of Arts and Sciences 1973–; Foreign Assoc. N.A.S. 1974–; Pres. Nishina Memorial Foundation 1979–; mem. Japan Acad. 1982–; Hon. D.Sc. (Chicago Univ.) 1978; Hon. Imperial Award, Japan Acad. 1969, Order of Culture, Japan 1973, Boltzmann Medal 1977. *Leisure interest:* reading. *Publications:*

several articles in scientific periodicals. *Address:* 1-6-5 Komagome Toshi-maku, Tokyo 170, Japan (Home). *Telephone:* 03 941 8748 (Home).

KUBRICK, Stanley; American film writer, producer and director; b. 26 July 1928, New York; m. Suzanne Harlan 1958; three d.; ed. City Coll. of New York; staff photographer Look 1946–50; produced, directed and photographed documentaries for RKO (Day of the Fight, Flying Padre) 1951; has produced, written and directed feature films since 1952; New York Critics' Best Film award for Dr. Strangelove 1964, Best Dir. award 1971; Acad. Award (Oscar) for best special visual effects in 2001: A Space Odyssey 1968. *Feature films directed:* Fear and Desire (also wrote, photographed) 1953, Killer's Kiss (also wrote) 1955, The Killing (also wrote) 1956, Paths of Glory (also co-writer) 1958, Spartacus 1960, Lolita 1962, Dr. Strangelove (also wrote, produced) 1963, 2001: A Space Odyssey (also co-writer, producer) 1968, A Clockwork Orange (also wrote screen-play, produced) 1971, Barry Lyndon (also produced) 1975, The Shining 1980, Full Metal Jacket (also co-writer) 1987. *Address:* c/o Loeb & Loeb, 10100 Santa Monica Boulevard, Suite 2200, Los Angeles, Calif. 90067, U.S.A.

KUČERA, Bohuslav, J.U.DR.; Czechoslovak politician; b. 26 March 1923, Lomnice; one d.; ed. Law Faculty. Charles Univ., Prague; Clerk, Velveta Nat. Enterprise, Varnsdorf 1948–49; Chief of Dept., Nopako Nat. Enterprise, Nová Paka 1949–50; Sec. of Club of Deputies of Czechoslovak Socialist Party 1950–54; Sec. of Presidium of Czechoslovak Socialist Party 1954–60, Gen. Sec. 1960–68; Chair. Socialist Party 1968–; Minister of Justice 1968–69; Minister without Portfolio of Fed. Govt. of Czechoslovak Socialist Repub. 1969–71; mem. Cen. Cttee. of Nat. Front; Deputy to Nat. Ass. 1960–69; Deputy, House of the People, Fed. Ass. 1969–, Vice-Chair., mem. Presidium, Fed. Ass. 1971; Chair. Govt. Cttee. for Prosecution of Nazi war criminals 1968–; Deputy Chair. Legislative Council, Govt. of Č.S.S.R. 1969–72; Deputy Chair. Constitutional and Legal Cttee. of Nat. Ass. 1965–68; Deputy of Czech. Nat. Council 1968–71; mem. Presidium of Cen. Cttee. Nat. Front of Č.S.S.R. 1971–; Vice-Chair. Czechoslovak del. to Interparl. Union 1971–; Chair. Benelux Cttee., Czechoslovak Soc. for Int. Relations 1973–; Chair., Czechoslovak Cttee. for European Security and Co-operation 1977–; Distinction for Merits in Construction 1958, Order of Labour 1965, Order of Victorious February 1973, Klement Gottwald Order 1983 and several other decorations. *Leisure interest:* literature. *Address:* Federal Assembly, Vinohradská 1, Prague 1, Czechoslovakia.

KUCZYNSKI, Pedro Pablo, D.ECON.; Peruvian economist and banker; b. Lima; ed. Markham School, Cambridge, Oxford and Princeton Univs.; exec., Cen. Bank of Peru, and posts in public admin. until 1969; went to U.S.A. 1969; fmr. Head Econ. Dept., IFC, Washington, D.C.; fmr. Adviser, Banco Cen. de Venezuela; fmr. Exec. Pres. Hake Mining Co., Guinea; taught Econ. and Finance, Univ. of Pittsburgh, U.S.A.; Pres., C.E.O. Halco Inc. 1977–80; Minister of Energy and Mines 1980–82; Pres. First Boston Int. 1982–83, Co-Chair. 1983–; Man. Dir. First Boston Corpn. 1982–. *Address:* Ministerio de Energía y Minas, s/n Av. de la Artes, San Borja, Peru.

KUDLOW, Lawrence A., B.A.; American economist and government official; b. 20 Aug. 1947, Englewood, N.J.; s. of Irving Howard and Ruth (née Grodnick) Kudlow; m. 1st Susan Cullman 1981, one d.; m. 2nd Judith Pond 1987; ed. Univ. of Rochester, Woodrow Wilson School of Public and Int. Affairs, Princeton Univ.; Economist, Fed. Reserve Bank of New York 1973–75; Chief Economist and Corporate Vice-Pres. Paine, Webber, Jackson, and Curtis, New York 1975–79; Chief Economist and Partner, Bear, Stearns and Co., New York 1979–81; Asst. Dir. for Econ. Policy, Office of Man. and Budget, Washington, D.C. 1981–82, Assoc. Dir. for Econs. and Planning 1982–83; Pres. and C.E.O. Lawrence Kudlow and Assocs., Washington D.C. 1983–84; Pres. and C.E.O. Rodman and Renshaw Economics Inc. 1984–86; Chief Economist and Man. Dir. Rodman and Renshaw Capital Group Inc. 1984–86; Chief Economist, Bear, Stearns and Co. 1986–. *Leisure interests:* tennis, golf. *Address:* 130 East 94th Street, New York, N.Y. 10028, U.S.A. (Home).

KUDRYASHOV, Oleg; Russian (graphic) artist; b. 1932, Moscow; ed. secondary school; exhibited in Moscow 1958, 1962 (Manège), 1965; left U.S.S.R. 1973, settled in London; exhbns. include: Barcelona, Paris Biennale, U.S.A., numerous exhbns. in London, exhbn. in Leeds 1987.

KUDRYAVTSEV, Vladimir Nikolaevich; Soviet jurist; b. 1923; served in Soviet Army 1941–45; mem. CPSU 1945–; ed. Mil. Law. Acad. 1945–49; on staff of Acad. 1950–56; teacher at Lenin Mil.-Political Acad. 1956–60; on staff of Mil. Coll. of U.S.S.R. Supreme Soviet 1960–63; Deputy Dir. of All-Union Inst. for Crime Prevention 1963–69, Dir. 1969–73; Dir. of U.S.S.R. Inst. of State and Law of Acad. of Sciences 1973–; corresp. mem. of U.S.S.R. Acad. of Sciences 1974–84, mem. 1984–, Vice-Pres. 1988–; elected to Congress of People's Deputies of the U.S.S.R. 1989; State Prize 1984. *Address:* Institute of State and Law, Moscow, Ul. Frunze 10, U.S.S.R.

KUDSI, Nazem el, PH.D.; Syrian former Head of State; b. 1906; ed. American Coll., Beirut, Damascus Univ. and Univ. of Geneva; Barrister in Aleppo 1930; Deputy for Aleppo 1936, 1947, 1955; Minister Plenipotentiary, Washington 1944–45; Prime Minister and Minister for Foreign Affairs 1950; Pres. Council of Ministers 1954–57; Leader, Populist Party; held political office during U.A.R. regime 1958–61; Pres. of the Syrian Arab Repub. 1961–63, retd. 1963. *Address:* Aleppo, Syria.

KUENHEIM, Eberhard von; German motor executive; b. 2 Oct. 1928, Juditten, Kreis Bartenstein; ed. Höhere Schule, Salem and Technische Hochschule, Stuttgart; Chair. Man. Bd. BMW AG, Munich 1970–; Chair. Supervisory Bd. Industrie-Werke Karlsruhe Ausberg, AG; mem. Supervisory Bd. Allianz Rückversicherung AG, Munich; Bayerische Vereinsbank AG, Munich. *Leisure interests:* sciences, hockey, walking, books on politics and modern history. *Address:* c/o Bayerische Motorenwerke AG, 8000 Munich 40, Petuelring 130, Federal Republic of Germany. *Telephone:* 38952500 (Office).

KUHARIĆ, H.E. Cardinal Franjo; Yugoslavian (Croatian) ecclesiastic; b. 15 April 1919, Pribić, near Zagreb; ordained priest 1945; Bishop of titular church of Meta 1964–; Archbishop of Zagreb 1970–; Pres. of Yugoslavian Episcopal Conf.; cr. Cardinal 1983. *Address:* Kaptol 31, PP 553, 41000 Zagreb, Yugoslavia. *Telephone:* (041) 275-132.

KUHLMANN, Kathleen Mary; American opera singer; b. 7 Dec. 1950, San Francisco; m. Haydn John Rawstron 1983; ed. Mercy High School, San Francisco and Univ. of San Francisco; student Chicago Lyric Opera School 1976–79; Resident Mezzo-soprano, Cologne Opera 1980–82; freelance 1982–; int. débuts: Teatro alla Scalla, Milan 1980, San Francisco Opera 1982, Royal Opera House, Covent Garden 1982, Teatro Regio Parma 1983, Glyndebourne Festival Opera 1983, Wiener Staatsoper 1983, Teatro Communale Pisa 1983, Chicago Lyric Opera 1984, Salzburger Festspiele 1985, Stuttgart Opera 1985, Hamburg State Opera 1985; Grand Prix (Belgium Radio/TV Competition). *Recordings: audio:* Andrea Chenier 1982, Lucia di Lammermoor 1983, Alcina 1985; *video:* Rigoletto 1981, La Cenerentola 1983. *Leisure interests:* cooking, playing snooker. *Address:* 37 Sydenham Park Road, London, S.E.26, England. *Telephone:* 01-699 5828.

KUHN, Heinrich Gerhard, D.PHIL., M.A., F.R.S.; British physicist; b. 10 March 1904, Breslau (then Germany); s. of Wilhelm and Martha (née Hoppe) Kuhn; m. Marie B. Nohl 1931; two s.; ed. Greifswald and Göttingen Univs.; research on atomic and molecular spectroscopy jointly with James Franck 1926–33; emigrated to England 1933; engaged in teaching and research at Clarendon Lab., Oxford 1933–71, Univ. Reader 1955 (now Emer.), Fellow, Balliol Coll. 1950 (Emer. Fellow 1971–); Prof. Emer. Göttingen Univ. 1962; Hon. D.Sc. (Aix-Marseille) 1958; Holweck Prize 1967. *Publications:* Atomspektren 1934, Atomic Spectra 1962; papers in professional journals. *Leisure interests:* gardening, walking, reading. *Address:* 25 Victoria Road, Oxford, OX2 7QF, England. *Telephone:* (0865) 515308.

KÜHN, Heinz; German politician; b. 18 Feb. 1912, Cologne; m. Marianne Kühn 1952; one s.; ed. Univs. of Cologne, Prague and Ghent; mem. Catholic Youth Movement "Neudeutschland", Socialist Youth Movement of Germany 1928; mem. Socialist Party (SPD) 1930; Chair. of Socialist Student Group, Cologne; political emigration and studies at Univs. of Prague and Ghent 1933; journalist and ed.-in-chief Rheinische Zeitung 1949–51; mem. Landtag, North Rhine-Westphalia 1948–54, 1962, Chair. SPD Parl. Party 1962–66, Minister-Pres. of North Rhine-Westphalia 1966–78; mem. Bundestag, mem. SPD Parl. Man. Cttee., Bundestag Foreign Affairs Comm. and Chair. Bundestag Comm. on German Schools and Insts. Abroad 1953–62; mem. Ass., Western European Union; mem. European Parl. 1979–84; Chair. Bundesrat 1971–72; Chair. SPD North Rhine-Westphalia 1962–73; mem. Presidium SPD 1966, Deputy Chair. 1973; Chair. Friedrich Ebert Stiftung 1983–; Deputy Chair. Admin. Bd. Westdeutscher Rundfunk. *Address:* Roteichenweg 5, 5000 Cologne 80, Federal Republic of Germany. *Telephone:* Düsseldorf 8371.

KUHN, Thomas S., M.A., PH.D.; American professor of philosophy; b. 18 July 1922, Cincinnati, Ohio; s. of Samuel Louis and Minette (née Stroock) Kuhn; m. 1st Kathryn Louise Muhs 1948 (divorced 1978); one s. two. d; m. 2nd Jehane Robin Burns 1982; ed. Harvard Coll., Harvard Univ.; Jr. Fellow, Harvard 1948–51, Instructor and Asst. Prof. 1951–56; Asst. Prof., Assoc. Prof. and Prof., Univ. of Calif. (Berkeley) 1957–64; Prof. and M. Taylor Pine Prof., Princeton 1964–79; Prof., M.I.T. 1979–83, Laurance S. Rockefeller Prof. of Philosophy 1983–; Guggenheim Fellow 1954–55; Center for Advanced Study in the Behavioral Sciences Fellow 1958–59., Pres., History of Science Soc. 1968–70; mem., Inst. for Advanced Study 1972–79, American Acad. of Arts and Sciences, American Philosophical Soc., N.A.S.; Behrman Award (Princeton) 1977, Sarton Medal (History of Science Soc.) 1982. Bernal Award (Soc. for Social Studies of Science) 1983. *Publications:* The Copernican Revolution: Planetary Astronomy in the Development of Western Thought 1957, The Structure of Scientific Revolutions 1962, Sources for History of Quantum Physics; an Inventory and Report 1966 (with J. L. Heilbron, P. Forman, L. Allen), The Essential Tension; Selected Studies in Scientific Tradition and Change 1977, Black-Body Theory and the Quantum Discontinuity, 1894–1912 1978. *Leisure interests:* cooking, riding roller coasters. *Address:* Department of Linguistics and Philosophy, Massachusetts Institute of Technology, 20D-213, Cambridge, Mass. 02139, U.S.A. *Telephone:* (617) 253-5344.

KÜHNE, Gunther Albert Hermann, DR.IUR., LL.M.; German professor of law; b. 25 Aug. 1939, Gelsenkirchen; s. of Friedrich and Gertrud (née Belgard) Kühne; ed. Univ. of Cologne and Columbia Univ., New York; part-time legal adviser to German mining cos. 1963–68; Research Asst. Bochum Univ. Law School 1967–70; Sr. Govt. official, Ministry of Econs.,

Bonn 1971–74; Sr. official German del. OECD, Paris 1972–73; Sr. Govt. official, Ministry of Justice, Bonn 1974–78; Lecturer Private Law, Private Int. and Comparative Law, Bochum Univ. 1971–79; Prof. of Mining and Energy Law, Dir. Inst. for Mining and Energy Law, Tech. Univ. Clausthal 1978–; Hon. Prof. of Law, Univ. of Göttingen 1986–. *Publications:* numerous books and articles on aspects of law, including Die Parteiautonomie im internationalen Erbrecht 1973, IPR-Gesetz-Entwurf (Private Int. Law Reform Draft) 1980, Memorandum on the State and Reform of German International Family Law 1980. *Address:* Arnold-Sommerfeld-Strasse 6, D-3392 Clausthal-Zellerfeld, Federal Republic of Germany. *Telephone:* 05323-722283.

KUIPERS, J. D., M.A., M.SC.ECON., D.SC.; Netherlands consultant; b. 9 July 1918, Timperley, England; s. of Johannes and Marion Kuipers-Sewell; m. Johanna Adriana de Roon 1940; three s.; ed. Univ. of Cambridge, L.S.E. and Univ. of Amsterdam; served British and Royal Netherlands Army 1940–45; Dir. Royal De Betuwe Co. 1945–65; Vice-Pres. Fed. of Netherlands Industry, Brussels 1970–75; Chair. Foreign Affairs Cttee., Council of Netherlands Industrial Feds., Brussels 1970–75; Prof., Strathclyde Univ. Business School 1974–80; mem. Econ. and Social Cttee. of EEC 1962–74, Pres. 1970–72; mem. Pres. Council, Union of Industrial Feds. of EEC 1964–75, Council of Business and Advisory Cttee. to OECD; Hon. LL.D. (Strathclyde) 1974; Kt. Order of Netherlands Lion, Officer Order of Orange Nassau, Commdr. Order Léopold II, Order Georges I, Order of Merit (Italy). *Publication:* Resale Price Maintenance in Great Britain 1951. *Leisure interests:* arts, history. *Address:* 7 avenue Paul Hymans, Brussels 1200, Belgium; Los Algarrobos PU 106, Javea, Alicante, Spain. (Homes.)

KUJIRAOKA, Hyosuke; Japanese politician; b. 15 Sept. 1915, Fukushima Prefecture; ed. Waseda Univ.; mem. Tokyo Metropolitan Assembly 1955–60; mem. House of Reps. 1963–, Chair. Standing Cttee. on Foreign Affairs 1976; Deputy Dir.-Gen. Prime Minister's Office 1968–70; Deputy Chief Cabinet Sec. 1976–77; Vice-Chair. Liberal-Democratic Party Exec. Council 1978–79; Minister of State and Dir.-Gen. Environment Agency 1980–81. *Publications:* two books on metropolitan government and party debates. *Address:* c/o Liberal-Democratic Party, 7, 2-chome, Hirakawacho, Chiyoda-ku, Tokyo, Japan.

KUKUŁKA, Józef, H.H.D.; Polish political scientist and politician; b. 3 Jan. 1929, Rączyna, Przemyśl Voivodship; s. of Jan and Kazimiera Kukułka; m. Krystyna Bolesta 1963; two s.; ed. Main School of Foreign Service, Warsaw 1953; Asst., then Lecturer, Main School of Foreign Service and Acad. of Political Sciences, Warsaw 1949–56; mem. United Peasants' Party (ZSL) 1949–; Deputy Pres. ZSL Warsaw Cttee. 1959–61; mem. Presidium of Gen. Bd., Rural Youth Union (ZMW) 1958–66, Chair. ZMW Nat. Students' Council 1958–62; Deputy Head, Research Centre for Peasant Movt. History and Ed.-in-Chief, "Roczniki Ruchu Ludowego" of ZSL Chief Cttee. 1960–62; scientific worker, Polish Inst. of Int. Affairs, Warsaw 1962–68; First Sec., Embassy, Paris 1968–70, Counsellor, Embassy, Paris 1970–72; Adviser to Minister of Foreign Affairs 1972–78; Staff Warsaw Univ. 1972–, in. Inst. of Political Sciences 1972–76, Dir. Int. Relations Inst. 1977–, Extraordinary Prof. 1977–85, Ordinary Prof. 1986–; mem. ZSL Chief Cttee. 1980–, Deputy Pres. ZSL Chief Cttee. May 1981–; Deputy Chair. Exec. Cttee., Nat. Council of Patriotic Movement for Nat. Rebirth (PRON) July 1984–; Deputy Chair. Foreign Affairs Comm. of Parl. 1985–; Sec. Polish Group, IPU 1985–; Chair. Polish-Belgian Group in Parl. 1985–; Officer's and Kt.'s Crosses of Order of Polonia Restituta, Gold Cross of Merit. *Publications:* numerous works on history of int. relations, including, Francja a Polska po Traktacie Weralskim 1919-1922 (France and Poland after Versailles Treaty 1919-1922) 1970, Współpraca polityczna państw wspólnoty socjalist-ycznej (Political Co-operation between Socialist Countries) 1976, Problemy teorii stosunków międzynarodowych (Problems of International Relations Theory) 1978, Międzynarodowe stosunki polityczne (International Political Relations) 1982. *Address:* Naczelny Komitet ZSL, ul. Grzybowska 4, 00-131 Warsaw (Office); ul. Powsińska 38 m. 3, 02-903 Warsaw, Poland (Home). *Telephone:* 20-60-21 (Office).

KUKURYKA, Stanisław Edward; Polish politician and lawyer; b. 14 June 1928, Zemborzyce, Lublin Voivodship; m.; two c.; ed. Maria Curie-Skłodowska Univ., Lublin; Head, Investment Dept. of Lublin Cooperative for Animal Products Sales, Lublin 1948–55; Head, Rural Bldg. Bd. in Lublin Voivodship Nat. Council 1955–58; Pres. Lublin Housing Co-operative 1958–65; Dir. Lublin Branch of Cen. Union of Housing Co-operatives 1965–66; Deputy Chair. Bd. of Cen. Union of Housing Co-operatives, Warsaw 1967–72, Chair. 1972–82; Deputy Chair. Dwelling Cttee. of Int. Co-operative Union 1983–; Deputy to Seym 1976–85; Minister of Building and Building Materials Industry 1982–85; Amb. to Libya 1986–; mem. Polish United Workers' Party (PZPR) 1962–, deputy mem. PZPR Cen. Cttee. 1980–81; Gold Cross of Merit 1962, Officer's and Kt.'s Cross of Order of Polonia Restituta and other decorations. *Publications:* numerous articles on housing. *Address:* Embassy of Poland, P.O. Box 519, Tripoli, Garden City, Libya.

KUŁAGA, Eugeniusz, M.A.; Polish diplomatist (retd.); b. 1 Nov. 1925, Auby, France; s. of Michał and Karolina Kułaga; m. Maria Hamerlak 1953; two d.; ed. Cen. School for Foreign Service, Warsaw; Second, then First Sec., Perm. Del. of Poland to UN 1952-55; Deputy Rep. ICSC, Vietnam 1955; Act. Rep., Laos 1956; Head, UN Div. Min. of Foreign Affairs,

Warsaw 1956–59; Deputy Rep. of Poland to UN, Geneva 1959–62; Amb. of Poland to Ghana, Mali, Dahomey, Sierra Leone 1962–65; Dir. of Dept. of Int. Orgs., Min. of Foreign Affairs, Warsaw 1965–69; Del. of Poland to several UN Gen. Assemblies; Perm. Rep. to UN 1969–75; Chair. Special Political Cttee. of Gen. Assembly 1969; Rep. UN Security Council 1970–71; Vice-Chair. Special Cttee. on Rationalization of Procedure and Organization of Gen. Assembly 1970–71; Vice-Chair. Special Cttee. on the Financial Situation of the UN 1972; Chair. UN Comm. on Human Rights 1972–75; Rep. Int. Comm. of Control and Supervision (ICCS) 1973–74; Vice-Chair. Ad-Hoc Cttee. on the World Disarmament Conf. 1974–75; Under-Sec. of State, Ministry of Foreign Affairs 1975–80; Amb. to France 1980–84; Chair. UN European Econ. Comm. 1978–85; Sr. Adviser to Ministry of Foreign Affairs 1985–86; Chair. Polish del., Conf. on Security and Co-operation in Europe, Vienna 1986; Gold Cross of Merit 1954, Medal of 10th Anniversary of People's Poland 1954, Commdr.'s, Officer's and Kt.'s Cross, Order of Polonia Restituta, Medal of 30th Anniversary of People's Poland 1974.

KULARATNAM, Karthigesapillai, M.A., PH.D., DR.SC.; Sri Lankan educationist, geographer and geologist; b. 28 May 1911; m. Poospadevi Kularatnam; Prof. Emer. and Dean, Univ. of Sri Lanka; taught in Univs. of Edinburgh, Sheffield, Birmingham, New York, Kansas City and Sir George Williams (Montreal); Pres. Inst. of Environmental Sciences; Dir. Commonwealth Geographical Bureau, Inst. of Population Eng.; Sr. Consultant, Population Div., UN/ESCAP; Pres. Ceylon Geographical Soc., Gemmologists Asscn., Soil Conservation Soc.; Past Pres. of Natural Sciences, Ceylon Asscn. for the Advancement of Science; Corresp. mem. World Fed. of Scientific Workers. *Publications:* several essays on geography, geology, Sri Lanka, etc. *Address:* 61 Abdul Caffoor Mawatha, Colombo 3, Sri Lanka.

KULCSÁR, Kálmán, D.IUR.; Hungarian legal scholar and sociologist; b. 27 June 1928, Erdőtelek; s. of Ödön Kulcsár and Margit Szücs; m. Dr. Erzsébet Balogh; one d.; ed. Eger and Pázmány Péter Univ. of Budapest; various Judical posts to mem. of the Supreme Court of Justice 1950–57; research worker, Hungarian Acad. of Sciences with Eötvös Loránd Univ. Budapest; sr. mem. Inst. of Political and Legal Sciences 1957–69; Ford Scholarship for study in USA 1965–66; Dir. Hungarian Acad. of Sciences Inst. of Sociology 1969–83; Prof. of Sociology of Law, Eötvös Loránd Univ., Budapest 1970–; Minister of Justice 1988–; corresp. mem. Hungarian Acad. of Sciences 1973, mem. 1980–, Deputy Gen. Sec. 1983–88; Pres. Hungarian Sociological Soc. 1983–; mem. Council of Int. Sociology Assn., Amsterdam 1983–; mem. editorial bd. International Journal of the Sociology of Law 1982–; State Prize 1985. *Publications include:* A jogszociológia problémái (Problems of the sociology of law) 1960, A szociológiai gondolkodás fejlődése (Development of the Sociological Thought) 1966, Társadalom, politika, jog (Society, Politics, Law) 1974; A jogszociológia alapjai (Foundations of the Sociology of Law) 1976, Gazdaság, társadalom, jog (Economy, Society, Law) 1983, Rechts-soziologische Abhandlungen 1982, People's Assessors in the Court 1983, Contemporary Hungarian Society 1984, Modernization and Hungarian Society 1986, Politics and Sociology of Law 1987; numerous studies in Hungarian and foreign trade papers. *Leisure interest:* memoirs by statesmen before and after World War II. *Address:* Ministry of Justice, Budapest V, Szalay utca 16. *Telephone:* 326-170.

KULIDZHANOV, Lev Aleksandrovich; Soviet film producer; b. 19 March 1924, Tbilisi; ed. All-Union Film Inst. (VGIK); producer, later dir., Gorky Film Studio 1955–; mem. CPSU 1962–; Chair. Organizing Cttee., U.S.S.R. Union of Film Workers 1964–65, First Sec. 1965–86; Chief rep. on State Cttee. of Council of Ministers of U.S.S.R. on Cinema 1963–64; Deputy to U.S.S.R. Supreme Soviet; mem. Comm. on Educ., Science and Culture, Soviet of Nationalities, U.S.S.R. Supreme Soviet 1966–; Chair. U.S.S.R. Mexico Friendship Soc. 1966–; mem. Cen. Auditing Comm. of CPSU 1966–76, cand. mem. Cen. Cttee. CPSU 1976–; Order of Lenin, Hero of Socialist Labour 1984. *Films include:* It Happened So 1956; The House in which I Live 1957; My Father's House 1959; The Lost Photo 1959; When Trees Were Big 1961; The Blue Book 1963; Crime and Punishment 1969; State Prize of the R.S.F.S.R. 1971. *Address:* Supreme Soviet, Moscow, U.S.S.R.

KULIKOV, Marshal Viktor Georgiyevich; Soviet army officer; b. 5 July 1921; ed. Frunze Military Acad., Acad. of General Staff; joined Soviet Army 1938; Commdr. of Platoon 1940, Chief of Staff tank battalion, regt., brigade 1941–45; various command posts in tank detachments 1945–48; Frunze Mil. Acad. 1948–53; Commdr. tank regt., Chief of Staff tank div., Deputy Commdr. of Army, Commdr. of Army 1953–67; Commdr. Kiev Mil. Area 1967–69; C.-in-C. Soviet Forces in Germany 1969–71; mem. CPSU 1942–; mem. Cen. Cttee. of CPSU April 1971–; Chief of Gen. Staff and First Deputy Minister of Defence 1971–77; C.-in-C. of Armed Forces of Warsaw Pact 1977–89; Order of Lenin 1983, Order of the Red Banner (three times), Hero of the Soviet Union and other decorations. *Address:* c/o Ministry of Defence, 34 Naberezhnaya M. Thoreza, Moscow, U.S.S.R.

KULKA, Konstanty Andrzej; Polish violinist; b. 5 March 1947, Gdańsk; m.; two c.; ed. Higher State School of Music, Gdańsk; participant in 2 music competitions: Paganini Competition, Genoa 1964, Diploma and Special Prize; Music Competition, Munich 1966 (1st Prize); since 1967 has given concerts all over the world and participates in many int. festivals including Lucerne, Prague, Bordeaux, Berlin, Granada, Barcelona, Brighton; many gramophone, radio and TV recordings; Minister of Culture and

Art Prize 1969, 1973, Minister of Foreign Affairs Prize 1977, Pres. of Radio and TV Cttee. Prize 1978, Prize Winner 33 Grand Prix du Disque Int. Sound Festival, Paris 1980; Gold Cross of Merit. *Leisure interests:* collecting gramophone records, bridge, collecting interesting kitchen recipes. *Address:* ul. Związku Walki Młodych 1 m. 44, 00-001 Warsaw, Poland. *Telephone:* 47-82-91 (Office).

KULLBERG, Rolf, M.SOC.SC. (ECON.); Finnish banker; b. 3 Oct. 1930, Pohja; s. of Harry Kullberg and Svea Kullberg; m. Märta Elisabeth Sourander 1953; three s.; Sales Man. Oy Fiskars Ab 1956–60; Chief of Dept. Union Bank of Finland 1961–67, Asst. Gen. Man. 1967–71; Head of Dept., Ministry of Finance 1971–72; mem. Bd. of Man. Union Bank of Finland 1973–74, Bank of Finland 1974–, Acting Deputy Gov. 1979–82, Deputy Gov. 1982–83, Gov. 1983–; mem. Supervisory Bd., Finnish Fund for Industrial Devt. 1979–; mem. Finnish Export Credit Ltd. 1982–, mem. Supervisory Bd. Finnish Export Credit 1983–, Econ. Council 1983–; mem. Bd. of Govs. IMF 1983–. *Publication:* Encyclopaedia of Money (ed. with K. Kara) 1970. *Address:* Bank of Finland, Snellmaninaukio, SF-00170 Helsinki, Finland. *Telephone:* 358-0-1831.

KUMAGAI, Tasaburo; Japanese politician; ed. Kyoto Univ.; Mem. of House of Councillors; fmr. Mayor of Kyoto; fmr. Parl. Deputy Minister of Int. Trade; fmr. Chair. House of Councillors Cabinet Cttee. on Revision of the Public Offices Election Law; Dir.-Gen. Science and Tech. Agency 1977–78; Liberal-Democratic Party. *Address:* c/o Science and Technology Agency, 2 Kasumigaseki 2-chome, Chiyoda-ku, Tokyo, Japan.

KUMAGAI, Yoshifumi, B.L.; Japanese business executive; b. 30 Nov. 1915, Shimani Pref.; m. Sumiko 1941; three s. one d.; ed. Tokyo Imperial Univ.; joined Head Office of Sumitomo Companies Group 1939; Ministry of Int. Trade and Industry 1940–69; Admin. Vice-Minister, Ministry of Int. Trade and Industry 1968; Sumitomo Metal Industries Ltd. 1971–, Man. Dir. 1971, Sr. Man. Dir. 1972, Exec. Vice-Pres. 1976, Pres. 1978–86, Chair. 1986–, Adviser to Pres. 1988–. *Leisure interest:* gardening. *Address:* 13 Shimodacho 667, Kohoku-ku, Yokohama-shi, Kanagawa, Japan. *Telephone:* 044-62-2693.

KUME, Tadashi; Japanese business executive; b. 1 Jan. 1932, Shizuoka Pref.; ed. Shizuoka Univ.; joined Honda Motor Co. Ltd. 1954; Dir. Honda Research and Devt. Co. Ltd., 1969, Dir. and Chief Eng. 1970, Man. Dir. 1971, Sr. Man. Dir. 1974, Pres. 1977; Sr. Man. Dir. and Rep. Dir. Honda Motor Co. Ltd. 1979–83 and Pres. Honda R & D Co. Ltd. 1979–81; C.E.O. Honda Motor Co. Ltd. 1983–. *Address:* Honda Motor Co. Ltd., No. 27-8, 6-chome, Jingumae, Shibuya-ku, Tokyo 150, Japan. *Telephone:* Tokyo (499) 0111.

KUME, Yutaka, B.E.; Japanese business executive; b. 20 May 1921, Tokyo; s. of Kinzaburo Kume and Chiyo Kume; m. Aya Kume 1947; one s. one d.; ed. Univ. of Tokyo; joined Nissan Motor Co. Ltd. 1946, dir. and mem. of Bd., concurrently Gen. Man. of Tochigi Plant 1973, Man. Dir. in charge of Office of Product and Eng. Strategy 1977, Exec. Man. Dir., and also in charge of Quality Admin. Div. 1982, Exec. Vice-Pres. in charge of Research and Devt., Diversified Operations and Corp. Planning Office, and concurrently Gen. Man. Quality Admin. Div. 1983, Pres. June 1985–; Exec. Dir. Japan Fed. of Employers' Asscns.; Dir. Japan Automobile Mfrs'. Asscn. Inc.; mem. Bd. of Dirs. Keidanren (Fed. of Econ. Orgs.), Japan Automobile Fed. *Leisure interests:* photography, golf, Haiku, reading. *Address:* 17-1, Ginza 6-chome, Chuo-ku, Tokyo (Office); 571 Unomori, Sagamihara City, Kanagawa Prefecture, Japan (Home).

KUMMER, Wolfgang, DR.TECH.; Austrian physicist; b. 15 Oct. 1935, Krems; s. of Dr Friedrich Kummer and Maria Kummer; m. Lore Pokorny 1960; ed. Gymnasium Krems and Technical Univ. Vienna; Asst. Tech. Univ. Vienna 1958–66; Dir. Inst. of High Energy Physics, Austrian Acad. of Sciences 1966–71; Prof. of Theoretical Physics, Technical Univ. Vienna 1968–; Head, Interuniv. Computer Center 1979–; Pres. CERN Council 1985–87; Visiting Prof. Univ. of Philadelphia 1973, Princeton Univ. 1975, Brookhaven Nat. Lab. 1977, 1980 etc.; mem. Austrian Acad. of Sciences; Culture Award, Fed. Country of Lower Austria 1971; Innitzer Award 1981. *Publications:* 85 scientific publs. on the theory of elementary particle physics. *Leisure interests:* music, tennis, skiing. *Address:* Institut für Theoretische Physik, Technische Universität Wien, Wiedner Hauptstrasse 8-10, 1040 Vienna (Office); Liebhartstalstrasse 31, 1160 Vienna, Austria (Home). *Telephone:* (0222) 58801/5690 (Office); (0222) 9488405 (Home).

KUMP, Ernest Joseph, M.A. (ARCH.); American architect; b. 29 Dec. 1911, Bakersfield, Calif.; s. of Ernest J. Kump, Sr. and Mary Petsche Kump; m. Josephine Miller Kump 1934; one s. one d.; ed. Univ .of Calif. (Berkeley) and Harvard Grad. School of Design; fmr. Prof. of Architecture, Columbia Univ. and has lectured at numerous univs.; founded own architectural firm 1934; Chair. Bd. of Dirs. Tekto Systems Research 1977–82; Sr. Partner, KUMP, Architecture Research Assocs. 1983–; work has included college and univ. campuses, civic centres, performing arts centres and other public bldgs. and new residential communities; consultant and panel or cttee. mem. for numerous orgs. including British Bldg. Comm., Carnegie Foundation and U.S. Govt.; Consulting Architect to Ronald Reagan Pres. Library Foundation, Calif. 1987; mem. Task Force on Arts and Humanities 1981; Hon. Fellow, R.I.B.A.; mem. Berlin Akad. der Künste; Fellow American Inst. of Architects (Architectural Firm Award 1970), Life mem.

R.S.A. London. *Publication:* A New Architecture for Man 1957. *Leisure interests:* inventing, philosophy, classical music, literature. *Address:* Schloss Matzen Castle, A-6230 Brixlegg, Austria; 17 Rue Chanoinesse, 75004 Paris, France.

KUNAYEV, Dinmohammed Akhmedovich; Soviet (Kazakh) politician and mining engineer; b. 12 Jan. 1912; ed. Moscow Inst. of Non-Ferrous Metals; Former Dir. Kounrad Mine, Kazakh S.S.R.; Vice-Chair. Council of Ministers Kazakh S.S.R. 1942-52, Chair. 1955-60, 1962-64; First Sec. Kazakh CP 1960-62, 1964-86; Cand. mem. Politburo Cen. Cttee. of CPSU 1966-1971, mem. 1971-87; Deputy to Supreme Soviet of the U.S.S.R. 1950-86 and Supreme Soviet of the Kazakh S.S.R.; mem. Presidium of Supreme Soviet of U.S.S.R. 1962-86; mem. CPSU Cen. Cttee. 1956-86; Acad. of Sciences of the Kazakh S.S.R. 1952-55; Hero of Socialist Labour, Order of Lenin (seven times), Hammer and Sickle Gold Medal (twice), Sixty Years of Armed Forces of U.S.S.R. Medal, Order of the October Revolution 1980 and other decorations. *Address:* Central Committee of Communist Party of the Kazakh S.S.R., Alma-Ata, Kazakh S.S.R., U.S.S.R.

KUNCEWICZOWA, Maria; Polish writer; b. 30 Oct. 1897, Samara, Russia; d. of Józef and Adela Szczepański; m. Jerzy Kuncewicz 1921 (died 1984); one s.; ed. Warsaw Univ., Jagellonian Univ., Cracow, and Univ. of Nancy; lived in France during World War II, in U.K. until 1956; Founder, Centre Writers in Exile; Prof. Polish Literature, Univ. of Chicago 1963-72; mem. Int. PEN Club; hon. mem. Lublin Scientific Soc. 1979-; Literary Prize of Warsaw 1937, Golden Laurel of Polish Acad. of Letters 1937, Pietrzak Prize 1969, State Prize 1st Class 1974; Medal of Merit (Kosciuszko Foundation, N.Y.) 1971, Prize and Medal, European Soc. of Culture (Polish Section) 1982, Albert Prize 1986. *Publications:* Przymierze z dzieckiem (Alliance with a Child) 1927, Twarz mężczyzny (Face of Man), Miłość Panieńska (Maiden Love), Dwa Księżyce (Two Moons) 1933, Dyliżans Warszawski (Warsaw Stage-Coach) 1935, Cudzoziemka (The Stranger) 1936, Dni Powszednie Państwa Kowalskich (Everyday) 1938, Miasto Heroda (Herod's Town) 1938, Klucze (The Keys) 1943, Zmowa Nieobecnych (The Conspiracy of the Absent) 1945, Leśnik (The Forester) (trans. into English, German, Hungarian) 1957, Dziękuję ci za różę (Thank you for the Rose) 1955 (play), W domu i w Polsce (At Home and in Poland) 1958, Odkrycie Patusanu (The Discovery of Patusan) 1958, Gaj oliwny (also written in English as The Olive Grove) 1961, The Modern Polish Mind (anthology) 1962, Don Kichote i nianki (Don Quixote and Nurses) 1965, Tristan 1946, 1967; Fantomy (Phantoms), Vol. I 1971, Natura, Vol. II 1975 (two vol. autobiography), Fantasia alla Polacca (essay) 1979, Tamto spojrzenie (That Other Look) (short stories) 1980, Rozmowy z Maria Kuncewicz 1982, Przeźrocza: Notatki włoskie (Slides: Roman notes) 1985. *Leisure interests:* music, travel. *Address:* ul. Małachowskiego 19, 24-120 Kazimieirz Dolny, Poland; c/o Witold Kuncewicz, Flint Hill, Virginia, 22627 U.S.A. *Telephone:* 102 (Poland); (703) 364 1841 (Virginia).

KUNDERA, Milan; Czechoslovak writer (also French nationality); b. 1 April 1929, Brno; s. of Dr. Ludvik Kundera and Milada Kunderová-Janosikova; m. Věra Hrabánková 1967; ed. Film Faculty, Acad. of Music and Dramatic Arts, Prague; Asst., later Asst. Prof., Film Faculty, Acad. of Music and Dramatic Arts, Prague 1958-69; Prof., Univ. of Rennes 1975-80; Prof. Ecole des hautes études en sciences sociales, Paris 1980-; mem. Union of Czechoslovak Writers 1963-69; mem. Editorial Bd. Literární noviny 1963-67, 1968; mem. Editorial Bd. Listy 1968-69; Klement Lukeš Prize 1963; Union of Czechoslovak Writers' Prize 1968, Czechoslovak Writers' Publishing House Prize 1969, Prix Médicis (for Life is Elsewhere) 1973, Premio letterario Mondello (for The Farewell Party) 1978, Commonwealth Award (for all his work) 1981, Prix Europa-Littérature 1982, Los Angeles Times Prize (for Unbearable Lightness of Being) 1984, Jerusalem Prize (for all his work) 1985, Nelly Sachs Preis (for all his work) 1987, Österreichische Staatspreis für Europäische Literatur 1988. *Publications:* Drama: The Owners of the Keys 1962, Jacques et son maître 1971-81; Short stories: Laughable Loves 1970; Novels: The Joke 1967, Life is Elsewhere 1973, La Valse aux adieux (The Farewell Party) 1976, Livre du rire et de l'oubli (The Book of Laughter and Forgetting) 1979, The Unbearable Lightness of Being 1984, The Art of the Novel 1987. *Address:* Ecole des hautes études en sciences sociales, 54 boulevard Raspail, Paris 75006, France.

KUNERALP, Zeki; Turkish diplomatist (retd.); b. 5 Oct. 1914, Istanbul; m. Necla Ozdilci 1943; two s.; ed. Univ. of Berne; entered Diplomatic Service 1940, served Bucharest 1943-47, Ankara (Ministry of Foreign Affairs) 1947-49, Prague 1949-52, NATO (Paris) 1952-57; Asst. Sec.-Gen. Ministry of Foreign Affairs 1957, Sec.-Gen. 1960; Ambassador to Switzerland 1960, to U.K. 1964-66; Sec.-Gen. Min. of Foreign Affairs 1966-69; Amb. to U.K. 1969-72, to Spain 1972-79; Hon. G.C.V.O. 1971. *Publication:* Sadece Diplomat (memoirs) 1981. *Address:* Fenerbahce Caddesi 85/B, Belvü Ap. D. 4, Kiziltoprak, Istanbul, Turkey.

KUNERT, Günter; German author; b. 6 March 1929, Berlin; s. of Adolf Kunert and Edith Warschauer; m. Marianne Todten 1951; Visiting Assoc. Prof. Univ. of Tex. (Austin) 1972; Writer-in-Residence Univ. of Warwick 1975; mem. Akad. der Künste, W. Berlin, Akad. für Sprache und Dichtung, Darmstadt; Heinrich Mann Prize, Akad. der Künste (E. Berlin) 1962; Becher Prize for Poetry 1973; Heinrich Heine Prize (City of Düsseldorf) 1985 etc. *Publications:* 55 volumes of poetry, prose, satire, essays, novels,

short stories, radio plays and lectures. *Leisure interest:* travel. *Address:* 2216 Kaisborstel, Schulstrasse 7, Federal Republic of Germany. *Telephone:* 04892/1414.

KÜNG, Hans, D.THEOL.; Swiss theologian and univ. professor; b. 19 March 1928, Sursee, Lucerne; ed. Gregorian Univ., Rome, Inst. Catholique and Sorbonne, Paris; ordained priest 1954; mem. practical ministry, Lucerne Cathedral 1957-59; Scientific asst. for Dogmatic Catholic Theol., Univ. of Münster/Westfalen 1959-60; Prof. Fundamental Theol., Univ. of Tübingen 1960-63; Prof. of Dogmatics and Ecumenical Theology and Dir., Inst. Ecumenical Research 1963-80, Prof. of Ecumenical Theology, Dir. Inst. of Ecumenical Research (under direct responsibility of Pres. and Senate Univ. of Tübingen) 1980-; Hon. LL.D. (St. Louis, Toronto), Hon. D.D. (Pacific School of Religion, Berkeley, Univ. Glasgow, Cambridge), Hon. L.H.D. (Chicago, Mich., Ann Arbor). *Publications:* The Council: Reform and Reunion 1961, That the World May Believe 1963, The Council in Action 1963, Justification: The Doctrine of Karl Barth and a Catholic Reflection 1964, (with new introductory chapter, and response of Karl Barth) 1981, Structures of the Church 1964, (with new preface) 1982, Freedom Today 1966, The Church 1967, Truthfulness 1968, Menschwerdung Gottes 1970, Infallible?—An Inquiry 1971, Why Priests? 1972, Fehlbar?—Eine Bilanz 1973, On being a Christian 1976, Signposts for the Future 1978, The Christian Challenge 1979, Freud and the Problem of God 1979, Does God Exist? 1980, The Church-Maintained in Truth 1980, Eternal Life? 1984, Christianity and the World Religions: Paths to Dialogue with Islam, Hinduism and Buddhism (with others) 1986, The Incarnation of God 1986, Church and Change: The Irish Experience 1986, Why I am still a Christian 1987, Theology for the Third Millennium: An Ecumenical View 1988, Christianity and Chinese Religions (with Julia Ching) 1989; ed. Journal of Ecumenical Studies, Revue Internationale de Théologie Concilium, Theological Meditations, Ökumenische Theologie. *Leisure interests:* watersport, skiing, classical music. *Address:* 74 Tübingen, Waldhäuserstr. 23, Federal Republic of Germany. *Telephone:* 62646.

KUNIN, Madeleine May, M.A., M.S.; American state governor; b. 28 Sept. 1933, Zürich, Switzerland; d. of Ferdinand May and Renee Bloch; m. Arthur S. Kunin 1959; three s. one d.; ed. Univ. of Mass., Columbia Univ. and Univ. of Vermont; reporter, Burlington Free Press, Vermont 1957-58; Asst. Producer, WCAX-TV, Burlington 1960-61; freelance writer and instructor in English, Trinity Coll. Burlington 1969-70; mem. Vermont House of Reps. 1973-78; Lt.-Gov. of Vermont 1979-82, Gov. 1985-; Fellow, Inst. of Politics, Kennedy School of Govt. Harvard Univ. 1983, Lecturer, Middlebury Coll., St. Michael's Coll. 1984; several hon. degrees and other distinctions; Democrat. *Publications:* The Big Green Book (with M. Stout) 1976; articles in professional journals, magazines and newspapers. *Address:* Office of the Governor, Pavilion Building, 5th Floor, Montpelier, Vt. 05602, U.S.A.

KUNITZ, Stanley J., M.A.; American writer and educator; b. 29 July 1905, Worcester, Mass.; s. of Solomon Z. Kunitz and Yetta Helen Jasspon; m. 1st Helen Pearce 1930, 2nd Eleanor Evans 1939, 3rd Elise Asher 1958; one d.; ed. Harvard Univ.; Ed. Wilson Library Bulletin 1928-42; service with U.S. Army, rising to rank of Staff Sergeant 1943-45; Prof. of Literature, Bennington Coll., Vt. 1946-49; Dir. of Seminar, Potsdam Summer Workshop in Creative Arts 1949-53; Lecturer and Dir. of Poetry Workshop, New School for Social Research, New York 1950-58; Dir. Poetry Workshop, The Poetry Center, New York, 1958-62; Lecturer, Columbia Univ. 1963-66; Adjunct Prof. School of the Arts (Columbia) 1967-85; Sr. Fellow in the Humanities (Princeton) 1978; Ed., Yale Series of Younger Poets, Yale Univ. Press 1969-77; Poetry Consultant of the Library of Congress 1974-76, hon. Consultant in American Letters 1976-82; mem. American Acad. of Arts and Letters, Nat. Inst. of Arts and Letters; Pres. Poets House, New York 1985-; Hon. Litt.D. (Clark Univ.) 1961, (Anna Maria College) 1977, (Worcester State Coll.) 1980; Hon. D. Hum.Litt. (State Univ. of New York) 1987; awards include Garrison Medal for Poetry 1926, Blumenthal Prize 1941, Levinson Prize 1956, Harriet Monroe Award 1958, Pulitzer Prize for Poetry 1959, Brandeis Creative Arts Poetry Medal 1965; Fellowship Award, Acad. of American Poets 1968, Lenore Marshall Award for Poetry 1980, Bollingen Prize in Poetry 1987, designated New York State Poet, with Walt Whitman Citation of Merit 1987; Sr. Fellowship Award, Nat. Endowment for the Arts 1984; Fellow, Yale Univ. 1969; Chancellor, Acad. of American Poets 1970-. *Publications* (Verse): Intellectual Things 1930, Passport to the War 1944, Selected Poems 1958; Editions: Living Authors 1931, Authors Today and Yesterday 1933, Junior Book of Authors 1934, British Authors of the XIX Century 1936, American Authors 1600-1900 1938, XX Century Authors 1942, British Authors Before 1800 1952, XX Century Authors (First Supplement) 1955, Poems of John Keats 1964, European Authors 1000-1900 1967, The Testing-Tree (verse) 1971, Poems of Akhmatova (translations) 1973, The Terrible Threshold (verse) 1974, Story under Full Sail (trans. of A. Voznesensky) 1974, The Coat Without a Seam (verse) 1974, A Kind of Order, a Kind of Folly 1975, Orchard Lamps (trans. of Ivan Drach) 1978, The Poems of Stanley Kunitz 1928-1978, 1979, The Wellfleet Whale and Companion Poems 1983, Next-to-Last Things: New Poems and Essays 1985, Ed. The Essential Blake 1987. *Address:* 37 West 12th Street, New York, N.Y. 10011, U.S.A.

KUNZ, Erich; Austrian opera singer; b. 20 May 1909; ed. High School for Music, Vienna; with Staatsoper, Vienna 1941-; Mozart Medal, Verdienstkreuz 1st Class for Arts and Sciences; Hon. mem. Vienna State Opera; Gold Medal of Honour for services to Vienna. *Address:* Grinzingerstrasse 35, 1190 Vienna, Austria. *Telephone:* 32-22-01.

KUNZE, Horst, DR. PHIL.; German librarian; b. 22 Sept. 1909, Dresden; m. 1941; two s. two d.; ed. Sächsische Landesbibliothek, Dresden and Deutsche Bücherei, Leipzig; Research Librarian, Landesbibliothek, Darmstadt 1939–42; Dir. Universitäts- und Landesbibliothek Sachsen-Anhalt, Halle 1947–50; Gen. Dir. Deutsche Staatsbibliothek 1950–76; Dir. Inst. of Library Science and Scientific Information, Humboldt-Univ. Berlin 1955–68; Full Prof. of Library Science, Univ. of Berlin 1954–75; Chair. Arbeitsgemeinschaft für das Kinder- und Jugendbuch 1959–75; Pres. Deutscher Bibliotheksverband 1964–68; Dr. h.c.; Nat. Prize and other decorations. *Publications:* Lieblingsbücher von dazumal 1938 (reprint 1965), Gelesen und geliebt (2nd edn.) 1963, Über das Registermachen 1964 (3rd edn. 1968), Schatzbehalter vom Besten aus der älteren deutschen Kinderliteratur (6th edn. 1981), Werner Klemkes gesammelte Werke 1968 (3rd edn. 1977), Lexikon des Bibliothekwesens (ed. with G. Rückl) 1969 (2nd edn. 2 vols. 1974–75), Bibliophilie im Sozialismus 1969, Alles für das Buch (coll. papers, 2nd edn.) 1976, Geschichte der Buchillustration in Deutschland: Das 15. Jahrhundert (2 vols.) 1975, Grundzüge der Bibliothekslehre (4th edn.) 1977, Im Mittelpunkt das Buch (collected papers) 1980, Das Grosse Buch vom Buch 1983, Spiegel proletarischer Kinder-und Jugend-Literatur 1870–1936 (with H. Wegehaupt) 1985. *Leisure interest:* books. *Address:* Regattastrasse 246, 19-05, 1180 Berlin, German Democratic Republic. *Telephone:* 6814809.

KUNZE, Reiner; German author; b. 16 Aug. 1933, Oelsnitz/Erzgeb.; s. of Ernst Kunze and Martha Kunze; m. Dr Elisabeth Kunze 1961; one s. one d.; ed. Univ. of Leipzig; mem. Bavarian Acad. of Fine Arts, Acad. of Arts, Berlin, German Acad. for Languages and Literature, Darmstadt, PEN Club; numerous awards and prizes including Literary Prize of Bavarian Acad. of Fine Arts 1973, Georg Trakl Prize (Austria) 1977, Andreas Gryphius Prize 1977, Georg Büchner Prize 1977, Bavarian Film Prize 1979, Eichendorff Literature Prize 1984; Bundesverdienstkreuz, Bayerischer Verdienstorden. *Publications:* Sensible Wege 1969, Der Löwe Leopold 1970, Zimmerlautstärke 1972, Brief mit blauem Siegel 1973, Die wunderbaren Jahre 1976, Auf eigene Hoffnung 1981, In Deutschland zuhaus 1984, Eines jeden einziges Leben 1986, Zurückgeworfen auf Sich Selbst 1989. *Address:* Am Sonnenhang 19, 8391 Obernzell 1-Erlau, Federal Republic of Germany.

KUO WEI-FAN, DR., M.ED.; Chinese educationalist and politician; b. 3 Sept. 1937, Tainan City; m. Mei-Ho L. Kuo 1969; one s. one d.; ed. Provincial Taiwan Normal Univ. and Univ. of Paris; Assoc. Prof. Grad. Inst. of Educ., Nat. Taiwan Normal Univ. 1967–70, Prof. 1970–72, 1977–78, Dir. 1978, Pres. Nat. Taiwan Normal Univ. 1978–84; Admin. Vice-Minister of Educ. 1972–77; Pres. Chinese Asscn. of Special Educ. 1973–75, 1979–81, Chinese Asscn. of Comparative Educ. 1981–82; Minister of State 1984–; Pres. Chinese Educ. Soc. 1985–87. *Leisure interests:* table tennis, tennis, music. *Address:* 1 East Chung Shiao Road, Taipei, Taiwan. *Telephone:* 3217713.

KURAISHI, Tadao; Japanese politician; b. 1900; ed. Hosei Univ.; mem. House of Reps.; Chair. House of Reps. Labour Affairs Cttee., Budget Cttee.; Minister of Labour 1955–56, 1958–59, of Agric. and Forestry 1966–67, 1970–71, 1973–74, of Justice 1979–80; Chair. Liberal-Democratic Party (LDP) Nat. Org. Cttee., Chair. Exec. Council LDP 1978–80. [*Deceased.*]

KURANARI, Tadashi; Japanese politician; b. 31 Aug. 1918; s. of the late Shohachiro Kuranari; m. Ryoko Kuranari; two s.; fmr. official in Nagasaki Prefectural Govt.; mem. House of Reps. for Nagasaki Meguro1958–, elected eleven times; Parl. Vice-Minister of Finance; Chair. Social and Labour Affairs Cttee. of House of Reps.; fmr. Chair. Council on Anti-Monopoly Problems (informal body); Minister of Econ. Planning Agency Nov.-Dec. 1974, 1977; Acting Chair. Policy Research Affairs Council of Liberal-Democratic Party (LDP) 1974–76; assoc. of Yasuhiro Nakasone (q.v.); Minister of Foreign Affairs 1986–87; Chair. Parl. League for Information, Industry and Devt., and for Japan-EEC Friendship. *Address:* 2-18-12 Daita, Setangaya-ku, Tokyo 155, Japan. *Telephone:* 508-7612.

KURDYUMOV, Georgiy Vyacheslavovich; Soviet metallurgist; b. 14 Feb. 1902, Rylsk, Kursk; m. Tatyana Ivanovna Kurdyumova 1926; one s.; ed. Leningrad Polytechnical Inst.; research with X-rays on quenched and tempered steel, Physical Tech. Inst., Leningrad 1924–32; Head, Phase Transformation Lab., Physical Tech. Inst., Dniepropetrovsk 1932–44; Prof. Metal Physics, Dniepropetrovsk Univ. 1933–41; Dir. Inst. of Metallography and Metal Physics, Cen. Research Inst. of Ferrous Metallurgy, Moscow 1944–78; Dir. Lab. of Metal Physics, Ukraine Acad. of Sciences, Kiev 1946–51, Dir. Inst. of Solid State Physics, U.S.S.R. Acad. of Sciences 1962–73; Deputy Academician, Sec. Dept. of Gen. Physics and Astronomy, U.S.S.R. Acad. of Sciences 1955–89; Hadfield Memorial Lecturer 1959; Lecturer, AJME Inst. of Metals 1962; Fellow, Metallurgical Soc., AJME 1965–; mem. Ukraine Acad. of Sciences 1939–, Corresp. mem. U.S.S.R. Acad. of Sciences 1946–53, mem. 1953–; mem. Acad. of Sciences, G.D.R. 1969; Hon. mem. Japan Inst. of Metallurgy 1976; Foreign Assoc. U.S.A. Nat. Acad. Eng. 1977; Dr. h.c. (Krakow Mineral Metallurgy Acad.) 1967; State Prize 1949, Hero of Socialist Labour 1969, Orders of Lenin (5), Red Banner of Labour (2), Grande Médaille (Chatelier) Metallurgical Soc. of

France 1966, Heyndenkmünze, German Soc. of Metallography 1973; D. K. Chernov Gold Medal, U.S.S.R. Acad. of Sciences 1979. *Publications:* Crystal Structure of Martensite 1926–29, Martensite-Austenite Lattice Relationships 1930, Heat Treatment of Steels in the Light of X-Ray Investigations 1932, Mechanism of the Phase Transformations in Eutectoid Alloys 1933, Reversible Martensitic Transformations in the Alloys of Cu with Al, Sn and Zn 1932–41, Theory of the Hardening and Tempering of Steel 1940, Diffusionless (Martensitic) Transformations 1948, Thermoelastic Equilibrium and Elastic Martensite Crystals 1948–49, Isothermal Austenite-Martensite Transformation at Low Temperatures 1948, Use of Radioactive Isotopes for the Study of Diffusion and the Interatomic Interactions 1955, Strengthening of Metals and Alloys 1958–62, Phenomena of Quenching and Tempering of Steels 1960, Anomalies of Axial Ratio of Martensite Lattice and Mechanism of the Austenite-Martensite Transformation 1975, Behaviour of Carbon Atoms in Martensite 1966–75, Transformations in Iron and Steel 1977, Nature of Martensitic Transformations 1976–80. *Leisure interests:* singing folk songs, swimming, gardening. *Address:* U.S.S.R. Academy of Sciences, 14 Leninsky Prospekt, Moscow, U.S.S.R.

KURIA, Most Rev. Manasses; Kenyan ecclesiastic; b. 22 July 1929, Limuru; m. Mary Nyambura Kuria 1947; two s. four d.; ed. St. Paul's United Theological Coll.; Archdeacon of Eldoret 1965; Asst. Bishop Nakuru Diocese 1970, Bishop of Nakuru 1976–80; Archbishop of Kenya and Bishop of Nairobi 1980–. *Address:* 26 State House Avenue, P.O. Box 40502, Nairobi, Kenya. *Telephone:* 28146 and 333324/5 (Office).

KURIEN, Verghese, M.SC., C.B.I.M.; Indian business executive; b. 26 Nov. 1921, Calicut; m. Susan Molly 1953; one d.; Chief Exec. Kaira Dist. Co-operative Milk Producers' Union Ltd., Anand 1950–73; mem. Bd. Gujarat Electricity Bd. 1960–68, Chair. 1965; Dir. Bank of Baroda until 1969, Life Insurance Corpn. of India Ltd. 1970–74, Cen. Bd. Reserve Bank of India 1972–83; Chair. of Bd. Inst. of Agric., Anand 1969–72; Vice-Chancellor, Gujarat Agricultural Univ. Dantiwada 1984–85; Hon. Chair. Nat Dairy Devt. Bd., Anand 1965–, Indian Dairy Corpn., Baroda 1970–, Bd. of Govs. Inst. of Rural Man. Anand 1979–, Tribhuvandas Foundation, Anand 1982–, Gujarat Co-operative Milk Marketing Fed. Anand 1983–, Nat. Co-operative Dairy Fed. of India Ltd. 1986–, and other public appts.; several awards and honours and four hon. degrees from univs. in U.S.A., Canada and Scotland. *Address:* National Dairy Development Board, 1 Amul Dairy, Anand 388001, India (Office). *Telephone:* 3001 (Office); 3000 (Home).

KURIHARA, Yuko; Japanese politician; b. 1921; previous posts include: Labour Minister; Dir.-Gen. Defence Agency; Chair. Cttee. on Finance and on Rules and Admin., House of Councillors; Chair. Cttee. on Budget and Special Cttee. on Security, House of Reps.; Sec.-Gen. Liberal Democratic Party (LDP); Minister of State (Dir.-Gen. Defence Agency) 1986–87; Liberal Democratic Party. *Address:* c/o House of Representatives, Tokyo, Japan.

KURKOTKIN, Marshal Semyon Konstantinovich; Soviet military official; b. 1917; ed. Acad. of Tank Troops, and Acad. of Gen. Staff; political instructor of a co., commdr. of a tank regt., then of a tank brigade 1941–58; command posts 1958–; mem. Cen. Cttee. of Byelorussian CP 1961–66; Deputy C.-in-C. of Soviet Forces in Germany, Commdr. of Transcaucasian Mil. Dist. 1966–71; Deputy to U.S.S.R. Supreme Soviet 1970–; Gen. 1972; Cand. mem. 1971–76, mem. Cen. Cttee. CPSU 1976–; mem. Cen. Cttee. and Politburo of Georgian CP 1971; C.-in-C. of Soviet Forces in Germany 1971–73; Marshal of Soviet Union 1983; now Deputy Minister of Defence, Chief of Rear Services of Armed Forces. *Address:* The Kremlin, Moscow, U.S.S.R.

KURMAZENKO, Aleksandr Kirilovich; Soviet foreign trade official; b. 8 Sept. 1917; ed. Dniepropetrovsk Metallurgical Inst. and Acad. of Foreign Trade; mem. CPSU 1945–; Official, Main Dept. of Soviet Property Abroad 1948–56; Official, Ministry of Foreign Trade 1956–58; Deputy U.S.S.R. Commercial Rep. in Italy 1958–61; U.S.S.R. Commercial Rep. in Turkey 1961–65; Chair. Techmashexport Trust 1966–79; Badge of Honour (three times). *Address:* c/o Techmashexport Trust, 35 Mosfilmovskaya ulitsa, Moscow, U.S.S.R.

KURODA, Mizuo; Japanese diplomatist; b. 1919, Osaka Pref.; m. Mitsuko Unno; two s.; ed. Tokyo Univ.; entered diplomatic service 1945; Third Sec., Washington, D.C. 1952–54; Treaty Bureau, Ministry of Foreign Affairs 1954–58; First Sec., London 1958–62; Pvt. Sec. to Prime Minister 1962–64; Dir. North East Asia Div., Asian Affairs Bureau, Ministry of Foreign Affairs 1964–66; Counsellor, Washington, D.C. 1966–67; Counsellor, Manila, also Consul-Gen. 1967–69, Minister 1969; Minister, Washington D.C. 1969–71; Deputy Dir.-Gen. UN Bureau, Ministry of Foreign Affairs 1971, Research and Planning Dept. 1972, Public Information Bureau 1973–76; Amb. to Yugoslavia 1976–78, to Egypt (also accred. to People's Democratic Repub. of Yemen) 1978–80, to Australia 1980–82; Perm. Rep. to UN 1983–86. *Leisure interests:* golf, music. *Address:* c/o Ministry of Foreign Affairs, Tokyo, Japan.

KUROKAWA, Kisho, M.TECH.; Japanese architect; b. 8 April 1934, Aichi Prefecture; s. of Miki and Ineko Kurokawa; m. Ayako Wakao; one s. one d.; ed. Kyoto and Tokyo Univs.; Pres. Kisho Kurokawa Architect & Assocs.; Chair. Urban Design Consultants Inc.; Adviser, Int. Design Conf. in Aspen, U.S.A.; Prin. Inst. of Social Eng.; Adviser, Ministry of Construction; Analyst, Japan Broadcasting Corpn.; mem. numerous govt.

cttees., Architectural Inst. of Japan, City Planning Inst. of Japan, Japan Architects' Asscn.; Life Fellow, Royal Soc. of Arts; Hon. Fellow, A.I.A., R.I.B.A.; Hon. Prof., Univ. of Buenos Aires; Visiting Prof. Tsinghua Univ., Beijing 1986; awarded The Madara, Bulgarian First Order 1979; Commandeur de l'Ordre de Lion de Finlande 1985; Gold Medal French Acad. of Architecture; Takamura Kotaro Design Prize and prizes in int. competitions in Peru, France, Fed. Repub. of Germany, Tanzania and Bulgaria, prize for conference city, Abu Dhabi, U.A.E. 1976, for Univ. New Town, Al Ain, U.A.E., and numerous Japanese architectural awards. *Works include:* Nitto Food Co. 1963, Cen. Lodge in Nat. Childrens Land 1964, Hans Christian Andersen Memorial Lodge 1964, Sagae City Hall 1967, Odakyu Rest House 1969, Takara, Toshiba and Theme Pavilions, Expo 1970, Nakagin Capsule Tower 1972, Head Offices of Fukuoka Bank 1975, Sony Tower 1976, Sports Centre, Italy, Fujisawa New Town 1976, Ishikawa Cultural Centre 1977, Head Office, Japanese Red Cross Society 1977, Nat. Ethnology Museum 1977, Kumamoto Municipal Museum 1978, Daido Insurance Bldg., Tokyo 1978, Hotel Vitostia the New Otani, Sofia, Bulgaria 1979, Shoto Club, Tokyo 1980, Fukuoka Prefectural Governmental Headquarters 1981, Suginami Ward Cen. Library, Tokyo 1982, Saitama Pref. Museum of Modern Art 1982, Nat. Bunraku Theatre 1983, Kanagawa Citizens' Mutual Aid Asscn. Bldg., Yokohama 1983, Wacoal Kojimachi Bldg., Tokyo, Roppongi Prince Hotel, Tokyo, Pavilions of IBM Japan, Toshiba, Mitsui, Foreign Reps., Electric Power 1984, Yasuda Fire Insurance Bldg., Automobile Mfrs.' Asscn. at Tsukuba Int. Science Exposition 1985, Yoshiundo Bldg. 1985, Koshi Kaikan Centre 1986, Nagoya Mun. Museum of Modern Art 1987, Central Plaza 1 and 2, Brisbane 1988. *Works in progress include:* Chinese-Japanese Youth Centre, Beijing, Rond Point Nord, Nîmes, France, Gateway Center, Los Angeles, Calif., Lotte Jamsil Leisure and Shopping Center Devt., Seoul, Vic. Cen., Melbourne. *Publications include:* Prefabricated House, Metabolism 1960 1960, Urban Design 1964, Action Architecture 1967, Homo-Movens 1969, Architectural Creation 1969, The Work of Kisho Kurokawa 1970, Creating Contemporary Architecture 1971, Conception of Metabolism, In the Realm of the Future 1972, The Archipelago of Information: The Future Japan 1972, Introduction to Urbanism 1973, Metabolism in Architecture, 1977, A Culture of Grays 1977, Concept of Space 1977, Concept of Cities 1977, Architecture and Design 1982, Thesis on Architecture 1982, A Cross Section of Japan 1983, Architecture of the Street 1983, Landscapes under the Road 1984, Prospective Dialogues for the 21st Century, Vols. 1-3 1985. *Leisure interest:* photography. *Address:* Aoyama Bldg. 11f., 1-2-3 Kita Aoyama, Minato-ku, Tokyo, Japan.

KUROKAWA, Takeshi, B.A.; Japanese trade unionist; b. 1 April 1928, Gunma Pref.; one s. one d.; ed. Chuo Univ.; Pres. Gen. Fed. of Pvt. Railway Workers' Union (Shitetsu Soren) 1980-88, Adviser 1988-; Vice-Pres. SOHYO 1980-83, Pres. 1983-. *Leisure interest:* reading. *Address:* 3-2-11 Kanda Surugadai, Chiyoda-ku, Tokyo, Japan. *Telephone:* (03) 251-0311.

KUROSAWA, Akira; Japanese film director; b. 23 March 1910; ed. Keika Middle School; joined Toho Film Co. as Asst. Dir. 1936; dir. his first film Sugata Sanshiro 1943; First Prize, Venice Film Festival for Rashomon, Silver Lion for The Seven Samurai, American Motion Picture Acad. Award for Rashomon, Golden Palm Award for Kagemusha; Order of the Yugoslav Flag; David di Donatello Award for Kagemusha; Order of Culture (Japan) 1985, British Film Inst. Fellowship 1986. *Films:* Sugata Sanshiro, Ichiban Utsukushiku, Torano Owofumu Otokotachi, Waga Seishun ni Kuinashi, Subarashiki Nichiyobi, Yoidore Tenshi, Shizukanaru Ketto, Norainu, Rashomon 1950, Hakuchi, Ikiru, The Seven Samurai 1954, Ikimono no Kiroku, Kumonosu Jio, Donzoko, Kakushi Toride no San Akunin, The Throne of Blood 1957, The Hidden Fortress 1958, The Bad Sleep Well 1959, Yojimbo 1961, Sanjuro 1962, High and Low 1962, Akahige, Redbeard 1964, Dodes'ka-den, Derzu Uzala 1976, Barkerousse 1977, Kagemusha 1979, Ran 1984, Dreams 1989. *Publication:* Something Like an Autobiography 1982. *Address:* 21-6 Seijo 2-chome, Matsubara-cho, Setagaya-ku, 157 Tokyo, Japan.

KUROWSKI, Zdzisław; Polish politician and state official; b. 14 April 1937, Janiec, Ciechanów, Voivodship; s. of Henryk and Lucyna Kurowski; m. Zofia Kurowska 1966; one s. one d.; ed. Main School of Agriculture, Warsaw; mem. of Peasant Youth Union (ZMW), Chair. Cen. Bd. 1966-71; mem. of Exec. of Warsaw Voivodship Cttee., Polish United Workers' Party (PZPR) 1964-66, Deputy mem. Cen. Cttee. 1968-71, mem. 1971-81, mem. Secr. of Cen. Cttee. 1975-80, Sec. Cen. Cttee. Sept. 1980-81; Deputy to Seym (Parl.) 1969-85; First Sec. Białystok Voivodship Cttee. of PZPR 1972-75; Chair. of Białystok Voivodship Nat. Council 1973-75; Chair. Cen. Bd. of Fed. of Polish Socialist Youth Unions 1975-77; fmr. mem. Presidium All-Poland Cttee. of Nat. Unity Front (OK FNJ); Chief, Dept. of Light Industry, Trade and Consumption of Cen. Cttee. PZPR 1977-80, of Organizational Dept. Feb.-Dec. 1980; Sec. of PZPR Cen. Cttee. 1980-81; Deputy Sec.-Gen. COMECON, Moscow 1982-86; official, Ministry of Foreign Econ. Co-operation 1987-. *Leisure interest:* hunting. *Address:* Ministerstwo Współpracy z Zagranicą, ul. Wiejska 10, 00-489 Warsaw, Poland.

KUROYEDOV, Vladimir Alexeyevich; Soviet politician; b. 1906; ed. Gorky Teachers' Training Inst.; teacher, Secondary School Dir., Deputy Head of Dept. of Educ., Gorky 1928-34; Dir. Gorky Automechanical Tech. Coll. 1934-39; mem. CPSU 1936-; Instructor, Gorky Regional Cttee. of CPSU 1939-40; Dept. Head, Central Cttee. of CP of Lithuania 1940-41;

Sec. Gorky City Cttee. CPSU and Ed. Gorkovskaya Kommuna (regional newspaper) 1941-46; Dept. Head, Cen. Cttee. of CPSU 1946-49; Sec. Sverdlovsk Regional Cttee., CPSU 1949-59; Chair. of Council for Russian Orthodox Church of U.S.S.R. Council of Ministers 1960-66; Chair. of U.S.S.R. Council of Ministers' Council for Matters of Religion 1966-85; Order of Red Banner of Labour.

KURSANOV, Andrey Lvovich, SC.D.; Soviet plant physiologist; b. 8 Nov. 1902, Moscow; s. of Lev. I. Kursanov and Ljubov J. Kursanova; m. 1928; one d.; ed. Moscow Univ. Cen. Inst. of Sugar Industry 1929-34; A. N. Bakh Inst. of Biochem. 1934-54; Dir. K. A. Timiriazev Inst. of Plant Physiology and Head of Lab. of Translocation of Substances 1952-88 (retd.); mem. U.S.S.R. Acad. of Sciences 1953-, Leopoldina German Acad. of Natural Science 1958-, Acad. of Agric. of France 1964-, foreign mem. Polish Acad. of Sciences; Hon. mem. German Botanical Soc. 1961-, American Acad. of Arts and Sciences 1962-; Hero of Socialist Labour 1969, Order of Lenin (four times), Red Banner of Labour (twice), Commdr. Ordre de Léopold II (Belgium). *Publications:* The Reversible Action of Enzymes in Living Plant Cells 1940, Synthesis and Transformation of the Tannins in Tea Leaves 1953, In France and W. Africa 1956, The Root System as an Organ of Metabolism 1957, The Interaction of Physiological Processes in Plants 1960, Metabolism and the Transport of Organic Substances in the Phloem 1963, Competition of Sugars for Penetrations into Cells 1964, Biochemical basis of transport and accumulation of Sucrose in the Sugar-beet plant, Translocations of Assimilates in the Plant (monograph) 1976, Scientist and Auditorium 1982, Assimilate Transport in Plants 1984. *Leisure interests:* fishing, boating. *Address:* K. A. Timiryazev Plant Physiology Institute, Academy of Sciences, 35 Botanicheskaja, Moscow 127273, U.S.S.R.

KURTÁG, György; Hungarian composer; b. 19 Feb. 1926, Lugos; ed. Budapest Music Acad. and in Paris; Deutsche Akad. Austauschdienst (West Berlin) 1971; Prof. of Composition, Music Acad. of Budapest; Erkel Prize (three times), Kossuth Prize 2nd Degree 1973, Merited Artist, Eminent Artist's title. *Compositions:* Concerto for Viola 1954, String Quartet 1959, Quintet for Wind Instruments 1959, Eight pieces for piano 1960, Signs (for solo viola) 1961, Eight duets for violin and dulcimer 1961, The Sayings of Peter Bornemissza (for soprano and piano) 1968, Four fragments for soprano, dulcimer and violin 1969, Four capriccios for soprano and chamber ensemble 1970, Splinters solo for cimbalom 1974, Four Pilinsky Songs, S. K. Remembrance Noise, Hommage à Mihály András, Twelve Microludes for String Quartet, Herdecker Eurythmie, Guitar pieces, The Little Fix, Grabstein für Stephan, Omaggio a Luigi Nono, Messages of the late Miss R. V. Troussova, Five Russian Choruses, Rimma Dalos Lieder, Attila József Fragments, Seven Lieder, Eight Choruses, Kafka Fragment. *Address:* 1064 Budapest VI, Rózsa Ferenc utca 46, Hungary. *Telephone:* 420-819.

KURTI, Nicholas, C.B.E., M.A., DR.PHIL., F.R.S.; British physicist; b. 14 May 1908, Budapest, Hungary; s. of Károly and Margit (née Pintér) Kurti; m. Georgiana Shipley 1946; two d.; ed. Minta Gymnasium, Budapest, Paris and Berlin Univs.; Asst. Breslau Tech. Univ. 1931-33; attached to Clarendon Lab., Oxford 1933-40, U.K. Atomic Bomb Project 1940-45; Demonstrator in Physics, Oxford Univ. 1945-60, Reader 1960-67, Prof. 1967-75, Emer. Prof. 1975-; Sr. Research Fellow, Brasenose Coll. 1947-67, Professorial Fellow 1967-75, Emer. Fellow 1975-; Vice-Pres. Royal Soc. 1965-67; Foreign Hon. mem. American Acad. of Arts and Sciences 1968; Hon. mem. Hungarian Acad. of Sciences 1970, Société Française de Physique 1974, Fachverband Deutscher Köche 1978; Foreign mem. Finnish Acad. of Sciences and Letters 1974, Acad. of Sciences of G.D.R. 1975; Holweck Prize and Medal (British and French Physical Socs.) 1955, Fritz London Award 1957, Hughes Medal, Royal Soc. 1969; Chevalier, Légion d'honneur. *Publications:* Papers on low temperature physics and magnetism, energy storage and conversion, culinary physics. *Leisure interest:* cooking. *Address:* Department of Engineering, Parks Road, Oxford, OX1 3PJ (Office); 38 Blandford Avenue, Oxford, OX2 8DZ, England (Home). *Telephone:* (0865) 273115 (Office); (0865) 56176 (Home).

KURTZ, Efrem; American conductor; b. 7 Nov. 1900, St. Petersburg (now Leningrad), Russia; m. Elaine Shaffer 1955 (died 1973); ed. St. Petersburg Conservatory and Stern Conservatory, Berlin; conductor, Berlin Philharmonic Orchestra 1921-24; Musical Dir. Stuttgart Philharmonic 1924-33; Guest conductor New York Philharmonic, NBC Symphony, San Francisco, Cleveland and Chicago Symphony Orchestras 1933-54; Musical Dir. Kansas City Symphony Orchestra 1941-46, Houston Symphony Orchestra 1948-54; during recent years has been guest conductor of major orchestras of Europe, Japan, Australia, Canada, Israel, U.S.A., U.S.S.R., South Africa and at numerous festivals; Commdr., Order of Merit of Italy, Medal of Honor of Bruckner Soc. of America, awarded golden disc by Columbia Records Inc. after three millionth sale of his recordings with the New York Philharmonic. *Leisure interests:* drawing, collecting (paintings, stamps, historical letters), mountaineering. *Address:* c/o 19 Air Street, Regent Street, London W1R 6QL, England. *Telephone:* 01-734 5459.

KURYOKHIN, Sergei; Soviet musician; b. 1955, Leningrad; ed. musical secondary school, Leningrad Conservatory, Inst. of Culture; expelled from both 1975; pianist-instrumentalist with rock-group Akvarium 1976-.

Recordings include: The Ways of Freedom (Leo Records) 1981, Akvarium (U.S.S.R.) 1987.

KUSAKABE, Etsuji; Japanese business executive; b. 31 Oct. 1923, Hyogo Pref.; s. of Yasutaro and Hisae Kusakabe; m. Masako Yoshikawa 1949; two s.; ed. Kyoto Univ.; Dir. The Furukawa Electric Co. Ltd. 1972, Man. Dir. 1975, Sr. Man. Dir. 1977, Vice-Pres. 1982, Pres. 1983–. *Leisure interest:* golf. *Address:* The Furukawa Electric Co. Ltd., 6-1, Marunouchi 2-chome, Chiyoda-ku, Tokyo 100, Japan. *Telephone:* 03 (286) 3011.

KUSCH, Polykarp, M.S., PH.D.; American physicist; b. 26 Jan. 1911, Blankenburg, Germany; s. of John Matthais Kusch and Henrietta (née Van der Haas) Kusch; m. 1st Edith Starr McRoberts 1935 (died 1959); thre d.; m. 2nd Betty Jane Pezzoni 1960; two d.; ed. Case Inst. of Tech. and Univ. of Illinois; Asst. in Physics, Univ. of Illinois 1931–36; Research Asst. Univ. of Minn. 1936–37; Instructor in Physics, Columbia Univ. 1937–41; Vacuum Tube Engineer, Westinghouse Electric Corpn. 1941–42; staff mem. Div. of War Research, Columbia Univ. 1942–44; mem. Tech. staff, Bell Telephone Labs. 1944–46; Assoc. Prof. of Physics, Columbia Univ. 1946–49, Prof. 1949–72, Vice-Pres. and Dean of Faculties 1969–70; Exec. Vice-Pres. for Acad. Affairs and Provost, Univ. of Columbia 1970–71; Prof. of Physics, Univ. of Texas, Dallas 1972–; Eugene McDermott Prof., UT System Chair. 1974–80; Regental Prof. UT System 1980–82, Regental Prof. Emer. 1982–; research in atomic, molecular and nuclear physics; mem. Nat. Acad. of Sciences, American Philosophical Soc.; Hon. D.Sc. (Case, Ohio, Ill., Colby, Gustavus Adolphus, Yeshiva, Columbia Univs., Incarnate Word Coll.); Nobel Prize in Physics (jointly with Prof. W. E. Lamb, q.v.) 1955. *Address:* University of Texas, Dallas, P.O. Box 830688, Richardson, Tex. 75083, U.S.A.

KUSHNER, Aleksandr Semyonovich; Soviet poet; b. 14 Sept. 1936, Leningrad; m.; ed. Leningrad Pedagogical Inst.; lecturer in literature 1959–69. *Publications include:* First Meeting 1957, First Impression 1962, Night Watch 1966, Omens 1969, Letter 1974, Direct Speech 1976, Voice 1978, Canvas 1981, Daydreams 1986, Hedge 1988. *Address:* U.S.S.R. Union of Writers, Ulitsa Vorovskogo 52, Moscow, U.S.S.R.

KUŚNIEWICZ, Andrzej, LL.M.; Polish writer and poet; b. 30 Nov. 1904, Kowenice, near Sambor; s. of the late Bolesław Kuśniewicz and Joanna Ostrawa-Tworkowska Kuśniewicz; m. Anna Kotaniec; ed. Jagiellonian Univ., Cracow 1935; Ministry of Foreign Affairs until 1939; participated in French Resistance Movement, later held in Neue Bremm and Mauthausen concentration camps; Consul Toulouse and Strasbourg and Consul Gen. Lille 1945–50; first work published 1955; worked for Polish Radio 1955–70; mem. Polish Writer's Assen. 1959–83, mem. Gen. Bd. 1978–83; mem. PEN Club 1970–, European Soc. of Culture (SEC) 1973–; Sub-Ed. Miesięcznik Literacki (Literary Monthly) 1966–82; mem. Union of Fighters for Freedom and Democracy; Médaille de la Guerre et Résistance 1947, Minister of Culture and Art Prize, 2nd Class 1965, Gold Cross of Merit 1965, Award of Meritorious Culture Worker 1968, Kt.'s Cross, Order of Polonia Restituta 1970, Minister of Culture and Arts Prize, 1st Class 1971, State Prize, 1st Class 1974, Alfred Jurzykowski Prize (U.S.A.) 1974, Order of Banner of Labour (2nd class) 1977, Seguier Prize (France) 1978, Diploma, Minister of Foreign Affairs 1979. *Publications:* poetry: Słowa o nienawiści 1956, Diabłu ogarek 1959, Czas prywatny 1962, Piraterie 1975, novels: Korupcja, Kryminał heroiczny 1961, Eroica 1963, W drodze do Koryntu 1964, Król obojga Sycylii 1970, Strefy 1971, Stan nieważkości 1973, Trzecie królestwo 1975, Lekcja martwego języka 1977, Witraż 1980, Moja historia literatury 1980; Mieszaniny obyczajowe 1985, Nawrócenie 1987; novels translated into numerous foreign languages. *Leisure interests:* film, tourism. *Address:* Ul. Juliana Bruna 28 m. 57, 02-594 Warsaw, Poland. *Telephone:* 25-18-71.

KÜSS, René; French surgeon and academic; b. 3 May 1913, Paris; s. of Georges Küss and Elise-Jeanne Amos; m. Josette Beneteau 1958, four d.; ed. Lycée Janson-de-Sailly and Univ. of Paris; surgeon in Paris hosps. 1950–; Prof. at Faculty of Medicine, Paris 1964–; Prof. of Urology, La Pitié-la Salpêtrière Coll. of Educ. and Research; Chair. and Founder, Société française de transplantation 1972; Chair. Int. Urological Soc. 1979–; mem. Académie de chirurgie 1964; mem. Académie nationale de médecine 1979; Officier, Légion d'honneur, Commandeur, Ordre nat. du Mérite, Croix de guerre 1939–45. *Leisure interest:* painting. *Address:* 63 ave. Niel, 75017 Paris, France.

KUSUMAATMADJA, Mochtar, LL.D.; Indonesian politician; b. Feb. 1929, Jakarta; ed. Univ. of Indonesia, Yale and Harvard Law Schools and Univ. of Chicago Law School; Minister of Justice 1974–77; Acting Foreign Minister 1977–78, then Minister of Foreign Affairs 1978–88; Indonesian rep. at Law of the Sea Conference, Geneva, and at Seabed Cttee. sessions, New York; involvement in numerous int. orgs. *Address:* c/o Ministry of Foreign Affairs, Jalan Taman Pejambon 6, Jakarta, Indonesia.

KUTAKOV, Leonid Nikolayevich; Soviet diplomatist; b. 1919, Moscow; m.; one s. one d.; ed. Moscow Inst. of History, Philosophy and Literature; Soviet Army, Second World War; Chief of Historical Diplomatic Div., Ministry of Foreign Affairs 1946–51; Pro-Rector Moscow State Inst. of Int. Relations 1952–55; Adviser to Dir. of Peking Inst. of Diplomacy, Chinese Ministry of Foreign Affairs 1955–57; Counsellor, Soviet Embassy, Japan 1957–59; Deputy Dir. Inst. of History of Acad. of Sciences of U.S.S.R. 1961–63; Rector, Moscow State Inst. of Int. Relations 1963–65;

Sr. Counsellor for Political Questions, Perm. Soviet Mission to UN 1965–68; Under Sec.-Gen. for Political and Security Council Affairs, UN Secr. 1968–73; mem. Exec. Bd. UNESCO 1974–. *Publications:* A New History of International Relations 1918–45 1952, History of Soviet-Japanese Diplomatic Relations 1962, The Portsmouth Peace Treaty 1905 1964, Foreign Policy and Diplomacy of Japan 1964, History of International Relations and Foreign Policy 1917–73, 1975, View from the 35th Floor 1975. *Address:* c/o Ministry of Foreign Affairs 1932–34 Smolenskaya-Sennaya Ploshchad, Moscow, U.S.S.R.

KUTI, Fela Anikulapo; Nigerian musician; b. 1938; studied law, London, England; formed his first group, Koola Lobitos, in London, then returned Lagos with group; opened The Shrine nightclub, introducing his own "Afro-beat" style; recorded 30 albums by 1975; imprisoned by mil. authorities 1977, subsequently in exile in Ghana, then returned to Nigeria; f. political party Movt. of the People (MOP) 1981; European tour 1984; arrested Sept. 1984 on charges of illegal currency exportation and sentenced to five years' imprisonment, released 1986; tours to U.S., Europe 1986; recording of Army Arrangement 1986. *Address:* The Shrine, Kalakuta, Lagos, Nigeria.

KUTSCHER, Hans, DR.IUR.; German judge; b. 14 Dec. 1911, Hamburg; m. Irmgard Schroeder 1946; two step-d.; ed. Univ. of Graz, Austria and Univ. of Freiburg/Br., Berlin; Civil Servant, Ministry of Commerce and Industry, Berlin 1939, Ministry of Transport, Baden-Württemberg 1946–51, Ministry of Foreign Affairs, Bonn 1951; Sec. Legal Cttee., Conf. Cttee., Bundesrat 1951–55; Judge of Fed. Constitutional Court 1955–70; Judge, Court of Justice of European Communities 1970–76, Pres. 1976–80; Hon. Prof. Univ. of Heidelberg 1965; Hon. Bencher, Middle Temple 1976, King's Inns, Dublin 1978; Grosskreuz des Verdienstordens (Fed. Repub. Germany) 1980. *Publications:* Die Enteignung 1938, Bonner Vertrag mit Zusatzvereinbarungen 1952, and numerous contributions in professional journals. *Leisure interests:* history, literature. *Address:* 7506 Bad Herrenalb-Neusatz, Federal Republic of Germany.

KUTTNER, Stephan George, J.U.D.; American (b. German) legal historian; b. 24 March 1907, Bonn, Germany; s. of the late Georg Kuttner and Gertrude Schocken; m. Eva Illch 1933; six s. three d.; ed. Univs. of Frankfurt and Berlin; Research Assoc., Vatican Library 1934–40; Prof. of History of Canon Law, Catholic Univ. of America, Washington 1940–64; T. L. Riggs Prof. of Roman Catholic Studies, Yale Univ. 1964–70; Founder and Pres. Inst. of Medieval Canon Law 1955–; Prof. Univ. of Calif. at Berkeley 1970– (Emer. 1975–), Dir. Robbins Collection of Canon Law 1970–88; Consultant, Papal Comm. for the Revision of Code of Canon Law 1967–83; Founder and Ed. Traditio: Studies in Ancient & Medieval History & Religion 1943–70, Monumenta Iuris Canonici 1965–, Bulletin of Medieval Canon Law 1971–; Dr. h.c. (Univ. of Bologna) 1952, (Louvain Univ.) 1955, (Univ. of Paris) 1959, (Univ. of Genoa) 1966, (Univ. of Salamanca) 1968, (Univ. of Strasbourg) 1970, (Univ. of Montpellier) 1972, (Univ. of Madrid) 1978, (Univ. of Cambridge) 1978, (Univ. of Würzburg) 1982 and others; Guggenheim Fellow, Prize for Distinguished Contribution to the Humanities, American Council of Learned Socs., Orden Pour le mérite für Wissenschaften und Künste. *Publications:* Kanonistische Schuldlehre 1935, Repertorium der Kanonistik 1937, Anglo-Norman Canonists 1951, Collected Essays (3 vols.) 1980–83. *Leisure interests:* music, hiking, swimming. *Address:* School of Law (Boalt Hall), University of California, Berkeley, Calif. 94720 (Office); 771 Euclid Avenue, Berkeley, Calif. 94708, U.S.A. (Home). *Telephone:* (415) 642-5081 (Office); (415) 526-7708 (Home).

KUUSKOSKI-VIKATMAA, Eeva Maija Kaarina, LIC.MED.; Finnish politician; b. 1946, Aura; s. of Tino Kuuskoski and Kirsti Kuuskoski; one d. (deceased); Medical Dir. Turku Health Centre 1973–; Asst. Dir. Paediatric Clinic, Helsinki Univ. Central Hosp. 1976–80; mem. Turku City Council 1973–80; M.P. 1979–; Minister of Social Affairs and Health 1983–87; Centre Party. *Leisure interests:* non-governmental health work, opera, handicraft. *Address:* c/o Töölonkatu 1C22, 00100 Helsinki, Finland.

KUWABARA, Takeo, B.A.; Japanese writer; b. 10 May 1904, Turuga; s. of Jitsuzo Kuwabara and Shin Uta; m. Tazu Tanaka 1933; one s. five d.; ed. Kyoto Univ.; Lecturer Kyoto Univ. 1931–42; Asst. Prof. Tohoku Univ. 1943–48; Prof. Kyoto Univ. 1948–68, Emer. Prof. 1968–; Dir. Univ. Inst. of Humanistic Studies 1959–63; mem. Science Council of Japan 1951–71, Vice-Pres. 1960–71; Vice-Pres. Japan PEN Club 1974–75, 1981–85; mem. Japanese Acad. of Arts 1977; Man of Cultural Merits (govt. award) 1979. *Publications:* Fiction and Reality 1943, Reflections on Contemporary Japanese Culture 1947, Some Aspects of Contemporary French Literature 1949, Introduction to Literature 1950, Conquest of Mount Chogolisa 1959, Studies on J.-J. Rousseau 1951, Studies on the Encyclopédie 1954, Studies on the French Revolution 1959, Studies on Chomin Nakae 1966, European Civilization and Japan 1974, Selected Works (in 10 vols.) 1980-81. *Leisure interest:* mountaineering. *Address:* 421, Tonodan-Yabunosita, Kamikyo-ku, Kyoto, 602 Japan. *Telephone:* 231-0261.

KUWAIT, H.H. The Ruler of (see Sabah, Sheikh Jaber al-Ahmad al-Jaber al-).

KUWAIZ, Abdullah Ibrahim el, M.A., M.B.A., PH.D.; Saudi politician and international official; b. 1939; two s. two d.; ed. Pacific Lutheran Univ., U.S.A., St. Louis Univ., U.S.A.; Accountant, Pensions Dept. 1959–67,

Economist, Ministry of Finance and Nat. Economy 1967-81 (Adviser 1977-81); Exec. Dir. Arab Monetary Fund, Abu Dhabi 1977-83; Co-Chair. Financial Co-operation Cttee., Euro-Arab Dialogue 1978-83; Asst. Under-Sec. for Econ. Affairs 1981-87; Deputy Minister of Finance and Nat. Economy, Saudi Arabia 1987-; Dir.-Gen. and Chair. of Bd. Arab Monetary Fund, Abu Dhabi 1987-; Asst. Sec.-Gen. for Econ. Affairs, Co-operation Council for the Arab States of the Gulf 1981-; mem. of Bd. and mem. Exec. Cttee., Gulf Int. Bank, Bahrain 1977-; mem. of Bd. Gulf Co-operation Council's Org. for Measures and Standards 1984-, Oxford Energy Inst., Oxford, U.K. 1985-, Int. Maritime Bureau, London 1985-88. *Publications:* numerous papers relating to oil affairs and econ. devt. delivered at symposia in N. America, Europe and the Middle East. *Address:* Arab Monetary Fund, P.O. Box 2818, Abu Dhabi, United Arab Emirates; Gulf Co-operation Council for Arab States, P.O. Box 7153, Riyadh 11462, Saudi Arabia. *Telephone:* Abu Dhabi 328873; Riyadh 4827777.

KUZIŃSKI, Stanisław, D.ECON.; Polish politician and economist; b. 8 Oct. 1923, Warsaw; s. of Jan and Zofia Kuziński; m. Hanna Kuzińska 1979; one s. two d.; ed. Main School of Planning and Statistics (SGPiS), Warsaw; worked in youth movement (ZWM) 1945-47, in Co-operative Research Inst., then in Inst. of Agric. Econ., Warsaw 1948-54; Insp. of Secretariat, Cen. Cttee. of Polish United Workers' Party (PZPR) 1954-56, Sec. of Warsaw Cttee. of PZPR 1956-57, Deputy Head of Econ. Dept. of Cen. Cttee. 1959-64, Head of Light Industry, Trade and Bldg. Dept., then of Econ. Dept., Cen. Cttee. 1964-72, mem. Cen. Cttee. 1970-71; Pres. Cen. Statistical Office (GUS) 1972-80; Extraordinary Prof. of Econ. Sciences 1982-; Chair. Foreign Trade Comm. of Seym 1957-71; Deputy to Seym 1957-76; Econ. Adviser to Seym 1985-; Fellow, Inst. of Econ. Sciences, Polish Acad. of Sciences 1972-; Prof., Inst. of Nat. Econ., Warsaw; Order of Banner of Labour, First Class, Commdr.'s Cross and Kt.'s Cross of Order of Polonia Restituta, Partisan Cross, Grunvald Cross, Third Class, Medal of 40th Anniversary of People's Poland. *Publications:* Economic Policy 1987, Industrial Policy 1988. *Address:* Al. I Armii WP 2/4 m. 52, 00-582, Warsaw, Poland. *Telephone:* 29-34-77.

KUZMIN, Iosif Iosifovich; Soviet engineer, politician and diplomatist; b. 19 May 1910, Astrakhan; ed. Leningrad Electrical Engineering Inst.; Engineer, later Chief Engineer, Moscow projector factory; mem. Party Control Comm., Cen. Cttee. CPSU (Kuibyshev Region) 1940; Deputy Chair. Party Control Comm., CPSU 1940-46; mem. Bureau of Agric. and Storage 1947-50, Deputy Chair. 1950-52; mem. Council of Ministers of U.S.S.R. 1947-57, Deputy Chair. 1957-59; on staff of Cen. Cttee. CPSU 1952-57; Chair. State Planning Cttee. of U.S.S.R. 1957-59; Chair. Scientific Econ. Council with rank of Minister 1959-60; Amb. to Switzerland 1960-63; Expert Consultant in Dept. of Int. Econ. Orgs., Ministry of Foreign Affairs 1963-. *Address:* Ministry of Foreign Affairs, 32-34 Smolenskaya-Sennaya ploshchad, Moscow, U.S.S.R.

KUZNETSOV, Viktor Ivanovich, DR.TECH.SC.; Soviet scientist; b. 27 April 1913, Moscow; ed. Leningrad Polytechnic Inst.; Engineer at a number of enterprises of Instrument-making Industry 1938-; mem. CPSU 1942; Corresp. mem. U.S.S.R. Acad. of Sciences 1958-68, Academician 1968-; research in field of automation and technical cybernetics; State Prize 1943, 1946; Order of Lenin (twice), Order of October Revolution, Order of the Red Banner and other decorations. *Address:* U.S.S.R. Academy of Sciences, 14 Leninsky Prospekt, Moscow, U.S.S.R.

KUZNETSOV, Vladimir Nikolayevich; Soviet diplomatist; b. 24 July 1916, Kliven village, Kursk region; ed. Chernyshevsky State Univ., Saratov; State Service till 1946; Employee, Third European Dept. 1946-49; Asst. then Head of Group, Gen. Secr., Ministry of Foreign Affairs 1949-56; Counsellor, Soviet Embassy, Netherlands 1956-60; Counsellor, First European Dept. Ministry of Foreign Affairs 1960-61; Counsellor-envoy, Soviet Embassy, Indonesia 1961-67; Envoy of South East Asia Dept., Ministry of Foreign Affairs 1967-68; Amb. to Malaysia 1968-73; Dir. of Admin. Services to the Diplomatic Corps 1974-80; Amb. to Burma 1980-85; Order of Patriotic War, 1st Class, Order of Red Banner of Labour (twice), Order of Friendship of Peoples, Order of Red Star, Order of Honour 1980 and medals. *Address:* c/o Ministry of Foreign Affairs, Moscow, U.S.S.R.

KUZNETSOV, Yuriy Ivanovich; Soviet diplomatist; mem. diplomatic service 1952-; with Embassy, Vietnam and Laos until 1965; Chief of South Asian Dept., U.S.S.R. Ministry of Foreign Affairs 1970-78; Amb. to Thailand 1978-85. *Address:* c/o Ministry of Foreign Affairs, Moscow, U.S.S.R.

KVAPIL, Radoslav; Czechoslovakian pianist. b. 15 March 1934, Brno; s. of Karel Kvapil and Marie Kvapilová; m. Eva Mašlaňová; one s.; ed. Gymnasium Dr. Kudely, Brno and Janáček Acad. of Musical Arts; first piano recital Brno 1954; 1st prize Janáček Competition 1958, Int. Competition, Czechoslovak Radio 1968; Prof. of Piano, Prague Conservatory 1963-73; concerts in countries throughout Europe, in U.S.A. and Japan 1963-; performed world premiere of Dvořák's Cypresses 1983; Hon. mem. Dvořák Soc., Prague; Hon. Vice-Pres. Dvořák Soc., London: Janáček Medal (Cultural Ministry). *Recordings include:* complete piano works of Dvořák 1967-69, of Janáček 1968-69, of Jan Jugo Voříšek 1973-74, complete polka cycles of Smetana 1970, Czech contemporary piano music 1970, complete studies and polkas and Sonata No. 1 of Martinů 1984, Piano Concerto by

A. Rejcha (first ever recording). *Leisure interest:* chess. *Address:* Kladská 5, 12000 Prague 2, Czechoslovakia. *Telephone:* (42) 2-257296.

KVIDAL, Mary; Norwegian politician; b. 4 July 1943; m.; fmr. Principal Hummelvik Primary School; mem. Malvik Municipal Council 1971-79, Municipal Exec. Cttee. 1975-79; Minister of Church and Educ. 1988-; Chair. Bd. Norwegian State Housing Bank; mem. Bd. Norwegian Broadcasting Corpn. *Address:* Ministry of Church and Education, Akersgt. 42, POB Dep., 0032 Oslo 1, Norway. *Telephone:* (2) 11-90-90.

KVITSINSKY, Youli Aleksandrovich; Soviet diplomatist; b. 28 Sept. 1936, Rzev; s. of Alexander Kvitsinsky and Maria Orlova; m. Inga Kuznetsova 1955; two d.; ed. Moscow Inst. of Int. Relations; served in Embassy in G.D.R. 1959-65, in Fed. Repub. of Germany 1978-81; head of Soviet del., negotiations on medium-range nuclear weapons until latter broken off Nov. 1983; subsequently responsible for negotiations on Strategic Defence Initiative (SDI) Geneva talks 1985; Amb. to Fed. Repub. of Germany 1986-; cand. mem. CPSU Cen. Cttee 1986-89, mem. April 1989-. *Leisure interest:* fishing. *Address:* Waldstr. 72, Bonn, Federal Republic of Germany. *Telephone:* 31-20-85.

KWAPONG, Prof. Alex. A., PH.D.; Ghanaian professor; b. 8 March 1927, Akropong, Akwapim; s. of E. A. and Theophilia Kwapong; m. Evelyn Teiko Caesar 1956; six d.; ed. Presbyterian junior and middle schools, Akropong, Achimota Coll. and King's Coll., Cambridge; Visiting Prof., Princeton Univ. 1962; fmr. Pro Vice-Chancellor and Head of Classics Dept., Ghana Univ., Vice-Chancellor 1966-75; Vice-Rector for Institutional Planning and Resource Devt. UN Univ. 1976-88; Lester B. Pearson Chair. in Devt. Studies, Dalhousie Univ. 1988-; mem. Political and Educ. Cttees., Nat. Liberation Council 1966, Fellow, Ghana Acad. of Arts and Sciences; Hon. D.Litt. (Warwick, Ife); Hon. LL.D. (Princeton); Order of Volta (Ghana). *Publications:* Higher Education and Development in Africa Today: A Reappraisal 1979; Under-development and the Challenges of the 1980s: The Role of Knowledge 1980, The Relevance of the African Universities to the Development Needs of Africa 1980, Medical Education and National Development 1987, Culture, Development and African Unity 1988, African Scientific and Technical Institution Building and the Role of International Co-operation 1988. *Address:* Dalhousie University, 1325 Edward Street, Halifax, Canada B3H 3J5. *Telephone:* (902) 424-2142.

KWAŚNIEWSKI, Aleksander, M.ECON.; Polish politican; b. 15 Nov. 1954, Białogard, Koszalin Voivodship; s. of Zdzisław Kwaśniewski and Aleksandra Kwaśniewski; m. Jolanta Konty 1979; one d.; ed. Gdańsk Univ.; former active leader of youth movt., including Chair. Univ. Council of Polish Socialist Students' Union (SZSP) at Gdańsk Univ., Head of Culture Dept. of SZSP Gen. Bd. 1979-80, mem. Exec. Cttee. of SZSP Chief Council 1980-81; Ed.-in-Chief of students' weekly Itd, Warsaw 1981-84; Ed.-in-Chief of daily Sztandar Młodych (Banner of Youth), Warsaw 1984-85; mem. Council of Ministers Nov. 1985-; Head Socio-Political Cttee. Oct. 1988-; Minister for Youth 1985-87; Chair. Cttee. for Youth and Physical Culture 1987-; mem. Polish United Workers' Party (PZPR). *Leisure interests:* sport, literature, films. *Address:* Komitet Młodzieży i Kultury Fizycznej, ul. Swietokrzyska 12, 00-916 Warsaw (Office); ul. Wiktorü Wiedeńskiej 1/7, 02-954 Warsaw, Poland (Home). *Telephone:* 26-21-72 (Office).

KY, Air Vice-Marshal Nguyen Cao (see Nguyen Cao Ky, Air Vice-Marshal).

KYNASTON, Nicolas; British organist; b. 10 Dec. 1941; s. of Roger Tewkesbury Kynaston and late Jessie Dearn Caecilia Kynaston (née Parkes); m. Judith Felicity Heron 1961 (divorced 1989); two s. two d.; ed. Westminster Cathedral Choir School, Downside, Accademia Musicale Chigiana, Siena, Conservatorio San Cecilia, Rome, Royal Coll. of Music; Westminster Cathedral Organist 1961-71; début recital, Royal Festival Hall 1966; recording début 1968; concert career 1971-, travelling throughout Europe, North America, Asia and Africa; Artistic Dir. J. W. Walker & Sons Ltd. 1978-82, Consultant 1982-83; consultant tutor Birmingham School of Music 1986-; Jury mem. Grand Prix de Chartres 1971, St. Albans Int. Organ Festival 1975; Pres. Inc. Assocn. of Organists 1983-85; Hon. F.R.C.O. 1976; records include 5 nominated Critic's Choice; EMI/CFP Sales Award 1974; Deutscher Schallplattenpreis 1978. *Leisure interests:* walking, church architecture. *Address:* 28 High Park Road, Kew Gardens, Richmond-upon-Thames, Surrey, TW9 4BH, England. *Telephone:* 01-878 4455.

KYO, Machiko, Japanese actress; b. 1924; began her career as a dancer with the Shochiku Girls' Opera Co., Osaka; film début in Saigo ni Warau Otoko (Last Laughter) 1949; has appeared in over 80 films including Rashomon 1950, Ugetsu Monogatari 1953, Gate of Hell 1954, Story of Shunkin 1955, Akasen Chitai (Street of Shame), Teahouse of the August Moon 1956, Yoru no Cho (Night Butterflies) 1957, Odd Obsession 1959, Floating Weeds 1959, A Woman's Testament 1960; Best Actress Award for Rashomon 1950; Jussie (Finland) Award 1957. *Address:* Uni Japan Film, 9-13 Ginza 5-chome, Chuo-ku, Tokyo, Japan.

KYPRIANOU, Demetrios, B.SC.; Cypriot broadcasting executive; b. 22 Nov. 1931, Nicosia; s. of Kyprianos and Eleni Kyprianou; m. Foula Ioannou 1956; one s. one d.; joined Cyprus Broadcasting Corpn. 1959, Dir. Commercial Div. 1968-82, Dir. Admin. and Finance 1982-84, Dir.-Gen. 1984-.

Publication: The Development of Industrial Relations in Cyprus. *Leisure interest:* farming. *Address:* Cyprus Broadcasting Corporation, P.O. Box 4824, Nicosia (Office); 3a Nikou Evagorou, Acropolis, Nicosia, Cyprus (Home). *Telephone:* 21652 (Home).

KYPRIANOU, Spyros; Cypriot lawyer and politician; b. 28 Oct. 1932, Limassol; s. of Achilleas and Maria (née Araouzou) Kyprianou; m. Mimi Papatheoklitou 1956; two s.; ed. City of London Coll. and Gray's Inn, London; called to the Bar 1954; f. Nat. Union of Cypriot Students in England (EFEKA), elected its first Pres. 1952–54; London Sec. to Ethnarch Makarios 1952–54; London Sec. of Ethnarchy 1954–56; journalist 1952–56; New York rep. of Ethnarchy 1956–57, London rep. 1957–59; mem. Cen. Cttee. of Nat. Dem. Front for Reconstruction (EDMA) 1959; Minister of Foreign Affairs 1960–72 (resigned); Pres. Cttee. of Foreign Ministers of Council of Europe April-Dec. 1967; led numerous Dels. to UN Gen. Ass., Security Council, also led talks on the association of Cyprus to the EEC; legal practice 1972–; mem. Cyprus Del. to UN Gen. Ass. 1974, *ad hoc* mem. to UN Security Council 1975; Founder and Chair. Democratic Party 1976–; Pres. House of Reps. 1976–77; Pres. of Cyprus 1977–88; Grand Star of the U.A.R. 1961, Grand Cross, Order of George I of Greece 1962, Grand Cross of Fed. Repub. of Germany 1962, Grand Cross, Order of Boyaca (Colombia) 1966, Grand Cross, Order of Merit (Chile) 1966, Order of St. Aikaterini of Sinai 1966, Grand Silver Cross of Austria 1973, Star of the Socialist Repub. of Romania 1979, Grand Cross of the Order of the Saviour (Greece) 1983, Collar of the Order of Isabel la Católica (Spain) 1987 etc. *Leisure interests:* literature, music, sports. *Address:* Elia Papakyriakou 29, Acropolis, Nicosia, Cyprus.

KYRIAZIDIS, Nicolas; Greek economist; b. 3 Sept. 1927, Athens; m. Ellie Kyrou 1960; one s. one d.; ed. Oxford, Illinois and Chicago Univs.; Head of Reports Section, Ministry of Co-ordination 1949; Dir. Monetary Policy Service 1950; Dir. Foreign and Trade Payments 1951–54; Asst. Econ. Adviser, Bank of Greece 1956–60, Alt. 1960–64; Deputy Dir.-Gen. Ministry of Co-ordination 1962–64; Econ. Adviser, Nat. Bank of Greece 1964–67; Senior Economist IMF 1968–70; Adviser to Govt. of Cyprus in negotiations for association with European Community 1971–73, 1978–82; Deputy Gov. Bank of Greece 1974–77; Amb. to U.K. 1982–86; Alternative Exec. Dir. IMF 1986–; took part in negotiations for EFTA 1957–58, for association between Greece and EEC 1959–61, led Greek Del. in accession negotiations 1976; mem. Board, Soc. for the Study of Greek Problems 1971–72; mem. Cttee. for Restoration of Democratic Legality 1973; Commdr. George I (Greece), Kt. Commdr. Léopold II (Belgium), Knight Commdr. Order of Merit of Italian Repub., Commdr. Order of Merit of Fed. Repub. of Germany. *Leisure interests:* reading, opera, collecting antiques. *Address:* 2 Misthou Street, Athens, Greece; International Monetary Fund, 700 19th Street, Washington, D.C. 20431, U.S.A. *Telephone:* (202) 623-6991.

KYUNG-WHA CHUNG (see Chung, Kyung-Wha).

L

LAAGE, Gerhart, DIPL. ING.; German architect and town planner; b. 19 April 1925, Hamburg; s. of Richard and Valerie (née Pitzner) Laage; m. Ursula Gebert 1959; one s. two d.; ed. Technische Hochschule, Brunswick; freelance architect 1954–; Prof. of Theory of Architectural Planning, Univ. of Hanover 1963–, Pro-rector and Rector 1973–75, Dean 1983–84; Adviser to Fed. Govt. on planning for city of Bonn 1977–82. *Publications:* Wohnungen von heute für Ansprüche von Morgen 1971, Planung und Mitbestimmung 1973, Planungstheorie für Architekten 1976, Wohnen beginnt auf der Strasse 1977, Handbuch für Architekturplanung 1978, Weder Traum noch Trauma 1978, Das Stadthaus—mehr als eine Bauform 1980, Kosten- und flächensparendes Bauen 1984, Warum wird nicht immer so gebaut 1985. *Address:* Universität Hannover, Institut für Architektur- und Planungstheorie, Schlosswender Strasse 1, D-3000 Hanover 1; Weidenallee 26a, 2000 Hamburg 36, Federal Republic of Germany. *Telephone:* 0511-762 3270 (Office); 040-44 13 23.

LABARDAKIS, Augoustinos; Greek ecclesiastic; b. 7 Feb. 1938, Voukoulies-Chania, Crete; s. of Emmanouil and Eurydike Labardakis; ed. theological schools in Chalki, Turkey, Salzburg, Münster, West Berlin; ordained as priest, Greek Orthodox Church, Fed. Repub. of Germany 1964, worked as priest, West Berlin 1964–72, ordained as Bishop 1972, as Greek Orthodox Metropolitan of the Fed. Repub. of Germany and Exarch of Cen. Europe Nov. 1980; Grosses Bundesverdienstkreuz. *Address:* Greek Orthodox Metropolis of Germany, Dietrich-Bonhoeffer-Strasse 2, P.O. Box 300409, 5300 Bonn, Federal Republic of Germany. *Telephone:* (0228) 462041.

LABARRÈRE-PAULÉ, André, D. ÉS L.; French academic and politician; b. 12 Jan. 1928, Pau; s. of Maximien Labarrère-Paulé and Catherine Bouilhat; ed. Ecole Henri-IV, Collège Beau-Frêne, Pau, Univ. of Paris; Teacher, Digne Lycée 1956–58; scholarship to Arts Council of Canada 1958–59; Prof. Faculty of Arts and of Admin. Sciences, Laval Univ., Quebec 1959–66; Prof. of History of Art, Ecole des Beaux-arts, Quebec 1964–66; Deputy (Pyrénées-Atlantiques) to Nat. Assembly 1967–68, re-elected 1973, 1978, 1986, Vice-Pres. Nat. Assembly 1973–74; Gen. Councillor, Pau-Ouest 1967–73, Jurançon 1973–81; teacher, Lycée Carnot, Paris 1968–70, Auch Lycée 1970–; mem. Political Bureau and Steering Cttee., Parti Socialiste 1969–; Mayor of Pau 1971, re-elected 1977; Regional Councillor for Aquitaine 1974–81, Pres. of Council 1979–81; Minister-Del. for Relations with Parl., attached to Prime Minister 1981–86. *Publications:* Pierre-Joseph-Olivier-Chauveau 1962, Les laïques et la presse pédagogique au Canada français 1836-1900 1965, Les secrets de l'écriture 1965, Monseigneur Leflêche 1970, Pau 1973. *Leisure interests:* geography, swimming. *Address:* 18 rue Vaneau, 75700 Paris (Office); El Patio, 103 avenue des Lilas, 64000 Pau, France (Home). *Telephone:* 556 80 00 (Office).

LABARTHE CORREA, Javier; Peruvian politician; b. 3 July 1924, Salaverry-Trujillo; ed. Escuela Naval, rising to rank Oficial de Marina; served with Marines for 7 years; worked in fishing industry 1950–67, becoming Dir. Soc. Nacional de Pesquería, Man. Dir. Empresa Pesquera San Andrés, Exec. Dir. Consorcio Nacional de Pesquería, Vice-Pres. Comité Mundial de Pesquería, FAO; elected Deputy to Nat. Ass. 1963; Pres. Comm. for Finance and the Budget; Vice-Pres. Chamber of Deputies 1967; Head of Operations, Banco Interamericano de Desarrollo 1975, Fisheries Rep. for Cen. America, Panama and Mexico 1975–80; re-elected Deputy in Nat. Ass. 1980–, Pres. Comm. for Water Transport, Pres. Comm. for the Economy and Finance 1985; Minister of Fisheries 1987–89. *Address:* c/o Ministerio de Pesquería, 3101 Av. Paseo de la República, Lima, Peru. *Telephone:* 704745.

LABIB, Abdel Rahman, B.SC.; Egyptian politician; b. 1924; Ministry of Public Utilities 1952; Chair. Housing and Construction Authority 1973–84; Minister of Housing 1985–87. *Address:* c/o Ministry of Housing, 1 Sharia Ismail Abaza, Cairo, Egypt.

LABIDI, Abdelwahab; Tunisian financier and consultant; b. 22 April 1929, Kef; s. of Mohamed and Khedija Labidi; m. Nicole Michel 1955; one s. two d.; ed. Collège Sidiki Tunis, Institut des Hautes Etudes, Tunis, Faculty of Law, Paris Univ; fmr. Gen. Man. Banque de Tunisie; Insp. Gen. Banque Nat. Agricole de Tunisie; Man. Soc. Tunisienne de Banque; Man. Dir. Nat. Devt. Bank of Niger 1964–69; Vice-Pres. African Devt. Bank 1969–70, Pres. 1970–76; Pres. African Devt. Fund 1973–76; Chair. Sifida (Geneva) 1973–77; Adviser to Scandinavian Bank Ltd. (London) 1977–; Adviser to Banque Worms (Paris) 1978–, to CEAO 1979–; mem. Exec. Cttee. Club de Dakar (Paris). *Address:* 56 boulevard Bineau, 92200 Neuilly sur Seine, France. *Telephone:* 7577470.

LABIS, Attilio; French ballet dancer and choreographer; b. 5 Sept. 1936, Vincennes; s. of Umberto and Renée (née Cousin) Labis; m. Christiane Vlassi 1959; two s.; ed. Ecole de danse académique of l'Opéra, Paris; mem. Corps de Ballet at the Paris Opera 1952, Premier Danseur 1959, Principal Premier Danseur 1960–65, Maître de ballet adjoint 1965–; Guest Dancer in London, Paris, Washington, Tokyo, Moscow, Kiev, Leningrad, Rome, Milan, Berlin, Munich, Stuttgart, Rio de Janeiro and Sydney; Chief Chore-

ographer at the Paris Opera; devised choreography for productions including Rencontre (TV) 1961, Arcades 1964, Iphigénie en Tauride 1965, Romeo and Juliet 1967, Spartacus 1973, Raymonda 1973; has created and interpreted numerous ballets including Giselle, Sleeping Beauty, Swan Lake, Don Quixote, Pièces Choréographiques (Peter Van Dijk), Pas de Dieux (Gene Kelly), Marines (Georges Skibine), Icare (Serge Lifar), Symphonie Concertante, Sarracenia (Michel Descombey), Renart, Pas de danse (music by Gluck); Chevalier des Arts et des Lettres. *Address:* 36 rue du Chemin-de-fer, 78380 Bougival, France.

LABOULAYE, François René de; French diplomatist; b. 16 June 1917, Washington, D.C., U.S.A.; s. of André and Marie (Hely d'Oissel) de Laboulaye; m. Antoinette de Vienne 1939; two s. two d.; ed. Landon School, Washington, D.C., Univ. of Paris; entered diplomatic career in Cen. Admin. 1943; at disposal of French Red Cross 1944; Third Sec., then Second Sec., Beirut, Lebanon 1944–46, Berlin and Bonn, Germany 1947–49; Central Admin., Africa, Middle East 1949–51; First Sec., then Counsellor, Ottawa, Canada 1951–54; Counsellor, Washington, U.S.A. 1954–57; at disposal of Compagnie Française des Pétroles 1958–62; First Counsellor, Moscow, U.S.S.R. 1962–65; Pres. Frantéco (Colour TV) 1965; in charge of North African Affairs 1965–68; Amb. to Brazil 1968–71, to Japan 1972–75; Dir. of Political Affairs, Central Admin. 1975–77; Amb. to U.S.A. 1977–82; Commdr. de la Légion d'honneur 1981, Commdr. Ordre national du Mérite 1975, Ambassadeur de France 1978; Order of the Rising Sun (First Class), Japan, Grand Cross, Order of Southern Cross, Brazil. *Address:* 97 rue du Bac, 75007 Paris, France.

LABUDA, Gerard; Polish historian; b. 28 Dec. 1916, Nowa Huta, Kartuzy district; s. of Stanisław Labuda and Anastazja Baranowska; m. Countess Alberta Wielopolska 1943; four s. one d.; ed. Poznań Univ. and Lund Univ., Sweden; Doctor 1944–46, Docent 1945–50, Extraordinary Prof. 1950–56, Prof. 1956–; Rector, Poznań Univ. 1962–65; Sec.-Gen. Poznań Soc. of Friends of Learning 1961–72, Pres. 1972–75; Ed. Roczniki Historyczne (Annals of History) 1969–; Corresp. mem. Polish Acad. of Sciences 1965–68, mem. 1968–, mem. Presidium 1972, Vice-Pres. 1984–86, 1987–; mem. Consultative Council attached to Chair. of State Council 1986–; Chair. Cttee. for Research on Poles Living Abroad, Polish Acad. of Sciences 1973–80; fmr. Chair. Poznań br. of Polish Acad. of Sciences; Fellow Wissenschaftskoll. zu Berlin-Inst. for Advanced Studies 1981–82; mem. European Soc. of Culture 1963–; Foreign mem. Akademie d. Wissenschaften d. DDR, Berlin 1978–; State Prizes (3rd class) 1949, 1951, (2nd class) 1970; Kt.'s Cross, Order of Polonia Restituta 1954, Officer's Cross 1960, Commdr.'s Cross with Star 1965; Palacki Medal (Czechoslovakia) 1968, Medals of 30th and 40th Anniversaries of People's Poland 1974 and 1985, Order of Banner of Labour, 1st Class 1976. *Publications:* Pierwsze państwo słowiańskie—państwo Samona (First Slavonic State—Samon's State) 1949, Fragmenty dziejów Słowiańszczyzny Zachodniej (Fragments of History of the West Slavs) vols. I-III 1960–74, Polska granica zachodnia: Tysiąc lat dziejów politycznych (The Western Frontier of Poland: A Thousand Years of Political History) 1971-1974, co-author, Słownik Starożytności Słowiańskich (Dictionary of Slavonic Antiquities), Historia Pomorza (History of Pomerania), Historia dyplomacji polskiej (Średniowiecze) (History of Polish Medieval Diplomacy) 1981, Dzieje zakonu Krzyżackiego W Prusach (History of the Order of the Teutonic Knights in Prussia) 1986; numerous articles. *Leisure interests:* sociology, linguistics. *Address:* Ul. Kanclerska 8, 60-327 Poznań, Poland. *Telephone:* 673-585.

LACANT, Jacques, D. ÉS L.; French university professor and literary critic; b. 10 May 1915, Paris; s. of Jean and Edmée (née Pontarlier) Lacant; m. Germaine Le Houérou 1948; three s. one d.; ed. Lycée Louis-le-Grand, Paris, and Ecole normale supérieure; attached to Econ. Del. 1942–44; broadcaster to Germany and Austria, Radiodiffussion Française 1944–45; Admin. in French occupation zone, Germany 1945–52; Dir. French Inst., Cologne 1952–60; Asst. Instructor, Sorbonne 1960–66; Head of Educ. Arts Faculty, Dijon Univ. 1966–69, Nanterre Univ. 1969; Prof. Paris X Univ., Prof. Emer. 1984–; mem. Higher Council of Univ. Bodies; Drama Critic; lecturer abroad; Vice-Pres. Défense de la Langue Française; Officier, Légion d'honneur; Officier des Palmes Académiques; Officier of Merit (Fed. Repub. of Germany); Laureate, Acad. Française 1976; Pierre Brisson Prize 1977; Grand Prix du Rayonnement Français, Acad. Française 1984. *Publications:* La Correspondence Wagner-Liszt 1943, L'Université de Fribourg 1947, Marivaux en Allemagne 1975, numerous works of literary history. *Leisure interest:* books. *Address:* 10 square du Croisic, 75015 Paris, France (Home). *Telephone:* 47 34 16 14.

LACAZE, Gen. Jeannou; French army officer; b. 11 Feb. 1924, Hué, Viet-Nam; s. of Jean Joseph and Andrée (née Momert) Lacaze; m. Henriette Bulot 1952; two s. two d.; entered mil. acad., Saint-Cyr 1945; joined infantry; served Foreign Legion, Algeria, Tunisia and the Far East; Major 11th demi-brigade parachutiste de choc 1959–63; Commdr. 2nd Foreign Parachute Regt. (for a time in Chad) 1967; Dir. of Intelligence, Service de documentation extérieure et de contre-espionage (SDECE) 1971–76; first mem. secret service to be made Gen.; Commdr. 11th Parachute Div. 1976–79; Inspecteur de l'infantrie Aug. 1979; Lieut.-Gen. Feb. 1980; Commdr. 1st mil. region and 3rd army corps, Commanding Officer, Paris Sept. 1980; Army Chief of Staff Jan. 1981–85; Special Counsellor, military relations with African continent countries 1985–; Grand Officier, Légion d'honneur; Croix de guerre, Croix de la Valeur militaire. *Leisure interests:* riding, sailing. *Address:* c/o Ministère de la Défense, 231 Boulevard St. Germain, 75007 Paris, France.

LACHARRIÈRE, Guy Ladreit de, DR.IUR., L. ÉS L.; French judge; b. 27 June 1919, Marseille; one d.; ed. Ecole des Sciences Politiques, Ecole de Langues Orientales Vivantes, Inst. de Droit Comparé, Paris; attached to French Embassy, Moscow 1946–48; Head, Office of Int. Orgs., Directorate-Gen. for Cultural Relations, Ministry of Foreign Affairs 1948–52; Perm. Del. to UNESCO and Sec.-Gen. French Del. to Gen. Conf. of UNESCO 1948–52; Asst. Dir. Dept. of Social Sciences 1952–57; served in, subsequently Asst. Dir. Dept. of Econ. Co-operation, Ministry of Foreign Affairs 1957–63, Dir. Dept. of UN and Int. Orgs. 1964–69, Dir. Legal Affairs 1969–79; Vice-Chair., Perm. Head of French Del. to Third UN Conf. on Law of the Sea 1973–; mem. Perm. Court of Arbitration 1975–; Judge, Int. Court of Justice, The Hague 1982–87; Conseiller d'Etat on special service; rep. France several times at sessions of organs of UN, in particular Sixth Cttee. of Gen. Ass., and in several int. arbitrations; teacher, Institut d'Etudes Politiques, Univ. of Paris 1954–, Institut des Hautes Etudes internationales, Ecole Nat. d'Admin., Hague Acad. of Int. Law 1973; Officier, Légion d'honneur; Commdr., Ordre nat. du Mérite. *Publications:* numerous works on international questions. *Address:* 11 quai de Bourbon, 75004 Paris, France (Home).

LACHER, Hans, LL.D.; Swiss diplomatist (retd.); b. 8 Aug. 1912, Basel; m. Daisy E. Bubeck 1941; one s.; ed. Basel and Paris Univs.; Swiss Foreign Office 1941–48; First Sec. Swiss Legation, Washington, D.C. 1948–53; Head of Swiss Del. Berlin 1954–61; Amb. to the Philippines 1961–63; Consul-Gen. New York 1963–69; Amb. to Fed. Repub. of Germany 1969–75. *Leisure interests:* history, photography, art. *Address:* Beim Goldenen Loewen 12, CH-4052 Basle, Switzerland.

LACHMANN, Peter Julius, SC.D., F.R.S., F.R.C.P., F.R.C.PATH.; British immunologist; b. 23 Dec. 1931, Berlin, Germany; s. of Heinz Lachmann and Thea Heller; m. Sylvia Stephenson 1962; two s. one d.; ed. Trinity Coll., Univ. of Cambridge and Univ. Coll. Hospital, London; Research Student, Dept. of Pathology, Univ. of Cambridge 1958–60, Research Fellow, Empire Rheumatism Council 1962–64, Asst. Dir. of Research, Immunology Div. 1964–71; Prof. of Immunology, Royal Postgraduate Medical School, Univ. of London 1971–75; Hon. Consultant Pathologist, Hammersmith Hosp. 1971–75; Dir. MRC Research Group on serum complement 1971–75; Sheila Joan Smith Prof. of Immunology, Univ. of Cambridge 1977–; Hon. Dir., MRC Molecular Immunopathology Unit 1980–; Hon. Consultant Clinical Immunologist, Cambridge Health Dist. 1976–; Visiting Investigator Rockefeller Univ., New York 1960–61, Scripps Clinic and Research Foundation, La Jolla, Calif. 1966, 1975, 1980, 1986, Basel Inst. for Immunology 1971, Fellow, Christ's Coll., Univ. of Cambridge 1962–71, 1976–; mem. Medical Advisory Cttee., British Council 1983–; Chair. Science Cttee. Asscn. Medical Research Charities 1988–; Chair. Medical Research Cttee. Muscular Dystrophy Group; Foundation Lecturer, Royal Coll. of Pathologists 1982; Langdon Brown Lecturer, Royal Coll. of Physicians 1986; Heberden Orator, British Soc. of Rheumatology 1986. *Publications:* Jt. Ed. Clinical Aspects of Immunology 3rd and 4th Edns. 1975, 1982. *Leisure interests:* keeping bees, walking in mountains. *Address:* Molecular Immunopathology Unit, Medical Research Council Centre, Hills Road, Cambridge, CB2 2QH (Office); 36 Conduit Head Road, Cambridge, CB3 0EY, England (Home). *Telephone:* (0223) 243237 (Office); (0223) 354433 (Home).

LACHS, Manfred, LL.M., LL.D., DR.JUR.; Polish international lawyer; b. 21 April 1914, Stanisławów; s. of Ignancy and Zofia Lachs; m. Halina Antonina; one d.; ed. Uniwersytet Jagiellónski, Cracow, Univ. of Vienna and L.S.E.; Dir. Legal and Treaties Dept., Ministry for Foreign Affairs 1947–60; Prof. Acad. of Political Sciences, Warsaw 1949–52; Prof. of Int. Law, Univ. of Warsaw 1952–; Minister 1956–60, Amb. 1960–66; Judge, Int. Court of Justice, The Hague 1967–, Pres. 1973–76; Polish Delegate, Paris Peace Conf. 1946; mem. Polish Del. to UN Gen. Ass. 1946–52, 1955–60, 1962–64, 1964–66; Rep. of Poland to UN Disarmament Cttee. 1962–64; Chair. Legal Cttee., UN Gen. Ass. 1949, 1951, 1955, Vice-Chair. 1952; mem. UN Int. Law Comm. 1962–, Rapporteur 1962, Chair. of its sub-cttee. on Succession of States and Govts., Special Rapporteur on sub-cttee.; Chair. UN Legal Comm. for Outer Space 1962–66; mem. Consultative Council attached to Chair. of State Council 1986–; Vice-Pres. Curatorium Hague Acad. of Int. Law; mem. Perm. Court of Arbitration, Inst. of Int. Law, Polish Acad. of Sciences, Acad. of Moral Sciences, Bologna, Mexican Acad. of Int. Law; Corresp. mem. Inst. de France; involved with various other UN orgs. and cttees.; Lecturer various acads., univs. and insts. in Europe and North and South America; Vice-Pres. Polish Club of Int. Relations 1988–; Distinguished Visiting Senior Fellow, New York Univ. 1970; Hon. mem. Int. Acad. of Astronautics, American Soc. of Int. Law; Foreign mem. Dutch Soc. of Sciences; Hon. Fellow Inst. of Social Studies, The Hague; Hon. Dr. (Algiers), Hon. Dr. jur. et pol. sc. (Budapest), Hon. LL.D. (Delhi), Hon. D.Sc. (Law) (Moscow), Hon. Dr. (State Univ. of New York, Nice, Cracow,

Bucharest, Dalhousie, New York, Brussels, Southampton, Sofia, Vancouver, Howard, London, Helsinki, Washington, Vienna, Silesian Univ., Katowice); Wateler Peace Prize 1977, Gold Medal for Outstanding Achievements in Law Making for Outer Space 1966, World Jurist Award 1975, Copernicus Prize 1984, Britannica Award for dissemination of learning and the enrichment of life 1987, Great Prize for Scientific Achievements, Polish Acad. of Sciences 1988; Commdr.'s Cross with Star and Officer's Cross of Polonia Restituta, Order of Banner of Labour (1st class) and other decorations. *Publications:* An Attempt to Define The Issues 1945, The Geneva Agreements on Indochina (in Polish) 1955 (Russian trans. 1956), Les Développements et Fonctions des Traités Multilatéraux: Recueil des Cours 1957, The Multilateral Treaties (in Polish) 1958 (Russian, Hungarian and Spanish trans.), The Polish-German Frontier (in English, French, Spanish and German) 1964, The International Law of Outer Space, A Law in the making, Recueil des Cours, The Hague 1964, The Law of Outer Space, An Experience in Contemporary Law-Making, Leyden 1972, Teachings and Teaching of International Law 1976, El Derecho del Espacio Ultraterrestre 1977, General Principles of International Law 1981, The Teacher in International Law 1982, The Development and General Trends of International Law in Our Time 1984, Rzecz o nauce prawa międzynarodowego 1986, and over 120 essays and articles. *Leisure interests:* walking, reading, science, science fiction. *Address:* The International Court of Justice, Peace Palace, The Hague 2517 KJ, Netherlands.

LACINA, Ferdinand; Austrian politician; b. 31 Dec. 1942, Vienna; s. of Anna and Ferdinand Lacina; m. Monika Lacina 1966; one s. one d.; ed. Hochschule für Welthandel, Vienna; various posts in Kammer für Arbeiter und Angestellte, Vienna 1964; Beirat für Wirtschafts- und Sozialfragen 1974; Dir. Dept. of Financial Planning, Österreichische Industrieverwaltungs-A.G. 1978; Dir. Pvt. Office of Fed. Chancellor Kreisky 1980; Sec. of State, Fed- Chancellery 1982; Fed. Minister of Transport Sept. 1984–Jan. 1985, of Public Economy and Transport 1985–86, of Finance 1986–89, Acting Minister of Employment and Social Affairs Feb. 1989–. *Publications:* Auslandskapital in Österreich (with O. Grünwald); articles in trade union newspapers and political and econ. journals. *Leisure interests:* literature, walking. *Address:* Ministry of Employment and Social Affairs, 1010 Vienna, Stubenring 1, Austria.

LACO, Karol, JU.DR., DR.SC.; Czechoslovak politician; b. 28 Oct. 1921, Sobotiště; ed. Faculty of Law, Comenius Univ., Bratislava; mem. of Faculty of Law, Comenius Univ. 1947–, Asst. Prof. 1952, Prof. 1963, Dean 1953–56, 1957–59, 1960–61; Deputy to House of Nations, Fed. Ass. 1968–71; Deputy to Slovak Nat. Council 1968–71; Deputy Prime Minister of Č.S.S.R. 1969–88; Chair. Legis. Council of Fed. Govt. 1969–; mem. Czechoslovak Pugwash Cttee. 1965–; Chair. Co-ordination Cttee. of Govt. of Č.S.S.R. for Nat. Cttees. 1970–; Deputy to House of the People, Fed. Ass. 1971–; mem. Czechoslovak Acad. of Sciences, Academician 1977–, Academician, Slovak Acad. of Science 1978–; Head Dept. State Law, Univ. of Komenský, Bratislava 1978–; Order of Labour 1969, 1971, Gold Medal Comenius Univ. 1969. *Publications:* The National Committees, the Core of the Political Basis of People's Democratic Czechoslovakia 1954, Constitutional Law No. 33/1956 on the Slovak National Organs 1956, The Social System of the Czechoslovak Socialist Republic 1960, Constitution of pre-Munich Č.S.R. and Constitution of Č.S.S.R. (Part I) 1966; textbooks and study aids; contributions to specialized journals. *Address:* Presidium of the Czechoslovak Government, Prague 1, nábř. kpt. Jaroše 4, Czechoslovakia.

LACOMBE, Américo Jacobina; Brazilian teacher (retd.); b. 7 July 1909; s. of Domingos Lourenço and Isabel Jacobina Lacombe; m. Gilda Masset Lacombe 1935; four s. one d.; ed. Colégio Jacobina, Rio de Janeiro, Colégio Arnaldo (Belo Horizonte), and Univ. of Rio de Janeiro; Sec. Nat. Council of Educ. 1931–39; Pres. Casa de Rui Barbosa 1939–81; fmr. Prof. of Brazilian History at Pontifical Univ. of Rio de Janeiro; mem. numerous Historical Insts., Portuguese Historical Acad. and Brazilian Acad. of Letters. *Publications:* Mocidade e Exilio de Rui Barbosa 1934, Paulo Barbosa e a Fundação de Petrópolis 1940, Um Passeio Pela História do Brasil 1942 (trans. Brazil: A Brief History 1954), O Pensamento Vivo de Rui Barbosa 1944, Brasil—Período Nacional 1956, Introdução ao Estudo da História do Brasil 1974, À Sombra de Rui Barbosa 1978, Afonso Pena e Seu Tempo 1986. *Address:* Rua Dezenove de Fevereiro 127/201, Code 22280, Botafogo, Rio de Janeiro, RJ, Brazil. *Telephone:* 246-3176 (Home).

LACOMBE, Henri; French oceanographer; b. 24 Dec. 1913, Nîmes; s. of Adrien Lacombe and Marguerite Llorens; m. Geneviève Geoffroy 1939; three s. four d.; ed. Lycée de Nice, Lycée Saint-Louis, Paris, and Ecole Polytechnique, Paris; Marine Hydrographical Engineer 1935–55; Hon. Prof. of Physical Oceanography, Muséum de Paris 1955–82, Dir. of scientific expeditions at sea—in the Mediterranean and Strait of Gibraltar; fmr. Pres. Int. Asscn. for the Physical Sciences of the Ocean 1970–75; Chair. UNESCO Intergovernmental Oceanographic Comm. 1965–67; mem. French Acad. of Sciences 1973–; Marine Acad. 1976–, Commdr. Ordre nat. du Mérite, Officier, Légion d'honneur, Croix de guerre, Commdr. Etoile d'Anjouan, Médaille d'Or Prince Albert 1er de Monaco 1976, etc. *Publications:* Etudes d'acoustique sous-marine 1946, Ouvrage sur courants de marée 1953, Mission hydrographique Maroc 1959; various studies on the movement of the sea 1949–84; Cours d'océanographie physique 1965, Les énergies de la mer 1968, 1979, Les mouvements de la mer 1971. *Address:*

Laboratoire d'Océanographie Physique du Muséum, 43 rue Cuvier, 75231 Paris Cédex 05 (Office); 20 bis avenue de Lattre de Tassigny, 92340 Bourg-La-Reine, France (Home). *Telephone:* 43-31-94-94 (Office); 46-64-23-22 (Home).

LACOSTE, Paul, O.C., PH.D.; Canadian university administrator; b. 24 April 1923, Montreal; s. of Emile and Juliette (née Boucher) Lacoste; m. 1st Louise Mackay (divorced), 2nd Louise Marcil 1973; one s. two d.; ed. Montreal, Chicago, Paris Univs.; Vice-Pres., Montreal Univ. 1966-75; Prof. Dept. of Philosophy, Montreal Univ. 1948-; lawyer 1960-; Pres. Asscn. des universités partiellement ou entièrement de langue francaise 1978-81, Fonds Int. de coopération universitaire 1978-81, Asscn. of Univs. and Colls. of Canada 1978-79, Conf. of Rectors and Principals of Quebec Univs. 1977-80, mem. Bd. Asscn. of Commonwealth Univs. 1977-80, Ecole polytechnique Montréal 1975-85, Clinical Research Inst. of Montreal 1975-, Ecole des hautes commerciales de Montréal 1982-85; Pres. Univ. of Montreal 1975-85; Officer of the Order of Canada 1977, Chevalier, Légion d'honneur 1985; Hon. L.L.D. (McGill Univ.) 1975, (Univ. of Toronto) 1978; Dr. h.c. (Laval Univ.). *Publications:* Justice et paix scolaire 1962, A Place of Liberty 1964, Le Canada au seuil du siècle de l'abondance 1969, Principes de gestion universitaire 1970, Education permanente et potentiel universitaire 1977. *Leisure interests:* reading, music, travel. *Address:* 356 Woodlea Avenue, Mont-Royal, P.Q. H3P 1R5, Canada. *Telephone:* (514) 343-7727 (Office); (514) 342-6150 (Home).

LACROIX, Christian Marie Marc; French artistic director of fashion; b. 16 May 1951, Arles; s. of Maxime Lacroix and Jeannette Bergier; ed. Lycée Frédéric Mistral, Arles, Univ. Paul Valéry, Montpellier, Univ. Paris-Sorbonne and Ecole du Louvre; Asst. Hermès 1978-79, Guy Paulin 1980-81; Artistic Dir. Jean Patou 1981-87, Christian Lacroix Feb. 1987-; Dé d'or 1986, 1988, Council of fashion designers of America. *Address:* 73 Faubourg Saint Honoré, 75008 Paris, France. *Telephone:* (1) 42 65 79 08.

LADAS, Ioannis; Greek army officer and politician (retd.); b. 9 Sept. 1920, Dyrrachion, Arcadia; s. of Elias and Chariklia Ladas; m. Ephrosyni Ladas 1949; one s. one d.; ed. Cadet Coll., Infantry School, Fort Menning Infantry School, U.S.A., Supreme War Coll. and Gen. Education School; commissioned 1940, Col. 1965; Chief of Hellenic Mil. Police 1966; participated in army coup 1967; retd. from army with rank of Brig. 1968; Sec.-Gen. Ministry of Public Order 1967-68, Ministry of Interior 1968-71; Deputy Minister of Regional Admin., Thessali dist. 1971-72; Minister of Social Services 1972-73; arrested Oct. 1974, sentenced to life imprisonment for high treason and 10 years' imprisonment for insurrection Aug. 1975.

LADER, Malcolm Harold, PH.D., M.D., D.SC., F.R.C.PSYCH.; British professor of clinical psychopharmacology; b. 27 Feb. 1936, Liverpool; m. Susan Packer 1961; three d.; ed. Liverpool Inst. High School and Liverpool and London Univs.; Research Asst. in Pharmacology, Univ. Coll. and Inst. of Psychiatry, London 1960-63; training in psychiatry 1963-66; external mem. of scientific staff on MRC 1966-; Reader Univ. of London 1973-78, Prof. 1978-; Consultant Psychiatrist, Bethlem Royal and Maudsley Hospitals 1970-; mem. various U.K. govt. advisory bodies; Heinz Karger Memorial Foundation Prize 1974. *Publications:* Clinical Anxiety 1971, The Psychophysiology of Mental Illness 1975, Psychiatry on Trial 1977, Introduction to Psychopharmacology 1980, Dependence on Tranquillizers 1984, Guide to the Use of Psychotropic Drugs 1986; numerous articles on psychopharmacology. *Leisure interests:* antiques, paintings. *Address:* Institute of Psychiatry, De Crespigny Park, Denmark Hill, London, SE5 8AF, England. *Telephone:* 01-703 5411.

LADGHAM, Bahi; Tunisian politician; b. 10 Jan. 1913, Tunis; joined Dept. of Interior 1933, subsequently moved to Finance Dept.; Sec.-Gen. Socialist Desturian Party (fmrly. Neo-Destur Party) 1953-73; Sec. of State for the Presidency and Sec. of State for Defence 1956-69; Prime Minister of Tunisia Nov. 1969-Nov. 1970; Chair. Arab Cttee. supervising the ceasefire between Jordanian Govt. and the Palestinians in Jordan Sept. 1970-April 1971; fmr. personal rep. of Pres. Bourguiba; resgnd. from Party and Nat. Ass. March 1973.

LADREIT DE LACHARRIERE, Marc; French business executive; b. 6 Nov. 1940, Nice; m. Sibylle Lucet; one s. two d.; ed. Ecole Nat. d'Admin.; Asst. Man. Banque de Suez et de l'Union des Mines 1970, Asst. Dir. 1971, Deputy Dir. 1973; Vice-Dir. Banque de l'Indochine et de Suez 1975, Corporate Affairs Dir. 1976; Financial Dir. L'Oreal 1976, Man. Dir. Admin. and Finance 1977, Vice-Pres. Man. Cttee. 1978, mem. Strategic Cttee., Dir. and Exec. Vice-Pres. 1984-; Chair. Geral, U.S.A.; Man. Dir. Regefi and Holdilux, Luxembourg; Vice-Chair. L'Oreal (G.B.), Editions Masson; Dir. Collection de l'Inst. de l'Entreprise; Lecturer, Inst. d'Etudes Politiques, Paris 1971, then Prof.; Adviser, Foreign Trade of France; numerous directorships; Chevalier, Légion d'honneur, Ordre Nat. du Mérite. *Leisure interests:* tennis, skiing. *Address:* L'Oreal, 41 rue Martre, 92117, Clichy (Office); 42 rue Hallé, 75014 Paris, France (Home). *Telephone:* (1) 47 31 11 45 (Office).

LÆSSØE, Jørgen, D.PHIL.; Danish professor of Assyriology; b. 2 June 1924, Dråby; s. of Albert and Karen (née Stroyer) Læssøe; m. Herdis Elsie Aaberg 1949; two s.; ed. Univ. of Copenhagen; Research Asst. Chicago Assyrian Dictionary, Oriental Inst., Univ. of Chicago 1948-51; Asst. Prof. Assyriology, Univ. of Copenhagen 1951-53, Assoc. Prof. 1953-57, Prof.

1957-87, Prof. Emer. 1987-; also Asst. Prof. of Assyriology, Univ. of California, Berkeley 1953-55; mem. (epigraphist) of the excavations at Nimrud, Iraq 1956-60, also at Tell Rimah, Iraq 1964; mem. Scandinavian Jt. Expedition to Sudanese Nubia 1961-63; Visiting Prof. of Assyriology, Univ. of California, Berkeley 1966-67; Visiting Fellow, All Souls Coll., Oxford 1970-71; mem. Royal Danish Acad.; Gold Medal Univ. of Copenhagen 1956; Knight of the Order of Dannebrog. *Publications:* Studies on the Assyrian Ritual and Series *bît rimki* 1955, The Shemshāra Tablets 1959, Fra Assyriens arkiver 1960 (English ed. People of Ancient Assyria 1963, Polish ed. Ludy Asyrii 1973), Babylon 1966, Det første assyriske imperium 1966; numerous specialist articles. *Leisure interests:* Horatio Nelson, Winston Churchill. *Address:* 77 Bredgade, DK-1260 Copenhagen K., Denmark. *Telephone:* 01 14 12 42.

LAFAURIE, Jean; French numismatist; b. 21 Nov. 1914, Bordeaux; m. Raymonde Forment 1938; Prof. Ecole pratique des Hautes Etudes de la Sorbonne; fmr. Dir. Soc. for Study of History of Paper Money; fmr. Keeper Cabinet des médailles, Nat. Library, Paris 1946; Dir. Revue Numismatique 1958-; Past Pres. Soc. Nat. Antiquaires de France, French Numismatic Soc.; Hon. mem. Int. Numismatic Comm., Inst. Grand-Ducal de Luxembourg, Académie Bavière, Royal Belgian, American, French, Netherlands and Swiss Numismatic Socs.; Royal Numismatic Soc. Medal, Archer M. Huntington Medal of American Numismatic Soc. and Royal Numismatic Soc., London. *Publications:* Les monnaies des rois de France (2 vols.) 1951, 1956, Les assignats et les papiers monnaies émis en France au XVIIIe. siècle 1981, Le trésor de deniers mérovingiens trouvé à Bais 1981, Monnaies romaines du Bas Empire, Monnaies mérovingiennes, Monnaies carolingiennes, Monnaies françaises; over 500 articles. *Address:* 3 rue de l'Abbé Guilleminault, 94130 Nogent-sur-Marne, France. *Telephone:* (1) 48.71.15.72.

LAFÉE, Alfredo; Venezuelan civil engineer and banker; b. 21 March 1921, Caracas; m. Ines Dominici de Lafée; four c.; ed. Venezuela Central Univ.; Engineer, public drainage and water supply dept. of Ministry of Public Works 1941-44, in charge of works inspection 1945-47; Chief of Technical Dept. Caracas Drainage Works, Nat. Inst. of Sanitary Works 1947-51; mem. (Ad Honorem) comm. for widening Avenida Sucre 1950-53; mem. Municipal Council 1958-59; Dir. of Construction, Caracas and Maracaibo Urban Devt. 1951-66; mem. Bd. of Venezuelan Chamber of Bldg. 1960-62, represented Bd. in numerous Fed. Comms. 1960-63, Pres. 1962-64; Dir.-Gen. Banco Hipotecario de la Vivienda Popular S.A. 1962-68, First Vice-Pres. and Dir. 1968-71; mem. El Conde Perm. Devt. Comm. 1963-64; mem. Council of Inter-american Fed. of Bldg. Industry 1962-64; Deputy Nat. Congress 1964-69; mem. Bd. Venezuelan Fed. of Chambers of Commerce and Industry (FEDECAMARAS) 1962-64, First Vice-Pres. 1964-67, Pres. 1967-69, Perm. Assessor 1969, Prin. mem. Bd. 1972; mem. Ad Honorem Comm. for enquiry into the working of the Stock Market 1969-71; M.P. for the State of Miranda 1969-71; mem. Bd. Cen. Office for Co-ordination and Planning (CORDIPLAN) 1970, Nat. Energy Council 1971, Bd. of Foreign Trade Inst. 1971, Nat. Banking Council 1971, Nat. Council of Asociación Pro-Venezuela 1971; Pres. Banco Central de Venezuela 1971-76; Governor, IMF 1971; Pres. Gov. Council of CEMLA 1972; Del. numerous int. confs.; Orden Francisco de Miranda 1st Class, Mérito Industrial del Brasil 2nd Class. *Address:* FEDECAMARAS, Edif. Fedecámaras, 5°, Avda. El Enpalme, Urb. El Bosque, Apdo. 2568, Caracas, Venezuela.

LAFFER, Arthur, M.B.A., PH.D.; American economist; ed. Yale Univ. and Stanford Univ.; fmr. faculty mem. Stanford Univ. and Univ. of Chicago; fmr. Chief Economist Office of Man. and Budget, Exec. Office of Pres., now mem. Pres.'s Econ. Policy Advisory Bd.; Prof. of Finance and Business Econs. Univ. of S. Calif., L.A. 1976-84, Charles B. Thornton Prof. 1979-84; Distinguished Prof. Pepperdine Univ. 1984-; mem. Bd. Dirs. Cttee. for Monetary Research and Educ.; Hon. mem. Bd. L.A. County Museum of Natural History; mem. Advisory Bd. Taxpayers Foundation; Commerce Assocs. Dean's Facility Award, Univ. of S. Calif. 1979, Teaching Excellence Award, Univ. of S. Calif. Assocs. 1980, John J. Knezevich Americanism Award 1979, Daniel Webster Award, Int. Platform Asscn. 1979. *Address:* 24255 Pacific Coast Highway, Malibu, Calif. 90265, U.S.A.

LAFFONT, Robert Raoul, L. EN D.; French publishing executive; b. 30 Nov. 1916, Marseille; s. of Raymond Laffont and Nathalie Périer; m. Hélène Furterer 1987; three s. two d.; ed. Lycée Périer, Marseille and Ecole des Hautes Etudes Commerciales, Paris; Lieut. 94th Regt. of Artillery, Montagne; f. Edns. Robert Laffont, Marseille 1941, transferred to Paris 1945, Pres., Chief Exec. 1941-86, Editeur-Fondateur Dec. 1986-; Chevalier, Légion d'honneur, Officier, Ordre nat. du Mérite. *Publication:* Robert Laffont, éditeur 1974. *Leisure interest:* football. *Address:* Editions Robert Laffont, 6 place Saint Sulpice, Paris 75006 (Office); 11 rue Pierre Nicole, Paris 75005, France (Home). *Telephone:* 43.29.12.33 (Office); 43.26.02.41 (Home).

LAFONTAINE, Oskar; German politician; b. 16 Sept. 1943, Saarlois; m.; ed. Univ. of Bonn; Mayor of Saarbrücken 1976-85; mem. Saarland Landtag (Regional Parl.), Minister-Pres. March 1985-; Chair. SPD Regional Asscn., Saar 1977; mem. SPD Cen. Cttee.; Vice-Chair. SPD 1987-; Social Democrat. *Publications:* Angst vor den Freunden 1983, Der andere Fortschritt 1985. *Address:* Staatskanzle, Am Ludwigsplatz 14, D-6600 Saarbrücken, Federal Republic of Germany. *Telephone:* (0681) 5006-01.

LAFORTE, Conrad, D. ÈS L., F.R.S.C.; Canadian university professor; b. 10 Nov. 1921, Kenogami, P.Q.; s. of Philippe Laforte and Marie-Mathilda Dallaire; m. Hélène Gauthier 1957; one d.; ed. Montréal Univ. and Laval Univ.; librarian and archivist, Folklore Archives, Laval Univ. 1951–73; Instructor CELAT, Laval Univ. 1965–67, Asst. Prof. 1967–73, Assoc. Prof. 1973–77, Prof. 1977–81, Titular Prof. Dept. of History and CELAT 1981–; Fellow Emer. CELAT, Laval Univ. 1984; several awards for folklore research etc. *Publications:* Le chanson folklorique et les écrivains du XIXe siècle 1973, Poétiques de la chanson traditionnelle française 1976, Catalogue de la chanson folklorique française (6 vols.) 1977–87, Menteries drôles et merveilleuses 1978, Survivances médiévales dans la chanson folklorique 1981. *Address:* Department of History, Université Laval, Sainte-Foy, P.Q., G1K 7P4 (Office); 949 rue Gatineau, Sainte-Foy, P.Q., G1V 3A2, Canada.

LÅG, Jul, DR.AGR.; Norwegian professor of soil science; b. 13 Nov. 1915, Flesberg; s. of Torsten S. Buind Låg and Jøran Låg; m. Ingrid Brenner 1956 (died 1979); one s. one d.; ed. Agric. Univ. of Norway; Prof. of Soil Science, Agric. Univ. of Norway 1949–85, Rector 1968–71; Chair. Agric. Council of Norway 1972–73; mem. Council, Int. Soc. of Soil Science 1977–79, Chair. Working Group on Soils and Geomedicine 1986–; Pres. Norwegian Acad. of Science and Letters 1976–84; corresp. mem. Soil Science Soc. of W. Germany; hon. mem. Soil Science Soc. of U.S.S.R.; mem. of Royal Norwegian Soc. of Science and Letters; mem. of Danish, Finnish, Polish and Swedish Acads.; mem. ed. bds. of Agrochimica (Italy), Geoderma (Netherlands), Ambio (Sweden), Soil Science (U.S.A.), Alexandria Science Exchange; Commdr. Cross of Icelandic Order; Copernicus Medal (Polish Acad.). *Publications:* eight books and 190 papers in soil science and related subjects. *Leisure interests:* skiing, literature. *Address:* Department of Soil Science, Agricultural University of Norway, P.O. Box 27, 1432 As-NLH, Norway. *Telephone:* 09-94 90 60.

LAGACOS, Eustache P.; Greek diplomatist (retd.); b. 4 June 1921, Athens; m. Claire Lagacos 1949; one d.; ed. Law Faculty of Athens Univ.; Mil. service 1946–49; Embassy Attaché, Ministry of Foreign Affairs 1949–51, Third Sec. 1951–52; Vice-Consul, Paris 1952; mem. Perm. Del. to NATO, Paris 1952–55; Foreign Ministry 1955; Consul, Istanbul 1956–59; Foreign Ministry 1959; Counsellor, Nicosia 1960–64; Foreign Ministry 1964, Chef de Cabinet 1965; Counsellor, London 1967; Minister Plenipotentiary 1969; Amb. to Cyprus 1972–74; Dir.-Gen. Econ. Affairs, Foreign Ministry 1974–76; Amb. to NATO, Brussels 1976–79, to U.K. 1979–82; Foreign Affairs Counsellor to Nea Democratia Party Leader. *Publications:* Two Lectures on G. Seferis (in Greek), The Cyprus Question 1950–74. *Leisure interest:* classical music. *Address:* 7 Kapsali Street, Athens 10674, Greece.

LAGARDE, Paul, D. EN D.; French professor of law; b. 3 March 1934, Rennes; s. of Gaston Lagarde and Charlotte Béquignon; m. Bernadette Lamberts 1962; two s. one d.; ed. Paris Univ.; Prof. Faculty of Law, Nancy 1961–69, Nanterre 1969–71; Prof. of Private Int. Law, Univ. of Paris I 1971–; Gen. Sec. Revue critique de droit international privé 1962, Ed.-in-Chief 1981; Pres. Comité Français de droit int. privé 1987–. *Publications:* Recherches sur l'ordre public en droit international privé 1959, Traité de droit international privé (with Henri Batiffol, q.v.), La nationalité française 1975, La réciprocité en droit international privé 1977, Le Principe de Proximité dans le Droit International Privé Contemporain 1987. *Address:* 32 bis boulevard Jean Jaurès, 92100 Boulogne-sur-Seine, France. *Telephone:* (1) 48.25.69.03.

LAGARDÈRE, Jean-Luc; French engineer and business executive; b. 10 Feb. 1928, Aubiet, Gers; s. of André Lagardère and Marthe Fourcade; one s.; ed. Lycée Buffon, Auch, Lycée Saint-Louis, Paris, École supérieure d'électricité; eng. then Head of Dept. Marcel Dassault Gen. aéronautique 1951–62; Admin., Dir.-Gen. Soc. Matra 1963–76, Pres., Dir-Gen. 1977–; Admin. Europe No. 1 Images et Son 1972, Vice-Pres., Del 1973, Pres., Del. 1981; Pres. Supervisory Bd. Europe No. 1 Télécie., Régie No. 1 1978–; Vice-Pres. Supervisory Bd. CERT 1978–; Admin. Manurhin 1978–; Pres., Dir.-Gen. Soc. Hachette 1981–; Man. of the Year, Nouvel Economiste 1979; Officier, Légion d'honneur, Commdr., Ordre nat. du Mérite. *Leisure interests:* football, tennis, skiing. *Address:* 4 rue de Presbourg, 75116 Paris, France (Office).

LAGASSE, Raphael; Belgian international official; b. 20 Dec. 1927, Brussels; ed. Catholic Univ. of Louvain; Sec.-Gen., Int. Org. of Employers 1960–; Belgian Civic and Mil. Orders. *Address:* 28 Chemin de Joinville, P.O. Box 68, 1216 Cointrin, Geneva, Switzerland (Office).

LA GENIÈRE, Renaud de; French financial administrator; b. 2 Sept. 1925, Le Mans; s. of Yves de la Genière and Marcelle Montigny; m. Juliette Massenet 1952; one s. two d.; ed. Faculté de Droit, Univ. of Paris, Ecole Libre des Sciences Politiques, Paris, Ecole Nat. d'Admin.; Inspecteur des Finances 1949; Technical Adviser to Antoine Pinay Cabinet 1958–59; Deputy Dir. Dept. of External Finance 1959; Deputy Dir. of the Budget 1960, Dir. 1966–74; lecturer Institut d'Etudes Politiques 1971–80; Deputy Gov. Banque de France 1974; Pres. Institut des Hautes Etudes Scientifiques 1978–85; Gov. Banque de France 1979–84; Pres. Compagnie Financière Suez 1986–; Commdr., Légion d'honneur, Croix de guerre. *Publication:* Le Budget 1976. *Address:* Compagnie financière de Suez, 1 rue d'Astorg, 75008 Paris (Office); 5 avenue de Bretteville, 92200 Neuilly-sur-Seine, Paris, France.

LAGERCRANTZ, Olof, PH.D.; Swedish journalist; b. 10 March 1911, Stockholm; s. of Carl and Agnes (née Hamilton) Lagercrantz; m. Martina Ruin 1939; three s. two d.; Cultural Ed., Dagens Nyheter 1951–60, Chief Ed. 1960–75; Prize of Nordic Council (jointly) 1965. *Publications:* Från helvetet till paradiset 1964, Den pågående skapelsen 1966, Att finnas till 1970, China-Report 1971, Tretton lyriker o fågeltruppen 1973, Enhörningen 1977, August Strindberg, a Biography 1979 (English and American edns. 1984), Min första krets (autobiog.) 1982, Om konsten att läsa och skriva 1985, Färd med Mörkrets Hjärta (on Joseph Conrad's Heart of Darkness) 1987; biographies and collections of poems and essays. *Leisure interest:* writing. *Address:* Box 28, 17011 Drottingholm, Sweden. *Telephone:* 08-7590651.

LAGERFELD, Karl; German fashion designer; b. 1938, Hamburg; ed. privately and at art school, Hamburg; fashion apprentice with Balmain and Patou 1959; freelance designer associated with Fendi, Rome 1963–, Chloe, Paris 1964–83, Chanel, Paris 1982–, Isetan, Japan; designer Karl Lagerfeld's Women's Wear, Karl Lagerfeld France Inc. 1983–; first collection under his own name 1984; Hon. Teacher, Vienna 1983; awarded Golden Thimble 1986. *Publication:* Lagerfeld's Sketchbook (with Anna Piaggi). *Address:* Avenue Champs-Élysées, 75008 Paris, France.

LAGERGREN, Gunnar Karl Andreas; Swedish judge; b. 23 Aug. 1912, Stockholm; m. Nina von Dardel 1943; one s. three d.; ed. Stockholm Univ.; Arbitrator, Int. Chamber of Commerce, Paris 1949–80; Judge, Stockholm Court of Appeal 1957–66; Pres. Court of Appeal for Western Sweden, Göteborg 1966–77; Judge, European Court of Human Rights, Strasbourg 1977–88; Pres. Comm. on Int. Commercial Practice of Int. Chamber of Commerce 1951–67; Pres. Supreme Restitution Court, Fed. Repub. of Germany 1964–; Chair. Italian-Somali Arbitration Tribunal in Mogadishu 1964; Chair. Indo-Pakistan Western Boundary Tribunal, Geneva 1965–69; Vice-Pres. Arbitration Comm. on Property Rights and Interests in Germany, Koblenz 1956–69; mem. Int. Court, Tangier 1953–56; mem. Permanent Court of Arbitration, The Hague 1966–; sole Arbitrator of the BP/Libya Concession Tribunal, Copenhagen 1972–75; Deputy Chair. Appeals Bd. of the Council of Europe 1981–87, Chair. 1987–; Pres. Iran-U.S.A. Claims Tribunal, The Hague 1981–84; Pres. Arbitral Tribunal for German External Debts, Koblenz 1982–; Pres. Egypt-Israel Taba Arbitration Tribunal, Geneva 1986–; Marshal of the Realm (Excellency) 1976–82; Dr. h.c. (Uppsala Univ.) 1965. *Address:* Dahlbergsvägen 22, 182 62 Djursholm, Sweden. *Telephone:* 8/7555826.

LAGU, Joseph; Sudanese army officer; b. 21 Nov. 1931; s. of Yakobo Yanga and Marini Kaluma; ed. Rumbek Secondary School, Mil. Acad. Omdurman; served in Sudanese Army 1960–63; joined South Sudan Liberation Movt. 1963, Leader SSLM 1969; signed peace agreement with Govt. of Sudan March 1972; Second Vice-Pres. of Sudan 1978–80, 1982–85; Pres. Supreme Exec. Council for the South 1978–80; Order of the Two Niles 1972. *Publication:* The Anya-Nya—what we fight for 1972. *Address:* c/o Office of the Second Vice-President, Khartoum, Sudan.

LAGUNA, Frederica de, PH.D.; American anthropologist; b. 3 Oct. 1906, Ann Arbor, Mich.; d. of Theodore and Grace Andrus de Laguna; ed. Phoebe Anna Thorne School, Bryn Mawr, Pa., Bryn Mawr Coll. and Columbia Univ.; on staff of Univ. of Penna Museum 1931–34; U.S. Soil Conservation Service 1935–36; Lecturer, Bryn Mawr Coll. 1938–41, Asst. Prof. 1941–42, 1946–49, Assoc. Prof. 1949–55, Prof. of Anthropology 1955–75; U.S.N.R. 1942–45; Chair. Dept. of Sociology and Anthropology, Bryn Mawr Coll. 1950–66, Chair. Dept. of Anthropology 1967–72, R. Kenan Jr. Prof. 1974–75, Prof. Emer. 1975–; Bryn Mawr Coll. European Fellowship 1927; Columbia Univ. Fellowship 1930–31; Nat. Research Council Fellow 1936–37; Rockefeller Post-War Fellow 1945–46; Viking Fund Fellow 1949, Social Science Research Council Faculty Fellow 1962–63; Hon. Fellow Rochester (New York) Museum of Arts and Sciences 1941; Fellow A.A.A.S., Arctic Inst. of N. America, American Anthropological Asscn. (Pres. 1966–67); mem. N.A.S.; Hon. Life Mem. Alaska Anthropological Asscn.; Hon. D.Hum.Litt. (Alaska); Lindback Award for Distinguished Teaching 1973; Distinguished Service Award, American Anthropological Asscn. 1986. *Publications:* The Archaeology of Cook Inlet, Alaska 1934, The Eyak Indians of the Copper River Delta, Alaska (with Kaj Birket-Smith) 1938, Chugach Prehistory: The Archaeology of Prince William Sound, Alaska 1956, Under Mount Saint Elias: The History and Culture of the Yakitat Tlingit 1972, Voyage to Greenland: A Personal Initiation into Anthropology 1977; contributions to learned journals. *Address:* Apt. 510, The Conway Arms, 830 Montgomery Avenue, Bryn Mawr, Pa. 19010, U.S.A. (Home). *Telephone:* (215) 526-5171 (College).

LAHNSTEIN, Manfred; German civil servant and politician; b. 1937, Rhineland; joined SPD 1959; at European Comm., Brussels, latterly as Chef de Cabinet to Commr. Wilhelm Haferkamp 1967–73; econ. adviser, Chancellery 1973; moved to Finance Ministry 1974, successively Div. Head and State Sec. in charge of Financial and Monetary Policy 1974–80; Chancellor's Chief Civil Servant 1980–82; Minister of Finance April-Oct. 1982; Pres. Electronic Media Group; mem. Bd. Dirs. Bertelsmann AG 1983–. *Address:* Carl-Bertelsmannstrasse 270, 4830 Gütersloh, Federal Republic of Germany.

LAI SHAOQI; Chinese painter and calligrapher; b. 1915, Puning Co., Guangdong Prov.; Chair. Anhui Prov. Fed. of Literary and Art Circles.

Address: Federation of Literary and Art Circles, Anhui Province, People's Republic of China.

LAIDIG, William Rupert, B.S.; American business executive; b. 3 Feb. 1927, Sterling, Ill.; s. of George Laidig and Margaret Anne Gnewuch; m. Lorraine Mae Grom 1952; one s. three d.; ed. Marquette Univ., Milwaukee; Mill Man., Nekoosa Papers Inc., Port Edwards, Wis. 1972-75; Vice-Pres., Resident Man., Great Southern Paper Co., Cedar Springs, Ga. 1975-80, Sr. Vice-Pres. 1979-80, Pres. 1980-84; Exec. Vice-Pres., Great Northern Nekoosa Corpn., Stamford, Conn. 1980-84, Pres., Chair. of Bd., C.E.O. 1984-. *Address:* 75 Prospect Street, P.O. Box 9309, Stamford, Conn. 06904, U.S.A. *Telephone:* (203) 359-4000.

LAIDLAW, Sir Christophor Charles Fraser, Kt.; British business executive; b. 9 Aug. 1922; s. of late Hugh Alexander Lyon Laidlaw and Sarah Georgina Fraser; m. Nina Mary Prichard 1952; one s. three d.; ed. Rugby School and St. John's Coll. Cambridge; served War of 1939-45, Europe and Far East, Maj. on Gen. Staff; joined British Petroleum Co. Ltd. (BP) 1948, BP rep. in Hamburg 1959-61, Gen. Man. Marketing 1963-67, Dir. BP Trading 1967, Pres. BP Belgium 1967-71, Dir. (Operations) 1971-72, Chair. BP Germany 1972-83, Man. Dir. BP Co. Ltd. 1972-81, Deputy Chair. 1980-81; Chair. BP Oil 1977-81, BP Oil Int. 1981, ICL 1981-84, Bridon PLC 1985-; Pres. ICL France 1983; Dres. Dalgety 1984-; Redland 1984-; Dir. Commercial Union Assurance Co. 1978-83, Barclays Bank Int. Ltd. 1980-87, Barclays Bank 1981-88, Barclays Merchant Bank 1984-87, Warden, Tallow Chandler Co., Boving & Co. Ltd. 1984- (Chair. 1984-86), Mercedes-Benz (U.K.) 1986-; Pres. German Chamber of Industry and Commerce 1983-86. *Leisure interests:* fishing, shooting. *Address:* c/o Bridon PLC, 20 New Bond Street, London, W1Y 9PF, England.

LAINE, Cleo (Mrs. Clementina Dinah Dankworth), O.B.E.; British singer; b. 28 Oct. 1927, Southall, Middx.; m. 1st George Langridge 1947 (dissolved 1957), one s.; m. 2nd John Philip William Dankworth (q.v.) 1958, one s. one d.; joined Dankworth Orchestra 1953; lead in Seven Deadly Sins, Edinburgh Festival and Sadler's Wells 1961; acting roles in Edinburgh Festival 1966, 1967; many appearances with symphony orchestras performing Façade (Walton) and other compositions; Julie in Show Boat, Adelphi Theatre 1971; title role in Colette, Comedy Theatre 1980; Desiree in A Little Night Music, Mich. Opera House, U.S.A. 1983; frequent tours and TV appearances, Europe, Australia and U.S.A.; Melody Maker and New Musical Express Top Girl Singer Awards 1956; Moscow Arts Theatre Award for acting role in Flesh to a Tiger 1958; top place in Int. Critics' Poll of American Jazz magazine Downbeat 1965; Woman of the Year (9th annual Golden Feather Awards) 1973; Edison Award 1974; Variety Club of G.B. Show Business Personality Award (with John Dankworth) 1977; TV Times Viewers' Award for Most Exciting Female Singer on TV 1978; Grammy Award for Best Jazz Vocalist-Female 1982; Best Actress in a Musical (Edwin Drood) 1986, also Tony Award 1986; Theatre World Award for Edwin Drood 1986; Hon. D.Mus. (with John Dankworth, Berklee Coll. of Music, Boston, U.S.A.) 1982. *Leisure interest:* painting. *Address:* International Artistes Representation, Regent House, 235 Regent Street, London, W.1, England. *Telephone:* 01-439 8401.

LAINE, Jermu Tapani; Finnish politician; b. 1931, Turku; Functionary, Ministry of Trade and Industry 1955-65; Lecturer in Commercial Studies, Valkeakoski 1965-69; Rector, Commercial Inst., Mänttä 1969-; municipal positions in Valkeakoski and Mänttä 1968-; Political Sec. to Prime Minister Sorsa 1972-73; Minister for Foreign Trade 1973-75; M.P. 1975-; Minister, Ministry of Finance 1982-83; Minister for Foreign Trade 1983-87; Social Democratic Party; Chair. Supervisory Bd. Valmet Og 1987-88. *Address:* c/o Ministry of Trade and Industry, Aleksanterinkatu 10, 00170 Helsinki 17, Finland.

LAINE, Pekka Ilmari, M.B.A.; Finnish business executive; b. 22 Oct. 1937, Helsinki; s. of Prof. Veikko Laine and Onerva Brusila; m. Helka Parviainen 1961; one s. one d.; Marketing Man., Finnpapier, Helsinki 1963-66, Man. Dir. Finnpapier, Frankfurt 1970-74; Commercial Sec., Finnish Embassy, Warsaw 1966-70; Dir. United Paper Mills Ltd., Paperitoute 1974-79, Dir. Tervasaari Paper Mill 1978-81; Vice-Man. Dir. Asko Oy, Plastic Industry, Lahti 1981-82; Man. Dir. Uponor Oy, Helsinki 1982-83; Man. Dir., Chair. Bd. Tervakoski Oy 1983-86; Man. Dir. Wärtsilä Marine Industries Inc., Helsinki 1986-; mem. Bd. of Industrial Mutual Insurance Co. 1984-. *Leisure interests:* hunting, jogging. *Address:* Wärtsilä Marine Industries Inc., P.O. Box 1090, SF-00101, Helsinki, Finland.

LAING, Gerald Ogilvie-, N.D.D.; British sculptor; b. 11 Feb. 1936, Newcastle upon Tyne; s. of Gerald Francis Laing and Enid Moody Laing née Foster; m. 1st Jenifer Ann Redway 1962 (divorced 1967); m. 2nd Galina Golikova 1969 (divorced 1983); m. 3rd Adaline Havemeyer Frelinghuysen 1988; two s. one d.; ed. Berkhamsted School, Royal Mil. Acad. Sandhurst and St. Martin's School of Art, London; Lieut., Royal Northumberland Fusiliers 1955-60; St. Martin's School of Art 1960-64; resident New York 1964-69; Hybrid, a project with Peter Phillips 1965-66; Artist in Residence, Aspen Inst. for Humanistic Studies, Colo. 1966, Aspen Center for Contemporary Art 1972; Artist in Residence, Tamarind Inst., Albuquerque, N.M. 1973; Visiting Assoc. Prof., Dept. of Art, Univ. of N.M., Albuquerque 1976-77; since 1978 has divided time between London, New York and Scotland; about 30 one-man exhbns. in U.K., U.S.A. and Fed. Repub. of

Germany; many group exhbns. in Europe, U.S.A., Japan and Brazil; works in many public collections including Museum of Modern Art and Whitney Museum, New York, Victoria & Albert Museum and Tate Gallery, London and Scottish Nat. Gallery of Modern Art, Edinburgh; major commissions: Callanish Univ. of Strathclyde, Glasgow 1971, Frieze of the Wise and Foolish Virgins, George St., Edinburgh 1979, Fountain of Sabrina, Broad Quay House, Bristol 1981, Portrait of Siaka Stevens, President of Sierra Leone 1986; Posthumous Portrait of Andy Warhol for Andy Warhol Foundation, N.Y. 1988; Civic Trust Award for restoration of Kinkell Castle 1971. *Publication:* Kinkell: The Reconstruction of a Scottish Castle 1974, 1985. *Leisure interests:* literature, philosophy, religion. *Address:* Kinkell Castle, Ross and Cromarty, Scotland IV7 8AT; 139 East 66th Street, New York, N.Y. 10021, U.S.A. *Telephone:* Dingwall (0349) 61485 (Scotland); (212) 628-5693 (U.S.A.).

LAING, Sir Hector, Kt.; British company executive; b. 12 May 1923, Edinburgh; s. of Hector Laing and Margaret Norris Grant; m. Marian Clare Laurie 1950; three s.; ed. Loretto School, Musselborough, and Jesus Coll., Cambridge; joined McVitie & Price Ltd. as a Dir. 1947, Chair. 1963-64; Dir. of United Biscuits Ltd. 1953, Man. Dir. 1964-; Chair. United Biscuits (Holdings) Ltd. 1972-; Council mem. Inst. of Dirs. 1969-75; mem. Intervention Bd. for Agric. Produce 1972-75; Chair. Food & Drink Industries Council 1977-79; Dir. Court of Bank of England 1973-, Royal Insurance Co. 1970-78, Allied-Lyons 1979-82, Exxon Corpn. (U.S.A.) 1984-; mem. Advisory Council, London Enterprise Agency 1981-; Dr. h.c. (Stirling) 1985, Hon. D. Litt. (Herriot Watt) 1986; Bronze Star (U.S.A.), Hambro Award 1979; Businessman of the Year 1979; Nat. Free Enterprise Award 1980. *Leisure interests:* gardening, walking, flying. *Address:* United Biscuits (UK) Ltd., Grant House, Syon Lane, Isleworth, Middx., TW7 5NN; High Meadows, Windsor Road, Gerrards Cross, Bucks., England. *Telephone:* (0753) 82437.

LAING, Sir (John) Maurice, Kt.; British building and civil engineering contractor (retd.); b. 1 Feb. 1918, Carlisle; s. of Sir John (William) Laing, C.B.E., and Lady Laing; m. Hilda Violet Richards 1940; one s.; ed. St. Lawrence Coll., Ramsgate; served with R.A.F. 1941-45; Dir. Bank of England 1963-80; Chair. Fed. of Civil Eng. Contractors 1959-60, Vice-Pres. 1960-77, Pres. 1977-80; Pres. British Employers' Confed. 1964-65; CBI 1965-66; Chair. Export Group for the Constructional Industries 1957-59, Pres. 1976-79; Hon. Pres. John Laing PLC 1982-87 and fmr. Deputy Chair. Laing Properties PLC; mem. U.K. trade missions to Middle East 1953, to Egypt, Sudan and Ethiopia 1955; mem. Export Credits Guarantees Advisory Council 1959-63, Econ. Planning Bd. 1961, Ministry of Transport Cttee. of Inquiry into major ports of Great Britain (Rochdale Cttee.) 1961-62, NEDC 1962-66; Visiting Fellow, Nuffield Coll. 1965-70; Gov. Admin. Staff Coll. 1966-72, Nat. Inst. of Econ. and Social Research 1964-82; Hon. LL.D. (Strathclyde) 1967; Commodore, Royal Ocean Racing Club 1973-75, Admiral 1976-82; AIMS Award 1980. *Leisure interests:* keen interest in church activities at home and abroad, sailing and swimming. *Address:* Reculver, 63 Totteridge Village, London, N20 8AG, England.

LAING, R(obert) Stanley, B.S.MECH.ENG., M.B.A.; American business executive; b. 1 Nov. 1918, Seattle; s. of Robert Vardy Laing and Marie (Scott) Laing; m. 1st Janet Emmott Orr 1947 (died 1986), one s. four d.; m. 2nd Eva Nofke 1986 (died 1988); m. 3rd Mary Wilshire 1988; ed. Univ. of Washington and Harvard Business School; Nat. Cash Register Co., Dayton, Ohio 1947-72; Special Asst. in Exec. Office 1947-49; Asst. to Comptroller 1949; Gen. Auditor 1950-53; Asst. Comptroller 1953-54; Comptroller 1954-60; Vice-Pres. (Finance) 1960-62, Exec. Vice-Pres. 1962-64, Pres. 1964-72; Dir. and Chair. Business Equipment Mfg. Assn. 1963-64; fmr. Dir. Gen. Mills Inc., Mead Corpn., NCR Corpn., Cincinnati Milacron Inc., B. F. Goodrich Co., Armco Corpn.; Dir. Amdahl Corpn., Sinclair Community Coll. Foundation; Order of Lateran Cross (Vatican). *Address:* 3430 South Dixie, Dayton, Ohio 45439 (Office); 650 W. David Road, Dayton, Ohio 45429, U.S.A. (Home). *Telephone:* 513-298-0884 (Office).

LAING, Ronald David, M.B., CH.B., D.P.M.; British psychiatrist; b. 7 Oct. 1927; s. of D. P. M. and Amelia Laing; ed. Univ. of Glasgow; Glasgow and West of Scotland Neurosurgical Unit 1951; Cen. Army Psychiatric Unit, Netley 1951-52; Psychiatric Unit, Mil. Hosp., Catterick 1952-53; Dept. of Psychological Medicine, Univ. of Glasgow 1953-56; Tavistock Clinic 1956-60; Tavistock Inst. of Human Relations 1960-, Prin. Investigator, Schizophrenia and Family Research Unit 1964-67; Fellow, Foundations Fund for Research in Psychiatry 1960-67; Dir. Langham Clinic for Psychotherapy 1962-65; Fellow, Tavistock Inst. of Medical Psychology 1963-64; Chair. Philadelphia Assen. Ltd. 1964-81. *Publications:* The Divided Self 1960, The Self and Others 1961, co-author Reason and Violence (introduced by J.-P. Sartre) 1964, co-author Sanity, Madness and the Family 1965, co-author Interpersonal Perception 1966, The Politics of Experience and the Bird of Paradise 1967, Knots 1970, The Politics of the Family 1971, The Facts of Life 1976, Do You Love Me? 1976, Conversations with Adam and Natasha 1977, Sonnets 1980, The Voice of Experience 1982, Conversations with Children (Vol. II), Wisdom, Madness and Folly 1985. *Address:* c/o G. Aitken, 29 Fernshaw Road, London, S.W.10, England; Aschauerweg 161, 5363 Going, Austria. *Telephone:* 43-5358-2119 (Home).

LAING, Stanley (see Laing, Robert Stanley).

LAINSON, Prof. Ralph, F.R.S.; British scientist; b. 21 Feb. 1927, Upper Beeding, Sussex; s. of Charles Harry Lainson and Anne Woods; m. 1st Ann Patricia Russell (divorced 1976), one s. two d.; m. 2nd Zéa Constante Lins 1978; ed. Steyning Grammar School, Univ. of London; lecturer in Medical Protozoology London School of Hygiene and Tropical Medicine 1955–59, Attached Investigator, Dept. of Medical Protozoology 1962–65; Officer-in-Charge Dermal Leishmaniasis Unit, Baking-Pot, Cayo Dist., Belize 1959–62; Dir. Wellcome Parasitology Unit, Inst. Evandro Chagas, Fundação Serviços de Saúde Pública, Pará, Brazil 1965–; Chalmers Medal 1971, Manson Medal 1983 Royal Soc. of Tropical Medicine and Hygiene, Oswaldo Cruz Medal, Conselho Estadual de Cultura do Pará (Brazil) 1973; Medalha Comemorativa do 10° Aniversario da Instalação do Conselho Estadual de Saúde do Pará (Brazil) 1983; Hon. Fellow, London School of Hygiene and Tropical Medicine 1982, Hon. Prof. Fed. Univ. of Pará 1982, Hon. mem. British Soc. of Parasitology 1984. *Publications:* author or co-author of approx. 200 articles in scientific journals. *Leisure interests:* fishing, collecting S. American Lepidoptera, music, philately. *Address:* Instituto Evandro Chagas, F.SESP., Avenido Almirante Barroso 492, 66.000 Belém, Pará (Office); Avenida Visconde de Souza Franco 1237 (Edificio 'Visconti'), Apartado 902, 66.000 Belém, Pará, Brazil. *Telephone:* 228-1022 (Office): 223-2382 (Home).

LAIRD, Gavin Harry, C.B.E.; British trade union official; b. 14 March 1933, Scotland; s. of James and Frances Laird; m. Catherine Gillies 1956; one d.; shop stewards' convener, Singer, Clydebank for seven years; Regional Officer, Amalgamated Eng. Union (fmrly. Amalgamated Union of Eng. Workers) 1972–75, Exec. Councillor for Scotland and N.W. England 1975–82, Gen. Sec. (Eng. Section) Oct. 1982–; mem. Exec. Council 1975–; mem. Scottish TUC Gen. Council 1973–75; mem. TUC Gen. Council 1979–82; part-time Dir. Highlands and Islands Devt. Bd. 1974–75; mem. Industrial Devt. Advisory Bd. 1979–; Arts Council 1983–86; part-time Dir. BNOC 1976–86; Chair. The Foundries E.D.C. Oct. 1982–; Dir. Bank of England 1986–; Dir. (non-exec.) Scottish TV PLC 1986–; Dir. (non-Exec.) FS Assurance April 1988–; mem. Council, Strathclyde Business School 1983–; Gov. London Business School 1988–; mem. Editorial Bd. European Business Journal. *Leisure interests:* reading, hill-climbing. *Address:* 35 Southlands Grove, Bromley, BR1 2DA, England.

LAIRD, Melvin Robert; American government official; b. 1 Sept. 1922, Omaha, Neb.; s. of Melvin and Helen (Connor) Laird; m. Barbara Masters 1945; two s. one d.; ed. Carleton Coll., Northfield, Minn; served in U.S. Navy in Pacific, Second World War; mem. Wisconsin Senate 1946–52, Chair. Wisconsin Legis. Council; mem. U.S. House of Reps. 1952–69, served on Appropriations Cttee., Chair. House of Republican Minority, mem. Coordinating Cttee., Vice-Chair. Republican Nat. Platform Council 1960, Chair. 1964; U.S. Sec. of Defense 1969–73; Counsellor to Pres. for Domestic Affairs 1973–74; Senior Counsellor for Nat. and Int. Affairs, Readers' Digest Assen. 1974–; mem. Bd. the Kennedy Center, George Washington Univ., Airlie Foundation, Nat. Defence and Energy Projects of American Enterprise Inst., Thomas Jefferson Center Foundation of Univ. of Virginia, World Rehabilitation Fund; Dir. Metropolitan Life Insurance Co., Northwest Airlines, Phillips Petroleum Co., Communications Satellite Corpn., Martin Marietta Corpn., Science Application Int. Corpn., Public Oversight Bd.; over 200 awards and hon. degrees, including Albert Lasker Medical Award, Statesman in Medicine Award (Airlie Foundation), The Harry S. Truman Award for distinguished service in defense; Presidential Medal of Freedom (U.S.A.), Order of Merit (1st Class) (Fed. Repub. of Germany), Commdr. Légion d'honneur (France); Republican. *Publications include:* A House Divided: America's Strategy Gap 1962, The Conservative Papers (Ed.) 1964, Republican Papers (Ed.) 1968. *Address:* Suite 212, 1730 Rhode Island Avenue, N.W., Washington D.C. 20036, U.S.A. (Office).

LAISTER, Peter, B.SC.TECH., A.M.C.T., F.INST.PET., F.INST.CHEM.ENG., C.ENG.; British business executive; b. 24 Jan. 1929, Birmingham; s. of late Horace Laister and Mrs I. L. Bates; m. 1st Barbara Cooke 1951, one s. one d.; m. 2nd Eileen A. Goodchild (née Town) 1958, one d.; ed. King Edward's School, Birmingham and Manchester Univ.; with Esso Petroleum Co. 1951–66; with British Oxygen Co. (now BOC Int.) 1966–75, Group Man. Dir. 1969–75, Chair. BOC Financial Corpn. (U.S.A.) 1974–75; Group Man. Dir. Ellerman Lines Ltd. 1976–79; Chair. Tollemache and Cobbold Breweries 1977–79, London and Hull Insurance 1976–79; Group Man. Dir. Thorn Electrical Industries (later Thorn EMI PLC) 1979–85, Chair. 1984–85; Gov. BUPA 1982–; non-exec. Dir. BMCL 1976–, Chair. 1984–; Dir. (non-exec.) Inchcape PLC 1982–, Fluor GB PLC 1985–: A. and P. Appledore 1986–; Dir. British Printing and Communications Corpn. (BPCC) PLC 1985–, Mirror Group Newspapers Ltd. 1985–, SelecTV 1987–; Chair. Park Hotels PLC 1985–, Premiere PLC 1985–, Oceonics PLC 1986–88, Tower Group 1985–, Contec PLC 1986–; mem. Council, Industrial Soc. 1971–86; mem. Industrial Devt. Advisory Bd. 1981–83, Univ. Coll. Council 1978–, B.I.M. Exec. Bd. 1983; Companion B.I.M.; Hon. Fellow UMIST; Chair. Foundation for Age Research 1982–. *Leisure interests:* private flying, boating and angling, gardening, photography. *Address:* Thatches, 92 Staines Road, Wraybury, Middx., England.

LAITHWAITE, Prof. Eric Roberts, D.SC., PH.D.; British scientist; b. 14 June 1921, Atherton, Lancs.; s. of Herbert and Florence (née Roberts) Laithwaite; m. Sheila Margaret Gooddie 1951; two s. two d.; ed. Kirkham Grammar School, Regent Street Polytechnic, Victoria Univ. of Manchester; served in R.A.F. 1941–46; Asst. Lecturer, Univ. of Manchester 1950–53, Lecturer 1953–57, Sr. Lecturer 1957–64; Prof. of Heavy Electrical Eng., Imperial Coll. of Science and Tech., London 1964–86, Emer. Prof. 1986–; Prof., Royal Inst. 1967–76; developer of the linear motor; Pres. Assen. for Science Educ. 1970; S. G. Brown Award and Medal (Royal Soc.) 1966; Nikola Tesla Award (Inst. of Electrical and Electronics Engineers) 1986. *Publications:* Propulsion without Wheels 1966, Induction Machines for Special Purposes 1966, The Engineer in Wonderland 1967, Linear Electric Motors 1971, Exciting Electrical Machines 1974, The Dictionary of Butterflies and Moths 1975, How to Invent (with M. W. Thring) 1977, Engineer through the Looking-Glass, Electric Energy (with L. L. Freris) 1980, Invitation to Engineering 1984, A History of Linear Electric Motors 1987, numerous papers and articles in learned journals. *Leisure interest:* entomology. *Address:* Department of Electrical Engineering, Imperial College, London, SW7 2BT, England. *Telephone:* 01-589 5111.

LAJOINIE, André; French politician; b. 26 Dec. 1929, Chasteaux, Corrèze; s. of Joseph Lajoinie and Maria Jauberty; m. Paulette Rouffiange 1960; one s.; mem. French Communist Party (PCF) 1948–, mem. Cen. Cttee. 1972–, mem. Politburo 1976–, in charge of agric. section 1976–; Dir. La Terre (weekly paper) 1977–; Deputy to Nat. Ass. 1978–; Pres. Communist group in Nat. Ass. 1981–. *Address:* Assemblée nationale, 75355 Paris, France.

LAJOUS MARTÍNEZ, Adrián, LL.B.; Mexican export official and international negotiator; b. 25 Jan. 1920, Buenos Aires, Argentina; s. of Adrian Lajous Nelson and Evangelina Martínez de Lajous; m. Luz Vargas de Lajous 1943; four c.; ed. Univ. of Mexico and New York Univ; Officer, private radio stations and networks 1941–49, Vice-Chair. Board, Nucleo Radio Mil. group of radio stations 1949; Gen. Counsel and Head of Credit Dept., Patronato del Ahorro Nacional 1950–52; Officer Banco Nacional de Comercio Exterior 1953–58; Dir.-Gen. Federación Interamericana del Algodón 1959–63; Minister-Counsellor, Mexican Embassy, Washington, D.C. 1956, Commercial Counsellor, London 1964; Export Man. Unión Nacional de Productores de Azúcar 1965–67; Mexican Rep. Int. Coffee negotiations 1962–67; Dir. Banco Nacional de Comercio Exterior 1976–79, Dir.-Gen. 1979–82; Chair. Board, Int. Sugar Org. 1969–; Exec. Dir. World Bank 1970–72; Dir.-Gen. Fondo de Equipamiento Industrial 1973–76; Dir.-Gen. Instituto Mexicano de Comercio Exterior 1976–79; Editorial newspaper columnist 1983–; Chair. Bd., Fundación Mexicana para la Planeación Familiar 1984–. *Leisure interest:* bridge. *Address:* Guadalquivir 68, México 5, D.F., Z.C. 065D Mexico. *Telephone:* 514-98-58.

LAKAS BAHAS, Ing. Demetrio Basilio; Panamanian administrator and politician; b. 29 Aug. 1925, Colón; s. of Basilio Demetrio Lakas and Zaharo Bahas de Lakas; m. Elizabeth Fannia Roger de Lakas 1959; two s. one d.; ed. Texas Wesleyan Coll. and Texas Technical Coll.; fmr. Dir. of Social Security; Pres. of Provisional Govt. Council 1969–72; Pres. of Panama 1972–78. *Leisure interests:* sailing, fishing. *Address:* c/o Palacio de las Garzas, Panama City, Panama.

LAKER, Sir Frederick Alfred, Kt.; British business executive; b. 6 Aug. 1922; m. 4th Jacqueline Harvey; ed. Simon Langton School, Canterbury; worked for Short Bros., Rochester 1938–40; Gen. Aircraft 1940–41; served with Air Transport Auxiliary 1941–46; with Aviation Traders 1946–60; British United Airways 1960–65; Chair. and Man. Dir. Laker Airways Ltd 1966–82; Dir. Skytrain Holidays 1982–83, Sir Freddie Laker Ltd. 1982–, Northeastern Int. Airlines Inc. (U.S.A.) 1984–; mem. Jockey Club 1979–; Chair. Guild of Air Pilots and Navigators Benevolent Fund; Hon. D.Sc. (City Univ.) 1979, (Cranfield Inst. of Tech.) 1980, Hon. LL.D. (Victoria Univ. of Manchester) 1981; Hon. Fellow (U.M.I.S.T.) 1978. *Address:* Furze Grove Farm, Chailey, East Sussex, England.

LAKING, Sir George (Robert), K.C.M.G., LL.B.; New Zealand diplomatist and public official; b. 15 Oct. 1912, Auckland; s. of Robert and Alice (née Wilding) Laking; m. Pat Hogg 1940; one s. one d.; ed. Auckland Grammar School, and Auckland and Victoria Univs.; Prime Minister's and External Affairs Depts. 1940–49; Counsellor, New Zealand Embassy, Washington 1949–54, Minister 1954–56; Deputy Sec. of External Affairs, Wellington 1956–58; Acting High Commr. for New Zealand in London 1958–61; Amb. to EEC 1960–61, to U.S.A. 1961–67; Perm. Head of Prime Minister's Dept. and Sec. of Foreign Affairs 1967–72; Parl. Commr. (Ombudsman) 1975–77, Chief Ombudsman 1977–84; Privacy Commr. 1977–78; mem. Human Rights Comm. 1978–84; Pres. Inst. of Int. Affairs; mem. Public and Admin. Law Reform Cttee. 1980–85; Chair. Legislation Advisory Cttee. 1986–; mem. Int. Council, Asia Soc. of New York. *Address:* 3 Wesley Road, Wellington, New Zealand. *Telephone:* 722-717 (Office); 728-454 (Home).

LAL, Bansi, LL.B.; Indian politician; b. 26 Aug. 1927, Golagarh, Bhiwani District; s. of Chaudhary Mohar Singh; m. Smt. Vidya Devi; two s. four d.; ed. Punjab Univ. and Law Coll., Jullundur; agriculturalist and advocate; started practice at Bhiwani 1956; took part in Praja Mandal Movement, Loharu State; Sec. Loharu Praja Mandal 1943–44; Gen. Sec. Tosham Mandal Congress Cttee. 1955; Pres. Mandal Congress Cttee., Kural 1959–60; mem. Punjab PCC 1959–62, Rajya Sabha 1960–66, Haryana Assembly 1967; Chief Minister Haryana 1968–75; Minister without portfolio, Govt.

of India Dec. 1975, Minister of Defence 1975–77; Minister of Railways 1985–86; Minister of Transport (Railways, Shipping, Transport and Civil Aviation) 1985–86; arrested on charges of corruption, expelled from Indian Nat. Congress April 1977, conduct during Emergency subject to Comm. of Enquiry July 1977; Hon. LL.D. (Kurukshetra Univ., Haryana) 1972, Hon. D.Sc. (Haryana Agric. Univ.) 1972. *Leisure interest:* reading. *Address:* Hansi Road, Bhiwani, Haryana State, India.

LAL, Bipen Behari, M.SC.; Indian fmr. state governor; b. 30 Jan. 1917, Allahabad, Uttar Pradesh; s. of Mr. and Mrs. Kishan Chand; m. Saroj Lal 1943; one s. one d.; ed. St. Stephens Coll. Delhi, Allahabad Univ., Harvard Univ.; Indian Civil Service 1941; magistrate successively in Gorakhpur, Varanasi and district of Hardoi and Dehra Dun 1942–51; successively Joint Sec. for Finance, Sec. for Finance, Commr. and Sec. for Irrigation and Power Govt. of Uttar Pradesh (U.P.); Chair. U.P. State Electricity Board; mem. U.P. Univs. Comm. and U.P. Pay Rationalization Comm.; Fellow, Harvard Univ. 1951–66; Chief Sec. Govt. of U.P. 1967–69; Addition Sec. Ministry of Finance, Govt. of India 1969–70, Sec. Dept. of Personnel 1970–71, Sec. Ministry of Industrial Devt. 1971–73, Sec. Ministry of Commerce 1973; Adviser to Gov. of U.P. 1973; Sec. of Planning Comm., Govt. of India 1973–74; Chief Exec. of Sikkim 1974–75, Gov. of Sikkim 1975–80. *Leisure interests:* reading, photography. *Address:* c/o Raj Bhavan, Gangtok-737 101, Sikkim, India. *Telephone:* 450 (Home).

LAL, Devendra, M.SC., PH.D., F.R.S.; Indian scientist; b. 14 Feb. 1929, Varanasi (Banaras); s. of the late Dr. Radhekrishna Lal; m. Aruna Damany 1955; ed. Harish Chandra High School, Banaras Hindu Univ., Varanasi, and Bombay Univ.; Assoc. Prof. Tata Inst. of Fundamental Research 1960–63, Prof. 1963–70, Sr. Prof. 1970–72, Visiting Prof., Univ. of Calif. 1965–66; Prof., Scripps Inst. of Oceanography, Univ. of Calif. 1967–; Dir. Physical Research Lab., Navrangpura 1972–83, Sr. Prof. 1983–89; Chair. working group on River Inputs to Ocean System 1977–81; Vice-Pres. Indian Acad. of Sciences, Bangalore 1978–82; Pres. Int. Asscn. for Physical Sciences of the Ocean 1979–82, Int. Union of Geodesy and Geophysics 1983–87, Indian Geophysical Union 1980–82; Foreign Sec. Indian Nat. Science Acad., New Delhi 1981–84; mem. Scientific Advisory Cttee. to the Cabinet 1979–83; mem. Joint Scientific Cttee. of WMO 1979–83; mem. Group of Experts on Scientific Aspects of Marine Pollution, UNESCO, Paris 1979–81; Foreign Assoc., N.A.S. (U.S.A.); Fellow, Indian Acad. of Sciences, Bangalore, Indian Nat. Science Acad., New Delhi, Centre of the Earth Sciences Studies, Cochin 1983; Founding mem. Third World Acad. of Sciences, Italy 1983; Assoc. Royal Astronomical Soc. 1984; mem. Int. Acad. of Astronautics 1985; Hon. D.Sc. (Banaras Univ., Varanasi) 1981; Krishnan Medal for Geochemistry and Geophysics 1965; Shanti Swarup Bhatnagar Award for Physical Sciences, Council of Scientific and Industrial Research 1967; Repub. Day Nat. Award, Padma Shri 1971; Fed. of Indian Chambers of Commerce and Industry Award in Science and Tech. 1974, Jawaharlal Nehru Award for Science 1986. *Publications:* over 200 articles in scientific journals; Early Solar System Processes and the Present Solar System (Ed.). *Leisure interests:* photography, painting, mathematical puzzles, chess. *Address:* Scripps Institution of Oceanography, GRD/A-020, University of California, San Diego, La Jolla, Calif. 92093, U.S.A. (Office); No. 20, Jayantilal Park, Amli Bopal Road, Village Makarba, Ahmedabad 380054, India (Home). *Telephone:* 619-534-2134 (Office); 401451 (Home).

LALBHAI, Arvind N., B.SC.; Indian industrialist; b. 3 April 1918, Ahmedabad; s. of Narottam Lalbhai and Sulochnaben Lalbhai; ed. Bombay Univ.; Head of Lalbhai Group in India; Chair. and Man. Dir. Arvind Mills Ltd., Ahmedabad; Chair. Anil Starch Products Ltd., Ahmedabad, Sussen Textiles Bearings Ltd., Baroda, Lalbhai Exports Ltd., Ahmedabad, Indo-Pharma Pharmaceuticals Works Ltd., Bombay, Gujarat High Tech Industries Ltd., Anup Eng. Ltd., Ahmedabad; Dir. Tata Chemicals Ltd., Grasim Industries Ltd., VXL India Ltd., J.K. Industries Ltd., Sirpur Paper Mills Ltd., etc.; fmr. Dir. State Bank of India; Past Pres. Fed. of Indian Chambers of Commerce 1981–82, Indian Cotton Mills' Fed. 1982–83, 1983–84, Gujarat Chamber of Commerce and Industry 1969, Ahmedabad Textile Mills' Asscn.; Pres. Sankat Nivaran Samiti, Gujarat, Nat. Asscn. for the Blind, Bombay; mem. Man. Cttee. several public and professional bodies, and hon. mem. of others. *Leisure interests:* travel, swimming. *Address:* Shalimar, Shahibag, Ahmedabad 380 004, India. *Telephone:* 374002 (Office); 66259 (Home).

LALIVE d'EPINAY, Jean-Flavien, M.A., LL.D. (brother of Pierre Lalive d'Epinay, q.v.); Swiss lawyer; b. 1 May 1915, La Chaux-de-Fonds; s. of Auguste Lalive and Mme. Lalive (née Nobs); m. Elisabeth Dusendschoen 1942; ed. Univ. of Geneva, Harvard and Columbia Univs.; attorney, Geneva 1941–46; Sec. of Bd., then Sec.-Gen. Jt. Relief Comm. IRC, Geneva 1947–53; First Sec. Int. Court of Justice, The Hague 1953–58; Gen. Counsel, UNRWA, Beirut 1958–61; Sec.-Gen. Int. Comm. of Jurists, Geneva; has taught at Acad. of Int. Law, The Hague, Acad. of American and Int. Law, Dallas, Tex.; mem. Inst. of Int. Law; now Sr. Partner, Lalive, Budin & Partners (attorneys-at-law), Geneva. *Publications:* Le droit de la neutralité et le problème des crédits consentis par les neutres aux belligérants 1942, Immunité de juridiction des Etats et des organisations internationales 1953, Contrats entre Etats et personnes privées 1983, other books and numerous articles on int. and comparative law in legal periodicals. *Address:* 20 rue Sénebier, Geneva, Switzerland (Office). *Telephone:* 29 46 66 (Office); 50 15 75 (Home).

LALIVE d'EPINAY, Pierre, B.A., PH.D. (brother of Jean-Flavien Lalive d'Epinay, q.v.); Swiss lawyer; b. 8 Oct. 1923, Chaux-de-Fonds; s. of Auguste Lalive and Mme. Lalive; m. Michèle-Hélène Villard 1957; ed. Geneva and Cambridge Univs.; Geneva Bar; Prof. of Law, Geneva Univ. 1955–, Dir. Dept. of Pvt. Law, Dean of Law School 1967–69; Prof. of Int. Business Law, Graduate Inst. of Int. Studies 1962–86, Hon. Prof. 1986–; Sr. Partner Lalive, Budin and Partners; Pres. ICC Inst. of Int. Business Law and Practice, Swiss Arbitration Asscn.; Visiting Prof. Columbia, Brussels and Cambridge Univs.; mem. Inst. of Int. Law, numerous Swiss Federal Comms. and dels.; D.Jur. h.c. (Lyon, Paris). *Publications:* more than 100 publs. on int. law (public, pvt.), arbitration, contracts and family law. *Address:* Senebier 20, Geneva (Office); Ermitage 47, Chene-Bougeries, Geneva, Switzerland (Home). *Telephone:* 29-46-66 (Office); 49-32-32 (Home).

LALL, Arthur Samuel, M.A.; Indian teacher and diplomatist (U.S. Citizen 1978–); b. 14 July 1911, Lahore; s. of Parmanand and Zoe (Lewis) Lall; m. Betty Goetz 1963; one d.; ed. Punjab and Oxford Univs.; Apptd. to Indian Civil Service and served in the Punjab and with central Govt.; Commercial Counsellor, High Comm., London 1947–51; Consul-Gen., with rank of Minister, New York 1951–54; Perm. Rep. to UN 1954–59; Chair. UN Mission to Samoa 1959; Amb. to Austria 1959–63; Lecturer, Cornell Univ. 1963–; Prof. of Int. Relations, Columbia Univ., New York 1965–75; Chair. Common Heritage Int.; Consultant, UN Inst. for Training and Research, New York; Del. to UN Econ. and Social Council and Trusteeship Council; Del. to numerous econ. confs. *Publications:* Modern International Negotiation 1966, How Communist China Negotiates 1968, The UN and the Middle East Crisis 1969, The Security Council in a Universal United Nations 1971, The Emergence of Modern India 1980, Multilateral Negotiation and Mediation 1985; numerous articles on int. affairs; short stories. *Leisure interest:* writing novels (two novels published). *Address:* 230 East 81st Street, New York, N.Y. 10028, U.S.A.

LALLA AICHA, H.R.H. Princess; Moroccan diplomatist; eldest daughter of the late King Mohammed V.; Amb. to U.K. 1965–69, to Italy 1969–73 (also accred. to Greece); Pres. Moroccan Red Crescent; Grand Cordon of Order of the Throne. *Address:* c/o Ministry of Foreign Affairs, Rabat, Morocco.

LALLEMENT, Jacques Georges Paulin, D. ÉS L.; French financial official; b. 21 Feb. 1922, Cloyes-sur-Marne; s. of Marcel Lallement and Georgette (née Janson); m. Aliette Lemarchand 1947; two s. one d.; ed. Inst. Saint-Etienne, Châlons-sur-Marne, Lycée Louis-le-Grand, Paris, and Ecole Nat. de la France d'Outre-Mer; Mission Chief, Financial Admin., French West Africa; Exec. Sec. for Econ. Affairs and Planning, Ministry of French Overseas Territories 1949–54; Departmental Dir. High Commr. of French Repub. in Pacific, Nouméa 1954–55; Attaché, departmental staff, Ministry of French Overseas Territories 1956, Tech. Adviser 1957–58; Insp. of Finances 1958, Insp.-Gen. 1976–; Sec.-Gen. Bureau of Geological Research and Mining 1958–62; Dir. Loan Policy, then Deputy Dir.-Gen. Caisse Nationale de Crédit Agricole 1965–72, C.E.O. 1975–81; C.E.O. Inst. de Développement Industriel 1972–75, later Pres., mem. Bd. 1975–84; Pres. Comm. on Agric. for 7th Nat. Plan 1975–78; Pres. Fed. French Insurance Cos. 1981–; Pres. Financial Comm. 1982–86, Econ. Comm. 1986; Exec. Vice-Pres. Conseil Nat. du Patronat Français; Chair. Bd. Société Financière pour l'Expansion des Télécommunications (FINEXTEL) 1982–; mem. Conseil nat. d'assurances 1981–; mem. Bd. Louis Dreyfus Bank 1982–, SCOA 1982–; mem. French Solar Energy Comm., Improvement Council of Ecole Supérieure des Mines de Paris; City Councillor, Cloyes-sur-Marne; Officier, Légion d'honneur, Commdr. Ordre nat. du Mérite, Commdr. Ordre nat. du Mérite agricole. *Leisure interests:* hunting, golf. *Address:* Fédération Française des Sociétés d'Assurances, 26 boulevard Haussmann, 75009 Paris (Office); 15 rue Raynouard, 75016 Paris, France (Home).

LALONDE, Brice; French politician; b. 10 Feb. 1946, Neuilly; s. of Alain Lalonde and Fiona Forbes; m. Patricia Raynaud 1986; one s. three d.; student leader 1968; Chair. Friends of the Earth 1972, French Branch 1978; Candidate for the Green Party, French Pres. Election 1981; Admin. European Environment Bureau 1983; Dir. Paris Office Inst. for European Environmental Policy 1987; Sec. of State for the Environment 1988–. *Address:* Ministry of the Environment, 45 Avenue Georges-Mandel, 75016 Paris, France (Office). *Telephone:* (1) 46 47 38 24.

LALONDE, Marc, Q.C., P.C., M.P., LL.L., M.A.; Canadian lawyer and fmr. politician; b. 26 July 1929, Ile Perrot; s. of J. Albert and Nora (St. Aubin) Lalonde; m. Claire Tétreau 1955; two s. two d.; ed. St. Laurent Coll., Montreal and Univs. of Montreal, Ottawa and Oxford; called to the Bar, Quebec 1955; Prof. of Commercial Law and Econs., Univ. of Montreal 1957–59; mem. Bd. of Dirs. Inst. of Public Law, Univ. of Montreal 1960–64; mem. Cttee. on Broadcasting 1964; Special Asst. to Minister of Justice, Ottawa 1959–60; Partner, Gélinas, Bourque, Lalonde & Benoit, Montreal 1960–68; Policy Adviser to Prime Minister 1967, Prin. Sec. to Prime Minister 1968–72; mem. Parl. 1972–84; Minister of Nat. Health and Welfare 1972–77, responsible for the Status of Women 1975–78, for Federal-Provincial Relations 1977–78, of Justice and Attorney-Gen. of Canada 1978–79, of Energy, Mines and Resources 1980–82, of Finance 1982–84; Chair. Hotel-Dieu de Montréal 1985–; Dir. Steinberg Inc. 1984–, Citibank Canada, Coronet Carpets Inc.; partner, Stikeman Elliott 1984–; Counsel before several Royal Comms., including Royal Comm. on Great Lakes Shipping;

Liberal. *Publication:* The Changing Role of the Prime Minister's Office 1971. *Leisure interests:* jogging, tennis, skiing, swimming, reading. *Address:* 5440 Légaré, Outremont, Que. H3T 1Z4, Canada (Home).

LALOR, Patrick Joseph; Irish politician; b. 21 July 1926, Dublin; s. of Joseph and Frances Lalor; m. Myra Murphy 1952; one s. three d.; ed. in Abbeyleix and Knockbeg Coll., Carlow; fmr. mem. Laois County Council and fmr. exec. mem. Retail Grocery, Dairy and Allied Trades Asscn. (RGDATA); mem. Dáil Eireann Oct. 1961–81; Parl. Sec. to Minister of Agric. and Fisheries 1965–66, to Minister for Transport, Power, Posts and Telegraphs 1966–69; Minister of Posts and Telegraphs 1969–70, for Industry and Commerce 1970–73; mem. Fianna Fáil, Chief Whip Parl. Party 1973–77; Parl. Sec. to the Taoiseach (Prime Minister) and to Minister of Defence Jan.-Dec. 1977, Minister of State at Depts. of the Taoiseach and of Defence 1979 (resgnd.); mem. of European Parl. 1979–, Leader of Fianna Fail Party in European Parl. 1979–, Vice-Pres. Group of European Progressive Democrats 1979–84; Quaestor 1979–82; Vice-Pres. of European Parl. 1982–; Vice-Pres. European Democratic Alliance Group 1984–86, European Renewal and Democratic Alliance Group 1986–; Grand Officier du Ouissam Alaouite (Morocco) 1981. *Leisure interests:* hurling, Gaelic football, golf, drama. *Address:* Main Street, Abbeyleix, Portlaoise, Co. Laois, Ireland. *Telephone:* 0502-31206.

LALOY, Jean Léonard, L. ÈS. L., DIPL.; French diplomatist and academic (retd.); b. 1 April 1912, Meudon; s. of late Louis Laloy and Susanik (Babaïan) Laloy; m. Karen Gjestland 1937; four s. three d.; ed. Université de Paris (Sorbonne); Attaché, Tallinn, Estonia 1937, Moscow 1940; Embassy Sec., Geneva 1943, Paris (Ministry of Foreign Affairs) 1945, Berlin, Frankfurt, Bonn 1947; Minister Plenipotentiary, Paris 1949, Dir. European Affairs 1956, Dir.-Gen. Cultural Relations 1974–78; Prof. Institut d'études politiques, Paris 1950–81, Ecole nationale d'admin. 1952–72; mem. Inst. de France (Académie des sciences morales et politiques, 1975; Commdr., Légion d'honneur, Grand-Officier, Ordre nat. du Mérite; Hon. K.C.M.G. *Publications:* Entre guerres et paix 1966, Le socialisme de Lenine 1967, Yalta–hier, aujourd'hui, demain 1988. *Address:* 25 rue Ernest Renan, Bellevue, 92190 Meudon; Rahon, 39120 Chaussin, France. *Telephone:* 1.45.34.22.92.

LALUMIÈRE, Catherine; French politician; b. 3 Aug. 1936, Rennes; specialist in public law; lecturer, Univ. of Paris; mem. Steering Cttee., Parti Socialiste 1979–; mem. Nat. Ass. for Gironde 1986–; Adviser to Pres. on civil service; Sec. of State for the Civil Service and Admin. Reforms May-June 1981, Minister for Consumer Affairs 1981–83, Sec. of State 1983–84, Minster for European Affairs 1984–86. *Address:* c/o Assemblée Nationale, 126 rue de l'Université, 75355 Paris; 37 Quai d'Orsay, 75700 Paris, France.

LAMA, Luciano, DOTT. IN SC. POL.; Italian trades union official; b. 14 Oct. 1921, Gambettola (Forli); s. of Domenico and Paganelli Noerri; m. Lora Bosi 1947; two d.; ed. Istituto Cesare Alfieri, Florence; Vice-Sec. Confederazione Generale Italiana del Lavoro (CGIL) 1947; Sec. Fed. of Chemical Workers 1951; Sec.-Gen. Fed. of Metal Workers (FIOM) 1957; Sec. Gen. Union of Italian Workers (CGIL) 1961, Sec.-Gen. 1970–85. *Address:* Confederazione Generale Italiana del Lavoro, Corso d'Italia 25, 00198 Rome, Italy.

LAMB, Denis; American diplomatist; b. 6 Sept. 1937, Cleveland, Ohio; m. Helen Turner 1960; one s.; ed. Columbia Univ., M.I.T.; pvt. business 1959–64; Vice-Consul, Foreign Service, Fort-de-France, Martinique 1965–66; Admin. Adviser, Mission to OECD, Paris 1966–69; Systems Analyst and Computer Systems Man. 1970–74; Science and Tech. Officer, OECD Desk Officer and Deputy Dir., Political-Econ. Office, Bureau of European Affairs 1974–77; Exec. Asst. to Deputy Sec. of State 1977–78; Deputy Chief of Mission to the EEC, Brussels 1978–82; Deputy Asst. Sec., Trade and Commercial Affairs 1982–86; Prin. Deputy Asst. Sec. in Bureau of Econ. and Business Affairs 1986–87; Perm. Rep. to OECD, Paris 1987–. *Address:* 19 Rue de Franqueville, 75016 Paris, France. *Telephone:* (331) 4524-7414.

LAMB, Willis Eugene, Jr., PH.D., SC.D., L.H.D.; American physicist; b. 12 July 1913, Los Angeles, Calif.; m. Karen Schaefer 1939; ed. Univ. of California; Instructor, Columbia Univ. 1938, Prof. of Physics 1948–52; Loeb Lecturer, Harvard 1953–54; Prof. of Physics, Stanford Univ. 1951–56; Wykeham Prof. of Physics and Fellow, New Coll., Univ. of Oxford 1956–62; Henry Ford II Prof. of Physics, Yale Univ. 1962–72, J. Willard Gibbs Prof. of Physics, Yale Univ. 1972–74; Prof. of Physics and Optical Sciences, Univ. of Arizona 1974–; mem. N.A.S.; Hon. Fellow, Royal Soc. Edinburgh; awarded Rumford Premium (American Acad. of Arts and Sciences) 1953; Hon. Sc.D. (Pennsylvania) 1953, Hon. L.H.D. (Yeshiva) 1964, Hon. Sc.D. (Gustavus Adolphus Coll.) 1975; Nobel Prize in Physics (shared with Prof. P. Kusch q.v.) 1955; Research Corpn. Award 1955; Guggenheim Fellow 1960. *Address:* Department of Physics, University of Arizona, Tucson, Ariz. 85721, U.S.A.

LAMBECK, Kurt, F.A.A., D. PHIL.; Australian professor of geophysics; b. 20 Sept. 1941, Loosdrecht, The Netherlands; s. of J. Lambeck and J. Weber; m. Bridget Marguerite Nicholls 1967; one s. one d.; ed. Univ. of N.S.W., Tech. Univ. of Delft, Tech. Univ. of Athens and Oxford Univ.; Geodesist, Smithsonian Astrophysical Observatory 1967–70; Dir. of Research, Paris Observatory 1970–73; Prof. of Geophysics, Univ. of Paris 1973–77, A.N.U. 1977–, Dir. Research School of Earth Sciences 1984–; Harold Jeffreys Lecturer Royal Astronomical Soc. 1989; Fellow American Union of Geophysics 1976; Hon. mem. European Geophysics Soc. 1988–; Macelwane Award, American Union of Geophysics 1976. *Publications:* The Earth's Variable Rotation 1980, Geophysical Geodesy 1988, numerous papers on geodesy and geophysics. *Address:* Research School of Earth Sciences, Australian National University, GPO Box 4, Canberra, A.C.T. 2601; 31 Brand Street, Hughes, A.C.T. 2605, Australia. *Telephone:* (062) 492487.

LAMBERT, Allen Thomas, O.C.; Canadian banker, b. 28 Dec. 1911, Regina, Sask.; s. of Willison A. and Sarah (Barber) Lambert; m.; one s. one d.; ed. Victoria Public and High Schools; joined Toronto Dominion Bank 1927; Supervisor, Head Office, Toronto 1949; Asst. Man., Montreal 1950; Supt. Head Office 1953, Asst. Gen. Man. 1953, Gen. Man. 1956, Vice-Pres. and Dir. 1956–, Pres. 1960–72, Chair. 1961–78, C.E.O. Toronto Dominion Bank 1972–78; Chair. Royal Comm. on Financial Man. and Accountability; Chair. and Dir. Trilon Financial Corpn.; Dir. of numerous cos. including Placer Dome Inc., Hudson Bay Mining and Smelting Co. Ltd. (Chair. 1983–), Lonvest Corpn., Raritan River Steel Co., Rolls-Royce Industries Canada Inc., Western Int. Communications Ltd., Royal Trustco Ltd., Inspiration Resources Inc., Dome Petroleum 1983–, Brascan Inc., Falconbridge Ltd. *Leisure interests:* golf, curling, fishing. *Address:* c/o The Toronto-Dominion Bank, P.O. Box 1, Toronto-Dominion Centre, Toronto M5K 1A2, Ont., Canada.

LAMBERT, Henry Uvedale Antrobus, M.A.; British banker; b. 9 Oct. 1925, London; s. of the late R. U. Lambert and M. F. Lambert; m. Diana Dumbell 1951; two s. one d.; ed. Winchester Coll., New Coll., Oxford; served R.N., war of 1939–45; with Barclays Bank Ltd. (now Barclays Bank PLC) 1948–, local Dir. Lombard Street 1957–59, Southampton 1959–69, Birmingham 1969–72, Vice-Chair. Barclays Bank Int. Ltd. 1972–79, Chair. 1979–83, Deputy Chair. Barclays Bank PLC 1979–85, Dir. 1966–; Deputy Chair. Agricultural Mortgage Corpn. PLC 1977–85, Chair. 1985–; Vice-Chair. Sun Alliance and London Insurance Group 1978–83, Deputy Chair. 1983–85, Chair. 1985–; Dir. British Airways 1985–; Fellow, Winchester Coll. *Leisure interests:* fishing, gardening, golf, naval history. *Address:* c/o Agricultural Mortgage Corporation PLC, AMC House, 27 Camperdown Street, London, E1 8DZ, England.

LAMBERT, Yves Maurice; French engineer and international official; b. 4 June 1936, Nancy, Meurthe-et-Moselle; s. of André Arthur Lambert and Paulette Franck; m. Odile Revillon 1959; three s. two d.; ed. Ecole Polytechnique, Paris, Nat. Civil Aviation School, Centre de Préparation à l'Admin. des Entreprises; Dir. Org. de Gestion et de Sécurité de l'Algérie (OGSA), Algeria 1965–68; Tech. Adviser to Minister of Transport, France 1969–72; Rep. of France to ICAO Council 1972–76; Sec.-Gen. ICAO Aug. 1976–; Chevalier, Ordre nat. du Mérite. *Address:* International Civil Aviation Organization, 1000 Sherbrooke Street West, Montreal, P.Q., H3A 2R2 (Office); 3216 The Boulevard, Westmount, P.Q., Canada (Home). *Telephone:* 285-8041/2 (Office).

LAMBO, (Thomas) Adeoye, O.B.E., M.B., CH.B., M.D., F.R.C.P., D.P.M.; Nigerian neuro-psychiatrist; b. 29 March 1923, Abeokuta; s. of the late Chief David Basil Lambo and Felicia Lambo; m. Dinah V. Adams 1945; three s. ed. Baptist Boys' High School, Abeokuta, Birmingham Univ., England, London Univ. Inst. of Psychiatry; Medical Officer, Nigerian Medical Services 1950–56; Govt. Specialist-in-charge, Aro Hospital for Nervous Diseases; Consultant Physician, Univ. Coll., Ibadan 1956–63; Prof. and Head of Dept. of Psychiatry and Neurology, Univ. of Ibadan 1963–71, Dean of Medical Faculty 1966–68; Vice-Chancellor, Univ. of Ibadan 1968–71; Asst. Dir.-Gen. WHO 1971–73, Deputy Dir.-Gen. Nov. 1973–; mem. Exec. Comm. World Fed. for Mental Health 1964–; Chair. Scientific Council for Africa, UN Advisory Cttee. for Prevention of Crime and Treatment of Offenders, Co-ordinating Bd. African Chairs of Tech. in Food Processing, Biotechnology, Nutrition and Health; Vice-Pres. World Asscn. of Social Psychiatry; mem. of numerous asscns. including Advisory Cttee. for Mental Health, WHO, Exec. Cttee. Council for Int. Org. for Medical Sciences, UNESCO, Expert Advisory Panel on Mental Health, WHO, WHO Advisory Cttee. for Health Research (Geneva), Royal Medico-Psychological Asscn., U.K., Pontifical Acad. of Sciences Int. Epidemiological Asscn., Int. Hosp. Fed., Nigerian Medical Council; Founding mem. African Acad. of Sciences; Assoc. mem. Int. Asscn. For Child Psychiatry and Allied Professions; Hon. mem. Swiss Acad. of Medical Sciences, Third World Acad. of Sciences (founding mem.); Hon. D.Sc. (Ahmadu Bello, Nigeria; Long Island, New York; Jos, Nsukka, Nigeria; McGill, Canada; Hacettepe, Ankara; Hanemann, Pa.), Hon. LL.D. (Birmingham, England; Kent State, Ohio; Pennsylvania, Pa.); Dr. h.c. (Benin, Aix-Marseille, France, Louvain, Belgium, Medical School of Univ. of Debrecen, Hungary); Haile Selassie African Research Award 1970; Nigerian Nat. Order of Merit 1979, Commdr. Order of the Niger 1979. *Publications:* Psychiatric Disorder among the Yorubas (co-author) 1963 and numerous articles in various medical journals. *Leisure interests:* collection of ethnographic material on Africa, of art of traditional and tribal religions, and of ancient books on the history of medicine, on literature and philosophy. *Address:* World Health Organization, Avenue Appia, 1211 Geneva 27 (Office); Chemin des Châtaigniers 27, 1292 Chambésy, Switzerland (Home). *Telephone:* 91-27-16 (Office); 58-19-42 (Home).

LAMBRAKIS, Christos; Greek journalist and newspaper proprietor; b. 24 Feb. 1934; ed. L.S.E.; Publr. and Ed. weekly Tachydromos (Courier) 1955–; succeeded father as propr. of dailies To Vima (Tribune), Ta Nea (News) and the weeklies Economicos Tachydromos (Economic Courier) 1957, Omada (The Team) 1958; Publr. monthly Epoches 1963; Pres. Greek Section, Int. Press Inst.; in prison (Folgentros Prison Island) Nov. 1967. *Address:* Lambrakis Press, Odos Christou Lada 3, Athens, Greece. *Telephone:* 3230-221; 3237-283.

LAMBSDORFF, Graf Otto Friedrich Wilhelm von der Wenge, D.IUR.; German government official and fmr. company executive; b. 20 Dec. 1926, Aachen; ed. Univs. of Bonn and Cologne; Mil. service, prisoner of war, seriously wounded 1944–46; admitted to bar at local and dist. courts of Düsseldorf 1960; activities in credit business, rising to power of attorney for a private bank 1955–71; mem. board of dirs. of an insurance co. 1971–77; mem. Bundestag 1972–; Fed. Minister of Econs. 1977–84; Chair. FDP 1988–; Dr. h.c. 1980; Free Democratic Party. *Address:* Fritz-Erler-Strasse 23, 5300 Bonn, Federal Republic of Germany. *Telephone:* 02221-761.

LAMBY, Werner, DR.JUR.; German business executive; b. 1 Oct. 1924, Oberwörresbach, Rheinland-Pfalz; s. of Peter and Anna Lamby; m. Gisela Bürfent 1956; three s.; ed. Univs. of Heidelberg and Mainz; Civil service 1952–73; mem Bd. VIAG Aktiengellschaft 1974–; Chair. Supervisory Bd. Saarbergwerke 1983– and mem. of various supervisory bds. *Address:* VIAG Aktiengellschaft 53 Bonn 1, Georg-von-Boeselager-Strasse 25, Postfach 626 (Office); 53 Bonn-Bad Godesberg, Lyngsbergstrasse 19, Federal Republic of Germany (Home).

LAMIZANA, Lieut.-Gen. Aboubakar Sangoulé; Burkinâbe army officer and politician; b. 1916, Dianra, Tougan; s. of Kafa and Diantoro Lamizana; m. Mouilo Kékélé Bintou 1947; six c.; served in French Army in Second World War, and later in N. Africa; joined Bataillon Autonome du Soudan Nigérien, Ségou 1947; with Centre d'Etudes Africaines et Asiatiques, Paris 1950; served in Indo-China; Joint Chief of Mil. Cabinet, Ivory Coast 1956–59; Capt. 1957; served N. Africa 1959–60; Chief of Staff, Army of Upper Volta (now Burkina Faso) 1961, Lt.-Col. 1964, Brig.-Gen. 1967, Maj.-Gen. 1970, Lieut.-Gen. 1973; led coup to depose Pres. Maurice Yaméogo Jan. 1966; Pres. of Upper Volta 1966–80 (deposed in coup); Prime Minister 1966–71, 1974–78; Minister of Defence 1966–67, of Foreign Affairs 1966–67, of Information, Youth and Sports 1966–67, of Justice 1974–75; Grand Croix, Ordre nat. de Haute-Volta, Légion d'honneur, Croix de guerre, Croix de Valeur Militaire, other foreign decorations. *Leisure interest:* sport.

LAMJAV, Banzraghiin; Mongolian politician; b. 1920; ed. Higher School for Party Cadres, Ulaanbaatar and Higher Party School of the CPSU Cen. Cttee.; Instructor at Prov. Cttee. of the Mongolian Revolutionary Youth League; served in army as a private, elected as Bureau secretary of the Youth League Cttee., worked as asst. and deputy chief of political dept. of regt., then a brigade; head of section Political Directorate, Mongolian People's Army (MPRP), then deputy chief of dept.; Deputy Chair. Party Cen. Cttee. of MPRP Cen. Cttee. 1954–56; First Sec. Party Cttee. of Zavkhan Aimak (Prov.) 1956–58; Instructor at the MPRP Cen. Cttee. 1958–62; Head of Personnel Dept. MPRP Cen. Cttee. 1962–86; concurrently First Deputy Chair. Party Control Cttee. of MPRP Cen. Cttee. 1979–86; Alt. mem. Political Bureau of MPRP Cen. Cttee. 1986–87, mem. 1987– and Chair. Party Control Cttee. MPRP Cen. Cttee. 1986–; Deputy to the Great People's Hural; mem. of Presidium of Great People's Hural 1976–86. *Address:* c/o Central Committee of the Mongolian People's Revolutionary Party, Ulaanbaatar, Mongolia.

LAMM, Donald Stephen, B.A.; American publisher; b. 31 May 1931, New York; s. of Lawrence W. Lamm and Aleen A. Lassner; m. Jean S. Nicol 1957; two s. one d.; ed. Fieldston School, Yale and Oxford Univs.; Counterintelligence Corps, U.S. Army 1953–55; joined W. W. Norton & Co. Inc. 1956, college rep. 1956–59, ed. 1959–, Dir. 1964–, Vice-Pres. 1968–76, Pres. 1976–, Chair. 1984–; mem. Advisory Council Inst. of Early American History and Culture 1979–82; mem. Council on Foreign Relations 1978–; Guest Fellow, Yale Univ. 1980, 1985; Trustee, The Roper Center 1984–; Fellow, Branford Coll. Yale Univ. 1985–; Pres. Bd. of Govs. Yale Univ. 1986–; Ida H. Beam Distinguished Visiting Prof. Univ. of Iowa 1987–88. *Publication:* Economics and the Common Reader 1989. *Leisure interests:* wilderness canoeing, skiing. *Address:* 500 Fifth Avenue, 6th Floor, New York, N.Y. 10110 (Office); Woods End Road, New Canaan, Conn. 06840, U.S.A. (Home). *Telephone:* (212) 354-5500 (Office); (203) 972-2896 (Home).

LAMM, Richard D., LL.B., C.P.A.; American lawyer and state governor; b. 8 Aug. 1935, Madison, Wis.; s. of A. E. Lamm; m. Dottie Lamm; one s. one d.; ed. Univs. of Wisconsin and California; Certified Public Accountant, Ernst & Ernst, Denver 1961–62; Lawyer, Colorado Anti-Discrimination Comm. 1962–63; Lawyer, Jones, Meiklejohn, Kilroy, Kehl & Lyons 1963–65; private practice 1965–74; mem. Colorado House of Reps. 1966–74; Assoc. Prof. of Law, Univ. of Denver 1969–74; Gov. of Colo. 1975–87; Montgomery Fellow (Visiting Prof.) Dartmouth Coll., N.H. 1987. *Publications:* The Angry West (with Michael McCarthy) 1982, 1988 (with Arnie Grossman) 1985, Megatraumas 1985, The Immigration Time Bomb 1985. *Leisure interests:* mountain climbing, reading. *Address:* Governor's Mansion, 400 East 8th Avenue, Denver, Colo. 80203, U.S.A.

LAMO DE ESPINOSA Y MICHELS DE CHAMPOURCÍN, Jaime; Spanish agronomic engineer and politician; b. 4 April 1941, Madrid; s. of Emilio Lamo de Espinosa and Maria Luisa Michels de Champourcin; m. Carmen Rocamora 1965; four d.; ed. Colegio de Nuestra Señora del Pilar, Escuela Técnica Superior de Ingenieros Agrónomos, Univ. of Madrid; Asst. Engineer, Study Group, Servicio Nacional de Concentración Parcelaria 1964–69; Tech. Dir. Fondo de Ordenación y Regulación de Productos y Precios Agrarios (FORPPA) 1969–73; Sub-commissar for Devt. Plan 1973; Dir. of Tech. Cttee., Ministry of Agric. 1974; Dir.-Gen. Food Industries 1974–76; Under-Sec. of Agric. 1976; Asst. to Third Vice-Pres. of Govt. 1977–78; Minister of Agric. and Fisheries 1978–81; Minister Asst. to Pres. Council of Ministers 1981–82; mem. Congress of Deputies for Castellón 1979–; mem. Unión de Centro Democrático (UCD); Chief UCD spokesman in Congress 1981–82; Pres. 20th FAO World Conf. 1979–81; Pres. Conf. of OECD Ministers of Agric. 1980; Prof., Int. Centre for Advanced Mediterranean Agronomic Studies, Montpellier, France (OECD) 1980; Gran Cruz del Mérito Agrícola, Gran Cruz del Mérito Civil, Encomienda del Mérito Agrícola; Cross of Merit (Fed. Repub. of Germany); Croix du Mérite Civil (France). *Publications:* Agricultura a tiempo parcial y minifundios, Reflexiones sobre la política de precios y su armonización con la política general agraria, Los latifundios y el desarrollo agrario, Interrelación de las políticas de precio y de estructura en la agricultura, La agricultura en una sociedad democrática. *Leisure interests:* reading, music, painting. *Address:* José Abascal 46, Madrid, Spain. *Telephone:* 441 34 15.

LAMONICA, Roberto de; Brazilian artist; b. 27 Oct. 1933; ed. Escola de Belas Artes de São Paulo and Museu de Arte Moderna, Rio de Janeiro; Prof. School of Fine Arts, Lima 1961–62, Univ. de Chile and Univ. Católica de Chile 1962–63, School of Fine Arts, Viña del Mar 1963–64; Prof. of Printmaking, Museum of Modern Art, Rio de Janeiro 1964–; has exhibited in Graphic Art Exhbns. all over the world; illustrations and covers for several books; numerous prizes. *Address:* Rua Anibal de Mendança 180, A.P. 202, Rio de Janeiro ZC-37, RJ, Brazil.

LAMONT, Most Rev. Donal, M.A.; Irish ecclesiastic; b. 27 July 1911, Ballycastle, Co. Antrim; s. of Daniel Lamont and Margaret Tumelty; ed. Terenure Coll., Dublin, Univ. Coll., Dublin, Collegio Sant'Alberto, Rome; professed in Carmelite Order 1930; ordained priest, Rome 1937; Superior Carmelite Mission Rhodesia 1946; Prefect Apostolic, Umtali (now Mutare, Zimbabwe) 1953; Bishop of Umtali 1957–82; attended Second Vatican Council 1962–65; mem. Vatican Secr. for Promoting Christian Unity 1962–75; Pres. Rhodesia Catholic Bishop's Conf. 1970–72, rep. at Roman Synods 1969, 1971, 1974; sentenced to prison and deported from Rhodesia March 1977; returned to Umtali Diocese after Independence 1980; resgnd. as Bishop of Diocese 1982, now Emer. Bishop of Mutare; Hon. LL.D. (Univs. of Notre Dame, Indiana, Seton Hall, N.J. Mount St. Mary's, Md., Marymount, N.Y.); People of God Award, Washington Theological Union. *Publication:* Speech from the Dock 1977. *Leisure interests:* reading, poetry, walking. *Address:* Terenure College, Dublin 6, Ireland. *Telephone:* 904621.

LAMOTHE, William E., B.A.; American business executive; b. 23 Oct. 1926, Brooklyn, New York; m. Pat LaMothe; six c.; ed. Fordham Univ.; Retail Sales Rep. New York Div. Kellogg Co. 1950, Asst. Gen. Sales Man. 1956, Co-ordinator Product Devt. 1958, Asst. to Pres. 1960, Vice-Pres. 1961, Exec. Vice-Pres. 1972, C.E.O. 1979–80, Chair. and C.E.O. Jan. 1980–; Dir. Burroughs Corpn., the Food and Drug Law Inst., and others. *Address:* Kellogg Co., P.O. Box 3599, Battle Creek, Mich., 49016-3599, U.S.A. (Office). *Telephone:* (616) 966 2000 (Office).

LAMOUR, Philippe, L. EN D.; French businessman; b. 12 Feb. 1903, Landrecies; s. of Emmanuel Lamour and Léonie Lamon; m. 2nd Geneviève Walter 1931; one s. four d.; Pres. and Gen. Man. Compagnie Nat. d'Aménagement de la Région du Bas-Rhône-Languedoc 1955–; Pres. Comm. Nat. de L'Aménagement du Territoire, Comité écon. et social de la région Languedoc-Roussillon, Conseil Supérieur du Plan; Féd. Nat. des Vins de Qualité Supérieure, Asscn. pour la Grande Traversée des Alpes; Pres. Féd. des Asscns. Viticoles de France (F.A.V.); Pres. de la Fondation des Pays de France, de l'Assoc. Nat. pour le Dévt. et l'Aménagement Foncier Agricole et Rural (A.N.D.A.F.A.R.); Vice-Pres. de l'Assoc. Mer du Nord-Méditerranée; Mayor of Ceillac. *Publications:* 60 millions de Français, Prendre le temps de vivre, L'écologie, oui, les écologistes, non, Le cadran solaire 1979, Les quatre verités 1980, Les hauts pays 1981. *Leisure interest:* alpinism. *Address:* Mas Saint-Louis-la-Perdrix, 30127 Bellegarde du Gard (Gard), France. *Telephone:* (66) 01-11-27.

LAMOUREUX, Hon. Lucien, P.C., Q.C., M.A.; Canadian politician and diplomatist (retd.); b. 3 Aug. 1920, Ottawa, Ontario; s. of Prime Lamoureux and Graziella Madore; m. Dr. Jur. Elisabeth Hoffmann; one d.; ed. Ottawa Univ. and Osgoode Hall Law School, Toronto; elected to House of Commons 1962, Deputy Speaker 1963–66, Speaker 1966–74; Amb. to Belgium and Luxembourg 1974–80, to Portugal 1980–85; Hon. LL.D. (Ottawa), Hon. Ph.D. (Univ. of Punjab); Hon. Lieut.-Col. S. D. G. Highlanders. *Address:* c/o Ministry of Foreign Affairs, Lester B. Pearson Building, 125 Sussex Drive, Ottawa, K1A 0G2, Canada.

LAMRANI, Mohammed Karim (see Karim-Lamrani, Mohammed).

LANC, Erwin; Austrian politician; b. 17 May 1930, Vienna; m. Melitta Fröhlich 1957 (deceased); one s. one d.; mem. Socialist Party 1948–; with

Fed. Ministry of Social Admin. 1949–55; Nat. Sec. Austrian Youth Hostels Asscn. 1955–59; mem. Diet and Municipal Council of Vienna 1960–; mem. Special Cttee. for Examination of Vienna Public Transport Co. 1961, Chair. 1964; Man. Information Bureau for Communal Financing 1965; mem. Parl. 1966–83; Pres. Viennese Workers' Asscn. for Sport and Physical Culture (ASKO) 1968–82; Minister of Transport 1973–77, of Interior 1977–83, of Foreign Affairs 1983–84; Man. Zentralsparkasse und Kommerzialbank, Vienna; Exec. Man. Z-Export und Handelsbank Ges.m.b.H., Vienna; Chair. Bd. of Advisers ICD-Austria; mem. Exec. Cttee. Austrian Socialist Party 1977–; Pres. Int. Handball Fed. Aug. 1984–. *Publications:* Volksaktie ohne make-up 1960, Gemeinden und Kapitalmarkt 1967. *Address:* Feldkellergasse 70, 1130 Vienna, Austria.

LANCASTER, Burt(on) Stephen; American actor; b. 2 Nov. 1913; ed. New York Univ.; Acrobat 1932–39; shop asst. and salesman 1939–42; army service 1942–45; appeared in plays A Sound of Hunting (New York) 1945, The Boys of Autumn 1981. *Films include:* The Killers 1946, Desert Fury 1947, Brute Force 1947, Sorry, Wrong Number 1948, All My Sons 1948, Criss Cross 1949, Rope of Sand 1949, The Flame and the Arrow 1950, Ten Tall Men 1951, The Crimson Pirate 1952, Come Back Little Sheba 1953, From Here to Eternity 1953, His Majesty O'Keefe 1954, Apache 1954, Vera Cruz 1954, The Kentuckian (also dir.) 1955, The Rose Tattoo 1955, Trapeze 1956, The Rainmaker 1956, Gunfight at the O.K. Corral 1957, Sweet Smell of Success 1957, Separate Tables 1958, The Devil's Disciple 1958, Run Silent, Run Deep 1958, The Unforgiven 1959, Elmer Gantry (Acad. Award) 1960, Judgment at Nuremberg 1961, Birdman of Alcatraz 1962, A Child is Waiting 1962, The Leopard 1963, Seven Days in May 1964, The Train 1964, The Hallelujah Trail 1965, The Professional 1966, The Swimmer 1967, The Scalphunters 1968, The Gypsy Moths 1969, Airport 1969, Lawman 1970, Valdez is Coming 1971, Ulzana's Raid 1972, Scorpio 1973, Executive Action 1973, The Midnight Man 1974, Conversation Piece 1974, 1900 1975, Moses 1976, Go Tell the Spartans 1977, Zulu Dawn 1979, Atlantic City 1980 (B.A.F.T.A. Award 1982), Local Hero 1983, The Ostreman Weekend 1983, Little Treasure 1985, On Wings of Eagles (TV) 1986, Tough Guys 1986, The Goldsmith's Shop 1987, Fathers and Sons 1988. *Address:* c/o ICM, 8899 Beverly Boulevard, Los Angeles, Calif. 90048, U.S.A.

LANCASTER, (Christopher Ronald) Mark, B.A.; British artist; b. 14 May, 1938, Holmfirth; s. of Charles Ronald Lancaster and Muriel Roebuck; ed. Holme Valley Grammar School, Bootham School, York, Univ. of Newcastle upon Tyne; Lecturer Univ. of Newcastle 1965–66, Bath Acad. of Art 1966–68; Artist in Residence King's Coll., Cambridge 1968–70; Artistic Advisor Merce Cunningham Dance Co., N.Y. 1980–84. *Address:* c/o Mayor Rowan Gallery, 31A Bruton Place, London, W1X 7AB, England. *Telephone:* 01-499 3011.

LANCASTER, Henry Oliver, M.D., PH.D., F.A.A.; Australian statistician (retd.); b. 1 Feb. 1913, Sydney; s. of Llewellyn B. Lancaster and Edith H. (née Smith) Lancaster; m. Joyce Mellon 1940; five s.; ed. Univ. of Sydney; Resident Medical Officer, Sydney Hosp. 1937–39; pathologist Royal Australian Army Medical Corps 1940–46; lecturer, Sr. Lecturer, Assoc. Prof. School of Public Health and Tropical Medicine, Sydney 1946–59; Rockefeller Fellow in Medicine, London School of Hygiene 1948–49; Prof. of Math. Statistics, Univ. of Sydney 1959–78, Prof. Emer. 1978–; T. R. Lyle Medal 1961, E. J. G. Pitman Medal 1980; Hon. Life mem. Statistical Soc. of Australia 1972, Australian Math. Soc. 1981; Hon. Fellow Royal Statistical Soc. 1975. *Publications:* Bibliography of Statistical Bibliographies 1968, The Chi-squared Distribution 1969, An Introduction to Medical Statistics 1974; over 140 articles on medical statistics and math. *Leisure interests:* reading, bowls. *Address:* Room 174, Fisher Building F04, University of Sydney, N.S.W. 2006, Australia. *Telephone:* (02) 692 3921.

LANCE, James Waldo, C.B.E., M.D., F.R.C.P., F.R.A.C.P., F.A.A.; Australian professor of neurology; b. 29 Oct. 1926, Wollongong, N.S.W.; s. of Waldo and Jessie (née Stewart) Lance; m. Judith L. Logan 1957; one s. four d.; ed. Geelong Grammar School, The King's School, Parramatta and Univ. of Sydney; Chair. Div. of Neurology, Prince Henry and Prince of Wales Hosps., Sydney 1961–; Prof. of Neurology, Univ. of N.S.W. 1975–; Pres. Australian Asscn. of Neurologists 1978–81; Vice-Pres. Australian Acad. of Sciences 1984–85; Harold G. Wolff Award of American Asscn. for Study of Headache 1967, 1983. *Publications:* Headache 1975, The Golden Trout 1978, A Physiological Approach to Clinical Neurology (with J. G. McLeod 1981), The Mechanism and Management of Headache 1982, Introductory Neurology (with J. G. McLeod) 1984. *Leisure interests:* swimming, trout fishing, skiing. *Address:* Department of Neurology, The Prince Henry Hospital, Little Bay, N.S.W. 2036; 15 Coolong Road, Vaucluse, N.S.W. 2030, Australia. *Telephone:* 661-0111 (Office); 337-5790 (Home).

LANCE, (Thomas) Bertram; American banker and politician; b. 3 June 1931, Gainesville, Ga.; s. of the late Dr. and of Mrs. T. J. Lance; m. LaBelle David 1950; four s.; ed. Univ. of Georgia, Louisiana State Univ., Rutgers Univ., New Brunswick, N.J., Emory Univ., Atlanta, Ga.; worked as teller, Calhoun First Nat. Bank, Ga. 1951, Pres. and C.E.O. 1963–74, Chair. 1974–77, 1981–86, Dir. 1958–77; Commr. Ga. Dept. of Transportation 1971–73; Dir. of the Office of Man. and Budget, Exec. Office of Pres. of U.S.A. Jan.-Sept. 1977; Presidential Campaign Man. for Walter Mondale 1984 (resgnd. Aug.); financial consultant Lance Co., Calhoun, Ga. 1977–; Invest-

ment Consultant, Bank of Credit and Commerce Int.; Head, Chair. of Private Enterprise, Ga. State Univ.; Dir. Ga. Conservancy; mem. Exec. Cttee. for Cen. Atlanta Progress, Ga. Advisory Council of Coll. of Industrial Man., Exec. Cttee. of Ga. Foundation for Ind. Colls.; Trustee Ga. State Univ., Reinhardt Coll., Waleska, Ga.; numerous civic, religious and charitable activities. *Address:* P.O. Box 637, Calhoun, Ga. 20701, U.S.A.

LANCHBERY, John Arthur, A.R.A.M., F.R.A.M.; British conductor and composer; b. 15 May 1923, London; s. of William E. Lanchbery and Violet S. Mewett; m. Elaine Fifield 1951; one d.; ed. Alleyn's School, Dulwich and Royal Acad. of Music; served R.A.C. 1943–45; Musical Dir. Metropolitan Ballet 1948–50; Sadler's Wells Theatre Ballet 1951–57; Royal Ballet 1957–72, Prin. Conductor 1959–72; Musical Dir. Australian Ballet 1972–77; American Ballet Theatre 1978–80. *Arrangements and composition of ballets include:* Pleasuredrome 1949, Eve of St. Agnes 1950, House of Birds 1955, La Fille Mal Gardée 1960, The Dream 1964, Don Quixote 1966, Giselle 1968, La Sylphide 1970, Tales of Beatrix Potter 1971, Tales of Hoffman 1972, Merry Widow 1975, Month in the Country 1976, The Turning Point 1977, Mayerling 1978, Rosalinda 1978, Papillon 1979, La Bayadere 1980, Peer Gynt 1981, Evil Under the Sun 1982, The Sentimental Bloke 1985, Le Chat Botté 1985, A Midsummer Night's Dream 1985, Hunchback of Notre Dame 1988, Robinson Crusoe (opéra comique) 1986; Bolshoi Theatre Medal 1961. *Leisure interests:* walking, reading. *Address:* c/o Roger Stone Management, West Grove, Hammers Lane, Mill Hill, London, NW7 4DY, England. *Telephone:* 01-855 0222.

LAND, Edwin Herbert, LL.D., L.H.D.; American scientist; b. 7 May 1909, Bridgeport, Conn.; s. of Harry M. and Matha G. Land; m. Helen Maislen 1929; two d.; ed. Norwich Acad. and Harvard Univ.; Founder Polaroid Corpn., Cambridge, Mass. 1937, Chair., Consultant Dir. Basic Research 1937–82, Dir. Basic Research 1937–80, Pres. 1937–80; Founder, Pres. and Dir. of Research The Rowland Inst. for Science, Cambridge, Mass. 1979–; developed first modern polarizers for light, sequence of subsequent polarizers, theories and practices for application of polarized light; during World War II developed optical systems for mil. use; created cameras, films that give instantaneous dry photographs in black and white and colour; mem. President's Science Advisory Cttee., President's Foreign Intelligence Advisory Board, Nat. Comm. on Technology, Automation and Econ. Progress 1964–66, Nat. Acad. of Eng., American Philosophical Soc., Nat. Acad. of Arts, Fellow American Acad. of Arts and Sciences (past Pres.), N.A.S., Photographic Soc. of America; Photographic Soc. of America, Royal Photographic Soc. of G.B.; Foreign mem. Royal Soc. 1986; Hon. mem. Royal Inst. of G.B., etc.; Visiting Inst. Prof. M.I.T. 1956–; William James Lecturer on Psychology, Harvard 1966–67; numerous hon. degrees; numerous medals incl. Presidential Medal of Freedom 1963, Nat. Medal of Science 1967, Wright Prize 1980. *Address:* The Rowland Institute of Science, 100 Cambridge Parkway, Cambridge, Mass. 02142; 163 Brattle Street, Cambridge, Mass. 02138, U.S.A. (Home).

LAND, Michael Francis, M.A., PH.D., F.R.S.; British professor of biology; b. 12 April 1942, Dartmouth; s. of Prof. F. W. Land and Mrs. N. B. Land; m. 1st Judith Drinkwater 1966 (divorced 1980), one s.; m. 2nd Rosemary Roper 1980, two d.; ed. Birkenhead School, Jesus Coll., Cambridge, Univ. Coll., London and Univ. of Calif., Berkeley (Miller Fellowship); Asst. Prof. Univ. of Calif., Berkeley 1969–71; Lecturer, School of Biological Sciences, Univ. of Sussex 1971–77, Reader 1977–84, Prof. of Biology 1984–; Visiting Prof. Univ. of Ore. 1980; Sr. Visiting Fellow, A.N.U., Canberra 1982–84. *Publications:* 55 articles and papers on aspects of vision in animals from visual optics to behaviour. *Leisure interests:* gardening, music. *Address:* School of Biological Sciences, University of Sussex, Brighton, BN1 9QG (Office); White House, Cuilfail, Lewes, Sussex, BN7 2BE, England (Home). *Telephone:* 0273-606755 (Office); 0273 476780 (Home).

LANDAIS, Hubert Léon; French museum administrator; b. 22 March 1921; s. of Pierre Landais and Odette Surmont; m. Madeleine Legris 1946; five s. one d.; ed. Ecole Nat. des Chartes, Ecole du Louvre; at the Louvre Museum 1946–, Attendant 1946–48, Curator Middle Ages, Renaissance, Modern objects d'art 1948–62, Asst. Curator to the Dir. of Museums 1962–63, Chief Curator Nat. Museums 1963–65, Dir. objects d'art dept. 1965–68, Inspector-Gen. of Museums 1968, Dir. of the Museums 1977–88, Sec.-Gen. 1962–73, Pres. French Cttee. 1973–, mem. Int. Council 1974–77; Pres. Réunion des musées nationaux 1977; Vice-Pres., Conseil d'admin. du musée de l'Armée; mem. Int. Council of Museums 1974–77, Pres. 1977–83; Commandeur de la Légion d'Honneur, Commdr. Ordre nat. du Mérite et des Arts et des Lettres. *Publications:* numerous articles on objects d'art, especially Renaissance works and porcelain, Dir. l'Univers des Formes. *Address:* 4 quai des Tuileries, 75001, Paris, France (Home).

LANDAU, Moshe, LL.B.; Israeli judge (retd.); b. 29 April 1912, Danzig (now Gdańsk, Poland); s. of Dr. Isaac Landau and Betty (née Eisenstädt); m. Leah Doukhan 1937; three d.; ed. London Univ.; went to Israel 1933; called to Palestine Bar 1937; Magistrate of Haifa 1940, District Court Judge, Haifa 1948; Justice, Supreme Court, Jerusalem 1953—(Presiding Judge, Eichmann Trial), Deputy Pres. 1976–80, Pres. 1980–82. *Leisure interest:* piano. *Address:* 10 Alharizi Street, Jerusalem, Israel. *Telephone:* 632757.

LANDAU, Peter, DR.JUR.; German professor of law; b. 26 Feb. 1935, Berlin; s. of Gerhard Landau and Ilse Lohr; m. Angelika Linnemann 1971;

one s. one d.; ed. Univs. of Berlin, Freiburg, Bonn and Yale Univ.; Prof. Univ. of Regensburg 1968–87; Prof. of Law, Univ. of Munich 1987–; mem. Bayerische Akad. der Wissenschaften. *Publications:* Die Entstehung des kanonischen Infamiebegriffs von Gratian bis zur Glossa ordinaria 1966, Ius patronatus 1975, Strafrecht, Strafprozess und Rezeption (ed. Landau and Schroeder) 1984. *Leisure interest:* art. *Address:* Leopold-Wenger-Institut für Rechtsgeschichte, 8000 Munich 22, Professor-Huber-Platz 2 (Office); Tsingtauer Strasse 103, 8000 Munich 82, Federal Republic of Germany (Home). *Telephone:* 089/2180-3263 (Office); 089/4300121 (Home).

LANDÁZURI RICKETTS, H.E. Cardinal Juan, D.C.L.; Peruvian ecclesiastic; b. 19 Dec. 1913, Arequipa; ed. Univs. of Arequipa and Antonianum, Rome; Franciscan Friar; Teacher of Canon Law; Ordained Priest 1939; Titular Archbishop of Roina 1952; cr. Cardinal 1962; Archbishop of Lima; Kt., Commdr. of Order of Malta and many honours. *Address:* Arzobispado, Plaza de Armas, Apartado Postal 1512, Lima 100, Peru.

LANDES, David S., PH.D.; American professor of history; b. 29 April 1924, New York; s. of Harry and Sylvia Landes; m. Sonia Tarnopol 1943; one s. two d.; ed. City Coll., New York, Harvard Univ.; Jr. Fellow, Soc. of Fellows, Harvard Univ. 1950–55; Asst. Prof. of Econs., Columbia Univ., New York 1952–55, Assoc. Prof. 1955–58; Fellow, Center for Advanced Study in Behavioral Sciences, Stanford, Calif. 1957–58; Prof. of History and Econs., Univ. of Calif., Berkeley 1958–64; Prof. of History, Harvard Univ. 1964–72, LeRoy B. Williams Prof. of History and Political Science 1972–75, Robert Walton Goelet Prof. of French History 1975–81, Prof. of Econs. 1977–, Coolidge Prof. of History 1981–; Chair. Faculty Cttee. on Social Studies 1981–; Pres. Council on Research in Econ. History 1963–66; Dir. Center for Middle Eastern Studies, Harvard Univ. 1966–68; Acting Dir. Center for West European Studies, Harvard Univ. 1969–70; Pres. Econ. History Assen. 1976–77; Ellen McArthur Lecturer, Univ. of Cambridge 1964; Visiting Prof., Univ. of Paris IV 1972–73, Univ. of Zürich and Eidgenössische Technisch Hochschule, Zürich 1978; Richards Lectures, Univ. of Va. 1978, Janeway Lectures, Princeton Univ. 1983; mem. Bd. of Eds., various journals of history; Fellow, N.A.S., American Acad. of Arts and Sciences, American Philosophical Soc., British Acad., Royal Historical Soc.; Overseas Fellow, Churchill Coll., Cambridge 1968–69; Visiting Fellow, All Souls, Oxford 1985; mem. American Historical Assen., Econ. History Assen. (also Trustee), Econ. History Soc., Soc. for French Historical Studies, Soc. d'Histoire Moderne and other socs.; Assoc. mem. Fondation Royaumont pour le Progrès des Sciences de l'Homme; Dr. h.c. (Lille) 1973. *Publications:* Bankers and Pashas 1958, The Unbound Prometheus 1968, Revolution in Time: Clocks and the Making of the Modern World 1983 and other books and articles on economic and social history. *Leisure interests:* antiquarian horology, squash, tennis. *Address:* Department of Economics, Harvard University, Cambridge, Mass. 02138 (Office); 24 Highland Street, Cambridge, Mass. 02138, U.S.A. (Home). *Telephone:* (617) 495-4849 (Office); (617) 354 6308 (Home).

LANDON, Howard Chandler Robbins, B.MUS.; American author and educator; b. 6 March 1926, Boston, Mass.; s. of William G. Landon and Dorothea LeB. Robbins; m. Else Radant 1957; ed. Lenox School, Mass., Swarthmore Coll. and Boston Univ.; corresp. The Times 1958–61; Hon. Professorial Fellow, Univ. Coll. Cardiff 1971–78, John Bird Prof. of Music 1978–; Prof. of the Humanities, Middlebury Coll., Vt. 1980–83; Verdienstkreuz für Kunst und Wissenschaft (Austria); Hon. D. Mus. (Boston) 1969, (Belfast) 1974, (Bristol) 1982. *Publications:* The Symphonies of Joseph Haydn 1955, Beethoven 1970, Joseph Haydn: Chronicle and Works (5 vols.) 1976–80, Haydn: A Documentary Study 1982, Mozart & the Masons 1983, Handel and his World 1984, 1791: Mozart's Last Year 1987; critical edns. of many of works of Haydn, Mozart and 18th century composers. *Leisure interests:* walking, swimming, cooking. *Address:* Château de Foncoussieres, 81800 Rubastens (Tarn), France. *Telephone:* 63.40.61.45.

LANDOWSKI, Marcel François Paul; French composer; b. 18 Feb. 1915, Pont-l'Abbé (Finistère); s. of the late Paul Landowski and Louise-Amélie Cruppi; m. Jacqueline Potier 1941; one s. two d.; ed. Lycée Janson-de-Sailly and Conservatoire nationale de musique de Paris; Dir. Conservatoire, Boulogne-sur-Seine 1960–65; Dir. of Music, Comédie Française, Paris 1961–66; Insp.-Gen. of Music, Ministry of Nat. Education, Dir.-Gen. of Cultural Affairs, City of Paris 1977; Founder, Orchestre de Paris 1967, Hon. Pres. 1975–; mem. Inst. de France (Acad. des beaux-arts, Life Sec. 1986) 1975, Officier, Légion d'honneur, Commdr. des Arts et des Lettres, Croix de guerre and numerous awards and prizes; compositions include: three symphonies, five operas (including Montsegur 1984), eight concertos, choral music (including Chant de Paix 1985), chamber music, film music and ballets. *Publications:* Honegger, Les Instruments de l'orchestre, Batailles pour la Musique. *Address:* 10 rue Max-Blondat, 92100 Boulogne-sur-Seine, France.

LANDRIEU, Moon, LL.B.; American lawyer and politician; b. 23 July 1930, New Orleans, La.; s. of Joseph and Loretta (Bechtel) Landrieu; m. Verna M. Satterlee 1954; four s. five d.; ed. Loyola Univ., New Orleans; admitted to La. Bar 1954; army service 1954–57; entered law firm Landrieu, Calogero & Kronlage, New Orleans 1957, partner 1958–69; mem. La. House of Reps. 1960–65; Councilman-at-large, City of New Orleans 1966–70; Mayor 1970–78; Pres., Joseph C. Canizaro (real estate development firm) 1978–79, rejoined 1981–; U.S. Sec. of Housing and Urban Devt. 1979–81; Counsel,

Rogers and Wells law firm, Washington, D.C. 1981–; Pres. U.S. Conf. of Mayors 1975–76; mem. Bd. of Dirs., Inter-American Municipal Org., Nat. Urban Coalition, Advisory Bd., Nat. League of Cities; B'nai B'rith Humanitarian award 1974. *Address:* 4301 Prieur Street, New Orleans, La. 70125, U.S.A.

LANDRY, Monique; Canadian politician; b. 25 Dec. 1937, Montreal; m. Jean-Guy Landry; four c.; ed. Univ. of Montreal; M.P. 1984–; mem. of several inter-parl. asscns.; fmr. Parl. Sec. to the Sec. of State and the Minister of Int. Trade, Minister for External Relations June 1986–; fmr. mem. Standing Cttee. on Communications and Culture, Jt. Cttee. on Official Languages Policy and Programs and the Standing Cttee. on Finance, Trade and Econ. Affairs, Canada-Europe Parl. Assen., Canada-France Inter-Parl. Assen., Canada-NATO Parl. Assen. *Address:* c/o Department of External Affairs, Lester B. Pearson Building, 125 Sussex Drive, Ottawa K1A 0G2, Canada. *Telephone:* (619) 994-6161; (613) 992-2659.

LANE, Baron (Life Peer), cr. 1979, of St. Ippollitts in the County of Hertfordshire; **Geoffrey Dawson Lane,** P.C., A.F.C.; British judge; b. 17 July 1918; s. of the late Percy Albert Lane; m. Jan Macdonald 1944; one s.; ed. Shrewsbury, Trinity Coll., Cambridge; served in R.A.F. 1943–45, Squadron Leader 1942; called to the Bar, Gray's Inn 1946, Bencher 1966; Q.C. 1962; Deputy Chair. Bedfordshire Quarter Sessions 1960–66, Recorder of Bedford 1963–66; mem. Parole Bd. 1970–72, Vice-Chair. 1972; a Judge, High Court of Justice, Queen's Bench Div. 1966–74; a Lord Justice of Appeal 1974–79; Lord of Appeal in Ordinary 1979; Lord Chief Justice of England April 1980–; Hon. Master of Bench, Inner Temple 1980; Hon. D.C.L. (Cambridge) 1984. *Address:* Royal Courts of Justice, Strand, London, W.C.2, England.

LANE, Anthony Milner, PH.D., F.R.S.; British research physicist; b. 27 July 1928, Wilts.; s. of Herbert W. and Doris R. Lane; m. 1st Anne S. Zissman 1952 (died 1980), 2nd Jill V. Parvin 1983; two s. one d.; ed. Trowbridge Boys' Grammar School, Univ. of Cambridge; with UKAEA 1954–, Deputy Chief Scientific Officer 1975–. *Publications:* research articles in theoretical physics. *Leisure interests:* churches, birds. *Address:* c/o UKAEA (TP424.4), Harwell, Didcot, Oxon. (Office); 6 Walton Street, Oxford, OX1 2HG, England (Home). *Telephone:* (0235) 24141, Ext. 3247 (Office); (0865) 56565.

LANE, Ronald Anthony Stuart, C.M.G., M.C., F.I.B.; British banker; b. 8 Dec. 1917, Bushey, Herts.; s. of Wilmot Ernest Lane and Florence Blakey; m. Anne Brenda Walsh 1948; one s. one d.; ed. Lancing Coll.; served with Chartered Bank of India, Australia and China in the Far East 1939–60; 7th Light Cavalry, Indian Army 1940–45; Chief Gen. Man. the Chartered Bank 1972; mem. Export Guarantees Advisory Council 1972 (Deputy Chair. 1977–78); mem. Council, Inst. of Bankers 1975; Man. Dir. Standard Chartered Bank Ltd. 1975–77, Vice-Chair. 1977–83, Deputy Chair. Chartered Trust Ltd. 1979–83. *Leisure interest:* sailing. *Address:* West Hold, by the Church, West Mersea, Essex, England. *Telephone:* (0206) 2563.

LANG, Andrew Richard, PH.D., M.INST.P., F.R.S.; British professor of physics; b. 9 Sept. 1924; s. of late Ernest F. S. Lang and Susannah (Gueterbock) Lang; unmarried; ed. Univ. Coll. of South-West, Exeter and Univ. of Cambridge; Research Dept. Lever Bros. Port Sunlight 1945–47; Research Asst. Cavendish Lab. 1947–48; North American Philips, Irvington-on-Hudson, New York 1952–53; Instr. Harvard Univ. 1953–54, Asst. Prof. 1954–59; Lecturer in Physics, Univ. of Bristol 1960–66, Reader 1966–79, Prof. 1979–87, Prof. Emer. 1987–; Charles Vernon Boys Prize, Inst. of Physics 1964. *Publications:* contributions to learned journals. *Address:* 1B Elton Road, Bristol, BS8 1SJ, England. *Telephone:* (0272) 739784.

LANG, Anton, DR.NAT.SC.; American (naturalized 1956) plant physiologist; b. 18 Jan. 1913, St. Petersburg (now Leningrad), Russia; s. of Dr. George Lang and Vera Davidov; m. Lydia Kamendrovsky 1946; two s. one d.; ed. High School, Berlin and Labes, Pomerania, and Univ. of Berlin; Scientific Asst., Kaiser Wilhelm (later Max Planck) Inst. of Biology, Berlin, later Tübingen, Germany 1939–49; Research Assoc., Genetics Dept., McGill Univ., Montreal 1949; Visiting Prof. Agronomy and Genetics Depts., Texas Agric. and Mech. Coll. 1950; Research Fellow and Senior Research Fellow, Div. of Biology, Calif. Inst. of Tech. Pasadena 1950–52; Asst. and Assoc. Prof., Dept. of Botany, Univ. of Calif., Los Angeles 1952–59; Prof. of Biology in charge of Earhart-Campbell Plant Research Labs., Calif. Inst. of Tech. 1959–65; Dir. MSU-DOE Plant Research Lab., Prof. Botany and Plant Pathology, Michigan State Univ., E. Lansing 1965–78, Prof. 1978–83, Prof. Emer. 1983–; Visiting Prof., Dept. of Botany and Plant Sciences, Univ. of Calif., Riverside 1984; Lady Davis Foundation Fellowship 1949; Lalor Foundation Fellowship 1950–52; Sr. Research Fellowship, Nat. Science Foundation 1948–49; mem. N.A.S. (Chair. Botany Section 1983–86), American Acad. of Arts and Sciences, Akademie Leopoldina; Chair. Nat. Research Council Cttee. on the Effects of Herbicides in Viet-Nam 1971–74; mem. President's Cttee. on Nat. Medal of Science 1976–78; Hon. mem. German Botanical Soc. 1982; Hon. LL.D. (Glasgow) 1981; Distinguished Faculty Award, Mich. State Univ. 1976, Stephen Hales Price and Charles Reid Barnes Life Membership Awards, American Soc. Plant Physiologists 1976, Merit Award, Botanical Soc. of America 1979, Silver Medal (Mass. Horticultural Soc.) 1979. *Publications:* Over 100 publs. on plant physiology (physiology of flowering, hormone physiology). *Leisure interests:* gardening, reading, music. *Address:* MSU/DOE Plant Research Laboratory, Michigan

State University, East Lansing, Mich. 48824 (Office); 1538 Cahill Drive, East Lansing, Mich. 48823-1312, U.S.A. (Home). *Telephone:* 517-351-5431 (Home); 517-355-5149 (Office).

LANG, Jack; French politician; b. 2 Sept. 1939, Mirecourt; s. of Roger Lang and Marie-Luce Bouchet; m. Monique Buczynski 1961; two d.; ed. Lycée Henri-Poincaré, Nancy, Univ. of Paris; Founder and Dir. World Festival of Univ. Theatre, Nancy 1963–72; Dir. Nancy Univ. Theatre 1963–72; Dir. Théâtre du palais de Chaillot 1972–74; Prof. of Int. Law 1976–; Dir. Educ. and Research Unit for econ. and legal sciences, Nancy 1977–; Councillor, Paris 1977–81; mem. Nat. Ass. for Loir-et-Cher 1986–; Special Adviser to First Sec., Parti Socialiste (PS) 1978–81, PS Nat. Del. for Culture 1979–81; Minister of Culture and Communications 1981–83, 1984–86, May 1988–, also Minister for Major Public Works and Bicentenary May 1988–, Minister del. 1983–84. *Address:* Assemblée nationale, 75355 Paris; 17 place des Vosges, 75004 Paris, France (Home).

LANG, Hon. Otto Emil, P.C., Q.C., B.A., LL.B., B.C.L., LL.D.; Canadian lawyer, politician and business executive; b. 14 May 1932, Handel, Sask.; s. of Otto T. Lang and Maria Theresa Wurm; m. 1st Adrian Ann Merchant 1963 (divorced 1988); three s. four d.; m. 2nd Deborah J. MacCawley 1989; ed. Univ. of Saskatchewan and Oxford Univ.; admitted to Saskatchewan Bar 1956, to Ontario, Yukon and Northwest Territories Bars 1972; Asst. Prof., Univ. of Saskatchewan, Faculty of Law 1956, Assoc. Prof. 1957, Prof. 1961, Dean of Law School 1961–68; M.P. for Saskatoon-Humboldt 1968–79; Minister without Portfolio 1968, with responsibility for Energy and Water Resources 1969, with responsibility for Canadian Wheat Bd. 1969–79; Minister of Manpower & Immigration 1970–72, of Justice 1972–75, of Transport responsible for Canadian Wheat Bd. 1975–79, of Justice and Attorney-Gen. Aug.–Nov. 1978; Pres. Asscn. of Canadian Law Teachers 1962–63; Vice-Pres. Saskatchewan Liberal Asscn. 1956–63; Fed. Campaign Chair. Liberal Party 1963–64; Past Pres. Saskatoon Social Planning Council; Exec. Vice-Pres. Pioneer Grain Co. Ltd. 1979–88; Chair. Transport Inst., Univ. of Manitoba 1988–; Campaign Chair. Winnipeg United Way 1983; Rhodes Scholar 1953; Knight of Malta 1962; Q.C. for Ontario 1972; Q.C. for Saskatchewan 1972. *Publication:* Contemporary Problems of Public Law in Canada (Ed.) 1968. *Leisure interests:* curling, bridge, golf. *Address:* 12 Kingsway, Winnipeg, Manitoba R3M 0G8, Canada.

LANG DAZHONG; Chinese state official; b. March 1933; alt. mem. 12th CCP Cen. Cttee. 1983–87, mem. 13th Cen. Cttee. 1987–; Chair. Dehong Dai and Jingpo Autonomous Pref., Yunnan Prov. 1983–. *Address:* Dehong Dai and Jingpo Autonomous Prefectural People's Government, Yunnan, People's Republic of China.

LANG PING; Chinese volleyball player; b. 1960, Beijing; leader Chinese Women's Volleyball team 1982–. *Address:* China Sports Federation, Beijing, People's Republic of China.

LÅNGBACKA, Ralf Runar, M.A.; Finnish theatre director; b. 20 Nov. 1932, Närpes; s. of Runar Emanuel Långbacka and Hulda Emilia Långbacka (née Backlund); m. Runa Birgitta Danielsson 1961; two s. one d.; ed. Åbo Akademi, Munich Univ. and Freie Univ., Berlin; Ed. Finnish Radio literary programmes 1955–56; Asst. and Dir. Lilla Teatern, Helsinki 1958–60; Man. and Artistic Dir. Swedish Theatre, Turku 1960–63; Dir. Finnish Nat. Theatre 1963–65; Artistic Dir. Swedish Theatre, Helsinki 1965–67; freelance Dir. in Finnish Nat. Opera, Helsinki, Municipal Theatre, Gothenburg, Sweden, Royal Dramatic Theatre, Stockholm, Sweden 1967–71; mem. Finnish State Comm. of Dramatic Art 1967–70; Artistic Dir. Municipal Theatre, Turku 1971–77; Head Finnish Dirs. Asscn. 1978–82; Artistic and Man. Dir. Municipal Theatre, Helsinki 1983–87, Artistic Prof. 1979–83, 1988–; Pres. Finnish Centre, Int. Theatre Inst. (ITI) 1983–; Corresp. mem. Akad. der Künste, Berlin 1979; The Critics Spurs 1963, Pro Finlandia 1973. *Publications:* Teaterikirja (The Theatre Book) (with Kalle Holmberg) 1977, Bland annat om Brecht (On Brecht and Others) 1981, Möten med Tjechov (Meetings with Chekhov) 1986, Denna långa dag, detta korta liv (This long day, this short life: poems) 1988 and articles. *Leisure interests:* music, mushrooms, sailing. *Address:* Hopeasalmenranta 1B, 00570 Helsinki 57, Finland. *Telephone:* 90-6849508.

LANGDON, Jervis, Jr.; American railroad executive; b. 28 Jan. 1905, Elmira, New York; s. of Jervis and Eleanor (Sayles) Langdon; m. Irene Fortner 1949; ed. Cornell Univ. and Univ. de Dijon, France; Asst. Gen. Attorney, Chesapeake and Ohio Railway 1936–38, Gen. Attorney 1938–41, Asst. Vice-Pres. (Traffic) 1941–42; U.S. Army Air Force 1942–45; Special Counsel, Asscn. of Southeastern Railroads 1947–53, Chair. 1953–56; Gen. Counsel, Baltimore and Ohio Railroad 1956–61, Pres. 1961–64; Chair. Chicago, Rock Island and Pacific Railroad 1964–65, Chair. and Pres. 1965–70; Trustee, Penn. Cen. Transport Co. 1970–74, Pres., C.E.O. 1974–76; Counsel, Alston, Miller and Gaines, Washington, D.C. 1976–; Legion of Merit. *Address:* Quarry Farm, P.O. Box 224, Elmira, N.Y. 14902, U.S.A. (Home).

LANGDON, Michael, C.B.E.; British bass singer; b. 12 Nov. 1920, Wolverhampton; s. of Mr. and Mrs. Henry Langdon; m. Vera Duffield 1947; two d.; ed. Bushbury Hill School, Wolverhampton; Prin. bass, Royal Opera House, Covent Garden 1951–; sang in Gloriana (Britten) at Royal Command Performance 1953; Promenade Concerts, Royal Albert Hall 1953–; int. engagements since 1961; T.V., radio, etc.; Dir. Nat. Opera Studio 1978–86,

Consultant 1986–87; leading bass roles in Fidelio, Der Rosenkavalier, The Abduction from the Seraglio, Don Carlos, Wozzeck, Don Giovanni, Faust, Das Rheingold, Die Walküre, Götterdämmerung, The Magic Flute, Falstaff, Tristan and Isolde, Tannhäuser, The Flying Dutchman, Billy Budd, Boris Godunov, The Bartered Bride, Aida, etc.; particularly well known as Baron Ochs in Der Rosenkavalier; Hon. Diploma (Guildhall School of Music and Drama) 1973. *Publication:* Notes from a Low Singer (autobiog.) 1982. *Leisure interests:* walking, swimming and association football (Wolves F.C.), plus reading science fiction and autobiographies. *Address:* 34 Warnham Court, Grand Avenue, Hove, East Sussex, England. *Telephone:* (0273) 733120.

LANGE, Rt. Hon. David Russell, LL.M., P.C.; New Zealand politician and fmr. lawyer; b. 1942, Otahuhu; m.; three c.; ed. Otahuhu Coll., Auckland Univ.; barrister and solicitor, sole practice at Kaikohe 1968, Auckland 1970–77; Labour Party M.P. for Mangere, Auckland 1977–; Opposition Spokesman on Justice 1978, Deputy Leader, Parl. Labour Party 1979–83, Leader 1983–; fmr. Opposition Spokesman on Foreign Affairs, Overseas Trade, Justice, Pacific Islands Affairs and Regional Devt.; Prime Minister July 1984–; Minister in Charge of the Security Intelligence Service 1984–87, Minister of Foreign Affairs 1984–87, Minister of Educ. Aug. 1987–. *Address:* Parliament House, Wellington (Office); 282 Massey Road, Mangere, Auckland, New Zealand (Home).

LANGE, Hermann, DR. JUR.; German professor of law; b. 24 Jan. 1922, Dresden; s. of Arno Lange and Käthe Lange; m. Ulrike Moser 1960; une s. one d.; ed. Kreuzgymnasium, Dresden and Univs. of Leipzig, Munich and Freiburg/Breisgau; Asst. Inst. of Legal History, Univ. of Freiburg/Breisgau 1949–53; Privatdozent, Freiburg/Breisgau 1953–55; Extraordinary Prof. Univ. of Innsbrück 1955–57; Prof. Univ. of Kiel 1957–62, Univ. of Mainz 1962–66, Univ. of Tübingen 1966– (now Emer.); mem. Akad. der Wissenschaften und Literatur, Mainz. *Publications:* Schadenersatz und Privatstrafe in der mittelalterlichen Rechtstheorie 1955, Familienrecht (Kommentar) 1962, Die Consilien des Baldus de Ubaldis 1974, Schadenersatz 1979. *Address:* 7400 Tübingen, Ferdinand-Christian-Baur-Strasse 3, Federal Republic of Germany. *Telephone:* 07071/61216.

LANGE, Jessica; American actress; b. 20 April 1949; d. of Al Lange and Dorothy Lange; m. Paco Grande 1970 (divorced 1982); one d. (with Mikhail Baryshnikov); one s. one d. (with Sam Shepard); ed. Univ. of Minn.; student of mime with Etienne DeCroux, Paris; Dancer Opera Comique, Paris; model, Wilhelmina Agency, N.Y. *Films include:* King Kong 1976, All That Jazz 1979, How to Beat the High Cost of Living 1980, The Postman Always Rings Twice 1981, Frances 1982, Tootsie 1982 (Acad. award for best supporting actress 1982), Country 1984, Sweet Dreams 1985, Crimes of the Heart 1986, Everbody's All American 1989, Far North 1989, Music Box; Star Showtime TV production Cat On A Hot Tin Roof 1984; in Summer stock production Angel On My Shoulder, N.C. 1980. *Address:* 8899 Beverly Boulevard, Los Angeles, California 90048, U.S.A.

LANGE, Otto Ludwig, DR. RER. NAT.; German professor of botany; b. 21 Aug. 1927, Dortmund; s. of Otto Lange and Marie (née Pralle) Lange; m. Rose Wilhelm 1956; two d.; ed. Univs. of Göttingen and Freiburg; Asst. Prof. Univ. of Göttingen 1953–61; Dozent Technische Universität Darmstadt 1961–63; Prof. Forest Botany Univ. Göttingen 1963–67; Prof. Botany Univ. of Würzburg 1967–; Visiting Scientist Utah State Univ. 1973, 1985, Australian Nat. Univ., Canberra 1978–79; Dir. Botanical Garden, Univ. of Würzburg; Antarctic Service Medal, U.S. Govt. 1972, Verdienstkreuz, (1st Class) Fed. Repub. of Germany 1985, Leibniz Prize, Deutsche Forschungsgemeinschaft 1986; Bulsan Prize for "Applied botany including ecology" 1988; mem. Deutsche Akad. der Naturforscher Leopoldina, Bayerische Akad. der Wissenschaften; Corresp. mem. Akad. der Wissenschaften Göttingen. *Publications:* Ed. (with others); 4 vols. of Physiological Plant Ecology in Encyclopaedia of Plant Physiology 1981–83, also scientific journals Oecologia, Photosynthetica, Flora, Trees, Acta Botanica, book series Ecological Studies; 250 scientific papers. *Address:* Lehrstuhl für Botanik der Universität Würzburg, Mittlerer Dallenbergweg 64, D-8700 Würzburg (Office); Leitengraben 37, D-8700 Würzburg, Federal Republic of Germany (Home). *Telephone:* 0931-73085 (Office); 0931-705249 (Home).

LANGE, Per; Danish writer; b. 30 Aug. 1901, Hørsholm, Denmark; s. of Sven Lange and Mimi Blad; m. Hanne Thiele 1942; one s. two d.; Freelance trans. and literary critic; former book critic of Berlingske Tidende; on staff of Sind og Samfund 1932–37; Literary adviser Gyldendals Forlag, Copenhagen 1946–. *Publications:* Poems: Kaos og Stjœrnen 1926, Forvandlinger 1929, Orfeus 1932, Relieffer 1943; Spejlinger (essays) 1953, Ved Musikkens Tœrskel (essays) 1957, Samtale med Æsel (essays) 1961, Om Krig og Krigsmœnd (essays) 1966, Dyrenes Maskerade (essays) 1969; also numerous trans. of English, French and American authors. *Leisure interest:* music. *Address:* Dr. Olgasvej 5, DK-2000 Frederiksberg, Denmark. *Telephone:* (01) 190056.

LANGELAND, Arne Lodvar; Norwegian diplomatist and international official; b. 24 Nov. 1928, Nötterö; m. Harriet Karen Lulla 1954; two s. three d.; ed. Univ. of Oslo; joined Foreign Service 1953; served in Del. to OEEC, NATO in Paris 1954–56, Embassy in Turkey 1957–59; Ministry of Foreign Affairs 1959–65; served in Del. to Geneva 1965–70; private business 1970–75; Deputy Sec.-Gen. EFTA 1976–78; Dir.-Gen., Ministry of Trade and Shipping, Oslo Nov. 1978–81, Sec.-Gen. 1981–82; Dir.-Gen. Export Council of Norway Dec. 1982–. *Address:* The Export Council of Norway, Drammensvn. 40, Oslo 2, Norway. *Telephone:* (02) 11.40.30.

LANGEMEIJER, Gerard Eduard, DR. JUR.; Netherlands lawyer; b. 3 Nov. 1903, Dieren; s. of Mr. and Mrs. E. G. Langemeijer; m. 1958; ed. Univ. of Leiden; called to the Bar 1928; Dist. Attorney, Rotterdam 1929–34; The Hague 1934–39; Judge, Amsterdam 1939–46; Prof. of Law, Leiden Univ. 1946–58; Asst. Attorney-Gen. Supreme Court 1947–57, Attorney-Gen. 1957–73; Pres. Royal Netherlands Acad. of Sciences and Letters 1963–68; Co-editor of Nederlands Juristenblad (Law Review). *Address:* Flat 7, Rozenhof, 8161 BD, Epe G, Netherlands.

LANGLAIS, Jean-François-Hyacinthe; French composer and organist; b. 15 Feb. 1907, La Fontenelle, Ille-et-Vilaine; s. of Jean Langlais and Flavie Canto; m. 1st Jeanne Sartre 1931 (deceased); one s. one d.; m. 2nd Marie-Louise Jaquet 1979, one d.; ed. Conservatoire de Paris (Premier Prix d'Orgue); blind from birth; taught at Institution Nationale des Jeunes aveugles de Paris 1930–68; Organist Sainte-Clotilde Basilica, Paris 1945–; Prof. of Organ, Schola Cantorum de Paris 1961–76; int. recitalist (300 concerts in U.S.A.); Grand Prix du Disque français. *Compositions:* more than 300 works for organ, 3 concertos for organ and orchestra, 13 Masses, vocal and instrumental works, both sacred and secular; Prix Madame René Coty for Missa Salve Regina 1955; Commandeur des Arts et Lettres; Officier de la Légion d'Honneur et des Palmes académiques; Dr. h.c. (Pittsburgh, Fort Worth and Washington D.C., U.S.A.). *Leisure interests:* loves animals, particularly dogs. *Address:* 26 rue Duroc, 75007 Paris, France. *Telephone:* (1) 4734 7205.

LANGLANDS, Robert Phelan, M.A., PH.D., F.R.S.; Canadian mathematician; b. 6 Oct. 1936, New Westminster; s. of Robert Langlands and Kathleen J. Phelan; m. 1956; two s. two d.; ed. Univ. of British Columbia, Yale Univ.; Instr., Assoc. Prof. Princeton Univ. 1960–67; Prof. Yale Univ. 1967–72; Prof. Inst. for Advanced Study, Princeton 1972–; several awards. *Publications:* Automorphic Forms on GL (2) (with H. Jacquet) 1970, Euler Products 1971, On the Functional Equations Satisfied by Eisenstein Series 1976, Base Change for GL (2) 1980, Les Débuts d'une Formule des Traces Stable 1983. *Leisure interests:* reading, travel. *Address:* School of Mathematics, Institute for Advanced Study, Princeton, N.J. 08540 (Office); 60 Battle Road, Princeton, N.J. 08540, U.S.A. (Home). *Telephone:* (609) 734-8106 (Office); (609) 921-7222 (Home).

LANGLEY, Maj.-Gen. Sir (Henry) Desmond (Allen), K.C.V.O., M.B.E.; British army officer (retd.); b. 16 May 1930, London; s. of Col. Henry Langley and Winsome (née Allen) Langley; m. Felicity Joan Oliphant 1950; one s. one d.; ed. Eton Coll. and Royal Mil. Acad., Sandhurst; commissioned Life Guards 1949; served in regimental and staff appts. in U.K., Egypt, Libya, Germany, Singapore and Malaysia; commanded the Life Guards 1969–71, Household Cavalry 1973–75, 4th Guards Armoured Brigade 1976–77, Gen. Officer commanding London Dist. and Maj.-Gen. commanding Household Div. 1979–83, Commdr. British Forces Cyprus and Admin. Sovereign Base Areas 1983–85; Gov. and Commdr.-in-Chief Bermuda 1988–. *Leisure interests:* horses, gardening, sailing, history. *Address:* Government House, Nassau, Bermuda.

LANGONI, Carlos G., D.ECON.; Brazilian banker; b. 23 July 1944, Rio de Janeiro; s. of Geraldo and Marina C. Langoni; m. Vera S. Langoni; two s. one d.; ed. Fed. Univ. of Rio de Janeiro and Univ. of Chicago; Prof. of Monetary Theory and Policy, Postgraduate School of Econs. (EPGE), Getúlio Vargas Foundation 1971; Research Prof., Econ. Research Inst., Univ. of São Paulo 1971; Technical Deputy Dir. EPGE 1972–73, Dir. 1974–79; Dir. Banking Activities, Cen. Bank of Brazil 1979, Pres. Cen. Bank 1980–83; mem. Nat. Monetary Council, Nat. Foreign Trade Council (CONCEX); Brazilian rep. as Alt. Gov. to IMF, mem. Bd. of Govs. IDB, Bd. of Govs. IBRD, Bd. of Govs. Financial Fund for the Devt. of River Plate Basin and of African Devt. Bank; Orders of Naval Merit, of Merit Brasilia and Aeronautico; Grande Medalha da Inconfidencia. *Publications:* Income Distribution and Brazilian Economic Development 1973, The Causes of Brazilian Economic Growth 1974, Transformation Economy 1975, The Economic Policy of Development 1978. *Leisure interest:* tennis. *Address:* c/o Edificio-sede do Banco Central do Brasil, 20.-70.074, Brasilia, Brasil. *Telephone:* (0612) 224-7753 or 224-1503.

LANGSLET, Lars Roar, M.A.; Norwegian politician; b. 5 March 1936, Nesbyen, Buskerud Co.; ed. Univ. of Oslo, in Paris, Munich and Harvard; Lecturer in History of Ideas, Oslo Univ. 1969; mem. Council Norwegian Broadcasting Corpn. 1970–74; deputy mem. Norwegian Language Council 1972–76; Gov. Fondation Européenne de la Culture 1972–; mem. Storting 1969–; mem. Cen. Exec. Conservative Party 1970–; Minister of Culture and Science 1981–86. *Address:* c/o Storting, Oslo, Norway.

LANGUETIN, Pierre; Swiss diplomatist and central banker; b. 30 April 1923, Lausanne; m. Florentina Lobo 1951; one s. one d.; ed. Univ. de Lausanne and L.S.E.; diplomatic career 1949–; in Div. of Exchange, OEEC, Paris; in Div. of Commerce, Fed. Dept. of Public Economy 1955–57, Head of Secr. 1957–61, Chief of Section IA 1961–63; Chief of Subdiv. 1963; has been concerned with problems of European econ. co-operation; Asst. Head of Bureau of Integration, Fed. Political Dept. and Dept. of Public Economy 1961–; Swiss Del. to Trade Cttee., OECD, Paris 1961–76, Vice-Pres.

1963–76; mem. Swiss Del. to UNCTAD Geneva 1964; Swiss Rep. at various int. orgs. 1965–66; Del. of Fed. Council for Trade Negotiations, title of Minister Plenipotentiary 1966–68; Head of Swiss Del. to EFTA Geneva 1967–77, title of Amb. 1968–74; Head of Swiss Del. to Second UNCTAD New Delhi 1968; Head of Swiss Del., Trade and Devt. Bd. 1967–70; Deputy Head of Swiss Negotiating Team with EEC 1970–72; Head of Swiss Del. to Exec. Cttee. in special session OECD 1972–76; Head of Swiss Del. for accession negotiations to Int. Energy Agency 1974, Rep. for Switzerland to Governing Bd. 1974–76; mem. Governing Bd. of Swiss Nat. Bank 1976–, Vice-Chair. 1981–84, Chair. 1985–88; Chair. Inst. for Public Admin. Studies, Lausanne 1988–; Vice-Chair. Sandoz S.A. 1988–; mem. Bd. of Dirs. Swiss Reinsurance Co. 1988–; mem. Advisory Bd. American Int. Group; mem. Int. Red Cross Cttee. 1988–; Dr. h.c. (Lausanne) 1979. *Address:* 37 Mulinenstrasse, 3006 Berne, Switzerland.

LANKESTER, Timothy Patrick, M.A.; British government official; s. of Robin P. A. Lankester and Jean D. Gilliat; m. Patricia Cockroft 1968; three d.; ed Monkton Combe School, St. John's Coll. Cambridge and Jonathan Edwards Coll., Yale; teacher St. Michael's Coll., Belize 1960–61; Fereday Fellow, St. John's Coll. Oxford 1965–66; Econ. IBRD, Washington, D.C. 1966–69, New Delhi 1970–73; HM Treasury 1973–78; Pvt. Sec. to Prime Minister Callaghan 1978–79, to Prime Minister Thatcher 1979–81; seconded to S. G. Warburg & Co. 1981–83; Under-Sec. HM Treasury 1983–85, Deputy Sec. 1988–; Dir. Ocean Transport & Trading PLC 1984–85; Econ. Minister, Washington, D.C. and U.K. Exec. Dir. IMF and IBRD 1985–88. *Leisure interests:* tennis, music, sailing. *Address:* H.M. Treasury, Parliament Street, London, SW1P 3AG, England.

LANOVOY, Vasiliy Semenovich; Soviet stage and film actor; b. 16 Jan. 1934; m. Irina Petrovna Kupchenko 1972; two s.; ed. Shchukin Theatre School; actor with Vakhtangov Theatre 1957–; mem. CPSU 1968–; Lenin Prize 1980, People's Artist of U.S.S.R. 1985. *Theatrical roles include:* Ognev in Korneichuk's Front, Prince Calaf in Gozzi's Princess Turandot, Caesar in Shaw's Anthony and Cleopatra, Sagadeev in Abdullin's Thirteenth President, Don Juan in Pushkin's The Stone Guest. Acted in films: War and Peace, Anna Karenina, The Strange Woman. *Leisure interests:* working as a narrator, hunting, sports. *Address:* Starokonyushenny, House 39, Flat 18, Moscow; Vakhtangov Theatre, Moscow, U.S.S.R.

LANSBURY, Angela; British actress; b. 1925, London; film debut in Gaslight 1944; numerous appearances on London and New York stage and on TV. *Films include:* Manchurian Candidate, In the Cool of the Day, Harlow, Moll Flanders, Bedknobs and Broomsticks, Death on the Nile, The Lady Vanishes, The Mirror Cracked, The Pirates of Penzance, Company of Wolves. *Address:* c/o William Morris, 31 Soho Square, London, W.1, England.

LANSDOWNE, 8th Marquess of; George John Charles Mercer Nairne Petty-Fitzmaurice, P.C.; British politician; b. 27 Nov. 1912; s. of the late Major Lord Charles Mercer Nairne and of Lady Violet Elliot; m. 1st Barbara Chase 1938 (died 1965), two s. two d. (one deceased); m. 2nd Mrs. Polly Carnegie (d. of Viscount Eccles, q.v.) 1969 (divorced 1978); m. 3rd Gillian Morgan 1978; ed. Eton Coll. and Christ Church, Oxford Univ.; Army service 1939–45, Major 1944, served with Free French Forces; Private Sec. to Rt. Hon. A. Duff Cooper, Amb. to France 1944–45; Lord-in-Waiting to H.M. The Queen 1957–58; Joint Parl. Under-Sec. of State, Foreign Office 1958–62; Chair. Intergovernmental Cttee. Malaysia Aug.-Dec. 1962; Minister of State for Colonial Affairs 1962–64; Pres. Franco-Scottish Soc.; Prime Warden Fishmongers' Co. 1967–68; Conservative. *Address:* Meikleour House, Perthshire, Scotland.

LANSING, Sherry, B.S.; American business executive; b. 31 July 1944, Chicago, Ill.; d. of Norton and Margot Lansing; ed. Northwestern Univ., Evanston, Ill.; mathematics teacher, Public High Schools, Los Angeles, Calif. 1966–69; model, TV commercials, Max Factor Co. and Alberto-Culver 1969–70; appeared in films Loving and Rio Lobo 1970; Exec. Story Ed., Wagner Int. 1970–73; Vice-Pres. for Production, Heyday Productions 1973–75; Exec. Story Ed., then Vice-Pres. for Creative Affairs, MGM Studios 1975–77; Vice-Pres., then Sr. Vice-Pres. for Production, Columbia Pictures 1977–80; Pres. 20th Century-Fox Productions 1980–83; independent producer, Jaffe-Lansing Productions, L.A. 1983–; producer Racing with the Moon 1984, Firstborn 1984, Fatal Attraction 1987. *Address:* Jaffe-Lansing Productions, 5555 Melrose Avenue, Los Angeles, Calif. 90038, U.S.A.

LANUSSE, Gen. Alejandro Agustín; Argentine army officer; b. 28 Aug. 1918, Buenos Aires; s. of Gustavo Lanusse and Albertina Gelly; m. Ileana Bell; five s. four d.; ed. Colegio Militar de la Nación and Escuela Superior de Guerra; Commdr. San Martin Regt.; Mil., Naval and Air Attaché, Mexico 1958–60; Chief of Staff, 3rd Cavalry Div. 1960; Deputy Dir. Escuela Superior de Guerra 1960–62; Commdr. 1st Armoured Cavalry Div. 1962–64; Army Command 1965–66; Commdr. 3rd Army, Córdoba 1967; C.-in-C. of Army 1968; C.-in-C. of the Armed Forces 1971–73; Pres. of Argentina 1971–73; detained May 1977, released June 1977.

LAO CHONGPIN; Chinese artist; b. 3 Nov. 1936, Xinxing City., Guangdong; s. of Lao Xianguang and Chen Ermei; m. Luo Yuying 1956; two s. one d.; ed. Fine Arts Dept., Cen. China Teachers' Coll.; has painted more than one thousand landscapes and human figures in Japan, Canada, France, Egypt, Yugoslavia, Democratic People's Repub. of Korea, Pakistan,

Burma, Jordan, Hungary, U.S.S.R., Albania 1973–; Dir. Poetry Inst. 1987–; mem. staff Chinese Exhbn. Agency, Ministry of Culture; mem. Chinese Artists' Assen., Advisory Cttee., Beijing Children's Fine Arts Research Acad., Chinese Poetry Assen., Int. Biographical Assen.; Hon. Dir. Hanlin Forest of Steles, Kaifeng; *Major works:* Harvest Time, Spring Ploughing, Harbour, Riverside, Arashiyama in Rain, Mosque in Lahore, Golden Pagoda of Rangoon, Pyramid and Sphinx, Autumn in Amman, Morning Glory on Seine River, Niagara Falls; Group exhbns. include Seven Star Cliff, Japan 1979, Scenery on Xinghu Lake, Mexico 1980, Drum Beaters, Hong Kong 1982, Panda, Wulongtang Waterfall, Belgium 1982, Scenery on Huangshan Mountain, Jordan 1983, Light Boats on the Yangtze River (Nat. Arts Museum, Romania) 1986, Scenes of Petra (Sact City Museum, Jordan) 1987, Waterfall of Lushan Mountain (Zacheta Art Museum, Poland) 1987; one-man show in 15 Chinese cities and provs. 1979–. *Publication:* An Album of Sketches of Life in Foreign Countries 1986. *Leisure interests:* travel, literature, poetry, caligraphy, swimming, table tennis, cultivating flowers. *Address:* China Exhibition Agency, Jia 25 Hao, Dongsi, Shitiao, Beijing, People's Republic of China. *Telephone:* 44.1556.

LAPESA MELGAR, Rafael; Spanish author and university professor; b. 1908, Valencia; s. of Prof. Rafael Lapesa and Ascensión Melgar de Lapesa; m. Pilar Lago Couceiro 1932; ed. Instituto Cardenal Cisneros and Madrid Univ.; engaged in research work at Centro de Estudios Históricos, Madrid, under guidance of Ramón Menéndez Pidal 1927–39; Prof. at Madrid Univ. 1947–78; has lectured as guest Prof. in Univs. of Princeton, Yale, Harvard, California, Pennsylvania, Wisconsin, La Plata, Puerto Rico, Colegio de México and Buenos Aires; mem. Real Acad. Española, Hispanic Soc. of America; corresp. mem. Acad. Argentina de Letras, Acad. Nac. de Letras de Uruguay, Acad. de Artes y Letras de Puerto Rico, etc.; hon. mem. Modern Language Assen. of America and American Assen. of Teachers of Spanish and Portuguese; Dr. h.c. (Toulouse, San Marcos, Lima, Valencia, Salamanca, Oviedo). *Publications:* Historia de la Lengua Española 1942, 1951, 1955, 1980, 1981, Asturiano y Provenzal en el Fuero de Avilés 1948, La trayectoria poética de Garcilaso 1948, 1968, La obra literaria del Marqués de Santillana 1957, De la Edad Media a nuestros días 1967, 1971, Poetas y prosistas de ayer y de hoy 1977, Estudios de Historia Lingüística Española 1984. *Address:* Residencia de Profesores, Ministro Ibáñez Martín 3, 28015 Madrid, Spain. *Telephone:* 243-77-66.

ŁAPICKI, Andrzej; Polish actor and director; b. 11 Nov. 1924, Riga; s. of Borys and Zofia Łapicki; m. Zofia Chrząszczewska 1947; one s. one d.; ed. Underground Inst. of Theatrical Art, Warsaw; Extraordinary Prof. 1979; Actor in Łódź: Polish Army Theatre 1945–48, Kameralny (Chamber) Theatre 1948–49; in Warsaw: Współczesny (Contemporary) Theatre 1949–64, 1972–81, Dramatyczny (Dramatic) Theatre 1964–66, 1982–83, Polski Theatre, Warsaw 1983–; Lecturer Higher State School of Drama, Warsaw 1953–, Asst. Prof. 1970–79, Extraordinary Prof. 1979–87, Ordinary Prof. 1987–, Dean Actors' Faculty 1971–81, Rector 1981–87; mem. SPATiF-ZASP (Assen. of Polish Theatre and Film Actors) until 1982 (Vice-Pres. 1976–79); Minister of Culture and Art Prize (1st Class), Pres. of Radio and TV Cttee. Prize (five times), Officer's and Kt.'s Cross Order of Polonia Restituta, Gold Cross of Merit and other distinctions. *Major parts:* about 100 theatre, 50 TV and 30 film parts; *major theatre roles:* The Respectable Prostitute, The Night of the Iguana, L'Ecole des femmes, Ring Round the Moon, Biedermann und die Brandstifter, Way of Life; *major films:* Everything for Sale, Pilatus und Andere, The Wedding, How Far from Here, How Near; dir. of about 30 TV and 20 theatre plays. *Address:* ul. Karłowicza 1/7 m. 50, 02-501 Warsaw, Poland.

LAPIERRE, Dominique; French journalist and author; b. 30 July 1931, Châtelaillon, Charente-Inférieure; s. of Jean Lapierre and Luce (Andreotti) Lapierre; m. 2nd Dominique Conchon; one d. (by first m.); ed. Lycée Condorcet, Paris and LaFayette Univ., Easton, U.S.A.; journalist and reporter, Paris Match 1954–67; f. and Pres. Action Aid for Leper Children of Calcutta. *Publications:* Un dollar les mille kilomètres 1949, Lune de miel autour de la terre 1953, En liberté sur les routes d'U.R.S.S. 1957, Russie portes ouvertes 1957, Les Caïds de New York 1958, Chessman m'a dit 1960; with Larry Collins: Is Paris Burning 1964?, I'll Dress You In Mourning 1967, O Jerusalem 1971, Freedom at Midnight 1975, The Fifth Horseman 1980; with Stephane Groueff: Les Ministres du Crime 1969, La Cité de la joie 1985, Les héros de la Cité de la joie 1986. *Address:* 26 avenue Kléber, 75116 Paris; Les Bignoles, 83350 Ramatuelle, France. *Telephone:* 4500 8556.

LAPIN, Sergey Georgiyevich; Soviet diplomatist and journalist; b. 15 July 1912, St. Petersburg (now Leningrad); ed. Univ. of Leningrad; mem. CPSU 1939–; journalist, editor, Vice-Chair. Radio Cttee. 1945–55; Diplomatic Service 1955; Head, Third European Dept. Ministry of Foreign Affairs 1955–56; Amb. to Austria 1956–60; Vice-Chair. State Comm. for Cultural Relations with Foreign Countries 1960; Minister of Foreign Affairs of R.S.F.S.R. 1960–62; Deputy U.S.S.R. Minister of Foreign Affairs 1962–65; mem. CPSU Central Cttee. 1966–; Amb. to People's Republic of China 1965–66; Dir.-Gen. of TASS 1967–70; Deputy to Supreme Soviet of U.S.S.R. 1970–; mem. Cttee. U.S.S.R. Parl. Group; Chair. U.S.S.R. State Cttee. for Television and Broadcasting 1970; Hero of Socialist Labour, Order of Lenin (three times), Order of Red Banner of Labour and other decorations. *Address:* U.S.S.R. State Committee for Television and Broadcasting, Pyatnitskaya ulitsa 25, Moscow, U.S.S.R.

LAPIS, Károly, PH.D.; Hungarian pathologist and clinical oncologist; b. 14 April 1926; s. of Károly Lapis and Eszter Földesi; m. Ibolya Keresztes; one s.; ed. Lóránd Eötvös Univ. Budapest; certified in clinical oncology 1980; Scientific worker Oncopathological Research Inst. 1954–63; Prof. Postgraduate Medical School, Budapest 1963–68; Prof. and Dir. 1st Inst. of Pathology and Experimental Cancer Research, Budapest 1968–; Gordon Jacob Fellow Chester Beatty Research Inst., London 1959–60; Eleanor Roosevelt Fellow, Paris 1963–64; Visiting Prof. Duke Univ. Medical School, Durham, N.C. 1972; Fogarty Scholar, Nat. Cancer Inst., Bethesda 1984–85; Corresp. mem. Hungarian Acad. of Sciences 1970, mem. 1979–; Foreign mem. Medical Acad. of the U.S.S.R. 1986–; Pres. 14th Int. Cancer Congress of the UICC, Budapest 1986; Vice-Pres. European Assoc. for Cancer Research 1979–85; mem. European Soc. of Pathology, French Electron Microscope Soc., German Cancer Soc., Corresp. mem. American Assen. for Cancer Research; Dir. Metastasis Research Soc. 1986–; Chief ed. Acta Morphologica, Hungarian Acad. of Sciences, Labour Order of Merit 1978. *Leisure interests:* tennis, gardening. *Publications:* Lymphknotengeschwülste (co-author) 1966, The Liver 1979, Mediastinal Tumors and Pseudotumors (co-author) 1984, Co-ed. Liver carcinogenesis 1979, Ultrastructure of Tumours in Man 1981, Regulation and Control of Cell Proliferation 1984, Tumour Progression and Markers 1982, Biochemistry and molecular genetics of cancer metastasis 1985. *Address:* First Institute of Pathology and Experimental Cancer Research, Semmelweis Medical University, 1085 Budapest, Üllői ut 26, Hungary. *Telephone:* 36 /1/ 334-931.

LAPORTE, William F., A.B., M.B.A.; American business executive; b. 3 Sept. 1913, New York; m. Ruth W. Hillard 1946; one s. two d.; ed. Princeton Univ., and Harvard Coll. of Business Admin.; Pres. Whitehall Pharmacal Co. 1950–57; Vice-Pres. American Home Products Corpn. 1957–60, Dir. 1957–, Pres. 1960–73, Chair. of Bd. 1965–81, Chair. Exec. Cttee. 1981–; Dir. Mfrs. Hanover Trust Co. 1965–82, American Standard Inc. 1975–, B. F. Goodrich Co. 1978–; Trustee, Dime Savings Bank of New York 1966–. *Address:* American Home Products Corporation, 685 Third Avenue, New York, N.Y. 10017 (Office); 435 East 52nd Street, New York, N.Y. 10022, U.S.A. (Home).

LAPORTE, Yves Michel Frédéric, M.D.; French professor of neurophysiology; b. 21 Dec. 1920, Toulouse; s. of Frédéric Laporte and Yvonne Grill; m. Béatrice Colomb de Daunant 1945; two d.; ed. Lycée de Toulouse, Faculté de Médecine, Toulouse and in U.S.A.; intern, Toulouse hosps. 1942; research, Inst. Nat. d'Hygiène 1947–49, 1951–53; Asst. Rockefeller Inst. New York 1949–51; Maître de conférences 1953–58; Prof. of Physiology, Univ. of Toulouse 1958–72; Prof. of Neurophysiology, Coll. de France 1972–; Admin. Coll. de France 1980–; mem. Acad. des Sciences; Chevalier, Légion d'honneur, Commdr. Ordre du Mérite; Grand Prix Scientifique, Ville de Paris; Prix du C.E.A. *Publications:* articles on muscle receptors, spinal cord and synaptic transmission in scientific journals. *Leisure interests:* tennis, bridge. *Address:* Laboratoire de Neurophysiologie, Collège de France, 75231 Paris Cedex 05 (Office); 4 rue Joseph Bara, 75006 Paris, France (Home). *Telephone:* 43.29.12.11. (Office).

LAPPAS, Alfons; German trade unionist; b. 3 June 1929, Wiesbaden; s. of Peter and Therese (née Klee) Lappas; m. Sigrid Albrecht 1954; one d.; ed. secondary school; Dist. Organizer of Horticulture, Agric. and Forestry Union, Fulda and Darmstadt 1951–57, Rheinland-Palatinate Organizer 1957–59, Head of Collective Bargaining Dept., Head Office 1959–61, mem. Exec. 1961–, Vice-Pres. 1966, Pres. 1968; mem. Exec., German Trade Union Confed. (Deutscher Gewerkschaftsbund—(DGB)) 1969; Dir. holding co. for enterprises of DGB 1977–, Chair. –1986; Pres. European Fed. of Agricultural Workers 1968–71; Alt. mem. European Confed. of Trade Unions 1969–77, Finance and Gen. Purpose Cttee., Int. Confed. of Trade Unions 1969–77; mem. Econ. and Social Cttee. of European Communities 1970–76, Pres. 1972–74, 1977. *Leisure interests:* modern literature, music, cross-country running. *Address:* Petunienweg 13, 6382 Friedrichsdorf, Federal Republic of Germany.

LAPPERT, Michael F., PH.D., D.SC., F.R.C.S., F.R.S.; British professor of chemistry; b. 31 Dec. 1928, Brno, Czechoslovakia; s. of Julius and Kornelie (née Beran) Lappert; m. Lorna McKenzie 1980; ed. Wilson's Grammar School and Northern Polytechnic, London; Asst. Lecturer, Northern Polytechnic, London 1952–53, Lecturer 1953–55, Sr. Lecturer 1955–59; Lecturer, Univ. of Manchester Inst. of Sciences and Tech. (UMIST) 1959–61, Sr. Lecturer 1961–64; Reader, Univ. of Sussex 1964–69, Prof. of Chem. 1969–; Science and Eng. Research Council Sr. Research Fellow 1980–85; Tilden Lecturer 1972–73; Chem. Soc. Award in Main Group Metal Chem. 1970; Award in Organometallic Chem. 1978; F.S. Kipping Award, American Chem. Soc. 1976. *Publications:* Metal and Metalloid Amides (jointly) 1979, Chemistry of Organo-Zirconum and -Hafnium Compounds (jointly) 1986; more than 450 papers in scientific journals. *Leisure interests:* golf, tennis, walking, theatre, opera. *Address:* 4 Varndean Gardens, Brighton, BN1 6WL, England. *Telephone:* (0273) 503661.

LAPSLEY, William W., M.S.; American business executive; b. 14 Jan. 1910, Selma, Ala.; s. of Robert Kay and Ethel Baine (Pearce); m. 1st June Louise English 1935 (died 1952), 2nd Frances Vivian Lynn 1953; one s. two d. two step s.; ed. U.S. Mil. Acad., Univ. of Calif. at Berkeley; Maj.-Gen. U.S. Army, retd. 1967; Programme Man. Foreign Management Dept., Kaiser Jeep Corpn., Taiwan; joined Consolidated Edison Co. of New York

Inc. 1969–, Vice-Pres. Cen. Services 1969, Senior Vice-Pres. 1970, Exec. Vice-Pres. Cen. Operations 1971–73, Pres. 1973–75, mem. Bd. of Trustees 1973–; mem. U.S. team that negotiated protocol to Columbia River Treaty with Canada 1961–62; Bronze Star with Oak Leaf Cluster, Legion of Merit, D.S.M. *Leisure interest:* golf. *Address:* 41 Willow Oak Road West, Seapines Plantation, Hilton Head, S.C. 29928, U.S.A. *Telephone:* (803) 671-4957.

LAPTEV, Ivan Dmitrievich, D.PHIL.SC.; Soviet journalist and editor; b. 1936; ed. Siberian Inst.; mem. CPSU 1960–; worked at Omsk River Port 1952–60; teacher 1960–61; instructor, Soviet Army Sports Club 1961–64, literary collaborator and special corresp. Sovietskaya Rossiya 1964–67; Consultant on Kommunist 1967–73; work with CPSU Cen. Cttee. 1973–78; Section Ed. Pravda 1978–82; Deputy Ed. Pravda 1982–84; Chief Ed. of Izvestiya 1984–; elected to Congress of People's Deputies of the U.S.S.R. 1989. *Address:* Izvestiya, Pushkinskaya pl. 5, Moscow, U.S.S.R.

LAQUEUR, Walter; American historian and political commentator; b. 26 May 1921, Breslau, Germany (now Wrocław, Poland); s. of Fritz Laqueur and Else (née Berliner); m. Barbara Koch 1941; two d.; Ed. Survey 1955–65; Dir. Inst. of Contemporary History and Wiener Library, London 1964–; Ed. Journal of Contemporary History 1965–; Prof. of History Brandeis Univ. 1967–72; Prof. of History, Tel Aviv Univ. 1970–; Prof. of Govt. Georgetown Univ. 1979–; Chair. Int. Research Council, Center for Strategic and Int. Studies, Washington D.C. 1973–; Ed. Washington Papers 1973–; Washington Quarterly 1978–; Visiting Prof. of History, Harvard 1977; Rockefeller Fellow, Guggenheim Fellow. *Publications:* Young Germany 1962, The Road to War 1967 1968, Europe Since Hitler 1970, A History of Zionism 1972, Confrontation 1974, Weimar 1974, Guerrilla 1976, Terrorism 1977, A Continent Astray: Europe 1970–78 1979, The Missing Years (novel) 1980, The Terrible Secret 1981, Farewell to Europe (novel) 1981, Germany Today 1985, A World of Secrets 1985, Breaking the Silence 1986, The Age of Terrorism 1987. *Leisure interest:* swimming. *Address:* Center for Strategic and International Studies, 1800 K Street, N.W., Washington, D.C., U.S.A.

LARA BUSTAMANTE, Fernando; Costa Rican lawyer and politician; b. 12 Jan. 1911, San José; s. of Ernesto Lara Iraeta and Angela Bustamante Castro; m. Ofelia Calvo; four s. four d.; ed. Liceo de Costa Rica and Escuela de Derecho; graduated in law 1934; Police Official, San José 1932–37; Official in Ministry of Educ. 1937–40; Dir. Jurisprudencia (law magazine) 1933–36; Deputy to Nat. Assembly 1942, re-elected 1946; mem. Editorial Comm. for Political Constitution 1948; Prof. Faculty of Law 1940–52; Deputy, First Sec., Legis. Assembly 1949; Minister of Foreign Affairs 1949–52, 1966–70; Pres. Colegio de Abogados de Costa Rica 1954–55; Deputy to Legis. Ass. 1958–62, 1966–; Pres. 1960–61; Sec.-Gen. Partido Unión Nacional 1958–66; decorations from Mexico, El Salvador, Panama, France, Italy, Vatican, Ecuador, Taiwan and Cuba. *Address:* Asamblea Legislativa, San José, Costa Rica.

LARAKI, Azeddine, PH.D.; Moroccan politician; b. 1929, Fez; ed. Faculty of Medicine, Paris; Cabinet Dir., Ministry of Nat. Educ. 1958, of Public Health 1959; Dir. Avicenne Hosp., Head of Respiratory Surgery and Pneumology 1960–, Prof. of Medicine 1967–; fmr. mem. Exec. Cttee. Istiqlal –1984; Minister of Nat. Educ. 1977–86; Prime Minister of Morocco Sept. 1986–; mem. Royal Acad. of Morocco. *Address:* Office of the Prime Minister, Rabat, Morocco.

LARAKI, Moulay Ahmed; Moroccan physician, diplomatist and politician; b. 15 Oct. 1931, Casablanca; ed. Univ. de Paris; with Ministry of Foreign Affairs 1956–57; Perm. Rep. to UN 1957–59; Head of Hosp. Services, Casablanca 1956–61; Amb. to Spain 1962–65, to Switzerland 1965–66, to U.S.A. and concurrently accred. to Mexico, Canada and Venezuela 1966–67; Minister of Foreign Affairs 1967–69; Prime Minister 1969–71; medical affairs 1971–74; Minister of State for Foreign Affairs 1974–77.

LARCO COX, Guillermo; Peruvian politician and engineer; b. 19 Feb. 1932; mem. Alianza Popular Revolucionaria Americana (APRA); Mayor of Trujillo 1964–66, 1967–68; civil engineer; Parl. Deputy for Dept. of La Libertad 1980–85; Senator 1985; Prime Minister of Peru 1987–88; Minister for Presidency 1987–88; Minister of Foreign Affairs 1989–. *Address:* Ministry of Foreign Affairs, Ucayali 363, Lima, Peru.

LARDY, Henry Arnold, PH.D.; American professor of biochemistry; b. 19 Aug. 1917, S. Dakota; s. of Nick and Elizabeth Lardy; m. Annrita Dresselhuys 1943; three s. one d.; ed. S. Dakota State Univ. and Univs. of Wis. and Toronto; Asst. Prof., Univ. of Wis. 1945–47, Assoc. Prof. 1947–50, Prof. 1950–66, Co-Dir. Inst. for Enzyme Research 1950–, Vilas Prof. of Biological Sciences 1966–; mem. Nat. Acad. of Sciences, American Acad. of Arts and Sciences, American Philosophical Soc., American Soc. Biological Chemists (Pres. 1964), Harvey Soc.; Hon. mem. Japanese Biochemical Soc.; Hon. D.Sc. (S. Dakota State Univ.) 1978; Paul Lewis Award in Enzyme Chem., American Chemical Soc. 1949, Neuberg Medal, American Soc. of European Chemists 1956, Wolf Foundation Prize in Agric. 1981, Nat. Award for Agricultural Excellence 1981, Amory Award, American Acad. of Arts and Sciences 1984, Carl Hartman Award, Soc. for the Study of Reproduction 1984, W. C. Rose Award American Soc. of Biochem. and Molecular Biology 1988, Hilldale Award, Univ. of Wis. 1988. *Publications:* The Enzymes (Co-Editor), 8 vols 1958–63; and research papers in biochemistry in scientific journals. *Leisure interests;* tennis, riding, retriever field

trials. *Address:* 1702 University Avenue, Madison, Wis. 53706; Thorstrand Road, Madison, Wis. 53705, U.S.A. (Home). *Telephone:* 608-262-3372 (Office); 608-233-1584 (Home).

LARENZ, Karl, D.JUR.; German university professor; b. 23 April 1903, Wesel; s. of Karl and Ida Larenz (née Pagenstecher); m. Irmgard Müller 1929; one s. three d.; ed. Univ. of Göttingen; Pvt. Tutor, Göttingen 1929–33; Prof. Univ. of Kiel 1933–60; Prof. Univ. of Munich 1960–71, Emer. Prof. 1971–. *Publications:* Die Methode der Auslegung des Rechtsgeschäfts 1930, Geschäftsgrundlage und Vertragserfüllung 1963, Methodenlehre der Rechtswissenschaft 1983, Richtiges Recht, Grundzüge einer Rechtsethik 1979, Lehrbuch des Schuldrechts 1987; Allgemeiner Teil des deutschen Bürgerlichen Rechts 1989. *Address:* Hubertusstrasse 18, 8000 Munich 19, Federal Republic of Germany. *Telephone:* (089) 176514.

LARKIN, Felix Edward, A.B., M.B.A., J.D., LL.D.; American business executive; b. 3 Aug. 1909, New York; s. of John A. Larkin and Maria C. Henry; m. Evelyn M. Wallace 1937; two s. one d.; ed. Fordham Univ., New York Univ. Graduate School of Business Admin. and St. John's Univ. School of Law; Law Sec. Court of Gen. Sessions, N.Y. 1939–47; Asst. Gen. Counsel, Dept. of Defense 1947–49, Gen. Counsel 1950–51; joined W. R. Grace & Co. 1951, Man. Industrial Relations Div., Vice-Pres. 1955, Exec. Vice-Pres. in charge of Corporate Admin. 1958, Dir. 1963–86, Dir. Emer. 1986–, Pres. and C.O.O. 1971–74, Chair. 1974–81, Chair. Exec. Cttee. 1981–86; Chair. Advisory Council Marine Midland Bank 1981–; Dir. Marine Midlands Banks Inc.; mem. Exec. Reserve Office of Sec. of Defense 1961–63; mem. Nat. Manpower Advisory Cttee, 1962–66; mem. Advisory Cttee. Foreign Service Inst., Washington, D.C. 1961–63; mem. Bd. of Trustees, Fordham Univ., Chair. 1970–77, Trustee Emer. 1978–; Dir. American Arbitration Assen.; mem. several boards. *Publication:* Uniform Code of Military Justice. *Leisure interest:* golf. *Address:* W. R. Grace & Co., Grace Plaza, 1114 Avenue of the Americas, New York, N.Y. 10036 (Office); 1030 Old White Plains Road, Mamaroneck, N.Y. 10543, U.S.A. (Home). *Telephone:* 212-819-7196 (Office).

LARKIN, Terence Alphonsus, B.E., B.SC. (TECH.); Irish business executive; b. 1 Feb. 1924, Newry; s. of Felix Larkin and Ellen Larkin; m. Eileen McGeown 1950; three s. one d.; ed. Univ. Coll. Dublin, Sheffield Univ.; Jt. Man. Dir. Irish Glass PLC 1965–85, Chief Exec. 1985–; Vice-Chair. Irish Plastic Packaging Ltd. 1985–; Chair. Consolidated Plastics 1987–; Pres. Confed. of Irish Industry 1986–; Chair. Governing Body Nat. Inst. for Higher Educ., Dublin 1982–; Fellow The Inst. of Engineers of Ireland 1987–; Council mem. Irish Man. Inst. 1986–; Dir. Irish Glass PLC 1988–; Bd. mem. Council of the Nat. Training Bd. ANCO 1972–82. *Leisure interest:* golf. *Address:* Irish Glass PLC, Charlotte Quay, Ringsend Road, Dublin 4 (Office); South Bank Road, Ringsend, Dublin 4, Republic of Ireland (Home). *Telephone:* 01-68 35 71 (Office).

LAROCHE, Emmanuel Pierre, D. ES. L., F.B.A.; French scholar; b. 11 July 1914, Clamart; s. of Jean Laroche and Valentine Coutris; m. 1st Jane Morel 1944 (divorced 1986), 2nd Lisbeth Franck 1988; two s. one d.; ed. Lycée Michelet, Vanves, Lycée Henri IV, Paris, Ecole Normale Supérieure; teacher at Chartres Lycée 1940–42; lecturer, Faculty of Letters, Nancy 1942–45; Prof., Faculty of Letters, Strasbourg 1946–73; Dir. of Studies (Religious Sciences), Ecole Pratique des Hautes Etudes 1954–84; Prof. (Chair of Languages and Civilization of Asia Minor), Coll. de France 1973–85, Hon. Prof. 1985–; Dir. Inst. français d'archéologie, Istanbul 1965–75; Ed. Revue Hittite et Asianique; Mem. de l'Inst. (Acad. des Inscriptions et Belles-Lettres); Foreign mem. Vienna and Ljubljana Acads. of Sciences, German Archaeological Inst., Turkish History Soc. *Publications:* ten books and 200 articles on the languages, history and civilizations of ancient Asia Minor. *Address:* 24 rue de Verneuil, 75007 Paris, France. *Telephone:* 42.61.04.13.

LAROSIÈRE DE CHAMPFEU, Jacques Martin Henri Marie de; French international civil servant; b. 12 Nov. 1929, Paris; s. of Robert and Hugayte (de Champfeu) de Larosière; m. France du Bos 1960; one s. one d.; ed. Lycée Louis-le-Grand, Paris Univ. and Ecole nat. d'admin.; Insp. adjoint 1958, Insp. des Finances 1960; Chargé de Mission in Inspectorate-Gen. of Finance 1961, External Finance Office 1963, Treasury 1965; Asst. Dir. Treasury 1967; Deputy Dir. then Head of Dept., Ministry of Econs. and Finance 1971; Principal Private Sec. to Valéry Giscard d'Estaing (then Minister of Econs. and Finance) 1974; Under-Sec. of Treas. 1974–78; Chair. Deputies Group of Ten 1976–78; Man. Dir. and Chair. Bd., IMF 1978–86; Gov. Banque de France Jan. 1987–; Insp. Gen. des Finances 1981; Dir. Renault 1971–74, Banque nat. de Paris 1973–78, Air France and Soc. nat. de chemins de fer français (S.N.C.F.) 1974–78, Soc. nat. industrielle aerospatiale 1976–78; Censeur Banque de France 1974–78, Crédit nat. 1974–78, Comptoir des Entrepreneurs 1973–75, Crédit foncier de France 1975–78; Vice-Pres. Caisse nat. des Télécommunications 1974–78; Officier, Légion d'honneur, Chevalier, Ordre nat. du Mérite. *Address:* Banque de France, rue de la Vrilliere, 75001 Paris, France.

LARQUIÉ, André Olivier, L. EN D.; French civil servant; b. 26 June 1938, Nay; s. of Henri Larquié and Simone Tauziede; ed. Lycée Louis-le-Grand and Univ. of Paris; Deputy Dir. Musique Art lyrique et Danse, Ministry of Culture and Communications 1978–, Official Rep. 1981–83, 1987; Govt. Commr. Centre nat. d'art et de Culture Georges Pompidou 1981–84; Pres.

Paris Opera 1983–87; Tech. Adviser to the Prime Minister May 1988–; Pres. Théâtre Contemporain de la Danse, Asscn. pour le Dialogue entre les Cultures; Chevalier Légion d'honneur, ordre national du Mérite, Palmes académiques, Commandeur des Arts et Lettres. *Publications:* official reports. *Leisure interests:* song and dance. *Address:* Hôtel de Matignon, 57 rue de Varenne, 75700 Paris, France (Office). *Telephone:* 42 75 80 41 (Office).

LARRABEE, Martin Glover, PH.D.; American professor of biophysics; b. 25 Jan. 1910, Boston, Mass.; s. of Ralph Clinton Larrabee and Ada Perkins Miller; m. 1st Sylvia Kimball 1932 (divorced 1944), one s.; m. 2nd Barbara Belcher 1944, one s.; ed. Harvard Coll. and Univ. of Pennsylvania; Research Asst. and Fellow, Univ. of Pa. 1934–40, Assoc., Asst. Prof., Assoc. Prof. 1941–49; Asst. Prof. of Physiology, Cornell Medical Coll., New York City 1940–41; Assoc. Prof. of Biophysics, Johns Hopkins Univ. 1949–63, Prof. of Biophysics 1963–; mem. Nat. Acad. of Sciences, American Physiological Soc., Biophysical Soc., Int. Soc. for Neurochem., American Soc. for Neurochem., Soc. for Neuroscience; Foreign Assoc. Physiological Soc., England; Hon. M.D. (Lausanne) 1974. *Publications:* About 60 technical papers and 60 abstracts covering original research in the circulatory, respiratory and nervous systems of mammals, especially on synaptic and metabolic mechanisms in sympathetic ganglia. *Leisure interests:* hiking, trail construction and maintenance, skiing. *Address:* Department of Biophysics, Johns Hopkins University, Baltimore, Md. 21218, U.S.A. *Telephone:* 301-338-7256 or 7245.

LARRE, René J.; French civil servant; b. 21 Feb. 1915, Pau; m. 1st Monique Bailac (deceased), three d.; m. 2nd Thérèse Allègre 1961; ed. Faculté de Droit and Ecole des Sciences Politiques, Paris; Inspector of Finance 1942–45; External Relations Dept., Ministry of Econ. Affairs 1946–50; Asst. Exec. Sec. Int. Materials Conf. 1951; Tech. Counsellor, French Embassy, Washington 1952–54; Tech. Adviser, Office of Minister of Finance 1955; Dir. Office of Sec. of State for the Budget 1956; Exec. Dir. IBRD 1957–67; Dir. Office of Minister of Finance 1957–58; Exec. Dir. EIB 1958–61; Financial Minister, French Embassy in Washington, D.C. 1961–67; Exec. Dir. IMF 1964–67; Dir. of Treasury, Ministry of Finance, Paris 1967–71; Gen. Man. BIS 1971–81; Counsellor to Schneider S.A. 1981–86; Chair. B.E., Finter Bank France 1987–; Commdr., Légion d'honneur. *Address:* 1 rue François 1e, Paris 8e, France (Office); 84 Lange Gasse, Basel, Switzerland (Home).

LARROCHA, Alicia de; Spanish concert pianist; b. 23 May 1923, Barcelona; d. of Eduardo and Teresa (de la Calle) de Larrocha; m. Juan Torra 1950; one s. one d.; ed. private school; first public recital, Barcelona 1928; first orchestral concert with Madrid Symphony Orchestra under Fernandez Arbós, Madrid 1935; concert tours in Europe, South America, U.S.A., Canada, Japan, South Africa, New Zealand, Australia; Dir. Academia Marshall, Barcelona 1959; mem. Bd. Dirs. Musica en Compostela 1968; Hon. Pres. Int. Piano Archives, New York 1969; corresp. mem. Hispanic Soc. of America, New York 1972; Gold Medal, Academia Marshall 1943, Harriet Cohen Int. Music Award 1956, Grand Prix du Disque Académie Charles Cros, Paris 1960, 1974, Paderewski Memorial Medal 1961, Orders of Civil Merit 1962, Isabel la Católica 1972, Edison Award, Amsterdam 1968, first Gold Medal, Mérito a la Vocación 1973, Grammy Award, U.S.A. 1974, 1975, Musician of the Year (Musical America Magazine) 1978, Edison Award, Amsterdam 1978, Gold Medal, Spanish Int. (U.S.A.) 1980.

LARRY, R. Heath, LL.D., J.D.; American steel company executive; b. Feb. 1914, Huntingdon, Pa.; s. of Ralph E. and Mabel (Heath) Larry; m. Eleanor Ketler 1938; three s.; ed. Grove City Coll., Univ. of Pittsburgh; Attorney, Nat. Tube Co. 1938–44, Sec., then Dir. 1944–48; Attorney, U.S. Steel Corpn. 1948–52, Asst. gen. solicitor 1952–58, Admin. Vice-Pres. Labour Relations 1958–66, Exec. Vice-Pres., asst. to Chair. 1966, Vice-Chair. Bd. of Dirs. 1969, retd. 1977; Pres. Nat. Asscn. of Mfrs. 1977–80; with Reed, Smith, Shaw & McClay, Washington 1980–; mem. Bd. of Visitors, Univ. Pittsburgh, Council on Foreign Relations, Ethics Resource Center, U.S.-U.S.S.R. Trade and Econ. Council, The Conf. Board, Foreign Policy Asscn., Business Cttee. for the Arts; Trustee of U.S. Council of Int. Chamber of Commerce Inc. *Leisure interests:* golfing, skiing, sailing. *Address:* 1150 Connecticut Avenue, Washington, D.C. 20036 (Office); Apt. A-3, S. Ballantrae, 4333 N. Ocean Boulevard, Delray Beach, Fla. 33444, U.S.A.

LARSEN, Helge, M.A.; Danish teacher and politician; b. 25 April 1915, Vester-Aaby; s. of Johs. Larsen and Kamilla Larsen; m. Tonny Lolk 1942; one s. one d.; ed. Univ. of Copenhagen; Sec. to Chief Ed. of Politiken (Vald. Koppel) 1942–44; Sec. Social Liberal Party 1943–48; teacher, Copenhagen 1946–49, Nykøbing Falster 1949–65; Headmaster of Gladsaxe Gymnasium 1965–68; mem. Folketing 1956–64, Nordic Council 1957–64; mem. Bd. Danish State Radio and TV 1959–68, 1974–78; Minister of Educ. 1968–71; mem. Cen. Educational Council 1974–82; Univ. Examiner in History 1975–85; Chair. Exec. Bd., Danish European Movt. 1982–. *Publications:* Kensgerninger om Sydslesvig (Facts on Southern Schleswig) 1946, Politiske Grundtanker, liberalisme og socialisme (Political Ideas, Liberalism and Socialism) 1948; contributor to Socialliberale Tanker (Social-liberal Ideas) 1950, De politiske Partier (Political Parties in Denmark) 1950, 1964, Kort besked om EF (Brief Information on the EEC), Det Radikale Venstre 1955–80 (Radical Liberal Party 1955–80) 1980, Avis, egn, folk, Holbaek Amts Venstreblad 1905–1980 (Newspaper, County, People, Newspaper of

Holbaek County 1905–1980) 1980, Egnens Avis i Folkeje, Skive Folkeblad 1906–81 (Skive Folkeblad, local newspaper owned by the people) 1981, Fra Liberalisme til radikalisme Københavns liberale Vaelgerforening 1883–1908 1985. *Address:* Malmøgade 12, 2100 Copenhagen, Denmark.

LARSEN, Kai, B.A., M.SC.; Danish professor of botany; b. 15 Nov. 1926, Hillerød; s. of Axel G. Larsen and Elisabeth Hansen; m. Supee Saksuwan 1971; ed. Univ. of Copenhagen; Asst. Scientist, Botany Dept. Univ. of Copenhagen 1952–55; Asst. Prof. Royal Danish School of Pharmacy 1955–62, Assoc. Prof. 1962–63; Prof. of Botany, Aarhus Univ. 1963–; founder, Botanical Inst. and Herbarium Jutlandicum, Aarhus; mem. Royal Danish Acad. and corresp. mem. of other int. socs.; Kt. Order of Dannebrog; Officer, Crown of Thailand. *Publications:* about 200 scientific books and articles on tropical botany, nature conservation. *Leisure interests:* classical music (playing piano). *Address:* Botanical Institute, Nordlandsvej 68, 8240 Risskov (Office); Graastenvej 6, Søften, 8382 Hinnerup, Denmark (Home).

LARSEN, Peder Olesen, DR.PHIL.; Danish research director; b. 7 Sept. 1934, Copenhagen; s. of Kristoffer O. Larsen and Vibeke Nordentoft; m. Lis Nielsen 1958; one s. two d.; ed. Univ. of Copenhagen; Research Assoc. Royal Veterinary and Agricultural Univ. Copenhagen 1958, lecturer 1961, Prof. of Organic Chem. 1968–88, Pro-rector 1981–85; Chair. Danish Natural Science Research Council 1973–75; Chair. Danish Council for Research Policy and Planning 1984–87; Chair. Danish Council for Research Policy and Planning 1984–87; Dir. Danish Research Admin. 1988–; mem. Royal Danish Acad. of Science and Letters. *Publication:* Research Policy in a Small Country 1981. *Address:* Danish Research Administration, Holmens Kanal 7, 1060 Copenhagen K (Office); Marievej 10A, 2, 2900 Hellerup, Denmark (Home). *Telephone:* 451 114 300 (Office); 451 610 572 (Home).

LARSON, Arthur, M.A., D.C.L., LL.D.; American lawyer, writer and politician; b. 4 July 1910, Sioux Falls; s. of Judge Lewis Larson and Anna B. (Huseboe); m. Florence Faye Newcomb 1935; one s. one d.; ed. Augustana Coll., Univ. of South Dakota and Pembroke Coll., Oxford; practised law Milwaukee, Wisconsin 1935–39; Asst. Prof. of Law, Univ. of Tenn. 1939–41; Div. Counsel, Office of Price Admin., Washington 1941–44; Head Scandinavian Branch, Foreign Econ. Admin., Washington 1944–45; Prof. of Law, Cornell Law School 1945–53; Dean Univ. of Pittsburgh Law School 1953–54; Under-Sec. of Labour, Washington 1954–56; Dir. U.S. Information Agency 1956–57; Speech Writer to Pres. 1957–58; Special Consultant 1958–61; Dir. Rule of Law Research Centre; James B. Duke Prof. of Law, Duke Univ., Durham N.C. 1959–; Consultant, U.S. Dept. of State; Consultant to Pres. on Foreign Affairs; Hon. Fellow, Pembroke Coll., Oxford. *Publications:* Towards World Prosperity (jt. author) 1947, Cases on Corporations (with R. S. Stevens) 1947, The Law of Workmen's Compensation, 10 vols. 1952, Know Your Social Security 1955, 1959, A Republican Looks at his Party 1956, What We Are For 1959, The International Rule of Law 1961, When Nations Disagree 1961, A Warless World 1963, Propaganda: Towards Disarmament in the War of Words (with J. B. Whitton) 1964, Vietnam and Beyond (with D. R. Larson) 1965, Eisenhower: The President Nobody Knew 1968, Population and Law (with L. T. Lee) 1971, Workmen's Compensation for Occupational Injuries and Death (2 vols.) 1972, The Law of Employment Discrimination (5 vols.) 1975, Workers' Compensation Law, Cases, Materials and Text 1984. *Leisure interests:* collecting and playing ancient stringed instruments, classical guitar, baritone soloist Duke Opera Group, wood and metal sculpture. *Address:* The Law School, Duke University, Durham, N.C. (Office); No. 1 Learned Place, Durham, N.C. 27705, U.S.A. (Home). *Telephone:* 919-684-3518 (Office); 919-489-4530 (Home).

LARSSON, Lars-Erik; Swedish musician; b. 15 May 1908, Åkarp; s. of Lilly and Vilner Larsson; m. Brita Holm 1936; one s.; ed. Stockholm, Vienna and Leipzig; at Royal Swedish Opera 1930–31; music critic 1933–37; conductor Swedish Broadcasting Co. 1937–54; Prof. Kungl. Musikhögskolan 1947–59; Dir. of Music, Uppsala 1961–65; mem. Council Swedish Asscn. of Composers. *Compositions:* three Concert Overtures, Sinfonietta for String Orchestra, Serenade for Strings, Divertimento, Pastoral Suite, Music for the Orchestra, Orchestral Variations, Three Orchestral Pieces, Lyric Fantasy, Due Auguri, Saxophone Concerto, Violin Concerto, 12 Concertinos, music to Shakespeare's The Winter's Tale; opera—The Princess of Cyprus; Disguised God and The Sundial and the Urn for solo, choir and orchestra, Missa Brevis and Three Quotations for unaccompanied choir; chamber music, songs and piano music.

LA SALLE, Roch; Canadian politician; b. 6 Aug. 1929, Saint-Paul-de-Joliette; m.; four c.; worked initially as butcher's apprentice, later turned to marketing, and held several man. positions; became Canada's youngest Mayor 1957, leader of town council, Crabtree, Joliette Co., Quebec 1957–65; M.P. for Joliette 1968–; Minister of Supply and Services 1979–80, of Public Works and Minister responsible for Nat. Capital Comm. 1984–86, Minister of State 1986–87; fmr. mem. numerous parl. cttees. including those for Agric., Regional Econ. Expansion, Health and Welfare. *Address:* House of Commons, Ottawa, Canada.

LASDUN, Sir Denys Louis, Kt., C.B.E., F.R.I.B.A.; British architect; b. 8 Sept. 1914; s. of Norman and Julie (née Abrahams) Lasdun; m. Susan Bendit 1954; two s. one d.; ed. Rugby School, Architectural Asscn., London; served with Royal Engineers 1939–45 (M.B.E.); practised with Wells Coates, Tecton, Drake; with Alexander Redhouse and Peter Softley 1960–

85; in pvt. practice with Peter Softley and Assocs. 1986-; Hoffman Wood Prof. of Architecture, Univ. of Leeds 1962-63; Assessor, Competitions for Belgrade Opera House 1971, and new Parl. Bldg., London 1971-72. *Works include (in London):* housing and schools for Bethnal Green and Paddington, HQ of Govt. of N.S.W., flats at 26 St. James's Place, Royal Coll. of Physicians, work for the Univ. of London (S.O.A.S.), Inst. of Educ., Law Inst., project for Courtauld Inst., Nat. Theatre and IBM Cen. London Marketing Centre, South Bank, office bldg., 6-12 Fenchurch St. *Other works include:* Fitzwilliam Coll. and Christ's Coll. extensions, Cambridge, devt. plan and bldgs. for new Univ. of East Anglia, Univs. of Leicester and Liverpool redevts.; EEC HQ for EIB Luxembourg, Hurva Synagogue, Old City of Jerusalem; Cannock Community Hosp., Genoa Opera House; Trustee, British Museum 1975-85; mem. CIAM and MARS Group 1935-59, Victoria and Albert Advisory Council 1973-83, Slade Cttee. 1976-, Arts Panel, Arts Council of G.B. 1980-84; mem. Acad. d'Architecture (Paris), Acad. Nazionale di San Luca (Rome) 1983; Hon. Fellow, AIA 1966, Bulgarian Inst. of Architects 1985, Int. Acad. of Architecture 1986; Hon. D.Arch (Manchester) 1966, Hon. F.R.C.P. 1975, Hon. D.Litt. (E. Anglia) 1974, (Sheffield) 1978; R.I.B.A. London Architecture Bronze Medallist 1960, 1964; Civic Trust Awards, Class 1 1967, Group A 1969, Special Award, São Paulo Biennale, Brazil 1969; Concrete Soc. Award 1977, R.I.B.A. Gold Medal 1977; R.I.B.A. Architectural Award for London Region 1978; Academician, Int. Acad. of Architecture, Bulgaria 1987. *Publications include:* An Architect's Approach to Architecture 1965 (R.I.B.A.), A Language and a Theme 1976 (R.I.B.A.), Architecture in an Age of Scepticism 1984 and contribs. to architectural and other papers. *Address:* 146 Grosvenor Road, London, SW1V 3JY, England.

LASHKARASHVILI, Tamara Vasiliyevna; Soviet politician; b. 1916, Georgia; ed. Tbilisi State Univ.; tech. instructor with railways 1932-37; mem. CPSU 1946; teacher and Prin. of a middle school 1937-51; Deputy Chief of a Dist. Cttee. of the Georgian S.S.R., Sec. of Tbilisi City Cttee., mem. of Cen. Cttee. of Georgian CP (educ.) 1951-60; Deputy to Supreme Soviet of Georgian S.S.R. 1955-66, 1975-; mem. of Cen. Cttee. of Georgian CP 1956; Minister of Educ. for Georgian S.S.R. 1960-76; Sec. Presidium of Supreme Soviet of Georgian S.S.R. 1976-. *Address:* Supreme Soviet of Communist Party of Georgian S.S.R., Tbilisi, Georgian S.S.R., U.S.S.R.

LASKARIS, Constantine; Greek trade unionist and politician; b. 1918, Athens; with Free Greek Armed Forces; mem. Gen. Confed. of Greek Workers; Adviser to OECD; mem. Exec. Cttee. of Labour Comm., EEC; Instructor Training School for Senior Police Officers 1963-67; Minister of Employment July-Oct. 1974, 1974-81; Founding mem., mem. of Board, Greek NATO Asscn. *Address:* c/o Ministry of Labour, Athens, Greece.

LASKO, Peter Erik, C.B.E., M.A., F.S.A., F.B.A., F.R.HIST.S.; British professor emeritus, writer and lecturer (retd.); b. 5 March 1924, Berlin, Germany; s. of Leo Lasko and Wally Lasko; m. Gwendoline Joan Norman 1948; three d.; ed. St. Martin's School of Art and Univ. of London; Asst. Keeper, Dept. of British and Medieval Antiquities, British Museum 1950-65; Prof., School of Fine Arts, Univ. of E. Anglia, Norwich 1965-74; Dir. and Prof. Courtauld Inst., Univ. of London 1975-85; Trustee, British Museum 1980-, Royal Armouries 1983-; Commr., Cathedrals Advisory Comm. 1980-, Royal Comm. on Historical Monuments of England 1984-. *Publications:* Ars Sacra 800-1200 1972, The Kingdom of the Franks 1971. *Leisure interest:* walking. *Address:* 53 Montagu Square, London, W1H 1TH, England. *Telephone:* 01-723 1843.

LASLETT, Peter, D.LITT., F.B.A.; British historical sociologist, writer and innovator; b. 18 Dec. 1915, Bedford; s. of Rev. S. H. R. Laslett and Eveline E. Alden; m. Janet Crockett Clark 1947; two s.; ed. Watford Grammar School, St. John's Coll., Cambridge; Royal Navy, R.N.V.R. 1940-45; Producer BBC Talks 1946-49; Reader in Politics and History of Social Structure, Cambridge Univ. 1966-; Dir. Cambridge Gp. for the History of Population and Social Structure 1964-; Fellow, Trinity Coll., Cambridge 1953-; mem. Working Party on Foundation of Open Univ. 1965-; Dir. Rank Xerox Unit on Ageing at the Cambridge Group. *Publications:* a series of works on John Locke the philosopher, The World We Have Lost 1965, Household and Family in Past Time 1972, Family Life and Illicit Love in Earlier Generations 1977, Bastardy and its Comparative History (Co-author) 1980. *Leisure interests:* book collecting, gardening. *Address:* Trinity College, Cambridge; Cambridge Group, 27 Trumpington Street, Cambridge, England. *Telephone:* (0223) 358201 (Coll.); (0223) 354248 (Cambridge Group).

LASSEN, Ulrik V., M.D.; Danish professor of physiology and business executive; b. 17 April 1930, Aalborg; s. of Tyge Lassen and Dorritt (née Henriques) Lassen; m. Ulla Regitze Lassen 1957; ed. Univ. of Copenhagen; Research Asst. Univ. of South California 1962-63; Assoc. Prof. of Physiology, Univ. of Copenhagen 1965-67, Prof. 1967-80; Exec. Vice-Pres. Research and Devt., Novo Industri A/S, Copenhagen 1980-84, Sr. Exec. Vice-Pres. 1984-; Gold Medal for experimental work in theoretical medicine, Univ. of Copenhagen. *Publications:* scientific papers on physiology. *Address:* Novo Industri A/S, Novo Allé, 2880 Bagsvaerd (Office); Skowmindevej 26, 2840 Holte, Denmark (Home). *Telephone:* 45 2 98 2333 (Office); 45 2 42 1412 (Home).

LASSILA, Jaakko Sakari, D.SC. (ECON); Finnish banker; b. 27 March 1928, Vaasa; s. of Dr. Yrjö Lassila and Tyyne (Hynynen) Lassila; m. Arnevi

Kytöniemi 1954; three s.; ed. Helsinki School of Econs. and Business Admin.; Alt. Exec. Dir. IBRD (World Bank), IFC, IDA 1960-62; Sec. Bank of Finland 1962-65; Dir. Central Fed. of Finnish Woodworking Industries 1965-67; Pres. Industrialization Fund of Finland Ltd. 1967-70; mem. Bd. Bank of Finland 1970-73; Pres. Pohjola Insurance Co. Ltd. 1974-83, Suomi-Salama Mutual Life Assurance Co. 1977-83; Chair. Bd. and C.E.O. Kansallis-Osake-Pankki 1983-; Grand Cross Order of Lion, Commdr. Order of White Rose of Finland (First Class), Order of Lion, Grand Cross Order of Merit of Fed. Repub. of Germany, Commdr. Order of Icelandic Falcon; Helsinki Medal. *Leisure interests:* fishing, farming. *Address:* Kansallis-Osake-Pankki, Aleksanterinkatu 42, 00100 Helsinki, Finland. *Telephone:* (3580) 1631.

LÁSZLÓ, Andor; Hungarian banker, university professor and economist; b. 24 Dec. 1914, Szombathely; s. of Samuel László and Margit Löwy; m. Agnes Vitéz 1941; one s.; ed. Budapest and Vienna Univs.; Hungarian Gen. Credit Bank, Budapest 1936; Office of State Banks until 1948; directed establishment of Hungarian Savings Bank System 1948; Deputy Chief, Credit Dept. Nat. Bank of Hungary 1948-49; Chief Banking and Credit Dept., Ministry of Finance 1949-54; Prof. Karl Marx Univ., Budapest 1950-; Gen. Man. Nat. Savings Bank 1954-61; Pres. Nat. Bank of Hungary 1961-75 (retd.); Sec. of State 1968-75 (retd.); Pres. Nat. Patriotic Front Finance Control Cttee.; various Hungarian honours. *Address:* Varázs utca 7-9, 1125 Budapest, Hungary. *Telephone:* 767-491.

LATARJET, Raymond, D.SC., M.D.; French research scientist; b. 17 Oct. 1911, Lyons; s. of André Latarjet and Suzanne Linossier; m. Jacqueline Bernard 1940; two s. one d.; ed. Lycée Ampère, Lyons and Univ. of Lyons; Asst. Prof. of Biophysics, School of Medicine, Lyons 1937-41; Head of Lab. (radiobiology), Inst. de Radium, Paris 1941-53, Head of Service 1953-81, Dir. (Biology) 1954-77, Hon. Dir. 1981-; mem. Acad. des Sciences; Commdr. Légion d'honneur; Dr. h.c. (Leeds, Rio de Janeiro etc.) *Publications:* Laponie 1943, D'Abord Vivre 1982, Novelettes 1987; nearly 200 scientific papers in radiation biology and cancer research. *Leisure interests:* sport, literature. *Address:* Institut Curie, 26 rue d'Ulm, 75005 Paris, France. *Telephone:* (1) 46 33 30 16.

LATERZA, Vito; Italian publisher; b. 11 Dec. 1926, Bari; m. Antonella Chiarini 1955; two c.; ed. Univ. of Florence; joined family-owned publishing house Gius. Laterza & Figli 1949, Gen. Man. 1975-. *Address:* Gius Laterza & Figli Spa, via Dante 51, 70121 Bari, Italy. *Telephone:* (080) 5213413.

LATHIÈRE, Bernard, L. EN D.; French aviation executive; b. 4 March 1929, Calcutta, India; s. of Jean and Lucienne (née Fagneaux) Lathière; m. Odette Duport 1957; one s.; ed. Lycée Montaigne and Lycée Henry-IV, Faculty of Law, Paris, Ecole nat. d'admin.; Deputy Insp. of Finances 1955, Insp. of Finances 1957; Rapporteur, Export Comm. 1958; Tech. Adviser to Minister of the Armed Forces 1959-60; Chargé de Mission, direction de la Construction 1961; Tech. Adviser to Minister of Public Works 1962-66; Asst. Man. Air Transport 1966-68, Man. 1968-74; Dir. Sud-Aviation 1968; Pres. French Del. on construction of Concorde, Airbus 1968-; Dir. Soc. Nat. Industrielle Aérospatiale (SNIAS) 1970, mem. Supervisory Council 1974-75, Adviser to Chair. of Bd. 1974-; Dir. Soc. nat. d'études et de construction de moteurs d'aviation (SNECMA) 1970-75; Deputy Govt. Commr. to Air France 1968-, to Union des transports aériens (U.T.A.) 1971-; Pres. and Chief Officer Airbus-Industrie 1975-85, Vice-Pres., Conseil de Surveillance 1985-86; Insp. Gen. of Finances 1979-; Pres. Centre français pour le commerce extérieur 1983-; Dir. Aéroports de Paris 1985-, Pres. 1986-; Officier, Légion d'honneur, Officier de l'Ordre nat. du Mérite, Médaille de l'aéronautique. *Address:* 5 avenue de Villiers, 75017 Paris, France.

LATIMER, Radcliffe Robertson, B.S., M.B.A.; Canadian company executive; b. 2 Oct. 1933, Florence, Ont.; s. of Canon Ralph and Grace Radcliffe Latimer; m. Jacqueline Verret 1982; two s. one d.; ed. McGill Univ., University of Western Ontario; Admin. Asst. CN Rail 1956-, Traffic Research Officer, General Rates Officer 1962, Vice-Pres., Marketing 1974-76, Pres. 1979; Man. of Research, Royal Securities Corpn. 1962-63; Exec. Vice-Pres., Algoma Cen. Railroad 1963-69; Vice-Pres., Operations, White Pass & Yukon Corpn. 1969-73; Exec. Vice-Pres., Grand Trunk Corpn. 1973-74; Pres. and C.E.O., TransCanada PipeLines 1979-; Dir. numerous cos. *Leisure interests:* golf, skiing. *Address:* 6 Highland Avenue, Toronto, Ont., M4W 2AE, Canada.

LATOUR-ADRIEN, Hon. Sir (Jean François) Maurice, Kt., LL.B.; Mauritian judge; b. 4 March 1915; s. of late Louis C. E. Adrien and Maria E. Latour; ed. Royal Coll., Mauritius, Univ. Coll., London and Middle Temple, London; called to the Bar, Middle Temple, and in Mauritius 1940; District Magistrate 1947-48; Crown Counsel 1948-60; Asst. Attorney-Gen. 1960-61; Solicitor-Gen. 1961-64; Dir. of Public Prosecutions 1964-66; Puisne Judge 1966; Chief Justice of the Supreme Court of Mauritius 1970-77; Acting Gov.-Gen. Feb. 1973, July-Aug. 1974, Jan.-Feb. 1975, June-Aug. 1975, July-Sept. 1976; Pres. Mauritius Red Cross 1978-; Vice-Pres. Mauritius Mental Health Asscn. 1978-85, Pres. 1986-; Dir. Mauritius Union Assurance Co. 1978-, Chair. 1983-84, 1985-; Dir. Mauritius Commercial Bank Ltd. 1980-83, 1984-87, Legal Consultant 1983-; Pres. War Memorial Bd. of Trustees 1978-84; Vice-Pres. I.D.E.F. (Institut de Droit d'Expression Française);

Kt. Order of St. Lazarus of Jerusalem 1969. *Address:* c/o Mauritius Union Assurance Co. Ltd., 4 Léoville l'Homme Street, Port Louis, Mauritius.

LATTANZIO, Vito, M.P., M.D.; Italian politician; b. 31 Oct. 1926, Bari; s. of Michele Lattanzio and the late Maria Concetta Mininni; m. Rosa Pellegrini 1956; one d.; ed. medical schools; mem. Chamber of Deputies; Under-Sec. of State for Labour and Social Security June–Nov. 1968; Under-Sec. of State for Industry and Commerce 1968–70; Under-Sec. of State for Defence 1970–74; Minister of Defence 1976–77; Minister of Transport 1977–78, of Civil Defence April 1988–; Pres. of the Bari Regional Direct Farmers' Fed.; Pres. of the Nat. Olive-Growers' Union; Pres. of the Perm. Comm. for Oleaginous Food Materials at EEC; mem. Comm. for Council, Presidential and Home Affairs; Gold Medal of the Italian Red Cross. *Publications:* several works on medicine and science. *Leisure interest:* swimming. *Address:* Via Fratelli Rosselli 32, 70100 Bari, Italy. *Telephone:* 80-334 340; and 80-339 760.

LATTEUR, Jean Pierre, D.JUR.; Belgian administrative official; b. 11 Feb. 1936, Charleroi; s. of Paul Latteur and Antoinette Haegeman; m. Marie Leytens 1961; one s. three d.; Admin. Sec. Sobeac S.A. 1960; Sec.-Gen. and Ed., Adic A.S.B.L. 1964; Consultant, Eurosurvey S.A. 1970; Asst. Gen. Man. Dechy S.A. 1971; Gen. Man. Portal S.A. 1975; Sec.-Gen. and Adviser, Fabrimetal A.S.B.L. 1985; Gen. Man. Fédération de l'Industrie Cimentière 1986–. *Publications:* La participation aux responsabilités dans l'entreprise 1965, L'homme et la révolution urbaine 1968. *Leisure interests:* riding, skiing. *Address:* Rue César Franck 46, 1050 Brussels, Belgium. *Telephone:* (322) 649-9850.

LATTIMORE, Owen, F.R.G.S.; American educator and writer; b. 29 July 1900, Washington, D.C.; s. of David Lattimore and Margaret Barnes Lattimore; m. Eleanor Holgate 1926 (died 1970); one s.; ed. St. Bees School, Cumberland, and Harvard Univ.; business and journalism, China 1919–25; research work for Social Science Research Council in Manchuria 1929–30, for Harvard-Yenching Inst. Peiping 1930–31, for Guggenheim Foundation 1931–33; research, China and Mongolia to 1937; Ed. of Pacific Affairs 1934–41; special political adviser to Generalissimo Chiang Kai-shek 1941–42; Dir. Pacific Operations, Office of War Information 1943–44; mem. Vice-Pres. Wallace's mission in Siberia and China 1944; Econ. Adviser American Reparations Mission in Japan 1945–46; Chief UN Tech. Aid Exploratory Mission to Afghanistan 1950; numerous visits to Mongolia 1961–78; Prof. of Chinese Studies, Leeds Univ. 1963–70, Emer. 1970–; mem. American Philosophical Soc., Royal Geographical Soc., Royal Soc. for Asian Affairs; Foreign mem. Acad. of Sciences Mongolian People's Repub.; Hon. mem. American Geographical Soc., Körosi Csoma Soc., Hungary; Hon. Litt.D. (Glasgow), Hon. Ph.D. (Copenhagen), Hon.D.Jur. (Brown); Cuthbert Peek Grant of Royal Geographical Soc. 1930, Gold Medal Geographical Soc. of Philadelphia 1933, Patron's Medal Royal Geographical Soc. 1942, Gold Medal, Univ. of Ind. 1974. *Publications:* The Desert Road to Turkestan 1928, High Tartary 1930, Manchuria: Cradle of Conflict 1932, The Mongols of Manchuria 1934, Inner Asian Frontiers of China 1940, Mongol Journeys 1941, America and China 1943, The Making of Modern China (with Eleanor Lattimore) 1944, Solution in Asia 1945, China, A Short History (with Eleanor Lattimore) 1947, The Situation in Asia 1949, Pivot of Asia 1950, Ordeal by Slander 1950, Nationalism and Revolution in Mongolia 1955, Nomads and Commissars 1962, Studies in Frontier History 1962, Silks, Spices and Empire (with Eleanor Lattimore) 1968, History and Revolution in China 1974. *Address:* 3 Larchfield, Gough Way, Barton Road, Cambridge, CB3 9LR, England.

LATTRE, André Marie Joseph de; French banker; b. 26 April 1923, Paris; m. Colette Petit 1947; three s. two d.; ed. Univs. de Paris à la Sorbonne and Grenoble, and Ecole libre des sciences politiques; Insp. of Finance 1946; with Ministry of Finance 1948–; Dept. of External Finance 1949–54, Sub-Dir. 1955–58; Alt. Exec. Dir. IMF 1954; Prof. Inst. d'Etudes Politiques, Paris 1958–83; Financial Adviser to Pres. of the Repub. 1958–60; Perm. Sec. Ministry of Finance 1960–61; Dir. of External Finance 1961; Censor, Bank of France 1962, Vice-Gov. 1966–74; Mission to India for Pres. IBRD 1965; Alt. Dir. BIS 1973; Pres. Crédit National 1974–82; World Bank Special Rep. to IDA 1983; Man. Dir. Inst. of Int. Finance, Washington 1983–86; Chair. Banque Française Standard-Chartered 1987–; Commandeur Légion d'honneur and foreign awards. *Publications:* Les Finances extérieures de la France 1959, Politique économique de la France depuis 1945 1967. *Leisure interests:* skiing, tennis. *Address:* 69 rue Perronet, 92200 Neuilly, France. *Telephone:* 46.24.79.00.

LAUBACH, Gerald D., PH.D.; American chemical industry executive; b. 21 Jan. 1926, Bethlehem, Pa.; m. Winifred Isabelle Taylor (died 1979); one s. two d.; ed. Newark High School, Delaware, Univ. of Pennsylvania and Massachusetts Inst. of Tech.; Research fellow M.I.T. 1950; joined Pfizer as research chemist 1950; Research Supervisor 1953–58, Man. Medicinal Products Research 1958–61, Dir. Dept. of Medicinal Chem. 1961–63, Group Dir. Medicinal Research 1963–64, Vice-Pres. Medicinal Products Research 1964–69, mem. Bd. of Dirs. 1968–; Pres. Pfizer Pharmaceuticals 1969–71; Exec. Vice-Pres. Pfizer Inc. 1971–72, Pres. 1972–; Dir. Millipore Corpn., CIGNA Corpn., Pharmaceutical Mfrs. Asscn.; mem. Presidential Comm. on Industrial Competitiveness Aug. 1983–; mem. Bd. of Business, Higher Educ. Forum; Fellow New York Acad. of Sciences; mem. American Asscn. for Advancement of Science, American Chemical Soc., American Manage-

ment Asscn., Soc. of Chemical Industry, Rockefeller Univ. Council, M.I.T. Visiting Cttee., Harvard Coll. Visiting Cttee., Corpn. Polytechnic Inst. of New York, Council on Health Care Tech. of Inst. of Medicine, and other professional and civic associations; Trustee Carnegie Inst. of Washington. *Address:* Pfizer Inc., 235 East 42nd Street, New York, N.Y. 10017 (Office); Lyme, Conn. 06371, U.S.A. (Home). *Telephone:* 212-573-2513.

LAUCKE, Sir Condor Louis, K.C.M.G.; Australian politician; b. 9 Nov. 1914, Greenock, S.A.; s. of Friedrich Laucke and Marie Jungfer; m. Rose Hambour 1942; one s. one d.; ed. Immanuel Coll., Adelaide, South Australian School of Mines; elected to S.A. House of Assembly for Barossa 1956, 1959, 1962; mem. Australian Senate for S.A. 1967–; Deputy Chair. of Senate Select Cttee. on Air Pollution 1968–69; leader Del. to IPU Conf., New Delhi 1969; mem. Select Cttee. on Off-Shore Petroleum Resources 1969–71; Chair. Standing Cttee. on the Social Environment 1971–73; mem. Fed. Parl. Exec. of Liberal Party 1972–74; mem. Standing Cttee. on Finance and Govt. Operations 1974–75, Estimates Cttee. C. (Media, Educ., Tourism, Recreation) 1974–75; Pres. of Australian Senate 1976–81; Lieut.-Gov. of S. Australia 1982–; Joint Pres. of Australian Group of IPU, of Australian Branch of Commonwealth Parl. Assen. *Address:* Australian Senate, Canberra, A.C.T.; Bunawunda, Greenock, S.A., Australia (Home). *Telephone:* 085 628143.

LAUDA, Andreas-Nikolaus ("Niki"); Austrian racing driver; b. 22 Feb. 1949, Vienna; s. of Ernst Peter and Elisabeth Lauda; m. Marlene Knaus 1976; two s.; competed in hill climbs 1968, later in Formula 3, Formula 2 and sports car racing; winner 1972 John Player British Formula 2 Championship; started Formula 1 racing in 1971; World Champion 1975, 1977, 1984, runner-up 1976; *Grand Prix wins:* 1974 Spanish (Ferrari), 1974 Dutch (Ferrari), 1975 Monaco (Ferrari), 1975 Belgian (Ferrari), 1975 Swedish (Ferrari), 1975 French (Ferrari), 1975 United States (Ferrari), 1976 Brazilian (Ferrari), 1976 South African (Ferrari), 1976 Belgian (Ferrari), 1976 British (Ferrari), 1977 South African (Ferrari), 1977 German (Ferrari), 1977 Dutch (Ferrari), 1978 Swedish (Brabham-Alfa Romeo); 1978 Italian (Brabham-Alfa Romeo); retd. 1979; winner of Victoria Sporting Club's Int. Award for Valour in 1977, following recovery from near-fatal crash in 1976 German Grand Prix at Nüburgring; now runs own airline in Austria; returned to racing 1981, won U.S. Formula 1 Grand Prix, British Grand Prix 1982, Dutch Grand Prix 1985; retd. again 1985. *Leisure interests:* music, skiing. *Address:* Hof, near Salzburg, Austria; St. Eulalia, Ibiza, Spain.

LAUDER, Estee; American business executive; b. New York; m. Joseph Lauder; two s.; Chair. Bd. Estee Lauder Inc. (cosmetics co.) 1946–; recipient of numerous awards inc. Neiman-Marcus Fashion Award 1962, Albert Einstein Coll. of Medicine Spirit of Achievement Award 1968, Harpers Bazaar Top Ten Outstanding Women in Business 1970, Médaille de Vermeil de la Ville de Paris 1979, Athena Award 1985; Hon. LL.D. (Univ. of Pa.) 1986. *Publication:* Estee: A Success Story 1985. *Address:* Estee Lauder Inc., 767 Fifth Avenue, New York, N.Y. 10153, U.S.A.

LAUDER, Ronald Stephen, B.S.; American business executive and diplomatist; b. 26 Feb. 1944, New York; s. of Joseph Lauder and Estee Lauder (q.v.); m. Jo Carole Knopf 1967; two d.; ed. Univ. of Pennsylvania, Univ. of Paris (Sorbonne), Univ. of Brussels; Estee Lauder N.V. Belgium 1965–67, Estee Lauder S.A. France 1967, Estee Lauder Sales Promotion Dir. 1968–69, Vice-Pres. Sales Promotion, Clinique 1969–72, Exec. Vice-Pres., Gen. Man. Clinique, Inc. 1972–75, Exec. Vice-Pres. Estee Lauder Int. 1975–78, Exec. Vice-Pres. Estee Lauder Inc., Chair. Estee Lauder Int. 1978–83; Deputy Asst. Sec. of Defense for European and NATO Policy 1983–86; Amb. to Austria 1986–87; Trustee, Museum of Modern Art; Chair. and Pres. Lauder Investments; Trustee Mount Sinai Hosp. Art Collection; Ordre du Mérit (France) Great Cross of the Order of Aeronautical Merit with White Ribbon (Spain), Dept. of Defense Medal for Distinguished Public Service. *Address:* Suite 850, 660 Madison Avenue, New York, N.Y. 10021, U.S.A. *Telephone:* (212) 572-6964.

LAUER, Reinhard, DR.PHIL.; German professor of Slavonic Philology; b. 15 March 1935, Bad Frankenhausen; s. of Erich Lauer and Rose Fischer; m. Stanka Ibler 1962; one d.; ed. Univs. of Marburg, Belgrade and Frankfurt and Freie Univ. Berlin; reader in German Language, Univ. of Zagreb 1960–62; Research Fellow, Univ. of Frankfurt 1962–69; Prof. of Slavonic Philology and Head of Dept. of Slavonic Philology, Univ. of Göttingen 1969–; mem. Göttingen Acad.; hon. mem. Bulgarian Philology Soc.; Valjavec Prize 1961. *Publications:* Heine in Serbien 1961, Gedichtform zwischen Schema und Verfall 1975, Europäischer Realismus 1980, M. Krleža und der deutsche Expressionismus 1984, Sprachen und Literaturen Jugoslaviens 1985, Poetika i ideologija 1987. *Leisure interests:* music, painting, ornithology. *Address:* Seminar für Slavische Philologie der Universität, Platz der Göttinger Sieben, 3400 Göttingen (Office); Baurat-Gerber-Strasse 18, 3400 Göttingen, Federal Republic of Germany. *Telephone:* 0551-394701 (Office); 0551-58210 (Home).

LAUGERUD GARCÍA, Gen. Kjell Eugenio; Guatemalan army officer and politician; b. 24 Jan. 1930, Guatemala City; s. of Pedro E. Laugerud and Catalina García; m. Helen Losi 1951; three s. two d.; Minister of Defence, Chief of Gen. Staff of Army 1970–74; Presidential Cand. of Movimiento de Liberación Nacional/Partido Institucional Democrático

(MLN/PID) March 1974; Pres. of Guatemala 1974–78; numerous awards, including Legion of Merit (U.S.A.) 1971, Gran Collar Orden del Quetzal (Guatemala) 1974, Gran Cruz Brillantes Orden de El Sol (Peru), Orden del Mérito (Chile) 1978, etc. *Leisure interests:* horseback riding, collecting small arms, military history. *Address:* c/o Oficina del Presidente, Guatemala City, Guatemala.

LAUGHTON, Sir Anthony Seymour, Kt., PH.D., F.R.S.; British oceanographic scientist; b. 29 April 1927; s. of Sydney T. Laughton and Dorothy (Chamberlain) Laughton; m. 1st Juliet A. Chapman 1957 (dissolved 1962), one s.; m. 2nd Barbara C. Bosanquet 1973, two d.; ed. Marlborough Coll. and King's Coll. Cambridge; RNVR 1945–48; John Murray Student, Columbia Univ. New York 1954–55; Nat. Inst. of Oceanography, now Inst. of Oceanographic Sciences 1955, fmr. Dir.; Royal Soc. of Arts Silver Medal 1958; Prince Albert 1er Monaco Gold Medal 1980. *Publications:* papers on marine geophysics. *Leisure interests:* music, gardening, sailing. *Address:* Okelands, Pickhurst Road, Surrey, England. *Telephone:* (042 879) 3941.

LAURA, Ernesto Guido; Italian film festival director; b. 4 May 1932, Villafranca, Veronese; s. of the late Manuel Laura and of Pia Romei Laura; m. Anna Maria Vercellotti 1958; two s.; ed. Dept. of Law, Catholic Univ., Milan; Co-Nat. Sec. Centri Universitari Cinematografici 1953–54; Admin. Nat. Sec. Federazione Italiana Circoli del Cinema 1954–55; Chief Ed. Bianco e Nero 1956–58, Filmlexicon 1968; Film Critic, Il Veltro 1958–; mem. Editorial Bd. Rivista del Cinematografo 1967–; Pres. Immagine, Centro Studi Iconografici 1968–; Dir. Venice Film Festival 1969–; has directed various film documentaries including Diario di Una Dama Veneziana 1958, Riscoperta di un Maestro 1960, Alla Ricera di Franz Kafka 1964, Spielberg 1964, Don Minzoni (Special Award) 1967. *Publications:* Il Film Cecoslovacca 1960, La Censura Cinematografica 1961, Ladri di Biciclette 1969. *Address:* 285 Via Conca d'Oro, 100141 Rome, Italy.

LAURAIN, Jean; French teacher and politican; b. 1 Jan. 1921, Metz-Grigy; s. of Lucien Laurain and Georgette Lapointe; m. Anne-Marie Jumeau 1946; two s. two d.; ed. Ecole des Frères, Lycée, Fabert, Metz, Univs. of Lyon, Nancy, Strasbourg; Philosophy Teacher, Lycée Robert-Schuman, Metz; Nat. Sec. Maisons des jeunes et de la culture 1970–75; Gen. Councillor, Metz 1973–79; Pres. Socialist Group of Moselle Gen. Council; Deputy (Moselle) to Nat. Ass. 1978–81, 1986–; mem. European Parl.; mem. Cultural, Family and Social Affairs Comm. 1978–81, 1986–; mem. Regional Council of Lorraine 1978–81; Minister for Ex-Serviceman 1981–83; Sec. of State attached to Minister of Defence responsible for Ex-Servicemen 1983–86; Officier des Palmes Académiques; Médaille d'honneur de la Jeunesse et des Sports. *Publication:* L'éducation populaire 1977. *Address:* 1 rue de la Haye, 57000 Metz (Office); 4 rue Pierre Perrat, 57000 Metz, France (Home).

LAURÉ, Maurice, D. EN D.; French banker and Inspector of Finances; b. 24 Nov. 1917, Marrakesh, Morocco; s. of Prosper Lauré and Marie-Thérèse Delpech; m. Marie-Claude Girard 1955; three s.; ed. Ecole Polytechnique and Paris Univ.; Transmissions Officer, French Army 1938–41; Telecommunications Engineer 1941–45; Gen. Insp. of Finances 1949–; Deputy Dir. of Taxes 1954–55; Govt. Commissioner, Banque d'Etat du Maroc 1955–58; Dir. of Financial Services and programmes, Ministry of Armed Forces 1958–60; Dir. Crédit National 1960–67; Dir.-Gen. Société Générale S.A. 1967–72, Chair. 1973–82; now Chair. Soc. Française de Nouvelles Galeries Réunies; Dir. numerous banks etc.; Commdr. Légion d'honneur, Médaille des Evadés, Commdr. Lion of Finland, Commdr. Ordre national de la Côte d'Ivoire. *Publications:* L'exposé de concours 1952, La taxe sur la valeur ajoutée 1953, Révolution, dernière chance de la France 1953, Traité de politique fiscale 1956, Au secours de la TVA 1957, Reconquérir l'espoir 1983. *Address:* 50 boulevard Haussmann, 75009 Paris (Office); 5 Square Cd. Claude Barrès, 92200 Neuilly-sur-Seine, France.

LAUREL, Salvador Hidalgo, LL.D.; Philippines politician; b. 18 Nov. 1928, Manila; s. of José P. Laurel; m. Celia Franco Daiz Laurel; eight c.; ed. Univ. of the Philippines and Yale Univ.; Senator 1967–73 until imposition of martial law; Prof. of Law and Jurisprudence; founded Legal Aid Soc. of the Philippines; mem. interim Nat. Ass. 1978; active in opposition politics since 1982; leader, United Nationalist Democratic Org. (UNIDO) 1981–, Union for Nat. Action Aug. 1988–; Vice-Pres. of Philippines Feb. 1986–; Prime Minister Feb.–March 1986; Minister of Foreign Affairs 1986–87. *Address:* Office of the Vice-President, Manila, Philippines.

LAURENS, André Antoine; French journalist; b. 7 Dec. 1934, Montpellier (Hérault); s. of André Laurens and Mme née Raymonde Balle; unmarried; ed. Lycée de Montpellier; journalist, L'Eclaireur Meridional (fortnightly), Montpellier 1953–54, Agence centrale de Presse, Paris 1958–62; mem. political staff, Le Monde 1963–69, Asst. to head of political dept. 1969–82; Dir. Le Monde 1982–84. *Publications:* Les nouveaux communistes 1972, D'une France à l'autre 1974, Le Métier politique ou la conquête du pouvoir 1980. *Address:* 34 rue de Clichy, 75009 Paris, France (Home).

LAURENT, Jacques; French author and journalist; b. 5 Jan. 1919, Paris; s. of Jean Laurent-Cely and Louise Deloncle; m. 3rd Elisabeth Nilsonn 1969; ed. Lycées Condorcet, Carnot and Charlemagne, Paris and Faculté des Lettres, Paris; f. Literary review La Parisienne 1953; Pres. Dir.-Gen. Arts (weekly magazine) 1954–59; has written screenplay for several films; mem. Académie française; Prix Goncourt for Les Bêtises 1971, Grand Prix

de Littérature, Acad. Française 1981, Prix Littéraire Prince Pierre de Monaco 1983. *Publications:* under pseudonym Cecil Saint-Laurent: Caroline chérie, Le fils de Caroline chérie, Lucrèce Borgia, Prénom Clotilde, Ici Clotilde, Les passagers pour Alger, Les agités d'Alger, Hortense 1914–18, A Simon l'honneur, L'histoire imprévue des dessous féminins, La Communarde, Demandez-moi n'importe quoi 1973, La Bourgeoise 1974, La Mutante 1978, Clarisse 1980, L'erreur 1986; as Jacques Laurent: Les corps tranquilles, Paul et Jean-Paul, Le petit canard, Mauriac sous de Gaulle 1964, Année 1940, Lettre ouverte aux étudiants, Les Bêtises 1971, Dix perles de culture 1972, Histoire Egoïste 1976, Roman du Roman 1977, Le Nu vêtu et dévêtu 1979, Les sous-ensembles flous 1981, Les dimanches de Mademoiselle Beaunon 1982, Stendhal comme Stendhal 1984, Clotilde Jolivet ou le hasard des rencontres 1985, Le dormeur debout 1986. *Leisure interest:* painting. *Address:* c/o Editions Grasset, 61 rue des Saints-Pères, Paris 6e (Office); 11 bis rue Chanel, 75007 Paris, France.

LAURENTS, Arthur; American playwright; b. 14 July 1918, New York; s. of Irving Laurents and Ada Robbins; ed. Cornell Univ.; Radio Script-Writer 1939–40; mem. Screenwriters Guild, Acad. Motion Picture Arts and Sciences; dir. La Cage aux Folles (Tony Award) 1983, Sydney (Best Dir. Award) 1985, London 1986, Birds of Paradise 1987; American Acad. of Arts and Letters Award (for play Home of the Brave) 1946; Writers Guild of America Award (for The Turning Point) 1977; Tony Award 1967, 1984; Drama Desk Award 1974, Screenwriters' Guild Award and Golden Globe Award (best screenplay) for Turning Point. *Publications:* novels: The Way We Were 1972, The Turning Point 1977; screenplays: The Snake Pit 1948, Rope 1948, Caught 1948, Anna Lucasta 1949, Anastasia 1956, Bonjour Tristesse 1958. *plays:* Home of the Brave 1946, The Bird Cage 1950, The Time of the Cuckoo 1952, A Clearing in the Woods 1956, Invitation to a March 1960, The Enclave 1973, Scream 1978; musical plays: West Side Story 1957, Gypsy 1959, Do I Hear a Waltz? 1964, Hallelulah Baby 1967; screenwriter, co-producer film The Turning Point 1977; writer and dir. of several Broadway plays including Anyone can Whistle 1964, The Enclave 1973. *Address:* Quogue, New York, N.Y. 11959, U.S.A.

LAURENZO, Vincent D., M.B.A.; American business executive; b. 31 May 1939, Des Moines, Ia.; s. of Vincent C. and Billie Jean Laurenzo; m. Sherrill S. Mullen 1961; five c.; ed. Notre Dame Univ. and Univ. of Mich.; with Ford Motor Co. 1961–66; joined Massey-Ferguson N. American Operations, Des Moines 1966, Gen. Financial Analysis Man. 1970, later Comptroller and Sr. Dir. of Finance; Gen. Plans and Controls Man. Head Office, Toronto 1971–72, Vice-Pres. and Comptroller 1978, Sr. Vice-Pres. Planning and Admin. 1980; Pres. Massey-Ferguson Ltd. (now Varity Corpn.) Dec. 1981–88, Pres. and Vice Chair. 1988–. *Address:* Varity Corporation, 595 Bay Street, Toronto, Ont. M5G 2C3, Canada. *Telephone:* (416) 593-3811.

LAUSBERG, Heinrich, DR. PHIL. HABIL.; German professor of philology (retd.); b. 12 Oct. 1912, Aachen; s. of Ludwig Lausberg and Barbara (née Mattar) Lausberg; m. Pia Müller 1942; one d.; ed. Univs. of Bonn and Tübingen; Ordinary Prof. Romance Philology, Univ. of Bonn 1946–49, Univ. of Münster 1949–72, Univ. of Paderborn 1972–81, Prof. Emer. 1981–; Commdr. Order of Merit, Italy, Officier Palmes Académiques, France. *Publications:* Mundarten Südlukanien 1939, Handbuch literarischer Rhetorik 1960, Johannes-Evangelium 1984–87. *Address:* Schreiberstrasse 14, D-4400 Münster, Federal Republic of Germany. *Telephone:* 0251 80509.

LAUSTSEN, Agnete, LL.D.; Danish politician; b. 25 Sept. 1935, Copenhagen; ed. Univ. of Copenhagen; mem. staff Ministry of Interior, subsequently Head of Office, Ombudsman for Consumer Affairs; mem. Folketing (Parl.) 1979–; Chair. Parl. Social Cttee. 1983–87; Minister of Health 1987–88, of Housing 1988–; fmr. Conservative mem. Copenhagen City Council. *Address:* Ministry of Housing, Slotsholmsgade 12, 1216 Copenhagen K, Denmark. *Telephone:* (01) 02-61-00.

LAUTENBERG, Frank R., B.S., D.H.L.; American business executive and politician; b. Jan. 1924, Paterson, N.J.; s. of Samuel and Mollie Lautenberg; m.; one s. three d.; ed. Columbia Univ.; f. Automatic Data Processing Inc., Clifton, N.J. 1952, Exec. Vice-Pres. Admin. 1961–69, Pres. 1969–, Chair. and C.E.O. 1975–; Senator from N.J. Jan. 1983–; Nat. Pres. American Friends of Hebrew Univ. 1973–74; Gen. Chair. and Pres. Nat. United Jewish Appeal 1975–77; Commr. Port Authority, New York; mem. Int. Bd. of Govs. Hebrew Univ., Jerusalem; mem. Pres.'s Comm. on the Holocaust; f. Lautenberg Center for Gen. and Tumor Immunology, Medical School, Hebrew Univ., Jerusalem 1971; fmr. Pres. Asscn. of Data Processing Service Orgs.; mem. Advisory Council, Columbia Univ. School of Business; Torch of Learning Award, American Friends of Hebrew Univ. 1971; Scopus Award 1975; Hon. D.H.L. (Hebrew Union Coll., Cincinnati and New York) 1977; Hon. Ph.D. (Hebrew Univ., Jerusalem) 1978; Democrat. *Address:* 405 Route 3, Clifton, N.J. 07015, U.S.A.

LAUTENSCHLAGER, Hans Werner; German diplomatist; b. 31 Jan. 1927, Tianjin, China; ed. German School, Shanghai and studied law and political science at Heidelberg and Hamburg, Germany and Basle, Switzerland; joined diplomatic service of Fed. Repub. of Germany 1955; served in Ministry of Foreign Affairs, participating in negotiations to set up EEC and EURATOM 1956–57; attached to EURATOM; Counsellor for Political Affairs, Embassy New Delhi 1964–68; Deputy Head, Soviet Affairs Div., Foreign Office 1968–69; Head of EEC Trade and Agricultural Policy Div.

1969–73; Dir. of Foreign Trade and European Econ. Integration 1973–75; Dir.-Gen. Ministry of Foreign Affairs 1975–79, State Sec., Ministry of Foreign Affairs 1979–84; Perm. Rep. to UN 1984–88. *Address:* c/o Ministry of Foreign Affairs, 5300 Bonn 1, Adenauerallee 99-103, Federal Republic of Germany.

LAUTI, Rt. Hon. Toaripi, P.C.; Tuvalu politician; b. 28 Nov. 1928, Papua New Guinea; m.; three s. two d.; ed. Queen Victoria School, Fiji, Wesley Coll., Paerata, N.Z., St. Andrew's Coll., Christchurch, Christchurch Teachers' Coll.; teacher in Tarawa, Gilbert Is. (now Kiribati) 1953–62; Labour Relations and Training Officer for Nauru and Ocean Is. Phosphate Comm. 1962–74; returned to Ellice Is. (now Tuvalu) 1974; Chief Minister of Tuvalu 1975–78, Prime Minister 1978–81; Leader of the Opposition 1981–; also fmr. Minister of Finance and Foreign Affairs. *Address:* Parliament House, Funafuti, Tuvalu.

LAUTMANN, Rüdiger, D.PHIL., D.JUR.; German professor of sociology; b. 22 Dec. 1935, Koblenz; s. of Kurt Lautmann; Research Asst. Univ. of Bielefeld, Dortmund 1968–71; Prof. of Sociology Univ. of Bremen, Law School 1971–82, Dept. of Sociology 1982–. *Publications:* Wert und Norm 1969, Die Funktion des Rechts in der modernen Gesellschaft (co-Ed.) 1970, Die Polizei (co-Ed.) 1971, Soziologie vor den Toren der Jurisprudenz 1971, Justiz—die stille Gewalt 1972, Seminar Gesellschaft und Homosexualität 1977, Lexikon zur Soziologie (co-Ed.) 1978, Rechtssoziologie—Examinatorium (co-Ed.) 1980, Der Zwang zur Tugend 1984, Die Gleichheit der Geschlechter und die Wirklichkeit des Rechts 1989. *Address:* D-200 Hamburg 52, Papenkamp 3, Federal Republic of Germany. *Telephone:* 040-825965.

LAUZANNE, Bernard, L. ÈS L.; French journalist; b. 22 June 1916, Paris; s. of Gaston Lauzanne and Sylvia Scarognino; m. Lucie Gambini 1949; two d.; ed. Lycée Condorcet and Univ. of Paris; war service and prisoner of war in Germany 1939–45; joined Radiodiffusion Française (R.T.F.) and worked on programme "Paris vous parle" 1945–59; Chief Sub-Ed., Le Monde 1945–59, News Ed. 1959–69, Asst. Ed. 1969–74, Ed. 1974–78, Man. Ed. 1978–83; Directeur de Collection Éditions Denoël 1983–; Pres. France-Japan Assen.; Chevalier Légion d'honneur Croix de guerre. *Leisure interests:* music, theatre, painting. *Address:* Éditions Denoël, 30 rue de l'Université, 75007 Paris (Office); 26 rue de Turin, 75008 Paris, France (Home).

LAVE, Lester B., PH.D.; American professor of economics; b. 5 Aug. 1939, Philadelphia, Pa.; m. Judith Rice 1965; one s. one d.; ed. Reed Coll., M.I.T. and Harvard Univ.; Asst. to Prof., Carnegie-Mellon Univ. 1963–, James Higgins Prof. of Econs. 1983–; Sr. Fellow, Brookings Inst. 1978–82; Visiting Asst. Prof. Northwestern Univ. 1965–66; consultant, Gen. Motors Research Labs., U.S. Depts. of Justice, Defense, Transportation, Health and Welfare, Environmental Protection Agency, Nuclear Regulatory Comm., Nat. Science Foundation, Office of Tech. Assessment; Pres. Soc. for Risk Analysis 1985–86. *Publications:* Technological Change 1966, Air Pollution and Human Health 1977, The Strategy of Social Regulation 1981, Scientific Basis of Health & Safety Regulation 1981, Clearing the Air 1981, Quantitative Risk Assessment 1982; more than 200 scientific articles. *Leisure interests:* swimming, skiing. *Address:* Graduate School of Industrial Administration, Carnegie-Mellon University, Pittsburgh, Pa. 15213, U.S.A. *Telephone:* 412-268-8837.

LAVENTHOL, David, M.A.; American publisher; b. 15 July 1933, Philadelphia; s. of Clare Howard; m. Esther Coons 1957; one s. one d.; ed. Yale Univ. and Univ. of Minnesota; Reporter, later News Ed. St. Petersburg Times 1957–63; City Ed. New York Herald Tribune 1963–66; Asst. Man. Ed. The Washington Post 1966–69; Assoc. Ed. Newsday 1969, Exec. Ed. 1969–70, Ed. 1970–78, Publr. and C.E.O. 1978–86; Group Vice-Pres. Times Mirror 1981–86, Sr. Vice-Pres. 1986, Pres. 1987–; Chair. Pulitzer Prize Board; Vice-Chair. Int. Press Inst.; Dir. Newspaper Advertising Bureau, American Press Inst., L.A. Times Washington Post/News Service, Times Mirror Foundation, United Negro Coll. Fund; mem. American Soc. of Newspaper Eds. Writing Awards Bd., American Newspaper Publr. Assen., Century Assen., Council on Foreign Relations. *Address:* Times Mirror Co., Times Mirror Square, Los Angeles, Calif. 90053 (Office); 800 West First Street, Los Angeles, Calif. 90012, U.S.A. (Home). *Telephone:* (213) 237 2900 (Office); (213) 617 2541 (Home).

LAVER, Rod(ney) George, M.B.E.; Australian tennis player; b. 9 Aug. 1938, Rockhampton, Queensland; s. of R. S. Laver; m. Mary Benson 1966; one s.; ed. Rockhampton Grammar School and High School; Professional player since 1963; Australian Champion 1960, 1962, 1969; Wimbledon Champion 1961, 1962, 1968, 1969; U.S.A. Champion 1962, 1969; French Champion 1962, 1969; first player to win double Grand Slam 1962, 1969; first player to win over U.S. $1 million in total prize money 1972; played Davis Cup for Australia 1958, 1959, 1960, 1961, 1962 and 1973 (first open Davis Cup). *Publications:* How to Play Winning Tennis 1964, Education of a Tennis Player 1971. *Leisure interests:* golf, fishing, skiing. *Address:* Rod Laver Tennis, 4029 Western Plaza Suite, 201B Newport Beach, Calif. 92660, U.S.A.

LAVIER, Bertrand; French artist; b. 14 June 1949, Châtillon-sur-Seine; s. of Jean Lavier and Geneviève Duteil; m. Gloria Friedmann 1984; ed. Ecole Nat. Supérieure d' Horticulture; landscape artist and town planner, Marne Lavallée New Town 1971–72; at Centre de Recherches et d'Etudes

sur le Paysage, Paris 1973–75; artist 1974–; first one-man exhbn., Centre Nat. d'Art contemporain, Paris 1975; subsequent exhbns. at Biennale, Venice 1976, Europa 79, Stuttgart 1979, Musée d'Art Moderne, Paris 1980, 1985, Galerie Massimo Minini, Milan 1982, Dokumenta 7, Kassel 1982, Noveau Musée, Lyon Villeurbanne 1983, Lisson Gallery, London 1984, Galerie Durand-Dessert, Paris 1984, Kunsthalle, Bern 1984, Museum of Modern Art, New York 1984, Biennales, Paris, São Paulo 1985, I.C.A. London 1986, Museum of Modern Art, Tokyo 1986, Musée des Beaux-Arts, Dijon 1986, Gallery Buchmann, Basel 1986, Biennale of Sydney 1986, John Gibson Gallery, New York 1986, Musée des Beaux Arts, Grenoble 1986, Stedjelik van Abbemuseum, Eindhoven 1987, Galerie Durand-Dessert, Paris 1987, Dokumenta 8, Kassel 1987; First Prize (Sculpture), Biennale, Budapest 1984. *Publication:* Bertrand Lavier présente la peinture des Martin de 1603 á 1984 1984. *Leisure interests:* hunting, motor-racing, tennis. *Address:* Galerie Durand-Dessert, 3 rue des Haudriettes, 75003 Paris; 21510 Aignay-le-Duc, France. *Telephone:* (80) 93.87.00; (80) 93.82.59.

LAVILLA ALSINA, Landelino; Spanish lawyer and government official; b. 1927, Lérida; ed. Univ. Complutense, Inst. Social León XIII; fmr. Tech. Adviser to Nat. Bd. of Railways and Road Transport, also Asst. to Tech. Secretariat of Prime Minister's Office; fmr. Under-Sec. for Industry; Chair. of Board, EDICA 1975–76; Minister of Justice 1976–79; Pres. Congress of Deputies 1979–82; mem. Council of State, Spanish Assen. for Admin. Sciences, Grupo Tácito. *Address:* c/o Congreso de los Diputados, Madrid, Spain.

LAVIN, Mary, M.A.; Irish writer; b. 12 June 1912, E. Walpole, Mass., U.S.A.; d. of Thomas Lavin and Nora Lavin (née Mahon); m. 1st William Walsh 1942 (died 1954), 2nd Michael MacDonald Scott 1969; three d.; ed. Loreto Convent, Dublin and Univ. Coll. Dublin (Nat. Univ. of Ireland); has lived in Ireland since childhood; Pres. Irish PEN 1964–65, 1985–86; Pres. Irish Acad. of Letters 1972–73; mem. Bd. of Govs. School of Irish Studies, Dublin 1974–; Trustee, Nat. Library of Ireland 1978–; James Tait Black Memorial Prize 1943; Guggenheim Fellowship 1959–60, 1960–61; Katherine Mansfield Prize 1961; Ella Lyman Cabot Award 1972; Eire Soc. Gold Medal 1974; Gregory Medal, "Supreme Literary Award of the Irish Nation" 1975; American Irish Foundation Literary Award 1979; Allied Irish Banks Literary Award 1981; Hon. D.Litt. (Univ. Coll. Dublin) 1968. *Publications:* Tales from Bective Bridge 1942, The Long Ago 1944, The House in Clewe Street 1945, The Becker Wives 1946, At Sallygap 1947, Mary O'Grady 1950, A Single Lady 1956, The Patriot Son 1956, A Likely Story 1957, Selected Stories 1959, The Great Wave 1961, The Stories of Mary Lavin, Vol. I 1964, In the Middle of the Fields 1967, Happiness 1969, Collected Stories 1971, The Second Best Children in the World (illustrated by Edward Ardizzone) 1972, A Memory 1972, The Stories of Mary Lavin, Vol. II 1973, The Shrine 1977, A Family Likeness 1985, The Stories of Mary Lavin, Vol. III 1985, The House in Clewe Street 1987. *Leisure interest:* work. *Address:* The Abbey Farm, Bective, Co. Meath; 5 Gilford Pines, Gilford Road, Sandymount, Dublin 4, Ireland. *Telephone:* 046-21243 (Bective); 692402 (Dublin).

LAVOIE, Léo; Canadian banker; b. 18 March 1913, Notre-Dame-du-Lac, P.Q.; s. of late Phydime Lavoie and Caroline Viel; m. Claire Maranda 1940; one d.; ed. St. François Xavier Coll., Rivière du Loup and Harvard Univ.; joined Provincial Bank of Canada 1930, Man. at Warwick, P.Q., and other branches 1940–55, Asst. to Pres. 1955, Asst. Gen. Man. 1955, Gen. Man. 1957, Dir. 1960, Vice-Pres. and Gen. Man. 1966, Pres. 1967–76, C.E.O. 1967–77, Chair. 1974–79; Chair. Canadair Ltd., Ciné-Monde Inc.; Dir. of several corpns., social and cultural orgs.; Hon. D.Sc.Comm. (Montreal Univ.) 1970. *Leisure interests:* travel, golf.

LAVROV, Vladimir Sergeyevich; Soviet diplomatist; b. 4 Oct. 1919, Moscow; m. Valentina Felixsovna 1948; one s. one d.; mem. diplomatic service 1947–; Asst. First Deputy Minister of Foreign Affairs 1953–56; Counsellor at Embassy, Washington 1956–59; Chargé d'Affaires, Yemen 1959–60; Deputy Chief of Second European Dept., U.S.S.R. Ministry of Foreign Affairs 1960–62, Chief 1962–64; Amb. to Kenya 1964–67, to Netherlands 1967–73, to Switzerland 1977–83, to Turkey 1983–87; Chief of Personnel Directorate, Ministry of Foreign Affairs 1973–77. *Publications:* (under pseudonym L. Vladimorov): The Diplomacy of the U.S.A. during the American-Spanish War 1957, The Beacon of Friendship 1962, Born in Flame: Kenya's Road to Independence 1972, Kenya: The Choice of Path 1979: articles on diplomacy. *Leisure interests:* reading, art, sports, photography. *Address:* c/o Embassy of the U.S.S.R., Karyagdı sok., 5, 06692 Kavaklıdere, Ankara, Turkey.

LAVRUSHIN, Vladimir, D.SC.; Soviet chemist; b. 15 May 1912; ed. Kharkov State Univ.; worked in shoe factory 1927–30; Kharkov State Univ. 1930–35; postgraduate course 1935; Army Service 1941–45; research and educ. work, Kharkov 1945–48; Prof. of Chemical Tech., later Organic Chem., Kharkov State Univ. 1948–, Asst. Rector 1956–61, Rector 1961–66, Dir. Inst. of Chem. 1967, Head Dept. of Organic Chem. 1970–89; Hon. D.Sc. (Manchester); Order of Lenin, Order of Red Star. *Publications:* contributions to the study of the halochromism of organic compounds. *Address:* Kharkov A.M. Gorky State University, Ploshchad Dzerzhinskogo 4, Kharkov, U.S.S.R.

LAW, Bob; British artist; b. 22 Jan. 1934, Brentford, Middx.; m. Georgina Cann 1965; one s. one d.; works include paintings and sculptures; exhibited in public collections at Tate Gallery, London, Victoria & Albert, London, Stedelijk Museum, Amsterdam, Museum of Modern Art, New York, the Panza Collection, Milan, City Art Gallery, Johannesburg, Arts Council of G.B., London, Southampton Art Gallery, Worcester Coll., Oxford, New Coll., Oxford; Arts Council of G.B. Award 1967, 1975, 1981. *Leisure interest:* clay pigeon shooting. *Address:* Karsten Schubert Gallery, 85 Charlotte Street, London, W1P 1LB; 17 Second Cross Road, Twickenham, TW2 5QY, England.

LAW, H.E. Bernard F.; American ecclesiastic; b. 4 Nov. 1931, Torreón; ordained 1961; Bishop of Springfield-Cape Girardeau 1973; Archbishop of Boston 1984–; cr. Cardinal by Pope John Paul II 1985. *Address:* 2101 Commonwealth Avenue, Brighton, Mass. 02135, U.S.A. *Telephone:* (617) 782-2544.

LAW, Admiral Sir Horace Rochfort, G.C.B., O.B.E., D.S.C.; British naval officer; b. 23 June 1911, Dublin, Ireland; s. of Samuel Horace Law and Mary Clay; m. Heather Valerie Coryton; two s. two d.; ed. Sherborne School; Capt., Royal Naval Coll., Dartmouth 1960; Flag Officer, Sea Training, Portland 1961; Flag Officer, Submarines 1963; Controller of the Navy 1965; C.-in-C. Naval Home Command 1970–72; First and Prin. Naval A.D.C. to H.M. The Queen 1970–72; fmr. mem. Security Comm.; Chair. R. & W. Hawthorn Leslie 1973–81; Pres. Royal Inst. of Naval Architects 1975–77; Chair. Church Army 1980–87. *Leisure interests:* sailing, gardening. *Address:* West Harting, near Petersfield, Hants., England. *Telephone:* 073-085-511.

LAW, Phillip Garth, A.O., C.B.E., M.SC., D.APP.SC., D.Ed., F.T.S., F.A.A., F.A.I.P., F.A.N.Z.A.A.S., F.R.G.S.; Australian scientist, antarctic explorer and educationist; b. 21 April 1912, Tallangatta, Victoria; s. of the late Arthur James Law and Lillie Law; m. Nel Allan 1941; ed. Ballarat Teachers' Coll. and Univ. of Melbourne; Science master in secondary schools 1933–38; Tutor in Physics Newman Coll., Melbourne Univ. 1940–45 and Lecturer in Physics 1943–47; Research Physicist and Asst. Sec. Scientific Instrument and Optical Panel, Ministry of Munitions 1940–45; Scientific Mission to New Guinea battle areas for the Australian Army 1944; Sr. Scientific Officer Aust. Nat. Antarctic Research Expeditions 1947–48, Leader 1949–66; Dir. Antarctic Div., Dept. of External Affairs 1949–66; Australian Observer Norwegian-British-Swedish Antarctic Expedition 1950; led expeditions to establ. first perm. Australian research station at Mawson, MacRobertson Land 1954 and at Davis, Princess Elizabeth Land 1957; exploration of coast of Australian Antarctica 1954–66; mem. gov. council Melbourne Univ. 1959–79, La Trobe Univ. 1964–74; Exec. Vice-Pres. Victoria Inst. of Colls. 1966–77; Chair. Australian Nat. Cttee. on Antarctic Research 1966–80; mem. Council of Science Museum of Victoria 1968–83; Pres. Royal Soc. of Victoria 1967, 1968; Pres. Graduate Union, Univ. of Melbourne 1972–77; Pres. Victorian Inst. of Marine Sciences 1978–80; Pres. Australia and N.Z. Scientific Exploring Soc. 1976–81, Patron 1982–; Hon. Fellow Royal Melbourne Inst. of Tech.; Award of Merit Commonwealth Professional Officers Assen. 1957, Clive Lord Memorial Medal Royal Soc. of Tasmania 1958, Founder's Medal Royal Geographical Soc. 1960, John Lewis Gold Medal Royal Geographical Soc. of Australia 1962, Vocational Service Award Melbourne Rotary Club 1970, James Cook Medal of the Royal Soc. of N.S.W. 1988, Gold Medal Australian Geographic Soc. 1988. *Publications:* ANARE (with Bechervaise) 1957, Antarctic Odyssey 1983, also numerous articles on antarctic exploration and research and papers on cosmic rays, thermal conductivity, optics and education. *Leisure interests:* music, tennis, skiing, swimming. *Address:* 16 Stanley Grove, Canterbury, Vic. 3126, Australia. *Telephone:* 882-5575.

LAWDEN, Derek Frank, M.A., SC.D.; British university professor; b. 15 Sept. 1919, Birmingham; s. of Joseph Lawden and Lily Lawden; m. Dorothy M. Smith 1940; three s.; ed. King Edward's Grammar School, Aston and St. Catharine's Coll. Cambridge; served R.A. 1940–46; Sr. Lecturer, Royal Mil. Coll. of Science 1948–51, Coll. of Tech. Birmingham 1951–55; Prof. of Math. and Head of Dept. Univ. of Canterbury, New Zealand 1956–67; Prof. of Mathematical Physics, Univ. of Aston 1967–76, Head of Mathematics 1977–83, Prof. Emer. 1983–; Hector Medal (Royal Soc. of N.Z.) 1964; Mechanics and Control of Flight Award (American Inst. of Aeronautics and Astronautics) 1967. *Publications:* Optimal Trajectories for Space Navigation 1963, Mathematical Principles of Quantum Mechanics 1967, Introduction to Tensor Calculus, Relativity and Cosmology 1982, Principles of Thermodynamics and Statistical Mechanics 1986. *Leisure interest:* contract bridge. *Address:* Newhall, Church Bank, Temple Grafton, Alcester, B49 6NU, England. *Telephone:* (0789) 773445.

LAWLER, James Ronald, M.A., D.U.P.; Australian academic; b. 15 Aug. 1929, Melbourne; m. Christine Labossière 1954; one s. one d.; ed. Univs. of Melbourne and Paris; lecturer in French, Univ. of Queensland 1955–56; Sr. Lecturer, Univ. of Melbourne 1956–62; Prof. of French, Head of Dept., Univ. of Western Australia 1963–71; Prof. of French, Chair., Univ. of Calif., Los Angeles 1971–74; McCulloch Prof. of French, Dalhousie Univ. 1974–79; Prof. of Romance Languages, Univ. of Chicago 1979–83; Edward Carson Waller Distinguished Service Prof., Univ. of Chicago 1983–; Visiting Prof. Collège de France 1985; Vice-Pres. Assen. Int. des Etudes Françaises 1974–; Carnegie Fellowship 1961–62; Commonwealth Interchange Visitor 1967; Guggenheim Fellowship 1974; Nat. Endowment of Humanities Fellowship 1984–85; Foundation Fellow, Australian Acad. of the Human-

ities; Officier, Palmes academiques; Prix Int. des Amitiés Françaises 1986. *Publications:* Form and Meaning in Valéry's Le Cimetière Marin 1959, An Anthology of French Poetry 1960, Lecture de Valéry: Une Etude de Charmes 1963, The Language of French Symbolism 1969, The Poet as Analyst: Essays on Paul Valéry 1974, Paul Valéry: An Anthology 1976, René Char: The Myth and the Poem 1978; Edgar Poe et les Poètes français 1989; Founding Ed.: Essays in French Literature 1964–, Dalhousie French Studies 1979–. *Address:* Wieboldt 214, 1050 East 59th Street, Chicago, Ill., U.S.A. *Telephone:* (312) 702 8481, (312) 702 8485.

LAWRENCE, Arnold Walter, M.A., F.S.A.; British archaeologist; b. 2 May 1900; ed. City of Oxford School, and New Coll., Oxford; Ur excavations 1923; Craven Fellow, Oxford 1924; Student of British Schools of Rome and Athens; Reader in Classical Archaeology Cambridge 1930; Literary executor of T. E. Lawrence 1935; Mil. Intelligence Middle East 1940; Scientific Officer R.A.F. 1942; with Ministry of Econ. Warfare 1943; Prof. of Classical Archaeology Cambridge Univ. 1944–51; Fellow of Jesus Coll. Cambridge 1944–51; Prof. of Archaeology, Univ. Coll. of Gold Coast and Dir. Nat. Museum of the Gold Coast 1951–57; Hon. Sec. and Conservator, Monuments and Relics Comm., Gold Coast 1952–57; Hon. F.B.A. *Publications:* Later Greek Sculpture and its Influence 1927, Classical Sculpture 1929, Herodotus annotated 1935, T. E. Lawrence by his Friends 1937, Greek Architecture 1957, 1967, 1974, (revised edn. by R.A. Tomlinson) 1983, Letters to T. E. Lawrence 1962, Trade Castles and Forts of West Africa 1963, Fortified Trade Posts 1969, Greek and Roman Sculpture 1972, The Cilician Kingdom of Armenia 1978 (with others), Greek Aims in Fortification 1980, etc. *Address:* c/o Barclays Bank, High Street, Pateley Bridge, Harrogate, HG3 5LA, North Yorks., England.

LAWRENCE, Henry Sherwood, M.D.; American physician and immunologist; b. 22 Sept. 1916, New York; s. of Victor J. and Agnes B. (Whalen) Lawrence; m. Dorothea W. Wetherbee 1943; two s. one d.; ed. New York Univ.; Instructor in Medicine, New York Univ. School of Medicine 1949–52, Asst. Prof. 1952–55, Assoc. Prof. 1955–61, Prof. of Medicine 1961–, Jeffrey Bergstein Prof. of Medicine 1979–, Head Infectious Disease and Immunology Div. 1959–; Co-Dir. New York Univ. Medical Services 1964–; Dir. Cancer Center 1974–79; Endowed Chair in Medicine, Jeffrey Bergstein Prof. of Medicine 1979; Commonwealth Foundation Fellow, Univ. Coll., London 1959; mem. N.A.S.; Hon. Fellow American Acad. of Allergy, Soc. Française d'Allergie, Royal Coll. Physicians and Surgeons (Glasgow); Harvey Soc. Lecturer 1973, Councillor 1974–77; Von Pirquet Award, American Coll. of Physicians Award, New York Acad. of Medicine Science Medal, American Coll. of Allergy Scientific Achievement Award, Infectious Diseases Soc. of America Bristol Award, Chapin Medal, City of Providence, Lila Gruber Award for Cancer Research, American Acad. of Dermatology, Dowling Lectureship Award, Alpha Omega Alpha Award, New York Univ. School of Medicine Alumni Scientific Achievement Award and Distinguished Teachers Award, New York Univ. Washington Square Coll. Alumni Achievement Award. *Publications:* Cellular and Humoral Aspects of Hypersensitivity (Ed.) 1959, Mediators of Cellular Immunity (Ed. with M. Landy) 1969, Cellular Immunology 1970, Immunobiology of Transfer Factor (Ed. with C. H. Kirkpatrick, D. Burger) 1983; articles in professional journals. *Leisure interests:* landscape painting, medieval English history. *Address:* Department of Medicine, New York University School of Medicine, 550 First Avenue, New York, N.Y. 10016 (Office); 343 East 30th Street, New York, N.Y. 10016, U.S.A. (Home). *Telephone:* (212) 340-6400 (Office); (212) 684-0997 (Home).

LAWRENCE, Peter Anthony, PH.D., F.R.S.; British biologist; b. 23 June 1941, Longridge; s. of Ivor D. Lawrence and Joy Liebert; m. Birgitta Haraldson 1971; ed. Univ. of Cambridge; Commonwealth Fellowship, U.S.A. 1965–67; Dept. of Genetics, Univ. of Cambridge 1967–69; Staff, MRC Lab. of Molecular Biology, Univ. of Cambridge 1969–, Jt. Head, Cell Biology Div., 1984–87; Medal of Zoological Soc. of London 1977. *Publications:* numerous scientific papers. *Leisure interests:* garden, golf, trees, fungi, theatre. *Address:* 9 Temple End, Great Wilbraham, Cambridge, CB1 5JF, England. *Telephone:* (0223) 880505.

LAWRENCE, Robert Swan; American physician; b. 6 Feb. 1938, Philadelphia; s. of Thomas George Lawrence and Catherine Swan Lawrence; m. Cynthia Starr Cole 1960; three s. two d.; ed. Harvard Coll. and Medical School; Medical Epidemiologist, Center for Disease Control, U.S. Public Health Service, Atlanta 1966–69; Asst. to Assoc. Prof. of Medicine, Dir. Div. of Community Medicine, N.C. Univ. School of Medicine 1970–74; Dir. Div. of Primary Care, Asst. to Assoc. Prof. of Medicine, Harvard Medical School 1974–, Charles Davidson Assoc. Prof. of Medicine 1981–; Assoc. Chief of Medicine, Cambridge Hosp. 1974–77, Chief of Medicine, Dir. Dept. of Medicine 1980–; Chair. U.S. Preventive Services Task Force, Dept. of Health and Human Services, U.S. Govt. 1984–; Maimonides Prize 1964; mem. Inst. of Medicine, N.A.S 1978. *Publications:* 45 articles in scientific journals. *Address:* Cambridge Hospital, 1493 Cambridge Street, Cambridge, Mass. 02139; 67 Silver Hill Road, Weston, Mass. 02139, U.S.A. (Home). *Telephone:* 617-498-1024 (Office); 617-894-5072 (Home).

LAWRENCE, Walter Nicholas Murray, M.A.; British underwriting agent; b. 8 Feb. 1935, London; s. of Henry Walter Neville Lawrence and Sarah Schuyler Lawrence (née Butler); m. Sally Louise O'Dwyer 1961; two d.; ed. Winchester Coll., Trinity Coll., Oxford; with C. T. Bowring and Co.

Ltd. 1957–62, 1976–84, Treaty Dept. 1957–62, Dir. 1976–84; with Harvey Bowring and Others 1962–84, Asst. Underwriter 1962–70, Underwriter 1970–84; Dir. C. T. Bowring (Underwriting Agencies) Ltd. 1973–84; Chair. Fairway Underwriting Agencies Ltd. 1979–85; mem. Lloyd's Underwriter's Non-Marine Asscn., Deputy Chair. 1977, Chair. 1978; served Cttee. of Lloyd's 1979–82, Deputy Chair. 1982, re-elected to the Council of Lloyd's 1984, Deputy Chair. 1984–87, Chair. 1988–; Dir., Chair. Murray Lawrence Holdings Ltd. 1988, Murray Lawrence Mems. Agency Ltd. 1988. *Leisure interests:* golf, opera, travel. *Address:* c/o Murray Lawrence & Partners, 32 Threadneedle Street, London, EC2R 8AY, England. *Telephone:* 01-588 7447.

LAWRENSON, Peter John, D.SC., F.ENG., F.R.S., F.I.E.E.E.; British electrical engineer and business executive; b. 12 March 1933, Prescot; s. of John Lawrenson and Emily Houghton; m. Shirley H. Foster 1958; one s. three d.; ed. Prescot Grammar School and Manchester Univ.; research eng. General Electric Co., Ltd. 1956–61; Lecturer, Univ. of Leeds 1961–65, Reader 1965–66, Prof. of Electrical Eng. 1966–, Head, Dept. of Electrical and Electronic Eng. 1974–84, Chair. Faculty of Science and Applied Science 1978–80; Chair. Switched Reluctance Drives Ltd. 1981–, Man. Dir. 1986–; other professional appointments; James Alfred Ewing Medal 1983, Royal Soc. Esso Medal 1985 and other awards. *Publications:* Analysis and Computation of Electromagnetic Field Problems 1973; other books and over 120 articles in the field of electrical eng., particularly electromagnetics and electromechanics. *Leisure interests:* squash, lawn tennis, bridge, chess, jewelery making. *Address:* Department of Electrical and Electronic Engineering, The University, Leeds, LS2 9JT (Office); Spen Watch, 318 Spen Lane, Leeds, LS16 5BA, England (Home). *Telephone:* (0532) 755849 (Home).

LAWS, Richard Maitland, PH.D., F.R.S., C.B.E.; British scientist; b. 23 April 1926, Whitley Bay; s. of Percy Malcolm Laws and Florence May Heslop; m. Maureen Isobel Holmes 1954; three s.; ed. Dame Allan's School, Newcastle, and St. Catharine's Coll., Cambridge; Biologist and Base Leader, Falkland Islands Dependencies Survey 1947–53; Whaling Insp., F/F Balaena 1953–54; Prin. Scientific Officer, Nat. Inst. of Oceanography, Godalming 1954–61; Dir., Nuffield Unit of Animal Ecology, Uganda 1961–67; Dir., Tsavo Research Project, Kenya 1967–68; Head, Life Sciences Div., British Antarctic Survey 1969–73; Dir., British Antarctic Survey, Cambridge 1973–87; Dir. Sea Mammal Research Unit, Cambridge 1977–87; Master, St. Edmund's Coll., Cambridge 1985–; Sec. Zoological Soc. of London 1984–88; mem. Council of the Senate, Univ. of Cambridge 1989–, Financial Bd. 1988–. *Publications:* Elephants and Their Habitats (co-author) 1975, Scientific Research in Antarctica (Ed.) 1977, Antarctic Ecology (Ed.) 1984, Antarctic Nutrient Cycles and Food Webs (co-ed.) 1985, Antarctica: The Last Frontier 1989. *Leisure interests:* walking, photography, painting. *Address:* St. Edmund's College, Cambridge, CB3 0BN; 3 The Footpath, Coton, Cambs., CB3 7PX, England (Home). *Telephone:* (0223) 350398 (Office); (0954) 210567 (Home).

LAW-SMITH, Sir (Richard) Robert, Kt., C.B.E., A.F.C.; Australian business executive and banker; b. 9 July 1914, Adelaide; s. of Walter Henry and Agnes (née Giles) Law-Smith; m. Joan Darling 1941; two d.; ed. St. Edward's School, Oxford, England, Adelaide Univ.; mem. Australian Nat. Airlines Comm. 1962, Vice-Chair. 1975–79, Chair. 1979–83; Dir. Qantas Airways Ltd. 1956–81, Vice-Chair. 1961–81; Chair. Victorian Branch Bd., Australian Mutual Provident Soc. 1977–84; Dir. Nat. Australian Bank Ltd. (fmrly. Nat. Commercial Bank Corpn. of Australia Ltd.) 1983–, Vice-Chair. 1968–78, Chair. 1978–86; Chair. Chase-NBA Group Ltd. (now First National Ltd.) 1980–; Dir. Broken Hill Pty. Co. Ltd. 1961–84, Australian Mutual Provident Soc., Victoria 1960–84, Prin. Bd. 1977–84, Commonwealth Aircraft Corpn. Ltd. 1965–84, Blue Circle Southern Cement Ltd. 1974–84. *Leisure interest:* farming. *Address:* Bolobek, Macedon, Vic. 3440, Australia. *Telephone:* 054 261 493.

LAWSON, John David, SC.D., F.INST.P., F.R.S.; British research physicist; b. 4 April 1923, Coventry; s. of Ronald and Ruth (née Houseman) Lawson; m. Kathleen Wyllie 1949; two s. one d.; ed. Wolverhampton Grammar School, St. John's Coll., Cambridge; TRE (now RSRE) Malvern, Aerials Group 1943–47; AERE Malvern, Accelerator Group 1947–51; AERE Harwell, Gen. Physics Div. 1951–62; Microwave Lab., Stanford, U.S.A. 1959–60; Rutherford Lab. (now Rutherford Appleton Lab.) 1962–, fmrly. Deputy Chief Scientific Officer, now retd., Hon. Scientist; Visiting Prof., Dept. of Physics and Astronomy, Univ. of Md. 1971; Technology Div., Culham Lab. 1975–76. *Publications:* The Physics of Charged Particle Beams 1977, 1988; numerous papers on applied physics. *Leisure interests:* travel, mountain walking, book collecting (especially science books). *Address:* 7 Clifton Drive, Abingdon, Oxon., OX14 1ET, England. *Telephone:* (0235) 21516.

LAWSON, Lesley (Twiggy), British model, singer and actress; b. 19 Sept. 1949, London; d. of William and Helen (née Reeman) Hornby; m. 1st Michael Whitney Armstrong 1977 (died 1983); one d.; m. 2nd Leigh Lawson 1988; ed. Brondesbury and Kilburn Grammar School; model 1966–76; Man. and Dir. Twiggy Enterprises Ltd. 1966–; own British TV series; has made several LP records. *Films include:* The Boy Friend 1971, W, There Goes the Bride 1979, Blues Brothers 1981, The Doctor and the Devils 1986, Club Paradise 1986, Madame Sousatzka 1987, Istanbul 1988, Young Charlie Chaplin (TV) 1989. *Play:* My One and Only 1983. *Publications:* Twiggy:

An Autobiography 1975, An Open Look 1985. *Leisure interests:* daughter Carly, music, design. *Address:* c/o Neville Shulman, 4 St. George's House, 15 Hanover Square, London, W1R 9AJ, England. *Telephone:* 01-486 6363.

LAWSON, Rt. Hon. Nigel, M.A., M.P.; British politician; b. 11 March 1932, London; s. of Ralph and Joan (née Davis) Lawson; m. 1st Vanessa Salmon (dissolved 1980), 2nd Thérèse Mary Maclear 1980; two s. four d.; ed. Westminster and Christ Church, Oxford; Sub Lieut., R.N.V.R. 1954–56; mem. editorial staff, Financial Times 1956–60; City Ed. Sunday Telegraph 1961–63; Special Asst. to Prime Minister 1963–64; Financial Times columnist and BBC broadcaster 1965; Ed. The Spectator 1966–70; regular contributor to Sunday Times and Evening Standard 1970–71, The Times 1971–72; Fellow, Nuffield Coll., Oxford 1972–73; Special Political Adviser, Conservative Party HQ 1973–74; M.P. for Blaby, Leics. 1974–; Opposition Whip 1976–77; Opposition spokesman on Treasury and Econ. Affairs 1977–79; Financial Sec. to the Treasury 1979–81; Sec. of State for Energy 1981–83, Chancellor of the Exchequer June 1983–; Finance Minister of the Year, Euromoney Magazine 1988. *Publications:* The Power Game (with Jock Bruce-Gardyne) 1976, Contributions to Britain and Canada 1976, The Coming Confrontation 1978 and various pamphlets. *Address:* 11 Downing Street, London, S.W.1, England.

LAWSON, Gen. Sir Richard George, K.C.B., D.S.O., O.B.E.; British army officer; b. 24 Nov. 1927, Hatfield; s. of John Lawson and Rebecca (née White) Lawson; m. Ingrid Montelin 1956; one s.; ed. St. Albans School, Birmingham Univ., Royal Mil. Acad., Sandhurst, Staff Coll., Camberley, U.S. Armed Forces Staff Coll., Royal Coll. of Defence Studies; Asst. Mil. Attaché, Baghdad 1957–61; Brigade Major, Royal Nigerian Army 1961–63; C.O. Independent Squadron (Berlin), Royal Tank Regiment 1963–64; Chief of Staff, South Arabian Army 1967; C.O. 5th Royal Tank Regiment 1968–69; Commdr. 20th Armoured Brigade 1972–73; G.O.C. 1st Armoured Div. 1977–79; G.O.C. Northern Ireland 1980–82; C.-in-C. Allied Forces, N. Europe 1982–86; Kt. Commdr., Order of St. Sylvester (Vatican), Leopold Cross (Belgium). *Publications:* Strange Soldiering 1963, All the Queen's Men 1967, Strictly Personal 1972. *Leisure interest:* sailing. *Address:* c/o Royal Bank of Scotland, Kirkland House, London, S.W.1, England.

LAWSON, Gen. Richard Laverne, B.S., M.P.A.; American air force officer; b. 19 Dec. 1929, Fairfield, Ia.; s. of Vernon C. and Wilma A. (née Rabel) Lawson; m. Joan Lee Graber 1949; two s. two d.; ed. Univ. of Iowa, Parsons Coll. George Washington Univ.; graduated Nat. War Coll., 1969; Deputy Commdr. Operations, 306th Bomb Wing, McCoy Air Force Base (A.F.B.), Fla. 1969–70; Commdr. 28th Bomb Wing, Elsworth A.F.B., S. D. 1970–71; Chief Strategic Div., Dir. of Operations DCS/Plans and Operations, U.S. Air Force (U.S.A.F.) HQ, Washington D.C. 1971–72, Deputy Dir. Strategic Operations Forces, Dir. of Operations 1972–73, Deputy Dir. Operations 1973; Mil. Asst. to Pres. White House, Washington, D.C. 1973–75; Dir. of Plans, Office of DCS/Plans and Operations, U.S.A.F. HQ, Washington, D.C. 1975–77; Commdr. 8th Air Force (Strategic Air Command), Barksdale AFB, La. 1977–78; Dir. J-5, Org. of Jt. Chiefs of Staff, Washington, D.C. 1978–80; U.S. Rep. to Mil. Cttee., NATO, Brussels, Belgium 1980–81; Chief of Staff, Supreme Headquarters Allied Powers Europe (SHAPE) 1981–83; Deputy C.-in-C., U.S. European Command (USEUCOM) July 1983–; Defense Distinguished Service Medal, Distinguished Service Medal O (oak leaf cluster), Legion of Merit O (oak leaf cluster); citation and unit decorations. *Leisure interests:* golf, squash. *Address:* Richard Wagner Strasse 39, Stuttgart 1, Federal Republic of Germany (Home). *Telephone:* (711) 246-085 (Home).

LAWZI, Ahmed Abdel Kareem al–; Jordanian politician; b. 1925, Jubeiha, nr. Amman; m.; ed. Teachers' Training Coll., Baghdad, Iraq.; Teacher, 1950–53; Asst. to Chief of Royal Protocol 1953–56; Head of Ceremonies, Ministry of Foreign Affairs 1957; mem. Parl. 1961–62, 1962–63; Asst. to Chief of Royal Court 1963–64; Minister of State, Prime Minister's Office 1964–65; mem. Senate 1965, 1967; Minister of the Interior for Municipal and Rural Affairs April–Oct. 1967; Minister of Finance Oct. 1970– Nov. 1971; Prime Minister 1971–73; Pres. Nat. Consultative Council 1978–79; various Jordanian and foreign decorations. *Address:* c/o Ministry of Foreign Affairs, Amman, Jordan.

LAX, Melvin, PH.D.; American physicist; b. 8 March 1922, New York; s. of Morris Lax and Rose Hutterer; m. 1949; two s. two d.; ed. New York Univ. and Mass. Inst. of Tech.; Research Physicist M.I.T. 1942–45, Research Assoc. 1947; Prof. of Physics, Syracuse Univ. 1947–55; Consultant Naval Research Lab. 1951–55; lecturer in Physics Princeton Univ. 1961, Oxford Univ. 1961–62; mem. Tech. Staff Bell Labs. 1955–72, Head Theoretical Physics Dept. 1962–64, Consultant 1972–; Consultant Army Research Office 1972–, Los Alamos Science Lab. 1975–; now Distinguished Prof. City Coll. of New York; Charles Hayden Scholar New York Univ.; Fellow American Physical Soc.; mem. N.A.S. *Publications:* Scattering and Radiation from Circular Cylinders and Spheres (with M. Morse, A. N. Lowan and H. Feshbach) 1946, Elementary Nuclear Theory (contrib.) 1947, Fluctuations and Coherence Phenomena in Classical and Quantum Physics (in Statistical Physics, Vol. 2) 1968, Symmetry Principles in Solid State and Molecular Physics 1974, and articles in journals. *Leisure interest:* tennis. *Address:* Department of Physics, City College, 138 Street and Convent Avenue, New York, N.Y. 10031 (Office); 12 High Street, Summit, N.J.

09901, U.S.A. (Home). *Telephone:* (212) 690-6864 (Office); (201) 273-6188 (Home).

LAX, Peter D., PH.D.; American mathematician; b. 1 May 1926, Budapest, Hungary; ed. New York Univ.; with Los Alamos Scientific Lab., Manhattan Project 1945-46; Asst. Prof., New York Univ. 1949; staff mem. Los Alamos Scientific Lab. 1950-58; Fulbright Lecturer in Germany 1958; Prof., New York Univ. 1958-, Dir. AEC Computing and Applied Math. Center 1964-72, Courant Inst. of Math. Sciences 1972-80, Courant Math. and Computing Lab. 1980-; Visiting Lecturer, Oxford Univ. 1969; mem. American Acad. of Arts and Sciences, N.A.S.; Foreign Assoc. French Acad. of Sciences; Pres. American Math. Soc. 1969-71; mem. Nat. Science Bd. 1980-86; foreign mem. Soviet Acad. of Sciences 1989; Chauvenet Prize, Math. Asscn. of America 1974; Norbert Wiener Prize, American Math. Soc. and Soc. of Industrial and Applied Math. 1975; Nat. Medal of Science 1986, Wolf Prize 1987; Hon. D.Sc. (Kent State) 1976; Dr. h.c. (Paris) 1979. *Publications:* papers in learned journals. *Address:* Courant Institute of Mathematics, New York University, 251 Mercer Street, New York, N.Y. 10012, U.S.A.

LAXALT, Paul; American lawyer and politician; b. 2 Aug. 1922, Reno, Nevada; s. of Dominique and Theresa (Alpetche) Laxalt; m. 1st Jackalyn Ross 1946 (divorced 1972); m. 2nd Carol Wilson 1976; one s. five d. one step-d.; ed. High School, Carson City, Univ. of Santa Clara, Calif., Denver Univ. School of Law; served in infantry in Second World War; became attorney 1949; joined Republican Party and was elected Dist. Attorney of Ormsby County 1950; Lieut.-Gov., Nevada 1962-67; Gov. of Nevada 1967-71; U.S. Senator from Nevada 1975-87, joined law firm Finley, Kumble, Wagner, Heine, Underberg, Manley, Myerson and Casey 1987-; Chair. Campaign to Elect Reagan as Pres. 1980, 1984; Co-Chair. Campaign to Elect Bush as Pres. 1988. *Leisure interests:* tennis, golf. *Address:* 1455 Pennsylvania Avenue, N.W., Wash., D.C. 20004, U.S.A.

LAXNESS, Halldor; Icelandic writer; b. 23 April 1902; s. of Gudjon H. Helgason and Sigridur Halldorsdottir; m. 1st Ingibjörg Einarsdittir 1930, one s.; m. 2nd Audur Sveinsdottir 1945, two d.; many of his novels have been translated into English; corresp. mem. Deutsche Acad. der Kunste 1955-; Hon. mem. Union of Icelandic Artists; Dr. h.c. (Edinburgh, Iceland); Nobel Prize for Literature 1955; Sonning Prize 1969. *Publications include:* Salka Valka 1931, Independent People (epic) 1935, The Atom Station 1948, The Honour of the House 1959, A Quire of Seven 1964, Christianity at the Glacier, World Light. *Leisure interests:* music, walking. *Address:* Gljúfrasteinn, 270 Mosfellsbaer; Vaka-Helgafell, Sidumula 29, 108 Reykjavik, Iceland.

LAYA, Jaime C., M.S.; Philippine banker and fmr. politician; b. 8 Jan. 1939, Manila; s. of late Juan C. Laya and of Silvina C. Laya; m. Alicia Sandoval 1966; one s. three d.; ed. Univ. of the Philippines, Georgia Inst. of Tech. and Stanford Univ., U.S.A.; fmr. consultant to various bodies; partner in accounting firm Sycip, Gorres, Velayo (SGV); mem. Cabinet 1974-81; Deputy Gov. Cen. Bank of Philippines 1974-79, Gov. 1981-84; Minister for the Budget 1979-81, of Educ., Culture and Sports 1984-86; arrested on a warrant requiring him as material witness against F. Marcos (q.v.) 1989; Deputy Dir. Nat. Econ. Devt. Authority (NEDA) 1974-79. *Leisure interests:* swimming, collecting antiques. *Address:* c/o Central Bank of the Philippines, Mabini Street, Manila, Philippines.

LAYARD, Peter Richard Grenville, B.A., M.SC.; British economist; b. 15 March 1934, Welwyn Garden City; s. of John Willoughby Layard and Doris Layard; ed. Cambridge Univ., London School of Economics; school teacher, London County Council 1959-61; Sr. Research Officer, Robbins Cttee. on Higher Educ. 1961-64; Deputy Dir. Higher Educ. Research Unit, L.S.E. 1964-74, lecturer, L.S.E. 1968-75, Reader 1975-80, Prof. of Econ. 1980-, Head, Centre for Labour Econ. 1974-; Consultant, Centre for European Policy Studies, Brussels 1982-86; mem. Univ. Grants Cttee. 1985-; Chair. Employment Inst. 1987-; Fellow Econometric Soc. *Publications:* Cost Benefit Analysis 1973, Causes of Poverty (with D. Piachaud and M. Stewart) 1978, Microeconomic Theory (with A. A. Walters) 1978, More Jobs, Less Inflation 1982, The Causes of Unemployment (Ed. with C. Greenhalgh and A. Oswald) 1984, The Rise in Unemployment (Ed. with C. Bean and S. Nickell) 1986, How to Beat Unemployment 1986, Handbook of Labor Economics (Ed. with Orley C. Ashenfelter) 1987. *Leisure interest:* walking. *Address:* Centre for Labour Economics, London School of Economics, Houghton Street, London, WC2A 2AE (Office); 18 Provost Road, London, NW3 4SZ, England (Home). *Telephone:* 01-405 7686 (Office).

LAYCRAFT, James Herbert, Q.C., LL.D.; Canadian judge; b. 5 Jan. 1924, Veteran, Alberta; s. of George Edward and Hattie Laycraft; m. Helen Bradley 1948; one s. one d.; ed. Univ. of Alberta; practised law 1952-75; Queen's Counsel 1964; Judge, Supreme Court Trial Div. 1975-79; Judge, Court of Appeal of Alberta 1979-85, Chief Justice of Alberta 1985-; Hon. LL.D. (Calgary) 1986. *Leisure interests:* hiking, fishing, skiing. *Address:* Court of Appeal of Alberta, Court of Appeal Building, 530—7th Avenue S.W., Calgary, Alberta T2P 0Y3, Canada. *Telephone:* (403) 297-7447.

LAYTON, Robert G., B.COM., F.C.A., F.C.W.A.; business executive; b. 16 May 1923; ed. Bromsgrove School, Univ. of London, Inst. of Chartered Accountants, England; Chartered Accountant, London and Birmingham 1939-47; Chief Accountant, Caracas Petroleum S.A., Caracas, Venezuela 1948; Controller, Van Reekum Paper Inc., New York 1948-50; Ford Motor Co., Finance Int. Div. 1950-54; Dir. of Finance, Ford Mexico 1954-57,

Ford Germany 1957-63, Gen. Man. 1963-67, Vice-Pres. Sales, Ford Europe 1967-68; Vice-Pres. Ford U.S., Latin America 1968-69; mem. Man. Bd. Dynamit Nobel A.G., Troisdorf 1970-73; Pres. Feldmühle A.G., Düsseldorf 1973-78; Commr. for Econ. Devt. in Berlin May 1978-; mem. Advisory Bd., Friedrich Simon Bank KG, Düsseldorf, Allianz Versicherung, Deutsche Industrie Kredit Bank, Kan-American Grundbesitz. *Address:* Berlin Economic Development Corpn., Budapester Strasse 1, 1000 Berlin 30, Federal Republic of Germany. *Telephone:* (030) 2636211.

LÁZÁR, György; Hungarian economist and politician; b. 15 Sept. 1924, Isaszeg; began as technical draughtsman; mem. CP 1945-; joined Nat. Planning Office 1948, Chief Dept. Head 1953, Vice-Pres. 1958, Pres. 1973-75; Minister of Labour 1970-73; Deputy Prime Minister 1973-75, Prime Minister 1975-87; Co-Pres. Nat. Youth Policy and Educ. Council 1970-74; mem. Int. Econ. Relations Cttee. 1973-75; mem. HSWP Cen. Cttee. 1976-88; Political Cttee. 1975-88, Deputy Gen. Sec. HSWP 1987-88; Labour Order of Merit (twice). *Publication:* Történelmi jelen (Historic Present) 1983.

LAZAR, Philippe; French research director; b. 21 April 1936, Paris; s. of Maximilien Lazar and Françoise Lazar; m. Monique Lazar 1960; one s. one d.; ed. Ecole Polytechnique, Paris; researcher, Nat. Inst. of Hygiene 1960, Dir. of Research INSERM (French Nat. Inst. of Health and Medical Research) 1964, Dir. Environmental Health Research Unit 1977, Chair. Scientific Council 1981, Dir.-Gen. INSERM 1982-; Visiting Prof. Harvard School of Public Health 1975; Rapporteur-Gen. Nat. Colloque on Research and Technology 1982; Chevalier du Mérite Nat.; Chevalier, Légion d'honneur. *Publications:* Eléments de probabilités et statistiques 1967, Méthodes statistiques en expérimentation biologique 1974. *Leisure interests:* arts, literature. *Address:* 101 rue de Tolbiac, 75654 Paris, Cedex 13, France. *Telephone:* 45.84.14.41.

LAZENBY, Alec, A.O., SC.D., F.T.S., F.I.BIOL.; Australian university vice-chancellor; b. 4 March 1927, U.K.; s. of G. and E. Lazenby; m. Ann J. Hayward 1957; one s. two d.; ed. Univ. Coll. of Wales and Univ. of Cambridge; Scientific Officer, Welsh Plant Breeding Station 1949-53; Demonstrator, Agricultural Botany, Univ. of Cambridge 1953-58, Lecturer in Agricultural Botany 1958-65, Fellow and Asst. Tutor, Fitzwilliam Coll. 1962-65; Foundation Prof. of Agronomy, Univ. of New England, N.S.W. 1965-70, Vice-Chancellor 1970-77; Dir. Grassland Research Inst. 1977-82; Visiting Prof. Reading Univ. 1978-82; Hon. Professorial Fellow, Univ. of Wales 1979-82; Vice-Chancellor, Univ. of Tasmania 1982-; Hon. D.Rur. Sci. (New England) 1981. *Publications:* Intensive Pasture Production (Jt. Ed.) 1972, Australian Field Crops (Jt. Ed.), Vol I 1975, Vol. II 1979, Australia's Plant Breeding Needs 1986, The Grass Crop (Jt. Ed.) 1988; papers on pasture plant breeding, agronomy and weed ecology in various scientific journals. *Leisure interest:* golf. *Address:* c/o University of Tasmania, GPO Box 252C, Hobart, Tasmania, Australia 7001. *Telephone:* 202002.

LE DUC THO; Vietnamese politician; b. (as Phan Dinh Khai) 10 Oct. 1911, Dich Le Village, Ha Nam Ninh Prov.; joined CP of Indochina 1929; arrested by French and exiled in Con Dao 1930-36; led revolutionary movement, Nam Dinh 1937-39; rearrested and imprisoned 1939-44; in charge of organizational work of Cen. Cttee. 1944; mem. CP Cen. Cttee., in charge of Bac Ky (Tonkin) Party Cttee., attended First Nat. Conf. CP, Tan Trao, mem. Cen. Cttee. and Standing mem. 1945-; in charge of Party organizational work 1945-48; Deputy Sec. Nam Bo (Cochinchina) Party Cttee. and of Party Cen. Office, S. Viet-Nam 1948; mem. Politburo 1955-86, Adviser to Cen. Cttee. of CP 1986; Head Reunification Comm. 1955-56; Head Cen. Organizational Dept. 1957-68; Deputy Sec. Party Cen. Office, S. Viet-Nam 1968; Special Adviser of Vietnamese Del. to Paris Conf. 1968-73; Head S. Viet-Nam Comm. Cen. Cttee. participation in commanding Ho Chi Minh campaign 1975; Deputy Rep. of CP and Govt. Comm., S. Viet-Nam after liberation 1975-76; Head S.-W. War Front 1977-79; mem. Cen. Mil. Comm. 1967-82; Deputy Chair. Nat. Defence Comm. of CP 1983; has attended several Communist Party congresses abroad; declined Nobel Peace Prize 1973. *Publications:* several political works and poems. *Address:* Central Committee of Communist Party of Viet-Nam, 1c boulevard Hoang Van Thu, Hanoi, Viet-Nam.

LE THANH NGHI; Vietnamese politician; Deputy Premier of Democratic Repub. of Viet-Nam 1974-76; Chair. State Planning Comm. 1974-80; mem. Nat. Defence Council, Socialist Repub. of Viet-Nam 1976-81; Deputy Premier, Socialist Repub. of Viet-Nam 1976-81, Vice-Pres. Council of State 1981; Sec.-Gen. Council of State 1982; fmr. mem. Politburo and Secretariat of CP of Viet-Nam. *Address:* Council of State, Hanoi, Viet-Nam.

LE VAN LUONG; Vietnamese politician; b. 1910, North Viet-Nam; mem. Politburo, Lao Dong party 1951-56; assoc. with Truong Chinh (q.v.); mem. Secr. and Politburo, CP of Viet-Nam 1976-82. *Address:* Central Committee of the Communist Party of Viet-Nam, No. 1-c boulevard Hoang Van Thu, Hanoi, Viet-Nam.

LEACH, Admiral of the Fleet Sir Henry (Conyers), G.C.B.; British naval officer; b. 18 Nov. 1923; s. of Capt. John Catterall Leach and Evelyn Burrell Lee; m. Mary Jean McCall 1958; two d.; ed. St. Peter's Court, Broadstairs, Royal Naval Coll., Dartmouth; served cruiser Mauritius, S. Atlantic and Indian Ocean 1941-42; battleship Duke of York (involved in Scharnhorst action) 1943-45, destroyers, Mediterranean 1945-46, gunnery

1947; gunnery appointments 1948–51; Gunnery Officer, cruiser Newcastle, Far East 1953–55; staff appointments 1955–59; commanded destroyer Dunkirk 1959–61; frigate Galatea (Capt. 27th Squadron and Mediterranean) 1965–67; Dir. of Naval Plans 1968–70; commanded Commando Ship Albion 1970; Asst. Chief of Naval Staff (Policy) 1971–73; Flag Officer First Flotilla 1974–75; Vice-Chief of Defence Staff 1976–77; C.-in-C. Fleet and Allied C.-in-C., Channel and Eastern Atlantic 1977–79; Chief of Naval Staff and First Sea Lord 1979–82; First and Prin. Naval ADC to the Queen 1979; Pres. R.N. Benevolent Soc., Naval Officers' Assen., Sea Cadet Assen.; Gov. Cranleigh School; Chair. St. Dunstan's, Royal Navy Club, King Edward VII Hosp.; Vice-Pres. SSAFA. *Leisure interests:* fishing, gardening. *Address:* Wonston Lodge, Wonston, Winchester, Hants., England.

LEACH, Sir Ronald George, Kt., G.B.E., F.C.A.; British chartered accountant; b. 21 Aug. 1907, London; s. of William T. Leach and Esther Leach; m. Margaret Alice Binns 1953; one s. one d.; ed. Alleyn's School, Dulwich; Deputy Financial Sec. Ministry of Food 1939–46; Sr. Partner, Peat, Marwick, Mitchell and Co. (Chartered Accountants) 1966–77; Pres. Inst. of Chartered Accountants in England and Wales 1969–70; Chair. Accounting Standards Cttee. 1970–76; mem. Cttee. on Coastal Flooding 1953, Inquiry into Shipping 1967–70; Chair. Consumer Cttee. for G.B. 1958–67, Bd. of Trade Cos. Act Accountancy Advisory Cttee. 1969–; Bd. of Trade Insp. into the affairs of Pergamon Press 1969; Dir. Standard Chartered Bank (Channel Islands) 1980– (Chair. 1980–), Int. Investment Trust of Jersey 1980–, Ann Street Brewery 1981–; mem. Nat. Theatre Bd. 1971–76, Council of Oxford Centre in Man. Studies; Hon. LL.D. (Lancaster) 1977. *Publication:* (with Prof. Edward Stamp) British Accounting Standards: the first ten years 1981. *Address:* La Rosière, St. Saviour, Jersey, Channel Islands. *Telephone:* (0534) 77039.

LEAF, Alexander, M.D.; American physician; b. 10 April 1920, Yokohama, Japan; s. of Dr. Aaron L. and Dora Hural Leaf; m. Barbara L. Kincaid 1943; three d.; ed. Univs. of Washington and Michigan; Intern, Mass. Gen. Hosp. 1943–44, mem. staff 1949–, Physician-in-Chief 1966–81, Physician 1981–; Resident, Mayo Foundation, Rochester, Minn. 1944–45; Research Fellow, Univ. of Mich. 1947–49; mem. Faculty, Medical School, Harvard Univ. 1949–, Jackson Prof. of Clinical Medicine 1966–81, Ridley Watts Prof. of Preventive Medicine 1980–; Visiting Fellow, Balliol Coll., Oxford 1971–72; mem. N.A.S., A.A.A.S., American Acad. of Arts and Sciences, American Coll. of Physicians, The Biochemical Soc. (U.K.), Inst. of Medicine 1978 etc. *Publications:* 170 articles in professional journals; Significance of the Body Fluids in Clinical Medicine, Youth in Old Age, Renal Pathophysiology. *Leisure interests:* music (flautist), jogging. *Address:* Medical Services, Massachusetts General Hospital, Boston, Mass. 02114 (Office); One Curtis Circle, Winchester, Mass. 01890, U.S.A. (Home). *Telephone:* 617-726 5910 (Office); (617) 729-5852.

LEAHY, Sir John H. G., K.C.M.G., M.A.; British diplomatist (retd); b. 7 Feb. 1928, Worthing, Sussex; s. of the late William H. G. and Ethel Leahy; m. Elizabeth Anne Pitchford 1954; two s. two d.; ed. Tonbridge School, Clare Coll., Cambridge, Yale Univ.; joined diplomatic service 1951, Third Sec., Singapore 1955–57; Second Sec., then First Sec., Paris 1958–62; First Sec., Teheran 1965–68; Counsellor, Paris 1973–75; attached to Northern Ireland Office, Belfast 1975–76; Amb. to South Africa 1979–82; Deputy Under-Sec. (Africa and the Middle East), FCO 1982–84; High Commr. in Australia 1984–88; mem. Court of Skinners' Co. 1988–. *Address:* Manor Stables, Bishopstone, Near Seaford, E. Sussex, BN25 2UD, England.

LEAHY, Patrick Joseph, J.D.; American lawyer and politician, b. 31 March, 1940, Montpelier, Vt.; s. of Howard and Alba (Zambon) Leahy; m. Marcelle Pomerleau 1962; two s. one d.; ed. St. Michael's Coll., Winooski, Vt., and Georgetown Univ. Law Center, Washington, D.C.; admitted to practise law, State of Vermont 1964, U.S. Supreme Court, Second Circuit Court of Appeals, New York, U.S. Fed. Dist. Court of Vt.; Senator from Vermont 1975–; Vice-Chair. Senate Intelligence Cttee. 1984–; mem. Vt. Bar Assen. 1964–; Vice-Pres. Nat. Dist. Attorney's Assen.; Distinguished Service Award of Nat. Dist. Attorneys' Assen. 1974. *Leisure interests:* photography, reading, hiking, cross country skiing. *Address:* 433 Russell Senate Office Building, Washington, D.C. 20510 (Office); 31 Green Acres Drive, Burlington, Vt., U.S.A. (Home).

LEAKEY, Mary Douglas, F.B.A.; British archaeologist; b. 6 Feb. 1913, London; d. of Erskine Edward Nicol and Cecilia Marion Frere; m. Louis Seymour Bazett Leakey 1936 (died 1972); three s. (including Richard Leakey, q.v.); ed. privately; fmr. Dir. of Research, Olduvai Gorge Excavations, Tanzania, Hon. mem. American Assen. for Arts and Sciences; Foreign mem. N.A.S. (U.S.A.); Hon. D.Sc. (Witwatersrand) 1968, (W. Mich.) 1980, (Chicago) 1981, (Cambridge) 1987, Hon. D.Soc.Sc. (Yale) 1976, Hon. D.Litt. (Oxford) 1981; Prestwich Medal, Geological Soc. of London (jointly with L. S. B. Leakey), Gold Medal of Soc. of Women Geographers, Hubbard Medal of Nat. Geographical Soc. (jointly with L. S. B. Leakey), Linnaeus Gold Medal, Royal Swedish Acad. 1978, Bradford Washburn Award, Boston 1980. *Publications:* Olduvai Gorge, Vol. III 1971, Africa's Vanishing Art: the Rock Paintings of Tanzania 1983, Disclosing the Past (autobiog.) 1984, Lactoli: a Pliocene Site in Northern Tanzania (with J. M. Harris) 1988, contributor to Background to Evolution in Africa, After the Australopithecines; various scientific papers in Nature. *Leisure interests:*

game watching, reading. *Address:* c/o National Museum, P.O. Box 30239, Nairobi, Kenya.

LEAKEY, Richard Erskine Frere, F.R.A.I.; Kenyan palaeontologist; b. 19 Dec. 1944, Nairobi; s. of the late Louis Leakey and of Mary Leakey (q.v.); m. Meave Gillian Epps 1971; three d.; ed. the Duke of York School, Nairobi; leader of expeditions to West Natron, Tanzania 1963, 1964, Baringo, Kenya 1966, Omo River, Ethiopia 1967 and East Rudolf, Kenya 1968–70; researcher on Origin of Man, Lake Turkana 1971–76, Bulok 1980, Rusinga Island 1983–84, W. Turkana 1984–85; Admin. Dir. Nat. Museums of Kenya 1968–74, Dir. 1974–; mem. Museum Bd. of Govs.; Trustee, Nat. Fund for the Disabled; Chair. East African Wildlife Soc. 1985–; Head Wildlife Conservation Dept. April 1989–; Chair. Wildlife Clubs of Kenya 1969–84, Kenya Exploration Soc. 1969–72, Foundation for Research into Origin of Man (U.S.A.), Trustee Foundation for Social Habilitation, Rockford Coll., Callman Memorial Foundation; Franklin Burr Prize 1965, 1973; Hon. D.Sc. (Wooster Coll.) 1978, (Rockford Coll.) 1984, Hon. D.Litt. (Kent) 1987. *Publications:* numerous articles on finds in the field of palaeontology in scientific journals, including Nature, Journal of World History, Science, American Journal of Physics and Anthropology, etc.; contrib. to General History of Africa (vol. I), Perspective on Human Evolution, and Fossil Vertebrates of Africa; Origins (book, with Roger Lewin), People of the Lake: Man, His Origins, Nature and Future (book, with Roger Lewin) 1979, The Making of Mankind (also Television Series) 1981, Human Origins 1982, One Life 1984. *Leisure interests:* sailing and cooking. *Address:* National Museums of Kenya, P.O. Box 40658, Nairobi (Office); P.O. Box 24926, Nairobi, Kenya (Home). *Telephone:* Nairobi 742161.

LEAL, H. Allan, O.C., Q.C., LL.M.; Canadian lawyer; b. 15 June 1917, Beloeil, P.Q.; s. of Frederick William and Marie Ange (Ranger); m. Muriel I. Clemens; two s. one d.; ed. McMaster and Harvard Univs. and Osgoode Hall Law School; called to Bar of Ont. 1948; practised law with Erichsen-Brown & Leal, Toronto 1948–50; lecturer, Osgoode Hall Law School 1950–56, Vice-Dean and Prof. 1956–58, Dean and Prof. 1958–66; mem. Ont. Law Reform Comm. 1964–, Chair. 1966–77, Vice-Chair. 1981–; Deputy Attorney-Gen. for Ont. 1977–81; Special Adviser to Premier on constitutional matters 1981–82; Chancellor, McMaster Univ. 1977–86; mem. or fmr. mem. numerous nat. and int. cttees., del. to int. legal confs. etc.; Rhodes Scholar 1940; Hon. LL.D. (McMaster) 1963, (York) 1978, (Dalhousie) 1983, Hon. D.C.L. (W. Ont.) 1982; Law Soc. Medal 1987. *Publications:* articles in legal journals. *Leisure interests:* sailing, fishing, golf, skiing. *Address:* 18 King Street, East Toronto, Ont. M5C 1C5, Canada.

LEALOFI IV, Chief Tupua Tamasese; Samoan politician and doctor; b. 8 May 1922, Apia; m. Lita 1953; five c.; ed. Fiji School of Medicine and postgraduate studies at Suva; Medical practitioner 1945–69; succeeded to Paramount Chief (Tama-a-Aiga) of Tupua Tamasese 1965; mem. Council of Deputies 1968–69; mem. Legis. Ass. 1970; Prime Minister of Western Samoa 1970–73, 1975–76; Minister of Internal and External Dist. Affairs, Labour and Audit, Police and Prisons 1975–76. *Leisure interests:* reading, golf. *Address:* Legislative Assembly, Apia, Western Samoa.

LEAN, Sir David, Kt., C.B.E.; British film director; b. 25 March 1908; s. of late Francis William le Blount Lean and Helena Annie Tangye; one s. by previous marriage; m. 2nd Ann Todd 1949 (divorced 1957); m. 3rd Leila Matkar 1960 (divorced 1978); m. 4th Sandra Hotz 1981 (divorced 1985); ed. Leighton Park School, Reading; entered industry with Gaumont-British as numberboard boy 1928; editor for Gaumont Sound News and British Movietone News; edited Escape Me Never, Pygmalion, 49th Parallel; co-directed with Noel Coward In Which We Serve 1942; directed This Happy Breed 1943, Blithe Spirit 1944, Brief Encounter 1945, Great Expectations 1946, Oliver Twist 1947, The Passionate Friends 1948, Madeleine 1949, The Sound Barrier (British Acad. Award) 1952, Hobson's Choice 1953, Summer Madness (American title Summertime) 1955, The Bridge on the River Kwai (U.S. Acad. Award, Best Picture) 1957, Lawrence of Arabia (U.S. Acad. Award, Italian Silver Award) 1962, Dr. Zhivago 1965, Ryan's Daughter 1970, A Passage to India 1984; Fellow, British Film Inst. 1983; Officier de l'Ordre des Arts et des Lettres; Dr. h.c. (Royal Coll. of Art, London) 1985. *Address:* c/o Film Producers' Association, 162 Wardour Street, London, W.1, England.

LEAR, Evelyn, American soprano; b. Brooklyn, New York; d. of Nina Quartin; m. 2nd Thomas Stewart (q.v.); two d. by previous marriage; ed. New York Univ., Hunter Coll., Juilliard Opera Workshop; Fulbright Scholarship for study in Germany 1957; joined Berlin Opera, début in Ariadne auf Naxos 1957; début in U.K. in Four Last Songs with London Symphony Orchestra 1957; début at Metropolitan Opera in Mourning Becomes Electra 1967; début at La Scala, Milan, in Wozzeck 1971; regular performances with leading opera cos. and orchestras in Europe and U.S.A.; guest appearances with Berlin Opera and Vienna State Opera; soloist with the leading American orchestras including New York Philharmonic, Chicago Symphony, Philadelphia Orchestra, Boston Symphony, San Francisco Symphony and Los Angeles Philharmonic, has given many recitals and orchestral concerts and operatic performances with Thomas Stewart; Concert Artists Guild Award 1955. *Major roles include:* Marie in Wozzeck, Marschallin in Der Rosenkavalier, Countess in The Marriage of Figaro, Fiordiligi in Così fan tutti, Desdemona, Mimi, Dido in The Trojans, Donna Elvira in Don Giovanni, Marina in Boris Godunov, Tatiana in Eugene

Onegin, Lavinia in Mourning Becomes Electra, title role in Lulu; appeared in film Buffalo Bill 1976. *Recordings Include:* Wozzeck, Lulu, The Flying Dutchman, The Magic Flute, Boris Godunov, Eugene Onegin, Bach's St. John Passion, Pergolesi's Stabat Mater, Der Rosenkavalier. *Address:* 414 Sailboat Circle, Lauderdale, Fla. 33326, U.S.A.

LEATHER, Sir Edwin Hartley Cameron, K.C.M.G., K.C.V.O.; British politician and administrator; b. 22 May 1919, Toronto, Canada; s. of Harold H. Leather, M.B.E., and Grace C. Leather; m. Sheila A. A. Greenlees 1940; two d.; ed. Trinity Coll. School, Royal Mil. Coll., Kingston, Canada; M.P. for N. Somerset 1950–64; mem. Exec. Cttee. British Commonwealth Producers' Asscn. 1960–63, British Caribbean Assen.; Chair. Horder Centres for Arthritics 1962–65, Nat. Union of Conservative and Unionist Assens. 1970–71; Canadian Rep. Exec. Cttee., British Commonwealth Ex-servicemen's League 1954–63; Chair. Bath Festivals Soc. 1960–65; with Yehudi Menuhin School and Orchestra 1965–, mem. Bd. of Dirs. 1967–, Deputy Chair. 1967–73; Gov. of Bermuda 1973–77; Chair. United World Colls. Cttee. of Bermuda, Menuhin Foundation of Bermuda; Dir. N. M. Rothschild (Bermuda), and other cos.; Hon. Fellow, Royal Soc. of Arts 1968; K.St.J. 1974; Hon. LL.D. (Bath) 1975; Nat. Inst. Social Sciences Gold Medal 1977. *Publications:* The Vienna Elephant, The Mozart Score, The Duveen Letter. *Leisure interests:* music, travel, reading. *Address:* Chelsea, Inwood Close, Paget, Bermuda. *Telephone:* (809) 236-0240.

LEATHERS, 2nd Viscount; Frederick Alan Leathers, M.A., F.R.S.A.; British company director; b. 4 April 1908; s. of late Viscount Leathers; m. 1st Elspeth Stewart 1940, two s. two d.; m. 2nd Lorna May Barnett 1983; ed. Brighton Coll., and Emmanuel Coll., Cambridge; mem. Baltic Exchange; fmr. underwriting mem. of Lloyd's, Gen. Cttee. of Lloyd's Register of Shipping; mem. Court Worshipful Co. of Shipwrights, Court Watermen's and Lightermen's Co.; Fellow, Inst. of Chartered Shipbrokers; mem. Inst. Petroleum; fmr. Chair. Wm. Cory and Son Ltd., Cory Mann George Ltd., Hull Blyth and Co. Ltd., St. Denis Shipping Co. Ltd., Cory Ship Towage Ltd., Smit and Cory Int. Port Towage Ltd.; Nat. Westminster Bank Ltd., Outer London Regional Bd.; Fellow, Royal Philatelic Soc. *Address:* Park House, Chiddingfold, Surrey, GU8 4TS, England. *Telephone:* (042 879) 3222.

LEAVER, Sir Christopher, G.B.E., K.ST.J., J.P., F.R.S.A.; British business executive; b. 3 Nov. 1937, London; s. of Robert Leaver and Audrey Kerpen; m. Helen Mireille Molyneux Benton 1975; one s. two d.; ed. Eastbourne Coll.; commissioned Royal Army Ordnance Corps 1956–58; mem. Retail Food Trades Wages Council; J.P., Inner London 1970; mem. Council, Royal Borough of Kensington and Chelsea 1970–73; Court of Common Council (Ward of Dowgate), City of London 1974, Sheriff, City of London 1979–80; Lord Mayor of London 1981–82; Chair. Russell and McIver Group of Cos. (Wine Merchants), Thames Line PLC, London Tourist Bd. Ltd.; Deputy Chair. Thames Water Authority; Dir. Thermal Scientific PLC; Bd. of Brixton Prison 1975–78; Bd. of Govs., City Univ. 1978–; Gov. Christ's Hospital School 1975, City of London Girls' School 1975–78, City of London Freemen's School 1980; Chair. Young Musicians' Symphony Orchestra Trust 1979–81; Trustee, London Symphony Orchestra; Hon. Liveryman, Farmers' Co. 1975–; Freeman Co. of Watermen and Lightermen; Chancellor, City Univ. 1981–82; Vice-Pres. Nat. Playing Fields Assen.; Bridewell Royal Hosp.; Hon. Col. 151 Regt. RCT(V); Trustee, Chichester Festival Theatre; Order of Oman; Fellow, Chartered Inst. of Transport. *Leisure interests:* gardening, music, travel, old motor cars. *Address:* The Rectory, St. Mary-at-Hill, London, EC3R 8EE, England; Le Bois L'Abbé, Epaignes, Lieurey, 27260 Cormeilles, Eure, France. *Telephone:* 01-283 3575 (London).

LEAVER, Christopher John, B.SC., PH.D., D.I.C., A.R.C.S., F.R.S.E., F.R.S.; British professor of plant molecular biology; b. 31 May 1942, Bristol; s. of Douglas P. Leaver and Elizabeth C. Leaver; m. Anne Huggins 1971; one s. one d.; ed. Imperial Coll. of Science London; Fulbright Scholar, Purdue Univ., Ind., U.S.A. 1966–68; Scientific Officer, ARC Unit of Plant Physiology, Imperial Coll. London 1968–69; Lecturer, Univ. of Edinburgh 1969–80, Reader 1980–86, S.E.R.C. Sr. Research Fellow, 1985–, Prof. of Plant Molecular Biology 1986–; Nuffield Commonwealth Bursary, Sr. Visiting Fellowship (S.E.R.C), CSIRO Div. of Plant Industry, Canberra 1975; EMBO Long-term Fellowship, Biozentrum, Basle 1980; Trustee, John Innes Foundation, Norwich 1984–; mem. editorial bd. of several int. scientific journals.; European Molecular Biology Org'g; Huxley Gold Medal, Imperial Coll. 1970; Tate & Lyle Award, Phytochemical Soc. of Europe 1984. *Publications:* Ed. several books; numerous papers in int. scientific journals. *Leisure interests:* walking, talking. *Address:* Department of Botany, The King's Buildings, University of Edinburgh, Mayfield Road, Edinburgh, EH9 3JH, Scotland. *Telephone:* 031-667 1081 (Ext. 3304).

LEBEDEV, Yevgeniy Alekseyevich; Soviet actor; b. 15 Jan. 1917, Balakovo; s. of Aleksey Mikhailovich Lebedev and Zinaida Ivanovna Lebedeva; m. Natalya Aleksandrovna Tovstonogova 1950; one s. one d.; ed. Moscow Theatre School; Tbilisi Russian Theatre for Youth 1940–49; Leningrad Theatre 1949–56; Leningrad Academic Bolshoi Drama Theatre 1956–; People's Artist of R.S.F.S.R. 1962, U.S.S.R. State Prize 1950, 1968, People's Artist of the U.S.S.R. 1968, R.S.F.S.R. State Prize 1980, Lenin Prize 1986, Hero of Socialist Labour 1987. *Main roles:* Mitya (Poverty is No Vice), Tikhon (Thunderstorm by A. N. Ostrovsky), Pavel Korchagin

(How the Steel is Tempered by N. Ostrovsky), Monakhov (Barbarians by M. Gorky), Arturo Ui (Brecht), Bessemenov (Citizens by Gorky), Rogožin (The Idiot by Dostoyevsky), Poprishtshin (Diary of a Madman by Gogol), Falstaff (Shakespeare), Shtshukaz (Sholokhov), Marmeladov (Crime and Punishment by Dostoyevsky), Holstomer (Tolstoy), Waller (D. L. Koburn), Serebryakov (Chekhov), etc.; cinema roles: Mercy Train 1964, The Last Month of Autumn 1965, Under Fire there is no Ford 1967, Crash, The Wood Engraver. *Publications:* My Bessemenov 1975, numerous short stories. *Leisure interests:* sculpture, wood engraving. *Address:* Leningrad Academic Bolshoi Drama Theatre, Petrovskaya ul. 4/2, Kv. 70, Leningrad 197046, U.S.S.R.

LEBEDEV, Yuriy Vladimirovich; Soviet diplomatist; b. 29 Sept. 1923, Orekhovo-Zuevo, Moscow Region; ed. Moscow State Inst. of Int. Relations; Soviet Army until 1946; entered diplomatic service 1962; Counsellor, then Counsellor-Envoy, Soviet Embassy, Cuba 1962–68; ranking official, Ministry of Foreign Affairs, U.S.S.R. 1968–69; Amb. to Peru 1969–77, to Uruguay Aug. 1978–. *Address:* Soviet Embassy, Boulevard España 2741, Montevideo, Uruguay.

LEBEGUE, Daniel Simon Georges, B.L.; French banker; b. 4 May 1943, Lyons; s. of Robert Lebegue and Denise (née Flachet) Lebegue; m. Chantal Biron 1970; one s. one d.; ed. Univ. of Lyons, Inst. for Political Sciences and Nat. School for Admin., Paris; civil servant, Ministry of Economy and Finance 1969–73; Financial Adviser, Embassy in Japan 1974–76; Head of Balance of Payments Section, Treasury 1976–79, Head of Monetary Funds Section 1979–80; Deputy Dir. of Savings and Financial Market 1980–81; Counsellor in charge of Economy and Finance, Prime Minister's Office 1981–83; Head of Dept. of Financial and Monetary Affairs at Treasury 1983–84, Head of Treasury 1984–87; Man. Dir. Banque Nat. de Paris Sept. 1987–; Prof. at Inst. for Political Sciences, Paris; Chevalier Ordre Nat. du Mérite. *Publication:* Treasury and Financial Policy, cours de droit 1985. *Leisure interests:* opera, cinema, cycling, hiking. *Address:* 16 boulevard des Italiens, 75009 Paris (Office); 25 rue de Bourgogne, 75007 Paris, France (Home). *Telephone:* 40.14.78.72 (Office).

LEBEL, Claude, French diplomatist; b. 18 Feb. 1914, Paris; s. of Jacques Lebel and Marie-Germaine Delavigne; m. Claudie de Schoutheete de Tervarent; two s. two d.; ed. Lycée Pasteur, Neuilly-sur-Seine, Faculté de Droit de Paris, Ecole Libre des Sciences Politiques; entered diplomatic service 1938; served Brussels 1938–39, Madrid 1941–42, Athens 1947–49, London 1949–55, Washington 1959–62; joined the Provisional French Govt. in Algiers 1943–44, served in Paris 1945–47, 1955–59, 1962–69; Amb. to Morocco 1970–74, to Switzerland 1975–79; Commdr., Légion d'honneur, Commdr. Ordre national du Mérite, Croix de guerre. *Address:* 11 *bis* boulevard de Beauséjour, 75016 Paris, France (Home). *Telephone:* (1) 45-27-60-73 (Home).

LEBENSTEIN, Jan; Polish painter; b. 5 Jan. 1930, Warsaw; ed. Warsaw Acad. of Fine Arts; one-man exhbns.: Musée d'Art Moderne and Galerie Lambert, Paris 1961, Galerie Pauli, Lausanne 1963, Galerie Lacloche, Paris 1965, exhbn. of series Créatures abominables, Carnet intime, Figury osiowe (Axial Figures) Cologne 1965, Galerie Desbière, Paris 1970; Collections: Nat. Gallery, Warsaw, Poznań, Cracow, Musée d'Art Moderne, Paris, Municipal Museum, Amsterdam, Museum of Modern Art, New York, São Paulo, San Francisco, Nat. Gallery of Modern Art, Belgrade; S. Guggenheim Prize 1958, Grand Prix, Biennale of Youth, Paris. *Works include:* Zwierzęta (The Animals), Pożegnanie (Leave-Taking), Przeciwstawienie (Opposition), Zwierzę zielone (The Green Animal), Bieg skamienały (The Petrified Run), Przebudzenie (Awakening), Affection, Figura na przekątnych (The Figure on the Diagonals), Affection, Figura w błękitnej (The Figure in a Blue Frame) (all series). *Address:* Living in France.

LEBER, Georg; German trade unionist and politician; b. 7 Oct. 1920, Obertiefebach; s. of Jakob Leber and Elisabeth (née Geis) Leber; m. Erna Maria Wilfing 1942; one s.; ed. primary and commercial schools in Limburg (Lahn); soldier 1939–45; joined trade union and Social Democrat Party (SPD) 1947; trade union leader, Limburg 1949; Chair. of local branch of SPD 1951; Ed. Der Grundstein (trade union paper) 1952; mem. Man. Cttee. Bau-Steine-Erden Trade Union 1953–57, Chair. 1957; mem. Man. Cttee. Fed. of German Trade Unions 1957; mem. Man. Cttee. of Int. Federation of Building and Timber Workers and Pres. Jt. Cttee. of Trade Unions of Building and Timber Trade in European Common Market 1957; mem. Bundestag 1957–82; mem. European Parl. 1958–59; mem. Man. Cttee. SPD Faction in Bundestag 1961, mem. Presidium 1968; Fed. Minister of Transport 1966–69, of Transport, Posts and Telecommunications 1969–72, of Defence 1972–78; Vice-Pres. German Bundestag 1979–; Dr. h.c. (Tübingen) 1980; Grosses Bundesverdienstkreuz mit Stern und Schulterband. *Address:* c/o Rathaus, 7850 Lörrach, Federal Republic of Germany.

Le BIGOT, Guillaume Charles René; French shipping executive; b. 24 Feb. 1909, Lorient, Morbihan; s. of Vice-Admiral J. Le Bigot and Louise Avenel; m. Pauline Coutret 1937; two s. three d.; ed. Ecole des Hautes Etudes Commerciales; Chief of Budgetary and Financial Section, Ministry of Armed Forces 1947–50; Chief of Liaison Mission with Allied Forces 1950–51; Chief of Div. of Budget and Finance, Allied Forces in Europe 1951–58; Ministerial Sec. for the Navy 1958–61; Mayor of Puget-sur-Argens 1959–77; Chair. Cie. des Messageries Maritimes 1961–66; Admin. Union des Transports Aériens (U.T.A.) 1961–66; Chair. French Cttee. of Lloyd's Register of Shipping 1971–79, Acad. de Marine 1980–81; Commdr. Légion d'honneur, Commdr. des Palmes académiques, Commdr. Legion of Merit. *Leisure interest:* viticulture. *Address:* 9 boulevard Suchet, 75016 Paris, France. *Telephone:* 504-65-73.

LEBLANC, Roméo A., P.C.; Canadian journalist and politician; b. 18 Dec. 1927, L'Anse-aux-Cormier, Memramcook, N.B.; s. of Philias and Lucie Leblanc; m. Joslyn Carter 1966; one s. one d.; ed. St.-Joseph and Paris Univs.; Press Sec. to Prime Minister Trudeau 1967–71; M.P. for Westmorland-Kent 1972–; Minister of Fisheries 1974–79, for the Environment 1976–79, of Fisheries and Oceans 1980–82, of Public Works 1982–84; Senator, Beauséjour, New Brunswick 1984–; Pres. First Session of Gen. Conf. of UNESCO 1979–80; Liberal. *Address:* House of Commons, Ottawa, Ont. K1A 0A6; P.O. Box 93, Grand Digne, N.B., Canada.

LEBLOND, Charles Philippe, L.ÈS S., M.D., PH.D., D.SC., F.R.S.C., F.R.S.; Canadian professor of anatomy; b. 5 Feb. 1910, Lille, France; s. of Oscar Leblond and Jeanne Desmarchelier; m. Gertrude Elinor Sternschuss 1936; three s. one d.; ed. Univs. of Lille, Paris, Montreal and the Sorbonne; Asst. in Histology, Medical School, Univ. of Paris 1934–35; Rockefeller Fellow, School of Medicine, Yale Univ. 1936–37; Asst. Laboratoire de Synthèse Atomique, Paris 1938–40; lecturer in Histology and Embryology, McGill Univ. 1942–43, Asst. Prof. of Anatomy 1943–46, Assoc. Prof. 1946–48, Prof. of Anatomy 1948–, Chair. Dept. of Anatomy 1957–75; Fellow Royal Soc. of Canada, Royal Soc. (London); mem. American Asscn. of Anatomists, Canadian Ass008 of Anatomists, American Soc. for Cell Biology, Histochemical Soc., Soc. for Experimental Biology and Medicine, and others; Hon. D.Sc. (Acadia, McGill, Montreal and York Univs.); Prix Saintour, French Acad. 1935; Flavelle Medal, Royal Soc. of Canada 1961, Gairdner Fed. Award 1965, American Coll. of Physicians Award 1966, Province of Quebec Biology Prize 1968, Officer of Order of Canada 1977, American Soc. for Cell Biology, E. B. Wilson Award 1982. *Publications:* The Use of Radioautography in Investigating Protein Synthesis (with K. B. Warren) 1965, and over 300 articles in scientific journals. *Leisure interests:* architecture, snowshoeing, gardening. *Address:* Department of Anatomy, McGill University, Strathcona Anatomy and Dentistry Building, 3640 University Street, Montreal, Quebec H3A 2B2 (Office); 68 Chesterfield Avenue, Montreal, Quebec, Canada (Home). *Telephone:* (514) 392-4931 (Office); (514) 486-4837 (Home).

LeBLOND, Richard Knight II; American banker; b. 16 Nov. 1920, Cincinnati, Ohio; s. of Harold R. and Elizabeth (Conroy) LeBlond; m. Sally C. Chapman 1948; six s. four d.; ed. Hill School, Pottstown, Pa., Princeton Univ., Columbia Univ., Graduate School of Business Admin., Harvard Business School; joined New York Trust Co. (now Chemical Bank) 1946, Asst. Treas. 1949, Asst. Vice-Pres. 1952, Vice-Pres. 1958, Sr. Vice-Pres. 1966, Exec. Vice-Pres. 1968, Dir. Chemical Bank and Chemical New York Corpn. 1972–, Vice-Chair. 1973–85, Sr. Adviser 1985–; Chair. Bd. of Dirs., Bedford Stuyvesant D and S Corpn. 1985; Dir. Home Life Insurance Co., Barnes Group Inc. *Leisure interests:* golf, tennis, squash, skiing, swimming. *Address:* Chemical Bank, 30 Rockefeller Plaza, Suite 6101, New York, N.Y. 10112 (Office); 194 Sunset Hill Road, New Canaan, Conn. 06840, U.S.A. (Home). *Telephone:* (212) 310-7080 (Office); (203) 966-4125 (Home).

LEBOTSA, Mohamane Masimole, B.SC. (HONS.)(RSA), M.SC. (ENG.), U.E.D.; Lesotho engineer and politician; b. 1927, Hlotse, Leribe; ed. Hlotse Govt. Intermediate School; teacher at Lesotho High School; Asst. Lecturer Fort Hare Univ. Coll.; Asst. Engineer, Sir William Halcrow & Partners (U.K.); joined Civil Service as Structural Engineer (Bldg. & Service Div.) 1963; asst. teacher and Prin. St. Agnes High School; Dir. of Works, Nat. Univ.; Minister of Works 1986–; ordained priest 1976; mem. ECLOF Cttees. *Address:* c/o The Military Council, Maseru, Lesotho, South Africa.

LEBOUDER, Jean-Pierre; Central African Republic politician; b. 1944; ed. Ecole nationale supérieure agronomique, Toulouse, France; Dir. Research Centre, Union cotonnière centrafricaine 1971–72, Dir.-Gen. 1974–76; Minister of Rural Devt. 1976, of Planning, Statistics and Int. Co-operation 1978–80; Prime Minister 1980–81. *Address:* c/o Office du Premier Ministre, Bangui, Central African Republic.

LEBOWITZ, Joel L., M.S., PH.D.; American professor of mathematics and physics; b. 10 May 1930, Taceva, Czechoslovakia; m. Estelle Mandelbaum 1953; ed. Brooklyn Coll. and Syracuse Univ.; Nat. Science Foundation Postdoctoral Fellow, Yale Univ. 1956–57; Asst. Prof. Stevens Inst. of Tech. 1957–59; Asst. Prof. Belfer Grad. School of Science, Yeshiva Univ. 1959–60, Assoc. Prof. 1960–65, Prof. of Physics 1965–77, Chair. Dept. of Physics 1968–76; Dir. Center for Mathematical Sciences Research and Prof. of Math. and Physics, Rutgers Univ. 1977–; mem. N.A.S., A.A.A.S., New York Acad. of Sciences, American Physical Soc.; Dr. h.c. Ecole Polytechnique Fédérale Lausanne and other distinctions. *Publications:* 297 scientific papers. *Address:* Department of Mathematics, Rutgers University, New Brunswick, N.J. 08903, U.S.A. *Telephone:* (201) 932-3117.

LE BRETON, David Francis Battye, C.B.E., M.A.; British diplomatist; b. 2 March 1931, London; s. of the late Lieut.-Col. F. H. Le Breton, M.C., and of Elisabeth Trevor-Battye; m. Patricia June Byrne 1961; one s. two d.; ed. Winchester, New Coll., Oxford; Colonial Admin. Service, Tanganyika 1953–63, Dist. Officer 1954, Pvt. Sec. to Gov. 1959–60, Magistrate 1962–63;

Commonwealth Relations Office 1963; Diplomatic Service 1965–88; First Sec., Zanzibar 1964, Lusaka 1964–68; FCO 1968–71; Head of Chancery, Budapest 1971–74; Commr. Anguilla 1974–78; Counsellor and Head of Chancery, Nairobi 1978–81; High Commr. in The Gambia 1981–84, Head Commonwealth Co-ordination Dept., FCO 1984–86, Head Nationality and Treaty Dept. 1986–87; Financial Adviser Allied Dunbar Assurance PLC 1988–. *Leisure interests:* travel, African affairs. *Address:* Brackenwood, French Street, Westerham, Kent, TN16 1PN, England.

LE BROCQUY, Louis, D.LITT., LL.D., H.R.H.A., F.S.I.A.D.; Irish artist; b. 10 Nov. 1916, Dublin; s. of the late Albert le Brocquy and Sybil de Lacy Staunton; m. 1st Jean Atkinson Stoney 1938, one d.; m. 2nd Anne Madden-Simpson 1958, two s.; ed. St. Gerard's School, Wicklow; founder mem., Irish Exhbn. of Living Art 1943; Visiting Instructor, Cen. School of Arts and Crafts, London 1947–54; Visiting Tutor, R.C.A., London 1955–58; mem. Irish Council of Design 1963–65; Dir. Kilkenny Design Workshops 1965–77; exhibits in Albright Museum, Buffalo, Carnegie Inst., Pittsburgh, Detroit Inst., Hirshhorn Museum, Washington, Kunsthaus, Zurich, Guggenheim Museum, New York, Uffizi Gallery, Florence, Columbus Museum, Ohio, San Diego Museum, Tate Gallery, London; retrospective exhbns.: Fondation Maeght, 1973, Musee D'Art Moderne, Paris 1976, New York State Museum 1981, Boston 1982, Palais des Beaux Arts, Charleroi 1982, Arts Council, Dublin 1987, Ulster Museum 1987, aegis Nat. Gallery of Victoria, Melbourne, Adelaide, Brisbane 1988, Musée Picasso, Antibes 1989; Premio Prealpina, Venice Biennale 1956; illustrated The Tain (trans. Kinsella) 1969, The Playboy of the Western World (Synge) 1970, The Gododdin (trans. O'Grady) 1978, Dubliners (Joyce) 1986; Stirrings Still (Samuel Beckett) 1988; Chevalier, Légion d'honneur 1974. *Address:* c/o Gimpel Fils, 30 Davies Street, London, W1Y 1LG, England.

LE BRUN, Christopher Mark, M.A., D.F.A.; British artist; b. 20 Dec. 1951, Portsmouth; s. of John Le Brun and Eileen B. Le Brun (née Miles); m. Charlotte Verity 1979; one s. one d.; ed. Portsmouth Southern Grammar School, Slade School of Fine Art and Chelsea School of Art; Visiting Lecturer, Brighton Polytechnic 1975–82, Slade School of Fine Art 1978–83, Wimbledon School of Art 1981–83; one-man exhbns. Nigel Greenwood Inc., London 1980, 1982, 1985, Gillespie-Laage-Salomon, Paris 1981, Sperone-Westwater, New York 1983, 1986, Fruitmarket Gallery, Edinburgh 1985, Arnolfini Gallery, Bristol 1985, Kunsthalle Basel 1986, D.A.A.D. Gallery, Berlin 1988, Rudolf Zwirner, Cologne 1988; has participated in group exhbns. in U.K., Europe and New York including Venice Biennale 1982, 1984, Zeitgeist Berlin 1982; work in several public collections including Tate Gallery, London and Museum of Modern Art, New York; Gulbenkian Printmakers Award 1983, D.A.A.D. Award, W. Berlin 1987–88 and other prizes. *Leisure interest:* cricket. *Address:* c/o Nigel Greenwood, 4 New Burlington Street, London, W1X 1FE, England. *Telephone:* 01-434 3795.

LEBRUN MORATINOS, H.E. Cardinal José Alí; Venezuelan ecclesiastic; b. 19 March 1919, Puerto Cabella, Valencia, Venezuela; ordained priest 1943; Titular Bishop of Arado 1956, Bishop of Maracay 1958–62, of Valencia 1962–80; given title of Archbishop 1972; Archbishop of Caracas 1980–; cr. Cardinal 1983. *Address:* Arzobispado, Apartado 954, Caracas 1010-A, Venezuela. *Telephone:* (02) 451611.

LEBURTON, Edmond Jules Isidore; Belgian politician; b. 18 April 1915, Lantremange (Waremme); ed. Liège Univ.; Prin. Controller of Labour 1936–46; Chef de Cabinet, Ministry of Labour and Social Welfare 1945–46; Commandant of Secret Army and mem. various resistance groups 1939–45; mem. House of Representatives 1946–81, Speaker 1977–79; Mayor of Waremme 1947–87; Prof. Ecole Provinciale de Service Social, Liège, and Ecole Provinciale d'Infirmières, Herstal; Prof., Institut d'Etudes Sociales de l'Etat, Brussels; Minister of Public Health and Family Welfare 1954–58, of Social Security 1961–65; Minister-Vice-Pres., Co-ordinator of Infrastructure Policy 1965–66; Minister for Econ. Affairs, 1969–71; Prime Minister 1973–74; Nat. Chair. Socialist Party 1971–73; Chair. Union Nationale des Mutualités Socialistes 1959–85; fmr. Pres. Bd. of Dirs. Le Peuple, Le Monde du Travail, Travail; fmr. Admin., Free Univ. of Brussels; Chair. Home Waremmien; Chair. or Hon. Pres. numerous charities; Arthur Jauniaux Prize for Social Action 1973; Arthur Gailly Medical and Social Prize 1981; Commdr. de l'Ordre de Léopold, Croix de guerre avec Palmes, Grand Cross Order of Leopold II, Hon. Capt. Resistance Movement, Grand Officer Order of Merit (Italy), Grand Cross Order of Orange-Nassau (Netherlands), Grand Officer Légion d'honneur, Ordre de l'Etoile Yugoslave avec Couronne d'Or and numerous other awards and decorations. *Publications:* Précis de sécurité sociale, Traité d'économie politique. *Address:* 36 Clos de Hesbaye, 4370 Waremme, Belgium (Home).

LECANUET, Jean Adrien François; French politician; b. 4 March 1920, Rouen; ed. Lycée Corneille, Rouen, Lycée Henri IV, Paris, and Univ. of Paris; Counsellor of State; Insp. Gen., Ministry of Information 1944; Dir. of the Cabinets of Ministry of Information, Merchant Marine, Nat. Econ., Interior 1946–51; mem. Nat. Assembly 1951–55; Sec. of State, Presidency Council 1955–58; Mayor of Rouen 1968, 1971, 1977, 1983; Senator 1959–73, 1977–; Pres. Senate Cttee. of Foreign Affairs; Pres. Centre Démocrate 1966–76, Centre des démocrates sociaux 1976–; Pres. UDF 1978–88; Minister of Justice 1974–76, also Minister of State 1974–77; Minister of Planning and Devt. 1976–77; mem. European Parl. June 1979–; Conseiller Gen. of Rouen 1958, 1964, 1970, 1976; Officier Légion d'honneur, Commdr. Ordre

St. Grégoire le Grand. *Publication:* Le Projet Réformateur (in collab.) 1973. *Address:* 59 boulevard du Château, Neuilly-sur-Seine, France (Home).

Le CARRÉ, John (see Cornwell, David John Moore).

LECAT, Jean-Philippe; French politician; b. 29 July 1935, Dijon; s. of Jean Lecat and Madeleine Bouchard; m. Nadine Irène Romm 1965; two d.; ed. Ecole Nationale d'Administration; mem. Council of State 1963–66, 1974–, Auditor 1963–; Chargé de Mission, Prime Minister's Office 1966–68; Deputy to the Nat. Ass., Beaune 1968–72, 1973, 1978–81; Nat. Del. for Cultural Affairs, Union des Démocrates pour la République 1970–71, Asst. Sec.-Gen. for Cultural Affairs and Information 1971–72; Spokesman of the Govt. 1972–73; Sec. of State for Econ. 1973–74; Minister of Information 1973–74, of Culture and Communication 1978–81; mem. Bourgogne Regional Council 1973–; Del. to Natural Resources Conservation Conf. 1975; Chargé de Mission, Pres. of Repub. 1976–78, and Spokesman of the Pres. 1976–81. *Publications:* Quand flamboyait la Toison d'or 1982, Beaune 1983, La Bourgogne 1985, La siècle de la toison d'or 1986. *Address:* 131 boulevard du général Koenig, 92200 Neuilly-sur-Seine, France.

LECERF, Olivier Marie Maurice; French industrialist; b. 2 Aug. 1929, Merville-Franceville; s. of Maurice and Colette (Lainé) Lecerf; m. Aline Bazin de Jessey 1958; two s. two d.; ed. Univ. of Paris, Centre d'Etudes Industrielles, Geneva; joined Ciments Lafarge 1956, marketing and man. responsibilities in Brazil and Canada 1956–65; Vice-Pres. Canada Cement Lafarge 1965–71; Vice-Chair. and Gen. Man. Ciments Lafarge 1973–74, Chair. and C.E.O. 1974–82; Vice-Chair. and C.O.O. Lafarge SA 1983, Chair. and C.E.O. 1984–; Chevalier, Légion d'honneur, Commandeur, Ordre nat. du Mérite. *Leisure interest:* tennis. *Address:* Lafarge Coppée, 28 rue Emile Menier, 75116 Paris (Office); 8 rue Guy de Maupassant, 75016 Paris, France (Home). *Telephone:* 47.04.11.00 (Office); 45-04-14-70 (Home).

LECHAT, Paul, M.D.; French professor of pharmacology; b. 14 Dec. 1920, Le Mans; s. of Robert Lechat and Louise Blondin; m. Gabrielle Guyader 1948; three s. one d.; ed. Univ. of Paris-Sorbonne; Assoc. Prof. of Pharmacology, Univ. of Paris 1958–66, Prof. 1966–, Dir. Inst. of Pharmacology 1967–; Expert WHO 1965–85; Pres. Int. Union of Pharmacology 1984–87; mem. British Pharmacological Soc. 1982–; mem. Acad. Nat. de Pharmacie de Paris 1962–, Acad. Nat de Médecine 1980–; Foreign mem. Acad. Royale Belgique de Médecine 1986–; Hon. Doctor (Lund); Chevalier Légion d'honneur, Officier ordre national du Mérite. *Publications:* Abrégé de pharmacologie médicale 1973, over 300 papers on pharmacology. *Address:* 15 rue de l'Ecole de Médecine, 75006 Paris (Univ.); 44 rue Saint-Didier, 75116 Paris, France (Home). *Telephone:* 46 33 51 32 (Univ.); 45 53 08 00 (Home).

LECHÍN OQUENDO, Juan; Bolivian politician and diplomatist; b. 1915; fmr. professional footballer; fmr. Minister of Mines; Pres. Bolivian Mine Workers' Confed.; fmr. Pres. of Senate; Vice-Pres. of Repub. 1960–64; Amb. to Italy 1962–63; exiled May 1965; fmr. Leader, Left Sector of Movimiento Nacionalista Revolucionario (MNR); sought asylum in Chile June 1967; Exec. Sec. Cen. Obrera Boliviana 1952–65, 1970, 1982–86; re-elected Exec. Sec. Fed. Sindical de Trabajadores Mineros de Bolivia 1970.

LECHÍN SUÁREZ, Lieut.-Gen. Juan; Bolivian army officer; b. 8 March 1921, Cochabamba; s. of Juan Alfredo Lechín and Julia Suárez de Lechín; m. Ruth Varela de Lechín 1947; one s. three d.; ed. Bolivian Military Acad., General Staff Coll. (Fort Leavenworth), U.S.A.; Chief of Operations, Bolivian Army H.Q.; Mil. and Air Attaché Bolivian Embassy Fed. Repub. of Germany; Commdr. 5th Infantry Div. (Bolivian); Pres. Bolivian Mining Corpn. and Minister of State; Commdr. 3rd Infantry Div. (Bolivian); Amb. to U.K., also accred. to Netherlands 1969–74; Minister for Planning and Co-ordination to the Pres. 1974–78; Chair. Nat. Advisory and Legis. Council 1980; Cóndor de los Andes (Bolivia), Grosses Verdienstkreuz (Fed. Repub. of Germany), Guerrillero José M. Lanza, Mérito Aeronáutico, Mérito Naval (Bolivia). *Publications:* essays on military history and geo-politics. *Address:* Casilla 4405, La Paz, Bolivia.

LeCLAIR, J. Maurice, C.C., M.D., C.M., M.SC.; Canadian business executive; b. 19 June 1927, Sayabec, Quebec; s. of François LeClair and Rose-Anna Chassé; m. Pauline Heroux; two s. four d.; ed. McGill Univ., Montreal and Univ. of Minnesota; entered gen. medicine, Shawinigan, Que. 1953; taught medicine, Univ. of Montreal 1962–68, Chair. Dept. of Medicine, later Dean of Medicine 1965–68; Deputy Minister of Health, Fed. Govt. 1970–74; Sec. Ministry of Science and Tech. 1974–76; Sec. of Treasury Bd. 1976–79; Vice-Pres. Planning and Finance, Canadian Nat. (group of transportation and communications cos.) 1979–82, Pres. and C.E.O. 1982–85, Chair. and C.E.O. 1985–; mem. Bd. of Dirs. Grand Trunk Corpn., Grand Trunk Western Railroad, Cen. Vermont Railway, Duluth, Winnipeg & Pacific Railway Co., CN France, etc.; Fellow, Royal Coll. of Surgeons of Canada, American Coll. of Physicians; Hon. doctorates (Sherbrooke) 1970, (McGill) 1971, (McMaster) 1976. *Leisure interests:* collecting antique clocks and watches. *Address:* P.O. Box 8100, Montreal, Quebec, H3C 3N4 (Office); 3120 Daulac Road, Westmount, Que. H3Y 2A2, Canada. *Telephone:* (514) 877-5746 (Office).

LECLANT, Jean, D. ÈS. L.; French professor of Egyptology; b. 8 Aug. 1920, Paris; s. of René Leclant and Laure Pannier; ed. Ecole Normale Supérieure, Paris and Inst. Français d'Archéologie Orientale, Cairo; Prof. Univ. of Strasbourg 1953–63, Sorbonne 1963–79, Collège de France 1979–;

Dir. of Studies, Ecole des Hautes Etudes 1963–; Sec. Acad. des Inscriptions et Belles Lettres (Inst. de France) 1983–; mem. Acad. des Sciences d'Outre-Mer and many other learned socs. in France and abroad; Officier, Légion d'honneur; Chevalier, Ordre du Mérite; Commdr. Ordre des Palmes Académiques; Officier, Ordre des Arts et Lettres; Chevalier du Mérite Militaire; Imperial Order of Menelik (Ethiopia), Grand Officier, ordre de la Repub. d'Egypte. *Publications:* Dans les Pas des Pharaohs 1958, Montouemhat, Prince de la Ville 1963, Recherches sur les Monuments Thébains 1965, Les Pharaons 1978–80 and more than 300 books and articles. *Address:* 77 rue Georges Lardennois, Paris 75019; 23 quai de Conti, Paris 75006, France. *Telephone:* 42 08 36 96; 43 26 92 82.

LECLERC, Edouard; French business executive; b. 20 Nov. 1926, Landerneau; s. of Eugène Leclerc and Marie Kerouanton; m. Hélène Diquélou 1950; one s. two d.; ed. seminaries in Paris, Uriage-les-Bains and Saint-Cirgues; pioneer of Leclerc supermarket chain (first opened Landerneau) 1949–, currently 512 branches; Pres. Asscn. nat. des centres Leclerc 1980–. *Publications:* Combat pour la distribution, La part de bonheur, Le soleil de l'Ouest. *Leisure interests:* archaelogy, writing. *Address:* La-Haye-Saint-Divy, B.P.23, 29220 Landerneau (Home), 11 rue Bélerit, 29220 Landerneau, France (Office).

Le CLÉZIO, Jean Marie Gustave; French-British writer; b. 13 April 1940, Nice; m. Rosalie Piquemal 1961; one d.; ed. Lycée and Univ. de Nice; travelled in Nigeria 1948, England (studied at Bristol and London Univs.), U.S.A. 1965; Chevalier des Arts et des Lettres; Prix Renaudot 1963, Grand Prix Paul Morand (Acad. française) 1980. *Publications:* Le procès-verbal (The Interrogation) 1963, La fièvre (Fever) (short stories) 1965, Le procès 1965, Le déluge 1966, L'extase matérielle (essay) 1967, Terra amata (novel) 1967, Le livre des fuites 1969, La guerre 1970, Haï 1971, Conversations 1971, Les géants 1973, Mydriase 1973, Voyages de l'autre côté 1975, Les prophéties du Chylam Balam 1976, Mondo et autres histoires, L'inconnu sur la terre 1978, Désert 1980, Trois villes saintes 1980, La ronde et autres faits divers 1982, Journal du chercheur d'or 1985, Voyage à Rodrigues 1986. *Address:* c/o Editions Gallimard, 5 rue Sébastien-Bottin, 75007 Paris, France.

LECOURT, Robert, L. EN D.; French lawyer and politician; b. 19 Sept. 1908, Pavilly; s. of Léon and Angèle (née Lépron) Lecourt; m. Marguerite Chabrerie 1932; one d.; ed. Coll. Saint-Jean-Baptiste-de-la-Salle, Rouen, and Law Faculty, Caen; Lawyer, Court of Appeal, Rouen 1928–32, Paris 1932–73; mem. Comité directeur du mouvement Résistance 1942–45, L'Assemblée consultative provisoire 1944–45; mem. two Constituent Assemblies 1945–46, Nat. Assembly 1946–58; Minister of Justice 1948–49, 1957–58; concerned with Constitutional Reform 1957–58; Minister of State for Overseas Relations 1959–69; Judge, European Court of Justice 1962–76, Pres. 1967–76; mem. Constitutional Council Sept. 1979–; Pres. Mouvement Républicain Populaire (MRP) 1946–48, 1952–57; Hon. Bencher, Gray's Inn; Hon. Dr. (Univ. of Exeter); Commdr., Légion d'honneur, Croix de guerre, Grand Cross of Belgium, Luxembourg, Fed. Repub. of Germany, Italy, Yugoslavia, Gabon, Madagascar and others. *Publications:* Le juge devant le Marché commun 1970, L'Europe des juges 1976, Concorde sans concordat 1978. *Address:* 11 boulevard Suchet, 75016 Paris, France (Home).

LE COUTEUR, Kenneth James, M.A., PH.D. (CANTAB.), F.A.A.; British academic; b. 16 Sept. 1920, Jersey, C.I.; s. of the late P. Le Couteur and E. Le Couteur; m. Enid Domville 1950; three d.; ed. Victoria Coll., Jersey and Cambridge Univ.; Scientific Officer Ministry of Aircraft Production 1941–45; Fellow St. John's Coll., Cambridge 1945–48; Turner and Newall Fellow, Manchester Univ. 1947–49; Sr. Lecturer and Reader Univ. of Liverpool 1949–56; Prof. of Theoretical Physics, Inst. of Advanced Studies, Australian Nat. Univ. 1956–85; Prof. Emer. 1985–. *Publications:* scientific articles. *Leisure interests:* fishing, sailing. *Address:* 12 Hutt Street, Yarralumla, A.C.T. 2600, Australia. *Telephone:* (062) 812013.

LEDDY, John Francis, O.C., M.A., M.LITT., D.PHIL., F.R.HIST.S., F.R.S.A.; Canadian university president (retd.); b. 16 April 1911, Ottawa; s. of John J. and Teresa F. (Dwyer) Leddy; m. Kathleen B. White 1938; no c.; ed. Univs. of Saskatchewan, Chicago and Oxford; mem. Dept. of Classics, Univ. of Sask. 1936–64, Prof. and Head 1946–64, Vice-Pres. (Academic) 1961–64; Pres. and Vice-Chancellor, Univ. of Windsor 1964–78, Prof. of Classical Studies 1970–78, Hon. Prof. 1978–; Hon. Fellow, Exeter Coll., Oxford 1983; numerous other professional appointments and mem. numerous dels. to int. confs.; 12 hon. degrees. *Publications:* The Humanities in an Age of Science 1961, The Humanities in Modern Education 1965; about 100 articles dealing especially with the ancient classics, the history of ideas, univ. educ. and int. educ. *Leisure interests:* travel, reading. *Address:* The Leddy Library, University of Windsor, Windsor, Ont., N9B 3P4 (Office); Apt. 1210, 1333 Ouellette Avenue, Windsor, Ont., N8X 4V4, Canada (Home). *Telephone:* (519) 253-4232 (Office); (519) 258-3589 (Home).

LEDERBERG, Joshua, PH.D.; American geneticist; b. 23 May 1925, Montclair, N.J.; s. of Zwi H. and Esther Goldenbaum Lederberg; m. Marguerite Stein Kirsch 1968; one s. one d.; ed. Columbia and Yale Univs.; Research Asst. in Zoology Columbia Univ. 1945–46; Research Fellow Yale Univ. 1946–47; Prof. of Genetics Univ. of Wis. 1947–59, Chair. Dept. of Medical Genetics 1957–59; Prof. of Genetics, Biology and Computer Science and Chair. Dept. of Genetics Stanford Univ. School of Medicine 1959–78;

Pres. Rockefeller Univ., New York City 1978–; Visiting Prof. of Bacteriology Univ. of Calif. at Berkeley 1950; Fulbright Visiting Prof. of Bacteriology Univ. of Melbourne 1957; Trustee and mem. numerous bds. and cttees.; mem. Bd. of Dirs. Inst. for Scientific Information, Phila., Procter & Gamble, Cincinnati, Ohio; scientific consultant and adviser to several cos.; mem. N.A.S.; Hon. life mem. New York Acad. of Sciences; Hon. mem. A.O.A.; Foreign mem. Royal Soc., London; Hon. Fellow New York Acad. of Medicine; Fellow A.A.A.S., American Philosophical Soc., American Acad. of Arts and Sciences; Hon. Sc.D. (Yale) 1960, (Wis., Columbia) 1967, (Yeshiva) 1970, (Mt. Sinai) 1979, (Rutgers) 1981, (New York) 1984; Hon. M.D. (Turin) 1969, (Tufts) 1985; Hon. Litt.D. (Jewish Theological Seminary) 1979; Hon. LL.D. (Pa.) 1979; Nobel Prize in Medicine (for studies on org. of the genetic material in bacteria) (with Beadle and Tatum) 1958. *Publications:* numerous papers and articles in various scientific and lay publications. *Address:* Rockefeller University, 1230 York Avenue, New York, N.Y. 10021, U.S.A. *Telephone:* (212) 570-8080.

LEDERMAN, Leon M., B.S., A.M., PH.D.; American professor of physics; b. 15 July 1922, New York, N.Y.; s. of Morris Lederman and Minna Rosenberg; m. Florence Gordon 1945; one s. two d.; ed. City Coll. of New York and Columbia Univ., New York; Prof. of Physics, Columbia Univ. 1958–, Eugene Higgins Prof. of Physics 1973–; Dir. Nevis Lab., Irvington, N.Y. 1960–67, 1968–; Dir. Fermi Nat. Accelerator Lab., Batavia, Ill. 1979–; Guest Scientist Brookhaven Nat. Labs. 1955–; J. S. Guggenheim Fellow 1958, Nat. Science Foundation Sr. Postdoctoral Fellow 1967, Sr. Scientific Visitor CERN 1971; Ed. Comments on Nuclear and Particle Physics 1967–72; mem. N.A.S., Fellow, American Physical Soc., American Asscn. of Arts and Science; Nat. Medal of Science 1965, other medals. *Publications:* About 100 articles in physics journals on general problems in elementary particle physics, including Observation of Parity Violations in Meson Decay and Observation of Two Neutrinos. *Address:* Department of Physics, Columbia University, 538 West 120th Street, New York, N.Y. 10027; and Nevis Laboratory, Irvington, N.Y.; 34 Overlook Road, Dobbs Ferry, N.Y. 10522, U.S.A. *Telephone:* 212-280-3366 (Columbia Univ.); and 914-591-8100 (Nevis Laboratory).

LEDESMA BARTRET, Fernando; Spanish politician; b. 1939, Toledo; m.; four c.; ed. Salamanca Univ.; mem. Justicia Democrática; worked in legal practice of Prof. Ruiz-Giménez 1964–65; counsel for the prosecution 1965–72; worked in Offices of the Public Prosecutor, Madrid and Barcelona; Prof. of Political Law, Pedralbes Univ., Barcelona; began judicial career, specializing in admin. suits 1972, worked in Territorial High Courts, Palma de Mallorca, Valladolid and Madrid, then Nat. High Court 1979; fmr. Head of Studies and Prof. of Political Law, Univ. of Palma de Mallorca; Asst. Prof. of Admin. Law, Valladolid; Tutor of Political Law, Universidad Nacional de Educación a Distancia; elected mem. of Consejo Gen. del Poder Judicial (CGPJ—Judicial Gen. Council) by Congress of Deputies; contributed to El País and Diario 16; mem. Editorial Bd. La Actualidad Jurídica and Poder Judicial (organ of CGPJ); Minister of Justice 1982–88. *Address:* c/o Ministerio de Justicia, San Bernardo 45–47, Madrid, Spain.

LEDGER, Philip Stevens, C.B.E., M.A., MUS.B., LL.D., F.R.C.M., F.R.C.O.; British musician; b. 12 Dec. 1937, Bexhill-on-Sea, Sussex; s. of late Walter Stephen and of Winifred Kathleen Ledger (née Stevens); m. Mary Erryl Wells 1963; one s. one d.; ed. Bexhill Grammar School, King's Coll., Cambridge; Master of the Music, Chelmsford Cathedral 1962–65; Dir. of Music, Univ. of East Anglia 1965–73, Dean of School of Fine Arts and Music 1968–71; an Artistic Dir. Aldeburgh Festival of Music and Arts 1968–; Conductor, Cambridge Univ. Musical Soc. 1973–82; Dir. of Music and Organist, King's Coll., Cambridge 1974–82; Prin. Royal Scottish Acad. of Music and Drama 1982–; John Stewart of Rannoch Scholar in Sacred Music; Silver Medal of Worshipful Company of Musicians, Hon. Fellow Royal Acad. of Music. *Publications:* (ed.) Anthems for Choirs 2 and 3 1973, Oxford Book of English Madrigals 1978, editions of Byrd, Handel and Purcell and carol arrangements. *Leisure interests:* swimming, theatre, membership of Sette of Odd Volumes. *Address:* The Royal Scottish Academy of Music and Drama, 100 Renfrew Street, Glasgow, G2 3DB, Scotland. *Telephone:* 041-332-4101.

LEDIG-ROWOHLT, Heinrich Maria; German publisher; b. 12 March 1908, Leipzig; s. of Ernst Rowohlt and Maria Ledig; m. Jane Scatcherd 1961; two d.; ed. Höhere Schule, Leipzig; bookselling and publishing apprenticeship Berlin 1925–28, Cologne 1929–30, London 1930–31; with Rowohlt Verlag 1930–; reopened publishing house under licence from U.S. Mil. Govt. 1945; Publr. youth magazine Pinguin 1946; Ed.-in-Chief and Publr. magazine Story 1946; Rowohlts Rotations Romane (rororo) 1950; shareholder Rowohlt Verlag 1945–, majority shareholder 1960–; Dir. Rowohlt Taschenbuch Verlag until 1970, Rowohlt Verlag until 1982; Chair. Rowohlt Verlag and Rowohlt Taschenbuch Verlag; Hon. D.Hum.Litt. (Washington Univ.); Grosses Verdienstkreuz des Verdienstordens 1974, Ehrenkreuz für Wissenschaft und Kunst (Austria) 1979, Commdr., Ordre des Arts et des Lettres 1984. *Publications:* Thomas Wolfe in Berlin; translations into German of works by Roald Dahl, John Updike, James Thurber, Harold Pinter. *Address:* Hamburger Strasse 17, D-2075, Reinbek 72721, Federal Republic of Germany.

LEDOUX, Paul Joseph, D. ÉS SC.; Belgian astrophysicist; b. 8 Aug. 1914, Forrières; s. of Justin and Ida Ledoux; m. Aline Michaux 1939 (deceased

1977); one d.; ed. Athénée Royal, Marche-en-Famenne, Univ. de Liège, Inst. for Theoretical Astrophysics, Oslo and Yerkes Observatory, Univ. of Chicago; served with Belgian Forces in U.K. and R.A.F. Meteorological Service 1941–46; Adviser, Service Météorologique, Régie des Voies Aériennes; mem. teaching staff, Univ. of Liège 1950–, Prof. 1959–; Visiting Prof., Univ. of Calif. (Berkeley) 1963, Monash Univ. 1967, Sussex Univ. 1969, Univ. of Colo. 1970; Sr. Foreign Scientist Fellow, Nat. Science Foundation, Univ. of Washington 1972; Chair. Observatory Programme Cttee., European Southern Observatory 1972–74, mem. Council ESO 1975–81, Pres. 1981–84; mem. Acad. Royale de Belgique, Acad. Européenne des Sciences, des Lettres et des Arts 1980; Assoc. Royal Astronomical Soc. 1974; Fellow, A.A.A.S. 1980–; Foreign Assoc. Acad. des Sciences, Paris 1984; Dr. h.c. (Brussels) 1970, (Leuven) 1985; Prix décennal du gouvernement Belge 1968, Prix Francqui 1964, Eddington Medal, Royal Astronomical Soc., U.K. 1972, J. Jansen Medal, Acad. des Sciences, Paris 1976. *Publications:* various articles in astrophysical journals on the problems of stellar structure, stellar stability and variable stars. *Leisure interests:* gardening, country walks. *Address:* Institut d'Astrophysique, avenue de Cointe 5, 4200 Ougrée (Office); rue de la Faille 55, 4000 Liège, Belgium (Home). *Telephone:* 041-52-99-80 (Office); 041-52-12-45.

LEDOUX, Pierre, D. EN D., H.E.C.; French banker; b. 30 Sept. 1914, Bordeaux; s. of René Ledoux and Jeanne Dupuy; m. Renée Boissin 1949; ed. Lycée de Bordeaux and Faculté de Droit, Paris; on special assignment with Financial Comm. in the Far East 1945; Financial Attaché, China 1946; Financial Attaché, French Embassy, Washington, D.C. 1947–48; Office of Prime Minister on special assignment concerning EEC 1949–50; Gen. Sec. and Man. Banque Nationale pour le Commerce et l'Industrie (BNCI) 1950–56, Pres. BNCI (Afrique) 1957–72, Pres. BNCI 1963–66; Pres. Banque Nationale de Paris 1966–71, Chair. 1971–79, Hon. Chair. 1979–; Chair. Banque Nationale de Paris Intercontinental 1972–79, Vice-Chair. 1979; mem. Comm. on Privatisation 1986–; Vice-Chair. Cie. Arabe et Int. d'Investissement, Banque Marocaine pour le Commerce et l'Industrie, Dir. Nord-Est, Banque Nationale de Paris PLC, French American Banking Corpn. Croix de guerre 1939–45, Commdr. Légion d'honneur. *Address:* Banque Nationale de Paris, 16 boulevard des Italiens, 75450 Paris Cedex 09 (Office); 8 avenue Pierre-ler-de-Serbie, 75116 Paris, France (Home). *Telephone:* 4244-45-46 (Office); 4720-85-72 (Home).

LEDUC, François Jacques; French diplomatist; b. 10 Nov. 1912, Paris; m. France Renaudin 1937; four s. three d.; ed. Lycée Louis-le-Grand, Univ. de Paris, and King's Coll., Cambridge; Econ. Section, Ministry of Foreign Affairs 1945–47; Resident, Tunis 1947–50; Ministry of Nat. Defence 1951–54; Mayor of Servon 1953–71, 1977–83; Minister-Counsellor, Bonn 1955–57, 1958–60, Brussels 1957–58; Dir. Admin. and Consular Affairs, Ministry of Foreign Affairs 1960–65; Chair. Compagnie européenne de radiodiffusion et de télévision (CERT) 1963–65; Amb. to Canada 1965–68, to Austria 1968–73; mem. of Board, Télédiffusion de France 1974–78, Institut National de l'Audiovisuel 1974–76, Soc. Monégasque d'Etudes et Radiocommunications (SOMERA) 1975–78, Agence France-Presse 1975; Maître de Confs. Univ. of Paris XIII Sciences économiques 1977; Prof. European Business School 1980; Commdr. Légion d'honneur, Medal of Freedom. *Publications:* L'Asile territorial (Annuaire Français de droit international XXIII 1977). *Address:* 4 rue Oudinot, 75007 Paris; and 77170 Servon, France. *Telephone:* 4273-36-51 (Paris).

LEDWIDGE, Sir William Bernard John, K.C.M.G., M.A.; British diplomatist and author; b. 9 Nov. 1915, London; s. of late Charles and of Eileen (née O'Sullivan) Ledwidge; m. 1st Anne Kingsley 1948 (divorced 1970); m. 2nd Flora Groult 1970; one s. one d.; ed. Cardinal Vaughan School, King's Coll., Cambridge and Princeton Univs.; Commonwealth Fund Fellow, Princeton 1937–39; Mil. Service 1941–45; Prin., India and Burma Office 1946–48, First Sec. Foreign Office 1948–49, Counsellor 1961–65; British Consul, St. Louis, U.S.A. 1949–52; First Sec. British Embassy, Afghanistan 1952–56; Political Adviser British Mil. Gov., Berlin 1956–61; Minister, British Embassy, Paris 1965–69; Amb. to Finland 1969–72 to Israel 1972–75; Chair. U.K. Cttee. for UNICEF 1976–; mem. Police Complaints Bd. 1977–82; Vice-Chair. U.K. Asscn. for Int. Year of Child 1979. *Publications:* Frontiers (novel) 1979, Nouvelles de la Famille (short stories) 1980, De Gaulle (biog.) 1982, De Gaulle et les Américains (history) 1984, Sappho (biography) 1987. *Leisure interests:* talking, drinking. *Address:* 19 Queen's Gate Terrace, London, S.W.7, England; 54 rue de Bourgogne, 75007 Paris, France. *Telephone:* 01-584 4132 (London); 4705-8026 (Paris).

LEE, Christopher Frank Carandini; British actor, author and director; b. 27 May 1922, London; s. of late Lieut.-Col. Geoffrey Trollope Lee and of Estelle Marie Carandini; m. Birgit Kroenke 1961; one d.; ed. Summer Fields Preparatory School, Wellington Coll.; served R.A.F. 1941–46; mentioned in despatches 1944; film industry 1947–; appeared in over 160 motion pictures; Officier, Ordre des Arts et des Lettres 1973; Officer St. John of Jerusalem 1986. *Publications:* Christopher Lee's Treasury of Terror, Christopher Lee's Archives of Evil 1975, 1976, Christopher Lee's The Great Villains 1977, Tall, Dark and Gruesome (autobiog.) 1977. *Films include:* Moulin Rouge 1953, The Curse of Frankenstein 1956, Tale of Two Cities 1957, Dracula 1958, The Hound of the Baskervilles 1959, The Mummy 1959, Rasputin the Mad Monk 1965, The Wicker Man 1973, The Three Musketeers 1973, The Private Life of Sherlock Holmes 1973, The Four Musketeers 1975, The Man With the Golden Gun 1975, To the Devil a

LEE INTERNATIONAL WHO'S WHO LEE

Daughter 1976, Airport 77 1977, Return from Witch Mountain, 1977, How the West Was Won 1977, Caravans 1977, The Silent Flute 1977, The Passage 1978, 1941 1978, Bear Island 1978, The Serial 1979, The Salamander 1980, An Eye for an Eye, Goliath Awaits, Charles and Diana, The Last Unicorn, The Far Pavilions, The House of the Long Shadows, The Return of Captain Invincible, The Howling Z, Behind the Mask, Roadstrip, Shaka Zulu, Mio my Mio, The Girl, Un Métier du Seigneur, Casanova, The Disputation (TV), Murder Story, Round The World in 80 Days (TV), For Better, For Worse, Return of the Musketeers. *Leisure interests:* music, travel, golf. *Address:* c/o James Sharkey and Associates Ltd., 13 Golden Square, London, W1R 3AG, England.

LEE, Edward Graham, Q.C., LL.M.; Canadian lawyer and diplomatist; b. 21 Nov. 1931, Vancouver, B.C.; s. of William C. Lee and Dorothy F. Graham; m. Beverly J. Saul 1955; three d.; ed. Univ. of British Columbia and Harvard Univ.; joined Canadian Dept. of External Affairs 1956; Second Sec. Djakarta 1959–61; Counsellor, London 1965–69; Dir. of Personnel, Dept. of External Affairs 1969–72, Legal Adviser 1973–75; Amb. to Israel 1975–79, to S. Africa 1982–86; Asst. Under-Sec. for U.S.A. Affairs 1979–82; Legal Adviser and Asst. Deputy Minister for Legal, Consular and Immigration, Dept. of External Affairs 1986–. *Publications:* numerous articles in Canadian legal journals. *Leisure interests:* skiing, swimming, reading. *Address:* Department of External Affairs, L.B. Pearson Building, 125 Sussex Drive, Ottawa, Ont., Canada.

LEE, Sir Henry Desmond Pritchard, Kt., M.A.; British university lecturer and schoolmaster; b. 30 Aug. 1908, Nottingham; s. of Canon H. B. Lee; m. Elizabeth Crookenden 1935; one s. two d.; ed. Arden House, Repton School, Cambridge Univ.; Tutor, Corpus Christi Coll., Cambridge Univ. 1935–48; Lecturer, Faculty of Classics 1937–48; Fellow, Corpus Christi Coll. 1933, Life Fellow 1948–68, 1978–; Regional Commrs. Office (Civil Defence) 1940–44; mem. Council of Senate, Cambridge Univ. 1944–48; Headmaster, Clifton Coll. 1948–54, Winchester Coll. 1954–68; Chair. Headmasters' Conf. 1959–60, 1967; Research Fellow, Wolfson Coll., Cambridge 1968–73, Hon. Fellow 1974; Pres. Hughes Hall, Cambridge 1974–78, Hon. Fellow 1978; Hon. D.Litt. (Nottingham). *Publications:* Zeno of Elea (text and trans.) 1935, Aristotle's Meteorologica (trans.) 1952, Plato's Republic (trans.) 1955, Plato's Timæus and Critias (trans.) 1971, Entry and Performance at Oxford and Cambridge 1966–71 1972, Wittgenstein: Lectures 1930–32 (ed.) 1980. *Leisure interests:* carpentry, reading. *Address:* 8 Barton Close, Cambridge, CB3 9LQ, England.

LEE, Gen. Honkon; Korean army officer and diplomatist; b. 11 Dec. 1920, Kongjoo, Choong Chung Nam-Do, Korea; s. of Kidong Lee and Jinsil Ahn; m. Kwiran Lee 1946; two s. four d.; ed. Japanese Imperial Mil. Acad., Japanese Field Artillery School and U.S. Infantry School; Supt. Korean Mil. Acad. 1946–48; Mil. Attaché, Washington 1949; Commdg. Gen., Eighth Repub. of Korea Army Div. 1949–50; Third Army Corps 1950–51, First Army Corps 1952–54; UN Command Del. to Korean Armistice 1951–52; Chair. Jt. Chiefs of Staff 1954–56, Chief of Staff 1956–58; Nat. Pres. Korean Veterans Asscn. 1958–61; Amb. to Philippines 1961–62, to U.K. 1962–67 (also to Scandinavian countries, Iceland, Malta and African countries concurrently); Amb. at large 1967–69; Chair. President's Advisory Comm. on Govt. Admin. 1969; Chair. Korea Anti-Communist League 1976–; Chair. Korea-British Soc. 1978–; decorations from Republic of Korea, U.S.A., France, U.K., Greece and Vatican. *Publications:* Nation's Destination 1950, Free Opinion (monthly publ.) 1976–. *Leisure interests:* horse riding, reading, music appreciation. *Address:* 51 Daeshin-Dong, Sudaemoon-Ku, Seoul, Republic of Korea. *Telephone:* 33-5233.

LEE, James E.; American oil executive, b. 13 Dec. 1921, Kiln, Mississippi; m. Kathleen Ruth Edwards 1943; two s. two d.; ed. Polytechnic Inst.; Gulf Oil Corpn. 1942–, served in various engineering and supervisory posts 1942–56; Project Adviser to Filoil Refinery Corpn., Manila 1959; Area Rep. Manila, Exec. Vice-Pres., Gen. Man. Orient Gulf Oil Co. 1962; Vice-Pres. of Refining, Pacific Gulf Oil Ltd., Japan 1963; Area Rep. and Co-ordinator for Far East 1964; Man. Dir. Kuwait, Kuwait Oil Co. 1966; Pres. Gulf Oil Co. (Eastern Hemisphere) 1969; Exec. Vice-Pres. Gulf Oil Corpn. 1972–73, Pres., Dir. 1973–81, Chair. and C.E.O. Dec. 1981–; Vice-Chair. Chevron Corpn. 1985–87; Trustee Carnegie-Mellon Univ. 1973 (Life Trustee 1979), Shady Side Acad. 1974; mem. Bd. American Petroleum Inst., Western Pennsylvania Hospital, La. Tech. Eng. Foundation 1973, Pittsburgh Theological Seminary 1976, Pittsburgh Nat. Bank 1978, Joy Manufacturing Co. 1979; mem. Council on Foreign Affairs Inc. 1979; Hon. D.S. (Louisiana Tech. Univ.) 1975; Gov's. Outstanding Mississippian Award 1973.

LEE, James Matthew, P.C., M.L.A.; Canadian politician; b. 26 March 1937, Charlottetown, P.E.I.; s. of James Matthew and Catherine (Blanchard) Lee; m. Patricia Laurie 1960; one s. two d.; ed. Queen's Square School, Charlottetown, St. Dunstan's Univ., Charlottetown; trained as architectural draughtsman; f. own real estate and devt. co. 1970; mem. Legis. Ass., for 5th Queen's 1975–; Minister of Social Services and Minister of Tourism, Parks and Conservation 1979–80, Minister of Health and Social Services and Minister responsible for Hospital and Health Services Comms. and the P.E.I. Addiction Services 1980–81, Premier and Pres. of Exec. Council of P.E.I. Nov. 1981; Progressive Conservative. *Leisure interest:* community activities. *Address:* P.O. Box 2000, Charlottetown, Prince Edward Island, C1A 7N8 (Office); 41 Centennial Drive, Sherwood, Prince Edward Island, Canada (Home).

LEE, Laurie, M.B.E., F.R.S.L.; British author and poet; b. 26 June 1914, Stroud, Gloucestershire; m. Catherine Francesca Polge 1950; one d.; ed. Slad Village School, and Stroud Central School; Script-writer with Crown Film Unit 1940–43; editor, Ministry of Information 1944–46; film-making in India 1946–47; caption-writer-in-chief, Festival of Britain 1950–51; travelling and writing 1951–; Atlantic Award 1947, William Foyle Poetry Prize 1956, W. H. Smith and Son Award (Cider with Rosie) 1960. *Publications:* The Sun My Monument (poems) 1944, The Bloom of Candles (poems) 1947, The Voyage of Magellan (radio play) 1948, A Rose for Winter (travel) 1955, My Many-Coated Man (poems) 1955, Cider with Rosie (autobiog.) 1959, The Firstborn (essay) 1964, As I Walked out one Midsummer Morning (autobiography) 1969, I Can't Stay Long (prose collection) 1975, Selected Poems 1983, Two Women 1983. *Leisure interests:* music, country pleasures. *Address:* 9/40 Elm Park Gardens, London, S.W.10, England. *Telephone:* 01-352 2197.

LEE, Yuan Tseh, PH.D.; American (b. Chinese) professor of chemistry; b. 29 Nov. 1936, Hsinchu, Taiwan; s. of Tse Fan Lee and Pei Tsai; m. Bernice W. Lee 1963; two s. one d.; ed. Nat. Taiwan Univ., Nat. Tsinghua Univ., Taiwan and Univ. of Calif., Berkeley; Asst. Prof. James Franck Inst. and Dept. of Chemistry, Univ. of Chicago 1968–71, Assoc. Prof. 1971–72, Prof. of Chem. 1973–74; Prof. of Chem. Univ. of Calif., Berkeley 1974–; Sloan Fellow 1969; Guggenheim Fellow 1976; Miller Professorship 1981; mem. American Acad. of Arts and Sciences; shared Nobel Prize for Chemistry 1986; E. O. Lawrence Award (U.S. Dept. of Environment), 1981, and many other awards and prizes. *Publications:* articles in professional journals. *Address:* Department of Chemistry, University of California (Berkeley), Calif. 94720, U.S.A. *Telephone:* 415-486-6154.

LEE HSIEN LOONG; Singapore politician; b. 1953; s. of Lee Kuan Yew (q.v.) and Kwa Geok Choo; m. 1st (deceased 1982), one s. one d.; m. 2nd Ho Ching 1985; one s.; ed. Nanyang Girls High School, Catholic High School, Nat. Jr. Coll., Cambridge, Harvard Univ.; nat. service 1971; Sr. Army course at Fort Leavenworth, U.S.A.; Asst. Chief of Gen. Staff (Operations) 1981–82, Chief of Staff (Gen. Staff) Singapore army 1982–84; resgnd. as Brig.-Gen. Aug. 1984; Political Sec. to Minister of Defence; M.P. for Teck Ghee Dec. 1984–; Minister of State for Defence and for Trade and Industry 1985–86, for Trade and Industry 1986–; Second Asst. Sec.-Gen. People's Action Party 1989–. *Leisure interests:* swimming, reading, jogging, computers. *Address:* Ministry of Trade and Industry, Treasury Building, Republic of Singapore. *Telephone:* 2259911.

LEE HUAN, M.A.; Chinese politician; b. 8 Feb. 1917, Hankow City; m.; two s. two d.; ed. Nat. Chengchi Univ. and Columbia Univ.; Dir. Shenyang Daily News 1946–48; Chief Sec., Deputy Dir.-Gen. and Dir.-Gen. China Youth Corps 1952–77; Prof. Nat. Chengchi Univ. 1962–79; Chair. Comm. for Youth Assistance and Guidance, Exec. Yuan 1967–72; Exec. Officer, Alumni Assscn. of Nat. Chengchi Univ. 1977–80; Pres. Nat. Sun Yat-sen Univ. 1979–84; Minister of Educ. 1984–87; Sec.-Gen. Cen. Cttee. Kuo-Min-Ta-Hui 1987–; Hon. Ph.D. (Tan Kok) 1978; Hon. LL.D. (Sun Kyun Kwan) 1981. *Address:* 23 Lane 4, Suwei Road, Taipei 100, Taiwan. *Telephone:* 3513111.

LEE KIM SAI, Dato'; Malaysian politician; b. 1 March 1937, Selangor; m.; fmr. teacher; mem. State Ass. for Rawang, Selangor 1974–82; M.P. for Ulu Selangor 1982–; Deputy Minister, Prime Minister's Dept. 1983; Minister of Labour 1986–; Sec.-Gen. Malaysian Chinese Asscn. (MCA) 1985–. *Address:* Ministry of Labour, Block B, Jalan Satu, Pusat Bandar Damansara, 50530 Kuala Lumpur, Malaysia.

LEE KUAN YEW, M.A.; Singapore politician and barrister; b. 16 Sept. 1923, Singapore; s. of Lee Chin Koon and Chua Jim Neo; m. Kwa Geok Choo 1950; two s. one d.; ed. Raffles Coll., Singapore, Fitzwilliam Coll., Cambridge; called to Bar, Middle Temple, London 1950, Hon. Bencher 1969; Advocate and Solicitor, Singapore 1951; one of founders of People's Action Party 1954, Sec.-Gen. 1954–; mem. Legis. Assembly 1955–; first Prime Minister Repub. of Singapore 1959, re-elected 1963, 1968, 1972, 1976, 1980, 1984; mem. Singapore Internal Security Council 1959–; M.P. Fed. Parl. of Malaysia 1963–65; Chair. Singapore Investment Corpn. 1981–; Fellow, Inst. of Politics, Harvard Univ. 1968; Hoyt Fellow, Berkeley Coll., Yale Univ. 1970; Hon. Fellow, Fitzwilliam Coll., Cambridge 1969, Royal Australasian Coll. of Surgeons 1973, R.A.C.P. 1974; Hon. LL.D. (Royal Univ. of Cambodia) 1965, (Hong Kong) 1970, (Liverpool) 1971, (Sheffield) 1971; Hon. C.H. 1970; Hon. G.C.M.G. 1972; Bintang Republik Indonesia Adi Pradana 1973, Order of Sikatuna (Philippines) 1974, Most Hon. Order of Crown of Johore (First Class), 1984, Hon. Freeman, City of London 1982, numerous other awards. *Leisure interests:* jogging, swimming. *Address:* Prime Minister's Office, Istana Annexe, Singapore 0923, Republic of Singapore. *Telephone:* 7375133.

LEE SAN CHOON; Malaysian politician; b. 1935, Pahang; M.P. 1959–83; Parl. Sec. 1963; Minister of Tech., Research and Co-ordination of New Villages 1973–75, of Labour and Manpower 1975–78, of Works and Public Utilities 1978–80, of Transport 1980–83; Pres. Malaysian Chinese Asscn. (MCA) 1974–83. *Address:* c/o Malaysian Chinese Association, P.O. Box 626, 67 Jalan Ampang, Kuala Lumpur, Malaysia.

LEE TA-HAI, B.SC.; Chinese politician and business executive; b. 10 Feb. 1919, Haicheng County, Liaoning; m.; two s.; ed. Nat. Southwest Associated Univ.; Eng. Kansu Oil Mining Admin., Nat. Resources Comm. 1942–46; Eng. Kaohsiung Refinery, Chinese Petroleum Corpn. 1946–55, Chief, Eng. Dept. 1955–61, Chief Eng. 1961–66; Construction Man. Mobil China Co. 1962–63; Project and Construction Man. China Gulf Oil Co. Ltd. 1963–65; Deputy Gen. Man. Kaohsiung Refinery 1966–72, Gen. Man. 1972–76, Pres. 1976–81; Chair. of Bd. Chinese Petroleum Corpn. 1981–85, China Gulf Oil Co. Ltd. 1980–85; Minister of Econ. Affairs 1985–88; Nat. Policy Adviser to the Pres. 1988–. *Address:* RM. 609, No 53, Jen-Ai Road, Sec. 3, Taipei 10628, Taiwan. *Telephone:* 71111776.

LEE TENG-HUI, PH.D.; Taiwan politician; b. 15 Jan. 1923, Tamsui; m. Tseng Wen-hui; two d.; ed. Kyoto Imperial Univ., Japan Nat. Taiwan Univ., Iowa State Univ. and Cornell Univ.; Instructor Nat. Taiwan Univ. 1948–52, 1953–57, Prof. of Econs. 1958–78; Research Fellow, Taiwan Provincial Co-operative Bank 1955–57; Specialist, Joint Comm. on Rural Reconstruction (JCRR) 1957–61, Sr. Specialist 1961, Head, Rural Economy Div. 1970–72; Consultant to JCRR and Minister without Portfolio 1972–78; Mayor of Taipei 1978–81; Gov. Taiwan Province 1981–84; Vice-Pres. of Repub. of China (Taiwan) 1984–88, Pres. Jan. 1988–. *Leisure interest:* golf. *Address:* Office of the President, Taipei, Taiwan.

LEE TSUNG-DAO, PH.D.; Chinese physicist; b. 25 Nov. 1926, Shanghai; ed. National Chekiang Univ., National Southwest Univ. (China) and Univ. of Chicago; Research Assoc. in Astronomy, Univ. of Chicago 1950; Research Assoc. and lecturer in Physics. Univ of California 1950–51; mem. Inst. for Advanced Study, Princeton, N.J. 1951–53; Asst. Prof. of Physics, Columbia Univ., New York 1953–55, Assoc. Prof. 1955–56, Prof. 1956–60, 1963–; Prof. Princeton Inst. for Advanced Study 1960–63; mem. N.A.S.; shared Nobel Prize for Physics 1957 with Prof. Yang Chen-ning (q.v.) for work on elementary particles; Albert Einstein Award in Science 1957. *Publications:* articles in physical journals. *Address:* Department of Physics, Columbia University, Morningside Heights, New York, N.Y. 10027; 25 Claremont Avenue, New York, N.Y. 10027, U.S.A. (Home).

LEE WON KYUNG; Korean politician; b. 15 Jan. 1922; ed. Tokyo Univ., Japan, Seoul Nat. Univ.; joined foreign service 1957, Chief Protocol Officer and Counsellor, Korean Embassy, Tokyo 1957–60, Vice-Minister of Foreign Affairs 1961–62, Minister of Culture and Information 1974–75, of Sports 1982–83, of Foreign Affairs 1983–86; Pres. Hapdong News Agency 1966–74; Chair. Doosan Industrial Co. 1976, Korean Foreign Service Asscn. 1980–82, Hapdong Inc. 1981; Vice-Chair. Korean Amateur Sports Asscn. 1971–74; mem. Korean Olympic Cttee. 1968–74, Vice-Chair. and Hon. Sec. 1971–74, Standing Adviser 1976–, Hon. Chair. 1978–; Vice-Chair. and Sec.-Gen. Seoul Olympic Organizing Cttee. 1981–88, mem. Exec. Cttee. 1982–88; Amb. to Japan 1988–; mem. Legis. Ass. 1981–. *Address:* Embassy of the Republic of Korea, 1-2-5 Minahi-Azabu, Minato-ku, Tokyo, Japan. *Telephone:* (03)-452-7611.

LEE YOCK SUAN, B.SC.; Singapore politician; b. 1946; m.; one s. one d.; ed. Queenstown Secondary Technical School, Raffles Institution, Imperial Coll., Univ. of London, U.K., Univ. of Singapore; Div. Dir (Projects), Econ. Devt. Bd. 1969–80; elected M.P. for Cheng San 1980; Deputy Man. Dir. Petrochemical Corpn. of Singapore (Pte.) Ltd. Jan.–Sept. 1981; Minister of State (Nat. Devt.) 1981–83, (Finance) 1983–84, Sr. Minister of State and Acting Minister for Labour 1985–86, Minister for Labour 1987–; Deputy Chair. People's Asscn. 1984–. *Leisure interest:* badminton. *Address:* Ministry of Labour, Havelock Road, Singapore 0105. *Telephone:* 5336141.

LEE YONG LENG, M.A., PH.D.; Singapore diplomatist; b. 26 March 1930, Singapore; s. of Lee Choon Eng and Lim Swee Joo; m. Wong Loon Meng 1957; one d.; ed. Univ. of Singapore and St. Antony's Coll., Oxford; Lecturer and Prof. Univ. of Singapore 1956–70, Prof. of Geography 1976–; High Commr. to U.K. 1971–75; Amb. to Denmark and Ireland 1974–75; Chair. Singapore Nat. Library Bd. 1977–81; Dir. Centre for Advanced Studies, Faculty of Arts and Social Sciences, Nat. Univ. of Singapore 1983–85. *Publications:* North Borneo 1965, Population and Settlement in Sarawak 1970, Land Use of Brunei, Sabah and Sarawak 1972, Southeast Asia and the Law of the Sea 1978, 1980, The Razor's Edge: Boundaries and Boundary Disputes in S.E. Asia 1980, Southeast Asia: Essays in Political Geography 1982. *Leisure interests:* reading, travel. *Address:* c/o National University of Singapore, Kent Ridge, Singapore. *Telephone:* Singapore 7756666.

LEE OF ASHERIDGE, Baroness (Life Peeress), cr. 1970, of the City of Westminster; **Jennie Lee,** P.C., M.A., LL.B.; British politician; b. 3 Nov. 1904, Lochgelly, Fife, Scotland; d. of James Lee and Euphemia Grieg; m. The Rt. Hon. Aneurin Bevan 1934 (died 1960); ed. Edinburgh Univ.; M.P. for North Lanark 1929–31, Cannock 1945–70; Parl. Sec. Ministry of Public Building and Works 1964–65; Minister for the Arts and Under-Sec. of State, Dept. of Educ. and Science 1965–67, Minister for the Arts and Minister of State, Dept. of Educ. and Science 1967–70; Dir. Tribune; mem. Cen. Advisory Cttee. on Housing; mem. Nat. Exec. Cttee., Labour Party 1958–70, Chair. 1967–68; Hon. Fellow Royal Acad. 1981; Hon. LL.D. (Cambridge) 1974; Hon. Dr. (Edinburgh) 1982. *Publications:* Tomorrow is a New Day 1939, Our Ally, Russia 1941, This Great Journey 1963, My

Life with Nye 1980. *Leisure interests:* reading, theatre, gardening. *Address:* 67 Chester Row, London, S.W.1, England.

LEES, Anthony David, PH.D., SC.D., F.R.S.; British entomologist; b. 27 Feb. 1917; s. of Alan H. Lees and Mary H. Bomford; m. Annzella P. Wilson 1943; one d.; ed. Clifton Coll. Bristol and Trinity Hall, Cambridge; mem. ARC Unit of Insect Physiology, Zoology Dept., Univ. of Cambridge 1945–67; Deputy Chief Scientific Officer and Prof. of Insect Physiology, ARC at Imperial Coll. Field Station, Ascot 1969–82, Prof. Emer. 1982–; Sr. Research Fellow, Imperial Coll. at Silwood Park 1982–; Pres. Royal Entomological Soc. 1973–75, Hon. Fellow 1984; Lalor Fellow 1956; Visiting Prof. Univ. of Adelaide 1966. *Publications:* scientific papers. *Leisure interests:* gardening, fossicking. *Address:* Wells Lane Corner, Sunninghill, Ascot, Berks., SL5 7DY, England.

LEES, David Bryan, F.C.A., F.R.S.A.; British business executive; b. 23 Nov. 1936, Aberdeen; s. of late Rear-Admiral D. M. Lees, C.B., D.S.O., and of C. D. M. Lees; m. Edith M. Bernard 1961; two s. one d.; ed. Charterhouse; articled clerk, Binder Hamlyn & Co. (Chartered Accountants) 1957–62, Sr. Audit Clerk 1962–63; Chief Accountant, Handley Page Ltd. 1964–68; Financial Dir. Handley Page Aircraft Ltd. 1969; Chief Accountant, GKN Sankey Ltd. 1970–72, Deputy Controller 1972–73, Dir., Sec., Controller 1973–76; Group Finance Exec. GKN Ltd. 1976–77, Gen. Man. Finance 1977–82; Finance Dir. GKN PLC 1982–87, Group Man. Dir. 1987–88, Chair. May 1988–; Pres. GKN North American Inc.; United Engineering Steels Ltd., GKN (U.K.) PLC. *Leisure interests:* walking, golf, opera, music. *Address:* GKN PLC, P.O. Box 55, Redditch, Worcs., B98 0TL, England. *Telephone:* 0527 517715 (Office).

LEES-MILNE, James, F.R.S.L., F.S.A.; British author; b. 6 Aug. 1908; s. of George Crompton Lees-Milne; m. Alvilde Bridges 1951; no c.; ed. Eton Coll. and Magdalen Coll. Oxford; Pvt. Sec. to 1st Baron Lloyd 1931–35; on staff, Reuters 1935–36; on staff, Nat. Trust 1936–66; Adviser on Historic Bldgs. to Nat. Trust 1951–66. *Publications:* The National Trust (ed.) 1945, The Age of Adam 1947, National Trust Guide: Buildings 1948, Tudor Renaissance 1951, The Age of Inigo Jones 1953, Roman Mornings (Heinemann Award) 1956, Baroque Italy 1959, Baroque in Spain and Portugal 1960, Earls of Creation 1962, Worcestershire: A Shell Guide 1964, St. Peter's 1967, English Country Houses: Baroque 1685–1714 1970, Another Self 1970, Heretics in Love 1973, Ancestral Voices 1975, William Beckford 1976, Prophesying Peace 1977, Round the Clock 1978, Harold Nicolson (Vol. I) 1980, (Vol. II) 1982 (Heinemann Award 1982), Images of Bath (with David Ford) 1982, The Country House (anthology) 1982, Caves of Ice 1983, The Last Stuarts 1983, Midway on the Waves 1985, The Enigmatic Edwardian 1986. *Address:* Essex House, Badminton, Avon, GL9 1DD, England. *Telephone:* (045 421) 288.

LEESE, John Arthur; British journalist; b. 4 Jan. 1930; s. of late Cyril Leese and May Leese; m. Maureen Jarvis 1959; one s. one d.; ed. Bishop Vesey's School, Warwicks.; Ed. Coventry Evening Telegraph 1964–70; Deputy Ed. Evening News 1970–76, Ed. 1980; Ed.-in-Chief and Publr. Soho News, New York 1981–82; Editorial Dir. Harmsworth Publishing 1975–82; Ed. You magazine and Ed.-in-Chief and Man. Dir. Associated Magazines 1983–86; Dir. Mail Newspapers 1983–; Ed. London Standard (now Evening Standard) 1986–. *Address:* The Evening Standard, 121 Fleet Street, London, EC4P 4DD, England. *Telephone:* 01-353 8000.

LEFEBVRE, Mgr. Marcel, S.T.D.; French ecclesiastic; b. 29 Nov. 1905, Tourcoing; s. of the late René Lefebvre and Gabrielle (née Watine); ed. Sacred Heart Coll., Tourcoing, and French Seminary, Rome; ordained R.C. priest 1929; entered Congregation of the Fathers of the Holy Ghost (missionary congregation); sent to Gabon as Missionary 1932; Superior Seminary, Mortain, France 1946; ordained Bishop Sept. 1947; Apostolic Vicar of Dakar, Senegal 1947; Apostolic Del. to French-speaking Africa 1948–59; Archbishop of Dakar 1948–62; mem. Cen. Preparatory Comm. for Second Vatican Council 1960–62; Bishop of Tulle, France 1962, resgnd. 1962; Titular Archbishop of Synnada in Phrygia 1962–83; excommunicated July 1988; Superior-Gen. Congregation of Fathers of the Holy Ghost 1962–68, resgnd.; f. Soc. of Saint Pius X 1969, Superior-Gen. 1970–83; mem. Acad. Berrichone, France; Hon. Ph.D. (Duquesne); Asst. at Pontifical Throne, Commdr. Order of Christ (Portugal), Grand Officier, Légion d'honneur, Officer of Equatorial Star. *Publications:* Un evêque parle (A Bishop Speaks) 1974, J'accuse le concile 1976, Lettre ouverte aux catholiques perplexes 1985, many articles on the current crisis in the Catholic Church. *Address:* Séminaire International Saint Pie X, 1908 Ecône, Valais, Switzerland. *Telephone:* (026) 6 29 27.

LE FLOCH-PRIGENT, Loïk; French business executive; b. 21 Sept. 1943, Brest; s. of Gerard Le Floch and Gabrielle Julienne; m.; one s. one d.; ed. Inst. Nat. Polytechnique, Grenoble and Univ. of Missouri; scientific and tech. research, D.G.R.S.T. 1969–78; Dir. of Cabinet of Industry Minister, Pierre Dreyfuss 1981–82; Dir.-Gen. Rhône-Poulenc 1982; Chair. and C.E.O. Rhône-Poulenc Group 1982–86; Dir. Crédit Nat. 1985–; mem. Admin. Council for public establishment of Grand Louvre 1986–; Chevalier, ordre nat. du Mérite. *Address:* Crédit National, 45 rue Saint-Dominique, 75007 Paris, France.

LEFRANÇOIS, Jacques; Belgian accountant; b. 1 March 1929, Seine Maritime, France; m.; one s. one d.; second accountant 1948–52; Publicity

Agent (Publi-Buro) 1952–68; mem. Congress of European People's (EFB-MFE) 1961–65; confidential employee 1966–78; World Citizen for Peace through Human Rights 1964; mem. Professional Union of Int. School of Detective Experts 1950–75; Pres. Group 'L'Homme Planétaire' 1970–88; mem. Flemish Asscn. of Journalists of Periodical Press 1970–88; Ed. Journal 14 Independant 1964–, Het Watervlietje 1975–88; Pres. Flemish Regions, Parti Progressiste Belge 1985–88; Belgian Ombudsman/Médiateur Belge 1986–88. *Address:* 9 rue Leo Baekelandstr., 2030 Anvers, Belgium.

Le GALLIENNE, Eva; American actress, director and author; b. 11 Jan. 1899, London, England; d. of Richard Le Gallienne and Julie Norregaard; ed. Coll. Sévigné, Paris; début in London in The Laughter of Fools 1915; in New York starred in Liliom 1922, The Swan 1923; f. Civic Repertory Theatre in New York 1926; played and produced there some 40 plays, including Ibsen's Master Builder, Hedda Gabler, John Gabriel Borkman, Chekhov's The Cherry Orchard, The Seagull, Sierra's The Cradle Song, Giraudoux's Siegfried, Dumas' Camille, Shakespeare's Romeo and Juliet and Twelfth Night, Barrie's Peter Pan, Molière's Would-be Gentleman, Carroll's Alice in Wonderland, etc.; subsequently appeared on Broadway in Rostand's L'Aiglon, Job's Uncle Harry, Shakespeare's Henry VIII, Ibsen's Rosmersholm and Ghosts, Williams' The Corn is Green; Elizabeth I in Schiller's Mary Stuart in New York and on tour 1958–60 and in Maxwell Anderson's Elizabeth The Queen on tour 1961–62; on tour in Chekhov's The Seagull and Anouilh's Ring Round the Moon 1962–63 and in The Trojan Women and The Mad Woman of Chaillot 1965–66; with A.P.A. Repertory Co., New York, in Ionesco's Exit the King, directed Chekhov's The Cherry Orchard 1967–68, Ibsen's A Doll's House, Seattle Rep. 1975; played in All's Well That Ends Well at the American Shakespeare Festival Theatre, Stratford, Conn. 1970, Mrs. Woodfin in The Dream Watcher at the White Barn Theatre 1975, Fanny Cavendish in The Royal Family at the Helen Hayes Theatre, New York 1976 and on the National Tour 1976–77, To Grandmother's House We Go (Biltmore Theatre, Broadway) 1981; Man. Dir. of American Rep. Theatre 1946–47; Hon. M.A. (Tufts), Hon. Litt.D. (Russell Sage and Mt. Holyoke Colls., Brown Univ.), D.H.L. (Smith Coll., Ohio Wesleyan Univ., Goucher Coll., Univ. of N.C., Bard Coll. and Fairfield Univ.); Gold Medal Soc. of Arts and Sciences, Gold Medal American Acad. of Arts and Letters, Cross of St. Olav (Norway), Handel Medallion 1976, ANTA Award 1977, Nat. Medal of Arts 1986. *Publications:* At 33 (autobiography) 1934, Alice in Wonderland (stage version, French edn.), Flossie and Bossie 1949, With a Quiet Heart 1953, Six Plays by Henrik Ibsen (trans.) 1958, Seven Tales by H. C. Andersen (trans.) 1959, The Wild Duck and other Plays by Ibsen (trans.) 1961, H. C. Andersen's The Nightingale (trans.) 1965, The Mystic in the Theatre: Eleonore Duse 1966, The Spider and Other Stories (Carl Evald) (trans.) 1980. *Address:* Bard College, Weston, Conn. 06883, U.S.A.

LEGATOWICZ, Aleksander, MATH. PHYS. SC.D.; Polish politician; b. 2 March 1923, Warsaw; m.; ed. Wawelberg and Rotwand Eng. School, Warsaw and Warsaw Univ.; worked in Roads and Bridges Construction Bureau, Warsaw, subsequently lecturer, Warsaw Tech. Univ. and Warsaw Univ., then scientific worker, Inst. of Nuclear Research, Świerk nr. Warsaw; now Asst. Prof., Econ. and Social Dept. of Łódź Univ. and Head of Foreign Trade Econs. Research Centre; Deputy to Seym (Parl.), mem. Seym Comms. of Econ., Budget and Finance, of Foreign Econ. Co-operation and of Water Econ.; mem. Council of State 1987–; mem. Consultative Council attached to Chair. of Council of State 1987–; mem. Polish Econ. Soc.; mem. Scientific Council of Polish Cybernetic Soc.; mem. Presidium of Polish Measurements and Automation Cttee., Cttee. of Econs. and Econ. Reform of Polish Fed. of Eng. Asscn.; for many years active mem. Polish Catholic Social Union, fmr. mem. Catholic Intelligentsia Club. *Address:* Kancelaria Rady Państwa, ul. Wiejska 2/4/6, 00-902 Warsaw, Poland.

LEGENDRE, André; French mining engineer; b. 28 Nov. 1918, Melun; s. of Marcel Legendre and Suzanne More; m. Françoise Fournier 1945; three s. three d.; ed. Ecole des Mines de Paris; Mining Eng., Metz 1945–50, Chief Mining Eng., Strasbourg 1951–53; Asst. Dir.-Gen. Marine-Firminy, then Dir. Gen., then Pres. 1954–75; Admin. at Marine-Wendel, and at Allevard Industries 1975–; Pres. Supervisory Council Dilling Iron- and Steelworks Soc.; Deputy Vice-Pres. the Franco-German Soc.; Chevalier, Légion d'honneur. *Address:* 28 Rue Dumont d'Urville, 75116 Paris (Office); 70 boulevard Flandrin, 75116 Paris, France (Home). *Telephone:* 45-00-36-55 (Office); 45 53 06 99 (Home).

LÉGER, H.E. Cardinal Paul Emile, L.TH., J.C.L.; Canadian ecclesiastic; b. 26 April 1904, Valleyfield; s. of Ernest Léger and Alda Beauvais; brother of the late Jules Léger (Gov.-Gen. of Canada 1974–78); ed. Grand Séminaire of Montreal and Paris; ordained at Montreal May 1929; Prof. Issy Séminaire (near Paris) 1931–32; Asst. Master of Novices, Saint-Sulpice, Paris 1932–33; Founder-Superior at Fukuoka Seminary, Japan 1933–39; Prof. Montreal Seminary of Philosophy 1939–40; Vicar-Gen. and Cathedral Pastor Valleyfield 1940–47; Rector of Canadian Coll., Rome 1947–50; elected to Episcopal See 1950 and enthroned as Archbishop of Montreal May 1950, resgnd. as Archbishop of Montreal Nov. 1967 to become missionary in leper colonies, W. Africa; elevated to Cardinal, with title of St. Mary of the Angels 1953; papal legate to closing of the Marian Year at Lourdes 1954, to crowning of statue of St. Joseph at Montreal 1955, to St. Anne de Beaupré Tercentenary P.Q. 1958; Paris priest St. Madeleine Sophie Barat 1974, resgnd.

1975; Co-Pres. Canada Foundation for Refugees 1979–; numerous hon. degrees; Kt. Grand Cross Légion d'honneur, Equestrian Order of Holy Sepulchre (Jerusalem), Sovereign Order of Malta, Order of Canada Medal, Grand Cross of Benemerencia (Portugal), Humanitarian Award of Variety Clubs Int., Pearson Medal for Peace Canada Assoc. UN, commemorative plate for exceptional contribution to human relations, Canadian Council for Christians and Jews, Velan Foundation Award. *Address:* 130 de l'Epée Avenue, Outremont, Que. H2V 3T2, Canada.

LEGO, Paul Edward, M.S.; American business executive; b. 16 May 1930, Sandy Ridge, Pa.; s. of Paul Irwin Lego and Sarah Elizabeth (Montgomery) Lego; m. Ann Sepety 1956; three s. one d.; ed. East Conemaugh High School, Pa., Univ. of Pittsburgh, Pa.; served U.S. Army 1948–52; various eng. and man. positions with Westinghouse Electric Corpn. 1956–77, Vice-Pres. and Gen. Man., Lamp Divs. 1977–80, Exec. Vice-Pres., Electronics and Control 1980–83, Control Equipment 1983–85, Sr. Exec. Vice-Pres., Corp. Resources 1985–88, Pres. and C.O.O. 1988–; Univ. of Pittsburgh Bicentennial Medallion of Distinction 1987. *Leisure interests:* golf, running, bridge, art. *Address:* Westinghouse Electric Corporation, Westinghouse Building, Gateway Center, Pittsburgh, Pa. 15222, U.S.A. *Telephone:* (412) 642-3052.

LE GOFF, Jacques Louis; French professor of history; b. 1 Jan. 1924, Toulon; s. of Jean Le Goff and Germaine Ansaldi; m. Anna Dunin-Wasowicz 1962; one s. one d.; ed. Lycées, Toulon, Marseilles and Louis-le-Grand, Paris, Ecole normale supérieure, Paris; history teacher 1950; Fellow of Lincoln Coll., Oxford 1951–52; mem. Ecole française de Rome 1953–54; Asst. at Univ. of Lille 1954–59; Prof., then Dir. of Studies, 6th Section, Ecole des hautes études (EHE) 1962–, Pres. Ecole des hautes études en sciences sociales (fmr. 6th Section of EHE) 1972–77; mem. Comité nat. de la recherche scientifique 1962–70, Comité des travaux historiques et scientifiques 1974–, Conseil supérieur de la Recherche 1985–87; Co-Dir. reviews Annales-Economies, sociétés, civilisations and Ethnologie Française 1972–; Grand Prix nat. 1987. *Publications:* Les Intellectuels au Moyen Age 1957, Le Moyen Age 1962, La Civilisation de l'occident médiéval 1964, Das Hochmittelalter 1965, Pour un autre Moyen Age 1978 (English trans.), Time, Work and Culture in the Middle Ages 1980, La naissance du purgatoire 1981, L'apogée de la chrétienté 1982, L'imaginaire médiéval 1985, La bourse et la vie 1986. *Leisure interests:* gastronomy and swimming. *Address:* Ecole des hautes études en sciences sociales, 54 blvd. Raspail, 75006 Paris (Office); 11 rue Monticelli, 75014 Paris, France (Home). *Telephone:* 222-79-11 (Office).

LEGORRETA VILCHIS, Ricardo; Mexican architect; b. 7 May 1931, México, D.F.; s. of Luis Legorreta and Guadalupe Vilchis; m. María Luisa Hernández 1956; three s. three d.; ed. Univ. of Mexico; Draughtsman and Chief Designer with José Villagran García 1948–55, Partner 1955–60; Prof. of Design, Univ. of Mexico 1959–62, Head of Experimental Group 1962–64; private practice 1961–63; f. Legorreta Arquitectos (LA) with Carlos Hernández, Ramiro Alatorre and Noe Castro 1963, Dir. 1963–; f. LA Diseños 1977, Pres. 1977–; mem. Int. Cttee., Museum of Modern Art, New York 1970; mem. Bd. of Judges, A.I.A. 1977; Emer. Fellow, Colegio de Arquitectos de México 1978, mem. Bd. of Judges 1980; mem. Pritzker Prize Jury 1984; Hon. mem. North American Inst. of Architects. *Publication:* Los muros de México (with Celanese Mexicana). *Leisure interests:* tennis, cycling, music. *Address:* Palacio de Versalles 285-A, Col. Lomas Reforma, Código Postal 11020, México 10, D.F. (Office); Palacio de Versalles 285-A, Col. Lomas Reforma, Código Postal 11020, México 10, D.F., Mexico (Home). *Telephone:* 596-04-11 (Office); 596-21-88 (Home).

Le GOY, Raymond Edgar Michel, M.A.; British civil servant; b. 1919, London; s. of J. A. S. M. N. Goy and May Callan; m. Silvia Ernestine Burnett 1960; two s.; ed. William Ellis School, London, Gonville and Caius Coll., Cambridge; British Army 1940–46; entered Civil Service 1947, Road Transport and Establishments Divs., Ministry of Transport 1947–48; U.K. Shipping Adviser in Japan, Far East and S.E. Asia 1948–52; various posts in shipping and highway divs., Ministry of Transport and Civil Aviation 1952–57; Dir. Goeland Co. 1953; Asst. Sec. Railways and Inland Waterways Div., Ministry of Transport and Civil Aviation 1958; Asst. Sec. Finance and Supply Ground Services and Aerodrome Management, Ministry of Aviation 1959–61, Dir. of Admin. Navigational Services 1961–62; Asst. Sec. Aviation Overseas Policy, Ministry of Aviation and Bd. of Trade 1962–67; Under-Sec. of Civil Aviation 1968–73; Head Del. to European Civil Aviation Conf.; Dir.-Gen. of Transport Comm. of EEC 1973–81, of EEC Comm. 1981–. *Publication:* The Victorian Burletta 1953. *Leisure interests:* theatre, music, race relations. *Address:* c/o Société Générale de Banque, 10 Rond Point Schumann, Brussels 1040, Belgium.

Le GRANGE, Louis, B.A., LL.B.; South African politician; b. 16 Aug. 1928, Ladybrand; m. Jessie Ortlepp Marais 1952; two s. two d.; joined Civil Service, Department of the Interior 1947, later moving to Dept. of Justice; practised as attorney, Potchefstroom from 1953; M.P. 1966, Deputy Minister of Information and the Interior 1975–78, Interior, Immigration and Public Works Feb. 1978, Minister of Public Works and Tourism 1978–79, of Law and Order 1979–86; Speaker, House of Ass. 1987–; Decoration for Meritorious Service. *Leisure interests:* target rifle shooting, golf. *Address:* Office of the Speaker, P.O. Box 15, Cape Town 8000, South Africa.

LEGRAS, Guy; French European Community official; b. 19 July 1938, Angers; s. of René Legras and Pauline Legras; m. Borka Oreb 1971; one s. one d.; ed. Faculté de Droit, Paris, Inst. d'Etudes Politiques, Paris and Ecole Nat. d'Admin.; joined Ministry of Foreign Affairs 1967; Cabinet of Sec. of State for Foreign Affairs 1968-71; Secr.-Gen. of Interministerial Cttee. (SGCI) for European Affairs (Prime Minister) 1971-74; Cabinet of Sec.-Gen. of OECD 1974-77; Counsellor, Perm. Rep. of France at European Communities, Brussels 1977-80; Asst. Sec.-Gen. SGCI 1980-82; Head, Dept. of Econ. Affairs, Ministry of Foreign Affairs 1982-85; Dir.-Gen. for Agric. Comm. of European Communities, Brussels 1985-; Officier du Mérite. *Address:* 1 avenue d L'Hippodrome, 1050 Brussels, Belgium.

LE GUIN, Ursula Kroeber, M.A.; American writer; b. 1929, Berkeley, Calif.; d. of Alfred L. and Theodora K. Kroeber; m. Charles A. Le Guin 1953; one s. two d.; ed. Radcliffe Coll., Columbia Univ.; taught French, Mercer Univ., Univ. of Ida. 1954-56; teacher, resident writer or visiting lecturer at numerous univs., including Univ. of Washington, Portland State Univ., Pacific Univ., Reading Univ., Univ. of Calif. at San Diego, Indiana Writers' Conf., Kenyon Coll., etc. 1971-; mem. Science Fiction Research Asscn., Authors' League, Writers' Guild W., PEN; Hon. D.Litt (Bucknell Univ., Lawrence Univ.), Hon. D.Hum.Litt. (Lewis and Clark Coll., Occidental Coll.), Distinguished Service Award (Univ. of Oregon). *Publications include: novels:* Rocannon's World 1966, City of Illusions 1966, The Left Hand of Darkness (Nebula Award, Hugo Award) 1969, A Wizard of Earthsea 1968, The Farthest Shore (Nat. Book Award) 1972, The Dispossessed (Hugo Award) 1974, The Word for World is Forest 1976, Malafrena 1979, The Beginning Place 1980, The Eye of the Heron 1983, Always Coming Home (Kafka Award 1986) 1985, Dancing at the Edge of the World 1988; *screenplay:* King Dog 1985; *short stories:* The Wind's Twelve Quarters 1975, Orsinian Tales 1975, The Compass Rose 1982, Buffalo Gals 1987; *poetry:* Wild Angels 1974, Hard Words 1981, In the Red Zone (with H. Pander) 1983, Wild Oats and Fireweed 1987; *for children:* A Visit from Dr. Katz 1988, Catwings 1988; Ed. Nebula Award Stories 1977, Interfaces 1980, Edges 1980. *Address:* c/o Virginia Kidd, Box 278, Milford, Pa. 18337, U.S.A.

LEGWAILA, Legwaila Joseph, M.A.; Botswanese diplomatist; b. 2 Feb. 1937, Mathathane; s. of Madume and Morongwa Legwaila; m. Pholile Matsebula 1975; three d.; ed. Bobonong School, Brussels School, S.A., Serowe Teacher Training Coll., Univ. of Calgary and Univ. of Alberta; Asst. Prin. External Affairs, Govt. of Botswana 1973-74; Sr. Pvt. Sec. to Pres. of Botswana 1974-80; Perm. Rep. to UN 1980-, High Commr. in Guyana 1981-, in Jamaica 1982-, Amb. to Cuba 1983-; *Publication:* Safari to Serowe (co-author) 1970. *Leisure interests:* music, cycling. *Address:* Botswana Mission to the United Nations, 103 East 37th Street, New York, N.Y. 10016, U.S.A. *Telephone:* (212) 889-2272 (Office); (914) 636-4858 (Home).

LEHEL, György; Hungarian conductor; b. 10 Feb. 1926, Budapest; s. of László Lehel and Klára Ladányi; m. Dr. Zsuzsa Markovits 1969; one s.; studied composition with Pál Kadosa and conducting with László Somogyi; Conductor Symphonic Orchestra of Hungarian Radio 1947-62, Chief Conductor and Music Dir. 1962-; propagates contemporary Hungarian music; has conducted in Czechoslovakia, Poland, Switzerland, Austria, U.S.S.R., Italy, Romania, France, Belgium, Norway, Finland, Sweden, German Dem. Repub., Fed. Repub. of Germany, Yugoslavia, Spain, Great Britain, U.S.A., Canada and Japan; Hon. D.Mus. (Chicago Conservatory) 1977; Liszt Prize 1955, 1962, Merited Artist of the Hungarian Repub. 1968, Kossuth Prize 2nd Degree 1973, Eminent Artist 1979; numerous recordings. *Leisure interests:* literature, arts. *Address:* Symphonic Orchestra of Hungarian Radio, Bródy Sándor u. 5-7, 1800 Budapest VIII; Normafa ut 17/A, H-1121, Budapest, Hungary (Home). *Telephone:* 366-283.

LEHMANN, Erich Leo, PH.D.; American professor of statistics; b. 20 Nov. 1917, Strasbourg, France; s. of Julius Lehmann and Alma Schuster; m. Juliet Popper Schaffer; one s. two d.; ed. High School, Zurich, Switzerland, Univ. of Cambridge, Univ. of Calif., Berkeley; mem. Dept. of Math. Univ. of Calif., Berkeley 1946-55, Dept. of Statistics 1955-, Chair. Dept. of Statistics 1973-76; Visiting Assoc. Prof. Columbia Univ. 1950, Stanford Univ. 1951-52, Visiting Lecturer Princeton Univ. 1951, Guggenheim Fellow 1955, 1966, 1979, Miller Research Prof. 1967, 1972; mem. N.A.S., American Acad. of Art and Sciences; fmr. Pres. Inst. Math. Statistics; Dr. h.c. (Leiden) 1985. *Publications:* Testing Statistical Hypotheses 1959, 1986, Basic Concepts of Probability and Statistics (with J. L. Hodges, Jr.) 1964, Nonparametrics: Statistical Methods based on Ranks 1975, Theory of Point Estimation 1983, Ed. Annals of Mathematical Statistics 1953-55. *Leisure interests:* music, reading, hiking. *Address:* Department of Statistics, University of California at Berkeley, Calif. 94720 (Office); 2550 Dana Street, Berkeley, Calif. 94704, U.S.A. (Home). *Telephone:* (415) 549-3596 (Office).

LEHMANN, Heinz E., O.C., M.D., F.R.S.C.; Canadian professor of psychiatry; b. 17 July 1911, Berlin, Germany; s. of Richard R. and Emmy (Grönke) Lehmann; m. Annette Joyal 1940; one s.; ed. Mommsen Gymnasium, Berlin, Univs. of Freiburg, Marburg, Vienna and Berlin; psychiatrist, Verdun Protestant Hosp. 1935-47; Clinical Dir. Douglas Hosp. Verdun 1947, Dir. of Research 1966-76; Prof. of Psychiatry, McGill Univ. 1965-81, Prof. Emer. 1981-; Dir. of Research Operations, Dept. of Research for Mental Health, State of New York 1979-80; Deputy Commr. of Research, Office of Mental Health, State of New York 1981-; hon. consultant to several

Canadian hosps.; Visiting Prof. Univ. of Cincinnati; Albert Lasker Award 1957. *Publications:* Handbook of Psychiatric Treatment in Medical Practice (co-author) 1962, Pharmacotherapy of Tension and Anxiety 1970, Experimental Approaches to Psychiatric Diagnosis 1971, three chapters in Comprehensive Textbook of Psychiatry; over 300 professional publs. on psychiatry and psychopharmacology. *Leisure interests:* skiing, scuba diving, astronomy, gem collecting, lapidary. *Address:* 1212 Pine Avenue W., Apt. 908, Montreal, Québec, H3G 1A9, Canada. *Telephone:* (514) 288-1006.

LEHMANN, Rosamond Nina, C.B.E.; British writer and critic; b. 3 Feb. 1907, Bourne End, Bucks.; d. of R. C. Lehmann and Alice Marie Davis; m. Hon. Wogan Philipps (later 2nd Lord Milford) 1928 (divorced 1942); one s. one d. (deceased); ed. Girton Coll., Cambridge; Int. Vice-Pres. Int. PEN; Fellow, Royal Soc. of Literature; Companion of Literature (R.S.L.) 1987, Companion, Ordre des Arts et Lettres. *Publications include:* (novels) Dusty Answer 1927, A Note in Music 1930, Invitation to the Waltz 1932, The Weather in the Streets 1936, The Ballad and the Source 1944, The Gypsy's Baby 1946, The Echoing Grove 1953, The Swan in the Evening 1967, A Sea-Grape Tree 1976, The Awakening Letters 1978; (play) No More Music 1939. *Leisure interests:* music, reading, travelling. *Address:* 30 Clareville Grove, London, S.W.7; Coachhouse Cottage, Yoxford, Saxmundham, Suffolk, England.

LEHN, Jean-Marie Pierre, D. ÈS SC.; French professor of chemistry; b. 30 Sept, 1939, Rosheim, Bas-Rhin; s. of Pierre and Marie (née Salomon) Lehn; m. Sylvie Lederer 1965; two s.; ed. Univ. of Strasbourg; various posts, C.N.R.S. 1960-66; post-doctoral research assoc. with Prof. R. B. Woodward, Harvard Univ. 1963-64; Asst. Prof., Univ. of Strasbourg 1966-70, Assoc. Prof. 1970, Prof. 1970-79; Visiting Prof. of Chem., Harvard Univ. 1972, 1974, E.T.H., Zurich 1977, Cambridge Univ. 1984, Barcelona Univ. 1985; Prof Coll. de France, Paris 1979-; mem. Inst. de France, Deutsche Akad. der Naturforscher Leopoldina, Accad. Nazionale dei Lincei; Foreign assoc. N.A.S.; foreign hon. mem. American Acad. of Arts and Sciences; Foreign mem. Royal Netherlands Acad. of Arts and Sciences 1983; shared Nobel Prize in Chemistry 1987; Gold, Silver and Bronze Medals of C.N.R.S.; Gold Medal, Pontifical Acad. of Sciences 1981; Paracelsus Prize, Swiss Chem. Soc. 1982, von Humboldt Prize 1983; Chevalier, Légion d'honneur, Ordre nat. du Mérite. *Publications:* about 257 scientific publications. *Leisure interest:* music. *Address:* Institut Le Bel, Université Louis Pasteur, 4 rue Blaise Pascal, 67000 Strasbourg; Collège de France, 11 place Marcelin Berthelot, 75005 Paris; 21 rue d'Oslo, 67000 Strasbourg, France (Home). *Telephone:* (88) 41-60-56 (Inst. le Bel); (1) 4329-12-11 (Coll. de France); (88) 61-34-11 (Home).

LEHTO, Olli Erkki, PH.D.; Finnish professor of mathematics; b. 30 May 1925, Helsinki; s. of Paul V. L. Lehto and Hilma Autio; m. Eva G. Ekholm 1954; one s. two d.; ed. Univ. of Helsinki; Docent, Univ. of Helsinki 1951-56, Assoc. Prof. 1956-61, Prof. of Math. 1961-88, Dean, Faculty of Science 1978-83, Rector 1983-88, Chancellor 1988-; Pres. Finnish Math. Soc. 1962-85; mem. Exec. Cttee. Int. Math. Union 1975-, Sec.-Gen. 1982-; mem. Gen. Cttee. Int. Council of Scientific Unions 1982-; Visiting Prof. at numerous univs. in Europe, N. America and Asia; PhD. h.c. (Turku) 1980. *Publications:* three monographs and 60 papers in mathematical journals. *Leisure interest:* butterflies. *Address:* Office of the Chancellor, University of Helsinki, Hallituskatu 6, SF-00170 Helsinki (Office); Ritarikatu 3 A 7, SF-00170 Helsinki, Finland (Home). *Telephone:* 358-0-191 2206 (Office); 358-0-662 526 (Home).

LEHTO, Sakari Tapani, B.LL., B.SC.(ECON.); Finnish business executive; b. 26 Dec. 1923, Turku; s. of Reino and Hildi Lehto; m. Karin Hildén 1950; three d.; ed. Helsinki School of Econs. and Helsinki Univ.; Chief Legal Counsellor and Dir. Foreign Activities, United Paper Mills Ltd. 1952-64; Man. Dir. and Pres. Fed. of Finnish Industries 1964-71; Pres. and C.E.O. Oy Partek Ab 1972-87, Vice-Chair. 1987-; Chair. Insurance Ltd. Sampo 1976-, Insurance Co. Kalera 1978-, Pensions Sampo 1985-; Minister of Foreign Trade 1975-76; mem. Finland Defence Bd. 1988-; Tech. Dr. (h.c.). *Address:* Oy Partek Ab, Söörnaiston Rantatse 23, 00500 Helsinki (Office); Puistokatu 9A5, 00140 Helsinki, Finland (Home). *Telephone:* 358 0 653447 (Home).

LEI JIEQIONG; Chinese jurist and politician; b. 1906, Guangdong Prov.; m. Yan Jingyao; ed. in U.S.A.; Prof. Yanjing Univ., 1951-; mem. Cttee. for Implementation Campaign of Marriage Laws 1953; Deputy Dir., Bureau of Foreign Experts Admin. under State Council 1956-; mem., Standing Cttee. 5th CPPCC 1978-83; mem. Standing Cttee. 6th NPC and Vice-Chair. of Cttee. 1983-88; Vice-Chair. 6th NPC 1986-88; Vice-Chair. 7th NPC 1988-. *Address:* Standing Committee of National People's Congress, Tian An Men Square, Beijing, People's Republic of China.

LEI YANG; Chinese diplomatist; b. 19 Feb. 1920, Xian, Shaanxi; m.; four s. two d.; Counsellor, PRC Embassy, Burma 1956-61; Dir. Training Dept. Ministry of Foreign Affairs 1962-65; Chargé d'affaires a.i., Poland 1969-72; Amb. to The Gambia 1975-79, to Nigeria 1980-85, mem. Council, Chinese People's Inst. of Foreign Affairs. *Leisure interests:* sports, calligraphy. *Address:* Ministry of Foreign Affairs, 225 Chaonei Street, Dongsi, Beijing, People's Republic of China.

LEIBLER, Kenneth Robert, B.A.; American business executive; b. 21 Feb. 1949, New York; s. of Max and Martha (née Dales) Leibler; m.

Marcia Kate Reiss 1973; two s. two d.; ed. Syracuse Univ. and Univ. of Pennsylvania; Options Man. Lehman Bros. 1972-75; Vice-Pres. Options American Stock Exchange, N.Y. 1975-79, Sr. Vice-Pres. Admin. and Finance 1979-81, Exec. Vice-Pres. Admin. and Finance 1981-85, Sr. Exec. Vice-Pres. 1985-86, Pres. 1986-; Instructor N.Y. Inst. of Finance; Dir. Securities Industry Automation Corpn.; mem. Finance Execs. Inst. of Securities Industry Asscn. American Stock Exchange Clearing Corpn. *Publication:* (contrib.) Handbook of Financial Markets: Securities, Options, Futures 1981. *Address:* 86 Trinity Place, New York, N.Y. 10006, U.S.A.

LEIBOWITZ, Joshua O., M.D.; Israeli professor of the history of medicine; b. 25 April 1895, Wilna, Russia; m. Hannah Janette Bing 1943; ed. Heidelberg Univ., Germany; Assoc. Prof. of History of Medicine 1957; Pres. Int. Acad. of the History of Medicine 1979-86, Hon. Pres. 1986-; Einhorn Prize (City of Tel Aviv) 1975. *Publications:* The History of Coronary Heart Disease 1970, Maimonides on the Causes of Symptoms 1974, Sefer Hanisyonot, attributed to Abraham Ibn Ezra . . . 1984. *Leisure interest:* old printed material on medicine and Jewish lore. *Address:* Yordei-Hasira Street 3, 93225 Jerusalem, Israel.

LEIDING, Rudolf Wilhelm Karl; German motor executive (retd.); b. 4 Sept. 1914, Busch, Kr. Osterburg/Altmark; m. Helga Petry 1965; one s. one d.; ed. engineering school; joined Volkswagenwerk, Wolfsburg after Second World War, Man. VW Plant, Kassel 1958, also Dir. Volkswagenwerk AG; Man. and Chair. Man. Bd., Auto Union G.m.b.H. (subsidiary of VW Group) 1965-68; Head, VW do Brasil (Brazilian subsidiary) 1968-71; Chair. Man. Bd., AUDI NSU Auto Union AG April-Sept. 1971; Chair. Man. Bd., Volkswagenwerk AG 1971-74; Hon. Dr.-Ing. (Tech. Univ. Berlin) 1976; Ordem de Rio Branco (Brazil) 1969, Ordem de Merito de Trabalho (Brazil) 1971, Bayerischer Verdienstorden 1973, Order of Tudor Vladimirescu (Romania) 1973. *Address:* Am Baunsberg 1, 3507 Baunatal 1, Federal Republic of Germany. *Telephone:* (0561) 49.23.01.

LEIFLAND, Leif, LL.B.; Swedish diplomatist; b. 30 Dec. 1925, Stockholm; s. of Sigfrid and Elna Leifland; m. Karin Abard 1954; one s. two d.; ed. Univ. of Lund; joined Ministry of Foreign Affairs 1952; served Athens 1953, Bonn 1955, Washington 1961, 1970; Sec. Foreign Relations Cttee., Swedish Parl. 1966-70; Under-Sec. for Political Affairs 1975-77; Perm. Under-Sec. of State for Foreign Affairs 1977-82; Amb. to U.K. 1982-; Hon. G.C.V.O. *Publications:* various articles on foreign policy and national security questions. *Address:* 27 Portland Place, London, W.1, England. *Telephone:* 01-724 2101.

LEIGH, Mike; British dramatist and film and theatre director; b. 20 Feb. 1943, Salford, Lancs.; s. of A. A. and P. P. (née Cousin) Leigh; m. Alison Steadman 1973; two s.; ed. R.A.D.A., Camberwell School of Arts and Crafts, Cen. School of Art and Design, London Film School; Golden Leopard (Locarno Film Festival) and Golden Hugo (Chicago Film Festival) 1972 for Bleak Moments, George Devine Award 1973, London "Evening Standard" and "Drama" London Critics' Choice best comedy awards 1981 for Goose-Pimples, Int. Critic's Prize, Venice Film Festival 1988 for High Hopes. *Plays:* The Box Play 1965, My Parents Have Gone to Carlisle, The Last Crusade of the Five Little Nuns 1966, Nenaa 1967, Individual Fruit Pies, Down Here and Up There, Big Basil 1968, Epilogue, Glum Victoria and the Lad with Specs 1969, Bleak Moments 1970, A Rancid Pong 1971, Wholesome Glory. The Jaws of Death, Dick Whittington and His Cat 1973, Babies Grow Old, The Silent Majority 1974, Abigail's Party 1977 (also television play), Ecstasy 1979, Goose-Pimples 1981, Smelling A Rat 1988. *Television films:* A Mug's Game, Hard Labour 1973, The Permissive Society, The Birth of the 2001 F.A. Cup Final Goalie, Old Chums, Probation, A Light Snack, Afternoon 1975, Nuts in May, Knock for Knock 1976, The Kiss of Death 1977, Who's Who 1978, Grown Ups 1980, Home Sweet Home 1981, Meantime 1983, Four Days in July 1984. *Feature films:* Bleak Moments 1971, The Short and the Curlies 1987, High Hopes 1988. *Radio play:* Too Much of a Good Thing 1979. *Address:* c/o A. D. Peters and Co. Ltd., 5th Floor, The Chambers, Chelsea Harbour, Lots Road, London, SW10 0XF, England. *Telephone:* 01-376-7676.

LEIGH GUZMÁN, Gen. Gustavo; Chilean air force officer; b. 19 Sept. 1920; m. Gabriela García Powdich; three s. one d.; ed. Liceo José Victorino Lastarria, Mil. Acad., Nat. Defence Acad.; postgraduate studies specializing in Supply and Maintenance, Command and Staff; Academic Instructor of Operations and Logistics; Deputy Commdr. Group 11 1953; Commdr. Group 10 1961; Commdr. of Supply Wing 1963; Air Attaché to U.S.A. 1964; Sec.-Gen. Chilean Air Force 1966; Dir. Aviation School 1968; Chief of Gen. Staff 1971-78; fmr. C.-in-C. of Chilean Air Force; mem. Mil. Junta 1973-78; many mil. decorations including Grand Mil. Merit Cross, Mil. Star, and Nat. Order of Merit (Paraguay), Legion of Merit (U.S.A.), Grand Cross for Aeronautical Merit (Spain), and others. *Address:* c/o Junta Militar de Gobierno, Santiago, Chile.

LEIGH-PEMBERTON, Rt. Hon. Robert (Robin), P.C., M.A., D.C.L.; British barrister, landowner and banker; b. 5 Jan. 1927, Lenham; s. of Robert Douglas Leigh-Pemberton, M.B.E., M.C., and Helen Isabel Payne-Gallwey; m. Rosemary Davina Forbes 1953; five s.; ed. St. Peter's Court, Broadstairs, Eton Coll., Trinity Coll., Oxford; Oppidan Scholar, Eton 1940-45; Grenadier Guards 1945-48; practised at the Bar 1953-60; Dir. Univ. Life Assurance Soc. 1968-78; Dir. Birmid-Qualcast PLC, Deputy Chair. 1970-75, Chair.

1975-77; Dir. Redland PLC 1972-83, Equitable Life Assurance Soc. 1978-83, Vice-Pres. 1982; Dir. Nat. Westminster Bank PLC 1972-74, Deputy Chair. 1974-77, Chair. 1977-83; Gov. Bank of England July 1983-; Dir. BIS 1983-; mem. Kent County Council 1961-77, Leader 1964-69, Chair. 1972-75; J.P. for Kent 1961-76; Deputy Lieut. for Kent 1969, Vice-Lord Lieut. 1972-82, Lord Lieut. 1982-; Gov. Wye Coll., London Univ. 1968-77; Hon. Master of the Bench, Inner Temple 1983; Deputy Pro-Chancellor of Kent Univ. 1969-78, Pro-Chancellor 1977-83; mem. Medway Ports Authority 1972-77, S.E. Econ. Planning Council 1971-74, Prime Minister's Cttee. on Standards in Local Govt. 1973-74, Cttee. of Enquiry into Teachers' Pay 1974, Cttee. to review Police Conditions of Service 1977-79, NEDC 1981-; Chair. City Communications Centre 1979-82, Cttee. of London Clearing Bankers 1982-83; Hon. D.C.L. (Kent) 1983, Hon. M.A. (Trinity Coll, Oxford) 1984; K.St.J. 1983, Order of Aztec Eagle, Mexico (First Class) 1985. *Leisure interests:* English country life, skiing, the arts. *Address:* Bank of England, Threadneedle Street, London, EC2R 8AH, England (Office). *Telephone:* 01-601 4444 (Office).

LEIGHTON, Robert Benjamin, M.S., PH.D.; American physicist; b. 10 Sept. 1919, Detroit, Mich.; s. of George B. Leighton and Olga O. Homrig; m. 1st Alice M. Winger 1943, two s.; m. 2nd Margaret L. Lauritsen 1977; ed. Calif. Inst. of Tech.; Research Fellow, Calif. Inst. of Tech. 1947-49, Asst. Prof. 1949-53, Assoc. Prof. 1953-59, Prof. of Physics 1959-85, Prof. Emer. 1985-, Chair. Physics, Math. and Astronomy Div. 1970-75, also mem. of staff of Hale Observations; mem. N.A.S., American Acad. of Arts and Sciences, American Physical Soc., American Astronomical Soc.; A.I.A.A. Award 1967. *Publications:* Principles of Modern Physics 1959, Feynman Lectures on Physics (co-author) 1963; 36 articles in professional journals. *Leisure interests:* astronomy, photography, optics, chamber music, reading, hiking. *Address:* California Institute of Technology, Pasadena, Calif. 91125, U.S.A.

LEIJON, Anna-Greta; Swedish politician; b. 30 June 1939, Stockholm; ed. Uppsala Univ.; social welfare officer, Uppsala Student Union 1963-64; Chair. Social Democratic Youth League 1964-65; at Nat. Labour Market Bd. 1964-72; mem. Stockholm County Council 1970-73; Chair. Northern Greater Stockholm Dist., Nat. Asscn. of Tenants' Saving and Building Socs.; head of Secr., Govt. Advisory Cttee. on Equal Opportunities 1973; M.P. 1973-; Minister without Portfolio at Ministry of Labour, also with responsibility for immigrant affairs 1973-76; mem. Bd. Socialdemokratiska Arbetarepartiet (Social Democratic Labour Party—SDLP) 1975-, mem. Exec. Cttee. 1981-82; Vice-Chair. Parl. Standing Cttee. on Labour Market Affairs 1979; Minister of Labour 1982-87, of Sexual Equality 1986-87, of Justice 1987-88; Pres. 70th Int. Conf., Geneva 1984. *Address:* c/o Ministry of Justice, Rosenbad 4, 103 33 Stockholm, Sweden.

LEINONEN, Tatu Einari, D.TECH.; Finnish professor of machine design; b. 21 Sept. 1938, Kajaani; m. Maria Tuovinen 1968; one s. two d.; lecturer, Tech. Inst. of Helsinki 1963; researcher, Tech. Research Centre of Finland 1965; Design Eng. State Railway Co. 1966; Prof. of Machine Design, Univ. of Oulu 1968-. *Address:* University of Oulu, Department of Mechanical Engineering, Linnanmaa, 90570 Oulu, Finland. *Telephone:* 358 81 352 423.

LEINSDORF, Erich; American musician; b. 4 Feb. 1912, Vienna, Austria; s. of Ludwig Julius and Charlotte (Loebl) Leinsdorf; m. 1st Anne Frohknecht 1939 (divorced 1968), 2nd Vera Graf 1968; three s. two d.; ed. Univ. of Vienna and State Acad. of Music, Vienna; Asst. Conductor, Salzburg Festival 1934-37; U.S.A. 1937-; Conductor, Metropolitan Opera 1937-43; Music Dir. and Conductor Cleveland Orchestra 1943; Music Dir. Philharmonic Orchestra, Rochester 1947-56; Dir. New York City Center Opera 1956, Metropolitan Opera 1957-62; Music Consultant, Metropolitan Opera Management 1958-62; Music Dir. Boston Symphony Orchestra 1962-69; Dir. Berkshire Music Center, Festival 1963-69; mem. Bd. of Dirs. American Arts Alliance; fmr. mem. Exec. Cttee. John F. Kennedy Center for the Performing Arts, Exec. Cttee. Corpn. for Public Broadcasting, Mass. Council on the Arts and Humanities; mem. Nat. Endowment on the Arts; Guest Conductor (since 1969) Teatro Colón, Buenos Aires, Metropolitan Opera, New York, Berlin Philharmonic, Chicago Symphony, Cleveland, Concertgebouw Amsterdam, New York Philharmonic, London Symphony, London Philharmonic, New Philharmonia, BBC Symphony Orchestras and Orchestre de Paris; Bayreuth, Netherlands, Edinburgh and Prague Festivals; Fellow, American Acad. of Arts and Sciences; Hon. music degrees (Rutgers and Baldwin-Wallace, Columbia and Williams Colls.). *Publication:* Cadenza—A Musical Career (autobiography) 1976, The Composer's Advocate 1981. *Address:* c/o Dodds, 209 East 56th Street, New York, N.Y. 10022, U.S.A.

LEITE, Antônio Dias, Jr.; Brazilian engineer and politician; b. 29 Jan. 1920, Rio de Janeiro; s. of Antônio Dias Leite and Georgeta Lahmeyer Leite; m. Manira Alcure Dias Leite 1944; two s. three d.; ed. Universidade Federal do Rio de Janeiro; Prof. of Econ., Univ. Federal do Rio de Janeiro; Under-Sec. for Econ. Affairs, Ministry of Finance 1963; Pres. Companhia Vale do Rio Doce 1967; Minister of Mines and Power 1969-74; Economy Eng. Consultant 1975. *Publications:* Caminhos do Desenvolvimento 1966, Politica Mineral e Energética 1973. *Address:* Universidade Federal do Rio de Janeiro, Ilha da Cidade Universitária, 250 Rio de Janeiro, RJ, Brazil.

LEITO, Ben M.; Netherlands Antilles economist and administrator; b. 6 Feb. 1923, Curaçao; m. Christine A. M. Koot 1951; two s. two d.; ed.

Curaçao and Netherlands; Jr. Officer Netherlands Antilles Dept. of Social and Econ. Affairs 1951; Officer Gen. Affairs Div., Curaçao 1952, Finance Div. 1953; mem. Curaçao Island Council 1955–63; mem. Netherlands Antilles Parl. 1959–62; Head of Finance Div., Curaçao 1961–65; Dir. Netherlands Antilles Dept. of Finance 1965–70; Pres. Supervisory Dirs. Bank of Netherlands Antilles 1965–70; Chair. Socio-Econ. Council of Netherlands Antilles 1967–70; Acting Lieut.-Gov. of Curaçao 1968–70; Acting Gov. of Netherlands Antilles 1969–70, Gov. 1970–83; mem. Council of State, Kingdom of Netherlands 1987–; several Netherlands and foreign decorations. *Address:* P.O. Box 19014, 3501 DA Utrecht, Netherlands.

LEJEUNE, Jérôme Jean Louis Marie, M.D., PH.D.; French geneticist; b. 13 June 1926, Montrouge; s. of Pierre Ulysse Lejeune and Marcelle Lermat; m. Birthe Bringsted 1959; two s. three d.; ed. Coll. Stanislas, Paris, Faculty of Medicine and Faculty of Sciences, Paris; Dir. de recherche, C.N.R.S. 1963–; Prof. of Fundamental Genetics, Faculty of Medicine, Paris 1964–; mem. Pontifical Acad. of Sciences 1974–; American Acad. of Arts and Sciences; Officier, Ordre nat. du Mérite; Kennedy Prize, Feltrinelli Prize. *Publications:* Discovery of the extra chromosome in Trisomy 21 (mongolism), research on human chromosomes, research on mental deficiency. *Leisure interest:* knowledge. *Address:* Institut de Progénèse, 45 rue des Saints-Pères, 75270 Paris Cedex 06 (Office); 31 rue Galande, 75005 Paris, France (Home). *Telephone:* 4329-21-77 (Office).

LEJEUNE, Michael L.; American (b. British) international finance official; b. 22 March 1918, Manchester; s. of F. Arnold and Gladys (née Brown) Lejeune; m. Margaret Werden Wilson 1947; two s. one d.; ed. Cate School, Carpinteria, Calif., Yale Univ., and Yale Univ. Graduate School; Teacher St. Paul's School, Concord, New Hampshire 1941; Volunteer in King's Royal Rifle Corps in British Army 1942–46; IBRD (now called World Bank) 1946–83, Personnel Officer 1948–50, Asst. to Loan Dir. and Sec. Staff Loan Cttee., Loan Dept. 1950–52, Chief of Div., Europe, Africa and Australasia Dept. 1952–57, Asst. Dir. of Operations, Europe, Africa and Australasia 1957–63, Asst. Dir. of Operations, Far East 1963–64; Dir. of Admin., World Bank, IDA and IFC 1964–67, Dir. Middle East and North Africa Dept. 1967–68; Dir. Europe, Middle East and North Africa Dept. 1968–69; Dir. Eastern Africa Dept. 1970–74, Exec. Sec. Consultative Group on Int. Agric. Research 1974–83; Sr. Adviser to Vice-Pres. Operations Policy 1983; Consultant 1983–. *Publication:* Partners Against Hunger: The Consultative Group on International Agricultural Research (with Warren C. Baum) 1986. *Address:* 80 Conejo Road, Santa Barbara, Calif. 93103, U.S.A. *Telephone:* (805) 963-6598.

LEJEUNE, Michel; French research director; b. 30 Jan. 1907, Paris; s. of Albert Lejeune and Marie Clairin; m. Suzanne Hubert 1931; two s. two d.; ed. Lycée Carnot and Lycée Louis-le-Grand, Paris and Ecole Normale Supérieure, Paris; Maître de conférences, Faculté des Lettres, Poitiers 1933–37; Prof. then Dean, Faculté des Lettres, Bordeaux 1937–46; Dir. of Studies, Ecole Pratique des Hautes Etudes (Section IV) 1946–; Prof. Faculté des Lettres de Paris, Sorbonne 1946–55; Deputy Dir. C.N.R.S. 1955–63, Dir. of Research 1963–77; mem. Inst. de France, Acad. des Inscriptions; mem. Rome, Brussels and London Acads.; Dr. h.c. (Louvain, Salamanca). *Publications:* approximately 250 articles and 20 books on ancient Indo-European languages. *Address:* 25 rue Gazan, 75014 Paris, France. *Telephone:* (1) 45 88 04 26.

LEJINS, Voldemars Petrovich; Soviet politician; b. 7 July 1920, Bugrysh, Udmurtian A.S.S.R.; ed. Moscow Tech. Inst. of Food Industry and Higher Party School of CPSU Cen. Cttee.; Soviet Army 1942–43; Section Chief, Dept. of Confectionery Industry, Food Ministry of Latvian S.S.R. 1945–46; Engineer, "Laima" confectionery factory, Riga 1946–49; Party work, Riga 1949–; Higher Party School of CPSU Cen. Cttee. 1956–58; Head, Main Dept. of Food Industry, Latvian Council of Nat. Econ. 1958–60; Second Sec. Riga Town Cttee. of CP of Latvia 1960–61, Sec. Cen. Cttee. 1961–70; Deputy to U.S.S.R. Supreme Soviet 1966–; U.S.S.R. Minister of Food Industry 1970–86; Cand. mem. Cen. Cttee. CPSU 1971–76, mem. 1976–; Order of Lenin (three times), Red Banner of Labour (twice), etc. *Address:* c/o Ministry of Food Industry, 29 Building 4, Prospekt Kalinina, Moscow, U.S.S.R.

LEKHANYA, Maj.-Gen. Justin; Lesotho army officer and politician; Commdr. of Lesotho Army; Head Mil. Council and Council of Ministers Jan. 1986–, Minister of Defence and Internal Security June 1986–, also Minister of Public Service, Youth and Women's Affairs, Food Man. Units and Cabinet Office. *Address:* c/o Military Council, Maseru, Lesotho.

LE LANNOU, Maurice; French professor; b. 8 May 1906, Plouha; s. of Théophile Le Lannou and Adèle Geffroy; m. Adrienne Trehiou 1934; two c.; ed. Ecole Normale Supérieure, Paris; Prof. Lycées in Brest and Rennes 1933–44; Prof. Univs. of Rennes and Lyon, Prof. Coll. de France 1969–76, Hon. Prof. 1976–; mem. Acad. des Sciences morales et politiques; Commandeur Légion d'honneur. *Publications:* Pâtres et paysans de la Sardaigne 1941, La Géographie humaine 1949, Géographie de la Bretagne 1952, Le Déménagement du Territoire 1967, Europe, terre promise 1977, La Bretagne et les Bretons 1978, Un Bleu de Bretagne, souvenirs d'un fils d'instituteur de la 3ème République 1979, Saint-Brieuc 1986. *Address:* 36 rue de la Glacière, 75013 Paris, France. *Telephone:* (16-1) 45 35 10 08.

LELONG, Pierre Alexandre; French politician and administrative official; b. 22 May 1931, Paris; s. of Prof. Marcel Lelong; m. Catherine Demargne 1958; four s. one d.; ed. Coll. Stanislas, Paris, Univ. of Paris and Ecole Nat. d'Administration; Ministry of Finance and Econ. Affairs 1958–62; Econ. Adviser to Prime Minister Pompidou 1962–67; Gen. Man. Fonds d'Orientation et de Régularisation des Marchés Agricoles (FORMA) 1967–68; M.P. for Finistère 1968–74; Sec. of State for Posts and Telecommunications 1974–75; Judge, Court of Accounts 1975–77; mem. European Court of Auditors 1977–, Pres. 1981–84; mem. European Court of Auditors 1984–. *Address:* 56 rue de l'Eglise, Walferdange, Luxembourg; Keremma, 29255 Tréflez, Finistère, France; 12 Rue Alcide de Crasperi, C1615 Luxembourg. *Telephone:* 43-98-203 (Luxembourg).

LELONG, Pierre Jacques, D. ÈS SC.; French academic; b. 14 March 1912, Paris; s. of Charles Lelong and Marguerite (née de Bronner) Lelong; m. Jacqueline Ferrand 1947; two s. two d.; ed. Ecole des Sciences Politiques; Science Faculty, Grenoble 1942–44; Prof. Science Faculty, Lille 1944–54, Université de Paris VI 1954–81; Research Counsellor for the Pres. of the Repub. 1959–62; Pres. du Comité Consultatif de la Recherche et de la Comm. du Plan 1961–63; mem. Comm. mathématique C.N.R.S., Pres. 1962–66; Officier Légion d'honneur; mem. Académie des Sciences 1986–. *Publications:* Fonctions plurisousharmoniques 1968, Function of Several Complex Variables 1986; numerous research papers and articles on the org. of research. *Address:* 9 place de Rungis, Paris 75013, France. *Telephone:* 45.81.51.45 (Home).

LELOUCH, Claude; French film director; b. 30 Oct. 1937, Paris; s. of Simon Lelouch and Charlotte Abeilard; m. Christine Cochet 1968 (divorced); one s. two d.; Pres. and Dir.-Gen. Société Les Films 13, 1966–; Chevalier, Ordre nat. du Mérite, Officier, Ordre des Arts et des Lettres; *films directed include:* l'amour des si..., La femme-spectacle, Une fille et des fusils, Les grands moments, Pour un maillot jaune, Un homme et une femme, (Palme d'or, Cannes 1966, Acad. Award 1966), Vivre pour vivre, Treize jours en France, La vie, l'amour, la mort, Un homme qui me plaît, Le Voyou, Smic, Smac, Smoc, co-dir. Visions of Eight 1973, L'Aventure c'est l'aventure, La bonne année 1973, (producer, dir., author) Toute une vie 1974, Mariage 1974, Le chat et la souris 1975, Le bon et les méchants 1975, Rendez-vous 1976, Si c'était à refaire 1976, Un autre homme, une autre chance 1977, Robert et Robert 1978, A nous deux 1979, Les uns et les autres 1981, Edith et Marcel 1983, Viva la vie 1984, Partir, revenir 1985, Un homme et une femme ... 20 ans après 1986, Les nouveaux bandits 1987. *Address:* 15 avenue Hoche, 75008 Paris, France. *Telephone:* 42-25-00-89.

LEM, Stanisław; Polish prose writer and essayist; b. 12 Sept. 1921, Lvov; ed. Lvov Med. Inst., Jagellonian Univ., Cracow; literary début with novel Człowiek z Marsa (Man from Mars) in weekly Nowy Świat Przygód, Katowice 1946; mem. Polish Astronautic Soc., mem. Poland 2000 Comm. of Polish Acad. of Sciences 1972–; mem. Science Fiction Research Asscn. and Science Fiction Writers of America; several literary awards. *Major works:* science-fiction novels include Astronauci (The Astronauts) 1951, Obłok Magellana (Magellan's Cloud) 1955, Eden 1959, Śledztwo (The Investigation-detective story) 1959, Powrót z gwiazd (Return from the Stars) 1961, Solaris 1961, Pamiętnik znaleziony w wannie (Memoirs Founded in a Bathtub) 1963, Niezwyciężony (The Invincible) 1964, Głos Pana (Master's Voice) 1968, Doskonała próżnia (A Perfect Vacuum) 1971, Bezsenność. Opowiadania 1971, Transfer 1975, Katar (The Chain of Chance, thriller) 1976, Maska (The Mask) 1976, Wizja lokalna 1982, Kongres Futurologiczny (Futurological Congress) 1983, Prowokacja 1984; *science fiction stories include:* Dzienniki gwiazdowe (The Star Diaries) 1957, Księga robotów (Book of Robots) 1961, Bajki robotów (Robots' Fairy-Tales) 1964, Cyberiada (Cyberiad) 1965, Opowieści o pilocie Pirxie (The Tales of Pirx the Pilot) 1967, Fantastyka i futurologia 1970, Golem XIV 1981, Fiasco 1987; *essays include:* Dialogi (The Dialogues) 1957, 1972, 1984, Summa technologiae 1964, 1967, 1974, 1984; series of novels; Czas nieutracony Part I-III 1955, autobiographical novel: Wysoki Zamek (High Castle) 1966; books translated into 25 languages. *Address:* Cracow, Poland.

LEMAEV, Nikolay Vasilevich, DR. TECH. SC.; Soviet oil specialist and politician; b. 1929; ed. Ufa Oil Inst.; operator, foreman, deputy chief-engineer in Novoufa oil refinery 1950–60; mem. CPSU 1955–; Deputy Dir. of Management of Chemical industry of Tatar region 1960–63; Dir., General Dir. of Nizhekamsky production unit 1963–85; U.S.S.R. First Deputy Mn. of Oil Refining and Oil Industry Oct. 1985–; mem. of CPSU Cen. Cttee. 1986–; Hero of Socialist Labour 1980. *Address:* The Kremlin, Moscow, U.S.S.R.

LEMAN, Alexander B., F.R.A.I.C., F.R.S.A.; Canadian architect and planner; b. 5 May 1926, Belgrade, Yugoslavia; s. of Boris E. and Nataly Leman; m. 1st Catherine B. Leman 1950 (deceased), 2nd N. Bella Leman 1968; two s. two d.; ed. Univ. of Belgrade; Prin. Partner, Leman Partners, architects and engineers 1956–; Pres. Leman Group Inc., Consultants on Human Settlements 1971–; Chair. of Bd. Royal Architectural Inst. of Canada Research Corpn. 1982–; Chair. Fourth World Congress on Conservation of Built and Natural Environments May 1988; Dir. Devt. of a new city for 185,000 people in Vancouver; Vice-Pres. Royal Architectural Inst. of Canada 1975–76; Progressive Architecture Award 1973. *Publications:* articles in professional journals. *Leisure interests:* travel, community activities.

Address: 131 Bloor W., The Colonnade, 521, Toronto, M5S 1R8, Canada (Home). *Telephone:* (416) 964-1865 (Home).

LEMAN, Paul H., O.C., A.B., LL.L.; Canadian business executive; b. 6 Aug. 1915, Pointe Claire, Québec; s. of J. B. Beaudry Leman and Caroline Beique; m. Jeannine Prud'homme 1939; two s. three d.; ed. Collège Sainte-Marie, Univ. of Montreal and Harvard Graduate School of Business Admin.; admitted to Québec Bar 1937; joined Aluminum Co. of Canada Ltd. 1938, Asst. Sec. 1943, Treas. 1949, Vice-Pres. 1952, Dir. 1963, Exec. Vice-Pres. 1964, Pres. 1969-75, Chair. 1975-; Treas. Saguenay Power Co. Ltd. 1945; Dir. Alcan Aluminium Ltd. 1968-, Exec. Vice-Pres. 1969, Pres. 1972-77, Vice-Chair. 1977-79; Dir. Export Devt. Corpn. 1969-74; Dir. Canadian Int. Paper, Crédit Foncier Franco-Canadien, Bell Canada; Trustee, Nat. Museums of Canada 1979-83; mem. Royal Comm. on Banking and Finance 1962-64. *Leisure interests:* golf, bridge. *Address:* Alcan Aluminium Ltd., 1 place Ville Marie, Montreal, H3C 3H2 (Office); 445 St. Joseph Boulevard W., Outremont, Québec, Canada H2V 2P8.

LeMAY, Gen. Curtis E.; American air force officer (retd.); b. 15 Nov. 1906, Columbus, Ohio; s. of Erving LeMay; m. Helen Estelle Maitland 1934; one d.; ed. Ohio State Univ.; held various mil. posts until outbreak of Second World War; in command of 305th Bombardment Group in England 1942; Commdg. Gen. Third Bombardment Div. 1943-44; transferred to Pacific theatre of war in command 20th Bomber Command 1944-45; Commdr. of the Mariana-based 21st Bomber Command 1945; Deputy Chief of Air Staff Research and Devt. 1945-47; Commdr. U.S.A.F. in Europe 1947-48; C.-in-C. Strategic Air Command 1948-57; Vice-Chief of Staff U.S.A.F. 1957-61, Chief of Staff 1961-64; American Ind. Party cand. for Vice-Pres. of U.S.A. 1968; several hon. degrees; Distinguished Service Cross, Distinguished Service Medal with three Oak Leaf Clusters, Silver Star, Distinguished Flying Cross with two Oak Leaf Clusters, Air Medal with three Oak Leaf Clusters, Medal for Humane Action and the Mackay Trophy, etc.; foreign decorations: British D.F.C., Commdr. Légion d'honneur and Croix de guerre with Palm Leaf (France), Belgian Croix de guerre with Palm Leaf, Brazilian Order of the Southern Cross, Commdr. Moroccan Order of the Ouissam Alaouite Chérifien, Russian Order of Patriotic War, Argentine Order of Aeronautical Merit. *Leisure interests:* hunting, shooting. *Address:* 773 Stradella Road, Los Angeles, Calif. 90024, U.S.A.

LEMBERG, Aleksandr Yanovich (b. Lembergs); Soviet ballet-master and choreographer; b. 1921, Latvia; ed. Nat. Opera and Ballet School of Riga; studied under L. N. Yegorova in Paris; soloist with Ballet de la Jeunesse 1938-39; soloist with State Acad. of Theatre, Opera and Ballet of Latvian S.S.R. 1939-68, chief ballet-master 1968-; *productions include:* Peer Gynt, Notre Dame de Paris, Scaramouche, Carmen Suite, Anthony and Cleopatra, In the Fire (Karlson); Dir. of Riga Ballet School 1964-68; Nat. Artist of Latvian S.S.R. 1971, Nat. Artist of U.S.S.R. 1982.

LEME, Hugo de Almeida; Brazilian agricultural specialist; b. 1917; ed. Escola Superior de Agricultura Luiz de Queiroz; Assoc. Prof., Escola Superior de Agricultura Luiz de Queiroz, Piracicaba, (Univ. de São Paulo) 1939-40, Prof. 1940, Full Prof. 1944, 1946-, Vice-Dir. 1958-60, Dir. 1960-64; Minister of Agric. 1964-66; mem. Council for Agric. Reform, State of São Paulo; has attended and organized numerous confs.; Ford Motor Co. Prize for work on the mechanization of agric. 1961. *Address:* c/o Ministério da Agricultura, Esplanada dos Ministérios, Bloco 8, Brasília, D.F., Brazil.

LEMELIN, Roger, C.C.; Canadian writer and publisher; b. 7 April 1919, Quebec City; s. of Joseph Lemelin and Florida Dumontier; m. Valéda Lavigueur 1945; three s. two d.; Guggenheim Fellowship 1946, Rockefeller Fellowship 1947; journalist Time, Life, Fortune magazines 1948-52; Pres. and Publr. La Presse daily 1972-82; mem. Royal Soc. of Canada 1949; Foreign mem. Acad. Goncourt 1974; Hon. D.Litt. (Laurentian Univ. of Sudbury, Ontario) 1976, Hon. LL.D. (Windsor) 1982; Prix David 1946, Canadian News Hall of Fame 1978. *Publications:* novels: Au pied de la pente douce 1944, Les Plouffe 1948, Pierre le magnifique 1952; short stories: Fantaisie sur les péchés capitaux 1949, Les voies de l'espérance 1979, La culotte en or 1980, Le Crime d'Ovide Plouffe 1982. *Leisure interests:* golf, fishing, reading, chess, travel. *Address:* La Presse, 7 St. James Street, Montreal, Quebec, H2Y 1K9 (Office); 4753 St. Felix Street, Cap Rouge, Quebec G0A 1K0, Canada (Home). *Telephone:* (418) 872-5114 (Home).

LEMERLE, Paul, L. ÈS L.; French civil servant; b. 18 May 1927, Paris; s. of P. E. Lemerle; m. Monique Roger-Machart 1960; three d.; ed. Univ. of Paris, Ecole Nationale d'Administration, M.I.T.; Insp.-Gen. of Finances 1953; service with Commissariat Gén. du Plan 1959-67; Dir. du Cabinet to Minister of Scientific Affairs 1967-68, of Social Affairs 1968-69, of Foreign Affairs 1969-73; with Inspection Générale des Finances 1973-77; Financial Counsellor, French embassies in the Near and Middle East 1977-80; Deputy Sec.-Gen. OECD 1980-85; Minister plenipotentiary, Econ. and Financial Counsellor, French Mission to UN, New York 1985-; Officier, Légion d'honneur. *Address:* French Mission to United Nations, 245 East 47th Street, New York, N.Y. 10017, U.S.A.; 58 rue D'Assas, 75006 Paris, France. *Telephone:* (212) 758-6979 (New York); 45.48.19.93 (Paris).

LEMIEUX, Joseph Henry, B.S.; American business executive; b. 3 Feb. 1931, Providence, R.I.; s. of Joseph C. Lemieux and Mildred L. Lemieux;

m. Frances J. Schmidt 1956; two s. two d.; ed. Stonehill Coll., Univ. of Rhode Island, Bryant Coll., Providence; joined Glass Container Div., Owens-Ill. as trainee 1957, numerous posts include Plant Comptroller 1961, Admin. Man. 1964, Plant Man. 1965-72, Vice-Pres. 1972-78, Group Vice-Pres. 1979-84, Exec. Vice-Pres. and Pres. Packaging Operations 1984-86, Pres and C.O.O. 1986-; Chair. Bd. of Dirs. Health Care and Retirement Corpn. of America 1986-; Outstanding Young Man of America, U.S. Jr. Chamber of Commerce 1965. *Leisure interests:* golf, tennis. *Address:* Owens-Illinois, Inc., One Sea Gate, Toledo, Ohio 43666, U.S.A. *Telephone:* 419-247 5800.

LEMIEUX, Raymond Urgel, O.C., PH.D., F.R.S. ; Canadian chemist; b. 16 June 1920, Lac La Biche, Alberta; s. of Octave Lemieux; m. Virginia Marie McConaghie 1948; one s. five d.; ed. Univ. of Alberta, Edmonton, and McGill Univ., Montreal; Research Fellow, Ohio State Univ. 1947; Asst. Prof., Univ. of Saskatchewan 1948-49; Sr. Research Officer, Nat. Research Council 1949-54; Prof. Univ. of Ottawa 1954-61; Prof. of Organic Chem., Univ. of Alberta 1961-81, Univ. Prof. 1980-85, Prof. Emer. 1985-; Pres.-elect Chemical Inst. of Canada 1983-84, Pres. 1984-85; Fellow, Chemical Inst. of Canada 1954, Royal Society of Canada 1955, Royal Soc. (London) 1967; Hon. D.Sc. (New Brunswick) 1967, (Laval) 1970, (Provence, France) 1972, (Ottawa) 1975, (Calgary) 1979, (Waterloo) 1980, (Newfoundland) 1981, (Quebec) 1982, (Queen's, Ont.) 1983, (McGill) 1984; Chemical Inst. of Canada Medal 1964, C. S. Hudson Award, American Chemical Soc. 1966, Officer Order of Canada 1968, Haworth Medal, Chemical Soc. of England 1978, Award of Achievement, Province of Alberta 1979, Diplôme d'Honneur, Groupe Français des Glucides, Lyons 1981, Killam Memorial Prize, The Canada Council 1981, Univ. of Alberta Research Prize, Sir Frederick Haultain Prize, Tishler Prize (Harvard Univ.) 1983. *Publications:* over 200 research papers mostly appearing in Canadian Journal of Chemistry. *Leisure interests:* golf, curling, fishing. *Address:* Department of Chemistry, University of Alberta, Edmonton, Alberta T6G 2G2 (Office); 7602 119 Street, Edmonton, Alberta T6G 1W3, Canada (Home).

LEMKE (VON SOLTENITZ), Helmut, DR. IUR.; German lawyer and politician; b. 29 Sept. 1907, Kiel; s. of Franz Lemke and Friederike Voigt; m. Annemarie Petersen 1933; two s., two d.; ed. Univs. of Kiel, Tübingen and Heidelberg; Naval officer in Second World War; Public Prosecutor; Mayor of Eckernförde, Schleswig, Lübeck; Barrister at Law; Minister of Educ., Schleswig-Holstein 1954-56, Minister of Interior 1955-63; Pres. German Fed. Council 1966-67 (as such for four months Acting Pres. Fed. Repub. of Germany); mem. State Diet 1955-83; mem. Bundesrat 1954-71; Minister-Pres. of Schleswig-Holstein 1963-71; Pres. of State Parl., Schleswig-Holstein 1971-83; Grand Cross of Fed. German Order of Merit and other decorations; Hon. Chair. CDU Schleswig-Holstein. *Leisure interests:* sailing, hunting. *Address:* Calvinweg 6, 2400 Lübeck, Schleswig-Holstein, Federal Republic of Germany. *Telephone:* 34929.

LEMMON, Jack; American actor; b. (as John Uhler Lemmon III) 8 Feb. 1925, Boston; s. of John Uhler Lemmon II and Mildred LaRue Noel; m. 1st Cynthia Boyd Stone 1950, one s.; m. 2nd Felicia Farr 1962, one d.; ed. Phillips Andover Acad., Harvard Univ.; actor, stage, radio and television 1948-; numerous Broadway appearances; Acad. Award 1956, 1974; Best Actor, Cannes Film Festival 1979, American Film Inst.'s Life Achievement Award 1988. *Films include:* It Should Happen to You 1953, Three for the Show 1953, Phffft 1954, My Sister Eileen 1955, Mister Roberts 1955, You Can't Run Away From It 1956, Fire Down Below 1957, Bell, Book and Candle 1958, It Happened to Jane 1958, Some Like it Hot 1959, The Apartment 1960, The Notorious Landlady 1962, Days of Wine and Roses 1962, Irma La Douce 1963, Under the Yum Yum Tree 1964, Good Neighbour Sam 1964, How to Murder Your Wife 1965, The Great Race 1965, The Fortune Cookie (British title Meet Whiplash Willie) 1966, Luv 1967, The Odd Couple 1968, The April Fools 1969, The Out-of-Towners 1969, Kotch (Dir. only) 1971, The War Between Men and Women 1972, Avanti 1972, Save The Tiger 1973, The Prisoner of Second Avenue 1974, The Front Page 1975, The Entertainer 1975, Alex and the Gypsy 1976, Airport 77 1977, The China Syndrome 1979, Tribute 1980, Buddy Buddy 1981, Missing 1982, Mass Appeal 1984, Macaroni 1986, Film Crisis 1986, That's Life 1986, Long Day's Journey Into Night 1986, Dad 1989. *Address:* 141 El Camino, Suite 201, Beverly Hills, Calif. 90212, U.S.A.

Le MOAL, Henri-Jean Alain, D.SC.; French university rector (retd.); b. 21 Dec. 1912, Plozévet, Finistère; s. of Jean Le Moal and Catherine Le Guellec; m. Suzanne Allée 1937; one d.; ed. Lycée La Tour d'Auvergne, Quimper and Univ. of Rennes; Mil. service 1938-44; Asst., Faculty of Science, Univ. of Rennes 1945-47, Chef de Travaux 1947-53, Asst. Prof. 1953-57, Prof. of Gen. Chem. 1957, Dean 1958-60, Rector, Acad. of Rennes 1960-70, Prof. of Gen. Chem. 1970-81, Prof. Emer.; mem. of Admin. Council, Asscn. des Universités partiellement ou entièrement de langue française (AUPELF) 1961-70, Admin. Council, Univ. de Rennes I 1977-83, Univ. de Haute-Bretagne (Rennes II) 1977-86, Admin. Council, Chancellerie des Universités de Bretagne 1986-; Pres. Rotary Club of Rennes 1972-73; Vice-Pres. Commission de Développement Economique de Bretagne 1965-74, Soc. Française d'Energie Nucléaire—Section Bretagne; Deputy Mayor of Rennes 1977-83; Hon. LL.D. (Exeter); Officier, Légion d'honneur, Commdr., Ordre des Palmes académiques, Commdr. de l'Ordre Nat. de la République de la Côte d'Ivoire, Commdr. de l'Ordre du Mérite

Sportif, Officier du Mérite pour la Recherche et l'Invention. *Publications:* (memoirs) Bulletin de la Société chimique de France; contributions to La Bretagne radicale, Le rotarien, Armor-Magazine, Ouest-France, Le Progrès, Saint-Germain-en-Laye. *Leisure interests:* scientific books and historical frescos. *Address:* 4 rue A. de Musset, 35700 Rennes, France. *Telephone:* 99-36-18-22.

LEMPER, Ute; German singer and actress; b. 4 July 1963, Munster; ed. Max-Reinhardt-Seminar, Vienna; leading role in Viennese production of Cats 1983; appeared in Peter Pan, Berlin, Cabaret, Dusseldorf and Paris (recipient of Molière Award 1987). Albums include: Ute Lemper Sings Kurt Weill 1988. *Address:* c/o Marek Liederberg-Konzertagentur, Hansallee 19, 6000 Frankfurt 1, Federal Republic of Germany.

LEMUS, Lieut.-Col. José María; Salvadorian army officer and politician; b. 1911; ed. School and Acad. of Military Staff, San Salvador, and Military Staff School, Camp Lee, U.S.A.; Under-Sec. of Defence 1948-49; Minister of the Interior 1949-55; Pres. of the Repub. of El Salvador 1956-60, deposed Oct. 1960; Gran Cordón Orden del Libertador (Venezuela), Gran Cruz Orden del Mérito Civil (Spain). *Publications:* many military and political works, including Pensamiento Social de Don Bosco, Simón Bolívar, Símbolos Patrios, etc. *Address:* Guatemala City, Guatemala.

LENAERT, Henri; Belgian banker; b. 3 Jan. 1915, Louvain; ed. Catholic Univ. of Louvain; Dept. Supervision of Banking, Banking Comm. 1942; Banking Auditor 1946; Man. Banque Centrale du Congo Belge et du Ruanda-Urundi 1951, Liquidator 1961; Sec.-Gen. Man., Gen. Admin. Dept., EIB 1962-86; lecturer, Catholic Univ. of Louvain 1955-. *Address:* Catholic University of Louvain, Place de L'Université 1, 1348 Louvain-La-Neuve, France.

LENÁRT, Jozef; Czechoslovak politician; b. 3 April 1923, Lipt. Porúbka; ed. Party Coll. Moscow; mem. Czechoslovak underground movement, Second World War; took part in Slovak rising 1944; mem. CP of Czechoslovakia 1943-; mem. Cen. Cttee. CP of Slovakia 1950-53, 1957-66; Leading Sec. Bratislava Regional Cttee. CP of Slovakia 1956-58; mem. Cen. Cttee. CP of Czechoslovakia 1958-; Sec. Cen. Cttee. Slovak CP 1958-62; Chair. Slovak Nat. Council 1962-63; Prime Minister of Czechoslovakia 1963-68; Alt. mem. Presidium of Cen. Cttee. of Czechoslovak CP 1968-69; mem. of Cen. Cttee. Secr. 1968-75; Deputy to Nat. Assembly 1960-69; Sec. Cen. Cttee. of CP of Czechoslovakia 1968-70, mem. Presidium of Cen. Cttee. 1970-; Deputy to House of the People, Fed. Assembly 1969-; Chair. Econ. Comm. Cen. Cttee. CP of Czechoslovakia 1969-70, 1988-; First Sec. and mem. Presidium and Secr. Cen. Cttee. CP of Slovakia 1970-; Deputy to Slovak Nat. Council 1971-; Chair. Cen. Cttee. Nat. Front of Slovak Socialist Repub. 1971-88; Deputy Chair. and mem. Presidium Cen. Cttee. Nat. Front of Č.S.S.R. 1971-; mem. Presidium, Fed. Assembly 1971-; Sec. for Econ. Devt. April 1988-; Order of Slovak Nat. Uprising 1945, Order of 25th February 1949, Commdr. of People's Militia in Slovakia 1970-, Decoration for Merit in Construction 1958, Order of the Nile 1965, Order of the Red Banner 1970, Order of Victorious February 1973, Order of the Repub. 1973, Hero of Socialist Labour 1983, Order of the October Revolution (U.S.S.R.) 1983, Klement Gottwald Order 1983. *Address:* Central Committee CP of Slovakia, Hlboká 2, Bratislava, Czechoslovakia.

LENDL, Ivan; Czechoslovak professional tennis player; b. 7 March 1960, Ostrava; winner, Italian Jr. Singles 1978, French Jr. Singles 1978, Wimbledon Jr. Singles 1978, Spanish Open Singles 1980, 1981, S. American Open Singles 1981, Canadian Open Singles 1980, 1981, WCT Tournament of Champion Singles 1982, WCT Masters Singles 1982, WCT Finals Singles 1982, Masters Champion 1984, French Open Champion 1984, 1986, U.S. Open Champion 1985, 1986, 1987, U.S. Clay Court Champion 1985, Italian Open Champion 1986, Australian Open Champion 1989; named World Champion (Int. Tennis Fed.) 1985, 1986. *Leisure interests:* golf, collecting art. *Address:* c/o U.S. Tennis Association, 51 East 42nd Street, New York, N.Y. 10017, U.S.A.

LENICA, Jan; Polish graphic artist and animator; b. 4 Jan. 1928, Poznań; m.; one c.; ed. Faculty of Arch. Warsaw Tech. Univ.; satirical drawings 1945-60, book illustration 1945-, poster 1950-, author of experimental animated cartoons 1957-, stage design 1963-; contributions to many journals including Szpilki; Int. Poster Biennale (1st Prize) 1966,Toulouse-Lautrec Prize, Paris, Max Ernst Prize for animated cartoon 1966, St. Marcus' Lion, Emil Cohl Prize and about 20 prizes at film festivals worldwide. *Major works:* book illustrations: Lokomotywa by J. Tuwim 1956, Population Explosion by Sauvy 1962; *posters:* Wages of Fear 1954, Phédre 1957, Il bidone 1957, Wozzeck 1964, Faust 1964, Othello 1968, Olympic Games 1969; *animated cartoons:* Once Upon a Time 1957, House (with W. Borowczyk) 1958, Monsieur Tête 1959, Labyrinth 1962, Rhinoceros 1963, A 1964, Adam 2 1968, Hell 1972, Ubu 1979. *Address:* ul. Nowy Świat 55, 00-042 Warsaw, Poland; 56 Av Emile Zola, 75015 Paris, France.

LENIHAN, Brian Joseph, B.A.; Irish politician; b. 17 Nov. 1930, Dundalk, Co. Louth; s. of Patrick J. Lenihan and Ann Scanlon; m. Ann Devine 1958; four s. one d.; ed. St. Mary's Coll., Athlone, Marist Brothers Secondary School, Athlone, Univ. Coll., Dublin, and King's Inns, Dublin; called to the Bar 1952, mem. Roscommon County Council and Roscommon Vocational Educ. Cttee. 1955-61; mem. Consultative Assembly of Council of Europe and of Legal, Political and Econ. Cttees. 1958-61; Parl. Sec. to Minister

for Lands 1961-64; Minister for Justice 1964-68, for Educ. 1968-69, for Transport and Power 1969-72, for Foreign Affairs 1972-73, 1979-81, March 1987-, for Fisheries (portfolio name changed to Fisheries and Forestry July 1978) 1977-79, for Agric. March-Dec. 1982; Deputy Prime Minister 1987-; mem. Seanad Éireann 1957-61, 1973-77, Dáil Éireann 1961-73, 1977-; Leader Fianna Fáil in Senate 1973-77; Deputy Leader, Fianna Fáil 1983-; Pres. Perm. Comm. European Org. for the Safety of Air Navigation (EUROCONTROL) 1969-70; mem. European Parl. 1973-77. *Address:* Department of Foreign Affairs, 80 St. Stephen's Green, Dublin 2 (Office); 24 Park View, Castleknock, Co. Dublin, Ireland (Home). *Telephone:* (01) 780822 (Office); Dublin 213453.

LENK, Hans Albert Paul, PH.D.; German professor of philosophy; b. 23 March 1935, Berlin; s. of Albert and Annemarie Lenk; m. Ulrike Reincke; two s. one d.; ed. Lauenburgische Gelehrtenschule, Ratzeburg, Freiburg and Kiel Univs., Tech. Univ. of Berlin; Asst. Prof. Tech. Univ. of Berlin 1962, Assoc. Prof. 1966, Prof. (Wissenschaftlicher Rat und Professor) 1969; Chair. and Prof. of Philosophy, Karlsruhe Univ. 1969-; Prof. Philosophy of Social Sciences and Theory of Planning, European Faculty of Land Use and Devt., Strasbourg 1983-; Dean, Coll. of Humanities and Social Sciences 1973-75; Visiting Prof. Univ. of Ill. 1973, Univ. of Mass. 1976, Univs. of São Paulo and Santa Maria, Brazil 1979, Belo Horizonte, Brazil 1980, Caracas 1981, Oslo 1983, Tokyo 1983, Madras 1986 and 3 Austrian univs. 1985; Green Honours Chair. Tex. Christian Univ., Fort Worth 1987; Pres. Int. Philosophic Soc. for Study of Sport 1980-81, Int. Olympic Union 1980-, European Forum, Baden 1980-; Vice-Pres. European Acad. of Sciences and Philosophy of Law 1986-; mem. American Acad. of Physical Educ., Nat. Olympic Cttee. for Germany, German UNESCO Comm.; Coach World Champion Eight Oar Crew 1966; Dr. h.c. (Deutsche Sporthochschule, Cologne) 1986; Hon. mem. Int. Olympic Acad.; four German, two European, one Olympic titles for rowing, Silver Leaf of Fed. Pres. 1959, 1960, Scientific Diem Plaque 1962, Sievert Award (Olympia International) 1973, Noel Baker Prize (UNESCO) 1978, Outstanding Academic Book Award 1979. *Leisure interests:* reading, running, writing, skiing, swimming. *Publications include:* Social Philosophy of Athletics 1979, Zur Sozialphilosophie der Technik 1982, Zwischen Wissenschaftstheorie und Sozial Wissenschaft 1985, Zur Kritik der Wissenschaftlichen Rationalität 1986, Zwischen Sozialpsychologie und Sozialphilosophie 1987, Kritik der Kleinen Vernunft. ä Einführung in die jokologische Philosophie 1987, more than 400 articles, some translated into 11 languages. *Address:* Universität (TH) Karlsruhe, Lehrstuhl für Philosophie, Kollegium am Schloss, Bau 11, D-7500 Karlsruhe 1 (Office); Neubrunnenschlag 15, D-7517, Waldbronn 1, Federal Republic of Germany (Home). *Telephone:* (07 21) 608-21 49 (Office); (072 43) 6 79 71 (Home).

LENK, Thomas; German sculptor and graphic artist; b. 15 June 1933, Berlin; s. of Franz and Anneliese (née Hoernecke) Lenk; m. Maria Bendig 1959; two d.; one-man shows in Wiesbaden 1958, Stuttgart 1962, 1965, 1968, 1970, 1974, 1977, 1981, Wuppertal 1963, Ulm 1964, 1970, Zürich 1966, 1969, Kassel 1966, New York, London, Milan 1967, Münster 1968, 1980, Darmstadt 1968, Detroit 1969, Bochum 1971, Essen 1971, 1973, Düsseldorf 1971, 1974, 1980, Saarbrücken 1971, 1982, Cologne 1976, Alexandria 1978, Tübingen 1980, Nürnberg, Munich 1983, Mannheim, Leverkusen, Linz 1985, Staatsgaleri, Stuttgart 1986; has participated in numerous group exhbns. in Germany, Switzerland, Italy, Belgium, Spain, Netherlands, Scandinavia, Yugoslavia, Poland, Canada, U.S.A. and Japan; exhibited at XXXV Venice Biennale 1970; Guest Prof., Heluwan Univ., Cairo 1978; Carnegie Int. Purchase Award 1967; Third Prize, Socha Piestanskych Parkov, Bratislava 1969, Prize of 2nd Norwegian Graphics Biennale 1974, Hon. Life mem., Art Gallery of Ont., Toronto 1988. *Address:* 7176 Tierberg, Gemeinde Braunsbach, Schloss Tierberg, Federal Republic of Germany. *Telephone:* (0 79 05) 362.

LENNEP, Jonkheer Emile van, DR.JUR.; Netherlands lawyer and economist; b. 20 Jan. 1915, Amsterdam; s. of Jonkheer Louis Henri van Lennep and Catharina Hillegonda Enschedé; m. Alexa Alison Labberton 1941; two s. two d.; ed. Amsterdam Univ.; Foreign Exchange Inst. 1941-45; Netherlands Bank 1945-48, 1950-51; Financial Counsellor to High Rep. of the Crown, Indonesia 1948-50; Head of Financial Dept. of Netherlands High Commr. in Indonesia 1949-50; Treas.-Gen. in Netherlands Ministry of Finance 1951-69; Sec.-Gen. OECD, Paris 1969-84; Special Amb. 1984-; Minister of State 1986; Chair. Monetary Cttee. EEC 1958-69; Del. to Devt. Assistance Cttee. OECD, Chair. Econ. Policy Cttee. (E.P.C.) OECD, Working Party No. 3, (E.P.C.), OECD 1961-69; mem. Advisory Council Rockwell Int., Ford Motor Co., Goldman, Sachs and Co., Nippon Telecommunications Co.; Commdr. Order of the Netherlands Lion, Order of Orange Nassau, K.St.J., Grand Cross (Star) of the Order of Merit of the Fed. Repub. of Germany, Grand Cross Order of the Falcon (Iceland), Order of the Flag (Yugoslavia), Order of the Lion (Finland), Order of the Sacred Treasure (Japan), Order of Don Henrique (Portugal), Ordre du Mérite (Luxembourg), Order of the Liberator (Venezuela), Grand Officier Légion d'honneur, Ordre de Léopold (Belgium), Ordre Léopold II (Belgium), Ordre de la Chêne (Luxembourg), Order of Merit (Italy). *Leisure interests:* music, sports. *Address:* Ruychrocklaan 444, 2597 EJ The Hague, The Netherlands. *Telephone:* 070-240916.

LENNINGS, Manfred, DR.ING.; German industrialist; b. 23 Feb. 1934, Oberhausen; s. of Wilhelm Lennings and Amanda Albert; m. Renate

Stelbrink 1961; one s. one d.; ed. Gymnasium Geislingen/Steige, Univ. of Munich and Bergakademie Clausthal; Chair. German Student Org. 1959-60; Asst. of Man. Bd., Gutehoffnungshütte Aktienverein 1964-67, Deputy mem. 1968, Chair. 1975-83; mem. Man. Bd., Deutsche Werft AG 1968-69; Chair. Man. Bd. Howaldtswerke-Deutsche Werft AG 1970-74; State Sec. for Armaments, Ministry of Defence 1983-; Dir. several cos.; Consultant Westdeutsche Landesbank 1984-. *Leisure interests:* modern art and literature, swimming, horse riding. *Address:* 4307 Kettwig, Schmachtenbergstrasse 142, 43 Essen 18, Federal Republic of Germany. *Telephone:* 45-45.

LENNKH, Georg, LL.D.; Austrian diplomatist; b. 8 Dec. 1939, Graz; s. of Friedrich and Elisabeth Lennkh; m. Annie Lechevalier 1966; one s. one d.; ed. Univ. of Graz, Johns Hopkins School of Advanced Informational Studies, Bologna and Univ. of Chapel Hill, N.C., U.S.A.; entered Fed. Ministry for Foreign Affairs 1965; served Tokyo 1968-72, Austrian Mission to UN, New York 1972-76, Dept. for Int. Orgs., Ministry of Foreign Affairs 1976-78; served Cabinet Office of Fed. Chancellor Kreisky, with responsibility for foreign relations 1978-82; Perm. Rep. to OECD 1982-. *Leisure interest:* skiing. *Address:* 3 rue Albéric Magnard, 75016 Paris, France.

LENNOX-BOYD, Simon Ronald Rupert (see Boyd of Merton, 2nd Viscount).

LENTON, Aylmer Ingram, PH.D.; British business executive; b. 19 May 1927, Leeds; s. of Albert and Olive (née Clegg) Lenton; m. Ursula Kathleen King 1951; one s. two d.; ed. Leeds Grammar School, Magdalen Coll., Oxford, and Univ. of Leeds; Devt. Dir. Richard Haworth and Co. Ltd. 1951-56; various tech. and managerial posts, British Nylon Spinners 1956-64; Man. Dir. South African Nylon Spinners (Cape Town) 1964-66; Dir. ICI Fibres 1966-67; with Bowater Corpn. Ltd. 1976-87, Man. Dir. 1981-87, Chair. 1984-87; Chair. John Heathcoat and Co. (Holdings) Ltd. 1984- (Man. Dir. 1967-75). *Leisure interests:* fencing, golf, walking.

LENZ, Siegfried; German writer; b. 17 March 1926; ed. High School, Samter, and Univ. of Hamburg; Cultural Ed. Die Welt 1949-51; freelance writer 1952-; Gerhart Hauptmann Prize 1961, Bremer Literaturpreis 1962, Kulturpreis, Goslar 1978 and numerous other prizes. *Publications* include novels: Es waren Habichte in der Luft 1951, Duell mit dem Schatten 1953, Der Mann im Strom 1957, 1958, Brot und Spiele 1959, Stadtgespräche 1963, Deutschstunde 1968, Das Vorbild 1973, Heimatmuseum 1978, Der Verlust 1981, Ein Kriegsende 1984; stories: So zärtlich war Suleyken 1955, Jäger des Spotts 1958, Das Feuerschiff 1960, Der Spielverderber 1965, Einstein überquert die Elbe bei Hamburg 1975; plays: Zeit der Schuldlosen 1961, Das Gesicht 1963, Haussuchung (radio plays) 1967. *Address:* Preusserstrasse 4, 2000 Hamburg 52, Federal Republic of Germany. *Telephone:* 880-83-09.

LENZ, Widukind, DR. MED.; German professor of human genetics; b. 4 Feb. 1919, Eichenau; s. of Fritz Lenz and Emmy Weitz; m. Almuth Thomsen von Krohn 1952; one s. one d.; Dir. Inst. of Human Genetics Hamburg Univ. 1962-65, Münster Univ. 1965-85; Dr. h.c.rer.nat. Tübingen Univ.; Otto-Heubner Medal 1964. *Publications:* Medizinische Genetik 1961, Humangenetik in Psychologie und Psychiatrie 1978. *Leisure interests:* art and philosophy. *Address:* Besselweg 22, 44 Münster, Federal Republic of Germany. *Telephone:* (0251) 861641.

LEÓN PORTILLA, Miguel, PH.D.; Mexican anthropologist and historian; b. 22 Feb. 1926, Mexico City; s. of Miguel León Ortiz and Luisa Portilla Nájera; m. Ascensión Hernández Triviño 1965; one d.; ed. Loyola Univ. of Los Angeles and Nat. Univ. of Mexico; Sec.-Gen. Inter-American Indian Inst. 1955-59, Asst. Dir. 1959-60, Dir. 1960-66; Asst. Dir. Seminar for Náhuatl Culture, Nat. Univ. of Mexico 1956-; Dir. América Indígena 1960-; Dir. Inst. of Historical Research, Nat. Univ. of Mexico 1963-78; Adviser, Int. Inst. of Different Civilisations 1960-; Perm. Rep. of Mexico to UNESCO, Paris 1987-; mem. Bd. Govs. Nat. Univ. Mexico 1976-; mem. American Anthropological Assen. 1960-, Mexican Acad. of the Language 1962-, Corresp. to Royal Spanish Acad. 1962-; mem. Société des Américanistes de Paris 1966-, Mexican Acad. of History 1969-; Corresp. mem. Royal Spanish Acad. of History 1969-; Guggenheim Fellow 1969; mem. Nat. Coll. of Mexico 1971-; American Anthropological Assen. Fifth Distinguished Lecturer 1974; Hon. Ph.D. (Southern Methodist Univ., Dallas, Tex.) 1980, (Univ. of Tel Aviv) 1987; Commendatore Repub. Italiana 1977, Serra Award 1978, Nat. Prize in the Social Sciences (Mexico) 1981, Manuel Gamio Anthropological Award 1983. *Publications:* La Filosofía Náhuatl 1956, Visión des los Vencidos 1959, Los Antiguos Mexicanos 1961, The Broken Spears, Aztec Account of the Conquest of Mexico 1962, Rückkehr der Götter 1962, Aztec Thought and Culture 1963, Literaturas Precolombinas de México 1964, Imagen del México Antiguo 1964, Le Crépuscule des Aztèques 1965, Trece Poetas del Mundo Azteca 1967, Pre-Columbian Literatures of Mexico 1968, Tiempo y Realidad en el Pensamiento Maya 1968, Testimonios Sudcalifornianos 1970, De Teotihuacan a los Aztecas 1971, The Norteño Variety of Mexican Culture 1972, The Voyages of Francisco de Ortega to California 1632-1636 1972, Time and Reality in the Thought of the Maya 1973, Historia Natural y Crónica de la Antigua California 1973, Il Rovescio della Conquista, Testimonianze Asteche, Maya e Inca 1974, Aztecs and Navajos 1975, Endangered Cultures: The Indian in Latin America 1975, Indian Place Names of Baja California 1977,

L'Envers de la conquête 1977, Los Manifestos en Náhuatl de Emiliano Zapata 1978, Toltecayotl, Aspectos de la Cultura Náhuatl 1980, Mesoamerican Spirituality 1980, Middle America 1981, Literaturas de Anahuac y del Imcario 1982, Mesoamerica before 1519 1984, Codex Fejérváry-Mayer, a Book of the Merchants, 1985, La Pensée Aztèque 1985, Libro de los Coloquios 1986, Das Alte Mexiko: Religion 1986, Huehuehtlahtolli, Testimonies of the Ancient Word 1988. *Leisure interests:* scouting and gardening. *Address:* Calle de Alberto Zamora 103, Coyoacán, México 21, D.F., Mexico; 42 Charles Floquet, 75007 Paris, France. *Telephone:* 548-15-10.

LEONARD, Rt. Rev. and Rt. Hon. Graham Douglas, P.C., M.A., D.D.; British ecclesiastic; b. 8 May 1921, Greenwich; s. of the late Rev. Douglas Leonard; m. Vivien Priscilla Swann 1943; two s.; ed. Monkton Combe School, Balliol Coll., Oxford, Westcott House, Cambridge; Capt. Oxon. and Bucks. Light Infantry 1941-45, Army Operational Research Group 1944-45; ordained Deacon 1947, Priest 1948; Curacies 1948-52; Vicar of Ardleigh 1952-55; Dir. Religious Educ., Diocese of St. Albans, Canon, St. Albans Cathedral 1955-58; Gen. Sec. Nat. Soc. and Gen. Sec. Church of England Schools Council 1958-62; Archdeacon of Hampstead, Rector of St. Andrew Undershaft and St. Mary Axe 1962-64; Bishop of Willesden 1964-73, of Truro 1973-81, of London 1981-; mem. Anglican/Orthodox Joint Doctrinal Comm. 1974-81; Chair. Church of England Bd. for Social Responsibility 1976-83, Churches Main Cttee. 1981-, BBC and IBA Cen. Religious Advisory Cttee. 1984-, Bd. of Educ. 1983-88, Polytechnics and Colls. Funding Council 1989-; Dean of H.M. Chapels Royal 1981-, Prelate of Order of British Empire 1981-, Prelate Imperial Soc. of Kts. Bachelor 1986-; Hon. D.D. (Episcopal Theological Seminary, Kentucky) 1974; Hon. D.Cn.L., Nashotah House 1983; Hon. S.T.D. (Siena Coll.) 1984; Hon. Bencher, Middle Temple 1981; Episcopal Canon of Jerusalem 1982. *Publications:* The Gospel is for Everyone 1971, God Alive: Priorities in Pastoral Theology 1981, Firmly I Believe and Truly 1985, Life in Christ 1986, contribs. to several theological works. *Leisure interest:* reading. *Address:* London House, 8 Barton Street, Westminster, London, SW1P 3NE, England. *Telephone:* 01-222 8661.

LEONARD, Hugh (John Keyes Byrne); Irish playwright; b. 9 Nov. 1926, Dublin; m. Paule Jacquet 1955; one d.; ed. Presentation Coll., Dún Laoghaire; worked as Civil Servant 1945-49; Script Ed. Granada TV, England 1961-63; Literary Ed., Abbey Theatre, Dublin1976-77; Programme Dir., Dublin Theatre Festival 1978-; stage plays include The Big Birthday 1957, A Leap in the Dark 1957, Madigan's Lock 1958, A Walk on the Water 1960, The Passion of Peter Ginty 1961, Stephen D 1962, The Poker Session 1963, Dublin 1 1963, The Saints Go Cycling In 1965, Mick and Mick 1966, The Quick and the Dead 1967, The Au Pair Man 1968, The Barracks 1969, The Patrick Pearse Motel 1971, Da 1973, Thieves 1973, Summer 1974, Times of Wolves and Tigers 1974, Irishmen 1975, Time Was 1976, A Life 1977, Moving Days 1981, The Mask of Moriarty 1984; writing for television includes Silent Song 1967, Nicholas Nickleby 1977, London Belongs to Me 1977, The Last Campaign 1978, The Ring and the Rose 1978, Strumpet City 1979, The Little World of Don Camillo 1980, Kill 1982, Good Behaviour 1982, O'Neill 1983, Beyond the Pale 1984, The Irish RM 1985, A Life 1986, Troubles 1987, Parnell 1988; films: Herself Surprised 1977, Da 1984, Widows' Peak 1984, Troubles 1984; Hon. D.H.L. (R.I.); Hon. D.Litt. (Trinity Coll., Dublin); Writers' Guild Award 1966, Tony Award, Critics Circle Award, Drama Desk Award, Outer Critics Award 1978. *Publications:* Home Before Night (autobiog.) 1979, Out After Dark 1988. *Leisure interests:* river cruising, conversation, travel, gastronomy, vintage movies. *Address:* 6 Rossaun, Pilot View, Dalkey, Co. Dublin, Ireland. *Telephone:* Dublin 809590.

LEONARD, Nelson Jordan, B.S., D.SC., PH.D.; American professor of chemistry; b. 1 Sept. 1916, Newark, N.J.; s. of Harvey Nelson Leonard and Olga Pauline Jordan; m. Louise Cornelie Vermey 1947; three s. one d.; ed. Lehigh, Oxford and Columbia Univs.; Research Asst., Univ. of Ill. 1942-43, Instructor 1943-44, Assoc. 1944-45, 1946-47, Asst. Prof. 1947-49, Assoc. Prof. 1949-52, Prof. of Chem. 1952-, Head of Div. of Organic Chem. 1954-63, and Prof. of Biochem. 1973-86; mem. Center for Advanced Study, Univ. of Ill. 1968-86, Reynold C. Fuson Prof. of Chem. 1981-86, R.C. Fuson Prof., Emer. 1986-; Fogarty Scholar-in-Residence, Nat. Inst. of Health, Bethesda 1989-90; Scientific Consultant and Special Investigator, Field Intelligence Agency Technical, U.S. Army and U.S. Dept. of Commerce, European Theater 1945-46; Ed. Organic Syntheses 1951-58, mem. Advisory Bd. 1958-, Bd. of Dirs. 1969-, Vice-Pres. 1976-80, Pres. 1980-88; mem. Exec. Cttee. Journal of Organic Chemistry 1951-54, mem. Editorial Bd. 1957-61; mem. Editorial Bd. Journal of the American Chemical Society 1960-72; mem. Advisory Bd. Biochemistry 1973-78; Sec., Div. of Organic Chem. of American Chemical Soc. 1949-54, Chair. 1956; mem. Advisory Panel for Chem. of Nat. Science Foundation 1958-61, Program Cttee. in the Basic Physical Sciences of Alfred P. Sloan Foundation 1961-66, Study Section in Medicinal Chem. of Nat. Insts. of Health 1963-67, Educational Advisory Bd. of John Simon Guggenheim Memorial Foundation 1969-88, Cttee. of Selection 1977-88, Advisory Cttee., Searle Scholars Program, Chicago Community Trust 1982-85; Visiting Prof. Univ. of Calif. at Los Angeles 1960; mem. N.A.S. 1955-; titular mem. Organic Chem. Div., Int. Union of Pure and Applied Chem. 1981-85, co-opted mem. 1985-, Sec. 1988-90; Fellow, American Acad. of Arts and Sciences 1961-; Foreign mem. Polish Acad. of Sciences; Swiss American Foundation Lecturer 1953,

1970, Julius Stieglitz Memorial Lecturer of Chicago Section of American Chemical Soc. 1962, Backer Lecturer, Univ. of Groningen 1972 and other lectureships; Hon. Sc.D. (Lehigh, Ill., Adam Mickiewicz Univ., Poland); American Chemical Soc. Award for Creative Work in Synthetic Organic Chem. 1963, Synthetic Organic Chemical Mfrs. Asscn. Medal 1970, Edgar Fahs Smith Award and Memorial Lecturer of Philadelphia Section of American Chem. Soc. and Univ. of Pa. 1975, Roger Adams Award in Organic Chemistry, American Chem. Soc. 1981. *Publications:* Numerous research articles in scientific journals. *Leisure interests:* skiing, swimming. *Address:* Department of Chemistry, University of Illinois, 1209 West California Street, Urbana, Ill. 61801; 606 West Indiana Avenue, Urbana, Ill., U.S.A. (Home). *Telephone:* 217-333-0363 (Office); 217-344-6266 (Home).

LEONARD, Ray Charles ("Sugar Ray"); American boxer; b. 17 May 1956, Wilmington, N.C.; s. of Cicero Leonard and Getha Leonard; m. Juanita Wilkinson 1980; one s.; amateur boxer 1970-77; won 140 of 145 amateur fights; world amateur champion 1974, U.S. Amateur Athletic Union champion 1974, Pan-American Games gold medallist 1975, Olympic gold medallist 1976; guaranteed record purse of $25,000 for first professional fight Feb. 1977; won North American welterweight title from Pete Ranzany August 1979; won World Boxing Council version of world welterweight title from Wilfred Benitez Nov. 1979; retained title against Dave Green March 1980, lost it to Roberto Durán (q.v.), Montreal, June 1980, regained it from Durán, New Orleans, Nov. 1980; world junior middleweight title, World Boxing Asscn. (W.B.A.) June 1981; won W.B.A. world welterweight title from Tommy Hearns to become undisputed World Champion Sept. 1981; 33 professional fights, 32 wins; retd. from boxing Nov. 1982; returned to the ring April 1987; won World middleweight title; commentator for Home Box Office TV Co.; now student, Univ. of Business Admin. *Address:* Box Office, Time Building, Rockefeller Center, New York, N.Y. 10020, U.S.A.

LEONE, Giovanni; Italian professor and politician; b. 3 Nov. 1908, Naples; s. of Mauro and Maria (Gioffrida) Leone; m. Vittoria Michitto 1946; four s. (one deceased); ed. Univ. of Naples; Prof. of Law, Univ. of Naples; elected to Constituent Assembly 1946, to Chamber of Deputies 1948 and 1953; Vice-Pres., Chamber of Deputies 1948-49, Pres. 1955-63; Prime Minister June-Nov. 1963, June-Dec. 1968; made life Senator 1967; Pres. of Italian Repub. 1971-78; Christian Democrat. *Address:* c/o Senato, Piazza Madama, Rome, Italy.

LEONE, Sergio; Italian film director; b. 3 Jan. 1930, Rome; m. Carla Ranalli. *Films include:* Colossus of Rhodes 1960, A Fistful of Dollars 1967, For a Few Dollars More 1967, The Good, The Bad and The Ugly 1968, Once Upon a Time in the West 1969, Fistful of Dynamite 1972, Once Upon a Time in America 1984.
[*Died 30 April*].

LEONHARD, Kurt Albert Ernst; German author, translator and editor; b. 5 Feb. 1910, Berlin; s. of Paul Leonhard and Erna Leonhard; m. Ilse Bliedner 1943; two d.; ed. Reformrealgymnasium, Berlin-Karlshorst and Univ. of Berlin; bookseller, author, art critic and publisher's reader 1937-41; mil. service 1941-46; freelance author, translator and lecturer 1946-; publisher's reader, Esslingen 1950-59; Prof. h.c. 1976; Verdienstmedaille, Baden-Württemberg 1984; Hon. mem. Stuttgart Acad. 1985. *Publications:* Die heilige Fläche 1947, Augenschein und Inbegriff 1953, Gegenwelt (poems) 1956, Cézanne (monograph) 1966, Picasso, Graphik 1966, Dante Alighieri (monograph) 1970, Wort wider Wort (poems) 1974, Das zehnte Loch (poems) 1983, Gegenbilder (poetry and prose) 1986, Zirkelschlüsse 1988. *Leisure interests:* travel, art, nature. *Address:* Auchtweg 24, 7300 Esslingen, Federal Republic of Germany. *Telephone:* 0711-384688.

LEONHARDT, Rudolf Walter, DR.PHIL.; German journalist; b. 9 Feb. 1921, Altenburg; s. of Rudolf and Paula (née Zeiger) Leonhardt; m. Ulrike (née Zoerb) Leonhardt; two s. one d.; ed. Berlin, Leipzig, Bonn, Cambridge and London; Lecturer in German, Cambridge Univ. 1948-50; Foreign Corresp. Die Zeit, London 1953-55, Cultural Ed. Die Zeit, Hamburg 1957-73, Deputy Editor-in-Chief 1974-. *Publications:* The Structure of a Novel 1950, Notes on German Literature 1955, 77 x England 1957 (trans. into Spanish 1964), Der Sündenfall der deutschen Germanistik 1959, Leben ohne Literatur? 1961, x-mal Deutschland 1961 (trans. into English, Italian, Spanish 1964), Zeitnotizen 1963, Junge deutsche Dichter für Anfänger 1964, Reise in ein fernes Land (with Marion Gräfin Dönhoff and Theo Sommer) 1964 (trans. into Japanese 1965); Kästner für Erwachsene 1966, Wer wirft den ersten Stein? 1969, Sylt für Anfänger 1969, Haschisch-Report 1970, Drei Wochen und drei Tage—Japan-Tagebuch 1970, Deutschland 1972, Argumente Pro und Contra 1974, Das Weib, das ich geliebet hab—Heines Mädchen und Frauen 1975, Journalismus und Wahrheit 1976, Lieder aus dem Krieg 1979, Sylt 1870-1920 1980, Hamburg 1985. *Leisure interest:* people. *Address:* Leuchtturmweg 42A, 2000 Hamburg 56, Federal Republic of Germany.

LEONHART, William, PH.D.; American diplomatist; b. 1 Aug. 1919, Parkersburg, W. Va.; s. of Harry Kempton Leonhart and Rae Corinne Kahn; m. Florence Lydia Sloan 1944; two d.; ed. Univ. of West Virginia, Princeton Univ. and Imperial Defence Coll., London; in office of Co-ordinator for Inter-American Affairs 1943-44; entered U.S. Foreign Service and assigned to Buenos Aires 1944, in Belgrade 1946-49, in Rome 1949-50,

in French Indo-China 1950-52, in Tokyo 1952-55; mem. Policy Planning Staff of Dept. of State 1955-57, concurrently Alt. Dept. of State Rep. on Nat. Security Council Planning Bd. 1956-57; in London 1958; Deputy Chief of Mission, Tokyo, with personal rank of Minister 1959; U.S. Amb. to Tanganyika (later Tanzania) 1962-65; Deputy to Special Asst., then Special Asst. to the Pres., The White House, Washington 1966-68; Special Asst. to Pres.-Elect's Personal Rep. for Foreign Policy Matters 1968-69; Amb. to Yugoslavia 1969-71; Deputy Commdt. Nat. War Coll., Fort Leslie J. McNair 1971-75; Vice-Pres. Nat. Defense Univ. 1975-77; Dept. of State 1977-79; mem. Sr. Intelligence Review Panel 1979-; Pres. Daval Foundation 1980-. *Address:* Suite 720, 600 Watergate, Washington, D.C. 20037 (Office); 2618 30th Street, N.W., Washington, D.C. 20008, U.S.A. (Home). *Telephone:* (202) 965-2464 (Home).

LEONOV, Col. Aleksey Arkhipovich; Soviet cosmonaut; b. 30 May 1934, Listianka, Kamerovo Region; s. of Arkhip and Yevdokia Leonov; m. Svetlana Leonova; two d.; ed. Chuguevsky Air Force School for Pilots and Zhukovsky Air Force Engineering Academy; Pilot 1956-59; cosmonaut training 1960; took part in flight of space-ship Voskhod 2, and moved 5 metres into space outside space-ship; mem. CPSU 1957-; Pilot-Cosmonaut of U.S.S.R.; Deputy Commdr. Gagarin Cosmonauts Training Center 1971; mem. Exec. Asscn. of Space Explorers 1985-; first man to walk in space 1965; took part in joint flight Soyuz 19-Apollo 1975; Chair. Council of Founders of Novosti Press Agency 1969-; Hon. Dr. S.Cs. Eng.; Hero of the Soviet Union (twice), Hero of Bulgaria, Hero of Vietnam, Order of Lenin (twice). *Leisure interests:* Union of Artists, U.S.S.R., shooting movies. *Address:* Zvezdny Gorodok, Moscow, U.S.S.R. *Telephone:* 526 28 40.

LEONOV, Leonid Maksimovich; Soviet writer; b. 31 May 1899, Moscow; ed. Moscow Univ.; Deputy to Supreme Soviet 1970; Dir. of Pushkin Dom (Pushkin House-U.S.S.R. Acad. of Sciences, Inst. of Russian Literature) 1972; Sec. of Bd., U.S.S.R. Union of Writers; mem. Acad. of Sciences of U.S.S.R.; State Prize 1942, Lenin Prize 1957; Order of Lenin (four times), Hero of Socialist Labour, Hammer and Sickle Gold Medal, Order of Red Banner of Labour, Order of Patriotic War, Merited Worker of Arts of R.S.F.S.R. *Publications:* Barsuki 1924, The Thief 1927, Sotj 1930, Skutarevsky 1932, Road to the Ocean 1936, The Ordinary Man 1941, Lenushka 1943, The Fall of Velikoshumsk 1944, The Golden Car 1946, Sazancha 1959, Mr. McKinley's Flight 1961, Evgenia Ivanovna 1963, Plays 1964, Sot' 1968, The Russian Forest 1973, In the War Years and After 1974, Moscow Publicistics 1976. *Address:* Union of Soviet Writers, 52 Ulitsa Vorovskogo, Moscow, U.S.S.R.

LEONTIEF, Wassily; American (b. Russian) economist; b. 5 Aug. 1906, St. Petersburg (now Leningrad); s. of Wassily and Eugenia Leontief (née Bekker); m. Estelle Helena Marks 1932; one d.; ed. Univs. of Leningrad and Berlin; Asst. Kiel Econ. Research Inst. 1927-28, 1930; Econ. Adviser to Chinese Govt., Nanking 1929; Nat. Bureau of Econ. Research, N.Y. 1931; Lecturer in Econs., Harvard Univ. 1931, Asst. Prof. 1933-38, Assoc. Prof. 1939-45, Prof. 1946-75; Dir. Inst. for Econ. Analysis, N.Y. Univ. 1975-85, Univ. Prof. 1983-; Consultant Dept. of Labour 1941-47, Office of Strategic Services 1943-45, UN 1961-62, 1980-, Dept. of Commerce 1966-82; mem. American Philosophical Soc., American Acad. of Arts and Sciences, Int. Statistical Inst., American Econ. Asscn., U.S. N.A.S. and several foreign acads.; Nobel Prize for Econs. 1973; Légion d'honneur 1967, Gold Medal of Paris 1974, Order of the Rising Sun (2nd Class), Japan 1984, Commdr. Ordre des Arts et des Lettres 1985. *Publications:* Structure of American Economy 1919-1920 (2nd edn.) 1953, Studies in the Structure of the American Economy 1953, Input-Output Economics 1966, 1986, Essays in Economics Vol. I 1966, 1985, The Future of the World Economy 1977, Essays in Economics Vol. II 1977, 1985, Military Spending: Facts and Figures, Worldwide Implications and Future Outlook 1983 (with F. Duchin), The Future of Non-Fuel Minerals in the U.S. and the World Economy 1983 (J. Koo, S. Nasar and I. Sohn), Collected Essays 1966 1985, The Future Impact of Automation on Workers 1986. *Address:* Institute for Economic Analysis, New York University, 269 Mercer Street, New York, N.Y. 10003, U.S.A. *Telephone:* (212) 998-7484.

LÉONTIEFF, Alexandre, D. EN SC. ECON.; Polynesian politician; b. 21 Oct. 1948, Tahiti; adviser to M. Gaston Flosse, Deputy and Mayor of Pirae 1977-82; mem. of Territorial Ass. French Polynesia (RPR) 1977-; Deputy to French Nat. Ass. 1986-; Minister of Economy, of the Sea and Tourism 1986-87; Pres. Govt. of Polynesia Dec. 1987-. *Address:* Office of the President, Papeete, French Polynesia.

LEONTIEVA, Valentina Mikhailovna; Soviet actress and broadcaster; b. 1923; ed. Stanislavsky Drama Studios, Moscow; worked for Lunacharsky Theatre, Tambov 1948-54; on staff of U.S.S.R. Cen. TV Network 1954-; Asst. Dir. 1954-55, announcer 1955-; covers important State occasions and appears in many TV shows; U.S.S.R. State Prize 1975, People's Artist of U.S.S.R. 1982.

LEOPOLD, Luna Bergere, PH.D.; American geologist and engineer; b. 8 Oct. 1915, New Mexico; s. of Aldo Leopold and Estella Bergere; m. 1st Carolyn Clugston 1940; m. 2nd Barbara Beck Nelson 1973; one s. one d.; ed. Harvard Univ. and Univs. of California and Wisconsin; U.S. Army 1941-46; Head Meteorologist, Pineapple Research Inst. of Hawaii 1946-50;

Hydraulic Engineer, U.S. Geological Survey, Washington, D.C. 1950–66, Chief Hydrologist 1956–66, Sr. Research Hydrologist 1966–71; Prof. of Geology, Univ. of Calif. 1973–; mem. N.A.S.; Hon. D.Sc. (St. Andrews) 1981; Kirk Bryan Award, Geological Soc. of America, Cullum Geographical Medal, American Geographical Soc., Distinguished Service Award, U.S. Dept. of Interior, Veth Medal, Royal Netherlands Geographical Soc., Rockefeller Public Service Award, Warren Prize, N.A.S. *Publications:* The Flood Control Controversy (with Thomas Maddock, Jr.) 1954, Fluvial Processes in Geomorphology 1964, Water 1974, Water in Environmental Planning (with Thomas Dunne) 1978 and over 100 scientific papers on water, hydrology and rivers. *Address:* Department of Geology, University of California, Berkeley, Calif. 94720; 400 Vermont Avenue, Berkeley, Calif. 94707, U.S.A. (Home).

LÉOTARD, François Gérard Marie; French politician; b. 26 March 1942, Cannes; s. of André Léotard and Antoinette Tomasi; m. 2nd France Reynier; ed. Lycées Charlemagne and Henri IV, Paris, Faculté de Droit and Inst. d'Etudes Politiques, Paris, and Ecole Nationale d'Administration; Sec. of Chancellery, Ministry of Foreign Affairs 1968–71; Admin. Town Planning 1973–75; Sous-préfet 1974; Mayor of Fréjus 1977–; Deputy to Nat. Ass. (UDF-PR) 1978–86, 1988–; Conseiller-General, Var 1980–; Pres. Parti Républicain 1982–; Vice-Pres. Union pour la Démocratie Française (UDF) 1983–84; Minister of Culture and Communications 1986–88; Chevalier, Ordre nat. du Mérite. *Address:* c/o Parti Républicain, 3 rue de Constantine, 75007 Paris, France.

LE PEN, Jean-Marie, L. EN D.; French politician; b. 20 June 1928, La Trinité-sur-Mer, Morbihan; s. of Jean-Marie Le Pen and Anne-Marie Hervé; m. Pierrette Lalanne, 1960; one s. two d.; ed. Coll. des jésuites Saint-François-Xavier, Vannes, Lycée de Lorient, Univ. de Paris; Pres. Corpn. des étudiants en droit de Paris 1949–51; Sub-Lieut. 1st foreign bn. of paratroopers, Indochina 1954; Political Ed. Caravelle 1955, Nat. Del. for Union de défense de la jeunesse française, then Deputy 1st Sector, La Seine; mem. Groupe d'union et de fraternité at Nat. Ass., independent Deputy for the Seine 1958–62; Gen. Sec. Front nat. combattant 1956, of Tixier Vignacour Cttee. 1964–65; Dir. Soc. d'études et de relations publiques 1963–; Pres. Front nat. 1972–; mem. Nat. Ass. 1986–; Pres. groupe des droites européennes au Parlement européen 1984–; Presidential cand. 1988; Croix de la Valeur militaire. *Address:* 6 rue de Beaune, 75007 Paris (Office); 8 parc de Montretout, 92210 Saint-Cloud, France (Home).

LE PENSEC, Louis; French politician; b. 8 Jan. 1937, Mellac; s. of Jean Le Pensec and Marie-Anne Hervé; m. Colette Le Guilcher 1963; one s.; Personnel Officer, Société nationale d'étude et de construction de moteurs d'aviation 1963–66, Société anonyme de véhicules industriels et d'équipements mécaniques 1966–69; Teacher of Personnel Man., Legal Sciences Teaching and Research Unit, Univ. of Rennes 1970–73; Mayor of Mellac 1971–; Deputy (Finistère) to Nat. Assembly 1973–81, 1983–88; Councillor for Finistère 1976–81; mem. Steering Cttee., Parti Socialiste 1977, Exec. Bureau 1979; Vice-Pres. Council of European Communes 1980; Minister for the Sea 1981–83, of Overseas Depts. and Territories May 1988–; First Vice-Pres. for Europe, Council of European Communities 1983–88; Head ASEAN Mission for External Trade. *Leisure interests:* reading, tennis, the sea. *Address:* Kerviguennou, 29130 Mellac, France (Home). *Telephone:* (98) 96 15 60 (Home).

LE PICHON, Xavier; French geologist; b. 18 June 1937, Vietnam; s. of Jean Le Pichon and Helene Tyl; m.; six c.; Research Asst. Columbia Univ., New York 1963; Scientific Adviser, Centre Nat. pour l'Exploitation des Océans (CNEXO) 1968; Head, Dept. of Oceanography, Centre Océanologique de Bretagne, Brest 1969; Scientific Adviser to Pres. CNEXO, Paris 1973; Prof. Univ. P. & M. Curie, Paris 1978; Dir. Dept. of Geology, Ecole Normale Supérieure, Paris 1984; Prof. Collège de France (Chair. of Geodynamics) 1986–; mem. Acad. des Sciences; Maurice Ewing Medal, American Geophysical Union 1984. *Publications:* Plate Tectonics (with others) 1973, Expédition Famous, à 3000m sous l'Atlantique (with C. Riffaud) 1976, Kaiko, voyage aux extrémités de la mer 1986. *Address:* Ecole Normale Supérieure, Département de Géologie, 24 rue Lhomond, 75231 Paris Cedex 05, France. *Telephone:* 43.29.12.25 (Ext. 35.12.).

LE PORS, Anicet; French economist and politician; b. 28 April 1931, Paris; s. of François Le Pors and Gabrielle Goguennec; m. Claudine Carteret 1959; one s. two d.; ed. Collège Arago, Paris, Ecole de la Météorologie nat., Univ. of Paris, Centre d'étude des programmes économiques; Meteorological Eng., Marrakesh, Morocco 1953, Paris 1957–65; trade union official (CGT) 1955–77; Consultant, World Meteorological Org., Léopoldville, Congo (now Kinshasa, Zaire) 1960; Sec. Communist section of Met. Office 1962; Head of Dept., Ministry of Economy and Finance 1965–; Sec. Cttee. of Cen. Admin., Parti Communiste Français (PCF) 1976–77, Head of Nationalizations, Industrial Policy and Insts. Dept., then of Int. Dept., PCF 1978, mem. Cen. Cttee. 1979; Head of Interministerial Comm., Univ. of Paris XIII 1976–77, and Ecole supérieure des Sciences Economiques et Commerciales 1978; Senator (Hauts-de-Seine) 1977–81; Minister-Del. for the Civil Service and Admin. Reforms, attached to Prime Minister 1981–83; Sec. of State in charge of Public and Admin. Reform 1983–84; Sr. mem. Council of State 1985–; Councillor-Gen. from Hauts-de-Seine 1985. *Publications:* Les transferts Etats-industries en France et dans les pays occidentaux 1976, Les béquilles du capital 1977, Marianne à

l'encan 1980, Contradictions 1984, L'état efficace 1985. *Leisure interests:* swimming, sailing. *Address:* Conseil d'Etat, place du Palais-Royal, 75001 Paris (Office); 187 boulevard de la République, 92210 Saint-Cloud, France (Home).

Le PORTZ, Yves; French financial executive; b. 30 Aug. 1920, Hennebont; m. Bernadette Champetier de Ribes 1946; five c.; ed. Univ. de Paris à la Sorbonne, Ecole des Hautes Etudes Commerciales, and Ecole Libre des Sciences Politiques; attached to Gen. Inspectorate of Finances 1943, Dir. Adjoint du Cabinet, Président du Conseil 1948–49, Sous-Dir., Chef de Service, Ministry of Finance and Econ. Affairs 1951; Dir. du Cabinet, Sec. of State for Finance and Econ. Affairs 1951–52; Dir. du Cabinet, Minister for Posts, Telegraphs and Telephones 1952–55; Dir. du Cabinet, Minister for Reconstruction and Housing 1955–57; French Del. to Econ. and Social Council of UN 1957–58; Dir.-Gen. of Finance for Algeria 1958–62; Dir.-Gen. Bank for Devt. of Algeria 1959–62; Vice-Pres. and Vice-Chair. Bd. Dirs. European Investment Bank (EIB) 1962–70, Pres. and Chair. 1970–84, Hon. Pres. 1984–; Pres. Supervisory Cttee., Bourse (Stock Exchange) Aug. 1984–; Insp.-Gen. of Finances 1971–84; Commdr., Légion d'honneur 1978. *Address:* Commission des Opérations de Bourse, 39–43 Quai André-Citroën, 75739 Paris Cedex 15, France (Office). *Telephone:* 45-78-33-33.

LEPPANEN, Urpo Olavi, M.POL.SC.; Finnish politician; b. 10 Feb. 1944, Polvijärvi; s. of Reino Olavi Leppanen and Tyyne Elina Leppanen; m. Sinikka Hurskainen 1985; research worker on accident prevention 1966–70; Asst. Faculty of Political Science, Univ. of Helsinki 1967–68; Sec. Finnish Rural Party 1972–77, 1979–84; M.P. 1979–; Minister of Labour 1983–87; Chair. SMP Parl. Group 1987–88. *Address:* c/o Parliament House, 00102 Helsinki (Office); Lapinlahdenk 14A7, 00180 Helsinki, Finland (Home).

LEPPARD, Raymond John, C.B.E., M.A.; British conductor and composer; b. 11 Aug. 1927, London; s. of A. V. Leppard and B. M. Beck; ed. Trinity Coll., Cambridge; Fellow of Trinity Coll., Univ. Lecturer in Music 1958–68; Music Dir., BBC Philharmonic (fmrly. BBC Northern Symphony) Orchestra 1973–80; Prin. Guest Conductor, St. Louis Symphony Orchestra 1984–; Music Dir. Indianapolis Symphony Orchestra 1987–; has conducted New York Philharmonic, Chicago Symphony, Philadelphia and Pittsburgh Symphony Orchestras, and Royal Opera, Covent Garden, English Nat. Opera, Metropolitan Opera, New York, New York City Opera and San Francisco Opera; realizations of Monteverdi's L'Incoronazione di Poppea, Il Ritorno d'Ulisse and L'Orfeo, and Cavalli's L'Ormindo, L'Egisto, La Calisto and L'Orione. *Publication:* Authenticity in Music 1989. *Leisure interests:* friends, theatre, reading. *Address:* c/o Colbert Artists Management, 111 West 57th Street, New York, N.Y. 10019; Orion House, Route 128, West Cornwall, Conn. 06796, U.S.A. (Home). *Telephone:* (212) 757 0782 (Agents); (203) 672 6222.

LEPRETTE, Jacques; French diplomatist; b. 22 Jan. 1920; m. Carina Leprette; one s. two d.; ed. Univ. of Paris and Ecole Nationale d'Administration; Ministry of Foreign Affairs (European Div.) 1947–49, Counsellor, Council of Europe 1949–52; Head Political Div., French Mil. Govt., Berlin 1952–55; Counsellor, French Embassy, U.S.A. 1955–59; Ministry of Foreign Affairs (African Div.) 1959–61; Amb. to Mauritania 1961–64; Dir. Int. Liaison Service for Information 1964–65; Minister-Counsellor, Washington 1966–71; Dir. of UN and int. org. affairs at the Foreign Office 1971–74; Asst. Dir. of Political Affairs 1975–76; Amb. and Perm. Rep. to UN 1976–81; Amb. and Perm. Rep. to EEC 1982–85; Ambassadeur de France; Commandeur, Légion d'honneur, Croix de guerre, Bronze Star Medal. *Address:* 36 rue Miollis, 75015 Paris, France (Home). *Telephone:* (1) 45-66-77-47.

LEPRINCE-RINGUET, Louis; French scientist; b. 27 March 1901, Alès-Gard; s. of Félix Leprince-Ringuet and Renée Stourm; m. Jeanne Motte 1929; three s. four d.; ed. Lycée Louis-le-Grand, Ecole Polytechnique and Ecole Supérieure d'Electricité et des P.T.T.; worked as engineer and did research on cosmic rays and fundamental particles physics; Prof. at Ecole Polytechnique 1936–69; Dir. of Lab. at Ecole des Hautes Etudes Pratiques; mem. Atomic Energy Comm. 1951–71; Prof. of Nuclear Physics at Collège de France 1959–72; Pres. CERN Scientific Council 1964–66; Pres. Union Catholique des Scientifiques Français 1948–63; Pres., Soc. Française de Physique 1956; mem. Acad. des Sciences (Physics) 1949–, Acad. Pontificale des Sciences 1956–; Acad. Française 1966–; Pres. Jeunesses Musicales de France 1971–83, Vice-Pres. 1983–; Pres. Mouvement Européen (France) 1974–; Grand Officier, Légion d'honneur, Grand Croix, Ordre nat. du mérite, Commdr. des Palmes académiques. *Publications:* Rayons cosmiques, Les inventeurs célèbres, Les grandes découvertes du XXe siècle, Des atomes et des hommes, La science contemporaine, Science et bonheur des hommes, L'aventure de l'électricité, Le grand merdier ou l'espoir pour demain, La Potion magique, les pieds dans le plat. *Leisure interests:* painting, tennis, skiing. *Address:* 86 rue de Grenelle, 75007 Paris, France. *Telephone:* (1) 43.54.04.45.

Le QUESNE, Sir (Charles) Martin, K.C.M.G.; British diplomatist (retd.); b. 10 June 1917, London; s. of the late C. T. Le Quesne, Q.C. and Eileen Pearce Gould; brother of Sir (John) Godfray Le Quesne (q.v.); m. Deirdre Noel Fisher 1948; three s.; ed. Shrewsbury, Exeter Coll., Oxford; served in Royal Artillery 1940–45; joined Foreign Service 1946; Second Sec., Baghdad 1947–48; First Sec. Foreign Office 1948–51; with Political Residency, Bahrain 1951–54; at British Embassy, Rome 1955–58; Foreign Office 1958–60; Chargé d'Affaires, Repub. of Mali 1960, Amb. 1961–64; Foreign Office 1964–68; Amb. to Algeria 1968–71; Deputy Under-Sec. of State, FCO 1971–74; High Commr. in Nigeria 1974–76; Dir. Barclay's Unicorn Group, Chair. Barclaytrust Int. Ltd; mem. States of Jersey 1978– (Deputy for parish of St. Saviour's); Chair. Establishment Trust 1984–. *Leisure interests:* gardening, books. *Address:* Beau Desert, St. Saviour's, Jersey. *Telephone:* (0534) 22076.

LE QUESNE, Sir (John) Godfray, Kt., Q.C., M.A.; British lawyer; b. 1924, London; s. of the late C. T. Le Quesne; brother of Sir (Charles) Martin Le Quesne (q.v.); m. Susan Mary Gill 1963; two s. one d.; ed. Shrewsbury School, Exeter Coll., Oxford; Pres. Oxford Union 1943; called to Bar, Inner Temple 1947; Q.C. 1962; Deputy Chair. Lincolnshire (Parts of Kesteven) Quarter Sessions 1963–71; Judge, Courts of Appeal, Jersey and Guernsey 1964–; Recorder 1971–; Chair. Monopolies and Mergers Comm. 1975–87; Chair. Council, Regent's Park Coll., Oxford 1958–87; Master of the Bench, Inner Temple 1969, Treasurer 1989. *Leisure interests:* music, railways. *Address:* 1 Crown Office Row, Temple, London, E.C.4, England. *Telephone:* 01-353 9292.

LE QUESNE, Sir Martin (see Le Quesne, Sir Charles Martin).

LÉR, Leopold, ING., C.SC.; Czechoslovak politician; b. 23 Oct. 1928, Ostrava; ed. Commercial Coll., Prague; Ministry of Finance 1951–62, Deputy Minister 1962, First Deputy Minister 1963, Minister of Finance of Czech Socialist Repub. 1969–73, Fed. Minister 1973–86; participated in work of CMEA and in formation of Int. Bank for Econ. Co-operation; Deputy, Czech Nat. Council 1971–76; Cand. of the Cen. Cttee. of CP of Czechoslovakia 1976–86; Chair. of Govt. Cttee. for Issues of Planned Man. of the Nat. Economy 1976–86; Deputy, House of the People, Fed. Assembly 1976–86; Chair. Algerian Cttee. attached to Czechoslovak Soc. for Int. Relations 1981–86; Deputy Chair. Econ. Research Council of C.S.S.R. 1983–86; Distinction for Merits in Construction 1973, Order of Labour 1978. *Address:* c/o Ministry of Finance, Letenská ulice, Prague 1, Czechoslovakia.

LERAY, Jean, D. ÈS SC., F.R.S.; French mathematician; b. 7 Nov. 1906, Nantes; m. Marguerite Trumier 1932; two s. one d.; ed. Ecole Normale Supérieure; Prof. Faculty of Sciences, Nancy 1936–41, Paris 1941–47; Prof. of Differential and Functional Equations, Collège de France 1947–78; mem. Inst. de France; Foreign Assoc. N.A.S.; Foreign mem. U.S.S.R. Acad. of Sciences, Accad. Naz. dei Quaranta, Accad. Naz. dei Lincei and Acad. of Sciences of Belgium, Boston, Göttingen, Milan, Palermo, Poland and Turin; Commdr. Légion d'honneur; Prix Feltrinelli 1971, Wolf Prize 1979. *Publications:* papers on math. and mechanics. *Address:* 6 avenue Jean Racine, 92330 Sceaux, France. *Telephone:* (1) 46-61-0321.

LERCHE, Peter Fritz Franz, DR.JUR.; German professor of law; b. 12 Jan. 1928, Leitmeritz; s. of Dr. Fritz and Karoline (née Artmann) Lerche; m. Dr. Ilse Lerche (Peschek) 1955; two s.; ed. Univ. of Munich; Prof. Freie Universität Berlin 1960; Prof. of Public Law, Univ. of Munich 1965; mem. Bavarian Acad. of Sciences; mem. Council of Science; First Pres. Union of German Lecturers in Public Law 1982; mem. numerous govt. comms. and attorney in governmental lawsuits, etc.; Bavarian Order of Merit, Maximiliansorden. *Publications:* Ordentlicher Rechtsweg und Verwaltungsrechtsweg 1953, Übermass und Verfassungsrecht 1961, Werbung und Verfassung 1967, Rundfunkmonopol 1970, Verfassungsrechtliche Fragen zur Pressekonzentration 1971, Verfassungsrechtliche Aspekte der 'inneren Pressefreiheit' 1974, Kernkraft und rechtlicher Wandel 1981, Städte und Kabelkommunikation 1982. *Leisure interest:* study of the hippopotamus. *Address:* Junkerstrasse 13, 8035 Gauting, Federal Republic of Germany. *Telephone:* 089/850 20 88.

le RICHE, William Harding, M.D., F.R.C.P.(C.), F.A.C.P.; Canadian physician and professor; b. 21 March 1916, Dewetsdorp, S. Africa; s. of Josef Daniel le Riche and Georgina Henrietta Guest le Riche (née Harding); m. Margaret Cardross Grant 1943; two s. three d.; ed. Univ. of Witwatersrand and Harvard Univ.; Intern. Zulu McCord Hosp., Durban, S. Africa 1944; Union Health Dept., Health Centre Service (Pholela, Natal and Knysna) 1945–49; Epidemiologist, Union Health Dept. 1950–52; Consultant, Dept. of Nat. Health and Welfare, Ottawa, 1952–54; Research Medical Officer, Physicians Services Inc., Toronto 1954–57; Staff, School of Hygiene, Univ. of Toronto 1957, Prof. of Public Health 1959, Prof. and Head of Dept. of Epidemiology and Biometrics 1962–75, Prof. of Epidemiology, Prof. Emer. 1982. *Publications:* Physique and Nutrition 1940, The Complete Family Book of Nutrition and Meal Planning 1976; co-author: The Control of Infections in Hospitals 1966, People Look at Doctors 1971, Epidemiology as Medical Ecology 1971, A Chemical Feast 1982. *Leisure interests:* writing books, photography, research, public speaking. *Address:* McMurrich Building, 12 Queen's Park Crescent West, Toronto, Ontario, M5S 1A8 (Office); 30 Golfdale Road, Toronto, Ont. M4N 2B6, Canada (Home). *Telephone:* 978-5664 (Office); 489-2298 (Home).

LE RIVEREND, Julio; Cuban historian; b. 1916, La Coruna; ed. Colegio de Mexico; fmr. adviser Banco Nacional; Deputy Minister of Educ. and Amb. of Cuba to UNESCO 1973–76; Vice-Pres. Acad. of Sciences; now Dir. Biblioteca Nacional de La Habana. *Publications:* works on Cuban economic history and the sugar cane industry. *Address:* Biblioteca Nacional de La Habana, Apdo Oficial No. 3, Plaza de la Revolución José Martí, Havana, Cuba.

LERNER, Max, A.B., A.M., PH.D.; American writer, b. 20 Dec. 1902, Ivenitz, Russia; s. of Benjamin and Bessie (Podbereski) Lerner; m. 1st Anita Marburg 1928, 2nd Edna Albers 1941; three s. three d. (one d. deceased); ed. Yale and Washington (St. Louis) Univs., Robert Brookings Graduate School of Econs. and Govt.; Asst. Ed. Encyclopædia of the Social Sciences 1927, later Man. Ed.; mem. Social Science Faculty Sarah Lawrence Coll. Bronxville (N.Y.) 1932–36; Chair. Faculty Wellesley Summer Inst. 1933–35; Dir. Consumers' Div. Nat. Emergency Council 1934; lecturer Dept. of Govt. Harvard Univ. 1935–36; Ed. The Nation 1936–38; Prof. of Political Science Williams Coll. 1938–43; Contrib. Ed. New Republic 1940–45; Editorial Dir. PM New York 1943–48; Columnist New York Star 1948–49; radio commentator WOR 1944–47; Columnist New York Post 1949–; Prof. of American Civilization, Brandeis Univ. 1949–73; Ford Foundation Prof. American Civilization, School of Int. Studies, New Delhi, India 1959–60; Internationally-syndicated newspaper columnist 1959–; Ford Foundation Research and Study Grant, Paris 1963–64; Visiting Prof. of American Civilization, Univ. of Florida 1973–75, Pomona Coll. 1974–75, Graduate School of Human Behaviour, U.S. Int. Univ. (San Diego) 1974–; Prof. Southwest Univ. Law School (Los Angeles) 1978–79; Prof. Univ. of Notre Dame 1982–84. *Publications:* It Is Later Than You Think 1938, Ideas Are Weapons 1939, Ideas for the Ice Age 1941, The Mind and Faith of Justice Holmes 1943, Public Journal 1945, The World of the Great Powers 1947, Actions and Passions 1948, America as a Civilisation 1957 (revised edn. 1987), The Unfinished Country 1959, Essential Works of John Stuart Mill 1961, Education and a Radical Humanism 1962, The Age of Overkill 1962, Tocqueville's Democracy in America 1966, Tocqueville and American Civilization 1969, Values in Education 1976, Ted and the Kennedy Legend 1980. *Address:* 25 East End Avenue, New York, N.Y. 10028, U.S.A.

LE ROY LADURIE, Emmanuel, D. ÈS L.; French historian; b. 19 July 1929, Les Moutiers en Cinglais; s. of Jacques Le Roy Ladurie and Léontine Dauger; m. Madeleine Pupponi 1956; one s. one d.; taught Lycée de Montpellier 1955–57, C.N.R.S. 1957–60, Faculté de Montpellier 1960–63, the Sorbonne 1970–71, University of Paris VII 1971–73, Collège de France 1973–; Gen. Admin. Bibliothèque Nat. Oct. 1987–; Dir. d'études, Ecole pratique des hautes études 1965–; Dr. h.c. (Univ. of Geneva); Hon. D.Litt. (Leeds) 1982, Hon. L.H.D. (East Anglia) 1985, Hon. D.Litt. (Durham) 1987. *Publications:* Les paysans de Languedoc 1966, Histoire du climat depuis l'an mil 1967, Montaillou, village occitan de 1294 à 1324 1975, Le territoire de l'historien 1973, Le carnaval de Romans 1579–80 1979, L'argent, l'amour et la mort en pays d'oc 1980, Parmi les historiens 1983, The French Peasantry 1450–1680. *Leisure interests:* cycling, swimming. *Address:* 88 rue d'Alleray, 75015 Paris, France (Home). *Telephone:* 4842 01 27.

LESCH, George H.; American businessman; b. 10 Oct. 1909, Washburn, Illinois; s. of William Lesch and Cora Held; m. Esther Barrett 1935; two d.; ed. Monmouth Coll. and Univ. of Illinois; worked in Home Office Accounting, Colgate-Palmolive 1932–36, mem. of European Auditing Staff 1936–39, Office Man., Mexico 1939–48, Vice-Pres. and Asst. Gen. Man. 1948, Exec. Vice-Pres. and Gen. Man. 1948–55; Pres. and Gen. Man. Mexican Co. (subsidiary of Colgate-Palmolive) 1955–56; Vice-Pres. Colgate-Palmolive Int., responsible for sales and advertising in U.K. and Europe 1956–57, Pres., Vice-Pres. and Dir. 1957–60; Pres., C.E.O., Colgate-Palmolive Co. 1960–61, Chair., Pres. 1961–70, Chair. 1970–75; mem. Bds. of Dirs. Amstar Corpn., F. W. Woolworth; Hon. LL.D. (Syracuse); Commdr., Order of Merit (Italy). *Address:* 2817 Casey Key Road, Nokomis, Fla. 34275, U.S.A.

LESKIEN, Hermann, DR.PHIL.; German university librarian; b. 23 Dec. 1939, Koenigsberg/Pr.; m. 1965; one s. one d.; ed. Univ. of Würzburg; library training, Bayerische Staatsbibliothek, Munich 1965–67; Head of Acquisition Dept. Univ. Library, Würzburg 1967–73; Head Univ. Library, Bamberg 1973–79, Munich 1979–. *Publications:* several articles in library journals. *Address:* Geschwister-Scholl-Platz 1, D-8000 Munich 22, Federal Republic of Germany. *Telephone:* (049)-89/2180 2420.

LESLIE, Donald S., Jr., B.A., M.B.A.; American business executive (retd.); b. 5 June 1925, Minn.; s. of Donald S. Leslie and Dorothy R. Leslie; m. Miriam Bennett 1953; two s. one d.; ed. Princeton Univ. and Harvard Business School; Weyerhaeuser 1949–51; Canadian Gulf Oil 1953–56; Hammermill Paper Co. 1956–87, Treasurer 1960–67, Dir. 1962–, Sr. Vice-Pres. 1969–70, Exec. Vice-Pres. 1970–83, Pres. 1983–85, Chair. of Bd. 1985–87; Dr. h.c. (Gannon). *Leisure interests:* tennis, skiing, biking, jogging. *Address:* Hammermill Paper Company, Box 10050, Erie, Pa. 16533, U.S.A. *Telephone:* (814) 456-8811.

LESLIE, Peter Evelyn, M.A., C.B.I.M., F.I.B.; British banker; b. 24 March 1931, Oxford; s. of Patrick Holt Leslie and Evelyn (née de Berry); m. Charlotte Chapman-Andrews 1975; two step-s. two step-d.; ed. Stowe School and New Coll. Oxford; joined Barclays Bank DCO 1955, served in Sudan, Algeria, Zaire, Kenya and the Bahamas; Gen. Man. Barclays Bank Ltd. 1973–76, Dir. 1979–; Sr. Gen. Man. Barclays Bank Int. 1980–83; Chief Gen. Man. Barclays Bank PLC 1985–87, Deputy Chair. 1987–; Chair. British Bankers' Assen. Exec. Cttee. 1978–79, mem. Export Guarantees Advisory Council 1978–81, Chair. 1987–; Chair. Overseas Devt. Inst. 1988–,

Commonwealth Devt. Corpn. July 1989–; mem. Inst. of Marketing; Gov. Stowe School 1983–. *Leisure interests:* natural history, historical research. *Address:* 54 Lombard Street, London, EC3P 3AH, England.

LESLIE, Robert Anthony; Belize diplomatist; b. 16 Aug. 1942; ed. Kalamazoo Coll., Mich., U.S.A. and Polytechnic Inst., London; staff reporter, then Ed. The Belize Times and contrib. to many other newspapers and magazines in Belize, U.K. and U.S.A.; Asst. Sec., Office of Personnel Services, Govt. of Belize 1970–71; Admin., Ministry of Lands 1971–73; Controller of Supplies, Ministry of Trade and Industry 1973–75; Asst. Sec., Foreign Affairs Unit 1975–77; Sec. of the Cabinet 1978–79; Perm. Sec. Ministry of Health, Housing, Co-operatives and Fisheries 1979–80; Perm. Sec. Ministry of Foreign Affairs 1980–81; apptd. Amb. Extraordinary and Plenipotentiary 1982; Minister to the U.S.A. and Chargé d'affaires at Embassy, Washington D.C. 1982–84; Perm. Rep. to UN 1984–86; a Rep. of Belize to 1981 and 1982 UN Gen. Ass.; mem. Belize del. to 1976, 1979 and 1983 Non-Aligned Summits. *Address:* c/o Ministry of Foreign Affairs, Belmopan, Belize.

LESOTHO, King of (see Moshoeshoe II).

LESSING, Doris May; British writer; b. 22 Oct. 1919, Kermanshah, Iran; d. of Captain Alfred Cooke Tayler and Emily Maude McVeagh; m. 1st F. A. C. Wisdom 1939–43, 2nd Gottfried Anton Nicolai Lessing 1944–49; two s. one d.; ed. Roman Catholic Convent, and Girls' High School, Salisbury, Southern Rhodesia; assoc. mem. American Acad. of Arts and Letters 1974; Nat. Inst. of Arts and Letters (U.S.A.) 1974; mem. Inst. for Cultural Research; Hon. Fellow MLA (U.S.A.); Somerset Maugham Award 1954; Prix Medici for Foreigners (France) 1976, The Austrian State Prize for European Literature 1981, The Shakespeare Prize (F.V.S. Foundation, Hamburg) 1982, W. H. Smith Award 1986. *Publications include:* The Grass is Singing 1950, Martha Quest 1952, A Proper Marriage 1954, Going Home 1957, The Habit of Loving 1958, Each His Own Wilderness (play) 1958, A Ripple from the Storm 1958, In Pursuit of the English (reportage) 1960, The Golden Notebook 1962, Play With a Tiger (play) 1962, A Man and Two Women 1963, Landlocked 1965, Particularly Cats 1967, The Four Gated City 1969, Briefing for a Descent into Hell 1971, The Story of a Non-Marrying Man (short stories) 1972, The Summer Before the Dark 1973, Collected Edn. African Stories (2 vols.) This Was the Old Chief's Country and The Sun Between Their Feet 1973, The Memoirs of a Survivor 1974, To Room Nineteen (collected stories, vol. 1), The Temptation of Jack Orkney (collected stories, vol. 2), Series: Canopus in Argos; Re: Colonised Planet Shikasta 1979, The Marriages Between Zones 3, 4 and 5 1980, The Sirian Experiments 1981, The Making of a Representative for Planet 8 1982, The Sentimental Agents in the Volyen Empire 1983, The Diary of a Good Neighbour, If the Old Could (published under the pseudonym Jane Somers, later published as The Diaries of Jane Somers by Doris Lessing) 1984, The Good Terrorist 1985, The Wind Blows Away our Words 1987, Prisons We Choose to Live Inside 1987, The Fifth Child 1988, The Libretto of the Making of the Representative for Planet 8 1988. *Address:* c/o Jonathan Clowes, 22 Prince Albert Road, London, NW1 7ST, England.

LESTER, Anthony Paul, Q.C., B.A., LL.M.; British lawyer; b. 3 July 1936, London; s. of Harry and Kate Lester; m. Catherine Elizabeth Debora Wassey 1971; one s. one d.; ed. City of London School, Trinity Coll., Cambridge, Harvard Law School; called to Bar, Lincoln's Inn 1963, Bencher 1985; Special Adviser to Home Sec. 1974–76; Q.C. 1975; Standing Adviser to Northern Ireland Standing Advisory Comm. on Human Rights 1975–77; Recorder, South-Eastern Circuit 1987; Chair. Interights 1983–; Hon. Visiting Prof., Univ. Coll. London 1983–; mem. Bd. of Overseers, Univ. of Pa. Law School 1977–, Council of Justice; mem. Standing Cttee. Court of Govs., L.S.E. 1980–; Gov. British Inst. of Human Rights; Chair. Bd. of Govs., James Allen's Girls' School 1987–; mem. Advisory Council, Policy Studies Inst. 1987–. *Publications:* Justice in the American South (Amnesty Int.) 1964, Race and Law (co-author) 1972 and articles on race relations, public affairs and international law. *Address:* 2 Hare Court, Temple, London, EC4Y 7BH, England. *Telephone:* 01-583 1770.

LESTER, Richard; American film director; b. 19 Jan. 1932, Philadelphia; s. of Elliott Lester and Ella Young; m. Deirdre V. Smith 1956; one s. one d.; ed. William Penn Charter School, Univ. of Pennsylvania; TV Dir., CBS 1952–54, ITV 1955–59; Composer 1954–57; Film Dir. 1959–; Acad. Award Nomination 1960; Grand Prix, Cannes Festival 1965; Best Dir. Rio de Janeiro Festival 1966; Gandhi Peace Prize, Berlin Festival 1969; Best Dir. Teheran Festival 1974. *Films directed:* The Running, Jumping and Standing Still Film 1959, It's Trad, Dad 1962, The Mouse on the Moon 1963, A Hard Day's Night 1963, The Knack 1965, Help! 1965, A Funny Thing Happened on the Way to the Forum 1966, How I Won the War 1967, Petulia 1969, The Bed Sitting Room 1969, The Three Musketeers 1973, Juggernaut 1974, The Four Musketeers 1974, Royal Flash 1975, Robin and Marian 1976, The Ritz 1976, Butch and Sundance: The Early Days 1979, Cuba 1979, Superman II 1980, Superman III 1983, Finders Keepers 1984, The Return of the Musketeers 1989. *Leisure interests:* tennis, music. *Address:* c/o Twickenham Film Studios, St. Margarets, Middlesex, England. *Telephone:* 01-892 4477.

LESZCZYCKI, Stanisław Marian, PH.D.; Polish geographer (retd.); b. 8 May 1907, Mielec; s. of Bronisław Leszczycki and Jadwiga Macharska; m.

Jadwiga Stella Sawicka 1950; one d. (deceased); ed. Jagiellonian Univ., Cracow; Asst. Jagiellonian Univ., Cracow 1928–39; imprisoned in Dachau and Sachsenhausen concentration camps during Second World War; Deputy to Seym (Parliament) 1945–52; Extraordinary Prof. of Anthropogeography, Jagiellonian Univ., Cracow 1945–48; Prof. of Econ. Geography, Warsaw Univ. 1948–70; Vice-Minister of Foreign Affairs 1946–50; Pres. Polish Geographical Soc. 1950–53; Pres. Nat. Geographical Cttee. 1956–68, 1972–77; Pres. Cttee. of Space Econ. and Regional Planning Polish Acad. of Sciences 1958–84; Dir. Geographical Inst., Polish Acad. of Sciences 1953–78, Prof. Emer. 1978; Corresp. mem. Polish Acad. of Sciences 1952–64, mem. 1964–; mem. Presidium of Polish Acad. of Sciences 1953–67, 1978–80; mem. Vice-Pres. Int. Geographical Union 1964–68, 1972–76, Pres. 1968–72; Lauréat d'Honneur 1988; Vice-Chair. State Council for Plan of Spatial Econ. of Poland 1972–83; mem. Polish Socialist Party 1945–48, Polish United Workers' Party 1948–; mem. and Chancellor World Acad. of Art and Science 1979–; Hon. mem. 20 European Geographical Socs.; Dr. h.c. (Prague) 1970, (Acad. Econ. Poznań) 1977, (Warsaw) 1987; 36 foreign and Polish decorations including Order of Banner of Labour 1st Class, Commdr. Cross with Star, Order Polonia Restituta, Hon. K.C.M.G., State Prize 2nd Class 1976, 1st Class 1986. *Publications:* numerous works on economic geography, spatial economy and regional planning. *Leisure interests:* photography, hiking, collecting old engravings and numismatics. *Address:* Karowa 18A m. 11, 00-324 Warsaw, Poland. *Telephone:* 260328.

LETSIE, Col. Joshua Sekhobe; Lesotho police officer and politician; b. 17 Nov. 1947, Makhalaneng, Maseru Dist.; s. of Chief Dinizulu Nako Letsie; ed. Maseru Secondary School; joined Police Mobile Unit (PMU) 1967, LPF Pvt. School 1977; PMU Adjutant to the Maj. Gen. 1977–82; promoted to Lieut.-Col. 1982; Chief Instructor LPF Training Wing 1983; Liaison Officer British Army Advisory and Training Team 1983–86; mem. Mil. Council of Lesotho; awarded Medal for Gallantry 1971, Medal for Meritorious Service 1985; Church Elder. *Leisure interests:* soccer, martial arts, music, reading, cinema. *Address:* The Military Council, Maseru, Lesotho, South Africa.

LETSIE, Col. Thaabe; Lesotho police officer and politician; b. 4 April 1940, Qeme, Ha Thaabe, Maseru Dist.; s. of Chief Sekhobe Letsie; ed. Maseru Secondary School, LPF High School; joined Lesotho Mounted Police (LMP) 1961, transferred to Police Mobile Unit (PMU) 1964, became Lt.-Col. 1978 and Air Wing Commdt.; Minister of Foreign Affairs March 1988–; mem. Mil. Council of Lesotho; mem. Lesotho Sports Council; sub-Deacon Anglican Church; awarded Medal for Meritorious Service 1976, Medal for Gallantry 1984. *Address:* The Military Council, Maseru, Lesotho, South Africa.

LEUSSINK, Hans, DR.ING., DIPL.ING.; German administrator; b. 2 Feb. 1912, Schüttorf/Hann; s. of Gerhard Leussink and Geertien Barkemeyer; m. Erika-Renate Hagemann 1941; ed. Technische Hochschule, Dresden and Technische Hochschule, Munich; Man. Soil Mechanics Inst., Technische Hochschule, Munich 1939–46; Construction eng. office 1946–54; Prof. and Dir. of Inst. for Soil Mechanics and Rock Mechanics, Univ. of Karlsruhe 1954–69, Rector, Technische Hochschule, Karlsruhe 1958–61; Pres. West German Conf. of Univ. Rectors, Bad Godesberg 1960–62; at Council of Europe, Strasbourg 1962–69; mem. German Scientific Council 1963–69, Chair. 1965–69; mem. Advisory Council for Science Policy of Fed. Govt. 1967–69; Dir. Krupp Foundation 1967–; Minister of Educ. and Science 1969–72; Dir. Volkswagen Foundation 1972–, Anglo-German Foundation 1973–, Friedrich Krupp GmbH 1974–; Sen. Max Planck Soc. 1972–; mem. J. McCloy Fund, N.Y. 1975–. *Leisure interests:* archaeology, gardening. *Address:* 7500 Karlsruhe 41, Strählerweg 45, Federal Republic of Germany. *Telephone:* 0721 42668.

LEUTWILER, Fritz, DR.ECON.SC.; Swiss banker; b. 30 July 1924, Ennetbaden; m. Andrée Cottier 1951; one s. one d.; ed. Univ. of Zürich; Sec. Asscn. for a Sound Currency 1948–52; with Swiss Nat. Bank 1952–84, Dir. First Dept. 1959–66, Deputy Gen. Man. Third Dept. 1966–68, Head Third Dept. 1968–74, Chair. Gov. Bd., Head First Dept. 1974–84; Chair. Bd. of Dirs. and Pres. Bank for Int. Settlements, Basle 1982–84; Adviser Robeco Group 1985–; Chair. BBC Brown Boveri AG 1985–; Mediator between South African Govt. and foreign banks 1985–86; Dr. h.c. (Berne) 1978, (Zurich) 1983, (Lausanne) 1984. *Address:* Weizenacher 4, 8126 Zumikon, Switzerland (Home).

LEVARD, Georges; French trade union official; b. 24 March 1912, Paris; m. Marguerite Pardini 1939; three s. two d.; ed. Conservatoire National des Arts et Métiers; mem. Nat. Cttee. for Productivity; mem. Econ. Council 1947–59, Vice-Pres. 1959–69; mem. Higher Council of the Plan; mem. several other councils; mem. Federal Bureau and Pres. of French and Democratic Confederation of Labour (C.F.T.C.) 1946–48, Asst. Sec.-Gen. 1948–53, Sec.-Gen. 1953–61, Pres. 1961–67; Pres. Section du travail et des relations professionnelles du Conseil Economique et Social 1974–79; mem. Bd. of Dirs. Banque Nationale de Paris; Conseiller d'Etat 1966–70; mem. Admin. Council Fondation de France 1969–, Ecole Nat. d'Administration 1971–76, Haut Conseil de la population 1978; Officier, Légion d'honneur. *Publications:* Chances et périls du syndicalisme chrétien, Eléments d'action syndicale, Rapport sur la réforme de l'entreprise. *Leisure interests:* country walks, history. *Address:* L'Ermitage, Turenne, 19500 Meyssac, France.

LEVELT, Willem J. M., PH.D.; Netherlands professor and administrator; b. 17 May 1938, Amsterdam; s. of Dr. W. H. Levelt and J. Levelt-Berger; m. Elisabeth C. M. Jacobs 1963; two s. one d.; ed. Leiden Univ.; Staff. mem. Inst. for Perception, Soesterberg 1962–65; Research Fellow Center for Cognitive Studies, Harvard Univ. 1965–66; Visiting Asst. Prof. Univ. of Illinois 1966–67; Prof. of Experimental Psychology, Groningen Univ. 1967–70, Nijmegen Univ. 1971–79, Hon. Prof. of Psycholinguistics 1980–; Leader Max-Planck Project Group for Psycholinguistics, Nijmegen 1976–79; Dir. Max-Planck-Inst. for Psycholinguistics, Nijmegen 1980–; Visiting Prof. Louvain Univ. 1967–70; mem. Inst. for Advanced Study, Princeton 1971–72; mem. Royal Netherlands Acad. of Sciences. *Publications:* On binocular rivalry 1968, Formal grammars in linguistics and psycholinguistics, 3 Vols. 1974, Speaking: From intention to articulation 1989. *Leisure interests:* playing the flute and traverso. *Address:* Max-Planck-Institute for Psycholinguistics, Wundtlaan 1, 6525 XD Nijmegen, The Netherlands. *Telephone:* (31) 80 521317.

LEVENE, Sir Peter Keith, K.B.E., B.A., F.R.S.A., C.B.I.M.; British civil servant; b. 8 Dec. 1941, Pinner, Middx.; s. of the late Maurice Levene and of Rose Levene; m. Wendy Ann Levene 1966; two s. one d.; ed. City of London School and Univ. of Manchester; joined United Scientific Holdings 1963, Man. Dir. 1968, Chair. 1982; Personal Adviser to Sec. of State for Defence 1984; Chief of Defence Procurement, Ministry of Defence 1985–; mem. S.E. Asia Trade Advisory Group 1979–83, Council, Defence Mfrs. Assen. 1982–85, Vice-Chair. 1983–84, Chair. 1984–85; Alderman, City of London 1984–; C.B.I.M. *Leisure interests:* skiing, travel, watching Association football. *Address:* Ministry of Defence, Main Building, Whitehall, London, SW1A 2HB, England. *Telephone:* 01-218 2928.

LEVENTAL, Valery Ya.; Soviet artist and stage designer for opera and ballet; b. 1942, Moscow; Honoured artist of R.S.F.S.R.; designs and sets for Cinderella, Romeo and Juliet, Anna Karenina, Khovanshchina, Prince Igor (Vilnius and Sofia), Tosca, Così fan tutte, Madam Butterfly, Otello, Till Eulenspiegel, Icarus, décor for experimental ballets of Maiya Plisetskaya (q.v.) and Vladimir V. Vasiliyev (q.v.); also for Love for Three Oranges (Berlin), War and Peace, Dead Souls (Bolshoi). *Theatrical designs:* Woe from Wit, The Bedbug, The Wedding (Gogol), The Marriage of Figaro, The Duenna, Macbeth (1979), The Seagull (1979), Boris Godunov.

LÉVÊQUE, Jean André Eugène; French aeronautical engineer; b. 30 April 1929, Béthune; s. of André and Elise (Forêt) Lévêque; m. Geneviève Cauwet 1953; two s.; ed. Ecole Polytechnique, Paris; with Air Navigation Directorate of Ministry of Public Works and Transport 1954–60, Eng. in Air Traffic Bureau 1954, Head of Airports Bureau 1956–60; Civil Aviation Tech. Adviser to Minister of Public Works and Transport 1960–63; Head of Div. in European Org. for the Safety of Air Navigation (EUROCONTROL), Brussels 1964–67; with Secretariat-General for Civil Aviation, Paris 1968–78, Tech. Adviser to Sec.-Gen. 1968–70, Acting Sec.-Gen., then Dir. of Air Navigation 1971–78; Dir.-Gen. EUROCONTROL 1978–83; Inspecteur Gen. for Civil Aviation; Chevalier, Légion d'honneur, Officier de l'Ordre national du Mérite, Médaille de l'Aéronautique. *Leisure interests:* skiing, table tennis. *Address:* 13 rue Gambetta, 92100 Boulogne, France (Home). *Telephone:* (1) 48-25-50-66.

LÉVÊQUE, Jean Maxime; French banker; b. 9 Sept. 1923, Paris; s. of Pierre Lévêque and Marthe Tisserand; m. Anne Charles-Laurent 1947; one s. two d.; ed. Lycée Buffon, Faculté de Droit, Paris, Ecole libre des sciences politiques and Ecole nat. d'admin.; Inspector of Finances 1950; external finance official 1950–56; temporary appt. IMF and IBRD 1956–58; Dir. European Investment Bank 1958–60; Adviser, Secr.-Gen. of Presidency of Repub. 1960–64; Sec.-Gen. Conseil Nat. du Credit 1960–64; Dir.-Gen. Credit Commercial de France 1964, Chief Exec. 1966, Vice-Pres. 1971, Pres. 1976, then Hon. Pres.; Pres. Union des Banques pour l'Equipement 1965, Vice-Pres. 1976–82; Pres. Dir.-Gen. Crédit Lyonnais 1986–; numerous other directorships and professional appts.; Officier, Légion d'honneur, Commdr. Ordre Nat. du Mérite; Croix de Guerre; Prix Renaissance 1983. *Publications:* Dénationalisations: mode d'emploi 1985, En première ligne 1986. *Address:* 16 rue Barbet-de-Jouy, 75007 Paris, France.

LEVER OF MANCHESTER, Baron (Life Peer), cr. 1979, of Cheetham in the City of Manchester; **Harold Lever**, P.C., LL.B.; British politician; b. 15 Jan. 1914, Manchester; s. of the late Bernard and Bertha Lever; m. Diane Zilkha 1962; three d. (and one d. by previous marriage); ed. Manchester Grammar School and Univ. of Manchester; M.P. 1945–79; Joint Parl. Under-Sec., Dept. of Econ. Affairs 1967; Financial Sec. to the Treasury 1967–69; Paymaster-Gen. 1969–70; Chair. Public Accounts Cttee. 1970–73; Opposition Front Bench Spokesman on European Affairs 1970–72, on Trade and Industry 1972–74; Chancellor of Duchy of Lancaster 1974–79; mem. Bd. Dirs. The Guardian 1979–, Manchester Evening News 1979–; mem. Cttee. of Inquiry into events leading to Argentine invasion of Falklands 1982; Chair. World Jewish Congress, Jerusalem 1981, Royal Acad. Fund-Raising Trust 1981–, London Interstate Bank Ltd. 1984–, Stormgard 1985–87; Joint Pres. European League for Econ. Co-operation 1982–; Chair. Authority Investments PLC 1984–86, Pres. 1986–; Hon. Fellow, Royal Acad. 1981; headed inquiry into problems of small firms; Labour. *Publication:* Debt and Danger: The World Financial Crisis (with Christopher Huhne) 1986. *Address:* House of Lords, London, S.W.1, England.

LEVERHULME, 3rd Viscount, cr. 1922, of the Western Isles; **Philip William Bryce Lever**, K.G., T.D.; British university chancellor; b. 1 July 1915; s. of 2nd Viscount and Marion Lever; m. Margaret Ann Moon 1937 (died 1973); three d.; ed. Eton Coll. and Trinity Coll., Cambridge; Lord Lieut. of City and County of Chester 1949–; Maj. Cheshire Yeomanry, now Hon. Col.; Pres. Council Liverpool Univ. 1957–63, Sr. Pro-Chancellor 1963–66, Chancellor 1980–; Advisory Dir. Unilever Ltd.; mem. Nat. Hunt Cttee. 1961 (Steward 1965–68); Deputy Sr. Steward Jockey Club 1970–73, Sr. Steward 1973–76; Council of King George's Jubilee Trust; Chair. Exec. Cttee. Animal Health Trust 1964; Hon. F.R.C.S. 1970, Hon. Assoc. Royal Coll. of Veterinary Surgeons 1975; Hon. LL.D. (Liverpool) 1967; Kt. of Order of St. John of Jerusalem. *Leisure interests:* shooting, hunting. *Address:* Badanloch, Kinbrace, Sutherland, Scotland; Thornton Manor, Thornton Hough, Wirral, Merseyside, L63 1JB; Flat 6, Kingston House East, Prince's Gate, Kensington, London, SW17 1LJ, England.

LÉVESQUE, Very Rev. Father Georges Henri, C.C., F.R.S.C.; Canadian ecclesiastic; b. 16 Feb. 1903, Roberval, Que.; s. of Georges Lévesque and Laura Richard; ed. Ecole des Frères Maristes (Roberval), Séminaire de Chicoutimi, Coll. des Dominicains (Ottawa) and Catholic Univ. of Lille; Dominican Novitiate 1923–24, ordained Priest 1928; in Europe 1930–33; Lecturer, Coll. des Dominicains d'Ottawa 1933–38, Univ. of Montreal 1935–38, Laval Univ. 1936–62; Founder and first Dean, Faculty of Social Sciences, Laval Univ. 1938–55; Founder-Pres. Quebec Co-operative Council 1939–44; Founder, Ed. Ensemble magazine 1939–44, Les Cahiers de la Faculté des Sciences Sociales 1941; Exec. on Advisory Council to Minister of Labour 1941–51; Predicator Generalis of his Order 1943; mem. Royal Comm. on the devt. of arts, sciences and letters in Canada 1949–51; Pres. Canadian Political Science Assen. 1951; Co-Dir. in India of the Int. Seminar of the World Univ. Service 1953; Rector of La Maison Montmorency 1955–63; Vice-Chair. Canada Council 1957–62; Fellow, Canadian Royal Soc. 1949; Founder, first Pres., Univ. Nat. du Rwanda 1963–71, Hon. Pres., Adviser 1971–; Dr. h.c. (Univs. of B.C., Manitoba, Antigonish, Toronto, W. Ont., St. Joseph, Saskatchewan, Ottawa, Laval, Sherbrooke, McGill, Montreal, Nat. Univ. of Rwanda, Univ. of Quebec at Chicoutimi); Molson Prize, Canada Council, Pearson Medal for Peace 1983, City of Quebec Medal 1984; Chevalier, Légion d'honneur, Companion of the Order of Canada, Commdr. de l'Ordre des Mille Collines, Ordre international de la Pleiade, Royal Bank Award 1982, Pearson Medal for Peace 1983, Institut des Affairs internationales Prize 1986, Fondation Edouard-Montpetit Medal 1986. *Publications include:* Capitalisme et Catholicisme 1936, Le pluralisme démocratique, condition de l'unité canadienne 1948, Culture et civilisation 1950, Humanisme et sciences sociales 1952, Le chevauchement des cultures 1955, Service social, Industrialisation et famille 1956, Youth and Culture To-day 1961, Le bilinguisme et les Universités 1961, Mon itinéraire sociologique 1974, La Première Décennie de la Faculté des Sciences Sociales à Laval 1982, Memoirs Vol. I 1983, Vol. II 1987. *Address:* 2715 Côte Ste.-Catherine, Montreal, Que. H3T 1B6, Canada.

LEVEY, Sir Michael (Vincent), Kt., L.V.O., F.B.A., F.R.S.L.; British art historian; b. 8 June 1927, London; s. of the late O. L. H. Levey and Gladys Mary Milestone; m. Brigid Brophy (q.v.) 1954; one d.; ed. Oratory School and Exeter Coll., Oxford; officer, British Army 1945–48; Asst. Keeper Nat. Gallery 1951–66, Deputy Keeper 1966–68, Keeper 1968–73, Deputy Dir. 1970–73, Dir. 1973–86; Slade Prof. of Art Cambridge Univ. and Fellow of King's Coll. Cambridge 1963–64; fmr. Chair. Nat. Dirs. Conf.; Hon. Fellow, Exeter Coll., Oxford; Foreign mem. Ateneo Veneto, Italy. *Publications:* Edited Nat. Gallery Catalogues: 18th Cent. Italian Schools 1956, The German School 1959, Painting in XVIIIth c. Venice 1959; From Giotto to Cézanne 1962, Later Italian Pictures in the Royal Collection 1964, Dürer 1964, A Room-to-room Guide to the National Gallery 1964, Rococo to Revolution 1966, Fifty Works of English and American Literature We Could do Without (with Brigid Brophy and Charles Osborne) 1967, Bronzino 1967, Early Renaissance 1967 (awarded Hawthornden Prize 1968), A History of Western Art 1968, Holbein's Christina of Denmark, Duchess of Milan 1968, 17th and 18th Cent. Italian Schools (Nat. Gallery Catalogue) 1971, Painting at Court 1971, The Life and Death of Mozart 1971, Art and Architecture in 18th Cent. France (co-author) 1972, High Renaissance 1975, The World of Ottoman Art 1976, The Case of Walter Pater 1978, Sir Thomas Lawrence (exhbn. catalogue) 1979, The Painter Depicted (Neurath Lecture) 1982, Tempting Fate (fiction) 1982, An Affair on the Appian Way (fiction) 1984, Giambattista Tiepolo 1986, The National Gallery Collection 1987 (Banister Fletcher Prize), Men At Work (fiction) 1989. *Address:* 185 Old Brompton Road, London, S.W.5, England.

LEVI, Arrigo, PH.D.; Italian journalist and political writer; b. 17 July 1926, Modena; s. of Enzo and Ida (Donati) Levi; m. Carmela Lenci 1952; one d.; ed. Univs. of Buenos Aires and Bologna; refugee in Argentina 1942–46; Negev Brigade, Israeli Army 1948–49; BBC European Services 1951–53; London Corresp. Gazzetta del Popolo and Corriere d'Informazione 1952–59; Moscow Corresp. Corriere della Sera 1960–62; news anchor man on Italian State Television 1966–68; special corresp. La Stampa 1969–73, Ed. in Chief 1973–78, special corresp. 1978–; columnist on int. affairs, The Times 1979–83; Leader Writer C. Della Sera 1988–; Premio Marconi, Premio Saint Vincent. *Publications:* Il potere in Russia 1965, Journey among the Economists 1972. *Address:* Piazza S. Carlo 206, 1-10121 Turin, Italy.

LEVI, Doro, PH.D.; Italian archaeologist; b. 1898, Trieste; s. of Eduardo and Eugenia Tivoli; m. Anna Cosadinou 1928; ed. Florence and Rome Univs.; mem. Italian Archaeological School, Athens 1921–23; conducted excavations in Crete 1924 and in Chiusi, Vetulonia, Volterra, Massa Marittima 1926–31; Insp. of Antiquities in Florence 1926, later Dir.; Organizer Italian Mission in Mesopotamia 1930, first expedition to Kakzu (Assyria) 1933; Lecturer Florence Univ. 1931; Prof. of Archaeology and History of Classical Art in Univ. of Cagliari 1935; Dir. of Art and Antiquities in Sardinia; Dir. Museums of Cagliari and Sassari 1935–38; mem. Inst. for Advanced Study, Princeton, N.J.; lectureships at Princeton and Harvard Univs. 1939–45; Guggenheim Fellow 1941–43; Dir. Italian Archaeological School at Athens 1947–77; conducted excavations at Phaistos, Gortyna, Crete, Iasos in Anatolia, etc.; mem. Accad. dei Lincei, Rome, Acad. of Athens, The New York Acad. of Sciences, Pontifical Archaeological Acad.; hon. mem. German Archaeological Inst.; hon. Vice-Pres. Greek Archaeological Soc.; Dr. h.c. (Athens). *Publications:* Arkades, Una Città Cretese all'alba della civiltà ellenica (Annuario Scuola It. di Atene X-XII), La necropoli etrusca del Lago dell' Accesa (in Monumenti Antichi Lincei XXXV) 1933, Corpus Vasorum Antiquorum: Florence I-II, Il Museo Civico di Chiusi 1935, Early Hellenic Pottery of Crete 1945, Antioch Mosaic Pavements 1947, L'ipogeo di S. Salvatore di Cabras in Sardegna 1949, L'arte romana 1950, L'archivio di cretule a Festòs, etc. (Annuario Scuola Atene XXXV-XXXVI 1957-58) and other papers in Annuario, Bollettino d'Arte, La Parola del Passato, The Recent Excavations at Phaistos 1964, Festòs e la civiltà minoica part I (4 vols.) 1976–77, part II (2 vols.) 1981, 1988. *Address:* 64 Veïkou Street, Athens, Greece. *Telephone:* 9220760.

LEVI, Edward Hirsch; American lawyer and university professor; b. 26 June 1911, Chicago; s. of Gerson B. and Elsa B. Hirsch; m. Kate Sulzberger 1946; three s.; ed. Univ. of Chicago and Yale; Asst. Prof. Univ. of Chicago Law School 1936–40, Prof. of Law 1945–75, Dean of Law Faculty 1950–62, Provost 1962–68, Pres. 1968–75, Pres. Emer. 1975–; Karl Llewellyn Distinguished Service Prof. in Jurisprudence (on leave) 1975–77; Glen A. Lloyd Distinguished Service Prof. in Law School and Coll. 1977–84, Prof. Emer. 1984–; Special Asst. to U.S. Attorney-Gen., Washington 1940–45; mem. Research Advisory Bd., Cttee. for Econ. Devt. 1951–54, Citizens' Comm. on Graduate Medical Educ. 1963–66; mem. White House Council on Domestic Affairs 1964, several comms. on internal affairs 1966–71, Council on Legal Educ. and Professional Responsibility, Nat. Comm. on Productivity and Work Quality 1970–74; Attorney-Gen. 1975–77; Trustee, Aspen Inst. for Humanistic Studies 1970–75, 1977–79, Council of Nat. Endowment for the Humanities 1974–75; mem. Bd. of Overseers Univ. of Pa. Law School 1978–80, Bd. of Trustees Nat. Humanities Center 1978– (Chair. 1979–83), Bd. of Trustees Aerospace Corpn. 1978–80, Bd. of The William Benton Foundation 1980–; Dir. MacArthur Foundation 1979–84, Foundation of Liberty 1979–, Inst. for Civil Justice 1979–81; lecturer, Salzburg Seminar in American Studies 1980, mem. Bd. 1986–; mem. Bd. of Govs., Univ. of Calif. Humanities Research Inst. 1988–; Fellow, American Acad. of Arts and Sciences, (Pres. 1986–89), American Philosophical Soc., American Bar Foundation; mem. Council of American Law Inst.; Hon. Trustee, Int. Inst. of Educ. *Publications:* Introduction to Legal Reasoning 1949, Four Talks on Legal Education 1952, Ed. Gilbert's Collier on Bankruptcy (with J. W. Moore) 1937, Elements of the Law (with R. S. Steffen) 1950, Points of View 1969, The Crisis in the Nature of Law 1969, The Place of Professional Education in the Life of the University 1971, The Collective Morality of a Maturing Society 1973. *Address:* The University of Chicago, 1116 East 59th Street, Harper Library, Chicago, Ill. 60637; 4950 Chicago Beach Drive, Chicago, Ill. 60615, U.S.A. (Home). *Telephone:* 312-702-8588.

LEVI-MONTALCINI, Rita; Italian research scientist; b. 22 April 1909, Turin; d. of Adamo Levi and Adele Montalcini; ed. Turin Univ. Medical School; engaged in neurological research in Turin and Brussels 1936–41, in a country-cottage in Piemonte 1941–43; in hiding in Florence during German occupation 1943–44; medical doctor working among war refugees in Florence 1944–45; resumed academic positions at Univ. of Turin 1945; worked in St. Louis, U.S.A. with Prof. Viktor Hamburger from 1947, Assoc. Prof. 1956, Prof. 1958–77; Dir. Inst. of Cell Biology of Italian Nat. Council of Research, Rome 1969–78, Guest Prof. 1979–; Nobel Prize for Medicine 1986 (with Stanley Cohen q.v.) for work on chemical growth factors which control growth and devt. in humans and animals. *Address:* Institute of Cell Biology, National Research Council of Italy, Piazzale Aldo Moro 7, 00185, Rome, Italy.

LEVI-SANDRI, Lionello, LL.D.; Italian politician and government official; b. 5 Oct. 1910, Milan; s. of Dario Levi and Carlotta Sandri; m. Bice Pederzini 1938; two s. two d.; fmr. Prof. of Labour Law, Univ. of Rome, fmr. official in Ministry of Labour and Transport; del. to numerous int. labour confs.; Pres. of Section, State Council 1964; mem. Comm. of the European Econ. Community, Brussels 1961–64, Vice-Pres. 1964–67, Vice-Pres. Combined Comm. of the European Communities 1967–70; Pres. State Council 1979–81, Pres. Emer. 1981–; Pres. Inst. "Corpo volontari della Libertà" 1983. *Publications:* I controlli dello Stato sulla produzione industriale 1938, Gli infortuni sul lavoro 1952, Linee di una teoria giuridica della previdenza sociale 1953, La tutela dell'igiene e della sicurezza del lavoro 1954, Lezioni di diritto del lavoro 1962, Codice delle leggi sul lavoro 1975, Istituzioni di legislazione sociale 1983, Il "Giallo" della Regia 1983. *Leisure*

interest: historical studies. *Address:* Largo dei Lombardi 21, 00186 Rome, Italy. *Telephone:* 687 8628.

LÉVI-STRAUSS, Claude; French anthropologist, university professor and writer; b. 28 Nov. 1908, Brussels, Belgium; s. of Raymond Lévi-Strauss and Emma Lévy; m. 1st Dina Dreyfus 1932; m. 2nd Rose Marie Ullmo 1946, one s.; m. 3rd Monique Roman 1954, one s.; ed. Lycée Janson de Sailly, Paris, and Univ. de Paris à la Sorbonne; Prof. Univ. of São Paulo, Brazil 1935–39; Visiting Prof. New School for Social Research, New York 1942–45; Cultural Counsellor, French Embassy to U.S.A. 1946–47; Assoc. Dir. Musée de l'Homme, Paris 1949–50; Dir. of Studies, Ecole Pratique des Hautes Etudes, Paris 1950–74; Prof. Collège de France 1959–82, Hon. Prof. 1983–; mem. Acad. Française; Foreign mem. Royal Acad. of the Netherlands, Norwegian Acad. of Sciences and Letters, American Acad. of Arts and Sciences, American Acad. and Inst. of Arts and Letters, British Acad.; Foreign Assoc. U.S. N.A.S.; Hon. mem. Royal Anthropological Inst., American Philosophical Soc., and London School of Oriental and African Studies; Dr. h.c. (Univ. of Brussels, Yale, Chicago, Columbia, Oxford, Stirling, Zaire, Mexico, Uppsala, Johns Hopkins, Quebec, Visva-Bharati Univ., India); Prix Paul Pelliot 1949; Huxley Memorial Medal 1965, Viking Fund Gold Medal 1966, Gold Medal Centre National de la Recherche Scientifique 1967; Erasmus Prize 1973; Grand Officier, Légion d'honneur, Commdr. Ordre Nat. du Mérite 1971. *Publications:* La vie familiale et sociale des indiens Nambikwara 1948, Les structures élémentaires de la parenté 1949, Tristes tropiques 1955, Anthropologie structurale 1958, Le totémisme aujourd'hui 1962, La pensée sauvage 1962, Le cru et le cuit 1964, Du miel aux cendres 1967, L'origine des manières de table 1968, L'homme nu 1971, Anthropologie structurale deux 1973, La voie des masques 1975, 1979, Le regard éloigné 1983, Paroles données 1984, La potière jalouse 1985, De Près et de Loin (with Didier Eribon) 1985. *Leisure interest:* country life. *Address:* Laboratoire d'Anthropologie Sociale, Collège de France, 52 rue du Cardinal Lemoine, 75005 Paris (Office); 2 rue des Marronniers, 75016 Paris, France (Home). *Telephone:* 46-33-24-50 (Office); 42-88-34-71 (Home).

LEVICK, William Russell, M.SC., F.A.A., F.R.S.; Australian medical scientist; b. 5 Dec. 1931, Sydney; s. of Russell L. S. and Elsie E. I. (Nance) Levick; m. Patricia J. Lathwell 1961; two s. one d.; ed. Univ. of Sydney; registered medical practitioner, N.S.W. 1957–; resident Medical Officer, Royal Price Alfred Hosp., Sydney 1957–58; Nat. Health and Medical Research Council Fellow, Univ. of Sydney 1959–62; C. J. Martin Travelling Fellow, Cambridge Univ. and Univ. of Calif. (Berkeley) 1963–64; Assoc. Research Physiologist, Univ. of Calif. (Berkeley) 1965–66; Sr. Lecturer in Physiology, Univ. of Sydney 1967; Professorial Fellow in Physiology, John Curtin School of Medical Research, Australian Nat. Univ., Canberra 1967–83, Prof. 1983–; Fellow, Optical Soc. of America 1982. *Publications:* articles on neurophysiology of visual system in int. scientific journals. *Leisure interest:* chess. *Address:* John Curtin School of Medical Research, Australian National University, G.P.O. Box 334, Canberra, A.C.T. 2601, Australia. *Telephone:* (61)-(62)-49-2525.

LEVIE, Dr. Simon Hijman; Dutch art historian; b. 17 Jan. 1925, Rheden; m. Mary Levie-Lion 1955; one s. two d.; ed. Univ. of Basel, Switzerland; worked as Keeper, Centraal Museum, Utrecht, and as Dir., Historical Museum, Amsterdam; now Dir. Gen. Rijksmuseum, Amsterdam; mem. Bd. Stichting Foundation Rembrandt Research Project. *Address:* Rijksmuseum, Hobbemastraat 21, 10712X Amsterdam; Chopinstraat 29, 1077GM Amsterdam, Netherlands (Home). *Telephone:* 020-73-21-21 (Office); 020-71-88-95 (Home).

LEVIN, Carl, J.D.; American politician; b. 28 June 1934, Detroit, Mich.; s. of Saul R. and Bess (née Levinson) Levin; m. Barbara Halpern 196.; three d.; ed. Central High School, Detroit, Swarthmore Coll., Pa., and Harvard Law School; Asst. Mich. Attorney Gen. and Gen. Counsel for Mich. Civil Rights Comm. 1964–67; Special Asst. Attorney Gen. and Chief Appellate Attorney for Defender's Office of Legal Aid and Defender Assoc. of Detroit 1968–69; elected to Detroit City Council 1969, re-elected as City Council Pres. 1973; U.S. Senator from Michigan 1979–. *Address:* 459 Russell Senate Office Building, Washington, D.C. 20510, U.S.A. *Telephone:* (202) 224-6221.

LEVIN, Harry (Tuchman), A.B.; American teacher and writer; b. 18 July 1912, Minneapolis, Minn.; s. of I. H. Levin and Beatrice Tuchman; m. Elena Zarudnaya 1939; one d.; ed. Univs. of Harvard and Paris; instructor in English, Harvard Univ. 1939–44; Assoc. Prof. 1944–48, Prof. 1948–55; Prof. of English and Comparative Literature 1955–60; Chair. Dept. of Comparative Literature 1946–51, 1953–54, 1960–61, 1963–69, 1972–73, 1977–78; Chair. Div. of Mod. Languages 1951–52, 1955–61; Irving Babbitt Prof. Comparative Literature 1960–83, Prof. Emer. 1983–; Visiting Prof. Univ. of Paris 1953, Salzburg Seminar in American Studies 1953, Univ. of Tokyo 1955, Univ. of Calif. (Berkeley) 1957, 1985, Princeton Univ. 1961, Ind. Univ. 1967, Cambridge Univ. 1967, Folger Shakespeare Inst. 1980, Univ. of Puerto Rico 1981, Chinese Univ. of Hong Kong 1982, Univ. of Ariz. 1984; Visiting Fellow All Souls, Oxford 1974; Chair. English Inst. 1957; Vice-Pres. Int. Comparative Literature Asscn. 1964–67; Pres. American Comparative Literature Asscn. 1965–68; Pres. Modern Humanities Research Asscn. 1976–77; George Eastman Visiting Prof., Oxford Univ. 1982–83; Fellow, Balliol Coll. 1982; Corresp. Fellow, British Acad. 1982; mem. American Inst. Arts and Letters 1960, American Acad. of Arts and

Sciences 1950-, American Philosophical Soc. 1961-, Royal Netherlands Acad. of Arts and Sciences; Hon. Litt., LL.D., L.H.D., Dr. h.c. (Univ. of Paris) 1974, Hon. M.A. (Oxford) 1982; Award of the American Inst. of Arts and Letters 1947; Award of American Council of Learned Socs. 1962; Chevalier Légion d'honneur. *Publications:* The Broken Column: A Study in Romantic Hellenism 1931, James Joyce: A Critical Introduction 1941, The Overreacher: A Study of Christopher Marlowe 1952, Symbolism and Fiction 1956, Contexts of Criticism 1957, The Power of Blackness: Hawthorne, Poe, Melville 1958, The Question of Hamlet 1959, The Gates of Horn: A Study of Five French Realists 1963, Refractions: Essays in Comparative Literature 1966, The Myth of the Golden Age in the Renaissance 1969, Grounds for Comparison 1972, Shakespeare and the Revolution of the Times: Perspectives and Commentaries 1976, Memories of the Moderns 1980, Playboys and Killjoys: An Essay on the Theory and Practice of Comedy 1987. *Leisure interests:* theatre, travel, Cape Cod. *Address:* 400 Boylston Hall, Harvard University, Cambridge, Mass. 02138 (Office); 14 Kirkland Place, Cambridge, Mass. 02138, U.S.A. (Home). *Telephone:* 617-495-2543 (Office); 617-876-0289 (Home).

LEVIN, (Henry) Bernard, B.SC.(ECON.); British journalist and author; b. 19 Aug. 1928; s. of late Phillip Levin and Rose Levin (née Racklin); ed. Christ's Hosp., L.S.E., Univ. of London; writer, regular and occasional, many newspapers and magazines, U.K. and abroad, including The Times, London, Sunday Times, Observer, Manchester Guardian, Truth, Spectator, Daily Express, Daily Mail, Newsweek, Int. Herald Tribune 1953-; writer and broadcaster for radio and TV 1952-; Pres. English Asscn. 1984-85, Vice-Pres. 1985-; numerous awards for journalism; Hon. Fellow (L.S.E.) 1977-; mem. Order of Polonia Restituta (by Polish Govt.-in-Exile) 1976. *Publications:* The Pendulum Years 1971, Taking Sides 1979, The Conducted Tour 1981, Speaking Up 1982, Enthusiasms 1983, The Way We Live Now 1984, Hannibal's Footsteps 1985, In These Times 1986, To the End of the Rhine 1987, All Things Considered 1989. *Address:* c/o Curtis Brown Ltd., 162-168 Regent Street, London, W.1, England.

LEVINE, David, B.F.A., B.S.; American artist; b. 20 Dec. 1926, Brooklyn; s. of Harry Levine; one s. one d.; ed. Temple Univ. and Hans Hoffman School of Painting; served U.S. Army 1945-46; one-man shows Forum Gallery, New York 1966-, Georgia Museum of Art 1968, Calif. Palace Legion of Honor 1968-69, 1971-72, 1983, Wesleyan Univ. 1970, Brooklyn Museum 1971, Princeton Univ. 1972, Galerie Yves Lambert, Paris 1972, Yale Univ. 1973, Hirshhorn Museum and Sculpture Garden, Washington 1976, Galerie Claude Bernard 1979, Philips Gallery 1980, Pierpont Morgan Library 1981, Santa Fe East Gallery 1983, Meredith Long, Houston 1984; Guggenheim Fellow 1967; recipient of several awards. *Address:* c/o Forum Gallery, 1018 Madison Avenue, New York, N.Y. 10021, U.S.A.

LEVINE, Jack; American artist; b. 3 Jan. 1915, Boston, Mass.; s. of Samuel and Mary (née Grinker) Levine; m. Ruth Gikow 1946 (died 1982); one d.; studied with Dr. Denman W. Ross, and H. K. Zimmerman; one-man exhibition Downtown Gallery, New York 1938; Artists 1942 Exhbn., Museum of Modern Art, New York 1943; exhibited at Jeu de Paume, Paris 1938; Carnegie Int. Exhbn. 1938, 1939, 1940; Retrospective Exhbns. Inst. of Contemporary Art, Boston 1953, Whitney Museum of American Art, New York 1955, Palacio de Bellas Artes, Mexico 1960; Dunn Int. Exhbn., Tate Gallery, London 1963; one-man exhbn. The Jewish Museum, New York 1978-79; pictures in Museum of Modern Art, William Hayes Fogg Museum (Harvard), Addison Gallery, Andover, Mass., Vatican Museum, etc.; mem. Nat. Acad. of Arts and Letters, American Acad. of Arts and Sciences; D.F.A. Colby Coll., Maine. *Address:* 68 Morton Street, New York, N.Y. 10014, U.S.A. *Telephone:* Yukon 9-5990.

LEVINE, James; American musician, conductor and pianist; b. 23 June 1943, Cincinnati, Ohio; s. of Lawrence M. Levine and Helen (Goldstein) Levine; ed. Walnut Hills High School, Juilliard School of Music; Asst. Conductor, Cleveland Orchestra 1964-70; Prin. Conductor, Metropolitan Opera, New York 1973-, Music Dir. 1976-, Artistic Dir. 1986-; Music Dir. Ravinia Festival 1973-, Cincinnati May Festival 1974-78; regular appearances as conductor and pianist in Europe and the U.S.A. with orchestras including Vienna Philharmonic, Berlin Philharmonic, Chicago Symphony, Philadelphia Orchestra, Salzburg and Bayreuth Festivals; conducted Metropolitan Opera premieres of I Vespri Siciliani (Verdi), The Rise and Fall of the City of Mahagonny (Weill), Lulu (Berg), Porgy and Bess (Gershwin), Le Rossignol (Stravinsky), Idomeneo, La Clemenza di Tito (Mozart); conductor Salzburg Festival premiere of Schönberg's Moses and Aaron 1987; Grammy awards for recordings of Mahler's Symphony No. 7, Brahms' A German Requiem, Verdi's La Traviata; Dr. h.c. (Univ. of Cincinnati), Cultural Award of New York City, St. Nicholas Soc. Medallion of Merit. *Address:* P.O. Box 698, Canal Street Station, New York, N.Y. 10013, U.S.A.

LEVINE, Rachmiel, B.A., M.D.; American physician and endocrinologist; b. 26 Aug. 1910, Poland; s. of Solomon and Bessie Levine; m. 1943; one s. one d.; ed. McGill Univ., Montreal, Canada; Asst. Dir. then Dir. Dept. of Metabolism and Endocrinology, Michael Reese Hosp., Chicago, U.S.A. 1939-42; lecturer in Physiology, Univ. of Chicago 1939-60; Chair. Dept. of Medicine, Michael Reese Hosp., Chicago 1950-60; Chair. Dept. of Medicine, New York Medical Coll. 1960-70; Medical Dir. City of Hope Medical

Center, Duarte, Calif. 1970-78, Emer. Medical Dir. and Dir. of Research 1978-; Hon. Pres. Int. Diabetes Asscn. 1970-; mem. N.A.S., American Acad. of Arts and Sciences; Banting Medal, American Diabetes Asscn. 1965, Thompson Medal, American Geriatrics Asscn. 1968. *Publications:* Carbohydrate Metabolism monograph, with S. Soskin) 1946, Advanced Metabolic Disorders (Ed., with R. Luft) 1964; about 300 scientific papers. *Leisure interests:* comparative literature, philosophy of science. *Address:* City of Hope Medical Center, 1500 E. Duarte Road, Duarte, Calif. 91010 (Office); 2024 Canyon Road, Arcadia, Calif. 91006, U.S.A. (Home).

LEVINE, Seymour, PH.D.; American university professor; b. 23 Jan. 1925, Brooklyn, New York; s. of Joseph Levine and Rose Reines; m. Barbara Lou McWilliams 1950; one s. two d.; ed. Univ. of Denver, New York Univ.; Asst. Prof., Div. of Research, Boston Univ. 1952-53; Postdoctoral Fellow, Michael Reese Hosp., Chicago 1953-55, Research Assoc. 1955-56; Asst. Prof., Dept. of Psychiatry, Ohio State Univ. 1956-60; Postdoctoral Fellow, Maudsley Hosp., London, England 1960-62; Assoc. Prof., Dept. of Psychiatry, Stanford Univ. 1962-69, Prof. 1969-, Dir. Stanford Primate Facility 1976-; Dir. Biological Sciences Research Training Program 1971-; Consultant, Foundation of Human Devt., Univ. Coll. Dublin, Ireland 1973-; Pres. Int. Soc. of Developmental Psychobiology 1975-76; Pres. Elect Int. Soc. of Psychoneuroendocrinology; Hoffheimer Research Award 1961, Research Career Devt. Award 1962, Research Scientist Award 1967. *Publications:* (Co-author) Stress, arousal and the pituitary-adrenal system 1979, chapters and articles on stress in animals and humans. *Leisure interests:* music, art, sports. *Address:* Department of Psychiatry and Behavioral Sciences, Stanford University School of Medicine, Stanford, Calif. 94305; 927 Valdez Place, Stanford, Calif. 94305, U.S.A. (Home). *Telephone:* (415) 723-5781 (Office); (415) 493-3956 (Home).

LEVINGSTON, Gen. Roberto Marcelo; Argentine army officer and politician; b. 10 Jan. 1920, San Luis; s. of Guillermo Levingston and Carmen Laborda; m. Betty Nelly Andrés 1943; two s. (one deceased) one d.; ed. Pius IX Coll., Nat. Mil. Coll., Army Intelligence School, Escuela Superior de Guerra and Center for High Mil. Studies; entered army as cadet, Nat. Mil. Coll. 1938, Sub-Lieut. 1941, Brig.-Gen. 1966; Army Information Officer 1947-50; mem. Gen. Staff 1951-57; Prof., Escuela Superior de Guerra 1958-62; Head of Army Information Services 1963-64; Dir.-Gen. Lemos School of Logistics 1965-66; Head of Intelligence of Jt. Chiefs of Staff 1967-68; Mil. Attaché Army del. to Interamerican Defense Bd. and Pres. Special Comm. on Acquisitions in U.S.A. 1969-70; Pres. and Prime Minister of Argentina 1970-71; Pres. Circle of Studies of Nat. Argentine Movement. *Publications:* political and military works. *Leisure interests:* reading of all kinds, particularly on politics, economics and military subjects, music and sport. *Address:* 11 de Septiembre 1735-17 A, Buenos Aires, Argentina. *Telephone:* 782-4433 (Home).

LEVINTHAL, Cyrus, PH.D.; American professor of biology; b. 2 May 1922, Philadelphia, Pa.; s. of Hon. Louis E. and Lenore C. Levinthal; m. Françoise Chassaigne Levinthal 1963; five c.; ed. Swarthmore Coll. and Univ. of California (Berkeley); Instructor, Dept. of Physics, Univ. of Mich. 1950-52, Asst. Prof. 1952-56, Assoc. Prof. 1956-57; Prof. of Biophysics, M.I.T. 1957-68; Chair. Dept. of Biological Sciences, Columbia Univ. 1968-71; William R. Kenan, Jr. Prof. of Biology 1968-; mem. N.A.S., American Acad. of Arts and Sciences, Inst. of Medicine. *Publications:* numerous articles in professional journals. *Address:* Department of Biological Sciences, 1011 Fairchild Building, Columbia University, New York, N.Y. 10027, U.S.A. (Office). *Telephone:* 212-854-2439.

LEVY, Bernard-Henri; French writer; b. 5 Nov. 1948, Beni-Saf, Algeria; s. of André Levy and Ginette Levy; m. Sylvie Bouscasse 1980; one s. one d.; ed. Ecole Normale Supérieure (rue d'Ulm), Paris; War Correspondent for Daily Combat 1971-72; lecturer in Epistemology, Univ. of Strasbourg, in Philosophy, Ecole Normale Supérieure 1973; mem. François Mitterrand's Group of Experts 1973-76; joined Editions Grasset as Ed. "nouvelle philosophie" series 1973; Ed. Idées section, Quotidien de Paris; Contrib. to Nouvel Observateur and Temps Modernes 1974; Co-founder Action Int. contre la Faim 1980. *Publications:* Les Indes Rouges 1973, La Barbarie à Visage Humain 1977, Le Testament de Dieu 1979, L'Idéologie Française 1981, Questions de Principe 1983, Le Diable en tête (Prix Médicis) 1984, Impressions d'Asie 1985, Questions de Principe Deux 1986, Eloge des Intellectuels 1987, Les Dernier jours de Charles Baudelaire (Prix Interallié) 1988. *Address:* 61 rue des Saint Pères, 75006 Paris, France. *Telephone:* 45.44.38.14.

LEVY, David; Israeli politician; b. 1938, Morocco; emigrated to Israel 1957; construction worker; joined Histadrut; elected to Knesset, representing Herut (Freedom) group of Gahal 1969- (subsequently of Likud Bloc); Likud cand. for Sec.-Gen. of Histadrut 1977, 1981; now Chair. Likud group in Histadrut; Minister of Immigrant Absorption 1977-78, of Construction and Housing Jan. 1978-; Deputy Prime Minister 1981-84, Dec. 1988-. *Address:* Ministry of Construction and Housing, 23 Hillel Street, Jerusalem, Israel.

LEVY, Maurice; French scientist and university professor; b. 7 Sept. 1922, Tlemcen, Algeria; s. of Jean and Noémie (née Fisse) Levy; m. Geneviève Villié 1962; two d. (and two s. one d. from previous marriage); ed. Lycée Bugeaud, Algiers and Univs. of Paris and Algiers; Physicist, Nat.

Centre of Scientific Research, Paris 1945–48; Research Fellow, Manchester Univ. 1948–50; mem. Inst. of Advanced Study, Princeton Univ. 1950–52, 1954–55, 1962; fmrly. Visiting Prof. Stanford and Rochester Univs., Calif. Inst. of Technology and Tata Inst. of Fundamental Research, Bombay; Prof. Bordeaux Faculty of Science 1953–54, Prof. Paris Faculty of Science 1954–59, Hon. Prof. of Theoretical Physics 1959–; served as Scientific Adviser to French Embassy, Wash. 1968–70; Dir. Programming Service for Research Orgs., Ministry of Industrial and Scientific Devt. 1971–74; Chair. Council of ESRO 1972–75; Pres. Nat. Center of Space Research 1974–76; Dir. Energy Programme, UN Univ. 1977–83; Dir. Nat. Museum for Tech. and Industry 1983–85; Pres., City of Science and Industry 1985–87; Pres. Dir.-Gen. Sofracin; Hon. D.Sc. (Lancaster, U.K.); Officier, Légion d'honneur, Commdr., Ordre nat. du Mérite. *Publications:* include studies on theoretical nuclear physics and on the theory of elementary particles. *Address:* 34 rue de Longchamp, 92200 Neuilly-sur-Seine, France (Home). *Telephone:* 47-45-78-01.

LEVY, Raymond Haïm, M.S.; French oil company executive; b. 28 June 1927, Paris; s. of Sam and Rachel Levy; m. Jacqueline Schwartz 1955; three s. one d.; ed. Ecole Polytechnique, Ecole des Mines de Paris, M.I.T.; engineer in coal mines in north of France 1952–53, in Public Mines Service 1953–57; Chief Eng., Régie Autonome des Pétroles (RAP) 1957–65; Gen. Man. of Exploration and Production, ERAP-ELF 1966–72, Dir.-Gen., Refining and Distribution 1973–; Gen. Man. ELF Union 1972–75; Vice-Pres. ERAP (Enterprise de recherches et d'activités pétrolières) 1976–; Chair. and Pres. ELF Union and SOCANTAR 1976–80; Chair. and Pres. ELF France 1975–80; Vice-Pres. and Gen. Man. SNEA (Soc. Nat. Elf Aquitaine) 1976–80; Pres., Dir.-Gen. USINOR 1982–84; Chair. Cockerill-Sambre 1985–86; Chair. Renault Inc. Dec. 1986–; Officier, Légion d'honneur, Officier, Ordre nat. du Mérite. *Address:* Renault Inc., 34 quai du Pont du Jour, 92109 Boulogne Cedex, France.

LEVY, Robert Isaac, M.D.; American professor of medicine; b. 3 May 1937, New York; s. of George Gerson Levy and Sarah Levinson; m. Ellen Marie Feis 1958; one s. three d.; ed. Cornell and Yale Univs.; Intern, Asst. Resident in Medicine, Yale-New Haven Medical Center 1961–63; Clinical Assoc., Molecular Diseases, Nat. Heart Inst. 1963–66, Chief Resident 1965–66, Attending Physician, Molecular Disease Branch 1965–81, Head, Section on Lipoproteins 1966–78, Deputy Clinical Dir. 1968–69, Clinical Service 1969–73, Chief Lipid Metabolism Branch 1970–74, Dir. Div. of Heart and Vascular Diseases 1973–75, Dir. of Nat. Heart, Lung and Blood Inst. 1975–81; Prof. of Medicine, Dean of School of Medicine and Vice-Pres. for Health Sciences, Tufts Univ. 1981–83; Prof. of Medicine, Columbia Univ. 1983–, Vice-Pres. for Health Sciences 1983–84, Sr. Advisor to Univ. 1984–86, Sr. Assoc. Vice-Pres. for Health Sciences 1985–87; Pres. Sandoz Research Inst. 1988–; Arthur S. Flemming Award 1975; Asscn. Health Foundation Humanitarian Award 1976; American Asscn. for Clinical Chemistry Award 1979; Donald D. Van Llyke Award in Clinical Chemistry 1980, Roger J. Williams Award in Preventive Nutrition 1985. *Publications:* over 280 scientific papers. *Address:* Columbia University College of Physicians and Surgeons, 630 W. 168th Street, New York, N.Y. 10032, U.S.A. *Telephone:* (212) 305 4138.

LEVY, Walter James, C.M.G., LL.D.; American oil consultant; b. 21 March 1911, Hamburg, Germany; s. of Moses and Bertha Levy (née Lindenberger); m. Augusta Sondheimer 1942 (deceased); one s. one d.; ed. Univs. of Berlin, Freiburg, Munich, Hamburg, Heidelberg and Kiel; Asst. to Ed., Petroleum Press Bureau, London 1937–41; Special Asst. and Chief, Petroleum Section, Office of Strategic Services; mem. of Enemy Oil Cttee. under Jt. Chiefs of Staff 1942–44; Special Asst. Office of Intelligence Research, Dept. of State 1945–48; Consultant, Office of Deputy Admin., Chief of Oil Branch, Econ. Co-operation Admin. 1948–49; Econ. Consultant N.Y. Sept. 1949–; Consultant ECA 1949–50; Consultant, President's Materials Policy Comm. 1951–; U.S. Oil Adviser, missions to Iran, July-Sept. 1951; Consultant, Nat. Security Resources Bd. 1952, Policy Planning Staff 1952–53; Consultant to Int. Co-operation Admin. 1956–57, to Dept. of State and Office of Civil and Defense Mobilization 1960–, to Dept. of State, Office of Under-Sec. and Asst. Secs. 1960–80; Oil Adviser to the Special Emissary and Pres. Kennedy to the Pres. of Indonesia 1963; Consultant to the EEC 1970; mem. Advisory Council to School of Advanced Int. Studies, Johns Hopkins Univ.; mem. Council on Foreign Relations Inc.; President's Cert. of Merit, recipient of special Plaque in appreciation for contribution to welfare of the U.S. (from Sec. of State) 1968; Dato Selia Laila Jasa, Brunei, Order of Taj (Iran), Insignia of Commdr.'s Cross of the Order of Merit (Fed. Repub. of Germany) 1979, Hon. C.M.G. (U.K.). *Publications:* Oil Strategy and Politics 1941–81 1982 and numerous articles in professional publications. *Address:* 30 Rockefeller Plaza, New York, N.Y. 10112; 300 Central Park West, New York, N.Y. 10024, U.S.A. (Home). *Telephone:* 212-586-5263 (Rockefeller Plaza).

LEWANDO, Sir Jan Alfred, Kt., C.B.E., C.B.I.M., F.R.S.A.; British business executive; b. 31 May 1909; s. of Maurice and Eugénie (née Goldsmid) Lewando; m. Nora Slavouski 1948; three d.; ed. Manchester Grammar School and Manchester Univ.; served British Army in Europe, Middle East and Far East 1939–45, British Army Staff in Washington D.C. and

British Ministry of Supply Mission 1941–45 (Lieut.-Col. 1943); with Marks & Spencer Ltd. 1929–70, Dir. 1954–70; mem. Export Council for Europe 1965–69, British Nat. Export Council 1969–71, Council of CBI 1971–75, European Steering Cttee. CBI 1968–71, British Overseas Trade Bd. 1972–77, British Overseas Trade Advisory Council 1975–77, European Trade Cttee. 1973–83; Vice-Chair. Clothing Export Council 1966–70; Pres. British Textile Confed. 1972–73; Vice-Chair. Comitextil, Brussels 1972–73; Chair. Carrington Viyella Ltd. 1970–75, Consolidated Textile Mills Ltd., Canada 1972–75, Gelvenor Textiles Ltd., South Africa 1973–75; Dir. Carrington Tesit, Italy 1971–75, Heal & Son Holdings Ltd. 1975–81 (Deputy Chair. 1977–81), Bunzl PLC 1975–85, W. A. Baxter & Sons Ltd. 1976–, Johnston Industries Inc., U.S.A. 1976–84, Royal Worcester Spode Ltd. 1978–79, Edgars Stores Ltd., South Africa 1976–82, Bunzl and Biach AG (Austria) 1979–80, Johnston Industries Ltd. 1980–84; Vice-Pres. Transport Trust 1975–; Chair. Appeal Cttee., British Inst. of Radiology 1979–84; Legion of Merit (U.S.A.) 1946; Companion Textile Inst. 1972–. *Address:* Davidge House, Knotty Green, Beaconsfield, Bucks., England. *Telephone:* (049 46) 4987.

LEWANDOWSKI, Bohdan, M.A.; Polish diplomatist; b. 29 June 1926, Ostrołęka; m. Helen M. Harris 1948 (separated 1980); two d.; ed. Acad. of Political Sciences, Warsaw, and Warsaw Univ.; Ministry of Foreign Affairs, Warsaw 1945–46; Polish Foreign Service in USA 1946–48; Head, N. America Section, Ministry of Foreign Affairs 1951–56; Deputy Dir. Dept. for U.K. and America 1956–60; Polish Rep. UN Security Council 1960; Perm. Rep. of Poland to UN 1960–66; Dir. of Research Bureau, Ministry of Foreign Affairs 1966–67; Deputy Head, Foreign Dept., Cen. Cttee. PZPR 1967–71; Dir.-Gen. Ministry of Foreign Affairs 1971–72; Under Sec.-Gen. of UN 1972–82; Consultant to UN Sec.-Gen. 1982–83; Sr. Adviser to UNDP Admin. 1982–; Consultant to Aspen Inst. for Humanistic Studies 1982–; Regents Prof., Univ. of Calif., San Diego 1984–; Visiting Prof., Diplomatic Acad., Vienna 1984, 1985, 1987, Carleton Coll. Northfield, U.S.A. 1986, Colo. Coll., Colo. Springs 1988–89; mem. Policy Bd., Inter-Action Council 1984–; mem. Governing Council, Center for Int. Studies, New York Univ. School of Law 1982–; Dr. h.c. (Kyung Hee Univ., Seoul) 1985; Gold Cross of Merit, Officer's Cross of Order of Polonia Restituta, Order of Banner of Labour (2nd Class). *Publications:* Polska w Organizacji Narodów Zjednoczonych 1970, Rola Organizacji Narodów Zjednoczonych w utrzymaniu międzynarodowego pokoju i bezpieczeństwa 1971, Organizacja Narodów Zjednoczonych we współczesnym świecie 1972. *Leisure interests:* music, theatre, sport. *Address:* Al. Róż 8, 00-556 Warsaw, Poland. *Telephone:* (22) 28 62 96.

LEWIN, Baron (Life Peer), cr. 1982, of Greenwich in Greater London; **Admiral of the Fleet Terence Thornton Lewin,** K.G., G.C.B., M.V.O., D.S.C., D.SC.; British naval officer; b. 19 Nov. 1920, Dover; s. of Eric Lewin; m. Jane Branch-Evans 1944; two s. one d.; ed. The Judd School, Tonbridge; war service in Home and Mediterranean Fleets in H.M.S. Valiant, H.M.S. Ashanti in Malta Convoys, N. Russian Convoys, invasion N. Africa and Channel (mentioned in despatches); Command, H.M.S. Corunna 1955–56; Commdr. H.M. Yacht Britannia 1957–58; Captain, Dartmouth Training Sqn. and H.M.S. Urchin, H.M.S. Tenby 1961–63; Dir. Naval Tactical and Weapons Policy Div. of Ministry of Defence 1964–65; Command, H.M.S. Hermes 1966–67; Asst. Chief of Naval Staff (Policy) 1968–69; Rear-Adm. 1968; Flag Officer, Second-in-Command, Far East Fleet 1969–70; Vice-Adm. 1970; Vice-Chief of Naval Staff 1971–73; Adm. 1973; C.-in-C. Fleet, NATO C.-in-C. Channel and C.-in-C. Eastlant 1973–75; C.-in-C. Naval Home Command 1975–77; Chief of Naval Staff and First Sea Lord 1977–79; Chief of Defence Staff 1979–82; Elder Brother, Trinity House 1975; Trustee, Nat. Maritime Museum 1981– (Chair. 1987–); Regional Dir. Lloyds Bank 1982; Pres. British Schools Exploring Soc. 1984, Shipwrecked Mariners' Soc. 1984; Hon. Freeman City of London. *Address:* House of Lords, London, S.W.1, England.

LEWINSKY, Herbert Christian, DR.IUR.; Austrian business executive; b. 20 Sept. 1928, Teschen, Czechoslovakia; s. of Wilhelm Lewinsky and Emmy Schaible; m. 1st Rosmarie Lewinsky 1953, 2nd Bettina Lewinsky 1985; one s. two d.; ed. Vienna Univ.; Head, Business Admin. Dept., Mobil Oil, Austria 1960, Pres. 1967, Retail Marketing Dept., Mobil Oil, U.S.A. 1963–64, Pres., Mobil Oil, Fed. Repub. of Germany 1972; Chair. and Pres. of Voest-Alpine AG 1986; Gold Medal (Austria) 1967. *Leisure interests:* music, tennis. *Address:* Voest-Alpine AG, Postfach 2, 4031 Linz, Austria.

LEWIS, Sir Allen (Montgomery), Kt., G.C.M.G., G.C.V.O., Q.C., LL.B.; Saint Lucia lawyer and politician; b. 26 Oct. 1909, Castries; s. of George Ferdinand Montgomery and Ida Louisa (née Barton) Lewis; m. Edna Leofrida Theobalds 1936; three s. two d.; ed. St. Mary's Coll., St. Lucia, and Univ. of London (external); legal practitioner in Royal Court, St. Lucia (later Supreme Court of Windward and Leeward Islands) 1931–59; Acting Magistrate, St. Lucia 1940–41; called to Bar, Middle Temple, London 1946; Acting Puisne Judge, Windward and Leeward Islands 1955–56; Commr. for reform and revision of laws of St. Lucia 1954–58; Q.C. 1956; Judge of Fed. Supreme Court 1959–62, of British Caribbean Court of Appeal 1962, of Court of Appeal, Jamaica 1962–67, Acting Pres. 1966; Acting Chief Justice of Jamaica 1966; Chief Justice, W. Indies Associated States Supreme Court 1967–72; Chair. Nat. Devt. Corpn., St. Lucia 1972–74; Gov.

of St. Lucia 1974-79, Gov.-Gen. of Saint Lucia 1979-80, 1982-87; Pres. W. Indies Senate 1958-59; Pres. Grenada Boy Scouts Asscn. 1967-72; mem. Castries Town Council 1942-56 (Chair. six times); mem. Legis. Council, St. Lucia 1943-51; Dir. St. Lucia Br. of British Red Cross Soc. 1955-59; Chancellor, Univ. of the W. Indies 1975-89; Rep. St. Lucia, Windward Islands and W. Indies at various confs., including Montego Bay 1947, Chaguaramas Comm. 1958; Coronation Medal 1953, Jubilee Medal 1977; Hon. LL.D. (Univ. of the W. Indies) 1974; K.St. J.; Grand Cross of Order of St. Lucia. *Publication:* Revised Edition of Laws of St. Lucia 1957. *Leisure interests:* gardening, swimming. *Address:* Beaver Lodge, P.O. Box 1076, Castries, Saint Lucia, West Indies. *Telephone:* (809) 45-27285.

LEWIS, Andrew Lindsay, Jr., B.S., M.B.A.; American business executive and politician; b. 3 Nov. 1931, Philadelphia, Pa.; s. of Andrew Lindsay and Lucille (Bricker) Lewis; m. Marilyn S. Stoughton 1950; two s. one d.; ed. Haverford Coll., Pa., Harvard Univ.; foreman, job supt., production man. and Dir. Henkels & McCoy, Inc., Blue Bell, Pa. 1955-60; Dir. of Marketing, Vice-Pres. (Sales) and Dir. American Olean Tile Co. Inc., Lansdale, Pa. 1960-68; Vice-Pres. and Asst. to Chair. Nat. Gypsum Co., Buffalo, N.Y. 1969-70; Chair. Simplex Wire and Cable Co., Boston, Mass. 1970-72; Pres. and C.E.O. Snelling and Snelling Inc. 1970-74; Lewis and Assocs. (Financial and Man. Consultants), Plymouth Meeting, Pa. 1974-81; U.S. Sec. of Transportation 1981-83; Dir. Campbell Soup Co. 1983-; Chair. Warner Amex Satellite Entertainment Co. 1983-86; Chair., Pres. and C.E.O. Union Pacific Corpn., New York City 1987-; Trustee Reading Co., operating freight and mass transit railroad network (now, with five other railroad lines, Consolidated Rail Corpn.) 1971-81; fmr. Dir. numerous cos.; Deputy Chair. Republican Nat. Cttee. Aug. 1980. *Address:* Union Pacific Corporation, 345 Park Avenue, New York, N.Y. 10154, U.S.A.

LEWIS, Sir Arthur (see Lewis, Sir William Arthur).

LEWIS, Bernard, B.A., PH.D., F.B.A., F.R.HIST.S.; British university professor; b. 31 May 1916, London; m. Ruth Hélène Oppenhejm 1947 (divorced 1974); one s. one d.; ed. Univs. of London and Paris; Lecturer in Islamic History, School of Oriental Studies, Univ. of London 1938; served R.A.C. and Intelligence Corps 1940-41; attached to Foreign Office 1941-45; Prof. of History of the Near and Middle East, Univ. of London 1949-74; Visiting Prof. of History, Univ. of Calif. at Los Angeles 1955-56, Columbia Univ. 1960, Ind. Univ. 1963, Princeton Univ. 1964, Univ. of Calif. at Berkeley 1965; Visiting mem. Inst. for Advanced Study, Princeton 1969; Cleveland E. Dodge Prof. of Near Eastern Studies, Princeton Univ. 1974-86, Prof. Emer. 1986-; Dir. Annenberg Research Inst., Philadelphia 1986-; Long-term mem. Inst. for Advanced Study 1974-86; Visiting Prof., Coll. de France 1980, École des Hautes Études en Sciences Sociales, Paris 1983, Cornell Univ. 1984; mem. American Acad. of Arts and Sciences 1983, American Historical Asscn. 1984; Assoc. mem. Inst. d'Egypte, Cairo 1969; Foreign mem. American Philosophical Soc. 1973; Hon. mem. Société Asiatique, Paris 1984, Ataturk Acad. of History, Language and Culture, Ankara 1984; Hon. Fellow S.O.A.S., London 1986; Hon. Dr. (Hebrew Univ., Jerusalem) 1974, (Tel-Aviv) 1979, (State Univ. of N.Y. Brighampton, Penn., Hebrew Union Coll., Cincinnati) 1987; Harvey Prize 1978. *Publications:* The Origins of Ismā'ilism 1940, Turkey Today 1940, British Contributions to Arabic Studies 1941, Handbook of Diplomatic and Political Arabic 1947, 1956, Land of Enchanters (Ed.) 1948, The Arabs in History 1950, Notes and Documents from the Turkish Archives 1952, The Emergence of Modern Turkey 1961, 1968, The Kingly Crown 1961, Historians of the Middle East (co-editor with P.M. Holt) 1962, Istanbul and the Civilization of the Ottoman Empire 1963, The Middle East and the West 1964, The Assassins 1967, Race and Colour in Islam 1971, Islam in History 1973, Ed. Islamic Civilization 1974, Islam from the Prophet Muhammad to the Capture of Constantinople (2 vols.) 1974, History— Remembered, Recovered, Invented 1975, The World of Islam (Ed.) 1976, Population and Revenue in the Towns of Palestine in the Sixteenth Century (with Amnon Cohen) 1978, The Muslim Discovery of Europe 1982, The Jews of Islam 1984, Semites and Anti-Semites 1986, As Others See Us (co.-ed.) 1986, The Political Language of Islam 1988. *Address:* Department of Near Eastern Studies, Princeton University, Princeton, N.J. 08544, U.S.A. *Telephone:* (609) 452-4280.

LEWIS, Charles Edwin; American professor of medicine; b. 28 Dec. 1928, Kansas City, Mo.; m. Mary Ann Gurera 1963; three s. one d.; ed. Univs. of Kansas and Cincinatti and Harvard Medical School; U.S.A.F. 1955-56; Fellow, The Kettering Lab. 1956-59; Asst. Prof. Epidemiology, Baylor Univ. 1959-61; Assoc. Prof. of Medicine, Univ. of Kansas 1962-64, Prof. and Chair. Dept. of Community Medicine 1964-69; Prof. and Head of Div. of Health Services and Prof. of Medicine, Univ. of Calif. Los Angeles (UCLA) 1970-72, Chief, Div. of Gen. Internal Medicine and Prof. of Nursing 1972-; mem. Inst. of Medicine (N.A.S.); Rosenthal Award (A.C.P.) 1980. *Publications:* more than 120 research publs. in journals and 15 chapters in books. *Leisure interests:* music, travel. *Address:* Department of Medicine, University of California at Los Angeles Center for Health Sciences, Los Angeles, Calif. 90024 (Office); 221 Burlingame Avenue, Los Angeles, Calif. 90049, U.S.A. (Home). *Telephone:* 213-825-6709 (Office).

LEWIS, Dan, PH.D., D.SC., F.R.S.; British geneticist; b. 30 Dec. 1910, Stoke-on-Trent; s. of Ernest Albert and Edith Jane Lewis; m. Mary P. E. Burry 1933; one d.; ed. High School, Newcastle under Lyme, and Univs. of

Reading and London; plant breeder, John Innes Inst. 1935, Head Dept. of Genetics 1947; Quain Prof. of Botany, Univ. Coll. London 1957-78, Prof. Emer. 1978-; Hon. Research Fellow, Univ. Coll. London 1978-; Visiting Prof. of Genetics, Univ. of Calif., Berkeley 1961, Delhi 1965, Singapore 1970; Visiting Prof., Queen Mary Coll., London 1978-; Pres. Genetical Soc. 1968-71; mem. Univ. Grants Cttee. 1968-74. *Publications:* Sexual Incompatibility in Plants and articles on genetics; Ed. Science Progress. *Leisure interests:* swimming, music. *Address:* Flat 2, 56/57 Myddleton Square, London, EC1R 1YA, England (Home).

LEWIS, David Sloan, Jr., B.S.; American business executive; b. 6 July 1917; s. of David Sloan Lewis, Sr. and Reuben (Walton) Lewis; m. Dorothy Sharpe 1941; three s. one d.; ed. Univ. of S. Carolina and Georgia Inst. of Technology; Aerodynamicist, Glenn L. Martin Co., Baltimore 1939-46, McDonnell Aircraft Corpn., St. Louis 1946-70, Chief Preliminary Design 1952-55, Sales Man. 1955-57, Vice-Pres. and Project Man. 1957-60, Sr. Vice-Pres. Operations 1960-61, Exec. Vice-Pres. 1961, Vice-Pres. and Gen. Man. 1961-62, Pres. 1962-67; Pres. McDonnell Douglas Co. and Chair. Douglas Aircraft Co. Div. 1967-70; Chair., C.E.O. Gen. Dynamics Corpn. 1970-85, Pres. 1970-80; Dir. Bankamerica Corpn., Ralston Purina Co.; Fellow, A.I.A.A.; mem. Bd. of Govs. Nat. Acad. of Eng.; mem. Bd. Cessna Aircraft Co. 1983-85; Hon. D.Sc. (Clarkson Coll. of Tech., Potsdam, New York), Hon. LL.D. (St. Louis Univ.). *Leisure interest:* golf. *Address:* c/o General Dynamics Corporation, Pierre Laclede Center, St. Louis, Mo. 63105, U.S.A.

LEWIS, Edward B., PH.D.; American professor of biology; b. May 20 1918, Wilkes-Barre; s. of Edward B. Lewis and Laura Histed Lewis; m. Pamela Harrah 1946; three s. (one deceased); ed. Minnesota Univ. and Calif. Inst. of Tech.; Instructor, Calif. Inst. of Tech. 1946-48, Asst. Prof. 1948-49, Assoc. Prof. 1949-56, Prof. 1956-66, 1966-; Rockefeller Foundation Fellow, Cambridge Univ. 1947-48; Sec. Genetics Soc. of America 1962-64, Vice-Pres. 1966-67, Pres. 1967; Guest Prof., Inst. of Genetics, Copenhagen Univ. 1975-76; mem. N.A.S. and American Acad. of Arts and Sciences; Hon. PH.D. (Umea, Sweden) 1981; Thomas Hunt Morgan Medal, Wolf Prize for Medicine (jtly. with John B. Gurdon, q.v.) 1989; Genetics Soc. of America 1983. *Address:* Biology Division 156-29, California Institute of Technology, Pasadena, Calif. 91125, U.S.A.

LEWIS, Geoffrey David, M.A., F.S.A.; British university teacher and museologist; b. 13 April 1933, Brighton, Sussex; s. of David and Esther Lewis; m. Frances May Wilderspin 1956; three d.; ed. Varndean Grammar School, Brighton, Univ. of Liverpool; Asst. Curator, Worthing Museum and Art Gallery 1950-60; Deputy Dir. (and Keeper of Antiquities) Sheffield City Museum 1960-65; Dir. Sheffield City Museums 1966-72, Liverpool City Museums 1972-74, Merseyside Co. Museums 1974-77; Dir. of Museum Studies, Univ. of Leicester 1977-; Hon. Lecturer in British Prehistory, Univ. of Sheffield 1965-72; Pres. Int. Council of Museums 1983-89, Chair. Advisory Cttee. 1974-80; Fellow Museums Asscn., London, Pres. 1980-81. *Publications:* The South Yorkshire Glass Industry 1964, Prehistoric and Roman Times in the Sheffield Area (Co-author) 1968, Manual of Curatorship (Co-Ed.) 1984; many articles relating to archaeology and museums. *Address:* Department of Museum Studies, University of Leicester, 105 Princess Road East, Leicester LE1 7LG; 4 Orchard Close, Wolvey, Hinckley, Leics., LE10 3LR, England (Home). *Telephone:* (0533) 523962 (Office).

LEWIS, Irving James, M.A.; American professor of public policy and community health; b. 9 July 1918, Boston; s. of Harry Lewis and Sarah H. Bloomberg; m. Rose Helen Greenwald 1941; one s. two d.; ed. Harvard Coll. and Chicago Univ.; Dept. Head Intergovernmental Comm. on European Migration, Geneva 1957-59; Deputy Chief Int. Div. Bureau of Budget, U.S. Govt. 1959-65, Chief Health and Welfare Div. 1965-67, Deputy Asst. Dir. 1967-68; Deputy Admin. for Health Services and Mental Health Admin., Dept. of Health, Educ. and Welfare 1968-70; Prof., later Prof. Emer., of Public Policy and Community Health, Albert Einstein Coll. of Medicine, New York 1970-; WHO Fellow 1977; Annual Career Service Award, Nat. Civil Service League 1969; Assoc. Fellow New York Acad. of Medicine; mem. Inst. of Medicine, N.A.S., N.Y. Bd. of Professional Medical Conduct, community health groups; Chair. N.Y. Medical Liability Reform Coalition. *Publications:* Co-author: Registration for Voting in the U.S. 1946, The Sick Citadel: The Academic Medical Centre and the Public Interest 1983; numerous health policy articles. *Leisure interests:* sports, music, literature, dancing. *Address:* Albert Einstein College of Medicine, Department of Epidemiology and Social Medicine, 1300 Morris Park Avenue, Bronx, New York, N.Y. 10461; 262 Monterey Avenue, Pelham, New York, N.Y. 10803, U.S.A. (Home). *Telephone:* (914) 738-1599 (Home).

LEWIS, Baron (Life Peer) cr. 1989, of Newnham; **Jack,** PH.D., F.R.S.C., F.R.S.; British professor of chemistry; b. 13 Feb. 1928; m. Elfreida M. Lamb 1951; one s. one d.; ed. Barrow Grammar School and Univs. of London and Nottingham; Lecturer, Univ. of Sheffield 1953-56, Imperial Coll. London 1956-57; Lecturer-Reader, Univ. Coll. London 1957-62; Prof. of Chem. Univ. of Manchester 1962-67, Univ. Coll. London 1967-70, Univ. of Cambridge 1970-; Hon. Fellow, Sidney Sussex Coll. Cambridge; Warden, Robinson Coll. Cambridge 1975-; mem. numerous cttees. etc.; Foreign mem. American Acad. of Arts and Sciences; Davy Medal, Royal Soc. 1985; Hon. D. Sc. (Leicester) 1988, seven other hon. degrees and other distinctions and awards. *Publications:* papers in scientific journals. *Address:*

Chemistry Department, University Chemical Laboratory, Lensfield Road, Cambridge, CB2 1EW, England.

LEWIS, Jerry (Joseph Levitch), American comedian; b. 16 March 1926; s. of Danny and Rachael Lewis; m. 1st Patti Palmer 1944 (divorced), six s.; m. 2nd Sandra Pitnick 1983; performed in nightclubs as a comedian before teaming with Dean Martin in 1946 at the 500 Club, Atlantic City, N.J.; made film début with Martin in My Friend Irma 1949; other films include: My Friend Irma Goes West 1950, That's My Boy 1951, Sailor Beware 1952, Jumping Jack 1952, The Stooge 1953, Scared Stiff 1953, The Caddy 1953, Living it Up 1954, Three Ring Circus 1954, You're Never Too Young 1954, Pardners 1956, Hollywood or Bust 1956, The Delicate Delinquent 1957, The Sad Sack 1958, Rock a Bye Baby 1958, The Geisha Boy 1958, Visit to a Small Planet 1960, The Bellboy 1960, Cinderfella 1960, The Errand Boy 1961, It's Only Money? 1964, The Patsy 1964, The Disorderly Orderly 1964, The Family Jewels 1965, Boeing-Boeing 1965, Three On a Couch 1966, Way Way Out 1966, The Big Mouth 1967, Don't Raise the Bridge, Lower the River 1968, Hook, Line and Sinker 1969, Which Way to the Front? 1970, One More Time 1971, The Day the Clown Cried 1971, Hardly Working 1981, King of Comedy 1981, Slapstick 1982, Smorgasbord 1982, Retenez-moi . . . ou je fais un malheur!, How Did You Get In 1985; Television appearances include: Startime, The Ed Sullivan Show and the Jazz Singer; Nat. Chair. Muscular Dystrophy Assçn. of America; Prof. of Cinema at Univ. of Southern Calif.; mem. Screen Directors Guild; Commdr. des Arts et Lettres 1984. *Leisure interests:* golf, sailing. *Address:* Plaza Vegas, Suite I, 3305 W. Spring Mountain Road, Las Vegas, NV 89102, U.S.A.

LEWIS, Hon. John Vernon Radcliffe, B.A.; Zimbabwean judge (retd.); b. 14 Feb. 1917, London, England; s. of Hon. Vernon Arthur Lewis and Ethel Amy Jameson; m. Erica E. W. Cook (died 1988); ed. Prince Edward School, Salisbury, Rhodesia, Rhodes Univ., S. Africa and Balliol Coll., Oxford, England; admitted as advocate, High Court of S. Rhodesia 1939; active service 1940–45; practising lawyer, Salisbury 1945–60; Queen's Counsel 1956; Judge of the High Court 1960; Judge of Appeal, Appellate Div. of the High Court 1970; Judge Pres. 1977; Acting Chief Justice 1980, 1981; retd. 1982. *Address:* 5 Maasdorp Avenue, Alexandra Park, Harare, N.12, Zimbabwe (Home). *Telephone:* 733551 (Home).

LEWIS, Lawrence Vernon Harcourt; Barbados development consultant and government official; b. 13 March 1932; m.; two s.; ed. Univ. of West Indies and Int. Inst. for Labour Studies, Geneva; various posts, Ministry of Finance and Planning 1957–71, Accountant-Gen. 1971–72, Deputy Financial Sec. 1973, Perm. Sec. Finance 1973–77; Perm Sec. Energy 1982; Chair. Barbados Savings Bank 1973–78, Barbados Mortgage Finance Corpn. 1977–83, Consulting Assocs. (Barbados) Ltd. 1977–, Insurance Corpn. of Barbados 1978–81; Pres. and C.E.O. Barbados Nat. Bank 1978–81; Exec. Dir. Nat. Petroleum Corpn. 1982–84 and many other directorships; Gov. for Barbados, Caribbean Devt. Bank 1973–81; Minister of State, Civil Services 1986–. *Address:* Ministry of Civil Services, Bay Street, St. Michael, Barbados.

LEWIS, Neville Brice, M.P.; Jamaican politician; b. 19 May 1936, Middle Quarters, St. Elizabeth; s. of Neville C. and Marie Lewis; m. Jasmin Lewis; one s. one d.; ed. Munro Coll., St. Elizabeth and Lincoln's Inn, London; accounting clerk, McCaulay's Motor Service, Kingston 1959–61; legal studies in London 1961; later worked in property management in London; returned to Jamaica 1976; M.P. for N.W. St. Elizabeth 1976–; Minister of Social Security 1980–83, of Local Govt. 1983–89; Jamaica Labour Party (Deputy Leader 1983–). *Address:* c/o Ministry of Local Government, Ocean Boulevard, Kingston, Jamaica.

LEWIS, Richard, C.B.E., F.R.A.M., F.R.M.C.M., L.R.A.M.; British opera singer; m. Elizabeth Robertson 1963; one s. (and one s. by previous marriage); ed. Royal Manchester Coll. of Music, Royal Acad. of Music; English début in Rape of Lucretia, Glyndebourne; created Troilus (Troilus and Cressida by Walton); sang in première of Stravinsky's Canticum Sacrum; guest appearances at Covent Garden, Edinburgh Festival, San Francisco Opera, Glyndebourne, Vienna State Opera and Teatro Colón, Buenos Aires; appearances in oratorio and recitals in Europe, America, Australia and New Zealand; numerous broadcasts and recordings; Pres. Inc. Soc. of Musicians 1975–76; Hon. D.Mus. (St. Andrews, Manchester). *Leisure interests:* painting, calligraphy, photography. *Address:* Combe House, 22 Church Street, Willingdon, England.

LEWIS, Samuel Winfield, M.A.; American diplomatist; b. 1 Oct. 1930, Houston; s. of Samuel W. Lewis and Sue Roselle Hurley Lewis; m. Sallie S. Smoot 1953; one s. one d.; ed. Yale and Johns Hopkins Univs.; Exec. Asst. American Trucking Asscn., Washington 1953–54; entered Foreign Service 1954; with Consulate, Naples 1954–55; Consul, Florence 1955–59; Officer-in-Charge Italian Affairs, Dept. of State 1959–61; Special Asst. to Under-Sec. of State 1961–63; Deputy Asst. Dir. U.S. AID Mission to Brazil 1964–66; Deputy Dir. Office for Brazil Affairs, Dept. of State 1967–68; senior staff mem. for Latin American Affairs, Nat. Security Council, White House 1968–69; Special Asst. for Policy Planning, Bureau of Inter-American Affairs 1969, to Dir.-Gen. Foreign Service 1969–71; Deputy Chief of Mission and Counsellor, U.S. Embassy, Kabul 1971–74; Deputy Dir. Policy Planning Staff, Dept. of State 1974–75, Asst. Sec. of State for Int. Organization

1975–77; Amb. to Israel 1977–85; Visiting Fellow, Princeton Univ. 1963–64; Diplomat-in-Residence, Johns Hopkins Foreign Policy Inst. 1985–87; Guest Scholar, The Brookings Institution, Washington, D.C. Jan.-Oct. 1987; Pres. U.S. Inst. of Peace 1987–; mem. Council on Foreign Relations, American Acad. of Diplomacy, The Middle East Inst., Cousteau Soc.; Chair. Bd. of Overseers, The Harry S. Truman Inst. for Advancement of Peace, Hebrew Univ. of Jerusalem; Sr. Int. Fellow, Dayan Centre for Middle Eastern and African Affairs, Tel Aviv Univ.; Hon. Ph.D.; Hon. D.Hum.Litt.; William A. Jump Award 1967; Meritorious Honor Award (Dept. of State, AID) 1967; Presidential Man. Improvement Award 1970; Distinguished Honor Awards 1977, 1985. *Publications:* Soviet and American Attitudes toward the Arab-Israeli Peace Process, in Super Power Rivalry in the Middle East 1987, The United States and Israel 1977–1988, in The Middle East: Ten Years after Camp David 1988. *Leisure interests:* tennis, scuba diving, nature photography. *Address:* 6232 Nelway Drive, McLean, Va. 22101, U.S.A.

LEWIS, Stephen; Canadian politician and commentator; b. 11 Nov. 1937, Ottawa; s. of David and Sophie Lewis; m. Michele Landsberg 1963; three c.; ed. Univ. of Toronto, Univ. of British Columbia; spent two years teaching and travelling in Africa; fmr. Dir. of Org., New Democratic Party (NDP), Prov. Leader 1970–77; M.P. for Scarborough W., Ont. Legis. 1963–78; Amb. and Perm Rep. of Canadian Mission to UN 1984–88; Fellow, Ryerson Polytechnical Inst. 1981–; Hon. LL.D (McMaster Univ.) 1979, (York Univ., Toronto) 1984; Gordon Sinclair ACTRA Award 1982; B'nai B'rith Human Rights Award 1983. *Publication:* Art Out of Agony 1983. *Address:* c/o Department of External Affairs, Lester B. Pearson Bldg., 125 Sussex Drive, Ottawa K1A 0G2, Canada.

LEWIS, Sir (William) Arthur, Kt., B.COM., PH.D., LL.D.; British economist; b. 23 Jan. 1915, Saint Lucia, West Indies; s. of George Ferdinand and Ida Louisa Lewis; m. Gladys Jacobs 1947; two d.; ed. L.S.E.; Lecturer, L.S.E. 1938–48; Prof. of Political Economy, Univ. of Manchester 1948–58; Prin., then Vice-Chancellor, Univ. of the West Indies 1959–63; Prof. of Political Economy, Princeton Univ. 1963–83, Prof. Emer. 1983–; Pres. Caribbean Devt. Bank 1970–73; Chair. Caribbean Research Council 1985–; mem. American Philosophical Soc., American Acad. of Arts and Sciences; Distinguished Fellow, American Econ. Asscn., Pres. 1983; Corresp. Fellow, British Acad.; shared Nobel Prize in Econs. 1979, Hon. D.S.C. Econ. (London Univ.) 1982, Hon. LL.D. (Yale) 1983, (Harvard) 1984. *Publications:* Economic Survey 1918–1939 1949, Overhead Costs 1949, The Theory of Economic Growth 1955, Politics in West Africa 1965, Development Planning 1966, Reflections on the Economic Growth of Nigeria 1968, Some Aspects of Economic Development 1969, Tropical Development 1880-1913 1971, The Evolution of the International Economic Order 1978, Growth and Fluctuations 1870-1913 1978, Racial Conflict and Economic Development 1985. *Leisure interest:* music. *Address:* Woodrow Wilson School, Princeton, N.J. 08540, U.S.A. *Telephone:* 452-4825.

LE WITT, Jan; British (b. Polish) artist; b. 3 April 1907, Czestochowa; s. of Aaron and Deborah (née Koblenz) Le Witt; m. Alina Prusicka 1939; one s.; settled in Britain 1937; one-man exhbns.: Soc. of Fine Arts, Warsaw 1930, London, Paris, Milan, Rome, New York, Philadelphia etc.; retrospective exhbns.: Musée d'Antibes, Chateau Grimaldi, Museum of Modern Art, Zacheta Palace, Warsaw, Sala Napoleonica, Venice; works at Musée d'Antibes, Musée Nat. d'Art Moderne, Paris, Nat. Museum, Warsaw, Nat. Museum, Jerusalem and others; mem. of Lewitt-Him Partnership 1933–54; originator of range of anti-invasion defences 1940; Co-designer of murals for Festival of Britain, Festival Clock, Battersea Park 1951; designed decors and costumes for Sadlers Wells Ballet, glass sculptures, Murano, Venice; designed tapestries for Abusson; Gold Medal, Vienna 1948, Gold Medal Triennale, Milan 1954; mem. Exec. Council Soc. Européene de Culture, Venice 1961–; Fellow Int. PEN 1978. *Publications:* Vegetabull 1956 and various review articles. *Leisure interests:* music, poetry. *Address:* 10 Highfield Avenue, Cambridge, CB4 2AL, England. *Telephone:* (0223) 311614.

LEWITT, Sol, B.F.A.; American artist; b. 1928, Hartford, Conn.; ed. Syracuse Univ.; Instructor Museum of Modern Art School 1964–67, Cooper Union 1967, School of Visual Arts, N.Y. 1969–70, New York Univ. 1970; one-man shows include: Guggenheim Museum 1971, Museum of Modern Art, N.Y. 1971, Walker Art Center 1972, Museum of Modern Art, Oxford 1973, Stedelijk Museum, Amsterdam 1974, Visual Arts Museum, N.Y. 1976, San Francisco Museum of Art 1975, Wadsworth Atheneum, Hartford 1981, Musée d'Art Contemporain, Bordeaux 1983; group exhbns. include Sculpture Annual, Whitney Museum of American Art, N.Y. 1967, Minimal Art, The Hague 1968, Stadtische Kunsthalle, Düsseldorf 1969, La Jolla Museum of Contemporary Art 1970, Tokyo Biennale 1970, Guggenheim Int., N.Y. 1971, Whitney Biennial N.Y. 1979, Hayward Gallery, London 1980, Int. Sculpture Exhbn. Basle 1980, Musée Nat. d'Art Moderne, Paris 1981, Art Inst. Chicago 1982, Museum of Modern Art, N.Y. 1983, Museum of Contemporary Art, Los Angeles 1986; also represented in a number of perm. collections. *Publications:* numerous articles for specialist magazines on sculpture, drawing and conceptual art. *Address:* c/o Susanna Singer, 50 Riverside Drive, New York, N.Y. 10024, U.S.A.

LEWY, Casimir, M.A., PH.D., F.B.A.; British philosopher; b. 26 Feb. 1919, Warsaw, Poland; s. of Ludwik Lewy and Izabela Rybier; m. Eleanor Ford 1945; three s.; ed. Mikolaj Rej School, Warsaw, Poland, Fitzwilliam House and Trinity Coll., Cambridge; Lecturer in Philosophy, Univ. of Liverpool 1945–52, Univ. of Cambridge 1952–72; Sidgwick Lecturer, Univ. of Cambridge 1955–72, Reader in Philosophy 1972–82; Fellow, Trinity Coll. Cambridge 1959–; Visiting Prof. of Philosophy, Univ. of Texas at Austin 1967, at Yale Univ. 1969. *Publications:* Meaning and Modality 1976; Editor G. E. Moore, Commonplace Book 1919–1953 1962; G. E. Moore, Lectures on Philosophy 1966; C. D. Broad, Leibniz 1975; C. D. Broad, Kant 1978; C. D. Broad, Ethics 1985; articles in philosophical journals. *Leisure interests:* reading, walking. *Address:* Trinity College, Cambridge, CB2 1TQ, England. *Telephone:* (0223) 338400.

LEY, Hermann Hubert, DR.SC.PHIL., DR.MED.DENT.; German philosopher and politician; b. 30 Nov. 1911, Leipzig; s. of Hermann and Agnes Ley (née Dietel); m. Christine Simon 1958; ed. Helmholtz School and Leipzig Univ.; four years prison for high treason between 1933–45; Prof. of Theoretical Pedagogics, Leipzig Univ. 1947–48, of Dialectics and Historical Materialism, Dresden Tech. High School 1948–56; Dir.-Gen. State Cttee. for Broadcasting and TV 1956–62; Prof. of Relations of Nat. Science and Philosophy, Humboldt Univ. Berlin; mem. CP 1930, Socialist Unity Party 1946–, Presidium of Deutscher Kulturbund 1962–; Dr. phil. h.c.; National Prize 1960, Karl Marx Prize 1974, Vaterländischer Verdienstorden in Silver 1959. *Publications:* Avicenna 1952, Mittasch 1953, Zur Entwicklungsgeschichte der europäischen Aufklärung 1955, Bemerkungen über Kant 1954, Bemerkungen zum Wesen echter Menschlichkeit (Auseinandersetzung mit Jakob Hommes) 1956, Vorreformatorische Bewegung in Deutschland 1956, Studie zur Geschichte des Materialismus in Mittelalter 1958, Dialektischer Widerspruch zu Lakebrink 1958, Dämon Technik 1960, Einige erkenntnistheoretische Probleme in Naturwissenschaft und Technik 1963, Geschichte der Aufklärung und des Atheismus I 1967, II 1970–71, III 1978–80, IV 1982, Vergleich der Geschichtsphilosophie von Hegel und Marx 1982, Kaiser Frederick II als Antichrist 1982, Gesetz und Bedingung in den Technischen- und Naturwissenschaften 1964, Struktur und Prozess in Nat. und Tech. 1966, Bildung und Erziehung 1966, Technik, Praxis, Philosophie 1967, Technik und Weltanschauung 1969, Kritische Vernunft und Revolution, Zur Kontroverse zwischen Hans Albert und Jurgen Habermas 1971, Zum Hegelverständnis unserer Zeit 1972, Zum Kantverständnis unserer Zeit 1975, Atheismus/Materialismus/ Politik 1978. *Leisure interests:* skiing, driving. *Address:* Ernst-Grube-Strasse 41C, 117 Berlin, German Democratic Republic. *Telephone:* 65-7-29-02.

LEYGUE, Louis Georges; French sculptor; b. 25 Aug. 1905, Bourg en Bresse; s. of Albert Leygue and Josephine Parisot; m. Marianne Cochet 1932; two s.; ed. Ecole Nat. Supérieure des Beaux Arts; Prof Ecole des Beaux Arts, Paris 1945–75, Ecole Normale Supérieure d'Enseignement Technique 1950–67; mem. Inst. de France; Pres. Acad. des Beaux Arts 1976, 1982; Pres. of Section, Confed. des Travailleurs Intellectuels 1970–; Officier, Légion d'honneur; Commdr. des Arts et des Lettres; Croix de Guerre avec palme and other decorations. *Works include:* decoration for French Embassy in Ottawa, phoenix at Univ. of Caen, Le Prisonnière Politique, Young Africa Monument, Abidjan, monumental fountain, Paris La Défense, statues for French Embassy, Tokyo and Lycée Français, Lisbon, Le Soleil, stainless steel sculpture on Nancy-Dijon autoroute 1983; bronzes in several private collections. *Address:* 6 rue du Docteur Blanche, 75016 Paris, France. *Telephone:* 42.24.82.78 and 42.88.53.55.

LEYSER, Karl Joseph, T.D., M.A., F.B.A., F.S.A., F.R.HIST.S.; British professor of medieval history; b. 24 Aug. 1920, Düsseldorf, Germany; s. of Otto Leyser and Emma Hayum; m. Henrietta Louise Valerie Bateman 1962; two s. two d.; ed. Hindenburg Gymnasium, Düsseldorf, St. Paul's School, London, Magdalen Coll. Oxford; war service, Pioneer Corps, then Capt., Black Watch (despatches) 1940–45; Fellow and Tutor in History, Magdalen Coll. Oxford 1948–84, Univ. Lecturer, CUF 1950–65, 1975–84, Emer. Fellow 1984–, Special Lecturer, Medieval European History 1965–75, Vice-Pres. Magdalen Coll. 1971–72; Chichele Prof. of Medieval History, Oxford 1984–88; Fellow All Souls Coll., Oxford 1984–88; Distinguished Visiting Prof., Univ. of Berkeley Calif., U.S.A. 1987; Lecturer Denys Hay Seminar in Medieval and Renaissance History, Univ. of Edinburgh 1986, Medieval Acad. of America 1987; Visiting Prof., Dept. of History, Harvard Univ. 1988; mem. Beirat, Max-Planck-Institut für Geschichte, Göttingen, German Historical Inst., London; mem. Kuratorium, Historisches Kolleg, Munich; Corresp. mem. Cen. Directorate, Monumenta Germaniae Historica. *Publications:* Rule and Conflict in an Early Medieval Society, Ottonian Saxony 1979, Medieval Germany and its Neighbours 1982. *Address:* Magdalen College, Oxford (Office); Manor House, Islip, Oxford, OX5 2SZ, England (Home). *Telephone:* Kidlington 3177.

LHERMITTE, François Augustin, D. EN MED.; French neurologist; b. 4 March 1921, Paris; s. of Jean Lhermitte and Marcelle Duflocq; m. Françoise Garçon 1952; four c.; ed. Lycée Condorcet, Faculty of Medicine, Paris; House Dr. then Dr., Paris 1944–55; Prof. of Neuropsychiatry, Hôpital de la Salpêtrière, Paris 1955–, and of Neurology 1962–, also Head Dept.; Médaille d'or des Hôpitaux de Paris 1954, Commdr., Légion d'honneur; numerous foreign decorations. *Publications:* over 300 publs. on neurological topics. *Address:* Hôpital de la Salpêtrière, 47 boulevard de l'Hôpital, 75013

Paris (Office); 14 rue de Tournon, 75006 Paris, France (Home). *Telephone:* 45.86.20.69 (Office).

LHO SHIN-YONG; Korean diplomatist and politician; b. 28 Feb. 1930, S. Pyongyang Prov.; ed. Law Coll. of Seoul Nat. Univ., Kentucky State Univ.; joined diplomatic service 1956, Dir. Planning and Man. Office, Ministry of Foreign Affairs 1967; Consul-Gen., Los Angeles, U.S.A. 1969–72; Amb. to India 1973, to Geneva 1976; Vice-Foreign Minister 1974, Foreign Minister 1980–82, Prime Minister 1985–87; Head, Agency of Nat. Security Planning 1982–85; Democratic Justice Party. *Address:* c/o Office of the Prime Minister, 77 Sejong-no, Chongno-ku, Seoul, Republic of Korea.

LI BAOHUA; Chinese party official; b. 1908, Luoting, Hebei; s. of Li Tachao; Alt. mem. 7th Cen. Cttee. of CCP 1945; Vice-Minister of Water Conservancy 1949–63 and of Electric Power 1958–63; mem. 8th Cen. Cttee. of CCP 1956; First Sec. CCP Anhui 1963–67; Third Sec. E. China Bureau, CCP 1965; First Political Commissar Anhui Mil. Dist. People's Liberation Army 1966; criticized and removed from office during Cultural Revolution 1967; mem. 10th Cen. Cttee. of CCP 1973, 11th Cen. Cttee. 1977; Second Sec. CCP Guizhou 1973; Chair. Guizhou Prov. Revolutionary Cttee. 1978–80; mem. State Council and Pres. People's Bank of China 1978–82; First Gov., IMF for China 1980–; mem. Cen. Advisory Comm. 1982–. *Address:* c/o People's Bank of China, Beijing, People's Republic of China.

LI BIN; Chinese army officer; Commdr. Gansu Mil. Dist. 1980–85; mem. Standing Cttee., CCP Prov. Cttee., Gansu 1983–. *Address:* People's Liberation Army Headquarters, Gansu Military District, Lanzhou, Gansu Province, People's Republic of China.

LI CHANG; Chinese party official; b. 12 Dec. 1914, Hu Nan Province; s. of Lei Chengwu and Tian Yangying; m. Feng Lanrui 1946; two s. three d.; ed. Qinghua Univ.; joined CCP 1936; mem. CCP Cttee., Qinghua Univ. 1936; Gen. Chief Pioneers of Nat. Liberation Vanguard Corps 1936–38; Dir. Org. Bureau, Cttee. for Youth Work, CCP Cen. Cttee. 1938–42; Sec. CCP Cttee., Beijing Co. and Lishan Co. 1943–46; Dir. Political Dept., 64th Army, PLA 1946–49; mem. E. China Mil. Admin. Council 1950; posts in New Democratic Youth League 1949–53; Pres. Harbin Polytech. Univ. 1953–64; Deputy for Harbin, 1st NPC 1954; Alt. mem. CCP 8th Cen. Cttee. 1956; Vice-Chair. Comm. for Cultural Relations with Foreign Countries, State Council 1964–75; Deputy for Shanghai and mem. Standing Cttee. 5th NPC 1978; Vice-Pres. and Deputy Sec., CCP Cttee., Acad. of Sciences July–Nov. 1975, Vice-Pres., Exec. Chair. of Presidium and Sec. CCP Cttee. 1977–82; Sec. CCP Cen. Comm. for Discipline Inspection 1983–85; mem. CCP Cen. Advisory Comm.; Chair. Bd. of Dirs. Experimental Univ. of Beijing, Wuling Univ.; Dir. Research and Consulting Centre for Regional Devt.; Gen. Consultant, Beijing Inst. for Devt. Strategy; Hon. Prof., Harbin Polytech. Univ. 1986. *Publications:* several articles on scientific research and tech. devt. *Leisure interests:* art, literature. *Address:* 34 Dong Zongbu Hutong, Beijing, People's Republic of China. *Telephone:* 557465.

LI CHANG'AN; Chinese party and state official; alt. mem. 12th CCP Cen. Cttee. 1982, mem. 1985; Deputy Sec. CCP Cttee., Shandong Prov. 1983–88; Gov. of Shandong 1985–88; Deputy Sec.-Gen. CCP State Council 1987–; Deputy Head State Flood Control Headquarters 1988–, Central Forest Fire Prevention 1987–; Vice-Chair. State Tourism Cttee. June 1988–. *Address:* State Council, Beijing, People's Republic of China.

LI CHANGCHUN; Chinese party and government official; b. 1944; ed. Harbin Polytechnic; Sec. Shenyang Mun. CCP Cttee. 1985–; Deputy Sec. Liaoning Prov. CCP Cttee. 1985–86; Gov. of Liaoning Prov. 1986–; alt. mem. CCP Cen. Cttee. 1985; mem. 1987–. *Address:* Central Committee of the Chinese Communist Party, Zhongnanhai, Beijing, People's Republic of China.

LI CHOH-MING, M.A., PH.D., LL.D., D.S.SC.; American (b. Chinese) educator and university professor; b. 17 Feb. 1912, Canton, China; s. of Kanchi and Mewching Tsui Li; m. Sylvia Lu 1938; two s. one d.; ed. Univ. of Nanjing, China, and Univ. of Calif. (Berkeley); Prof. of Econs., Nankai, Southwest Associated and Nat. Cen. Univs., China 1937–43; mem. Chinese Special Mission to U.S.A., Canada and U.K. 1943–45; Deputy Dir. Gen. Chinese Nat. Relief and Rehabilitation Admin. (CNRRA) 1945–47; Chief Del. of Republic of China to UN Econ. Comm. for Asia and the Far East 1947–49; Chair. Bd. of Trustees for Rehabilitation Affairs, Nat. Govt. of China 1949–50; Expert on the UN Population Comm. and Statistical Comm. 1952–57; Lecturer, Assoc. Prof. and Prof. of Business Admin. and fmr. Dir. of Centre for Chinese Studies, Univ. of Calif. (Berkeley) 1951–73, Prof. Emer. 1974–; Vice-Chancellor Chinese Univ. of Hong Kong 1963–78; Sr. Consultant SRI Int. 1979; Pres. Assen. of Southeast Asian Insts. of Higher Learning 1968–70; Dir. Asian Workshop on Higher Educ. 1969; mem. Bd. of Trustees, Asian Inst. of Tech. 1973–87; mem. Editorial Bds. Asian Economic Review, Asian Survey, Modern Asian Studies; Life Fellow, Royal Econ. Soc., R.S.A., London; mem. American Econ. Assen., Assen. for Asian Studies (U.S.A.) and other socs.; Dr. of Laws h.c. (Univs. of Hong Kong, Michigan, Western Ontario, Marquette, Chinese Univ. of Hong Kong), Hon. Dr. of Social Sciences (Pittsburgh); Elise and Walter A. Haas Int. Award, Univ. of Calif. 1974, Clark Kerr Award 1979; Hon.

Prof. Tsinghua Univ. (Peking), Zhongshan Univ. (Canton), Nankai Univ. (Tientsin) 1983–; Hon. C.B.E. 1967, Hon. K.B.E. 1973. *Publications:* Economic Development of Communist China 1959, Statistical System of Communist China 1962; Ed.: Industrial Development in Communist China 1964, Asian Workshop on Higher Education—Proceedings 1969, The First Six Years 1963-69 1971, The Emerging University 1970-74 1975, A New Era Begins, 1975-78 1979, The Li's Chinese Dictionary 1980. *Leisure interests:* Chinese calligraphy, tennis. *Address:* 81 Northampton Avenue, Berkeley, Calif. 94707, U.S.A.

LI DA, Gen.; Chinese army officer; b. 1905, Meixian Co., Shaanxi Prov.; ed. Moscow Mil. Acad., U.S.S.R.; joined Red Army 1931, CCP 1932; Staff Officer, Red 6th Army, on Long March 1934-36; Staff Officer, 129th Div. 1937-45; Chief of Staff, Cen. Plains Field Army 1947, Chinese People's Volunteers in Korea 1953-54; Vice-Minister of Nat. Defence 1954-59; Gen. 1955; Chair. Nat. Defence Sports Asscn. 1958-67; criticized and removed from office during Cultural Revolution 1967; Deputy Chief of Cen. Staff, People's Liberation Army 1972-80; mem. Cen. Advisory Comm. 1982-; Chair. PLA All-Army Sports Guidance Comm. 1978-; Adviser, Mil. Comm., Cen. Cttee. 1980-; mem. 10th Cen. Cttee. of CCP 1973, 11th Cen. Cttee. 1977. *Address:* People's Republic of China.

LI DELUN; Chinese orchestral conductor; b. 6 June 1917, Beijing; s. of Li Yuxiang and Tie Jingou; m. Li Jue 1947; one s. two d.; Artistic Dir. and Conductor, Symphony Orchestra of China Cen. Philharmonic Soc.; Vice-Pres. China Musicians' Asscn.; Hon. Dir. Beijing Symphony Orchestra. *Leisure interests:* photography, calligraphy. *Address:* Cultural Philharmonic Society, 11-1 Hepingjie (Peace Street), 100013 Beijing, People's Republic of China. *Telephone:* 421-1504.

LI DENGYING; Chinese politician; b. 17 Feb. 1914, N. Shaanxi Prov.; mem. Standing Cttee., CCP Cttee., N. Sichuan Dist. 1950; Dir. Organizing Dept., CCP Cttee., N. Sichuan 1950; Deputy Dir. Rural Work Dept., S.W. China Bureau, Cen. Cttee. 1952-54; Deputy Dir. 7th Gen. Office, State Council 1954-60; Dir. Rural Work Dept., N.W. China Bureau, and mem. Standing Cttee., N.W. China Bureau; Chair. Cttee. for Water and Soil Conservation in Middle Reaches of Yellow River, State Council 1961-66; Vice-Chair. Provincial Revolutionary Cttee., Shaanxi 1977-78; Sec. CCP Cttee., Gansu 1978-; Vice-Chair. People's Congress, Gansu 1978-80; Gov. Gansu 1980-83; Chair. People's Congress, Gansu 1983-86; mem. Presidium 6th NPC 1983-87; mem. Cen. Advisory Comm. 1987-. *Address:* Lanzhou, Gansu Province, People's Republic of China.

LI DESHENG, Gen.; Chinese army officer; b. 1916, Xinxian Co., Henan Prov.; Commdr., Red 4th Front Army on Long March 1934-36; Div. Commdr. 2nd Field Army, People's Liberation Army 1949; Gen. PLA 1964; Commdr. Anhui Mil. Dist., PLA 1967; Chair. Anhui Revolutionary Cttee. 1968; Alt. mem. Politburo, 9th Cen. Cttee. of CCP 1969; Dir., Gen. Political Dept., PLA 1969-74; First Sec. CCP Anhui 1971-73; mem. Standing Cttee. of Politburo and Vice-Chair. 10th Cen. Cttee. of CCP 1973-75; mem. Politburo 11th Cen. Cttee. of CCP 1977; mem. Politburo 12th Cen. Cttee. of CCP 1982-85; Commdr. Shenyang Mil. Region, PLA 1974-85, Head, Leading Group for the Prevention and Treatment of Endemic Disease in N. China, Cen. Cttee. 1977-; First Sec. CCP Cttee., PLA Shenyang Mil. Region 1978-85; mem. Standing Cttee., Cen. Advisory Comm. 1985-; Political Commissar, Leading Group of All-Army Financial and Econ. Discipline Inspection 1985-; Hon. Pres. Beijing Inst. of Modernization Admin. Aug. 1986-. *Address:* Shenyang Military Region, People's Republic of China.

LI DING; Chinese theatre director; b. 1927; Dir. China Children's Art Theatre; Vice-Pres. China Asscn. for Advancement of Int. Friendship. 1987-; *productions include:* Changing Expressions. *Address:* China Children's Art Theatre, Beijing, People's Republic of China.

LI DINGZHONG; Chinese traditional medicine practitioner; b. 1930 Beijing; ed. Beijing Medical Univ. 1952; noted for Point Magnetic Theory 1954; Dir. Inst. of Dermatology 1953-. *Publication:* Jimluo Phenomena I 1984. *Address:* Chinese Institute of Dermatology, Beijing, People's Republic of China.

LI DONGYE; Chinese politician and party official; b. 1918, Pinglu Co., Shanxi Prov.; Dir. Social Work Dept., Prov. CCP Cttee., Rehe 1949; Dir. Public Security Dept., Rehe People's Govt. 1950; Deputy Chief Procurator N.E. China Branch, Supreme People's Procuracy 1950; Dir. Political and Judicial Dept., Liaoning 1958; Sec. CCP Cttee., Liaoning 1960-68; disappeared during Cultural Revolution; Vice-Minister of Metallurgical Industry 1979; Sec. CCP Cttee., Anshan Iron and Steel Co. 1979-; Minister of Metallurgical Industry 1982-85; mem. 12th Cen. Cttee. 1982-87; mem. Cen. Advisory Comm. 1987-; Adviser Financial and Econ. Leading Group, CCP Cen. Cttee. 1985-. *Address:* State Council, Beijing, People's Republic of China.

LI FANG; Chinese political scientist; b. 7 March 1925 Changde City, Hunan Prov.; s. of Li Xin Zhai and Wang Fu Ying; m. Zhang Cun Li 1954; one s. one d.; ed. Nanjing Univ.; Prof. of Public Admin., Beijing Inst. of Political Science, Chinese Acad. of Social Sciences 1980-. *Publications:* Outline of Public Administration, numerous articles on science and literature. *Address:* Department of Public Administration, Institute of Political Science, 5 Jianguomennei Dajie, Beijing, People's Republic of China.

LI FENG; Chinese party and state official; b. 1921, Xushui, Hebei; m. Zhang Wenying; one s. three d.; county, then municipal dir.; Deputy Sec.-Gen., Hebei Prov. CCP Cttee. 1958; Deputy Gov., Hebei Prov. 1978-86; alt. mem. CCP 12th Cen. Cttee.; Adviser, Hebei Prov. People's Govt. 1986-. *Address:* Hebei Provincial People's Government, Hebei, People's Republic of China. *Telephone:* 25951.

LI FENGPING; Chinese politician; Dir. Public Security Dept., People's Govt., Zhejiang Prov. 1949, Council mem. 1951; Vice-Gov. Zhejiang 1951; Sec. CCP Cttee., Zhejiang 1957-63, 1966–Cultural Revolution, Anhui 1963-66; purged 1968; Sec. CCP Cttee., Zhejiang 1978-83; Vice-Chair. Prov. Revolutionary Cttee., Zhejiang 1979; Gov. Zhejiang 1979-83; Chair. Prov. People's Congress 1983-; mem. Cen. Advisory Comm. 1987-. *Address:* Office of the Governor, Hangzhou, Zhejiang Province, People's Republic of China.

LI FUSHAN; Chinese artist and engraver; b. June 1940, Quinhuangdao, Hebei; s. of Li Yinchang and Wang Lihui; m. Lei Suoxia 1961; one s. two d.; worked at Quinhuangdao Cultural Centre 1959-62, at Shanhaiguan Cultural Centre 1962-; his works are in pvt. collections in Canada, U.S.A., Italy, N.Z. and countries in S.E. Asia; Dir. Quinhuangdao Arts Asscn.; mem. Hebei br. China Arts Asscn., Hebei Prov. Research Asscn. of Etched Plates. *Leisure interests:* classical literature, photography. *Address:* Shanhaiguan Cultural Centre, Quinhuangdao, Hebei Province, People's Republic of China. *Telephone:* Quinhuangdao 51418.

LI GANG; Chinese state official; Gen. Man. China Automotive Industry Corpn. 1982, Chair. of Bd. 1985-; alt. mem. 12th CCP Cen. Cttee. 1982-87. *Address:* China Automotive Industry Corporation, Beijing, People's Republic of China.

LI GENSHEN; Chinese engineer and party official; b. 1931; Dir. and Chief Engineer, No. 3 Research Inst., No. 7 Research Acad., China Shipbldg. Industrial Corpn.; mem. Standing Cttee. Heilongjiang Prov. CCP Cttee. 1983-, Sec.-Gen. 1984, Deputy Sec. 1985-86; Sec. Harbin Mun. CCP Cttee. 1985, Chair. 1985-; mem. CCP Cen. Cttee. 1987-. *Address:* Municipal Committee of the Chinese Communist Party, Harbin, Heilongjiang Province, People's Republic of China.

LI GUIXIAN; Chinese party official; b. 1938, Gaixian Co., Liaoning Prov.; ed. Mendeleyev Chemical Tech. Inst., Moscow; Vice-Gov., Liaoning 1982-83; Sec. CCP Cttee., Liaoning 1985-; mem. CCP Cen. Cttee. 1985-; Gov. PRC Cen. Bank April 1988-. *Address:* Liaoning Provincial Chinese Communist Party, Shenyang, Liaoning, People's Republic of China.

LI GUOHAO, ENG.D.; Chinese bridge engineer; b. 13 April 1913, Meixian Co., Guangdong Prov.; ed. Shanghai Tongji Univ., Darmstadt Polytech. Inst., Germany; Chair. Nanjing Changjiang River Bridge Tech. Advisory Cttee. 1958-66; council mem. Shanghai People's Govt. 1955-; Vice-Pres. Shanghai Tongji Univ. 1962-66, 1977-79; in disgrace during Cultural Revolution 1966-76; Pres. Shanghai Tongji Univ. 1979-83; Vice-Pres. Society of Civil Eng. of China 1979; received Goethe Medal from Goethe Inst., Fed. Repub. of Germany 1982; Chair. Shanghai CPPCC 1981-; Hon. Pres. Tongji Univ. 1984-. *Publications:* The Torsion Theory of Truss Girders-Torsion, Stability and Vibration of Truss Bridges 1977, and 7 other monographs and 50 papers. *Address:* Room 4, 354, Tongji Xincun, Siping Road, Shanghai, People's Republic of China. *Telephone:* 455290 (Shanghai).

LI GUOWEN; Chinese author; b. 1930, Yancheng, Jiangsu; Head Literary and Artistic Creation Section, Tianjin Railway Art Troupe 1950-53; and ed., Propaganda Dept. All-China Railway Trade Union 1954-57; criticized as a "rightist" 1957; construction worker 1957-76. *Publications include:* The First Cup of Bitter Wine 1980, Spring in Winter 1982.

LI HENG (LI XIAOFANG), PH.D.; Chinese astronomer; b. 22 Dec. 1898, Chengdu City, Sichuan Prov.; ed. Univ. of Paris; Prof. Shangdong Univ. 1933-37; Prof. Huaxi Univ. and Sichuan Univ. 1937-50; Dir. Shanghai Observatory, Academia Sinica 1951-81; Vice-Pres. Astronomy Society of China 1962-; Hon. Dir. Shanghai Observatory 1982-. *Address:* Shanghai Observatory, Shanghai, People's Republic of China.

LI HONGREN; Chinese artist; b. 1931, Beijing; s. of Li Shixin and Wang Huizhen; m. Li Yu-Shu 1958; one s. one d.; Prof. and Dir. Studio of Lithography. *Leisure interest:* drama. *Address:* Central Institute of Fine Arts, Beijing 100005, People's Republic of China.

LI HUA; Chinese woodcut artist; b. 6 March 1907, Canton, Kwangtung Prov.; s. of Li Sui-Feng and Liang; m. Zung Yu-Ren 1953; one d.; Prof. and Head Graphic Dept., Cen. Acad. of Fine Arts 1950-; Pres. Chinese Graphic Artists' Asscn. 1980-; Deputy Dir. Art Bureau, Ministry of Culture 1983-. *Works include:* Two Horses, Camel, Antique Vases with White Plum Blossoms, Morning Song, Antique Vase with Lotus Flowers, Two Flowers with Interwoven Stalks. *Publication:* On Illustrations of Literary

Works. *Leisure interest:* music. *Address:* Central Academy of Fine Arts, Beijing, People's Republic of China.

LI HUAJI; Chinese mural artist, painter and university professor; b. 16 Feb. 1931, Beijing; s. of Li Jue-Tian and Zhang Yun-Zheng; m. Quan Zhenghuan 1959; two d.; mem. Acad. Cttee. and Dir. Mural Painting Dept., Cen. Acad. of Fine Arts; Vice-Dir. Mural Painting Cttee., Artists' Asscn. of China; important murals include Hunting (Harbin Swan Hotel), 5,000 Years of Culture (Beijing Nat. Library). *Leisure interests:* classical music, Beijing opera. *Address:* Central Academy of Fine Arts, Beijing, People's Republic of China. *Telephone:* 554731-226.

LI HUAMIN, Maj.-Gen.; Chinese military official; b. 1915, Lintao Co., Gansu Prov.; Commdr. 21st Div. of the 7th Column, Northeast Field Army 1948; Deputy Commdr. 44th Corps, 4th Field Army 1949; Commdr. 54th Corps in the Korean War 1953; Chief-of-Staff Guangzhou Mil. Region 1963; Deputy Commdr. Wuhan Mil. Region 1968-77; alt. mem. 9th CCP Cen. Cttee. 1969; 12th Cen. Cttee. 1982-85; Deputy Commdr. Shenyang Mil. Region 1978-85; mem. Cen. Advisory Comm. 1985-. *Address:* Central Advisory Commission, Chinese Communist Party, Beijing, People's Republic of China.

LI HUIFEN; Chinese electronics engineer and party official; b. 1941; ed. Qinghua Univ.; alt. mem. 12th CCP Cen. Cttee. 1982; Deputy Man. and Chief Engineer, Radio Equipment Joint Co., Tianjin 1982; Vice-Mayor Tianjin Municipal People's Govt. May 1988-; Deputy for Zhejiang to 6th NPC 1983; alt. mem. 13th CCP Cen. Cttee. 1987-. *Address:* Radio Equipment Joint Company, Tianjin, People's Republic of China.

LI JIANZHEN; Chinese party official; b. 1904, Fengshun Co., Guangdong; joined CCP 1927; propagandist 11th Red Army 1927; worked in Fujian Soviet Govt. 1930-33; Leader Women's Squad, 1st Cadre Co. during Long March ; Dir. Women's Dept., Shaanxi-Gansu Special Regional Soviet Govt. 1937; Sec. CCP Changting Cty. Cttee., Fujian 1945; mem. Exec. Council Democratic Women's Fed. 1949-53; mem. Cen. S. China Mil. and Admin. Council (CSMAC) 1949; Sec. Women's Work Cttee. Cen. S. China Sub-Bureau, CCP Cen. Cttee. 1949-54; Vice-Chair. Land Reform Cttee., Prov. People's Govt., Guangdong 1950; mem. Land Reform Cttee., CSMAC 1950; Deputy for Guangdong, 1st NPC 1954; mem. People's Council, Guangdong 1955; First Sec. Secr. CCP Cen. Guangdong Dist. Cttee. 1955; Alt. mem. CP Cen. Cttee., 8th Party Congress 1956-Cultural Revolution; Sec. Control Cttee., CCP Cttee., Guangdong 1958-Cultural Revolution; Sec. Secr. CCP Cttee., Guangdong 1958-Cultural Revolution; Deputy for Guangdong, 2nd NPC 1958, 3rd NPC 1964; mem. Control Cttee., Cen. Cttee. 1963; disappeared during Cultural Revolution; Vice-Chair. Prov. Revolutionary Cttee., Guangdong 1973-79; Alt. mem. CCP Cen. Cttee., 11th Party Congress 1977-82; Sec. CCP Cttee., Guangdong 1979-83; Sec. Discipline Inspection Cttee., Guangdong 1979-83; Chair. Prov. People's Congress, Guangdong 1979-83; mem. Cen. Advisory Comm. 1982-87. *Address:* Office of the Chairman, People's Congress, Guangdong, People's Republic of China.

LI JIJUN; Chinese army officer; alt. mem. 12th CCP Cen. Cttee. 1982, mem. 1985; Deputy Dir. of a Dept. under the Acad. of Mil. Science 1982; Deputy Dir. Gen. Office, CPC Cen. Mil. Comm. Feb. 1988-; mem. 13th CCP Cen. Cttee. 1987-. *Address:* Academy of Military Science, Beijing, People's Republic of China.

LI JIULONG; Chinese army officer; took part in Jinzheng Campaign of Korean War 1953; Commdr., 160th Div., 54th Army 1972; Commdr., 54th Army 1980; Commdr. Jinan Mil. Region, PLA 1985-; mem. CCP Cen. Cttee. 1985-. *Address:* Jinan Military Region Headquarters, Jinan, Shandong, People's Republic of China.

LI JUNFENG; Chinese sports organizer; b. Gaocheng, Co. Hebei; ed. Beijing Physical Culture Inst.; Vice Pres. Nat. Wushu Coach Cttee. 1985-. *Address:* State Physical Culture and Sports Commission, Beijing, People's Republic of China.

LI KA-SHING; Hong Kong industrialist, financier and property developer; b. 1928; m. Chong Yuet-ming; two s.; moved with family from mainland to Hong Kong 1940; salesman for toy mfg. co. 1942-1950; est. Cheung Kong plastics factory 1950; acquired Hutchison Whampoa trading and industrial conglomerate 1979; owner or shareholder numerous cos. Hong Kong and Canada. *Address:* Hutchison Whampoa Ltd, Hutchison House, 22nd Floor, 10 Harcourt Road, Hong Kong.

LI KERAN; Chinese artist and professor of fine arts; b. 26 March 1907, Xuzhou, Jiangsu; s. of Li Huichun and Li Lishi; m. 1st Su E 1925 (died 1939), three s. one d.; m. 2nd Zou Peizhu 1944, two s. one d.; learned traditional landscape painting from age of 13, then studied sketching and oil painting West Lake Art Acad., Hangzhou; also studied Shanghai Specialised School of Fine Arts and Dept. of Research, State Acad. of Fine Arts, Xihu; thorough study of traditional painting in middle age; teacher, pvt. Specialized School of Fine Arts, Xuzhou 1932-37; Researcher, Art Section of Wuhan Political Dept. and Cttee. of Cultural Activities 1938-43; Lecturer, State Specialized School of Fine Arts at Peking 1946-49; Pres. Research Inst. of Chinese Paintings 1981-; has travelled throughout China painting landscapes, including Spring Rain in South China, The Lijiang River, Lofty Mountain and Heavy Forest; works exhibited in Beijing, Shanghai and other cities in China, in East Berlin 1957, Prague

1959, Tokyo and Osaka 1981 and 1983, Taiwan 1986; paintings in collections in China, Europe, U.S.A. and Japan; old home in Xuzhou now a permanent museum; Vice-Chair. Chinese Artists' Asscn. Nov. 1979-; mem. China Fed. of Literary and Art Circles, Chinese People's Political Consultative Conf.; Corresp. mem. Acad. of Art and Science, G.D.R.; Hon. Pres. Huang Binhong Studies Inst., Beijing Research Inst. of Landscape Painting, Beijing Social Welfare Foundation; Consultant, Chinese Asscn. for the Advancement of Int. Friendship; Hon. Vice-Pres. Chinese Youth Calligraphy and Painting Research Inst.; Nat. Award for Fine Arts 1985. *Publications:* Learn Traditional Landscape Painting, On the Art of Li Keran, etc. *Leisure interests:* Chinese operas, music, jinghu. *Address:* Central Academy of Fine Arts, Beijing, People's Republic of China. *Telephone:* 86.0423 (Home).

LI KEYU; Chinese costume designer; b. 15 May 1929, Shanghai; m. Yuan Mao 1955; ed. Cen. Acad. of Fine Arts; Chief Costume Designer of Cen. Ballet; Deputy Dir. Chinese Soc. of Stage Design; mem. Bd. All-China Artists' Asscn., Chinese Dancers' Asscn.; Deputy Dir. China Export Garments Research Centre; she has designed costumes for many works, including Swan Lake, Le Corsaire, The Maid of the Sea, The Fountain of Bakhchisarai, La Esmeralda, The Red Detachment of Women, The East is Red, The New Year Sacrifice (Ministry of Culture costume design prize), Zigeunerweisen (Ministry of Culture costume design prize), Othello (for Peking Opera, Beijing's costume design prize), Tang Music and Dance, Zheng Ban Qial (Houston Ballet), Fu (Hongkong Ballet); winner sole costume design prize, 4th Japan World Ballet Competition, Osaka 1984. *Publications:* two vols. of sketches. *Address:* 21 Gong-jian Hutong, Do-An-Men, Beijing, People's Republic of China. *Telephone:* 447474.

LI KONGZHENG; Chinese diver; b. 1959; Guangxi Prov.; ed. Texas Univ., U.S.A.; youngest diving gold medallist at Asian Games 1984; bronze medallist 1984 Olympics; gold medallist World Univ. Games 1987. *Address:* China Sports Federation, Beijing, People's Republic of China.

LI KWOH-TING, B.S.; Chinese government official; b. 28 Jan. 1910, Nanking; s. of P. L. Li and Jean Liu; m. Pearl Sung 1937; one s.; ed. Nat. Central Univ., China, and Cambridge Univ., England; Supt. Tze Yu Iron Works, Chungking 1942-45; Pres. Taiwan Shipbuilding Corpn. 1951-53; mem. Industrial Devt. Comm., Econ. Stabilisation Bd. 1953-58; Publisher of The Industry of Free China (monthly) 1954-71; Sec.-Gen. Council for U.S. Aid 1958-63; Convener of Industrial Planning and Co-ordination Group of Ministry of Econ. Affairs 1958-63; Head of Industrial Devt. and Investment Center 1958-63; Vice-Chair. Council for Int. Econ. Cooperation and Devt. 1963-73; Minister of Econ. Affairs 1965-69, of Finance 1969-76, of State 1976-; Sr. Adviser to the Pres. 1988-; mem. Nat. Security Council 1967-; Vice-Chair. Nat. Reconstruction Planning Cttee. 1967-72; mem. Council of Academia Sinica 1981-; Gov. Int. Bank for Reconstruction and Devt. 1969-76; mem. Council for Econ. Planning and Devt., Nat. Taiwan Univ. 1977-; Hon. D.Sc. (Nat. Cen. Univ.) 1983; Distinguished Service Award, New York Chinese Inst. of Engineers; Ramon Magsaysay Award for Govt. Service 1968, and decorations from Repub. of Korea, Spain, Repub. of Viet-Nam, Jordan, Madagascar, Paraguay, Thailand and Gabon. *Publications:* Symposium on Nuclear Physics, British Industries, Japanese Shipbuilding Industry, The Growth of Private Industry in Free China, Economic Policy and Economic Development, The Experience of Dynamic Economic Growth in Taiwan, My Views on Taiwan Economic Development: A Collection of Essays 1975-80, Prospects for Taiwan's Economic Development—a Collection of Essays from 1980-1984 1985, The Economic Transformation of Taiwan 1976-88, The Evolution of Policy Behind Taiwan's Development Success 1988. *Leisure interest:* golf. *Address:* 3 Lane 2, Tai-an Street, Taipei, Taiwan. *Telephone:* 737-7711, 737-7717 (Office); 351 5595 (Home).

LI LANQING; Chinese party and government official; b. 1932; ed. Shanghai Fudan Univ.; Vice-Mayor Tianjin 1983-85; Vice-Minister Foreign Econ. Relations and Trade 1986-; alt. mem. Cen. Cttee. of CCP 1987-. *Address:* Central Committee of the Chinese Communist Party, Zhongnanhai, Beijing, People's Republic of China.

LI LI'AN; Chinese party official; b. 19 July 1920, Wutai County, Shanxi; s. of Zhoa Xu Cheng and Wang Yong Di; Deputy Dir., Office of Personnel Admin. Dept., Cen. Govt. 1952-54; Deputy Dir., a section, Org. Dept., Cen. Cttee. CCP 1954-55; Dir., a section, Finance and Commerce Dept. 1956-60, Dir., a section, and Deputy Dir. Org. Dept. 1961-64; Sec. CCP Cttee., Heilongjiang 1964-66, 1973-81; Deputy for Heilongjiang, 5th NPC 1978-81; Second Sec. CCP Cttee., Heilongjiang 1981-83; First Sec. 1983-; First Sec., CCP Cttee., Harbin City 1981-83; mem. Cen. Cttee. CCP 1982-87; mem. Cen. Advisory Comm. 1987-; Vice-Pres. Prov. Party School, Heilongjiang 1978-83. *Address:* Office of the CCP Committee, Harbin, Heilongjiang, People's Republic of China.

LI LIGONG; Chinese party official; b. 20 Feb. 1925, Jiaocheng, Shanxi; s. of Li Zhengliang and Li Shi; m. Xie Bin; two s. three d.; Sec. CCP County Cttee., Sec. CCP Pref. Cttee., Sec. Communist Youth League of Shanxi Prov., mem. Cen. Cttee. Communist Youth League 1953-65; Sec. Communist Youth League, Beijing Municipal Cttee. 1966; Vice-Dir. Beijing Municipal Revolutionary Cttee. 1977; Sec. CCP Beijing Municipal Cttee. 1978-81;

Exec. Sec. CCP Shanxi Prov. Cttee. 1981–83, Sec. 1983–; mem. CCP Cen. Comm. for Inspecting Discipline 1979–82; mem. 12th Cen. Cttee. CCP 1982, 13th Cen. Cttee. 1987–. *Leisure interests:* swimming, fencing, tennis, hiking. *Address:* General Office of the Chinese Communist Party Shanxi Provincial Committee, Taiyuan, Shanxi, People's Republic of China. *Telephone:* 224451.

LI LIN; Chinese physician; b. 31 Oct. 1923, d. of Li Siguang; m. Zou Chenglu; ed. Birmingham Univ., Cambridge Univ.; returned to China 1951; researcher, Mechanics Lab., Academia Sinica 1951–57; won a collective prize for research in spherical graphite 1956; Research Fellow, Beijing Atomic Energy Inst. 1958–; Research Fellow, Physics Inst., Academia Sinica 1978–; mem. Dept. of Math. and Physics under Academia Sinica 1985–. *Address:* Physics Institute, Zhong Guan Cun, Beijing 100080, People's Republic of China. *Telephone:* 284091 (Beijing).

LI LING; Chinese musician; b. 28 Dec. 1913, Taishan Co., Guangdong Prov.; ed. Yan'an Lu Xun Art Coll.; joined CCP 1941; Art Dir., Cen. Song and Dance Ensemble 1963–66; in disgrace during Cultural Revolution 1966–77; Dir. Cen. Philharmonic Soc. 1979–; Vice-Chair. Chinese Musicians' Asscn. 1981–; Sec. Fed. Literary and Art Circles of China 1982–. *Address:* Chinese Musicians Association, Beijing, People's Republic of China.

LI LINGWEI; Chinese badminton player; b. 1964; won women's single title at 3rd World Badminton Championships, Copenhagen 1982; elected 7th in list of ten best Chinese athletes 1984; won Women's Singles and Women's Doubles (co-player Wu Dixi) at 5th ALBA World Cup, Jakarta 1985; won Women's Singles at World Badminton Grand Prix finals. Tokyo 1985. *Address:* China Sports Federation, Beijing, People's Republic of China.

LI LUYE; Chinese diplomatist; b. 1925, Beijing; served as Chief of Gen. Affairs of Foreign Affairs Office, Yunnan Prov. Govt., Second Sec., Chinese Embassy in Sri Lanka, Section Chief and Div. Chief, First Asian Dept. of Foreign Ministry, Deputy Dir. Inst. of Int. Studies, Deputy Dir. and Dir. Dept. of Int. Orgs. of the Foreign Ministry, Perm. Rep. of China to UN, Geneva Office, now to UN, New York; took part 11th UN Special Session on Econ. Affairs 1980, Ministerial Preparatory Meeting and Summit Meeting of Cancun Int. Conf. on Co-operation and Devt. 1981, 38th Session of Econ. and Social Comm. for Asia and Pacific 1982, and 40th Session of UN Gen. Ass. *Address:* Permanent Mission of the People's Republic of China to the United Nations, 155 West 66th Street, New York, N.Y. 10023, U.S.A.

LI MENGHUA; Chinese politician; b. 1922, Pingshan Co., Hebei Prov.; Dir. S.W. Office, Youth Fed. 1953; mem. Cen. Cttee., New Democratic Youth League 1953; mem. Nat. Cttee., Youth Fed. 1953–57, Vice-Chair. Youth Fed. 1958; Vice-Chair. Physical Culture and Sports Comm., State Council 1960–67; purged 1967; Cadre, State Council 1973; Vice-Chair. Physical Culture and Sports Comm., State Council 1978–81, Chair. 1981–; Vice-Pres. All-China Sports Fed. 1979–86, Pres. March 1986–; Pres. Weidi Asscn. 1979; Vice-Pres. Chinese Olympic Cttee. 1980–86, Pres. March 1986–; Minister, Physical Culture and Sports Comm. 1981–; Sec. Party Group, Physical Culture and Sports Comm., State Council 1986–; mem. Cen. Cttee. of CCP 1982–. *Address:* c/o State Council, Beijing, People's Republic of China.

LI MING; Chinese state official; b. Nov. 1927, Tienjin; m. 1954; two s. one d.; Engineer, Dept., Dir., Anshan Iron and Steel Complex 1949–81; Chief Engineer, Pres. Panzhihua Iron and Steel Complex 1968–81; Gen. Dir., Leading Office, Shanghai Baoshan Steel Plant Project, Dir. Baoshan Steel Plant 1983–88, Chair. Aug. 1988–; mem. Hainan Mil. and Admin. Council 1949; council mem. Guangzhou Mun. People's Govt. 1950; Deputy Commdr., Liuzhou South Dist., Guangxi Mil. Dist. 1952; Deputy for Guangxi to 1st NPC 1954, 2nd NPC 1958, 3rd NPC 1964; Deputy Dir.-Gen., Gen. Admin. of Civil Aviation 1964, and 1978; Vice-Chair. Aviation Asscn. 1964; Deputy for PLA to 5th NPC 1978; Vice-Minister of Metallurgical Industry 1982–; Vice-Chair. Liaoning Prov. Cttee. Jan. 1988–; alt. mem. 12th CCP Cen Cttee. 1982–85, mem. 1985–87; alt. mem. 13th CCP Cen. Cttee. 1987–. *Leisure interest:* swimming. *Address:* Ministry of Metallurgical Industry, 46, West Dongsi Xidajie, Beijing, People's Republic of China. *Telephone:* 557431-4305 (Office).

LI NING; Chinese gymnast; b. 1963, Liuzhou, Guangxi Zhuang Autonomous Region; winner, Men's Individual Event, 6th World Cup Gymnastics Competition Oct. 1982; 9th Asian Games Nov. 1982.

LI PENG; Chinese politician; b. 1928, Chengdu City, Sichuan Prov.; s. of the late Li Shuoxun and Zhao Jhentao; m. Zhu Lin 1958; two s. one d.; ed. Moscow Power Inst.; Vice-Minister of Electric Power Industry 1980–81, Minister 1981–82; Vice-Premier of State Council 1983–; Vice-Minister of Water Conservancy and Electric Power 1982–85; Minister in Charge of State Educ. Comm. 1985–88; Acting Prime Minister 1987–88; Prime Minister of People's Repub. of China April 1988–; mem. 12th Cen. Cttee. of CCP 1982–87, 13th Cen. Cttee. 1987–; mem. Political Bureau 1985–87, Standing Cttee. 1987–; mem. Secr. CCP Cen. Cttee. 1985–87. *Address:* c/o State Council, Beijing, People's Republic of China.

LI QI; Chinese party ideologue; b. 1908, Shanxi; Dir. CCP Party Literature Research Centre 1982–; mem. 6th NPC 1984, mem. Standing Cttee. 1986–; Vice-Pres. All-China Sports Fed. 1979; Pres. Middle Schools' Sports Asscn. 1979–; Adviser, Marxist-Leninist Inst. 1984–; *Address:* Chinese Academy of Social Sciences, Beijing, People's Republic of China.

LI QIANG; Chinese politician and telecommunications specialist; b. 1911, Hunan; mem. 6th Exec. Cttee., Nat. Fed. of Trade Unions 1948–53; Dir. Radio Bureau, Ministry of Post and Telecommunications 1950; Commercial Attaché, Embassy in Moscow 1952–54; mem. Scientific Planning Comm., State Council 1957; Deputy Dir. Bureau for Econ. Relations with Foreign Countries, State Council 1961; Vice-Chair. Comm. for Econ. Relations with Foreign Countries 1965–67; Vice-Minister of Foreign Trade 1968–73; mem. 9th Cen. Cttee. of CCP 1969; Minister of Foreign Trade 1973–81; mem. 10th Cen. Cttee. of CCP 1973, 11th Cen. Cttee. 1977–82; Vice-Chair. Credentials Cttee. 5th Nat. People's Congress 1979–83; Adviser to State Council 1981; Pres. China Romania Friendship Asscn. 1984–. *Address:* People's Republic of China.

LI QIAOXIAN; Chinese diver; b. 1967, Guangdong Prov.; women's springboard gold medallist World Univ. Games. *Address:* China Sports Federation, Beijing, People's Republic of China.

LI QIMING; Chinese party official; b. 1908, Shanxi; Deputy Dir. Public Security Dept. Shaanxi-Gansu-Ningxia Border Govt. 1944; Deputy Dir. Social Work Dept. Northwest China Bureau, CCP Cen. Cttee. 1947; Deputy Dir. Public Security Dept. Northwest Mil. and Admin. Council 1950–53, Dir. 1953–56; mem. Standing Cttee. CCP Prov. Cttee. Shaanxi 1956–61; Sec. CCP Prov. Cttee. Shaanxi 1961–68; Acting Gov. Shaanxi 1963, Gov. 1963–68; criticised and removed from posts during the Cultural Revolution 1968–77; Vice-Chair. Yunnan Revolutionary Cttee. 1977; mem. 11th CCP Cen. Cttee. 1977, 12th Cen. Cttee. 1982–87; mem. Cen. Advisory Comm. 1987–; Sec. CCP Prov. Cttee. Yunnan 1977–78, Standing Sec. 1978–79, 2nd Sec. 1979–83; Chair. Yunnan Prov. CPPCC 1980–85; Dir. Yunnan Party School 1981; Perm. Vice-Chair., Yunnan Prov. Guiding Cttee. for Party Consolidation 1983–; Chair. Children's Activities Centre Admin. Cttee. 1986–. *Address:* Yunnan Chinese Communist Party Provincial Committee, Kunming, People's Republic of China.

LI QING; Chinese politician; b. 1920, Ninghe Co., Hebei Prov.; Dir. State Navigation Bureau 1956; Dir. Chinese Shipping Register 1973; Dir. State Bureau for Harbour Superintendency 1975–76; Vice-Minister of Communications 1979–82, Minister 1982–84, Adviser to Ministry 1984–; Adviser, Law Comm., NPC 1986–; Vice-Chair. Bd. of Dirs. China Merchant Steam Navigation Co. 1981. *Address:* c/o State Council, Beijing, People's Republic of China.

LI QINGWEI; Chinese party and government official; Vice-Gov. of Henan 1956–Cultural Revolution; Vice-Chair. Prov. Revolutionary Cttee., Henan 1977–79; Deputy Sec. CCP Cttee., Henan 1978–79; Vice-Gov. of Henan 1979–83; Sec. CCP Cttee., Henan 1980–83, Deputy Sec. 1983; Gov. of Shaanxi 1983–87; Deputy Dir.-Gen. Econ., Tech. and Social Devt. Research Centre 1987–; mem. Cen. Advisory Comm. 1987–. *Address:* Office of the Governor, Taiyuan, Shaanxi Province, People's Republic of China.

LI QUN; Chinese woodcut artist; b. 25 Dec. 1912, Lingshi Co., Shanxi; s. of Hao Changxu and Ren Shuangzhi; m. Liu Pingdu 1935; four s. four d.; mem. Standing Council, Chinese Artists' Asscn. *Leisure interests:* swimming, tennis, social dancing. *Address:* Shanxi Province Branch, Chinese Artists' Association, Taiynan, Shanxi, People's Republic of China. *Telephone:* 440386.

LI RENLIN; Chinese politician; b. 1918, Anhui; took part in Long March 1934–35; Sec. Enshi Dist. CCP Cttee. 1950; Council mem. People's Govt., Hubei Prov. 1950; Deputy Dir. Industrial and Communication Political Dept., Cen. Cttee. 1966–67; purged 1967; Dir. Capital Construction Eng. Corps 1977–; Vice-Chair. State Capital Construction Comm., State Council 1978–82; mem. Presidium CPPCC 1983–. *Address:* c/o State Council, Beijing, People's Republic of China.

LI RUI; Chinese party official; cadre in Hunan 1950; Asst. Minister of Water Conservancy and Electrical Power 1955–58; in political disgrace 1967–79; Vice-Minister, 4th Ministry of Machine Building 1979–82; Vice-Minister, Power Industry 1979–82; Dir. State Bureau of Computers 1980–; mem. 12th Cen. Cttee. CCP 1982–85; mem. Cen. Advisory Comm. 1987–; Deputy Head Org. Dept. CCP 1983. *Publications:* The Early Revolutionary Activities of Comrade Mao Zedong, Some Fundamental Problems Concerning the Total Utilization Plan for the Yellow River. *Address:* Central Committee of the Chinese Communist Party, Beijing, People's Republic of China.

LI RUIHUAN; Chinese party and government official; b. 1935; Vice-Chair. Beijing Trade Union 1973; Dir.-Gen. Work Site for Mao Zedong Memorial Hall, Beijing 1977; Deputy for Beijing, 5th NPC 1978; Sec. Communist Youth League 1978–; mem. Standing Cttee., 5th NPC 1978–; Deputy Mayor Tianjin 1981, Acting Mayor 1982, Mayor Tianjin 1982–; Sec. CCP Cttee., Tianjin 1982–83, Deputy Sec. 1983–87, Sec. Sept. 1987–; Vice-Pres.

All-China Youth Fed. 1980; mem. CCP Cen. Cttee. 1982–, Politburo 1987–; named Nat. Model Worker 1979. *Address:* People's Republic of China.

LI RUISHAN; Chinese state official; b. Hebei Prov.; Deputy Dir. Financial and Econ. Affairs Cttee., Hunan People's Govt. 1954; Deputy Sec. CCP Cttee., Hunan Prov. 1955, Dir. Rural Work Dept. 1954, Sec. 1956–68; First Sec., Changsha Municipality 1959–68; Chair. Revolutionary Cttee., Hunan 1968–78; mem. 9th CCP Cen. Cttee. 1969; First Political Commissar, Shaanxi Mil. Dist. 1969–78; Political Commissar, Lanzhou Mil. Region 1969–76; First Sec. CCP Cttee., Shaanxi Prov. 1971–78; Deputy for Shaanxi to 5th NPC 1978; Vice-Minister, State Agricultural Comm. 1979–82; Vice-Minister, State Econ. Comm. 1982–85; Adviser, State Econ. Comm. 1985–; alt. mem. 12th CCP Cen. Cttee. 1982–87; Deputy Head, State Leading Group to Direct Construction of Gansu Prov. Corridor Commercial Grain Basin 1983. *Address:* State Economic Commission, Beijing, People's Republic of China.

LI SENMAO; Chinese state and railways official; joined CCP 1946; Vice-Minister of Railways in charge of Transport and Factories 1982–; mem. 12th CCP Cen. Cttee. 1982–87, alt. mem. 13th Cen. Cttee. 1987–. *Address:* Ministry of Railways, 10, Fuxing Road, Beijing, People's Republic of China. *Telephone:* 863855 (Office).

LI SHOUSHAN; Chinese party official; alt. mem. 12th CCP Cen. Cttee. 1982, 13th Cen. Cttee. 1987–; Sec. CCP Cttee., Tacheng Pref., Xinjiang Autonomous Region 1982; mem. CCP Standing Cttee., Xinjiang 1983–85; Deputy Sec. CCP Regional Cttee., Xinjiang 1985–. *Address:* Xinjiang Autonomous Regional Chinese Communist Party, Urumqi, Xinjiang, People's Republic of China.

LI SHUIQING; Chinese army officer and party official; b. 1905; joined CCP 1935; Political Commissar nr. Beijing 1942; Div. Commdr. 20th Army 1948; Chief of Staff 67th Army 1952, Deputy Commdr. 1954, Commdr. (also of Qingdao Garrison) 1957; Deputy Commdr. Jinan Mil. Region 1968; mem. 9th Cen. Cttee. CCP 1969, 10th Cen. Cttee. 1973, 11th Cen. Cttee. 1977; Cadre Prov. Revolutionary Cttee., Shandong 1970; Mil. Leader Jinan Mil. Region 1970–71; Minister 1st Ministry of Machine-Building 1971–76; Deputy Commdr. Nanjing Mil. Region 1976–77; Commdr. PLA 2nd Artillery Corps 1978–82; Vice-Minister of Communications 1979–82; mem. Presidium CPPCC 1983–. *Address:* State Council, Beijing, People's Republic of China.

LI SHUZHENG; Chinese party official and fmr. youth leader; Deputy Dir. Foreign Relations Dept., Communist Youth League 1962; Alt. Sec. Communist Youth League 1964; Sec. Women's Fed. 1978–80; dir. of a Bureau under Int. Liaison Dept., CCP Cen. Cttee., Deputy Dir. Int. Liaison Dept. 1981–; alt. mem. 12th CCP Cen. Cttee. 1982, 13th Cen. Cttee. 1987. *Address:* International Liaison Department, Chinese Communist Party Central Committee, Beijing, People's Republic of China.

LI SONGWAN; Chinese tennis player; b. 1958, Beijing; ed. Beijing Univ.; Nat. Tennis Champion 1983–86. *Address:* Institute of Sports, Beijing, People's Republic of China.

LI SUJIE; Chinese athlete; gold medallist in women's 10 kilometre walk at 1987 World Univ. Games. *Address:* Chinese Sports Federation, Beijing, People's Republic of China.

LI TIEYING; Chinese state official; b. 1937; s. of late Li Weihan; fmr. deputy dir. of an electronics research inst.; Sec. CCP Cttee., Shenyang Municipality 1981; alt. mem. 12th CCP Cen. Cttee. 1982, mem. 1985; mem. Politburo, 13th Cen. Cttee. CCP 1987–; Sec. CCP Cttee., Liaoning Prov. 1983–86; Minister of Electronics Industry 1985–88; Minister in charge of State Educ. Comm. April 1988–; of State Comm. for Econ. Reconstruction 1987–88; Chair. Cen. Patriotic Public Health Campaign Cttee. *Address:* State Education Commission, Beijing, People's Republic of China.

LI TINGDONG; Chinese geologist; b. 1932; Pres. Acad. of Geological Sciences 1982–. *Address:* Chinese Academy of Sciences, Beijing, People's Republic of China.

LI XIANJI; Chinese woodcut artist; b. 1943, Xian, Shaanxi; s. of Li Yuting and Lu Jingui; m. Sun Julan 1969; one s. one d.; ed. Polytech. School at Xian Fine Arts Inst.; mem. Chinese Woodcut Artists' Assćn. (Vice-Pres. Shaanxi Branch); mem. Chinese Bookplate Research Soc.; Dean, Fine Arts Research Studio, Shaanxi Prov. Art Research Inst.; has published large no. of woodcuts, many of which have been exhibited in China and abroad and have won prizes. *Address:* Shaanxi Provincial Art Research Institute, Xian, People's Republic of China.

LI XIANNIAN; Chinese politician; b. 1909, Huangan, Hubei; m. Lin Jiamei; joined CCP 1927; Political Commissar 30th Army, 4th Front Red Army 1935; Commdr. 5th Column, New 4th Army 1938; mem. 7th Cen. Cttee. of CCP 1945; Gov. of Hubei 1949; Commdr. Political Commissar Hubei Mil. Dist., PLA 1949; Vice-Premier, State Council 1954–80; Minister of Finance 1954–75; mem. Politburo, 8th Cen. Cttee. of CCP 1956; Sec. Secr. of Cen. Cttee., CCP 1958–66; Vice-Chair. State Planning Comm. 1962; mem. Politburo, 9th Cen. Cttee. of CCP 1969, Politburo, 10th Cen. Cttee. 1973, Politburo, 11th Cen. Cttee. 1977, Politburo, 12th Cen. Cttee.

CCP 1982–87; Vice-Chair. CCP; Pres. of People's Repub. of China 1983–88; Chair. CPPCC 7th Nat. Cttee. 1988–; Hon. D.Econs. (Bangkok) 1985; Star of Socialist Repub. of Romania 1984. *Address:* People's Republic of China.

LI XIMING; Chinese party and government official; b. 1936, Hebei; ed. Xinghua Univ.; Sec. CCP Cttee., Shijingshan Power Plant; identified as govt. cadre 1975; Vice-Minister of Water Conservancy and Electric Power 1976–79; Vice-Minister of Electric Power Industry 1979–82; Minister of Urban and Rural Construction and Environmental Protection 1982–84; mem. 12th Cen. Cttee., CCP 1982–87; mem. Politburo 13th Cen. Cttee. CCP 1987–; First Political Commissar PLA Garrison, Beijing 1984–; CCP First Sec. Beijing; Vice-Chair. Cen. Patriotic Public Health Campaign Cttee., CCP Cen. Cttee. 1983; Vice-Chair. Environmental Protection Cttee., State Council 1984–; Pres. Urban Devt. Scientific Research Soc. 1984–; Vice-Chair. Cen. Greening Cttee. 1983–. *Address:* c/o State Council, Beijing, People's Republic of China.

LI XINLIANG; Chinese soldier and party official; Commdr. Autonomous Region Mil. Dist., Guangxi Prov. 1983–86; mem. CCP Cen. Cttee. 1987–. *Address:* Central Committee of the Chinese Communist Party, Zhongnanhai, Beijing, People's Republic of China.

LI XIPU; Chinese party official; Gen. Man. Xi'an Aircraft Mfrs. 1975–81; mem. Shaanxi Prov. CCP Cttee., Dir. Industry-Transportation Dept. 1981; mem. 12th CCP Cen. Cttee. 1982; Sec. CCP Cttee. Shaanxi 1983; Deputy Dir. Advisory Cttee. Shaanxi 1986–; Chair. Shaanxi Prov. 7th People's Congress Standing Cttee. May 1988–. *Address:* Shaanxi Provincial Chinese Communist Party, Xian, Shaanxi, People's Republic of China.

LI XIUFU; Chinese footballer; mem. women's nat. team. *Address:* China Sports Federation, Beijing, People's Republic of China.

LI XUANHUA; Chinese army officer; fmr. Dir. Political Dept., Urumqi Mil. Region, PLA; Political Commissar, Lanzhou Mil. Region, PLA 1985–; Sec. Party Cttee., Lanzhou Mil. Area 1985–. *Address:* Lanzhou Military Region Headquarters, Lanzhou, Gansu, People's Republic of China.

LI XU'E; Chinese state and aerospace official; b. 1929; ed. Qinghua Univ.; Vice-Minister of Space Industry 1982–85; Minister of Astronautics (Space) Industry 1985–88; Vice-Minister State Science and Tech. Comm. May 1988–; Chair. Bd. of Dirs. China Science and Tech. Consultant Corpn. 1983–; mem. 12th CCP Cen. Cttee. 1982. *Address:* c/o Ministry of Space Industry, Beijing, People's Republic of China.

LI XUEZHI; Chinese politician; b. Ningxia; joined CCP 1935; CCP Sec. of Chinhua Admin. Dist., Zhejiang prior to Cultural Revolution; Sec. Ningxia Hui Autonomous Regional Cttee. 1977–79; alt. mem. CCP 11th Cen. Cttee. 1979; First Sec., CCP Ningxia Hui Autonomous Regional Cttee. 1979–; First Political Commissar, Ningxia PLA Mil. Dist. 1981–86; mem. 12th Cen. Cttee. CCP 1982–87. *Address:* c/o Ningxia Hui Autonomous Regional Cttee., Ningxia, People's Republic of China.

LI YAN (Zhuang bei); Chinese painter; b. Nov. 1943, Beijing; s. of Li Ku Chan and Li Hui Wen; m. Sun Yan Hua 1972; one d.; Prof., Qi Bai Shi Correspondence Coll. of Art, Beijing; Vice-Prof. Cen. Inst. of Arts and Crafts; Vice-Pres. Flowers and Birds Painting Asscn., Beijing, Li Ku Chan Museum; mem. Chinese Artists' Asscn.; specializes in painting figures, animals and mountains and water scenes, and in calligraphy; over 10,000 sketches and paintings from life, 3,000 exercises in Chinese painting 1956–; works have been exhibited in Sweden, U.S.A., Canada, Japan, Singapore, Philippines, Hong Kong, Tanzania; gave lectures at Hong Kong Univ. 1980; subject of TV films by Shen Zhen TV 1986 and Swedish TV 1986; important works include Chinese Emperor, Zhou Wen Emperor, Lao Zi, Confucian Worry about Taoism, Lao Zi and Einstein, Five-Colour Earth, Start Sailing, A Swarm of Monkeys, Cat and Chrysanthemum, Tiger Cub; several magazine articles on art. *Leisure interests:* writing poetry, Qigong, The Book of Changes. *Address:* No. 2-1, Building 15, Nan sha Go, San Li He, Xi Cheng District, Beijing, People's Republic of China. *Telephone:* 863844; 8011038.

LI YAOWEN, Gen.; Chinese army officer and diplomatist; b. 1918, Rongcheng Co., Shandong Prov.; Political Commissar, 26th Corps, 3rd Field Army 1949; served in Korea 1950; Deputy Dir. Political Dept., Jinan Mil. Region 1955, Dir. 1958; Deputy Political Commissar, Jinan Mil. Region 1964; mem. Standing Cttee., Revolutionary Cttee., Shandong Prov. 1967; unspecified mil. leader, Jinan Mil. Region 1969; recalled to Beijing 1970; Amb. to Tanzania 1972–76, concurrently to Madagascar 1973–74; alt. mem. 11th CCP Cen. Cttee. 1977–82; Political Commissar, Nat. Defence Scientific and Technological Comm. 1977–82, PLA Navy 1981–; mem. 12th CCP Cen. Cttee. 1982–87, mem. Cen. Advisory Comm. 1987–. *Address:* PLA Navy Headquarters, Beijing, People's Republic of China.

LI YUNCHANG; Chinese soldier and party official; b. 1908, Hebei Prov.; Commdr. Anti-Japan United Forces Fengrun County, Hebei Prov. 1937; Commdr. 4th Column Shanxi-Qahar-Hebei Mil. Area 1938; Commdr. Hebei-Rehe-Liaoning Mil. Area 1945; N.E. Region mem. CPPCC 1949; Vice-Chair. Cen. Aviation Corpn. 1949; Vice-Minister of Communications 1949–; First Sec. Rehe CCP Cttee. 1949–52; Standing Cttee. CPPCC 1959–63; Standing Cttee. Control Cttee. of CCP Cen. Cttee. 1963–; CCP del. to CPPCC Dec. 1964; Standing Cttee. CPPCC 1965; purged 1966, rehabilitated 1979; mem. Standing Cttee. CPPCC 1979; mem. Cen. Advisory Cttee. CCP Cen. Cttee. 1987-. *Address:* Central Advisory Committee of the Central Committee of the Chinese Communist Party, Zhongnanhai, Beijing, People's Republic of China.

LI YUNCHUAN; Chinese diplomatist; b. 1919, Shandong; Sec.-Gen. Machine Building Trade Union 1956; Chair. Machine Building Trade Union 1960; Dir. Int. Liaison Dept., China Fed. of Trade Unions 1963; Amb. to Dahomey 1965-66, to N. Korea 1970-76, to Switzerland 1976-84. *Address:* c/o Ministry of Foreign Affairs, Beijing, People's Republic of China.

LI ZEMIN; Chinese party official; Deputy Sec. Shenyang Mun. CCP Cttee. Liaonong Prov. 1985-; Deputy Sec. Liaoning Prov. CCP Cttee. 1985-86; mem. CCP Cen. Cttee. 1987-. *Address:* Central Committee of the Chinese Communist Party, Zhongnanhai, Beijing, People's Republic of China.

LI ZEWANG; Chinese diplomatist; official in Embassy, Moscow 1959-60; with Oceania Dept. Ministry of Foreign Affairs 1964-65; Amb. to Hungary 1973-76, to Poland 1977-83, to Romania 1983-85, to U.S.S.R. 1985-87; Vice-Pres. China-U.S.S.R. Friendship Assen. Aug. 1988-. *Address:* China-U.S.S.R. Friendship Association, Beijing, People's Republic of China.

LI ZHENGWU; Chinese academic; Pres. Soc. of High Energy Physics 1980-. *Address:* Chinese Academy of Sciences, Beijing, People's Republic of China.

LI ZHUANG; Chinese journalist; Dir. of Gen. Editing Dept., Deputy Ed.-in-Chief, People's Daily 1963-66; in political disgrace 1966-76; Deputy Ed.-in-Chief, People's Daily 1976-83; mem. Cen. Inspection Discipline Comm. CCP 1982-87; Ed.-in-Chief People's Daily 1983-86. *Address:* People's Daily, Beijing, People's Republic of China.

LI ZHUN; Chinese (Mongolian) writer; b. 17 May 1928, Luo Yang, Henan; s. of Li Jun-Ren and Yang Fen; m. Dong Bing; four s. two d.; Cttee. mem., Presidium of Writers' Union of China and of Film Specialists' Union of China 1984-; Vice-Pres. Soc. of Film Literary Inst. 1980-. *Publications:* five collections of short stories, including The Biography of Li Shuang-Shuang; novels, including The Yellow River Flows to the East (Mao Dun Literature Prize); over 20 film scripts, including The Herdsmen (Hundred Flowers Award) and The Wreath at the Foot of the Mountain (Golden Rooster Award). *Leisure interests:* calligraphy, painting, drama. *Address:* 2-401A, No. 15 Hu Fang Road, Beijing, People's Republic of China. *Telephone:* 336700.

LI ZIQI; Chinese party official; Dir. Light Industry Bureau, Prov. Govt., Gansu 1980-; Leading Sec. CCP Cttee., Gansu 1983-; mem. 12th CCP Cen. Cttee. 1982, 13th Cen. Cttee. 1987. *Address:* Chinese Communist Party Headquarters, Lanzhon, Gansu Province, People's Republic of China.

LIANG BUTING; Chinese politician; b. 1921, Fengxian Co., Jiangsu Prov.; Sec. Gen. Secr., Cen. Cttee. of Communist Youth League; mem. Exec. Cttee., 8th Session All-China Fed. of Trade Unions 1957-64; Deputy Dir. Office of Agric. and Forestry, State Council 1964; disappeared during Cultural Revolution; mem. Standing Cttee. and Second Sec. Gen. of Qinghai Prov. Cttee., CCP, mem. Cen. Cttee. CCP 1979-80; First Sec. Gen. Qinghai Prov. Cttee., CCP First Political Commissar of Qinghai Prov. Mil. Region 1980-83; Sec. Gen. Shandong Prov. Cttee., CCP 1983-; Gov. Shandong Prov. 1983-; mem. 12th Cen. Cttee. CCP 1983, 1985, 13th Cen. Cttee. 1987-. *Address:* Jinan, Shandong Province, People's Republic of China.

LIANG CHENGYE; Chinese state official; b. April 1924, Chongzuo County, Guangxi; s. of Liang Chaoji and Ye Shi; m. Li Pianquin 1949; two s. one d.; CCP local leader, Wuzhou, Beihai, and Nanning cities, Guangxi, before 1978; Deputy to NPC and Mayor of Guilin City 1978; Vice-Chair. Guangxi People's Govt. 1980-84; alt. mem. 12th CPC Cen. Cttee. 1980-84; Adviser to Guangxi People's Govt. 1985-. *Leisure interest:* swimming. *Address:* The People's Government of Guangxi, Zhuang Autonomous Region, Nanning, Guangxi, People's Republic of China.

LIANG DONG-CAI (D.C.LIANG); Chinese molecular biophysicist and protein crystallographer; b. 29 May 1932, Guangzhou; Prof., Inst. of Biophysics, Chinese Acad. of Sciences (Dir. 1983-86); mem. Chinese Acad. of Sciences 1980-; Fellow Third World Acad. of Sciences 1985-; Vice-Chair. Nat. Natural Science Foundation of China 1986-; mem. Cttee. on Biomacromolecule Crystallography of Int. Soc. of Crystallography 1981-84; Pres. Chinese Biophysics Soc. 1983-86; Vice-Pres. Chinese Biochemistry Soc. 1987-. *Address:* Institute of Biophysics, Chinese Academy of Sciences, Beijing 100080, People's Republic of China. *Telephone:* Beijing 285529.

LIANG LINGGUANG; Chinese politician and government official; b. 31 Oct. 1916, Yongchun Co., Fujian Prov.; m. Zhu Han-Zhang 1939; two d.; fmr. administrator in Fujian; Minister of Light Industry 1977-80; First Sec. CPC Cttee., Guangzhou Municipality 1980-83; Sec. CCP Cttee. Guangdong Prov. 1980-85; Mayor of Guangzhou 1981-86; Gov. Guangdong Prov. 1983-85; mem. 12th CCP Cen. Cttee. 1982-85; Chair. Hong Kong China Travel Service Group 1986-; Pres. Jinan Univ. 1983-; mem. Preparatory Cttee. for 6th Nat. Games 1985-; Chair. Prov. Advisory Cttee., Guangdong 1985-.

Leisure interest: Chinese and foreign literature. *Address:* Office of the Governor, Guangdong, People's Republic of China.

LIANG NING; Chinese mezzo-soprano; b. 1952; winner, 1st Int. Mirjam Helin Vocal Competition, Helsinki 1984. *Address:* Guangzhou Philharmonic Society, Guangzhou, People's Republic of China.

LIANG XIANG; Chinese government official; Sec. Mun. CCP Cttee. and Mayor of Canton 1960-66; Vice-Chair. Canton Revolutionary Cttee. 1976; mem. Guangdong Prov. CCP Cttee., Vice-Chair. Guangdong Prov. Revolutionary Cttee., 2nd Sec. Canton Municipal CCP Cttee. 1977; Gov. Hainan Prov. People's Govt. Aug. 1988-; Deputy Sec. Hainan Prov. Cttee. Sept. 1988-; fmr. Mayor of Shenzhen City; Deputy Head of preparatory group for establishing Hainan as a prov. 1987-. *Address:* Office of the Special Economic Zone Administration, Haikou City, Hainan, People's Republic of China.

LIANG XIAOSHENG; Chinese writer; b. 1949, Harbin; worker on land reclamation project; local newspaper reporter; Chinese language student, Fudan Univ. 1975; mem. Chinese Writers' Assen., Chinese Film-makers' Assen.; and official of Chinese Film Script-writers' Assen.; Film Script Ed., Beijing Film Studio. *Publications:* four anthologies of short stories, an anthology of medium-length novels and two novels, most of which have been adapted as films or TV plays; works include: This is a Strange Land, Literary Accomplishments, Blizzard at Midnight (all of which have won All-China Short Novel Prizes), For the Harvest, TV play based on Blizzard at Midnight (awarded All-China TV Playscript Grand Prize). *Address:* Editorial Department, "Creative Cinema", 19 Xi-lu, Bei-huan, Beijing, People's Republic of China.

LIANIS, Georgios, PH.D.; Greek engineer and politician; b. 1926 Naousa; ed. Athens Polytechnic Univ. and Imperial Coll., London; teaching and research posts at Brown, Rhode Island, Purdue Univs., Univ. of Washington (Seattle), Patras Univ. and Lehigh Univ., Pa. 1956-76; Prof. of Tech. Mechanics, Thessalonika Univ. 1976-81; founding mem. Pasok; Under-Sec. for Educ. and Religious Affairs 1981-82; Minister for Research and Tech. 1982-85. *Publications:* 55 articles in scientific journals on mechanical properties of plastics, missile dynamics, theories of thermodynamics and relativity, etc. *Address:* c/o Ministry of Research and Technology, Odos Zalokosta 10, Athens, Greece.

LIAO BINGXIONG; Chinese cartoonist; b. 1915, Canton; Vice-Chair. Guangdong branch, Chinese Artists' Assen. *Exhibitions include:* Spring and Autumn in Cats' Kingdom 1945, A 50 Years' Retrospective 1982. *Publication:* Bingxiong's Cartoons 1932-82. *Address:* Chinese Artists Association, Beijing; 2 Hu Bian Village, Renmin Bai Road, Guangzhou, People's Republic of China. *Telephone:* 33979-26 (Guangzhou).

LIAO HANSHENG, Lieut.-Gen.; Chinese government official; b. 1911, Sangzhi Co., Hunan Prov.; Political Commissar 6th Div., 2nd Front Army 1934; Political Commissar, Div. 2nd Front, Red Army 1936; Political Comm. 716 Regiment, 120th Div., 8th Route Army; Political Commissar 1st Column, N.W. Liberation Army 1947; Political Commissar 2nd Army Group, CCP Red Army 1949; Chair. Qinghai Mil. & Admin. Cttee. 1949; Political Commissar, Qinghai Mil. Area 1949; Vice-Chair., Qinghai People's Provincial Govt. 1949-56; Deputy Commdr. Qinghai Mil. Area 1950; mem. N.W. Mil. and Admin. Cttee. 1950; mem. N.W. Admin. Cttee. 1953; Deputy Political Commissar N.W. Mil. Area 1954; Deputy for PLA to 1st NPC 1954; mem. Nat. Defence Council 1954; rank of Lieut.-Gen. 1955; Alt. mem. CCP 8th Cen. Cttee. 1956; Pres. Mil. Acad. of PLA 1957; responsible person PLA Units, Nanjing 1957, Beijing 1962; Deputy for Beijing PLA Units to 3rd NPC 1964; mem. Presidium 3rd NPC 1964; Sec. CCP N. China Bureau 1965; detained in Beijing Garrison HQ, 1967; Branded a 3-Anti Element 1967; resumed activities 1972; Vice-Pres. Acad. of Mil. Science 1974; First Political Commissar PLA Nanjing Mil. Region 1978-80, PLA Shenyang Units 1980-85; mem. 12th CCP Cen. Cttee. 1982-85; Vice-Chair. Standing Cttee.; 6th Nat. People's Congress 1983-; Chair. Cen. Patriotic Public Health Campaign Cttee. 1983-; Chair. Foreign Affairs Cttee.; mem. Presidium 6th NPC 1986-; Chair. Credentials Cttee., NPC 1986-. *Address:* People's Liberation Army, Shenyang, People's Republic of China.

LIAO HUI; Chinese army officer; Deputy Commdr., Anhui Mil. Dist. 1973-81; mem. 12th CCP Cen. Cttee. 1985, 13th Cen. Cttee. 1987; Dir. Overseas Chinese Affairs Office, State Council 1984-; mem. 21st Century Comm. for China-Japan Friendship 1984; Hon. Vice-Chair. Zhonghai Inst. of Agricultural Tech. 1987-. *Address:* Anhui Military District Headquarters, Hefei, Anhui, People's Republic of China.

LIAO KAIMING; Chinese woodcut artist; b. 16 Oct. 1940, Chong-qing, Sichuan; s. of Liao Yuyan and Li Canming; m. Zheng Zhimin 1968; one s.; self-taught artist; Leader China Art Gallery; mem. China Artists' Assen. China Woodcut Artists' Assen.; currently establishing China Folk Art Gallery; many works in galleries and pvt. collections in China, Hong Kong, Japan, U.S.A. etc. *Publication:* Liao Kai-Ming's Woodcut Album. *Leisure interests:* listening to music, reading literature, swimming, fishing, playing chess and ping pong. *Address:* No. 1 Wu Si Da Road, China Art Gallery, Beijing, People's Republic of China. *Telephone:* 44.2906.

LIAO ZHIGAO; Chinese party official; b. *circa* 1908, Jianning, Sichuan; ed. Qinghua Univ., Beijing; Dir. Political Dept., N. Shaanxi 1947; Political Commissar Xikang Mil. Dist., People's Liberation Army 1950-55; Gov. of Xikang Provisional Govt. 1950-55; Vice-Gov. of Sichuan 1955-58; Sec. CCP Sichuan 1956-65, First Sec. 1965-68; Alt. mem. 8th Cen. Cttee. of CCP 1956; Sec. S.W. Bureau, CCP 1964-68; criticized and removed from office during Cultural Revolution 1968; Alt. mem. 10th Cen. Cttee. of CCP 1973; First Sec. CCP Fujian 1975-82; First Political Commissar, Fujian Mil. Dist. 1975-82; Chair. Fujian Prov. People's Congress 1979-82; mem. 11th Cttee. of CCP 1977; First Political Commissar PLA Fuzhou Mil. Region 1980-82; Adviser, Org. Dept., Cen. Cttee. CCP 1982-; mem. Cen. Advisory Comm. 1982-. *Address:* People's Republic of China.

LIAQUAT ALI KHAN, Begum Raana (widow of late Liaquat Ali Khan, fmr. Prime Minister of Pakistan), M.A., B.T.; Pakistani diplomatist; b. 13 Feb. 1905, Almora, India; ed. Univs. of Lucknow and Calcutta; Founder Pres. All-Pakistan Women's Asscn., Nat. Guard, Naval Reserve and Cottage Industry Projects; chair. various educational, hospital and social work groups; del. to UN Gen. Ass. 1952; mem. ILO Expert Cttee. on Recommendations 1955; Amb. to the Netherlands 1954-61, to Italy 1961-66, to Tunisia 1961-64; Gov. Sind Prov. 1973-76; UN Human Rights Award 1978. *Address:* Quaid-e-Millat House, H.M.I., Bath Island, Karachi, Pakistan. *Telephone:* 532709.

LIBANIO CHRISTO, Carlos Alberto (Frei Betto); Brazilian Dominican brother and writer; b. 25 Aug. 1944, Belo Horizonte; s. of Antonio Carlos Vieira Christo and Maria Stella Libanio Christo; ed. Univ. of Brazil, Escola Dominicana de Teologia and Seminario São Leopoldo; Nat. leader, Catholic Young Students 1962-64; political prisoner 1964; newspaper and magazine ed. 1966-69; political prisoner 1969-73; organizer of basic Church communities 1973-79; teacher, popular educ. 1977-; works as writer and teacher with Workers' Pastoral 1979-. *Publications include:* Oração na Ação, Letters from a Prisoner of Conscience, Les Frères de Tito, Against Principalities and Powers, Fidel and Religion. *Address:* Rua Atibaia 420, 01235 São Paulo, S.P., Brazil. *Telephone:* 011-65-1473 (Office); 62-2324.

LIBERAKI, Margarita; Greek novelist and dramatist; b. 1919, Athens; s. of Themistuclis and Sapho Liberaki; m. Georges Karapanos 1941 (divorced); one d.; ed. Athens Univ.; lives in Paris and Greece, writes in Greek and French; plays performed at Festival d'Avignon, Festival of Athens. *Publications:* The Trees 1947, The Straw Hats 1950, Trois étés 1950, The Other Alexander 1952, The Mystery 1976; plays: Kandaules' Wife 1955, The Danaids 1956, L'autre Alexandre 1957, Le saint prince 1959, La lune a faim 1961, Sparagmos 1965, Le bain de mer 1967, Erotica 1970, Zoe 1985; film scripts: Magic City 1953, Phaedra 1961. *Leisure interest:* painting. *Address:* 7 rue de L'Eperon, 75006 Paris, France; 2 Strat. Sindesmou, Athens, Greece. *Telephone:* 46-33 05-92 (Paris).

LIBERIA-PETERS, Maria; Netherlands Antilles politician; m.; leader Nat. Volkspartij (Nat. People's Party); Prime Minister of Netherlands Antilles 1984-85, March 1988-. *Address:* Office of the Prime Minister, Fort Amsterdam, Willemstad, Curaçao, Netherlands Antilles.

LICHFIELD, 5th Earl of, cr. 1831; **Thomas Patrick John Anson,** F.R.P.S.; British photographer; b. 25 April 1939; s. of Viscount Anson and Princess Anne of Denmark; m. Lady Leonora Grosvenor 1975 (divorced 1986); one s. two d.; ed. Harrow School, Sandhurst; army service, Grenadier Guards 1957-62; now works as photographer; Fellow British Inst. of Professional Photographers. *Publications:* The Most Beautiful Women 1981, Lichfield on Photography 1981, A Royal Album 1982, Patrick Lichfield's Unipart Calendar Book 1982, Patrick Lichfield Creating the Unipart Calendar 1983, Hot Foot to Zabriskie Point 1985, Lichfield on Travel Photography 1986, Not the Whole Truth 1986, Lichfield in Retrospect 1988. *Address:* Shugborough Hall, Stafford, England. *Telephone:* (0889) 881-454.

LICHNEROWICZ, André, D. ÈS SC.; French mathematician; b. 21 Jan. 1915, Bourbon; s. of Jean Lichnerowicz and Antoinette Gressin; m. Suzanne Magdelain 1942; three s.; ed. Lycée Louis-le-Grand, Paris, Ecole Normale Supérieure, Paris, and Univ. de Paris; research assignments, Centre National de Recherche Scientifique 1938-41; mem. staff, Univ. of Strasbourg 1941-46, Full Prof. 1946-49; Full Prof. Univ. de Paris 1949-52, Prof. of Mathematical Physics, Collège de France 1952-; mem. Acad. des Sciences, Accad. Naz. dei Lincei, Rome, Acad. Real de Ciencias, Madrid, Acad. Royale de Belgique, Pontifical Acad. of Sciences; Dr. h.c. (Univ. of Waterloo) 1977, (Univ. of Liege) 1982, (Univ. of Coimbra) 1984; Commdr. Légion d'honneur; Commandeur de l'Ordre du Mérite et des Palmes académiques; Médaille Copernic de l'Acad. Polonaise des Sciences 1973; Prix int. Fubini 1955. *Publications:* Algèbre et analyse linéaire 1946, Eléments de calcul tensoriel 1949, Théories relativistes de la gravitation 1954, Théorie globale des connexions 1955, Géométrie des groupes de transformation 1958, Relativistic hydrodynamics and magnetohydrodynamics 1967. *Leisure interests:* philosophy, gardening, tennis. *Address:* 6 avenue Paul Appell, 75014 Paris, France. *Telephone:* 4540-5166.

LICHTENBERG, Paul; German banker; b. 10 Dec. 1911, Bonn; Hon. Chair. Supervisory Bd. Rheinische Hypothekenbank, Frankfurt; Chair. Supervisory Bd., Commerzbank AG, Frankfurt (Main)/Düsseldorf; Vice-Chair. Supervisory Bd., Allianz Lebensversicherungs-AG, Stuttgart; mem. Supervisory Bd. BBC Brown, Boveri & Cie AG, Mannheim, Kaufhof AG,

Cologne; Admin. Bd. Deutsches Atomforum e.V., Bonn; Gelsenwasser AG, Gelsenkirchen, RWE Rheinisch-Westfälisches Elektrizitätswerk AG, Essen. *Address:* Commerzbank AG, Neue Mainzer Strasse 32-36, D-6000 Frankfurt am Main (Office); Breite Strasse 25, 4000 Düsseldorf, Federal Republic of Germany. *Telephone:* 069-13620 (Frankfurt); 8271 (Düsseldorf).

LICHTENSTEIN, Roy, M.F.A.; American painter and sculptor; b. 27 Oct. 1923, New York, N.Y.; s. of Milton and Beatrice (Werner) Lichtenstein; m. 1st Isabel Wilson 1949 (divorced), two s.; m. 2nd Dorothy Herzka 1968; ed. Art Students League, New York, Ohio State Univ.; cartographical draughtsman, U.S. Army 1943-46; Instructor, Fine Arts Dept., Ohio State Univ. 1946-51; product designer for various cos., Cleveland 1951-57; Asst. Prof., Fine Arts Dept., N.Y. State Univ. 1957-60, Rutgers Univ., New Brunswick, N.J. 1960-63; works in Pop Art and other themes derived from comic strip techniques; one-man shows include Carlebach Gallery, New York 1951, Leo Castelli Gallery 1962, 1963, 1965, 1967, 1971-75, 1977, 1979, 1981, 1983, Galerie Illeana Sonnabend, Paris 1963, 1965, 1970, 1975, Venice Biennale 1966, Pasadena Art Museum, Calif. 1967, Walker Art Center, Minneapolis 1967, Stedelijk Museum, Amsterdam 1967, Tate Gallery, London 1967, Kunsthalle, Berne 1968, Guggenheim Museum, New York 1969, Nelson Gallery, Kansas City, Mo. 1969, Museum of Contemporary Art, Chicago 1970, Galerie Beyeler, Basel 1973, Centre Nat. d'Art Contemporain, Centre Beaubourg, Paris 1975, Seattle Art Museum 1976, 1981, Portland Center for the Visual Arts 1980, St. Louis Art Museum 1981; Fort Worth Art Museum 1981, Musée des Arts Décoratifs, Paris 1981, Seibu Museum, Takanawa 1983; group exhbns. include Six Painters and the Object, Guggenheim Museum 1963, Venice Biennale 1966, U.S. Pavilion Expo 1967, Montreal, São Paulo Biennale 1968, 36th Biennial Exhibition of Contemporary American Art at Corcoran Gallery of Art, Washington 1979, and numerous others in Europe and U.S.A. *Address:* P.O. Box 1369, Southampton, New York, N.Y. 11968, U.S.A.

LICKLIDER, J(oseph) C(arl) R(obnett), PH.D.; American psychologist; b. 11 March 1915, St. Louis, Mo.; s. of Joseph Parron Licklider and Margaret Robnett; m. Louise Carpenter Thomas 1945; one s. one d.; ed. Washington Univ., St. Louis and Univ. of Rochester; Research Assoc. and Fellow, Psycho-Acoustic Lab., Harvard; Lecturer in Psychology, Harvard 1946-50; Assoc. Prof. M.I.T. 1950-57, Acoustics Lab. 1951-55, Group Leader Lincoln Lab. 1952-55, Visiting Prof., M.I.T. 1965-66, Prof. of Electrical Eng. 1967-; with Bolt Beranek and Newman 1957-62, Vice-Pres. 1961-62, Head, Psychoacoustics Dept., Engineering Psychology Dept. and Information Systems Research Dept., Dir. Information Processing Research and Behavioural Science, Advanced Research Projects Agency, Dept. of Defense 1962-64; Consultant to I.B.M., Dir. of Research 1964-67; Assoc. Dir. Project MAC, Dir. 1968-70; with Dept. of Defense 1974-75; fmr. Pres. Acoustical Soc. of America, Soc. of Eng. Psychologists; Fellow, American Acad. of Arts and Sciences; mem. Nat. Acad. of Sciences, Assen. for Computing Machinery. *Publications:* Libraries of the Future, and numerous papers on psychoacoustics, communications theory, man-computer interaction, information storage and retrieval. *Address:* 40 Pleasant View Road, Arlington, Mass. 02174, U.S.A. *Telephone:* 617-646-0680.

LIDDIARD, Richard England, C.B.E., M.A.; British commodity broker; b. 21 Sept. 1917, Nainital, India; s. of late Edgar S. and Mabel A. Liddiard; m. Constance L. Rook 1943; one s. three d.; ed. Oundle School and Worcester Coll., Oxford; joined C. Czarnikow Ltd. 1946, Chair. 1958-74, Chair. Czarnikow Group Ltd. 1974-84; Chair. Sugar Assen. of London 1960-78; Vice-Chair. London Commodity Exchange 1971, Chair. 1972-75; Chair. British Fed. of Commodity Assens. 1963-71, Vice-Chair. 1971-77; Chair. Lion Mark Holdings Ltd. 1984-. *Leisure interests:* reading, golf. *Address:* Lion Mark Holdings Ltd., 66 Mark Lane, London, E.C.3; Oxford Lodge, 52 Parkside, Wimbledon, London, S.W.19, England (Home). *Telephone:* 01-480 6677 (Office); 01-946 3434 (Home).

LIDMAN, Sara; Swedish writer; b. 30 Dec. 1923; d. of Andreas and Jenny (née Lundman) Lidman; ed. Uppsala Univ.; first four books deal with life in sparsely populated N. Sweden; in S. Africa 1960, in Kenya 1962-64, in N. Viet-Nam 1965. *Publications include:* Tjärdalen 1953, Hjortronlandet 1955, Aina 1956, Regnspiran 1958, Bära mistel 1960, Jag o min son 1961, Med fem diamanter 1964, Samtal i Hanoi 1966, Gruva 1968, Vänner o uvänner 1969, Marta, Marta 1970, Fåglarna i Nam Dinh 1973, Libretto till två baletter, Inga träd skall väcka dig 1974, Balansen 1975, Din tjänare hör 1977.

LIEBERMAN, Joseph I., B.A., J.D.; American politician; b. 24 Feb. 1942, Stamford, Conn.; s. of Henry and Marcia (née Manger) Lieberman; m. Hadassah Freilich 1983; two s. one d.; ed. Yale Univ.; called to Bar, Conn. 1967; mem. Conn. Senate 1971-81, Senate Majority Leader 1975-81; Partner Lieberman, Segaloff & Wolfson, New Haven 1972-83; Attorney Gen. State of Conn., Hartford 1983-88, Senator for Conn. 1989-; Trustee Wadsworth Atheneum, Univ. of Bridgeport; Democrat. *Publications:* The Power Broker 1966, The Scorpion and the Tarantula 1970, The Legacy 1981, Child Support in America 1986. *Address:* Senate Building, Washington, D.C. 20510, U.S.A.

LIEBERMAN, Seymour, PH.D.; American professor of biochemistry; b. 1 Dec. 1916, New York; s. of Samuel D. Lieberman and Sadie Levin; m. Sandra Spar 1944; one s.; ed. Brooklyn Coll., New York, Univ. of Illinois and Standford Univ., Calif.; Prof. of Biochemistry, Coll. of Physicians and Surgeons, Columbia Univ. 1962–87, Prof. Emer. 1987–; Program Officer The Ford Foundation 1974–75; Pres. St. Luke's-Roosevelt Inst. for Health Sciences 1981–, Assoc. Dean 1984–; mem. N.A.S. 1977–; Roussel Prize (France) 1984; Dale Medal 1986. *Publications:* A Heuristic Proposal for Understanding steroidogenic Processes 1984, Detection in Bovine Brain of Sulfate Esters of Cholesterol and Sitosterol 1985 and more than 150 other publs. *Leisure interest:* tennis. *Address:* College of Physicians and Surgeons, Columbia University, 630 W. 168 Street, New York, N.Y. 10032, U.S.A.

LIEBERMANN, Rolf; Swiss musician and administrator; b. 14 Sept. 1910; ed. Zürich Conservatoire, and Univ. of Zürich; mem. Musical Dept. Swiss Radio Corpn. 1945–50; Head of Orchestra Dept. Swiss Radio Station Beromünster 1950–57; Musical Dir. N. German Broadcasting System, Hamburg 1957–59; Gen. Man. State Opera, Hamburg 1959–72; Gen. Man. Théâtre Nat. de l'Opéra, Paris 1973–80; Guest Prof. Mozarteum, Salzburg 1982; Dr. h.c. (Spokane and Berne); Commdr. Légion d'honneur 1974. *Works,* operatic: Leonore 1952, Penelope 1954, School for Wives 1955; orchestral: Polyphonic Studies 1943, Une des Fins du Monde 1943, Volkslieder Suite, Furioso 1947, Symphony No. 1 1949, The Song of Life and Death 1950, Concerto for Jazzband and Symphony Orchestra 1954, Concerto pour machines à écrire et machines à calculer 1964, Symphonie des Echanges (for business machines) 1964. *Address:* c/o Théâtre National de l'Opéra, Place de l'Opéra, 75009 Paris, France.

LIECHTENSTEIN, Prince of (see Franz Josef).

LIED, Finn; Norwegian scientist, administrator and politician; b. 12 April 1916, Fana; ed. Norwegian Technological Univ., Trondheim and Cambridge Univ.; Norwegian Armed Forces 1942–45; later Research Fellow and Head of Norwegian Defence Research Establishment, Dir. 1957–83; Minister of Industry 1971–72; Chair. Exec. Cttee. Royal Norwegian Council for Industrial Research 1958–79, Bd. of Dirs. Norwegian Telephone and Telegraph Admin. 1969–81; Chair. of Bd. Den Norske Stats Oljeselskap A/S 1974–84; mem. Norwegian Acad. of Science and Letters at Oslo, Norwegian Acad. of Tech. Sciences, Swedish Scientific Acad. of Engineers. *Publications:* textbooks on radio technique and various papers on ionosphere physics and applied research in general. *Address:* Institute for Energy Technology, N-2007 Kjeller, Norway.

LIEN CHAN, M.SC., PH.D.; Chinese politician; b. 27 Aug. 1936, Tainan City; m.; two s. two d.; ed. Nat. Taiwan Univ. and Univ. of Chicago; Assoc. Prof. Nat. Taiwan Univ. 1968–69, Prof. and Chair. Dept. of Political Science and Dir. Graduate Inst. of Political Science 1969–75; Amb. to El Salvador 1975–76; Dir. Dept. of Youth Affairs, Cen. Cttee. Kuomintang 1976–78; Deputy Sec.-Gen. Cen. Cttee. Kuomintang 1978, mem. Cen. Standing Cttee. 1983–; Chair. Nat. Youth Comm., Exec. Yuan 1978–81; Minister of Communications 1981–87; Vice-Premier 1987–88; Minister of Foreign Affairs 1989–; Pres. The Chinese Asscn. of Political Science 1979–82. *Address:* Ministry of Foreign Affairs, 2 Chieh Shou Road, Taipei 10016, Taiwan. *Telephone:* 3119292.

LIENDO, Maj.-Gen. Horacio Tomás; Argentine army officer and politician; b. 17 Dec. 1924, Córdoba; ed. Mil. Coll.; first post with 4th Bn., Communications; with 6th Motorized Bn., Communications; as Capt., entered Army War Coll. 1954, later Gen. Staff Officer; served in Communications Inspection, Army Gen. Staff, and, as Second-in-Command, 4th Bn., Communications; rank of Major 1959; 61st Communications Command; under orders of Mil. Attaché, U.S.A. 1962; rank of Lieut.-Col. 1965, Col. 1970, Gen. 1980; Minister of Labour 1976–79; Chief of Staff, Armed Forces 1979–81; Minister of the Interior March-Nov. 1981; Pres. of Argentina (a.i.) Nov.-Dec. 1981.

LIEPA, Maris-Rudolf Eduardovich; Soviet ballet dancer; b. 27 July 1936, Riga; s. of Eduard and Lilia Liepa; m. Margareta; one s. one d.; ed. Bolshoi Theatre Ballet School, Moscow; soloist with Latvian Theatre of Opera and Ballet, Riga 1955–56; soloist with Moscow Stanislavsky and Nemirovich-Danchenko Theatre Ballet Co. 1956–60; soloist with Bolshoi Theatre Ballet 1959–; Teacher Bolshoi Theatre Ballet School 1963–; People's Artist of U.S.S.R. 1976; Lenin Prize Winner 1970, Nijinsky Prize 1971, Marius Petipa Prize 1977. *Main roles include:* Jean de Brien (Raimonda), Konrad (Corsair), Siegfried (Swan Lake), Vatslav (Fountain of Bakhchisarai), Phoebus (Esmeralda), the Poet (Straussiana), Basilio (Don Quixote), Albert (Giselle), Armen (Gayane), Spartacus, Crassus (Spartacus), Prince Desire (Sleeping Beauty), Romeo (Romeo and Juliet), Farkhad (Legend of Love), Spectre de la Rose (Spectre de la rose), Vronsky (Anna Karenina), Karenin (Anna Karenina), José (Carmen), Prince Lemon (Chipolino), leading role in These Wonderful Sounds 1978; *film roles:* Prince Vseslav (Lion's Tomb), Jack Wheeler (The Fourth Man); *TV roles:* Hamlet, Henrie, Mouse King and Nutcracker Prince (Nutcracker) 1977, roles in Benefice 1978, Galateja 1978. *Leisure interest:* swimming.
[*Died 25 April 1989.*]

LIEPMANN, Hans Wolfgang, PH.D.; American professor of aeronautics and applied physics; b. 3 July 1914, Berlin, Germany; s. of Wilhelm and Emma (Leser) Liepmann; m. 1st Kate Kaschinsky 1939 (dissolved); m. 2nd Dietlind Wegener Goldschmidt 1954; two s.; ed. Univ. of Zürich; Research

Fellow, Univ. of Zürich 1938–39, Calif. Inst. of Tech. 1939–45; Asst. Prof. Calif. Inst. of Technology 1945–46, Assoc. Prof. 1946–49, Prof. of Aeronautics and Applied Physics 1949–76, Charles Lee Powell Prof. of Fluid Mechanics and Thermodynamics 1976–83; Theodore von Kármán Prof. of Aeronautics 1983–85, Prof. Emer. 1985–; Dir. Graduate Aeronautical Labs. 1972–85; mem. Nat. Acad. of Sciences, Nat. Acad. of Eng., Int. Acad. of Astronautics, A.A.A.S.; First Dryden Lecturer, A.I.A.A. 1968, Hon. Fellow 1974; Hon. Fellow, Indian Acad. of Sciences 1985; Hon. D.Eng. (Tech. Univ., Aachen) 1985; Ludwig Prandtl Ring, German Soc. for Aeronautics and Astronautics 1968; Warner Medal, American Soc. of Mechanical Engineers 1969, Monie A. Ferst Award, Sigma Xi 1978, Michelson-Morley Award, Case Inst. of Tech. 1979, Fluid Dynamics Prize, American Physical Soc. 1980, Nat. Medal of Science 1986. *Publications:* Aerodynamics of a Compressible Fluid (co-author) 1947, Elements of Gasdynamics (co-author) 1957, Free Turbulent Flows 1961, many articles in professional journals. *Leisure interest:* tennis. *Address:* Mail Stop 105-50, California Institute of Technology, Pasadena, Calif. 91125; 555 Haverstock Road, La Canada-Flintridge, Calif. 91011, U.S.A. (Home). *Telephone:* (818) 356-4535 (Office); (818) 790-2264 (Home).

LIESNER, Hans Hubertus, C.B., M.A.; British economist and civil servant; b. 30 March 1929, Naumburg, Germany; s. of Curt Liesner and Edith (née Neumann); m. Thelma Seward 1968; one s. one d.; ed. Univ. of Bristol, Nuffield Coll., Oxford; Asst. Lecturer, later Lecturer in Econs., London School of Econs. and Political Science 1955–59; Lecturer in Econs., Univ. of Cambridge, Fellow, Dir. of Studies in Econs., also Asst. Bursar of Emmanuel Coll. 1959–70; Under-Sec. (Econ.), H.M. Treasury 1970–76; Chief Econ. Adviser, Dept. of Trade and Industry (fmrly. Depts. of Trade, Industry and Prices and Consumer Protection) 1976–. *Publications:* The Import Dependence of Britain and Western Germany 1957, Case Studies in European Economic Union: the Mechanics of Integration (with J. E. Meade and S. J. Wells) 1962, Atlantic Harmonisation: Making Free Trade Work 1968, Britain and the Common Market: the effect of entry on the pattern of manufacturing production (with S. S. Han) 1971. *Leisure interests:* skiing, ciné photography, gardening, walking. *Address:* Department of Trade and Industry, 1 Victoria Street, London, SW1H 0ET, England. *Telephone:* 01-215 4258.

LIFSON, Shneior, PH.D.; Israeli scientist; b. 18 March 1914, Tel Aviv; m. Hanna Stern; three c.; ed. Hebrew Univ.; mem. kibbutz 1932–43; served in Science Unit, Israel Defence Forces 1948–49; Weizmann Inst. of Science, attached to Polymer Dept. 1949, Chair. Scientific Council 1961–63, Head, Chemical Physics Dept. 1963–79, Science Dir. 1963–67, Dean Faculty of Chem. 1975–77; Rector, Everyman's Univ., Israel 1974–75; mem. Council for Higher Educ., Israel Science Teaching Centre, Comm. of Molecular Biophysics of Int. Union of Pure and Applied Biophysics, European Molecular Biology Org., Advisory Bd. Biopolymers, Current Contents and Editorial Bd. Journal of Statistical Physics (U.S.A.); Weizmann Prize 1958, Israel Prize 1969. *Publications:* numerous scientific papers. *Address:* c/o 15 Neve Weizmann, Rehovot, Israel. *Telephone:* 951721/589.

LIGACHEV, Gen. Yegor Kuzmich; Soviet party official and politician; b. 1920; ed. Moscow Inst. of Aviation and CPSU Higher Party School; Engineer 1943–49; joined CPSU 1944; Party and Local Govt. Official Novosibirsk 1949–55; Vice-Chair. Novosibirsk Regional Soviet of Working People's Deputies 1955–58; Sec. Novosibirsk Regional Cttee. CPSU 1959–61, with Cen. Cttee. CPSU 1961–65; First Sec. Tomsk Regional Cttee. CPSU 1965–; Cand. mem. Cen. Cttee. CPSU 1966–76, mem. 1976–, mem. Politburo April 1985–; Deputy to Supreme Soviet 1966–; Sec. Cen. Cttee. in Charge of Personnel and Ideology 1983–88; in Charge of Agric. 1988–; elected to Congress of People's Deputies of the U.S.S.R. 1989; fmr. Chair. Comm. for Youth Affairs, Soviet of the Union; mem. Mil. Council and Head of Political Div. of Soviet Troops in Germany 1985–88; Head of Political Section of U.S.S.R. Armed Forces 1985–88; Gen. 1988. *Address:* Tomsk Regional Committee, Communist Party of the Soviet Union, Tomsk, U.S.S.R.

LIGETI, György Sándor; Austrian (Hungarian-born) composer; b. 28 May 1923, Dicsöszentmárton; s. of Dr. Sándor Ligeti and Dr. Ilona Somogyi; m. Dr. Vera Spitz 1957; one s.; ed. Budapest Acad. of Music; studied with Ferenc Farkas and Sándor Veress, Budapest Acad. of Music; taught Budapest Acad. of Music 1950–56; left Hungary 1956; Guest Prof., Stockholm Acad. of Music 1961–71; Composer-in-Residence, Stanford Univ., Calif. 1972; worked in Electronic Studios, Cologne, Fed. Repub. of Germany; active in music composition, Cologne, Vienna, Stockholm, Berlin and Darmstadt; Prof. of Composition, Hamburg Music Acad. 1973–; mem. Swedish Royal Acad. of Music 1964, Acad. of Arts, Berlin 1968, Free Acad. of Arts, Hamburg 1972, Bavarian Acad. of Fine Arts, Munich 1978, American Acad. and Inst. of Arts and Letters 1984; Orden pour le mérite, Bonn 1975, Grawemeyer Award 1986; Commdr., Ordre Nat. des Arts et Lettres, France 1988. *Works include:* Artikulation (tape piece) 1958, Apparitions (orchestral) 1958–59, Atmosphères (orchestral) 1960, Volumina (organ) 1961–62, Poème Symphonique for 100 metronomes 1962, Aventures for three singers and seven instrumentalists 1962, Requiem for soprano, mezzo-soprano, two choirs and orchestra 1963–65, Lux Aeterna for 16-part chorus 1966, Concerto for 'cello and orchestra 1966, Lontano (orchestral) 1967, Continuum (harpsichord), Ten pieces for wind quintet 1968, Ramifications for string orchestra or 12 solo strings 1968–69, String Quartet No. 2

1968, Melodien (orchestral) 1971, Monument, Selbstportrait, Movement (for two pianos) 1976, Le Grand Macabre (opera) 1974-77, Trio (violin, horn, piano) 1982, 3 Phantasien nach Hölderlin (chorus) 1982, Hungarian Etudes (chorus) 1983, 6 Piano Etudes 1985, Piano Concerto 1985-88, Nonsense Madrigals for 6 Singers 1988. *Address:* Himmelhofgasse 34, A-1130 Vienna, Austria; Mövenstrasse 3, D-2000 Hamburg 60, Federal Republic of Germany.

LIGGINS, Graham Collingwood, C.B.E., M.B., CH.B., PH.D., F.R.S., F.R.C.S.(E.), F.R.A.C.S.; New Zealand professor of obstetrics and gynaecology; b. 24 June 1926, Thames, N.Z.; s. of James Bull Liggins and Isabella Graham Liggins née Mandeno; m. Cecilia Ward 1954; two s. two d.; ed. Auckland Grammar School and Univs. of Auckland and Otago; Registrar in Obstetrics, Gen. Hosp., Newcastle upon Tyne, England 1954-58; Consultant Obstetrician and Gynaecologist, Nat. Women's Hosp., Auckland, N.Z. 1960-86; Prof. (fmrly. Assoc. Prof.) of Obstetrics and Gynaecology, Univ. of Auckland 1968-86, Prof. Emer. 1986-; mem. Royal Coll. of Gynaecologists, London, Fellow Royal N.Z. Coll. of Gynaecologists, Fellow Royal Soc. of N.Z.; Hector Medal, Royal Soc. of N.Z. 1980; Hon. M.D. (Lund) 1983. *Publications:* 200 papers. *Leisure interests:* sailing, fishing, forestry. *Address:* University of Auckland, Private Bag, Auckland 1 (Office); 3/38 Awatea Road, Auckland 1, New Zealand (Home). *Telephone:* 609.856 (Office); 775.127 (Home).

LIGHT, Walter Frederick, B.SC.; Canadian business executive; b. 24 June 1923, Cobalt, Ont.; s. of Herbert Light and Rosetta Elizabeth (Hoffman) Light; m. Margaret Anne Wylie Miller 1950; two d.; ed. Queen's Univ., Ont.; joined Bell Canada 1949, Vice-Pres. Eng. 1967, Vice-Pres. Operations 1969, Exec. Vice-Pres. Operations 1970; Pres. Northern Telecom Ltd. 1974-79, C.E.O. 1979-, Chair. 1984-85; Dir. Northern Telecom Ltd., The Procter & Gamble Co., Air Products and Chemicals Inc., Inco Ltd., Shell Canada Ltd., Moore Corpn. Ltd., The Royal Bank of Canada, Rolls-Royce Industries Canada Inc., NewTel Enterprises Ltd, SNC Group. Inc., Rockliffe Research and Tech. Inc. *Leisure interests:* antiques, swimming. *Address:* Bell Trinity Square, Floor 10, South Tower, Toronto, Ont. M5G 2E1 (Office); 7 Nanton Avenue, Toronto, Ont. M4W 2Y8, Canada (Home). *Telephone:* (416) 581-3888 (Office).

LIGHTHILL, Sir James, Kt., F.R.AE.S., F.R.S.; British college provost and fmr. professor of mathematics; b. 23 Jan. 1924, Paris, France; s. of Ernest B. and Marjorie (née Holmes) Lighthill; m. Nancy A. Dumaresq 1945; one s. four d.; ed. Trinity Coll., Cambridge; Sr. Lecturer, Manchester Univ. 1946-50, Beyer Prof. of Applied Maths. 1950-59; Dir. Royal Aircraft Establishment 1959-64; Royal Soc. Research Prof., Imperial Coll., London 1964-69; Physical Sec. Royal Soc. 1965-69; Lucasian Prof. of Maths., Univ. of Cambridge 1969-79; Provost, Univ. Coll. London 1979-89; Pres. Int. Comm. on Mathematical Instruction 1971-74; Int. Union of Theoretical and Applied Mechanics 1984-88; mem. Advisory Council on Research and Devt. 1978-81; Hon. foreign mem. American Acad. of Arts and Sciences, American Philosophical Soc., A.I.A.A., U.S. Nat. Acad. of Sciences and Nat. Acad. of Eng., Acad. des Sciences (France), Koninklijke Akad. van Wetenschappen; 19 hon. doctorates; Royal Medal, Royal Soc.; Gold Medal, Royal Astronautical Soc., Modesto Panetti Prize, Timoshenko Medal, Harvey Prize, Gold Medal, Inst. of Mathematics and its Applications 1982. *Publications:* Higher Approximations in Aerodynamic Theory 1954, Fourier Analysis and Generalised Functions 1958, Mathematical Biofluiddynamics 1975, Waves in Fluids 1978, An Informal Introduction to Theoretical Fluid Mechanics 1986, articles in collective works and learned journals. *Leisure interests:* music, swimming. *Address:* c/o University College, Gower Street, London, WC1E 6BT, England. *Telephone:* 01-387 7050.

LIIKANEN, Erkki Antero, M. POL. SC.; Finnish politician; b. 19 Sept. 1950, Mikkeli; m. Hanna-Liisa Issakainen 1971; mem. Parl. 1972-; Minister of Finance 1987-; mem. Social Democratic Party (SDP) Cttee. 1978-, Gen. Sec. 1981-87; Chair. Supervisory Bd. Outokumpu Oy 1983-. *Address:* Ministry of Finance, Snellmaninkatu 1A, 00170 Helsinki, Finland. *Telephone:* (90) 1601.

LIKENS, Gene E., M.S., PH.D.; American ecologist; b. 6 Jan. 1935, Pierceton, Ind.; s. of Colonel and Josephine Likens; m. Phyllis Craig 1983; four c.; ed. Manchester Coll., Ind., Univ. of Wisconsin; graduate asst. in Zoology, Univ. of Wis. 1957-61, Project Asst. Jan.-June 1962, Research Assoc. June-Nov. 1962; Instructor in Zoology, Dartmouth Coll. Sept.-Dec. 1961, Instructor in Biological Sciences Feb.-Sept. 1963, Asst. Prof. 1963-66, Assoc. Prof. 1966-69; Assoc. Prof., Section of Ecology and Systematics, Cornell Univ. 1969-72, Prof. 1972-83, Charles A. Alexander Prof. of Biological Sciences 1983, Adjunct Prof. Sept. 1983-, Acting Chair. 1973-74, Chair. 1982-83; Prof. of Biology, Yale Univ. March 1984-; Visiting Prof., Univ. of Va. 1978-79; Vice-Pres., The New York Botanical Garden Sept. 1983-; Dir. Inst. of Ecosystem Studies Sept. 1983-, Mary Flagler Cary Arboretum 1983-; mem. A.A.A.S. (Fellow 1965), American Acad. of Sciences 1979-, N.A.S. 1981-, Ecological Soc. of America (Vice-Pres. 1978-79, Pres. 1981-1982), American Soc. of Limnology and Oceanography (Vice-Pres. 1975-76, Pres. 1976-77), American Polar Soc., etc.; Hon. D.SC. (Manchester Coll.) 1979, (Rutgers Univ.) 1985; numerous awards. *Publications:* over 280 professional articles; Biochemistry of a Forested Ecosystem, Pattern and Process in a Forested Ecosystem, Limnological Analyses, An Ecosystem Approach to Aquatic Ecology. *Leisure interests:*

canoeing, fishing. *Address:* Institute of Ecosystem Studies, The New York Botanical Garden, Box AB, Millbrook, N.Y. 12545, U.S.A. *Telephone:* 914-677-5343.

LIKHACHEV, Dmitriy Sergeyevich, D.SC.; Soviet professor of Russian literature; b. 28 Nov. 1906, St. Petersburg (now Leningrad); s. of Sergey Likhachev and Vera Likhacheva; m. Zinaida Makarova 1936; two d.; ed. Leningrad State Univ.; Ed. in a publishing house 1932-38; Assoc. Inst. of Russian Literature (Pushkin House) of U.S.S.R. Acad. of Sciences 1938-, Head of Section of Early Russian Literature 1954-, Academician 1970-; lecturer, Kazan State Univ. 1942-43; Prof. Leningrad State Univ. 1946-53; Pres. Soviet Cultural Fund 1987-; Hon. mem. Bulgarian Acad. of Sciences, Hungarian Acad. of Sciences, Serbian Acad. of Sciences and Arts; corresp. foreign mem. Austrian Acad. of Sciences; corresp. mem. British Acad.; Dr. h.c. (Oxford, Edinburgh and Toruń Univs.); State Prize 1952, 1969. *Publications include:* National Self-Awareness in Ancient Russia 1945, The Culture of Old Russia at the Time of the Formation of the Centralised State 1946, Russian Chronicles 1947, The Emergence of Russian Literature 1952, The Image of Man in the Literature of Old Russia 1958, The 'Slovo o Polku Igoreve' (authoritative text) 1961; The Culture of the Russian People from the 10th to the 17th Centuries 1961, Russian Culture of the Time of Andrei Rublev 1962, Textology 1962, The Poetics of Old Russian Literature 1967, The Artistic Heritage of Old Russia 1971, The Evolution of Russian Literature from the 10th to the 17th Centuries 1973, A Great Heritage: The Classical Works of Old Russian Literature 1975, The World of Laughter in Ancient Russia 1975, The 'Laughing World' of Old Russia 1976, Russische Literatur und europäische Kultur des 10-17 Jahrhunderts 1977, The Slovo and the Culture of the Time 1977, The Poetics of Ancient Russian Literature 1978, and several Russian titles. *Leisure interests:* Problems of town-buildings (theory) and the history of Petersburg-Leningrad. *Address:* U.S.S.R. Academy of Sciences, 14 Leninsky Prospekt, Moscow V-71, U.S.S.R.

LILJESTRAND, Maj.-Gen. Bengt Tson, M.A., DIPL.C.E.I.; Swedish army officer; b. 26 Feb. 1919, Stockholm; ed. Uppsala Univ., Centre d'Etudes Industrielles, Geneva and Inst. Univ. de Hautes Etudes Internationales, Geneva; Instructor, Royal Nat. Defence Coll. 1960-62; Co-ordination Office, Defence Dept. 1962-63; Defence Staff, Org. and Total Defence Section 1964-66; Commdr. Boden Artillery Regt. 1968-69; Chief of Staff, Western Region 1969-73; Dir., Gen. Staff Coll. of Armed Forces 1973-74; Chief of Staff UN Truce Supervision Org. in Palestine 1974-75; Commdr. UN Emergency Force 1975-76; Dir. Nat. Defence Inst. 1978-84, Inst. Univ. des Hautes Etudes Int., Geneva 1985-; Columnist for Stockholms Tidningen 1980-84; Commdr. 1st Class Royal Swedish Order of the Sword, Commdr. Order of the White Rose of Finland (1st Class), Kt. Finnish Order of Freedom. *Address:* 8 Les Vergers de La Gottaz, 1110 Morges, Switzerland.

LILL, John Richard, O.B.E., F.R.C.M.; British pianist; b. 17 March 1944, London; s. of George Lill and the late Margery (née Young) Lill; ed. Leyton County High School and Royal Coll. of Music; gives recitals throughout the world and has appeared as soloist with many leading orchestras; Prof., Royal Coll. of Music; Fellow, Trinity Coll. of Music, London, London Coll. of Music; Hon. D.Sc. (Univ. of Aston), Hon. D.Mus. (Exeter Univ.); numerous prizes include First Prize, Int. Tchaikovsky Competition, Moscow 1970; recordings include complete Beethoven piano sonatas. *Leisure interests:* chess, amateur radio, walking. *Address:* c/o Harold Holt Ltd., 31 Sinclair Road, London, W14 0NS, England. *Telephone:* 01-603 4600.

LILLEE, Dennis K., M.B.E.; Australian cricketer; b. 18 July 1949; played for Western Australia 1969-; for Haslingden, Lancashire League, England 1971, for Northants, England 1988-; 57 test matches for Australia -Feb. 1982; leading wicket-taker in test matches with 332 (passed previous record of 309 on 27 Dec. 1981) and leading wicket-taker in England/Australia test matches with 167 in 29 tests -Aug. 1981, retd. from test cricket Jan. 1984 with 355 test wickets. *Publications:* My Life in Cricket 1982, Over and Out 1985. *Address:* c/o W.A.C.A., W.A.C.A. Ground, Nelson Crescent, East Perth 6000, Western Australia.

LILLEY, James Roderick, M.A.; American diplomatist; b. 15 Jan. 1928, Tsingtao, China; s. of late Frank W. Lilley and Inez Bush; m. Sally Booth 1954; three s.; ed. Phillips Exeter Acad., Yale Univ. and George Washington Univ.; Adjunct Prof. School of Advanced Int. Studies, Johns Hopkins Univ. 1978-80; Consultant, Hunt Oil, Dallas, Tex. 1979-81; East Asian Dir. Nat. Security Council, White House, Washington, D.C. Jan.-Nov. 1981; Dir. American Inst. in Taiwan, Taipei 1982-84; Consultant, Otis Elevator Co., Farmington, Conn. 1984-85; Deputy Asst. Sec. of State, East Asian and Pacific Affairs, Dept. of State 1985-86; Amb. to Republic of Korea 1986-89, to China 1989-; Distinguished Intelligence Medal. *Leisure interests:* swimming, bicycling. *Address:* 3 Xiu Shui Bei Jie, Beijing, People's Republic of China; American Embassy, APO San Francisco, Calif. 96301, U.S.A.

LILLY, Frank, PH.D.; American professor of genetics; b. 28 Aug. 1930, Charleston, W. Va.; s. of Frank O. Lilly and E. Verna Zimmerman Lilly; unmarried; one adopted s.; ed. West Virginia Univ., Univ. of Paris, Cornell Medical School; Asst. Prof. Albert Einstein Coll. of Medicine 1967-70, Assoc. Prof. 1970-74, Prof. 1974-, Chair. Dept. of Genetics 1976-89; mem.

Nat. Bd. of Dirs. Leukemia Soc. of America 1966-71, 1984-87; mem. Scientific Advisory Cttee. Cancer Research Inst., Inc. 1979-, Wistar Inst. 1980-; mem. Bd. of Dirs. Gay Men's Health Crisis 1984-87; mem. Presidential Comm. on Human Immunodeficiency Virus Epidemic 1987-88; Fellow New York Acad. of Sciences 1977; mem. N.A.S. 1984. *Publications:* 120 scientific articles and reviews on oncology, virology, genetics and immunology in scientific journals. *Leisure interests:* music, gardening, reading. *Address:* 444 Central Park West, New York, N.Y. 10025, U.S.A.

LIM, Kim, D.F.A.; British sculptor and printmaker; b. 16 Feb. 1936, Singapore; m. William Turnbull 1960; two s.; ed. St. Martin's School of Art and Slade School of Art, London; one-woman exhbns. in London, Oxford, Southampton, Harrogate and Singapore since 1966; has participated in numerous group exhbns. in Britain, Europe, Canada and Japan including British Pavilion, Expo '67, Montreal 1967, Nagoaka Prize Exhbn., Japan 1967, Open Air Sculpture, Middelheim, Antwerp 1969, Hayward Annual, Hayward Gallery, London and British Sculpture 1951-80, Whitechapel Gallery, London 1982; work in several public collections inc. Tate Gallery, London, Nagoaka Museum of Modern Art and I.B.M. New York.

LIM CHONG EU, M.B., CH.B.; Malaysian politician; b. 28 May 1919, Penang; m. Goh Sing Yeng; two s. two d.; ed. Penang Free School, Edinburgh Univ.; Medical Officer (Flight Lieut.) Malayan Auxiliary Air Force 1951-54; private medical practice; mem. Penang State Settlement Council 1951; Radical Party 1952-58; mem. Fed. Council for Penang 1955-57, Alliance Chief Whip; Pres. Malayan Chinese Assen. (M.C.A.) 1958-59, resigned as Pres. 1959, left M.C.A. 1960; Chair. pro tem. Cttee. of United Democratic Party 1962-63, Gen. Sec. 1963-66, Pres. 1966-68; Deputy Chair. Gerakan Rakyat Malaysia 1968-71, Pres. 1971-80, Chair. Tanjong Br. 1969-80, Hon. Adviser and mem., Cen. and Cen. Working Cttees. 1980-; M.P. for Kota, Penang State Ass., for Tanjong, House of Reps. 1964-1969, 1974, for Kota, Penang State Ass. 1978, 1982; Chief Minister of Penang 1969, 1974, 1978, 1982-; Chair. Penang State Goodwill Cttee. 1969-, State Operations Cttee. 1969-, Penang Devt. Corpn. 1970-; Chair. Barisan Nat., Penang 1978; first Chair. of Jaycees, Jaycees Senator 1955; Chair. Bd. of Trustees Silver Jubilee Home, Penang and Prov. Wellesley, Penang Free School, Penang Scouts Council; Patron of Penang and Prov. Wellesley Welfare Council 1955; mem. Malayan Medical Council 1964; mem. Malayan Medical Assen. House Cttee., Pres. Northern Branch of Malayan Medical Assen. 1968-69, fmr. mem. Exec. Council; fmr. Pres. Penang Medical Practitioners' Soc., Hon. mem. 1969-; Hon. LL.D. (Univ. of Science, Malaysia) 1976; Freeman of George Town, Penang 1984; resigned Presidency of Parti Gerakan Rakyat Malaysia, elected Hon. Life Adviser, appointed mem. Cen. Working Cttee. and Cen. Cttee. 1980. *Leisure interests:* shooting, tennis, contract bridge, fishing, golf. *Address:* Pejabat Ketua Menteri, Komtar, Peti Surat 3006, Penang, Malaysia.

LIM KENG YAIK, Dato' Dr., M.B., B.CH.; Malaysian politician; b. 8 April 1939, Tapah, Perak; m. Wong Yoon Chuan; three c.; ed. Queen's Univ., Belfast; Senator 1972-78; Minister with Special Functions 1972-73, of Primary Industries 1986-; mem. State Exec. Council, Perak 1978-86; mem. Parl. 1986-; Pres. Gerakan 1980-. *Address:* Ministry of Primary Industries, 6th-8th Floors, Menara Daya Bumi, 50654 Kuala Lumpur, Malaysia.

LIM KIM SAN; Singapore politician; b. 30 Nov. 1916, Singapore; s. of Choon Huat and Wee Geok Hwan Lim; m. Pang Gek Kim 1939; two s. four d.; ed. Anglo-Chinese School, Raffles Coll., Singapore; Dir. United Chinese Bank Ltd., Chair. Batu Pahat Bank Ltd., and Pacific Bank Ltd. 1940-; mem. and Deputy Chair. Public Service Comm., Singapore 1959-63; Chair. Housing Devt. Bd. 1960-63; Deputy Chair. Econ. Devt. Bd. 1961-63; Minister for Nat. Devt. 1963-65, for Finance 1965-67, for the Interior and Defence 1967-70, for Educ. 1970-72, for the Environment 1972-75, of Nat. Devt. 1975-78, for Communications 1975-79, for the Environment 1979-81; Acting Pres. March 1989; Chair. Port of Singapore Authority 1979-; Chair. Public Utilities Bd. 1971-78, Bd. Trustees, Consumers' Co-operative Ltd. 1973; Man. Dir. The Monetary Authority of Singapore April 1981-82; mem. of Dewan Ra'ayat; Exec. Chair. Singapore Press Holdings Ltd. 1988; Darjah Utama Temasek (Order of Temasek) 1962, Ramon Magsaysay Award for community leadership 1965 and others. *Leisure interest:* golf. *Address:* Port of Singapore Authority, PSA Building, 460 Alexandra Road, Singapore 0511 (Office); 81 Dalvey Road, Singapore 1025 (Home).

LIM PIN, M.A., M.D., F.R.C.P., F.R.C.P.E., F.R.A.C.P., F.A.C.P.; Singapore university vice-chancellor; b. 12 Jan. 1936, Penang, Malaysia; m. Shirley Loo Ngai Seong 1964; two s. one d.; ed. Raffles Inst., Singapore and Cambridge Univ.; Registrar, King's Coll. Hosp., London 1965; Medical Officer, Ministry of Health, Singapore 1965-66; Lecturer in Medicine, Univ. of Singapore 1966-70, Sr. lecturer 1971-73, Assoc. Prof. of Medicine 1974-77, Prof. and Head of Dept. 1978-81, Deputy Vice-Chancellor 1979-81, Vice-Chancellor 1981-; Commonwealth Medical Fellow, The Royal Infirmary, Edinburgh 1970; Dir. Neptune Orient Lines, Singapore 1981-, Nat. Univ. Hosp., Singapore; mem. Nat. Productivity Council, Cttee. on Nat. Computerisation, Econ. Devt. Bd.; mem. Bd. of Govs., Inst. of East Asian Philosophies, Inst. of Policy Studies; Chair. Applied Research Corpn. 1982-; Eisenhower Fellow 1982; Hon. Fellow, Coll. of General Practitioners, Singapore; Rep. of Singapore Public Admin. Medal (Gold) 1984, Officier, Ordre des Palmes Académiques 1988. *Publications:* numerous articles in medical journals.

Address: National University of Singapore, Kent Ridge, Singapore 0511, Singapore. *Telephone:* 7756666.

LIMANN, Hilla, PH.D.; Ghanaian diplomatist and politician; b. 1934, Gwollu, Upper Region; m.; five c.; ed. Govt. Teacher Training Coll., L.S.E., Univ. of Paris; mem. Tumu Dist. Council 1952-55, Chair. 1953-55; mem. Ghana Constitutional Comm. formulating 1969 Constitution; Head of Chancery and Official Sec. Embassy in Lomé; mem. dels. to many int. confs. incl. OAU, Non-aligned States Conf., ILO, WHO, IAEA; Pres. of Ghana 1979-81; fmr. Leader People's Nat. Party; under arrest 1982-83; Hon. G.C.M.G. 1981, Hon. Fellow L.S.E. 1982.

LIMERICK, 6th Earl of, cr. 1803 (Ireland); **Patrick Edmund Pery,** K.B.E., M.A., C.A.; British merchant banker; b. 12 April 1930, London; s. of 5th Earl of Limerick (Edmund Colquhoun Pery) and Angela Olivia (née Trotter); m. Sylvia Rosalind Lush; two s. one d.; ed. Eton and New Coll., Oxford; Nat. Service Comm. with 2nd Dragoon Guards 1948-50; Territorial Army Comm. with City of London Yeomanry 1950-61; qualified as Chartered Accountant with Peat, Marwick, Mitchell & Co. 1953-58; joined Kleinwort Sons & Co. 1958; Dir. Kleinwort Benson Ltd. 1966-72, 1974-83, Vice-Chair. 1983-85, Deputy Chair. 1985-88; Dir. Kleinwort, Benson, Lonsdale PLC 1982-; mem. Council, London Chamber of Commerce and Industry 1968-79; London Dir. Commercial Bank of Australia Ltd. 1969-72; Parl. Under-Sec. of State for Trade 1972-74; Pres. Assen. of British Chambers of Commerce 1974-77, Vice-Pres. 1977-; mem. British Overseas Trade Bd. 1975- (Chair. 1979-83); Chair. Cttee. for Middle East Trade 1975-79, Mallinson-Denny Ltd. 1979-81, British Invisible Exports Council 1984-, Polymeters Response Int. 1988-; Dir. Brooke Bond Group PLC 1981-84, De La Rue Co. PLC 1983-; Chair. of Court City of London Polytechnic 1982-; Dir. T. R. Pacific Investment Trust PLC 1976-; Pres. Ski Club of Great Britain 1974-81, Inst. of Export 1983-; Vice-Pres. Alpine Ski Club 1974-76, Pres. 1985-87; Pres. Anglo-Swiss Soc. 1984-; mem. Council, Royal Inst. of Int. Affairs 1980-85. *Publications:* numerous specialist articles. *Leisure interests:* mountaineering, skiing, boating. *Address:* Chiddinglye, West Hoathly, East Grinstead, Sussex; 30 Victoria Road, London, W8 5RG, England. *Telephone:* Sharpthorne 810214 (Sussex); 01-937 0573 (London).

LIMONOV, Eduard; Ukrainian poet and writer; b. 1952, Dzerzhinsk, Gorky Dist.; m. Yelena Limonova 1971; first wrote poetry at age of 15; in Kharkov 1965-67, moved to Moscow in 1967, where acquired reputation of "unofficial" poet; forced to leave U.S.S.R. 1974; settled in New York 1975. *Publications include:* verse and prose in Kontinent, Ekho, Kovcheg, Apollon -1977 (in trans. in England, U.S.A., Austria and Switzerland), It's Me—Eddie (novel) 1979 and Russian (Russkoye) (verse) 1979. *Address:* c/o Index Publishers, New York, N.Y., U.S.A.

LIN, Chia-Chiao, B.SC., M.A., PH.D.; American applied mathematician; b. 7 July 1916, Fukien, China; s. of Kai and Y. T. Lin; m. Shou-Ying Liang 1946; one d.; ed. Nat. Tsing Hua Univ., Univ. of Toronto, Calif. Inst. of Technology; Asst. Prof. of Applied Maths., Brown Univ. 1945-46, Assoc. Prof. 1946-47; Assoc. Prof. of Maths., M.I.T. 1947-53, Prof. 1953-66, Inst. Prof. of Applied Maths. 1966-; Guggenheim Fellow 1954-55, 1960; Pres. Soc. for Industrial and Applied Maths. 1973; mem. N.A.S.; John von Neumann Lecturer, Soc. for Industrial and Applied Maths. 1967. *Publications:* The Theory of Hydrodynamic Stability 1955, Turbulent Flow, Theoretical Aspects 1963. *Leisure interest:* astronomy. *Address:* Department of Mathematics, Massachusetts Institute of Technology, Cambridge, Mass, 02139, U.S.A.

LIN CHIN-SHENG, B.L.; Chinese government official; b. 4 Aug. 1916; ed. Law Coll., Tokyo Imperial Univ.; Magistrate, Chiayi Co. Govt. 1951-54; Chair. Yunlin Co. HQ, Kuomintang (Nationalist Party of China) 1954-57; Magistrate, Yunlin Co. Govt. 1957-64; Dir. Cheng-Ching Lake Industrial Waterworks 1964-67; Commr. Taiwan Prov. Govt. 1966-70; Sec.-Gen. Taiwan Provincial HQ, Kuomintang 1967-68, Chair. Taipei Municipal HQ 1969-70, Deputy Sec.-Gen. Cen. Cttee. 1970-72, mem. Standing Cttee. of Cen. Cttee. 1976-; Minister of the Interior 1972-76, of Communications 1976-81, without Portfolio 1981-84; Vice-Pres. Examination Yuan 1984-; mem. Standing Cttee. of Kuomintang Cen. Cttee. 1976-; Order of the Brilliant Star. *Address:* 25 Lane 62, Hsinsheng North Road, Sec. 3, Taipei, Taiwan.

LIN FENGMIAN; Chinese artist; b. 1900, Meixian Co., Guangdong Prov.; ed. in France and Germany; Dir. Nat. Art Coll., Beijing 1928; Dir. Hangzhou Art Coll. 1930-; mem. Nat. Cttee., China's Fed. of Literary and Art Circles 1983-. *Address:* Shanghai Artists' Association, Shanghai, People's Republic of China.

LIN HUJIA; Chinese government official; b. 1916, Shandong; Chair. Culture and Educ. Cttee., CCP Zhejiang Prov. Cttee. 1951; Council mem. Zhejiang People's Prov. Govt. 1951; Vice-Sec. CCP Zhejiang Prov. Cttee. 1955, Sec. 1957-64; a leading mem. Nat. Planning Cttee. 1965; branded a rightist opportunist 1967; Vice-Chair. Nat. Planning Cttee. 1973; Sec. Shanghai CCP Cttee. 1977; Vice-Chair. Shanghai Revolutionary Cttee. 1977; mem. Presidium CCP 11th Cen. Nat. Congress 1977-; mem CCP 11th Cen. Cttee. 1977-. First Sec. Tianjin Municipal CCP Cttee. 1978; Chair. Tianjin Municipal Revolutionary Cttee. 1978; First Sec. Beijing CCP Cttee. 1978; Chair. Beijing Revolutionary Cttee. 1978-80; Mayor, Beijing 1980-81; Minister of Agric. 1981-82, of Agric., Animal Husbandry and Fishery 1982-83, Adviser 1983-; mem. CCP 12th Cen. Cttee. 1982-85; Head, State Leading Group to Direct Construction at Gansu Prov. Corridor 1983-; Head, Leading Group for Agricultural Construction in the Sanxi Area (Gansu and Ningxia Prov.), State Council 1983-; mem. Cen. Advisory Comm. 1985-; Adviser, Leading Group for Econ. Devt. in Poor Areas 1986-. *Address:* The State Council, Beijing, People's Republic of China.

LIN JIANQING; Chinese party official; Deputy Dir. Research Cen. under CCP Cen. Cttee. Secr. 1982-87; alt. mem. 12th CCP Cen. Cttee. 1982-87. *Address:* Research Centre, Secretariat of the Chinese Communist Party Central Committee, Beijing, People's Republic of China.

LIN LANYING, PH.D.; Chinese scientist; b. 18 Dec. 1917, Futian Co., Fujian Prov.; ed. Fujian Xiehe Univ., Pennsylvania Univ., U.S.A.; returned to China 1957; Research Fellow, Semiconductors Inst. Academia Sinica 1959-; Vice-Chair., Youth Fed. of China 1962-66; mem. Standing Cttee. 3rd NPC 1964-66; Deputy, 4th NPC 1974-78; Deputy Dir., Semiconductors Inst. 1977-; mem. Standing Cttee. 5th NPC 1978-83, 6th NPC 1983-88; mem. Dept. of Tech. Sciences, Academia Sinica 1985-. *Address:* Room 401, Building 809, Haidian Huang Zhuang, Beijing 100080, People's Republic of China. *Telephone:* 284942 (Beijing).

LIN LIN; Chinese writer; b. 27 Sept. 1910, Zhao'an Co., Fujian Prov.; s. of the late Lin Hede and Zhen Yilian; m. 1st Wu Lanjiao 1930 (died); m. 2nd Chen Ling 1950, two s. two d.; ed. Zhao'an middle school, Chinese Univ., Beijing, Waseda Univ. Tokyo, Japan; joined Left-Wing Movt. in Literature, 1934-36; returned to Shanghai 1936; Ed., Jiuwang Daily, Shanghai 1937, Guangzhou 1938-39, Guilin 1940-41; Chief Ed. of Huaqiao Guide, Manila, Philippines 1941-47; Prof., Dept. of Chinese Literature, Dade Coll., Hongkong 1947-49; Cultural Counsellor, Embassy, New Delhi, India 1955-58; mem. Standing Cttee. of the Sino-African Friendship Asscn. 1960-66; Vice-Chair., Asscn. for Friendship with Foreign Countries 1973-; Advisor, Soc. for Study of Sino-Japanese Relations 1984-. *Publications:* Poems of India 1958, The Sea and the Ship 1987. *Address:* Room 402, Bldg. 22, Congwenmen Dongdajie Street, 100062 Beijing, People's Republic of China.

LIN LIYUN; Chinese state official; b. 1933, Taizhong, Taiwan; ed. Kobe, Japan, Beijing Univ.; council mem. Sino-Japanese Friendship Asscn. 1973-; mem. 10th CCP Cen. Cttee. 1973; mem. Standing Cttee. 4th NPC 1975; Deputy for Taiwan to 5th NPC 1978, 6th NPC 1983; Vice-Pres. Women's Fed. 1978-; Pres. Fed. of Taiwan Compatriots 1981-; mem. 12th CCP Cen. Cttee. 1982-; mem. Presidium 6th NPC 1986-; Standing Cttee. NPC 1984-; mem. Credentials Cttee. NPC 1984-; mem. Overseas Chinese Cttee. NPC 1986-; mem. Working Group for Unification of the Motherland 1984-; Vice-Pres. China Int. Cultural Exchange Centre 1984-; Vice-Pres. All-China Sports Fed. 1979-. *Address:* Chinese Communist Party Central Committee, Beijing, People's Republic of China.

LIN MOHAN; Chinese writer; mem. Nat. Council, China Fed. of Literature and Arts 1953-; Deputy Dir. Propaganda Dept. CCP 1959-66; Vice-Minister of Culture 1959-67; in political disgrace 1966-77; Vice-Minister of Culture 1978-82; Vice-Chair. China Fed. of Literature and Arts 1979-; Chair. Nat. Council on Cultural and Art Work for Children 1981-86; Adviser to Ministry of Culture 1982-86; mem. Presidium CPPCC 1983-; mem. CPPCC Nat. Cttee. 1983-; Chair. China Asscn. for Advancement of Int. Friendship 1985-87, Adviser Feb. 1987-; Adviser, Arts Educ. Cttee. of State Comm. of Educ. 1986-. *Address:* Ministry of Culture, Beijing, People's Republic of China.

LIN PING; Chinese diplomatist; b. 1920, Zhejiang; m. Zhi Ni; Asst. Sino-American Ambassadorial Talks, Warsaw 1955; Deputy Dir. America and Australia Dept., Ministry of Foreign Affairs 1959; Head Chinese Trade Mission, Chile 1965-70; Amb. to Chile 1971-73; Dir. American and Oceanian Affairs Dept., Ministry of Foreign Affairs 1973-78; Amb. to Australia 1978-83, to Papua New Guinea 1980; Vice-Chair. Shandong Prov. People's Congress 1983-. *Address:* c/o Ministry of Foreign Affairs, Beijing, People's Republic of China.

LIN RUO; Chinese party official; b. 1924, Chaoan, Guangdong Prov.; ed. Zhonshan Univ.; joined CCP 1945; Dir. Nanfang ribao 1980; mem. 12th CCP Cen. Cttee. 1982-; Sec. CCP Cttee., Zhanjiang Pref. 1982-; Sec. CCP Cttee., Guangdong Prov. 1983-. *Address:* Guangdong Provincial Chinese Communist Party, Guangzhou, Guangdong, People's Republic of China.

LIN, See-Yan, M.A., M.P.A., PH.D., F.I.B., F.I.S.; Malaysian banker; b. 3 Nov. 1939, Ipoh, Malaysia; ed. Univ. of Malaya in Singapore, Harvard Univ.; Tutor in econs., Univ. of Malaya 1961-63, Harvard Univ. 1970-72, 1976-77; Statistician, Dept. of Statistics 1961-63; Econ. Adviser, Minister of Finance 1966-69; Dir. Malaysian Rubber Exchange and Licensing Bd. (MRELB) 1974-85; mem. Council on Malaysian Invisible Trade (COMIT) 1981-85, Econ. Panel of the Prime Minister 1982-87, Capital Issues Cttee. (CIC) 1985-86; Chief Economist, Bank Negara Malaysia (Cen. Bank of Malaysia) 1973-77, Econ. Adviser 1977-80, Deputy Gov. 1980-; Chair. Credit Guarantee Corpn. Malaysia Berhad (CGC), Malaysian Insurance Inst. (MII); Deputy Chair. Industrial Bank of Malaysia Berhad (Bank Industri); Dir. Malaysia Export Credit Insurance Berhad (MECIB), Govt. Officers Housing Corpn., Seacen Research and Training Centre, Malaysian Wildlife Conservation Foundation; mem. Malaysia Program Advisory Council, US-

ASIAN Centre for Tech. Exchange, Commonwealth Group of Experts on the Debt Crisis 1984, IMF Working Party on Statistical Discrepancy in World Currency Imbalances 1985-87, IMF Cttee. of Balance of Payments Compilers 1987; Pres. Malaysian Econ. Asscn.; Eisenhower Fellow 1986. *Publications:* numerous articles in academic, banking and business journals. *Address:* Bank Negara Malaysia, Jalan Kuching, POB 10922, 50929 Kuala Lumpur, Malaysia.

LIN WENXI; Chinese artist; b. 1933, Changxian C., Zhejiang; ed. Yucai School, Shanghai, Fine Arts Inst., Huangzhou 1953; teacher Fine Arts Inst., Shaanxi 1958. *Works include:* Be Happy Together, Four Generations of Peasants, A Girl from Northern Shaanxi, Tibetan Youth. *Address:* People's Republic of China.

LIN YANG-KANG, B.A.; Chinese politician; b. 10 June 1927, Nantou County; s. of Lin Chih-Chang and Lin Chen Ruan; m. Chen Ho 1945; one s. three d.; ed. Nat. Taiwan Univ.; Chair. Yunlin County H.Q., Kuomintang 1964-67; Magistrate, Nantou County 1967-72; Commr. Dept. of Reconstruction, Taiwan Provincial Govt. 1972-76; Mayor of Taipei 1976-78; Gov. Taiwan Prov. 1978-81; Minister of Interior 1981-84; Vice-Premier of Taiwan 1984-87; Pres. Judicial Yuan 1987-. *Leisure interests:* hiking, reading and studying, music, films. *Address:* 124 Chungking South Road, Sec. 1, Taipei, Taiwan.

LIN YINCAI; Chinese politician; Vice-Minister of Chemical Industry 1982-; alt. mem. 12th CCP Cen. Cttee. 1982-87, mem. 13th Cen. Cttee. 1987. *Address:* Ministry of Chemical Industry, Beijing, People's Republic of China.

LIN ZHAOHUA; Chinese theatre director; b. 1 July 1936, Tianjin; s. of Lin Baogui and Zhang Shuzhen; m. He Binzhu 1964; one s. one d.; Vice-Pres. and Dir. Beijing People's Art Theatre 1984-; mem. Standing Cttee., China Theatre Asscn. 1984-. *Productions include:* Warning Signal, The Red Heart, Just Opinion, Bus Stop 1983, Marriages and Funerals 1984, Amadeus 1985, Wild Man 1985, Schweyk in the Second World War, A Grandfather's Nirvana, Farmland is Greenspread Again. *Publications:* Stage Art of Warning Signal (ed.) 1985, Stage Art of Marriages and Funerals, Peace Lake. *Leisure interest:* Chinese yoga. *Address:* Beijing People's Art Theatre, Beijing, People's Republic of China. *Telephone:* 55.0091 (Office); 421.4081 (Home).

LIN ZHUN; Chinese judge; b. Sept. 1927, Fujian Prov.; Deputy Section Chief, Ministry of Internal Affairs, Cen. People's Govt. 1953-59; Sec. Supreme People's Court 1959-65; Research Fellow, Supreme People's Court 1966-78; Vice-Pres. Criminal Court, Supreme People's Court 1978-81, Dir. Research Dept.; Vice-Pres. Supreme People's Court 1982-. *Address:* Supreme People's Court, Beijing, People's Republic of China.

LINACRE, Sir (John) Gordon (Seymour), Kt., C.B.E., A.F.C., D.F.M., C.B.I.M.; British newspaper executive; b. 23 Sept. 1920; s. of John J. Linacre and Beatrice B. Linacre; m. Irene A. Gordon 1943; two d.; ed. Firth Park Grammar School, Sheffield; served R.A.F. rank of Squadron Leader 1939-46; journalistic appts. Sheffield Telegraph/Star 1937-47; Kemsley News Service 1947-50; Deputy Ed. Newcastle Journal 1950-56, Newcastle Evening Chronicle 1956-57; Ed. Sheffield Star 1958-61; Asst. Gen. Man. Sheffield Newspapers Ltd. 1961-63; Exec. Dir. Thomson Regional Newspapers Ltd., London 1963-65; Man. Dir. Yorkshire Post Newspapers Ltd. 1965-83, Deputy Chair. 1981-83, Chair. 1983-; Dir. United Newspapers PLC 1969-, Jt. Man. Dir. 1981-83, Deputy Chair. 1981-, Chief Exec. 1983-88; Deputy Chair. Express Newspapers PLC 1985-88; also fmr. Chair. United Provincial Newspapers Ltd., Sheffield Newspapers Ltd., Lancashire Evening Post Ltd., Northampton Mercury Co. Ltd., East Yorkshire Printers Ltd. etc.; Dir Yorkshire TV; many other professional and public appts.; Commendatore, Ordine al Merito della Repubblica Italiana. *Address:* White Windows, Staircase Lane, Bramhope, Leeds, LS16 9JD, England. *Telephone:* Arthington 842751.

LIND, Nathalie, LL.B.; Danish lawyer and politican; b. 1 Oct. 1918, Copenhagen; d. of Aage Lind and Ane Johanne Lind (née Bjørndahl); m. 1st Erik Tfelt-Hansen 1943 (died 1962), 2nd Erik Langsted 1968; two s.; Sec. Mothers' Aid Inst., Copenhagen 1943-44; Asst. Chief Constable, Ålborg 1945-48; barrister Ålborg 1949; Asst. to Public Prosecutor, Ålborg 1949; M.P. for Co. of Frederiksborg 1964-66, for Co. of Ribe 1968-82; mem. Exec. Cttee. of Liberal Party 1967-68; Minister of Social Affairs 1968-71; Minister of Justice 1973-75, 1978-79; Minister of Cultural Affairs 1973-75; mem. Danish Radio and TV Bd. 1966-68, 1978; Chair. Law Cttee. and Pres. Danish Del. to Nordic Council 1978; Vice-Chair. Danish Liberal Parl. Group 1978; Judge in Court of Appeal of Social Affairs; Chair. Women's Debating Soc., Ålborg 1947-55; Chair. Copenhagen Section of Danish Women's Soc. 1959-62; Nat. Chair. of Danish Women's Soc. 1966-68; Gwanghwa Medal (Korea); Commdr. of 1st degree of Order of Dannebrog, Order of Yugoslav Flag (with ribbon). *Leisure interests:* literature, history, grandchildren. *Address:* Marielystvej 26, DK-2000 Copenhagen F, Denmark. *Telephone:* (01) 744101.

LINDAUER, Martin, DR.RER.NAT.; German professor of zoology; b. 19 Dec. 1918, Wäldle; s. of Matthias and Katharina Lindauer; m. 1st Franziska Fleck 1943; two s. one d.; m. 2nd Rosemarie Angerbauer; ed. Univ. of Munich; Prof. Univ. of Munich 1961, Univ. of Frankfurt 1963, Univ.

of Würzburg 1973–87; Vice-Pres. Univ. of Würzburg 1976–82; Fellow Rockefeller Foundation; Prather Lecturer Harvard Univ., Prof.-at-large Cornell Univ.; mem. Akad. der Wissenschaften und Literatur, Mainz, Deutsche Akad. der Naturforscher Leopoldina, Halle, American Acad. of Arts and Sciences, Nat. Acad. of Sciences, American Philosophical Soc., Accad. Nazionale dei Lincei, Rome; Dr. h.c. (Zurich, Umeå and Saarbrücken). *Publication:* Communication among Social Bees. *Leisure interests:* mountain climbing, music. *Address:* Zoologisches Institut (II) der Universität, Röntgenring 10, D-8700 Würzburg, Federal Republic of Germany. *Telephone:* 0931-31695.

LINDBLOM, Seppo Olavi, LIC.POL.SC.; Finnish politician and bank executive; b. 9 Aug. 1935, Helsinki; s. of Olavi and Aura (née Sammal) Lindblom; m. Anneli Johanson 1958; four d.; ed. Univ. of Helsinki; Man. br. office, Finnish Workers' Savings Bank 1948–60; scientist, Bank of Finland 1960-68; Sec. to Prime Minister 1968–70; Head, Labour Inst. for Econ. Research 1970–72; Minister in Ministry of Trade and Industry 1972; Head, Dept. of Nat. Econ. Ministry of Finance 1973–74; Nat. Conciliator for Incomes Policy 1973–74; Dir. Bank of Finland 1974–87, mem. Bd. of Man. 1982–87; Minister of Trade and Industry 1983–87; Chief Gen. Man. Postipankki Ltd. 1988–. *Leisure interests:* music, activity in sports orgs. *Address:* Postipankki Ltd., Unioninkatu 20, 00007 Helsinki, Finland. *Telephone:* 1641.

LINDENSTRAUSS, Joram, PH.D.; Israeli professor of mathematics; b. 28 Oct. 1936, Tel-Aviv; m. Naomi Salinger 1962; one s. three d.; ed. Hebrew Univ., Jerusalem; Sr. Lecturer in Math., Hebrew Univ. 1965, Assoc. Prof. 1967, Prof. 1970–; Visiting Prof. Univs. Yale, Washington, California, Texas, Inst. Mittag Leffler, Inst. for Advanced Study, Princeton; mem. Israel Acad. of Science and Humanities; Israeli Prize in Math. 1981. *Publications:* Absolutely summing operators in Lp spaces and their applications (with A. Pelczynski) 1968, The dimension of almost spherical sections of convex bodies 1977, Classical Banach spaces, Vols. I–II, 1977, 1979. *Address:* 36 Habanai Str., Jerusalem, Israel. *Telephone:* (02) 522-762.

LINDERBERG, Jan Erik, F.D.; Danish professor of theoretical chemistry; b. 27 Oct. 1934, Karlskoga, Sweden; s. of David Lindberg and Sara Bäckström; m. Gunnel Björstram 1957; two s.; ed. Uppsala Univ.; Docent, Uppsala Univ. 1964–68; Prof. of Theoretical Chem. Aarhus Univ. 1968–. *Publications:* Role of Correlation in Electronic Systems 1964, Propagators in Quantum Chemistry (co-author), Quantum Science (with others) 1976. *Leisure interest:* orienteering. *Address:* Janus la Cours gade 20, 8000 Aarhus C, Denmark. *Telephone:* 06 12 46 33 (Office); 06 12 02 41 (Home).

LINDEROTH, Karl-Axel, M.B.A.; Swedish insurance company managing director; b. 7 Aug. 1927, Jönköping; m. Gun Ryberg 1955; one s. one d.; ed. Gothenburg School of Econs.; Finance Dir. Co-operative Co. 1952–54; Man. Consultant Volvo 1955; Man. Consultant Swedish Council of Personnel Admin. 1956–59; Exec. Vice-Pres. Finance and Personnel COOP Sweden 1959–76; Man. Dir. Svenska Personal—Pensionskassan (insurance co. owned by Swedish labour orgs.) 1976–; mem. Cen. Cttee. of Int. Cooperative Alliance 1972–76; mem. Bd. Int. Co-operative Bank 1972–80, Sydkraft AB 1972–76, Swedish Pension Fund 1972–77, Uddeholm AB 1977–, Incentive AB 1976–, AB Diligentia 1977–82, Swedish Insurance Orgs. 1976–; Chair. Bd. Statsföretag AB (Swedish State Co.) 1978–82; Chair. Bd. of Swedish Man. Inst. 1978–. *Leisure interests:* sailing, skiing, tennis, YMCA (mem. YMCA President's Cttee. 1965–73). *Address:* Svenska Personal—Pensionskassan, Regeringsgatan 107, S-103 73 Stockholm, Sweden. *Telephone:* 08-787 30 00.

LINDH, Sten, LL.B., B.A.; Swedish diplomatist and industrialist; b. 24 Oct. 1922; s. of Ernst and Elisabeth (née Larsson) Lindh; m. Maikki Birgitta Velander 1945; two s. one d.; ed. Kalmar Grammar School, Stockholm Univ. and Stockholm Business School; entered Swedish Foreign Service 1945, served Washington, Paris, London, Geneva and Brussels; Ministry of Finance 1950–51; Head of Dept., Ministry of Foreign Affairs 1959, 1961–63; Head of EFTA Secr., Geneva 1960; Amb. to the European Econ. Communities and Perm. Rep. to Council of Europe 1964–67; Amb. en disponibilité 1968; Pres. Euroc A.B. (fmrly. Skånska Cement A.B.) 1968–82, Chair. 1982–83, Dir. 1984–; Dir. Liberian American-Swedish Minerals Co., Swedish Lamco Syndicate 1968–82, Skanska A.B. (fmrly. Skanska Cementgjuteriet A.B.) 1969–, Skandinaviska Enskilda Banken A.B. 1969–83 (Vice-Chair. 1983), Gränges A.B. 1970–81, A.B. Cardo 1972–86, Protorp A.B. 1975–, Fed. of Swedish Industries 1975–83; Pres. European Cement Asscn. 1976–79; Dir. Int. Man. Inst. (Geneva) 1981–86; Int. Rep. Skanska AB, London 1984–88; mem. Royal Soc. of Letters, Lund Univ. *Address:* Chemin du Préau 2, CH 1009 Pully, Switzerland. *Telephone:* (021) 280-258.

LINDH, Ylva Anna Maria, B.L.; Swedish politician and youth worker; b. 19 June 1957, Stockholm; d. of Staffan Lindh and Nancy Lindh; ed. Sanobro School, Enkoping, Univ. of Uppsala; Pres. of the Nat Council of Swedish Youth 1981–83; M.P. and mem. Standing Cttee. on Taxation 1982–85; Pres. of the Social Democratic Youth League 1984–; Pres. Govt. Council of Alcohol and Drug Politics 1986–; Vice-Pres. Int. Union of Socialist Youth 1987–. *Leisure interests:* theatre, music, novels. *Address:* c/o S.S.U., Box 11544, 10061 Stockholm, Sweden.

LINDHARD, Jens; Danish professor of theoretical physics; b. 26 Feb. 1922, Tystofte; s. of the late Erik Lindhard and Agnes Lindhard (née Nielsen); unmarried; ed. Univ. of Copenhagen; Prof. Univ. of Aarhus 1956–;

mem. Royal Danish Acad. of Sciences and Letters 1962–, Pres. 1981–88; mem. Danish Acad. of Tech. Sciences 1962–; mem. Hollandsche Maatschappij der Wetenschappen 1983–; Rigmor and Carl Holst-Knudsen's Prize 1965; C. G. Filtenborg's Award 1978; H. C. Ørsted Medal 1974, Danish Physical Soc. Award 1988. *Address:* J. F. Willumsensvej 4, 8270 Højbjerg (Home); Institute of Physics, University of Aarhus, 8000 Aarhus C, Denmark (Office). *Telephone:* 45-86-12 88 99 ext. 265 (Office).

LINDHARDT, Poul Georg, D.TH.; Danish university professor; b. 12 Dec. 1910, Nakskov; s. of G. W. Lindhardt and Caroline Christensen; m. Gerda Winding 1937; four s.; ed. Univ. of Copenhagen; ordained 1934, Minister in various parishes 1934–42; Asst. Lecturer Univ. of Copenhagen 1939–41, Aarhus Univ. 1941–42; Prof. of Church History, Aarhus Univ. 1942–80, Dean of Faculty of Divinity 1944, 1948, 1953, 1957, 1962, 1969–71; Minister of Our Lady's Church, Aarhus 1945–80. *Publications:* Konfirmationens Historie i Danmark 1936, Danmark og Reformkoncilierne 1942, Bibelen og det danske Folk 1942, Den nordiske Kirkes Historie 1945, Dines Pontoppidan 1948, Morten Pontoppidan I 1950, II 1953, Grundtvig, An Introduction 1951, Vækkelser og kirkelige retninger 1951, Det evige Liv 1953, En dansk Sognepræst 1954, Fem Aalborg-Bisper 1954, Religion og Evangelium 1954, Kirken igaar og idag 1955, 15 Prædikener 1956, Danmarks kirkehistorie 1849-1901, To Højkirkemænd, Repliker, Helvedsstrategi 1958, F. C. Krarups Breve til Lyder Brun 1959, Stat og kirke 1960, Biskop Chr. Ludwigs visitatsdagbog 1960, Paaskud og Prædikener 1963, Grundtvig 1964, Det religiøse liv i senmiddelalderen 1966, Den danske reformations historie 1966, Den danske kirkes historie 1901-65, 1966, Nederlagets Maend 1968, Brudstykker af en postil 68, Thomas Skat Rørdam 1969, Konfrontation 1974, Gentagelse 1975, Regeneration 1977, Dansk Kirkekundskab 1979, Eftertryk 1980, Optryk 1981, Sådan set (memoirs) 1981, Skandinaviske Kirchengeschichte seit dem 16. Jahrhundert 1982, Kirchengeschichte Skandinaviens 1983, 12 Praedikener 1984. *Address:* Tagmosevej 7, 8541 Skødstrup, Denmark. *Telephone:* 06 99 11 91.

LINDLEY, Sir Arnold Lewis George, Kt., D.SC., C.G.I.A., F.ENG., F.I.MECH.E., F.I.E.E.; British electrical manufacturing executive; b. 13 Nov. 1902, London; s. of George Dilnot Lindley and Charlotte Hooley; m. 1st Winifred May Lindley 1927 (deceased), one s. one d.; m. 2nd Mrs. Phyllis Rand 1963; ed. Woolwich Polytechnic; Chief Engineer, British Gen. Electric Co. (B.G.E.C.), S. Africa 1933–45, Dir. and Man. 1945–49; Dir. E. Rand Eng. Co. 1943–49; Gen. Man. Erith Works, Gen. Electric Co. (G.E.C.), England 1949–58, Dir. G.E.C. 1953–64, Asst. Man. Dir. 1958–59, Man. Dir. 1959–61, Chair. 1961–64; Chair. Eng. Industry Training Bd. 1964–74; Deputy Chair. Motherwell Bridge (Holdings) Ltd. 1965–84; Pres. British Electrical and Allied Mfg. Asscn. 1961–63; Int. Electrical Asscn. 1962–64, Inst. Mech. Eng. 1968–69; Chair. Council of Eng. Insts. 1969–72; Fellow, Woolwich Polytechnic; mem. Design Council 1971–77. *Leisure interests:* golf, sailing. *Address:* Heathcote House, 18 Nab Lane, Shipley, West Yorkshire, England (Home). *Telephone:* Shipley 598484 (Home).

LINDNER, Carl Henry; American business executive; b. 22 April 1919, Dayton, Ohio; s. of Carl Henry and Clara (née Serrer) Lindner; m. Edith Bailey 1953; three s.; co-founder United Dairy Farmers 1940; Pres. American Finance Corpn., Cincinnati 1959–84, Chair. 1959–; C.E.O. 1984–; Chair., C.E.O., Chair. Exec. Cttee. United Brands Co., N.Y. 1984–; Chair. Penn Cen. Corpn., Greenwich, Conn. 1983–, Chair. and C.E.O. Great American Communications Co. 1987–; mem. bd. of Dirs. Mission Inst., bd. of Advisers Business Admin. Coll., Univ. of Cincinnati. *Address:* American Financial Corpn., 1 E. Fourth Street, Cincinnati, Ohio 45202; Fisher Foods Inc., 5300 Richmond Road, Bedford Heights, Ohio 44146, U.S.A.

LINDNER, Gerhard; German diplomatist; b. 26 Feb. 1930, Thalheim; m. Edeltraut Lindner; two s.; ed. Leipzig Univ.; entered diplomatic service 1956, Counsellor, Czechoslovakia 1964, Finland 1965–68, Head of G.D.R. Trade Mission in Denmark 1970–71; Amb. to Australia 1977–81, to U.K. 1984–; holds several awards and medals. *Leisure interests:* sport, classical music. *Address:* Embassy of the German Democratic Republic, 34 Belgrave Square, London, S.W.1, England. *Telephone:* 01-235 9941.

LINDON, Jérôme; French publisher; b. 9 June 1925, Paris; s. of Raymond Lindon and Thérèse Baur; m. Annette Rosenfeld 1947; two s. one d.; ed. Lycée Pasteur, Neuilly-sur-Seine, Lycée Mignet, Aix-en-Provence; Pres., Dir. Gen. Editions de Minuit 1948–, has published novels of the "nouveau roman" (Beckett—Nobel Prizewinner 1969, Robbe-Grillet, Butor, Nathalie Sarraute, Simon—Nobel Prizewinner 1985, Pinget, Marguerite Duras, etc.). *Address:* Editions de Minuit, 7 rue Bernard Palissy, 75006 Paris, France. *Telephone:* 42-22-37-94.

LINDQVIST, Bengt, M.A.; Swedish politician; b. 3 June 1936, Helsingborg; m. Gun Lindqvist; two d.; former teacher of the visually handicapped; head of research and projects concerning the educational problems of the blind, Univ. of Uppsala and language producer, Swedish Broadcasting Corpn. 1969–73; Exec. Chair. Swedish Fed. of the Visually Handicapped 1975–85; Chair. Cen. Cttee. Nat. Asscns. of the Handicapped and various int. assignments 1977–85; mem. Parl. 1982–85; Minister at Ministry of Health and Social Affairs (with responsibility for Family Planning, the Disabled and the Elderly) 1985–. *Address:* Ministry of Health and Social Affairs, Jakobsgt. 26, 103 33 Stockholm, Sweden.

LINDSAY, Jack, O.A., B.A., F.R.S.L., D.LITT.; British author; b. 20 Oct. 1900, Melbourne, Australia; s. of the late Norman Lindsay and of Catharine Parkinson; m. Meta Waterdrinker 1958; one s. one d.; ed. Queensland Univ.; earlier work mainly verse; began series of translations of Greek and Latin poets; went to England 1926; Man. and Ed. Fanfrolico Press until 1930; began novel-writing and direct historical work in 1930s; first historical novel 1934; served in Signals and in War Office 1941–45; Fellow, Royal Soc. of Literature; Fellow, Australian Acad. of Humanities 1982–; D.Litt. (Queensland); Gold Medal Australian Soc. of Literature 1960; Soviet Order Znak Pocheta 1968. *Publications include:* poetry: Fauns and Ladies, Passionate Neatherd, Hereward (verse drama); William Blake, The Romans, Arthur and his Times, Short History of Culture, Byzantium into Europe, Daily Life in Roman Egypt, Origins of Alchemy, Origins of Astrology, The Clashing Rocks, Helen of Troy, The Normans, The Troubadors, Decay and Renewal; trans. Lysistrata, Women in Parliament, complete works of Petronius, Latin Medieval Poets, I am a Roman; Ed. Metamorphosis of Aiax (Sir John Harington, 1596), Loving Mad Tom (Bedlamite verses), Parlement of Pratlers (J. Eliot; 1593); art criticism: Life of Turner, Cézanne, Courbet, Hogarth, Gainsborough; history: 1764: The Writing on the Wall, The Monster City, Defoe's London 1978, The Crisis in Marxism 1981; biographies: John Bunyan, George Meredith, Charles Dickens, William Morris, J. M. W. Turner, William Hogarth; autobiography: Life Rarely Tells, The Roaring Twenties, Fanfrolico and After; novels: Rome For Sale, Caesar is Dead, The Barriers are Down, Time to Live, 1649, Lost Birthright, We Shall Return, Rising Tide, All on the Never-Never (film Live Now Pay Later), Masks and Faces, Choice of Times, Thunder Underground. *Leisure interests:* field archaeology, bricklaying, tree-planting. *Address:* 56 Maids Causeway, Cambridge, England.

LINDSAY, John Vliet; American lawyer and politician; b. 24 Nov. 1921, New York City; s. of George and Eleanor (Vliet) Lindsay; brother of Robert V. Lindsay (q.v.); m. Mary Harrison 1949; one s. three d.; ed. The Buckley School, St. Paul's School, Concord, Yale Univ., and Yale Law School; admitted to New York Bar 1949, D.C. Bar 1957; mem. Webster and Sheffield, New York 1948–55, 1974–; Exec. Asst. to U.S. Attorney-Gen. 1955–57; mem. U.S. House of Reps. 1959–65; Mayor of New York 1966–73; fmr. Commentator on ABC-TV programmes; New York Int. Trade Rep. 1981–; Int. Rep. of Mayor's Cttee. for New York 1983–; Chair. Vivian Beaumont Theater, New York 1984–; Hon. LL.D. (Williams Coll.) 1968, (Harvard) 1968. *Publications:* Journey into Politics 1966, The City 1970, The Edge 1976. *Address:* 1 Rockefeller Plaza, New York, N.Y. 10020, U.S.A.

LINDSAY, Robert V.; American banker; b. 1 Jan. 1926, New York City; s. of George and Eleanor (Vliet) Lindsay; brother of John V. Lindsay (q.v.); m. Nancy A. Dalley 1950; two s. one d.; ed. Yale Univ.; joined Morgan Guaranty Trust Co. 1949, Asst. Treas. 1954, Asst. Vice-Pres. 1955, Vice-Pres. 1960, Sr. Vice-Pres. 1969, Exec. Vice-Pres. 1976, Chair. 1979–80, Pres. 1980–87, Chair. Int. Council 1987–; Chair. of Exec. Cttee. and Dir. J. P. Morgan & Co. Inc. 1979–; Dir. St. Joe Minerals Corpn., Chubb Corpn., Russell Reynolds Assocs. 1983–; mem. Bd. of Dirs. Philharmonic Symphony Soc. of New York, Inc. 1977–85; Trustee Guggenheim Memorial Foundation 1983–; Chair. Foreign Policy Assen. 1986–. *Address:* Morgan Guaranty Trust Co., 23 Wall Street, New York, N.Y. 10015 (Office); 296 Altamont Road, Millbrook, New York, N.Y. 12545, U.S.A. (Home).

LINDSLEY, Donald Benjamin, A.B., M.A., PH.D.; American professor of psychology and physiology; b. 23 Dec. 1907, Brownhelm, Ohio; s. of Benjamin Kent Lindsley and Martha Elizabeth Jenne; m. Ellen Ford 1933; two s. two d.; ed. Wittenberg Univ. and Univ. of Iowa; Instructor in Psychology, Univ. of Ill. 1932–33; Nat. Research Council Fellow, Harvard Medical School 1933–35; Research Assoc., W. Reserve Univ. Medical School 1935–38; Asst. Prof. Brown Univ. and Dir. Psychology and Neurophysiology Lab., Bradley Hosp. 1938–46; Dir. Radar Research Project, Office of Scientific Research and Devt., Yale Univ., Camp Murphy and Boca Raton Air Force Base, Fla. 1943–45; Prof. of Psychology, Northwestern Univ. 1946–51; Prof. of Psychology, Physiology and Psychiatry, Univ. of Calif., Los Angeles 1951–77, Prof. Emer. 1977–, mem. Brain Research Inst., Univ. of Calif., Los Angeles 1960–, Chair. Dept. of Psychology 1959–62; Phillips Visiting Lecturer, Haverford Coll. 1961; Pillsbury Visiting Lecturer, Cornell Univ. 1963; Special Visiting Lecturer, Michigan State Univ. 1964; mem. Amazon Neurobiological Expedition on Research Vessel Alpha Helix 1967; Visiting Lecturer, Univ. of Sydney, Australia 1972 and 10 South African univs. 1969; Lashley Lecturer, Queens Coll., N.Y. 1979; mem. Nat. Acad. of Sciences, American Acad. of Arts and Sciences, Soc. of Experimental Psychologists, Int. Brain Research Org., American Physiological Soc., Soc. for Neuroscience (Annual Donald B. Lindsley Prize in Behavioral Neuroscience est. in his name 1978); Hon. mem. American Electroencephalographic Soc. 1980; Hon. mem. of Great Distinction, Western Electroencephalography Soc.; Hon. Fellow Univ. of Calif. at Los Angeles School of Medicine 1986; Foreign mem. Finnish Acad. of Science and Letters 1987; William James Lecturer, Harvard 1958; Guggenheim Fellow 1959; Hon. D.Sc. (Brown Univ.) 1958, (Wittenberg Univ.) 1959, (Trinity Coll.) 1965, (Loyola Univ.) 1969; Ph.D. h.c. (Johannes Gutenberg Univ., Mainz) 1977; Presidential Certificate of Merit for Second World War Research Work; Distinguished Scientific Contribution Award, American Psychological Assen.; Distinguished Scientific Achievement Award, Soc. Psychophysiological Research 1984, Ralph Gerard Prize (jtly.), Soc. for Neuroscience 1988. *Publications:* 250 publs., including scientific works in journals and 40 chapters in books; subjects: emotion, electro-encephalography, neurophysiology, perception, attention, brain function, developmental neurology, autonomic function, sleep and wakefulness, conditioning and learning, etc. *Leisure interests:* music, photography, gardening, golf, travel. *Address:* Department of Psychology, University of California, Los Angeles, Calif. 90024 (Office); 471 23rd Street, Santa Monica, Calif. 90402, U.S.A. (Home). *Telephone:* 213-825-2517 (Office); 213-395-8026 (Home).

LINDSTROM, Torsten L., M.SC.; Swedish company executive; b. 21 Sept. 1921, Kiruna; s. of Sigurd and Henny (Andersson) Lindstrom; m. Else Maj Mortberg 1945; one d.; ed. Royal Inst. of Tech., Stockholm; Asst. Prof. Electrical Eng., Royal Inst. of Tech. 1946–60; joined ASEA AB 1961, Man. Low-Voltage Switchgear and Controlgear Design Dept. 1961–63, Gen. Man. Low-Voltage Switchgear and Controlgear Div. 1964–66, Exec. Vice-Pres. in charge of Research and Product Devt. 1967–75, Pres. of ASEA AB 1976–80, Group Exec. Officer 1980–81; Kt. of Royal Order of Vasa; Hon. D.Tech. 1979. *Publications:* articles on electrotechnical subjects. *Leisure interests:* outdoor life, music. *Address:* ASEA Stockholm Office, P.O. Box 7373, S-103 91 Stockholm (Office); Sankt Johannesgatan 23 F, S-75235 Uppsala, Sweden (Home). *Telephone:* 08/24 59 50 (Office); 018/14 28 23 (Home).

LINDSTROM, Ulla; Swedish politician; b. 15 Sept. 1909, Stockholm; d. of Nils and Gull (née Magnell) Wohlin; m. Martin Lindstrom 1947; ed. Univ. of Stockholm; teacher 1933; Ed. teachers' weekly publ. 1934–46; Ed. weekly publ. on housing 1934–44; elected Stockholm Municipal Council 1942; elected Senate 1946–70; Chair. Govt. Cttees. on the Furniture Industry, the Shoe Industry, and on the Distribution of Consumer Goods 1946, 1948, 1955; Expert, Trade Dept. 1946–54; Minister without Portfolio 1954–66; mem. Swedish Del. to UN 1947–66; Chair. Swedish Save the Children Fed. 1970–78; mem. Nat. Campaign Cttee. against Nuclear Power; Labour Party. *Address:* Fleminggatan 56, Stockholm, Sweden.

LINDT, Auguste Rudolph, LL.D.; Swiss diplomatist (retd.); b. 5 Aug. 1905, Berne; s. of August Ludwig Lindt and Lina Mathilda Rüfenacht; ed. Univs. of Geneva and Berne; special news corresp. in Manchuria, Liberia, Palestine, Jordan, the Persian Gulf, Tunisia, Rumania and Finland 1932–40; served in Swiss Army 1940–45; special del. of the Int. Red Cross, Berlin 1945; Press Attaché and Counsellor Swiss Legation, London; Perm. Observer from Switzerland to the UN 1953–56; fmr. Chair. UNICEF; Pres. UN Opium Conf. 1953; UN High Commr. for Refugees 1956–60; Swiss Amb. to U.S.A. 1960–63; Del. Swiss Fed. Council for Technical Co-operation 1963–66; Amb. to U.S.S.R. 1966–69, to India and Nepal 1969–70; Int. Red Cross Commr. for Nigeria-Biafra relief operation 1968–69; Pres. Int. Union for Child Welfare 1971–77; Adviser to Pres. of Rwanda 1973–75; Hon. Dr. (Geneva). *Publication:* Special Correspondent with Bandits and Generals in Manchuria 1933, Genoräle hungern nie, Geschichte einer Hilfsaktion in Afrika 1983. *Leisure interests:* gardening, mountaineering. *Address:* Jolimontstrasse 2, 3006 Berne, Switzerland. *Telephone:* 43 31 54.

LINDWALL, Raymond Russell, M.B.E.; Australian cricketer and florist; b. 3 Oct. 1921, Mascot, Sydney, N.S.W.; s. of Arthur and Catherine Lindwall; m. Margaret Rose Robinson 1951; one s. one d.; fast right-arm bowler; played for Australia in 61 Test Matches 1946–60, took 228 wickets (114 against England), scored 1,502 runs; now proprietor of florist's business. *Leisure interests:* golf, swimming. *Address:* 3 Wentworth Court, Endeavour Street, Mt. Ommaney, Brisbane 4074, Queensland, Australia.

LING, James J.; American business executive; b. 1922, Hugo, Okla.; s. of Henry William Ling and Mary (née Jones) Ling; ed. St. John's College, Shreveport; Pres. Ling Electrics 1946–58, Chair. 1958–60; Pres. Chair. Exec. Cttee. Ling Temco Electronics 1960–61; Chair. Exec. Cttee. Ling-Temco-Vought Inc. 1961–63, Chair. of Bd. and C.E.O. 1963–70; partner Bear, Stearns & Co., New York; Dir. Southwest Research Inst., Chief Exec. Forum, Knights of Malta; Pres. Matrix Inc.; mem. Hudson Inst.; Regent of Texas Technological Univ.; fmr. mem. Visiting Cttee. MIT, Bd. of Dirs. Univ. of Dallas; fmr. Pres. Council, Calif. Inst. of Tech.; Horatio Alger Award 1962, Hon. LL.D., Hon. D.B.A. *Address:* 2820 Southland Center, Dallas, Tex. 75201 (Office); 14 Royal Way, Dallas, Tex. 75229, U.S.A. (Home).

LING LIONG SIK, Dato', M.B., B.S.; Malaysian politician; b. 18 Sept. 1943, Kuala Kangsar, Perak; m. Datin Ee Nah Ong 1968; two c.; ed. King Edward VII School, Royal Mil. Coll. and Univ. of Singapore; Parl. Sec. Ministry of Local Govt. and Fed. Territory 1976–77; Deputy Minister of Information 1978–82, of Finance 1982–84, of Educ. 1985–86; Minister of Transport 1986–; Deputy Pres. Malaysian Chinese Assen. 1985–87, Pres. 1987–. *Leisure interests:* reading, golf. *Address:* Ministry of Transport, 7th Floor, Wisma Perdana, Jalan Dungun Bukit Damansara, 50616 Kuala Lumpur, Malaysia.

LING QING; Chinese diplomatist; b. 1 April 1923, Beijing; m. Zhang Lian; one d.; ed. Yanjing Univ.; entered diplomatic service 1945; Dir. and Deputy Dir., Depts. of European and American Affairs, Int. Orgs. and Int. Law of Foreign Ministry; Amb. to Venezuela 1975–78; Perm. Rep. to UN 1980–85; Chair. or Vice-Chair., Del. to 1st, 2nd, 3rd UN Confs. on Law of the Sea, 10th Special Session UN Gen. Ass., Conf. on Indochinese Refugees, Geneva 1979, 36th Session ESCAP, Int. Conf. on Kampuchea, New York 1981, 35th-39th UN Gen. Ass. Sessions 1980-84; Vice-Pres. Chinese People's Asscn. for Friendship with Foreign Countries 1986-; Vice-Chair. CPCCC 6th Fujian Prov. Cttee. 1988-. *Address:* 1 Taijichang Street, Beijing, People's Republic of China.

LING YUN; Chinese government official; b. 1917; Vice-Minister of Public Security, 1964-66; Deputy for Shanghai, 3rd NPC 1964; leading mem. Ministry of Public Security 1975-78; Deputy for Shanghai, 5th NPC 1978; Vice-Minister of Public Security 1978-83; Minister of State Security 1983-85. *Address:* c/o Ministry of State Security, Beijing, People's Republic of China.

LINI, Father Walter Hadye, C.B.E.; Vanuatu ecclesiastic and politician; b. 1942, Pentecost; m. Mary B. Ketu 1970; four s. two d.; ed. for Anglican priesthood, Solomon Islands and New Zealand; ordained deacon 1968; ordained priest 1970; Deputy Chief Minister and Minister of Social Services, New Hebrides (now Vanuatu) Jan.-Nov. 1979; Chief Minister and Minister of Justice 1979-80; Prime Minister of Vanuatu July 1980-; Pres. Vanuaaku Pati (VP), formerly the Nat. Party. *Publication:* Beyond Pandemonium 1980. *Address:* Office of the Prime Minister, P.O. Box 110, Port Vila, Vanuatu.

LINK, Arthur A.; American politician; b. 24 May 1914, Alexander, N.D.; s. of John Link and Anna Mencl; m. Grace Johnson 1939; five s. one d.; ed. N.D. Agricultural Coll.; mem. Randolph Township Bd. for 28 years and McKenzie Co. Welfare Bd. for 21 years; served on local school bd. for 18 years and was mem. of co. and state Farm Security Admin. Cttee.; State Rep., N.D. Legislature for 24 years; Speaker 1965; served as Minority Floor Leader for seven terms, and on legislative cttees. on Educ., Finance and Taxation, Business and Industry, and Labour Relations; Chair. N.D. State Advisory Council for Vocational Educ. 1969-71; Chair. Second Interim Cttee. on Legislative Procedure and Arrangements and of the Subcttee. on Educ. of the Legislative Research Cttee.; U.S. House of Reps., mem. for Second (West) District of N.D. 1970, mem. Agricultural Cttee. and the Livestock and Grains, Domestic Marketing and Consumer Relations subcttees.; mem. of the House District of Columbia Cttee., serving on the Judiciary and the Business, Commerce and Fiscal Affairs subcttees.; co-sponsor of the Melcher Farm Bill; Gov. of North Dakota 1973-81; Dir. Bismarck State Bank; Chair. Midwestern Govs.' Conf. 1978; mem. Exec. Cttee., Nat. Govs.' Asscn. 1978; Chair. Agric. Cttee., Nat. Govs.' Asscn. 1979; Chair. Resolutions Cttee., Farmers' Union Grain Terminal Asscn. annual meeting for three years; bd. mem. Williston Univ. Center Foundation; fmr. bd. mem. McKenzie Co. Museum and Lewis and Clark Trail Museum. *Leisure interests:* camping, fishing, horseriding, reading. *Address:* Alexander, N.D. 58831, U.S.A. (Home).

LINK, Christoph, D.JUR.; German/Austrian professor of law; b. 13 June 1933, Dresden; s. of Hellmuth Link and Gerda Link; m. Eva Link 1957; one s. one d.; ed. Kreuzschule Dresden and Univs. of Marburg, Cologne and Munich; Prof. Vienna 1971-77, Salzburg 1977-79, Hon. Prof. 1979-, Göttingen 1979-86; Prof. of State Admin. and Church Law, Univ. of Erlangen and Dir. Hans-Liermann-Inst. für Kirchenrecht 1979-; mem. Akad. der Wissenschaften, Göttingen. *Publications:* Die Grundlagen der Kirchenverfassung im lutherischen Konfessionalismus des 19. Jahrhunderts 1966, Herrschaftsordnung und bürgerliche Freiheit 1979, Kirchen und privater Rundfunk (with A. Pahlke) 1985. *Address:* Hans-Liermann-Institut für Kirchenrecht, 8520 Erlangen, Hindenburgstrasse 34 (Office); Hindenburgstrasse 47, 8520 Erlangen, Federal Republic of Germany (Home). *Telephone:* 09131-852242 (Office); 09131-209335 (Home).

LINNANE, Anthony William, D.SC., PH.D., F.R.S., F.A.A.; Australian professor of biochemistry; b. 17 July 1930, Sydney; s. of late W. P. Linnane; m. 1st Judith Neil 1956 (dissolved 1979), one s. one d.; m. 2nd Daryl Woods 1980, one s. one d.; ed. Sydney Univ., Univ. of Wisconsin; Postdoctoral Fellow, Univ. of Wis. 1956-58; Lecturer, then Sr. Lecturer, Sydney Univ. 1958-62; Reader, Monash Univ. 1962, Prof. of Biochem. 1965-, Dir. Centre of Molecular Biology and Medicine 1984-; Visiting Prof., Univ. of Wis. 1967-68; Pres. Australian Biochemical Soc. 1974-76, Fed. of Asian and Oceanic Biochemical Socs. 1975-77, 12th Int. Congress of Biochem., Perth 1982; Treas.-elect, Int. Union of Biochemistry 1988. *Publications:* Autonomy and Biogenesis of Mitochondria and Chloroplasts 1971; over 200 publs.; Ed.-in-Chief Biochemistry International. *Leisure interests:* tennis, reading, horseracing. *Address:* Department of Biochemistry, Monash University, Clayton, Vic. 3168 (Office); 25 Canterbury Road, Camberwell, Vic. 3124, Australia (Home). *Telephone:* (Melbourne) 565-3721 (Office); 8824-384 (Home).

LINNEMANN, Hans, D.ECON.; Netherlands economist; b. 7 May 1931, Rotterdam; s. of Philippus Linnemann and Johanna Verkaik; m. Alida J. van Noort 1956; three s. one d.; ed. Netherlands School of Econs.; Staff mem. Netherlands Econ. Inst. 1951-58; UN Expert, Ecuador 1959-60, Egypt 1962-63; Staff mem. Netherlands School of Econs. 1960-62, 1964-66; Asst. Prof. American Univ. of Cairo 1963-64; Prof. of Devt. Econs. Inst. of Social Studies, The Hague 1966-70, Free Univ. of Amsterdam 1970-; mem. Royal Netherlands Acad. of Sciences. *Publications:* An Analysis and Projection of the Exports of Ecuador 1960, An Econometric Study of International Trade Flows 1966, MOIRA-Model of International Relations in Agriculture (with others) 1979, Export-Oriented Industrialization in Developing Countries (ed.) 1987. *Leisure interests:* chess, coin collecting, jogging. *Address:* Patryslaan 70, 2261 EG Leidschendam, The Netherlands. *Telephone:* 27 64 88.

LINNER, Carl Sture, M.A., PH.D.; Swedish international civil servant; b. 15 June 1917, Stockholm; s. of Carl W. Linner and Hanna Hellstedt; m. Clio Tambakopoulos 1944; two s.; ed. Stockholm and Uppsala Univs.; Assoc. Prof. of Greek, Uppsala Univ. 1943; Del. to Int. Red Cross, Greece 1943-45; Dir. A.B. Electrolux, Stockholm 1945-50; Dir. Swedish Employers' Confed. 1950-51; Exec. Vice-Pres. A.B. Bahco, Stockholm 1951-57; Pres. Swedish Lamco Syndicate 1957; Exec. Vice. Pres. and Gen. Man. Liberian-American-Swedish Minerals Co., Monrovia 1958-60; Chief UN Civilian Operations, later UN Mission, in the Congo 1960-61; Special Rep. of UN Sec.-Gen. in Brussels and London 1962; UN Rep. in Greece, Turkey, Israel and Cyprus 1962-65, in London 1965-68, in Tunis 1968-71, UNDP, New York 1971-73; Resident Rep. UNDP in Egypt 1973-77; Sr. Consultant, FAO 1977-; mem. Royal Swedish Acad. of Letters, History and Antiquities, Royal Acad. of Arts and Sciences, Uppsala; Star of Africa, Order of Phoenix, Prince Carl Medal. *Publications:* Syntaktische und lexikalische Studien zur Historia Lausiaca des Palladios 1943, Giorgos Seferis 1963, Roms Konungahävder 1964, Fredrika Bremer i Grekland 1965, W. H. Humphreys' First Journal of the Greek War of Independence 1967, Thucydides 1978, Min odyssé 1982, Bysantinska porträtt 1984, Homeros 1985, Bistånd till Afrika 1985, Disaster Relief for Development 1986, Hellenika 1986, En värld utan gränser 1988, Den gyllene lyran: Archilochos, Sapfo, Pindaros 1989. *Leisure interests:* poetry, sports. *Address:* 24 Phokylidou, 10 673 Athens, Greece. *Telephone:* 3614754.

LINOWITZ, Sol Myron, LL.B.; American lawyer and diplomatist; b. 7 Dec. 1913, Trenton, N.J.; s. of Joseph and Rose (née Oglenskye) Linowitz; m. Evelyn Zimmerman 1939; four d.; ed. Hamilton Coll., and Cornell Univ. Law School; Asst. Gen. Counsel, Office of Price Admin., Washington 1942-44; Officer, Office of Gen. Counsel, Navy Dept. 1944-46; fmr. Partner, Harris, Beach, Wilcox, Dale & Linowitz; Gen. Counsel, Chair. Bd. and Chair. Exec. Cttee. Xerox Corpn. 1958-66; Chair. Bd. and C.E.O. Xerox Int. 1966; Chair. Nat. Urban Coalition 1970-75; Pres. Fed. City Council 1974-78; mem. Council on Foreign Relations, American Jewish Cttee.; U.S.A. Amb. to OAS and U.S. Rep. on the Inter-American Cttee. of the Alliance for Progress 1966-69; Sr. Partner Coudert Brothers (Int. Law firm) 1969-84, Sr. Counsel 1984-; co-negotiator, Panama Canal Treaties 1977; personal Amb. of Pres. Carter to Middle East negotiations 1979-81; Chair. Presidential Cttee. on World Hunger 1978-79; Head of Comm. for U.S.-Latin American Relations; Co-Chair. Inter-American Dialogue; Fellow, American Acad. of Arts and Sciences; Chair. American Acad. of Diplomacy; Trustee, Cornell Univ., Hamilton Coll., Johns Hopkins Univ., American Assembly; hon. degrees (LL.D. and L.H.D.) from more than 35 colls. and univs. *Publications:* This Troubled Urban World 1974, The Making of a Public Man (a memoir) 1985. *Leisure interest:* violin. *Address:* 1627 I Street N.W., Washington, D.C. 20006 (Office); 2325 Wyoming Ave., Washington, D.C. 20008, U.S.A.

LINSKENS, Hansferdinand, DR.PHIL.; German professor of botany; b. 22 May 1921, Lahr; s. of late Albert W. Linskens and Maria E. Bayer; m. Ingrid M. Rast 1954; two s. two d.; ed. Univs. of Berlin, Cologne and Bonn, Eidgenössische Tech. Hoschschule, Zürich; Battelle Memorial Fellow, ETH, Zürich 1952-53; Privat Dozent, Univ. of Cologne 1954-56; Prof. of Botany, Univ. of Nijmegen, Netherlands 1957-86, Dean, Faculty of Science 1980-85; Prof. of Geobotany, Univ. of Eichstätt 1986-; mem. Royal Dutch Acad., Deutsche Akad. der Naturforscher Leopoldina, Linnean Soc. of London, Royal Belgian Acad., New York Acad. of Science etc.; NATO stipendiary, Lisbon 1960; Visiting Prof. Marine Biological Lab. Woods Hole, Mass. 1966, 1968, Univ. of Siena 1988, 1989; K. Heyer Prize for Ecology 1984; Dr. h.c. (Lille) 1982, (Siena) 1985. *Publications:* Papierchromatographie in der Botanik 1958, Pollen Physiology and Fertilization 1964, Fertilization in Higher Plant 1974, Cellular Interaction (with J. Heslop-Harrison) 1985; Modern Methods in Plant Analysis (series) 1966-. *Leisure interests:* history of science, collecting autographs. *Address:* Oosterbergweg 5, 6573 Beek, Netherlands; Goldberglein 7, 8520 Erlangen, Federal Republic of Germany. *Telephone:* 08895-41652 (Beek); 09131-440517 (Erlangen).

LINTOTT, Sir Henry (John Bevis), K.C.M.G.; British diplomatist; b. 23 Sept. 1908; s. of the late Henry John Lintott and of Edith Lunn; m. Margaret Orpen 1949; one s. one d.; ed. Edinburgh Acad., Edinburgh Univ., and King's Coll., Cambridge; Customs and Excise Dept. 1932-35; Bd. of Trade 1935-48; Ministry of Econ. Warfare 1939-40; Office of Minister of State, Cairo 1941; Deputy Sec.-Gen. OEEC 1948-56; Deputy Under-Sec. of State, Commonwealth Relations Office 1956-63; High Commr. in Canada 1963-68; Dir. The Metal Box Co. 1968-73, Glaxo Holdings Ltd. 1968-. *Address:* 47 Granchester Street, Cambridge, CB3 9HZ, England. *Telephone:* (0223) 312410.

LIONAES, Aase; Norwegian politician; b. 10 April 1907, Oslo; d. of Erling and Anna Lionaes; m. Kurt Jonas 1938; one d.; ed. Univ. of Oslo and L.S.E.; mem. Storting (Parl.) 1953-; Vice-Pres. of the Lagting (Upper House) 1965-69, of the Odelsting (Lower House) 1969-77; mem. Govt. del. to UN 1946-65; mem. Nobel Peace Prize Cttee. 1948-, Pres. 1968-79; Hon.

LL.D. (Oxford Coll., Ohio); Labour. *Address:* Pans Vei nr. 8, Ulvøya, N. Oslo, Norway. *Telephone:* 282408.

LIONS, Jacques L.; French scientist; b. 2 May 1928, Grasse; s. of Honoré and Anne (née Muller) Lions; one s.; ed. Ecole normale supérieure, Paris; Centre Nat. de la Recherche Scientifique (CNRS) 1950–54; Prof. Univ. of Nancy 1954–62, Univ. of Paris 1962–73, Coll. de France 1973–; Pres. Centre Nat. d'Etudes Spatiales (CNES), Paris 1984–, Conseil Scientifique d'Electricité de France 1986–; Hon. Prof. Ecole Polytechnique; Dr. h.c. (Madrid, Liège, Academia Sinica, Edinburgh, Göteborg, Santiago de Compostela, Fudan, Wuhan Univs.); mem. Acad. of Sciences, Paris 1973, Brasilia Acad. of Sciences, Soc. Royale de Science, Liège; Foreign mem. Inst. Lombardo, U.S.S.R. Acad. of Sciences, Acad. of Arts, Sciences and Letters, Boston, Int. Acad. of Astronautics, Acad. Europaea; Officier, Légion d'honneur, Commdr., ordre nat. du Mérite. *Publications:* 20 books on analysis, optimal control, partial differential equations and numerical analysis. *Address:* Centre National d'Etudes Spatiales, 2 place Maurice Quentin, 75039 Paris Cedex 01 (Office); 7 rue Paul Barruel, 75015 Paris, France (Home).

LIOTARD-VOGT, Pierre Alberto; French business executive; b. 14 Dec. 1909, London, England; s. of Alfred and Enrica (Cerasoli) Liotard-Vogt; divorced; two s.; ed. School of Higher Business Studies, Paris; with Nestlé Co., Switzerland 1933; with Société des Produits Alimentaires et Diététiques (Nestlé Products in France) 1936; factory man. 1938; Man. Head Office 1940, Gen. Man. 1942, Pres. 1965; Dir. Nestlé Alimentana S.A. 1967, Man. Dir. 1968–75, Chair. 1973–82; mem. Int. Advisory Cttee. Chase Manhattan Bank, New York 1973–83; Dir. L'Oréal, Paris 1974–, Labruyère and Eberlé, Mâcon 1976–82, L'Air Liquide, Paris 1978–; Commdr., Légion d'honneur, Croix de guerre. *Address:* 55 avenue Nestlé, 1800 Vevey (Office); Novavilla, 1807 Blonay, Switzerland (Home). *Telephone:* 021-51-01-12 (Office); 021-53-10-86 (Home).

LIPATOV, Vil Vladimirovich; Soviet author; b. 1927, Chita; ed. Tomsk Pedagogical Inst.; first works published 1956; mem. CPSU 1957–; Order of the Red Banner 1977. *Publications include:* The Six 1958, The Captain of the Smelyi 1969, Your Own Burden You Don't Feel 1959, The Wisdom Tooth 1961, The Death of Yegor Suzun 1963, The Stranger 1964, etc. *Address:* c/o U.S.S.R. Union of Writers, ulitsa Vorovskogo 52, Moscow, U.S.S.R.

LIPKIN, Semen Izrailevich; Soviet poet and translator; b. 19 Sept. 1911, Odessa; ed. Moscow Econ. Inst.; served in Soviet Army 1941–45; Rudaki State Prize 1967, People's Poet of Kalmuk A.S.S.R. 1968; resgnd. from Union of Writers 1980. *Translations include:* Dzangar (Kalmuk epic) 1940, Geser (Buryat epic) 1968, Mahabharata (Indian epic) 1969, also from classical Tadzhik, Uzbek and Kirghiz writers; *poetry:* Eyewitness 1967, A Nomadic Flame 1984.

LIPKOWSKI, Count Jean-Noël de, L. EN D.; French politician and diplomatist; b. 25 Dec. 1920, Paris; s. of Henri and Irène (née Marie) de Lipkowski; m. Nadine Hecquet d'Orval 1963; one s. one d.; ed. Ecole libre des sciences politiques; served as paratrooper in Free French Forces, Second World War; entered diplomatic service 1945; attached to Cen. Admin. for Asia-Oceania; Third Sec. for Far East, Nanking; Attaché to French Embassy, Nanking 1947–49, to Cen. Admin. 1950–52; Sec. of Foreign Affairs 1951; Deputy Consul, Madrid; Deputy Dir., Cabinet of the Resident-Gen. of France in Tunis and later in Rabat; Counsellor 1956; Deputy to Nat. Assembly for Seine-et-Oise 1956–58; Chargé d'Affaires, French Embassy, Beirut 1958; Political Adviser, Cie. française de l'Afrique occidentale; Deputy for Charente-Maritime 1962, 1967–68, 1973, 1978, 1981, 1986; Mayor of Royan 1965–, re-elected 1971, 1977, 1982; Sec. of State for Foreign Affairs with rank of Minister 1968–72, 1973–74; Minister of Co-operation Jan.-Aug. 1976; Deputy to European Assembly 1976–81; Counsellor to Jacques Chirac 1981–; now Special Envoy of Prime Minister for Asia; Officier, Légion d'honneur, Croix de guerre. *Address:* 44 rue du Bac, 75007 Paris, France.

LIPP, Robert I., B.A., J.D.; American banker; b. 1938; m.; ed. Williams Coll., Harvard Univ., New York Univ.; with Chemical Bank, N.Y. 1963–86, Sr. Trainee 1963–65, Asst. Control Div. 1965–66, Asst. Controller 1966–67, Asst. Vice-Pres. Corp. Planning 1967–69, Sr. Vice-Pres. Deputy Head Operations 1972–74, Exec. Vice-Pres. Head Operations Div. 1974–79, Sr. Exec. Vice-Pres. 1979–83, Pres. Chemical Bank 1983–86; Vice-Pres. Corp. Planning, Treas. Chemical N.Y. Corpn. 1969–70, Man. Operations Div. 1970–72; Exec. Vice-Pres. Consumer Financial Services Group, Commercial Credit Co., Baltimore 1986–; bd. of Dirs. Greater N.Y. Fund; mem. Man. Team Commercial Credit Corpn., San Antonio; Trustee Jackie Robinson Foundation. *Address:* Commercial Credit Corporation, 300 Saint Paul Plaza, Baltimore, Md. 21202, U.S.A.

LIPSCOMB, William Nunn Jr., PH.D.; American professor of chemistry; b. 9 Dec. 1919, Cleveland, Ohio; s. of Dr. William Lipscomb and Edna Porter Lipscomb; m. Mary Adele Sargent 1944; one s. one d.; ed. Univ. of Kentucky and Calif. Inst. of Tech.; Asst. Prof. of Physical Chem., Univ. of Minn. 1946–50, Assoc. Prof. 1950–54, Acting Chief, Physical Chem. Div. 1952–54, Prof. and Chief, Physical Chem. Div. 1954–59; Prof. of Chem., Harvard Univ. 1959–71, Chair. Dept. of Chem. 1962–65, Abbott and James Lawrence Prof. of Chem. 1971–; Dir. Midland Dow Chemical Co., Mich.

1982–; Overseas Fellow of Churchill Coll., Cambridge 1966; mem. N.A.S., American Acad. of Arts and Sciences, Acad. Européenne des Sciences, des Arts et des Lettres, Paris 1980; Foreign mem. Royal Netherlands Acad. of Arts and Sciences 1976–; Hon. mem. The Chemical Soc., London 1972; Int. Assen. of Bioinorganic Scientists 1979, Int. Acad. Quantum Molecular Science 1980; Pres. American Crystallographic Soc. 1955; Dr. h.c. Munich 1976, Hon. D.Sc. (Long Island Univ.) 1977, (Rutgers Univ.) 1979, (Gustavus Adolphus Coll.) 1980, (Marietta Coll.) 1981; Hon. Fellow, Royal Soc. of Chemistry; Harrison Howe Award in Chem. 1958, Award for Distinguished Service in the Advancement of Inorganic Chem. 1968, Ledlie Prize, Harvard Univ. 1971, Peter Debye Award in Physical Chem., A.C.S. 1973, Nobel Prize in Chem. 1976, Distinguished Alumni Award, Calif. Inst. of Technology 1977, Senior U.S. Scientist Award, Alexander von Humboldt-Stiftung 1979. *Publications:* Boron Hydrides 1963, Nuclear Magnetic Resonance Studies of Boron and Related Compounds (with G. R. Eaton) 1969, Crystallography in North America 1983; and papers on structure and function of enzymes and natural products in inorganic chem. and theoretical chem. *Leisure interests:* chamber music, tennis. *Address:* Gibbs Chemical Laboratory, Harvard University, 12 Oxford Street, Cambridge, Mass. 02138 (Office); 44 Langdon Street, Cambridge, Mass. 02138, U.S.A. (Home). *Telephone:* 617-495-4089 (Office); 617-492-2673 (Home).

LIPSET, Seymour Martin, PH.D.; American professor of political science and sociology; b. 18 March 1922, New York; s. of Max Lipset and Lena Lippman; m. Elsie Braun 1944; two s. one d.; ed. City Coll. of New York and Columbia Univ.; Asst. Prof. Univ. of Calif., Berkeley 1948–50; Asst. then Assoc. Prof. and Asst. Dir. Bureau of Applied Social Research, Columbia Univ. 1950–56; Prof. of Sociology, Univ. of Calif. (Berkeley) 1956–66; George D. Markham Prof. of Govt. and Sociology, Harvard Univ. 1966–75; Caroline S. G. Munro Prof. of Political Science and Sociology and Sr. Fellow, The Hoover Inst., Stanford Univ. 1976–; Fellow, N.A.S., American Acad. of Arts and Sciences; MacIver Award 1962; Gunnar Myrdal Award 1970; Fellow Guggenheim Foundation 1971–72; Rawson Award 1986. *Publications:* Agrarian Socialism 1950, Political Man: The Social Bases of Politics 1960, The First New Nation 1963, Revolution and Counterrevolution 1968, Rebellion in the University (with W. Schneider) 1972, The Confidence Gap: Business, Labor and Government in the Public Eye 1983, Consensus and Conflict 1985, Unions in Transition (ed.) 1986. *Leisure interests:* swimming, reading, walking, politics. *Address:* The Hoover Institution, Stanford University, Stanford, Calif. 94305 (Office); 650 Gerona Road, Stanford, Calif. 94305, U.S.A. (Home). *Telephone:* 415-497-4741 (Office); 415-853-0316 (Home).

LIPSKI, Witold, D.AGRIC.SC.; Polish politician and journalist; b. 15 June 1925, Dębowiec, Częstochowa Voivodship; s. of Karol Lipski and Otylia Lipski; m. 1947; two s.; ed. Main School of Commerce, Warsaw, Main School of Planning and Statistics, Warsaw and Main School of Farming, Warsaw; soldier of Peasant Battalions in Włoszczowa Dist. during Nazi occupation 1943–44; mem. Peasant Party (SL) 1946–49, United Peasant Party (ZSL) 1949–, mem. Main Bd. 1964–84, mem. Main Bd. Presidium 1971–84, Chair. Foreign Relations Comm. ZSL 1984–; Ed., Head of Section, Deputy Ed.-in-Chief Iskry State Publishing House, Warsaw 1951–56, Man. Ed. 1957, Deputy Ed.-in-Chief 1957–65, Ed.-in-Chief monthly Wieś Współczesna 1965–80, 1981–; Deputy to Seym (Parl.) 1972–; Deputy Chair. Seym Comm. of Foreign Affairs 1972–85; Sec. Bd. of Polish Group of Interparl. Union; mem. Council of State 1985–; mem. Jt. Comm. of Reps. of Govt. and Church 1981–; Deputy Chair. Assen. Polonia 1977–; mem. Presidium, Polish Club of Int. Relations 1988–; Chair. Parl. Friendship Assen. between Poland and Italy; Commdr.'s Cross of Order of Polonia Restituta, Order of Banner of Labour (2nd Class), Partisan Cross, Cross of Valour and other decorations. *Leisure interests:* modern history, swimming. *Address:* ul. Wiejska 4/6, 00-902 Warsaw, Poland. *Telephone:* 281993.

LIPSKÝ, Oldřich; Czechoslovak film director; b. 4 July 1924, Pelhřimov; ed. Charles Univ., Prague; founder, actor, dir. and art man., Theatre of Satire, Prague 1945–49; actor, scenarist, asst. dir. 1949–54; dir. Film Studios Barrandov, Prague 1954–; numerous prizes from film festivals, title Artist of Merit 1974, National Artist 1979. *Films:* Circus 1954, The Exemplary Cinema of Jaroslav Hašek 1956, A Star Travels to the South 1958, Circus on the Road 1960, A Man from the First Century 1961, Lemonade Joe 1964, Happy End 1966, I've Killed Einstein, Gentlemen 1969, Four Murders is Enough, Dear 1970, Straw Hat 1971, Six Bears with Onion 1972, Three Men on a Journey 1973, Joachim, Throw Him into the Machine 1974, Circus in a Circus 1975, Hand me my Pen, Mareček 1976, Long Live the Ghosts 1977, Dinner for Adele 1977, The Secret of a Castle in the Carpathians 1981, Cordial Greetings from the Earth 1962, The Three Veterans 1983; founder and dir. of a professional ice show.

LIPSON, Henry, C.B.E., M.A., M.SC.TECH., D.SC., F.R.S.; British professor emeritus of physics (retd.); b. 11 March 1910, Liverpool; s. of Israel and Sarah Lipson; m. Jane Rosenthal 1937; one s. two d.; ed. Hawarden County School and Univ. of Liverpool; Oliver Lodge Fellowship, Liverpool 1933–36; D.S.I.R. Grant, Manchester 1936–37; Jr. Scientific Officer, Nat. Physical Lab. 1937–38; Asst. in Crystallography, Univ. of Cambridge 1938–45; Head, Dept. of Physics, Manchester Coll. of Tech. 1945–77, Prof. 1954–77. *Publications:* 9 books (in collaboration). *Leisure interests:* hospital voluntary work, Independent Crossword, D.I.Y., grandchildren, nuclear disarmament. *Address:* 22 Cranmer Road, Manchester, M20 0AW, England. *Telephone:* (061-445) 4517.

LIPWORTH, Maurice Sydney, B.COM., LL.B.; British barrister and administrator; b. 13 May 1931, Johannesburg, South Africa; m. Rosa Liwarek 1957; two s.; ed. King Edward VII School, Johannesburg, Univ. of Witwatersrand; practising barrister, Johannesburg 1956-64; Non-Exec. Dir. Liberty Life Assen. of Africa Ltd. 1956-64; Exec. Private Trading Cos. 1964-67; Exec. Dir. Abbey Life Assurance PLC 1968-70; Vice-Pres. and Dir. Abbey Int. Corpn. Inc. 1968-70; one of co-founders and Dir. Allied Dunbar Assurance PLC 1970-88, Deputy Man. Dir. 1977-79, Jt. Man. Dir. 1979-84, Deputy Chair. 1984-88; Dir. J. Rothschild Holdings PLC 1984-87, BAT Industries PLC 1985-88; Chair. Monopolies and Mergers Comm. 1988-. *Leisure interests:* music, theatre, tennis. *Address:* New Court, 48 Carey Street, London, WC2A 2JT, England. *Telephone:* 01-831 6111.

LISETTE, Gabriel; French international official; b. 2 April 1919, Puerto Bello, Panama; s. of Gabriel Lisette and Hortense Zachée; m. Yeyon Darrotchetche 1945; three s. one d.; ed. Lycée Carnot (Point-à-Pitre, Guadeloupe), Lycée Henri IV (Paris) and Ecole Nat. de la France d'Outremer; Admin. France d'Outre-mer 1944-46; Deputy from Chad to Nat. Assembly, Paris 1946-51, 1956-59; Territorial Counsellor, Chad 1952-59; Pres. Chad Govt. Council 1957-58; Deputy Chad Legis. Assembly 1959-60; Pres. Council of Ministers, Repub. of Chad 1958-59, Vice-Pres. 1959-60; Minister-Counsellor to French Govt. 1959-60; Admin.-in-Chief of Overseas Affairs (France); Mayor of Fort-Lamy (now N'Djamena) 1956-60; French Govt. Perm. Rep. to UN Econ. Comm. for Latin America (ECLA) 1960-79; Plenipotentiary Minister 1979; Pres. Parti Progressiste Tchadien 1946-60, Mutualité d'Outre-mer et de l'Extérieur 1963, Union Nat. Interprofessionalle Mutualiste et sociale (France) 1981-; Vice-Pres. Fondation Félix Houphouët-Boigny 1974-, Vice-Pres. Comité français contre la faim; mem. Conseil de Direction du Comité français pour la campagne mondiale contre la faim 1970-, Conseil d'Admin. de la Féd. Nat. de la Mutualité Française 1978-; First Citizen of Honour of Chad, Officier Légion d'honneur, Commdr. Ordre nat. du Mérite français, Grand Officier Ordre nat. de la République de Côte d'Ivoire, Grand Officier Ordre nat. de la République du Niger, Commdr. Etoile de la Grande Couronne, Chevalier Ordre du Mérite Centrafricain. *Publications:* Le Combat du rassemblement démocratique africain (1983). *Leisure interests:* reading, the sea. *Address:* 3 boulevard de Courcelles, 75008 Paris, France.

LISNYANSKAYA, Inna L'vovna; Soviet writer; b. 1928, Baku; first works published 1949; resigned from Union of Writers 1980. *Publications include:* This Happened to Me 1957, Faithfulness 1958, Not Simply Love 1963; contributed to the literary almanack Metropole 1979, Verse 1970-83, 1984, On the Edge of Sleep 1984.

LISSMANN, Hans Werner, F.R.S.; British biologist; b. 30 April 1909, Nikolaeff, Russia; s. of Robert and Ebba Lissmann; m. Corinne Foster-Barham 1949; one s.; ed. Univ. of Hamburg; Research Assoc. Hungarian Biological Research Inst. Tihany 1932-33; visiting research worker, Dept. of Zoology, Univ. of Cambridge 1934-37, Asst. in Research 1938-47, Asst. Dir. of Research 1947-55, Lecturer 1955-66, Reader in Experimental Zoology 1966-77, Dir. Sub-Dept. of Animal Behaviour 1969-77, now Emer. Reader; Fellow and Dir. of Studies Trinity Coll., Cambridge 1955-77. *Publications:* Animal Movement, Sense Organs, Nervous System, Electric Fish. *Leisure interests:* travel, gardening. *Address:* Department of Zoology, Cambridge (Office); 9 Bulstrode Gardens, Cambridge, CB3 0EN, England (Home). *Telephone:* (0223) 356126.

LISSOUBA, Pascal, D. ÈS SC.; Congolese politician; b. 15 Nov. 1931, Tsinguidi, Congo (Brazzaville); s. of Albert Lissouba and Marie Bouanga; m. 2nd Jocelyne Pierrot 1967; one s. six d.; ed. secondary education in Nice, France, and Ecole Supérieure d'Agriculture, Tunis; fmr. agricultural specialist; Prime Minister of Congo (Brazzaville) 1963-66, concurrently Minister of Trade and Industry and Agric.; Prof. of Genetics, Brazzaville 1966-71, concurrently Minister of Planning 1968, Minister of Agric., Waterways and Forests 1969; Dir. Ecole Supérieure des Sciences, Brazzaville 1971; imprisoned for life for organization of assassination of Pres. Ngouabi March 1977. *Leisure interests:* geology, music. *Address:* Ouesso District, Congo People's Republic.

LIST, Robert Frank; American politician; b. 1 Sept. 1936, Visalia, Calif.; s. of Franklin Way and Alice A. (née Dove) List; m. Kathryn Sue Geary 1962; one s. two d.; ed. Hastings School of Law, Univ. of Calif.; admitted to Nevada Bar 1962; dist. attorney, Carson City 1966-70; Attorney Gen. 1970-78; Gov. of Nevada 1979-83; Chair. Western Governors' Conf. 1980-, Nat. Governors' Assen. Cttee. on Crime Prevention and Public Safety 1979-83; mem. Nev. Crime Comm. 1968-; Nat. Gambling Comm. 1972-, U.S.A.F. Acad. Bd. of Visitors; Exec. Cttee. of the Republican Governors' Assen. 1979-; fmr. mem. Exec. Cttee. of Nat. Assoc. of Attorneys Gen. *Leisure interests:* flying, skiing, fishing, hunting, tennis. *Address:* c/o Office of the Governor, Capitol Complex, Carson City, Nevada 89710, U.S.A.

LIST, Roland, DR.SC.NAT., F.R.S.C.; Canadian (b. Swiss) UN agency official; b. 21 Feb. 1929, Frauenfeld, Thurgau, Switzerland; s. of August Joseph List and Anna Kaufmann; m. Gertrud K. Egli 1956; two c.; ed. Swiss Fed. Inst. of Tech., Zurich; Head, Hail Section, Swiss Fed. Inst. for Snow and Avalanche Research, Davos 1952-63; Prof. of Physics (Meteorology), Dept.

of Physics, Univ. of Toronto 1963-82, Assoc. Chair. Dept. of Physics 1969-73; Chair. Exec. Cttee. Panel of Experts on Weather Modification, WMO, Geneva 1969-82, Deputy Sec.-Gen. WMO 1982-84; mem. or chair. many Canadian and Swiss nat. cttees.; mem. Canadian Meteorological and Oceanic Soc., American Meteorological Soc., Royal Meteorological Soc., etc.; Sesquicentennial Medal, Univ. of Leningrad 1970; Patterson Medal, Canadian Meteorological Soc. *Publications:* over 140 papers and many reports in the field of cloud physics, weather modification and classical physics. *Address:* 58 Olsen Drive, Don Mills, Ont. M3A 3J3, Canada.

LISTAU, Thor; Norwegian politician; b. 3 June 1938, Svolvaer, Lofoten Islands; ed. Univ. of Denver; electrotechnician and radio communications specialist, Norwegian Army; served Defence Research Station, Kirkenes, Finnmark 1961, later Chief; technical courses, U.S.A.F. 1966-70; mem. Storting 1973-; Minister of Fisheries 1981-86; Conservative. *Address:* c/o Ministry of Fisheries, Drammensveien 20, Pb. 8118, Oslo, Norway.

LISTOV, Gen. Vladimir Vladimirovich; Soviet industrialist and politician; b. 4 Dec. 1931, Tomsk; ed. Kirov Polytechnical Inst., Tomsk; technician and foreman, factory in Voroshilovgrad 1955; technician, head of workshop, Deputy Dir., Dir., factory in Kemerovo 1956-64; mem. CPSU 1962-; Head of Dept., First Sec., Kemerovo City Cttee. of CPSU 1964-70; Head of directorate of Chemical Industry Ministry of the U.S.S.R. 1964-70, Deputy Minister 1971-77, Minister 1980-86; Head of Dept. of Chemical Industry, Cen. Cttee. of the CPSU 1977-80; Deputy Head Political Section of Soviet Army and Armed Forces 1980-82; mem. Mil. Council and Head Political Section of Soviet Troops in Germany 1985-; Deputy to the Supreme Soviet of the U.S.S.R.; Laureate of the State. *Address:* c/o Ministry of Defence, Moscow, U.S.S.R.

LISTOWEL, the 5th Earl of, cr. 1822; **William Francis Hare,** P.C., G.C.M.G., PH.D.; British philosopher and politican; b. 28 Sept. 1906; m. 1st Judith de Marffy-Mantuano 1933 (divorced 1945), one d.; m. 2nd Stephanie Sandra Yvonne Wise 1958 (divorced 1963), one d.; m. 3rd Mrs. Pamela Read 1963, two s. one d.; ed. Eton and Balliol Coll., Oxford, and London Univ.; Labour mem. London Co. Council for E. Lewisham; Chief Whip Labour Party and Deputy Leader House of Lords, Parl. Under-Sec. of State India Office 1944-45; Postmaster-Gen. 1945-47; Sec. of State for India and Burma April-Aug. 1947; Sec. of State for Burma, 1947-48; Minister of State for the Colonies 1948-50; Jt. Parl. Sec., Ministry of Agric. and Fisheries 1950-51; Gov.-Gen. of Ghana 1957-60; Chair. of Cttees., House of Lords 1965-76; Pres. Voluntary Euthanasia Soc., Council for Aid to African Students; Jt. Pres. Anti-Slavery Soc. for Protection of Human Rights; Jawaharlal Nehru Lecture 1980. *Publications:* The Values of Life 1931, A Critical History of Modern Aesthetics 1933 (2nd edn. as Modern Aesthetics: An Historical Introduction 1967). *Address:* 10 Downshire Hill, London, N.W.3, England.

LISULO, Daniel Muchiwa, B.A. (HONS.), LL.B.; Zambian lawyer and politician; b. 6 Dec. 1930, Mongu; m. Mary Mambo 1968 (died 1976); three s. two d.; ed. Loyola Coll. of Madras Univ., Law Faculty of Delhi Univ., India; active in independence struggle 1953-63; with Anglo-American Corpn. (Cen. Africa) 1963-64; Asst. Solicitor, Ellis & Co., Lusaka 1964-67; Advocate, Lisulo & Co. 1968-, later Sr. Partner; Dir. Bank of Zambia 1964-77; mem. and Chair. Local Govt. Service Comm. 1964-72; mem. Nat. Comm. on One Party System in Zambia; Dir. various cos.; mem. Cen. Cttee. United Nat. Independence Party (UNIP) 1972-; Minister of Legal Affairs and Attorney-Gen. 1977-78; Prime Minister of Zambia 1978-81; Chair. Social and Cultural Sub-Cttee., UNIP 1981-82, Appointments and Disciplinary Sub-Cttee. 1982, now Head Political and Legal Sub-Cttee.; Chair. ZIMCO (Zambia Industrial and Mining Corpn. Ltd.) 1979-81; mem. Nat. Assembly; also Legal Counsel of UNIP. *Leisure interests:* swimming, hunting, boating, soccer. *Address:* c/o United National Independence Party, Freedom House, P.O. Box 302, Lusaka; Lisulo and Co., Lusaka, Zambia. *Telephone:* 218727, 218170 (Freedom House); 214715, 214997 (Lisulo and Co.).

LITHERLAND, Albert Edward, PH.D., F.R.S.; Canadian professor of physics; b. 12 March 1928, Wallasey, England; s. of Albert Litherland and Ethel Clement; m. Anne Allen 1956; two d.; ed. Wallasey Grammar School and Liverpool Univ.; Scientific Officer, Atomic Energy of Canada 1955-66; Prof. of Physics, Toronto Univ. 1966-79, Univ. Prof. 1979-; Gold Medal, Canadian Assen. of Physicists 1971, Rutherford Medal and Prize, Inst. of Physics 1974; Guggenheim Fellow 1986. *Publications:* numerous scientific papers. *Leisure interests:* reading, travel. *Address:* 3 Hawthorn Gardens, Toronto, Ont., M4W 1P4, Canada. *Telephone:* (416) 923-5616.

LITTLE, Ian Malcolm David, M.A., D.PHIL., F.B.A.; British economist; b. 18 Dec. 1918, Rugby; s. of Brig.-Gen. M. O. Little and Iris H. (née Brassey); m. Doreen Hennessey 1946 (died 1984); one s. one d.; ed. Eton and New Coll., Oxford; R.A.F. officer 1939-46; Fellow, All Souls Coll., Oxford 1948-50, Trinity Coll., Oxford 1950-52, Nuffield Coll., Oxford 1952-76, Fellow Emer. 1976-; Deputy Dir. Econ. Section, H.M. Treasury 1953-55; mem. M.I.T. Center for Int. Studies, India 1958-59, 1965; Vice-Pres. OECD Devt. Centre, Paris 1965-67; mem. Bd. British Airports Authority 1969-74; Prof. Econs. of Underdeveloped Countries, Univ. of Oxford 1971-76; Special Adviser, IBRD, Washington, D.C. 1976-78; Project Dir. Twentieth Century Fund, New York 1978-81; Consultant, IBRD 1984-85; Hon. D.Sc.

(Edinburgh). *Publications:* A Critique of Welfare Economics 1950, The Price of Fuel 1952, Aid to Africa 1964, Economic Development, Theory, Practice and International Relations 1982; jt. author of several other books. *Address:* 7 Ethelred Court, Dunstan Road, Headington, Oxford, OX3 9DA, England. *Telephone:* (0865) 61028.

LITTLEWOOD, Joan (Maud); British theatre director and artist; Dir. Theatre of Action, street theatre co., Manchester 1931–37; Founder, Theatre Union, Manchester, introducing the Individual Work System 1937–39; freelance writer, banned from BBC and Entertainments Nat. Service Asscn. for political opinions 1939–45; founded Theatre Workshop with Gerry Raffles 1945, Artistic Dir. 1945–75, tours in U.K. and Europe with original works 1945–53, Theatre Royal, Stratford, London, E.15 1953–75; invited to Theatre of the Nations, Paris yearly from 1955; transfers to West End, London and Broadway, New York 1960–61; Centre Culturel, Hammamet, Tunisia 1965–67; Image India, Calcutta 1968; created children's entertainments outside Theatre Royal Stratford 1968–75; working in France 1975–; Seminar, Relais Culturel, Aix-en-Provence 1976; mem. French Acad. of Writers 1964–; Best Production of the Year (three times), Theatre of the Nations, Paris; Dr. h.c. (Open Univ.) 1977; Gold Medal for production of Lysistrata, Berlin, German Democratic Repub. 1958; Olympic Award, Taormina 1959, Soc. of West End Theatre Award 1983. *Productions include:* Oh, What a Lovely War! (with Gerry Raffles) 1963; film Sparrers Can't Sing 1962. *Address:* 1 place Louis Revol, 38200 Vienne, France.

LITTMAN, Mark, Q.C.; British barrister-at-law and business executive; b. 4 Sept. 1920, London; s. of Jack and Lilian Littman; m. Marguerite Lamkin 1965; no c.; ed. Owen's School, L.S.E. and Queens Coll., Oxford; Lieut. R.N.V.R. 1941–46; called to Bar, Middle Temple 1947; Dir. Rio Tinto-Zinc Corpn. 1968–; Pres. Bar Asscn. for Commerce, Finance and Industry 1974–80; mem. Bar Council 1973–75, mem. of Senate of the Inns of Court and the Bar 1974–75; Deputy Chair. British Steel Corpn. 1970–79; Dir. Commercial Union Assurance Co. Ltd. 1970–81, Granada Group Ltd. 1977–, British Enkalon Ltd. 1972–80; Amerada Hess Corpn. 1973–86, Envirotech Corpn 1974–78, Burton Group PLC 1983–; Treas. Middle Temple 1988; Bencher of the Middle Temple 1970; mem. Royal Comm. on Legal Services 1976; mem. Int. Council for Commercial Arbitration 1978–; mem. Court of Govs., L.S.E. 1980–; Vice-Chair. London Int. Arbitration Trust 1980–. *Address:* 79 Chester Square, London, S.W.1, England. *Telephone:* 01-730 2973.

LITVAK KING, Jaime, M.A., PH.D.; Mexican archaeologist; b. 10 Dec. 1933, Mexico City; s. of Abraham Litvak and Eugenia King; m. 1st Elena Kaminski 1954 (divorced 1968), one d.; m. 2nd Carmen Aguilera 1972 (divorced 1978); ed. Univ. Nacional Autónoma de México; Asst. Dept. of Prehistory, Inst. Nacional de Antropología e Historia 1960–63, Researcher 1963–66; Lecturer Escuela Nacional de Antropología e Historia 1963–74; Head Sección de Maquinas Electronicas, Museo Nacional de Antropología 1966–68; Asst. Research Fellow, Anthropological Section, Univ. Nacional Autónoma de México 1968–72, Full Research Fellow 1972–74, Head of Section 1973; Dir. Inst. for Anthropological Research, Univ. Nacional Autónoma de México 1973–85, Dir.-Gen. for Academic Projects 1985–86; Chair. Anthropology, Univ. of the Americas 1986–88; Joint Chair. Archaeology, Escuela Nacional de Antropología 1966–67, Chair. 1969–71; Co-Ed. Antropología Matemática 1968–74; Research Ed. American Antiquity 1971–74; Advisory Ed. Mesoamerican Archaeology, Abstracts in Anthropology 1973–74; Visiting Prof., Univ. of Minn. 1981, Univ. of New Mexico 1985–86; Mellon Prof. of Humanities, Tulane Univ. 1988; Gen. Sec. Mexican Anthropological Soc. 1970–76, 1981–83; mem. Mexican Scientific Research Acad. 1972–, Nat. Researcher, Class III, Mexico; mem. Bd. of Dirs. Museum Computer Network 1982–; Fray Bernardino de Sahagun (Mexican Nat. Award for Anthropology) 1970, Nat. Researcher, Mexican Scientific Research Acad. 1984. *Publications:* El Valle de Xochicalco 1970, Cihuatlán y Tepecoacuilco 1971, Xochicalco: Un Asentamiento Urbano Prehispanico 1974, Ancient Mexico 1985, Todas las piedas tienen su 2000 años 1985, etc. *Address:* Instituto de Investigaciones Antropológicas, Universidad Nacional Autónoma de México, Ciudad Universitaria, Villa Obregón, 04510 México, D.F., Mexico.

LITVINOV, Pavel Mikhailovich; Russian physicist and dissident activist; b. 1940, Moscow; (grandson of fmr. People's Commissar for Foreign Affairs M. M. Litvinov); m. M. Rusakovskaya; two c.; employed in Lomonosov Inst. of Chemical-Tech., Moscow 1968; author of various samizdat documents protesting trials of dissidents; sentenced to 5 years exile 1968–73; released 1973; expelled from U.S.S.R. 1974. *Publications include:* The Demonstration on Pushkin Square 1967, Letters and Telegrams to Pavel Litvinov Dec. 1967–May 1968, 1969, Self-Awareness 1976.

LITVINOV, Sergey K.; Soviet health official; b. 4 Sept. 1938, Moscow; m.; two d.; ed. Second Medical Inst., Moscow; hospital work, Inst. of Parasitology and Tropical Medicine, Moscow; began career in epidemiology at same inst.; health work in developing countries 1965–68; WHO Medical Officer responsible for epidemiological services project, Ghana 1973–78; work on WHO Immunization Programme, Geneva 1978; Deputy Chief External Relations Bd., Ministry of Health, U.S.S.R. until 1983; an Asst. Dir.-Gen. WHO 1983–87. *Address:* c/o World Health Organization, Avenue Appia, 1211 Geneva 27, Switzerland.

LITWINISZYN, Jerzy, ENG.K.D.; Polish scientist; b. 2 Aug. 1914, Płoki; m.; two c.; ed. Acad. of Mining and Metallurgy, Cracow; scientist, Acad. of Mining and Metallurgy, Cracow 1945–, Doctor of Tech. Sciences 1947–50, Asst. Prof. 1950–54, Extraordinary Prof. 1954–58, Ordinary Prof. 1958–; Corresp. mem. Polish Acad. of Sciences 1956–66, mem. 1966–, Scientific Sec., Cracow Branch 1972–75, mem. Acad. Presidium 1959, Vice-Pres. 1977–, Chair. Cracow branch 1980–; Dir. Strata Mechanics Research Inst., Cracow 1959–; mem. Acad. of Eng. of Mexican Inst. of Culture 1976; Hon. Prof. Changsha Inst. of Mining 1986, Xrangton Mining Inst. 1986; State Prize 2nd Class 1953, 1st Class 1968, Officer's and Commdr.'s Cross of Order Polonia Restituta, Order of Banner of Labour (Second Class) 1977. *Publications:* over 200 works on hydromechanics, mechanics of rocks, loose mediums and strata. *Address:* Strata Mechanics Research Institute, Polish Academy of Sciences, Ul. Reymonta 27, 30-059 Cracow; ul. Jaracza 5 m. 9, 31-143 Cracow, Poland (Home). *Telephone:* 3728-84 (Office), 2264-59 (Home).

LIU, Ts'un-yan, PH.D., D.LIT.; Australian professor of Chinese; b. 11 Aug. 1917, Peking, China; s. of Tsung-ch'üan Liu (deceased) and Huang Yü-shu Liu (deceased); m. Chiang Szuyung 1940; one s. one d.; ed. Univs. of Peking, London and Hong Kong; Chair. Chinese Panel, Queen's Coll., Hong Kong 1952–59; lecturer Northcote Training Coll., Hong Kong 1959–62; Sr. Lecturer Govt. Evening School, Hong Kong 1959–62; Sr. Lecturer, Reader in Chinese, A.N.U. 1962–66, Prof. and Head of Dept. of Chinese 1966–82, Dean Faculty of Asian Studies 1970–72, 1973–75, Prof. Emer. 1983–, Univ. Fellow 1983–85; Visiting Prof. Columbia Univ. 1966, Harvard-Yenching Inst. 1969, Hawaii Univ. 1969, Univ. of Paris (Sorbonne) 1973, Univ. of Malaya 1976, Chinese Univ. of Hong Kong 1976–77, Waseda Univ. 1981, Nat. Univ. of Singapore 1984–85; Hon. D. Litt. (Yeungnam Univ., South Korea) 1972. *Publications:* Buddhist and Taoist Influences on Chinese Novels 1962, Chinese Popular Fiction in Two London Libraries 1967, Selected Papers from the Hall of Harmonious Wind 1976, Chinese Middlebrow Fiction from the Ch'ing and Early Republican Era 1984, New Excursions from the Hall of Harmonious Wind. *Leisure interests:* singing, Beijing opera. *Address:* 66 Condamine Street, Turner, A.C.T. 2601, Australia.

LIU ANYUAN; Chinese party and military official; Political Cttee., Canton Mil. Region 1985–86; Political Commissar 1987–; mem. CCP Cen. Cttee. 1987–. *Address:* Central Committee of the Chinese Communist Party, Zhongnanhai, Beijing, People's Republic of China.

LIU BINGYAN, Maj.-Gen.; Chinese government official; b. 19 March 1915, Li Xian County, Hebei; s. of Liu Jing-di and Zhang Nai; m. Li Zai-yun; four c.; ed. Beijing Univ.; joined CCP 1937; Specially Apptd. Official of 1st Independent Regt., Middle Hebei People's Self Defence Corps. 1937–38, Organizational Section Chief, then Dir. Political Dept. 1938; Regimental Commdr. Middle Hebei 5th Mil. Sub-area 32nd Regt. 1938, Vice-Chief of Staff 9th Mil. Sub-area HQ 1941, Chief of Staff 10th Mil. Sub-area, then Commdr. 1942; Chief of Staff Middle Hebei 2nd Column, Brigade Commdr., 2nd Brigade 1945; Brigade Commdr. 20th Brigade 1947, Div. Commdr. N. China Mil. Area 205 Div. 1949; Chief of Staff N. China Mil. Area Air Defences Army HQ 1951; Sec. of Party Cttee., CCP and Acting Commdr.; Chief of Staff Chinese People's Air Defences Army, mem. Standing Party Cttee., CCP; Sec. Party Cttee., CCP and Vice-Dir. 5th Acad. of Ministry of Nat. Defence 1957; Vice-Minister, 3rd Ministry of Machine Building, Dir.-Gen. Bureau of Missiles, mem. Leading Party Group, CCP 1960; Vice-Minister 7th Ministry of Machine Building, mem. Party Cttee., CCP 1965; Standing Vice-Minister 8th Ministry of Machine Building, Vice-Sec. Leading Party Group, CCP 1975; Sec. Prov. Party Cttee. of Hebei, CCP 1981–82, 1982–83; Acting Chair. Hebei Prov. 1982–83, Chair. Prov. People's Congress and Sec. of Leading Party Group, CCP 1983–85; mem. Finance and Econs. Cttee. of NPC 1985–; Deputy to 1st, 5th and 6th NPC. *Leisure interests:* the progress of spaceflight, calligraphy. *Address:* Provincial People's Congress, Shijiazhuang, Hebei Province, People's Republic of China. *Telephone:* 25921.

LIU CHIEH; Chinese diplomatist; b. 16 April 1906; ed. Oxford and Columbia Univs.; Foreign Service 1931–; Chinese Del. to League of Nations 1932–39; Counsellor, Chinese Embassy, London 1933–40, Minister, Washington 1940–45; Vice-Minister for Foreign Affairs 1945–47; Amb. to Canada 1947–63; mem. Chinese Del. to UN 1946; Pres. UN Trusteeship Council 1948; mem. Int. Law Comm. 1961–66; Perm. Rep. of China to UN 1962–71; Amb. to Philippines 1972–75; Presidential Adviser 1975–; Chair. Research and Planning Comm., Ministry of Foreign Affairs 1975–. *Address:* c/o Ministry of Foreign Affairs, Taipei, Taiwan.

LIU CHUN; Chinese diplomatist and state official; b. 1918, Huanghua Co., Hebei Prov.; Dir. Political Dept. PLA Armoured Force 1960; Amb. to Laos 1962–70, to Turkey 1972–76, to Tanzania 1976–79, to Seychelles 1978–79, to Egypt 1980–; Dir. Asia Dept. Ministry of Foreign Affairs 1971; Man. China Nat. Seed Corpn. 1982–; mem. Standing Cttee. CPPCC 1987–. *Address:* China National Seed Corporation, 16 Donghuan North Road, Beijing, People's Republic of China. *Telephone:* 593619.

LIU DANIAN; Chinese historian; Deputy Ed. Historical Research 1954–60; Deputy Dir. Inst. of Modern Chinese History, Chinese Acad. of Sciences (later Social Sciences) 1954–66, Dir. 1978–82, Hon. Dir. 1982–; mem. and Exec. Chair. Chinese Asscn. of History 1982–; Vice-Pres. Sun Yat-sen Society 1984–; Del. to 3rd NPC and mem. 4th, 5th and 6th Standing Cttee.

of NPC. *Publications:* The History of America's Invasion of China, General Descriptions on the History of Taiwan, Problems of Modern History in China, Speech on History at the University of Tokyo, Chinese Modern History (Ed.-in-Chief of Vols. 1, 2 and 3). *Address:* Institute of Modern History, Chinese Academy of Social Sciences, 1 Dongchang Hutong, Wangfu Dajie, Beijing, People's Republic of China.

LIU DANZHAI; Chinese traditional artist; b. 4 March 1931, Wenzhou, Zhejiang; m. Wang Weilin 1953; one s. one d.; also known as Liu Xiaosu, Liu Hun and Hai Yun Sheng; noted for "ren wu hua" (figure painting); teacher Wenzhou Westlake Elementary School 1949-51; Painter, Shanghai Books Publs. 1951-56; Art Ed. Shanghai Educational Publishing House 1956-72; Painter, Shanghai People's Fine Arts Publishing House 1972-83; Prof. Shanghai Teachers' Univ. 1985-; Visiting Prof. Wenzhou Univ. 1985-; Artist, Shanghai Acad. of Chinese Arts 1956-; Art Counsellor, Shanghai Jiaotong Univ. 1981-; mem. Chinese Artists' Assen. 1953-, mem. Bd. of Dirs., Shanghai Br. 1953-; exhibitions: (Liu Xiaosu) Wenzhou 1941, 1946; (Liu Danzhai) Shanghai 1979, Hongzhou 1984, Ishimaki, Japan 1985; works in Nat. Museum of Fine Arts, Nat. Museum of History, Beijing and in many pvt. collections in Asia, Europe and N. America; Nat. First Award for Prints 1981; First Award for Chinese Prints (Japan) 1981; Hon. Prize for Chinese Sport Art (Chinese Olympic Cttee.) 1985. *Publications:* Images of a Dream of Red Mansions 1979, The 12 Beauties of Jinling from A Dream of Red Mansions (prints) 1981, Album of Chinese Poets 1983, Liu Danzhai: One Hundred Illustrations for 'Strange Studio' 1985, A Dream of Red Mansions 1985, Liu Danzhai (monograph) 1987, Liu Danzhai: Selections from Picture-Story Book 1987. *Leisure interests:* poetry, travel, stone collecting. *Address:* 165 Reijing No. 1 Road, No. 29, Shanghai, People's Republic of China. *Telephone:* 374658.

LIU DAOSHENG, Lieut.-Gen.; Chinese soldier and party official; b. 1915, Chaling Co., Hunan Prov.; ed. Red Army Acad., Ruijin; joined CCP 1930; Political Dept. of 22nd Div. Guangdong-Jiangxi Mil. Region 1934; Long March veteran; Political Cttee. 4th Mil. Sub-Dist. Shanxi-Hebei-Chahar Mil. Region 1938, Commdr. 10th Mil. Sub-Dist. 1940; Deputy Dir. Political Dept. Shanxi-Cahar-Hebei Field Army 1947; Dir. Political Dept. Navy HQ 1950-; Jiangsu Prov. deputy to 2nd NPC Sept. 1958; Deputy Commdr. PLA Navy 1958-66; PLA deputy to 3rd NPC Sept. 1964; purged 1966; rehabilitated 1972; Deputy Commdr. PLA Navy 1973-78, 1st Deputy Commdr.-in-Chief 1978-; alt. mem. CCP Cen. Cttee. 1977; Pres. Sports Navigation Assen. 1979-; Sec. Beijing Mun. CCP Cttee. June-Sept. 1981; mem. Cen. Advisory Cttee. of CCP Cen. Cttee. 1982-. *Address:* Central Advisory Committee of the Central Committee of the Chinese Communist Party, Zhongnanhai, Beijing, People's Republic of China.

LIU FANGREN; Chinese party official; Deputy Sec. Jiangxi Prov. CCP Cttee. 1985-86; alt. mem. CCP Cen. Cttee. 1987-. *Address:* Central Committee of the Chinese Communist Party, Zhongnanhai, Beijing, People's Republic of China.

LIU FUZHI; Chinese party and government official; b. 1917, Meixian Co., Guangdong Prov.; Deputy Head Security Dept., Political Dept., Shanxi-Chahar-Hebei Field Army 1948; concurrently Deputy Head 3rd Office, Head Secr., and Dir. 1st Section, Social Dept., N. China Bureau 1949; Deputy Dir.-Gen., Ministry of Public Security 1949; Vice-Minister of Public Security 1964-67; disappeared during Cultural Revolution; Vice-Minister of Public Security 1972; disappeared 1973-78; Vice-Minister of Culture 1978-79, of Public Security -Nov. 1978; First Deputy Sec.-Gen. Legal Comm., Standing Cttee. 5th NPC 1979, Vice-Chair. 1980; Minister of Justice 1982-83; mem. 12th Cen. Cttee., CCP 1982-85; Sec.-Gen. Cen. Comm. Politics and Law, Cen. Cttee. CCP 1982-; Minister of Public Security 1983-87; Procurator Gen. April 1988-; mem. Cen. Advisory Cttee. 1985-; Hon. Pres. Law Soc. 1986-, Nat. Lawyers' Assen. 1986-. *Address:* State Council, Beijing, People's Republic of China.

LIU GUANGTAO, Maj.-Gen.; Chinese politician; b. 1920, Sanyuan Co., Shaanxi Prov.; m. Wei Shenghua; Divisional Political Commissar in Fourth Field Army, PLA 1949; Political Commissar of Fortieth Army, PLA 1961, of Heilongjiang Mil. Dist. PLA 1969; Vice-Chair. Heilongjiang Revolutionary Cttee. 1970; Deputy Political Commissar, Shenyang Mil. Region, PLA 1970; Second Sec. of CCP Cttee., Heilongjiang 1971; First Political Commissar of Heilongjiang Mil. Dist. PLA 1971; Alt. mem. 10th Cen. Cttee., CCP 1973, mem. 11th Cen. Cttee. 1977; First Sec. CCP Heilongjiang March-Dec. 1977; Sr. Political Commissar, Heilongjiang March-Dec. 1977, disappeared Dec. 1977. *Address:* People's Republic of China.

LIU GUIQIAN; Chinese party official; alt. mem. 12th CCP Cen. Cttee. 1982; Deputy Sec. CCP Cttee., Inner Mongolia Autonomous Region 1983-85. *Address:* Inner Mongolia Autonomous Regional Chinese Communist Party, Hohhot, Inner Mongolia, People's Republic of China.

LIU GUISU; Chinese economist; b. 1948, Changsha, Hunan; fmr. Man. Hunan Cigarette Factory; mem. Hunan Prof. Econ. Com. 1985. *Address:* Hunan Provincial People's Government, Changsha, People's Republic of China.

LIU GUOFAN; Chinese party official; mem. Standing Cttee. Ningxia Autonomous Region CCP Cttee. 1983-, Deputy Sec. 1985-; alt. mem. CCP Cen. Cttee. 1985-. *Address:* Central Committee of the Chinese Communist Party, Zhongnanhai, Beijing, People's Republic of China.

LIU GUOGUANG; Chinese party official and economist; b. 23 Nov. 1923, Nanjing; s. of Liu Zhihe and Zhiang Shulang; m. Liu Shulang 1948; two s. one d.; Vice-Pres. Chinese Acad. of Social Sciences 1982-; Prof. Beijing Univ.; Alt. mem. 12th Cen. Cttee., CCP 1982-87, Alt. mem. 13th Cen. Cttee. 1987-; Vice-Chair. Guidance Cttee. for State Examinations for Econ. Managerial Personnel 1983-. *Publications include:* The Problem of Reproduction Under Socialism, Some Theoretical Questions Concerning the Overall Balance of the National Economy, Some Theoretical Problems Concerning the Reform of the Management System of the National Economy, Problems Concerning China's Strategy of Economic Readjustment, Economic Reform and Economic Readjustment, Developing Marxist Theory in the Practice of Reform. *Leisure interest:* music. *Address:* Academy of Social Sciences, Beijing, People's Republic of China. *Telephone:* 5007435.

LIU HAIQING; Chinese army officer; b. 1914, Pingjiang, Hunan Prov.; joined Red Army 1928; took part in Long March serving with 3rd Front Army; Commdr., 115th Div., 8th Route Army 1937; Commdr., Regt. of Northeast Field Army 1945 (after 1949 4th Field Army); in Korea, Chief of Staff, later Deputy Commdr., 112th Div., 38th Army 1950-55; Commdr., 113th Div., 38th Army 1955; rank of Maj.-Gen. 1963; Deputy Commdr., 38th Army 1966; Sec. CCP Cttee., Hebei Prov. 1971; Deputy Commdr., Beijing Mil. Region 1972-77; Deputy Commdr., Xinjiang Mil. Region 1981-82, Commdr. 1985-; Deputy Commdr. Lanzhou Mil. Region 1985-; alt. mem. 12th CCP Cen. Cttee. 1982, 1985-87. *Address:* Xinjiang Military Region Headquarters, Urumqi, Xinjiang Autonomous Region, People's Republic of China.

LIU HAISU (PAN JIFANG); Chinese artist and art historian; b. 16 March 1896, Jiangsu; s. of Liu Kia Feng and Liu Hoong-Shiin; m. Hsia I-Chiao 1944; four s. three d.; ed. Shengzheng Acad.; studied Inst. of Backdrop Painting, Shanghai 1910; f. Shanghai Acad. of Painting and Fine Arts 1912, Dir until 1952; leader of modern art in China during 4 May period; in France 1929-31, Japan 1919 and 1927, France, Germany, Netherlands and Switzerland 1933-35, France 1986; Pres. E. China Coll. of Arts 1952-57; Pres., Prof., Nanjing Acad. of Fine Arts 1979-84, Hon. Pres. 1984-; has exhibited in Paris, London and Tokyo, lectured at China Inst. Frankfurt and various other European cities; fmr. mem. Int. Artists Assen. of Berlin; mem. Nat. Joint Men of Letters and Artists Soc., Standing Cttee. of CPCC, Accad. Italia, Accad. d'Europa, Accad. of Bedriacense; Life mem. American Biographical Inst. Research Assen.; awards include Silver Cup award of Emperor of Japan (1927), Prize of Honour, Int. Exposition Centenary Independence (Belgium) 1930, Diploma of Merit, Accademia d'Italia 1931, Gold Medal for artistic merit of the Int. Parl. for Safety and Peace, U.S.A. (1982), Oscar Gold Prize (Italy) 1985, World Gold Flame Prize (U.S.A. World Parl.) 1986, and several other prizes. *Publications include:* On the Six Principles of Chinese Painting 1931, Theory on Painting 1931, On Modern Painting 1936, A General Statement on Sources of Chinese Traditional Painting 1936. *Leisure interests:* enjoying reading, travelling, nature, drawing, collecting cultural relics. *Address:* Nanjing Academy of Fine Arts, 15 Hoo Qu Road, Nanjing (Office); 512 Fushing Road Central, Shanghai, People's Republic of China (Home). *Telephone:* 203346 (Home).

LIU HANG; Chinese artist; b. 18 March 1932, Huang Shan Guan Qian, Zhaoyuan Co., Shandong; s. of Liu Anbin and Wang Shi; m. Bao Ning 1957; one d.; Vice-Pres. Zhejiang Traditional Chinese Painting Acad. 1983-; Vice-Chair. Zhejiang Artists' Assen. 1986-. *Works include:* Spring rain was falling upon a small town (publ. in The Collection of Prints of Zhejiang Province for 50 Years), Marching on in the snowfield (in collection of Museum of Western and Eastern Art of the Ukraine, U.S.S.R.), Snow scene at West Lake and Taking a rest (both exhibited U.S.S.R., Japan, Egypt). *Leisure interests:* reading foreign and Chinese classic works of literature. *Address:* Zhejiang Members of Literature and Art Association, No. 1 Sui'an Road, Hangzhou, Zhejiang, People's Republic of China. *Telephone:* 24594.

LIU HONG; Chinese business executive; b. Fuzhou; Man. Dir. Xiamen S.E. Electronics Industry Co. 1984-; Dir. Fujian Prov. Computer Research Inst. 1985-. *Address:* Xiamen Southeast Electronics Industry Company, Xiamen, People's Republic of China.

LIU HONGKUAN; Chinese artist; b. 1938, Hebei; teacher Beijing Children's Palace 1983-. *Address:* Beijing Children's Palace, Beijing, People's Republic of China.

LIU HONGRU; Chinese banker; b. 1930, Yushu, Jilin; ed. Northeast Mil. Coll., Chinese People's Univ., Moscow Univ., Moscow Financial Coll.; Deputy Gov. Agricultural Bank of China 1979; Deputy Gov. People's Bank of China 1980-, Vice-Chair. Council People's Bank of China 1983-; Alt. Gov. IMF Sept. 1986-; Vice-Minister State Comm. for Restructuring the Economy May 1988-; Part time Prof., Beijing, Qinghua and Nankai Univs.; Pres. Financial and Banking Inst. of China; alt. mem. 13th CCP Cen. Cttee. 1987-. *Address:* Head Office, People's Bank of China, Beijing, People's Republic of China.

LIU HUANZHANG; Chinese sculptor; b. 1930, Leting County, Hebei; Assoc. Prof., Sculpture Studio, Beijing Cen. Acad. of Fine Arts. *Address:* Central Academy of Fine Arts, Beijing, People's Republic of China.

LIU HUAQING, Gen.; Chinese naval officer; b. 1916, Dawu Co., Hubei Prov.; Head, Political Dept., 11th Corps, 2nd Field Army 1949; transferred to Navy 1950; Rear-Admiral, PLA, Luda (Port Arthur and Dairen) 1958; Vice-Chair. Scientific and Technological Comm. for Nat. Defence 1967, First Vice-Chair. 1968; mem. Cultural Revolution Group, PLA 1967; disappeared during Cultural Revolution; Vice-Minister, State Scientific and Technological Comm., State Council 1978-80; Asst. to Chief of PLA Gen. Staff 1979-80; Deputy Chief of Staff, PLA 1980-, Commdr. PLA Navy Oct. 1982-; mem. 12th CCP Cen. Cttee. 1982-85; mem. Cen. Advisory Cttee. 1985-. *Address:* c/o People's Liberation Army, Beijing, People's Republic of China.

LIU JIANZHANG; Chinese politician; Dir. Railway Admin. Bureau, Zhengzhou 1951-52; mem. Nat. Cttee. of Supply and Marketing Co-operatives 1954; Vice-Minister of Railways 1954-66, 1975-81; Vice-Pres. All-China Sports Fed. 1971-; mem. Patriotic Health Campaign Cttee., under Cen. Cttee. 1978-; Acting Minister of Railways July-Sept. 1981, Minister 1981-82; Pres. Railway Soc. 1980-, Chinese Railway Veterans Assen. 1981-; Adviser to Ministry of Railways 1982-85; mem. Cen. Advisory Cttee. 1983-. *Address:* c/o State Council, Beijing, People's Republic of China.

LIU JIE; Chinese politician; mem. People's Govt., Henan Prov. 1949-54; Deputy Sec. CCP Cttee., Henan 1950; Dir. Industry Dept., Cen.-South China Mil. and Admin. Council 1950-52; Vice-Minister of Geology 1952-57; Deputy Dir. 3rd Gen. Office, State Council 1955-57; Vice-Minister, Second Ministry of Machine Building 1959-60, Minister 1960; mem. 4th CPPCC 1964; Vice-Chair. Prov. Revolutionary Cttee., Henan 1978-79; mem. Standing Cttee., CCP, Henan 1978-79; Gov. Henan 1979-81; Standing Sec. CCP Cttee., Henan 1979-81, First Sec. 1981-83, Sec. 1983-85; First Political Commissar, PLA Henan Mil. Dist. 1982-; Pres. Cycling Assen. 1979-; mem. Cen. Advisory Comm. 1987-. *Address:* Provincial Communist Party Committee, Zhengzhou, Henan Province, People's Republic of China.

LIU JINGSONG; Chinese army officer; Commdr., Shenyang Mil. Region, PLA 1985—; mem. CCP Cen. Cttee. 1985-. *Address:* Shenyang Military Region Headquarters, Shenyang, Liaoning, People's Republic of China.

LIU KEMING; Chinese academic; b. 28 July 1919, Liaoning; Prof., Beijing Univ. 1979-; Dir. Soviet Research Inst. 1976-; Dir. Inst. of Soviet and East European Studies 1980-82; Prof., Coll. of Foreign Affairs 1985-; Vice-Pres. Chinese Soc. of Soviet and East European Studies 1982-. *Address:* Chinese Academy of Social Sciences, P.O. Box 1103, Beijing, People's Republic of China.

LIU LANTAO; Chinese party, government and military official; b. Liu Zhenfang, 1904, Mizhi, Shaanxi Prov.; ed. San Min No. 2 School, Mizhi, Beijing Univ.; m. Liu Sufei; joined CCP 1928; Sec. CCP Shaanxi Special Cttee. 1930; imprisoned in N. Shaanxi Aug.-Oct. 1930; Hebei CCP Prov. Cttee., Tianjin 1931; imprisoned in Beijing July 1931; Sec. Beiyue CCP Dist. Cttee., Shanxi-Chahar-Hebei Mil. Dist. 1940; alt. mem. 7th CCP Cen. Cttee. 1945; Pres. N. China People's Univ. 1950-; Third Sec. N. Region CCP Cttee. 1952-54, Chair. 1951-54; mem. State Planning Comm. of Govt. Admin. Council 1952-54; mem. Cttee. for Drafting Electoral Law 1953; mem. Standing Cttee. 1st NPC 1954; mem. 1st. CPPCC Decl. 1954; Deputy Sec. Gen. CCP Cen. Cttee. Nov. 1955; visits to GDR, Romania and U.S.S.R. Dec. 1955-Feb. 1956; Presidium 8th CCP Nat. Congress Sept. 1956; Deputy Sec., Secr. of CCP Control Comm. 1956-63; alt. Sec., Secr. of 8th CCP Cen. Cttee. 1956-66; mem. CCP Control Cttee. Standing Cttee. 1961-63; First Sec. N. Region CCP Cttee. 1963-66; mem. 4th CPPCC 1964-, Vice-Chair. 1965; purged Jan. 1967, rehabilitated 1978; mem. 11th CCP Cen. Cttee. 1979; mem. Cen. Advisory Cttee. of CCP Cen. Cttee. 1982-. *Address:* Central Advisory Committee of the Central Committee of the Chinese Communist Party, Zhongnanhai, Beijing, People's Republic of China.

LIU LIFENG; Chinese army officer; Political Commissar, PLA 2nd Artillery 1983-, *Address:* People's Liberation Army Headquarters, Beijing, People's Republic of China.

LIU LIN; Chinese state, army and party official; b. 1918; Sec. CCP Cttee. Nanjing Municipality 1958; Chief of Staff, Jiangsu Mil. Dist. 1965; Deputy Commdr. Jiangsu Mil. Dist. 1977; Vice-Gov., Jiangsu 1979-81; First Sec. CCP Cttee. Nanjing Municipality 1981; Second Sec. CCP Cttee. Jiangsu 1982-83; mem. 12th CCP Cen. Cttee. 1982-87; Chair. CCP Jiangsu Prov. Consultative Cttee. 1984; Chair. Advisory Cttee. 1983-. *Address:* Jiangsu Provincial Chinese Communist Party, Nanjing, Jiangsu, People's Republic of China.

LIU MINGHUI; Chinese politician; b. 1914, Jiangxi Prov.; Dir. Public Security Bureau, Chongqing Municipality; Council mem. People's Govt., Chongqing Municipality; Deputy Commdr. and Commdr. of Chongqing Garrison 1949; Sec. Secr. CCP Cttee., Yunnan 1955-66; criticized without loss of position 1967; Vice-Chair. Prov. Revolutionary Cttee., 1968-79; Deputy Sec. CCP Cttee., Yunnan Prov. 1972-75, Sec., Second Sec. 1975-79, Sec. CCP Cttee., Gov. Yunnan 1979-83; Chair. Prov. People's Congress,

Yunnan 1983; alt. mem. 11th Cen. Cttee. CCP, 13th Cen. Cttee. 1982-87; mem. Cen. Advisory Comm. 1987-; Deputy to 3rd, 4th, 5th, 6th NPC. *Address:* People's Government of Yunnan Province, Kunming, Yunnan, People's Republic of China.

LIU NIANQU; Chinese composer; b. 24 Nov. 1945, Shanghai; Exec. Deputy Dir. Shanghai Mun. Bureau of Culture; Art Inspector Gen. Shanghai Int. Arts Festival 1987. *Address:* Shanghai Municipal Bureau of Culture, 709 Ju Lu Road, Shanghai, People's Republic of China.

LIU SHAHE; Chinese poet; b. 1931, Chengdu, Sichuan Prov.; ed. Sichuan Univ.; mem. editorial staff The Stars (poetry magazine) -1957 and 1979-; satirical poem Verses of Plants (1957) led to his political persecution 1957-79. *Publications include:* Farewell to the Big Star. *Address:* People's Republic of China.

LIU SHAOHUI; Chinese artist; b. 27 Aug. 1940, Szechuan; s. of Liu Veizheng and Xiong Wenying; m. Yang Yijing; one s. one d.; ed. Cen. Inst. of Applied Arts, Beijing; fmr. Dir. Art Layout Office, Yunnan People's Publishing House; now mem. Chinese Artists Assen., engaged in design and research; exhbns. in Italy, Hong Kong, Japan, Singapore; works at Guilin Arts Garden; Prize of Nat. Art Works of Excellence 1981 and 1983; main designer for film Fire Boy (1st Prize, Asia Film Festival, Japan 1985). *Works include:* Zhaoshutun—Legend of a Dai Prince, An Elementary Theory on Binding and Layout of Books. *Address:* Lijiang Publishing House, Guilin, People's Republic of China.

LIU SHAOTANG; Chinese writer; b. 29 Feb. 1936, Scholar Village, Tongxian County, Beijing; s. of Liu Tongjiu and Bo Lizhen; m. Zeng Caimei 1955; one s. two d.; ed. Beijing Univ. 1954; sent down to the countryside 1958; mem. Standing Cttee. Beijing People's Congress; Dir. Chinese Writers' Assen., Man. Dir. Beijing Writers' Assen. *Publications:* Green Branches and Leaves 1952, The Sound of Oars on the Grand Canal 1954, Summer 1956, Catkin Willow Flats 1980, The Liuxiang Melon Hut 1981, Some Families of a Hamlet 1982, An Encounter in Green Vine Lane 1983, The Suburbs of Beijing 1984, Bean Shed, Melon Hut, Drizzle 1985, In these Years: Story-telling by Jing Liuting 1986, The Sweet Grass within Reach 1987, Rural Marriage: Grass of Spring and Flames of War 1988. *Leisure interest:* Beijing opera. *Address:* Beijing Writers' Association, Beijing, People's Republic of China.

LIU SHILAN; Chinese chess player; b. 1962; China's first woman chess grand master.

LIU SHUQING; Chinese diplomatist; Second Sec. Embassy, U.S.S.R. 1960; Amb. to Poland 1972-77, to Norway 1977-80, to Bangladesh 1980-83; Vice Foreign Minister 1984-; Head Chinese del. to 6th Round of Sino-Indian Negotiations 1985, to 3rd China-Bhutan Boundary Talks 1985. *Address:* Ministry of Foreign Affairs, Beijing, People's Republic of China.

LIU SHUSHENG; Chinese party official; alt. mem. 12th CCP Cen. Cttee. 1982-87; Deputy Sec. CCP Cttee., Yunnan Prov. 1981, 1983-, Chair. 1988-. *Address:* Yunnan Provincial Committee of Chinese Communist Party, Kunming, Yunnan, People's Republic of China.

LIU TIANFU; Chinese politician; b. 1926; Second Sec. Dist. CCP Cttee., West Guangdong Dist. 1952; Deputy Dir. Gen. Office, Cen.-South China Mil. Region 1953; Dir. Industry Dept., CCP Cttee., Guangdong Prov. 1957; Vice-Chair. Scientific Work Cttee., People's Govt., Guangdong 1958; Vice-Gov. Guangdong 1958—Cultural Revolution; Alt. mem. Secr., CCP Cttee., Guangdong 1960-62; Sec. CCP Cttee., Guangdong 1962; Alt. mem. Secr., Cen.-South China Bureau, Cen. Cttee. 1965—Cultural Revolution; Vice-Chair. Provincial Revolutionary Cttee., Guangdong 1973-79; mem. Standing Cttee., CCP Cttee., Guangdong 1973-77; Sec. CCP Cttee., Guangdong 1977; Vice-Gov. Guangdong 1979-81, Gov. 1981-83; mem. Cen. Advisory Cttee. 1982-. *Address:* c/o Office of the Provincial Governor, Guangzhou, Guangdong, People's Republic of China.

LIU WEI; Chinese politician and party official; b. 1912, Hubei; Dir. 8th Bureau, Ministry of Public Security 1952; Asst. to Minister of Geology 1955-57; Vice-Minister 2nd Ministry of Machine Building 1961-78, Minister 1978-82; mem. 11th Cen. Cttee. CCP 1977; mem. Standing Cttee. NPC 1983-, Credentials Cttee. 1983, Foreign Affairs Cttee. 1986-, Financial and Econ. Cttee.; Head China-Greece Friendship Group 1985-. *Address:* c/o State Council, Beijing, People's Republic of China.

LIU WEIMING; Chinese party official and youth leader; Vice-Chair. Revolutionary Cttee., Guangdong Prov. 1975-78; alt. mem. 11th CCP Cen. Cttee. 1977, and 12th Cen. Cttee. 1982-87; Sec. Communist Youth League 1978-82; Vice-Chair. Youth Fed. 1979-, Acting Chair. 1981-83; mem. Standing Cttee. CCP Prov. Cttee., Guangdong 1986-, Vice-Gov. Jan. 1988-. *Address:* Chinese Communist Youth Federation, Beijing, People's Republic of China.

LIU XIAN; Chinese woodcut artist; b. 7 July 1915, Lanfeng Co., Henan; s. of Wang Zhangyi and Liu Fen; m. Wang Zhuojuin 1937; one d.; ed. Imperial Acad. of Fine Arts, Tokyo, studied under Lu Xun; teacher Lu Xun Acad. of Literature and Art, Yenan 1939; Dir. Research Dept. Nat. Art Gallery, Beijing. *Works include:* Illustrations of wood engravings for Call To Arms, Midnight, Crime and Punishment, Rise Up, China! A Hundred Flowers (novels), Wild Grass (essays). *Publications include:*

Selection of Wood Engravings by Liu Xian, and over 20 others. *Leisure interests:* music, travel. *Address:* National Art Gallery, Beijing, People's Republic of China. *Telephone:* 44-3119.

LIU XIAOQING; Chinese actress; b. 1952, Chengdu City, Sichuan Prov.; m. Chen Guojun; ed. Sichuan Music School; 10th Hundred Flowers Best Actress Award for Furong Zhen (Lotus Town) 1987; 11th Hundred Flowers Best Actress Award for Yuanye (Champain) 1988. *Address:* Beijing Film Studio, 19 Bei Sanhuan Xilu, Beijing, People's Republic of China. *Telephone:* 2010011 (Beijing).

LIU XIAOYI; Chinese sculptor; b. 26 Nov. 1944, Shandong; s. of Liu Xuean and Sun Xianling; m. Liu Huixian 1974; one d.; ed. Beijing No. 4 Middle School, Secondary School of Arts and Crafts, Cen. Acad. of Arts and Design; stage artist, Art Troupe of the Army 1970; Cadre, Ministry of Electronics Industry 1977; Art Ed., China Youth magazine 1979–. *Publications:* Chinese Handiwork Techniques (with Liu Huixian) 1988; numerous illustrations, designs, handicraft products and articles on handiwork techniques. *Leisure interest:* music. *Address:* China Youth Magazine, Beijing, People's Republic of China. *Telephone:* 484931.

LIU XINWU; Chinese writer; b. 4 June 1942, Chengdu, Sichuan; s. of Liu Tien Yen and Wang Yun Tao; m. Lu Xiaogo 1970; one s.; lived in Beijing since 1950; ed. Beijing Teachers' Coll.; school teacher 1961–76; ed. Beijing Publishing House 1976–80; Ed.-in-Chief People's Literature Jan. 1987–; professional writer since 1980; mem. Standing Cttee., China All Nation Youth Fed.; mem. Council, Chinese Writers' Asscn. *Publications:* short stories: Class Counsellor (Nationwide Short Story Prize 1977), The Position of Love 1978, I Love Every Piece of Green Leaves (Nationwide Short Story Prize 1979), A Scanning over the May 19th Accident 1985; medium-length novels: Ru Yi (As You Wish) 1980, Overpass 1981; novel: Drum Tower (Mao Dun Literature Prize 1984). *Leisure interests:* reading, travelling, painting, stamp collecting, music, gardening. *Address:* People's Literature, 52 Dong Si Ba Tiao (No. 8 Lane of Dongsi), Beijing (Office); 122 Building Unit 1 No. 7, Jin Soong District, Beijing, People's Republic of China. *Telephone:* 781292 (Home).

LIU XIYAO, Maj.-Gen.; Chinese party and government official; b. 1916, Changsha City, Hunan Prov.; Deputy Sec. CCP Hubei Prov. 1953–54; Vice-Chair. State Technological Comm. 1957–59, State Scientific and Technological Comm. 1959–67; Alt. mem. 9th Cen. Cttee. of CCP 1969; Dir. Scientific and Educ. Group, State Council 1972–77; Alt. mem. 10th Cen. Cttee. of CCP 1973; 11th Cen. Cttee. 1977; Minister, Second Ministry of Machine Bldg. 1975; Minister of Educ. 1977–79, Vice-Gov., Sichuan Prov. 1979–83; Sec. CCP Cttee. 1980–81; mem. CPPCC Nat. Cttee. 1986–; mem. Standing Cttee. CCP Cttee. Sichuan. *Address:* Office of the Provincial Vice-Governor, Chengdu, Sichuan Province, People's Republic of China.

LIU YAZHOU; Chinese writer; b. 1953; ed. Wuhan Univ.; Council mem. Chinese Writers' Asscn.; mem. Chinese Literature Foundation; Chinese del. to UN Paris Conf. to commemorate Int. Year of Peace. *Publications include:* The Demon Directed War, Two Generations of Truly Great. *Address:* Zhongnanhai, Beijing, People's Republic of China.

LIU YI; Chinese party and government official; b. 1930, Rushan Co., Shandong Prov.; cadre State Council 1974; Deputy for Beijing Municipality, 5th NPC 1978; Deputy Dir.-Gen. Office, State Council 1978; Dir. Counsellor's Office, State Council 1977–; mem. Cttee. to Examine Proposals at 2nd Session of 5th NPC 1979; Pres. Soc. of Refrigeration 1980–; Minister of Commerce 1982–88; Dir. Nat. Tourism Admin. May 1988–; Vice-Chair. State Tourism Cttee. June 1988–; Alt. mem. 12th Cen. Cttee., CCP 1982, 13th Cen. Cttee. 1987. *Address:* State Tourism Committee, Beijing, People's Republic of China.

LIU YING; Chinese party official; b. 1905; m. Zhang Wenhan (deceased); joined CCP 1925; veteran of Long March. *Address:* Chinese Communist Party, Zhong Nan Hai, Beijing, People's Republic of China.

LIU YINXIN; Chinese botanist; ed. N.W. China Agric. Coll.; first woman to visit Tengger Desert, N. China 1953; specialises in sand control experimentation; retd. 1985, continues to write. *Publications:* two volumes of a three volume study of Chinese Desert Flora. *Address:* Spapoto Sand Control Station, Tengger Desert, People's Republic of China.

LIU YOUFA; Chinese party official; cadre of United Front Work Dept. under CCP Cen. Cttee. 1973–77; alt. mem. 12th CCP Cen. Cttee. 1982–87. *Address:* c/o Chinese Communist Party Central Committee, Beijing, People's Republic of China.

LIU YUJIE; Chinese party official and youth leader; Sec. Henan Prov. Branch, Communist Youth League 1979–; alt. mem. 12th CCP Cen. Cttee. 1982, 13th Cen. Cttee. 1987. *Address:* Chinese Communist Youth League, Henan Branch, Zhengzhou, Henan, People's Republic of China.

LIU ZHEN, Col.-Gen.; Chinese party and military official; b. 1915, Xiaogan Co., Hubei Prov.; m. Li Ling; ed. Anti-Japan Military and Political Coll., Yan'an; Dir. Gen. Supply 4th Front Army HQ and Red 25th Army, wounded at Yuan Zhai Gou 1935; Political Cttee. Red 15th Army Corps 1936; brigade commdr. New 4th Army 1941–42; Commdr. 39th Army, N.E. Field Army, Tianjin 1949; Council mem. N.E. People's Govt. 1950–53; PLA Gen. 1955, Col. Gen. 1957; Mil. Friendship Del. to U.S.S.R. 1957; mem.

8th CCP Cen. Cttee. 1958; Vice-Commdr. PLA Air Force 1959; Pres. PLA Air Force Acad. 1965; Deputy Sec. Gen. Hubei Prov. CCP Cttee. 1965; purged 1967, rehabilitated 1973; mem. 11th CCP Cen. Cttee. 1977; Commdr. Xinjiang Mil. Region 1977–79; Second Sec. Xinjiang Autonomous Region CCP Cttee. 1978–79; mem. 12th CCP Cen. Cttee. 1982; Vice-Chair. Shaanxi Prov. People's Congress 1984; mem. Cen. Advisory Cttee. of CCP Cen. Cttee. 1987–. *Address:* Central Advisory Committee of the Central Committee of the Chinese Communist Party, Zhongnanhai, Beijing, People's Republic of China.

LIU ZHENGWEI; Chinese party official; mem. 12th CCP Cen. Cttee. 1982; Sec. CCP Cttee., Nanyang Pref., Henan 1982–83; Sec. CCP Cttee., Henan Prov. 1983, Deputy Sec. 1983–; mem. 13th CCP Cen. Cttee. 1987. *Address:* Henan Provincial Chinese Communist Party, Zhengzhou, Henan, People's Republic of China.

LIU ZHENHUA, Gen.; Chinese army officer; b. 1921, Tai'an Co., Shandong Prov.; m. Liu Junxiao; Amb. to Albania 1971–76; Vice-Minister Foreign Affairs 1976–79; Deputy Political Commissar, Shenyang Mil. Region 1980–82; mem. 12th Cen. Cttee. CCP 1982; mem. 13th Cen. Cttee. 1987; Political Commissar, Shenyang Mil. Region 1982–88, Beijing Mil. Region Jan. 1988–. *Address:* People's Liberation Army, Beijing Units, Beijing, People's Republic of China.

LIU ZHENG; Chinese government official; b. 1929; Gov. of Hunan Prov. 1983–85; Deputy Sec. CCP Provincial Cttee. 1983–. *Address:* Office of the Governor, Hunan Province, People's Republic of China.

LIU ZHIJIAN, Lieut.-Gen.; Chinese army officer and party official; b. 1912, Pingjiang Co., Hunan Prov.; joined Communist Youth League 1930; mem. Co. Political Cttee., 3rd Army Group, Red Army 1930; Deputy Political Commissar and Dir. Political Dept. 4th Army Group, Red Army 1949; Dir. Propaganda Dept., Gen. Political Dept., People's Revolutionary Mil. Council 1950; Dir. Propaganda Dept., PLA Gen. Political Dept. 1954; Deputy Dir. PLA Gen. Political Dept. 1958; Lieut.-Gen. 1958; Deputy for PLA, 3rd NPC 1964; mem. Nat. Defence Council 1965; Deputy Head Cultural Revolution Group, State Council 1965; disappeared 1967–74; Political Commissar, Kunming Mil. Region 1975–79; Alt. mem. 11th Cen. Cttee., CCP 1977; First Political Commissar, PLA Kunming Mil. Region; Second Sec. CCP Cttee., PLA Kunming Mil. Region 1979–80; First Sec. CCP Cttee., PLA Kunming Mil. Region 1980–; mem. 12th Cen. Cttee., CCP 1982–85; mem. Cen. Advisory Comm. 1987–. *Address:* First Political Commissar, Kunming Military Region, People's Republic of China.

LIU ZHONGGUI; Chinese politician; Mil. Attaché, Hanoi 1963; Deputy C.O. Army in Guangxi 1965, Political Commissar, Second Sec., Cttee. for Guangxi Zhuang Autonomous Region, Deputy Chair. 1970. *Address:* c/o Office of the Political Commissar, Nanning, Guangxi Zhuang Autonomous Region, People's Republic of China.

LIU ZIHOU; Chinese party official; b. 1911, Hebei; joined CCP 1937; Deputy Gov. of Hubei 1952–54, Gov. 1954–56; Second Sec. CCP Hubei 1953–56; Dir. Sanmen Gorge Construction Bureau 1956–58; Gov. of Hebei 1958–68; Sec. CCP Hebei 1958–64; Alt. mem. 8th Cen. Cttee. of CCP 1956; Sec. N. China Bureau, CCP 1963–68; Second Sec. CCP Hebei Revolutionary Cttee. 1964–68; First Vice-Chair. Hebei Revolutionary Cttee. 1968, Chair. 1970–79; mem. 9th Cen. Cttee. of CCP 1969; First Sec. CCP Hebei 1971–80; mem. 10th Cen. Cttee. of CCP 1973, 11th Cen. Cttee. 1977; First Political Commissar Hebei Mil. Dist.; mem. CCP Nat. Comm. 1986–. *Address:* People's Republic of China.

LIVELY, Penelope Margaret; British author; b. 17 March 1933; d. of Roger Low and Vera Greer; m. Jack Lively 1957; one s. one d.; ed. St. Anne's Coll., Oxford. *Publications:* Astercote 1970, The Whispering Knights 1971, The Wild Hunt of Hagworthy 1971, The Driftway 1972, The Ghost of Thomas Kempe 1973 (Carnegie Medal), The House in Norham Gardens 1974, Going Back 1975, Boy Without a Name 1975, A Stitch in Time 1976 (Whitbread Award), The Stained Glass Window 1976, Fanny's Sister 1976, The Presence of the Past (non-fiction) 1976, The Road to Lichfield 1977, The Voyage of QV66 1978, Nothing Missing but the Samovar and other stories 1978 (Southern Arts Literature Prize), Treasures of Time 1979 (Nat. Book Award), Fanny and the Monsters 1979, Judgement Day 1980, Fanny and the Battle of Potter's Piece 1980, The Revenge of Samuel Stokes 1981, Next to Nature, Art 1982, Perfect Happiness 1983, Corruption 1984, According to Mark 1984, Uninvited Ghosts and other stories 1984, Pack of Cards (short stories) 1986, Debbie and the Little Devil 1987, A House Inside Out 1987, Moon Tiger 1987 (Booker-McConnell Prize), Passing On 1989; television and radio scripts. *Leisure interests:* gardening, landscape history, talking, listening. *Address:* Duck End, Great Rollright, Chipping Norton, Oxon., OX7 5SB, England. *Telephone:* (0608) 737565.

LIVINGSTONE, Ken(neth) Robert; British politician; b. 17 June 1945, London; s. of Robert Moffat Livingstone and Ethel Ada Kennard; m. Christine Pamela Chapman 1973 (divorced 1982); no c.; ed. Tulse Hill Comprehensive School, Phillipa Fawcett Coll. of Educ.; Technician, Cancer Research Unit, Royal Marsden Hospital 1962–70; Councillor, Borough of Lambeth 1971–78, of Camden 1978–82, of Greater London Council 1973–86 (Leader 1981–86); M.P. for Brent East June 1987–; joined Labour Party

1969, mem. Regional Exec. 1974–, Nat. Exec. Council 1987–. *Publication:* If Voting Changed Anything They Would Abolish It 1987. *Leisure interests:* science fiction, cinema, natural history. *Address:* House of Commons, Westminster, London, S.W.1, England.

LIZICHEV, Gen. Aleksey Dmitrievich; Soviet government official; b. 22 June 1928, Vologda Dist.; ed. Moscow Mil. School; mem. CPSU 1949–; political komsomol work, later asst. to Head of Political Admin., Northern Mil. Dist. later Leningrad Mil. Dist. 1949–61; Asst. for komsomol work to Head of Main Political Admin., Soviet Army and Navy 1961–65; cand. mem. 1962–65, mem. Cen. Cttee. All-Union Komsomol 1966–; Head of Political Admin. Army Corps, Volga Mil. District; Deputy Head, then First Deputy Head of Political Admin., Moscow Mil. Dist. 1965–71; First Deputy Head of Political Admin. to Soviet Troops in Germany 1971–75; Head of Political Admin. and mem. of Mil. Council of Transbaikal Mil. Dist. 1975–80; deputy to R.S.F.S.R. Supreme Soviet 1975–85; Deputy Head of Main Political Admin. on questions of ideology, Soviet Army and Navy 1980–82, Head 1985–; Head of Political Admin., Troops in Germany 1982–85; Deputy to Council of Nationalities, U.S.S.R. Supreme Soviet 1984–; rank of Gen. of Soviet Army 1986–; elected to Congress of People's Deputies of the U.S.S.R. 1989; Order of the Red Star (twice). *Publications:* numerous publications on komsomol work in the army. *Address:* Ministry of Defence, Moscow, U.S.S.R.

LJUBIČIĆ, Gen. Nikola; Yugoslav politician and army officer; b. 1916, Karane, Serbia; ed. High Mil. Acad.; one of organizers of Titovo Užice uprising; joined CP of Yugoslavia 1941; active in Resistance movement; held various mil. and political posts after 2nd World War, including Chief, Mil. School and Commanding Officer, 1st Army Region; Fed. Ass. Deputy 1963–67; Fed. Sec. for Nat. Defence, rank of Gen. 1967–82; elected mem. Cen. Cttee. of the League of Communists of Yugoslavia 5 times, Presidency Central Cttee. League of Communists of Yugoslavia 3 times; elected mem. Cen. Cttee. and mem. Presidency of the League of Communists of Serbia at League's 9th Congress; Pres. Presidency of Socialist Repub. of Serbia 1982–84; 1941 Partisan Memorial Medal; Order of the Nat. Hero. *Address:* Federal Executive Council, Bul. Lenjina 2, 11075 Novi Beograd, Yugoslavia.

LJUNGGREN, Olof, LL.B.; Swedish publisher and business executive; b. 5 Jan. 1933, Eskilstuna; s. of Lars and Elisabeth Ljunggren; m. 1st Lena Carlsöö; m. 2nd Margreth Bäcklund; three s.; ed. Univ. of Stockholm; Sec. Tidningarnas Arbetsgivareförening (Swedish Newspaper Employers' Asscn.) 1959–62, Pres. and C.E.O. 1962–66; Deputy Pres. and C.E.O. Allers Förlag AB 1967–72, Pres. and C.E.O. 1972–74; Pres. and C.E.O. Svenska Dagbladet 1974–78; Pres. and C.E.O. Svenska Arbetsgivareföreningen (Swedish Employers' Confed.) 1978–; Chair. of Bd. Askild & Kärnekull Förlag AB 1971–74, Nord Artel AB 1971–78, Förlags AB Tifa & Tryckeri AB Tifa 1975–78, Skivklubben Musik för alla AB 1976–78, Centralförbundet Folk och Försvar (Vice-Chair. 1978–83) 1983–86, Rådet för Personal- och Arbetslivsfrågor (PArådet) (The Swedish Council for Personnel Admin.) 1980–81, Svenska Management Gruppen AB 1981–85, Richard Hägglöf Fondkommission AB 1984–87; mem. numerous other bds.; Knight Commdr. Order of the White Rose of Finland 1982, The King's Medal of the 12th Dimension with the Ribbon of the Order of the Seraphim 1987, Kommendörskorset av Den Kgl. Norske Fortjenstorden. *Address:* Skeppargatan 7, 114 52 Stockholm, Sweden. *Telephone:* 08-660 08 51.

LJUNGQVIST, Bengt, B.A.; Swedish lawyer and business executive; b. 13 Aug. 1937, Stockholm; m. 1st Sylvia Elmstedt 1961 (divorced 1977), 2nd Christina (née Hedén) Ljungqvist 1978; two s. two d.; ed. Stockholm Univ.; joined Malmström and Malmenfelt Advokatbyrå, Stockholm 1967, Partner 1971–; Pres. Bd. of City Planning, Danderyd 1976–85, Communal Council, Danderyd 1986–; mem. Swedish Bar Asscn. 1983–, Vice-Pres. 1985–; mem. Council Int. Bar Assen. 1984–. *Address:* Malmström and Malmenfelt Advokatbyrå, Hovslagargatan 5 B, 111 48 Stockholm (Office); Sigurdvagen 18, 182 64 Djursholm, Sweden (Home). *Telephone:* (08) 755 31 96 (Home).

LLERAS CAMARGO, Alberto; Colombian journalist, politician and writer; b. 3 July 1906; Editorial staff of El Espectador and El Tiempo, Bogotá 1925–30; Sec.-Gen. of Partido Liberal and Ed. La Tarde 1930; Chair. House of Reps. 1932; Sec. Colombian Del. to Pan-American Conf., Montevideo 1934; Sec.-Gen. exec. branch of Colombian Govt. 1934–35; Minister of Govt. 1935; Del. to Inter-American Conf. for Maintenance of Peace, Buenos Aires 1936; Minister of Educ. 1936; Minister of Govt. 1936–38; Ed. El Liberal 1938–43; elected Senator 1943; Amb. to U.S.A. and Minister of Govt. 1943; Minister of Foreign Affairs 1945; head of Colombian Del. to Conf. of Chapultepec, Mexico and UN Conf., San Francisco 1945; Pres. of Colombia 1945–46; Ed. Semana 1946–47; Sec.-Gen. of OAS 1947–54; Pres. Univ. de los Andes 1954–55; Pres. of Colombia 1958–62; produced study of Alliance for Progress 1963; Hon. Ph.D. (Univ. de los Andes) 1957, Hon. Degree (Johns Hopkins Univ.) 1960; Hon. LL.D. (Harvard); Human Rights Prize (Congreso Judío Latinoamericano) 1976, Orden Centenario 1976, Theodore Brent Prize. *Address:* Bogotá, Colombia.

LLERAS RESTREPO, Carlos; Colombian lawyer and politician; b. 12 April 1908, Bogotá; s. of Federico Lleras Acosta; m. Cecilia de la Fuente 1933; two s. two d.; ed. Univ. Nacional de Colombia; Lawyer 1930–; Deputy 1931; Minister of Treasury 1938–43; Prof. of Public Finance, Law Faculty,

Univ. Nacional 1939; Pres. of Partido Liberal 1941, 1948–50, mem. Triumvirate 1950, Leader 1961–73; Senator 1942–52, 1958–59, 1962–; Pres. Colombian Del. to Bretton Woods Conf. 1944; mem. various Colombian Dels. to UN Comms.; Vice-Pres. Econ. and Social Council, UN 1946; in Europe 1959–60; Pres. Colombian Del. to Geneva Conf. 1964; Pres. of Colombia 1966–70; Chair. FAO Special Cttee. on Agrarian Reform 1970–71; Leader Partido Liberal 1972–73; Consultant Inter-American Bank of Devt. (IADB) 1973–74; Ed. and Dir. Nueva Frontera 1974–. *Publications:* La Estadística Nacional 1938, De la República a la Dictadura 1955, Crónicas y Coloquios del Bachiller Cleofás Pérez 1962, 1964, Hacia la Restauración Democrática y el Cambio Social 1963, Comercio Internacional 1966, Messages of the President of the Republic to the National Congress 1967–70, Borradores para la Historia de la República Liberal 1975; five vols. of discourses on political, financial and administrative subjects 1966–70 and many articles. *Address:* Carrera 7A, No. 17-01, Bogotá, D.E., Colombia.

LLESHI, Maj.-Gen. Haxhi; Albanian politician; b. 1913; fought with resistance against Italian and German occupations 1939–45; mem. provisional Govt. 1944; Minister of the Interior 1944–46; Maj.-Gen. Albanian Army; Pres. Presidium of the People's Assembly (Head of State) 1953–82; mem. Cen. Cttee. Albanian Workers' Party 1953–. *Address:* c/o Kuvendi Popullore, Tirana, Albania.

LLEWELLYN, John; American scientist; b. 22 April 1933, Cardiff, U.K.; s. of John and Morella (Roberts) Llewellyn; m. Valerie Davies-Jones; one s. one d.; ed. Univ. Coll., Cardiff, Wales; Research Fellow, Nat. Research Council of Canada 1958–60; Assoc. Prof. School of Eng. Science, Florida State Univ. 1964–72; selected by NASA as scientist-astronaut 1967; Dean, School of Eng. Science, Florida State Univ. 1970–72; Prof. Depts. of Chemical and Mechanical Eng., Coll. of Eng., Univ. of South Fla., Tampa 1973–; Co-ordinator, Scientist in the Sea Project 1973; aquanaut Nat. Oceanographic Atmospheric Admin; Scientific consultant on marine environment, energy and industrial computer applications; Pres. J. Vector Inc., K. Vector Inc.; mem. Royal Inst. of Chem., A.I.A.A., Radiation Research Soc. *Publications:* Principles and Applications of Digital Devices 1983, Basic Elements of Digital Systems 1983. *Leisure interests:* sailing, underwater exploration. *Address:* 3010 St. Charles Drive, Tampa, Fla. 33618, U.S.A.

LLOREDA CAICEDO, Rodrigo; Colombian politician; b. 2 Sept. 1942, Cali; s. of Alvaro Lloreda and Mercedes Caicedo; m. María E. Piedrahita 1974; two s. three d.; ed. Pontificia Univ. Javeriana; Gov. Valle del Cauca 1968–70; Dir. El Pais, Cali 1970–78; Senator 1978–; Minister of Educ. 1978–80, of Foreign Affairs 1982–84; Vice-Pres. of Columbia 1984–86; Amb. to U.S.A. 1984–86; del. to several int. confs.; Gran Cruz de la Orden de Boyacá and decorations from Venezuela, Mexico, Panama, Chile, Honduras and Spain. *Publications:* El Sistema Presidential de Gobierno, La Juventud en el Gobierno, Reforma de la Educatión Superior, La Nueva Politica Internal de Colombia 1984, Una Gestion por Colombia 1986. *Leisure interests:* reading, music, tennis. *Address:* Cra 16 No. 36-55, Bogota, Colombia. *Telephone:* 2450903.

LLOYD, Christine Marie Evert (see Evert, Christine Marie).

LLOYD, Clive; Guyanese cricketer; b. 31 Aug. 1944, Georgetown, British Guiana (now Guyana); left-handed batsman, right-arm medium-paced bowler; in W. Indies Test team, tour to India 1966–67; played for Lancashire 1968–74, capt. West Indies 1974–88; scored 126 against Warwickshire at Lord's 1972; captained World Cup winning team 1975; scored 201 not out in 120 minutes against Glamorgan 1976; made 6,000 Test runs by 1983.

LLOYD, Geoffrey Ernest Richard, PH.D., F.B.A.; British professor of philosophy; b. 25 Jan. 1933, London; s. of William Ernest Lloyd and Olive Irene Neville Lloyd; m. Janet Elizabeth Lloyd 1956; three s.; ed. Charterhouse and King's Coll., Cambridge; Univ. Asst. Lecturer in Classics, Cambridge 1965–67, Univ. Lecturer 1967–74, Reader in Ancient Philosophy and Science 1974–83, Prof. 1983–; Master, Darwin Coll., Cambridge Oct. 1989–; Fellow King's Coll. 1957–, Japan Soc. for the Promotion of Science; Sarton Medal 1987. *Publications:* Polarity and Analogy 1966, Aristotle, the Growth and Structure of his Thought 1968, Early Greek Science: Thales to Aristotle 1970, Greek Science after Aristotle 1973, Hippocratic Writings (Ed.) 1978, Aristotle on Mind and the Senses (Ed.) 1978, Magic, Reason and Experience 1979, Science, Folklore and Ideology 1983, Science and Morality in Greco-Roman Antiquity 1985, The Revolutions of Wisdom 1987. *Leisure interest:* travel. *Address:* 2 Prospect Row, Cambridge, CB1 1DU, England. *Telephone:* (0223) 355970.

LLOYD, George Walter Selwyn; British composer and conductor; b. 28 June 1913, St. Ives, Cornwall; s. of William A. C. Lloyd and Constance Priestley née Rawson; m. Nancy Kathleen Juvet 1937; studied privately and with Albert Sammons for violin, Harry Farjeon for composition and C. H. Kitson for counterpoint; conducted Symphony No. 1, Bournemouth Municipal Orchestra 1933, No. 2, Eastbourne Municipal Orchestra 1935, opera Iernin at Lyceum Theatre, London 1935, Symphony No. 3, BBC Symphony Orchestra 1935; opera The Serf at Covent Garden 1938; war service in Royal Marine Band aboard cruiser HMS Trinidad, severely shell-shocked 1942; opera John Socman commissioned for Festival of Britain, first performed Bristol 1951; grew carnations and mushrooms in Dorset, composing only intermittently, due to poor health 1951–73; Symphony No.

8 performed, BBC 1977 and subsequently many other works performed; conducted Fourth Piano Concerto, Royal Festival Hall, London 1984; now actively engaged in composing and conducting; Symphony No. 11 commissioned by Albany Symphony Orchestra, New York, first performance Nov. 1986. *Publications:* The Vigil of Venus 1981, A Miniature Triptych 1981, Royal Parks 1985, Diversions on a Bass Theme 1986, Aubade 1987. *Leisure interest:* reading. *Address:* 199 Clarence Gate Gardens, Glentworth Street, London, NW1 6AU, England. *Telephone:* 01-262 7969.

LLOYD, John Nicol Fortune, M.A.; British journalist; b. 15 April 1946; s. of Christopher Lloyd and Joan A. Fortune; m. 1st Judith Ferguson 1974 (divorced 1979), 2nd Marcia Levy 1983; one s.; ed. East Fife Comprehensive School and Univ. of Edin.; Ed. Time Out 1972-73; reporter, London Programme 1974-76; Producer, Weekend World 1976-77; industrial reporter, labour corresp., industrial and labour ed. Financial Times 1977-86; Ed. New Statesman 1986-87; with Financial Times 1987-. *Publications:* The Politics of Industrial Change (with Ian Benson) 1982, The Miners' Strike: Loss without Limit (with Martin Adeney) 1986, In Search of Work (with Charles Leadbeater) 1987. *Leisure interests:* opera, hill walking, squash. *Address:* c/o Financial Times, Greystoke Place, London, EC4, England.

LLOYD, Seton, C.B.E., M.A., F.B.A., F.S.A., A.R.I.B.A.; British archaeologist; b. 30 May 1902, Birmingham; s. of John Eliot Howard and Florence Louise Lloyd; m. Ulrica Fitzwilliams Hyde 1944 (died 1987); two s. one d.; ed. Uppingham and Architectural Asscn.; Asst. to Sir Edwin Lutyens, P.R.A. 1927-28; excavated for Egypt Exploration Soc., Egypt 1929-30, for Oriental Inst., Univ. of Chicago in Iraq 1930-37, for Univ. of Liverpool in Turkey 1937-39; Technical Adviser, Govt. of Iraq, Directorate-Gen. of Antiquities 1939-49; Dir. British Inst. Archaeology at Ankara 1949-61, Hon. Sec. 1964-74, Pres. 1974-; Prof. of Western Asiatic Archaeology, London Univ. 1962-69, Emer. Prof. 1969-; Pres. British School of Archaeology in Iraq 1978; Lawrence of Arabia Memorial Medal (Royal Soc. for Asian Affairs) 1971, Gertrude Bell Memorial Medal, British School of Archaeology in Iraq 1978; Certificate of Merit, Turkey 1973. *Publications:* Mesopotamia 1934, Sennacherib's Aqueduct at Jerwan 1935, The Gimilsin Temple 1940, Presargonid Temples 1942, Ruined Cities of Iraq 1942, Twin Rivers 1943, Foundations in the Dust 1948, Early Anatolia 1956, Art of the Ancient Near East 1961, Beycesultan 1962, Mounds of the Near East 1963, Early Highland Peoples of Anatolia 1967, Archaeology of Mesopotamia 1978, The Interval (memoirs) 1986. *Leisure interest:* Near Eastern archaeology. *Address:* Woolstone Lodge, Faringdon, Oxon., England. *Telephone:* (036 782) 248.

LLOYD-JONES, David Mathias, B.A.; British (Welsh) musician; b. 19 Nov. 1934, London; s. of the late Sir Vincent Lloyd-Jones and of Margaret Alwena Mathias; m. Anne Carolyn Whitehead 1964; two s. one d.; ed. Westminster School, Magdalen Coll., Oxford; Chorus Master, New Opera Co. 1961-64; conducted at Bath Festival 1966, City of London Festival 1966, Wexford Festival 1967-70, Scottish Opera 1968, Welsh Nat. Opera 1968, Royal Opera, Covent Garden 1971, Sadler's Wells Opera Co. (now English Nat. Opera) 1969-; Artistic Dir. Opera North 1977-; also conductor for TV operas (Eugene Onegin, The Flying Dutchman, Hansel and Gretel), for operas in Amsterdam and Paris, and has appeared with most British symphony orchestras; Hon. D.Mus. (Leeds) 1986. *Publications:* Boris Godunov—Translation, Vocal Score, Eugene Onegin—Translation, Vocal Score, Boris Godunov—Critical Edition of Original Full Score, numerous contributions to publs. including Grove's Dictionary of Music and Musicians, Musik in Geschichte und Gegenwart, Music and Letters, The Listener. *Leisure interests:* theatre, French cuisine, rose growing. *Address:* Opera North, Leeds Grand Theatre, Leeds LS1 6NZ; 94 Whitelands House, Cheltenham Terrace, London, SW3 4RA, England (Home). *Telephone:* (0532) 439999; (0532) 584490.

LLOYD-JONES, Peter Hugh Jefferd, M.A., F.B.A.; British classical scholar; b. 21 Sept. 1922, St. Peter Port, Guernsey; s. of Brevet-Major W. Lloyd-Jones, D.S.O., and Norah Leila Jefferd; m. 1st Frances Elisabeth Hedley 1953 (dissolved 1981); two s. one d.; m. 2nd Mary R. Lefkowitz 1982; ed. Lycée Français du Royaume-Uni (London), Westminster School, and Christ Church, Oxford; Fellow, Jesus Coll., Cambridge 1948-54; Fellow and E.P. Warren Praelector in Classics, Corpus Christi Coll., Oxford 1954-60; Regius Prof. of Greek and Student of Christ Church 1960-89; Chancellor's Prize for Latin Prose, Ireland and Craven Scholarships 1947; J. H. Gray Lecturer, Cambridge 1961; Visiting Prof. Yale Univ. 1964-65, 1967-68; Sather Prof. of Classical Literature, Univ. of Calif. at Berkeley 1969-70; Alexander White Visiting Prof. Univ. of Chicago 1972; Visiting Prof., Harvard Univ. 1976-77; Corresp. mem. Acad. of Athens, American Acad. of Arts and Sciences, Rheinisch-Westfälische Akad. der Wissenschaften, Accad. di Archeologia Lettere e belle Arti di Napoli; Hon. D.Hum.Litt. (Chicago) 1970, Hon. D.Phil. (Tel Aviv) 1984. *Publications:* Appendix to Aeschylus (Loeb Classical Library) 1957, Menandri Dyscolus (Oxford Classical Texts) 1960; Greek Studies in Modern Oxford 1961, The Justice of Zeus 1971, (ed.) Maurice Bowra: a Celebration 1974, Females of the Species 1975, Myths of the Zodiac 1978, Mythical Beasts 1980, Blood for the Ghosts 1982, Classical Survivals 1982, Supplementum Hellenisticum (with P. J. Parsons) 1983; translated Greek Metre 1962, Aeschylus Agamemnon, The Libation-Bearers and The Eumenides 1970; edited The Greeks 1962,

Tacitus 1964; articles and reviews in classical periodicals. *Address:* 15 West Riding, Wellesley, Mass. 02181, U.S.A. *Telephone:* (617) 237-2212 (U.S.A.).

LLOYD WEBBER, Andrew; British composer; b. 22 March 1948; s. of the late Dr. William Southcombe Lloyd Webber and of Jean H. Johnstone; m. 1st Sarah Jane Tudor (née Hugill) 1971 (divorced 1983), one s. one d.; m. 2nd Sarah Brightman 1984; ed. Westminster School; f. The Really Useful Co.; owns Aurum Press; Tony Award (for Evita) 1980, two Tony Awards (for Cats) 1983; Laurence Olivier Award 1986. *Works* (with lyrics by Timothy Rice): Joseph and the Amazing Technicolour Dreamcoat 1968, Jesus Christ Superstar 1970, Jeeves (with Alan Ayckbourn) 1975, Evita 1976 (stage version 1978), Tell me on a Sunday (with Don Black) 1979 (stage version 1982 with ballet of Variations), Cats (based on T. S. Eliot's Old Possum's Book of Practical Cats) 1981, Song and Dance (a Concert for the theatre) 1982, Starlight Express (with Richard Stilgoe) 1984, Requiem Mass 1985, The Phantom of the Opera (Tony Award for Best Musical 1988) (with Charles Hart) 1986, Aspects of Love 1989. *Film Scores:* Gumshoe 1971, The Odessa File 1974, Jesus Christ Superstar 1974; composed Variations (based on A minor Caprice No. 24 by Paganini) 1977. *Producer:* Daisy Pulls it Off 1983, The Hired Man 1984. *Publication:* Evita (with Timothy Rice) 1978, Joseph and the Amazing Technicolour Dreamcoat (with Timothy Rice) 1982. *Leisure interest:* architecture. *Address:* 20 Greek Street, London, W1V 5LF, England.

LLOYD WEBBER, Julian, A.R.C.M.; British cellist; b. 14 April 1951, London; s. of late Dr. William S. Lloyd Webber and of Jean H. Johnstone; m. Celia M. Ballantyne 1974; no c.; ed. Univ. Coll. School and Royal Coll. of Music; debut at Queen Elizabeth Hall 1972; debut with Berlin Philharmonic Orch. Feb. 1984; appears at major int. concert halls and has undertaken concert tours to many parts of Europe, North and South America, Australasia, Singapore and Japan; numerous television appearances and broadcasts in U.K., Netherlands, Africa, Germany, Scandinavia, France, Belgium, Spain, Australasia and U.S.A.; recordings include world premieres of Britten's 3rd Suite for Solo Cello, Bridge's Oration, Dvorak Concerto, Rodrigo's Cello Concerto, Holst's Invocation, Haydn's Cello Concerto No. 4, Sullivan's Cello Concerto, Vaughan Williams' Fantasia on Sussex Folk Tunes, brother Andrew Lloyd Webber's Variations which won gold and silver discs, Elgar's Cello Concerto (British Phonographic Industry Award for Best Classical Recording 1986). *Publications:* Frank Bridge, Six Pieces 1982, Young Cellist's Repertoire (3 vols.) 1984, Travels with my Cello 1984, Song of the Birds 1985, Recital Repertoire for Cellists 1986. *Leisure interests:* turtle keeping, Orient Football Club, topography (especially British). *Address:* c/o Kaye Artists Management, Kingsmead House, 250 Kings Road, London, SW3 6NR, England. *Telephone:* 01-376-3456.

LLUCH MARTÍN, Ernest; Spanish politician; b. 31 Jan. 1937, Vilassar de Mar; m.; three d.; ed. Univ. of Barcelona; f. Convergència Socialista; Parl. Spokesman for Socialistes de Catalunya group; worked for Banca Catalana and in town planning dept., Barcelona City Council; holds Chair of History of Econ. Ideas, Univ. of Barcelona; Minister of Health 1982-86, of Health and Consumer Affairs 1986; mem. Círculo de Economía and Economía Crítica; mem. jury Premi d'Honor de les Lletres Catalanes (Catalan arts prize). *Leisure interest:* reading. *Publication:* El pensament econòmic a Catalunya 1760-1840 1973. *Address:* c/o Ministerio de Sanidad, Paseo del Prado 18-20, Madrid, Spain (Office).

LOACH, Kenneth, B.A.; British film director; b. 17 June 1936, Nuneaton; s. of John Loach; m. Lesley Ashton 1962; three s. (one deceased) two d.; ed. King Edward VI School, Nuneaton, St. Peter's Hall (now Coll.), Oxford; BBC trainee, Drama Dept. 1963; freelance film dir. 1963-; Hon. D.Litt. (St. Andrews). *Films:* Poor Cow 1967, Kes 1969, In Black and White 1970, Family Life 1971, Black Jack 1979, Looks and Smiles 1981, Fatherland 1986. *Television:* Diary of a Young Man 1964, Three Clear Sundays 1965, The End of Arthur's Marriage 1965, Up the Junction 1965, Coming Out Party 1965, Cathy Come Home 1966, In Two Minds 1966, The Golden Vision 1969, The Big Flame 1970, After a Lifetime 1971, The Rank and File 1972, Days of Hope (four films) 1975, The Price of Coal 1977, The Gamekeeper 1979, Auditions 1980, A Question of Leadership 1980, The Red and the Blue 1983, Questions of Leadership 1983, Which Side are You on? 1984, The View from the Woodpile 1988. *Address:* c/o Central Independent Television, 46 Charlotte Street, London, W.1; c/o Judy Daish Associates, 83 Eastbourne Mews, London, W2 6LQ, England.

LOANE, Most Rev. Marcus Lawrence, K.B.E., M.A., D.D.; Australian ecclesiastic; b. 14 Oct. 1911, Waratah, Tasmania; s. of the late K. O. A. Loane; m. Patricia Knox 1937; two s. two d.; ed. The King's School, Parramatta, Univ. of Sydney, and Moore Theological Coll., Sydney; Resident Tutor and Chaplain, Moore Theological Coll., Sydney 1935-58, Vice-Prin. 1939-53, Prin. 1954-58; Canon, St. Andrew's Cathedral 1949-58; Bishop Co-adjutor, Diocese of Sydney 1958-66; Archbishop of Sydney and Metropolitan of New South Wales 1966-82, Primate of Australia 1978-82; Hon. D.D. (Wycliffe Coll., Toronto) 1958. *Publications:* Oxford and the Evangelical Succession 1951, Cambridge and the Evangelical Succession 1952, Masters of the English Reformation 1955, Life of Archbishop Mowll 1959, Pioneers of the Reformation in England 1963, Sons of the Covenant 1963, Makers of Our Heritage 1967, The Hope of Glory 1968, This Surpassing Excellence 1969, They Were Pilgrims 1970, By Faith We Stand 1971, They Overcame

1971, The King is Here 1973, Hewn from the Rock (lectures) 1976, This is My Son 1977, The God who Acts 1978, Makers of Puritan History 1981. *Leisure interest:* walking. *Address:* 18 Harrington Avenue, Warrawee, N.S.W. 2074, Australia.

LOBASHEV, Vladimir Mikhailovich; Soviet nuclear physicist; b. 29 July 1934, Leningrad; s. of Mikhail Ephimovitch Lobashev and Nina Vladimirovna Evropeitseva; m. Musa Romanovna Lobasheva; two s. two d.; ed. Leningrad Univ.; mem. CPSU 1970-; mem. of staff of Physical-Tech. Inst. 1957-72, Scientific Leader, Moscow Meson Factory Programme, Head, Experimental Physics Div. of Inst. for Nuclear Research at U.S.S.R. Acad. of Sciences, Leader, Lab. for Weak Interaction Study, Leningrad Inst. for Nuclear Physics 1972-; Corresp. mem. of U.S.S.R. Acad. of Sciences 1970-. *Address:* Institute for Nuclear Research, U.S.S.R. Academy of Sciences, 60th Anniversay October Revolution prospect 7a, 117312, Moscow, U.S.S.R. *Telephone:* 135-77-60 (Moscow); 298-35-38 (Leningrad).

LOBKOWICZ, Nicholas, DR.PHIL.; American political philosopher; b. 9 July 1931, Prague, Czechoslovakia; s. of Prince Jan Lobkowicz and Countess Marie Czernin; m. Countess Josephine Waldburg-Zeil 1953; three s. two d.; ed. Collegium Maria Hilf, Switzerland, Univs. of Erlangen and Fribourg; Assoc. Prof. of Philosophy, Univ. of Notre Dame, Ind. 1960-67; Prof. of Political Theory and Philosophy, Univ. of Munich 1967-, Dean School of Arts and Letters 1970-71, Rector Magnificus 1971-76, Pres. Univ. of Munich 1976-82; Pres. Catholic Univ. of Eichstätt 1984-; mem. Bd. of Dirs. Fed. Inst. of Int. and E. European Studies, Cologne 1972-75; mem. of Senate, W. German Rectors' Conf. 1976-82, Perm. Cttee. European Rectors' Conf. 1979-84, Council Int. Fed. of Catholic Univs. 1984-; founding mem. Int. Metaphysical Asscn.; mem. Cen. Cttee. of German Catholics 1980-84; mem. Ukrainian Acad. of Arts and Science (U.S.A.) 1979-; W. Europe Advisory Cttee. to Radio Free Europe/Radio Liberty 1980-; Pres. Freier Deutscher Autorenverband 1985-; mem. Pontifical Council for Culture 1982-; Pres. Czechoslovak Christian Acad. in Rome 1983-; Hon. D.H.L. (Wayne State Univ.); Hon. D.LL. (Univ. of Notre Dame); Dr.phil. h.c. (Seoul and Ukrainian Univ., Munich); Hon. Citizen Dallas, Tex. *Publications:* Theory and Practice 1967, Ende aller Religion? 1976, Marxismus und Machtergreifung 1978, Wortmeldung zu Staat, Kirche, Universität 1981, Irrwege der Angst 1983, Das europäische Erbe 1984, Das Konzil 1986, Geistige Wende 1987. *Leisure interest:* hunting. *Address:* Katholische Universität, 8078 Eichstätt, Federal Republic of Germany. *Telephone:* (08421) 20230.

LOBO, José Carlos; Mozambique diplomatist and former teacher; b. 14 Sept. 1942, Quelimane; s. of Carlos Lobo Chibaia and Catarina Carlos Ernesto; m. Iveth Venichand Lobo 1978; two c.; ed. California State Univ., U.S.A.; joined Mozambique Liberation Front (FRELIMO) in Tanzania 1964; Teacher and Dean of Students at Mozambique Inst., Dar es Salaam 1965-66; studied at Calif. State Univ., U.S.A. until 1973; Headmaster, FRELIMO Secondary School, Bagamoyo, Tanzania 1974-75; Headmaster, FRELIMO Secondary School, Ribaue, Mozambique 1975; Dir. of Int. Orgs. and Confs. Dept., Ministry of Foreign Affairs 1975-76; Perm. Rep. to UN 1976-83; mem. Cen. Cttee. FRELIMO 1983-; Minister of Mineral Resources 1983-84; mem. of People's Ass. 1983-; Vice-Minister of Foreign Affairs 1984-; FRELIMO 20th Anniversary Medallion. *Address:* c/o Ministry of Foreign Affairs, Maputo, Mozambique.

LØCHEN, Einar; Norwegian lawyer and diplomatist; b. 6 April 1918; m. Aud Sohnsen 1950; one s. one d.; ed. Oslo Univ., London School of Econs., Chicago Univ., Univ. of California; asst. judge 1945-46; Lawyer 1946-49; Asst. Adviser to Norwegian Ministry of Foreign Affairs 1949-51; Fellow of Chr. Michelsens Institutt, Bergen 1951-55; Counsellor to Norwegian Ministry of Foreign Affairs 1955-58; Perm. Rep. to Council of Europe 1958-63; Sec. Norwegian Del. to Nordic Council 1958-72; Judge, Norwegian Court of Appeal 1974, Norwegian Supreme Court 1977-. *Publications:* Norway's Views on Sovereignty 1955, A Comparative Study of Certain European Parliamentary Assemblies 1958, Norway in European Atlantic Co-operation 1964. *Address:* Møllebokken 1, Grini, Oslo 1, Norway.

LOCK, Thomas Graham, C.B.I.M.; British business executive; b. 19 Oct. 1931, Cardiff; s. of Robert H. and Morfydd (née Thomas) Lock; m. Janice O. B. (née Jones) 1954; two d.; ed. Whitchurch Grammar School, Univ. Coll. of S. Wales and Monmouthshire Coll. of Advanced Tech. (Aston) and Harvard Business School; Instructor Lieut. R.N. 1953-56; joined Lucas Industries Ltd. 1956; Production Foreman, Lucas Electrical Ltd. 1957-59, Factory Man. 1959-61; Dir. Girling Bremsen GmbH 1961-66; Overseas Operations Dir. Girling Ltd. 1966-73; Gen. Man. and Dir. Lucas Service Overseas Ltd. 1973-79; Man. Dir. Industrial Div. Amalgamated Metal Corpn. PLC 1979-83, Chief Exec. 1983-; Dir. (non-exec.) Evode Group PLC, Marshalls Universal PLC until June 1986; Fellow Inst. of Metals; Chartered Engineer; Freeman, City of London. *Leisure interests:* sailing, music, skiing. *Address:* Amalgamated Metal Corporation PLC, Adelaide House, London Bridge, London, EC4R 9DT (Office); The Cottage, Fulmer Way, Gerrards Cross, Bucks., SL9 8AJ, England (Home). *Telephone:* 01-626 4521 (Office); 0753 883200 (Home).

LOCKE, Edwin Allen, Jr., A.B.; American industrialist, banker and diplomatist; b. 8 June 1910, Boston, Mass.; s. of Edwin A. and Elizabeth Ferguson Locke; m. 1st Dorothy Q. Clark 1934 (divorced); two s. one d.;

m. 2nd Karin Marsh 1952; one s.; ed. Harvard Univ.; with Paris Branch, Chase Nat. Bank, N.Y. 1933-35, London Branch 1935-36, New York 1936-40; served in Office of Co-ordinator of Purchases, Advisory Comm. to Council of Nat. Defense 1940-41; Asst. Deputy Dir. Priorities Div., Office of Production Man. 1941; Deputy Chief Staff Officer Supply Priorities and Allocation Bd. 1941-42; Asst. to Chair. War Production Bd. 1942-44; Exec. Asst. to Personal Rep. of the Pres. 1944-45; Personal Rep. of the Pres., Washington and China 1945-46, Special Asst. to the Pres. March-Dec. 1946; Vice-Pres. of the Chase Nat. Bank, New York 1947-51; Trustee, China Medical Bd. Inc. 1947-80; apptd. Special Rep. of Sec. of State, with personal rank of Amb. to co-ordinate econ. and tech. assistance programmes in the Near East 1951-53; Pres. and Dir. Union Tank Car Co. 1953-63; Dir. Harris Trust and Savings Bank 1955-63; Dir. Federal Home Loan Bank of Chicago 1956-63, Chair. 1961-63; mem. special Presidential mission to Liberia and Tunisia; Pres. and Dir. Modern Homes Construction Co. 1963-67, Coastal Products Corpn. 1963-67; Dir. Manpower Inc. 1961-75, Warner Nat. Corpn. 1969-77, Nat. American Life Insurance Co. of Pa. 1968-85, Bankers Nat. Life Insurance Co. 1982-85, Nat. American Insurance Co. of New York 1981-85; Pres. and C.E.O. First City Fed. Savings Bank 1985-86; financial consultant and investment banker 1986-; Pres. and C.E.O. American Paper Inst. 1968-77; Pres. Econ. Club of New York 1977-85. *Address:* 321 East 48th Street, New York, N.Y. 10017, U.S.A.

LOCKHART, James, B.MUS., F.R.C.O.(CHM), F.R.C.M.; British conductor and music director; b. 30 Oct. 1930, Edinburgh; s. of Archibald C. Lockhart and Mary B. Lawrence; m. Sheila Grogan 1954; two s. one d.; ed. George Watson's Coll., Edin., Univ. of Edinburgh and Royal Coll. of Music; Asst. Conductor, Yorkshire Symphony Orchestra 1954-55; Repetiteur and Asst. Conductor, Städtische Bühnen Münster 1955-56, Bayerische Staatsoper, Munich 1956-57, Glyndebourne Festival Opera 1957-59; Dir. Opera Workshop, Univ. of Texas 1957-59; Repetiteur and Asst. Conductor, Royal Opera House, Covent Garden 1959-60, Conductor 1962-68; Conductor, Sadler's Wells Opera 1961-62; Prof. Royal Coll. of Music 1962-72; Musical Dir. Welsh Nat. Opera 1968-73; Generalmusikdirektor, Staatstheater Kassel 1972-80, Rheinische Philharmonie, Koblenz and Theater der Stadt Koblenz 1981-; Prin. Guest Conductor, BBC Concert Orchestra 1982-87; Dir. of Opera, Royal Coll. of Music 1986-. *Leisure interests:* driving fast cars, swimming, hill-walking. *Address:* 5400 Koblenz, Layer Strasse 47, Federal Republic of Germany; 105 Woodcock Hill, Harrow, Middx., HA3 0JJ, England. *Telephone:* (0261) 40 12 57 (Germany); 01-907 2112 (England).

LOCKSPEISER, Sir Ben, K.C.B., M.A., D.SC., F.I.MECH.E., F.ENG., F.R.S.A., F.R.AE.S., F.R.S.; British scientist; b. 9 March 1891, London; s. of Leon and Rose Lockspeiser; m. 1st Elsie Shuttleworth 1920 (died 1964), 2nd Mrs. M. A. Heywood 1966 (died 1984); one s. two d.; ed. Sidney Sussex Coll., Cambridge; Asst. Dir. Scientific Research, Ministry of Aircraft Production 1939, Deputy Dir. 1941, Dir. 1943; Dir.-Gen. Scientific Research (Air) Ministry of Supply 1946; chief scientist to Ministry of Supply 1946-49; Sec. Dept. of Scientific and Industrial Research 1949-56; Pres. European Org. for Nuclear Research 1955-57; Hon. Fellow Sidney Sussex Coll., Cambridge. *Leisure interests:* gardening and music. *Address:* Birchway, 15 Waverley Road, Farnborough, Hants., England. *Telephone:* (0252) 543021.

LOCKWOOD, David, B.SC., PH.D., F.B.A.; British university professor; b. 9 April 1929, Holmfirth, Yorks.; s. of Herbert Lockwood and Edith Annie Lockwood née Lockwood; m. Leonore Davidoff 1954; three s.; ed. Honley Grammar School, L.S.E.; Trainee, Victoria Textiles, Honley, Yorks. 1944-47; Nat. Service, Intelligence Corps, Austria 1947-49; Univ. of London Postgraduate Studentship in Econs. 1952-53; Asst. Lecturer and Lecturer in Sociology, L.S.E. 1953-60; Rockefeller Fellow, Univ. of Calif. (Berkeley), U.S.A. 1958-59; Univ. Lecturer, Faculty of Econs. and Fellow of St. John's Coll. Cambridge 1960-68; Visiting Prof., Dept. of Sociology, Columbia Univ., U.S.A. 1966-67; Prof., Dept. of Sociology, Univ. of Essex 1968-; Visiting Prof., Delhi School of Econs., India 1975; mem. Social Science Research Council, Chair. Sociology and Social Admin. Cttee. 1973-76. *Publications:* The Blackcoated Worker 1958, The Affluent Worker in the Class Structure, 3 vols. (jtly.) 1968-69; numerous articles in journals and symposia. *Leisure interest:* swimming. *Address:* University of Essex, Wivenhoe Park, Colchester, CO4 3SQ; 82 High Street, Wivenhoe, Essex, England. *Telephone:* (0206) 862286 (Univ.); (0206) 223530 (Home).

LOCKWOOD, Sir Joseph Flawith, Kt.; British businessman; b. 14 Nov. 1904, Southwell, Notts.; s. of Joseph Agnew and Mabel Lockwood; Man. flour mills in Chile 1924-28; Tech. Man. Henry Simon Ltd. in Paris and Brussels 1928-33; Dir. Henry Simon Ltd., Manchester 1933; Dir. Henry Simon, Buenos Aires and Chair. Henry Simon (Australia) Ltd., etc. 1945; Chair. EMI (fmrly. Electrical and Musical Industries) Ltd. 1954-74; Vice-Pres. Cen. School of Speech and Drama; Dir. South Bank Theatre Bd. 1968-84, Chair. 1977-84; Chair. Industrial Reorganization Corpn. 1969-71; Chair. Royal Ballet 1971-85. *Publications:* Provender Milling: the Manufacture of Feeding Stuffs for Livestock 1939, Flour Milling (in English, French, Spanish, German and Serbo-Croat) 1945. *Leisure interests:* walking, reading. *Address:* c/o National Westminster Bank, Southwell, Notts., England.

LODGE, David John, PH.D., F.R.S.L.; British professor of modern English Literature; b. 28 Jan. 1935; s. of William F. and Rosalie M. (née Murphy)

Lodge; m. Mary F. Jacob 1959; two s. one d.; ed. St. Joseph's Acad., Blackheath and Univ. Coll., London; British Council, London 1959-60; Asst. Lecturer in English, Univ. of Birmingham 1960-62, Lecturer 1963-71, Sr. Lecturer 1971-73, Reader 1973-76, Prof. of Modern English Literature 1976-87, Hon. Prof. 1987-; Harkness Commonwealth Fellow, 1964-65; Visiting Assoc. Prof. Univ. of Calif. (Berkeley) 1969; Henfield Writing Fellow, Univ. of E. Anglia 1977; Fellow, Univ. Coll. London 1982; Yorkshire Post Fiction Prize 1975; Hawthornden Prize 1976. *Publications:* novels: The Picturegoers 1960, Ginger, You're Barmy 1962, The British Museum is Falling Down 1965, Out of the Shelter 1970, Changing Places 1975, How Far Can You Go? 1980 (Whitbread Book of Year Award), Small World 1984, Nice Work 1988 (Sunday Express Book of the Year Award); four vols. of criticism. *Leisure interests:* tennis, television, cinema. *Address:* Department of English, University of Birmingham, Birmingham, B15 2TT, England. *Telephone:* (021)-472 1301.

LODGE, Geoffrey Arthur, PH.D., F.I.BIOL., F.R.S.A., F.R.S.E.; British professor of animal science; b. 18 Feb. 1930, Newcastle; s. of Capt. Arthur Lodge and Winifred R. Lodge; m. Thelma Calder 1956; one s. two d.; ed. Newcastle Royal Grammar School and Univs. of Durham and Aberdeen; Scientific Officer, Rowett Research Inst. Aberdeen 1954-59; Sr. Scientific Officer 1959-61; Lecturer, Animal Production, Univ. of Nottingham 1961-66, Reader 1966-68; Sr. Research Scientist, Animal Research Inst. Ottawa 1968-74, Prin. Research Scientist 1974-78; Prof. and Principal, Aberdeen School of Agric. 1978-86; Prof. of Animal Science, Sultan Qaboos Univ., Oman 1986-. *Publications:* Nutrition of the Young Pig (with Lucas) 1961, Growth and Development of Mammals (with Lamming) 1968; book chapters and over 100 other scientific publs. *Leisure interests:* food, malt whisky, travel, farming. *Address:* Sultan Qaboos University, P.O. Box 32484, Al Khod, Oman.

LOEB, John Langeloth, Jr., A.B., M.B.A.; American banker and diplomatist; b. 2 May 1930, New York; s. of John Langeloth and Frances (née Lehman) Loeb; one s. one d.; ed. Hotchkiss School, Harvard Univ.; with Loeb, Rhoades and Co., New York 1956-, Gen. Partner, mem. Man. Cttee. 1959-73, Man. Partner, Pres. 1971-73, Limited Partner 1973-; Chair. Bd. Holly Sugar Co., Colo. 1969-71; Special Adviser on Environmental Matters to Nelson A. Rockefeller (Gov. of New York) 1967-73; Amb. to Denmark 1981-83; del. to UN Gen. Ass. 1983-84; Hon. LL.D. (Georgetown Univ.) 1980. *Address:* 375 Park Avenue, Suite 807, New York, N.Y. 10152, U.S.A.

LOEHNIS, Anthony David, C.M.G., B.A.; British banker; b. 12 March 1936, London; s. of Sir Clive and Rosemary (née Ryder) Loehnis; m. Jennifer Forsyth Anderson 1965; three s.; ed. Eton Coll., New Coll., Oxford, Harvard School of Public Admin.; in Diplomatic Service 1960-66; with J. Henry Schroder Wagg and Co. Ltd. 1967-80 (seconded to Bank of England 1977-79); Assoc. Dir. Bank of England 1980-81, Exec. Dir. (Overseas Affairs) 1981-89; Group Exec. Dir., Vice-Chair. S. G. Warburg and Co. 1989-. *Address:* 1 Finsbury Avenue, London, EC2M 2PA, England. *Telephone:* (01) 606-1066.

LOFSTAD, Knut; Norwegian business executive and mechanical engineer; b. 30 April 1927, Aker; s. of Nils Lofstad and Margit Iversen; m. Anne-Lise Ravnsborg-Gjertsen 1960; one s. one d.; ed. Univ. of Wisconsin; Sales Engineer, A/S G. Hartmann 1950-61; Sales Man., Man. Dir. Eureka 1962-; Man. Dir. Thune Eureka 1969-81; Dir.-Gen. Fed. of Norwegian Industries 1982-. *Leisure interests:* skiing, hunting. *Address:* Drammensveien 40, 0225 Oslo 2/P.O.B. 2435-Solli, 0202 Oslo 2 (Office); Ankerveien 18, 0390 Oslo 3, Norway (Home). *Telephone:* 02-55 56 10 (Office); 02-14 18 32 (Home).

LOGACHEV, Nikolay Alekseyevich, D.MIN.SCI.; Soviet geologist and academic; b. 7 Oct. 1929, Novoshipunovo Village, Altai; s. of Aleksey and Marina Logachev; m. Tamara Kashkina 1948; one s. one d.; ed. Irkutsk Univ.; research at Inst. of Geology, Siberian Div. of Acad. of Sciences 1952-59; mem. CPSU 1959-; sr. researcher, head of lab. at Inst. of the Earth's Crust, Siberian Div. of Acad. of Sciences 1959-73; Deputy Chair. of Presidium of East Siberian Branch, Siberian Div. of Acad. of Sciences 1973-76; Dir. of Inst. of Earth's Crust 1976-; simultaneously Chair. of Presidium of East Siberian Br., Siberian Div. of Acad. of Sciences 1977-; mem. Supreme Soviet of U.S.S.R. 1979-(89); corresp. mem. of U.S.S.R. Acad. of Sciences 1979-84, mem. 1984-; State Prize 1978. *Leisure interest:* nature. *Address:* Institute of the Earth's Crust, Lermontov Street 128, Irkutsk 664033, U.S.S.R. *Telephone:* 464000.

LOGINOV, Vadim Petrovich; Soviet diplomatist; b. 1927, Leningrad; First Sec. of Leningrad Komsomol 1955-58; Sec. of U.S.S.R. Komsomol 1958-61; First Sec. of Vyborg City Cttee. of CPSU 1962-65; First Sec., Counsellor Embassy in U.S.A. 1968-71; Minister-Counsellor Embassy in Poland 1971-74; Head of Fourth European Dept., Ministry of Foreign Affairs 1974-78, Amb. to Angola 1978-83; Head of Fifth European Dept., Ministry of Foreign Affairs 1983-85; Vice-Minister of Foreign Affairs 1985-; cand. mem. CPSU Cen. Cttee. 1986-. *Address:* c/o Ministry of Foreign Affairs, Moscow, U.S.S.R.

LOGUNOV, Anatoly Alekseyevich; Soviet nuclear physicist; b. 30 Dec. 1926, Obsharovka, Kuibyshev Dist.; ed. Moscow Univ.; mem. CPSU 1960-; mem. of staff of Moscow Univ. 1951-56; Deputy Dir. of Lab. for Theoretical Physics at Inst. of Nuclear Research, Dubna 1956-63, Prof. 1961-; Dir. of Serpukhov Inst. of Higher Energies 1963-74; mem. U.S.S.R. Acad. of

Sciences; main research on quantum theory of the field and physics of elementary particles; Vice-Pres. of U.S.S.R. Acad. of Sciences 1974-; Deputy to Supreme Soviet 1974-; Rector of Moscow Univ. 1977-; Cand. mem. to Cen. Cttee. CPSU 1981-86, mem. 1986-; Order of Lenin and various medals. *Address:* U.S.S.R. Academy of Sciences, Leninsky Pr. 14, Moscow V-71, U.S.S.R.

LOHIA, Renagi Renagi, M.A.; Papua New Guinea diplomatist; b. 15 Oct. 1945, Tubesereia; m.; five c.; ed. Univ. of Papua New Guinea and London Univ.; Research Asst. Univ. of Papua New Guinea 1970-73, Sr. Tutor 1973, Lecturer in Education 1974-82, Pro Vice-Chancellor 1976, Deputy Vice-Chancellor 1977, Vice-Chancellor 1977-82; Chair. Public Services Comm. 1982-83; Special Asst. Dept. of Foreign Affairs 1985-87; Perm. Rep. to UN 1983-85, 1988-; mem. Govt. Cttee. Five Years Education Plan 1974; Chair. Educational Planning Cttee., Univ. of Papua New Guinea 1974-75; Education Faculty Rep. Jt. Cttee. on Teacher Education 1975-76. *Address:* Permanent Mission of Papua New Guinea to the United Nations, 100 East 42nd St, Room 1005, New York, N.Y. 10017, U.S.A. *Telephone:* (212) 682-6447.

LOHR, Helmut H. W., DR.OEC, DIPL. ING.; German engineer and business executive; b. 7 April 1931, Munich; s. of Eduard and Gertrud (Schnitzler) Lohr; m. Franziska Wiedemann 1959; two d.; ed. Munich Tech. Univ., Harvard Business School, U.S.A.; worked for Int. Switching Systems Dept. (FTZ), Deutsche Bundespost 1959; joined Standard Elektrik Lorenz AG 1965, Dir. 1974, Man. Dir. 1976-; Dir. Alcatel NV, Brussels (Vice-Pres. 1987-), Compagnie Générale d'Electricité, Paris (mem. Supervisory Bd. 1987-); Pres. ZVEI (German Electrical and Electronic Mfrs. Asscn.); Vice-Pres. BDI (Fed. Asscn. of German Industry); arrested on suspicion of tax evasion Jan. 1989; Hon. British Consul Gen.; Hon. Consul Gen. of Repub. of Indonesia. *Address:* Lorenzstrasse 10, 7000 Stuttgart 40, Federal Republic of Germany. *Telephone:* 0711-8211.

LOHSE, Eduard, D.THEOL.; German ecclesiastic; b. 19 Feb. 1924, Hamburg; s. of Dr. Walther Lohse and Dr. Wilhelmine Lohse (née Barrelet); m. Roswitha Flitner 1952; two s. one d.; ed. Bethel/Bielefeld and Göttingen; Pastor, Hamburg 1952; Privatdozent, Faculty of Protestant Theology, Mainz 1953; Prof. of New Testament, Kiel 1956, Göttingen 1964; Bishop of Hanover 1971-88; Pres. of the Council of the Evangelical Church in Germany 1979-85; mem. Göttingen Akad. der Wissenschaften; Hon. D.Theol. (Mainz) 1961, (Glasgow) 1983. *Publications:* Märtyrer und Gottesknecht 1955, Die Offenbarung des Johannes 1960, Die Texte aus Qumran 1964, Die Geschichte des Leidens und Sterbens Jesu Christi 1964, Die Briefe an die Kolosser und an Philemon 1968, Umwelt des Neuen Testaments 1971, Entstehung des Neuen Testaments 1972, Die Einheit des Neuen Testaments 1973, Grundriss der neutestamentlichen Theologie 1974, Die Urkunde der Christen 1979, Die Vielfalt des Neuen Testaments 1982, Die Ethik der Bergpredigt 1984, Kleine Evangelische Pastoralethik 1985, Theologische Ethik des Neuen Testaments 1988. *Leisure interest:* music. *Address:* Haarstrasse 6, 3000 Hannover 1, Federal Republic of Germany. *Telephone:* (0511) 8001-88/89.

LØKEN, Johan Christen; Norwegian farmer and politician; b. 27 July 1944, Heradsbygd, Hedmark; s. of Asbjørn and Tora Løken; m. Randi Øxseth Løken 1970; ed. Norwegian Coll. of Agric.; fmr. consultant, Norwegian Fed. of Industries and Norwegian Agric. Research Council; farmer, Heradsbygd, Elverum; mem. Elverum Municipal Council 1971-79, mem. Hedmark County Council 1979-81; Chair. Council, Norwegian Regional Devt. Fund 1978-81; proxy mem. Storting 1977-81, mem. 1981-; Minister of Agric. 1981-83; mem. Finance Cttee.; Chair. Cttee. of EFTA Parliamentarians; Conservative. *Address:* Stortinget, 0026 Oslo 1 (Office); 2433 Heradsbygd, Norway (Home). *Telephone:* (02) 313050 (Office); (064) 18382 (Home).

LOKOLOKO, Sir Tore, G.C.M.G., O.B.E.; Papua New Guinea politician; b. 21 Sept. 1930, Iokea, Gulf Province; s. of Paramount Chief Lokoloko Tore and Kevau-Sarufa; m. Lalahaia Meakoro 1950; four s. six d.; elected to House of Assembly (now Nat. Parl.) as Opposition mem. for Kerema (Gulf Province); Gov.-Gen. of Papua New Guinea 1977-83; Chair. Indosuez Niugine Bank 1983-89; K.St.J. *Leisure interests:* golf, fishing. *Address:* c/o Indosuez Niugine Bank, Burns House, Port Moresby, Papua New Guinea.

LOLLI, Ettore; Italian financier; b. 23 June 1908, Bologna; s. of Fausto and Ada (née Leoni) Lolli; ed. Rome Univ.; joined Società Romana di Elettrica as transmission line engineer 1930, advanced to gen. man. position in 1940s; with American Gas and Service Corpn. 1940-45; joined Italian Embassy and helped set up Deltec, official channel for econ. relations between Italy and U.S.A. 1945-50; joined Banca Nazionale del Lavoro 1950, organized its New York office, Vice-Dir.-Gen. 1966; Chief Exec. Officer, Riunione Adriatica di Sicurtà S.p.A. 1966-68, Chair. 1969-83, Hon. Chair. 1983-; Chair. Int. Advisory Bd., Banca Nazionale del Lavoro 1983-; Vice-Chair. Mfrs. Hanover Ltd., BNL Investment Bank PLC 1986-, Lavoro Bank A.G. (Zurich) 1987-; mem. Int. Advisory Bd., Kreditanstalt Vienna 1982-84; mem. Bd. British Olivetti Ltd. and of numerous other European and North American cos. and banks. *Address:* 70 Eaton Square, London, S.W.1, England. *Telephone:* 01-235 5617.

LOLLOBRIGIDA, Gina; Italian actress; b. 4 July 1927, Sibiaco; d. of Giovanni and Giuseppina Mercuri; m. Milko Skofic 1949; one s.; ed. Liceo Artistico, Rome; first screen role in Pagliacci 1947; has since appeared in numerous films including Campane a Martello 1948, Cuori senza Frontiere 1949, Achtung, banditi! 1951, Enrico Caruso 1951, Fanfan la Tulipe 1951, Altri Tempi 1952, The Wayward Wife 1952, Les belles de la nuit 1952, Pane, amore e fantasia 1953, La Provinciale 1953, Pane, amore e gelosia, La Romana 1954, Il Grande Gioco 1954, La Donna più Bella del Mondo 1955, Trapeze 1956, Notre Dame de Paris 1956, Solomon and Sheba 1959, Never So Few 1960, Go Naked in the World 1961, She Got What She Asked For 1963, Woman of Straw 1964, Le Bambole 1965, Hotel Paradiso 1966, Buona Sera Mrs. Campbell 1968, King, Queen, Knave 1972. *Publications:* Italia Mia (photography) 1974, The Philippines. *Leisure interest:* photography. *Address:* Via Appia Antica 223, 1-00178 Rome, Italy.

LOM, Herbert; British actor; b. 11 Sept. 1917, Prague, Czechoslovakia; theatre work in Prague before coming to England in 1939; joined the Old Vic theatre co.; entered films 1940; worked with BBC European Section 1940–46. *Films include:* Tomorrow We Live 1941, The Young Mr. Pitt 1942, The Dark Tower 1943, Night Boat to Dublin 1945, Appointment With Crime 1946, Good Time Girl 1947, Cage of Gold 1950, Star of India 1953, The Ladykillers 1955, War and Peace 1955, Passport to Shame 1958, North-West Frontier 1959, El Cid 1961, The Phantom of the Opera 1962, A Shot in the Dark 1963, Marrakesh 1965, Gambit 1966, Doppelganger 1968, The Picture of Dorian Gray 1970, Return of the Pink Panther 1974, The Pink Panther Strikes Again 1976, Charleston 1976, Revenge of the Pink Panther 1977, Trail of the Pink Panther 1981, Curse of the Pink Panther 1983, Dead Zone 1984, Memed My Hawk 1984, King Solomon's Mines 1985, Whoops Apocalypse, Going Bananas, Scoop 1986, Coast of Skeletons, Master of Dragonard Hill 1987. *Television appearances include:* The Human Jungle 1963, Hawaii Five-O 1971, The Acts of Peter and Paul 1980, Lace 1985. *Publication:* Enter a Spy, the Double Life of Christopher Marlowe 1978. *Address:* c/o Duncan Heath Ltd., Paramount House, 162 Wardour Street, London, W.1, England.

LOMAKIN, Viktor Pavlovich; Soviet politician and diplomatist; b. 1926; ed. Kuybyshev Polytechnic, and Moscow Industrial Inst.; Deputy Sec., Sec. of party cttee. of factory 1949–58; mem. CPSU 1953–; Second, First Sec. of Komsomolsk-na-Amur City Cttee., First Sec. of Khabarovsk CPSU District Cttee. 1958–67; work for CPSU Cen. Cttee. 1967–69; First Sec. of Primorskoy District Cttee. 1969–84; Amb. to Czechoslovakia 1984–; mem. of CPSU Cen. Cttee. 1971–; Deputy to U.S.S.R. Supreme Soviet, Hero of Socialist Labour 1981. *Address:* U.S.S.R. Embassy, Pod Kaštany 1, 160 00 Prague 6, Czechoslovakia.

LOMAKO, Pyotr Fadeyevich; Soviet metallurgist and government official; b. 12 July 1904; ed. Moscow Inst. of Non-Ferrous Metals and Gold; mem. CPSU 1925–; Engineer, Dir. of Plant, Man. of Trust in Non-Ferrous Metallurgy 1932–39; Deputy Minister of Non-Ferrous Metallurgy 1939–40, Minister 1940–48, 1950–53, 1954–57; Deputy Minister of Metallurgical Industry 1948–50, 1953–54; Deputy to U.S.S.R. Supreme Soviet 1946–50, 1954–; Chair. Krasnoyarsk Nat. Econ. Council 1957–61; mem. CPSU Cen. Cttee. 1961–; Deputy Chair. CPSU Cen. Cttee. Bureau for R.S.F.S.R. 1961–62; Deputy Chair. U.S.S.R. Council of Ministers and Chair. State Planning Cttee. (Gosplan) 1962–65; Minister of Non-Ferrous Metal Industry 1965–86; Deputy to Supreme Soviet; Order of Lenin (six times), Order of the Oct. Revolution and other decorations. *Address:* c/o U.S.S.R. Ministry of Non-Ferrous Metal Industry, 5-7 Ploshchad Nogina, Moscow, U.S.S.R.

LOMAX, Alan, B.A.; American collector of folk songs, radio, television and film producer/director, and musical anthropologist; b. 31 Jan. 1915, Austin, Texas; s. of John A. and Bess B. Lomax; m. 1st Elizabeth Harold 1937, 2nd Antoinette Marchand 1962; one d.; ed. Univ. of Texas, Harvard and Columbia Univs.; American Folk Music Library of Congress 1937–42; CBS 1939–44; Decca 1947–49; Research at Univ. of W. Indies 1962, Columbia 1963–; Dir. Cantometrics Project, Dept of Anthropology, Columbia Univ. 1963–, American Patchwork Project, Choreometrics Project; Fellow, American Folklore Soc., A.A.A.S. (1979); Pres. American Film Research Inst., American Anthropological Asscn.; many lectures, radio programmes and over 100 recordings of folk and primitive music; Ed., World Library Folk and Primitive Music, Columbia Records (19 vols.) 1951–57 and other series; Nat. Medal of Arts 1986. *Publications:* Harriett and her Harmonium, Mister Jelly Roll 1949, The Rainbow Sign 1959, Folk Songs of North America 1960, Penguin Book of American Folk Songs 1961, Folk Song Style and Culture 1968, 3,000 Years of Black Poetry (with R. Abdul) 1969; Co-ed. with John A. Lomax: American Ballads and Folk Songs 1934, Negro Folk Songs as Sung by Leadbelly 1936, Cowboy Songs 1937, Our Singing Country 1938, Folk Song U.S.A. 1946, Cantometrics: A Method in Musical Anthropology (audio-cassettes and handbook) 1977, World Dance and Movement Style (with Forrestine Paulay) and many articles. *Films:* Dance and Human History, Step Style, Palm Play (with Forrestine Panlay), Land where the Blues Began, The Longest Trail (Dir. and Ed.) 1984. *Leisure interests:* travel, the sea. *Address:* Cantometrics, 215 West 98th Street, 12-E, New York, N.Y. 10025, U.S.A.

LOMBARD, Jacques; French mining engineer and business executive; b. 12 July 1923, Auxerre; s. of Henri Lombard and Juliette Chapron; m. Arlette Drougard 1946; one s. two d.; Insp. of collieries, Bassin du Nord

and Pas de Calais 1945–53; Insp.-Gen. in commercial man. 1956; Asst. Business Dir. 1960; Dir. Sté. des Automobiles Peugeot 1964–74; mem. Bd. then Pres. Automobiles Citroën 1975–82, Vice-Pres., Dir.-Gen. 1982–; Chevalier, Légion d'honneur; Officier, Ordre Nat. du Mérite. *Leisure interest:* tennis. *Address:* 62 boulevard Victor-Hugo, 92208 Neuilly-sur-Seine, France.

ŁOMNICKI, Tadeusz; Polish actor and theatre director; b. 18 July 1927, Podhajce; s. of Marian and Jadwiga (née Kleinberger) Lomnicki; m. Maria Bojarska 1984; two s.; ed. Studio Theatrical School, Cracow, State Coll. of Theatrical Arts, Warsaw; Old Theatre, Cracow 1945–46; Wyspiański's Theatre, Katowice 1946–47; Słowacki's Theatre, Cracow 1947–49; Współczesny Theatre, Warsaw 1949–74; Narodowy Theatre 1974–75; Polski Theatre 1981–83; Studio Theatre 1984–; Pro-Rector, State Coll. of Theatrical Arts, Warsaw 1969–72, Rector 1972–81, Extraordinary Prof. 1972–; Dir. Teatr na Woli, Warsaw 1976–81; acts in films and TV; Deputy mem. Cen. Cttee. Polish United Workers' Party 1971–75, mem. 1975–81, mem. Varsovian Cttee. 1979–81, left the party 1981; mem. Presidium Cen. Board, Soc. for Polish-Soviet Friendship 1974–81 (left the soc.); Order of Banner of Labour 2nd Class, State Prize 1st Class 1968, 1978, Golden Prize for the Best Male Actor, Int. Film Festival, Moscow 1969; Golden Mask for Best Polish Actor 1970, Solidarity Cultural Prize 1986. *Roles include:* title role in The Resistible Rise of Arturo Ui, Edgar in Play Strindberg, Solony in Three Sisters, Prisypkin in The Bed-Bug by Majakovsky, Fool in Twelfth Night, Batarzeff in Minutes of Certain Meeting by Gelman (also dir.), Orestes in Iphigenie of Tauris, Goya in When Reason Sleeps by A. R. Vallejo, Stakh in Generation and Manager in Man of Marble (films), title role in Kordian by Słowacki, Jan and Anzelm in The First Day of Freedom by Kruczkowski (also dir.), Orestes in Iphigenie of Tauris, Goya in When Reason Sleeps by A. R. Vallejo, Batarzeff in Minutes of Certain Meeting by Gelman (also dir.), Bukar in A Performance of Hamlet by Brešan, Galileo Galilei in Life of Galileo by Brecht, Salieri in Amadeus, Krapp in Krapp's Last Tape, Father in Affabulazione by Pasolini; Pres. Starzyński in Anywhere You Are, Mr. President (film), Fior in operetta by Gombrowicz (W. Berlin); dir. To the Boneyard by Różewicz, The Two Gentlemen of Verona. *Publications:* Noah and his Menagerie 1948, Spotkania teatralne (The Theatre Meetings) 1984. *Address:* Ul. Piwna 21/23 m.2, 00-625 Warsaw, Poland.

LOMONOSOV, Vladimir Grigoryevich; Soviet politician; b. 20 June 1928, Mikhailovskoe, Khabavosk Oblast; ed. Moscow Steel Inst.; Asst. Foreman, Moscow Hammer and Sickle Iron Works 1953–58; mem. CPSU 1950–; Sec. Kalinin raion Cttee., Moscow, CPSU 1958–62; Head, Cen. Asian Bureau, CPSU Dec. 1962–65; Second Sec. Cen. Cttee. of CP of Uzbekistan 1965–76; mem. Bureau of Cen. Cttee. of CP of Uzbekistan 1965–76, CPSU Cen. Cttee. 1966–; Deputy to U.S.S.R. Supreme Soviet 1966–; Chair. U.S.S.R. State Cttee., Council of Ministers 1976–78, U.S.S.R. State Cttee. on Labour and Social Questions 1978–83; Vice-Chair. Planning and Budgetary Comm., Soviet of the Union; Order of Lenin (3 times), Order of October Revolution and other decorations. *Address:* c/o State Committee on Labour and Social Questions, Moscow, U.S.S.R.

LONCAR, Budimir; Yugoslav politician; Deputy Fed. Sec. for Foreign Affairs -1988, Fed. Sec. Feb. 1988–. *Address:* Federal Secretariat for Foreign Affairs, 11000 Belgrade, Kneza Milosa 24, Yugoslavia. *Telephone:* (011) 682555.

LONDON, Irving Myer, M.D.; American physician; b. 24 July 1918, Malden, Mass.; s. of Jacob A. London and Rose Goldstein; m. Huguette Piedzicki 1955; two s.; ed. Harvard Coll. and Harvard Medical School; Instructor, Assoc. Asst. Prof., Assoc. Prof. of Medicine, Columbia Univ. Coll. of Physicians and Surgeons 1947–55; Prof. and Chair. Dept. of Medicine, Albert Einstein Coll. of Medicine 1955–70; Prof. of Biology, M.I.T. 1969–; Dir. Harvard-M.I.T. Div. of Health Sciences and Technology 1969–85; Visiting Prof. of Medicine, Harvard Medical School 1969–72; Prof. of Medicine at Harvard Univ. and M.I.T. 1972–, Grover M. Hermann Prof. of Health Sciences and Tech. M.I.T. 1977–; Dir. Whitaker Coll. of Health Sciences, Tech. and Management, M.I.T. 1978–83, Johnson and Johnson 1982–; mem. Nat. Acad. of Sciences; Hon. D.Sc. (Univ. of Chicago); Theobald Smith Award in Medical Sciences (A.A.A.S.). *Publications:* numerous publications on the metabolism of erythrocytes and of haemoglobin 1948–. *Address:* Harvard-M.I.T. Div. of Health Sciences and Technology, 77 Massachusetts Avenue, Cambridge, Mass. 02139, U.S.A. *Telephone:* (617) 253-4030 (Office).

LONG, Gerald, B.A., C.B.I.M.; British journalist; b. 22 Aug. 1923, York; s. of Fred Harold and Sabina (Walsh) Long; m. Anne Hamilton Walker 1951; two s. three d.; ed. St. Peter's School, York, and Emmanuel Coll., Cambridge; served with British Army 1943–47; Reuters 1948–81, Corresp. in France, Germany and Turkey 1950–60, Asst. Gen. Man. 1960–63, Chief Exec. 1963–81, Gen. Man. 1963–73, Man. Dir. 1973–81; Chair. Visnews Ltd. 1968–79; Man. Dir. Times Newspapers Ltd. 1981–82; Deputy Chair. News Int. 1982–84; Chair. Exec. Cttee. Int. Inst. of Communication Ltd. 1973–78; Dir. Maxwell Media S.A. (France) 1987–; Exec. Dir. Journalists in Europe 1987–; mem. Design Council 1974–77; F.B.I.M. 1978; Commdr. Royal Order of the Phoenix (Greece) 1964, Grand Officier, Order of Merit (Italy) 1973, Commdr. Order of the Lion of Finland 1979, Chevalier, Légion d'honneur (France) 1979, Commdr.'s Cross, Order of Merit of the Fed. Repub. of Germany 1983. *Leisure interest:* cooking. *Address:* 15 rue d'Aumale, 75009

Paris (Home); 51 route de Caen, St.-Martin-des-Entrées, 41400 Bayeux, France (Home). *Telephone:* 48 74 67 26. (Paris); 31.92.47.12 (Bayeux).

LONG, Joan Dorothy, B.A.(HONS.), A.M.; Australian film producer; b. Victoria; d. of Francis C. Boundy and Katherine H. Robinson; m. Martin M. Long 1953; one s. one d., two steps s.; ed. Geelong High School and Melbourne Univ.; editing asst. Commonwealth film Unit 1948–51, film dir. 1952–53; home occupations 1954–63; freelance scriptwriter 1963–67, 1974–76; staff scriptwriter, Film Australia 1967–73; Man. Dir. Limelight Productions Pty. Ltd. 1975–; feature film producer 1976–; fmr. mem. Council, Australian Film and Television School, Interim Bd. to Australian Film Comm.; Chair. Nat. Film and Sound Archive Advisory Cttee. 1984–85; AWGIE Awards 1970, 1971, 1973; Vittoria de Sica Award 1980; wrote script for The Pictures that Moved 1968, The Passionate Industry (also Dir.) 1972, Paddington Lace 1970; screenplay for Caddie 1975; screenplay and producer, The Picture Show Man 1976; co-producer Puberty Blues 1981; producer Silver City 1984, Emerald City (play) 1987/88. *Publications:* The Pictures that Moved (with M.Long) 1982. *Leisure interests:* reading, history, jazz, gardening, the Bush. *Address:* 81 Bent Street, Lindfield, 2070, N.S.W., Australia. *Telephone:* 02/46 4078.

LONG, Marceau, L. ÈS L., L. EN D.; French civil servant; b. 22 April 1926, Aix-en-Provence, Bouches-du-Rhône; s. of Lucien Long and Marcelle Seymard; m. Josette Niel, 1946; two s. three d.; ed. Lycée Mignet, Univ. of Aix-en-Provence. École nat. d'administration; at Council of State 1952–57, 1975–, Vice-Pres. Feb. 1987–, apptd. auditor 1952, master of petitions 1957, Sec.Gen. to Govt. 1975–82, Counsellor of State on long-term secondment 1976–; apptd. Govt. Comm. 1957, Tech. Counsellor to Cabinet, Sec. of State on Tunisian and Moroccan Affairs, then Foreign Affairs, then Judicial Counsellor to French Embassy, Morocco 1958, Dir.-Gen. Admin. and Public Offices 1961–67, Sec. Gen. Admin. Ministry of Armies 1967–73, mem. Atomic Energy Cttee. 1975–82; Pres. Dir. Gen. Organisation de la radio et de la télévision françaises (O.R.T.F.) 1973–74; Pres.-Dir.-Gen. Cie. Air-Inter 1982–84; Pres.-Dir.-Gen. Cie. Air France 1984–87; lecturer Inst. d'études politiques de Paris, École nat. d'admin. 1963–68 (Chair. Bd. of Govs. 1987–); Admin. Crédit industriel et commercial bank 1982–87, Soc. de Gestion de participations aéronautiques 1985–; mem. numerous admin. councils and cttees.; Commdr., Légion d'honneur, Commdr. ordre nat. du Mérite. *Publications:* numerous contribs. to magazines and books on public office and law. *Address:* 22 avenue Noël, 94100 Saint-Maur-des-Fossés, France (Home).

LONG, Olivier, D.EN D., D.ÈS SC.POL.; Swiss diplomatist; b. 1915, Petit-Veyrier, Geneva; s. of Dr. Edouard Long and Dr. Marie Landry; m. Francine Roels 1946; one s. two d.; ed. Faculté de Droit and Ecole des Sciences Politiques à Paris and Univ. de Genève; with Int. Red Cross 1941–46; Foreign Affairs Dept., Berne 1946–49; Washington Embassy 1949–53; Div. of Commerce, Berne 1954–55; Govt. Del. for Commercial Agreements 1955–66; Head of Swiss Del. to European Free Trade Assen. (EFTA) 1960–66; Amb. to United Kingdom and Malta 1967–68; Dir.-Gen. GATT 1968–80; Prof. Graduate Inst. of Int. Studies Geneva 1962–85, mem. Int. Red Cross Cttee. 1980–; Pres. Inst. of Advanced Studies in Public Admin., Lausanne 1981–88; Trustee, Foundation for Int. Conciliation, Geneva 1984–. *Publications:* Law and Its Limitations in the GATT Multilateral Trade System 1987, Le Dossier Secret des Accords d'Evian–Une Mission Suisse Pour la Paix en Algérie 1988. *Leisure interests:* music, reading, skiing, swimming. *Address:* 6 rue Constantin, 1206 Geneva, Switzerland.

LONG, Russell B.; American lawyer and politician; b. 3 Nov. 1918, Shreveport, La.; s. of Huey Pierce Long and Rose McConnell; m. 2nd Carolyn Bason 1969; two d. by previous marriage; ed. Fortier High School and Louisiana State Univ.; served U.S. Navy 1942–45; in private legal practice 1945–48, Exec. Counsel to Gov. of Louisiana 1948; U.S. Senator from Louisiana 1948–86, Senate Majority Whip 1965–69; Chair. Finance Cttee. 1966–81; partner Long Law Firm, Washington and Baton Rouge 1987–; Democrat. *Address:* Long Law Firm, 1455 Pennsylvania Avenue, N.W., Washington, D.C. 20004, U.S.A.

LONGFORD, Countess of; Elizabeth Pakenham, C.B.E., F.R.S.L.; British writer; b. 30. Aug 1906, London; d. of N. B. Harman, F.R.C.S., and Katherine Chamberlain; m. Francis A. Pakenham (now Earl of Longford, q.v.) 1931; four s. four d. (one deceased); ed. Headington School, Oxford, and Lady Margaret Hall, Oxford; Parliamentary Candidate (Labour) Cheltenham 1935, Oxford 1950; Trustee Nat. Portrait Gallery 1967–78; mem. Advisory Bd., Victoria and Albert Museum 1969–75, Advisory Bd., British Library 1976–80; Hon. D.Litt. (Sussex) 1970; James Tait Black Prize for Victoria R.I. 1964; Yorkshire Post Book of the Year Prize for Wellington: The Years of the Sword 1969. *Publications:* Jameson's Raid 1959, Victoria R.I. 1964, Wellington: The Years of the Sword 1969, Wellington: Pillar of State 1972, Winston Churchill 1974, The Royal House of Windsor 1974, Byron's Greece (with photographer Jorge Lewinski) 1975, Byron 1976, Wilfred Scawen Blunt 1978, Louisa, Lady in Waiting to Queen Victoria and Queen Alexandra 1980, The Queen Mother 1981, Eminent Victorian Women 1981, Elizabeth R 1983, The Pebbled Shore: The Memoirs of Elizabeth Longford 1986, The Oxford Book of Royal Anecdotes (ed.) 1989. *Leisure interests:* Victoriana, gardening. *Address:* 18 Chesil Court, Chelsea Manor Street,

London, S.W.3; Bernhurst, Hurst Green, Sussex, England. *Telephone:* 01-352 7794 (London); (058 086) 248.

LONGFORD, 7th Earl of (cr. 1785); **Francis Aungier Pakenham** (cr. Baron 1945), K.G., P.C., M.A.; British politician and writer; b. 5 Dec. 1905; s. of 5th Earl of Longford; m. Elizabeth Harman (now Countess of Longford, q.v.) 1931; four s. four d. (one deceased); ed. Eton Coll. and New Coll., Oxford; Tutor, Univ. Tutorial Courses, Stoke-on-Trent 1929–31; with Conservative Party Econ. Research Dept. 1930–32; Lecturer in Politics, Christ Church, Oxford 1932; Student in Politics, Christ Church 1934–46 and 1952–64; Prospective Parl. Labour Candidate for Oxford City 1938; served Bucks. Light Infantry 1939–40; personal asst. to Sir William Beveridge 1941–44; Lord-in-Waiting 1945–46; Parl. Under-Sec. to War Office 1946–47; Chancellor of the Duchy of Lancaster 1947–48; Minister of Civil Aviation 1948–51; First Lord of the Admiralty May-Oct. 1951; Lord Privy Seal and Leader of House of Lords 1964–65, 1966–68; Sec. of State for Colonies 1965–66; Chair. Nat. Youth Employment Council 1968–71; fmr. Chair. Matthew Trust, Chair. Nat. Bank Ltd. 1955–62; Chair. Sidgwick and Jackson Ltd. (Publishers) 1970–80, Dir. 1980–85; Jt. Founder and Dir. The Help Charitable Trust 1986. *Publications:* Peace by Ordeal (The Anglo-Irish Treaty of 1921), Born to Believe 1953, The Causes of Crime 1958, Five Lives 1963, Humility 1969, De Valéra (with T. P. O'Neill) 1970, The Grain of Wheat 1974, The Life of Jesus Christ 1974, Abraham Lincoln 1974, Kennedy 1976, Francis of Assisi: A Life for All Seasons 1978, Nixon 1980, Ulster 1981, Pope John Paul II (biog.) 1982, Diary of a Year 1982, Eleven at No. 10: A Personal View of Prime Ministers 1931–84, 1984, One Man's Faith 1984, The Search for Peace 1985, The Bishops: A Study of Leaders in the Church today 1986, Saints 1987, A History of the House of Lords 1989. *Address:* Bernhurst, Hurst Green, Sussex; The Help Charitable Trust, 39/41 New Oxford Street, London, WC1A 1BH, England. *Telephone:* (058 086) 248; 01-352 7794 (London).

LONGMIRE, William Polk, Jr., M.D.; American physician; b. 14 Sept. 1913, Sapulpa, Okla; s. of William Polk and Grace M. (née Weeks) Longmire; m. Jane Jarvis Cornelius 1939; one s. two d.; ed. Univ. of Oklahoma, Johns Hopkins Univ.; Intern Surgery Johns Hopkins Hosp., Baltimore 1938–39, resident surgery 1944, Surgeon-in-Charge Plastic Out-Patient Clinic 1946–48, Surgeon 1947–48, Instructor, Asst. Prof., Assoc. Prof. Surgery 1943–48; Prof. of Surgery Univ. of California 1948–81, Prof. Emer. 1981–, Chair. Dept. 1948–76; Surgery Consultant Wadsworth VA Hosp., Los Angeles County Harbor Hosp. 1948–; Guest Prof. of Surgery Free Univ. of Berlin 1952–54; Visiting Prof. of Surgery Mayo Graduate School of Medicine 1968, Royal Coll. of Physicians and Surgeons of Canada 1968; mem. Conf. Cttee. on Graduate Educ. in Surgery 1959–66 (Chair. 1964–66); Chair. Surgery Training Cttee. N.I.H. 1969–70; Wade Visiting Prof. Royal Coll. of Surgeons, Edinburgh 1972; Surgeon Gen. U.S. Army 1961–; Ed. Advances in Surgery 1975–76; Ed. Bd. Annals of Surgery 1965–; Hon. M.D. (Athens) 1972, (Northwestern Univ.) 1976, (Lund) 1976; Fellow American Coll. of Surgeons; Hon. Fellow Assen. Surgeons of Great Britain and Ireland, Int. Soc. of Surgery, etc.; mem. Deutsche Gesellschaft für Chirurgie. *Address:* University of California Medical Center, Los Angeles, Calif. 90024 (Office); 10102 Empyrean Way, Building 8, Unit 203, Los Angeles, Calif. 90067, U.S.A. (Home).

LONGO, Pietro, B.L.; Italian politician; b. 29 Oct. 1935, Rome; s. of Leonardo L. and Rosa (née Fazio) Longo; m. Fernanda Parrini; ed. high school; mem. Youth Fed., Partido Socialista Italiano (PSI) 1951; head of Political Secr. of Pietro Nenni (Vice-Pres. Council of Ministers) 1964–68; mem. Chamber of Deputies 1968–72, 1976–87; mem. Chamber's Foreign Affairs Comm.; involved in reforming Partido Socialista Democratico (PSDI), mem. Party Nat. Political Office, Nat. Vice-Sec. 1972–78, Nat. Sec. 1978–85; Minister of the Budget 1983–84; Leader, Assen. for Devt. in the Mezzogiorno (SVIMEZ); Leader of Admin. Council of the Ente Nazionale per l'Energia Elettrica (ENEL); mem. Leaders' Council of the Centro Studi Investimenti Sociali (CENSIS). *Publications:* various studies on problems of S. Italy. *Address:* c/o Partito Socialista Democratico, Via Santa Maria in Via 12, 00187 Rome, Italy.

LONGUET-HIGGINS, Hugh Christopher, M.A., D.PHIL., F.R.S., F.R.S.E.; British university professor; b. 11 April 1923, Lenham, Kent; s. of the late Henry H. L. Longuet-Higgins and Albinia Cecil Bazeley; brother of Michael Selwyn Longuet-Higgins (q.v.); ed. Winchester Coll., and Balliol Coll., Oxford; Research Fellow Balliol Coll. 1947–48; Research Assoc. Univ. of Chicago 1948–49; Lecturer and Reader in Theoretical Chem., Victoria Univ. of Manchester 1949–52; Prof. of Theoretical Physics King's Coll., London Univ. 1952–54; Fellow, Corpus Christi Coll. and Prof. of Theoretical Chem., Univ. of Cambridge 1954–67; Royal Soc. Research Prof., Univ. of Edinburgh 1968–74, Univ. of Sussex 1974–, Harrison Memorial Prize 1950; F.R.S. 1958; Gov. of BBC 1979–84; Foreign mem. American Acad. of Arts and Sciences 1961; Foreign Assoc. U.S. Nat. Acad. of Sciences 1968–; Life Fellow, Corpus Christi Coll., Cambridge, Hon. Fellow, Balliol Coll., Oxford 1969, Wolfson Coll., Cambridge 1977; Dr. h.c. (Univ. of York) 1973, (Univ. of Essex) 1981, (Univ. of Bristol) 1983. *Publications include:* The Nature of Mind (Gifford Lectures) 1972, Mental Processes 1987, and about 200 papers in scientific journals. *Leisure interest:* music. *Address:* Centre for Research on Perception and Cognition, Laboratory of Experimental Psychology, University of Sussex, Falmer, Brighton, BN1 9QY, England. *Telephone:* (0273) 606755.

LONGUET-HIGGINS, Michael Selwyn, M.A., PH.D., F.R.S.; British research scientist; b. 8 Dec. 1925, Lenham, Kent; s. of the late Henry H. L. Longuet-Higgins and Albinia Cecil Bazeley; brother of Hugh Christopher Longuet-Higgins (q.v.); m. Joan R. Tattersall 1958; two s. two d.; ed. Winchester Coll., Trinity Coll., Cambridge Univ.; Research Fellow, Trinity Coll., Cambridge 1951-55, Commonwealth Fund Fellow, Scripps Inst., La Jolla, 1951-52; Research Scientist, Nat. Inst. of Oceanography 1954-67; Visiting Prof. M.I.T. 1958; Visiting Prof. Inst. of Geophysics, Univ. of Calif. 1961-62; Visiting Prof. Univ. of Adelaide 1963-64; Prof. of Oceanography, Oregon State Univ., Corvallis 1967-69; Royal Soc. Research Prof., Cambridge Univ. (joint appointment with Inst. of Oceanographic Sciences) July 1969-; Foreign Assoc. N.A.S. 1979-; Hon. LL.D. (Glasgow) 1979; Hon. D.Tech. (Tech. Univ. of Denmark) 1979; Fellow, Royal Soc. 1963, Sverdrup Gold Medal of American Meteorological Soc. 1983; Int. Coastal Eng. Award, American Soc. of Civil Engineers 1984. *Publications:* Contributions to scientific journals on physics and math. of the sea, especially ocean waves and currents. *Leisure interests:* music, gardening, mathematical toys. *Address:* Department of Applied Mathematics and Theoretical Physics, Cambridge University, Silver Street, Cambridge; Institute of Oceanographic Sciences, Wormley, Godalming, Surrey; Gage Farm, Comberton, Cambridge, CB3 7DH, England. *Telephone:* (022 026) 2346 (Home).

LOOIJEN, Anthony IJ. A., LL.M.; Netherlands international official; b. 26 Sept. 1921, Goes; m. Maria E. Westerveld 1955; two d.; ed. Leiden Univ.; worked in Ministry of Finance 1946-63; Financial Counsellor to Perm. Rep. to EEC 1963-70; mem. Cttees. of European Devt. Fund and European Agricultural Fund 1963-70; Dir. External Financial Relations Dept. of Ministry of Finance 1970-76; alt. mem. Werner Cttee. on European Econ. and Monetary Union 1970; mem. Bd., European Investment Bank 1971-76; Exec. Dir. World Bank (IBRD) representing Cyprus, Israel, Netherlands, Romania, Yugoslavia 1976-83; Verdienstorden (Fed. Repub. of Germany) 1964; Commdr. Ordre Nat. (Ivory Coast) 1965; Officer, Order of Orange Nassau 1969; Commdr. Order of Merit (Luxembourg) 1971; Order of Netherlands Lion 1976. *Address:* 5829 Midhill Street, Bethesda, Md. 20034, U.S.A. (Home).

LOOMIS, Henry, A.B.; American broadcasting executive and fmr. government official; b. 19 April 1919, Tuxedo Park, N.Y.; s. of Alfred Lee Loomis and Ellen Holman Farnsworth Loomis; m. 1st Mary Paul Macleod 1946, two s. two d.; m. 2nd Jacqueline C. Williams 1974; ed. Harvard Univ. and Univ. of California; U.S. Navy 1940-45; Asst. to the Pres., M.I.T. 1947-50; Asst. to Chair. of Research and Devt. Bd., Dept. of Defense, Washington, D.C. 1950-51; Consultant, Psychological Strategy Bd., Washington, D.C. 1951-52; mem. Staff, Pres. Cttee. on Int. Information 1953; Chief, Office of Research and Intelligence, U.S. Information Agency, Washington, D.C. 1954-57; Staff Dir. to Special Asst. to Pres. for Science and Tech., White House 1957-58; Dir. Broadcasting Service (Voice of America), U.S. Information Agency, Washington, D.C. 1958-65; Deputy U.S. Commr. of Educ., Dept. of Health, Educ. and Welfare, Washington, D.C. 1965-66; Partner, St. Vincent's Island Co., New York 1966-69; Deputy Dir. U.S. Information Agency, Washington, D.C. 1969-72; Pres. Corpn. for Public Broadcasting 1972-78; Rockefeller Public Service Award in Foreign Affairs 1963; Distinguished Service Award, U.S. Information Agency 1963. *Leisure interests:* sailing, hunting, fishing, skiing. *Address:* 5068 Yacht Club Road, Jacksonville, Fla. 32210, U.S.A.

ŁOPATKA, Adam, D.JUR.; Polish lawyer and politician; b. 10 Nov. 1928, Szlachcin Wielkopolska; s. of Stanislaw and Franciszka Łopatka; m. 1952; two s.; ed. Poznań Univ.; teacher, Poznań Univ. (now Adam Mickiewicz Univ.) 1950-74, Pro-Dean Law and Admin. Faculty 1962-64, Dean 1964-66, Asst. Prof. 1962-68, Dir. Inst. of Political Sciences 1967-72; Extraordinary Prof. 1968-73, Ordinary Prof. 1973-, Dir. Inst. for State and Law of Polish Acad. of Sciences, Warsaw 1969-87; Prof. Inst. for Fundamental Problems of Marxism-Leninism of Cen. Cttee. of Polish United Workers' Party (PZPR) 1975-87; mem. Polish Lawyers' Asscn. 1960-, Pres. 1972-81; Vice-Pres. Int. Assen. of Lawyers Democrats 1974-84; mem. Internal Acad. of Comparative Law 1976-, Exec. Cttee., Institut International des Droits de l'Homme 1976-, Exec. Cttee., Int. Assen. of Philosophy of Law and Social Philosphy 1975-; Polish del. to UN Comm. on Human Rights 1978-83; Deputy to Seym 1976-85, Chair. Seym Legis. Comm. 1976-80, Chair. Seym Comm. for Workers' Self-govt. Matters 1981-82, Vice-Chair. PZPR Deputies Club 1980-82; Minister, Chief of the Bureau for Denominational Affairs 1982-87; First Pres. Supreme Court 1987-; mem. PZPR 1953-, deputy mem. PZPR Cen. Cttee. 1971-80, mem. 1986-; Kt.'s Cross of Order of Polonia Restituta 1969, Order of Banner of Labour (2nd Class) 1975 (and 1st Class) and other decorations; UN Prize for outstanding achievements in the field of Human Rights 1988. *Publications:* about 300 articles on theory of state and law; Kierownicza rola partii komunistycznej w stosunku do państwa socjalistycznego 1960, Państwo socjalistyczne a związki zawodowe 1962, Wstęp do prawoznawstwa 1968, Organizacja społeczeństwa socjalistycznego w Polsce (co-author) 1968, Podstawowe prawa i obowiązki obywateli PRL (co-author) 1969, Ustrój polityczny PRL (co-author) 1981. *Address:* Sąd Najwyższy PRL, ul. Ogrodowa 6, 00-958 Warsaw; ul. Partyzantów 4 m.2, 00-629 Warsaw, Poland. *Telephone:* 20-39-75 (Office); 25-79-07 (Home).

LOPES, Henri; Congolese politician and author; b. 12 Sept. 1937, Léopold-ville, Belgian Congo (now Kinshasa, Zaire); s. of Jean-Marie Lopes and Micheline Vulturi; m. Nirva Pasbeau 1961; one s. three d.; ed. France; Minister of Nat. Educ. 1968-71, of Foreign Affairs 1971-73; mem. Political Bureau, Congolese Labour Party 1973; Prime Minister and Minister of Planning 1973-75, of Finance 1977-80; UN Asst. Dir.-Gen. for Programme Support 1982-86, UNESCO Asst. Dir.-Gen. for Culture and Communication 1986-; mem. du Haut Conseil de la Francophonie; Commdr. du Mérite Congolais, etc.; Prix littéraire de l'Afrique noire 1972, Prix SIMBA de littérature 1978, Prix de littérature du Président (Congo). *Publications:* Tribaliques (short stories), La Nouvelle Romance (novel), Learning to be (with others), Sans tam-tam (novel) 1977, Le Pleurer Rire (novel) 1982; author of nat. anthem. *Address:* UNESCO, 7 Place de Fontenoy, 75700 Paris, France (Home). *Telephone:* 45.68.43.75 (Home).

LOPES-GRAÇA, Fernando; Portuguese composer and writer; b. 17 Dec. 1906, Tomar; s. of Silverio Lopes-Graça and Emilia da Conceição Lopes-Graça; ed. Lisbon Conservatoire, Univs. of Lisbon, Coimbra and Paris; Professor, Instituto de Música (Coimbra) 1932-36, Acad. de Amadores de Música (Lisbon) 1940-54, 1980-. *Compositions include:* two piano concertos 1940, 1953, six piano sonatas 1934, 1939, 1952, 1961, 1977, 1981, Glosas (piano) 1949-50, Cuatro Canciones de Federico García Lorca (for baritone and chamber instrumental ensemble) 1954, Trois Danses Portugaises pour orchestre 1941, Sinfonia per Orchestra 1944, Estelas Funerárias 1948, Suite Rústica No. 1 (for Orchestra) 1950, 24 Preludes (piano) 1952-58, Concertino (for piano, brass, strings and percussion) 1956, História Trágico-Marítima, for baritone, fem. chorus and orch. 1943-60, Gabriela, Cravo e Canela (overture) 1960, Prelude and Fugue (violin solo) 1961, Canto de Amor e de Morte (orch.) 1961, Poema de Dezembro (orch.) 1961, Para uma Criança que vai Nascer (for strings) 1961, Mar de Setembro (cycle for voice and piano) 1962, Concertino for Viola and Orchestra 1962, In Memoriam Bela Bartok (8 suites for piano) 1959-64, First String Quartet 1964, 9 Cantigas de Amigo (for voice and chamber instrumental ensemble) 1964, Four Sketches (for strings) 1965, Concerto da camera col violoncello obbligato 1965, Quatorze Anotações (for string quartet) 1966, D. Duardos e Flérida (cantata-melodrama in two parts for narrator, mezzo-soprano, alto, tenor, chorus and orchestra) 1966-69, Prelúdio e Baileto, Partita (for guitar) 1968, 1971, Four Pieces (for harpsichord) 1971, Requiem pelas vítimas do fascismo em Portugal (for soloists, chorus and orchestra) 1978, Sinfonietta (Homenagem a Haydn) 1980, Sete Predicações d'Os Lusiadas (for tenor, baritone, male chorus and twelve wind instruments) 1980, Sete Apotegmas (for oboe, viola, double bass and piano) 1981, Second String Quartet 1982, Dez Novos Sonetos de Camões (voice and piano) 1984, Dançares (ballet) 1984, In Praise of Peace (orchestra) 1986, Tre Equali (for double-bass) 1986, Cantos de Mágoa e Desalento, Nove Odes de Ricardo Reis, Quatro Momentos de Alvaro de Campos (voice and piano) 1987. *Publications include:* Reflexões sobre a Música 1941, Introdução à Música Moderna 1942, Música e Músicos Modernos 1943, A Música Portuguesa e os seus Problemas (Vol. I) 1944, (Vol. II) 1959, Talia, Euterpe e Terpsicore 1945, A Canção Popular Portuguesa 1954, Dicionário de Música (Vol. I) 1956, (Vol. II) 1958, Igor Stravinsky and Bela Bartok 1959, Musicália 1960, Nossa Companheira Música 1964, Páginas Escolhidas de Crítica e Estética Musical 1967, Disto e Daquilo 1973, A Música Portuguesa e os seus Problemas (Vol. III) 1974, Um artista intervem, Cartas com alguma moral 1974, Escritos musicólogicos 1977, and translations of Rousseau, Mann, Keller, Mörike, Percy Buck, Alan Bush, Haskell, Romain Rolland, Balzac. *Address:* El Mio Paraiso, 2°, Ave. da República, 2775 Parede, Portugal. *Telephone:* 2472824.

LÓPEZ, Salvador P.; Philippine journalist, diplomatist and educationist; b. 27 May 1911, Currimao, Ilocos Norte; s. of Bernabe P. López and Segunda Sinang; m. 1st Maria Luna 1936 (died 1986); two d.; m. 2nd Adelaida Escobar 1986; ed. Univ. of the Philippines; columnist, Magazine Ed. and Assoc. Ed. Philippines Herald 1933-41; Radio News Commentator 1940-41; Philippine Army Service 1942-46; Diplomatic Service 1946-; Adviser on Political Affairs, Philippine Mission to UN 1946-48, Sr. Adviser 1948-49, Chargé d'affaires a.i. 1950-52, Acting Perm. Rep. to UN 1953-54; Minister to France 1955-56, concurrently Minister to Belgium and Netherlands 1955-59, to Switzerland 1957-58, Amb. to France 1956-62, concurrently Perm. Rep. to UNESCO 1958-62, Minister to Portugal 1959-62; Under-Sec. of Foreign Affairs, Philippines 1962-63; Sec. of Foreign Affairs 1963-64; Perm. Rep. to UN 1964-68, concurrently Amb. to U.S.A. 1968-69; Perm. Rep. to UN 1986-88; Pres. Univ. of the Philippines 1969-75, Prof. 1975-86; Chair. Philippine chapter, Int. PEN 1978-86; Consultant UN Univ., Tokyo 1979-81; numerous decorations and hon. degrees. *Publications:* Literature and Society 1941, Freedom of Information 1953, English for World Use 1954, The United States— Philippines Colonial Relationship 1966, Human Rights and the Constitution 1970, The Philippines Under Martial Law 1974, New Directions in Philippine Foreign Policy 1975, Reflections on Human Rights in the Philippines 1977, The Philippines into the 21st Century 1979, Aspects of International Intellectual Co-operation 1980. *Leisure interests:* classical music, reading.

LÓPEZ ARELLANO, Gen. Oswaldo; Honduran air force officer and politician; b. 30 June 1921; ed. School of Mil. Aviation and Flight Training, U.S.A.; joined armed forces 1939, Lieut. 1947, Col. 1958; Chief of Armed Forces 1956-75; mem. Mil. Junta, Chief of Mil. Govt. of Honduras, Minister of Nat. Defence, Minister of Public Security 1963-66; Pres. of Honduras 1966-71, 1972-75; now Pres. Servicio Aéreo de Honduras, Transportes

Aéreos Nacionales; several decorations. *Address:* Servicio Aéreo de Honduras, Apdo 129, Tegucigalpa, D.C., Honduras.

LOPEZ-COBOS, Jesus, D.PHIL.; Spanish orchestral conductor; b. 25 Feb. 1940, Toro; s. of Lorenzo Lopez and Gregoria Cobos; m. 2nd Karin Lopez-Cobos 1982 (died 1986); two s.; m. 3rd 1987; ed. Madrid Univ. (philosophy), Madrid Conservatory (composition) and Vienna Acad. (conducting); worked with major orchestras including London Symphony, Royal Philharmonic, Philharmonia, Concertgebouw, Vienna Philharmonic, Vienna Symphony, Berlin Philharmonic, Hamburg NDR, Munich Philharmonic, Cleveland, Chicago Symphony, New York Philharmonic, Philadelphia, Pittsburgh Symphony; conducted new opera productions at La Scala, Milan, Covent Garden, London and Metropolitan Opera, New York; recordings include Donizetti's Lucia di Lammermoor, Rossini's Otello and recital discs with José Carreras; Gen. Musikdirektor, Deutsche Oper, Berlin 1981–(91); Prin. Guest Conductor London Philharmonic Orchestra 1981–86; Prin. Conductor and Artistic Dir., Spanish Nat. Orchestra 1984–(89); Music Dir., Cincinnati Symphony Orchestra 1986–(90); First Prize, Besançon Int. Conductors' Competition 1969; Prince of Asturias Award (Spanish Govt.) 1981, Founders Award, American Soc. of Composers, Authors and Publrs. 1988. *Address:* c/o Terry Harrison Artists, 9a Penzance Place, London W11 4PE, England. *Telephone:* 01-221 7741.

LÓPEZ DE LETONA Y NÚÑEZ DEL PINO, José María; Spanish politician; b. 26 Nov. 1922, Burgos; m.; three c.; Road Engineer until 1949; Technical Eng. Dir. Vías y Construcciones S.A. 1952–54, Dir.-Gen. 1954–60; associated with Westinghouse Air Brake Co. and affiliated cos. in Spain and Europe 1960–65; Sub-Commissary to Social and Econ. Devt. Plan 1966; Minister of Industry 1969–74; Gov. Bank of Spain 1976–78; Vice-Chair., Man. Dir. Banco Español de Crédito 1986–; mem. Cortes; Pres. Asociación de Empresas Constructoras de Ambito Nacional (SEOPAN); Chair. Bank of Madrid, Rank Xerox Española, S.A.; man. several industrial corpns.; Grand Cross, Carlo III, Isabel la Católica, Merito Civil. *Address:* Banco Español de Crédito, Paseo de la Castellana 7, 28046 Madrid, Spain. *Telephone:* 261 53 88.

LÓPEZ-GARCÍA, Antonio; Spanish artist; b. 1936, Tomelloso; m. María Moreno; ed. Escuela de Bellas Artes de San Fernando, Madrid; travelled in Italy and Greece 1955, 1958; one-man exhbns. in Madrid 1957, 1961, Staempfli Gallery, New York 1965, 1968–69, Paris, Turin 1972; group exhbns. in Madrid 1955, 1964, World Fair Exhbn., New York 1964, Carnegie Int., Pittsburgh 1965, 1967, European tour of Contemporary Spanish Art exhbn. 1968, 1969; Prize of Diputación de Jaén 1957, Prize of Fundación Rodríguez Acosta 1958, Molino de Oro Prize of Exposición Regional de Valdepeñas 1959. *Address:* c/o Marlborough Fine Art Ltd., 6 Albemarle Street, London, W.1, England.

LOPEZ-IBOR, Juan José, M.D.; Spanish professor of psychiatry; b. 17 Dec. 1941, Madrid; s. of Juan J. López-Ibor Sr. and Socorro Alino; m. Cristina Alcocer 1967; four c.; ed. Madrid and Frankfurt Univs. and St. Bartholomew's Hosp., London; Asst. Prof. of Psychiatry, Madrid Univ. 1962–72; Head Prof. of Psychiatry, Oviedo Univ. 1972–73, Salamanca Univ. 1973–77, Alcalá de Henares Univ. 1982–; Head, Psychiatric Unit, Ramón y Cajal Hosp. 1977–; Pres. Spanish Psychiatry Soc. 1978–80; Pres. Int. Coll. of Psychosomatic Medicine 1985; Temporary Adviser WHO 1984–; hon. mem. World Psychiatric Asscn. *Publications:* Los Equivalentes Depresivos 1972, 1978, El Cuerpo y la Corporalidad 1974, Las Depresiones 1976, Tratado de Psiquiatría 1982, 1984. *Leisure interests:* skiing, water skiing. *Address:* Avenue Nueva Zelanda 44, E-28035 Madrid, Spain. *Telephone:* (91) 216-2740 and (91) 216-2840.

LÓPEZ MICHELSEN, Alfonso; Colombian lawyer and politician; b. 30 June 1913, Bogotá; s. of Alfonso López Pumarejo (Pres. of Colombia 1934–38, 1942–45) and María Michelsen; m. Cecilia Caballero de López; ed. London, Brussels, Colegio Mayor de Nuestra Señora del Rosario, Bogotá, Santiago (Chile) and Georgetown Univ., Washington, D.C., U.S.A.; fmr. Teacher at Univ. Nacional de Colombia, Univ. Libre de Bogotá and Colegio Mayor de Nuestra Señora del Rosario; legal practice; spent seven years as emigré in Mexico 1952–58; later an Ed. of El Liberal (weekly); mem. Chamber of Deputies 1960–62, 1962–66; Founder, Leader of moderate wing of Movimiento Revolucionario Liberal 1958–67; joined Partido Liberal 1967, Leader 1982; Gov. of César Dept. 1967–68; Minister of Foreign Affairs 1968–70; Pres. of Colombia 1974–78. *Publications:* Introduction to the Study of the Colombian Constitution 1942, Benjamín Constant or the Father of Bourgeois Liberalism 1946, Colombian Inquiries, The Elected (novel). *Address:* c/o Partido Liberal, Avda. Jiménez 8-56, Bogotá, Colombia.

LÓPEZ-PORTILLO Y PACHECO, José; Mexican lawyer and politician; b. 16 June 1920, Mexico City; s. of José López-Portillo y Weber; m. Carmen Romano; one s. two d.; ed. Law Nat. Faculty, Univ. Nacional Autónoma de México, Univ. de Chile; Prof. of Gen. Theory on the State, Univ. Nacional Autónoma de México 1954, Assoc. Prof. of Political Sciences 1956–58; Founder Prof. in Admin. Sciences Doctorate, Comm. School of the Nat. Polytechnical Inst. 1961; with Partido Revolucionario Institucional (PRI) 1959–64; Technical Assoc., Head Office of Ministry of Patrimony 1960; Co-ordinator Border Urban Devt. Cttee. 1962; mem. Intersecretarial Comm. for Nat. Devt. 1966; Under-Sec. of the Presidency 1968; Under-

Sec. Ministry of Patrimony 1970; Gen. Dir. Electricity Fed. Comm. 1972–73; Sec. for Finances and Public Credit 1973–75; Pres. of Mexico 1976–82; fmr. Gov. for Mexico, IMF; Order Nacional do Cruzeiro do Sul (Brazil) 1978. *Publications:* Valoración de la Estatal, Génesis y Teoría del Estado Moderno, Quetzalcoatl, Don Q. *Address:* c/o Palacio de Gobierno, México, D.F., Mexico.

LÓPEZ RODÓ, Laureano; Spanish lawyer, government official and university professor; b. 18 Nov. 1920, Barcelona; s. of Laureano López and Maria Teresa Rodó; ed. Univ. de Barcelona, Univ. de Madrid; Prof. Admin. Law, Univ. de Santiago de Compostela 1945–53, Univ. de Madrid 1953–; Technical Sec.-Gen. Office of the Pres. 1956–62; Pres. and founder Escuela Nacional de Administración Pública; Commr. for the Devt. Plan 1962, also Minister without Portfolio 1965–73; Minister for Foreign Affairs 1973–74; Amb. to Austria 1974–77; Pres. Int. Inst. of Admin. Sciences; Councillor Superior Council for Scientific Investigation; M.P.; del. to numerous int. congresses; mem. Interparl. Union, Real Academia de Ciencias Morales y Políticas, Academia de Ciencias Económicas y Financieras, Academia de Jurisprudencia y Legislación, Int. Social Science Council of UNESCO; Dr. h.c. (Univ. de Coimbra, Portugal, Univ. of Aix-en-Provence, France). *Address:* Calle de Alcalá 73, 28009 Madrid, Spain.

LÓPEZ TRUJILLO, H.E. Cardinal Alfonso; Colombian ecclesiastic; b. 8 Nov. 1935, Villahermosa, Ibague; ordained priest 1960; Titular Bishop of Boseta with personal title of Archbishop 1971–; Archbishop of Medellín 1979–; Pres. Latin American Conf. of Bishops; Pontifical Comm. for Latin America (CELAM); mem. Sacred Congregation for the Doctrine of the Faith, Secr. for Non-believers; cr. Cardinal 1983. *Address:* Arzobispado, Calle 57, N. 48-28, Medellín, Colombia. *Telephone:* 317980.

LORA TAMAYO, Manuel; Spanish chemist; b. 1904, Jerez de la Frontera; m. Amelia D'Ocon; eleven c.; Prof. of Organic Chem., Seville 1933–43; fmr. Prof. of Organic Chem., Madrid; Minister of Educ. 1962–68; Pres. Higher Council for Scientific Research 1967; Dir. Nat. Centre of Organic Chem.; mem. Acad. of Pharmacy, Nat. (now Royal) Acad. of Exact, Physical and Natural Sciences 1968–, Pres. 1974, Hon. Pres. 1985; Hon. mem. Pontificia Acad. Rome, Acad. of Science Lisbon, Heidelberg, Argentina, Puerto Rico; Hon. mem. various scientific socs.; fmr. Pres. Royal Spanish Soc. of Physics and Chem.; mem. Int. Union Pure and Applied Chem.; Dr. h.c. Paris. *Address:* Real Academia de Ciencias Exactas, Físicas y Naturales, Valverde 22 y 24, Madrid, Spain.

LORANC, Władysław, H.H.D.; Polish politician and journalist; b. 5 Dec. 1930, Bierna; s. of Jan Loranc and Julia Loranc; m.; one d.; ed. Philology Faculty of Jagellonian Univ., Cracow; mem. youth orgs. Polish Pathfinders' Union 1945–49, Polish Youth Union 1948–54; mem. Polish United Workers' Party (PZPR) 1952–; Asst., Sr. Asst. Jagellonian Univ., Cracow 1953–57; functionary, Science and Educ. Dept. of PZPR Voivodship Cttee., Cracow 1957–68; journalist of Polish Radio, Cracow 1968–71; functionary, Science and Educ. Dept. of PZPR Cen. Cttee. 1971–72; Deputy Chair. Polish Radio and TV Cttee. 1972–73; Under-Sec. of State, Ministry of Culture and Art 1974–81; Chair. Polish Radio and TV Cttee. 1981–82; Head, Ideology Dept. of PZPR Cen. Cttee. 1982–87; Minister and Head of Office for Denominational Affairs 1987–; mem. Atheists' and Free-Thinkers' Asscn., subsequently Soc. for Dissemination of Lay Culture 1956–; mem. Polish-Soviet Friendship Soc. 1952–; mem. Polish Journalists' Asscn. 1968–81, Journalists' Asscn. of People's Poland 1982–; Officer's Cross of Order of Polonia Restituta, Gold Cross of Merit and other decorations. *Publications:* about 350 articles, 10 books including monographs on artists Marian Konieczny and Czesław Rzepiński, Marksistowski pogląd na świat 1974, Sztuka i społeczeństwo w programach leterackich i artystycznych polskiego modernizmu 1975, Kultura i świat robotniczy 1980, Stare upiory w najnowszych dziejach Polski 1987. *Leisure interests:* reading belle-lettres and philosophy, gardening. *Address:* Urząd do spraw Wyznań, ul. Krakowskie Przedmieście 50, 00-325 Warsaw, Poland.

LORANT, Stefan; American author and editor; b. 22 Feb. 1901, Budapest, Hungary; m. Laurie Robertson 1963 (divorced 1978); two s.; started career as film cameraman in Vienna; Ed. Das Magazin Berlin 1925; Ed. Bilder Courier Berlin 1925, Ufa Magazin Berlin 1926, Münchner Illustrierte Presse 1928–33; in "protective custody" following Hitler's accession to power; upon release came to England where he founded Weekly Illustrated 1934, Lilliput (Ed. 1937–40), Picture Post (Ed. 1938–40); now in U.S.A.; LL.D. (Knox Coll.), D.Litt. (Syracuse Univ.); M.A. (Harvard). *Publications:* Wir vom Film 1928, I was Hitler's Prisoner 1935, Chamberlain and the Beautiful Llama 1940, The United States (ed.) 1940, Lincoln: His Life in Photographs 1941, The New World 1946, F.D.R.: A Pictorial Biography 1950, The Presidency 1951, Lincoln, a Picture Story of Life 1952 (revised and enlarged 1957, 1969), The Life of Abraham Lincoln 1954, The Life and Times of Theodore Roosevelt 1959, Pittsburgh: The Story of an American City (revised, Bicentennial edn.) 1964 (revised enlarged edns. 1975, 1980, 1988), The New World: The First Pictures of America 1946, Sieg Heil! An Illustrated History of Germany from Bismarck to Hitler 1974, The Glorious Burden: The American Presidency from George Washington to James Earl Carter Jr. 1976, The Years Before Hitler 1988, I Lived Six Lives (autobiography) 1988, Mark, I Love You (memorial) 1989. *Address:* "Farview", Lenox, Mass. 01240, U.S.A.

LORD, Alan, C.B., B.A.; British business executive; b. 12 April 1929, Rochdale, s. of Frederick and Ann (née Whitworth) Lord; m. Joan Ogden 1953; two d.; ed. Rochdale Grammar School and St. John's Coll., Cambridge; Admin. Civil Servant, Inland Revenue 1950–59; H.M. Treasury 1959–62; Principal Private Sec. to First Sec. of State 1962–63; Commr. Inland Revenue 1969, Deputy Chair. Bd. 1971–73; Principal Finance Officer, Depts. of Industry, Trade and Prices 1973–75; Second Perm. Sec. H.M. Treasury 1975–77; Man. Dir. Dunlop Int. Ltd. 1978–79; Exec. Dir. Dunlop Holdings PLC 1978–79, Man. Dir. and C.E.O. 1980–84, Deputy Chair. and C.E.O. of Lloyds March 1986–; Non-Exec. Dir. Allied-Lyons PLC 1979–86; Dir. Bank of England 1983–86, Dunlop Olympic, Australia; Gov. Nat. Inst. of Econ. and Social Research (NIESR) 1978–; Fellow, Plastics and Rubber Inst. *Publication:* A Strategy for Industry (Sir Ellis Hunter Memorial Lecture, Univ. of York 1976), Earning an Industrial Living (Johnian Soc. Lecture 1985). *Leisure interest:* gardening. *Address:* Mardens, Hildenborough, Tonbridge, Kent, England. *Telephone:* (0732) 832268.

LORD, Winston, B.A.; American civil servant and diplomatist; b. 14 Aug. 1937, New York; s. of Oswald Bates and Mary (Pillsbury) Lord; m. Bette Bao 1963; one s. one d.; ed. Yale Univ., Fletcher School of Law and Diplomacy and Tufts Univ.; mem. Staff Congressional Relations, Politicomil. and Econ. Affairs, U.S. Dept. of State, Washington 1962–64, Geneva 1965–67; mem. staff Int. Affairs, U.S. Dept. of Defense, Washington 1967–69; mem. staff Nat. Security Council, Washington 1969–73, Special Asst. to Asst. to Pres. on Security Affairs 1970–73; Dir. Policy Planning Staff, U.S. Dept. of State, Washington 1973–77; Pres. Council on Foreign Relations 1977–85; Amb. to People's Repub. of China 1985–89; mem. Bd. of Dirs. Atlantic Council of U.S.A., Center for Int. Relations, Americas Soc. *Address:* 740 Park Avenue, New York, N.Y. 10021, U.S.A. (Home).

LOREN, Sophia; Italian actress; b. 20 Sept. 1934, Rome; d. of Riccardo Scicolone and Romilda Villani; m. Carlo Ponti (q.v.) 1957; two s.; ed. Scuole Magistrali Superiori; first screen appearance as an extra in Quo Vadis; has appeared in many Italian and other films including E Arrivato l'Accordatore 1951, Africa sotto i Mari (first leading role), La Tratta delle Bianche, La Favorita 1952, Aida 1953, Il Paese dei Campanelli, Miseria e Nobiltà, Il Segno di Venere 1953, Tempi Nostri 1953, Carosello Napoletano 1953, L'Oro di Napoli 1954, Attila 1954, Peccato che sia una canaglia, La Bella Mugnaia, La Donna del Fiume 1955, Boccaccio 1970, Matrimonio All'Italiana; and in the following American films: The Pride and the Passion 1955, Boy on a Dolphin, Legend of the Lost 1956, Desire Under the Elms 1957, That Kind of Woman 1958, Houseboat 1958, The Key 1958, The Black Orchid 1959, It Started in Naples, Heller in Pink Tights 1960, The Millionairess 1961, Two Women 1961, El Cid 1961, Madame Sans Gêne 1962, Yesterday, Today and Tomorrow 1963, The Fall of the Roman Empire 1964, Lady L 1965, Operation Crossbow 1965, Judith 1965, A Countess from Hong Kong 1965, Arabesque 1966, More than a Miracle 1967, The Priest's Wife 1970, Sunflower 1970, Hot Autumn 1971, Man of La Mancha 1972, Brief Encounter (TV) 1974, The Verdict 1974, The Voyage 1974, The Cassandra Crossing 1977, A Special Day 1977, Firepower 1978, Brass Target 1979, Blood Feud 1981, Two Women 1989; Chair. Nat. Alliance for Prevention and Treatment of Child Abuse and Maltreatment; Venice Festival Award for The Black Orchid 1958, Cannes Film Festival Award for best actress (Two Women) 1961. *Publications:* Eat with Me 1972, Sophia Loren on Women and Beauty 1984. *Address:* Chalet Daniel Burgenstock, Luzern, Switzerland.

LORENTE DE NÓ, Rafael, M.D.; American (naturalized) physiologist; b. 8 April 1902, Zaragoza, Spain; s. of Francisco Lorente and Maria de Nó (de Lorente); m. Hede Birfield 1931; one d.; ed. Univ. of Madrid; Asst. Inst. Cajal, Madrid 1921–29; Head, Dept. of Otolaryngology, Valdecilla Hosp. Santander 1929–31; went to U.S. 1931; neuroanatomist, Cen. Inst. for the Deaf, St. Louis 1931–36; Assoc. physiologist, Rockefeller Inst., New York 1936–38, Assoc. mem. 1938–41, mem. 1941–72; Visiting Prof. Univ. of Calif. (Los Angeles) 1972–82; mem. N.A.S., American Physiological Soc., American Neurological Soc.; hon. mem. American Otological Soc., American Acad. of Arts and Sciences. *Publications:* A Study of Nerve Physiology 1947, The Primary Acoustic Nuclei 1981, and articles in scientific journals. *Address:* 5066 N. Pueblo Villas Drive, Tucson, Ariz. 85704, U.S.A. *Telephone:* (602) 293-5179.

LORENTZ, Stanisław, PH.D.; Polish art historian and museum administrator; b. 28 April 1899, Radom; s. of Karol Lorentz and Maria Schoen; m. Irene Nasfeter 1927 (died 1983); two d.; ed. Warsaw Univ.; Lecturer, Vilno Univ. 1929–35, Warsaw Univ. 1935–39; Dir. Nat. Museum, Warsaw 1935–82; Dir.-in-Chief, Museums and Conservation of Monuments Dept., Ministry of Culture and Art 1945–51; Extraordinary Prof. of Art History, Warsaw Univ. 1947–51, Prof. 1951–69, Emer. 1969–; M.P. 1965–69; Pres. Centre Int. d'Etudes pour la Conservation et la Restoration des Biens Culturaux 1965–70; Pres. Polish Nat. Cttees. of Int. Council of Museums and of Int. Council of Monuments and Sites, mem. Int. Exec. Cttee. of ICOM; Pres. Int. Consultative Cttee. of ICOMOS; Vice-Pres. Polish Nat. UNESCO Cttee.; Pres. Soc. of Friends of Warsaw 1965–; Corresp. mem. Polish Acad. of Sciences 1952–64, mem. 1964–; mem. Acad. of Fine Arts, Venice 1955, Bordeaux 1971; Hon. mem. Int. Union of Art Historians 1970; Dr. h.c. (Bordeaux) 1961, (Nancy) 1966; Herder Prize 1964, Polish State Prize 1964, City of Kiel Cultural Prize (Fed. Repub. of Germany) 1973,

hon. Gold Award of League for Friendship of Nations (G.D.R.) 1978, Alfred Jurzykowski Foundation Award (New York) 1979, Special State Prize 1979; Gold Cross of Merit 1936, Virtuti Militari 1939, Commdr.'s Cross with Star of Order Polonia Restituta 1947, Order of the Banner of Labour 1st Class 1955, Order of the Builders of People's Poland 1969; also has other Polish and foreign awards from Italy, France, Mexico, etc. *Publications:* Jan Krzysztof Glaubitz architekt wileński XVIII w. 1937, Natolin 1948, Victor Louis à Varsovie 1958, Relazioni artistiche fra l'Italia e la Polonia 1961, Jabłonna 1961, What remained of the Royal Palace in Warsaw 1971, Guide to Polish Museums and Collections 1971, 1974, Le Château Royal de Varsovie 1973, Pałac Prymasowski w Warszawie 1982, Architekt Szreger 1986, Album Wileńskie 1986, Walka o Zamek 1986 and numerous other works in Polish, French and English. *Address:* c/o Muzeum Narodowe, Aleje Jerozolimskie 3, 00-495 Warsaw, Poland. *Telephone:* 29-30-93.

LORENTZEN, Annemarie Røstvik; Norwegian politician; b. 23 Sept. 1921, Grense Jakobselv, Finnmark; teacher, Hammerfest Secondary School 1947–49; mem. Hammerfest Municipal Council 1951–63; Chair. W. Finnmark Labour Party 1961–65; mem. Labour Party Nat. Exec. 1961–69; mem. Norwegian Broadcasting Council 1963–70, many parl. cttees.; mem. Storting (Parl.) for Finnmark 1961–; mem. Standing Cttee. on Defence 1969–73; Minister of Communications 1973–76, of Consumer Affairs and Govt. Admin. 1976–78; Amb. to Iceland 1978–86; Labour. *Address:* c/o Ministry of Foreign Affairs, P.O. Box 8114, Dep., Oslo 1, Norway.

LORENZ, (Hermann Clemens) Werner, DR.IUR.; German professor of law; b. 15 Nov. 1921, Lichtenstein; s. of Dr. Rudolf Lorenz and Gabriele Sonntag; m. Dr. Gerda Weber 1957; three s.; ed. Univs. of Heidelberg and Oxford; lecturer in Law, Univ. of Heidelberg 1957; Prof. of Law, Univ. of Würzburg 1958–65; Prof. of Int. and Comparative Law, Univ. of Munich 1965–, Dean, Faculty of Law 1967–69, Dir. Inst. of Int. Law 1983–86; Pres. Int. Asscn. of Legal Science 1987–; Dr. h.c. (Copenhagen) 1985. *Publications:* Vertragsabschluss und Parteiwille im internationalen Obligationenrecht Englands 1957, Unjust Enrichment 1979, Contracts for Work and Labour and Building Contracts 1980; numerous essays in law journals and Festschriften. *Leisure interests:* literature, playing the piano, skiing. *Address:* Lochhamer Strasse 34, 8032 Graefelfing, Federal Republic of Germany. *Telephone:* 089-853089.

LORENZ, Siegfried; German politician; b. 26 Nov. 1930, Annaberg; m.; two c.; ed. Karl Marx Univ., Leipzig; mem. Berlin City Council 1958–67; mem. Cen. Council of Free German Youth 1959–74; Dir. Youth Dept. of Cen. Cttee. of Socialist Unity Party (SED) 1966–76; cand. mem. Cen. Cttee. SED 1967–71, mem. 1971–; mem. Politburo of SED 1986–; Deputy to Volkskammer (Parl.) 1963–, Chair. Youth Exec. of Volkskammer 1966–76; numerous decorations including Karl Marx Order, Vaterländische Verdienstorden, Banner of Labour. *Address:* Karl-Marx-Stadt, Karl-Marx-Allee 12, German Democratic Republic. *Telephone:* 6550.

LORENZEN, Paul Peter Wilhelm, DR.RER.NAT.; German professor of philosophy; b. 24 March 1915, Kiel; s. of Dr. Max Rosenkranz and Lisa Moehlmann; m. Kaethe Dalchow 1939; one d.; ed. Univs. of Kiel, Berlin and Göttingen; Asst. Prof. of Math. Bonn 1939; Research Fellow, Univ. of Cambridge 1948–49; Prof. of Philosophy, Univ. of Kiel 1956–62; guest mem. Inst. for Advanced Studies, Princeton, N.J. 1957–58; Prof. of Philosophy, Univ. of Erlangen 1962–80; Visiting professorships in Oxford, Moscow, Stanford, Austin (Tex.) and Boston; mem. Akad. der Wissenschaften, Göttingen; Dr. h.c. (Rio de Janeiro) 1973, (Boston) 1985. *Publications:* Einführung in die operative Logik und Mathematik 1955, Formale Logik 1958, Die Entstehung der exakten Wissenschaften 1960, Metamathematik 1962, Differential und Integral 1965, Normative Logic and Ethics 1969, Elementargeometrie 1984, Grundbegriffe technischer und politischer Kultur 1985, Lehrbuch der konstruktiven Wissenschaftstheorie 1987. *Address:* Charlottenburger Strasse 19, 3400 Göttingen, Federal Republic of Germany. *Telephone:* 7993018.

LORENZO, Francisco A., B.A., M.B.A.; American airlines executive; b. 19 May 1940, New York; s. of Olegario and Ana (née Mateos) Lorenzo; m. Sharon Neill Murray 1972; ed. Columbia Univ. and Harvard Univ.; Financial Analyst TransWorld Airlines 1963–65; Man. Financial Analysis Eastern Airlines 1965–66; Founder, Chair. of Bd. Lorenzo, Carney & Co., N.Y. 1966–; Chair. of Bd. Jet Capital Corpn., Houston 1969–; Pres. Texas Int. Airlines Inc. 1972–80, Chair. Exec. Cttee. 1980–; Pres. Texas Air Corpn. 1980–85, Chair., C.E.O. 1986–; Chair. N.Y. Airlines 1980–87, Continental Airlines Corpn., Houston 1982–, Eastern Air Lines Inc., Miami 1987–; Chair. Bd. of Dirs. Eastern Airlines (in receivership April 1989). *Address:* Eastern Airlines Inc., Miami International Airport, Miami, Fla. 33148, U.S.A.

LORIMER, George Huntly, PH.D., F.R.S.; British scientist; b. 14 Oct. 1942; s. of Gordon Lorimer and Ellen Lorimer; m. Freia Schulz-Baldes 1970; one s. one d.; ed. George Watson's Coll. Edinburgh and Univ. of St. Andrews, Univ. of Illinois, Michigan State Univ.; scientist, Max-Planck Society, Berlin, 1972–74; Research Fellow, Inst. for Advanced Studies, Canberra 1974–77; Research Leader, Cen. Research Dept., E.I. Du Pont de Nemours & Co. 1978–; scientist, Soc. for Environmental Research, Munich 1977. *Leisure interests:* philately, music. *Address:* 2025 Harwyn Rd, Wilmington, Del. 19810, U.S.A. *Telephone:* (302) 695-4584 (Office); (302) 475-6748 (Home).

LORIMER, Sir (Thomas) Desmond, Kt.; British chartered accountant and business executive; b. 20 Oct. 1925; s. of Thomas Berry Lorimer and Sarah Ann Lorimer; m. Patricia Doris Samways 1957; two d.; ed. Belfast Tech. High School; chartered accountant 1948, practised 1952-74; Sr. Partner, Harmood, Banner, Smylie & Co., Belfast 1960; Chair. Lamont Holdings PLC 1973-; Dir. Ruberoid PLC 1972-88, Northern Bank Ltd. 1983-, Chair. 1985-; Dir. Irish Distillers PLC 1986-, Old Bushmills Distillery 1986-; Chair. Industrial Devt. Bd. for Northern Ireland 1982-86; Fellow Inst. of Chartered Accountants in Ireland, Pres. 1968-69; Chair. Ulster Soc. of Chartered Accountants 1960, Northern Ireland Housing Exec. 1971-75; mem. Review Body on Local Govt. in Northern Ireland 1970. *Leisure interests:* gardening, golf. *Address:* Windwhistle Cottage, 6A Circular Road West, Cultra, Holywood, Co. Down, BT18 0AT, Northern Ireland. *Telephone:* (023 17) 3323.

LORIOD, Yvonne; French pianist; b. 20 Jan. 1924, Houilles; d. of Gaston and Simone (née Bilhaut) Loriod; m. Olivier Messiaen (q.v.) 1961; Prof. of Piano, Conservatoire National de Musique, Paris; specializes in interpretation of complete works including Bach's Well-Tempered Klavier, Beethoven sonatas, Mozart piano concertos, works of Chopin and Debussy and complete works of Olivier Messaien; first performances in Paris of Bartok's 1st and 2nd concertos, Schoenberg concerto and works by Messiaen, Jolivet, Boulez and other contemporary composers; Officier, Légion d'honneur; Officier des Arts et Lettres; 7 Grand Prix du Disque. *Address:* C.S.N.M., 14 rue de Madrid, 75008 Paris, France.

LORSCHEIDER H.E. Cardinal Aloisio; Brazilian ecclesiastic; b. 8 Oct. 1924, Linha Geraldo, Porto Alegre; ordained priest 1948; Bishop of Santo Angelo 1962-73; Archbishop of Fortaleza 1973-; cr. Cardinal 1976; mem. Sacred Congregation for the Clergy, for Religious Orders and Secular Insts., Secr. for Non-Christians; entitled S. Pietro in Montorio. *Address:* Arcebispado, C.P. 9, 60000 Fortaleza, Ceará, Brazil. *Telephone:* 26.6503.

LOSONCZI, Pál; Hungarian politician; b. 18 Sept. 1919, Bolhó, County Somogy; agricultural labourer; mem. CP 1945-; set up Red Star Co-operative Farm, Barcs 1948; MP 1953-; Minister of Agric. 1960-67; Chair. Nat. Council of Co-operative Farms 1965-67; Pres. of Presidential Council 1967-87; mem. Cen. Cttee. Hungarian Socialist Workers' Party 1975-89, Political Cttee. 1975-87; mem. Presidium of Nat. Council of Patriotic People's Front; Kossuth Prize 1956; Hero of Socialist Labour and Order of Merit of the Hungarian People's Repub. 1954, Order of the October Revolution (U.S.S.R.) 1979. *Publication:* Erősödő népi-nemzeti egység, békés egymásmellett élés (Strengthening Popular National Unity, Peaceful Co-existence) 1985. *Address:* The Presidential Council, H-1357 Budapest, Kossuth tér 1, Hungary. *Telephone:* 121-754.

LOTMAN, Yuriy Mikhailovich; Soviet scholar and structuralist; b. 28 Feb. 1922, Petrograd (now Leningrad); s. of Mikhail and Aleksandra Lotman; m. Zara Mints 1950; three s.; ed. Leningrad Univ.; Prof. of Russian Literature at Tartu (fmrly. Dorpat) State Univ., Estonian S.S.R. 1963-; Leader of Semiotics Summer Schools 1962, 1964, 1968, 1970; Corresp. Fellow, British Acad. 1977; Vice-Pres. Int. Asscn. for Semiotic Studies; Hon. mem. Semiotic Soc. of America 1977; mem. Modern Language Asscn. of America 1986, Norwegian Acad. *Publications:* Lectures on Structural Poetics 1964 (Eng. trans. 1968), The Structure of the Literary Text 1970, Analysis of the Poetic Text: Verse Structure 1972, Semiotics of Film 1973, Ansätze zur Theorie und Methodologie der Literatur und Kunst 1974, Semiotica e Cultura (with B. A. Uspenskij) 1975, Tipologia della cultura 1975, Pushkin's Novel in Verse "Eugene Onegin" 1975, Semiotica dell'arte e della Cultura 1980, Kunst als Sprache 1981, Aleksander Pushkin: A Biography 1981, L'Asimmetria e il dialogo nelle strutture pensanti 1985, Creation of Karamzin 1987; over 300 articles and works on eighteenth- and early nineteenth-century Russian literature and on structuralism and semiotics. *Address:* Tartu State University, Tartu, Ülikooli 18, Estonia, U.S.S.R.

LOTON, Brian Thorley, B.MET.E.; Australian business executive; b. 17 May 1929, Perth; s. of late Sir Thorley Loton; m. Joan Kemelfield 1956; two s. two d.; ed. Hale School, Perth, Trinity Coll., Melbourne Univ.; started as Cadet, Broken Hill Pty. Co. Ltd. 1954, Tech. Asst. to Production Superintendent 1959, Asst. Chief Engineer 1961, Gen. Man. Planning and Devt. 1969, Dir. 1969-82, Man. Dir. 1982-, C.E.O. 1985-; Gen. Man., Newcastle Steelworks 1970, Exec. Gen. Man. Steel Div. 1973, Dir. 1976, Chief Gen. Man. 1977; Dir. BHP, Elders IXL Ltd., Woodside Petroleum Ltd.; Deputy Chair. Defence Industry Cttee.; Pres. Australian Mining Industry Council 1983-84; mem. Faculty of Eng., Melbourne Univ. 1980-83, Dept. of Immigration and Ethnic Affairs Advisory Cttee. 1980-82, mem. and Councillor Australian Inst. of Mining and Metallurgy, fmr. mem. Australian Science and Tech. Council 1977-80; Fellow, A.I.M., Inst. of Dirs. in Australia, Australian Acad. of Tech. Sciences; Hon. Fellow, Inst. of Engineers Australia; mem. Bd. Int. Iron and Steel Inst.; Int. Counsellor, The Conf. Bd. 1984-. *Address:* c/o P.O. Box 86A, Melbourne, Victoria, Australia 3001. *Telephone:* 60-0701.

LOTT, Felicity Ann, B.A., F.R.A.M.; British singer; b. 8 May 1947, Cheltenham; d. of John A. Lott and Whyla Lott (née Williams); m. 1st Robin Golding 1973 (divorced), 2nd Gabriel Woolf 1984; one d.; ed. Pate's Grammar School for Girls, Cheltenham, Royal Holloway Coll., Univ. of London and Royal Acad. of Music; début English Nat. Opera 1975, Glyndebourne 1977; has sung prin. roles Covent Garden, Glyndebourne, English Nat. Opera, Welsh Nat. Opera, Scottish Nat. Opera, Paris Opera, Brussels, Hamburg, Munich, Chicago; wide recital repertoire; founder mem. Songmakers' Almanac; concert tour Australia 1985; recordings include St. Matthew Passion (Bach), Messiah (Handel), Sacred Music by Vivaldi, Complete Mélodies of Ravel, Louise (Charpentier), French songs. *Leisure interests:* reading, gardening. *Address:* c/o Lies Askonas Ltd., 186 Drury Lane, London, WC2B 5RY, England. *Telephone:* 01-405 1808/9.

LOTT, Trent, B.P.A., J.D.; American politician; b. 9 Oct. 1941, Grenada, Miss.; s. of Chester P. and Iona (née Watson) Lott; m. Patricia E. Thompson 1964; one s. one d.; ed. Univ. of Mississippi; called to Miss. Bar 1967; Assoc. Bryan & Gordon, Pascagoula, Miss. 1967; Admin. Asst. to Congressman Colmer 1968-73; mem. 93rd-100th Congresses from 5th Dist. Miss., Repub. Whip 97th and 98th Congresses; Senator for Miss. 1989-; named as observer from House to Geneva Arms Control talks; mem. American Bar Asscn.; recipient Golden Bulldog award, Guardian of Small Business award; Republican. *Address:* U.S. Senate, Washington, D.C. 20515, U.S.A.

LOUCHHEIM, Katie S.; American government official; b. 28 Dec. 1903, New York; d. of Leonard B. and Adele Scofield (née Joseph); m. Walter C. Louchheim 1926; two d.; ed. Rosemary Hall, and Columbia Univ.; Asst. to Dir. of Public Information, UNRRA 1942-46; Democratic Nat. Committeewoman D.C. 1956-61; Dir. Women's Activities, Democratic Nat. Cttee. 1953-60; Vice-Chair. Democratic Nat. Cttee. 1956-60; Special Consultant to Promote the Role of Women in Int. Cultural Exchange Matters, State Dept. 1961-62; Deputy Asst. Sec. of State for Public Affairs 1962-63; mem. Defense Advisory Cttee. on Women in the Armed Services 1955-62; Deputy Asst. Sec. of State for Community Advisory Services 1964-66, for Educ. and Cultural Affairs 1966-69; American Nat. Red Cross 1966-; mem. Arthur and Elizabeth Schlesinger Library on History of Women in America, Radcliffe Coll. 1964-; mem. First Lady's Cttee. on Beautification 1965-68, Arts Council, M.I.T. 1974, Visiting Comm., School of Foreign Service, Georgetown; Chair. Fed. Woman's Award 1962-68; U.S. mem. Exec. Bd. with rank of Amb., UNESCO, Paris 1968-69; Hon. D.Lit. Drexel Inst. of Technology 1964; Hon. D.Hum.Litt. Franklin Pierce Coll. 1967. *Publications:* With or Without Roses (poems) 1966, By the Political Sea 1970. *Leisure interest:* writing poetry and articles for magazines. *Address:* 2824 O Street, N.W., Washington, D.C. 20007, U.S.A. *Telephone:* 212-337-1096.

LOUDON, Aarnout Alexander, LL.M.; Netherlands business executive; b. 10 Dec. 1936, The Hague; m. Talitha Adine Charlotte Boon 1962; two s.; ed. Univ. of Utrecht; joined Bank Mees & Hope 1964, Head, New Issues Dept. 1967; joined Akzo Group 1969, Dir. cen. staff dept. Finance 1971; Finance Dir. Astral (subsidiary of Akzo Coatings), France 1972; Pres. Akzo, Brazil 1975-77; mem. Man. Bd. Akzo N.V. 1977, Deputy Pres. 1978, mem. Exec. Cttee. 1979, Pres. 1982-. *Leisure interests:* horseback riding, skiing. *Address:* Akzo N.V., P.O. Box 186, Velperweg 76, 6800 LS Arnhem (Office); Kluizenaarsweg 6, 6881 BS Velp, Netherlands (Home). *Telephone:* 085-663651 (Office); 085-646606 (Home).

LOUDON, Jonkheer John Hugo; Netherlands oil executive (retd.) and company director; b. 27 June 1905, The Hague; s. of Jonkheer Hugo Loudon and Anna P. A. van Marken; m. Baroness Marie Cornelie van Tuyll van Serooskerken 1931 (died 1988); three s.; ed. Univ. of Utrecht; joined N.V. De Bataafsche Petroleum Mij., The Hague 1930, served Venezuela, The Hague, U.S.A. 1930-44; Gen. Man. Royal Dutch/Shell interests, Venezuela 1944-47; Man. Dir. Royal Dutch Petroleum Co., N.V. De Bataafsche Petroleum Mij., Shell Petroleum Co. Ltd. 1947; Pres. Royal Dutch Shell Group 1952-65, Chair. 1965-76; Chair. Int. Advisory Cttee., Chase Manhattan Bank 1965-77; Chair. Int. Council European Inst. of Business Admin., Fontainebleau; fmr. Chair. Netherlands Econ. Inst., Rotterdam; fmr. Chair. European Advisory Council Ford Motor Co.; Dir. Russell Reynolds Assocs. Inc., New York; fmr. Dir. Orion Bank Ltd.; Bd. mem., Wright Investors' Service, Bridgeport, U.S.A. 1987-; Pres. Trustees, World Wildlife Fund 1977-81, fmr. mem. Int. Council; mem. Council, Rockefeller Univ., New York; fmr. mem. Int. Jury of the Alexander S. Onassis Foundation, Athens, Advisory Bd. Yale School of Org. and Man., Yale; Trustee, Pierpont Morgan Library, New York; fmr. Trustee, Ford Foundation; Hon K.B.E. (U.K.), Kt., Order of the Netherlands Lion, Grand Officer, Order of Orange-Nassau, Officer, Légion d'honneur, and other decorations. *Leisure interest:* yachting. *Address:* 48 Lange Voorhout, 2514 EG The Hague (Office); Koekoeksduin, 5 Vogelenzangseweg, 2111 HP Aerdenhout, The Netherlands (Home); *Telephone:* (070) 345 3755 (Office); (023) 245924 (Home).

LOUEKOSKI, Matti Kalevi; Finnish politician; b. 14 April 1941, Oulu; m. Pirjo Hiltunen 1969; Sec.-Gen. Union of Finnish Student Corpns. 1967-69; official at Ministry of Finance and Ministry of Interior 1969-70; Counsellor of Higher Educ. 1970-72; Special Adviser, Office of the Council of State 1975-76; established own law firm 1978; Dir. Finnish Workers' Savings Bank 1979-; mem. Parl. 1976-79, 1983-; Minister of Educ. 1971-72; Minister without Portfolio Feb.-Sept. 1972; Minister of Justice 1972-75, 1987-; Social Democratic Party. *Address:* Ministry of Justice, Eteläesplanadi 10, 00130 Helsinki, Finland. *Telephone:* (90) 18251.

LOUET, Philippe Marie Alexandre Gabriel, L. EN D.; French diplomatist; b. 7 July 1933, Paris; s. of Michel Louet and Marguerite (née Perrin); m. 1st Hélène Delorme, one s.; m. 2nd Penelope Wilkinson 1974; two s.; ed. Coll. Saint-Martin, Pontoise, Lycée Janson-de-Sailly, Inst. d'études politiques de Paris, Ecole nat. d'admin.; Dir. of Political Affairs, Ministry of Foreign Affairs 1962-66; second, later first Sec. to Perm. Rep. of France to the EEC 1966-71; Foreign Affairs Adviser 1968; Tech. Adviser, Ministry of Industrial and Scientific Devt. 1971-74, Ministry of Foreign Affairs 1974, Deputy Dir. for Spatial and Atomic Matters 1976-81; Asst. to Perm. Rep. to the UN 1981-86; Amb. to Turkey 1986-88; Perm. Rep. to the EEC, Brussels Nov. 1988-; Chevalier, Légion d'honneur, Officier, ordre nat. du Mérite. *Leisure interest:* sailing. *Address:* Permanent Representative of France to the European Communities, 40 boulevard du Régent, 1000 Brussels, Belgium.

LOUGH, John, M.A., PH.D., F.B.A.; British professor of French; b. 19 Feb. 1913, Newcastle upon Tyne; s. of the late Wilfred Gordon Lough and Mary Turnbull Lough; m. Muriel Alice Barker 1939; one d.; ed. Royal Grammar School, Newcastle upon Tyne, St. John's Coll., Cambridge, Sorbonne, Paris; Asst., later Lecturer in French, Univ. of Aberdeen 1937-46, Univ. of Cambridge 1946-52; Prof. of French, Univ. of Durham 1952-78, Emer. 1978-; Hon. Dr. (Clermont), Hon. D.Litt. (Newcastle upon Tyne). *Publications:* Locke's Travels in France 1953, Paris Theatre Audiences in the 17th and 18th Centuries 1957, Essays on the Encyclopédie 1968, Writer and Public in France 1978, The Philosophes and Post-Revolutionary France 1982, France Observed in the Seventeenth Century by British Travellers 1985, France on the Eve of Revolution: observations by British Travellers 1763-1788 1987, John Graham Lough (1798-1876), a Northumbrian Sculptor (with E. Merson) 1987. *Leisure interest:* gardening. *Address:* 1 St. Hild's Lane, Durham, DH1 1QL, England. *Telephone:* (091) 384-8034.

LOUGHEED, Hon. (Edgar) Peter, LL.B., M.B.A. Q.C.; Canadian politician; b. 26 July 1928, Calgary, Alberta; s. of late Edgar D. and Edna (Bauld) Lougheed; m. Jeanne Rogers 1952; two s. two d.; ed. public and secondary schools, Calgary, Univ. of Alberta and Harvard Univ.; Sec., Mannix Co. 1956, Gen. Counsel 1958, Vice-Pres. 1959, Dir. 1960-62; private legal practice 1962-; with Bennett Jones, Barristers and Solicitors 1985-; Prov. Leader, Progressive Conservative Party of Alberta 1965-85; mem. Alberta Legis. Ass. 1967-85; Leader of Opposition 1967-71; Premier of Alberta 1971-85; mem. Int. Advisory Council, Morgan Grenfell 1986-; Hon. D.Jur. St. Francis Xavier Univ. *Leisure interests:* skiing, golf, the symphony. *Address:* c/o 307 Legislative Building, Edmonton, Alberta T5K 2B6, Canada (Office).

LOUGHRAN, James; British conductor; b. 30 June 1931, Glasgow; s. of James and Agnes (née Fox) Loughran; m. 1st Nancy Coggon 1961, two s.; m. 2nd Ludmila Navratil 1985; ed. Glasgow, Bonn, Amsterdam and Milan; Assoc. Conductor, Bournemouth Symphony Orchestra 1962-65; debut Royal Opera House, Covent Garden 1964; Principal Conductor BBC Scottish Symphony Orchestra 1965-71; Prin. Conductor and Musical Adviser, Hallé Orchestra 1971-83, Conductor Laureate 1983-; debut New York Philharmonic with Westminster Choir 1972; Prin. Conductor Bamberg Symphony Orchestra 1979-83; Chief Guest Conductor BBC Welsh Symphony Orchestra 1987; Guest Conductor of prin. orchestras of Europe, America, Australia and Japan; first recorded complete Beethoven Symphonies with London Symphony Orchestra as contribution to Beethoven Bicentenary Celebrations 1969-70; recordings with Hallé, London Philharmonic, Philharmonia, BBC Symphony and Scottish Chamber Orchestras; Fellow Royal Northern Coll. of Music 1976, Royal Scottish Acad. of Music and Drama 1983; Hon. D.Mus. (Sheffield) 1983; First Prize, Philharmonia Orchestra Conducting Competition 1961, Gold Disc EMI 1983. *Leisure interest:* unwinding. *Address:* c/o Harold Holt Ltd., 31 Sinclair Road, London, W14 0NS, England. *Telephone:* 01-603 4600.

LOUIS, John Jeffry, Jr.; American business executive and diplomat; b. 10 June 1925, Evanston, Ill.; s. of John Jeffry Louis and Henrietta (Johnson) Louis; m. Josephine Peters 1953; one s. two d.; ed. Deerfield Acad., Mass., Northwestern Univ., Evanston, Ill., Williams Coll., Williamstown, Mass., Dartmouth Coll., Hanover, N.H.; served in U.S. Army 1943-45; Account Exec., Needham, Louis & Brorby Inc. 1952-58; Dir. Int. Marketing Dept., Johnson's Wax 1958-61; Chair. Bd. KTAR Broadcasting Co. 1961-68, Combined Communications Corp. 1968-79; Dir. Johnson's Wax 1961-, Baxter Travemol Labs. 1984-, Gannett Co. Inc. 1984-, Air Wisconsin 1984-; Amb. to U.K. 1981-83; Trustee, Evanston Hosp. 1959-81 (Chair. 1962-68), Deerfield Acad. 1963-81, Northwestern Univ., Williams Coll. 1979-81; Hon. Master of the Bench Inner Temple. *Leisure interests:* golf, tennis, skiing. *Address:* Suite 510, One Northfield Plaza, Northfield, Ill. 60093, U.S.A. *Telephone:* (312) 446-9191.

LOUIS, Pierre, D. ÈS L.; French professor and university official; b. 1 Aug. 1913; m. Andrée Bouillon 1940; two s. one d.; ed. Lycée Henri IV, Univ. of Paris and Fondation Thiers; fmr. Dir. of Studies, Faculty of Letters, Rennes, Faculty of Letters, Lyon; fmr. Prof., Faculty of Letters, Lyon; Rector, Acad. of Clermont-Ferrand 1954, Acad. of Lyon 1960-76; Conseiller d'Etat en service extraordinaire 1976-80; Pres. Acad. of Sciences, Belles-Lettres and Arts of Lyon 1982-; Dir. Research Group on History of Scientific Language 1983-; Officier de la Légion d'honneur, Commdr., Ordre des Palmes académiques, Commdr. de l'Ordre nat. du Mérite.

Publications: Vie d'Aristote, other works on Aristotle and history of science. *Address:* 18 rue Guilloud, 69003 Lyon, France. *Telephone:* 78-53-51-73.

LOUISY, Rt. Hon. Allan (Fitzgerald Laurent), P.C., C.B.E.; Saint Lucia politician; fmr. Judge Supreme Court of Grenada; Leader of St. Lucia Labour Party 1974-82; Prime Minister of Saint Lucia, Minister of Finance, Home Affairs, Information and Tourism 1979-81, Minister without Portfolio May 1981-Jan. 1982, Minister of Legal Affairs Jan.-May 1982. *Address:* Laborie, Castries, Saint Lucia, West Indies.

LOULY, Lieut.-Col. Mohamed Mahmoud Ould Ahmed; Mauritanian army officer and politician; Minister for Control and Investigation July 1978-Jan 1979, in charge of the Perm. Secr. of the Mil. Cttee. for Nat. Recovery (CMRN) Jan.-March 1979, for the Civil Service and Higher, Technical and Vocational Training March-May 1979; Pres. of Mauritania 1979-80. *Address:* c/o Office du Président, Comité de Redressement National, Nouakchott, Mauritania.

LOUNASMAA, Olli Viktor, M.S. D.PHIL. (OXON.); Finnish professor of cryogenics; b. 20 Aug. 1930, Turku; s. of Aarno and Inki (née von Hellens) Lounasmaa; m. Inkeri Kupiainen 1951; two d.; ed. Univs. of Helsinki, Turku and Oxford; Resident Research Assoc., Argonne Nat. Lab., Chicago 1960-65; Prof. of Tech. Physics, Helsinki Univ. of Technology 1965-70; Research Prof. Acad. of Finland 1970-; Dir. Low Temperature Lab., Helsinki Univ. of Tech. 1968-; Visiting Prof. in U.S.A., Japan, India, West Germany; Chair. Ministry of Educ. Working Groups on basic research 1980, 1984; fmr. Pres. Comm. on Cryophysics, Int. Inst. of Refrigeration; fmr. Chair. Very Low Temperature Physics Comm., Int. Union of Pure and Applied Physics; mem. Int Cryogenic Engineering Comm.; mem. Exec. Cttee. European Physical Soc.; editorial bds. 4 scientific journals; mem. Finnish Acad. of Tech. Sciences 1965, Finnish Acad. of Arts and Sciences 1969, Royal Swedish Acad. of Sciences 1974, Societas Scientiarum Fennica 1976; Hon. Fellow Indian Cryogenics Council 1976; Fellow American Physical Soc. 1986; awarded Homén Prize 1969, Emil Aaltonen Foundation Prize 1973, Finnish Cultural Foundation Prize 1978, Fritz London Memorial Award 1984; Commdr. Order of the Lion of Finland. *Publications:* Experimental Principles and Methods Below 1K; 170 scientific papers. *Address:* Low Temperature Laboratory, Helsinki University of Technology, Espoo 15 (Office); Ritokalliontie 21 B, Helsinki 33, Finland (Home). *Telephone:* 358-0-4512957 (Office); 358-0-481541 (Home).

LOURDUSAMY, H.E. Cardinal Simon; Indian ecclesiastic; b. 5 Feb. 1924, Kalleri, Pondicherry; ordained 1951; consecrated Bishop (Titular Church of Sozusa, Libya) 1962; Titular Archbishop of Philippi 1964; Archbishop of Bangalore 1968-71; cr. Cardinal 1985; Sec. Congregation for the Evangelization of Peoples 1973-85; Pres. Pontifical Missionary Work. *Address:* Congregation for the Eastern Churches, Palazzo dei Convertendi, Via della Conciliazione 34, 00193 Rome (Office); Palazzo Propaganda Fide, Piazza di Spagna 48, 00187, Rome, Italy (Home).

LOURIÉ, Sylvain, PH.D.; French educationist; b. 9 Oct. 1928, Paris; s. of Michel and Sarah (née Krynker) Lourie; m. 1st Sofia Sjostrandh 1956 (divorced 1972), one s.; m. 2nd Dominique Luccioni 1974, two d.; ed. Lycée Carnot, Lycée du Parc Imperial, Forest Hills High School, New York, Lehigh Univ., Bethlehem, Pa., Columbia Univ., Sorbonne, Econ. and Social Devt. Inst., Univ. of Paris.; Political Affairs Officer, UN Comm. for India and Pakistan 1948-50; Area Officer (Asia), UN Tech. Assistance Admin. 1950-52; Deputy Sec.-Gen. Nat. Foundation of Political Science, Paris 1957-65; Head of Tech. Co-operation Personnel Bureau, Ministry of Foreign Affairs 1960-62; Head of Special Research Staff, Ministry of Co-operation 1962-65; Asst. Dir. Educ. Financing Div., UNESCO 1965-68, Sr. Economist World Bank Comm. on Int. Devt. 1968-69, Dir. Educ. Planning and Policy Div. 1969-73, Educ. Adviser to Govts. in Central America, including Panama 1973-78, Agency Rep. UNDP Inter-Agency Task Force 1978-79, Sec. CCSQ/OPS 1978-79, Special Adviser Educ. Sector, UNESCO 1981-; Visiting Prof. Univ. of Aix-Marseille II 1979-80; Dir. Int. Inst. of Educ. Planning 1982-. *Publications:* Education and Development: Strategy and Decision-making in Central America 1985, studies and articles on aspects of educational strategy. *Address:* International Institute of Educational Planning, 7-9 rue Eugène Delacroix, 75116 Paris (Office); 27 avenue du 11 novembre 1918, 92310 Meudon-Bellevue, France (Home). *Telephone:* 45 04 28 22 (Office); (1) 4626-186 (Home).

LOUSTAU-LALANNE, Bernard Michel; Seychelles lawyer and diplomatist; b. 20 June 1938, Mahé; s. of J. A. M. and Madeleine (née Boullé) Loustau-Lalanne; m. Daphne Elizabeth Temple-Brown 1974; one s. one d.; ed. Seychelles Coll., Vic., St. Mary's Coll., Southampton, Imperial Coll., London; Barrister, Middle Temple 1969; Asst. Insp. N. Rhodesia Police, Ndola 1962-64; Crown Counsel, Attorney-General's Chambers, Seychelles 1970-73; Sr. State Counsel and Official Notary 1973-76; Attorney-Gen. 1976-78; High Commr. in U.K. (also Amb. to U.S.A.) 1978-81; Int. Rep. Performing Right Soc. Ltd. 1980-; Commr. Int. Whaling Comm. 1978-. *Leisure interests:* tennis, windsurfing, reading. *Address:* 2 Albert Mansions, Loughborough Street, London, W.1, England. *Telephone:* 01-935 4092.

LOUTFY, Aly, PH.D.; Egyptian professor of economics and government minister; b. 6 Oct. 1935, Cairo; s. of Mahmoud Loutfy; m. Eglal Mabrouk 1966; one s.; ed. Ain Shams and Louzan Univs.; joined staff, Faculty of

Commerce Ain Shams Univ. 1957, Prof. and Chair. Dept. of Econs. June 1980–; Prof. High Inst. of Co-operative and Admin. Studies; Part-time Prof. Inst. of Arab Research and Studies, Cairo; mem. Bd. of Dirs. Bank of Alexandria 1977–78, Bank of Commerce and Devt. (Cairo) 1981–; mem. Legis., Political Science and Econ. Asscn. 1977, Delta Sugar Co. 1978, Bank of Commerce and Devt. June 1980–; Minister of Finance 1978–80; Prime Minister of Egypt 1985–86; Speaker of the Shoura Council Nov. 1986–; Ideal Prof. Award, Egyptian Univs. 1974, Gold Mercury Int. Award 1979. *Publications:* Economic Evolution, Economic Development, Economic Planning, Studies on Mathematical Economics and Econometrics, Financing Problems in Developing Countries, Industrialization Problems in Under-Developed Countries; 30 research papers in economics in Arabic, French and English. *Leisure interests:* tennis, reading, travel. *Address:* 29 Ahmed Heshmat Street, Zamalek, Cairo, Egypt (Home). *Telephone:* 3416068.

LOUTIT, John Freeman, C.B.E., F.R.C.P., F.R.S.; British medical researcher (retd.); b. 19 Feb. 1910, Perth, W. Australia; s. of John Freeman Loutit and Margaret Loutit; m. Thelma Salisbury 1941; one s. two d.; ed. Church of England Grammar School, Guildford, W. Australia, Univs. of W. Australia, Melbourne, Oxford, London; Rhodes Scholar, Univ. of W. Australia 1930; various appts., London Hosp. 1935–39; Dir. S. London Blood Supply Depot 1940–47; Dir. MRC Radiobiology Unit, Harwell 1947–69, External Staff 1969–75, Visitor, 1975–, Hon. Consultant 1988–; Officer, Order of Orange-Nassau 1951; Hon. V.M.D. (Stockholm) 1965, Hon. D.Sc. (St. Andrews) 1988. *Publications:* Irradiation of Mice and Men 1962, Tissue Grafting and Radiation (jtly.) 1966. *Leisure interests:* gardening, cookery. *Address:* Medical Research Council Radiobiology Unit, Harwell, Didcot, Oxon. OX11 0RD (Office); Lyking, 22 Milton Lane, Steventon, Abingdon, Oxon. OX13 6SA, England (Home). *Telephone:* (0235) 831379.

LOUVIER, Alain; French composer and conductor; b. 13 Sept. 1945, Paris, France; s. of René Louvier and Marthe (née Fournier) Louvier; one s. one d.; ed. Centre Nat. de Télé-Enseignement, Conservatoire Nat. Supérieur de Musique, Paris; Dir. Conservatoire Nat. de Région, Boulogne-Billancourt 1972–86; Dir. Conservatoire Nat. Supérieur de Musique, Paris 1986–; Rome Prize 1968, Arthur Honegger Award 1975, Paul Gilson Award 1981. *Works include:* Chant des limbes (for orchestra) 1969, 3 Atmosphères (for clarinet and orchestra) 1974, le Clavecin non tempéré 1978, Messe des Apôtres 1978, Casta Diva (with Maurice Béjart) 1980, Poèmes de Ronsard (for voice ensemble and chamber orchestra) 1984. *Publication:* l'Orchestre. *Leisure interests:* botany and entomology. *Address:* CNSMP, 14 rue de Madrid, 75008 Paris (Office); 26 rue de la Belle Feuille, 92100 Boulogne-Billancourt, France (Home).

LOUW, Raymond; South African publisher and editor; b. 13 Oct. 1926, Cape Town; s. of George K. E. and Helen K. Louw (née Finlay); m. Jean Ramsay Byres 1950; two s., one d.; ed. Parktown High School, Johannesburg; reporter on Rand Daily Mail 1946–50, Worthing Herald 1951–52, North-Western Evening Mail 1953–54, Westminster Press Provincial Newspapers (London) 1955–56; Night News Ed. Rand Daily Mail 1958–59, News Ed. 1960–65, Ed. 1966–77; News Ed. Sunday Times 1959–60; Chair. S.A. Morning Newspaper Group 1975–77; Gen. Man. S.A. Associated Newspapers 1977–82; Chair. Media Defence Trust 1989–; mem. Exec. Bd., Int. Press Inst., London, 1979–87; Ed. Southern Africa Report; Pringle Medal for services to journalism 1976. *Leisure interests:* sailing, walking, travel, wildlife. *Address:* Southern Africa Report, P.O. Box 261579, Excom, Johannesburg 2023; 23 Duncombe Road, Forest Town, Johannesburg, South Africa (Home). *Telephone:* 011-646-8790 (Office).

LOVE, Andrew Henry Garmany, M.D., F.R.C.P., F.R.C.P.I.; British professor of medicine; b. 28 Sept. 1934, Bangor, Northern Ireland; s. of Andrew Love and Martha Love; m. Margaret Jean Lennox 1963; one s.; ed. Queen's Univ. of Belfast; Lecturer in Physiology, Queen's Univ. Belfast 1960–63, in Medicine 1963–65; Physician and Guest Investigator U.S. Naval Medical Research Unit, Taipei, Taiwan 1965–66; Hon. Consultant SEATO Cholera Research Labs., Dacca 1967–73; Prof. of Gastroenterology, Queen's Univ. Belfast 1973–83, Medicine 1983–, Dean of Faculty of Medicine 1981–86; mem. Gen. Medical Council 1981–, Exec. Cttee. Asscn. of Medical Deans of Europe 1985–, Research Cttee. Ulster Cancer Foundation 1983–; Hans Sloane Trustee 1981–; Irish Amateur Golf Champion 1956. *Publications:* various contributions to medical literature. *Leisure interests:* golf, sailing, horse riding, gardening. *Address:* Department of Medicine, Queen's University Institute of Clinical Science, Grosvenor Road, Belfast, BT12 6BJ (Office); The Lodge, New Road, Donaghadee, Co. Down, BT21 0DU (Home). *Telephone:* 0232-240503, Ext. 2707 (Office); (0247) 883507 (Home).

LOVE, Howard McClintic; American business executive; b. 5 April 1930, Pittsburgh, Pa.; s. of George Hutchinson Love and Margaret (née McClintic); m. Jane Vaughn 1956; two s. three d.; ed. Colgate Univ. (Hamilton, N.Y.) and Harvard Univ.; man. trainee, Great Lakes Steel Div., Nat. Steel Corpn., Ecorse, Mich. 1956–58; Operating Man. Great Lakes Div. 1958–63; Asst. Gen. Man. Sales, Midwest Steel Div. 1963–64, Great Lakes Steel Div. 1964–65; Asst. to Pres. 1965–66, Pres. Midwest Steel Div. 1966–82; Pres. Granite City, Ill., Steel Div. 1972–, Corp. Pres., C.O.O. 1975–, C.E.O. 1980–; C.O.O., Nat. Steel Corpn. (now Nat. Intergroup) 1975–, C.E.O. 1980–81, Chair. 1981–; Chair. Nat. Pipe and Tube Co. 1974–; Dir. Monsanto Co., St. Louis, Gould Inc., United Financial Corpn. of Calif., Trans. World Corpn.; Pittsburgh Symphony Orchestra; Trustee Colgate

Univ., Children's Hospitals, Pittsburgh, Pittsburgh Ballet Theatre Inc.; mem. Exec. Cttee. American Iron and Steel Inst., Allegheny Conf. on Community Devt. *Address:* 1440 Bennington Avenue, Pittsburgh, Pa. 15217, U.S.A. (Home).

LOVEDAY, Harold Maxwell, M.B.E.; Australian diplomatist; b. 12 Sept. 1923, Sydney; s. of R. T. Loveday; m. Cynthia Nelson 1962; one s. one d.; ed. Sydney Univ. and Canberra Univ. Coll.; joined Dept. of Foreign Affairs as a career Foreign Service Officer 1945; served in Shanghai and Nanking 1946–50, Bonn and Berlin 1953–54, Rep. of Korea 1954–55; served in Kuala Lumpur 1955–56, 1964; Counsellor, Embassy in Washington, D.C. 1959–62; Australian Commr., South Pacific Comm. 1962–66; Asst. Sec. Dept. of Foreign Affairs 1962–66, Amb. to Indonesia 1966–69; Amb. and Perm. Rep. to UN Office in Geneva 1969–72; Acting Dir.-Gen. Australian Devt. Assistance Agency 1973–74; High Commr. to Canada 1975–77; Amb. to Fed. Repub. of Germany 1977–82; Head, Cultural Relations and Visits, Dept. of Foreign Affairs and Trade 1983–. *Leisure interests:* tennis, golf, skiing. *Address:* c/o Department of Foreign Affairs and Trade, Canberra, Australia.

LOVELL, Sir (Alfred Charles) Bernard, Kt., F.R.S., O.B.E., PH.D., M.SC.; British radio astronomer; b. 31 Aug. 1913, Oldland Common, Glos.; s. of Gilbert and Emily Laura Lovell (née Adams); m. Mary Joyce Chesterman 1937; two s. three d.; ed. Bristol Univ.; Asst. Lecturer in Physics, Univ. of Manchester 1936–39, Lecturer 1945–47, Sr. Lecturer 1947–49, Reader 1949–51, Prof. of Radio Astronomy 1951–81, Emer. Prof. 1981–; with Telecommunications Research Est. 1939–45; Founder and Dir. Nuffield Radio Astronomy Labs., Jodrell Bank 1945–81; Fellow, Royal Soc. 1955; Hon. Foreign mem. American Acad. of Arts and Sciences 1955, Hon. mem. New York Acad. of Sciences 1960; Pres. Royal Astronomical Soc. 1969–71, British Asscn. 1974–75; Vice-Pres. Int. Astronomical Union 1970–76; mem. Aeronautical Research Council 1955–58, Science Research Council 1965–70; Master Worshipful Co. of Musicians 1986–87; Hon. Fellow, Royal Swedish Acad. 1962, Inst. of Electrical Engineers 1967, Inst. of Physics 1975; Hon. Freeman City of Manchester 1977, Hon. LL.D. (Edinburgh) 1961, (Calgary) 1966, Hon. D.Sc. (Leicester) 1961, (Leeds) 1966, (Bath, London) 1967, (Bristol) 1970, Hon. D.Univ. (Stirling) 1974, (Surrey) 1975; Royal Medal of Royal Soc. 1960; Daniel and Florence Guggenheim Int. Astronautics Award 1961; Ordre du Mérite pour la Recherche et l'Invention 1962; Polish Order of Merit 1975; Maitland Silver Medal, Inst. of Structural Engineers 1964; Churchill Gold Medal, Soc. of Engineers 1964, Benjamin Franklin Medal, Royal Soc. of Arts 1980, Gold Medal, Royal Astronomical Soc. 1981. *Publications:* Science and Civilisation 1939, World Power Resources and Social Development 1945, Radio Astronomy 1952, Meteor Astronomy 1954, The Exploration of Space by Radio 1957, The Individual and the Universe (The Reith Lectures 1958), The Exploration of Outer Space 1962, Discovering the Universe 1963, Our Present Knowledge of the Universe 1967; Ed. (with Tom Margerison) The Explosion of Science: The Physical Universe 1967, The Story of Jodrell Bank 1968, The Origins and International Economics of Space Exploration 1973, Out of the Zenith: Jodrell Bank 1957–1970 1973, Man's Relation to the Universe 1975, P. M. S. Blackett—a Biographical Memoir 1976, In the Centre of Immensities 1978, Emerging Cosmology 1981, The Jodrell Bank Telescopes 1985, Voice of the Universe 1987, Pathways to the Universe (with Sir Francis Graham-Smith) 1988. *Leisure interests:* music, gardening, cricket. *Address:* Nuffield Radio Astronomy Laboratories, Jodrell Bank, Macclesfield, Cheshire; The Quinta, Swettenham, Nr. Congleton, Cheshire, England (Home). *Telephone:* (0477) 71321.

LOVELOCK, Sir Douglas, K.C.B.; British civil servant; b. 7 Sept. 1923, London; s. of late Walter Lovelock and Irene Lovelock; m. Valerie Margaret Lane 1961; one s. one d.; ed. Bec. School, London; entered Treasury 1949; Ministry of Supply 1952, Pvt. Sec. to Perm. Sec. 1953–54, Prin. 1954; Pvt. Sec. to Minister of Aviation 1961–63, Asst. Sec. 1963; Under-Sec. (Contracts) Minister of Tech., subsequently Minister of Aviation Supply 1968–71; Asst. Under-Sec. of State (Personnel) at Ministry of Defence 1971–72; Deputy Sec. at Dept. of Trade and Industry 1972–74; Depts. of Trade, Industry, Prices and Consumer Protection 1974–77; Chair. Bd. Customs and Excise 1977–83; First Church Estate Commr. 1983–; Chair. Civil Service Benevolent Fund 1980–83, Cen. Bd. of Finance of Church of England 1983–, Review of Citizens' Advice Bureaux Service 1983–84. *Leisure interests:* gardening and rugby football. *Address:* The Old House, 91 Coulsdon Road, Old Coulsdon, Surrey, England.

LOVELOCK, James Ephraim, PH.D., A.R.I.C., F.R.S.; British scientist; b. 26 July 1919; s. of Tom A. Lovelock and Nellie A.E. (March) Lovelock; m. Helen M. Hyslop 1942; two s. two d.; ed. Strand School, London and Univs. of London and Manchester; staff scientist, Nat. Inst. for Medical Research 1941–61; Rockefeller Fellow, Harvard Univ. 1954–55, Yale Univ. 1958–59; Prof. of Chemistry Baylor Univ. Coll. of Medicine, Tex. 1961–64; independent scientist 1964–; Visiting Prof. Univ. of Reading 1967–; Pres. Marine Biological Asscn. 1986–; Hon. Sc.D. (E. Anglia) 1982. *Publications:* Gaia 1979, The Great Extinction (with M. Allaby) 1983, The Ages of Gaia (with M. Allaby) 1988; numerous papers and patents. *Leisure interests:* walking, painting, computer programming, reading. *Address:* Coombe Mill, St. Giles on the Heath, Launceston, Cornwall, PL15 9RY, England.

LOW, Sir Alan Roberts, Kt., M.A.; New Zealand banker (retd.); b. 11 Jan. 1916, Blenheim; s. of Benjamin and Sarah Low; m. Kathleen Mary Harrow 1940; one s. two d.; ed. Timaru Boys' High School and Canterbury Univ. Coll.; joined Reserve Bank of N.Z. 1938; Mil. Service 1942–44; Econ. Adviser, Reserve Bank of N.Z. 1951, Asst. Gov. 1960–62, Deputy Gov. 1962–67, Gov. 1967–77; Chair. Dairy Products Prices Authority 1977–; Past Pres. N.Z. Asscn. of Economists. *Publications:* No Free Lunch 1983, Where Do We Go for Lunch 1984. *Leisure interests:* gardening, music. *Address:* 171 Muritai Road, East Bourne, New Zealand.

LOW, Francis Eugene, B.S., M.S., PH.D.; American physicist; b. 27 Oct. 1921, New York; s. of Bela Low and Eugenia Ingerman Low; m. Natalie Sadigur 1948; three c.; ed. Harvard Coll. and Columbia Univ.; Asst. and Assoc. Prof., Univ. of Ill. 1952–57; Prof. of Physics, M.I.T. 1957–67, Karl Taylor Compton Prof. of Physics 1968–, Dir. Center for Theoretical Physics 1973–77, Dir. Lab. for Nuclear Science 1979–80, Provost 1980–85, Inst. Prof. 1985–; Guggenheim and Fulbright Fellow; Loeb Lecturer, Harvard Univ.; mem. N.A.S., American Acad. of Arts and Sciences. *Leisure interests:* piano, composing music, skiing, tennis, flying, problems of impact of science on society. *Address:* Room 6-301, Massachusetts Institute of Technology, Cambridge, Mass. 02139; 28 Adams Street, Belmont, Mass. 02178, U.S.A. *Telephone:* (617) 484-1889.

LOW, Stephen, PH.D.; American diplomatist; b. 2 Dec. 1927, Cincinnati, Ohio; s. of Martin and Margaret (Friend) Low; m. Helen Carpenter 1954; three s.; ed. Yale Univ. and Fletcher School of Law and Diplomacy, Tufts Univ.; joined Foreign Service 1956, served in Uganda and Senegal; Special Asst. to Deputy Under-Sec. of State for Political Affairs, Dept. of State 1965–67; Counsellor for Political Affairs, Brasilia 1968–71; Dir. of Brazilian Affairs, State Dept. 1971–74; Nat. Security Council, White House 1974–76; Amb. to Zambia 1976–79, to Nigeria 1979–81; diplomat in residence, Univ. of California, Santa Barbara 1981–82; Dir. Foreign Service Inst., Dept. of State 1982–87; Dir. Bologna Center, Johns Hopkins School of Advanced Int. Studies 1987–. *Address:* The Bologna Center, Via Belmeloro 11, 40126 Bologna, Italy.

LOWE, Douglas Ackley; Australian politician; b. 15 May 1942, Hobart; s. of Ackley Reginald and Dulcie Mary Lowe; m. Pamela June Grant 1963; two s. two d.; ed. St. Virgil's Coll.; worked as electrical fitter, Electrolytic Co.; State Sec. Tasmanian Section, Australian Labour Party 1965–69, State Pres. 1974–75; mem. Tasmania House of Ass. for Franklin 1969–81, Independent 1981–86; Minister for Housing 1972–74; Chief Sec. 1974–76; Deputy Premier 1975–77; Minister for Planning and Reorganization 1975–76, for Industrial Relations 1976–79, for Planning and Environment 1976, for Health 1976–77; Premier of Tasmania 1977–81; Minister for Manpower Planning 1977–79, for Economic Planning and Development 1979–80, for Energy 1979, Treas. 1980–81; elected to Tasmanian Legis. Council May 1986–; del. to Australian Constitutional Convention; Queen's Silver Jubilee Medal 1977. *Publication:* The Price of Power 1984. *Address:* 15 Tooma Avenue, Chigwell, Tasmania 7011, Australia (Home).

LOWENSTEIN, Otto Egon, PH.D., D.PHIL., F.R.S., F.R.S.E.; British professor of zoology (retd.); b. 24 Oct. 1906; s. of Julius Lowenstein and Mathilde Heusinger; m. 1st Elsa B. Ritter, two s.; m. 2nd Gunilla M. Dohlman (died 1981), one step s.; m. 3rd Maureen Josephine McKernan; ed. Neues Realgymnasium, Munich and Univ. of Munich; Asst. Univ. of Munich 1931–33; Research Scholar, Univ. of Birmingham 1933–37; Asst. Lecturer, Univ. Coll. Exeter 1937–38; Sr. Lecturer, Univ. of Glasgow 1938–52; Mason Prof. of Zoology and Comparative Physiology, Univ. of Birmingham 1952–74; Hon. Sr. Research Fellow, Pharmacology Dept. Birmingham Univ. Medical School 1976–. *Publications:* Revision of the 6th edn. of A Textbook of Zoology (Parker and Haswell) Vol. I; The Senses 1966; papers in journals. *Leisure interests:* music, golf, painting. *Address:* 22 Estria Road, Birmingham, B15 2LQ, England. *Telephone:* (021) 440 2526.

LÖWHAGEN, Birger, M.SC.; Swedish business executive; b. 3 Sept. 1924, Hallsberg; s. of Fritz Löwhagen; m. Kerstin Svensson 1953; two d.; ed. Univ. of Gothenburg; Project Man., Skanska (bldg. contractor), Gothenburg 1957–60, Man. Road Construction Div., Malmö 1961–64, Vice-Pres. 1964–68, Exec. Vice-Pres. 1969, mem. Bd. of Dirs. 1979–, Exec. Vice-Pres. Int. Div. 1980, First Exec. Vice-Pres. 1980, Pres. of Skanska 1981–86; mem. Bd. of Dirs. Svenska Handelsbanken, Sandvik AB, AB W. Sonesson, Evroc, Swedish Employers Confed., SBEF (Fed. of Swedish Bldg. Contractors). *Leisure interests:* golf, tennis, hunting. *Address:* Skånegatan 5, S-216 11 Malmö, Sweden. *Telephone:* 040-15.92.03 (Home).

LOWRY, Baron (Life Peer), cr. 1979, of Crossgar in the County of Down; **Robert Lynd Erskine Lowry,** Kt., Q.C., M.A., LL.D.; British judge; b. 30 Jan. 1919, Dublin, Ireland; s. of late William Lowry (Rt. Hon. Mr. Justice Lowry) and Catherine Hughes (Lynd) Lowry; m. Mary Audrey Martin 1945; three d.; ed. Royal Belfast Acad. Inst., Jesus Coll. Cambridge; served in H.M. Forces 1940–46, commissioned Royal Irish Fusiliers 1941, Major 1945; called to the Bar of Northern Ireland 1947, Bencher of Inn of Court of Northern Ireland 1955, Q.C. 1956, Justice of High Court 1964, Lord Chief Justice of Northern Ireland 1971–88; Lord of Appeal in Ordinary Aug. 1988–; mem. Joint Law Enforcement Comm. 1974; Privy Counsellor 1974; Chair. Northern Ireland Constitutional Convention 1975–76; Hon.

Bencher Middle Temple and King's Inns Dublin; Hon. Fellow Jesus Coll. Cambridge; Int. Showjumping Judge 1973–; Hon. LL.D. (Queens' Univ.) 1980; Hon. D.Litt. (New Univ. of Ulster) 1981. *Leisure interests:* golf, showjumping. *Address:* White Hill, Crossgar, Co. Down, Northern Ireland. *Telephone:* (0936) 397.

LOWRY, Bates, PH.B., M.A., PH.D.; American art historian and museum director; b. 21 June 1923, Cincinnati, Ohio; m. Isabel Barrett 1946; two d.; ed. Univ. of Chicago; Asst. Prof. Univ. of Calif. 1954–57; Asst. Prof. New York Univ., Inst. of Fine Arts 1957–59; Prof., Chair. Art Dept. Pomona Coll. 1959–63, Prof. Brown Univ. 1963–68, Chair. Dept. of Art 1965–68; Dir. Museum of Modern Art, New York 1968–69; mem. Inst. for Advanced Study 1971; Prof., Chair. Art Dept., Univ. of Mass., Boston 1971–80; mem. Bds. of Dirs. Soc. of Architectural Historians 1959–61, 1963–65, College Art Asscn. 1962–65; Ed.-in-Chief, Art Bulletin 1965–68; Ed. College Art Asscn. Monographs Series 1957–59, 1965–68; Chair. Nat. Exec. Cttee., Cttee. to Rescue Italian Art (CRIA) 1966–76; Pres. The Dunlap Soc. 1974–; Dir. Nat. Bldg. Museum, Washington, D.C. 1980–87; Distinguished Visiting Prof., Univ. of Delaware 1988–89; Hon. mem. Accademia del Disegno (Florence); Trustee, American Fed. of Arts; Guggenheim Fellowship 1972; Govs. award for Fine Arts, Rhode Island 1967; Grand Officer Star of Solidarity of Italy 1968. *Publications:* The Visual Experience 1961, Renaissance Architecture 1962, The Architecture of Washington, D.C. 1977–80, Building a National Image 1985. *Address:* 4501 Connecticut Avenue, N.W., Washington, D.C. 20008, U.S.A.

LOWRY, Sir (John) Patrick, (Pat), Kt., C.B.E., F.R.S.A., B.COM.; British administrator; b. 31 March 1920; s. of John McArdle and Edith Mary Lowry; m. Sheilagh Mary Davies 1952; one s. one d.; ed. Wyggeston Grammar School, Leicester, London School of Econs.; Statistical Clerk, Eng. Employers' Fed. 1938; served Army 1939–46; various posts in Eng. Employers' Fed. 1946–70, Dir. 1965–70; Dir. of Industrial Relations, British Leyland Motor Corpn. 1970, Bd. Dir. 1972; Dir., Personnel, British Leyland Ltd. 1975–77, Personnel and Admin. 1977–78, Personnel and External Affairs 1978–81; Chair. Advisory, Conciliation and Arbitration Service (ACAS) 1981–87; Pres. Inst. of Personnel Man. 1987–; mem. U.K. Employers' Del., ILO 1962, 1963, 1967, Court of Inquiry, Barbican and Horseferry Road Bldg. Disputes 1967, Grunwick Dispute 1977; Pres. Inst. of Supervisory Man. 1972–74; Hon. LL.D. (Leicester) 1984. *Leisure interests:* theatre, gardening, fishing. *Address:* Ashfield, Snowdenham Links Road, Bramley, Guildford, Surrey, England. *Telephone:* (0483) 893289.

LOWRY, Oliver Howe, PH.D., M.D.; American professor of pharmacology; b. 18 July 1910, Chicago, Ill.; m. 1st Norma van Ness 1935 (deceased), 2nd Adrienne Kennedy; three s. two d.; ed. Northwestern Univ. and Univ. of Chicago; Instructor, Dept. of Biological Chem., Harvard Medical School 1937–42; at Div. of Physiology and Nutrition, Public Health Research Inst., New York 1942–47; Prof. of Pharmacology, Washington Univ. School of Medicine 1947– (Head of Dept. 1947–76, Dean 1955–58); Commonwealth Fund Fellow, Carlsberg Lab. Denmark 1939–40; mem. Editorial Bd. Journal of Neurochemistry; mem. Nat. Advisory Gen. Medical Sciences Council of Nat. Insts. of Health, Scientific Advisory Cttee. of Nat. Foundation, Scientific Advisory Bd. of Scripps Clinic and Research Foundation; mem. of many socs. including N.A.S., A.A.A.S., Royal Danish Acad. of Science, Harvey Soc., A.C.S.; Hon. D.Sc. (Washington) 1981; Midwest Award of A.C.S. 1962, Merit Award of Northwestern Univ. 1963, John Scott Award 1963, Distinguished Service Award of Medical Alumni Asscn. of Univ. of Chicago 1965, Borden Award of Asscn. of American Medical Colls. 1966. *Publications:* 245 papers in Journal of Biological Chemistry, Journal of Neurochemistry, other scientific journals 1939–88. *Address:* Washington University School of Medicine, 660 S. Evelid, St. Louis, Mo. 63110, U.S.A. *Telephone:* 314-362-7055.

LOYN, Henry Royston, D.LITT., F.S.A., F.R.HIST.S., F.B.A.; British professor of history; b. 16 June 1922, Cardiff, Wales; s. of the late Henry George Loyn and of Violet Monica Loyn; m. Patricia Beatrice Haskew 1950; three s.; ed. Cardiff High School, Univ. Coll., Cardiff; Asst. Lecturer, Dept. of History, Univ. Coll., Cardiff 1946, Lecturer 1949, Sr. Lecturer 1961, Reader 1966, Prof. of Medieval History 1969–77, Dean of Students 1968–70, 1975–76, Fellow 1981; Prof. of History, Westfield Coll., Univ. of London 1977–87, Vice-Prin. 1980–86; Pres. Historical Asscn. 1976–79, Glamorgan Historical Asscn. 1975–77, Cardiff Naturalists' Soc. 1975–76, Soc. for Medieval Archaeology 1983–86; Vice-Pres. Soc. for Medieval Archaeology 1971–74, Soc. of Antiquaries 1983–87, Royal Historical Soc. 1983–86; mem. Ancient Monuments Bd. for England 1982–84; W.N. Medlicott Medal for service to History, Historical Asscn. 1986. *Publications:* Anglo-Saxon England and the Norman Conquest 1962, Norman Conquest 1965, Norman Britain 1966, Alfred the Great 1967, A Wulfstan MS, Cotton, Nero Ai 1971, British Government and Administration (Ed. with H. Hearder) 1974, The Reign of Charlemagne (with J. Percival) 1975, The Vikings in Britain 1977, Medieval Britain (with Alan and Richard Sorrell) 1977, The Governance of England (Vol. 1) 1984; introduction, facsimile ed. Domesday Book 1987; contribs. to English Historical Review, Antiquaries Journal and Medieval Archaeology. *Leisure interests:* natural history, gardening. *Address:* Westfield College, Kidderpore Avenue, London, NW3 7ST, England. *Telephone:* 01-435 7141.

LOZOYA-SOLIS, Jesús; Mexican pediatric surgeon; b. 3 March 1910, Parral, Chihuahua; s. of late Leodegario Lozoya and late Josefa Solis; m. 1st Susana Thalmann 1937 (divorced 1958); 2nd Margarita Prieto de Lozoya 1959; four s. one d.; ed. Mil. Medical School of Mexico, Western Reserve Univ. Hosp., Cleveland, Ohio, Harvard Univ. Children's Hosp.; founder of pediatric surgery in Mexico 1940-52; Hosp. Infantil of Mexico 1940-52; Asst. Prof. Pediatrics and Surgical Pediatrics 1940; Pres. Mexican Soc. of Pediatrics 1948-50; Pres. Mexican branch American Acad. of Pediatrics 1944-46; Pres. Laboratorios Infan of Mexico 1949-; Pres. Mexican Soc. Pediatric Surgery 1958-60; founder and first Pres. Pan-American Pediatric Surgery Assen. 1966-68, World Symposium Pediatric Surgery 1965-68, World Fed. Pediatric Surgeons 1974; founder of Dept. of Pediatrics of Armed Forces of Mexico 1940 (Prof. Emer. Mexico Mil. Medical School), Nat. Inst. for the Protection of Children 1958; Senator of the Repub. 1952-55; Gov. of Chihuahua 1955-56; Gen. of Mexican Army 1949 (retd. 1977); Guest Prof. of Pediatric Surgery at numerous Univs.; mem. American Acad. of Paediatrics 1944, American Coll. of Surgeons 1945, American Mil. Surgeons Assen., Mediterranean Acad.; hon. mem. American Pediatric Surgical Assen., Pacific Assen. of Pediatric Surgeons, and many pediatric surgery assens.; Pres. organizing cttee. World Fed. of Pediatric Surgery Assens. 1972-74; Pediatric Surgery Adviser to Int. Pediatric Assen. 1980-83; Chevalier, Hospitalare of Malta 1976, Medical Benefactor 1976. *Publications:* Paediatria Quirúrgica 1959, México ayer y hoy, visto por un pedíatra mexicano 1965, La escuela médico militar de México 1977, and numerous articles. *Leisure interests:* history, philosophy, anthropology, writing, lecturing, gardening, travelling, riding. *Address:* Calzada Tlalpan 4515, México 22, D.F., Mexico. *Telephones:* 5730094, 5732200/01/02/03.

LU DADONG; Chinese politician; Sec. Dist. CCP Cttee., Leshan, Sichuan 1950; Dir. Industrial Dept., Municipal CCP Cttee., Chongqing 1954, Deputy Sec. Chongqing Municipal CCP Cttee. 1955-57, Sec. 1957-72; Vice-Chair. Municipal Revolutionary Cttee., Chongqing 1968-74; alt. mem. 11th CCP Cen. Cttee. 1969-73; mem. Standing Cttee., Prov. Revolutionary Cttee., Sichuan 1972-77; Second Sec. Municipal CCP Cttee., Chongqing 1972-76, First Sec. 1976; Chair. Municipal Revolutionary Cttee., Chongqing 1974; Sec. Provincial CCP Cttee., Sichuan 1977-79, Standing Sec. 1979-80, Second Sec. 1980-83; Vice-Chair. Provincial Revolutionary Cttee., Sichuan 1977-79; mem. 11th Cen. Cttee., CCP 1977-82, 12th Cen. Cttee. 1982-85, 12th Cen. Advisory Cttee. 1985-87; Gov. Sichuan Prov. 1979-83; mem. Standing Cttee., CCP Cttee., Sichuan 1983-; Vice-Chair. Advisory Cttee., CCP Cttee., Sichuan 1983. *Address:* Office of the Provincial Governor, Chengdu, Sichuan Province, People's Republic of China.

LU DONG; Chinese politician; fmr. Minister of Metallurgical Industry; Minister, Third Ministry of Mechanical Industry 1978-81; Vice-Minister of State Econ. Comm. 1982-84, Minister 1984-; mem. Leading Group for Scientific Work, State Council 1983-; Deputy Head, Leading Group for Devt. of Electronics Industry 1984-; mem. Presidium CPPCC 1983-; Pres. Industrial Econs. Soc. 1984-; mem. Cen. Advisory Comm. of CCP 1987-. *Address:* State Economic Commission, Sanlihe, Fuxingmenwei, Beijing, People's Republic of China.

LU GONGXUN; Chinese party official; b. 1935; alt. mem. 12th CCP Cen. Cttee. 1982, 13th Cen. Cttee. 1987; Sec. CCP Cttee., Zuoyun Co., Shanxi Prov. 1982-83; mem. CCP Cttee., Shanxi 1983-, Deputy Sec. 1988-. *Address:* Shanxi Provincial Chinese Communist Party, Taiyuan, Shanxi, People's Republic of China.

LU JI; Chinese musician; b. 23 April 1909, Hunan; s. of Lu Xing and Yi Zong-Ying; m. Guan Li-Ren 1942; two s. two d.; Chair. Chinese Musicians' Assen. 1949-85, Hon. Chair. 1985-; Vice-Dir. Cen. Conservatory 1949-57; mem. Standing Cttee. NPC 1978-; mem. Educ., Science, Culture and Public Health Cttee. NPC 1983-; Hon. mem. Int. Music Council 1985-; mem. Presidium 6th NPC 1986-. *Leisure interest:* visual arts appreciation. *Address:* Chinese Musicians' Association, 203 Chao-Nei Street, Beijing, People's Republic of China.

LU JIAXI, B.S.C., PH.D.; Chinese scientist; b. 26 Oct. 1915, Xiamen, Fujian; s. of Lu Dongqi and Lu Guo Wanqing; m. Lu Wu Xunyu; five s. two d.; Prof. Xiamen Univ. 1946-60, Fuzhov Univ. 1960-; Vice-Pres. Fuzhou Univ. 1960-81, Hon. Pres. 1981-87; Prof. Fujian Inst. of Research and Structure of Matter, Chinese Acad. of Sciences 1960-, Dir. 1960-83, Hon. Dir. 1983-; Hon. Pres. Fuzhou Univ. 1961; Deputy to NPC 1964, 1978-82; mem. CPPCC Standing Cttee. 1983-; removed from office during Cultural Revolution 1967-78; Vice-Chair. 9th Cen. Cttee. Chinese Peasants' and Workers' Democratic Party 1983-; Dir. Fujian Inst. on Structure of Matter, Chinese Acad. of Sciences, Pres. Chinese Acad. of Sciences 1981-87, Chinese Chemical Soc. 1982; Vice-Chair. China Assen. for Science and Tech. 1986-; Hon. Pres. Soc. of Gerontology 1986-. *Address:* Chinese Academy of Sciences, Beijing, People's Republic of China. *Telephone:* 868361, Ext. 412.

LU LIANGSHU; Chinese agronomist; Pres. Acad. of Agricultural Sciences 1982-, Chinese Assen. of Agricultural Science Socs. 1982-; alt. mem. 12th Cen. Cttee. CCP 1982; Vice-Chair. Scientific and Technological Cttee., Ministry of Agric., Animal Husbandry and Fisheries 1983-. *Address:* Academy of Agricultural Sciences, Beijing, People's Republic of China.

LU MAOZENG; Chinese agronomist and party official; b. 1928, Jiangsu Prov.; alt. mem. 12th CCP Cen. Cttee. 1982-87, mem. 13th Cen. Cttee.

1987-; Vice-Pres. Shandong Agricultural Science Acad. 1982-; Deputy Sec. CCP Cttee., Shandong 1983-. *Address:* Shandong Provincial Agricultural Science Academy, Jinan, Shandong, People's Republic of China.

LU PEIJIAN; Chinese bank executive; b. 1928, Jiangsu; Vice-Minister of Finance 1978-82; Pres. People's Bank of China 1982-85, Chair. Council 1984-85; Auditor-Gen. of Audit Admin. 1985-; Gov. of IMF 1982; mem. 12th Cen. Cttee. CCP 1982, 13th Cen. Cttee. 1987. *Address:* People's Bank of China, San Li Ho, West City, Beijing, People's Republic of China.

LU QIHUI; Chinese sculptor; b. April 1936, Shanghai; d. of Ren Jin; m. Fang Zenxian 1961; one s. one d.; ed. Sculpture Dept., Cen. Art Acad., E. China Branch; worked in China Sculpture Factor, E. China Branch 1955-61; teacher, Shanghai Art School 1961-65; Professional Sculptor, Shanghai Oil Painting and Sculpture Inst. 1965-, Assoc. Prof. 1984-; mem. Chinese Artists' Assen. *Works include:* Monument to the Yi Jiang Shan Island Liberation 1956, sculpture at Agric. Exhbn. Hall, Xian 1958, Statue of Child Labourers, for Shanghai Workers' Union 1974, sculpture for Chairman Mao Memorial Hall 1977, Statue of Lu Xun, Shanghai 1979, Angrily Seeking Verses against the Reign of Terror 1980, Statue of the Geologist Li Siguang 1984, Bada, an Ancient Chinese Artist 1987 (exhibited New York in Contemporary Oil Paintings from the P.R.C.). *Leisure interest:* Chinese painting. *Address:* 1520 Hong Qao Road, Shanghai (Office); 2, 9 Hen Shan Road, Shanghai, People's Republic of China (Home). *Telephone:* 512761 (Office).

LU QIN'AN; Chinese cultural official; b. 1941; ed. Anhui Univ.; Sec.-Gen. Beijing Catholic Patriotic Assen. 1985-. *Address:* Beijing Catholic Patriotic Association, Xuanwumen Catholic Church, Beijing, People's Republic of China.

LU SHENGZHONG; Chinese artist; b. 1952, Pinggu Co., Shandong Prov.; ed. Cen. Acad. of Fine Arts; specializes in Chinese folk arts. *Address:* Central Academy of Fine Arts, Beijing, People's Republic of China.

LU YANSHAO; Chinese artist; b. 26 June 1909, Jiading Cty., Shanghai; s. of Lu Yunbo and Zhu Xuan; m. Zhu Yanyin 1929; three s. two d.; Prof. Zhejiang Acad. of Fine Arts; Bd. Dir. All-China Artists' Assen.; Pres. Zhejiang Landscape Soc.; mem. NPC. *Publications:* Some Opinions on Landscape Painting 1980, Manual of Lu Yanshao's Studio Drawings 1985, Lu Yanshao's Autobiography 1985. *Address:* Zhejiang Academy of Fine Arts, 218 Nanshan Road, Hangzhou, People's Republic of China. *Telephone:* 28701.

LÜ ZHENGCAO, Col.-Gen.; Chinese army officer and politician; b. 1905, Haicheng Co., Liaoning Prov.; ed. Northeast Mil. Acad.; joined Army 1921; Regimental Commdr. in Kuomintang Army 1933; joined CCP 1936; Commdr. Northeast Railway Protection Corps 1948; Vice-Minister of Railways 1949-61; Commdr. PLA Railway Corps 1950; Act. Minister of Railways 1961-65, Minister 1965-66; criticized and removed from office during Cultural Revolution 1967; Political Commissar, PLA Railway Corps 1976-79, First Political Commisar 1979-81; mem. 11th Cen. Cttee. of CCP 1977; Pres. Tennis Assen. 1977-; Hon. Pres. Chinese Railways Veterans Assen. 1981-. *Address:* People's Republic of China.

LÜ ZHIXIAN; Chinese diplomatist; Dir. Propaganda Dept., Provincial CCP Cttee., Zhejiang 1954; Sec.-Gen. Zhejiang CCP Cttee. 1958; First Sec. CCP Cttee., Jinhua Special District, Zhejiang 1958; Chancellor, Hangzhou Univ. 1964; Amb. to Mauritania 1965-67, to Hungary 1970-73, to People's Repub. of the Congo 1973-76, to Democratic People's Repub. of Korea 1976-82; Vice-Minister of Culture 1982-87; Vice-Pres. Assen. for Cultural Exchanges with Foreign Countries April 1987-; Vice-Chair. Nat. Comm. for UNESCO 1983-. *Address:* c/o Ministry of Culture, Donganmen North Street, Beijing, People's Republic of China.

LUAN JUJIE; Chinese fencing champion; b. 1958, Nanjing; Women's Individual Foils Champion of China 1977; winner, Women's Foil World Cup, Fed. Repub. of Germany 1984; winner, Women's Individual Foil, Los Angeles Olympics 1984. *Address:* Nanjing Sports Training School, Nanjing, Jiangsu, People's Republic of China.

LUBAC, Cardinal H.E. Henri Sonier de; French theologian; b. 20 Feb. 1896, Cambrai Nord; s. of Maurice Sonier de Lubac and Gabrielle de Beaurepaire; Prof. Catholic Theology Faculty, Univ. of Lyon 1929-61; Hon. Prof. 1961-; cr. Cardinal 1983; Deacon of St. Maria in Domnica 1984-; mem. Acad. Moral Science and Politics 1958-; Officier Légion d'Honneur, Croix de guerre 1914-18; Dr. h.c. (American Univ. of Notre Dame, Univ. of Innsbruck, Catholic Univ. of Chile). *Publications:* Catholicisme 1938, Corpus Mysticum 1944, Proudhon et le Christianisme 1945, le Fondement théologique des missions 1946, Surnaturel 1946, Histoire et Esprit 1950, Aspects du Bouddhisme (2 vols) 1951, 1955, Rencontre du Bouddhisme et de l'Occident 1952, Méditation sur l'Eglise 1953, Paradoxes, nouveaux Paradoxes 1946, 1955, Sur les Chemins de Dieu 1956, Exégèse médiévale (4 vols) 1959-64, la Pensée religieuse du Père Teilhard de Chardin 1962, la Prière du Père Teilhard de Chardin 1964, l'Eglise dans la crise actuelle 1969, la Structure du Symbole des Apôtres, Teilhard et notre temps 1971, les Eglises particulières dans l'Eglise universelle 1972, Dieu se dit dans l'histoire, 1974, Pic de la Mirandole 1975, Teilhard posthume, réflexions et souvenirs 1977, la Postérité spirituelle de Joachim de Flore 1979, 1981, La Révélation divine 1983, Théologies d'occasion 1984, Correspondance commentée entre G. Marcel et G. Fessard 1985, Entretien autour de Vatican II 1985, Lettres de M. Etienne Gilson au P. de Lubac 1986, Résistance Chrétienne à l'antisémitisme 1988. *Address:* 42 rue de Grenelle, 75007 Paris, France.

LUBACHIVSKY, H.E. Myroslav Ivan; Soviet (Ukranian) ecclesiastic; b. 24 June 1914, Dolyna; ordained 1938; consecrated Archbishop Metropolitan of Philadelphia of the Ukrainians 1979; Coadjutor to Archbishop Major of Luiv of the Ukrainians 1980, Major Archbishop 1984; cr. Cardinal by Pope John Paul II 1985. *Address:* Piazza Madonna dei Monti 3, 00184 Rome, Italy. *Telephone:* (06) 48.57.78.

LUBBERS, Rudolph Frans Marie; Netherlands politician; b. 7 May 1939, Rotterdam; m.; two s. one d.; ed. Erasmus Univ., Rotterdam; Sec. to Man. Bd., Lubbers Hollandia Eng. Works 1963-65, Co-Dir. 1965; mem. Bd. Netherlands Christian Employers' Fed., Fed. of Mechanical and Electrical Eng. Industries; mem. Programmes Advisory Council of Catholic Broadcasting Assocn.; Minister of Econ. Affairs 1973-77; mem. Second Chamber of States-Gen. (Parl.) May 1977-; Prime Minister of the Netherlands Nov. 1982-; mem. Christian Democratic Appeal. *Address:* Office of the Prime Minister, The Hague, Netherlands.

LUBIN, Steven, B.A. M.S. PH.D.; American pianist and fortepianist; b. 22 Feb. 1942, New York; m. 1974; one s.; ed. Harvard Univ., Juilliard School, New York Univ.; piano studies with Lisa Grad, Nadia Reisenberg, Seymour Lipkin, Rosina Lhevinne, Beveridge Webster; recital and concert tours U.S.A., U.K. and Austria; f. The Mozartean Players 1978; mem. Faculty Juilliard School 1964-65, Aspen Music School 1967, Cornell Univ. 1971-75, Vassar Coll. 1971-75, School of the Arts, State Univ. of N.Y.-Purchase 1975-; recordings on Arabesque, Decca and Spectrum labels. *Publications:* articles in The New York Times, Keynote, Ovation and Keyboard Classics on modern pianos and fortepianos. *Address:* c/o J. B. Keller, 250 West 57th Street 1130, New York, N.Y. 10107, U.S.A. *Telephone:* (212) 315-2430.

LUBIS, Mochtar; Indonesian journalist; b. 7 March 1922, Padang, Sumatra; s. of Raja Pandapotan and Mandailing Sumatra; m. Siti Halimah 1945; two s. one d.; joined Indonesian Antara News Agency 1945; publisher daily Indonesian Raya 1949-61, Ed. 1956-51, 1966; published and edited The Times of Indonesia 1952; now Dir.-Gen. Press Foundation of Asia, Manila, Philippines; Vice-Chair. The Jakarta Acad.; Chair. Yayasan Obor Indonesia (books); Nat. Literary Award 1953; Pres. Magsaysay Award for the Press 1958, Golden Pen of Freedom, Int. Fed. of Publishers 1967, Press Foundation of Asia; Vice-Chair. Jakarta Acad.; mem. Bd. Int. Press Inst.; mem. UNESCO Comm. for Communication Problems; Dir.-Gen. Press Foundation of Asia; Chair. Obor Indonesia Foundation. *Publications:* Pers and Wartawan, Tak Ada Esok, Si Djamal (short stories), Djalan Ada Udjung, Korean Notebook, Perkenalan Di Asia Tenggara, Melawat Ke Amerika, Stories from Europe, Indonesia Dimata Dunia, Stories from China, A Road with No End (novel) 1952, Twilight in Djakarta 1963, Tiger! Tiger!, Subversive Notes, Love and Death 1976, Indonesia, Land under the Rainbow (history), Land under the Sun (a report on Indonesia Today) 1983, Bromocorah (short stories) 1987. *Leisure interests:* painting, ceramics, sculpture, orchids, tennis, sailing, flying, gardening. *Address:* Jalan Bonang No. 17, Jakarta 10320, Indonesia. *Telephone:* 331128.

LUBOTSKY, Mark; Netherlands violinist; b. 18 May 1931, Leningrad; one s.; ed. Moscow Conservatoire under Prof. A. Jampolsky and David Oistrakh; winner of int. competitions, Berlin, Salzburg, Moscow 1951-58; concert violinist appearing in Europe, Australia, U.S.A., Japan and Israel 1959-; Prof. of Violin, Amsterdam Conservatoire and Hamburg Hochschule. *Address:* Overtoom 329 III, 1054 JM Amsterdam, Netherlands. *Telephone:* (020) 855256.

LÚCAN, Matej, PH.DR.; Czechoslovak politician; b. 11 Jan. 1928, Gotovany; ed. Comenius Univ., Bratislava; Head of Dept., Cen. Cttee., CP of Slovakia 1951-52, 1953-63; mem. Cen. Cttee., CP of Slovakia 1958-68, 1969-71; Head of Dept. of Marxism-Leninism, Comenius Univ., Bratislava 1952-53; mem. Presidium, Slovak Nat. Council 1963-68; Commr. for Educ. and Culture, Slovak Nat. Council 1963-67, for Educ. 1967-68; Minister of Educ. of Slovak S.R. 1969-70; Perm. Rep. to Int. Office for Educ. 1964-68; Deputy Premier, Czechoslovak S.R. 1970-; mem. House of Nations, Fed. Assembly 1970-; mem. Cen. Cttee., CP of Czechoslovakia 1970-; Vice-Premier 1971-; Chair. State Cttee. for Culture, Scientific and Health Regulations with Foreign Countries 1971-, Govt. Population Comm. 1971-; Deputy Chair. Govt. Cttee. for Science and Tech. 1971-; Chair,. Cttee. for Physical Educ. and Sport of Czechoslovak Govt. 1981-, Cttee. for Klement Gottwald State Prizes 1981-; Order of Labour 1970, Order of Victorious February 1978. *Address:* Presidium of Czechoslovak Government, nábřeží kpt. Jaroše 4, Prague 1, Czechoslovakia.

LUCAS, Sir Cyril (Edward), Kt., C.M.G., D.S.C., F.R.S.E., F.R.S.; British marine scientist; b. 30 July 1909, Hull, Yorks.; s. of Archibald Lucas and Edith Lucas; m. Sarah A. Rose 1934 (died 1974); two s. one d.; ed. Hull Grammar School and Univ. Coll. Hull; Research Biologist, Univ. Coll. Hull 1931, Head, Dept. of Oceanography 1942; Dir. of Fisheries Research, Scotland (Dept. of Agric. and Fisheries for Scotland) and Dir. Marine Lab. Aberdeen 1948-70; U.K. expert or del. to various int. confs. on marine fisheries and conservation 1948-; Hon. D.Sc. (Hull) 1975, Hon. LL.D. (Aberdeen) 1977.

Publications: papers in scientific journals. *Address:* 16 Albert Terrace, Aberdeen, AB1 1XY, Scotland. *Telephone:* Aberdeen 645568.

LUCAS, George, B.A.; American film director; b. 1944, Modesto, Calif.; ed. Univ. Southern Calif.; with Warner Bros. Studio; Asst. to Francis Ford Coppola on The Rain People, also dir. documentary on making of that film; dir., co-author screenplay films THX-1138 1970, American Graffiti 1973; dir., author screenplay Star Wars 1977, also novel of same title 1977; Exec. Producer More American Graffiti 1979, The Empire Strikes Back 1980, Raiders of the Lost Ark 1981, Return of the Jedi 1982, Indiana Jones and the Temple of Doom 1984, Howard the Duck 1986, Labyrinth 1988, Willow 1988, Tucker: The Man and His Dream 1988; co. exec. producer Mishima 1985, Indiana Jones and the Last Crusade 1989; Grand Prize for THX, Nat. Student Film Festival 1967. *Address:* Lucasfilm Ltd., P.O. Box 2009, San Rafael, Calif. 94912, U.S.A.

LUCAS, Georges, L. EN D.; French publisher; b. 29 Aug. 1915, Rennes; s. of René and Madeleine (Bazin) Lucas; m. Evelyne Torres 1941; one s.; Man. Dir. and Pres. Livraria Bertrand-Amadora, Lisbon 1948-75; Dir. Editions Robert Laffont 1967, Man. Dir. 1967-75, 1978-81; Vice-Pres. and Man. Dir. Banque Franco-Portuguaise d'Outre-Mer 1966-73; Chair. and Man.-Dir. Librairie Larousse 1979-83, Adviser 1984-86; Conseiller Nat. du Commerce Extérieur 1973; Chevalier, Légion d'honneur, Croix de Guerre. *Address:* 5 avenue Emile Deschanel, 75007 Paris, France.

LUCAS GARCÍA, Gen. Fernando Romeo; Guatemalan politician; Minister of Nat. Defence 1975-76; Pres. of Guatemala July 1978-82; Cand. for Partido Revolucionario and Partido Institucional Democrático.

LUCE, Charles F., LL.B.; American business executive and lawyer; b. 29 Aug. 1917, Platteville, Wis.; m. Helen G. Oden; two s. two d.; ed. Univ. of Wisconsin Law School and Yale Law School; admitted to Wis. Bar 1941, Ore. Bar 1945, Wash. Bar 1946, New York Bar 1981; Law clerk to Mr. Justice Hugo Black, Supreme Court 1943-44; Attorney, Bonneville Power Admin., Portland, Ore. 1944-46; in private law practice, Walla Walla, Wash. 1946-61; Bonneville Power Administrator 1961-66; Under-Sec. of the Interior 1966-67; Chair. Bd. of Trustees, Consolidated Edison Co. of New York Inc. 1967-82, C.E.O. 1967-81; partner Preston, Ellis and Holman, Portland 1982-86; Special Counsel Metropolitan Life Insurance Co. 1987-; mem. Bd. of Dirs. Metropolitan Life Insurance Co., UAL Inc., United Airlines Inc., GAB Business Services Inc.; mem. Bd. of Trustees, Columbia Univ.; mem. Advisory Bd., Barclays Int. 1983-; mem. various advisory cttees., etc. *Address:* Metropolitan Life Insurance Co., 1 Madison Avenue, New York, N.Y. 10010, U.S.A.

LUCE, Henry, III; American journalist, publisher and foundation administrator; b. 28 April 1925, New York; s. of Henry R. Luce and Lila Hotz Tyng; m. 1st Patricia Potter 1947 (divorced 1954), one s. one d.; m. 2nd Claire McGill 1960 (died 1971), three step s.; m. 3rd Nancy Bryan Cassiday 1975 (died 1987), two step s. (one deceased); ed. Brooks School and Yale Univ.; served U.S.N.R. 1943-46; Commr.'s Asst., Hoover Comm. on Org. Exec. Branch of Govt. 1948-49; Reporter, Cleveland Press 1949-51; Washington Corresp. Time Inc. 1951-53, Time writer 1953-55, Head New Bldg. Dept. 1956-60, Asst. to Publr. 1960-61, Circulation Dir. Fortune and Architectural Forum 1961-64, House and Home 1962-64, Vice-Pres. 1964-80, Chief London Bureau 1966-68, Publr. Fortune 1968-69, Publr. Time 1969-72; Pres. Assocn. of American Corresps. in London 1968; Vice-Pres. for Corporate Planning, Time Inc. 1972-80; Dir. Time Inc. 1967-; Pres. Henry Luce Foundation 1958-; mem. American Council for UN Univ.; Trustee, United Bd. for Christian Higher Educ. in Asia, Eisenhower Exchange Fellowships, Yale-China Assocn., Princeton Theological Seminary, Center of Theological Inquiry, Coll. of Wooster, American Fed. of Arts, Int. Leadership Center Foundation, China Inst. in America, Temple of Understanding, A Christian Ministry in the Nat. Parks, Pan American Devt. Foundation; mem. Long Range Planning and Devt. Cttee., American Acad. of Religion, Visiting Cttee. to Harvard Divinity School; Pres. The New Museum of Contemporary Art; Hon. L.H.D. (St. Michael's Coll., Long Island Univ.). *Address:* Suite 504, 720 Fifth Avenue, New York, N.Y. 10019 (Office); 4 Sutton Place, New York, N.Y. 10022 (Home), Fishers Island, New York, N.Y. 06390 (Home), Mill Hill Road, Mill Neck, N.Y. 11765, U.S.A. (Home).

LUCE, Rt. Hon. Richard Napier, P.C., M.P.; British politician; b. 14 Oct. 1936; s. of late Sir William Luce, G.B.E., K.C.M.G. and of Margaret (née Napier) Luce; m. Rose Nicholson 1961; two s.; ed. Wellington Coll. and Christ's Coll., Cambridge; Dist. Officer, Kenya 1960-62; Brand Man. Gallaher Ltd. 1963-65; Marketing Man. Spirella Co. of G.B.; Dir. Nat. Innovations Centre 1968-71; Chair. IFA Consultants Ltd. 1972-79, Selanex Ltd. 1973-79, Courtenay Stewart Int. Ltd. 1975-79; mem. European Advisory Bd. Corning Glass Int. 1975-79; mem. Parl. for Arundel and Shoreham 1971-74, for Shoreham 1974-; Parl. Under-Sec. of State 1979-81; Minister of State, FCO 1981-82, 1983-85; Minister of State (Minister for the Arts) Privy Council Office 1985-; Conservative. *Leisure interests:* tennis, walking, reading. *Address:* House of Commons, London, S.W.1, England.

LUCE, R(obert) Duncan, PH.D.; American mathematical psychologist; b. 16 May 1925, Scranton, Pa.; s. of Robert R. and Ruth Downer Luce; m. 1st Gay Gaer 1950, 2nd Cynthia Newby 1967; one d.; m. 3rd Carolyn A. Scheer 1988; ed. M.I.T.; Member of Staff, Research Lab. of Electronics

M.I.T. 1950-53; Asst. Prof. of Sociology and Mathematical Statistics, Columbia Univ. 1954-57; Fellow Center for Advanced Study in the Behavioral Sciences 1954-55, 1966-67, 1987-88; Lecturer in Social Relations, Harvard Univ. 1957-59, Prof. of Psychology 1976-83, Victor S. Thomas Prof. of Psychology 1984-88, Emer. 1988-; Distinguished Prof. of Cognituve Sciences Univ. of Calif. at Irvine 1988-; Prof. of Psychology, Univ. of Pa. 1959-68, Benjamin Franklin Prof. 1968-69; Visiting Prof. Inst. for Advanced Study, Princeton, N.J. 1969-72; Prof. of Social Science, Univ. of Calif., Irvine 1972-75; mem. N.A.S., American Acad. of Arts and Sciences, Soc. of Experimental Psychologists; American Psychological Asscn. Distinguished Scientific Contribution Award. *Publications:* Games and Decisions (with H. Raffa), Individual Choice Behavior, Handbook of Mathematical Psychology (Jt. Ed.), Contemporary Developments in Mathematical Psychology (Jt. Ed.), Foundations of Measurement Vols. I, II, III (with D. H. Krantz, P. Suppes and A. Tversky), Response Times, Stevens' Handbook of Experimental Psychology (Jt. Ed.) and over 140 articles in scientific journals. *Address:* Social Science Tower, University of Calif. at Irvine, Calif. 92717; 7 Urbino, Irvine, Calif. 92720, U.S.A. (Home). *Telephone:* (717) 856-6239 (Office); (717) 838-8108 (Home).

LUCEBERT (pseudonym of L. J. Swaanswijk); Netherlands painter and poet; b. 15 Sept. 1924; ed. School of Applied Arts, Amsterdam; mem. Experimental COBRA group; has lived and worked in Berlin (with Bertolt Brecht) 1954, Bulgaria 1955, France 1964 and Spain 1965; first one-man exhbn., Galerie Espace, Haarlem 1958, also Stedelijk Museum, Amsterdam 1959, and Marlborough New London Gallery 1963; retrospective exhbn. Stedelijk Museum, Amsterdam 1969, 1987; Amsterdam Poetry Prize 1954, Premio Marzotto 1962, Graphic Art Prize, Biennale Carrara 1962, Del Naviglio Prize, Venice Biennale 64, P.C. Hooft Prize 1967, Combined Belgian-Dutch Prize for Literature 1983. *Publications:* Collected Poems 1974, Harvest in a Labyrinth 1981, Swamprider from Paradise 1982; trans.: Wir sind Gesichter 1972, Die Silbenuhr 1981, Antologia 1978, Skola Amsterdamska 1986. *Address:* Boendermakerhof 10, 1861 TB Bergen N-H, Netherlands. *Telephone:* 02208-13551.

LUCEY, Patrick Joseph; American politician and diplomatist; b. 21 March 1918, LaCrosse, Wis.; s. of Gregory and Ella (McNamara) Lucey; m. Jean Vlasis 1951; two s. one d.; ed. St. Thomas Coll., Minneapolis and Univ. of Wisconsin; Founder/owner, Lucey Realty 1954-70; State legislator 1948-50; State Chair. Wisconsin Democratic Party 1957-63; Lieut.-Gov. State of Wisconsin 1964-66, Gov. 1971-77; Amb. to Mexico 1977-80; several hon. degrees; Democrat. *Address:* c/o Department of State, 2201 C Street, N.W., Washington, D.C. 20520, U.S.A.

LUCHINSKY, Petr Kirillovich, CAND.PHIL.SC.; Soviet politician; b. 1940; ed. Kishinev Univ. and CPSU Cen. Cttee. Higher Party School; served in Soviet Army 1962-63; Komsomol work for Cen. Cttee. of Moldavian CP 1963-64; mem. CPSU 1964-; First Sec. of Belt, City Komsomol Cttee. 1964-65; Head of Section, Second Sec., First Sec. of Cen. Cttee. of Moldavian Komsomol 1965-71; Sec. of Cen. Cttee. of Moldavian CP 1971-76; First Sec. of Kishinev City Cttee. 1976-78; Deputy Head, First Sec., of CPSU Cen. Cttee. 1978-86; Second Sec. of Cen. Cttee. of Tadzhik CP 1986-; Cand. mem. of CPSU Cen. Cttee. 1986-; Deputy to U.S.S.R. Supreme Soviet. *Address:* Central Committee of Tadzhik CP, Dushanbe, Tadzhik S.S.R., U.S.S.R.

LUCHKO, Klara Stepanovna; Soviet actress; b. 1925; graduated from VGIK in 1948; worked in films 1948-; mem. of CPSU 1966; People's Artist of U.S.S.R. 1985. *Roles include:* Dasha Shelest in Cossacks from the Kuban (U.S.S.R. State Prize 1955), Viola in Twelfth Night, Jadwiga in Red Leaves, Claudia Puvlyakov in film The Gipsies (TV).

LUCHSINGER, Fred W., PH.D.; Swiss journalist; b. 9 July 1921, St. Gallen; s. of Caspar and Lina Luchsinger-Schwyter; m. Dorette Walther 1950; one s. two d.; ed. Literargymnasium, Kantonschule St. Gallen, Univs. of Zürich and Basel, and Yale Univ.; with Neue Zürcher Zeitung 1949-, Foreign News Dept. 1949, Bonn Corresp. 1955-63, Foreign Ed. 1963, Ed.-in-Chief 1968-84. *Publications:* Der Basler Buchdruck als Vermittler italienischen Geistes 1953, Die Neue Zürcher Zeitung im Zeitalter des Zweiten Weltkrieges 1955, Bericht über Bonn: deutsche Politik 1955-1965 1966, Realitäten und Illusionen, Internationale Politik 1963-83 1983. *Address:* c/o Neue Zürcher Zeitung, Postfach, 8021 Zürich, Switzerland. *Telephone:* 258 11 11.

LUCIO PAREDES, Antonio José, DR.JUR.; Ecuadorean diplomatist; b. 13 Dec. 1923; ed. Univ. Central del Ecuador and Pontifícia Univ. Católica de Rio de Janeiro; joined Ministry of Foreign Affairs 1944; Third Sec., Rio de Janeiro 1949-52; Consul-Gen., Madrid 1955-56; Counsellor 1956-60; Counsellor, del. of Ecuador to OAS 1960-62; Prof. of Diplomatic Law, Inst. Ecuatoriano de Derecho Internacional 1965-66; Prof. of Consular Law, School of Political and Admin. Sciences, Univ. Central 1967-68; Under-Sec.-Gen. Ministry of Foreign Affairs 1967-68; Amb. to Belgium 1968-71, to France 1976-80, to the Netherlands 1980-85; Minister of Foreign Affairs 1972-75; del. to numerous int. confs.; Gran Cruz, Orden Nacional al Mérito (Ecuador) and decorations from thirteen other countries. *Address:* c/o Ministry of Foreign Affairs, Avenida 10 de Agosto y Carrión, Quito, Ecuador. *Telephone:* 528-830.

LUCIUS, Wulf D. von, DR.RER.POL.; German scientific publisher; b. 29 Nov. 1938, Jena; s. of late Tankred R. von Lucius and of Annelise Fischer; m. Akka Achelis 1967; three s.; ed. Heidelberg, Berlin and Freiburg; mil. service 1958-60; Asst. Inst. of Econometrics, Freiburg 1965-66; worked in several publishing houses and as public accountant 1966-69; partner and Exec. Officer, Gustav Fischer Verlag (family-owned publishing co.) 1969-; mem. Bd. of Exec. Officers, German Publrs. Asscn. (Börsenverein) 1976-86; Pres. Stiftung Buchkunst 1986-, Herbert Hoffmann Foundation for Research into the History of the Book Trade 1987-. *Publications:* numerous articles on publishing, copyright and book history. *Leisure interests:* collecting fine print and art books. *Address:* Wollgrasweg 49, 7000 Stuttgart 72 (Office); Ameisenbergstrasse 22, 7000 Stuttgart 1, Federal Republic of Germany. *Telephone:* 0711-458030 (Office); 0711-264386 (Home).

LUCKHOO, Sir Lionel Alfred, K.C.M.G., C.B.E., Q.C.; Guyanese barrister and diplomatist; b. 2 March 1914, Guyana; s. of Edward Luckhoo, O.B.E., and Evelyn Luckhoo; m. Sheila Chamberlin; two s. three d.; ed. Queen's Coll., Georgetown, Guyana, and Middle Temple, London; mem. Legis. Council, British Guiana 1949, State Council 1952; mem. Exec. Council and Minister without Portfolio 1953; mem. Interim Govt. 1953; mem. Georgetown Municipality for fifteen years; Mayor of Georgetown four times; Chair. Georgetown Sewage and Water Comms., Public Health Comm., Fire Comm., Chair. numerous other Cttees.; Pres. four Trade Unions; rep. Guyana at several confs. throughout world; High Commr. for Guyana in U.K. 1966-70, for Barbados 1966-70, Amb. of Guyana and Barbados to France, Fed. Repub. of Germany and Netherlands 1967-70; retd. from diplomatic service 1972; Amb. and Special Envoy to Pres. of Guyana 1981-; official interpreter to the Courts; pvt. law practice 1972- ("World's Most Successful Advocate", 245 murder acquittals without a single conviction to date, 1981, Guinness Book of Records); Pres. Guyana Olympic Cttee.; Chair. Red Cross Guyana. *Publications:* The Fitzluck Theory of Horse Breeding 1952, I Believe 1968, Life After Death 1975, Sense of Values 1975, God is Love 1975, Christ is Coming, Xmas Story, My dear Atheist 1977, Dear Boys and Girls 1978, Dear Adults 1979, God and Science 1980, Dear Muslims 1980, The Question Answered 1984, The Verdict is Yours 1985. *Leisure interests:* horse racing, cricket, magic, chess, bridge, short story writing. *Address:* Lot 1, Croal Street, Georgetown, Guyana.

LUDER, Owen (Harold), C.B.E., F.R.S.A.; British architect, planner and environmentalist; b. 7 Aug. 1928, London; s. of late Edward Charles Luder and of Ellen Clara Luder; m. Rose Dorothy (Doris) Broadstock 1951; one s. (deceased) four d.; ed. Brixton School of Building, Regent St. Polytechnic Evening School of Architecture, Brixton School of Architecture; f. Owen Luder Partnership 1957, Sr. Partner until 1978 (when partnership became an unlimited co.), Chair. and Man. Dir. 1958-87; f. Owen Luder Consultants 1988; Council mem. R.I.B.A. 1967-, Hon. Treas. 1975-78, Pres. 1981-83, now Past Pres.; Pres. Norwood Soc. 1982-; Sec./Treas. Commonwealth Asscn. of Architects 1985-87; Consultant to Nat. Coal Bd. for environmental, architectural and planning issues on Vale of Belvoir Coal Mining Project, U.K. 1975-, Consultant for many commercial devt. schemes; R.I.B.A. Architecture Bronze Medal 1963; Town Planning and Housing Council Silver Jubilee Award 'Housing in the 80's'; various architectural, design and civic trust awards and commendations. *Publications:* Promotion and Marketing for Building Professionals 1988; frequent contributions to nat. and tech. publications. *Leisure interests:* golf, photography, writing, Arsenal Football Club. *Address:* 418 Premier House, 10 Greycoat Place, London, S.W.1, England. *Telephone:* 01-222 8866.

LUDLUM, Robert, B.A.; American author; b. 25 May 1927, New York; s. of George Hartford Ludlum and Margaret Wadsworth; m. Mary Ryducha 1951; two s. one d.; ed. Wesleyan Univ.; actor and theatrical producer, New York 1952-69; novelist 1969-. *Publications:* The Scarlatti Inheritance 1971, The Osterman Weekend 1972, The Matlock Paper 1973, The Rhinemann Exchange 1974, The Gemini Contenders 1976, The Chancellor Manuscript 1977, The Holcroft Covenant 1978, The Matarese Circle 1979, The Bourne Identity 1980, The Parsifal Mosaic 1982, The Aquitaine Progression 1983, The Icarus Agenda 1988. *Address:* Dell Publishing, 1 Dag Hammarskjold Plaza, New York, N.Y. 10017, U.S.A.

LUDWICZAK, Dominik; Polish farmer and politician; b. 1939, Mirosławki, Poznań Voivodship; runs own specialized farm; mem. United Peasants' Party (ZSL) 1974-; Pres. ZSL Village Circle, Trzebaw, Poznań Voivodship 1976-82; Pres. ZSL Town and Commune Cttee., Steszew, Poznań Voivodship 1982-; mem. ZSL Chief Cttee. Dec. 1980-, mem. Presidium ZSL Chief Cttee. July 1982-, Deputy Pres. ZSL Chief Cttee. March 1984-; Deputy to Seym (Parl.) 1985-; mem. Nat. Council of Patriotic Movt. for Nat. Rebirth (PRON) May 1983-. *Address:* Naczelny Komitet ZSL, ul. Grzybowska 4, 00-131 Warsaw, Poland. *Telephone:* 20-02-51.

LUDWIG, Christa; Austrian mezzo-soprano opera singer; b. 16 March 1928, Berlin, Germany; d. of Anton Ludwig and Eugenie Besalla-Ludwig; m. 1st Walter Berry (q.v.) 1957 (divorced 1970), one s.; m. 2nd Paul-Emile Deiber 1972; opera debut at 18, guest appearance at the Athens Festival in Epidauros 1965; joined Vienna State Opera 1955, Hon. mem. 1981; Hon. mem. Vienna Konzerthaus; appearances at Festivals in Salzburg, Bayreuth, Lucerne, Holland, Prague, Saratoga, Stockholm; guest appearances in season in Vienna, New York, Chicago, Buenos Aires, Scala Milano, Berlin, Munich; numerous recitals and soloist in concerts; recordings of Lieder and complete operas including Norma (with Maria Callas), Lohengrin, Cosí fan tutte, Der Rosenkavalier, Carmen, Götterdämmerung, Die Walküre, Herzog Blaubarts Burg, Don Giovanni, Die Zauberflöte, Figaros Hochzeit, Capriccio, Fidelio; winner of Bach-Concours, record award for Fricka in Walküre, and Des Knaben Wunderhorn; awarded title of Kammersängerin by Austrian Govt. 1962; Prix des Affaires Culturelles, for recording of Venus in Tannhäuser, Paris 1972; Silver Rose (Vienna Philharmonic) 1980; Golden Ring (Staatsoper, Vienna) 1980; Golden Gustav Mahler Medal 1980, Hugo Wolf Medal 1980, Goldenes Ehrenzeichen (Salzburg). *Leisure interests:* music, archaeology, reading, home movie making, cooking, sewing, fashion, shopping, weaving, rug knitting and travelling. *Address:* 14 Rigistrasse, 6045, Meggen, Switzerland (Home).

LUEDERITZ, Alexander, DR.IUR.; German professor of law; b. 19 March 1932, Göttingen; s. of Heinrich and Gertrud Luederitz; m. Renate née Wessling 1960; one s. one d.; ed. Cologne and Lausanne Schools of Law; mem. of the Bar 1961–65; Prof. of Law, Frankfurt Univ. 1966–70, Dean, Faculty of Law 1969–70; Prof. of Law and Dir. Inst. for Int. and Foreign Private Law, Univ. of Cologne 1971–, Dean, Faculty of Law 1979–80; Visiting Prof. Univ. of Calif., Berkeley 1982; Fellow, American Council of Learned Socs. *Publications:* Auslegung von Rechtsgeschäften 1966, Commentary on German Conflicts Law (Corporation, Agency, Torts) 1984, International Sales 1987, International Privatrecht 1987; articles in learned journals. *Leisure interests:* hiking, stamp collecting. *Address:* Kellerhardtsweg 12, D-5064 Roesrath, Federal Republic of Germany. *Telephone:* (0)2205-3124.

LUELLEN, Charles J., B.S.; American oil executive; b. 18 Oct. 1929, Greenville, S.C.; s. of John B. and Dorothy C. (née Bell) Luellen; m. Jo S. Riddle 1953; two d.; ed. Univ. of Indiana; Sales Rep. Ashland Oil, Inc., Ky. 1952–70, Vice-Pres. Sales 1970–72, Group Vice-Pres. Sales 1972–80, Pres., C.O.O. 1986–; Pres. Ashland Petroleum Co. 1980–86; mem. Bd. of Dirs. American Petroleum Inst., Washington 1982–, Asphalt Inst., Washington 1974–76; mem. Energy and Natural Resources Cttee. U.S. Chamber of Commerce 1987–, Nat. Chamber Foundation, Washington 1987, Indiana Univ. Fellows. *Address:* Ashland Oil Inc., P.O. Box 391, Ashland, Ky. 41114 (Office); 4400 Oak Hollow Drive, Ashland, Ky. 41101, U.S.A. (Home).

LUERS, William Henry, M.A.; American diplomatist and art gallery president; b. 15 May 1929, Springfield, Ill.; s. of Carl U. and Ann L. Luers; m. Wendy Woods Turnbull 1979; three s. one d. by previous marriage; ed. Hamilton Coll., Columbia and Northwestern Univs.; Foreign Service Officer Dept. of State 1957; Vice-Consul, Naples, Italy 1957–60; Second Sec. Embassy, Moscow 1963–65; Political Counsellor, Caracas, Venezuela 1969–73; Deputy Exec. Sec., Dept. of State 1973–75; Deputy Asst. Sec. for Inter-American Affairs, Washington 1975–77, Deputy Asst. Sec. 1977–78; Amb. to Venezuela 1978–82, to Czechoslovakia 1983–86; Pres. Metropolitan Museum of Art, New York 1986–; mem. Council on Foreign Relations, Int. Inst. for Strategic Studies, London. *Address:* Metropolitan Museum of Art, Fifth Avenue and 82nd Street, New York, N.Y. 10028, U.S.A.

LUERSSEN, Frank Wonson, M.S.; American business executive; b. 14 Aug. 1927, Reading, Pa.; s. of George V. Luerssen and of Mary Ann Swoyer; m. Joan M. Schlosser 1950; one s. four d.; ed. Pennsylvania State Univ., Lehigh Univ., Bethlehem, Pa.; Metallurgist, Research and Devt. Inland Steel Co., various man. positions in research 1952–58, Vice-Pres. Research 1968–77, Vice-Pres. Steel Manufacturing 1977–78, Pres. and Dir. Inland Steel Co. 1978–83, Chair., Pres., C.E.O. 1982– and Dir. Jan. 1983–; mem. A.I.M.E., American Soc. for Metals, Metallurgical Soc., American Iron and Steel Inst., Asscn. of Iron and Steel Engineers, Nat. Acad. of Eng., Soc. of Automotive Engineers, Metals Soc. (G.B.), Visiting Cttee., Northwestern Univ. Tech. Inst., W. Soc. of Engineers and of other socs. and cttees.; Fellow, American Soc. for Metals; has registered five patents concerned with metal production processes; Howe Memorial Lecture A.I.M.E. 1984, Distinguished Alumnus (Penn State Univ.) 1984. *Leisure interests:* golf, gardening, sailing. *Address:* 30 West Monroe Street, Chicago, Ill. 60603 (Office); 8226 Parkview Avenue, Munster, Ind. 46321, U.S.A. (Home). *Telephone:* (312) 899 3905 (Office); (219) 838 5672 (Home).

LUFT, Friedrich; German journalist; b. 24 Aug. 1911, Berlin; s. of Prof. Fritz and Mary (née Wilson) Luft; m. Heide Thilo 1940; ed. Univs. of Berlin and Königsberg (Kaliningrad); drama and film critic Die Neue Zeitung 1945–55, Süddeutsche Zeitung 1955–62, Die Welt 1955–, Berliner Morgenpost 1976–; weekly commentator on theatre and film for Radio RIAS, Berlin 1946–; mem. PEN Club; F.R.S.A.; Prof. h.c. 1976; Ordre des Arts et des Lettres 1984. *Publications:* Luftballons 1939, Tagesblätter von Urbanus 1947, Puella auf der Insel 1947, Köpfe (with Fritz Eschen) 1957, Altes-Neues Berlin 1959, Kritische Jahre, Berliner Theater 1945–61 1961, Luftsprünge (essays) 1961, Stimme der Kritik 1965, Zille, Mein Photo-Milieu (ed.) 1967, Stimme der Kritik II, Theaterereignisse seit 1965. *Address:* Maienstrasse 4, 1000 Berlin 30, Federal Republic of Germany. *Telephone:* 0311-245873.

LUGAR, Richard Green, M.A.: American politician; b. 4 April 1932, Indianapolis, Ind.; s. of Marvin L. Lugar and Bertha Green Lugar; m. Charlene Smeltzer 1956; four s.; ed. Shortridge High School, Denison Univ., Ohio, Pembroke Coll., Oxford Univ.; Rhodes Scholar, Pembroke Coll., Oxford

1956; served U.S.N. 1957–60; Vice-Pres. and Treas. Thomas Green & Co. Inc. 1960–67, Sec.-Treas. 1968–; Treas. Lugar Stock Farms Inc. 1960–; mem. Bd. of Trustees, Denison Univ. 1966–, Advisory Bd., Ind. Univ., Purdue Univ. at Indianapolis 1969–75, Bd. of Trustees of Ind. Cen. Univ. 1970; Vice-Chair. 1975, Visiting Prof. of Political Science, Dir. of Public Affairs 1975–76; mem. Visiting Cttee. of Harvard–M.I.T. Joint Centre for Urban Studies 1973–; mem. Bd. of Dirs., Indianapolis Centre for Advanced Research 1973–76; mem. Indianapolis Bd. of School Commrs. 1964–67, Vice-Pres. 1965; Mayor of Indianapolis 1968–75; del. and keynote speaker, Ind. Republican Convention 1968, del. 1972; del. mem. Platform Cttee., Repub. Nat. Convention 1968, del., keynote speaker and mem. Platform Cttee. 1972; Candidate for U.S. Senate 1974, Senator from Indiana 1977–; mem. Advisory Comm. on Intergovernmental Relations 1969–75, Vice-Chair. 1970–75; mem. Advisory Bd. of U.S. Conf. of Mayors 1969–75; mem. Pres. Model Cities Advisory Task Force 1969–70, State and Local Govt. Advisory Cttee. of Office of Econ. Opportunity 1969–73, Nat. Advisory Comm. on Criminal Justice Standards and Goals 1971–73; Pres. of Advisory Council, Nat. League of Cities 1971, mem. Council 1972–75; Chair. Nat. Republican Senatorial Cttee. 1983–84; Chair. Foreign Relations Cttee. 1985–87; mem. Bd. of Dirs. of Westview Osteopathic Hosp. 1969–76, also of Indianapolis Symphony Orch.; mem. Nat. Acad. of Public Admin., Rotary Club of Indianapolis and other civic orgs., Hon. Doctorates from 20 colls. and univs. in U.S.A. 1970–78; Exceptional Service Award, Office of Econ. Opportunity 1972, Fiorello La Guardia Award, New School of Social Research 1975. *Leisure interests:* music, reading, running, golf, tennis. *Address:* 306 Hart Senate Office Building, Washington, D.C. 20510, U.S.A. *Telephone:* (202) 224-4814.

LUHMANN, Niklas, DR.SC.POL.; German sociologist; b. 8 Dec. 1927, Lüneburg; s. of Wilhelm Luhmann and Dora née Gurtner; m. Ursula von Walter 1960 (died 1977); two s. one d.; ed. Univ. of Freiburg in Breisgau and Harvard Univ.; Ministry of Cultural Affairs, Lower Saxony 1954–62; Research Fellow, School for Admin. Sciences, Speyer 1962–65; Chief of Dept., Inst. for Social Research, Dortmund 1965–68; Prof. of Sociology, Univ. of Bielefeld 1968–; Visiting Prof. New School of Social Research, New York 1975. *Publications:* Funktionen und Folgen formaler Organisation 1964, Grundrechte als Institution 1965, Legitimation durch Verfahren 1969 , Rechtssoziologie 1972, Zweckbegriff und Systemrationalität 1968, Soziologisch. Aufklärung (3 vols.) 1970, 1975, 1981, Funktion der Religion 1977, Trust and Power 1979, Gesellschaftsstruktur und Semantik (2 vols.) 1980–81, Politische Theorie im Wohlfahrtsstaat 1981, Ausdifferenzierung des Rechts 1981, The Differentation of Society 1982, Liebe als Passion 1982, Soziale Systeme 1984, Ökologische Kommunikation 1986. *Address:* Marianne Weber str. 13, D-4811 Oerlinghausen, Federal Republic of Germany. *Telephone:* 05202/5336.

LUHOVY, Ladislav; Czechoslovak politician; b. 1931; ed. Slovak Technical Univ., Bratislava; mem. Cen. Cttee. C.P. of Czechoslovakia and mem. Econ. Comm. 1976–; Minister of Gen. Eng. 1986–88. *Address:* c/o Ministry of General Engineering, Prague, Czechoslovakia.

LUJAN, Manuel, Jr., B.A.; American politician; b. 12 May 1928, San Ildefonso, N.M.; s.of Manuel Lujan and Lorenzita (née Romero) Lujan; m. Jean Kay Couchman 1948; two s. two d.; ed. Santa Fe Coll., St. Mary's Coll., Calif.; Insurance executive, Santa Fe, Albuquerque 1948–; mem. 91st-100th Congresses from 1st N.M. Dist. 1969–; nominated Sec. of the Interior Dec. 1988; mem. Interior and Insular Affairs Cttee., Energy and Environment Subcttee., Science and Tech. Cttee. *Address:* Office of the Secretary of the Interior, C Street between 18th and 19th Streets, N.W., Washington, D.C. 20240; 1323 Longworth Office Building, Washington, D.C. 20515, U.S.A.

LUKÁCS, János; Hungarian politician; b. 1935, Püspökszenterzsébet; worked as a mason; ed. H.S.W.P. Political Academy; joined the Party 1953; various leading functions in youth movt.; First Sec. Communist Youth Fed. County Baranya Cttee. 1964–72; Sec., later First Sec. H.S.W.P. Municipal Party Cttee. of Pécs 1972–80, Co. Baranya Cttee. 1980–; mem. H.S.W.P. 1985–; Sec. 1987–; mem. Political Cttee. 1988–89. *Address:* Hungarian Socialist Workers Party, Central Committee, 1387 Budapest, Széchenyi rakpart 19, Hungary. *Telephone:* 111-400.

LUKE, 2nd Baron, cr. 1929, of Pavenham; **Ian St. John Lawson Johnston,** K.C.V.O.; British business executive; b. 7 June 1905, London; s. of 1st Baron and Hon. Edith Laura; m. Barbara Anstruther-Gough-Calthorpe 1932; four s. one d.; ed. Eton Coll., Trinity Coll., Cambridge; Pres., Inc. Sales Managers Assen. 1953–56, Advertising Assen. 1955–58, London Chamber of Commerce 1952–55; fmr. Chair. Bovril Ltd., Argentine Estates of Bovril Ltd., Virol Ltd.; Life Pres. (fmr. Chair.) Electrolux Ltd. 1978–; Chair. Nat. Playing Fields Assen. 1950–76, Vice-Pres. 1977–; Chair. Gateway Bldg. Soc. 1978–86; Dir. Ashanti Goldfields Corpn. Ltd.; mem. Int. Olympic Cttee. 1951–88; Hon. mem. Int. Olympic Cttee. 1988–; Nat. Vice-Pres. Royal British Legion; Pres. Inst. of Export 1973–83; Hon. Fellow, Queen Mary College, Univ. of London 1980; extensive farming interests, Bedfordshire. *Leisure interest:* gardening. *Address:* Odell Castle, Odell, Bedfordshire, MK43 7BB, England. *Telephone:* 0234-720-240.

LUKE, Eben Livesey, B.A., B.L.; Sierra Leone judge; b. 7 May 1930, Freetown; s. of late Samuel E. Luke and Rebecca Luke; m. Rachel E.

Macauley 1959; ed. Methodist Boys' High School, Freetown, Univ. of Southampton, and Lincoln's Inn, London; called to bar 1956; in private legal practice in Sierra Leone 1957-70; Puisne Judge 1970; Justice, Supreme Court of Sierra Leone 1971; Acting Chief Justice 1976-78, Chief Justice 1979-86; Pres. Sierra Leone Bar Asscn. 1970; Justice, Gambia Court of Appeal 1972-; del. to several int. confs. and mem. various comms. and cttees.; Officer, Order of the Repub. of Sierra Leone. *Leisure interests:* golf, reading. *Address:* c/o Chief Justice's Chambers, Law Courts, Freetown, Sierra Leone.

LUKINOV, Ivan Illarionovich, D.ECON.SC.; Soviet economist; b. 5 Oct. 1927, Belgorod Region; s. of Illarion Ivanovich Lukinov and Praskyorya Alexeyevna Lukinova; m. Tatyana Borisovna Kozminskaya 1956; one s. one d.; ed. Agric. Tech. Coll., Kharkov Agric. Inst.; mem. CPSU 1953-; worked for Ukrainian Acad. of Sciences Inst. of Econ. 1951-56; head of a section of Cen. Cttee. of Ukrainian CP 1956-67; head of section at Ukrainian Inst. of Econs. 1965-67; Dir. of Schlichter Ukrainian Inst. of Econ. 1967-76; Prof. 1968; Dir. Inst. of Econs., Ukrainian Acad. of Sciences 1976-, Acad. Sec. 1976-80; Vice-Pres. of Ukrainian Acad. of Sciences 1979-; mem. of U.S.S.R. Acad. of Sciences 1984-. *Leisure interests:* tennis, skiing. *Address:* Academy of Sciences of the Ukrainian SSR, Vladimirskaya 24, 252601 Kiev 30; Institute of Economics, Academy of Sciences of the Ukrainian SSR, Panas Myrny Street 26, 252011 Kiev 11, U.S.S.R.

LUKMAN, Rilwanu, B.SC., C.ENG.; Nigerian business executive and government minister; b. Feb. 1938, Zaria, Kaduna State; ed. Govt. Coll. Zaria (now Barewa), Nigerian Coll. of Arts, Science and Tech. (now Ahmadu Bello Univ.), Royal School of Mines, Imperial Coll. of Science and Tech., Univ. of London, Inst. of Prospecting and Mineral Deposits, Univ. of Mining and Metallurgy, Leogen, Austria; Asst. Mining Engineer, A.G. Stataghruvor, Sweden 1962-64; Inspector of Mines and Sr. Inspector of Mines, Jos 1964-67, Acting Asst. Chief Inspector of Mines 1968-70; Gen. Man. Cement Co. of Northern Nigeria Ltd., Sokoto 1970-74, Gen. Man. and Chief Exec. Nigerian Mining Corpn., Jos 1978-84; Fed. Minister of Mines, Power and Steel, Lagos 1984-85, of Petroleum Resources, Lagos 1986-; Pres. OPEC 1986-; Fellow Institution of Mining and Metallurgy, London (currently Overseas mem. of Council, representing Nigeria); Hon. Fellow Imperial Coll.; Fellow and Corp. mem. Nigerian Mining and Geosciences Soc. (fmrly. Nigerian Mining, Geological and Metallurgical Soc.), Past. Pres., now mem. Council; mem. Asscn. of Geoscientists for Int. Devt. (mem. Council, Vice-Pres.); mem. Soc. of Mining Engineers of AIME. *Address:* NNPC Headquarters, Falomo Office Complex, Ikoyi-Lagos, Nigeria. *Telephone:* 681146.

ŁUKOSZ, Edward, MECH.ENG.; Polish politician, b. 1929, Czechowice; ed. Ural Polytechnic Inst.; employee, Mechanical Appliances Works, Poręba, nr. Zawiercie 1956-61; Chief Eng., Andrychów Machine Works 1961-63; Gen. Dir. Design Office of Construction and Tech. of Machine Tools and Tools, Warsaw 1963-64; Dir. for tech. matters and Gen. Dir. Union of Machine Tools and Tools Industry, Warsaw 1964-73; Dir. of Unit for Eng. Industry, Planning Comm. attached to Council of Ministers 1973-82; Minister of Metallurgy and Eng. Industry 1982-84; Deputy Chair. Planning Comm. attached to Council of Ministers 1984-86; Counsellor-Minister Plenipotentiary, Embassy in Moscow 1986-; mem. Polish United Workers' Party (PZPR). *Address:* Embassy of the Polish People's Republic. ul. Klimashkina 4, Moscow, U.S.S.R. *Telephone:* 254-01-05.

LUKYANIENKO, Vladimir Matveyevich; Soviet oil construction engineer and official; b. 1937; ed. Kharkov Polytechnic; engineer 1961-73; mem. CPSU 1963-; Dir. of Frunze Machine-Construction Works, Suma 1973-86; U.S.S.R. Minister of Chemical and Oil Machine Construction 1986-; Cand. mem. of CPSU Cen. Cttee. 1986-; Deputy to U.S.S.R. Supreme Soviet; State Prize 1980; Hero of Socialist Labour 1985. *Address:* Ministry of Chemical and Oil Machine Construction, Moscow, U.S.S.R.

LUKYANOV, Anatoliy Ivanovich, D.JUD.SC.; Soviet official; b. 7 May 1930; ed. Moscow Univ.; mem. CPSU 1955-; Chief Consultant on Legal Comm. of U.S.S.R. Council of Ministers 1956-61; Deputy Head of Dept. of Presidium of U.S.S.R. Supreme Soviet 1969-76, Head of Secr. 1977-83; mem. of editorial staff of Sovietskoe gosudarstvo i pravo 1978-; mem. Cen. Auditing Comm. CPSU 1981-86; Deputy of R.S.F.S.R. Supreme Soviet 1984-; Head of Gen. Dept. of Cen. Cttee. CPSU 1985-87, Sec. of Cen. Cttee. 1987-88; Cand. mem. Political Bureau 1988-; First Vice-Chair. of Presidium, U.S.S.R. Supreme Soviet 1988-; Chief Adviser on Legal Reform in U.S.S.R. 1986-; mem. Cen. Cttee. CPSU 1987-; Order of October Revolution 1980. *Publications include:* many articles and books on Soviet legal system and Soviet constitution. *Address:* Central Committee of the Communist Party of the Soviet Union, Staraya pl. 4, Moscow, U.S.S.R.

LUMET, Sidney; American film director; b. 25 June 1924, Philadelphia; s. of Baruch Lumet and Eugenia Wemus; m. 1st Rita Gam (divorced); m. 2nd Gloria Vanderbilt 1956 (divorced 1963); m. 3rd Gail Jones 1963 (divorced 1978); m. 4th Mary Gimbel 1980; two d.; ed. Columbia Univ.; started as a child actor, later theatrical dir. and teacher; Assoc. Dir. CBS 1950, Dir. 1951-57; Hon. Life mem. Directors Guild of America. *Films include:* Twelve Angry Men 1957, Stage Struck 1958, That Kind of Woman 1959, The Fugitive Kind 1960, A View from the Bridge 1961, Long Day's Journey into Night 1962, The Pawnbroker 1963, Fail Safe 1964, The Hill

1965, The Group 1965, The Deadly Affair 1966, Bye, Bye Braverman 1968, The Seagull 1968, The Appointment 1969, Blood Kin 1969, The Offence, The Anderson Tapes 1972, Child's Play 1973, Serpico 1973, Lovin' Molly 1974, Murder on the Orient Express 1974, Dog Day Afternoon 1975, Network 1976, Equus 1977, The Wiz 1978, Just Tell Me What You Want 1980, Prince of the City 1981, Deathtrap 1982, The Verdict 1982, Daniel 1983, Garbo Talks 1984, Power 1986, The Morning After 1987, Running on Empty 1988, Family Business 1989. *Play:* Caligula 1960. *Address:* c/o LAH Film Corporation, 1775 Broadway, New York, N.Y. 10019, U.S.A.

LUMINA, Machila Joshua, M.SC.; Zambian politician; b. 8 July 1939, Mazabuka, Zambia; s. of Mweene and Muiinia (née Chikoko) Lumina; m. Jane Nkhoma 1961; three s. four d.; ed. Munali Secondary School, Canius Coll. and Univ. of Warsaw; research in agronomy 1968-70; Chief Agricultural Research Officer 1970-72; Gen. Man. Tobacco Bd. of Zambia 1972-74; Minister of State in various ministries 1974-78; Minister of Planning 1978-79, of Finance Jan.-Dec. 1979, of Labour and Social Services 1979-80, of Nat. Comm. for Devt. Planning 1980-82. *Leisure interests:* reading, football, indoor games, hunting. *Address:* Bbata Cooperative, Box 231, Kafue, Zambia.

LUMLEY, Joanna; British actress; b. 1 May 1946, Kashmir; TV appearances include: Release, Mark II Wife, Comedy Playhouse, It's Awfully Bad for Your Eyes Darling, Satanic Rites of Dracula 1973, Coronation Street, The Protectors, General Hospital 1974-75, The New Avengers 1976-77, Steptoe & Son, Are You Being Served?, The Cuckoo Waltz, Up The Workers, Sapphire and Steel 1978; stage appearance in London in Noel Coward's Blithe Spirit 1986. *Films include:* Some Girls Do, Tam Lin, The Breaking of Bumbo, Games That Lovers Play, Don't Just Lie There Say Something, On Her Majesty's Secret Service, Trail of the Pink Panther, Curse of the Pink Panther, That Was Tory, Mistral's Daughter. *Address:* c/o M.L.R., 200 Fulham Road, London, S.W.10, England.

LUMSDEN, Sir David James, Kt., M.A., D.PHIL., MUS.B., F.R.C.M., F.R.S.A., R.A.M., F.R.S.A.M.D., F.R.C.O.; British musician; b. 19 March 1928, Newcastle upon Tyne; s. of Albert Lumsden and Vera May Lumsden (née Tate); m. Sheila Daniels 1951; two s. two d.; ed. Dame Allan's School, Newcastle upon Tyne, Selwyn Coll. Cambridge (organ scholar); Asst. Organist, St. John's Coll. Cambridge 1951-53; Organist and Choirmaster St. Mary's, Nottingham 1954-56; Founder and Conductor Nottingham Bach Soc. 1954-59; Rector Chori Southwell Minster 1956-59; Dir. of Music, Keele 1958-59; Prof. of Harmony, R.A.M. 1959-61; Fellow and Organist New Coll. Oxford and Lecturer, Faculty of Music, Oxford Univ. 1959-76; Principal RSAMD Glasgow 1976-82; Prin. R.A.M. 1982-; Conductor Oxford Harmonic Soc. 1961-63; Organist Sheldonian Theatre 1964-76; Harpsichordist to the London Virtuosi 1972-75; Pres. Inc. Asscn. of Organists 1966-68; Visiting Prof. Yale Univ., U.S.A. 1974-75; Conductor Oxford Sinfonia 1967-70; Choragus Oxford Univ. 1968-72; Pres. Inc. Soc. of Organists 1966-68, Royal Coll. of Organists 1986-88; Chair. Nat. Youth Orchestra 1985-, Nat. Early Music Asscn. 1986-; mem. Bd. English Nat. Opera 1984-; Hon. Fellow, Selwyn Coll., Cambridge 1986-. *Publications:* An Anthology of English Lute Music 1954, Thomas Robinson's Schoole of Musicke 1603 1971, Music for the Lute (Gen. Ed.) 1965-. *Leisure interests:* reading. theatre, photography, travel. *Address:* Royal Academy of Music, Marylebone Road, London, NW1 5HT (Office); 47 York Terrace East, London, NW1 4PT; Melton House, Cambridgeshire, England (Home). *Telephone:* 01-935 5461 (Office); 01-935 5937 (Home).

LUMSDEN, James Alexander, M.B.E., LL.B.; Scottish solicitor and company director; b. 24 Jan. 1915, Arden, Dunbartonshire; s. of the late Sir James Robert Lumsden and of Lady Lumsden (née Henrietta Macfarlane Reid); m. Sheila Cross 1947; three s.; ed. Rugby School and Corpus Christi Coll., Cambridge Univ.; Partner, Maclay Murray & Spens (Solicitors), Glasgow and Edinburgh 1947-82; Dir. Burmah Oil Co. Ltd. 1957-76, Chair. 1971-75; Dir. Bank of Scotland 1958-85, The Weir Group PLC 1957-84, Murray Western Investment Trust PLC, and other cos. *Leisure interests:* shooting and other country pursuits. *Address:* Bannachra, by Helensburgh, Dunbartonshire, Scotland (Home). *Telephone:* (038 985) 653 (Home).

LUND, Henning, D.PHIL.; Danish professor of chemistry; b. 15 Sept. 1929, Copenhagen; s. of Prof. Hakon Lund and Bergljot I. G. (née Dahl) Lund; m. Else Margrethe (née Thorup) Lund 1953; one s. three d.; ed. Aarhus Katedralskole and Tech. Univ. of Copenhagen; Research Chemist Leo Pharmaceutical Products 1952-60; Research Fellow Harvard Univ. 1954-55; Asst. Prof. of Chemistry 1960, Prof. 1964-; Visiting Prof. Japan 1960, France 1964; Chair. UNESCO workshop for European Co-operation in Organic Electro-chemistry 1976-81; Section Co-Chair. Int. Soc. of Electrochemistry 1973-78, 1986-, Nat. Sec. 1986-; Pres. Learned Soc., Univ. of Aarhus 1973-79; mem. Danish Research Council for Tech. Sciences 1977-82, Vice-Chair. 1980-82; mem. Royal Danish Acad. of Sciences and Letters 1979; Bjerrums Gold Medal 1969. *Publications:* Elektrodereaktioner i Organisk Polarografi og Voltammetri 1961, Encyclopaedia of Electrochemistry of the Elements, Vols. 11-15 1978-84, Organic Electrochemistry (Co-Ed.) 1983. *Leisure interests:* music, literature, jogging. *Address:* Department of Chemistry, University of Aarhus, 8000 Aarhus (Univ.); Vinkelvej 8A, 8240 Risskov, Denmark (Home). *Telephone:* 06202711-6658 (Univ.).

LUND, John Walter Guerrier, C.B.E., D.SC., F.R.S.; British botanist; b. 27 Nov. 1912; s. of George E. Lund and Kate (Hardwick) Lund; m. Hilda M. Canter 1949; one s. one d.; ed. Sedbergh School and Univs. of Manchester and London; Demonstrator in Botany, Univ. of Manchester, Queen Mary Coll. London and Chelsea Polytechnic 1935–38; Temporary Lecturer in Botany, Univ. of Sheffield 1936; Staff Biologist, West Midland Forensic Science Lab. Birmingham 1938–45; Botanist, Windermere Lab. Freshwater Biological Assen. 1945–78. *Publications:* articles in scientific journals. *Leisure interest:* gardening. *Address:* Ellerbeck, Ellerigg Road, Ambleside, Cumbria, LA22 9EU, England. *Telephone:* (0966) 32369.

LUNDBERG, Arne S., DR.TECH.; Swedish business executive; b. 14 May 1911, Luleå; m.; one s. two d.; journalist 1929–44; specialist in Ministry of Communications 1944–47, Perm. Sec., Ministry of Communications 1947–51; Sec.-Gen., Ministry for Foreign Affairs 1951–56; Man Dir. Luossavaara-Kiirunawaara AB 1957–76; Chair. AB Svensk Exportkredit 1962–78, Swedish Mine-Owners' Assen. 1963–75, Byggherreföreningen 1964–80, Norrbottens Järnverk AB 1967–70 (mem. Bd. 1960–70), Sveriges Investeringsbank 1967–82, Oljeprospektering AB (OPAB) 1969–80, Petroswede AB 1973–80, Berol Kemi AB (petrochemical) 1973–78, Svenska Petroleum AB 1975–81, Statsraff AB 1975–80, Swede Sorb Corpn. 1984–87, Sanpox 1987–, Miljöförbättring AB 1985–; Vice-Chair. Post-och Kreditbanken 1966–82; mem. Bd. Swedish Ironmasters' Assen. 1962–76; mem. Swedish Acad. of Eng. Sciences (IVA) 1962–, Pres. 1974–76. *Leisure interests:* music, hunting, sailing. *Address:* Östermalmsgatan 50, 11426 Stockholm, Sweden. *Telephone:* 08-20 18 85.

LUNDBERG, Bo Klas Oskar, Dr. in Aeronautics; Swedish aircraft designer and aeronautical scientist; b. 1 Dec. 1907, Karlskoga; s. of Ehrenfried and Fanny Lundberg; m. Svea Maria Johansson 1935; two s. two d.; ed. Hudiksvalls Läroverk and Royal Inst. of Tech., Stockholm; Designer Test Pilot, AB Svenska Järnvägsverkstäderna, Aeroplanavdelningen, Linköping 1931–35, Sparmanns flygplanverkstad, Stockholm 1935–37; Asst. Insp. at the Bd. of Civil Aviation, Stockholm 1937–38; Chief, Aeronautical Dept., Götaverken, Gothenburg 1939; Chief Designer, J-22 Fighter, Royal Air Bd. 1940–44; Chief, Structures Dept., Aeronautical Research Inst. of Sweden 1944–47, Dir.-Gen. 1947–67, Aviation Consultant 1967–; F.R.Ae.S., Hon. Fellow A.I.A.A., Fellow Canadian Aeronautics and Space Inst., Socio Onorario, Instituto Internazionale delle Comunicazioni; mem. A.A.A.S., Fellow Royal Swedish Acad. of Eng. Sciences; Thulin Medal, Silver 1948, Gold 1955, Flight Safety Foundation Air Safety Award 1960, Sherman Fairchild Certificate of Merit 1963, Monsanto Aviation Safety Award 1963, Carl August Wicander Gold Medal 1966. *Publications include:* Fatigue Life of Airplane Structures (18th Wright Brothers Lecture) 1954, Should Supersonic Airliners be Permitted? 1961, Some Special Problems Connected with Supersonic Transport 1961, Speed and Safety in Civil Aviation (3rd Daniel and Florence Guggenheim Memorial Lecture) 1962, The Allotment of Probability Shares (APS) Method, A Guidance for Flight Safety Measures 1966, Economic and Social Aspects of Commercial Aviation at Supersonic Speeds 1972, Why the SST Should Be Stopped Once and For All 1973; numerous articles and papers mainly on the problems of aircraft safety and supersonic transport. *Leisure interests:* golf, tennis. *Address:* Gubbkärrsvägen 29/9, 16151 Bromma, Sweden. *Telephone:* 08-87-75-92.

LUNDBERG, Henry; Swedish chemical engineer and business executive; b. 11 July 1931, Boliden; s. of Karl and Dagmar Lundberg; m. 2nd Tua Forsström 1981; seven c.; Mining Div. Boliden AB 1951, Gen. Man. Smelting Div. 1967, Man. Dir. Boliden Metall AB 1975; Exec. Vice-Pres. SSAB Swedish Steel Corpn. 1980, Pres. and C.E.O. 1981–87; mem. Bd. Fed. of Swedish Industries, Swedish Employees' Confed. (SFO), Swedish Iron Masters' Assen.; mem. Exec. Cttee. Int. Iron and Steel Inst. (IISI), Viscaria Copper Co.; mem. Advisory Council, Royal Swedish Acad. of Eng. Sciences; Chair. Audit Cttee. IISI, Swedish Iron and Steel Works' Assen., Swedish Inst. of Steel Construction, Tibnor Group. *Leisure interests:* hunting, orienteering, skiing. *Address:* Stavgårdsgatan 5, S-161 37 Bromma, Sweden.

LUNDEEN, Robert West, B.S.; American business executive; b. 25 June 1921, Astoria, Ore.; s. of Arthur Robert and Margaret Florence Lundeen; m. Betty Charles Anderson 1942; two s. one d.; ed. Oregon State Univ., Univ. of Chicago; joined Dow Chemical Co. 1946, Research and Devt. Engineer Pittsburg, Calif. 1946–51, Process Design and Project Supervision 1951–56, Man. Planning 1956–61; transferred to Dow Chemical Int., Midland, Mich. 1961, Dir. Business Devt. 1963–66; Pres. Dow Chemical Pacific, Hong Kong 1966–78, Dow Chemical Latin American, Coral Gables, Fla. 1978–86; Exec. Vice-Pres. Dow Chemical Co., Midland, Mich. 1978–86, Chair. 1982–86, Dir. 1973–87; Chair. Tektronix Inc. 1987–; Dir. Chemical Bank and Trust Co., Midland; mem. American Inst. of Chemical Engineers, American Chemical Soc., Soc. of Chemical Industry; Trustee, Cttee. for Econ. Devt.; mem. Advisory Council on Japan-U.S. Econ. Relations; Dir. U.S.A.-U.S.S.R. Trade and Econ. Council; mem. Visiting Cttee. Graduate School of Business Admin., Univ. of Mich., Advisory Bd. for Dept. of Chemical Eng., Univ. of Calif., Bd. of Visitors, School of Foreign Service, Georgetown Univ., N.J. Inst. of Tech.; Trustee, Ore. Univ. Foundation; Bronze Star 1945; Order of Industrial Service Merit (Silver Tower), Repub. of Korea 1977. *Leisure interests:* tennis, sailing. *Address:* Tektronix Inc., P.O. Box 500, Beaverton, Ore. 97007, U.S.A.

LUNDQVIST, Svante; Swedish politician (retd.); b. 20 July 1919, Eskilstona; s. of Karl and Matilda Lundqvist; m. Maj- Britt Bernhardsson; one s. two d.; mem. Riksdag (Parl.) 1959–; mem. Exec. Social Democratic Party 1960–; Minister without Portfolio 1965, Minister of Communications 1967, of Physical Planning and Local Govt. 1969, of Agric. 1973–76, 1982–86. *Leisure interests:* music, sport. *Address:* Socialdemokratiska Arbetarepartiet, Sveavägen 68, 105 60 Stockholm, Sweden.

LUNDSTROM, Hans Olof; Swedish economist and civil servant; b. 29 April 1927, Ystad; m. 1st Eva Lundquist 1959; one s. one d.; m. 2nd Marianne Svennilson 1982; ed. Stockholm School of Economics, Institut d'Etudes Politiques, Paris and College of Europe, Bruges; Bank of Sweden 1952–61; Head of Section for Devt. Assistance, Ministry of Finance 1962–64, Head of Int. Secr. 1965–66; Under-Sec. of State for Econ. Affairs 1967–68; Under-Sec. of State, Ministry of Industry 1969–72; Deputy Gov. Bank of Sweden 1973–79; Exec. Dir. IBRD 1980–82; Chair. Review Comm. on the Swedish Concessional Credit System, Ministry of Foreign Affairs 1983; Exec. Dir. IMF 1985–87; Consultant Ministry of Foreign Affairs and Swedish Int. Devt. Authority 1987–. *Publications:* Capital Movements and Economic Integration 1960, Policy-Related Assistance 1988; numerous articles on Swedish econ. policy and int. affairs. *Address:* Seglarvägen 13, 13333 Saltsjöbaden, Sweden. *Telephone:* 08-7170763.

LUNENBERG, Engelbartus; Netherlands administrator; b. 11 Aug. 1922; s. of Albert J. Lunenberg and Maria P. van der Woerd; m. Bella Leonie Stein Pinto 1969; ed. Netherlands School of Econs. (now Erasmus Univ.), Rotterdam; Dir. UNESCO Centre, Nat. Comm. for UNESCO, Amsterdam 1951–53; Dept. of Foreign Relations, Ministry of Educ., Science and Culture 1953–54; Deputy Dir. Int. Statistical Inst. 1954–55, Dir. 1955–87, Sec., Treas. 1972–87, Dir. Emer. 1987–; Exec. Dir. Int. Assen. for Statistical Computing 1977–87; Exec. Sec. Bernoulli Soc. for Math. Statistics and Probability 1963–87; Sec.-Treas. Int. Assen. for Regional and Urban Statistics 1957–87; Exec. Dir. Int. Assen. for Official Statistics 1985–87; mem. Exec. Cttee., Int. Assen. of Survey Statisticians 1973–87; Hon. F.R.S.S.; Officer, Order of Oranje Nassau (Netherlands), Gold and Silver Star, Order of the Sacred Treasure and Officer, Order of the Rising Sun (Japan). *Leisure interest:* gardening. *Address:* 340 Parkweg, 2271 BJ Voorburg, Netherlands (Home). *Telephone:* 070-871296 (Home).

LUNENFELD, Bruno, M.D., F.R.C.O.G.; Israeli endocrinologist and university professor of life sciences; b. 11 Feb. 1927, Vienna, Austria; s. of David Lunenfeld and Ernestine Lunenfeld; m. Susanne Aron 1951; two s.; ed. British Inst. of Eng. Tech., Medical School, Univ. of Geneva, Switzerland; Acting Chief, Endocrine Research and Devt., Tel-Hashomer 1962–64; Scientist, Weizman Inst. of Science 1961–66; Assoc. Prof. and Head Dept. of Biology, Bar-Ilan Univ. 1964–69, Prof. Ordinarius and Head Dept. of Life Sciences 1969–71, Prof. of Life Sciences 1971; Dir. Inst. of Endocrinology, Sheba Medical Centre 1964, Chair. Div. of Labs. 1977–81, Chair. Research and Ethical Cttee. 1977–81; mem. Expert Cttee. on Biological Standardization, WHO 1967–87; Counsellor External Relations to Minister of Health and Head Dept. of Int. Relations, Ministry of Health 1981–85; Acting Chief Scientist, Ministry of Health 1984–86; mem. Nat. Council for Research and Devt. 1985–87; Visiting Prof., Yale School of Medicine, U.S.A. 1986–87; mem. Nat. Council for Health and Social Affairs 1985–87; Sec. Israel Endocrine Soc. 1974–79; Pres. Israel Fertility Assen. 1979–83; mem. Exec. Bd. Scientific Council, Israel Medical Assen., Exec. Council of Int. Cttee. for Research in Reproduction, Exec. Council Medical Examination Bd., Exec. Council of Int. Andrology Soc., Exec. Council of Int. Soc. of Gynaecological Endocrinology; Pliskin Prize, Israel Trade Union Sick Fund 1962, Yaffeh Prize, Ministry of Health 1963, U.S. Public Health Service Special Recognition Award 1983. *Publications:* Infertility, Diagnosis and Treatment of Functional Infertility 1978, Ovulation Induction 1982, Diagnosis and Management of Male Infertility 1984, Ovulation Induction and In Vitro Fertilization 1986, Infertility in Male and Female 1986; 25 chapters in books; 250 papers in scientific journals; 112 published lectures and abstracts. *Leisure interest:* sailing. *Address:* Institute of Endocrinology, Sheba Medical Centre, 52 621 Tel-Hashomer (Office); 6/58 Elijahu Hakim Street, 69120 Tel Aviv, Israel (Home). *Telephone:* 972.3.5302 802 (Office); 972.3.425 434 (Home).

LUNKOV, Nikolai Mitrofanovich; Soviet diplomatist; b. 7 Jan. 1919, Pavlovka, Ryazan Region; ed. Lomonosov Tech. Inst., Moscow; Diplomatic Service 1943–; Asst. Minister of Foreign Affairs 1951–52; Deputy Political Counsellor, Soviet Control Comm. in Germany 1952–54; Counsellor, Stockholm 1954–57; Deputy Head, Dept. of Int. Orgs., Ministry of Foreign Affairs 1957, 3rd European Dept. 1957–59; Head of Scandinavian Div., Ministry of Foreign Affairs 1959–62; Amb. to Norway 1962–68; Head of Dept. of Cultural Relations with Foreign Countries 1968–73; Amb. to U.K. (also accred. to Malta) 1973–80, to Italy 1980–; mem. Cen. Auditing Comm. CPSU 1976–; Cand. mem. Cen. Cttee., CPSU 1981–. *Address:* Embassy of the U.S.S.R., Via Gaeta 5, Rome, Italy.

LUNS, Joseph Marie Antoine Hubert, G.C.M.G., C.H., D.C.L., LL.D.; Netherlands politician and diplomatist; b. 28 Aug. 1911, Rotterdam; m. Baroness Elisabeth Van Heemstra; one s. one d.; ed. Amsterdam and Brussels, Univs. of Leiden, Amsterdam, London and Berlin; Ministry of Foreign Affairs 1938–40; Attaché, Dutch Legation, Berne 1940–41, Lisbon 1941–42, Second Sec. 1942–43; Second Sec. Netherlands Ministry for Foreign Affairs,

London 1943–44; Second, then First Sec. Dutch Embassy, London 1944–49; Perm. Del. to UN 1949–52; Co-Minister for Foreign Affairs 1952–56; Minister of Foreign Affairs 1956–71; Pres. NATO Council 1958–59; Sec.-Gen. NATO 1971–83; Hon. Fellow, L.S.E.; Kt. Grand Cross of the Order of the Netherlands Lion, Officer Order of Orange-Nassau, Charlemagne Prize 1967, Hon. C.H. (U.K.) 1971, Ataturk Int. Peace Prize, and foreign awards. *Publications:* Several studies on Netherlands Navy in British and Portuguese magazines and articles about current political problems in various magazines, incl. International Affairs and Atlantic Review. *Leisure interests:* swimming, walking, reading. *Address:* 117 Avenue Franklin Roosevelt, 1050 Brussels, Belgium.

LUO BIN JI; Chinese writer; b. Feb. 1917, Jilin; s. of Zhang Qing Shan and Zhang Jin Ying; m. Zou Min Cai 1949; one s. one d.; began writing in Shanghai 1936; articles for magazine Feng Huo (The Flames of War) 1937; Head, Chengxian Co. Propaganda Dept., Chinese CP 1938, Ed. Propaganda Dept., New Fourth Army 1940; Sec.-Gen. Northeast Cultural Soc. 1945; twice arrested for political reasons 1944, 1947; Chief. Ed. Zhan Qi magazine 1939, Wen Xue Bao Magazine 1941; Head, Culture and Educ., Shandong Prov. Cttee. 1950–52; Screenwriter, Beijing Film Bureau 1953–57; Council mem. Chinese Writers' Asscn., Vice-Chair. Beijing Branch 1979–. *Publications:* On the Border Line 1939, Childhood 1944, A Biography of Xiao Hong 1947, Spring over Bei-wang-yuan and other stories 1947, Old Wei Jun and Fang Fang and other stories 1958, A Trading Post in the Mountains and other stories 1963, Selected Short Stories 1980, Selected Short Stories and Novelettes 1982, New Textual Research of Inscriptions on Bronze Objects 1987 and several critical and historical works. *Leisure interests:* fishing, reading, stamp collecting, go weiqi (Chinese board game). *Address:* Beijing Branch, Chinese Writers' Association, Beijing, China.

LUO GAN, DIP.ENG.; Chinese party and state official; b. 14 July 1935, Jinan, Shandong; m. He Zuozhi 1965; one s. one d.; ed. Leipzig Univ.; metallurgical and casting engineer; Vice-Gov. Henan Prov. 1981–83; Minister of Labour April 1988–; alt. mem. 12th CCP Cen. Cttee. 1982–87, mem. 13th Cen. Cttee. 1987–; Sec. CCP Cttee., Henan 1983–85; Vice-Pres. All-China Fed. of Trade Unions 1983–. *Address:* Ministry of Labour, Beijing, People's Republic of China.

LUO GUIBO; Chinese party and government official; b. 1908, Jiangxi Prov.; m. Li Hanzhen 1937; ed. France; joined CCP 1927; took part in Long March 1934–35; Head Propaganda Section, Political Dept., CCP 120th Div. and Sub-bureau Cen. Cttee., Shanxi-Suiyuan 1938; Political Commissar 358th Brigade, 8th Route Army 1939; Political Commissar New Army Provisional HQ, Shanxi 1939; mem. Mil. Control Comm., Taiyuan 1949; Dir. Gen. Office, People's Revolutionary Mil. Council 1950–54; Amb. to N. Viet-Nam 1954–57; Alt. mem. 8th Cen. Cttee., CCP 1956–69; Vice-Minister of Foreign Affairs 1958–79; Second Sec. CCP Cttee., Shanxi 1979–83; Gov. of Shanxi Prov. 1979–83; mem. Cen. Advisory Comm., Cen. Cttee. 1983–. *Address:* Shanxi Province, People's Republic of China. *Telephone:* 346937, 346090.

LUO PINGAN; Chinese artist; b. 12 April 1945, Xian; s. of Luo Deyu and Tian Cuilan; m. Qi Juyan 1967; two s.; mem. China Artists' Asscn., Shaanxi Br.; Artist of Shaanxi Imperial Art Gallery (traditional Chinese painting); Vice-Pres. Changan Imperial Art Acad.; 2nd exhbn. of paintings, sponsored by China Art Gallery and Research Inst. of Traditional Chinese Painting, Beijing, Feb. 1988. *Leisure interests:* literature and music. *Address:* 32 North Street, Xian, Shaanxi Province, People's Republic of China. *Telephone:* 2-5333.

LUO QINGCHANG; Chinese politician; b. 1920, Hubei; Deputy Dir. Premier's Office, State Council 1954–65; Deputy Sec.-Gen. State Council 1965–75; mem. 10th Cen. Cttee. CCP 1973 and 12th 1982–87; mem. Cen. Advisory Comm. 1987–; Head, Investigation Dept. CCP 1978–; *Address:* Central Committee of Chinese Communist Party, Beijing, People's Republic of China.

LUO SHANGCAI; Chinese party and state official; alt. mem. 12th CCP Cen. Cttee. 1982, 13th Cen. Cttee. 1987; First Sec. CCP Cttee., South Guizhou Buyi and Miao Autonomous Pref. 1982–; Vice-Gov., Guizhou Prov. 1983–88; Vice-Chair. Guizhou Prov. People's Congress Jan. 1988–; Deputy for Guizhou to 6th NPC 1983. *Address:* Guizhou Provincial People's Government, Guiyang, Guizhou, People's Republic of China.

LUO TIAN; Chinese party and government official; Vice-Gov. Guangdong 1961–Cultural Revolution; Vice-Chair. Prov. Revolutionary Cttee., Guangdong 1975–79; Sec. CCP Cttee., Hainan Island 1976; Vice-Chair. Prov. People's Congress, Guangdong 1979–83; First Political Commissar, Hainan Mil. Area 1981–85; First Sec. Hainan Admin. Area 1981–84; Chair. Prov. People's Congress, Guangdong 1983–; mem. Presidium 6th NPC 1986–; mem. China-Britain Friendship Group 1985–. *Address:* Provincial People's Congress, Guangdong Province, People's Republic of China.

LUO YUCHUAN; Chinese party and government official; b. 1908; also known as Luo Yuming; Sec. Hebei CCP Cttee, Shanxi-Chabar-Hebei sub-bureau of CCP Cen. Cttee. 1948; Vice-Minister of Agric. 1949; Vice-Gov. Hebei Prov. 1949–50; Vice-Gov. Pingyuan 1950–52; Vice-Minister of Forestry 1952–56; Timber Industry 1956–58, of Forestry 1958–67, of Agriculture and Forestry 1977–79; mem. 2nd NPC Oct. 1958; Presidium

Nat. Conf. of Outstanding Groups and Workers in Agric. Nov. 1958; mem. 3rd NPC 1964; purged 1967, rehabilitated 1974; cadre in Ministry of Agric. and Forestry 1976; mem. 5th NPC Feb. 1978; Minister of Forestry 1979–; mem. Cen. Advisory Cttee. of CCP Cen. Cttee. 1987–. *Address:* Central Advisory Committee of the Central Committee of the Chinese Communist Party, Zhongnanhai, Beijing, People's Republic of China.

LUPINACCI, Julio César; Uruguayan diplomatist; b. 1929; m.; four c.; ed. Law School of Univ. of Uruguay; fmr. Prof. of Int. Public Law, Univ. of Uruguay; fmr. teacher at Mil. School and Naval War School of Uruguay; post in Legal Affairs Dept. of OAS, Washington D.C. 1967–69; joined Ministry of Foreign Affairs as Legal Adviser 1969, subsequently Dir. of Foreign Policy, Dir. of Legal Affairs, and Under-Sec.; Amb. to Venezuela 1976, to Chile 1982–85; headed Uruguayan del. to Third UN Conf. on the Law of the Sea; Sec.-Gen. of meeting of Foreign Ministers of Rio de la Plata Basin 1985; Perm. Rep. of Uruguay to UN, New York 1985–88; has lectured worldwide. *Publications:* numerous papers on UN issues. *Address:* c/o Ministry of Foreign Affairs, Colonia 1218, Montevideo, Uruguay.

LUPU, Petre; Romanian politician; b. 25 Oct. 1920, Iași; m. Nesia Lupu; one s. one d.; ed. Acad. Ştefan Gheorghiu; mem. Romanian Communist Party (RCP) 1936–; Sec. Iași Dist. Cttee. of Union of Communist Youth (U.C.Y.) 1939; imprisoned for anti-fascist activities 1940–44; Sec. of Oltenia Region Cttee. of RCP 1944–45; Sec. Cen. Cttee. of U.C.Y. 1945–50; Deputy to Grand Nat. Assembly 1948–; mem. Cen. Cttee. of RCP 1955–84, Alt. mem. Exec. Political Cttee. 1965–69, mem. 1969–80; Chair. State Cttee. of Org. and Salary Problems 1966–69; Minister of Labour 1969–77; Chair. Cen. Party Coll. 1977–84; Amb. to Venezuela and Trinidad and Tobago 1984–88, to Portugal 1988–; Hero of Socialist Labour 1971. *Address:* Romanian Embassy, Rua de São Caetano 5, 1200 Lisbon, Portugal.

LUPU, Radu, M.A.; Romanian pianist; b. 30 Nov. 1945, Galați; s. of Mayer Lupu and Ana Gabor; ed. High School, Brașov, Moscow Conservatoire, U.S.S.R.; first piano lessons 1951; won scholarship to Moscow 1961; entered Moscow Conservatoire 1963, graduated 1969; First Prize, Van Cliburn Competition 1966; First Prize, Enescu Int. Competition, Bucharest 1967; First Prize, Leeds Int. Competition 1969; a leading interpreter of the German classical composers; now lives in Britain and appears frequently with all the major orchestras; has toured Eastern Europe with London Symphony Orchestra; American debut 1972; gave world première of André Tchaikowsky Piano Concerto, London 1975; records for Decca (incl. complete Beethoven cycle with Israel Philharmonic and Zubin Mehta 1979). *Address:* c/o Terry Harrison Artists, 9a Penzance Place, London, W11 4PE, England. *Telephone:* 01-221 7741.

LURAGHI, Giuseppe; Italian business executive; b. 12 June 1905, Milan; s. of Felice Luraghi and Giuditta Talamona; m. Maria Magdalena Poli 1927; two s. three d.; ed. Univ. Commerciale Luigi Bocconi, Milan; started career in textile industry; with Pirelli Group 1930–50; Gen. Man. Finmeccanica Group 1951–56, and Dir. several subsid. and affiliated cos.; Chair. and Man. Dir. Lanerossi S.p.A. 1956–60; Chair. Bd. of Dirs. Alfa Romeo S.p.A., Milan 1960–74, COGIS (Compagnia Generale Interscambi 1960–73, SICA 1967–74, Alfa Romeo-ALFASUD 1968–74, Necchi S.p.A. 1974–79, SOFIST (Società Finanziazia Sviluppo Tessile) 1975–80, Mondadori Editore S.p.A. 1977–83, Finservizi S.p.A. 1980; Dir. Club degli Editori 1980–82. *Publications:* Le macchine della libertà, Capi si diventa, Due Milanesi alle piramidi, Miracolo a Porta Ticinese, Castelli di Carte. *Address:* Via Revere 2, 20123 Milan, Italy. *Telephone:* 02-75422300.

LURIA, Salvador Edward, M.D.; American professor of biology; b. 13 Aug. 1912, Turin, Italy; s. of David and Ester (Sacerdote) Luria; m. Zella Hurwitz 1945; one s.; ed. Univ. of Turin; Research Fellow, Inst. of Radium, Paris 1938–40; Research Asst., Columbia Univ. Medical School, N.Y. 1940–42; Guggenheim Fellow, Vanderbilt and Princeton Univs. 1942–43; Instructor in Bacteriology, Ind. Univ., Bloomington 1943–45, Asst. Prof. 1944–47, Assoc. Prof. 1947–50; Prof. of Bacteriology, Univ. of Ill., Urbana 1950–59; fmr. Chair. Dept. of Microbiology, M.I.T., Prof. 1959–64, Sedgwick Prof. of Biology 1964–70, Inst. Prof. 1970–; Dir. Center for Cancer Research 1972–; non-resident Fellow, Salk Inst. for Biol. Studies 1965–; ed. Virology 1955–; Jessup Lecturer, Columbia Univ.; Nieuwland Lecturer, Univ. of Notre Dame; mem. Nat. Acad. of Sciences; Pres. American Soc. for Microbiology; Nobel Prize for Medicine (with Max Delbrück and A. D. Hershey, q.v.) 1969. *Publication:* Life: The Unfinished Experiment (Nat. Book Award) 1974. *Research interests:* bacterial genetics; bacterial viruses; structure of bacterial cell wall and membrane. *Address:* Department of Microbiology, Massachusetts Institute of Technology, Cambridge, Mass. 02139; 48 Peacock Farm Road, Lexington, Mass. 02173, U.S.A. (Home).

LURIE, Alison, A.B.; American novelist; b. 3 Sept. 1926, Chicago; d. of Harry Lawrence and Bernice Stewart Lurie; m. Jonathon Peale Bishop 1948 (divorced 1985); three s.; ed. Radcliffe Coll.; lecturer in English, Cornell Univ. 1969–73, Adjunct Assoc. Prof. 1973–76, Assoc. Prof. 1976–79, Prof. 1979–; Yaddo Foundation Fellow 1963, 1964, 1966, 1984, Guggenheim Fellow 1965, Rockefeller Foundation Fellow 1967; Literature Award, American Acad. of Arts and Letters 1978, Pulitzer Prize in Fiction 1985. *Publications:* V. R. Lang: a Memoir 1959, Love and Friendship 1962, The Nowhere City 1965, Imaginary Friends 1967, Real People 1969, The War Between the Tates 1974, Only Children 1979, The Language of Clothes

1981, Foreign Affairs 1985, The Man with a Shattered World 1987, The Truth about Lorin Jones 1988. *Address:* Department of English, Cornell University, Ithaca, New York, N.Y. 14850, U.S.A.

LURIE, Ranan Raymond; American political cartoonist; b. 26 May 1932, Port Said, Egypt; s. of Joseph and Rose (Sam) Lurie (parents Israeli citizens); m. Tamar Fletcher 1958; two s. two d.; ed. Herzelia Coll., Tel-Aviv, and Jerusalem Art Coll.; Corresp. Maariv Daily 1950-52; Features Ed. Hador Daily 1953-54; Ed.-in-Chief Tavel (weekly magazine) 1954-55; staff political cartoonist Yedioth Aharonot Daily 1955-66, Honolulu Advertiser 1979; went to U.S.A. (invited by Life Magazine) 1968, naturalized 1974; political cartoonist, Life Magazine, New York 1968-73; political cartoonist interviewer Die Welt, Bonn 1980-81; Contrib. New York Times 1970-72; Contrib. Ed. and political cartoonist, Newsweek Int. 1974-76; Ed., political cartoonist, Vision Magazine of S. America 1974-76; syndicated United Features Syndicate 1971-73; syndicated nationally by Los Angeles Times and internationally by New York Times to over 260 newspapers 1973-75; syndicated nationally by King Features Syndicate, internationally by Editors Press Syndicate (345 newspapers) 1975-, in U.S.A. by Universal Press Syndicate 1982-; lecturer, Univ. of Hawaii, American Program Bureau, Boston; political cartoonist, The Times, London 1981-83; Sr. Political Analyst and cartoonist, The Asahi Shimbun, Tokyo 1983-84; Sr. Analyst and political cartoonist, U.S. News and World Report, Washington 1984-85; Chief Editorial Dir. Editors' Press Service 1985-; inventor of first animated electronic television news cartoon; joined MacNeil/Lehrer News Hour as daily political cartoonist/analyst, appearing on 275 TV stations; creator of Taiwan's official new nat. cartoon symbol "Cousin Lee"; cr. Japan's nat. cartoon symbol "Taro San"; fine arts shows in Israel, Canada, U.S.A. 1960-75, including Expo 1967, Canada, Dominion Gallery, Montreal, Canada, Lim Gallery, Tel Aviv 1965, Overseas Press Club, New York 1962, 1964, 1975, U.S. Senate, Washington, Honolulu Acad. Fine Arts 1979; exhibited in numerous group shows including Smithsonian Inst. 1972; trained as Parachute Officer, French Foreign Legion 1955, served as Combat Paratroop Maj., Israeli Army Reserve 1950-67; recipient highest Israeli journalism award 1954; U.S. Headliners Award 1972; named Outstanding Editorial Cartoonist of Nat. Cartoonist Soc. 1972-78; Salon Award, Montreal Cartoon 1971; New York Front Page Award 1972, 1974, 1977, certificate of Merit of U.S. Publication Designers 1974, Hon. mention Overseas Press Club 1979, winner of John Fischetti Political Cartoon Award 1982; listed in Guinness Book of World Records as most widely syndicated political cartoonist in the world, Toastmasters' Int. and Leadership Award 1985; mem. Asscn. of Editorial Cartoonists, Nat. Cartoonists' Soc. of America; Hon. Assoc. mem. Asahi Shimbun. *Publications:* Among the Suns 1952, Lurie's Best Cartoons (Israel) 1961, Nixon Rated Cartoons (New York Times) 1973, Pardon Me, Mr. President (New York Times) 1974, Lurie's Worlds (U.S.A.) 1980, So sieht es Lurie (Germany) 1981, Lurie's Almanac (U.K.) 1982, (U.S.A.) 1983, Taro's International Politics, Taro-San No Kokusai Seijigaku (Japan) 1984, Lurie's Middle East 1986, Lurie's Mideast Almanac (Israel) 1986, Lurie's Fareast Views (China) 1987; creator The Expandable Painting 1969. *Address:* Trump Tower, 721 Fifth Avenue, New York, N.Y. 10022, U.S.A. *Telephone:* (212) 9800 855.

LURIE, Richard; South African stockbroker; b. 30 March 1918, Johannesburg; s. of the late A. C. Lurie; m. Lois Harris 1949; three s.; ed. King Edward VII School, Johannesburg, Univ. of the Witwatersrand; joined Johannesburg Stock Exchange 1946, mem. Exchange Cttee. 1960, Vice-Pres. 1970-72, 1976-77, Pres. of Exchange 1972-74, 1978-82. *Address:* c/o Johannesburg Stock Exchange, P.O. Box 1174, Johannesburg, South Africa.

LUSAKA, Paul John Firmino; M.A., LL.D.; Zambian diplomatist; b. 10 Jan. 1935, Broken Hill (now Kabwe); s. of Firmino Lusaka and Rebecca Mutakwa; m. Joan Gay 1963; four c.; ed. Univ. of Minnesota, Univ. of Basutoland and McGill Univ.; Graduate Asst. Lecturer, Univ. of Basutoland 1960; Second Sec. 1964-65, First Sec. 1965 to U.K.; Deputy High Commr. to U.K. 1965-68; Amb. to U.S.S.R. (also accred. to Yugoslavia, Romania, Czechoslovakia) 1968-72; Perm. Rep. to UN 1972-73, 1979-86 (also accred. as High Commr. to Canada, Jamaica, Guyana, Trinidad and Tobago, and Barbados, and Amb. to Cuba); Pres. UN Council for Namibia 1973, 1979-; Minister of Rural Devt. 1973-77, of Power, Transport and Communications 1977-78, of Health 1978; Chair. of Nat. Council of United Nat. Independence Party (UNIP) 1976-79; Chair. UNIP Gen. Conf. 1978; Pres. UN Security Council 1979; Pres. ECOSOC 1981; Pres. UN Gen. Ass. 1984-85 (39th Session); Special Asst. (Political) to Pres. 1986-87; Roving Amb. 1987-; Insignia of Honour (Yugoslavia) 1970, Citation by Univ. of Minnesota 1985, Citation by CORE, Brooklyn, New York 1985. *Address:* c/o Ministry of Foreign Affairs, Lusaka, Zambia.

LUSCHIKOV, Anatoliy Pavlovich; Soviet politician; b. 1917; ed. Kuybyshev Agric. Inst.; active service in Soviet Army 1941-46; mem. CPSU 1942; work on Saratov District Cttee. 1946-52; First Sec. of Romanov Regional Cttee. 1952-54; Head of Section of Balashov District Cttee. 1954-57; work with CPSU Cen. Cttee. 1957-60; Sec. of Bryansk Dist. Cttee. 1960-62; Deputy Head of Section of CPSU Cen. Cttee. 1962-71, Asst.-Sec. 1971-; Asst. to General Sec. of CPSU Cen. Cttee. 1985-; mem. of CPSU Cen. Cttee. 1986-; Deputy to U.S.S.R. Supreme Soviet. *Address:* The Kremlin, Moscow, U.S.S.R.

LUSCOMBE, David Edward, PH.D., F.B.A., F.S.A., F.R.HIST.S.; British historian; b. 22 July 1938, London; s. of Edward Dominic Luscombe and Norah Luscombe; m. Megan Phillips 1960; three s. one d.; ed. St. Michael's Convent School, Finchley Catholic Grammar School, London and King's Coll., Cambridge; Fellow, King's Coll. 1962-64, Churchill Coll., Cambridge 1964-72; Prof. of Medieval History, Univ. of Sheffield 1972-, Dean of Faculty of Arts 1985-87; mem. Governing Body, later the Asscn. of St. Edmund's House, Cambridge 1971-84; Vice-Pres. Société int. pour l'étude de la philosophie médiévale 1987-. *Publications:* The School of Peter Abelard, Peter Abelard's Ethics, Church and Government in the Middle Ages (Jt. Ed.) 1976, Petrus Abaelardus (1079-1142): Person, Werk, und Wirkung (Jt. Ed.) 1980; articles in learned journals. *Leisure interests:* playing cricket, walking a spaniel. *Address:* Department of History, The University, Sheffield, S10 2TN; 4 Caxton Road, Sheffield, S10 3DE, England (Home). *Telephone:* (0742) 768 555 (Office); (0742) 686 355 (Home).

LUSH, The Hon. Sir George Hermann; Australian judge (retd.); b. 5 Oct. 1912, Melbourne; s. of J. F. Lush and D. L. E. Lush (née Putmann); m. Winifred Betty Wragge 1943; three d.; ed. Carey Grammar School, Ormond Coll., Univ. of Melbourne; admitted to practice 1935; war service, Middle East and New Guinea 1940-45; Lecturer in Mercantile Law, Melbourne Univ. 1947-55; Q.C., Vic. 1957, Tasmania 1958; mem. Overseas Telecommunications Comm. 1961-66; Pres. Medico-Legal Soc., Victoria 1962-63; Chair. Victorian Bar Council and Pres. Australian Bar Asscn. 1964-66; Judge Supreme Court of Vic. 1966-83; Chair. Ormond Coll. Council 1981-; Chair. Bar Disciplinary Tribunal 1981-; Chancellor Monash Univ. 1983-. *Leisure interests:* tennis, cricket, the countryside. *Address:* 37 Rochester Road, Canterbury, Vic. 3126, Australia. *Telephone:* (03) 836 8275.

LUSHEV, Gen. Petr Georgevich; Soviet army officer; b. 18 Oct. 1923, Poboishche, Archangel Dist.; ed. jr. lieuts'. courses 1941-42, infantry officers' courses 1945-47, Stalin Mil. Acad. for Tanks, Moscow, until 1954, Mil. Acad. of Gen. Staff, Moscow until 1966; commdr. of a platoon, commdr. of a co. served on Volkhov and Leningrad fronts, in Leningrad blockade, wounded, 1942-45; mem. CPSU 1951-; First Deputy Commdr. 1969-71, Commdr. of Soviet First Army in Germany, Dresden 1971-73; First Deputy C.-in-C. Group of Soviet Troops in Germany 1973-75; Deputy to Estonian S.S.R. Supreme Soviet 1975-80; Commdr. of Volga Mil. Dist. 1975-77; Commdr. of Cen. Asian Mil. Dist. 1977-80; Deputy to Council of the Union, U.S.S.R. Supreme Soviet 1979-; Commdr. Moscow Mil. Dist., Chief of Moscow Garrison 1980-85; mem. Cen. Cttee. CPSU 1981-; rank of Army General 1981; C.-in-C. Group of Soviet Troops in Germany 1985-; First Deputy Minister of Defence 1986-89; C.-in-C. Warsaw Pact Forces Feb. 1989-; elected to Congress of People's Deputies of the U.S.S.R 1989, Order of Lenin, Order of Red Banner, Order of Red Star (twice), Hero of Soviet Union, numerous medals. *Address:* The Kremlin, Moscow, U.S.S.R.

LUSIGNAN, Guy de, M.A.; French international financial official; b. 17 March 1929, Paris; s. of Georges Roux de Lusignan and Helle Zaharoff; m. 1st Françoise Aubert 1951 (divorced 1954); m. 2nd Suzanne Landre 1956 (divorced 1981), two s. one d.; m. 3rd Martine Lacroix 1981, one d.; ed. Janson de Sailly, Paris and Univs. of Paris and Strasbourg; Press Attaché, Embassy, Copenhagen 1952-54; with French Productivity Agency, Paris 1955-59; Comm. for Tech. Co-operation in Africa South of the Sahara (CCTA), Brazzaville and Lagos 1959-62; Chief of Econ. Studies Div., Organisme de Mise en Valeur des Ressources du Sous-Sol Saharien, Algiers 1963-64; Programme Co-ordinator, World Bank/FAO Co-operative Programme, Rome 1964-68; joined World Bank 1968 and worked on operations in Zaire, Rwanda, Burundi and Madagascar, Div. chief for Algeria, Greece, Iran, Israel, Lebanon, Oman, Portugal and Tunisia 1971; Dir. World Bank Resident Mission in Saudi Arabia 1979-81; World Bank Special Rep. to UN, New York 1981-83; Deputy Dir. World Bank Econ. Devt. Inst. (EDI) 1983. *Publications:* ILO 1919-59 1959, French Speaking Africa since Independence 1969; numerous articles in historical reviews in the 1950s. *Leisure interests:* classical music, opera, cooking, Middle East history. *Address:* 1243 34th Street N.W., Washington, D.C. 20007, U.S.A.

LUSINCHI, Dr Jaime; Venezuelan politician and paediatrician; b. 27 May 1924, Clarines, Anzoátegui; m. Gladys Castillo (divorced 1988); five c.; ed. Univ. del Oriente, Univ. Central; active mem. Acción Democrática (AD) Party 1941-; Pres. Legis. Ass. for Anzoátegui and regional Gen. Sec. 1948-52; arrested during presidency of Gen. Marcos Pérez Jiménez; in exile in Argentina, Chile and U.S.A. 1952-58; returned to Venezuela 1958; mem Rómulo Betancourt's electoral comm. 1958, mem. Nat. Exec. Ctte. of AD 1958-, Dir. Int. Affairs 1958-61, Deputy for Anzoátegui 1959-67, Pres. Parl. Gp. 1968-78, Senator for Anzoátegui 1979-83, Presidential Cand. 1977, Sec.-Gen. AD 1980-83, Party Leader 1980-84; Pres. of Venezuela 1984-89; Paediatrician, Lincoln Hosp., Bellevue Medical Centre, New York 1958; mem. American Acad. of Pediatrics. *Address:* Oficina del Presidente, Caracas, Venezuela.

LUSSER, Markus, D.IUR.; Swiss lawyer and banker; b. 8 April 1931, Altdorf, Uri; m. Elisabeth Degen 1965; one s.; ed. Univs. of Berne and Paris; Sec. (later Deputy Dir.) Swiss Bankers' Assn., Basel 1958-75, Dir. 1976-78, Del., Admin. Bd. 1979-80; mem. Governing Bd., Swiss Nat. Bank, Zurich 1981-84; mem. and Vice-Chair. Gov. Bd. Swiss Nat. Bank, Berne 1985-88; Chair. Gov. Bd. Swiss Nat. Bank, Zurich May 1988-. *Address:*

Schweizerische Nationalbank, Börsenstrasse 15, CH-8022 Zurich, Switzerland.

LÜST, Reimar, DR.RER.NAT.; German physicist; b. 25 March 1923, Barmen; s. of Hero and Grete (née Strunck) Lüst; m. 1st Dr. Rhea Kulka 1953; two s.; 2nd Nina Grunenberg 1986; ed. Univs. of Frankfurt/M and Göttingen; Research Physicist, Max Planck Insts. Göttingen and Munich 1950–60, Enrico Fermi Inst., Univ. of Chicago 1955–56, Princeton Univ. 1956; Head, Dept. for Extraterrestrial Physics, Max Planck Inst. for Physics and Astrophysics 1960, Dir. Inst. of Extraterrestrial Physics 1963–72; Visiting Prof., Univ. of New York 1959, M.I.T. 1961, Calif. Inst. of Tech. 1962, 1966; Chair. German Research Council 1969–72, Deutsche Gesellschaft für Luft- und Raumfahrt 1968–72; Pres. Max-Planck-Gesellschaft June 1972–84; Dir. Gen. European Space Agency 1984–; mem. Int. Acad. Astronautics, Royal Astronomical Soc., Bavarian Acad. Sciences; Hon. Foreign mem. American Acad. of Arts and Sciences, Austrian Acad. of Sciences; Hon. mem. Heidelberg Acad. of Sciences, Senat Max-Planck-Gesellschaft, Deutsche Gesellschaft für Luft- und Raumfahrt; Corresp. mem. Real Acad. de Ciencias Exactas, Fisicas y Naturales de Madrid; Fellow Imperial Coll. of Science and Tech.; Officier Ordre des Palmes Académiques; Officier l'Ordre Nat. de la Légion d'Honneur; Bayerischer Maximiliansorden für Wissenschaft und Kunst, Grosses Verdienstkreuz mit Stern des Verdienstordens der Bundesrepublik Deutschland; Daniel and Florence Guggenheim Int. Astronautics Award, Personality of the Year 1986, Tsiolkowsky Medal (U.S.S.R. Fed. of Cosmonauts) 1987 and numerous other awards. *Publications:* articles on space research, astrophysics and plasmaphysics. *Leisure interests:* history, tennis, skiing. *Address:* European Space Agency, 8–10 rue Mario Nikis, F-75738 Paris (Office); 215 rue de l'Université, 75007 Paris, France (Home). *Telephone:* 42.73.74.04 (Office).

LUSTIG, Arnošt; Czechoslovak writer; b. 21 Dec. 1926, Prague; s. of Emil and Terezie Lustig (née Löwy); m. Věra Weislitz 1949; one s. one d.; ed. Coll. of Political and Social Sciences, Prague; in concentration camps at Terezín, Auschwitz and Buchenwald, Second World War; Radio Prague corresp. in Arab-Israeli war 1948, 1949; Radio Prague reporter 1948–58; Ed. Mladý svět (weekly) 1958–59, screenplay writer for Studio Barandov 1960–68, for Jadran-Film Yugoslavia 1969–70; naturalized American citizen 1979; mem. Cen. Cttee. Union of Czechoslovak Writers 1963–69, mem. Presidium 1963–69; mem. Int. Writing Program 1970–71; Visiting Lecturer Univ. of Iowa 1971–72; Visiting Prof. Drake Univ., Iowa 1972–73; Prof. of Literature and Film, American Univ., Washington, D.C. 1973–; Klement Gottwald State Prize 1967; Bne'i Brit'h Prize 1974; Nat. Jewish Book Award 1980, 1986; Emmy, The Nat. Acad. of Television Arts and Sciences 1986; Hon. Dr. Hebrew Letters, Spertus Coll. of Judaica, Chicago 1986. *Publications:* Démanty noci (Diamonds of the Night—short stories, two of which were filmed 1961, 1964) 1958, Blue Day (story, filmed for TV) 1960, Night and Hope (short stories) 1958, filmed as Transport z ráje (Transport from Paradise) 1962, Modlitba za Kateřinu Horovitzovou (A Prayer for Katerina Horovitzova—novel, filmed for TV) 1964, Dita Saxova (novel 1962, filmed 1968), The Street of Lost Brothers 1962, Prague Crossroads 1964, The Man the Size of a Stamp 1965 (radio plays), Nobody will be Humiliated (long stories) 1965, The White Birches in Autumn (novel) 1966, Bitter Smell of Almonds (novel) 1968, Darling (novel) 1969, Darkness Casts No Shadow (novel) 1976, Children of Holocaust (3 vols., collected stories) 1977–78 and 1986; TV documentaries: Theresienstadt (U.S.A.) 1965, Stolen Childhood (Italy) 1966; text for symphonic poem Night and Hope (with Otmar Macha) 1963, The Beadle of Prague (text for a cantata, music by Herman Berlinski) 1983; The Holocaust and the Film Arts (essay with Josef Lustig) 1980, The Precious Legacy (screenplay for documentary) 1984, The Unloved (from the diary of seventeen years' old Pearl Sch.—novel) 1985, Indecent Dreams 1988. *Leisure interests:* swimming, travelling, skiing, soccer. *Address:* 4000 Tunlaw Road N. W., Apartment 825, Washington, D.C. 20007, U.S.A. *Telephone:* 202-3385357.

LUSTIGER, H.E. Cardinal Jean-Marie, M.PH., L. EN. THEOL.; French ecclesiastic; b. 17 Sept. 1926, Paris; s. of Charles and Gisèle Lustiger; ed. Carmelite Seminary, Inst. Catholique de Paris and Université de Paris (Sorbonne); worked one year in factory, Decazeville; Chaplain to the students, Sorbonne 1954–69; Dir. Centre Richelieu, Paris 1959–69; Parish Vicar, Sainte-Jeanne-de-Chantal, Paris 1969–79; Bishop of Orléans 1979–81; Archbishop of Paris Jan. 1981–, cr. Cardinal Feb. 1983. *Publications:* Sermons d'un curé de Paris 1978, Pain de vie, Peuple de Dieu 1981, Habt Vertrauen 1982, Osez vivre, Osez croire 1985, Premiers pas dans la prière 1986, Six sermons aux élus de la Nation 1986, The Mass 1987, Le choix de Dieu 1987, The Lord's Prayer 1988. *Address:* Maison diocésaine, 8 rue de la Ville-l'Evêque, 75008 Paris, France.

LUSZTIG, George, M.A., PH.D., F.R.S.; British professor of mathematics; b. 20 May 1946, Timisoara, Romania; m. Michal Abraham 1972; two d.; ed. Univ. of Bucharest and Princeton Univ.; Visiting mem. Inst. for Advanced Study, Princeton, N.J. 1969–71; Research Fellow, Dept. of Math., Univ. of Warwick 1971–72, Lecturer 1972-74, Prof. 1974-78; Prof. of Math. M.I.T. 1978–; Guggenheim Fellowship 1982; Cole Prize in Algebra (American Math. Soc.) 1985. *Publications:* The Discrete Series of GLn over a Finite Field, 1974, Characters of Reductive Groups over a Finite Field 1984, *Address:* 106 Grant Avenue, Newton, Mass. 02159, U.S.A.

LUTFI, Aly, (see Loutfy, Aly).

LUTOSŁAWSKI, Witold; Polish composer and conductor; b. 25 Jan. 1913, Warsaw; s. of Józef and Maria Lutosławski; m. Maria-Danuta Dygat 1946; ed. Warsaw Conservatoire; mem. Swedish Royal Acad. of Music 1963–; Hon. mem. Freie Akademie der Künste Hamburg 1966–, Int. Soc. for Contemporary Music 1969–, Polish Composers' Union 1971–, American Acad. of Arts and Letters, Nat. Inst. of Arts and Letters 1975, R.A.M. 1976–, Guildhall School of Music 1978, Wiener Konzerthausgesellschaft 1980–; Extraordinary mem. Akademie der Künste Berlin 1968–; Corresp. mem. Deutsche Akad. der Künste, Berlin (D.D.R.) 1970–, Bayerische Akademie der schönen Künste, Munich 1973; mem. European Acad. of Arts, Sciences and Humanities 1980–; mem. Acad. européenne des Sciences des Arts et des Lettres; Foreign assoc. Acad. des Beaux Arts (Paris) 1979, Acad. Royale des Sciences, des Lettres et des Beaux Arts (Brussels) 1987; Hon. mem. Acad. Nazionale di Santa Cecilia (Rome) 1987; Vice-Pres. Polish Composers' Union 1973–79; Hon. D.Mus. (Cleveland Inst. of Music) 1971, (Glasgow Univ.) 1977, Dr. h.c. (Univ. Warsaw) 1973, (Lancaster Univ.) 1975, (Copernicus Univ., Toruń) 1980, (Durham Univ.) 1983, (Jagiellonian Univ., Cracow) 1984, (Royal Northern Coll., Manchester) 1987, (Queen's Univ., Belfast) 1987, Hon. Dr. Fine Arts (Northwestern Univ. Evanston-Chicago) 1974, Hon. D. Hum. Litt. (Baldwin-Wallace, Berea, Ohio) 1987; Hon. D. Mus. (Cambridge) 1987; City of Warsaw Music Prize 1948, Polish Music Festival Prize 1951, State Prizes 1952, 1955, 1964, 1978 (First Class), Prime Minister's Prize for Children's Music 1954, Polish Composers' Union's Prize 1959 and 1973, Minister of Culture's Prize 1962, Koussevitzky Int. Recording Award 1964; Plaque of the Freie Akad. der Künste, Hamburg 1966, Gottfried-von-Herder Prize, Vienna 1967; Sonning Music Prize, Copenhagen 1967; Award Int. Rostrum of Composers, UNESCO 1958, 1964, 1968; Prize ad honorem of Pres. of France 1971; Maurice Ravel Prize 1971, Prize Sibelius de Wihuri 1973, City of Warsaw Prize 1975, Order of Builders of People's Poland 1977, Award of Polish Cen. European Soc. of Culture (SEC) 1979, Ernst von Siemens Musikpreis 1983, Solidarity Award 1984; Univ. of Louisville Grawemeyer Award for music composition for Symphony No. 3 1985, UNESCO and Int. Music Council Award 1985, The Prize of Queen Sophia (Spain) 1985, Gold Medal of the Royal Philharmonic Soc. 1985; The Int. Record Critics' Award for Symphony No. 3 1986, High Fidelity Grammy Award 1987, Commdr. des arts et des lettres, Paris 1982. *Works include:* Symphonic Variations 1938, Variations on a Theme of Paganini (two pianos) 1941, Folk Melodies (piano) 1945, Symphony 1947, Overture (string orch.) 1949, Little Suite for Orchestra 1951, Silesian Triptych (voice and orch.) 1951, Bucoliques for Piano 1952, Dance Preludes (clarinet) 1953, Concerto for Orchestra 1954, Musique Funèbre (string orch.) 1958, Five Songs (female voice and instruments) 1958, Jeux vénitiens 1961, Trois poèmes d'Henri Michaux (choir and orch.) 1963, String Quartet 1964, Paroles tissées (tenor and chamber orch.) 1965, Second Symphony 1967, Livre pour orchestre 1968, Concerto for Cello and Orchestra 1970, Preludes and Fugue for 13 Solo Strings 1972, Les espaces du sommeil (for baritone voice and orchestra) 1975, Mi-parti (for orchestra) 1976, Novelette (for orchestra) 1979, Epitaph (for oboe and piano) 1979, Double Concerto (for oboe, harp and chamber orchestra) 1980, Grave for cello and piano 1981, Symphony No. 3 1983, Chain 1 for Chamber Orchestra 1983, Partita for violin and piano 1984, Chain 2 for violin and orchestra 1985, Chain 3 for symphony orchestra 1986, Concerto for piano and orchestra 1988; chamber, piano, vocal and children's music; compositions for theatre, films and radio. *Leisure interests:* literature, other arts, yachting. *Address:* ul Śmiała 39, 01-523 Warsaw, Poland. *Telephone:* 39 23 90.

LUTTINEN, Vilho Matti; Finnish politician; b. 1936, Haapavesi; held various positions in food production industry for 13 years; Sec. Lahti Social Democratic Communal Org. 1965–69; Sec. and Head of Dept. Lahti Cooperative Store 1969–75; mem. Lahti City Council 1969–, Lahti City Bd. 1971, 1973–75; M.P. 1975–; Chair. Econ. Cttee. of Parl. 1983; Minister, Ministry of the Interior 1983–84; Minister of Transport and Communications 1984–87; Social Democratic Party. *Address:* c/o Ministry of Transport and Communications, Aleksanterinkatu 3D, 00170 Helsinki 17, Finland.

LUTTWAK, Edward Nicolae, PH.D.; American academic, defence consultant and writer; b. 4 Nov. 1942, Arad, Romania; s. of Joseph Luttwak and Clara Baruch; m. Dalya Iaari 1970; one s. one d.; ed. elementary schools in Palermo and Milan, Carmel Coll., Wallingford, U.K., London School of Econs. and Johns Hopkins Univ.; Lecturer, Univ. of Bath, U.K. 1965–67; Consultant, Walter J. Levy S.A. (London) 1967–68; Visiting Prof. Johns Hopkins Univ. 1974-76; Sr. Fellow, Georgetown Univ. Center for Strategic and Int. Studies 1977–87; Chair. of Strategic and Int. Studies, Strategy Center 1987–; Consultant to Office of Sec. of Defense 1975–, to Policy Planning Council, Dept. of State 1981–, Nat. Security Council 1987–, Dept. of Defense 1987–; Prin., Edward N. Luttwak Inc. Defense Consultants 1981–; mem. editorial Bd. of The American Scholar, Journal of Strategic Studies, The National Interest, Géopolitique, The Washington Quarterly. *Publications:* Coup d'Etat 1968, Dictionary of Modern War 1972, The Israeli Army 1975, The Political Uses of Sea Power 1976, The Grand Strategy of the Roman Empire 1978, Strategy and Politics: Collected Essays 1979, The Grand Strategy of the Soviet Union 1983, The Pentagon and the Art of War 1985, Strategy and History: collected essays 1985, International Security Yearbook 1984/85 (with Barry M. Brechman) 1985, On the Meaning of Victory 1986, Strategy: The Logic of War and Peace

1987. *Leisure interests:* hunting, fishing. *Address:* 4510 Drummond Avenue, Chevy Chase, Md. 20815, U.S.A. *Telephone:* 301-656-1972.

LUTZ, Robert A., M.B.A.; American (b. Swiss) business executive; b. 2 Dec. 1932, Zurich; s. of Robert H. and Marguerite Lutz; m. Heide-Marie Schmid 1980; four d.; ed. Univ. of Calif. (Berkeley); Capt. U.S. Marine Corps 1954–59; Research Assoc. IMEDE, Lausanne 1962–63; Senior Analyst, Forward Planning, Gen. Motors, New York 1963–65; Staff Asst., Man. Dir.'s Staff, Adam Opel AG (GM) 1965–66; various man. positions, GM (France) 1966–69; Asst. Domestic Gen. Sales Man., Merchandising, Adam Opel AG 1969, Dir. of Sales and mem. Management Bd. 1969–70; Vice-Pres. (Sales) and mem. Management Bd., BMW AG 1970–74; Gen. Man. Ford of Germany 1974–76; Vice-Pres. (Truck Operations), Ford of Europe 1976–77; Pres. Ford of Europe 1977–79; Vice-Pres. Ford Motor Co. and Chair. of Bd., Ford of Europe 1979–82; Exec. Vice-Pres. Ford Int. Automotive Operations 1982–86, Exec. Vice-Pres. N. American Truck Operations 1986; Head Int. Operations Chrysler 1986–, Exec. Vice-Pres. 1986–88, Pres. 1988–. *Address:* Chrysler Motors Corporation, 12000 Chrysler Drive, Highland Park, Mich. 48288, U.S.A.

LUVSANGOMBO, Sonomyn; Mongolian politician; b. 1924; ed. Higher Mil. School, Ulaanbaatar, Acad. of Mil. Eng., U.S.S.R. and Higher School of Civil Eng.; army technician, instructor, divisional supply officer 1948–56; Sr. Engineer, Ministry of Construction 1956–59; Deputy and First Deputy Minister of Construction and Construction Materials Industry, Deputy Chair. State Construction Cttee. 1959–71; Chair. Exec. Cttee. of Ulaanbaatar People's Deputies' Hural (Ass.) 1971–72; Deputy Chair. Council of Ministers 1972–82, Chair. 1984, now Deputy-Chair.; Minister of Public Security 1982–84; Chair. State Cttee. for Construction, Architecture and Tech. Control 1984–; Deputy to People's Great Hural (Assembly); Cand. mem. Mongolian People's Revolutionary Party Cen. Cttee. 1966–71, mem. Cen. Cttee. 1971–, cand. mem. Politburo Jan. 1982–; Order of the Pole Star, Order of the Red Banner of Labour. *Address:* Government Palace, Ulaanbaatar, Mongolia.

LUVSANRAVDAN, Namsrayn; Mongolian politician; b. 5 Feb. 1923; schoolmaster 1943–45; Head of dept. in Ministry of Educ. 1945–50: Head of dept. in Ulaanbaatar City Cttee., Mongolian People's Revolutionary Party (MPRP) 1950–53, Second Sec. Ulaanbaatar City Cttee., MPRP 1953–55, 1958–60; mem. Presidium, People's Great Hural (Assembly) 1963–81, Deputy Chair. 1963–66, 1969–71, 1977–81; First Sec. Ulaanbaatar Cttee., MPRP 1960–63; cand. mem. Political Bureau, MPRP Cen. Cttee. 1960–71, mem. Political Bureau 1971–81; Chair. Party Control Cttee. of MPRP Cen. Cttee. 1963–81; Amb. to Romania 1981–84; Order of Sühbaatar. *Address:* c/o Ministry of Foreign Affairs, Ulaanbaatar, Mongolia.

LUXEMBOURG, Grand Duke of (see Jean).

LUXON, Benjamin Matthew, C.B.E., F.G.S.M.; British musician; b. 24 March 1937, Redruth, Cornwall; s. of Maxwell Luxon and Lucille Grigg; m. Sheila Amit; two s. one d.; ed. Truro School, Westminster Training Coll., Guildhall School of Music and Drama; always a freelance artist; sang with English Opera Group 1963–70; has sung with Royal Opera House, Covent Garden, and Glyndebourne Festival Opera 1971–, Boston Symphony Orchestra 1975–, Netherlands Opera 1976–, Frankfurt Opera House 1977–; performs as recitalist with piano accompanist David Willison; folk-singing partnership with Bill Grofut 1976–; has recorded for all major record cos.; Hon. mem. R.A.M.; Hon. D.Mus. (Exeter Univ.); Bard of Cornish Gorseth. *Leisure interests:* most sports, English watercolours of 18th and 19th centuries. *Address:* Bylands House, Dunstable Road, Redbourn, Herts., England.

LUYT, Sir Richard Edmonds, G.C.M.G., K.C.V.O., D.C.M., M.A., LL.D.; South African (sometime British) administrator; b. 8 Nov. 1915, Cape Town, South Africa; s. of Richard Robins Luyt and Wilhelmina Roberta Frances Edmonds; m. 1st Jean Mary Wilder 1948 (died 1951), one d.; 2nd Eileen Betty Reid 1956; two s.; ed. Diocesan Coll., Rondebosch, Univ. of Cape Town and Trinity Coll., Oxford; Colonial Service, N. Rhodesia 1940, 1946–53; War Service 1940–45; Labour Commr., Kenya 1954–57; Perm. Sec. Kenya Govt. 1957–60, Sec. to Cabinet 1960–61; Chief Sec. Govt. of N. Rhodesia 1962–64; Gov. and C.-in-C., British Guiana 1964–66; Gov.-Gen. of Guyana May-Oct. 1966; Prin. and Vice-Chancellor Univ. of Cape Town 1968–80; Pres. Civil Rights League (of South Africa). *Leisure interests:* cricket, tennis, rugby, swimming, gardening, turtles, tortoises. *Address:* Allandale, Alma Road, Rosebank, 7700 Cape Province, South Africa. *Telephone:* 68-66-765.

LUZ, Hans; German landscape architect; b. 10 June 1926, Stuttgart; s. of Karl Luz and Frieda (née Sieling) Luz; m. Gretel Reinhardt 1952; three s. one d.; ed. in garden design and improvement; general experience 1948–56, planning depts. 1958–73, teacher Technischen Universität Stuttgart 1973–75, at present freelance landscape architect and partner in Büro Luz; mem. Akademie der Künste Berlin 1975–, Deutschen Akademie für Städtebau und Landesplanung 1980–, Akademie der Künste Mannheim 1984–; Chair. Landesgruppe Baden-Württemberg des Bundes Deutscher Landschaftsarchitekten 1982–84; Paul-Bonatz-Preis 1958, 1977, BDLA-Preis 1977, 1987, Fritz-Schumacher-Preis 1980. *Publications:* lectures and articles, Stuttgarter Gärten 1980. *Address:* Luz & Partner, Dinkelstrasse 40, 7000 Stuttgart 70, Federal Republic of Germany (Office). *Telephone:* (0711) 454066 (Office).

LWIN, U; Burmese diplomatist and politician; b. 10 Dec. 1912; m.; two s. two d; fmr. officer, Burma army; Mil. Adviser, Burma Del. to UN Gen. Assembly 1953; Amb. to Fed. Germany 1966–71, also to Netherlands 1969–71; Perm. Rep. to UN 1971–72; Minister for Planning and Finance 1972–75, for Information 1975–77; Deputy Prime Minister 1974–77; withdrew from Cen. Cttee. of Burma Socialist Programme Party 1977.

LWOFF, André Michel; French scientist; b. 8 May 1902; ed. Lycée Voltaire, Univ. de Paris à la Sorbonne; joined Institut Pasteur 1921, Asst. 1925–29, Head of Lab. 1929–38, Head Dept. of Microbial Physiology 1938–68, mem. Bd. of Dirs. 1966–72; Prof. Microbiology, Univ. de Paris 1959–68; Head Cancer Research Inst., Villejuif 1968–72; Pres. French Family Planning Movement 1970–; mem. numerous French and foreign scientific socs.; mem. Acad. des Sciences 1976–; Foreign mem. Nat. Acad. Sciences U.S.A. 1955, Foreign mem. Royal Soc. London 1958, Foreign mem. U.S.S.R. Acad. of Medicine; Nobel Prize for Medicine (jointly with F. Jacob and J. Monod) 1965, Einstein Award 1967; Médaille de la Résistance, Grand Croix, Légion d'honneur. *Publications include:* Biological Order 1962, Jeux et combats 1981. *Address:* 69 avenue de Suffren, 75007 Paris, France.

LYAKHOV, Vladimir Afanasevich; Soviet cosmonaut; b. 1941; ed. Kharkov Aviation School for Pilots, Gagarin Mil. Acad.; mem. CPSU 1963–; served in Soviet Air Force 1964–; Cosmonaut 1967–; Commdr. of spaceship Soyuz-32, 1979, and Soyuz T-9 which connected up with orbital station Salyut-7; space-walked 1983; Hero of Soviet Union (twice).

LYGO, Adm. Sir Raymond Derek, K.C.B., F.R.AE.S., F.R.S.A., C.B.I.M.; British business executive; b. 15 March 1924, Ilford, Essex; s. of Edwin and Ada E. Lygo ; m. Pepper van Osten 1950; two s. one d.; ed. Ilford County High School and Clarkes Coll., Bromley; The Times 1940; naval airman, Royal Navy 1942; served V.S.N. 1949–51; C.O. 759 Squadron 1951–53, 800 Squadron 1954–56, H.M.S. Lowestoft 1959–61, H.M.S. Juno 1967–69, C.O. H.M.S. Ark Royal 1969–71; Vice-Chief of Naval Staff 1975–77, Chief of Naval Staff 1977–78; joined British Aerospace 1978, Man. Dir. Hatfield/Lostock Div. 1978–80, Chair. and Chief Exec. Dynamics Group 1980–82; Man. Dir. British Aerospace PLC Jan. 1983–, mem. Bd. 1980–, Chief Exec. June 1985–; Chair. Royal Ordnance PLC 1987; Pres. Soc. of British Aerospace Cos. 1984–85, Vice-Pres. 1985–; Freeman City of London, Liveryman Coachmakers. *Leisure interests:* building, gardening, joinery. *Address:* British Aerospace PLC, 11 Strand, London, WC2N 5JT, England. *Telephone:* 01-389 3925.

LYMPANY, Moura, C.B.E., F.R.A.M.; British concert pianist; b. 18 Aug. 1916, Saltash, Cornwall; d. of John and Beatrice Johnstone; m. 1st Colin Defries 1944 (divorced 1950); m. 2nd Bennet H. Korn 1951 (divorced 1961); one s. (deceased); ed. Belgium, Austria, England; first performance, Harrogate 1929; has played in U.S.A., Canada, South America, Australia, New Zealand, India and most European countries including the U.S.S.R.; Commdr. Order of Crown (Belgium) 1980. *Leisure interests:* gardening, reading, tapestry. *Address:* c/o Ibbs and Tillett, 450/452 Edgware Road, London, W.2, England; 4 Boulevard du Ténao, Monte Carlo, Monaco. *Telephone:* (93) 30 73 29.

LYNCH, Frank William; American aerospace executive; b. 26 Nov. 1921, San Francisco ; s. of James G. Lynch and Med Kelly; m. Marilyn Hopwood 1950; two d.; ed. Principia Acad., Principia Coll. and Stanford Univ.; Research Eng., Boeing Airplane Co., Seattle, Wash. 1948–50; Eng. Dept. Man. Northrop Corpn., Hawthorne, Calif. 1950–57 ; Div. Vice-Pres. (Eng.) Lear-Siegler Corpn., Anaheim, Calif. 1957–59; Vice-Pres. (Eng.) Nortronics Div., Northrop Corpn., Los Angeles, Calif. 1959–61, Vice-Pres. and Gen. Man. Electronic Systems Div. 1961–62, Electro-Mechanical Div. 1962–74, Sr. Vice-Pres. Operations 1974–78, Sr. Vice-Pres. and Group Exec. Tactical and Electronic Systems Group 1978–82, Pres. and C.O.O. 1982–87, Vice-Chair. 1987–. *Leisure interest:* sailing. *Address:* Northrop Corporation, 1800 Century Park East, Los Angeles, Calif. 90067; 1933 Altura Drive, Corona del Mar, Calif. 92625, U.S.A. *Telephone:* (213) 553-6262 (Office); (714) 673-7352 (Home).

LYNCH, John Mary, B.L.; Irish lawyer and politician; b. 15 Aug. 1917, Cork; s. of Daniel Lynch and Norah O'Donoghue; m. Mairin O'Connor 1946; ed. North Monastery, Cork, Univ. Coll., Cork, and King's Inns, Dublin; mem. Civil Service (Dept. of Justice) 1936–45; called to Bar 1945; mem. of Dáil Éireann (Parl.) 1948–81; Alderman, Cork Corpn. 1950–57; Parl. Sec. to Govt. and to Minister for Lands 1951–54; Minister for Educ. 1957–59; Minister for Industry and Commerce 1959–65, for Finance 1965–66; Vice-Pres. Council of Europe 1958, Pres. European Council (EEC) July-Dec. 1979; Pres. Int. Labour Conf. 1962; Taoiseach (Prime Minister) 1966–73, 1977–79; Pres. Fianna Fáil (Republican Party) 1966–79; Leader of the Opposition 1973–77; Dir. Irish Distillers Group 1980–86, Jefferson Smurfit Group PLC 1980–, Algemene Bank Nederland (Ireland) Ltd. 1980–87, Hibernian Insurance PLC 1980–; Chair. Galway Irish Crystal 1984–; Hon. LL.D. (Dublin Univ.) 1967, (Nat. Univ. of Ireland) 1969, Hon. D.C.L. (Belmont Abbey, Univ. Coll., N. Carolina, U.S.A.) 1971, (Rhode Island Coll.) 1981; Grand Cross of Belgian Order of the Crown 1968, Robert Schumann Gold Medal 1973, Mérite Européen Gold Medal 1981. *Leisure interests:* reading, music (operatic and folk), swimming, boating, inshore sea fishing. *Address:* 21 Garville Avenue, Rathgar, Dublin 6, Ireland (Home).

LYNCH, Patrick, M.A., M.R.I.A.; Irish university professor and public administrator (retd.); b. 1917, Dublin; s. of Daniel and Brigid Lynch; m. Mrs. Mary Crotty 1965 (died 1982); ed. Univ. Coll., Dublin; joined Irish Civil Service 1941; served Finance Dept. 1941–48; Asst. Sec. Dept. of Prime Minister 1950–52; Lecturer, Nat. Univ. of Ireland 1952–66; Chair. Aer Lingus 1954–75, Capital Investment Advisory Cttee.; Dir. Provincial Bank of Ireland 1959–66; Chair. Inst. of Public Admin. 1973–76, Medico-Social Research Bd. 1966–72; Dir. Allied Irish Banks 1966–84; Dir. OECD Govt. Surveys on Investment in Educ. and Research and Devt. 1962–66; mem. Governing Body, Univ. Coll., Dublin 1964–76; mem. Senate Nat. Univ. of Ireland 1972–77; Fellow Commoner, Peterhouse, Cambridge; Assoc. Prof. of Political Econ. (Applied Econs.) 1966–75, Prof. 1975–80; Treas. Royal Irish Academy 1971–80; mem. Nat. Science Council 1967–77, Higher Educ. Authority 1968–72, Club of Rome 1973, Patron British-Irish Asscn. 1973, EEC Group EMU 1980 1974–75, Exec. Council, European Science Foundation 1975–77; Chair. Econ. and Social Research Inst. 1983–88; Deputy Chair. Allied Irish Banks 1976–84; Dir. Allied Irish Finance Co. 1976–82; Jt. Deputy Chair. Co-operation North 1981–84; Dr. h.c. (Brunel) 1976, LL.D. h.c. (Dublin) 1979, Dr. Econ. Sc. h.c. (Nat. Univ.) 1985. *Publications:* The Economics of Independence 1959, Planning for Economic Development (with C. F. Carter) 1959, Guinness's Brewery in the Irish Economy (with J. Vaizey) 1960, The Role of Public Enterprises in Ireland 1961, essay on The Irish Economy in Conor Cruise O'Brien introduces Ireland 1969, Ireland in the War Years and after (ed. Nowlan and Williams) 1969, Ireland in the International Labour Organization (with B. Hillery) 1970, Economics of Educational Costing (with J. Vaizey) 1971, Readings in Public Administration (ed. with B. Chubb) 1971, essay in Travel and Transport in Ireland (ed. K. B. Nowlan) 1973, Whither Science Policy 1979. *Leisure interest:* talking. *Address:* 68 Marlborough Road, Dublin 4, Ireland.

LYNDEN-BELL, Donald, M.A., PH.D., F.R.S.; British professor of astrophysics; b. 5 April 1935; s. of late Lieut.-Col. L. A. Lynden-Bell and of M. R. Lynden-Bell; m. Ruth M. Truscott 1961; one s. one d.; ed. Marlborough Coll. and Clare Coll. Cambridge; Harkness Fellow, Calif. Inst. of Tech. and Hale Observatories 1960–62, Visiting Assoc. 1969–70, Research Fellow, then Fellow and Dir. of Studies in Math. Clare Coll., Cambridge 1960–65; Asst. Lecturer in Applied Math. Univ. of Cambridge 1962–65; Prin. Scientific Officer, later Sr. Prin. Scientific Officer, Royal Greenwich Observatory, Herstmonceux 1965–72; Prof. of Astrophysics, Univ. of Cambridge 1972–; Dir. Inst. of Astronomy, Cambridge 1972–77, 1982–87; Pres. Royal Astronomical Soc. 1985–87; Hon. D.Sc. (Sussex) 1987, (Cambridge) 1987; Eddington Medal 1984. *Publications:* contributions to Monthly Notices of Royal Astronomical Soc. *Leisure interests:* hill-walking, golf, squash racquets. *Address:* Institute of Astronomy, The Observatories, Madingley Road, Cambridge, CB3 0HA, England. *Telephone:* (0223) 62204.

LYNG, Richard Edmund, PH.B.; American government official; b. 29 June 1918, San Francisco; s. of Edmund J. Lyng and Sarah C. (McGrath) Lyng; m. Bethyl Ball 1944; two d.; ed. Univ. of Notre Dame; With Ed. J. Lyng Co., Modesto, Calif. 1945–66, Pres. 1949–66; Dir. Calif. Dept. of Agric. 1967–69; Asst. Sec. U.S. Dept. of Agric. 1969–73, Deputy Sec. 1981–86, Sec. for Agric. 1986–89; Dir. Commodity Credit Corpn. 1969–73, Vice-Chair. 1981–; Pres. American Meat Inst. 1973–79; Dir. Nat. Livestock and Meat Bd. 1973–76, Tri-Valley Growers 1975–81; mem. numerous advisory bds., etc. *Address:* c/o Department of Agriculture, 14th Street and Independence Avenue, S.W., Washington, D.C. 20250, U.S.A.

LYNN, James Thomas; American lawyer and former government official; b. 27 Feb. 1927, Cleveland, Ohio; s. of Fred R. and Dorothea E. Lynn; m. Joan Miller 1954; one s. two d.; ed. Euclid Cen. High School, Adelbert Coll. of Western Reserve Univ., Harvard Law School; joined Cleveland law firm, Jones, Day, Cockley and Reavis 1951, Partner 1960–69; Gen. Counsel Dept. of Commerce 1969–71, Under-Sec. 1971–73; Sec. of Housing and Urban Devt. 1973–75; Dir. Office of Man. and Budget 1975–77; partner in law firm Jones, Day, Reavis and Pogne 1977; Dir. Aetna Life & Casualty Co., Vice-Chair. 1984–85, Chair., C.E.O. 1985–; Pres. Fed. City Council, Washington, D.C. 1978–. *Address:* 151 Farmington Avenue, Hartford, Conn. 06115, U.S.A. (Office).

LYNN, Dame Vera, D.B.E.; British singer; b. 20 March 1917; d. of Bertram Welch and Ann Welch; m. Harry Lewis 1941; one d.; ed. Brampton Road School, East Ham; joined singing troupe 1928; ran dancing school 1932; broadcast with Joe Loss and joined Charlie Kunz band 1935; singer with Ambrose Orchestra 1937–40, then went solo; voted most popular singer in Daily Express competition 1939; own radio show Sincerely Yours 1941–47; sang to troops abroad during Second World War, named "Forces' Sweetheart"; appeared in Applesauce, London 1941; post-war radio and TV shows and numerous appearances abroad including Denmark, Canada, South Africa and Australia; most successful record Auf Wiederseh'n; Pres. Printers' Charitable Corpn. 1980; Hon. Citizen Nürnberg 1974; Freedom of City of London 1978, Commdr. Order of Orange-Nassau (Holland), Burma Star Medal and War Medal 1985, Variety Club Int. Humanitarian Award. *Publication:* Vocal Refrain (autobiog.) 1975. *Leisure interests:* gardening, painting, sewing, swimming.

LYON, John David Richard, M.A.; British business executive; b. 4 June 1936, London; s. of F. A. Lyon and E. G. Lyon; m. 1st Nicola M. E. Bland 1960 (marriage dissolved 1986); two s.; m. 2nd Lillis Lanphier 1987; ed. Wellington Coll., Magdalen Coll. Oxford and Harvard Business School; 1st Bn. The Rifle Brigade 1954–56; Courtaulds PLC 1959–70; Rank Org. PLC 1970–71; Man. Dir. Redland Roof Tiles, Redland PLC 1971–76, Dir. Redland PLC 1976–80, Deputy Man. Dir. 1980–82, Group Man. Dir. 1982–87; C.E.O. Bowater Industries 1987–; mentioned in despatches, Kenya 1954. *Leisure interests:* deer stalking and gardening. *Address:* Redland House, Reigate, Surrey, RH2 0SJ, England. *Telephone:* (07372) 42488.

LYON, Mary Frances, B.A., PH.D., SC.D., F.R.S., F.I.BIOL.; British geneticist; b. 15 May 1925, Norwich; d. of Clifford James and Louise Frances (née Kirby) Lyon; ed. Woking Grammar School, Girton Coll., Cambridge; on Medical Research Council (MRC) Scientific Staff, Inst. of Animal Genetics Edinburgh 1950–55; Scientific Staff MRC Radiobiology Unit, Harwell 1955–, Head of Genetics Section 1962–87; Clothworkers Visiting Research Fellow, Girton Coll., Cambridge 1970–71; Foreign Assoc. Nat. Acad. of Sciences 1979; Foreign Hon. mem. American Acad. of Arts and Sciences 1980; Francis Amory Prize, American Acad. of Arts and Sciences 1977, Royal Medal, Royal Soc. 1984, San Remo Int. Prize for Genetics 1985, Gairdner Int. Award 1985, William Allan Award, American Soc. of Human Genetics 1986. *Publications:* papers on genetics in scientific journals. *Address:* Medical Research Council Radiobiology Unit, Chilton, Didcot, Oxon. OX11 0RD, England. *Telephone:* (0235) 834393.

LYON, Stanley Douglas, B.SC.ENG., A.M.I.C.E., C.B.I.M.; British engineer and industrialist; b. 22 June 1917, Edinburgh; s. of Ernest Hutcheon Lyon and late Helen Wilson Lyon; m. May Alexandra Jack 1941; three s.; ed. George Heriot's School and Edinburgh Univ.; joined ICI Ltd. 1946, Dyestuffs Div. 1946, Eng. Dir. Wilton Works 1957, Production Dir. Agricultural Div. 1962, Deputy Chair. Agricultural Div. 1964, Chair. Agricultural Div. 1966, Dir. ICI Ltd. 1968, Deputy Chair. 1972–77. *Leisure interests:* golf, tennis, gardening. *Address:* Ghyll Close, 32 West Lane, Danby, Whitby, North Yorkshire, England. *Telephone:* (0287) 60505.

LYON, Hon. Sterling, P.C., Q.C.; Canadian politician; b. 30 Jan. 1927, Windsor, Ont.; s. of late David Rufus Lyon and Ella Mae (Cuthbert) Lyon; m. Barbara Lyon 1953; five c.; ed. Univs. of Manitoba and Winnipeg; reporter, Winnipeg Free Press 1948–49; called to the Bar 1953; Crown Attorney, Manitoba Dept. of Attorney-Gen. and legal practice 1953–58; mem. Man. Legis. Ass. 1958–69, 1976–86; Attorney-Gen. 1958–63, 1966–69; Minister of Municipal Affairs 1960–61, of Mines and Natural Resources 1963–66; Govt. House Leader 1966–69; Leader, Man. Progressive Conservative Party 1975–83; Leader of Opposition, Man. 1977, 1981–83; Premier of Man. 1977–81; Minister of Dominion-Provincial Affairs 1977–81; Judge Manitoba Court of Appeal 1986–; Trustee, North American Wildlife Foundation. *Leisure interests:* reading, wildlife conservation, hunting, fishing, gardening. *Address:* The Lawcourts, Winnipeg, Man. R3C 0V8, Canada. *Telephone:* (204) 9452050.

LYONS, Bernard, C.B.E., J.P., D.L.; British company executive; b. 30 March 1913, Leeds; s. of Samuel Henry and Sophie (née Niman) Lyons; m. Lucy Hurst 1938; three s. one d.; ed. Leeds Grammar School; mem. Leeds City Council 1951–65; Chair. Yorkshire and N.E. Conciliation Cttee. of Race Relations Bd. 1968–70; mem. Community Relations Comm. 1970–72; Man. Dir. UDS Group PLC 1972–79, Chair. 1972–82; Life Pres. Leeds Jewish Representative Council; J.P. Leeds 1960; mem. Court and Council of Univ. of Leeds 1962–65; mem. Dept. of Trade Advisory Cttee. on Retail Distribution 1968–70; D.L. West Riding of Yorkshire 1971; Hon. LL.D. (Leeds Univ.) 1973. *Publications:* The Thread is Strong 1982, The Narrow Edge 1985. *Leisure interests:* farming, forestry, travelling, writing. *Address:* Upton Wood, Fulmer, Bucks., England; 2784 South Ocean Boulevard, Palm Beach, Fla., U.S.A. *Telephone:* Fulmer 2404; (305) 582-2227 (U.S.A.).

LYONS, Sir John, Kt., PH.D., F.B.A.; British professor of linguistics; b. 23 May 1932, Manchester; s. of Michael Austin Lyons and Mary Bridget O'Sullivan; m. Danielle Jacqueline Simonet 1959; two d.; ed. St. Bede's Coll. Manchester and Christ's Coll. Cambridge; Lecturer in Comparative Linguistics, S.O.A.S., Univ. of London 1957–61; Lecturer in Linguistics and Fellow of Christ's Coll., Univ. of Cambridge 1961; Prof. of Gen. Linguistics, Univ. of Edin. 1964–76; Prof. of Linguistics, Univ. of Sussex 1976–84, Dean, School of Social Sciences 1979–81, Pro-Vice-Chancellor 1981–84, Visiting Prof. of Linguistics 1984–; Master of Trinity Hall, Cambridge 1984–; Hon. Fellow Christ's Coll. Cambridge 1985; Hon. mem. Linguistic Soc. of America; Dr. h.c. (Univ. Catholique, Louvain) 1980, Hon. D.Litt. (Reading) 1986. *Publications:* Structural Semantics 1963, Introduction to Theoretical Linguistics 1968, Chomsky 1970, 1977, New Horizons in Linguistics 1970, Semantics 1 and 2 1977, Language and Linguistics 1980, Language, Meaning and Context 1981. *Address:* Master's Lodge, Trinity Hall, Cambridge, England. *Telephone:* (0223) 332540.

LYONS, Lawrence Ernest, B.A., PH.D., F.A.A.; Australian professor of physical chemistry; b. 26 May 1922, Sydney; s. of Ernest Lyons and Doris Lyons; m. Alison Hargreaves 1956; two s.; ed. Sydney Boys' High School and Univs. of Sydney and London; lecturer to Reader in Chem. Univ. of Sydney 1945–63; Prof. of Physical Chem. Univ. of Queensland 1963–87,

Prof. Emer. 1987–; Dir. New Univ. Colls. Council 1960–87; Visiting Prof. Univ. of British Columbia 1967, Waterloo Univ. 1986; Leverhulme Sr. Fellow, Tokyo Univ. 1971; mem. Nat. Energy Research, Devt. and Demonstration Council 1978–81, Australian Nat. Comm. for Unesco 1982–84; Burfitt Prize 1968; Smith Medal 1968. *Publications:* co-author of Organic Semiconductors, (Part A) 1967, (Part B) 1983. *Leisure interests:* reading, tennis. *Address:* 2172 Moggill Road, Kenmore, Queensland 4069, Australia. *Telephone:* 07-3781614.

LYSSARIDES, Vassos, M.D.; Cypriot politician; b. 1920, Lefkara; m. Barbara Cornwall; ed. Univ. of Athens; mem. House of Reps. 1960–, Pres. 1985–; Pres. Socialist Party of Cyprus (EDEK) 1969–; Sec.-Gen. Int. Cttee. of Solidarity with the Struggle of the Peoples of Southern Africa; Vice-Pres. Presidium, Afro-Asian Peoples' Solidarity Org.; Hon. Pres. Nicosia Medical Asscn. Hippocrates. *Address:* House of Representatives, Nicosia, Cyprus.

LYSYK, Hon. Kenneth Martin, Q.C., B.A., L.L.B., B.C.L.; Canadian judge and university professor; b. 1 July 1934, Weyburn, Sask.; s. of Michael Lysyk and Anna (née Maradyn) Lysyk; m. Patricia Irene Kinnon 1959; three d.; ed. McGill Univ., Univ. of Sask., Oxford Univ.; Lecturer, Asst. Prof., Assoc. Prof. and Prof., Faculty of Law, Univ. of B.C. 1960–70, Dean and Prof. of Law 1976–82; Adviser, P.C. Office (Constitutional Review Section), Govt. of Canada, Ottawa 1969–70; Prof., Faculty of Law, Univ. of Toronto 1970–72; Deputy Attorney Gen., Govt. of Sask. 1972–76; Chair., Alaska Highway Pipeline Inquiry 1977; Judge, Supreme Court of B.C. 1983–; Dir., Potash Corpn. of Sask. (Crown Corpn.) 1975–82; arbitrator in labour relations, B.C. and Ont. 1966–82; advisory work for fed. and prov. govts. *Leisure interest:* sport. *Address:* The Law Courts, 800 Smithe Street, Vancouver, B.C. V6Z 2E1 (Office); 3157 Point Grey Road, Vancouver, B.C. V6K 1B3, Canada (Home).

LYTHGOE, Basil, F.R.S.; British professor of organic chemistry; b. 18 Aug. 1913; s. of Peter W. Lythgoe and Agnes Lythgoe; m. Kathleen C. Hallum 1946; two s.; ed. Leigh Grammar School and Manchester Univ.; Asst. Lecturer, Manchester Univ. 1938; Univ. Lecturer, Cambridge 1946; Fellow, King's Coll. Cambridge 1950; Prof. of Organic Chem. Univ. of Leeds 1953–78, now Emer. *Publications:* papers in Journal of Chemical Soc. *Leisure interest:* mountaineering. *Address:* 113 Cookridge Lane, Leeds, LS16 0JJ, England. *Telephone:* (0532) 678837.

LYTTELTON, Humphrey Richard Adeane; British bandleader and journalist; b. 23 May 1921, Eton, Bucks.; s. of the late Hon. George William Lyttelton; m. 1st Patricia Mary Braithwaite 1948 (dissolved 1952), one d.; m. 2nd Elizabeth Jill Richardson 1952, two s. one d.; ed. Sunningdale School, Eton Coll.; Grenadier Guards 1941–46; Camberwell Art School 1947–48; formed own band 1948; cartoonist for London Daily Mail 1949–53; freelance journalist and leader of Humphrey Lyttelton's Band 1953–; recorded Parlophone 1950–60, Columbia 1960–63, Black Lion 1973–83, Calligraph Records (own label) 1983–, contrib. Melody Maker 1954–61, Reynolds News 1955–62, Sunday Citizen 1962–67, Harpers and Queen (Restaurant column) 1968–76, Punch; Compère BBC jazz programmes: Jazz Scene, Jazz Club, Jazz 625 (TV); frequent television appearances; Pres. Soc. for Italic Handwriting 1981–; Hon. D. Litt. (Warwick) 1987, (Loughborough) 1988, (Durham) 1989. *Publications:* I Play as I Please 1954, Second Chorus 1958, Take it from the Top 1975, The Best of Jazz—Basin Street to Harlem

1978, Humphrey Lyttelton's Jazz and Big Band Quiz 1979, The Best of Jazz 2—Enter the Giants 1981, Why No Beethoven? the diary of a vagrant musician 1984. *Leisure interests:* birdwatching, calligraphy. *Address:* BBC Light Music Department, Broadcasting House, Portland Place, London, W1A 4WW; Alyn Close, Barnet Road, Arkley, Herts., England. *Telephone:* 01-580 4468.

LYTTLETON, Prof. Raymond Arthur, M.A., F.R.S., F.R.A.S.; British professor of theoretical astronomy; s. of William John Lyttleton and Agnes Kelly; m. Meave Marguerite Hobden; ed. King Edward's Grammar School, Five Ways, King Edward's School, Birmingham, Clare Coll., Univ. of Cambridge; Lecturer in Math., Univ. of Cambridge 1937–59, Stokes Lecturer 1954–59, Reader in Theoretical Astronomy 1954–69 (resgnd.); Prof. Emer., Fellow of St. John's Coll., mem. Inst. of Astronomy 1967–; Experimental Officer Ministry of Supply 1940–42; Tech. Asst. to Scientific Adviser to Army Council, War Office 1943–45; Visiting Prof. Brandeis Univ. 1965–66, Brown Univ. 1967–68, Halley Lecturer 1970, Milne Lecturer 1978, Univ. of Oxford; mem. Council Royal Soc. 1959–61; Geophysical Sec. Royal Astronomical Soc. 1949–60, mem. Council 1950–61, 1969–72; Pres. Milne Soc. 1977–88; Hopkins Prize Cambridge Univ. Philosophical Soc. 1951, Gold Medal Royal Astronomical Soc. 1959, Royal Medal Royal Soc. 1965. *Publications:* The Comets and their Origin 1953, The Stability of Rotating Liquid Masses 1953, The Modern Universe 1956, Rival Theories of Cosmology 1960, Man's View of the Universe 1961, Mysteries of the Solar System 1968. A Matter of Gravity (play) 1968, The Earth and its Mountains 1982, Co-Ed. and contrib. Cambridge Encyclopaedia of Astronomy 1977, numerous papers in scientific journals. *Leisure interests:* golf, motoring, music, wondering about it all. *Address:* St. John's College, Cambridge, Institute of Astronomy, Madingley Road, Cambridge (both Offices); 48 St. Alban's Road, Cambridge, CB4 2HG, England (Home). *Telephone:* (0223) 61621, (0223) 337548 (Offices); (0223) 354910 (Home).

LYUBIMOV, Yuriy Petrovich; Soviet actor and theatrical director; b. 30 Sept. 1917, Yaroslavl'; ed. Vakhtangov Theatre Studio; served in Soviet Army 1940–47; mem. CPSU 1947–(84); teacher and Dir. Shchukin Drama School (Vakhtangov Theatre) 1953–63; Dir. Moscow Theatre of Drama and Comedy (Taganka) 1964–84; left the Soviet Union 1984, returned 1987; awards include State Prizes 1952, People's Artist of the U.S.S.R. 1954. *Roles include:* Oleg Koshevoy (The Young Guard by Fadeyev), Shubin (On the Eve by Turgenev), Chris (All My Sons by A. Miller), Benedict (Much Ado About Nothing), Mozart (The Little Tragedies by Pushkin); prominent in Soviet films 1947–, including Robinson Crusoe. *Productions include:* The Good Woman of Szechwan 1963, Ten Days that Shook the World 1965, Mother (Gorky) 1969, Hamlet 1972, Crime and Punishment (London) 1983, The Devils (London, Paris) 1985, Boris Godunov (Moscow) 1987.

LYUBSHIN, Stanislav Andreyevich; Soviet film actor; b. 6 April 1933; ed. Shchepkin Theatre School; worked with various Moscow theatres: Sovremenvik, Taganka, Yermolova, Malaya Bronnaya 1959–80; one of prin. actors with Moscow Arts Theatre 1980–; film debut 1959; R.S.F.S.R. People's Artist 1981. *Films include:* No Sackings Today 1959, I am Twenty Today 1965, Sword and Shield 1968, Red Square 1970, Defence Counsel 1977, Call Me into the Faraway 1978, Three Years 1980 (dir. with D. A. Dolinin), Encounter 1981. *Address:* Moscow Arts Theatre, Moscow, U.S.S.R.

M

NOTE: All names beginning Mc and Mac are treated as if they began Mac.

MA, Yo Yo, B.A.; American 'cellist; b. 7 Oct. 1955, Paris; of Chinese parentage; m. Jill A. Hornor 1978; one s. one d.; ed. Harvard Univ. and 'cello studies with his father, with Janos Scholz and at Juilliard School of Music, New York; first public recital at age of five; winner Avery Fisher Prize 1978 since when he has performed under many distinguished conductors with all the major orchestras of the world including Berlin Philharmonic, Boston Symphony, Chicago Symphony, Israel Philharmonic, London Symphony Orchestra and New York Philharmonic; regularly participates in festivals of Tanglewood, Ravinia, Blossom, Salzburg and Edinburgh; also appears in chamber music ensembles with artists such as Emanuel Ax, Leonard Rose, Pinchas Zukerman, Gidon Kremer and Yehudi Menuhin; received 1984 Grammy Award for his recording of the six Bach Suites for Unaccompanied 'Cello; second Grammy Award 1985; records for CBS Masterworks; Dr. h.c. (Northeastern) 1985. *Address:* c/o ICM Artists Ltd., 40 W. 57th Street, New York, N.Y. 10019, U.S.A. *Telephone:* (212) 556-5600.

MA CHI-CHUANG; Chinese politician; b. 14 Oct. 1912, Nankung Co., Hopeh; m.; two d.; ed. Chinese Naval Acad., Advanced Research Inst., Kuomintang and Chinese Armed Forces Staff Coll.; C.-in-C. Chinese Navy 1952–54; Asst. Chief-of-Staff, Ministry of Nat. Defence 1954–55, Deputy Minister 1955–59, 1965–72; C.-in-C. Combined Service Forces 1959; Exec. Vice-Chief, Gen. Staff, Ministry of Nat. Defence 1959–65; Amb. to Thailand 1972–75; Chair. China Steel Corpn. 1975–78; Sec.-Gen. Exec. Yuan 1978; Sec.-Gen. to Pres. 1978–84; Minister of State 1984–86; Rep. Tokyo Office, Assen. of East Asian Relations 1986–. *Leisure interest:* golfing. *Address:* Shirokanedai 5-20-2, Minato-ku, Tokyo 106, Japan. *Telephone:* (03) 280-7851.

MA CHUNG-CH'EN (see Ma Zhongchen).

MA DAYOU, PH.D.; Chinese acoustician; b. 1 March 1915, Chaoyang Co., Guangdong Prov.; ed. Beijing Univ., Harvard Univ.; Prof., Qinghua Univ., Kunming 1940–45; Beijing Univ. 1946–52; Prof., Harbin Industrial Univ. 1952–55; Research Prof. and Deputy Dir., Inst. of Physics, Inst. of Electronics and Acoustics, Academia Sinica 1955–66; mem. Chinese Written Language Reform Cttee., Beijing 1980–; Deputy Head, Postgraduate School, Univ. of Science and Tech., Beijing 1981–; mem., Dept. of Tech. Sciences, Academia Sinica 1985–; permanent mem., CPPCC 7th Nat. Cttee. 1988–. *Address:* Room 403, Bldg. 810, Huang Zhuang, Haidian, Beijing, People's Republic of China. *Telephone:* 281957 (Beijing).

MA FENG; Chinese writer; b. 1922, Shanxi Prov.; ed. Lu Xun Acad. of Literature and Art, Yanan; joined 8th Route Army and Communist Party 1938; first short story (First Reconnaissance) published 1942; mem. China-Britain Friendship Assen. 1983–; Vice-Chair. CPPCC Provincial Cttee., Shanxi 1986–; Chair. Soc. of Chinese Folk Literature May 1987–. *Publications include:* Heroes of Lüliang (with Xi Rong), Liu Hulan (novel), The Young People of One Village (film script), and numerous short stories, including The Marriage Ceremony (Nat. Short Story Award Winner 1980). *Address:* People's Republic of China.

MA GUORUI; Chinese (Hui nationality) party official; b. Ningxia; Deputy Commdr. of an army div. 1939; Deputy Sec. CCP Cttee., Hebei 1950, Acting Sec. 1952, Second Sec. 1953; Vice-Chair. Hebei CPPCC 1954, Chair. 1955; mem. Prov. People's Council 1955; Sec. Secr., CCP Cttee., Hebei 1957; mem. Standing Cttee., Control Cttee. Cen. Cttee. 1963; Deputy for Hebei, 3rd NPC 1964; Sec. Control Cttee., Cen. Cttee. 1967; disappeared during Cultural Revolution; Vice-Chair. Municipal Revolutionary Comm., Nanjiang 1977; Deputy for Jiangsu, 5th NPC 1978; Deputy Sec. Cen. Discipline Inspection Comm., Cen. Cttee. 1978, Sec. 1982–87. *Address:* c/o Communist Party Central Committee, Beijing, People's Republic of China.

MA HONG; Chinese economist; b. 1920, Shanxi; Vice-Pres. Chinese Acad. of Social Sciences 1979–82, Pres. 1982–; Dir. Gen. Tech. and Econ. Research Centre, State Council 1983–; Adviser, State Comm. for Restructuring Econ. System 1984–85, China-Japan Personnel Exchange Cttee. 1985–; Pres. Assoc. Correspondence Univ. for Econ. Man. 1983–; Ed. Contemporary China Magazine 1982–. *Address:* Chinese Academy of Social Sciences, Beijing, People's Republic of China.

MA HUI; Chinese army officer; b. 1915, Yongxin Co., Jiangxi Prov.; m. Ding Bao Tian 1943; two s. five d.; joined Red Army 1930; Div. Commdr. 1948; Maj.-Gen. People's Liberation Army 1955; Deputy Commdr. Hebei Mil. Dist., PLA 1960, Commdr. 1964; Vice-Chair. Hebei Revolutionary Cttee. 1968–79; Sec. CCP Cttee. Hebei 1971–82; mem. 11th Cen. Cttee. of CCP 1977; Vice-Chair. Prov. People's Congress 1980–83; Deputy Commdr. PLA, Beijing Mil. Region 1980–83, Hebei Region 1980–83. *Address:* Beijing, People's Republic of China.

MA JIRONG; Chinese party official; b. Oct. 1914, Shandong Prov.; m. Fang Wenjian 1941; three s. two d.; Dir. Admin. Office, Nanjing Mil. Control Comm. 1949; Sec.-Gen. Prov. People's Govt. Yunnan 1950; Sec.

CCP Cttee. Kunming 1951; Deputy Sec. CCP Cttee. Yunnan 1955, Sec. 1956; Deputy for Yunnan, 2nd NPC 1958; Sec. CCP Cttee. Gansu 1965; removed from office 1966; Vice-Chair. Prov. Revolutionary Cttee. Gansu 1977–78; Sec. CCP Cttee. Gansu 1978; Sec. CCP Cttee. Jiangxi 1979; Vice-Chair. Prov. Revolutionary Cttee. Jiangxi 1979; Vice-Chair. Prov. CPPCC Cttee. Jiangxi 1979–83; Chair. Prov. People's Congress, Jiangxi 1983–85. *Address:* General Office, Yunnan Provincial Chinese Communist Party Committee, Kunming, Yunnan Province, People's Republic of China.

MA MING; Chinese mine worker and party official; b. 1937; Head Ma Wanshui Production Group, Longyan Iron-ore Mine 1966; alt. mem. 10th CCP Cen. Cttee. 1973, 11th Cen. Cttee. 1977, 12th Cen. Cttee. 1982–87; Head, Tunnelling Team, Longyan Iron-ore Mine, Hebei 1974; Vice Minister of Metallurgical Industry 1976–82; C.-in-C. Jiangxi copper base, Guixi 1980. *Address:* Ministry of Metallurgical Industry, 46 West Dongsi Street, Beijing, People's Republic of China. *Telephone:* 557031.

MA SHIJUN; Chinese ecologist; b. 5 Dec. 1915, Shandong; m. Yue Fong Wu 1951; one s. two d.; Prof. Inst. of Zoology 1979–; Pres. Ecological Soc. 1979–; Chair. Nat. Cttee. for IUBS; Hon. Dir. Research Center for Ecoenvironmental Sciences. *Publications:* Improvement and protection of the environment in China, General Ecology 1989. *Leisure interest:* Beijing opera. *Address:* Central Institute of Zoology, Academy Sinica, 19 Zhongguancun Lu, Haidian, Beijing 100080, People's Republic of China.

MA SIZHONG; Chinese party and state official; Deputy for Ningxia Autonomous Region to 3rd NPC 1964; alt. mem. 11th CCP Cen. Cttee. 1977, 12th Cen. Cttee. 1982, mem. 13th CCP Cen. Cttee. 1987; Vice-Chair. Revolutionary Cttee., Ningxia 1977–79; mem. CCP Cttee., Ningxia 1979; Vice-Chair. Ningxia 1980–88, Chair. May 1988–. *Address:* Ningxia Autonomous Regional People's Government, Ningxia, People's Republic of China.

MA SZU-CHUNG (see Ma Sizhong).

MA WENRUI; Chinese politician; b. 1909, Shaanxi; Cadre, N.W. China Bureau, CCP 1949–54; Minister of Labour 1954–65; alt. mem. 8th Cen. Cttee. 1956; criticized and removed from office 1967; Vice-Minister of State Planning Comm. 1977; mem. 11th Cen. Cttee. 1977; First Sec. CCP Shaanxi 1979–84; Chair. Shaanxi Prov. People's Congress 1979–83; First Political Commr., Shaanxi Mil. Dist. 1979–85; Deputy for Shaanxi to 6th NPC 1983; mem. 12th Cen. Cttee., CCP 1982–85; mem. CPPCC Nat. Cttee. 1984–. *Address:* People's Republic of China.

MA XIN; Chinese (Hui nationality) party official; Council mem. and Deputy Dir. Agric. and Forestry Dept., Prov. People's Govt., Rehe; Chair. Planning Cttee., Autonomous Regional People's Council, Ningxia 1959; Vice-Chair. Ningxia 1954; State Council 1969; Vice-Chair. Autonomous Regional Revolutionary Cttee., Ningxia 1977; mem. Cen. Comm. for Inspecting Discipline Cen. Cttee. 1978; Chair. Autonomous Regional People's Govt., Ningxia 1980–83: Deputy for Ningxia, 5th NPC 1978; Sec. CCP Cttee., Ningxia 1980, mem. Presidium CPPCC Nat. Cttee. 1983–; Head Work Group for Nationalities CPPCC 1983–. *Address:* Chinese Communist Party Committee, Yinchuan, Ningxia Hui Autonomous Region, People's Republic of China.

MA XINGYUAN; Chinese politician; b. 23 Nov. 1917, Shanxi Prov.; s. of Ma Xianghe and Chen Funi; m. Zheng Huilan 1945; three s. two d.; Dir. Org. Dept., Longqi Prefecture 1950–52; Sec. CCP Cttee. Longqi Pref. 1952–56; Deputy Dir. Rural Work Dept., Provincial CCP Cttee., Fujian 1956–64; Dir. Agric., Forestry and Water Dept. 1964–79; Sec. CCP Cttee., Fujian 1975, 1979–86; mem. 11th Cen. Cttee., CCP 1974–; Vice-Chair. Prov. Revolutionary Cttee., Fujian 1978–79; Gov. Fujian 1979–83; mem. 12th Cen. Cttee., CCP 1982–87; mem. Cen. Advisory Comm. 1987–. *Address:* c/o Fujian People's Government, Fuzhou, People's Republic of China.

MA YUAN; Chinese judge; b. June 1930, Liaoning Prov. PRC; teacher Dept. of Law, Beijing Univ. 1955–62; Judge Civil Court, Supreme People's Court 1981–82; mem. Standing Cttee. All China Women's Fed.; Vice-Pres. Civil Court, Supreme People's Court 1982–85, Vice-Pres. Supreme People's Court 1985–. *Address:* Supreme People's Court, Beijing, People's Republic of China.

MA YUHUAI; Chinese party and government official; b. 1917, Renqiu Co., Hebei Prov.; ed. Tongren Middle School, Baoding; Chair. Shanxi-Chahar-Hebei Border Region; Chair. Beijing Islam Work Cttee. –1949; Pres. Islam Coll. 1949–; mem. Nationalities Affairs Comm., Govt. Admin. Council 1949–54; Vice-Chair. China Islamic Assen. 1953–68; Nat. People's Congress Nationalities Cttee. 1954–68; head of Islamic del. to Mecca July 1955; head of cultural visit to Egypt Feb. 1956; Vice-Pres. China-Indonesia Friendship Assen. 1955–60; signatory to China-Syria Cultural Co-operation Protocol and Exec. Plan June 1956; head of Islamic del. to Afro-Asian

Islamic Conf. Feb. 1958; Vice-Chair. Preparatory Comm. Ningxia Autonomous Region 1958; Vice-Chair. Ningxia Autonomous Region CCP Cttee. 1958-67; Sec., Secr. Ningxia CCP Works Cttee. 1959-68; Council mem. China-Africa People's Friendship Assen. 1960-68; head of Islamic del. to 24th Congress of Assen. of Islamic Teachers, Indonesia Dec. 1962, Afro-Asian Islamic Conf. Feb. 1965; purged 1968, rehabilitated 1977; Vice-Chair. Ningxia Autonomous Region Revolutionary Cttee. Oct.-Dec. 1977; Sec. Ningxia Autonomous Region CCP Cttee. 1978-81; Deputy Dir. All China Greening Cttee. 1983-; alt. mem. CCP Cen. Cttee. 1987-. *Address:* Central Committee of the Chinese Communist Party, Zhongnanhai, Beijing, People's Republic of China.

MA ZHONGCHEN; Chinese party official; alt. mem. 12th CCP Cen. Cttee. 1982, 13th Cen. Cttee. 1987; Sec. CCP Cttee., Tai'an Municipality, Shandong Prov. 1982-; Vice-Gov. Shandong 1988-. *Address:* Tai'an Municipal Chinese Communist Party, Tai'an, Shandong, People's Republic of China.

MAAG, Peter; Swiss conductor; b. 10 May 1919, St. Gall; s. of Otto and Nelly Maag; m.; one s.; ed. theology and philosophy studies at Zürich and Basel Univs.; studied piano with Alfred Cortot; began conducting in small theatre; Asst. to Wilhelm Furtwängler; Asst. to Ernest Ansermet, Orchestre de la Suisse Romande; Düsseldorf Opera 1952-55; Chief Conductor Bonn Opera 1956-59, Volksoper, Vienna 1962, Teatro Regio, Turin 1974, Berne Symphony Orchestra 1984-; fmr. Prin. Guest Conductor Radiotelevisione Italiana (RAI), Orquesta Nacional, Madrid; regular guest conductor at La Scala, Milan, Metropolitan Opera, New York, Teatro Colón, Buenos Aires, Venice, Royal Opera House, Covent Garden; First Guest Conductor, Orchestra da Camera di Padova e del Veneto (ex Solisti Veneti), Teatro le Fenice, Venice; also at various festivals incl. Aix-en-Provence, Zürich, Netherlands, Vienna, Salzburg; Toscanini Medal, Parma 1969, Verdi Medal 1973. *Leisure interest:* theology. *Address:* Secretariat Peter Maag, Dina Thoma-Tennenbaum, 23, Jennershausweg, 3098 Köniz-Bern, Switzerland.

MAALØE, Ole Urban, M.D.; Danish professor of microbiology; b. 15 Aug. 1914, Copenhagen; s. of Carl Urban Maaløe and Betsy Skårup; m. Aase Johansen 1938; two s. one d.; Dir. of Dept. of Biological Standards, State Serum Inst., Copenhagen 1948-58; Head of Univ. Inst. of Microbiology, Copenhagen 1958; Co-Ed. Journal of Molecular Biology 1965-70; Chair. of ICSU standing Cttee. on Safeguard of the Pursuit of Science 1977-80; mem. council of fifteen that founded European Molecular Biology Org. (EMBO) 1964; mem. Danish Pugwash Group 1960-, Danish Science Advisory Council 1970-72, Royal Danish Acad. of Sciences and Letters 1960-, Vice-Pres. 1976-81; American Acad. of Arts and Sciences 1968-; mem. Exec. Cttee. Int. Cell Research Org. 1978-, Advisory Cttee. for Max-Planck-Inst. for Molecular Genetics, Berlin 1979-; Anders Jahre Prize, Univ. of Oslo 1968. *Publications:* On the Relation Between Alexin and Opsonin 1946; Control of Macromolecular Synthesis (with N. O. Kjeldgaard) 1966, Control of Ribosome Synthesis (Alfred Benzon Symposium IX, editor with N. O. Kjeldgaard) 1976, Regulation of Proteinsynthesizing Systems (in Biological Regulation and Devt.) 1979, Growth of the Bacterial Cell (jt. author). *Leisure interests:* books, paintings. *Address:* Ahlmanns Alle 38, 2900 Hellerup, Copenhagen, Denmark (Home). *Telephone:* (45) 1-620485 (Home).

MAAZEL, Lorin, F.R.C.M.; American conductor and musician; b. 6 March 1930, Neuilly, France; s. of Lincoln and Marie Varencove Maazel; m. 3rd Dietlinde Turban 1986; one s.; one s. three d. by previous marriages; ed. under Vladimir Bakaleinikoff and at Univ. of Pittsburgh; début as conductor 1938; Conductor, American Symphony Orchestras 1939-; violin recitalist; European début 1953; festivals include Bayreuth, Salzburg, Edinburgh; tours include South America, Australia, U.S.S.R. and Japan; Artistic Dir. Deutsche Oper Berlin 1965-71; Musical Dir. Radio Symphony Orchestra, Berlin 1965-75; Assoc. Prin. Conductor, New Philharmonia Orchestra, London 1970-72; Dir. Cleveland Orchestra 1971-82, Conductor Emer. 1982-86; Prin. Guest Conductor London Philharmonia 1976-80; Dir. Vienna State Opera 1982-84, Music Dir. Pittsburgh Symphony Orchestra 1988-; Music Dir. Orchestre Nat. de France 1988-; Hon. D.Mus. (Pittsburgh) 1968; D.Hum.Litt. (Beaver Coll.) 1973; Officier, Légion d'honneur 1981; Finnish Commdr. of the Lion; Portuguese Commdr.; Bundesverdienstkreuz (Germany). *Leisure interests:* swimming, tennis, reading. *Address:* c/o Helga Hazelrig, Holbeinstr. 14, D-8000 Munich, Federal Republic of Germany.

MABE, Manabu; Brazilian (b. Japanese) painter; b. 1924, Kumamoto-Ken; s. of Soichi and Haru Mabe; m. Yoshino Mabe 1951; three s.; abstract painter; exhbns. in countries all over the world; one-man exhbn., Museum of Fine Arts, Houston, Tex. 1970; Leiner Prize for Contemporary Arts 1957, Braun Prize 1959, Best Nat. Painter, São Paulo Bienal 1959, Fiat Prize Venice Biennale 1960, First Prize American Biennale, Cordoba 1962. *Leisure interest:* collecting pre-Columbian objects of art. *Address:* Rua das Canjeranas 321, Jabaquara, São Paulo, SP, Av. Irerê, 146 Planalto Paulista, CEP 04064, São Paulo, SP, Brazil.

MABROUK, Ezzidin Ali, LL.M.; Libyan politician; b. 28 May 1932; ed. Cairo Univ. and Univ. Coll., London; Public Prosecutor, Tripoli 1956; subsequently Judge, Summary Court, Tripoli, Pres. Tripoli Court and Counsellor of Supreme Appeal Court; Sr. Legal Adviser, Org. of Petroleum Exporting Countries (OPEC); Minister of Petroleum, Libya 1970-77; Sec. for Petroleum, Gen. People's Cttee. 1977-80; Chair. Org. of Arab Petroleum Exporting Countries 1979; under house arrest Jan. 1980-.

MABUS, Raymond Edwin, Jr., M.A., J.D.; American politician; b. 10 Nov. 1948, Starkville, Miss.; s. of Raymond Edwin Mabus, Sr. and Lucille M. Mabus; m. Julia Gates Hines 1987; ed. Univ. of Mississippi, Johns Hopkins Univ., Harvard Univ.; called to Texas Bar 1976, Washington, D.C. 1978, Mississippi 1982; Law Clerk U.S. Circuit Court of Appeals, Montgomery, Ala. 1976-77; Legal Counsel to House of Reps., D.C. 1977-78; Assoc. Fried, Fran et al., Washington, D.C. 1979-80; Gov.'s Legislative Aide, State of Miss., Jackson 1980-83; State Auditor, State of Miss. 1984-88; Gov. of Miss. 1988-; Woodrow Wilson Scholarship, Johns Hopkins Univ. 1969; Democrat. *Leisure interests:* spectator sports, walking, reading. *Address:* 400 High Street, P.O. Box 139, Jackson, Miss. 39205 (Office); 300 East Capitol Street, P.O. Box 139, Jackson, Miss. 39205, U.S.A. (Home). *Telephone:* (601) 359-3100 (Office); (601) 359-3175 (Home).

MACADAM, Sir Peter, Kt.; British business executive; b. 9 Sept. 1921, Buenos Aires, Argentina; s. of the late Francis Macadam and Marjorie Mary Browne; m. Ann Musson 1949; three d.; ed. Buenos Aires, Stonyhurst Coll., Lancashire; war service with Queens Bays 1941-46; joined British-American Tobacco Co. (BAT) Group in Argentina 1946; Chair., Gen. Man. Commander S.A. (BAT subsidiary) 1955-58; marketing post in Chile 1958-59; Personal Asst. to BAT Dir., London 1959-60; Chair., Gen. Man. BAT Co. (Hong Kong) Ltd. 1961-62; Dir. BAT Group 1963-, Chair.'s Policy Cttee. 1970-, Chair. Tobacco Div. Bd. of Man. 1973-75, Chair. BAT Co. Ltd. 1976, BAT Industries Ltd. (parent co. of BAT Group following merger) 1976-82; Chair. British Nat. Cttee. of Int. Chamber of Commerce 1978-85; Dir. Nat. Westminster Bank 1978-84; Chair. Libra Bank Ltd. 1984-; Pres. Canning House 1982-87. *Leisure interests:* golf, shooting. *Address:* Layham Hall, Layham, Nr. Hadleigh, Suffolk, IP7 5LE, England (Home). *Telephone:* (0473) 822137.

McAFEE, Jerry, SC.D.; American petroleum company executive (retd.); b. 3 Nov. 1916, Port Arthur, Tex.; s. of Almer McDuffie McAfee and Marguerite Calfee McAfee; m. Geraldine Smith 1940; three s. one d.; ed. Univ. of Texas, M.I.T.; Research Chemical Eng., Universal Oil Products Co. 1940-45; Tech. Specialist, Gulf Oil Corpn. 1945-49; Dir., Chem. Div., Gulf Research and Devt. Co. 1950-51, Asst. Dir. of Research 1951-53, Vice-Pres. and Assoc. Dir. of Research 1954-55; Vice-Pres. Eng. Gulf Oil Corpn. 1955-60, Vice-Pres. Exec., Tech. Adviser 1960-64, Dir. Planning and Econ. 1962-64; Sr. Vice-Pres. of Gulf Oil Corpn. and Co-ordinator, Gulf Eastern Co., London, U.K. 1964-67; Exec. Vice-Pres. British American Oil Co., Toronto, Canada 1967-69; Pres. and C.E.O., Gulf Oil Canada Ltd. 1969-76; Chair. and C.E.O, Gulf Oil Corpn. 1976-81. *Leisure interests:* tennis, fishing, reading. *Address:* 4 Indian Hill Road, Pittsburgh, Pa. 15238, U.S.A.

McANALLY, Ray, B.A.; Irish actor and theatre director; b. Donegal; ed. Univ. of Dublin; studied for priesthood; joined Abbey Theatre 1947, Life mem. 1954-; became freelance actor 1962; ran own co., Old Quay Productions; returned to Abbey Theatre 1980; has appeared in over 500 plays, 16 films (roles include Gen. Karpov in The Fourth Protocol and Altamirano in The Mission) and 70 TV plays; Dir. The Loves of Cass McGuire, All My Sons, Of Mice and Men, A Very British Coup etc. *Address:* The Abbey Theatre, Dublin, Ireland.

MACAPAGAL, Diosdado; Philippine politician; b. 28 Sept. 1910; ed. Santo Tomás Univ.; Diplomatic Service 1946-49, Second Sec., Washington, D.C. 1948; mem. House of Reps. 1949-57; Vice-Pres. of the Philippines 1957-61, Pres. 1961-65; Chair. Liberal Party 1957-61; Pres. Constitutional Convention 1971. *Address:* 92 Cambridge Circle, North Forbes Park, Makati, Rizal, The Philippines.

MACARRÓN JAIME, Ricardo; Spanish painter; b. 9 April 1926, Madrid; m. Alicia Macarrón Jaime 1951; two d.; ed. Escuela Superior de Bellas Artes de San Fernando, Madrid and scholarship in Paris; Prof. of Drawing and Painting, Escuela Superior de Bellas Artes, Madrid; has painted many portraits of royalty and nobility; mem. Royal Soc. of Portrait Painters 1962; numerous one-man exhbns. in Spain and abroad including two in London and one in New York; represented at Museo de Arte Contemporáneo, Madrid, Univ. of Oslo and Fundación Guell, Barcelona, portraits at the Royal Soc. of Portrait Painters; numerous awards. *Leisure interests:* walking in the country, hunting, playing chess. *Address:* Agustín de Bethencourt No. 7, Madrid 3, Spain.

MacARTHUR, Douglas, II; American diplomatist (retd.), lecturer and businessman; b. 5 July 1909, Bryn Mawr, Pa.; s. of Arthur MacArthur and Mary Hendry McCalla; m. Laura Louise Barkley 1934 (deceased 1987); one d.; ed. Milton Acad. and Yale Univ.; U.S. Army 1933-35; Foreign Service 1935-72; Vancouver 1935-36; Foreign Service School 1936; Italy 1937-38, Paris 1938-40, Lisbon 1940, Vichy 1940-42; interned by Nazis 1942-44; Asst. Political Adviser SHAEF 1944; Paris 1944-48, Brussels 1948-49; Chief, W. European Div., Dept. of State 1949-51; Political Adviser to Gen. Eisenhower at SHAPE 1951-52; Counsellor of the Dept. of State 1953-56; Amb. to Japan 1957-61, to Belgium 1961-65; Asst. Sec. of State for Congressional Relations 1965-67; Amb. to Austria 1967-69; Amb. to Iran 1969-72; Business Consultant and Dir. of several European and

American cos. 1972-. *Leisure interests:* shooting, hiking. *Address:* 2101 Connecticut Avenue, N.W., Washington, D.C., U.S.A. *Telephone:* (202) 387-5662.

McBAIN, Ed (see Hunter, Evan).

McBRIDE, William Griffith, A.O., C.B.E., M.D., F.R.A.C.O.G., M.C.T.; Australian medical practitioner; b. 25 May 1927, Sydney; s. of John McBride and Myrine Griffith; m. Patricia Glover 1957; two s. two d.; ed. Canterbury Boys' High School, Sydney, Conservatorium of Music, Sydney, Univ. of London, Univ. of Sydney; Medical Officer, St. George Hosp. 1950, Consultant Obstetrician and Gynaecologist 1958-; Medical Officer, Launceston Gen. Hosp. 1951; Medical Officer, Women's Hosp., Sydney 1952-53; Medical Supt. 1955-57, Consultant Obstetrician 1966-83; Consultant Gynaecologist, Bankstown Hosp., Sydney 1957-66; Consultant Obstetrician and Gynaecologist, Royal Hosp. for Women 1983-; examiner in Obstetrics and Gynaecology Univs. of Sydney and N.S.W.; mem. American Coll. of Toxicology; Fellow of the Senate, Univ. of Sydney 1974-; mem. Faculty of Medicine Univ. of Sydney 1966-; mem. WHO Cttee. on Safety of Contraceptives 1971, Australian Opera Council 1984-; Dir., Foundation 41 Research Lab. 1972-; Dir., Australian Opera 1979-82; mem. American Coll. of Toxicologists, Soc. for Risk Analysis; Gold Medal and B.P. Prize (L'Institut de la Vie) 1971. *Leisure interests:* surfing, tennis, riding, golf. *Address:* Foundation 41, 365 Crown Street, Sydney 2010, Australia. *Telephone:* 332-3394.

McBRIDE, William James, M.B.E.; Irish rugby football player and banker; b. 6 June 1940, Toomebridge; s. of William James McBride and Irene Patterson; m. Penny Michael 1966; one s. one d.; ed. Ballymena Acad.; first played rugby for Ireland against England 1962; five Lions tours, S. Africa 1962, New Zealand 1966, S. Africa 1968, New Zealand 1971, S. Africa 1974; holder of 63 int. caps (world record); 17 Test appearances for Lions (record); toured Argentina 1970 and Australia 1967 for Ireland; Asst. Bank Man. 1974-. *Leisure interests:* gardening, fishing. *Address:* Gorse Lodge, Ballyclare, Co. Antrim, Northern Ireland, United Kingdom. *Telephone:* Ballyclare 2710.

McBRIEN, Rev. Richard Peter, M.A., S.T.D.; American ecclesiastic and professor of theology; b. 19 Aug. 1936, Hartford, Conn.; s. of late Thomas H. McBrien and of Catherine Botticelli; ed. St. Thomas Seminary, Bloomfield, St. John Seminary, Brighton, Mass. and Pontifical Gregorian Univ., Rome; Prof. of Theol. and Dean of Studies Pope John XXIII Nat. Seminary, Weston, Mass. 1965-70; Prof. Boston Coll., Newton, Mass. 1970-80; Prof. and Chair. Dept. of Theol., Univ. of Notre Dame, Ind. 1980-; John Courtney Murray Award, Catholic Theol. Soc. of America 1976, Christopher Award for Catholicism (book) 1981. *Publications:* Do We Need the Church? 1969, Church: The Continuing Quest 1970, The Remaking of the Church 1973, Catholicism (two vols.) 1980, Caesar's Coin: Religion and Politics in America 1987. *Leisure interests:* reading, films. *Address:* Department of Theology, University of Notre Dame, Notre Dame, Ind. 46556, U.S.A. *Telephone:* (219) 239-7811.

McCABE, John, C.B.E., MUS.B., F.R.M.C.M., F.L.C.M., F.R.C.M., R.A.M.; British musician; b. 21 April 1939, Huyton, Lancs. (now Merseyside); s. of Frank and Elisabeth (Herlitzius) McCabe; m. 1st Hilary Tann 1968 (divorced 1974); m. 2nd Monica Smith 1974; ed. Liverpool Inst. High School for Boys, Manchester Univ., Royal Manchester Coll. of Music, Staatliche Hochschule für Musik, Munich; Pianist-in-residence, University Coll., Cardiff 1965-68; Pres. Inc. Soc. of Musicians 1983-84; Dir. London Coll. of Music Sept. 1983-; Chair. Asscn. of Professional Composers 1985-86; travels worldwide as pianist-composer; Royal Manchester Inst. Medal 1962, Royal Philharmonic Prize 1962, Special Citation, Koussevitsky Recording Foundation 1974, Award for service to British music, Composers Guild 1975; Fellow of London Coll. of Music, Royal Nat. Coll. of Music. *Publications:* Rachmaninov, Bartok's Orchestral Music, Haydn's Piano Sonatas, and numerous articles on music. *Compositions include:* The Chagall Windows, Variations on a theme of Hartmann, Notturni ed Alba, Concerto for Orchestra, Cloudcatcher Fells, operas, ballets, symphonies, concertos, much orchestral and chamber music, vocal works and keyboard music; numerous piano recordings including complete piano works of Haydn and Nielsen. *Leisure interests:* books, films, cricket, snooker. *Address:* c/o London College of Music, 47 Great Marlborough Street, London, W.1, England.

McCAIN, John Sidney III, D.F.C.; American politician; b. 29 Aug. 1936, Panama Canal Zone, Panama; s. of John Sidney McCain and Roberta Wright; m. Cindy Hensley 1980; three s. one d.; ed. U.S. Naval Acad. and Nat. War Coll.; Ensign, U.S. Navy 1958, Capt. 1977; Dir. Navy Senate Liaison Office, Washington 1977-81; Bd. Dirs. Community Assistance League, Phoenix 1981-82; mem. 99th Congress from 1st Ariz. Dist.; Senator from Arizona Jan. 1987-; various decorations including Legion of Merit, Silver Star, Purple Heart Vietnamese Legion of Honour; Republican. *Address:* U.S. Senate Office, 210 Hart Building, Washington, D.C. 20510, U.S.A.

McCANCE, Robert Alexander, C.B.E., PH.D., F.R.C.P., F.R.S.; British physician; b. 9 Dec. 1898, Belfast, N. Ireland; s. of John Stoupe Finlay McCance and Mary Bristow; m. Mary Lindsay (MacGregor) 1922; one s. one d.; ed. Mourne Grange, Co. Down, St. Bees School, Cumberland, Sidney Sussex Coll., Cambridge; Royal Naval Air Service, including service with Grand

Fleet 1917-19; undergraduate studies 1919-22; Biochemical research 1922-25; qualified in medicine 1927; Asst. Physician in charge of Biochemical Dept., King's Coll. Hospital 1934; Reader in Medicine, Cambridge Univ. 1938; Prof. of Experimental Medicine, Cambridge Univ. 1945-67; Fellow of Sidney Sussex Coll., Cambridge; Dir. Dept. of Experimental Medicine, Medical Research Council, 1945-67; Dir. Infant Malnutrition Unit, M.R.C., Kampala 1967-69; Triennial Gold Medal, West London Medico-Chirurgical Society 1949; hon. mem. American Pediatric Soc., Asscn. of American Physicians, Swiss Soc. for Research in Nutrition; Conway Evans Prize 1960, James Spence Medal, British Paediatric Assen. 1961; Hon. D.Sc. (Belfast) 1964; Hon. F.R.C.O.G. *Publications:* Breads White and Brown: Their Place in Thought and Social History (jointly) 1956, Maintenance and Stability in the Newly-born 1959, Composition of Foods (jointly) 1960. *Leisure interest:* field observation. *Address:* 32 Havenfield, Arbury Road, Cambridge, CB4 2JY, England. *Telephone:* (0223) 329377.

McCANDLESS, Bruce, II; American astronaut; b. 8 June 1937, Boston, Mass.; s. of the late Rear-Adm. Bruce McCandless and late Mrs. Sue Worthington Bradley McCandless Inman; m. Bernice Doyle 1960; one s. one d.; ed. U.S. Naval Acad. and Stanford Univ.; flight training, Pensacola, Fla. and Kingsville, Tex.; weapons system and carrier landing training, Key West, Fla. 1960; carrier duty, Fighter Squadron 102 1960-64; instrument flight instructor, Attack Squadron 43, Naval Air Station, Apollo Soucek Field, Oceana, Va.; graduate studies in electrical eng., Stanford Univ. until 1966; selected by NASA as astronaut April 1966; Co-investigator Astronaut Manoeuvring Unit Experiment on Skylab 1968-74; back-up crew for first Skylab Mission 1973; Mission Specialist on STS-11, first flight of manned manoeuvring unit; Mission Specialist on STS-61J, space telescope deployment. *Leisure interests:* electronics, scuba diving, sailing, photography. *Address:* NASA Johnson Space Center, Houston, Tex. 77058, U.S.A. *Telephone:* 713-483-2712.

McCANN, H.E. Cardinal Owen, D.D., PH.D.; South African ecclesiastic; b. 26 June 1907, Cape Town; s. of late Edward McCann and Susan Mary Plint; ed. St. Joseph's Coll., Rondebosch, Univ. of Cape Town and Pontificium Collegium Urbanianum de Propaganda Fide; ordained priest 1935; Titular Bishop of Stettorio 1950; Archbishop of Cape Town 1951-84; named Asst. at the Papal Throne 1960; cr. Cardinal 1965; Hon. D.Litt. (Cape Town), Hon. D.Hum.Litt. (Me.) 1984. *Address:* Archdiocesan Chancery, Cathedral Place, 12 Bouquet Street, Cape Town, South Africa. *Telephone:* 415-2417.

McCARTHY, Eugene Joseph, M.A.; American politician and writer; b. 29 March 1916, Watkins, Minn.; s. of late Michael J. McCarthy and Anna Baden McCarthy; m. Abigail Quigley 1945; one s. three d.; ed. St. John's Univ., Collegeville, Minn. and Minnesota Univ.; successively Prof. of Econs. and Educ., St. John's Univ., Collegeville, Minn.; Civilian Tech. Asst., War Dept. Mil. Intelligence Division; Acting Chair. Sociology Dept., St. Thomas Coll., St. Paul, Minn.; mem. U.S. House of Reps. (Fourth Minn. district) 1949-58; Senator from Minnesota 1959-70; Liberal Independent cand. for Presidency 1976; Adlai Stevenson Prof. of Political Science, New School for Social Research 1973-74; syndicated columnist 1977-; Dir. Harcourt Brace Jovanovich Inc.; Hon. LL.D. (St. Louis) 1955; Cardinal Newman Award 1955. *Publications:* Frontiers in American Democracy 1960, Dictionary of American Politics 1962, A Liberal Answer to the Conservative Challenge 1964, The Limits of Power: America's Role in the World 1967, The Year of the People 1969, Other Things and the Aardvark (poems) 1970, The Hard Years 1975, Mr. Raccoon and his friends (children's stories) 1977, America Revisited 1978, Ground Fog and Night (poetry) 1979, A Political Bestiary (co-author) 1979, The Ultimate Tyranny 1979, Gene McCarthy's Minnesota 1982, The View from Rappahanock 1984, Up 'Til Now: A Memoir of the Decline of American Politics 1987. *Address:* Box 22, Woodville, Va., U.S.A.

McCARTHY, Mary; American writer; b. 21 June 1912, Seattle, Washington; d. of Roy Winfield McCarthy and Therese (née Preston) McCarthy; m. 1st Harold Johnsrud 1933; m. 2nd Edmund Wilson 1938, one s.; m. 3rd Bowden Broadwater 1946; m. 4th James West 1961; ed. Vassar Coll.; Theatre critic Partisan Review 1937-57; Instructor Bard Coll. 1945-46, Sarah Lawrence Coll. 1948; Stevenson Chair. of Literature, Bard Coll., 1986-; mem. American Acad. of Arts and Letters; four hon. degrees; Horizon award (for The Oasis) 1948, Guggenheim Fellowships 1949 and 1959, Nat. Acad. of Arts and Letters award 1957, Nat. Medal for Literature 1984, Macdowell Award 1984. *Publications:* The Company She Keeps (novel) 1942, The Oasis (re-issued as A Source of Embarrassment) (novel) 1949, Cast a Cold Eye (short stories) 1950, The Groves of Academe (novel) 1952, A Charmed Life (novel) 1955, Venice Observed 1956, Sights and Spectacles (theatre criticism) 1956, Memories of a Catholic Girlhood (memoirs) 1957, The Stones of Florence 1959, On the Contrary 1962, The Group 1963 (film 1966), Vietnam 1967, Hanoi 1968, The Writing on the Wall (literary essays) 1970, Birds of America (novel) 1971, Medina 1972, The Mask of State—Watergate Portraits 1974, The Seventeenth Degree 1974, Cannibals and Missionaries 1979, Ideas and the Novel 1980; Occasional Prose 1985, How I Grew (autobiog.) 1987; numerous essays, short stories, reviews, etc. in The New Yorker, Harper's, Encounter, The New York Review of Books and other magazines. *Address:* 141 rue de Rennes, Paris, France; Castine, Me. 04421, U.S.A.

McCARTHY, Rt. Hon. Sir Thaddeus (Pearcey), Kt., K.B.E., P.C.; British judge; b. 24 Aug. 1907; s. of Walter McCarthy; m. Joan Margaret Miller 1938; one s. three d.; ed. St. Bede's Coll., Christchurch and Victoria Coll., Wellington, N.Z.; war service 1939–45; barrister and solicitor 1945–57; Judge of Supreme Court 1957–; Judge of the Court of Appeal of New Zealand, 1963–76, Pres. 1973–76; Chair. N.Z. Press Council 1978–; Chair. Royal Comm. on State Services 1961–62, on Salary and Wage Fixing Procedures in the State Services, 1968, on Social Security 1969, on Salaries and Wages in the State Services 1972, on Nuclear Power Generation 1976–78, on Maori Land Courts 1979–; Chair. Security Review Authority and Commr. of Security Appeals 1977–; Chair. Advisory Cttee., N.Z. Computer Centre 1977–86; Chair., Winston Churchill Memorial Trust 1966–76, Queen Elizabeth Nat. Trust 1978–84; Fellow N.Z. Inst. of Public Admin. 1984; Hon. LL.D. (Vic. Univ. of Wellington) 1978. *Leisure interests:* golf, sailing. *Address:* 383 Fergusson Drive, Heretaunga, New Zealand. *Telephone:* 286322.

McCARTNEY, Paul, M.B.E.; British songwriter and performer; b. 18 June 1942, Liverpool; s. of James McCartney; m. Linda Eastman 1969; one s. three d.; ed. Stockton Wood Road Primary School, Speke, Joseph Williams Primary School, Gateacre, and Liverpool Inst.; plays guitar, piano and organ; taught himself to play trumpet at age of 13; wrote first song 1956, wrote numerous songs with John Lennon; joined pop group The Quarrymen 1956; appeared under various titles until formation of The Beatles 1960; appeared with The Beatles in the following activities: performances in Hamburg 1960, 1961, 1962, The Cavern, Liverpool 1960, 1961; worldwide tours 1963–66; attended Transcendental Meditation Course at Maharishi's Acad., Rishikesh, India Feb. 1968; formed Apple Ltd., parent org. of The Beatles Group of Cos. 1968; left The Beatles after collapse of Apple Corps. Ltd. 1970; formed MPL group of cos. 1970; first solo album McCartney 1970; formed own pop group Wings 1971–; tours of Britain and Europe 1972–73, U.K. and Australia 1975, Europe and U.S.A. 1976, U.K. 1979; albums with the Beatles: Please Please Me 1963, With the Beatles 1963, A Hard Day's Night 1964, Beatles for Sale 1965, Help! 1965, Rubber Soul 1966, Revolver 1966, Sgt. Pepper's Lonely Hearts Club Band 1967, Magical Mystery Tour 1967, The Beatles (White Album) 1968, Yellow Submarine 1969, Abbey Road 1969, Let it Be 1970; subsequent albums: Ram 1971, Wildlife 1971, Red Rose Speedway 1973, Band on the Run 1973, Venus and Mars 1975, Wings at the Speed of Sound 1976, Wings Over America 1976, London Town 1978, Wings Greatest 1978, Back to the Egg 1979, McCartney II 1980, Tug of War 1982, Pipes of Peace 1983, Give My Regards to Broad Street 1984, Press to Play 1986, All the Best 1987; two Grammy Awards for Band on the Run (incl. Best Pop Vocal Performance) 1975, Ivor Novello Award for Best Selling British Record 1977–78 for single Mull of Kintyre, for Int. Hit of the Year 1982 for single Ebony and Ivory, for Outstanding Services to British Music 1989; Guinness Book of Records "Triple Superlative Award" (43 songs each selling more than 1 million copies, holder of 60 gold discs, estimated sales of 100 million albums and 100 million singles) 1979; Freeman of Liverpool 1984; Hon. Dr. (Sussex) 1988; composed soundtrack music for The Family Way 1966, James Paul McCartney 1973, Live and Let Die 1973, The Zoo Gang (TV series) 1973; Films by The Beatles: A Hard Day's Night 1964, Help! 1965, Yellow Submarine (animated colour cartoon film) 1968, Let it Be 1970; TV film Magical Mystery Tour 1967; Wings over the World (TV) 1979, Rockshow 1981; Give My Regards to Broad Street (wrote and dir.) 1984, Rupert and the Frog Song (wrote and produced) 1985 (BAFTA Award Best Animated Film), Press to Play 1986. *Address:* c/o MPL Communications Ltd., 1 Soho Square, London, W1V 6BQ, England.

McCARTY, Maclyn, A.B., M.D.; American medical research scientist; b. 9 June 1911, South Bend. Ind.; s. of Earl Hauser and Hazel Beagle McCarty; m. 1st Anita Davies 1934 (divorced 1966), 2nd Marjorie Steiner 1966; three s. one d.; ed. Kenosha High School, Wis., Stanford and Johns Hopkins Univs.; Intern and Asst. Resident in Paediatrics, Johns Hopkins Hosp. 1937–40; Fellow in Medicine, New York Univ. 1940–41; Fellow in Medical Sciences of Nat. Research Council (with O. T. Avery), Rockefeller Inst. for Medical Research (now Rockefeller Univ.) 1941–42, Active Duty (U.S.N.R.) Naval Research Unit 1942–46, Assoc. and Assoc. Physician 1946–48, Assoc. mem. and Assoc. Physician 1948–50, mem. (Prof.) 1950–81, Physician in Chief to the Hosp. 1960–74, Vice-Pres. 1965–78, John D. Rockefeller, Jr. Prof. 1977–81, Prof. Emer. 1981–; Vice-Pres. Helen Hay Whitney Foundation, Chair. Scientific Advisory Cttee. 1960–; Ed. Journal of Experimental Medicine 1963–; 1st Waterford Biomedical Award 1977; Robert Koch Gold Medal (Fed. Repub. of Germany) 1981, Order of Repub., First Degree (Egypt) 1982; Commdr.'s Cross of the Order of Merit (Fed. Repub. of Germany) 1984, Kovalenko Medal, N.A.S. 1988. *Publications:* The Transforming Principle: Discovering that Genes are made of DNA 1985, numerous scientific papers, mainly in Journal of Experimental Medicine. *Leisure interests:* travel, reading. *Address:* The Rockefeller University, 1230 York Avenue, New York, N.Y. 10021, U.S.A. *Telephone:* (212) 570-8158.

McCAUGHEY, (John) Davis, A.C., M.A., F.A.C.E.; Australian university teacher and administrator; b. 12 July 1914, Belfast, Northern Ireland; s. of John McCaughey and Lizzie McCaughey; m. Jean Middlemas Henderson 1940; three s. two d.; ed. Pembroke Coll., Cambridge, New College, Edinburgh, Presbyterian College, Belfast; ordained in Presbyterian Church in Ireland 1942; Study Sec. Student Christian Movt. of G.B. & Ireland 1946–52; Prof. of New Testament Studies, Ormond Coll., Univ. of Melbourne 1953–64, Master Ormond Coll. 1959–79, Deputy Chancellor Univ. of Melbourne 1978–79, 1982–85; Pres. of Uniting Church in Australia 1977–79; Gov. of Vic. 1986–. *Publications:* Christian Obedience in the University 1958, Diversity and Unity in the New Testament Picture of Christ 1969, Piecing Together a Shared Vision 1988; articles in Colloquium, Australian Biblical Revue. *Leisure interests:* reading, listening, golf. *Address:* Government House, Melbourne, 3004 Vic., Australia. *Telephone:* (03) 650 9971.

McCLELLAND, Douglas, A.C.; Australian politician; b. 5 Aug. 1926; s. of the late A. McClelland and of Gertrude Amy Cooksley; m. Lorna B. McNeill 1950; one s. two d.; ed. Parramatta Commercial Boys' High School, Metropolitan Business Coll.; joined 2nd Australian Imperial Forces 1944; Court Reporter 1949–61; mem. N.S.W. Labor Party Exec. 1957–61; Senator for N.S.W. 1962–87; Minister for the Media 1972–75; Special Minister of State June-Nov. 1975; Man. Govt. Business in Senate 1972–75; Labor Party Spokesman on Admin. Services 1976–77; Deputy Leader of Labor Party in Senate 1977–81; Deputy Pres. of Senate 1981–83; Pres. of the Senate 1983–87; High Commr. to U.K. 1987–; mem. Senate Select Cttee. on the Encouragement of Australian Production for TV 1962–63, Joint Cttee. on Broadcasting of Parl. Proceedings 1965, Joint Select Cttee. on the New and Perm. Parl. House 1967, Senate Select Cttee. on Medical and Hosp. Costs 1968, Senate Standing Cttee. on Health and Welfare 1970, on Finance and Govt. Relations 1977. *Address:* Australian High Commission, Aldwych, Strand, London, England.

McCLELLAND, W. Craig, B.A., M.B.A.; American business executive; b. 21 April 1934, Orange, N.J.; s. of late William N. McClelland and Pauline L. McClelland; m. Alice Garrett McClelland 1956; three d.; ed. Princeton Univ. and Harvard Graduate School; Pres. Watervliet Paper Co. 1969–73; Vice-Pres. Hammermill Paper Co. 1973–80, Sr. Vice-Pres. 1980–83, Exec. Vice-Pres. and Dir. 1983–84, Pres., C.E.O. and Dir. Hammermill Paper Co. (subsidiary of Int. Paper Co.) 1985–86, 1987–88; Dir. and Exec. Vice-Pres. Int. Paper Co. 1987–88; Exec. Vice-Pres. and Dir. Union Camp Corpn. 1989–; Dir. Allegheny Ludlum Corpn., Quaker State Corpn., PNC Financial Corpn. *Address:* 242 Mill Road, Erie, Pa. 16505, U.S.A. (Home). *Telephone:* (814) 838-8713 (Home).

McCLINTOCK, Barbara, PH.D.; American scientist; b. 16 June 1902; ed. Erasmus Hall High School, Brooklyn, New York and Cornell Univ.; Instructor in Botany, Cornell Univ. 1927–31; Fellow, Nat. Research Council 1931–33; Fellow, Guggenheim Foundation 1933–34; Research Assoc., Cornell Univ. 1934–36; Asst. Prof. Univ. of Missouri 1936–41; mem. staff, Carnegie Inst. of Washington 1941–47, Distinguished Service mem. 1967–; Visiting Prof. Calif. Inst. of Tech. 1953–54; Andrew D. White Prof.-at-Large, Cornell Univ. 1965–; Consultant, Agricultural Science Program, The Rockefeller Foundation 1962–69; mem. N.A.S., American Philosophical Soc., American Acad. of Arts and Sciences, Genetics Soc. of America (Pres. 1945), Botanical Soc. of America, A.A.A.S., American Inst. of Biol. Science, American Soc. of Naturalists; Hon. D.Sc. (Univs. of Rochester and Missouri, Smith Coll., Williams Coll. and Western Coll. for Women); Achievement Award, Assen. of Univ. Women 1947; Award of Merit, Botanical Soc. of America 1957, Kimber Genetics Award, Nat. Acad. of Sciences 1967, Nat. Medal of Science 1970; Lifetime Laureate, MacArthur Foundation 1981; Albert Lasker Medical Research Award 1981; Nobel Prize for Medicine and Physiology 1983. *Address:* Carnegie Institution of Washington, Cold Spring Harbor Laboratory, N.Y. 11724, U.S.A.

McCLOSKEY, Robert James, B.S.; American diplomatist; b. 25 Nov. 1922, Philadelphia, Pa.; s. of Thomas and Anna (Wallace) McCloskey; m. Anne Taylor Phelan 1961; two d.; ed. Temple Univ. and George Washington Univ.; served U.S. Marine Corps 1942–45; hotel work 1945–50; newspaper reporter 1952–55; joined U.S. Foreign Service 1955; assigned Hong Kong 1955–57; Public Officer, State Dept. 1957–58; Press Officer, Office of News 1958–60; U.S. Mission to XV Session, UN Gen. Assembly 1960–62; Special Asst. Bureau of Public Affairs, State Dept. 1962–63; Deputy Dir. Office News 1963–64; Dir. 1964–66; Dept. Asst., Sec. of State 1966–68; Deputy Asst. Sec., Special Asst. to Sec. for Press Relations, Office of Press Relations 1968–73; Amb. to Cyprus 1973–74; Amb.-at-Large and Asst. Sec. for Congressional Relations 1974–76; Amb. to Netherlands 1976–78, to Greece 1978–81; Ombudsman, Washington Post 1981–; with Int. Catholic Relief Services, New York 1983. *Address:* 111 Hesketh Street, Chevy Chase, Md. 20815, U.S.A. *Telephone:* (301) 652-4635.

McCLURE, Donald S., PH.D.; American professor of chemistry; b. 27 Aug. 1920, Yonkers, New York; s. of Robert H. McClure and Helen Campbell; m. Laura Lee Thompson 1949; two s. one d.; ed. Yonkers High School and Univs. of Minnesota and Calif. (Berkeley); War Research Div. Columbia Univ. 1942–46; Instr. in Chem. Univ. of Calif. (Berkeley) 1948–50, Asst. Prof. 1950–55; RCA Labs. Princeton, N.J. 1955–62; Prof. of Chem. Univ. of Chicago 1962–67, Princeton Univ. 1967–; mem. N.A.S., American Acad. of Arts and Sciences; Guggenheim Fellow, Univ. of Oxford 1972–73; Humboldt Fellow 1982; Irving Langmuir Award 1979. *Publications:* numerous articles in professional journals. *Address:* Department of Chemistry, Princeton University, Princeton, N.J. 08544 (Office); 23 Hemlock Circle,

Princeton, N.J. 08540, U.S.A. (Home). *Telephone:* 609-452-4980 (Office); 609-924-0830 (Home).

McCLURE, James A., DR. JUR.; American lawyer and politician; b. 27 Dec. 1924, Payette, Idaho; s. of W. R. and Marie McClure; m. Louise Miller; two s. one d.; ed. Univ. of Idaho Coll. of Law; pvt. law practice; Prosecuting Attorney for Payette County; State Senator from Payette County for three terms; Ida. Senate Majority Leader 1965-66; mem. U.S. House of Reps. 1966-72; U.S. Senator from Idaho Jan. 1973-; re-elected to U.S. Senate 1978; Chair. Senate Energy and Nat. Resources Cttee. 1981-, Republican Conf. of the Senate, Interior Sub-Cttee. of Appropriations Cttee.; mem. Senate Rules and Admin. Cttee., Senate Steering Cttee.; mem. Naval Acad. Visitors' Bd., Kennedy Center Bd. of Trustees, Bd. of Visitors, Duke Univ. School of Environmental Studies, Bd. of Govs., Council of Nat. Policy; Dr. h.c. (Univ. of Idaho) 1981. *Address:* 361 Dirksen Senate Building, Washington, D.C. 20510, U.S.A.

McCOLOUGH, Charles Peter, M.B.A.; American business executive; b. 1 Aug. 1922, Halifax, Canada; s. of Reginald Walker McColough and Barbara Theresa Martin McColough; m. Mary Virginia White 1953; four s. one d.; ed. Osgoode Hall Law School, Toronto, Canada, Dalhousie Univ., Halifax, Canada and Harvard Graduate School of Business Admin.; Sales Man. Lehigh Navigation and Coal 1951-54; various exec. positions, Xerox Corpn. 1954-60; Vice-Pres. for Sales, Xerox Corpn. 1960-63, Exec. Vice-Pres. of Operations 1963-66, Pres. 1966-71, Chief Exec. 1968-82, Chair. 1971-85, Chair. Exec. Cttee. 1985-87; Dir. Xerox Corpn., Rank Xerox Ltd. (London), Fuji Xerox Co. Ltd. (Tokyo), Citibank and Citicorp (New York), Council on Foreign Relations, New York Stock Exchange, Union Carbide Corpn.; mem. Business Council; Hon. LL.D. (Dalhousie) 1970. *Leisure interests:* skiing, sailing. *Address:* Xerox Corporation, P.O. Box 1600, Stamford, Conn. 06904, U.S.A. *Telephone:* 203-329-8711 (Office).

McCONNELL, Albert Joseph, M.A., SC.D.; Irish mathematician and university administrator; b. 19 Nov. 1903; m. 1st Hilda McGuire 1934 (died 1966); m. 2nd Jean McConnell 1983 (died 1985); ed. Ballymena Acad., Trinity Coll., Dublin, and Univ. of Rome; Lecturer in Mathematics, Trinity Coll., Dublin 1927-30, Fellow 1930-52; Prof. of Natural Phil., Univ. of Dublin 1930-57; Visiting Prof. Univ. of Alexandria 1946-47; Univ. of Kuwait 1970; Provost of Trinity Coll., Dublin 1952-74; mem. Council of State 1973-; Chair. Governing Bd. and mem. Council, School of Theoretical Physics, Dublin Inst. for Advanced Studies 1975-; mem. Royal Irish Acad.; Hon. Fellow, Oriel Coll., Oxford; Hon. D.Sc. (Belfast, Ulster), Hon. Sc.D. (Columbia), Hon. LL.D. (Nat. Univ. of Ireland). *Publications:* The Mathematical Papers of Sir William Rowan Hamilton, Vol II (with A. W. Conway) 1940, Applications of the Absolute Differential Calculus 1931, Applications of Tensor Analysis 1957. *Address:* Seafield Lodge, Seafield Road, Killiney, Dublin, Ireland.

McCONNELL, Harden M., PH.D.; American professor of chemistry; b. 18 July 1927, Richmond, Va.; s. of Harry R. McConnell and Frances (née Coffee) McConnell; m. Sofia Glogovac 1956; two s. one d.; ed. George Washington Univ., California Inst. of Tech. and Univ. of Chicago; with Dept. of Physics, Univ. of Chicago, Nat. Research Fellow 1950-52; Shell Devt. Co., Emeryville, Calif. 1952-56; Asst. Prof. of Chem., Calif. Inst. of Tech. 1956-58, Assoc. Prof. of Chem. 1958-59, Prof. of Chem. 1959-63, Prof. of Chem. and Physics 1963-64; Prof. of Chem. Stanford Univ. 1964-79, Robert Eckles Swain Prof. of Chemistry 1979-, Chair. Dept. of Chem.; f. Molecular Devices Corpn. 1983; Fellow, American Physical Soc., Biophysical Soc., American Soc. of Biological Chemists, American Assen. for the Advancement of Science 1982; mem. A.C.S., Nat. Acad. of Sciences, Int. Acad. of Quantum Molecular Science, A.A.A.S., several bds. Neuroscience Research Program, M.I.T.; Harkins Lecturer, Univ. of Chicago 1967, Falk-Plant Lecturer, Columbia Univ. 1967, Renaud Foundation Lecturer 1971, Peter Debye Lecturer, Cornell Univ. 1973, Harvey Lecturer, Rockefeller Univ. 1977, A. L. Patterson Lecturer, Inst. for Cancer Research, Philadelphia 1978, Pauling Lecturer, Stanford Univ. 1981, Remsen Memorial Lecturer, Maryland Section A.C.S. 1982, Prof. du Collège de France 1986, Le Bel Lecturer, Strasbourg 1986, Swift Lecturer, Calif. Inst. of Tech. 1986; Venable Lecturer Univ. of N. Carolina 1987, Linus Pauling Distinguished Lecturer, Oregon State Univ. 1987; Calif. Section Award of A.C.S. 1961, Nat. A.C.S. Award in Pure Chem. 1962, Harrison Howe Award 1968, Irving Langmuir Award in Chemical Physics 1971, Alumni Achievement Award (George Washington Univ.) 1971, Dickson Prize for Science (Carnegie-Mellon Univ.) 1982, Distinguished Alumni Award (Calif. Inst. of Tech.) 1982, Wolf Prize in Chemistry 1983-84, ISCO Award 1984; Pauling Medal, Puget Sound and Oregon A.C.S. Sections 1987, Wheland Medal, Univ. of Chicago 1988, N.A.S. Award in Chemical Sciences 1988. *Publications:* over 300 scientific publs. in the field of chem., chemical physics, biophysics and immunology. *Leisure interest:* mathematics. *Address:* Department of Chemistry, Stanford University, Stanford, Calif. 94305, U.S.A. (Office). *Telephone:* 415-497-2857.

McCONNELL, James Desmond Caldwell, PH.D., F.R.S.; British professor of the physics and chemistry of minerals; b. 3 July 1930; s. of Samuel D. McConnell and Cathleen McConnell; m. Jean Elspeth Ironside 1956; one s. two d.; ed. Queen's Univ. of Belfast and Univ. of Cambridge; demonstrator, Univ. of Cambridge 1955, lecturer 1960, Reader 1972-82; Fellow, Churchill Coll., Cambridge 1962-82, Extraordinary Fellow 1983-; Head of Dept. of Rock Physics, Schlumberger Cambridge Research 1983-86. *Publications:* Principles of Mineral Behaviour (with A. Putnis) 1980, numerous papers in physics and mineralogical journals. *Leisure interests:* local history, hill walking and singing. *Address:* 8 The Croft, Old Headington, Oxford, OX3 9BU, England. *Telephone:* Oxford 69100.

McCORMACK, Mark Hume, LL.B.; American lawyer and business executive; b. 6 Nov. 1930; s. of Ned H. and Grace W. McCormack; m. 1st Nancy Breckenridge McCormack 1954; two s. one d.; m. 2nd Betsy Nagelsen 1986; ed. Princeton and Yale Univs. and William and Mary Coll.; admitted to Ohio bar 1957; Assoc. Arter, Hadden, Wykoff & Van Duzer 1957-63, Partner 1964-; started Int. Management Group 1962, Chair. and C.E.O. 1964-; commentator for televised golf, B.B.C. *Publications:* The World of Professional Golf 1967, Arnie: The Evolution of a Legend 1967, The Wonderful World of Professional Golf 1973, What they don't teach you at Harvard Business School 1984. *Leisure interest:* golf. *Address:* No. 1300, One Erieview Plaza, Cleveland, Ohio 44114 (Office); 2830 Lander Road, Pepperpike, Cleveland, Ohio 44124, U.S.A. (Home).

McCORMICK, Brooks; American business executive; b. 1917, Chicago; s. of Chauncey and Marion (Deering) McCormick; m. Hope Baldwin 1940; ed. Groton School, Yale Univ.; joined Int. Harvester Co. 1940; various posts 1942-50; Joint Man. Dir. Int. Harvester Co. of G.B. Ltd. 1951-54; Dir. of Mfg., Int. Harvester Co. 1954-57, mem. of Bd. 1958-80, Pres. 1968-77; C.E.O. 1971-77, Chair. 1977-79, Chair. Exec. Cttee. 1979-80, Dir. Nov. 1980-; mem. Business Council 1976-; Trustee, Art Inst., Chicago Community Trust; Life Trustee, Rush-Presbyterian St. Luke's Medical Center; Chevalier, Légion d'honneur 1980. *Address:* International Harvester Company, Room 560, 401 N. Michigan Avenue, Chicago, Ill. 60611, U.S.A.

MacCORMICK, (Donald) Neil, M.A., LL.D., F.B.A., F.R.S.E.; British professor of law; b. 27 May 1941, Glasgow; s. of John MacDonald MacCormick and Margaret Isobel Miller; m. Caroline Rona Barr 1965; three d.; ed. High School of Glasgow, Univ. of Glasgow, Balliol Coll., Oxford; Lecturer in Jurisprudence, Queen's Coll., Dundee, St. Andrews Univ. 1965-67; Fellow and Tutor in Jurisprudence, Balliol Coll., Oxford 1967-72; Regius Prof. of Public Law and the Law of Nature and Nations, Univ. of Edinburgh 1972-, Dean of the Faculty of Law 1973-76, 1985-88; Pres. Soc. of Public Teachers of Law 1983-84; mem. Nat. Council of Scottish Nat. Party 1978-84, 1985-86; Dr. h.c. (Uppsala Univ.) 1986. *Publications:* Legal Reasoning and Legal Theory 1978, H. L. A. Hart 1981, Legal Right and Social Democracy 1982, An Institutional Theory of Law 1986, The Scottish Debate (ed.) 1970, The Legal Mind (ed.) 1986. *Leisure interests:* gardening, hill-walking, dinghy sailing, politics (Scottish Nat. Party), piping. *Address:* Faculty of Law, University of Edinburgh, Old College, South Bridge, Edinburgh, EH8 9YL, Scotland. *Telephone:* 031-667 1011, ext. 4260.

McCOWEN, Alec, C.B.E.; British actor; b. 26 May 1925, Tunbridge Wells; s. of Duncan McCowen and Mary Walkden; ed. Skinners School, Tunbridge Wells, and Royal Acad. of Dramatic Art; mem. Nat. Theatre; Evening Standard (now The Standard) Best Actor 1968, 1973, 1982; Variety Club Stage Actor 1970; Old Vic Theatre: played Touchstone, Ford, Richard II, Mercutio, Malvolio, Oberon 1959-60; with R.S.C.: played Fool in King Lear 1964, Hadrian VII 1968, The Philanthropist 1970, The Misanthrope 1972, Dr. Dysart in Equus 1972, Henry Higgins in Pygmalion 1974, Ben in The Family Dance 1976; with Prospect Co.: Antony in Antony and Cleopatra 1977; solo performance of St. Mark's Gospel 1978, 1981; Frank in Tishoo 1979; Malvolio in Twelfth Night (TV) 1980; with Nat. Theatre: Crocker-Harris in The Browning Version, Arthur in Harlequinade, Capt. Corcoran in H.M.S. Pinafore 1981, Adolf Hitler in The Portage to San Cristobal of AH 1982, solo performance in Kipling 1983, Reilly in The Cocktail Party 1986, Nicolai in Fathers and Sons 1987, Vladimir in Waiting for Godot 1987, Modern Love 1988; Dir.: Definitely the Bahamas 1987. *Films:* Frenzy 1971, Travels with my Aunt 1973, Stevie 1978, The Assam Garden 1985, Personal Services 1986, Henry V 1989. *T.V.:* Private Lives 1976, Mr. Palfrey of Westminster 1984. *Publications:* Young Gemini 1979, Double Bill 1980 and Personal Mark 1984. *Leisure interests:* music and gardening. *Address:* c/o Jeremy Conway, Eagle House, 109 Jermyn Street, London, SW1 76HB, England.

McCRACKEN, Paul Winston, PH.D.; American economist; b. 29 Dec. 1915, Richland, Ia.; s. of late C. Sumner McCracken and Mary (Coffin) McCracken; m. E. Ruth Siler 1942; two d.; ed. William Penn Coll. and Harvard Univ.; mem. Faculty, Foundation School, Berea Coll., Kentucky 1937-40; economist, Dept. of Commerce, Washington 1942-43; Financial Economist, Dir. of Research, Fed. Reserve Bank of Minneapolis 1943-48; Assoc. Prof. School of Business Admin., Univ. of Mich. 1948-50, Prof. 1950-66, Edmund Ezra Day Univ. Prof. of Business Admin. 1966-86, Prof. Emer. 1986-; mem. Council of Econ. Advisers, Washington 1956-59, Chair. 1969-72; mem. Pres.'s Cttee. to Fight Inflation 1980-. *Publications:* Hypothetical Projection of Commodity Expenditures, Northwest in Two Wars, Future of Northwest Bank Deposits, Rising Tide of Bank Lending, Balance of Payments and Domestic Prosperity, Economic Progress and the Utility Industry. *Address:* 2564 Hawthorn Road, Ann Arbor, Mich. 48104, U.S.A.

McCREA, Sir William Hunter, Kt., PH.D., SC.D., F.R.S.; British mathematician and astronomer; b. 13 Dec. 1904, Dublin; s. of the late Robert Hunter

McCrea and the late Margaret Hutton; m. Marian Nicol Core Webster 1933; one s. two d.; ed. Chesterfield Grammar School, Cambridge and Göttingen Univs.; Lecturer in Math., Edinburgh Univ. 1930-32; Reader in Math., Univ. of London and Asst. Prof. Imperial Coll. of Science 1932-36; Prof. of Math., Queen's Univ. of Belfast 1936-44; Temporary Prin. Experimental Officer, Admiralty 1943-45; Prof. of Math., Univ. of London (Royal Holloway Coll.) 1944-66; Comyns Berkeley Bye-Fellow, Caius Coll., Cambridge 1952-53; Visiting Prof. of Astronomy, Univ. of Calif. 1956, 1967, Case Inst. of Tech. 1964; Research Prof. of Theoretical Astronomy, Univ. of Sussex 1966-72, Emer. 1972-; Fellow of Imperial Coll. of Science and Tech., London 1967-; Georges Lemaître Prof., Univ. of Louvain 1969; Royal Soc. Leverhulme Visiting Prof. Cairo 1973; Visiting Prof. of Astronomy, Univ. of British Columbia, Vancouver 1975-76; Visiting Prof. Univ. of Istanbul 1977-78; William Evans Visiting Prof. Univ. of Otago, N.Z. 1979; Pres. Royal Astronomical Soc. 1961-63, Treas. 1976-79; Pres. Math. Asscn. 1973-74, Hon. mem. 1985; mem. Akad. Leopoldina, Halle; Keith Prize, Royal Soc. of Edinburgh, Gold Medal, Royal Astronomical Soc. 1976; Hon. D.Sc. (Nat. Univ. of Ireland, Queen's Univ. Belfast, Univ. of Sussex), Sc.D. (Dublin), Dr. h.c. (Nat. Univ. of Córdoba, Argentina), Hon. Fellow Royal Holloway Coll. 1984-. *Publications:* Relativity Physics 1935, Analytical Geometry of Three Dimensions 1942, Physics of the Sun and Stars 1950, trans. of A. Unsöld's The New Cosmos 1969, Cosmology 1969, The Royal Greenwich Observatory 1975, and numerous papers in mathematical and astronomical journals. *Leisure interests:* travel and walking. *Address:* Astronomy Centre, University of Sussex, Falmer, Brighton BN1 9QH (Office); 87 Houndean Rise, Lewes, Sussex BN7 1EJ, England (Home). *Telephone:* (0273) 606755 (Office); (0273) 473296 (Home).

McCREDIE, Andrew Dalgarno, M.A., D.PHIL., F.A.H.; Australian professor of musicology; b. 3 Sept. 1930, Sydney; s. of Harold A. McCredie and Marjorie C. (née Dalgarno) McCredie; m. Xenia Rosner 1965; ed. Univ. of Sydney, Royal Acad. of Music, London, Univs. of Copenhagen, Stockholm, Hamburg; Sr. Research Fellow, Univ. of Adelaide 1965-69, Sr. Lecturer in Musicology 1970-73, Reader in Musicology 1974-77, Prof. 1978-; Visiting Lecturer Univs. of Amsterdam, Utrecht 1964, Western Australia 1970, City Univ. of New York 1974, Yale, Pennsylvania 1977, Ljubljana, Bologna, Marburg, Frankfurt, Cracow, Warsaw 1978, Copenhagen, Belfast (Queen's Univ.), Hamburg, Munich, Zentral Inst. für Musikforschung (Berlin), Berne, Basle, Zurich 1983, Melbourne, Stockholm, Tübingen 1986, Heidelberg, Saarbrücken, Queen's Univ. Kingston, Ont., Brandeis (Boston), City Univ. of New York 1987; mem. Council Int. Musicological Soc. 1977-87; Adviser Musica Antiqua Europae Orientalis 1977-; advisory, corresp., ed. appts. Int. Review of Aesthetics and Sociology of Music 1981-, Current Musicology 1987-, Studies in Music 1980; Edward J. Dent Medal 1974, Paderewski Medal-Bydgoszcz Philharmonia 1982. *Publications:* Musical Composition in Australia (3 vols.) 1969, Karl Amadeus Hartmann: Catalogue of all his works with biography 1981 (trans. German), Miscellanea Musicologica, Adelaide (Ed.) 1966-, Paperbacks on Musicology (Gen. Ed.) 1978-. *Leisure interests:* travel, books, art and antiques. *Address:* Faculty of Music, University of Adelaide, Adelaide, S.A. (Office); 8 Hawker Avenue, Belair, S.A., Australia (Home). *Telephone:* 228.5138, 228.5286 (Office); 278.3950 (Home).

McCRUM, Michael William, M.A.; British headmaster and university administrator; b. 23 May 1924; s. of Capt. C. R. McCrum, R.N. (retd.) and Ivy I. H. (née Nicholson) McCrum; m. Christine M. K. fforde 1952; three s. one d.; ed. Sherborne School and Corpus Christi Coll., Cambridge; Asst. Master, Rugby School 1948-50; Fellow, Corpus Christi Coll., Cambridge 1949, Second Tutor 1950-51, Tutor 1951-62, Master Oct. 1980-; Headmaster of Tonbridge School 1962-70; Head Master of Eton Coll. 1970-80; Gov. King's School, Canterbury 1980-, Rugby School 1982-; Vice-Chancellor Cambridge Univ. 1987-89. *Publication:* Select Documents of the Principates of the Flavian Emperors AD 68-96 1961. *Address:* Master's Lodge, Corpus Christi College, Cambridge, CB2 1RH, England. *Telephone:* (0223) 59418.

McCULLIN, Donald; British photographer; b. 9 Oct. 1935, London; s. of Frederick and Jessica McCullin; m. Christine Dent 1959 (marriage dissolved 1987); two s. one d. and one s. by Laraine Ashton; ed. Tollington Park Secondary Modern, Hammersmith Art and Crafts School; R.A.F. Nat. Service; photographer with Observer for four years; photographer with Sunday Times, London for eighteen years; freelance 1980-; has covered eight wars—Viet-Nam, Cambodia, Biafra, Congo, Israel, Cyprus, Chad, Lebanon—and many famine areas; has travelled to 64 countries; World Press Photographer 1964, Warsaw Gold Medal 1964, Granada TV Award 1967, 1969, Two Gold, One Silver Art Director Awards, U.K. *Publications:* The Destruction Business 1971, The Concerned Photographer II 1972, Is Anyone Taking Notice? 1973, Hearts of Darkness 1980, Battle Beirut—A City in Crisis 1983, Perspectives 1987, Skulduggery 1987. *Leisure interests:* walking in countries, collecting Victorian children's books, looking at things and people. *Address:* Holly Hill House, Batcombe, Shepton Mallet, Somerset, BA4 6BL, England.

McCULLOCH, Frank Waugh, LL.B.; American lawyer, teacher, arbitrator and government official; b. 1905, Evanston, Ill.; s. of Frank Hathorn McCulloch and Catharine Waugh McCulloch; m. Edith F. Leverton 1937; two s.; ed. Williams Coll. and Harvard Law School; Legal Practice 1930-35;

Industrial Relations Sec., Council for Social Action, Congregational-Christian Churches, Chicago 1935-46; Dir. Labor Educ. Div., Roosevelt Univ., Chicago 1946-49; Admin. Asst. to U.S. Senator Paul H. Douglas 1949-61; Chair. Nat. Labor Relations Bd. 1961-70; Visiting Prof. of Law, Univ. of N. Carolina 1971; mem. Center for Advanced Studies, Univ. of Virginia 1971-74, Prof. of Law 1971-76, Scholar in Residence 1976-; Visiting Prof. Cornell Univ. Industrial and Labor Relations School 1976; mem. Public Review Bd., United Automobile Workers 1971-88; mem. Admin. Conf. of U.S. 1968-70, Comm. of Experts on the Application of Conventions and Recommendations, Int. Labour Office 1974-85; Anglo-American Admin. Law Exchange 1969, Comm. on Public Employee Rights (Va.) 1972-76; State Employee Labor Relations Council (Ill.) 1973-82, Migrant Legal Action Program Bd. 1973-85, Industrial Devt. Authority, Albermarle County (Va.) 1977-87; Consultant, President's Personnel Man. Project 1977; Hon. LL.D. (Olivet Coll., Chicago Theological Seminary, Williams Coll.). *Publication:* The National Labor Relations Bd. (with T. Bornstein) 1974. *Leisure interests:* music, travel, social and community action. *Address:* 104 Falcon Drive, Charlottesville, Va. 22901, U.S.A. (Home). *Telephone:* 804-295-7371 (Home).

McCUNE, Francis Kimber; American business executive; b. 10 April 1906, Santa Barbara, Calif.; s. of Thomas H. McCune and Vernon K. McCune; m. Mary Harper Waddell 1969; two d.; ed. California Univ.; with Gen. Electric Co. 1928-67, Asst. Gen. Man., Nucleonics Dept. 1949, Gen. Man. Atomic Products Div. 1954, Vice-Pres. 1954-67, Vice-Pres. Eng. 1960, Vice-Pres. Business Studies 1965-67; Vice-Pres. and Dir. American Standards Asscn. 1965; Hon. Dir. and Past Pres. Atomic Industrial Forum Inc.; Chair. N.Y. State Gen. Advisory Cttee. on Atomic Energy 1959-62; Pres. U.S.A. Standards Inst. 1967-69; Hon. mem. Nat. Acad. Eng.; Hon. mem. Woods Hole Oceanographic Inst.; mem. Nat. Research Council 1969-71; life mem. and Fellow of I.E.E.E.; Charter mem. American Nuclear Soc.; mem. A.S.M.E.; Howard Coonley Medal 1970. *Leisure interests:* fishing, hunting, boating, golf. *Address:* 470 Magellan Drive, Sarasota, Fla. 34243, U.S.A. *Telephone:* (813) 755-7177.

McCUNE, William James, Jr.; American engineer; b. 2 June 1915, Glens Falls, N.Y.; s. of William James McCune and Brunnhilde Decker McCune; m. 1st Janet Waters 1940; one d.; m. 2nd Elisabeth Johnson 1946; one s. two d.; ed. M.I.T.; joined Polaroid Corpn. 1939, Gen. Eng. Man. 1954-63, Asst. Gen. Man. and Vice-Pres. 1963-69, Exec. Vice-Pres. 1969-75, Pres. 1975-83, C.O.O. and mem. Bd. of Dirs. 1975-, C.E.O. 1980-85, Chair. July 1982-; mem. Nat. Acad. of Eng.; Fellow, American Acad. of Arts and Sciences. *Leisure interests:* skiing, cycling. *Address:* Polaroid Corporation, 549 Technology Square, Cambridge, Mass. 02139, U.S.A. *Telephone:* (617) 577-3411.

McCURDY, Richard Clark; American oil executive; b. 2 Jan. 1909, Newton, Ia.; s. of Ralph B. McCurdy and Florence (Clark) McCurdy; m. Harriet Sutton 1933; three s. one d.; ed. Stanford Univ.; with Shell Oil Co., Ventura, Calif. 1933, Jr. Engineer, later Engineer, Los Angeles, Bakersfield, Coalinga, Long Beach 1935-42, Washington Office 1942-43, Chief Exploitation Engineer, Pacific Coast Production Area 1943-45, Acting Div. Man. San Joaquin Production Div. Bakersfield 1945-47; Asst. Man., later Man., Western Div. Royal Dutch/Shell Group companies in Venezuela 1947-50, Gen. Man. 1950-53; Pres. Shell Chemical Co. (div. of Shell Oil Co.) 1953-65, Pres. and C.E.O. Shell Oil Co. 1965-69; Assoc. Admin. Org. and Man., NASA, Washington, D.C. 1970-73, Consultant 1974-; fmr. Chair. Bd. of Dirs. Mfg. Chemists' Asscn.; Trustee Stanford Univ., etc.; Chair. Bd. of Trustees, Hood Coll. 1968-86, Emer. 1986-; Trustee Rensselaer Polytechnic Inst. 1974-86, Hon. Trustee 1986-; mem. Soc. of Chemical Industry, American Physical Soc., and American Inst. of Mining and Metallurgical Engineers; Distinguished Service Medal, NASA 1972. *Leisure interest:* sailing. *Address:* Contentment Island, Darien, Conn. 06820, U.S.A. (Home).

McDANIEL, Boyce Dawkins, PH.D.; American physicist; b. 11 June 1917, Brevard, N.C.; s. of Allen Webster McDaniel and Grace Dawkins; m. Jane Chapman Grennell 1941; one s. one d.; ed. Ohio Wesleyan Univ., Case Inst. of Tech. and Cornell Univ.; Staff mem. Radiation Lab., M.I.T. 1943; Los Alamos Scientific Lab. 1943-46; Asst. Prof. of Physics, Cornell Univ. 1946-48, Assoc. Prof. 1948-56, Prof. 1956-87, Emer. 1987-; on sabbatical leave at Australian Nat. Univ., Canberra 1953-54, Laboratorio Nazionale di Frascati, Italy 1959-60; Assoc. Dir. Lab. of Nuclear Studies, Cornell Univ. 1960-67, Dir. 1967-85; Resident Collaborator, Brookhaven Nat. Lab. 1966-; Floyd E. Newman Prof. in Nuclear Studies 1977-; Head accelerator section, Nat. Accelerator Laboratory 1975-; mem. N.A.S. 1981; Trustee, Associated Univs. Inc. 1963-75, Univs. Research Asscn. Inc. 1971-77, 1983; Physicist Fermi Nat. Accelerator Lab. 1972, 1974, 1980; Fulbright Research Award 1953, 1959; Guggenheim Award 1959; Fellow, American Physical Soc. *Address:* Laboratory of Nuclear Studies, Cornell University, Ithaca, N.Y. 14850; 26 Woodcrest Avenue, Ithaca, N.Y. 14850, U.S.A. *Telephone:* (607) 255-2301 (Office).

MACDERMOT, Niall, O.B.E., Q.C.; British international jurist; b. 10 Sept. 1916, Dublin, Ireland; s. of Henry MacDermot, K.C. and Gladys née Lowenadler; m. 1st Violet Denise Maxwell 1940 (dissolved); one s.; m. 2nd Ludmila Benvenuto 1966; ed. Rugby School, Balliol Coll., Oxford; called to the Bar 1946, M.P. (Labour) for Lewisham N. 1957-59, for Derby N. 1962-70;

Deputy Chair. Bedfordshire Quarter Sessions 1962; Recorder of Newark 1963–64; Financial Sec. to H.M. Treasury 1964–67; Minister of State for Planning and Land 1967–68; Recorder of Crown Court 1972–74; Master of Bench, the Inner Temple 1970–; Trustee Tate Gallery 1969–76; Sec.-Gen. Int. Comm. of Jurists 1970–; Chair. Special Non-Governmental Orgs. Cttee. on Human Rights, Geneva 1973–86, Vice-Chair. 1986–; mem. Bd. Int. Alert 1985–; mem. Advisory Council Interights 1984–. *Address:* International Commission of Jurists, P.O. Box 120, 109 route de Chêne, 1224 Chêne Bougeries, Geneva, Switzerland. *Telephone:* 49-35-45.

McDERMOTT, Edward Aloysious, B.A., IUR.D.; American lawyer, educator and government official; b. 28 June 1920, Dubuque, Ia.; m. Naola Spellman 1945; three s. one d.; ed. Loras Coll. and State Univ. of Iowa; Prof. of Business Law, Loras Coll., Dubuque, Iowa 1946–48; Prof. of Econs., Clarke Coll., Dubuque 1948–50; Partner law firm O'Connor, Thomas, McDermott and Wright, Dubuque 1951–61; Chief Counsel U.S. Senate Sub-cttee. on Privileges and Elections 1950–51; Deputy Dir. Office of Civil and Defense Mobilisation, The White House 1960–61; Dir. Office of Emergency Planning, Exec. Office of the Pres. 1962–65; mem. Nat. Security Council; Chair. Emergency Planning Cttee.; U.S. Rep. Sr. Civil Emergency Planning Cttee., NATO 1962–65; mem. President's Cttee. on Econ. Impact on Defense and Disarmament; mem. Advisory Comm., Fed. Emergency Man. Admin. 1980–85; Chair. President's Petroleum Policy Cttee. 1963; Sr. Adviser, President's Reorganization Project 1977–79; Partner Law Firm Hogan and Hartson, Washington D.C., 1965–; Pres. John Carroll Soc. 1972, Knights of Malta 1979–82; Chair. Lombardi Cancer Research Center; mem. Bd. of Advisers, Industrial Coll. of Armed Forces, Washington 1965–70; mem. Bd. of Regents, Univ. Santa Clara (Calif.), Lynchburg Coll. (Virginia), Coll. of Notre Dame, Loras Coll. (Dubuque) 1975–79; Trustee, Colgate Univ. (New York); mem. Bd. of Dirs. American Irish Foundation; mem. Maynooth Coll. (Ireland) Cttee.; mem. Council of Hosp. of St. John and Elizabeth (U.K.); mem. of Bd. Religious Educators Foundation; Fellow, American Bar Asscn.; official of legal, civic and charitable orgs.; Kt. of Holy Sepulchre. *Address:* Columbia Square, 555 13th Street N.W., Washington, D.C. 20004 (Office); 5400 Albemarle St., Bethesda, Md. 20816, U.S.A. (Home). *Telephone:* 301-229-8755 (Home); (202) 331-4637 (Office).

MacDERMOTT, Hon John Clarke; British judge; b. 1927; s. of Baron MacDermott and Louise Palmer Johnston; m. Margaret H. Dales; four d.; ed. Campbell Coll. Belfast, Trinity Hall, Cambridge and Queen's Univ. Belfast; called to Bar, Inner Temple and N. Ireland 1949; Q.C. (N. Ireland) 1964; Judge, High Court of N. Ireland 1973–87; Lord Justice 1987–. *Address:* Royal Courts of Justice, Belfast; 6 Tarawood Holywood, Co. Down, N. Ireland.

MCDONAGH, Enda; Irish professor of moral theology; b. 27 June 1930, Co. Mayo; s. of Patrick McDonagh and Mary Kelly; ed. St. Jarlath's Coll., Tuam, St. Patrick's Coll., Maynooth, Gregorianum Univ., Rome and Univ. of Munich; Prof. of Moral Theology (and Canon Law), St. Patrick's Coll. 1958–, Dir. Postgraduate Studies in Theology 1970–76, Dean of Faculty of Theology 1973–79; lecturer in Irish School of Ecumenics, Dublin 1970–; Husking Prof. of Theology, Univ. of Notre Dame, U.S.A. 1979–81; Ferguson Lecturer, Univ. of Manchester March 1978; Leverhulme Research Fellow, Univ. of Cambridge 1978. *Publications:* Roman Catholics and Unity 1963, Religious Freedom 1967, Invitation and Response 1972, Gift and Call 1975, Social Ethics and the Christian 1979, Doing the Truth 1979, Church and Politics: The Case History of Zimbabwe 1980, The Making of Disciples 1982, Between Chaos and New Creation 1987, ed. and contrib. The Meaning of Christian Marriage 1963, Moral Theology Renewed 1965, Truth and Life 1968. *Leisure interests:* poetry and music. *Address:* St. Patrick's College, Maynooth, Co. Kildare, Ireland. *Telephone:* 285222.

McDONAGH, Robert; Irish diplomatist; b. 23 March 1924, Tralee, Co. Kerry; m.; four c.; ed. Presentation Coll., Glasthule, Co. Dublin and Univ. Coll. Dublin; served in Office of the Revenue Commrs. and in Depts. of Industry and Commerce and Supplies; entered Dept. of Foreign Affairs as Third Sec. 1949; served in Irish missions at Madrid 1951, Washington D.C. 1952 and Stockholm 1957; Sec., Dept. of Foreign Affairs 1955, 1958, 1961; Chargé d'Affaires a.i., Copenhagen 1962; Counsellor, Dept. of Foreign Affairs 1965, Asst. Sec. 1970; Amb. to Fed. Repub. of Germany 1973–76, to Italy, Turkey and Libya 1978–83; Deputy Sec., Dept. of Foreign Affairs 1976–77, Sec. 1977–78; Perm. Rep. to UN 1983–. *Address:* Permanent Mission of Ireland to the United Nations, 19th Floor, 1 Dag Hammarskjöld Plaza, 885 Second Floor, New York, N.Y. 10017, U.S.A.

McDONALD, Alonzo L., B.A., M.B.A.; American business executive; b. 5 Aug. 1928, Atlanta, Ga.; s. of Alonzo L. McDonald Sr. and Lois Burrell McDonald; m. Suzanne Moffitt 1959; two s. two d.; ed. Emory Univ., Atlanta, Ga., and Graduate School of Business Admin., Harvard Univ.; reporter Atlanta Journal 1948–50; Man. Sales and Service Activities, Air Conditioning Div., Westinghouse Corpn. 1956–60; joined McKinsey & Co. Inc. 1960, Man. Dir. and C.E.O. 1973–76; Amb. and Head of U.S. Del. to Tokyo Round of Multilateral Trade Negotiations, Geneva 1977–79; Amb. and Deputy U.S. Special Trade Rep. (later acting Special Trade Rep.), Washington, D.C. 1979; Asst. to the Pres. and White House Staff Dir., Washington, D.C. 1979–81; Pres. The Bendix Corpn. 1981–83; Dir. IBJ Bank & Trust Co., Chicago Pacific Corpn., Lafarge Corpn., Scientific Atlanta; Chair. Avenir Group Inc., 1983–; Sr. Lecturer, Harvard Graduate School of Business Admin. 1981. *Publications:* numerous articles in business publications. *Address:* Avenir Group, Inc., 5505 Corporate Drive, Suite 400, Troy, Mich. 48098, U.S.A.

MACDONALD, Hon. Donald Stovel, P.C., LL.M.; Canadian politician and lawyer; b. 1 March 1932, Ottawa, Ont.; s. of Donald A. Macdonald and Marjorie I. Stovel; m. Ruth Hutchison 1961 (deceased 1987); four d.; ed. Ottawa public schools, Ashbury Coll., Ottawa, Univs. of Toronto and Cambridge, and Osgoode Hall and Harvard Law Schools; with McCarthy and McCarthy, Barristers, Toronto 1957–62; M.P. 1962–78; Parl. Sec. to Minister of Justice 1963–65, to Minister of Finance 1965, to Sec. of State for External Affairs 1966–68, to Minister of Industry 1968; Minister without Portfolio 1968; Pres. Privy Council and Govt. House Leader 1968; Minister of Nat. Defence 1970–72, of Energy, Mines and Resources 1972–75, of Finance 1975–77; partner, firm McCarthy & McCarthy, Toronto 1977–; High Commr. to the U.K. Oct. 1988–; Chair. Royal Comm. on the Econ. Union and Devt. Prospects for Canada 1982–85; Dir. Du Pont Canada Inc., McDonnell Douglas Corpn., McDonnell Douglas Canada Ltd., Bank of Nova Scotia, Alberta Energy Co. Ltd.; Miron Inc., MacMillan Bloedel Ltd.; Rowell Fellowship, Canadian Inst. of Int. Affairs 1956; Hon. LL.D. (St. Lawrence Univ.), Hon. D.Eng. (Colorado School of Mines). *Leisure interests:* fishing, cross-country skiing, tennis. *Address:* Canada High Commission, Macdonald House, 1 Grosvenor Square, London, W1X 0AB, England; 29 Dunvegan Road, Toronto, Ont., M4V 2P5, Canada (Home). *Telephone:* 960-1223 (Home).

McDONALD, Sir Duncan, Kt., C.B.E., D.ENG., D.SC., F.R.S.E.; British chartered engineer and business executive; b. 20 Sept. 1921, Inverkeithing, Scotland; s. of Helen Orrick and Robert McDonald; m. Jane Anne Guckian 1955; three s. one d.; ed. Dunfermline High School and Edinburgh Univ.; Graduate Eng., British Thomson Houston 1942–54; Chief Transformer Designer, Bruce Peebles Ltd. 1954–59, Chief Eng. 1959–62, Man. Dir. 1962–74; Dir. Reyrolle Parsons 1973; Chair. and Chief Exec. Reyrolle, Bruce Peebles Industries, Bushing Co. 1974–76; Chief Exec. Reyrolle Parsons 1976; Group Man. Dir. NEI Ltd. 1977–80, Chair. and Chief Exec. NEI PLC 1980–83, Chair. 1983–86; Dir. General Accident, Barclays (Scotland), Northern Rock (Scotland); Fellow Herriot Watt Coll.; Vice-Pres. and Fellow Scottish Council for Devt. and Industry, mem. of Court Herriot Watt Univ.; Hon. F.I.E.E. *Leisure interests:* golf, gardening, fishing. *Address:* Duncliffe, 15 Kinellan Road, Edinburgh, EH12 6ES, Scotland. *Telephone:* (031) 337 4814.

McDONALD, Edward Lawson, M.A., M.D., F.R.C.P., F.A.C.C.; British cardiologist; b. 8 Feb. 1918; s. of Charles S. McDonald and Mabel D. McDonald; m. (divorced); one s.; ed. Felsted School, Clare Coll. Cambridge, Middlesex Hosp., Univ. of London and Harvard Univ.; Consultant Cardiologist, Nat. Heart Hosp., London 1961–, King Edward VII Hosp. for Officers, London 1968–, King Edward VII Hosp. Midhurst 1970–; mem. Most Honourable Order of Crown of Johore. *Publications:* Medical and Surgical Cardiology 1969, Very Early Recognition of Coronary Heart Disease (Ed.) 1978; contributions to learned journals. *Leisure interests:* art, skiing, mountain walking, sailing. *Address:* 9 Upper Wimpole Street, London, W1M 7TD, England. *Telephone:* 01-935 7101.

MACDONALD, Rev. Fergus, M.A., B.D.; British ecclesiastic; b. 2 March 1936, Evanton, Scotland; s. of Rev. John A. Macdonald and Dr. May F. (née Urquhart) Macdonald; m. Dolina M. Mackay 1961; one s. four d.; ed. Univ. of Edinburgh, Free Church Coll., Edinburgh; Asst. Minister Hope Street Free Church, Glasgow 1960–62; Minister St. Andrew's Evangelical Presbyterian Church, Lima, Peru 1962–67; Minister Cumbernauld Free Church of Scotland 1968–81; Gen. Sec. Nat. Bible Soc. of Scotland 1981–; Moderator of Gen. Assembly of Free Church of Scotland 1987–88; Ed. The Instructor 1973–81. *Publication:* Prospects for Scotland (with Peter Brierley) 1985. *Leisure interests:* gardening, D.I.Y. *Address:* 7 Hampton Terrace, Edinburgh, EH12 5XU (Office); 113 St. Alban's Road, Edinburgh, EH9 2PQ, Scotland (Home).

MACDONALD, Hon. Flora Isabel, P.C.; Canadian politician; b. 3 June 1926, North Sydney, N.S.; d. of George Frederick and Mary Isabel (née Royle) Macdonald; ed. North Sydney High School, Empire Business Coll. and National Defence Coll., Kingston; held various secretarial posts in Canada and U.K.; Exec. Dir. Progressive Conservative Headquarters 1957–66; admin. officer and tutor Dept. of Political Studies Queen's Univ. 1966–72; Nat. Sec. Progressive Conservative Assen. of Canada 1966–69; mem. Parl. for Kingston and the Islands, Ont. 1972–88; Opposition Spokesman for Indian Affairs and Northern Devt. 1972–79; Sec. of State for External Affairs 1979–80; Minister for Employment and Immigration 1984–86, of Communications 1986–88; Dir. Canadian Political Science Assen.; Dir. Canada Trust Co.; Chair. Nat. Ballet School; mem. Canadian Inst. of Public Affairs, Canadian Inst. of Int. Affairs, Canadian Civil Liberties Assen.; Progressive Conservative. *Leisure interest:* speedskating. *Address:* 502-350 Driveway, Ottawa, Ont., K2P 1E2 (Home). *Telephone:* (613) 238-1098.

McDONALD, (Francis) James; American business executive (retd.); b. 3 Aug. 1922, Saginaw, Mich.; s. of Francis J. McDonald and Mary C. Fordney; m. Betty Ann Dettenthaler 1944; two s. one d.; ed. Gen. Motors Inst.; served to rank of Lieut. U.S.N. 1944–46; joined Saginaw Malleable Iron

Plant 1946, Man. -1955; Plant Man. Cen. Foundry Div., Defiance, Ohio 1955-56; Works Man. Transmission Div., Detroit 1956-63, Gen. Man. 1963-65; Works Man. Pontiac Motor Div., Pontiac, Mich. 1965-68; Dir. Manufacturing Operations, Chevrolet Motor Div. 1968-69; Gen. Man. Pontiac Motor Div., Vice-Pres. and mem. Admin. Cttee. Gen. Motors 1969; Gen. Man. Chevrolet Motor Div. 1972-74; Exec. Vice-Pres., mem. Bd. of Dirs. and Exec. Cttee. Gen. Motors 1974; overall responsibility for Power Products Group 1978; mem. Finance Cttee. 1979-; responsible for Overseas Group 1980; Pres. and C.O.O. Gen. Motors and Chair. Exec. and Admin. Cttees. 1981-87; Chair. Beaumont Hosp. Foundation 1987-; mem. Bd. of Dirs. and Exec. Compensation and Audit Cttees. H. J. Heinz Co.; mem. Soc. of Automotive Engineers, Detroit Engineering Soc. *Address:* c/o 3044 West Grand Boulevard, Detroit, Mich. 48202, U.S.A. *Telephone:* (313) 556-3504.

MACDONALD, Gordon James Fraser, PH.D.; American geophysicist; b. 30 July 1929, Mexico, D.F.; s. of Gordon J. MacDonald and Josephine Bennett; m. 1st Marcelline Kuglen 1960 (deceased), two s. one d.; m. 2nd Betty Ann Kipniss, one s.; ed. Harvard Univ.; Staff Assoc. Geophysics Lab., Carnegie Inst., Washington 1955-58; Consultant, U.S. Geological Survey 1955-60; Assoc. Prof. of Geophysics, M.I.T. 1955-58; Prof. Geophysics, Univ. of Calif. at Los Angeles 1958-68, Dir. Atmospheric Research Lab. 1960-66, Assoc. Dir. Inst. of Geophysics and Planetary Physics 1960-68; Vice-Pres. Research Inst. for Defense Analyses 1966-67, Exec. Vice-Pres. 1967-68, Trustee 1966-70; Vice-Chancellor for Research and Graduate Affairs, Univ. of Calif., Santa Barbara 1968-70, Prof. of Physics and Geophysics 1968-70; mem. Council on Environmental Quality, Washington 1970-72; Consultant, NASA 1960-70; mem. Space Science Bd., Nat. Acad. Sciences 1962-70, President's Science Advisory Cttee. 1965-69, Lunar and Planetary Missions Bd. 1967-70, Defense Science Bd., Dept. of Defense 1966-70; Consultant, Dept. State 1967-70; Henry R. Luce Prof. of Environmental Studies and Policy, Dartmouth 1972-79; mem. Advisory Panel on Nuclear Effects, Office of Tech. Assessment 1975-77; Trustee, Mitre Corpn. 1968-70, 1972-77, mem. Exec. Cttee. 1972-77; Distinguished Visiting Scholar 1977-79, Chief Scientist 1979-83, Vice-Pres. and Chief Scientist 1983-; mem. American Math. Soc., Nat. Acad. Sciences, Royal Astronomical Soc., American Mineral Soc., etc.; Fellow American Acad. Arts and Sciences, A.A.A.S.; American Acad. of Arts and Sciences Monograph Prize in Physics and Biological Sciences 1959, James B. Macelwane Award, American Geophysical Union 1965. *Publications:* Rotation of the Earth (with Walter Munk) 1960, The Long-Term Impacts of Increasing Atmospheric Carbon Dioxide Levels 1982, and articles in scientific journals. *Address:* c/o Mitre Corporation, 7525 Colshire Drive, McLean, Va. 22102, U.S.A. *Telephone:* (703) 883-6726.

MACDONALD, Ian Grant, M.A., F.R.S.; British professor of mathematics; b. 11 Oct. 1928, London; s. of Douglas G. and Irene A. (née Stokes) Macdonald; m. Margaretha Van Goethem 1954; two s. three d.; ed. Winchester Coll. and Trinity Coll., Cambridge; Asst. Prin., Prin., Ministry of Supply 1952-57; Asst. Lecturer, Manchester Univ. 1957-60; Lecturer, Exeter Univ. 1960-63; Fellow and Tutor in Math., Magdalen Coll., Oxford 1963-72; Fielden Prof. of Pure Math. Manchester Univ. 1972-76; Prof. of Pure Math., Queen Mary Coll., London 1976-. *Publications:* various monographs and papers in mathematical journals. *Address:* School of Mathematical Sciences, Queen Mary College, Mile End Road, London, E1 4NS (Office); 8 Blandford Avenue, Oxford, OX2 8DY, England (Home). *Telephone:* 01-980 4811 (Office); (0865) 515373 (Home).

MCDONALD, James, M.S.E.E.; American engineer and business executive; b. 17 Feb. 1940, Louisville, Ky.; s. of Matthew and Irene McDonald; m. Paula McDonald 1970; three c.; ed. Univ. of Kentucky; with IBM 1963-84, Devt. Man., Copier Products 1975-76, Systems Man. 1976-78, Lab. Dir. Office Systems Div., Boulder, Colo. 1978-80, Gen. Man. Industrial Automation Business Unit 1980-84; Pres. and C.O.O. Gould 1984-88, Chief Exec. 1986-88. *Leisure interests:* golf, tennis. *Address:* Gould Inc., 10 Gould Center, Rolling Meadows, Ill. 60008 (Office); Box 414, Caesar Drive, Borrington Hill, Ill. 60010, U.S.A.

MACDONALD, J(ames) Ross, B.A., S.M., PH.D., D.SC.; American physicist; b. 27 Feb. 1923, Savannah, Ga.; s. of John Elwood Macdonald and Antonina Jones Hansell; m. Margaret Milward Taylor 1946; two s. one d.; ed. Williams Coll., Mass. Inst. of Tech. and Oxford; mem. staff Digital Computer Lab., M.I.T. 1946-47; Physicist Armour Research Foundation 1950-52; Assoc. Physicist Argonne Nat. Lab. 1952-53; Adjunct Assoc. Prof. of Biophysics Univ. of Tex. Southwestern Medical School 1954-71, Adjunct Prof. 1971-74; Research Physicist Texas Instruments, Inc. 1953-55; Dir. Solid State Physics Research 1955-61, Physics Research Lab. 1961-63, Cen. Research Labs. 1963-72; Dir then Asst. Vice-Pres. Corp. Research and Eng. 1967-68, Vice-Pres. 1968-73; Man. Objectives, Strategies and Tactics System 1972-73; Vice-Pres. Corp. Research and Devt. 1973-74, Consultant 1974-78; William Rand Kenan, Jr. Prof. of Physics Univ. of N.C. 1974-; Consultant Simmonds Precision Products 1978-83, Dir. 1979-83; Chair. Cttee. on Educ., American Physical Soc. 1973-75, Ad Hoc Cttee. on Applied Physics 1974, Cttee. on Application of Physics 1975-78; Chair. Cttee. on Professional Concerns 1976-78; mem. N.A.S., Nat. Acad. of Eng., New York Acad. of Sciences, Audio Eng. Soc., Electrochemical Soc., American Inst. of Physics (mem. Corp. Assocs. Advisory Cttee. 1969-74, Governing Bd.

1975-78); mem. numerous cttees. and comms; Achievement Award, IRE 1962, Meritorious Services Award, I.E.E.E. Acoustics, Speech and Signal Processing Group 1974, George E. Pake Prize, American Physical Soc. 1985; I.E.E.E. Edison Medal 1988. *Publications:* more than 175 articles in professional journals. *Address:* Department of Physics and Astronomy, University of North Carolina, Chapel Hill, N.C. 27514 (Office); 308 Laurel Hill Road, Chapel Hill, N.C. 27514, U.S.A. (Home). *Telephone:* (919) 962 3012 (Office); (919) 967 5005 (Home).

McDONALD, John W., Jr., DR. JUR.; American lawyer, diplomatist and international official; b. 18 Feb. 1922, Koblenz, Germany; s. of John Warlick McDonald and Ethel Mae Raynor; m. 1st Barbara Jane Stewart 1943 (divorced); one s. three d.; m. 2nd Christel Meyer 1970; ed. Univ. of Illinois, Nat. War Coll., Washington, D.C.; admitted to Ill. Supreme Court Bar 1946, to U.S. Supreme Court 1951; Legal Div., U.S. Office of Mil. Govt., Berlin 1947; Asst. District Attorney, U.S. Mil. Govt. Courts, Frankfurt 1947-50; Sec. Law Cttee., Allied High Comm. 1950-52; mem. Mission to NATO and OECD, Paris 1952-54; Office of Exec. Sec. Dept. of State 1954-55; Exec. Sec. to Dir. of Int. Co-operation Admin. 1955-59; U.S. Econ. Co-ordinator for CENTO Affairs, Ankara 1959-63; Chief, Econ. and Commercial Sections, Cairo 1963-66; Deputy Dir. Office of Econ. and Social Affairs, Dept. of State 1967-68, Dir. 1968-71; Co-ordinator, UN Multilateral Devt. Programmes, Dept. of State 1971-74, Acting Deputy Asst. Sec. for Econ. and Social Affairs 1971, 1973; Deputy Dir.-Gen. Int. Labour Org. (ILO) 1974-78; Pres. Int. Telecommunications Satellite Org. (INTELSAT) Conf. on Privileges and Immunities 1978; Amb. to UN Conf. on TCDC 1978; Sec.-Gen. 27th Colombo Plan Ministerial Meeting 1978; U.S Co-ordinator for UN Decade on Drinking Water and Sanitation 1979-; Amb. to UNIDO III 1979-80; Chair. Fed. Cttee. for UN Int. Year of Disabled Persons; Amb. to UN World Assembly on Ageing 1981-82; co-ordinator for Multilateral Affairs, Center for the Study of Foreign Affairs, U.S. Dept. of State 1983-87; Pres. Iowa Peace Inst. 1988-; People-to-People Cttee. for the Handicapped, Countdown 2001, World Cttee.: UN Decade of 87; del. to many int. confs.; Bd. of Dirs. Global Water; Chair. American Asscn. for Int. Ageing; Disabled Persons; Professorial Lecturer in Law, The George Washington Univ. Nat. Law Center 1987-; mem. Cosmos Club, American Foreign Service Asscn., U.S. Asscn. for the Club of Rome; Superior Honour Award, Dept. of State 1972, Presidential Meritorial Service Award 1984. *Publications:* The North-South Dialogue and the United Nations 1982, How To Be a Delegate 1984, International Negotiations 1985, Perspectives on Negotiation: Four Case Studies 1986, Conflict Resolution: Track Two Diplomacy 1987, U.S.-Soviet Summitry 1987, U.S. Base Rights Negotiations 1989. *Leisure interests:* reading, tennis, fencing, skiing. *Address:* Iowa Peace Institute, Box 480, Grinnell, Ia. 50112 (Office); 2 College Park Road, Grinnell, Ia. 50112, U.S.A. (Home). *Telephone:* (515) 236-4880 (Office); (515) 236-7900 (Home).

McDONNELL, Sanford N., M.S.; American business executive; b. 12 Oct. 1922, Little Rock, Ark.; s. of William A. and Carolyn C. McDonnell; nephew of James S. McDonnell; m. Priscilla Robb 1946; one s. one d.; ed. Princeton Univ., Univ. of Colorado and Washington Univ.; joined McDonnell Aircraft Co. 1948, Vice-Pres. (Project Man.) 1959, F4H Vice-Pres. and Gen. Man. 1961, mem. Bd. of Dirs. 1962-67, mem. Finance Cttee. 1962, Exec. Cttee. 1963; Vice-Pres. Aircraft Gen. Man. 1965, Pres. 1966; Dir. McDonnell Douglas Corpn. 1967, Vice-Pres. March 1971; Exec. Vice-Pres. McDonnell Aircraft Co. March 1971; Pres. McDonnell Douglas Corpn. 1971-72, Pres. 1972-80, C.E.O. 1972-88, Chair. 1980-88; mem. Bd. of Govs. Aerospace Industries Asscn. Nov. 1974-; Fellow, American Inst. of Aeronautics and Astronautics and mem. many other professional orgs.; mem. Bd. of Dirs. First Union Bankcorpn. in St. Louis; mem. Nat. Exec. Bd., Boy Scouts of America. *Address:* McDonnell Douglas Corporation, P.O. Box 516, St. Louis, Mo. 63166 (Office); 24 Oakleigh Lane St. Louis, Mo. 63124, U.S.A. (Home).

McDOUGALL, Barbara Jean, P.C., B.A. (HONS); Canadian politician and financial analyst; b. 1937, Toronto; m; ed. Univ. of Toronto; fmr. business journalist and writer for newspapers and TV; fmr. Vice-Pres. Dominion Securities Ames Ltd., A. E. Ames and Co. Ltd.; fmr. Investment Analyst, Odlum Brown Ltd., Vancouver; Exec. Dir. Canadian Council of Financial Analysts 1982, 1983; Govt. Affairs and Financial Consultant 1982-83; Campaign Man. for the Hon. David Crombie (q.v.), Fed. elections 1979, 1980; Pres. Rosedale Progressive Conservative Asscn. 1981-82; Minister of State for Finance 1984-86, for Privatization and responsibility for the Status of Women 1986-87, Minister for Privatisation and Regulatory Affairs 1987-88, of Employment and Immigration 1988-; fmr. Chair. Vancouver Art Gallery; fmr. Chair. Community Occupational Therapy Assocs., Salvation Army Red Shield Appeal; fmr. Dir. Second Mile Club, Toronto; Progressive Conservative. *Address:* House of Commons, Ottawa, Ont., K1A 0A6, Canada.

MacDOUGALL, Sir (George) Donald (Alastair), C.B.E., F.B.A., LL.D., LITT.D., D.SC.; British economist; b. 26 Oct. 1912, Glasgow, Scotland; s. of Daniel MacDougall and Beatrice Miller; m. 1st Bridget Bartrum 1937 (dissolved 1977), one s. one d.; m. 2nd Laura Margaret, Lady Hall 1977; ed. Balliol Coll., Oxford; Asst. Lecturer, Leeds Univ. 1936-39; mem. Sir Winston Churchill's Statistical Branch 1939-45 and 1951-53; Fellow Wadham Coll., Oxford 1945-50, Nuffield Coll. 1947-64, Hon. Fellow, Wadham Coll. 1964-,

Nuffield Coll. 1967–; Reader in Int. Econs., Oxford 1951–52; Econ. Dir. OEEC, Paris 1948–49; Econ. Dir. Nat. Econ. Devt. Office 1962–64; Dir.-Gen. Dept. of Econ. Affairs 1964–68; Head of Govt. Econ. Service and Chief Econ. Adviser to Treasury 1969–73; Chief Econ. Adviser Confed. of British Industry 1973–84; Pres. Royal Econ. Soc. 1972–74; Chair. EEC Study Group on Role of Public Finance in European Integration 1975–77. *Publications:* The World Dollar Problem 1957, Studies in Political Economy (2 vols.) 1975, Don and Mandarin: Memoirs of an Economist 1987, and other books and articles on economic matters. *Leisure interest:* fishing. *Address:* 86A Denbigh Street, London, SW1V 2EX, England.

MACDOUGALL, Patrick Lorn, M.A., F.C.A.; British banker; b. 21 June 1939, Edinburgh; s. of the late J. A. Macdougall; m. 1st Alison Offer 1967 (divorced 1982); two s.; m. 2nd Bridget Young 1983; two d.; ed. Millfield School and Univ. Coll. Oxford; called to the Bar, Inner Temple 1962; Hambros Bank Ltd. 1962–63; Arthur Andersen & Co. 1963–67; N. M. Rothschild & Sons 1967–70; Dir. Rothschild Intercontinental Bank (renamed Amex Bank 1975) 1970–72, Deputy Man. Dir. 1972–75, Man. Dir. 1975–77, Chief Exec. 1977–78; Exec. Dir. Jardine Matheson & Co. Hong Kong 1978–85, Standard Chartered PLC 1988–; Chief Exec. Standard Chartered Merchant Bank Ltd., London 1985–; mem. Int. Advisory Bd. Creditanstalt-Bankverein, Vienna 1982–85. *Leisure interests:* skiing, golf, bridge. *Address:* Standard Chartered Merchant Bank Ltd., 33/36 Grace-church Street, London, EC3V 0AX (Office); 40 Stevenage Road, London, SW6 6ET, England (Home). *Telephone:* 01-623 8711 (Office); 01-736 3506 (Home).

McDOWALL, Robert John Stewart, D.SC., M.D., M.R.C.P., F.R.C.P. (Edin.); British physiologist; b. 1892, Auchengaillie; s. of Robert McDowall and Fanny Grace Stewart; m. 1st Jessie Mary Macbeth 1921 (died 1963); two d.; m. 2nd Jean Esther Rotherham 1964; ed. Edinburgh Univ.; Asst. Lecturer in Physiology, Edinburgh Univ. 1919–21; Lecturer in Experimental Physiology and Pharmacology, Leeds Univ. 1921–23; Lecturer in Applied Physiology, London School of Hygiene 1927–29; served in R.A.M.C. 1914–18, also 1940–41; Prof. of Physiology, King's Coll., London Univ. 1923–59, Prof. Emer. 1959–, Fellow; Deputy Asst. Dir. of Medical Services, Egyptian Expeditionary Force; fmr. Examiner for London, Edinburgh, Bristol, Manchester, Durham, Sheffield, Aberdeen, and Leeds Univs., Royal Coll. of Physicians and Royal Coll. of Surgeons (England, Ireland, India, Australia, Egypt and Scotland); Pres. Physiology section of British Assen. 1936; Chair. and founder mem. Medical Advisory Cttee. Asthma Research Council; Pres. European Congress of Allergy 1959; Hon. Fellow several Allergy Socs.; Arris and Gale Lecturer, Royal Coll. of Surgeons 1933; Oliver Sharpey Lecturer, Royal Coll. of Physicians 1941; Parkin Prize 1935, Cullen Prize 1938, Gold Medal, Univ. of Edinburgh 1936, Medal of Honour, Univ. of Ghent 1951. *Publications:* The Science of Signs and Symptoms in Relation to Modern Diagnosis and Treatment, Handbook of Physiology, The Control of the Circulation of the Blood 1938, A Biological Introduction to Psychology 1941, Sane Psychology 1943, The Whiskies of Scotland 1967; Ed. The Mind. *Leisure interests:* golf, chess, curling (internationalist). *Address:* Lea Rig, Crede Lane, Bosham, Nr. Chichester, West Sussex, PO18 8PD, England. *Telephone:* (0243) 572482.

McDOWALL, Roddy; British actor; b. 17 Sept. 1928, London; ed. St. Joseph's School, London; with Twentieth Century-Fox Film Corpn., Hollywood, Calif. 1940–. *Films include:* Man Hunt 1941, How Green was My Valley 1941, My Friend Flicka 1943, Lassie Come Home 1943, Macbeth 1950, The Longest Day 1962, Cleopatra 1963, Lord Love a Duck 1966, Planet of the Apes 1967, Beneath the Planet of the Apes 1970, Escape from the Planet of the Apes 1971, Conquest of the Planet of the Apes 1972, The Poseidon Adventure 1972, Battle for the Planet of the Apes 1973, Funny Lady 1975, Embryo, The Cat From Outer Space, Laserblast, Rabbit Test, Circle of Iron, Scavenger Hunt, The Devil's Widow (dir.), Class of 1984, Doing Time on Planet Earth 1987, Overboard 1987, Fright Night Part 2 1988; TV films: Flood, A Taste of Evil, The Elevator. *TV appearances include:* Hollywood Squares, Kraft Theater, Goodyear Playhouse, U.S. Steel Hour, Run for your Life, Ironside, Harry O, Love American Style, McCloud, Macmillan and Wife, Miracle on 34th Street 1973, Planet of the Apes 1974. *Stage appearances include:* Misalliance, Escapade, Doctor's Dilemma, No Time for Sergeants, Camelot, The Astrakhan Coat, Mean Johnny Barrows (all Broadway). *Address:* 222 North Cannon Drive, Beverly Hills, Calif. 90210, U.S.A.

McDOWELL, David Keith, M.A.; New Zealand diplomatist; b. 30 April 1937, Palmerston North; m.; four c.; ed. Victoria Univ. of Wellington; joined Ministry of Foreign Affairs 1959, Head, UN and African and Middle East Divs. 1973, Dir. of External Aid 1973–76, Head, Econ. Div. 1980–81, Special Asst. to Sec. Gen., Commonwealth Secr., London 1969–72; High Commr. to Fiji 1977–80, to India, Nepal and Bangladesh 1983–85; Asst. Sec. of Foreign Affairs for Asia, Australia and the Americas 1981–85; First Sec., Perm. Mission to UN 1964–68, Perm. Rep. 1985–. *Address:* Permanent Mission of New Zealand to the United Nations, One United Nations Plaza, 25th Floor, New York, N.Y. 10017, U.S.A. *Telephone:* 826-1960.

McDOWELL, Malcolm (Malcolm Taylor); British actor; b. 13 June 1943, Leeds; m. Mary Steenburgen 1980; one s. one d.; began career with the R.S.C. at Stratford 1965–66; early television appearances in such series as Dixon of Dock Green, Z Cars; stage appearance in Entertaining Mr. Sloane

(London) 1976. *Films include:* If. . . . 1969, Figures in a Landscape 1970, The Raging Moon 1971, A Clockwork Orange 1971, O Lucky Man 1973, Royal Flash 1975, Aces High 1976, Voyage of the Damned 1977, Caligula 1977, The Passage 1978, Time After Time 1979, Cat People 1981, Blue Thunder 1983, Get Crazy 1983, Britannia Hospital 1984, Gulag 1985, The Caller 1987, Sunset 1987, Class of 1999. *Plays include:* Holiday 1987. *Address:* c/o I.C.M., 8899 Beverly Blvd., Los Angeles, Calif. 90048, U.S.A.

MacEACHEN, Hon. Allan J., P.C., M.A.; Canadian politician; b. 6 July 1921, Inverness, N.S.; ed. St. Francis Xavier Univ., Univs. of Toronto and Chicago, and M.I.T.; Prof. of Econs., St. Francis Xavier Univ. 1946–48, later Head, Dept. of Econs. and Social Sciences; mem. House of Commons 1953–58, 1962–84; M.P. for Cape Breton Highlands-Inverness, N.S. 1953–; Special Asst. and Consultant on Econ. Affairs to Lester Pearson 1958; Minister of Labour 1963–65; Minister of Nat. Health and Welfare 1965–68, of Manpower and Immigration 1968–70, of Finance 1980–82; Pres. Privy Council 1970–74; Sec. of State for External Affairs 1974–76, Sept. 1982–84; Pres. Privy Council and Govt. Leader of House 1976–79, also Deputy Prime Minister 1977–79, 1980–84; Leader of Senate 1984, Leader of the Opposition in the Senate 1984–; Co-Chair. Conf. on Int. Econ. Co-operation 1975–77; Gov. IMF 1980–82 (Chair. Interim Cttee. 1981–82); Hon. D.Iur. (St. Francis Xavier Univ.) 1964, Hon. D.C.L. (Acadia Univ.) 1966, Hon. L.H.D. (Loyola Coll., Baltimore, Md.) 1966, Hon. LL.D. (St. Mary's Univ.) 1973, (Dalhousie Univ.) 1974, (Wilfrid Laurier Univ.) 1976; Liberal. *Address:* The Senate, Ottawa, K1A 0A4, Ontario (Office); R.R.1, Whycocomagh, Nova Scotia, Canada (Home).

MACEDO, Air Marshal Joelmir Campos de Araripe; Brazilian air force officer; b. Rio de Janeiro; joined Brazilian Army 1928, transferred to Air Force 1941; a pioneer of the Govt. air service linking the remote areas of Brazil to provincial capitals, Correio Aereo Nacional (CAN); has held posts of Dir. Galcão Air Factory, Pres. Nat. Engines Plant, Dir. of Air Routes, Pres. Co-ordinating Cttee. for Rio de Janeiro Int. Airport; Minister of Aeronautics 1974–79. *Address:* c/o Ministério da Aeronática, Brasília, Brazil.

MACEK, Josef, PHDR., CSC.; Czechoslovak historian; b. 8 April 1922, Řepov; ed. Charles Univ., Prague, and State Archive School, Prague; Prof., Coll. of Political and Econ. Sciences 1949; Dir. Historical Inst., Czechoslovak Acad. of Sciences 1952–69; Corresponding mem. Czechoslovak Acad. of Sciences 1952–60, mem. 1960, Academician 1960–; Chair. Czechoslovak Soc. for Dissemination of Political and Scientific Knowledge 1957–65; mem. Ideological Comm., Cen. Cttee. CP of Czechoslovakia 1963–69; Deputy to Nat. Assembly 1964–69; mem. Presidium World Peace Council 1962–70; Chair. Czechoslovak Peace Cttee. 1966–68, mem. Presidium 1968–70; Deputy to House of the People, Fed. Assembly Jan.-Dec. 1969; Cand. mem. Cen. Cttee. CP of Czechoslovakia 1962–66, mem. 1966–69, Inst. of Czech Language 1970–75, Inst. of Archaeology 1975–; State Prize 1952, Czechoslovak Peace Prize 1967. *Publications:* mainly on history of Hussite Movement in Bohemia, including Husitské revoluční hnutí (Hussite Revolutionary Movement) 1952 (State Prize), Der Tiroler Bauernkrieg und M. Gaismair 1965, Renaissance and Reformation, Il Rinascimento italiano 1972, Jean Hus et les traditions Hussites 1973, La Riforma Populare 1973, La Revolución Husita 1975, Machiavelli e il Machiavellismo 1980, Histoire de la Bohême 1984. *Address:* Institute of Archaeology, Letenská 4, Prague (Office); Kaděrákovská 1, Prague, Czechoslovakia. *Telephone:* 322013.

McELROY, William David, PH.D.; American professor and scientist; b. 22 Jan. 1917, Rogers, Tex.; s. of William D. McElroy and Ora Shipley McElroy; m. 1st Nella Winch 1940 (divorced), two s. two d.; m. 2nd Marlene Anderegg DeLuca 1967, two s.; ed. Reed Coll. and Stanford and Princeton Univs.; Instructor in Biology, Johns Hopkins Univ. 1946, Asst. Prof. 1946–48, Assoc. Prof. 1948–51, Dir. McCollum-Pratt Inst. 1949–64, Prof. of Biology 1951–69, Chair. Dept. of Biology 1956–69; Harvey Lecturer, New York Acad. of Sciences 1957; Exec. Ed. Archives of Biochemistry and Biophysics 1958–69; Ed. Biochemical and Biophysical Research Communications 1959–; Chair. AIBS Microbiology Advisory Cttee., Office of Naval Research 1952–57; mem. President's Science Advisory Cttee. 1962–67, Bd. of Dirs. of Nat. Insts. of Health 1966–; Dir. U.S. Nat. Science Foundation 1969–72; Chancellor, Univ. of Calif., San Diego 1972–80, Prof. 1980–; mem. Soc. of Biological Chemists (Pres. 1963–64), American Acad. of Arts and Sciences, A.A.A.S., Pres. 1975, Chair. Bd. of Dirs. 1977, American Inst. of Biological Sciences (Pres. 1968), N.A.S., etc.; numerous hon. degrees; Barnett Cohen Award, American Soc. of Bacteriology 1958, Rumford Prize, American Acad. of Arts and Sciences 1964. *Publications:* Cell Physiology and Biochemistry 1961; Ed. with B. Glass: Copper Metabolism 1950, Phosphorus Metabolism (2 vols.) 1951–52, Mechanism of Enzyme Action 1954, Amino Acid Metabolism 1955, Inorganic Nitrogen Metabolism 1956, The Chemical Basis of Heredity 1957, The Chemical Basis of Development 1958, Light and Life 1961; Ed. with C. P. Swanson: Foundations of Modern Biology (series) 1961–64; co-editor: Analytical Biochemistry. *Leisure interests:* golf, music, tennis. *Address:* Department of Biology, University of California, San Diego, La Jolla, Calif. 92067, U.S.A.

McENROE, John Patrick; American lawn tennis player; b. 16 Feb. 1959, Wiesbaden, Fed. Repub. of Germany; s. of John P. McEnroe I and Katy McEnroe; m. Tatum O'Neal (q.v.) 1986; two s.; ed. Trinity High School, N.J., and Stanford Univ., Calif.; amateur player 1976–78, professional

1978–; U.S.A. singles Champion 1979, 1980, 1981, 1984; U.S.A. doubles Champion 1979, 1981; Wimbledon Champion (doubles) 1979, 1981, 1983, 1984 (singles) 1981, 1983, 1984; WCT Champion 1979, 1981, 1983, 1984, 1989; Grand Prix Champion 1979, 1983, 1984; played Davis Cup for U.S.A. 1978, 1979, 1980, 1981, 1982, 1983, 1984, 1985; only player to have reached the Wimbledon semi-finals (1977) as pre-tournament qualifier. *Leisure interest:* music. *Address:* c/o U.S. Tennis Association, 51 East 42nd Street, New York, N.Y. 10017, U.S.A.

McENTEE, Peter Donovan, C.M.G., O.B.E.; British soldier, colonial civil servant and diplomatist; b. 27 June 1920, England; s. of Ewen Brooke McEntee and Caroline Laura Clare Bayley; m. Mary Elisabeth Sherwood 1945; two d.; ed. Haileybury Coll., Herts.; served in King's African Rifles 1939–45; H.M. Overseas Civil Service 1946–63; Dist. Commr., later Prin. of Kenya Inst. of Admin.; H.M. Diplomatic Service 1963–67, First Sec., Lagos 1964–67; Commonwealth Office, later FCO 1967–72; Consul-Gen., Karachi 1972–75; Gov. and C.-in-C., Belize 1976–80; mem. Council, Royal Commonwealth Soc. for the Blind, Royal Overseas League. *Leisure interests:* music, natural history, golf, reading. *Address:* Woodlands, Church Lane, Danehill, Sussex, RH17 7EU.

McEWAN, Angus David, B.E., M.ENG.SC., PH.D., F.A.A.; Australian oceanographer; b. 20 July 1937, Alloa, Scotland; s. of David R. McEwan and Anne Marion McEwan; m. Juliana K. Britten 1961 (divorced 1982); two d.; ed. Melbourne High School, Caulfield Tech. Coll., Melbourne Univ., Cambridge Univ.; engineer, Aeronautical Research Labs., Melbourne 1956–58, Research Scientist 1961–62, 1966–69; Research Scientist, Program Leader, Chief Research Scientist, Div. of Atmospheric Research, CSIRO, Aspendale, Vic. 1972–81, Foundation Chief, Div. of Oceanography, Hobart 1981–; Hon. Research Prof. Univ. of Tasmania 1988; mem., Chair., Int. Oceanography Div. (IOC), Scientific Cttee. for Oceanic Research (SCOR), Cttee. on Climatic Changes; Australian Nat. Del., ASEAN, IOC, SCOR and numerous other nat. bodies and cttees.; Queen Elizabeth Fellow 1969–71; Rossby Fellow (Woods Hole Ocean. Inst.) 1975. *Publications:* scientific articles on geophysical fluid dynamics. *Leisure interests:* sailing, sketching, woodwork. *Address:* Box 1538, Hobart, Tasmania 7001; 300 Sandy Bay Road, Sandy Bay, Tasmania 7005, Australia. *Telephone:* (61) 02-206212; (61) 02-234912.

McEWAN, Geraldine; British actress; b. 9 May 1932, Old Windsor, Berks.; d. of Donald and Norah McKeown; m. Hugh Cruttwell 1953; one s. one d.; ed. Windsor County Girls' School; first engagement with Theatre Royal, Windsor 1949; London appearances in Who Goes There? 1951, Sweet Madness, For Better, For Worse, Summertime; Shakespeare Memorial Theatre, Stratford on Avon 1956, 1958, 1961 playing Princess of France (Love's Labours Lost), Olivia (Twelfth Night), Ophelia (Hamlet), Marina (Pericles), Beatrice (Much Ado about Nothing); played in School for Scandal, U.S.A. 1962, The Private Ear and The Public Eye, U.S.A. 1963; mem. Nat. Theatre 1965–71, and has played in Armstrong's Last Goodnight, Love for Love, A Flea in Her Ear, The Dance of Death, Edward II, Home and Beauty, Rites, The Way of the World, The White Devil, Amphitryon 38, Dear Love 1973, Chez Nous 1974, The Little Hut 1974, Oh Coward! (musical) 1975, On Approval 1975, Look After Lulu 1978, The Browning Version 1980, Harlequinade 1980, The Provoked Wife 1980–81, The Rivals (Evening Standard Drama Award for Best Actress), You Can't Take It With You 1983–84, A Lie of the Mind 1987, Lettice and Lovage 1988–89; Dir. As You Like It 1988; TV: The Prime of Miss Jean Brodie (TV Critics Best Actress Award) 1978, L'Elégance 1982, The Barchester Chronicles 1982, Come Into the Garden, Maude 1982, Mapp and Lucia 1985–86, Foreign Body (film) 1986, Henry V (film). *Address:* c/o Marmont Management Ltd., 303-308 Regent Street, London, W.1, England.

McEWAN, Ian, M.A.; British author; b. 21 June 1948, Aldershot, Hants.; s. of David McEwan and Rose Moore; m. Penny Allen 1982; two s. and two step-d.; ed. Woolverstone Hall, Univs. of Sussex and E. Anglia; Somerset Maugham Prize 1975; Primo Letterario, Prato 1982; Whitbread Fiction Prize 1987. *Publications:* First Love, Last Rites 1975, In Between the Sheets 1978, The Cement Garden 1978, The Imitation Game 1980, The Comfort of Strangers 1981, Or Shall we Die? 1983, The Ploughman's Lunch 1983, The Child in Time 1987, Soursweet (screenplay) 1987. *Address:* c/o Jonathan Cape, 32 Bedford Square, London, WC1B 3EL, England.

McFADZEAN, Baron (Life Peer), cr. 1966, of Woldingham; **William (Hunter) McFadzean,** K.T., C.A., C.I.E.E., J.DIP.M.A.; British chartered accountant; b. 17 Dec. 1903, Stranraer; s. of the late Henry McFadzean; m. Eileen Gordon 1933; one s. two d. (one adopted); ed. Stranraer Acad. and High School, and Glasgow Univ.; Chartered Accountant, Chalmers Impey & Co. 1927–32; joined British Insulated Cables Ltd. as Accountant 1932, apptd. Financial Sec. 1937, Exec. Man. 1942; on amalgamation of British Insulated Cables Ltd. and Callender's Cable & Construction Co. Ltd. in 1945 apptd. to the Bd. of BICC, also Exec. Dir.; Deputy Chair. 1947, Chief Exec. Dir. 1950, Man. Dir. 1954–61, Chair. 1954–73, Hon. Pres. 1973–; Dir. Midland Bank Ltd. 1959–81, Deputy Chair. 1968–77; Dir. Midland Bank Trust Co. Ltd. 1959–67, English Electric Co. Ltd. 1966–68, Steel Co. of Wales Ltd. 1966–67, Canadian Imperial Bank of Commerce 1967–74 (now Dir. Emer.), Home Oil Co. Ltd. 1972–77, Standard Broadcasting Corpn. Ltd. 1976–79; Deputy Chair. RTZ/BICC Aluminium Holdings Ltd. 1967–73; Dir. Anglesey Aluminium Ltd. 1968–73, The Canada Life Assurance Co. 1969–79 (now Hon. Dir.); Dir. The Canada Life Assurance Co. (G.B.) 1971- (Deputy Chair. 1971–82); Deputy Chair. Canada Life Unit Trust Managers Ltd. 1971– (Chair. 1971–82); Chair. Standard Broadcasting Corpn. (U.K.) Ltd. 1972–79, Home Oil (U.K.) Ltd. 1972–78; mem. Council Inst. of Dirs. 1954–74, Ministry of Labour Advisory Bd. on Resettlement of Ex-Regulars 1957–60, Bd. of Trade Advisory Council on Middle East Trade 1958–60; Pres. Fed. British Industries 1959–61; Chair. Council of Industrial Feds. of European Free Trade Asscns. 1960–63, Export Council for Europe 1960–64, Hon. Pres. 1964–71; Pres. British Electrical Power Convention 1961–62; mem. Ministry of Transport Shipping Advisory Panel 1962–64; Vice-Pres. British/Swedish Chamber of Commerce 1963–74; Pres. British Nuclear Forum 1964–66; mem. Court of British Shippers' Council 1964–74; (Pres. 1968–71); Chair. British Nat. Export Council 1964–66, Pres. 1966–68; Chair. Commonwealth Export Council 1964–66; Vice-Pres. Middle East Asscn. 1965, 1986, City of London Soc. 1965–72; mem. Council Anglo-Danish Soc. 1965–75, Chair. 1969–84, Hon. Pres. 1975–; mem. Advisory Cttee. for The Queen's Award to Industry 1965–67, Chair. Review Cttee. for 1970; mem. Council CBI 1965–74; Pres. The Coal Trade Benevolent Asscn. 1967–68; mem. Council Foreign Bondholders 1968–74; Pres. The Electrical and Electronics Industries Benevolent Asscn. 1968–69; Deputy Chair. Nat. Nuclear Corpn. Ltd. 1973–80; Companion I.E.E. 1956; Grand Officer Order of Infante Dom Henrique (Portugal) 1972, Grand Commdr. Order of the Dannebrog (Denmark) 1974. *Leisure interests:* travelling, golf, gardening. *Address:* 16 Lansdown Crescent, Bath, Avon, BA1 5EX; and 114 Whitehall Court, London, SW1A 2EL, England. *Telephone:* (0225) 335487; 01-930 3160 (London).

McFADZEAN OF KELVINSIDE, Baron (Life Peer), cr. 1980, of Kelvinside in the district of the City of Glasgow; **Francis (Frank) Scott McFadzean,** M.A.; British oil and airline executive (retd.); b. 26 Nov. 1915, Troon, Ayrshire; m. Isabel McKenzie Beattie 1938; one d.; ed. Glasgow Univ. and L.S.E.; fmr. civil servant, Bd. of Trade and the Treasury; later worked for Malayan Govt. and Colonial Devt. Corpn. in Far East; joined Shell 1952, held various posts in Middle East, Far East and London; Dir. Shell Int. Petroleum Co. 1962, Shell Oil Co. 1972–76; Dir. Shell Transport and Trading Co. Ltd. 1964–86, Man. Dir. 1971, Chair. 1972–76, subsequently non-Exec. Dir.; Man. Dir. Royal Dutch/Shell Group of Cos. 1964–76; Man. Dir. Shell Petroleum Co. Ltd. 1964–72, Chair. 1972–76; Man. Dir. Bataafse Petroleum Maatschappij N.V. (now Shell Petroleum N.V.) 1964–72, Chair. Shell Int. Marine Ltd. 1966–76; Chair. Shell Canada Ltd. 1970–76; Dir. Beecham Group 1974–86, British Airways 1975–79, Chair. and Chief Exec. 1976–78, Part-time Chair. 1978–79; Chair. and Chief Exec. Rolls-Royce Ltd. 1980–83; non-Exec. Dir. Coats Patons Ltd. 1979–86; Visiting Prof. of Econs., Univ. of Strathclyde 1967–76; Chair. Trade Policy Research Centre 1971–82; mem. Steering Bd., Strathclyde Div., Scottish Business School 1970–76; Hon. LL.D. (Strathclyde) 1970, Hon. Fellow, L.S.E. 1974; Commdr., Order of Orange-Nassau. *Publications:* Galbraith and the Planners 1968, Energy in the Seventies 1971, The Operation of a Multi-National Enterprise 1971, Towards an Open World Economy (with others) 1972, The Economics of John Kenneth Galbraith 1977, Global Strategy for Growth—A Report on North-South Issues (with others) 1981. *Address:* House of Lords, Westminster, London, S.W.1, England.

McFALL, Richard Graham; British commodity merchant; b. 31 Jan. 1920, Blundellsands, Lancs.; s. of Henry Joseph Marshall McFall and Sarah Gertrude McFall; m. Louise Mitford 1945; one s. one d.; ed. Clifton Coll., Bristol; joined Pacol Ltd. 1938; served Hon. Artillery Co. 1939–40; Asst. Sec., then Sec. W. African Produce Control Bd. 1941–45; Motor and Air Products Ltd. 1946–48; rejoined Pacol Ltd. 1949, Dir. 1951–79; Chair. London Cocoa Terminal Market Asscn. 1954–55, Cocoa Asscn. of London Ltd. 1958–59; Dir. Gill & Duffus Group Ltd. 1962–82, Man. Dir. 1965–71, Chair. 1971–76, Vice-Chair. 1976–78; Chair. Fleming Enterprise Investment Trust PLC 1980–86. *Leisure interests:* travel, golf. *Address:* Springfold Cottage, Green Dene, East Horsley, Surrey, KT24 5RG, England (Home). *Telephone:* (048 65) 3282 (Home).

MACFARLANE, Alan Donald James, D.PHIL., PH.D., M.A., F.B.A.; British academic; b. 20 Dec. 1941, Assam, India; s. of Donald Macfarlane and Iris Macfarlane; m. 1st Gillian Ions 1965, 2nd Sarah Harrison 1981; one d.; ed. Sedbergh School, Worcester Coll., Oxford, London School of Econs. and School of Oriental & African Studies, London Univ.; Sr. Research Fellow, in History, King's Coll. Cambridge 1971–75; Lecturer in Social Anthropology, Univ. of Cambridge 1975–81, Reader in Historical Anthropology 1981–; Fellow, King's Coll., Cambridge 1981–; Rivers Memorial Medal 1984. *Publications:* Witchcraft in Tudor and Stuart England 1970, Family Life of Ralph Josselin 1970, The Diary of Ralph Josselin (Ed.) 1976, Resources and Population 1976, The Origins of English Individualism 1977, The Justice and the Mare's Ale 1981, Marriage and Love in England 1986, The Culture of Capitalism 1987. *Leisure interests:* gardening, walking, music. *Address:* King's College, Cambridge, CB2 1ST; 25 Lode Road, Lode, nr. Cambridge, CB5 9FR, England. *Telephone:* (0223) 811976.

MacFARLANE, Alistair George James, C.B.E., D.SC., PH.D., SC.D., F.R.S., F.ENG.; British professor of engineering; b. 9 May 1931; s. of George R. MacFarlane; m. Nora Williams 1954; one s.; ed. Hamilton Acad., Univ. of Glasgow, Univ. of London, Univ. of Manchester; with Metropolitan-Vickers, Manchester 1953–58; Lecturer Queen Mary Coll., Univ. of London 1959–65, Reader 1965–66; Reader in Control Eng. UMIST 1966–69, Prof. 1969–74;

Prof. of Eng. Univ. of Cambridge 1974–; Fellow Selwyn Coll., Cambridge 1974–, Vice-Master 1980–; Chair. Cambridge Control Ltd. 1985–; mem. Council SERC 1981–85, Computer Bd. 1983–. *Publications:* Engineering Systems Analysis 1964, Dynamical System Models 1970, (with I. Postlethwaite) A Complex Variable Approach to the Analysis of Linear Multivariable Feedback Systems 1979, (Ed.) Frequency-Response Methods in Control Systems 1979, (Ed.) Complex Variable Methods for Linear Multivariable Feedback Systems 1980, (with S. Hung) Multivariable Feedback: a quasi-classical approach 1982, (with G. K. H. Pang) An Expert Systems Approach to Computer-Aided Design of Multivariable Systems 1987. *Address:* Selwyn College, Cambridge (Office); 9 Dane Drive, Newnham, Cambridge CB3 9LP, England (Home).

MACFARLANE, Sir George Gray, C.B., B.SC., DR.ING., F.ENG.; British consultant scientist; b. 8 Jan. 1916, Airdrie; s. of the late John Macfarlane; m. Barbara Grant Thomson 1941; one s. one d.; ed. Airdrie Acad., Glasgow Univ., Tech. Hochschule, Dresden, Germany; Telecommunications Research Establishment 1939–60; Deputy Dir. Nat. Physical Lab., Teddington 1960–62; Dir. Royal Radar Establishment, Malvern 1962–67; Controller of Research, Ministry of Tech. and Ministry of Aviation Supply 1967–71; Controller of Research and Devt. Establishments and Research, Ministry of Defence 1971–76; mem. Post Office Bd. 1978–81; mem. British Telecom Bd. 1981–87; now in private consultancy; mem. Nat. Enterprise Bd. 1980–85, Nat. Research Devt. Corpn. 1981–85; Fellow, Inst. of Math. and its Applications; Trustee Imperial War Museum 1978–; Vice-Pres. Fellowship of Eng. 1983–86; Hon. F.I.E.E. 1988; Hon. LL.D. (Glasgow). *Publications:* articles in Proceedings of the Physical Society, Physics Review, Proceedings of the Institution of Electrical Engineers, Philosophical Magazine. *Leisure interests:* gardening, walking. *Address:* Red Tiles, Orchard Way, Esher, Surrey, England. *Telephone:* (0372) 63778.

McFARLANE, Ian Dalrymple, M.B.E., M.A., F.B.A.; British academic (retd.); b. 7 Nov. 1915, Newcastle-upon-Tyne; s. of James Blair McFarlane and Valérie Edith Liston Dalrymple; m. Marjory Nan Hamilton 1939; one s. one d.; ed. Westminster School, St. Andrews Univ., Univ. of Paris; war service in Black Watch 1939–45; P.O.W. 1940–45; lecturer, Univ. of Cambridge 1945–61; Fellow Gonville and Caius Coll., Cambridge 1947–61, Sr. Tutor 1956–61; Prof. of French, Univ. of St. Andrews 1961–70; Prof. of French Literature, Univ. of Oxford (Professorial Fellow, Wadham Coll.) 1971–83, Prof. Emer. 1983–; Visiting Fellow, Univ. of Virginia 1983; Pres. Int. Asscn. of Neo-Latin Studies 1979–82; Pres. Modern Humanities Research Asscn. 1986; Officier des Palmes Académiques 1971; Hon. D.Litt. (St. Andrews) 1982; Dr. h.c. (Univ. of Tours) 1983. *Publications:* Renaissance France 1470–1589 1974, Buchanan 1981, Critical edition of Maurice Scèves Délie 1966, The Entry of Henry II into Paris 1549 1982. *Leisure interests:* music, cricket. *Address:* Wadham College, Oxford, England.

MACFARLANE, Sir Norman Somerville, Kt.; British business executive; s. of Daniel Robertson Macfarlane and Jessie Lindsay Somerville; m. Marguerite Mary Campbell 1953; one s. four d.; ed. Glasgow High School; f. N. S. Macfarlane and Co. Ltd. 1949, Chair. and Man. Dir. 1973–; Chair. Scottish Industrialists Council 1975–; Dir. Glasgow Chamber of Commerce 1976–79; Chair. The Fine Art Soc. PLC 1976–; Underwriting mem. of Lloyds 1978–; Dir. American Trust PLC 1980–, Chair. 1984–; Dir. Clydesdale Bank PLC 1980–; Dir. Edinburgh Fund Mans. PLC 1980–; Dir. Gen. Accident Fire and Life Assurance Corpn. PLC 1984–; Chair. Guinness Co. 1987–89, Jt. Deputy Chair. May 1989–; United Distillers PLC 1987–; Dir. Scottish Ballet 1975–, Vice-Chair. 1983–87; Pres. Royal Glasgow Inst. of the Fine Arts 1976–; Dir. Scottish Nat. Orchestra 1977–82; Bd. Scottish Devt. Agency 1979–; Gov. Glasgow School of Art 1976–; Chair. Govs., High School of Glasgow 1979–; mem. Court, Glasgow Univ. 1979–; Trustee, Nat. Heritage Memorial Fund 1984–. *Leisure interests:* golf, cricket, theatre, art. *Address:* Macfarlane Group (Clansman) PLC, Sutcliffe Road, Glasgow, G13 1AH, Scotland.

MCFARLANE, Robert Carl, M.S.; American government official; b. 12 July 1937, Washington, D.C.; s. of William McFarlane and Alma Carl; m. Jonda Riley 1959; one s. two d.; ed. U.S. Naval Acad. and Inst. des Hautes Etudes, Geneva; U.S. Marine Corps, Second Lieut. rising to Lieut.-Col. 1959–79; White House Fellow, Exec. Asst. Council to Pres. for Legis. Affairs 1971–72; Mil. Asst. to Henry Kissinger (q.v.) 1973–75; Exec. Asst. to Asst. to Pres. for Nat. Security Affairs 1975–76; Special Asst. to Pres. 1976–77; Research Fellow Nat. Defence Univ., Washington, D.C. 1977–78; mem. Professional Staff Senate Comm. on Armed Services 1979–81; Counsellor Dept. of State 1981–82; Deputy Asst. to Pres., Nat. Security Affairs 1982–83; Personal Rep. of U.S. Pres. in Middle East July–Oct. 1983; Asst. to Pres. for Nat. Security Affairs 1983–85; received 2 year suspended sentence for illegal activity in Iran Contra Scandal March 1988; fined $5,000 on each of four charges and ordered to do 200 hours Community Service; Distinguished Service Medal and other medals and awards. *Publications:* At Sea Where We Belong 1971, Crisis Revolution (co-author) 1978, The Political Potential of Parity 1979. *Address:* 3414 Prospect Street, N.W. Washington, D.C. 20007-3218, U.S.A. (Home).

McGAHERN, John; Irish writer; b. 12 Nov. 1934, Dublin; s. of Francis McGahern and Susan McManus; m. Madeline Green 1973; ed. Presentation Coll., Carrick-on-Shannon, St. Patrick's Coll. and Univ. Coll. Dublin; Primary School Teacher 1955–64; Research Fellow, Univ. of Reading, England 1968–71; Northern Arts Fellow, Univs. of Durham and Newcastle upon Tyne, England 1974–76; Visiting Prof., Colgate Univ., New York, U.S.A. 1969, 1972, 1977, 1980, 1983; Literary Fellow, Trinity Coll., Dublin 1988; mem. Irish Acad. of Letters; Fellow Royal Literary Soc.; mem. Aosdana; AE Memorial Award; Macauley Fellowship, Arts Council of G.B. Award; Soc. of Authors Travelling Fellowship; American Irish Award. *Publications:* The Barracks 1963, The Dark 1965, Nightlines 1970, The Leavetaking 1975, Getting Through 1978, The Pornographer 1979, High Ground 1985, The Rockingham Shoot 1987. *Address:* c/o Faber & Faber, 3 Queen Square, London, WC1 3AU, England.

McGEE, Gale William, PH.D.; American professor and politician; b. 17 March 1915, Lincoln, Neb.; m. Loraine Baker 1939; two s. two d.; ed. Nebraska State Teachers' Coll., Univs. of Colorado and Chicago; High School teacher 1936–40; History Instructor, Neb. Wesleyan Univ. 1940–43, Iowa State Coll. 1943–44, Univ. of Notre Dame 1944–45, Univ. of Chicago 1945–46; Prof. of History, Univ. of Wyoming 1946–58; Senator from Wyoming 1958–77; U.S. Perm. Rep. to OAS 1977–81; Pres. Gale W. McGee Assocs. 1981–, ALESA (American League for Export and Security Assistance) 1986–; Sr. Consultant, Hill and Knowlton Inc. 1987–; Chair. Senate Post Office and Civil Service Cttee.; mem. Senate Appropriations and Foreign Relations Cttees., Nat. Comm. on Food Marketing; Hon. LL.D. (Wyoming, Eastern Kentucky, American Univ. Washington, Allegheny); Hon. L.H.D. (Seton Hall); Golden Fleece Award 1966; Torch of Liberty Award 1966; several other awards; Democrat. *Publication:* The Responsibilities of World Power 1968. *Address:* 7205 Marbury Road, Bethesda, Md. 20817, U.S.A.

McGHEE, George C., D.PHIL.; American government official and business executive; b. 10 March 1912, Waco, Tex.; s. of George Summers McGhee and Magnolia Spruce; m. Cecilia DeGolyer 1938; two s. four d.; ed. Southern Methodist Univ., Dallas, Univ. of Oklahoma, Oxford Univ. and Univ. of London; Subsurface Geologist, The Atlantic Refining Co. 1930–31; Geophysicist, Continental Oil Co. 1933–34; Vice-Pres. Nat. Geophysical Co., Dallas 1937–39; Partner DeGolyer, MacNaughton and McGhee 1940–41; independent explorer for and producer of oil 1940–; Sr. Liaison Officer OPM and WPB 1941–43; U.S. Deputy Exec. Sec. Combined Raw Materials Bd. 1942–43; Special Asst. to the Under-Sec. of State for Econ. Affairs 1946–47; Co-ordinator for Aid to Greece and Turkey, Dept. of State 1947–49; Special Rep. of Sec. of State to Near East on Palestine Refugee problem with personal rank of Minister 1949; Special Asst. to Sec. of State 1949; Asst. Sec. Near East, South Asian and African Affairs 1949–51; Amb. to Turkey 1951–53; Adviser N.A.T.O. Council, Ottawa 1951; Dir. Inst. of Inter-American Affairs, Inter-American Educ. Foundation 1946–51; Dir. U.S. Commercial Co. 1946; Dir. Foreign Service Educ. Foundation 1947–; Consultant, Nat. Security Council 1958–59; Counsellor, Dept. of State and Chair. Policy Planning Council Jan.-Nov. 1961; Under-Sec. of State for Political Affairs 1961–63; Amb. to Fed. Repub. of Germany 1963–68; Amb. at Large 1968–69; Dir. Panama Canal Co. 1962–63, Mobil Oil Co. 1969–82, Procter & Gamble Co. 1969–82, American Security & Trust Co. 1969–82, Trans World Airlines 1976–82; Chair. of Bd. Saturday Review/World 1973–76; Chair. Smithsonian Assocs. 1976–78; Owner McGhee Production Co.; Dir. of Trustees, Robert Coll., Istanbul 1953–61, Brookings Inst. 1954–61, Cttee. for Econ. Devt. 1957–, Aspen Inst. Humanistic Studies 1958–, Vassar Coll. 1959–61, Duke Univ. 1962–78; Chair. Business Council for Int. Understanding 1969–74; Chair. English Speaking Union, U.S.A. 1970–74, Deputy Chair. Int. Council of the English Speaking Union 1974; Chair. Nat. Trust for Historic Preservation 1971–75, Int. Man. and Devt. Inst. 1972–, Fed. City Housing Corpn. 1972–, Piedmont Environmental Council; Trustee, George C. Marshall Research Foundation, American Council on Germany, The American Univ., The Asia Foundation 1974–; Dir. Atlantic Council 1975–, Atlantic Inst. for Int. Affairs 1977–, Cordier Fellow, Advisory Council, Columbia Univ. 1977–; Pres. Fed. City Council 1970–74, etc.; mem. Bd. Nat. Civil Service League 1967–71, Salzburg Seminar 1969–71; mem. Japan-U.S. Econ. Advisory Council 1970–74, American Petroleum Inst., American Asscn. Petroleum Geologists, Soc. of Exploring Geophysicists, American Inst. Mining and Metallurgical Engineers, Council on Foreign Relations (New York), American Foreign Service Asscn., Acad. of Political Science, Washington Inst. of Foreign Affairs, Dept. of Conservation and Econ. Devt., Club of Rome; mem. Bd. of Trustees, American Univ. 1981–, Council of American Ambs. 1984–, Visiting Cttee. for Arthur M. Sackler Gallery at Smithsonian Inst. 1986–; Vice-Chair. Bd. of Dirs. Inst. for the Study of Diplomacy, Georgetown Univ.; served in U.S.N.R. 1943–46; Lieut.-Col. U.S.A.F. Reserve 1949–; Hon. Fellow, Queen's Coll., Oxford 1968; Hon. LL.D. (Tulane Univ.) 1957, (Maryland Univ.) 1965; Hon. D.C.L. (Southern Methodist Univ.) 1953; Hon. D.Sc. (Univ. of Tampa) 1969; Legion of Merit; Asiatic Ribbon with three battle stars; mem. Order Hospital St. John of Jerusalem 1972–, numerous other awards. *Publications:* Envoy to the Middle World 1983, Ed. Diplomacy for the Future 1987. *Address:* 2808 N Street, N.W., Washington, D.C. 20007, U.S.A. *Telephone:* (202) 338-8472 (Home).

McGILL, Archie Joseph, Jr., B.A.; American business executive; b. 29 May 1931, Winona, Minn.; s. of Archibald Joseph and Anne (Lettner) McGill; m. Jeanne Sullivan 1974; four s. three d.; ed. St. Mary's Coll., Winona; served U.S.A.F. 1951–54; with IBM Corpn. 1956–69; Founder and Chair. McGill Assocs., White Plains 1970–73; Dir. Market Man. AT&T

Co. 1973-78, Vice-Pres. Business Marketing 1978-83; Pres. Advanced Information Systems American Bell Inc. 1983, Chardonnay Inc. 1985-; Chair. and C.E.O. Rothschild Ventures Inc. 1983-; Dir. MSI Data; mem. Special Advisory Cttee. Pres.'s Council on Physical Fitness and Sports 1981; Bd. of Dirs. Fertility Research Foundation 1983- and of numerous other cos. *Leisure interests:* golf, skiing, racing. *Address:* 289 Mount Harmony Road, Bernardsville, N.J. 07924, U.S.A. *Telephone:* (201) 221-1850.

McGILL, William James, PH.D.; American university president; b. 27 Feb. 1922, New York; s. of William E. and Edna (née Rankin) McGill; m. Ann Rowe 1948; one s. one d.; ed. Fordham Coll. and Fordham and Harvard Univs.; Instructor, Fordham Univ. and Boston Coll., then Teaching Fellow at Harvard Univ.; at Lincoln Lab., M.I.T. 1951, Asst. Prof. 1954; Asst. Prof. of Psychology, Columbia Univ., N.Y. 1956-58, Assoc. Prof. 1958-60, Prof. 1960-65, Pres. 1970-80, Pres. Emer. 1980-; Prof. of Psychology, Univ. of Calif. at San Diego, at same time serving as mem. and Chair. of Cttee. on Educ. Policy and as mem. of Academic Council of Academic Senate and of Chancellor's Senate Council 1965-68, Chair. of state-wide Academic Senate and Chancellor of Univ. of Calif. at San Diego 1968-70; Chair. Carnegie Comm. on Future of Public Broadcasting 1977-79; Dir. American Telephone and Telegraph Co. 1972-80, American Council on Educ. 1972-78, McGraw Hill Co. 1973-, Texaco Inc. 1973-80, Lounsbery Foundation 1980-, Occidental Petroleum Co. 1981-, Weingart Foundation 1983-; Trustee Trinity School 1972-80, United World Coll. of the American West 1982-; Assoc. Ed., Journal of Mathematical Psychology 1964-, Perception and Psychophysics 1966-70; Consulting Ed., Psychological Bulletin 1966-70, Psychometrika 1965-70; Fellow, A.A.A.S. 1963, American Psychological Asscn. 1967, mem. Soc. of Experimental Psychologists, Gov. Bd. Psychonomic Soc. 1965-71, American Statistical Asscn., Psychometric Soc. (also on Bd. of Trustees 1967-), Biometric Soc.; Achievement Award of Fordham Univ. 1968; Gold Medal, Nat. Inst. of Social Sciences 1980. *Publications:* Over 35 studies and reviews. *Address:* 2624 Costebelle Drive, La Jolla, Calif. 92037, U.S.A.

McGILLICUDDY, John Francis, LL.B.; American banker; b. 30 Dec. 1930, Harrison, N.Y.; s. of Michael McGillicuddy and Anna Munro; m. Constance Burtis 1954; three s. two d.; ed. Princeton Univ. and Harvard Law School; Sr. Vice-Pres. Mfrs. Hanover Trust Co. 1966, Exec. Vice-Pres. and Asst. to Chair. 1969, Vice-Chair. and Dir. Jan. 1970-71, Pres. 1971-82, Chair., C.E.O. 1979-; Dir. Dart and Kraft Inc., Westinghouse Electric Corpn., Continental Corpn., A.M.F., Inc.; Pres. Nat. Multiple Sclerosis Soc. 1977-; Trustee, Princeton Univ. *Address:* Manufacturers Hanover Trust Co., 270 Park Avenue, New York, N.Y. 10022 (Office); Hilltop Place, Rye, N.Y. 10580, U.S.A. (Home). *Telephone:* (212) 286-5381 (Office).

McGOVERN, George Stanley, PH.D.; American politician; b. 19 July 1922, Avon, S. Dakota; s. of Rev. J. C. McGovern and Frances McLean McGovern; m. Eleanor Faye Stegeberg 1943; one s. four d.; ed. Dakota Wesleyan Univ. and Northwestern Univ.; served U.S.A.F., Second World War; Teacher, Northwestern Univ. 1948-50; Prof. of History and Political Science, Dakota Wesleyan Univ. 1950-53; Exec. Sec. S. Dak. Dem. Party 1953-56; mem. U.S. House of Reps. 1957-61, served Agricultural Cttee.; Dir. "Food for Peace" Programme 1961-62; Senator from South Dakota 1963-81; partner John Kornmeier Assocs., Washington 1981-; lecturer, North-Western Univ., Chicago 1981; Dem. cand. for U.S. Presidency 1972, 1984; Chair. Americans for Common Sense 1981-. *Publications:* The Colorado Coal Strike 1913-14 1953, War Against Want 1964, Agricultural Thought in the Twentieth Century 1967, A Time of War, a Time of Peace 1968, The Great Coalfield War (with Leonard Guttridge) 1972, An American Journey 1974, Grassroots (autobiog.) 1978. *Address:* P.O. Box 5591, Friendship Station, Washington, D.C. 20016, U.S.A.

McGOVERN, R. Gordon, M.B.A.; American business executive; b. 22 Oct. 1926, Norristown, Pa.; s. of James Joseph and Marian (née Stritzinger) McGovern; m. Julia Hull Merrow 1955; one s. three d.; ed. Williams Coll., Holy Cross Coll., Brown Univ., Providence, R.I., and Graduate School of Business Admin., Harvard Univ.; Production Planner and Scheduler, Merck Inc., N.J. 1950-54; Lieut. U.S. Army 1952-54; Production Trainee, Pepperidge Farm Inc., Downingtown, Pa. 1956-57, successively Production Supervisor, Asst. Plant Man., Div. Man. 1957-63, Dir. Marketing, Bakery Div., then Vice-Pres. Marketing 1963-68, Pres. Pepperidge Farm Inc. 1968-80; Exec. Vice-Pres. Campbell Soup Co., Camden, N.J. 1980, Pres. 1980-, also C.E.O. *Leisure interests:* vegetable gardening, travel, sports (tennis). *Address:* Campbell Soups Co., Campbell Place, Camden, N.J. 08101; 182 Lounsbury Road, Ridgefield, Conn. 06877, and 527 Pine Street, Philadelphia, Pa. 19106, U.S.A. (Homes).

McGRATH, James A., P.C.; Canadian politician and administrator; b. 11 Jan. 1932, Buchans, Newfoundland; m. Margaret Smart; one s. five d.; Service R.C.A.F. 1950; radio and TV post; Prov. Sec. Conservative Party 1955-57; M.P. for St. John's East 1957-65, 1968-84; Parl. Sec. to Minister of Mines and Tech. Surveys 1962-63; Exec. Asst. to Leader of the Opposition, Senate 1963-65; Pres. Progressive Conservative Asscn., Newfoundland 1965-68; mem. successive Shadow Cabinets 1968-79, 1980-84; Minister of Fisheries and Oceans 1979-80; Chair. Special Cttee. on Reform of House of Commons 1984; Vice-Chair. Canadian Br. Commonwealth Parl. Asscn. 1984; Gov. of Newfoundland 1986-; Hon. LL.D. (St. Francis Xavier);

Queen's Jubilee Medal; Kt. Sovereign Order of Malta, Kt. St. J. *Address:* Government House, St. John's, Newfoundland, Canada.

McGRATH, Most Rev. Archbishop Marcos Gregorio, S.T.D.; Panamanian ecclesiastic; b. 10 Feb. 1924, Panama; ed. La Salle Mil. Acad., Catholic Univ., Chile, Univ. Notre Dame, Holy Cross Theology Coll. and Catholic Inst., Paris; Dean Theological Coll., Catholic Univ., Santiago 1959-61, Auxiliary Bishop, Panama 1961-64, Bishop 1964-69; Archbishop of Panama 1969-; mem. Doctrinal Comm., 2nd Vatican Council 1962-65; Vice-Pres. Council of Latin America Bishops 1967-72; Hon Dr. (Notre Dame), (Georgetown), (Louvain). *Publications:* articles in theological journals and others on int. affairs. *Address:* Apartado 6386, Panama 5, Republic of Panama. *Telephone:* 62-9669 (Office); 26-4792 (Home).

McGREGOR, Sir Ian Alexander, Kt., C.B.E., F.R.C.P., F.F.C.M., D.T.M. & H., F.R.S., F.R.S.E.; British medical scientist; b. 26 Aug. 1922, Cambuslang, Lanarks.; s. of John McGregor and Isabella Taylor; m. Nancy J. Small 1954; one s. one d.; ed. Rutherglen Acad. and St. Mungo's Coll., Glasgow; mem. scientific staff, M.R.C. Human Nutrition Unit 1949-53; Dir. M.R.C. Labs., The Gambia 1954-74, 1978-80; Head, Lab. of Tropical Community Studies, Nat. Inst. for Medical Research (M.R.C.), Mill Hill, London 1974-77; Liverpool Univ. Professorial Fellow, Liverpool School of Tropical Medicine 1981-87, Visiting Prof. 1987-; mem. scientific staff M.R.C. at Liverpool School of Tropical Medicine 1981-84; mem. various advisory cttees. etc. including WHO Advisory Panel on Malaria 1961-, Chair. WHO Expert Cttee. on Malaria 1985; several awards and hon. degrees. *Publications:* Ed. (with W. H. Wernsdorfer) Malaria, 2 vols. 1988; some 160 papers on malaria and other aspects of health in the tropics. *Leisure interests:* ornithology, fishing, gardening. *Address:* The Liverpool School of Tropical Medicine, Pembroke Place, Liverpool, L3 5QA (Office); The Glebe House, Greenlooms, Hargrave, Chester, CH3 7RX, England (Home). *Telephone:* Tarvin 40973 (Home).

MacGREGOR, Sir Ian Kinloch, Kt., B.SC.; American (British-born) business executive; b. 21 Sept. 1912, Kinlochleven, Scotland; m. Sibyl Spencer 1942; one s. one d.; ed. George Watson's Coll., Edinburgh, Hillhead High School, Univ. of Glasgow; Trainee Man. British Aluminium Co.; with William Beardmore Co., Glasgow; participated in mission of Ministry of Supply to N. America 1940; seconded to U.S. Army Ordnance Corps 1941; joined CWC Foundry Co. 1945; Gen. Man. Manning, Maxwell and Moore Inc. 1952; Vice-Pres. Climax Molybdenum Co. 1957 (merged later with American Metal Co.); Exec. Vice-Pres. Amax Inc. 1965, Pres. 1966-69, C.E.O. 1966-77, Chair. 1969-77, Hon. Chair. 1977-82; Deputy Chair. BL Ltd. 1977-80 (Dir. 1975-80); Partner Lazard Frères & Co., New York 1978-, non-exec. Dir. 1986-; Chair. British Steel Corpn. 1980-83, non-exec. Dir. 1983-; Chair. Nat. Coal Bd. (now British Coal) 1983-86, C.E.O. 1983-86; Chair. Alumax 1974-82; Chair. and C.E.O. Highland Express 1987-, Clyde Cable Vision 1987-, North Sea Assets 1987, Trusthouse Forte Inc. 1988-; Dir. (non-exec.) Norman Broadbent Int. 1986-; Dir. Atlantic Assets Trust; fmr. Dir. Brunswick Corpn., American Cyanamid, LTV Corpn., Botswana RST; fmr. Pres. ICC; Hon. degrees from Univs. of Glasgow, Strathclyde, Bristol, Montana State, Rochester, Denver, Wyoming, Colorado School of Mines, TriState Coll., Ind.; awarded Rand Gold Medal 1978, Jackling Gold Medal 1979, Fritz Gold Medal 1981, Bessemer Gold Medal 1983; Chevalier, Légion d'Honneur 1972. *Publication:* The Enemies Within 1986. *Leisure interests:* golf, fishing. *Address:* Lazard Frères and Co. Ltd., 21 Moorfields, London, EC2P 2HT, England.

MacGREGOR, Rt. Hon. John Roddick Russell, O.B.E., P.C., M.A., LL.B.; British politician; b. 14 Feb. 1937; s. of the late Dr. N. S. R. MacGregor; m. Jean Mary Elizabeth Dungey 1962; one s. two d.; ed. Merchiston Castle School, Edin., St. Andrews Univ., King's Coll., London; Univ. Admin. 1961-62; Editorial Staff, New Society 1962-63; Special Asst. to Prime Minister, Sir Alec Douglas-Home 1963-64; Conservative Research Dept. 1964-65; Head of Pvt. Office of Rt. Hon. Edward Heath (Leader of Opposition) 1965-68; Conservative M.P. for South Norfolk 1974-; an Opposition Whip 1977-79; a Lord Commr. of H.M. Treasury 1979-81, Parl. Under-Sec. of State, Dept. of Industry 1981-83; Minister of State, Minister of Agric., Fisheries and Food 1983-85, Sec. of State June 1987-; Chief Sec. to H.M. Treasury 1985-87; with Hill Samuel & Co. Ltd. 1968-79, Dir. 1973-79; Chair. Fed. of Univ. Conservative and Unionist Asscns. 1959, Bow Group 1963-64; First Pres. Conservative and Christian Democratic Youth Community 1963-65. *Leisure interests:* music, reading, travelling, gardening, conjuring. *Address:* House of Commons, London, SW1A 0AA, England.

McGREGOR OF DURRIS, Baron (Life Peer), cr. 1978; **Oliver Ross McGregor,** M.A., B.SC.(ECON.); British sociologist and social historian; b. 25 Aug. 1921, Durris, Scotland; s. of late William McGregor and Anne Olivia Ross; m. Nellie Weate 1944; three s.; ed. Worksop Coll., Univ. of Aberdeen, London School of Econs.; Simon Sr. Research Fellow, Univ. of Manchester 1959-60; Prof. of Social Insts., Univ. of London 1964-85, Head of Dept. of Sociology, Bedford Coll. 1964-77; Joint Dir. Rowntree Legal Research Unit 1966-84; Dir. of Centre for Socio-Legal Studies, Univ. of Oxford 1972-75; Fellow, Wolfson Coll., Oxford 1972-75; Chair. Advertising Standards Authority 1980-; mem. Cttee. on the Enforcement of Judgment Debts 1965-69, Cttee. on Statutory Maintenance Limits 1966-68, Cttee. on Land Use 1967, Independent TV Authority's Gen. Advisory Council

1967–72, Countryside Comm. 1968–80, Lord Chancellor's Advisory Cttee. on Legal Aid 1969–78; mem. Cttee. on One-Parent Families 1969–74; Pres. Nat. Council for One Parent Families 1975–; Ind. Trustee of Reuters 1984–, Chair. Reuters Founders Share Co. 1987–; mem. Royal Comm. on the Press 1974, Chair. 1975–77; Pres. Nat. Asscn. of Citizens' Advice Bureaux 1981–86; Hon. Fellow, L.S.E. 1977; Hon. LL.D. (Bristol) 1986. *Publications:* Divorce in England 1957, Ed. Lord Ernle, English Farming Past and Present (6th edn.) 1960, Separated Spouses 1970, Social History and Law Reform 1981. *Leisure interest:* book collecting. *Address:* House of Lords, London, S.W.1; Advertising Standards Authority, 2–16 Torrington Place, London, WC1E 7HH (Office); Far End, Wyldes Close, London, NW11 7JB, England (Home). *Telephone:* 01-580 5555 (Office); 01-458 2856 (Home).

MacGREGOR, (Robert) Neil; British editor and gallery director; b. 16 June 1946; s. of Alexander Rankin and Anna Fulton Scobie (née Neil) MacGregor; ed. Glasgow Acad., New Coll., Oxford, Ecole Normale Supérieure, Paris, Univ. of Edinburgh, Courtauld Inst. of Art; lecturer, Univ. of Reading 1976; Ed. The Burlington Magazine 1981–86; Dir. Nat. Gallery 1987–; mem. Faculty of Advocates, Edinburgh 1972. *Publications:* numerous articles in Apollo, The Burlington Magazine, Connoisseur, etc. *Address:* 10 Pembridge Crescent, London, W.11, England.

MacGUIGAN, Hon. Mark R., PH.D., LL.M., J.S.D., LL.D.; Canadian judge and fmr. politician and professor of law; b. 17 Feb. 1931, Charlottetown, P.E.I.; s. of Hon. Mark R. MacGuigan and Agnes V. Trainor; m. 1st (divorced); two s. one d.; m. 2nd Patricia Robinson 1987; ed. Queen Square School, Prince of Wales Coll., St. Dunstan's Univ. Charlottetown, Univ. of Toronto, Osgoode Hall, Columbia Univ.; Dean, Faculty of Law, Univ. of Windsor 1967–68; Asst. Prof. of Law, Univ. of Toronto 1960–63, Assoc. Prof. 1963–66; Prof. of Law, Osgoode Hall, 1966–67; mem. Special Cttee. on Hate Propaganda 1965; Advisor to Special Counsel on Constitution 1967–68; Founding Dir. Canadian Civil Liberties Asscn. 1964, Chair. 1966–67; mem. House of Commons 1968–84; Parl. Sec. to Ministry of Manpower and Immigration 1972–74, to Ministry of Labour 1974–75; Sec. of State for External Affairs 1980–82; Minister of Justice and Attorney-Gen. for Canada 1982–84; Judge, Federal Court of Appeal 1984–. *Address:* 23 Linden Terrace, Ottawa, Ont., K1S 1Z1, Canada.

McGUIGAN, Hon. Thomas Malcolm, Q.S.O.; New Zealand parliamentarian and business consultant; b. 20 Feb. 1921, Christchurch; m. Ruth Deacon 1946; two s. one d.; ed. Christchurch Boys' High School, Christchurch Tech. Evening School; served in Navy 1941–45; secretarial and accountancy posts in commerce 1946–54; House Man. Christchurch Hosp. 1955–57; Sr. Admin. Officer, Princess Margaret Hosp., Christchurch 1958–69; M.P. 1969–75; Minister of Railways, Electricity and Civil Defence 1972–74, of Health and Public Trust Office 1974–75; J.P. 1953–; Pres. New Zealand Football Asscn. 1974–75; mem. Canterbury Hosp. Bd. 1980–, mem. New Zealand Bd. of Health 1985–. *Leisure interests:* golf, cricket, fishing, football, reading, music. *Address:* 71 Main Road, Christchurch 8, New Zealand.

MACH, Stanisław, M.ECON., C.SC.; Polish politician; b. 22 April 1938, Przychody, near Olkusz; economic studies; Chief Mechanic, Cart Factory, Sianów 1960–61, Voivodship Amalgamation of Establishments for Mechanization of Agric., Koszalin 1961–63; Branch Sec. Main Tech. Org. (NOT), Koszalin 1963–68; Deputy Chair. Voivodship Council of Trade Unions, Koszalin 1968–71; mem. Polish United Workers' Party (PZPR) 1961–; First Sec. PZPR Dist. Cttee., Kołobrzeg 1971–72; Chair. Presidium, Voivodship Nat. Council (WRN), Koszalin 1972–73, Voivode, Koszalin 1973–75; First Sec. PZPR Voivodship Cttee., Słupsk 1975–77; Chair. Presidium, WRN Słupsk 1975–77; Deputy mem. PZPR Cen. Cttee. 1975–81; Deputy to Seym (Parl.) 1976–80; Minister of Light Industry 1977–80; Deputy Chair. Council of Ministers 1980–81; Vice-Pres. Supreme Chamber of Control 1985–; decorations include Knight's Cross of Order Polonia Restituta. *Address:* Najwyższa Izba Kontroli, ul. Filtrowa 57, 02-052 Warsaw, Poland. *Telephone:* 25-44-81, 25-32-71 (Office).

MACHADO, Paulo de Almeida; Brazilian medical doctor; b. Minas Gerais; active in planning public health and sanitary services; Dir. Nat. Inst. for Research in the Amazon Region until 1974; Minister of Health 1974–78. *Address:* c/o Ministério da Saúde, Esplanada dos Ministérios, Bloco 11, Brasília, D.F. Brazil.

MACHARSKI, H.E. Cardinal Franciszek; Polish ecclesiastic; b. 20 May 1927, Cracow; ed. Jagiellonian Univ., Cracow, Fribourg Univ., Switzerland; ordained priest 1950; engaged in pastoral work 1950–56; taught pastoral theology Pontifical Faculty of Theology, Cracow 1962–68; Rector, Cracow Seminary 1970–78; Archbishop of Cracow Jan. 1979–; cr. Cardinal 1979, entitled S. Giovanni a Porta Latina; mem. Sacred Congregation for the Clergy 1979–, Sacred Congregation for Catholic Educ. 1981–, Sacred Congregation for Bishops 1983–, Council for Public Affairs 1984–; Vice-Pres. of Polish Bishop's Conf. 1979–; mem. Episcopate Cttee. for Gen. Ministry 1979–; Vice-Chair. Scientific Council of Polish Episcopate 1981–, Episcopate Cttee. for Ministry of Working People 1981–; Chair. Episcopate Cttee. for Laity 1981–, Episcopate Cttee. for Catholic Science 1983–. *Address:* Ul. Franciszkańska 3, 31-004 Cracow, Poland. *Telephone:* 22-98-27.

MÂCHE, François-Bernard, D. ES. L.; French composer and professor of musicology; b. 4 April 1935, Clermont-Ferrand; s. of Henry Mâche and Marie-Antoinette Bédabourg; m. Marie-Luce Staib 1973; one d.; ed. Ecole Normale Supérieure and Conservatoire nat. supérieur de Paris; teacher of classical philology 1962–63; Prof. of Musicology, Univ. of Strasbourg 1983–; Prix Italia 1977; Grand Prix national de la Musique 1988; Officier Ordre des Arts et Lettres. *Major works:* Volumes 1960, La Peau du Silence 1962–66, Rituel d'oubli 1969, Danaé 1970, Korwar 1972, Naluan 1974, Uncas 1986, Eridan 1987, Aliunde 1988, Tempora 1989, Cassiopée 1989. *Publications:* Les mal entendus 1978, Musique, mythe, nature 1983. *Leisure interests:* skin-diving, translations from modern Greek. *Address:* 83 rue Vieille du Temple, 75003 Paris, France (Home). *Telephone:* (1) 42 78 46 57 (Home).

McHENRY, Donald F., M.SC.; American diplomatist; b. 13 Oct. 1936, St. Louis, Mo.; m. Mary Williamson (divorced 1978); one s. two d.; ed. Illinois State Univ., Southern Illinois and Georgetown Univs.; taught Howard Univ., Washington 1959–62; joined dept. of State 1963, Head Dependent Areas Section, Office of UN Political Affairs 1965–68; Asst. to U.S. Sec. of State 1969; Special Asst. to Dept. Counsellor 1969–71; lecturer, School of Foreign Service, Georgetown Univ., Guest Scholar, Brookings Inst. and Int. Affairs Fellow, Council on Foreign Relations (on leave from State Dept.) 1971–73; resigned from State Dept. 1973; Project Dir. Humanitarian Policy Studies, Carnegie Endowment for Int. Peace, Washington 1973–76; served Pres. Carter's transition team 1976–77; Amb. and Deputy Perm. Rep. to UN 1977–79, Perm. Rep. 1979–81; Research Prof., School of Foreign Service, Georgetown Univ. 1981–; Dir. Int. Paper Co., Coca Cola Co., The First Nat. Bank of Boston, First Nat. Boston Corp., Inst. for Int. Econs., The American Ditchley Foundation, AT & T; mem. Council on Foreign Relations; mem. Editorial Bd. of Foreign Policy Magazine; mem. Nat. Advisory Council Harriman Inst. for Advanced Study of the Soviet Union, Columbia Univ.; Trustee Mount Holyoke Coll., The Ford Foundation, Phelps-Stokes Fund, The Brookings Inst.; Gov. American Stock Exchange; Superior Honor Award, Dept. of State 1966. *Publication:* Micronesia: Trust Betrayed 1975. *Address:* c/o The School of Foreign Service, Georgetown University, Washington, D.C. 20057, U.S.A.

MACIEJEWICZ, Janusz, M.ENG.; Polish politician and economic administrator; b. 22 Sept. 1931, Przeworsk, Przemyśl Voivodship; ed. Technical Univ. of Gliwice; Asst. Mining Faculty of Silesian Tech. Univ., Gliwice 1952–55; employee in mining 1955–, Head of Technological Arrangements Section and Head of Mechanical Treatment Dept. of coal-mine Zabrze 1955–65; managerial posts in Copper Mining and Metallurgy Works, Lubin 1965–84, including mining units Lubin and Rudna, supervisional inspector, Head, Mechanical Treatment Dept., Chief Eng. for ores separation, Dir. for investment matters 1976–81, Gen. Dir. of Copper Mining and Metallurgy Works 1981–84; Minister of Metallurgy and Eng. Industry 1984–87; Chair. Voivodship Council of Polish Fed. of Engineering Asscns., Legnica; mem. Polish United Workers Party (PZPR); Officer's Cross, Order of Polonia Restituta and other decorations.

McILRAITH, Rt. Hon. George James, P.C., Q.C., M.P.; Canadian lawyer and politician; b. 29 July 1908, Lanark, Ont.; s. of James McIlraith and Kate McLeod; m. Margaret Summers 1935; one s. three d.; ed. Osgoode Hall, Toronto; mem. House of Commons 1940–72; Parl. Asst. to Minister of Reconstruction 1945, to Minister of Trade and Commerce 1948, to Minister of Defence Production 1951; Canadian rep. to UN 1946; Minister of Transport 1963–64; Pres. of Privy Council and Pres. of Treasury Bd. 1964; Govt. House Leader 1964–67; Minister of Public Works 1965–68; Solicitor-Gen. of Canada 1968–70; Senator 1972–83; Liberal. *Leisure interests:* golf, fishing. *Address:* 550 Wilbrod Street, Ottawa, K1N 6N2, Canada.

McILWAIN, Henry, D.SC., PH.D.; British university professor; b. 20 Dec. 1912, Newcastle-on-Tyne; s. of John McIlwain and Louisa Widdowson; m. 1st Valerie Durston 1940 (deceased 1977); m. 2nd Marjorie Crennell 1979; two d.; ed. King's Coll., Durham Univ. and Queen's Coll., Oxford; with British Medical Research Council 1937–47; Sr. Lecturer and Reader in Biochem., London Univ. 1948–55, Prof. Inst. of Psychiatry 1955–80; Dr. h.c. (Univ. d'Aix-Marseilles) 1974; Visiting Prof. St. Thomas's Hospital Medical School 1980–86; Hon. Sr. Research Fellow, Pharmacology Dept., Birmingham Univ. 1987–. *Publications:* Biochemistry and the Central Nervous System 1955, 5th edn. (with H. S. Bachelard) 1985, Chemotherapy and the Central Nervous System 1957, Chemical Exploration of the Brain 1963, Practical Neurochemistry (with R. Rodnight) 1975. *Leisure interests:* contemporary arts, travel. *Address:* 68 Cartway, Bridgnorth, Shropshire, WV16 4BG, England. *Telephone:* 0746 761353.

McINNES, Stewart D., LL.B.; Canadian lawyer and politician; b. 24 July 1937, Halifax, N.S.; s. of Donald McInnes and Constance B. (Rowan-Legg) McInnes; m. Shirley Bowness 1984; one s. one d.; ed. Dalhousie Univ.; Sr. Partner, McInnes, Cooper & Robertson-Halifax 1961–84; Minister of Supply and Services 1985–86, Minister of Public Works 1986–89, with responsibility for Mortgage and Housing Corpn. 1986–87; fmr. N.S. squash champion. *Leisure interests:* tennis, skiing, gardening. *Address:* 490 Francklyn Street, Halifax, N.S. B3H 1A9, Canada.

MACINNIS, Joseph Beverley, C.M., M.D.; Canadian marine research scientist; b. 2 March 1937, Barrie, Ont.; s. of Allistair MacInnis and Beverly

Saunders; m. Deborah J. Ferris 1971; one s. three d.; ed. Univs. of Toronto and Pennsylvania; Pres. Undersea Research Ltd. and has held consulting contracts for U.S. Navy, Smithsonian Inst., IBM, Canadian Ministry of State for Science and Tech. and Canadian Dept. of Environment; est. SUBLIMNOS, Canada's first underwater manned station programme 1969; led 14 scientific expeditions into Arctic 1970-79, and during third expedition, SUB-IGLOO, world's first polar dive station established under ice; co-ordinated diving programme for ICE Station LOREX 1979; led team which discovered remains of English barque Breadalbane, sunk in 1853, 700 miles north of Artic Circle in 340 feet of water, world's most noteworthy shipwreck discovered to date 1980; host, The New Wave (CBC television series) 1975-76, The Newfoundlanders: Voices from the Sea 1978; scientific consultant, Mysteries of the Sea (ABC) 1979; co-ordinator, Shot Point 260 (Texaco Canada film), Breakthrough (Dome Petroleum film) 1979; has lectured and shown his films in all parts of world including Israel, Germany, Australia, the Philippines, U.S.S.R. and Singapore; mem. Canadian Environmental Advisory Council, Canadian Council of Fitness and Health; Fellow, Royal Canadian Geographical Soc.; Hon. LL.D.; Hon. F.R.C.P. *Publications:* Underwater Images, Underwater Man; more than 30 scientific papers and articles in Scientific American, National Geographic Magazine etc. *Address:* 178 Balmoral Avenue, Toronto, Ont. M4V 1J6, Canada. *Telephone:* (416) 921-1652.

MacINTOSH, Frank Campbell, M.A., PH.D., F.R.S., F.R.S.C.; Canadian physiologist; b. 1909, Baddeck, N.S.; s. of Rev. C. C. and Beenie A. (Matheson) MacIntosh; m. Mary MacLachlan MacKay 1938; two s. three d.; ed. Dalhousie and McGill Univs.; mem. research staff, Nat. Inst. for Medical Research, London 1938-49; Drake Prof. of Physiology, McGill Univ. 1949-78, Chair. of Dept. 1949-65, Prof. Emer. 1980-; several hon. degrees. *Publications:* contributions to scientific journals. *Address:* Department of Physiology, McGill University, 3655 Drummond Street, Montreal, P.Q., Canada, H3G 1Y6. *Telephone:* (514) 481-7939.

MACINTOSH, Sir Robert Reynolds, M.D., F.R.C.S., F.F.A.R.C.S., F.R.C.O.G., D.A.; British anaesthetist; b. 17 Oct. 1897, Timaru, New Zealand; s. of C. N. Macintosh; ed. New Zealand and Guy's Hospital; Prof. of Anaesthetics Oxford Univ. 1937-65; hon. consultant in Anaesthetics, R.A.F.; Hon. Fellow Pembroke Coll., Oxford, Royal Soc. of Medicine; Hon. D.Sc. (Univ. of Wales; Medical Coll., Ohio), Hon. M.D. (Buenos Aires, Aix-Marseilles and Poznań); Order of Mil. Merit (Spain), Order of Liberty (Norway). *Publications:* Essentials of General Anæsthesia, Physics for the Anæsthetist, Local Anæsthesia, Brachial Plexus, Lumbar Puncture and Spinal Analgesia. *Address:* 326 Woodstock Road, Oxford, England. *Telephone:* (0865) 55471.

McINTOSH, Sir Ronald Robert Duncan, K.C.B., M.A.; British businessman; b. 26 Sept. 1919, Whitehaven; s. of late Dr. T. S. McIntosh, F.R.C.P.; m. Doreen MacGinnity 1951; ed. Charterhouse, Balliol Coll., Oxford; joined Bd. of Trade 1947; Counsellor, British High Comm., New Delhi 1957-61; Deputy Sec. Dept. of Econ. Affairs 1966-68, Cabinet Office 1968-70, Dept. of Employment 1970-72, Treasury 1972-73; Dir.-Gen. Nat. Econ. Devt. Office 1973-77; Chair. APV Holdings (now APV BAKER) PLC 1982-; Dir. S. G. Warburg and Co. 1978-, London and Manchester Group PLC, Foseco Minsep PLC 1978-; Gov., Nat. Inst. of Econ. and Social Research; mem. CBI Council; C.B.I.M.; Hon. D.Sc. (Aston). *Leisure interest:* sailing. *Address:* APV House, Manor Royal, Crawley, RH10 2GZ; 24 Ponsonby Terrace, London, S.W.1, England. *Telephone:* (0293) 51777.

McINTYRE, Donald Conroy, C.B.E., O.B.E.; British bass opera singer; b. 22 Oct. 1934, Auckland, N.Z.; s. of George D. and Hermyn McIntyre; m. Jill Redington 1961; three d.; ed. Mt. Albert Grammar School, Auckland, Auckland Teachers' Training Coll. and Guildhall School of Music, London; Prin. Bass, Sadler's Wells Opera 1960-67; with Royal Opera House, Covent Garden 1967-; annual appearances at Bayreuth Festival 1967-81; frequent int. guest appearances: roles include: Wotan and Wanderer (Der Ring), Dutchman (Der Fliegende Holländer), Telramund (Lohengrin), Barak (Die Frau ohne Schatten), Pizzaro (Fidelio), Golaud (Pelléas et Mélisande), Kurwenal (Tristan and Isolde), Gurnemanz, Klingsor and Amfortas (Parsifal), Heyst (Victory), Jochanaan (Salome), Macbeth, Scarpia (Tosca), the Count (Marriage of Figaro), Nick Shadow (The Rake's Progress), Hans Sachs (Die Meistersinger), Dr. Schöne (Woyzeck), Cardillac (Cardillac Hindemith), Rocco (Fidelio); recordings include Pelléas et Mélisande, Oedipus Rex, Il Trovatore, etc. *Leisure interests:* sport (particularly golf, tennis and swimming), gardening, languages. *Address:* c/o Ingpen & Williams, 14 Kensington Court, London, W.8 (Office); Foxhill Farm, Jackass Lane, Keston, Bromley, Kent, BR2 6AN, England (Home). *Telephone:* (0689) 55368.

MacINTYRE, Duncan, P.C., D.S.O., O.B.E., E.D.; New Zealand farmer and politician; b. 1915, Hastings; s. of A. MacIntyre; m. Diana Hunter; two s. three d.; ed. Larchfield School, Scotland, Christ's Coll., Christchurch; farming 1933-39, 1947-; served Second World War in Middle East, Italy and Japan as mem. N.Z. Cavalry Regt. 1939-45; after war commanded 1st Battalion Hawke's Bay Regt., the N.Z. Scottish Regt., 2nd Infantry Brigade and 4th Armoured Brigade in Territorial Army 1949-60; Territorial mem. of N.Z. Army Bd. 1960; M.P. for Hastings 1960-72, for Bay of Plenty 1975-78, for East Cape 1978-84; Minister of Lands, Minister of Forests, Minister in Charge of the Valuation Dept. 1966-72, of Maori and Island

Affairs 1969-72, of the Environment Feb.-Dec. 1972, of Maori Affairs 1975-79, of Agric. and in Charge of the Rural Banking and Finance Corpn. 1975-84, of Fisheries 1978-84; Deputy Prime Minister 1981-84; Deputy Leader Nat. Party Feb. 1981-; mem. Parl. Select Cttee. on Privileges; fmr. Chair. Soil Conservation Cttee., Hawkes Bay Catchment Bd.; fmr. Area Del. Hawkes Bay Branch of Federated Farmers. *Address:* Taikura, RD4, Waipukurau, New Zealand.

MacINTYRE, Iain, M.B., CH.B., PH.D., D.SC., F.R.C.P.; British professor of chemical pathology; b. 30 Aug. 1924, Glasgow; s. of John MacIntyre and Margaret Fraser Shaw; m. Mabel Wilson Jamieson 1947; one d.; ed. Jordanhill Coll. School, Univs. of Glasgow and London; Asst. Clinical Pathologist, United Sheffield Hosps. and Hon. Demonstrator in Biochemistry, Univ. of Sheffield 1948-52; Registrar in Chemical Pathology, Royal Postgraduate Medical School, Hammersmith Hosp., London 1952-54, Sir Jack Drummond Memorial Fellow 1954-56, Asst. Lecturer in Chemical Pathology 1956-59, Lecturer 1959-63, Reader 1963-67, Prof. of Endocrine Chem. 1967-82, Dir. Endocrine Unit 1967-, Prof. of Chemical Pathology, Univ. of London and Dir. Chemical Pathology 1982-; Visiting Scientist, N.I.H., Bethesda, Md., U.S.A. 1960-61; Visiting Prof. of Medicine, Univ. of Calif., San Francisco 1964, Univ. of Melbourne 1980; Dir. of Chemical Pathology, Hammersmith and Queen Charlotte's Hosps.; Hon. Consultant Pathologist, Hammersmith Hosp.; Fellow, Royal Coll. of Pathologists; Hon. M.D. (Turin); Gairdner Int. Award, Toronto 1967. *Publications:* numerous articles on endocrinology. *Leisure interests:* tennis, chess, music. *Address:* Department of Chemical Pathology, Royal Postgraduate Medical School, Hammersmith Hospital, Ducane Road, London, W12 0NN; Great Broadhurst Farm, Broad Oak, Nr. Heathfield, East Sussex, TN21 8UX, England. *Telephone:* 01-740-3227 (Office); (0435) 883 515 (Home).

McINTYRE, James T., Jr., J.D.; American lawyer and administrator; b. 17 Dec. 1940, Vidalia, Ga.; m. Maureen Ball; three d.; ed. Univ. of Georgia; employed by Univ. of Georgia's Inst. of Gov. 1964; practised law, Athens, Ga. 1964; Gen. Counsel to Ga. Municipal Assen. 1966-70; Deputy State Revenue Commr. 1970-72; Dir. Georgia Office of Planning and Budget 1972-77; Deputy Dir. Office of Man. and Budget, Exec. Office of Pres. of U.S.A. Feb.-Dec. 1977, Dir. 1977-80; partner Hansell, Post, Brandon & Dorsey 1981-; Legal counsel Ga. Reorganization and Man. Improvement Study 1971; Project Dir. State and Local Gov. Co-ordination Study 1972; mem. State Bar of Ga. *Address:* Hansell, Post, Brandon & Dorsey, 1915 I Street NW, 5th Floor, Washington, D.C. 20006, U.S.A.

McINTYRE, Very Rev. John, C.V.O., M.A., B.D., D.LITT., D.H.L., F.R.S.E.; British ecclesiastic and university professor; b. 20 May 1916, Glasgow; s. of John C. McIntyre and Annie Summers; m. Jessie B. Buick 1945; two s. one d.; ed. Bathgate Acad. and Univ. of Edinburgh; Minister, Church of Scotland, Fenwick Parish Church 1943-45; Hunter Baillie Prof. of Theology St. Andrew's Coll. Univ. of Sydney 1946, Prin. 1950-56; Prof. of Divinity, Univ. of Edinburgh 1956-86, Dean Faculty of Divinity and Prin. New Coll. 1968-74, Acting Prin. and Vice-Chancellor 1973-74, 1979; Chaplain to H.M. The Queen in Scotland 1974-86, Chaplain Extraordinary 1974, 1986-; Dean, Order of the Thistle 1974-; Moderator, Gen. Ass. of Church of Scotland 1982; Vice-Pres. Royal Soc. of Edinburgh 1983-86; Fulbright Visiting Prof. Union Theological Seminary, New York 1953; Warfield Lecturer, Princeton Theol. Seminary 1966; Laidlaw Lecturer, Knox Coll. Toronto 1987; Dr. h.c. (Edin.) 1987. *Publications:* St Anselm and his Critics 1954, The Christian Doctrine of History 1957, On the Love of God 1962, The Shape of Christology 1967, Faith, Theology and Imagination 1987. *Leisure interest:* travel. *Address:* 22/4 Minto Street, Edinburgh, EH9 1RQ, Scotland. *Telephone:* 031-667 1203.

MacIVER, Loren; American artist; b. 2 Feb. 1909; m. Lloyd Frankenburg 1929; ed. Art Students League; One Man exhbns., East River Gallery, New York 1938, Pierre Matisse Gallery, New York 1940-44, 1949, 1956, 1961, 1966, 1970, 1981, 1987, Museum of Modern Art Travelling Exhbn. 1941, Vassar Art Gallery 1950, Wellesley Coll. 1951, Whitney Museum 1953, Dallas Museum of Fine Arts 1953, Beaux Arts Museum, Lyons 1968, Musée Nat. d'Art Moderne, Paris 1968, Musée des Ponchettes, Nice 1968, Montclair Museum 1975, etc.; rep. in numerous exhbns. including Fantastic Art, Dada, Surrealism 1938, Art in Our Time 1939, State Dept. Exhbn. in Europe 1946, Dunn Int. Exhbn., Tate Gallery, London 1963, Venice Biennale 1961; First Prize, Corcoran Art Gallery 1957; Chicago Art Inst. 1961, Univ. of Ill. 1962; Ford Foundation Grant 1960; mem. Nat. Inst. of Arts and Letters; Purchase Prize, Krannert Art Museum, Univ. of Ill. 1963; Mark Rothko Foundation Award 1972, Guggenheim Fellowship 1976; Francis J. Greenberger Award 1987. *Address:* c/o Pierre Matisse Gallery, 41 East 57th Street, New York, N.Y. 10022, U.S.A.

McIVOR, Donald K., B.SC.; Canadian business executive; b. Winnipeg; ed. Univ. of Manitoba; joined Imperial Oil from univ. as geophysical trainee, Alberta; various operational and research positions in exploration, Imperial and affiliated cos. 1950-58; various positions, including Asst. to Exploration Man., Supervisor, Exploration Planning, and Man. Exploration Research, Calgary 1958-68; assignments, Angola and France, Standard Oil of N.J. evaluation teams; one year with Jersey Production Research Co., Tulsa, Okla., U.S.A.; Asst. Man., later Man., Corporate Planning Dept., Imperial Oil, Toronto 1968-69; Exploration Man. Imperial Oil 1970; Nat. Defence Coll. 1972-73; Sr. Vice-Pres. and Dir. Imperial Oil 1973-75, Exec.

Vice-Pres. 1975; Vice-Pres. Exxon Corpn. with responsibility for Oil and Gas exploration and production 1977-81; Deputy Chair. and Dir. Imperial Oil Ltd. 1981-82, Chair. and C.E.O. Jan. 1982-; Dir. Royal Bank of Canada, Montreal 1982-, Business Council on Nat. Issues, Toronto Symphony, C.D. Howe Inst.; mem. Canadian Soc. of Petroleum Geologists; *Address:* Imperial Oil Ltd., 111 St. Clair Avenue West, Toronto, Ont., M5W 1K3, Canada. *Telephone:* (416) 968-4111.

McKANE, William, M.A., PH.D., D.LITT., D.D., F.B.A., F.R.S.E.; British academic; b. 18 Feb. 1921, Dundee; s. of Thomas and Jemima S. McKane; m. Agnes M. Howie 1952; three s. two d.; ed. Univs. of St. Andrews and Glasgow; R.A.F. 1941-45; Lecturer in Hebrew, Univ. of Glasgow 1953, Sr. Lecturer 1956; Prof. of Hebrew and Oriental Languages, Univ. of St. Andrews 1968-, Dean, Faculty of Divinity 1973-77; Prin. St. Mary's Coll., St. Andrews 1982-86; Burkitt Medal (British Acad.) 1985; Hon. D.D. (Edinburgh) 1984. *Publications:* Prophets and Wise Men 1965, Proverbs, A New Approach 1970, Studies in the Patriarchal Narratives 1979, Jeremiah 1-25 (int. critical commentary) 1986; articles in British and European journals. *Leisure interests:* hill-walking, golf. *Address:* The University of St. Andrews, Fife, KY16 9JU; 51 Irvine Crescent, St. Andrews, Fife, KY16 8LG, Scotland. *Telephone:* (0334) 76161 (Ext. 7119); (0334) 73797.

MACKAY, Elmer MacIntosh, P.C., Q.C., B.A., LL.B., M.P.; Canadian politician; b. 5 Aug. 1936, Hopewell, N.S.; s. of Gordon Mackay and Laura MacIntosh; m. Laura MacAulay; one d., four from previous marriage; ed. Acadia Univ., Wolfville, Nova Scotia, Dalhousie Univ., Halifax; called to Bar, Nova Scotia 1961; mem. House of Commons 1971-83, 1984-; Minister of Regional Econ. Expansion and responsible for Canada Housing and Mortgage Corpn. 1979; Sr. Advisor to Leader of Opposition 1983; Solicitor Gen. of Canada 1984-85; Minister of Nat. Revenue 1985-89, of Public Works, for the Atlantic Canada Opportunities Agency Jan. 1989-; Progressive Conservative Party. *Address:* House of Commons, Ottawa, Ont., K1A 0A2 (Office); R.R.1, Hopewell, Picton Co., Nova Scotia, B0K 1C0, Canada (Home).

MACK, Connie (Cornelius McGillicuddy), III; American politician; b. 29 Oct. 1940, Philadelphia; s. of Cornelius M. and Susan (née Sheppard) McGillicuddy; m. Ludie Priscilla 1960; one s. one d.; ed. Univ. of Florida, Sun Bank, Ft. Myers, Fla.; Vice-Pres. Business Devt. First Nat. Bank, Ft. Myers 1968-71; Sr. Vice-Pres., Dir. Sun Bank, Cape Coral, Fla. 1971-75; Pres., Dir. Florida Nat. Bank, Cape Coral 1972-82; mem. U.S. House of Reps. from Fla. 1983-89, Senator, Fla. 1989-; Dir. Fed. Reserve Bd., Miami 1981-82; mem. Bd. of Dirs., Chair. Palmer Drug Abuse Program, Cape Coral; mem. Bd. of Dirs. Cape Coral Hosp.; Republican. *Address:* U.S. Senate, Washington, D.C. 20515, U.S.A.

McKAY, Robert B., B.S., J.D.; American teacher of law; b. 11 Aug. 1919, Wichita, Kan.; s. of John B. and Ruth G. McKay; m. Kate Warmack 1954 (deceased 1986); two d.; ed. Univ. of Kansas and Yale Univ.; Asst. and Assoc. Prof. of Law, Emory Univ. 1950-53; Assoc. Prof. then Prof. of Law, New York Univ. 1953-, Dean, School of Law 1967-75; Dir. Justice Program, Aspen Inst. 1975-80, Sr. Fellow 1980-; Vice-Pres. American Judicature Soc. 1980-; many awards and prizes. *Publication:* Reapportionment 1965. *Leisure interest:* civic affairs. *Address:* New York University School of Law, 40 Washington Square South, New York, N.Y. 10012 (Office); 29 Washington Square West, New York, N.Y. 10011, U.S.A. (Home). *Telephone:* 998-6189 (Office); 475-3076 (Home).

MACKAY OF CLASHFERN, Baron (Life Peer), cr. 1979, of Eddrachillis in the District of Sutherland; **James Peter Hymers Mackay,** P.C., M.A., LL.B., F.R.S.E.; British advocate; b. 2 July 1927, Scotland; s. of James Mackay and Janet Hymers; m. Elizabeth Gunn Hymers 1958; one s. two d.; ed. George Heriot's School, Edinburgh, Univ. of Edinburgh; Lecturer in Math., Univ. of St. Andrews 1948-50; Major Scholar, Trinity Coll., Cambridge 1947, Sr. Scholar 1951; admitted to Faculty of Advocates 1955, Vice-Dean 1973-76, Dean 1976-79; Lord Advocate 1979-84; Sheriff Prin., Renfrew and Argyll 1972-74; Commr. Northern Lighthouses 1972-84; Dir. Stenhouse Holdings Ltd. 1976-78; Senator of Coll. of Justice in Scotland 1984-85; Lord of Appeal in Ordinary 1985-87; Lord Chancellor Oct. 1987-; Part-time mem. Scottish Law Comm. 1976-79; mem. Insurance Brokers' Registration Council 1978-79; Fellow, Int. Acad. of Trial Lawyers; Hon. Fellow, Inst. of Taxation, Inst. of Civil Engineers; Hon. LL.D. (Edinburgh, Dundee, Strathclyde, Aberdeen), Hon. D.Iur. (Cambridge) 1989. *Publication:* Armour on Valuation for Rating (Sr. Ed.) 1961, 1971. *Leisure interest:* walking. *Address:* House of Lords, Westminster, London, S.W.1, England. *Telephone:* 01-219 3232.

McKEE, James W., Jr., B.COMM; American businessman; b. 19 Aug. 1922, Pittsburgh, Pa.; s. of James W. McKee and Mary Isabel Welch; m. Jayne A. Finnegan 1947; one s. two d.; ed. McGill Univ.; Cost Accountant, CPC Italian affiliate 1947-50; Financial Man. CPC Brazilian affiliate 1950-58; Pres. CPC Cuban affiliate 1958-59; Man. CPC Brazilian affiliate 1959-64; Exec. Asst. CPC Int. 1964; Comptroller, CPC Int. 1964-65, Vice-Pres. (Finance) 1965-69, Dir. 1968, Pres. and Chief Admin. Officer 1969-80, C.E.O. 1972-84, Chair. 1979-87; Dir. Fidelity Union Bancorpn. 1969, Marine Midland Banks Inc., Melville Corpn., Singer Co.; Co-Chair. The Conference Bd. 1982-; Trustee U.S. Council of Int. Chamber of Commerce, Council of the Americas, Cttee. for Econ. Devt., Conf. Bd.; mem. Bd. Fellows Fairleigh Dickinson Univ.; mem. Advisory Council Johns Hopkins Univ.

School of Advanced Int. Studies, Center of Brazilian Studies, Cruzeiro do Sol (Brazil). *Leisure interests:* golf, reading. *Address:* c/o CPC International Inc., International Plaza, Englewood Cliffs, N.J. 07632, U.S.A.

McKEE, John Angus; Canadian business executive; b. 31 Aug. 1935, Toronto, Ont.; s. of John W. McKee and Margaret E. Phippen; m. Susan E. Harley; one s. one d.; ed. Trinity Coll. School, Port Hope, Ont. and Univ. of Toronto; joined the Patiño Mining Corpn. 1962, Asst. to Pres. 1963, Vice-Pres. (Corporate Devt.) 1966; Man. Dir. Consolidated Tin Smelters Ltd. 1968-71; Pres. J. A. McKee and Assocs. Ltd. 1971-; Pres. and C.E.O. Canadian Occidental Petroleum Ltd.; Dir. Stone and Webster Canada Ltd., Stone and Webster Inc. (U.S.A.), Teradyne Canada Ltd., CVI Ltd. and others; mem. Bd. of Govs., Trinity Coll. School, Port Hope. *Leisure interests:* skiing, shooting. *Address:* 803, 94 Cumberland Street, Toronto, Ont., M5R 1A3 (Office); 9 Dunloe Road, Toronto, Ont., M4V 2W4, Canada (Home).

MacKELLAR, Michael John Randal, B.SCI.AGR., M.A.; Australian politician; b. 27 Oct. 1938; s. of Geoffrey Neil and Colleen Randal MacKellar; m. Robin Morey Smith 1969; ed. Sydney Church of England Grammar School, Sydney Univ., Balliol Coll., Oxford; New South Wales Dept. of Agric. 1961-69; mem. for Warringah, N.S.W., House of Reps. 1969-; mem. Council of Australian Nat. Univ. 1970-75; mem. House of Reps. Select Cttee. on Wildlife Conservation 1971-72; mem. Joint Parl. Cttee. on Foreign Affairs and Defence 1972-74, 1983-, Joint Standing Cttee. on Public Accounts 1972-74, on Electoral Reform 1985, on the Nat. Crime Authority 1985-; mem. first Australian Parl. Del. to People's Repub. of China 1973; Parl. Sec. to Leader of Opposition 1973-74; Shadow Minister for Immigration 1974-75; Minister for Immigration and Ethnic Affairs Dec. 1975-79; Minister Assisting the Treas. 1978-79, Minister for Health 1979-82, Minister Assisting the Prime Minister 1979-80; Minister for Home Affairs and Environment Feb.-March 1981; Shadow Minister for Foreign Affairs 1983-84, for Science and Special Minister of State 1984-85; leader of del. to UN Habitat Conf. 1976; Chair. House of Reps. Standing Cttee. on Environment and Conservation 1982-83; mem. N.S.W. Advisory Cttee. for Australian Broadcasting Comm. 1973-75; mem. Advisory Council of CSIRO 1984; mem. Council, Royal Blind Soc., N.S.W. 1970-; Liberal Party. *Leisure interests:* tennis, cricket, golf, reading, photography. *Address:* Parliament House, Canberra, A.C.T. 2600 (Office); 1 Lewis Street, Balgowlah Heights, N.S.W. 2093, Australia. (Home).

McKELLEN, Ian Murray, C.B.E., B.A.; British actor; b. 25 May 1939, Burnley, Lancs.; s. of Denis Murray and Margery (Sutcliffe) McKellen; ed. Bolton School, St. Catharine's Coll., Cambridge; First stage appearance as Roper (A Man for All Seasons), Belgrade Theatre, Coventry 1961; numerous other parts include title-roles in Henry V, Luther, Ipswich 1962-63; Aufidius (Coriolanus), Arthur Seaton (Saturday Night and Sunday Morning), title-role in Sir Thomas More, Nottingham Playhouse 1963-64; London début as Godfrey (A Scent of Flowers), Duke of York's Theatre 1964; Claudio (Much Ado About Nothing), Protestant Evangelist (Last Goodnight), Capt. de Foenix (Trelawny of the Wells), Nat. Theatre Co. 1965; Alvin (A Lily in Little India), Hampstead and St. Martin's 1965-66; Andrew Cobham (Their Very Own and Golden City), Royal Court 1966; title-part in O'Flaherty, V.C. and Bonaparte (The Man of Destiny), Mermaid 1966; Leonidik (The Promise), Oxford Playhouse, Fortune, and Henry Miller (Broadway début) 1966-67; Tom (The White Liars), Harold Gorringe (Black Comedy), Lyric 1968; Richard II (Edinburgh Festival 1969), Edward II, Hamlet, Prospect Theatre Co. 1968-71; British tour, Mermaid and Piccadilly Theatres; Darkly (Billy's Last Stand), Theatre Upstairs 1970; Capt. Plume (The Recruiting Officer), Corporal Hill (Chips With Everything), Cambridge Theatre Co. 1970; Svetlovidov (Swan Song), Crucible, Sheffield 1971; founder-mem. Actors' Co., Edinburgh Festival 1972 and touring as Giovanni ('Tis Pity She's A Whore), Page-Boy (Ruling the Roost), Prince Yoremitsu (The Three Arrows), title-role in Michael, the Wood Demon, Footman (The Way of The World), then Knots, Shaw Theatre, Edgar (King Lear), Brooklyn Acad., and Giovanni, Wimbledon 1973-74; début with R.S.C. as Dr. Faustus (Edinburgh Festival) 1974; title-role in The Marquis of Keith, Philip the Bastard (King John), Aldwych 1974-75; Colin (Ashes), Young Vic. 1975; Aubrey Bagot (Too True to Be Good), also at Globe, Romeo, Macbeth, Bernick (Pillars of the Community), Face (The Alchemist) Stratford season 1976; Langevin (Days of the Commune) 1976-78; organized R.S.C. British tour of Twelfth Night (Toby Belch) and Three Sisters (Andrei); Max (Bent), Royal Court and Criterion 1979, Amadeus (New York) 1980, Short List (Hampstead Theatre Club), Cowardice (Ambassadors) 1983; int. tour of one-man show Acting Shakespeare (L.A. and Ritz Theatre, New York) 1984, (London) 1987; Assoc. Dir. Nat. Theatre of Great Britain (also actor) 1984-86; Venice Preserv'd (Pierre), Coriolanus; Wild Honey (Platonov); McKellen/Petherbridge Nat. Theatre Group: Duchess of Malfi (Bosola), Real Inspector Hound (Hound), The Critic (Mr Puff), The Cherry Orchard (Lopakhin); Wild Honey (Va. Theatre, New York), U.S.A. Shakespeare tour 1987; Henceforward (Vaudeville Theatre) 1988-89; *Films include:* Alfred the Great 1969, The Promise 1969, A Touch of Love 1969, Priest of Love 1981, The Keep 1982, Plenty, Zina 1985, Scandal 1988. *TV appearances include:* David Copperfield 1965, Ross 1969, Richard II, Edward II and Hamlet 1970, Hedda Gabler 1974, Macbeth, Every Good Boy Deserves Favour, Dying Day 1979, Acting Shakespeare 1981, Walter, The Scarlet Pimpernel 1982, Walter and June

1983; Clarence Derwent Award 1964; Variety and Plays and Players awards 1966; Actor of the Year (Plays and Players) 1976; Soc. of W. End Theatres Award for Best Actor in Revival 1977, for Best Comedy Performance 1978, for Best Actor in a New Play 1979, Tony Award 1981, Drama Desk 1981, Outer Critics Circle Award 1981; Royal TV Soc. Performer of the Year 1983; Laurence Olivier Award 1984; Evening Standard Best Actor Award 1984; council mem. British Actors' Equity 1970-71. *Address:* c/o James Sharkey, 3rd Floor Suite, 15 Golden Square, London, W1R 3AG, England. *Telephone:* 01-434 3801.

McKELVEY, Edward Neil, O.C.; Canadian barrister and solicitor; b. 1 May 1925, Saint John; s. of Fenwin M. McKelvey and Margaret L. McKelvey; m. Joan B. Belyea 1948; two s.; ed. Saint John High School, Khaki Univ. of Canada and Dalhousie Univ.; admitted to N.B. Bar 1949; partner McKelvey, Macaulay, Machum 1955-; appointed Queen's Counsel 1960; Pres. Canadian Bar Asscn. 1973-74, Int. Bar Asscn. 1978-80; Dir. Bell Canada 1973-83, BCE Inc. 1983-, CIP Inc. 1982-88, Canadian Pacific Forest Products Ltd. 1988-, Royal Trustco Ltd. 1988-; mem. Bd. of Gov., Dalhousie Univ. 1978-; Fellow American Coll. of Trial Lawyers 1975-, Int. Acad. of Trial Lawyers 1986-; Hon. LL.B. (Dalhousie), D.C.L. (N.B.); Jubilee Medal 1977. *Leisure interest:* boating. *Address:* 44 Chipman Hill, P.O. Box 7289, Station "A", Saint John, N.B. E2L 4S6 (Office); 14 Beach Crescent, Saint John, N.B., E2K 2E3, Canada (Home).

McKENNA, Frank Joseph, M.L.A., LL.B.; Canadian lawyer and politician; b. 19 Jan. 1948, Apohaqui, N.B.; s. of Durward McKenna and Olive Moody; m. Julie Friel; two s. one d.; ed. St. Francis Xavier Univ., Queen's Univ. and Univ. of N.B.; Special Asst. to Pres., Privy Council 1971; Research Asst. Constitutional Law Unit, PMO 1973; partner, Martin, Lordon, McKenna, Martin & Bowes; mem. N.B. Bar Asscn., Canadian Bar Asscn.; mem. Legis. Ass. 1982-; Leader, N.B. Liberal Party 1985-; Premier, Prov. of N.B. 1987-; Vanier Award 1988; Hon. LL.D. (Univ. of N.B.) 1988. *Leisure interests:* jogging, baseball. *Address:* P.O. Box 6000, Fredericton, N.B., E3B 5H1, Canada.

McKENNA, Stephen Francis, D.F.A.; Irish painter; b. 20 March 1939, Ashford, Middx.; s. of the late Maj. James McKenna and Violet (née Kinnear) McKenna; one s.; ed. Cardinal Vaughan Memorial School, London, De La Salle Coll., Hong Kong, Andover Grammar School, St. Illtyd's Coll., Cardiff, Welbeck Coll., Royal Mil. Acad., Sandhurst, Slade School of Fine Art; Sr. Lecturer in Painting, Canterbury Coll. of Art 1965-68; Visiting Lecturer, Goldsmiths Coll., Univ. of London 1968-72; lived in Bonn 1971-79, Brussels 1979-84; invited to Berlin by Kunstler Programm DAAD 1984; in London, Donegal and Umbria 1985-; one-man exhbns. include: Edward Totah Gallery, London 1985, 1986, 1988, Gallery Seno, Milan, Kunsthalle, Düsseldorf 1986; Raab Gallery, Berlin, ICA, London, Sander Gallery, N.Y. 1985, Van Abbemuseum Eindhoven, Gallery Springer, Berlin 1984, Museum of Modern Art, Oxford, Gallery Isy Brachot, Brussels, Gallery Swajcer, Antwerp 1983, Orchard Gallery, Derry 1981, 1988, Barry Barker Gallery, London 1978, 1979; works in numerous public collections. *Publications:* numerous catalogues; texts: 'On Landscape' 1984, Parables of Painting 1980. *Leisure interest:* conversation. *Address:* Crocknafeola, Killybegs, County Donegal, Ireland.

McKENNA, Thomas Patrick (T.P.); Irish actor; b. 7 Sept. 1931, Cavan; s. of Ralph and Mary McKenna; m. May White 1956; four s. one d.; joined Abbey Theatre Co., Dublin 1954, Hon. Life Mem. 1966. *Films include:* Siege of Sidney Street, Girl with Green Eyes, Ferry Cross the Mersey, Young Cassidy, Ulysses, Charge of the Light Brigade, Anne of the Thousand Days, Perfect Friday, Villain, Straw Dogs, Portrait of the Artist as a Young Man, A Child's Voice, Exposure, The Outsider, Silver Dream Racer, The Scarlet and the Black, To the Lighthouse, Mehmed my Hawk, Doctor and the Devils, Honour, Profit and Pleasure, Cat's Eyes, Anything Legal Considered, O.S.S., Strong Medicine, Pascali's Island, Red Scorpion, Valmont. *Television includes:* Jack the Ripper, Dr. Who and several British and American TV serials. *Leisure interests:* sport, music. *Address:* c/o Joy Jameson Ltd., 7 West Eaton Place Mews, London, S.W.1 (Agent); 28 Claverley Grove, London, N3 2DH, England (Home). *Telephone:* 01-346 4118 (Home).

McKENNA, Virginia; British actress; b. 7 June 1931, London; m. Bill Travers; three s. one d.; f. Zoo Check Charitable Trust 1984; film debut in The Second Mrs Tanqueray; stage appearances have included The King And I 1983, Hamlet (RSC) 1985, Winnie 1988; has appeared in numerous TV plays and films and in documentary The Lion at World's End 1971. *Films include:* Father's Doing Fine, The Cruel Sea, Simba, The Ship that Died of Shame, A Town Like Alice, The Smallest Show on Earth, The Barretts of Wimpole Street, Carve Her Name With Pride, The Passionate Summer, Wreck of the Mary Deare, Two Living, One Dead, Born Free, Ring of Bright Water, An Elephant Called Slowly, Waterloo, Swallows and Amazons, The Disappearance, Holocaust-2000. *Publications:* On Playing with Lions (with Bill Travers), Some Of My Friends Have Tails; Co-Ed. and Contrib. Beyond the Bars. *Address:* c/o Derek Webster, A.I.M., 5 Denmark Street, London, W.C.2, England.

McKENNON, Keith Robert, B.S.; American business executive; b. 25 Dec. 1933, Condon, Ore.; s. of Russell McKennon and Lois Edgerton; m. Patricia Dragon 1961; three s.; ed. Pendleton High School, Golden Gate Coll. and

Oregon State Univ.; joined Dow Chemical U.S.A. 1955; Dir. Public Affairs, The Dow Chemical Co. 1978, Vice-Pres. 1980, Vice-Pres. Agricultural Products 1982; Vice-Pres. Product Dept. Man. Dow Chemical U.S.A. Jan. 1983; Group Vice-Pres. Global Agricultural Products, Legal, Employee Relations and Public Affairs, The Dow Chemical Co. April 1983; mem. Bd. of Dirs. The Dow Chemical Co. 1983-, Group Vice-Pres. and Dir. of Research and Devt. 1985, Exec. Vice-Pres. 1987-; Pres. Dow Chemical U.S.A. 1987-; Dir. Chemical Bank and Trust Co., Chemical Financial Corpn., Dowell Schlumberger Inc., Dow Corning Corpn., Nat. Legal Center for the Public Interests etc. *Leisure interests:* tennis, fishing, reading. *Address:* Dow Chemical U.S.A., 2020 Willard H. Dow Center, Midland, Mich. 48674, U.S.A. *Telephone:* (517) 636-3989.

McKENZIE, Sir Alexander, K.B.E.; New Zealand businessman; b. 26 Oct. 1896, Invercargill; m. Constance Mary Howard 1935; two s. two d.; ed. Southland Boys' High School; began career as farmer; served army 1914-18 war; with The Govt. Life Insurance, Invercargill; joined N.Z. Forest Products Ltd. 1922, which he helped establish in N.Z., Australia and U.K., Business Man. for N.Z. 1929; founded own business 1932; a Dir. of 3 cos.; Sharebroker and mem. Auckland Stock Exchange 1961-; mem. N.Z. Nat. Party, Pres. 1951-62; fmr. Chair. Auckland Div. of Party. *Leisure interests:* surfing, bowling, gardening, trout-fishing. *Address:* 1/46 King Edward Parade, Devonport, Auckland, New Zealand.

McKENZIE, Dan Peter, M.A., PH.D., F.R.S.; British geologist; b. 21 Feb. 1942, Cheltenham; s. of W. S. and N. M. (née Fairbrother) McKenzie; m. Indira M. Misra 1971; one s.; ed. Westminster School and King's Coll., Cambridge; Fellow, King's Coll. 1965-, Sr. Asst. in Research, Dept. of Earth Sciences, Univ. of Cambridge 1969-73, Asst. Dir. of Research 1973-79, Reader in Tectonics 1979-85, Prof. of Earth Sciences 1985-; Foreign Assoc. N.A.S.; Balzan Prize 1981. *Publications:* papers in professional journals. *Leisure interest:* gardening. *Address:* Bullard Laboratories, Madingley Rise, Madingley Road, Cambridge, CB3 0EZ, England. *Telephone:* (0223) 337177.

MACKENZIE, Ian, D.S.O., M.A.; South African business executive; b. 7 Sept. 1914; s. of late George Mackenzie; m. Anne McNab Lindsay 1944; two s. two d.; ed. Glenalmond, Scotland, Pembroke Coll., Oxford; service in Royal Scots Fusiliers 1939-46, rank of Lieut.-Col.; Chair. African Finance Corpn. Ltd., African Finance Corpn. Investment Ltd., Rank Xerox Ltd., Messina Ltd., NMA Administrators Ltd.; Pres. The Urban Foundation, 1820 Foundation; mem. Board of Gov. of Rhodes Univ.; Kt. of the Mil. and Hospitalier Order of St. Lazarus of Jerusalem, Auditor-Gen. of the S.A. Bailiwick; *Address:* P.O. Box 3437, Johannesburg 2000, South Africa.

McKENZIE, Rev. John Lawrence, S.T.D.; American ecclesiastic; b. 9 Oct. 1910, Brazil, Ind.; s. of Harry J. McKenzie and Myra Belle Daly; Teacher St John's Coll., Toledo 1935-36, West Baden Coll., 1942-60, Loyola Univ., Ill. 1960-65, Univ. of Chicago 1965-66, Univ. of Notre Dame 1966-70, DePaul Univ. 1970-78; John Courtney Murray Theology Award, Catholic Press Award. *Publications:* Dictionary of the Bible 1966, Second Isaiah 1968, A Theology of the Old Testament 1974. *Address:* 447 West Tenth Street, Claremont, Calif. 91711, U.S.A. *Telephone:* (714) 626-0431.

MACKENZIE, Maxwell Weir, O.C., C.M.G., LL.D., B.COM.; Canadian business executive; b. 30 June 1907, Victoria, B.C.; s. of Hugh Mackenzie and Maud Weir; m. Jean Fairbairn 1931; two s. two d.; ed. Trinity Coll. School, McGill Univ.; joined McDonald, Currie & Co., Chartered Accountants, Montreal, and admitted to Soc. of Chartered Accountants of Prov. of Quebec 1929; became partner in firm 1935; called to Foreign Exchange Control Bd. and transferred to Wartime Prices and Trade Bd. 1942, apptd. Deputy Chair. of Bd. 1943; returned to McDonald, Currie & Co. 1944; apptd. mem. of Royal Comm. on Taxation of Annuities and Family Corpns. 1944; Deputy Minister of Trade and Commerce 1945-51; Deputy Minister of Defence Production 1951-52; Exec. Vice-Pres. Canadian Chemical & Cellulose Co. Ltd. 1952-54; Pres. Canadian Chemical & Cellulose Co. Ltd. 1954-59, Chemcell Ltd. 1959-63; Chair. Finance Cttee., Chemcell Ltd. and Columbia Cellulose Co. Ltd. 1967-68; Chair. Royal Comm. on Security 1966-68; Dir. The Canadian Imperial Bank of Commerce 1955-77 (now Emer. Dir.), Celanese Corpn. of America 1959-67, The Royal Trust Co. 1960-67, Canron Ltd. 1961-78, Imperial Life Assurance Co. of Canada 1962-75, RCA Victor Co. Ltd. (name changed to RCA Ltd. 1968) 1963-76, Int. Multi-foods Corpn. 1964-77; mem. Econ. Council of Canada 1963-71; Pres. N.B. Multiplex Corpn. 1971-76; Pres. Montreal Joint Hosp. Inst. 1971-73; Dir. C. D. Howe Research Inst. 1973-79; Chair. Comm. of Inquiry into the Marketing of Beef and Veal Jan. 1975; Hon. LL.D. (McGill Univ.) 1973. *Leisure interests:* woodwork, gardening, skiing. *Address:* 383 Maple Lane, Rockcliffe Park, Ottawa, K1M 1H7, Canada.

MACKENZIE STUART, The Hon. Lord (Alexander John), B.A., LL.B.; British judge; b. 18 Nov. 1924, Aberdeen; s. of Prof. A. Mackenzie Stuart, Q.C. and Amy Margaret Dean; m. Anne Burtholme Millar 1952; four d.; ed. Fettes Coll., Edinburgh, Cambridge and Edinburgh Univs.; Royal Engineers 1942-47; admitted to Faculty of Advocates 1951; Standing Jr. Counsel, Scottish Home Dept. 1956-57, Inland Revenue, Scotland 1957-63; Q.C. 1963; Keeper of Advocates Library 1970-72; Sheriff-Prin. of Aberdeen, Kincardine and Banff 1971-72; Senator, Coll. of Justice, Scotland 1972; Judge, Court of Justice of European Communities 1973-88, Pres. 1984-88;

Dr. h.c. (Stirling), Hon LL.D. (Exeter, Edinburgh, Glasgow, Aberdeen, Cambridge, Birmingham). *Address:* 7 Randolph Cliff, Edinburgh, EH3 7TZ, Scotland.

McKERCHER, Robert Hamilton, Q.C., B.A., LL.M.; Canadian lawyer; b. 6 May 1930, Saskatoon, Sask.; s. of Stewart McKercher and Etta Marie McKercher; m. Margaret Louise Wilton 1952; two s. one d.; ed. Univ. of Saskatchewan, Harvard Law School, Univ. of Toronto; Sr. Partner, McKercher, McKercher, Stack, Korchin and Laing, Saskatoon; mem., Canadian Bar Asscn. Nat. Exec. 1978-81, Nat. Treas. 1981-82, Nat. Vice-Pres. 1982-83, Nat. Pres. 1983-84; Dir. Bank of Montreal; Pres., Law Soc. of Sask. 1977-78; Vice-Pres., Canadian Bar Asscn., Sask. Branch 1966-68; Bencher, Law Soc. of Sask. 1973-79; Fellow, Foundation for Legal Research of Canada; Fellow, American Coll. of Trial Lawyers. *Leisure interests:* pure bred Black Angus herd, grain farming, golf, fishing. *Address:* 300-374 Third Avenue South, Saskatoon, Sask. S7K 1M5, Canada. *Telephone:* (306) 653-2000.

McKERN, Leo Reginald, A.O.; Australian actor; b. 16 March 1920, Sydney; s. of Norman W. McKern and Vera Martin; m. Jane Holland 1946; two d.; ed. Sydney Tech. High School; eng. apprentice 1935-37; artist 1937-40; army service 1940-42; actor since 1944; came to England 1946; Confed. of Shipbldg. and Eng. unions tour, Germany; Arts Council tours 1947; Old Vic 1949-52; Shakespeare Memorial Theatre 1952-54; Old Vic last season 1962-63; New Nottingham Playhouse 1963-64; has since appeared regularly on London stage, including Boswell for the Defence 1989; *films:* The French Lieutenant's Woman 1983, Ladyhawke 1984, The Chain 1985, Travelling North 1986; *television:* Rumpole of the Bailey 1977-, Reilly-Ace of Spies 1983, Monsieur Quixote, Murder with Mirrors 1985, The Master Builder 1987. *Publication:* Just Resting (memoir) 1983. *Leisure interests:* photography, sailing, environment. *Address:* c/o I.C.M. Ltd., 388/396 Oxford Street, London, W1N 9HE, England.

McKERNAN, John Rettie, J.D.; American politician; b. 20 May 1948, Bangor, Maine; s. of John Rettie McKernan Sr. and Barbara Guild; one s.; m. 2nd Olympia Snowe 1989; ed. Dartmouth Coll. and Southern Maine Univ.; Attorney, Sterns and Finnegan, Bangor, Maine 1974-76, Verrill and Dana, Portland, Maine 1976-82; mem. 98th-99th Congresses from 1st Dist. Maine 1982; Gov. of Maine Jan. 1987-; mem. Pres. Comm. on Presidential Scholars 1981; Republican. *Address:* Office of the Governor, State House, Station 1, Augusta, Maine, U.S.A.

MACKERRAS, Sir Charles, Kt., C.B.E., F.R.C.M.; British conductor; b. 17 Nov. 1925, Schenectady, U.S.A. of Australian parentage; s. of Alan and Catherine Mackerras; m. Judith Wilkins 1947; two d.; ed. Sydney Grammar School, N.S.W. Conservatoire, and Prague Acad. of Music; Principal Oboist Sydney Symphony Orchestra 1943-46; Conductor Sadler's Wells 1948-53, BBC Concert Orchestra 1954-56; guest conductor in Europe, Canada, Australia, S. Africa 1957-66; guest opera conductor at Covent Garden, English Nat. Opera, Sadler's Wells, Berlin State Opera, Hamburg State Opera, Vienna State Opera, etc. 1956-66; First Conductor, Hamburg State Opera 1966-69; Musical Dir., English Nat. Opera 1970-77, Chief guest conductor 1978-80; Chief guest conductor, BBC Symphony Orchestra 1976-79; Chief Conductor Sydney Symphony Orchestra 1982-85; Prin. Guest Conductor Royal Liverpool Philharmonic Orchestra 1986-88; Musical Dir. Welsh Nat. Opera 1987-; Assoc. Artist English Nat. Opera 1980; guest conductor with U.S. Symphony Orchestras, Boston, Chicago, Cincinnati, Dallas, Los Angeles, St. Louis, New York Philharmonic, San Francisco Opera, Houston Opera, Metropolitan Opera, Paris Opéra, Cologne Opera, Deutsche Oper, W. Berlin, Royal Opera House Covent Garden, Vienna State Opera, Geneva and Zürich Opera, Australian Opera; Evening Standard Award for Most Outstanding Achievement in Opera 1977; Janáček Medal 1978; Gramophone awards 1978, 1980, 1983, 1984; Gramophone Record of the Year and Grammy Award for Best Opera Recording 1981: Janacek's House of the Dead. *Arrangements:* Ballets: Pineapple Poll 1951, Lady and the Fool 1954, Melbourne Cup 1965, many recordings notably Janáček and Handel series. *Publications:* musical articles in various magazines. *Leisure interests:* languages, yachting. *Address:* 10 Hamilton Terrace, London, NW8 9UG, England. *Telephone:* 01-286 4047.

MACKEY, George Whitelaw, PH.D.; American mathematician; b. 1 Feb. 1916, St. Louis, Mo.; s. of William Sturges Mackey and Dorothy Frances Allison; m. Alice Willard 1960; one d.; ed. Rice and Harvard Univs.; Instructor in Math., Ill. Inst. of Tech. 1942-43; Faculty Instructor in Math., Harvard Univ. 1943-46 (on leave for war work April 1944-Sept. 1945), Asst. Prof. of Math 1946-48, Assoc. Prof. 1948-56, Prof. 1956-69, Landon T. Clay Prof. of Math. and Theoretical Science 1969-85, Prof. Emer. 1985-; Walker Ames Visiting Prof., Univ. of Washington, Summer 1961; George Eastman Visiting Prof. at Oxford 1966-67; Visiting Prof. Tata Inst. of Fundamental Research, Bombay 1970-71; Assoc. Prof. Univ. of Paris VI 1978; Visiting Prof. Univ. of Calif., Berkeley 1984; mem. Inst. for Advanced Study, Princeton 1942, 1977, Math. Sciences Research Inst., Berkeley, Calif. 1983-84, A.A.A.S., N.A.S., American Philosophical Soc.; Guggenheim Fellow 1949-50, 1961-62, 1970-71. *Publications:* Mathematical Foundations of Quantum Mechanics 1963, Lectures on the Theory of Functions of a Complex Variable 1967, Induced Representations and Quantum Mechanics 1968, The Theory of Unitary Group Representations 1976, Unitary Group Representations in Physics, Probability and Number Theory 1978, articles in mathematical journals. *Leisure interests:* conversation, reading, music. *Address:* Department of Mathematics, Harvard University, Cambridge, Mass. 02138; 25 Coolidge Hill Road, Cambridge, Mass. 02138, U.S.A.

MACKEY, James Patrick, B.A., B.D., S.T.L., D.D., PH.D.; Irish professor of theology and ecclesiastic; b. 9 Feb. 1934, Ireland; s. of Peter Mackey and Esther Morrissey; m. Noelle Quinlan 1973; one s. one d.; ed. Mount St. Joseph Coll., Nat. Univ. of Ireland, Pontifical Univ., Maynooth and Queen's Univ., Belfast; ordained priest 1958; lecturer in Philosophy Queen's Univ. 1960-66, Philosophy and Theol. St. John's Coll., Waterford 1966-69; Assoc. Prof. of Philosophical and Systematic Theology Univ. of San Francisco 1969-73, Prof. 1973-79; Visiting Prof. Univ. of Calif. Berkeley 1974-75; Thomas Chalmers Prof. of Theology Univ. of Edinburgh 1979-, Dean of Faculty of Divinity 1984-88; British Acad. Research Scholarship 1964-65; scripted and presented TV series The Hall of Mirrors 1984, The Gods of War 1986. *Publications:* Life and Grace 1966, Morals, Law and Authority (ed.) 1969, The Problems of Religious Faith 1974, Jesus, The Man and the Myth 1979, The Christian Experience of God as Trinity 1983, Religious Imagination (ed.) 1986, Modern Theology 1987, An Introduction to Celtic Christianity 1989, etc. *Leisure interest:* sailing. *Address:* 10 Randolph Crescent, Edinburgh, EH3 7TT (Home); New College, Mound Place, Edinburgh, EH1 2LX, Scotland (Office). *Telephone:* (031) 225-9408 (Home); (031) 225-8400 (Office).

McKINLEY, John K., M.S.; American business executive (retd.); b. 24 March 1920, Tuscaloosa, Ala.; s. of Virgil P. McKinley and Mary E. Key; m. Helen Heare 1946; two s.; ed. Univ. of Alabama; joined Texaco as chemical engineer 1941; Asst. Dir. of Research, Texaco Research Lab., Beacon, N.Y. 1957; Asst. to Vice-Pres. 1959; Man. Commercial Devt. Processes, Research and Tech. Dept., Beacon 1960; Gen. Man. Petrochemical Dept., New York 1960-67; Vice-Pres. in charge of Petrochemical Operations and of Supply and Distribution 1967-71; Sr. Vice-Pres. for Worldwide Refining, Petrochemicals, and Supply and Distribution Jan.-April 1971; Pres. Texaco Inc. 1971-80, Chair., and C.E.O. 1980-86; Dir. Texaco Inc. 1971-, Apollo Computer Inc. 1987-, Manufacturers Hanover Corpn. 1980-, Manufacturers Hanover Trust 1980-, Martin Marietta 1985-, Merck and Co. Inc. 1982-; Man. Dir. Metropolitan Opera Asscn. 1980-; mem. A.C.S.; Fellow, A.I.Ch.E.; Andrew Wellington Cordier Fellow, Columbia Univ.; Hon. LL.D. (Alabama 1972, Troy State Univ. 1974); George Washington Honor Medal, Freedoms Foundation 1972, Alabama Business Hall of Fame 1982. *Address:* One Canterbury Green, Stamford, Conn. 06901, U.S.A. *Telephone:* (203) 967-3000.

McKINNEY, James Russell; Canadian diplomatist (retd.); b. 28 June 1925, New Brunswick; s. of George Melbourne and Margaret Jane McKinney; m. Chloe Constance MacLeod 1955; two s. one d.; ed. Dalhousie Univ.; joined Dept. External Affairs 1949, posted Belgrade 1951-54; Chargé d'Affaires, Djakarta 1957, First Sec., later Counsellor, Copenhagen 1959, Ottawa 1962-66; High Commr., Trinidad and Tobago and Barbados, Canadian Commr. to West Indies Assoc. States 1966-69; Amb. and Perm. Rep. to OECD 1969-72; Minister, Embassy, Washington 1972-77; Dir.-Gen. Bureau of U.S. Affairs, Dept. of External Affairs, Ottawa 1977; Asst. Under-Sec. of State for External Affairs 1980-82; Amb. to Mexico 1982-85. *Leisure interests:* yachting, fishing. *Address:* 762 Eastbourne Avenue, Ottawa, Ont., K1K 0H7, Canada.

McKINNEY, Robert Moody, B.A.; American newspaper publisher and diplomatist; b. 28 Aug. 1910, Shattuck, Okla.; s. of Edwin McKinney and Eva Moody; m. 1st Louise Trigg 1943, one d.; m. 2nd Marie-Louise de Montmollin 1970; ed. Univ. of Oklahoma; War Service, U.S. Navy 1942-45; Ed. and Publr., The New Mexican 1949-; Pres. The New Mexican Inc. 1950-; Chair. Taos Publs. Corpn., New Mexico Econ. Devt. Comm. 1949-51; Asst. Sec. U.S. Dept. of Interior 1951-52; Chair. Panel to report to Congress on impact of Peaceful Uses of Atomic Energy 1955-56; Perm. U.S. Rep. to Int. Atomic Energy Agency, Vienna 1957-58; U.S. Rep. to 2nd Int. Conf. on Peaceful Uses of Atomic Energy 1958; rapporteur, Cttee. on Scientific and Tech. Co-operation, Atlantic Congress, London 1959; apptd. by Joint Cttee. of U.S. Congress to review int. atomic policies and programmes of U.S.A. 1959-60; Amb. to Switzerland 1961-63; Exec. Officer, Presidential Task Force on Int. Investments 1963-64; Vice-Chair. Advisory Cttee. on Financial Investments 1966; U.S. Rep. Int. Centre for Settlement of Investment Disputes, Washington 1967-73; Chair. Presidential Industry-Gov. Special Task Force on Travel 1968; Pres. Robert Moody Foundation 1986-; mem. Foreign Policy Assen.; Chair. Bd. of Visitors and Governors, Oklahoma Univ.; mem. American Soc. of Newspaper Eds., Council on Foreign Relations; Distinguished Service Citation 1965; Hon. LL.D. (New Mexico); Democrat. *Publications:* Hymn to Wreckage: A Picaresque Interpretation of History 1947, The Scientific Foundation for European Integration, Reappraising the European Energy Problem, On Increasing the Effectiveness of Western Science and Technology, all 1959, The Red Challenge to Technological Renewal 1960, Review of the International Atomic Policies and Programs of the United States 1960, The Bolshoi Ballet's Last Tour 1983, The Toad and the Water Witch 1985, Variations on a Marxist Interpretation of Culture 1986, The Bolshoi Ballet's Last Tour 1986. *Leisure interest:* farming. *Address:* P.O. Box 1705, Santa Fe, N.M. 87501 (Office); Wind Fields, Rt. 1, Box 64, Middleburg, Va. 22117, U.S.A. (Home).

MACKINTOSH, Allan Roy, PH.D. (CANTAB.); Danish professor of physics; b. 22 Jan. 1936, England; s. of Malcolm R. and Alice (née Williams) Mackintosh; m. Jette Stannow 1958; one s. two d.; ed. Nottingham High School, Univ. of Cambridge; Assoc. Prof. of Physics, Iowa State Univ. 1960–66; Research Prof., Tech. Univ. of Denmark 1966–70; Prof. of Physics, Univ. of Copenhagen 1970–; Dir. Risø Nat. Lab. 1971–76, NORDITA (Nordic Inst. for Theoretical Physics) 1986–88; mem. ed. bds. Journal of Physics, Journal of Magnetism and Magnetic Materials, Physica Scripta; mem. Royal Danish Acad. of Sciences and Letters, Danish Acad. of Tech. Sciences, Danish Physical Soc., European Physical Soc., Inst. of Physics, American Physical Soc.; Knight of the Order of Dannebrog 1975, First Class 1984; F.H. Spedding Award 1986; Fil. Dr. h.c. (Uppsala) 1980. *Publications:* approx. 70 articles on solid state physics. *Leisure interests:* squash, music, reading. *Address:* H.C. Ørsted Institute, Universitetsparken 5, DK 2100 Copenhagen (Office); H. Thomsensvej 4, DK 3460 Birkerød, Denmark (Home). *Telephone:* 1 35 31 33 (Office); 2 81 50 38 (Home).

MACKINTOSH, Nicholas John, D.PHIL., F.R.S.; British professor of experimental psychology; b. 9 July 1935; s. of Dr. Ian Mackintosh and Daphne Mackintosh; m. 1st Janet Ann Scott 1960; one s. one d.; m. 2nd Bundy Wilson 1978; two s.; ed. Winchester and Magdalen Coll., Oxford; lecturer, Univ. of Oxford 1964–67; Resident Prof., Dalhousie Univ. 1967–73; Prof., Univ. of Sussex 1973–81; Prof. of Experimental Psychology and Professorial Fellow of King's College, Cambridge 1981–; Resident Fellow, Lincoln Coll., Oxford 1966–67; Visiting Prof., Univ. of Pennsylvania 1965–66, Univ. of Hawaii 1972–73, Bryn Mawr Coll. 1977; Ed. Quality Journal of Experimental Psychology 1977–84. *Publications:* Fundamental Issues in Associative Learning (ed. with W. K. Honig) 1969, Mechanisms of Animal Discrimination Learning (with N. S. Sutherland) 1971, the Psychology of Animal Learning 1974, Conditioning and Associative Learning 1983, papers in psychological journals. *Address:* King's College, Cambridge, CB2 1ST, England. *Telephone:* (0223) 351386.

McKISSICK, Floyd Bixler, Sr., A.B., LL.B.; American lawyer; b. 9 March 1922; m. Evelyn Williams 1941; one s. three d.; ed. Morehouse Coll., Atlanta, UNC/Chapel Hill, North Carolina Coll., Durham; U.S. Army 1941–45; admitted to N.C. Bar 1952; U.S. Supreme Court 1955; licensed to practise before the F.C.C.; Fed. Dist. Court of Appeals and U.S. Customs Court; Nat. Chair. Congress of Racial Equality (CORE) 1963–66, Nat. Dir. 1966–68; Columnist Amsterdam News, New York; Pres. Floyd B. McKissick Enterprises Inc. 1968–74; Pres. and Developer Soul City (new town) 1974–80; ordained Minister of Gospel 1979; mem. U.S. Comm. on Civil Rights Advisory Cttee., Asscn. of Trial Lawyers, American Bar Asscn.; founder and Chair. Nat. Conf. of Black Lawyers of Republicans; founder Nat. Asscn. of Black Manufacturers; Vice-Pres. N.C. Black Leadership Conf.; Co-founder and Pres. N.C. Center for the Study of Black History, Inc. 1987; Dir. N.C. Chapter of PUSH; mem. Southern Christian Leadership Conf.; Gen. Counsel Cen. Orphanage of N.C.; fmr. Pastor First Baptist Church of Soul City, N.C.; Adjunct Prof. Shaw Univ. Divinity School; Hon. M. Div. (Shaw Univ. Divinity School) 1985; Ike Smalls Award, NAACP; Life mem. NAACP; currently practising law as McKissick and Jones, P.A. *Publications:* Is Integration Necessary? A Black Manifesto, Constructive Militancy 1966, Genocide 1967, Three-Fifths of a Man 1968. *Address:* P.O. Box 128, Soul City, Manson, N.C. 27553; 205 E. McClanahan Street, P.O. Box 931, Oxford, N.C. 27565, U.S.A. (Home). *Telephone:* (919) 693-7393.

MACKNIGHT, Anthony Dunstan Crawford, M.D., PH.D., B.M., F.R.S.N.Z.; New Zealand professor of physiology; b. 5 July 1938, Auckland; s. of William Crawfurd Macknight and Leila (née Maher) Dunstan; m. Jocelyn Mabel Mulinder 1959; three s. three d.; ed. Lindisfarne Coll., Univ. of Otago Medical School; intern, Auckland Hosp. 1964; Research Officer, Medical Research Council of N.Z., Dunedin 1965–69; USPHS Post-Doctoral Research Fellow in Medicine, Harvard Medical School, Boston, U.S.A. 1969–71; lecturer in Physiology, Univ. of Otago Medical School 1971–72; Sr. Lecturer in Physiology 1973–77, Assoc. Prof. and Asst. Dean 1978–79; Visiting Fellow in Medicine, Harvard Medical School, Mass. Gen. Hosp., Boston, U.S.A. 1977; Wolff Harris Prof. of Physiology, Univ. of Otago Medical School 1980–; Sr. Research Scholar 1977. *Publications:* Epithelial Ion and Water Transport 1981 (Ed.); approx. 80 reviews, chapters and original scientific papers on aspects of epithelial transport and cell volume regulation. *Leisure interests:* listening to music, gardening, cricket, reading. *Address:* 6 Tui Street, St. Leonards, Dunedin, New Zealand. *Telephone:* (64) 24-710-094.

McKNIGHT, Hon. William Hunter; Canadian politician; b. 12 July 1940, Elrose, Sask. m. Beverley Ogden; two c.; ed. Wartime and Elrose, Sask.; fmr. farmer and business exec.; M.P. 1979, fmr. Chair. House Standing Cttee. on Agric., fmr. mem. Transport Cttee., Man. and mem's. Services Cttee., Finance, Trade and Econ. Affairs Cttee., fmr. Progressive Conservative Party spokesperson on Canadian Wheat Bd., on Int. Trade, fmr. Deputy Opposition House Leader; Progressive Conservative Party Minister of Labour 1984–86, of Indian Affairs and Northern Devt. 1986–89, of Defence Jan. 1989–. *Address:* Department of Defence, 101 Colonel By Drive, Ottawa, Ont., K1A 0J2, Canada.

McKUEN, Rod; American author and composer; b. 29 April 1933, Oakland, Calif; has appeared in numerous films, concerts and on TV, composer of film scores and background music for TV shows; composer-lyricist of many songs; Pres. of numerous record and book cos.; mem. Bd. of Dirs. American Nat. Theatre of Ballet, Animal Concern; mem. Bd. of Govs. Nat. Acad. of Recording Arts and Sciences; mem. A.S.C.A.P., Writers Guild, A.F.T.R.A., M.P.A., NARAS; Pres. of American Guild of Variety Artists (AGVA); mem. Bd. of Dirs. Calif. Music Theater; Grand Prix du Disque 1966, 1974, 1975, 1982, Golden Globe 1969, Motion Picture Daily Award 1969; Los Angeles Shrine Club Award 1975, Freedoms Foundation 1975, Horatio Alger Award 1976; Brandeis Univ. Literary Trust Award 1981, Freedoms Foundation Patriot Medal 1981, Salvation Army Man of the Year 1983, Rose d'Ore, Cannes 1986, Myasthenia Gravis Community Service Award 1986. *Works include:* Symphony Number One, Concerto for Guitar and Orchestra, Concerto for Four Harpsichords, Seascapes for Piano and Orchestra, Adagio for Harp and Strings, Piano Variations, Concerto Number Three for Piano and Orchestra 1972, The Plains of My Country (ballet) 1972, The City (orchestral suite) 1973, Ballad of Distances (orchestral suite) 1973, Bicentennial Ballet 1975, Symphony Number Three 1975, over 200 record albums. *Film scores:* Joanna 1968, The Prime of Miss Jean Brodie 1969, Me, Natalie 1969, A Boy Named Charlie Brown 1970, Come to Your Senses 1971, Scandalous John 1971, Wildflowers 1971, The Borrowers 1973, Lisa Bright and Dark 1973, Awareness of Emily 1976, The Unknown War 1979, Man to Himself 1980, Portrait of Rod McKuen 1982, Death Rides this Trail 1983, The Living End 1983. *Publications:* And Autumn Came 1954, Stanyan Street and Other Sorrows 1966, Listen to the Warm 1967, Twelve Years of Christmas 1968, In Someone's Shadow 1969, With Love 1970, Caught in the Quiet 1970, Fields of Wonder 1971, The Carols of Christmas 1971, And to Each Season 1972, Beyond the Boardwalk 1972, Come to Me in Silence 1973, America—An Affirmation 1974, Seasons in the Sun 1974, Alone, Moment to Moment 1974, The McKuen Omnibus 1975, Celebrations of the Heart 1975, My Country 200 1975, I'm Strong but I Like Roses, Sleep Warm, Beyond the Boardwalk 1976, The Sea Around Me … The Hills Above 1976, Finding My Father (biographical) 1977, Coming Close to Earth 1977, Hand in Hand … 1977, Love's Been Good to Me 1979, We Touch the Sky 1979, Looking for a Friend 1980, An Outstretched Hand 1980, The Power Bright and Shining 1980, Too Many Midnights 1981, Rod McKuen's Book of Days 1981, The Beautiful Strangers 1981, The Works of Rod McKuen, Vol. 1, Poetry 1982, Watch for the Wind … 1982, Rod McKuen—1984 Book of Days 1983, The Sound of Solitude 1983, Suspension Bridge 1984, Another Beautiful Day 1985, Valentines 1986, Intervals 1986. *Address:* P.O. Box G, Beverly Hills, Calif. 90213, U.S.A.

McLAGLEN, Andrew V.; British film director; b. 28 July 1920, London. *Films include:* Gun the Man Down 1956, Man in the Vault 1956, The Abductors 1957, Freckles 1960, The Little Shepherd of Kingdom Come 1961, McLintock 1963, Shenandoah 1965, The Rare Breed 1966, Monkeys, Go Home! 1967, The Way West 1967, The Ballad of Josie 1968, The Devil's Brigade 1968, Bandoleroi 1968, Hellfighters 1969, The Undefeated 1969, Chisum 1970, One More Train to Rob 1971, Fool's Parade 1971, Something Big 1971, Cahill, U.S. Marshal 1973, Mitchell 1975, The Log of the Black Pearl 1975, Stowaway to the Moon 1975, Banjo Hackett: Roamin' Free 1976, The Last Hard Men 1976, Murder at the World Series 1977, Breakthrough Sergeant Steiner 1978, The Wild Geese 1979, North Sea Hijack 1980, The Sea Wolves 1981, Deprisa, Deprisa 1981, Sweet Hours 1982, Antonieta 1982, The Shadow Riders 1982, The Blue and the Gray 1982, Carmen 1983, Travis McGee 1983, Sahara 1983. *Address:* c/o Tom Chasin, 190 North Canon Drive, Beverly Hills, Calif. 90210, U.S.A.

MacLAINE, Shirley; American film actress, writer and film director; b. 24 April 1934, Richmond, Va.; d. of Ira Beaty and Kathlyn MacLean; m. Steve Parker; one d.; ed. grammar school and Lee High School, Washington; fmr. chorus girl and dancer; Star of the Year Award (Theater Owners of America) 1967; Best Actress Award for role in Desperate Characters, Berlin Film Festival 1971. *Films include:* The Trouble With Harry, Artists and Models, Around The World in 80 Days, Hot Spell, The Matchmaker, Can-Can, Career, The Apartment, Two For The Seesaw, The Children's Hour, Irma La Douce, What A Way To Go, The Yellow Rolls-Royce, Gambit, Woman Times Seven, The Bliss of Mrs. Blossom, Sweet Charity, Two Mules For Sister Sara, Desperate Characters, The Possessions of Joel Delaney, The Turning Point 1977, Being There 1979, Loving Couples 1980, The Change of Seasons 1981, Slapstick 1981, Terms of Endearment (Acad. Award for Best Actress) 1984, Out on a Limb 1987, Madame Sousatzka (Golden Globe Award for Best Actress) 1989, Steel Magnolias 1989, Waiting for the Light; *revues:* If My Friends Could See Me Now 1974, To London With Love 1976, London 1982; *Video:* Shirley MacLaine's Inner Workout 1989; *Produced and co-directed* The Other Half of the Sky—A China Memoir 1973; *producer and star of* Amelia 1975. *Publications:* Don't Fall Off the Mountain 1971, The New Celebrity Cookbook 1973, You Can Get There From Here 1975 (Vols. 1 and 2 of autobiog.), Out on a Limb (Vol. 3) 1983, Dancing in the Light 1985 (Vol. 4), It's All in the Playing (Vol. 5) 1987, Going Within (Vol. 6) 1989. *Address:* c/o ICM, 8899 Beverly Boulevard, Los Angeles, Calif. 90048, U.S.A.

MacLANE, Saunders, PH.D.; American mathematician; b. 4 Aug. 1909, Norwich, Conn.; s. of Donald B. MacLane and Winifred A. Saunders; m. 1st Dorothy M. Jones 1933 (died 1985); two d.; m. 2nd Osa Skotting Segal 1986; ed. Yale Coll., Univ. of Chicago, Göttingen Univ.; Benjamin Peirce

Instructor in Math., Harvard Univ. 1934–36; Instructor Cornell Univ. 1936–37, Chicago Univ. 1937–38; Asst. Prof., Harvard Univ. 1938–41, Assoc. Prof. 1941–46, Prof. 1946–47; Prof. Univ. of Chicago 1947–62, Max Mason Distinguished Service Prof. in Math., Univ. of Chicago 1963–82, Prof. Emer. 1982–; mem. Nat. Acad. of Sciences, Vice-Pres. 1973–81; Vice-Pres. American Philosophical Soc. 1968–71; mem. Nat. Science Bd. 1974–80; Pres. American Math. Soc. 1973–74; Hon. Sc.D., Hon. LL.D. *Publications:* Survey of Modern Algebra (with G. Birkhoff) 1941, Homology 1963, Algebra (with G. Birkhoff) 1967, Categories for the Working Mathematician 1972, Mathematics: Form and Function 1985. *Leisure interests:* sailing, skiing, photography. *Address:* Department of Mathematics, The University of Chicago, 5734 University Avenue, Chicago, Ill. 60637 (Office); 5712 South Dorchester Avenue, Chicago, Ill. 60637, U.S.A. (Home). *Telephone:* (312) 962-7330 (Office).

McLAREN, Digby Johns, O.C., M.A., PH.D., F.R.S., F.R.S.C.; Canadian geologist; b. 11 Dec. 1919, N. Ireland; s. of James and Louie (née Kinsey) McLaren; m. Phyllis Matkin 1942; two s. one d.; ed. Sedbergh School, Yorks., Queens' Coll., Cambridge, and Univ. of Michigan; Capt. Royal Artillery 1940–46; geologist, Geol. Survey of Canada 1948–80, Dir.-Gen. 1973–80; Dir. Inst. of Sedimentary and Petroleum Geology 1967–73; Asst. Deputy Minister, Science and Tech., Dept. of Energy, Mines and Resources 1980–81, Sr. Scientific Adviser 1980–84; Prof. Dept. of Geology, Univ. of Ottawa 1981–88; Chair. Int. Geological Correlation Prog., UNESCO/IUGS 1976–80, adviser in earth science to Dir.-Gen. of UNESCO 1980–; Foreign Assoc., U.S. Nat. Acad. of Sciences; Pres. Geological Soc. of America 1982; Chair. and Organiser of two Dahlem Confs. (Berlin) on Resources and World Devt. 1986; Pres. Royal Soc. of Canada 1987–; Hon. D.Sc. (Ottawa) 1980; Gold Medal (Science), Professional Inst. 1979; Leopold von Buch Medal, Geological Soc. of Germany 1983; Logan Medal, Geological Asscn. of Canada 1987. *Publications:* Resources and World Development (ed.) 1987; over 80 papers, bulletins, memoirs and maps on regional geology, western and Arctic Canada, paleontology, time, historical geology, evolution, extinction, etc. *Leisure interests:* gardening, orchid culture, skiing, music. *Address:* 248 Marilyn Avenue, Ottawa, Ont. K1V 7E5, Canada. *Telephone:* (613) 737-4360.

McLAUGHLIN, Ann Dore, B.A.; American government official; b. 16 Nov. 1941, Newark; d. of Edward J. Lauenstein and Marie Koellhoffer; m. John J. McLaughlin 1975; ed. Marymount Coll.; supervisor, network commercial schedule, ABC, New York 1963–66; Dir. Alumnae Relations, Marymount Coll. 1966–69; Account Exec. Meyers-Infoplan Int. Inc., New York 1969–71; Consultant, Literary Agent, Perla Meyers Int. Kitchen, New York 1970–71; Dir. of Communications, Presidential Election Cttee. 1971–72; Asst. to Chair. and Press Sec. Presidential Inaugural Cttee. 1972–73; Dir. Office of Public Affairs, EPA, Washington 1973–74; Govt. Relations and Communications Exec. Union Carbide Corpn. 1974–77; Public Affairs, Issues Man., Counselling, McLaughlin & Co. 1977–81; Asst. Sec. for Public Affairs, Treasury Dept. 1981–84; Under-Sec. Dept of Interior 1984–87, Sec. of Labor 1987–89; other public appts. *Address:* c/o Department of Labor, 200 Constitution Avenue, N.W., Washington, D.C. 20210, U.S.A.

McLAUGHLIN, William Earle, O.C.; Canadian banker; b. 16 Sept. 1915, Oshawa, Ont.; s. of Frank McLaughlin and Frankie L. Houldon; m. Ethel Wattie 1940; one s. one d.; ed. Queen's Univ.; joined Royal Bank of Canada 1936, Asst. Man., London, Ont. 1942, Head Office 1945, Man. Montreal Branch 1951, Asst. Gen. Man. 1953, Asst. to Pres. 1959, Gen. Man. 1960, Pres. and Dir. 1960; Chair. The Royal Bank of Canada 1962–80, fmr. Pres., fmr. C.E.O. 1979; Dir. and Trustee of numerous cos. and orgs.; Chancellor, Concordia Univ.; Kt. of Grace, Venerable Order of the Hosp. of St. John of Jerusalem. *Leisure interest:* reading. *Address:* 67 Sunnyside Avenue, Westmount, Quebec, H3Y 1C3, Canada (Home).

MacLAURIN, Sir Ian Charter, Kt., F.R.S.A.; British retailing company executive; b. 30 March 1937, Blackheath; s. of Arthur and Evelina MacLaurin; m. Ann Margaret Collar 1962; one s. two d.; ed. Malvern Coll., Worcs.; joined Tesco as a Trainee Man. 1959; Dir. Tesco Stores (Holdings) Ltd. 1970, Man. Dir. 1974–, Deputy Chair. 1983–85, Chair. July 1985–; non-exec. Dir. Enterprise Oil 1984, Guinness PLC 1986; Fellow Inst. of Marketing 1987; Freeman of City of London 1981; mem. MCC; mem. Lords Taverners and Worshipful Co. of Carmen; Hon. D.Univ. (Stirling) 1986. *Leisure interests:* cricket, golf. *Address:* Tesco PLC, Tesco House, Delamare Road, Cheshunt, Herts., England. (Office). *Telephone:* (0992) 32222 (Office).

McLAY, James Kenneth, LL.B.; New Zealand lawyer and politician; b. 21 Feb. 1945, Auckland; s. of late Robert McLay and Joyce Evelyn Dee; m. Marcy Farden 1983; ed. King's Coll. and Univ. of Auckland; Officer, Territorial Force 1967–70; began practice as solicitor 1971, practised solely as barrister from 1974; Ed. Recent Law 1969–70; mem. Parl. for Birkenhead 1975–; Attorney-Gen. and Minister of Justice 1978–84; Deputy Prime Minister 1984; Deputy Leader of Opposition 1984; Leader of Opposition 1984–86; Man. Dir. and Prin. J. K. McLay Ltd. 1986–; Nat. Party. *Leisure interest:* trout fishing. *Address:* Parliament Buildings, Wellington, New Zealand.

MACLEAN, Baron (Life Peer), cr. 1971, of Duart and Morvern in the County of Argyll; **Maj. Charles Hector Fitzroy Maclean,** Bt., K.T., P.C., G.C.V.O., K.B.E.; Scottish army officer and scout; b. 5 May 1916; s. of the late

Hector F. and Winifred Joan (née Wilding) Maclean; m. Elizabeth Mann 1941; one s. one d.; served Scots Guards; Boy Scouts Assen., Chief Commr. for Scotland 1954–59, Chief Scout, U.K. 1959–71, Commonwealth 1959–75; Lord Chamberlain 1971–84; Lord High Commr. to Church of Scotland 1984, 1985; Perm. Lord in Waiting 1984–; Chancellor, Royal Victorian Order 1971–84; Lord Lieut. of Argyll 1954–; Chief Steward, Hampton Court Palace 1985–; Dir. Distillers Co.; Chief of Clan Maclean; awarded Royal Victorian Chain 1984. *Publication:* Only 1979. *Leisure interest:* travelling. *Address:* Duart Castle, Isle of Mull, Scotland. *Telephone:* (068 02) 309.

McLEAN, Colin, C.M.G., MBE., M.A.; British diplomatist; b. 10 Aug. 1930, Dundee, Scotland; m. Huguette Leclerc 1953; one s. one d.; ed. Fordyce Acad., Fettes Coll., St. Catharine's Coll., Cambridge; served 0 Battery, Rocket Troop, 2nd. Regt. Royal Horse Artillery 1953–54; Dist. Officer, Kenya 1955–63, Vice-Prin., Kenya Inst. of Admin. 1963–64; with diplomatic service 1964–, served FCO, then Wellington, then Bogotá, then FCO, then Oslo 1964–81, Head of Trade Relations and Exports Dept., FCO 1981–83, High Commr. in Uganda 1983–86; Perm. Rep. of U.K. to Council of Europe (with status of Amb.) 1986–. *Leisure interests:* climbing, sailing, squash. *Address:* c/o Foreign and Commonwealth Office, King Charles Street, London, SW1A 2AH, England. *Telephone:* 01-233 3000.

McLEAN, Don; American singer, instrumentalist and composer; b. 2 Oct. 1945, New Rochelle, N.Y.; s. of Donald McLean and Elizabeth Bucci; m. Patrisha Shnier 1987; ed. Villanova Univ. and Iona Coll.; Pres. Benny Bird Corpn., Inc.; mem. Hudson River Sloop Singers 1969; solo concert tours throughout U.S.A., Canada, Australia, Europe, Far East etc.; numerous TV appearances; composer of film scores for Fraternity Row, Flight of Dragons; composer of over 200 songs including Prime Time; recordings include Tapestry 1970, American Pie 1971, Don McLean 1972, Playin' Favorites 1973, Homeless Brother 1974, Solo 1976, Prime Time 1977, Chain Lightning 1979, Castles in the Air, etc.; recipient of many gold discs in U.S.A., Australia, U.K. and Ireland; Israel Cultural Award 1981. *Publications:* Songs of Don McLean 1972, The Songs of Don McLean (Vol. II) 1974.

MACLEAN, Sir Fitzroy, Bart., C.B.E.; British author; b. 11 March 1911, Cairo, Egypt; s. of Charles Maclean and Gladys Royle; m. Veronica Fraser (d. of 16th Baron Lovat) 1946; two s.; ed. Eton and Cambridge Univ.; entered Diplomatic Service 1933; served Paris 1934–37, Moscow 1937–39; enlisted in Cameron Highlanders 1941; joined 1st Special Air Service Regiment 1942; Capt. 1942, Lt.-Col. 1943, Brig. 1943; Commdr. British Mil. Mission to Yugoslav Partisans 1943–45; Conservative M.P. for Lancaster Div. 1941–59, for Bute and N. Ayr 1959–74; Parl. Under-Sec. to State and Financial Sec. War Office 1954–57; Pres. G.B.-U.S.S.R. Assen. 1959–77, Past Pres. 1977–; Hon. LL.D. (Dalhousie) 1971, (Dundee) 1984; Croix de guerre, Order of Kutuzov (U.S.S.R.), Partisan Star (1st Class), Order of Yugoslav Star with Ribbon 1981. *Publications:* Eastern Approaches 1949, Disputed Barricade 1957, A Person from England 1958, Back to Bokhara 1959, Jugoslavia 1969, A Concise History of Scotland 1970, The Battle of the Neretva 1970, To the Back of Beyond 1974, To Caucasus 1976, Take Nine Spies 1978, Holy Russia 1979, Tito 1980, The Isles of the Sea 1985, Portrait of the Soviet Union 1988, Bonnie Prince Charlie 1988. *Address:* Strachur House, Strachur, Argyll, Scotland. *Telephone:* Strachur 242.

MacLEAN, Wing Commdr. J. Angus, D.F.C., B.SC., C.D., LL.D., M.L.A., P.C.; Canadian farmer and retd. politician; b. 15 May 1914, Lewes, P.E.I.; s. of George Allen and Sarah MacLean; m. Gwendolyn Esther Burwash 1952; two s. two d.; ed. local schools in P.E.I., Mount Allison Acad., Summerside High School, Univ. of British Columbia and Mount Allison Univ.; served with R.C.A.F. 1939–47; cand. Fed. Elections 1945 and 1949; mem. House of Commons 1951–76; Minister of Fisheries 1957–63; Leader Progressive Conservative Party, P.E.I. 1976–81; mem. P.E.I. Legislature 1976–81; Premier of P.E.I. 1979–81; Officer Order of St. John of Jerusalem 1982. *Address:* Lewes, Belle River, R.R. 3, Prince Edward Island C0A 1B0, Canada.

McLEAN, Rev. Walter Franklin, P.C.; Canadian religious official and politician; b. 26 April 1936, Leamington, Ont.; m. Barbara Scott 1961; four s.; ed. Victoria Coll., Univ. of British Columbia, Knox Coll., Univ. of Toronto, Univ. of Edinburgh; co-founder CUSO (fmrly. first Nigerian Coordinator); fmr. Exec. Dir. Man. Centennial Corpn.; fmr. Minister of Knox Presbyterian Church, Waterloo; Alderman for City of Waterloo 1976–79; M.P. 1979–; fmr. mem. Standing Cttee. on Communications and Culture, on External Affairs, on Nat. Defence; fmr. mem. Special Sub-Cttee. on Latin America and Caribbean; fmr. spokesperson for status of women; spokesperson for Sec. of State 1981, Sec. of State 1984–85, Minister of State (Immigration) and Minister Responsible for the Status of Women 1984–86; Progressive Conservative Party. *Address:* House of Commons, Ottawa, Ont., K1A 0A2, Canada. *Telephone:* (613) 731-8725.

McLEAN, William F., B.SC. (HONS.); Canadian business executive (retd.); b. 30 Oct. 1916, Toronto; ed. Univ. of Toronto Schools, Univ. of Toronto and in U.S.A.; Research Chemist, Canada Packers Ltd. 1939, in charge of all Plants and Equipment 1949, Dir. and Vice-Pres. 1950, mem. Exec. Cttee. 1952, Pres. Canada Packers Ltd. 1954–78, Chair. and C.E.O. 1978–82; served with Royal Canadian Air Force 1942–46; mem. Bd. of Govs.,

Roy Thomson Massey Hall Corpn. *Address:* 30 St. Clair Avenue West, Suite 1200, Toronto, Ont. M4V 3A2, Canada.

MacLEHOSE OF BEOCH, Baron (Life Peer), cr. 1982, of Maybole in the District of Kyle and Carrick and of Victoria in Hong Kong; **(Crawford) Murray MacLehose,** K.T., G.B.E., K.C.M.G., K.C.V.O., K.ST.J.; British diplomatist and administrator; b. 16 Oct. 1917, Glasgow; s. of Hamish A. and Margaret Bruce MacLehose; m. Margaret N. Dunlop 1947; two d.; ed. Rugby School and Balliol Coll., Oxford; served with R.N.V.R. 1939–45; entered diplomatic service 1947; Acting Consul, Hankow 1947, Acting Consul-Gen. 1948; Foreign Office 1950; First Sec., Prague 1951; seconded to Commonwealth Relations Office for service in Wellington 1954; returned to Foreign Office and transferred to Paris 1956; Counsellor 1959; Political Adviser, Hong Kong; Counsellor, Foreign Office 1963; Prin. Pvt. Sec. to Sec. of State 1965–67; Amb. to Repub. of Viet-Nam 1967–69, to Denmark 1969–71; Gov. of Hong Kong 1971–82; Dir. Nat. Westminster Bank 1982–; Chair. Scottish Trust for Physically Handicapped 1982–, Margaret Blackwood Housing Asscn. 1982–, Victoria League for Commonwealth Friendship 1983–87, S.O.A.S. 1985–; Hon. Ph.D. (York) 1983, Hon. D.L. (Strathclyde) 1984. *Leisure interests:* fishing, sailing, farming. *Address:* Beoch, Maybole, Ayrshire, Scotland.

MacLENNAN, Hugh, C.C., PH.D.; Canadian author and professor; b. 20 March 1907, Glace Bay, N.S.; s. of Dr. Samuel MacLennan and Katherine MacQuarrie; m. 1st Dorothy Duncan 1936 (died 1957); m. 2nd Frances Aline Walker 1959; ed. Dalhousie Univ., Oriel Coll., Oxford, Princeton Univ.; Classics Master, Lower Canada Coll., Montreal 1935–45; writing 1945–; part-time Assoc. Prof., McGill Univ. 1951–63, Assoc. Prof. 1964–66, Full Prof. of English Literature 1966–79, Emer. Prof. 1979–82 (retd.); Gov.-Gen.'s Award for Literature (five times); Hon. LL.D., Hon. D.Litt., Hon. D.C.L., from various univs. *Publications:* novels: Barometer Rising 1941, Two Solitudes 1945, The Precipice 1948, Each Man's Son 1951, The Watch That Ends the Night 1959, Return of the Sphinx 1967, Voices in Time 1980; non-fiction: Oxyrhynchus: an Economic and Social Study 1935, Cross Country 1949, Thirty and Three (essays) 1954, Scotchman's Return and Other Essays 1960, Seven Rivers of Canada 1961, The Colour of Canada 1967, Rivers of Canada 1972, Voices in Time 1980. *Leisure interests:* swimming, gardening. *Address:* 1535 Summerhill Avenue, Montreal, P.Q., Canada.

McLENNAN, Sir Ian Munro, K.C.M.G., K.B.E., B.E.E.; Australian engineer; b. 30 Nov. 1909, Stawell, Victoria; m. Dora Haase Robertson 1937; two s. two d.; ed. Scotch Coll., Melbourne and Melbourne Univ.; Asst. Gen. Man. Broken Hill Pty. Co. Ltd. 1947–50, Gen. Man. 1950–56, Dir. 1953–77, Sr. Gen. Man. 1956–59, Chief Gen. Man. 1959–67, Man. Dir. 1967–71, Chair. and Dir. of Admin. 1971–77; Chair. BHP-GKN Holdings Ltd. 1970–78, Tubemakers of Australia Ltd. 1973–79, Interscan Australia Pty. Ltd. 1978–84, Henry Jones (IXL) Ltd. 1980–81, Elders-IXL Ltd. 1982–85; Dir. ICI Australia Ltd. 1976–79, ANZ Banking Group Ltd. 1976–82, Chair. 1977–82; Councillor Australasian Inst. of Mining and Metallurgy (Pres. 1951, 1957, 1972); mem. and Deputy Chair. Immigration Planning Council 1949–67; mem. Int. Council of Morgan Guaranty Trust Co., New York 1973–79, General Motors Australian Advisory Council 1979–82, CSIRO Advisory Council 1979–81; Pres. Australian Acad. of Tech. Sciences 1976–83, Foundation Pres. 1983–; Pres. Australia Japan Business Co-operation Cttee. 1977–85; Gov. Ian Clunies Ross Memorial Foundation 1961, Chair. Bd. of Dirs. 1966–85; Chair. Queen Elizabeth II Silver Jubilee Appeal for Young Australians 1978–81; Councillor of Bd. Royal Agricultural Soc. of Victoria 1978–; Hon. Fellow, Inst. of Engineers, Australia 1982; Australasian Inst. of Mining and Metallurgy Medal 1959, Inst. of Production Engineers' James N. Kirby Award 1964, Australian Inst. of Engineers Award 1968, American Inst. of Mining, Metallurgical and Petroleum Engineers Charles F. Rand Memorial Gold Medal Award 1978, Distinguished Int. Man. Award 1981, Australian Inst. of Man., Bessemer Gold Medal (The Metals Soc., U.K.) 1982. *Leisure interests:* farming, golf. *Address:* 140 William Street, Melbourne, 3000 (Office); Apartment 3, 112 Walsh Street, South Yarra, Vic. 3141, Australia (Home). *Telephone:* 609 3880 (Office); 266 3651 (Home).

MACLENNAN, Robert Adam Ross, M.A., LL.B.; British politician and barrister-at-law; b. 26 June 1936, Glasgow; s. of Sir Hector Maclennan and Lady Maclennan; m. Helen Cutter Noyes 1968; one s. one d. one step-s.; ed. Glasgow Academy, Balliol Coll., Oxford, Trinity Coll., Cambridge, Columbia Univ., New York; M.P. 1966–; Parl. Pvt. Sec. to Sec. of State for Commonwealth Affairs and Minister without portfolio 1967–70, Parl. Under-Sec. of State for Prices and Consumer Protection 1974–79; Opposition Spokesman on Scottish Affairs 1970–71, on Defence 1971–72, on Foreign Affairs 1980–81; resigned from Labour Party 1981; founder mem. SDP 1981; SDP Spokesman on Agriculture 1981–87, on Home and Legal Affairs 1983–87, on Econ. Affairs 1987; Leader SDP 1987–88; Jt. Leader SLD 1988; mem. Public Accounts Cttee. 1979–; mem. SDP Nat. and Policy Cttees.; Gladstone Memorial Prize 1957; Lee Prize, Gray's Inn 1961. *Leisure interests:* music, theatre, books and the 2,800 square miles of his constituency. *Address:* House of Commons, London, SW1A 0AA, England; 74 Abingdon Villas, London, W8 6XB, England (Home); Hollandmake, Barrock, Caithness, KW14 8SY, Scotland. *Telephone:* 01-219-4133 (Office).

McLEOD, James Graham, O.A., M.B., D.PHIL., F.A.A.; Australian professor of neurology and medicine; b. 18 Jan. 1932, Sydney; s. of Hector R. McLeod and Dorothy S. (née Craig) McLeod; m. Robyn E. Rule 1963; two s. two d.; ed. Univ. of Sydney, Oxford Univ., Univ. of London, Harvard Univ.; Sr. Lecturer, Univ. of Sydney 1967–69, Assoc. Prof. 1970–72, Bosch Prof. of Medicine 1972–, Bushell Prof. of Neurology 1978–; Visiting Medical Officer, Royal Prince Albert Hosp., Sydney 1965–, Head, Dept. of Neurology 1978–; mem. Bd. of Dirs. Royal North Shore Hosp., Sydney (Vice-Chair.) 1978–86; Pres. Australian Asscn. of Neurologists 1980–83; Rhodes Scholar 1953–56; Nuffield Travelling Fellow 1964–65; Sir Arthur Sims Travelling Prof. 1983–84; Fellow Australian Acad. of Tech. Science and Eng. 1987. *Publications:* A Physiological Approach to Clinical Neurology (with J. W. Lance, q.v.), Introductory Neurology (with J. W. Lance, q.v.) 1983. *Leisure interests:* swimming, boating. *Address:* Department of Medicine, University of Sydney, Sydney, N.S.W. 2006 (Office); 52 Northwood Road, Northwood, N.S.W. 2066, Australia (Home). *Telephone:* 692 3385 (Office); 427 5130 (Home).

McLUCAS, John Luther, PH.D.; American scientist and government official; b. 22 Aug. 1920, Fayetteville, N.C.; s. of John Luther and Viola Conley McLucas; m. 1st Patricia Newmaker Knapp 1946 (divorced); two s. two d.; m. 2nd Harriet D. Black 1981; ed. Davidson Coll., Tulane Univ. and Pennsylvania State Univ.; U.S. Navy 1943–46; Physicist, U.S. Air Force, Cambridge Research Center 1946–47; Physics Dept., Pennsylvania State Univ. 1947–49; Electronics Engineer Haller, Raymond and Brown Inc. 1949–50, Vice-Pres. and Tech. Dir. 1950–57; Pres. HRB-Singer Inc. 1957–62; Chair. Pennsylvania State Univ. Industrial and Professional Advisory Council 1957–62; Deputy Dir. of Research and Eng. (Tactical Warfare Programs) U.S. Dept. of Defense 1962–64; Asst. Sec.-Gen. for Scientific Affairs, NATO 1964–66; Pres. The Mitre Corpn. 1966–69; Under-Sec. Air Force 1969–73, Sec. Air Force 1973–75; Admin. Fed. Aviation Admin. 1975–77, Pres. Comsat Gen. Corpn., Washington 1977–79, Exec. Vice-Pres. COMSAT 1979–80, Pres. COMSAT World Systems Div. 1980–83, Exec. Vice-Pres. and Chief Strategic Officer 1983–85; Chair. ISY Int. Space Year Comm. of U.S. 1987–; Chair. Bd. Arthur C. Clarke Foundation of U.S.A., Questech Inc.; Chair. Bd. Wolf Trap Foundation for Performing Arts; mem. Air Force Scientific Advisory Bd. 1967–69, 1977–84, Nat. Acad. Eng. 1969, A.I.A.A., Bd. of Dirs. C-COR Electronics Inc.; NASA Advisory Comm. 1987–; F.I.E.E.E.; Hon. D.Sc. (Davidson Coll.) 1974; Dept. of Defense Distinguished Civilian Service Award 1964, 1973 (First Bronze Palm), 1975 (Silver Palm); NASA D.S.M. 1975. *Leisure interests:* golf, bicycling. *Address:* Questech Inc., 6858 Old Dominion Drive, McLean, Va. 22101, U.S.A.

MACMAHON, Brian, M.D., PH.D., D.P.H.; American epidemiologist; b. 12 August 1923, Sheffield, England; s. of Gladys and Desmond MacMahon; m. Heidi Graber 1948; two s. two d.; ed. Univ. of Birmingham, England and Harvard Univ.; Ship Surgeon, Alfred Holt & Co. 1946–48; Lecturer, Prof., State Univ. of New York, Downstate Medical Center 1953–58; Prof. and Chair., Dept. of Epidemiology, Harvard School of Public Health 1958–; Hon. M.D. (Athens) 1976, Hon. Sc.D. (State Univ. of New York) 1985; Edwards Memorial Medal, Univ. of Wales 1974, Lemuel Shattack Award, Mass. Public Health Asscn. 1983, Prix Antoine Laccassagne Soc. Nat. Française pour la Lutte contre le Cancer 1986. *Publications:* Epidemiology: principles and methods 1960, Preventive Medicine and Public Health 1967. *Address:* Department of Epidemiology, Harvard School of Public Health, 677 Huntington Avenue, Boston, Mass. 02115; 89 Warren Street, Needham, Mass. 02192, U.S.A. (Home).

McMAHON, Sir Christopher William "Kit", Kt., M.A.; British banker; b. 10 July 1927, Melbourne, Australia; s. of late Dr. J.J. and Margaret McMahon; m. 1st Marion E. Kelso 1956; two s.; m. 2nd Alison Braimbridge 1982; ed. Melbourne Grammar School, Univ. of Melbourne and Magdalen Coll., Oxford; Econ. Asst., H.M. Treasury 1953–57; Econ. Adviser, British Embassy, Washington, D.C. 1957–60; Fellow and Tutor in Econs., Magdalen Coll., Oxford 1960–64; Adviser, Bank of England 1964–66, Adviser to Govs. 1966–70, Exec. Dir. 1970–80, Deputy Gov. March 1980–85; Deputy Chair. and Chair. (desig.) Midland Bank PLC 1986–87, Chair. April 1987–; Dir. Eurotunnel 1987–, Midland Montagu Holdings 1987–; Chair. OECD Working Party Three; mem. Steering Cttee., Consultative Group on Int. Econ. and Monetary Affairs (Group of Thirty) 1978–84; mem. Court London Univ. 1984–; Trustee, Whitechapel Art Gallery 1984–; Royal Opera House Trust 1984–. *Publications:* Sterling in the Sixties 1964, Techniques of Economic Forecasting 1965. *Leisure interests:* gardening, walking. *Address:* Midland Bank PLC, 27–32 Poultry, London, EC2P 2BX, England.

McMAHON, John Alexander, J.D.; American hospital association executive; b. 31 July 1921, Monongahela, Pa.; s. of late John H. McMahon and of Jean A. McMahon; m. 1st Betty Wagner 1947 (divorced 1977), 2nd Ann F. Willets 1977; one s. three d.; ed. Duke Univ., Harvard Univ. Business School and Harvard Law School; Prof. of Public Law and Govt. and Asst. Dir. Inst. of Govt., Univ. of N.C. 1948–59; Gen. Counsel, Sec.-Treas. N.C. County Commissioners, Chapel Hill 1959–65; Vice-Pres. Special Devt. Hospital Savings Asscn., Chapel Hill 1965–67; Pres. N.C. Blue Cross and Blue Shield, Chapel Hill 1968–72; Pres. American Hospital Asscn. 1972–86; Prof. and Chair. Dept. of Health Admin., Duke Univ. 1986–; Chair. Bd. Trustees Duke Univ. 1971–83, Chair. Emer. 1983–; Hon. LL.D. (Wake

Forest) 1948; Hon. D.Sc. (Georgetown) 1985. *Leisure interests:* golf, reading. *Address:* Box 3018 Medical Center, Durham, N.C. 27710 (Office); 181 Montrose, Durham, N.C. 27707, U.S.A. (Home). *Telephone:* 919-684-4188 (Office); 919-489-5231 (Home).

McMANNERS, John, M.A., F.B.A.; British professor of ecclesiastical history; b. 25 Dec. 1916, Ferryhill, Co. Durham; s. of Rev. Canon Joseph McManners and Ann McManners; m. Sarah Carruthers Errington 1951; two s. two d.; ed. Oxford and Durham Univs.; mil. service in Royal Northumberland Fusiliers (rank of Maj.) 1939–45; Fellow St. Edmund Hall, Oxford 1948–56, Hon. Fellow 1983; Prof. of History, Univ. of Tasmania 1956–59, Univ. of Sydney, Australia 1959–66, Univ. of Leicester 1967–72; Regius Prof. of Ecclesiastical History, Univ. of Oxford 1972–84; Fellow and Chaplain, All Souls Coll., Oxford 1984–; Dir. d'études associé, Ecole Pratique des Hautes Etudes, Sec. IV, Paris 1980–81; Trustee Nat. Gallery 1970–78; mem. Doctrine Comm. Church of England 1978–81; Fellow Australian Acad. of the Humanities 1970; Hon. D.Litt. (Oxford) 1980, (Durham) 1984; Wolfson Literary Award 1982; Officer of the Order of King George I of The Hellenes 1945. *Publications:* French Ecclesiastical Society under the Ancien Régime—Angers 1960, Men, Machines and Freedom 1966, The French Revolution and the Church 1969, Church and State in France 1870–1914 1972, Death and and Enlightenment 1981; contrib. to New Cambridge Modern History Vols. VI and VIII, Ed. Oxford Illustrated History of Christianity 1989. *Leisure interest:* tennis. *Address:* All Souls College, Oxford, OX1 4AL; 71 Cunliffe Close, Oxford (Home). *Telephone:* (0865) 57589 (Home).

McMANUS, Jason Donald, B.A., M.P.A.; American journalist; b. 3 March 1934, Mission, Kan.; s. of John A. McManus and Stella F. Gosney; m. 1st Patricia A. Paulson 1958 (divorced 1966), one s.; m. 2nd Deborah H. Murphy 1973, two d.; ed. Davidson Coll., Princeton Univ. and Univ. of Oxford (Rhodes Scholar); Common Market Bureau Chief, Time Magazine, Paris 1962–64; Assoc. Ed. Time Magazine, New York 1964–68, Sr. Ed. 1968–75, Asst. Man. Ed. 1975–78, Exec. Ed. 1978–83; Corporate Ed. Time Inc. 1983–85; Man. Ed. Time Magazine 1985–87; Ed.-in-Chief, Time Inc. 1987–; Hon. Litt. D. (Davidson Coll.) 1979. *Address:* Time Inc., Time & Life Building, Rockefeller Center, New York, N.Y. 10020, U.S.A. *Telephone:* (212) 522-3753.

McMICHAEL, Sir John, Kt., F.R.S., M.D., F.R.C.P., F.A.C.P.; British emeritus professor of medicine; b. 25 July 1904; s. of James McMichael and Margaret Sproat; m. 1st Joan K. Macpherson (dissolved 1941), 2nd Sybil E. Blake (died 1965), four s.; m. 3rd Sheila M. Howarth; ed. Kirkcudbright Acad. and Edinburgh Univ.; Beit Memorial Fellow 1930–34; Johnston and Lawrence Fellow, Royal Soc. 1937–39; Univ. teaching appointments, Aberdeen, Edinburgh, London; Dir. Dept. of Medicine, Postgraduate Medical School of London 1946–66, British Postgraduate Medical Federation 1966–71; Morgan Prof., Nashville 1964; mem. Medical Research Council 1949–53; Hon. mem. American Medical Assen. 1947, Medical Soc. Copenhagen 1953, Norwegian Medical Soc. 1954, Assen. of American Physicians 1959, Finnish Acad. of Sciences and Letters 1963, U.S. Nat. Acad. of Sciences 1974; foreign mem. Royal Acad. of Medicine, Belgium; numerous lectureships; Trustee, Wellcome Trust 1960–77; Vice-Pres. Royal Soc. 1969–70; Cullen Prize, Royal Coll. of Physicians (Edinburgh) 1953, Jacobs Award, Dallas 1958, Moxon Medal, Royal Coll. of Physicians 1960, Gairdner Award, Toronto 1960, Wihuri Int. Prize, Finland 1968, Krug Award of Excellence 1980. *Publications:* Pharmacology of the Failing Human Heart 1951; numerous papers on: splenic anaemia 1931–35, cardiac output in health and disease 1938–47, lung capacity in man 1938–39, liver circulation and liver disease 1932–43. *Leisure interest:* gardening. *Address:* 2 North Square, London, NW11 7AA, England. *Telephone:* 01-455 8731.

McMILLAN, Edwin M(attison), PH.D.; American physicist; b. 18 Sept. 1907, Redondo Beach, Calif.; s. of Edwin Harbaugh and Anna Marie (née Mattison) McMillan; m. Elsie Blumer 1941; two s. one d.; ed. California Inst. of Tech. and Princeton Univ.; Nat. Research Fellow, Univ. of Calif. 1933–34, Research Assoc. 1935, Asst. Prof. 1935–41, Assoc. Prof. 1942–46, Prof. of Physics at Univ. of Calif., Berkeley 1946–73, Prof. Emer. 1973–; mem. Gen. Advisory Cttee. U.S. Atomic Energy Comm. 1954–58; Dir. E. O. Lawrence Radiation Lab., Univ. of Calif. 1958–71; Dir. Lawrence Berkeley Lab. 1971–73; Dir. San Francisco Palace Arts and Sciences Foundation 1968–; mem. High Energy Physics Comm., Int. Union for Pure and Applied Physics 1960–66; Trustee, Rand Corpn. 1959–69, Univ. Research Assen. 1969–74; mem. Nat. Acad. of Sciences (Chair. Class I 1968–71); Guest Prof. CERN, Geneva 1974; D.Sc. h.c. (Rensselaer Polytechnic Inst.) 1961, (Gustavus Adolphus Coll.) 1963; Research Corpn. Scientific Award 1951, Nobel Prize in Chemistry (with G. T. Seaborg) 1951, Atoms for Peace Prize (with V. Veksler) 1963, Alumni Distinguished Service Award, Calif. Inst. of Tech. 1966. *Address:* Lawrence Berkeley Laboratory, Univ. of California, Berkeley, Calif. 94720 (Office); 1401 Vista Road, El Cerrito, Calif. 94530, U.S.A. (Home).

MACMILLAN, Jake, PH.D., D.SC., F.R.S.; British professor of organic chemistry; b. 13 Sept. 1924, Scotland; s. of John MacMillan and Barbara Lindsay; m. Anne Levy 1952; one s. two d.; ed. Lanark Grammar School and Glasgow Univ.; Assoc. Research Man., ICI 1962–63; Lecturer in Organic Chem., Bristol Univ. 1963–68, Reader 1968–78, Personal Chair. 1978–83, Head of Dept. and Alfred Capper Pass Prof. of Organic Chem. 1983–;

Flintoff Medal 1978 and Hugo Muller Medal 1989, Royal Soc. of Chem.; Research Medal, Int. Plant Growth Substance Assen. 1982; Charles Reid Barnes Award, American Soc. of Plant Physiology. *Publications:* over 250 papers on organic chemistry and plant hormones. *Leisure interests:* gardening, theatre, golf. *Address:* School of Chemistry, University of Bristol, Bristol, BS8 1TS (Office); 1 Rylestone Grove, Bristol, BS9 3UT, England (Home). *Telephone:* (0272) 303678 (Office); (0272) 620535 (Home).

MacMILLAN, Sir Kenneth, Kt.; British ballet director; b. 11 Dec. 1929; m. Deborah Williams 1974; one d.; ed. Great Yarmouth Grammar School; Choreographer 1953–; Resident Choreographer, Royal Ballet until 1966, 1977–; Dir. of Ballet, Deutsche Oper, Berlin 1966–70; Dir. The Royal Ballet 1970–77; Artistic Adviser, American Ballet Theatre, New York 1984–; Dr. h.c. (Edinburgh) 1976. *Major Choreography:* Romeo and Juliet, Song of the Earth, Rite of Spring, Las Hermanas, The Invitation, Diversions, The Fairy's Kiss, Danses concertantes, Agon, Solitaire, Noctambules, House of Birds, Images of Love, The Seven Deadly Sins, Anastasia, Cain and Abel, Olympiad, Checkpoint, Triad, Pavane, Manon 1974, Elite Syncopations 1974, The Four Seasons 1975, Rituals, Requiem, Mayerling 1978, My Brother, My Sisters, La Fin du Jour, Isadora 1981, Orpheus 1982, Dance of Death 1983, Different Drummer 1984; dir. plays: The Chairs and the Lesson 1982, The Dance of Death 1983, The Kingdom of Earth 1984. *Leisure interest:* cinema. *Address:* c/o Royal Opera House, Covent Garden, London, W.C.2., England.

McMILLAN, Hon. Thomas Michael; Canadian politician and political scientist; b. 15 Oct. 1945, Charlottetown, P.E.I.; m. Katherine Jean Hambly; two d.; ed. Univ. of Prince Edward Island, Queen's Univ., Univ. of New Brunswick, Trent Univ.; served as Special Asst. to fmr. Leader of Progressive Conservative Party, Robert Stanfield, then Exec. Dir. to Leader's Policy Advisory Cttee,; fmr. Sr. Research Assoc. Nat Cttee. on Canadian Studies; fmr. Exec. Officer Ont. Human Rights Comm.; fmr. Chair. Book and Periodical Devt. Council of Canada; M.P. 1979–; fmr. mem. Communications and Culture Cttee., Fisheries and Forestry Cttee., Special Cttee. on Acid Rain; fmr. Deputy House Leader for Question Period; Minister of State for Tourism 1984–85; Minister for the Environment 1985–88; Progressive Conservative Party. *Address:* House of Commons, Ottawa, Ont., K1A 0A2, Canada.

McMURRAY, Joseph Patrick Brendan; American economist; b. 3 April 1912, Bronx, New York; s. of Bartholomew and Catherine O'Carvell; m. 2nd Rose-Marie Barker McMurray; six s. three d.; ed. Jamaica High School, Queens, New York, Brooklyn Coll., and New School for Social Research; Economist, Gov. Agencies 1940–44; Econ. Consultant, U.S. Senate Labor and Educ. Comm. 1945–47; Admin. Asst. to U.S. Senator Wagner 1947–48; Consultant and Staff Dir. U.S. Senate Banking and Currency Comm. 1948–54; Exec. Dir. New York City Housing Authority 1954–55; Commr. of Housing, N.Y. 1955–59; Pres. Queensborough Community Coll. 1959–61; Chair. Fed. Home Loan Bank Bd. 1961–65; Pres. of Queens Coll., Flushing, New York 1965–71, Coll. of New Rochelle, New York 1971–73; special assistant to Speaker, House of Reps., now Econ. Consultant, Ameribond Securities Assocs.; Trustee, Bowery Savings Bank, New York; Bd. of Advisors, Instructional Television, New York; mem. Mayor's Rent Guidelines Bd., New York 1969–. *Publication:* Ways and Means of Providing Housing for Families Unable to Afford Rentals or Mortgage Payments Necessary to Adequate Private Housing 1960. *Leisure interests:* reading, fishing and golf. *Address:* 767 3rd Avenue, 500 Park Avenue, New York, N.Y. 10017 (Office); 907 6th Street, S.W., Apartment 815, Washington, D.C. 20024, U.S.A. (Home).

MacNABB, Byron Gordon; American research and development engineer (retd.); b. 14 Aug. 1910, Gary, Ind.; s. of Walter S. and Leila B. (née Mogle) MacNabb; m. 1st Iris L. Cook 1939 (divorced 1977); one d.; m. 2nd Kathryn F. Naylor 1978; ed. Rose-Hulman Inst. Tech., Terre Haute, and Illinois Inst. of Tech.; worked for Carnegie-Illinois Steel Corpn., S. Chicago 1930–43; U.S.N. officer 1943–48; Asst. to Dir. of Research for Sandia Corpn., Albuquerque, working on A-bomb 1948–50; Asst. to Dir. of Research, Pullman Standard Car Co. 1950–53; Operations Man. for Cambridge Corpn., working on H-bomb 1953–55; joined Convair-Astronautics (now Gen. Dynamics/Convair) 1955; Operations Man. at Air Force Missile Test Center, Cape Canaveral 1955–58, Dir. of Operations 1962–63; Dir. of Test Eng., Gen. Dynamics/Astronautics, San Diego 1963–65; Operations Man. Gen. Dynamics/Convair, Cape Kennedy 1965–66; responsible for launch of first Intercontinental Ballistic Missile, first four American astronauts to orbit Earth (Mercury Program), first payload to the Moon (Ranger), first fly-by of Venus and Mars (Mariner), first soft landing on the Moon (Surveyor), first hydrogen-propelled rocket (Centaur); Man. Tests and Operations, Advanced Interplanetary Programs, Gen. Electric Co., Missile & Space Div. 1966–68; Consulting Engineer Gen. Electric, Space and Re-entry Systems 1968–75; Presidential Citation for devt. of first anti-kamakazi anti-aircraft weapon, and other awards. *Address:* 1120 Everglade Drive, Cheyenne, Wyoming 82001, U.S.A. *Telephone:* 307-632-7762.

McNALLY, Derek, PH.D.; British lecturer in astronomy; b. 28 Oct. 1934, Belfast; s. of David McNally and Sarah (née Long) McNally; m. Shirley Allen 1959; one s. one d.; ed. Royal Belfast Acad. Inst., Queen's Univ., Belfast and Royal Holloway Coll., London; Sec. Royal Astronomical Soc. 1966–72, Vice-Pres. 1972–73; Asst. Dir. Univ. of London Observatory

1966–; Sr. Lecturer in Astronomy, Univ. Coll., London 1970–; Asst. Gen. Sec. Int. Astronomical Union 1985–88, Gen. Sec. 1988–91. *Publications:* Positional Astronomy 1974, numerous articles in astronomical journals. *Leisure interests:* natural history, music, travel. *Address:* International Astronomical Union, Institut d'Astrophysique, 98 bis Boulevard Arago, 75014 Paris, France; University of London Observatory, Mill Hill Park, London, NW7 2QS, England. *Telephone:* (1) 43 25 83 58; 01-959 0421.

McNAMARA, Robert Strange, LL.D.; American businessman, government official and international civil servant; b. 9 June 1916, San Francisco; s. of Robert James McNamara and Clara Nell Strange; m. Margaret Craig McNamara (died 1981); one s. two d.; ed. Univ. of California and Harvard Univ.; Asst. Prof. in Business Admin., Harvard Univ. 1940–43; served Army, Air Force 1943–46; Exec. Ford Motor Co. 1946–61, Vice-Pres. 1955–60, Pres. 1960–61; U.S. Sec. of Defense 1961–68; Pres. IBRD (World Bank) 1968–81; Admin. Royal Dutch Shell 1981–; Dir. The Washington Post Co. July 1981–, Bank of America 1981–, Corning Glass Works 1981–, TWA 1981–; Chair. Overseas Devt. Council Jan. 1982–; Adviser Robeco Group 1982–; mem. Steering Cttee. on IBRD Reorganisation 1987–; mem. Ford Foundation, Brookings Inst., Calif. Inst. of Tech., Urban Inst.; mem. American Acad. of Arts and Sciences, Advisory Council, Int. Reporting Systems 1981–83, Barbara Ward Fund 1982–; Hon. LL.D. (St. Andrews) 1981; Hon. D.C.L. (Oxford) 1987; Legion of Merit; U.S. Medal of Freedom (with distinction) 1968, Albert Einstein Peace Prize 1983, Franklin D. Roosevelt Freedom Medal 1983, Onassis Award 1988. *Publications:* The Essence of Security: Reflections in Office 1968, One Hundred Countries— Two Billion People 1973, The McNamara Years at the World Bank 1981, Blundering into Disaster. *Address:* 2412 Tracy Place, Washington, D.C. 20008, U.S.A. (Home).

MacNAUGHTON, Angus Athole, C.A.; Canadian business executive; b. 15 July 1931, Montreal; s. of Athole Austin and Emily Kidder (née MacLean) MacNaughton; m. Penelope Bower Lewis 1957; one s. one d.; ed. Lakefield Coll. School, Ont., Lower Canada Coll., Montreal, McGill Univ.; joined Coopers & Lybrand as auditor 1949–55; joined Genstar as Accountant 1955, Asst. Treas. 1956, Treas. 1961, Vice-Pres. 1964, Exec. Vice-Pres. 1970, Pres. 1973–76, Dir., Vice-Chair. and C.E.O. 1976–84, C.E.O. 1984–86, Pres. 1984–; Dir. Canadian Pacific Enterprises, Royal Trust Co., Sun Life Assurance Co. of Canada, Dart Containerline Inc., Canadian Commercial Corpn. *Leisure interests:* skiing, tennis, water skiing. *Address:* Suite 3800, Four Embaradero Centre, San Francisco, Calif. 94111, U.S.A.

MacNAUGHTON, Donald Sinclair, LL.B.; American business executive; b. 14 July 1917, Schenectady, N.Y.; s. of William MacNaughton and Marion (Colquhoun) MacNaughton; m. Winifred Thomas 1941; two s.; ed. Syracuse Univ. and Syracuse Univ. School of Law; Teacher of History, Pulaski (N.Y.) Acad. and Cen. School 1939–42; admitted to N.Y. Bar 1948; pvt. law practice, Pulaski 1948–54; Deputy Sup. of Insurance, N.Y. State 1954–55; with Prudential Insurance Co. of America 1955–70, Chair. of Bd. and C.E.O. 1970–78; C.E.O. Hosp. Corpn. of America 1978–82, Chair. of Bd. Oct. 1978–85, Chair. H.C.A. Foundation 1985–; Chair. Exec. Cttee. Healthtrust, Inc. 1987–; Chair. Bd. of Trustees for Meharry Medical Coll.; Dir. Exxon Corpn., Equicor Equitable HCA Corpn., Third Nat. Corpn., Vanderbilt Univ., New York Stock Exchange, SunTrust Banks, Inc. *Leisure interests:* golf, boating, reading. *Address:* HealthTrust, Inc., 4525 Harding Road, Nashville, Tenn. 37205 (Office); 108 Belle Brook Circle, Nashville, Tenn. 37205, U.S.A. (Home). *Telephone:* (615) 298-6322 (Office).

MACNAUGHTON, Sir Malcolm Campbell, Kt., M.D., F.R.C.O.G., F.R.C.P., F.R.S.E.; British professor of obstetrics and gynaecology; b. 4 April 1925, Glasgow; s. of James Hay Macnaughton and Mary Robieson Hogarth; m. Margaret-Ann Galt 1955; two s. three d.; ed. Glasgow Acad. and Glasgow Univ.; Sr. Lecturer, Obstetrics and Gynaecology, Dundee and St. Andrews Univs. 1961–70; Muirhead Prof. of Obstetrics and Gynaecology, Glasgow Univ. 1970–; Pres. Royal Coll. of Obstetricians and Gynaecologists, London 1984–87; Hon. Fellow Scottish Coll. of Obstetricians and Gynaecologists, Royal Australian Coll. of Obstetricians and Gynaecologists, American Coll. of Obstetricians and Gynaecologists. *Publications:* Combined Textbook of Obstetrics and Gynaecology 1976, The Ovary 1976, Medical Gynaecology 1985. *Leisure interests:* walking, fishing, curling, sailing. *Address:* Beechwood, 15 Boclair Road, Bearsden, Glasgow, G61 2AF, Scotland. *Telephone:* 041-942-1909.

McNEE, Sir David Blackstock, Kt., F.B.I.M., F.R.S.A.; British retd. police officer; b. 23 March 1925, Glasgow; s. of John McNee and late Mary McNee (née Blackstock); m. Isabella Clayton Hopkins 1952; one d.; ed. Woodside Sr. Secondary School, Glasgow; Deputy Chief Constable, Dunbartonshire Constabulary 1968–71; Chief Constable, City of Glasgow Police 1971–75; Chief Constable, Strathclyde Police 1975–77; Commr., Metropolitan Police 1977–82; Dir. Fleet Holdings 1983–86; Chair. (non-exec.) Scottish Express Newspapers 1983–; Orr Pollock & Co. Ltd. (Greenock Telegraph), Craig M. Jeffrey Ltd. (Helensburgh Advertiser), Integrated Security Services Ltd.; Adviser Bd. British Airways 1982–87; Dir. (non-exec.) Clydesdale Bank PLC, Trusthouse Forte PLC; Pres. Royal Life Saving Soc. 1982–, Nat. Bible Soc. of Scotland 1983–, Glasgow City Cttee., Cancer Relief 1987–; Freeman, City of London 1977; C.B.I.M. 1980; Order of St. John 1974, Commdr. 1977; Hon. Col. 32 (Scottish) Signal Regt. (Volunteers)

1988–; Queen's Police Medal 1975. *Publication:* McNee's Law 1983. *Leisure interests:* fishing, golf, music.

MacNEIL, Cornell Hill; American opera singer; b. 24 Sept. 1922, Minneapolis, Minn.; s. of Walter Hill and Harriette Belle (Cornell) MacNeil; m. 1st Margaret Gavan 1947 (divorced 1972), two s. three d.; m. 2nd Tania Rudensky 1972; ed. Julius Hartt School of Music, Univ. of Hartford, West Hartford, Conn. *Appeared on Broadway in:* Sweethearts 1947, Where's Charley 1949; operatic début as John Sorel in world premiere of The Consul (Menotti) 1950; début with New York City Opera as Germont in La Traviata 1953, at La Scala, Milan, as Charles V in Ernani 1959, at Metropolitan Opera, New York in title-role of Rigoletto 1959; has appeared in leading opera houses of Europe, U.S.A., S. America; Pres. American Guild of Musical Artists 1971–77; Alumnus of Year, Hartt School of Music 1976; Grammy Award for best opera recording (La Traviata) 1984; Medal of Achievement, Acad. of Vocal Arts 1985. *Leisure interests:* cooking, woodwork, gardening.

McNEIL, Frederick Harold; Canadian banker; b. 17 Nov. 1916, Saskatoon, Sask.; s. of Harold and Jean McNeil (née Swan); m. Marian Doreen Williams 1943; two s. one d.; ed. Univs. of Manitoba and Saskatchewan; Journalist 1945–54; Man. Consultant, Braun & Co. 1954–56; Dir. Man. Services, Powell River Co. 1956–60; Dir. Org. Personnel and Admin. Planning, Ford Motor Co. of Canada 1960–65; Gen. Man. Personnel Planning, Bank of Montreal 1966–67, Vice-Pres. Org. and Personnel 1967–68, Exec. Vice-Pres. Admin. 1968–70, Exec. Vice-Pres., Gen. Man. 1970–73, Pres., C.O.O. 1973–74, Deputy Chair. and C.E.O. Jan.-Dec. 1975, Chair. 1975–81, C.E.O. 1975–79, Dir. 1960–86; Chair. and Dir. Encor Energy Corpn. Ltd.; Dir. The Bowfort Group, Mancal Ltd., Gendis Inc. Air Force Cross. *Leisure interests:* ranching, riding. *Address:* Suite 3200, 1st Canadian Center, 350 7th Avenue, S.W., Calgary, Alberta T2P 3N9, Canada.

MACNEISH, Richard Stockton, M.A., PH.D., F.B.A.; American archaeologist; b. 29 April 1918, New York; s. of Harris Franklin MacNeish and Elizabeth Stockton; m. Phyllis Diana Walter 1965; two s.; ed. Colgate Univ., Univ. of Chicago, Harvard; Sr. Archaeologist, Nat. Museum of Canada 1949–63; Head, Dept. of Archaeology, Univ. of Calgary 1963–69; Dir., Peabody Foundation for Archaeology 1969–83; Sr. Research Prof., Boston Univ. 1983–86; Dir. Andover Foundation for Archaeological Research 1986–; participated in and supervised archaeological digs in Mexico, Canada, Honduras, Guatemala, Peru, Belize, etc.; Fellow, American Anthropological Asscn., Arctic Inst. for N. America, American Acad. of Arts and Sciences –1971; mem. A.A.A.S., Int. Congress of Americanists, N.A.S.; Fellow Soc. for American Archaeology; numerous awards and honours, including Hon. LL.D (Simon Fraser Univ.) 1980, Spinden Medal for Archaeology 1964, Alfred Vincent Kidder Award 1971, Cornplanter Medal for Iroquois Research 1977. *Publications:* numerous articles and reports; The Origins of Agriculture and Settled Life, Macroblades and Megablades in Ancient Belize, Classic and Post-Classic States in Prehistoric Mexico, The Science of Archaeology 1976. *Leisure interest:* sports. *Address:* 3 Longwood Drive, Unit 1, Andover, Mass. 01810, U.S.A. *Telephone:* (508) 475-1326.

McNERNEY, Walter J., B.S., M.H.A.; Irish professor of health policy; b. 8 June 1925, New Haven, Conn.; s. of Robert F. McNerney and Anna Shanley McNerney; m. Shirley H. McNerney 1948; four s. one d.; ed. Yale Univ. and Univ. of Minnesota; Asst. to co-ordinator of Hosps. and Clinics of Medical Center, Univ. of Pittsburgh 1950–53; Instr. and Asst. Prof. Graduate School of Public Health, Univ. of Pittsburgh 1950–55; Assoc. Prof. School of Business Admin. Univ. of Mich. 1955–58, Prof. and Founding Dir. Bureau of Hospital Admin. 1958–61; Pres. Blue Cross Assn. 1961–78, Blue Cross and Blue Shield Asscns. 1978–81; Herman Smith Prof. of Health Policy, Kellogg Graduate School of Management, Northwestern Univ. 1982–; Man. Partner, Walter J. McNerney & Assocs. (man. consultants) 1982–; several awards. *Publications:* three books, two monographs, several book chapters and over 50 articles. *Leisure interests:* golf, tennis, sailing. *Address:* Northwestern University, Kellogg Graduate School of Management, Hospital & Health Services Management Program, 2001 Sheridan Road, Evanston, Ill. 60208 (Office); 675 Blackthorn Road, Winnetka, Ill. 60093, U.S.A. (Home).

McNICOL, George Paul, F.R.S.E., M.D., PH.D., F.R.C.P., F.R.C.P.G., F.R.C.PATH., F.R.S.A.; British university vice-chancellor; b. 24 Sept. 1929, Glasgow; s. of M. W. McNicol and Elizabeth (Harper) McNicol; m. Dr. Susan Ritchie 1959; one s. two d.; ed. Hillhead High School, Glasgow and Univ. of Glasgow; Regimental Medical Officer, R.A.M.C. 1953–55; Registrar, Univ. Medical Unit, Stobhill Gen. Hospital 1955–57; Registrar, Univ. Dept. of Medicine, Royal Infirmary, Glasgow 1957–59, Hon. Sr. Registrar 1961–65, Lecturer in Medicine 1963–65, Hon. Consultant Physician 1966–71, Sr. Lecturer in Medicine 1966–70, Reader in Medicine 1970–71; Prof. of Medicine and Hon. Consultant Physician, Leeds Gen. Infirmary 1971–81; Chair. Bd. of Faculty of Medicine, Univ. of Leeds 1978–81; Prin. and Vice-Chancellor, Univ. of Aberdeen 1981–; mem. Aberdeen Local Bd. Bank of Scotland 1983–; Harkness Fellow, Washington Univ. 1959–61; other professional appts.; foreign corresp. mem. Belgian Royal Acad. of Medicine; Hon. F.A.C.P. *Publications:* approximately 200 publications in biomedical literature in the field of haemostasis and thrombosis. *Leisure interests:* skiing, sailing. *Address:* Chanonry Lodge, 13 The Chanonry, Old Aberdeen, AB2 1RP, Scotland.

McNULTY, Anthony, C.B.E.; British barrister and human rights lawyer; b. 25 May 1911, Warwick; s. of Canon B. McNulty and Mrs. M. McNulty; ed. Winchester Coll., Magdalen Coll., Oxford; called to Bar, Middle Temple 1932; war service in Army in N. Africa and Italy and in Mil. Govt., Vienna 1939–46; Asst. Legal Adviser, Colonial Office 1947–50; London Man. and Dir. of pvt. business firm 1950–54; Sec., European Comm. of Human Rights, Council of Europe, Strasbourg 1954–76; Dir. British Inst. of Human Rights Jan. 1977–. *Address:* Whites Club, 37 St. James's Street, London, S.W.1, England. *Telephone:* 01-492 1242.

MACOVESCU, George, LL.B.; Romanian politician (retd.) and writer; b. 28 May 1913, Joseni, Buzău Dist.; s. of Nicolae and Maria Macovescu; m. Emilia Grigorescu 1963; one s. one d.; ed. Bucharest Univ.; Sec.-Gen. Information Ministry 1945–47, Chargé d'affaires London 1947–49, Dir., Ministry of Foreign Affairs 1949–52, Dir.-Gen. of Cinematography 1955–59; Minister, Washington 1959–61; Deputy Minister of Foreign Affairs 1961–67, First Deputy Minister 1967–72, Minister 1972–78; Prof., Faculty of Romanian Language and Literature, Bucharest Univ. 1949–; mem. Romanian CP 1936–, mem. Cen. Cttee. 1969–84; mem. Grand Nat. Assembly 1969–85; mem. Acad. of Social and Political Sciences 1970–; mem. Writers' Union of the Socialist Repub. of Romania (Pres. 1977–81); Sec. Bucharest Writers' Asscn. 1972–77. *Publications:* Viața si opera lui Alexandru Sahia (The Life and Work of Alexandru Sahia) 1950, Contradicții în Imperiul Britanic (Contradictions in the British Empire) 1950, Teoria literarii (Theory of Literature) 1963, Vîrstele Timpului (The Ages of Time) 1971, Catargele înalte (Tall Masts) 1972, Gheorghe Lazăr 1973, Farmecul pămîntului (Charm of the Earth) 1977, Parfumul amar al pelinului verde (The Bitter Fragrance of the Green Mugwort) 1982, Semnul Dintre Ochi (The Mark Between the Eyes) 1983, Undeva, Toamna, Cîndva ... (Somewhere, Sometime, The Autumn ...) (poems) 1985, Walt Whitman—Carl Sandburg: Poems (selected and trans. into Romanian) 1987, Trecînde anotimpuri (Passing Seasons) 1988. *Address:* Strada Herăstrău 31, Bucharest, Romania.

McPHERSON, Harry Cummings, Jr., B.A., LL.B.; American lawyer and government official; b. 22 Aug. 1929, Tyler, Tex.; s. of Harry Cummings and Nan (née Hight) McPherson; m. 1st Clayton Read 1952 (divorced 1981); two s.; m. 2nd Patricia McPherson 1981; ed. Tyler High School, Texas, Southern Methodist Univ., Dallas, Univ. of the South, Tennessee, Columbia Univ. and Univ. of Texas Law School; U.S. Air Force 1950–53; admitted to Texas Bar 1955; Asst. Gen. Counsel, Dem. Policy Cttee., U.S. Senate 1956–59, Assoc. Counsel 1959–61, Gen. Counsel 1961–63; Deputy Under Sec. for Int. Affairs, Dept. of Army 1963–64; Asst. Sec. of State for Educational and Cultural Affairs 1964–65; Special Asst. and Counsel to Pres. Johnson 1965–69; Special Counsel to the Pres. 1966–69; Vice-Chair. John F. Kennedy Center for Performing Arts 1969–76, Gen. Counsel 1977–; pvt. law practice, Washington, D.C. 1969–; Chair. Task Force on Domestic Policy, Democrat Advisory Council of Elected Officials 1974; mem. Pres.'s Comm. on the Accident at Three Mile Island 1979; Pres. Federal City Council, Washington, D.C. 1983–. *Publication:* A Political Education 1972. *Address:* 1660 L Street, N.W., Washington, D.C. 20036 (Office); 10213 Montgomery Avenue, Kensington, Md. 20895, U.S.A. (Home).

McPHERSON, James M., PH.D.; American historian; b. 11 Oct. 1936, Valley City, N.D.; s. of James M. McPherson and Miriam O. McPherson; m. Patrician Rasche 1958; one d.; ed. Gustavus Adolphus Coll. and Johns Hopkins Univ.; Instructor Princeton Univ. 1962–65, Asst. Prof. 1965–66, Assoc. Prof. 1966–72, Prof. of History 1972–82, Edwards Prof. of American History 1982–; Anisfield-Wolf Award in Race Relations 1965; Guggenheim Fellow 1967–68; Huntington Seaver Fellow 1987–88. *Publications:* The Struggle for Equality: Abolitionists and the Negro in the Civil War and Reconstruction 1964, The Negro's Civil War 1965, The Abolitionist Legacy 1975, Ordeal by Fire: The Civil War and Reconstruction 1982, Battle Cry of Freedom: The Civil War Era 1988. *Leisure interests:* tennis, bicycling, sailing. *Address:* Department of History, Princeton University, Princeton, N.J. 08544 (Office); 15 Randall Road, Princeton, N.J. 08540, U.S.A. (Home). *Telephone:* 609-452-4173 (Office); 609-924-9226 (Home).

MacPHERSON, Sir Keith Duncan, F.A.S.A.; Australian business executive; b. 12 June 1920; s. of late Duncan Macpherson; m. Ena McNair 1946; three s. two d.; with The Herald and Weekly Times Ltd. 1938–, Co. Sec. 1959–64, Asst. Gen. Man. 1965–67, Gen. Man. 1967–70, Dir. 1974–86, Chief Exec. 1975–85, Chair. of Dirs. 1977–86, Consultant 1986–; Dir. South Pacific Post Pty. Ltd. (New Guinea Newspapers) 1965–70; W. Australian Newspapers Ltd. 1970–86, Chair. 1977–86; Dir. Davies Brothers Ltd. 1975–86; New Nation Publishing 1974–82; Tasman Pulp and Paper Co. Ltd. 1977–78; Qld Press Ltd. 1978–86, Deputy Chair. 1981–83, Chair. 1983–86; Queensland Newspapers Pty. Ltd. 1978–, Deputy Chair. 1981–83; Vice-Chair. Australian Newsprint Mills Holdings Ltd. 1976–78, Chair. 1978–86; Pres. Australian Newspapers Council 1968–70; Chair. Newspaper Proprietors' Asscn. of Melbourne 1968–70; Chair. Media Council of Australia 1969–70. *Leisure interests:* swimming, gardening. *Address:* 24 Balwyn Road, Canterbury, Vic. 3126, Australia (Home). *Telephone:* 836-8571.

McPHERSON, Melville Peter, B.A., M.B.A.; American lawyer and government official; b. 27 Oct. 1940, Grand Rapids, Mich.; s. of Donald McPherson and Ellura E. (Frost) McPherson; one s. one step s.; Peace Corps volunteer, Peru 1966; with Internal Revenue Service, Washington 1969–75; Special Asst. to Pres. and Deputy Dir. Presidential Personnel White House,

Washington 1975–77; mem. Vorys, Sater, Seymour & Pease, Washington 1977–81; Acting Counsel to Pres., White House 1981; Admin. U.S. Int. Devt. Co-operation Agency (USAID), Washington 1981–87; Exec. Vice-Pres. Bank of America 1988–; mem. Bd. for Int. Food and Agric. Devt. 1977–80, Bd. American Council of Young Political Leaders 1978–81; Republican Chair. Del. Selection Cttee. 1976; mem. Washington Bar Asscn. *Address:* Bank of America, 555 California Street, San Francisco, Calif. 94137, U.S.A.

MACQUARRIE, Rev. John, T.D., PH.D., D.LITT., D.D., F.B.A.; British priest and professor of theology; b. 27 June 1919, Renfrew, Scotland; s. of John Macquarrie and Robina Macquarrie (née McInnes); m. Jenny Fallow Welsh 1949; two s. one d.; ed. Renfrew High School, Paisley Grammar School and Univ. of Glasgow; British Army Chaplain 1945–48; Incumbent, St. Ninian's Church, Brechin 1948–53; Lecturer in Systematic Theology, Univ. of Glasgow 1953–62; Prof. of Systematic Theology, Union Theological Seminary, New York, U.S.A. 1962–70; Hon. Curate, St. Mary's, Manhattanville, New York 1965–70; Lady Margaret Prof. of Divinity, Oxford Univ. and Canon of Christ Church Oxford 1970–86; Gifford Lecturer, Univ. of St. Andrews 1983–84; Consultant, Lambeth Conferences 1968, 1978, Gov. St. Stephen's House, Oxford 1970–, Pusey House, Oxford 1975. *Publications:* An Existentialist Theology 1955, Twentieth Century Religious Thought 1963, Principles of Christian Theology 1966, God-Talk 1967, Existentialism 1972, In Search of Humanity 1982, In Search of Deity 1984, Theology, Church and Ministry 1986. *Leisure interests:* hill walking, the language and literature of Scottish Gaelic. *Address:* 206 Headley Way, Oxford, OX3 7TA, England. *Telephone:* (0865) 61889.

McQUILLIN, Robert, M.SC., F.G.S., F.R.S.E.; British geologist; b. 28 May 1935, Brampton, Cumberland; s. of George Hay McQuillin and Thomasina McQuillin (née White); m. Angela Walker Battersby 1958; two s.; ed. White House School, Brampton, Univs. of Durham and London; British Geological Survey Applied Geophysics Unit 1957–66; set up new Marine Geophysics Unit for survey of U.K. Continental Shelf 1966–84; U.K. Tech. Adviser, Cttee. for the Co-ordination of Offshore Prospecting in the South Pacific 1982–84; Deputy Dir. Marine Surveys and Energy Div. 1984–85; Chief Geophysicist Britoil PLC 1985, Chief Scientist 1986–88, Scientific Adviser BP/Britoil 1988–; Visiting Prof., Univ. of Glasgow 1988–; Lyell Fund award, Geological Soc. of London. *Publications:* Exploring the Geology of Shelf Seas (with D. A. Ardus) 1977, Introduction to Seismic Interpretation (with M. Bacon and W. Barclay) 1977, 1984; numerous scientific articles. *Leisure interests:* squash, literature. *Address:* Britoil PLC, 301 St Vincent Street, Glasgow, G2 5DD; 94 Liberton Drive, Edinburgh, EH16 6NR, Scotland. *Telephone:* (041) 225 2896 (Office); (031) 664 2193 (Home).

MACRÉAMOINN, Seán, M.A.; Irish broadcasting executive (retd.); b. 27 Nov. 1921, Birmingham, England; s. of James Macréamoinn and Wilhelmina (Bruen) Redmond; m. Patricia Louisa Hall 1952; one s. two d.; ed. High School, Clonmel, Jesuit School, Galway, Univ. Coll., Galway; Third Sec., Dept. of Foreign Affairs 1946–47; writer/producer, RTE (Irish Radio & TV) 1947–74, Head of Radio Programmes 1974–76, Head of Int. Relations 1976–86; Hon. LL.D. (Nat. Univ. of Ireland) 1987; Hon. Druid, Welsh Gorsedd 1980. *Publications:* Vatacáin II agus an Reabhlóid Chultúrtha (in Gaelic) 1987, The Synod on the Laity: An Outsider's Diary 1987; Ed: Pleasures of Gaelic Poetry 1984, Freedom to Hope 1985, The Laity in Ireland 1986. *Leisure interests:* writing, reading, music, theatre. *Address:* 37 Eden Park Drive, Dublin 14, Ireland. *Telephone:* (353-1) 981 707.

McSHANE, Edward James, PH.D.; American mathematician; b. 10 May 1904, New Orleans, La.; s. of Dr. Augustus McShane and Harriet Kenner (Butler) McShane; m. Virginia Haun 1931; one s. (deceased) two d.; ed. Tulane Univ. and Univ. of Chicago; Instructor, Princeton 1933–34, Asst. Prof. 1934–35; Prof. Univ. of Virginia 1935–57, Alumni Prof. 1957–74, Alumni Prof. Emer. 1974–; mem. Nat. Acad. of Sciences, American Philosophical Soc.; Hon. Sc.D. (Tulane); Distinguished Service Award, Math. Asscn. of America 1964, Chauvenet Prize 1952. *Publications:* Integration 1944, Exterior Ballistics (with J. L. Kelley and F. V. Reno) 1953, Order-Preserving Maps and Integration Processes 1953, Real Analysis (with T. A. Botts) 1959, Stochastic Calculus and Stochastic Models 1974, Unified Integration 1983; various research papers. *Leisure interests:* photography, music, painting. *Address:* Department of Mathematics, University of Virginia, Charlottesville, Va. 22903 (Office); 209 Maury Avenue, Charlottesville, Va. 22903, U.S.A. (Home). *Telephone:* 804-924-7127 (Office); 804-293-8956 (Home).

McSHARRY, Deirdre Mary; Irish journalist; b. 4 April 1932, London, England; d. of the late Dr. John McSharry and of Mary O'Brien; ed. Trinity Coll., Dublin Univ.; actress at Gate Theatre, Dublin 1953–55; writer with The Irish Times 1953; mem. staff Evening Herald, Dublin 1955–56; with book dept. Metropolitan Museum of Art, New York 1956; Reporter Women's Wear Daily, New York 1957–59; mem. staff Woman's Own 1959–62; Fashion Ed. Evening News 1962; Woman's Ed. Daily Express 1963–67; Fashion Ed. The Sun 1967–71; Fashion Ed. Cosmopolitan 1972, Ed. 1973–85; Ed.-in-Chief Country Living 1986–; Ed. of the Year (Periodical Publrs. Asscn.) 1981, 1987. *Leisure interests:* architecture, the arts, gardening. *Address:* c/o Country Living, 72 Broadwick Street, London, W1V 2BP, England. *Telephone:* 01-439 7144 (Office).

MacSHARRY, Ray; Irish politician; b. 29 April 1938, Sligo; m. Elaine Neilan; three s. three d.; ed. Summerhill Coll., Sligo; fmr. haulier, auctioneer, farm-owner; mem. Sligo County Council and Sligo Corpn. 1967–78; mem. Dail 1969–; Minister of State, Dept. of Finance and Public Service 1977–79; Minister for Agriculture 1979–81; Tanaiste and Minister for Finance March-Nov. 1982; mem. European Parl. 1984–; Minister for Finance and Public Service 1987–88; EEC Commr. with responsibility for Agric. and Rural Devt. Jan. 1989–; Fianna Fail. *Address:* Commission of the European Communities, 200 rue de la Loi, 1049 Brussels, Belgium (Office); Alcantara, Pearse Road, Sligo, Republic of Ireland (Home).

McSWINEY, James Wilmer; American business executive; b. 13 Nov. 1915, McEwen, Tenn.; s. of James S. and Delia (Conroy) McSwiney; m. Jewel Bellar 1940; one s. one d.; ed. Hume Fogg High School, Nashville; Asst. Sec. and Treas., Brunswick Pulp & Paper Co. (subsidiary of Mead Corpn.) 1944–54; Exec. Asst. to Pres. The Mead Corpn. 1954–57, Vice-Pres. 1957, Group Vice-Pres. and Gen. Man. 1961, Exec. Vice-Pres. 1963, Pres., C.E.O. and Chair Exec. Cttee. 1968–71, Chair. of Bd. and C.E.O. 1971–78, Chair. 1978–82, Chair. Exec. Cttee. 1978–81, C.E.O. 1980–81. *Leisure interests:* golf, swimming. *Address:* The Mead Corporation, Mead World Headquarters, Courthouse Plaza Northeast, Dayton, Ohio 45463 (Office); 396 West D'Ayllon Street, Sea Island, Ga. 31561, U.S.A. (Home). *Telephone:* 513-222-6323 (Office); (912) 638-5262 (Home).

McTIERNAN, Rt. Hon. Sir Edward A., P.C., K.B.E., B.A., LL.B.; Australian lawyer (retd.); b. 16 Feb. 1892, Glen Innes, N.S.W.; s. of the late Patrick McTiernan and of Isabella McTiernan (née Diamond); m. Kathleen Lloyd 1948; ed. Sydney Univ.; barrister 1916; mem. N.S.W. Legislature 1920–27; Attorney-Gen. 1920–22 and 1925–27; mem. Fed. Parl. 1929–30; Justice of High Court of Australia 1930–76; Privy Chamberlain of Sword and Cape 1928. *Leisure interests:* music, literature. *Address:* "Breffni", 36 Chilton Parade, Warrawee, N.S.W., Australia. *Telephone:* 483103.

McVITTIE, George Cunliffe, O.B.E., PH.D., F.R.S.; British professor of astronomy; b. 5 June 1904; s. of Frank S. McVittie; m. Mildred Bond Strong 1934 (died 1985); no c.; ed. Edinburgh Univ. and Christ's Coll., Cambridge; Asst. Lecturer, Leeds Univ. 1930–34; lecturer in Applied Math., Liverpool Univ. 1934–36; Reader in Math., King's Coll., London 1936–48; Prof. of Math., Queen Mary Coll., London 1948–52; Prof. of Astronomy, Univ. of Illinois 1952–72, Emer. Prof. 1972–; Hon. Prof. of Theoretical Astronomy, Univ. of Kent 1972–85; war service with Meteorological Office and Dept. of the Foreign Office 1939–45; Jt. Ed. of The Observatory 1938–48; Jt. Exec. Ed. of Quarterly Journal of Mechanics and Applied Math. 1947–51; Pres. Comm. on Galaxies, Int. Astronomical Union 1967–70; Sec. American Astronomical Soc. 1961–69; Hon. D.Sc. (Kent) 1985; Minor Planet 2417 named "McVittie" by Int. Astronomical Union 1984. *Publications:* Cosmological Theory 1937, General Relativity and Cosmology 1956, Fact and Theory in Cosmology 1961, Ed. Problems of Extra-galactic Research 1962; papers on Relativity and its astronomical applications, etc., in numerous journals. *Address:* 74 Dover Rd, Canterbury, Kent, CT1 3AY, England.

McWHERTER, Ned R.; American politician; b. 15 Oct. 1930, Palmersville, Tenn.; s. of Harmon R. McWherter and Lucille Smith; one s. one d.; mem. Tenn. House of Reps. 1968–87, Speaker 1973–87; Gov. of Tennessee Jan. 1987–; Chair. Bd. Eagle Distributors Inc., Weakley Gas and Oil Co.; Dir. Weakley Co. Bank, People's Bank; Democrat. *Address:* State Capitol, Nashville, Tenn., U.S.A.

McWHIRTER, Norris Dewar, C.B.E., M.A.; British publisher and broadcaster; b. 12 Aug. 1925, London; s. of William Allan McWhirter and Margaret Williamson; m. Carole Eckert 1957 (died 1987); one s. one d.; ed. Marlborough Coll. and Trinity Coll., Oxford; Sub-Lieut. R.N.V.R. 1943–46; Dir. McWhirter Twins Ltd. (facts and figures agency) 1950–; Chair. William McWhirter & Son Ltd. (electrical eng.) 1955–86; Athletics Corresp. The Star 1951–60, The Observer 1951–67, Editor, Athletics World 1952–56; Dir. Guinness Superlatives (now Guinness Publs.) Ltd. 1954–, Man. Dir. 1954–76; BBC TV commentator Olympic Games 1960–72; contested general elections, Orpington, Kent (Conservative) 1964, 1966; co-founder, Chair. Redwood Press Ltd. 1966–72; mem. Sports Council 1970–73; Dir. Gieves Group Ltd. 1972–; Presenter BBC TV series "The Record Breakers" 1972–88; co-founder and Vice-Chair. The Freedom Asscn. 1975–83, Chair. 1983–. *Publications:* Get To Your Marks 1951, Guinness Book of World Records (Ed. and Compiler of 270 editions in 31 languages to 1989, Advisory Ed. 1986–) 1955–86; Dunlop Book of Facts 1964, 1966, Guinness Book of Answers, 6th ed. 1987, Ross, Story of a Shared Life 1976. *Leisure interests:* skiing, family tennis, athletics, exploring islands. *Address:* Guinness Publishing Ltd., 33 London Road, Enfield, Middx., England. *Telephone:* 01-367 4567.

McWILLIAM, (Frederick) Edward, C.B.E.; British sculptor; b. 30 April 1909; s. of William Nicholson McWilliam; m. Elizabeth Marion Crowther 1932 (died 1988); two d.; ed. Campbell Coll., Belfast and Slade School of Fine Art; served in R.A.F. 1939–45; mem. of Staff, Slade School 1947–66; mem. Art Panel, Arts Council of G.B. 1960–68; one-man exhbns. since 1939 at London, Hanover and Waddington Galleries, London, Dawson Gallery, Dublin, Felix Landau Gallery, L.A.; retrospective exhbns. Belfast, Dublin, Londonderry, London; has exhibited in int. open-air exhbns. London, Antwerp, Arnhem, Paris; work included in British Council touring exhbns. to U.S.A., Canada, Germany, S. America; Fellow Univ. Coll. London; Hon.

D.Lit. (Belfast) 1964. *Address:* 8A Holland Villas Road, London, W14 8BP, England.

MACK SMITH, Denis, M.A., F.B.A.; British historian and writer; b. 3 March 1920, London; s. of Wilfrid Mack Smith and Altiora Mack Smith; m. Catharine Stevenson 1963; two d.; ed. Cambridge Univ.; Fellow and Tutor, Peterhouse, Cambridge 1947–62, Hon. Fellow 1986; Sr. Research Fellow, All Souls Coll., Oxford 1962–86; Sub-Warden 1984–86; Extraordinary Fellow Wolfson Coll., Oxford 1987–; Foreign Hon. mem. American Acad. of Arts and Sciences; Commendatore of Italian Order of Merit; Serena, Duff Cooper, Wolfson, Thirlwall, Elba, Mondello, Nove Muse and Rhegium Julii Prizes. *Publications:* Cavour and Garibaldi in 1860 1954, Italy: A Modern History 1959, revised 1969, Medieval and Modern Sicily 1968, The Making of Italy 1968, Victor Emanuel, Cavour and the Risorgimento 1971, Mussolini 1981, Cavour 1985, A History of Sicily (jtly.) 1986; Jt. Ed. Nelson History of England 1962. *Address:* White Lodge, Osler Road, Headington, Oxford, England.

MADAN, Bal Krishna, PH.D.; Indian economist and banker (retd.); b. 13 July 1911, Sahowala, Punjab; s. of Shivram Madan and Jamnadevi Chhabra; m. Savitri Pahwa 1935; four s.; ed. Univ. of Punjab, Lahore; Lecturer in Econs., Univ. of Punjab 1936–37; Officer for Enquiry into Resources, Punjab Govt. 1937–39; Econ. Adviser to Punjab Govt. 1940–41; Dir. of Research, Reserve Bank of India, Bombay 1941–45; Sec. of Indian del. to Bretton Woods 1944; Deputy Sec. Indian Tariff Bd. 1945; mem. Indian Legis. Assembly and Assembly Cttee. on Bretton Woods Agreement 1946; Alt. Exec. Dir., IMF 1946–48, IBRD 1947–48; Exec. Dir. IMF 1948–50, 1967–71; mem. Indian Del., First Commonwealth Finance Ministers' Conf. London 1949; mem. UN Cttee. on Domestic Financing of Econ. Devt. 1949; Econ. Adviser to Reserve Bank of India 1950; mem. Finance Comm., Indian Govt. 1952; mem. Taxation Enquiry Comm. 1953–54; mem. Experts Group on UN Special Fund for Econ. Devt. 1955; Prin. Adviser to Reserve Bank of India 1957, Exec. Dir. 1959, Deputy Gov. 1964–67; mem. Governing Body Indian Investment Centre 1960–67; Dir. Industrial Finance Corpn. of India 1961–64, Life Insurance Corpn. of India 1964–67; Chair. Steering Group on Wages, Incomes and Prices Policies 1964–66; Pres. Soc. of Agricultural Econs. 1957, Indian Econ. Asscn. 1961; Vice-Chair. Industrial Devt. Bank of India 1964–67; Chair. Bonus Review Cttee., Indian Govt. 1972–74; Chair. Man. Devt. Inst. 1973–80; mem. Bd. of Govs., Nat. Council of Applied Econ. Research 1975–, Nat. Inst. of Public Finance and Policy 1977–; Dir. Hindustan Electro-Graphites Ltd. 1979–, Springs India Ltd. 1981–. *Publications:* India and Imperial Preference—A Study in Commercial Policy 1939, Aspects of Economic Development and Policy 1964, Real Wages of Industrial Labour in India 1977, Report on the Study of Debt-Equity Ratio Norms 1978, Towards Monetary Cooporation in South Asia 1986. *Leisure interests:* golf, reading. *Address:* B-100, Greater Kailash-1, New Delhi 110048, India. *Telephone:* 6419006.

MADDOCKS, Arthur Frederick, C.M.G., M.A.; British diplomatist (retd.); b. 20 May 1922, Stockport, Cheshire (now Greater Manchester); s. of Frederick William and Celia Elizabeth (Beardwell) Maddocks; m. Margaret Jean Crawford Holt 1945; two s. one d.; ed. Manchester Grammar School, Corpus Christi Coll., Oxford; Army Service 1942–46; Foreign (later Diplomatic) Service 1946–; served Washington, D.C. 1946–48, Foreign Office 1949–51, Bonn, Fed. Repub. of Germany 1951–55, Bangkok, Thailand 1955–58, Del. to OEEC 1958–60, Foreign Office 1960–64, Del. to EEC 1964–68, Hong Kong 1968–72, Ottawa 1972–76; Amb. to OECD 1977–82 (Chair. Exec. Cttee. 1980–82); mem. OECD Appeals Tribunal 1984–. *Address:* Lynton House, 83 High Street, Wheatley, Oxford OX9 1XP, England.

MADELIN, Alain, L. EN D.; French lawyer and politician; b. 26 March 1946, Paris; lawyer, Paris office, Fed. Nat. des Républicains Indépendants (FNRI) 1968–; mem. Nat. Secr. FNRI 1977–; Deputy to Nat. Ass. (UDF-PR) 1978–86; Minister of Industry, Posts and Telecommunications and Tourism 1986–88. *Address:* 13 rue de Fleurimont, 35600 Redon, France.

MADHAVAN, Ananthanarayanan, M.A.; Indian diplomatist; b. 9 Oct. 1933; s. of M. Ananathanarayanan; m. Girija Madhavan 1959; one s.; ed. Loyola Coll., Madras Univ., Trinity Coll., Cambridge; joined Foreign Service 1956; Third, later Second Sec. Embassy, Rangoon 1958–60, Embassy, Berne 1961–64; Deputy Sec. Ministry of External Affairs, New Delhi 1965–68, Jt. Sec. 1977–80; served in Embassy, Peking 1968–70; Counsellor, High Comm. of India, London 1970–73; Commr., Hong Kong 1973–77; Deputy Chief of Mission, Embassy, Moscow 1982–85; Amb. to Japan 1985–88, to Fed. Repub. of Germany May 1988–; Fellowship Center for Int. Affairs, Harvard 1980. *Leisure interests:* music, literature, history, philosophy. *Address:* Embassy of India, Adenauerallee 262-264, 5300 Bonn 1, Federal Republic of Germany. *Telephone:* (0228) 5405100.

MADIA, Chunilal Kalidas; Indian writer; b. 12 Aug. 1922; ed. Bhagwatsinhji High School, Dhoraji, Gujarat, and H.L. Coll. of Commerce, Ahmedabad; writes mainly in Gujarati; Editorial Staff Prabhat and Navsaurashtra 1942–44; Ed. Varta (short story monthly) 1943; Editorial Staff, Janmabhoomi Group of Newspapers, Bombay 1945–50; Language Ed., U.S. Information Service, Bombay 1950–62; now Ed. Ruchi (literary and cultural magazine); Literary Ed. Sandesh (Gujarati daily); Official Del. 35th PEN Congress of World Writers, Ivory Coast 1967; Narmad Gold Medal for

Best Play Writing 1951; Ranajitram Gold Medal for Outstanding Creative Writing 1957; numerous other prizes. *Publications:* (in Gujarati): novels: Vyajano Varas, Velavelani Chhanyadi, Liludi Dharati, Kumkum Ane Ashaka; short stories: Ghooghavatan Pur, Padmaja, Champo Ane Kel, Tej Ane Timir, Roop-Aroop, Antasrota; plays: Rangada, Vishavimochan, Raktatilak, Shoonyashesh; poems: Sonnet (collected sonnets); criticism: Granthagarima, Shahamrig, Suvarnamrig; in Malayalam: Gujarati Kathakal. *Address:* B-213, Chandralok, Manav Mandir Road, Malabar Hill, Bombay 6, India. *Telephone:* 36-8245.

MADIGAN, Sir Russel Tullie, Kt., O.B.E., M.E., LL.B., F.S.A.S.M., M.AUS.I.M.M., F.T.S.; Australian business executive; b. 22 Nov. 1920, Adelaide; s. of the late C. T. Madigan; m. 1st Margaret Symons 1942 (deceased); four s. one d.; m. 2nd Satsuko Tamura 1981; ed. Univ. of Adelaide; joined Zinc Corpn. 1946; Gowrie scholarship in Canada and U.S.A. 1947-49; Underground Man. Zinc Corpn. Ltd., NBHC Ltd. 1956-59; Gen. Man., Gen. Mining Div., CRA Ltd., (Conzinc Rio Tinto Australia Ltd.) 1960-64, Dir. 1968-; Deputy Chair. 1978-87; Man. Dir. Hamersley Iron 1965-71, Chair. 1971-81; Chair. Blair Athol Coal Pty. Ltd. 1971-80, Interstate Oil Ltd. 1972-81, Hamersley Holdings Ltd., 1971-81; Dir. Rio Tinto Zinc Corpn., Ltd. 1971-85, Nat. Commercial Union Ltd. 1969-; Dir. APV Holdings 1983-87; Chair. APV Asia Pacific Ltd. 1983-87; Australian Mineral Foundation 1984, Australia-Japan Foundation 1977-81, Muswellbrook Energy and Minerals Ltd. 1987-, Australian Nat. Pacific Co-operation Cttee. 1986-; mem. Export Devt. Council 1970-76, Consultative Cttee. on Relations with Japan 1977-82; Life mem. of Pacific Basin Econ. Council; Councillor Australian Acad. of Tech. Sciences and Eng. 1978-, Treas. 1985-; Pres. Australian Inst. of Int. Affairs 1984-. *Leisure interests:* flying, farming. *Address:* Muswellbrook Energy and Minerals Ltd., 2nd Floor, 135 Collins Street, Melbourne, Vic. (Office); 99 Spring Street, Melbourne, Vic. 3000, Australia (Home). *Telephone:* 650 5322 (Office); 654 3854 (Home).

MADONNA, Madonna Louise Veronica Ciccone; American singer and film actress; b. 1958, Detroit; m. Sean Penn 1985 (divorced 1989); ed. Alvin Ailey Dance School; has sold over 55 million records worldwide (20 million albums, 35 million singles); toured U.K. 1983, 1987, France 1987, Fed. Germany 1987; appeared in play Speed-the-Plow 1988; Commercial for Pepsi Cola 1989; *albums:* Madonna—the First Album, Like a Virgin, True Blue, You Can Dance; *singles include:* Everybody, Burning Up, Holiday, Borderline, Like a Virgin, Material Girl, Into the Groove, Dress You Up, Crazy for You, Papa Don't Preach, La Isla Bonita, Who's That Girl?, True Blue, Like a Prayer; *films include:* Desperately Seeking Susan, Shanghai Surprise, Who's That Girl?, Bloodhounds of Broadway.

MADRID HURTADO, Miguel de la (see De La Madrid Hurtado, Miguel).

MADSEN, Ib Henning, PH.D.; Danish professor of mathematics; b. 12 April 1942, Copenhagen; s. of Henning Madsen and Gudrun (née Davids-Thomsen) Madsen; m. 1st Benedicte Rechnitzer 1963 (divorced 1982); m. 2nd Ulla Lykke Jorgensen 1984; two s.; ed. Univ. of Copenhagen and Univ. of Chicago; Research Stipend Aarhus Univ. 1965-70; Research Instructor Univ. of Chicago 1971-72; Assoc. Prof. Aarhus Univ. 1971-83, Prof. 1983-; ed. Acta Mathematica 1988-; mem. Royal Danish Acad. of Sciences 1978, Inst. for Advanced Study, Princeton 1986-87; Rigmor and Carl Holst-Knudsen Science Prize 1982. *Address:* Department of Mathematics, Aarhus University, 8000 Aarhus C. (Univ.); Vestervang 2, 222, DK-8000 Aarhus C, Denmark (Home). *Telephone:* 456-127188 (Univ.); 456-133905 (Home).

MADSEN, Mette; Danish writer and politician; b. 3 July 1924, Pandrup, north Jutland; d. of Holger Fruensgaard; a professional writer, including collections of poetry; M.P. 1971-; Chair. of Supervisory Cttee. Royal Theatre 1978-; mem. of Presidium Folketing; Minister for Ecclesiastical Affairs 1984-88; Liberal. *Address:* c/o Ministry of Ecclesiastical Affairs, Frederiksholms Kanal 21, 1220 Copenhagen K, Denmark. *Telephone:* (01) 14-62-63.

MADUBUIKE, Ihechukwu, PH.D.; Nigerian writer, lecturer and politician; b. 9 July 1944, Isuochi-Okigwe; ed. Duke Town Secondary School, Calabar, Lavel Univ., Quebec, State Univ. of New York, Buffalo, Univ. of Paris (Sorbonne); Asst. Prof. State Univ. of New York, Buffalo 1972-74, Ohio State Univ., Columbus 1974-76; Principal lecturer Alvan Ikoku Coll. of Educ., Owerri; Fed. Minister of Educ. 1979-81. *Publications:* A Handbook of African Names 1976, The Sociology of the Senegalese Novel 1980, Towards the Decolonization of the African Novel (co-author) 1980, IGBO Poetry 1980. *Address:* c/o Federal Ministry of Education, Lagos, Nigeria.

MAEDA, Kazuo, D.ENG.; Japanese company executive; b. 13 Feb. 1919, Yamaguchi; s. of Riyozo and Chiyo Maeda; m. Gensho Hiroko; ed. Kyushu Imperial Univ.; joined Mitsui Eng. and Shipbuilding Co. Ltd. 1943, Man. Hull Construction Dept. Tamano Shipyard 1963, Gen. Man. Shipbuilding Div. 1966, Dir. 1968, Gen. Man. Shipbuilding Div. Chiba/Tamano Shipyard 1968, Chiba Shipyard 1972, Man. Dir. 1974, Gen. Man. of Admin. Headquarters, also of Research and Devt. Headquarters 1974; Exec. Man. Dir. 1976, Exec. Sr. Man. Dir. 1977, Pres. Mitsui Eng. and Shipbuilding Co. Ltd. June 1979-; Medal of Honour with Purple Ribbon 1977. *Publication:* A Study on Modernization, Rationalization and Labor Saving of the Shipbuilding Industry: Development of ROTAS SYSTEM 1976. *Leisure interests:* travelling, go, golf. *Address:* Mitsui Engineering and Shipbuilding

Co. Ltd., 6-4 Tsukiji 5-chome, Chuo-ku, Tokyo (Office); 3-1, Hiroo 2-chome, Shibuya-ku, Tokyo, Japan (Home). *Telephone:* (03) 544-3001 (Office); (03) 499-1413 (Home).

MAEGAARD, Jan Carl Christian, DR.PHIL; Danish musicologist and composer; b. 14 April 1926, Copenhagen; s. of late Johannes H. Maegaard and Gerda Glahnson; m. Kirsten Andersen 1973; two d.; ed. Royal Danish Conservatory and Univ. of Copenhagen; freelance musician 1949-56; music critic for various newspapers 1952-60; teacher of theory and music history, Royal Danish Conservatory 1953-58; Asst. Prof. Univ. of Copenhagen 1959, Assoc. Prof. 1961-71, Prof. 1971-; Visiting Prof. State Univ. of New York at Stony Brook 1974; Prof. of Music. U.C.L.A. 1978-81; consultant to music dept. Danish State Radio 1962-78, Chief Consultant 1982-; Chair. Music Cttee. State Endowment for the Arts 1968-71; mem. Bd. Danish State Radio and Television 1970-74; mem. Danish and Norwegian Acads. *Compositions include:* Elegy of Equinox (for voice, 'cello and organ), Five Preludes (solo violin), Trio Serenade (piano trio), Chamber Concerto No. 2, Due tempi (for orchestra), Musica riservata I (string quartet). *Publications:* Musikalsk Modernisme 1964, Præludier til Musik af Schönberg 1976, Indføring i Romantisk Harmonik I-II 1980, 1986; numerous articles. *Address:* Musikvidenskabeligt Institut, Klerkegade 2, 1308 Copenhagen K (Office); Duevej 14, 6, 2000 Frederiksberg, Denmark (Home). *Telephone:* 01-141335 (Office); 01-880780 (Home).

MAEGRAITH, Brian Gilmore, C.M.G., T.D., M.A., M.B., M.SC., F.R.C.P. (L. & E.), F.R.A.C.P., D.PHIL.; Australian university professor; b. 26 Aug. 1907, Adelaide; s. of A. E. R. Maegraith; m. Lorna Langley 1934; one s.; ed. St. Peter's and St. Mark's Colls., Univ. of Adelaide, Magdalen and Exeter Colls., Univ. of Oxford; Medical Fellow and Tutor in Physiology, Exeter Coll. Oxford 1934-40; Univ. Lecturer and Demonstrator in Pathology, Oxford 1937-44, Dean of Medical School 1938-44; Lieut.-Col. R.A.M.C., O.C. Malaria Research Unit, War Office 1939-45; mem. Medical Research Council Malaria Cttee. 1943-46; Tropical Medicine Research Bd. (Medical Research Council) 1959-69, Council Royal Soc. of Tropical Medicine 1947-51, Vice-Pres. 1949-51, 1957-69, Pres. 1969-71; Dean of School, Liverpool School of Tropical Medicine 1944-75, Vice-Pres. 1975-, Prof. Tropical Medicine 1944-72, Prof. Emer. 1972-, Hon. Sr. Research Fellow, Dept. of Tropical Pediatrics 1978; Consulting Physician in Tropical Medicine, Royal Infirmary, Liverpool; Nuffield Consultant in Tropical Medicine, W. Africa 1949; Consultant Faculty of Tropical Medicine, Bangkok 1959-, and S.E.A.M.E.O. Tropical Med 1966-; Chair. Council of European Insts. of Tropical Medicine 1969-72, Hon. Life Pres. 1972-; Maurice Bloch Lecturer, Glasgow, Heath Clark Lecturer, London 1970, Craig Lecturer, U.S. Soc. of Tropical Medicine, Cohen Lecturer, History of Medicine, Liverpool 1979; Hon. Fellow London School of Hygiene and Tropical Medicine 1979-; Hon. mem Belgian, American, Canadian, French and German Societies of Tropical Medicine; Hon. D.Sc. (Bangkok), Emer. M.D. (Athens); Chalmers Gold Medal, Royal Soc. of Tropical Medicine 1951, Le Prince Medal, American Society of Tropical Medicine 1955, Bernhard Nocht Medal (Hamburg) 1957, Mary Kingsley Medal 1973; Kt. Order of St. Lazarus of Jerusalem 1977; Hon. Fellow, St. Mark's Coll. 1956-; Commdr., Exalted Order of White Elephant (Thailand) 1982. *Publications:* Pathological Processes in Malaria 1948, Clinical Tropical Diseases 1953, Tropical Medicine for Nurses 1954, Clinical Methods in Tropical Medicine 1962, Exotic Diseases in Practice 1965, Management and Treatment of Diseases in the Tropics 1970, One World 1973. *Leisure interests:* music, painting, writing. [Died 2 April 1989.]

MAEHLER, Herwig Gustav Theodor, PH.D., F.B.A.; German papyrologist; b. 29 April 1935, Berlin; s. of Ludwig Maehler and Lisa Maehler; m. Margaret Anderson 1963; two d.; ed. Katharineum, Lübeck and Univs. of Hamburg, Tübingen and Basle; British Council Scholarship, Oxford 1961-62; Research Asst. Dept. of Classics, Univ. of Hamburg 1962-63, Dept. of Manuscripts, Hamburg Univ. Library 1963-64; Keeper of Greek Papyri, Egyptian Museum, West Berlin 1964-79; Lecturer in Classics, Freie Universität Berlin 1975-79; Reader in Papyrology, Univ. Coll. London 1979-81, Prof. 1981-; Visiting Fellow, Inst. for Advanced Studies in the Humanities, Edinburgh 1977; corresp. mem. German Archaeological Inst. *Publications:* Die Auffassung des Dichterberufs im frühen Griechentum bis zur Zeit Pindars 1963, Die Handschriften der S. Jacobi-Kirche Hamburg 1967, Urkunden römischer Zeit 1968, Papyri aus Hermupolis 1974, Die Lieder des Bakchylides (2 vols.) 1982; Greek Bookhands of the Early Byzantine Period (with G. Cavallo) 1987; editions of Bacchylides and Pindar. *Leisure interests:* chamber music (viola), horse riding (dressage). *Address:* Department of Greek, University College London, Gower Street, London, WC1E 6BT (Office); 2 Oswald Road, St. Albans, Herts., AL1 3AQ, England.

MAFATLAL, Arvind N.; Indian industrialist; b. 27 Oct. 1923, Ahmedabad; s. of late Navinchandra Mafatlal and of Vijayalaxmi N.; m. Sushila A. Mafatlal; two s. one d.; ed. St. Xavier's High School and Sydenham Coll. of Commerce and Econs., Bombay; joined Mafatlal Group of Cos. 1941, Chair. 1955-; Dir. Tata Eng. and Locomotive Co. Ltd., and others; Chair. Nat. Organic Chem. Industries Ltd., Polyolefins Industries Ltd., Mafatlal Eng. Industries Ltd., Shri Sadguru Seva Singh Trust; Trustee Bharatiya Agro-Industries Foundation, Uruli Kanchan Employers' Del. to 43rd Session, ILO Conf.; mem. Durga Prasad Khaitan Memorial Gold Medal 1966, Business Leadership Award (Madras Man. Asscn.) 1971, Sir Jehangir Ghandy Medal for Industrial Peace (Xavier Labour Relations Inst.) 1979. *Leisure interest:* golf. *Address:* Mafatlal House, Backbay Reclamation, Bombay 400 020 (Office); 10 Altamount Road, Bombay 400 026, India (Home). *Telephone:* 202-69-44 (Office); 36-83-50 (Home).

MAGA, Hubert Coutoucou; Benin politician; b. 10 Aug. 1916; ed. Ecole Normale de Gorée; headmaster of school at Nabitingou until 1951; Gen. Counsellor of Dahomey 1947; Grand Counsellor of Art 1948–57; Deputy for Dahomey to French Nat. Assembly 1951–58; Under-Sec. for Labour, Gaillard Cabinet; Minister of Labour in Dahomey 1958–59, Premier 1959–63, Pres. 1960–63; under restriction 1963–65; Head of State, also Minister of Interior and of Defence 1970–72; under house arrest 1972; released April 1981; mem. Dahomeyan Democrat Group; awards incl. Grand-Croix, Légion d'honneur, Mérite Social and Etoile Noire de Bénin. *Address:* Cotonou, Benin.

MAGALHÃES PINTO, José de; Brazilian banker, business executive and politician; b. 28 June 1909, Santo Antônio do Monte; m. Berenice Catão de Magalhães Pinto 1932; three s. three d.; ed. Free School of Law, Belo Horizonte; Dir. Banco da Lavoura, Minas Gerais 1929–35; Pres. Assoc. Commercial, Minas Gerais 1935–37; Pres. Fed. Comércio, Minas Gerais 1937; Founder and Chair. of Bd. Banco Nacional de Minas Gerais 1944; Fed. Deputy 1940–60; Gov. of Minas Gerais 1960–65; mem. Chamber of Deputies 1945–60, 1966–70, 1979–82, 1982–86; Minister of Foreign Affairs 1967–69; Pres. União Democrática Nacional (UDN); mem. Senate 1970–78; Pres. Nat. Congress; Prof. at Econ. Univ. of Minas Gerais; Dr. h.c.(Univ. Rural de Viçosa); Homem de Visão do Ano 1979 and other Brazilian and foreign decorations. *Address:* Avenida Atlântica 2016, Apt. 401 Copacabana, Rio de Janeiro, RJ, CEP 22021; and SQS 309, BC, ap. 402, CEP 7000D Brasília D.F., Brazil. *Telephone:* 236-4838 (Rio de Janeiro); 243-8782 (Brasília).

MAGALOFF, Nikita; Swiss pianist; b. 8 Feb. 1912, St. Petersburg (now Leningrad), Russia; s. of Dimitri and Barbara Magaloff; m. Irène Szigeti 1939; one d.; ed. Conservatoire nat. de musique, Paris and with Joseph Szigeti; Prof. of Virtuosity, Geneva Conservatoire 1949–59; numerous concerts all over the world since 1939, including tours of S. America and tour round the world 1960; particularly well known as Chopin interpreter; numerous invitations to play in the major European int. music festivals; frequent mem. of jury in European Int. Piano Competitions. *Compositions include:* Sonatina for Violin and Piano Toccata for Piano and Songs; has recorded complete piano works of Chopin. *Leisure interests:* sightseeing, chess. *Address:* 1815 Baugy/Clarens (Vaud), Switzerland. *Telephone:* (021)-643186.

MAGAÑA BORJA, Dr. Alvaro; Salvadorean politician; b. 1926; fmr. lawyer and economist; Dir. state mortgage bank for 17 years; worked abroad for OAS; Sec. of State for Housing 1960s; Pres. of El Salvador 1982–84. *Address:* c/o Oficina del Presidente, San Salvador, El Salvador.

MAGARIÑOS D., Victor; Argentine painter; b. 1 Sept. 1924, province of Buenos Aires; s. of José Magariños and Antonia Mahia Sánchez; m. Hilda Mans; ed. Escuela nacional de artes visuales; founded Grupo Jóven 1946; First one-man exhbn. Galería Juan Cristóbal 1950, also at Inst. de Arte Moderno 1950–51, Pres. Argentine Cttee. of Int. Asscn. for Plastic Arts, UNESCO 1958; Scholarship to France 1951, to U.S.A. 1965; mem. (with gold medal) Acad. delle Arti e de Laboro Perme (Italy); represented at Biennali: São Paulo 1951–55, Venice 1956; also at Concrete Art Exhbn. Museum of Modern Art 1963, El Nuevo Arte Argentino, Walker Art Center, Minneapolis, A Decade of Latin-American Art, Guggenheim Museum 1965–66, Museum of Modern Art, New York, Museo Nacional de Bellas Artes, Museo de Arte Moderno, Buenos Aires, Centro de Arte y Comunicación, Argentina, Premio d'Italia 1986, Museo de Arte Moderno, Brussels 1986, Milan Prize 1988. *Address:* Los Talleres, Estaf. No. 5, C.P. 7167, Pinamar, Argentina.

MAGARIÑOS MORALES DE LOS RÍOS, Gustavo; Uruguayan international civil servant; b. 31 Dec. 1922, Montevideo; s. of Mateo M. Pittaluga and Margarita M. de los Ríos; m. Ivonne Pagani 1947; one s. one d.; ed. Univ. de la República; Econ. Counsellor, Uruguayan Embassy, London, and Econ. Adviser, Ministry of Foreign Affairs 1954–59; Dir. of Commercial and Econ. Dept., Uruguayan Embassy, Buenos Aires 1959–62; Dir. of Dept. of Negotiation, Latin American Free Trade Asscn. (LAFTA) 1962, Asst. Exec. Sec. LAFTA 1962–67, Perm. Exec. Sec. 1967–73; Gen. Dir. Dept. of Trade 1974–76; Amb. to Argentina and Rep. to River Plate Basin Cttee. 1976–78; Amb. to EEC, Belgium and to Luxembourg 1979–84. *Leisure interests:* sport, classical literature. *Address:* c/o Ministry of Foreign Affairs, Montevideo, Uruguay.

MAGEE, Reginald Arthur Edward, M.B., B.CH., B.A.O., F.R.C.S.I., F.R.C.O.G., F.R.A.C.S. (Hon); British obstetrician and gynaecologist; b. 18 Aug. 1914, Belfast; s. of James Magee and Eleanor Magee; m. Gwladys S. Chapman 1945; two d.; ed. Campbell Coll. Belfast and Queen's Univ. Belfast; Consultant Obstetrician and Gynaecologist, Ulster Hosp. for Women and Children and Consultant Obstetrician and Gynaecologist, Royal Victoria Hosp. and Royal Maternity Hosp. Belfast 1948–79; Acting Dist. Medical Admin. Officer, Royal Group of Hosps., Belfast 1979–84; Pres. Royal Coll.

of Surgeons in Ireland 1986–88 (Vice-Pres. 1984–88); numerous other professional appts.; mem. for S. Belfast (Official Unionist Party), Northern Ireland Ass. 1973; Adviser, Sunningdale Conf. 1973. *Leisure interests:* riding, horse breeding, travel, photography. *Address:* Montpellier, 96 Malone Road, Belfast BT9 5HP, Northern Ireland.

MAGHOUR, Kamal Hassan; Libyan diplomatist and politician; ed. Cairo Univ. Law School; Legal Adviser to the oil industry in Libya 1970; has represented Libya at Int. Court of Justice, The Hague; Amb. to UN 1972–76, to France 1976–78, to People's Repub. of China 1978–81; Head Petroleum Secretariat 1982–84. *Address:* c/o Petroleum Secretariat, P.O. Box 256, Tripoli, Libya.

MAGHRABI, Mahmoud Sulaiman; Libyan politician; b. 1935; ed. George Washington Univ., U.S.A.; helped to organize strikes of port workers June 1967, for which he was sentenced to four years imprisonment and deprived of Libyan nationality; released Aug. 1969; following the coup of Sept. 1969 became Prime Minister, Minister of Finance and Agric., and of Agricultural Reform until Jan. 1971; Perm. Rep. to UN 1971–72; Amb. to UK 1973–77. *Address:* c/o Ministry of Foreign Affairs, Tripoli, Libya.

MAGISTRETTI, Vico; Italian architect, industrial designer and interior decorator; b. 6 Oct. 1920, Milan; s. of Piergiulio and Luisa Tosi Magistretti; one s. one d.; ed. Ginnasio Liceo Parini and Politecnico di Milano; industrial design for Artemide, Cassina S.p.A., Habitat-Conran, Knoll Int., Azucena, La Rinascente, De Padova I.C.F., Montina Fratelli, Oca Brazil, Asko Finlandia, Poggi, Carrara & Matta, Spalding (U.S.A.), Rosenthal-Selb (G.D.R.), Fiat Auto S.p.A. etc.; lectures at Venice architectural school, Barcelona Coll. of Architecture, Vienna, Toronto, Frankfurt, London, Belfast etc.; has participated in numerous exhbns. *Publications:* articles in journals, magazines and newspapers. *Leisure interest:* golf. *Address:* via Conservatorio 20, Milan, Italy. *Telephone:* 702.964.

MAGLOIRE, Gen. Paul; Haitian officer and politician; b. 1907; ed. Cap Haiti High School; taught at Lycée National Philippe Guerrier, Cap Haiti 1929–30; entered army as cadet 1931; Lieut. 1931; Head of Mil. School 1934; Asst. District Commdr., Cap Haiti 1935–37; Maj. 1938; District Commdr. 1938–41; Chief of Police, Port-au-Prince, and Commdr. of Palace Guard 1944; mem. provisional Mil. Govt. and Minister of Interior 1946 and 1950; Pres. of Haiti 1950–56; Orders of Honneur et Mérite, Brevet de Mérite, etc. *Address:* Living in U.S.A.

MAGNÉLI, Arne, FIL.DR.; Swedish chemist; b. 6 Dec. 1914, Stockholm; s. of Agge and Valborg (née Hultman) Magnéli; m. Barbro Wigh 1946; two s. one d.; ed. Univs. of Stockholm and Uppsala; Research Asst., Univ. of Uppsala 1941–50; Docent in Chemistry 1950–53; Assoc. Prof. of Inorganic and Physical Chemistry 1953–61, Univ. of Stockholm, Prof. of Inorganic Chemistry 1961–80, Prof. Emer. 1981–; mem. Exec. Cttee., Int. Union of Crystallography 1972–81, Pres. 1975–78; Sec. Nobel Cttee. for Physics 1966–73, for Chemistry 1966–86, mem. Swedish Natural Science Research Council 1965–71; mem. Bd. of Dirs., Nobel Foundation 1973–85; Chair. Swedish Nat. Cttee. for Chemistry 1984–; mem. Royal Swedish Acad. of Sciences, Royal Soc. of Sciences (Uppsala); Dr. h.c. (Univ. Pierre et Marie Curie, Paris) 1988; Bergstedt Prize 1947; Bjurzon Prize 1950; Norblad-Ekstrand Medal 1954; Bror Holmberg Medal 1980; Gregori Aminoff Prize 1989; Commdr. Ordre nat. du Mérite; Officier des Palmes Académiques. *Publications:* about 100 research articles in chemical crystallography and solid state inorganic chemistry. *Address:* Arrhenius Laboratory, University of Stockholm, S-106 91, Stockholm; Odensgatan SA, S-752 22 Uppsala, Sweden (Home). *Telephone:* (08) 162417 (Office); (018) 118650 (Home).

MAGNUSON, Warren Grant; American lawyer and politician; b. 12 April 1905, Moorhead, Minnesota; m. Jermaine Elliot Peralta Magnuson; one d.; ed. Public School, Minnesota, Univ. of North Dakota, North Dakota State Univ. and Univ. of Washington; Special Prosecuting Attorney 1931; elected to Washington State Legislature 1933–34; Asst. U.S. Dist. Attorney 1934; Prosecuting Attorney, King County, Washington 1934–36; served in House of Reps. 1937–44; Senator from Washington 1944–81, Chair. Senate Appropriations Cttee. 1978–81; served as Lieut.-Commdr. in U.S.N. during Second World War; Hon. D.Jur.(Gonzaga Univ.) 1966, (Seattle) 1967, (St. Martin's Coll.) 1967, (Gallaudet Coll.) 1972, (Alaska) 1973; Hon. Dr. Public Admin. (Puget Sound) 1967; Hon. Dr.rer.Pol. (Univ. of the Pacific) 1970; awards include Metropolitan Bd. of Trade World Trade Award 1961, American Coll. of Cardiology Distinguished Service Award 1972, Albert Lasker Award for Public Service in Health 1973, Nat. Consumer League Consumer of the Year 1978. Democrat. *Publications:* The Dark Side of the Marketplace (with Jean Carper) 1968, How Much for Health? (with Elliot A. Segal) 1974.

MAGNUSSEN, Einar, CAND. ECON.; Norwegian economist and politician; b. 5 June 1931, Ålesund; s. of Gustav Magnussen and Selma Giske; m. Aase Bjørg Andersen 1956; two s. one d.; ed. Oslo Univ.; Economist, Norges Bank 1957–60; worked on team preparing Norwegian Econ. Long Term Programme, Ministry of Finance 1960–61; Economist, IMF 1962–65; Head, Monetary Policy Div., Norges Bank 1965–68; Econ. Adviser, Bank of Tanzania 1968–70; Dir. Monetary Policy Dept., Norges Bank 1970–73; Under-Sec. of State, Ministry of Commerce and Shipping 1973–74, Minister 1974–76; Exec. Dir., World Bank (IBRD) 1976–79; Man. Dir. Norwegian

Export Council 1979–82; Chair. Norwegian Petroleum Price Bd. 1976–87; Dir. Norges Bank 1983–. *Address:* Norges Bank, Bank pl. 2, Oslo 1 (Office); Ulvøya, Box 62, Oslo 1, Norway (Home). *Telephone:* (02) 316071 (Office).

MAGNUSSON, Thor Eyfeld; Icelandic museum director; b. 18 Nov. 1937, Hvammstangi; s. of Magnus Richardson and Sigridur Thordardottir; m. Maria V. Heiddal 1964; two s. one d.; ed. Univ. of Uppsala; Asst. Curator, Nat. Museum 1964, Dir. 1968–. *Address:* National Museum, Box 1489, 121 Reykjavik (Office); Bauganes 26, 101 Reykjavik, Iceland (Home). *Telephone:* (91) 28888.

MAGOMETOV, Col. Gen. Soltan Kekezevich; Soviet tank-troop officer; Deputy Commdr. Transbaikal Mil. District 1974–. *Address:* c/o Ministry of Defence, Moscow, U.S.S.R.

MAGOWAN, Peter Alden, M.A.; American business executive; b. 5 April 1942, New York; s. of Robert Anderson and Doris Merrill Magowan; ed. Stanford Univ., Oxford Univ., Johns Hopkins School of Advanced Int. Studies; Store Man., Washington, D.C., Safeway Stores, 1968–70, Dist. Man., Houston, Tex. 1970, Retail Operations Man., Phoenix, Ariz. 1971–72, Div. Man., Tulsa, Okla. 1973–76, Man., Int. Div., Toronto, Canada 1976–78, Western Regional Man., San Francisco, Calif. 1978–79, Dir., Safeway Stores, Inc. 1979, Chair. of the Bd. and C.E.O. 1980–, Pres. and C.O.O. March 1988–, also Chair. Exec. Cttee.; Dir. of U.S. Chamber of Commerce, The Hudson Inst., Pacific Gas and Electric Co., Food Marketing Inst., Chrysler Corpn.; mem. Advisory Council, Johns Hopkins School of Advanced Int. Studies; Trustee, Johns Hopkins Univ.. *Address:* Safeway Stores Inc., 4th and Jackson Streets, Oakland, Calif. 94660, U.S.A. *Telephone:* 415-891-3300.

MAGRI, Charles George; British boxer; b. 20 July 1956, Tunisia; s. of André and Rose (née Tonna) Magri; m. Jacqueline Britton 1979; one d.; ed. Cardinal Griffin Secondary School, Stepney, London; Amateur Boxing Asscn. (A.B.A.) light-flyweight champion 1974, A.B.A. flyweight champion 1975, 1976, 1977; rep. England and Great Britain; boxed in Olympic Games, 1976; professional boxer 1977–84; won vacant British flyweight title in third professional fight Dec. 1977 (new British record); won European title from Franco Udella May 1979, retained it v. Manuel Carrasco Dec. 1979, Giovanni Camputaro June 1980, Rodriguez Cal 1981 and 1982; world flyweight champion 1983; 29 professional fights, 27 wins. *Leisure interest:* helping schoolboy and junior boxers. *Address:* c/o British Boxing Board of Control, 2 Ramilles Buildings, Hills Place, London, W.1, England.

MAH SOO-LAY; Chinese politician; b. 3 Aug. 1909, Kiangsu; m. Weilin Wu; ed. Meiji Univ., Japan, Univ. of Santo Tomas, Philippines; Ed. Minkuo Daily News, Singapore 1931–33, New China Herald, Manila 1936–38; Chief Ed. and Dir. Front Daily News, Shanghai 1938–49; Chief Ed. and Dir. Chinese Commercial Daily News, Djakarta 1953–58; Head of Third Div., Kuomintang (KMT) Cen. Cttee. in charge of Overseas Chinese Affairs 1962–72, KMT Sec.-Gen. 1985–87; Chair. CTV 1987–; Chair. Grand Alliance for the Reunification of China under the Three Principles of the People 1988–; Chair. Broadcasting Corpn. of China 1972–85; Rep. to Asscn. of E. Asia Relations, Tokyo, 1973–85; mem. Legis. Yuan 1948–. *Address:* 120 Chungyang Road, Nankang, Taipei, Taiwan.

MAHACHI, Moven Enock, M.P.; Zimbabwean farmer and politician; b. 13 June 1948, Rusape; s. of Prisca Mahachi and Enock Mahachi; m. Rashiwe Mahachi 1970; one s. three d.; ed. Univ. of London, Univ. of South Africa; Vice-Chair. Cold Comfort Farm Soc. 1970–71; Man. Dir. Nyafonu Devt. Co. 1971–74; serving 15-year sentence as political prisoner 1974–79; Z.A.N.U. (PF) Prov. Admin. Manicaland Prov. 1979–80; Deputy Minister of Land Resettlement and Rural Devt. 1980–82, Minister 1982–85; M.P. for Manicaland Prov. 1980–85, for Makoni West and mem. Cen. Cttee. 1985–; Minister of Land, Agriculture and Rural Resettlement 1985–88, of Home Affairs Jan. 1988–; Deputy Sec. for Production, Z.A.N.U. (PF) Politburo. *Leisure interests:* soccer, farming, squash, hunting, fishing. *Address:* P.O. Box 5, Ruwa, Harare, Zimbabwe. *Telephone:* 883169.

MAHASANDANA, Suli; Thai politician; b. 19 March 1919, Nonthaburi Prov.; ed. Chulalongkorn Univ., Bangkok; Royal Thai Air Force 1942–48 rank of Flying Officer; joined ESSO Standard Thailand Ltd., apptd. Dir. and Gen. Sales Man. 1969; f. Siam City Cement Co. Ltd., Dir. and Gen. Man. until 1980; Minister in Prime Minister's Office 1981–88. *Address:* c/o Office of the Prime Minister, Nakhon, Pathom Road, Bangkok 10300, Thailand.

MAHATHIR BIN MOHAMED, Dr.; Malaysian politician; b. 20 Dec. 1925, Alur Setar, Kedah; m. Dr. Siti Hasmah binti Haji Mohd Ali 1956; three s. two d.; ed. Sultan Abdul Hamid Coll. and Univ. of Malaya in Singapore; Medical Officer, Kedah, Langkawi and Perlis 1953–57; private practice 1957–64; mem. UMNO (now Umno Baru) Supreme Council 1965–69, 1972– (Pres. 1981–), mem. Supreme Council 1972–; mem. House of Reps. for Kota Setar Selatan 1964–69, for Kubang Pasu 1974–; mem. Senate 1973; Chair. Food Industries of Malaysia Sdn. Bhd. 1973; Minister of Educ. 1974–77, of Trade and Industry 1977–81, of Defence 1981–86, of Home Affairs Oct. 1986–, of Justice 1987–; Deputy Prime Minister 1976–81, Prime Minister of Malaysia July 1981–. *Publication:* The Malay Dilemma 1969. *Address:* Office of the Prime Minister, Jalan Dato Onn, Kuala Lumpur, Malaysia.

MAHBUBANI, Kishore; Singapore diplomatist; b. 24 Oct. 1948; ed. Univ. of Singapore and Dalhousie Univ., Canada; joined Ministry of Foreign Affairs 1971, Deputy Dir. 1979–82; Chargé d'affaires to Cambodia 1973–74; Counsellor at Singapore Embassy in Malaysia 1976–79; mem. of Singapore dels. to several sessions of UN Gen. Ass. and int. confs. 1979–83; Deputy Chief at Washington D.C. Embassy 1982–84; Perm. Rep. of Singapore to UN, New York 1984–89. *Address:* c/o Ministry of Foreign Affairs, 250 North Bridge Road, 07-00 Raffles City Tower, Singapore 0617.

MAHBUBUZZAMAN, Mohammad, B.A.; Bangladeshi politician; b. 1929, Rajshahi; s. of late Alhaj Mohammad Karim Baksh; m.; two s.; ed. Dhaka Univ., Univ. of London, Univ. of Southern California; served in various admin. posts in E. Pakistan, then different Ministries of the Govt. of Bangladesh; Adviser to Pres. 1986–87; Minister of Agric. 1987–88. *Address:* c/o Ministry of Agriculture, Dhaka, Bangladesh.

MAHDI, Sadiq Al (Since 1978 known as **Sadiq Abdul Rahman**); Sudanese politician; b. 1936; great grandson of Imam Abdul-Rahman El Mahdi, s. of late Siddik El Mahdi; ed. Comboni Coll., Khartoum and St. John's Coll., Oxford; Leader, Umma Mahdist (now New Nat. Umma) Party 1961–; Prime Minister 1966–67, May 1986–; Minister of Defence 1986–89; arrested on a charge of high treason 1969; exiled April 1970; returned to Sudan and arrested Feb. 1972, released April 1974; exiled 1974–77; led unsuccessful coup against fmr. Pres. Nimeri July 1976, returned to Sudan Sept 1977; reconciliation with Pres. Nimeri 1977; mem. Cttee. Sudanese Socialist Union (SSU) 1978–79; mem. Nat. Ass. 1986–; led mediation mission in U.S. hostages in Iran Crisis Jan. 1980; Visiting Fellow St. Anthony's Coll., Oxford 1983; returned to prison Sept. 1983, released Dec. 1984. *Publication:* Problems of the South Sudan. *Address:* Office of the Prime Minister, Khartoum, Sudan.

MAHDI AL TAJIR, Mohamed; Dubai administrator and diplomatist; b. 26 Dec. 1931, Bahrain; m. Zohra Al-Tajir 1956; five s. one d.; ed. Bahrain Govt. School and Preston Grammar School, Lancs., England; Department of Port and Customs, Govt. of Bahrain, Dir. 1955–63; Dir. Dept. of His Highness the Ruler's Affairs and Petroleum Affairs March 1963–; Dir. Nat. Bank of Dubai Ltd. 1963–; Dir. Dubai Petroleum Co. April 1963–; Dir. Dubai Nat. Air Travel Agency Jan. 1966–; Dir. Qatar-Dubai Currency Bd. Oct 1965–73; Chair. South Eastern Dubai Drilling Co. April 1968–; Dir. Dubai Dry Dock Co. 1973–; Amb. of the United Arab Emirates to U.K. 1972–82, 1983–86, also accred. to France 1972–77; Hon. Citizen of State of Texas, U.S.A. 1963. *Address:* P.O. Box 207, Dubai, United Arab Emirates.

MAHFUZ, Nagib; Egyptian author; b. 11 Dec. 1911, Gamaliya, Cairo; m.; c.; ed. Univ. of Cairo; Civil servant 1934; successively with Univ. of Cairo, Ministry of Waqfs, Dept. of Arts and Censorship Bd.; fmr Dir.-Gen., then Adviser, Cinema Org. of Egypt; contrib. to Al Ahram; State Prize for 1st vol. Bain al-Kasrain 1957, Nobel Prize for Literature 1988. *Publications:* novels: Khan al Khalili 1946, Midaq Alley 1947, The Castle of Desire (Vol. I) 1956, Between the Two Castles (Vol. II) 1957, The Sugar Bowl (Vol. III) 1957 (trilogy Bain al-Kasrain), The Thief and the Dogs 1961, Quails in Autumn 1962, The Road 1964, The Beggar 1965, Gossip by the Nile 1966, Miramar 1967, Children of Gebelani (novel) 1980, High Mile Ribbon 1988; Short story collections: The Whisper of Madness 1938, God's World 1963, At the Sign of the Black Cat 1969, Under the Umbrella 1969, A Story Without Beginning or End 1971, Mirrors (Contemporary History) 1972. *Address:* c/o Cinema Organization, TV Building, Maspero Street, Cairo, Egypt.

MAHGOUB, Mohammed Ahmed; Sudanese lawyer and politician; b. 1908; ed. Gordon Coll. and Khartoum School of Law; practising lawyer; fmr. mem. Legis. Assembly; accompanied Umma Party Del. to UN 1947; mem. Constitution Amendment Comm.; non-party candidate in Gen. Election 1954; Leader of the Opposition 1954–56; Minister of Foreign Affairs 1956–58, 1964–65, Prime Minister 1965–66, 1967–69; practising solicitor 1958–64. *Publications:* Democracy on Trial 1974, and several vols. of poetry (in Arabic). *Address:* 60c Prince's Gate, Exhibition Road, London, S.W.7, England.

MAHINDRA, Keshub, B.SC.; Indian business executive; b. 9 Oct. 1923, Simla; s. of late Kailash Chandra Mahindra and Savitri Mahindra; m. Sudha Y. Varde 1956; three d.; ed. Univ. of Pennsylvania, U.S.A.; Pres. Assocn. of Indian Automobile Mfrs. 1964–65, Bombay Chamber of Commerce and Industry 1966–67, Assoc. Chamber of Commerce and Industry 1969–70, Maharashtra Econ. Devt. Council 1969–70; Chair. Indian Council of Trade Fairs and Exhbns. 1964–69, Indian Soc. of Advertisers 1968–71; Chair. Mahindra and Mahindra Ltd., Remington Rand of India Ltd., Otis Elevator Co. (India) Ltd.; Dir. Bombay Dyeing and Mfg. Co. Ltd., WIMCO Ltd., Bombay Burmah Trading Corpn. Ltd., Tata Iron and Steel Co. Ltd., Tata Chemicals Ltd., Housing Devt. Finance Corpn. Ltd., The Industrial Credit and Investment Corpn. of India Ltd., The Atul Products Ltd., Mahindra Ugine Steel Co. Ltd., The North Borneo Timbers Berhard, Malaysia; Pres. Employers' Fed. of India; Vice-Pres. M. Visvesvaraya Industrial Research and Devt. Centre, Nat. Soc. for Clean Cities; Chair. Nat. Assocn. for the Blind, IDBI Polytechnic; Trustee Urban Design Research Inst.; Foundation mem. Int. Man. Inst., Geneva; Modi Enterprises Man of the Year Award 1980, Giants Int. Business Leadership Award 1972–82, Madras Man. Assocn.

Business Leadership Award 1983, Companion of the British Inst. of Management, Chevalier Légion d'honneur. *Leisure interests:* golf, tennis, photography, reading. *Address:* Mahindra and Mahindra Ltd., Gateway Building, Apollo Bunder, Bombay 400 039 (Office); St. Helen's Court, Pedder Road, Bombay 400 026, India (Home). *Telephone:* 2021031 (Office); 364106 (Home).

MAHLER, Dr. Halfdan, M.D.; Danish health official; b. 21 April 1923, Vivild; m. Dr. Ebba Fischer-Simonesen; two s.; ed. Univ. of Copenhagen; Planning Officer, Mass Tuberculosis Campaign, Ecuador 1950–51; joined WHO 1951; Sr. WHO Officer attached to Nat. TB Programme, India 1951–61; Visiting Prof., postgraduate medical schools, Rome and Prague 1961–; Chief Medical Officer, Tuberculosis Unit, WHO HQ, Geneva 1962–69, also Sec. to WHO Expert Panel on TB; Dir. Project Systems Analysis 1969; Asst. Dir.-Gen. WHO, responsible for Div. of Family Health, Div. of Org. of Health Services, Div. of Research in Epidemiology and Communication Science 1970–73, Dir.-Gen. 1973–88; Pres. Int. Planned Parenthood Fed. April 1989–; Fellow, Royal Coll. of Physicians 1981; various hon. fellowships and memberships; Hon. LL.D. (Nottingham) 1975, Hon. M.D. (Karolinska Inst., Stockholm) 1977, Hon. Dr. (Univ. des Sciences Sociales, Toulouse) 1977, Hon. Dr. of Public Health (Seoul Nat. Univ.) 1979, Hon. Dr. of Science (Lagos) 1979, Hon. M.D. (Warsaw Medical Acad.) 1980, (Charles Univ., Prague) 1982, (Mahidol Univ., Bangkok) 1982; Dr. h.c. (Gand Univ., Belgium) 1983, (Nat. Univ. of Nicaragua) 1983; numerous awards. *Publications:* several publications relating to the epidemiology and control of TB and to the utilization of operational research in health care delivery systems. *Leisure interests:* sailing, skiing. *Address:* Regent's College, Inner Circle, Regent's Park, London, NW1 4NS, England.

MAHMUD, Anisul Islam, M.SC., M.A.; Bangladesh barrister and politician; b. 1947, Chittagong; m.; one s. one d.; ed. Dhaka and Islamabad Univs. and Univ. of Essex; Lecturer in Econs. Dhaka Univ. 1969–70; Sr. Research Assoc. in Econs. Univ. of East Anglia 1972–73; Lecturer in Econs. Hatfield Coll., U.K. 1973–77; called to Bar, Lincoln's Inn, London 1975; mem. Jatiya Sangsad 1979; Minister of Irrigation, Water Devt. and Flood Control 1985–88, of Educ. 1988, of Foreign Affairs Dec. 1988–. *Leisure interests:* photography, travel, cricket. *Address:* Ministry of Foreign Affairs, Topkhana Road, Dhaka, Bangladesh.

MAHMUD, Air Vice-Marshal Sultan; Bangladeshi army officer and government official; b. Noakhali Dist.; s. of Nurul Huda; m.; two s.; ed. Armanitola Govt. High School, Dhaka, Pakistan Air Force Public School, Sargodha, U.S.A.F. Air Command and Staff Coll. and Academic Instructors' School, also Iran, U.S.S.R.; joined Pakistan Air Force 1960, served Liberation war, then Pioneer Commdr. First Bangladeshi air force Contingent, then engaged in reconstruction of Air Force, then Commdr. Air Force bases at Basher, Matiur Rahman, Air Force Acad., then at Air HQ, Dir. of Operations, then Asst. Chief-of-Staff; Chief of Air Staff 1981–87; apptd. Deputy Chief Martial Law Admin. 1981–86; Minister for Energy and Mineral Resources 1981-85, Minister for Industry, Commerce, Jute and Textiles –July 1985, for Industry 1985–86; Bir Uttam. *Leisure interest:* football. *Address:* c/o Ministry of Commerce and Industries, Shilpa Bhaban, Motijhed C/A, Dhaka, Bangladesh.

MAHMUD HUSAIN, Syed Abul Basher; Bangladesh fmr. judge; b. 1 Feb. 1916; s. of late Abdul Mutakabbir Abul Hasan; m. Sufia Begum 1936; three s. five d.; ed. Shaistagonj High School, M.C. Coll., Sylhet, Dhaka Univ.; Pleader, Judge's Court, Habiganj 1940–42; Additional Govt. Pleader, Habiganj 1943–48; Advocate, Dhaka High Court Bar 1948–51; Attorney, Fed. Court of Pakistan 1951–53, Advocate 1953–58, Sr. Advocate of Supreme Court of Pakistan 1958–65; Asst. Govt. Pleader, High Court of E. Pakistan 1952–56, Sr. Govt. Pleader and later acting Advocate-Gen. of E. Pakistan 1956–65; Judge, High Court of E. Pakistan 1965–72, of Bangladesh 1972, of Appellate Div. of High Court 1972, of Appellate Div. of Supreme Court 1972–75; Chief Justice 1975–76, Chief Justice of Supreme Court 1976–81; Councillor, Assam Prov. Muslim League 1944–47, All-India Muslim League 1945–47, All-Pakistan Muslim League 1947–55; mem. Constituent Assembly of Pakistan 1949–54, Commonwealth Parl. Assocn. 1950–54, Interparl. Union 1950–54, Pakistan Tea Bd. 1951–54, Exec. Council of Dhaka Univ. 1952–54, Bar Council of Dhaka High Court 1958–66. *Address:* 56/1 Shab Saheb Lane, Narinda, Dhaka, Bangladesh. *Telephone:* 281986.

MAHON, Sir (John) Denis, Kt., C.B.E., M.A., F.B.A.; British art historian; b. 8 Nov. 1910; s. of the late John Fitzgerald Mahon and Lady (Alice Evelyn Browne) Mahon; ed. Eton and Christ Church, Oxford; Trustee of the Nat. Gallery 1957–64, 1966–73; mem. Advisory Panel, Nat. Art Collections Fund 1975–; specialist in 17th Century paintings; mem. Cttee. of the Biennial Exhbns., Bologna, Italy; Hon. D. Litt. (Newcastle) 1969; Medal for Bènemeriti della Cultura for services to criticism and history of Italian art 1957, Archiginasio d'Oro, City of Bologna 1968, Serena Medal for Italian Studies, British Acad. 1972; Corresp. Fellow Accad. Raffaello, Urbino 1968, Ateneo Veneto 1987; Hon. Citizen, Cento 1982. *Publications:* Studies in Seicento Art and Theory 1947, numerous articles in publs. on history of art. *Address:* 33 Cadogan Square, London, S.W.1, England. *Telephone:* 01-235-7311.

MAHONEY, Hon. Patrick Morgan, P.C., B.A., LL.B.; Canadian politician and judge; b. 20 Jan. 1929, Winnipeg; s. of Paul Morgan Mahoney and

Joan Ethel Tracy Patrick; m. Mary A. Sneath 1958; two s. two d.; ed. Univ. of Alberta; admitted to Alberta Bar 1952; M.P. 1968–72; Parl. Sec. to Minister of Finance 1970–72; Minister without Portfolio Jan.-Oct. 1972; apptd. Q.C. 1972; Judge of Trial Div., Fed. Court of Canada 1973; Judge Fed. Court of Appeal 1983; Judge of Court Martial Appeal Court of Canada Nov. 1973–, Chief Justice 1982–; fmr. Pres. Western Football Conf., Canadian Football League. *Address:* 3 Coltrin Place, Ottawa K1M 0A5, Ont., Canada.

MAHONEY, Richard John, B.S.; American business executive; b. 30 Jan. 1934, Springfield, Mass.; s. of late Maurice Edward Mahoney and of Marion Loretta Kennedy; m. Barbara M. Barnett 1956; three s.; ed. Univ. of Mass.; joined Monsanto Co. as product devt. specialist, then in sales, eng. and tech. service positions; Market Man. for new products, Plastic Products and Resins Div. 1965–67; Market Man. bonding products, then Div. Sales Dir., plastic products, Kenilworth, N.J. 1967–71; Sales Dir. Agricultural Div., St. Louis, Mo. 1971–74; Dir. Int. Operations, Monsanto Agricultural Products Co. 1974–75, Gen. Man. Overseas Div. 1975, Vice-Pres. and Man. Dir. Oct. 1975; Vice-Pres. and Man. Dir. Monsanto Plastics and Resins Co. 1976, Exec. Vice-Pres. 1977–80, Pres. 1980–81, Pres. and Chief Operating Officer 1981–83, Pres. and C.E.O. 1983–86, Chair and C.E.O. 1986–; Dir. Metropolitan Life Insurance Co., Fisher Controls Int., U.S./U.S.S.R. Trade and Econ. Council, G. D. Searle & Co., Council for Aid to Educ.; mem. Advisory Bd., St. John's Mercy Medical Center, Bd. of Mans. Cen. Inst. for the Deaf; Trustee Washington Univ., St. Louis; mem. The Business Round Table, The Business Council. *Address:* 800 North Lindbergh Boulevard, St. Louis, Mo. 63167 (Office). *Telephone:* 314 694-3756 (Office).

MAIDOU, Henri; Central African Republic banker and politician; b. 14 Feb. 1936, Bangui; fmr. Pres. Banque Centrale des Etats de l'Afrique de l'Ouest; Minister of Nat. Educ., Youth, Sports and Arts 1970–1973, of Nat. Health and Social Affairs 1973–74; Minister of State charged with Town Planning and Territorial Devt. 1974–76, with Nat. Educ. and Educational Reform April-Sept. 1976; Second Deputy Prime Minister, charged with Nat. Educ. and Admin. Reform Sept.–Dec. 1976, with Nat. Educ., Youth, Sports, Arts and Culture 1976–78; Prime Minister 1978–79; Vice-Pres. of Central African Repub. 1979–80; imprisoned Aug.-Oct. 1980; Leader, Parti Républicain du Progrès 1981 (political parties banned Sept. 1981).

MAIHOFER, Werner; German politician; b. 20 Oct. 1918, Konstanz; m. Margrit Schiele 1942; five d.; ed. Secondary School, Konstanz and Freiburg Univ.; Prof., Univ. of the Saarland 1955, Dean of Faculty of Law and Econs. 1956-57, Rector 1967–69; Prof. Univ. of Bielefeld 1970, Dir. Centre for Interdisciplinary Research 1971; mem. Bundestag 1970–80; Fed. Minister without Portfolio 1972; Fed. Minister of the Interior 1974–78; Pres. European Univ. Inst., Fiesole 1981–87; mem. Presidium Int. Asscn. Legal and Social Philosophy; Dr. h.c. (Nancy) 1968; Grand Cross, Order of Léopold II (Belgium), Grosses Verdienstkreuz mit Stern und Schulterband 1977; Freie Demokratische Partei (FDP). *Publications:* Der Handlungsbegriff im Verbrechenssystem 1953, Recht und Sein 1954, Rechtsstaat und menschliche Würde 1968, Demokratie im Sozialismus 1968. *Leisure interests:* yachting, skiing, music. *Address:* c/o European University Institute, Badia Fiesolana, Via dei Roccettini 5, San Domenico di Fiesole, 50016 Florence, Italy.

MAILER, Norman Kingsley, B.S.; American writer; b. 31 Jan. 1923, Long Branch, N.J.; s. of Isaac Barnett Mailer and Fanny Schneider; m. 1st Beatrice Silverman 1944 (dissolved 1951), one d.; m. 2nd Adele Morales 1954 (dissolved 1962), two d.; m. 3rd Lady Jeanne Campbell 1962 (dissolved 1963), one d.; m. 4th Beverly Rentz Bentley 1963 (divorced 1980), two s. one d.; m. 5th Carol Stevens (divorced 1980), one d.; m. 6th Norris Church 1980; one s.; ed. Harvard Univ.; served in U.S. Army 1944–46; Co-founder New York weekly Village Voice 1955; mem. Editorial Bd. of Dissent magazine 1953–69, American Acad. of Arts and Letters 1984–; Pres. of PEN (U.S. Chapter) 1984–86; Dir. films: Wild 90 1967, Beyond the Law 1967, Maidstone 1968, Tough Guys Don't Dance 1986; Nat. Book Award for Arts and Letters 1969; Pulitzer Prize for Non-Fiction 1969, for Fiction 1980; 14th Annual Award for outstanding service to the arts, McDowell Colony 1973; acted in film Ragtime 1981. *Publications:* The Naked and The Dead 1948, Barbary Shore 1951, The Deer Park 1955 (dramatized 1967), Advertisements for Myself 1959, Deaths for the Ladies (poems) 1962, The Presidential Papers 1963, An American Dream 1964, Cannibals and Christians 1966, Why are we in Vietnam? (novel) 1967, The Armies of the Night 1968, Miami and the Siege of Chicago 1968, Moonshot 1969, A Fire on the Moon 1970, The Prisoner of Sex 1971, Existential Errands 1972, St. George and the Godfather 1972, Marilyn 1973, The Faith of Graffiti 1974, The Fight 1975, Some Honourable Men 1976, Genius and Lust—A Journey Through the Writings of Henry Miller 1976, A Transit to Narcissus 1978, The Executioner's Song 1979, Of Women and Their Elegance 1980, The Essential Mailer (selections) 1982, Pieces and Pontifications 1982, Ancient Evenings (novel) 1983, Tough Guys Don't Dance (novel) 1983; contributions to numerous magazines. *Address:* c/o Rembar, 19 W. 44th Street, New York, N.Y. 10036, U.S.A.

MAILLARD, Pierre; French diplomatist; b. 24 June 1916, Laval; s. of Adrien and Hélène (née Coliette) Maillard; m. Evelyn George 1943; one s.; ed. Ecole Normale Supérieure; Letters and Law faculties, Paris Univ.; entered diplomatic service 1942, attaché to French Embassy, Berne 1942–

43, mem. representation of French Liberation Cttee. 1943; Head, French Office for Refugees in Switzerland 1944; Head of Office of Sec.-Gen. for German and Austrian Affairs 1945; Second Sec., London 1946; Ministry of Foreign Affairs 1948; Asst. to French Deputy at negotiation of Peace Treaty with Austria 1949; First Sec., Vienna 1950; served Secr. of Confs. 1952; Head of Sarre Service 1953; Head of Levant Service 1954; Political Dir. Council of Europe 1958; Minister, Diplomatic Counsellor to Gen. Secr. of Presidency 1959-64; Asst. Sec.-Gen. for Nat. Defence 1964-68; mem. Bd. of Dirs. Nat. Centre for Space Studies 1965-69; Amb. to UNESCO 1970-75; Diplomatic Counsellor to the Govt. 1976-79; mem. Bd. of Dirs. Agence Havas 1976-79; Amb. to Peking 1979; Amb. to Canada 1979-81; Ambassadeur de France 1981-; membre Council d'Admin. de l'Institut français des relations internationales 1982-83; Pres. de l'Asscn. pour la défense du français et du patrimoine linguistique européen 1983; Officier, Légion d'honneur, Commdr., Ordre nat. du Mérite, Chevalier des Palmes académiques, Commdr. de l'Etoile noire. *Publications:* Articles in La Revue de la Défense nationale, La Revue de l'Institut Charles de Gaulle, l'Appel, La Revue des deux mondes, etc. *Address:* 3 square de Latour-Maubourg, 75007 Paris, France (Home).

MAILLART, Ella; Swiss traveller and writer; b. 20 Feb. 1903, Geneva; d. of Paul and Dagmar Klim; ed. Geneva; travelled Russia, Turkestan, Manchuria, Tibet, Iran, Afghanistan, Ladakh, Yemen, S. Korea, China, etc.; in S. India 1940, Nepal 1951; Fellow Royal Geographical Soc., London; Hon. mem. Alpine Club, Ski Club G.B.; Sir Percy Sykes Medal 1955, Prix quadriennal Ville de Genève 1987. *Publications:* Parmi la jeunesse russe 1932, Des monts célestes aux sables rouges (Turkestan Solo) 1934, Oasis interdites (Forbidden Journey) 1937 (English, French), The Cruel Way 1947 (published in Dutch, Swedish, French, Spanish and German) (all recently reprinted in French, English and German edns.); Gypsy Afloat 1942, Cruises and Caravans 1942 (published in French, German), Ti-Puss (in English, French and German), The Land of the Sherpas. *Leisure interests:* skiing, sailing, travels, gardening in the Alps. *Address:* 10 avenue Vallette, Geneva; and Chandolin Sur Sierre, Switzerland. *Telephone:* 022 (Geneva) 46 46 57.

MAILLET, Pierre Paul Georges; French professor of economics; b. 7 July 1923, Paris; s. of Marcel Maillet and Madeleine Cuvinot; m. Monique Chassagne 1956; two s. one d.; ed. Ecole Polytechnique, Paris; Budget Forecasting Dept., Ministry of Finance 1954-60; Dir. of Econ. Studies, ECSC 1960-67; Dir. of Scientific Policy, EEC 1967-71, Dir. of Budget 1971-73, Hon. Dir.-Gen. of EEC 1973-; Prof. of Econ. Sciences, Univ. of Lille 1973-; fmr. Pres. French Asscn. for Econ. Science; fmr. mem. Exec. Cttee., Int. Econ. Assen.; Sec.-Gen. Confed. of European Econ. Assens.; Chevalier des Palmes Académiques. *Publications:* 8 books on econs., Europe, etc. *Leisure interest:* travel. *Address:* Université de Lille I, UER Sciences Economiques et Sociales, 59 655 Villeneuve d'Ascq, Cedex (Office); 8 rue Richepanse, 75001 Paris, France (Home).

MAINA, Charles Gatere, B.A.; Kenyan civil servant; b. 1 March 1931, Nyeri; s. of Chief Gideon Gatere Wagithu and Nyamahiga Kinyugo; m. 1st Muringo Wangari Kariuki 1959, three d.; m. 2nd Florence Wachuka Ikundo 1974, one s. two d.; ed. in Kianjogu, Tumutumu, Kagumo and Makerere; teacher, 1959-61; District Educ. Officer 1962; Prov. Educ. Officer 1962-64; Asst. Chief Educ. Officer 1964-66; Deputy Sec. for Educ. 1966-68; Prin., Kenya Inst. of Admin. 1968-71; mem. Council, Univ. Coll., Dar es Salaam 1969-70; Univ. of Nairobi 1969-76; mem. Agricultural Educ. Comm. 1967, Working Party on Higher Educ. in E. Africa 1968; Sec.-Gen. E. African Community 1971-74; Perm. Rep. to UN 1974-82; Man. Dir. A. T. & H. Ltd. 1982-. *Leisure interests:* swimming, tennis, golf. *Address:* African Tours and Hotels Ltd., Box 30471, Nairobi, Kenya.

MAIRE, Edmond; French trades union official; b. 24 Jan. 1931, Epinay-sur-Seine; m. Raymonde Le Goff 1954; three c.; ed. Conservatoire Nat. des Arts et Métiers; Technician, chemical industry; Perm. Sec. of Union of Chemical Industries of Parisian branch of the Conféd. Française Démocratique du Travail (C.F.D.T.) 1958-60; Perm. Sec. of Fed. of Chemical Industries of C.F.D.T. 1960-70, Sec.-Gen. 1964-70; mem. Exec. Comm. of C.F.D.T., in charge of professional and social action; Sec.-Gen. of C.F.D.T. 1971-88; Deputy Dir. Villages-Vacances-Familles (VVF) 1989-. *Address:* Tour Montparnasse, 33 avenue du Maire, 75755 Paris Cédex 15, France.

MAIRIE, Simone, L. ès L.; Cameroon diplomatist; b. 28 Dec. 1939, Mokolo; m.; ed. Univ. of the Sorbonne and Inst. of Overseas Studies; with Diplomatic Service 1963-, First Sec., Paris 1963-65, Second Counsellor 1965-67, Chief UN Service in Foreign Office 1968-70, Dir.-in-Charge of European, American and Oceania Affairs, several missions abroad, also mem. del. to UN Gen. Ass. 1971-82, Perm. Rep. to UN, New York Dec. 1982-85; Nat. Order of Merit. *Address:* c/o Ministry for Foreign Affairs, Lomé, Cameroon.

MAIS OF WALBROOK, Baron (Life Peer), cr. 1967; **Alan Raymond Mais,** G.B.E., E.R.D., T.D., J.P., F.ENG., F.I.C.E., F.I.ARB., F.R.I.C.S., F.I.STRUCT.E.; British business executive; b. July 1911; s. of the late Capt. E. Mais; m. Lorna Aline Boardman 1936; two s. one d.; ed. Banister Court, Hants, and Coll. of Estate Man., Univ. of London; Commissioned Regular Army Reserve of Officers, Royal W. Kent Regt. 1929; transferred Royal Eng. 1931; Maj. 1939, Lieut.-Col. 1941, Col. 1944; served British Expeditionary Force, France 1939-40 (despatches); Special Forces, Middle East, Iraq

and Persia 1941-43 (despatches); Normandy and N.W. Europe 1944-46 (despatches), O.B.E. (mil.) 1944; CRE 56th Armoured Div., Territorial Army 1947-50; Command, Eng. Group, Army Emergency Reserve 1951-54, Deputy Dir. Eng. Stores 1954-58; Civil eng. posts with Richard Costain and Co. 1931-38; private practice, A. R. Mais & Partners, Structural Eng. and Surveyors 1938-39, 1946-48; Dir. Trollope & Colls Ltd. (contractors) and subsidiaries 1948, Asst. Man. Dir. 1953, Man. Dir. 1957, Deputy Chair. 1961, Chair. and Man. Dir. 1963, retd. 1968; Dir. Nat. Commercial Bank of Scotland 1966-69, Royal Bank of Scotland 1969-82, Slag Reduction Co. Ltd., William Sindall Ltd. 1969-81; Chair. City of London Insurance Co. Ltd. 1970-77, Hay MSL Consultants 1971-81, Peachey Property Corpn. 1976-81, Chair. 1978-81; fmr. Pres. London Master Builders' Assen.; mem. Land Comm. 1967-69; D.L., Greater London 1951-76; Sheriff, City of London 1969-70; Lord Mayor of London 1972-73; D.L., Kent 1976-; Chancellor City Univ. 1972-73, Pro-Chancellor 1979-84; Pres. London Chamber of Commerce and Industry 1975-78; mem. House of Lords Select Cttee. on EEC 1974-81; mem. Court and Council of City Univ.; Commr. of Income Tax 1972-84; Treas. Royal Masonic Hosp. 1973-86; Hon. B.Sc.; Hon. D.Sc. (City) 1972, (Ulster) 1982; Order of Patriotic War (1st Class) U.S.S.R. 1942, Order of the Aztec Eagle, Mexico 1973, Order of Merit, Mexico 1973; K. St. J. *Publications:* Yerbury Foundation Lecture, R.I.B.A. 1960, Bossom Foundation Lecture 1971. *Leisure interests:* family, travel and enjoying retirement. *Address:* Griffins, Sundridge Avenue, Bromley, Kent, England.

MAISEL, Sherman Joseph, PH.D.; American economist; b. 8 July 1918, Buffalo, N.Y.; s. of Louis Maisel and Sophia (née Beck) Maisel; m. Lucy Cowdin 1942; one s. one d.; ed. The Nichols School, Harvard Coll. and Harvard Univ.; Economist, Fed. Reserve Bd. 1939-41; U.S. Army 1941-45; mem. staff, U.S. del. to Interallied Reparations Agency 1945-46; Prof. of Business Admin. Univ. of Calif. (Berkeley) 1948-65, 1972-86, Econ. Consultant 1973-; mem. Bd. of Govs. Fed. Reserve System 1965-72; Co-Dir. Nat. Bureau of Econ. Research-West 1973-77; Fellow, Inst. for Advanced Study in the Behavioral Sciences, Stanford 1972-73; Pres. American Finance Assen. 1973. *Publications:* Housebuilding in Transition 1953, Fluctuations, Growth and Forecasting 1957, Financing Real Estate 1965, Managing the Dollar 1973, Real Estate Investment and Finance 1976, Risk and Capital Adequacy in Commercial Banks 1981, Macroeconomics: Theories and Policies 1982, Real Estate Finance 1987, and various pamphlets. *Address:* School of Business Administration, Barrows Hall, University of California, Berkeley, Calif. 94720 (Office); 2164 Hyde Street, San Francisco, Calif. 94109, U.S.A. (Home). *Telephone:* (415) 771-9650 (Home).

MAISKY, Mischa (Michael); Israeli concert cellist; b. 10 Jan. 1948, Riga, U.S.S.R.; m. Maryanne Kay Lipman 1983; ed. Moscow Conservatory (with Mstislav Rostropovich), Univ. of Southern California; debut with Leningrad Philharmonic Orchestra 1965; debut with Pittsburg Symphony Orchestra at Carnegie Hall 1973; debut at Royal Festival Hall 1976; debut at Berlin Philharmonic Hall 1978; numerous TV, film and video appearances all over the world; All-Soviet prize-winner 1965, Int. Tchaikovsky Competition 1966; also winner of Cassada Competition, Florence 1973 and Rostropovich Competition, Paris 1981; Grand Prix du Disque, Paris 1985; Record Acad. Prize, Tokyo 1985; recordings include Six Suites for Solo Cello (Bach), Three Sonatas for Cello and Piano (Bach), Concerto in A minor Op. 102 for Violin, Cello and Orchestra (Brahms), Concerto for Cello and Orchestra in A Minor (Schumann). *Leisure interests:* music, chess computing. *Address:* 52 Chemin de l'Ariel, 78380 Bouqival, France. *Telephone:* 3918-0300.

MAISONROUGE, Jacques G.; French computer executive; b. 20 Sept. 1924, Cachan (Seine); s. of Paul and Suzanne (née Cazas) Maisonrouge; m. Françoise Féron 1948; one s. four d.; ed. Ecole Centrale de Paris and Columbia Univ.; joined IBM France June 1948; studied electronics U.S.A. 1948-49; Asst. to Sales Man. IBM France 1954-56; Man. of Market Planning and Research, IBM Europe 1956-58, Regional Man. IBM Europe 1958-59, Asst. Gen. Man. IBM Europe 1959-62; Vice Pres. IBM World Trade Corpn., New York 1962-64, Pres. IBM Europe, Paris 1964-67; Pres. IBM World Trade Corpn. and Vice-Pres. IBM Corpn., New York 1967-72; IBM Sr. Vice-Pres. 1972-84; C.E.O., IBM World Trade Corpn., 1973-74; Chair. and C.E.O., IBM World Trade Europe/Middle East/Africa Corpn. 1974-81; Chair. of the Bd., IBM World Trade Corpn., 1976-84; mem. Bd. of Dirs., IBM World Trade Europe/Middle East/Africa Corpn. 1981-; mem. Bd. of Dirs. IBM Corpn. 1983-84; mem. Bd. of Dirs. IBM Switzerland, L'Air Liquide, Moet Hennessey, Philip Morris, Inc. (USA) 1964-86; Dir.-Gen. and Sr. Civil Servant, Industry Ministry 1986-87; Chair. of the Bd., French Centre for Foreign Trade; mem. American Chamber of Commerce in France and numerous other socs.; Chair. of the Bd. of Trustees, Ecole Cen. des Arts et Manufactures; Officier Legion d'honneur, Commdr. de l'Ordre Nat. du Mérite, Officier des Palmes Académiques and several foreign decorations. *Address:* 90 rue de la Faisanderie, 75116 Paris, France.

MAITAMA-SULE, Alhaji Yusuf; Nigerian diplomatist; b. 1929; trained as teacher and taught in secondary school 1948-55; Visiting teacher 1955-58; elected mem. Fed. House of Reps. 1954, Chief Party Whip in House 1955-56; Chief Information Officer, Kano Native Authority 1958-59; Fed. Minister of Mines and Power 1959-66; Leader del. to Conf. of Independent African States, Addis Ababa 1960 (proposed resolution at conf. that led to creation of Org. of African Unity (OAU)); mem. first Nigerian del. to UN

1960; Commr. for Local Govt., then in Ministries of Forestry, Co-operatives and Community Devt., and Information 1967; Chief Public Complaints Commr. 1975–78; Pres.'s Rep., Lancaster House Talks on Zimbabwe, London 1979; Perm. Rep. to UN 1981–83; Minister of Nat. Guidance 1983–84. *Address:* c/o Ministry of National Guidance, Lagos, Nigeria.

MAITLAND, Sir Donald James Dundas, G.C.M.G., O.B.E., M.A.; British civil servant (retd.); b. 16 Aug. 1922, Edinburgh; s. of Thomas D. Maitland and Wilhelmina S. Dundas; m. Jean Marie Young 1950; one s. one d.; ed. George Watson's Coll. and Edinburgh Univ.; Army Service 1941–47; joined Diplomatic Service 1947; Consul, Amara 1950; British Embassy, Baghdad 1950–53; Private Sec. to Minister of State, Foreign Office 1954–56; Dir. Middle East Centre for Arab Studies, Lebanon 1956–60; Foreign Office 1960–63; Counsellor, British Embassy, Cairo 1963–65; Head, News Dept., Foreign Office 1965–67; Prin. Private Sec. to Foreign and Commonwealth Sec. 1967–69; Amb. to Libya 1969–70; Chief Press Sec. to Prime Minister 1970–73; Perm. Rep. to UN 1973–74; Deputy Under-Sec., FCO 1974–75; mem. British Overseas Trade Bd. 1974–75; U.K. mem. Commonwealth Group on Trade, Aid and Devt. 1975; U.K. Perm. Rep. to European Communities 1975–79; Deputy Perm. Under-Sec. FCO 1979–80; Perm. Under-Sec. of State, Dept. of Energy 1980–82; Chair. Ind. Comm. World-wide Telecommunications Devt. 1983–85; Govt. Dir. Britoil 1983–85; Dir. Slough Estates 1983–, Northern Eng. Industries 1986–; Adviser, British Telecom 1985–86; Deputy Chair. Independent Broadcasting Authority (IBA) 1986–89; Chair. Health Educ. Authority 1989–; Chair. U.K. Cttee. World Communications Year 1983; mem. Commonwealth War Graves Comm. 1983–87; Chair. Christians for Europe 1984–. *Leisure interests:* music, hill-walking. *Address:* Murhill Farm House, Limpley Stoke, Bath, BA3 6HH, England.

MAITLAND SMITH, Geoffrey; British accountant and business executive; b. 27 Feb. 1933; s. of Philip John Maitland Smith and Kathleen Goff; ed. Univ. Coll. School, London; Partner, Thornton Baker & Co., Chartered Accountants 1960–70; Dir. Sears Holdings PLC (now Sears PLC); 1971–, Chief Exec. 1978–88, Jt. Chair. 1984–85, Chair. 1985–; Chair. British Shoe Corpn. 1984–, Mallet PLC 1986–; Deputy Chair. Lewis's Investment Trust Ltd. 1978–85 (Chair. 1985–), Selfridges Ltd. 1978–85 (Chair. 1985–), Garrard & Co. 1978–85 (Chair. 1985–), Mappin & Webb Ltd. 1978–85 (Chair. 1985–), Butler Shoe Corpn., U.S.A. 1981–84, (Chair. 1984–); Dir. Asprey and Co. PLC 1980–, Cen. Ind. Television 1983–85, Courtaulds PLC 1983–, Imperial Group PLC 1984–86, Midland Bank PLC 1986–; Hon. Vice-Pres. Inst. of Marketing 1987–; mem. Council, Univ. Coll. School; Liveryman, Worshipful Co. of Gardeners. *Address:* 40 Duke Street, London, W1A 2HP, England (Office). *Telephone:* 01-408 1180.

MAJALI, Abdel Salam, M.D., D.L.C., F.A.C.S., DH.C.; Jordanian university president; b. 1925, Karak; s. of Attallah Majali and Khadeejeh Serougi; m. Joan M. Lachlan 1956; two s. one d.; ed. Medical Coll., Syrian Univ., Damascus; Dir.-Gen. and Ear, Nose and Throat Consultant, The Royal Medical Services, Jordanian Armed Forces, Amman 1960–69; Minister of Health 1969–71; Pres. Univ. of Jordan, Amman 1971–76, 1980–; Minister of Educ. and Minister of State for Prime Ministry Affairs 1976–79; Chair. and mem. UN Univ. Council, Tokyo 1977–83; Fellow, American Coll. of Surgeons; Dr.h.c. (Hacettepe Univ., Ankara) 1974; Jordan Independence Medal; Medal of St. John of Jerusalem and other decorations. *Address:* University of Jordan, Amman (Office); P.O. Box 913, Amman, Jordan (Home). *Telephone:* 843555 (Office); 812909 (Home).

MAJDALANI, Nassim Mikail; Lebanese banker and politician; b. 1912, Beirut; ed. American Univ. of Beirut and Université de Lyon; Barrister 1937–44; Deputy for Beirut 1957, 1960, 1964; Vice-Pres. of Council of Ministers and Minister of Justice 1960–61, 1964–65; mem. of Admin. Council of Bank N. Majdalani, Beirut; Minister of Economy 1968–69; Minister of Foreign Affairs 1969–71; Deputy Speaker, Chamber of Deputies 1971–75; Grand Cordon, Order of Tunisia; Medal of Order of St. Vladimir. *Address:* Chambre des Députés, Place de l'Etoile, Beirut, Lebanon (Office).

MAJEKODUNMI, Chief The Hon. Moses Adekoyejo, C.M.G., LL.D., M.A., M.D., F.R.C.P.I., F.M.C.O.G., M.A.O., D.C.H., L.M.; Nigerian physician and administrator; Chief Otun of Egbaland, Chief Maiyegun of Lagos, Chief Bashegun of Ede, Chief Agba-Akin of Oshogbo, Chief Kaiyero of Akure, Chief Maiyegun of Iwo, Chief Asipa of Iragbiji; b. 17 Aug. 1916, Abeokuta; s. of Chief J. B. Majekodunmi, Chief Otun of Egba Christians and Alice Oladunni (Soetan); m. 1st Nola C. Maclaughlin 1943 (divorced 1963), five s. three d.; m. 2nd Katsina Saratu Atta 1964; ed. Abeokuta Grammar School, St. Gregory's Coll., Lagos, Trinity Coll., Dublin; House Physician, Nat. Children's Hosp., Dublin 1941–43; Medical Officer, Nigeria 1943–49; Consulting Obstetrician, Massey Street Maternity Hosp., General Hosp. and Creek Hosp., Lagos 1949–60; Sr. Specialist Obstetrician, Nigerian Federal Gov. Medical Services 1949–60; Senator and Leader of Senate 1960; Minister of State for the Army 1960–61, Fed. Minister of Health 1961–66; Fed. Minister of Health and Information 1965; Admin. for W. Nigeria 1962; Pres. 16th World Health Assembly 1963; Int. Vice-Pres., 3rd World Conf. on Medical Educ., New Delhi 1966; Chancellor Ogun State Univ. 1986–; mem. Bd. of Govs., St. Gregory's Coll., Lagos; Medical Dir. and Chair. Bd. of Govs., St. Nicholas Hosp., Lagos 1967–; Chair. Bd. Dirs. Lion Bldgs. Ltd.; Dir. Abbott Labs. (Nigeria) Ltd., Swiss Nigeria Chemical Co., Johnson and Johnson (Nigeria) Ltd.; Trustee, J. K. Randle Memorial Hall, Lagos; mem.

Soc. Gynaecology and Obstetrics, Nigeria; Hon. LL.D. (Trinity Coll., Dublin), Hon. D.Sc. (Lagos), (Ogun State Univ.). *Publications:* Premature Infants: Management and Prognosis 1943, Behold the Key (play) 1944, Partial Atresia of the Cervix Complicating Pregnancy 1946, Sub-Acute Intussusception in Adolescents 1948, Thiopentone Sodium in Operative Obstetrics 1954, Rupture of the Uterus involving the Bladder 1955, Effects of Malnutrition in Pregnancy and Lactation 1957, Medical Education and the Health Services: A Critical Review of Priorities in a Developing Country 1966. *Leisure interests:* riding, squash, swimming. *Address:* St. Nicholas Hospital, 57 Campbell Street, P.O. Box 3015, Lagos, Nigeria (Office); 3 Kingsway, Ikoyi, Lagos (Home). *Telephone:* 637639 (Office); 681660 (Home).

MAJEWSKI, Janusz; Polish film director and scriptwriter; b. 5 August 1931, Lvov; s. of Tadeusz and Maria Taschké; m. Zofia Nasierowska 1960; one d. one s.; ed. Cracow Polytechnic, State School of Drama and Film, Łódź 1960; feature film set designer 1955–60; short film dir. 1961–67, feature film dir. 1967–; Asst. Prof. in Higher State School of Film, TV and Drama, Łódź, Prof. Nov. 1987–; mem. editorial bd., monthly Kino 1966–81; mem. Polish Film-makers Assen., Sec. Gen. Bd. 1970–74, Pres. 1983–; mem. ZAiKS Authors Assen.; Nat. Council of Culture 1984–; Visiting Prof. Kansas Univ. 1985–86; numerous awards and citations at nat. film festivals in Cracow, Gdańsk and Łagów and at int. film festivals; several Polish awards including Gold Cross of Merit 1975 and Kt's. Cross Order of Polonia Restituta 1981. *Major works: shorts:* Rondo (Rondeau) 1959, Album Fleischera (Fleischer's Album) 1963, Pojedynek (Duel) 1964, Avatar 1965; *feature films:* Sublokator (The Lodger) 1966, Lokis 1970, Zazdrość i medycyna (Jealousy and Medicine) 1973, Zaklęte rewiry (Hotel Pacific) 1975, Sprawa Gorgonowej (The Gorgonowa Case) 1977, Lekcja martwego języka (Lesson in the Dead Language) 1979, Epitafium dla Barbary Radziwiłłówny (The Epitaph for Barbara Radziwiłłówna) 1983, Mrzonka (Daydream) 1985, C. K. Dezerterzy (Deserters) 1986, Prisoner of Rio 1988, Czarny wawáz (The Black Canyon) 1989; also TV plays, TV series Królowa Bona (Bona the Queen) 1982. *Leisure interests:* music, travel, sport, objet d'art and antique collecting. *Address:* ul. Trębacka 3, 00-074 Warsaw (Office); ul. Forteczna 1a, 01-540 Warsaw, Poland (Home). *Telephone:* 27-67-85 (Office); 39-23-12 (Home).

MAJEWSKI, Władysław, D.SC.TECH.; Polish politician; b. 6 April 1933, Warsaw; teacher, Warsaw Tech. Univ. 1954–70; scientific worker, Telecommunications Inst., Warsaw 1970–81, extraordinary Prof., recently Vice Dir. of Inst.; Minister of Telecommunications 1981–87; mem. Democratic Party Cen. Cttee. 1985–; Officer's Cross of Order of Polonia Restituta, Gold Cross of Merit and other decorations. *Publications:* numerous scientific works on telecommunications.

MAJKA, Jerzy Józef, M.A.; Polish journalist; b. 17 Jan. 1930, Wadowice; s. of Józef Majka and Jaina Majka; m. Ewa Kłusiewicz 1979; one s. two d.; ed. Warsaw Univ.; employee on Boards of Polish Youth Union Cracow, Warsaw 1949–53; Deputy Ed.-in-Chief Świat Młodych 1954–56; Deputy Head Polish Pathfinders' Assen. 1957–67; Ed.-in-Chief Świat Młodych 1968–79, First Sec. of Polish United Workers' Party (PZPR) at Workers' Publishing Co-operative Prasa-Książka-Ruch 1980–81; Head Information Dept. of PZPR Cen. Cttee. 1981–85; Ed.-in-Chief Trybuna Ludu 1985–; mem. PZPR 1948–; mem. Cen. Cttee. PUWP 1986–; Chair. Polish-Mongolian Soc.; mem. Presidium Main Bd. of Polish-Soviet Soc.; Commdr's., Officer's and Companion's Cross of Order of Polonia Restituta and other decorations. *Leisure interests:* hiking, angling. *Address:* Redakcja Trybuny Ludu, Pl. Starynkiewicza 7, 02-015 Warsaw, Poland.

MAJOR, Jean-Louis, L.PH., M.A., PH.D.; Canadian author and academic; b. 16 July 1937, Cornwall, Canada; s. of Joseph Major and Noella Daoust; m. Bibiane Landry 1960; one d.; ed. Univ. of Ottawa and Ecole Pratique des Hautes Etudes; Lecturer, Dept. of Philosophy, Univ. of Ottawa 1961–65, Prof. Dept. de Lettres Françaises 1965–; Visiting Prof. Dept. of French, Univ. of Toronto 1970–71; Coordinator, Corpus d'editions critiques and Bibliothèque du nouveau monde 1980–; mem. Royal Soc. of Canada, Acad. des Lettres et Sciences Humaines. *Publications include:* Saint-Exupéry, l'écriture et la pensée 1968, Le jeu en étoile 1978, Entre l'écriture et la parole 1984, and a critical edn. of Cocteau's Léone. *Address:* Département des Lettres Françaises, University of Ottawa, Ottawa, Ont., K1N 6N5 (Office); P.O. Box 357, St. Isidore, Ont., KOC 2BO, Canada (Home). *Telephone:* (613) 564-4218 (Office).

MAJOR, Rt. Hon. John, P.C., A.I.B.; British banker and politician; b. 29 March 1943, Merton; s. of late Thomas Major and Gwendolyn Major; m. Norma Major 1970; one s. one d.; ed. Rutlish Grammar; sr. exec. Standard Chartered Bank PLC to 1979; M.P. for Huntingdon 1979–; Parl. Pvt. Sec. to Home Office Minister 1981–83; Govt. Whip 1983–84; Lord Commr. of Treasury 1984–85; Under-Sec. of State for Social Security 1985–86; Minister for Social Security and the Disabled 1986–87; Chief Sec. to Treasury June 1987–. *Leisure interests:* cricket and opera. *Address:* House of Commons, London, SW1A 0AA, England. *Telephone:* 01-219 4568.

MAJOR, Kathleen, M.A., F.B.A.; British academic (retd.); b. 10 April 1906, London; d. of George Major and Gertrude Blow; ed. St. Hilda's Coll., Oxford; Librarian, St. Hilda's Coll., Oxford 1931–35; Archivist to Bishop of Lincoln 1936–45; Lecturer, and subsequently Reader in Diplomatic,

Univ. of Oxford 1945-55; Prin., St. Hilda's Coll., Oxford 1955-65; Part-time Prof. of History, Univ. of Nottingham 1966-71. *Publications:* Registrum Antiquissimum of the Cathedral Church of Lincoln Vol. IV (jt. Ed.), V–X (sole Ed.) 1938-73; Acta Stephani Langton 1950. *Leisure interest:* reading. *Address:* 21 Queensway, Lincoln, LN2 4AJ, England. *Telephone:* (0522) 25370.

MAKAREZOS, Nikolaos; Greek army officer and politician; b. 1919, Gravia; s. of John Makarezos and Catherine N. Tsonou; m. Chariclia G. Mattheou 1941; one s. one d.; ed. graduate schools, Evelpidon Mil. Coll., War Coll. and British and U.S. artillery schools; commissioned 1941; mem. Army Gen. Staff and Prof. Evelpidon Mil. Coll. and Higher War Coll. 1961; Mil. Attaché, Greek Embassy, Bonn 1961-63, Chief of Operations, 1st Army Corps, 1966; Minister of Co-ordination 1967-71; retd. from army 1967; Second Deputy Prime Minister 1971-73; arrested Oct. 1974; sentenced to death for high treason and insurrection Aug. 1975 (sentence commuted to life imprisonment).

MAKAROV, Askold Anatolevich; Soviet ballet-dancer and teacher; b. 3 May 1925; s. of Olga Anatolevna Makarova; m. Petrova Ninel Alexandrovna 1959; one s.; ed. Leningrad Ballet School (under V. I. Ponomarev); mem. CPSU 1958-; dancer with Kirov Ballet 1943-70; Ballet-master at Leningrad Conservatoire 1970-76, Prof. 1976-; Artistic Dir. of Leningrad Ballet 'Choreographic Miniatures', 1976-; People's Artist of U.S.S.R. 1983. *Address:* c/o Leningrad Ballet Company Choreographic Miniatures, 15 Mayakovsky Street, Leningrad, U.S.S.R.

MAKAROVA, Inna Vladimirovna; Soviet actress; b. 28 July 1926, Taiga, Kemerovo district; ed. All-Union Film Inst.; U.S.S.R. State Prize 1949; Order of Red Banner of Labour, People's Artist of R.S.F.S.R., Order of Merit R.S.F.S.R. 1967. *Roles include:* Katya (Vysota) 1957, Varya (My Dear Man) 1958, Nadya (Girls) 1962, Dusya (Women) 1966, Nonna (The Rumyantsev Affair) 1956, Anfisa (Balsaminov's Wedding) 1965 and many others.

MAKAROVA, Natalia; Soviet ballerina; b. 1940, Leningrad, U.S.S.R.; m. 3rd Edward Karkar 1976; one s.; ed. Vagonova Ballet School, Leningrad; mem. Kirov Ballet 1959-70; sought political asylum, London 1970; Prin. Dancer, American Ballet Theatre Oct. 1970-; Guest Artist, Royal Ballet 1972; Guest Artist, London Festival Ballet 1984; Honoured Artist of R.S.F.S.R.; best known for performance of Giselle. *Publications:* A Dance Autobiography 1979, On Your Toes 1984. *Address:* American Ballet Theatre, 888 Seventh Avenue, New York, N.Y. 10019, U.S.A.

MAKASA, Kapasa; Zambian politician; b. 29 Jan. 1922, Chinsali Dist.; m. Delila C. Makasa; three s. two d.; ed. Lubwa Mission and Public Admin., Oxford Univ.; Church Elder, Church of Scotland (now United Church of Zambia), Lubwa; teacher, Mufulira Mine School 1943; Clerk, Mine Office, Copper Belt Prov. 1944-45; Teacher under African Methodist-Episcopal Church, Choma 1945-46; Teacher, Chinsali 1947-53; mem. Chinsali Welfare Assen. 1947; Chair. African Nat. Congress (ANC) (N. Rhodesia) 1950; Prov. Pres. ANC (N.R.) N. Prov. 1953-58; imprisoned for conducting boycott, N. Rhodesia 1955-56; Div. Pres., Zambian Nat. Congress (ZANC), N. Prov. 1958; restricted to Solwezi Dist. by Colonial Govt. 1960; Div. Pres. ZANC, Luapula Prov. 1960-61; United Nat. Independence Party (UNIP) Rep., Tanganyika (now Tanzania) and Chair. Refugees Cttee. 1961-62; Regional Sec., Katete, Chadza Region, E. Prov., Zambia 1963; M.P. for Chinsali North and Parl. Sec., Ministry of Agric. 1963; Resident Minister N. Prov. 1964-68; Cabinet Minister of N.W. Prov. and Amb. to Ethiopia 1969; Cabinet Minister to Luapula Prov. 1971-72; High Commr. to Tanzania and Amb. to Rwanda, Burundi and Malagasy Repubs. 1972-75; High Commr. to Kenya, concurrently Amb. to Rwanda and Burundi 1975-80; Chair. Zambia Agricultural Devt. Bank Sept. 1983-, Small Industries Devt. Org. (SIDO) 1987-; Chair. (part-time) Lima Bank; mem. Cen. Cttee. UNIP 1978-; mem. Katongo Mukulu Multi-purpose Co-operative Union 1980-, Lusaka City Council Credit Union 1980-. *Publications:* March to Political Freedom, Umsungu wa Musonko (in Bemba). *Address:* SIDO House, P.O. Box 35373, Lusaka, Zambia. *Telephone:* 219801.

MAKEKA, Thabo, LL.B., LL.M.; Lesotho lawyer and diplomatist; b. 11 June 1947, Qacha's Nek, Lesotho; s. of Pascal Mokena and Sarah (née Matsokolo) Makeka; m. Felleng Mamakeka 1975; three s.; ed. Univs. of Lesotho, Edinburgh and Columbia; part-time lecturer in Law, Lesotho Univ. 1970-76; practised law, Advocate of High Court of Lesotho 1970-72; Legal and Treaties Officer, Ministry of Foreign Affairs 1972-74, Legal Adviser (Int. Law) 1974-75; Deputy Sr. Perm. Sec. Cabinet 1976; Perm. Sec. for Foreign Affairs 1976; Amb. to U.S.A. and Mexico 1976-79, Amb. and Perm. Rep. to UN 1979-80, 1983-; Deputy Sr. Perm. Sec. and Deputy Sec. to Cabinet 1980-83; High Commr. to Bahamas, Trinidad and Tobago 1985-87; Prin. Sec., Ministry of Employment, Social Welfare and Pensions 1987-88; Advocate of the High Court 1988-; Exec. Dir. Union of Employers 1988-. *Leisure interests:* film, theatre, reading, tennis, table tennis. *Address:* P.O. Box 1691, Maseru, Lesotho.

MAKENETE, Strong Thabo, M.B.; Lesotho physician and politician; b. 3 Dec. 1923, Ha Patlo Phamotse, Leribe Dist.; ed. St. Peter's Secondary School, Rosettenville; joined Civil Service as Medical Officer 1951, then Sr. Medical Officer, Dir. of Health and Perm. Sec. for Health; in pvt. medical practice 1970-86; Minister of Health 1986-; Pres. Lesotho Medical,

Dental and Pharmacy Council 1971-; Chair. Lesotho Planned Parenthood Assen.; Distinguished Order of Mohlomi 1976. *Address:* c/o The Military Council, Maseru, Lesotho.

MAKEYEV, Evgeny Nikolaevich; Soviet diplomatist; b. 28 April 1928, Kirov; m. Leniana Makeyeva 1950; two d.; ed. Moscow Inst. of Int. Relations; entered diplomatic service 1950; served in People's Republic of China 1950-53; Official Ministry of Foreign Affairs 1953-60, Deputy Head European Dept. 1967-68, Head 1968-71, Head Dept. of Int. Econ. Org. 1980-86; first Sec., counsellor Perm. Mission to the UN 1960-64, Deputy Perm. Rep. 1964-67, with rank of Amb. 1971-80; Perm. Rep. to UN Office, Geneva Sept. 1986-; Order of the Red Banner of Labour (twice), Order of People's Friendship, Order of Badge of Honour, numerous medals. *Address:* Permanent Mission of the U.S.S.R. to UN Office, 15 avenue de la paix, 1202 Geneva, Switzerland. *Telephone:* (022) 331870.

MAKEYEV, Valentin N.; Soviet politician; b. 10 April 1930, Kaliningrad, Moscow Region; ed. S. Ordzhonikidze Eng. and Econ. Inst. of Moscow; Insp. of a dept. of the Ministry of Culture 1953; at Moscow Eng. and Econ. Inst. as post-graduate student, Asst. Lecturer, Chief Lecturer, then Vice-Rector 1954-64; mem. CPSU 1956-; Second Sec. of the Bauman region CPSU Cttee. of Moscow 1964-69, First Sec. 1969-76; Sec., then Second Sec. Moscow City Cttee., CPSU 1976-80; a Vice-Chair. U.S.S.R. Council of Ministers 1980-83; mem. CPSU Cen. Cttee.; Deputy to Supreme Soviet (9th and 10th convocations). *Address:* c/o Presidium of the Supreme Soviet, The Kremlin, Moscow, U.S.S.R.

MAKHKAMOV, Kakhar Makhkamovich; Soviet party official and politician; b. 1932, Tadzhikistan; ed. Leningrad Mining Inst.; engineer, party-worker, then dir. of an ore-extraction works in Tadzhikistan 1953-61; Pres. of Leninabad mining exec. cttee. 1961-63; mem. CPSU 1957-; Pres. of Tadzhikistan State Planning Comm. of Council of Ministers of Tadzhikistan 1963-65; Deputy Pres. of Council of Ministers and of Tadzhikistan Gosplan 1965-82; Pres. of Council of Ministers of Tadzhikistan S.S.R. 1982-85; First Sec. of Cen. Cttee. of Tadzhik CP 1985-; mem. CPSU Cen. Cttee. 1986-; Deputy to Supreme Soviet. *Address:* Council of Ministers, Frunze, Tadzhikistan, U.S.S.R.

MAKHULU, Walter Paul Khotso; British ecclesiastic; b. 2 July 1935, Johannesburg, S.A.; s. of Paul Makhulu; m. Rosemary Makhulu 1966; one s. one d.; ed. Pimville Govt. School, Johannesburg, Khaiso Secondary School, Coll. of the Resurrection and St. Peter, S.A., St. Andrews Coll., Birmingham; Area Sec. for Eastern Africa and African Refugees, Comm. on Inter-Church Aid Refugee and World Service, World Council of Churches 1975-79; Bishop of Botswana 1979-; Archbishop of Cen. Africa 1980-; Pres. All Africa Conf. of Churches 1981-86; Pres. World Council of Churches 1983; Hon. Curate Holy Trinity, Geneva; Hon. D.D. (Kent) 1988; Officier, l'Ordre des Palmes Academiques 1981. *Leisure interests:* music, international affairs. *Address:* P.O. Box 769, Gaborone, Botswana. *Telephone:* 353779 (Office).

MAKI, Fumihiko, M.ARCH.; Japanese architect; b. 6 Sept. 1928, Tokyo; m. Misao 1960; two d.; ed. Univ. of Tokyo, Cranbrook School of Art, Michigan and Harvard Univ.; Assoc. Prof. Washington Univ. 1956-62, Harvard Univ. 1962-66; lecturer, Dept. of Urban Eng., Univ. of Tokyo 1964-, Prof. of Architecture 1979-; Prin. Partner, Maki and Assocs. 1964-; mem. of Trilateral Comm. 1975-; Visiting Prof. at Berkeley, Univ. of Calif. 1970, Los Angeles, Univ. of Calif. 1977, Colombia Univ. 1977, Tech. Univ. of Vienna 1978; mem. Japan Inst. of Architecture; Hon. Fellow, American Inst. of Architects 1980; awards include Gold Medal of Japan Inst. of Architects 1964, 1st prize in Low Cost Housing Int. Competition, Lima 1969, art award from Mainichi Press 1969. *Major works include:* Toyoda Memorial Hall, Nagoya Univ. 1960, Rissho Univ. Campus 1966, Nat. Aquarium, Okinawa 1975, Tsukuba Univ. Complex 1976, Hillside Terrace Housing Complex 1978, The Royal Danish Embassy in Tokyo 1979. *Publications:* Investigations in Collective Form 1964, Movement Systems in the City 1965, Metabolism 1960, Structure in Art and Science (contrib.) 1965. *Leisure interests:* reading, chess. *Address:* 16-22, 5-chome Higashi-Gotanda, Shinagawa-ku, Tokyo, Japan.

MAKK, Károly; Hungarian film director; b. 22 Dec. 1925; s. of Kálmán Makk and Emma Szmolka; m. Andrea Zsiga-Kis; one s. one d.; ed. Budapest Univ. of Sciences, Univ. of Dramatic and Cinematic Arts; asst. lecturer 1953, lecturer 1959-; mem. Univ. Council; worked as assistant dir. MAFILM Studio 1946-53, dir. 1954-; Guest lecturer Istituto Centro Sperimentale per Film, Roma 1976 and German Film Acad., München 1973-74; Merited Artist and Eminent Artist titles, Balázs Béla prize, Kossuth prize 1973. *Productions:* Liliomfi 1955, Ház a sziklák alatt (House under the Rocks); 39-es dandár (The Brigade No. 39) 1959; Megszállottak (The Fanatics) 1962, Elveszett paradicsom (The Lost Paradise) 1963, Az utolsó előtti ember (The Last but One) 1963, Isten és ember előtti (Before God and Man) 1968, Szerelem (Love) (1971 International Journalist Fed. Award and Jury's Special Award of Cannes), Macskajáték (Catsplay) 1973, Egy erkölcsös éjszaka (A very moral night) 1977, Két történet a félmultból (Two stories from the Recent Past), A téglafal mögött (Behind the Brickwall), Philemon and Baucis, 1981, Egymásra nézve (Another Way) (1984 Int. Critiques Award and Best Female Performance of Cannes), Játszani kell (Playing for Keeps) 1984, Az utolsó kézirat (The last Manuscript) 1987.

Address: 1022 Budapest, Hankóczy Jenő utca 15, Hungary. *Telephone:* 351-010.

MAKKI, Mohammed Hassan, D.ECON.; Yemeni politician and diplomatist; b. 22 Dec. 1933; ed. Univs. of Bologna and Rome; Adviser, Ministry of Econ. 1960-62, Deputy Minister 1962, Minister 1963-64; Minister of Foreign Affairs April-Sept. 1966, 1967-68; Amb. to Italy 1968-70, 1977-79, to Fed. Repub. of Germany 1970-72; Deputy Prime Minister 1972-74; Prime Minister March-June 1974; Deputy Prime Minister for Econ. Affairs June-Oct. 1974, 1980-84; Deputy Prime Minister Nov. 1985-; Perm. Rep. to UN 1974-76, Amb. to U.S.A. (also accred. to Canada) 1975-76. *Address:* Office of the Deputy Prime Minister, San'a, Yemen Arab Republic.

MAKSIMOV, Leonid Aleksandrovich, DR. PHYS. SC.; Soviet theoretical physicist; b. 1931; ed. Moscow Univ.; Senior Asst. Researcher, Kurchatov Inst. of Atomic Energy 1955-85, Head of Laboratory 1985-; Prof. 1981; Lenin Prize 1986. *Address:* I.V. Kurchatov Institute of Atomic Energy, Ul. Kurchatova 46, Moscow, U.S.S.R.

MAKSIMOV, Vladimir Yemelyanovich; Soviet writer; b. 1932; ed. secondary school; began publishing 1952; an editor of October 1965-67; expelled from Union of Writers 1973; allowed to visit France but deprived of Soviet citizenship 1974; Ed. of dissident magazine Kontinent 1974-. *Publications:* Verse 1956, Story in Pages from Tarusa 1961, Man Alive (play) 1965, stories, novels, plays for October 1965-67, We Adore the Earth 1970, The Seven Days of Creation (Frankfurt) 1971, (English trans. 1977), The Quarantine (Frankfurt) 1973, Farewell from Nowhere 1974, Collected Works (6 vols., Frankfurt) 1973-79.

MAKSIMOV, Gen. Yuriy Pavlovich; Soviet army officer and politician; b. 30 June 1924, Kryukovka, Michurinsk Region, Tambov Dist.; ed. Frunze Mil. Acad., Moscow; served in Soviet Army 1942-; mem. CPSU 1943-; commdr. of a machine gun co. 1943-45; officer on Gen. Staff in an operational area, commdr. of a bn. 1945-57; at Mil. Acad. of Gen. Staff, Moscow 1965 (Gold Medal); commdr. of a regt., then chief of staff of a div., commdr. of a div. 1957-69; First Deputy Commdr. of an army unit 1969-73; First Deputy Commdr., Turkestan Mil. Dist. and Chief of Tashkent Garrison 1973-79; on Gen. Staff of U.S.S.R. Armed Forces 1976-78; First Deputy Commdr., Turkestan Mil. Dist. 1978-79; Commdr. of Turkestan Mil. Dist. 1979-; Deputy to Council of Nationalities, Deputy to the Council of the Union, U.S.S.R. Supreme Soviet 1979-; mem. of Politburo of Uzbek Cen. Cttee. of Uzbek CP 1981-; mem. of Cen. Cttee. of Uzbek CP 1981; cand. mem. of Cen. Cttee. CPSU 1981-86, mem. 1986-; Army Gen. 1982-; Commdr. Southern Theatre of Operations 1984-85; C.-in-C. of Strategic Rocket Forces, U.S.S.R. Deputy Minister of Defence 1985-; Orders of Red Banner (thrice), Order of Red Star, Orders of Patriotic War (twice), Order of Lenin 1982, Hero of Soviet Union 1982, Certificate of Honour Presidium of Uzbek S.S.R. Supreme Soviet 1984, many medals and foreign orders. *Address:* Ministry of Defence, The Kremlin, Moscow, U.S.S.R.

MAKSIMOVA, Yekaterina Sergeyevna; Soviet ballet dancer; b. 1 Feb. 1939, Moscow; ed. Bolshoi Theatre Ballet School; joined Bolshoi Theatre Ballet Co. 1958; Honoured Artist of R.S.F.S.R., Gold Medal, Varna (int. competition) 1964, Pavlova Prize of Paris Acad. of Dance 1969; People's Artist of U.S.S.R. 1973; Order of Red Banner. *Main roles:* Masha (Nutcracker), Katerina (Stone Flower), Seventh Waltz, Prelude (Chopiniana), Maria (Fountain of Bakhchisarai), Giselle (Giselle), Mavka (Song of the Forest by Zhukovsky), Jeanne (Flames of Paris), the Muse (Paganini by Rachmaninov), Lizzie (Thunder Road by Karayev), Cinderella (Cinderella), Aurora (Sleeping Beauty), Kitri (Don Quixote), Frigina (Spartacus by Khachaturyan), leading role in Hussars' Ballad by Khrennikov. *Address:* c/o State Academic Bolshoi Theatre of U.S.S.R., 1 Ploshchad Sverdlova, Moscow, U.S.S.R.

MAKSYMIUK, Jerzy; Polish conductor, composer and pianist; b. 9 April 1936, Grodno; ed. Warsaw Conservatory; fmr. Conductor, Polish Nat. Radio Symphony Orchestra, Katowice; Conductor, Teatr Wielki, Warsaw 1970-72; f. Polish Chamber Orchestra 1972; Prin. Conductor BBC Scottish Symphony Orchestra, Glasgow 1983-; guest conductor Calgary Symphony, Nat. Arts Centre (Ottawa), English Chamber, Scottish Chamber, City of Birmingham Symphony, London Symphony and other orchestras; has toured Europe, U.S.A., Canada, Japan, Israel and Australia with Polish Chamber Orchestra. *Address:* c/o Centrum Sztuki Studio, 00-901 Warsaw, Poland; c/o BBC Scottish Symphony Orchestra, BBC, Queen Margaret Drive, Glasgow, G12 8BG, Scotland. *Telephone:* 20-43-69 (Warsaw); 041-330 2345 (Glasgow).

MAKTOUM, Sheikh Hamdan bin Rashid al-; United Arab Emirates politician; b. 1945; s. of Rashid bin Said bin Said al-Maktoum (q.v.); Deputy Prime Minister U.A.E. 1971-73, Minister of Finance and Industry 1973-; Pres. Dubai Municipal Council. *Address:* Ministry of Finance and Industry, P.O. Box 433, Abu Dhabi, United Arab Emirates.

MAKTOUM, Sheikh Maktoum bin Rashid al-; United Arab Emirates politician; b. 1943; s. of Rashid bin Said al-Maktoum (q.v.); m. 1971; Deputy Ruler of Dubai; Prime Minister, U.A.E. 1971-79, Deputy Prime Minister 1979-. *Address:* Office of the Deputy Prime Minister, P.O. Box 831, Abu Dhabi, United Arab Emirates.

MAKTOUM, Sheikh Muhammad bin Rashid al-; United Arab Emirates politician; b. 1946; s. of Rashid bin Said al-Maktoum (q.v.); ed. Mons Officer Cadet Training Coll.; Minister of Defence Dec. 1971-. *Address:* Ministry of Defence, P.O. Box 2838, Dubai, United Arab Emirates.

MAKTOUM, H.H. Sheikh Rashid bin Said al-; Ruler of Dubai; b. 1914; ed. privately; succeeded his father, Said bin Maktoum, as 4th Sheikh 1958; Vice-Pres. United Arab Emirates (UAE) Dec. 1971-; Prime Minister April 1979-. *Address:* Royal Palace, Dubai, United Arab Emirates.

MALABO, Capt. Cristino Seriche Bioke (see Bioke Malabo, Capt. Cristino Seriche).

MALAGODI, Giovanni Francesco, DR.IUR.; Italian politician; b. 12 Oct. 1904; ed. Rome Univ.; Joint Gen. Man. Banca Commerciale Italiana 1933, Gen. Man. 1947; Gen. Man. Banque Française et Italienne pour l'Amérique du Sud 1937; Econ. and Financial Adviser, Ministry of Foreign Affairs 1947; Chair. OEEC Manpower Cttee. 1950; Deputy for Milan 1953- (re-elected 1958, 1963, 1968, 1972, 1976); Senator for Milan 1979-; Sec.-Gen. Partito Liberale Italiano 1954-72, Chair. 1972; Minister of Treasury 1972-73; Vice-Chair. Liberal Int. 1956-58, 1966, Chair. 1958-66, Hon. Chair. 1973-; Commdr. Ordine al Merito della Repubblica Italiana; Liberal. *Publications:* Le Ideologie Politiche 1927, Rapporto sull'Emigrazione 1952, Massa non Massa 1963, Liberalismo in Commino 1965, Sarnano-Libertà Nuova 1967. *Address:* Via Frattina 89, Rome, Italy.

MALAN, Gen. Magnus André de Merindol, B.SC.; South African army officer; b. 30 Jan. 1930, Pretoria; m. Magrietha Johanna Van der Walt 1962; two s. one d.; ed. Univ. of Pretoria; rank of Gen., S. African Defence Force; Chief of Defence Staff 1976-; Minister of Defence Aug. 1980-; medals include Star of South Africa 1975, Southern Cross Decoration 1977, Pro Patria Medal 1977. *Address:* Defence Headquarters, Private Bag X414, Pretoria 0001, South Africa.

MALAN, Pedro, PH.D.; Brazilian economist; b. 19 Feb. 1943, Rio de Janeiro; s. of Elysio S. Malan and Regina S. Malan; m. 1st Ana María Toledo Piza Rudge; m. 2nd Catarina Gontijo Souza Lima 1980; one s. one d.; ed. St. Ignatius School, Rio de Janeiro, Polytechnic School of Catholic Univ. of Rio de Janeiro, School of Econs. and Univ. of California, Berkeley; with Inst. of Applied Research, Brazilian Ministry of Planning 1967-69, 1973-79, 1981-83; Faculty of Econs., Catholic Univ. of Rio de Janeiro Jan.-Dec. 1979; Head Int. Trade and Finance Section, Inst. of Applied Econ. Research 1980-83; Dir. Policy Analysis and Research Div. Centre of Transnat. Corpns, UN, New York 1983-84, Dept. of Int. Econs. and Social Affairs 1985-86; Exec. Dir. World Bank, Washington, D.C. Oct. 1986-; Fed. of São Paulo Industries Prize for book External Economic Policy and Industrialization in Brazil. *Publications:* The Structure of Protection in Brazil (with J. Bergsman) 1971, The Brazilian Economy in the 1970s: Old and New Developments (with R. Bonelli) 1977, Brazilian External Debt and its Implications 1978, Structural Models of Inflation and Balance of Payments Disequilibria in Semi-Industrialized Economies (with John R. Wells) 1984, Financial Integration with the World Economy, The Brazilian Case 1982, Relações Internacionais do Brasil no Periodo 1946-64 1984, Debt, Trade and Development: the crucial years ahead 1985. *Leisure interests:* literature, classical music, diplomatic and financial history, swimming, tennis. *Address:* 1818 H St., N.W., Washington, D.C. 20433 (Office); 2241 48th Street, N.W., Washington, D.C. 20007, U.S.A. (Home).

MALATESTA, Lamberto; Italian chemist; b. 20 June 1912, Milan; s. of Dr. Giuseppe Malatesta and Clara Tombolan Fava; m. Rachele Pizzotti 1947; one s. two d.; ed. Milan Univ.; Asst. to the Chair of Industrial Chem., Milan Univ. 1937, Reader 1940, Lecturer 1942, Chair. Prof. of Analytical Chem. 1948-51, of Gen. and Inorganic Chem. 1951-87, Dir. Istituto di Chimica Generale 1951-82, Dir. Dept. Inorganic Chem. 1982-87, Dir. of a Centre of Consiglio Nazionale delle Ricerche 1970-82; Dir. Gazzetta Chimica Italiana 1971-84; Pres. Società Chimica Italiana 1971-73, 1981-83; Pres. of Div. of Inorganic Chem., IUPAC 1975-77, Pres. Chemical Sciences Cttee., Nat. Research Council (CNR) 1976-81; Fellow, Accad. Nazionale dei Lincei, Istituto Lombardo Accad. di Scienze e Lettere; Hon. Fellow, Chemical Soc. (London); Prize of the Pres. of Italian Repub. 1963; Gold Medal for Educ., Culture and Art 1974. *Publications:* General Chemistry (in Italian) 1965, Inorganic Chemistry (in Italian) 1968; co-author: Isocyanide Compounds of Metals 1968, Zerovalent Compounds of Metals 1974; about 140 original papers in scientific journals. *Leisure interests:* swimming, playing bridge. *Address:* Via Carpaccio 2, 20133 Milan, Italy. *Telephone:* 236-0350.

MALAUD, Philippe, L. EN D.; French politician and diplomatist; b. 2 Oct. 1925, Paris; s. of Jaques Malaud and Odette (née Desruol du Tronçay); m. Chantal de Gorguette d'Argoeuves 1951; one d.; ed. Lycée Lamartine, Mâcon, Lycée Janson-de-Sailly, Paris Univ., Ecole Libre des Sciences Politiques; joined cen. admin. of Foreign Office 1947; Embassy Attaché, Warsaw 1949; 2nd Sec., Cairo 1952; studied Ecole Nat. d'Admin. 1954-56; Personnel Dept. Foreign Office 1957; Deputy Chief 1958-61, then Chief of Cabinet of Foreign Ministry under Couve de Murville 1961-67; Dir. Cabinet A. Bettencourt, Sec. of State for Foreign Affairs 1967-68; elected Deputy for Saône-et-Loire, Nat. Ass. 1968, 1973, 1978; Sec. of State for the Civil Service and Information 1968-73; Minister of Information 1973, of Civil Service 1973-74; Ministre Plenipotentiaire, Foreign Office 1975; Mayor of

Dompierre-les-Ormes 1965, 1971, 1972, 1978; Gen. Councillor for Canton of Matour 1967, 1973, 1979, 1985; Pres. of Gen. Council of Saône-et-Loire 1970-79; European Pres. World Fed. of Twin Towns 1973-; Political Dir. Nouveaux Jours 1975-; Pres. of Nat. Centre of Independents and Peasants 1980; Vice-Pres. R.D.E. Group, European Parl., Strasbourg; mem. European Parl. 1984-; Chevalier, Légion d'honneur, Ordre du Mérite; Commdr., American Legion. *Leisure interest:* history. *Address:* 18 place des Vosges, 75116 Paris, France.

MALAVOLTA, Euripedes, D.SC.; Brazilian agricultural biochemist; b. 13 Aug. 1929, Araraquara, São Paulo; s. of Antônio Malavolta and Lucia Canassa Malavolta; m. Leila M. B. Malavolta 1953; two s. three d.; ed. Escola Superior de Agricultura, Luiz de Queiroz (Univ. de São Paulo) and Univ. of California (Berkeley), U.S.A.; Instructor in Agricultural Chem., Univ. de São Paulo 1949, Private Docent 1951, Prof. of Agricultural Biochem. 1958-; Research Assen. Univ. of Calif. 1952-53, Visiting Prof. 1959-60; Vice-Dean, Escola Superior de Agricultura, Luiz de Queiroz, Univ. de São Paulo 1966-67, Dean 1967, Dean Inst. of Physics and Chem. (São Carlos) 1972-76; State Council of Educ.; mem. Brazilian Acad. of Sciences, São Paulo Acad. of Sciences, Int. Cttee. of Plant Analysis and Fertilizer Problems. *Publications:* Elements of Agricultural Chemistry 1954, Manual of Agricultural Chemistry 1959, On the Mineral Nutrition of Some Tropical Crops 1962. *Leisure interests:* reading, gardening. *Address:* Escola Superior de Agricultura Luis de Queiroz, Universidade de São Paulo, Piracicata, 13400 São Paulo, SP (Office); Travessa Portugal, 146 Piracicata, 13400 São Paulo, SP, Brazil (Home). *Telephone:* 0194-332915 (Office); 0194-223948 (Home).

MALAYSIA, The Yang di Pertuan Agung (Supreme Head of State) of (see Perak, H.R.H. the Sultan of).

MALCOLM, Dugald, C.M.G., C.V.O., T.D.; British diplomatist (retd.); b. 22 Dec. 1917, London; s. of Major-Gen. Sir Neill Malcolm, K.C.B., D.S.O.; m. Mrs. Peter Atkinson Clark 1957 (died 1976); one step-d. one d.; ed. Eton and New Coll., Oxford; Armed Forces 1939-45; Foreign Service 1945-; served Lima, Bonn, Seoul and London; Vice-Marshal of Diplomatic Corps 1957-65; Amb. to Luxembourg 1966-70, to Panama 1970-74; Minister to the Vatican 1975-77; mem. Queen's Bodyguard for Scotland (Royal Company of Archers). *Address:* Flat 11, 33 Cranley Gardens, London, SW7 3BD, England. *Telephone:* 01-244 7079.

MALCOLM, George (John), C.B.E., M.A., B.MUS.; British harpsichordist, pianist and conductor; b. 28 Feb. 1917, London; s. of George Hope Malcolm; ed. Wimbledon Coll., Balliol Coll., Oxford, and Royal Coll. of Music; originally trained as concert pianist; Master of Music, Westminster Cathedral 1947-59, trained Boys' Choir for which Benjamin Britten wrote Missa Brevis Op. 63; harpsichordist, pianist and conductor making frequent tours especially in Europe; Artistic Dir., Philomusica of London 1962-66; F.R.C.M.; Hon. mem. R.A.M.; Hon. Fellow Balliol Coll., Oxford; Hon. D. Mus. (Sheffield) 1978; Hon. F.R.C.O. 1988; Cobbett Gold Medal, Worshipful Co. of Musicians 1960, Papal Kt., Order of St. Gregory the Great 1970. *Address:* 99 Wimbledon Hill Road, London, SW19 7QT, England. *Telephone:* 01-947 6672.

MALEBO, Vincent Moeketse; Lesotho local government officer and politician; b. 26 Nov. 1931, Bogate, Maseru Dist.; ed. Basutoland High School, Basutoland Training Coll., Morija, South Devon Tech. Coll.; joined Civil Service 1955, Interpreter and Elections Educator 1958-60, Sr. Interpreter for Colonial Admin. 1962-64; launched Radio Lesotho 1964; Dir. Information and Broadcasting 1965; Counsellor at High Comm. in London and Perm. Mission at UN 1967-68; Prin. Asst. Sec., Ministry of Justice 1970-72; Chief of Protocol and Perm. Sec.; Minister of Information and Broadcasting 1986-. *Address:* c/o The Military Council, Maseru, Lesotho.

MALECELA, John William Samuel; Tanzanian diplomatist and politician; b. 1934; ed. Bombay Univ. and Cambridge Univ.; Admin. Officer, Civil Service 1960-61; Consul in U.S.A. and Third Sec. to the UN 1962; Regional Commr., Mwanza Region 1963; Perm. Rep. to the UN 1964-68; Amb. to Ethiopia 1968; E. African Minister for Communications, Research and Social Services, E. African Community 1969-72; Minister of Foreign Affairs 1972-75, of Agric. 1975-80, of Mines 1980-81; of Transport and Communications 1982-86; Vice-Chair. Desert Locust Control Org. for East Africa; mem. Commonwealth Group on S. Africa 1985; Order of Merit of First Degree, Egypt; First Order of Independence, Equatorial Guinea. *Address:* c/o Ministry of Transport and Communications, Dar es Salaam, Tanzania.

MALECKI, Ignacy, D.ENG.; Polish physicist; b. 18 Nov. 1912, Pokiewna; s. of Jan and Emilia Malecki; m. 1st Maria Gąssowska 1946; one s. one d.; m. 2nd Wanda Malecka 1982; Prof., Tech. Univ., Gdańsk 1945-50, Warsaw 1950-; Dir. Inst. of Fundamental Tech. Problems, Polish Acad. of Sciences 1953-62 and 1973-82, Chair. Council for Tech. Affairs 1957-60; Vice-Pres. Int. Council of Scientific Unions (ICSU) 1963-70; Chair. Polish Nat. Pugwash Cttee. 1964-69; Vice-Chair. Polish Cttee. for UNESCO Affairs; Dir. Dept. of Science and Promotion of Basic Sciences, UNESCO 1969-72; mem. Polish United Workers' Party 1948-; mem. Polish Acad. of Sciences 1953-, mem. Presidium 1956-81; mem. Gen. Cttee., Int. Council of Scientific Unions 1976-80; Scientific Adviser to Polish Acad. of Sciences 1983-; mem. Acoustic Assen. of S. America; Hon. mem. Spanish Acoustic Assen. 1973; Pres. Int. Comm. on Acoustics 1966-71; Vice-Pres. Fed. of Acoustical Socs.

of Europe 1978; mem. editorial staff "Outlook on Science Policy" (Oxford) 1980-; Gold Cross of Merit 1946, 1954; Officer's and Commdr.'s Cross of Order Polonia Restituta 1957, 1964; State Prize 1953, 1966; Dr. h.c. (Budapest) 1964; Order of Banner of Labour 2nd Class 1969, 1st Class 1977; Cyril and Metody Order (Bulgaria) 1970; Medal of French Acoustic Assen. 1971; Medal of 30th Anniversary of People's Poland 1974; N. Copernicus Medal, Polish Acad. of Sciences 1975; Commdr. des Palmes Acad. (France) 1986; Dr. h.c. Acad. of Mining, Cracow, Tech. Univ., Budapest. *Publications:* Akustyka radiowa i filmowa (Radio and Film Acoustics) 1950, Naukowe podstawy zastosowania metod ultradźwiękowych w górnictwie i geologii (Scientific Bases of Applying Ultrasonic Methods in Mining and Geology) 1956, Problemy koordynacji badań naukowych (Co-ordination of Scientific Researches) 1960, Teoria fal i układów akustycznych (Theory of Acoustic Waves and Systems) 1966, Podstawy teoretyczne akustyki kwantowej (Theoretical Basis of the Quantum Acoustic) 1972, etc. also ed. of quarterly science reviews. *Leisure interest:* gardening. *Address:* Polska Akademia Nauk, Pałac Kultury i Nauki, Warsaw (Office); Asfaltowa 11 m. 12, 02-527 Warsaw, Poland (Home). *Telephone:* 26-58-27 (Office); 49-11-43 (Home).

MALEK, Gustavo, PH.D.; Argentine politician and chemical engineer; b. 29 March 1929, Buenos Aires; s. of Agustín and Ester Szana de Malek; m. Esther Mercedes Perramón 1956; four s. one d.; ed. Univ. Nacional del Sur; lecturer in chemical and industrial eng., Univ. Nacional del Sur 1950-60; Dir. Laboratorio de la Curtiembre "La Normandie", S.A.I.C. 1955-58; Head of Research Lanera San Blas, S.A.I.C. 1958-68; Asst. Prof. of Industrial Eng., Univ. Nacional del Sur 1961-62, Prof. of Industrial Eng. and Head, Laboratorio de Lanas (Wool Research Lab.) 1963-69, Academic Sec. 1968-70, Rector 1970-71; served on numerous cttees. of Univ. Nacional del Sur; Minister of Educ. and Culture 1971-73; Dir. Regional Office (Uruguay) UNESCO for Science and Tech. of Latin America and Caribbean 1976-; mem. Argentine Chem. Soc., Argentine Assen. of Textile Chemists and many other nat. and foreign socs. in field of textile chemistry; various prizes and decorations. *Publications:* many articles on chemistry in the textile industry. *Leisure interest:* fishing. *Address:* Bulevar Artigas 1320, P.O.B. 859, Montevideo, Uruguay. *Telephone:* 41-18-07.

MALEK, Reda; Algerian diplomatist and politician; b. 1931, Batna; s. of Malek Ahmed and Ladjouze Zoulikha; m. Rafida Cheriet 1963; two s. one d.; ed. in Algiers and Paris; Editor-in-Chief El-Moudjahid (weekly newspaper of F.L.N.); mem. Algerian delegation to negotiations of Evian 1961-62, Drafting Cttee. of Program of Tripoli setting out F.L.N. political programme 1962, Drafting Cttee. of Nat. Charter 1976; Amb. to Yugoslavia 1963-65, to France 1965-70, to U.S.S.R. 1970-77, to U.K. 1982-84; Minister of Information and Culture 1978-79; involved in negotiations for release of 52 American hostages in Iran 1980-81; Harold Weill Medal (New York Univ.). *Address:* 2 rue Ahmed Bey, Algiers, Algeria.

MALEKOU, Paul, L. EN D.; Gabonese politician; b. 17 Nov. 1938, Fougamou; m. Odette Maroundou 1965; ten c.; ed. Univs. of Lille and Paris, Inst. des Hautes Etudes d'Outre-Mer, and admin. course, Strasbourg; Head, Interregional Service for Labour, Centre-Gabon, Port-Gentil 1963-64; Minister of Labour and Social Affairs 1964-65, of Nat. Educ., Youth and Sports, subsequently of Co-ordination in charge of Nat. Educ. 1965-68; Minister Del. at the Presidency, in charge of Co-ordination and Foreign Affairs Jan.-July 1968, for State Controls 1984; Minister of Public Works and Transport 1968-69, of Public Works and charged with Special Functions at the Presidency 1969-70, of Public Works, Housing and Urbanism 1970; Minister of State in charge of Public Works, Housing and Urbanism 1970-74, concurrently of Land Registry 1972-74; Dir.-Gen. Agence pour la Sécurité de la Navigation Aérienne en Afrique et au Madagascar 1974-; Pres. Coll. des Hauts Conseillers de l'Etat 1983-; Minister of State for State Control 1984-87; Man. Dir. Soc. Nat. des Bois du Gabon 1987-; Chair. Bd. of Dirs. Société d'Energie et d'Eau du Gabon 1988-; Special Adviser to Pres. of Repub. 1988-; Commdr., Etoile equatoriale, Palmes académiques, Ordre nat. Guinéen, Légion d'honneur, Grand Officier, Ordre nat. du Lion (Senegal), Ordre nat. de l'Etoile equatoriale (Gabon), Ordre nat. de la République Italienne, Ordre de Malte and numerous other decorations. *Leisure interests:* hunting, fishing, flying. *Address:* B.P. 2825, Libreville, Gabon. *Telephone:* 76 78 00; 73 36 11.

MALERBA, Luigi; Italian author and scriptwriter; b. 11 Nov. 1927, Berceto (Parma); s. of Pietro and Maria Olari; m. Anna Lapenna 1962; two s.; ed. Liceo Classico Romagnosi di Parma, and Faculty of Law, Univ. of Parma; Dir. of review Sequenza 1948-51; Advertising Man. of review Discoteca 1956-60, Ed. 1960-65; Premio Selezione Campiello for Il Serpente 1966; Golden Nymph Award for best TV film, Int. TV Festival, Monte Carlo for Ai poeti non si spara; Premio Sila for Salto mortale 1969; Prix Médicis (France) for best non-French novel for Salto mortale 1970. *Publications:* La scoperta dell' alfabeto 1963, Il serpente 1966, Salto mortale 1968, Storie dell'Anno Mille (with Tonino Guerra, illustrations by Adriano Zannino) 1969-71, Il protagonista 1973, Le rose imperiali 1974, Mozziconi 1975, Storiette 1977, Le parole abbandonate 1977, Pinocchio con gli stivali 1977, Il pataffio 1978, C'era una volta la città di Luni 1978, La storia e la gloria 1979, Dopo il pescecane 1979, Le galline pensierose 1980, Diario di un sognatore 1981, Storiette tascabili 1984, Cina Cina 1985, Il pianeta azzurro 1986, Testa d'argento 1988. *Leisure interests:* agriculture and protection of nature. *Address:* Via Tor Millina 31, Rome, Italy.

MALFATTI, Franco Maria; Italian politician; b. 13 June 1927, Rome; Nat. Del. of Youth Movt. of Christian Dem. Party until 1952; worked in headquarters of Christian Dem. Party 1952-64; mem. Chamber of Deputies 1958-; Under-Sec. of State for Foreign Affairs June-Dec. 1968; Minister of State Participations 1968-69; Minister for Posts and Telecommunications 1969-70, of Educ. 1973-78, of Finance 1978-79, of Foreign Affairs 1979-80; fmr. mem. of numerous parl. cttees. on finance, educ., home and foreign affairs, etc.; Pres. of combined Comm. of European Communities 1970-72. *Address:* Camera dei Deputati, Rome, Italy.

MALFATTI DI MONTETRETTO, Baron Francesco; Italian diplomatist (retd.); b. 13 Jan. 1920, Vienna; s. of Giuseppe Malfatti di Montetretto and Felicita Newickluf; m. Adonella Brenciaglia 1945; two s.; ed. Lycée Janson-de-Sailly, Paris, and Univ. of Rome; Army Officer 1939-43; Resistance Movement 1943-45; on mission to London 1945; Sec. to Deputy Prime Minister 1946; Vice-Chef de Cabinet Ministry of Foreign Affairs 1946; Sec. Italian Mission for Econ. Negotiations with U.S. 1947; entered Diplomatic Service 1947; Consul in Geneva 1948; Consul-Gen., Munich 1949, also on mission to Berlin 1949; then Ministry of Foreign Affairs posts; Counsellor, Italian Embassy, Paris 1956, Minister-Counsellor 1958-63; later Chef de Cabinet, Ministry of Foreign Affairs; Diplomatic Counsellor to Pres. of Repub. 1965-69; Amb. to France 1969-77; Sec.-Gen. Ministry of Foreign Affairs 1977-85; Vice-Pres. Societa Italiana Vetro 1985-; Grand Cross, Légion d'honneur, mil. awards for bravery in the war and in the Resistance. *Leisure interests:* painting, history, tennis, antiques, politics. *Address:* Piazza del Popolo 3, Rome, Italy. *Telephone:* 3611-788.

MALHOTRA, R. N.; Indian financial official; b. 1926; ed. Punjab and Lucknow Univs.; mem. Indian Admin. Service 1951-; Head Depts. of Taxes, Finance, and Planning, Govt. of Madhya Pradesh; Fiscal Adviser IMF 1970-75; in charge of External Finance, Dept. of Econ. Affairs, Govt. of India; fmr. Sec. Dept. of Econ. Affairs, Ministry of Finance; fmr. Alt. Sec. World Bank, ADB, African Devt. Fund; Exec. Dir. IMF 1982-85. *Address:* c/o Ministry of Foreign Affairs, New Delhi, India.

MALHOUTRA, Manmohan; Indian international official; b. 15 Sept. 1937, Izatnagar; s. of Col. Gopal Das Malhoutra and Shukla Malhoutra; m. Leela Nath 1963; two d.; ed. Delhi Univ., Balliol Coll., Oxford; entered Indian Admin. Service 1961; mem. Prime Minister's Secr. 1966-73; joined Commonwealth Secr. 1974; Dir. Sec.-Gen.'s Office and Int. Affairs Div. 1977-82, Asst. Commonwealth Sec.-Gen. Nov. 1982-; Conf. Sec. to Commonwealth Heads of Govt. Meetings, London 1977, Lusaka 1979, Melbourne 1981, also at Asia-Pacific Regional Heads of Govt. Meetings; led Commonwealth Secr. team assisting Observer Group at elections in Zimbabwe and Uganda 1980; Sec. Commonwealth Southern Africa Cttee.; Head of Secr. of Commonwealth Group of Eminent Persons on Southern Africa 1986; mem. Editorial Bd. of the Round Table, Commonwealth Journal of Int. Affairs. *Leisure interests:* reading, music, tennis. *Address:* Commonwealth Secretariat, Marlborough House, London, SW1Y 5HX, England. *Telephone:* 01-839 3411.

MALIETOA TANUMAFILI II, H.H., C.B.E.; Samoan politician; b. 4 Jan. 1913; ed. Wesley Coll., Auckland, New Zealand; Adviser, Samoan Govt. 1940; mem. N.Z. del. to UN 1958; fmr. mem. Council of State; Joint Head of State of Western Samoa 1962-63, Sole Head (O le Ao o le Malo) April 1963-; Fautua of Maliena. *Address:* Government House, Vailima, Apia, Western Samoa, South Pacific.

MALIK, Gunwantsingh Jaswantsingh, M.A.; Indian diplomatist; b. 29 May 1921, Karachi; s. of late Shri Jaswant Singh Malik and Balwant Kaur (Bhagat) Malik; m. Gurkirat Kaur 1948 (dissolved 1982); two s.; R.A.F. 1943-46; Indian Foreign Service 1947-79, Second Sec., Indian Embassy, Brussels 1948-50, Addis Ababa 1950; Under-Sec. Ministry of External Affairs 1950-52; First Sec. and Chargé d'affaires Argentina 1952-56; in Japan 1956-59; Counsellor (Commercial) and Asst. Commr. Singapore 1959-63; Dir. Ministry of Commerce 1963-64; Jt.-Sec. Ministry of External Affairs 1964-65; Amb. to Philippines 1965-68, to Senegal, concurrently to the Ivory Coast, Mauritania, The Gambia and Upper Volta 1968-70, to Chile (also accred. to Peru, Ecuador and Colombia) 1970-74, to Thailand 1974-77, to Spain 1977-79; Leader trade del. to S. America 1964; mem. del. to ECAFE 1965, to Group of 77 in Lima 1971, to Gov. Body of UNDP 1971, to UNCTAD III 1972, to ESCAP 1975; Chair. Tech. and Drafting Cttee., ESCAP 1976; Deputy Chair. Cttee. of the Whole 1977; Dir. Indian Shaving Products 1986-; Sec. Assen. Indian Diplomats 1983-84, Vice-Pres. 1985-86, Pres. 1986-87; Vice-Chair. Delhi Chapter Soc. for Int. Diplomats. *Publications:* numerous literary, political and economic articles. *Leisure interests:* photography, writing, touring. *Address:* 21A Nizamuddin West, New Delhi, India. *Telephone:* 61 9785.

MALINEN, Pekka Kullervo M.A.; Finnish diplomatist; b. 11 June 1921, Viipuri; m. Hilkka Malinen 1945; ed. Univ. of Helsinki; Man. Dir. Oulu Chamber of Commerce 1948-50; Econ. Ed. Kaleva 1950-52; Sec. Gen. Finnish People's Party 1952-60; Minister of Defence, Minister of Social Affairs 1957; entered Foreign Service 1960; Amb. to Cairo 1969-74; Dir. Gen. Ministry of Foreign Affairs 1975-78; Amb. to the OECD, Paris 1978-83; Amb. to Algeria 1983-85, to Portugal 1985-. *Address:* Embassy of Finland, Rua Miguel Lupi 12, 1200 Lisbon, Portugal.

MALINGA, Norman Zombodze Magugu, M.A.; Swazi diplomatist; b. 17 Nov. 1938, Zombodze; s. of Joel Mashehsa and Dora Malinga; m.; three c.; ed. Mphumulo Teacher Training Coll., Natal, Fordham Univ. and Columbia Univ., U.S.A.; school teacher 1962-65; Librarian/Warden, Staff Training Inst., Swaziland 1965-68; Asst. Establishment Officer, Staff Training Inst. 1968; Asst. Sec., Dept. of Foreign Affairs 1968-70; Swaziland Counsellor in E. Africa 1970-71; Dir. of Broadcasting and Information 1971-72; Perm. Rep. to UN 1972-86. *Leisure interests:* painting, soccer. *Address:* c/o Ministry of Foreign Affairs, PO Box 518, Mbabane, Swaziland.

MALINOWSKI, Roman, DR.ECON.SC.; Polish politician; b. 26 Feb. 1935, Białystok; s. of Antoni and Maria Malinowski; m. Mirona Malinowski 1960; two s.; ed. Main School of Planning and Statistics, Warsaw; former activist in Polish Youth Union (ZMP); worked in Union of Peasants' Co-operatives, then in Cen. Statistical Office, Warsaw 1956-58, in Cen. Union of Saving-Loan Co-operatives, Warsaw 1958-63; worked in Chief Cttee. United Peasants' Party (ZSL) 1963-69; Deputy Chair. Cen. Union of Co-operative Creameries 1969-71; Chair. Presidium of Voivodship Nat. Council, then Voivode, Łódź 1971-75; mem. ZSL 1956-, Deputy Chair. ZSL Voivodship Cttee., Łódź 1971-75, mem. Secr. of Chief Cttee., ZSL 1975-76, Sec. of Chief Cttee., ZSL 1976-80, mem. Presidium of Chief Cttee., ZSL 1976-, Chair. Supreme Exec. Cttee. 1981-; Deputy to Seym 1976-; Minister of Food Industry and Purchases April-Oct. 1980; a Deputy Chair. Council of Ministers 1980-85; Chair. Council of Food Econ. 1981-85; mem. Presidium, Provisional Nat. Council of Patriotic Movement for Nat. Rebirth (PRON) 1982-83, mem. Nat. Council PRON 1983-; Speaker (Marshal) of Seym 1985-; Order of Banner of Labour (1st Class); Kt.'s and Officer's Cross, Order of Polonia Restituta, and other decorations. *Address:* c/o Kancelaria Semju PRL, ul. Wiejska 4/6, 00-902 Warsaw, Poland.

MALINVAUD, Edmond, L. EN D.; French economist; b. 25 April 1923, Limoges; s. of Auguste Malinvaud and Andrée Ballet; m. Elizabeth Compagnon 1952; two d.; ed. Lycée Gay-Lussac, Limoges, Lycée du Parc, Paris, Univ. of Paris, Ecole polytechnique; Dir. Inst. nat. de statistique et des études économiques 1948-66, Insp. Gen. 1966-74, Man. Dir. 1974-87; Prof. Collège de France 1987-; Researcher, Cowles Foundation for Research in Econs., Chicago 1951; Dir. of Studies, Ecole pratique des hautes études 1957-; Prof., Univ. of Calif. at Berkeley 1961, 1967; Dir. Ecole nat. de la statistique et de l'admin. économique 1962-66, Dir.-Gen. 1974-; Chair. Int. Econometric Soc. 1963: Assoc. Prof., Law Faculty, Univ. of Paris 1969-71; Vice-Chair. Soc. de Statistique de Paris 1971-73, Chair. 1974; Dir. of Econ. Projections, Ministry of Econ. and Finance 1972-74; mem. Bd. Banque de France 1972-; Dir. Banque nat. de Paris 1973-81; Vice-Pres. Assen. française des sciences économiques 1985-87; Chair. Int. Econ. Assen. 1974-77; Chair. Int. Statistical Inst. 1979-81; Dr. h.c. (Univs. of Basle, Louvain, Helsinki); Commdr., Légion d'honneur, Commdr., Ordre nat. du mérite, Médaille d'argent, C.N.R.S. *Publications:* Initiation à la compatibilité nationale 1957, 1961, 1964, Méthodes statistiques de l'écon-ométrie 1964, 1969, Leçons de théorie micro-économique 1968-71, La croissance française 1972, Réexamen de la théorie du chômage 1980, Théorie macroéconomique 1981, Essais sur la théorie du chômage 1983. *Address:* 42 avenue de Saxe, 75007, Paris, France (Home).

MALIȚA, Mircea, PH.D.; Romanian academic; b. 20 Feb. 1927, Oradea; ed. Univ. of Bucharest; Dir. Library of the Romanian Acad. 1950-56; Deputy Minister of Foreign Affairs 1962-70; Minister of Educ. 1970-72; Adviser to the Pres. of Romania 1972-77; Amb. to Switzerland 1980-82, to the U.S.A. 1982-85; Prof. (Math.) Univ. of Bucharest 1985-; mem. Romanian Writer's Union 1969-, Romanian Acad. of Social and Political Studies 1970-; Corresp. mem. Romanian Acad. 1972-; Chair. Cttee. on Future Studies 1976-; mem. World Acad. of Art and Science, Club of Rome, World Future Studies Fed., European Center for Research and Documentation in Social Sciences, Vienna, Int. Foundation for Devt. Alternatives (Nyon, Switzerland), Int. Council for Science Policy Studies, New Delhi, New York Acad. of Sciences; *Main works:* Cronica anului 2000 (Chronicle of the Year 2000) 1969; Diplomația. Scoli și instituții (Diplomacy. Schools and Institutions) 1970, Romanian Diplomacy. Historical Outlook, 1970, Aurul cenușiu (Grey Gold) 3 vol. 1971, 1972, 1973, Teoria și practica negocierilor (Theory and Practice of Negotiations) 1972, Idei în mers (Ideas in March) 1975, Zidul și iedera (The Wall and the Ivy) 1977; Mathematical Approaches to International Relations, 3 vol. 1977-78. *Main works* (co-ed.): Mathematics of Organization 1971, Programarea nelineară (Nonlinear Programming) 1973, Coalition and Connection in Games 1982, Mecanisme de reglementare pașnică a diferendelor între state (Means of Peaceful Settlement of Disputes between States) 1982. *Address:* Sos. Kiseleff 24, Bucharest, Romania.

MALJERS, Floris; Netherlands business executive; b. 12 Aug. 1933, Middelburg; m. J. H. de Jongh 1958; two s. one d. (deceased); ed. Univ. of Amsterdam; joined Unilever 1959; Man. Dir. Unilever, Colombia 1964, Unilever, Turkey 1966; Man. Dir. Vdberg & Jurgens, Netherlands 1970; mem. Parent Bd. of Unilever and Head of Man. Edible Fats Group 1974; Chair. Unilever N.V. 1984-, Vice-Chair. Unilever PLC 1984-. *Address:* c/o Unilever N.V., Postbus 760, 3000 DK Rotterdam, Netherlands. *Telephone:* 010-4645911.

MALKOVICH, John; American actor; b. 9 Dec. 1953, Christopher, Ill.; m. Glenne Headley 1982; ed. Eastern Illinois and Illinois State Univs.; co-founder Steppenwolf Theatre, Chicago 1976; *theatre appearances include:*

True West 1982, Death of a Salesman 1984, Burn This 1987; Dir. Balm in Gilead 1984–85, Arms and the Man 1985, Coyote Ugly 1985, The Caretaker 1986. *Film appearances include:* Places in the Heart 1984, The Killing Fields 1984, Eleni 1985, Making Mr. Right 1987, The Glass Menagerie 1987, Empire of the Sun 1987, Miles from Home 1988, Dangerous Liaisons 1989. *Address:* Steppenwolf Theatre, 2851 North Halstead Street, Chicago, Ill. 60657 (Office); 40 West 57th Street, New York, N.Y. 10019, U.S.A.

MALLE, Louis; French film director; b. 30 Oct. 1932; m.; one s.; m. 2nd Candice Bergen (q.v) 1980; two d.; Asst. to Commdr. Cousteau on La Calypso 1953–55; co-producer Le Monde du Silence 1955; tech. collaborator with Robert Bresson for Un condamné à mort s'est échappé. *Films:* Ascenseur pour l'échafaud 1957 (Prix Louis-Delluc 1958), Les amants 1958 (Special Jury Prize, Venice Film Festival 1958), Zazie dans le métro 1960, Vie privée 1962, Le feu follet (special Jury Prize, Venice Film Festival 1963), Viva María 1965, Le voleur 1966, William Wilson 1967, Calcutta 1968, Le souffle au coeur 1971, Humain trop humain 1974, Lacombe Lucien (Best Film Award, Soc. of Film and TV Arts) 1974, Black Moon 1975, Pretty Baby 1978, Atlantic City 1980, My Dinner with André 1980, Alamo Bay 1984, God's Country 1985, And the Pursuit of Happiness 1986, Au revoir les enfants (co-dir. with Candice Bergen) 1987 (Cesar Award 1988, European Film Award 1988, Best Film Dir., BAFTA 1989). *Publications:* Le Souffle au Coeur 1971, Lacombe Lucien 1974. *Leisure interest:* bicycle racing. *Address:* Nouvelles éditions de films, 15 rue du Louvre, 75001 Paris, France.

MALLEA, Eduardo; Argentine writer and journalist; b. 14 Aug. 1903, Bahía Blanca; s. of Narciso S. Mallea and Manuela Aztiria; m. Helena Muñoz Larreta 1944; ed. Colegio Nacional and Faculty of Law, Buenos Aires; mem. Bd. of Dirs. of Sur and of Realidad; fmr. Pres. Argentine Soc. of Writers; literary Ed. on staff of La Nación; First Nat. Prize for Literature 1946, 1970; mem. Argentine Acad. of Letters; fmr. Amb. to UNESCO; Hon. D.Hum.Litt. (Ann Arbor Univ., Michigan). *Publications:* Cuentos para una Inglesa Desesperada 1926, Nocturno Europeo, Conocimiento y Expresión de la Argentina 1935, La Ciudad junto al Río Inmóvil 1936, Historia de una Pasión Argentina 1937, Fiesta en Noviembre 1938, Meditación en la Costa 1940, El Sayal y la Púrpura 1941, Todo Verdor Perecerá 1941, La Bahía de Silencio 1940, Las Aguilas 1941, Rodeada está de sueño 1944, El retorno 1946, El Vínculo 1946, Los Enemigos del Alma 1950, La Torre 1951, Chaves 1953, La sala de espera 1953, Notas de un novelista 1954, Simbad 1957, El gajo de enebro 1957, Posesión 1959, La razón humana 1960, La vida blanca 1960, Las travesías 1962, La barca de hielo 1967, La Penúltima Puerta 1970, Gabriel Andaral 1971, Triste piel del universo 1971. [*Deceased.*]

MALLET, Robert Albert Marie Georges, D. ÈS L., D.EN D.; French university rector and author; b. 15 March 1915, Paris; m. 1st Francine Leullier 1944 (divorced); two c.; m. 2nd Yvonne Noviant 1985; ed. Faculté des Lettres and Faculté de Droit, Paris; Dir., Ecole Nat. des Lettres, Tananarive, Malagasy Repub. 1959, subsequently Dean, Faculty of Letters, Madagascar; Rector, Acad. d'Amiens 1964–68, Univ. of Paris 1969–80; Pres. Assen. des universités partiellement ou entièrement de langue française 1972–75, Hon. Pres. 1975–; Pres. Comité perm. des mondialistes de France 1978–; Pres. Jury du Prix Apollinaire; mem. Universal Movement for Scientific Responsibility (Pres. 1974–), Acad. royale de Belgique; Commdr., Légion d'honneur, Commdr. des Arts et Lettres, Croix de guerre, Commdr., Palmes académiques, Ordre nat. Malagasy; Silver Medal, City of Paris 1952; Prix de la Critique 1955; Grand prix de poésie, Acad. française 1977, Prix des libraires 1987. *Publications:* poems: Le poème du sablier, La rose en ses remous, Quand le miroir s'étonne, Silex éclaté, l'Espace d'une fenêtre, etc.; plays: Le filandier, Satire en trois temps cinq mouvements, Le train de nuit, L'équipage au complet; novels: Région inhabitée, Ellynn; numerous other publications. *Address:* 18 rue de la Glacière, 75013 Paris, France.

MALLOUM, Brig.-Gen. Félix; Chad army officer; b. 1932, Fort-Archambault (now Sarh); ed. Mil. Schools, Brazzaville, Fréjus, Saint-Maixent; served in French Army, Indo-China 1953–55, Algeria; joined Chad Nat. Army; Lieut.-Col. 1961, Capt. 1962, Col. 1968; fmr. Head of Mil. Corps at the Presidency; Chief of Staff of the Army Dec. 1972–Sept. 1972; C.-in-C. of the Armed Forces 1972–73; under house arrest June 1973, released April 1975 after coup deposed Pres. Tombalbaye; Head of State, Chair. Supreme Mil. Council 1975–79, Pres. Council of Ministers, Minister of Defence and Ex-Servicemen 1975–79; resigned March 1979 after signing Kano Peace Agreement with Front Nat. du Tchad.

MALONE, Thomas Francis, SC.D.; American geophysicist; b. 3 May 1917, Sioux City, Iowa; s. of John and Mary (Hourigan) Malone; m. Rosalie A. Doran 1942; six c.; ed. S. Dakota State School of Mines and Tech. and M.I.T.; mem. of Staff M.I.T. 1941–43, Asst. Prof. 1943–51, Assoc. Prof. 1951–54; Dir. Travelers Weather Service and Travelers Weather Research Center for Travelers Insurance Co., Hartford, Conn. 1954–56, Dir. of Research 1956–69, Second Vice-Pres. 1964–66, Vice-Pres. 1966–68, Sr. Vice-Pres. 1968–70; Dean of Graduate School, Univ. of Connecticut 1970–73; Dir. Holcomb Research Inst., Butler Univ. 1973–83, Dir. Emer. 1983–; Sec.-Gen. Scientific Cttee. on Problems of Environment 1970–72; Pres. Inst. of Ecology 1978–81; Vice-Pres. Int. Council of Scientific Unions

1970–72, Treas. 1978–84; Foreign Sec. Nat. Acad. of Sciences 1978–82, Chair. Bd. 1981–84; Scholar in Residence St. Joseph Coll., Conn. 1983–; Fellow, Nat. Sciences Resources for the Future 1983–; Exec. Scientist, Connecticut Acad. of Science and Eng. 1987–; Pres. American Geographical Union 1961–, Sigma Xi. The Scientific Research Soc. 1988–89; Hon. D.Eng., Hon. L.H.D.; Hon. Sc.D. (Bates Coll.) 1988; Losey Award, Inst. of Aerospace Sciences 1960; Charles Franklin Brooks Award 1964 and Cleveland Abbe Award 1968 (American Meteorological Soc.), Int. Meteorological Soc. Prize 1984, World Meteorological Org. Gold Medal 1984. *Publications:* numerous articles in scientific journals. *Address:* St. Joseph College, 1678 Asylum Avenue, P.O. Box 71, West Hartford, Conn. 06117 (Office); 5 Bishop Road, West Hartford, Conn. 06119, U.S.A. (Home). *Telephone:* (203) 232-4571, Ext. 312 (Office); (203) 236-2426 (Home).

MALOTT, Deane Waldo, LL.D., D.C.S.; American university president; b. 10 July 1898, Abilene, Kan.; s. of Michael H. and Edith G. (Johnson) Malott; m. Eleanor S. Thrum 1925; one s. two d.; ed. Kansas and Harvard Univ.; Asst. Dean, Harvard Business School 1923–29, Assoc. Prof. of Business 1933–39; Vice-Pres. Hawaiian Pineapple Co., Honolulu 1929–33; Chancellor, Univ. of Kan. 1939–51; Pres. Cornell Univ. 1951–63, Pres. Emer. 1963–; Consultant, U.S. Army Air Corps. 1943–45; Chair. Emer. Pacific Tropical Botanical Garden; mem. Business Council 1944–; Trustee, Teagle Foundation 1951–84; Consultant to Assen. of American Colls. 1963–69; Dir. Advisory Bd. Norstar Bank, Ithaca; Commons Dir. Norstar Trust Co.; Dir. William Allen White Foundation, Univ. of Kansas Endowment Assen.; Hon. LL.D. (Washburn, Bryant Coll., Hamilton Coll., Calif., Juniata Coll., Univ. of N.H., Emory, Liberia), D.C.S. (Pittsburgh), D.H.L. (Long Island). *Publications:* (with Philip Cabot) Problems in Public Utility Management 1927, (with J. C. Baker) Introduction to Corporate Finance 1936, (with J. C. Baker and W. D. Kennedy) On Going into Business 1936, Problems in Agricultural Marketing 1938, (with B. F. Martin) The Agricultural Industries 1939. *Address:* 322 Wait Avenue, Cornell University, Ithaca, N.Y. 14850, U.S.A. *Telephone:* (607) 255-4010.

MALOTT, Robert H., M.B.A.; American business executive; b. 6 Oct. 1926, Boston; m. Elizabeth Malott; one s. two d.; ed. Kansas Univ., Harvard Graduate School of Business Admin., New York Univ. Law School; Asst. to Dean, Harvard Graduate School of Business Admin. 1950–52; joined FMC Corpn. 1952, Controller Niagara Chemical Div. 1955, Man. Dapon Dept. of Organic Chemicals Div. 1959, Div. Man. 1963, Vice-Pres. American Viscose Div. 1965, Vice-Pres. FMC 1966, Exec. Vice-Pres., Planning 1967, Man. Machinery Divs., Dir. 1970, mem. Exec. Cttee. 1971, Pres. and C.E.O. 1972–, Chair. of Bd. 1973–; Dir. Standard Oil Co. (Ind.), Bell & Howell Co., Continental Illinois Corpn., Data Documents Inc.; mem. Business Council, Mfg. Chemists Assen., Exec. Council of Harvard Business School Assen., Nat. Council for U.S.-China Trade, Conf. Bd., Stanford Research Inst. Council. *Address:* FMC Corporation, 200 East Randolph Drive, Chicago, Ill. 60601, U.S.A.

MALOY, Robert, A.M., S.T.D.; American library director and medievalist; b. 12 July 1935, Cleveland, Ohio; s. of Harry J. and E. M. (Barnes) Maloy; ed. Cathedral Latin School, Cleveland, Univs. of Dayton, Chicago and Fribourg; Asst. Prof. of Church History, Univ. of Dayton, Ohio 1967–71; Visiting lecturer and Consultant, Univ. of Notre Dame 1971–72; Asst. Prof., Rosary Coll. Grad. Library School, Chicago 1971–72; Library Dir. and Assoc. Prof. of Church History, School of Theology, Claremont and Claremont Graduate School 1972–75; Library Dir. and Assoc. Prof. of History, Union Theological Seminary, New York 1975–79; mem. Bd. of Trustees and Advisers, Missionary Research Library Inc., New York 1975–79, Smithsonian Science Information Exchange, Washington, D.C. 1979–82, Rhode Island School of Design 1980–, Wake Forest Univ., N.C. 1982–, etc.; Dir. of Libraries, Smithsonian Inst. 1979–87; Hon. Litt.D. (Rosary Coll.) 1982. *Publication:* Sermonary of Ildephonsus of Toledo: scholarship and manuscripts 1971. *Address:* P.O. Box 524, Washington, D.C. 20560, U.S.A. (Home). *Telephone:* (202) 265-0800 (Home).

MALPAS, Robert, C.B.E., B.SC.; British business executive; b. 9 Aug. 1927; s. of Cheshyre and Louise Marie Marcelle Malpas; m. Josephine Dickenson 1956; ed. Taunton School, St. George's Coll., Buenos Aires, Argentina, Durham Univ.; joined ICI Ltd. 1948; C.E.O. ICI Europa Ltd. 1973; Dir. ICI 1975; resigned from ICI to become Pres. Halcon Int. Inc., New York 1978; mem. (non-exec.) Bd. BOC Group 1981, Eurotunnel 1987–; Halcon bought by Texas Eastern 1982; a Man. Dir. British Petroleum (BP) Jan. 1983–; mem. Eng. Council 1983– (Vice-Chair. 1984–); Order of Civil Merit, Spain 1968. *Leisure interests:* theatre, opera, reading, music, sports. *Address:* Britannic House, Moor Lane, London, EC2Y 9BU, England.

MALQINHU; Chinese (Mongolian) writer; b. 1930, Liaoning; Pres. Minority Writers' Soc. Dec. 1985–, Minority Literature Foundation Dec. 1986–. *Publications:* On the Kolchin Grasslands, The Barren Grasslands; *Address:* Nationalities' Literature, Beijing, People's Republic of China.

MALTBY, John Newcombe, M.A.; British business executive; b. 10 July 1928, Esher; s. of Air Vice-Marshal Sir Paul Maltby; m. Lady Sylvia Harris 1956; one s. two d.; ed. Wellington Coll., Clare Coll., Cambridge; with Royal Dutch Shell 1951–69; founder and Man. Dir. Panocean Shipping and Terminals Ltd. 1969–79; Dir. Burmah Oil Co. 1980–82, Deputy Chair. 1982–83, Chair. June 1983–; Chair. Dover Harbour Bd. 1989–; Dir. various public cos. *Leisure interests:* history, gardening, sailing. *Address:* Broadford House, Stratfield Turgis, Basingstoke, Hants., RG27 0AS, England.

MALTER, Arnold S., J.D.; American lawyer; b. 13 March 1934, New York; s. of Emanuel H. Malter and Harriet Misbin; m. 1st Sheila Zonis 1957, 2nd Ana Sulek 1977; one s. one d.; ed. Univ. of Calif. Los Angeles and Univ. of Southern Calif.; Pres. Arnold S. Malter (a professional corpn.); mem. State Bar of Calif., Int. Bar Assen., A.B.A., L.A. County Bar Assen., Wilshire Bar Assen., Inter-American Bar Assen., Foreign Trade Assen., British American Chamber of Commerce, German American Chamber of Commerce and numerous other trade and juridical assens. etc.; Dir. and Legal Adviser, All Asia Bar Assen. 1984–; Dir. Int. Inst. of L.A., Liberty Int. *Publications include:* Companies, Council and Illegal Payments 1978, Sales Representative and Other Agents: An American View 1979, Expropriation of Real Property 1980, Consumer Protection-Overkill 1981; articles and reports. *Leisure interests:* travel, photography. *Address:* Suite 1432, 123 S. Figueria, Los Angeles, Calif. 90017, U.S.A.

MALTSEV, Nikolay, M.SC.(TECH.); Soviet politician; b. 10 March 1928, Maikop, Krasnodar Kray; ed. Grozny Oil Inst.; mem. CPSU 1953–; Head of Oil Industry, Perm. Council of Nat. Econ. 1961–63; Head Permneft Assen. 1963–72; First Deputy Minister of Oil Industry 1972–77, Minister of Oil Industry 1977–85; Cand. mem. Cen. Cttee. CPSU 1981–; Deputy to U.S.S.R. Supreme Soviet (7th–10th Convocations); Order of the October Revolution 1978, Hero of Socialist Labour 1971, Order of Lenin (twice), and other decorations. *Address:* c/o Ministry of the Oil Industry, nab. Morisa Toreza 26/1, Moscow, U.S.S.R.

MALTSEV, Viktor Fyodorovich; Soviet engineer and diplomatist; b. 22 June 1917, Dnepropetrovsk, Ukraine; ed. Moscow Inst. of Railway Engineers; with Ministry of Railways 1941–61; mem. CPSU 1945–; Chair. Soviet of Irkutsk Region, E. Siberia 1961–67; Amb. to Sweden 1967–71, to Finland 1971–73, to India 1974–77, to Yugoslavia 1986–; First Deputy Minister of Foreign Affairs 1978–86; Cand. mem. CPSU Cen. Cttee. 1971–76, mem. 1986–89. *Address:* Soviet Embassy, Deligradska 32, Belgrade, Yugoslavia.

MALULA, H.E. Cardinal Joseph-Albert; Zairian ecclesiastic; b. 17 Dec. 1917, Kinshasa (then Léopoldville); ed. Petit Séminaire, Bolongo, Grand Séminaire, Kabwe; Vicar in Parish of Christ-Roi; Auxiliary Bishop of Léopoldville 1959–64; Archbishop of Kinshasa 1964–; cr. Cardinal 1969; Chevalier, Ordre du Léopard. *Address:* B.P. 8431, Kinshasa 1, Zaire. *Telephone:* 69221.

MAMAEVA, Nina Vasilevna; Soviet actress; b. 1923; ed. Leningrad Theatre Inst.; chief mem. of Leningrad Youth Theatre 1946–; acted in numerous roles, including Anya (Chekhov's Cherry Orchard), Juliet (Romeo and Juliet); worked with the Pushkin Academic Theatre 1954–, in numerous celebrated roles, including Ophelia (Hamlet), Nina (Chekhov's Seagull), Leo (Cocteau's Les Parents terribles). *Address:* Pushkin Academic Theatre, Leningrad, U.S.S.R.

MAMALONI, Solomon; Solomon Islands politician; b. 1943, Arosi, San Cristobal; ed. King George VI School, Malaita, Te Aute Coll., N.Z.; joined British Colonial Admin. Service, Honiara 1966; Exec. Officer in Civil Service, then clerk to Legis. Council 1970; M.P. for Makira 1970–76, for W. Makira 1976–77, 1980–; Chief Minister, (British) Solomon Islands 1974–76; Prime Minister of Solomon Islands 1981–85, March 1989; f. and Leader People's Progress Party (merged with Rural Alliance Party to form People's Alliance Party 1979), Parl. Leader People's Alliance Party 1980–; Man. Dir. Patosha Co. 1977; Grand Gwanghwa Medal, Order of Diplomatic Service Merit (Repub. of Korea). *Publications:* AEDO, Census Day (radio plays) 1978. *Address:* Office of the Prime Minister, P.O. Box GO1, Honiara, Guadalcanal, Solomon Islands. *Telephone:* 22208.

MAMBA, Sir George Mbikwakhe, Kt.; Swaziland diplomatist; b. 5 July 1932; s. of Ndabazebelungu Mamba and Getrude Mthwalose Thwala; m. Sophie Sidzandza Sibande 1960; three s. two d.; ed. Franson Christian High School, Swazi Nat. High School, Morija Teacher Training Coll., Cambridge Inst. of Educ., Nairobi Univ., Kenya; Head Teacher Makhonza Mission School 1956–60; Teacher Kwaluseni Cen. School 1961–65; Head Teacher Enkamheni Cen. School 1966–67; Insp. of Schools, Manzini Dist. 1969–70; Welfare and Aftercare Officer, Prison Dept. 1971–72; Counsellor, Swaziland High Comm., Nairobi 1972–77; High Commr. in U.K. 1978–88, concurrently High Commr. to Malta, Amb. to Denmark, Norway and Sweden and Perm. Del. to UNESCO; Vice-Pres. Swaziland Nat. Union of Teachers 1966–67; Minister of Foreign Affairs 1988–; Field Commr. Swaziland Boy Scouts Assen. 1967–68, Chief Commr. 1971–72. *Publication:* Children's Play 1966. *Leisure interests:* scouting, reading. *Address:* Ministry of Foreign Affairs, P.O.B. 518, Mbabane, Swaziland.

MAMERT, Jean Albert; French public servant; b. 26 March 1928; m. Monique Petit 1966; one s. one d.; ed. Lycée et Faculté de Droit, Montpellier, Inst. d'Études Politiques, Paris, Ecole Nat. d'Admin., Paris; Auditor 1955–, later Master of Requests, Council of State 1962–; Tech. Counsellor of Govt. for Constitutional Problems, 1958–59, Sec.-Gen. Constitutional Consultative Cttee. 1958; Chief of Prime Minister's Office Jan.-July 1959; Sec.-Gen. Econ. and Social Council 1959–72; Dir.-Gen. Cino del Duca 1978–; mem. EEC Econ. and Social Cttee. 1970–74; with Michelin Group 1972–78, Pres. Pneumatiques Michelin S.A., Spain 1974–78; Dir.-Gen. Editions Mond-

iales 1978–80; Pres. Société Lorraine de matériel minier et métallurgique (S.L.M.M.) 1980–; Dir. France-Soir 1983–; Dir. Avenir-Publicité 1984–; Gen. Del. Assen. Nat. des Sociétés par Action 1986–. *Address:* 15 rue du Général Catroux, 75017 Paris (Office); 89 rue de l'Assomption, 75016 Paris, France.

MAMET, David Alan, B.A.; American playwright and director; b. 30 Nov. 1947, Chicago; s. of Bernard Morris Mamet and Lenore June (née Silver) Mamet; m. Lindsay Crouse 1977; ed. Goddard Coll., Plainfield, Vermont; Artist-in-residence Goddard Coll. 1971–73; Artistic Dir., St. Nicholas Theatre Co., Chicago 1973–75; Guest Lecturer, Univ. of Chicago 1975, 1979, N.Y. Univ. 1981; Assoc. Artistic Dir. Goodman Theatre, Chicago 1978; Assoc. Prof. of Film, Columbia Univ. 1988; Dir. (films) House of Games 1986, Things Change 1987; recipient Outer Critics Circle Award for contrib. to American theatre 1978. *Publications:* The Duck Variations 1971, Sexual Perversity in Chicago 1973 (Village Voice Obie Award 1976), The Reunion 1973, Squirrels 1974, American Buffalo (Village Voice Obie Award 1976) 1976, (N.Y. Drama Critics Circle Award 1977), A Life in the Theatre 1976, The Water Engine 1976, The Woods 1977, Lone Canoe 1978, Prairie du Chien 1978, Lakeboat 1980, Donny March 1981, Edmond 1982 (Village Voice Obie Award 1983), The Disappearance of the Jews 1983, The Shawl 1985, Glengarry Glen Ross (Pulitzer prize for Drama, N.Y. Drama Critics Circle award) 1984, Speed-the-Plow 1987; (screenplays) The Postman Always Rings Twice 1979, The Verdict 1980, The Untouchables 1986, House of Games 1986, Things Change (with Shel Silverstein) 1987, We're No Angels 1987; (childrens' books) Mr. Warm and Cold 1985, The Owl (with Lindsay Crouse) 1987; (essay) Writing in Restaurants 1986. *Address:* Columbia University, Morningside Heights, New York, N.Y. 10027, U.S.A.

MAMIAKA, Gen. Raphaël; Gabonese politician; b. 12 Nov. 1936, Lambaréné; ed. Inst. d'Enseignement Secondaire, Paris, Ecole d'Officiers de Gendarmerie Nat., Melun, France, Univ. of Paris; Sub-Lieut. of Gendarmerie 1964, Lieut. 1966, Capt. 1968, Commdt. 1970; served French Army in Cen. Congo, Oubangui-Chari, Far East and Algeria; fmr. Commdr. Gendarmerie of Ndeu-N'Tem, Moanda and N'Gounie; Sec. of State for the Interior in charge of the Prison Service Feb.-Dec. 1969; Sec. of State at the Presidency in charge of the Interior 1969–70; Minister of the Interior 1970–73, of Public Health and Population 1973–75, 1978–81, of Public Works and Buildings 1975–76, of Justice 1976–78, of Social Affairs, Veterans, War Victims and Women's Promotion 1978–80; Commdr., Légion d'honneur and other nat. and foreign decorations. *Address:* c/o Ministry of Public Health, Libreville, Gabon.

MAMLIN, Gennadiy Semenovich; Soviet author; b. 1925, Simferopol; first works published 1950; writes mainly for children. *Publications include:* Nikita Snegiryov 1956, But with Alyoshka We Are Friends 1961, Miracle at Noon 1964, Fireworks 1965. *Address:* U.S.S.R. Union of Writers, Moscow, U.S.S.R.

MAMMI, Oscar; Italian politician; b. 25 Oct. 1926, Rome; fmr. Nat. Sec. Italian Union of Bank Employees; elected mem. Rome City Council 1962, 1966, 1971; mem. Nat. Exec., Italian Republican Party 1959–; M.P. for Rome-Viterbo-Latina-Frosinone 1968–; Under-Sec. of State, Ministry of Industry and Trade in second Rumor Govt. and in Colombo Govt.; Chair. Republican Group in eighth Legislature; Minister of Parl. Relations 1986–87, of Posts and Telecommunications July 1987–. *Address:* Camera dei Deputati, Rome, Italy.

MAMO, Sir Anthony Joseph, K.ST.J., O.B.E., Q.C., LL.D., B.A.; Maltese judge and former Head of State; b. 9 Jan. 1909, Birkirkara; s. of late Joseph and Carola (née Brincat) Mamo; m. Margaret Agius 1939; one s. two d.; ed. Archbishop's Seminary, Malta and Royal Univ. of Malta; mem. Statute Law Revision Comm. 1936–42; Crown Counsel 1942–51; Prof. of Criminal Law, Royal Univ. of Malta 1943–57; Deputy Attorney-Gen. 1952–54; Attorney-Gen. 1955; Chief Justice and Pres. of H.M. Court of Appeal 1957; Pres. H.M. Constitutional Court 1964; Pres. H.M. Court of Criminal Appeal 1967; Gov.-Gen. of Malta 1971–74; Pres. of the Repub. 1974–76; Hon. LL.D. (Libya) 1971; Hon. D.Litt. (Malta) 1969. *Publications:* lectures on criminal law and criminal procedure delivered at the Royal Univ. of Malta. *Leisure interest:* reading. *Address:* 49 Stella Maris Street, Sliema, Malta. *Telephone:* 330708.

MAMULA, Adm. Branko; Yugoslav naval officer and politician; b. 1921, Slavsko Polje, Vrgin Most, Croatia; m.; two s.; ed. mil. schools; Political Commissar Bn., Brigade, Maritime Dist. Sector and Maritime Command, Northern Adriatic, World War II; after war, Political Commissar Fleet and Maritime Zone, Head of Operational Dept., Navy Command, Asst. Commdr. Navy, Commdr. Mil.-Naval Region, Head Naval Div., Asst. Fed. Sec. for Nat. Defence, Commdr. Navy; mem. Cen. Cttee. Yugoslav League of Communists, 11th Congress; Chief of Gen. Staff, Yugoslav People's Army 1979–; mem. Council for Nat. Defence, Presidency 1979–; Fed. Sec. for Nat. Defence 1982–88. *Publications:* Navies at High and Narrow Seas 1975 and numerous articles on naval and military matters. *Leisure interest:* hunting. *Address:* Federal Secretariat for National Defence, Kneza Miloša 35, 11000 Belgrade, Yugoslavia.

MAN, Ivan Aleksandrovich; Soviet sailor and polar explorer; b. 23 Sept. 1903, Mogilev Region, Byelorussia; ed. Leningrad Naval Polytechnic; Nat. Navigation Safety Inspector; Commdr. of cargo steamers Pravda, Transbalt in the Arctic Ocean, and of the liners Ukraina, Rossia in the Black

Sea; Capt. of diesel-electric ship Ob, flagship of the Soviet Antarctic Expedition 1955; sailed to Mirny in the Antarctic 1955, 1956, 1957; Capt. of liner Gruzia 1961-62, Peter Veliki 1962-64, research ship Professor Vize, Antarctic 1968; Chief Specialist in Navigation, Ministry of Merchant Marine 1964-; Orders of Lenin, Patriotic War (1st Class), Red Banner of Labour (twice), Badge of Honour and other decorations. *Address:* Ministry of Merchant Marine, Moscow, U.S.S.R.

MANAC'H, Étienne Manoël; French diplomatist (retd.); b. 3 Feb. 1910, Plouigneau; s. of François-Marie and Mme. (née Colleter) Manac'h; m. Mme. Denise Lorenzet 1969; two s. one d.; ed. Faculté des Lettres, Paris; Free France Del. to Turkey 1941-42, Head of Mission to Balkans 1942-44, Consul-Gen. in Istanbul 1944; First Sec., French Embassy, Prague 1945, Consul-Gen., Bratislava 1946-51; Counsellor and Deputy Dir., Ministry of Foreign Affairs 1951, Head of E. European Services 1953; Tech. Counsellor to Minister of Foreign Affairs 1957-58; Dir. of Cabinet to Minister of State, Guy Mollet 1958-59; Minister plenipotentiary 1960; Dir. for Asia and Oceania of Cen. Admin. 1960-69; Amb. to People's Repub. of China 1969-75; Hon. Pres. Assen. Démocratique des Français à l'Etranger; mem. du Conseil de l'Ordre nat. de Légion d'honneur 1982; Grand Officier, Légion d'honneur; Grand Croix Ordre nat. du Mérite. *Publications:* Mémoires d'Extrême-Asie (Vols. I, II, III). *Address:* Manoir de Lezaven, 29123 Pont-Aven, France. *Telephone:* 98-06-03-55.

MANASSEH, Leonard Sulla, O.B.E., R.A., F.R.I.B.A., R.W.A.; British architect; b. 21 May 1916; s. of Alan Manasseh and Esther (née Elias); m. 1st 1947 (divorced 1956), two s.; m. 2nd Sarah Delaforce 1957, two s. one d. (deceased); ed. Cheltenham Coll., The Architectural Assen. School of Architecture; Asst. Architect, CREN London and Guy Morgan & Partners; teaching staff, Architectural Assen. and Kingston School of Art 1941-43; served Fleet Air Arm 1943-46; Asst. Architect, Herts. County Council 1946-48; Sr. Architect, Stevenage New Town Devt. Corpn. 1948-50; partner, Leonard Manasseh Partnership (fmrly. Leonard Manasseh and Partners) 1950-; teaching staff, Architectural Assen. 1951-59; opened office in Singapore and Malaysia with James Cubitt & Partners 1953-54; mem. Council, Architectural Assen. 1959-66, Pres. 1964-65, Council of Industrial Design 1965-68, Council R.I.B.A. 1968-70, 1976-82 (Hon. Sec. 1979-81), Council, Nat. Trust 1977-, Ancient Monuments Bd. 1978-84, Bd., Chatham Historic Dockyard Trust 1984-; Pres. Franco-British Union of Architects 1978-79; R.A. Rep. Bd. of Govs. Dulwich Schools Foundation and Surveyor to Picture Gallery 1987. *Work includes:* houses, housing and schools, industrial work, conservation plan for Beaulieu Estate, Nat. Motor Museum, Beaulieu, Wellington Country Park, Stratfield Saye, Pumping Station, Weymouth, British Museum refurbishment, additions to Old Royal Observatory, Greenwich. *Publications:* Office Buildings (with 3rd Baron Cunliffe) 1962, Snowdon Summit Report (Countryside Comm.) 1974, Eastbourne Harbour Study (Trustees, Chatsworth Settlement) 1976; planning reports and studies. *Leisure interests:* photography, travel, sketching, watching aeroplanes, being optimistic. *Address:* 6 Bacon's Lane, Highgate, London, N6 6BL, England. *Telephone:* 01-340 5528.

MANATT, Charles Taylor, B.S., J.D.; American lawyer and politician; b. 9 June 1936, Chicago, Ill.; s. of William Price and Lucille (Taylor) Manatt; m. Margaret K. Klinkefus 1957; two s. one d.; ed. Ia. State and George Washington Univs.; legis. asst. to congressman, Washington, D.C. 1959-60; admitted to Calif. Bar 1962; practiced Los Angeles 1962-63, Beverly Hills, Calif. 1963-64, Van Nuys, Calif., and Los Angeles 1964-; mem. firm Manatt, Phelps, Rothenburg and Tunney, Los Angeles; Chair. Democratic Cttee., Calif. 1971-73, 1975-77; mem. Democratic Exec. Cttee. 1976-; mem. Democratic Nat. Cttee. 1976-, Chair. 1981-85, Chair. Nat. Finance Council 1978. *Address:* Democratic National Committee, 1625 Massachusetts Avenue, N.W., Washington D.C. 20036, U.S.A.

MANCERA AGUAYO, Miguel, M.A.ECONS.; Mexican economist and banking executive; b. 18 Dec. 1932, Mexico, D.F.; s. of Rafael Mancera and Luisa Aguayo; m. Sonia Corcuera 1959; five s.; ed. Instituto Tecnológico de México and Yale Univ.; Banco de Comercio S.A. 1953-56; economist Public Investments Comm. under Presidency of Repub. 1957-58; economist Banco de México 1958-62, Admin. of FOMEX (Export Finance and Export Credit Guarantee Fund) 1962-67, Man. Int. Affairs 1967-71, Deputy Dir. Banco de México 1971-73, Gen. Deputy Dir. 1973-82, Dir. Gen. (Gov.) 1982, Jan. 1983-. *Address:* Banco de México, Avenida 5 de mayo No. 2, 06059 México, D.F. (Office); Salvador Novo No. 94, Coyoacán, 04000 México (Home). *Telephone:* 512.22.66/512.33.23 (Office); 554.17.83 (Home).

MANCHAM, Sir James Richard Marie, Kt., F.R.S.A.; British (b. Seychelles) lawyer and politician; b. 11 Aug. 1939, Victoria, Mahé; s. of Richard and Evelyne (née Tirant) Mancham; m. 1st Heather Jean Evans 1963 (dissolved 1974); one s. one d.; m. 2nd Catherine Olsen 1985; one s.; ed. Univ. of Paris and Middle Temple, London; Called to the Bar, Middle Temple 1961; mem. Legis. Council of the Seychelles 1961; mem. Govt. Council 1967; founder and leader, Social Dem. Party 1964; mem. Legis. Ass. 1970-76, of Nat. Ass. 1976-77; Chief Minister 1970-75, Prime Minister 1975-76; Pres. of the Republic of Seychelles 1976-77 (deposed by coup); int. trade consultant 1981-; Hon. K.B.E. 1976; Officier, Légion d'honneur 1976 and numerous medals and decorations. *Publications:* Reflections and Echoes from the Seychelles, Paradise Raped 1983, Gallow: The Undiscovered Paradise 1984, New York's Robin Island 1985. *Leisure interests:* travel, water sports,

tennis, writing. *Address:* c/o Lloyds Bank Ltd., 81 Edgware Road, London, W2 2HY, England.

MANCHESTER, William, B.A., A.M.; American writer; b. 1 April 1922, Attleboro, Mass.; s. of William Raymond Manchester and Sallie Thompson Manchester; m. Julia Brown Marshall 1948; one s. two d.; ed. Univ. of Massachusetts, Dartmouth Coll., and Univ. of Missouri; Reporter Daily Oklahoman 1945-46; Reporter, Foreign Corresp., War Corresp. Baltimore Sun 1947-55; Man. Ed. Wesleyan Univ. publs. 1955-64; Fellow, Wesleyan Univ. Center for Advanced Studies 1959-60, Wesleyan Univ. E. Coll. 1968-86; mem. faculty, Wesleyan Univ. 1968-69, Writer-in-Residence 1975-, Adjunct Prof. of History 1979-; Hon. Fellow Yale Univ. 1988; Pres. Bd. of Trustees, Univ. of Mass. Library 1970-72; B.A. (Univ. of Mass.) 1946, M.A. (Univ. of Mo.) 1947, L.H.D. (Univ. of Mass.) 1965; L.H.D. (Univ. of New Haven) 1979; Purple Heart 1945; Guggenheim Fellow 1959; Dag Hammarskjöld Int. Prize in Literature 1967, Overseas Press Club Award 1968, Univ. of Missouri Award 1969, President's Cabinet Award (Univ. of Detroit) 1980, McConaughty Award (Wesleyan Univ.) 1980, Troy Medal (Univ. of Mass.) 1980, Lincoln Literary Award 1983, Blenheim Award 1986. *Publications:* Disturber of the Peace 1951, The City of Anger 1953, Shadow of the Monsoon 1956, Beard the Lion 1958, A Rockefeller Family Portrait 1959, The Long Gainer 1961, Portrait of a President 1962, The Death of a President 1967, The Arms of Krupp 1968, The Glory and the Dream 1974, Controversy and Other Essays in Journalism 1976, American Caesar 1978, Goodbye Darkness 1980, The Last Lion: Winston Spencer Churchill 1874-1932, (vol. 1), Visions of Glory (vol. 2) 1983, The Caged Lion 1932-40, (vol. 3) 1988, Alone 1987, One Brief Shining Moment 1983, This is Our Time 1988. *Leisure interest:* photography. *Address:* c/o Don Congdon Associates, 177 East 70th Street, New York, N.Y. 10021; Box 329 Wesleyan University, Middletown, Conn. 06457, U.S.A. *Telephone:* (203) 347-9411, Ext. 388; and (203) 346-4789 (Conn.).

MANCINI, Giacomo; Italian politician; b. 21 April 1916; ed. Univ. of Turin; mem. Partito Socialista Italiano (PSI) 1943-; Dir. Socialist Fed. of Cosenza 1946-48; mem. Chamber of Deputies 1948-; mem. Directorate PSI 1953-, Dir. of Party Org. 1959, later Asst. Sec.; Minister of Public Health 1963-64, of Public Works 1964-70; Sec. Unitarian Socialist Party 1970-72; Minister for Southern Devt. March-Oct. 1974. *Address:* via Liceo 26, 1-87100 Cosenza, Italy.

MANCINI, Giuseppe Federico, LL.D.; Italian professor of law and advocate; b. 23 Dec. 1927, Perugia; s. of Ettore Mancini and Fulvia Lina Valigi; m. Vittoria Ghigi 1956; two d.; ed. Bologna, Bordeaux, Paris and Chicago Univs.; Lecturer (Libero docente) in Labour Law 1956; Lecturer Univ. of Urbino 1956-62; Visiting Prof. of Italian Politics, Johns Hopkins Bologna Center 1957-76; Supply Lecturer in Labour Law, Univ. of Bologna 1962; taught a course at Univ. of N. Carolina and gave seminars in Devt. of Govt. Harvard Univ. 1965; Prof. of Labour Law Univ. of Bologna 1965-79; Prof. Faculty of Pol. Science, Rome Univ. 1979-82; mem. Consiglio Superiore della Magistratura (Gen. Council of the Judiciary) 1976-81; Advocate-Gen., Court of Justice of the European Communities, Luxembourg 1982-, First Advocate-Gen. 1985-86, Judge 1988-; Dr. h.c. (Univ. of Cordoba, Spain) 1984. *Publications:* La responsabilità contrattuale del prestatore di lavoro 1958, Il recesso unilaterale e i rapporti di lavoro 1962, Giuffrè (Vol. I) 1962, (Vol. II) 1965, Lo Statuto dei diritti dei lavoratori, Commentario (with G. Ghezzi, L. Montuschi and U. Romagnoli), Costituzione e movimento operaio 1976, Terroristi e riformisti 1981. *Leisure interests:* swimming, science fiction. *Address:* Court of Justice of the European Communities, Kirchberg, Luxembourg. *Telephone:* 4303-2224 (Office).

MANCINI, Henry; American composer and conductor of film music; b. 16 April 1924, Cleveland, Ohio; s. of Quinto Mancini and Anna Mancini; m. Ginny O'Connor 1948; one s. two d.; ed. Juilliard School of Music, New York and composition studies under Krenek, Castelnuovo-Tedesco and Sendrey; joined music dept. of Universal Int. studios 1952; film scores include Breakfast at Tiffany's, The Pink Panther, Days of Wine and Roses, Two for the Road, "10", Victor/Victoria, Santa Claus—The Movie, The Glass Menagerie, Sunset; composed music for television series Peter Gunn 1957, Mr Lucky 1960; has conducted numerous concerts of his music with the world's leading orchestras; recipient of four Acad. Awards (Oscars), 20 Grammy Awards; four hon. doctorates from U.S. univs. *Leisure interests:* photography, skiing. *Address:* 9229 Sunset Boulevard, Suite 304, Los Angeles, Calif. 90069, U.S.A.

MANCUSO, Frank G.; American film industry executive; m. Fay Mancuso; one s. one d.; joined Paramount Pictures Corpn., Buffalo, N.Y. 1962; Vice-Pres. and Gen. Sales Man. Paramount Pictures Corpn. of Canada Ltd., Toronto 1970-72, Pres. and subsequently head of Paramount's Western Div., Los Angeles, U.S.A. 1972-76; Vice-Pres., Gen. Sales Man. Paramount's Motion Picture Div., New York 1976-78, Sr. Vice-Pres. 1978-79, Exec. Vice-Pres. in charge of Distribution and Marketing 1979-80; Pres. Paramount Distribution 1980-83; Pres. Motion Picture Group of Paramount Pictures Corpn. 1983-84; Chair. and C.E.O. Paramount Pictures Corpn. 1984-; Vice-Pres. Variety Clubs Int. and of Motion Picture Pioneers; Chair. of Bd. of Will Rogers Memorial Fund; Sherrill G. Corwin Human Relations Award, American Jewish Cttee. 1985. *Address:* Paramount Pictures Corporation, 1 Gulf & Western Plaza, New York, N.Y. 10023; 5555 Melrose Avenue, Los Angeles, Calif. 90038, U.S.A.

MANDEL, Marvin; American former state governor; b. 19 April 1920, Baltimore, Md.; s. of late Harry Mandel and of Rebecca Cohen; m. 1st Barbara Oberfeld 1941 (divorced 1974), one s. one d.; m. 2nd Jeanne Blackistone Dorsey 1974; ed. Baltimore City Coll. and Univ. of Maryland; Army Service 1942–44; subsequently partner in law firm Mandel, Gilbert, Rocklin and Franklin until 1969; mem. Md. House of Delegates 1952–69, Speaker 1963–69; Gov. of Maryland 1969–77; mem. Baltimore, Md. and American Bar Asscns.; Hon. LL.D. (Univ. of Md. and Towson State Coll.); Herbert Lehman Ethics Award 1969, 1970 and other honours; found guilty of political corruption Aug. 1977; sentenced to four years' imprisonment Oct 1977; in prison 1980–81; Democrat. *Leisure interests:* pipe-collecting, hunting, sport. *Address:* c/o State Capitol, Annapolis, Md., U.S.A.

MANDELA, Nelson Rolihlahla; South African lawyer and politician; b. 1918, Umtata, Transkei; m. Winnie Mandela (q.v.); ed. Univ. Coll. of Fort Hare, Univ. of the Witwatersrand; s. of Chief of Tembu tribe; legal practice, Johannesburg 1952; Nat. organizer African Nat. Congress (ANC); on trial for treason 1956–61 (acquitted 1961); arrested 1962, sentenced to five years' imprisonment Nov. 1962; on trial for further charges 1963–64, sentenced to life imprisonment June 1964; Hon. LL.D. (Nat. Univ. of Lesotho) 1979; Jawaharlal Nehru Award (India) 1979, Bruno Kreisky Prize for Human Rights 1981, Freedom of City of Glasgow 1981, Hon. Citizen of Rome 1983, Simon Bolivar Int. Prize (UNESCO) 1983; Hon. LL.D. (City Coll. of City Univ. of New York) 1983, (Lancaster) 1984, (Strathclyde) 1985, (Calcutta) 1986; Third World Prize 1985, Sakharov Prize 1988, Freeman of Dublin 1988. *Publication:* No Easy Walk to Freedom 1965. *Address:* Pollsmoor Prison, Cape Town, South Africa.

MANDELA, (Nomzano) Winnie; South African politician; b. 1934, Bizana, Pondoland, Transkei; m. Nelson Mandela (q.v.) 1958; active mem. of African Nat. Congress (ANC) until its banning in 1960; has campaigned constantly on behalf of her husband gaoled for life for political activities since 1964; held in solitary confinement 1969–70; named a 'banned person' by S. African authorities 1976; Third World Prize 1985. *Address:* Soweto, Transvaal, South Africa.

MANDELBAUM, Moshe Y., PH.D.; Israeli economist and banker; b. 3 March 1933, Jerusalem; s. of Yechiel Mandelbaum and Debora Mandelbaum; m. Sara Salomon 1957; two s. one d.; ed. Mizrahi Teachers' Coll., Jerusalem, Hebrew Univ. and Vanderbilt Univ., Nashville, Tenn.; Price Commr. and Deputy Dir.-Gen. Ministry of Commerce and Industry 1971–74, Dir.-Gen. 1974–77; Vice-Chair. Industrial Devt. Bank of Israel Ltd. 1978–81; fmr. Chair. Israel Foreign Trade Risk Insurance Corpn., Diamond Inst., Public Price Cttee.; mem. Foreign Affairs Advisory Council, Jerusalem Town Council; Sr. Lecturer, Dept. of Econs., Bar-Ilan Univ.; Deputy Gov. Bank of Israel 1981–82, Gov. 1982–86. *Publications:* numerous articles in economic journals. *Address:* Miltel, 9A Rothchild Avenue, Tel Aviv, Israel.

MANDELSTAM, Stanley, PH.D., F.R.S.; British professor of physics; b. 12 Dec. 1928, Johannesburg, S. Africa; s. of Boris Mandelstam and Beatrice née Liknaitzky; ed. Univs. of Witwatersrand, Cambridge and Birmingham; Boese Postdoctoral Fellow, Columbia Univ., U.S.A. 1957–58; Asst. Research Physicist, Univ. of Calif. (Berkeley) 1958–60; Prof. of Math. Physics, Univ. of Birmingham 1960–63; Prof. of Physics, Univ. of Calif. (Berkeley) 1963–; Prof. Associé. Univ. de Paris Sud 1979–80, 1984–85. *Publications:* papers on theoretical particle physics. *Leisure interests:* reading, music. *Address:* Department of Physics, University of California, Berkeley, Calif. 94720 (Office); 1800 Spruce Street, Berkeley, Calif. 94720, U.S.A. (Home). *Telephone:* (415) 642-5237 (Office); (415) 540-5318 (Home).

MANDIL, Claude; French engineer, administrative official and business executive; b. 9 Jan. 1942, Lyons; s. of Léon Mandil and Renée née Mizraki; m. Annick Goubelle 1966; five s.; ed. Lycée Pasteur de Neuilly and Ecole Polytechnique; Mining Engineer, Metz 1967–71, Rennes 1971–74; Délégation à l'Aménagement du Territoire et à l'Action régionale (DATAR) 1974–77; Inter-dept. Dir. and Regional Del. Agence nat. de Valorisation de la Recherche, Anvar 1978–81; Tech. Adviser to Prime Minister 1981–82; Dir.-Gen. Inst. of Industrial Devt. (IDI) 1983, Pres. 1984–; Dir. Cie. Boussac-Saint-Frères, Régie nat. des Usines Renault 1983–; Chevalier, Ordre nat. du Mérite. *Leisure interest:* music. *Address:* 4 rue Ancelle, 92200 Neuilly-sur-Seine (Office); 39 boulevard de la Reine, 78000 Versailles, France.

MANDUCA, John A.; Maltese journalist and diplomatist; b. 14 Aug. 1927, Notabile; s. of Capt. Philip dei Conti Manduca and Emma (née Pullicino) Manduca; m. Sylvia Parnis 1954; two s. two d.; ed. St. Edward's Coll.; joined Allied Malta Newspapers Ltd. 1945, Deputy Ed. 1953; Malta corresp. The Daily Telegraph and Sunday Telegraph (London) 1946–62; attached to BBC 1963, Chief Exec., Malta Broadcasting Authority 1963–68; Dir. and Man. Malta TV Service Ltd. 1968; Man. Dir. Rediffusion Group of Cos. in Malta 1971–76; Chair. Tourist Projects Ltd. 1976–; Dir.-Gen. Confed. of Pvt. Enterprises 1983–87; High Commr. for Malta in London 1987–; Amb. to Norway, Sweden and Denmark 1988–. *Publications:* Tourist Guide to Malta and Gozo, Connoisseur's Guide to City of Mdina, Tourist Guide to Harbour Cruises, Gen. Ed. Malta Who's Who 1987, and others. *Leisure interests:* melitensia, current affairs, reading. *Address:* Malta High Commission, 16 Kensington Square, London, W8 5HH, England; Beaulieu,

Bastion Square, Notabile (Mdina), Malta (Home). *Telephone:* 01-938 1712 (Office); 674009 (Home).

MÁNDY, Iván; Hungarian writer; b. 23 Dec. 1918, Budapest; s. of Gyula Mándy and Ilona Alfay; m. Dr. Judit Simon; sport reporter then full-time writer 1939–; Baumgarten Prize 1948, József Attila Prize 1969, Déry Prize 1986, Kossuth Prize 1988. *Works include:* novels and short novels: Csőszház (Park keeper's shelter) 1943, Franciakulcs (Screw spanner) 1948, A huszonegyedik utca (Twentyfirst street) 1949, Tabulya feleségei (Tabulya's wives) 1959, A pálya szélén (On the side line) 1963, Mi van Verával? (What about Vera?) 1970, Egy ember álma (Someone's dream) 1971, Mi az, Öreg? (What's on Old Man?) 1972, Magukra maradtak (Things abandoned) 1986; short stories: Vendégek a palackban (Guests in the bottle) 1949, Idegen szobák (Strange rooms) 1957, Az ördög konyhája (The devil's kitchen) 1965, Régi idők mozija (Movie of yore) 1967, Egyérintő (Touch and run) 1969, Előadók, társszerzők (Speakers, co-authors) 1973, Fél hat felé (About five thirty) 1974, Zsámboky mozija (Zsámboky's movie) 1975, Átkelés (Traversing) 1984, Tájak, az én tájaim (Scenes, my own scenes) 1985; juvenile books: Egy festő ifjúsága (A painter's young days) 1955, Csutak szinre lép (Csutak enters) 1957, Csutak és a szürke ló (Csutak and the grey horse) 1959, Csutak a mikrofón előtt (Csutak and the microphone) 1961, A locsolókocsi (The sprinkling cart) 1964, A pincér éjszakája (The waiter's night) 1977; *film scripts:* Sziget a szárazföldön (Isle on land), Lányarcok a tükörben (Girls' faces in the mirror), Régi idők focija (Football of yore), Diákszerelem (Puppy love); radio play: Ha köztünk vagy, Holman Endre (Endre Holman, are you with us?). *Leisure interest:* watching football. *Address:* 1054 Budapest, Aulich utca 7, Hungary. *Telephone:* 325-696.

MANEKSHAW, Field-Marshal Sam Hormuzji Framji Jamshedji, M.C.; Indian army officer; b. 3 April 1914, Amritsar; s. of Dr. H. F. J. Manekshaw and Mrs. H. F. J. Manekshaw; m. Silloo Manekshaw 1939; two d.; ed. Sherwood Coll., Nainital, Indian Mil. Acad., Dehra Dun; commissioned 1934; active service in Waziristan, N.W. Frontier Provs. 1940–41; W.W.II Burma 1942 wounded in action, awarded immediate Mil. Cross; graduated Staff Coll., Quetta 1943; served as Brigade Maj. Razmak Brigade, Waziristan 1943–44; Instructor Staff Coll., Quetta 1944; active service in Burma and French Indo-China 1945–46; Gen. Staff Officer Grade I, Mil. Operations Directorate, Army H.Q. 1946–47, Brig. 1947; Dir. Mil. Operations 1948–52; Commdr. 167 Infantry Brigade 1952–54; Col. 8th Gurkha Rifles 1953–; Dir. Mil. Training 1954–55; Commdr. Infantry School, Mhow 1955–56; attended Imperial Defence Coll., London 1957; promoted Maj.-Gen. and appointed G.O.C. 26 Infantry Div. in Jammu and Kashmir 1957; Commdt. Defence Services Staff Coll., Wellington 1958–62; G.O.C. IV Corps. 1962–63; G.O.C.-in-C. Western Command 1963–64, Eastern Command 1964–69; Chief of the Army Staff 1969–73; promoted Field-Marshal Jan. 1973; masterminded Pakistan's defeat in Indo-Pakistan War 1971; Gen. of Nepalese Army 1970; Chair. of six cos.; dir. of ten cos.; awarded Padma Bhushan 1967, Padma Vibhushan 1971, U.S. Order of Merit 1970. *Leisure interests:* fishing, gardening, music. *Address:* Stavka Springfield, Coonor, The Nilgiris, South India.

MĂNESCU, Corneliu; Romanian politician and diplomatist (retd.); b. 8 Feb. 1916, Ploieşti, Romania; s. of Constantin and Elena Mănescu; m. Dana Dobrescu 1950; one d.; ed. Law Coll., Bucharest; mem. Democratic Students Front, Romanian CP 1936–; Deputy Minister of Armed Forces 1948–55; Deputy Chair. State Planning Cttee. 1955–60; Chief of Political Dept. Ministry of Foreign Affairs 1960; Amb. to Hungary 1960–61; Minister of Foreign Affairs 1961–72; mem. Cen. Cttee. of the Romanian CP 1965–84; Deputy to Grand Nat. Ass. 1965–80; Head of Romanian Del. to UN Gen. Assembly 1961–72; Pres. 22nd Session of UN Gen. Assembly 1967–68; Pres. of Romanian Interparl. Group 1973–77; Vice-Pres. of Nat. Council of Socialist Unity Front 1973–77; Chair. Grand Nat. Ass. Comm. for Foreign Policy and Int. Co-operation 1973–77; Amb. to France 1977–82; Romanian Perm. Del. to UNESCO 1979–82; Star of Romania (1st Class), Grand Officier, Légion d'honneur, and other Romanian and foreign decorations. *Address:* Şos Kiselef, No. 22, Bucharest, Romania.

MĂNESCU, Manea; Romanian university professor, economist and politician; b. 9 Aug. 1916, Brăila; m. Maria Munteanu; one s.; Gen. Dir. Cen. Statistical Office 1951–55; Minister for Finance 1955–57; Chair. Labour and Wages State Cttee. and First Vice-Chair. of State Planning Cttee. 1957–68; mem. Union of Communist Youth 1932, Romanian Communist Party (RCP) 1936–, mem. Cen. Cttee. RCP 1960–79, 1982–, Sec. 1965–72; Alt. mem. Exec. Political Cttee. 1966–68, mem. 1968–79, 1982–; mem. Perm. Praesidium 1971–74; mem. Standing Exec. Cttee. 1974–83; mem. Grand Nat. Assembly 1961–80, 1982–; Chair. Econ. and Financial Standing Comm. 1961–69; Chair. Econ. Council 1968–72; Chair. State Planning Cttee. 1972–74; Pres. Nat. Council of Agric. 1976–79, Nat. Cttee. of Sociology; Vice-Pres. State Council 1969–72, 1982–; Vice-Chair. Council of Ministers 1972–74, Chair. (Prime Minister) 1974–79; Vice-Pres. Supreme Council for Econ. and Social Devt. 1974–79 and 1982–87, First Vice-Pres. 1987–; Vice-Pres. Socialist Unity Front 1974–80; Corresp. mem. Romanian Acad. 1955–74, mem. 1974–, Pres. Bd. of Economy and Sociology, Pres. Cybernetics Comm.; mem. Acad. of Social and Political Sciences 1970, World Acad. for Cybernetics, Int. Inst. of Statistics, The Hague, Statistical Soc. of Paris; Hero of Socialist Labour 1971, Order of Victory of Socialism 1974,

Légion d'honneur. *Publications:* Economic Computation 1963, Directions and Trends in Economic Cybernetics 1968, Mathematical Modelling in Economics 1970, Mathematical Programming in the Oil Industry 1970, The Socio-Economic Progress of Romania 1971, The Social Present and Future of Romania 1974, Romania in the Seventies 1976, Romania's National Wealth 1977, Economic Cybernetics 1980, Cybernetics—Applications in Economy 1982, National Wealth 1983, Applied Cybernetics for the Economic and Social Development of the Country 1983, National Income 1984, The Computerization and Simulation of the Industrial Process in the Oil Industry 1986, Cybernetics and the technico-scientific revolution 1988. *Leisure interest:* painting. *Address:* Str. Anton Cehov 8, Bucharest Sector 1, Romania.

MANESSIER, Alfred; French artist; b. 5 Dec. 1911, Saint-Ouen; s. of Nestor and Blanche (née Tellier) Manessier; m. Thérèse Simonnet 1938; one s. one d.; ed. Lycée d'Amiens and Paris Schools of Fine Art; has designed and executed stained glass for churches at Bresseux (Jura), Arles, Basel, etc.; rep. at numerous exhbns., including the Brussels Int. Exhbn. 1958, Dunn Int. Exhbn., London 1963; Caracas Int. Painting Prize, Carnegie Prize 1955, Venice Biennale Prize 1962; Chevalier, Légion d'honneur, Officier, Ordre nat. du Mérite, Officier des Arts et des Lettres. *Address:* rue du Haut-Martin, Emance, 78120 Rambouillet, France.

MANGAKIS, Georgios Alexandros; Greek lawyer and politician; b. 1922; Lecturer in Penal Law, Univ. of Athens 1955–69; political prisoner 1969–72; lecturer in Criminal Law, Univ. of Heidelberg 1972–74; Minister of Public Works 1974; Deputy for Athens, EKND Party 1974–77; supporter of Pasok 1978–; Minister of Justice 1982–85, 1985–86, of Health and Welfare July-Sept. 1987. *Address:* c/o Ministry of Health and Welfare, Odos Zalokosta 10, Athens, Greece.

MANGELSDORF, Paul C., M.S., SC.D.; American scientist; b. 20 July 1899, Atchison, Kan.; s. of August and Mary Brune Mangelsdorf; m. Helen Parker 1923; two s.; ed. Kansas State Coll. and Harvard Univ.; Asst. Geneticist, Conn. Agricultural Experimental Station 1921–26; Agronomist, Texas Agricultural Experimental Station 1927–40, Asst. Dir. 1936–40, Vice-Dir. 1940; Asst. Dir. Botanical Museum, Harvard Univ. 1940–45, Dir. 1945–67, Prof. of Econ. Botany 1940–67, Fisher Prof. of Natural History 1962–68, Emer. Prof. 1968–; Consultant in Agric., Rockefeller Foundation 1941–54 and periodically since; lecturer in Botany, Univ. of N.C. 1968–; mem. American Philosophical Soc., N.A.S.; Hon. D.Sc. (Park Coll.) 1960, (Saint Benedict's Coll.) 1965, Hon. LL.D. (Kansas State). *Publications:* Genetics and Morphology of some Endosperm Characters in Maize 1926, Origin of Indian Corn and its Relatives (with R. G. Reeves) 1939, Races of Maize in Mexico (with E. J. Wellhausen et al.) 1951, Races of Maize in Columbia (with L. M. Roberts et al.) 1957, Races of Maize in Central America (with E. J. Wellhausen et al.) 1957, Races of Maize in Peru (with Alexander Grobman et al.) 1961, Campaigns against Hunger (with E. C. Stakman and R. Bradfield) 1967, Corn, Its Origins, Evolution and Improvement 1974 and over 100 articles. *Address:* 510 Caswell Road, Chapel Hill, N.C. 27514, U.S.A. (Home).

MANGLA, Professor P. B.; Indian professor of library and information science; b. 5 July 1936, India; s. of Radha Krishan; m. Raj Mangla 1961; one s. one d.; ed. Univ. of Delhi, Columbia Univ., New York, London; Prof. and Head of Dept. of Library Sciences, Univ. of Tabriz, Iran 1970–72, Visiting Prof. 1974–75; UNESCO expert, Guyana 1978–79; Prof. and Head of Dept. of Library and Information Sciences, Univ. of Delhi 1972–, Dean Faculty of Arts 1976–78, 1984–87, Chair. Bd. of Research Studies 1979, various other admin. posts in Delhi and numerous other univs. 1972–; Chair. Manpower Devt. Cttee. of Nat. Information System in Science and Tech. 1977–; Sr. Vice-Pres. and founder-mem. Indian Asscn. of Academic Librarians 1981–83; mem. Bd. Int. Fed. of Library Asscns. and Insts. 1983– (Vice-Pres. 1987–(89)), Inst. of Information Scientists; Nat. Prof. of the U.G.C. 1984–86; Hon. Fellow Indian Library Asscn.; awarded Int. Library Movt. Award (India) 1984. *Publications:* author/ed. of numerous books and specialist reviews in India and overseas including Journal of Library and Information Science, Education for Information, Amsterdam, Review in Library and Information Science, U.S.A., LIBRI (Copenhagen); several memorial lectures. *Leisure interests:* gardening, outdoor pursuits. *Address:* 19/4 Cavalry Lines, Delhi University Campus, Delhi 110007, India. *Telephone:* 2523752 (home).

MANGLAPUS, Raul S.; Philippines lawyer and politician; b. 20 Oct. 1918, Manila; s. of Valentin Manglapus and Justina Sevilla; m. Pacita Lao 1948; five c.; ed. Ateneo de Manila, Univ. of Santo Tomas and Georgetown Univ.; wartime broadcaster; prisoner-of-war 1942–44; Chief Broadcasting Div. Office of Pres. Sergio Osmena 1945–46; Prof. of Constitutional Law, Ateneo de Manila 1948–54; Under-Sec. of Foreign Affairs 1954–57; Sec. for Foreign Affairs 1957; f. Party for Philippine Progress (with M. P. Manahan) 1957, Grand Alliance Party 1959; coalesced with Liberal Party 1961; elected Senator 1961–67; founded Christian Social Movt. 1968; elected Del. to Constitutional Convention 1970, leader of progressive opposition in Convention 1971–72; granted political asylum in U.S.A. 1973; founded Movt. for a Free Philippines 1973; Ford Foundation Fellowship, Visiting Prof. and Sr. Research Assoc. Cornell Univ. 1973–74; Sr. Assoc. Carnegie Endowment for Int. Peace, Washington, D.C. 1974–75; Adjunct Prof. for Int. Relations, School of Int. Service, American Univ. 1977–80; lecturer in Int. Relations, Labour Studies Program, D.C. Consortium of Univs. 1978; Vice-Pres. Christian Democrats Int. 1980; Pres. Democracy Int. (org. of exiles in U.S.A.) 1983; Fellow, Harvard Univ. 1985; returned to Philippines 1986; fmr. Vice-Pres. Int. Center for Devt. Policy, Washington D.C.; Sec. for Foreign Affairs Oct. 1987–; Senator of the Philippines 1987–; recipient of several grants, awards and decorations. *Publications:* five books and numerous articles in major U.S. newspapers and magazines. *Address:* Department of Foreign Affairs, Manila, Philippines.

MANGOPE, Chief Lucas Manyane: South African (Bophuthatswana) tribal chief and politician; b. 27 Dec. 1923, Motswedi, Zweerust; s. of Manyane and Semakaleng Mangope; m. Leah Tscholofelo Dolo 1950; four s. three d.; ed. St. Peter's Coll. and Bethel Coll.; worked in the Dept. of Bantu Admin. and Devt., later taught at Motswedi; succeeded his father as Chief of the Bahurutshe-Boo-Manyane Sept. 1959; Vice-Chair. Tswana Territorial Authority 1961–68, Chief Councillor, Exec. Council 1968–72; Chief Minister of Bophuthatswana 1972–77; fmr. Prime Minister, Minister of Finance, Minister of Law and Order; Pres. Dec. 1977–. *Leisure interests:* soccer, tennis, choral music. *Address:* Department of the Presidency, Private Bag X2005, Mafikeng, Bophuthatswana, South Africa. *Telephone:* (01401) 29-2010.

MANGWAZU, Timon Sam, M.A.; Malawi diplomatist; b. 12 Oct. 1933, Kasungu; s. of Sam Isaac Mangwazu and Malita Nyankhata; m. Nelly Kathewera 1958; three s. three d.; ed. Inyati Boys' Inst. (London Missionary Soc.) Bulawayo, Tegwani Methodist Secondary School, Plumtree, Ruskin Coll., and Brasenose Coll. Oxford; Nyasaland Civil Service 1956; Sec.-Gen. Nyasaland African Civil Servants Asscn. 1961; Asst. Registrar of Trade Unions 1963; First Sec. British Embassy in Vienna 1964; Amb. of Malawi to German Fed. Repub., later accred. to Norway, Sweden, Denmark, Netherlands, Belgium, Switzerland, Austria 1964–67; Malawi High Commr. in U.K. 1967–69, concurrently Amb. to Holy See, Portugal, Netherlands and Belgium; reading Econs. and Politics at Brasenose Coll., Oxford 1969–72; Amb. to EEC, Belgium and the Netherlands 1973–78; Chair. Nat. Bank of Malawi 1980–86; Perm. Rep. to UN 1986–; Deputy Man. Dir. Press Group of Cos. 1978–80, Man. Dir. Jan.-Nov. 1980; Group Man. Dir. Nov. 1980; Malawi Independence Medal, Malawi Repub. Medal, Knight Commdr. Cross of Order of Merit of Fed. Repub. of Germany. *Leisure interest:* angling. *Address:* Permanent Mission of Malawi to the United Nations, 767 Third Avenue, New York, N.Y. 10017, U.S.A.; Press (Holdings) Ltd., P.O. Box 1227, Blantyre, Malawi.

MANIGAT, Leslie; Haitian politician and academic; b. 16 Aug. 1930, Port-au-Prince; m. 2nd Mirlande Manigat 1970; f. School of Int. Studies at Univ. of Haiti, first Dir.; fmr. Research Assoc. Johns Hopkins Univ., Washington; fmr. Prof. Inst. of Political Studies, Paris; then with Univ. of West Indies, Trinidad and Tobago; with Simon Bolivar Univ., Caracas 1978; returned from 23 years in exile 1986; Pres. of Haiti Jan. 1988, overthrown June 1988.

MANIKFAN, Hussein; Maldivian diplomatist; b. 16 June 1936; m.; six c.; served in civil service, Ministry of Educ., Dept. of Information, Ministry of Finance and Office of the Pres. of the Repub. 1953–58; Sec. Ministry of Trust and Public Endowment 1958; teacher, Ministry of Educ. 1959; served in Ministry of Home Affairs, Dept. of Posts and Telecommunications and at Pres.'s Official Residence 1959–74; Sec. Dept. of Electricity 1974; mem. Maldives Parl. 1970–; Under-Sec. Ministry of Transport 1978; Dir. Unit, Male' Int. Airport 1978; Man. Dir. Govt. Fishing Corpn. 1982; Deputy Minister of Trade and Industries 1982–88; Perm. Rep. to UN March 1988–. *Address:* Permanent Mission of the Republic of Maldives to the United Nations, 820 Second Avenue, Suite 800c, New York, N.Y. 10017, U.S.A. *Telephone:* (212) 599-6195.

MANILOW, Barry; American singer, composer; b. 17 June 1949, New York; s. of Harold and Edna Manilow; ed. New York Coll. Music; worked in mailroom, CBS; film ed. WCBS-TV; Dir. Music Ed Sullivan's Pilots; Dir. Music, Conductor and Producer for Bette Midler; singer and composer; appeared in TV film Copacabana 1985; *songs include:* Mandy, I Write the Songs, At the Copa, Looks Like We Made It, Can't Smile Without You, Even Now, Could it be Magic, and others; Producer of Year 1975; Ruby Award, After Dark magazine 1976; Photoplay Gold Medal Award 1976; Tony Award (jt.) 1977. *Publication:* Sweet Life: Adventures on the Way to Paradise 1987. *Address:* c/o International Creative Management, 40 West 57th Street, New York, N.Y. 10019, U.S.A.

MANIUSIS, Iuozas (see Manushis).

MANKIEWICZ, Frank, M.A., LL.B.; American public affairs executive; b. 16 May 1924, New York; s. of Herman J. and Sara Mankiewicz; m. Holly Mankiewicz 1952 (divorced); two s.; m. 2nd Patricia O'Brien 1988; ed. Columbia Univ. and Univ. of Calif., Berkeley; mem. Calif. Bar; practised as lawyer, Los Angeles 1955–61; served with Peace Corps as Country Dir., Lima, Peru and later as Regional Dir. for Latin America; Press Sec. to late Senator Robert F. Kennedy 1966–68; syndicated columnist (with Tom Braden), Washington and co-presenter, nightly newscast on CBS television affiliate 1968–71; Campaign Dir. presidential campaign of George McGovern 1972; Pres. Nat. Public Radio 1977–83; Exec. Vice-Pres. Gray and Co. (now Hill and Knowlton) 1983–; Univ. of Calif. (L.A.) Public Service Award; Hon. D.H.L. (Lincoln Univ.). *Publications:* Perfectly Clear: Nixon from Whittier to Watergate 1973, U.S. *v.* Richard Nixon: The Final Crisis 1975, With Fidel: A Portrait of Castro and Cuba 1975, Remote Control: Television and the Manipulation of American Life 1978. *Leisure interests:* baseball, literature, U.S. political history. *Address:* Hill and Knowlton, 901 31st Street, N.W., Washington, D.C. 20007, U.S.A. *Telephone:* (202) 333-7400.

MANKIEWICZ, Joseph Leo, B.A.; American film writer, director and producer; b. 11 Feb. 1909, Wilkes-Barre, Pa.; s. of Frank and Johanna Blumenau Mankiewicz; m. 2nd Rosa Stradner 1939 (died 1958), 3rd Rosemary Matthews 1962; two s. one d.; one s. by previous marriage; ed. Columbia Univ.; Asst. Corresp. in Berlin for Chicago Tribune; writer, Paramount Pictures 1929-33; Founding mem. and Sec. Screen Writers' Guild 1933; writer and producer, M.G.M. 1933-43; writer, director and producer, Twentieth-Century Fox 1943-51; Pres. Screen Directors' Guild 1950; directed La Bohème at Metropolitan Opera House 1952; Formed own co., Figaro Inc., 1953, dissolved, 1961; Fellow, Yale Univ. 1979-; Acad. of Motion Picture Arts and Sciences Award (Oscar) best screen-play and director 1949 and 1950; British Film Acad. Award and New York Film Critics' Award (for All About Eve) 1951; Commdr., Order of Merit from Italian Republic for contribution to the Arts, Erasmus Award, Rotterdam 1984, D. W. Griffith Award for lifetime achievement, Dirs. Guild of America 1986, Alexander Hamilton Medal, Columbia Coll., New York 1986, Leone d'Oro (Golden Lion) Award, Venice Film Festival 1987. *Films include:* Script: Skippy, Million Dollar Legs 1932, If I Had a Million, Manhattan Melodrama, Forsaking All Others 1934; Produced: Fury 1936, Three Comrades 1937, Huckleberry Finn 1939, The Philadelphia Story 1940, Woman of the Year 1942, The Keys of the Kingdom; Script and Dir.: Dragonwyck 1946, The Late George Apley 1947, The Ghost and Mrs. Muir 1947, Escape, A Letter to Three Wives 1948 (Acad. Award for script and direction 1949), No Way Out 1950, All About Eve (Acad. Award for script and direction) 1950, People Will Talk 1951, Julius Caesar 1953, The Barefoot Contessa 1954, Guys and Dolls 1955, The Quiet American (also prod.) 1957, Cleopatra 1963, The Honey Pot 1967, There Was a Crooked Man 1970; Dir.: House of Strangers 1949, Five Fingers 1952, Suddenly Last Summer 1959, Sleuth 1972. *Address:* 491 Guard Hill Road, RFD 1, Bedford, N.Y. 10506, U.S.A.

MANKOWITZ, Wolf, M.A.; British writer and theatrical producer; b. 7 Nov. 1924, Bethnal Green, London; s. of Solomon Mankowitz and Rebecca Brick; m. Ann Margaret Seligmann 1944; four s.; ed. East Ham Grammar School, and Downing Coll., Cambridge; extensive work in journalism, radio, television and films and as a theatrical producer; is also an expert in English Ceramics; Hon. Consul to the Repub. of Panama in Dublin 1971; Adjunct Prof. of English, Univ. of New Mexico 1982-86, Adjunct Prof. of Theatre Arts 1987-88. *Films:* Make me an Offer 1954, A Kid for Two Farthings 1954, The Bespoke Overcoat 1955 (Venice Film Festival Award, British Film Acad. Award, Hollywood Oscar), Expresso Bongo 1960, The Millionairess 1960, The Long and the Short and the Tall 1961, The Day the Earth Caught Fire 1961 (British Film Acad. Award), Waltz of the Toreadors 1962, Where the Spies are 1965, Casino Royale 1967, The Assassination Bureau 1969, Bloomfield (screenplay and production) 1970, Black Beauty 1971, Treasure Island 1972, The Hebrew Lesson (wrote and directed, Critics' Prize, Cork Int. Film Festival) 1972, The Hireling (Grand Prix, Cannes) 1973, Almonds and Raisins 1984. *Plays:* The Boychik 1954, The Bespoke Overcoat 1955, The Mighty Hunter, Expresso Bongo (musical) 1958, Make Me an Offer (musical) 1959, Belle (musical) 1961, Pickwick (musical) 1963, Passion Flower Hotel (musical) 1965, The Samson Riddle 1972, The Hebrew Lesson 1978, Samson and Delilah 1978, Casanova's Last Stand 1980, Iron Butterflies 1980, The Devil in Texas 1984. *Television includes:* Conflict series, East End, West End series, The Killing Stones play-cycle 1958, A Cure for Tin Ear 1965, The Battersea Miracle 1966, Dickens of London series 1976. *Publications:* Novels: Make Me an Offer 1952, A Kid for Two Farthings 1953, Laugh till You Cry 1955, My Old Man's a Dustman 1956, Cockatrice 1963, The Biggest Pig in Barbados 1965, Penguin Wolf Mankowitz 1967, Raspberry Reich 1978, ¡Abracadabra! 1980, The Devil in Texas 1984, Gioconda 1987, The Magic Cabinet of Prof. Smucker 1988; Short stories: The Mendelman Fire 1957, The Blue Arabian Nights 1972, The Day of the Women and the Night of the Men 1975; Plays: The Bespoke Overcoat and Other Plays 1955, Expresso Bongo 1961, The Samson Riddle 1972; Histories: The Portland Vase 1953, Wedgwood 1953, An Encyclopedia of English Pottery and Porcelain 1957, Dickens of London (TV script also) 1976; Biography: The Extraordinary Mr. Poe 1978, Mazeppa 1981; also The Wolf Mankowitz Reader (collection) 1961. *Leisure interests:* alternative living styles, sleeping. *Address:* Bridge House, Ahakista, Co. Cork, Ireland. *Telephone:* Kilcrohane 11.

MANLEY, Albert Leslie; South African diplomatist; b. 1945, Cape Town; m.; two s.; ed. Univ. of Orange Free State; entered Dept. of Foreign Affairs 1969, Desk Officer for Middle E. 1974-76, Planning Section of Ministry, Pretoria and Cape Town 1981-82, other posts 1982-87; Vice-Consul in Lourenco Marques (now Maputo) 1970-74; Counsellor for Political Affairs at Embassy, London 1977-81; Perm. Rep. to UN, New York 1987-88, Geneva 1988-. *Address:* Permanent Mission of South Africa to United Nations, 65 rue du Rhone, Geneva 1204, Switzerland.

MANLEY, Michael Norman, B.SC.ECON.; Jamaican politician, journalist and trade unionist; b. 10 Dec. 1923, Kingston; s. of the late Norman W.

Manley, Q.C. (Prime Minister of Jamaica, 1955-62), and Edna Swithenbank Manley; m. Beverley Anderson 1972; two s. three d.; ed. Jamaica Coll. and L.S.E.; with BBC 1950-51; Assoc. Ed., Public Opinion 1952-53; Sugar Supervisor, Nat. Workers' Union 1953-54, Island Supervisor and First Vice-Pres. 1955-84, Pres. 1984-; positions in numerous other unions and Labour cttees.; mem. Senate 1962-67; mem. House of Reps. for Cen. Kingston 1967-83; Leader of People's Nat. Party Feb. 1969-, mem. Exec. 1952-, Leader of the Parl. Opposition 1969-72, 1980-89; Prime Minister March 1972-80, Feb. 1989-; Minister of External Affairs 1972-75, of Econ. Affairs 1972-75, of Defence 1972-80, of Youth and Community Devt. 1974-75, of Nat. Mobilization and Human Resources Devt. 1977-79, of Information, Broadcasting and Culture 1978-80, of Agric. 1979-80; Jamaican Rep. on Exec. Council Caribbean Congress of Labour; Hon. Dr. of Laws (Morehouse Coll., Atlanta) 1973; UN Special Award for contrib. to struggle against Apartheid 1978; Joliot Curie Medal, World Peace Council 1979; Order of the Liberator (Venezuela) 1973, Order of Mexican Eagle 1975, Order of Jose Marti (Cuba) 1976. *Publications:* Politics of Change 1974, A Voice at the Workplace 1975, Search for Solutions 1976, Jamaica: Struggle in the Periphery 1982, A History of West Indies Cricket 1988. *Leisure interests:* reading, music, gardening, boxing, tennis, cricket. *Address:* People's National Party, 89 Old Hope Road, Kingston 6, Jamaica.

MANN, Frederick (Francis) Alexander, C.B.E., LL.D., D.JUR., F.B.A.; British lawyer; b. 11 Aug. 1907; s. of Richard and Ida (née Oppenheim) Mann; m. Eleonore Ehrlich 1933 (died 1980); one s. two d.; ed. Univs. of Geneva, Munich, Berlin and London; Asst. Faculty of Law, Univ. of Berlin 1929-33; int. law consultant, London 1933-46; solicitor 1946; mem. Legal Div. Allied Control Council (British Element), Berlin 1946; mem. Lord Chancellor's Standing Cttee. for Reform of Private Int. Law 1952-64; mem. numerous working parties of Law Comm.; Partner, Herbert Smith & Co. 1957-83, now consultant; Hon. Prof. of Law, Univ. of Bonn 1960-; has lectured at Acad. of Int. Law, The Hague at and numerous univs. in U.K., Europe and U.S.A.; mem. numerous cttees., etc.; mem. Inst. de Droit Int.; Hon. mem. American Soc. of Int. Law; Alexander von Humboldt Prize 1984; Grosses Bundesverdienstkreuz mit Stern; Hon. Dr.Jur. (Kiel) 1978, (Zürich) 1983. *Publications:* The Legal Aspect of Money 1938, Studies in International Law 1973, Foreign Affairs in English Courts 1986, Further Studies in International Law 1989; numerous articles on international law, the conflict of laws and monetary law in legal publications. *Leisure interests:* music, walking. *Address:* Flat 4, 56 Manchester Street, London, W.1, England. *Telephone:* 01-487 4735.

MANN, Golo, DR.PHIL.; Swiss historian of German origin; b. 27 March 1909, Munich, Germany; s. of Thomas and Katja (née Pringsheim) Mann; ed. Schloss Salem, Univs. of Munich, Berlin and Heidelberg; Reader in German Literature and History, Ecole Normale Supérieure, St. Cloud 1933-35, Rennes Univ. 1935-36; Ed. Mass und Wert, Zürich 1937-40; Prof. of Modern History Olivet Coll. (Mich.) 1942-43; U.S. Army 1943-46; Prof. of History Claremont Men's Coll. (Calif.) 1947-57; Visiting Prof. Münster Univ. 1958 and 1959; Prof. of History, Stuttgart Tech. Hochschule 1960-64; mem. American Acad. of Arts and Sciences 1977, Deutsche Akad. für Sprache und Dichtung, Darmstadt, Bayerische Akademie der Schönen Künste, Munich, Vereinigung deutscher Wissenschaften; Berlin Fontane Prize 1962, Mannheim Schillerpreis 1964, Büchner Prize 1968, Gottfried Keller-Preis 1969, Schiller-Gedächtnispreis, Stuttgart 1977, Bayerisches Maximiliansorden für Kunst, Goethe Prize 1985; Orden pour le Mérite. *Publications:* Friedrich von Gentz: Geschichte eines europäischen Staatsmannes 1947, Vom Geist Amerikas 1954, Aussenpolitik (with H. Pross, vol. in Fischer-Lexikon) 1958, Deutsche Geschichte des 19. und 20. Jahrhunderts 1958, Politische Entwicklung Europas und der Vereinigten Staaten 1815-1871 (in Propyläen Weltgeschichte) 1960, Geschichte und Geschichten 1961, Wallenstein (biography) 1971, Gentz 1973, Zwölf Versuche (essays), Wallenstein, Bilder zu seinem Leben 1973, Zeiten und Figuren (essays) 1979, Erinnerungen und Gedanken: Eine Jugend in Deutschland 1986; publisher of Propyläen Weltgeschichte 1960-64 and of Neue Rundschau 1962-. *Leisure interests:* hiking, dogs. *Address:* Alte Landstrasse 39, Kilchberg am Zürichsee, Switzerland. *Telephone:* Zürich 715-46-66.

MANN, Robert Wellesley, S.B., S.M., SC.D.; American professor of engineering design and biomedical research; b. 6 Oct. 1924, Brooklyn, New York; s. of Arthur Wellesley Mann and Helen Rieger Mann; m. Margaret Florencourt Mann 1950; one s. one d.; ed. M.I.T.; Draftsman Bell Telephone Labs. 1942-43, 1946-47; Technician (3rd) U.S. Army Signal Corps 1943-46; Research Engineer and Supervisor Design Div. Dynamic Analysis and Control Lab., M.I.T. 1951-56, Asst. Prof. of Mechanical Eng. 1953-58, Head Eng. Design Div. Dept. of Mechanical Eng. 1957-66, 1982-83, Assoc. Prof. of Mechanical Eng. 1958-63, Prof. 1963-70, Germeshausen Prof. 1970-72, Prof. of Eng. 1972-74, Whitaker Prof. of Biomedical Eng. 1974-; Prof. Harvard-M.I.T. Div. of Health Sciences and Tech. 1973-; Dir. Newman Lab. for Biomechanics and Human Rehabilitation 1975-; Dir. Bioeng. Programmes, Whitaker Coll., M.I.T. 1986-; mem. N.A.S., Nat. Acad. of Eng., Inst. of Medicine; Fellow American Acad. of Arts and Sciences, Inst. of Electrical and Electronics Engineers, American Soc. of Mechanical Engineers, A.A.A.S.; Gold Medal, American Soc. of Mechanical Engineers, Lissner Award for Outstanding Bioeng.; New England Award; Goldenson Award for Outstanding Scientific Research for the Physically Handicapped; James R. Killian Jr. Faculty Achievement Award, M.I.T. *Publications:*

over 200 professional publications and four patents on missile research, engineering design, computer-aided design, biomedical eng., human rehabilitation, synovial joint biomechanics and the etiology of osteoarthritis. *Leisure interests:* gardening, crafts, sailing, flying, tennis. *Address:* Massachusetts Institute of Technology, Room 3-144, 77 Massachusetts Avenue, Cambridge, Mass. 02139 (Office); 5 Pelham Road, Lexington, Mass. 02173, U.S.A. (Home). *Telephone:* (617) 253-2220 (Office); (617) 862-4318 (Home).

MANN, Thaddeus Robert Rudolph, C.B.E., M.D., SC.D., PH.D., F.R.S.; British physiologist and biochemist; b. 4 Dec. 1908, Lwów, Poland; s. of William Mann and Emilia (née Quest); m. Cecilia Lutwak, M.D., PH.D., 1934; ed. Univs. of Lwów and Cambridge; commenced biochemical research 1933, first in field of muscle biochem. (working with J. K. Parnas); carried out studies on various enzymes, e.g. peroxidase, polyphenoloxidase, carbonic anhydrase (with D. Keilin) 1935–39; studied biochem. of mould fungi 1939–44; studied biochem. of semen and of male reproductive tract 1944–; Fellow of Royal Soc. 1951; Dir. Agricultural Research Council Unit of Reproductive Physiology and Biochem., Cambridge 1954–76; Fellow of Trinity Hall, Cambridge 1961–; Prof. of Physiology of Reproduction, Univ. of Cambridge 1967–76; Visiting Prof., Univ. of Adelaide 1976; Visiting Scientist, Nat. Inst. of Health, U.S.A. 1977–82; Sr. Lalor Fellow, Woods Hole 1960; mem. Polish Acad. of Sciences 1980; Corresp. mem. Belgian Royal Acad. of Medicine 1971; Hon. mem. Belgian Royal Acad. of Medicine 1984, European Soc. of Human Reproduction and Embryology; Dr. h.c. (Cracow, Hanover and Ghent); Knight of Italian Order of Merit, Amory Prize, American Acad. of Arts and Sciences, Marshall Medal, Soc. for the Study of Fertility, Distinguished Andrology Award, American Soc. of Andrology 1979. *Publications:* Biochemistry of Semen 1954, Biochemistry of Semen and of the Male Reproductive Tract 1964, Male Reproductive Function and Semen: Themes and Trends in Physiology, Biochemistry and Investigative Andrology (with Cecilia Lutwak-Mann) 1981, Spermatophores-Development, Structure, Biochemical Attributes and Role in Transfer of Spermatozoa 1984; about 270 publs. in fields of biochemistry of muscle, blood, plants, fungi, spermatozoa and reproductive organs. *Address:* 1 Courtney Way, Cambridge, CB4 2EE, England. *Telephone:* (0223) 355891.

MANN, Yuri Vladimirovich, DR.PHIL.SC.; Soviet literary scholar and historian; b. 9 June 1929, Moscow; m. Galina Mann 1956; two s.; ed. Moscow Univ.; Prof. of Russian Literature, Gorky Inst. of World Literature. *Publications include:* Russian Philosophical Aesthetics 1820s–1830s 1969, The Poetics of Russian Romanticism 1976, The Poetics of Gogol 1978, In Search of a Live Soul—Gogol's Dead Souls 1984. *Address:* Astrakhansky pereulok, 5, kv. 99, Moscow 129010, U.S.S.R.

MANNING, Rt. Hon. Ernest Charles, P.C., C.C.; Canadian politician; b. 20 Sept. 1908, Carnduff, Sask.; s. of George Henry Manning and Elizabeth Mara Dickson; m. Muriel Aileen Preston 1936; two s.; ed. Rosetown, Sask.; mem. Legis. Ass. (Social Credit), Alberta 1935–68; Prov. Sec. and Minister of Trades and Industry, Alberta Govt. 1935–43, Prov. Treas. 1944–55, Minister of Mines and Minerals 1952–62, Attorney-Gen. 1955–68, Premier 1943–68; Chair. Manning Consultants Ltd., Fluor Canada Ltd.; Dir. Coal Valley Investment Corpn. *Address:* P.O. Box 2317, Edmonton, Alberta T5J 2P4, Canada. *Telephone:* (403) 482-5768.

MANNING, Jane, F.R.A.M., G.R.S.M.; British concert and opera singer; b. 20 Sept. 1938, Norwich; d. of Gerald Manning and Lily Thompson; m. Anthony Payne 1966; ed. Norwich High School for Girls, R.A.M., London and Scuola di Canto, Cureglia, Switzerland; London début concert 1964; since then active world-wide as freelance soprano soloist with special expertise in contemporary music; more than 350 BBC broadcasts; regular tours of U.S.A. since 1981, and of Australia since 1978; appearances at all leading European festivals and concert halls; New York début 1983; more than 250 world premières including several operas; Founder/Artistic Dir. Jane's Minstrels (ensemble) 1988; also active as lecturer; many recordings including complete vocal works of Messiaen; Visiting Prof., Mills Coll., Oakland, Calif. 1981, 1982, 1983, 1986; visiting lecturer, univs. in U.K., U.S.A., Australia, N.Z. and Scandinavia; Hon. D. Univ. (York) 1988; Special Award for Services to British Music, Composers' Guild of G.B. 1973. *Publication:* New Vocal Repertory 1986. *Leisure interests:* cooking, ornithology, cinema, philosophy. *Address:* 2 Wilton Square, London, N.1, England. *Telephone:* 01-359 1593.

MANNING, Patrick Augustus Mervyn, B.SC.; Trinidad and Tobago politician; b. 17 August 1946, Trinidad; s. of Arnold Manning and Elaine Manning; m. Hazel Anne-Marie Kinsale 1972; two s.; ed. Presentation Coll., San Fernando and Univ. of the West Indies; refinery operator Texaco, Trinidad 1965–66; Parl. Sec. 1971–78, Minister 1978–86; Minister of Information, and of Industry and Commerce 1981, of Energy 1981–86; Leader of the Opposition 1986–, Leader People's Nat. Movt. 1987–. *Leisure interests:* chess, reading. *Address:* Chepstow House, 36 Frederick St, Port-of-Spain (Office); 4–5 Union Park East Road, Gopaul Lands, Marabella, Trinidad (Home). *Telephone:* 625-3342 (Office); 658-5838 (Home).

MANNING, Robert Joseph; American journalist; b. 25 Dec. 1919, Binghamton, N.Y.; s. of Joseph James Manning and Agnes Pauline Brown; m. Margaret Marinda Raymond 1944; three s.; U.S. Army service 1942–43; Nieman Fellow, Harvard Univ. 1945–46; State Dept. and White House Corresp. United Press. 1944–46, Chief UN Corresp. United Press. 1946–49;

Writer, Time magazine 1949–55, Senior Ed. 1955–58, Chief, London Bureau, Time, Life, Fortune, Sports Illustrated magazines 1958–61; Sunday Ed., New York Herald Tribune 1961–62; Asst. Sec. of State for Public Affairs, U.S. Dept. of State 1962–64; Exec. Ed. Atlantic Monthly 1964–66, Ed.-in-Chief 1966–80; Vice-Pres. Atlantic Monthly Co. 1966–80; Ed.-in-Chief Boston Publishing Co. 1981–87; Pres., Ed.-in-Chief Bobcat Books Inc., Boston 1987–; Fellow, Kennedy Inst. of Politics, Harvard Univ. 1980. *Address:* 143 Newbury Street, Boston, Mass. 02116; 191 Commonwealth Avenue, Boston, Mass. 02116, U.S.A. (Home).

MANNING, H.E. Cardinal Timothy; American (Irish born) ecclesiastic (retd.); b. 15 Nov. 1909, Balingeary, Cork, Ireland; s. of Cornelius and Margaret Manning; ed. St. Patrick's Seminary, Menlo Park, Gregorian Univ., Rome; ordained 1934; consecrated titular Bishop of Lesvi 1946, transferred to Fresno 1967; titular Archbishop of Capri and Coadjutor Archbishop of Los Angeles 1969–70; Archbishop of Los Angeles 1970–85; cr. Cardinal by Pope Paul VI 1973. *Address:* c/o Archbishop's House, 1531 West 9th Street, Los Angeles, Calif. 90015, U.S.A.

MANQOUR, Sheikh Nasir Hamad al-, B.A.; Saudi Arabian diplomatist; b. 1927, Riyadh; ed. Cairo Univ.; Attaché, Foreign Ministry 1952; Dir. of Educ. in Najd 1954, Asst. Dir.-Gen. of Educ. 1955, Dir.-Gen. 1956, Dir.-Gen. Ministry of Educ. 1957; Rector, Riyadh Univ. 1958; Minister of State for Cabinet Affairs and Minister of Labour and Social Affairs 1959; Amb. to Japan 1964, to Sweden 1968, to Spain 1973, to U.K. 1980–, to Ireland 1982; King Abdulaziz Order (Second Class); Gran Cruz, Orden del Mérito Civil (Spain), Grand Cordon, Order of Brilliant Star (Republic of China). *Address:* Embassy of Saudi Arabia, 30 Belgrave Square, London, SW1X 8QB, England. *Telephone:* 01-235 0831.

MANSAGER, Felix Norman; American business executive; b. 30 Jan. 1911, Dell Rapids, S. Dak.; s. of Hoff and Alice Qualseth Mansager; m. Geraldine Larson 1931; one s. two d.; ed. Colton High School; joined Hoover Co. as Salesman 1929; Gen. Sales Man., The Hoover Co. 1959, Vice-Pres. (Sales) 1959–61, Exec. Vice-Pres. and Dir. The Hoover Co. 1961–63, Hoover Group 1963–66, Pres. and Chair. 1966–75, Hon. Chair. 1975–; Prof. School of Business Univ. of Akron 1978–82; Trustee at Large, Independent Coll. Funds of America, Pilgrims of the U.S.; Trustee Graduate Theological Union (Calif.), Fellow, British Inst. of Man.; mem. and Gov. Ditchley Foundation; mem. Asscn. of Ohio Cdres., Council on Foreign Relations, The Newcomen Soc. in N. America, Ohio Foundation of Ind. Colls.; Hon. LL.D. (Capital Univ., Columbus, Ohio and Strathclyde Univ., Scotland), Hon. L.H.D. (Malone Coll.), PD.D. (Walsh Coll.) 1974, H.H.D. (Wartburg Coll.) 1976; Medal of Honour, Vaasa Univ.; Chevalier, Order of Léopold (Belgium), Grand Dukes of Burgundy, Kt. 1st Class, Order of St. Olav (Norway) 1971; British Inst. of Marketing Award 1971; Canton Chamber of Commerce Award of Appreciation 1971; Chevalier, Légion d'honneur; Hon. K.B.E. 1976, Order of Merit of Repub. of Italy. *Leisure interests:* reading, golf. *Address:* 3421 Lindel Court, N.W. Canton, Ohio 44718, U.S.A.

MANSER, Michael John, R.I.B.A.; British architect; b. 23 March 1929, London; s. of Edmund G. and Augusta M. Manser; m. Josephine Bernini 1953; one s. one d.; ed. School of Architecture, The Polytechnic of Cen. London; Chair. Manser Assocs. Ltd. (architects) 1961–; architectural corresp. The Observer 1964–66; engaged on wide variety of architectural projects including private housing, industrial buildings, research labs., schools, swimming pools, commercial and domestic renovation and refurbishment, hotel alterations in Paris and factory extensions in Netherlands; Pres. R.I.B.A. 1983–85; Civic Trust Award 1967, Civic Trust Commendation 1973, European Architectural Heritage Award 1975, Dept. of Environment Good Design in Housing Award 1975, Structural Steel Design Award 1976, R.I.B.A. Award Commendation 1977; Hon. Fellow, Royal Architectural Inst. of Canada 1984. *Publications:* Planning Your Kitchen (co-author); contributions to nat. and tech. press. *Leisure interests:* architecture, music, gardening, boats, books. *Address:* Manser Associates Ltd., 8 Hammersmith Broadway, London, W6 7AL, England. *Telephone:* 01-741 4381.

MANSERGH, (Philip) Nicholas (Seton), O.B.E., D.PHIL., D.LITT., LITT.D., F.B.A.; Irish historian; b. 27 June 1910, Tipperary; s. of Philip St. George Mansergh; m. Diana Mary Keeton 1939; three s. two d.; ed. Coll. of St. Columba, Dublin and Pembroke Coll. Oxford; Sec. Oxford Univ. Politics Research Cttee. and Tutor in Politics 1937–40; Empire Div., Ministry of Information 1941–46, Dir. 1944–46; Asst. Sec., Dominions Office 1946–47; Abe Bailey Research Prof. of Commonwealth Affairs, Royal Inst. of Int. Affairs 1947–53; Smuts Prof. of the History of the British Commonwealth, Cambridge Univ. 1953–70; Fellow of St. John's Coll. Cambridge 1955–69, 1979–, Master 1969–79; Ed.-in-Chief, India Office Records on the Transfer of Power in India (12 vols.) 1967–82; Hon. Fellow Pembroke Coll. Oxford and Trinity Coll. Dublin. *Publications:* The Irish Free State: its Government and Politics 1934, The Government of Northern Ireland 1936, The Commonwealth and the Nations 1948, The Coming of the First World War 1949, Survey of British Commonwealth Affairs (2 vols.) 1931–39 and 1939–52 1952 and 1958, Documents and Speeches on Commonwealth Affairs 1931–62 (Ed.) 1953–63, South Africa 1906–61 1962, The Irish Question 1840–1921 1975, The Commonwealth Experience 1982. *Leisure interest:*

gardening. *Address:* The Lodge, Little Shelford, Cambridge, CB2 5EW, England.

MANSFIELD, Eric Harold, M.A., SC.D., F.I.M.A., F.ENG., F.R.AE.S., F.R.S.; British structural research scientist; b. 24 May 1923, Croydon, Surrey; s. of Harold G. and Grace Pfundt Mansfield; m. 1st Mary O. P. Douglas 1947 (dissolved 1973), 2nd Eunice Shuttleworth-Parker 1974; two s. one d.; ed. St. Lawrence Coll., Ramsgate, Trinity Hall, Cambridge; various grades, Structures Dept., Royal Aircraft Est., Farnborough 1943-83, Chief Scientific Officer 1980-83; Visiting Prof. Univ. of Surrey 1984-; aeronautical consultant 1984-; mem. British Nat. Cttee. for Theoretical and Applied Mechanics 1973-79, Gen. Ass. Int. Union of Theoretical and Applied Mechanics 1976-80; Bronze Medal, Royal Aeronautical Soc. 1967. *Publications:* Bending and Stretching of Plates 1964, Bridge: the Ultimate Limits 1986, articles in professional journals. *Leisure interests:* bridge, philately, palaeontology, snorkling. *Address:* Manatoba, Dene Close, Lower Bourne, Farnham, Surrey, GU10 3PP, England.

MANSFIELD, J(ohn) Kenneth; American government official; b. 1921; ed. Northwestern Univ. and Yale Univ.; Instructor in Int. Relations, Yale Univ. 1949-50; Chief of Staff, Mil. Applications Sub. Cttee., Jt. Congressional Cttee. on Atomic Energy 1950-56; combustion engine firm 1956-59; Staff Dir. U.S. Senate Sub-Cttee. on Nat. Policy Machinery 1959-62; Insp. Gen. Foreign Assistance, Dept. of State 1962-69, Deputy Dir. Operations, Office of Gen. Scientific Affairs 1969-. *Address:* Office of General Scientific Affairs, Department of State, Washington D.C. 20520, U.S.A. (Office).

MANSFIELD, Michael Joseph, A.M.; American politician and diplomatist; b. 16 March 1903, New York; s. of Patrick and Josephine O'Brien Mansfield; m. Maureen Hayes 1932; one d.; ed. Univ. of Montana; fmr. mining engineer; Prof. of History and Political Science, Univ. of Montana 1933-42; mem. House of Reps. 1943-52, Senator (Democrat, Montana) 1952-76; Majority Whip 1957-61; Leader of Senate 1961-76; Amb. to Japan 1977-89; Dr. h.c. (Soka) 1986; Nelson Rockefeller Public Service Award 1988. *Address:* Missoula, Mont., U.S.A.

MANSFIELD, Peter, PH.D., F.R.S.; British professor of physics; b. 9 Oct. 1933, London; s. of late S. Mansfield and R. L. Mansfield; m. Jean M. Kibble 1962; two d.; ed. William Penn School, Peckham and Queen Mary Coll., London; Research Assoc. Dept. of Physics, Univ. of Ill. 1962; lecturer, Univ. of Nottingham 1964, Sr. Lecturer 1967, Reader 1970, Prof. of Physics 1979-; MRC Professorial Fellow 1983-88; Sr. Visitor, Max Planck Inst. for Medical Research, Heidelberg 1972-73; Fellow, Queen Mary Coll. 1985; Pres. Soc. for Magnetic Resonance in Medicine 1987-88; Royal Soc. Wellcome Foundation Gold Medal and Prize 1985; Duddell Medal, Inst. of Physics 1988 and other awards. *Publications:* NMR Imaging in Biomedicine 1982; some 150 scientific publs. in learned journals. *Leisure interests:* reading, walking, languages, DIY. *Address:* 68 Beeston Fields Drive, Bramcote, Nottingham, NG9 3DD, England.

MANSFIELD, Sir Philip Robert Aked, K.C.M.G.; British diplomatist (retd.); b. 9 May 1926; s. of Philip Theodore Mansfield; m. Elinor Russell MacHatton 1953; two s.; ed. Winchester, Pembroke Coll., Cambridge; Grenadier Guards 1944-47; Sudan political service 1950-54; entered diplomatic service 1955; served Addis Ababa, Singapore, Paris, Buenos Aires; Counsellor and Head of Rhodesia Dept., FCO 1969-72; Royal Coll. of Defence Studies 1973; Counsellor and Head of Chancery 1974-75; Deputy High Commr. in Kenya 1976; Asst. Under-Sec. of State, FCO, and Commr. for British Indian Ocean Territory 1976-79; Amb. and Deputy Perm. Rep. to UN 1979-81; Amb. to Netherlands 1981-84; Consultant, Rank Xerox 1987-, BPB Industries 1987-. *Leisure interests:* sailing, bird watching, gardening. *Address:* Gill Mill, Stanton Harcourt, Oxford, England. *Telephone:* (0993) 2554.

MANSFIELD, Terence Arthur, PH.D., F.R.S.; British professor of biology; b. 18 Jan. 1937, Ashby-de-la-Zouch; s. of Sydney W. Mansfield and Rose (née Sinfield) Mansfield; m. Margaret M. James 1963; two s.; ed. Univ. of Nottingham, Univ. of Reading; Research Fellow Reading Univ. 1961-65; lecturer and Prof. Univ. of Lancaster 1965-87; Dir. Inst. of Environmental and Biological Sciences Lancaster Univ. 1987-. *Publications:* Physiology of Stomata (co-author) 1968, Effects of Air Pollutants on Plants (Ed.) 1976, Stomatal Physiology (co-Ed.) 1981. *Address:* Institute of Environmental and Biological Sciences, University of Lancaster, Bailrigg, Lancaster, LA1 4YQ, England. *Telephone:* 0524-65201 (Office).

MANSHARD, Walther, DR. RER. NAT.; German university professor and UN official; b. 17 Nov. 1923, Hamburg; s. of Otto and Ida Manshard; m. Helga Koch 1951; one d.; ed. Univ. of Hamburg; Asst. lecturer, Univ. of Southampton, U.K. 1950-52; lecturer, Univ. of Ghana 1952-60; Dozent, Univ. of Cologne 1960-63; Prof. Univ. of Giessen 1963-70; Prin. Dir. UNESCO Dept. of Environmental Sciences 1970-73; Prof., Head of Dept. Univ. of Freiburg 1973-77, 1980-; Vice-Rector, UN Univ., Tokyo 1977-80; Sec.-Gen. and Treas. Int. Geographical Union 1976-84. *Publications:* Die geographischen Grundlagen der Wirtschaft Ghanas 1961, Tropisches Afrika 1963, Agrargeographie der Tropen 1968, Afrika–Südlich der Sahara 1970, Tropical Agriculture 1974, Die Städte des tropischen Afrika 1977, Renewable Natural Resources and the Environment 1981. *Address:* Geographisches Institut, University of Freiburg, Werderring 4, 7800 Freiburg

i. Br.; Schwarzwaldstrasse 24, 7812 Bad Krozingen, Federal Republic of Germany.

MANSHOLT, Sicco Leendert; Netherlands politician; b. 13 Sept. 1908, Ulrum, Groningen, Netherlands; m. H. Postel 1937; four c.; ed. School for Tropical Agric., Deventer; studied agric.; worked on Dutch farms 1924-34, tea plantations in Netherlands East Indies (now Indonesia) 1934-36; returned to Netherlands and worked on Wieringermeer Polder from 1937; during the German occupation organized important illegal work, particularly for the food supply of western provinces and worked on behalf of concentration camp victims; commanded a section of the forces of the Interior after the capitulation; became Burgomaster of Wieringermeer; Minister of Agric., Fisheries and Food in Schermerhorn Cabinet 1945-46; in Beel Cabinet 1946-48, in Drees Cabinet 1948, 1951, 1952 and 1956-58; Head of the Netherlands Del. to UN for Agric., and took part in negotiations for creation of Benelux Union 1946; prepared Mansholt Plan for Agricultural Section of European Econ. Community 1953; Vice-Pres. EEC Comm. 1958-67; Vice-Pres. Combined Exec. of EEC, ECSC and Euratom 1967-72, Pres. 1972-1973; mem. UN Eminent Persons Group to Study Multinationals 1973; Dr. h.c. in Agric. (Inst. of Agric., Wageningen, Gembloux); Grand Croix, Ordre de la Couronne de Belgique, Grand Cross, Order of the Netherlands Lion and numerous other foreign awards; Robert Schuman Prize 1968. *Address:* Oosteinde 18, 8351 HB Wapserveen, Netherlands. *Telephone:* 05213-1313.

MANSUR, Mallikarjun; Indian classical singer; b. 31 Dec. 1910, Mansur; s. of Bheemraiappa Mansur and Neelamma Mansur; m. Gangambika Mansur; one s. seven d.; ed. elementary educ.; joined drama co. 1919; started sangeet lessons with Neela Kanth Bua 1922; first gramophone record 1933; mem. Legis. Council, Karnataka State 1985-; Padmashri Award 1970; Padmabhusan award 1975 and many other awards. *Publications:* Sangeet Ratna, Ananna Rasayatre. *Leisure interests:* shivapooja, sangeet, reading. *Address:* Mruthunjaya Nilava, A.I.R. Road, Dharwar, 580008, India. *Telephone:* 8906.

MANT, Arthur Keith, M.D., B.S., M.R.C.S., F.R.C.P., F.R.C. PATH., D.M.J. PATH.; British professor of forensic medicine; b. 11 Sept. 1919, Purley, Surrey; s. of George A. Mant and Elsie M. Slark; m. Emma O. H. Smith 1947; two s. one d.; ed. Denstone Coll. Staffs. and Univ. of London; rank of Maj., R.A.M.C. 1945-48; Research Fellow, Dept. of Forensic Medicine, Guy's Hosp. London 1949-55, lecturer 1955-66, Head of Dept. 1972-74; Reader in Forensic Medicine, Univ. of London 1966-74, Prof. 1974-84, Prof. Emer. 1984-; Sr. Lecturer in Forensic Med. King's Coll. Hosp. 1965-67, Hon. Consultant 1967-84; Visiting Lecturer, St. Mary's Hosp. 1955-84; Visiting Prof. Univ. of Jordan and Nihon Univ. Tokyo; Gerin Medal 1978; H. Ward Smith Memorial Award 1984. *Publications:* Forensic Medicine 1960, Modern Trends in Forensic Medicine 1973, Taylor's Principles and Practice of Medical Jurisprudence (13th Edn.) 1984; over 100 scientific papers. *Leisure interests:* orchidology, fly fishing. *Address:* 29 Ashley Drive, Walton-on-Thames, Surrey, KT12 1JT, England. *Telephone:* (0932) 225005.

MANTELET, Jean; French industrialist; b. 10 Aug. 1900, Paris; s. of Alexis Mantelet and Apolline Gremy; m. Fernande Moulat, 1929; ed. Chambre de commerce et d'industrie, Paris; mfr. of agric. pulverisers 1922-31; invented Moulin-Légumes 1932, first electrified small household appliances 1956; Pres.-Dir.-Gen. Moulinex 1932-72, Chair. Bd. Dirs. 1973-; Pres.-Dir.-Gen. Soc. of Financial Man. and Investment 1969-; Counsellor on French External Trade 1951-73, Hon. Counsellor 1973-; Commdr., Légion d'honneur, du Mérite commercial. *Leisure interest:* yoga. *Address:* 15 rue Jules-Ferry, 93170 Bagnolet, France (Office).

MANUEL, Robert; French actor and producer; b. 7 Sept. 1916, Paris; s. of Henri and Alice (née Kahn) Manuel; m. 1st Léone Mail (divorced), two d.; m. 2nd Claudine Coster 1963, one s. one d.; ed. Lycée Carnot and Nat. Conservatoire of Dramatic Art, Paris; Comédie-Française 1936-63, hon. mem. 1967-; Prof., Nat. Conservatoire of Dramatic Art and Conservatoire de la rue Blanche; Lecturer and Dir. Théatre Marigny 1964-; film actor and dir. of many TV programmes; Mayor of Roquebrune-sur-Argens 1971-74; Commdr. Ordre nat. du Mérite, Officier, Légion d'honneur, Ordre des Arts et des Lettres, des palmes académiques and many other awards. *Plays produced include:* Les trois valses, Les cloches de Corneville, Mamzelle Nitouche, Les précieuses ridicules, On ne saurait penser à tout, Mariage forcé, Bidule, Les croulants se portent bien, La grève des amoureux, Gigi, Une femme qui ne cache rien, La maison de Zaza, la Purée, J'y suis, j'y reste, Le marchand de soleil, Chat en poche 1986, La galipette 1987; also numerous films, television. *Publications:* Qu'allais-je faire dans cette galère?, Merci Molière, Le Juste Milieu. *Leisure interest:* Molière artefacts. *Address:* La Maison du Buisson, 78370 Plaisir, France.

MANYAKIN, Sergei Iosifovich; Soviet politician; b. 1923; ed. Stavropol Agric. Inst.; active service with Soviet Army 1941-43; mem. CPSU 1945-; Senior Agronomist, Dir. of agric. inst., Pres. of collective farm in Stavropol District 1948-57; work for Stavropol CPSU District Cttee. 1957-60; Pres. 1960-61; Inspector for CPSU Cen. Cttee. 1961-; First Sec. of Omsk District Cttee. 1961-87; Pres. of U.S.S.R. Cttee. of National Control 1987-; mem. of CPSU Cen. Cttee. 1961-; Deputy to U.S.S.R. Supreme Soviet; Hero of Socialist Labour 1983. *Address:* The Kremlin, Moscow, U.S.S.R.

MANZONI, Giacomo, MUS.M.; Italian composer; b. 26 Sept. 1932, Milan; m. Eugenia Tretti 1960; one s; ed. Bocconi Univ., Milan, Univ. of Tübingen and Conservatorio Verdi, Milan; Ed. Il Diapason (music review) 1956; music critic, l'Unita 1958–66; music ed. Prisma 1968; mem. editorial staff, Musica Realtà 1980–; Prof. Conservatorio Verdi 1962–64, 1974–, Conservatorio Martini, Bologna 1965–68, 1969–74; *compositions include:* Atomtod 1965, Per M. Robespierre 1975, Parole de Beckett 1971, Masse: omaggio a E. Varèse 1977, Ode 1982, Scene Sinfoniche per il Dr. Faustus 1984, Dedica (su testi di Maderna) 1985. *Publications:* A. Schoenberg 1975, essays on Monteverdi, Dallapiccola, Th. Mann etc. and translations. *Address:* Viale Papiniano 31, 20123 Milan, Italy. *Telephone:* 02/4817955.

MANZÙ, Giacomo; Italian sculptor; b. 22 Dec. 1908; s. of Angelo and Maria Manzoni; divorced; three s. (deceased); began his career working in a gilder's then a plasterer's studio; attended evening classes in plastic arts; Prof. of Sculpture Accad. Brera, Milan 1940–54, Salzburg Int. Sommerakad. 1954–60; Exhbn. of paintings and drawings, Hanover Gallery, London 1965, of Sculpture 1969; numerous exhbns. worldwide, most recently Tokyo 1982, 1983, Oslo and tour of Norway 1986, Florence 1986; museum devoted to his work in Ardea; Sculpture Prize, Venice Biennale 1948; major works include main door of Salzburg Cathedral, Porta delle Morte, San Pietro in Vaticano, Rome and Porta della Pace e della Guerra, St. Laurenz Church, Rotterdam; mem. Acad. des Beaux Arts, des Arts et des Lettres, American Acad. of Arts and Letters, Akademie der Kunst etc.; Hon. Dr. (R.C.A.) London 1971; Lenin Peace Prize 1966. *Publications:* La Porta di San Pietro 1964, Un artista e il Papa 1968. *Address:* 00040 Ardea, Rome, Italy.

MAO LIRUI; Chinese educationalist; b. 1905; s. of Mao Lun and Mao Zhong; m. Peng Gi Wao 1920; two s. two d.; ed. Univ. of Nanking, King's Coll. London and Univ. of Michigan, U.S.A.; taught at secondary schools; Prof. of Educ. Univs. of Honan, Nanjing, Beijing 1937–. *Publications:* The History of Education in China (8 edns.), Thoughts of China. *Leisure interest:* television. *Address:* Beijing Normal University, Beitaipingzhuang, Beijing, People's Republic of China. *Telephone:* 201 2255; 201 2288 (Office); 2810 (Home).

MAO ZHIYONG; Chinese party official; b. 1929, Yueyang Co., Hunan Prov.; joined CCP 1938; Chair. Yueyang Co. Revolutionary Cttee. 1968–70, Sec. 1970–; Vice-Chair. Hunan Peasants Asscn. 1973–77; Sec. Hunan Prov. CCP Cttee. 1973–77; mem. 11th CCP Cen. Cttee. 1977; Chair. Hunan Prov. CPPCC Cttee. 1977–79; Chair. Hunan Prov. Revolutionary Cttee. 1977–79; First Sec. Political Cttee. of Mil. Dist., Hunan; mem. 5th NPC 1978–80; Head of CCP party workers del. to Romania Aug. 1979; Goodwill del. to Japan April 1980; mem. 12th CCP Cen. Cttee. Sept. 1982; Presidium of 12th CCP Nat. Congress Sept. 1982; Head of Party Group for Party Rectification, Hunan Prov. CCP Cttee. 1983; mem. CCP Cen. Cttee. 1987–; Sec. Jiangxi Prov. Cttee. April 1988–. *Address:* Central Committee of the Chinese Communist Party, Zhongnanhai, Beijing, People's Republic of China.

MAPA, Placido, PH.D.; Philippines economist and banker; b. 24 June 1932; s. of Placido Mapa and Loreto Ledesma; m. Maria Corazon Tinio 1962; two s. seven d.; ed. Ateneo de Manila, St. Louis Univ. and Harvard; Deputy Dir.-Gen. Program Implementation Agency 1964–65; Under-Sec. of Finance 1965; Dir.-Gen. Presidential Econ. Staff 1966–70; Chair. Nat. Econ. Council 1970; Alt. Exec. Dir. IBRD 1970–74, Exec. Dir. 1979–80; Exec. Dir. IMF 1972; Pres. Philippine Commercial and Industrial Bank 1974–76; Chair. Devt. Bank of the Philippines 1976–79; Dir.-Gen. Nat. Econ. Devt. Authority 1981–83; Minister of Econ. Planning, Minister of State for Finance 1981–83; mem. Nat. Ass. 1981–83; Pres. Philippine Nat. Bank 1983–86; Gran Cruz, Orden de San Carlos (Colombia). *Leisure interest:* tennis. *Address:* c/o Philippine National Bank, P.O. Box 1844, Escolta, Metro Manila 2804, Philippines.

MAR GREGORIOS, Most Rev. Benedict, M.A., D.D.; Indian ecclesiastic; b. 1 Feb. 1916, Kallooppara; s. of late Idicula Mar Gregorios and Annamma Mar Gregorios; ed. St. Joseph's Coll. Tiruchirapalli; Prin., Mar Ivanios Coll. Trivandrum 1949; Auxiliary Bishop of Archdiocese of Trivandrum 1953, Archbishop of Trivandrum and Head of Malankara Catholic Hierarchy 1955–; Pres. Catholic Bishops' Conf. of India; Chair. Catholic Bishops' Conf. of Kepala; mem. Bishops' Synod, Rome. *Leisure interests:* astronomy, agriculture. *Address:* Archbishop's House, Trivandrum, 695004 Kerala, India. *Telephone:* 77642; 77643; 77331.

MARA, the Rt. Hon. Ratu Sir Kamisese Kapaiwai Tuimacilai, P.C., G.C.M.G., K.B.E., M.A.; Fiji politician; b. 13 May 1920; s. of the late Tui Nayau and Adi Lusiana Qolikoro; m. Adi Lala Mara 1951; three s. five d.; ed. Queen Victoria School and Cen. Medical School, Suva, Fiji, Sacred Heart Coll., Otago Univ., Oxford Univ., and London School of Econs.; joined British Colonial Service 1950; Admin. Officer, Dist. Officer and Commr., Fiji 1951–61; mem. Legis. Council, Fiji 1953–; mem. Exec. Council, Fiji 1959–61; mem. for Natural Resources 1964–66; f. Alliance Party 1960; Leader, Fiji Del. Constitutional Conf., London 1965; Chief Minister 1967–70; Prime Minister 1970–87, Prime Minister and Minister of Foreign Affairs 1977–87, Dec. 1987–, and of Foreign Affairs and the Public Service Dec. 1987–; Leader of Opposition April–May 1987; Adviser on Foreign Affairs Gov. Gen.'s Interim Govt. May-Sept. 1987; Hon. Fellow Wadham Coll. 1971; Hon. LL.D. (Guam, Otago, New Delhi, Papua New Guinea); Hon.

Dr. Political Science (Yonsei Univ., Korea) 1978; Hon. Dr. Univ. (Univ. of S. Pacific) 1980; Pacific Man of the Year 1984; K. St. J., Grand Master, Order of the National Lion (Senegal) 1975, Order of Diplomatic Service Merit (Repub. of Korea) 1978. *Leisure interests:* fishing, golf. *Address:* 6 Berkley Crescent, Suva, Fiji. *Telephone:* 314905.

MARADONA, Diego; Argentine footballer; b. Lanus, 1960; one d. (by Claudia Villafane); with Boca Juniors, Argentina –1982; then with Barcelona Football Club; with Naples Football Club 1984–; founded Maradona Producciones; fmr. Amb. for UNICEF. *Address:* Naples Football Club, Naples, Italy.

MARAINI, Dacia; Italian author; b. 13 Nov. 1936; d. of Fosco Maraini (q.v.) and Alliata Topazia; ed. Collegio S.S. Annunziata, Florence and Rome; Prix Formentor for L'Età del Malessere (The Age of Discontent) 1962. *Publications:* La Vacanza 1962, L'Età del Malessere 1962, Crudeltà All' Aria Aperta (poems) 1966, A Memoria (novel) 1967, La famiglia normale (one-act play) 1967, Il ricatto a teatro (play) 1968, Memoirs of a Female Thief 1973, Donna in Guerra (novel) 1975, Mangiami' Pure (poems) 1980, I Sogni di Clitennestra (5 plays) 1981, Lettere a Marina (novel) 1981, Lezioni d'Amore (6 plays) 1982, Dimenticato di Dimenticare (poems) 1983, Isolina (novel) 1985, Devour me too (short stories) 1987, La Bionda, la bruna e l'asino (essays) 1987. *Address:* Via Beccaria 18, 00196 Rome, Italy. *Telephone:* 3611795.

MARAINI, Fosco, D.S.C.; Italian writer; b. 15 Nov. 1912; s. of Antonio Maraini and Yoi Crosse (father of Dacia Maraini, q.v.); m. Alliata Topazia 1935 (divorced); three d.; ed. Univ. of Florence; Asst. Prof., Univ. of Hokkaido, Japan 1938–41; Reader in Italian, Univ. of Kyoto 1941–43; civil internee (as anti-Fascist) in Japan 1943–45; returned to Italy 1946; Fellow, St. Antony's Coll., Oxford; lecturer in Japanese, Univ. of Florence; writing and research on anthropology and ethnology of Asia. *Publications:* Secret Tibet 1953, Meeting with Japan 1959, Karakoram 1961, Hekura 1962, Where Four Worlds Meet 1964, Japan: Patterns of Continuity 1971, Tokyo (Great Cities of the World, Time-Life series) 1977. *Leisure interests:* music, skiing, mountaineering. *Address:* Viale Magalotti 6, Florence, Italy.

MARAIS, Jean; French actor; b. 11 Dec. 1913, Cherbourg; s. of Alfred and Marie-Louise (née Vassord) Villain-Marais; one s.; ed. Lycées Condorcet and Janson-de-Sailly, and Conservatoire Maubel; acting career 1933–; served French Army 1939–40 and 1944–45; Pres. Union des Artistes 1974–; Chevalier, Légion d'honneur, Officier, Ordre nat. du Mérite, Officier des Arts et des Lettres, Croix de guerre; Grande Médaille de vermeil de la ville de Paris 1973. *Films include:* La belle et la bête, L'éternel retour, Aux yeux du souvenir, Le secret de Mayerling, Orphée, Le château de verre, Julietta, Elena et les hommes, Typhon sur Nagazaky, La vie à deux, Amour de poche, Les nuits blanches, Chaque jour a son secret, Versailles Le Bossu, Austerlitz, Le testament d'Orphée, Le capitan, La Princesse de Clèves, Les mystères de Paris, Patate, Fantomas, Le Saint prend l'affût, La provocation, Peau d'âne, Parking, Next of Kin. *Theatre:* Britannicus, Mithridate, Andromaque, La machine infernale, Les parents terribles, Pygmalion, César et Cléopâtre, etc.; television appearances in Renaud et Armide 1969, Robert Macaire 1970, Joseph Balsam 1973, Karatekas and Co. 1973. *Publications:* Mes quatre vérités 1957, Histoire de ma vie 1975, Contes 1978. *Address:* c/o Jean Nainchrick, 31 Champs-Elysées, 75008 Paris, France.

MARAMIS, Johan Boudewijn Paul, DRS.; Indonesian diplomatist; b. 23 Jan. 1922, Limbung, Celebes; m. Niny Rosalie Krumpis; three s. three d.; ed. Univ. of Leyden, Netherlands; served in Directorate of Econ. Affairs, Ministry of Foreign Affairs 1951–54; First Sec., Teheran 1954–58; Deputy Head, Directorate of UN Affairs, Ministry of Foreign Affairs 1958–60; Counsellor, Indonesian Mission to UN 1960–65; Head, Directorate of Int. Orgs., Ministry of Foreign Affairs 1965–69; mem. Del. to UN Gen. Assembly 1966–68; Deputy Perm. Rep. to UN 1969–72, Rep. UN ECOSOC 1968, Vice-Pres. 1969, Pres. 1970; Amb. to Belgium and Luxembourg and Chief Indonesian Mission to EEC 1972–73; Exec. Sec. UN ESCAP 1973–81. *Address:* c/o Ministry of Foreign Affairs, Jalan Taman Pejambon 6, Jakarta, Indonesia.

MARAMZIN, Vladimir Rafailovich; Soviet writer; b. 1934, Leningrad; m.; graduated Leningrad Electro-Tech. Inst.; engineer at Leningrad factory 1958–65; began literary career 1962 and became mem. trade union of Publishing House "The Soviet Writer"; dissident activities 1968–, including publication of several short stories in *samizdat*; arrested for his works 1974 and tried 1975; sentenced to five years of camps on probation; left U.S.S.R. 1975; ed. literary magazine in Paris 1976–. *Publications:* (apart from *samizdat*) include Tyanitolkai (selection of stories from 1960s and 1970s) 1981.

MARANDA, Pierre Jean, M.A., L.PH., PH.D., F.R.S.C.; Canadian professor of anthropology; b. 27 March 1930, Quebec; s. of Lucien Maranda and Marie-Alma Rochette; m. Elli-Kaija Köngäs 1962 (deceased); two s.; ed. Laval Univ., Quebec, Univ. of Montreal and Harvard Univ.; Asst. Prof. of Classics, Univ. Laval 1955–58; Research Fellow, Harvard Univ. 1966–70; Dir. of Research Ecole Pratique des Hautes Etudes, Paris 1968–69; Assoc. Prof. of Anthropology Univ. of B.C. 1969–71, Prof. 1971–75; Prof. Collège de France, Paris 1975; Research Prof. Laval Univ. 1976–; Visiting Prof. Fed. Univ. of Rio de Janeiro 1983; Dr. h.c. (Memorial Univ., Newfoundland)

1985; Médaille du Collège de France 1975. *Publications:* Structural Models in Folklore and Transformational Essays (with E.K. Köngäs) 1963, French Kinship: Structure and History 1974, Mythology 1974, Soviet Structural Folkloristics 1974, Dialogie conjugal 1985, DISCAN: A Computer Programme for Discourse Analysis 1987, plus over 60 articles in scientific journals. *Leisure interests:* skiing, swimming, tennis, bridge, music, art. *Address:* Département d'Anthropoligie, Université Laval, Quebec, G1K 7P4, Canada. *Telephone:* (418) 656-7687.

MARAVALL HERRERO, José María; Spanish politician and university professor; b. 7 April 1942, Madrid; s. of José Antonio and María Teresa Maravall Herrero; m. Maria Jesús 1966; two c.; ed. Univ. of Madrid, Univ. of Oxford; fmr. mem. Frente de Liberación Popular and Federación Universitaria de Estudiantes; Research Fellow, St. Antony's Coll. 1973–74; Prof. Sociology Dept., Univ. of Warwick 1974–78; joined Partido Socialista Obrero Español 1974, Sec. of Educ., Fed. Exec. 1979; Chair. of Political Sociology, Universidad Complutense de Madrid 1978; Minister of Educ. and Science 1982–88; mem. Parl. 1986–. *Publications:* Trabajo y Conflicto Social 1967, El Desarollo Económico y la Clase Obrera 1970, Sociología de lo Posible, Dictadura y Disentimiento Político (Dictatorship and Political Dissent) 1978, La Política de la Transición (The Transition to Democracy in Spain) 1982, La Reforma de la Enseñanza 1985. *Leisure interests:* travelling, cinema, walking, swimming. *Address:* c/o Ministerio de Educación y Ciencia, Alcala 34/36, Madrid 14, Spain (Office).

MARCEAU, Félicien (pseudonym of Louis Carette); French writer; b. 16 Sept. 1913, Cortenberg, Belgium; s. of Louis Carette and Marie Lefèvre; m. 2nd Bianca Licenziati 1953; ed. Coll. de la Sainte Trinité à Louvain and Univ. de Louvain; Prix Interallié for Les élans du coeur 1955; Prix Goncourt for Creezy 1969; Prix Prince Pierre de Monaco 1974; Grand Prix du Théâtre 1975; mem. Acad. Française 1975. *Publications:* Novels: Chasseneuil 1948, L'Homme du Roi 1952, Bergère Légère 1953, Creezy 1969, Le corps de mon ennemi 1975, Appelez-moi Mademoiselle 1984, la Carriole du Père Juniet 1985, Les passions partagées 1987; plays: L'oeuf 1956, La bonne soupe 1958, La preuve par quatre 1965, Un jour j'ai rencontré la vérité 1967, Le babour 1969, L'ouvre-boîte 1972, L'homme en question 1973, A nous de jouer 1979; essays: Balzac et son monde 1955, Le roman en liberté 1977, Une insolente liberté: Les aventures de Casanova 1983; memoirs: Les années courtes 1968. *Leisure interest:* painting. *Address:* c/o Les Editions Gallimard, 5 rue Sébastien-Bottin, 75007 Paris, France. *Telephone:* 4544-39-19.

MARCEAU, Marcel; French mime; b. 22 March 1923, Strasbourg; s. of Charles and Anne (née Werzberg) Mangel; m. 1st Huguette Mallet (divorced), two s.; m. 2nd Ella Jaroszewicz 1966 (divorced); m. 3rd Anne Sicco 1975 (divorced), two d.; ed. Lille and Strasbourg Lycées; Dir. Compagnie de Mime Marcel Marceau 1948–64; annual world tours, and numerous television appearances throughout the world; created Don Juan (mime drama) 1964, Candide (ballet), Hamburg 1971; creator of the character "Bip"; Head Ecole de Mimodrame Marcel Marceau Aug. 1978–; Officier, Légion d'honneur, Officier, Ordre nat. du Mérite, Commdr. des Arts et des Lettres; Hon. degrees from Princeton and Oregon Univs. *Mimes include:* Le manteau, Exercices de style (both filmed), Mort avant l'aube, Le joueur de flûte, Moriana et Galvau, Pierrot de Montmartre, Les trois perruques, etc.; other films: Pantomime, Un jardin public, Le fabricant de masques, Paris qui rit, Paris qui pleure, Barbarella, Silent Movies 1976. *Publications:* Les sept péchés capitaux, Les rêveries de Bip, Alphabet Book, Counting Book, L'histoire de Bip, The Third Eye, Pimporello. *Leisure interests:* painting, poetry, fencing. *Address:* c/o Compagnie de Mime Marcel Marceau, 21 rue Jean-Mermoz, 75008 Paris, France. *Telephone:* 225-06-05.

MARCELLIN, Raymond, D.EN D.; French politician and lawyer; b. 19 Aug. 1914, Sézanne; s. of Gustave and Anaïs (née Gominard) Marcellin; ed. Meaux Coll., Paris and Strasbourg Univs.; Barrister, Cour d'Appel, Paris 1945–; elected Deputy for Morbihan, Nat. Ass. 1946, 1951, 1956, 1958, 1962, 1967, 1968, 1973, 1981; Under-Sec. of State of the Interior 1948–49; Sec. of State of Industry and Commerce 1949–50, of the Pres. of the Council 1952, of Information 1952–57, of Public Functions and Admin. Reform 1957–62; Minister of Public Health and Population 1962–66, of Industry 1966–67; Minister under Prime Minister, Responsible for Planning 1967–68; Minister of Interior 1968–74, of Agric. and Rural Devt. March–May 1974; Vice-Pres. Fed. nat. des républicains indépendants 1966–, Pres. Fed. bretonne des républicains indépendants 1968–; Pres. Conseil général du Morbihan 1964–, Conseil régional de Bretagne; Mayor of Vannes 1965–77; Senator for Morbihan 1974–81; Vice-Pres. Conseil régional de Bretagne 1986–; Deputy for Morbihan 1981–; Croix de guerre, Médaille des Evadés, etc. *Publication:* L'ordre public et les groupes révolutionnaires 1969. *Address:* Assemblée nationale, 75355 Paris (office); 8 boulevard de Latour Maubourg, 75007 Paris, France (Home).

MARCHAIS, Georges; French politician; b. 7 June 1920, La Hoquette; s. of René and Germaine (née Boscher) Marchais; m. 1st Paulette Noetinger 1941 (divorced); three d.; m. 2nd Liliane Garcia Marchais; one s.; fmr. metal worker; Sec. Metal-workers Union, Issy-les-Moulineaux 1946, Union des syndicats de travailleurs de la métallurgie de la Seine 1953–56; joined French CP 1947, mem. Cen. Cttee. 1956, mem. Political Bureau 1959, Sec. Cen. Cttee. 1961, Deputy Sec.-Gen. 1970, Sec.-Gen. Dec. 1972–; elected

Deputy for Val-de-Marne, Nat. Ass. 1973, 1978, 1981, 1986; mem. European Parl. 1979–; Presidential Cand. 1981. *Publications:* Qu'est-ce que le parti communiste français? 1970, Les communistes et les paysans (co-author) 1972, Le défi démocratique 1973, La politique du parti communiste français 1974, Parlons franchement 1977, Réponses 1977, L'espoir au présent 1980. *Address:* Parti Communiste Français, 2 place du Colonel Fabien, 75019 Paris, France. *Telephone:* 202-70-10.

MARCHAIS, Pierre Julien, D. EN MED.; French neuropsychiatrist; b. 21 April 1924, Paris; s. of Julien Marchais and Emilienne Marchais; m. Bernadette Somma 1954; one s. three d.; ed. Faculté de Médecine and Faculté des Sciences, Paris; Intern, Centre National d'Orientation des Prisons de Fresnes, Hôpitaux Psychiatriques de la Seine and Hôpital Foch; Asst. doctor, Centre Nat. des Prisons de Fresnes 1954; Asst. Hôpital Foch, Suresnes 1954, Head of Dept. 1960, Head Doctor, Psychiatric Service 1970–; Sec.-Gen. Soc. Medico-Psychologique 1983–; many other professional appts.; Prix de l'Acad. Nat. de Médecine (Prix Ritti) 1972; Prix de l'Acad. Française (Prix Bordin) 1973. *Publications:* 12 books and numerous articles in medical journals. *Leisure interests:* music, painting, skiing, swimming, philosophy of science. *Address:* 33 rue Lacépède, 75005 Paris, France. *Telephone:* 4535.49.07.

MARCHAL, Jean, D.EN D.; French academic; b. 25 June 1905, Colombey-les-Belles; s. of Albert Marchal and Emma Tassard; m. Gabrielle Perrin 1935; seven c.; ed. Lycée de Nancy and Facultés de Droit, Nancy and Paris; Prof. Faculté de Droit, Nancy 1935–48; Prof. Faculté de Droit et des Sciences Economiques, Paris 1948–72; Prof. Inst. d'Etudes Politiques, Paris, Ecole Nat. d'Admin.; Dir. of Research, Ecole pratique des Hautes Etudes, Sorbonne; mem. Inst. de France (Acad. des Sciences Morales et Politiques); Commdr. Légion d'honneur; various prizes. *Publications:* ten books. *Leisure interests:* mountaineering, skiing, tennis. *Address:* 9 Villa Davoust, 92600 Asnières, France.

MARCHAND, André Marius; French painter; b. 10 Feb. 1907, Aix-en-Provence; s. of Henri Marchand and Madeleine Cécile Michel de l'Hospital; m. 2nd Odile Vivier 1968; ed. Coll. of Aix-en-Provence, Bouches du Rhône, and studied in Pais; has exhibited in Paris since 1934; in Holland 1936, Cambridge 1939, Washington, Boston and Chicago 1939, Rio de Janeiro 1945, Brussels 1945, 1968, Canada 1946, New York 1946, Berne 1948, Geneva 1948, 1967, Stuttgart 1948, London, Stockholm, Avignon 1949, Innsbruck 1950; Bienal in São Paulo 1951; exhbns. in museums in Holland and Belgium 1951, in London (Wildenstein Galleries) 1952, in Switzerland and Germany 1953; in New York (Wildenstein Gallery) 1954, Venice Biennale 1954, in Mexico and Guatemala 1967, in Baden Baden 1974; work on perm. exhbn. in Musée d'Art Moderne, Galerie Maeght, Galerie Louis Carré (Paris), and in Grenoble, Arles, Algiers, Toulouse, The Hague, Liège, Eindhoven, Turin, Tokyo; a founder mem. and exhibitor in Salon de Mai 1945–; illustrated (lithographs) Les nourritures terrestres (André Gide), Le visionnaire (Julien Green), etc. and designed for the works of Darius Milhaud and Jacques Audiberti; lithographs for Petite cosmogonie portative (Raymond Queneau) 1955; Paul Guillaume Prize 1937, Arche Prize for design 1952. *Address:* 31 bis rue Campagne Première, 75014 Paris, France. *Telephone:* 4842-35-31, 4320-96-97.

MARCHANDISE-FRANQUET, Jacques; French lawyer and company executive; b. 6 July 1918, Paris; s. of Paul Marchandise and Mme Franquet; m. Jacqueline Feuillette 1940; three s. two d.; ed. Ecole Libre des Sciences Politiques; training as barrister 1939; sous-préfet, Dir. of office of Commissaire of the Repub., Laon 1944; auditeur, Council of State 1946; head of office of Minister for War Veterans 1948; legal adviser, Caisse Cen. de la France d'Outre-mer 1948; Chargé de mission for Minister of France Overseas 1952, head of office 1953–54; Maître des Requêtes, Council of State 1954, Maître des Requêtes Honoraire 1962; legal adviser, office of Pres. of Council of Ministers 1954–55; Asst. Dir. to Dir.-Gen., Bureau of Mines of France Overseas 1955; Sec.-Gen. Fria (int. aluminium production corpn.) 1956–60, Vice-Pres. 1967, Pres. 1969, Vice-Pres. Friguia (part-nationalized successor to Fria) 1976–; Dir. Pechiney 1960, Asst. Dir.-Gen. 1970, Dir. délégué to Pechiney Ugine Kuhlmann 1971–75; Dir. Aluminium de Grèce 1961, Pres. 1968–75; Vice-Pres. and Dir.-Gen. Librairie Hachette 1975, Pres. and Dir.-Gen. 1976–81; Pres. and Dir.-Gen. Soc. Frialco 1982–; Pres. Groupement de l'Industrie chimique 1981–; Pres. Franco-American Foundation 1982–, Institut pour l'histoire de l'Aluminium 1986–; Dir. Banque de Paris et des Pays-Bas 1978–, S.A. Philips Industrielle 1982–, Cie. Générale des Eaux 1984–; Commdr., Légion d'honneur, Ordre des Palmes académiques, Officier, Ordre nat. du Mérite, Croix de guerre. *Address:* 38 avenue Hoche, 75008 Paris (Office); 25 ter boulevard de La Saussaye, 92200 Neuilly, France (Home). *Telephone:* 4563-28-30 (Office).

MARCHUK, Guri Ivanovich; Soviet mathematician and politician; b. 8 June 1925, Petro-Khersonets Village, Orenburg Region; ed. Leningrad State Univ.; Sr. Research Assoc., Head of Dept., Inst. of Physics and Energetics, Obninsk 1953–62; Inst. of Maths. of Siberian Br. of U.S.S.R. Acad. of Sciences 1962–64; Dir. Computing Centre of Siberian Br. of U.S.S.R. Acad. of Sciences 1964–79; Deputy Chair. U.S.S.R. Council of Ministers and Chair. State Cttee. for Science and Tech. 1980–86; Pres. U.S.S.R. Acad. of Sciences 1986–; Deputy Chair., Chair. of Presidium of Siberian Br. of U.S.S.R. Acad. of Sciences 1964–79; Lenin Prize 1961; Order of Lenin (three times); State Prize 1979 and other decorations;

Corresp. mem. U.S.S.R. Acad. of Sciences 1962–68, mem. 1968–; mem. CPSU Cen. Cttee. 1986–. *Publications:* works on problems of computational mathematics and physics of atmosphere. *Address:* Leninsky prosp. 14, Moscow, U.S.S.R.

MARCHUK, Ivan Ivanovich; Soviet diplomatist; b. 14 Nov. 1922, Kozychanka, Kiev region, Ukraine; ed. Univ. of Kiev; Diplomatic Service 1947–; Counsellor, Conakry 1959–62; Deputy Head of Press Dept., U.S.S.R. Ministry of Foreign Affairs 1962–64; Amb. to Burundi 1964–67; on staff of Ministry of Foreign Affairs 1967–70; Amb. to Ecuador 1970–75; on staff of Ministry of Foreign Affairs 1975–77; Amb. to Chad 1977–79, to Zaire 1979–84. *Address:* c/o Ministry of Foreign Affairs, Moscow, U.S.S.R.

MARCINKEVICIUS, Iustinas Moteiaus; Soviet (Lithuanian) poet, playwright and translator; b. 1930, Vazhatkiemis, Lithuania; ed. Univ. of Vilnius; began literary career 1953; mem. CPSU 1957–; awards include State Prizes (twice), Komsomol Prize of Lithuanian S.S.R., People's Poet of Lithuania. *Publications include:* I Ask to Speak 1955, The Twentieth Spring 1955, The Pine that Laughed 1961, Blood and Ashes 1961, Hands that Share out the Bread 1963, The Wall 1965; plays: Mindaugas, The Cathedral, Mazhvydas; Collections of poetry.

MARCINKUS, Most Rev. Paul Casimir; American ecclesiastic; b. 15 Jan. 1922; ordained as a Roman Catholic priest 1947; Asst. Pastor, St. Cristina's Parish, Chicago 1947–52; joined Vatican State Secr. 1952; served as papal diplomatist in Canada and Bolivia; Gen. Man. Istituto per le Opere di Religioni (Vatican Bank) 1969–71, Chair. 1971–89; Pro-Pres. Pontifical Comm. for the Vatican City State 1981–; Titular Archbishop of Orta 1981–. *Address:* Via della Nocetta 63, 00164, Rome, Italy.

MARCKER, Kjeld Adrian, PH.D.; Danish molecular biologist; b. 27 Dec. 1932, Nyborg; s. of Kjeld A. C. Marcker and Minna C. Callesen; m. Anne Birgit Hansen 1964; two s. one d.; ed. Nyborg Gymnasium and Univ. of Copenhagen; Dept. of Physical Chem., Univ. of Copenhagen 1958; Carlsberg-Wellcome Fellow, MRC Lab. of Molecular Biol., Cambridge 1962, mem. staff 1964; Fellow, King's Coll. Cambridge 1968; Prof. in Molecular Biology, Aarhus Univ. 1970–; mem. Royal Danish Acad., Danish Acad. of Tech. Science; Novo Medical Prize 1971; Anders Jahre Medical Prize 1973. *Publications:* articles in scientific journals. *Leisure interests:* soccer, bird-watching, history. *Address:* Department of Molecular Biology and Plant Physiology, University of Aarhus, C. F. Møllers Alle 130, 8000 Aarhus C; Toftevej 1, 8250 Egå, Denmark (Home). *Telephone:* 06220118 (Home).

MARCOPOULOS, Christos, D.SC.; Greek nuclear chemist and politician; b. 25 Dec. 1925, Athens; s. of Antony Marcopoulos and Paraskevi Vergopoulou; m. 1st Sapfo Mazaraki 1954 (divorced 1960), one s.; m. 2nd Kleopatra Papadopoulou 1974, two s.; ed. Varvakios High School, Teachers' Acad., Athens, Univ. of Athens, Leicester Coll. of Tech., U.K.; Nat. State Chem. Lab. 1956–59; Group Leader, Greek Atomic Energy Comm. 1962–69, Dir. Radio-immunochem. 1977–81; Asst. Prof., Nat. Tech. Univ. of Athens 1965; Sr. Researcher, Imperial Coll., London 1968; Visiting Scientist, Tech. Hochschule, Darmstadt, Fed. Repub. of Germany; Visiting Prof., Univ. of Bologna 1973; Pres. Hellenic Nuclear Soc. 1975–81; mem. Steering Cttee., European Nuclear Soc. 1979–81; mem. Cen. Cttee., Panhellenic Socialistic Movement (PASOK) 1975–; mem. European Parl. 1981–84; Amb.-at-Large for West European Countries 1984–85; mem. Nat. Parl. of Greece 1985– (Pres. Foreign Affairs Cttee. 1986–87); Pres. Panhellenic Movement for Nat. Independence, World Peace and Disarmament 1981–, Head of Greek Parl. Del. in Council of Europe 1986–88 (Vice-Pres. Parl. Ass. 1987–88); Minister in charge of Int. Orgs. 1988–. *Publications:* Organic Chemistry (2 vols.) 1963 and 1971, Inorganic Chemistry (2 vols.) 1968 and 1971, Introduction to Modern Chemistry 1973 and over 50 articles on nuclear disarmament and peace. *Leisure interests:* swimming, classical music. *Address:* 34 Eratous Street, Holargos, Athens, Greece (Home). *Telephone:* 36 41 230 (Office), 65 29 696 (Home).

MARCOS, Ferdinand Edralin; Philippine lawyer and politician; b. 11 Sept. 1917; m. Imelda Romualdez (Marcos, q.v.); one s. two d.; ed. Univ. of the Philippines; Lieut., later Capt. in the Philippines Army and U.S. Forces in the Far East during Second World War; led own unit in anti-Japanese resistance; Special Asst. to Pres. Manuel Roxas 1946–47; mem. House of Reps. 1949–59, Senate 1959–66; Pres. of Senate 1963–65; Pres. of the Philippines 1965–86 (re-elected 1969, 1981), Prime Minister 1973–81; Leader Kilusan Bagong Lipunan (New Society Movement) 1981–86; forced to leave for Hawaii March 1987, indicted for embezzlement 1988; Dag Hammarskjöld Award 1968; numerous war decorations. *Leisure interest:* golf. *Address:* Honolulu, Hawaii, U.S.A.

MARCOS, Imelda Romualdez; Philippine politician and social leader; b. c. 1930; m. Ferdinand E. Marcos (q.v.); one s. two d.; Gov. of Metro Manila 1975–86; Roving Amb.; visited Beijing 1976; took part in negotiations in Libya over self-govt. for southern provinces 1977; leader Kilusan Bagong Lipunan (New Society Movement) 1978–81; mem. Batasang Pambansa (Interim Legis. Assembly) 1978–83; Minister of Human Settlements 1978–79, 1984–86, of Human Settlements and Ecology 1979–83; mem. Cabinet Exec. Cttee. 1982–84; Chair. Southern Philippines Devt. Authority 1980–86; indicted for embezzlement 1988. *Address:* Honolulu, Hawaii, U.S.A.

MARCUS, Rudolph Arthur; American professor of chemistry; b. 21 July 1923, Montreal, Canada; s. of Myer and Esther Marcus; m. Laura Hearne 1949; three s.; ed. McGill Univ.; worked for Nat. Research Council of Canada 1946–49; Univ. of N. Carolina 1949–51; Asst. Prof. Polytech. Inst. of Brooklyn 1951–54, Assoc. Prof. 1954–58, Prof. 1958–64; Prof. Univ. of Ill. 1964–68; Arthur Amos Noyes Prof. of Chem., Calif. Inst. of Tech. 1978–; Visiting Prof. of Theoretical Chem., Oxford Univ. 1975–76; temp. mem. Courant Inst. of Mathematical Sciences, New York Univ. 1960–61; mem. Council, Gordon Research Confs. 1965–68, Chair. Bd. of Trustees and mem. Bd. 1966–69; Chair. Div. of Physical Chem., American Chemical Soc. 1964–65; mem. Exec. Cttee. American Physical Soc. Div. of Chemical Physics 1970–72; mem. Advisory Bd. American Chemical Soc. Petroleum Research Fund 1970–72; mem. Review Cttee. Argonne Nat. Laboratory Chem. Dept. 1966–72 (Chair. 1968–69), Brookhaven Nat. Lab. 1971–73, Radiation Lab., Univ. of Notre Dame 1976–78; mem. Nat. Research Council/N.A.S., Cttee. on Climatic Impact; Chair. Cttee. on Kinetics of Chemical Reactions 1975–77, Panel on Atmospheric Chem. 1975–78, Cttee. on Chemical Sciences 1977–79, Cttee. Survey Opportunities in Chem. 1982–86, Advisory Cttee. for Chem. Nat. Science Foundation 1977–80, Review Cttee. Chem. Depts. Princeton Univ. 1972–78, Polytech. Inst. of N.Y. 1977–80, Calif. Inst. of Tech. 1977–78; mem. editorial bds., Journal of Chemical Physics 1964–66, Annual Review of Physical Chem. 1964–69, Journal of Physical Chem. 1968–72, 1980–84, Accounts of Chemical Research 1968–73, Int. Journal of Chemical Kinetics 1976–80, Molecular Physics 1977–80, Chemical Physics Letters 1980–, Laser Chem. 1983–, Advances in Chemical Physics 1984–, Theoretica Chimica Acta 1985–, Work Scientific Publishing 1987–, Int. Reviews in Physical Chem. 1988–; mem. N.A.S.; Fellow, American Acad. of Arts and Sciences, Co-Chair. Exec. Cttee. Western Section; Foreign mem. Royal Society, London; mem. Int. Acad. Quantum Molecular Science; Prof., Fellow Univ. Coll., Oxford Univ. 1975–76; Assoc. mem. Center for Advanced Studies, Univ. of Ill. 1968–69; Anne Molson Prize for Chem. 1943; Nat. Science Foundation Sr. Post-Doctoral Fellowship 1960–61; Alfred P. Sloan Fellowship 1960–63; Fulbright-Hays Sr. Scholar 1971–72; Alexander von Humboldt Foundation Sr. U.S. Scientist Award 1976; Irving Langmuir Award in Chem. Physics (American Chemical Soc.) 1978, R. A. Robinson Medal, Faraday Div., Royal Soc. of Chem. 1982, C. F. Chandler Medal (Univ. of Columbia) 1983, Wolf Prize 1985, Peter Debye Award in Physical Chem. (American Chemical Soc.) 1988, Willard Cribbs Medal (American Chemical Soc.) 1988, Centenary Medal, Faraday Div., Royal Soc. Chem. 1988; Hon. D.Sc. (Chicago) 1983, (Polytechnic Univ.) 1986, (Gothenborg) 1987, (McGill Univ.) 1988; numerous university guest lectureships. *Publications:* numerous articles in scientific journals, especially Journal of Chemical Physics. *Leisure interests:* music, history, tennis and skiing. *Address:* California Institute of Technology, Pasadena, Calif. 91125, U.S.A.

MARCUS, Ruth Barcan, M.A., PH.D.; American professor of philosophy; b. 2 Aug. 1921, New York; d. of Samuel Barcan and Rose Post; m. Jules A. Marcus 1942 (divorced 1976); two s. two d.; ed. New York and Yale Univs.; Research Assoc. Inst. for Human Relations, Yale Univ. 1945–47; Assoc. Prof. Roosevelt Univ. 1959–64; Prof. and Chair. Dept. of Philosophy, Univ. of Ill. 1964–70; Prof. Northwestern Univ. 1970–73; Reuben Post Halleck Prof. of Philosophy, Yale Univ. 1973–; Adviser, Oxford Univ. Press New York 1980–; Fellow, Center for Advanced Studies, Stanford Univ. 1979, Inst. for Advanced Study in the Humanities, Univ. of Edinburgh 1983, Wolfson Coll. Oxford 1985, 1986, Clare Hall, Cambridge 1988; Fellow, American Acad. of Arts and Sciences; mem. and Vice-Pres. Int. Inst. de Philosophie, Paris; Chair. Nat. Bd. of Officers, American Philosophical Asscn. 1977–83; Pres. Assen. for Symbolic Logic 1983–86; Medal, Coll. de France 1986; mem. numerous editorial bds. *Publications:* The Logical Enterprise (ed. with A. Anderson and R. Martin) 1975, Logic Methodology and Philosophy of Science 1986; articles in professional journals. *Address:* Department of Philosophy, Box 3650, Yale University, New Haven, Conn. 06520 (Office); 311 St. Ronan Street, New Haven, Conn. 06511, U.S.A. (Home). *Telephone:* 203-432-1665 (Office); 203-787-3074 (Home).

MARCUS, Stanley, B.A.; American business executive; b. 20 April 1905, Dallas; s. of late Herbert Marcus, Sr. and Minnie Lichtenstein Marcus; m. 1st Mary Cantrell 1932 (deceased), one s. two d.; m. 2nd Linda Cumber 1979; ed. Amherst Coll., Harvard Univ., and Harvard Business School; joined Neiman-Marcus 1926, Sec., Treas. and Dir. 1928, Merchandise Man. of Sports Shop 1928, Merchandise Man. of all Apparel Divs. 1929, Exec. Vice-Pres. 1935–50, Pres. 1950–72, Chair. of Bd. 1972–75, Chair. Exec. Cttee. 1975–77, Chair. Emer. 1977–; with Stanley Marcus Consultancy Services; owner Somesuch Press; fmr. Hon. Dir., Consultant and Corporate Vice-Pres. Carter Hawley Hale Stores Inc., Los Angeles; Dir. Republic of Texas Corpn., New York Life Insurance Co., Jack Lenor Larsen Inc., New York, Center for the Book Library of Congress; Dir. Dallas Symphony Soc. (Pres. 1948–49), N. Tex. State Comm.; founding mem. Business Cttee. for the Arts; fmr. mem. of many cttees. and asscns.; mem. Gov. Bd., Common Cause 1976–79; mem. Exec. Cttee., Nat. Council for Arts and Educ.; mem. Bd. of Publs. of Southern Methodist Univ.; mem. Bd. Dirs. and Chair. Internat (marketing co.); Dir. Center for Study of Democratic Insts.; Trustee, Southern Methodist Univ.; Hon. Trustee, Cttee. for Econ. Devt.; fmrly. held many similar civic offices; mem. Texas Inst. of Letters 1976; Hon. D.H. (Southern Methodist Univ.) 1965, Hon. Dr. Arts and

Letters (N. Tex. State Univ.) 1982; numerous awards from U.S.A., Austria, Denmark, U.K., Italy, Belgium, France. *Publications:* Minding the Store 1974, My Fashion Business 1976, Quest for the Best 1979, His & Hers: The Fantasy World of the Nieman-Marcus Catalogue 1982 and numerous articles in the press. *Leisure interests:* collecting primitive books, books on typography, collecting African and other primitive art. *Address:* 4800 Republic Bank Tower, Dallas, Tex. 75201 (Office); 1 Nonesuch Road, Dallas, Tex. 75214, U.S.A. (Home).

MARCZEWSKI, Jan; French university professor; b. 27 May 1908, Warsaw, Poland; s. of Witold Marczewski and Rose Szymanska; m. Janine-Victoire Wroblewska 1930; one s.; ed. Lycée Henri Poincaré, Nancy, Univs. of Nancy, Strasbourg and Paris à la Sorbonne; early career in Polish Consular Service 1926-40; War Service with Polish Army in France; Scientific Dir. Inst. de Science Economique Appliquée, Paris, and mem. Higher Council for Nat. Revenue 1946-50; Prof. Inst. Political Studies, Paris, Scientific Dir. E. European Section of Nat. Foundation of Political Sciences, and Founder and Dir. Preparation Centre, Univ. of Caen 1952-59, Hon. Prof. 1959-; Prof. of Econs., Univ. of Paris I 1959-77, Hon. Prof. 1977-; Hon. Pres. French Econ. Asscn., Soc. of Political Econ.; Scientific Dir. Europe de l'Est et Union Soviétique 1952-59; Vice-Pres. Féd. Int. Libre des Déportés et Internés de la Résistance; Chevalier, Légion d'honneur, Croix de guerre, Krzyż Walecznych (Poland). *Publications:* Politique monétaire et financière du IIIe Reich 1941, Planification et croissance économique des démocraties populaires 1956, La conjoncture économique des Etats-Unis 1850-1960 1961, L'Europe dans la conjoncture mondiale 1963, Comptabilité nationale 1965, Introduction à l'histoire quantitative 1966, Crise de la planification socialiste 1973, Inflation et chômage en France, explication quantative 1977, Vaincre l'inflation et le chômage 1978, La crise de l'économie mondiale 1983, The Concept of Macroeconomic Cost and Its Utility 1986 and numerous articles on econ. theory and history. *Leisure interests:* skiing, sailing, swimming. *Address:* 53 boulevard Suchet, Paris 75016, France. *Telephone:* 4525-57-03.

MARDALL, Cyril Leonard, (b. Sjöström), F.R.I.B.A.; British architect; b. 21 Nov. 1909, Helsinki, Finland; s. of Einar and Phyllis (née Mardall) Sjöström; m. June Park 1948; one s. one d.; ed. Nya Svenska Laroverket, Helsinki, Northern Polytechnic School of Architecture, Architectural Asscn. Inc., London; Consultant Architect, Govt. of Sweden House Exporting Cttee. 1937-39; Lieut. R.N.V.R. 1940-43; UN Relief and Rehabilitation Asscn. 1943-44; Consulting Architect to Air Ministry on System Building 1939-40; founder partner Yorke, Rosenberg, Mardall (architects) 1944-75; C. Mardall and June Park Consultancy for work in Finland, Netherlands, W. Indies and Ireland 1975-; Commdr., Order of Lion of Finland. *Publications:* The Architecture of Yorke, Rosenberg, Mardall 1944 to 1972. *Address* 5 Boyne Terrace Mews, London, W11 3LR, England. *Telephone:* 01-221 6199.

MÅRDH, Per-Anders, M.D., PH.D.; Swedish university professor and physician; b. 9 April 1941, Stockholm; s. of Gustav-Adolf Mårdh and Inga-Greta (née Bodin) Mårdh; m. Ingrid Ekstrand 1967; one s. one d.; ed. Univ. of Lund; Assoc. Prof. Univ. of Lund 1973; Dir. WHO Collaboration Centre for Sexually Transmitted Diseases, Univ. of Lund 1980-85, then Uppsala Univ. 1985-; Prof. Clinical Bacteriology, Univ. of Uppsala 1984-; mem. of Priority Cttee., Swedish Medical Research Council 1984-; founder and Bd. mem., BioCarb AB, Science Park, Lund 1982; Fernström's Award for young prominent research workers 1982. *Publications:* as Ed.: Genital Infections and Their Complications 1975, Chlamydia trachomatis in Genital and Related Infections 1982, Chlamydial Infections 1982, International Perspectives on Neglected Sexually Transmitted Diseases 1983, Gas Chromatography/Mass Spectrometry in Applications in Microbiology 1984, Sexually Transmitted Diseases 1984, Bacterial Vaginosis 1984, Coagulase-negative Staphylococci 1986, Infections in Primary Health Care 1986; Author: Chlamydia 1988. *Leisure interests:* art, skiing. *Address:* Department of Clinical Bacteriology, University of Uppsala, Box 552, 751 22 Uppsala, Sweden. *Telephone:* 018-663902.

MARÉCHAL, (Robert Gaston) André, D. ÈS SC.; French optical physicist (retd.); b. 10 Dec. 1916, La Garenne; s. of Victor Maréchal and Henriette Maréchal; m. 1st Jacqueline Poullain 1967; one s. one d.; m. 2nd Lucienne Chenaud 1977; m. 3rd Christine Villeneuve 1981; ed. Ecole Normale Supérieure, Ecole Supérieure d'Optique; Asst. Prof Univ. of Paris, Inst. d'Optique 1943-50, Lecturer 1950-55, Full Prof. 1955-85, Prof. Emer. 1985-; Délegué Gén. for Scientific Research 1961-68; Pres. Int. Comm. of Optics 1962-66; Dir. Inst. d'Optique 1968-84; mem. Acad. of Sciences 1981-; Pres. MESUCORA 1985-; Commdr Légion d'honneur, Thomas Young Medal 1965, Mees Medal 1977; Hon. mem. Optical Soc. of America 1986. *Publications:* numerous scientific papers relating to modern problems of optics. *Leisure interests:* music, mountaineering, travel. *Address:* 25 rue de Chazelles, 75017 Paris, France (Home). *Telephone:* 47.66.75.41 (Home).

MAREE, John B., B.COMM., A.M.P.; South African business executive; b. 13 Aug. 1924, Middelburg, Cape; s. of Dr. John Maree; m. Joy du Plessis 1950; two s.; ed. Univ. of the Witwatersrand and Harvard Business School; Industrial Div., Union Free State Mining and Finance Corpn. 1951-67; Man. Dir. and Deputy Chair. Calan Ltd., Chair. Bldg. and Construction Div. 1982-; joined Barlow Rand as Exec. Chair. of Rand Mines Property 1970, Exec. Dir. 1974; Chair. Atomic Energy Corpn., 1986; seconded to

Dept. of Defence 1979-82; Star of S.A. 1985; Alexander Aitken Medal, one of top 5 Businessmen of the Year 1981. *Leisure interests:* golf, gardening. *Address:* Barlow Rand Ltd., P.O. Box 78 2248, Sandton 2196; 52 4th Road, Hyde Park, Sandton 2146, South Africa (Home). *Telephone:* 788-8512 (Home).

MAREI, Sayed Ahmed; Egyptian politician; b. 26 Aug. 1913; m. Soad Marei 1941; two s. one d.; ed. Faculty of Agric., Cairo Univ.; worked on his father's farm after graduation; subsequently with import-export, pharmaceutical, seed, and fertilizer companies; mem. Egyptian House of Commons 1945-49; Del. mem. Higher Cttee. for Agrarian Reform 1952-; Chair. of Bd., Agricultural Co-operative Credit Bank 1955-56; initiated "Supervised Credit System"; Minister of State for Agrarian Reform 1936-57; Minister of Agric. and Agrarian Reform 1957-58; Cent. Minister for Agric. and Agrarian Reform in the U.A.R. 1958-61; later Deputy Speaker U.A.R. Nat. Ass.; Pres. Bank Misr, Cairo 1963-67; Minister of Agric. 1967-70, and of Agrarian Reform 1968-70; Deputy Premier of Agric. and Land Reform, Land Reclamation 1970-72; Sec. Arab Socialist Union 1972-73; Asst. to Pres. 1973-75, 1978-; Sec.-Gen. UN World Food Conf., Rome 1974, Pres. World Food Council 1975-77; Speaker, People's Ass. 1975-78. *Publications:* Agrarian Reform in Egypt (in English), Agriculture in the U.A.R. Enters a New Era (in English), Problems of Agrarian Reform and the Population Explosion, Food Production in Developing Countries: Possibilities and Means, Agriculture in Egypt (in English), The World Food Crisis (in English) 1976; reports on Agricultural Missions to Syria, U.S.S.R., Italy, U.S.A. and Iraq. *Address:* 9 Sharia Shagaret el-Door, Zamalek, Cairo, Egypt. *Telephone:* 400166.

MARENGO, Pier Carlo; Italian banker; b. 29 Jan. 1926, Turin; two d.; ed. Univ. of Turin; joined Credito Italiano 1946, apptd. Officer 1953, Vice-Rep. to Bank's Rep. Office, New York 1955, U.S. Rep. 1965, returned to Head Office, Milan 1971, Deputy Gen. Man. 1973, Gen. Man. 1982, Man. Dir. 1985-; mem. Finance Comm. and Comm. for Int. Monetary Relations, Italian Section, ICC, Exec. Cttee. and Dir. Mediobanca, Exec. Cttee. and Dir. Associazione Sindacale fra le Aziende di Credito; Deputy Chair. Associazione Bancaria Italiana; Chair. Politico-Econ. and Monetary Comm., Centre Européen de l'Entreprise Publique, Brussels; Grande Ufficiale dell'Ordine al Merito. *Address:* Credito Italiano, Direzione Centrale, Piazza Cordusio, 20123 Milan, Italy. *Telephone:* 02-88621.

MARGÁIN, Hugo, B.; Mexican lawyer and diplomatist; b. 13 Feb. 1913, Mexico City; m. Margarita Charles 1941; three s. (one deceased) three d.; ed. Univ. Nacional Autónoma de México; Prof. Univ. Nacional Autónoma de México 1947-51; Dir.-Gen. Sales Tax Bureau 1951, Income Tax Bureau 1952-59; Asst. Sec. for Admin. Ministry of Industry and Commerce 1959-61; Under-Sec. for Industry and Commerce 1961-64; Pres. Nat. Comm. for Distribution of Profits 1963-64; Chair. Nat. Comm. on Profit Sharing 1963; Amb. to the U.S.A. 1964-70; Minister of Finance 1970-73; Amb. to U.K. (also accred. to Iceland) 1973-76, to the U.S.A. 1977-82. *Publications:* Importance of Fiscal Law in the Economic Development 60, An Adequate Public Administration 61, World Tax Series Taxation in Mexico 1957, and numerous financial and taxation articles. *Address:* c/o Ministerio de Relaciones Exteriores, Avenue Nonoalco, Matelolco, México 3, D.F., Mexico.

MARGARET ROSE, H.R.H. The Princess, Countess of Snowdon, C.I., G.C.V.O., G.C.ST.J.; b. 21 Aug. 1930, Glamis Castle, Angus, Scotland; sister of H.M. Queen Elizabeth II (q.v.); married Antony Armstrong-Jones (now 1st Earl of Snowdon, q.v.) 1960 (divorced 1978); son, Viscount Linley, b. 1961; daughter, Lady Sarah Frances Elizabeth, b. 1964; Pres. Royal Ballet; Grand Cross, Order Crown of Belgium; Hon. D.Mus. (London), Hon. LL.D. (Keele). *Address:* 10 Kensington Palace, London, W8 4PU, England.

MARGÉOT, H.E. Cardinal Jean; Mauritian ecclesiastic; b. 3 Feb. 1916, Port-Louis; ordained 1938, elected bishop of Port-Louis 1969, consecrated 1969; cr. Cardinal 1988. *Address:* Evêché, rue Mgr. Gonin, Port-Louis, Mauritius. *Telephone:* (08) 5663.

MARGERIE, Emmanuel Jacquin de, L.EN D.; French diplomatist; b. 25 Dec. 1924, Paris; s. of Roland and Jenny (née Fabre-Luce) Jacquin de Margerie; m. Hélène Hottinguer 1953; one s. one d.; ed. Aurore Univ., Shanghai, Inst. d'études politiques, Paris, Ecole nat. d'administration; Sec. European section, Ministry of Foreign Affairs 1951-54; Sec. London Embassy 1955-59, First Sec., Moscow 1959-61; Deputy Dir. E. European section, Ministry of Foreign Affairs 1961-67; First Counsellor, Tokyo 1967-70, Minister Plenipotentiary 1970, First Counsellor, Washington 1970, Minister-Counsellor 1971-72; Dir. European Dept., Ministry of Foreign Affairs 1972-74; Dir. of French Museums 1975-77; Amb. to Spain 1977-81, to U.K. 1981-84, to U.S.A. 1984-; Officier, Légion d'honneur, Officier, Ordre nat. du Mérite, Commdr. Ordre des Arts et des Lettres; Grand Cross, Order of Isabel la Católica (Spain). *Address:* French Embassy, 2535 Belmont Road, N.W., Washington, D.C. 20008, U.S.A.; 9 rue Bonaparte, 75006 Paris, France. *Telephone:* (202) 328-2600 (Washington).

MARGETSON, Sir John (W. D.), K.C.M.G.; British diplomatist (retd.); b. 9 Oct. 1927, Edinburgh, Scotland; s. of Very Rev. W. J. and Mrs. Margetson; m. Miranda Coldstream 1963; one s. one d.; ed. Blundell's School, St. John's Coll., Univ. of Cambridge; Lieut. Life Guards 1947-49; Colonial Admin. Service, Tanganyika 1951-60, Pvt. Sec. to Gov. 1956-57; entered diplomatic service 1960, at The Hague, then in Saigon, then mem. del. to

NATO; Amb. to Viet-Nam 1978-80; Deputy Perm. Rep. and Amb. to UN, New York 1983-84; Amb. to Netherlands 1984-87; Dir. John S. Cohen Foundation 1988-; Chair. Royal School of Church Music 1988-; World Family (Foster Parents Plan, U.K.) 1988-. *Leisure interest:* music. *Address:* c/o Coutts and Co., 1 Old Park Lane, London, W1Y 4BS, England.

MARGOLIASH, Emanuel, M.D.; American biochemist; b. 10 Feb. 1920, Cairo, Egypt; s. of Wolf Margoliash and Bertha Margoliash (née Kotler); m. Sima Beshkin 1944; two s.; ed. Mission Laïque Française, Cairo, American Univ. of Beirut, Lebanon; Research Fellow, Dept. of Experimental Pathology, Hebrew Univ., Jerusalem 1945-48; served as Medical Officer in the Israel Army 1948-49; Sr. Asst. in Experimental Pathology, Cancer Research Labs., Hadassah Medical School, Hebrew Univ., Jerusalem 1951; worked under Prof. D. Keilin, Molteno Inst., Univ. of Cambridge, England 1951-53; Acting Head, Cancer Research Labs., Hadassah Medical School, Hebrew Univ., Jerusalem 1954-58, Lecturer in Experimental Pathology, 1955; worked at Nobel Inst., Dept. of Biochem. under a fellowship of the Dazian Foundation for Medical Research 1958; Research Assoc., Dept. of Biochem., Univ. of Utah Coll. of Medicine, Salt Lake City, Utah, U.S.A. 1958-60; Research Assoc., McGill-Montreal Gen. Hospital Research Inst., Montreal, Canada 1960-62; Research Fellow and Head, Protein Section, Dept. of Molecular Biology, Abbott Labs., North Chicago, Ill. 1962-71; Professorial Lecturer, Dept. of Biochem., Univ. of Chicago, Ill. 1964-71; Prof. of Biochem. and Molecular Biology, Northwestern Univ., Evanston, Ill. 1971-; mem. Nat. Acad. of Sciences and numerous scientific socs.; Fellow, American Acad. of Arts and Sciences; mem. Editorial Bd. of Journal of Biological Chem. 1966-72, Biochemical Genetics 1966-80, Journal of Molecular Evolution 1971-82, Biochem. Int. 1981-; mem. Int. Union of Biochem. Cttee. on Nomenclature 1962-, Advisory Cttee., Mich. State Univ. Atomic Energy Comm. Plant Research Lab. 1967-72; Co-Chair. Gordon Research Conf. on Proteins 1967; Keilin Memorial Lectureship of the Biochemical Soc. 1970; Harvey Soc. Lectureship 1970-71; mem. Publs. Cttee., American Soc. of Biological Chemists Inc. 1973-76; Chair. Dept. of Biochem., Molecular Biology and Cell Biology, Northwestern Univ. 1979-82; mem. of Exec. Cttee. of U.S. Bioenergetics Group of the Biophysical Soc. 1980-; Rudi Lemberg Fellow, Australian Acad. of Science 1981; Guggenheim Fellow 1983. *Publications:* more than 200 scientific papers and volumes. *Address:* Department of Biochemistry, Molecular Biology and Cell Biology, Northwestern University, Evanston, Ill. 60201; 353 Madison Avenue, Glencoe, Ill. 60022, U.S.A.

MARGRAVE, John, B.S., PH.D.; American professor of chemistry; b. 13 April 1924, Kansas City; s. of Orville Frank Margrave and Bernice J. Hamilton Margrave; m. Mary Lou Davis 1950; one s. one d.; ed. Univ. of Kansas, Lawrence; AEC Postdoctoral Fellow, Univ. of Calif., Berkeley 1951-52; Instructor, Assoc. Prof. then Prof. of Chem., Univ. of Wis. 1952-63; Prof. of Chem., Rice Univ. 1963-, Chair. Dept. of Chem. 1967-72, E. D. Butcher Chair. 1986-, Dean of Advanced Studies and Research, Rice Univ. 1972-80, Vice-Pres. 1980-86; consultant to govt. agencies and pvt. industry; Pres. MarChem Inc. 1969-, High Temperature Science Inc. 1968-; Vice-Pres. for Research, Houston Area Research Center (HARC) 1986-; Chair. Cttee. on Chemical Processes in Severe Nuclear Accidents, Nat. Research Council 1987-; mem. A.A.A.S., American Chemical Soc., American Physical Soc., Chemical Soc. (U.K.) and other socs.; Fellow American Inst. of Chemists; mem. N.A.S.; Alfred P. Sloan Research Fellow 1956-57, 1957-58; Guggenheim Research Fellow 1961; numerous awards include American Chemical Soc. Award in Inorganic Chem. 1967, Award in Fluorine Chem. 1980, Distinguished Alumnus Award 1981; mem. numerous advisory cttees. and editorial bds. *Address:* 5012 Tangle Lane, Houston, Tex. 75506 (Home); Rice University, P.O. Box 2692, Houston, Tex. 77252, U.S.A. (Office). *Telephone:* (713) 527-4813 (Office).

MARGRETHE II, H.M. Queen of Denmark; b. 16 April 1940; d. of late King Frederik IX and of Queen Ingrid; m. Count Henri de Laborde de Monpezat (now Prince Henrik of Denmark) 1967; two s.; ed. Univs. of Copenhagen, Aarhus and Cambridge, The Sorbonne, Paris, and London School of Econs.; succeeded to the throne 14 Jan. 1972; has undertaken many official visits abroad with her husband, travelling extensively in Europe, the Far East, North and South America; illustrated The Lord of the Rings 1977-78, Norse Legends as Told by Jorgen Stegelmann 1979, Bjarkemaal 1982; Hon. LL.D. (Cambridge) 1975, (London) 1980; K.G. 1979. *Publications:* (Trans.) All Men are Mortal (with Prince Henrik) 1981, The Valley 1988, The Fields 1989. *Address:* Amalienborg Palace, Copenhagen, Denmark.

MARGULIS, Lynn, PH.D.; American biologist; b. 5 March 1938, Chicago, d. of Morris and Leona Wise Alexander; m. 1st Carl Sagan 1957; m. 2nd T. N. Margulis 1967; three s. one d.; ed. Univs. of Chicago, Wisconsin and Calif. at Berkeley; Research Assoc. Dept. of Biology, Brandeis Univ. 1963-64, Lecturer 1963-65, Biology Co-ordinator, Peace Corps, Colombia Project 1965-66; Consultant and Staff mem. The Elementary Science Study, Educational Services 1963-67; Adjunct Asst. Prof. Dept. of Biology, Boston Univ. 1966-67, Asst. Prof. 1967-71, Assoc. Prof. 1971-77, Prof. 1977-, Univ. Prof. 1986-; Visiting Prof. Dept. of Marine Biology, Scripps Inst. of Oceanography Jan.-March 1980, Dept. of Geology and Planetary Science Calif. Inst. of Tech. 1980, Dept. of Microbiology, Universidad Autónama de Barcelona, Spain 1986; NASA-Ames Planetary Biology and

Microbial Ecology Summer Research Programme 1980, 1982, 1984; Guggenheim Foundation Fellow 1979; Sherman Fairchild Distinguished Scholar, Calif. Inst. of Tech. 1977; mem. N.A.S.; Fellow A.A.A.S.; NASA Public Service Award 1981. *Publications:* Origin of Eukaryotic Cells 1970, Origins of Life I (Ed.) 1970, Origins of Life II (Ed.) 1971, Origins of Life: Planetary Astronomy (Ed.) 1973, Origins of Life: Chemistry and Radioastronomy (Ed.) 1973, Limits of Life (Ed. with C. Ponnamperuma) 1980, Symbiosis in Cell Evolution 1981, Early Life 1982, Five Kingdoms: An Illustrated Guide to the Phyla of Life on Earth (with Schwartz) 1982, Origins of Sex (with D. Sagan) 1986, Microcosmos: Four billion years of evolution from our bacterial ancestors (with D. Sagan) 1986. *Leisure interests:* fiction, ballet, Spain, pre-Columbian Mexican culture. *Address:* Department of Biology, Boston University, 2 Cummington Street, Boston, Mass. 02215, U.S.A. *Telephone:* (617) 353-2443.

MARIAM, Lt.-Col. Mengistu Haile; Ethiopian army officer and politician; b. 1937; m. Wubanchi Bishaw; ed. Holeta Mil. Acad.; served in Army's Third Div., attaining rank of Maj.; mem. Armed Forces Co-ordinating Cttee. (Derg) June 1974-; took leading part in overthrow of Emperor Haile Sellassie Sept. 1974, Head of Derg Exec. Cttee. Nov. 1974; First Vice-Chair. Provisional Mil. Admin. Council (PMAC) 1974-77, Chair. (Head of State) Feb. 1977-; Pres. of Democratic Repub. of Ethiopia Sept. 1987-; Chair. PMAC Standing Cttee.; Chair. Council of Ministers Dec. 1976-, OAU 1983-84; Sec.-Gen. Workers' Party of Ethiopia Sept. 1984-. *Address:* c/o Provisional Military Administrative Council, Addis Ababa, Ethiopia.

MARIATEGUÍ, Sandro; Peruvian politician; Senator of Acción Popular (AP) Party; Prime Minister and Minister of Foreign Affairs April-Oct. 1984. *Address:* c/o Oficina del Primer Ministro, Lima, Peru.

MARIE, Aurelius John Baptiste Lamothe, M.B.E.; Dominica lawyer and politician; b. 23 Dec. 1904, Portsmouth, Dominica; s. of Bright Percival Marie and Lily Marie; m. Bernadette Dubois 1964; one s.; fmr. magistrate; Pres. of Dominica Feb. 1980-83. *Leisure interests:* gardening, reading, hiking. *Address:* c/o Office of the President, Roseau, Dominica.

MARIN, Jean (pseudonym of Yves Morvan); French journalist; b. 24 Feb. 1909, Douarnenez; s. of Henri Edouard and Octavie Eugénie Angèle (née Michaux) Morvan; m. 1st Ulla Malm Rasmussen (divorced), one s.; m. 2nd Maria Dupont 1964; ed. Britanny and Paris; naval officer 1930-38; broadcast for Free French from London during World War II; mem. Conseil Municipal de Paris 1945-53, Vice-Pres. 1946-47; Pres., Dir.-Gen. Agence France Presse 1954-75; Pres. European Alliance of Information Agencies 1961-69; Dir. Publicis, Inter-France Quotidiens 1975-; Grand-Officier, Légion d'honneur, Croix de guerre, Hon. K.B.E. 1975 and other honours. *Address:* 133 avenue des Champs-Elysées, 75008 Paris, France.

MARIN, Manuel; Spanish international official; b. 1949; ed. Coll. of Europe, Bruges and Univ. of Nancy; joined Spanish Socialist Party 1975; M.P. for Ciudad Real, La Mancha 1977; EEC Commr. for Social Affairs, Employment, Educ. and Training 1986-89, for Co-operation and Devt., Fisheries Jan. 1989-. *Address:* 200 rue de la Loi, 1049, Brussels, Belgium.

MARINI-BETTOLO, Giovanni Battista, DR.CHEM.; Italian professor of chemistry; b. 27 June 1915, Rome; s. of Rinaldo and Evelina (Bettolo); m. Luisa Piva 1945; four c.; ed. Univ. of Rome; Asst. Univ. of Rome 1938-46; Prof. of Chem., Catholic Univ., Santiago 1947-48; Prof., Faculty of Chem., Univ. of Montevideo 1948-49; Research Prof., Istituto Superiore di Sanita, Rome 1950-60, Head, Dept. of Biochem. 1961-68, Dir. 1964-71; Prof. of Chem. Univ. of Rome 1971-; Chair. European Pharmaceutical Comm. 1964-68; Pres. Accad. Naz. delle Scienze 1981-89; Pres. Pontifical Acad. of Sciences 1988-. *Publications:* numerous articles. *Address:* 00196 Rome, Via Principessa Clotilde 1, Italy.

MARIOLOPOULOS, Elias, M.A., D.U.P., D. ÈS SC.; Greek meteorologist; b. 1900, Athens; m. Catherine Canaguini 1938; ed. Univs. of Athens, Cambridge, London and Paris; Chief, Meteorological Dept. Nat. Observatory, Athens 1925-28; Prof. of Meteorology, Univ. of Thessaloniki 1928-39; Prof. of Meteorology, Univ. of Athens 1939, Rector Univ. of Athens 1959-61; mem. Acad. of Athens; Pres. Nat. Observatory, Athens 1942, Pres. Nat. Cttee. of Geophysics and Geodesy; mem. Int. Climatological Comm.; several Greek and foreign decorations. *Publications:* Climate of Greece (Greek), Atlas Climatique de la Grèce (French), Distribution des Eléments météorologiques en Grèce, Climate of Athens, Dodecanese, Climate of Different Regions of Greece, etc. *Address:* 48 Aghias Lavras Street, Patissia, Athens 11141, Greece.

MARJAI, József; Hungarian politician; b. 18 Dec. 1923, Budapest; s. of József Marjai and Erzsébet Bihary; four s.; joined workers movt. 1939, Communist Party 1943; took job with Foreign Ministry 1948, leader of various depts.; Amb. to Switzerland, Czechoslovakia and Yugoslavia; Deputy Foreign Minister 1970, Sec. of State 1973, Amb. to Moscow 1976; elected mem. Hungarian Socialist Workers Party Cen. Cttee. 1976; Deputy Prime Minister 1978-88, Minister of Trade 1987-88; Hungarian Perm. Rep. to CMEA 1978; Pres. Econ. Cttee. of Council of Ministers 1980; Pres. Comm. for Internal Econ. Relations of Council of Ministers 1987; Pres. Nat. Tourism Bd. 1988-; Order of Merit for Socialist Fatherland, Labour Order of Merit (three times), Memorial Plaque for Worker-Peasant Power. *Publication:* Egyensúly, realitás, reform (Balance, Reality, Reform) 1984.

Address: Prime Minister's Office, Budapest V, Kossuth Lajos tér 1, Hungary.

MARJORIBANKS, Sir James Alexander Milne, K.C.M.G., M.A.; British diplomatist; b. 29 May 1911, Edinburgh; s. of Thomas Marjoribanks and Mary Ord Logan; m. Sonya Alder 1936 (died 1981); one d.; ed. Edinburgh Acad., Edinburgh Univ., Strasbourg Univ., and Univ. degli Studi, Florence; entered Foreign Office 1934; early service in Beijing, Hankou, Marseilles, Jacksonville, Florida, New York, Bucharest, Canberra 1934-52; Deputy Head Del. to High Authority of European Coal and Steel Community 1952-55; Cabinet Office, London 1955-57; Econ. Minister, Bonn 1957-62; Asst. Under-Sec. Foreign Office 1962-65; Amb. to the EEC and Head of Del. 1965-71; Dir. Distillers Co. Ltd. 1971-76; Chair. Scotland in Europe 1979-; Vice-Pres. Scottish Council (Devt. and Industry); Gen. Council Assessor to Edinburgh Univ. Court 1975-79; Governing mem. Inveresk Research Int. Foundation 1978-. *Leisure interests:* mountaineering, golf. *Address:* 13 Regent Terrace, Edinburgh EH7 5BN; Lintonrig, Kirk Yetholm, Roxburghshire, TD5 8PH, Scotland.

MARK, Alan Francis, PH.D., F.R.S.N.Z.; New Zealand professor of botany; b. 19 June 1932, Dunedin; s. of Cyril L. Mark and Frances E. Marshall; m. Patricia K. Davie 1957; two s. two d.; ed. Mosgiel District High School, Univ. of Otago and Duke Univ., N. Carolina; Otago Catchment Bd., Dunedin 1959-61; Sr. Research Fellow, Hellaby Indigenous Grasslands Research Trust 1961-65, Adviser in Research 1965-; Lecturer, Univ. of Otago 1960, Sr. Lecturer 1966, Assoc. Prof. 1969, Prof. of Botany 1975-; Visiting Asst. Prof. Duke Univ. 1966; Fulbright Travel Award 1955; James B. Duke Fellowship 1957; Loder Cup 1975. *Publications:* New Zealand Alpine Plants (with N. M. Adams) 1973, about 100 scientific papers. *Leisure interests:* nature conservation, enjoying the outdoors. *Address:* Department of Botany, University of Otago, Box 56, Dunedin (Office); 205 Wakari Road, Helensburgh, Dunedin, New Zealand (Home). *Telephone:* 024-797573 (Office); 024-63229 (Home).

MARK, Herman F., PH.D.; American professor of chemistry; b. 3 May 1895, Vienna, Austria; s. of Herman C. and Lili Mueller Mark; m. Mary Schramek 1922 (died 1970); two s.; ed. Univ. of Vienna; Instructor, Univ. of Berlin 1921; Research Fellow, later Group Leader, Kaiser Wilhelm Inst. für Faserstoff-Chemie 1922-26; Research Chemist, I.G. Farben-Industrie 1927-28, Group Leader 1928-30, Asst. Research Dir. 1930-32, concurrently Assoc. Prof. of Physical Chem., Tech. Univ., Karlsruhe; Prof. of Chem. and Dir. First Chemical Inst., Univ. of Vienna 1932-38; Research Man. Canadian Int. Paper Co., Canada 1938-40; Adjunct Prof. of Organic Chem., Polytech. Inst. of Brooklyn 1940, Prof. 1942, Dir. Polymer Research 1946, Inst. Dean 1961-65, Dean Emer. 1965-; at Dept. of Textile Chem., N.C. State Univ., Raleigh 1974-; Ed. Journal of Polymer Science and other scientific publications; mem. N.A.S., American Chemical Soc., American Inst. of Chemists, A.A.A.S.; Fellow, American Physical Soc., New York Acad. of Sciences, American Acad. of Arts and Sciences; numerous hon. degrees and other awards. *Address:* 333 Jay Street, Brooklyn, N.Y. 11201, U.S.A.

MARK, Reuben, A.B., M.B.A.; American business executive; b. 21 Jan. 1939, Jersey City, N.J.; s. of Edward Mark and Libbie (née Berman) Mark; m. Arlene Slobzian 1964; two s. one d.; ed. Middlebury Coll. and Harvard Univ.; with Colgate-Palmolive Co., New York 1963-, Pres., Gen. Man. Venezuela 1972-73, Canada 1973-74, Vice-Pres., Gen. Man. Far East Div. 1974-75, Household Products Div. 1975-79, Group Vice-Pres. Domestic Operations 1979-81, Exec. Vice-Pres. 1981-83, C.O.O. 1983-84, Pres. 1983-, C.E.O. 1984-, Chair. 1986-; lecturer in Business Admin., Univ. of Conn. 1977; mem. Bd. of Dirs. Soap and Detergent Asscn. *Address:* Colgate-Palmolive Co., 300 Park Avenue, New York, N.Y. 10022, U.S.A.

MARK, Sir Robert, G.B.E., M.A.; British fmr. police official; b. 13 March 1917, Manchester; s. of the late John and Louisa Hobson Mark; m. Kathleen Mary Leahy 1941; one s. one d.; ed. William Hulme's Grammar School, Manchester; Constable to Chief Supt., Manchester Police 1937-42, 1947-56; Chief Constable of Leicester 1957-67; Asst. Commr., Metropolitan Police (London) 1967-68, Deputy Commr. 1968-72, Commr. 1972-77; Royal Armoured Corps 1942-47, Lieut. Phantom (GHQ Liaison Regt.) N.W. Europe 1944-45, Maj. Control Comm. for Germany 1945-47; mem. Standing Advisory Council on Penal System 1966; Assessor to Lord Mountbatten's Inquiry into Prison Security 1966; mem. Advisory Cttee. on Police in N. Ireland 1969; Dir. Automobile Asscn. 1977-87, Control Risks Ltd. 1981-87; Visiting Fellow Nuffield Coll., Oxford 1970-78; Lecture tour of N. America for World Affairs Council and FCO Oct. 1971; Dimbleby Memorial Lecturer, BBC TV 1973; Queen's Police Medal 1965; Hon. LL.M. (Leicester) 1966, Hon. D.Litt. (Loughborough) 1976, Hon. LL.D. (Liverpool) 1978, (Manchester) 1978; K.St.J.; Hon. Freeman City of Westminster 1977. *Publications:* Numerous articles in the national press and in legal and police journals; Edwin Stevens Lecture to the Laity at the Royal Society of Medicine 1972, Policing a Perplexed Society 1977, In the Office of Constable (autobiog.) 1978. *Address:* Esher, Surrey, KT10 8LU, England.

MARKERT, Clement L., PH.D.; American biologist; b. 11 April 1917, Las Animas, Colo.; s. of Edwin John Markert and Sarah Esther Norman; m. Margaret Rempfer 1940; two s. one d.; ed. Univ. of Colo., Univ. of Calif. at Los Angeles, Johns Hopkins Univ. and Calif. Inst. of Tech.; Asst. Prof.

of Zoology, Univ. of Mich. 1950-56, Assoc. Prof. 1956-57; Prof. of Biology, Johns Hopkins Univ. 1957-65; Prof. of Biology, Yale Univ. 1965-86, Chair. Dept. of Biology 1965-71; Dir. Yale Center for Research in Reproductive Biology 1974-86; Distinguished Univ. Research Prof. North Carolina State Univ. 1986-; mem. N.A.S. 1967-, Nat. Inst. of Medicine 1974-; American Acad. of Arts and Sciences; mem. Bd. Scientific Advisors, La Jolla Cancer Research Foundation 1977-86; mem. Bd. Scientific Advisors, Jane Coffin Childs Memorial Fund for Medical Research 1979-86; Trustee Bermuda Biological Station for Research 1959-83, Life Trustee 1983-, trustee BIOSIS 1976-81, Chair. of Bd. 1981; numerous editorial posts on biological journals. *Publications:* Over 100 articles, several books. *Leisure interests:* skin diving, ranching. *Address:* Department of Animal Science, North Carolina State University, Raleigh, N.C. 27695 (Office); 7308 Mevan Court, Raleigh, N.C. 27613, U.S.A. (Home). *Telephone:* (919) 737-2768 (Office).

MARKEZINIS, Spyros; Greek lawyer, historian and politician; b. 1909, Athens; s. of Basil Markezinis and Helen Flora Markezinis; m. Ieta Xydis 1943; one s. one d.; ed. Univ. of Athens; Legal Adviser to late King George II of the Hellenes 1936-46; served in Greek Nat. Resistance 1941-44; M.P. for the Cyclades 1946, for Athens 1952-67; f. New Party 1947 (dissolved 1951); Minister without Portfolio 1949; Minister for Co-ordination and Econ. Planning until 1954; formed Progressive Party 1955, re-formed 1977; Prime Minister Oct.-Nov. 1973; Kt., Gold Cross George I, D.S.M., Kt. Commdr. St. Saba; Grand Cross, Order of Phoenix (Greece), Légion d'honneur, Al Merito della Repubblica Italiana, First Class of the Fed. Repub. of Germany; Order of St. Mark of the Patriarchate of Alexandria and of Constantinople. *Publications:* The Divorce, From War to Peace 1949, The Supreme Ruler in Contemporary Democracies, The King, the Royal Family and their Private Lives, The King as International Representative, Political History of Modern Greece (1828-1936) (8 vols.), Political History of Greece in the Last Fifty Years (4 vols.) (1988). *Leisure interests:* books, chess. *Address:* 26 Isiodou Street, Athens, Greece. *Telephone:* 724-56-56/57/58.

MARKHAM, Kenneth Ronald, PH.D., F.R.S.N.Z.; New Zealand research chemist; b. 19 June 1937, Christchurch; s. of Harold W. Markham and Alicia B. Markham; m. E. P. Eddy 1966; two d.; ed. Victoria Univ. of Wellington, Melbourne Univ.; Tech. Trainee, Dominion Lab., Wellington 1955-62; Scientist Chem. Div., DSIR, Lower Hutt 1962-65; Post-Doctoral Fellow, Botany Dept., Univ. of Texas 1965-66, Asst. Prof. 1967; Scientist, Organic Chem. Section, Chem. Div., DSIR 1968-75, Section Leader, Natural Products Section 1976-, Group Leader Chem. Div. 1980-87; Monsato Chemicals Research Fellow 1960, Easterfield Award (Royal Inst. of Chem.) 1971, Sr. Research Fellow (Chem. Div. DSIR) 1987. *Publications:* The Systematic Identification of Flavonoids (with Maby and Thomas) 1970, Techniques of Flavonoid Chemistry 1982; 10 invited chapters on flavonoids and spectroscopy 1974-87, over 150 scientific papers on phytochem. and its interpretation in int. journals 1960-87. *Leisure interests:* philately, swimming, stock market, world news. *Address:* Chemistry Division, Department of Scientific and Industrial Research, Private Bag, Petone (Office); 8 Dowling Grove, Silverstream, New Zealand (Home). *Telephone:* 690 577 (Office); 285 991 (Home).

MARKIEWICZ, Władysław; Polish sociologist; b. 2 Jan. 1920, Ostrów Wielkopolski; s. of Józef and Bronisława Markiewicz; m. Ludgarda Trzybińska 1949; one s. one d.; ed. Poznań Univ.; Doctor 1959-61, Docent 1961-66, Assoc. Prof. 1966-72, Prof. 1972-; imprisoned in Mauthausen-Gusen concentration camp 1941-45; active mem. youth orgs. 1947-50; mem. PZPR 1948-, mem. Comm. for investigation into social conflicts, PZPR Cen. Cttee. 1981-84; mem. Voivodship Nat. Council, Poznań 1949-54; Dir. Inst. of Sociology, Poznań Univ. 1957-71; Vice-Dir. Western Inst., Poznań 1962-66, Dir. 1966-72; Head, Dept. of Sociology of Labour and Org., Warsaw Univ. 1972-76; Ed.-in-Chief Studia Socjologiczne (quarterly) and Polish Western Affairs; Vice-Chair. Polish Cttee. of UNESCO; Pres. Polish Sociological Soc. 1968-72; Corresp. mem. Polish Acad. of Sciences 1971-76, Ordinary mem. 1976-, mem. Presidium 1981-, Sec., Dept. of Social Sciences 1972-83, Vice-Pres. 1984-; mem. Polish Cttee. of Pugwash confs.; Gold Cross of Merit, Kt.'s and Officer's Cross, Order of Polonia Restituta, Medals of 10th and 30th Anniversaries of People's Poland, Order of Banner of Labour (2nd Class 1974, 1st Class 1986), Gold Award of Polish Teachers' Asscn. *Publications:* Przeobrażenia świadomości narodowej reemigrantów polskich z Francji 1960, Społeczeństwo i socjologia w Niemieckiej Republice Federalnej 1966, Sociology in People's Poland 1970, Propedeutyka nauki o społeczeństwie 1971, Socjologia a służba społeczna 1972, Konflikt społeczny w PRL 1983, Spraw polskich splatanie 1986; numerous articles. *Address:* ul. Wiejska 18 m. 13, 00-490 Warsaw, Poland. *Telephone:* 20-45-53 (Office); 29-80-30 (Home).

MARKING, Sir Henry Ernest, K.C.V.O., C.B.E., M.C., F.B.I.M.; British lawyer and fmr. company director; b. 11 March 1920, Saffron Walden, Essex; s. of Isaac and Hilda Jane Marking; ed. Saffron Walden Grammar School, Univ. Coll., London, Middle East Centre for Arab Studies, Jerusalem; army service, The Sherwood Foresters 1940-45, Adjutant 1944-45; admitted Solicitor 1948; Asst. Solicitor Cripps, Harries, Hall & Co., Tunbridge Wells 1948-49; Asst. Solicitor British European Airways (BEA) 1949, Sec. BEA 1950, C.E.O. 1964-71, Chair. and C.E.O. 1971-72; mem. Bd. of British Overseas Airways Corpn. (BOAC) 1971-72; Group Man. Dir. British Airways 1972-74, Deputy Chair. and Man. Dir. 1974-77, mem. Bd. 1977-81; mem. Bd. British Tourist Authority 1969-77, Chair. 1977-84; Chair.

Rothmans (U.K.) Ltd. 1979–86, Holiday Care Service 1981–86; Dir. Barclays Bank Int. 1977–86, Rothmans Int. Ltd. 1979–86; Gov. Bell Educational Trust 1984–; Trustee, London City Ballet 1978–87; Trustee and Vice-Chair. Leonard Cheshire Foundation 1962–. *Address:* 6a Montagu Mews North, London, W1H 1AH, England. *Telephone:* 01-935 3305.

MARKO, Ján, ING.; Czechoslovak politician; b. 6 Sept. 1920, Točnica, Slovakia; ed. School of Econs., Bratislava Univ.; office worker, Production Man., Dir. Slovak Magnesite Works, Lovinobaňa 1947–54; Finance Commr. 1954–59; Deputy Chair. of Bd. of Commrs. 1959–60; Dir. of Slovak Magnesite Works, Košice 1960–62; Deputy Minister-Chair. of State Comm. for Co-ordination of Science and Tech., Prague 1962–63; Slovak Comm. for Investment Bldg. 1963–65; Commr.-Chair., Minister, Slovak Comm. for Tech. 1965–68; Minister of Foreign Affairs, Fed. Govt. of Č.S.S.R. 1969–71; mem. Slovak Nat. Council 1954–71; mem. Cen. Cttee. of CP of Czechoslovakia 1954–62, 1969, Alt. mem. 1962–66; Deputy Chair. Slovak Nat. Council 1965–68; mem. Cen. Cttee. of Czechoslovak-Soviet Friendship Union 1966–70; mem. Cen. Cttee. CP of Slovakia 1966–68; Deputy to House of Nations, Fed. Ass. 1968–71, 1981–, First Vice-Chair. Fed. Ass. 1971–, Deputy to House of the People 1971–81; Presidium mem. Fed. Ass., Č.S.S.R. 1971; Chair. Czechoslovak Group of Inter-Parl. Union 1971–; mem. Presidium Č.S.S.R. Cttee. for European Security 1972–; Chair. Czechoslovak Cttee. for the Protection of the Rights of the Chilean People 1974–; Order of Labour 1970, Order of Republic 1980, and other decorations. *Address:* Federal Assembly, Prague 1, Vinohradská 1, Czechoslovakia.

MARKO, Miloš, JU.DR., DR.SC.; Czechoslovak journalist, broadcasting official and politician; b. 4 March 1922, Hronská Dúbrava; s. of Pavel and Alžběta Marko; m. Magda Kirchhoffová 1948; two d.; ed. Comenius Univ. Bratislava; journalist on various Slovak dailies; Asst. Ed.-in-Chief Pravda 1948–52, Ed.-in-Chief 1953–58; Ed.-in-Chief Predvoj 1958–60; Corresp. of the Czechoslovak News Agency in Moscow 1960–64; Asst. Prof. of Journalism, Comenius Univ., Bratislava 1962–; Regional Dir. Czechoslovak Radio, Bratislava 1964–67; Gen. Dir. Czechoslovak Radio, Prague 1967–68; mem. Ideological Comm., Cen. Cttee. of CP of Slovakia 1971–; Gen. Man. Czechoslovak Radio, Slovakia 1969–73; Vice-Chair. and mem. Presidium Union of Slovak Journalists 1969–72, Chair. 1972–82; Chair. Cen. Union of Journalists of Č.S.S.R. 1969–72, Vice-Chair. 1972–82; Vice-Chair. Cen. Cttee., Union of Slovak Journalists 1982–; mem. Presidium Cen. Cttee. Czechoslovak-Soviet Friendship Union 1969–; mem. Cen. Cttee. CP of Slovakia 1971–; Deputy to Slovak Nat. Council 1971–; Gen. Man. Czechoslovak TV, Slovakia 1973–84; Deputy Gen. Man. Czechoslovak TV 1973–84; Corresp. mem. Slovak Acad. of Sciences 1984–; Order of Labour 1970, Order of Victorious February 1982; Klement Gottwald Prize 1973. *Address:* Czechoslovak TV, Mlýnská dolina, Bratislava; Obrancov mieru 24, Bratislava, Czechoslovakia. *Telephone:* 471-12 (Home).

MARKÓJA, Dr. Imre; Hungarian lawyer and politician; b. 1931, Hetes, County Somogy; ed. in Eötvös Lóránd Univ. Budapest; joined Hungarian CP 1948, Hungarian Socialist Workers' Party 1956 and worked on the staff of Party organ Társadalmi Szemle; Deputy Minister of Justice 1963; Secr. of State in Ministry of Justice 1973; Minister of Justice 1978–88; mem. Nat. Council Patriotic Peoples' Front, Bd. Hungarian Lawyers Fed., Cttee. for Law and Political Science Hungarian Acad. of Sciences; Labour Order of Merit. *Address:* c/o Ministry of Justice, 1055 Budapest, Szalay utca 16, Hungary. *Telephone:* 326-170.

MARKOV, Dmitriy Fyodorovich; Soviet philologist; b. 5 Nov. 1913, Preslav, Zaporozphye region, Ukraine; ed. Kharkov Univ.; School Teacher 1936–38; Postgraduate 1938–41; Army Service 1941–44; Head of Chair. Pedagogical Inst. Sumy 1944–56; mem. CPSU 1948–; Sr. Research Assoc. 1956–63; Head of Sector Inst. of Slavonic and Balkan Studies, U.S.S.R. Acad. of Sciences 1969–; Corresp. mem U.S.S.R. Acad of Sciences 1966–; Foreign mem. Bulgarian Acad. of Sciences; Dimitrov Prize 1972; Order of Red Banner and other decorations. *Publications:* Main works devoted to Bulgarian literature and a study of the laws of the 20th century literary process among the western and southern Slavs. *Address:* U.S.S.R. Academy of Sciences, 14 Leninsky Prospekt, Moscow, U.S.S.R.

MARKOV, Georgiy Mokeyevich; Soviet author and state official; b. 1911, Novo-Kuskovo, Tomsk Dist.; Komsomol posts 1927–31; ed. of various newspapers in Siberia 1931–35; Head of "Literary Studio" at Irkutsk City Library 1935–41; corresp. of a front newspaper 1941–45; literary activity 1945–; mem. CPSU 1946–; Sec. U.S.S.R. Writers' Union 1956–71, First Sec. 1971–86; mem. Cen. Auditing Comm. 1966–71; mem. Cen. Cttee. of CPSU 1971–; Deputy, mem. and Sec. to Legis. Comm. of U.S.S.R. Supreme Soviet 1970–74; mem. Presidium of U.S.S.R. 1980; Order of Lenin, Hammer and Sickle Gold Medal 1984. *Works include:* The Strogovs 1939–46, The Salt of the Earth 1954–60, Father and Son 1963–64, Friendship between Nations 1966, Siberia 1969–73, The Coming Century 1981–86. *Address:* U.S.S.R. Union of Writers, ul. Vorovskogo 52, Moscow, U.S.S.R.

MARKOV, Leonid Vasilevich; Soviet stage and film actor; b. 1927; Theatre-Studio School, Lenin Komsomol Theatre, Moscow; acted with the co. 1950–60; with Pushkin Drama Theatre, Moscow 1960–65; with Mossovet Theatre 1965–; People's Artist of U.S.S.R. *Roles include:* Arbenin in Lermontov's Masquerade, Protasov in Tolstoy's The Living Corpse, Porfiry Petrovich in Petersburg Dreams (after Dostoevsky), and others. *Films*

include: Our Debts, My Sweet and Friendly Beast Zmeyelov. *Address:* Mossovet Theatre, Moscow, U.S.S.R.

MARKOV, Moisey Aleksandrovich; Soviet theoretical physicist; b. 13 May 1908, Rasskazovo, Tambov Region; ed. Moscow, Univ.; Associate, Physics Inst., U.S.S.R. Acad. of Sciences 1934–; Chair. of Group Jt. Inst. for Nuclear Research 1951–; Dir. Inst. of Semi-Conductors, U.S.S.R. Acad. of Sciences until 1962; Corresp. mem. U.S.S.R. Acad. of Sciences 1953–66, mem. 1966–; Sec. Dept. of Nuclear Physics of U.S.S.R. Acad. of Sciences 1967–; Chair. Interdepartmental Comm. on Nuclear Physics 1971–; Order of Lenin (three times), Hammer and Sickle Gold Medal, Hero of Socialist Labour and other decorations; Hon. D.Sc. (Bristol) 1988. *Address:* U.S.S.R. Academy of Sciences, 14 Leninsky Prospekt, Moscow, U.S.S.R.

MARKOVA, Dame Alicia, D.B.E. (Lilian Alicia Marks); British prima ballerina; b. 1 Dec. 1910, London; d. of Arthur Tristman Marks and Eileen Barry; ed. privately; first appeared in Dick Whittington at the Kennington Theatre 1920; studied under Astafieva and appeared with Legat Ballet Group 1923; taken into Russian Ballet by Serge Diaghilev 1924, studied under Enrico Cecchetti and toured with the co. until Diaghilev's death in 1929 (Song of a Nightingale created for her); Prima Ballerina, Rambert Club 1931–34; first Prima Ballerina of Vic-Wells (now the Royal Ballet) 1933–35; formed Markova-Dolin Ballet Co 1935 and toured U.K. till 1938; with Ballet Russe de Monte Carlo 1938–41; and Ballet Theatre 1941–44; toured North and Cen. America with Markova-Dolin group 1944–45; many guest appearances 1946–47; concerts with Dolin in U.S.A., Far East and South Africa 1947–49; formed Festival Ballet company with Dolin 1950–52; guest artist with Teatro Colón in Buenos Aires 1952, Sadler's Wells, Ballet Theatre, Marquis de Cuevas Ballet and Metropolitan Opera 1953; Royal Winnipeg Ballet 1953; with de Cuevas Ballet in London 1954; with Royal Danish Ballet 1955; Scala Milan, Municipal Theatre Rio de Janeiro 1956; Royal Ballet Covent Garden 1957; Italian Opera Season, Drury Lane, Festival Ballet Tour 1958, and Season 1959; appearances with Royal Ballet and Festival Ballet 1960; with the Metropolitan Opera Co. 1954–58; British Prima Ballerina Assoluta; Dir. Metropolitan Opera Ballet of New York 1963–69; Distinguished Lecturer on Ballet at Cincinnati Univ. 1970, Prof. of Ballet and Performing Arts 1970–; produced Les Sylphides, Australian Ballet 1976, London Festival Ballet 1977, Northern Ballet Theatre 1978, Royal Ballet School 1978, Royal Winnipeg Ballet 1979; "Masterclass" BBC TV series 1980; Pres. London Ballet Circle 1981–, All England Dance Competition 1983–, Arts Educational Trust Schools 1984–, London Festival Ballet 1986–; Vice-Pres. Royal Acad. of Dancing 1958–; Guest Prof., Royal Ballet School 1972–; Gov. Royal Ballet 1973–; Prof. Yorkshire Ballet Seminars 1973–; Guest Prof. de Danse, Paris Opera Ballet 1975; Guest Prof., Australian Ballet 1976; Pres. Int. Dance Competition, Paris 1986; Hon. Dr. Music (Leicester) 1966, Hon. Mus.D. (E. Anglia Univ.) 1982. *Publications:* Giselle and I 1960, Markova Remembers 1986. *Leisure interest:* music. *Address:* c/o Barclay's Bank, 1–3 Brompton Road, London, SW3 1EB, England.

MARKOVIĆ, Ante; Yugoslav politician; b. 1924, Konjic; ed. Zagreb Univ.; Sec. League of Communist Youth; Engineer, Designer and Head Test Dept., Rade Koncar factory, Dir.-Gen. 1961–86; Pres. Exec. Council of Croatia 1982–86; Pres. Presidency of Croatia May 1986–88; Pres. Federal Exec. Council March 1989–. *Address:* Federal Executive Council, 11070 Belgrade, bul. Lenjina 2, Yugoslavia.

MARKS, Leonard Harold, B.A., LL.B.; American lawyer and government official; b. 5 March 1916; m. Dorothy L. Ames 1948; two s.; ed. Univ. of Pittsburgh, and Univ. of Pittsburgh Law School; Faculty Fellow, Univ. of Pittsburgh Law School 1938–39, Asst. Prof. 1939–42; Asst. Prof. Nat. Univ. Law School, Washington, D.C. 1943–50; Asst. to Gen. Counsel, Fed. Communications Comm., Washington, D.C. 1943–46; Partner, Cohn and Marks (law firm), Washington, D.C. 1946–65, 1969–; Dir. Communications Satellite Corpn. 1963–65; Dir. U.S. Information Agency 1965–69; Pres. Broadcasters' Club of Washington, Int. Home Library Foundation, Int. Rescue Cttee. 1973–79; Chair. Int. Telecommunications Satellite Conf., U.S. Del., Washington, D.C. 1969, U.S. Advisory Comm. on Int. Educational and Cultural Affairs 1974–78, Nat. Savings and Trust Co. 1977–; Pres. Honor America Cttee. 1977–; Vice-Chair. Foreign Policy Assen. 1979–81, Chair. 1981–. *Address:* 1333 New Hampshire Avenue, N.W., Washington, D.C. 20036 (Office); 2833 McGill Terrace, N.W., Washington, D.C. 20008, U.S.A. (Home). *Telephone:* (202) 293-3860 (Office); (202) 232-7214 (Home).

MARKS, Paul Alan, M.D.; American oncologist and cell biologist; b. 16 Aug. 1926, New York; s. of Robert R. Marks and Sarah (Bohorad) Marks; m. Joan Harriet Rosen 1953; two s. one d.; ed. Columbia Coll. and Columbia Univ.; Fellow, Columbia Coll. of Physicians and Surgeons 1952–53, Assoc. 1955–56, mem. of Faculty 1956–82, Dir. Haematology Training 1961–74, Prof. of Medicine 1967–82, Dean Faculty of Medicine and Vice-Pres. Medical Affairs 1970–73, Dir. Comprehensive Cancer Center 1972–80, Vice-Pres. Health Sciences 1973–80, Prof. of Human Genetics and Devt. 1969–82, Frode Jensen Prof. of Medicine 1974–80; Prof. of Medicine and Genetics, Cornell Univ. Coll. of Medicine, New York 1981–; Attending Physician Presbyterian Hosp., New York 1967–83; Pres. and C.E.O. Memorial Sloan-Kettering Cancer Center 1980–; Attending Physician Memorial Hosp. for Cancer and Allied Diseases 1980–; mem. Sloan-Kettering Inst. for Cancer Research 1980–; Adj. Prof. Rockefeller Univ. 1980–; Physician, Rockefeller

Univ. Hosp. 1980–; Gov. Weizmann Inst. 1976–; Dir. Revson Foundation 1976–; Dr. h.c. (Urbino, Italy). *Publications:* over 200 articles in scientific journals. *Address:* Memorial Sloan-Kettering Cancer Center, 1275 York Avenue, New York, N.Y. 10021 (Office); Beach Hill Road, Bridgewater, Ct. 06752, U.S.A. (Home).

MARLAND, Sidney P., Jr., M.A., PH.D.; American educationist and fmr. government official; b. 19 Aug. 1914, Danielson, Conn.; s. of Sidney P. Marland, Sr. and Ruth Johnson; m. Virginia Partridge 1940; one s. two d.; ed. Univ. of Conn. and New York Univ.; Teacher of English, William Hall School, West Hartford, Conn. 1938–41; U.S. Army Service (rising to rank of Col., Infantry) 1941–47; Supt. of Schools, Darien, Conn. 1948–56, Winnetka, Ill. 1956–63, Pittsburgh, Pa. 1963–68; Pres. Inst. for Educational Devt., New York City 1968–70; fmr. mem. Presidential Advisory Council on Educ. of Disadvantaged Children and for Office of Econ. Opportunity; U.S. Commr. of Educ. 1970–72; Asst. Sec. for Educ., Health, Educ. and Welfare Dept. 1972–73; Pres. Coll. Entrance Examination Bd. 1973–78, Pres. Emer. 1978–; Chair. Ed. Bds. Scholastic Magazines 1978–; Co-Chair. Nat. Advisory Council, Statue of Liberty/Ellis Island Student Centennial Campaign 1983–; mem. Bd. Dirs. Nat. Manpower Inst., The Atlantic Cos., Scholastic Magazines Inc., Mutual of N.Y., The American College; fmr. Visiting Prof. and Lecturer at Harvard, Northwestern Univ., Teachers Coll., Columbia Univ., and Nat. Coll. of Educ.; fmr. Visiting Prof. Univ. of Conn., New York Univ.; mem. and Vice-Chair. Conn. Bd. Govs. for Higher Educ. 1983–; Distinguished Service Cross, Legion of Merit, Bronze Star. *Publications:* Winnetka: The History and Significance of an Educational Experiment (with Carleton W. Washburne), Career Education: A Proposal for Reform 1974, The College Bd. and the Twentieth Century 1975, and numerous monographs, book contributions and journal articles. *Leisure interest:* growing Christmas trees. *Address:* North Bigelow Road, Hampton, Conn. 06247, U.S.A. *Telephone:* (203) 455-0080.

MARLER, Peter Robert, PH.D.; American biologist; b. 24 Feb. 1928, London, England; s. of Robert A. and Gertrude Hunt Marler; m. Judith G. Gallen 1954; one s. two d.; ed. Univ. Coll. London and Univ. of Cambridge; Research Fellow, Jesus Coll., Cambridge 1954–56; Asst. Prof., later Prof., Univ. of Calif., Berkeley 1957–66; Prof. The Rockefeller Univ. 1966–; Sr. Research Zoologist, New York Zoological Soc. 1966–72; Dir. Inst. for Research in Animal Behaviour 1969–72; Dir. Rockefeller Univ. Field Research Center 1972–81; mem. N.A.S.; mem. Council Smithsonian Inst. 1979–; Fellow, American Acad. of Arts and Sciences, A.A.A.S. 1965, New York Zoological Soc., American Psychological Asscn. 1975; Guggenheim Fellow 1964–65; mem. American Philosophical Soc. 1983. *Publications:* Mechanisms of Animal Behaviour (with W. J. Hamilton) 1966, Handbook of Behavioral Neurobiology 3: Social Behavior and Communication (with J. G. Vandenbergh) 1979, The Biology of Learning (ed. with H. S. Terrace), (Eds. J. P. Rauschecker and P. Marler) Imprinting and Cortical Plasticity 1987. *Leisure interests:* gardening, natural history. *Address:* Rockefeller University, New York, N.Y. 10021, U.S.A.

MARÓTHY, László; Hungarian politician; b. 1942, Szeghalom; ed. Univ. of Agronomy; joined Communist Youth League 1960, Hungarian Socialist Workers' Party 1965; Sec. County Pest Communist Youth Cttee. 1968–70; First Sec. Municipal Party Cttee. of Szentendre; First Sec. Hungarian Communist Youth League Cen. Cttee. 1973–80; mem. HSWP Cen. Cttee. 1973–, Party Political Cttee. 1975–88; First Sec. Budapest Metropolitan Party Cttee. 1980–84; M.P. 1981–; Vice-Pres. Council of Ministers 1984–87; Chair. Nat. Planning Office 1986–87; Minister for Environment and Water Man. Dec. 1987–. *Address:* Ministry for Environment and Water Management, 1011 Budapest, Fő utca 44–50, Hungary. *Telephone:* 154-840.

MAROUF, Taha Muhyiddin, LL.B.; Iraqi politician and diplomatist; b. 1924, Sulaimaniyah; s. of Muhyiddin and Fatima Marouf; ed. Coll. of Law, Univ. of Baghdad; worked as lawyer; joined Diplomatic Service 1949; Minister of State 1968–70; Minister of Works and Housing 1968; Amb. to Italy, concurrently non-resident Amb. to Malta and Albania 1970–74; Vice-Pres. of Iraq April 1974–; mem. Higher Cttee. of Nat. Progressive Front 1975–; Chair. African Affairs Bureau of Revolutionary Command Council 1976–. *Address:* Office of the Vice-President of the Republic, National Assembly Building, Baghdad, Iraq.

MARPLES, Brian John, M.A., M.SC.; British professor of zoology (retd.); b. 31 March 1907, Hessle, Yorks.; s. of George Marples and Anne Marples; m. Mary Joyce Ransford 1931; two s.; ed. St. Bees School and Exeter Coll., Oxford; Asst. Lecturer in Zoology Univ. of Manchester 1929–36, Univ. of Bristol 1936–37; Prof. of Zoology Univ. of Otago, N.Z. 1937–67; Fellow Royal Soc. of N.Z. *Publications:* various papers on zoological and archaeological topics. *Leisure interests:* zoology and archaeology. *Address:* 1 Vanbrugh Close, Old Woodstock, Oxford, OX7 1YB, England. *Telephone:* Woodstock 811056.

MARQUARD, William A.; American business executive; b. 6 March 1920, Pittsburgh, Pa.; s. of William Albert and Ann (née Wild) Marquard; m. Margaret Thoben 1942; one s. two d.; ed. Univ. of Pennsylvania; fmrly. held positions with Westinghouse Electric Corpn.; joined the Mosler Safe Co. (purchased by American Standard 1967) 1952, Vice-Pres. 1956, Sr. Vice-Pres. and Dir. 1961, Pres. 1967–70; Sr. Exec. Vice-Pres., C.O.O. and Dir. American Standard Oct. 1970, Pres. 1971–83, C.E.O. 1971, Chair. of

Bd. 1979–86; Dir. NL Industries, Inc., Shell Oil Co., Houston, Chemical N.Y. Corpn. and Chemical Bank, Allied Stores Corpn., N.Y. Life Insurance Co.; sr. mem. Conf. Bd.; mem. Business Cttee. for the Arts, British-N. American Cttee., Bd. of Trustees, Foundation of Univ. of the Americas (Mexico); Trustee, Citizens Budget Comm. Inc., Cttee. for Econ. Devt., N.Y. Infirmary, Washington Opera; Hon. D.H. *Address:* American Standard, 40 West 40th Street, New York, N.Y. 10018, U.S.A. *Telephone:* (212) 840-5100.

MARQUARDT, Klaus Max, DR.RER.POL.; German business executive; b. 18 Dec. 1926, Berlin; s. of Dr. Arno and Ruth Marquardt; m. Brigitte Weber; three d.; ed. Realgymnasium Berlin, Univ. Berlin and Tech. Univ. Berlin; mem. Bd. ARAL AG –1971, Chair. 1971–86; Pres. Petroleum Econ. Asscn. 1979–; Chair. Supervisory Bd., Westfalenbank AG, Bochum; mem. Supervisory Bd., Gerling-Konzern Zentrale Vertriebs AG, Cologne, Dortmunder-Ritterbrauerei AG. *Address:* ARAL Aktiengesellschaft, 4630 Bochum, Wittenerstrasse 45, Federal Republic of Germany (Office). *Telephone:* 0234-3152200 (Office).

MARQUEZ, Gabriel García (see García Márquez, Gabriel).

MÁRQUEZ DE LA PLATA IRARRAZAVAL, Alfonso; Chilean politician; b. 19 July 1933; m. Maria de la Luz Cortes Heyermann 1957; one s. one d.; ed. Universidad Católica de Chile; Vice-Chair. Sociedad Nacional de Agricultura 1969–73, Chair. 1973–77; Chair. Banco de Santiago 1977–78; Minister of Agric. 1978–80; mem. Govt. Legislative Comm. 1981–83; Dir. A.F.P. Provida 1981–83, Compañia de Cervecerias Unidas 1981–83, Banco de Credito e Inversiones 1981–83; Co-Proprietor and Admin. Sociedad Agrícola Caren Ltda.; Govt. Minister-Sec.-Gen. 1983–84, Minister of Labour and Social Security 1984–88. *Address:* La Capitania 103, Santiago, Chile. *Telephone:* 211-66-84.

MARR, Geoffrey Vickers, D.SC., PH.D., F.INST.P., F.R.S.E.; British professor of natural philosophy; s. of John Marr and Florrie (Vickers) Marr; m. Jean Tebb 1954; two s. one d.; ed. Darlington Queen Elizabeth Grammar School and Univs. of Manchester and Reading; Postdoctoral Fellow, Dept. of Physics, Univ. of Western Ont. 1954–57; Assoc. Inst. of Physics 1956; Lecturer, Eaton Electronics Lab. Dept. of Physics, McGill Univ. 1957–59; Physicist, English Electric, Nuclear Power Div. Whetstone, Leicester 1959–61; Fellow, J. J. Thomson Lab. Dept. of Physics, Univ. of Reading 1961–63, Lecturer, Dept. of Physics 1963–68, Reader 1968–81; Prof. of Natural Philosophy and Head, Dept. of Physics, Aberdeen Univ. 1981–; mem. numerous cttees. etc.; Chartered Physicist. *Publications:* Photoionization Processes in Gases 1967, Plasma Spectroscopy 1968, An Introduction to the Theory of Photoelectron Spectroscopy for Experimentalists 1975, Feasibility Study European Synchrotron Radiation Facility III Instrumentation 1979, Handbook of Synchrotron Radiation, Vol. 2 1987. *Leisure interests:* walking, painting, bee-keeping. *Address:* Department of Physics, Frazer-Noble Building, Aberdeen University, Aberdeen, AB9 2UE, Scotland. *Telephone:* (0224) 272495.

MARRE, Sir Alan Samuel, K.C.B., M.A.; British fmr. public servant; b. 25 Feb. 1914, London; s. of Joseph and Rebecca (née Green) Marre; m. Romola Mary Gilling 1943; one s. one d.; ed. St. Olave's Grammar School, Southwark and Trinity Hall, Cambridge; Asst. Prin., Ministry of Health 1936, Prin. 1941, Asst. Sec. 1946, Under-Sec. 1952; Under-Sec. Ministry of Labour 1963; Deputy Sec. Ministry of Health 1964, Ministry of Labour (later Dept. of Employment and Productivity) 1966; Second Perm. Under-Sec. of State, Dept. of Health and Social Security 1968–71; Parl. Commr. for Admin. (Ombudsman) 1971–76, Health Service Commr. 1973–76; mem. Council on Tribunals 1971–76; mem. Comm. for Local Admin. 1974–76; Chair. Age Concern England 1977–80, Crown Housing Asscn. 1978–; Vice-Chair. Advisory Cttee. on Distinction Awards 1979–85; Gen. Gov. British Nutrition Foundation 1981–, Chair. 1983–85; Pres. The Maccabaeans 1982–; Chair. Rural Dispensing Cttee. 1983–87. *Leisure interests:* reading, walking. *Address:* 44 The Vale, London NW11 8SG, England. *Telephone:* 01-458 1787.

MARRINER, Sir Neville, Kt., C.B.E., F.R.C.M.; British musician and conductor; b. 15 April 1924, Lincoln; s. of Herbert H. and Ethel M. Marriner; m. Elizabeth M. Sims 1958; one s. one d.; ed. Lincoln School, Royal Coll. of Music; f. and Dir. Acad. of St. Martin in the Fields 1959–; Musical Dir. L.A. Chamber Orchestra 1969–78; Dir. S. Bank Festival of Music 1975–78, Dir. Meadowbrook Festival Detroit 1979; Music Dir. Minn. Orchestra 1979–86, Stuttgart Radio Symphony Orchestra 1984–, Barbican Summer Festival 1985–87; Tagore Gold Medal, six Edison Awards (Netherlands), two Mozart Gemeinde Awards (Austria), Grand Prix du Disque (France) (three times). *Address:* 67 Cornwall Gardens, London, S.W.7, England.

MARRIS, Stephen Nicholson, M.A., PH.D.; British international economist; b. 7 Jan. 1930, London; s. of Eric Denyer Marris and Phyllis May Marris; m. Margaret Swindells 1955; two s. one d.; ed. Bryanston School and King's Coll., Cambridge; Parker of Waddington Research Student, King's Coll., Cambridge 1952–53; Nat. Inst. of Econ. and Social Research, London 1953–54; with Org. for European Econ. Co-operation, later named Org. for Econ. Co-operation and Devt. (OECD) 1956–83, Econ. Adviser to the Sec.-Gen. 1975–83; Sr. Fellow, Inst. for Int. Econs., Washington, D.C. 1983–88; Visiting Research Prof., Int. Econs., Brookings Inst., Washington, D.C. 1969–70; Hon. Dr. (Stockholm Univ.) 1979. *Publications:* Managing the

World Economy: Will We Ever Learn? 1984, Deficits and the Dollar: The World Economy at Risk 1985. *Leisure interest:* sailing. *Address:* 8 Sentier des Pierres Blanches, 92190 Meudon, France.

MARSALIS, Wynton; American trumpeter; b. 18 Oct. 1961, New Orleans; ed. Berks. Music Centre, Tanglewood, Juilliard School, New York; joined Art Blakey's big band; in addition to regular appearances in many countries with his own jazz quintet, he follows a classical career and has performed with the world's top orchestras; numerous int. awards, including the Grand Prix du Disque and Grammy Award in both jazz and classical categories in 1983. *Address:* c/o Van Walsum Management Ltd., 40 St. Peter's Road, London, W6 9BH, England. *Telephone:* 01-741 5881.

MARSH, Baron (Life Peer), cr. 1981; of Mannington in the County of Wiltshire; **Richard William Marsh,** Kt., P.C.; British politician and public servant; b. 14 March 1928; m. 1st Evelyn Mary Andrews 1950 (divorced 1973), two s.; m. 2nd Caroline Dutton 1973 (died 1975); m. 3rd Felicity McFadzean 1979; ed. Jennings School, Swindon, Woolwich Polytechnic and Ruskin Coll., Oxford; Health Services Officer, Nat. Union of Public Employees 1951–59; mem. Clerical and Admin. Whitley Council for Health Service 1953–59; M.P. for Greenwich 1959–71; Parl. Sec. Ministry of Labour 1964–65; Jt. Parl. Sec. Ministry of Tech. 1965–66; Minister of Power 1966–68, of Transport 1968–69; Dir. Michael Saunders Man. Services 1970–71, Nat. Carbonising Ltd. 1970–71, Concord Rotaflex 1970–71; Chair. British Railways Bd. 1971–76, Newspaper Publishers Asscn. Ltd. 1976–, Allied Investments Ltd. 1977–82, British Iron & Steel Consumers' Council 1977–82, Lee Cooper Licensing Services 1980–83, Dual Fuel Systems 1981–, Lee Cooper Group 1983–, TV-am 1983– (Deputy Chair. 1981–83), Lopex PLC 1986–; Dir. Imperial Life of Canada UK 1983–; Chair. British Industry Cttee. on S.A. Ltd. 1989–. *Publication:* Off the Rails (memoirs) 1978. *Address:* Newspaper Publishers Association Ltd., 6 Bouverie Street, London, EC4Y 8AY, England. *Telephone:* 01-583 8132.

MARSH, Derick Rupert Clement, PH.D., F.A.H.A.; Australian professor of English; b. 26 March 1928, Bloemfontein, S.A.; s. of late Clement Marsh and Lillian (née Gradwell) Marsh; m. 1st Nicola Carter 1954 (deceased); m. 2nd Elizabeth Lawson 1964 (divorced); m. 3rd Ann Blake James 1984; two s. two d.; ed. Univ. of Natal, Pietermaritzburg; lecturer and Sr. Lecturer Univ. of Natal 1955–60; Sr. Lecturer English Dept. Univ. of Sydney 1961–66; Foundation Prof. of English, La Trobe Univ., Melbourne 1966–76, Prof. of English 1981–89, Emer. 1989–; Prof. Univ. of Western Australia 1977–80; Visiting Prof. Queen's Univ., Kingston, Ont. 1964–65; Visiting Fellow Wolfson Coll., Cambridge 1976. *Publications:* The Recurring Miracle 1962, Poetry: Reading and Understanding 1966, Shakespeare's Hamlet 1970, Passion Lends Them Power 1976. *Leisure interests:* reading, listening to music, walking. *Address:* English Department, La Trobe University, Bundoora, Vic. 3083 (Office); 20 Kasouka Road, Camberwell, Vic. 3124, Australia (Home). *Telephone:* 479 2390 (Office); 813 3430 (Home).

MARSHAK, Robert E., PH.D.; American university professor; b. 11 Oct. 1916, New York City; s. of Harry and Rose Marshak; m. Ruth Gup 1943; one s. one d.; ed. Columbia Coll. and Cornell Univ.; Univ. of Rochester 1939–70, Chair. and Harris Prof., Dept. of Physics and Astronomy 1950–64, Distinguished Univ. Prof. 1964–70; mem. School of Math., Inst. for Advanced Studies, Princeton 1948; visiting lecturer to numerous univs. and colls. throughout the world 1940–67; Avco Visiting Prof., Cornell Univ. 1959, Buhl Visiting Prof., Carnegie Mellon Univ. 1968, Distinguished Visitor Univ. of Texas 1970; Pres. City Coll. of New York 1970–79; Distinguished Prof., Virginia Polytech. Inst. 1979–87, Emer. 1987–; Physicist, Radiation Lab., M.I.T., Montreal Atomic Energy Lab., Los Alamos Scientific Lab. 1942–46; Chair. Fed. of American Scientists 1947–48; Vice-Chair. N.Y. State Advisory Comm. on Atomic Energy 1957–58; Trustee, Atoms for Peace Awards 1958–70, Univ. Research Asscn. 1968–70; mem. various univ. cttees. etc.; Consultant to IAEA on establishment of Int. Center for Theoretical Physics, Trieste 1961–63; American mem. of Science Council, Int. Center for Theoretical Physics 1967–75, 1984–; Sec. Comm. of High Energy Physics, Int. Union of Pure and Applied Physics 1957–63; mem. Jt. Cttee. on U.S.-Japan Science Co-operative Program 1968–72; mem. American Acad. of Arts and Sciences (Chair. Cttee. on World Univ. and Int. Science Foundation 1969–71, mem. Council 1985–), N.A.S. (Chair. Advisory Cttee. for Soviet Union and E. Europe 1963–66, Head of Del. to Poland 1964, to Yugoslavia 1965, Rep. on Nat. Comm. for UNESCO Exec. Cttee. 1970–73, Council 1971–74, Assoc. Ed. Proceedings of N.A.S. 1980–86); mem. Interim Bd. for Int. Foundation of Science, Stockholm 1972–75; mem. Council, American Physical Soc. 1965–69, Exec. Cttee. 1968–69, Vice-Chair. (and Chair. Div. of Particles and Fields) 1969–70, Vice-Pres. 1981, Pres. 1983; Guggenheim Fellow 1953–54, 1960–61, 1967–68; first Niels Bohr Visiting Prof., Inst. of Math. Sciences, Madras (India) 1963; Hon. degrees (Uktal Univ., India 1977, City Univ. of New York 1979, City Coll. of New York 1980); New York Acad. of Sciences Prize in Astronomy 1940, Oppenheimer Memorial Prize 1982, Alexander von Humboldt Award (Fed. Repub. of Germany) 1985, Clark Kerr Medal (Univ. of Calif., Berkeley) 1987. *Publications:* Our Atomic World (with E. C. Nelson and L. I. Schiff) 1946, Messon Physics 1952, Introduction to Elementary Particle Physics (with E. C. G. Sudarshan) 1961, Perspectives in Modern Physics (editor) 1966, Advances in Particle Physics (joint editor, 2 vols.) 1968, 1969, Theory of Weak Interactions in Particle Physics (with

Riazuddin and C. P. Ryan) 1969, Academic Renewal in the 1970s: Memoirs of a City College President. *Leisure interests:* hiking, music. *Address:* 202 Fincastle Drive, Blacksburg, Va. 24060, U.S.A. *Telephone:* (703) 951-8090.

MARSHALL, Alexander Badenoch, M.A.; British business executive; b. 31 Dec. 1924, Dunfermline, Fife, Scotland; s. of David Marshall; m. Mona K. D. Kirk 1961; two s. one d.; ed. Glenalmond and Worcester Coll., Oxford; served R.N. 1943–46; with the P & O Group 1947–79, C.E.O. 1972–79; Chair. Bestobell PLC 1979–85; Dir. Commercial Union Assurance Co. PLC 1970–, Chair. May 1983–; Dir. The Maersk Co. Ltd., Vice-Chair. 1983–87, Chair. 1987–; Dir. Royal Bank of Canada 1985–, Chair. RBC (UK) Holdings Ltd. 1988–; Vice-Chair. The Boots Co. PLC 1985–; Chair. U.K.-S. Africa Trade Asscn. 1982–85; Co-Chair. British N. American Cttee. 1985–. *Leisure interests:* gardening, hill-walking, sheep. *Address:* Crest House, Woldingham, Surrey, CR3 7DH, England. *Telephone:* (088385) 2299.

MARSHALL, Cedric Russell, M.P.; New Zealand politician. b. 1936, Nelson; m.; two s. one d.; ed. Nelson Coll., Christchurch Teachers' Coll., Trinity Theological Coll., Auckland; teacher at various schools 1955–58; Methodist Minister in Christchurch 1960–66, Masterton 1967–71; M.P. for Wanganui 1972–; Minister of Educ. and for the Environment 1984–86, of Educ. and of Conservation 1986–87, of Foreign Affairs Aug. 1987–, Disarmament and Arms Control 1987–89, Pacific Island Affairs 1989–; Chief Opposition Whip 1978–79; Labour. *Leisure interests:* classical music, genealogy. *Address:* House of Representatives, Wellington, New Zealand.

MARSHALL, David Saul, LL.B.; Singapore diplomatist and fmr. politician; b. 12 March 1908, Singapore; s. of Saul Nassim Mashaal and Flora Ezekiel; m. Jean Mary Gray 1961; one s. three d.; ed. Raffles Institution, Middle Temple and Univ. of London; worked in Singapore as sharebroker, salesman and sec. to a shipping co. 1924–32; then studied law in England and began legal career in Singapore 1937–; joined Singapore Volunteer Corps 1938; imprisoned by Japanese 1942–45; founder Sec. War Prisoners Asscn.; mem. Jewish Welfare Bd.; founder mem. Labour Front; Chief Minister of Singapore 1955–56; mem. Singapore Legis. Ass. 1961–63; Del. to XXIII Session of UN Gen. Ass. 1968; Chair. Singapore Inst. of S.E. Asian Studies 1970–74; Amb. to France 1978– (also accred. to Portugal March 1981–, to Spain Sept. 1981–); Perm. Rep. to UNESCO 1978–85; mem. ICC Court of Arbitration Nov. 1985–. *Address:* Embassy of Singapore, 12 square de l'avenue Foch, Paris 75116, France. *Telephone:* 4500-33-61.

MARSHALL, Geoffrey, PH.D., F.B.A.; British academic; b. 22 April 1929, Chesterfield; s. of Leonard William and Kate Marshall; m. Patricia Anne Woodcock 1957; two s.; ed. Arnold School, Blackpool, Univs. of Manchester and Glasgow; Research Fellow, Nuffield Coll., Oxford 1955–57; Fellow and Praelector in Politics, Queen's Coll. Oxford 1957–; Visiting Prof.-at-large, Cornell Univ. 1985–; mem. Oxford City Council 1964–74; Sheriff of City of Oxford 1970. *Publications:* Parliamentary Sovereignty and the Commonwealth 1957, Some Problems of the Constitution (with G. C. Moodie) 1959, Police and Government 1965, Constitutional Theory 1971, Constitutional Conventions 1984. *Leisure interest:* middle-aged squash. *Address:* Queen's College, Oxford, England. *Telephone:* (0865) 279176.

MARSHALL, J. Howard, II, A.B., LL.B.; American business executive; b. 24 Jan. 1905, Philadelphia, Pa.; s. of S. Furman and Annabelle T. Marshall; m. 1st Eleanor Pierce 1931; two s.; m. 2nd Bettye M. Bohanan 1961; ed. George School, Haverford Coll., and Yale School of Law; Instructor and Asst. Cruise Dir. Floating Univ. Inc. 1926–27, Cruise Dir. 1928–29; Asst. Dean and Asst. Prof. of Law, Yale School of Law 1931–33; Special Asst. to Attorney-Gen. and Asst. Solicitor, U.S. Dept. of Interior, and mem. Petroleum Admin. Bd. 1933–35; Counsel, Standard Oil Co. of Calif. 1935–37; Assoc., Pillsbury, Madison and Sutro (Corporate Attorneys) 1937–38, Partner 1938–44; Dir., Pacific City Lines, Inc. 1938–41; Vice-Pres. and Dir. Long Beach Oil Devt. Corpn. 1939–42; Chief Counsel and Asst. Deputy Admin., Petroleum Admin. for War 1941–44; mem. Mil. Petroleum Advisory Bd. 1944–50, 1954–59; Gen. Counsel, U.S. Del., Allied Comm. on Reparations 1945; Pres. Dir. Ashland Oil and Refining Co. 1944–51; Exec. Vice-Pres. and Dir. Signal Oil and Gas Co. 1952–60; Pres. and Dir. Union Texas Natural Gas Corpn. 1961–62; Pres. Union Texas Petroleum 1962–67; Exec. Vice-Pres. and Dir. Allied Chemical Corpn. 1965–67; Chair. Bd. The Petroleum Corpn. 1968–87; Chair. Bd. and Pres. Marshall Petroleum Inc. 1985; Vice-Pres. Haverford Coll.; fmr. dir. Nat. Industries Inc.; Dir. American Petroleum Inst., Texas Commerce Bank (Houston), Presidio Corpn. 1987–; Dir. and Chair. Exec. Cttee. Coastal Corpn. 1973–; Dir. and mem. Exec. Cttee. MKT Railroad, etc. *Address:* P.O. Box 42808-L, Houston, Tex. 77042 (Office); 11100 Meadowick, Houston, Tex. 77024, U.S.A. (Home). *Telephone:* (713) 690-4321 (Office).

MARSHALL, Margaret Anne; British concert and opera singer; b. 4 Jan. 1949, Stirling; d. of Robert and Margaret Marshall; m. Dr Graeme G. K. Davidson 1970; two d.; ed. High School of Stirling and Royal Scottish Acad. of Music and Drama; first opera appearance in Orfeo ed Euridice, Florence 1977; has since sung at La Scala, Covent Garden, Glyndebourne, Scottish Opera, Barcelona, Hamburg, Cologne and Salzburg; concert performances in major European and U.S. cities and festivals with major orchestras; First Prize, Munich Int. Competition 1974; numerous recordings. *Leisure interests:* squash, golf, cooking. *Address:* 46 Borestone Place, Stirling, FK7 0PL, Scotland. *Telephone:* (0786) 74921.

MARSHALL, Sir Peter, K.C.M.G.; British diplomatist; b. 30 July 1924, Reading; s. of late R. H. and Winifred Marshall; m. Patricia R. Stoddart 1957 (died 1981); one s. one d.; ed. Tonbridge School and Corpus Christi Coll., Cambridge; R.A.F.V.R. 1943-46; served H.M. Foreign (later Diplomatic) Service 1949-83; Aide to British Amb., Washington, D.C. 1952-56; Head of Chancery, Baghdad 1961, Bangkok 1962-64, Paris 1969-71; Deputy Dir. Treasury Centre for Admin. Studies 1965-66; Counsellor, U.K. Mission, Geneva 1966-69; Head, Financial Relations Dept., FCO 1971-73, Asst. Under-Sec. of State 1973-75; Minister, U.K. Mission to UN, New York 1975-79; Perm. Rep. U.K. Mission, Geneva 1979-83; Commonwealth Deputy Sec.-Gen. (Econ.) 1983-88; Chair. Royal Commonwealth Soc. 1988-. *Leisure interests:* music, golf. *Address:* 1 Caroline Close, London, W2 4RW, England (Home). *Telephone:* 01-229 3069 (Home).

MARSHALL, Ray, PH.D.; American economist and government official; b. 22 Aug. 1928, Oak Grove, La.; m. Patricia Williams 1947; one s. three d.; ed. Millsaps Coll., Miss., Louisiana State Univ., Univ. of Calif. at Berkeley; Fulbright Research Scholar, Finland; post-doctoral research, Harvard Univ.; Instructor San Francisco State Coll.; Assoc. Prof. and Prof. Univs. of Miss., Ky., La.; Prof. of Econs., Texas Univ. 1962-67, Prof. of Econs. 1969-, and fmrly. Dir. Center for Study of Human Resources, Chair. Dept. 1970-72, Prof. of Econs. and Public Affairs, Lyndon B. Johnson School of Public Affairs 1981-; Rapoport Prof. Econs. and Public Affairs, Univ. of Tex. at Austin; Pres. Southern Econ. Asscn.; Chair. State Jobs Training Council (Tex.); U.S. Sec. of Labor 1977-81; Trustee Carnegie Corpn. *Publications:* The Negro Worker 1967, The Negro and Apprenticeship 1967, Cooperatives and Rural Poverty in the South 1971, Human Resources and Labor Markets 1972, Anthology of Labor Economics 1972, Rural Workers in Rural Labor Markets 1974, Human Resources and Labor Markets 1975, Labor Economics: Wages, Employment and Trade Unionism 1976, The Role of Unions in the American Economy 1976, An Economic Strategy for the 1980's, 1981, Work and Women in the Eighties 1983, Unheard Voices: Labor and Economic Policy in a Competitive World 1987. *Address:* LBJ School of Public Affairs, University of Texas, Austin, Tex. 78712, U.S.A.

MARSHALL, Thurgood; American lawyer and government official; b. 2 July 1908, Baltimore, Md.; s. of William and Norma Marshall; m. 1st Vivian Burey 1929 (deceased), 2nd Cecilia Suyat 1955; two s.; ed. Lincoln Univ., Pa., and Howard Univ. Law School, Washington, D.C.; admitted Md. Bar 1933; Dir.-Gen. Nat. Asscn. for Advancement of Colored People Legal Defense and Educ. Fund 1940-61; Judge, Second Circuit Court of Appeals 1961-65; Solicitor-Gen. of U.S.A. 1965-67; Assoc. Justice, U.S. Supreme Court 1967-; Spingarn Medal 1946; mem. Bd. of Dirs. John F. Kennedy Library; mem. American Bar Asscn., Assn. of the Bar of the City of New York, Nat. Bar Assn., N.Y.C. County Lawyers Assn.; Living History Award; numerous hon. degrees, awards, medals and citations. *Address:* U.S. Supreme Court, 1 First Street, N.E., Washington, D.C. 20543, U.S.A. *Telephone:* (202) 479-3000.

MARSHALL OF GORING, Baron (Life Peer) cr. 1985, of South Stoke in the County of Oxfordshire, **Walter Charles Marshall,** Kt., C.B.E., PH.D., F.R.S.; British physicist; b. 5 March 1932, Wales; s. of Frank and Amy Marshall; m. Ann Vivienne Sheppard 1955; one s. one d.; ed. Birmingham Univ.; Scientific Officer, Atomic Energy Research Establishment, Harwell 1954-57; Research Physicist, Univ. of Calif. and Harvard Univ. 1957-59; Group Leader, Solid State Theory, A.E.R.E., Harwell 1959-60, Head, Theoretical Physics Div. 1960-66, Deputy Dir. 1966-68, Dir. 1968-75; Dir. Research Group, U.K. Atomic Energy Authority 1969-75; mem. Nat. Research Devt. Corpn. Bd. 1969-75; mem. UKAEA 1972-82, Deputy Chair. 1975-81, Chair. 1981-82; Chief Scientist, Dept. of Energy 1974-77; Chair. Cen. Electricity Generating Bd. July 1982-; mem. NEDC 1984-; Foreign Assoc. Nat. Acad. of Eng. (U.S.A.) 1979; Fellow Royal Swedish Acad. of Eng. Sciences; Hon. Fellow Welding Inst. 1987; Maxwell Medal, Henry DeWolf Smyth Nuclear Stateman Award 1985. *Publications:* The Theory of Neutron Scattering (with Dr. S. W. Lovesey) 1971, Nuclear Power Technology 1984, research papers on magnetism, neutron scattering and solid state theory. *Leisure interests:* origami, gardening. *Address:* The Central Electricity Generating Board, Sudbury House, 15 Newgate Street, London, EC1A 7AU, England.

MARSHAM, Thomas Nelson, C.B.E., PH.D., F.ENG., F.R.S.; British physicist (retd.); b. 10 Nov. 1923, Liverpool; s. of Capt. Thomas B. Marsham, C.B.E. and Jane W. (Nelson) Marsham; m. Sheila M. Griffin 1958; two s.; ed. Merchant Taylors School and Univ. of Liverpool; Ocean Steam Ship Co. 1941-46; Oliver Lodge Fellow, Univ. of Liverpool 1951-53; Dept. of Atomic Energy, Ministry of Supply 1953-55; joined UKAEA 1955, Reactor Man. Calder Hall Nuclear Power Station 1955-57, Deputy Gen. Man. Windscale and Calder Works 1958-64, Dir. Tech. Policy, Reactor Group 1964-77, Man. Dir. Northern Div. 1977-87, mem. Bd. 1979-; Non-Exec. Dir. British Nuclear Fuels PLC 1979-87; Royal Soc. Esso Medal 1978. *Publications:* papers on nuclear physics in scientific journals. *Leisure interests:* sailing, rugby football. *Address:* Fairfield, Eskdale, Holmbrook, Cumbria, England (Home). *Telephone:* 094 03-252.

MARSTON, Robert Quarles, B.S., M.D.; American science administrator; b. 12 Feb. 1923, Toano, Va.; s. of Warren and Helen Smith Marston; m. Ann Carter Garnett 1946; two s. one d.; ed. Virginia Mil. Inst., Medical Coll. of

Virginia and Oxford Univ.; Intern, Johns Hopkins Univ. 1949-50; Asst. Resident, Vanderbilt Univ. Hospital, Nashville, Tenn. 1950-51; Asst. Resident, Medical Coll. of Va., Richmond 1953-54, Asst. Prof. of Medicine 1954-57, Dean in Charge of Student Affairs 1959-61; Asst. Prof. of Bacteriology and Immunology, Univ. of Minn. 1958-59; Dir. of Univ. of Miss. Medical Center and Dean of School of Medicine, Jackson, Miss. 1961-65; Vice-Chancellor, Univ. of Miss. and Dean of School of Medicine 1965-66; Assoc. Dir. Nat. Insts. of Health, Bethesda, Md., and Dir. of Regional Medical Programs 1966-68, Dir. Nat. Insts. of Health 1968-73; Scholar-in-Residence Univ. of Va. 1973-74; Pres. Univ. of Fla. 1974-84, Pres. Emer., Prof. of Medicine 1984-; Adjunct Prof. of Fish and Aquaculture 1986-; mem. Bd., Johnson and Johnson; Rhodes Scholar 1947-49, Markle Scholar 1954-59; mem. Exec. Cttee. Nat. Assn. of State Univs. and Land Grant Colls., Council Inst. of Medicine, Assn. of American Physicians; Hon. mem. Nat. Medical Assn. 1969, American Hospital Assn. 1969; Distinguished Fellow Inst. of Medicine, N.A.S. 1973; Distinguished mem. Assn. of American Medical Colls.; Hon. Fellow, Lincoln Coll.; five Hon. degrees. *Publications:* Numerous articles in the field of infectious diseases, medical educ., and admin. of health programmes. *Leisure interests:* sailing, camping, music, reading. *Address:* University of Florida, Gainesville, Fla. 32611 (Office); Route 1, Box 20a, Alachua, Fla. 32615, U.S.A. (Home).

MARSZAŁEK-MŁYŃCZYK, Krystyna, M.A.; Polish politician; b. 9 April 1930, Białystok; m.; one c.; ed. Faculty of Romance Philology, Catholic Univ. of Lublin; journalist in regional and cultural journals 1955-68, Ed.-in-Chief, Kontrasty (monthly) 1968-73; mem. Democratic Party (SD) 1959-, mem. Presidium of SD Voivodship Cttee., Białystok 1962-76, Sec. SD Voivodship Cttee. Białystok 1974-76, mem. SD Cen. Cttee. 1965-81, mem. Presidium of SD Cen. Cttee. and Sec. Cen. Cttee. 1976-81; mem. Presidium of Chief Council, Soc. for Connections with Poles Living Abroad (Polonia), mem. Gen. Bd. of Soc. for Polish-Russian Friendship and numerous social and cultural societies; Deputy to Seym 1965-85, Chair. Seym Comm. of Culture and Art 1980-85; mem. Council of State 1980-83; Deputy Chair. Council for Family Matters of Council of Ministers 1981-84; Cultural Attaché Polish Embassy, Paris and Dir. of Polish Inst., Paris 1984-86; Under-Sec. of State, Ministry of Culture and Art 1986-; Kt.'s Cross, Order of Polonia Restituta, Gold Cross of Merit and other decorations. *Address:* Ministry of Culture and Art, Krakowskie Przedmieście 15, 00-071 Warsaw, Poland.

MÁRTA, Ferenc, D.CHEM.; Hungarian chemist; b. 12 Jan. 1929, Kiskundorozsma; s. of Ferenc Márta and Matild Forrai; m. 1954; one d.; Head of Dept. of Physics and Chem., Attila József Univ., Szeged 1962, Rector 1967-73; Corresp. mem. Hungarian Acad. of Sciences 1970, full mem. 1976-, Gen. Sec. 1975-80, mem. Presidium, Vice-Pres. 1985-, Gen. Dir. of Acad.'s Cen. Research Inst. for Chem.; mem. Presidium of Nat. Cttee. on Technological Devt., Council of Assn. of Hungarian Chemists; Foreign mem. Soviet and Czechoslovakian Acad. of Sciences; Hon. Dr. Odessa State Univ. 1975; Order of Labour (Silver 1964, Gold 1973), State Prize 1985. *Address:* Central Research Institute for Chemistry of the Hungarian Academy of Sciences, 1025 Budapest, Pusztaszeri ut 59/67, Hungary. *Telephone:* 152-868.

MARTELLI, Claudio; Italian politician; b. 1944; Deputy Leader of Socialist Party (PSI) 1978-. *Address:* c/o Italian Socialist Party (PSI), Via del Corso 476, 00186 Rome, Italy. *Telephone:* (06) 67781.

MARTENS, Wilfried, D.EN D.; Belgian politician; b. Sleidinge, 19 April 1936; m. Lieve Verschroeven; two d.; ed. Louvain Univ.; fmr. Leader Vlaamse Volksbeweging; Adviser to Harmel Cabinet 1965, to Vanden Boeynants Cabinet 1966; Minister of Community Problems 1968; Pres. Christelijke Volkspartij (CVP) 1972-79; mem. Parl. for Ghent-Eeklo 1974; co-founder Europese Volkspartij (EVP); Prime Minister 1979-81, 1981-85, 1985-. *Address:* 16 rue de la Loi, 1000 Brussels; 24 Désiré Van Monckhovenstraat, 9000 Ghent, Belgium.

MARTENSON, Jan; Swedish United Nations official; b. 14 Feb. 1933, Uppsala; m.; four c.; ed. Univ. of Uppsala; held various Foreign Ministry and diplomatic posts until 1966; Head Section UN Dept. Ministry for Foreign Affairs, Stockholm 1966-67, Head Information Dept. 1973-75; Deputy Dir. Stockholm Int. Peace Research Inst. 1968-69; Sec.-Gen. Swedish Prep. Cttee. for UN Conf. on Human Environment 1970-72; Chef de Cabinet for King of Sweden 1975-79; Asst. Sec.-Gen. Centre for Disarmament UN Dept. of Political and Security Council Affairs 1979-82, Under-Sec.-Gen. for Disarmament Affairs 1983-87; Chair. UN Appointments and Promotions Bd. 1984-86; Sec.-Gen. Int. Conf. on Relationship between Disarmament and Devt. 1987; Dir.-Gen. UN Office, Geneva 1987-; Head UN Centre for Human Rights, Geneva 1987-; Co-ordinator UN Second Decade Against Racism 1987. *Publications:* some 25 books, articles on disarmament and human rights. *Address:* Palais des Nations, 1211 Geneva 10, Switzerland. *Telephone:* (022) 346011.

MARTIN, Archer John Porter, C.B.E., M.A., PH.D., F.R.S.; British chemist; b. 1 March 1910, London; s. of Dr. William A. P. and Lillian K. Martin; m. Judith Bagenal 1943; two s. three d.; ed. Bedford School and Peterhouse, Cambridge; Research, Cambridge, Physical Chemical Lab., Nutritional Lab. 1933-38; Wool Industries Research Assn., Leeds 1938-46; Boots' Pure Drug Co. Research Dept., Nottingham 1946-48; mem. staff Medical

Research Council 1948–52; Head of Physical Chem. Div., Nat. Inst. for Medical Research, Mill Hill, London, 1952–56; Chemical Consultant 1956–59; Dir. Abbotsbury Laboratories Ltd. 1959–70; Consultant to Wellcome Foundation Ltd. 1970–73; Extraordinary Prof. Eindhoven Technological Univ., Holland 1964–74; MRC Professorial Fellowship of Chem., Univ. of Sussex 1973–78; Robert A. Welch Prof. of Chem., Univ. of Houston, Tex. 1974–79; Visiting Prof. Ecole Polytechnique Fédérale de Lausanne 1980–83; Berzelius Gold Medal of Swedish Medical Soc. 1951; shared Nobel Prize in Chem. 1952; Hon. Fellow (Cambridge) 1974; John Scott Award 1958, John Price Wetherill Medal 1959, Franklin Inst. Medal 1959, Leverhulme Medal 1963, Kolthoff Medal 1969, Callendar Medal 1971, Randolf Major Medal (Conn. Univ.) 1979, Fritz Pregl Award (Austria) 1985, Order of the Rising Sun, 2nd Class (Japan) 1972; Achievement Award The Worshipful Co. of Scientific Instrument Makers 1972; Hon. D.Sc. (Leeds) 1968, (Glasgow) 1972, (Urbino) 1985. *Address:* 47 Roseford Road, Cambridge, CB4 2HA, England.

MARTIN, Dean (Dino Crocetti); American actor and singer; b. 17 June, 1917, Steubenville, Ohio; s. of Guy Crocetti; m. 1st Elizabeth Ann MacDonald 1940 (divorced 1947), one s., three d.; m. 2nd Jeanne Bieggers 1969 (divorced), two s. one d.; m. 3rd Catherine Mae Hawn 1973 (divorced 1976); (one s. deceased); an amateur prize fighter before becoming a singer; first partnered with Jerry Lewis (q.v.) in 1946 at the 500 Club, Atlantic City N.J.; made film début with Lewis in My Friend Irma 1949; other films include: My Friend Irma Goes West 1950, That's My Boy 1951, Sailor Beware 1952, Jumping Jack 1952, The Stooge 1953, Scared Stiff 1953, The Caddy 1953, Living it Up 1954, Three Ring Circus 1954, You're Never Too Young 1954, Pardners 1956, Hollywood or Bust 1956, The Young Lions 1958, Some Came Running 1958, Rio Bravo 1959, Who Was That Lady? 1960, Bells Are Ringing 1960, Sergeants Three 1962, Toys in the Attic 1963, Who's Been Sleeping in My Bed? 1963, What a Way to Go 1964, Robin and the Seven Hoods 1964, Kiss Me Stupid 1964, The Sons of Katie Elder 1965, The Silencers 1966, Murderer's Row 1967, The Ambushers 1967, Bandolero 1968, How to Save a Marriage 1968, Five Card Stud 1968, The Wrecking Crew 1968, Airport 1969, Something Big 1971, Showdown 1973, Mr. Ricco 1975, Cannonball Run 1981, Cannonball Run II 1984; television appearances include: Dean Martin Show, Dean's Place 1975, Dean Martin's Celebrity Roast; has played in many nightclubs, especially in Las Vegas. *Address:* c/o Mort Viner, 8899 Beverly Boulevard, Los Angeles, California 90048, U.S.A.

MARTIN, Edmund Fible, B.S., ENG.D.; American steel executive; b. 2 Nov. 1902; ed. Stevens Inst. of Technology; with Bethlehem Steel Corpn. mills, Bethlehem 1922–70, Supt. 1928–39, Asst. Supt. Saucon Div. Bethlehem plant 1939–46, Asst. Gen. Man. Lackawanna, N.Y., plant of Bethlehem Steel 1946–50, Gen. Man. 1950–58; Vice-Pres. Steel Div., Bethlehem Steel Corpn. 1958–60; Dir. Bethlehem Steel Corpn. 1958–70, Pres. 1960–63, Vice-Chair. 1963–64, Chair. and Chief Exec. 1964–70; Trustee Nat. Industrial Conf. Bd. 1960–70, Stevens Inst. of Tech., Lehigh Univ., St. Luke's Hospital Bethlehem; Hon. Dir. American Iron and Steel Inst. (Chair. and C.E.O. 1967–69), J. P. Morgan & Co. Inc., Morgan Guaranty Trust Co., New York, The Pennsylvania Soc., Bethlehem Area Foundation; Hon. Dr. Eng. (Buffalo) 1961, Hon. LL.D. (Moravian Coll.) 1964, (Lehigh) 1966, (Valparaiso) 1967; Hon. Eng.D. (Stevens Inst. of Tech.) 1967; Kt. Commdr., Royal Order of the North Star, Sweden; Southern Cross (Brazil), Grand Band, Order of the Star of Africa (Liberia); numerous other awards. *Address:* Suite 310, 437 Main Street, Bethlehem, Pa. 18018, U.S.A.

MARTIN, H.E. Cardinal Jacques; French ecclesiastic; b. 26 Aug. 1908, Amiens; ordained 1934, elected bishop of Nabulus, Palestine 1964, consecrated 1964, Archbishop 1986; cr. Cardinal 1988; Prefect Emer. of the Casa Pontificia. *Address:* 00120 Vatican City, Rome, Italy. *Telephone:* (06) 698-3718.

MARTIN, James Grubbs, PH.D.; American politician; b. 11 Dec. 1935, Savannah, Ga.; s. of Arthur M. and Mary J. (Grubbs) Martin; m. Dorothy A. McAulay 1957; two s. one d.; ed. Davidson (N.C.) Coll. and Princeton Univ.; Assoc. Prof. of Chem. Davidson Coll. 1960–72; mem. 93rd–98th Congresses from N.C.; Gov. of North Carolina Jan. 1985–; Republican. *Address:* Governor's Mansion, Raleigh, N.C., U.S.A. Ohio 43615, U.S.A.

MARTIN, Sir (John) Leslie, Kt., R.A., M.A., PH.D., F.R.I.B.A.; British architect; b. 17 Aug. 1908; s. of the late Robert Martin; m. Sadie Speight; one s. one d.; ed. Manchester Univ. School of Architecture; Asst. Lecturer, Manchester Univ. 1930–34; Dir. Hull School of Architecture 1934–39; Prin. Asst. Architect L.M.S. Railway 1939–48; Deputy Architect, London County Council 1948–53, Architect 1953–56; Prof. of Architecture, Cambridge Univ. 1956–72, Prof. Emer. 1973–; Fellow, Jesus Coll., Cambridge 1956–72, Hon. Fellow 1973–; Council mem. R.I.B.A. 1952–58, Vice-Pres. 1955–57; Slade Prof. Oxford 1965–66; Ferens Prof. Hull 1966–67; Visiting Prof. of Architecture, Yale Univ. 1973–74; Lethaby Prof. Royal Coll. of Art, London 1981–82; mem. Royal Fine Art Comm. 1958–72; Hon. mem. Asscn. of Finnish Architects; Corresp. mem. Nat. Acad. S. Luca, Rome; Hon. LL.D. (Leicester, Manchester, Hull and Essex); awards include Soane Medal 1930 and London Bronze Architectural Medal 1954; R.I.B.A. Distinction in Town Planning; Royal Gold Medal (Arch.) 1973, Order of Santiago da Espada (Portugal). *Publications:* Joint Ed. Cambridge Architectural and Urban

Studies; Buildings and Ideas from the Studio of Leslie Martin 1933–83. *Address:* Church Street Barns, Great Shelford, Cambridge, England. *Telephone:* (0223) 842399.

MARTIN, Sir Leslie (see Martin, Sir (John) Leslie).

MARTIN, Ludwig Markus; German lawyer; b. 25 April 1909, Martinszell, Bavaria; s. of Joachim and Maria Endrass Martin; m. Renate Borgmeyer 1943; two s. two d.; ed. Univ. of Munich; Assessor, Munich High Court 1937–39; Scientific Asst., Supreme Court, Leipzig 1939; Military Service 1939–46; Chair. Santhofen Court 1946–50; Civil Rights Dept., Fed. Ministry of Justice 1950–; Fed. Attorney 1952–53; Fed. Judge, Fed. Supreme Court 1953–63; Fed. Attorney-Gen. 1963–74, Pres. German Section, Int. Comm. of Jurists; Pres. German-Italian Asscn. of Jurists *Leisure interests:* walking, swimming, photography, music, reading. *Address:* Postfach 51 02 29, 7500 Karlsruhe 51, Federal Republic of Germany.

MARTIN, Hon. Paul Joseph James, P.C., C.C., Q.C., M.A., LL.M.; Canadian lawyer and politician; b. 23 June 1903, Ottawa, Ont.; s. of Phillip Ernest and Lumina Marie Chouinard Martin; m. Eleanor Adams 1937; one s. one d.; ed. St. Alexandre Coll., Ironsides, Que., St. Michael's Coll., Osgoode Hall Law School, Toronto, Univ. of Toronto, Harvard Law School, Trinity Coll., Cambridge, and Geneva School of Int. Studies; Lecturer in Political Science, Assumption Coll., Univ. of Western Ontario 1931–34; senior partner firm of Martin, Laird, Easton & Cowan 1934–63; M.P. for Essex East 1935–68; K.C. 1937; Del. to L.N. Ass. 1938; Parl. Asst. to Minister of Labour 1943; Chair. Canadian Govt. Del. and Chair. Employment Comm. ILO Conf., Philadelphia 1944; Sec. of State of Canada 1945–46; Minister of Nat. Health and Welfare 1946–57; Sec. of State for External Affairs 1963–68; Sr. Minister and Leader of Govt. in Senate 1968–74; High Commr. in U.K. 1974–80; Del. to 1st, 4th, 7th, 10th, 18th, 19th and 20th General Assemblies of the UN. to 1st Session of Econ. and Social Council (London) 1946 and to 3rd and 5th Sessions (New York 1946 and 1947); Pres. NATO 1965–66; Del. Consultative Cttee., Colombo Plan, Wellington, N.Z. 1956; Chancellor, Wilfrid Laurier Univ. 1972–76; Hon. mem. Acad. Political Science, New York; Hon. Col. Windsor Regt.; Hon. LL.D., D.C.L., Dr. Humanities, LL.D. (Cambridge) 1980; Grande Médaille d'Or de l'Ordre international du Bien public (France) 1971; Hon. Capt. Air Canada 1979; Christian Culture Award 1956; Liberal. *Publications:* A Very Public Life (autobiography) (2 vols.), and several other books. *Address:* 2021 Ontario Avenue, Windsor, Ont., Canada (Home).

MARTIN, Preston, M.B.A., PH.D.; American government official; b. 5 Dec. 1923, Los Angeles; s. of Oscar and Gaynell (Horne) Martin; one s.; ed. Univ. of S. California and Indiana Univ.; Savings and Loan Commr., State of Calif. 1967–69; Chair. of Bd. Fed. Home Loan Bank Bd. 1969–72; Chair. and C.E.O. PMI Mortgage Insurance Co. (subsidiary of Sears Roebuck and Co.) 1972–80, Seraco Enterprises Inc. (subsidiary of Sears Roebuck) 1980–82; Vice-Chair. Bd. of Govs., Fed. Reserve System 1982–86. *Publications:* Principles and Practices of Real Estate 1959. *Leisure interests:* tennis, bicycling. *Address:* 20th and Constitutional Avenue, N.W. Washington, D.C. 20007, U.S.A.

MARTIN, Roger Léon René; French businessman; b. 8 April 1915, Asnières; s. of Gilbert Martin and Andrée Eugénie (Portemer); m., two s. one d.; m. 2nd Renée Guernier, one s. two d. (previous marriage); ed. Ecole Polytechnique and Ecole Nat. Supérieure des Mines; Ingénieur des Mines, Nancy 1941–42; Asst. to Steel Industry Dir., Dept. of Industry (French Govt.) 1942–46; Lecturer Ecole Nat. des Mines 1945–53; joined Compagnie de Pont-à-Mousson 1948, Asst. Gen. Man. 1953, Gen. Man. 1959–64, Pres. and Gen. Man. 1964–70; Pres. Cie. de Saint-Gobain Pont-à-Mousson 1970–80, Hon. Chair. 1980–; Dir. L'Oréal, Certainteed, Pont-à-Mousson S.A.; Commdr. Légion d'honneur. *Publication:* Patron de droit divin 1984. *Address:* Compagnie de Saint-Gobain, "Les Miroirs", 18 avenue d'Alsace, 92400 Courbevoie (Office); 86 rue d'Assas, 75006 Paris, France. *Telephone:* (1) 47 62 30 00.

MARTÍN FERNANDEZ, Miguel; Spanish banker; b. 9 Nov. 1943, Jerez de la Frontera; m. Anne Catherine Cleary 1972; one s. two d.; ed. Univ. Complutense, Madrid; Head Budget and Finance Sections, Ministry of Finance 1969–72, Deputy Dir. 1972–76; Controller, World Bank, Latin American Region 1976–77, Alt. Exec. Dir. for Spain, Italy and Portugal, World Bank 1977–78; Dir.-Gen. Treasury, Ministry of Finance 1978–79; Under-Sec. for Budget and Public Expenditure 1979–81; Pres. Inst. for Official Credit 1982; Head Cen. Office for Trade Balances, Banco de España 1983–84; Under-Sec. Economy and Finance 1984–86; Dir.-Gen. Banco de España 1986–; Gran Placa de la Orden del Mérito Postal, Encomienda del Mérito Agrícola. *Address:* Banco de España, Calle Alcalá 50, 28014 Madrid, Spain. *Telephone:* 446.90.55.

MARTÍN VILLA, Rodolfo; Spanish engineer, trade union official and politician; b. 3 Oct. 1934, Santa María del Páramo, León; m. María Pilar Pena Medina; two c.; ed. Escuela de Ingeniería Industrial, Madrid; Leader of Madrid Section, Sindicato Español Universitario, Nat. Leader 1962–64; Sec.-Gen. Syndical Org. 1969–74; mem. Council of the Realm; Nat. Econ. Adviser, Nat. Inst. of Industry; Nat. Econ. Adviser, Banco de Crédito Industrial, later Pres.; Civil Gov. of Barcelona and Prov. Head of Falangist Movement 1974–75; Minister for Relations with Trade Unions 1975–76, of the Interior 1976–79, of Territorial Admin. 1980–82; First Deputy Prime

Minister 1981–82; mem. Corps. of Financial and Tax Inspectors, Inland Revenue; fmr. mem. special group of industrial engineers assisting Treasury. *Address:* Jerez 4, 28016 Madrid, Spain.

MARTINA, Dominico (Don) F.; Netherlands Antilles politician; fmr. finance officer, Govt. of Curaçao; head, govt. social affairs dept.; f. Movimentu Antiyas Nobo 1979; M.P. 1979–; Prime Minister of Netherlands Antilles 1979–84, 1985–88. *Address:* c/o Office of the Prime Minister, Fort Amsterdam, Willemstad, Curaçao, Netherlands Antilles.

MARTINEAU, Rt. Hon. Paul, P.C., Q.C.; Canadian lawyer and politician; b. 10 April 1921, Bryson, Quebec; s. of Alphonse Martineau and Lucienne Lemieux; m. Hélène Neclaw 1946; two d.; legal practice at Campbells Bay, Que. 1950–, at Hull, Que. 1966–; fmr. Crown Attorney for District of Pontiac, Quebec; M.P. 1958–65; Parl. Asst. to Prime Minister 1959–61; Deputy Speaker of House of Commons 1961–62; Minister of Mines and Tech. Surveys 1962–63; mem. Royal Comm. on Admin. of Justice 1967–70; Puisne Judge Superior Court Prov. of Quebec 1980–; Progressive Conservative. *Leisure interests:* painting, writing, travelling, hiking. *Address:* Palais de Justice, 1 Notre Dame Street East, Montreal, Que.; 1204 Mountain Road, Aylmer, Quebec J9H 5E1, Canada (Home). *Telephone:* (514) 873-7433 (Office); (819) 827-2065 (Home).

MARTINET, Gilles, L. ÈS L.; French journalist, politician and diplomatist; b. 8 Aug. 1916, Paris; m. Iole Buozzi 1938; two d.; Ed.-in-Chief, Agence France Presse 1944–49, Observateur 1950–61; Dir. Observateur 1960–64; mem. Bd. of Dirs., Nouvel Observateur 1964–, Matin 1975–; Dir., Faire (monthly) 1975–; Deputy Sec.-Gen. Parti Socialiste Unifié 1960–67; Nat. Sec. Parti Socialiste 1976–79; mem. European Parl. 1979–81; Amb. to Italy 1981–84; Hon. Ambassadeur de France 1984. *Publications:* Le marxisme de notre temps 1961, La conquête des pouvoirs 1971, Les cinq communismes 1971, Le système Pompidou 1973, L'avenir depuis vingt ans 1975, Les sept syndicalismes 1977, Cassandre et les tueurs, cinquante ans d'une histoire française 1986. *Address:* 12 rue Las Cases, 75007 Paris, France.

MARTINEZ, Robert, B.S., M.A.; American state governor; b. 25 Dec. 1934, Tampa; s. of Serafin Martinez and Ida (née Carreno) Martinez; ed. Univ. of Tampa and Univ. of Illinois; Pres. Cafe Sevilla Spanish Restaurant 1975–83; Mayor of Tampa 1979–86; Gov. of Florida 1987–; mem. Fla. task force on medical malpractice U.S. Conf. of Mayors; Pres.'s Advisory Cttee. on Intergovernmental Relations. *Address:* Office of the Governor, The Capitol, Tallahassee, Fla. 32301-8047, U.S.A.

MARTINEZ, Victor Hipolito; Argentine lawyer, law professor and politician; b. 24 Nov. 1924, Cordoba; m. Fanny Munte; three s.; ed. Univ. of Cordoba; Rep. to the Prov. Ass. of Cordoba 1967; Mayor of Cordoba 1963–66; Dir. of newspaper Los Principios 1970–72; Vice-Pres. of Argentina Dec. 1983–. *Address:* Senado de la Nacion Argentina, Hipolito Yrigoyen 1849, C.P. 1089, Buenos Aires, Argentina.

MARTÍNEZ DE PERÓN, María Estela (Isabelita); Argentine politician and fmr. dancer; b. 6 Feb. 1931, La Rioja Province; m. Gen. Juan Domingo Perón (Pres. of Argentina 1946–55, 1973–74) 1961 (died 1974); joined troupe of travelling folk dancers; danced in cabaret in several S. American countries; lived in Spain 1960–73; returned to Argentina with Juan Perón, became Vice-Pres. of Argentina 1973–74, Pres. 1974–76 (deposed by mil. coup); Chair. Peronist Party 1974–85; detained 1976–81; settled in Madrid, Spain.

MARTÍNEZ ESTERUELAS, Cruz, LL.D.; Spanish politician and lawyer; b. 4 Feb. 1932, Barcelona; s. of Cruz and Presentación Martínez Esteruelas; m. Encarnación Oliveras y Gajo 1958; one s. two d.; ed. Deusto Univ., Bilbao and Univ. Complutense de Madrid; State attorney and Parl. Counsel; Dir.-Gen. Patrimonio del Estado, Ministry of Finance 1962–65; Chief Exec. Legal Advisory Bd., Secr.-Gen. of the Falangist Movement 1965–68; mem. Cortes 1968; Minister of Devt. Planning July-Dec. 1973, of Educ. and Science 1973–75; Dir. March Foundation 1970–73; Pres. Industrias Quimicas Procolor S.A. 1977–; Pres. Unión del Pueblo Español (UDPE); Gran Cruz de Carlos III, Grand Cross of Civil Merit, Order of Cisneros, and many other decorations. *Publications:* La Enemistad Politica 1971, Estudios de Sociologia Politica, Administración y economia en una nueva constitución de los EE.UU. 1973, Monarquia y cambio social 1974, Cartas para el humanismo social 1976. *Address:* Monte Esquinza 26, 28010 Madrid, Spain.

MARTÍNEZ SOMALO, H.E. Cardinal Eduardo; Spanish ecclesiastic; b. 31 March 1927, Banos de Rio Tobia; ordained 1950; elected Bishop of Tagora 1975, consecrated 1975, then Archbishop; cr. Cardinal 1988; an Under-Sec. of State to the Vatican. *Address:* 00120 Vatican City, Rome, Italy.

MARTINI, H.E. Cardinal Carlo Maria; Italian ecclesiastic; b. 15 Feb. 1927, Turin; ordained priest 1952; Archbishop of Milan 1980–; mem. Synod of Bishops; Consultant to Sacred Congregations for the Bishops, Doctrine of Faith, Religions, People's Evangelisation and Catholic Educ.; cr. Cardinal 1983. *Address:* Palazzo Arcivescovile, Piazza Fontana 2, 20122 Milan, Italy. *Telephone:* (02) 85561.

MARTINI, Fritz, DR. PHIL. HABIL.; German university professor; b. 5 Sept. 1909, Magdeburg; m. Ruth Hoelscher 1938; two s. one d.; ed. Univs. of Zürich, Graz, Heidelberg, Grenoble, Berlin; Extraordinary Prof. of Literary Science and Aesthetics, Tech. Univ., Stuttgart 1943–49, Ordinary Prof. 1949–75; mem. Presidium Deutsche Akad. für Sprache und Dichtung, Darmstadt. *Publications include:* Heinrich von Kleist und die geschichtliche Welt 1939, Deutsche Literaturgeschichte, Das Wagnis der Sprache, Was war Expressionismus?, Das Zeitalter des Realismus 1960. *Address:* Grüneisenstrasse 5, Stuttgart 7000, Federal Republic of Germany. *Telephone:* 245064.

MARTINI-URDANETA, Alberto, DR.RER.POL., D.SC.S.; Venezuelan lawyer, politician and diplomatist; b. 2 April 1930, Trujillo; m.; five c.; ed. Cen. Univ. of Venezuela; Clerk at Third Court of First Instance, Fed. Dist. 1949–51, Sec. Labour Third Court of First Instance 1954–62; Substitute Judge, Labour Court of First Instance 1956, Judge 1957; Legal Counsellor to Ministry for Foreign Relations 1958; f. mem. (1956) and Sec.-Gen. Venezuelan Inst. of Social Legislation 1960–69; Pres. Venezuelan Industrial Bank 1971; Minister of Labour 1972–74; Dir.-Gen. Venezuelan Inst. for Social Legis. 1978–79; Perm. Rep. to UN and other int. orgs., Geneva 1979–81, Perm. Rep. to UN, New York 1981–84; Chair. numerous int. cttees. and orgs., including several ILO cttees. and confs. *Publications:* numerous articles on labour and social matters. *Address:* c/o Ministerio de Relaciones Exteriores, Caracas, Venezuela.

MARTINS, António Gentil da Silva; Portuguese paediatric and plastic surgeon; b. 10 July 1930, Lisbon; s. of António da Silva Martins and Maria Madalena Gentil da Silva Martins; m. Maria Guilhermina Ivens Ferraz Jardim da Silva Martins; three s. five d.; ed. Univ. of Lisbon; intern, Hospitais Civis, Lisbon; Registrar, Alder Hey Children's Hosp., Liverpool; founder and Head, Paediatric Dept. Instituto Portugues de Oncologia de F. Gentil 1960–85, consultant paediatric surgeon 1985–; paediatric surgeon, Hosp. D. Estefania (Children's Hosp.), Lisbon 1965, Dir. of Paediatric Surgery 1987–; Assoc. Prof. of Paediatric Surgery, Faculty of Medical Sciences, Lisbon 1984–; Pres. Portuguese Soc. of Plastic and Reconstructive Surgery 1968–74, Ordem dos Medicos (Portuguese Medical Asscn.) 1978–86, Portuguese Asscn. of Paediatric Surgeons 1975–84, World Medical Asscn. 1981–83, Southern Branch Portuguese League Against Cancer 1988–(91); mem. Exec. Council World Fed. of Asscns. of Paediatric Surgeons 1983–89; mem. numerous professional socs. etc.; awarded Silver Plate for film on separation of Siamese twins; Grande Oficial da Ordem do Infante D. Henrique and other awards. *Publication:* Textbook on Plastic Surgery of the Ibero-Latin-American Foundation of Plastic Surgery (co-author) 1986. *Leisure interests:* target-shooting, volleyball, tennis, collecting stamps and coins, music, photography. *Address:* Av. António Augusto Aguiar 22 1 Dto, 1000 Lisbon (Office); Rua D. Francisco Manuel de Melo 1 3°, Lisbon 100, Portugal (Home). *Telephone:* 560807 (Office); 651436/657642 (Home).

MARTINS, Peter; American ballet director, choreographer, and former dancer; b. Oct. 27 1946, Copenhagen, Denmark; m. Lise la Cour (divorced 1973); one c.; pupil of Vera Volkova and Stanley Williams with Royal Danish Ballet; Dir. N.Y. City Ballet; Teacher, School of American Ballet 1975, N.Y. Ballet 1975, Ballet Master 1981–83, Co-Ballet Master-in-Chief 1983–; Artistic Adviser, Pa. Ballet 1982–; mem. Royal Danish Ballet 1965–67, Prin. Dancer (including Bournonville repertory) 1967; Guest Artist, N.Y. Ballet 1967–70, Prin. Dancer 1970–83; Guest Artist Regional Ballet Cos. U.S., also Nat. Ballet, Canada, Royal Ballet, London, Grand Theatre, Geneva, Paris Opera, Vienna State Opera, Munich State Opera, London Festival Ballet, Ballet Int., Royal Danish Ballet; *choreographed Broadway musicals include:* Dream of the Twins (co-choreographer) 1982, On your Toes 1982, Song and Dance 1985; *works choreographed include:* Calcium Light Night 1977, Tricolore (Pas de Basque Section) 1978, Rossini Pas de Deux 1978, Tango-Tango (ice ballet) 1978, Dido and Aeneas 1979, Sonate di Scarlatti 1979, Eight Easy Pieces 1980, Lille Suite 1980, Suite from Histoire de Soldat 1981, Capriccio Italien 1981, The Magic Flute 1981, Symphony No. 1 1981, Delibes Divertissement 1982, Piano-Rag-Music 1982, Concerto for Two Solo Pianos 1982, Waltzes 1983, Rossini Quartets 1983, Tango 1983, A Schubertiad 1984, Mozart Violin Concerto 1984, Poulenc Sonata 1985, La Sylphide 1985, Valse Triste 1985, Eight More 1985, We Are the World 1985, Eight Miniatures 1985, Ecstatic Orange, Tanzspiel 1988; Dance magazine award 1977; Cue's Golden Apple award 1977, Award of Merit, Phila. Art Alliance 1985. *Publications:* Far From Denmark (autobiog.) 1982. *Address:* New York City Ballet, New York State Theatre, Lincoln Center, Plaza New York, New York 10023, U.S.A.

MARTINS, Rudolf, LL.D.; Austrian diplomatist (retd.); b. 9 Feb. 1915, Zürich; s. of Martin and Carola (née Dobolschek) Martins; ed. Humanistisches Gymnasium (Vienna XIII), and Univ. of Vienna; with Fed. Chamber of Commerce, Vienna 1946–47; Austrian Trade Commr. for Switzerland and Liechtenstein and Sec. of Austrian Chamber of Commerce for Switzerland, Zürich 1947–49; with Fed. Chamber of Commerce, Vienna 1949–59; Counsellor, Adviser on Multilateral Trade and Commerce, Ministry of Foreign Affairs 1959–63; Counsellor, Head of Dept. for Multilateral Trade and Commerce Questions, Ministry of Trade and Reconstruction 1963–65; Amb. and Perm. Austrian Rep. to Office of UN and UN Specialized Agencies, Geneva, and Leader of Austrian Del. to European Free Trade Asscn. (EFTA) 1965–68, 1972–76; Envoy Extraordinary and Minister Plenipotentiary, Head of Dept. for Multi-lateral Trade and Commerce Questions, Ministry of Foreign Affairs 1968–72; Office of the Sec.-Gen. Ministry of

Foreign Affairs 1977; Consul-Gen. of Austria at Zagreb 1978–80; Hon. Amb. for Life 1980; Goldenes Ehrenzeichen für Verdienste um die Republik Österreich. *Publications:* Statesmanship in Civil War (Spain's President Manuel Azaña), A Dualism in Multilateral Economic Policies–GATT and UNCTAD, A Meditation on Mediaeval Bosnia. *Leisure interests:* music, linguistics. *Address:* Schloss Schönbrunn 39, A-1130 Vienna, Austria (Home).

MARTINSON, Ida Marie, PH.D.; American professor of nursing; b. 8 Nov. 1936, Mentor, Minn.; m. Paul Martinson 1962; one s. one d.; ed. St. Luke's Hosp. School of Nursing, Duluth, Minn. and Univs. of Minnesota and Illinois; Instructor in Tuberculosis Nursing, St Luke's Hosp., Duluth 1957–58; Instructor in Nursing, Thornton Jr. Coll., Harvey, Ill. 1967–69; Asst. Prof. and Chair. of Research, Univ. of Minn. School of Nursing 1972–74, Assoc. Prof. and Dir. of Research 1974–77, Prof. and Dir. of Research 1977–82; Prof. and Head. Dept. of Family Health Care Nursing, Univ. of Calif., San Francisco 1982–; Fellow American Acad. of Nursing; mem. Inst. of Medicine, N.A.S. 1981–, mem. Governing Council 1984–86; Pres. Children's Hospice Int. 1986–88; Co-founder of Children's Cancer Foundation, Taiwan. *Publications:* Home care: a manual for implementation of home care for children dying of cancer 1978, Home care: A manual for parents (with D. Moldow) 1979; more than 80 articles in journals, 35 book chapters (1986) and one film; ed. of several books on home nursing. *Leisure interests:* skiing, walking, reading. *Address:* Room N411Y, Department of Family Health Care Nursing, University of California, San Francisco, Calif. 94143, U.S.A. *Telephone:* (415) 476-4558.

MARTONO; Indonesian politician; b. 17 May 1925, Karanganyar, Cen. Java; ed. Univ. of Gajah Mada, Yogyakarta and Univ. of Leiden; Head, Div. C, Bureau of Higher Educ., Dept. of Educ. and Culture 1954–60; Cultural Attaché, Tokyo 1960–64; sr. official, Dept. of Educ. and Culture 1964–71; Exec. Chair. Multipurpose Co-operatives (KOSGORO) 1964–71; Head, Jt. Secr. of Functional Groups (GOLKAR) and KOSGORO'S mother org. 1973; Jr. Minister for Transmigration 1978–83; Minister of Transmigration 1983–88. *Address:* Ministry of Transmigration, Jln. Letjen, Haryono MT, Jakarta, Indonesia.

MARTRE, Jean François Henri; French telecommunications and space engineer; b. 6 Feb. 1928, Bélesta; s. of Marius Martre and Paule Maugard; m. Odette Coppier 1953; three d.; ed. Ecole Polytechnique; telecommunications eng. 1952–59; Deputy Head of telecommunications service in the production of armaments 1961–64, Head of Bureau Département Electronique, then Head Industrial Bureau of the Cen. Service of Telecommunications to the Ministerial Del. for Armaments 1964–66, Deputy Dir. Industrial Affairs 1966, Dir. of Programmes and Industrial Aspects of Armaments 1971–74, Gen. Eng. First Class for Armaments 1974, Gen. Del. for Armaments 1977–83, State Admin. Société Nat. Industrielle Aérospatiale 1974–77, also SNECMA, Société Française d'Equipements pour la Navigation Aérienne; mem. Atomic Energy Cttee. 1977–83; Pres. and Dir.-Gen. Société Aérospatiale 1983–; Vice-Pres. Surveillance Council for the Airbus Industry 1983–; Officier, Légion d'honneur, Commandant, Ordre nat. du Mérite, Médaille de l'Aéronautique. *Leisure interests:* skiing, sailing. *Address:* 37 blvd. de Montmorency, 75016 Paris, France (Office).

MARTY, H.E. Cardinal François, D.THEOL.; French ecclesiastic; b. 18 May 1904, Pachins; s. of François Marty and Zoé Gineste; ed. Collège de Graves et de Villefranche de Rouergue (Aveyron), Grand Séminaire de Rodez (Aveyron) and Inst. Catholique de Toulouse; ordained 1930; Priest, Villefranche and Rodez 1932–40, Curé, Bournazel, Rieupeyroux and Millau 1940–51; Vicar-Gen., Rodez 1951–52; Bishop of Saint-Flour 1952; Archbishop of Reims 1960–68; Archbishop of Paris 1968–81; cr. Cardinal March 1969; Prés. de la Conférence épiscopale de France May 1969–75; Chevalier, Légion d'honneur. *Publications:* Dieu est tenace 1973, Evangile au présent 1974, Prophètes de la joie 1978, L'evêque dans la ville 1979, Cardinal Marty, Chronique vécue de l'église de France 1980. *Address:* Monastère de Monteils, 12200 Villefranche-de-Rouergue, France.

MARTY, Martin E., M.DIV., PH.D., S.T.M.; American ecclesiastic and professor of religious history; b. 5 Feb. 1928, West Point, N.E.; s. of Emil A. Marty and Anne Louise Wuerdemann Marty; m. 1st Elsa Schumacher 1952 (died 1981), 2nd Harriet Lindemann 1982; four s., one step-d.; ed. Concordia Seminary, St. Louis, Lutheran School of Theology, Chicago and Univ. of Chicago; Lutheran Minister 1952–63; Fairfax M. Cone Distinguished Service Prof. Univ. of Chicago 1963–; Ed., now Sr. Ed., The Christian Century 1956–; Pres. Park Ridge Center 1985–; Pres. American Soc. of Church History 1971, American Catholic History Assen. 1981, American Acad. of Religion 1988; Nat. Book Award for Righteous Empire 1972. *Publications:* 40 books and numerous articles on religious history, theology and cultural criticism. *Leisure interests:* good eating, baroque music, calligraphy. *Address:* 239 Scottswood Road, Riverside, Ill. 60546, U.S.A. *Telephone:* 312-442-9453.

MARTYNENKO, Vladimir Nikiforovich; Soviet (Ukrainian) diplomatist; b. 6 Oct. 1923, Zhitomir, Ukrainian S.S.R.; m. Galina Gribovska 1951; one d.; ed. Kiev Univ.; Soviet Army 1941–46; Ukrainian Soc. for Friendship and Cultural Relations with Foreign Countries 1951–56; Ukraine Diplomatic Service 1956–; Embassy of U.S.S.R. to Canada 1965–68; Deputy Minister of Foreign Affairs of Ukraine 1968–73, 1979–80, Minister 1980–;

Ukrainian Perm. Rep. to UN 1973–79; UN Special Comm. Against Apartheid 1973–79; Vice-Pres. ECOSOC 1978; Vice-Pres. UN Gen. Ass. 1981. *Address:* c/o Ministry of Foreign Affairs, Kiev, Ukrainian S.S.R., U.S.S.R.

MARTYNOV, Nikolay Vasiliyevich; Soviet politician; b. 26 April 1910, Moscow; ed. Moscow Energy Inst.; Mem. CPSU 1932; Engineer 1934–41; Deputy Commissar for Munitions U.S.S.R. 1941–46; Deputy Minister then First Deputy Minister of Agricultural Machine Building, U.S.S.R. 1946–53; Dept. Head, Ministry of Automobile, Tractors, and Agricultural Machine Building 1954–55, Deputy Minister 1955–57; First Deputy Chair. Tashkent Nat. Econ. Council 1957–59, Chair. 1959–60; Chair. Uzbekistan Nat. Econ. Council 1960–63; Sec. Cen. Cttee. of CP of Uzbekistan 1963–65; mem. Cen. Auditing Comm. CPSU 1961–66; First Deputy Chair. U.S.S.R. Council of Ministers State Cttee. for Material and Equipment Supplies 1965–76; Chair. State Cttee. for Material and Tech. Supply 1976–86; Deputy to Supreme Soviet 1962–; Vice-Chair. U.S.S.R. Council of Ministers 1976–85; mem. Comm. for Industry; U.S.S.R. State Prize, Hero of Socialist Labour, Order of Lenin (four times) and other decorations. *Address:* c/o U.S.S.R. Council of Ministers State Committee for Material and Equipment Supplies, Orlikovsky pereulok 5, Moscow, U.S.S.R.

MARUYAMA, Masao, LL.D.; Japanese professor of history of political ideas; b. 22 March 1914, Osaka; m. Yukari Koyama 1944; ed. Faculty of Law, Imperial Univ. of Tokyo; Asst., Faculty of Law, Univ. of Tokyo 1937–40, Prof. of East Asian Political Theory 1950–71, Prof. Emer. 1974–; Distinguished Visiting Scholar, Harvard Univ. 1961–62; Fellow, St. Antony's Coll., Oxford 1962–63, Inst. for Advanced Study, Princeton 1975–76; mem. Japan Acad. 1978–; Foreign Corresp. mem. British Acad. 1982–; Hon. LL.D. (Harvard) 1973; Hon. D. Lit. (Princeton) 1973. *Publications:* Thought and Behaviour in Modern Japanese Politics, Studies in the Intellectual History of Tokugawa Japan, Das Denken in Japan. *Address:* 2-44-5, Higashicho, Kichijōji, Musashino-shi, Tokyo, Japan. *Telephone:* 0422-22-4102.

MARX, György; Hungarian physicist; b. 26 May 1927, Budapest, s. of Dr. István Marx and Julia László; m. Edit Koczkás 1952; two s. one d.; ed. Roland Eötvös Univ., Budapest; started as staff member, Univ. Inst. for Theoretical Physics; Univ. Prof. 1964–; Leading Prof., Dept. of Atomic Physics 1970–; Corresp. mem. Hungarian Acad. of Sciences 1970–, mem. 1982–; Corresp. mem. Int. Acad. of Astronautics, Paris 1969–78, mem. 1978–; Hon. Prof. Univ. of Vienna 1968–; Vice-Pres. Int. Union for Pure and Applied Physics, Int. Comm. of Physics Educ., Int. Astronomical Union Comm. for Bio-astronomy, Int. Group for Research in Teaching of Physics; initiator Int. Neutrino Conf. series; Consultant, UNESCO; principal fields: particle, nuclear and astrophysics; discoverer of lepton charge conservation; Kossuth Prize 1956; Labour Order of Merit; Golden Degree 1968. *Leisure interests:* education, space, archaeology. *Publications:* Életrevaló atomok (Atoms in Action) 1978, Jövőidőben (Future Tense) 1979, Atomközelben (Atom at Close Range) 1981, and six other books; 200 papers in Hungarian and 150 in foreign scientific journals. *Address:* Department of Atomic Physics, Eötvös University, Puskin 5, H-1088 Budapest, Hungary. *Telephone:* 36-1-187902.

MASALIEV, Absamat Masalevich; Soviet party official; b. 1933; ed. Moscow Mining Inst.; mem. CPSU 1960; asst. chief engineer of mining works 1958–61; party work in Kirghizia 1961–69; head of section of Cent. Cttee. of Kirghiz CP and Pres. of Frunze City Exec. Cttee. 1969–74; Sec. of Cen. Cttee. of Kirghiz CP 1974–79; First Sec. of Issyk-Kul dist. party cttee. 1979–85; work for Cen. Cttee. of CPSU 1985–; First Sec. of Cen. Cttee. of Kirghiz CP 1985–; mem. of Cen. Cttee. of CPSU 1986–. *Address:* Central Committee Communist Party of Kirghiz, Frunze, U.S.S.R.

MASANI, Minoo; Indian author, publicist and business consultant; b. 20 Nov. 1905, Bombay; s. of Sir Rustom and Lady Manijeh Masani; ed. Elphinstone Coll., Bombay, and London School of Econs.; Barrister of Lincoln's Inn; founder and Joint Sec., Congress Socialist Party 1934–39; mem. Bombay Municipal Corpn. 1935–45, Mayor 1943–44; mem. Indian Legis. Ass. 1945–47, Constituent Ass. of India 1947–48; Amb. to Brazil 1948–49; mem. Lok Sabha (lower house of Parl.) 1949–52, 1957–62, 1963–71; Chair. Public Accounts Cttee. 1967–69, Minorities Comm. 1978, UN Sub-Comm. on Discrimination and Minorities 1950–52; Gen. Sec., Swatantra Party 1960–67, Pres. 1970–71; Patron, Liberal Int.; Chair. World Fed. of Socs. for Right to Die, Soc. for Right to Die with Dignity, India. *Publications:* Our India, Socialism Reconsidered, Your Food, Picture of a Plan, Plea for the Mixed Economy, Our Growing Human Family, Communist Party of India–a Short History, Congress Misrule and the Swatantra Alternative, J.P.; Mission Partly Accomplished, Bliss Was It in That Dawn, Against the Tide. *Leisure interests:* reading and writing. *Address:* 148 Mahatma Gandhi Road, Bombay 400 023, India. *Telephone:* 243268, 243649.

MASCALL, Rev. Eric Lionel, D.D., F.B.A.; British ecclesiastic and academic (retd.); b. 12 Dec. 1905, Sydenham, England; s. of John R. S. Mascall and S. Lilian Grundy; ed. Latymer Upper School, Pembroke Coll., Cambridge and Ely Theological Coll.; ordained in Church of England 1932; parochial work until 1937; Sub-Warden, Lincoln Theological Coll. 1937–45; Student and Tutor, Christ Church, Oxford 1945–62; Prof. of Historical Theology, King's Coll., London 1962–73, Fellow 1968–, now Prof. Emer.; Hon. Canon of Truro Cathedral 1974–84, Canon Emer. 1984–; Bampton Lecturer,

Oxford 1956, Columbia Univ. 1958; Gifford Lecturer, Edinburgh Univ. 1970–71; mem. Oratory of the Good Shepherd; Hon. D.D. (St. Andrews) 1967. *Publications:* He Who Is 1943, 1966, Corpus Christi 1953, 1965, Existence and Analogy 1949, Christ, the Christian and the Church 1946, Christian Theology and Natural Science 1956, The Recovery of Unity 1958, The Secularization of Christianity 1965, The Openness of Being 1971, Theology and the Gospel of Christ 1977, Whatever Happened to the Human Mind? 1980, Jesus, Who He is and How We Know Him 1985, Compliments of the Season 1985, The Triune God 1986. *Leisure interest:* reading. *Address:* Saint Mary's House, Kings Mead, East Blatchington, Seaford, East Sussex, BN25 2ET, England.

MASCHLER, Thomas Michael; British publisher; b. 16 Aug. 1933; s. of Kurt Leo Maschler and Rita Masseron; m. Fay Coventry 1970; one s. two d.; ed. Leighton Park School; Production Asst., André Deutsch 1955–56; Editor, MacGibbon and Kee 1956–58; Fiction Editor, Penguin Books 1958–60; Editorial Dir., Jonathan Cape 1960–70, Chair. 1970–; Dir. Random House 1987–; Assoc. Producer The French Lieutenant's Woman (film) 1981. *Publications:* Ed. Declarations 1957, New English Dramatists Series 1959–63. *Address:* 32 Bedford Square, London, WC1B 3SG, England. *Telephone:* 01-255 2393.

MASEFIELD, Sir Peter Gordon, Kt., M.A., C.ENG., F.R.AE.S., F.C.INST.T., F.B.I.M., C.I.MECH.E.; British engineer and administrator; b. 19 March 1914, Trentham, Staffordshire; s. of late Dr. W. Gordon Masefield, C.B.E., M.R.C.S., L.R.C.P. and Marian Ada Lloyd-Owen; m. Patricia Doreen Rooney 1936; three s. one d.; ed. Westminster School, Chillon Coll., Switzerland and Jesus Coll., Cambridge; on Design Staff, Fairey Aviation Co. Ltd. 1935–37; Asst. Tech. Ed. The Aeroplane 1937–39, Tech. Ed. 1939–43; war corresp. and air corresp. The Sunday Times 1940–43; Personal Adviser on Civil Air Transport to Lord Privy Seal and Sec. of Civil Aviation Cttee. of War Cabinet 1943–45; British Civil Air Attaché, British Embassy, Washington, D.C. 1945–46; Dir.-Gen. of Long-Term Planning and Projects, Ministry of Civil Aviation 1947–48; Chief Exec. and mem. of Bd. British European Airways 1949–56; Man. Dir. Bristol Aircraft Ltd. 1956–60, British Executive and General Aviation Ltd., Beagle Aircraft Ltd. 1960–67 (Chair. 1968–70); Chair. London Transport Exec. 1980–82; Dir. Pressed Steel Co. Ltd. 1960–67; Pres. Inst. of Transport 1955–56; mem. Aeronautical Research Council 1956–60, Pres. Royal Aeronautical Soc. 1959–60; Chair. Air Transport Section, London Chamber of Commerce 1962–65; Chair. British Airports Authority 1965–71; Chair. Royal Aero Club of the U.K. 1968–70; Vice-Chair. United Service and Royal Aero Club 1970–71; Chair. Imperial War Museum 1977–78; Chair. Project Man. Ltd. 1972–; Pres. Nigerian-British Chamber of Commerce 1977–81, London Transport Int. Services 1981–; Dir. Nationwide Building Soc. 1973–86, London Transport Exec. 1973–82, Worldwide Estates Ltd. 1972–, Worldwide Properties Ltd.; Deputy Chair. Caledonian Airways Ltd. 1978–; Chair. Royal Soc. of Arts 1977–79, Vice-Pres. 1980; Chair. Brooklands Trust Museum Feb. 1987–; mem. CAA Flight Time Limitations Bd., Bd. of London Transport Exec.; Hon. Fellow, Inst. Aeronautics and Astronautics (U.S.A.), Canadian Aeronautics and Space Inst.; Hon. D.Sc. (Cranfield), D.Tech. (Loughborough). *Publication:* To Ride the Storm 1982. *Leisure interests:* reading, writing, gardening, photography, flying. *Address:* Rosehill, Doods Way, Reigate, Surrey, RH2 0JT, England. *Telephone:* (07372) 42396.

MASEKELA, Hugh; South African trumpeter; b. near Johannesburg 1939; in voluntary exile since early 1960s, in U.K., U.S.A., Ghana, Nigeria, Guinea and Botswana. *Recordings include:* Home is Where the Music Is (with Dudu Pukwana, in London) 1972, I Am Not Afraid (with Hedzoleh Soundz) Technobush 1985. *Address:* Botswana.

MASERI, Attilio, M.D., F.R.C.P.; Italian physician; b. 12 Nov. 1935; s. of Adriano Maseri and Antonietta Albini; m. Countess Francesca Maseri Florio di Santo Stefano 1960; one s.; ed. Classical Lycee Cividale, Padua Univ. Medical School; Research Fellow Univ. of Pisa 1960–65, Colombia Univ., New York, U.S.A. 1965–66, Johns Hopkins Univ., Baltimore, U.S.A. 1966–67; Asst. Prof., Univ. of Pisa 1967–70, Prof. of Internal Medicine 1970, Prof. of Cardiovascular Pathophysiology, Prof. of Medicine (Locum) 1972–79, Sir John McMichael Prof. of Cardiovascular Medicine, Royal Postgraduate Medical School, Hammersmith Hosp., Univ. of London 1979–; Fellow American Coll. of Cardiology; Life mem. The Johns Hopkins Soc. of Scholars. *Publications:* Myocardial Flood Flow in Man 1972, Primary and Secondary Angina 1977, Perspectives on Coronary Care 1979; articles in major int. cardiological and medical journals. *Leisure interests:* skiing, tennis, sailing. *Address:* Flat 3, 51 Lennox Gardens, London, SW1X 0DF, England. *Telephone:* 01-584 9223

MASHEKE, Gen. Malimba; Zambian army officer and politician; fmr. Army Commdr.; Minister of Defence 1985–88, of Home Affairs 1988–89; Prime Minister of Zambia March 1989–. *Address:* Office of the Prime Minister, P.O. Box 30208, Lusaka, Zambia. *Telephone:* Lusaka 218282.

MASHHOUR, Mashhour Ahmad; Egyptian engineer and company executive; b. April 1918; m.; one s. two d.; ed. Faculty of Eng., Cairo Univ., Staff Officers' Coll.; Ministry of Transport 1941; Army Eng. 1942; eng. studies in Corps of Engs., British Army 1943–44; tech. studies in Corps of Engs., U.S. Army; lecturer, U.A.R. Acad. of War 1948–52; Officer, Corps of Engs., Egyptian Army; Dir. of Transit Dept., Suez Canal Authority

1956; Del. Chair. of Canaltex Co. and mem. Bd. of Dirs. of Timsah Ship Building Co., Ismailia; Chair. and Man. Dir. Suez Canal Authority 1965–; Sec.-Gen. of Arab Socialist Union, Governorate of Ismailia 1965–71; mem. People's Ass. 1976–; mem. Nat. Council of Production; Repub. Medal (1st Class), Mil. Service Medal (1st Class), Liberation Medal, Palestine Medal, Order of Merit (1st Class), Commdr. Légion d'honneur, Order of Polonia Restituta, Mono-Grand Officier (Togo); Gold Mercury Int. Award 1979. *Address:* Suez Canal Authority, Irshad Building, Ismailia, Egypt. *Telephone:* Ismailia 2201.

MASHOLOGU, Mothusi Thamsanga; Lesotho diplomatist; b. 7 March 1939, Morija; s. of Bennie and Sarah Mashologu; m. Debrah Mokhitli 1968; one s. two d.; ed. Univ. Coll. of Fort Hare, S.A., Univ. of Rhodesia and Nyasaland, Queens Univ., Belfast, and L.S.E.; Teacher at Basutoland Training Coll. and at Basutoland High School 1960–64; Asst. Sec., Ministry of External Affairs and Asst. Sec. in Cabinet Office 1965–66; Counsellor, Perm. Mission of Lesotho to UN 1966–68; Prin. Asst. Sec. and Acting Perm. Sec., Ministry of Foreign Affairs 1968–69; Amb. to U.S.A. 1969–73, also Perm. Rep. to UN 1969–71; Sec. to Cabinet 1974–75; Pro-Vice-Chancellor, Nat. Univ. of Lesotho Oct. 1975–76, Vice-Chancellor 1976–80; High Commr. to Canada 1980–85; Prin. Sec. for Foreign Affairs 1985–86; Govt. Sec. 1986–. *Leisure interests:* music, theatre, tennis. *Address:* c/o Ministry of Foreign Affairs, P.O.B. 527, Maseru 100, Lesotho.

MASINA, Giulietta; Italian actress; b. 22 Feb. 1921, Bologna; m. Federico Fellini (q.v.); ed. Univ. of Rome; began acting career in radio plays; in films since 1941. *Films:* Senza Pietà 1947, Luci del Varietà 1948, Persiane Chiuse, Cameriera Bella Presenza Offresi..., Europa 1951, Wanda la Peccatrice, Lo Sceicco Bianco 1952, Sette Ore di Guai, Il Romanzo della mia Vita, Ai Margini della Metropoli, Donne Proibite, Via Padova 1946, Cento Anni d'Amore, La Strada 1954, Il Bidone 1955, Buonanotte Avvocato!, Le Notte di Cabiria 1957, Fortunella 1958, Nella Città l'Inferno 1959, Giulietta degli spiriti 1965, The Madwoman of Chaillot 1969, Frau Holle 1985.

MASIRE, Dr. Quett Ketumile Joni, LL.D., J.P.; Botswana politician; b. 23 July 1925; m. Gladys Olebile 1957; three s. three d.; ed. Kanye and Tiger Kloof; founded Seepapitso Secondary School 1950; reporter, later dir., African Echo 1958; mem. Bangwaketse Tribal Council, Legis. Council; fmr. mem. Exec. Council; founder mem. Botswana Democratic Party (BDP); mem. Legis. (now Nat.) Ass. March 1965; Deputy Prime Minister 1965–66; attended Independence Conf., London Feb. 1966; Vice-Pres. and Minister of Finance 1966–80, and of Devt. Planning 1967–80, Pres. of Botswana July 1980–; Chair. SADCC; Hon. LL.D. (Sussex) 1986; Naledi Ya Botswana (Star of the Nation) 1986. *Address:* State House, Private Bag 001, Gaborone (Office); P.O. Box 70, Gaborone, Botswana (Home). *Telephone:* 355444 (Office); 353391 (Home).

MASLENNIKOV, Nikolay Ivanovich; Soviet politician; b. 1921; ed. Gorky Industrial Inst.; served in Soviet Army 1931–43; party work in Gorky Dist. 1944–45; mem. CPSU 1951–; Chief Mechanic, Dept. Head, Sec. of CPSU Cttee., Chief Engineer of Krasnaya Etna Works in Gorky 1948–61; Second Sec. Gorky City Cttee. of CPSU 1961–66, First Sec. 1966–68; First Sec. Gorky Dist. Cttee. of CPSU 1968–74; mem. U.S.S.R. Supreme Soviet 1970–; mem. Cen. Cttee. of CPSU 1971–; Deputy Chair. R.S.F.S.R. Council of Ministers 1974–; Chair. State Planning Cttee. for R.S.F.S.R. 1974–. Hero of Socialist Labour. *Address:* Council of Ministers of the R.S.F.S.R., Moscow, U.S.S.R.

MASLOV, Viktor Pavlovich, D.PHY.MATH.SC.; Soviet mathematician and academic; b. 1930, Moscow; m. Le Vu Ann 1977; one s. two d.; ed. Moscow Univ.; post-graduate 1953–56; asst. 1956–64, dean 1964–67, Sr. research asst. 1967–73 at Moscow Univ.; concurrently teacher at Moscow Inst. of Electronic Machine-Construction 1968–73, Head of Dept. 1973, mem. of U.S.S.R. Acad. of Sciences 1984–; specialized in theory of differential equation; U.S.S.R. State Prize 1978; Lenin Prize 1986; Lyapunov Gold Medal (U.S.S.R. Acad. of Sciences) 1983. *Address:* c/o U.S.S.R. Academy of Sciences, Moscow V-71, Leninsky Pr. 14, U.S.S.R.

MASLYUKOV, Yuriy Dmitrievich; Soviet politician; b. 30 Sept. 1937, Leninabad, Tadzhik S.S.R.; ed. Leningrad Inst. of Maths.; engineer, chief engineer at technological-scientific research inst. 1962–70; mem. CPSU 1966–; chief engineer, Izhevsk machine-bldg. plant 1970–74; Head of Admin., U.S.S.R. Ministry of Defence Industry 1974–82; First Deputy Chair. of U.S.S.R. Gosplan (with special responsibility for armaments) 1982–85; Deputy to Council of Nationalities, U.S.S.R. Supreme Soviet 1984–; Deputy Chair. of U.S.S.R. Council of Ministers, First Deputy Chair. Feb. 1988–; Chair. of Mil.-Industrial Comm. 1985–88; Head Econ. Planning Comm. 1988–; mem. Cen. Cttee. CPSU 1986–; Order of October Revolution, Order of the Red Banner Badge of Honour (for achievements in defence industry). *Address:* Central Committee of the Communist Party of the Soviet Union, Staraya pl. 4, Moscow, U.S.S.R.

MASOL, Vitaliy Andreyevich, CAND. TECH. SC.; Soviet politician; b. 1928; ed. Kiev Polytechnic; senior engineer 1951–63; mem. CPSU 1956–; Dir. of machine-construction plant 1963–71; General Dir. of production unit of heavy machine-construction factories in Kramatov (Ukraine) 1971–72; First Deputy Pres. of Gosplan for Ukrainian SSR 1972–79; Deputy Pres. of Council of Mins. for Ukraine 1979–87, Pres. 1987–; mem. of CPSU Cen.

Auditing Cttee. 1981-86; mem. Cen. Cttee. CPSU April 1989-; Deputy to U.S.S.R. Supreme Soviet. *Address:* Council of Ministers, Ukrainian CP, Kiev, Ukrainian SSR, U.S.S.R.

MASON, The Hon. Sir Anthony Frank, A.C., K.B.E., B.A., LL.B.; Australian justice; b. 21 April 1925; s. of F. M. Mason; m. Patricia Mary McQueen 1950; two s.; ed. Sydney Grammar School, Univ. of Sydney; Flying Officer, R.A.A.F. 1944-45; admitted to the Bar, N.S.W. 1951-; Q.C. 1964; Commonwealth Solicitor-Gen. 1964-69, Judge, Court of Appeal of the Supreme Court, N.S.W. 1969-72, Justice of the High Court 1972-87, Chief Justice 1987-; Vice-Chair. UN Comm. of Int. Trade Law 1968; Pro-Chancellor, A.N.U. 1972-75; Hon. LL.D. (A.N.U.), (Univ. of Sydney). *Leisure interests:* gardening, tennis. *Address:* Chief Justice's Chambers, High Court of Australia, P.O. Box E435, Queen Victoria Terrace, A.C.T., Australia. *Telephone:* (062) 706 955.

MASON, Sir (Basil) John, Kt., C.B., D.SC., F.R.S.; British meteorologist; b. 18 Aug. 1923, Docking, Norfolk; s. of late John Robert and Olive Mason; m. Doreen Sheila Jones 1948; two s.; ed. Fakenham Grammar School and Univ. Coll., Nottingham; Commissioned, Radar Branch, R.A.F. 1944-46; Shirley Research Fellow, Univ. of Nottingham 1947; Asst. lecturer in Meteorology, Imperial Coll., London 1948-49, lecturer 1949; Warren Research Fellow, Royal Soc. 1957; Visiting Prof. of Meteorology, Univ. of Calif. 1959-60; Prof. of Cloud Physics, Imperial Coll. of Science and Tech., Univ. of London 1961-65; Dir.-Gen. Meteorological Office 1965-83, Pres. Royal Meteorological Soc. 1968-70; mem. Exec. Cttee. World Meteorological Org. 1965-75, 1977-83; Chair. Council, Univ. of Surrey 1971-75; Pro-Chancellor Univ. of Surrey Sept. 1979-85; Pres. Inst. of Physics 1976-78; Treas. and Sr. Vice-Pres. Royal Soc. 1976-86; Dir. Fulmer Research Inst. 1976-78; Pres. B.A.A.S. 1982-83; Dir. Royal Soc. Project on Acidification of Surface Waters 1983-; mem. Advisory Bd. Research Councils 1983-86; Pres. UMIST 1986-; Chair. ICSU/WMO Scientific Cttee. for World Climate Research Prog., Co-ordinating Cttee. for Marine Science and Tech. 1987-; Hon. Fellow Imperial Coll. of Science and Tech. 1974, UMIST 1979; Hon. D.Sc. (Nottingham) 1966, (Durham) 1970, (Strathclyde) 1975, (City Univ.) 1980, (Sussex) 1983, (E. Anglia) 1988; Hugh Robert Mill Medal, Royal Meteorological Soc. 1959; Charles Chree Medal and Prize, Physical Soc. 1965; Bakerian Lecture, Royal Soc. 1971; Halley Lecture, Oxford Univ. 1977; Rumford Medal, Royal Soc. 1972; Glazebrook Medal and Prize, Inst. of Physics 1974; Symons Memorial Gold Medal, Royal Meteorological Soc. 1975; Naylor Prize and Lectureship 1979. *Publications:* The Physics of Clouds 1957, Clouds, Rain and Rain-making 1962. *Leisure interests:* music, foreign travel. *Address:* Centre for Environmental Technology, Imperial College, London, S.W.7; 64 Christchurch Road, East Sheen, London, S.W.14, England (Home). *Telephone:* 01-589 5111; 01-876 2557 (Home).

MASON, Sir Frederick Cecil, K.C.V.O. C.M.G.; British diplomatist (retd.); b. 15 May 1913, London; s. of late Ernest Mason and late Sophia Charlotte Dodson; m. Karen Rørholm 1941; two s. one d.; ed. City of London School and St. Catharine's Coll., Cambridge; Vice-Consul, Antwerp 1935-36, Paris 1936-37, Léopoldville 1937-39; Consul Faeroe Islands 1940-42, Colón, Panama 1942-45; First Sec., British Embassy, Santiago, Chile 1946-48; Press Attaché, Oslo 1948-50; Asst. Labour Adviser, Foreign Office 1950-53; First Sec., U.K. Control Comm., Bonn 1953-55; Commercial Counsellor, Athens 1955-57; Econ. Counsellor, Teheran 1957-60; Head, Econ. Relations Dept., Foreign Office 1960-64; Under-Sec. Ministry of Overseas Devt. 1964-65, Commonwealth Office 1966; Amb. to Chile 1966-70; Under-Sec. FCO 1970-71; Amb. and Perm. Rep. UN, Geneva 1971-73; U.K. mem. Int. Narcotics Control Bd., Geneva 1974-77; Dir. New Court Natural Resources Ltd. 1973-83; Chair. Anglo-Chilean Soc. 1976-81; Grand Cross, Chilean Order of Merit "Bernardo O'Higgins". *Leisure interests:* walking, ball games, painting. *Address:* The Forge, Ropley, Hampshire, England.

MASON, Sir John (see Mason, Sir Basil John).

MASON, Sir John (Charles Moir), K.C.M.G.; British business executive and fmr. diplomatist; b. 13 May 1927, Manchester; s. of late Charles M. Mason and Madeline Mason; m. Margaret Newton 1954; one s. one d.; ed. Manchester Grammar School and Peterhouse, Cambridge; army service 1944-48, Korea 1950-51; joined diplomatic service 1952; Second Sec., Rome 1954-56, Warsaw 1956-59; Foreign Office 1959-61; First Sec. (Commercial), Damascus 1961-65; Foreign Office 1965-68; Dir. of Trade Devt. and Deputy Consul-Gen., New York 1968-71; Head, European Integration Dept., FCO 1971-72; seconded as Under-Sec. Export Credits Guarantee Dept. 1972-75; Asst. Under-Sec. of State, FCO 1975-76; Amb. to Israel 1976-80; High Commr. in Australia 1980-84; Chair. Lloyds Bank NZA Ltd., Sydney 1985-, Lloyds Int. Ltd. 1987-, Thorn-EMI (Australia) Ltd. 1985-, Vickers Shipbuilders (Australia) Ltd. 1985-, Multicon Ltd. 1987, Prudential (Australia) Ltd. 1987-, Prudential Finance Ltd. 1987-, Prudential Funds Man. Ltd. 1987-; Bd. of Advisers Spencer Stuart and Assocs., Sydney 1985-; Pres. Heart Foundation N. Shore Hosp., Sydney 1985-; Dir. Wellcome (Australia) Ltd. 1985-, Nat. Bank of New Zealand 1985-, Churchill Memorial Trust 1985-, Fluor (Australia) Ltd., Melbourne 1985-, Pirelli (Australia) Ltd. 1986-. *Address:* 147 Dover Road, Dover Heights, Sydney, N.S.W. 2030, Australia; c/o Lloyds Bank PLC, 6 Pall Mall, London, S.W.1, England. *Telephone:* 371-7863 (Sydney).

MASON, Philip, C.I.E., O.B.E.; British writer and administrator; b. 19 March 1906, London; s. of Dr. H. A. Mason; m. Eileen Mary Hayes 1935; two s.

two d.; ed. Sedbergh, Oxford Univ.; Mem. Indian Civil Service 1928-47; Under-Sec., War Dept. 1933-36; Deputy Commr., Garhwal 1936-39; Deputy Sec., Defence Co-ordination and War Depts. 1939-42; Sec., Chiefs of Staff Cttee., India, and Head of Conf. Secr., S.E. Asia Command 1942-44; represented War Dept., Cen. Ass. 1946; Joint Sec., War Dept. 1944-47; Dir. of Studies in Race Relations, Chatham House, London 1952-58, Dir. Inst. of Race Relations, London 1958-69; Chair. Nat. Cttee. for Commonwealth Immigrants 1964-65, BBC Advisory Council for Immigrants 1965-74; Exec. U.K. Council for Overseas Student Affairs 1969-75; Hon. Fellow, School of Oriental and African Studies, Univ. of London 1970; Hon. D.Sc. (Soc.) (Bristol) 1971, D.Litt. (Oxon.) 1972. *Publications* (as Philip Woodruff): Call the Next Witness 1945, The Wild Sweet Witch 1947, Whatever Dies 1948, The Sword of Northumbria 1948, The Island of Chamba 1950, Hernshaw Castle 1950, Colonel of Dragoons 1951, The Men Who Ruled India: Vol. I The Founders 1953, Vol. II The Guardians 1954; (as Philip Mason): An Essay on Racial Tension 1954, Christianity and Race 1956, The Birth of a Dilemma 1958, Year of Decision 1960, Common Sense about Race 1961, Prospero's Magic 1963, Patterns of Dominance 1970, Race Relations 1970, How People Differ 1971, A Matter of Honour 1974, Kipling—The Glass, The Shadow and The Fire 1975, The Dove in Harness 1976, A Shaft of Sunlight 1978, Skinner of Skinner's Horse 1979, The English Gentleman 1982, A Thread of Silk 1984, The Men Who Ruled India 1985. *Leisure interest:* reading. *Address:* 4 Mulberry House, Church Street, Fordingbridge, Hants, England. *Telephone:* 0425-54495.

MASON, Sir Ronald, K.C.B., F.R.S., PH.D.; British professor of chemical physics and industrialist; b. 22 July 1930, Wales; s. of David John and Olwen Mason (née James); m. 1st E. Pauline Pattinson 1953; m. 2nd E. Rosemary Grey-Edwards 1979; three d.; ed. Quaker's Yard Grammar School and Univs. of Wales and London; Research Assoc., Univ. Coll. London 1953-60; Lecturer, Imperial Coll. London 1960-63; Prof., Univ. of Sheffield 1963-70; Prof., Univ. of Sussex 1970-; Chief Scientific Adviser, Ministry of Defence 1977-83; Pro-Vice-Chancellor, Univ. of Sussex 1977-78; many visiting professorships in Australia, Canada, France, Israel, New Zealand and U.S.A. 1965-83, Int. Relations, Univ. Coll. of Wales; Defence Consultant and Lecturer 1983-; Chair. Hunting Ltd. 1986-87, Systems Integration Tech. Ltd. 1987-; Dir. Thomson (UK) Holdings Ltd.; Pres. British Hydromechanics Research Asscn. 1986-; Chair. Council for Arms Control, London; mem. UN Disarmament Studies Comm. 1983-86; Hon. D.Sc. (Wales) 1986; medals of various learned societies. *Publications:* many scientific research publs. on structural chem. and chemical physics of surfaces, author/ed. of 10 monographs, papers on defence policies and technology. *Leisure interest:* gardening. *Address:* 905 Nelson House, Dolphin Square, London, S.W.1; Chestnuts Farm, Weedon, Bucks, HR22 4NH, England. *Telephone:* 01-834 7343.

MASON, Stephen Finney, F.R.S., D.PHIL., D.SC.; British professor of chemistry; b. 6 July 1923, Leicester; s. of Leonard Stephen and Christine Harriet Mason (née Finney); m. Joan Banus 1955; three s.; ed. Wyggeston School, Leicester and Wadham Coll., Oxford; Demonstrator, Museum of History of Science, Oxford 1947-53; Research Fellow in Medical Chem. Australian Nat. Univ. 1953-56; Reader in Chemical Spectroscopy Exeter Univ. 1956-64; Prof. of Chem. Univ. of East Anglia 1964-70; Prof. of Chem. King's Coll., Univ. of London 1970-87, Prof. Emer. 1987-. *Publications:* A History of the Sciences: main currents of scientific thought 1953, Molecular Optical Activity and the Chiral Discriminations 1982. *Leisure interest:* history and philosophy of science. *Address:* Chemistry Department, University of London, King's College, Strand, London, WC2R 2LS, England. *Telephone:* 01-836 5454.

MASON, Sydney, F.S.V.A.; British business executive; b. 30 Sept. 1920; s. of Jacob Mason and Annie Foreman; m. Rosalind Victor 1945; Man. Land Securities PLC 1943-49, Dir. 1949-, Chair. and Jt. Man. Dir. Hammerson Property Investment and Devt. Corpn. PLC 1958-; mem. Gen. Council British Property Fed. 1974-; Exec. Chair. Lewis W. Hammerson Memorial Home for the Elderly 1959-80; Exec. mem. Norwood Orphanage 1958-76 (Chair. 1968-76); Liveryman Worshipful Co. of Masons 1971. *Leisure interest:* painting. *Address:* Bolney Court, Lower Shiplake, Henley-on-Thames, Oxon. RG9 3NR, England. *Telephone:* (073 522) 2095.

MASON OF BARNSLEY, Baron (Life Peer), cr. 1987, of Barnsley in South Yorkshire; **Roy Mason,** P.C.; British politician; b. 18 April 1924, Barnsley, Yorks; s. of Joseph and Mary Mason; m. Marjorie Sowden 1945; two d.; ed. Carlton Junior School, Royston Sr. School, and London School of Econs. (T.U.C. Course); branch official, Nat. Union of Mineworkers 1947-53; mem. Yorkshire Miners' Council 1949-53; M.P. for Barnsley (now Barnsley Cen.) 1953-87; Minister of State (Shipping), Bd. of Trade 1964-67; Minister of Defence (Equipment) 1967-68; Postmaster-Gen. April-June 1968; Minister of Power 1968-69; Pres. Bd. of Trade 1969-70; Sec. of State for Defence 1974-76, for Northern Ireland 1976-79; Opposition Spokesman for Agric., Fisheries and Food 1979-81; Labour. *Address:* House of Lords, Westminster, London, S.W.1; 12 Victoria Avenue, Barnsley, S. Yorks., England (Home).

MASRI, Ahmad Fathi, Al-; Syrian diplomatist; b. 1932, Damascus; m.; two c.; ed. Damascus Univ.; Attorney 1954-57; Auditor Ministry of Finance 1957; joined diplomatic service, U.A.R. Ministry of Foreign Affairs, Cairo 1958; Consul, Baghdad 1960; Deputy Dir. Cultural Dept., Ministry of

Foreign Affairs, Damascus 1962-65; Chargé d'affaires Cyprus 1965-67; served in Western European Dept., Ministry of Foreign Affairs, Damascus 1967-69; Counsellor to the UN 1969-72, Deputy Perm. Rep. 1972-75; Dir. Dept. of Int. Org. 1975-78, 1983-88; Dept. of Cultural Affairs, Foreign Ministry 1975-78; Chargé d'affaires, Santiago 1978-83; Deputy Perm. Rep. to the UN 1982-83, Perm. Rep. Feb. 1988-. *Address:* Permanent Mission of Syria to the United Nations, 820 Second Ave, 10th Floor, New York, N.Y. 10017, U.S.A. *Telephone:* (212) 661-1313.

MASRI, Taher Nashat, B.B.A.; Jordanian diplomatist; b. 5 March 1942, Nablus; s. of Mashat Masri and Hadiyah Solh; m. Samar Bitar 1968; one s. one d.; ed. North Texas State Univ., with Cen. Bank of Jordan 1965-73; M.P., Nablus Dist. 1973-75; Minister of State for Occupied Territories Affairs 1973-74; Amb. to Spain 1975-78, also accred. to Belgium 1978-80, to France 1978-83, to U.K. 1983-84; Perm. Del. to UNESCO 1978-83; Minister of Foreign Affairs 1985-88; Minister of State for Econ. Affairs April 1989-; Order of Al-Kawkab (Jordan) 1974, Gran Cruz de Mérito (Spain) 1977, Order of Isabela la Católica (Spain) 1978, Commdr., Légion d'honneur 1981. *Address:* c/o Ministry of Foreign Affairs, P.O. Box 35217, Amman, Jordan.

MASSAUX, Mgr. Edouard, D.THEOL.; Belgian university rector; b. 27 Sept. 1920, Neufchâteau; ed. Univ. Gregorienne pontificale, Rome, Univ. Catholique de Louvain and Fonds Nat. de la Recherche Scientifique (FNRS); ordained priest 1944; Prof., Faculty of Theology, Univ. Catholique de Louvain 1953, Asst. Librarian 1960, Librarian 1961, Pro-Rector 1965, Rector 1969-86; mem. Exec. and Bd. of Dirs., FNRS, Pres. 1975-76, 1981-82; mem. Admin. Council, Inst. Interuniversitaire des Sciences Nucléaires; mem. exec. cttee., or council, Fonds de la Recherche Scientifique Medicale, Fonds de la Recherche Fondamentale Collective, Conseil Nat. de la Politique Scientifique and numerous other inter-univ. orgs., etc.; Pres. Belgian Univs. Rectors' Conf. 1973-74; mem. Societas Novi Testamenti, Acad. Luxembourgeoise, Soc. Scientifique de Bruxelles; Commdr., Ordre de Léopold; Officier, Légion d'honneur; Médaille civique and decorations from Luxembourg and Burundi. *Address:* place de l'Université 1, B 1348 Louvain-la-Neuve, Belgium.

MASSÉ, Marcel, B.A., B.PHIL.ECON.; Canadian civil servant; b. 23 June 1940, Montreal; m. Josée M'Baye 1965; three s. one d.; ed. Univ. of Montreal, McGill Univ., Montreal, Univ. of Warsaw, Poland, Oxford Univ., England; called to Bar, Quebec 1963; Admin. and Econs Div., World Bank, Washington, D.C. 1967-71; Econ. Adviser, Privy Council Office, Ottawa 1971-73; Deputy Minister of Finance, Prov. of N.B. 1973-74, Chair. Cabinet Secr. 1974-77; Deputy Sec. Cabinet for Fed. Prov. Relations, Ottawa 1977-79, Deputy Sec. Cabinet (Operations), Privy Council Office 1979, Sec. to the Cabinet and Clerk of the Privy Council Office 1979-80; Pres. Canadian Int. Devt. Agency, Ottawa 1980-82; Under-Sec. of State for External Affairs, Ottawa 1982-85; Exec. Dir. IMF, Washington 1985-; Hon. D.C.L. (Acadia Univ.) 1983; Hon. LL.D. (New Brunswick) 1984. *Publication:* An Evaluation of Investment Appraisal Methods. *Leisure interest:* reading. *Address:* 700 19th Street, N.W., Washington, D.C. 20431, U.S.A.

MASSE, Marcel; Canadian politician; b. 23 May 1936, Saint-Jean-De-Matha, Quebec; s. of Rosaire Masse and Angeline Clermont; m. Cecile Martin 1960; one s. one d.; ed. Ecole normale Jacques-Cartier, Univ. of Montreal, Sorbonne, City of London Coll., European Inst. of Business Admin.; fmr. teacher of Ancient History, Lanaudière Regional School Bd.; Dir. Lavalin (Eng. Co.) 1974-84 (also Project Dir. for UNDP, Vice-Pres., Vice-Pres. of Marketing and Commercial Devt.); mem. Quebec Nat. Ass. 1966-73 (held portfolios of Minister of State for Educ., Minister Responsible for Public Service, for Inter-Governmental Affairs, Minister of Planning and Devt.); Minister of Communications 1984-85, 1985-86, of Energy, Mines and Resources 1986-89, of Communications Jan. 1989-; fmr. Pres. Wilfrid Pelletier Foundation; Dir. numerous orgs. including Montreal Symphony Orchestra, Canadian Writers' Foundation, Canadian Refugee Foundation, Lanaudière Summer Festival, Club de Dakar, Jeunesses Musicales du Canada; Progressive Conservative. *Leisure interests:* reading, music, fishing, skiing. *Address:* House of Commons, Ottawa, Ont., K1A 0AZ (Office); 300 Slater Street, Ottawa, Ont., K1A 0C8, Canada (Home).

MASSEVITCH, Alla Genrikhovna, D.SC.; Soviet astronomer; b. 9 Oct. 1918, Tbilisi; d. of Henrik Massevitch and Natalie Zhgenti; m. Joseph Friedlander 1942, one d.; ed. Moscow Industrial Pedagogical Inst., Moscow Univ.; Assistant Prof. of Astrophysics Moscow Univ. 1946-48, Prof. 1948-; Vice-Pres. Astronomical Council, Soviet Acad. of Sciences 1952-88, Chief Scientific Researcher 1988-; in charge of optical (visual, photographic and laser ranging) tracking of Soviet space vehicles; Chair. Working Group I, Cttee. for Space Research (COSPAR) 1961-66; Vice-Pres. Comm. 44 JAU (Extraterrestrial Astronomy) 1961-67; Pres. Comm. 35 JAU (Internal Structure of Stars) 1967-70; Deputy Sec.-Gen. UNISPACE -1982, Pres. of Section Satellite Tracking for Geodesy, Inter-Cosmos Co-operation 1968-; Vice-Pres. Inst. for Soviet-American Relations 1967; Vice-Pres. Bd. Soviet Peace Cttee. 1967; Foreign mem. Royal Astronomical Soc. 1963, Indian Nat. Acad. of Sciences 1980, Austrian Acad. of Sciences 1985; mem. Int. Acad. of Astronautics 1964; U.S.S.R. State Prize 1975. *Publications:* 123 papers on internal structure of stars, stellar evolution and optical tracking of satellites, mainly in Astronomical Journal of the U.S.S.R., Publications of the Sternberg Astronomical Inst. and Scientific Information

of the Astronomical Council 1945-. *Leisure interests:* collecting coffee machines and cookery books. *Address:* Astronomical Council of the U.S.S.R. Acad. of Sciences, 48 Pjatnitskaja Street, Moscow 109017; 1 Vosstania Square 403, Moscow 123242, U.S.S.R. *Telephone:* 231-3980, 255-4962.

MASSEY, Vincent, PH.D., F.R.S.; Australian professor of biochemistry; b. 28 Nov. 1926, Berkeley; s. of Walter and Mary A. Massey; m. Margot E. Grünewald 1950; one s. two d.; ed. Univs. of Sydney and Cambridge; Research Officer, McMaster Animal Health Lab., CSIRO, Sydney 1946-50; Ian McMaster Fellow, Univ. of Cambridge 1950-53, ICI Fellow 1953-55; Research Officer, Henry Ford Hosp., Detroit 1955-57; Lecturer, then Sr. Lecturer, Univ. of Sheffield 1957-63; Prof. of Biological Chem. Univ. of Michigan, Ann Arbor 1963-; Visiting Prof. Univ. of Ill. 1960, Univ. of Konstanz 1973-74, Guest Prof. 1975-; Guest Prof. Inst. of Applied Biochem., Mitake 1985, Yokohama City Univ. 1988. *Publications:* over 300 research papers and reviews in scientific journals and books. *Leisure interests:* walking, sailing, gardening. *Address:* Department of Biological Chemistry, University of Michigan, Ann Arbor, Mich. 48109, U.S.A. *Telephone:* (313) 764-7196.

MASSIP, Roger; French journalist; b. 6 Nov. 1904, Montauban; s. of Jean Massip; m. Renée Castaings-Lahaille 1930; ed. Univ. of Paris; Corresp. Agence Havas Bucharest 1931-34, Le Petit Parisien Warsaw 1934-37, Asst. Foreign Ed. of latter 1937-40; Ed. underground newspaper Libération 1942-44, Asst. Ed. Libération 1944-47; Foreign Ed. Le Figaro 1947-75, leader writer 1975-; Sec.-Gen. Assen. for Study of Problems of Europe 1976-; Officier, Légion d'honneur, Officier de la Résistance, Officier, Orders of Vasa and Dannebrog, Hon. C.B.E. *Publications:* Que sera la nouvelle société des nations? 1945, Voici l'Europe 1958, De Gaulle et l'Europe 1963, La Chine est un miracle 1973, Il y a quarante ans 1978, Caramanlis, un Grec hors du commun 1982. *Address:* Le Figaro, 37 rue du Louvre, 75002 Paris, France.

MASSON, Jacques, L. EN D.; French banker; b. 17 April 1924, Paris; s. of Georges Masson and Yvonne née Poutot; m. Annie Bedhet 1946; one s. two d.; ed. Faculté de Droit, Paris, Ecole Nat. d'Organisation Economique et Sociale and Centre de Perfectionnement dans l'Administration des Affaires; joined Banque Nat. de Paris (BNP) 1950, Asst. Dir. 1963, Dir. in charge of Paris branches 1964, Dir. 1972, Asst. Dir.-Gen. 1978, Dir.-Gen. 1982; Pres. Natio Equipment; mem. Bd. (representing BNP), Locindus, Codetel, Banexi; Dir. U.F.B., Printemps S.A., Silec, Nouvelles Galeries, UFCA, Devanlay; mem. supervisory bd., SOVAC; Chevalier, Légion d'honneur. *Address:* 19 avenue Léopold II, 75016 Paris, France (Home). *Telephone:* 42 44 23 52.

MASSON, Paul Jean-Marie, L. EN D.; French civil servant and diplomatist; b. 21 July 1920, Ussel (Corrèze); s. of Jean and Marie (née Vidal) Masson; m. Simone Ageron 1943; one s. one d.; ed. Ecole Nat. de la France d'Outre-mer.; career in W. Africa 1945-60; fmr. Sec.-Gen. Guinea; High Commr. to Upper Volta 1958-60; Dir.-Gen. Bureau pour le développement de la production agricole 1961-67; mem. French dels. to FAO Confs. 1961, 1963, 1965; Préfet du Lot 1967-71; Dir. du Cabinet, Minister of Defence 1971-73; Préfet de la Région Centre, Préfet du Loiret 1973-76, Préfet de la Région Aquitaine, Préfet de la Gironde 1976-78; Dir. du Cabinet Civil et Mil., Minister of Defence 1978-79; Dir. Pechiney Ugine Kuhlman 1979-83; Vice-Pres. Soc. Aluminium de Grèce (A.D.G.) 1979-83; Senator from the Loiret (R.P.R.) 1983-; Commdr. Légion d'honneur; Commdr. du Mérite agricole, Commdr. Ordre nat. du Mérite, Officier Palmes académiques. *Publications:* Bilateral Assistance—Help, Trade or Strategy. *Address:* Sénat, Palais du Luxembourg, 75291 Paris, France. *Telephone:* (1) 42 34-26-96.

MASSOUD, Ahmed Shah; Afghan guerrilla commander; b. 1953; ed. Engineering Dept., Kabul Polytechnic; became a guerrilla 1975; guerrilla commdr. in Panjsher Valley 1979-; fmr. mem. Muslim Youth League; mem. Jamiat-i-Islami.

MASSU, Gen. Jacques; French retired army officer; b. 5 May 1908, Châlons/Marne; s. of Charles and Marie (née Lefèvre) Massu; m. 1st Suzanne Rosambert 1948 (died 1977); one s. two d.; 2nd Catherine Drouin 1978; ed. Ecole Spéciale Mil. de St. Cyr; joined Free French Forces Aug. 1940; took part in all the campaigns of Gen. Leclerc's 2nd Armoured Div.; Commdr., Hanoi, Indochina 1945-47, 1st Demibrigade, Colonial Parachute Commandos, 4th A.O.F. Brigade 1951-54; Gen. of Brigade 1955; as Commdr. 10th Parachute Div., directed airborne operation and landing at Port Said, Nov. 1956; Mil. Commdr. Dept. of Algiers Jan. 1957-60; headed the first Cttee. of Public Safety set up in Algiers and called upon Gen. de Gaulle to assume power May 1958; Commdr. Algiers Army Corps 1958-60; retd. 1960; Mil. Gov. of Metz 1961-66; C.-in-C. French Troops in Germany 1966-69; Grand-Croix, Légion d'honneur, Compagnon de la Libération, Croix de guerre, D.S.O., etc. *Publications:* memoirs: La vraie bataille d'Alger (Vol. 1) 1971, Le torrent et la digue (Vol. 11) 1973, Sept ans avec Leclerc (Vol. III) 1974, Verité sur Suez 1956 (Vol. IV) 1978, L'aventure Viet Minh (Vol. V) 1980, Baden 68 1983. *Leisure interests:* riding, hunting, shooting. *Address:* Le Prieuré, Conflans sur Loing, 45700 Villemandeur, France. *Telephone:* (38) 94-71-46.

MASSY-GREENE, Sir (John) Brian, Kt., M.A., F.A.I.M.; Australian business executive; b. 20 April 1916, Tenterfield, N.S.W.; s. of late Sir Walter

Massy-Greene, K.C.M.G., and Lula May Lomax; m. Margaret E. R. Sharp 1942; two s. two d.; ed. Sydney C. of E. Grammar School, Geelong Grammar School and Clare Coll., Cambridge; joined Metal Mfrs. Ltd. 1939; Lieut., AIF, New Guinea 1942-45; transferred to Austral Bronze Co. Pty. Ltd. (subsidiary of Metal Mfrs.) Gen. Man. 1953-62; Gen. Man. Dir. Consolidated Gold Fields Australia Ltd. 1962-66, Chair. and Man. Dir. 1966-76, Dir. Consolidated Gold Fields Ltd., London 1963-76; Chair. The Bellambi Coal Co. Ltd. 1964-72, Goldsworthy Mining Ltd. 1965-76, The Mount Lyell Mining & Railway Co. Ltd. 1969-76, Lawrenson Alumsac Holdings Ltd. 1964-73; Dir. Assoc. Minerals Consolidated Ltd. 1962-76, Commonwealth Mining Investments (Australia) Ltd. 1962-72, 1978-, Dalgety Australia Ltd. 1968-78, Zip Holdings Ltd. 1964-73, Nat. Mutual Life Asscn. Ltd. 1977-85, Hazelton Air Services Holdings Ltd. (Group) 1984-, Santos Ltd. 1984-; Chair. Pacific Dunlop Ltd. 1979-86, Dir. 1968-86; Chair. Commonwealth Banking Corpn. 1985-88, Dir. 1968-88; mem. Exec. Cttee. Australian Mining Industry Council 1967-76 (Pres. 1971), Mfg. Industries Advisory Council 1968-75, N.S.W. Advisory Cttee., C.S.I.R.O. 1968-75; Fellow Inst. of Engineers of Australia, Australian Inst. of Mining and Metallurgy. *Leisure interests:* farming, fishing, flying. *Address:* 1/7 Quambi Place, Edgecliff, N.S.W. 2027, Australia.

MASTER, Simon Harcourt; British publisher; b. 10 April 1944, Caterham; s. of Humphrey R. Master and Rachel B. Plumbly; m. Georgina M. C. Batsford 1969; two s.; ed. Ardingly Coll. Sussex; Publishing Dir. Pan Books Ltd. 1973-80, Man. Dir. 1980-87; Chief Exec. Random House U.K. and Exec. Vice-Pres. Random House Int. Group 1987-. *Leisure interests:* gardening, golf, classic cars, scuba diving. *Address:* 32 Bedford Square, London, WC1B 3JN; 13 Patten Road, London, SW18 3RH; Pendower, Polzeath, Cornwall, England. *Telephone:* 01-874 2204; (020 886) 3462.

MASTERSON, Valerie, C.B.E.; British opera and concert singer; b. Birkenhead; d. of Edward Masterson and Rita McGrath; m. Andrew March; one s. one d.; has sung with D'Oyly Carte Opera, Glyndebourne, Royal Opera House, Covent Garden and English Nat. Opera, and on TV and radio; also in major opera houses abroad including Paris, Aix-en-Provence, Toulouse, Munich, Geneva, San Francisco and Chicago; title roles include La Traviata, Manon, Semele, Merry Widow, Louise, Lucia di Lammermoor, Mireille; other leading roles in Faust, Alcina, Die Entführung aus dem Serail, Nozze di Figaro, Così fan Tutte, La Bohème, Magic Flute, Julius Caesar, Rigoletto, Orlando, Der Rosenkavalier, Xerxes, Pearl Fishers, Die Fledermaus etc.; recordings include Julius Caesar, La Traviata, Elisabetta d'Inghilterra, Bitter Sweet, Ring Cycle and various Gilbert and Sullivan discs. *Leisure interests:* tennis, swimming, ice-skating. *Address:* c/o Music International, 13 Ardilaun Road, London, N5 2QR, England.

MASTROIANNI, Marcello; Italian film actor; b. 28 Sept. 1924; ed. Univ. of Rome; films include Una Domenica d'Agosto 1949, Le Notti Bianche 1957, I Soliti Ignoti 1958, Bell' Antonio 1960, La Dolce Vita 1960, La Notte 1961, A Very Private Affair 1961, Divorce—Italian Style 1961, 8½ 1963, Family Diary 1963, Yesterday, Today and Tomorrow 1964, Fantasmi a Roma 1964, Casanova 70 1965, Marriage—Italian Style 1965, The Organizer 1965, The 10th Victim 1965, Ciao Rudy 1966, Lo Straniero 1967, Viaggio di G. Mastorna 1967, Shout Louder, I don't Understand, L'Etranger 1967, The Man with the Balloons 1968, Diamonds for Breakfast 1968, Leo the Last 1970, The Priest's Wife 1970, Drama of Jealousy 1970 (Prize for Best Actor, Cannes 1970), Sunflower 1970, The Pizza Triangle 1970 What? 1972, La Grande Bouffe 1973, Salut L'Artiste 1973, Massacre in Rome 1973, Touche Pas la Femme Blanche 1974, Allonsanfan 1975, Gangster Doll (Per le Antiche Scale) 1975, Bye-Bye Monkey 1978, La Cité des Femmes 1979, Blood Feud 1981, The New World 1981, Storia di Piera, Macaroni 1986, Oci Ciornie 1987, Dark Eyes (Best Actor Cannes Film Festival) 1987, Intervista 1987, The Beekeeper 1988; European Film Award 1988. *Address:* c/o Avv. Cav. Via Maria Adelaide 8, Rome, Italy.

MASUOKA, Hiroyuki; Japanese politician; b. 3 Feb. 1923; ed. Waseda Univ.; with Masuoka-gumi Steel Bldg. Co., Pres. 1952-; mem. House of Reps. 1967-; Parl. Vice-Minister for Health and Welfare 1972-73, for Transport 1973-74; Chair. of House of Reps. Transport Cttee. 1978-, of Finance Cttee. 1979-80; Minister of Health and Welfare 1984-85; Liberal Democratic Party. *Leisure interests:* golf, painting. *Address:* c/o Ministry of Health and Welfare, 1-2, Kasumigaseki, Chiyoda-ku, Tokyo 100, Japan.

MASUR, Kurt; German conductor; b. 18 July 1927, Silesia, Poland; ed. Hochschule für Musik, Leipzig; theatre conductor in Erfurt and Leipzig 1948-55, conductor, Dresden Philharmonic 1955-58, Chief Conductor 1967-72; Gen. Musical Dir., Mecklenburg State Theatre 1958-60; Prin. Musical Dir., Komische Oper in East Berlin 1960-64; Conductor, Leipzig Gewandhaus Orchestra 1970; has toured extensively in Europe and the U.S.A.; début in U.S.A. with Cleveland Orchestra 1974.

MASUREL, Jean-Louis Antoine Nicolas, M.B.A.; French industrialist; b. 18 Sept. 1940, Cannes; s. of Antoine and Anne-Marie (née Gallant) Masurel; m. 1st 1964, two d.; m. 2nd 1987; ed. Hautes Etudes Commerciales, Graduate School of Business Admin., Harvard Univ.; with Morgan Guaranty Trust Co., New York, last position Sr. Vice-Pres. New York 1964-80; Sr. Exec. Vice-Pres. Banque de Paris & des Pays Bas 1980-82; Deputy Pres. Banque Paribas Aug. 1982-83; Man. Dir. Moët-Hennessy 1983-, Vice-Chair. 1987-; Man. Dir. LVMH Moët-Hennessy Louis Vuitton 1987-; Dir.

Peugeot S.A., Cogedim, BGP-SIB, Tuffier & Assocs.; Gov. American Hosp. in Paris. *Leisure interests:* windsurfing, skiing. *Address:* LVMH Moët-Hennessy Louis Vuitton, 5 boulevard de Latour-Maubourg, 75007 Paris; 31 rue Raynouard, 75016 Paris, France.

MASUROK, Yuri; Soviet opera singer; b. Ukraine; ed. Lvov Inst. and Moscow Conservatoire; awards include Prague Spring Vocal Competition 1960, Int. Enesco Singing Competition, Bucharest, 1961, First Prize at World Fair, Montreal, 1967; début with Bolshoi Opera 1963, Prin. of the co. 1964-; has performed world-wide, including in France, U.S.A., U.K.; *roles include:* Eugene (Eugene Onegin), Prince Yeletsky (The Queen of Spades), Andrei (War and Peace), Figaro (The Barber of Seville), Scarpia (Tosca) and Escamillo (Carmen) and especially Verdi repertoire, including Anckarström (A Masked Ball) and Rodrigo (Don Carlos).

MASURSKY, Harold, M.S.; American geologist; b. 23 Dec. 1923, Fort Wayne, Ind.; s. of Louis Masursky and Celia Ochstein; m.; four c.; with U.S. Geological Survey 1951-, Head Astrogeologic Studies Br. 1967-71, Chief Scientist U.S. Geological Survey, Flagstaff, Ariz. 1971-75, Sr. Scientist 1975-; Lunar Orbiter Surveyor Missions 1965-67; Team Leader TV experiment (Mariner to Mars) 1971; Co-investigator Apollo Field Geological Team, Apollos 16 and 17; mem. Apollo orbital photographic team; Leader Viking Mars Missions Site Selection Team 1975; mem. imaging teams Voyager (Jupiter, Saturn, Uranus, Neptune) 1977; Chair. Venus Pioneer Mission 1978; Co-Chair. Operational Group Galileo Mission 1981; Leader Radar Team, Magellan Mission 1981; mem. Space Science Advisory Comm. 1978-81, Solar System Exploration Comm. 1980-86; mem. Space Science Bd. 1982-85; Pres. Comm. B. COSPAR; Sec. Co-ordinating Comm. of Moon and Planets; Assoc. Ed. Icarus Geophysical Review; Fellow Geological Soc. of America, A.A.A.S., American Geophysical Union, Int. Astronomical Union, American Astronomical Asscn.; Hon. D.Sc. (Arizona) 1981. *Address:* U.S. Geological Survey, 2255 N. Gemini St., Flagstaff, Ariz. 86001, U.S.A.

MATA, Eduardo; Mexican conductor; b. 5 Sept. 1942, Mexico City; m. Carmen Cirici-Ventalló 1968; one s. one d.; ed. Nat. Conservatory of Music, and has studied under Carlos Chavez; Music Dir., Guadalajara Symphony Orchestra 1964; Musical Dir. and Conductor, Orquesta Filarmonica, Nat. Univ., Mexico 1966-75; Conductor and Musical Advisor, Phoenix Symphony Orchestra 1969-77; Artistic Dir., 'Pueblo Ciudad' Musical 1975, Nat. Symphony Orchestra in Mexico City 1975, San Salvador Festival 1975, Pueblo Music Festival 1975-; Nat. Opera in Mexico City 1983-85; Conductor, Casals Festival 1976; Music Dir., Dallas Symphony Orchestra 1977-; Golden Lyre Award (Mexican Union of Musicians) 1964; Elias Sourasky Prize in the Arts (Mexico) 1975; appointed to Colegio Nacional. *Works:* numerous recordings and compositions. *Address:* P.O. Box 26207, Dallas, Tex. 75226, U.S.A.

MATANE, Sir Paulias Nguna, Kt., C.M.G., O.B.E.; Papua New Guinea diplomatist; b. Sept. 1931, Viviran, Rabaul; s. of Ilias and Elta (Toto) Matane; m. Kaludia Peril 1957; two s. two d.; senior positions in Dept. of Educ. 1957-69; mem. Public Service Bd. 1969; Head, Dept. of Lands, Surveys and Mines 1969, of Business Devt. 1970-75; Amb. to U.S.A. and Mexico 1975-80, Perm. Rep. to UN 1975-81, High Commr. in Canada 1977-81; Sec., Dept. of Foreign Affairs and Trade 1980-85; Chair. Cttee. on the Philosophy of Educ. for Papua New Guinea 1986, Cocoa Industry and Investigating Cttee. of Cocoa Quality in Papua New Guinea 1987; Chair. of Dirs. Triad Pacific (PNG) Pty. Ltd. 1987; mem. Nat. Investment and Devt. Authority, Nat. Tourism Authority, Nat. Citizenship Advisory Cttee., Univ. of Papua New Guinea Council; Hon. D.Tech. (Papua New Guinea) 1985; Hon. D.Phil. (Papua New Guinea) 1985; 10th Independence Anniversary Medal 1985, UN 40th Anniversary Medal. *Publications:* My Childhood in New Guinea, A New Guinean Travels through Africa, Two New Guineans Travel through South East Asia, What Good is Business?, Aimbe the Magician, Aimbe the Challenger, Aimbe the School Dropout, Aimbe the Pastor, Kum Tumun of Minj, Two Papua New Guineans Discover the Bible Lands 1987, To Serve with Love 1987. *Leisure interests:* reading, squash, writing, travel. *Address:* P.O. Box 680, Rabaul, Papua New Guinea. *Telephone:* 921268.

MATANO, Robert Stanley; Kenyan politician; b. 28 April 1925, Mazeras; s. of Stanley Robert Mwendar and Alice Dzame Mwendar; m. Ruth Kwekwe Rupia 1951; three s. three d.; ed. Alliance High School, Kikuyu, Makarere Univ. Coll.; Asst. Educ. Officer in Naivasha, Rift Valley 1954-55, in Mombasa 1955-56; studies in admin. of educ. at Cardiff, U.K. 1956; Asst. Minister for Coast Prov. 1957-60; Asst. Minister Foreign Health and Home Affairs 1961; election to Legis. Council (KADU) for Kwale West; Parl. Sec. Ministry of Educ. 1961-62; election to House of Reps. 1963; Vice-Pres. Coast Regional Ass. 1963-65; Asst. Minister Foreign Affairs 1964, Health 1965, Home Affairs 1966; Asst. Sec.-Gen. KANU 1966; Asst. Minister Home Affairs 1969-73; Minister of Information and Broadcasting 1973-74, of Co-operative Devt. 1974-76, of Local Govt. 1976-78, of Social Services and Housing 1980-81, for Co-operative Devt. 1981-83, of Information and Broadcasting 1983-85; mem. KADU 1960-64; mem. KANU 1964-, Acting Sec.-Gen. 1972-78, Sec.-Gen. 1978-79; Chair. Child Welfare Soc. 1963; Pres. Miji Tribal Union. *Leisure interests:* fishing, scouting. *Address:* c/o Ministry of Information and Broadcasting, Nairobi, Kenya.

MATANZIMA, Chief Kaiser; South African (Transkei) lawyer and politician; b. 1915, St. Mark's Dist.; s. of the late Mhlobo Matanzima; m.

Nozuko Jayinja 1954; four s. five d.; ed. Lovedale Missionary Institution and Fort Hare Univ. Coll.; Chief, Amahale Clan of Tembus, St. Mark's District 1940; mem. United Transkeian Gen. Council 1942-56; Perm. Head Emigrant Tembuland Regional Authority and mem. Exec. Cttee. Transkeian Territorial Authority 1956-58; Regional Chief of Emigrant Tembuland 1958-61; Presiding Chief Transkeian Territorial Authority 1961-63; Chief Minister of Transkei 1963-76, Prime Minister 1976-79; Pres. Repub. of Transkei 1979-85; Leader, Transkei Nat. Party 1987-88; Chancellor, Univ. of Transkei 1977-88; Freeman of Umtata 1982; Hon. LL.D. (Fort Hare). *Publications:* Independence My Way 1977. *Address:* Qamata, Bizana District, Transkei, South Africa.

MATES, Leo; Yugoslav diplomatist; b. 1911; ed. Univ. of Zagreb; Chief Ed. Tanjug Agency of Yugoslavia 1945; entered Foreign Service 1945; Counsellor for Information, Yugoslav Embassy, London, and later Dir. U.N. Dept. Ministry of Foreign Affairs 1947-48, Asst. Minister of Foreign Affairs 1948; Del. to U.N. Gen. Ass. 1946-48, 1951-55, Perm. Rep. 1953; Amb. to U.S.A. 1954-58; Sec.-Gen. to Pres. 1958-61; Asst. to Sec. of State for Foreign Affairs 1961-62; Dir. Inst. for Int. Politics and Econs., Belgrade 1962-79. *Address:* c/o Institute for International Politics, P.O. Box 750, 11000 Belgrade, Yugoslavia.

MATHÉ, Georges, M.D.; French professor of medicine; b. 9 July 1922, Sermages; s. of Adrien and Francine (née Doridot) Mathé; m. Marie-Louise Servier 1954; one d.; ed. Lycée Banville, Moulins, and Univ. de Paris; Head of Clinic, Medical Faculty, Paris Univ. 1952-53, Prof. of Cancer Research Fac. Medicine, Paris 1956-67; Head, Dept. of Haematology, Inst. Gustave-Roussy 1961-; Tech. Counsellor, Ministry of Health 1964-66; Dir. Inst. de Cancérologie et d'Immunogénétique 1965-; Prof. of Experimental Cancerology, Faculté de Médecine, Univ. de Paris-Sud, Villejuif 1966-; Ed.-in-Chief Biomedicine; Co-ed. Cancer Chemotherapy and Pharmacology, Cancer Immunology and Immunotherapy; mem. Cen. Cttee. Rassemblement pour la Répub.; Prés. Comité Consultatif de la Recherche Scientifique et Tech. 1972-, Medical Oncology Soc.; mem. Royal Soc. of Medicine, New York Acad. of Sciences; Médaille d'or des hôpitaux de Paris; Chevalier, Légion d'honneur; Officier, Ordre nat. du Mérite. *Publications:* Le métabolisme de l'eau (with J. Hamburger) 1952, La greffe (with J. L. Amiel) 1962, Aspects histologiques et cytologiques des leucémies et hématosarcomes (with G. Sémar) 1963, L'aplasie myélolymphoide de l'irradiation totale (with J. L. Amiel) 1965, Sémiologie médicale (with G. Richet) 1965 (3rd edn. 1977), La chimiothérapie des cancers 1966 (3rd edn. 1974), Le cancer 1967, Bone Marrow Transplantation and White Cells Transfusions (with J. L. Amiel and L. Schwarzenberg) 1971, La santé—est-elle au dessus de nos moyens? (with Catherine Mathé) 1970, Natural History and Modern Treatment of Hodgkin's Disease (with M. Tubiana) 1973, Histocytological typing of the neoplastic diseases of the haematopoietic and lymphoid tissues (with H. Rappaport) 1973, Cancérologie générale et clinique à l'usage du practicien et de l'étudiant (with A. Cattan) 1974, Le temps d'y penser 1974, Cancérologie à l'usage du practicien et de l'étudiant 1976, Immunothérapie active des cancers: immunoprévention et immunorestauration 1976, Cancer Active Immunotherapy; Immunoporphylaxis and Immunorestoration: An Introduction 1976, Cancer Chemotherapy: Its Role in the Treatment Strategy of Hematologic Malignancies and Solid Tumors (with A. Clarysse and Y. Kenis) 1976, Dossier Cancer 1977, L'homme qui voulait être guéri 1985. *Address:* Institut de Cancérologie et d'Immunogénétique, Hôpital Paul-Brousse, 14 Avenue Paul-Vaillant-Couturier, 94800 Villejuif (Office); Le Fonbois, 10 Rue du Bon Puits, Arpajon, 91290 La Norville, France (Home). *Telephone:* 46.77.00.00 (Office); 64.90.03.58 (Home).

MATHEALIRA, Morena Lechesa, D.P. ADMIN.; Lesotho politician; b. 20 June 1928, Ha Mopeli, Butha-Buthe; ed. Ohlanga High School, Lesotho High School, Roma Coll.; joined Dist. Commr.'s Office, Leribe; clerk Tsikoane Local Court; Office of Paramount Chief Matsieng; installed as Area Chief of Peka 1961 and Ward Chief 1976; served as Senate Chief Whip 1985 and Alt. mem.; Minister of Tourism, Sports and Culture 1986-; mem. of Land Tribunal. *Address:* c/o The Military Council, Maseru, Lesotho.

MATHER, Sir Kenneth, Kt., C.B.E., D.SC., LL.D., F.R.S.; British geneticist and former university vice-chancellor; b. 22 June 1911, Nantwich; s. of R. W. Mather; m. Mona Rhodes 1937; one s.; ed. Nantwich and Acton Grammar School and Univs. of Manchester and London; Lecturer in Galton Laboratory, Univ. Coll. London 1934-37; Rockefeller Research Fellow, California Inst. of Tech. and Harvard Univ. 1937-38; Head of Genetics Dept., John Innes Horticultural Inst. 1938-48; Prof. of Genetics Univ. of Birmingham 1948-65; Vice-Chancellor Univ. of Southampton 1965-71; Hon. Prof. of Genetics Univ. of Birmingham 1971-84, Emer. Prof. 1984-; mem. Agricultural Research Council 1949-54, 1955-60, 1969-79, Science Research Council 1965-69, Govt. Advisory Cttee. on Irradiation of Food 1967-74, Genetic Manipulation Advisory Group (D.E.S.) 1976-78; Weldon Medal, Univ. of Oxford 1962; Darwin Medal, Royal Soc. 1964. *Publications:* The Measurement of Linkage in Heredity 1938, Statistical Analysis in Biology 1943, Biometrical Genetics 1949, The Elements of Genetics (with C. D. Darlington) 1949, Genes, Plants and People (with C. D. Darlington) 1950, Human Diversity 1964, Elements of Biometry 1967, Biometrical Genetics (2nd edn. with J. L. Jinks) 1971, (3rd edn. with J. L. Jinks) 1982, Genetical Structure

of Populations 1973, Introduction to Biometrical Genetics (with J. L. Jinks) 1977. *Address:* School of Biological Sciences, University of Birmingham, P.O. Box 363, Birmingham, B15 2TT (Office); 296 Bristol Road, Birmingham, B5 7SN, England. (Home). *Telephone:* 021-414-5884 (Office); 021-472-2093 (Home).

MATHER, Leonard Charles, C.B.E., B.COM., F.I.B., F.C.I.S.; British banker; b. 10 Oct. 1909, Cheshire; s. of Richard and Elizabeth Mather; m. Muriel Armor Morris 1937; ed. Oldershaw School, Wallasey; Jt. Gen. Man. Midland Bank Ltd. 1958-63, Asst. Chief Gen. Man. 1964-66, Deputy Chief Gen. Man. 1966-68, Dir. 1968-, Chief Gen. Man. 1968-72, Vice-Chair, 1972-74; Chair. United Dominions Trust Ltd. 1974-81; Dir. Midland Bank Trust Co. 1968-74, Midland and Int. Banks Ltd. 1969-74, Montagu Trust Ltd. 1969-74, European Banks Int. Co. S.A. 1970-72, Clydesdale Bank Ltd. 1972-74, Northern Bank Ltd. 1972-74, Northern Bank Devt. Corpn. Ltd. 1972-74, European Banking Co. Ltd. 1973-74; Chair. European Banks Int. Co. S.A. 1972-74; Chair. Int. Commodities Clearing House; Deputy Chair. Euro-Pacific Finance Corpn. Ltd. 1971-74; Deputy Chair. Inst. of Bankers 1967-69, Pres. 1969-70, Life Vice-Pres. 1970-, Hon. Fellow 1974; Hon. D. Litt. (Loughborough) 1978; Inst. of Bankers' Prize. *Publications:* The Lending Banker 1955, Banker and Customer Relationship and the Accounts of Personal Customers 1956, The Accounts of Limited Company Customers 1958, Securities Acceptable to the Lending Banker 1960. *Leisure interests:* golf, bridge, theatre. *Address:* Rochester House, Parkfield, Seal, Sevenoaks, Kent, England (Home). *Telephone:* 0732-61007 (Home).

MATHESON, Sir (James Adam) Louis, K.B.E., C.M.G., PH.D., F.T.S., F. ENG.; Australian engineer, university professor and administrator; b. 11 Feb. 1912, Huddersfield, Yorks., England; s. of William and Lily Edith Matheson; m. Audrey Elizabeth Wood 1937; three s.; ed. Bootham School, York and Manchester Univ.; Lecturer, Birmingham Univ. 1938-46; Prof. Civil Eng., Univ. of Melbourne 1946-50; Beyer Prof. of Eng., Manchester Univ. 1951-59; Vice-Chancellor, Monash Univ., Victoria, Australia 1959-76; mem. Mission on Tech. Educ. to the W. Indies 1957, Ramsay Cttee. on Devt. of Tertiary Educ. in Victoria 1961-63, Commonwealth Scientific and Industrial Research Org. Advisory Council 1962-67, Royal Comm. into Failure of Kings Bridge 1962-63; Trustee Inst. of Applied Science of Victoria, now Science Museum of Victoria 1964-83; mem. Council Inst. of Engineers, Australia 1965-81, Pres. 1975-76; mem. Council Inst. of Civil Engineers 1966-68; Vice-Pres. Inst. Structural Engineers 1967-68; mem. Interim Council Univ. of Papua New Guinea 1965-68; Chair. Papua New Guinea Inst. of Tech. Council 1966-73, now Papua New Guinea Univ. of Tech., Chancellor 1973-75; Chair. Australian Science and Tech. Council 1975-76, mem. 1977-78; Chair. Australian Vice-Chancellors Cttee. 1967-68, Asscn. of Commonwealth Univs. 1967-69, Buildings Cttee. Commonwealth Schools Comm. 1976-81, Newport Power Station Review 1977, Victorian Planning and Finance Cttee. Commonwealth Schools Comm. 1979-83, Sorrento Harbour Inquiry 1984, 1987, St. Kilda Harbour Inquiry 1986; mem. Enquiry Post-Secondary Educ., Victoria 1976-78; Nauru Phosphate Corpn. 1977-80; Fellow Australian Acad. of Tech. Sciences, Hon. Fellow Inst. Civil Engineers, Inst. of Engineers, Australia; Hon. D.Sc. (Hong Kong), Hon. LL.D. (Manchester, Melbourne and Monash Univs.); Kernot Medal 1970, Peter Nicol Russell Medal 1976. *Publications:* Hyperstatic Structures (2 vols.) 1959, Still Learning 1980, papers on technical and educational subjects. *Leisure interests:* music, woodcraft. *Address:* 26/166 West Toorak Road, South Yarra, Victoria 3141, Australia. *Telephone:* (03) 266 4957, (03) 787 1931.

MATHEWS, (Forrest) David, PH.D.; American educationalist; b. 6 Dec. 1935, Grove Hill, Ala.; s. of Forrest Lee and Doris Mathews; m. Mary Chapman 1960; two d.; ed. Univ. of Alabama and Columbia Univ.; Infantry Officer U.S. Army Reserves 1959-67; Pres. Univ. of Ala. 1969-80, Lecturer and Prof. of History 1969-80; Sec. of Health, Educ. and Welfare 1975-77; Chair. Nat. Council for Public Policy Educ. 1981-; mem. numerous advisory bds., etc.; Trustee Nat. March of Dimes 1977-85, John F. Kennedy Center for Performing Arts 1975-77, Woodrow Wilson Int. Center for Scholars 1975-77, Miles Coll. 1978-, Teachers Coll., Columbia Univ. 1977-; Pres. and C.E.O. Kettering Foundation 1981-; numerous awards and hon. degrees. *Publications:* works on history of Southern U.S.A., higher educ. in public policy, including The Changing Agenda for American Higher Education. *Leisure interest:* gardening. *Address:* 6050 Mad River Road, Dayton, Ohio 45459, U.S.A. *Telephone:* (513) 434-7300.

MATHEWS, Ian Richard; British journalist; b. 29 Jan. 1933, Mitcham, Surrey; s. of late George James and Dorothy Mathews; m. Joyce Pamela Morris 1957; one s. one d.; ed. Sir Joseph Williamson's Mathematical School, Rochester, Kent; local govt. clerk, Maidstone, Kent 1949; clerk Guy's Hosp., London 1952-54; writer Royal Fleet Auxiliary 1954-55; with Kent & Sussex Courier Group of Newspapers 1955-59; Express & Echo, Exeter 1959-60; News Ltd., Adelaide, S. Australia 1960-63; joined Canberra Times 1963, subsequently Chief Sub-Ed., News Ed., Asst. Ed. 1963-72, Ed. 1972-85, Ed.-in-Chief 1985-; mem. Nat. Consultative Cttee. on Peace and Disarmament 1985-, Australian Bicentennial ACT and Island Territories Council, Educ. and Publicity Cttee. of the Nat. Health and Medical Research Council, Social Issues Cttee. of Royal Australasian Coll. of Physicians 1987-. *Leisure interests:* travelling, letter writing. *Address:* The Canberra Times, 18 Mort Street, 2601 Canberra (Office); 4 Stone

Place, Garran, 2605 A.C.T., Australia (Home). *Telephone:* (062) 802 201 (Office); (062) 814025 (Home).

MATHIAS, Charles McC., Jr.; American lawyer and politician; b. 24 July 1922, Frederick, Md.; s. of Charles McC. Mathias, Sr., and Theresa Trail Mathias; m. Ann Hickling Bradford 1958; two s.; ed. public schools, Frederick, Md., Haverford Coll., Yale Univ. and Univ. of Maryland; apprentice seaman 1942, commissioned Ensign 1944, sea duty, Pacific 1944–46; Capt. U.S. Naval Reserve retd.; admitted to Maryland Bar 1949, to U.S. Supreme Court Bar 1954; Asst. Attorney-Gen. of Maryland 1953, 1954; City Attorney, Frederick, Md. 1954–59; mem. Md. House of Dels. 1958; mem. U.S. House of Reps. 1960–68; U.S. Senator from Maryland 1969–87; Milton S. Eisenhower Distinguished Professorship in Public Policy, Johns Hopkins School for Advanced Int. Studies 1987–; Republican; Chair. Senate Rules and Admin. Cttee. 1981–87. *Address:* c/o Jones, Day, Reavis & Pogue, 655 15th Street, N.W., Washington, D.C. 20005 (Office); 3808 Leland Street, Chevy Chase, MD. 20815, U.S.A. (Home).

MATHIAS, Peter, C.B.E., M.A., D.LITT., LITT.D., F.B.A., F.R.HIST.S.; British professor of economic history; b. 10 Jan. 1928, Somerset; s. of John Samuel Mathias and Marion Helen Love; m. Elizabeth Ann Blackmore 1958; two s. one d.; ed. Colstons Hosp., Bristol, Jesus Coll. Cambridge and Harvard Univ., U.S.A.; Research Fellow, Jesus Coll. 1953–55; Lecturer, History Faculty, Cambridge Univ. 1955–68, Tutor and Dir. of Studies, Queens' Coll., Sr. Proctor, Cambridge Univ. 1965–66; Chichele Prof. of Econ. History, Oxford Univ. and Fellow of All Souls Coll. 1969–87; Master of Downing Coll., Cambridge 1987–; Pres. Int. Econ. History Assen. 1974–78, Hon. Pres. 1978–; Vice-Pres. Royal Historical Soc. 1975–80; Hon. Treas. British Acad. 1979–, Econ. History Soc. 1967–; Pres. Business Archives Council 1984–; mem. Advisory Bd. of the Research Councils 1983–; Chair. History of Medicine Panel, Wellcome Trust 1980–88; Curator Bodleian Library, Oxford 1972–87; Foreign mem. Royal Danish Acad., Royal Belgian Acad.; Hon. Litt.D. (Buckingham), (Birmingham). *Publications:* Brewing Industry in England 1700–1830 1959, Retailing Revolution 1967, Tradesmen's Tokens 1962, The First Industrial Nation 1969, 1983, The Transformation of England 1979. *Leisure interest:* travel. *Address:* Master's Lodge, Downing College, Cambridge, CB2 1DQ, England. *Telephone:* (0223) 334806.

MATHIAS, William (James), C.B.E., D.MUS., F.R.A.M.; British composer and professor of music; b. 1 Nov. 1934, Whitland, Dyfed, Wales; s. of James Hughes Mathias and Marian (née Evans); m. Margaret Yvonne Collins 1959; one d.; ed. Univ. Coll. of Wales, Royal Acad of Music; lecturer, Univ. Coll. of North Wales 1959–68; sr. lecturer, Univ. of Edinburgh 1968–69; Prof. and Head of Music Dept., Univ. Coll. of North Wales 1970–88; mem. Welsh Arts Council 1974–81 (Chair. Music Cttee. 1982–), Int. Soc. for Contemporary Music 1976–80, Bd. of Govs., Nat. Museum of Wales 1973–78, British Council Music Advisory Cttee. 1974–83, Welsh Advisory Cttee. 1979–, BBC Cen. Music Advisory Cttee. 1979–86; Artistic Dir. North Wales Music Festival 1972–; Vice-Chair. British Arts Festivals Assen. 1983–88, Vice-Pres. 1988–; Gov. Nat. Youth Orchestra of G.B. 1985–; Hon. D. Mus. (Westminster Choir Coll., Princeton) 1987; Arnold Bax Soc. Prize 1968, John Edwards Memorial Prize 1982. *Compositions: Orchestral:* Symphony 1969, Piano Concerto No. 2 1964, Piano Concerto No. 3 1970, Harp Concerto 1973, Clarinet Concerto 1976, Celtic Dances 1974, Divertimento for Strings 1961, Serenade 1963, Prelude Aria, and Finale 1966, Vistas 1977, Laudi 1978, Helios 1978, Requiescat 1978, Vivat Regina (for brass band) 1978, Dance Variations 1979, Investiture Anniversary Fanfare 1979, Reflections on a theme by Tomkins 1981, Symphony No. 2 1983, Organ Concerto 1984, Horn Concerto 1984, Anniversary Dances 1985. *Chamber music:* Violin Sonata 1963, Piano Sonata No. 1 1965, String Quartet No. 1 1970, String Quartet No. 2 1981, Wind Quintet 1976, Zodiac Trio 1977, Clarinet Sonatina 1978, Concertino 1977, Violin Sonata No. 2 1984. *Choral and vocal:* Wassail Carol 1965, Three Medieval Lyrics 1966, Ave Rex, 1970, A Babe is born 1971, A Vision of Time and Eternity (for contralto and piano) 1974, Ceremony after a Fire Raid 1975, This Worlde's Joie (for soli, chorus and orchestra) 1975, Elegy for a Prince (for baritone and orchestra) 1976, The Fields of Praise (for tenor and piano) 1977, A Royal Garland 1978, A May Magnificat 1980, Shakespeare Songs 1980, Songs of William Blake (for mezzo and orchestra) 1980, Rex Gloriae (four Latin motets) 1982, Te Deum (for soli, chorus and orchestra) 1982, Lux Aeterna (for soli, chorus and orchestra) 1982, Salvator Mundi (carol sequence) 1982, Veni, Sancte Spiritus 1985. *Organ:* Variations on a Hymn Tune 1963, Partita 1963, Postlude 1964, Processional 1965, Chorale 1967, Toccata Giocosa 1968, Jubilate 1975, Fantasy 1978, Canzonetta 1978, Antiphonies 1982. *Anthems and church music:* O Sing unto the Lord 1965, Make a Joyful Noise 1965, Festival Te Deum 1965, Communion Service in C 1968, Psalm 150 1969, Lift up your heads 1970, O Salutaris Hostia 1972, Gloria 1972, Magnificat and Nunc Dimittis 1973, Missa Brevis 1974, Communion Service (Series III) 1976, Arise, shine 1978, Let the People Praise Thee, O God (anthem composed for the Marriage of The Prince and Princess of Wales) 1981, Praise ye the Lord 1982, All Wisdom is from the Lord 1982, Except the Lord Build the house 1982, A Grace 1983, Jubilate Deo 1983, O How Amiable 1983, Tantum Ergo 1983, Angelus 1983, Let Us Now Praise Famous Men 1984, Alleluia! Christ is Risen 1984, Missa Aedis Christi—in memoriam William Walton 1984, Salve Regina 1986, O clap your Hands 1986, Let All the World in Every Corner Sing 1987,

Rejoice in the Lord 1987, I Will Lift up Mine Eyes unto the Hills 1987, Cantate Domino 1987, Thus Saith God the Lord, An Orkney Anthem 1987, O Lord our Lord 1987, As Truly as God is Our Father 1987, The Heavens Declare 1988. *Opera:* The Servants (Libretto by Iris Murdoch (q.v.) 1980. *Address:* Y Graigwen, Cadnant Road, Menai Bridge, Anglesey, Gwynedd, LL59 5NG, Wales. *Telephone:* 0248 712392.

MATHIESEN, Matthias (Árnason), CAND. JURIS; Icelandic lawyer and politician; b. 6 Aug. 1931, Hafnarfjördur; s. of Árni M. and Svava E. Mathiesen; m. Sigrún Thorgilsdóttir 1956; two s. one d.; ed. Univ. of Iceland; Chief Exec. Hafnarfjördur Savings Bank 1958–67, Chair 1967; Advocate, Supreme Court 1967–74; mem. Althing (Parl.) 1959–, Speaker Lower Chamber 1970–71; Rep. of Althing to Nordic Council 1965–74, mem. Presidium 1970–71, 1973–74, Pres. 1970–71, 1980–81; Del. North Atlantic Ass., NATO 1963–69, 1972, Chair. Icelandic Del. 1964–67, Pres. of Ass. 1967–68; Dir. Nat. Bank of Iceland 1961–74, 1980–83; Icelandic mem. of Bd. of Govs. World Bank Group (IBRD, IDA, IFC) 1983–85; Minister of Finance 1974–78, Minister of Commerce (including Banking), and of Nordic Co-operation 1983–85, for Foreign Affairs 1985–87, of Communications 1987–; mem. Cen. Cttee., Independence Party 1965–. *Address:* Hringbraut 59, Hafnarfjördur, Iceland (Home). *Telephone:* (91) 5-02-76 (Home).

MATHIEU, Georges Victor Adolphe, L. ÈS L.; French artist; b. 27 Jan. 1921, Boulogne; s. of Adolphe Mathieu d'Escaudoeuvres and Madeleine Dupré d'Ausque; ed. Facultés de droit et des lettres, Lille; Teacher of English; Public Relations Man., United States Lines; exhibited at Paris 1950, New York 1952, Japan 1957, Scandinavia 1958, England, Spain, Italy, Switzerland, Germany, Austria and South America 1959, Middle East 1961–62, Canada 1963; special exhbn. of work held at Musée Municipal d'Art Moderne, Paris 1963; exhbn. of 100 paintings, Galerie Charpentier, Paris 1965; designed gardens and buildings for B.C. transformer factory, Fontenay-le-comte 1966; 16 posters for Air France exhibited at Musée Nat. d'Art Moderne, Paris 1967; exhbn. of 10 tapestries at Musée de la Manufacture Nat. des Gobelins 1969; designed 18 medals for Paris Mint 1971, new 10F coin 1974; works exhibited in numerous countries including shows in Antibes 1976, Ostend 1977, Grand Palais, Paris 1978, Wildenstein Gallery, New York, Dominion Gallery, Montreal 1979, Musée de la Poste, Paris 1980, Galerie Kasper, Morges, Switzerland 1983, Théâtre municipal de Brives 1984; retrospective show, Palais des Papes, Avignon 1985; Galerie Calvin, Geneva 1985, Wally Findlay Galleries 1986, Galerie Schindler, Berne 1986, Galerie du Luxembourg 1986; creator of "Tachism"; mem. Acad. of Fine Arts; Officier, Légion d'honneur, des Arts et des Lettres; Ordre de la Couronne de Belgique. *Principal works:* Hommage à la Mort 1950, Hommage au Maréchal de Turenne 1952, Les Capétiens Partout 1954, La Victoire de Denain 1963, Hommage à Jean Cocteau 1963, Paris, Capitale des Arts 1965, Hommages aux Frères Boisserée 1967, Hommage à Condillac 1968, La prise de Berg op Zoom 1969, Election de Charles Quint 1971, Matta-Salums 1978, La Libération de Paris 1980, La libération d'Orléans par Jeanne d'Arc 1982, Monumental sculpture in Neuilly 1982, in Chareton 1982, Ceiling-painting in Boulogne-Billancourt town hall 1983, Massacre des 269 1985. *Publications:* Au-delà du Tachisme, Le privilège d'Etre, De la Revolte à la Renaissance, La Réponse de l'Abstraction lyrique, L'abstraction prophétique. *Address:* 23 Quai Conti, 75006 Paris; 11 bis Avenue Leopold II, Paris 75016, France.

MATHIS, Edith; Swiss soprano; b. 11 Feb. 1938, Lucerne; ed. Lucerne Conservatoire; début Lucerne 1956; sang with Cologne Opera 1959–62; appeared Salzburg Festival 1960, Deutsche Oper, W. Berlin 1963; début Glyndebourne (Cherubino in Nozze di Figaro) 1962, Covent Garden (Susanna in Nozze di Figaro) 1970, Metropolitan Opera House, New York (Pamina in The Magic Flute) 1970; mem. Hamburg State Opera 1960–75. *Address:* c/o Bueker-Management, Postfach 1169, D-Hannover 1, Federal Republic of Germany; c/o Ingpen & Williams Ltd., 14 Kensington Court, London, W8 5DN, England. *Telephone:* 01-937 5158 (London).

MATHIS-EDDY, Darlene, PH.D.; American professor of English and poet; b. 19 March 1937, Elkhart, Ind.; d. of the late William Eugene Mathis and Fern Roose Paulmer Mathis; m. Spencer Livingston Eddy, Jr. 1964 (died 1971); ed. Goshen Coll. and Rutgers Univ.; Instructor in English, Douglass Coll. 1962–64; Instructor in English, Rutgers Univ. 1964, 1965, Rutgers Univ. Coll. (Adult Educ.) 1967; Asst. Prof. in English, Ball State Univ. 1967–71, Assoc. Prof. 1971–75, Prof. 1975–; mem. Comm. on Women for the Nat. Council of Teachers of English 1976–79; Poetry Ed. BSU Forum; Woodrow Wilson Nat. Fellow 1959–62 and numerous other fellowships. *Publications:* Leaf Threads, Wind Rhymes 1986, The Worlds of King Lear 1971, Weathering 1988; Contributing Ed. Snowy Egret; numerous poems in literary reviews; articles in American Literature, English Language Notes, etc. *Leisure interests:* gardening, music, antiques, reading, sketching, photography, bird watching, cooking. *Address:* Department of English, Robert Bell Building, Office No. 248, Ball State University, Muncie, Ind. 47306; 1409 West Cardinal Street, Muncie, Ind. 47303, U.S.A. (Home).

MATIN, M. A., F.R.C.S.; Bangladesh politician; b. 1 Dec. 1937, Pabna; ed. Dhaka Medical Coll.; worked in Royal Eye Hosp. and King's Coll. Hosp., London 1964–67; Assoc. Prof. of Ophthalmology, Inst. of Postgraduate Medicine and Research, Dhaka 1967–72, Prof., then Head of Dept. 1972–; Hon. Col. and Consultant Ophthalmologist, Combined Mil. Hosp., Dhaka 1976; M.P. 1979–; Minister of Civil Aviation and Tourism 1979, Minister of

Youth Devt. and of Health and Population Control 1981, Minister of Home Affairs 1981–82, Minister of Commerce 1984, Minister of Works 1985, Deputy Prime Minister in charge of Ministry of Home Affairs 1986–88; Deputy Prime Minister 1988–; Minister of Health and Family Planning 1988, March 1989–, of Home Affairs 1988–89; fmr. Sec.-Gen. and Pres. Bangladesh Ophthalmological Soc. and Pres. Bangladesh Medical Services Asscn.; Vice-Chair. Bangladesh Medical Research Council and Vice-Pres. Bangladesh Coll. of Physicians and Surgeons; Alim Memorial Gold Medal; Int. Award, Asian Pacific Acad. of Ophthalmology 1981. *Address:* Ministry of Health and Family Planning, 3rd Floor, Bangladesh Secretariat, Dhaka, Bangladesh.

MATLOCK, Jack Foust Jr., M.A.; American diplomatist; b. 1 Oct. 1929, Greensboro; s. of Jack Foust Matlock and Nellie McSwain; m. Rebecca Burrum 1949; four s. one d.; ed. Duke and Columbia Univs. and Russian Inst.; Instructor, Dartmouth 1953–56; joined foreign service, State Dept. 1956, Official in Washington 1956–58, Embassy Official, Vienna 1958–60, Consul Gen., Munich 1960–61, Embassy Official, Moscow 1961–63, Accra, Ghana 1963–66, Zanzibar 1967–69, Dar es Salaam 1969–70, Country Dir. for U.S.S.R., State Dept. 1971–74, Deputy Chief of Mission, Embassy in Moscow 1974–78, Diplomat-in-Residence, Vanderbilt Univ. 1978–79, Deputy Dir., Foreign Service Inst., Washington 1979–80, Amb. to Czechoslovakia 1981–83, to U.S.S.R., Feb. 1987–; Special Asst. to Pres. and Sr. Dir. European and Soviet Affairs, Nat. Security Council 1983–87. *Publication:* Ed. Index to J.V. Stalin's Works 1971. *Address:* Embassy of the U.S.A., 19/23 ulitsa Chaikovskogo, Moscow, U.S.S.R. *Telephone:* (095) 252-24-51.

MATOKA, Peter Wilfred, M.A.; Zambian politician and diplomatist; b. 8 April 1930, Mwinilunga, N.W. Prov.; m. Grace J. Mukahlera 1957; two s. one d.; ed. primary and secondary schools, Fort Hare Univ. Coll. and American Univ., Washington, D.C.; Civil Servant 1955–63; Minister of Information and Postal Services 1964–65, of Health 1965–66, of Works 1967, of Power, Transport and Works 1968; Minister for Luapula Prov. 1969; High Commr. of Zambia in U.K. 1969–70, concurrently accredited to the Vatican; mem. Cen. Cttee., United Nat. Independence Party (UNIP) 1971–; Minister for the S. Prov. 1970–71, of Health 1971–72, of Local Govt. and Housing 1972–75, of Devt. Planning and Public Works 1975–77, of Econ. and Tech. Co-operation 1977–79; Sr. Regional Adviser UN Econ. Comm. for Africa, Addis Ababa 1979–83; Zambian High Commr. in Zimbabwe 1984–89; Chair. Social and Cultural Sub-Cttee. of Cen. Cttee. of UNIP; Kt. of St. Gregory (Vatican) 1964; Kt., Egypt and Ethiopia. *Leisure interests:* fishing, bird shooting, group discussion and photography. *Address:* Freedom House, P.O. Box 30302, Lusaka (Office); 1806 Kasangula Road, Roma Township, Lusaka, Zambia (Home). *Telephone:* 218170 (Office).

MATSEBULA, Mhlangano Stephen; Swazi business executive and farmer; b. 16 July 1925, Maphalaleni, Mbabane; s. of Khwane and Simpompoza Matsebula; m. 1st Fihliwe Zwane 1952, one s. six d.; m. 2nd Ntombana Motsa 1972; ed. High School; Regional Sec., Swazi Commercial Amadoda; Exec. mem. Imbokodvo Nat. Movt.; mem. House of Ass. 1967, Minister of State for Foreign Affairs 1972–78, Minister for Labour and Public Service 1983–86, Minister in the Prime Minister's Office 1986–87; mem. of the Border Adjustment Cttee. 1972–, Special Research Team, Border Adjustment Issue with S. Africa. 1980–83. *Publication:* Students at the University of Swaziland and the Law 1985. *Leisure interests:* handicrafts, reading, football. *Address:* PO Box 216, Mbabane, Swaziland. *Telephone:* 84506.

MATSUI, Masanao, D. SC.; Japanese professor and consultant; b. 9 Dec. 1917, Nagano; m. Chie Shirai 1946; one s. one d.; ed. Imperial Univ. of Tokyo; Assoc. Prof. Univ. of Tokyo 1953–56, Prof. 1956–78, Dean Faculty of Agriculture 1971–77; Prin. Scientist Inst. of Physical and Chemical Research 1967–78;·Pres. Tachikawa Coll., Tokyo 1979–83, Agricultural Chemical Soc. of Japan 1979–81, Asscn. of Agricultural Socs. of Japan 1984–; mem. Japan Acad. 1985–; Purple Ribbon Medal 1979, Japan Acad. Prize 1981, 2nd Order of Merit 1988. *Leisure interest:* golf. *Address:* 3-18-8 Wada, Suginami-ku, Tokyo, Japan. *Telephone:* (03) 383 8223.

MATSUKATA, Masanobu; Japanese business executive; b. 13 Aug. 1907; ed. Keio Univ.; with Tokyo Gas, Electric and Eng. Co. Ltd. 1932; Head of Gen. Affairs Dept. Tokyo Automobile Industry Co. Ltd., Hino Plant 1940; Head of Sales Dept., Hino Heavy Industry Co. Ltd. 1942, Head of Supply Div. 1943, Dir. and Gen. Man. 1945; Man. Dir. Hino Industry Co. Ltd. 1946; Sr. Man. Dir. Hino Diesel Industry Co. Inc. 1950, Vice-Pres. 1954; Pres. Hino Motors Ltd. 1961–74, Chair. 1974–; now also Chair. Hino Motor Sales Ltd., Sitsui Seiki Kogyo Co. Ltd., Teikoku Auto Industry Co. Ltd.; Dir. Sawafuji Electrical Co. Ltd., Auto Industry Employers' Asscn., Japan Automobile Mfrs. Asscn. Inc., Japan Ordinance Asscn., Japan Automobile Chamber of Commerce; Financial Dir. Japan Fed. of Employers' Asscns.; Blue Ribbon Medal. *Leisure interests:* golf, floriculture. *Address:* Hino Motors Ltd., Hinodai 3-1-1, Hino City, Tokyo, Japan. *Telephone:* 03-272-4811 (Office).

MATSUKAWA, Michiya, M.A.; Japanese economist; b. 22 Dec. 1924, Aizuwakamatsu; s. of Tomiyasu and Kou Matsukawa; m. Ryoko Sakakibara 1953; two d.; ed. First Sr. High School, Tokyo, Tokyo Imperial Univ. and Univ. of Illinois, U.S.A.; with Ministry of Finance 1947–80; Private Sec. to Minister of Finance 1958–60; Consul in Charge of Financial Matters, New York 1960–61; First Sec., later Counsellor, Japanese Embassy, Washington, D.C. 1965–68; Dir.-Gen. Int. Finance Bureau 1973–74; Deputy Vice-Minis-

ter of Finance 1974–75; Dir.-Gen. Finance Bureau 1975–76; Vice-Minister for Int. Affairs 1976–78, Special Adviser to Minister 1978–80; Chair. Nikko Research Center·Co. 1982–, Chair. Nikko Int. Capital Man. Co. Ltd. 1984–; now Sr. Adviser to Pres. Nikko Securities Co. Ltd.; mem. Investment Cttee. UN 1981–. *Leisure interests:* reading, classical music, golf. *Address:* 1-38-4 Takada, Toshima-ku, Tokyo 171, Japan. *Telephone:* 03-982-1819.

MATSUMOTO, Ken, M.A.; Japanese business executive; b. 2 Feb. 1935, Shanghai, China; s. of Shigeharu and Hanako Matsumoto; m. Junko Masuda 1969; one s.; ed. Gakushuin High School, Swarthmore Coll., U.S.A., Univ. of Tokyo; mem. Bd. of Dirs., Auburn Steel Co. Inc., Auburn, N.Y. 1973–77; Sr. Man. Export Dept.-I, Nippon Steel Corpn. 1977–84; Dir. Research Div., The Fair Trade Center 1984–; awarded Bancroft Scholarship. *Leisure interests:* tennis, skiing. *Address:* 5-11-38, Miyazaki, Miyamae-ku, Kawasaki-shi, Kanagawa-ken, 213 Japan. *Telephone:* 044-854-0693.

MATSUNAGA, Hikaru; Japanese politician; b. 23 Nov. 1928; ed. Chuo and Waseda Univs.; public prosecutor and lawyer; mem. House of Reps. 1969–; Parl. Vice-Minister for Justice 1974–75; Parl. Vice-Minister for Int. Trade and Industry; Minister of Educ. 1984–85; Liberal Democratic Party. *Leisure interests:* baseball, golf. *Address:* c/o Ministry of Education, 3-2, Kasumigaseki, Chiyoda-ku, Tokyo 100, Japan.

MATSUNAGA, Masanao; Japanese international financial official; b. 5 Nov. 1924, Ottawa, Canada; m. Hiroko Matsunaga 1960; one s. two d.; ed. Faculty of Law, Tokyo Univ.; Ministry of Finance 1948–63; Financial Attaché Embassy in Brussels 1963–65, Paris 1965–68; Dir. Second Insurance Div. of Insurance Dept., Banking Bureau in Ministry of Finance 1968–70; Dir. Int. Orgs. Div. of Int. Finance Bureau 1970–71, Int. Co-ordination Div. 1971–73; Dir.-Gen. Nagoya Regional Tax Admin. 1973–74; Deputy Dir.-Gen. Int. Finance Bureau, Ministry of Finance 1974–75, with Securities Bureau 1975–76; Exec. Dir. for Japan, IMF 1976–79; Councillor, Ministry of Finance 1979–80; Chair. Sumitomo Trust Int. Ltd., London; Adviser, Sumitomo Trust and Banking Co. *Address:* Sumitomo Trust and Banking Co. Ltd., 1-4-4 Marunouchi, Chiyoda-ku, Tokyo, Japan.

MATSUNAGA, Spark Masayuki, J.D.; American politician; b. 8 Oct. 1916, Kukuiula, Kauai, Hawaii; s. of Kingoro and Chiyono Fukushima Matsunaga; m. Helene Hatsumi Tokunaga 1948; five c.; ed. Univ. of Hawaii, Harvard Law School; served U.S. Army from Second Lieut. to Capt. 1941–45; Veterans' Counsellor, U.S. Dept. of Interior 1945–47; Head of Priority Claimants' Div., War Assets Admin. 1947–48; admitted to Hawaii bar 1952; Asst. Public Prosecutor, City and County of Honolulu 1952–54; practised law in Honolulu 1954–62; mem. Hawaii House of Reps. 1954–59, Majority Leader 1959; mem. U.S. House of Reps. 1963–76, mem. Rules Cttee., Deputy Chief Whip; U.S. Senator from Hawaii Jan. 1977–; Democrat; mem. Hawaii statehood dels. to Congress 1950, 1954, Pacific War Memorial Comm. 1959–62, American and Hawaii Bar Asscns., Japan-America Soc.; Bronze Star, Purple Heart with Oak Leaf Cluster. *Publication:* Rulemakers of the House. *Address:* United States Senate, Capitol Hill, Washington, D.C. 20510; 4020, Glenrose Street, Kensington, Maryland, U.S.A. (Home).

MATSUNO, Raizo; Japanese politician; b. 12 Feb. 1917; ed. Keio Univ.; fmrly. with Hitachi Ltd.; Japanese Navy, Second World War; fmr. Pres. Johoku Brewing Co.; fmr. Private Sec. to Prime Minister (Mr. Yoshida); fmr. mem. House of Reps. (resigned 1979); fmr. Parl. Vice-Minister, Ministry of Welfare; Dir.-Gen. Prime Minister's Office; Minister of Labour 1959–60; Minister of State in charge of Defence Agency 1965–66; Minister of Agric. 1966–67; Chair. Policy Affairs Research Council, Liberal-Democratic Party 1974–79; Chair. Liberal-Democratic Party Sept.-Dec. 1976; Liberal-Democrat. *Address:* 84 Imazato Shirogane, Shiba, Minato-ku, Tokyo, Japan.

MATSUSHITA, Konosuke; Japanese businessman; b. 27 Nov. 1894, Wasa Village, Wakayama Prefecture; s. of Masakusu and Tokue Matsushita; m. Mumeno Iue 1915; one d.; founded Matsushita Electric Housewares Mfg. Works 1918, inc. into Matsushita Electric Industrial Co. Ltd. 1935, fmr. Pres., Chair. 1961–73, Adviser, mem. of Bd. 1973–; Pres. Matsushita Communication Industrial Co. Ltd. 1958–66, Chair. 1966–70, Dir. 1970–; Pres. Matsushita Real Estate Co. Ltd. 1952–; Pres. Matsushita Electronics Corpn. 1952–66, Chair. 1966–71, Dir. 1971–; Chair. Kyushu Matsushita Electric Co. Ltd. 1955–74, Adviser 1974–; Chair. Matsushita Reiki Co. Ltd. (formerly Nakagawa Electric Co. Ltd.) 1951–77, Dir. 1974–77, Adviser to the Bd. 1977–; Chair. Matsushita Electric Works Ltd. 1951–71, Dir. 1971–; Adviser Matsushita Electric Trading Co. Ltd.; Chair. Matsushita Electric Corpn. of America 1959–74, Dir. 1974–75; Chair. Victor Co. of Japan Ltd. 1962–70, Exec. Adviser 1970–74, Adviser 1974–; Vice-Pres. Electronic Industries Asscn. of Japan 1958–68; Exec. Dir. Fed. of Econ. Orgs. of Japan 1956–73, Hon. mem. 1973–; mem. Int. Chamber of Commerce 1962–66, Adviser 1966–; mem. Advisory Cttee. Japan Nat. Railway 1962–71; founded Matsushita School of Govt. and Man. April 1980; Blue Ribbon Medal 1956; Commdr., Order of Orange-Nassau (Netherlands) 1958, Rising Sun 1965, Commdr. Ordre de la Couronne (Belgium) 1972, Panglima Mangku Negara and Tan Sri from King of Malaysia 1979, First Class Order of the Rising Sun (Japan) 1981; Hon. LL.D. (Waseda, Keio and Doshisha Univs.). *Publications:* What I Do, and What I Think, The Dream of My Work and the Dream of Our Life, The Words of Peace and Happiness through Prosperity, My View Towards Prosperity, My Thoughts on Man,

Looking Back on the Past and Forward to Tomorrow, Reflections on Business, Reflections on Management, A Way to Look at and Think about Things, Why?, Japan at the Brink, A Plan to Give Japan More Space, 21st Century Japan. *Leisure interest:* performance of tea ceremony. [*Died 27 April 1989.*]

MATSUSHITA, Masaharu, B.IUR.; Japanese businessman; b. 17 Sept. 1912, Tokyo; s. of Eiji Matsushita and Shizuko Hirata; m. Sachiko Matsushita; two s. one d.; ed. Tokyo Imperial Univ.; Mitsui Bank 1935-40; Matsushita Electric Industrial Co. Ltd. 1940-, Auditor 1944-47, Dir., mem. Bd., 1947-49, Exec. Vice-Pres. 1949-61, Pres. 1961-77, Chair. Bd. 1977-; Dir. Matsushita Electronics Corpn. 1952-72, 1985-, Chair. 1972-85; Auditor, Matsushita Real Estate Co. Ltd. 1952-68, Dir. 1968-; Dir. Matsushita Communication Industrial Co. Ltd. 1958-70, Chair. 1970-86; Dir. Matsushita Seiko Co. Ltd. 1956-87, Kyushu Matsushita Electric Co. Ltd. 1955-87, Matsushita Reiki Co. Ltd. (formerly Nakagawa Electric Inc.) 1961-87, Matsushita Electric Corpn. of America 1959-74 (Chair. 1974-); Pres. Electronics Industries Asscn. of Japan 1968-70; Rep. Dir., Kansai Cttee. for Econ. Devt. 1962-, Dir. 1975-; mem. Standing Cttee., Osaka Chamber of Commerce 1966-; Standing Dir., Kansai Econ. Fed. 1970-, Vice-Pres. 1977-; Blue Ribbon Medal 1972; Commdr. of Order of Orange-Nassau (Netherlands) 1975. *Address:* 2-23 Natsugi-cho, Nishinomiya, Hyogo Pref., Japan.

MATSUYAMA, Akira, B.ENG.; Japanese business executive; b. 24 Jan. 1912, Nagasaki Pref.; m.; one s. two d.; ed. Tokyo Univ.; Dir. East Japan Oil Devt. Co. Ltd. 1972-, Cen. Kagaku K.K. 1974-, Arctic Oil Co. Ltd. 1981-; Chair. Tonen Petrochemical Co. Ltd. 1975-, Nippon Unicar Co. Ltd. 1980-; Pres. Toa Nenryo Kogyo K.K. 1976-86, Chair. 1986-, Tonen Tanker K.K. 1978-. *Leisure interest:* golf. *Address:* c/o Toa Nenryo Kogyo K.K., 1-1, Hitotsubashi 1-chome, Chiyoda-ku, Tokyo 100, Japan. *Telephone:* 03 286-5001.

MATSUZAWA, Takuji; Japanese banker; b. 17 July 1913, Tokyo; s. of Takanori and Tameko Matsuzawa; m. Toshiko Yoshioka 1942; one s. one d.; ed. Tokyo Imperial Univ.; joined The Yasuda Bank Ltd. 1938 (name changed to The Fuji Bank Ltd. 1948), Chief Man. Planning and Co-ordination Div. 1959-61, Dir. and Chief Man. Planning and Co-ordination Div. 1961-63, Man. Dir. 1963-71, Deputy Pres. 1971-75, Chair. of Bd. 1975-, Pres. The Fuji Bank Ltd. 1975-81, Chair. 1981-87; Chair. of Research and Policy Cttee., Japan Cttee. for Econ. Devt. (Keizai Doyukai) 1973-75; Exec. mem. Bd. Japan Fed. of Econ. Orgs. (Keidanren) 1975-, Chair. Cttee. on Fiscal and Monetary Policies 1980-86; mem. Japanese Govt. Econ. Council Cttee. 1977-; Pres. Fed. of Bankers Assens. 1978-79; Chair. Inquiry and Audit Bd. Japanese Nat. Railways 1983-, Cttee. on Admin. Reform 1986-, Cttee. on Int. Coordination of Econ. Policies 1986-; Vice-Chair. Japan Federation of Econ. Orgs. 1986-; Order of Sacred Treasure (First Class) 1983. *Leisure interests:* playing golf, reading, theatre-going. *Address:* 8-7, 2-chome Shoto, Shibuya-ku, Tokyo, Japan (Home).

MATTAR, Dr. Ahmad, PH.D., M.A.; Singapore politician and scientist; b. 13 Aug. 1939, Singapore; ed. Geylang English School, Raffles Inst., Univ. of Singapore, Univ. of Sheffield; Asst. Lecturer for Math. and Science Div., Singapore Polytechnic 1964-69, Lecturer 1969; Lecturer in Applied Acoustics Dept. of Building Science, Univ. of Singapore (now Nat. Univ. of Singapore) 1971, now Sr. Lecturer; M.P. for Leng Kee and Parl. Sec. to Minister for Educ. 1972-76, M.P. for Brickworks 1976-80, 1980-84, 1984-88, 1988-; Minister of State for Social Affairs, and Acting Minister for Social Affairs 1977-80, Sr. Minister of State for Social Affairs and Acting Minister for Social Affairs 1981-84, Minister June 1984-; Minister for Environment 1985-88, Sept. 1988-; Minister-in-charge of Muslim Affairs; mem. World Supreme Council for Mosques, Saudi Arabia; Pres. Council on Education of Muslim Children. *Publications:* Engineering Science (2 vols.), Environmental Factors in the Design of Building Fenestrations (Co-author). *Address:* Ministry of the Environment, Environment Building, 40 Scotts Road, Singapore 0923. *Telephone:* 7319764.

MATTEOLI, Jean, LIC. EN DROIT; French business executive; b. 20 Dec. 1922, Montchanin; s. of Joseph and Jeanne Pernot Matteoli; m. Christiane Gibassier 1946; four s. two d.; Asst. with Special Functions to Cabinet of Commr. of the Repub. of Bourgogne-Franche Comté 1945-46, to Cabinet of Administrator of French Occupied Zone in Germany 1946-48, to Collieries of Nord and Pas-de-Calais 1948-68; Dir. External Relations, Sec. of Exec. Council 1957-68; Commr. for the Industrialisation of Nord Pas-de-Calais 1968-72; Pres. Dept. Bureau for Industrialization of Ardennes 1970-72; Pres. Dir.-Gen. SICCA (Soc. Industrielle et Commerciale des Charbonnages) 1972-79; Pres. Exec. Council Charbonnages de France 1973-79; Vice-Pres. Supervisor Council CDF CHIMIE (Soc. Chimique des Charbonnages) 1976-79; Pres. Dir. Gen. Soc. d'Aménagement et d'Equipement, Corsica 1977-79; Minister of Labour and Participation 1979-81; Industrial Advisor 1981-; Deputy Mayor of Paris and Distinguished Councillor, Ile-de France 1983; Pres., Comité nat. de l'organisation française 1984-; mem. Bd. Radiotechnique 1984-; Pres. Dir.-Gen. Soc. de Tréfileries d'Alsace 1985-; mem. of Bd., Grindlays Bank 1986-, Banque Scalbert Dupont 1986-; Pres. Conseil Econ. et Social 1987-; Croix de guerre, Médaille de la Résistance, Commdr. Légion d'honneur. *Leisure interest:*

painting. *Address:* 11 rue Magellan, 75008 Paris, France (Home). *Telephone:* 47.23.42.07 (Office).

MATTEOTTI, Gianmatteo; Italian journalist and politician; b. 17 Feb. 1921, Rome; s. of Giacomo and Titta Velia Matteotti; m. Giuliana Candiani 1954; two d.; ed. Ginnasio-Liceo "Terenzio Mamiani", Rome, and Univ. of Rome; Sec., Fed of Socialist Youth 1944-46; Deputy to Constituent Ass. 1946-48; Deputy to Parl. 1948-68; Nat. Sec. Partito Socialista Democratico Italiano 1954-57, mem. Directorate 1963-66, mem. Secr. 1970-; Minister of Tourism and Culture 1970-72; Minister of Foreign Trade 1972-74. *Publications:* La classe operaia sotto il fascimo 1944. *Leisure interests:* archaeology, music, numismatics. *Address:* Via Luciani 1945, 00197 Rome, Italy. *Telephone:* 804478.

MATTHAU, Walter; American actor; b. 1 Oct. 1920, New York; s. of Milton and Rose Matthau; m. Carol Marcus 1959; two s. one d.; ed. New York; New York Drama Critics Award 1951, 1958; Antoinette Perry Award 1961, 1964; Acad. Award for The Fortune Cookie; British Soc. of Film and TV Arts Award for Pete 'n' Tillie and Charlie Varrick. *Stage appearances in:* Anne of a Thousand Days 1948, The Liar 1949, Season in the Sun 1950, Fancy Meeting You Again 1951, Twilight Walk 1951, One Bright Day 1951, In Any Language 1952, The Grey-Eyed People 1952, The Ladies of the Corridor 1953, Will Success Spoil Rock Hunter 1955, Once More with Feeling 1958, Once There Was a Russian 1960, A Shot in the Dark 1961, My Mother, My Father and Me 1963, The Odd Couple 1964. *Films include:* The Kentuckian 1955, Bigger than Life 1956, A Face in the Crowd 1957, Slaughter on Tenth Avenue 1957, Ride a Crooked Trail 1958, Lonely are the Brave 1962, Charade 1963, Fail Safe 1964, Mirage 1965, The Fortune Cookie (British title Meet Whiplash Willie) 1966, A Guide for the Married Man 1967, The Odd Couple 1968, The Secret Life of an American Wife 1968, Candy 1968, Hello Dolly 1969, Cactus Flower 1969, A New Leaf 1971, Plaza Suite 1971, Kotch 1971, Pete 'n' Tillie 1972, Charley Varrick 1973, The Laughing Policeman 1973, Earthquake 1974, The Taking of Pelham One Two Three 1974, The Front Page 1975, The Sunshine Boys 1975, The Bad News Bears 1976, Casey's Shadow 1978, House Calls 1978, California Suite 1979, Hopscotch 1980, Little Miss Marker 1980, First Monday in October 1980, Buddy Buddy 1981, I Ought to be in Pictures 1981, Movers and Shakers 1984, Pirates 1986, The Couch Trip 1987. *Address:* 10100 Santa Monica Boulevard, Los Angeles, Calif. 90067.

MATTHEI AUBEL, Gen. Fernando; Chilean air force officer and politician; b. 11 June 1925, Osorno; m. Elda Fornet Fernández 1951; three s. two d.; ed. German Colls., Osorno and Santiago, Air Force School; Second Lieut. 1948, Lieut. 1951, Capt. 1954, Squadron Commdr. 1960, Adjutant to C.-in-C. Air Div. and mem. Personal Staff 1961, attended course at Maxwell Squadron Officer School, U.S.A. 1965, Group-Commdr. 1966, Sub-Dir. Air Force Acad. 1967, No. 7 Air Force Group Commdr. 1968, Air Force Attaché, Chilean Embassies in U.K. and Sweden, resident London 1971, Air Force Col. 1972, Head of Mission in London 1972, Dir. Air Force Acad. 1974, Dir. of Operations, Gen. Staff of Air Force 1974, Air Force Brig.-Gen. 1975, Minister of Public Health 1976-78, C.-in-C. Air Force and mem. Mil. Junta 1978-; numerous mil. decorations. *Address:* Oficina del Presidente, Santiago, Chile.

MATTHEWS, Baron (Life Peer) cr. 1980, of Southgate in the London borough of Enfield; **Victor Collin Matthews;** British company executive; b. 5 Dec. 1919, London; s. of A. Matthews and Mrs. J. Matthews; m. Joyce Geraldine Pilbeam 1942; one s.; ed. London; Chair., Trafalgar House Devt. Holdings Ltd. 1970-83, The Cunard Steam-Ship Co. PLC 1971-83, Eastern Int. Investment Trust Ltd. 1974-, Trafalgar Offshore Ltd. 1975-, The Ritz Hotel (London) Ltd. 1976-83, Trafalgar House Construction Holdings Ltd. 1977-83, Cunard Line Ltd. 1978-83, Cunard Cruise Ships Ltd. 1978-83, Fleet Publishing Int. Holdings Ltd. 1978-85, Fleet Holdings PLC 1982-85, Evening Standard Co. Ltd. 1980-85; Chair. (Chief Exec. 1977-82) Express Newspapers PLC 1977-85; Vice-Chair., Export Group for the Constructional Industries 1977-79, Pres. 1979-; Dir. Paternoster Devt. Ltd. 1969-, Assoc. Container Transportation (Australia) Ltd. 1972-83, Cunard Crusader World Travel Ltd. 1974-, Associated Communications Corpn. Ltd. 1977-82, Racecourse Holdings Trust Ltd. 1977-, Goldquill Ltd. 1977-83, Darchart Ltd. 1980-83, Garmaine Ltd. 1980-83, TV-am 1984-; Group Man. Dir. Trafalgar House Ltd. 1968-77, Deputy Chair. Trafalgar House PLC 1973-85, Group Chief Exec. 1977-83; Fellow, British Inst. of Man. 1978-. *Leisure interests:* horse-racing (owner and breeder), golf, cricket. *Address:* Waverley Farm, Mont Arthur, St. Brelades, Jersey, Channel Islands.

MATTHEWS, Drummond Hoyle, PH.D., F.R.S.; British marine geophysicist; b. 5 Feb. 1931, London; s. of Charles Bertram Matthews and Enid Mary Hoyle; m. Rachel E. McMullen 1963 (divorced 1981); one s. one d.; ed. Bryanston School, King's Coll., Cambridge; Geologist with British Antarctic Survey 1955-57; Research Fellow, King's Coll., Cambridge 1960-66; Sr. Asst. in Research, Dept. of Geophysics, Cambridge 1966-71, Asst. Dir. of Research, Reader in Marine Geology 1971-82, Sr. Research Assoc. 1982-; Dir. British Inst. Reflection Profiling Syndicate (BIRPS) 1982-; Int. Balzan Prize 1982, Hughes Medal 1982, Fellow of the American Geophysical Union 1982. *Publications:* some 80 scientific articles. *Leisure interests:* walking, sailing. *Address:* BIRPS, Bullard Laboratories, Madingley Rise, Madingley Road, Cambridge, CB3 OE2, England (Office).

MATTHEWS, Horatio Keith, C.M.G., M.B.E.; retd. British diplomatist; b. 4 April 1917; s. of the late Horatio and Ruth (née McCurry) Matthews; m. Jean Andrée Batten 1940; two d.; ed. Epsom Coll. and Gonville and Caius Coll., Cambridge; served in ICS in Madras Presidency 1940-47; joined foreign service 1948; First Sec., Lisbon 1949-51, Bucharest 1953-54; Imperial Defence Coll. 1955; Political Officer with Middle East Forces, Cyprus 1956-59; Counsellor, Canberra 1959-61; Political Adviser to Gen. Officer Commanding, Berlin 1961-64; Insp. Foreign Office 1964, Diplomatic Service 1965; Minister, Moscow 1966-67; High Commr. to Ghana 1968-70; Under-Sec.-Gen. for Admin. and Management, UN Secr. 1970-72; Asst. Under-Sec. of State, Ministry of Defence 1973-74; J.P., Isle of Wight 1975-. *Address:* Elm House, Bembridge, Isle of Wight, PO35 5UA, England. *Telephone:* Bembridge 872327.

MATTHEWS, Sir Peter Alec, Kt., A.O.; British business executive; b. 21 Sept. 1922, Duncan, Vancouver Island, B.C., Canada; s. of Major Alec B. Matthews and Elsie Lazarus Barlow; m. Sheila D. Bunting 1946; four s. one d., ed. Shawnigan Lake School, Vancouver Island, and Oundle School; army service 1940-46; joined Stewarts and Lloyds Ltd. 1946, Dir. of Research and Tech. Devt. 1962-68, mem. Research and Devt., British Steel Corpn. 1968-70; Man. Dir. Vickers PLC 1970-79, Chair. 1980-84; Dir. British Aircraft Corpn. (Holdings) 1971-77; Vice-Pres. Eng. Employers' Fed. 1971-82, Pres. 1982-84; Council mem. CBI 1971-77; Deputy Chair. British Steel Corpn. 1973-76; mem. British Overseas Trade Bd. 1973-77; mem. Export Credits Advisory Council 1973-77; Dir. Lloyds Bank PLC 1974-, Chair. Cen. London Regional Bd. 1978-; mem. Nat. Research Devt. Corpn. 1974-80; Dir. British Electric Traction Co. PLC 1976-87; mem. Advisory Council on Applied Research and Devt. 1977-80; Dir. Pegler-Hattersley PLC 1977-87 (Chair. 1979-86); Dir. Lloyds Bank U.K. Man. 1979-, Lloyds and Scottish 1983-, Sun Alliance and London Insurance PLC 1979-, Lead Industries Group 1980- (renamed Cookson Group 1982), Hamilton Oil G.B., PLC 1981-; Pres. Sino-British Trade Council 1983-86; Chair. Univ. Coll. London Council; Chair. Export Credits Guarantee Dept. Review Cttee. 1983; Hon. Fellow Univ. Coll. London 1982; companion, British Inst. of Management. *Leisure interests:* sailing, gardening. *Address:* Ladycross House, Dormansland, Surrey, RH7 6NP, England.

MATTHEWS, Peter Bryan Conrad, M.D., D.SC., F.R.S.; British professor in physiology; b. 23 Dec. 1928, Cambridge; s. of the late Sir Bryan Matthews; m. Margaret Rosemary Blears 1956; one s. one d.; ed. Marlborough Coll., King's Coll. Cambridge and Oxford Univ. Clinical School; Lecturer in Physiology Univ. of Oxford 1961-77, Reader 1978-87, Prof. of Sensorimotor Physiology 1987-; Tutor of Christ Church, Univ. of Oxford 1958-87, Student 1958-; Sir Lionel Whitby Medal, Cambridge Univ. 1959; Robert Bing Prize, Swiss Acad. of Medical Science 1971. *Publications:* Mammalian Muscle Receptors and their Central Actions 1972 and papers on neurophysiology in various scientific journals. *Address:* University Laboratory of Physiology, Parks Road, Oxford, OX1 3PT, England. *Telephone:* Oxford 272500.

MATTHEWS, Peter Hugoe, LITT.D., F.B.A.; British academic; b. 10 March 1934, Oswestry; s. of John Hugo Matthews and Cecily Eileen Elmsley Hagarty; m. Lucienne Marie Jeanne Schleich 1984; one step-s. one step-d.; ed. Montpellier School, Paignton, Clifton Coll., St. John's Coll., Cambridge; lecturer, Univ. Coll. of N. Wales, Bangor 1960-65, at Ind. Univ., Bloomington 1963-64; Lecturer, Reader and Prof., Univ. of Reading 1965-80; Visiting Prof. Deccan Coll., Poona 1969-70; Sr. Research Fellow King's Coll., Cambridge 1970-71; Fellow, Nias Wassenaar, Holland 1977-78; Prof. and Head of Dept. of Linguistics, Univ. of Cambridge, and Fellow of St. John's Coll. 1980-, Praelector 1987-. *Publications:* Inflectional Morphology 1972, Morphology 1974, Generative Grammar and Linguistic Competence 1979, Syntax 1981. *Leisure interests:* cycling, bird watching. *Address:* St. John's College, Cambridge, CB2 1TP (Office); 10, Fendon Close, Cambridge, CB1 4RU, England (Home); 112 ave. Victor Hugo, Luxembourg. *Telephone:* (0223) 335010 (Office); (0223) 247553 (Home).

MATTHEWS, Richard Ellis Ford, PH.D., F.R.S.N.Z., F.R.S.; New Zealand biologist; b. 20 Nov. 1921, Hamilton, N.Z.; s. of Gerald W. Matthews and Ruby M. Matthews; m. Lois A. Bayley 1950; three s. one d.; ed. Mount Albert Grammar School, Auckland Univ. Coll. and Univ. of Cambridge; N.Z. Army (Artillery) 1941-45; Sr. Mycologist, Dept. of Scientific and Industrial Research, Auckland 1949-54, Sr. Prin. Scientific Officer 1954-61; Prof. of Microbiology, Univ. of Auckland 1962-87; Fellow, N.Z. Inst. of Chem.; Sc.D. (Cambridge) 1964; Order of N.Z. *Publications:* Plant Virus Serology 1957, Plant Virology 1970, 1981. *Leisure interests:* gardening, bee-keeping, sea-fishing. *Address:* Department of Cellular and Molecular Biology, University of Auckland, Private Bag, Auckland 1; 1019 Beach Road, Torbay, Auckland 10, New Zealand (Home). *Telephone:* 737999 (Office); 4037709 (Home).

MATTHEWS, Robert Charles Oliver, C.B.E., M.A., F.B.A.; British economist; b. 16 June 1927, Edinburgh; s. of Oliver Harwood Matthews and Ida Finlay; m. Joyce Lloyds 1948; one d.; ed. Edinburgh Acad. and Corpus Christi and Nuffield Colls., Oxford; Asst. Univ. Lecturer, then Lecturer, Cambridge 1949-65; Drummond Prof. of Political Economy 1965-75, All Souls Coll., Oxford; Master of Clare Coll., Cambridge 1975-; Prof. of Political Economy, Cambridge 1980-; Chair. Social Science Research Council 1972-75; Fellow, St. John's Coll., Cambridge 1950-65, All Souls Coll.,

Oxford 1965-75; Hon. Fellow, Corpus Christi Coll., Oxford; Hon. D.Litt. (Warwick Univ.) 1981. *Publications:* A Study in Trade Cycle History 1954, The Trade Cycle 1958, Economic Growth: A Survey (with F. H. Hahn) 1964, Economic Growth: Trends and Factors (ed.) 1981, British Economic Growth 1856-1973 (with C. H. Feinstein and J. Odling-Smee) 1982, Slower Growth in the Western World (ed.) 1982, Contemporary Problems of Economic Policy (ed., with J. R. Sargent) 1983 and articles in learned journals. *Leisure interest:* chess problems. *Address:* Master's Lodge, Clare College, Cambridge, CB2 1TL, England. *Telephone:* (0223) 333200.

MATTHIESSEN, Peter, B.A.; American writer; b. 22 May 1927, New York; s. of Erard A. Matthiessen and Elizabeth (née Carey) Matthiessen; m. 1st Patricia Southgate 1951 (divorced); m. 2nd Deborah Love 1963 (deceased); three s. one d.; m. 3rd Maria Eckhart 1980; ed. The Sorbonne, Paris, Yale Univ.; Trustee New York Zoological Soc. 1965-78; mem. Nat. Inst. of Arts and Letters. *Publications:* Race Rock 1954, Partisans 1955, Raditzer 1960, Wildlife in America 1959, The Cloud Forest 1961, Under the Mountain Wall 1963, At Play in the Fields of the Lord 1965, The Shore Birds of North America 1967, Oomingmak: The Expedition to the Musk Ox Island in the Bering Sea 1967, Sal si Puedes 1969, Blue Meridian 1971, The Tree Where Man Was Born 1972, The Wind Birds 1973, Far Tortuga 1975, The Snow Leopard 1978, Sand Rivers 1981, In the Spirit of the Crazy Horse 1983, Indian Country 1984, Midnight Turning Grey 1984, Nine-Headed Dragon River 1986, Men's Lives 1986, Partisans 1987.

MATTHIESSEN, Poul Christian, DR. POL.; Danish professor of demography; b. 1 Feb. 1933, Odense; s. of Jens P. E. Matthiessen and Laura C. Nielsen; m. Ulla Bay 1986; two d.; research asst. Copenhagen Telephone Co. 1958-63; lecturer in Statistics, Univ. of Copenhagen 1963-70, Prof. of Demography 1971-; mem. European Population Cttee., Nat. Advisory Bd. at WHO Collaborating Centre, Arhus; mem. Royal Danish Acad. *Publications:* Infant Mortality in Denmark 1931-60 1964, Growth of Population: Causes and Implications 1965, Demographic Methods (Vol. I-III) 1970, Some Aspects of the Demographic Transition in Denmark 1970, The Limitation of Family Size in Denmark (Vol. I-III) 1985. *Leisure interests:* literature, history, architecture. *Address:* Institute of Statistics, University of Copenhagen, Studiestraede 6, 1455 Copenhagen K (Office); Prs. Alexandrines Alle 4, 2920 Charlottenlund, Denmark (Home). *Telephone:* 45 1 91 21 66 Ext. 341 (Office); 45 1 64 09 48 (Home).

MATTHÖFER, Hans; German politician; b. 25 Sept. 1925, Bochum; m. Traute Mecklenburg 1951; ed. Univs. of Frankfurt/Main and Madison, Wis., U.S.A.; Mem. of Social Democratic Party (SPD) 1950-; mem. Econ. Dept. IG Metall 1953, Head of Educ. and Training Dept. 1961; mem. OECD Mission to Washington and Paris 1957-61; mem. Bundestag (Parl.) 1961-87; mem. Bundestag Cttees. for Econ., Econ. Co-operation, Law, Foreign Affairs; Parl. Sec. of State, Ministry of Econ. Co-operation 1972-74; mem. Exec. Cttee. SPD 1973-85, mem. Presidency and Treas. 1985-87; Minister for Research and Tech. 1974-78, of Finance 1978-82, of Posts and Telecommunications April-Oct. 1982; Chair. BG-AG Holding Co. Feb. 1987-; Chair. and C.E.O. Beteiligungs-gesellschaft für Gemeinwirtschaft AG, Frankfurt/Main 1987-; Vice-Pres. Latin America Parliamentarians' Group 1961, 1983; mem. hon. Presidium of German Section, Amnesty Int.; Pres. Deutsche Stiftung für Entwicklungsländer (Foundation for Overseas Devt.) 1971-73; Vice-Chair. Enquiry Comm. on Tech. Assessment of Bundestag 1984-86; Publisher of Vorwärts 1985-. *Publications:* Der Unterschied zwischen den Tariflöhnen und den Effektivverdiensten in der Metallindustrie der Bundesrepublik 1956, Technological Change in the Metal Industries 1961/62, Der Beitrag politischer Bildung zur Emanzipation der Arbeitnehmer—Materialien zur Frage des Bildungsurlaubs 1970, Streiks und streikähnliche Formen des Kampfes der Arbeitnehmer im Kapitalismus 1971, Für eine menschliche Zukunft—Sozialdemokratische Forschungs- und Technologiepolitik 1976, Humanisierung der Arbeit und Produktivität in der Industriegesellschaft 1977, 1978, 1980, numerous articles on trades unions, research, technology, development, politics, economics and finance. *Leisure interests:* chess, reading. *Address:* Schreyerstrasse 38, 6242 Kronberg/Taunus, Federal Republic of Germany. *Telephone:* 79334.

MATTHUS, Siegfried; German composer; b. 13 April 1934, Mallenuppen, E. Prussia; s. of late Franz Matthus and of Luise Perrey; m. Helga Spitzer 1958; one s.; ed. Hochschule für Musik, Berlin, Acad. of Arts and Music, Berlin (masterclass with Hanns Eisler); composer and consultant, Komische Oper, Berlin 1964-; mem. Acad. of Arts of G.D.R., Acad. of Arts of W. Berlin, Acad. of Arts, Munich; Nat. Prize 1972, 1984. *Compositions include:* seven operas, one oratorio, concertos, orchestral and chamber music etc. *Leisure interests:* swimming, jogging, carpentry. *Address:* Elisabeth Weg 10, 1100 Berlin; Seepromenade 15, 1291 Stolzenhagen, German Democratic Republic. *Telephone:* 482-7362 (Berlin).

MATTINGLY, Mack Francis; American business executive and fmr. politician; b. 7 Jan. 1931, Anderson, Ind.; s. of Joseph Hilbert and Beatrice Wayts Mattingly; m. Carolyn Longcamp 1957; two d.; ed. Indiana Univ.; served U.S.A.F. 1951-55; Production Scheduler, Arvin Industries, Columbus, Ind. 1957-59; Man. IBM Corpn. 1959-; del. to Republican Nat. Convention 1964, 1976; Republican cand. for U.S. House of Reps. 1966; mem. Exec. Cttee. Ga. Republican Party 1966-, Vice-Chair. 1972-75, Chair.

1975–77; Republican U.S. Senator from Georgia 1981–87; Asst. Sec.-Gen. for Defence Support, NATO, Brussels 1987–, Chair. Conf. of Nat. Armaments Dirs.; fmrly. mem. Exec. Cttee. Republican Nat. Cttee.; mem. American Legion, Glynco Steering Cttee.; Good Conduct Medal, American Theater Medal. *Publications:* articles and speeches on NATO's conventional arms needs, in Wall Street Journal and other publs. *Address:* 23 avenue du Manoir, 1180 Brussels, Belgium; 4315 10th Street, East Beach, St. Simons Island, Ga. 31522, U.S.A. (Home).

MATUTE AUSEJO, Ana María; Spanish writer; b. 26 July 1925, Barcelona; d. of Facundo Matute and Mary Ausejo; m. 1952 (dissolved 1963); one s.; ed. "Damas Negras" French Nuns Coll.; collaborated on literary magazine Destino; Visiting lecturer, Indiana Univ. 1965–66, Oklahoma Univ. 1969–; Writer-in-Residence, Univ. of Virginia 1978–79; mem. Hispanic Soc. of America; "Highly Commended Author", Hans Christian Andersen Jury, Lisbon 1972. *Publications:* Los Abel 1947, Fiesta Al Noroeste (Café Gijon Prize) 1952, Pequeño Teatro (Planeta Prize) 1954, Los niños tontos 1956, Los Hijos Muertos (Nat. Literary Prize and Critics Prize) 1959, Primera Memoria (Nadal Prize) 1959, Tres y un sueño 1961, Historias de la Artamila 1961, El Rio 1963, El Tiempo 1963, Los Soldados lloran de noche 1964 (Fastenrath Prize 1969), El Arrepentido y otras Narraciones 1967, Algunos Muchachos 1968, La Trampa 1969, La Torre Vigia 1971, Olvidado Rey Gudu 1974; *Children's books:* El Pais de la Pizarra 1956, Paulina 1961, El Sal Tamontes Verde 1961, Caballito Loco 1961, El Aprendiz 1961, Carnavalito 1961, El Polizon del "Ulises" (Lazarillo Prize) 1965. *Leisure interests:* painting, drawing, the cinema. *Address:* Provenza, 84-At. 3a, Barcelona 29, Spain. *Telephone:* 239-72-13.

MATUTES, Abel; Spanish international official; b. 31 Nov. 1941, Ibiza; s. of Antonio and Carmen Matutes; m. Nieves Praks; one s. three d.; ed. studies in law and economics; fmr. entrepreneur in tourism and property in island of Ibiza; EEC Commr. for Credits and Investments, Small and Medium Sized Enterprises and Financial Eng. 1986–89, for American Policy, Latin American Relations Jan. 1989–; Nat. Vice-Pres. political party Alianza Popular. *Leisure interests:* tennis, sailing. *Address:* 200 rue de la Loi, 1049 Brussels, Belgium.

MATVEYEV, Aleksey Nikolayevich; Soviet scientist; b. 22 March 1922, Moscow; s. of Nikolay Matveyev and Nadyezhda Metlova; m. E. Zamchalova 1951; two d.; ed. Moscow State Univ.; Sr. Scientific Worker, Moscow State Univ. 1954–60, Prof. of Theoretical Physics 1960–64, Head of Chair of Gen. Physics 1969–; Head of Dept. of Univs., Ministry of Higher Educ., R.S.F.S.R. 1960–62; Asst. Dir.-Gen. for Science, UNESCO 1964–69; Order of Red Banner (twice), Order of the Patriotic War, Order of Alexander Nevsky, Order of Red Banner of Labour (twice), Order of Honour. *Publications:* Electrodynamics and Theory of Relativity 1964, Quantum Mechanics and Structure of Atoms 1965, Mechanics 1976, Electrodynamics 1980, Molecular Physics 1981.

MATVEYEVA, Novella Nikolaevna; Soviet poet and chansonnier; b. 7 Oct. 1934, Pushkin, nr. Leningrad; d. of Nikolai Nikolaevitch Matveyer-Bodryi and Nadejda Timofeevna Matveyeva (Orleneva); m. Ivan Semjonovitch Kiuru 1963. *Publications:* Lirika 1961, Little Ship 1963, Selected Lyrics 1964, The Soul of Things 1966, Reflection of a Sunbeam 1966, School for Swallows 1973, River 1978, The Song's Law 1983, The Land of the Surf 1983, Selected Works 1986, Praising the Labour 1987, An Indissoluble Circle 1988, Poems 1988; (play) The Foretelling of an Eagle (in Theatre magazine) 1988. *Recordings:* A Gipsy Girl 1966, What a Strong Wind! 1966, Poems and Songs 1973; (with Ivan Kiuru) The Music of Light 1984, My Small Raven 1985, Ballads 1985, A Red-haired Girl 1986. *Leisure interests:* listening to the radio (plays, classical music), reading. *Address:* Art Theatre, 2-42, 103009 Moscow, U.S.S.R. *Telephone:* 292-33-61.

MAUDE OF STRATFORD-UPON-AVON, Baron (Life Peer) cr. 1983 of Stratford-upon-Avon in the County of Warwickshire; **Angus Edmund Upton Maude,** Kt., T.D., M.A.; British politician and author; b. 8 Sept. 1912, London; s. of Col. Alan H. and Dorothy M. Maude; m. Barbara E. E. Sutcliffe; two s. two d.; ed. Rugby School and Oriel Coll., Oxford; financial journalist 1933–39; war service (prisoner of war 3½ years) 1939–45; Deputy Dir. Political and Econ. Planning 1949–50; Conservative M.P. 1950–58, 1963–83; Paymaster Gen. 1979–80; Dir. Conservative Political Centre 1951–55; Ed. The Sydney Morning Herald 1958–61; Deputy Chair. Conservative Party 1975–79; Chair. Conservative Party Research Dept. 1975–79. *Publications:* The English Middle Classes (with Roy Lewis) 1949, Professional People (with Roy Lewis) 1952, Biography of a Nation (with Enoch Powell, q.v.) 1956, and editor of One Nation 1950 and Change is our Ally 1954 (booklets on social policy by nine M.P.s), Good Learning 1964, South Asia 1966, The Common Problem 1969. *Address:* Old Farm, South Newington, nr. Banbury, Oxon., England. *Telephone:* 01-219 4467 (Office).

MAULDE, Bruno Guy André Jean de, L. EN D.; French banker; b. 27 March 1934, Toulouse; s. of Guy de Maulde and Suzanne Mazars; m. Dominique Le Henaff 1958; three d.; ed. Inst. of Political Studies, Toulouse, Nat. Coll. of Admin.; Insp. des Finances 1962–; Adviser, External Econ. Relations Dept., Finance Ministry 1967–68; Alt. Exec. Dir. IMF for France 1968–70; Financial attaché, Embassy, U.S.A. 1968–70, in New York 1970–71; French Treasury Adviser 1971–74, Asst. Dir. 1974–77, Deputy Dir.

1977–78; Deputy Man. Dir. Caisse Nat. de Crédit Agricole 1979–81; Financial Minister, Embassy of France, and Exec. Dir. IMF and IBRD, Washington 1981–85; Chair. and C.E.O. Crédit du Nord 1986–; Dir of various corpns. and public insts.; Chevalier, Légion d'honneur, l'Ordre nat. du Mérite, Croix de la Valeur Militaire, Officier du Mérite Agricole. *Leisure interest:* yachting. *Address:* Crédit du Nord, 6 et 8 boulevard Haussmann, 75009 Paris (Office); 4 rue Michelet, 75006 Paris, France (Home).

MAULNIER, Thierry (pseudonym of Jacques Louis André Talagrand); French writer; b. 1 Oct. 1909, Alès; s. of Joseph Talagrand and Virginie Gibrac; m. Marcelle Tassencourt 1941; m. Lycée Louis-le-Grand, Paris and Ecole Normale Supérieure; journalist on l'Action française, later Figaro 1930–; playwright 1942–; dramatic critic Combat and La revue de Paris; founded (with François Mauriac) La table ronde; mem. Acad. Française 1964–, Cttee. for TV programmes O.R.T.F. 1965–74; Pres. Asscn. France-Etats-Unis 1967–; Grand Prix de Litterature de l'Acad. Française 1959, Prix Pelman de la presse 1959, Grand Prix André Arnoux 1973; Commdr., Légion d'honneur. *Plays:* Antigone 1944, La course des rois 1947, Jeanne et les juges 1949, Le profanateur 1952, Oedipe-Roi (adaptation) 1952, La maison de la nuit 1953, La condition humaine (adaptation) 1954, Procès à Jésus (adaptation) 1958, Le sexe et le néant 1960, Signe du feu (adaptation) 1960; Dir. la Thébaïde, Paris 1964, Le soir du conquérant, Paris 1970, L'etrangeté d'être 1982, Le monde a pris le large à partir de Paris (with G. Prouteau) 1983, Le dieu masqué 1985. *Prose works include:* La crise est dans l'homme 1932, Nietzsche 1933, Racine 1934, Introduction à la poésie française 1939, Violence et conscience 1945, La face de méduse du communisme 1952, Cette Grèce où nous sommes nés 1965, La défaite d'Hannibal, La ville au fond de la mer 1967, Lettre aux Américains 1968, L'honneur d'être juif 1970 (with G. Prouteau), Le sens des mots 1976, Les vaches sacrées. *Address:* 3 rue Yves-Carriou, 92430 Marnes-la-Coquette, France.

MAUMENEE, Alfred Edward, M.D.; American professor of ophthalmology; b. 19 Sept. 1913, Mobile, Ala.; s. of Alfred Edward Maumenee and Lulie Radcliff; m. 1st Anne Elizabeth Gunnis 1949, one s. one d.; m. 2nd Irene Hussels 1972, two s.; ed. Philips High School, Birmingham, Alabama Univ. and Medical School, Cornell Univ. School of Medicine; served to Lieut. in U.S. Navy 1944–46; Intern and Asst. Resident in Ophthalmology Johns Hopkins Hosp. 1939–42, Chief Resident 1942–43; Assoc. Prof. of Ophthalmology, Johns Hopkins Univ. 1946–48; Prof. of Surgery in Ophthalmology, Stanford Univ. 1948–55; Prof. of Ophthalmology, Johns Hopkins Univ. 1955; Visiting Prof. to numerous univs. 1958–; Assoc. Ophthalmologist, Johns Hopkins Hosp. 1946–48; Clinical Staff, Mount Zion Hosp. and Children's Hosp., San Francisco 1949–55; Consultant in Ophthalmology, San Francisco Hosp. and Laguna Honda Hosp. 1948–55; Civilian Consultant, Letterman Army Hosp. and U.S. Naval Hosp., Oakland, Calif. 1948–55, Walter Reed Army Hosp., U.S. Naval Hosp., Bethesda, Md., Clinical Center, Nat. Insts. of Health 1955; Chair. Div. of Ophthalmology, Stanford Univ. Hosp. 1948–55; Dir. Wilmer Inst. Johns Hopkins Hosp. 1955–59; Consultant, Baltimore City Hospitals 1959–; Civilian Consultant to Surgeon-Gen., U.S. Navy for Postgraduate Medical Training 1963–; Consultant, U.S. Public Health Service Hosp., Wyman Park 1965–, N.A.S. 1974–; mem. and hon. mem. numerous medical socs.; Pres. American Acad. of Ophthalmology and Otolaryngology 1971; Vice-Pres. Int. Council of Ophthalmology 1977; mem. Bd. of Dirs. Pan-American Ophthalmological Foundation 1967– (Chair. 1974); mem. Editorial Staff, American Journal of Ophthalmology 1955–, Pres. Bd. Dirs. 1975–; Assoc. Ed. A.M.A. Archives of Ophthalmology 1952–54, Highlights of Ophthalmology 1954, Investigative Ophthalmology 1963–74; Corresp. Ed., Transplantation Bulletin 1953–57; mem. Editorial Advisory Board, Audio-Digest Ophthalmology 1963–; William Holland Wilmer Prof. Emer. of Ophthalmology, Dir. Emer. Dept. Ophthalmology, Johns Hopkins Univ. 1979–; Hon. Sc.D. (Illinois) 1974; Hon. F.R.C.S. (Edinburgh) 1971; numerous awards including The Howe Medal, American Ophthalmology Soc. 1969, Francis I. Proctor Research Medal 1972, John M. McLean Gold Medal Award 1976, Distinguished Service Award, U.S. Navy Dept. 1977, Gradle Medal for Teaching (Pan-American Asscn. Ophthalmology) 1979, Krieger Prize on Ophthalmology (Sinai Hosp. of Baltimore) 1979, Gonin Medal, Lausanne Univ. 1982. *Publications:* Co-Author: Ophthalmic Pathology. An Atlas and Textbook 1952, Atlas of Strabismus 1967, Second Edn. 1973; Ed.: First and Second Symposia on Uveitis, Council for Research in Glaucoma and Allied Diseases 1959, 1961; Co-Editor: Progress in Ophthalmology and Otolaryngology 1952, Immunopathology of Uveitis 1964; 221 scientific articles. *Leisure interests:* golf, tennis, fishing. *Address:* 601 N. Broadway, Baltimore, Md. 21205 (Office); 1700 Hillside Road, Stevenson, Md. 21153, U.S.A. (Home).

MAUNG MAUNG GYEE, U, B.A.; Burmese diplomatist; b. 15 Feb. 1921; m.; four c.; ed. Univ. of Rangoon; officer, Burma Defence Army in the Burmese independence movt.; Ministry of Foreign Affairs 1948; served in embassies in Paris, Washington, D.C., Tokyo, Peking, Rome and Kathmandu as Third, Second and First Sec. and Counsellor; Dir.-Gen. Int. Orgs. and Econ. Dept., Ministry of Foreign Affairs; Perm. Rep. of Burma to UN 1977–81, 1985–; fmr. Amb. to Sri Lanka. *Address:* Permanent Mission of Burma to the United Nations, 10 East 77th Street, New York, N.Y. 10021, U.S.A.

MAUNG MAUNG KHA, U; Burmese politician; mem. Cen. Exec. Cttee. Burma Socialist Programme Party (BSPP); Minister for Industry and

Labour 1973–74, for Industry 1974–75, for Mines 1975–77, Prime Minister of Burma 1977–88; mem. State Council 1977–88. *Address:* c/o Office of the Prime Minister, Rangoon, Burma. *Telephone:* (01) 83742.

MAURER, Ion Gheorghe, LL.D., D.JUR.; Romanian jurist and politician (retd.); b. 23 Sept. 1902, Bucharest; s. of Josef and Jeane Maurer; m. Elena Stanescu 1949; one s.; ed. Craiova Military School and Bucharest Univ.; joined Romanian Communist Party 1936; imprisoned in concentration camp for political activities; Under Sec. of State for Transport 1944–46, Ministry of Nat. Economy 1946–47; mem. Cen. Cttee. Romanian Workers' Party (now Romanian CP) 1945–74, Political Bureau of Cen. Cttee. 1960–65, Exec. Political Cttee. of Cen. Cttee. 1965–74, Perm. Presidium 1965–74; Deputy Minister of Industry and Trade 1948; Minister for Foreign Affairs 1957–58; mem. Grand Nat. Ass. 1948–75; Chair. Presidium Grand Nat. Ass. (Head of State) 1958–61; Chair. Council of Ministers 1961–74; mem. Defence Council of Romania 1969–74; mem. Romanian Acad. 1955–, Acad. of Social and Political Sciences 1970–; fmr. Dir. Inst. of Juridical Research 1954–58; Hero of Socialist Labour 1962, Order "Victoria Socialismului" 1971, Hero of Socialist Republic of Romania 1972, etc. *Address:* Bul. Aviatorilor 104, Bucharest, Romania. *Telephone:* 184069.

MAURER, H.E. Cardinal José (Josef) Clemente; German ecclesiastic; b. 13 March 1900, Püttlingen, Trier; ordained priest 1925; Titular Bishop of Cea 1950–51; fmr. Archbishop of Sucre, Bolivia; cr. Cardinal 1967; entitled Ss. Redentore e S. Alfonso in via Merulana. *Address:* Arzobispado, Casilla 205, Sucre, Bolivia. *Telephone:* 4109.

MAURIAC, Claude, D.IUR.; French writer; b. 25 April 1914; s. of late François Mauriac; m. Marie-Claude Mante 1951; two s. one d.; ed. Lycée Janson-de-Sailly; Sec. to Gen. de Gaulle 1944–49; Film Critic Figaro Littéraire; weekly literary column "La Vie des Lettres" in Le Figaro; Contrib. to L'Express 1972, Le Monde 1978, Le Matin 1986–; Admin. Soc. Figaro-Edition 1972–; Prix Sainte-Beuve for André Breton 1949, Prix Médicis for Le dîner en ville 1959. *Publications non-fiction:* Conversations avec André Gide 1951, Une amitié contrariée 1970, Une certaine rage 1977, L'éternité parfois 1978, Laurent Terzieff 1980, Qui peut le dire? 1985; *Essais include:* Aimer Balzac 1945, Malraux ou le mal du héros 1946, André Breton 1949, Marcel Proust par lui-même 1953, Hommes et idées d'aujourd'hui 1953, La littérature contemporaine 1958, Un autre de Gaulle 1944–54 1971; *Novels:* Toutes les femmes sont fatales 1957, Le dîner en ville 1959, La marquise sortit à cinq heures 1961, L'agrandissement 1963, L'oubli 1966, Le Bouddha s'est mis à trembler 1979, Un coeur tout neuf 1980, Radio Nuit 1982, Zabé 1984; *Plays:* La conversation 1964, Théâtre 1968; *Memoirs:* Le temps immobile, vol. I 1974, Les espaces imaginaires, vol. II 1975, Et comme l'espérance est violente, vol. III 1976, La terrasse de Malagar, vol. IV 1977, Aimer de Gaulle, vol. V 1978, Le rire des pères dans les yeux des enfants, vol. VI 1981, Signes, rencontre et rendezvous, vol. VII 1983, Bergère ô tour Eiffel, vol. VIII 1985, Mauriac et fils, vol. IX 1986, Qui peut le dire? 1985, François Mauriac: sa vie, son œuvre 1985. *Address:* 24 quai de Béthune, 75004 Paris, France.

MAUROY, Pierre; French politician; b. 5 July 1928, Cartignies; s. of Henri Mauroy and Adrienne Bronne; m. Gilberte Deboudt 1951; one s.; ed. Lycée de Cambrai, Ecole normale nationale d'apprentissage, Cachan; Nat. Sec. Jeunesses socialistes 1950–58; Tech. Teacher, Colombes 1952; Sec.-Gen. Syndicat des collèges d'enseignement tech. section, Féd. de l'Educ. Nationale 1955–59; Fed. Sec. for the North, Section Française de l'Internationale Ouvrière 1961, mem. Political Bureau 1963, Deputy Sec.-Gen. 1966; mem. Exec. Cttee., Féd. de la gauche démocratique et socialiste 1965–68; Gen. Councillor, Cateau 1967–73; Vice-Pres. Gen. Council, Nord Département 1967–73; Municipal Councillor, Lille 1971, First Deputy Mayor 1971, Mayor 1973–; First Sec. and Nat. Co-ordinating Sec., Northern Fed., Parti Socialiste 1971–79; Deputy (Nord) to Nat. Ass. 1973–81, 1986–; Pres. Regional Council, Nord-Pas-de-Calais 1974; Pres. Nat. Fed. Léo Lagrange youth centres 1972–81, Hon. Pres. 1981–; mem. European Parl. 1979–81, Vice-Pres. Political Cttee.; Political Dir. Action socialiste Hebdo newspaper 1979–81; Prime Minister of France 1981–84; Pres. World Fed. of Twinned Towns 1984–; Grand-croix, Ordre nat. du Mérite, Grand cordon de l'ordre de la Répub. de Tunisie. *Publications:* Héritiers de l'avenir 1977, C'est ici le chemin 1982, A gauche 1985. *Address:* Assemblée nationale, 75355 Paris; 17–19 rue Voltaire, 59800 Lille, France (Home).

MAURSTAD, Toralv; Norwegian actor and theatre director; b. 24 Nov. 1926, Oslo; s. of Alfred and Tordis Maurstad; m. Eva Henning 1956; one s.; ed. Universitet i Uppsala and Royal Acad. of Dramatic Art, London; début in Trondheim 1947; Oslo Nye Teater 1951; Oslo Nat. Theatre 1954; Man. Dir. Oslo Nye Teater (Oslo Municipal Theatre) 1967–78; Man. Dir. Nat. Theatre 1978–; Oslo Critics Award. *Plays acted in or directed include:* Young Woodley 1949, Pal Joey 1952, Peer Gynt 1954, Long Day's Journey 1962, Teenage Love 1963, Hamlet 1964, Arturo Ui (in Bremen, Germany) 1965, Brand (Ibsen) 1966, Of Love Remembered (New York) 1967, Cabaret 1968, Scapino 1975, Two Gentlemen of Verona 1976, The Moon for Misbegotten 1976, Same Time Next Year 1977, Twigs 1977 (also TV production), Sly Fox 1978, Whose Life is it Anyway? 1979, Masquerade|1980, Amadeus 1980, Much Ado about Nothing 1981, Kennen Sie die Milchstrasse? 1982, Duet for One 1982, Hamlet 1983. *Films:* Line 1960, Kalde Spor 1962, Song of Norway 1970, After Rubicon 1987. *Leisure interests:* skiing, hunting, fishing. *Address:* Nationaltheatret, Stortingsgt. 15, Oslo 1, Norway.

MAVROMMATIS, Andreas V.; Cypriot diplomatist and barrister; b. 9 June 1932, Larnaca; s. of Vladimiros and Marthe (Andreou) Mavrommatis; m. Mary Cahalane 1955; one s. three d.; ed. Greek Gymnasium, Limassol, Lincoln's Inn, London; practising advocate 1954–58; Magistrate 1958–60; Dist. Judge 1960–70; Minister of Labour and Social Insurance 1970–72; Special Adviser on Foreign and Legal Affairs to Pres. of Cyprus 1972–75; Perm. Rep. to UN Office at Geneva 1975–78, to UN, New York 1979–82; Greek Cypriot Interlocutor in Intercommunal Talks 1982–; Chair. UN Cttee. on Human Rights; fmr. Pres. ECOSOC; Chair. UN Cttee. on Relations with the Host Country. *Publication:* Treaties in Force in Cyprus. *Leisure interests:* reading, walking. *Address:* 43, Demosthenis Severis Avenue, Nicosia, Cyprus. *Telephone:* (21) 40-2466.

MAVROS, George, LL.D.; Greek lawyer and politician; b. 1909, Castellorizon; m. 1953; one s.; ed. Athens and Berlin Univs.; Lawyer Athens 1932–; Asst. Prof. of Int. Law, Univ. of Athens 1937–; M.P. 1946–; Under-Sec. of State for Justice 1945–46, Minister of Justice 1946; Minister of National Econ. (Trade and Industry) 1949–50, of Finance 1951, of Defence 1952; Gov. for Greece to IBRD 1949–52; Minister of Co-ordination 1963–64; Gov. Nat. Bank of Greece 1964–66; under house arrest April-Oct. 1968; fmr. Pres. Centre Union Party, Pres. Centre Union-New Forces Party 1974–78; arrested and deported to Yiaros island March 1974, released May 1974; Deputy Prime Minister, Minister of Foreign Affairs July-Oct. 1974; mem. Parl. 1974–; Pres. Democratic Centre Union Party (EDIK) 1974–79, Nov. 1980; Leader of Opposition Party 1974–77. *Publications:* Walker's Private International Law 1929, Problems in the Differentiation of Real Property and Chattels in the International Law on Wills 1936, Naval Privileges in International Law 1937. *Leisure interests:* classical music, golf, swimming. *Address:* 8 Akadimias Street, Athens 134, Greece.

MAXIMOS V HAKIM (fmrly. **Archbishop George S. Hakim**), D.D.; Lebanese ecclesiastic; b. 18 May 1908, Tanta, Egypt; s. of Salim Hakim and Eugenie Gazaleh; ed. St. Louis School, Tanta, Holy Family Jesuit School, Cairo and St. Anne Seminary, Jerusalem; Teacher Patriarchal School, Beirut 1930–31; Rector and Princ. Patriarchal School, Cairo 1931–43; Archbishop of Acre, Haifa, Nazareth and all Galilee 1943–67; elected Greek Catholic Patriarch of Antioch and all the East, Alexandria and Jerusalem Nov. 1967; founded Le Lien (French) Cairo 1936, Ar-Rabita (Arabic) Haifa 1943; Commdr. Légion d'honneur; Dr. h.c. (Laval Univ., Canada, Algiers Univ. and many U.S. univs.). *Publications:* Pages d'Evangile lues en Galilée (trans. into English, Dutch and Spanish) 1954, Life of Jesus (Arabic) 1980, Paroissien Byzantin (Arabic and French) 1980. *Address:* Greek Catholic Patriarchate, P.O. Box 50076, Beirut, Lebanon; P.O. Box 22249, Damascus, Syrian Arab Republic; Daher 16, Cairo, Arab Republic of Egypt. *Telephone:* (Beirut) 413111; (Damascus) 114568; (Cairo) 904697.

MAXWELL, Ian, M.A.; British/French publisher; b. 15 June 1956, Maisons Laffitte, France; s. of Robert Maxwell (q.v.) and Elisabeth Meynard; ed. Marlborough Coll. and Balliol Coll., Oxford; Man. Dir. Pergamon Press France 1980–81; Jt. Man. Dir. Pergamon Pres. GmbH 1980–; Marketing Dir. Pergamon Press Inc. 1982–83; Dir. Sales Devt. BPCC PLC 1985–86; Dir. Group Marketing BPCC PLC (now Maxwell Communication Corpn. PLC) 1986–; Chair. Agence Centrale de Presse, Paris 1987–; Dir. TFI TV station, Paris 1987–; C.E.O. Maxwell Pergamon Publrs. 1988–; Chair. Derby Co. Football Club 1984–87. *Leisure interests:* skiing, water skiing, watching football. *Address:* Agence Centrale de Presse, 26 rue du Sentier, Paris 75002, France (Office); Headington Hill Hall, Oxford, OX3 OBB, England (Home). *Telephone:* 40 26 11 11 (Office); (0865) 64881 (Home).

MAXWELL, (Ian) Robert, M.C.; British publisher and politician; b. 10 June 1923, Selo Slatina, Czechoslovakia; s. of Michael and Ann Hoch; m. Elisabeth Meynard 1945; four s. five d. (one s. and one d. deceased); self-educated; served in Second World War 1939–45; German Section of Foreign Office 1945–47; f. and Publisher Pergamon Press, Oxford, New York, Paris 1949–; Chair. Mirror Group Newspapers Ltd., Publisher of Daily Mirror, Daily Record, Sunday Mail, Sunday Mirror, The People, Sporting Life, Sporting Life Weekender 1984–, London Daily News 1987, China Daily in Europe 1986–, Moscow News (English edn.) 1988–; Publisher and Ed.-in-Chief The European Publisher 1988–; Chair. Maxwell Communication Corpn. PLC (fmnly. The British Printing & Communication Corpn. PLC) 1981–; Chair. British Cable Services Ltd. (Rediffusion Cablevision) 1984–; Chair., Chief Exec. The British Newspaper Printing Corpn. PLC 1983–, Macmillan Inc. 1988–; Chair. Pergamon Media Trust PLC 1986–, Pergamon Press PLC 1986–, BPCC PLC 1986–, MTV Europe 1987–, Maxwell Communications Corpn. Inc., New York 1987–; Dir. SelecTV PLC 1982–, Pergamon AGB PLC (fmrly. Hollis PLC) 1982– (Chair. 1988), Cen. TV PLC 1983–, Solicitors' Law Stationery Soc. PLC 1985–, Mirrorvision 1985–, Clyde Cablevision Ltd. 1985–, Premiere 1986–, Philip Hill Investment Trust 1985–, Reuters Holdings PLC 1986–, TF1 1987–, Agence Centrale de Presse 1987–, Maxwell Media, Paris 1987–; Chair. The Macmillan Foundation 1988–; Pres. State of Israel Bonds (UK) 1988–; acquired Sphere Books March 1989; MP (Labour) for Buckingham 1964–70; Chair. Labour Nat. Fund Raising Foundation 1960–69, Working Party on Science, Govt. and Industry 1963–64; mem. Council of Europe 1968; mem. Council of Newspaper Publrs. Asscn. 1984–; Chair. G.B.-Sasakawa Foundation 1985–; Pres. European Satellite TV Broadcasting Consortium 1986–; Chair. Commonwealth Games (Scotland 1986) Ltd., Oxford United Football Club 1982-87, Derby County Football Club 1987-; Chair. Nat. AIDS Trust fundraising group 1987-89; Dir. Bishopsgate Trust Ltd. 1984; Treasurer Round House Trust Ltd. 1965-83; Trustee Int. Centre for Child Studies; co-produced films: Mozart's Don Giovanni, Salzburg Festival 1954, Bolshoi Ballet 1957, Swan Lake 1968; Producer children's TV series DODO the Kid from Outer Space 1968; Kennedy Fellow, Harvard Univ. 1971; mem. Club of Rome 1979- (Exec. Dir. British Group); mem. Senate Univ. of Leeds 1986-; mem. Bd. of Trustees, Polytechnic Univ. of New York 1987-; Hon. mem. Acad. of Astronautics 1974; Hon. D.Sc. (Moscow State Univ.) 1983, (Polytechnic Univ. of New York) 1985; Hon. LL.D. (Aberdeen) 1988; Royal Swedish Order of the Polar Star (Officer 1st Class) 1983, Bulgarian People's Repub. Order Stara Planina (1st Class) 1983, Commdr. Order of Merit with Star, Polish People's Repub. 1986, Order of the White Rose of Finland (1st Class) 1988. *Publications:* The Economics of Nuclear Power 1965, Public Sector Purchasing 1968, Man Alive (jt. author) 1968; Gen. Ed. Leaders of the World series 1980-. *Leisure interests:* chess, football. *Address:* Holborn Circus, London, EC1A 1DQ; Headington Hill Hall, Oxford, OX3 0BB, England; 866 Third Avenue, New York, N.Y. 10022, U.S.A. *Telephone:* 01-353 0246 (London); (0865) 64881 (Oxford); (212) 702-2000 (New York).

MAXWELL DAVIES, Sir Peter (see Davies, Sir Peter Maxwell).

MAY, Elaine; American actress, film director and entertainer; b. 1932, Philadelphia; d. of Jack Berlin; ed. high school; m. 1st Marvin May (divorced), one d.; m. 2nd Sheldon Harnick (divorced); appeared on radio and stage as child; performed Playwright's Theatre, Chicago; appeared in student production Miss Julie, Univ. of Chicago; with Mike Nichols (q.v.) and others in improvisatory theatre group, The Compass (nightclub), Chicago -1957; improvised nightclub double-act with Mike Nichols, appeared New York Town Hall 1959; An Evening with Mike Nichols and Elaine May, Golden Theatre, New York 1960-61; numerous TV and radio appearances; weekly appearance NBC radio show Nightline. *Films:* Luv 1967, A New Leaf (also dir.) 1972, The Heartbreak Kid (dir.) 1973, Mikey and Nicky (dir.) 1976 (writer, dir. remake 1985), California Suite 1978, Heaven Can Wait (co-author screenplay) 1978. *Publication:* Better Part of Valour (play) 1983, Hotline 1983. *Address:* c/o Directors Guild of America, 110 West 57th Street, New York. N.Y. 10019, U.S.A.

MAY, Georges, PH.D.; American (born French) university professor; b. 7 Oct. 1920, Paris; s. of Lucien and Germaine May; m. Martha Corkery 1949; two d.; ed. Univs. of Paris, Montpellier and Illinois; mem. Faculty of Dept. of French, Yale Univ. 1946-; Instructor, Asst. Prof., Assoc. Prof., Prof. 1946-; Chair. Dept. of French 1978-79; Dean of Yale Coll. 1963-71; Sterling Prof. of French 1971-; Provost of Yale Univ. 1979-81; mem. bd. American Council of Learned Socs. 1979-, Chair. 1982-; Vice-Pres. Conseil Int. de la Philosophie et des Sciences Humaines 1982-84; mem. bd. Union Académique Internationale 1983-, Vice-Pres. 1985-; Guggenheim Foundation Fellow 1950, 1984; Chevalier de la Légion d'honneur 1971. *Publications:* Tragédie cornélienne, tragédie racinienne 1948, D'Ovide à Racine 1949, Quatre Visages de D. Diderot 1951, Diderot et la Religieuse 1954, J.-J. Rousseau par Lui-même 1961, Le dilemme du roman au XVIIIe siècle 1963, L'Autobiographie 1979, Les Mille et une nuits d'Antoine Galland, ou le Chef-d'oeuvre invisible 1986. *Leisure interests:* reading, drawing. *Address:* 177 Everit Street, New Haven, Conn. 06511, U.S.A. *Telephone:* (203) 562 5535.

MAY, Prof. Robert McCredie, PH.D., F.R.S.; Australian professor of biology; b. 1 Aug. 1936, Sydney; s. of Henry W. May and Kathleen M. McCredie; m. Judith Feiner 1962; one d.; ed. Sydney Boys' High School, Univ. of Sydney; Gordon Mackay Lecturer in Applied Math., Harvard Univ. 1959-61; at Univ. of Sydney 1962-73, Sr. Lecturer in Theoretical Physics 1962-64, Reader 1964-69, Personal Chair 1969-73; Prof. of Biology, Princeton Univ. 1973-88; Royal Soc. Research Prof., Dept. of Zoology, Oxford Univ. and Imperial Coll., London 1988-; Visiting Prof. of Biology, Imperial Coll., Univ. of London 1975-88; Visiting appointments at Harvard Univ. 1966, Calif. Inst. of Tech. 1967, UKAEA Culham Lab., U.K. 1971, Magdalen Coll., Univ. of Oxford 1971, Inst. for Advanced Study, Princeton Univ. 1972, King's Coll., Univ. of Cambridge 1976; Fellow, Merton Coll., Oxford 1988; Croonian Lecturer, MacArthur Award, Weldon Memorial Prize, Hitchcock Lecturer, John M. Prather Lecturer, Edgeworth David Medal. *Publications:* Stability and Complexity in Model Systems 1973, Exploitation of Marine Communities (ed.) 1974, ed. Theoretical Ecology: Principles and Applications 1981 (2nd edition), Population Biology of Infectious Diseases 1982, Ed. Exploitation of Marine Communities 1984. *Leisure interests:* tennis, running, hiking. *Address:* Department of Biology, Princeton University, Princeton, N.J. (Office); 25 Scott Lane, Princeton, N.J., U.S.A. (Home). *Telephone:* (609) 452-3830 (Office); (609) 924-8528 (Home).

MAYALL, Nicholas Ulrich, PH.D.; American astronomer; b. 9 May 1906, Moline, Ill.; s. of Edwin L. Mayall, Sr. and Olive Ulrich; m. Kathleen Czarina Boxall 1934; one s. one d.; ed. Univ. of Calif. at Berkeley; Teaching Fellow in Astronomy, Univ. of Calif. at Berkeley 1928-29, Martin Kellog Fellow in Astronomy 1931-33; Asst. (Computer) Mount Wilson Observatory, Pasadena, Calif. 1929-31; Observing Asst. Lick Observatory 1933-35, Asst. Astronomer 1935-42, Assoc. Astronomer 1945-49, Astronomer 1949-60; Staff mem. at Radiation Laboratory, M.I.T. 1942-43; Resident Assoc.,

Calif. Inst. of Tech., Pasadena 1943-45; Observatory Dir. Kitt Peak Nat. Observatory, Tucson, Ariz. 1960-71; mem. American Astronomical Soc., American Acad. of Arts and Sciences, American Philosophical Soc., Astronomical Soc. of the Pacific (Pres. 1942, 1958-59, Dir. 1956-62), N.A.S. (Chair. Astronomy Section 1958-61, Draper Fund Cttee. 1959-62, and on Space Science Bd. 1964-70, now mem. Emer.), Int. Astronomical Union (Pres. Comm. Extragalactic Nebulae 1958-61), Royal Astronomical Soc., London; corresp. mem. Acad. des Sciences, Inst. de France, Paris; Regional Trustee, Univs. Research Assn. (Fermi Nat. Accelerator Lab.) 1971-78. *Publications:* Numerous scientific papers including The Radial Velocities of Fifty Globular Star Clusters (Astrophysical Journal, Vol. 104) 1946, Redshifts and Magnitudes of Extragalactic Nebulae (with M. L. Humason and A. R. Sandage, in Astronomical Journal, Vol. 61) 1956, Photoelectric Photometry of Galactic and Extragalactic Star Clusters (with G. E. Kron, in Astronomical Journal, Vol. 65) 1960, The Expansion of Clusters of Galaxies (with J. Neyman and others, in Proceedings of the 4th Berkeley Symposium on Mathematical Statistics, Vol. 3) 1962. *Leisure interests:* music, reading, photography. *Address:* 7206 E. Camino Vecino, Tucson, Ariz. 85715, U.S.A.

MAYDAR, Damdinjavyn; Mongolian politician; b. 15 Aug. 1916; ed. Moscow and Novosibirsk; Chair. State Planning Comm. 1947-53; Deputy Chair. Council of Ministers 1953-72; First Deputy Chair. Council of Ministers 1972-84; Chair. State Construction Cttee. 1959-63, 1967-68; Deputy Chair. State Cttee. for Foreign Econ. Relations 1963-67; Chair State Cttee. for Science and Tech. 1971; Chair. Soc. for Protection of Nature and the Environment 1975-; Deputy Chair. State Rural Construction Comm. 1971; Deputy to People's Great Hural (Ass.); mem. Political Bureau of Mongolian People's Revolutionary Party (MPRP) Cen. Cttee. 1958-61, 1966-.

MAYER, H.E. Cardinal Augustin, O.S.B.; German ecclesiastic; b. 23 May 1911; ordained 1935; consecrated Bishop (Titular See of Satrianum) 1972, then Archbishop; cr. Cardinal 1985; Pres. Pontifical Comm. "Ecclesia Dei". *Address:* Città del Vaticano, Rome, Italy.

MAYER, Charles James, B.SC.; Canadian politician and farmer; b. 21 April 1936, Saskatoon, Sask.; m. Muriel Elaine Van Cleave; three d.; ed. Univ. of Saskatchewan; farmer, Carberry, Man.; M.P. 1979-; fmr. Caucus spokesperson on Agric., on the Canadian Wheat Bd.; fmr. Chair. Man. Progressive Conservative Party Caucus; fmr. mem. Standing Cttee. on Agric., on Econ. Devt., on Finance, on Trade and Econ. Affairs, on Miscellaneous Estimates, on Standing Orders and Procedures; Minister of State for The Canadian Wheat Bd. 1984-87, Minister of State (Grains and Oilseeds) 1987-, of Western Econ. Diversification Jan. 1989-; mem. Agricultural Inst. of Canada; Fed. Progressive Conservative Party. *Address:* House of Commons, Ottawa, Ont., K1A 0A6, Canada.

MAYER, Christian (pseudonym Carl Amery); German author; b. 9 April 1922, Munich; s. of Dr. Anton Mayer and Anna (née Schneller); m. Marijane Gerth 1950; three s. two d.; ed. Humanistisches Gymnasium, Freising and Passau, Univ. of Munich and Catholic Univ. of America, Washington, D.C.; freelance author 1949-; Dir. of City Libraries, Munich 1976-77; mem., fmr. Chair. German Writers' Asscn.; co-founder, German Literary Fund 1980; Chair. E. F. Schumachergesellschaft 1980. *Publications:* novels: Der Wettbewerb 1954, Die Grosse Deutsche Tour 1958, Das Königsprojekt 1974, Der Untergang der Stadt Passau 1975, An den Feuern der Leyermark 1979; essays: Die Kapitulation 1963, Fragen an Welt und Kirche 1967, Das Ende der Vorsehung 1972, Natur als Politik 1976, Leb Wohl Geliebtes Volk der Bayern 1980, G. K. Chesterton oder Der Kampf gegen die Kälte 1981, Der Wallfahrer 1986; various radio essays, radio plays, translations, etc. *Leisure interests:* gardening, cooking. *Address:* Drächslstrasse 7, 8000 Munich 90, Federal Republic of Germany. *Telephone:* 45 14 97.

MAYER, Hans; German university professor; b. 19 March 1907; ed. Univs. of Cologne, Bonn, Berlin, and Graduate Inst. of Int. Studies, Geneva; emigrated from Germany 1933; research at Int. Inst. of Social Research, New York, and Graduate Inst. of Int. Studies, Geneva 1933-40; literary and dramatic critic in Switzerland 1939-45; Chief Ed. Frankfurt Radio 1945-47; lecturer in Sociology and the History of Culture, Akad. der Arbeit, Frankfurt 1947-48; Prof. of History of Culture, Univ. of Leipzig 1948-50, Prof. of the History of German Literature 1950-64; Prof. of German Literature and Language Tech. University, Hanover 1965-73; Prof. Emer. 1975-; Prof. and Dir. of Inst. for the History of German Literature 1955; mem. Exec. Deutsche Goethe-Gesellschaft, Deutsche Schiller-Gesellschaft, Deutsche Schiller-Stiftung, PEN Club; Hon. Prof. Univ. of Tübingen 1975; mem. Acad. of Arts, Berlin 1964- (Dir. of Literature 1971); Hon. mem. Modern Languages Assn. of America 1975; Humane Letters Dr. h.c., (Wisconsin) 1972, D. Phil. h.c. (Brussels) 1969; German Nat. Prize for Science 1955; Literaturpreis der deutschen Kritiker 1965, Medal of Collège de France 1974, Grosser Literaturpreis der Stadt Köln 1980. *Publications:* Von der dritten zur vierten Republik: Geistige Strömungen in Frankreich 1939-1945 1945, Georg Büchner und seine Zeit 1946, Thomas Mann, Werk und Entwicklung 1950, Studien zur deutschen Literaturgeschichte 1954, Schiller und die Nation 1954, Deutsche Literatur und Weltliteratur: Reden und Aufsätze 1957, Richard Wagner 1959, Von Lessing bis Thomas Mann 1959, Bertolt Brecht und die Tradition 1961, Aragon, Die Karwoche (trans. from the French), Heinrich von Kleist, Der geschichtliche Augenblick 1962, Meisterwerke deutscher Literaturkritik (Ed.) (four vols.) 1962–76, Ansichten zur Literatur der Zeit 1962, Dürrenmatt und Frisch, Anmerkungen 1963, Zur deutschen Klassik und Romantik 1963, Anmerkungen zu Brecht 1965, Anmerkungen zu Richard Wagner 1966, Grosse deutsche Verrisse (Ed.) 1967, Zur deutschen Literatur der Zeit: Zusammenhänge, Schriftsteller, Bücher 1967, Das Geschehen und das Schweigen, Aspekte der Literatur 1969, Der Repräsentant und der Märtyrer, Konstellationen der Literatur 1971, Brecht in der Geschichte 1971, Goethe, ein Versuch über den Erfolg 1974, Aussenseiter 1975, Richard Wagner in Bayreuth 1976, Richard Wagner, Mitwelt und Nachwelt 1978, Doktor Faust und Don Juan 1979, Thomas Mann 1980, Versuche über die Oper 1981, Ein Deutscher auf Widerruf (memoirs, two vols.) 1982–84. *Address:* Neckarhalde 41, 7400 Tübingen, Federal Republic of Germany.

MAYER, Peter; American publisher; b. Hampstead, London; ed. Colombia Univ., Christ Church, Oxford; graduate Fellow, Indiana Univ.; Fulbright Fellow, Freie Universität Berlin 1959; worked with Orion Press before joining Avon books for 14 years; briefly with Pocketbooks; Chief. Exec. Penguin Books Ltd., London 1978–; Fellow Ind. Univ. *Publication:* The Pacifist Conscience (ed) 1966. *Address:* Penguin Books, 27 Wright's Lane, London, W.8, England.

MAYER-KUCKUK, Theo, DR.RER.NAT.; German nuclear physicist; b. 10 May 1927, Rastatt; m. Marianne Meyer 1965; two s.; ed. Univ. of Heidelberg; Research Fellow, Max Planck Institut für Kernphysik, Heidelberg 1953–59, Scientific mem. 1964; Research Fellow, Calif. Inst. of Tech., Pasadena 1960–61; Dozent, Univ. of Heidelberg 1962, Tech. Univ. Munich 1963; Prof. of Physics, Univ. of Bonn 1965–, Dir. Inst. of Nuclear and Radiation Physics 1965–; Vice-Pres. Int. Union of Pure and Applied Physics (IUPAP) 1984–; mem. Acad. of Sciences of Nordrhein-Westfalen 1982; Röntgenpreis, Univ. of Giessen 1964. *Publications:* Kernphysik (4th edn.) 1983, Atomphysik 1985, research papers and review articles in physics journals. *Leisure interest:* sailing. *Address:* Institut für Strahlen- und Kernphysik der Universität Bonn, Nussallee 14, D 5300 Bonn (Office); Hardtweg 51, D 533 Königswinter 41, Federal Republic of Germany (Home). *Telephone:* (0228) 732201 (Office); (02223) 22380 (Home).

MAYHEW, Baron (Life Peer), cr. 1981, of Wimbledon in Greater London; **Christopher Paget Mayhew,** M.A.; British politician, writer and director; b. 12 June 1915, London; s. of Sir Basil Mayhew, K.B.E. and Dorothea Mary Paget; m. Cicely Elizabeth Ludlam 1949; two s. two d.; ed. Haileybury Coll. and Christ Church, Oxford; M.P. for South Norfolk 1945–50; Parl. Private Sec. to Lord Pres. of Council 1945–46; Under-Sec. of State for Foreign Affairs Oct. 1946–50; M.P. for Woolwich East 1951–74; Minister of Defence for the Navy 1964–66; Chair. ANAF Foundation, Middle East Int. Publrs. Ltd.; Pres. Democrats Action Group on Electoral Reform, Parl. Asscn. for Euro-Arab Co-operation; Labour until 1974; joined Liberal Party 1974, Spokesman on Defence. *Publications:* Planned Investment 1939, Those in Favour 1951, Men Seeking God 1955, Commercial Television: What is to be Done? 1959, Co-existence Plus 1962, Britain's Role Tomorrow 1967, Party Games 1969, Europe—The Case for Going In (jointly) 1971, Publish It Not … (with Michael Adams) 1975, The Disillusioned Voter's Guide to Electoral Reform 1976, Time to Explain 1987. *Leisure interests:* music, golf. *Address:* 39 Wool Road, Wimbledon, London, S.W.20, England. *Telephone:* 01-946 3460 (Home).

MAYHEW, Rt. Hon. Sir Patrick Barnabas Burke, Kt., P.C., M.A., Q.C., M.P.; British barrister and politician; b. 11 Sept. 1929, Cookham, Berks.; s. of A. G. H. Mayhew and Sheila M. B. Roche; m. Jean Elizabeth Gurney 1963; four s.; ed. Tonbridge School and Balliol Coll., Oxford; Pres. Oxford Union Soc. 1952; called to Bar (Middle Temple) 1955; apptd. Q.C. 1972; M.P. (Conservative) for Royal Tunbridge Wells 1974–; Parl. Sec., Dept. of Employment 1979–81; Minister of State, Home Office 1981–83; Solicitor-Gen. 1983–87; Attorney-Gen. 1987–. *Leisure interests:* country pursuits, sailing. *Address:* House of Commons, London, SW1A 0AA, England.

MAYOR ZARAGOZA, Federico, DR.PHAR.; Spanish biologist, university official and politician; b. 27 Jan. 1934, Barcelona; s. of Federico Mayor and Juana Zaragoza; m. Maria Angeles Menéndez 1956; two s. one d.; ed. Univ. Complutense of Madrid; Prof. of Biochemistry, Faculty of Pharmacy, Granada Univ. 1963; Rector, Granada Univ. 1968–72; Prof. of Biochemistry, Autonomous Univ., Madrid; Chair. Severo Ochoa Molecular Biology Centre (Higher Council of Scientific Research) 1974–78; Under-Sec. Ministry of Educ. and Science 1974–75; mem. Cortes (Parl.) for Granada 1977–78; Chair. Advisory Cttee. for Scientific and Tech. Research 1974–78; Deputy Dir.-Gen. UNESCO 1978–81, Dir.-Gen. Nov. 1987–; Minister for Educ. and Science 1981–82; Dir. Inst. of the Sciences of Man, Madrid 1983–87; mem. European Parl. 1987; mem. Club of Rome 1981–; Academician, Royal Acad. of Pharmacy; mem. European Acad. of Arts, Sciences and Humanities, Int. Cell Research Org. (ICRO), A.A.A.S., The Biochemical Soc. (U.K.), Policy Bd., Interaction Council, Vienna, French Soc. of Biological Chem., American Chemical Soc. and numerous other orgs.; Grand Cross, Alfonso X El Sabio, Orden Civil de la Sanidad, Carlos III, Caro y Cuervo (Colombia); Commdr. Placa del Libertador (Venezuela); Grand Officier, Ordre Nat. du Mérite (France). *Publications:* Mañana Siempre es tarde 1987; numerous specialized works, transls., articles. *Leisure interests:* tennis, poetry.

Address: Office of the Director-General, UNESCO, 7 place de Fontenoy, 75700 Paris, France.

MAYORETS, Anatoly Ivanovich; Soviet politician; b. 1929; ed. Zaporozhye Mechanical Eng. Inst.; mem. of CPSU 1957–; Dir. of Zaporozhye Transformer Plant 1962–65; Deputy Minister of Electrical Eng., then First Deputy Minister 1965–80, Minister of Electrical Eng. of U.S.S.R. 1980–85, of Electric Power Devt. and Electrification March 1985–; Cand. mem. of CPSU Cen. Cttee. 1981–86, mem. 1986–; Deputy to U.S.S.R. Supreme Soviet (10th convocation); State Prize 1978. *Address:* Ministry of Electric Power Development and Electrification, Moscow, U.S.S.R.

MAYOUX, Jacques Georges Maurice Sylvain; French banker and businessman; b. 18 July 1924, Paris; s. of Georges Mayoux and Madeleine de Busscher; one s. one d.; ed. Ecole des Hautes Etudes Commerciales, Ecole Libre des Sciences Politiques, Faculté de Droit et des Lettres de Paris; studied at Ecole Nat. d'Admin. 1949–51; Personal adviser to Minister of Finance 1958, Asst. Gen. Sec. Comité Interministeriel pour les Questions de Coopération Economique Européenne 1958–63; mem. Gen. Council, Banque de France 1963–73; Gen. Man. Caisse Nat. de Crédit Agricole 1963–75; Prof., Inst. d'Etudes Politiques 1964–72; Chair., Gen. Man. Agritel 1972–75, SACILOR (Aciéries et laminoirs de Lorraine) 1978–82, SOLLAC (Soc. Lorraine de laminage continu) 1980–82; Pres. SOLMER 1980–81, Soc. Générale S.A. 1982–86 (Hon. Pres. 1986–), Cen. Cttee. for Rural Renovation 1971, Fondation H.E.C. 1978–80; Pres. French-Canadian Chamber of Commerce 1986–; Insp. Général des Finances 1976–87; mem. Supervisory Bd. Harpener Gesellschaft 1980–; Chevalier, Légion d'honneur; Commdr., Phoenix (Greece). *Address:* 60 avenue Henri-Martin, 75061 Paris, France.

MAYR, Ernst, PH.D.; American professor of biology; b. 5 July 1904, Kempten, Germany; s. of Otto Mayr and Helene Pusinelli; m. Margarete Simon 1935; two d.; ed. Univs. of Greifswald and Berlin; Asst. Curator, Univ. of Berlin 1926–32; Assoc. Curator, Whitney-Rothschild Collection of American Museum of Natural History 1932–44, Curator 1944–53; Alexander Agassiz Prof. of Zoology, Harvard Univ. 1953–75, Emer. 1975–; Dir. Museum of Comparative Zoology 1961–70; Visiting Prof., Univ. of Minn. 1949, 1974, Univs. of Pavia and Wash. 1951–52; lecturer, Columbia Univ. 1941, 1950, Philadelphia Acad. of Sciences 1947, Univ. of Calif. at Davis 1967; expeditions to Dutch New Guinea, Mandated Territory of New Guinea and Solomon Islands 1928–30; nine U.S. and foreign Hon. doctorates; Fellow, American Acad. of Arts and Sciences; mem. N.A.S., American Philosophical Soc.; Corresp. Fellow, Zoological Soc. of India; Foreign mem. Royal Soc.; Hon., Foreign and Corresp. mem. of 19 foreign socs.; numerous awards including Leidy Medal of Acad. of Natural Sciences, Philadelphia 1946, Wallace Darwin Medal of Linnean Soc., London 1958, Daniel Giraud Eliot Medal of N.A.S. 1967, Centennial Medal of American Museum of Natural History 1969, Nat. Medal of Science 1970, Linnean Medal 1977, Balzan Prize 1983, Darwin Medal, Royal Soc. 1984, Sarton Medal 1986. *Publications:* List of New Guinea Birds 1941, Systematics and the Origin of Species 1942, Birds of the Southwest Pacific 1945, Birds of the Philippines 1946, Methods and Principles of Systematic Zoology 1953, The Species Problem (Editor, American Assen. for the Advancement of Science Publication No. 50) 1957, Animal Species and Evolution 1963, Principles of Systematic Zoology 1969, Populations, Species and Evolution 1970, Evolution and the Diversity of Life 1976, The Evolutionary Synthesis (ed.) 1980, The Growth of Biological Thought 1982, Toward a New Philosophy of Biology 1988 and 560 articles in journals. *Leisure interests:* natural history, history of biology. *Address:* Museum of Comparative Zoology, Harvard University, Cambridge, Mass. 02138 (Office); 11 Chauncy Street, Cambridge, Mass. 02138, U.S.A. (Home). *Telephone:* 495-2476 (Office); 354-6769 (Home).

MAYRHOFER, Manfred, DR. PHIL.; Austrian professor of linguistics; b. 26 Sept. 1926, Linz; s. of late Josef Mayrhofer and Irma Fischer; m. Ingrid Gaissmayer 1984; two d.; ed. Univ. of Graz; Dozent 1951; Prof. Univ. of Würzburg 1958, Univ. of the Saar 1962; Prof. of Indo-European Linguistics, Univ. of Vienna 1966–88, now Prof. Emer.; mem. eleven acads. of sciences; Hon. D. Lit. (Illinois) 1985. *Publications:* twelve books including The Old Iranian Names 1979, Etymological Dictionary of Old Indo-Aryan 1986. *Address:* 1190 Vienna, Bauernfeldgasse 9/2/6, Austria. *Telephone:* 36 25 00.

MAYS, Colin Garth, C.M.G., B.A.; British diplomatist; b. 16 June 1931, Middlesbrough; s. of William A. Mays and Sophia M. Pattinson; m. Margaret P. Lloyd 1956; one s.; ed. Acklam Hall School and St. John's Coll. Oxford; Foreign Office 1955–56; served Sofia 1956–58, Baghdad 1958–60, Bonn 1960–65, Prague 1969–72; Commercial Counsellor, Bucharest 1977–80; seconded to PA Man. Consultants Ltd. 1980–81; Diplomatic Service Overseas Inspector 1981–83; High Commr. in the Seychelles 1983–86, in the Bahamas 1986–. *Leisure interests:* sailing, swimming, travel. *Address:* c/o Foreign and Commonwealth Office, King Charles Street, London, SW1A 2AH, England. *Telephone:* 01-270 3000.

MAYSTADT, Philippe, L. EN D.; Belgian politician; b. 14 March 1948, Petit-Rechain; m.; three c.; Adviser, Office of Minister for French Affairs 1974; Deputy for Charleroi 1977–; Sec. of State for French Region 1979–80; Minister of Civil Service and Scientific Policy 1980–81, for the Budget, Scientific Policy and Planning 1981–85, of Econ. Affairs 1985–88; Minister of Finance 1988–. *Address:* Ministry of Finance, 12 rue de la Loi, 1000 Brussels, Belgium. *Telephone:* (02) 233-81-11.

MAZANKOWSKI, Hon. Donald Frank, P.C., M.P.; Canadian politician; b. 27 July 1935, Viking, Alta.; s. of the late Frank Mazankowski and Dora Lonowski; m. Lorraine E. Poleschuk 1958; three s.; ed. High School; mem. Parl. 1968–; Minister of Transport and Minister responsible for Canadian Wheat Board 1979; Minister of Transport 1984–86; Deputy Prime Minister, Pres. of the Queen's Privy Council for Canada 1986–; Pres. Treasury Bd. 1987–88; Minister responsible for Privatization, Regulatory Affairs and Operations 1988, of Agric. Jan. 1989–; Progressive Conservative Party; Hon. D.Eng. (Tech. Univ. of Nova Scotia) 1987. *Leisure interests:* fishing, golf. *Address:* House of Commons, Ottawa, Ont., K1A 0A6 (Office); P.O. Box 1350, Vegreville, Alta., T0B 4L0, Canada (Home).

MAZAR, Benjamin, D.PHIL.; Russian-born Israeli archaeologist; b. 28 June 1906; m. Dina Shimshi (deceased) 1932; ed. Berlin and Giessen Univs; settled in Palestine 1929; joined staff of Hebrew Univ., Jerusalem 1943, Prof. of Biblical History and Archaeology of Palestine 1951–77, Rector 1952–61, Pres. 1953–61; Hon. Chair. Israel Exploration Soc.; Dir. excavations Ramat Rahel 1932, Beth Shearim 1936–40, 1956, Beth Yerah 1942–43, Tell Qasile 1948–50, 1959, Ein Gedi 1960, 1962, 1964, 1965, Old City of Jerusalem 1968–77; Hon. mem. British Soc. for Old Testament Study, American Soc. of Biblical Literature and Exegesis; mem. Admin. Council, Int. Asscn. of Univs.; Hon. D.H.L. Hebrew Union Coll. (Jewish Inst. of Religion, U.S.A.), Jewish Theological Seminary of America; Hon. Dr. h.c. (Hebrew Univ. of Jerusalem) 1975, (Weizmann Inst.) 1984, (Univ. of Haifa and Beersheba); Award of Govt. of Israel 1968. *Publications:* Untersuchungen zur alten Geschichte Syriens und Palästinas 1930, History of Archaeological Research in Palestine 1936, History of Palestine from the early days to the Israelite Kingdom 1938, Beth Shearim Excavations 1936–40 1940, Historical Atlas of Palestine: Israel in Biblical Times 1941, Excavations at Tell Qasile 1951, Ein Gedi 1964, The World History of the Jewish People Vol. II 1967, The Western Wall and the Ophel Hill 1974, The Mountain of the Lord 1976, Canaan and Israel 1980; Chair. Editorial Bd. Encyclopaedia Biblica 1950–82. *Address:* 9 Abarbanel Street, Jerusalem, Israel. *Telephone:* 39857.

MAZEAUD, Pierre; French politician; b. 24 Aug. 1929, Lyon; m. 1st Marie Prohom 1953 (divorced 1960), two d.; m. 2nd Sophie Hamel 1967, two d.; Judge of Tribunal of Instance, Lamentin, Martinique 1961; in charge of Conf., Faculty of Law, Paris 1955–; Tech. Adviser to Prime Minister 1961; Judge of Tribunal of Great Instance, Versailles 1962; Tech. Adviser to Minister of Justice 1962; Tech. Adviser to Minister of Youth and Sports 1967–68; Deputy for Hauts-de-Seine 1968–73, for Haute-Savoie 1986–; Vice-Pres. Groupe des députés sportifs 1968; Minister responsible for Youth and Sport 1973–76; Counsellor of State 1976–; Pres. Law Comm. of Assemblée Nationale 1987–88; Mayor, Saint-Julien-en-Genevois 1979–; climbed Everest 1978 (oldest man to climb Everest); Chevalier, Légion d'honneur; R.P.R. *Publications:* Montagne pour un homme nu 1971, Everest 1978, Sport et Liberté 1980, Nanga Parbat—montagne cruelle. *Address:* Assemblée nationale, 75355 Paris; 8 rue Charlemagne, 75004 Paris, France (Home).

MAZIA, Daniel, PH.D.; American biologist; b. 18 Dec. 1912, Scranton, Pa.; s. of Aaron Mazia and Bertha Kurtz; m. Gertrude Greenblatt 1938; two d.; ed. Univ. of Pennsylvania; Nat. Research Council Fellow 1937–38; Asst. Prof., Assoc. Prof., Univ. of Missouri 1938–42; Capt. U.S. Army Air Force 1942–45; Assoc. Prof., Prof., Univ. of Missouri 1945–50; Prof. of Zoology, Univ. of Calif., Berkeley 1951–53; Prof. Marine Biology Lab., Woods Hole 1980–; Prof. of Biological Sciences, Hopkins Marine Station of Stanford Univ. 1980–; mem. N.A.S.; Exec. Ed. Experimental Cell Research; Hon. Ph.D. (Stockholm) 1976; E. B. Wilson Medal, American Soc. for Cell Biology 1981. *Publications:* Mitosis and the Physiology of Cell Division 1961, Ed. General Physiology of Cell Specialization 1963, 160 articles in field of cell biology. *Address:* Hopkins Marine Station, Pacific Grove, Calif. 93950, U.S.A.

MAZRUI, Ali A., M.A., D.PHIL.; Kenyan professor of political science; b. 24 Feb. 1933, Mombasa; s. of Al'Amin Ali Mazrui and Safia Suleiman Mazrui; m. Molly Vickerman 1962 (divorced 1982); three s.; ed. Columbia Univ., New York, Univs. of Manchester and Oxford; Lecturer in Political Science, Makerere Univ., Uganda 1963–65, Prof. of Political Science 1965–72, Dean of Social Sciences 1967–69; Assoc. Ed. Transition Magazine 1964–73, Co-Ed. Mawazo Journal 1967–73; Visiting Prof. Univ. of Chicago 1965; Research Assoc. Harvard Univ. 1965–66; Dir. African Section, World Order Models Project 1968–73; Visiting Prof. Northwestern Univ., U.S.A. 1969, McGill and Denver Univs. 1969, London and Manchester Univs. 1971, Dyason Lecture Tour of Australia 1972; Vice-Pres. Int. Political Science Asscn. 1970–73, Int. Congress of Africanists 1967–73, Int. Congress of African Studies 1978–; Fellow, Center for Advanced Study in the Behavioral Sciences, Stanford 1972–73; Prof. of Political Science, Univ. of Michigan 1973–; Sr. Visiting Fellow, Hoover Inst. on War, Revolution and Peace, Stanford 1973–74; Dir. Centre for Afro-American and African Studies 1979–81; Research Prof. Univ. of Jos, Nigeria 1981–86; Andrew D. White Prof.-at-Large, Cornell Univ. 1986–; Reith Lecturer 1979; Presenter BBC TV series The Africans 1986; mem. World Bank's Council of African Advisers; Int. Org. Essay Prize 1964, Northwestern Univ. Book Prize 1969. *Publications:* Towards a Pax Africana 1967, On Heroes and Uhuru-Worship 1967, The Anglo-African Commonwealth 1967, Violence and Thought 1969, Co-Ed. Protest and Power in Black Africa 1970, The Trial of Christopher Okigbo 1971, Cultural Engineering and Nation Building in East Africa 1972, Co-Ed. Africa in World Affairs: The Next Thirty Years 1973, A World Federation of Cultures: An African Perspective 1976, Political Values and the Educated Class in Africa 1978, Africa's International Relations 1978, The African Condition (Reith Lectures) 1980, Nationalism and New States in Africa (Co-author) 1984, The Africans: A Triple Heritage 1986, The Culture of World Politics 1989. *Leisure interests:* travel, dining out, swimming, reading thrillers. *Address:* Center for Afro-American and African Studies, University of Michigan, Ann Arbor, Mich. 48109; 2104 Pauline, No. 307, Ann Arbor, Mich. 48103, U.S.A.

MAZUROV, Kiril Trofimovich; Soviet politician; b. 7 April 1914; ed. Gomel Highway Technicum and Higher Party School; Technician, road and bridge-building 1933–36; served Soviet Army 1936–39; engaged in Communist Youth League activities, Gomel and Brest Oblasts 1939–40; mem. CPSU 1940–; served Army 1941; resistance work 1942; Sec. Communist Youth League of Byelorussia 1943–47; Official of Cen. Cttee., CP of Byelorussia 1947–48; 1st Sec. Minsk City Party Cttee. 1949–50, Regional Cttee. 1950–53; Deputy to U.S.S.R. Supreme Soviet 1950–; Chair. Byelorussian Council of Ministers 1953–56; mem. CPSU Cen. Cttee. 1956–81; First Sec. CP of Byelorussia 1956–65; First Vice-Chair. U.S.S.R. Council of Ministers 1965–78; Cand. mem. Presidium of Cen. Cttee. of CPSU 1957–65, mem. 1965–66, mem. Politburo 1966–78; Order of Lenin (four times) and other decorations. *Address:* U.S.S.R. Council of Ministers, The Kremlin, Moscow, U.S.S.R.

MBASOGO, Lieut.-Col. Teodoro Obiang Nguema; Equatorial Guinea army officer and politician; ed. in Spain; fmr. Deputy Minister of Defence; overthrew fmr. Pres. Macias Nguema in coup; Pres. of Equatorial Guinea Aug. 1979–; Head Supreme Mil. Council 1979–; Minister of Defence 1986–. *Address:* Oficina del Presidente, Malabo, Equatorial Guinea.

M'BAYE, Kéba; Senegalese judge; b. 5 Aug. 1924, Kaolack; s. of Abdoul M'baye and Coura M'bengue; m. Mariette Diarra 1951; three s. five d.; ed. Ecole Nat. de la France d'Outre-mer; Judge of Appeal, Supreme Court of Senegal, First Pres. 1964–; fmr. Chair. Int. Comm. of Jurists, Chair. Comm. on Codification of Law of Civil and Commercial Liabilities; Vice-Chair. Exec. Cttee., Int. Inst. of Human Rights (René Cassin Foundation); mem. Supreme Council of Magistrature, Int. Penal Law Asscn. (and Admin. Council), Int. Criminology Asscn., Société de Législation comparée, Int. Olympic Cttee. (mem. Exec. Bd. 1985–); Judge, Int. Court of Justice, The Hague Feb. 1982– (Vice-Pres. 1987–); fmr. mem. various UN bodies, fmr. mem. or Chair. Comm. on Human Rights and other such cttees. and in various symposia organized by Int. Assn. of Legal Sciences, Red Cross, Unidroit and UNESCO; fmr. Pres. and mem. Int. Cttee. on Comparative Law, Int. African Law Assn., Int. Cttee. for Social Science Documentation; Hon. Pres. World Fed. of UN Assns. *Publications:* numerous publs. on Senegalese law, the law of black Africa and human rights. *Leisure interest:* golf. *Address:* International Court of Justice, Peace Palace, 2517 KJ The Hague, Netherlands. *Telephone:* (70) 92-44-41.

M'BOW, Amadou-Mahtar, L. ÉS L.; Senegalese educationist; b. 20 March 1921, Dakar; m. Raymonde Sylvain 1951; one s. two d.; ed. Faculté des Lettres, Univ. de Paris; Prof., Coll. de Rosso, Mauritania 1951–53; Dir. Service of Fundamental Educ. 1953–57; Minister of Educ. and Culture 1957–58; Prof. Lycée Faidherbe, St. Louis 1958–64; Ecole Normale Supérieure, Dakar 1964–66; Minister of Educ. 1966–68; Minister of Culture, Youth and Sports 1968–70; Asst. Dir.-Gen. for Educ., UNESCO 1970–74; Dir.-Gen. UNESCO 1974–87; Hon. Prof., Faculty of Humanities, Ind. Univ. of Santo Domingo (Dominican Repub.), Ecole Normale Supérieure, Dakar 1979, Nat. Independent Univ. of Mexico 1979, Escuela Superior de Administración y Dirección de Empresas, Barcelona 1984; mem. Acad. du Royaume du Maroc; Assoc. mem. Acad. of Athens; 46 hon. doctorates, 35 decorations, freedom of 11 cities (1987) including Dr. h.c. (Univ. of the Andes, State Univ. of Mongolia, State Univ. of Haiti, Khartoum, Sri Lanka, Tribhuvan Univ. Nepal, Pontifical Catholic Univ. of Peru, Buenos Aires, Granada, Sherbrooke, W. Indies, Open Univ. U.K., Belfast, Sofia, Nairobi, Philippines, Malaya, Venice, Uppsala, Moscow, Paris); Grand Cross of the Order of the Liberator (Venezuela), Grand Cross of the Order of the Sun (Peru), Commdr. and Grand Officier Ordre National (Ivory Coast), Commdr. des Palmes académiques (France), Officier, Ordre du Mérite (Senegal), Commdr. de l'Ordre national de Haute Volta, Bintang Jasa Utama (Order of Merit, Indonesia), Kawkab Star (Jordan), Order of Merit (Syria) and numerous other decorations; Prix "Terre des Hommes", Canada. *Publications:* numerous monographs, articles in educational journals, textbooks, etc. *Address:* B.P. 5276, Dakar-Fann, Senegal; B.P. 434, Rabat, Morocco.

MBUMBA, Nathaniel; Zairian nationalist leader; b. c. 1941; ed. American Methodist Missionary School; fmrly. worked as driver for Gécamines Co.; under Moïse Tshombe became Commdr. of Gendarmerie; went into exile in Angola after Mobutu took power; among founders of Front de Libération Nat. du Congo (FLNC) June 1968; Leader of FLNC in invasions of Zaire 1977 and 1978.

MEACHER, Michael Hugh, M.P.; British politician; b. 4 Nov. 1939, Hemel Hempstead, Herts.; s. of late George H. and Doris M. (née Foxell) Meacher; m. 1st Molly C. (née Reid) 1962 (divorced 1985); two s. two d.; m. 2nd Lucianne Craven 1988; ed. Berkhamsted School, New Coll., Oxford and London School of Econs.; Lecturer in Social Admin., Univ. of York and L.S.E. 1966–70; M.P. for Oldham West 1970–; Jr. Minister, Dept. of Industry 1974–75, Dept. of Health and Social Security 1975–76, Dept. of Trade 1976–79; mem. Nat. Exec. Cttee. of Labour Party 1983–, Shadow Spokesman for Health and Social Security 1983–87, for Employment 1987–; cand. for deputy leadership of Labour Party 1983; mem. Child Poverty Action Group and other voluntary orgs. *Publications:* Taken for a Ride: Special Residential Homes for the Elderly Mentally Infirm: A Study of Separatism in Social Policy 1972, Socialism with a Human Face 1982; over 1,000 articles on econ., industrial and social policy, regional devt., defence issues, the Welfare State, media reform, civil service reform, the police, etc. *Leisure interests:* sport, music, reading. *Address:* 5 Cottenham Park Road, London, S.W.20, England.

MEADE, James Edward, C.B., F.B.A., M.A.; British economist; b. 23 June 1907, Swanage, Dorset; s. of Charles Hippisley Meade and Kathleen (née Cotton-Stapleton); m. Elizabeth Margaret Wilson 1933; one s. three d.; ed. Malvern Coll., Oriel Coll., Oxford and Trinity Coll., Cambridge; Fellow and Lecturer in Econs., Hertford Coll., Oxford 1930–37, Bursar 1934–37; mem. Financial Section and Econ. Intelligence Service, LN; Ed. LN World Econ. Survey 1938–40; mem. Econ. Section Cabinet Office 1940–45, Dir. 1946–47; Prof. of Commerce with special reference to Int. Trade, L.S.E. 1947–57; Prof. of Political Economy, Univ. of Cambridge 1957–69; Nuffield Sr. Research Fellow, Christ's Coll., Cambridge 1957–74; Gov., Nat. Inst. of Econ. and Social Research 1947–, L.S.E. 1960–74, Malvern Coll. 1972–; Research Assoc., Dept. of Applied Econs., Cambridge Univ. 1979–; Visiting Prof. of Econs. and Finance in Australian Nat. Univ. 1956; Pres. Section F of British Assen. for the Advancement of Science 1957; Chair. Econ. Survey Mission to Mauritius 1960; Pres. Royal Econ. Soc. 1964–66; Chair. Inst. for Fiscal Studies Cttee. on U.K. Tax Structure 1975–77; mem. Council, Royal Econ. Soc. (Vice-Pres. 1966–); Hon. Fellow L.S.E., Oriel Coll., Hertford Coll., Oxford, Christ's Coll., Trinity Coll., Cambridge; Dr. h.c. (Basel, Hull, Essex, Oxford, Bath); Hon. D.Litt. (Glasgow) 1985; shared Nobel Prize (with Bertil Ohlin) for Econ. Science 1977. *Publications:* Public Works in their International Aspect 1933, The Rate of Interest in a Progressive State 1933, Economic Analysis and Policy 1936, Consumers' Credits and Unemployment 1937, The Economic Basis of a Durable Peace 1940, Planning and the Price Mechanism 1948, The Theory of International Economic Policy, Vol. I 1951, Vol. II 1955, A Geometry of International Trade 1952, Problems of Economic Union 1953, The Theory of Customs Unions 1955, The Control of Inflation 1958, A Neo-Classical Theory of Economic Growth 1961, Efficiency, Equality and the Ownership of Property 1964, The Stationary Economy 1965, The Growing Economy 1968, The Theory of Indicative Planning 1970, The Controlled Economy, The Theory of Economic Externalities 1973, The Intelligent Radical's Guide to Economic Policy 1975, The Just Economy 1976, Wage-Fixing 1982, Demand-Management (with D. Vines and J. Maciejowski) 1983, Alternative Systems of Business Organization and of Workers' Remuneration 1986, The Collected Papers of James Meade, vol. 3: International Economics 1989. *Address:* 40 High Street, Little Shelford, Cambridge CB2 5ES, England. *Telephone:* Cambridge 842491.

MEADMORE, Jean Georges, LL.M.; French diplomatist; b. 17 Oct. 1922, Tientsin, China; m. Nicole Robin 1954; two s.; ed. Law Faculty, Paris Univ. and Ecole des Langues Orientales; Attaché, Embassy in Nanking, Repub. of China 1948–49; Vice-Consul at Consulate-Gen. in Seoul, Korea 1949–50; deported to North Korea 1950–53; Second Sec., Wellington, New Zealand 1954–57; Ministry of Foreign Affairs 1957–61; Consul-Gen., Kobe, Japan 1961–65; Ministry of Foreign Affairs 1965–69; First Counsellor, Dakar, Senegal 1969–73; Ministry of Foreign Affairs, Personnel Section 1973–76; Amb. to Benin 1976–78; Minister Plenipotentiary 1978–; Head of codes and signals dept., Ministry of Foreign Affairs 1978–79, Dir. of Dept. for French Abroad 1979–82; Amb. to Luxembourg 1982–84; Inspector Gen., Foreign Affairs 1984–; Officier, Légion d'honneur, Commdr., Ordre nat. du Mérite. *Address:* Inspection générale, 37 quai d'Orsay, 75700 Paris; 14 clos de Verrières, 91370 Verrières-le-Buisson, France.

MEADOWS, Bernard William; British sculptor; b. 19 Feb. 1915, Norwich; s. of W. A. F. Meadows and E. M. Meadows; m. Marjorie Winifred Payne 1939; two d.; ed. City of Norwich School, Norwich School of Art and Royal Coll. of Art; exhibited Venice Biennale 1952, 1964, British Council exhbns., N. and S. America, Germany, Canada, New Zealand, Australia, Scandinavia, Finland and France; open-air exhbns. of Sculpture, Battersea Park, London 1952, 1960, 1963, 1966, Paris 1956, Holland Park 1957, Antwerp 1953, 1959, Arnhem 1958, British Pavilion, Brussels 1958, São Paulo Bienal 1958, Carnegie Inst., Pittsburgh 1959–61; one-man exhibitions London and New York 1957–; works in Tate Gallery, Victoria and Albert Museum and collections in Europe, America and Australia; mem. Royal Fine Art Comm. 1971–76; Prof. of Sculpture, Royal Coll. of Art, London 1960–80. *Publication:* 34 etchings and box (for Molloy by Samuel Beckett) 1967. *Address:* 34 Belsize Grove, London, N.W.3, England.

MEAGHER, Blanche Margaret, O.C., M.A.; Canadian diplomatist, retd.; b. 27 Jan. 1911, Halifax; d. of John Nicholas Meagher and Blanche C. Seals;

ed. St. Patrick's High School, Mount St. Vincent Coll., and Dalhousie Univ., Halifax, Nova Scotia; teacher, Halifax Public Schools 1932–42; Dept. of External Affairs 1942–, served Ottawa, Mexico, London, Tel Aviv, Vienna, Kenya, Uganda, Stockholm; Amb. to Israel 1958–61, concurrently High Commr. in Cyprus 1961; Amb. to Austria 1962–66; Gov. from Canada, IAEA 1962–66, Chair. Bd. of Govs., 1964–65; High Commr. to Kenya 1967–69, to Uganda 1967–69; Amb. to Sweden 1969–73; Diplomat-in-Residence, Dalhousie Univ., Halifax, Nova Scotia Sept. 1973–74; mem. Bd. of Trustees, Nat. Museums of Canada 1975–79, Bd. of Govs. Atlantic School of Theology 1976–82, Nova Scotia Coll. of Arts and Design 1984–; D.C.L. h.c. *Address:* 6899 Armview Avenue, Halifax, Nova Scotia, Canada. *Telephone:* 423-0895.

MEANEY, Audrey Lilian, PH.D., F.S.A., F.A.H.A.; British academic; b. 19 March 1931, Leyton, London; d. of Harry Charles Savill and Gladys Eliza (née Johnson) Savill; m. Neville Kingsley Meaney 1960 (divorced 1983); two s. one d.; ed. Brentwood Co. High School, Essex, St. Anne's Coll., Oxford and Girton Coll., Cambridge; English teacher Stover School, Devon 1953–55; lecturer in English Univ. of New England, N.S.W. 1959–68; temp. lecturer in English Language Univ. of Sydney 1960–61, 1963–64, 1966–67; lecturer in Early English Macquarie Univ., N.S.W. 1968–69, Sr. Lecturer 1970–83, Assoc. Prof. 1983–; Visiting Research Fellow Humanities Research Centre 1978; Pres. Australia and N.Z. Assen. for Medieval and Renaissance Studies 1981–84. *Publications:* A Gazetteer of Early Anglo-Saxon Burial Sites in England 1964, The Anglo-Saxon Cemeteries at Winnall, Winchester, Hants. (with S. C. Hawkes) 1970, Anglo-Saxon Amulets and Curing Stones 1981 and contrib. to Anglo-Saxon England 13 1984. *Leisure interests:* bush walking, embroidery and stained glass. *Address:* School of English, Macquarie Univ., N.S.W. 2109, Australia (Office); 108 Yallambee Road, Berowra, N.S.W. 2081, Australia (Home). *Telephone:* 805-8749 (Office).

MEANEY, Sir Patrick Michael, Kt.; British company director; b. 6 May 1925, London; s. of the late Joseph and Ethel Meaney; m. Mary June Kearney 1967; one s.; ed. Wimbledon Coll., Northern Polytechnic; mil. service 1941–47; joined Thomas Tilling Ltd. (now Thomas Tilling PLC) 1951, Chair. and Chief Exec. 1973–83; Dir. Cable and Wireless PLC 1978–84, Rank Org. PLC 1979– (Chair. Rank Org. PLC Nov. 1983–), A. Kershaw & Sons PLC (Chair. 1983–), Midland Bank PLC 1980– (Deputy Chair. 1984–), I.C.I. PLC 1981–, M.E.P.C. PLC 1986–, Horserace Betting Levy Bd. (Deputy Chair. 1985–), Metropolitan and Country Racecourse Man. Holdings 1985–, Racecourse Tech. Services Ltd. 1985–, Cement Roadstone PLC 1985–; Head Govt. Review 1981; mem. Council, British North America Cttee. 1979, CBI 1979–, R.S.A. 1987–, BESO 1987; Pres. Inst. of Marketing 1981–; Advisory Bd. World Econ. Forum 1979–. *Leisure interests:* sport, education, music. *Address:* Harefield House, Sandridge, Hertfordshire, AL4 9EG, England.

MÉBIAME, Léon; Gabonese politician; b. 1 Sept. 1934, Libreville; ed. Coll. Moderne, Libreville, Centre de Préparation aux Carrières Administratives, Brazzaville, Ecole Fédérale de Police, Ecole Nat. de Police, Lyon, France; posted to Chad 1957–59; Police Supt. 1960; further studies at Sûreté Nat. Française, Paris; Deputy Dir. Sûreté Nat., Gabon 1962–63, Dir. 1963–67; successively Head of State for the Interior, Minister Del. for the Interior and Minister of State in charge of Labour, Social Affairs and the Nat. Org. of Gabonese Women 1967; Vice-Pres. of the Govt., Keeper of the Seals and Minister of Justice Jan.-July 1968; Vice-Pres. of the Govt. in charge of Co-ordination 1968–75, Pres. Nat. Consultative Council 1972; Prime Minister April 1975–, Minister of Co-ordination, Housing and Town Planning 1975–76, of Land Registry 1976–78, of Co-ordination, Agric., Rural Devt., Waters and Forests 1978–79, in Charge of State Corpns. 1980–82, for Merchant Marine and Civil Service 1982–83; Commdr. Etoile Equatoriale; Grand Officier, Order nat. de Côte d'Ivoire, du Mérite Centrafricain; Chevalier, Etoile Noire du Bénin. *Address:* Office du Premier Ministre, B.P. 546, Libreville, Gabon.

MECHANIC, David, M.A., PH.D.; American professor of behavioural sciences; b. 21 Feb. 1936, New York; s. of Louis Mechanic and Tillie (Penn) Mechanic; two s.; ed. City Coll. of N.Y. and Stanford Univ.; mem. Faculty, Univ. of Wis. 1960–79, Prof. of Sociology 1965–73, John Bascom Prof. 1973–79, Dir. Center for Medical Sociology and Health Services Research 1971–79, Chair. Dept. of Sociology 1968–70; Prof. of Social Work and Sociology, Rutgers Univ. 1979–, Univ. Prof. and Dean Faculty of Arts and Sciences 1981–84, Univ. Prof. and Rene Dubos Prof. of Behavioral Sciences 1984–, Dir. Inst. for Health, Health Care Policy and Aging Research 1985–; mem. various advisory panels etc.; mem. Inst. of Medicine of N.A.S.; Guggenheim Fellowship 1977–78; Distinguished Medical Sociologist Award, American Sociology Assen. 1983, Distinguished Service Award, Melvyn H. Motolinsky Research Foundation 1987, Bd. of Trustees Award for Excellence in Research, Rutgers Univ. 1987. *Publications:* author of nine books and about 200 papers and chapters and ed. of seven books on sociological and health care subjects. *Address:* Institute for Health, Health Care Policy and Aging Research, Rutgers University, 30 College Avenue, New Brunswick, N.J. 08903, U.S.A. *Telephone:* (201) 932-8415.

MECKLINGER, Ludwig, PROF. DR. MED. HABIL.; German lawyer, doctor and politician; b. 14 Nov. 1919, Buchdorf; Col. of NVA (People's Army), G.D.R. 1958–64; Prof. of Social Hygiene, Univ. of Greifswald 1964–; Deputy

Minister 1964–69; State Sec. 1969–71; Minister of Health 1971–89; Prof. Dr. sc. med; Dr. h.c.; Dipl. jur; Vaterländischer Verdienstorden in Bronze, Silver and Gold and other decorations. *Address:* Ministerium für Gesundheitswesen, Rathausstrasse 3, 1020 Berlin, German Democratic Republic.

MECKSEPER, Friedrich; German painter and printmaker; b. 8 June 1936, Bremen; s. of Gustav Meckseper and Lily Ringel-Debatin; m. Barbara Müller 1962; one s. two d.; ed. State Art Acad., Stuttgart, State Univ. for the Visual Arts, Berlin; numerous one-man and group exhbns. in Europe, U.S.A., Australia and Japan; represented in many major museums of contemporary art and at print biennials world-wide; Prof. of Art, Int. Summer Acad., Salzburg 1977–79; Guest lecturer, London 1968; German-Rome Prize 1963, Prize of the 7th Biennale, Tokyo 1970, of the 6th Biennale, Fredrikstad 1982. *Leisure interests:* locomotives, steamboats, ballooning, paintings, etchings, books. *Address:* Landhausstrasse 13, D-1000 Berlin 31, Federal Republic of Germany.

MEDAK, Peter; British film director; b. Budapest, Hungary. *Films directed include:* Negatives 1968, A Day in the Death of Joe Egg 1970, The Ruling Class 1973, Third Girl From the Left 1973, Ghost in the Noonday Sun 1975, The Odd Job 1978, The Changeling 1979, Zorro, Zorro, The Gay Blade 1981, Breaking Through 1984, The Men's Club; has also dir. several films and series for U.S. TV. *Address:* 2439 Inverness Avenue, Los Angeles, Calif. 90027, U.S.A.

MEDARIS, Maj.-Gen. J. Bruce, A.I.A.A.; American army officer (retd.) and clergyman; b. 12 May 1902, Milford, Ohio; s. of William R. Medaris and Jessie LeSourd; m. 1st Gwendolynn Hunter 1920 (divorced 1930), one d.; m. 2nd Virginia Smith 1931 (died 1984), one s. one d.; ed. Ohio State Univ; U.S. Marine Corps in First World War 1918–1919; army service 1921–27; management and business in S. America and U.S.A. 1928–39; recalled to U.S. Army 1939; served in N. Africa, Sicily, France, Germany and Central Europe; Chief U.S. Army Mission to Argentina 1948–52; Commdg. Gen., Army Ballistic Missile Agency, Redstone Arsenal 1956–58; in Command of launch of satellite Explorer 1 Jan. 1958; Commdg. Gen., U.S. Army Ordnance Missile Command 1958–60; Pres. Lionel Corpn. 1960–62, Vice-Chair. 1962–63; Chair. Bd. Electronic Teaching Labs., Washington 1960–61; Chair. Exec. Cttee. All-State Devt. Corpn., Miami 1962–63; Pres. Medaris Management Inc. 1963–70, Chair. of Bd. 1970–78; Chair. Radio Free Europe; Bd. of Dirs. Pan American Funds 1973–75; ordained Deacon, Episcopal Church 1969, Priest 1970; Chaplain and Missioner, Order of St. Luke 1972–; Assoc. Rector, Episcopal Church of the Good Shepherd 1973–79; Chair. Bd., World Center for Liturgical Studies 1973–74; Priest Assoc. Comm. of St. Mary 1976–80; Soc. of the Holy Cross 1979–83; Rector, Anglican Church of the Incarnation 1979–81, Rector Emer. 1981–; Canon Missioner, Diocese of the South, Anglican Catholic Church 1981–83, Canon Theologian 1983–84, Archdeacon 1984–86, Archdeacon Emer. 1986–; Pres. Mountain Center for Renewal 1987–; Vicar Anglican Mission of the Holy Cross 1987–; mem. Inst. of Electrical and Electronics Engineers (N.Y.), Explorer's Club; Fellow A.I.A.A.; Distinguished Fellow American Coll. of Nuclear Medicine; U.S. Ordnance Corps Hall of Fame; Hon. Sc.D. (Alabama, N.M. State, Rollins Coll.); Hon. LL.D. (Chattanooga, Pa. Mil. Coll.); Hon. S.Sc. D. (Fla. Inst. Tech.); D.S.M. (one Oak Leaf Cluster), Soldiers Medal, Legion of Merit (two Oak Leaf Clusters), Croix de guerre avec palme, Couronne de Chêne (Luxembourg), Légion d'honneur, George Washington Medal of the Freedom Foundation, Crozier Gold Medal, American Ordnance Asscn., Medal of San Martin (Argentina), Life mem. American Legion. *Publications:* Count Down for Decision 1960, The Faith Once Delivered to the Saints (A Catechism for the Anglican Catholic Church) 1988, religious tapes. *Leisure interests:* golf, fishing. *Address:* P.O.B. 1531, Highlands, N.C. 28741; 1050 Cottontail Lane, Maitland, Fla. 32751, U.S.A. *Telephone:* (704) 526 3964 (Highlands).

MEDBERRY, Chauncey Joseph, III, B.A.; American banker; b. 9 Oct. 1917, Los Angeles, Calif.; s. of Chauncey Joseph Medberry, Jr. and Geneva Raymond; m. Thirza Cole 1958; two s. two d.; ed. Univ. of Calif., Los Angeles and Univ. of Munich; Lieut. U.S. Navy 1943–46; joined Bank of America 1939, Dir. BankAmerica Corpn., Bank of America, San Francisco 1971–, Chair. Bd. 1971–81, Chair. Exec. Cttee. 1981–82; Dir. Getty Oil Co., Los Angeles 1971–, Georgia Pacific Corpn. Portland and Atlanta, Los Angeles World Affairs Council 1971–, Los Angeles Philharmonic Assen. 1971–, Los Angeles Chamber of Commerce 1971–72, Calif. Chamber of Commerce 1979–82, Assen. of Reserve City Bankers 1979–82; Pres. Los Angeles Clearing House Assen. 1973–74; Chair. Bd. of Overseers Inst. for Civil Justice (Rand Corpn.) 1980–; Vice-Chair. Nat. Advisory Council, Salvation Army; Trustee, Cttee. for Econ. Devt. 1971–, Calif. Inst. of the Arts 1972–, Hosp. of the Good Samaritan 1972–, Calif. Inst. of Tech. 1973–, BankAmerica Realty Investors, Inc., San Francisco 1982–; Daniel, Mann, Johnson & Mendenhall, Los Angeles 1982–; mem. Pres.'s Advisory Cttee. for Foreign Negotiation 1975–80; Award for Distinguished Service and Outstanding Professional Achievement, Univ. of Calif., Los Angeles 1971; C. J. Medberry Chair in Man., Graduate School of Univ., of Calif., Los Angeles 1982. *Address:* Bank of America, 555 South Flower Street, Los Angeles, Calif. 90071, U.S.A.

MEDEARIS, Donald Norman, Jr., M.D.; American professor of pediatrics; b. 22 Aug. 1927, Kansas City; s. of Donald N. and Gladys (Sandford) Medearis; m. Mary E. Marble 1956; two s. two d.; ed. Univ. of Kansas and Harvard Medical School; Asst. Prof. of Microbiology, Johns Hopkins School of Medicine 1959–63, Assoc. Prof. of Microbiology 1963–65, Asst. Prof. of Pediatrics 1958–63, Assoc. Prof. of Pediatrics 1963–65; Chair. Dept. of Pediatrics, Univ. of Pittsburgh 1965–69, Prof. of Pediatrics 1965–74, Dean, School of Medicine 1969–74; Medical Dir. Children's Hospital of Pittsburgh 1965–69; Dir. Dept. of Pediatrics, Cleveland Metro. Gen. Hosp. 1974–77; Prof. of Pediatrics, Case Western Reserve 1974–77; Chief, Children's Services, Mass. Gen. Hospital 1977–; Charles Wilder Prof. of Pediatrics, Harvard Medical School 1977–; mem. Pres. Comm. for Study of Ethnic Problems in Medicine, Biomedical and Behavioural Research 1979–82; Fellow, A.A.A.S.; mem. Inst. of Medicine, N.A.S. *Publications:* articles in professional journals. *Address:* Chief of Children's Services, Massachusetts General Hospital, Fruit Street, Mass. 02114, U.S.A. *Telephone:* 617-726-2900.

MEDELCI, Mourad; Algerian politician; b. 30 April 1943, Tlemcen; m.; five c.; Asst. Financial Dir. SONELGAZ 1965; Financial Dir. Industrial Co-operation Body 1966, SNERI 1968; Pres. SOMERI 1971; Dir.-Gen. SNTA 1977, SNERI 1979; Sec. Gen. Ministry of Commerce 1980–88; Minister of Commerce 1988–; Pres. Bd of Dirs Fonds de participations des industries diverses. *Address:* 44 rue Muhammad Belouizdad, Algiers, Algeria. *Telephone:* (2) 63-33-66.

MEDGYESSY, Péter; Hungarian economist and politician; b. 1942, Budapest; ed. Karl Marx Univ. of Political Economy, Budapest; joined the HSWP 1965; started to work and served throughout in the Ministry of Finance; held various leading posts, especially in charge of taxing and pricing ; contributed to modernizing the system of econ. and financial regulations; mem. Int. Inst. of State Financing 1973–; Bd. mem. Finance Section of Hungarian Econ. Soc. 1982–; Minister of Finance 1987; Deputy Chair. Council of Ministers 1987–; Chair. Planning and Econ. Cttee. Dec. 1987–. *Address:* Vice-Premier's Office, Building of Parliament, Kossuth Lajos tér 1, Budapest, Hungary. *Telephone:* 123-500.

MEDICI, Giuseppe; Italian agricultural economist and politician; b. 24 Oct. 1907; ed. Univs. of Milan and Bologna; Prof. of Agricultural Econs., Univ. of Perugia 1935, of Turin 1936–47; Pres. Istituto Nazionale di Economia Agraria, Rome 1947–62; mem. Italian dels. to ECA international confs.; Pres. Ente Maremma (Land Reform Agency) 1951–53; Prof. Univ. of Naples 1952, Univ. of Rome 1960; mem. of the Senate (Christian Democrat); Minister of Agric. 1954–55, of the Treasury 1956–58, of the Budget 1958–59, of Educ. 1959–60; Minister without Portfolio (with responsibilities for Admin. Reform) 1962–63, Minister of the Budget June-Nov. 1963, Minister of Industry and Commerce 1963–65; Minister of Foreign Affairs June-Dec. 1968, 1972–73; Chair. Montedison 1977; Gov. EIB 1958; Pres. Senate Comm. for Foreign Affairs 1960–62; Pres. World Food Conf., Rome 1974. *Publications include:* Principii di Estimo 1948 (abridged edn. in English Principles of Appraisal 1953), Italy: Agricultural Aspects 1949, I Tipi d'Impresa dell' Agricoltura 1951, Agricoltura e Disoccupazione Vol. I 1952, Land Property and Land Tenure in Italy 1952, Lezioni di Politica Economica 1967. *Address:* c/o Montedison, Foro Bonaparte 31, Milan, Italy.

MEDLEY, Charles Robert Owen, C.B.E., R.A.; British artist and designer; b. 19 Dec. 1905, London; s. of C. D. and A. G. (née Owen) Medley; ed. Gresham's School, Holt and Slade School of Fine Art; mem. London Group 1929; Art Dir. Group Theatre; Designer for plays by T. S. Eliot, W. H. Auden, Christopher Isherwood, Louis MacNeice, etc. 1933–40; War Artist 1940–45; Head of Stage Design, Slade School 1949–58; Head, Camberwell Dept. of Fine Art 1958–65; Chair. Faculty of Painting, British School at Rome 1966–77; exhibited Tate Gallery, Victoria and Albert Museum, Liverpool, Birmingham, York, Southampton; Retrospective exhbns. Whitechapel 1963, Museum of Modern Art, Oxford 1984; First Prize, Arts Council, Festival of Britain 1951; *Publications:* Simon Agonistes (with 25 screen prints) 1979, Drawn from the Life (memoir) 1983. *Address:* 10 Gledhow Gardens, London, SW5 0AY, England. *Telephone:* 01-373 4481.

MEDVE, Dr. László; Hungarian doctor and politician; b. 1928, Vámosgyörk; ed. Budapest Univ. of Medicine; joined Hungarian CP 1945; asst. medical officer at Hospital of Lengyeltóti 1952–54; Sr. exec. Ministry of Health 1954–63, head of dept. scientific council 1963–67, sec. Party Cttee. 1967–70; Sub.-dept. leader of Hungarian Socialist Workers Party Cen. Cttee. 1970-74; Deputy Minister of Health 1974–81; Sec. of State 1981–84, 1987–; Minister of Health 1984–87; Labour Order of Merit 1973, 1978. *Address:* c/o Ministry of Health, Arany János utca 6–8, Budapest V., Hungary. *Telephone:* 323-100.

MEDVED', Aleksandr Vasilevich; Soviet wrestler; b. 16 Sept. 1937, Belaya Tserkov', Kiev Dist.; Honoured Master of Sports 1964; dean at Minsk Radio Eng. Inst.; mem. CPSU 1965; Olympic champion 1964, 1968, 1972; champion of Europe (1966, 1968, 1971–72), champion of U.S.S.R. (eight times 1961–70) many times world champion in free-style middleweight and heavy-weight wrestling; Order of Lenin.

MEDVEDEV, Roy Aleksandrovich, PH.D.; Soviet historian and sociologist; b. 14 Nov. 1925, Tbilisi; s. of Aleksandr Romanovich Medvedev and Yulia Medvedeva; twin brother of Zhores Medvedev (q.v.); m. Galina A. Gaidina 1956; one s.; ed. Leningrad State Univ., Acad. of Pedagogical Sciences of U.S.S.R.; mem. CPSU –1969, 1989–; Teacher of History, Ural Secondary

School 1951–53; Dir. of Secondary School in Leningrad region 1954–56; Deputy to Ed.-in-Chief of Publ. House of Pedagogical Literature, Moscow 1957–59; Head of Dept., Research Inst. of Vocational Educ., Acad. of Pedagogical Sciences of U.S.S.R. 1960–70, Senior Scientist 1970–71; freelance author 1972–. *Publications:* Vocational Education in Secondary School 1960, Faut-il réhabiliter Staline? 1969, A Question of Madness (with Zhores Medvedev) 1971, Let History Judge 1972, On Socialist Democracy 1975, Qui a écrit le "Don Paisible"? 1975, La Révolution d'octobre était-elle inéluctable 1975, Solschenizyn und die Sowjetische Linke 1976, Khrushchev—The Years in Power (with Zhores Medvedev) 1976, Political Essays 1976, Problems in the Literary Biography of Mikhail Sholokhov 1977, Samizdat Register 1978, Philip Mironov and the Russian Civil War (with S. Starikov) 1978, The October Revolution 1979, On Stalin and Stalinism 1979, On Soviet Dissent 1980, Nikolai Bukharin—The Last Years 1980, Leninism and Western Socialism 1981, An End to Silence 1982, Krushchev 1983, All Stalin's Men 1984, China and Superpowers 1986, L'URSS che cambia (with G. Chiesa) 1987, and over 200 professional and general articles. *Address:* c/o Z. A. Medvedev, National Institute for Medical Research, The Ridgeway, Mill Hill, London, NW7 1AA, England; Abonement Post Box 258, Moscow A-475, U.S.S.R.

MEDVEDEV, Vadim Andreyevich; Soviet official; b. 1929; ed. Leningrad Univ.; mem. CPSU 1952–; on staff of Univ. 1951–56; Asst. Prof. at Leningrad Eng. Inst. of Rail Transport 1956–61; Head of a faculty at Leningrad Tech. Inst. 1961–68; Sec. of Leningrad CPSU City Cttee. 1968–70; Deputy Head of Propaganda Dept. of Cen. Cttee. CPSU 1970–78; mem. of Cen. Auditing Comm. of CPSU 1976–86; Rector of CPSU Cen. Cttee. Acad. of Social Sciences 1978–; Head of Section, CPSU Cen. Cttee. 1983–; Sec. CPSU Cen. Cttee. 1986; Sec. in Charge of Ideology and Propaganda 1988–; cand. mem. Cen. Cttee. CPSU 1986–88, mem. 1988–; mem. Political Bureau 1988–; Order of October Revolution. *Address:* The Kremlin, Moscow, U.S.S.R.

MEDVEDEV, Zhores Aleksandrovich, PH.D.; British biologist; b. 14 Nov. 1925, Tbilisi, U.S.S.R.; s. of Aleksandr Romanovich Medvedev and Yulia Medvedeva; twin brother of Roy Medvedev (q.v.); m. Margarita Nikolayevna Buzina 1951; two s.; ed. Timiriazev Acad. of Agricultural Sciences, Moscow, Inst. of Plant Physiology, U.S.S.R. Acad. of Sciences; Scientist, later Sr. Scientist, Dept. of Agrochemistry and Biochemistry, Timiriazev Acad. 1951–62; Head of Lab., Molecular Radiobiology, Inst. of Medical Radiology, Obninsk 1963–69; Sr. Scientist All-Union Scientific Research Inst. of Physiology and Biochemistry of Farm Animals, Borovsk 1970–72; with Nat. Inst. for Medical Research, London 1973–; mem. New York Acad. of Sciences, American Gerontological Soc., Biochemical Soc., Genetic Soc.; Book award of the Moscow Naturalist Soc. 1965, Aging Research Award of U.S. Aging Assen. 1984, René Schubert Preis in Gerontology 1985. *Publications:* Protein Biosynthesis and Problems of Heredity, Development and Ageing 1963, Molecular-Genetic Mechanisms of Development 1968, The Rise and Fall of T. D. Lysenko 1969, The Medvedev Papers 1970, A Question of Madness (with Roy Medvedev) 1971, Ten Years After 1973, Khrushchev—The Years in Power (with Roy Medvedev) 1976, Soviet Science 1978, The Nuclear Disaster in the Urals 1979, Andropov 1983, Gorbachev 1986, Soviet Agriculture 1987, The Legacy of Chernobyl 1989, and over 200 papers and articles on gerontology, genetics, biochemistry and other topics. *Leisure interests:* social research and writing, travel. *Address:* c/o National Institute for Medical Research, The Ridgeway, Mill Hill, London NW7 1AA (Office); 4 Osborn Gardens, London, NW7 1DY, England (Home). *Telephone:* 01-959 3666 (Office); (01) 346-4158 (Home).

MEEK, Paul Derald, B.S.; American business executive; b. 15 Aug. 1930, McAllen, Tex.; s. of William Van Meek and Martha Mary (née Sharp) Meek; m. Betty Catherine Robertson 1954; four d.; ed. Univ. of Texas, Austin; with Tech. Dept. Humble Oil & Refining Co., Baytown, Tex. 1953–55; Cosden Oil & Chem. Co. 1955–76, Pres. 1968–76; Dir. American Petrofina Inc., Dallas 1968–, Vice-Pres., C.O.O. 1976–83, Pres., C.E.O. 1983–86, Chair. Bd., Pres., C.E.O. 1984–86, Chair. Bd. 1986–; mem. Advisory Council Coll. Eng. Foundation, Univ. of Texas 1979–; Co-Chair. Industrial Div. United Way of Metropolitan Dallas 1981–82; Trustee Southwest Research Inst.; mem. American Petroleum Inst., Dallas Wildcat Comm. (Chair. 1987–88). *Publication:* (contrib.) Advances in Petroleum Chemistry and Refining 1957. *Address:* Fina Oil & Chemical Co., P.O. Box 2159, 8350 N. Central Expressway, Dallas, Tex. 75221, U.S.A.

MEESE, Edwin, LL.B.; American lawyer and government official; b. 1931; m. Ursula Meese; two c.; ed. Yale Univ. and Univ. of Calif. at Berkeley; taught law, Univ. of San Diego Law School, Dir. Center for Criminal Justice Policy and Man.; sr. position under Gov. Reagan, State House, Sacramento, Calif.; Reagan's Campaign Chief of Staff, presidential elections 1980, Dir. Transition Org. 1980–81; Counsellor to Pres. Reagan and Man. Nat. Security Council, Domestic Policy and Cabinet Staffs 1981–85; Attorney Gen. of U.S.A. 1985–88; Distinguished Fellow, Heritage Foundation, Washington 1988–; Distinguished Visiting Fellow, Hoover Inst., Stanford Univ., Calif. 1988–; Harvard Univ. John F. Kennedy School of Govt. Medal 1986. *Leisure interest:* collecting models of police patrol cars. *Address:* The Heritage Foundation, 214 Massachusetts Avenue, N.E., Washington, D.C. 20002, U.S.A.

MEGARRY, Rt. Hon. Sir Robert (Edgar), M.A., LL.D., F.B.A.; British judge (retd.); b. 1 June 1910, Croydon, Surrey; s. of Robert Lindsay Megarry and Irene Clark; m. Iris Davies 1936; three d.; ed. Lancing Coll., Trinity Hall, Cambridge; Solicitor 1935–41, certificate of honour and called to the Bar, Lincoln's Inn 1944, in practice 1945–67, Q.C. 1956–67, Asst. Reader in Equity in the Inns of Court 1946–51, Reader 1951–67, judge, Chancery Div. of High Court 1967–76, Vice-Chancellor 1976–82, Vice-Chancellor of the Supreme Court 1982–85; Prin., Ministry of Supply 1940–44, Asst. Sec. 1944–46; Bencher, Lincoln's Inn 1962, Treas. 1981; Dir. of Law Soc.'s Refresher Courses 1944–47; Book Review Ed. and Asst. Ed., Law Quarterly Review 1944–67; Visiting Prof. New York Univ. School of Law 1960–61, Osgoode Law School, Toronto 1964; Regents' Prof., U.C.L.A. 1983; mem. Gen. Council of the Bar 1948–52, Lord Chancellor's Law Reform Cttee. 1952–73, Senate of the Inns of Court and the Bar 1966–70, 1980–82, Advisory Council on Public Records 1980–85; Chair. Notting Hill Housing Trust 1967–68, Friends of Lancing Chapel 1969–, Inc. Council of Law Reporting 1972–87; Pres. Soc. of Public Teachers of Law 1965–66, Selden Soc. 1976–79, Lancing Club 1974–; Hon. Life mem., Canadian Bar Assen., American Law Inst.; the Visitor, Essex Univ. 1983–, Clare Hall, Cambridge 1984–88; Hon. LL.D. (Hull) 1963, (Nottingham) 1979, (Law Soc. of Upper Canada) 1982, (London) 1988. *Publications:* The Rent Acts 1939, A Manual of the Law of Real Property 1946, The Law of Real Property (with Prof. H. W. R. Wade) 1957, Miscellany-at-Law 1955, Lawyer and Litigant in England 1962, A Second Miscellany-at-Law 1973. *Leisure interests:* heterogeneous. *Address:* Institute of Advanced Legal Studies, 17 Russell Square, London, WC1B 5DR; 5 Stone Buildings, Lincoln's Inn, London, WC2A 3XT, England. *Telephone:* 01-637 1731; 01-405 7641.

MEGSON, Claude Walter, M.ARCH.; New Zealand architect; b. 29 July 1936, Whangarei; s. of Cecil Wallace Megson and Anne Storey; m. Cherie Elizabeth Willson 1968; ed. Whangarei Boys High School, Auckland Univ.; began architectural practice 1963; Sr. lecturer Auckland Univ. School of Architecture 1969–; Nat. Award of Merit (Jopling House), N.Z. Inst. of Architects 1967, Bronze Medal (Wong House), N.Z. Inst. of Architects 1969, Architectural Design Awards of Architectural Assen. for Shopping Complex 1969, Town Houses 1971, Architect's Own House 1972. *Major works include:* Wade House 1963, Jopling House 1965, Wong House 1967, Mrkusich Town Houses 1968, Good House 1969, Todd House 1970, Barr House 1973, Cocker Town Houses 1974. *Leisure interests:* classical music, photography, modern art, gardening. *Address:* University of Auckland, Private Bag, Auckland 1; 27 Dingle Road, St. Heliers, Auckland 5, New Zealand (Home). *Telephone:* 556-822.

MÉHAIGNERIE, Pierre; French engineer and politician; b. 4 May 1939, Balazé; s. of Alexis and Pauline (Boursier) Méhaignerie; m. Julie Harding 1965; one s. one d.; ed. Lycée Saint-Louis, Paris, Ecole nationale supérieure agronomique, Rennes; engineer, Génie Rural des Eaux et Forêts, Tunisia 1965–67; technical counsellor, Ministry of Agric. 1969–71, Ministry of Cultural Affairs 1971–73; mem. Nat. Ass. for Ille-et-Vilaine 1973–76, 1981–86; County Councillor for Vitré-Est 1976–, elected Mayor of Vitré April 1977; Sec. of State to Minister of Agric. 1976–77; Minister of Agric. 1977–81; mem. European Parl. 1979; Vice-Pres. Union pour la démocratie française; Pres. Conseil Gen. d'Ille et Vilaine March 1982–, Centre des démocrates sociaux 1982–; Minister of Housing, Transport and Urban Affairs 1986–88; Commdr. du Mérite agricole. *Address:* Ministère de l'Equipement, du Logement, de l'Aménagement du territoire et des transports, 246 boulevard Saint-Germain, 75007 Paris; 76 rue du Rachapt, 35500 Vitré, France (Home).

MEHEDEBI, Bahsir; Tunisian politician and diplomatist; b. 1912; Amb. to Lebanon, Kuwait, Libya 1965–70; Sec.-Gen. Ministry of Foreign Affairs 1970–71; Minister of Defence 1971–72; Amb. to U.K. 1972–74, to Morocco 1974–76; mem. Political Bureau, Socialist Destour Party 1971–. *Address:* Parti Socialiste Destourien, blvd. 9 Avril 1938, Tunis, Tunisia.

MÉHES, Lajos; Hungarian politician; b. 23 July 1927, Budapest; worked as engine fitter; joined workers' movement 1944, CP 1945; finished Party Acad. 1952; First Sec. Budapest Dist. 14 Party Cttee. 1961–62; Sec. Budapest Party Cttee. 1962–64; First Sec. Communist Youth League Cen. Cttee. 1964–70; gen. secr., Iron Workers' Union 1970–78; Pres. Metal Workers' Int. Union 1974–78; First Sec. Budapest Metropolitan Party Cttee. 1978–80; mem. Presidential Council 1978–80; mem. HSWP Cen. Cttee. 1966–88, HSWP Political Cttee. 1980–85; Minister of Industry 1980–83; Gen. Sec. Cen. Council of Trades Unions 1983–85; M.P. 1967–; Order of the Hungarian People's Repub. 1950, Labour Order of Merit 1954, 1965, 1974. *Address:* Central Council of Trade Unions, 1415 Budapest VI, Dózsa György ut 84/b, Hungary. *Telephone:* 225-840.

MEHROTRA, Ram Charan, D.PHIL., D.SC., PH.D.; Indian professor of chemistry; b. 16 Feb. 1922, Kanpur, Uttar Pradesh; s. of the late R. B. and Mrs. Chameli Mehrotra; m. Suman Mehrotra 1944; one s. two d.; ed. Allahabad Univ., London Univ.; lecturer Allahabad Univ. 1944–54; Reader Lucknow Univ. 1954–58; Prof. Gorakhpur Univ. 1958–62; Dean Faculty of Science 1959–62; Prof. Rajasthan Univ. 1962–82, Prof. Emer. 1982–, Dean Faculty of Science 1962–65, Vice-Chancellor 1968–69, 1972, 1973, Dir., Special Assistance Programme 1979–; Vice-Chancellor Delhi Univ. 1974–79; Pres. Chem. Section, Indian Science Congress 1967, Indian Chemical Soc. 1976–77, Indian Science Congress Assen. 1979, Vigyan Parishad, Allahabad

1979–83; Vice-Pres. Indian Nat. Science Acad. 1977–78; mem. Bd. and Governing Body CSIR 1963–66, 1976–80, Chem. Advisory Cttee. Atomic Energy Establishment 1963–67, Univ. Grants Review Cttee. 1974–77, Inorganic Chem. Div., Int. Union of Pure and Applied Chem. 1977–81, Univ. Grants Comm. 1982–85, Comm. on Status of Teachers 1983–84; Inorg. Nomenclature Comm. 1981–; Fellow, Nat. Acad. of Sciences, Allahabad, Royal Inst. of Chem., U.K., Indian Nat. Science Acad., Indian Acad. of Sciences; D.Sc. h.c. (Meerut Univ.); E. G. Hill Memorial Prize, Allahabad Univ. 1949, Sir S. S. Bhatnagar Award 1965, Fed. of FICCI Award for Science and Tech. 1975, Seshadri Award of Indian Nat. Science Acad. 1976, P. C. Ray Memorial Award, Indian Chemical Soc. 1977, J. C. Ghosh Medal, Indian Chemical Soc. 1986, 1st Fed. of Asian Chemical Soc. Award 1987, Platinum Jubilee Award of the Indian Science Congress by the Prime Minister of India 1988, and numerous other awards and distinctions. *Publications:* textbooks, research papers and three treatises in chemistry. *Leisure interests:* photography and writing popular articles on science and technology. *Address:* c/o Chemistry Department, University of Rajasthan, Jaipur 302004, India. *Telephone:* 60088 (Office); 76275 (Home).

MEHTA, Zubin; Indian conductor; b. 29 April 1936, Bombay; s. of Mehli Nowrowji and Tehmina Daruvala Mehta; m. 1st Carmen Lasky 1958 (divorced); one s. one d.; m. 2nd Nancy Diane Kovack 1969; ed. Vienna Acad. of Music, studied under Hans Swarowsky; first professional conducting in Belgium and Yugoslavia; Chief Conductor of Montreal Symphony; Music Dir. Los Angeles Philharmonic Orchestra 1961–78; Music Dir. New York Philharmonic Orchestra 1979–(91); Music Dir. Israel Philharmonic 1968–, appointed Dir. for Life 1981; Dir. Florence Maggio Musicale 1986–; conductor at festivals of Holland, Prague, Vienna, Salzburg and Spoleto; debut at La Scala, Milan 1966; conducts regularly with the Vienna, Berlin and Philadelphia Orchestras; winner of Liverpool Int. Conductors' Competition 1958; Music Dir. Maggio Musicale, Florence 1969; Dr. h.c. Tel Aviv Univ., Weizmann Inst. of Science, The Hebrew Univ. of Jerusalem, Jewish Theological Seminary, Westminster Choir Coll.; Fellow, Brooklyn Coll., Colgate Univ.; Padma Bhushan (India), Commendatore (Italy), Médaille d'Or Verméil (City of Paris). *Address:* c/o New York Philharmonic Orchestra, Avery Fisher Hall, New York, N.Y. 10023, U.S.A.; 19A Air Street, London, W.1, England.

MEIER, Richard Alan, B.ARCH.; American architect; b. 12 Oct. 1934, Newark, N.J.; s. of Jerome and Carolyn (née Kaltenbacher) Meier; m. Katherine Gormley 1978; one s. one d.; ed. Cornell Univ.; with Frank Grad & Sons, N.J. 1957, Davis, Brody & Wisniewski, New York 1958–59, Skidmore, Owings & Merrill 1959–60, Marcel Breuer & Assocs. 1960–63; Prof. Architectural Design Cooper Union 1962–73; Prin. Architect, Richard Meier & Assocs., New York 1963–80, Richard Meier & Partners 1980–; Visiting Critic Pratt Inst. 1960–62, 1965, Princeton 1963, Syracuse Univ. 1964; Architect American Acad. in Rome 1973–74; Visiting Prof. of Architecture Yale Univ. 1975, 1977, Harvard 1977; Eliot Noyes Visiting Critic in Architecture 1980–81; mem. Advisory Council Cornell Univ.; mem. Jerusalem Comm.; exhbns.: XV Triennale, Italy 1973, Princeton Univ., Biennale Italy 1976, Cooper Union, Cooper Hewitt Museum, New York 1976–77, Leo Castelli Gallery, New York 1977, Museum of Modern Art, New York 1981, Nat. Gallery, Athens 1982–83 and others; *major works:* Smith House, Darien, Conn. 1967, Bronx Devt. Center 1977, Renault Head., France 1981, High Museum of Art, Atlanta, Ga. 1983, Museum fur Kunsthandwerk, Germany 1984 and others; A.I.A. Awards: 1968–71, 1974, 1976, 1977, 1983, 1984 Award of Merit 1965, 1970, 1973, New York Chapel Dist. Architects Award 1982, 1984; Pritzker Architect Prize 1984, R.I.B.A. Gold Medal 1988; Officier, Ordre des Arts et lettres (France) 1984. *Address:* 136 East 57th Street, New York, N.Y. 10022, U.S.A. *Telephone:* (212) 593-1170.

MEIGGS, Russell, M.A., F.B.A.; British lecturer in ancient history (retd.); b. 20 Oct. 1902, London; s. of William H. Meiggs; m. Pauline Gregg 1941; two d.; ed. Christ's Hospital and Keble Coll., Oxford; Fellow, Keble Coll., Oxford 1930–39; Fellow and Tutor in Ancient History, Balliol Coll., Oxford 1939–70, Hon. Fellow 1970–; Univ. Lecturer in Ancient History 1939–70; Praefectus, Holywell Manor 1945–69; Kipling Fellow, Marlborough Coll., Vermont, U.S.A. 1967; Visiting Prof. Swarthmore Coll., Pa. 1960, 1970–71, 1974, 1977–78; Foreign mem. American Philosophical Soc.; Hon. D.H.A. (Swarthmore). *Publications:* Home Timber Production 1935–45, 1949, Roman Ostia 1960, A Selection of Greek Historical Inscriptions (with David Lewis) 1969, The Athenian Empire 1972, Bury's History of Greece, 4th edn. (ed.) 1975, Trees and Timber in the Ancient Mediterranean World 1983 etc. *Leisure interests:* gardening, America. *Address:* Balliol College, Oxford; The Malt House, Garsington, Oxford, England (Home).

MEIJLER, Frits Louis, PH.D.; Netherlands cardiologist; b. 29 April 1925, Den Ham; s. of Gerzon S. Meijler and Anna Content; m. Annemarie P. Schendstok 1953; two s. one d.; ed. Almelo High School and Univ. of Amsterdam; served in Royal Dutch Army 1947–49; staff mem. Wilhelmina Gasthuis, Amsterdam 1962–67; Head, Dept. of Cardiology, Utrecht Univ. Hosp. 1968–83; Chair. Scientific Council and Dir. Interuniv. Cardiology Inst. of the Netherlands, Utrecht 1983–; mem. Royal Netherlands Acad. of Sciences, British Cardiac Soc., European Soc. of Cardiology, Dutch Cardiac Soc. (Hon.); Fellow American Coll. of Cardiology, American Heart Assen., Int. Group Research in Cardiac Metabolism; House Order of

Orange 1976, Order of the Dutch Lion 1986, Morawitz Prize 1987. *Publications:* numerous articles on cardiology and related subjects. *Leisure interests:* photography, swimming, hiking. *Address:* ICIN, P.O.B. 19258, Utrecht (Office); De Meijlpaal, Ravelijn 1, 4351 TB Veere, Netherlands (Home). *Telephone:* 31 30 373870 (Office); 31 1181 1747 (Home).

MEINER, Richard; German publisher; b. 8 April 1918, Dresden; s. of Felix Meiner and Elisabeth (née Gensel) Meiner; m. Ursula Ehlert 1947; one s. one d.; mil. service 1937–45; f. Richard Meiner Verlages, Hamburg 1948, Chief Exec. Felix Meiner Verlages until 1964; Man. Dir. Verlage Richard Meiner and Felix Meiner 1964–81, Felix Meiner Verlag GmbH, Hamburg 1981–; Mil. Medal; Gold Medal of Union of German Booksellers 1983; Medal of Honour of German Booksellers, Leipzig 1987, Hon. Fellow German Soc. for Philosophy in Germany 1988. *Publications:* Verlegerische Betretung der Philosophische Bibliothek, Corpus Philosophorum Teutonicorum Medii Aevi, G.W.F. Hegel, Gesammelte Werke. Krit. Ausgabe, G.W.F. Hegel, Vorlesungen, Kant-Forschungen, Nicolai de Cusa Opera omnia. Krit. Ausgabe, Handbuch PRAGMATIK, Studien zum achtzehnten Jahrhundert und weitere philosophische Reihen und Einzelmonographien. *Leisure interests:* tennis, skiing. *Address:* Felix Meiner Verlag GmbH, Richardstrasse 47, D-2000 Hamburg 76, Federal Republic of Germany. *Telephone:* (040) 29 48 70.

MEINWALD, Jerrold, M.A., PH.D.; American professor of chemistry; b. 16 Jan. 1927, New York, N.Y.; s. of Dr. Herman Meinwald and Sophie Baskind; m. 1st Dr. Yvonne Chu 1955 (divorced 1979); two d.; m. 2nd Dr. Charlotte Greenspan 1980; one d.; ed. Brooklyn and Queen's Colls., Univ. of Chicago and Harvard Univ.; Instructor in Chem. Cornell Univ. 1952–54, Asst. Prof. 1954–58, Assoc. Prof. 1958–61, Prof. 1961–72, Act. Chair. of Chem. 1968; Prof. of Chem. Univ. of Calif., San Diego 1972–73; Prof. of Chem. Cornell Univ. 1973–80, Goldwin Smith Prof. of Chem. 1980–; Chemical Consultant, Schering Corpn. 1957–, Norwich Eaton Pharmaceutical Co. 1958–, Cambridge Neuroscience Research Inc. 1987–; mem. of Visiting Cttee. for Chem., Brookhaven Nat. Lab. 1969–73; numerous lectureships U.S.A., Canada, U.K., Australia, N.Z., France, Czechoslovakia, Switzerland, Belgium 1964–; mem. Medicinal Chem. Study Section "A" of Nat. Insts. of Health 1964–66, Chair. 1966–68; Editorial Bd. of Organic Reactions 1967–78, Journal of Chemical Ecology 1974–, Insect Science and its Application 1979–; Chair. Div. of Organic Chem., American Chemical Soc. 1968; Alfred P. Sloan Foundation Fellow 1958–62, Guggenheim Fellow 1960–61, 1976–77, Nat. Insts. of Health Special Postdoctoral Fellow 1967–68, Fogarty Int. Scholar 1980–84; Distinguished Scholar-in-Residence, Hope Coll., Holland, Mich. 1984; N.A.S. Exchange Scholar to Czechoslovakia 1987; Research Dir. Int. Centre of Insect Physiology and Ecology, Nairobi 1970–77; Advisory Bd., Petroleum Research Fund 1970–73, Advisory Bd., Research Corpn. 1978–83, Advisory Council Dept. of Chem. Princeton Univ. 1978–82, Advisory Bd. Chem. Section, Nat. Science Foundation 1979–82; Organizing Chair. Sino-American Symposium on the Chemistry of Natural Products, Shanghai 1980, UNESCO's Working Group on Co-operation in the Field of Natural Products Chemistry 1982–, Chemistry Program Cttee., Alfred P. Sloan Foundation 1985–; mem. Nat. Acad. of Sciences, American Philosophical Soc.; Fellow, American Acad. of Arts and Sciences, A.A.A.S., American Assn. for the Advancement of Science, Japan Soc. for the Promotion of Science; Pres. Int. Soc. of Chemical Ecology 1988–89; Edgar Fah Smith Award (American Chemical-Soc.) 1977, E. Guenther Award, American Chem. Soc. 1984, Distinguished Scientist-Lecturer Award, Kalamazoo Section of American Chem. Soc. 1985, A. C. Cope Scholar Award, American Chem. Soc. 1989. *Publications:* Advances in Alicyclic Chemistry Vol. I (Co-Author) 1966, Co-Ed. Explorations in Chemical Ecology 1987, Co-Author Pheromone Biochemistry 1987; over 200 research articles in major chem. journals; *Leisure interests:* playing flute, baroque flute and recorder. *Address:* Department of Chemistry, Cornell University, Ithaca, N.Y. 14853, U.S.A. *Telephone:* 607-255-3301.

MEISNER, Cardinal Joachim; German ecclesiastic; b. 25 Dec. 1933, Breslau; s. of Walter and Hedwig Meisner; ed. Univ. of Erfurt, Pastoral Seminary at Neuzelle; ordained as priest 1962, Chaplain of St. Ägidien, Heiligenstadt 1963–66, St. Crucis, Erfurt 1966, Rector of the Diocese of Erfurt 1966–75, Suffragan Bishop, Erfurt 1975–80, Bishop of Berlin April 1980–89; cr. Cardinal Feb. 1983; Archbishop of Cologne and Primate of Germany Feb. 1989–. *Publications:* Das Auditorium Coelicum am Dom zu Erfurt 1960, Nachreformatorische katholische Frömmigkeitsformen in Erfurt 1971, various articles in magazines. *Leisure interest:* Christian art. *Address:* Marzellenstr. 32, 5000 Cologne 1, Federal Republic of Germany. *Telephone:* 1642-1.

MEISTER, Alton, B.S., M.D.; American professor of biochemistry; b. 1 June 1922, New York, N.Y.; s. of Morris and Florence G. Meister; m. Leonora Garten Meister 1943; two s.; ed. Harvard Coll. and Cornell Univ. Medical Coll.; Intern and Asst. Resident, New York Hospital, N.Y. 1946, Chief biochemist 1971–; Commissioned Officer (Biochemical research), Nat. Insts. of Health, Bethesda, Md. 1947–55; Prof. and Chair. Dept. of Biochem., Tufts Univ. School of Medicine, Boston, Mass. 1955–67; Prof. and Chair. Dept. of Biochem., Cornell Univ. Medical Coll. 1967–; Visiting Prof. of Biochem., Univ. of Washington, Seattle 1959, Univ. of Calif. (Berkeley) 1961; Assoc. ed. Journal of Biological Chem. 1977–; mem. N.A.S., Inst. of Medicine of American Nat. Acad. of Sciences; Fellow, American Acad. of

Arts and Sciences; Paul Lewis Award, American Chem. Soc. 1954, William C. Rose Award in Biochemistry, American Soc. of Biological Chemists 1984. *Publications:* Biochemistry of the Amino Acids 1965; various papers and scientific reviews on amino acids, enzymes, and glutathione. *Address:* Department of Biochemistry, Cornell University Medical College, 1300 York Avenue, New York, N.Y. 10021, U.S.A. *Telephone:* (212) 472-6212.

MEISTERMANN, Georg; German professor and painter; b. 16 June 1911, Solingen; s. of Artur Meistermann and Sophia Meistermann (née Kaltenhauser); m. Prof. Dr. phil. Edeltrud Linder 1959; ed. Volkes u. Höhere Schule, Kunstakademie of Düsseldorf; until 1945 work censored by Gestapo, much destroyed; exhbns. in Wuppertal, Hamburg 1944, 1945; teacher Frankfurt Stadelschüle 1952-55; Prof. Kunstakademie of Düsseldorf 1955-60, Karlsruhe (also seconded to Munich) 1960-76; Pres. Deutsch. Kuntsterbundes 1967-72; numerous awards and prizes including Grosses Bundesverdienstkreuz 1959, Romanus-Guardini Prize 1984. *Works on view:* stained glass windows: Rundfunkhaus, St. Gereon, Cologne; Catholic Church, Kissingen; Kaiser-Friedrich Church, Berlin; Deutsche Bank, Frankfurt; National Museum, Nuremberg; churches in Mayen, Schweinfurt, Sobernheim; Mural paintings: Church Regina Martyrum, Berlin, Staatstheater, Karlsruhe, churches in Würzburg, Trier. *Address:* Christian-Gau-Strasse 30, 5000 Cologne, Federal Republic of Germany. *Telephone:* 0221 492225 (Cologne); 06597 2727.

MEIXNER, Josef, DR.PHIL.; German professor of physics; b. 24 April 1908, Percha, nr. Munich; s. of Karl and Maria (née Bartl) Meixner; m. Hildegard L. Diemke 1933; three s.; ed. Univ. of Munich; Asst. Univ. of Giessen 1934-37, Lecturer 1937-39; Lecturer Univ. of Berlin 1939-42; Extraordinary Prof. Tech. Univ. of Aachen 1942, Ordinary Prof. 1949-74, Prof. Emer. 1974; Visiting Prof. 7 U.S. Univs. and Univ of Hokkaido; Dr. rer. nat. h.c. (Cologne) 1968; Fellow Rheinische-Westfalischen Akademie der Wissenschaften. *Publication:* Mathieusche Funktionen und Sphäroid-Funktionen (with F.W. Schäfke) 1954, 150 scientific papers. *Address:* Am Blockhaus 31, 5100 Aachen, Federal Republic of Germany. *Telephone:* 0241-71821.

MELAMID, Aleksandr; Soviet dissident artist; b. 1943, Moscow; initial artistic training at Moscow Art School; originator (with Vitaliy Komar (q.v.)) of 'Sots-art'; mem. of U.S.S.R. Union of Artists, expelled for "distortion of Soviet reality and non-conformity with the principles of Socialist realism" 1972; emigrated to U.S.A. 1979. *Principal works include:* Young Marx 1976, Colour Writing 1972, Quotation 1972, Post Art 1973, Factory for Producing Blue Smoke 1975, Poster Series 1980; some work shown at Ronald Feldman Gallery, New York 1976; two-man exhbn. (with Vitaliy Komar (q.v.)) at same gallery 1985. *Address:* Ronald Feldman Gallery, New York, U.S.A.

MELCHER, John; American politician; b. 6 Sept. 1924, Sioux City, Ia.; m. Ruth Klein 1945; three s. two d.; ed. Univ. of Minnesota, Iowa State Univ.; served U.S. Army 1943-45; Yellowstone Valley Veterinary Clinic, Forsyth, Mont.; Alderman, Forsyth 1953-55, Mayor 1955-61; mem. from Rosebud County, Montana House of Reps. 1961-62, 1969, Montana Senate 1963-67; mem. U.S. House of Reps. from 2nd District of Montana 1969-76; U.S. Senator from Montana 1977-89; Purple Heart, Combat Infantry Badge; Democrat. *Address:* Forsyth, Mont. 59327, U.S.A. (Home).

MELIKISHVILI, Georgiy Aleksandrovich; Soviet (Georgian) historian; b. 30 Dec. 1918, Tbilisi; s. of Aleksandr and Yekaterina Melikishvili; m. Yelena Iosifovna Dochanashvili 1942; one s. two d.; ed. Tbilisi Univ.; works deal with the ancient history of the Near East and Transcaucasia; Prof. Tbilisi Univ.; Dir. of Historical Inst. of Georgian Acad. of Sciences 1965; mem. CPSU 1946-; mem. Acad. of Sciences of Georgian S.S.R. 1960-; Lenin Prize 1957. *Publications:* Nairi-Urartu 1954, Urartian Inscriptions in Cuneiform Characters 1960, History of Ancient Georgia 1959, The Most Ancient Settlers of the Caucasus 1965, Die urartäische Sprache 1971. *Address:* c/o Academy of Sciences, Rizhskaya ulitsa 3, kv. 37, Tbilisi 380030, U.S.S.R. *Telephone:* 22-10-06.

MELLANBY, Kenneth, C.B.E., B.A., PH.D., SC.D.; British environmental consultant and editor; b. 26 March 1908, Barrhead, Scotland; s. of Prof. A. L. Mellanby; m. 1st Helen Nielson Dow 1933 (dissolved), 2nd Jean Louie Copeland 1949; one s. one d.; ed. Barnard Castle School, King's Coll., Cambridge, and London Univ.; Research work London School of Hygiene and Tropical Medicine 1930-36, Wandsworth Fellowship 1934; Sorby Research Fellow of the Royal Soc. 1936; Univ. Lecturer Sheffield 1936; Army Service (Major, R.A.M.C.) 1942-45; Deputy Field Dir. M.R.C. Scrub Typhus Comm. in S.E. Asia; Univ. Reader in Medical Entomology, London School of Hygiene and Tropical Medicine 1945-47; research worker 1953-55; Principal Univ. Coll. Ibadan, Nigeria 1947-53; Head of Dept. of Entomology, Rothamsted Experimental Station 1955-61; Dir. Monks Wood Experimental Station, Huntingdon 1961-74; Chair. Council for Environmental Science and Eng. 1981-; Pres. Inst. of Biology, British Asscn. Section D; Ed. Environmental Pollution; Hon. D.Sc. (Ibadan, Bradford, Leicester, Sheffield); Hon. Dr. Univ. (Essex); Hon. Prof. of Biology (Leicester); Hon. Prof. Polytechnic of Cen. London; Hon. Professorial Fellow (Univ. Coll., Cardiff); First Charter Award, Inst. of Biology 1981. *Publications:* Scabies 1943, Human Guinea Pigs 1945, The Birth of Nigeria's University 1958, Pesticides and Pollution (New Naturalist) 1967, The Mole

(New Naturalist) 1971, The Biology of Pollution 1972, Can Britain Feed Itself? 1975, Talpa, The Story of a Mole 1976, Farming and Wildlife (New Naturalist) 1981, (Ed.) Air Pollution, Acid Rain and the Environment 1988. *Leisure interests:* gardening, wine and food. *Address:* 38 Warkworth Street, Cambridge, CB1 1ER, England. *Telephone:* Cambridge 328733.

MELLERS, Wilfrid Howard, O.B.E., M.A., D.MUS., D.PHIL.; British composer, author and university professor; b. 26 April 1914, Leamington; s. of Percy Wilfrid Mellers and Hilda Maria Lawrence; m. 1st Vera Hobbs 1943; m. 2nd Peggy Pauline Lewis 1950; three d.; m. 3rd Robin Hildyard 1987; ed. Leamington Coll. and Downing Coll. Cambridge; Supervisor in English Studies and Lecturer in Music, Downing Coll. 1945-48; Staff Tutor in Music, Extramural Dept., Univ. of Birmingham 1948-60; Distinguished Andrew Mellon Visiting Prof. of Music, Univ. of Pittsburgh, U.S.A. 1960-63; Prof. and Head of Dept. of Music, Univ. of York 1964-81, now Emer.; Part-time Prof., Guildhall School of Music, London, City Univ., London and Keele Univ. 1981-; Hon. D. Phil. (City) 1981; many compositions published. *Publications:* François Couperin and the French Classical Tradition 1950, Man and his Music 1957, Music in a New Found Land (themes and developments in American music) 1964, Harmonious Meetings 1964, Twilight of the Gods: The Beatles in Retrospect 1973, Bach and the Dance of God 1981, Beethoven and the Voice of God 1984, A Darker Shade of Pale: a backdrop to Bob Dylan 1984, Angels of the Night: Women Jazz and Pop Singers in the Twentieth Century 1986, The Masks of Orpheus 1986. *Address:* Oliver Sheldon House, 17 Aldwark, York, YO1 2BX, England. *Telephone:* (0904) 38686.

MELLES, Carl; Austrian conductor; b. 15 July 1926, Budapest; m. Gertrud Dertnig 1963; one s. one d.; ed. Gymnasium and Acad. of Music, Budapest; conducts all the major orchestras of Europe including Vienna and Berlin Philharmonic, New Philharmonia London, Scala Milan; guest appearances at Flanders, Salzburg and Bayreuth Festivals and Vienna State Opera; concert tours in Europe, Japan, S. Africa; Franz Liszt Prize, Budapest 1954, Prize of Italian Record Critic Asscn. for Dallapiccola's Il Prigioniera 1974. *Recording:* Classical Excellence, Hollywood, Florida with the Austria Broadcast Symphonie Orchestra. *Address:* Grünbergstrasse 4, 1130 Vienna, Austria.

MELLINK, Machteld Johanna, PH.D.; Netherlands archaeologist; b. 26 Oct. 1917, Amsterdam; d. of Johan Mellink and Machteld Kruyff; ed. Amsterdam and Utrecht Univs.; Field Asst. Tarsus excavations 1947-49; Asst. Prof. of Classical Archaeology Bryn Mawr Coll. 1949-53, Assoc. Prof., Chair. Dept. of Classical and Near Eastern Archaeology 1953-62, Prof. 1962-88; staff mem. Gordion excavations organized by Pennsylvania Univ. Museum 1950, during which the putative tomb of King Midas was discovered 1957; Field Dir. excavations at Karataş-Semayük in Lycia 1963-; excavator archaic and Graeco-Persian painted tombs near Elmali 1969-; Pres. Archaeological Inst. of America 1981-84; Vice-Pres. American Research Inst. in Turkey 1980-, Pres. 1988-; Hon. LL.D. (Pennsylvania) 1987. *Publications:* Hyakinthos 1943, A Hittite Cemetery at Gordion 1956; Archaeology in Anatolia (reports in American Journal of Archaeology) 1955-; Co-author Frühe Stufen der Kunst 1974; Ed. Dark Ages and Nomads 1964, Ed. Troy and the Trojan War 1986.. *Address:* Bryn Mawr College, Bryn Mawr, Pa. 19010, U.S.A. *Telephone:* (215) 526-5339.

MELLISH, Baron (Life Peer) cr. 1985, of Bermondsey in Greater London; **Robert Joseph Mellish,** P.C., M.P.; British politician; b. 3 March 1913; m.; five s.; ed. elementary schools; Army Service 1939-45; Labour M.P. Rotherhithe Div. of Bermondsey 1946-50; Parl. Private Sec. and Financial Sec. to Admiralty 1946-49; M.P. for Bermondsey 1950-74, for Southwark, Bermondsey 1974-82; Parl. Private Sec. to Minister of Supply 1950-51, to Minister of Pensions 1951; Joint Parl. Sec. Minister of Housing and Local Govt. 1964-67; Minister of Public Building and Works 1967-69; Parl. Chief Whip, Labour Party 1969-70; Minister of Housing May-June 1970; Opposition Chief Whip 1970-74; Govt. Chief Whip 1974-76; Chair. London Regional Labour Party 1956-77; left Labour Party 1982; Vice-Chair. London Docklands Urban Devt. Corpn. 1981-; Hon. Fellow, Q.M.C., Univ. of London; Kt. Commdr. of St. Gregory. *Address:* West India House, Millwall Dock, London, E14 9TJ, England.

MELLON, Sir James, K.C.M.G., M.A.; British diplomatist; b. 25 Jan. 1929, Glasgow, Scotland; m. 1st Frances Murray 1956 (d. 1976); one s. three d.; m. 2nd Philippa Shuttleworth (née Hartley) 1979; ed. Glasgow Univ.; in Govt. Service 1953-, Dept. of Agric. for Scotland 1953-60; Agricultural Attaché, Copenhagen and The Hague 1960-63; Foreign Office 1963-64, Head of Chancery, Dakar 1964-66; U.K. Del. to European Communities 1967-72; Counsellor 1970; Head of Science and Tech. Dept. FCO 1973-75; Commercial Counsellor, East Berlin 1975-76; Head of Trade Relations and Exports Dept. FCO 1976-78; High Commr. in Ghana (also accred. to Togo) 1978-83; Amb. to Denmark 1983-86; Consul-Gen. New York and Dir.-Gen. of Trade and Investment, U.S.A. 1986-88; Chair. Scottish Homes 1989-. *Publication:* A Danish Gospel 1986. *Address:* c/o Foreign and Commonwealth Office, King Charles' Street, London, S.W.1, England. *Telephone:* 01-233 3000.

MELLON, Paul, M.A.; American business and foundation executive; b. 11 June 1907, Pittsburgh; s. of Andrew W. Mellon and Nora McMullen; m. 1st Mary Conover 1935 (died 1946); one s. one d.; m. 2nd Rachel Lambert

Lloyd 1948; ed. Choate School, Yale Univ. and Cambridge Univ.; Trustee Nat. Gallery of Art, Washington 1945-85, Pres. 1963-79, Chair. 1979-85, Hon. Trustee 1985-; Trustee The Andrew W. Mellon Foundation (successor to merged Old Dominion Foundation and Avalon Foundation), New York; Trustee, A. W. Mellon Educational and Charitable Trust, Pittsburgh; Hon. K.B.E. 1974, Hon. L.H.D. 1967, Hon. D.Litt. (Oxford) 1961, Hon. LL.D. (Carnegie Inst. of Tech.) 1967; Nat. Medal of Arts 1985, and numerous other awards and medals. *Address:* 1729 H Street, Washington, D.C. 20006, U.S.A.

MELLOR, David Hugh, M.A., PH.D., M.S., F.B.A.; British professor of philosophy; b. 10 July 1938, London; s. of S. D. and E. N. (née Hughes) Mellor; ed. Newcastle Royal Grammar School, Manchester Grammar School and Pembroke Coll., Cambridge; Harkness Fellowship in Chem. Eng., Univ. of Minnesota 1960-62, M.I.T. School of Chem. Eng. Practise 1962; Tech. Officer, Imperial Chemical Industries (ICI) 1962-63; research student in philosophy 1963-68; Fellow, Pembroke Coll., Cambridge 1964-70; Fellow, Darwin Coll., Cambridge 1971-, Vice-Master 1983-87; Asst. Lecturer in Philosophy, Univ. of Cambridge 1965-70, Lecturer 1970-83, Reader in Metaphysics 1983-86, Prof. of Philosophy 1986-; Visiting Fellow in Philosophy, Australian Nat. Univ. 1975; Radcliffe Fellow in Philosophy 1978-80, Visiting Prof. Auckland Univ. 1985; Pres. British Soc. for the Philosophy of Science 1985-87. *Publications:* The Matter of Chance 1971, Real Time 1981; numerous articles on philosophy of science, metaphysics and philosophy of mind. *Leisure interest:* theatre. *Address:* 25 Orchard Street, Cambridge, CB1 1JS, England. *Telephone:* 0223-460332.

MELMON, Kenneth; American professor of medicine and pharmacology; b. 20 July 1934, San Francisco; s. of Abe Melmon and Jean Kahn; m. Elyce Ester Melmon 1957; one s. one d.; ed. Stanford Univ. and California Medical School, San Francisco; Clinical Assoc., Nat. Heart and Lung Inst. 1961-64; Chief Resident in Medicine, Washington Univ. 1964-65; Chief of Section of Clinical Pharmacology, Calif. Univ. (San Francisco) 1965-68, Chief of Div. 1968-78; Chair., Dept. of Medicine, Stanford Univ. 1978-84, Prof. of Medicine and Pharmacology 1978-; mem. Nat. Bd. of Medical Examiners 1987-; Burroughs Wellcome Clinical Pharmacology Scholar; Guggenheim Fellow 1971. *Publications:* Ed. Cardiovascular Therapeutics 1974, Clinical Pharmacology 1978; Assoc. Ed. The Pharmacological Basis of Therapeutics 1980; over 250 scientific papers. *Leisure interests:* backpacking, swimming, business, photography, bicycling, woodworking. *Address:* Stanford University Medical Center, Room S 025, Stanford, Calif. 94305, U.S.A. *Telephone:* 415 723 5187.

MELNICHENKO, Afanasiy Kondratevich; Soviet politician; b. 1923; Soviet army 1941-44; Pharmaceutical Inst. 1950; U.S.S.R. Ministry of Health 1952-59; Dir. Central Apothecary Research Inst. 1959-70; Vice-Chair. Moscow City Soviet 1970-75; Minister of U.S.S.R. Medical Industry 1975-86; mem. Cen. Auditing Comm. of CPSU 1976-; Deputy to U.S.S.R. Supreme Soviet 1979-. *Address:* The Kremlin, Moscow, U.S.S.R.

MELNIKOV, Aleksandr Grigorevich; Soviet official and industrial construction specialist; b. 21 Oct. 1930; ed. Moscow Engineers' Inst. for Construction; engineer 1953-55; Komsomol work 1955-59; mem. CPSU 1957-; party work in Tomsk Dist. 1959-70; Head of a Dept., Second Sec. Tomsk Dist. Cttee. CPSU 1970-83; Deputy of R.S.F.S.R. Supreme Soviet 1980-85; First Sec. Tomsk Regional Cttee CPSU; mem. of Mil. Council for Siberian Mil. Dist. 1983-86; Deputy of Comm. on Construction and Construction Materials Industry, Deputy Chair. 1984-86; Deputy of Council of the Union U.S.S.R. Supreme Soviet 1984-; Head of Dept. of Construction of Cen. Cttee. CPSU 1986-; mem. Cen. Cttee. CPSU 1986-; numerous publications and awards. *Address:* Central Committee of the Communist Party of the Soviet Union, Staraya pl. 4, Moscow, U.S.S.R.

MELNIKOV, Vitaly Vyacheslavovich; Soviet film director; b. 1 May 1928; ed. All-Union State Inst. of Cinema (VGIK) under S.I. Yutkevich and M.I. Romm; series of documentary films 1953-64; R.S.F.S.R. Artist of Merit, 1977. *Films include:* Barbos Visits Bobik, 1965, Chukotka's Boss 1967, Mum's got Married 1970, Hello and Goodbye! 1973, Xenia, Fyodor's Favourite Wife 1974, The Elder Son 1975, Marriage 1978, October Holiday 1979, Two Lines in Small Handwriting 1981 (Venice Film Festival Prize), Unicum 1984.

MELNIZKY, Walter, DR. JUR.; Austrian judge; b. 1 Dec. 1928, Vienna; s. of Ernst Melnizky and Maria Melnizky; m. Gertrude Melnizky 1953; two d.; ed. Univ. of Vienna; Judge 1954-57, 1962-69; Public Prosecutor 1957-62; Gen. Prosecutor 1969-86; Pres. Supreme Court 1987-; Pres. Automobilclub Austria 1980-; Syndicus Assen. of Public Experts 1988-; Komturkreuz des Burgenlandes. *Publications:* numerous juridical essays, especially on traffic law and criminal law. *Leisure interests:* classical music, opera. *Address:* Justizpalast, 1016 Vienna, Office); 1190 Vienna, Hannplatz 4/14, Austria (Home). *Telephone:* 96-22-821 (Office); 36-73-74 (Home).

MELROSE, Donald Blair, D. PHIL., F.A.A.; Australian professor of physics; b. 13 Sept. 1940, Hobart, Tasmania; s. of late Andrew B. Melrose and of Isla L. Luff; m. Sara C. Knabe 1969; one s. one d.; ed. N. Sydney Boys' High School, John Curtin High School, Fremantle and Univs. of W. Australia, Tasmania and Oxford; Research Fellow, Univ. of Sussex 1965-66; Research Assoc. Belfer Grad. School of Science, Yeshiva Univ., New York 1966-68; Research Fellow, Center for Theoretical Physics, Univ. of Md.

1968-69; Sr. Lecturer in Theoretical Physics, Australian Nat. Univ. 1969-72, Reader 1972-79; Prof. of Theoretical Physics, Univ. of Sydney 1979-; Rhodes Scholar 1962; Pawsey Medal (Australian Acad. of Science) 1974, Lyle Medal (Australian Acad. of Science) 1987, Walter Boas Medal (Australian Inst. of Physics) 1986. *Publications:* Plasma Physics (2 vols.) 1980, Instabilities in Space and Laboratory Plasmas 1986; over 150 papers in scientific publs. *Leisure interests:* rugby union, surfing, jogging, squash. *Address:* School of Physics, University of Sydney, N.S.W. 2006 (Office); 10 Balfour Street, Wollstonecraft, N.S.W. 2065, Australia (Home). *Telephone:* (02) 6922538 (Office); (02) 4383635 (Home).

MELVILL JONES, Geoffrey, M.A., M.B., F.R.S., F.R.S.C., F.R.AE.S.; British/Canadian professor of applied physiology; b. 14 Jan. 1923, Cambridge, England; s. of Benett Melvill Jones and Dorothy Laxton Jotham; m. Jenny Marigold Burnaby; two s. two d.; ed. King's Coll. Choir School, Cambridge, Dauntsey's School, Wilts., Cambridge Univ. and Middx. Hosp.; House Surgeon Middx. Hosp., London 1950; House Surgeon in Otolaryngology, Addenbrooke's Hosp., Cambridge 1950-51; Medical Scientist R.A.F. 1951-55; Scientific Officer Medical Research Council 1955-61; Assoc. Prof. Dept. of Physiology, McGill Univ., Montreal 1961-68, Prof. 1968-, Hosmer Research Prof., Faculty of Medicine 1978-, Dir. Aerospace Medical Research Unit 1961-88; Visiting Prof. Stanford Univ. 1971-72, Coll. de France 1979; Assoc. mem. Dept. of Neurology and Neuro-Surgery, Montreal Neurological Inst., McGill Centre for Studies In Age and Aging, Montreal Gen. Hosp.; Fellow Canadian Aeronautical and Space Inst., Aerospace Medical Assen.; Harry G. Armstrong Lecture Award 1968; Arnold D. Tuttle Award 1971, Quinquennial Gold Medal, Bárány Soc. 1988, Wilbur Franks Award, Canadian Soc. for Aerospace Medicine 1988. *Publications:* Mammalian Vestibular Physiology (with V. J. Wilson) 1979, Adaptive Mechanisms in Gaze Control (Co-Ed. with A. Berthoz) 1985, over 100 scientific publications. *Leisure interests:* outdoor activities, music, reading. *Address:* Aerospace Medical Research Unit, McGill University, 3655 Drummond Street, Montreal, Quebec H3G 1Y6, Canada. *Telephone:* (514) 392-4217, (514) 392-4216.

MELVILLE, Sir Harry (Work), K.C.B., PH.D., D.SC., LL.D., D.C.L., D.TECH., F.R.I.C., F.R.S.; British chemist; b. 27 April 1908, Edinburgh; s. of Thomas Melville and Esther Burnett Melville; m. Janet Marian Cameron 1942; two d.; ed. George Heriot's School, Edinburgh, Edinburgh Univ. and Trinity Coll., Cambridge; Fellow Trinity Coll., Cambridge 1933-43; Asst. Dir. Colloid Science Laboratory, Cambridge Univ. 1938-40; Prof. of Chemistry, Aberdeen Univ. 1940-48; Scientific Adviser to Chief Supt. Chemical Defence, Min. of Supply 1940-43; Supt. Radar Research Station 1943-45; Mason Prof. and Dir. of Chemistry Dept., Birmingham Univ. 1948-56; mem. Advisory Council for Scientific and Industrial Research 1946-51; mem. Scientific Advisory Council, Ministry of Supply 1949-51, 1953-56; Advisory Council on Scientific Research and Development 1953-56; mem. Scientific Advisory Council, British Electricity Authority 1949-56; mem. Scientific Advisory Council, Ministry of Power 1954-60; mem. Advisory Council on Research and Devt., Ministry of Power (now Dept. of Trade and Industry) 1960-, Chair. 1970-74; mem. Nuclear Safety Advisory Cttee. DTI 1972-; Sec. Dept. of Scientific and Industrial Research 1956-65; Chair. Science Research Council 1965-67; Prin. Queen Mary Coll., London 1967-76; Cttee. of Managers, Royal Inst. of G.B. 1976-; Hon. degrees from Univs. of Aberdeen, Bradford, Exeter, Birmingham, Essex, Liverpool, Leeds, Kent, Heriot-Watt. *Publication:* Experimental Methods in Gas Reactions 1938. *Address:* Norwood, Dodds Lane, Chalfont St. Giles, Bucks., England. *Telephone:* Chalfont St. Giles 2222.

MELVILLE, Sir Leslie Galfreid, K.B.E., B.EC.; Australian economist; b. 26 March 1902, Marsfield; m. Mary Maud Scales 1925; two s.; ed. Church of England Grammar School, Sydney, and Univ. of Sydney; Public Actuary of South Australia 1924-28; Prof. of Econs., Univ. of Adelaide 1929-31; mem. of Cttees. on S. Australian Finances 1927-30; mem. of Cttees. on Australian Finances and Unemployment 1931 and 1932; Financial Adviser to Australian Dels. at Imperial Econ. Conf. 1932, and to Australian Del. at World Econ. Conf. 1933; mem. Australian Financial and Econ. Advisory Cttee. 1939; Chair. Australian Del. to UN Monetary Conf., Bretton Woods 1944; mem. Advisory Council of Commonwealth Bank 1945-50; Chair. UN Sub-Comm. on Employment and Econ. Stability 1947-50; Asst. Gov. (Central Banking) Commonwealth Bank of Australia; Exec. Dir. IMF and World Bank Nov. 1950-53; Vice-Chancellor, A.N.U. Canberra 1953-60; mem. Bd., Reserve Bank 1959-63, 1965-75; Chair. Commonwealth Grants Comm. 1966-74, mem. 1979-82; Chair. Tariff Bd. 1960-63; Devt. Advisory Service, Int. Bank for Reconstruction and Devt. 1963-65; Hon. LL.D. (Toronto) 1958, (A.N.U.) 1978; Hon. D.Sc.Econ. (Sydney) 1980. *Address:* 71 Stonehaven Crescent, Canberra, Australia. *Telephone:* 811838.

MEMMI, Albert; Tunisian writer; b. 15 Dec. 1920, Tunis; s. of François Memmi and Marguerite née Sarfati; m. Germaine Dubach 1946; two s. one d.; ed. Lycée Carnot, Tunis, Univ. of Algiers and Univ. de Paris à la Sorbonne; Teacher of Philosophy, Tunis 1955; Dir. Psychological Centre, Tunis 1956; Researcher, C.N.R.S., Paris 1959-; Asst. Prof. Ecole pratique des hautes études 1959-66, Prof. 1966-70; Prof., Inst. de Psychanalise, Paris 1968-; Prof. Univ. of Paris 1970-, Dir. Social Sciences Dept. 1973-76, Dir. Anthropological Lab.; Vice-Pres. Fed. Int. des Ecrivains francophones 1985; mem. Acad. des Sciences d'Outre-mer; Vice-Pres. Pen Club 1977-80;

Chevalier Légion d'honneur; Commdr. Ordre de Nichan Iftikhar; Officier Palmes académiques, Officier Arts et Lettres, Officier Ordre République Tunisienne, Prix de Carthage 1953, Prix Fénéon 1953, Prix Simba 1978. *Publications include:* The Pillar of Salt 1953, Strangers 1955, Colonizer, Colonized 1957, Portrait of a Jew 1962, Anthologie des écrivains nordafricains 1965, Les français et le racisme 1965, The Liberation of the Jew 1966, Dominated Man 1968, Decolonisation 1970, The Scorpion 1970, Jews and Arabs 1974, Entretien 1975, La terre intérieure 1976, Le désert 1977, The Dependence 1979, Le racisme 1982, Ce que je crois 1985, L'Écriture colorée 1986, Les écrivains francophones du Maghreb 1987, Le Pharaon 1988. *Address:* 5 rue Saint Merri, 75004 Paris, France. *Telephone:* 42-78-84-79, 42-78-02-63.

MEN HUIFENG; Chinese taiji master; Assoc. Prof. Beijing Sports Inst. *Address:* Beijing Sports Institute, Beijing, People's Republic of China.

MENDE, Erich, DR.IUR.; German politician; b. 28 Oct. 1916, Gross-Strehlitz; s. of Max and Anna (née Krawietz); m. Margot Hattje 1948; three s. one d.; ed. Gross-Strehlitz Coll. and Univs. of Cologne and Bonn; Army service 1936–45; studied law, Univs. of Cologne and Bonn 1945–48, studied political science, Univ. of Cologne 1948–49; co-founder of the Free Democratic Party (FDP), British Occupied Zone 1945, mem. Exec. Cttee. Fed. Org. of FDP 1949–70; mem. Bundestag 1949–80; Whip, Parl. Group of FDP and mem. Exec. Cttee. 1950–53; Deputy Chair. Parl. Group of FDP 1953–57, Chair. 1957–63; Chair. FDP 1960–68; Fed. Minister for All-German Affairs and Deputy Fed. Chancellor 1963–66; left FDP to join Christian Democratic Union (CDU) Oct. 1970; Kt. of the Iron Cross. *Publications:* Die Freie Demokratische Partei—Daten, Fakten, Hintergründe 1972, Das verdammte Gewissen Zeuge der Zeit 1921–1945 1982, Die neue Freiheit (1945–1961) 1984, Von Wende zu Wende (1962–1982) 1986. *Leisure interests:* historical literature, music, swimming, riding, walking. *Address:* Am Stadtwald 62, 5300 Bonn 2, Federal Republic of Germany. *Telephone:* Bad Godesberg 314486.

MÉNDEZ MONTENEGRO, Dr. Julio César; Guatemalan law professor and politician; b. 23 Nov. 1915, Guatemala City; s. of Marcial Méndez Mendoza and Mélida Montenegro de Méndez; m. Sara de la Hoz de León 1950; two s. one d.; Prof. of Law, fmr. Dean of Faculty of Law, Univ. de San Carlos de Guatemala; Pres. Colegio de Abogados; fmr. Under-Sec. of Admin. and of Foreign Affairs; fmr. Gen. Sec. to the Presidency of the Repub.; Pres. of Guatemala 1966–70; mem. Partido Revolucionario; author of numerous works on law.

MENDIS, Vernon Lorraine Benjamin, B.A., M.PHIL., PH.D.; Sri Lankan diplomatist; b. 5 Dec. 1925, Colombo; s. of S. H. and Letitia Mendis; m. Padma Rajapatirana 1953; one s.; ed. Prince of Wales Coll., Moratuwa, Royal Coll., Colombo, Univ. of Ceylon; entered Diplomatic Service 1949; attached to High Comm., London; Third Sec., Washington, D.C. 1951; Official Sec., Tokyo 1953; Chargé d'affaires, Paris 1955; First Sec., Moscow 1958; Chief of Protocol, Ministry of Foreign Affairs 1960, Counsellor for Foreign Relations 1961; Counsellor, High Comm. in London 1963–66; Deputy High Commr., New Delhi 1966–69; Dir.-Gen. Ministry of Foreign Affairs 1970–74; High Commr. in Canada and concurrently Amb. to Cuba 1974–75; High Commr. in U.K. 1975–78; Amb. to France, Switzerland and the Vatican 1978–80; Sec.-Gen. Conf. of Non-Aligned Countries, Colombo 1962, Summit Conf. of Non-Aligned Countries, Colombo 1976; Chair. Commonwealth Sanctions Cttee. 1977; Chair. Asia Group, UNESCO 1979, Rep. in Egypt and Sudan 1980–85; Chair. Telecommunications Bd. of Sri Lanka 1986–. *Publications:* The Advent of the British to Ceylon 1760–1815, Currents of Asian History 1000-1500 1980, Foreign Relations of Sri Lanka—Earliest Times to 1965, British Governors and Colonial Policy in Sri Lanka 1984, The Indo-Sri Lanka Accord of July 1987. *Leisure interests:* bird watching, hiking, films, writing. *Address:* Sri Lanka Telecommunications Board, Suite 1/101 BMICH, Colombo 7 (Office); 45 1/2, Elibank Road, Colombo 5, Sri Lanka (Home). *Telephone:* 598016 (Office); 501111 (Home).

MENDOZA, June, R.P.; British (b. Australian) portrait painter; b. Melbourne; d. of John Morton and Dot Mendoza; m. Keith Mackrell; one s. three d.; ed. Lauriston School for Girls, Melbourne, St. Martin's School of Art, London; portraits include H.M. Queen Elizabeth II, H.M. Queen Elizabeth, the Queen Mother, H.R.H. The Prince of Wales, H.R.H. The Princess of Wales, Rt. Hon. Margaret Thatcher, M.P., Prime Ministers of Fiji, Australia, Philippines, Pres. of Iceland and many other govt., academic and industrial personalities, internationally-known musicians, large boardroom and family groups; large canvas for the House of Commons (440 portraits) of the House in session, for Australian House of Reps. (170 portraits) for Parl., Canberra; has made numerous TV appearances and lectures regularly in U.K. and overseas; mem. Royal Soc. of Portrait Painters, Royal Inst. of Oil Painters, Contemporary Portrait Soc.; Hon. mem. Soc. of Women Artists; Hon. D.Litt. *Address:* 34 Inner Park Road, London, SW19 6DD, England.

MENEM, Carlos Saul, D.JUR.; Argentinian politician; b. 2 July 1935, Anillaco, La Rioja; m. Zulema Fatima Yoma; one s. one d.; f. Juventud Peronista (Peron Youth Group), La Rioja Prov. 1955; Legal Adviser, Confederación General del Trabajo, La Rioja Prov. 1955–70; cand. Prov. Deputy 1962; Pres. Partido Justicialista, La Rioja Prov. 1963–; cand. Gov. La Rioja Prov. 1963, elected Gov. 1973, re-elected 1983, 1987; cand. for

Pres. Argentine Repub. for Partido Justicialista 1989. *Address:* Gobernador de la Provincia de la Rioja, Argentina.

MENEMENCIOĞLU, Turgut; Turkish diplomatist; b. 1914, Istanbul; s. of Muvatfak and Kadriye Menemencioğlu; m. Nermin Moran 1944; two s.; ed. Robert Coll., Istanbul and Geneva Univ.; Turkish Ministry of Foreign Affairs 1939–; Perm. Del., European Office UN, Geneva 1950–52; Counsellor, Turkish Embassy, Washington 1952; Dir.-Gen. Econ. Affairs, Ministry of Foreign Affairs 1952–54; Deputy Perm. Rep. to UN 1954–60; Amb. to Canada 1960; Perm. Rep. to UN 1960–62; Amb. to U.S.A. 1962–67; Sec.-Gen. of CENTO (Cen. Treaty Org.) 1967–72; Adviser to Minister of Foreign Affairs 1971–72, Sr. Political Adviser 1978–80; Amb. to U.K. 1972–78; Turkish Rep. Turkish-Greek Cultural Relations Cttee. 1982. *Address:* Inünü Cad 31/12, Taksim, Istanbul, Turkey.

MENG YING; Chinese diplomatist; m. Wang Hongyu; Counsellor, Embassy, Burma 1950, Mongolia 1956–61; Deputy Dir. West Asia and African Dept., Ministry of Foreign Affairs 1961–63; Amb. to Zanzibar 1963–64; Deputy Dir. Asia Dept., Ministry of Foreign Affairs 1964; Amb. to Cen. African Repub. 1964–66, to Mongolia 1978; Vice-Pres. China-Mongolia Friendship Group 1985–, Pres. July 1987–. *Address:* c/o Ministry of Foreign Affairs, Beijing, People's Republic of China.

MENGES, Chris; British cameraman and film director; m. 2nd Judy Freeman 1978; five c. from 1st marriage; TV cameraman on documentaries filmed in Africa, Asia, S. America; cameraman The Killing Fields (Acad. Award), The Mission; Dir. A World Apart.

MENGISTU HAILE MARIAM (see Mariam, Mengistu Haile).

MENK, Louis W.; American railroad executive; b. 8 April 1918, Englewood, Colo.; s. of Louis Albert Menk and Daisy Deane Frantz; m. Martha Jane Swan 1942; one s. one d.; ed. S. Denver High School, Denver and Harvard; messenger, telegrapher, Union Pacific Railroad 1937–40; from telegrapher to Chair. and Pres. St. Louis-San Francisco Railroad 1940–65; Pres. and Dir. Burlington Lines 1965–66; Pres. and Dir. Northern Pacific Railway Co. 1966–70; Pres. and Dir. Burlington Inc. March 1970–71, Chair. of Bd., C.E.O. and Dir. 1971–78, Chair. of Bd. and Dir. June 1978; Chair. Int. Harvester Co. 1982–84 (C.E.O. May–Nov. 1982); Dir. numerous other companies; mem. Bd. of Trustees, Univ. of Denver, Business Roundtable, New York; mem. Business Council, Washington D.C., Bd. of Trustees, Conference Board; Seley Award 1970; Hon. LL.D., Drury Coll. 1965, Univ. Denver 1966, Monmouth Coll. 1967. *Address:* 34815 North Arroyo, Carefree, Ariz. 85377, U.S.A. (Home).

MENNE, W. Alexander, DR.; German company director (retd.); b. 20 June 1904, Dortmund; m. Marianne Müller 1945; one d.; mem. Bundestag, FDP 1961–69, May-Dec. 1972; Chair. Econ. Cttee. of Bundestag 1965–69; Man. Dir. Glasso Paint Products, London 1929–39; Dir. Glasruit-Werke AG, Hamburg 1939–51, Farbwerke Hoechst AG, Frankfurt 1952–69; mem. bd. of various cos. and banks; Vice-Pres. Fed. of German Industry, Cologne 1949–68, mem. Bd. 1968–; Pres. Asscn. of Chemical Industry, Frankfurt 1946–56, mem. Bd. 1956–; mem. Foreign Trade Advisory Bd. at Ministry of Economics; mem. bd. Anglo German Foundation 1973–; Pres. German-American Steuben-Schurz Soc. 1954–75, Hon. Pres. 1975–; Grand Cross Order of Merit with Star (Fed. Repub. of Germany). *Leisure interests:* golfing, hunting, fishing. *Address:* 6242 Kronberg/Ts., Im Brühl 37, Federal Republic of Germany (Home). *Telephone:* 06173/1866.

MENNINGER, Karl Augustus; American psychiatrist; b. 22 July 1893, Topeka, Kan.; s. of Charles Frederick and Flora Knisely Menninger; m. 1st Grace Gaines 1916 (dissolved 1941), one s. two d.; m. 2nd Jeanetta Lyle 1941, one d.; ed. Washburn Coll., Indiana Univ., Univ. of Wisconsin and Harvard Univ. Medical School; Chief of Staff, Menninger Clinic 1925–, Dir. Dept. of Educ., Menninger Foundation 1946–62, Dean, Menninger School of Psychiatry 1946–69, Chair. Menninger Foundation 1954–; Pres. American Psychoanalytic Assn. 1941–43; Chair. Cttee. on Reorganization, American Psychiatric Assn. 1944–49; Dir. Nat. Citizens Comm. for Public Schools 1953–55; mem. Editorial Bd., Journal of American Psychoanalytic Assn. 1954–56; Vice-Pres. American Soc. of Criminology 1960–62; Consultant, Bureau of Prisons, Dept. of Justice 1956, Forbes Air Force Base 1960–73; Chair. Educ. Cttee., Topeka Inst. for Psychoanalysis 1960–70; Sr. Consultant Topeka State Hospital, Topeka Veterans Admin. Hospital; Prof. Univ. of Health Sciences, Chicago Medical School; mem. Chicago Council on Foreign Relations, Presidential Task Force, Prisoner Rehabilitation 1969, also mem. numerous bds., asscns. and acads.; Hon. mem. Royal Medico-Psychological Assn., Environmental Research Foundation; mem. Bd. of Trustees Fund for Advancement of Camping; Hon. D.Sc.(Washburn Univ., Univ. of Wisconsin) 1965, Hon. L.H.D. (Park Coll., DePaul Univ.) 1974, Hon. LL.D. (Jefferson Medical Coll., Parsons Coll., Kansas State Univ.) 1962, (Saint Benedict's Coll., Baker Univ., Kansas) 1965, (Okla. Univ.) 1966, (Pepperdine Univ.) 1973, Hon. dr. of Public Service (Bowling Green State Univ., Ohio) 1982, D.S. (Harvard) 1986; numerous awards. *Publications:* Human Mind 1930, Man Against Himself 1938, Love Against Hate 1942, A Guide to Psychiatric Books 1956, A Manual for Psychiatric Case Study 1962, Theory of Psychoanalytic Technique 1958 (revised 1973), A Psychiatrist's World 1959, The Vital Balance 1963, The Crime of Punishment 1968, Whatever Became of Sin 1973, Sparks (with Lucy Freeman) 1973. *Leisure interests:* horticulture, soil conservation, wildlife preservation, chess, recorded music, American Indians, wines. *Address:* The Menninger Foundation, Box 829, Topeka, Kansas 66601 (Office); 1819 Westwood Circle, Topeka, Kansas 66604, U.S.A. (Home). *Telephone:* (913) 2345002.

MENON, Chelat Achutha, B.A., B.L.; Indian politician; b. 27 Jan. 1913, Trichur; s. of M. Achutha Menon; m. Lakshmykutty Amma 1943; one s. two d.; District Court Pleader, Trichur; took part in congress and trade union activities; restricted for one year for anti-war speech 1940; joined CP and detained for communist activities 1942; Sec. District Cttee. of CP 1943–47; underground 1948–52; elected to Travancore-Cochin Legislative Ass. 1952; mem. Kerala Legis. Ass. 1957, later Finance Minister; mem. Rajya Sabha 1968–69; Chief Minister of Kerala 1969–77. *Publications:* Translation of Short History of the World by H.G. Wells, Soviet Nadu, A Kissan Text Book, Kerala State—Possibilities and Problems, translation of Man Makes Himself by Gordon Child, Sheafs from Memory. *Leisure interest:* literature. *Address:* Saketham, Trichur, India. *Telephone:* 22693.

MENON, Mambillikalathil Govind Kumar, M.SC., PH.D., F.R.S.; Indian physicist; b. 28 Aug. 1928, Mangalore; s. of Kizhekepat Sankara Menon and Mambillikalathil Narayaniamma; m. Indumati Patel 1955; one s. one d.; ed. Jaswant Coll., Jodhpur, Royal Inst. of Science, Bombay, Univ. of Bristol; Research Assoc., Univ. of Bristol 1952–53; Sr. Award of Royal Comm. for Exhbn. of 1851, Univ. of Bristol 1953–55; Reader, Tata Inst. of Fundamental Research, Bombay 1955–58; Assoc. Prof. 1958–60, Prof. and Dean of Physics Faculty 1960–64, Sr. Prof. and Deputy Dir. (Physics) 1964–66, Dir. Tata Inst. of Fundamental Research 1966–75; Chair. Electronics Comm. and Sec. to Govt. of India Dept. of Electronics 1971–78; Scientific Adviser to Minister of Defence, Dir.-Gen. Defence Research and Devt. Org. and Sec. for Defence Research 1974–78; Dir.-Gen. Council of Scientific and Industrial Research 1978–81; Sec. to Govt. of India, Dept. of Science and Tech. 1978–82; Chair. Comm. for Additional Sources of Energy 1981–82; Chair. Science Advisory Cttee. to Cabinet 1982–85; Scientific Adviser to P.M. 1986–, and mem. Govt. Planning Comm. (with rank of Minister of State) 1982–; Pres. Int. Council of Scientific Unions 1988–; Fellow, Indian Acad. of Sciences (Pres. 1974–76), Indian Nat. Science Acad. (Pres. 1981–82); Pres. Indian Science Congress Asscn. 1981–82, Pres. India Int. Centre, New Delhi 1983–; Int. Union of Pure & Applied Physics (IUPAP); Chair. Cosmic Ray Comm. 1973–75; Vice-Pres. 1981–87; Pres. Asia Electronics Union 1973–75; Vice-Pres. Third World Acad. of Sciences 1983–; mem. Pontifical Acad. of Sciences, Rome; Hon. Fellow N.A.S., India (Pres. 1987–); Inst. of Electronics and Telecommunications Eng. of India, Indian Inst. of Science, Bangalore; Nat. Inst. of Educ.; Hon. mem. Inst. of Electrical and Electronic Engineers Inc.; Foreign Hon. mem. American Acad. of Arts and Sciences, U.S.S.R. Acad. of Sciences; Hon. Pres. Asia Electronic Union; Hon. Dr. Eng. (Stevens Inst. of Tech., U.S.A.); Hon. D.Sc. (Jodhpur, Delhi, Sardar Patel, Roorkee, Banaras Hindu, Jadavpur, Sri Venkateswara, Allahabad, Andhra, Utkal and Aligarh Muslim Univs., and I.I.T., Madras); Shanti Swarup Bhatnagar Award for Physical Sciences, Council of Scientific and Industrial Research 1960; Repub. Day (Nat.) Awards, Govt. of India; Padma Shri 1961, Padma Bhushan 1968, Padma Vibhushan 1985, Khaitan Medal, Royal Asiatic Soc. 1973; G. P. Chatterjee Award of Indian Science Congress Asscn. 1984, Award for Professional Excellence 1984, Pandit Jawaharlal Nehru Award for Sciences 1983, Om Prakash Bhasin Award for Science and Tech. 1985, C.V. Raman Medal of Indian Nat. Science Acad. 1985, Fourth J. C. Bose Triennial Gold Medal of Bose Inst. *Publications:* 110 papers on cosmic ray and elementary particle physics. *Leisure interests:* bird-watching, photography. *Address:* Planning Commission, Room 125, Yojana Bhavan, Parliament Street, New Delhi 110001 (Office); 1 Motilal, Nehru Marg, New Delhi 110011, India (Home). *Telephone:* 382148 (Office); 301 8974 (Home).

MENON, Nedyam Balachandra, B.A.; Indian diplomatist; b. 18 March 1921, South India; s. of K. M. R. Menon; m. Aneet Menon 1947; three s. one d.; ed. Allahabad Univ.; Indian Navy 1943–46; Indian Embassy, The Hague 1949; Indian Mil. Mission, Berlin 1951; Indian Embassy, Katmandu 1954; High Comm. of India, Ottawa 1957; Indian Embassy, Washington 1959; Ministry of External Affairs Dir. (China Div.) 1961; Nat. Defence Coll. 1964; Indian Embassy, Bangkok and Perm. Del. to ECAFE 1965; Deputy High Commr., Kuala Lumpur 1966; Political Officer for Sikkim and Bhutan 1967–70; Amb. to Indonesia 1970–73; Jt. Sec. Ministry of External Affairs 1973–75; Amb. to Turkey 1975–76, to Nepal 1976–79. *Address:* c/o Ministry of External Affairs, New Delhi, India.

MENON, Vatakke Kurupath Narayana, M.A., PH.D.; Indian radio official; b. 27 June 1911, Trichur, Kerala; s. of Parameswaran Nambudiripad; m. Rekha Devi Mukherji 1945; one d.; ed. Univ. of Madras and Edinburgh Univ.; Script Writer, Producer and Adviser for E. Services of BBC during Second World War; returned to India 1947; Dir. of Broadcasting, Baroda State 1947–48; joined All-India Radio as Dir. of Staff Training 1948, became Dir. of Delhi, Madras and Calcutta Stations, Dir. of External Services and Deputy Dir.-Gen.; Sec. Nat. Acad. of Music, Dance and Drama, India 1963–65; Dir.-Gen. All-India Radio 1965–68; Pres. Int. Music Council (UNESCO) 1966–68, 1976–78; mem. Faculty of Music, Delhi Univ.; Exec. Dir. Nat. Centre for the Performing Arts, Bombay 1968–82; Vice-Chair. Int. Inst. for Comparative Music Studies, Berlin; Hon. Exec. Dir. Homi Bhabha Fellowship Council 1968–82; Hon. mem. Int. Music Council 1980;

Fellow Sangeet Natak Akad. 1981, Chair. 1982–88; Trustee Int. Broadcasting Inst. 1969–77; Scholar-in-Residence, Aspen Inst. for Humanistic Studies 1973; Padma Bhushan 1969. *Publications:* Development of William Butler Yeats 1942, 1960, Kerala, a Profile 1961, Balasaraswathi 1963, The Communications Revolution 1976. *Leisure interest:* mass communication media. *Address:* Sangeet Natak Akademi, Rabindra Bhavan, New Delhi 110 001, India. *Telephone:* 386648 (Office).

MENOTTI, Gian Carlo; Italian composer; b. 7 July 1911, Cadegliano; ed. Curtis Inst. of Music, Philadelphia, Pa.; went to U.S.A. 1928; mem. teaching staff Curtis Inst. of Music 1941–45; Hon. B.M. (Curtis Inst. of Music); Guggenheim Award 1946, 1947; Pulitzer Prize 1950, 1955; Kennedy Center Award 1984; Hon. Assoc. Nat. Inst. of Arts and Letters 1953; Founder and Pres. Festival of Two Worlds, Spoleto, Italy. *Compositions include:* Operas: Amelia Goes to the Ball, The Old Maid and the Thief, The Island God, The Telephone, The Medium, The Consul, Amahl and the Night Visitors, The Labyrinth (own libretti), The Saint of Bleecker Street 1954, The Last Savage 1963, Martin's Lie 1964, Help, Help, The Glotolinks (space opera for children) 1968, The Most Important Man in the World 1971, Tamu Tamu 1973, Arrival 1973, La Loca 1979, St. Teresa 1982, Goya 1986; Song of Hope (cantata) 1980, The Boy Who Grew Too Fast (opera) 1982, Goya (opera) 1986; Ballet: Sebastian; Film: The Medium (producer); Vanessa (libretto) 1958, The Unicorn, The Gorgon and the Manticore—a Madrigal Fable, Maria Golovin 1959, The Last Superman 1961, The Death of a Bishop of Brindisi (cantata) 1963; chamber music, songs, etc. *Address:* c/o Thea Dispeker, 59 East 54th Street, New York, N.Y. 10022, U.S.A.

MENSAH, Joseph Henry, M.SC.; Ghanaian politician; b. 31 Oct. 1928; ed. Achimota Coll., Univ. Coll. of Gold Coast (now Univ. of Ghana), L.S.E. and Stanford Univ.; Asst. Insp. of Taxes 1953; Research Fellow, Univ. Coll. of Gold Coast 1953–57; lecturer in Econs., Univ. of Ghana 1957–58; Economist, UN H.Q., New York 1958–61; Chief Economist, Prin. Sec. and Exec. Sec. of Nat. Planning Comm. Ghana 1961–65; Economist, UN Dir., Div. of Trade and Econ. Co-operation and Econ. Comm. for Africa (ECA) 1965–69; Commr. of Finance April-July 1969; M.P. for Sunyani (Progress Party) 1969–72; Minister of Finance 1969–72, and of Econ. Planning 1969–71; arrested Jan. 1972, released July 1973; re-arrested 1975; sentenced to eight years' imprisonment with hard labour Oct. 1975, released June 1978.

MENSCHING, Horst Georg, DR. RER. NAT.; German professor of geography; b. 5 June 1921, Porta Westfalia; s. of Georg Mensching and Christine (née Kahre) Mensching; m. 1st Anne Würdemann 1949 (divorced); m. 2nd Ute Esselborn 1983 (deceased); ed. Universität Göttingen; Asst. Inst. of Geography, Univ. of Göttingen 1949–52; Prof. of Geography, Univ. of Würzburg 1952–62; Full Prof. of Geography, Technische Universität Hannover 1962–74; Univ. of Hamburg 1974–85; mem. Acad. of Sciences, Göttingen 1974, Acad. Leopoldina, Halle, Vienna 1974, Hon. mem. Acad. of Hungary 1985; Nachtigal Medal for Studies in Africa, Rüppell Medal, Geographical Soc. of Frankfurt. *Publications:* Geography of Morocco 1957, Geography of Tunisia 1968, North Africa and Middle East 1973, Sahel-Zone 1985; over 200 scientific articles. *Address:* Heinz Hilpert Strasse 10, 3400 Göttingen, Federal Republic of Germany. *Telephone:* (0551) 485007.

MENSHOV, Vladimir Valentinovich; Soviet film director and actor; b. 17 Sept. 1939; ed. Moscow Arts Theatre Studio School, All-Union State Inst. of Cinema (VGIK) 1970; R.S.F.S.R. State Prize 1978, U.S.S.R. State Prize 1981, R.S.F.S.R. Artist of Merit 1984. *Leading roles in* A Man in his Place 1973, Last Meeting 1974, Personal Opinions 1977 etc; *Films include:* Loss (Rozygrysh) 1977, Moscow does not Believe in Tears 1980, Love and Doves 1984.

MENTER, Sir James Woodham, Kt., PH.D., F.R.S.; British university principal and physicist; b. 22 Aug. 1921; s. of late Horace Menter and Jane Anne Lackenby; m. Marjorie Jean Whyte-Smith 1947; two s. one d.; ed. Dover Grammar School and Peterhouse, Cambridge; Experimental Officer, Admiralty 1942–45; Researcher, Univ. of Cambridge 1946–54; Tube Investments Research Labs., Dir. of Research and Devt. 1965–76; Dir. Tube Investments Research Labs. 1961–68, Tube Investments PLC 1965–86, Round Oak Steelworks Ltd. 1967–76, British Petroleum PLC 1976–87, Steetley PLC 1981–85; mem. SRC 1967–72; Vice-Pres. Royal Soc. 1971–76, Treas. 1972–76; Deputy Chair. Advisory Council Applied Research and Devt. 1976–79; Man. Royal Inst. 1981–84, Vice-Pres. 1983–85, Chair. Council 1984–85; Fellow, Churchill Coll., Cambridge; Pres. Inst. of Physics 1970–72, Metals Soc. 1976; Prin. Queen Mary Coll., Univ. of London 1976–86, Fellow 1986–; Hon. D. Tech. (Brunel) 1974, Bessemer Medal, Iron and Steel Inst. 1973, Glazebrook Medal and Prize, Inst. of Physics 1977. *Publications:* scientific papers, proceedings of Royal Society, Advances in Physics, Inst. Iron and Steel, and others. *Leisure interest:* fishing. *Address:* Carie, Rannoch Station, Perthshire, Scotland. *Telephone:* 01-488 3393.

MENTES, Cevdet; Turkish judge and politician; b. 1915, Bitlis; ed. Istanbul Univ.; fmr. public prosecutor and judge, mem. Supreme Court of Appeal 1958, Pres. 1972; Minister of Justice 1980–82. *Address:* c/o Ministry of Justice, Adalet Bakanlığı, Bakanlıklar, Ankara, Turkey.

MENTESHASHVILI, Tengiz Nikolayevich; Soviet (Georgian) politician; Second Sec. Politburo, Cen. Cttee. of Georgian Komsomol 1959–61; mem. Cen. Cttee. of Georgian CP 1964–66, 1976–, Second Sec. 1973–76; First

Sec. Tbilisi Cttee. of Georgian CP 1976-; mem. Politburo, Cen. Cttee. of Georgian CP 1976-; Sec. Presidium of Supreme Soviet of U.S.S.R. 1982-. *Address:* Central Committee of the Georgian Communist Party, Tbilisi, Georgia, U.S.S.R.

MENTRÉ, Paul; French civil servant and diplomatist; b. 28 June 1935, Nancy; s. of Paul Mentré and Cécile de Loye; m. 1st Sabine Brundsaux 1958 (divorced 1975), two d.; m. 2nd Gaëlle Bretillot 1975, two s.; ed. Ecole Polytechnique, Ecole Nat. d'Admin.; Insp. of Finance 1960; Special Asst., French Treas. 1965-70; Deputy Dir. of the Cabinet of the Minister of Finance (M. Giscard d'Estaing) 1971-73; Under-Sec. Ministry of Economy and Finance 1971-72; Dir. Crédit National 1973-75, Crédit lyonnais 1973-; Gen. Del. for Energy 1975-78; Financial Minister, French Embassy in Washington, D.C. 1978-82; Exec. Dir. IMF and World Bank 1978-81; Insp.-Gen. of Finance 1981; Man. Dir. Crédit National 1986-; Chevalier, Ordre nat. du Mérite (France); Saudi Royal Order. *Publications:* Imaginer l'Avenir, Gulliver Enchaîné 1982, articles on economic issues in Le Figaro, Le Monde and Les Echos. *Leisure interests:* tennis, skiing. *Address:* 80 boulevard Flandrin, Paris 75016, France (Home).

MENUHIN, Sir Yehudi, O.M., K.B.E.; British (b. American) violinist; b. 22 April 1916, New York, U.S.A.; s. of Moshe and Marutha Menuhin; m. 1st Nola Ruby Nicholas 1938; one s. one d.; m. 2nd Diana Rosamund Gould 1947; two s.; ed. privately in America and Europe; studied with Sigmund Anker, Louis Persinger, Georges Enesco (in Romania) and with Adolph Busch in Basel; New York debut 1925, Paris 1927 and Berlin 1929 (with Bruno Walter and the Berlin Philharmonic); first world tour 1935, in retirement 1935-37, subsequently appeared as soloist in orchestras under Toscanini, Furtwängler, Stokowski, Koussevitsky, Beecham, Paul Paray, Walter, Mitropoulos, etc.; has undertaken much research and restoration of neglected compositions; gave numerous benefit concerts during and after World War II; since 1945 has toured extensively all over the world and has made documentary musical films in Europe and America; Pres. Trinity Coll. of Music, London; f. the Yehudi Menuhin School, Surrey 1963; yearly festival at Gstaad 1957-, Bath 1959-68, Windsor 1969-72; founder Chair. Live Music Now 1977; Pres. Royal Philharmonic Orchestra 1982-; Prin. Guest Conductor English String Orchestra 1988-; records for His Master's Voice; appeared in film, Raga (with George Harrison and Ravi Shankar) 1974; Pres. Trinity Coll. of Music 1971, Elgar Soc. 1984-; Assoc. mem. Acad. des Beaux-Arts 1986; Hon. Fellow, St. Catharine's Coll., Cambridge 1970, R.I.B.A. 1978, Royal Northern Coll. of Music 1979; Hon. mem. R.A.M., Guildhall School of Music 1972, Royal Scottish Acad. 1981; Hon. D.Mus. (Oxford, Belfast, Leicester, London, Cambridge, Ottawa, Paris, Surrey, San Francisco Conservatory of Music), Hon. LL.D. (St. Andrews, Liverpool, Sussex, Bath), Hon. D.Lit. (Warwick, Leicester), Hon. Doctorate (California); Mozart Medal 1965, Nehru Award for Peace and Int. Understanding (India) 1970, Sonning Music Prize, Denmark 1972, 30th Anniversary Medal of Israel Philharmonic Orchestra, Canadian Music Council Gold Medal, Rosenberger Medal of Univ. of Chicago, Peace Prize of German Booksellers 1979, George Washington Award, American Hungarian Foundation 1980, City of Jerusalem Medal, Gold Medal Royal Philharmonic Soc., Albert Medal (R.S.A.) 1981, Mendelssohn Prize 1986, Kennedy Center Honor 1986, Golden Viotti Prize (Italy) 1987; Grand Chevalier, Légion d'Honneur 1985, Ordre des Arts et des Lettres (France); Commdr., Order of Orange-Nassau (Netherlands); Hon. Swiss Citizen 1970, Freedom of Cities of Edinburgh and Bath, Hon. Citizenship of Ville d'Avray; Ernst-Reuter-Plakette (W. Berlin); Médaille d'Or de la Ville de Paris, Royal Order of Phoenix, Greece, Légion d'honneur, Order of Leopold, Order of Crown, Belgium, Order of Merit, Germany, Hon. K.B.E. (U.K.). *Publications:* The Violin—Six Lessons with Yehudi Menuhin 1971, Theme and Variations 1972, The Violin 1976, Violin and Viola (with William Primrose) 1976, Sir Edward Elgar: my musical grandfather (essay) 1976, Unfinished Journey (autobiography) 1977, Conversations with Menuhin, The Music of Man 1980 (co-author), The King, the Cat and the Fiddle 1983, Life Class 1986, The Compleat Violinist: Thoughts, Exercises and Reflections of a Humanist Violinist 1986. *Address:* c/o Anglo-Swiss Artists' Management, 4 and 5 Primrose Mews, Regent's Park Road, London, NW1 8YL, England.

MENZE, Clemens, DR.PHIL.; German professor of pedagogy; b. 20 Sept. 1928, Tietelsen, Höxter; s. of Clemens Menze and Elisabeth Menke; m. Dr. med. Sigrun Schütz 1968; one d.; ed. Univ. of Cologne; research asst. 1957-63; Asst. Prof. of Pedagogy 1963-65; Adviser in govt. service 1965-67; Prof. and Head, Pedagogical Seminar, Univ. of Cologne 1967-, Rector 1975-77. *Publications:* Wilhelm von Humboldts Lehre und Bild vom Menschen 1965, Die Bildungsreform Wilhelm von Humboldts 1975, Bildung und Bildungswesen (essays) 1980. *Address:* Pädagogisches Seminar, Universität Köln, Albertus-Magnus-Platz, 5000 Köln 1 (Office); Paul-Gerhardt-Strasse 8, 5303 Bornheim-Walberberg, Federal Republic of Germany (Home).

MENZIES, Arthur Redpath, B.A., M.A.; Canadian diplomatist (retd.) and consultant in external affairs; b. 29 Nov. 1916, Changte, Honan, China; s. of Dr. James Mellon and Annie Belle (née Sedgwick) Menzies; m. Sheila Isabel Halliday Skelton 1943; one s. one d.; ed. Canadian Acad., Kobe, Japan, Univ. of Toronto and Harvard Univ.; Dept. of External Affairs 1940-, Second Sec., Havana 1945-46; Head of American and Far East

Div., Dept. of External Affairs, Ottawa 1948-50; Head of Canadian Liaison Mission, Tokyo 1950, later Chargé d'Affaires, Tokyo; Head, Far Eastern Div., Dept. of External Affairs 1953-58; High Commr. in Malaya 1958-61, concurrently Amb. to Burma 1958-61; Head of Defence Liaison (I) Div., Dept. of External Affairs 1962-65; High Commr. in Australia 1965-72, concurrently High Commr. to Fiji 1970-72; Perm. Rep. to N. Atlantic Council 1972-76; Amb. to People's Repub. of China 1976-80, concurrently to Socialist Repub. of Viet-Nam until 1979; Amb. for Disarmament 1980-82. *Leisure interests:* travel, Chinese archaeology, tennis. *Address:* 445 Maple Lane, Rockcliffe, Ottawa, Ont. K1M 1H8, Canada. *Telephone:* 745-9018.

MENZIES, Sir Peter (Thomson), M.A., F.INST.P., C.I.E.E., F.R.S.A.; British business executive; b. 15 April 1912, Chichester, Sussex; s. of John C. Menzies and Helen S. Aikman; m. Mary McPherson Alexander Menzies 1938; one s. one d.; ed. Musselburgh Grammar School and Univ. of Edinburgh; Inland Revenue Dept. 1933-39; Treasurer's Dept., Imperial Chemical Industries (I.C.I.) Ltd. 1939-47, Asst. Treasurer 1947-52, Deputy Treasurer 1952-56, Finance Dir. 1956-67, Deputy Chair. 1967-72; Chair. Imperial Metal Industries Ltd. 1964-72, Electricity Council 1972-77; Dir. Commercial Union Assurance Co. 1962-82; Part-time mem. Cen. Electricity Generating Bd. 1960-72; Dir. Nat. Westminster Bank Ltd. 1968-82; Pres. Int. Union of Producers and Distributors of Electrical Energy (UNIPEDE) 1973-76; Vice-Pres. and Chair. London Exec. Cttee. The Scottish Council (Devt. and Industry) 1977-82; General Treas. and Vice-Pres. B.A.A.S. 1981-86. *Address:* Kit's Corner, Harmer Green, Welwyn, Herts., England. *Telephone:* 043-871 4386.

MEO, Jean Alfred Emile Edouard; French civil servant; b. 26 April 1927, Vosne Romanée, Côte d'Or; s. of Gaston Meo and Marcelle Lamarche; m. Nicole Odelin 1955; one s. two d.; ed. Lycée Henri IV, Ecole Polytechnique, Ecole Nat. Supérieure des Mines, Inst. d'Etudes Politiques; operations engineer, Lorraine Basin coalfields 1952-53; Head of sub-regional mineralogical admin., Lille, teacher at Inst. Industriel du Nord 1954-56; tech. adviser to Minister of Finance 1957; worked in office of Gen. de Gaulle 1958, in Secr. of Presidency 1959-60; Chief Engineer Corps des Mines 1966-; Asst. Man. Dir., later Man. Dir. Union Générale des Pétroles 1964-72 (name changed to Elf Union 1967); Asst. Man. Dir. div. of refining and distribution, ERAP 1966-72 (name changed to Elf-Aquitaine); mem. Bd. of Dirs. and Man. Dir. SOCANTAR 1970-72; Deputy Man. Dir. France-Editions et Publications 1972-74; Chair. and Man. Dir. Agence Havas and Avenir Publicité 1974-76; Jt. Sec.-Gen. Rassemblement pour la République (RPR) 1979-81; mem. European Parl. 1981-82; Conseiller de Paris 1983; Ingénieur Général Corps des Mines 1983; Chair. Institut Français du Pétrole 1986-; Chevalier, Légion d'honneur. *Address:* 1 & 4 avenue de Bois Préau, 92506 Rueil Malmaison (Office); 9 Villa Saïd, 75116 Paris, France (Home).

MER, Francis Paul, L. ÈS SC. ECON.; French business executive; b. 25 May 1939, Pau, Basses Pyrénées; s. of René Mer and Yvonne Casalta; m. Catherine Bonfils 1964; three d.; ed. Lycée Montesquieu, Bordeaux, Ecole Nationale Supérieure des Mines, Paris and Ecole Polytechnique; mining engineer, Ministry of Industry 1966; tech. adviser, Abidjan 1967-68; Chair. Inter-ministerial Cttee. on European Econ. Co-operation 1969-70; Head of Planning, Saint-Gobain Industries 1971; Dir. of Planning, Compagnie Saint-Gobain-Pont-à-Mousson 1973; Dir. of Planning, later Dir.-Gen. Saint-Gobain Industries 1973; Dir. Société des Maisons Phénix 1976-78; Asst. Dir.-Gen. Saint-Gobain-Pont-à-Mousson 1978-82, Pres.-Dir.-Gen. de Pont-à-Mousson SA 1982-86; Pres.-Dir.-Gen. SACILOR and USINOR 1986-. *Address:* Sacilor, 29 le Parvis, Cedex 34, 92072 Paris-La-Défense, France.

MERBAH, Kasdi (Abdallah Khalef), L.EN D.; Algerian politician; b. 1938; joined underground resistance 1956, named Head Operational Information, Gen. Staff of Armée de Libération Nat. 1960; took part in independence negotiations 1961-62; Dir. of Mil. Security 1962-78; mem. Political Bureau, Cen. Cttee., Front de Libération Nat. 1979-80, 1984-; Sec.-Gen., Ministry of Defence 1979, Deputy Minister 1979-80; Minister of Heavy Industry 1982-84, of Agric. 1984-88, of Health Feb.-Nov. 1988; Prime Minister Nov. 1988-. *Address:* Office of the Prime Minister, Algiers, Algeria.

MERCADO JARRIN, Gen. Luis Edgardo; Peruvian army officer and politician; b. 19 Sept. 1919, Barranco, Lima; s. of Dr. Alejandro Mercado Ballón and Florinda Jarrín de Mercado; m. Gladys Neumann Teran de Mercado 1951; one s. four d.; ed. primary and secondary school, Colegio la Libertad de Moquegua, Escuela Militar de Chorrillos; commissioned 1940, Gen. of Div. Jan. 1970-; Prof. Escuela Militar, Escuela de Artillería, Escuela Superior de Guerra, Centro de Altos Estudios Militares, etc.; Dir. of Army Intelligence; del. of Peruvian Army to several inter-American army confs.; guest lecturer to U.S. Army, Fort Holabird and Fort Bragg; Commdt.-Gen. Centro do Instrucción Militar del Perú 1968; Minister of Foreign Affairs 1968-71; Army Chief of Staff Jan.-Dec. 1972; Prime Minister and Minister of War 1973-75; awards include Grand Cross of Orden Militar de Ayacucho and Orden al Mérito Militar, Orden del Sol and orders from Colombia, Portugal, Argentina, Bolivia, Brazil and Venezuela. *Publications:* La Política y la Estrategia Militar en la Guerra Contrasubversiba en América Latina, El Ejército de Hoy en Nuestra Sociedad en Período de Transición y en el Campo Internacional, El Ejército y la Empresa; contributor to magazine of Interamerican Defence Coll., U.S.A., Revista Militar del Perú, Brazilian Military Journal. *Leisure interests:*

tennis, riding, classical music, reading (contemporary military philosophy, sociology and economics). *Address:* Avenida Velasco Astete 1140, Chacarrilla del Estanque, Lima, Peru. *Telephone:* 256823.

MERCER, Robert Edward, B.E.; American company executive; b. 29 March 1924, Elizabeth, N.J.; s. of George W. and Margaret E. Mercer; m. Mary Magdalene Deuel; three s. two d.; ed. Yale Univ.; Pres., Kelly-Springfield Tire Co. 1974–76; Vice-Pres., Marketing, Goodyear Tire and Rubber Co. 1976, Exec. Vice-Pres. and Pres. Tire Div. 1976–78, Pres. and C.O.O. Goodyear Tire and Rubber Co. 1980–82, Chair., C.E.O. 1983–; Chair. Goodyear Int. Corpn. 1983–; mem. Bd. of Dirs. Manufacturers Hanover Corpn., CPC Int., General Electric Co.; mem Bd. of Trustees American Graduate School of Man.; Chair. Council of Better Business Bureaus 1985–88, U.S. Savings Bonds Nat. Sales Campaign 1986; mem. Advisory Council, Stanford Research Inst. Int. *Leisure interests:* baseball, golf. *Address:* Goodyear Tire and Rubber Co., 1144 East Market Street, Akron, Ohio 44316 (Office); 514 North Portage Path, Akron, Ohio 44303, U.S.A. (Home). *Telephone:* (216) 796-4014 (Office); (216) 864-8462 (Home).

MERCHANT, Ismail, B.A., M.B.A.; Indian film producer; b. 25 Dec. 1936, Bombay; s. of Noormohamed Haji Abdul Rehman and Hazra Memon; ed. St. Xavier's Coll., Bombay, New York Univ.; f. Merchant Ivory Productions (with James Ivory q.v.) 1961. *Films:* The Creation of Woman 1960, The Householder 1963, Shakespeare Wallah 1965, The Guru 1969, Bombay Talkie 1970, Adventures of a Brown Man in Search of Civilization, Savages 1972, Helen, Queen of the Nautch Girls 1973, Mahatma and the Mad Boy 1974, Autobiography of a Princess, The Wild Party 1975, Sweet Sounds 1976, Roseland 1977, Hullabaloo Over Georgie and Bonnie's Pictures 1978, The Europeans 1979, Jane Austen in Manhattan 1980, Quartet 1981, Heat and Dust 1982, The Bostonians, The Courtesans of Bombay 1983, A Room with a View 1986, Maurice 1987, Hullaballoo in Old Jaypoore 1988, Slaves of New York 1988, The Deceivers 1988, Mr and Mrs Bridge 1989. *Publication:* Ismail Merchant's Indian Cuisine 1986. *Leisure interests:* cooking, racquetball, cycling, squash. *Address:* 400 East 52nd Street, New York, N.Y. 10022, U.S.A. (Home). *Telephone:* (212) 759-3694.

MERCIER, Pierre; French doctor of medicine; b. 6 Aug. 1910, Auxerre, Yonne; s. of Abel and Louise (née Thomas) Mercier; m. Yvonne Magniat 1936; one s. one d.; ed. Lycée Auxerre and Faculté de Médecine, Univ. of Paris; Asst. Hôpital Raymond-Poincaré 1938–51; successively research worker, lab. head and section head, Inst. Pasteur, Paris 1938–51; Dir. Inst. Pasteur, Athens 1951–62; Attaché French Embassy, Athens 1951–62; Asst. Sec.-Gen. Inst. Pasteur 1963–66, Sec.-Gen. Jan.-June 1966, Dir. 1966–71, Hon. Dir. 1971–; Tech. Adviser to Minister of Health 1971–80; mem. Acad. de Médecine; Pres. Fondation Franco-Américaine du Mont Valérien; Hon. mem. Acad. Médicine de Belgique; Officier, Légion d'honneur, Officier, Order of George I and Commdr., Order of Phoenix (Greece), Chevalier, Ordre de Léopold; Médaille des Epidémies; Croix rouge française. *Publications:* over 200 works from 1934–62. *Address:* 11 bis avenue Emile-Deschanel, 75007 Paris, France.

MERCOURI, Melina; Greek actress and politician; b. 18 Oct. 1925; m. Jules Dassin (q.v.). *Films include:* Stella 1955, He Who Must Die 1956, Gipsy and the Gentleman, Never on Sunday 1959, Phaedra 1961, The Victors 1963, Light of Day 1963, Les pianos mécaniques 1964, A Man Could Get Killed 1966, 10.30 p.m. Summer 1966, Gaily, Gaily 1970, Promise at Dawn 1970, Once Is Not Enough 1975, Nasty Habits 1976, Maya and Brenda 1977, A Dream of Passion 1978; song and dance version of Never on Sunday called Illya Darling, Broadway 1967, Lysistrata (musical) 1972, played Medea in The Medea (production on Mount Lycabettos, Greece), Sweet Bird of Youth 1979, Clytaemnestra in Oresteia 1980; mem. Parl. (PASOK) for the Port of Piraeus 1977–; Minister of Culture and Sciences 1981–85, of Culture, Youth and Sports 1985–; Tregene Prize 1984. *Publication:* I was Born Greek (autobiography) 1971. *Address:* c/o Ministry of Culture and Sciences, Odos Aristidou 14, Athens, Greece.

MERCURE, Jean; French actor and theatrical director; b. 27 March 1909, Paris; s. of David-Gaston and Jeanne (née Horwitz) Libermann; m. Aline Jeannerot 1936; one d.; ed. Lycée Rollin, Paris; Dir. Théâtre de la Ville, Paris; has directed and played leading roles in The Flashing Stream, Skipper Next to God, Miss Mabel, Living Room, La volupté de l'honneur, Tea and Sympathy, Sur la terre comme au ciel, Sud, Cardinal d'Espagne, Vol de nuit, Six personnages en quête d'auteur 1968, L'engrenage 1969, La guerre de Troie n'aura pas lieu 1971, Les possédés 1972, The National Health, La visite de la vieille dame 1976, Zoo ou l'assassin philantrope 1975, La Maison des coeurs brisés 1978, Make and Break 1981, Volpone 1985; also producer/dir. opera, Opéra de Paris and Aix-en-Provence Festival; Grand Prix de la Mise en Scène 1953, Prix de la meilleure réalisation lyrique for Vol de Nuit 1960; Commdr., Légion d'honneur, Commdr. des Arts et Lettres. *Publications:* French adaptations of Skipper Next to God (J. de Hartog), Sur la terre comme au ciel (with R. Thieberger) (Hochwälder), Le silence de la mer (Vercors), Thunder Rock (Ardrey), The Living Room, The Potting Shed (Greene) and The Royal Hunt of the Sun (Shaffer), Gin Game (Coburn). *Address:* 12 villa Léandre, 75018 Paris, France. *Telephone:* 42-64-21-14.

MEREDITH, William (Morris Meredith), A.B.; American poet and educationalist; b. 9 Jan. 1919, New York; s. of William Morris and Nelley (née

Keyser) Meredith; ed. Princeton Univ.; reporter New York Times 1940–41; Instructor in English and Creative Writing Princeton Univ. 1946–50; Asst. Prof. in English Univ. of Hawaii 1950–51; mem. Faculty Conn. Coll. 1955–, Prof. of English 1965–83; Dir. Conn. Coll. Humanities-Upward Bound Program 1964–68; Poetry Conservator Library of Congress 1978–80; Chancellor Acad. of American Poets 1964–; mem. Nat. Inst. of Arts and Letters; Air Medal with Oak Leaf Cluster; awarded Loines Prize Nat. Inst. of Arts and Letters 1966, Van Wyck Brooks Award 1971, Int. Nicola Vaptsarov Prize in Literature, Sofia 1979, Pulitzer Prize for Poetry 1988. *Publications:* poems: Love Letter from an Impossible Land 1944, Ships and Other Figures 1948, The Open Sea and Other Poems 1958, Shelley 1962, The Wreck of the Thresher and Other Poems 1964, Winter Verse 1964, Alcools (trans.) 1964, Earth Walk: New and Selected Poems 1970, Hazard, The Painter 1975, The Cheer 1980, Partial Accounts: New and Selected Poems 1987. *Address:* Connecticut College, P.O. Box 1498, New London, Conn. 06320, U.S.A.

MERIKAS, George, M.D.; Greek professor of medicine; b. 5 May 1911, Andreas; s. of Emmanuel Merikas and Helen (née Kritikou) Merikas; m. Irene (née Koutsogianni) Merikas 1945 (died 1971); two s. one d.; ed. Medical School, Univ. of Athens; Assoc. Prof. of Medicine, Univ. of Athens 1953, Prof. 1970–78; Dir. Dept. of Medicine, Evangelismos Hosp., Athens 1960–70; Fulbright Grant, Univ. of Cincinnati Medical School 1964–65; mem. Acad of Athens 1978–, Pres. 1988–; Pres. Nat. Aids Cttee. in Greece 1988–; mem. Accad. Tiberina, New York Acad. of Sciences, Asscn. for the Advancement of Sciences. *Publications:* Hepatitis Associated Antigen in Chronic Liver Disease 1970, Australia Antigen in the Liver 1972, Hepatitis B Core Antigen and Antibody in Primary Liver Cancer 1975, Internal Medicine, 2 Vols. 1976, Cholesterol Gall-Stone Dissolution by CDC 1976. *Leisure interests:* literature, history. *Address:* 6 Nasileos Irakliou Str., 10682 Athens, Greece. *Telephone:* (01) 8210719.

MERIKOSKI, Veli Kaarlo, DR. IUR.; Finnish politician and university professor; b. 2 Jan. 1905, Pyhtaa; s. of Kaarlo Merikoski and Salli Nevalainen; m. Wava Margit Winge 1941 (died 1968); two s. one d.; ed. Helsinki Univ.; Asst. teacher of Public Law, Helsinki Univ. 1936, Prof. of Admin. Law 1941–69, Dean, Faculty of Law 1947–51; mem. High Court of Impeachment 1950–71; Chair. Union of Finnish Lawyers 1946–51, 1956–58; Chair. Finnish People's Party 1958–61; Minister of Foreign Affairs 1962–63; mem. Hague Int. Court of Arbitration 1966–; Chancellor of Turku School of Economics 1974–77; mem. Finnish Acad. of Science and Letters; Pres. Int. Asscn. of Universities 1970–75, Hon. Pres. 1975–; numerous awards and decorations. *Publications:* Freedom of Association 1935, The Concept of Dispensation 1936, The System of Government Grants 1938, Textbook of Finnish Public Law, Vol. I 1944, Vol. II 1946, Lectures on the Legal Aspect of Social Welfare 1948, The Rule of Law 1953, Juridical Position of Universities and Student Organisations 1954, Précis du droit public de la Finlande 1954, The Citizen's ABC-book 1955, Finnish Public Law, Vol. I 1952, Vol. II 1962, Le pouvoir discrétionnaire de l'administration 1958, The System of Legal Protection in Administration 1959, University Autonomy 1966, The Politicization of Public Administration 1969, The Question of University Administration in Finland 1969–1970 1970. *Address:* Urheilutie 15 A 2, 02700 Kauniainen, Finland. *Telephone:* 50-25-15.

MERILLON, Jean-Marie; French diplomatist; b. 12 Feb. 1926; s. of Robert Mérillon and Marguerite Dubourg; m. Jacqueline Plasschaert 1961; one s.; ed. Ecole Nat. d'Admin.; served at Ministry of Foreign Affairs 1952–68; Amb. to Jordan 1968–73, to S. Vietnam 1973–75, to Greece 1975–77; Dir. of Political Affairs 1977–79; Amb. to Algeria 1979–81, to NATO 1982–85, to Switzerland 1985–. *Address:* Schosshaldenstrasse 46, 3006 Bern, Switzerland (Office); 80 boulevard de Courcelles, 75017 Paris, France (Home).

MERINO CASTRO, Admiral José Toribio; Chilean naval officer; b. 14 Dec. 1915; m. Gabriela Margarita Riofrío Bustos 1952; three d.; ed. Naval Acad.; specialized as Gunnery Officer, Naval Acad.; naval service on Maipo 1936, Rancagua 1939; Instructor Blanco Encalada 1940; Div. Officer Almirante Latorre 1943; Asst. F.C. Officer U.S.S. Raleigh, Pacific Theater 1944; Artillery Officer, Serrano 1945; Commdr. of Corvette Papudo 1952; Tech. Adviser of Armaments 1955; Commdr. of destroyer Williams 1962, Riveros 1963; Vice-Chief of Gen. Staff 1964; C.-in-C. of the Fleet 1970–71; C.-in-C. of First Naval Zone 1972–73; C.-in-C. of the Navy and mem. of the Govt. Junta 1973; Armed Forces Medal III, II, I, Grand Star of Merit, Cross for Naval Merit, Decoration of Pres. of Repub. (Chile). *Address:* c/o Naval Headquarters, Santiago, Chile.

MERITT, Benjamin Dean, A.B., A.M., LL.D., PH.D., D.LITT., L.H.D.; American philologist; b. 31 March 1899, Durham, N.C.; s. of Arthur H. and Cornelia (Dean) Meritt; m. 1st Elizabeth Kirkland 1923, 2nd Lucy T. Shoe 1964; two s.; ed. Hamilton Coll., American School of Classical Studies, Athens, and Princeton Univ.; Instructor in Greek, Univ. of Vermont 1923–24, Brown Univ. 1924–25; Asst. Prof. of Greek, Princeton Univ. 1925–26; Asst. Dir. American School of Classical Studies, Athens 1926–28, Visiting Prof. 1932–33, 1969–70, Annual Prof. 1936, 1954–55; Assoc. Prof. of Greek and Latin, Univ. of Michigan 1928–29, Prof. 1929–33; Dir. Athens Coll. 1932–33; Francis White Prof. of Greek, Johns Hopkins Univ. 1933–35; Prof. Inst. for Advanced Study, Princeton 1935–69, Prof. Emer.; Eastman Prof. Oxford 1945–46; Sather Prof. Univ. of Calif. 1959; Visiting Prof. Univ. of

Texas 1971–72, Visiting Scholar 1973–; Foreign mem. Acad. of Athens; Fellow American Acad. of Arts and Sciences; hon. councillor, Greek Archaeological Society; mem. American Philological Assen. 1922–, Pres. 1953; corresp. mem. Royal Flemish Acad.; mem. American Philosophical Soc.; corresp. mem. British Acad.; hon. mem. Soc. for the promotion of Hellenic Studies; mem. German Archaeological Inst.; Commdr. Royal Order of Phoenix (Greece) and Commdr., Royal Order of George I (Greece). *Publications:* The Athenian Calendar in the Fifth Century 1928, Supplementum Epigraphicum Græcum, Vol. V (with Allen B. West) 1931, Corinth, Vol. VIII, Part I, Greek Inscriptions 1931, Athenian Financial Documents 1932, The Athenian Assessment of 425 B.C. (with Allen B. West) 1934, Documents on Athenian Tribute 1937, The Athenian Tribute Lists (with H.T. Wade-Gery and M.F. McGregor), Vol. I 1939, Vol. II 1949, Vol. III 1950, Vol. IV 1953, The Chronology of Hellenistic Athens (with W.K. Pritchett) 1940, Epigraphica Attica 1940, The Athenian Year 1961, Agora XV: The Athenian Councillors (with John S. Traill) 1974. *Address:* 712 West 16th Street, Austin, Tex. 78701, U.S.A. *Telephone:* 512-476-3103.

MERKELBACH, Reinhold, D.PHIL.; German professor of classics; b. 7 June 1918, Grenzhausen; s. of Paul Merkelbach and Gertrud Stade; m. Lotte Dorn 1941; one s. two d.; ed. Schondorf Gymnasium, Univs. of Munich and Hamburg; Asst. at Classics Inst. Univ. of Cologne 1950–57, Prof. 1961–83, Prof. Emer. 1983–; Prof. Erlangen Univ. 1957–61; mem. Rheinisch-Westfälisch Akad. der Wissenschaften 1979–; Corresp. mem. British Acad. 1986–; Dr. h.c. Univ. of Besançon, France 1978. *Publications:* Untersuchungen zur Odyssee 1951, Die Quellen des griechischen Alexanderromans 1954, Roman und Mysterium im Altertum 1961, Isisfeste 1962, (with M. West) Fragmenta Hesiodea 1968, (with F. Solmsen and M. West) Hesiodim Opera 1970, Mithras 1984, Die Hirten des Dionysos 1988, Platons Menon 1988, many edns. of Greek inscriptions, Ed. of Zeitschrift für Papyrologie und Epigraphik, Epigraphica anatolica, Beiträge zur klassischen Philologie. *Address:* University of Cologne, Institut für Altertumskunde, Kringsweg 9/IV, 5000 Köln 41; Parkstrasse 2, 8139 Bernried, Federal Republic of Germany. *Telephone:* 0221 470 2357 (Office); 02204 60717; 08158 8324.

MERLE D'AUBIGNÉ, Robert Aimé; French surgeon; b. 23 July 1900, Neuilly; s. of Charles Merle d'Aubigné and Lucy Maury; m. 1st Anna de Gunzburg 1932, one s. one d.; m. 2nd Christine Maroger 1975; ed. Lycée Pasteur, Univ. of Paris; hosp. surgeon 1936–39; Capt. in medical corps 1939–41; active in Resistance; Prof. of Orthopaedic and Reconstructive Surgery, Univ. of Paris 1948–70; Surgeon, Cochin Hospital 1948–60; Dean of Faculty, Cochin 1968–69; mem. Acad. des Sciences 1966–, Inst. de France, Acad. of Surgery, Nat. Acad. of Medicine and many French and int. learned socs.; Hon. F.R.C.S., Hon. F.R.C.S.(E), Hon. F.A.C.S.; Grand Officier Légion d'honneur, Officier Ordre de la Résistance, Croix de guerre. *Publications:* Précis de pathologie chirurgicale 1948, Affections traumatiques 1951, Chirurgie du paralysé 1960, Chirurgie de rhumatisme 1970, Technique chirurgicale orthopédique 1974. *Leisure interests:* mountaineering, sailing, farming. *Address:* 4 rue Croix-Saint-Antoine, 77116 Ury, France.

MERLONI, Dott. Vittorio; Italian industrialist; b. 30 April 1933, Fabriano, Ancona; Pres. Merloni Elettrodomestici S.p.A. 1970–; Confederazione Generale dell'Industria Italiana (Confindustria) 1976–, Pres. 1980–84; Dir. Harvard Business School 1981; mem. two dels. to China; mem. Consiglio Nazionale dell'Economia e del Lavoro (Nat. Council of Economy and Labour); Cavaliere di Gran Croce al merito della Repubblica. *Address:* Confindustria, Viale dell'Astronomia 30, 00144 Rome (Office); Via Aristide Merloni 45, 1-60044 Fabriano, Ancona, Italy (Home). *Telephone:* 06-59031 (Office).

MERMAZ, Louis; French politician; b. 20 Aug. 1931, Paris; teacher lycée le Mans, lycée Lakanal, Sceaux; junior lecturer in contemporary history, Univ. of Clermont-Ferrand; Sec.-Gen. Convention des institutions républicaines 1965–69; mem. Socialist Party Exec. Cttee. 67–; mem. Nat. Assembly for Isère 1967–68, March 1973–; Mayor of Vienne 1971–; Conseiller gén. Canton of Vienne-Sud 1973–; Pres. Conseil gén. of Isère 1976–85; Chair. Socialist Party Exec. Cttee. 1979; Minister of Transport May–June 1981, May–June 1988; Pres. Nat. Ass. 1981–86. *Address:* c/o Assemblée nationale, 126 rue de l'Université, 75355 Paris; Mairie, place de l'Hôtel de ville, 38200 Vienne, France.

MERRICK, David; American theatrical producer; b. 27 Nov. 1912, St. Louis; s. of Samuel and Celia Margulios; m. Etan Aronson; ed. St. Louis Univ.; producer of numerous plays on Broadway, including Fanny 1954, The Matchmaker 1955, Look Back in Anger, Romanoff and Juliet, Jamaica 1957, The Entertainer, The World of Suzie Wong, La plume de ma tante, Epitaph for George Dillon, Maria Golovin 1958, Destry Rides Again, Gypsy, Take Me Along 1959, The Good Soup, Vintage '60', Irma la Douce, A Taste of Honey, Becket, Do Re Me 1960, Carnival 1961, Sunday in New York 1961, Ross 1961, I Can Get it for You Wholesale 1962, Stop the World, I Want to Get Off 1962, Tchin Tchin 1962, Oliver! 1962, Rehearsal 1963, Hello Dolly 1964, Pickwick 1965, Inadmissible Evidence 1965, Cactus Flower 1965, Marat/Sade 1965, Don't Drink the Water 1966, I do! I do! 1966, Philadelphia, Here I Come 1966, Rosencrantz and Guildenstern Are Dead 1967, How Now, Dow Jones 1967, The Happy Time 1967, Promises Promises 1968, 40 Carats 1968, Play It Again Sam 1969, Private Lives

1969, Child's Play 1970, A Midsummer Night's Dream, Four on a Garden, The Philanthropist 1971, There's One in Every Marriage, Vivat, Vivat Regina!, Moonchildren, Sugar 1972, Child's Play 1972, Out Cry 1973, Mack and Mabel 1974, Dreyfus in Rehearsal 1974, Travesties, The Red Devil Battery Sign, Very Good Eddie 1975; produced films The Great Gatsby 1974, Semi-Tough 1977, Rough Cut 1980.

MERRIFIELD, (Robert) Bruce; American biochemist; b. 15 July 1921, Texas; s. of George and Lorene Merrifield; m. Elizabeth Furlong 1949; six c.; ed. Univ. of California, Los Angeles (U.C.L.A.); Chemist, Park Research Foundation 1943–44; Teaching Asst., Chem. Dept. U.C.L.A. 1944–47, Research Asst., Medical School 1948–49; Asst. to Assoc. Prof. Rockefeller Inst. 1949–66, Prof. of Biochem. 1966–; developed solid phase peptide synthesis; mem. Nat. Acad. of Sciences; Nobel Guest Prof. 1968; Lasker Award 1969, Gairdner Award 1970, Intra-Science Award 1970, A.C.S. Award 1972, Nichols Award 1973, Pierce Award 1979, Nobel Prize for Chem. 1984 for devt. of method of extracting peptides and proteins. *Publications:* 150 articles in various scientific journals. *Leisure interests:* tennis, camping, hiking. *Address:* Rockefeller University, New York, N.Y. 10021; 43 Mezzine Drive, Cresskill, N.J. 07626, U.S.A. (Home). *Telephone:* (212) 570-8244 (Office); (201) 567-0329 (Home).

MERRILL, James, B.A.; American author; b. 3 March 1926, New York; s. of Charles Edward and Hellen (née Ingram) Merrill; ed. Amherst Coll.; served with U.S. Army 1944–45; mem. Nat. Inst. of Arts and Letters; numerous awards include Bollingen Prize for Poetry 1973, Nat. Book Award for Poetry 1979. *Publications (poetry):* First Poems 1951, The Country of a Thousand Years of Peace 1959, Water Street 1962, Nights and Days 1967 (Nat. Book Award), The Fire Screen 1969, Braving the Elements 1972, The Yellow Pages 1974, Divine Comedies 1976 (Pulitzer Prize), Mirabell: Books of Numbers 1978. *Prose:* The Seraglio 1957, The (Diblos) Notebook 1965, Scripts for the Pageant 1980, The Changing Light at Sandover 1982, Santonini Stopping the Leak 1982, Souvenirs 1984, Bronze 1984, Late Settings 1985. *Plays:* The Immortal Husband 1956, The Bait 1960. *Address:* 107 Water Street, Stonington, Conn. 06378, U.S.A. (Home).

MERRILL, Maurice Hitchcock, A.B., LL.B., S.J.D.; American lawyer and university teacher; b. 3 Oct. 1897, Washington, D.C.; s. of George Waite and Mary Lavinia (Hitchcock) Merrill; m. Orpha Roberts 1922 (died 1971); one d.; ed. Univ. of Oklahoma and Harvard Univ.; served in U.S. Army 1918; taught in Univ. of Okla. 1919–22; practised law in Tulsa, Okla. 1922–26; Assoc. Prof. of Law, Univ. of Idaho 1925–26; Asst. Prof. of Law, Univ. of Nebraska 1926–28, Prof. of Law 1928–36; Prof. of Law, Univ. of Okla. 1936–50, Research Prof. of Law 1950–68, Research Prof. Emer. 1968, Act. Dean 1945–46; law practice Norman, Okla. 1968–; Gen. Counsel, Okla. Assen. of Municipal Attorneys 1971–; mem. Judicial Council of Okla. 1945–46, 1947–65; Commr. from Okla. to Nat. Conf. of Commrs. on Uniform State Laws 1944–, mem. Exec. Cttee. 1961–68, Vice-Pres. 1963–67, Chair. Okla. del. 1949–; mem. Panel of Labor Arbitrators U.S. Conciliation Service 1946–; mem. Nat. Acad. of Arbitrators, Perm. Ed. Bd. for Uniform Commercial Code 1963–75; Bd. of Advisers S.W. Inst. of Local Govt. Law 1968–75; mem. Special Comm. on Constitutional Revision (Okla.) 1969–70; Fellow, American Bar Foundation 1956–; Hon. D.Hum.Litt. (Okla. Christian Coll.) 1974; Hatton W. Sumners Award 1964; Distinguished Service Citation, Univ. of Okla. 1968; Okla. Hall of Fame 1970; President's Award, Okla. Bar Assen. 1972. *Publications:* Law of Covenants Implied in Oil and Gas Leases 1926, Nebraska Annotations to Restatement of Contracts (with William Sternberg and Lester B. Orfield) 1932, Nebraska Annotations to Restatement of Agency 1933, Oklahoma Annotations to Restatement of Agency 1940; mem. Bd. of Eds. and Ed. for Volume III (The Nation and the States), Selected Essays on Constitutional Law 1938, Cases and Materials on Administrative Law 1950, Law of Notice 1952, Administrative Law (American Case-book Series) 1954, The Public's Concern with the Fuel Minerals 1960, Lawyer from Wewoka Switch 1983. *Leisure interests:* writing, gardening. *Address:* 302 Law Center Building, 300 W. Timberdell Road, University of Oklahoma, Norman, Okla. 73019 (Office); 800 Elm Avenue, Norman, Okla. 73069, U.S.A. (Home). *Telephone:* 325-4373 (Office); 321-6585 (Home).

MERRILL, Richard Austin, M.A., LL.B.; American lawyer and professor of law; b. 20 May 1937, Logan, Utah; s. of Milton R. Merrill and Bessie A. Merrill; m. Elizabeth Duvall 1961; one s. one d.; ed. Colombia Coll., Oxford Univ., and Columbia Univ. School of Law; Law Clerk to Judge Carl McGowan, U.S. Court of Appeals, Dist. of Columbia Circuit 1964–65; in pvt. law practice with Covington & Burling, Washington, D.C. 1965–69; Assoc. Prof., Univ. of Va. School of Law 1969–72, Prof. 1972–75, Assoc. Dean 1974–75, Daniel Caplin Prof. 1977–85, 1988–, Arnold Leon Prof. 1985–88, Dean 1980–88; Chief Counsel U.S. Food and Drug Admin. 1975–77; mem. Bd. of Eds. Food Drug Cosmetic Law Journal, Journal of Regulatory Pharmacology and Toxicology, Bd. of Advisers Environmental Law Reporter, Bd. of Trustees Environmental Law Inst., Food and Drug Law Inst., Inst. of Medicine (Council), N.A.S., Bd. on Toxicology and Environmental Health Hazards; Fellow American Bar Foundation. *Publications:* Food and Drug Law: Cases and Materials (with Peter Barton Hutt) 1980, Federal Regulation of Cancer Causing Chemicals 1982, Risk Quantitation and Regulatory Policy: Banbury Report 19 (Co-Ed.) 1985,

Administrative Law: The American Public Law System: Cases and Materials (with Jerry L. Mashaw) 1985; numerous articles. *Leisure interests:* tennis, squash, golf, gardening, travel. *Address:* University of Virginia School of Law, Charlottesville, Va. 22901; 501 Wellington Place, Charlottesville, Va. 22901, U.S.A. (Home).

MERRILL, Robert; American baritone; b. 4 June 1919, Brooklyn, New York; s. of Abraham Miller and Lillian (née Balaban) Merrill; m. Marion Machno 1954; one s. one d; debut at Metropolitan Opera as Germont (La Traviata) 1945; has since appeared throughout U.S.A. and Europe in most of the baritone repertoire including: Gérard (André Chénier), Renato (A Masked Ball), Figaro (The Barber of Seville), Rodrigo (Don Carlos), Scarpia (Tosca), Amonasro (Aida) and Rigoletto; many concert and television appearances; frequent recordings. *Publications:* Once More from the Beginning 1965, Between Acts 1976, The Divas 1978. *Leisure interests:* art and golf. *Address:* c/o RMAI, 79 Oxford Road, New Rochelle, N.Y. 10804, U.S.A.

MERRITHEW, Gerald S., B.A., B.ED.; Canadian politician; b. 23 Sept. 1931, Saint John, N.B.; m. Gloria McLean; six c.; ed. Fredericton Teachers' Coll., Univ. of New Brunswick; 16 years' service in Canadian Army Militia (rank of Lieut.-Col., Commanding Officer, Royal N.B. Regt.), now Hon. Lieut.-Col., First Bn., Royal N.B. Regt.; mem. N.B. Legislature 1972-84, N.B. Minister of Educ. 1974-76, of Commerce and Devt. 1976-82, of Natural Resources, responsible for energy policy 1982-84, Govt. House Leader 1978-84; M.P., House of Commons, Minister of State for Forestry and Mines 1984-88, of Veterans' Affairs Jan. 1989-; Chair. Maritime Foresty Complex Corpn., Forestry Protection Ltd.; Exec. Mem. Army Cadet League of N.B.; mem. Red Cross Youth Advisory Bd., Council of St. John Art Club, N.B. Rifle Asscn., N.B. Black Powder Assn. *Address:* 434 Confederation Building, Ottawa, Ont. K1A 0A6 (Office); 3 Kennington Street, East Saint John, N.B. E2J 2Z1, Canada (Home).

MERSZEI, Zoltan, LL.D., D.SC.; Canadian company executive; b. 30 Sept. 1922, Budapest, Hungary; m. 1946; three s. one d.; ed. Jozsef Nador Polytechnicum, Budapest, Fed. Polytechnic Inst., Zürich, Northwood Inst., Albion Coll.; Pres. of Dow Chemical Europe 1965-75; Mem., Bd. of Dirs., Dow Chemical Co. 1968, Vice-Pres. and mem. of Exec. Cttee. 1971, Exec. Vice-Pres. 1975, Pres. and C.E.O 1976-78, Chair. 1978-79; Chair., Dow Chemical of Canada 1975; Pres. and C.O.O. Occidental Petroleum Co. 1979-80, Vice-Chair. 1979-86, Consultant 1986-; Pres. ENOXY (subsidiary of ENI (Ente Nazionale Idrocarburi) and Occidental Petroleum) 1981-83; C.E.O. Hooker Chemical Corpn. 1979-; bd. mem., Dow Banking Corpn., Handelsbank; Hon. LL.D. (Northwood Inst.) 1976, Hon. D.Sc. (Albion Coll.) 1978, Hon. D.Chem.Eng. (Veszprem Univ., Hungary) 1983; mem. exec. cttee. American Section Soc. of Chemical Industry; U.S.A. govt. 'E' award, Grand Cross of the Order of Merit (Spain), Commdr. Order of Orange Nassau (Netherlands). *Leisure interest:* skiing. *Address:* Dallhold Investments Pty. Ltd., R and I Tower, Level 33, 108 St. George's Terrace, Perth 6000, Western Australia (Office); 583 Lake Avenue, Greenwich, Connecticut 06830, U.S.A. (Home). *Telephone:* (61) 9-324-8200 (Office); (203) 869-0628 (Home).

MERTENS DE WILMARS, Josse Marie Honoré Charles, Baron D.L., D.POL.SC.; Belgian lawyer; b. 12 June 1912, St. Niklaas; s. of Albert Mertens and Jeanne Meert; m. Betty van Ormelingen 1939; eight c.; ed. Abbey School St. Andries, Bruges, Univ. of Louvain; mem. Bar 1935-67; Assessor, Conseil d'Etat 1948-51; M.P. 1951-61; Prof. of Law, Univ. of Louvain 1967-81; Judge, Court of Justice of European Communities 1967-84, Pres. 1980-84; Knight, Order of Léopold, Grand Croix Ordre de la Couronne, Grosskreuz Deutsche Verdienstorde, Grootkruis Orde Oranje Nassau, Grand Croix Ordre Couronne de Chêne. *Address:* Jan Van Ryswycklaan 192, 2020 Antwerp, Belgium. *Telephone:* 0032-32-380768 (Home).

MERTIN, Klaus, DR.RER.POL.; German banker; b. 9 March 1922; Chair. of Supervisory Bd. Deutsche Bank Berlin AG, Berlin, Dierig Holding AG, Augsburg; Deputy Chair. of Supervisory Bd. Deutsche Centralbodenkredit-A.G., Berlin, Cologne; mem. of Supervisory Bd. A.G. für Industrie und Verkehrswesen, Frankfurt, Badenwerk AG, Karlsruhe, Daimler-Benz AG, Stuttgart, Gerling-Konzern-Versicherungs-Beteiligungs AG, Cologne, Heidelberger Druckmaschinen AG, Heidelberg, Karstadt AG, Essen, Rheinmetall Berlin AG, Düsseldorf, Salamander AG, Kornwestheim, Schindler Aufzügefabrik GmbH, Berlin; mem. of Advisory Bd. Barmenia Versicherungen, Wuppertal; mem. of Admin. Council Deutsche Bank Compagnie Financière Luxembourg, Luxembourg; mem. of Exec. Council Schott Glaswerke, Mainz. *Address:* Deutsche Bank AG, Taunusanlage 12, 6000 Frankfurt am Main, Federal Republic of Germany.

MERTON, Patrick Anthony, M.D., F.R.S.; British professor of human physiology; b. 8 Oct. 1920, Kent; s. of Gerald Merton; m. Anna Gabriel Howe 1951; one s. three d.; ed. Beaumont, Trinity Coll., Cambridge, St. Thomas's Hosp.; MRC Neurological Research Unit, London 1946-57, Physiological Lab., Cambridge 1957-; Fellow Trinity Coll., Cambridge 1962-; Prof. of Human Physiology, Cambridge Univ. 1984-88; Hon. Consultant Nat. Hosp., London 1979-. *Publications:* scientific papers in Journal of Physiology and Brain. *Address:* 12 Lansdowne Road, Cambridge, CB3 0EU, England. *Telephone:* (0223) 359991.

MERTON, Robert K., PH.D.; American professor of sociology; b. 5 July 1910, Philadelphia, Pa.; ed. Temple Univ. and Harvard Univ.; Tutor and Instructor in Sociology, Harvard Univ. 1936-39; Assoc. Prof. and Prof. Tulane Univ. 1939-41; Asst. Prof. to Prof., Columbia Univ. 1941-63, Giddings Prof. of Sociology 1963-74, Univ. Prof. 1974-79; Emer. and Special Service Prof. 1979-; Assoc. Dir., Bureau of Applied Social Research, Columbia Univ. 1942-70; Chair. Centre for the Social Sciences, Columbia Univ. 1976-; Adjunct Prof. Rockefeller Univ. 1979-; George Sarton Prof. of Historical Sciences, Univ. of Ghent, Belgium 1986-; mem. N.A.S., American Philosophical Soc., American Acad. of Arts and Sciences, Nat. Acad. of Educ., World Acad. of Arts and Sciences; Pres. American Sociological Asscn. 1957, Sociological Research Asscn. 1968, Eastern Sociological Soc. 1969; Pres. Soc. for Social Studies of Science 1975-76; mem. John Simon Guggenheim Memorial Foundation Educ. Advisory Bd. 1964-, Chair. 1971-79; Foreign mem., Royal Swedish Acad. of Sciences 1977; numerous hon. degrees; Prize for Dist. Scholarship in Humanities, American Council of Learned Socs.; Lectureship in Recognition of Outstanding Scientific Achievement, Nat. Insts. of Health; Talcott Parsons Prize in Social Sciences, American Acad. of Arts and Sciences 1979; Commonwealth Trust Award of Distinguished Service in Sociology 1979, American Sociological Asscn. Career of Distinguished Scholarship Award 1980, Memorial Sloan-Kettering Cancer Centre Award for outstanding support of biomedical science 1981, J. D. Bernal Award for Social Studies of Science 1982, MacArthur Prize Fellow 1983-88, first Who's Who in America Achievement Award in Social Science 1984. *Publications:* Science, Technology and Society in 17th-Century England 1938, 1971, Mass Persuasion 1946, Social Theory & Social Structure 1949, 1968, Continuities in Social Research 1950, Reader in Bureaucracy 1952, Focused Interview 1956, Student-Physician 1957, Freedom to Read 1957, Sociology Today 1959, Contemporary Social Problems 1961, 1971, 1976, On the Shoulders of Giants 1965, On Theoretical Sociology 1968, Social Theory and Functional Analysis 1969, Sociology of Science 1973, Sociological Ambivalence 1976, Toward a Metric of Science 1978, The Sociology of Science in Europe 1977, (ed. with James Coleman and Peter Rossi) Qualitative and Quantitative Social Research: Papers in Honor of Paul Lazarsfeld 1979, The Sociology of Science: An Episodic Memoir 1979, Sociological Traditions from Generation to Generation 1980 (ed. with M. W. Riley), Continuities in Structural Inquiry 1981 (ed. with Peter Blau), Social Research and the Practicing Professions 1982. *Address:* 415 Fayerweather Hall, Columbia University, New York, N.Y. 10027, U.S.A. *Telephone:* (212) 280-3696.

MERTZ, Edwin Theodore, PH.D.; American consultant in biochemistry and nutrition; b. 6 Dec. 1909, Missoula, Mont.; s. of Gustav Henry and Louise (Sain) Mertz; m. 1st Mary Ellen Ruskamp 1936, one s. one d.; m. 2nd Virginia T. Henry 1987; ed. Univs. of Montana and Illinois; Research Biochemist, Armour and Co., Chicago 1935-37; Instructor in Biochemistry, Univ. of Ill., Urbana 1937-38; Research Assoc. in Pathology, Univ. of Iowa 1938-40; Instructor in Agricultural Chem., Univ. of Mo. 1940-43; Research Chemist, Hercules Powder Co. 1943-46; Prof. of Biochemistry, Purdue Univ., W. Lafayette, Ind. 1946-76, Emer. 1976-, Consultant in Biochemistry and Nutrition, INTSORMIL Project, Dept. of Agronomy, Purdue Univ. 1980-; co-discoverer of High Lysine Corn; mem. N.A.S.; Hon. D.Agr. (Purdue) 1977, Hon. D.Sc. (Montana) 1979; several awards. *Publications:* Elementary Biochemistry 1979 and over 100 scientific articles in field of biochemistry and nutrition. *Leisure interest:* playing jazz piano music. *Address:* Department of Agronomy, Purdue University, West Lafayette, Ind. 47907; 143 Tamiami Trail, West Lafayette, Ind. 47906, U.S.A. (Home). *Telephone:* (317) 494-4772 (Office); (317) 463-3624 (Home).

MERZAGORA, Cesare; Italian industrialist and politician; b. 9 Nov. 1898, Milan; s. of Luigi Merzagora and Elisa Fenini; m. Giuliana Benucci 1933; one s. four d.; served in First World War 1915-18; Dir. Banca Commerciale Italiana in Bulgaria 1920-27; also Italian Consul at Philippopolis; founder of anti-fascist newspaper La Voce d'Italia, suppressed in 1924; Dir. of banking institutes in foreign countries 1927-38; Dir. of Pirelli and associated firms 1938; mem. of Liberation Movement in Northern Italy; Pres. of its Cen. Econ. Comm.; Minister of Foreign Trade in fourth and fifth De Gasperi Cabinets 1947-49; Senator (Independent, Milan) 1948-; Pres. of the Senate 1953-67, Life Senator 1963-; Acting Pres. of Italy Aug.-Dec. 1964; Chair. Assicurazioni Generali 1968-79, Hon. Chair. 1979-; Chair. Montedison 1970. *Address:* Piazza Madama, 1-00100, Rome, Italy. *Telephone:* 856-267.

MERZBAN, Mohammed Abdullah, M.A.; Egyptian politician; b. 20 Jan. 1918, Fayoum; m.; ed. Fouad Univ. and Harvard Univ.; Lecturer, Faculty of Commerce, Cairo Univ. until 1956; Sec.-Gen. Ministry of Industry 1956-58; Gen. Man. Industrialization Authority 1958-60; Chair. Al-Nasr Org. 1960-61; Chair. Spinning & Weaving Org. 1961-66; Chair. Bank of Cairo 1966-68; Minister of Supply and Home Trade 1968-70, of Economy and Foreign Trade 1970-73; Acting Minister of Supply and Home Trade 1971-73; Deputy Prime Minister 1972-73; Pres. Investrade. *Publications:* Financial Management, Sales Management, Mathematics of Marketing. *Address:* c/o Investrade, 5 Talaat Harb Street, Cairo, Egypt. *Telephone:* 740188, 740219.

MESELSON, Matthew Stanley, PH.B., PH.D., F.A.A.A.S.; American professor of biochemistry; b. 24 May 1930, Denver, Colo.; s. of Hymen Avram and

Ann Swedlow Meselson; m. 1st Sarah Leah Page 1969, two d.; m. 2nd Jeanne Guillemin 1986; ed. Univ. of Chicago, Univ. of California (Berkeley) and California Inst. of Tech.; Research Fellow, Calif. Inst. of Tech. 1957-58, Asst. Prof. of Physical Chem. 1958-59, Sr. Research Fellow in Chemical Biology 1959-60; Assoc. Prof. of Biology, Harvard Univ. 1960-64, Prof. of Biology 1964-76, Thomas Dudley Cabot Prof. of Nat. Sciences 1976-; Chair. Fed. of American Scientists 1986-88; mem. Inst. of Medicine, N.A.S., American Acad. of Arts and Sciences, Acad. Santa Chiara, American Philosophical Soc., mem. Council on Foreign Relations; foreign mem. Royal Soc., Acad. des Sciences; Hon. D.Sc. (Oakland Coll.) 1966, (Columbia) 1971, (Chicago) 1975; Prize for Molecular Biology, N.A.S. 1963, Eli Lilly Award in Microbiology and Immunology 1964; Hon. Sc.D. (Yale) 1987; Public Service Award, Fed. of American Scientists 1972 Alumni Medal, Univ. of Chicago Alumni Assn. 1971, Alumni Distinguished Service Award, Calif. Inst. of Tech. 1975, Lehman Award of N.Y. Acad. of Sciences 1975, Leo Szilard Award, American Physical Soc. 1978, Presidential Award of N.Y. Acad. of Sciences 1983; MacArthur Fellow 1984-89. *Publications:* numerous papers on the biochemistry and molecular biology of nucleic acids, and on arms control of biological and chemical weapons, in various numbers of Proceedings of N.A.S. and of Scientific American, etc. *Address:* Sherman Fairchild Building, 7 Divinity Avenue, Harvard University, Cambridge, Mass. 02138, U.S.A. *Telephone:* (617) 495-2264.

MESHBERG, Lev, Soviet artist; b. 1933, Odessa; ed. Odessa Art College; mem. of Union of Soviet Artists 1960; participated in more than forty one-man and group exhbns. in U.S.S.R.; first prizes at All-Union Art Exhbns. 1965, 1967; work represented in Tretyakov Gallery, Moscow and Russian Museum, Leningrad; emigrated to U.S.A. 1973.

MESHEL, Yeruham; Israeli trade unionist; b. 24 Nov. 1912, Pinsk, Russia; m. Rachel Frank 1939; one s. one d.; emigrated to Palestine 1933; Sec. Metal Workers' Union, Tel-Aviv, mem. Tel-Aviv Labour Council Exec. 1945; mem. Trade Union Centre of Histadrut Exec. Cttee., Chair. Industrial Workers' Div. 1950-60, mem. Cen. Exec. Bureau 1960-, Chair. Trade Union Centre 1961, Deputy Sec.-Gen. Histadrut 1964-74, Head of Histadrut Social Security Centre and Arab Workers' Dept., Acting Sec.-Gen. 1973, Sec.-Gen. 1974-84; Chair. Inst. of Labour Research in memory of P. Lavon 1984-; mem. Cen. Cttee. of Mapai 1961-; mem. Secr. Israel Labour Party 1964; mem. Knesset 1977-; Vice-Pres. ICFTU, Vice-Pres. Asian Regional Org., ICFTU; rep. to numerous int. labour confs. *Address:* Nehardea Street 3, Tel-Aviv; 16 Sanhedrin Street, Shikun Bavly, Tel-Aviv, Israel. *Telephone:* (03) 238122.

MESKILL, Thomas Joseph, B.S.; American lawyer and politician; b. 30 Jan. 1928, New Britain, Conn.; s. of late Thomas Joseph Meskill and of Laura Ryan Meskill; m. Mary T. Grady; three s. two d.; ed. New Britain Senior High School, Trinity Coll., Hartford, Univ. of Connecticut Law School and New York Univ. School of Law; Asst. Corpn. Counsel, New Britain 1960-62; Mayor of New Britain 1962-64; Corpn. Counsel 1965-66; elected to Congress 1966, 1968; Gov. of Connecticut 1970-75; Judge U.S. Circuit Court 1975-; mem. American Bar Assn.; Republican; *Address:* 84 Randeckers Lane, Kensington, Conn. 06037, U.S.A. *Telephone:* (203) 523-7014.

MESNIL DU BUISSON, Robert Du, Count, D. ÈS L., D. EN D.; French archaeologist; b. 19 April 1895, Bourges; s. of late Léon Count du Mesnil du Buisson and Berthe Roussel de Courcy; m. 1st Jeanne Le Clerc de Pulligny 1923 (died 1964), four s. two d.; m. 2nd Pauline Husson de Sampigny 1965; Dir. French Archaeological Missions in Syria, Egypt and France; Dir. Excavation at Palmyra 1965-; Pres. Soc. Nat. des Antiquaries de France 1946-47; Pres. Soc. Historique et Archéologique de l'Orne 1947-55; Hon. Pres. 1956-; Pres. Soc. du Manoir d'Argentelles 1957-; Dir. du Centre Culturel et Touristique de l'Orne 1967-; Vice-Pres. Soc. d'Ethnographie de Paris 1960-69, Pres. 1969-; Dir.-Founder of cultural review of Orne region Au Pays d'Argentelles 1976-; Commdr. Légion d'honneur 1966, Croix de guerre, Médaille de la Résistance, Officier des Palmes académiques; Lauréat de l'Inst. de France 1940, 1958, 1963; Médaille d'Or de la Soc. d'Encouragement au Progrès 1973, Croix du Combattant de l'Europe 1974. *Publications:* Les ruines d'El-Mishrifé au Nord-Est de Homs 1927, La technique des fouilles archéologiques 1933, Le site archéologique de Mishrifé-Qatna 1935, Les noms et signes égyptiens désignant des vases 1935, Souran et Tell Masin 1935, Le site de Qadesh 1936, Inscriptions juives de Doura-Europos 1937, Inventaire des inscriptions palmyréniennes de Doura-Europos 1939, Les peintures de la Synagogue de Doura 245-246 ap. J-C. 1939, Les tessères et monnaies de Palmyre 1944, Les ouvrages du siège à Doura-Europos 1945, Le site archéologique d'Exmes (Uxoma) 1946, Le sautoir d'Atargatis et la chaîne d'amulettes 1947, Baghouz, l'ancienne Corsôte 1948, Une voie commerciale de haute antiquité dans l'Orne 1951, Les dieux et les déesses en forme de vase dans l'antiquité orientale, La palissade gauloise d'Alençon 1952, L'alcôve royale dite "Lit de Justice d'Argentelles" 1953, Un constructeur du Château de La Celle-Saint-Cloud, Jacques Jérémie Roussel 1954, Saint-Germain-en-Laye 1954, Poissy 1955, Chantilly 1957, Une famille de Chevaliers de Malte, les Costart 1960, Plaques de cheminées de l'Orne 1947-76, Les tessères et les monnaies de Palmyre de la Bibliothèque Nationale 1962, Inscriptions sur jarres de Doura-Europos 1959, Origine et évolution du panthéon de Tyr, Les Chausson de la Salle 1963, Le dieu-Griffon à Palmyre

et chez les Hittites 1963, Les origines du panthéon Palmyrénien 1964, Le dieu Ousô sur des monnaies de Tyr 1965, Le drame des deux étoiles du matin et du soir dans l'antiquité orientale 1967, Le décor des deux cuves de Tell Mardikh 1967, Le Manoir d'Argentelles, Guide du visiteur, Origines phéniciennes des Dioscures, Le décor asiatique du couteau de Gebel el-Arak 1969, Etudes sur les dieux phéniciens hérités par l'Empire Romain 1970, Nouvelles études sur les dieux et les mythes de Canaan 1973, Géographie et astronomie mythiques, Les voyages de Gilgamesh 1974, Le mythe de la Tour de Babel 1976, Le cylindre-sceau archaïque de Byblos réexaminé 1976, Origine et évolution de la ville de Sées 1977, Les clans et les tribus de la fondation de Rome, Origine des deux Léopards de Normandie 1983. *Leisure interests:* preservation of buildings and art objects in the Orne region of France. *Address:* Château de Champobert, par 61310 Exmes (Orne), France. *Telephone:* 33-39-93-61.

MESSAGER, Annette; French artist; b. 30 Nov. 1943, Berck-sur-Mer; d. of André and Marie L. (née Chalessin) Messager; unmarried; ed. Ecole Nationale Supérieure des Arts Décoratifs; one-man exhbns. include Munich and Grenoble 1973, Musée d'Art Moderne, Paris 1974, 1984, Rheinisches Landesmuseum, Bonn 1976, 1978, Galerie Seriaal, Amsterdam 1977, Holly Solomon Gallery, New York 1978, Galérie Gillespie-Laage, Paris 1979, 1980, Fine Arts Gallery, Univ. of Calif. and Irvine San Franciso Museum of Modern Art 1981, PS 1, New York, Galerie Hans Mayer, Düsseldorf 1981, Artist's Space, New York 1982, Musée des Beaux-Arts, Calais, Galérie Gillespie-Laage-Salomon, Paris 1983, Vienna and Zurich 1984, Riverside Studio, London 1985, Galerie Gillespie-Laage-Salomon, Sydney 1985, Galerie Laage Salomon, Paris 1988, Consortium Dijon 1988, Centre d'Art Contemporain, Castres 1988; Chevalier, Ordre des Arts et des Lettres. *Address:* 146 boulevard Camelinat, 92240 Malakoff, France. *Telephone:* 253.45.77.

MESSER, Thomas M., M.A.; American museum director; b. 9 Feb. 1920, Bratislava, Czechoslovakia; s. of Richard and Agatha (Albrecht) Messer; m. Remedios Garcia Villa 1948; ed. Thiel Coll. (Greenville, Pa.), Boston, Paris and Harvard Univs.; Dir., Roswell Museum, New Mexico 1949-52; Asst. Dir. in charge of Nat. Exhibitions Programme, American Fed. of Arts 1952-53, Dir. of Exhbns. 1953-55, Dir. 1955-56, Trustee 1972-; Dir., Boston Inst. of Contemporary Art 1957-61, Solomon R. Guggenheim Museum, New York 1961-88; First Vice-Pres. American Fed. of Arts 1973-75; Pres. Assn. of Art Museum Dirs. 1974-75; Chair. Int. Cttee. for Museums and Collections of Modern Art, Int. Council of Museums 1974-77, Hon. Chair. 1977-80; Chair. Int. Exhbns. Cttee. 1976-78, US/ICOM (Nat. Cttee. of Int. Council of Museums) 1978-; Adjunct Prof., Harvard Univ. 1960; Adjunct Prof. of Art History, Barnard Coll. 1966, 1971; Sr. Fellow, Center for Advanced Studies, Wesleyan Univ. 1966; Trustee Center for Inter-American Relations 1974-, Exec. Council Int. Council of Museums 1980-; Vice-Chair. U.S. Int. Council of Museums Cttee. of American Assn. of Museums, Washington, D.C. 1979-81; Pres. MacDowell Colony Inc. 1977-80; Dir. and Trustee, Solomon R. Guggenheim Foundation 1980-, Peggy Guggenheim Collection, Venice 1980-; Trustee, Wooster School, Americas Soc. 1981-; mem. Visiting Cttee. on Art Museums, Harvard Univ., Port Authority of New York and New Jersey Cttee. on Art, Art Advisory Cttee. UNESCO 1980-, Computerization Advisory Cttee. Getty Trust 1982-; fmr. mem. Museum Advisory Panel of Nat. Endowment for the Arts, Art Advisory Panel to Commr. of Internal Revenue Service 1974-77, Bd. of Visitors, School of Visual Arts, Boston Univ. 1977-79; Dr. Fine Arts h.c., (Univ. of Mass.); Kt., Royal Order of St. Olav (Norway); Officer's Cross of Order of Merit (Federal Repub. of Germany) 1975; Officer of Order of Leopold II (Belgium) 1978, Chevalier Légion d'honneur 1980, Austrian Cross of Honour for Science and Art 1981. *Publications:* The Emergent Decade: Latin American Painters and Paintings in the 1960's 1966, Edvard Munch 1973; Museum Catalogues on: Vasily Kandinsky, Paul Klee, Edvard Munch, Egon Schiele, etc.; articles and contributions to numerous art journals. *Leisure interests:* the theatre, literature, music. *Address:* 1105 Park Avenue, New York, N.Y. 10028, U.S.A. (Home). *Telephone:* (212) 860-1312.

MESSIAEN, Olivier; French composer and organist; b. 10 Dec. 1908, Avignon, Vaucluse; s. of Pierre Messiaen and Cécile Sauvage; m. 1st Claire Delbos (died 1959), one s.; m. 2nd Yvonne Loriod 1961 (q.v); Organist, Trinité, Paris 1931-; Co-founder Jeune-France movement 1936; Prof. Ecole Normale and Schola Cantorum 1936-39; Prof. of Harmony, Paris Conservatoire 1941-47, of Analysis, Aesthetics and Rhythm 1947-, of Composition 1966-; mem. Institut de France, Akad. der Künste, Berlin, Bayerische Akad. der Wissenschaften, Munich, Royal Acads. of Sweden, London and Madrid, American Acad. of Arts and Letters; Erasmus Prize 1971; Sibelius Prize 1971, Von Siemens Prize 1975, Leonie Sonning Prize 1977, Bach Prize, Hamburg 1979, Wolf Foundation Prize (shared) 1982, Liebermann "Prix d'Honneur" 1983, Prix Inamori de Kyoto 1985; Grand Croix (Légion d'honneur) 1986, Grand Croix de l'Ordre nat. du Mérite, Commdr. des Arts et des Lettres. *Compositions include:* Le banquet céleste for organ 1928, Préludes for piano 1929, Le diptyque for organ 1929, L'Ascension for organ 1933, La Nativité du Seigneur for organ 1935, Poèmes pour Mi for voice and piano 1936, Chants de terre et de ciel for voice and piano 1938, Les Corps glorieux for organ 1939, Quatuor pour la fin du Temps for violin, cello, clarinet and piano 1941, Visions de l'Amen for two pianos 1943, Vingt regards sur l'Enfant Jésus for piano 1944, Trois petites

Liturgies de la présence divine for choir and orchestra 1944, Harawi song cycle 1945, Turangalîla Symphonie for piano, onde martenot and orchestra 1946–48, Cinq rechants for choir a capella 1949, Etudes de rythme for piano 1949, Messe de la Pentecôte for organ 1949, Livre d'orgue 1951, Réveil des oiseaux 1953, Oiseaux exotiques 1955, Catalogue d'oiseaux for piano 1956–58, Chronochromie for large orchestra 1959, Sept Haïkaï for piano and small orchestra 1963, Couleurs de la Cité céleste for piano and orchestra 1964, Et Exspecto Resurrectionem Mortuorum for orchestra 1965, La Transfiguration de notre Seigneur Jésus-Christ for choir, orchestra and seven instrumental soloists 1969, Des canyons aux etoiles for piano and orchestra 1970–74, Saint François d'Assise (opera) 1983, Le livre du Saint-Sacrement 1986, Petites Esquisses d'oiseaux (for piano) 1986, Un Vitrail et des Oiseaux 1987. *Address:* Eglise de la Trinité, 3 rue de la Trinité, 75009 Paris, France.

MESSMER, Pierre Auguste Joseph, LL.D.; French politician and overseas administrator; b. 20 March 1916, Vincennes; s. of Joseph and Marthe (née Farcy) Messmer; m. Gilberte Duprez 1947; ed. Faculté de droit de Paris; mil. service 1937–45, with "Free French" forces 1940–45; Sec.-Gen. Interministerial Cttee. for Indochina 1946; Dir. of Cabinet High Comm. in Indochina 1947–48; Gov. Mauritania 1952, Ivory Coast 1954–56; High Commr. Cameroon 1956–58; High Commr.-Gen. French Equatorial Africa 1958, French West Africa 1958–60; Minister for the Armed Forces 1960–69; elected Deputy for Moselle, Nat. Assembly 1968, 1969, 1973, 1978, 1981, 1986; Minister of State for Overseas Depts. and Territories Feb.-July 1972; Prime Minister 1972–74; mem. European Parl. 1979–84; Pres. R.P.R. Group in Nat. Ass. 1986–; Grand Officier, Légion d'honneur, Compagnon de la Libération, Croix de guerre, Médaille de la Résistance. *Address:* Assemblée Nationale, 75355 Paris; 1 rue de Général-Delanne, 92200 Neuilly-sur-Seine, France.

MESSNER, Zbigniew, D.ECON.SC.; Polish economist and politician; b. 13 March 1929, Stryj; m.; two d.; ed. Higher School of Econs., Katowice; teacher Higher School of Econs. (now Econs. Acad.), Katowice, Asst. 1950–54, lecturer 1954–68, Asst. Prof. 1968–72, Extraordinary Prof. 1972–77, Ordinary Prof. 1977–, Pro-Rector 1968–75, Rector 1975–82; Dir. Inst. of Data Processing Orgs. 1972–77; mem. Polish Econ. Soc., Vice-Pres. Main Bd. 1971–81; Chair. Voivodship Nat. Council, Katowice 1980–83; mem. Polish United Workers' Party (PZPR) 1953–, mem. PZPR Town Cttee., Katowice 1975–81, First Sec. PZPR Voivodship Cttee., Katowice 1982–83, mem. PZPR Cen. Cttee. 1981–, mem. Political Bureau of PZPR Cen. Cttee. 1981–88, mem. PZPR Cen. Cttee. Comm. for Investigation into Social Conflicts in the History of Polish People's Repub. 1981–83; Vice-Chair. Council of Ministers 1983–85, Chair. 1985–88; Deputy Chair. Comm. for Econ. Reform 1984–85, Chair 1986–88; Deputy to Seym 1985–; mem. Council of State Dec. 1988–; Dr. h.c. (Martin Luther Univ., Halle) 1986; numerous Prizes of Ministry of Science, Higher Educ. and Tech.; Kt.'s and Commdr's Cross of Polonia Restituta 1973, Order of Banner of Labour (1st Class), Nat. Educ. Comm. Medal 1973, Award Meritorious Teacher of People's Poland 1974, Hon. Miner of Polish People's Repub. 1983, Gold Order of Friendship of Nations Star (G.D.R.) 1986. *Publications:* Rachunek kosztów produkcji w przedsiębiorstwie przemysłowym 1963, Informacja ekonomiczna a zarządzanie przedsiębiorstwem 1971, Rachunek kosztów jako instrument operatywnego zarządzania przedsiębiorstwem przemysłowym 1972, Rachunkowość a zarządzanie przedsiębiorstwem (co-author) 1976, Organizacja przetwarzania danych (co-author) 1978. *Leisure interest:* gardening. *Address:* Komitet Centralny PZPR, ul. Nowy Swiat 6/12, 00-920 Warsaw, Poland.

MESTEL, Leon, B.A., PH.D., F.R.S.; British professor of astronomy; b. 5 Aug. 1927, Melbourne, Australia; s. of Rabbi Solomon Mestel and Rachel née Brodetsky; m. Sylvia L. Cole 1951; two s. two d.; ed. West Ham Secondary School, London and Trinity Coll., Cambridge; ICI Research Fellow, Univ. of Leeds, 1951–54; Commonwealth Fund Fellow, Princeton Univ. Observatory 1954–55; Univ. Asst. Lecturer in Math., Cambridge 1955–58, Univ. Lecturer 1958–66; Fellow, St John's Coll., Cambridge 1957–66; Visiting mem. Inst. for Advanced Study, Princeton 1961–62; J. F. Kennedy Fellow, Weizmann Inst. for Science, Israel 1966–67; Prof. of Applied Math., Univ. of Manchester 1967–73; Prof. of Astronomy, Univ. of Sussex 1973–. *Publications:* papers, reviews, conf. reports on different branches of theoretical astrophysics. *Leisure interests:* reading, music. *Address:* Astronomy Centre, University of Sussex, Falmer, Brighton, BN1 9QH; 13 Prince Edward's Road, Lewes, BN7 1BJ, England. *Telephone:* 0273 678071 (Office), 0273 472731 (Home).

MESTIRI, Mahmoud; Tunisian diplomatist; b. 25 Dec. 1929, Tunis; s. of Mohamed Mestiri and Zohra Lasram; divorced; one s. one d.; ed. Inst. d'Etudes Politiques, Univ. de Lyons; served in several Tunisian Dels. to UN; Alt. Rep. to UN 1958, 1959; Head of Tunisian special Diplomatic Mission to Congo (Leopoldville) 1960; Asst. to Personal Rep. of UN Sec.-Gen. to Govt. of Belgium 1961; Deputy Perm. Rep. of Tunisia to UN 1962–65; Sec.-Gen. for Foreign Affairs, Tunis 1965–67; Perm. Rep. to UN 1967–69; Chair. UN Special Cttee. on the Granting of Independence to Colonial Countries and Peoples 1968–69; Amb. to Fed. Germany 1971–73, to U.S.S.R., also accred. to Poland 1973–76; Perm. Rep. to UN 1976–80; Sec. d'Etat aux Affaires Etrangères 1984–86; Minister of Foreign Affairs 1987–88; Amb. to Egypt 1989–. *Leisure interests:* ping-pong, swimming, watching football. *Address:* c/o Ministry of Foreign Affairs, Tunis, Tunisia.

MESTVIRISHVILI, Mirian Alekseyevich, DR. PHYS. SC.; Soviet theoretical physicist; b. 1934; ed. Tbilisi Univ.; Postgraduate, Junior Research Asst., Georgian Acad. of Sciences Cybernetics Inst. 1958–63; Junior, Senior Researcher with United Inst. for Nuclear Research, Dubna 1963–70; Head of Laboratory of Acad. of Sciences Inst. of High Energy Physics 1970–86; Prof. 1983; Head of Laboratory of Faculty of Nuclear Physics, Moscow Univ., 1986–; Lenin Prize 1986; *Address:* Moscow University, Moscow, U.S.S.R.

MESYATS, Valentin Karpovich; Soviet politician; b. 1 May 1928, Prokopyevsk, Kamerovo Region; m. Irina Mesyats; three d.; ed. Timiryazev Agricultural Acad., Moscow; Chief Agronomist, Dir. Motor Tractor Station, Moscow District 1953–58; mem. CPSU 1955–; engaged in party and state work 1958–63; Second Sec. for Agric., Moscow District Cttee. CPSU 1963–64, Sec. 1964–65; Second Sec. Cen. Cttee. CPSU, Kazakhstan 1971–76; Deputy Minister of Agric. R.S.F.S.R. 1965–71; Minister of Agric. U.S.S.R. 1976–85; CCP Chief, Moscow Region Nov. 1985–; mem. Cen. Cttee. CPSU 1981–; Chair. All-Union Council of Collective Farms 1976–; mem. Presidium of Supreme Soviet, Kazakhstan S.S.R. 1971–76; Deputy U.S.S.R. Supreme Soviet 1984; Chair. Mandate Comm. of the Soviet of the Union 1972–76; Order of Lenin. *Leisure interests:* sports. *Address:* Council of Ministers, The Kremlin, Moscow; 1/11, Orlikov per., Moscow, U.S.S.R. (Home).

MESZAROS, Marta; Hungarian film director; b. 1931, Budapest; d. of Laszlo Meszaros; m. 2nd Jan Nowicki; ed. Moscow Film School; emigrated to U.S.S.R. with family in 1936 but now lives in Budapest where she has made films for over 30 years. *Films include:* Diary for My Children, Diary for My Loves.

METCALF, Robert Lee, M.A., PH.D.; American entomologist; b. 13 Nov. 1916, Columbus, Ohio; s. of Clell Lee and Cleo Esther (née Fouch) Metcalf; m. Esther Jemima Rutherford 1940; two s. one d.; ed. Univ. of Illinois and Cornell Univ.; Asst. Entomologist, Tenn. Valley Authority, Wilson Dam 1943–44, Assoc. Entomologist 1944–46; Asst. Entomologist Univ. of Calif., Riverside 1946–49, Assoc. Entomologist 1949–53, Prof. of Entomology and Entomologist 1953–68, Chair. Entomology Dept. 1951–63, Vice-Chancellor 1963–66; Prof. of Entomology, Univ. of Ill. 1968–, Prof. Center for Advanced Study 1981–; Principal Scientist, Ill. Nat. History Survey 1970–; mem. N.A.S., Entomological Soc. of America (Pres. 1958), A.C.S., A.A.A.S., American Mosquito Control Assen., WHO Expert Cttee. on Insecticides; Consultant to WHO, AID, U.S. Dept. of Agric., U.S. Tenn. Valley Authority; Faculty Research Lecturer, Univ. of Calif., Riverside, Calif. 1959; Fellow of American Acad. of Arts and Sciences; Order of Cherubini, Univ. of Pisa, Italy 1966; Int. Award Pesticide Chem. 1972; Charles F. Spencer Award, A.C.S. 1966; Chancellor's Award for Excellence in Research, Univ. of Calif., Riverside 1967, Memorial Lecture Award 1979, CIBA-Geigy Award, Entomological Soc. of America, Founders Award, Soc. of Environmental Toxicology 1983, DuBors Award Soc. Toxicology 1987. *Publications:* Destructive and Useful Insects, Organic Insecticides—Their Chemistry and Mode of Action; Co-Ed. Advances in Environmental Sciences Technology; approx. 400 scientific pubs. mainly on chemistry and toxicology of insecticides, insect physiology and toxicology, medical entomology, insect control. *Address:* Department of Entomology, University of Illinois, Urbana, Ill. 61801 (Office); 1902 Golfview Drive, Urbana, Ill. 61801, U.S.A. (Home). *Telephone:* (217) 333-3649 (Office); (217) 367-3081 (Home).

METCALFE, Stanley Gordon, M.A.; British business executive; b. 20 June 1932, Horsforth; s. of Stanley Hudson Metcalfe and Jane Metcalfe; m. Sarah Harter 1968; two d.; ed. Leeds Grammar School, Pembroke Coll., Oxford; trainee, Ranks Hovis McDougall (RHM) 1956–59; Dir. Stokes & Dalton, Leeds 1963–66; Man. Dir. McDougalls 1966–69; Dir. Cerebos Ltd. 1969–70; Man. Dir. RHM Overseas Ltd. 1970–73, RHM Cereals Ltd. 1973–80; Dir. Ranks Hovis McDougall PLC 1979–, Man. Dir. 1981–, Chief Exec. 1984–, Deputy Chair. 1987–; Pres. Nat. Assen. of British and Irish Millers 1978. *Leisure interests:* cricket, golf, theatre. *Address:* The Oast House, Lower Froyle, Alton, Hants., GU34 4LX, England. *Telephone:* (0420) 22310.

METTLER, Ruben Frederick, B.S., M.S., PH.D.; American electrical engineer and business executive; b. 23 Feb. 1924, Shafter, Calif.; s. of Henry F. and Lydia Mettler; m. Donna Jean Smith 1955; two s.; ed. California Inst. of Tech.; Assoc. Dir. of Radar Div., Hughes Aircraft Co. 1949–54; Asst. to Asst. Sec. of Defense for Research and Devt. 1954–55; Assoc. Dir. of Guided Missile Research Div. and Thor Program Dir., The Ramo-Woolridge Corpn. 1955–57; Vice-Pres. The Ramo-Woolridge Corpn. 1957–58; Exec. Vice-Pres. Space Technology Labs. 1958–62; Pres. TRW Systems Group (formerly Space Technology Labs.) 1962–68; Exec. Vice-Pres. TRW Inc. 1965–68, Exec. Vice-Pres. and Asst. Pres. 1968–69, Pres. 1969–77, Chair. and C.E.O. 1977–88 and Chair., Exec. Cttee. 1978–88; Chair. Nat. Alliance of Business (NAB) 1978–79; mem. Bd. of Dirs, Bank of America, Goodyear Tire and Rubber Co., Inc., Merck and Co., Inc.; mem. Bd. of Trustees Caltech Associates, Emergency Cttee. for American Trade (ECAT), Business Council, Rockefeller Univ. Council, James Smithson Soc., Cleveland Cultural Resources Study Cttee., Einstein Memorial Steering Cttee. of Nat. Acad. of Sciences; Trustee: Cttee. for Econ. Devt. (CED), Nat. Safety Council, Cleveland Clinic Foundation, Nat. Fund for Minority Eng. Students; mem. Nat. Acad. of Eng.; Fellow, Inst. of Electrical and

Electronics Engineers, American Inst. of Aeronautics and Astronautics, American Astronautical Soc.; mem. Advisory Bd. Council for Financial Educ.; Outstanding Young Electrical Engineer 1954; S. Calif. "Engineer of the Year" 1964; Distinguished Service Award, Caltech 1966; Distinguished Civilian Meritorious Award, Dept. of Defense 1969; Nat. Human Relations Award (Nat. Conf. of Christians and Jews) 1979; Excellence in Man. Award (Industry Week Magazine) 1979. *Publications:* several book length classified reports on airborne electronic systems; holds joint patent for major interceptor fire control system. *Address:* 23555 Euclid Avenue, Cleveland, Ohio 44117, U.S.A. (Home). *Telephone:* (216) 383-3070.

METZ, Johann Baptist, DR. PHIL., DR. THEOL.; German professor of theology; b. 5 Aug. 1928, Auerbach; s. of Karl M. Metz and Sibylle Müller; ed. Univs. of Bamberg, Innsbrück and Munich; Prof. of Fundamental Theology, Univ. of Münster 1963–; mem. founding comm. of Univ. of Bielefeld 1966; consultant to Papal Secr. Pro Non Credendibus 1968–73; Adviser to German Diocesan Synod 1971–75; awards from Univ. of Innsbrück and Boston Coll., Mass. *Publications:* several books on theological themes. *Address:* Katholisch-Theologische Fakultät, Seminar für Fundamentaltheologie, Johannisstrasse 8–10, 4400 Münster (Office); Kapitelstrasse 14, 4400 Münster, Federal Republic of Germany. *Telephone:* 0251/83-2631 (Office); 0251/36662 (Home).

METZ, Paul; Luxembourg engineer (retd.); b. 4 June 1918, Dudelange; s. of Norbert Metz and Marie Wurth; m. Marie-Anne Goedert 1946; two s. one d.; ed. Univ. of Louvain and Aachen Tech. Hochschule; steelworks engineer Aciéries Réunies de Burbach-Eich-Dudelange (ARBED) at Burbach Div. 1943–44, at Esch-Belval Div. 1945–54, at Dudelange Div. 1954–55; Dept. Man., Dudelange Div. 1955–62, Man. of Div. 1962–67; Man. of Esch-Belval Div. 1967–69; H.Q. Man. ARBED HQ 1969–72, Asst. Gen. Man. 1972–76, Gen. Man. HQ 1977–78, Gen. Man. and mem. Bd. 1978–83, mem. Bd. 1983–; mem. Bd. Sidmar S.A.; Hon. Chair. Paul Wurth S.A., Métallurgique et Minière de Rodange-Athus S.A. (MMRA); D.Ing. h.c. (RUTH) Aachen; numerous decorations include Kt., Order of Merit of Luxembourg, Officer, Order of Oak Crown, Titre de Résistant (Luxembourg), Order of Tudor Vladimirescu (Romania), Commdr., Order of Merit of Italian Repub., Grand Golden Award of Order of Merit of the Austrian Repub., Hon. C.B.E. (U.K.), Commdr. Order of the Oak Crown, Commdr. Order of Leópold II (Belgium), Silver Tower of the Order of Industrial Merit (Repub. of Korea), Encomienda, Merito Civil (Spain), Grand Officier, Order of the Oak Crown, Bessemer Gold Medal, The Metals Soc. (London). *Publications:* various articles on refractories and steel-making. *Leisure interests:* fishing, literature. *Address:* 18 rue J. P. Brasseur, Luxembourg Ville, Grand-Duché de Luxembourg. *Telephone:* 450542.

METZENBAUM, Howard Morton, LL.B.; American politician, lawyer and company executive; b. 4 June 1917, Cleveland; s. of Charles I. and Anna (Klafter) Morton; m. Shirley Turoff 1946; four d.; ed. Ohio State Univ.; mem. War Labour Bd. 1942–45, Ohio Bureau for Code Revision 1949–50; mem. Ohio House of Reps. 1943–46, Ohio Senate 1947–50; alt. del. to Democratic Nat. Convention 1964, del. 1968; mem. Ohio Democratic Exec. Cttee. 1966–, Finance Cttee. 1969–; U.S. Senator from Ohio Jan. 1977–; Chair. Bd. Airport Parking Co. of America 1958–66, ITT Consumer Services Corpn. 1966–68; Chair. Exec. Cttee. ComCorp 1969–74, 1975–; Trustee, Mount Sinai Hosp., Cleveland 1961–, Treas. 1966–; mem. Bd. of Dirs., Council of Human Relations; mem. United Cerebral Palsy Asscn., Nat. Council on Hunger and Malnutrition, American, Ohio, Cuyahoga and Cleveland Bar Asscns., American Asscn. of Trial Lawyers. *Address:* 140 Russell Senate Office Building, Washington, D.C. 20510; 1700 Investment Plaza, Cleveland, Ohio 44114 (Office); 18500 North Park Boulevard, Shaker Heights, Ohio 44118, U.S.A. (Home).

MEULEMANS, Ludovicus; Belgian banker; b. 1924; Ministry of Finance 1948; Treasury, Dept. for Financial and Monetary Relations with other countries, Adviser 1962–71, Prin. Adviser 1971–75, Insp. Gen. 1975–85, Dir.-Gen. Treasury 1986–88; Alt. Gov., Inter-American Bank 1976–88, African Devt. Fund 1974–88, African Devt. Bank 1983–88; Vice-Pres. EIB 1988–; mem. EIB's Bd. Dirs. 1976–88; Govt. Commr. to Belgo-Luxembourg Exchange Inst. 1969–88, Inst. de Réescompte et de Garantie 1988; Minister of Finance Rep., Bd. Dirs. Office Nat. du Ducroire 1965–88, Creditexport 1976–88, Soc. d'Investissement Int. 1976–88; mem. EEC Monetary Cttee. 1966–76, 1988–. *Address:* European Investment Bank, 100 blvd. Konrad Adenauer, 2950 Luxembourg.

MEVALD, Josef; Czechoslovak politician; b. 1932, Velke Hamry, Jablonec nad Nisou; mem. CP of Czechoslovakia (CPCZ) 1951–; active Party worker in youth movt. and trade unions; Leading Sec. Plzen City Party Cttee. 1971, W. Bohemian Party Regional Cttee. 1975–; mem. Cen. Cttee. CPCZ 1976–, mem. Secr. 1988–; Deputy to Chamber of Nations, Fed. Assembly; Order of Labour, Order of Victorious February etc. *Address:* Central Committee of the Communist Party, Prague, Czechoslovakia.

MEXANDEAU, Louis Jean; French teacher and politician; b. 6 July 1931, Wanquetin; s. of Hilaire Mexandeau and Jeanne Canel; m. Michèle Cusin 1960; one s. two d.; ed. Lycée d'Arras, Univs. of Lille and Paris, Inst. d'Etudes Politiques, Paris; mem. Nat. Bureau, Syndicat Nat. de l'Enseignement Secondaire 1955–57; History and Geography Teacher, Lycée Malherbe, Caen 1961–73; Founder and Sec. for Calvados, Convention des

Institutions Républicaines 1966–71, mem. Perm. Cttee. and Nat. Political Bureau 1969–71; First Fed. Sec. Calvados section, Parti Socialiste (PS) 1971–73; Deputy (Calvados) to Nat. Assembly 1973–81, 1986–; PS Nat. Del. for Educ. 1975–81; Minister of Posts and Telecommunications 1981–83; Minister Del. attached to the Minister of Industrial Redeployment in charge of Posts and Telecommunications 1983–85, Minister 1985–86. *Publications:* Les Capétiens 1972, Plan socialiste pour l'éducation nationale 1977. *Address:* 38 rue de Bretagne, 14000 Caen, France (Home).

MEYER, Armin Henry; American diplomatist; b. 19 Jan. 1914, Fort Wayne, Ind.; s. of Rev. Armin Paul Meyer and Leona Buss; m. Helen Alice James 1949; one d.; ed. Lincoln Junior Coll., Capital Univ., Columbus, Ohio, Capital Univ. Theological Seminary and Ohio State Univ., Columbus, Ohio; Asst. Prof. and Dean of Men, Capital Univ. 1935–41; Radio Technician, Douglas Aircraft Co., Eritrea 1942–43; News Ed., Office of War Information, Cairo 1943–44; Public Affairs Officer, American Embassy, Baghdad 1944–48; Public Affairs Adviser, Dept. of State 1948–52; First Sec., Beirut 1952–55, Counsellor, Kabul 1955–57; Deputy Dir. Office of South Asian Affairs, Dept. of State 1957–58, Office of Near Eastern Affairs 1959–61, Deputy Asst. Sec. of State for Near Eastern and South Asian Affairs 1961; Amb. to Lebanon 1961–65, to Iran 1965–69, to Japan 1969–72; Special Asst. to Sec. of State 1972–73; Chair. of Cabinet Cttee. to Combat Terrorism 1972–73; Visiting Prof. American Univ. 1974–75; Dir. of Ferdowsi Project, Georgetown Univ. Washington D.C. 1975–79; Woodrow Wilson Visiting Fellow, private Middle East Consultant, Adjunct Prof. Georgetown Univ. 1975–; mem. Bd. of Dirs. Washington Inst. of Foreign Affairs 1978–, Pres. 1988–; hon. degrees (Capital Univ.) 1957, (Lincoln Coll.) 1969, (S. Dakota Tech.) 1972, (Wartburg Coll.) 1972, (Ohio State Univ.) 1972; Order of the Rising Sun (First Class), Japan 1982; Hall of Excellence, Ohio Fed. of Independent Colls. 1989. *Publication:* Assignment Tokyo 1974, Education in Diplomacy (Co-author) 1987. *Leisure interest:* amateur radio. *Address:* 4610 Reno Road, N.W., Washington, D.C. 20008, U.S.A. *Telephone:* (202) 244-7737.

MEYER, Charles Appleton, B.A.; American businessman and government official (retd.); b. 27 June 1918, Boston, Mass.; s. of George von Lengerke and Frances (née Saltonstall) Meyer; m. Suzanne Seyburn; two d.; ed. Harvard Univ.; served as Capt. U.S. Army, Second World War; Asst. to Chair. of Bd. of Sears, Roebuck and Co. for Latin American Affairs 1947; Pres. of a Sears Latin American subsid., Bogotá 1953–55; Vice-Pres. in charge of Latin American Operations, Sears, for five years; Dir. Eastern Operations, Sears, Roebuck and Co. 1966–69; Asst. Sec. of State for Inter-American Affairs and U.S. Co-ordinator, Alliance for Progress 1969–72; Vice-Pres. Corporate Planning, Sears, Roebuck & Co. 1973–78, Sr. Vice-Pres., Public Affairs 1978–81; Adviser to U.S. Del. to Econ. Conf. of OAS 1957; fmr. mem. Nat. Advisory Comm. on Inter-American Affairs; fmr. Chair. Latin American Cttee., Business Advisory Council; fmr. Chair. Advisory Bd. Export-Import Bank; fmr. Dir. numerous companies. *Address:* 135 South LaSalle Street, Chicago, Ill. 60603 (Office); 1320 North Sheridan Road, Lake Forest, Ill. 60045, U.S.A. (Home).

MEYER, Gen. Edward C.; American army officer; b. 11 Dec. 1928, St. Marys, Pa.; ed. U.S. Mil. Acad.; 2nd Light Infantry, U.S. Army 1951; served with 40th Infantry Div., Korea; Commdr. Infantry Co., Staff Officer Bn.; Infantry Instructor, Fort Benning, Ga.; Commdr. Airborne Co. 101st Airborne Div., Fort Campbell, Ky.; served on Allied Staff, SHAPE; served on Dept. Army Staff, Office of Chief of Staff, Washington, D.C.; 1st Cavalry Div., Divisional Chief of Staff; Jt. Staff, Washington, D.C.; Fed. Exec. Fellow, Brookings Inst., Washington, D.C.; Asst. Divisional Commdr., 82nd Airborne Div.; Deputy Commandant Army War Coll.; Deputy Chief of Staff (Operations and Planning), Europe; Commanding Gen. 3rd Infantry Div., Fed. Repub. of Germany; Asst. Deputy Chief of Staff (Operations and Planning), Washington, D.C. 1975–76, Deputy Chief of Staff 1976–79; Chief of Staff U.S. Army 1979–83; Exec. Vice-Pres. Parks-Jaggers Aerospace Co. 1983.

MEYER, Emmanuel R.; Swiss business executive (retd.); b. 6 April 1918; ed. Zürich State Commercial Coll.; practical training at Swiss Nat. Bank; joined Swiss Aluminium Ltd. (Alusuisse) 1942, exec. positions in subsidiaries in Hungary, Fed. Germany, Italy and U.S.A. 1942–56; transferred to head office 1956, Chief Exec. 1960, Deputy Chair. and Man. Dir. 1964, Chair. and Man. Dir. 1966–83, Chair. 1983–85. *Address:* c/o Alusuisse, Feldeggstrasse 4, P.O. Box 8034, Zürich, Switzerland.

MEYER, Jean Léon André; French actor and director; b. 11 June 1914, Paris; s. of Léon Meyer and Mathilde Magnin; m. Pierrette-Martine de Kerpezdron-Laveissière 1942; two s.; ed. Conservatoire Nat. d'Art Dramatique; worked at Comédie Française as actor, director, pensionnaire from 1937, Sociétaire 1942–59, Hon. Sociétaire 1959–; Prof. Conservatoire Nat. d'Art Dramatique; Artistic Dir. Ecole Nat. Supérieure des arts et technique du théâtre; Artistic Dir. Théâtre du Palais-Royal 1960; Dir. Théâtre Michel 1964–71; Co-Dir. Théâtre des Célestins, Lyons 1968–; mem. Acad. de Neuilly; Officier, Légion d'honneur; Officier des Arts et des Lettres. *Directed* (Plays): Port-Royal, Les caves du Vatican, Le dindon, La Célestine, Don Giovanni, Donogoo, Cycle Molière, Les contes d'Hoffman, La ville dont le prince est enfant, l'Ecole des maris 1975, Topaze, Noix de coco 1984, Gigi 1985, La prise de Berg op Zoom 1986; (films): Le bourgeois gentilhomme, Le mariage de Figaro, Tartuffe, Les femmes savantes, La ville dont le prince est enfant; Les affaires sont les affaires (television) 1974. *Publications:* Molière, Gilles Shakespeare ou les aventures de Jean Perrin, Etudes des oeuvres complètes de Molière; (plays): Mic-Mac 1962, L'âge idiot 1963, Le vice dans la peau 1965, La courte paille 1967. *Address:* 3 boulevard des Sablons, 92000 Neuilly-sur-Seine, France (Home).

MEYER, Klaus, DR. PHIL.; German diplomatist; b. 10 April 1928, Cologne; s. of late Hans Meyer and of Elfriede Meyer; m. Ingeborg Buhrow 1955; three s. one d.; ed. Univs. of Göttingen and Paris; joined German diplomatic service 1955; served Paris 1956–57; Deputy Chef de Cabinet, President of Comm. of European Community (EC), Brussels 1959–67; Dir. Office of Fed. Chancellor, Bonn 1967–69; post with EC Comm. 1969–77, Gen. Dir. for Devt. 1977–82; Amb. to Czechoslovakia 1982–85; Amb. and Perm. Rep. to OECD, Paris 1985–; Bundesverdienstkreuz. *Address:* 5 rue Léonard de Vinci, 75116 Paris, France.

MEYER, Robert Kenneth, PH.D., F.A.H.A.; American logician; b. 27 May 1932, Sharon Hill, Pa.; s. of the late Frank A. Meyer and Helen M. Mooney; m. 1st Bette Jane Gottschalk 1954 (died 1963), 2nd Barbara Lee Edwards 1963 (died 1973); three s. six d.; ed. Sharon Hill High School, Lehigh Univ., Princeton Theological Seminary, Kyoto School of Japanese Language Univ. of Pittsburgh; Asst. Minister Union Congregational Church, N.J. 1956–57; Missionary United Church of Christ 1957–62; Asst. Prof. of Philosophy and Math., West Virginia Univ. 1965–66; Asst. Prof. of Philosophy, Rice Univ. 1966–67, Bryn Mawr Coll. 1967–69, Indiana Univ. 1969–72, Visiting Assoc. Prof. Univ. of Toronto 1972–73, Univ. of Pittsburgh 1973–74; Postdoctoral Fellow in Philosophy, A.N.U. 1974–76, Sr. Research Fellow 1976–81, Sr. Fellow 1981–, Co-ordinator Automated Reasoning Project 1986–. *Publications:* Class Church and Labor Evangelism 1961, E, R, and Gamma (with J. M. Dunn) 1969, Semantics of Entailment (with R. Routley) 1973, Intuitionism, entailment, negation 1974, Solution to the P-W problem (with E. P. Martin) 1982, Relevant logics and their rivals (with R. Routley, V. Plumwood, R. T. Brady) 1983, Automated theorem-proving in non-classical Logics (with P. B. Thistlewaite, M. A. McRobbie) 1988. *Leisure interests:* chess, astronomy, personal computing. *Address:* Automated Reasoning Project, I-Block, Australian National University, Canberra, ACT 2601 (Univ.); 3 Rawlings Place, Fadden, ACT 2904, Australia (Home). *Telephone:* (062) 49-2209 (Univ.); (062) 92-5078 (Home).

MEYER-CORDING, Dr. Ulrich; German economist; b. 22 May 1911, Dresden; m. Dr. Gisela Cording 1950; one s.; ed. high school, Dresden and Univs. of Grenoble, Berlin, Kiel, Exeter and Leipzig; Lawyer, Stuttgart 1948–50; Ministerial Adviser, Ministry of Justice, Bonn 1950–57; Ministerial Man. in Ministry of Atomic Affairs 1957–58; Ministerial Dir. and Head of European Dept., Ministry of Commerce 1958–64; Prof. of Commercial and Business Law, Univ. of Cologne 1958–; Vice-Chair. European Investment Bank, Brussels 1964–72; Dir. Rheinische Hypothekenbank, Cologne 1972–77. *Publications:* Das Recht der Banküberweisung 1951, Monopol und Marktbeherrschung als Rechtsbegriffe 1954, Die Vereinsstrafe 1957, Die Rechtsnormen 1971. *Leisure interests:* literature, sport. *Address:* Hinter Hoben 6, 5300 Bonn 1, Federal Republic of Germany. *Telephone:* 23 28 10.

MEYER-LANDRUT, Andreas, PH.D.; German diplomatist; b. 31 May 1929, Tallinn, Estonia (now part of U.S.S.R.); s. of Bruno and Käthe (née Winter) Meyer-Landrut; m. Hanna Karatsony von Hodos 1960; one s. one d.; ed. Univs. of Göttingen and Zagreb; entered foreign service 1955, in Moscow, Brussels and Tokyo 1956–68, Amb. to Congo (Brazzaville) 1969; in Foreign Office, Bonn 1971–80, Head of Sub-Dept. for Policy towards E. Europe and G.D.R. 1974–78, Dir. Dept. of Relations to Asia, Near and Middle East, Africa and Latin America 1978–80, Amb. to U.S.S.R. 1980–83, 1987; State Sec. to Foreign Office 1983–87. *Address:* Adenauerallee 99–103, 5300 Bonn 1; Lukas-Cranach Strasse 3, 5300 Bonn 2, Federal Republic of Germany.

MEYERS, Franz, DR.JUR.; German lawyer and politician; b. 31 July, 1908, Mönchengladbach; s. of Franz and Emma (née Havenstein) Meyers; m. 1st Alberte Mertens 1937; m. 2nd Wilhelmine Esterhues 1985; ed. Univs. of Freiburg and Cologne; lawyer 1934–; mem. Diet of North-Rhine-Westphalia 1950–70; Mayor of Mönchengladbach 1952; Minister of Interior of North-Rhine-Westphalia 1952–56; mem. Bundesrat 1952–56, Bundestag 1957–58; Minister-Pres., North-Rhine-Westphalia 1958–66; Pres. Bundesrat 1961–62; fmr. Chair., now mem., Supervisory Bd., Klöckner-Werke AG; Pres. German Leisure Assocn.; Grosskreuz des Verdienstordens der Bundesrepublik Deutschland, Bayerische Verdiensterden and numerous foreign decorations. *Address:* 4050 Mönchengladbach, Bergstrasse 137, Federal Republic of Germany.

MEYERS, Gerald Carl, M.S.; American business executive; b. 5 Dec. 1928, Buffalo, N.Y.; s. of Meyer and Berenice Meyers; m. Barbara Jacob Meyers 1958; one s. two d.; ed. Carnegie Inst. of Tech. (now Carnegie-Mellon Univ.), Pittsburgh, Pa.; with Ford Motor Co., Detroit 1950–51, Chrysler Corpn., Detroit and Geneva 1954–62; with American Motors Corpn. 1962–, Dir. Purchasing Analysis 1962, Dir. Operations Control 1963–65, Dir. Automotive Manufacturing Staff 1965–67, Vice-Pres. Automotive Manufacturing 1967, Vice-Pres. Product Devt. Group 1968–72, Group Vice-Pres. (Product) 1972–75, Exec. Vice-Pres. 1975, Dir. 1976–, Pres. and C.O.O. 1977, Pres. and C.E.O. 1977–, Chair. 1978–82; Trustee, Carnegie-Mellon

Univ.; Chevalier, Légion d'honneur 1981. *Leisure interests:* jogging, sailing. *Address:* 5600 West Maple Road, Suite C-304, West Bloomfield, Mich. 48033 (Office); Bloomfield Hills, Mich. 48013, U.S.A. (Home).

MEYERSON, Martin, SC.D.; American university president; b. 14 Nov. 1922, New York; s. of S. Z. and Etta (née Berger) Martin; m. Margy Ellin Lazarus; two s. one d.; ed. Columbia Univ., Harvard Univ.; Asst. Prof. of Social Sciences, Univ. of Chicago 1948; successively Research Dir., Exec. Dir., Vice-Pres., Vice-Chair., American Council to Improve Our Neighbourhoods; Assoc. Prof., Prof., Univ. of Pa. Inst. for Urban Studies and Dept. of City and Regional Planning 1952–57; Adviser on urban problems for UN in Indonesia, Japan and Yugoslavia 1958–66; Frank Backus Williams Prof. of City Planning and Urban Research, Harvard Univ. 1957–63; Dir. Joint Center for Urban Studies of M.I.T. and Harvard Univ. 1957–63; Dean Coll. of Environmental Design, Univ. of Calif. (Berkeley), Acting Chancellor 1963–66; Pres. State Univ. of New York at Buffalo, Prof. of Policy Sciences 1966–70; Pres. Univ. of Pa. 1970–80, Pres. Emer. 1980–; mem. Int. Council for Educ. Devt. 1971–; American Dir., Int. Asscn. Univs. 1975–; Chair. Univ. of Pa. Foundation 1981–, Prof. 1981–; Gov. Centre for Environmental Studies, London; fmr. Gov. American Inst. of Planners; Fellow A.A.A.S., American Acad. of Arts and Sciences; Hon. LL.D. (Queens Univ., Canada, D'Youville Coll., Alfred Univ., Rutgers Univ., Univ. of Pa., Stonehill Coll.), Hon. D.Sc. (Chattanooga); Hon. Prof. Nat. Univ. of Paraguay. *Publications:* Co-Author Politics, Planning and the Public Interest 1955, Housing, People and Cities 1962, Face of the Metropolis 1963, Boston 1966, Conscience of the City (Editor) 1970, Gladly Learn and Gladly Teach 1977. *Address:* Room 225, Van Pelt Library, University of Pennsylvania, Philadelphia, Pa. 19104 (Office); 2016 Spruce Street, Philadelphia, Pa. 19103, U.S.A. (Home).

MEYNELL, Laurence W.; British writer; b. 9 Aug. 1899, Wolverhampton; s. of Herbert and Agnes Meynell; m. 1st Shirley Darbyshire 1932 (deceased), one d.; m. 2nd Joan Henley 1966; ed. St. Edmund's Coll., Ware; fmr. schoolmaster, land agent; served with R.A.F.; Literary Ed. Time and Tide 1958–60; Past Pres. Johnson Soc. *Publications:* Blue Feather 1928, On the Night of the 18th 1936, The Door in the Wall 1936, The Dandy 1938, The Hut 1938, Dark Square 1940, Strange Landing 1946, The Evil Hour 1947, The Bright Face of Danger 1948, The Echo in the Cave 1949, Party of Eight 1950, Famous Cricket Grounds 1951, The Man No One Knew 1951, The Frightened Man 1952, Too Clever by Half 1953, Builder and Dreamer (Life of I. K. Brunel) 1953, Man of Speed (Life of C. S. Rolls) 1953, Give me the Knife 1954, Under the Hollies 1954, Policeman in the Family 1954, Bridge under the water 1955, Where is She Now? 1955, Great Men of Staffordshire 1955, Life of James Brindley 1956, Life of T. Telford, The Breaking Point 1957, One Step from Murder 1958, The Abandoned Doll 1960, The House in Marsh Road 1960, The Pit in the Garden 1961, Virgin Luck 1962, Sleep of the Just 1963, More Deadly than the Male 1964, Scoop 1965, The Suspect Scientist 1965, Die by the Book 1966, The Mauve Front Door 1967, Week End in the Scampi Belt 1967, Death of a Philanderer 1968, The Curious Crime of Miss Julia Blossom 1970, The Fatal Flaw 1971, A Little Matter of Arson 1971, Death by Arrangement 1972, The End of the Long Hot Summer 1972, A View from the Terrace, The Fortunate Miss East 1973, Hooky and the Crock of Gold 1974, The Fairly Innocent Little Man 1974, The Lost Half Hour 1976, Papersnake 1978; and under the pseudonym of Robert Eton: The Pattern 1934, The Bus Leaves for the Village 1936, Palace Pier 1938, The Legacy 1939, The Faithful Years, The Corner of Paradise Place, St. Lynn's Advertiser 1946, The Dragon at the Gate 1948; as Stephen Tring (for children): The Old Gang 1951, Barry Gets His Wish 1952, Barry's Exciting Year 1952, Penny Dreadful 1952, Penny Penitent 1953, Penny Triumphant 1954, Penny Dramatic 1955, Penny in Italy 1957, Penny and the Pageant, Nurse Ross Takes Over 1958, Nurse Ross Saves the Day 1960, The Vision Splendid 1976, The Sisters 1979, Hooky and the Prancing Horse 1980, The Lady Who Wasn't 1980, The Visitor 1983, Silver Guilt 1983, False Gods 1984, The Open Door 1984, The Affair at Barwold 1985, Hooky Catches a Tartar 1986, The Abiding Thing 1986, The Rivals 1988, Hooky Hooked 1988. *Leisure interests:* writing, reading.
[*Died 14 April 1989.*]

MEZA, Roberto; Salvadorean civil engineer and diplomatist; b. 25 Nov. 1937, Santa Ana; m. Maruca de Meza 1960; six c.; ed. Univ. Nacional de El Salvador, Univ. José Simeón Cañas and Univ. of Michigan; mem. and occasional Acting Mayor, San Salvador Town Council 1968; Dir. of Marketing Bd. of City of San Salvador 1970–71; Advisor to Minister of Interior 1980–82; Dir. Inst. of Public Housing 1982; Vice-Pres. Cen. Elections Bd. 1983–84; Dir. Administración Nacional de Telecommunicaciones (ANTEL) 1984–85; Minister of Public Works 1985–86; Perm. Rep. of El Salvador to UN 1986–; Dir. Roberto Meza-Ingenieros 1961–80, Roberto Meza-Consultories 1980–83; also dir. of several other pvt. cos. *Leisure interests:* reading, theatre, music, travel. *Address:* Permanent Mission of El Salvador to United Nations, 46 Park Ave., New York, N.Y. 10016 U.S.A. *Telephone:* (212) 679-1616.

MEZHELAITIS, Eduardas (Beniaminovich); Soviet-Lithuanian poet and writer; b. 1919; writer 1935–; mem. Lithuanian CP 1943–; Exec. Ed. of Lithuanian Komsomol newspaper, Sec. Central Cttee. of Lithuanian Komsomol 1940–46; literary & editorial work 1946–54, Sec. Lithuanian

Writers' Union 1954-59, then Chair. 1959-; Deputy 1955-, and Deputy Chair., Pres. of Supreme Soviet, Latvian SSR 1975; mem. Central Cttee. Latvian CP 1960-; Lenin Prizewinner 1962; Order of Lenin and several others; Hero of Socialist Labour. *Publications include:* Lyric Poetry 1943, Wind from Homeland 1946, Poets of Soviet Lithuania 1953 (anthology) 1953, Strange Stories 1957, Sun in Amber 1961, Man 1961, Southern Panorama 1963, Bread & the Word 1965, Moths 1966, Carousel 1967, Here is Lithuania 1968, Horizons 1970, Amber Bird 1972, Low-flying Fowl 1979, Collected Works (3 Vols.) 1979 and others.

MEZHIROV, Aleksandr Petrovich; Russian poet; b. 29 Sept. 1923, Moscow; m. Elena Jaschenko 1945; one d.; ed. Gorky Inst.; first published verse 1947; State Prize for Poetry. *Publications include:* Returns 1955, Poems and Translations 1962, Ladoga Ice 1965, Selected Works (2 vols.) 1981, The Blind Turning 1983. *Address:* U.S.S.R. Union of Writers, ul. Vorovskogo 52, Moscow, U.S.S.R.

MICALLEF, Daniel, M.D.; Maltese politician; b. 1928; seven c.; ed. St. Aloysius Coll., Royal Univ. Malta; elected mem. Legis. (Christian Workers' Party) 1962-66; M.P. 1971-; mem. Council of Europe 1971-74; mem. Investment Cttee. Cen. Bank 1980; Speaker House of Reps. 1982; fmr. Minister of Educ. and the Environment; Labour Party. *Leisure interests:* gardening, archaeology, reading. *Address:* House of Representatives, Valletta, Malta.

MICHAEL, George; British singer, composer and producer; b. 25 June 1963, Finchley; s. of Jack Kyriacus Panayiotou and Lesley Panayiotou; ed. Bushey Meads School; has sold millions of records; creating promotional video for Coca-Cola 1989; Ivor Novello Award for Best Songwriter 1985, 1989, British Rock Industry Award for Best Male Artist 1988; Grammy Award for Best Album (Faith) 1989; debut in group The Executive 1979; formed (with Andrew Ridgeley) Wham, numerous consecutive hits; toured U.K., France, U.S.A., China, etc.; launched solo career 1986; *singles include:* with Wham: Wham Rap, Young Guns Go For It, Bad Boys, Club Tropicana, Wake Up before You Go Go; solo: I Knew You Were Waiting (for me) with Aretha Franklin, q.v.), Careless Whisper, A Different Corner, I Want Your Sex, Faith, Father Figure; *albums include:* Fantastic, Make It Big, Music From The Edge of Heaven, Final, Faith (solo). *Address:* c/o Columbia Records, 1801 Century Park West, Los Angeles, Calif. 90067, U.S.A.

MICHAEL, James Henry, PH.D., F.A.A.; Australian mathematician; b. 3 April 1920, Port Augusta, S. Australia; s. of Charles Michael and Susan V. M. Willoughby; m. Patricia Hartley 1952; one s. one d.; ed. Univ. of Adelaide; Lecturer, Sr. Lecturer, Univ. of Adelaide 1958-65, Reader 1965-67, Prof. 1968-69, Reader in Pure Math. 1970-83; Visiting Assoc. Prof. Purdue Univ. 1960-61, 1964-65; Nuffield Fellow 1956; Fulbright Fellow 1960. *Publications:* articles in mathematical journals. *Leisure interests:* rifle shooting, golf, skiing. *Address:* 31 Shakespeare Avenue, Tranmere, South Australia 5073. *Telephone:* (08) 31 9748.

MICHAELIDES, Constantinos M.; Cypriot politician and fmr. diplomatist; b. 26 Dec. 1937, Limassol; m. Olivia Phasouliotis; two s. one d.; studied law and political science in Greece; joined Diplomatic Service 1961, served various posts at Embassy in Athens, Dir. Diplomatic Office of Minister of Foreign Affairs 1969-72, Counsellor, Cairo 1973-78, Special Diplomatic Adviser to Pres. of Repub. 1978-80, apptd. to rank of Amb. 1980; Acting Dir.-Gen. of Ministry of Interior; Minister of Interior 1982-88; Silver Cross of the Phoenix 1962, Holy Cross of St. Marcus, First Order 1979, Grand Cross of Honour 1983. *Address:* c/o Ministry of the Interior, Nicosia, Cyprus.

MICHAŁEK, Zbigniew, AGRIC.ENG.; Polish politician; b. 18 Aug. 1935, Pszów; ed. Higher School of Agric., Cracow; employee State Farms in Opole Voivodship; Deputy Head, State Farm, Wojnowice 1958-60, Head, Dir. State Farm, Rychnów 1960-69, Dir. Agricultural Complex, Głubczyce 1969-; agricultural practice at Faculty of Agric. Mechanization of Purdue Univ., Indiana 1965-66; mem. Polish Youth Union 1949-53; mem. Polish United Workers' Party (PZPR) 1953-, mem. PZPR Voivodship Cttee., Opole 1980-81, mem. PZPR Cen. Cttee. 1981-, Sec. PZPR Cen. Cttee. 1981-, Chair. Agric. Comm. of PZPR Cen. Cttee. 1981-86; Chair. Comm. of Agric., Food and Forestry Econ. of PZPR Cen. Cttee. 1986; alt. mem. Political Bureau, PZPR Cen. Cttee. 1986-, mem. 1988-; Chair. Editorial Council "Chłopska Droga" 1986-; Kt.'s Cross of Order of Polonia Restituta, Gold and Silver Cross of Merit. *Address:* Komitet Centralny PZPR, ul. Nowy Świat 6, 00-497 Warsaw, Poland.

MICHAŁOWSKA-GUMOWSKA, Joanna, H.H.D.; Polish politician; b. 28 Nov. 1945, Vilnius, U.S.S.R.; ed. Food Industry Tech. School, Gdańsk, Gdańsk Univ.; worked in mill plants; teacher of Polish language since 1971; Instructress of PZPR District Cttee., Gdańsk-Centre 1973-74; Head of Dist. Centre for Party Work, Gdańsk 1974-75; Head of Centre for Information, Analyses and Programming Party Work of PZPR Voivodship Cttee., Gdańsk 1982-85; Sec. PZPR Voivodship Cttee., Gdańsk 1982-85; Deputy Chair. Voivodship Council of Patriotic Movt. for Nat. Rebirth (PRON), Gdańsk; Councillor of Voivodship Nat. Council, Gdańsk; Minister of Educ. 1985-87; Gold Cross of Merit and other decorations.

MICHALSKI, Jan, SC.D.; Polish chemist; b. 7 June 1920, Łódź; s. of Edward Michalski and Lucyna Jungowska; m. Maria Wejchert 1944; two

s. two d.; ed. Warsaw Tech. Univ., Jagiellonian Univ. Cracow, Cambridge Univ. U.K.; scientific worker, Łódź Tech. Univ. 1945-; Assoc. Prof. 1958-64, Prof. 1964-; Corresp. mem. Polish Acad. of Sciences 1962-69, mem. 1969-, Sec. of Third Dept. 1972-77, mem. of Presidium 1969-, Chair. Łódź branch 1978-; Dir. Centre of Molecular and Macromolecular Studies of Polish Acad. of Sciences, Łódź; Overseas Fellow, Churchill Coll., Cambridge Univ. 1964-; mem. Editorial Bd. of Tetrahedron, Tetrahedron Letters, Journal of Physical Organic Chem. and other scientific journals; mem. Polish Chemical Soc., American Chemical Soc., Royal Soc. of London, Int. Union of Pure and Applied Chem. (mem. of Exec. Cttee. 1977-85), and others; Fellow, Acad. of Sciences, Berlin 1978-, French Acad. of Sciences/Institut de France 1984; State Prize (1st Class) 1978; Knight's Cross, Order of Polonia Restituta 1958, Commdr.'s Cross 1974, Commdr.'s Cross with Star 1983, Medal of City of Paris 1969, Medal of 30th and 40th Anniversary of People's Poland 1974, Copernicus Medal of Polish Acad. of Sciences, Śniadecki Medal of Polish Chemical Soc. *Publications:* over 300 papers on organic chemistry of phosphorus-sulphur and related compounds, synthetic, mechanistic, stereochemical and biological aspects. *Leisure interest:* hiking. *Address:* Ul. Brzeźna 6 m. 3, 90-303 Łódź, Poland. *Telephone:* 84-31-20 (Office); 36-01-72 (Home).

MICHAUD, Jean-Claude Georges; French broadcasting executive; b. 28 Oct. 1933; s. of Maurice Michaud and Suzanne Michaud; m. Annette Chasserot 1957; two c.; ed. Lycée Louis-le-Grand, Paris and Ecole Normale Supérieure, Paris; Counsellor, Ministry of Educ. 1961-62, Ministry of Information 1962-64; Asst. Dir. Television ORTF 1964-68, Counsellor to Dir.-Gen. 1968-70; man. position, Librairie Hachette 1970-73; Deputy Dir. for External Affairs and Co-operation, ORTF 1973-74; Dir. of Int. Affairs and Co-ordination, Télédiffusion France 1975-80, Dir. of Commercial Affairs 1982-83, Overseas Dir. 1983-85; Pres.-Dir.-Gen. Soc. Française Radio-Télévision d'Outre-Mer (RFO) 1986-. *Publication:* Teoria e Storia nel Capitale di Marx 1960. *Leisure interests:* walking, skiing, reading. *Address:* 5 avenue du Recteur Poincaré, 75026 Paris (Office); 18 rue Gaston de Caillavet, 75025 Paris, France (Home). *Telephone:* 45 24 71 03 (Office).

MICHEL, François Claude, L. EN D.; French diplomatist; b. 30 July 1928, Saint-Denis, Réunion; s. of Claude Michel and Emilie Cabanne de Laprade; m. Jeanine Maurice 1953; four s.; ed. Faculté de Droit, Paris, Ecole nat. de la France d'Outre-Mer; Admin. Cameroon 1951-56; attached to the Ministry of Foreign Affairs 1959-60; Sec. French Embassy, Yaoundé 1960, Ankara 1963, Addis Ababa 1966-68; Liaison Officer with Org. for African Unity, UN Econ. Comm. for Africa, and French Del. for links with EEC 1968-71; Second Counsellor, Tananarive 1971-72, Dublin 1972-75; Amb. to Haiti 1983-86; Dir. of Cabinet for Sec. of State for Foreign Affairs 1986-88; Chevalier Légion d'honneur, Chevalier de l'ordre national du Mérite. *Address:* 57 rue du Docteur Blanche, 75016 Paris, France (Home).

MICHEL, Joseph; Belgian lawyer; b. 25 Oct. 1925, Saint-Mard; m.; three s. two d.; ed. Catholic Univ. of Louvain; Pres. Young Christian Democrats of Virton 1949; Councillor of Virton 1958; Mayor of Virton 1970; mem. House of Reps. 1961-; Minister of Interior 1974-77, 1986-88, of Educ. (French) 1977-79, of Civil Service and Decentralization 1987-88; Deputy Prime Minister 1986; political columnist Avenir du Luxembourg. *Publication:* Economic History of the Province of Luxembourg during the Nineteenth Century 1954. *Address:* 76 avenue Bouvier, 6760 Virton, Belgium. *Telephone:* (063) 577404 (Virton).

MICHEL, Louis, PH.D.; French physicist; b. 4 May 1923, Roanne; s. of Alfred Michel and Camille Nugue; m. Thérèse Vallet 1947; two s. four d.; ed. Ecole Polytechnique, Paris and Univ. of Paris/Sorbonne; explosives engineer 1946-58; research, Univ. of Manchester 1948-50, Inst. for Teoretisk Fysik, Copenhagen 1950-53, Inst. for Advanced Study, Princeton 1953-55; Prof. Univ. of Lille 1955-58, Univ. of Paris 1958-62; Prof. Inst. des Hautes Etudes Scientifiques, Bures-sur-Yvette 1962-; mem. Inst. for Advanced Study, Princeton 1953-55; mem. Acad. des Sciences; Chevalier, Légion d'honneur; Prize Robin (Soc. Française de Physique) 1975; Leigh Page Prize Lecturer (Yale Univ.) 1976; Wigner Medal 1984; Dr. h.c. (Louvain, Barcelona). *Publications:* one book and 120 publs. in scientific journals. *Leisure interest:* music. *Address:* Champ Secret, 91440 Bures-sur-Yvette, France. *Telephone:* (331) 69 07 69 49.

MICHEL, Robert Henry, B.S., L.H.D.; American politician; b. 2 March 1923, Peoria, Ill.; s. of Charles Michel and Anna (née Baer) Michel; m. Corinne Woodruff 1948; four s.; ed. Bradley Univ., Lincoln Coll.; Admin. Asst. to mem. of Congress 1949-56; mem. 85th-99th Congresses, 18th Dist. Ill. 1957-; House Minority Leader 97th and 100th Congresses 1981-; Del. Republican Nat. Convention 1964-; Chair. Nat. Republican Congressional Cttee. 1973-74. *Address:* 2112 Rayburn House Office Building, Washington, D.C. 20515, U.S.A.

MICHELANGELI (Arturo Benedetti Michelangeli); Italian concert pianist; b. 5 Jan. 1920; ed. privately and Conservatorio G. Verdi in Milan; taught by Paolo Chiuieri in Brescia, then by Giovanni Anfassi in Milan; studied violin, organ and composition at the Conservatoire in Milan; winner of Grand Prix of Geneva 1939; given concerts throughout world; Academician of Accad. Sta. Cecilia, Rome, and Accad. Cherubini, Florence;

Gold Medal of Italian Republic. *Address:* c/o Kazuko Hillyer International Inc., 250 West 57th Street, New York, N.Y. 10019, U.S.A.

MICHELIN, François; French industrialist; b. 3 July 1926, Clermont-Ferrand; s. of Etienne and Madeleine (née Calliès) Michelin; m. Bernadette Montagne 1951; Man. Dir. Compagnie Générale des Etablissements Michelin, "Michelin & Cie." 1959–66, Jt. Man. Dir. 1966–; Man. Dir. Cie. Financière Michelin; Admin. Soc. anonyme Automobiles Citroën 1968–. *Address:* Usines Michelin, place des Carmes-Déchaux, 63000 Clermont-Ferrand (Office); 12 cours Sablon, 63000 Clermont-Ferrand, France (Home).

MICHELL, Allan Henry (Mike); Canadian banker; b. 4 Aug. 1930, St. John, N.B.; s. of Reginald Charles and Annie (Woodman) Michell; m. Jeannine Paquette 1970; one s. four d.; joined Royal Bank of Canada, Moncton, N.B. 1947, served various posts in Montreal and Toronto, appt. Exec. Officer 1972, Gen. Man., Ontario-W. Dist. 1976, Exec. Vice-Pres., Canada Div. 1978, Sr. Exec. Vice-Pres., Financial Control and Admin. 1983, Vice-Chair. 1986–; Dir. The Royal Bank of Canada, Royal Bank Realty Inc., Canadian Realty Corpn. Ltd., Ralston Purina Canada Inc.; mem. Bd. of Govs. Concordia Univ.; mem. Financial Execs. Inst.; Dir. Council for Canadian Unity. *Address:* The Royal Bank of Canada, 1 Place Ville Marie, Montreal, Quebec, H3C 3A9, Canada. *Telephone:* (514) 874-5823.

MICHELL, Keith; actor; b. 1 Dec. 1928, Adelaide, Australia; s. of Joseph and Maud (née Aslat) Michell; m. Jeanette Sterk 1957; one s. one d.; ed. Port Pirie High School, Adelaide Univ., Old Vic. Theatre School; started career as art teacher; first stage appearance Playbox, Adelaide 1947; with Young Vic. Theatre Co. 1950–51, first London appearance in And So To Bed 1951; Artistic Dir., Chichester Festival Theatre 1974–77; Top Actor Award 1971, British Film Award 1973, Logie Award 1974, and numerous others. *Stage appearances include:* Troilus and Cressida 1954, Romeo and Juliet 1954, Macbeth 1955, Don Juan 1956, Irma La Douce 1958, The Art of Seduction 1962, The Rehearsal 1963, Robert and Elizabeth 1964, The King's Mare 1966, Abelard and Heloise 1970, Hamlet 1972, Dear Love 1973, The Crucifer of Blood 1979, Captain Beaky Christmas Show 1981–82, The Tempest 1982, On the Rocks 1982, Amadeus 1983, La Cage aux Folles 1984–85, Jane Eyre 1986, Portraits 1987, The Royal Baccarat Scandal 1988. *Television include:* The Six Wives of Henry VIII 1972, Keith Michell in Concert at Chichester 1974, Captain Beaky and His Band, Captain Beaky, Vol. 2, The Story of the Marlboroughs, Jacob and Joseph, The Story of David, The Tenth Month, The Day Christ Died. *Television/Video:* The Gondoliers, The Pirates of Penzance, Ruddigore. *Films include:* Dangerous Exile, The Hell Fire Club, Seven Seas to Calais, The Executioner, House of Cards, Prudence and the Pill, Henry VIII and his Six Wives, Moments. *One-Man Art Shows:* Jamaica paintings 1960, New York 1962, Portugal 1963, Outback in Australia 1965, Don Quixote series, New York 1969, Abelard and Héloïse 1972, Hamlet 1972. *Publications:* Shakespeare Sonnet series of lithographs 1974, Captain Beaky (illustrated poems) 1975, Captain Beaky Vol. 2 1982, Alice and Wonderland 1982, Keith Michell's Practically Macrobiotic Cookbook 1987. *Address:* c/o London Management and Representation Ltd., 235 Regent Street, London, W.1, England.

MICHELL, Robert H., PH.D., F.R.S.; British university professor; b. 16 April 1941, Yeovil; s. of Rowland C. Michell and Elsie L. (Hall) Michell; m. June Evans 1967 (divorced 1971); one s. one d.; ed. Crewkerne School and Univ. of Birmingham; Research Fellow, Birmingham Univ. 1965–66, 1969–70, Harvard Medical School 1966–68; Lecturer, Birmingham Univ. 1970–81, Sr. Lecturer 1981–84, Reader 1984–86, Prof. of Biochemistry 1986–87, Royal Soc. Research Prof. 1987–; other professional appts.; CIBA Medal, Biochemical Soc. 1988. *Publications:* Membranes and their Cellular Functions (with J. B. Finean and R. Coleman) 1974, 1978, 1984, Membrane Structure (ed. with J. B. Finean) 1981, Inositol Lipids and Transmembrane Signalling (ed. with M. J. Berridge) 1988, Inositol Lipids in Cell Signalling (ed. with A. H. Drummond and C. P. Downes) 1989. *Leisure interests:* birdwatching, photography, modern literature, wildernesses. *Address:* Department of Biochemistry, University of Birmingham, P.O. Box 363, Birmingham, B15 2TT (Office); 59 Weoley Park Road, Selly Oak, Birmingham, B29 6QZ, England (Home). *Telephone:* 021-414 5413 (Office); 021-472 1356 (Home).

MICHELMORE, Laurence, PH.D.; American international official; b. 1909, Philadelphia, Pa.; s. of John and Lily Elwert Michelmore; m. Janet Brownlee Hunter 1936; two d.; ed. Univ. of California and Harvard Univ.; Admin. Officer, Los Angeles Country Relief Admin. 1934–35, Idaho Works Progress Admin. 1935–36; Asst. Prof., Wayne Univ. 1936–42; Research Dept. Detroit Bureau of Governmental Research 1936–42; Staff, U.S. Budget Bureau 1942–46; UN Secr. 1946–71, Deputy Controller 1952–55, Sr. Dir. Tech. Assistance Bd. 1955–59, Deputy Dir. of Personnel 1959–63, Personal Rep. of Sec.-Gen. on Malaysia 1963; Commr. Gen. of UN Relief and Works Agency (UNRWA) 1964–71. *Address:* 4924 Sentinel Drive, Bethesda, Md. 20816, U.S.A. *Telephone:* (301) 320-4441.

MICHELSEN, Axel, DR. PHIL.; Danish professor of biology; b. 1 March 1940, Haderslev; s. of Erik Michelsen and Vibeke Michelsen; m. Ulla West-Nielsen 1980; two s. one d.; ed. Univ. of Copenhagen; Asst. Prof. of Zoophysiology and Zoology, Univ. of Copenhagen 1963–72; Prof. of Biology Odense Univ. 1973–; Chair. Danish Science Research Council 1975–78,

Danish Nat. Cttee. for Biophysics 1980–, Danish Nat. Cttee. for ICSU 1986–, Max-Planck Gesellschaft Fachbeirat 1978–82; Dir. Carlsberg Foundation 1986–; mem. Royal Danish Acad., Akad. der Naturforscher Leopoldina. *Publications:* The Physiology of the Locust Ear 1971, Sound and Life 1975, Time Resolution in Auditory Systems 1985. *Leisure interests:* wines, beekeeping, gardening. *Address:* Institute of Biology, Odense University, 5230 Odense M (Office); The Carlsberg Foundation, 35 H.C. Andersens Boulevard, 1553 Copenhagen V (Office); Læssøegade 204, 5230 Odense M, Denmark (Home). *Telephone:* 9-158600; 1-142128 (Office); 9-117568 (Home).

MICHELSEN, Hans Günter; German playwright; b. 1920, Hamburg; mil. service and P.O.W. 1939–49; began to write 1949; now freelance writer in Augsburg; Förderpreis des Niedersächsischen Kunstpreises, Hanover 1963, Förderpreis des Gerhart-Haupt-mann-Preises, Berlin 1963, Gerhart-Hauptmann-Preis, Berlin 1965, Literaturpreis der Freien Hansestadt Bremen 1967. *Publications:* plays: Stienz 1963, Feierabend 1 and 2 1963, Lappschiess 1964, Drei Akte 1965, Helm 1965, Frau L 1966, Planspiel 1969, Sein Leben 1975, Alltag 1978, Terror 1979; radio plays: Episode 1958, Kein schönes Land 1966, Ein Ende 1969, Himmelfahrt 1972. *Address:* Suhrkamp-Verlag, Postfach 2446, 6000 Frankfurt am Main, Federal Republic of Germany. *Telephone:* 726744.

MICHENER, Charles Duncan, B.S., PH.D.; American biologist (entomology); b. 22 Sept. 1918, Pasadena, Calif.; s. of Harold and Josephine Rigden Michener; m. Mary Hastings 1941; three s. one d.; ed. Univ. of California, Berkeley; Technical asst. in Entomology, Univ. of Calif. 1939–42; Asst. Curator, Lepidoptera and Hymenoptera, American Museum of Natural History, New York 1942–46, Assoc. Curator 1946–48, Research Assoc. 1949–; Curator, Snow Entomological Museum, Univ. of Kansas 1949–89, Dir. 1974–83; Assoc. Prof. Entomology, Univ. of Kansas 1948–50, Prof. 1950–89, Prof. Emer. 1989–; Chair. Dept. of Entomology 1949–61, 1972–75, Watkins Dist. Prof. of Entomology 1959–89, of Systematics and Ecology 1969–89; State Entomologist, S. Div. of Kansas 1949–61; Ed. Evolution 1962-64; American Ed. Insectes Sociaux (Paris), 1954–55, 1962–; Assoc. Ed. Annual Review of Ecology and Systematics 1970–; Pres. Soc. for the Study of Evolution 1967, Soc. of Systematic Zoology 1969, American Soc. of Naturalists 1978, Int. Union for the Study of Social Insects 1977–82 (Vice-Pres. Western Hemisphere Section 1979–80); mem. American Acad. of Arts and Sciences, Nat. Acad. of Sciences; Corresp. mem. Acad. Brasileira de Ciencias; Guggenheim Fellow to Brazil 1955–56, Africa 1966–67; Fellow Royal Entomological Soc. of London, American Asscn. for the Advancement of Sciences; Fulbright Scholar, Australia 1957–58; Morrison Prize, N.Y. Acad. of Sciences 1943; Founder's Award, American Entomological Soc. 1981. *Publications:* Comparative external morphology, phylogeny and a classification of the bees (Hymenoptera) 1944, American social insects (with M. H. Michener) 1951, The nest architecture of the sweat bees (with S. F. Sakagami) 1962, A classification of the bees of the Australian and S. Pacific regions 1965, The social behaviour of the bees 1974, Kin Recognition in Animals (Co-Ed. and Contrib.) 1987. *Leisure interests:* travel, field work. *Address:* Snow Entomological Museum, Snow Hall, University of Kansas, Lawrence, Kansas 66045; 1706 West 2nd Street, Lawrence, Kansas 66044, U.S.A. (Home). *Telephone:* (913) 864-4610 (Office); (913) 843-4598 (Home).

MICHENER, Rt. Hon. (Daniel) Roland, P.C., C.C., C.M.M., C.D., Q.C., B.C.L., M.A.; Canadian lawyer, business executive and fmr. Governor-General; b. 19 April 1900, Lacombe, Alberta; s. of late Edward and Mary Edith (Roland) Michener; m. Norah Evangeline Willis; three d.; ed. Univ. of Alberta and Oxford Univ.; Barrister, Middle Temple (England) 1923, Ontario 1924; practising lawyer, Lang, Michener and Cranston, Toronto 1924–57; mem. Ontario Legis. for St. David, Toronto 1945–48, Prov. Sec. 1946–48; Progressive Conservative mem. of House of Commons 1953–62; Speaker of House of Commons 1957–58, 1958–62; High Commr. in India 1964–67; Gov.-Gen. and Commdr.-in-Chief of Canada 1967–74; Chancellor and Prin. Companion of the Order of Canada 1967; Chancellor and Commdr., Order of Mil. Merit 1972; Royal Victorian Chain 1973; Prior for Canada, and Kt. of Justice of Most Venerable Order of the Hosp. of St. John of Jerusalem 1967; Gen. Sec. for Canada for Rhodes Scholarships 1936–64; mem. of Council, Commonwealth Parl. Asscn. 1959–61; Chair. Manitoba Royal Comm. on Local Govt. and Finance 1962–64; Chancellor Queen's Univ., Kingston 1974–80; Chair. Bd. Metropolitan Trust Co. 1974–76; Chair. Bd. Teck Corpn. Ltd. 1974–81; Public Gov. Toronto Stock Exchange 1974–76; Dir E.L. Financial Corpn. 1974–76; assoc. counsel Lang, Michener, Cranston, Farquharson and Wright; Chair. H.R.H. The Duke of Edinburgh's Fifth Commonwealth Study Conf., Canada 1980; fmr. Gov. Toronto Western Hospital, Univ. of Toronto; fmr. Pres. Lawyers Club, Empire Club, Bd. of Trade Club, Toronto; fmrly. Hon. Counsel and Chair. of Exec. Cttee., Canadian Inst. of Int. Affairs, Pres. 1974–79; Co-Chair. Canadian Foundation for Refugees 1979–81; fmr. Hon. Counsel Red Cross Ontario Div.; fmr. Chair. of Exec. Canadian Asscn. for Adult Educ.; Hon. Fellow Hertford Coll., Oxford 1961, Acad. of Medicine 1967, Royal Coll. of Physicians and Surgeons of Canada 1968, Royal Architectural Inst. of Canada 1968, Trinity Coll., Toronto 1968, Frontier Coll., Toronto 1972, Royal Soc. of Canada 1975, Royal Canadian Mil. Inst., Heraldry Soc. of Canada; Hon. mem. Canadian Medical Asscn. 1968; Hon. Life Bencher Law Soc. of Canada 1968; Hon. Master World Masters Games, Toronto 1985; numerous hon. degrees. *Address:* P.O. Box 10, First Canadian Place,

Toronto, Ont. M5X 1A2 (Office); 24 Thornwood Road, Toronto, Ont., M4W 2S1, Canada (Home).

MICHENER, James Albert, A.B., A.M.; American writer; b. 3 Feb. 1907, New York; m. 1st Patti Koon 1935 (divorced 1948); m. 2nd Vange Nord 1948 (divorced 1955); m. 3rd Mari Yoriko Sabusawa 1955; ed. Swarthmore Coll., Colorado State Coll. of Education, Ohio State Univ., Univs. of Pennsylvania, Virginia, Harvard and St. Andrews (Scotland); teacher 1929–36; Prof. Colo. State Coll. of Educ. 1936–41; Assoc. Ed., Macmillan Co. 1941–49; U.S. Naval Reserve 1944–45; mem. Advisory Cttee. on the Arts, U.S. State Dept. 1957; mem. Bd. Int. Broadcasting 1984–; Chair. Pres. Kennedy's Food for Peace Program 1961; mem. U.S. Advisory Comm. on Information 1971; Pulitzer Prize for Tales of the S. Pacific 1947; Einstein Award 1967; Medal of Freedom 1977, Gold Medal (Spanish Inst.) 1980. *Publications:* Unit in the Social Studies 1940, Tales of the South Pacific 1947, The Fires of Spring 1949, Return to Paradise 1951, The Voice of Asia 1951, The Bridges at Toko-ri 1953, Sayonara 1954, Floating World 1955, The Bridge at Andau 1957, Rascals in Paradise (with A. Grove Day) 1957, Selected Writings 1957, The Hokusai Sketchbook 1958, Japanese Prints 1959, Hawaii 1959, Report of the County Chairman 1961, Caravans 1963, The Source 1965, Iberia 1968, Presidential Lottery 1969, The Quality of Life 1970, Kent State 1971, The Drifters 1971, The Fires of Spring 1972, A Michener Miscellany 1973, Centennial 1974, Sports in America 1976, Chesapeake 1978, The Covenant 1980, Space 1982, Poland 1983, Texas 1985, Legacy 1987, Alaska 1988. *Address:* Barker Library, Univ. of Texas, Austin, Texas 78731, U.S.A.

MICHENER, Roland (see Michener, Daniel Roland).

MICHNA, Waldemar, AGRIC.SC.D.; Polish politician and agricultural economist; b. 1929, Gniadówka, Lublin Voivodship; m.; one d.; ed. Main School of Farming, Warsaw; active in youth org.; mem. Wici Rural Youth Union, Puławy 1946–48, then Polish Youth Union (ZMP), including Deputy Chair. ZMP Dist. Bd., Puławy, next Instructor ZMP Voivodship B., Lublin; mem. Gen. Bd. of Rural Youth Union 1956–63; after graduation Asst., Dept. of Agrarian Policy of Main School of Farming, Warsaw, subsequently Dist. Agronomist in Agricultural Machines State Centre, Lubaszcz; mem. Polish United Peasant Party (ZSL); Instructor, ZSL Chief Cttee. 1954–56; Adviser, subsequently Dir. of Office of Deputy Chair. of Council of Ministers 1956–73; at the same time scientific worker of Main School of Farming, Warsaw, Asst. Prof., next Extraordinary Prof.; Head, Economic-Agricultural Dept. of ZSL Chief Cttee. 1973–78; Pres., ZSL Warsaw Capital Cttee. 1979; Deputy to Seym (Parl.) 1980–85; Deputy Minister of Environmental Protection and Natural Resources 1984–87, Minister 1987–88; Officer's Cross of Polonia Restituta Order and other decorations. *Address:* c/o Ministerstwo Ochrony Środowiska i Zasobów Naturalnych, ul. Wawelska 52/54, 00-922 Warsaw, Poland.

MICHON, John Albertus, PH.D.; Netherlands university professor and consultant; b. 29 Oct. 1935, Utrecht; s. of late J. J. Michon and of S. Ch. A. de Ruyter; ed. Utrecht Mun. Gymnasium and Univs. of Utrecht and Leiden; Research Assoc. Inst. for Perception, Soesterberg 1960–73, Head, Dept. of Road User Studies 1969–73; Co-founder, Netherlands Psychonomics Foundation 1968, Sec. 1968–72, Pres. 1975–80; Prof. of Experimental Psychology and Traffic Science, Univ. of Groningen 1971–, Dir. Inst. for Experimental Psychology 1971–86, Chair. Traffic Research Center 1977–, Chair. Dept. of Psychology 1978, 1983–86, Assoc. Dean, Faculty of Social Sciences 1983–86; Pres. Int. Soc. for the Study of Time 1983–86; Co-founder, mem. Bd. European Soc. for Cognitive Psychology 1984–; Vice-Chair. Nat. Council for Road Safety 1977–86; Ed.-in-Chief, Acta Psychologica 1971–74; Visiting Prof. Carnegie Mellon Univ. Pittsburgh, Pa. 1986–87; mem. Royal Netherlands Acad. of Arts and Sciences; NATO Science Fellowship, NIAS Fellowship. *Publications:* Timing in Temporal Tracking 1967, Sociale Verkeerskunde 1976, Handboek der Psychonomie 1976, 1979, Beïnvloeding van Mobiliteit 1981, Time, Mind and Behavior 1985, Guyau and the Idea of Time 1988, Handboek der Sociale Verkeerskunde 1989; approx. 200 articles and chapters in scientific journals and books. *Leisure interests:* visual arts (painting, graphics), music (bassoon playing). *Address:* Institute for Experimental and Occupational Psychology, University of Groningen, P.O. Box 14, 9750 AA Haren (Office); Traffic Research Centre, P.O. Box 69, 9750 AB Haren (Office); Rijksstraatweg 251, 9752 CB Haren, The Netherlands (Home). *Telephone:* 50-636472 (Office); 50-636758 (Office); 50-347718 (Home).

MICKELSON, George S., B.S., J.D.; American governor; b. 31 Jan. 1941, Mobridge, S. Dak.; s. of George T. Mickelson and Madge Mickelson; m. Linda McCahren; two s. one d.; partner McCann, Martin and Mickelson 1968–83, Mickelson, Erickson and Helsper 1983–86; State Attorney, Brookings Co. 1970–74; mem. S. Dak. House of Reps. 1975–80, Speaker 1979–80, Gov. S. Dak. State 1986–; Chair. S. Dak. Bd. of Charities and Corrections 1980–84; mem. American Bar Asscn., Asscn. of Trial Lawyers of America, American Judicature Soc.; Republican. *Address:* Office of the Governor, 500 E. Capitol, Pierre, S. Dak. 57501, U.S.A.

MIDDENDORF, J. William, II, B.S., M.B.A.; American diplomatist and government official; b. 22 Sept. 1924, Baltimore, Md.; s. of Henry Stump and late Sarah Boone Middendorf; m. Isabelle J. Paine 1953; two s. two d.; ed. Holy Cross Coll., Harvard Univ. and New York Graduate School of Business Admin.; U.S. Navy service during Second World War; in Credit Dept. of Bank of Manhattan Co. (now Chase Manhattan Bank) 1947–52; Analyst, brokerage firm of Wood Struthers and Co. Inc., New York 1952–58, Partner 1958–62; Sr. Partner investment firm of Middendorf, Colgate and Co., New York 1962–69; U.S. Amb. to the Netherlands 1969–73; Under-Sec. of the Navy 1973–74, Sec. 1974–76; Pres. and C.E.O. of First American Bankshares, Washington, D.C. 1977–81; U.S. Amb. to O.A.S. 1981–85, to EEC 1985–87; Chair. Middendorf, Ansary and Co. Inc. 1987–; Chair. Presidential Task Force on Project Econ. Justice 1985–86; State Dept. Superior Honor Award 1974, Dept. of Defense Distinguished Public Service Award 1975, 1976, U.S. Navy Public Service Award 1976, Grand Master of Order of Naval Merit (Brazil) 1974, Distinguished Service Medal (Brazil) 1976, Order of Arab Repub. of Egypt (Class A) 1979, Grand Officer of the Order of Orange Nassau Netherlands 1985, Ludwig Von Mises Inst. Free Market Award 1985; U.S. Nat. Sculling Champion in Masters Div. 1979, won a world masters championship in rowing at the 1985 Toronto Masters Games. *Compositions:* has composed seven symphonies, an opera and numerous marches and concerti. *Publications:* Investment Policies of Fire and Casualty Insurance Companies. *Address:* Middendorf, Ansary and Co. Inc., 1725 K Street, N.W., Suite 808, Washington, D.C. 20006, U.S.A.

MIDDLEDITCH, Edward, M.C., R.A., A.R.C.A.; British artist; b. 23 March 1923; s. of Charles H. Middleditch and Esme Buckley; m. Jean K. Whitehouse 1947; one d.; ed. Mundella School, Nottingham, King Edward VI Grammar School, Chelmsford and Royal Coll. of Art; army service 1942–47; eleven exhbns. London 1954–74; Head of Fine Art Dept., Norwich School of Art 1964–; Keeper of the Royal Acad. Schools 1985–; contrib. to numerous group exhbns. including Venice Biennale 1956, Pittsburgh Int. 1958, English Landscape Tradition in the 20th Century 1969, 25 Years of British Painting 1977, The Forgotten Fifties 1984; paintings in Tate Gallery, Victoria & Albert Museum, Nat. Gallery of Australia, Nat. Gallery of Canada and many other public and pvt. collections; Gulbenkian Foundation Scholarship 1962. *Address:* c/o New Arts Centre, 41 Sloane Street, London, S.W.1, England.

MIDDLETON, Christopher, M.A., D.PHIL.; British professor of Germanic languages and literature; b. 10 June 1926, Truro; s. of Hubert S. Middleton and Dorothy M. Miller; m. 1953 (divorced); one s. two d.; ed. Felsted School and Merton Coll. Oxford; Lektor in English, Univ. of Zürich 1952–55; Asst. Lecturer in German, King's Coll. Univ. of London 1955–57, lecturer 1957–66; Prof. of Germanic Languages and Literature Univ. of Texas at Austin 1966–; Sir Geoffrey Faber Memorial Prize 1964, Guggenheim Poetry Fellowship 1974–75; Nat. Endowment for Humanities Poetry Fellowship 1980; Tieck-Schlegel Translation Prize 1985, Max Geilinger Stiftung Prize 1987, etc. *Publications:* Torse 3, poems 1948–61 1962, Nonsequences/Selfpoems 1965, Our Flowers and Nice Bones 1969, The Lonely Suppers of W.V. Balloon 1975, Carminalenia 1980, III Poems 1983, Two Horse Wagon Going By 1986; vols. of prose, essays etc. *Address:* Germanic Languages, Batts Hall 216, University of Texas at Austin, Austin, Tex. 78712, U.S.A. *Telephone:* 512-471-4123.

MIDDLETON, Donald King, C.B.E.; British diplomatist (retd.); b. 24 Feb. 1922; Ministry of Health 1958–61; Commonwealth Relations Office 1961; First Sec. (Information), Lagos 1961–65; Commonwealth Office (later FCO) 1966; First Sec. and Head of Chancery, Saigon 1970–72; Deputy High Commr., Ibadan 1973–75; Chargé d'Affaires, Phnom-Penh 1975; on loan to N. Ireland Office, Belfast 1975; High Commr. in Papua New Guinea 1977–81; mem. Council Voluntary Service Overseas 1982–. *Address:* Stone House, Ledgemoor, Hereford, HR4 8RN, England.

MIDDLETON, Drew, B.S.; American journalist; b. 14 Oct. 1913, New York; s. of Elmer Thomas and Jean (née Drew) Middleton; m. Estelle Mansel-Edwards 1943; one d.; ed. Syracuse Univ.; sports Ed. Poughkeepsie (N.Y.) Eagle News 1936; reporter Poughkeepsie Evening Star 1936–37; sports writer N.Y. office Assoc. Press 1939; war corresp. attached to B.E.F. France and Belgium 1939–40, to R.A.F. 1940–41, to U.S. Army and Navy, Iceland 1941–42, Allied Forces, London 1942; staff of New York Times, London 1942; corresp. North Africa and Mediterranean area and Allied H.Q. Algiers 1942–43; with U.S. Eighth Air Forces and R.A.F. Bomber Commd. 1943–44; U.S. First Army and SHAEF 1944–45; Frankfurt, Berlin and Int. Mil. Trials, Nuremberg 1945–46; Chief Corresp. New York Times in U.S.S.R. 1946–47, Germany 1947–53, London 1953–62, Paris 1962–65, UN (New York) 1965–69, European Affairs Corresp. 1969–70, Mil. Affairs Corresp. 1970–; Hon. D.Litt. (Syracuse Univ.) 1963; U.S. Medal of Freedom 1948; Hon. O.B.E. (Mil. Div.) 1947, Hon. C.B.E. 1985. *Publications:* Our Share of Night 1946, The Struggle for Germany 1949, The Defence of Western Europe 1952, The British 1957, The Sky Suspended 1960, The Supreme Choice: Britain and the European Community 1963, The Crisis in the West 1965, Retreat from Victory 1973, Where has last July Gone? 1974, Can America Win the Next War 1975, Submarine 1976, The Duel of the Giants: China and Russia in Asia 1978, Crossroads of Modern War 1983, This War Called Peace (jtly) 1984, Invasion of the United States (with Gene Braun) 1985, Southeast Asia 1985. *Address:* c/o New York Times, 229 W. 43rd Street, New York, N.Y. 10036, U.S.A.

MIDDLETON, Sir George Humphrey, K.C.M.G.; British diplomatist; b. 21 Jan. 1910; s. of George Close Middleton and Susan Sophie (née Harley); m. Marie Elisabeth Camille Françoise Sarthou; one s., one step s. one step d.; ed. St. Lawrence Coll., Ramsgate, and Magdalen Coll., Oxford; entered Consular Service 1933; Vice-Consul, Buenos Aires; Third Sec., Asunción 1934, in charge of Legation 1935, New York 1936; Consul at Lemberg (Lwów) 1939; in charge of Vice-Consulate, Cluj 1939–40, Genoa 1940, Madeira 1940, Foreign Office 1943; Second Sec., Washington 1944; First Sec. 1945; Foreign Office 1947; Counsellor 1949; Counsellor, British Embassy, Teheran 1951; Chargé d'Affaires 1951 and 1952; Deputy High Commr. for U.K., Delhi 1953–56; Amb. to the Lebanon 1956–58; Political Resident in Persian Gulf 1958–61; Amb. to Argentina 1961–64, to United Arab Repub. 1964–65; mem. ad hoc Cttee. for UN Finances 1966; Consultant Ind. Reorganisation 1966–68; fmr. Chief Exec. British Industry Road Campaign; Chair. Michael Rice (Overseas) Ltd. 1969–76, Overseas Medical Supplies Ltd., C. E. Planning Ltd., Mondial Expatriate Services Ltd.; Dir. Liberty Life Assurance Co. Ltd., Britarge Ltd., Decor France Ltd.; Fellow, Royal Soc. of Arts; Chair. Bahrain Soc., British Moroccan Soc. *Leisure interests:* talking, walking. *Address:* 1 Carlyle Square, London, SW3 6EX, England. *Telephone:* 01-352 2962.

MIDDLETON, Sir Peter Edward, G.C.B., M.A.; British civil servant; b. 2 April 1934; m. Valerie Ann Lindup 1964; one s. one d.; ed. Sheffield City Grammar School, Sheffield Univ.; Bristol Univ.; Sr. Information Officer, H.M. Treasury 1962, Prin. 1964, Asst. Dir., Centre for Admin. Studies 1967–69, Pvt. Sec. to Chancellor of Exchequer 1969–72, Treasury Press Sec. 1972–75, Head, Monetary Policy Div. 1975, Under-Sec. 1976, Deputy Sec. 1980–83, Perm. Sec. 1983–; mem. Council Manchester Business School 1985–; Gov. London Business School 1984–, Ditchley Foundation 1985–; Visiting Fellow, Nuffield Coll., Oxford 1981; Hon. D.Litt. (Sheffield) 1984. *Address:* Her Majesty's Treasury, Parliament Street, London, S.W.1, England.

MIDWINTER, John Edwin, O.B.E., PH.D., F.R.S., F.ENG., F.I.E.E., F.I.E.E.E., F.INST.P.; British professor of optoelectronics; b. 8 March 1938, Newbury, Berks.; s. of late H. C. Midwinter and of V. J. (née Rawlinson) Midwinter; m. Maureen A. Holt 1961; two s. two d.; ed. King's Coll., London; Sr. Scientific Officer, Royal Radar Establishment 1967–68; Sr. Research Physicist, Perkin-Elmer Corpn., U.S.A. 1968–70; Head, Fibre Optic Devt. British Telecom Research Labs. 1971–77, Head Optical Communications Technology 1977–84; British Telecom Prof. of Optoelectronics, Univ. Coll., London 1984–; IEE-J.J. Thompson Medal 1987. *Publications:* Applied Non-Linear Optics 1972, Optical Fibers for Transmission 1977. *Leisure interests:* walking, skiing, writing. *Address:* Department of Electronic and Electrical Engineering, University College, Torrington Place, London, WC1E 7JE, England. *Telephone:* 01-388 0427.

MIELKE, Erich; German shipping clerk and politician; b. 28 Dec. 1907, Berlin; m.; two c.; joined Communist Youth League 1921, CP 1925; fought in Spanish civil war 1936–39; emigrated to U.S.S.R. 1939–45; State Sec., G.D.R. Ministry of State Security 1950–53, 1955–57; Deputy State Sec. for State Security, Ministry of the Interior 1953–55; Minister of State Security 1957–; mem. Volkskammer (People's Chamber) 1958–; mem. Cen. Cttee. Socialist Unity Party (SED) 1950–, cand. mem. Politburo 1971–76, mem. 1976–; Col.-Gen. 1959, Gen. 1980; Vaterländischer Verdienstorden in Gold (twice), Karl-Marx-Orden and many other decorations. *Address:* Ministry of State Security, 113 Berlin, Normannenstrasse 22, German Democratic Republic.

MIELKE, Frederick William, Jr., A.B., J.D.; American business executive (retd.); b. 19 March 1921, New York; s. of Frederick William and Cressida (née Flynn) Mielke; m. Lorraine Roberts 1947; two s.; ed. Univ. of Calif., Stanford Univ.; admitted to Calif. Bar 1950; law clerk to Assoc. Justice John W. Shenk, Calif. Supreme Court 1949–51; with Pacific Gas and Electric Co., San Francisco 1951–86; Exec. Vice-Pres. 1976–79, Chair. and C.E.O. 1979–86, now mem. Bd.; Pres. United Way of Bay Area 1986–88; Dir. Pacific Gas Transmission Co., Alberta and Southern Gas Co., Natural Gas Corpn., Calif., Edison Electric Inst.; Trustee, Stanford Univ. 1977–87; mem. American and Calif. Bar Asscns., Pacific Coast Electric and Gas Asscns. *Address:* Pacific Gas and Electric Co., 245 Market Street, San Francisco, Calif. 94106, U.S.A.

MIESEL, Karl; German banker; b. 22 July 1933; m.; one s. one d.; ed. Heidelberg Univ.; with Deutsche Bank AG –1986; Speaker of Exec. Bd., Schweizerische Kreditanstalt (Deutschland) AG 1986–. *Leisure interests:* table tennis, biking. *Address:* Schweizerische Kreditanstalt (Deutschland) AG, Kaiserstrasse 30, 6000 Frankfurt/Main 1, Federal Republic of Germany. *Telephone:* 069-2691-0.

MIĘSOWICZ, Marian, PH.D.; Polish physicist; b. 21 Nov. 1907, Lwów (now Lvov, U.S.S.R.); s. of Jan and Józefa Mięsowicz; m. Stanisława Potocka 1932; two d.; ed. Jagiellonian Univ. Cracow; Doctor 1932–39, Docent 1939–46, Extraordinary Prof. 1946–48, Prof. 1948–; Corresp. mem. Polish Acad. of Sciences 1959–64, mem. 1964–, Vice-Pres. 1969–77, mem. Presidium 1977–80, Chair. Cracow Branch 1970–80; Deputy to Seym (Parl.) 1972–80; Dir. Inst. of Nuclear Eng. of Acad. of Mining and Metallurgy, Cracow 1961–77; Head, Dept. of High Energy Physics, Inst. of Nuclear Physics, Cracow 1970–82; Chair. Scientific Council of Inst. of Nuclear

Research, Świerk, Inst. of Technics and Nuclear Physics of Acad. of Mining and Metallurgy, Cracow; mem. European Physical Soc., Società Italiana di Fisica, American Physical Soc.; Dr. h.c. (Jagiellonian Univ.) 1975, (Acad. of Mining and Metallurgy, Cracow) 1979; Gold Cross of Merit 1946; State Prize, 3rd Class 1950, 2nd Class 1964, Special State Prize 1979; Knight's Cross, Order of Polonia Restituta 1954, Commdr.'s Cross 1958, with Star 1974; Order of Banner of Labour, 1st Class 1962; Order of Builders of People's Poland 1974; Medal of 30th and 40th Anniversary of People's Poland 1974. *Publications:* numerous works in professional journals. *Leisure interest:* colour photography. *Address:* Ul. Mikołajska 6 m. 7, 31-027 Cracow, Poland. *Telephone:* 2262-27 (Home).

MIFSUD BONNICI, Carmelo, LL.D., M.P.; Maltese lawyer and politician; b. 17 July 1933, Cospicua; s. of Lorenzo Mifsud Bonnici and Catherine Buttigieg; ed. Lyceum, Univ. of Malta, Univ. Coll. London; legal consultant, Gen. Workers' Union 1969; Deputy Leader, Maltese Labour Movt. 1980–82, Leader desig. 1982, Leader Labour Party 1984–; mem. Parl. 1982–; Minister of Labour and Social Services 1982–83; Sr. Deputy Prime Minister and Minister of Educ. 1983–84; Prime Minister of Malta and Minister of the Interior and of Educ. 1985–87; Lecturer in Industrial and Fiscal Law, Univ. of Malta 1969–. *Leisure interest:* reading. *Address:* House of Representatives, Valletta, Malta.

MIFSUD BONNICI, Ugo, LL.D., M.P.; Maltese lawyer and politician; b. 8 Nov. 1932, Cospicua; s. of Carmelo Bonnici; m. Gemma Bianco; two c.; ed. Royal Univ. of Malta; practising lawyer 1955–; mem. Parl. 1966–; Pres. Gen. Council and Admin. Council of Nationalist Party 1977; Minister of Educ. 1987–. *Publications:* articles in political journals. *Address:* Ministry of Education, Lascaris, Valletta, Malta. *Telephone:* 221401.

MIFUNE, Toshiro; Japanese actor and film producer, b. 1 April 1920, Chintago, China; m. Takeshi Shiro 1950; two s. one d.; Pres. Mifune Productions Co. Ltd.; first screen appearance in Shin Baka Jidai (These Foolish Times) 1947; played leading role in Rashomon 1950; other films in which he has played important roles include Yoidore Tenshi (Drunken Angel) 1948, Shichinin no Samurai (The Seven Samurai) 1954, Miyamoto Musashi (The Legend of Musashi) 1954, The Lower Depths 1957, Throne of Blood 1957, Kumonosu-Jo, Muhomatsu No Issho (The Rickshawman) 1958, Kakushitoride No San Akunin (The Hidden Fortress) 1958, Nippon Tanjo (The Three Treasures) 1959, Taiheiyo No Arashi (The Storm of the Pacific), Yojimbo 1961, Tsubaki Sanjuro, Rebellion, Akahige 1965, Grand Prix 1966, Admiral Yamanoto 1968, Hell in the Pacific 1968, Furinkazan 1969, Red Sun 1971, Paper Tiger 1974, The Battle of Midway 1975, Shogun 1981, The Equals 1981, Inchon 1941, The Challenge 1982. *Leisure interests:* hunting, yachting, flying, riding. *Address:* Mifune Productions Co. Ltd., 9-30-7, Seijyo, Setagayaku, Tokyo, Japan. *Telephone:* 484 1111.

MIGDAL, Arkadiy Baynusovich; Soviet theoretical physicist; b. 11 March 1911, Lida, Byelorussia; s. of Baynus K. Migdal and Rashel' A. Pupko; m. Tat'yana Soboleva 1944; one s. one d.; ed. Leningrad Univ.; Prof. Moscow Eng. and Physics Inst. 1944–; worked in Inst. of Atomic Energy, U.S.S.R. Acad. of Sciences 1945–71, Inst. of Theoretical Physics, U.S.S.R. Acad. of Sciences 1971–; Corresp. mem. U.S.S.R. Acad. of Sciences 1953–66, mem. 1966–; Order of Lenin; Order of Red Banner of Labour and other decorations. *Publications:* Theory of Finite Fermi Systems 1965, Approximation Methods in Quantum Mechanics 1966, Nuclear Methods: The Quasiparticle Theory 1968, The Qualitative Methods of Quantum Theory 1975. *Leisure interests:* sculpture, skin-diving. *Address:* U.S.S.R. Academy of Sciences, 14 Leninsky Prospekt, Moscow, U.S.S.R.

MIGUEL, Gen. Mário Firmino; Portuguese army officer and government official; b. 11 March 1932, Sintra; s. of João Francisco Miguel and Domingas da Conceição Firmino Miguel; m. Maria Luisa de Carvalho Pereira Miguel 1967; one s. one d.; ed. Zaragoza Mil. Acad., Spain, Higher Mil. Studies at Staff Course, Portugal, Ecole Supérieure de Guerre, Paris; Commdr. No. 2 Infantry Regt. 1954–55; Instructor in Army School 1955–56, 1958–59; Officer in Mil. Command, Portuguese India 1956–58; Commdr. at Mil. Acad. 1959–61; Officer in combat zone, Angola 1961–63; served in office of Army Chief of Staff 1966–70; Prof., Inst. of Higher Mil. Studies 1963–70; Head of Operations Dept., Gen. Command in Portuguese Guinea (now Guinea-Bissau) 1970–72; Asst. in office of Army Chief of Staff 1972–73; Prof., Inst. of Higher Mil. Studies 1972–75; Minister of Nat. Defence May–Sept. 1974, 1976–78; Chief of 4th Dept., HQ of Mil. Area of Angola 1975; Asst. to Army Chief of Staff 1975–76; Dir. Infantry Branch 1980–81; Commdr. S. Mil. Region 1981–82; Dir. Army Staff Personnel Dept. 1982–; Deputy Chief of Staff 1984–87, Chief of Staff 1987–; Silver Medal of Mil. Appraisal (in combat), Silver Medal for Distinguished Service (in combat), Medal of Mil. Merit, Grand Cross of Mil. Order of Avis, Medal for Exemplary Conduct, Order of Mil. Merit (Spain), (Brazil), Order of Southern Cross (Brazil). *Publications:* articles and essays on mil. subjects. *Address:* Calçada do Conde de Penafiel 34, 1 Esq., Lisbon, Portugal. *Telephone:* 864368.

MÍGUEZ-BONINO, Rev. José, PH.D.; Argentine clergyman, professor of theology and international church official; b. 5 March 1924, Santa Fé; s. of José Míguez Gándara and Aurelia Bonino; m. Noemi Nieuwenhuize 1947; ed. Facultad Evangélica de Teología, Emory Univ., Union Theological Seminary, New York; Methodist minister in Bolivia, later in Argentina

1945–; Prof. of Theology, Facultad Evangelica de Teología, Buenos Aires 1954–70, Rector 1960–70; Prof. of Systematic Theology and Ethics, Protestant Inst. for Higher Theological Studies, Buenos Aires 1970–, Dean of Post-Graduate Studies 1973–; mem. Cen. Cttee. of World Council of Churches (WCC) 1968–75, a Pres. Presidium of WCC 1976–82; Visiting Prof., Facoltà Valdese de Teologia, Rome 1963, Union Theological Seminary, New York 1967–68, Selly Oak Coll., Birmingham, U.K. 1974, Faculté de Théologie Protestante, Strasbourg Univ. 1981; Observer at II Vatican Council 1962–64; Hon. PH.D. (Candler School of Theol., Free Univ. of Amsterdam 1980), Hon. D.D. (Aberdeen) 1987. *Publications:* Concilio abierto 1968, Integración humana y unidad cristiana 1968, Ama y haz lo que quieras 1972, Theology in a Revolutionary Situation (trans. in Dutch, German, Italian) 1975, Espacio para ser hombres 1975, Christians and Marxists 1976, Toward a Christian Political Ethic 1983, articles in Concilium, Expository Times, Evangelische Kommentare. *Address:* F. Madero 591, 1706 Villa Sarmiento (Haedo), Buenos Aires, Argentina. *Telephone:* 6542184.

MIGULIN, Vladimir Vasiliyevich, D.SC.; Soviet physicist; b. 10 July 1911, Furmanov, Ivanov Region; s. of Vasiliy Alekseyevich and Polina Migulin; m. 2nd Marianna Nikolayevna Sokolova; two s. one d.; ed. Faculty of Physics and Mechanics of Polytechnical Inst. of Leningrad; Engineer in Research Inst. of Leningrad 1932–34; Sr. Research Fellow, Chief of Div. Physical Inst. of the Acad. of Sciences of U.S.S.R., Moscow, 1934–51; Asst. lecturer 1935–38, lecturer 1939–46, Prof. 1947–54, 1957–, Deputy Dean of the Faculty of Physics 1954–57, Moscow Univ.; Dir. Inst. of Physical Research at Suchumi 1951–54; Deputy Dir.-Gen. Int. Atomic Energy Agency for the Div. of Training and Tech. Information 1957–59; Ed. Moscow Univ. Bulletin, Physics and Astronomy section 1960–69; Chief, Div. of Inst. of Radio-engineering and Electronics, Acad. of Sciences of U.S.S.R. 1962–69; Dir. Inst. of Terrestrial Magnetism, the Ionosphere and Radio Wave Propagation (IZMIRAN), Acad. of Sciences of U.S.S.R. 1969–89, Adviser 1989–; Vice-Pres. URSI 1972–78, Chair. Soviet Nat. Cttee. URSI 1969–; mem. Popov Soc. on Radio Tech. and Electrocommunications 1979–80, Hon. mem. 1980–, Chair. History Comm. 1986–; Corresp. mem. U.S.S.R. Acad. of Sciences 1970–, Chair. Scientific Council on Solar-Terrestrial Physics 1986–; mem. CPSU 1945–; U.S.S.R. State prize for scientific works 1946, 1953; Order of Lenin (twice); several Orders of the Soviet Union and French-Soviet and U.S.-Soviet medals. *Publications:* include numerous books, papers and articles in scientific journals on investigations of electrical oscillations in non-linear and parametric systems, investigations of the propagation of radio waves by interference methods and circuit theory and investigations of new methods of receiving of mm and sub-mm e-m waves and ionospheric radio wave propagation. *Leisure interests:* skiing, tourism, music. *Address:* IZMIRAN, c. Troitsk Moscow Region, 142092, U.S.S.R. *Telephone:* 232-19-21.

MIHAJLOV, Mihajlo; Yugoslav author, scholar and human rights administrator; b. 26 Sept. 1934, Pančevo; s. of Nicholas Mihajlov and Vera Daniloff; ed. High School, Sarajevo, and Zagreb Univ.; served armed forces 1961–62; freelance writer and translator, magazines, newspapers and radio 1962–63; Asst. Prof. of Modern Russian Literature, Zagreb Univ. 1963–65; freelance writer, western press 1965–66, 1970–74; imprisoned 1966–70, 1974–77; lectures, U.S.A., Europe and Asia 1978–79; Visiting Lecturer, Yale Univ. 1981; Visiting Prof. of Russian Literature and Philosophy, Univ. of Va. 1982–83; Visiting Prof. Ohio State Univ. 1983–84, Univ. of Siegen 1984, Univ. of Glasgow 1985; Commentator on Ideological Matters, Radio Free Europe/Radio Liberty Inc. 1986–; Vice-Pres. Democracy Int.; Co-Chair. Democracy Int. Comm. to Aid Democratic Dissidents in Yugoslavia; mem. Editorial Bd. int. magazine Kontinent 1975–84, Tribuna Magazine, Paris and Forum Magazine, Munich, Contrib. Ed. Religion in Communist Dominated Areas, New York; mem. Int. PEN (French branch 1977, American 1982); Fellow, Nat. Humanities Cen.; mem. Int. Helsinki Group, Cttee. for the Free World; mem. Bd. Int. Gesselschaft für Menschenrechte 1982–, Bd. of Consultants, Centre for Appeals for Freedom 1980, Social Democrats U.S.A., Advisory Bd. CAUSA Int. 1986; Trustee, World Constitution and Parl. Assen. 1982–; Special Analyst for Intellectual and Ideological Events in the Soviet Union and Eastern Europe, Research Div. of Radio Free Europe 1985–86; Int. League for Human Rights Award 1978; Council against Communist Aggression Award 1975, 1978; Ford Foundation Award for the Humanities 1980. *Publications:* Moscow Summer 1965, Russian Themes 1968, Underground Notes 1976, 1982, Unscientific Thoughts 1979, Planetary Consciousness 1982, and hundreds of articles in newspapers, magazines and scholarly books. *Leisure interests:* classical music, motoring. *Address:* RFE/RL Inc., 1201 Connecticut Avenue, N.W., Washington, D.C. 20036 (Office); 1510 Third Street, N.W., Washington, D.C. 20001, U.S.A. *Telephone:* (202) 451-6900 (Office); (202) 232-5161 (Home).

MIHÁLIK, Vojtech; Czechoslovak (Slovak) poet and politician; b. 30 March 1926, Dolná Streda; ed. Comenius Univ., Bratislava; Slovak Writers' Publishing House, Bratislava 1949–51; mem. editorial staff Československý voják 1952–54; Sec. Union of Slovak Writers 1954–60; Ed.-in-Chief, Slovak Writers' Publishing House 1960–64; Slovak Centre of Publishing and Book Trade 1964; Deputy to Slovak Nat. Council 1964–, mem. Presidium 1968–69; First Sec. Union of Slovak Writers 1965–67, Chair. 1969–, mem. Presidium 1975–; mem. Cen. Cttee. of CP of Slovakia 1966–68, 1969–71, alt. mem. 1971–76, mem. 1976–81; mem. Presidium Fed. Ass. 1969–71, Deputy Chair.

of Fed. Ass. and Chair. of House of Nations 1969–71, Deputy to House of Nations 1971–; mem. Communità Europea degli Scrittori (COMES) 1962–; Chair. Cttee. for Educ. and Culture, Slovak Nat. Council 1969–70; Chair. Cultural Cttee., House of Nations, Fed. Ass. 1971–76; Dir. Slovensky Spisovatel (Slovak Writer) Publishing House 1977–; Artist of Merit 1966, Order of Labour 1976, Nat. Artist 1978. *Publications:* Sixteen vols. of poetry including: The Plebeian Shirt 1950, The Singing Heart 1952 (State Prize), Archimedes Circles 1960, The Rebel Job 1960 (Prize of Czechoslovak Union of Writers 1961), Appassionata 1965 (Prize of the Slovak Writers' Publishing House), Black Autumn 1970, The Thirteenth Room 1976; Man against Blindness 1974 (critical essays); translations of Greek, Latin, Polish, French, Spanish and American poetry; Medal of World Peace Council 1980. *Address:* Bratislava, Hollého 15, Czechoslovakia.

MIHÁLY, András; Hungarian composer and professor of chamber music; b. 6 Nov. 1917, Budapest; s. of Dezső Mauthner and Erzsébet Grosz; m. 2nd Klára Pfeifer 1951, 3rd Csilla Varga; three s.; ed. Berzsenyi Gymnasium and F. Liszt Conservatoire of Music, Budapest; first violoncello solo in orchestra of Budapest Opera House 1946–47; Gen. Sec. of Budapest Opera 1948–49; Prof. of Chamber Music, F. Liszt Music Acad., Budapest 1950–; Reader of Contemporary Music, Musical Dept., Hungarian Broadcasting Corpn. 1959–; Leader New Hungarian Chamber Ensemble; Dir. Hungarian State Opera 1978–86; Kossuth Prize 1955; Erkel Prize 1950, 1965; Liszt Prize 1972, Labour Order of Merit (Golden Degree) 1970, Eminent Artist of Hungary, "For Socialist Hungary" Order of Merit 1977. *Works include:* Concerto for Violoncello and Orchestra 1953, Concerto for Pianoforte and Orchestra 1954, Fantasy for Wind Quintet and String Orchestra 1955, Songs on the Poems of James Joyce 1958, Concerto for Violin and Orchestra 1959, String Quartet 1960, Symphony 1962, Together and Alone (opera in two acts) 1965, Musica per 15 1974, String Quartet No. 3 1975, Musica per Viola 1975. *Leisure interest:* reading. *Address:* Vérhalom tér 9b, 1025 Budapest II, Hungary. *Telephone:* 352-295.

MIHARA, Asao; Japanese politician; b. 20 Aug. 1909, Fukuoka; Deputy Speaker of Fukuoka Prefectural Assembly; elected eight times to House of Reps. 1963–; Parl. Deputy Dir.-Gen. of Defence Agency; Parl. Deputy Chief Cabinet Sec.; Vice-Chair. of Diet Policy Cttee. of Liberal Democratic Party (LDP); Chair. House of Reps. Cabinet Cttee.; Minister of Educ. Nov.-Dec. 1974; Minister of State, Dir.-Gen. of Defence Agency 1976–77; Minister of State, Dir.-Gen. of Prime Minister's Office and of Okinawa Devt. Agency 1978–79; Chair. Security Research Council 1980–84. *Address:* Shugiin-Giinkaikan Room 331, 2-1-2 Nagata-cho, Chiyoda-ku, Tokyo, Japan. *Telephone:* (03) 5087081.

MIJATOVIĆ, Cvijetin; Yugoslav politician; b. 1913, Lopare; s. of Ilija and Staka Mijatović; m. Mira Stupica; two d.; ed. Belgrade Univ.; mem. Yugoslav CP (now League of Communists of Yugoslavia, LCY) 1933–; party work Bosnia and Hercegovina 1937, Serbia 1940; participated in partisan uprising 1941; Gen. of Yugoslav Army during war; numerous post-war LCY posts; fmr. Deputy Prime Minister of Bosnia and Hercegovina; fmr. Amb. to U.S.S.R.; fmr. Minister of Educ. (Bosnia and Hercegovina); fmr. Dir. and Ed.-in-Chief, The Communist; mem. Exec. Cttee. of Cen. Cttee. LCY 1964; mem. Exec. Bureau, LCY; mem. Collective Presidency of Yugoslavia 1974–84 (Pres. 1980–81); numerous Yugoslav decorations. *Publications:* numerous articles in political journals. *Leisure interests:* hunting, fishing, mountaineering. *Address:* c/o Presidency of SFR of Yugoslavia, Bulevar Lenjina 2, Belgrade, Yugoslavia.

MIKANAGI, Kiyohisa; Japanese diplomatist; b. 13 Jan. 1921, Ise City; s. of Kiyotake and Isao Mikanagi; m. Mochiko Katori; one s. one d.; ed. Univ. of Tokyo; Dir. Co-ordination Div., Reparations Dept., Asian Affairs Bureau, Ministry of Foreign Affairs 1962, Int. Co-operation Div., Econ. Co-operation Bureau 1965, Planning Div., Econ. Co-operation Bureau 1966; Counsellor, Japanese Embassy, Indonesia 1967; Asst. Vice-Minister for Admin., Ministry of Foreign Affairs 1969, Dir.-Gen. Econ. Co-operation Bureau 1972; Exec. Dir. Japan Int. Co-operation Agency 1974; Amb. to the Philippines 1977, to Canada 1981–84; Amb. to the Republic of Korea 1985–87; Pres. Foreign Service Training Inst., Ministry of Foreign Affairs 1979. *Leisure interest:* swimming. *Address:* 725 Acacia Avenue, Rockcliffe Park, Ottawa, Ont. K1M 0M8, Canada (Home).

MIKHALEVICH, Vladimir Sergeyevich; Soviet mathematician; b. 10 March 1930, Kiev; s. of Sergey Konstantinovich Mikhalevich and Ljudmila Ananjevna Mitnik; m.; one s. two d.; ed. Kiev Univ.; teacher at Kiev Univ. 1955–58; Sr. researcher, head of dept. of Computing Centre of Ukrainian Acad. of Sciences 1958–60; deputy dir. 1962–82; mem. CPSU 1963–; dir. of Inst. of Cybernetics of Acad. of Sciences of Ukrainian S.S.R. 1982–; concurrently teacher at Kiev Univ. Inst. of Econ. 1959–; head of dept. of Moscow Physico-Tech. Inst. 1982–; Deputy to U.S.S.R. Supreme Soviet; mem. of U.S.S.R. Acad. of Sciences 1984–; Ukrainian S.S.R. State Prize 1973, U.S.S.R. State Prize 1981; specializes in econ. cybernetics, theory of optimal solutions, and systems analysis. *Leisure interests:* hunting, fishing. *Address:* Glushkov Institute of Cybernetics of the Academy of Sciences of the U.S.S.R., Prospect Glushkova 20, 25 22 07, Kiev-207, U.S.S.R.

MIKHALKOV, Nikita Sergeyevich; Soviet film director; b. 1945, Moscow; s. of Mikhalkov Sergej Vladimirovitch and Konchalovskaya Natalia Petrovna; m. 1st Anastasya Vertinskaya 1966; m. 2nd Tatyana Mikhalkova

1973; two s. two d.; studied at Shchukin Theatre, then Directors' Faculty, U.S.S.R. State Film Inst. under Mikhail Romm; first worked as actor in films: Strolling around Moscow, A Nest of Gentlefolk, The Red Tent; *films directed:* A Quiet Day at the End of the War, At Home Among Strangers, A Stranger at Home 1975, The Slave of Love 1976, An Unfinished Piece for Mechanical Piano 1977, Five Evenings 1978, Several Days in the Life of I. I. Oblomov 1979, Kinsfolk 1982, Without Witnesses 1983, Dark Eyes 1987, The Barber of Siberia; play: An Unfinished Piece for Mechanical Piano, Rome 1987. *Leisure interests:* sport, hunting. *Address:* Mosfilm, 1 Mosfilmovskaya ul., Goskino, Moscow, U.S.S.R.

MIKHALKOV, Sergey Vladimirovich; Soviet poet, playwright and children's writer; b. 12 March 1913, Moscow; ed. Literary Inst. Moscow; began writing 1928, verses for children 1935; joint author (with El-Registan) Soviet Anthem 1943; mem. CPSU 1950–; Chief Ed. Fitil 1962–; First Sec. Moscow Branch, R.S.F.S.R. Union of Writers 1965–70, Chair. of Union 1970–; Deputy to Supreme Soviet of R.S.F.S.R. 1967–70, to U.S.S.R. Supreme Soviet 1970–; mem. Comm. for Youth Affairs, Soviet of Nationalities; fmr. Corresp. mem. Acad. of Pedagogical Sciences, Academician 1970–; three Orders of Lenin, Hero of Socialist Labour 1973, Red Banner, Red Banner of Labour, Red Star, Lenin Prize 1970, four State Prizes, Merited Worker of Arts of R.S.F.S.R. 1967. *Publications:* Dyadya Styopa (Uncle Steve) 1936 and Collected Works (poems, stories, plays) in two vols.; *Film script:* Frontovye podrugi (Frontline Friends) 1941; *Plays:* Tom Kenti (after Mark Twain) 1938, Krasnyi galstuk (Red Neckerchief), Selected Works 1947, Ilya Golovin, Ya khochu domoi (I Want to Go Home) 1949, Raki (Lobsters) 1952, Zaika-Zaznaika 1955, Basni Mikhalkova 1957, Sombrero 1958, Pamyatnik Sebe (A Monument to Oneself) 1958, Dikari (Campers) 1959, Collected Works (4 Vols.) 1964, Green Grasshopper 1964, We are Together, My Friend and I 1967, In the Museum of Lenin 1968, Fables 1970, Disobedience Day 1971, The Funny Bone (articles) 1971, Collected Works (3 vols.) 1970–71, Selected Works 1973, Bibliographical Index 1975. *Address:* U.S.S.R. Union of Writers, ulitsa Vorovskogo 52, Moscow, U.S.S.R.

MIKHALKOV-KONCHALOVSKY, Andrey Sergeyevich; Soviet film director and script-writer; b. 1937, Moscow; s. of Sergey Mikhalkov; ed. U.S.S.R. State Inst. of Cinema, Moscow 1961. *Films include:* Roller and Violin (with A. Tarkovsky) 1959, The First Teacher 1965, The Story of Asya Klyachina, who Loved but Did Not Marry 1966, A Nest of Gentlefolk 1969, Uncle Vanya 1971, Romance of Lovers 1974, Maria's Lovers, Runaway Train, Duet for One; script-writer (with Tarkovsky) Andrei Rublev 1969. *Address:* 1 Mosfilmovskaya, Moscow, U.S.S.R. (Office).

MIKHEYEV, Vladimir Andreyevich, DR. PHYS. SC.; Soviet physicist; b. 1942; ed. Kharkov Polytechnic; researcher 1964–; mem. CPSU 1981–; Senior Scientific Asst., Head of Laboratory of Ukrainian Acad. of Sciences Physics Inst., for the Study of Low Temperatures 1981–; Lenin Prize 1986. *Address:* c/o Ukrainian SSR Academy of Sciences, Ul. Vladimirskaya 54, Kiev, U.S.S.R.

MIKKELSEN, Richard; Danish banker; b. 27 April 1920, Copenhagen; m. Ester Overgaard 1944; at Banken for Slagelse og Omegn 1937–45; apptd. Asst. Danmarks Nationalbank 1945, Asst. Head of Div. 1945–61, Asst. Head Dept. 1961, Head Dept. 1961, Dir. 1966, Deputy Gov. 1971, Gov. 1982–; Attaché, Danish-OECD Del., Paris 1955–57; mem. Bd. European Monetary Agreement 1970–72; Industrial Mortgage Fund 1971–81; mem. Bd. Mortgage Credit Council, Supervisor 1972–81; mem. Bd. Export Finance Corpn. 1975–; mem. Steering Cttee. and Bd. Employees Capital Pension Fund 1980–; mem. Monetary Cttee. of EEC 1982–; mem. Nordic Cttee. for Financial Matters 1982–; Master of Econs. *Address:* Danmarks Nationalbank, Havnegade 5, 1093, Copenhagen K, Denmark. *Telephone:* 01-14-14-11.

MIKÓ, András; Hungarian opera producer; b. 30 June 1922, Budapest; m. Éva Rehák; studied music and designing; started at State Opera Budapest; Chief Producer Budapest Operetta Theatre 1951–52; chief producer Budapest Opera 1963–87; Prof. of Operatic Stage Acting, Acad. of Music, Budapest 1950–; produced operas on open-air stage Margaret Island, Budapest and Summer Festival plays in Szeged, Covent Garden of London, Bolshoi Theatre of Moscow, Copenhagen, Turin, Rome, Brussels, Cologne, Helsinki, Berlin and others; Liszt Prize 1961, title of Merited Artist 1967, Eminent Artist 1987, Kossuth Prize 1975. *Address:* Hungarian State Opera, Népköztársaság utja 22, Budapest VI (Office); Uri utca 44/46, Budapest I, Hungary (Home). *Telephone:* 312-550 (Office), 560-382 (Home).

MIKULIĆ, Branko; Yugoslav politician; b. 1928, Gornji Vakuf, Bosnia and Herzegovina; ed. Faculty of Econs.; with nat. liberation struggle 1943, mem. League of Communist Youth 1944, mem. League of Communists 1945–; fmr. Sec. of Party Asst. Cttees. in various dists.; fmr. Pres. Sarajevo Dist.; Sec. Cen. Cttee. League of Communists of Bosnia and Herzegovina 1965–67; Pres. Exec. Council of Ass., Bosnia-Herzegovina 1967–69; Chair. Cen. Cttee. League of Communists of Bosnia-Herzegovina, mem. Presidency Cen. Cttee. League of Communists 1969–78; Pres. Presidency Bosnia-Herzegovina 1982; mem. Presidency of Yugoslavia 1984; Pres. Fed. Exec. Council 1986–89; mem. Cen. Cttee. League of Communists 1989; Chair. Organizing Cttee. 14th Winter Olympic Games 1984, Pres.; numer-ous Yugoslav and foreign decorations. *Address:* Novi Beograd, Lenjina 2, Yugoslavia.

MIKULSKI, Barbara Ann, B.A.; American politician; b. 20 July 1936, Baltimore; d. of William Mikulski and Christina Eleanor Kutz; ed. Mount St. Agnes Coll. and Maryland Univ.; Baltimore Dept. Social Services 1961–63, 1966–70; York Family Agency 1964; VISTA Teaching Center 1965–70; Teacher, Mount St. Agnes Coll. 1969; Teacher, Community Coll., Baltimore 1970–71; Democratic Nominee to U.S. Senate 1974, to House of Reps. 1976; mem. 96th–99th Congresses from 3rd Md. Dist.; Senator from Maryland Jan. 1987–; Hon. LL.D. (Goucher Coll.) 1973, (Hood Coll.) 1978; mem. Democratic Nat. Strategy Council; mem. Nat. Bd. of Dirs. Urban Coalition; mem. Nat. Asscn. of Social Workers; Democrat. *Address:* U.S. Senate, Office of Senate Members, Washington, D.C. 20510, U.S.A.

MILČINSKI, Janez, J.D., M.D.; Slovenian professor of forensic medicine (retd.); b. 3 May 1913, Ljubljana; s. of Fran Milčinski and Marija Krejči; m. 1st Marija Jeras 1945 (divorced 1952); m. 2nd Viktorija Vida Červ 1953, two d.; ed. Univs. of Ljubljana and Zagreb; Asst. Inst. for Pathology, Ljubljana 1941–43; surgeon, Partisan Liberation Army, rank of Maj., Yugoslavia 1943–45; Head, Prof. of Forensic Medicine, Univ. of Ljubljana 1945–83, Dean, Faculty of Medicine 1962–64, Univ. Rector 1973–76; Pres. Slovenian Acad. of Sciences and Arts 1976–; decorations from Yugoslavia, Italy, France; Avnoj Prize 1973; Prior h.c. Ordre de Saint Fortunat 1987; Dr. h.c. (Ljubljana) 1979; Dr. med. h.c. (Leipzig) 1987. *Publications:* Legal Medicine 1956, Medical Expertise, (Vol. I) 1970, (Vol. II) 1981, Medical Ethics and Deontology 1982. *Leisure interests:* old books and maps, photography. *Address:* Slovenska akademija znanosti in umetnosti, Novi trg 3, 61000 Ljubljana (Office); Beethovnova 12, 61000 Ljubljana, Yugoslavia (Home). *Telephone:* (3861) 331 130 (Office); (3861) 210 839 (Home).

MILEDI, Ricardo, M.D., F.R.S., M.R.I.; Mexican professor of biophysics; b. 15 Sept. 1927, Mexico D.F.; m. Ana Mela Garces 1955; one s.; ed. Universidad Nacional Autónoma de Mexico; Research Fellow, Instituto Nacional de Cardiología, Mexico 1954–56; Visiting Fellow, John Curtin School of Medical Research, Canberra, Australia 1956–58; Hon. Research Assoc., Dept. of Biophysics, Univ. Coll. London 1958–59, Lecturer 1959–62, Reader 1962–65, Prof. of Biophysics 1965–75, Foulerton Research Prof. of the Royal Soc. 1975–85, Foulerton Research Prof. and Head of Dept. of Biophysics 1978–85; Distinguished Prof., Dept. of Psychobiology, School of Biological Sciences, Univ. of Calif., Irvine 1984–; Fellow, Third World Acad. of Sciences, American Acad. of Arts and Sciences; Hon. mem. Hungarian Acad. of Sciences; King Faisal Foundation Int. Prize for Science. *Publications:* numerous published papers. *Address:* Laboratory of Cellular and Molecular Neurobiology, Department of Psychobiology, University of California, Irvine, Calif. 92717, U.S.A. *Telephone:* (714) 856-5693.

MILEIKOWSKY, Curt, DR.TECH.; Swedish business executive; b. 1 May 1923, Stockholm; s. of Gregor Mileikowsky and Margit Wallis; m. Ulla B. Varenius 1947; two s.; ed. Royal Inst. of Tech.; Research engineer, ASEA, Ludvika 1946; Research Asst. to Prof. Lise Meitner 1946–47, Nobel Inst. of Physics 1948–54, ASEA, Västerås 1954; Man. Nuclear Power Dept., ASEA 1958, Exec. Vice-Pres. for Sales 1962; Pres. SAAB, Linköping 1968–78, SAAB-SCANIA, Linköping 1969–78; Chair. Bd. Swedish Export Credit Corpn. *Publications:* Scientific and tech. publs. in Sweden and U.S.A. *Address:* Måsvaegen 8C, S-183 51 Taeby, Sweden (Home).

MILES, Baron (Life Peer), cr. 1979, of Blackfriars in the County of London; **Bernard Miles,** Kt., C.B.E.; British actor and director; b. 27 Sept. 1907; s. of Edwin James and Barbara (née Fletcher) Miles; m. Josephine Wilson 1931; one s. two d.; ed. Uxbridge County School and Pembroke Coll., Oxford; first stage appearance 1930; written for, directed, and acted in films 1937–; West End stage appearances 1938–; music-hall stage appearances 1950–; founded Mermaid Theatre, North London 1950, formed Mermaid Theatre Trust, opened Mermaid Theatre in City of London 1959; Hon. Fellow, Pembroke Coll., Oxford 1969; mem. Cttee. of Managers, Royal Inst. of Great Britain; Hon. D.Litt. (City Univ.) 1974; *Publications:* The British Theatre 1947, God's Brainwave 1972, Favourite Tales from Shakespeare 1976, Curtain Calls (ed. with J. C. Trewin) 1981. *Address:* House of Lords, London, SW1A 0PW, England.

MILES, Frank Stephen, C.M.G., M.A., M.P.A.; British diplomatist (retd.); b. 7 Jan. 1920, Edinburgh; s. of late Harry and Mary Miles; m. Joy Theaker 1953; three d.; ed. Daniel Stewart's Coll. Edinburgh, St. Andrews Univ., Harvard Univ.; served with Fleet Air Arm, Lt. (A) RNVR 1942–46; Scottish Home Dept. 1948; Foreign and Commonwealth Office 1948–80; diplomatic posts in New Zealand 1949–52, Pakistan 1954–57, Ghana 1959–62, Uganda 1962–63; Deputy High Commr. in Tanzania 1963–65; Acting High Commr. in Ghana March–April 1966; Consul-Gen. St. Louis 1967–70; Deputy High Commr. in Calcutta 1970–74; High Commr. in Zambia 1974–78, in Bangladesh 1978–79; Dir. of Studies, Royal Inst. of Public Admin. 1980–83; Dist. Councillor, Tandridge, Surrey 1982–, mem. Limpsfield Parish Council 1983– (Chair. 1987–). *Leisure interests:* cricket, tennis, golf. *Address:* Maytrees, 71 Park Road, Limpsfield, Oxted, Surrey, RH8 0AN, England. *Telephone:* (0883) 713132.

MILES, John Wilder, M.S., PH.D.; American professor of applied mechanics and geophysics; b. 1 Dec. 1920, Cincinnati, Ohio; s. of Harold Miles and Cleopatra (Morton) Miles; m. Herberta Blight 1943; three d.; ed. Calif.

Inst. of Tech.; Instructor Calif. Inst. of Tech. 1943–44; Radiation Lab., M.I.T. 1944; Eng. Lockheed Co. 1944–45; Prof. of Eng. and Geophysics, Univ. of Calif., L.A. 1945–61; Prof. of Applied Math., Australian Nat. Univ. 1962–64; Prof. of Applied Mechanics and Geophysics, Univ. of Calif., San Diego 1965, Vice-Chancellor, Academic Affairs 1980–83; mem. American Acad. of Arts and Sciences, N.A.S.; Fulbright Fellow, 1951, 1959; Guggenheim Fellow 1958–59, 1969; Overseas Fellow, Churchill Coll. 1980–; Timoshenko Medal 1982. *Publications:* 310 papers in professional journals. *Leisure interests:* amateur radio, cycling, swimming. *Address:* Institute of Geophysics and Planetary Physics, Mail Code A-025, University of California, San Diego, La Jolla, Calif. 92093, U.S.A. *Telephone:* (619) 452-2885.

MILES, Sarah; British actress; b. 31 Dec. 1941; ed. Royal Acad. of Dramatic Art, London; first film appearance in Term of Trial 1962; with Nat. Theatre Co. 1964–65; Shakespeare stage season 1982-83. *Films include:* Those Magnificent Men in Their Flying Machines 1964, I Was Happy Here 1966, The Blow-Up 1966, Ryan's Daughter 1970, Lady Caroline Lamb 1972, The Hireling 1973, The Man Who Loved Cat Dancing 1973, Great Expectations 1975, Pepita Jiminez 1975, The Sailor Who Fell From Grace With the Sea 1976, The Big Sleep 1978, Venom 1981, Hope and Glory 1987, White Mischief 1988; *plays include:* Asylum 1988. *Address:* c/o William Morris Ltd., 147–149 Wardour Street, London, W1V 3TB, England. *Telephone:* 01-734 9361.

MILEWSKI, Gen. Mirosław, M.A.; Polish politician; b. 1 May 1928, Lipsk, Suwałki Voivodship; in security apparatus 1944-, posts in dist. and voivodship security cells and in Ministry of Internal Affairs, fmr. Dir. of Dept.; Under-Sec. of State, Ministry of Internal Affairs 1971–80, Minister of Internal Affairs 1980–81; Div. Gen. 1979; Deputy Chair. Gen. Bd. and mem. Chief Council of Union of Fighters for Freedom and Democracy (ZBoWiD); mem. PZPR, deputy mem. PZPR Cen. Cttee. 1971–80, mem. Cen. Cttee. 1980–85, Sec. 1981–85, mem. Political Bureau of PZPR Cen. Cttee. 1981–85; mem. PZPR Cen. Cttee. Comm. for Investigation into Social Conflicts in the History of People's Poland 1981–83; Chair. Law and Law Enforcement Comm. PZPR Cen. Cttee. 1981–85; Order of Banner of Labour (1st Class), Commdr.'s and Kt.'s Cross, Order of Polonia Restituta, Grunvald Cross (3rd Class).

MILI, Mohamed Ezzedine; Tunisian telecommunications engineer and international official; b. 4 Dec. 1917, Djemmal; m. Mlle. Zouhir 1950; three s. two d.; ed. Teacher's Training Coll., Tunis, Ecole Normale Supérieure, Paris, Sorbonne and Ecole Nat. Supérieure des Télécommunications, Paris; joined Posts, Telegraphs and Communications (P.T.T.) Admin. 1948; Chief Engineer and Dir.-Gen. of Telecommunications, Ministry of P.T.T. 1957; Tunisian del. to ITU confs. 1956–, mem. ITU Admin. Council 1960–65, Chair. of 19th session 1964; Deputy Sec.-Gen. ITU 1965–67, Sec.-Gen. 1967–82; Sr. mem. I.E.E.E.; Officer, Order of Independence of Tunisia, Commdr. Order of the Tunisian Repub., Commdr. Swedish Order of Vasa, Grand Cross Order of Duarte, Sanchez y Mella with Silver star (Dominican Repub.), Honour Merit Medal (Paraguay), Grand Star of Order of Merit of Telecommunications (Spain), Commdr. of the Order of Leopold (Belgium), Officier, Légion d'honneur, Philip Reis Medal (Fed. Repub. of Germany), Diploma of Honour (Int. Council of Archives) 1978, I.E.E.E. Award for Public Service in the Field of Telecommunications 1984. *Leisure interests:* reading scientific publications, youth movements. *Address:* 5 route de Mon Idée, 1226 Thônex, Geneva, Switzerland (Home). *Telephone:* 022-48-79-19.

MILINGO, Most Rev. Archbishop Emmanuel, DIP.ED.; Zambian ecclesiastic; b. 13 June 1930; s. of Yakobe Milingo and Tomaida Lumbiwe; ed. St. Mary's Presbyteral School, Fort Jameson and Kasina Jr. Seminary and Kachebere Major Seminary, Nyasaland (now Malawi); Curate, Minga Mission 1958–61; studied Pastoral Sociology (Diploma), Rome 1961–62; Univ. Coll. Dublin, Ireland (Dip. Ed.) 1962–63; Parish Priest, St. Ann's Mission, Chipata 1963–66; Sec. for Mass Media, Zambia Episcopal Conf. 1966–69; Archbishop of Lusaka 1969–83; Special Del. to Pontifical Comm. for Pastoral Care of Migrants, Refugees and Pilgrims 1983-. *Publications:* Amake Joni, Demarcations, The World in Between, The Flower Garden of Jesus the Redeemer, My Prayers are not heard. *Leisure interests:* writing and preaching to make Jesus Christ known and loved. *Address:* Pontificia Commissione per la Pastorale delle Migrazioni e del Turismo, Palazzo San Calisto, Vatican City, Italy.

MILLAN, Rt. Hon. Bruce, P.C.; British politician; b. 5 Oct. 1927; m. Gwendoline Fairey 1953; one s. one d.; ed. Harris Acad., Dundee; worked as Chartered Accountant 1950–59; M.P. for Craigton Div. of Glasgow 1959–83, for Govan div. of Glasgow 1983-88; EEC Commr. for Regional Policy Jan. 1989-; Parl. Under-Sec. of State for Defence (R.A.F.) 1964–66, for Scotland 1966–70; Minister 'of State, Scottish Office 1974–76, Sec. of State for Scotland 1976–79; Opposition Spokesman for Scotland 1979–83; Hon. D.Iur. (Dundee) 1989; Labour. *Address:* 10 Beech Avenue, Dumbreck, Glasgow, G41, Scotland (Home). *Telephone:* 041-427 6483 (Home)

MILLAR, Fergus Graham Burtholme, M.A., D.PHIL., F.B.A., F.S.A.; British academic; b. 5 July 1935, Edinburgh s. of J. S. L. Millar and J. B. Taylor; m. Susanna Friedmann 1959; two s. one d.; ed. Edinburgh Acad., Loretto School, Trinity Coll., Oxford; Fellow, All Souls Coll., Oxford 1958–64; Fellow and Tutor in Ancient History, The Queen's Coll., Oxford 1964–76;

Prof. of Ancient History, Univ. Coll., London 1976–84; Camden Prof. of Ancient History, Univ. of Oxford 1984-; Fellow, Brasenose Coll., Oxford 1984-; Corresp. mem. German Archaeological Inst. 1977. *Publications:* several historical studies. *Address:* Brasenose College, Oxford, OX1 4AJ (Office); 80 Harpes Road, Oxford, OX2 7QL, England (Home). *Telephone:* (0865) 248641 (Office); (0865) 515782 (Home).

MILLAR, Sir Oliver Nicholas, K.C.V.O., F.B.A.; British art historian and administrator; b. 26 April 1923, Standon, Herts.; s. of Gerald and Ruth Millar; m. Delia Mary Dawnay 1954; one s. three d.; ed. Rugby School and Courtauld Inst. of Art, Univ. of London; Asst. Surveyor of the King's Pictures 1947–49, Deputy Surveyor of the King's (Queen's from 1952) Pictures 1949–72, Surveyor 1972–88; Dir. of the Royal Collection 1987-; Trustee Nat. Portrait Gallery 1972-; mem. Reviewing Cttee. on Export of Works of Art 1975–87, Exec. Cttee. Nat. Art Collections Fund 1986–, Man. Cttee. Courtauld Inst. 1986-. *Publications:* English Art 1625–1714 (with M. D. Whinney) 1957, Abraham van der Doort's Catalogue 1960, Tudor, Stuart and Georgian Pictures in the Collection of H.M. The Queen 1963, 1969, Inventories and Valuations of the King's Goods 1972, The Queen's Pictures 1977; numerous catalogues including William Dobson 1951, Age of Charles I 1972, Sir Peter Lely 1976, Van Dyck in England 1982 and for The Queen's Gallery. *Leisure interests:* drawing, gardening, cricket, golf. *Address:* Yonder Lodge, Penn, Bucks., England. *Telephone:* (049 481) 2124.

MILLARD, Sir Guy Elwin, K.C.M.G., C.V.O.; British diplomatist (retd.); b. 22 Jan. 1917; s. of Col. Baldwin Salter and Phyllis Mary (née Tetley) Millard; m. 1st Anne Mackenzie 1946; one s. one d.; m. 2nd Judy Dugdale 1964; two s.; joined Foreign Office 1939; navy service 1940–41; Foreign Office 1941–45; Paris 1945–49; Ankara 1949–52; Imperial Defence Coll. 1953; Foreign Office 1954–55; Private Sec. to Prime Minister 1955–57; Office of Paymaster-Gen. 1957–59; Counsellor, Teheran 1959; Foreign Office 1962–64; Deputy Perm. Rep. NATO 1964–67; Amb. to Hungary 1967–69; Minister, Washington, D.C. 1970–71; Amb. to Sweden 1971–74, to Italy 1974–76; Chair. British-Italian Soc. 1977–83; Grand Officer, Order of Merit (Italy) 1981. *Address:* Fyfield Manor, Southrop, Glos., England. *Telephone:* (036 785) 234.

MILLARD, Naomi Adeline Helen, PH.D.; South African marine biologist; b. 16 July 1914, Cape Town; d. of Harold Bokenham and Adeline Kate Bokenham née Thompson; m. Pierce Arthur Newton Millard 1938; one s. one d.; ed. Girls' High School, Wynberg, Univ. of Cape Town; Museum Asst., Zoology Dept., Univ. of Cape Town 1937–39, Jr. Lecturer 1940–43, Asst. Lecturer 1944–46, Full Lecturer 1946–59, Sr. Lecturer 1959–70; Marine Biologist, S. African Museum 1971–77; fmr. Sec. Zoological Soc. of Southern Africa and fmr. Ed.; Purcell Memorial Prize 1939; Univ. Fellowship 1952–55, 1964–67; Fellow Royal Soc. of S.A.; Hon. Life mem. and Medallist, Zoological Soc. of Southern Africa. *Publications:* The Dissection of the Spiny Dogfish and the Platanna (with J.T. Robinson) 1945, Monograph on the Hydroida of Southern Africa (Ann. S.A.Mus. 68: 1975); contribs. to The Normal Table of Xenopus Gaevis, Animal Life in Southern Africa and Marion and Prince Edward Islands; 43 other research publs. on hydroids, estuaries, fish morphology, xenopus anatomy, littoral ecology. *Leisure interests:* mountain climbing, sailing various crafts. *Address:* Silvermine Village, Private Bag 1, Noordhoek 7985, South Africa. *Telephone:* 89-1774.

MILLE, Hervé; French journalist; b. 23 Sept. 1909, Constantinople (now Istanbul), Turkey; s. of Dominique and Louise (née Hérault) Mille; Ed. Eclaireur de Nice and Paris Soir 1928-32; London correspondent of Paris Soir 1933-35; Editorial Dir. Paris Soir, Paris Midi, Marie Claire, Match 1937-39, Sept jours, Lyon 1941-43; Dir. Paris Match 1949-69, Marie Claire 1954-69; Man. and Dir. Télé-sept-jours 1960-70, then Hon. Dir.-Gen. *Address:* 32 avenue George V, 75008 Paris, France. *Telephone:* 47.20.17.75.

MILLER, Andrew, M.A., PH.D., F.R.S.E.; British academic; b. 15 Feb. 1936, Kelty, Fife; s. of William Hamilton Miller and Susan Anderson (née Auld) Miller; m. Rosemary Singleton Hannah Fyvie 1962; one s. one d.; ed. Beath High School, Univ. of Edinburgh; Asst. Lecturer in Chem., Univ. of Edinburgh 1960–62; Post-Doctoral Fellow, CSIRO Div. of Protein Chem., Melbourne 1962–65; Staff Scientist MRC Lab. of Molecular Biology, Cambridge 1965–66; Lecturer in Molecular Biophysics, Oxford Univ. 1966–83; First Dir. European Molecular Biology Lab., Grenoble Antenne, France 1975–80; Prof. of Biochem., Edinburgh Univ. 1984-; mem. Science and Eng. Research Council Biological Sciences Cttee. 1982–85; Council mem., Inst. Laue-Langevin, France 1981–85; mem. Univ. Grants Cttee. Biological Sciences Cttee. 1985–; Dir. of Research, European Synchrotron Radiation Facility, Grenoble; Fellow Wolfson Coll., Oxford 1967–83. *Publication:* Minerals in Biology (Co-Ed.) 1984. *Leisure interests:* reading, walking, music. *Address:* Department of Biochemistry, Hugh Robson Building, George Square, Edinburgh, Scotland. *Telephone:* 031-6671011 (Ext. 2336).

MILLER, Arjay, B.S.; American business executive; b. 4 March 1916, Shelby, Neb.; s. of Rawley John Miller and Mary Gertrude Schade; m. Frances M. Fearing 1940; one s. one d.; ed. Univ. of California; Teaching Asst. Univ. of Calif. Berkeley 1937–40; Research Technician, Calif. State Planning Bd. 1941; Economist, Fed. Reserve Bank of San Francisco 1941–43; U.S.A.F. 1943–46; Asst. Treas. Ford Motor Co. 1947–53, Controller 1953–57, Vice-Pres. and Controller 1957–61, Vice-Pres. (Finance) 1961–62, Vice-Pres. (Staff-Group) 1962–63, Dir. 1962–, Pres. 1963–68, Vice-Chair. 1968–69; Dean Graduate School of Business, Stanford Univ. 1969–79, Dean Emer. 1979–; Trustee of several insts. and mem. of various cttees.; Dir. Litton Industries Inc., Utah Int. Inc., Washington Post Co., Ford Motor Co., Santa Fe Southern Pacific Corpn.; Hon. D.Jur. (Calif., Nebraska, Washington (St. Louis) Univs., Whitman Coll., Ripon Coll.). *Publication:* An Economic and Industrial Survey of the Los Angeles and San Diego Areas (with Arthur G. Coons) 1941. *Leisure interests:* archaeology, golf, hunting, forestry. *Address:* 225 Mountain Home Road, Woodside, Calif. 94062, U.S.A.

MILLER, Arthur, A.B.; American playwright; b. 17 Oct. 1915, New York; s. of Isidore and Augusta (Barnett) Miller; m. 1st Mary Grace Slattery 1940 (divorced 1956), one s. one d.; 2nd Marilyn Monroe 1956 (divorced 1961); 3rd Ingeborg Morath 1962, one d.; ed. Univ. of Michigan; received Hopwood Award for play-writing, Univ. of Mich. 1936 and 1937, Theatre Guild Nat. Award 1938, New York Drama Critics Circle Award 1947 and 1949, Pulitzer Prize for Drama 1949, Antoinette Perry Award 1953, American Acad. of Arts and Letters Gold Medal for Drama 1959, Anglo-American Award 1966, Creative Arts Award, Brandeis Univ. 1970, Kennedy Centre Award 1984, Hon. D.Litt. (Univ. of E. Anglia) 1984; Pres. Int. PEN Clubs Org. 1965–69. *Publications:* The Man Who Had All the Luck 1943, Situation Normal 1944, Focus 1945, All My Sons 1947, Death of a Salesman 1949, The Crucible 1953, A View From The Bridge 1955, A Memory of Two Mondays 1955, Collected Plays 1958, The Misfits (screenplay) 1959, After the Fall 1964, Incident at Vichy 1964, I Don't Need You Any More (short stories) 1967, The Price (play) 1968, In Russia (with Inge Morath) 1969, The Creation of the World and Other Business (play) 1972, Up From Paradise 1974, The American Clock 1980, Playing for Time (play) 1981, Elegy for a Lady (play) 1983, Some Kind of Love Story (play) 1983, Salesman in Beijing (journal) 1984, Two Way Mirror 1985, Danger: Memory! (plays) 1986, The Archbishop's Ceiling 1986, Timebends: A Life (autobiog.) 1987, Everybody Wins (screenplay) 1989. *Address:* c/o Kay Brown, ICM, 40 W. 57th Street, New York, N.Y. 10019, U.S.A.

MILLER, C. Arden, M.D.; American professor of maternal and child health; b. 19 Sept. 1924, Shelby, Ohio; s. of Harley H. Miller and Mary Thuma; m. Helen Lloyd Meihack 1948; four c.; ed. Oberlin Coll. and Yale Univ. School of Medicine; House Officer, New Haven Hosp., Conn. 1948–51; mem. Faculty, Dept. of Pediatrics, Univ. of Kansas Medical Center 1951–66, Dean of Medical School and Dir. Medical Center 1960–66; Prof. of Pediatrics, Maternal and Child Health, School of Public Health, Univ. of N.C., Chapel Hill 1966–, Vice-Chancellor Health Sciences 1966–71, Chair. Dept. of Maternal and Child Health 1977–87; Markle Scholar in Medical Science; Sedgwick Medal, American Public Health Assen. 1986, Fulbright Grant to review perinatal care in Western Europe 1986; mem. Inst. of Medicine of N.A.S., Nat. Acad. of Medicine; Robert Felix Award in Community Medicine; Martha Mae Eliot Award in Public Health. *Publications:* Local Health Departments, 15 Case Studies 1981, Monitoring Child Health, Key Indicators 1986; Infant Mortality in the U.S., in Scientific American July 1985. *Leisure interest:* gardening. *Address:* Department of Maternal and Child Health, School of Public Health, The University of North Carolina at Chapel Hill, Chapel Hill, N.C. 27514; 908 Greenwood Road, Chapel Hill, N.C. 27514, U.S.A. (Home). *Telephone:* (919) 966-2017 (Office); (919) 942-4320 (Home).

MILLER, Donald C., A.M., PH.D.; American business executive; b. 31 March 1920, Geneseo, Ill.; s. of Otto H. Miller and Mary M. Miller; m. Marjorie Morgan; two s. one d.; ed. Univ. of Ill.; Asst. Prof. of Econs., Univ. of Calif., Los Angeles 1949–51; Economist and Chief of Govt. Finance Section, Bd. of Govs., Fed. Reserve System, Washington, D.C. 1951–58; joined Continental Ill. Nat. Bank and Trust Co. 1958; Second Vice-Pres. Bond Dept. 1958, Vice-Pres. 1959–66, Head 1966–68, Sr. Vice-Pres. 1968–71, Exec. Vice-Pres. 1971; Exec. Vice-Pres. CICorpn. 1972, and Treas. 1974; mem. Corporate Office 1976; Vice-Chair. and Dir. CICorpn. and Continental Bank, also Chief Financial Officer and Treas. CICorpn. 1976; Vice-Chair. and Chief Financial Officer, Continental Ill. Corpn. and Continental Ill. Nat. Bank and Trust Co. of Chicago May 1980–; Dir. Royal Group Inc. 1973–, A. E. Staley Mfg. Co. 1977–; mem. Robert Morris Assocs. 1977–; Dir. Chamber of Commerce of the U.S. 1979–, and Chair. its Banking, Monetary and Fiscal Cttee. 1979–80; mem. Int. Monetary Affairs Cttee., U.S. Council of Int. Chamber of Commerce; Treas. Nat. Tax Assen.-Tax Inst. of America 1961–. *Publications:* Taxes, the Public Debt, and Transfers of Income; articles in financial and economic journals. *Address:* c/o News Bureau, Continental Illinois Corporation, Corporate Communications Division, 231 South La Salle Street, Chicago, Ill. 60693, U.S.A.

MILLER, Edward, M.A., F.B.A.; British academic (retd.); b. 16 July 1915, Acklington, Northumberland; s. of Edward and Mary Lee Miller; m. Fanny Zara Salingar 1941; one s.; ed. King Edward VI Grammar School, Morpeth, Northumberland and St. John's Coll. Cambridge; Fellow of St. John's Coll. (Fellowship suspended during war service) 1939–65; war service in Durham Light Infantry, R.A.C. and Control Comm. for Germany 1940–46; Asst. Lecturer, then Lecturer in History, Cambridge Univ. 1946–65, Warden of Madingley Hall 1961–65; Prof. of Medieval History, Sheffield Univ. 1965–71; Master of Fitzwilliam Coll. Cambridge 1971–81; Hon. Fellow St. John's

and Fitzwilliam Colls. Cambridge; Hon. Litt.D. (Sheffield) 1972. *Publications:* The Abbey and Bishopric of Ely 1951, Portrait of a College 1961, Medieval England: Rural Society and Economic Change (with J. Hatcher) 1978; Jt. Ed. Cambridge Economic History of Europe Vol. III 1963, 2nd edn. Vol. II 1987; Historical Studies of the English Parliament, 2 vols. 1970; contribs. to and articles in The Victoria County Histories, The Cambridge Economic History of Europe and various historical collections and journals. *Leisure interests:* buildings that are old enough and a passive interest in season in cricket and rugby football. *Address:* 36 Almoners Avenue, Cambridge, CB1 4PA, England. *Telephone:* (0223) 246794.

MILLER, Frank, P.ENG., M.P.P.; Canadian politician; b. 14 May 1927, Toronto; s. of Percy Frank and Margaret Stuart (née McKean) Miller; m. Ann McArthur Norman 1950; three s. one d.; ed. Regal Rd. School, Oakwood Coll. Inst., Toronto, Gravenhurst High School, McGill Univ.; Research Eng. Rubberset Co. Ltd.; Gravenhurst 1949; Production Eng. Alcan, Arvida, Quebec 1951; Chem. teacher, St. Andrew's Coll., Aurora 1953; Sales Eng. and Branch Man. Scarfe & Co. Brantford and Montreal 1956–60; Pres. Gordon Motor Sales Muskoka Ltd. 1962–69; Pres. Pineland Lodge, Port Carling 1970–73; Pres. Patterson Kaye Lodge, Bracebridge 1960–82, Tamwood Lodge 1964–82, Councillor, Bracebridge 1967–70; M.P.P. for Muskoka Prov. 1971–, Parl. Asst. to Ont. Minister of Health 1972–74, Minister of Health 1974–77, Minister of Natural Resources 1977–78; Treas. of Ont. and Minister of Econs. 1978–83; Minister of Industry and Trade 1983–85; Premier of Ont. 1985, Leader of the Opposition 1985–; mem. Bd. of Dirs. Nat. Trust Co. 1986–, National Vic. & Grey Trustees Ltd. 1986–, Chrysler Canada Ltd. 1986–; mem. Assen. of Prof. Engs., Ont.. Conservative Party. *Leisure interests:* skiing, golf. *Address:* 355 Wellington Street North, Bracebridge, Ont., POB 1CO, Canada (Home).

MILLER, George A., PH.D.; American professor of psychology; b. 3 Feb. 1920, Charleston, W. Va.; s. of George E. and Florence (née Armitage) Miller; m. Katherine James 1939; one s. one d.; ed. Univ. of Alabama and Harvard Univ.; Assoc. Prof. of Psychology, M.I.T. 1951–55, Visiting Prof. 1976–; Assoc. Prof. Psychology, Harvard Univ. 1955–58, Prof. 1958–68, Co-Dir. Center for Cognitive Studies 1960–67, Chair. Dept. of Psychology 1964–67; Visiting Prof., The Rockefeller Univ. 1967–68, Prof. of Psychology 1968–80, Adjunct Prof. 1980–82; Prof. of Psychology, Princeton Univ. 1979–, James S. McDonnell Distinguished Univ. Prof. 1982–; Ed. Psychological Bulletin 1980–82; Pres. American Psychological Assen. 1968–69; Chair. Special Cttee. on Biochemistry, Princeton 1982–83; mem. N.A.S.; mem. educational advisory bd. John Simon Guggenheim Foundation 1982–86, Advisory Cttee. Center for Study of Language and Communication, Stanford Univ. 1983–; Pres. Eastern Psychological Assen. 1961–62; Dr. h.c. (Univ. Catholique de Louvain) 1976; Hon. D.Sc.S (Yale Univ.) 1979, Hon. D.Sc. (Columbia Univ.) 1980; Distinguished Scientific Contribution Award, American Psychological Assen. 1963, Warren Medal, Soc. of Experimental Psychology 1972, New York Acad. of Sciences Award in Behavioral Sciences 1982. *Publications:* Language and Communication 1951, Psychology 1962, Language and Perception (Co-author) 1976, Spontaneous Apprentices 1977, Language and Speech 1981. *Address:* Department of Psychology, Green Hall, Princeton University, Princeton, N.J. 08544 (Office); 478 Lake Drive, Princeton, N.J. 08540, U.S.A. (Home). *Telephone:* (609) 452-5973 (Office).

MILLER, G. (George) William, B.S., J.D.; American business executive; b. 9 March 1925, Sapulpa, Okla.; s. of James Dick and Hazel Deane (née Orrick) Miller; m. Ariadna Rogojarsky 1946; ed. U.S. Coast Guard Acad., New London, Univ. of Calif. School of Law, Berkeley; served as line officer in Pacific area, stationed in China for a year; lawyer with Cravath, Swaine and Moore, New York, N.Y. 1952–56; joined Textron Inc. as Asst. Sec. 1956, Vice-Pres. 1957–60, Pres. 1960–74, Chief Exec. Officer 1968–78, Chair. 1974–78; Chair. Fed. Reserve Bd. 1978–79, Sec. of the Treasury 1979–81; Chair. G. William Miller & Co. Inc. 1983–; Dir. Federated Dept. Stores, Repligen Corpn., Private Satellite Network, Georgetown Industries Inc., Harman Int., Supervisory Cttee. of the Schroder Venture Trust; mem. The Business Council and the Conference Bd. *Address:* 1215 19th Street, N.W., Washington, D.C. 20036, U.S.A.

MILLER, Jack Richard, A.B., M.A., J.D.; American lawyer, judge and politician; b. 6 June 1916, Chicago, Ill.; s. of Forest W. and Blanche M. Miller; m. Isabelle Margaret Browning 1942; one s. three d.; ed. Creighton Univ., Catholic Univ., Washington, D.C., Columbia Univ.; U.S.A.F. in Second World War; Brig.-Gen. U.S.A.F. Reserve (retd.); Attorney, Office of Chief Counsel, Internal Revenue Service (Fed. Govt.) 1947–48; Lecturer in Taxation, George Washington Univ. 1948; Asst. Prof. of Law, Notre Dame Univ. Coll. of Law 1948–49; mem. Iowa House of Reps. 1955–56, Iowa State Senate 1957–60, U.S. Senator from Iowa 1961–73; Judge, U.S. Court of Customs and Patent Appeals 1973–82; U.S. Circuit Judge, Court of Appeals (Fed. Circuit) 1982–; Hon. LL.D. (Iowa Wesleyan Coll., Loras Coll., Creighton Univ., Yonsei Univ., Korea); Republican. *Publications:* various articles on law, taxation and patents. *Leisure interests:* golf, fishing, hunting. *Address:* 6710 Maybole Place, Temple Terrace, Fla. 33617, U.S.A. *Telephone:* (813) 985-8823.

MILLER, Jacques Francis, A.O., M.B., PH.D., D.SC., B.A., F.A.A., F.R.S.; Australian medical research scientist; b. 2 April 1931, Nice, France; s. of late Maurice Miller and Fernande Debarnot; m. Margaret D. Houen 1956; ed. Univs. of

Sydney and London; Jr. Resident Medical Officer, Royal Prince Alfred Hosp., Sydney 1956; pathological research, Univ. of Sydney 1957; cancer research, Chester Beatty Research Inst., London 1958–65; Head, Experimental Pathology and Thymus Biology Unit, Walter and Eliza Hall Inst., Melbourne 1966–; various other professional appts.; Foreign Assoc., N.A.S.; numerous awards and honours. *Publications:* over 280 papers in scientific journals, mostly on immunology and cancer research. *Leisure interests:* art, photography, music, literature. *Address:* P.O. Royal Melbourne Hospital, Parkville, Vic. 3050 (Office); 5 Charteris Drive, East Ivanhoe, Vic. 3079, Australia (Home). *Telephone:* 3471511 (Office); 493481 (Home).

MILLER, James Clifford, III, PH.D.; American government official; b. 25 June 1942, Atlanta, Ga.; s. of James Clifford Miller and Annie Moseley; m. Demaris Humphries 1961; one s. two d.; ed. Univs. of Georgia and Virginia; Asst. Prof. Ga. State Univ. Atlanta 1968–69; Economist, U.S. Dept. of Transport 1969–72; Assoc. Prof. of Econs. Texas A & M Univ. 1972–74; Economist, U.S. Council of Econ. Advisers, Washington, D.C. 1974–75; Asst. Dir. U.S. Council of Wage and Price Stability 1975–77; Resident Scholar, American Enterprise Inst. 1977–81; Admin., Office of Information and Regulatory Affairs, Office of Man. and Budget and Exec. Dir. Presidential Task Force on Regulatory Relief 1981; Chair Fed. Trade Comm., Washington 1981–85; Dir. Office of Man. and Budget 1985–89; Thomas Jefferson Fellow 1965–66; DuPont Fellow 1966–67, Ford Foundation Fellow 1967–68. *Publications:* Why the Draft? The Case for a Volunteer Army 1968, Economic Regulation of Domestic Air Transport; Theory and Policy 1974, Perspectives on Federal Transportation Policy 1975, Benefit–Cost Analyses of Social Regulation 1979, Reforming Regulation 1980. *Address:* c/o Office of Management and Budget, Old Executive Building, Washington, D.C. 20503, U.S.A.

MILLER, Jonathan Wolfe, C.B.E., M.B., B.CH.; British stage and film director and physician; b. 21 July 1934, London; s. of late Emanuel Miller; m. Helen Rachel Collet 1956; two s. one d.; ed. St. Paul's School, St. John's Coll., Cambridge and Univ. Coll. Hosp. Medical School, London; co-author of and appeared in Beyond the Fringe 1961–64; dir. John Osborne's Under Plain Cover, Royal Court Theatre 1962, Robert Lowell's The Old Glory, New York 1964 and Prometheus Bound, Yale Drama School 1967; dir. at Nottingham Playhouse 1968–69; dir. Oxford and Cambridge Shakespeare Co. production of Twelfth Night on tour in U.S.A. 1969; Research Fellow in the History of Medicine, Univ. Coll., London 1970–73; Assoc. Dir. Nat. Theatre 1973–75; mem. Arts Council 1975–76; Visiting Prof. in Drama, Westfield Coll., Univ. of London 1977–; Exec. Producer Shakespeare TV series 1979–81; Artistic Dir. Old Vic; Dir. Research Fellow in Neuropsychology, Univ. of Sussex; Dir. of the Year, Soc. of West End Theatre Awards 1976; Fellow, Univ. Coll. London 1981–, Hon. Fellow, St. John's Coll. Cambridge; Dr. h.c. (Open Univ.) 1983; Hon. D.Litt. (Leicester) 1981, (Kent) 1985; Silver Medal (Royal Television Soc.) 1981. *Productions:* for Nat. Theatre, London: The Merchant of Venice 1970, Danton's Death 1971, The School for Scandal 1972, The Marriage of Figaro 1974; other productions The Tempest, London 1970, Prometheus Bound, London 1971, The Taming of the Shrew, Chichester 1972, The Seagull, Chichester 1973, The Malcontent, Nottingham 1973, The Family in Love, Greenwich Season 1974, Arden Must Die (opera) 1974, The Importance of Being Earnest 1975, The Cunning Little Vixen 1975, All's Well That Ends Well, Measure For Measure, Greenwich Season 1975, Three Sisters 1977, The Marriage of Figaro (English Nat. Opera) 1978, Arabella (opera) 1980, Falstaff (opera) 1980, 1981, Otello (opera) 1982, Rigoletto (opera) 1982, 1984; Fidelio (opera) 1982, 1983, Don Giovanni (opera) 1985, The Mikado (opera) 1986, Tosca (opera) 1986, Long Day's Journey into Night 1986, Taming of the Shrew 1987, The Tempest 1988, Turn of the Screw 1989, King Lear 1989; films: Take a Girl Like You 1969 and several films for television including Whistle and I'll Come to You 1967, Alice in Wonderland 1967, The Body in Question (series) 1978, Henry the Sixth, part one 1983, States of Mind (series) 1983, Subsequent Performances 1986, The Emperor 1987. *Publications:* McLuhan 1971, Freud: the Man, his World, his Influence 1972, The Body in Question 1978, Subsequent Performances 1986. *Address:* 63 Gloucester Crescent, London, N.W.1, England.

MILLER, Karl Fergus Connor; British professor of English Literature; b. 2 Aug. 1931; s. of William and Marion Miller; m. Jane E. Collet 1956; two s. one d.; ed. Royal High School, Edin. and Downing Coll., Cambridge; Asst. Prin., H.M. Treasury 1956–57; BBC TV producer 1957–58; Literary Ed. The Spectator 1958–61, New Statesman 1961–67; Ed. The Listener 1967–73; Lord Northcliffe Prof. of Modern English Literature, Univ. Coll., London 1974–; Ed. London Review of Books 1979–. *Publications:* Cockburn's Millennium 1975, Doubles: studies in literary history 1985, ed. of several anthologies, etc. *Leisure interest:* football. *Address:* 26 Limerston Street, London, S.W.10, England. *Telephone:* 01-352 1735.

MILLER, Lajos; Hungarian baritone; b. 23 Jan. 1940, Szombathely; s. of Lajos Miller and Teréz Sebestyén; m. Zsuzsa Dobránszky; one s.; studied at Music Acad. of Budapest under Jenö Sipos;. mem. Hungarian State Opera 1968–; won Grand Prix of Fauré singing contest, Paris 1974 and first prize of "Toti dal Monte" singing contest of Treviso, Italy 1975; awarded Liszt Prize 1975, Kossuth Prize 1980; has sung with maj. cos. in France (Aix-en-Provence, Paris, Lyons), Fed. Repub. of Germany (Bonn, Berlin, Cologne, Munich, Hamburg), Italy (Rome, Milan—La Scala, Trieste),

Monaco, Switzerland (Geneva, Basle), Austria (Vienna Staatsoper), G.B. (Edinburgh Festival), U.S.A. (New York Carnegie Hall, Houston and Philadelphia), Belgium (Brussels, Liège), Venezuela (Caracas). *Operatic roles include:* Verdi: Renato Rodrigo, Simon Boccanegra, Don Carlos, Conte di Luna, Miller, Germont; Gluck: Orpheus, Orestes; Mozart: Don Giovanni, Giordano, Carlo Gérard, Leoncavallo, Silvio; Rossini: Figaro; Tchaikovsky: Eugene Onegin, Yeletsky; Puccini: Scarpia; Bizet: Escamillo; Berio: Commandante Ivo; Donizetti: Enrico. *Recorded roles:* Don Carlos (Ernani), Simon Boccanegra, Lycidas, Sharpless (Madame Butterfly), Fanuel. *TV films:* Enrico (Lucia di Lammermoor), Marcello (Tabarro), Silvio (Pagliacci), Loth (Madarasz 'Loth). *Leisure interests:* tennis, surfing. *Address:* Balogh Ádám utca 28 1026 Budapest; State Opera, Népköztársaság utja 22, 1061 Budapest, Hungary. *Telephone:* 312-550.

MILLER, Morris, M.SC.; Canadian economist; b. 15 June 1924, Montreal; s. of Louis Miller and Sophie Miller (née Weiner); m. Claire Benzvy 1953; one s. two d.; ed. McGill Univ., L.S.E., England; Sr. Economist, World Bank, Washington D.C., U.S.A. 1968–74; Sr. Policy Adviser, Treasury Board, Govt. of Canada 1974–76, Sr. Econ. Adviser, Dept. of Energy, Minerals and Resources 1976–78, Chief, Task Force on Federalism, Privy Council 1979; Deputy Dir.-Gen., UN Conf. on New and Renewable Sources of Energy, New York, U.S.A. 1980–81; Exec. Dir. World Bank 1982–85. *Address:* c/o Ministry of Finance, Place Bell, Ottawa, K1A 0G5, Canada.

MILLER, Neal Elgar, M.A., PH.D.; American professor of psychology; b. 3 Aug. 1909, Milwaukee, Wis.; s. of Irving Miller and Lily Miller; m. Marion E. Edwards 1948; one s. one d.; ed. Univ. of Washington, Stanford and Yale Univs.; Asst. in Research, Dept. of Psychology, Yale Univ. 1933–35; Social Science Research Council Fellow, Vienna Psychoanalytic Inst. 1935–36; Research Asst. in Psychology, Inst. of Human Relations, Yale Univ. 1936–41, Research Assoc. 1941–42; Officer in charge of Research, Psychological Research Unit, Army Air Corps, Nashville, Tenn. 1942–44; Dir. of Psychological Research Project (Pilot), H.Q. Flying Training Command, Randolph, Tex. 1944–46; Research Assoc. in Psychology (Assoc. Prof.), Inst. of Human Relations, Yale Univ. 1946–50, Prof. of Psychology 1950–52, James Rowland Angell Prof. of Psychology 1952–66; Prof. The Rockefeller Univ. 1966–80, Prof. Emer. 1980–; Clinical Prof. of Psychology in Medicine, Cornell Univ. Medical Coll. 1970–73, Adjunct Prof. 1973–75; Research Affiliate, Yale Univ. 1985–; mem. N.A.S., American Acad. of Arts and Sciences, American Philosophical Soc., Inst. of Medicine and numerous professional socs. and orgs.; recipient of Nat. Medal of Science 1965, six hon. degrees and numerous other awards and prizes. *Publications:* 250 publs. *Leisure interests:* gardening, hiking. *Address:* Department of Psychology, P.O. Box 11A Yale Station, New Haven, Conn. 06520-7447, U.S.A. *Telephone:* (203) 432-4524.

MILLER, Paul Lukens, A.B.; American investment banker; b. 6 Dec. 1919, Philadelphia, Pa.; s. of Henry C.L. and Elsie (Groff) Miller; m. Adele Olyphant 1950; one s. three d.; ed. William Penn Charter School, Philadelphia, and Princeton Univ.; First Boston Corpn. 1946–, Vice-Pres. 1955–64, Pres. 1964–78; Dir. Aluminum Co. of America, Cummins Engine Co., Inc., McLean Industries Inc., Int. Income Property Inc. *Address:* First Boston Corporation, Park Avenue Plaza, New York, N.Y. 10055, U.S.A. *Telephone:* (212) 909-2222.

MILLER, Sir Peter North, Kt., M.A.; British insurance broker; b. 28 Sept. 1930, London; s. of Cyril T. and Dorothy N. Miller; m. 1st Katharine Mary 1955 (divorced 1977), 2nd Boon Lian (Leni) Tan 1979; two s. one d.; ed. Rugby School and Lincoln Coll. Oxford; joined Thos. R. Miller & Son (Insurance) 1953, Partner 1959, Sr. Partner 1971–, Chair. of Group 1971–83, 1988–; mem. Cttee. Lloyds Insurance Brokers' Assen. 1973–77, Deputy Chair. 1974–75, Chair. 1976–77; mem. Cttee. on Invisible Exports 1975–77; mem. Insurance Brokers' Registration Council 1977–81; mem. Cttee. of Lloyd's 1977–80, 1982–; Chair. of Lloyds 1984–87; Chair. British Cttee. of Bureau Veritas 1980–. *Leisure interests:* all forms of sport (except cricket), particularly running, riding, tennis and sailing, wine, music. *Address:* Garratt, Coombe End, Kingston-upon-Thames, Surrey, KT2 7DQ, England (Home). *Telephone:* 01-942 6724 (Home).

MILLER, Robert Stevens, Jr., A.B. M.B.A., J.D.; American business executive; b. 4 Nov. 1941, Portland, Ore.; s. of Robert Stevens Miller and Barbara Weston Miller; m. Margaret Rose Kyger 1966; three s.; ed. Stanford Univ. and Harvard Law School; mem. financial staff, Ford Motor Co., Dearborn, Mich. 1968–71; Investment Man., Ford Motor de Mexico, Mexico City 1971–73; Dir. of Finance, Ford Asia Pacific, Melbourne, Australia 1974–77; Vice-Pres. (Finance), Ford Motor de Venezuela, Caracas 1977–79; Vice-Pres.-Treas., Chrysler Corpn., Detroit, Mich. 1980–81, Exec. Vice-Pres. (Finance) 1981–85, Vice-Chair. of Bd. 1985–; mem. Int. Advisory Bd., Creditanstalt Bankverein, Vienna, Austria. *Leisure interest:* model railroading. *Address:* P.O. Box 1919, Detroit, Mich. 48288 (Office); 4834 Chipping Glen, Bloomfield Hills, Mich. 48013, U.S.A. (Home). *Telephone:* (313) 956-2592 (Office); (313) 644-1535 (Home).

MILLER, Stanley Lloyd, PH.D.; American educator and chemist; b. 7 March 1930, Oakland, Calif.; s. of Nathan Harry Miller and Edith (Levy) Miller; ed. Univs. of California (Berkeley) and Chicago; F. B. Jewett Fellow, Calif. Inst. of Tech. 1954–55; Instructor and Asst. Prof., Dept. of Chem., Coll. of Physicians and Surgeons, Columbia Univ. 1955–60; Asst.,

Assoc. then Full Prof., Dept. of Chem., Univ. of Calif., San Diego 1960–; mem. N.A.S.; Hon. Councillor, Higher Council of Scientific Research of Spain; Oparin Medal, Int. Soc. for the Study of the Origin of Life. *Publication:* The Origins of Life on the Earth (with L. E. Orgel) 1974. *Address:* University of California, San Diego, Department of Chemistry, B-017, La Jolla, Calif. 92093, U.S.A. *Telephone:* (619) 534-3365.

MILLER, Terence George, T.D., M.A., F.G.S.; British geologist; b. 16 Jan. 1918, Cambridge; s. of George Frederick Miller and Marion Johnston; m. Inga Catriona Priestman 1944; one s. three d.; ed. Perse School and Jesus Coll., Cambridge; Army Service 1939–46; Univ. Demonstrator in Geology, Univ. of Cambridge 1948–53; Lecturer and Sr. Lecturer in Geology, Univ. of Keele 1953–65; Prof. of Geography, Univ. of Reading 1965–67; Prin., Univ. Coll. of Rhodesia 1967–69; Dir. Polytechnic of N. London 1971–80; Harkness Scholarship 1948. *Publications:* Geology 1950, Geology & Scenery in Britain 1953; papers in Journal of Palaeontology, Palaeontology, Geological Magazine, Nature, etc. 1947–66. *Leisure interests:* walking, sailing, beachcombing. *Address:* 9 Shute Hill, Mawnan Smith, Falmouth, Cornwall, TR11 5HQ, England. *Telephone:* (0326) 250691.

MILLER, Walter Geoffrey Thomas, M.A.; Australian diplomatist; b. 25 Oct. 1934, Tasmania; s. of Walter T. Miller and Gertrude S. Galloway; m. Rachel C. Webb 1960; three s. one d.; ed. Launceston High School and Univs. of Tasmania and Oxford; served in Australian missions in Kuala Lumpur, Djakarta, and at UN, New York; Deputy High Commr., India 1973–75; Amb. to Repub. of Korea 1978–80; Head, Int. Div. Dept. of the Prime Minister and Cabinet, Canberra 1982; Deputy Sec. Dept. of Foreign Affairs 1985–86; Amb. to Japan 1986–; Rhodes Scholar 1956. *Leisure interests:* international relations, literature, ballet, tennis, reading, golf. *Address:* Australian Embassy, 1-14 Mita, 2-chome, Minato-ku, Tokyo 108, Japan. *Telephone:* 453-0251.

MILLER, William (see Miller, George William).

MILLET, Pierre Georges Louis, D. EN D.; French industrial officer; b. 11 April 1922, St. Maurice, Seine; s. of Gaston and Alice (née Bouillot) Millet; m. Monique Fulconis 1945; one s. two d.; ed. Ecole Nationale d'Administration; Ministry of Finance 1948–51, 1955–57; Deputy Dir. Int. Inst. of Patents 1952–54; Dir. of Contingency Fund and mem. Monetary Cttee., EEC 1958–60, Dir. of Econ. Policy and Devt. 1960–61; mem. Admin. Bd., European Investment Bank 1960–61; Dir.-Gen. of Home Market, EEC 1961–65; Asst. Dir. of Foreign Econ. Relations, Ministry of Finance 1965–66; Deputy Vice-Pres. Union des industries chimiques 1966–71; Dir.-Gen. Service d'Exploitation Industrielle des Tabacs et des Allumettes (SEITA) 1972–78; Regional Treasurer, Paymaster-Gen. Haute-Normandie and Seine-Maritime 1978–; mem. Admin. Council for the ports of Rouen and Le Havre 1978–; Officier, Légion d'honneur, Commdr., Ordre nat. du Mérite. *Address:* quai Jean-Moulin, 76037 Rouen Cedex (Office); 1 avenue Jacques-Cartier, 76100 Rouen (Home); 17 avenue d'Italie, 75013 Paris, France (Home).

MILLIGAN, Spike (Terence Alan); British actor and author; b. 16 April 1918, Ahmednagar, India; s. of L. A. Milligan and Florence Mary Winifred Kettleband; m. 1st Patricia Margaret Ridgway (deceased 1978); one s. three d.; m. 2nd Shelagh Sinclair 1983; ed. Poona, St. Paul's High School, Rangoon, and Brownhill Boys School, Catford; first broadcast as a comedian in Opportunity Knocks 1949; appeared in and wrote scripts for The Crazy People radio series, BBC 1951; appeared in and wrote The Goon Show radio series. *TV appearances include:* A Show Called Fred, Son of Fred 1956, World of Beachcomber, Q5, Oh in Colour, A Milligan for all Seasons, Marty Feldman's Comedy Machine (also co-wrote: Golden Rose and special comedy award, Montreux 1972), The Melting Pot 1975, Q7 1977, Q8 1978, Q9 1979, There's a lot of it about 1982, Last Laugh Before TV-AM (own show). *Films include:* Postman's Knock 1961, The Bed-Sitting Room 1969, The Magic Christian 1971, The Devils 1971, The Cherry Picker 1972, Digby the Biggest Dog in the World 1972, The Three Musketeers 1973, The Great McGonagall 1975, The Last Remake of Beau Geste 1977, The Hound of the Baskervilles 1978, Monty Python's Life of Brian 1978, History of the World, Part One 1980, Yellowbeard 1982. *Publications:* Dustbin of Milligan 1961, Silly Verse for Kids 1963, Puckoon 1963, The Little Pot Boiler 1965, A Book of Bits 1965, Milliganimals 1968, The Bedside Milligan 1968, The Bed-Sitting Room (co-author) 1969, The Bald Twit Lion 1970, Adolf Hitler, My Part in his Downfall 1971, Milligan's Ark 1971, Small Dreams of a Scorpion 1972, The Goon Show Scripts 1972, More Goon Show Scripts 1973, Rommel: Gunner Who? 1973, Badjelly the Witch 1973, Book of the Goons 1974, The Great McGonagall Scrapbook (with J. Hobbs) 1975, The Milligan Book of Records 1975, Dip the Puppy 1975, Transports of Delight 1975, William McGonagall, the truth at last 1976, Monty, His Part in my Victory 1976, Goblins (with illustrations by Heath Robinson) 1978, Mussolini, His Part in my Downfall 1978, Open Heart University 1978, Spike Milligan's Q Annual 1979, Ubu Roi (play) 1980, Get in the Q Annual 1980, Indefinite Articles and Scunthorpe 1981, Unspun Socks from a Chicken's Laundry 1981, The Goon Cartoon 1982, The 101 Best and Only Limericks of Spike Milligan 1982, Sir Nobonk and the terrible, awful, dreadful, naughty, nasty Dragon 1982, More Goon Cartoons 1983, The Melting Pot 1983, 'There's a Lot of it About' 1983, Vol. 5, War Memoirs, Where Have All the Bullets Gone 1985, Further Transports of Delight 1985, Floored Masterpieces and Worse Verse 1985, Vol. 6, Goodbye Soldier

1986, The Looney, An Irish Fantasy (novel) 1987, The Mirror Running (serious poetry) 1987, Starting Verse for All the Family 1987, The Lost Goon Shows 1987, Milligan's War 1988, William McGonagall meets George Gershwin 1989; TV Writer of the Year Award 1957. *Leisure interests:* restoration of antiques, oil painting, water colours, gardening, eating, drinking, talking, sleeping, wine, jazz. *Address:* Spike Milligan Productions, 9 Orme Court, London, W.2, England. *Telephone:* 01-727 1544.

MILLIKEN, Frank Roscoe; American mining executive; b. 25 Jan. 1914, Malden, Mass.; s. of Frank R. and Alice (née Gould) Milliken; m. Barbara Kingsbury 1935; two s.; ed. Massachusetts Inst. of Technology; Chief Metallurgist, Gen. Eng. Co., Salt Lake City 1936–41; Asst. Man. Titanium Div. Nat. Lead Co. 1941–52; Vice-Pres. (Mining Operations), Kennecott Copper Corpn. 1952–58, Exec. Vice-Pres. 1958–61, Dir. 1958–, fmr. Pres., C.E.O. 1961–79, Chair. 1978–79; Dir. Braden Copper Co., Peabody Coal Co., Chase Brass and Copper Co., Quebec Iron and Titanium Corpn.; mem. American Mining Congress, Mining and Metallurgy Soc. of America, American Inst. of Mining, Metallurgy and Petroleum Engineers, etc. *Address:* c/o Kennecott Copper Corporation, 161 East 42nd St., New York, N.Y. 10017, U.S.A.

MILLOT, Georges, D. ÈS. SC.; French professor in earth sciences; b. 24 May 1917, Troyes; s. of Marius Millot and Madeleine Merlin; m. Marie-Louise Ferré 1939; two s. five d.; ed. Ecole Normale Supérieure; Prof. of Geology, Univ. of Nancy 1947–54; Sub-Man. Ecole Nat. Supérieure de Géologie Appliquée, Nancy 1948–52; Prof. of Geology, Univ. Louis Pasteur, Strasbourg 1954–81; Head, Inst. of Geological Sciences, Strasbourg 1954–81; Dir. Centre de Sédimentologie et de Géochemie de la Surface (CNRS), Strasbourg 1965–81; Scientific Adviser for Earth Sciences, Ministry of Educ. 1969–76; Pres. Nat. French Cttee. of Geology 1981–86; mem. Acad. des Sciences, Inst. de France; Assoc. mem. Belgian Acad.; Officier, Légion d'Honneur, Ordre Nat. du Mérite; Commdr. des Palmes Académiques; Dr. h.c. (Madrid, Pavia, Neuchâtel). *Publications:* some 200 publs., including 4 books. *Leisure interests:* epistemological and historical readings. *Address:* Institut de Géologie, 1 rue Blessig, 67084 Strasbourg Cedex, France. *Telephone:* 88 35 85 37.

MILLS, Donald Owen, B.SC.(ECON.); Jamaican diplomatist; b. 23 July 1921, Mandeville; s. of the late Albert Maxwell Mills and Josephine Mills; m. Sonia McPherson 1967; two s. two d.; ed. Jamaica, and L.S.E.; entered civil service 1939; with the Treasury 1941–50; Cen. Bureau of Statistics 1950–55, Deputy Dir. 1955; with Jamaica Cen. Planning Unit 1957–68, Dir. 1962; Registrar Univ. of West Indies 1965–66; Perm. Sec. Ministry of Devt. of the Bahamas 1968–70; Alt. Exec. Dir. for Jamaica, Canada, Ireland, Barbados, IMF 1971–72; Perm. Rep. to UN 1973–81; Pres. UN Econ. and Social Council 1978, Chair., Group of 77 at UN 1977–78, Pres. UN Security Council Jan. 1979, March 1980; mem. Bd. of Trustees, UN Inst. for Training and Research 1980–, Steering Cttee. (North-South Round Table); mem. Bd., Centre for Research on new Int. Econ. Order, Bd. of Trustees Assen. of Caribbean Univs. and Research Insts., Governing Council and Exec. Cttee., Soc. for Int. Devt.; has represented Jamaica at many conferences, active participant in conferences, seminars outside of UN. *Leisure interests:* music, collecting musical instruments. *Address:* c/o Ministry of Foreign Affairs, Trade and Industry, 85 Knutsford Blvd., Kingston 5; 11 Lady Kay Drive, Kingston, Jamaica (Home). *Telephone:* 925-6870 (Home).

MILLS, Sir Frank, K.C.V.O., C.M.G.; British diplomatist (retd.); b. 3 Dec. 1923, Nuneaton; s. of Joseph Francis and Louisa Mills; m. Trilby Foster 1953; one s. two d.; ed. King Edward VI School, Nuneaton, Emmanuel Coll., Cambridge; served R.A.F.V.R. 1942–45; Commonwealth Relations Office 1948; service in Pakistan 1949–51, South Africa 1955–58, Malaysia 1962–64, Singapore 1964–66, India 1972–75; Private Sec. to Parl. Under-Sec. of State, Commonwealth Relations Office (CRO) 1952–53; Prin. Private Sec. to Sec. of State, CRO 1960–62; FCO 1966–71, Dir. of Communications 1978–81; High Commr. in Ghana 1975–78, in Bangladesh 1981–83; Chair. Camberwell Health Authority 1984–, Royal Commonwealth Soc. for the Blind 1985–. *Leisure interests:* golf, sailing, music, history. *Address:* c/o Camberwell Health Authority, King's College Hospital, Denmark Hill, London, SE5 9RS, England. *Telephone:* 01-274 6692.

MILLS, Hayley Cathrine Rose Vivien; British actress; b. 18 April 1946, London; d. of Sir John Mills (q.v.) and Lady Mills (Mary Hayley Bell); m. Roy Boulting (q.v.) 1971 (divorced 1977); two s.; ed. Elmhurst Ballet School, Inst. Alpine Vidamanette; first film appearance in Tiger Bay 1959; on contract to Walt Disney; films include Pollyanna 1960, The Parent Trap 1961, Whistle Down the Wind 1961, Summer Magic 1962, In Search of the Castaways 1963, The Chalk Garden 1964, The Moonspinners 1965, The Truth about Spring 1965, Sky West and Crooked 1966, The Trouble with Angels 1966, The Family Way 1966, Pretty Polly 1967, Twisted Nerve 1968, Take a Girl Like You 1970, Forbush and the Penguins 1971, Endless Night 1972, Deadly Strangers 1975, The Diamond Hunters 1975, What Changed Charley Farthing? 1975, The Kingfisher Caper 1975, Appointment with Death 1987; first stage appearance as Peter Pan 1969, appeared in The Wild Duck 1970, Trelawny 1972, A Touch of Spring 1975, My Fat Friend 1978, Hush and Hide 1979, The Importance of Being Earnest (Royal Festival Theatre, Chichester), The Summer Party 1980, Talley's Folly 1982; TV appearance: The Flame Trees of Thika 1981, Parent Trap

II 1986; Silver Bear Award, Berlin Film Festival 1958, British Acad. Award; Special Oscar (U.S.A.). *Publication:* My God (with Marcus Maclaine) 1988. *Leisure interests:* riding, reading, children, cooking, scuba-diving.

MILLS, Sir John, Kt., C.B.E.; British actor; b. 22 Feb. 1908, North Elmham, Suffolk; s. of Lewis Mills; m. Mary Hayley Bell 1941; one s. two d. (Hayley Mills, q.v.); ed. Norwich High School; debut in chorus of The Five O'Clock Girl 1929; appeared in repertory 1929–30; appeared as The Aunt in Charley's Aunt, London, 1930; has since appeared in numerous West End productions including the following plays by his wife Mary Hayley Bell: Men in Shadow 1942, Duet for Two Hands 1945, Angel 1947, The Uninvited Guest 1952; mem. Council Royal Acad. of Dramatic Art (RADA) 1965–; mem. Bd. Govs. of British Film Inst.; Chair. Stars Org. for Spastics 1975; Patron, Life mem. Variety Club; numerous theatre and film awards include Best Actor of the Year (for Of Mice and Men) 1939, Best Actor (for Great Expectations) 1947, Venice Film Festival Best Actor Award (for Tunes of Glory) 1960, San Sebastian Film Festival Best Actor Award (for The Family Way) 1968; Acad. Award (Oscar) for role in Ryan's Daughter 1971. Other stage appearances include: Noel Coward's Cavalcade 1931 and Words and Music 1932, Give me a Ring 1933, Jill Darling 1934, Red Night 1936, A Midsummer Night's Dream, She Stoops to Conquer, The Damascus Blade 1950, Figure of Fun 1951, The Uninvited Guest 1952, Ross (Broadway production) 1961, Powers of Persuasion 1963, Veterans 1972, At the End of the Day 1973, Good Companions (musical) 1974, Great Expectations (musical) 1975, Separate Tables 1977, Goodbye, Mr. Chips (musical) 1982, The Housekeeper 1983, Little Lies 1983 and 1984, The Petition 1986, My Fair Lady 1986. *Film appearances include:* The Midshipmaid, Those Were the Days, Doctor's Orders, Royal Cavalcade, Tudor Rose, O.H.M.S., Goodbye Mr. Chips (1937), Four Dark Hours, Black Sheep of Whitehall, The Young Mr. Pitt, In Which We Serve, Waterloo Road, This Happy Breed, The Way to the Stars, Scott of the Antarctic, The History of Mr. Polly, The Rocking Horse Winner, Morning Departure, Hobson's Choice, The Colditz Story, Above Us The Waves, Escapade, War and Peace, The Baby and the Battleship, Round the World in 80 Days, Dunkirk, Ice Cold in Alex, Monty's Double, Summer of the Seventeenth Doll, Tiger Bay, Swiss Family Robinson, Tunes of Glory, The Singer Not the Song, Flame in the Streets, Tiara Tahiti, King Rat, The Chalk Garden, Operation Crossbow, The Wrong Box, The Family Way, Chuka, Cowboy in Africa, Adam's Woman, Lady Hamilton, Oh! What a Lovely War, Run Wild, Run Free, A Black Veil for Lisa, Ryan's Daughter, Dulcima, Young Winston, Oklahoma Crude, The Human Factor, Trial by Combat, The Big Sleep, Thirty-Nine Steps, Zulu Dawn, Dr. Strange, Love Boat, Quatermass (TV), Young at Heart (TV) 1980/82, A Woman of Substance (TV), The Masks of Death (TV), Murder with Mirrors (TV), Gandhi 1980, Sahara 1983, A Woman of Substance, Tribute to Her Majesty (film documentary) 1986, A Tale of Two Cities (TV) 1989, Ending Up (TV) 1989. *Publications:* Up in the Clouds Gentlemen Please 1980, Book of Famous Firsts 1984. *Leisure interests:* skiing, golf, painting. *Address:* c/o I.C.M. Ltd., 388/396 Oxford Street, London, W.1, England.

MILLS, Wilbur Daigh; American politician; b. 24 May 1909, Kensett; s. of A.P. Mills and Abbie Lois Daigh Mills; m. Clarine Billingsley 1934; two d.; ed. Hendrix Coll. and Harvard Law School; admitted to Ark. Bar 1933, private legal practice, Searcy; County and Probate Judge, White County 1934–38; Cashier, Bank of Kensett 1934–35; mem. U.S. House of Reps. for Arkansas 1939–77, Chair. Ways and Means Cttee. 1958–74; Tax counsel, Shea and Gould, New York 1977, Washington 1981–; Democrat. *Leisure interests:* reading, crossword puzzles. *Address:* Shea and Gould, 1775 Pennsylvania Avenue, N.W., 700, Washington, D.C. 20006, U.S.A. (Office). *Telephone:* 202-833 9850 (Office).

MILLSAPS, Knox, PH.D.; American engineer; b. 10 Sept. 1921, Birmingham, Ala.; s. of Knox Taylor Millsaps and Millie May Joyce; m. Lorraine Marie Hartle 1956; one s. three d.; ed. Auburn Univ. and Calif. Inst. of Tech.; Assoc. Prof. Ohio State Univ. 1947–48; Physicist Wright Air Devt. Center 1948–49, Mathematician 1950–51, Chief Mathematician 1952–55; Prof. of Physics, Auburn Univ. 1949–50, 1951–52; Prof. of Mechanical Eng., M.I.T. 1955–56; Chief Scientist, Air Force Missile Devt. Center, U.S.A.F. 1956–60; Exec. Dir. Air Force Office of Scientific Research, U.S.A.F. 1961–62; Research Prof. of Aerospace Eng., Univ. of Fla. 1963–68, Prof. of Eng. 1986–88, Chair. Dept. of Eng. Sciences 1973–86; Head, Prof. Mechanical Eng., Colorado State Univ. 1968–73. *Leisure interests:* gardening, crinums, camellias. *Address:* P.O. Box 13857, Gainesville, Fla. 32604, U.S.A. *Telephone:* 904-372-3018.

MILNE, Alasdair David Gordon, B.A.; British broadcasting official; b. 8 Oct. 1930; s. of Charles Gordon Shaw Milne and Edith Reid Clark; m. Sheila Kirsten Graucob 1954; two s. one d.; ed. Winchester Coll., New Coll., Oxford; served with 1st Bn., Gordon Highlanders 1949; joined BBC 1954, Deputy Ed. 1957–61, Ed. of Tonight Programme 1961–62, Head of Tonight Productions 1963–65; Partner Jay, Baverstock, Milne & Co. 1965–67; rejoined BBC 1967, Controller BBC Scotland 1968–72, Dir. of Programmes, BBC TV 1973–77, Man. Dir. TV 1977–82, Deputy Dir.-Gen. BBC 1980–82, Dir.-Gen. 1982–87; Pres. Commonwealth Broadcasting Assen. 1984–87; Dr. h.c. (Stirling) 1983; Hon. Fellow New College, Oxford; Cyril Bennet Award 1987. *Publication:* DG: The Memoirs of a British Broadcaster 1988. *Leisure interests:* piping, salmon fishing, golf, tennis. *Address:*

c/o Midland Bank, Charing Cross Branch, 455 Strand, London, WC2R 0RH, England.

MILNE, Denys Gordon ('Tiny'), C.B.E., M.A.; British petroleum industry executive; b. 12 Jan. 1926, Shetlands; s. of Dr. George Gordon Milne and Margaret Campbell; m. Pamela Mary Senior 1951; two s. one d.; ed. Epsom Coll., Brasenose Coll., Oxford; Colonial Admin. Service, Northern Nigeria 1951–54; joined BP Group 1955, Regional Man., Kano, N. Nigeria 1955, then Sales Man., Ghana, then Gen. Man., Nigeria; returned to London 1965; Regional Co-ordinator, U.K. and Ireland 1966–71, also Dir. Shell-Mex and BP, Chair. Lubricants Producers Ltd.; Dir. Alexander Duckham & Co. Ltd. 1966–71, Chair. 1976–81; Shareholders' Rep. in Southern Africa 1971; First Chair. BP Southern Africa Ltd. 1975; returned to London as Deputy Man. Dir. BP Oil Ltd. 1975; Chief Exec. and Man. Dir. BP Oil Ltd. 1976–81; Pres. Inst. of Petroleum 1977–79; Vice-Pres. U.K. Petroleum Industry Assen. 1978–79, Pres. 1979–81; Chair. Occupational and Environmental Health Spar Ltd. 1986–; Stag Petroleum Co. Ltd. 1986–; mem. Advisory Cttee. on Energy Conservation 1979–81, Scottish Econ. Council 1978–81; Dir. Silkolene Lubricants Ltd. 1981–, Fluor (G.B.) Ltd. 1981–; Chair. Exec. Unit Business in the Community 1981–84; Dir. Weir Group PLC 1983–. *Leisure interests:* gardening, sailing. *Address:* Westbury, Old Lane, St. John's, Crowborough, Sussex, England. *Telephone:* (08926) 2634.

MILNE, Sir John Drummond, Kt.; British business executive; b. 13 Aug. 1924, Manchester; s. of Frederick John Milne and Minnie E. Milne; m. Joan Akroyd 1948; two s. two d.; ed. Stowe School, Trinity Coll. Cambridge and R.M.C. Sandhurst; served Coldstream Guards; joined Associated Portland Cement Mfrs. 1948, Asst. to Dir. in charge of overseas investment 1953; Pres. Ocean Cement Ltd., Van., B.C. 1957; Dir. Associated Portland Cement Mfrs. Ltd. 1964, Dir. in charge of overseas investments 1968; Man. Dir. and Chief Exec. Associated Portland Cement Mfrs. Ltd. (now known as Blue Circle Industries PLC) 1975; Chair. and Man. Dir. Blue Circle Industries PLC 1983–87, non-exec. Chair. 1987–; Chair DRG 1987–; Dir. Royal Insurance PLC 1982–. *Leisure interests:* golf, shooting, skiing. *Address:* Chilton House, Chilton Candover, Nr. Alresford, Hants., England.

MILNE, Malcolm Davenport, M.D., F.R.C.P., F.R.S.; British professor of medicine (retd.); b. 22 May 1915, Woodley, Cheshire; s. of Alexander Milne and Clara Lilian Gee; m. Mary Thorpe 1941; one s. one d.; ed. Univ. of Manchester; House Physician, Manchester Royal Infirmary 1939–40; served with R.A.M.C. 1940–46; Sr. Registrar in Medicine, Manchester 1946–49 Lecturer 1949–52; at Post-graduate Medical School, London 1952–61; Prof. of Medicine, Univ. of London 1961–81, Prof. Emer. 1981–. *Publications:* numerous scientific papers on nephrology, metabolism and the biological transport of small organic molecules. *Leisure interests:* horticulture, haute cuisine, pure mathematics. *Address:* 19 Fieldway, Berkhamsted, Herts., HP4 2NX, England.

MILNE-WATSON, Sir Michael, Bt., Kt., C.B.E.; British company executive; b. 16 Feb. 1910, London; s. of Sir David Milne-Watson, 1st Bart., and the late Lady Olga (Herbert) Milne-Watson; m. Mary Lisette Bagnall 1940; one s.; ed. Eton and Balliol Coll., Oxford; Gas Light and Coke Co. 1933–49, Gov. 1946–49; Chair. North Thames Gas Bd. 1949–64; Chair. Richard Thomas & Baldwins Ltd. 1964–67; mem. Org. Cttee. Nat. Steel Corpn. 1966–67, Deputy Chair. (Admin.) Nat. (now British) Steel Corpn. 1967–69; Chair. William Press Group of Companies 1969–74; Gov. British United Provident Assen. (BUPA), Chair 1976–81; Dir. Industrial and Commercial Finance Corpn. Ltd. 1963–80, Commercial Union Assurance Co. Ltd. 1968–81, Finance for Industry Ltd. 1974–80; mem. of Council, Reading Univ. 1972–80 (Pres. 1975–80), Soc. of British Gas Industries Guild 1970–71, Pipeline Industries Guild 1971–72; mem. R.N.V.R. 1943–45, Liveryman, Grocers Company 1947–. *Address:* 39 Cadogan Place, London, SW1X 9RX; Oakfield, Mortimer, Berks., RG7 3AP, England. *Telephone:* 01-235 3467 (London).

MILNER, Aaron Michael; Zambian politician; b. 31 May 1932; ed. Embakwe Mission, Plumtree, Rhodesia; Minister of State for the Cabinet and Civil Service; Minister of State for Presidential Affairs 1967–70; Minister of Transport, Power and Works Jan.-Nov. 1970; Sec.-Gen. to Govt. 1970–73, also Minister of Prov. and Local Govt. and Culture 1971–73; Minister of Defence Aug.-Dec. 1973, of Home Affairs 1973–77; fmr. Chair. Zambia Copper Mines; currently farming. *Address:* c/o Ministry of Home Affairs, Lusaka, Zambia.

MILNER, Anthony Francis Dominic, D.MUS., F.R.C.M.; British composer, writer and teacher; b. 13 May 1925, Bristol; ed. Douai School, Woolhampton, Berks. and Royal Coll. of Music, London; Tutor in Music Theory and History at Morley Coll., London 1954–65; part-time Teacher, R.C.M. 1961–80; Extension Lecturer in Music, Univ. of London 1954–65; Lecturer in Music, King's Coll., London Univ. 1965–71, Sr. Lecturer in Music, Goldsmith's Coll. 1971–74, Prin. Lecturer 1974–80; Prin. Lecturer, R.C.M. 1980–; lectured on variety of musical topics in over 70 univs. and colls. in U.S.A. and Canada 1964–; Dir. and Harpsichordist, London Cantata Ensemble 1954–65; Kt. Order of St. Gregory (Papal Award) 1985. *Compositions:* Symphony No. 1 1972, Symphony No. 2 1978, Symphony No. 3 1987, Orchestral Variations 1958, Oratorio: The Water and the Fire 1961, cantatas, chamber music, choral and vocal music, etc. *Leisure interests:*

reading, travel. *Address:* 147 Heythorp Street, Southfields, London, SW18 5BT, England.

MILNES, Sherill, M.MUS.ED.; American opera singer; b. 10 Jan. 1935, Hinsdale, Ill.; s. of James Knowlton and Thelma Roe Milnes; m. 2nd Nancy Stokes 1969; one s. (one s. one d. by first marriage); ed. Drake Univ., Northwestern Univ.; studied with Boris Goldovsky, Rosa Ponselle, Andrew White, Hermanes Baer; with Goldovsky Opera Co. 1960-65, New York City Opera Co. 1964-67, debut with Metropolitan Opera, New York 1965, leading baritone 1965-; has performed with all American city opera cos. and major American orchestras 1962-73; performed in Don Giovanni, Vespri Siciliani and all standard Italian repertory baritone roles, Metropolitan Opera and at San Francisco Opera, Hamburg Opera, Frankfurt Opera, La Scala, Milan, Covent Garden, London, Teatro Colón, Buenos Aires, Vienna State Opera, Paris Opera and Chicago Lyric Opera; recordings for RCA Victor, London Decca, EMI Angel, Phillips, Deutsche Grammophon, 60 albums 1967-; most recorded American opera singer 1978; Chair. of Bd. Affiliate Artists Inc.; three hon. degrees, Order of Merit (Italy) 1984. *Leisure interests:* table tennis, swimming, horse riding. *Address:* c/o Herbert Barrett, 1860 Broadway, New York, N.Y. 10023, U.S.A.

MIŁOSZ, Czesław; American (Polish-born) writer; b. 30 June 1911, Szetejnie, Lithuania; s. of Aleksander and Weronika (Kunat) Miłosz; ed. Univ. of Wilno (now Vilnius, U.S.S.R.); helped form literary group Zagary; first collection of poems published 1933; studied in Paris 1934-35; programmer with Polish Nat. Radio 1935-39; active in Polish resistance, World War II; brought out "underground" an anti-Nazi anthology of poems Pieśń niepodległa (Invincible Song) and other publications; diplomatic service, Washington Embassy, later Paris 1946-50; went into exile, Paris 1951; with Polish emigrant publishing house Instytut Literacki, Paris 1951-60, still writes for house magazine Kultura; went to U.S.A. 1960, became naturalized American 1970; Prix Littéraire Européen (jointly) for novel Zdobycie władzy (first published in French as La prise du pouvoir) 1953; Visiting Lecturer, Univ. of Calif. at Berkeley 1960, Prof. of Slavic Languages and Literatures 1960-78, Prof. Emer. 1978-; hon. doctorate (Univ. of Michigan, Ann Arbor) 1977; mem. American Acad. and Inst. of Arts and Letters; Polish PEN Club award for poetry translation 1974; Books Abroad/Neustadt Prize 1978; Nobel Prize for Literature 1980. *Publications include: poetry:* Swiatło dzienne (Daylight) 1953, Traktat poetycki (Poetic Treatise) 1957, Król Popiel i inne wiersze (King Popiel and Other Poems) 1962, Gucio zaczarowany (Bobo's Metamorphosis) 1964, Miasto bez imienia (City Without a Name) 1969, Gdzie słońce wschodzi i kedy zapada (From Where the Sun Rises to Where it Sets) 1974, Bells in Winter (poems) 1978; *prose:* Zniewolony umysł (The Captive Mind) 1953, Zdobycie władzy (The Usurpers) 1955, Dolina Issy (The Issa Valley) 1955, Native Realm: a Search for Self-Definition 1968, Emperor of the Earth: Modes of Eccentric Vision (essays) 1977, The History of Polish Literature 1969; translations into Polish: The Gospel According to St. Mark, The Book of Psalms; into English: Post-war Polish Poetry 1965; Ziemia Ulro (The Land of Ulro) 1977, The Separate Notebooks (poems) 1984, The Unattainable Earth (poems) 1986, Collected Poems 1988; numerous essays, translations. *Address:* c/o Department of Slavic Languages and Literature, University of California, Berkeley, Calif. 94720, U.S.A.

MILOW, Keith; British artist; b. 1945, London; ed. Camberwell School of Art and Royal Coll. of Art; experimental work at Royal Court Theatre, London 1968; teacher, Ealing School of Art 1968-70; Artist in Residence, Leeds Univ. (Gregory Fellowship) 1970; worked in New York (Harkness Fellowship) 1972-74; teacher, Chelsea School of Art 1975; teacher, School of Visual Arts, New York City 1981-85; lives and works in New York; many one-man exhbns. in England, U.S.A., Belgium, France, Netherlands and Switzerland; many group exhbns. in several countries; works in public collections in 6 countries including Tate Gallery and Victoria and Albert Museum, London, Guggenheim Museum and Museum of Modern Art, New York; Calouste Gulbenkian Foundation Visual Arts Award 1976; equal First Prize Tolly Cobbold/Eastern Arts 2nd Nation Exhbn. 1979; Arts Council of G.B. Major Award. *Address:* 32 West 20th Street, New York, N.Y. 10011, U.S.A. *Telephone:* (212) 929 0124.

MILSOM, Stroud Francis Charles, Q.C., F.B.A.; British academic; b. 2 May 1923, Merton, Surrey; s. of Harry Lincoln Milsom and Isobel Vida Collins; m. Irene Szereszewski 1955; ed. Charterhouse School, Trinity Coll. Cambridge and Univ. of Pennsylvania Law School (as Commonwealth Fund Fellow); Fellow, Trinity Coll. 1948-55; Fellow, Tutor and Dean, New Coll. Oxford 1956-64; Prof. of Legal History, L.S.E. 1964-76; Prof. of Law, Cambridge Univ. and Fellow of St. John's Coll. 1976-; called to Bar 1947, Hon. Bencher, Lincoln's Inn 1970, Q.C. 1985; Literary Dir. Selden Soc. 1964-80, Pres. 1985-88; mem. Royal Comm. on Historical Manuscripts 1975-; Foreign mem. American Philosophical Soc.; Hon. LL.D. (Glasgow) 1981, (Chicago) 1985; Ames Prize, Harvard 1972; Swiney Prize, R.S.A. 1974. *Publications:* Novae Narrationes 1963, Introduction to reissue of History of English Law (Pollock and Maitland) 1968, Historical Foundations of the Common Law 1969, 1981, Legal Framework of English Feudalism 1976, Studies in the History of the Common Law 1985. *Address:* St. John's College, Cambridge, CB2 1TP; 113 Grantchester Meadows, Cambridge, CB3 9JN, England (Home). *Telephone:* (0223) 354100 (Home).

MILSTEIN, César, PH.D., F.R.S.; British molecular biologist; b. 8 Oct. 1927, Bahia Blanca, Argentina; m. Celia Prilleltensky 1953; ed. Colegio Nacional, Bahia Blanca, Universidad de Buenos Aires, Instituto de Química Biológica and Univ. of Cambridge; British Council Fellowship, Dept. of Biochemistry, Cambridge Univ. 1958-60; on Scientific Staff, MRC 1960-61; Head of Molecular Biology Div., Instituto Nacional de Microbiología, Buenos Aires, Argentina 1961-63; on Scientific Staff of MRC Lab. of Molecular Biology, Cambridge 1963-, Head, Div. of Protein and Nucleic Acid Chem. 1983-; Fellow, Darwin Coll., Cambridge 1981-; Hon. Fellow Fitzwilliam Coll. Cambridge; many awards including Nobel Prize in Physiology or Medicine 1984, Ciba Medal and Prize 1978, Wolf Prize in Medicine, Wolf Foundation, Israel 1980, Robert Koch Prize and Medal, Fed. Repub. of Germany 1980, Royal Soc. Wellcome Foundation Prize 1980, Jimenez Diaz Memorial Award, Spain 1981, Gairdner Foundation Annual Award, Canada 1981, Royal Medal, Royal Soc. 1982. *Publications:* papers in various scientific journals. *Leisure interests:* theatre, walking, outdoor cookery. *Address:* Medical Research Council Laboratory of Molecular Biology, Hills Road, Cambridge, CB2 2QH (Office); 292A Hills Road, Cambridge (Home). *Telephone:* (0223) 248011 (Office); (0223) 245677 (Home).

MILSTEIN, Nathan; American (Russian-born) violinist; b. 31 Dec. 1904, Odessa; s. of Miron Milstein and Maria (Bluestein) Milstein; m. Thérèse Weldon 1945; one d.; ed. St. Petersburg Conservatoire under Leopold Auer; début 1919; gave recitals with Vladimir Horowitz; left Russia 1925; studied with Eugène Ysaÿe, Brussels; U.S. début with Philadelphia Orchestra, conducted by Stokowski 1929; became U.S. citizen 1942; extensive tours Europe, N., Cen. and S. America 1920-; Grammy Award 1975; Hon. mem. Acad. of St. Cecilia, Rome 1963; Commdr., Légion d'honneur; Ehrenkreuz (Austria). *Address:* c/o Shaw Concerts Inc., 1995 Broadway, New York, N.Y. 10023, U.S.A.; 17 Chester Square, London, S.W.1, England.

MILTON, (John Charles) Douglas, M.A., PH.D., F.R.S.C.; Canadian physicist; b. 1 June 1924, Regina, Sask.; s. of W. Milton and Frances C. McDowall; m. Gwendolyn M. Shaw 1953; two s. two d.; ed. Univ of Manitoba and Princeton Univ.; Asst. Research Officer, Atomic Energy of Canada Ltd., Chalk River Nuclear Labs. 1951-56, Assoc. Research Officer 1957-61, Sr. Research Officer 1962-69, Prin. Research Officer 1967-82, Head Nuclear Physics Branch and Dir. Physics Div. 1983-86, Acting Dir. of Research 1983-86, Vice-Pres. Physics and Health Sciences Div. 1986-; Visiting Scientist, Lawrence Berkeley Labs. 1960-62, Centre d'Etudes de Bruyère-le-Châtel 1965-66; Dir. de Recherche, CNR Strasbourg 1965; Fellow American Physical Soc.; mem. Canadian Assen. of Physicists. *Publications:* over 50 scientific papers and reviews. *Leisure interests:* music, gardening, woodwork. *Address:* Physics and Health Sciences Division, AECL, Chalk River, Ont. K0J 1J0 (Office); 3 Alexander Place, Deep River, Ont. K0J 1P0, Canada (Home).

MILTON-THOMPSON, Godfrey James, M.A., M.B., F.R.C.P.; British naval surgeon; b. 25 April 1930, Birkenhead, Cheshire; s. of late Rev. James Milton-Thompson and May L. Hoare; m. Noreen H. F. Fitzmaurice 1952; three d.; ed. Eastbourne Coll., Queens' Coll. Cambridge and St. Thomas's Hospital, London; joined R.N. 1955, Sr. Specialist in Medicine, R.N. Hospital, Malta 1962-66; Consultant Physician, R.N. Hospital, Plymouth 1966-69, 1971-75; Hon. Research Fellow, St. Mark's Hospital 1969-70; Prof. of Naval Medicine 1975-80; promoted Surgeon Capt. 1976; Royal Coll. of Defence Studies 1981; Deputy Medical Dir.-Gen. (Naval) 1982-84; Medical Dir.-Gen. (Naval) 1984-; Deputy Surgeon-Gen. (Research and Training) 1985-87; promoted Surgeon Rear Admiral 1984, Surgeon Rear Adm. (Operational Medical Services) 1984; Surgeon Gen., Defence Medical Services in the rank of Surgeon Vice-Adm. 1988-; Hon. Physician to H.M. the Queen 1982-; Errol-Eldridge Prize 1974; Gilbert Blane Medal 1976; Commdr. Order of St. John. *Publications:* contributions to medical and scientific literature on gastroenterology. *Leisure interests:* fishing, literature, collecting East Anglian paintings. *Address:* c/o The Naval Secretary, Old Admiralty Building, Whitehall, London, S.W.1, England.

MIMS, Cedric Arthur, M.D., F.R.C.PATH.; British professor of microbiology; b. 9 Dec. 1924, London; s. of A. H. and Irene Mims; m. Valerie Vickery 1952; two s. two d.; ed. Mill Hill School, Univ. Coll. London, Middx. Hosp. Medical School; Medical Research Officer, E. African Virus Research Inst., Entebbe 1953-56; Research Fellow and Professorial Fellow, John Curtin School of Medical Research, Australian Nat. Univ., Canberra 1957-72; Rockefeller Foundation Fellow, Children's Hosp. Medical Center, Boston 1963-64; Visiting Fellow, Wistar Inst., Philadelphia 1969-70; Prof. of Microbiology Guy's Hosp. Medical School, London 1972-. *Publications:* The Biology of Animal Viruses (jt. author) 1974, The Pathogenesis of Infectious Disease 1976, Viral Pathogenesis and Immunology (with D. O. White) 1984, numerous scientific papers. *Leisure interests:* writing, walking. *Address:* Sheriff House, Hammingden Lane, Ardingly, Sussex, RH17 6SR, England. *Telephone:* (0444) 892243.

MINÁČ, Vladimír, Czechoslovak writer; b. 10 August 1922, Klenovec, Rimavská Sobota Dist.; s. of Jan Mináč and Zuzana (née Karkus) Mináč; m. Mária Mináč (née Dénes) 1945; one s. two d.; ed. Philosophical Faculty, Comenius Univ., Bratislava 1940-44; participation in the Slovak Nat. Uprising 1944-45, then confined in concentration camp; ed. Obrana ľudu, Bratislava 1946-49; Sec. Union of Slovak Writers 1949-51; Cttee. mem.

Union of Slovak Writers 1949–; Chief Ed. Kultúrny život 1951–52; script-writer, Czechoslovak Film 1952–53; Chief Ed. Kultúrny život 1953–55; Chief Ed. Slovenské pohľady 1956; professional writer 1957–; Deputy, Nat. Assembly 1964–69; alt. mem. of the Cen. Cttee. of the CP of Czechoslovakia, 1966–68; mem. 1968–71; Deputy, Czechoslovak Fed. Assembly House of the People 1969–71; mem. Cen. Cttee. of the CP of Slovakia, 1971–; Deputy, Slovak Nat. Council, 1971–; Presidium mem. Union of Slovak Writers 1972–; Chair. Matica slovenská 1974–; Presidium mem. Union of Czechoslovak Writers, 1977–; Cttee. Deputy Chair. Czechoslovak Foreign Inst. 1980–; Deputy Chair. Union of Slovak Writers 1982–. *Work:* Death Strikes in the Mountains 1948, Yesterday and Tomorrow 1949, Break-through 1950, At the Turn 1954, triology The Generation—The Long Time of Waiting 1958, The Living and the Dead 1959, The Bells Ring the Day 1961, You Are Never Alone 1962, Time and Books 1962, Records 1964, Who Marches along the Road 1966, The Happiness Maker 1966, Paradoxes 1966, Blowing in the Embers 1971, Selected Disputes of J. M. Hurban 1974, Texts and Contexts 1978, Portraits 1986; *film stories and screenplays:* The Fight Will End Tomorrow 1951, Mária Justinová 1951, Untilled Fields 1954, Captain Dabač 1959; State Prize of Klement Gottwald 1955, 1962, Artist of Merit 1966, Order of Labour 1968, Order of the Red Star 1974, Nat. Artist 1975, Order of Victorious February 1982. *Address:* Matica slovenská, Pugačevova 2, 812 51 Bratislava, Czechoslovakia. *Telephone:* 334265.

MINAH, Francis Misheck, LL.M.; Sierra Leonean lawyer and politician; b. 19 Aug. 1929, Pujehun; m. Gladys Emuchay; four c.; ed. Methodist Boys' High School, Freetown, King's Coll. (London Univ.), Grays Inn, London; Pres. Sierra Leone Students' Union of Great Britain and Ireland 1960–62; mem. House of Reps. 1967–87; Minister of Trade and Industry 1973–75, of Foreign Affairs 1975–77, of Justice 1977–78; Attorney-Gen. 1978; Minister of Finance 1978–80, of Health 1980–82; Attorney-Gen. and Minister of Justice 1982–84; First Vice-Pres. 1985–87; UNESCO Fellowship to study community devt. in India and Liberia; Barrister-at-law; under house arrest April 1987–.

MINCER, Jacob, PH.D.; American professor of economics; b. 15 July 1922, Tomaszow, Poland; m. Flora Kaplan 1951; two d.; ed. Emory Univ., Atlanta, Ga., Columbia Univ., New York; Prof. of Econs., Columbia Univ. 1962–; Research Staff, Nat. Bureau of Econ. Research 1960–; Fellow American Statistical Asscn., Econometric Soc.; mem. American Acad. of Arts and Sciences, Nat. Acad. of Educ. *Publications:* Economic Forecasts and Expectations (Ed. and Author) 1969, Schooling, Experience and Earnings 1974, Trends in Women's Work and Wages (Ed. and Author) 1985; numerous articles in professional journals. *Leisure interests:* music, literature, sports. *Address:* Economics Department, Columbia University, New York, N.Y. 10027; 448 Riverside Drive, New York, N.Y. 10027, U.S.A. (Home). *Telephone:* (212) 280-3676 (Office); (212) 663-4897.

MINIĆ, Miloš; Yugoslav lawyer and politician; b. 28 Aug. 1914, Čačak, Serbia; s. of Dragomir and Jovanka Minić; m. Milka Minić 1936; two d.; mem. League of Communist Youth 1935, League of Communists of Yugoslavia 1936; one of the organizers of Nat. Liberation War, Serbia 1941; Public Prosecutor Serbia 1945–50; Minister in Govt. of Serbia 1950–53; Pres. People's Cttee. of Belgrade 1955–57; Pres. Exec. Council of Serbia 1957–62; Vice-Pres. Fed. Exec. Council 1963–65; Pres. Assembly of Serbia 1967–69; Vice-Pres. Fed. Assembly 1969–72; Vice-Pres. Fed. Exec. Council 1962–65 and Fed. Sec. for Foreign Affairs 1972–78; mem. Council of the Fed.; mem. Cen. Cttee. of League of Communists of Yugoslavia 1952–86, mem. Presidium of Cen. Cttee. 1974–82; mem. Standing Conf. of League of Communists of Yugoslavia; 1941 Partisan Memorial Medal and other decorations. *Publications:* Foreign Policy of Yugoslavia 1973–79, Contemporary World and Security of SFRY 1985, various papers on int. politics. *Address:* Savez Komunista Jugoslavije, Bulevar Lenjina 6, Novi Beograd; 11000 Beograd, Kumanovska 23, Yugoslavia.

MININ, Viktor Ivanovich; Soviet diplomatist; b. 4 Jan. 1926, Moscow; ed. Moscow State Inst. of Int. Relations; Diplomatic Service 1948–; with Balkan Countries Dept., Ministry of Foreign Affairs 1948–52; Second Sec. Soviet Embassy, Albania 1952–55; Ministry of Foreign Affairs 1955–57; Sec., First Sec. Soviet Embassy, Canada 1957–61; Counsellor, S.E. Asia Dept. Ministry of Foreign Affairs 1963–65; Counsellor, Soviet Embassy, Turkey 1965–68; Amb. to Kingdom of Laos 1968–72; Head of Middle East Dept., U.S.S.R. Ministry of Foreign Affairs 1973–78; Amb. to Guinea 1978–82, to Iraq 1982–; Order of Badge of Honour. *Address:* Embassy of U.S.S.R., 140 Mansour Street, Karradat Mariam, Baghdad, Iraq.

MINKOWSKI, Alexandre, M.D., F.R.A.P., F.R.C.P. (U.K.); French professor of neonatalogy; b. 5 Dec. 1915, Paris; s. of Eugene Minkowski and Francoise Minkowski; m. Mary Ann Wade 1952; four c.; ed. Paris Univ.; Chef de Clinique 1945–46; Rockefeller Fellow 1946–47; Head, Dept. of Intensive Care 1962; Prof. of Neonatalogy, Paris Univ. 1962–, Full Prof. 1970–87; mem., the American Pediatric Soc. and British Neonatalogy Soc.; Officier, Légion d'honneur, Croix de Guerre 1939–45. *Publications:* eight books and several scientific essays. *Leisure interests:* tennis, skiing, music. *Address:* 182 rue de Rivoli, Paris 19, France. *Telephone:* 4 234 1911.

MINNELLI, Liza; American actress and singer; b. 12 March 1946; d. of late Vincente Minnelli and Judy Garland; m. 1st Peter Allen 1967

(divorced 1970), 2nd Jack Haley, Jr. 1974 (divorced 1979); m. 3rd Mark Gero 1979. *Films:* Charlie Bubbles 1968, The Sterile Cuckoo 1969, Tell Me that You Love Me, Junie Moon 1971, Cabaret (played Sally Bowles) 1972 (Acad. Award for Best Actress, The Hollywood Foreign Press Golden Globe Award, the British Acad. Award and David di Donatello Award, Italy), Lucky Lady 1976, A Matter of Time 1976, New York, New York 1977, Arthur 1981, Rent-a-Cop 1988, Arthur 2: On the Rocks 1988. *TV Specials:* Liza, Liza with a Z (Emmy Award) 1972, Goldie and Liza Together 1980, Baryshnikov on Broadway 1980 (Golden Globe Award), A Time to Live 1985 (Golden Globe Award). *Theatre:* Best Foot Forward 1963, Flora, the Red Menace 1965 (Tony Award), Chicago 1975, The Act 1977–78 (Tony Award), Liza at the Winter Garden 1973 (Special Tony Award), The Rink 1984. *Recordings:* Liza with a Z, Liza Minnelli: The Singer, Liza Minnelli: Live at the Winter Garden, Tropical Nights, The Act, Liza Minnelli: Live at Carnegie Hall, The Rink, Liza Minnelli at Carnegie Hall. *Address:* c/o Creative Management Associates, 40 West 57th Street, New York, N.Y. 10022, U.S.A.

MINNETT, Harry Clive, O.B.E., B.SC., B.E., F.A.A.; Australian radiophysicist and electrical engineer; b. 12 June 1917, Sydney; s. of Frederick H. Minnett and Elsie M. Garnsey; m. Margaret B. Rooney 1955; one s. one d.; ed. Sydney High School and Univ. of Sydney; joined Radiophysics Lab. CSIRO 1940; Leader Antenna Research Group, CSIRO Div. of Radiophysics 1962–71; Acting Project Man. Anglo-Australian Telescope 1969–71; Eng. Dir. Interscan Microwave Landing System project 1972–78; Chief, CSIRO Div. of Radiophysics 1978–81; consultant and Deputy Chief. Exec. Inter-scan Int. Ltd. 1982–86; consultant, Australian Telecommunications and Electronics Research Bd. 1986–87; freelance consultant 1987–; Fellow, Australian Acad. of Technological Sciences, Fellow, Inst. of Eng. (Australia). *Publications:* professional papers. *Leisure interests:* golf, walking, travel, genealogy. *Address:* CSIRO Division of Radiophysics, P.O. Box 76, Epping, N.S.W. 2121; 88 Neerim Road, Castle Cove, N.S.W. 2069, Australia. *Telephone:* (02) 868-0222 (Office); (02) 406-4425 (Home).

MINNIGERODE, Gunther, Freiherr von, DR.RER.NAT.; German physicist; b. 6 Oct. 1929, Osterode/Harz; s. of Werner Freiherr von Minnigerode and Margarete von Drachenfels; m. Ulrike Göllerich 1972; two step-s.; ed. Univ. of Göttingen; Asst. Univ. of Göttingen 1959–66, lecturer 1966–67; Prof. of Applied Physics Univ. of Cologne 1967–73; Prof. of Experimental Physics, Univ. of Göttingen 1973–; mem. Göttingen Acad. *Publications:* articles on low temperature physics and solid state physics in professional journals. *Leisure interest:* farming. *Address:* I. Physikalisches Institute, Bunsenstrasse 9, 3400 Göttingen (Office); Hermann Föge Weg 10, 3400 Göttingen, Federal Republic of Germany (Home). *Telephone:* (0551) 397601 (Office); (0551) 58828 (Home).

MINOTIS, Alexis; Greek theatre producer and actor; b. 1906, Canea, Crete; s. of Stylianos and Styliani Minotis; m. Katina Paxinou 1940 (deceased); acting on Greek stage since 1925; mem. Nat. Theatre of Greece 1930–; Artistic Dir. of Nat. Theatre to 1967, Gen. Dir. 1974–80, Pres. Bd. of Dirs. 1980–82; has played principal roles in and produced most classical plays from Aeschylus to Pirandello; has made many tours outside Greece with Nat. Theatre; produced Cherubini's opera Medea, with Callas in leading role, for Dallas (Texas) Civic Opera, at Covent Garden, London and at La Scala, Milan; Ancient Greek Drama Festivals at Epidaurus and Athens 1955–; produced Oedipus Rex, Hecuba Medea 1955–58, Oedipus at Colonus, Antigone 1962 at Théâtre des Nations, Paris; produced Friedrich Dürrenmatt's Visit of the Old Lady, Royal Theatre, Greece 1961; played Oedipus in Oedipus Rex, London 1966; formed own theatre co. in Athens with Katina Paxinou 1967, and since produced works by O'Neil, O'Casey, Strindberg, Lorca, Brecht, Ibsen, Büchner and Shakespeare, played Shy-lock in The Merchant of Venice 1971–72; produced Danton's Death (Büchner), Nat. Theatre of Greece 1974; produced and acted in Oedipus at Colonus (Sophocles), Epidaurus Festival 1975, 1976, 1986, toured the play to Moscow, Leningrad, New York and Boston 1976, to Dodoni Theatre and Herodus Atticus Theatre, Athens 1986; produced and acted in John Gabriel Borkman (Ibsen), Nat. Theatre of Greece 1976, End Game (Beckett), Philoctetes (Sophocles); directed and acted in King Lear 1977; toured with Prometheus Bound and Phoenician Women to Japan and China 1979–80, with Prometheus Bound in Moscow 1980; dir. and acted in Cardinal of Spain (de Montherlant), Nat. Theatre of Greece 1982, The Persians (Aeschylus), Epidaurus 1984; dir. and acted in Father (Strindberg), Nat. Theatre of Greece 1988, Phoenician Women, Epidaurus Ancient Theatre 1988; several Greek and foreign decorations. *Leisure interest:* writing articles, books, etc. *Address:* Lykiou 13, Athens, Greece. *Telephone:* 7215687.

MINOW, Newton N., J.D.; American lawyer; b. 17 Jan. 1926, Milwaukee, Wis.; s. of Jay A. and Doris (Stein) Minow; m. Josephine Baskin 1949; three d.; ed. Northwestern Univ.; Law Clerk to Supreme Court Chief Justice Vinson 1951; Admin. Asst. to Gov. of Illinois 1952–53; served Stevenson's law firm 1955–57, Partner 1957–61; Chair. Fed. Communications Comm. 1961–63; Exec. Vice-Pres. Gen. Counsel Encyclopaedia Britannica, Chicago 1963–65; mem. Bd. of Trustees, Rand Corpn. 1965–75, 1976–86, Chair. 1970–72; Partner, Sidley & Austin (fmrly. Leibman, Williams, Bennett, Baird & Minow) 1965–; Hon. Chair. and Dir. Chicago Educational TV Asscn; Dir. Aetna Casualty and Surety Co. of Ill., Aetna

Life Insurance Co. of Ill., Chicago Pacific Corpn. 1984-89, Sara Lee Corpn., Carnegie Corpn. of New York; Professorial Lecturer, Northwestern Univ., Medill School of Journalism; mem. Int. Advisory Bd., Pan American World Airways; Dir. Foote, Cone and Belding Communications, CBS Inc., Encyclopaedia Britannica; Trustee Northwestern Univ. 1975-87, Univ. of Notre Dame; Chair. Arthur Andersen & Co. Public Review Bd. 1974-83; Chair. Public Broadcasting Service 1978-80; Hon. LL.D. (Northwestern Univ.) 1965, (Wisconsin) 1963, (Brandeis) 1963, (Columbia Coll.) 1972; Democrat. *Publications:* Presidential Television (co-author), Equal Time: The Private Broadcaster and the Public Interest (co-author) 1976. *Address:* Sidley & Austin, 1 First National Plaza, Chicago, Ill.; 179 E. Lake Shore Drive, Chicago, Ill., U.S.A. (Home). *Telephone:* (312) 853-7555 (Office).

MINOWA, Noboru, M.D.; Japanese politician; b. 5 March 1924, Hokkaido; ed. Hokkaido Univ.; mem. House of Reps. 1967-; Parl. Vice-Minister of Defence 1972-73; Chair. Standing Cttee. on Transport, House of Reps. 1978-79; Deputy Sec.-Gen. Liberal-Democratic Party 1980; Minister of Posts and Telecommunications 1981-82. *Publication:* book on defence. *Address:* c/o Liberal-Democratic Party, 7, 2-chome, Hirakawacho, Chiyoda-ku, Tokyo, Japan.

MINTAREDJA, Hadji Mohamad Sjafa'at, LL.M.; Indonesian lawyer and diplomatist; b. 17 Feb. 1921, Bogor, Java; s. of Mohamad Sjafe'i Mintaredja and Halimah Emon; m. Siti Romlah Abdulkadir 1945; four s. three d.; ed. Gadjahmada Univ., Leiden Univ., Netherlands, and Univ. of Indonesia, Jakarta; mem. Bd. of many nat. youth movements 1936-44; founder Himpunan Mahasiswa Islam; Judge, Court in Bandung 1944-46; Chief, Legal Dept., Foreign Exchange Control 1950-55; in private business (import, export, banking and industry) 1957-65; Pres. and Dir. of two state construction companies 1966-68; mem. of Bd. Muhammadiyah 1965-71; Chair. Partai Muslimin Indonesia 1970; Minister of State 1968-71; Minister of Social Affairs 1971-78; Gen. Exec. Chair. Partai Persatuan Pembangunan 1973-78; Amb. to Turkey 1980-84. *Publications:* Moslem Society and Politics in Indonesia 1971; many articles in Indonesian magazines and journals. *Leisure interests:* sports, reading, driving cars. *Address:* c/o Ministry of Foreign Affairs, Jalan Taman Pejambon 6, Jakarta, Indonesia.

MINTER, Alan; British boxer (retd.); b. 17 Aug. 1951, Penge, London; s. of Sidney and Anne Minter; m. Lorraine Bidwell 1974; one s. one d.; ed. Sarah Robinson School, Ifield; amateur boxer 1965-72; Amateur Boxing Assoc. (A.B.A.) champion 1971; Olympic bronze medallist 1972; 145 amateur fights, 125 wins; professional boxer 1972-82; won British middleweight championship 1975; won Lonsdale Belt outright 1976; won European championship from Germano Valsecchi Feb. 1977, lost it to Gratien Tonna Sept. 1977; forfeited British title Feb. 1977, regained it Nov. 1977; won vacant European title v. Angelo Jacopucci July 1978, retained it v. Tonna Nov. 1978; relinquished British title Nov. 1978; won world middleweight title from Vito Antuofermo, Las Vegas March 1980 (first British boxer to win a world championship in U.S.A. for 63 years); retained title v. Antuofermo June 1980, lost it to Marvin Hagler Sept. 1980; lost European title to Tony Sibson Sept. 1981; retd. from boxing Feb. 1982. *Leisure interest:* golf. *Publication:* Minter: An Autobiography 1980.

MINTOFF, Dominic, B.SC., B.E.&A., M.A.; Maltese politician; b. 6 Aug. 1916, Cospicua; s. of Lawrence Mintoff and Concetta née Farrugia (deceased); m. Moyra de Vere Bentinck 1947; two d.; ed. Univs. of Malta and Oxford; civil engineer in Great Britain 1941-43; practised in Malta as architect 1943-; rejoined and helped reorganize Maltese Labour Party 1944; elected to Council of Govt. and Exec. Council 1945; mem. Legis. Assembly 1947-; Deputy Leader of Labour Party, Deputy Prime Minister and Minister for Works and Reconstruction 1947-49; resigned Ministry, Leader of Labour Party 1949-85; Prime Minister and Minister of Finance 1955-58; Leader of the Opposition 1962-71; Prime Minister 1971-84, also Minister of Foreign and Commonwealth Affairs 1971-81 (redesignated Ministry of Foreign Affairs 1978) of the Interior 1976-81, 1983-84; Special Adviser to Prime Minister 1985-87; Chair. Malta Counter Trade Co. Ltd. *Publications:* several scientific, literary and artistic works. *Leisure interests:* swimming, water skiing, bocci, horse riding. *Address:* "The Olives", Xintill Street, Tarxien, Malta.

MINTON, Yvonne Fay, C.B.E.; Australian mezzo-soprano; b. 4 Dec. 1938, Sydney; d. of R. T. Minton; m. William Barclay 1965; one s. one d.; ed. Sydney Conservatorium of Music and studied in London with H. Cummings and Joan Cross; sang with several opera groups in London; début Covent Garden 1965, Prin. Mezzo-soprano 1965-71; U.S. début, Metropolitan Opera, New York (Octavian in Der Rosenkavalier) 1973; Guest Artist, Cologne Opera 1969-, Australian Opera 1972-73, also with Hamburg State Opera, and at Bayreuth, Paris, Salzburg, Chicago and San Francisco; recordings include Der Rosenkavalier, Figaro, La Clemenza di Tito, Mozart's Requiem, Elgar's The Kingdom; many concert appearances; created role of Thea in Tippett's The Knot Garden 1970; Hon. R.A.M. *Leisure interests:* reading, gardening. *Address:* c/o Ingpen and Williams, 14 Kensington Court, London, W.8, England. *Telephone:* 01-937 5158.

MINTZ, Shlomo; Israeli (Russian-born) violinist; b. 30 Oct. 1957, Moscow; s. of Abraham Mintz and Eve (Labko) Mintz; m. Corina Ciacci; one s.; ed. Juilliard School of Music, New York; went to Israel when very young;

many concert tours; Premio Accademia Musicale Chigiana, Siena, Italy 1984. *Recordings include:* Violin Concertos by Mendelssohn and Bruch (Grand Prix du Disque, Diapason d'Or) 1981, J. S. Bach Complete Sonatas and Partitas for Solo Violin, The Miraculous Mandarin by Bartok (with Chicago Symphony Orchestra, conducted by Abbado), Compositions and Arrangements by Kreisler (with Clifford Benson, piano), Twenty-four Caprices by Paganini, Two Violin Concertos by Prokofiev (with London Symphony Orchestra, conducted by Abbado), The Four Seasons by Vivaldi (with Stern, Perlman, Mehta). *Address:* ICM Artists Ltd., 40 West 57th Street, New York, N.Y. 10019, U.S.A.

MIODOWICZ, Alfred; Polish metallurgist, trade union leader; b. 28 June 1929, Poznań; s. of Alfred Miodowicz and Elżbieta Miodowicz; m. Aldona Miodowicz; active mem. Fighting Youth Union 1947-48, Polish Youth Union (ZMP) 1948-52, including Chair. ZMP Voivodship Bd. Cracow; mem. trade unions 1948-; blast-furnace worker, W. Lenin Ironworks, Cracow-Nowa Huta 1952-, active mem. Works Council in the 1960s, mem. Polish United Workers' Party (PZPR) 1959-; Founding mem. Polish Ergonomical Soc. 1977; mem. Polish Fed. of Eng. Asscns.; Chair., Fed. of Metallurgists' Trade Unions 1983-87; Chair. Programme Comm. of Initiative Group, All-Poland Trade Union Agreement (OPZZ) 1984, Chair. OPZZ Nov. 1984-; Deputy to Seym (Parl.) 1985-; mem. Seym Comm. of Econ. Plan, Budget and Finance; mem. Council of State 1985-86; mem. PZPR Cen. Cttee. 1986-, mem. Political Bureau PZPR Cen. Cttee. 1986-; Chair. Comm. for Civic Proposals, Complaints and Signals of PZPR Cen. Cttee.; mem. Gen. Council and Bureau of WFTU 1986-; Kt's and Commdr.'s Cross Order of Polonia Restituta, Gold Cross of Merit, Meritorious Metallurgist of Polish People's Repub. *Leisure interests:* jogging, skiing, roller-skating. *Address:* Ogólnopolskie Porozumienie Związków Zawodowych, ul. Kopernika 36/40, 00-328 Warsaw, Poland. *Telephone:* 26-46-76 (Office).

MIQUEL, Pierre Gabriel Roger; French social historian, broadcaster and administrator; b. 30 June 1930, Montluçon, Allier; s. of Jean Miguel and Suzanne Montagne; m. Maryvonne Jaume 1956; three s.; ed. Lycée de Montluçon, Lycée Henri-IV, Paris, Univ. de Paris; teacher, Lycée d'Avignon 1955-56, de Melun 1956-57, Carnot, Paris 1958-59; Asst. Faculté des lettres, Univ. de Paris 1961-64, Asst. lecturer, Nanterre 1964-70; lecturer Faculté des lettres, Univ. de Lyon 1970-71, Head Dept. Humanities 1971-72, Head Dept. TV Documentaries 1972-74; lecturer Inst. d'etudes politiques, Paris 1970-70; Prof. of Mass Communications, Sorbonne 1975-, fmr. Admin. Bibliothèque Nat.; at Ministry of Works 1957-58, Ministry of Co-operation 1959-61; Head of Documentaries Antenne 2 1975-; Pres. Inst. pratique de journalisme 1978-; Chevalier Palmes académiques, Légion d'honneur, Officer, Arts et Lettres, Diplome d'études superieures de philosophie, Agrégé d'histoire, Docteur d'Etat. *Publications:* numerous books on social and media history, including L'affaire Dreyfus 1959, Poincaré 1961, La paix de Versailles et l'opinion politique française 1971, Histoire de la radio et de la télévision 1973, Histoire de la France 1976, La véritable histoire des Français 1977, Les oubliés de l'histoire 1978, Les guerres de religion 1980, La quatrième république 1982, La grande guerre 1983, Histoire de la radio et de la télévision, au temps de la grande guerre 1984, La seconde guerre mondiale 1986. *Leisure interest:* collecting replicas (in tin) of soldiers of the First Empire. *Address:* 24 rue de la Gare, 77135 Pontcarré, France (Home).

MIRDHA, Ram Niwas, M.A.; Indian politician; b. 24 Aug. 1924, Rajasthan; ed. Allahabad and Lucknow Univs.; mem. Rajasthan State Legis. Ass. 1953, Minister of Agric., Irrigation and Transport 1954, Speaker of Ass. 1957-67; mem. Rajya Sabha 1970, Deputy Chair. 1977-80, Minister of State in Ministry of Home Affairs 1970-74, Minister of Defence Production 1974-75, Minister of Supply and Rehabilitation 1975-77, Minister of State and Irrigation 1983-84, Minister of State for External Affairs 1984, Minister of State for Ministry of Communications 1984-86, Minister of Textiles Feb. 1988-, of Health and Family Welfare 1989-; Rep. of India at several int. confs.; Pres. Indian Fed. of UN Asscns., Hon. Pres. World Fed. of UN Asscns.; fmr. Pres. All India Council of Sports; Chair. Nat. Acad. of Arts 1976-80. *Address:* Ministry of Textiles, Udyog Bhavan, New Delhi 110011, India. *Telephone:* (11) 301 1409, 301 6540.

MIRGHANI, AHMAD ALI AL-; Sudanese politician; mem. Democratic Unionist Party; Pres. Sudan Governing Council May 1986. *Address:* Democratic Unionist Party, Khartoum, Sudan.

MIRICIOIU, Nelly; Romanian opera singer; b. 31 March 1952, Adjud; d. of Voicu Miricioiu and Maria Miricioiu; ed. Conservatoire G. Enesco, Iassy; professional début as Queen of the Night in The Magic Flute in Romania 1970; western European début as Violetta in Scottish Opera production of La Traviata 1981; début at Convent Garden as Nedda in Pagliacci 1982, at La Scala as Lucia in Lucia di Lammermoor 1983; has since appeared at many of the other opera houses of the world including Verona, San Francisco, Vienna, Berlin, Hamburg, Madrid, Florence, and in recitals and concerts; repertoire includes Mimi (La Bohème), Julietta (I Capuleti e I Montecchi), Gilda (Rigoletto), Marguerite and Elena (Mephistofele), Michaela (Carmen), Marguerite (Faust), Violetta (La Traviata), Manon Lescaut; repertoire also includes Anna Bolena and Lucrezia Borgia (by Donizetti), Norma (Bellini), Tancredi (Rossini); made 1st recording, recital Wigmore Hall, London 1986; winner of 10 int. competitions. *Leisur* *interests:* literature, television, cooking, socializing. *Address:* 53 Midhurst Avenue, Muswell Hill, London, N10, England. *Telephone:* 01-883 8596.

MIRO ROMERO, Pilar; Spanish film director; b. 20 April 1940, Madrid; Dir.-Gen. of Cinematography, Ministry of Culture 1982–85; Dir. Gen. Ente Publico Radiotelevision Española 1986–89; has directed for film, TV, stage and opera; various hons. and awards. *Films directed:* La Peticion 1976, El Crimen de Cuenca 1979, Gary Cooper-Que Estas en Los Cielos 1981, Hablamos-Esta Noche 1982, Werther 1986. *Leisure interest:* opera. *Address:* Plaza del Rey, 28004 Madrid, Spain.

MIRONOV, Vasiliy Petrovich; Soviet politician and industrial specialist; b. 16 Jan. 1925; ed. Polytech. Inst., Donetsk; fitter in metal-construction plant 1943–47; party work for Ukrainian komsomol in Donetsk 1947–55; mem. CPSU 1949–; party organizer in industrial trust 1955–57; First Sec., Kirov. Regional Cttee., Ukrainian CP 1960–61; Chair., Exec. Cttee., Donetsk City Workers' Soviet 1961–76; Deputy to Ukrainian S.S.R. Supreme Soviet 1971–82; First Sec., Donetsk City Cttee. Ukrainian CP 1976–82; mem. Cen. Cttee. of Ukrainian CP 1976–; First Sec., Donetsk Dist. Cttee. and mem. Mil. Council, Kiev Mil. Dist. 1982–; cand. mem. Politburo of Cen. Cttee. Ukrainian CP 1983–84, mem. 1984–; Deputy to Council of Nationalities, U.S.S.R. Supreme Soviet; mem. of Cen. Cttee. CPSU 1986–. Order of Lenin 1985, U.S.S.R. State Prize. *Address:* Central Committee of the Communist Party of the Soviet Union, Stenaya pl. 4, Moscow, U.S.S.R.

MIRONOVA, Zoya Vasiliyevna; Soviet chemical engineer and diplomatist (retd.); b. 26 Feb. 1912, Yadrin, Chuvash; ed. Moscow Inst. of Chemical Tech.; Deputy Mayor of Moscow 1951–59; then Deputy Perm. Soviet Rep. to UN and Soviet Rep. on UN Cttee. on Women's Rights; then at Ministry of Foreign Affairs, Moscow; Perm. Rep. of U.S.S.R. at UN European Office and other int. orgs. in Geneva 1966–83; rank of Amb.; State Prize (for work on producing a rare metal and its compounds) 1950; Red Banner of Labour (twice), Badge of Honour, Order of the October Revolution, etc. *Address:* The Kremlin, Moscow, U.S.S.R.

MIROSHKIN, Oleg Semenovich; Soviet politician and diplomatist; b. 1928; ed. Moscow Oil Inst.; mechanic, Deputy Dir. of W. Kazakh Geological Exploration Div. 1957–70; mem. CPSU 1959–; Head of Section of Guryev District Cttee. of Kazakh CP 1970–73; Second Sec., Mangyshlak District Cttee. 1973–76; Sec., Second Sec., Cen. Cttee. of Kazakh CP 1976–79; Amb. to Zambia 1987–; mem. of CPSU Cen. Cttee. 1981–; Deputy to U.S.S.R. Supreme Soviet. *Address:* U.S.S.R. Embassy, Plot 6407, Diplomatic Triangle, P.O.B. 32355, Lusaka, Zambia.

MIRREN, Helen; British actress; b. 26 July 1945; London; first experience with Nat. Youth Theatre culminating in appearance as Cleopatra in Antony and Cleopatra, Old Vic 1965; joined Royal Shakespeare Co. (RSC) 1967 to play Castiza in The Revenger's Tragedy and Diana in All's Well that Ends Well. *Other roles include:* Cressida in Troilus and Cressida, RSC, Stratford 1968; Hero in Much Ado About Nothing, Stratford 1968; Win-the-Fight Littlewit in Bartholomew Fair, Aldwych 1969; Lady Anne in Richard III, Stratford, Ophelia in Hamlet, Julia in The Two Gentlemen of Verona, Stratford 1970 (the last part also at Aldwych); Tatyana in Enemies, RSC, Aldwych 1971; title role in Miss Julie, Elyane in The Balcony, The Place 1971; with Peter Brook's Centre Internationale de Recherches Théâtrales, Africa and U.S.A. 1972–73; Lady Macbeth, RSC, Stratford 1974 and Aldwych 1975; Maggie in Teeth 'n' Smiles, Royal Court 1975; Nina in The Seagull and Ella in The Bed Before Yesterday, Lyric for Lyric Theatre Co. 1975, Antony and Cleopatra, The Roaring Girl, RSC, Barbican 1983, Extremities (Evening Standard Award) 1984, Madame Bovary 1987, Two Way Mirror 1989. *Films include:* Age of Consent 1969, Savage Messiah, O Lucky Man! 1973, Caligula 1977, The Long Good Friday, Excalibur 1981, Cal (Best Actress, Cannes) 1984, 2010 1985, White Nights 1986, Heavenly Pursuits 1986, The Mosquito Coast 1987, Pascali's Island 1988, Bethune: The Making of a Hero 1989, The cook, the thief, his wife and her lover 1989; Dir. Othello, Johannesburg. *TV includes:* Miss Julie, The Apple Cart, The Little Minister, As You Like It, Mrs. Reinhardt, Soft Targets 1982. *Address:* c/o Al Parker, 55 Park Lane, London, W.1, England.

MIRRLEES, James Alexander, M.A., PH.D., F.B.A.; British professor of economics; b. 5 July 1936, Scotland; s. of the late George B. M. Mirrlees; m. Gillian M. Hughes 1961; two d.; ed. Edinburgh Univ. and Trinity Coll., Cambridge; Adviser, M.I.T. Center for Int. Studies, New Delhi 1962–63; Asst. Lecturer in Econs. and Fellow, Trinity Coll., Univ. of Cambridge 1963, Univ. Lecturer 1965; Research Assoc. Pakistan Inst. of Devt. Econs. 1966–67; Fellow, Nuffield Coll. and Edgeworth Prof. of Econs. Univ. of Oxford 1968–; Adviser to Govt. of Swaziland 1963; Visiting Prof. M.I.T. 1968, 1970, 1976, 1987; Ford Visiting Prof., Univ. of Calif., Berkeley 1986; mem̄ Treasury Cttee. on Policy Optimization 1976–78; Pres. Econometric S⸏⸏ ̇2; Foreign Hon. mem. American Acad. of Arts and Sciences; Hon. ̇ ̇erican Econ. Asscn.; Hon. D.Litt. (Warwick) 1982. *Publications:* ᶜ three books and articles in academic journals. *Leisure interests:* ̇l, computing. *Address:* Nuffield College, Oxford (Office); 11 ̇ ̇rive, Oxford, OX2 7NT, England (Home). *Telephone:* (0865) ̇(0865) 52436 (Home).

̇ ̇ard Mikhailovich; Soviet composer; b. 1921; ed. Yere- ̇ ̇teacher Komitas Conservatory, Yerevan, Armenia

1948–; Prof. 1965–; mem. CPSU 1952; Pres. of Union of Composers of Armenian S.S.R. 1957–; Sec. of U.S.S.R. Union of Composers 1962–; mem. Cen. Cttee. of Armenian CP 1964–; Minister of Posts and Telecommunications, Armenian S.S.R. 1983–; Deputy of Supreme Soviet of Armenian S.S.R.C.P.; named Armenian People's Artist 1963; U.S.S.R. People's Artist 1981. *Compositions include:* Soviet Armenia (cantata); To the Heroes of the War (Symphonic poem), Symphony of Light (ballet), string quartet, romances, instrumental pieces, songs, film-music. *Address:* Demirchyan Street 25, Apt. 9, 37500 Yerevan, Armenian S.S.R., U.S.S.R.

MISCHNICK, Wolfgang; German politician; b. 29 Sept. 1921; s. of Walter Mischnick and Marie Rölig; m. Christine Dietzsch 1949; two s. one d.; ed. High School, Dresden; co-founder, Liberal Democratic Party, Dresden 1945; town official, Dresden 1946–48; mem. Cen. Cttee. of Liberal Democratic Party, Soviet Zone 1946–48; fled to Fed. Germany 1948; mem. Prov. Assembly, Hesse, 1954–57, Parl. Leader of FDP; Fed. Chair. FDP Youth Movement and Ed. Stimmen der jungen Generation 1954–57; mem. Bundestag 1957–; Deputy Chair. FDP, Hesse 1957–67, Chair. 1967–77; Fed. Minister for Refugees 1961–63; Deputy Chair. FDP 1964–, FDP Chair. in Bundestag 1968–. *Address:* Bundeshaus, Görresstrasse 15, 5300 Bonn, Federal Republic of Germany.

MISHIN, Vasiliy Pavlovich; Soviet engineer; b. 18 Jan. 1917, Orekhovo-Zuevo, Moscow Region; ed. Moscow Aviation Inst.; specialist in applied mechanics; Prof. Moscow Aviation Inst. 1959–; Deputy of Supreme Soviet R.S.F.S.R. 1966–; mem. CPSU 1943–; Corresp. mem. U.S.S.R. Acad. of Sciences 1958–66, mem. 1966–; Hero of Socialist Labour 1956; Order of Lenin (three), Order of October Revolution and other decorations. *Publications:* numerous articles in the field of applied mathematics. *Address:* U.S.S.R. Academy of Sciences, 14 Leninsky Prospekt, Moscow, U.S.S.R.

MISHIN, Viktor Maksimovich; Soviet politician; b. 1943; ed. V. V. Kuybyshev Inst. of Eng. and Construction, Moscow; factory work 1961–67; mem. CPSU 1967–; engineer 1967–68; Second Sec. of Moskvoretsky, First Sec. of Sovietsky Moscow City Komsomol Cttees. 1968–71; First Sec. Moscow City Komsomol Cttees. 1971–73, Head of Section 1973–78; mem. Politburo of All-Union Komsomol Cen. Cttee. 1978–, Sec. 1978–82, First Sec. 1982–; mem. Presidium of U.S.S.R. –1986. *Address:* All-Union Komsomol Central Committee, Kremlin, Moscow, U.S.S.R.

MISHRA, Brajesh Chandra; Indian diplomatist; b. 29 Sept. 1928; entered Indian Foreign Service 1951; Third Sec., Karachi; Second Sec., Rangoon; First Sec., Brussels; Under-Sec. Ministry of Foreign Affairs 1956–57, Deputy Sec. 1957–60; First Sec., then Counsellor, Perm. Mission of India at UN, New York 1964–69; Minister and Chargé d'affaires, Peking 1969–73; Amb. and Perm Rep. to UN, Geneva 1973–77; Amb. to Indonesia 1977–79; Perm. Rep. to UN 1979–81; Consultant to UN from Govt. of India April 1981–; UN Commr. for Namibia and Asst. Sec.-Gen. 1982–87. *Address:* c/o Ministry of Foreign Affairs, New Delhi 110011, India.

MIŚKIEWICZ, Benon, H.H.D.; Polish historian and politician; b. 27 May 1930, Baranowicze; s. of Stanisław and Stanisława Miśkiewicz; m. Alina Jankowska 1954; four d.; ed. Poznań Univ.; teacher industrial school, Inowrocław 1949–50; lecturer, mil. school of Poznań Univ. 1951–55 and of Higher School of Physical Training, Poznań 1955–57; teacher, Adam Mickiewicz Univ., Poznań 1955–, Asst. Prof. 1964–70, Pro-Rector 1968–72, Rector 1972–81, Head, Mil. History Research Centre 1969–, Extraordinary Prof. 1970–76, Ordinary Prof. 1976–; Chair. Mil. History Comm. of Historical Sciences Cttee., Polish Acad. of Sciences 1978–86; Minister of Science, Higher Educ. and Tech. 1982–84, of Science and Higher Educ. 1985–87; mem. Polish United Workers' Party (PZPR) 1949–; State Prize (1st Class), Prizes of Minister of Nat. Defence and of Minister of Science, Higher Educ. and Tech.; Kt.'s, Commdr.'s and Commdr.'s with Star Cross Order of Polonia Restituta, Order of Banner of Labour (2nd Class) and other decorations. *Publications:* O metodyce badań historyczno-wojskowych 1960, Studia nad obroną polskiej granicy zachodniej w okresie wczesnofeudalnym 1961, Rozwój stałych punktów oporu w Polsce do połowy XV wieku 1964, Program rozwoju nauki historyczno-wojskowej w Polsce 1976, Z problematyki Szkolnictwa Wyższego, Dydaktyka i Wychowanie, Kształcenie, Kadr, Organizacja, Wybór Prac, Poznań 1980, Uniwersytet Poznański—fakty, refleksje, wspomnienia 1983, Wstęp do badań historycznych 1985. *Leisure interest:* hunting. *Address:* Waliszewo 4, 62-265 Stawno, Poland.

MISSOFFE, François; French industrialist and politician; b. 13 Oct. 1919, Toulon; s. of Jacques and Simone (née Tardieu) Missoffe; m. Hélène de Mitry 1948; two s. six d.; ed. Prytanée militaire de La Flèche; army service 1940–46; UNR (Union for the New Republic); elected Deputy for Seine, Nat. Assembly 1958, 1962, for Paris 1967, 1968, 1973; Gen. Treas. UNR 1959; Sec. of State for Domestic Trade April-Oct. 1962, Minister of Repatriation 1962–64; Amb. to Japan 1964–66; Minister for Youth and Sports 1966–68; Special Envoy of the French Govt. in Asiatic Countries 1973; Pres. A.C.E.C.O. (Assen. pour la Compensation des Echanges Commerciaux), Trans Pacific Fund; Pres., Dir.-Gen. Union pour le Financement des régions et de la mer 1986–; Pres. Supervisory Bd. Pirelli; Dir. Banque Demachy; Officier, Légion d'honneur; Croix de guerre; Médaille de la Résistance. *Address:* 38 rue Boileau, 75016, Paris, France (Home).

MISTLER, Jean; French writer; b. 1 Sept. 1897, Sorèze; s. of Albert and Mme. (née d'Auriol de Montagut) Mistler; m. Stéphane Baillot 1927; one d.; ed. Lycées de Carcassonne and Henri IV, Paris and Ecole normale supérieure; Cultural Attaché, Budapest, and Priv. Dozent Univ. of Budapest; Head of Section, Ministry of Foreign Affairs 1926; Deputy for Aude, Nat. Assembly 1928-40; Under-Sec. of State for Fine Arts 1932; Minister of Posts, Telecommunications and Commerce 1933-34; Pres. of Comm. for Foreign Affairs 1936-40; Co-Dir. Editions du Rocher 1944-47; Dir.-Gen. Maison du livre français 1947-60; writer on music and literature, L'aurore 1954-79; Dir. Dept. of Gen. Literature, Librairie Hachette 1964-68; Dir. Soc. Fulmen, Cie. Européenne d'accumulateurs, Cie. électrofinancière, Cie. Industrielles des Téléphones; mem. Acad. française 1966-, Perm. Sec. 1973-85, Vice-Pres. Inst. de France 1973; mem. Conseil supérieur des lettres, admin. cttee. Centre national des lettres 1974-; mem. Haut Comité de la langue française 1975-. *Publications include:* Châteaux en Bavière 1925, La vie d'Hoffmann 1927, Vienne 1931, La maison du Docteur Clifton 1932, Dictées de la nuit 1943, Le vampire 1944, La femme nue et le veau d'or 1945, La symphonie inachevée, Hoffmann le fantastique 1950, A Bayreuth avec Richard Wagner 1960, Epinal et l'imagerie populaire, Le 14 Juillet, Le bout du monde 1964, Les orgues de Saint Sauveur, Gaspard Hauser, La route des étangs, Le naufrage du Monte-Christo, L'ami des pauvres 1974, Gare de l'est 1975, Bon poids 1976, Hugo et Wagner face à leur destin 1977, Richard Wagner et Bayreuth 1980, Sous la Coupole 1981, Faubourg Antoine 1982, Le jeune homme qui rôde 1984, and numerous articles for L'aurore 1954-, and Revue de Paris 1928-40. *Address:* L'Académie Française, 23 quai de Conti, 75006 Paris; 1 rue de Seine, 75006 Paris, France.

MISTRY, Dhruva, M.A.; Indian sculptor; b. 1 Jan. 1957, Kanjari; s. of Pramodray Mistry and Kantaben Mistry; ed. Univ. of Baroda and R.C.A., London; artist in residence Churchill Coll., Cambridge 1984-85; Freelance Sculptor working at Nigel Greenwood Gallery, London; sculptor in residence, Victoria and Albert Museum, London 1988; one-man exhbns. at Kettle's Yard Gallery, Cambridge 1985, Arnolfini, Bristol 1986, Mostyn Art Gallery, Llandudno 1986, Walker Art Gallery, Liverpool 1986, Nigel Greenwood Gallery, London 1987, Collins Gallery, Strathclyde 1988; Public collections Tate Gallery, British Council, Arts Council, Victoria and Albert Museum, Walker Art Gallery, Nat. Museum of Wales. *Publications:* (exhbn. catalogues) Sculptures and Drawings 1985, Cross-sections 1988. *Leisure interests:* photography, reading, walking. *Address:* The Cottage, Dodds Farm, Ingatestone, Essex, CM4 0NW, England. *Telephone:* (0277) 35 44 36.

MITA, Katsushige, B.E.E.; Japanese business executive; b. 6 April 1924, Tokyo; s. of Yoshitaro and Fuji Mita; m. Toriko Miyata 1957; two d.; ed. Univ. of Tokyo; joined Hitachi Ltd. 1949; Gen. Man. Omika Works Aug.-Nov. 1971, Kanagawa Works 1971-75; Dir. 1975; Man. Computer Group 1976-78, Exec. Man. Dir. 1977-79, Sr. Exec. Man. Dir. 1979-80, Exec. Vice-Pres. 1980-81; Pres. and Rep. Dir. Hitachi Ltd. June 1981-; Pres. Electronic Industries Asscn. of Japan 1987-. *Leisure interests:* golf, gardening. *Address:* 2423-277, Nara-machi, Midori-ku, Yokohama-shi, Kanagawa-ken, 227, Japan (Home). *Telephone:* 045 961 7733.

MITCHELL, Alexander George, C.B.E., M.A., PH.D.; Australian academic; b. 13 Oct. 1911, Kempsey, N.S.W.; s. of Robert George Mitchell and Martha Matilda (née Keast) Mitchell; m. Una Marion White 1937; two d.; ed. Smith Town Public School, Morpeth Public School, Maitland Boys High School, Univ. of Sydney, Sydney Teachers' Coll., Univ. of London; lecturer in English, Univ. of Sydney 1940, McCaughey Prof. of Early English Literature and Language 1948, Deputy Vice-Chancellor, 1961; Vice-Chancellor, Macquarie Univ., Sydney 1964; Deputy Chair., State Cttee. on Tech. and Further Educ., N.S.W. 1975; Deputy Chancellor, N.S.W. Inst. of Tech. 1981; D.Litt. h.c. (Macquarie Univ.); Fellow Australian Coll. of Educ. *Publications:* The Pronunciation of English in Australia, Lady Meed and the Art of Piers Plowman 1957, Spoken English 1958, The Speech of Australian Adolescents (with A. Delbridge) 1965. *Address:* 1/202 Longueville Road, Lane Cove, N.S.W. 2066, Australia.

MITCHELL, Arthur; American dancer and choreographer; b. 27 March 1934, New York; s. of Arthur and Willie Mae Mitchell; ed. School of American Ballet; Prin. New York City Ballet 1955-; Dir. and Choreographer Dance Theater of Harlem 1969-; with John Butler Co. 1955, William Dollar's Ballet Theatre Workshop; Choreographer (with Rod Alexander) Shinbone Alley, Newport Jazz Festival; Dancer, Choreographer and Actor Spoleto Festival of Two Worlds 1960; teacher Dance Karel Shook Studio, Melissa Hayden School, Cedarhurst, Long Island, Jones-Haywood School of Ballet, Washington; Annual Award for Excellence, John F. Kennedy Center for Performing Arts 1980, American Dance Guild Award 1982, Pres.'s Cabinet Award, Univ. of Detroit 1983; has appeared in numerous productions. *Address:* Dance Theater of Harlem, 466 West 152nd Street, New York, N.Y. 10031, U.S.A. (Office).

MITCHELL, Basil George, M.A., D.D., F.B.A.; British academic; b. 9 April 1917, Bath; s. of George William Mitchell and Mary Mitchell; m. Margaret Collin 1950; one s. three d.; ed. King Edward VI School, Southampton and The Queen's Coll., Oxford; served R.N. 1940-46; Lecturer Christ Church, Oxford 1946-47; Fellow and Tutor Keble Coll., Oxford 1947-67; Nolloth Prof. of the Philosophy of the Christian Religion, Oxford Univ. and Fellow

of Oriel Coll. 1968-84, Prof. Emer. 1984-; Stanton Lecturer, Cambridge Univ. 1959-62; Edward Cadbury Lecturer, Birmingham Univ. 1966-67; Gifford Lecturer, Glasgow Univ. 1974-76; Visiting Prof. Princeton Univ., U.S.A. 1963, Colgate Univ., U.S.A. 1976; Nathaniel Taylor Lecturer, Yale Univ., U.S.A. 1986; mem. Church of England Doctrine Comm. 1978-85; Chair. Ian Ramsey Centre, Oxford 1985-; Hon. D.D. (Glasgow); Hon. D.Lit.Hum. (Union Coll., Schenectady). *Publications:* Faith and Logic (Ed.) 1957, Law, Morality and Religion in a Secular Society 1967, The Philosophy of Religion (Ed.) 1971, The Justification of Religious Belief 1973, Morality: Religious and Secular 1980. *Leisure interests:* gardening, travel. *Address:* Oriel College, Oxford, OX1 4EW, England.

MITCHELL, Sir Derek, K.C.B., C.V.O.; British banker and fmr. civil servant; b. 5 March 1922, Wimbledon; s. of the late Sidney Mitchell and Gladys Mitchell; m. Miriam Jackson 1944; one s. two d.; ed. St. Paul's School, London and Christ Church, Oxford; served, Royal Armoured Corps and HQ London District 1942-45; served in H.M. Treasury 1947-63, Principal Private Sec. to Chancellor of the Exchequer 1962-63; Principal Private Sec. to Prime Minister 1964-66; Deputy Under-Sec. of State, Dept. of Econ. Affairs 1966-67, Ministry of Agric., Fisheries and Food 1967-69; Econ. Minister, British Embassy, Washington and Exec. Dir. IBRD, IMF, etc. 1969-72; Second Perm. Sec. (Overseas Finance) H.M. Treasury 1973-77; Sr. Adviser, Shearson Lehman Brothers International 1979-88; Dir. Guinness Mahon 1977-78, Bowater Corpn. 1979-84, Bowater Industries PLC 1984-, Bowater Inc. 1984-, Standard Chartered PLC 1979-; mem. Nat. Theatre Bd. 1977-; Treas. Nat. Theatre Foundation 1982-; mem. Council of Univ. Coll., London 1978-82, Port of London Authority 1979-82, The Observer Ltd. Aug. 1981-; Trustee Nuffield Prov. Hosps. Trust 1978-. *Leisure interests:* opera, concerts, theatre, travelling. *Address:* 9 Holmbush Road, Putney, London, SW15 3LE, England. *Telephone:* 01-788 6581.

MITCHELL, Duncan, M.SC., PH.D.; South African professor of physiology; b. 10 May 1941, Germiston; s. of Thomas and Maud K. (née Abercrombie) Mitchell; m. Lily May Austin 1966; one s. one d.; ed. St. John's Coll., Johannesburg, Univ. of Witwatersrand; mem. scientific staff, Research Org. of Chamber of Mines of South Africa 1964-73, Nat. Inst. for Medical Research, London 1973-75; Prof. of Physiology and Head of Dept., Medical School, Univ. of Witwatersrand 1976-; F.R.S. (S.A.). *Publications:* over 100 papers in thermal physiology. *Leisure interests:* nature conservation, ballet. *Address:* Physiology Dept., Medical School, University of the Witwatersrand, Parktown 2193, South Africa. *Telephone:* (11) 647-2359.

MITCHELL, (Edgar) William John, C.B.E., F.R.S., F.INST.P.; British university professor; b. 25 Sept. 1925, Kingsbridge; s. of late Edgar Mitchell and Caroline Mitchell; m. 1st 1948; one s.; m. 2nd Margaret Constance Davies 1985; one step-s., one step-d.; ed. Sheffield and Bristol Univs.; Research Physicist, Metropolitan Vickers 1946-51, Bristol Univ. 1948-50; Research Fellow, Reading Univ. 1951, Lecturer 1952-56, Reader 1956-61, Prof. 1961-78, Deputy Vice-Chancellor 1976-78; Prof. Experimental Philosophy, Head of Clarendon Lab., Oxford Univ. 1978-88; Personal Chair., Clarendon Lab. 1988-; Chair. U.K. Science and Eng. Research Council 1985-; Fellow, Wadham Coll., Oxford. *Publications:* numerous scientific papers. *Leisure interests:* opera, mountains, food. *Address:* Science and Engineering Research Council, Polaris House, North Star Avenue, Swindon, SN2 1ET, Wilts., England. *Telephone:* (0793) 411000.

MITCHELL, George Francis, M.A., M.SC., F.R.S.; Irish landscape archaeologist; b. 15 Oct. 1912, Dublin; s. of late David W. Mitchell and Frances E. Kirby; m. Lucy M. Gwynn 1940 (died 1987); two d.; ed. High School, Dublin and Trinity Coll., Dublin; various teaching and admin. posts, Trinity Coll., Dublin 1934-65, Prof. of Quaternary Studies 1965-77; Pres. Int. Union for Quaternary Research 1969-73, Royal Irish Acad. 1976-79; hon. mem. and medallist several learned socs,; Hon. D.Sc. (Belfast, Nat. Univ. of Ireland); Fil. Dr. h.c. (Uppsala). *Publications:* Treasures of Irish Art 1977, Shell Guide to Reading the Irish Landscape 1986, Man and Environment in Valencia Island, Co. Kerry 1989. *Leisure interest:* archaeological field-walking. *Address:* School of Botany, Trinity College, Dublin 2 (Office); Townley Hall, Drogheda, Co. Louth, Republic of Ireland (Home). *Telephone:* 01-772941 (Office); 041-34615 (Home).

MITCHELL, George John, B.A., LL.B.; American lawyer and politician; b. 20 Aug. 1933, Waterville, Me.; s. of George J. Mitchell and Mary (née Saad) Mitchell; called to Bar 1960; Trial Attorney U.S. Dept. of Justice, Washington 1960-62; Exec. Asst. to Senator Edmund Muskie (q.v.) 1962-65; partner Jensen & Baird, Portland 1965-77; U.S. Attorney for Maine 1977-79; U.S. Dist. Judge 1979-80; U.S. Senator from Maine 1980-; Chair. Maine Democratic Cttee. 1966-68; mem. Nat. Cttee. Maine 1968-77; Democrat. *Address:* 176 Russell Senate Building, Washington, D.C. 20510, U.S.A.

MITCHELL, James Fitzallen; St. Vincent and the Grenadines politician, agronomist and hotelier; b. 1931, Bequia, Grenadines; s. of Reginald Fitzgerald and Lois Mitchell; m. Patricia Parker 1965; three d.; ed. St. Vincent Grammar School, Imperial Coll. of Tropical Agric., Trinidad and Univ. of British Columbia; Chief Agricultural Officer, St. Vincent 1958-60; Ed. Pest Control Articles and News Summaries, Ministry of Overseas Devt., London 1960-66; joined St. Vincent Labour Party (SVLP) 1966;

M.P. for the Grenadines 1966-72; Minister of Trade, Agric., Labour and Tourism 1967-72 (resgnd.); expelled from SVLP 1972; M.P. (as an ind.) for the Grenadines 1972-79, re-elected in by-election July 1979-; Premier of St. Vincent 1972-74; Prime Minister of St. Vincent and the Grenadines July 1984-, also Minister of Foreign Affairs; f. New Democratic Party 1975. *Address:* Prime Minister's Office, Kingstown, St. Vincent.

MITCHELL, James Richard, P.C., T.D.; Irish politician; b. 19 Oct. 1946, Dublin; s. of Peter Mitchell and Eileen Whelan; m. Patricia Kenny 1973; two s. three d.; ed. Trinity Coll., Dublin; Peace Commr. 1973; mem. Dublin City Council 1974-81; Lord Mayor of Dublin (youngest in post's 800-year history) 1976-77; Alderman, Dublin City Council 1979-81; mem. Dáil Eireann (House of Reps.) for Dublin Ballyfermot 1977, for Dublin West 1981; Shadow Minister for Labour 1977-81, for Public Service Jan.-June 1981; Minister for Justice 1981-82, for Transport, Posts and Telegraphs 1982-84, for Communications 1984-87; Fine Gael Front Bench Spokesman on Social Welfare 1987-1988; Fine Gael Front Bench Spokesman on Labour 1988-. *Publication:* Working Together: A Policy for Industrial Relations. *Leisure interests:* reading, athletics, canoeing, football. *Address:* c/o Dail Eireann, Dublin, Ireland.

MITCHELL, Joan, M.F.A.; American painter; b. 1926, Chicago; d. of James Herbert Mitchell and Marion (née Strobel) Mitchell; ed. Smith Coll., Art Inst., Chicago; one-person shows: Stable Gallery, New York 1952-64, Galerie Fournier, Paris 1967-78, Everson Museum, Syracuse 1972, Whitney Museum, New York 1974, Art Club, Chicago 1974, Carnegie Museum, Pittsburgh 1974, Corcoran Gallery of Art, Washington 1975, Xavier Fourcade Gallery 1981, etc.; group shows include: Acad. of Fine Arts, Philadelphia 1966, Museum of Modern Art, New York 1967, Univ. of Ill. 1967, Jewish Museum, New York 1967, Massachusetts Inst. of Tech., Haus der Kunst, Munich 1981-82, Richard Gray Gallery, Chicago 1981-82, Xavier Fourcade Gallery, New York 1982, Hirshhorn Museum and Sculpture Garden 1980, Biennial Whitney Museum 1983, Museum of Art, Fort Lauderdale 1986; also represented in perm. collections in Europe and across America; recipient Creative Arts citation, Brandeis Univ. 1973; Art Inst. of Chicago Travelling Fellow 1947. *Address:* c/o Xavier Fourcade Gallery, 36 E. 75th Street, New York, N.Y. 10021, U.S.A.

MITCHELL, John Wesley, D.SC., F.R.S.; American solid state physicist; b. 3 Dec. 1913, New Zealand; s. of John W. Mitchell and Lucy R. Snowball; m. 1st Jo Overstreet Long 1968-76, 2nd Virginia Jacobs Hill 1976; one step d. of fmr. marriage; ed. Canterbury Univ. Coll., Christchurch, N.Z. and Univ. of Oxford; Sr. Scientific Officer, Armament Research and Devt. Establishment, Ministry of Supply, U.K. 1940-45; Lecturer in Physics, Univ. of Bristol 1945-47, Reader in Experimental Physics 1947-59; Prof. of Physics, Univ. of Va. 1959-65, William Barton Rogers Prof. of Physics 1965-79, Sr. Research Fellow and Prof. Emer. 1979-; Dir. Nat. Chemical Lab. 1963-64; hon. mem. Soc. of Photographic Scientists and Engs., Soc. of Photographic Science and Tech. of Japan; corresp. mem. Deutsche Gesellschaft für Photographie; several awards for photographic science. *Publications:* more than 100 publications in scientific journals on theory of photography sensitivity, plastic deformation of metals, and other areas of solid state physics. *Leisure interests:* foreign languages, colour photography. *Address:* Department of Physics, University of Virginia, Charlottesville, Va. 22901 (office); 327 Kent Road, Charlottesville, Va. 22903, U.S.A. (Home). *Telephone:* (804) 924-3781 (Office); (804) 293-3771. (Home).

MITCHELL, Joni (Roberta Joan Anderson); Canadian singer, songwriter; b. 7 Nov. 1943, Fort Macleod, Alberta; d. of William A. and Myrtle (née McKee) Anderson; m. 1st Chuck Mitchell 1965 (divorced), m. 2nd Larry Klein 1982; ed. Alberta Coll.; *albums include:* Songs to a Seagull, Clouds, Ladies of the Canyon, Blue, For the Roses, Court and Spark, Miles of Aisles, The Hissing of Summer Lawns, Hejira, Don Juan's Reckless Daughter, Mingus, Shadows and Light 1980, Dog Eat Dog 1986, Chalk Mark in a Rainstorm 1988; *songs include:* Both Sides Now, Michael from Mountains, Urge for Going, Circle Game; Jazz Album of Year and Rock-Blues Album of Year for Mingus, Downbeat Magazine 1979. *Address:* c/o Geffens Records Distribution, Warner Bros., 3300 Warner Blvd., Burbank, Calif 91510, U.S.A.

MITCHELL, Joseph (Quincy); American journalist and writer; b. 27 July 1908, Fairmont, N.C.; s. of Averette Nance and Elizabeth A. (née Parker) Mitchell; m. Therese D. E. Jacobsen 1931; two d.; ed. Univ. of North Carolina; reporter New York World 1929-30, New York Herald Tribune 1930-31, New York World Telegram 1931-38; contrib. to New Yorker magazine 1938-; recipient N.C. Gold Medal for Literature 1984; mem. American Acad., Inst of Arts and Letters (Sec. 1972-74), Soc. of Architectural Historians, Soc. of Industrial Archaeology, Friends of Cast-Iron Architecture, James Joyce Soc., Gypsy Lore Soc. *Publications:* My Ears Are Bent 1938, McSorley's Wonderful Saloon 1943, Old Mr. Flood 1948, The Bottom of the Harbor 1960, Apologies to the Iroquois 1960, Joe Gould's Secret (with Edmund Wilson) 1965. *Address:* The New Yorker, 25 W. 43rd Street, New York, N.Y. 10036 (Office); 44 W. 10th Street, New York, N.Y. 10011, U.S.A. (Home).

MITCHELL, Julian; British author; b. 1 May 1935; s. of the late William Moncur Mitchell and of Christine Mitchell (née Browne); ed. Winchester and Wadham Coll., Oxford; mem. Literature Panel, Arts Council 1966-69;

John Llewellyn Rhys Prize 1965; Somerset Maugham Award 1966. *Publications: novels:* Imaginary Toys 1961, A Disturbing Influence 1962, As Far As You Can Go 1963, The White Father 1964, A Circle of Friends 1966, The Undiscovered Country 1968; *biography:* Jennie: Lady Randolph Churchill (with Peregrine Churchill); *plays:* Half Life 1977, The Enemy Within 1980, Another Country 1981 (SWET Award 1982, filmed 1984), Francis 1983, After Aida (or Verdi's Messiah) 1986; television plays and adaptations; translation of Pirandello's Henry IV. *Address:* 2 Castle Rise, Llanvaches, Newport, Gwent, NP6 3BS, Wales. *Telephone:* (0633) 400848.

MITCHELL, Keith Claudius, M.S., PH.D.; Grenada politician; ed. Presentation Coll., Grenada, Univ. of West Indies, Howard Univ. and American Univ., Washington; cand. for Grenada Nat. Party in 1972 elections; Gen. Sec. New Nat. Party (NNP) 1984-89, Leader Jan. 1989-; Minister of Communication, Works, Public Utilities, Transportation, of Civil Aviation and Energy 1984-87, of Communications, Works, Public Utilities, Co-operatives, Community Devt., Women's Affairs and Civil Aviation March 1988-; Capt. Grenada Nat. Cricket Team 1971-74. *Address:* Ministry of Communications, St. George's, Grenada.

MITCHELL, Peter Dennis, PH.D., F.R.S.; British biochemist; b. 29 Sept. 1920, Mitcham; s. of Christopher Gibbs Mitchell; m. Helen ffrench 1958; three s. one d.; ed. Queen's Coll., Taunton, Jesus Coll. Cambridge; worked in Department of Biochem., Univ. of Cambridge 1943-55, Demonstrator 1950-55; Dir. Chemical Biology Unit, Dept. of Zoology, Univ. of Edinburgh 1955-63, Sr. Lecturer 1961-62, Reader 1962-63; Dir. of Research, Glynn Research Inst. 1964-87, Chair. and Hon. Dir. the Glynn Research Foundation 1987-; Foreign Assoc., Nat. Acad. of Sciences, U.S.A. 1977; Hon. Fellow, Royal Soc. of Edinburgh 1979, Jesus Coll. Cambridge 1980; Hon. mem. Soc. Gen. Microbiology 1984, Japanese Biochemical Soc. 1984; Hon. Dr.rer.nat. (Tech. Univ., Berlin) 1976; Hon. D.Sc. (Exeter) 1977, (Chicago) 1978, (Liverpool) 1979, (Bristol) 1980, (Edinburgh) 1980, (Hull) 1980; Hon. Sc.D. (East Anglia) 1981, (Cambridge) 1985; D. Univ., (York) 1982; Fritz Lipmann Lecturer, Gesellschaft für Biological Chem. 1978; C.I.B.A. Medal and Prize, Biochemical Soc., England, for outstanding research 1973; Warren Triennial Prize (jointly), Trustees of Mass. Gen. Hospital, Boston 1974; Louis and Bert Freedman Foundation Award, New York Acad. of Sciences 1974; Wilhelm Feldberg Foundation Prize 1976; Lewis S. Rosenstiel Award, Brandeis Univ. 1977; Medal of Federation European Biochemical Socs. 1978; Nobel Prize for Chemistry 1978; Copley Medal, Council of the Royal Soc. for formulation and devt. of chemiosmotic theory of energy transduction 1981, Medal of Honour, Athens Municipal Council 1982, Croonian Lecturer, The Royal Soc. 1987. *Publications:* Chemiosmotic Coupling in Oxidative and Photosynthetic Phosphorylation 1966, Chemiosmotic Coupling and Energy Transduction 1968 and papers in scientific journals. *Leisure interests:* family life, home building and creation of wealth and amenity, restoration of buildings of architectural and historical interest, music, thinking, understanding, inventing, making, sailing. *Address:* Glynn House, Bodmin, Cornwall, PL30 4AU, England. *Telephone:* (020882) 540.

MITCHELL, Dame Roma Flinders, D.B.E.; Australian judge and university administrator; b. 2 Oct. 1913, Adelaide; d. of Harold Flinders and Maude I. V. (née Wickham) Mitchell; ed. St. Aloysius Coll., Adelaide and Univ. of Adelaide; admitted to Bar, S. Australia 1934, Q.C. 1962; Judge, Supreme Court of S. Australia 1965-83; Chair. Criminal Law and Penal Methods Reform Cttee. of S. Australia 1974-81; Chair. Parole Bd. of S. Australia 1974-81; Chair. Human Rights Comm. 1981-86, South Australia Council on Child Protection 1988-; Chancellor, Univ. of Adelaide 1983-. *Leisure interests:* swimming, walking, theatre, opera. *Address:* 256 East Terrace, Adelaide, S.A. 5000, Australia. *Telephone:* 223-5373.

MITCHISON, Prof. John Murdoch, F.R.S., F.R.S.E.; British zoologist and university professor; b. 11 June 1922; s. of Lord Mitchison and Naomi M. Haldane (Naomi Mitchison, q.v.); m. Rosalind Mary Wrong 1947; one s. three d.; ed. Winchester Coll., Trinity Coll., Univ. of Cambridge; Army Operational Research 1941-46; Sr. and Research Scholar, Trinity Coll., Univ. of Cambridge 1946-50, Fellow 1950-54; Lecturer in Zoology, Univ. of Edinburgh 1953-59, Reader in Zoology 1959-62, Prof. of Zoology 1963-88, Dean of Faculty of Science 1984-85, Univ. Fellow 1988-; J. W. Jenkinson Memorial Lecturer, Univ. of Oxford 1971-72; mem. Edinburgh Univ. Court 1971-74, 1985-88; mem. Council Scottish Marine Biological Assen. 1961-67; mem. Exec. Cttee. Int. Soc. for Cell Biology 1964-72; mem. Biology Cttee. S.R.C. 1976-79, Science Bd. 1976-79; mem. Royal Comm. on Environmental Pollution 1974-79; mem. Working Group of Biological Manpower Dept. of Ed. and Science 1968-71; Pres. British Soc. for Cell Biology 1974-77; mem. Advisory Cttee. on Safety of Nuclear Installations, Health and Safety Exec. 1981-84; Fellow Inst. Biology 1963. *Publications:* The Biology of the Cell Cycle 1971, numerous papers in scientific journals. *Address:* Department of Zoology, West Mains Road, Edinburgh, EH9 3JY (Office); Great Yew, Ormiston, East Lothian, EH35 5NJ, Scotland (Home). *Telephone:* (0875) 340530.

MITCHISON, Naomi, C.B.E.; British novelist and farmer; b. 1 Nov. 1897, Edinburgh; d. of late John Scott Haldane and Louisa Kathleen Trotter; m. Gilbert Richard Mitchison 1916; three s. two d.; ed. Dragon School, Oxford; Ed. Outline for Boys and Girls 1932; Labour candidate for Scottish Univs. 1935; mem. Bakgatla tribe (S.E. Botswana); Hon. D.Litt. (Strathclyde) 1983, (Stirling), (Dundee). *Publications:* The Conquered 1923, When the Bough Breaks 1924, Cloud Cuckoo Land 1925, Black Sparta 1928, Anna Comnena 1928, Nix-Nought-Nothing 1928, Barbarian Stories 1929, The Corn King and the Spring Queen 1931, The Delicate Fire 1932, We Have Been Warned 1935, The Fourth Pig 1936, Socrates (with R. H. S. Crossman) 1937, Moral Basis of Politics 1938, The Kingdom of Heaven 1939, As it Was in the Beginning (with L. E. Gielgud) 1939, The Blood of the Martyrs 1939, Among You Taking Notes 1945, Re-Educating Scotland 1945, The Bull Calves 1947, Men and Herring (with D. Macintosh) 1949, The Big House 1950, Lobsters on the Agenda 1952, Travel Light 1952, Swan's Road 1954, Graeme and the Dragon 1954, Land the Ravens Found 1955, Chapel Perilous 1955, Little Boxes 1956, Behold Your King, The Far Harbour 1957, Other People's Worlds, Five Men and a Swan 1958, Judy and Lakshmi 1959, Rib of the Green Umbrella 1960, The Young Alexander 1960, Karensgaard 1961, Memoirs of a Spacewoman 1962, The Fairy Who Couldn't Tell a Lie 1963, When We Become Men 1964, Return to the Fairy Hill 1966, Friends and Enemies 1966, African Heroes 1968, The Family at Ditlabeng 1969, The Africans: A History 1970, Sun and Moon 1970, Cleopatra's People 1972, A Danish Teapot 1973, A Life for Africa 1973, Sunrise Tomorrow 1973, Small Talk (autobiog.) 1973, All Change Here 1975, Solution Three 1975, Snake! 1976, The Two Magicians 1979, The Knife and other poems 1979, You May Well Ask: A Memoir 1920-40 1979, Images of Africa 1980, The Vegetable War 1980, Mucking Around 1981, What Do You Think Yourself? 1982, Not By Bread Alone 1983, Among You Taking Notes 1985, Early in Arcadia 1987. *Address:* Carradale House, Carradale, Argyll, Scotland.

MITCHISON, (Nicholas) Avrion, D.PHIL., F.R.S.; British professor of zoology and comparative anatomy; b. 5 May 1928, London; two s. three d.; ed. Leighton Park School and Univ. of Oxford; Lecturer, later Reader in Zoology, Univ. of Edinburgh 1956-62; Head, Div. of Experimental Biology, Nat. Inst. for Medical Research, Mill Hill 1962-71; Jodrell Prof. of Zoology and Comparative Anatomy, Head Dept. of Zoology and Cell Biology, Univ. Coll. London 1970-; Hon. Dir. Imperial Cancer Research Fund, Tumour Immunology Unit, Univ. Coll. London; Paul Ehrlich Prize; Hon. M.D. (Edin.). *Address:* University College London, Department of Biology, Medawar Building, Gower Street, London, WC1E 6BT (Office); 14 Belitha Villas, London, N.1, England (Home).

MITCHUM, Robert Charles Duran; American actor; b. 6 Aug. 1917, Bridgeport, Conn.; s. of James and Anne Mitchum; m. Dorothy Spence 1940; two s. one d.; settled in Calif. 1937; joined Long Beach Theatre Guild; worked as radio writer, shoe salesman; began film acting 1943; formed DRM Productions 1955, later Talbot Productions; named "best actor of the year" by Nat. Bd. of Review 1960. *Films include:* The Story of G.I. Joe 1945, Till the end of Time 1946, Undercurrent 1946, The Locket 1946, Pursued 1947, Crossfire 1947, Desire Me 1947, Out of the Past 1947, Rachel and the Stranger 1948, Blood on the Moon 1948, The Red Pony 1949, The Big Steal 1949, Holiday Affair 1949, Where Danger Lives 1950, My Forbidden Past 1951, His Kind of Woman 1951, The Racket 1951, Macao 1952, One Minute to Zero 1952, The Lusty Men 1952, Angel Face 1953, White Witch Doctor 1953, Second Chance 1953, She Couldn't Say No 1954, River of No Return 1954, Track of the Cat 1954, Not as a Stranger 1955, The Night of the Hunter 1955, The Man with the Gun 1955, Foreign Intrigue 1956, Bandido 1956, Heaven Knows Mr. Alison 1957, Fire Down Below 1957, The Enemy Below 1957, Thunder Road 1958, The Hunters 1958, The Angry Hills 1959, The Wonderful Country 1959, Home from the Hill 1960, A Terrible Beauty 1960, The Grass is Greener 1960, The Sundowners 1960, The Last Time I Saw Archie 1961, Cape Fear 1962, The Longest Day 1962, Two for the Seesaw 1962, The List of Adrian Messenger 1963, Rampage 1963, Man in the Middle 1964, What a Way to Go 1964, Mr. Moses 1965, The Way West 1967, El Dorado 1967, Anzio 1968, Villa Rides 1968, Five Card Stud 1968, Secret Ceremony 1968, Young Billy Young 1969, The Good Guys and the Bad Guys 1969, Ryan's Daughter 1971, The Wrath of God 1972, The Friends of Eddie Coyle 1973, The Yakusa 1974, Battle of Midway 1975, Farewell My Lovely 1975, The Amsterdam Kill 1975, The Last Tycoon 1976, The Big Sleep 1977, Breakthrough, The Ambassador 1984, Mr North 1988. *Address:* c/o Triad Artists Inc., 10100 Santa Monica Boulevard, 16th Floor, Los Angeles, Calif. 90067, U.S.A.

MITFORD, Jessica; American (b. British) writer; b. 11 Sept. 1917; d. of 2nd Baron Redesdale; m. 1st Esmond Marcus David Romilly (died 1941), one d.; m. 2nd Robert Edward Treuhaft, one s.; went to U.S.A. 1939; Distinguished Prof. San Jose State Univ. Sept. 1973-Jan. 1974. *Publications:* Hons and Rebels (autobiography) 1960, The American Way of Death 1963, The Trial of Dr. Spock 1970, The American Prison Business 1973, A Fine Old Conflict 1977, The Making of a Muckraker (essays) 1979, Faces of Philip: A Memoir of Philip Toynbee 1984, Grace Had An English Heart: The Story of Grace Darling, Heroine and Victorian Superstar 1988. *Address:* 6411 Regent Street, Oakland, Calif. 94618, U.S.A.

MITRA, Chittaranjan, S.M., D.I.I.SC., D.SC.(ENG.); Indian engineer and educationalist; b. 13 Feb. 1926, Allahabad, Uttar Pradesh; s. of late Iswar Chandra Mitra and of late Sova (née Bose) Mitra; m. Sandhya Ghosh 1951; one s. one d.; ed. Allahabad Univ., Bombay Univ., Indian Inst. of Science, Bangalore, M.I.T., and Columbia Univ., New York; Instructor and Researcher, M.I.T.; Researcher, Columbia Univ., New York; Process Engin-

eer, Foster-Wheeler Corpn., New York; Industrial Adviser in Chemical Eng., Govt. of Uttar Pradesh (U.P.); Dir. Harcourt Butler Technological Inst., Kanpur, U.P.; Dir. Birla Inst. of Tech. and Science, Pilani; Pres. Asscn. of Indian Univs., New Delhi; Chair. Bd. of Chem. Eng. and Chem. Tech., All India Council for Tech. Educ., New Delhi; Chair. Vidya Vihar, Municipal Bd., Pilani; Chair. Asscn. of Commonwealth Univs., London; mem. Corpn. Visiting Cttee. in Chemical Eng., M.I.T., U.S.A., Steering Cttee. United World Colls. and Int. Baccalaureate Office, London, U.K., World Council and Ass. on Co-operative Educ., London, Gen. Ass. of Indian Council for Cultural Relations, Draft Action Plan Cttee. of Govt. of India for Implementation Strategies of the New Educ. Policy, Senate of Indian Inst. of Tech., New Delhi, of Indian Inst. of Tech., Kanpur; Founding mem. Gen. Body and mem. Exec. Bd., Int. Educational Consortium, New Delhi; Inst. of Engineers (India) Sir Ganga Ram Memorial Prize 1974-75, Watumull Foundation (U.S.A.) Honor Summus Medal for contribs. in field of educ. 1987. *Publications:* Challenge and Response—Towards a New Education Policy and Beyond 1986. *Address:* Birla Institute of Technology and Science, Pilani, Rajasthan 333 031, India. *Telephone:* 90 (Office); 115 (Home).

MITRA, Sombhu; Indian actor and stage director; b. 22 Aug. 1915; ed. Ballygunge Govt. High School and St. Xavier's Coll., Calcutta; joined Stage, Calcutta 1939; Producer-Dir.-Actor, Indian People's Theatre Asscn. 1943-46; Producer-Dir.-Actor Bohurupee (non-commercial theatre) 1948-; Fellow Sangeet Natak Akademie, New Delhi; Grand Prix Karlovy Vary Film Festival 1957; Nat. Honour Padma Bhushan 1970, Ramon Magsasay Award 1976. *Productions include:* Four Chapters (Tagore) 1951, An Enemy of the People (Ibsen) 1952, Red Oleanders (Tagore) 1954, The Doll's House (Ibsen) 1958, Sacrifice (Tagore) 1961, The King of the Dark Chamber (Tagore) 1964, Oedipus Rex (Sophocles) 1964, Baki Itihas 1967, Pagla Ghora 1971. *Publications:* Abhinay-Natak-Mancha 1957, Putul Khela 1958, Kanchanranga 1961, Ghurnee 1967, Raja Oidipous 1969, Prasanga Natya 1973. *Address:* 96 Park Street, Calcutta 700017, India.

MITROPOLSKY, Yuriy Alekseyevich; Soviet mathematician; ed. Kiev Univ.; Dir. of Ukrainian Acad. of Sciences Inst. of Maths. 1958-; Academician-Sec. of Dept. of Maths. and Cybernetics of Ukrainian Acad. of Sciences 1963-; Acad. of U.S.S.R. Acad. of Sciences; Lenin Prize 1965. *Address:* Department of Mathematics and Cybernetics, Ukrainian Academy of Sciences, Kiev, U.S.S.R.

MITSUBAYASHI, Yataro; Japanese politician; b. 1918; previous posts include: Chair. Saitama Prefectural Ass.; Parl. Vice-Minister of Home Affairs and of Posts and Telecommunications; Chair. Cttee. on Educ. and Cttee. on Transport, House of Reps.; Deputy Sec.-Gen. Liberal Democratic Party (LDP); Minister of State (Dir.-Gen. Science and Tech. Agency, Chair. Atomic Energy Comm.) 1986-87; Liberal Democratic Party. *Address:* c/o House of Representatives, Tokyo, Japan.

MITSUDA, Hisateru, PH.D.; Japanese professor of nutritional chemistry; b. 27 May 1914, Osaka; s. of Kyuji Mitsuda and Ai Omura; m. Kiku Minamioji 1939; one s. one d.; ed. Kyoto Univ.; Asst. Prof. Dept. of Agricultural Chem. Kyoto Univ. 1938-44, Assoc. Prof. Inst. for Chemical Research 1944-52, Prof. of Nutritional Chem. Inst. for Chemical Research 1952-55, Dept. of Agricultural Chem. 1955-67, Dept. of Food Science and Tech. 1967-68, Prof. Emer. 1978-; Pres. Koshien Univ. 1978-83; Dir. Foundation of Interdisciplinary Research, Inst. of Environmental Sciences 1978-, Pres. 1981-; mem. Japan Acad.; Int. Award, Inst. of Food Technologists 1974, Japan Acad. Award 1980, Agricultural and Food Award, American Chem. Soc. 1981. *Publications:* book chapters. *Leisure interest:* sport. *Address:* Nishi-iru, Shichihonmatsu, Itsutsujidori, Kamigyo-ku, Kyoto 602 (Office); 64 Takanawate-cho, Kamigamo, Kita-ku, Kyoto 603, Japan (Home). *Telephone:* 075-464-5252 (Office); 075-781-1612 (Home).

MITSUI, Shingo, DR.AGR.SC.; Japanese agricultural scientist; b. 1 Jan. 1910, Tokyo; s. of Kenkyo Mitsui and Takeno Mitsui; m. Kikuko Mitsui 1935; one s. one d.; ed. Univ. of Tokyo; Sr. Chemist, Dept. of Agricultural Chem. Nat. Agricultural Experiment Station of Ministry of Agric. and Forestry 1932-45, Dir. of Dept. of Soil and Fertilizer 1945-48; Asst. Prof. (Fertilizer and Plant Nutrition) Faculty of Agric., Univ. of Tokyo 1948-52, Prof. (Fertilizer and Plant Nutrition) 1952-63, Dean of Dept. of Chemical Sciences of Graduate School 1963-65, Prof. Emer. 1970-; mem. Scientific Advisory Cttee. of Int. Atomic Energy Agency (IAEA) 1965-; Lecturer, FAO Int. Training Centre on Fertilizer and Soil for Rice, India 1952; Councillor Japan Radio Isotope Asscn. and Scientific Expert to Atomic Energy Comm. Japan 1955-; Dir. Fertilizer Research Inst. 1969-; Del. to numerous int. confs. on rice cultivation and peaceful uses of atomic energy; mem. Japan Acad. 1983-; Hon. mem. Agricultural and Biological Soc. of Japan 1981-, Soc. of Soil, Science and Plant Nutrition, Japan 1981-; Prize of Japan Acad. and others. *Publications:* Dynamic Studies on the Nutrients Uptake by Crop Plants (with others) Parts 1-45 1951-64, Inorganic Nutrition Fertilization and Soil Amelioration for Lowland Rice 1954, Efficient Use of Urea Fertilizer in Japan 1965, The Denitrification in Wet-Land Rice Soil—its Recognition and Impact 1978. *Leisure interests:* golf, violin, choral singing. *Address:* Higashi Fushimi 2-2-25, Hoya-shi, Tokyo, Japan. *Telephone:* 0424-63-1453.

MITTAG, Günter, DR.RER.OEC.; German politician; b. 8 Oct. 1926, Stettin (now Szczecin, Poland); ed. Stettin, and Transport Coll., Dresden; fmr.

Railway Inspector; mem. SED 1946–, Cand. mem. Cen. Cttee. 1958–62, mem. 1962–; Head of Transport Section of SED Cen. Cttee. 1953–58; cand. mem. Politburo (SED) 1963–66, mem. 1966–, Sec. Cen. Cttee. 1962–73, 1976–; Sec. Econ. Comm. of Politburo (SED) 1958–61, Deputy Chair. and Sec., G.D.R. Econ. Council 1961–62, Head of Bureau for Industry and Building 1963; Chair. Cttee. on Industry, Construction and Transport 1963–; mem. Volkskammer 1963–79; mem. State Council 1963–71, 1978–, Vice-Chair. 1984–; First Deputy Chair. Council of Ministers 1973–76; Vaterländischer Verdienstorden in Silber 1959, Gold 1964; Karl-Marx-Orden 1976; Order of Banner der Arbeit and other decorations. *Publications:* Die politische Ökonomie des Sozialismus und ihre Anwendung in der DDR 1969. *Address:* Sozialistische Einheitspartei Deutschlands, 102 Berlin, Am Marx-Engels-Platz 2, German Democratic Republic.

MITTERER, Otto; Austrian politician; b. 22 Oct. 1911, Vienna; m. Ilse Pichler; one d.; ed. grammar school and business college; family wholesale clock firm 1932–40, 1940–; mil. service 1940–45; entered politics, mem. Austrian Econ. Union 1947, Chair. Trade Section 1955; Minister of Trade and Industry, 1968–70; Pres. Vienna Chamber of Commerce; mem. of the Nat. Council 1968–, Vice-Chair. 1984–; Kommerzialrat 1956; Grosse Silberne Ehrenmedaille, Vienna Chamber of Commerce 1959; Grosses Silbernes Ehrenzeichen for Services to the Repub. of Austria 1963. *Leisure interests:* riding, skiing, skating, film making, theatre, cinema. *Address:* Vienna 1, Goldschmiedgasse 10, Austria.

MITTERRAND, François Maurice Marie; French politician; b. 26 Oct. 1916, Jarnac, Charente; s. of Joseph and Yvonne (née Lorrain) Mitterrand; brother of Gen. Jacques Mitterrand (q.v.); m. Danielle Gouze 1944; two s.; ed. Collège Saint-Paul, Angoulême, Univ. of Paris; served 1939–40; taken prisoner, escaped back to France where active in P.O.W. and resistance movements; missions to London and Algiers 1943; Sec.-Gen. Org. for P.O.W.s, War Victims and Refugees 1944–46; journalist and mem. Paris Bar 1954; Deputy for Nièvre, Nat. Ass. 1946–58, 1962–81; Conseiller Général, Montsauche Dist. 1949; Minister for Ex-Servicemen, Sec. of State to Presidency of the Council, then Minister of State 1947–54; Nat. Pres. Union Démocratique et Socialiste de la Résistance 1951–52; Del. to Council of Europe July-Sept. 1953; Minister of the Interior 1954–55; Minister of State for Justice 1956–57; Political Ed. Le Courrier de la Nièvre; Councillor-Gen. for canton of Montsauche 1949–85; Pres. Gen. Council, Nièvre Dept. 1964–; Mayor of Château-Chinon 1959–; Senator for Nièvre 1959–62; Pres. of Fed. of Democratic and Socialist Left 1965–68; First Sec. Socialist Party 1971–81; Vice-Pres. The Socialist Int. 1972–; Cand. for Pres. of France 1965, 1974; Pres. of France 1981–; Grand Maître, Légion d'honneur, Croix de guerre, Rosette de la Résistance, Grand Cross Order of St. Charles (Monaco) 1984, Simon Wiesenthal Centre Prize 1984; Dr. h.c. (New York Univ.) 1988. *Publications:* Aux frontières de l'union française, La Chine au défi 1961, Le coup d'état permanent 1964, Ma part de vérité 1969, Un socialisme du possible 1971, La rose au poing 1973, La paille et le grain 1975, Politique 1977, L'abeille et l'architecte 1978, Ici et maintenant 1980, The Wheat and the Chaff: The Personal Diaries of the President of France 1971–81, Réflexions sur la politique extérieure de la France 1986 and many articles. *Leisure interest:* table tennis. *Address:* Palais de l'Elysée, 55–57 rue du Faubourg Saint-Honoré, 75008 Paris; 22 rue de Bièvre, 75005 Paris, France (Home). *Telephone:* (1) 42-92-81-00 (Elysée).

MITTERRAND, Gen. Jacques; French aerospace executive; b. 21 May 1918, Angoulême, Charentes; s. of Joseph and Yvonne (née Lorrain) Mitterrand; brother of François Mitterrand (q.v.); m. Gisèle Baume 1948; two d.; ed. St. Paul Coll., Angoulême, St. Louis Lycée, Paris, St. Cyr Mil. Acad.; served in Air Force 1937–75; participated in devt. and institution of French Nuclear Force; mem. Del. to NATO Perm. Group, Washington, D.C. 1961–64; Gen., Asst. Commdr. French Strategic Air Forces 1965–67, Commdr. 1970–72; Deputy Chief of Staff of Air Force 1968, of Armed Forces 1968–70; Insp. Gen. of Air Force 1972–75; mem. Supreme Air Council 1970–75; Chair. Bd. and Chief Exec., Soc. Nat. Industrielle Aérospatiale (SNIAS) 1975–81; Counsellor to Chair. French Atomic Energy Agency 1975; First Vice-Chair. French Aerospace Industries Assen. (GIFAS), Chair. 1981–84; Chair. Assen. Européenne des Constructeurs de Matériel Aérospatial (AECMA) 1978–83; Pres. Office Gén. de l'Air 1984–; Vice-Chair. Supervisory Bd. of Airbus Industry; Vice-Pres. Turbomeca 1983–; mem. Bd. Inst. of Air Transport; Grand Croix, Légion d'honneur, Croix de guerre, Croix de la Valeur militaire, Croix du Combattant; Médaille de l'Aéronautique. *Address:* 10 bis rue Paul Baudry, 75008 Paris, France (Home).

MIYAI, Jinnosuke, M.A.; Japanese business executive and university official; b. 22 Oct. 1921, Kagawa; m. Takeko Inoue 1948; one d.; ed. The Sixth High School, Univs. of Tokyo and Chicago; Vice-Pres. Shell Sekiyu K.K. 1971–81, Shell Kosan K.K. 1971–81; Dir. Showa Sekiyu K.K. 1974–81; Pres. Shin Nishi Nihon Sikiyu Kaihatsu K.K. 1977–81; Vice-Pres. Showa Yokkaichi Sekiyu K.K. 1982–83, Pres. 1983–85; Pres. Japan Productivity Centre 1985–; Dir. Meiji Gakuin Univ. 1978–84; Hon. Research Fellow Stirling Univ. 1981–; Hon. O.B.E. *Address:* 240 Yabe-cho, Totsuka-ku, Yokohama 244, Japan. *Telephone:* (045) 861-4112.

MIYAKE, Issey; Japanese couturier; b. Hirishito 1938; f. Miyake Design Studio, Tokyo 1970; int. exhbns.; exhbn. A UN at Musée des Arts Decoratifs, Paris 1988.

MIYAKE, Shigemitsu; Japanese banker; b. 27 Feb. 1911, Osaka; s. of Shigetaka and Fumi (Ito) Miyake; m. Hina Inoue 1935; one s. two d.; ed. Tokyo Imperial Univ.; with Bank of Japan 1933–67, Dir. 1962–67; Deputy Pres. Tokai Bank Ltd. 1967–68, Pres. 1968–69, Chair. and Pres. 1969–75; Chair. 1975–86, Chair. Bd. 1986–88, Chair. Emer. 1988–; Exec. Dir. Japan Man. Orgs. 1970–; Exec. Dir. Fed. of Japan Econ. Orgs. 1971–87; Chair. Bd., Cen. Japan Railway Co. Ltd. 1987–; Pres. Nagoya Chamber of Commerce and Industry 1974–81, Adviser 1981–; Vice-Pres. Japan Chamber of Commerce and Industry 1974–81; Adviser Bank of Japan 1974–82; Order of the Sacred Treasure (First Class) 1982; Blue Ribbon Medal 1974. *Address:* Tokai Bank Ltd., 3-21-24 Nishiki, Naka-ku, Nagoya; Sanoh Mansion 302, 1-12-2, Mikanyama-cho, Mizuho-ku, Nagoya, Japan (Home). *Telephone:* 052-211-1111 (Office), 052-833-7921 (Home).

MIYAMOTO, Kenji; Japanese writer and politician; b. 17 Oct. 1908, Yamaguchi; s. of Sutekichi and Miyo Miyamoto; m. Sueko Miyamoto 1956; two c.; ed. Tokyo Imperial Univ.; mem. Japanese CP 1931–, (imprisoned 1933–45), mem. Cen. Cttee. 1933–, Gen. Sec. of Cen. Cttee. 1958–70, Chair. Presidium Cen. Cttee. 1970–82, Chair. Cen. Cttee. 1982–; mem. House of Councillors 1977–. *Publications:* Problems of Democratic Revolution 1947, Advance Towards Freedom and Independence 1949, Twelve Years' Letters 1952, World of Yuriko Miyamoto 1954, Prospects of Japanese Revolution 1961, The Path of Our Party's Struggle 1961, Actual Tasks and the Japanese Communist Party 1966, Selections from Literary Critiques of Kenji Miyamoto 1966–80, The Road towards a New Japan 1970, Standpoint of the Japanese Communist Party 1972, Dialogues with Kenji Miyamoto 1972, Kenji Miyamoto with Pressmen 1973, Abashiri Note 1975, Interviews with Kenji Miyamoto 1975, Kenji Miyamoto on Our Time 1975, Documentation of Trials of Kenji Miyamoto 1976, Dialogues with Kenji Miyamoto (sequel) 1977, Kenji Miyamoto on Contemporary Politics 1978, Kenji Miyamoto on the 1980s 1981–83, Now is turn for JCP 1983, Dialogues on Development in the World and Japan 1984, Road to elimination of Nuclear Weapons 1985, People in Retrospect 1985, Selected Works (in English) 1985–87, Consensus on Non-nuclear Government 1986. *Leisure interest:* shogi (Japanese chess). *Address:* Central Committee of the Japanese Communist Party, Sendagaya 4-chome 26, Shibuya-ku, Tokyo, Japan. *Telephone:* 403-6111.

MIYAZAKI, Hiromichi; Japanese diplomatist; b. 1921, Tokyo; m.; two s.; ed. Tokyo Univ.; entered diplomatic service 1944; Minister in del. to OECD 1967; Consul-Gen., Berlin 1971; Dir.-Gen. Bureau of Econ. Affairs 1972; Amb. to Algeria 1976; Deputy Minister of Foreign Affairs 1977–80; Amb. and Perm. Rep. to OECD 1980–82; Amb. to Fed. Repub. of Germany 1982–87. *Address:* c/o Ministry of Foreign Affairs, 2-2 Kasumigaseki, Chiyoda-ku, Tokyo 100, Japan.

MIYAZAKI, Kagayaki; Japanese chemical executive; b. 19 April 1909, Nagasaki Prefecture; s. of Matunosuke and Sue Miyazaki; m. Sumiko Miyasaki 1937; one s. one d.; ed. Tokyo Univ.; Exec. Dir. Japan Fed. of Employers' Assens. 1949–; Pres. Asahi Chemical Industry Co. Ltd. 1961–85, Chair. Bd. 1985–; Exec. Dir. Fed. of Econ. Orgs. 1961–; mem. Export and Import Trading Council 1969–73; Pres. Japan Textile Fed. 1980–; mem. Customs Tariff Council 1970–; Hon. Adviser Japan Chemical Fibres Assen. 1971–77, Pres. 1977–80, 1985–; mem. Japan External Trade Operational Council 1971–. *Leisure interest:* walking. *Address:* Asahi Chemical Industry Co. Ltd., 1-2 Yurakucho 1-chome, Chiyoda-ku, Tokyo; 26-8 Funabashi 1-chome, Setagaya-ku, Tokyo, Japan. *Telephone:* 429-2027.

MIYAZAWA, Kiichi; Japanese politician; b. 8 Oct. 1919, Tokyo; m. Yoko Miyazawa 1943; two c.; ed. Tokyo Imperial Univ.; Finance Ministry 1942–52, Pvt. Sec. to Minister of Finance 1949; mem. House of Councillors 1953–65; Parl. Vice-Minister of Educ. 1959–60; Minister of State, Dir.-Gen. of Econ. Planning Agency 1962–64, 1966–68, 1977–78; mem. House of Reps. 1967–; Minister of Int. Trade and Industry 1970–71, of Foreign Affairs 1974–76, of Finance 1986–88; Deputy Prime Minister and Minister of Finance 1987–88; Minister of State, Chief Cabinet Sec. 1980–82; Chair. Exec. Council LDP 1984–86. *Publications:* Tokyo-Washington no Mitsudan (Tokyo-Washington secret talks) 1956, Shakaito tono taiwa (Dialogue with the Socialist Party), Utsukushii Nippon heno Chosen (Challenge for Beautiful Japan) 1984. *Leisure interests:* Noh theatre, reading. *Address:* 6-34-1 Jingu-mae, Shibuya-ku, Tokyo 150, Japan.

MIZERE, N. T., B.A.; Malawi diplomatist; b. 5 Jan. 1940; m.; four c.; ed. Delhi, India, and Blantyre, Malawi; began career as lab. asst. and bank clerk 1959; Asst. Dist. Commr., Blantyre 1966–67; Admin. Officer, Treasury 1967–71; First Sec. and Head of Chancery, Embassy in S. Africa 1971–74; Under-Sec. Ministry of Local Govt.; Amb. to S. Africa and High Commr. (non-resident) in Lesotho 1974–77; Sr. Deputy Sec. Ministry of Trade, Industry and Tourism 1977–78; Amb. to EEC and Belgium and Amb. (non-resident) to Netherlands 1978; Amb. to Fed. Repub. of Germany 1979–80, Amb. (non-resident) to Switzerland, Austria and Sweden 1979–81, High Commr. in U.K. 1980–81; Perm. Rep. to UN 1981–86. *Address:* c/o Ministry of Foreign Affairs, P.O. Box 30315, Lilongwe, Malawi.

MIZUNO, Seiichi, D.LITT.; Japanese professor of oriental culture; b. 24 March 1905, Kobe; s. of Torata and Fuji Mizuno; m. Takayo Mizuno 1931; one s.; ed. Kyoto Univ.; studied Chinese archaeology in Peking 1929–31; Research mem. of Research Inst. of Oriental Culture 1931–48; Prof. of

Research Inst. for Humanities, Kyoto Univ. 1948-68, Prof. Emer. 1968-; mem. Specialist Cttee. of Protection for Nat. Properties 1959-; awards include Asahi-Sho and Onshi-Sho. *Publications:* Inner Mongolia and the Region of the Great Wall (with N. Egami) 1935, Study of Cave-Temples at Lung-men, Honan (with T. Nagahiro) 1941, Tsushima (with others) 1952, Yun-kang (with T. Nagahiro) (16 vols.) 1950-55, Bronze and Jades of Ancient China 1959, Bronze and Stone Sculpture of China 1960, Horyuji Monastery 1965. *Address:* 91 Jodoji-Kamibambacho, Sakyo-ku, Kyoto 606, Japan. *Telephone:* 771-6564.

MKAPA, Benjamin William, B.A.; Tanzanian journalist and politician; b. 12 Nov. 1938, Ndanda; s. of William Matwani and Stephania Nambanga; m. Anna Joseph Maro 1966; two s.; ed. Makerere Univ. Coll.; Admin. Officer 1962; Foreign Service Officer 1963; Man. Ed. Tanzania Nationalist and Uhuru 1966, The Daily News and Sunday News 1972; Press Sec. to Pres. 1974; founding Dir. Tanzania News Agency 1976; Minister of Foreign Affairs 1977-80, of Information and Culture 1980-82; High Commr. to Canada and Amb. to U.S.A. 1982-84; Minister of Foreign Affairs 1984-; M.P. for Nanyumbu Oct. 1985-. *Leisure interest:* reading. *Address:* Ministry of Foreign Affairs, P.O. Box 9000, Dar-es-Salaam, Tanzania.

MKHATSHWA, Smangaliso, PH.D., TH.M.; South African ecclesiastic; b. 26 June 1939, Barberton; ordained priest 1965; Gen. Sec. SACBC 1980-88; Patron of the United Democratic Front 1983; Gen.-Sec. Inst. for Contextual Theology 1988-; Dr. h.c. (Tubingen, Fed. Germany). *Leisure interests:* tennis, music, theatre. *Address:* St. Charles Lwanga, P.O. Box 27764, Sunnyside, 0132; Institute for Contextual Theology, P.O. Box 32047, Braamfontein 2017, South Africa. *Telephone:* (01214) 2120; (339) 2513-38-62.

MLADENOV, Peter Toshev; Bulgarian politician; b. 22 Aug. 1936, Toshevtsi, Vidin; ed. Moscow State Inst of Int. Relations; Sec., subsequently First Sec., Vidin District Cttee., League of Young Communists 1963-66; Sec. Cen. Cttee. League of Young Communists 1966-69; First Sec. Vidin Dist. Cttee., Bulgarian CP 1969-71; cand. mem. Politburo, Cen. Cttee. Bulgarian CP 1974-77, mem. 1977-; Deputy to Nat. Assembly; Minister of Foreign Affairs Dec. 1971-. *Address:* Ministry of Foreign Affairs, 1113 Sofia, Al. Zhendov St. 2, Bulgaria.

MŁYŃCZAK, Tadeusz Witold, M.ENG.; Polish politician; b. 7 Oct. 1934, Poznań; ed. Poznań Tech. Univ.; worked in H. Cegielski Plants, Poznań, then scientific worker, Poznań Tech. Univ. 1953-57; Chief Technologist in Mechanized Railway Works Establishment, Poznań 1958-61; Deputy Chair. Presidium Nat. Council of City of Poznań 1973-74; Chair. Bd. of Cen. Union of Handicrafts 1974-76; mem. Presidium Supreme Co-operative Council 1975-76; Deputy Chair. Council of State March 1976-; Chair. Soc. for Connection with Poles Living Abroad (Polonia) March 1977-; mem. Presidium of All-Poland Cttee. of Nat. Unity Front 1977-83; mem. Democratic Party (SD) 1958-, Sec. SD Town and Dist. Cttee. Poznań 1961-66, Sec. SD Voivodship Cttee., Poznań 1966-74, mem. SD Cen. Cttee. 1969-81, 1985-, mem. Presidium of Cen. Cttee. 1974-81, Chair. Cen. Cttee. 1976-81, Chair. SD Warsaw Cttee. Feb.-April 1985, Chair. SD Cen. Cttee. 1985-89; Deputy to Seym 1965-; Deputy Chair. Gen. Bd. Polish Mechanical Engineers' Asscn. 1976-80; mem. Nat. Council of Patriotic Movt. for Nat. Rebirth 1985-; Order of Banner of Labour (1st Class), Commdr.'s and Kt.'s Cross, Order of Polonia Restituta, and other decorations. *Leisure interests:* aquatics, travelling. *Address:* Kancelaria Rady Państwa, ul. Wiejska 4/6, 00-902 Warsaw, Poland.

MO WENXIANG; Chinese politician; Vice-Minister, Third Ministry of Machine-Building 1978-81, Minister 1981-82, of Aviation Ind. (now Aeronautics Industry) 1982; mem. 12th Cen. Cttee. CCP 1982-87; mem. Presidium 6th NPC 1986-; mem. Educ., Science and Public Health Cttee., NPC 1986-; Head China-Sudan Friendship Group 1985-; Chair. Bd. of Dirs., China Nat. Aero-Tech. Import and Export Corpn. Sept. 1986-. *Address:* 67 Jiaonan Street, Beijing, People's Republic of China.

MO YINGFENG; Chinese writer; b. 12 Jan. 1938, Taojiang County, Hunan; s. of Mo Liangzai and Liu Xiangxious m. 1st 1965 (divorced 1980), 2nd Ouyang Huiling 1981; two d.; ed. Hubei Art College (music composition); joined PLA 1961, demobilized 1970; scriptwriter, Hunan Xiaoxiang Film Studio 1978; began publishing short stories in 1972; Vice-Chair. Hunan Writers' Asscn., mem. Bd., China Writers' Asscn. 1983-. *Publications include:* A General's Lament, Dream of the Utopian World (new trend novel) 1987. *Leisure interests:* music, calligraphy. [Died 17 February 1989.]

MOALLA, Mansour, L. EN D., L. ES L., LL.D.; Tunisian economist; b. 1 May 1930, Sfax; s. of Slaiem Moalla and Emna Chaabouni; m. Leila Skandrani 1961; four c.; ed. Inst. des Etudes Politiques, Ecole Nat. d'Admin., Paris; Insp. des Finances 1956; Tech. Adviser, Ministry of Finance 1957-58; Dir.-Gen. Banque Cen. de Tunisie 1958-61; Dir. of Admin., Office of the Pres. 1961-63; Dir. Ecole Nat. d'Admin. (ENA) 1963-67; Under-Sec. of State, Ministry of Commerce and Industry 1967-68; Sec. of State (then Minister) for Posts, Telegraphs and Telecommunications (PTT) 1969-70; Deputy Minister in charge of the Nat. Plan 1970-71, Minister 1971-74; Chair., Gen. Man. Banque Int. Arabe de Tunisie 1976-80, Groupe des Assurances Tunisie 1976-80, Hon. Pres. 1983-; Minister of Planning and Finance

1980-83; mem. Cen. Cttee., Political Bureau, Destour Socialist Party 1971-; Grand Cordon, Order of the Repub.; Grand Cordon Order of Independence. *Leisure interests:* agriculture, swimming. *Address:* Banque Internationale Arabe de Tunisie, 70-72 Avenue Habib Bourguiba, Tunis (Office); 3 rue Mendès-France, Carthage, Tunisia (Home). *Telephone:* 340733 (Office); 275513 (Home).

MOBBS, Sir (Gerald) Nigel, Kt.; British business executive; b. 22 Sept. 1937, Birmingham; s. of Gerald Aubrey Mobbs and Elizabeth Lanchester; m. Hon. Pamela Jane Berry 1961; one s. two d.; ed. Marlborough Coll. and Christ Church, Oxford; numerous directorships including Barclays Bank PLC 1979-, Woolworth Holdings PLC 1982-, The Charterhouse Group PLC 1974-84, Cookson Group PLC 1985-, Slough Estates PLC; Chair. and Chief Exec. Slough Estates PLC 1976-; Vice.Pres. Asscn. of British Chambers of Commerce 1976-; Chair. Univ. of Buckingham. *Leisure interests:* hunting, skiing, golf, riding, travel. *Address:* 234 Bath Road, Slough, Berks., SL1 4EE, England. *Telephone:* (0753) 37171.

MOBERLY, Sir John Campbell, K.B.E., C.M.G.; British diplomatist (retd.); b. 27 May 1925, Exmouth, Devon; s. of the late Sir Walter Moberly and Lady Moberly (née Gwendolen Gardner); m. Patience Proby 1959; two s. one d.; ed. Winchester Coll. and Magdalen Coll., Oxford; war service in R.N. 1943-47; entered Foreign (later Diplomatic) Service 1950; service at Foreign Office and in Bahrain and Kuwait 1950-59; British Political Agent in Doha, Qatar 1959-62; First Sec., Athens 1962-66; with FCO 1966-68; Canadian Nat. Defence Coll., Kingston, Ont. 1968-69; Counsellor, Washington, D.C. 1969-73; Dir. Middle East Centre for Arab Studies, Shemlan, Lebanon 1973-75; Amb. to Jordan 1975-79; Asst. Under-Sec. FCO 1979-82; Amb. to Iraq 1982-85; C.St.J. 1979. *Leisure interests:* skiing, mountains, swimming. *Address:* 35 Pymers Mead, West Dulwich, London, SE21 8NH; The Cedars, Temple Sowerby, Penrith, Cumbria, CA10 1RZ, England. *Telephone:* 01-670 2680 (London); (07683) 61437 (Cumbria).

MOBERLY, Sir Patrick Hamilton, K.C.M.G., M.A.; British diplomatist (retd.); b. 2 Sept. 1928, London; s. of George Hamilton Moberly; m. Mary Penfold 1955; two s. one d.; ed. Winchester Coll., Trinity Coll., Oxford; entered Foreign Service 1951; served in Embassy, Baghdad 1953-57, Prague 1957-59; Foreign Office 1959-62; Embassy, Dakar 1962-64; with Ministry of Defence 1964-66; Foreign and Commonwealth Office (FCO) 1967-69; Canada (Nat. Defence Coll.) 1969-70; Embassy, Tel-Aviv 1970-74; FCO 1974-81, Asst. Under-Sec. of State 1976-81; Amb. to Israel 1981-84, to S. Africa 1984-87. *Address:* c/o Foreign and Commonwealth Office, London, SW1A 2AH, England.

MOBUTU SESE SEKO, Marshal (Joseph-Désiré Mobutu); Zairian politician; b. 14 Oct. 1930; ed. Léopoldville (now Kinshasa) and Coquilhatville (now Mbandaka); m. 1980; Sergeant-Maj. Accountancy Dept., Force Publique, Belgian Congo 1949-56; course at Inst. of Social Studies, Brussels; journalist, Léopoldville; mem. Mouvement Nat. Congolaise; del. Brussels Round Table Conf. on Congo independence 1959-60; Sec. of State for Nat. Defence, Lumumba cabinet 1960; Chief of Staff, Congo Army 1960; took over supreme power in name of army and suspended all political activity for three months Sept. 1960; appointed a Coll. of High Commrs. to take over govt.; Maj.-Gen. and C.-in-C. of Congolese Forces 1961-65, Lieut.-Gen. and Pres. of Congo (now Zaire) Nov. 1965-, also Pres. of Cabinet Oct. 1966-, concurrently Minister of Foreign Affairs 1966-72, Minister for Territorial Security, of Nat. Defence, and for Veterans' Affairs and Justice; adopted present name Jan. 1972; rank of Marshal 1982; Hon. LL.D. (Duquesne Univ., U.S.A.) 1970; Order of the Source of the Nile (Uganda) 1972. *Address:* Présidence de la République, Kinshasa, Zaire; Villa les Miguettes, Savigni, Switzerland. *Telephone:* Lausanne 971061.

MOCHALIN, Fyodor Ivanovich; Soviet party official; b. 1920; ed. Moscow Textile Inst.; Soviet Army 1943-44; craftsman in a spinning and weaving mill and chief engineer of a textile trust 1944-47; mem. CPSU 1952-; worked at Ministry of Light Industry Kazakh S.S.R. 1947-57; Deputy Chair. of Econ. Council of South Kazakhstan 1957-59; head of a dept. at Cen. Cttee. of Kazakh CP 1959-64; Second Sec. of Alma Ata Regional Cttee. of Kazakh CP 1964-65; First Sec. of Alma Ata City Cttee. of Kazakh CP 1965-73; Deputy to Supreme Soviet of U.S.S.R. 1966-; Head of Section of Cen. Cttee. CPSU 1973-; Head of Dept. of Light and Food Industry with Cen. Cttee. CPSU 1974-; mem. Cen. Auditing Comm. of CPSU 1976-81; cand. mem. Cen. Cttee. CPSU 1981-. *Address:* The Kremlin, Moscow, U.S.S.R.

MOCK, Alois, LL.D.; Austrian politician; b. 10 June 1934, Euratsfeld; s. of August and Mathilde Mock; m. Edith Partik 1963; ed. Univ. of Vienna, Johns Hopkins Univ., Bologna, and Free Univ., Brussels; mem. Austrian mission to OECD 1962-66; Private Sec. to Fed. Chancellor 1966, Head of Private Office 1968; Minister of Educ. 1969-70; mem. Parl. 1970-; Leader, Austrian People's Party (ÖVP) 1979-89; Leader of Opposition 1979-87; Vice-Chancellor and Minister of Foreign Affairs 1987-89; Chair. European Democratic Union, Vienna 1979-; Chair. Int. Democratic Union, London 1983-. *Publication:* Standpunkte 1983. *Address:* c/o Österreichische Volkspartei, Kärntnerstrasse 51, 1010 Vienna, Austria. *Telephone:* 0 222/52 26 21.

MÓD, Péter; Hungarian politician and diplomatist; b. 21 May 1911, Nagyalásony; s. of György Mód and Viktoria Mendel; m. 1st Irén Stettinger 1937

(died 1949), 2nd Irén Simon 1954; one s. two d.; ed. Univ. of Budapest, Univ. of Paris; volunteer, French Army 1939–40; French Resistance 1940–45; entered Hungarian diplomatic service 1947; Counsellor, Paris 1949; Dir. Municipal Library "Ervin Szabó", Budapest; Head, Near and Middle East Dept., Ministry of Foreign Affairs 1956; Head, Perm. Mission to the UN 1956–62; First Deputy Foreign Minister 1961–68; Amb. to France 1968–74; Chair. Hungarian UN Soc. 1975–; Perm. Rep. to UNESCO, Paris 1976–85; Chair. Hungarian Asscn. for UNESCO 1986–; Red Banner Order of Labour 1974 and many other Hungarian and foreign decorations. *Leisure interests:* literature, serious music. *Address:* Zichy Géza-u. 5, 1146 Budapest XIV, Hungary. *Telephone:* 428-391.

MODAI, Itzhak; Israeli politician; b. 1926, Tel-Aviv; m.; one s. one d.; ed. Geulah High School, Tel-Aviv, Technion Univ., Haifa, Univ. of London and Hebrew Univ. of Jerusalem; served Palestine Police Force 1943; served Israeli armed forces (Lieut.-Col.) 1948–50; Mil. Attaché, London 1951–53; Mil. Commdr., Gaza, Six-Day War 1967; chemical factory construction and industrial co. admin. 1951–73; Minister of Energy, Infrastructure and Communications 1978–81, without Portfolio 1981–82, of Energy 1982–83, of Finance 1984–85, of Justice 1985–86, without Portfolio 1987–88, of Econs. and Planning Dec. 1988–; mem. inner Cabinet; Pres. Israel-America Chamber of Commerce, Gov. IMF 1984–; Likud Party. *Address:* 1 Kaplan Street, Kiryat Ben-Gurion, POB 883, Jerusalem, Israel.

MODI, Vinay Kumar, B.TECH.CHEM.ENG.; Indian industrialist; b. 31 May 1943, Modinagar; s. of the late Rai Bahadur Gujar Mal Modi and of Dayawati Modi; m. Chander Bala 1965; one s. one d.; ed. Scindia School, Gwalior, Indian Inst. of Tech., Kanpur; Man. Dir. Modi Industries Ltd. 1965–; Vice-Chair., Man. Dir. Modi Rubber Ltd. 1976–; Pres. Modi Cement Ltd. 1979–; Sr. Vice-Chair. Bombay Tyres Int. Ltd. 1981–; various awards from govt. for export performance; prizes from several asscns. *Publications:* various articles on steel, tyres and cement production. *Leisure interests:* golf, tennis, billiards. *Address:* Modi Bhavan, Civil Lines, Modinagar 201204, India.

MODIANO, Patrick Jean; French novelist; b. 30 July 1945, Boulogne-Billancourt; s. of Albert Modiano and Luisa Colpyn; m. Dominique Zehrfuss 1970; two d.; ed. schools in Biarritz, Chamonix, Deauville, Thônes, Barbizon, coll. in Paris; Prix Roger Nimier 1968, Prix Felix Fénéon 1969, Grand Prix de l'Académie Française 1972, Prix Goncourt 1978; Chevalier des Arts et des Lettres. *Publications:* La place de l'étoile 1968, La ronde de nuit 1969, Les boulevards de ceinture 1972, Lacombe Lucien (screenplay) 1973, La polka (play) 1974, Villa triste (novel) 1975, Interrogatoire d'Emmanuel Berl 1976, Livret de famille (novel) 1977, Rue des boutiques obscures 1978, Une Jeunesse 1981, Memory Lane 1981, De si Braves Garçons (novel) 1982, Poupée blonde 1983, Quartier perdu 1985, Dimanches d'Août 1986, Une aventure de Choura 1986, La Fiancée de Choura 1987, Remise de peine (novel) 1988, Catherine Certitude 1988, Vestiaire de l'Enfance (novel) 1989. *Address:* c/o Editions Gallimard, 5 rue Sébastien Bottin, 75007 Paris, France.

MODIGLIANI, Franco, D.JUR., D.SC.; American professor of economics; b. 18 June 1918, Rome, Italy; s. of Enrico Modigliani and Olga Flaschel; m. Serena Calabi 1939; two s.; ed. Liceo Visconti, Univ. of Rome, New School for Soc. Research, New York; Lecturer, New School for Soc. Research, New York, 1943–44, Asst. Prof. of Math. Econ. and Econometrics 1946–48; Assoc. Prof. of Econs., Univ. of Ill. 1949–50, Prof. 1950–52; Prof. of Econs. and Industrial Admin., Carnegie Inst. of Tech. 1952–60; Prof. of Econs., Northwestern Univ. 1960–62; Prof. of Econs. and Finance, M.I.T. 1962–, Inst. Prof. 1970–; Academic Consultant, Bd. of Govs., Fed. Reserve System 1966–, mem. Cttee. on Monetary Statistics, 1974–76; Sr. Advisor, Brookings Panel on Econ. Activity 1971–; Vice-Pres. Int. Econ. Assen. 1976–83, Hon. Pres. 1983–; Pres. American Finance Assen. 1981; fmr. Pres. Econometric Soc., American Econ. Assen.; mem. N.A.S., American Acad. of Arts and Sciences; LL.D. h.c. (Univ. of Chicago) 1967, Dr. Econs. h.c. (Univ. Catholique de Louvain, Belgium) 1974, Dr. of Econs. and Commerce h.c. (Istituto Universitario di Bergamo) 1979; Hon. D.Hum. Litt. (Bard Coll., New York) 1985, (Brandeis Univ.) 1986; Journal of Business Award 1961, Graham and Dodd Award 1975, 1980, Nobel Prize for Economic Science 1985. *Publications:* National Incomes and International Trade 1953, Planning Production, Inventories and Work Force 1960, Role of Anticipations and Plans in Economic Behavior and Their Use in Economic Analysis and Forecasting 1961, New Mortgage Designs for Stable Housing in an Inflationary Environment 1975, The Collected Papers of Franco Modigliani (three vols.) 1980. *Leisure interests:* sailing, swimming, skiing, tennis. *Address:* Massachusetts Institute of Technology, Sloan School of Management, Room E52-443, 50 Memorial Drive, Cambridge, Mass. 02139 (Office); 25 Clark Street, Belmont, Mass. 02178, U.S.A. (Home). *Telephone:* (617) 253-7153 (Office); (617) 484-8419 (Home).

MÖDL, Martha; German singer; ed. Munich and Nuremberg Conservatoires; numerous appearances at German and foreign opera houses, and at Bayreuth Festivals 1951–; mem. Staatsoper Stuttgart 1953–. *Address:* 8082 Grünwald, Perlacherstrasse 19, Federal Republic of Germany.

MODZELEWSKI, Kazimierz; Polish craftsman and politician; b. 7 Nov. 1934, Lad. Sochaczew Dist.; m. (wife deceased); two d.; blds. supervisor in Mil. Bldg. Enterprise 1951–57; has run family workshop (repair and blds.

works) 1957–; for many years active in handicraft co-operative; Chair. Craft Nat. Council 1981–; mem. Democratic Party (SD) 1978–; mem. Presidium of SD Cen. Cttee. 1985–, Deputy Chair. SD Cen. Cttee. 1985–; M.P. 1985–; mem. Tribunal of State; active in Patriotic Movt. of Nat. Rebirth (PRON), mem. PRON Nat. Council; Kt.'s Cross of Order of Polonia Restituta, Bronze and Silver Cross of Merit, Jan Kiliński Gold Medal; Crafts Hon. Award and other decorations. *Leisure interests:* gardening, table tennis, chess. *Address:* Centralny Komitet SD, ul. Rutkowskiego 9, 00-021 Warsaw (Office); ul. Krasickiego 12b, 02-611 Warsaw, Poland (Home); *Telephone:* 31 61 61 (Office).

MOE, George Cecil Rawle, Q.C., M.A., LL.M.; Barbadian barrister-at-law and fmr. politician; b. 12 March 1932, Barbados; s. of Cecil S. and Odessa M. (née Marshall) Moe; m. Olga Louise Atkinson 1957; two s. one d.; ed. Harrison Coll., Oxford Univ. and Columbia Univ., New York; called to the Bar, Middle Temple, London; Magistrate 1960–62; Act. Asst. Legal Draftsman 1962–63; Act. Crown Counsel 1963–66; Sr. Crown Counsel 1967–71; Acting Perm. Rep. to UN 1970–71; Attorney-Gen. and Minister of Legal Affairs 1971–76, also Minister of External Afairs 1972–76; Leader of Senate 1972–76; pvt. practice 1976–79; Puisne Judge (Belize) 1979–81, Chief Justice (Belize) 1982–85; Justice of Appeal, Eastern Caribbean Supreme Court 1985–. *Leisure interests:* music, cricket, gardening, swimming. *Address:* Court of Appeal Chambers, P.O. Box 1093, Castries, Saint Lucia.

MOE, Thorvald, PH.D.; Norwegian diplomatist; b. 1940; m.; two c.; ed. Stanford Univ.; has held various sr. posts in Ministry of Finance; Dir.-Gen. Econ. Policy Dept. Ministry of Finance 1978–86; Amb. to OECD 1986– *Address:* Permanent Mission of Norway to Organization for Economic Co-operation and Development, 2 rue André Pascal, 75775 Paris Cedex 16, France.

MOERSCH, Karl; German journalist and politician; b. 11 March 1926, Calw/Württ.; s. of Karl F. Moersch; m. Waltraut Schweikle 1947; one s.; ed. Univ. of Tübingen; journalist in Ludwigshafen, Bad Godesberg (Deutscher Forschungsdienst) and Frankfurt (Ed. of Die Gegenwart) 1956–58; Head of Press Dept., Freie Demokratische Partei (FDP) 1961–64; free-lance journalist 1964–; fmr. mem. Bundestag; Parl. Sec. of State, Minister of State, Ministry of Foreign Affairs 1970–76; mem. Exec. Bd. of UNESCO 1980–85. *Publications:* Kursrevision–Deutsche Politik nach Adenauer 1978, Europa für Anfänger 1979, Sind wir denn eine Nation? 1982, Bei uns im Staate Beutelsbach 1984, Geschichte der Pfalz 1987, and numerous newspaper articles, etc. *Address:* Ludwigsburg-Ossweil, Aalener Strasse 10, Federal Republic of Germany. *Telephone:* 07141/861686.

MOERTEL, Charles George, M.D., M.S.; American physician; b. 17 Oct. 1927, Milwaukee; s. of Charles Henry and Alma Helen (née Soffel) Moertel; m. Virginia Claire Sheridan 1952; three s. one d.; ed. Univ. of Illinois, Univ. of Minnesota; resident in internal medicine Mayo Foundation, Rochester, Minn. 1954–57, Consultant Mayo Clinic 1957–, Chair. Dept. of Oncology 1975–86, Dir. Mayo Comprehensive Cancer Center 1975–86; Prof. of Medicine Mayo Medical School 1972–76, Prof. of Oncology 1976–, Purvis and Roberta Tabor Prof. 1981–; mem. Oncologic Drugs Advisory Cttee. FDA, Cancer Advisory Cttee. AMA, bd. scientific counselors Nat. Cancer Inst., Colorectal Cancer Advisory Cttee. American Cancer Soc., American Soc. Clinical Oncology, Soc. Clinical Trials, American Assen. Cancer Research, Soc. Surgical Oncology, American Gastroenterologic Assen.; mem. editorial bd.: Cancer 1974–, Cancer Medicine 1978–, Current Problems in Cancer 1978–83, Journal Soviet Oncology 1979–, Cancer Research 1979–84, Int. Journal Radiation Oncology and Biological Physics 1981–, Journal Clinical Oncology 1986–, Journal Medical and Pediatric Oncology 1986–; decorated Knight of Malta; recipient Heath Memorial Award, M.D. Anderson Hosp. Tex. 1986; Cancer Research Award, Assen. of Community Cancer Centers 1987; Dr. h.c. (Grenoble) 1987. *Publications:* Multiple Primary Malignant Neoplasms 1966, Advanced Gastro-intestinal Cancer, Clinical Management and Chemotherapy 1969. *Address:* 200 SW 1st Street, Rochester, Minn. 55905 (Office); 1009 Skyline Lane, SW Rochester, Minn. 55902, U.S.A. (Home).

MOERTONO, Maj.-Gen. Amir; Indonesian politician and retd. army officer; ed. Mil. School of Law, Jakarta; Staff Officer with Dept. of Defence during 1950s; attended intelligence course with Lightning Div. of U.S. Army 1959; worked with Sekber Golkar (now Golongan Karya) (Secr. of Functional Groups forming a political front) 1964–; Brig.-Gen. 1969; Asst. for Socio-Political Affairs, Hankam (Ministry of Defence and Security) 1969; Maj.-Gen. 1971; Chair. Golongan Karya 1972, Gen. Chair. 1973; retd. from Army 1972. *Address:* Golongan Karya, Jakarta, Indonesia.

MOFFATT, Henry Keith, SC.D., F.R.S.; British professor of mathematical physics; b. 12 April 1935, Edin.; s. of Frederick Henry Moffatt and Emmeline Marchant Fleming; m. Katharine (Linty) Stiven 1960; two s. (one deceased) two d.; ed. Edinburgh and Cambridge Univs.; Asst. Lecturer, then Lecturer, Cambridge Univ. 1961–76, Prof. of Mathematical Physics 1980–; Fellow of Trinity Coll., Cambridge 1961–76, 1980–, Tutor 1971–74, Sr. Tutor 1975; Prof. Applied Mathematics, Bristol Univ. 1977–80; Visiting Prof. at various int. univs. 1965–; Dr. h.c. (INPG Grenoble) 1987; Smiths Prize 1960. *Publications:* Magnetic Field Generation in Electrically Conducting Fluids 1978; Ed. Journal of Fluid Mechanics 1966–83. *Leisure* *interests:* French country cooking, hill walking. *Address:* 6 Banhams Close, Cambridge, CB4 1HX, England. *Telephone:* (0223) 63338.

MOFFATT, John, M.A., D.PHIL.; British physicist; b. 12 Oct. 1922; s. of Jacob Moffatt and Ethel Moffatt; m. Una Lamorna Morris 1949; one d.; ed. Keighley Boys' Grammar School, Magdalen Coll., Oxford; research scientist in radar, Thomson-Houston Co. Ltd., Rugby 1942–46; Sr. Research Fellow, Clarendon Lab., Oxford 1950–65, lecturer Dept. of Nuclear Physics 1965–87, Fellow and Praelector in Physics, The Queen's Coll. 1950–, Sr. Tutor 1972–76, Provost 1987–. *Publications:* articles on physics in scientific journals. *Address:* The Queen's College, Oxford, OX1 4AW, England. *Telephone:* (0865) 279120.

MOFFO, Anna; opera singer; b. Wayne, Pa., U.S.A.; d. of Nicholas and Regina (Cinti) Moffo; m. Robert Sarnoff 1974; ed. Curtis Inst.; m. Robert Sarnoff 1974; appeared in TV opera Madam Butterfly, Italy; singer opera houses in Paris, London, Salzburg, Vienna, Milan, numerous others abroad; American debut at Lyric Opera Co., Chicago 1957, Metropolitan Opera Co., New York 1959; appeared Voice of Firestone telecast 1957; *operatic roles (soprano) include;* Norma, La Bohème, Mignon, Rigoletto, Falstaff, Madam Butterfly, The Barber of Seville, La Traviata, Thaïs, The Daughter of the Regiment, Stiffelio, Tosca, Hansel and Gretel, Faust, Don Pasquale, Romeo and Juliet, The Magic Flute, Turandot, La Juive, The Marriage of Figaro, Otello, Il Trovatore, Luisa Miller, La Belle Hélène, The Gypsy Princess; recital tours, U.S.; numerous recordings; Order of Merit (Italy); Young Artists award, Philadelphia Orchestra; Fulbright award for study in Europe; Liebe Augustin Award. *Address:* c/o Columbia Artists Management, 165 West 57th Street, New York, N.Y. 10019, U.S.A.

MOFFORD, Rose; American politician; b. 10 June 1922, Globe, Ariz.; Sec. in Ariz. State Treasury 1941–43; Ariz. State Tax Commr. 1943–54; Wesley Bolinger Ariz. Sec. of State 1954–55; Asst. Sec. of State of Ariz., Phoenix 1955–75; Asst. Dir. of Revenue State of Ariz. 1975–77; Sec. of State 1977–88, Gov. 1988–; Democrat. *Address:* State Capitol, Phoenix, Ariz. 85007, U.S.A.

MOGAE, Festus Gontebanye, M.A.; Botswana financial administrator; b. 21 August 1939, Serowe; s. of Dihabano and Dithunya Mogae; m. Barbara Gemma Modise 1968; two d.; ed.Moeng Secondary School, North West London Polytechnic, Univs. of Oxford and Sussex; Planning Officer, Ministry of Devt. 1968–69, Ministry of Finance and Devt. Planning 1970–71, Sr. Planning Officer 1971–72, Dir. Econ Affairs 1972–74; Perm. Sec. 1975–76; Alt. Exec. Dir. of IMF 1976–78, Exec. Dir. 1978–80; Alt. Gov. for Botswana, IMF 1971–72, African Devt. Bank 1971–76, IBRD 1973–76; Dir. Botswana Devt. Corpn. 1971–74 (Chair. 1975–76), De Beers Botswana Mining Co. Ltd. 1975–76, Bangwato Concessions Ltd. 1975–76, B.C.L. Sales Ltd. 1975–76, Bank Botswana 1975–76 (Gov. –1982); Gov. IMF 1981–82; Perm. Sec. to Pres. of Botswana 1982–; Rep., Commonwealth Fund for Tech. Co-operation 1971–. *Leisure interests:* reading, tennis, music. *Address:* State House, Private Bag 001, Gaborone, Botswana.

MOGWE, Archibald Mooketa, M.B.E., B.A., P.M.S., P.H., M.P.; Botswana politician and teacher; b. 29 Aug. 1921, Kanye; s. of Rev. M. T. and Mary (née Leepo) Mogwe; m. Lena Mosele Senakhomo 1953; one s. two d.; ed. schools in Bechuanaland Protectorate, teacher training in S. Africa, Univs. of Reading and Oxford; teacher 1944–57; Educ. Officer 1957–64; transferred to Secr. 1964, Perm. Sec. 1966; worked in Foreign Office 1966–, Sr. Perm. Sec., Sec. to Cabinet and Head of Public Service 1968–74; Minister of Foreign Affairs 1974–84, of Mineral Resources and Water Affairs 1984–. *Leisure interests:* soccer, classical music, shooting. *Address:* Ministry of Mineral Resources and Water Affairs, Private Bag 0018, Gaborone, Botswana.

MOHALE, Albert Steerforth, M.A.; Lesotho diplomatist; b. 26 April 1928, Mohale's Hoek; s. of Solomon Setlolela and Alice Majobo Mohale; m. Catherine Setlogelo 1961; three d.; ed. Pius XII Univ. Coll., South Africa and Univ. of St. Francis Xavier, Canada; fmr. teacher, Basutoland and South Africa; Lecturer and Deputy Dir. Extension Dept., Pius XII Univ. Coll. 1960–61; Co-operative Training Officer, Basutoland 1961, later Asst. Registrar of Co-operative Socs.; Supernumerary Head of Govt. Training Section 1965; Amb. to U.S.A., High Commr. to Canada and Perm. Rep. to UN 1966–69; High Commr. to Kenya 1969; Perm. Sec. Public Service Dept. 1969–70, Ministry of Agric. 1970–71, Ministry of Interior 1971; Minister of Transport and Communications 1975–76, of Agric. 1976–77, of Educ., Youth Sports and Culture 1977–80; Gen. Man. Lesotho Nat. Devt. Corpn., Special Adviser 1975–; Man. Dir. Lesotho Nat. Bus Service 1975–. *Leisure interest:* tennis. *Address:* c/o Ministry of Education, P.O. Box MS. 47, Maseru, Lesotho. *Telephone:* 3040 (Home).

MOHAMED KAMIL, Abdallah; Djibouti politician; b. 1936, Obock; ed. Inst. of Politicial Studies, Paris; mem. of Union Démocratique Afar in opposition to Ali Arif Bourhan 1965–66; fmr. Sec.-Gen. of the Govt.; Pres. Conseil du Gouvernement July 1976–May 1977; Minister for the Plan and Devt. May-June 1977; Minister of Foreign Affairs July 1977–Feb. 1978; Prime Minister Feb.-Sept. 1978, also Minister of Defence; Chair. Special Comm. of Afars Jan. 1978. *Address:* c/o Conseil du Gouvernement, Djibouti, Republic of Djibouti.

MOHAMMAD, Lieut.-Gen. Nazar; Afghan politician; b. 1935, Herat Prov.; ed. Mil. Univ. of Kabul, Mil. Acad. of the U.S.S.R.; fmr. Commdr. in the air force, Deputy to the Minister of Communications and Defence Minister; mem. People's Democratic Party of Afghanistan 1974, mem. Cen. Cttee. 1983–, cand. mem. of Politburo 1985; First Vice-Chair. of Council of Ministers 1986–88; Order of the Red Banner. *Address:* c/o Council of Ministers, Kabul, Afghanistan.

MOHAMMED, Kamaluddin, M.P.; Trinidadian politician; b. 1927, Trinidad; s. of late Fazal Mohammed and Kajiman Khartoum; m. Saleema Muzaffar 1952; four s. two d.; ed. San Juan Church Missionary School and privately; County Councillor 1952–56; mem. Legis. Council 1956; Minister of Agric., Lands and Fisheries 1956–61, of Public Utilities 1961–67, of West Indian Affairs 1967–73, of External Affairs 1970–73, of Health and Local Govt. 1973–81, of Agric., Lands and Food Production 1981–86; founder mem. People's Nat. Movt., Deputy Political Leader 1971–; Leader House of Reps.; Gen. Sec. Trinidad Islamic Asscn.; Pres. World Health Assembly 1978–79. *Address:* Mohammedville, San Juan, Trinidad.

MOHAMMED ZAHIR SHAH; fmr. King of Afghanistan; b. 15 Oct. 1914; m. Lady Homira, 4 Nov. 1931; children: Princess Bilqis, Prince Ahmad Shah, Princess Maryam, Prince Mohammed Nadir, Prince Shah Mahmoud, Prince Mohammed Daoud, Prince Mirvis; ed. Habibia High School, Istiqlal Coll. (both in Kabul), Lycée Janson-de-Sailly and Lycée of Montpellier, France; graduated with honours; attended Infantry Officers' School, Kabul 1932; Asst. Minister in Ministry of Nat. Defence 1932–33; acting Minister of Educ. 1933; crowned King 8 Nov. 1933; deposed 17 July 1973, abdicated 24 Aug. 1973.

MOHIEDDIN, Zakaria; Egyptian army officer and politician; b. 7 May 1918; s. of late Abdul Magid Mohieddin and Zeinab Abdul Magid; m. Naila Moustafa 1950; one s. two d.; ed. Mil. Coll. and Staff Officers' Coll., Cairo; fmr. lecturer Mil. Coll. and Staff Officers' Coll. and Dir.-Gen. Intelligence; mem. Revolutionary Council 1952; Minister of the Interior 1953–58; Minister of the Interior U.A.R. 1958–62, Vice-Pres. U.A.R. and Chair. Aswan Dam Cttee. 1961–62; mem. Nat. Defence Cttee. 1962–69, Presidency Council 1962–64; mem. Exec. Cttee. Arab Socialist Union 1964–69; Deputy Prime Minister 1964–65, 1967–68; Prime Minister and Minister of the Interior 1965–66. *Leisure interests:* fishing, shooting, rowing, poultry farming. *Address:* 52 El-Thawra Street, Dokki, Cairo, Egypt. *Telephone:* 700 602.

MOHN, Reinhard; German publisher; b. 29 June 1921; ed. high school; army service 1939–43; P.O.W. in N. Africa and U.S.A. 1943–46; Pres. and C.E.O. Bertelsmann A.G. 1947–81, Chair. Supervisory Bd. 1981–. *Address:* Bertelsmann A.G., 4830 Gütersloh 1, Federal Republic of Germany.

MOHORITA, Vasil; Czechoslovak politician; b. 19 Sept. 1952, Prague; ed. Komsomol Coll., Moscow and CPCZ Political Coll., Prague; joined Communist Party of Czechoslovakia (CPCZ) 1970, mem. Cen. Cttee. 1988–; Chair. Youth Union's Czech Cen. Cttee. 1987–; mem. Czech Nat. Front Presidium; Deputy, Czech Nat. Council. *Address:* Central Committee of Communist Party of Czechoslovakia, Nábř. Ludvíka Svobody 12, 125 11 Prague, Czechoslovakia.

MOHRT, Michel, L. EN D.; French writer and editor; b. 28 April 1914, Morlaix; s. of Fernand and Amélie (née Gélébart) Mohrt; m. Françoise Jarrier 1955; one s.; ed. Law School, Rennes; lawyer, Marseilles Bar until 1942; Prof. Yale Univ. 1947–52; Ed. and Head English Translations Section Les Editions Gallimard 1952–; mem. Acad. Française 1985; Chevalier, Légion d'honneur, Croix de guerre; Grand Prix du roman de l'Académie française for La Prison Maritime 1962; Grand Prix de la Critique Littéraire 1970; Grand Prix de Litterature de l'Académie française 1983. *Publications:* Novels: Le répit, Mon royaume pour un cheval 1949, Les nomades, le serviteur fidèle, La prison maritime 1961, La campagne d'Italie 1965, L'ours des Adirondacks 1969, Deux Américaines à Paris 1974, Les moyens du bord 1975, La guerre civile 1986, Le Télésiège 1989; essays: Les intellectuels devant la défaite de 1870, Montherlant, homme libre 1943, Le nouveau roman américain 1956, L'air du large 1969, L'Air du Large II 1988; plays: Un jeu d'enfer 1970 (narration), La maison du père 1979, Vers l'Ouest 1988. *Leisure interest:* sailing. *Address:* c/o Editions Gallimard, 5 rue Sébastien-Bottin, 75007 Paris; 4 bis rue du Cherche-Midi, 75006 Paris, France (Home). *Telephone:* 42-22-42-12 (Home).

MOI, Daniel arap; Kenyan politician; b. 1924, Sacho, Baringo district; ed. African Mission School, Kabartonjo A.I.M. School and Govt. African School, Kapsabet; teacher 1945–57; Head Teacher, Govt. African School, Kabarnet 1946–48, 1955–57, teacher Tambach Teacher Training School, Kabarnet 1948–54; African Rep. mem., Legis. Council 1957–63; Chair. Kenya African Democratic Union (KADU) 1960–61; mem. House of Reps. 1961–; Parl. Sec., Ministry of Educ. April-Dec. 1961; Minister of Educ. 1961–62, Local Govt. 1962–64, Home Affairs 1964–67; Pres. Kenya African Nat. Union (KANU) for Rift Valley Province 1966–67; Vice-Pres. of Kenya 1967–78, concurrently Minister of Home Affairs; Pres. of Kenya and C.-in-C. of the Armed Forces Oct. 1978–; Chair. OAU 1981–82; mem. Rift Valley Educ. Bd., Kalenjin Language Cttee.; Chair. Rift Valley Provincial Court; Kt. of Grace, Order of St. John 1980. *Address:* Office of the President, P.O. Box 30510, Nairobi, Kenya.

MOINOT, Pierre, L. ES L.; French civil servant; b. 29 March 1920, Fressines, Deux-Sèvres; m. Madeleine Sarrailh 1947; one s. four d.; ed. Univs. de Paris, Caen and Grenoble; Sr. Civil Servant 1946–; Tech. Adviser, Pvt. Office of André Malraux 1959–61; Dir. Theatres and Cultural Action 1960–62; Admin. Union générale cinématographique 1960–; Pres. Comm. on advances in long films 1964–72, Comm. on Audiovisual Problems 1981–; French Del. to UNESCO 1966; Dir.-Gen. of Arts and Letters 1966–69; Chief Adviser, Audit Office 1967, Pres. 1978, Attorney-Gen. 1983–86; mem. Acad. française 1982–; Prix du Roman de l'Académie française, Prix Sainte-Beuve, Prix des libraries de France, Prix Fémina 1979; Commdr., Légion d'honneur, Croix de guerre, Médaille des blessés, Commdr. des Arts et des Lettres, Bronze Star Medal, Chevalier des Palmes académiques, Officier du Mérite agricole and other decorations. *Publications:* Armes et bagages 1951, La chasse royale 1954, La blessure 1956, Le sable vif 1963, Héliogabale 1971, Mazarin 1978, Le guetteur d'ombre 1979, Jeanne d'Arc 1988. *Leisure interests:* hunting, carpentry. *Address:* 44 rue du Cherche-Midi, 75006 Paris, France (Home). *Telephone:* 45-44-19-47.

MOISEYEV, Igor Aleksandrovich; Soviet choreographer; b. 21 Jan. 1906, Kiev; m. 1st Tamara Alekseevna Seifort 1918, one d.; m. 2nd Irina Alekseevna Chagadaeva; ed. Bolshoi Theatre School of Choreography; artist and ballet master at the Bolshoi Theatre 1924–39; Dir. of the Choreographic Dept. of the Theatre of People's Art 1936; was one of the organizers of the U.S.S.R. Festival of Folk Dancing; Art Dir. of the Folk Dance Ensemble of the U.S.S.R. 1937–; People's Artist of the U.S.S.R. 1953; State Prizewinner 1942, 1947, 1952; Lenin Prizewinner 1967; two Orders of Red Banner of Labour; Order of Lenin; Hero of Socialist Labour 1976 and other decorations. *Publications:* articles on choreography of national dance. *Address:* Moiseyev Dance Company of the U.S.S.R., 20 Ploshchad Mayakovskogo, Moscow, U.S.S.R. *Telephone:* 299-63-28.

MOISEYEV, Gen. Mikhail; Soviet chief of staff; b. 1938; mem. CPSU; specialist in Soviet mil. ideology and training; First Deputy Minister of Defence; Chief of Staff Dec. 1988–; elected to Congress of People's Deputies of the U.S.S.R. 1989. *Address:* Ministry of Defence, Moscow, U.S.S.R.

MOISEYEV, Lieut.-Gen. Nikolay Andreyevich; Soviet military official; b. 1934; ed. Cen. Cttee. Higher Party School and Lenin Mil.-Politican Acad.; Komsomol and party work in Soviet Army 1952–68; mem. CPSU 1955–; Head of Political Div., First Deputy Head of Political Section of Army 1968–79; First Deputy Head of Mil. Council, Head of Political Wing of Armed Forces 1979–85; mem. of Mil. Council, Head of Political Wing of Soviet Forces in Germany 1985–; Lieut.-Gen. 1982–; mem. of CPSU Cen. Auditing Cttee. 1986–. *Address:* c/o CPSU Central Auditing Comittee, Moscow, U.S.S.R.

MOISEYEVA, Olga Nikolayevna; Soviet ballerina and teacher; b. 25 Dec. 1928, Leningrad; m. Igor Lvovich Rogachev 1958; ed. Leningrad Ballet School (under A. Ya. Vaganova); Dancer with Kirov Ballet 1947–73. *Major roles:* Odette-Odile in Swan Lake, Princess Florina in Sleeping Beauty, Giselle, Kitri in Don Quixote, Aegina in Spartacus, Gayane in Gayane, etc.; Teacher at Kirov 1972–81; Sr. ballet-master with Kirov 1981–. *Leisure interest:* planting flowers. *Address:* c/o Kirov Ballet, Teatralnaya ploshchad, Leningrad, U.S.S.R.

MOJSOV, Lazar, D.IUR.; Yugoslav journalist, politician and diplomatist; b. 19 Dec. 1920, Negotino, Macedonia; s. of Dono and Efka Mojsov; m. Liljana Jankov 1945; two d.; ed. Belgrade Univ.; fmr. mem. Anti-Fascist Assembly for the Nat. Liberation of Macedonia; fmr. Public Prosecutor, Macedonia; Minister of Justice, Macedonia 1948–51; Dir. New Macedonia 1953–58; Pres. Supreme Court of Macedonia 1953; fmr. Head of Press Dept., Fed. Govt of Macedonia; mem. Yugoslav Fed. Parliament and Parliament of Macedonia; mem. Exec. Bd., Socialist League of Working People of Yugoslavia; mem. Exec. Cttee. of Cen. Cttee., Macedonian League of Communists; mem. Cen. Cttee. League of Communists of Yugoslavia –1989 (Pres. of Presidium 1980–81); Amb. to U.S.S.R. 1958–61; Dir. Inst. for Study of Workers' Movements 1961–62; Dir. and Chief Ed. Borba 1962–64; Pres. Int. Cttee. of Fed. Conf. of Socialist Alliance of Working People of Yugoslavia 1965; Amb. to Austria 1967–69; Perm. Rep. to UN 1969–74; Chair. Security Council 1973; Deputy Fed. Sec. for Foreign Affairs 1974–78, Fed. Sec. 1982–84; mem. Collective State Presidency of Yugoslavia 1984–86, Vice-Pres. 1986–87, Pres. 1987–88; Pres. 32nd UN Gen. Assembly 1977; Partisan Memorial medal 1941; Order of Merit for Exceptional Achievements First Class, Order of Merit for Services to the Nation, First and Third Class, Order of Brotherhood and Unity. *Publications:* The Bulgarian Working Party (Communist) and the Macedonian National Question 1948, Vasil Glavinov: First Propagator of Socialism in Macedonia 1949, Concerning the Question of the Macedonian National Minority in Greece 1954. *Leisure interest:* philately. *Address:* c/o Office of the Vice-President, Collective State Presidency, Belgrade, Yugoslavia.

MOKANU, Aleksandr Aleksandrovich; Soviet party official and politician; b. 1934, Moldavia; ed. Kishinev Agric. Inst.; engineer 1956–57; worked at Agric. Inst., Kishinev 1957–61; worked in the construction office of a tractor works in Kishinev 1961–67; mem. CPSU 1968; Dir. of a machine-construction plant for wine production 1967–71; Pres. of Lenin regional exec. cttee. 1971–74; First Deputy Pres. of Kishinev City Soviet 1974–77; First Sec. of Rybnits, then Tiraspol regional and city cttees. of Moldavian

CP 1977–85; Minister of Housing for Moldavian S.S.R. 1985; Pres. of Presidium of Supreme Soviet of Moldavian S.S.R. Dec. 1985–; Deputy Pres. of Presidium of Supreme Soviet of S.S.R. 1986–. *Address:* U.S.S.R. Supreme Soviet, Kremlin, Moscow, U.S.S.R.

MOKHANTŜO, Col. Philip Monyane; Lesotho politician; b. 14 Dec. 1946, Ha Koali, Quthing Dist.; joined Lesotho Paramil. Force (fmr. Police Mobile Unit) 1966; ed. LPF Pvt. School; qualified as fixed wing and helicopter pilot 1979; mem. Maseru LPF Air Squadron; Minister of Transport and Telecommunications 1986–; Police Medal for Meritorious Conduct. *Address:* c/o The Military Council, Maseru, Lesotho.

MOKODOPO, Jean-Paul; Central African Republic diplomatist and politician; Amb. to Yugoslavia 1970–73, to Nigeria 1982–; Minister Del. to the Presidency charged with Territorial Admin. April-Oct. 1973; Minister of Planning and Int. Co-operation 1973–76 (with Statistics 1974–76, also with Territorial Admin. April-Sept. 1976); Minister of Public Health Sept.-Dec. 1976, of Foreign Affairs 1976–79. *Address:* Embassy of the Central African Republic, Plot 137, Ajao Estate, New Airport, Oshodi, Lagos, Nigeria.

MOKOROANE, Morena Moletsane; Lesotho teacher and politician; b. 22 Aug. 1932, Ha Mokoroane, Mohale's Hoek Dist.; ed. Siloe Intermediate School, Morija Training Coll.; teacher, Siloe Parish; joined Basutoland Congress Party (BCP) 1962; Sec., then Deputy Leader of the party in Mohale's Hoek Dist.; Vice-Chair., then Chair. of Mohale's Hoek Dist. Council 1962–65; Opposition M.P. until dissolution in 1970; Opposition Leader Interim Nat. Ass. 1973, also Chair. Public Accounts Cttee. until 1984; Minister of Trade and Industry 1986–. *Address:* c/o The Military Council, Maseru, Lesotho.

MOKRZYŃSKI, Jerzy Bogusław; Polish architect; b. 22 Sept. 1909, Rzeszów; s. of Józef Mokrzyński and Helena Tabaczkowska; m. Maria Połczyńska-Armółowicz 1945; one d.; ed. Warsaw Polytechnic; Sr. Designer-Private Atelier 1936–39, and in Office of Gen. Architecture 1945–80; mem. Polish Asscn. of Architects (SARP) 1936–, Vice-Pres. Cen. Bd. 1952–56; mem. Co-ordination Cttee. of Competition Judges, Collective Judge and mem. for many years; mem. and Chair. Sec. Architecture ZAiKS Asscn. of Authors 1948–, mem. and Expert Cttee. of Tourism 1954–79; participation in 58 competitions, 44 first prizes and awards with W. Kłyszewski (q.v.) and E. Wierzbicki (q.v.) and many of them constructed, for instance: Univ. in Łódź 1937, Bank of Investment in Poznań 1938, Building for Asscn. "Polonia" in Warsaw 1938, Social Home in Starachowice 1938, Savings Bank in Warsaw 1946, Polish United Workers' Party Building in Warsaw 1951, Architects Rest Home in Zakopane 1956, Railway Station in Katowice 1959, Polish Pavilions for Expositions in New Delhi 1959 and Thessaloniki 1959, 1960, Exposition Pavilion in Poznań 1966, Museum Contemporary Art in Skopje, Yugoslavia 1970, Recreation Centre in Romanowo 1968, Social and Cultural Centre in Krynica 1969, Office Building in Katowice 1970, Hotel and Museum in Wilderness Białowieża 1971, Seamen's Home in Szczecin 1972, Tourist Hotel in Łowicz 1974, Philharmonic Hall and Music School in Rzeszów 1978, Puppet Theatre in Białystok 1979, Museum in Tatra Mts. Nat. Park in Zakopane 1980 and many others; Participant Int. Union of Architects' The Hague 1955, Moscow 1958, Mexico 1978, Warsaw 1981; State Award third 1951, second 1955 and first Grade 1974; Golden Badge Rebuilding Warsaw 1958; Hon. Award SARP and ZAiKS 1968; Hon. Badge SARP Katowice and Szczecin 1973, Golden Medal Ministry of Building 1975, Hon. Badge of Culture 1978, Ministry of Building Award 1983; Officer's Cross Order of Polonia Restituta 1957, Order of Banner of Labour 2nd Class 1969. *Publications:* Tourist Facilities 1962, 1972, Vacation Houses 1977, Architecture of Leisure Time 1988. *Leisure interests:* travel, nature, tourism. *Address:* ul. Marszałkowska 140 m. 18, 00 061 Warsaw, Poland. *Telephone:* 26 26 83.

MOKRZYSZCZAK, Włodzimierz, M.ENG.; Polish politician; b. 3 August 1938, Ostrowiec Świętokrzyski; ed. Transport Faculty of Warsaw Tech. Univ.; employee Polish State Railways 1961–76, Vice-Dir. Gdańsk Region of Polish State Railways 1974, Dir. Olsztyn Region 1974–76; mem. Polish United Workers' Party (PZPR) 1959–, Sec. PZPR Voivodship Cttee., Olsztyn 1976–81, First Sec. 1981; mem. PZPR Cen. Cttee. 1981–86, alt. mem. Political Bureau of PZPR Cen. Cttee. 1981–86, mem. Political Bureau PZPR Cen. Cttee. 1986–88, Sec. PZPR Cen. Cttee 1981–86, Chair. Cen. Control and Revisional Comm. of PZPR 1986–; Amb. to Czechoslovakia 1988–; Kt.'s Cross Order of Polonia Restituta and other decorations. *Address:* Embassy of the Polish People's Republic, Valdstejnska 8, Praha 1, Mala Swana, Czechoslovakia.

MOLAPO, Charles Dube, LL.B.; Lesotho politician; b. 25 Dec. 1918, Leribe District; ed. Cape Town Univ.; Attorney-at-Law, Basutoland 1954–64, subsequently Sec.-Gen. Basutoland Nat. Party and mem. Legis. Assembly; nominated to Senate 1965; Minister of Devt., Commerce and Industry 1965–67; High Commr. in Kenya and Roving Amb. in Africa 1968–69; Minister of Health, Educ. and Social Welfare 1971–74, of Justice 1974–75, of Foreign Affairs 1975–81, 1982–83, of Information and Broadcasting 1981–83; Pres. Basotho Democratic Alliance (BDA) 1984–85.

MOLAPO, Mooki Vitus; Lesotho diplomatist; b. 2 June 1937; m.; four c.; ed. Inkamana High School, Natal, Pius XII Coll., Univ. of South Africa, Univ. of Dar es Salaam, and Univ. of West Indies, Trinidad and Tobago; teacher, Maseru secondary school 1965; Information Officer, Dept. of

Information, Maseru 1966; chief announcer, Radio Lesotho 1966–67; First Sec. Lesotho Embassy, Washington 1967–70; Chief of Protocol, Ministry of Foreign Affairs 1970–71; Perm. Rep. to UN 1971–74, 1976–78; del. to UN Gen. Assembly 1967–75, and rep. at many other int. confs.; Amb. to Iran 1974–76, also accred. to Romania, Yugoslavia, the Vatican City, United Arab Emirates; Minister of Commerce and Industry 1978–81, of Foreign Affairs 1981–82. *Publication:* The Dawns are Quiet Here 1975. *Address:* c/o Ministry of Foreign Affairs, Maseru, Lesotho.

MOLDOVAN, Roman; Romanian politician and economist; b. 14 Dec. 1911, Daia, Mureş County; s. of Elisei and Ana Moldovan; m. Elena Moldovan 1938; two d.; Univ. Prof.; Corresp. mem. Acad. of Socialist Repub. of Romania 1963–; Deputy to Grand Nat. Assembly; mem. Cen. Cttee. of Romanian CP 1965–79; Chair. State Planning Cttee. 1965; Chair. Nat. Council of Scientific Research and Deputy Chair. Council of Ministers 1965–67; Chair. State Cttee. for Prices 1967–69; Vice-Pres. Econ. Council 1969–71; Vice-Pres. Acad. of Social and Political Sciences 1970–; Chair. Romanian Chamber of Commerce and Industry 1972–77. *Publications include:* Formation and Movement of Capital in Romania 1940, Planned Management of National Economy in Romanian People's Republic 1959, Logic, Methodology and Philosophy of Science 1973, Les changements structuraux économiques et sociaux dans le processus d'édification du socialisme 1974; Co-author: Romania's Economic Development 1944–1974, Romania's Industry 1944–1964. *Leisure interests:* mountains, tourism. *Address:* Romanian Chamber of Commerce and Industry, Bd. Nicolae Bălcescu 22, Bucharest, Romania. *Telephone:* 15-47-07.

MOLDT, Ewald; German diplomatist; b. 22 April 1927, Greifswald; ed. Deutsche Akademie fur Staats- und Rechtswissenschaften; mem. Socialist Unity Party (SED) 1946–; G.D.R. diplomatic service 1952–; 1st Sec., G.D.R. Embassy in Romania 1958–59, Amb. 1965–71; Counsellor, Embassy in Poland 1959–63; Head of Press Section, Ministry of Foreign Affairs 1963–65; Deputy Minister of Foreign Affairs 1970–; Chair. G.D.R. UNESCO Comm. 1973–; Head G.D.R. Perm. Mission in Fed. Repub. of Germany 1978–88; Verdienstorden in Silber und Bronze and other decorations. *Address:* Ministry of Foreign Affairs, 1020 Berlin, Manx-Engell-Platz 2, German Democratic Republic.

MOLIN, Yuriy Nikolaevich; Soviet chemist and physicist; b. 3 Feb. 1934; ed. Moscow Inst. of Physics and Tech.; worked in U.S.S.R. Acad. of Sciences Inst. of Chemistry and Physics 1957–59; in various posts in U.S.S.R. Acad. of Sciences Inst. of Chem. Kinetics and Combustion 1959–, Dir. 1974–; teacher in Univ. of Novosibirsk 1966–; mem. U.S.S.R. Acad. of Sciences, Lenin Prize 1986. *Address:* c/o Academy of Sciences of the U.S.S.R., Moscow V-71, Leninsky Pr. 14, U.S.S.R.

MOLINA BARRAZA, Col. Arturo Armando; Salvadorian army officer and politician; b. 6 Aug. 1927, San Salvador; s. of Mariano Molina and Matilde Barraza de Molina; m. María Elena Contreras de Molina; four s. one d.; ed. Escuela Militar, El Salvador, Escuela Superior de Guerra, Mexico, Escuela de Infanteria, Spain; Section and Co. Commdr., Escuela Militar; Artillery Garrison, Asst. Dir. Escuela de Armas, Section and Dept. Chief, Staff HQ; Del. 6th Conf. of American Armed Forces, Peru 1965, 7th Conf. Buenos Aires; Gen. Co-ordinator, 2nd and 3rd Confs. of Defence Council of Cen. American States; Dir. Exec. Comm. for Shipping; Dir. Nat. Cttee. of Caritas, El Salvador; Pres. of El Salvador 1972–77.

MOLINARI, Ricardo E.; Argentine writer; b. 23 March 1898; s. of Juan Lauriano Molinari and Maria Esther de Molinari; m. Amelia Vegazo; ed. secondary school; has received every poetry prize in Argentina. *Publications include:* El Huésped y la Melancolía 1946, Días donde la Tarde es un Pájaro 1954, Unida Noche 1957, El Cielo de las Alondras y las Gaviotas 1963, Una sombra antigua Canta 1966, La Hoguera Transparente 1970, La Escudilla 1973, Las Sombras del Pájaro Tostado (complete works) 1974. *Address:* Julián Alvarez 2092, Piso 4°, Codigo Postal 1425, Buenos Aires, Argentina. *Telephone:* 826-1821.

MÖLK, Ulrich, DR.PHIL.; German professor of Romance literature; b. 29 March 1937, Hamburg; m. 1962; ed. Univs. of Hamburg and Heidelberg; Prof. of Romance Literature, Univ. of Giessen 1967; Prof. of Romance Literature Univ. of Göttingen and Dir. Inst. für Lateinische und Romanische Philologie des Mittelalters 1974–; mem. Acad. of Göttingen. *Publications:* Guiraut Riquier, Las cansos 1962, Trobar clus 1968, Répertoire métrique de la poésie lyrique française 1972, Trotzki, Literaturkritik 1973, Trobadorlyrik 1982, Flaubert, Une Nuit de Don Juan, Edition 1984, Vita und Kult des hl. Metro von Verona 1987. *Address:* Hainholzweg 44A, 3400 Göttingen, Federal Republic of Germany. *Telephone:* (0551) 4 79 78.

MOLL, Kurt; German bass; b. 11 April 1938, Buir; m. Ursula Pade 1968; one d.; ed. Staatliche Hochschule für Musik, Cologne; operatic début Cologne; subsequently sang operatic roles at Aachen, Mainz, Wuppertal, Hamburg; appeared Bayreuth 1968, Salzburg 1970, La Scala, Milan 1972, Covent Garden, London 1975, Metropolitan Opera, New York 1978. *Address:* Billwerder Billdeich 500, 2050 Hamburg 80, Federal Republic of Germany.

MOLLAT du JOURDIN, Michel Jacques, D. ES L.; French professor and author; b. 13 July 1911, Ancenis; s. of Emmanuel Mollat du Jourdin and Jeanne Bonamy; m. Annick Deshais du Portail 1933; three s. two d.; ed. Ecole Saint Stanislas and Univ. of Rennes; School Teacher Lycées Lorient, Rouen and Paris 1935–45; Prof. Univ. of Besancon 1948–50, Lille 1950–58, Paris-Sorbonne 1958–79, Prof. Emer. 1979–; Dir. of Studies Ecole pratique des Hautes Etudes 1969–; Pres. Comm. Int. d'Histoire Maritime 1960–80; mem. Acad. de Marine, Acad. des Inscriptions et Belles Lettres; Assoc. mem. Real Acad. de Historia (Spain), Acad. Royale Flamande (Belgium), Acad. de Marinha (Portugal); Corresp. Fellow Medieval Acad. of America, Soc. of Nautical Research; Chevalier Légion d'honneur, Commandeur Palmes académiques, Grand Oficier ordre de l'Infant Henri le Navigateur; Grand Prix Gobert 1952, Médaille d'argent du C.N.R.S. 1978, Grand Prix Geographical Soc. of Paris. *Publications include:* le Commerce maritime normand à la fin du Moyen Age 1952, Les Affaires de Jacques Coeur 1952, Genèse médiévale de la France moderne (XIV-XVᵉs) 1970, Etudes sur l'économie et la société de l'Occident médiéval XII-XVᵉs. 1977, Etudes d'histoire maritime 1977, L'Image du Noir dans l'Art occidental (with J. Devisse) 1979, Histoire des Hôpitaux (with J. Imbert) 1982, Giovanni et Girolamo Verrazano, navigateurs de Francois 1er 1982, Les Explorateurs du XIIIᵉ au XVIᵉs. Premiers regards sur des mondes nouveaux 1984, Jacques Coeur ou l'esprit d'enterprise au XVs. 1988, Les routes millénaires (Antiquité et Moyen Age) 1988, over 150 articles in int. reviews, contributions to numerous encyclopaedias. *Leisure interest:* gardening. *Address:* 1 rue Bausset, 75015 Paris; Lutig Noz, pointe du Trec'h, 56780 Ile-aux-Moines, France. *Telephone:* (1) 48 28 88 31; 97 26 35 47.

MÖLLER, Erwin; German business executive; b. 23 Jan. 1939; m.; ed. Tech. Univ. of Darmstadt; Chair. Supervisory Bd. Metaleurop S.A., Foutenay-sous-Bois, VTG Vereinigte Tanklager und Transportmittel GmbH, Hamburg; Chair. Exec. Bd. Preussag A.G.; mem. Supervisory Bd. Hannoversche Lebensversicherung AG, Hannover, Kabelmetal Electro GmbH, Hannover, Salzgitter Stahl GmbH, Düsseldorf; mem. Governing Council DSL Bank, Bonn; Chair. Bd., Dir. Amalgamated Metal Corp. PLC, London; Hon. Consul Grand-Duchy of Luxembourg. *Address:* Preussag Aktiengesellschaft, P.O. Box 4827, Karl-Wiechert-Allee 4, D-3000 Hannover 61, Federal Republic of Germany. *Telephone:* (0511) 566-1413.

MØLLER, Hans Bjerrum, DR.PHIL.; Danish physicist; b. 11 May 1932, Copenhagen; s. of Oscar B. Møller and Erna Ch. Christensen; m. Inger J. Thorshaug; three c.; ed. Tech. Univ. of Denmark and Univ. of Copenhagen; scientist; Risø Nat. Lab. 1956–62, Nat. Lab. Brookhaven, U.S.A. 1958–62; Euratom Research Centre, Ispra, Italy 1962–63; Head, Physics Dept. Risø 1968; Dir. of Research, Risø Nat. Lab. 1982, Man. Dir. 1987–; mem. Royal Danish Acad., Danish Acad. of Technical Sciences. *Publications:* articles in int. scientific pubs. *Address:* Risø National Laboratory, DK-4000 Roskilde (Office); Kirsebaerhaven 12, DK-4000 Roskilde, Denmark (Home).

MØLLER, Maersk Mc-Kinney; Danish shipowner; b. 13 July 1913, Copenhagen; s. of Arnold Peter and Chastine Estelle Mc-Kinney Møller; m. Emma Marie Neergaard Rasmussen 1940; three d.; Partner A. P. Møller 1940–, Sr. Partner 1965–; Chair. Steamship Co. of 1912 Ltd., Steamship Co. Svendborg Ltd., Steamship Co. of 1960 Ltd., Maersk Line A/S, Odense Steel Shipyard Ltd., Dansk Industri Syndikat A/S, Maersk Olie og Gas A/S. *Address:* Esplanaden 50, 1098 Copenhagen K, Denmark.

MOLLISON, Patrick Loudon, C.B.E., M.D., F.R.S.; British professor of haematology and medical author; b. 17 March 1914, London; s. of William M. Mollison and Beatrice M. Walker; m. 1st Margaret D. Peirce 1940 (dissolved 1965), 2nd Jennifer A. Jones 1973; three s.; ed. Univ. of Cambridge and St. Thomas's Hosp. Medical School, London; worked in London Blood Transfusion Service for Medical Research Council 1939–43, then in R.A.M.C.; Dir. M.R.C. Blood Transfusion Research Unit (later Experimental Haematology Unit) at Postgrad. Medical School after demobilization; in charge of Haematology Dept. at St. Mary's Hosp., London 1960–79; Prof. of Haematology, Univ. of London 1962–79; various other professional appointments; several awards and honours. *Publications:* Blood Transfusion in Clinical Medicine 1951; some 120 papers in scientific journals. *Leisure interests:* opera, gardening, golf. *Address:* 60 King Henry's Road, London, NW3 3RR, (Home); N. London Blood Transfusion Centre, Deansbrook Road, Edgware, Middlesex, England (Office). *Telephone:* (01) 722-1947 (Home); 952-5511 (Office).

MOLLO, Joe Kaibe, B.A.; Lesotho diplomatist; b. 7 May 1944; s. of Kaibe and Masera Mollo; m. Matseliso Thabane 1972; one s. two d.; ed. Eagles' Peak High School, Univ. of Botswana, Lesotho and Swaziland, Univ. of Saskatchewan and Carleton Univ.; Asst. Sec. Ministry of Finance 1971–73; Commr. of Co-operatives 1973–75; Deputy Perm. Sec. Ministry of Finance 1975–76; High Commr. to Canada 1976–80; Perm. Sec. Ministry of Finance 1980–82; High Commr. to U.K. 1982–83; Amb. to Denmark 1983–86, also accred. to Sweden, Norway, Finland, Iceland, G.D.R., Poland and U.S.S.R.; Man. Dir. Trading Corpn. of Lesotho. *Leisure interests:* jogging, watching football, reading, music, dancing. *Address:* Trading Corporation of Lesotho, P/Bag, A120 Maseru, Lesotho.

MOLLOY, Robert M., B.COMM.; Irish politician; b. July 1936, Salthill, Galway; s. of Michael Edward and Rita (Stanley) Molloy; m. Phyllis Barry 1972; two s. two d.; ed. St. Ignatius Coll., Univ. Coll., Galway; mem. Dáil

Éireann (House of Reps.) 1965–, House Cttee. of Public Accounts 1965–69, House Cttee. on Constitution 1967; Parl. Sec. to Minister for Educ. 1969–70; Minister for Local Govt. 1970–73, for Defence 1977–79; mem. Galway Co. Council 1967–70, 1974–77, 1985–, Galway Borough Council 1967–70, 1985–; Mayor of Galway 1968–69; Chair. Galway Harbour Bd. 1974–77, 1985–, Lough Corril Navigation Trustees 1985–; Chair. House Cttee. on Bldg. Land; mem. House Cttee. on State-Sponsored Bodies 1982–87; mem. Governing Body, Univ. Coll., Galway 1977; mem. Exec., Inter-Parl. Assen.; Dir. Salthill Failte Ltd. 1985–; Progressive Democrat. *Leisure interests:* swimming, sailing, golf. *Address:* Dail Eirean, Dublin 2; St. Mary's, Rockbarton, Salthill, Galway, Ireland. *Telephone:* 01-795419 (Dublin), 091-21765 (Galway).

MOLLWO, Erich, DR.PHIL., DR.PHIL.HABIL.; German academic (retd.); b. 23 June 1909, Göttingen; s. of Dr. Ludwig Mollwo and Erika (née Voigt) Mollwo; m. Lotte Kern 1937; one s. one d.; ed. Univs. of Göttingen and Munich; Univ. Asst., Göttingen 1934–44, Asst. Prof. 1944–48; Prof. Erlangen Univ. 1948, now Emer.; mem. Acad. of Sciences Munich, corresp. mem. New York Acad. of Sciences. *Publications:* Masers and Lasers (with W. Kaale) 1966, scientific articles. *Leisure interests:* music, tennis. *Address:* Rathsberger Strasse 63, 8520 Erlangen, Federal Republic of Germany.

MOLOM, Tsendiyn; Mongolian politician; b. 1932; ed. Financial and Econ. Tech. School, Ulan Bator and a higher school of econs. in U.S.S.R.; Teacher; Dir. Financial and Econ. Tech. School, Ulan Bator; Head of a Dept., Ministry of Finance 1958–60; Deputy Minister of Finance 1961–63; Perm. Mongolian Rep. on Bd. on Int. Bank for Econ. Co-operation 1963–65; Trade Rep. in U.S.S.R. 1965–68; First Deputy Minister of Finance 1968–69; Minister of Finance 1969–79; Deputy Chair. Council of Ministers 1979–83; Chair. People's Control Cttee. 1979–83; Alt. mem. Cen. Cttee. Mongolian People's Revolutionary Party (MPRP) 1971–76, mem. 1976–; Deputy to People's Great Hural (Assembly). *Address:* c/o Government Palace, Ulaanbaatar, Mongolia.

MOLOMJAMTS, Demchigiyn; Mongolian politician; b. 24 Nov. 1920; ed. Inst. of Finance and Econs., U.S.S.R.; Deputy Minister of Finance 1946–48, Minister 1948–57; Deputy Chair. Council of Ministers 1957–58, First Deputy Chair. 1959–65; Chair. State Planning Comm. 1958–59; Chair. for Foreign Econ. Relations 1963–65; Perm. Rep. to CMEA (Comecon) 1963–65; Deputy to People's Great Hural (Assembly), Cttee. of Council of Ministers; alt. mem. Political Bureau of Mongolian People's Revolutionary Party (MPRP) Cen. Cttee. 1957–59, mem. Political Bureau 1959–; Sec. MPRP Cen. Cttee. 1964–. *Address:* Central Committee of the Mongolian People's Revolutionary Party, Ulaanbaatar, Mongolia.

MOLONEY, Thomas Walter, M.B.A., M.PH.; American foundation executive; b. 8 Feb. 1946, New York; s. of Thomas Walter Moloney and Anne Heney; ed. Columbia Univ.; Program Dir. Nat. Center for the Deaf-Blind, New York 1971–72; Special Asst. to Dir. and Dean, Cornell Univ. Medical Center 1973–74; Asst. Vice-Pres. Robert Wood John Foundation 1975–80; Visiting Lecturer, Princeton Univ. 1975–80; Sr. Vice-Pres., The Commonwealth Fund, New York 1980–; mem. Bd. Dirs. New England Medical Center, Boston 1982–; mem. Bd. Grantmakers in Health, New York, Chair. 1984–; mem. Nat. Bd. of Medical Examiners 1986–; Fellow of the American Acad. of Arts and Sciences; mem. Inst. of Medicine, N.A.S. *Publications:* Ed. New Approaches to the Medicaid Crisis 1983; numerous articles. *Address:* The Commonwealth Fund, 1 East 75th Street, New York, N.Y. 10021 (Office); 72 Norwood Avenue, Upper Montclair, N.J. 07043, U.S.A. *Telephone:* (212) 535-0400 (Office).

MOLTMANN, Günter, DR.PHIL.; German historian; b. 18 Dec. 1926, Hamburg; s. of Alexander and Maria (née Sailer) Moltmann; m. Joetta M. Laing 1960; three s.; ed. Heinrich Hertz Gymnasium, Hamburg and Univs. of Hamburg and Marburg; Dir of Studies, Heinrich Hertz Gymnasium, Hamburg 1956–61; Fulbright Fellowship, School of Advanced Int. Studies, Washington, D.C. 1959–60; Lecturer in American History, Univ. of Hamburg 1961–67; Prof. of History and Political Educ., Teachers' Acad., Bielefeld 1961–67; American Council of Learned Socs. Fellow, Univ. of Chicago 1965–66; Prof. of Medieval and Modern History, Univ. of Hamburg 1967–; Visiting Prof., Indiana Univ. 1970–71; Research Fellow, Charles Warren Center for Studies in American History, Harvard Univ. 1973; Pres. German Assen. for American Studies 1975–78; Dir. Research Project, German Immigration to the U.S.A. 1978–84; Ed. Amerikastudien 1973–. *Publications:* Amerikas Deutschlandpolitik im Zweiten Weltkrieg 1958, Atlantische Blockpolitik im 19. Jahrhundert 1973, Aufbruch nach Amerika; Friedrich List und die Auswanderung aus Baden und Württemberg 1816/17 1979, Germans to America; 300 Years of Immigration 1683–1983 1982; numerous articles on the history of U.S.-German relations. *Address:* Historisches Seminar, Universität Hamburg, Von-Melle-Park 6, D-2000 Hamburg 13 (Office). Steenbargkoppel 27, D-2000 Hamburg 65, Federal Republic of Germany. *Telephone:* (040) 6070306.

MOLYNEAUX, James Henry, P.C., M.P.; Northern Irish politician; b. 28 Aug. 1920, Crumlin; s. of William Molyneaux and Sarah Gilmore; unmarried; ed. Aldergrove School, Co. Antrim; served R.A.F. 1941–46; mem. Antrim Co. Council 1964–73; Vice-Chair. Eastern Special Care Hosp. Man. Cttee. 1966–73; Chair. Antrim Branch Northern Ireland Assen. for Mental

Health 1967–70; Hon. Sec. S. Antrim Unionist Assen. 1964–70; M.P. for Antrim South 1970–83, for Lagan 1983–; Vice-Pres. Ulster Unionist Council 1974; Leader Ulster Unionist Party, House of Commons 1974–; Leader Ulster Unionist Party 1979–; mem. Northern Ireland Ass. 1982–; fmr. J.P. (resgnd. 1987); Deputy Grand Master of Orange Order and Hon. Past Grand Master of Canada; Sovereign Grand Master, Commonwealth Royal Black Inst. 1971. *Leisure interests:* music, gardening. *Address:* House of Commons, London, S.W.1; Aldergrove, Crumlin, County Antrim, Northern Ireland. *Telephone:* 01-219 4520 (London); (08494) 22545 (Crumlin).

MOMIN, Abdul; Bangladesh diplomatist; b. 1 March 1921, Noakhali; s. of the late Janab Abdul Ghani and Musammat Obaidunnessa Bibi; m. Seema Sabir 1947; one d.; ed. Presidency Coll., Calcutta, Calcutta Univ.; Administrative Service, Pakistan 1946–50; Officer on Special Duty, Ministry of Foreign Affairs, Karachi 1950–51; Third Sec., Rangoon 1951–53; Vice-Consul, Akyab (Arakan, Burma) 1953–54; Second Sec. (later First Sec.), Washington, D.C. 1954–57; Political Sec., Baghdad Pact Secr., Iraq 1957, Under-Sec., Ministry of Foreign Affairs 1957–58; Asst. High Commr., Shillong, India 1958–61; First Sec., Brussels 1962–63; Chargé d'affaires, Lisbon 1964–67; Dir. Ministry of Foreign Affairs 1967–70; Amb. to Argentina 1970–71; Sec. Ministry of Foreign Affairs, Bangladesh 1972; High Commr. in Canada 1972–76, concurrently to Cuba; Amb. to People's Repub. of China 1976–80, concurrently to Democratic People's Repub. of Korea and Viet-Nam 1977–80, to France (also accred. to Spain) 1980–84; Perm. Del. to UNESCO Aug. 1980, also accred. to Portugal and Morocco March 1981. *Leisure interests:* photography, contract bridge, music. *Address:* c/o Ministry of Foreign Affairs, Dhaka, Bangladesh.

MOMOH, Maj.-Gen. Joseph Saidu, O.B.E.; Sierra Leone army officer and head of state; b. 26 Jan. 1937, Binkolo, Northern Prov. m. Hannah V. Wilson; two d.; ed. West Africa Methodist Collegiate Secondary School, Officers' Training School, Ghana, School of Infantry, Hythe, U.K., Nigeria Defence Acad., Kaduna, Mons Officers' Cadet School, Aldershot, U.K. and Mil. Training Dept., Zaria, Nigeria; commissioned, Royal Sierra Leone Mil. Forces 1963, Deputy Asst. Adjutant and Quartermaster-Gen. 1968, Commdr. First Bn. 1969, Acting Force Commdr. 1971, Brig. 1973, Maj.-Gen. 1983; mem. Parl. 1973–85; Minister of State 1973–85; Pres. of Sierra Leone 1985–; Minister of Defence and Public Services 1986–; Order of the Rokel; Order of Nat. Security Merit (Repub. of Korea); Hon. D.C.L. *Leisure interests:* reading, sport. *Address:* Office of the President, Freetown, Sierra Leone.

MOMPER, Walter; German politician; b. 21 Feb. 1945, Sulingen; mem. Berlin Chamber of Deputies 1975–; Party Whip SPD, Berlin 1985–89; Gov. Mayor of Berlin March 1989–. *Address:* Fichtestrasse 15, 1000 Berlin 61, Federal Republic of Germany.

MONDALE, Walter Frederick, LL.B.; American lawyer and politician; b. 5 Jan. 1928, Ceylon, Minn.; s. of Rev. and Mrs. Theodore Sigvaard Mondale; m. Joan Adams 1955; two s. one d.; ed. Minnesota public schools, Macalester Coll., Univ. of Minnesota and Univ. of Minnesota Law School; admitted to Minn. Bar 1956, pvt. practice 1956–60; Attorney-Gen., Minn. 1960–64; U.S. Senator from Minnesota 1964–77; Vice-Pres. of the U.S. 1977–81; mem. Nat. Security Council 1977–81; Regent Smithsonian Inst. 1977–; Counsel with firm Winston and Strawn 1981–; mem. Bd. Control Data 1981–, Columbia Pictures 1981–; Democrat-Farm Labor Party; Democratic Cand. for Presidency 1984. *Publication:* The Accountability of Power: Towards a Responsible Presidency 1976. *Leisure interest:* fishing. *Address:* 2200 First Bank Place, East Minneapolis, Minn. 55402, U.S.A.

MONDJO, Nicolas; Congolese diplomatist; b. 24 June 1933, Fort Rousset; ed. Inst. des Hautes-Etudes d'Outre Mer, Paris; fmr. Dir. of Admin., Ministry of the Interior; Amb. to France; Perm. Rep. to EEC; Minister of Foreign Affairs 1968–69; Dir. of Cabinet of Pres. of Repub. 1969–70; Perm. Rep. to UN 1970–82; del. to XXII and XXIII sessions of UN Gen. Ass.; del. to various int. confs. *Address:* c/o Ministry of Foreign Affairs, Lomé, Cameroon.

MONERAWELA, Chandra, B.A.(ECON.); Sri Lankan diplomatist; b. 8 Sept. 1937, Kandy; m. Rupa De Silva 1965; one s. two d.; ed. Trinity Coll., Kandy and Univ. of Ceylon, Peradeniya; joined Sri Lanka Overseas Service 1961; served People's Repub. of China 1964–67, Washington, D.C. 1967–70; Chief of Protocol, Ministry of Foreign Affairs 1970–74, Dir. Econ. Affairs 1980–83; Chargé d'Affaires, Thailand and Perm. Rep. to ESCAP and UN agencies, Bangkok 1974; High Commr. in Singapore 1984, in U.K. May 1984–. *Leisure interests:* cricket, rugby, golf, gardening. *Address:* Sri Lanka High Commission, 13 Hyde Park Gardens, London, W2 2LU, England. *Telephone:* 01-262 1841.

MONFORT, Silvia; French actress, writer, director; b. 7 June 1923, Paris; d. of Charles Favre-Bertin and Marguerite (née Calle) Favre-Bertin; m. Maurice Clavel (died 1976); ed. Lycées Victor-Hugo and Victor-Duruy, Paris; Dir. Centre Culturel de Paris; f. 1st Circus School 1974. *Stage appearances include:* la Mort de Danton, Si je vis, le Voyageur sans bagage, le Cid, Cinna, le Mariage de Figaro, Lady Godiva, Electre, la P... respectueuse, Soudain l'été dernier, Pucelle, Phèdre 1973, Pourquoi la robe d'Anna ne veut pas redescendre 1974, Lucrèce Borgia 1975, la Dame de la mer 1977, la Fourmi dans le corps 1979, la Duchesse d'Amalfi 1982, Chaud et froid 1983, les Perses, la Panne 1984, la Milliardaire 1985, Bajazet

1985, la Tour de Nesle 1986. *Films include:* les Misérables, le Cas du docteur Laurent, Du Rififi chez les femmes, la Française et l'amour, Mandrin. *TV appearances include:* Bajazet 1958, Bérénice 1959, la Machine infernale 1963, le Roi Lear 1965, la Guerre de Troie n'aura pas lieu 1968; Croix de guerre, Chevalier Légion d'honneur, Officier Arts et Lettres; Bronze Star Medal, Médaille d'or des Arts, Sciences et Lettres, Médaille de vermeil de la Ville de Paris. *Publications:* Il ne m'arrivera rien, Aimer qui vous aima, le Droit chemin, les Mains pleines de doigts, les Anes rouges, l'Amble 1971. *Leisure interest:* mountain climbing. *Address:* 106 rue Brancion, Paris 75015, France (Office). *Telephone:* (1) 45 33 66 70 (Office).

MONGE, Luis Alberto: Costa Rican politician; b. 29 Dec. 1925, Palmares; ed. Univs. of Costa Rica and Geneva; mem. Cen. de Trabajadores Rerum Novarum 1947, subsequently Pres.; fmr. Vice-Pres. Inter-American Labor Confed. (CIT); militant mem. Nat. Liberation Army 1948; mem. Nat. Constituent Ass. (Social Democrat) 1949; co-founder Nat. Liberation Party 1951, Sec.-Gen. for 12 years; worked for ILO, Geneva for 3 years; Sec.-Gen. Interamerican Labor Org. (ORIT) for 6 years; served at Ministry of the Presidency, Govt. of José Figueres 1955; mem. Legis. Ass. 1958, 1970, Pres. of Congress 1970–74; Prof. Inter-American School of Democratic Educ. and Dir. Center of Democratic Studies for Latin America (CEDAL); Pres. of Costa Rica 1982–86. *Address:* c/o Office of the President, San José 1, Costa Rica.

MONGO BETI (pseudonym of Alexandre Biyidi-Awala); Cameroonian writer and teacher; b. 1932, Mbalmayo; s. of Oscar Awala and Régine Alomo; m. Odile Marie Jeanne Lebossé 1963; two s. one d.; ed. Lycée de Yaoundé, Univ. d'Aix-en-Provence and Sorbonne, Paris; exiled from Cameroon, became teacher and writer in Paris; undertook research in sociology, Paris Univ. 1957–59; currently Prof. Lycée Corneille, Rouen; founder of bi-monthly journal, Peuples Noirs-Peuples Africains 1978; Prix Sainte-Beuve for Mission Terminée 1958. *Publications:* Le pauvre Christ de Bomba 1956 (trans. in English), Mission terminée 1957 (trans. in English), Le roi miraculé 1958 (trans in English), Main basse sur le Cameroun, autopsie d'une décolonisation (political essay) 1972 (banned in France), Remember Ruben 1974, Perpétue et l'habitude du malheur 1974, La ruine presque cocasse d'un polichinelle (novel) 1979. *Address:* 6 rue d'Harcourt, 76000 Rouen, France. *Telephone:* (35) 70 14 56.

MONGUNO, Alhaji Shettima Ali; Nigerian educationist and politician; b. 1926, Borno; s. of Rahma and Fanna Monguno; m. Ashe Meta 1948; two s. five d.; ed. Bornu Middle School, Bauchi Teacher Training Coll., Katshina Higher Coll., Nigerian Coll. of Arts, Science and Tech., Zaria and Univ. of Edinburgh; Native Authority Educ. Sec., Northern Nigeria 1959; Councillor for Educ., Borno Native Authority Council; mem. Fed. Ass. 1959; Fed. Minister of Int. Affairs 1965–66; Fed. Commr. for Industries 1967–71, for Mines and Power 1971–75; del. from XVI to the XXV sessions of UN Gen. Ass. and other int. confs.; Pres. of OPEC 1972; Councillor for Natural Resources and Co-operatives, Borno Local Authority 1975–76; Pro-Chancellor and Chair., Gov. Council of Calabar Univ. 1976–80; Pro-Chancellor, Univ. of Nigeria 1980–85; Chair. Metropolitan Council 1977–79; mem. Constituent Ass. 1977–78; active in many voluntary orgs.; various int. awards. *Leisure interests:* reading, cycling. *Address:* c/o University of Nigeria, Nsukka, Anambra State, Nigeria.

MONICELLI, Mario; Italian film director; b. 16 May 1915; ed. Università degli Studi, Pisa; fmr. Asst. to Pietro Germi; writer of film Riso Amaro; film dir. 1949–; Golden Lion, Venice Film Festival; Silver Medal, Berlin Film Festival; Silver Laurel Medal, San Francisco Film Festival. *Films include:* Guardie e Ladri 1948, The Big Deal of Madonna Street 1955, The Great War 1958, The Organiser 1960, Casanova '70 1963, L'Armata Brancaleone 1965, Vogliamo i Colonnelli, Romanzo popolare, Caro Michele, Amici miei, Un borghese piccolo piccolo, Viaggio con Anita, Temporale Rosy, Camera d'Albergo 1979, Il Marchese del Grillo 1980, 2nd part of Amici Miei (1982). *Address:* Via del Babuino 135, 06 6780448 Rome, Italy.

MONNERVILLE, Gaston Charles François, L. ES L., D. EN D.; French public servant; b. 2 Jan. 1897, French Guiana; s. of Saint-Yves Monnerville and Françoise Orville; m. Marie-Thérèse Lapeyre 1923; ed. Faculty of Law, Toulouse; admitted to Bar of Toulouse 1918, Paris 1921; Sec. of Lawyers' Conf., Paris 1923; Pres. of Union of Young Lawyers at the Paris Court 1927; Deputy for Guiana 1932; Mayor of Cayenne 1935; mem. of Radical and Radical-Socialist Party; Vice-Pres. of Party 1938; Under-Sec. of State for Colonies 1937, 1938; served in Navy in Second World War; after Armistice was active in resistance movement 1940–44; mem. of Consultative Ass. 1944; Pres. of Comm. of Overseas France; re-elected for Guiana to Constituent Ass. 1945 and 1946; Del. of France to UN Ass.; Councillor of the Repub. 1946; Senator for Lot 1948, 1955, 1958, 1965; Pres. of Council of the Repub. 1947–58; Pres. Senate of the Repub. 1958–68, Senate of the Community 1959–60; mem. Constitutional Council 1974–83; Pres. Gen. Council of Lot Dept. 1951–70, Hon. Pres. 1970–; Mayor of Saint-Céré (Lot) 1964–71; mem. Council of Paris Univ. 1959–69; Pres. Assoc. des Secrétaires et Anciens Secrétaires de la Conférence des Avocats, Paris 1963, 1964; mem. Soc. des Gens de Lettres 1968, Hon. Pres. Assen. Int. pour la Culture Française; Croix de guerre 1940; Medal of the Resistance with Rosette; Officier, Légion d'honneur, Commander des Arts et Lettres, and several mil. decorations. *Publications:* L'enrichissement sans cause

1921, Le Sénat 1965, Clemenceau 1968, Histoire générale de l'Afrique (with others) 1972, Témoignage, Vol. I 1975, Vingt-Deux Ans de Présidence 1980. *Leisure interests:* swimming, walking, skiing, golf, music. *Address:* 27 avenue Raymond-Poincaré, 75116 Paris, France.

MONNET, Bertrand; French architect (retd.); b. 31 Jan. 1910, Paris; s. of René Monnet and Marie Nourry; m. Madeleine Roitel 1940; one s. one d.; ed. Collège Stanislas, Paris, Ecole Nat. Supérieure des Beaux Arts; Chief Architect, Historic Monuments 1942–82, Deputy Inspector-Gen. 1968–82; fmr. Pres. Té (Compagnie des architectes en chef des monuments historiques), Union Franco-Britannique des Architectes; mem. Académie d'Architecture; Officier Légion d'honneur, Commandeur des Arts et des Lettres, de St. Gregoire-le-Grand. *Major restorations:* Cathedral and Palace of Rohan, Strasbourg 1946–82, Hotel Nat. des Invalides, Paris, 1975–82. *Major works:* Palais des Droits de l'Homme, Strasbourg, Nat. Necropolis and Nat. Deportation Memorial, Struthof, Lower Rhine; numerous scientific insts., lycées, colls. and schools, Ardennes psychiatric hosp., Harlisheim church, admin. bldgs., housing etc. *Publications:* numerous lectures in French, German and English; numerous articles. *Leisure interests:* pleasure boating, writing, drawing. *Address:* 1 rue Cognacq-Jay, 75007 Paris, France. *Telephone:* 45.51.76.11.

MONNIER, Claude Michel, PH.D.; Swiss journalist; b. 23 March 1938, Rwankéri, Rwanda; s. of Henri Monnier and Olga Pavlov; m. Estela Troncoso Balandrán 1958; two s.; ed. Univs. of Geneva and Mexico, Graduate Inst. of Int. Studies, Geneva; educational tour in Asia and America 1956–58; Research Fellow, Swiss Nat. Fund for Scientific Research, Tokyo 1963–66; Tokyo Corresp. Journal de Genève 1963–66, Foreign Ed. 1966–70, Ed.-in-Chief 1970–80; Ed. Le Temps Stratégique, Geneva 1982–; mem. Bd. French speaking Swiss TV and radio 1989–. *Publications:* Les Américains et sa Majesté l'Empereur: Etude du conflit culturel d'où naquit la constitution japonaise de 1946 1967. *Leisure interests:* walking, light aircraft flying. *Address:* chemin de Saussac 2, 1256 Troinex, Geneva, Switzerland (Home). *Telephone:* (022) 43 95 55 (Home).

MONOD, Jérôme; French businessman; b. 7 Sept. 1930, Paris; s. of Olivier and Yvonne (née Bruce) Monod; m. Françoise Gallot 1963; three s.; ed. Ecole nat. d'admin.; Auditeur, Cour des Comptes 1957; Rapporteur, Study mission of Sec.-Gen. for Algerian affairs 1958; Chargé de mission, Prime Minister's Office 1959–62; Conseiller Référendaire à la Cour des Comptes 1963; Chief Exec. Dél. à l'Aménagement du Territoire 1967–75; Special Asst. to Prime Minister Jacques Chirac 1975–1976; Sec.-Gen. Rassemblement pour la République 1976–78; Chair. Bd., Centre Français du Commerce Extérieur 1980–83; Pres. French Canadian Chamber of Commerce in Paris 1984–86; Admin. and Vice-Chair. Cie. lyonnaise des Eaux et de l'Eclairage 1979–; Chair. and Man. Dir. Soc. lyonnaise des Eaux 1980–; Vice-Chair. Soc. Gen. des eaux de Barcelone, Agbar Corpn. (Spain) 1981–; mem. Bd. of Dirs. Aqua-Chem Inc. (U.S.A.), Cie. Française des Pétroles, Cie. Financière de Suez, HAVAS; Vice-Chair. General Waterworks Corpn. (U.S.A.) 1983–; Officier, Légion d'honneur, Officier des Arts et des Lettres, Chevalier des Palmes académiques. *Publications:* L'aménagement du territoire 1971, Transformation d'un pays: pour une géographie de la liberté 1974, Propositions pour la France 1977. *Leisure interests:* swimming, climbing. *Address:* 94 rue du Bac, 75007 Paris, France (Home).

MONOD, Théodore André, D. ÈS SC.; French zoologist; b. 9 April 1902, Rouen; s. of Rev. Prof. Wilfred and Dorina Monod; m. Olga Pickova 1930; two s. one d.; ed. Ecole Alsacienne and Paris Univ.; Asst. Museum nat. d'histoire naturelle, Paris 1922, Prof. 1942, then Hon. Prof. 1974–; Dir. Inst. Français d'Afrique Noire, Dakar 1938–65; Dean, Faculty of Sciences, Dakar Univ. 1957–58; mem. Inst. de France (Acad. des Sciences) 1963–, Acad. des Sciences d'Outremer 1949–, Acad. de Marine 1957–; Dr. h.c. (Univs. of Cologne and Neuchâtel); Gold Medal, Soc. de Géographie, Royal Geographical Soc. and American Geographical Soc.; Haile Selassie Prize for African Research; Officier, Légion d'honneur, Order des Palmes académiques, Order of Golden Ark, Commdr. Order of Christ, Mérite Saharien, Mérite Nat. Mauritanie, Ordre Nat. Sénégal. *Publications:* Méharées, L'hippopotame et le philosophe, Bathyfolages, Les déserts 1973, L'émeraude des Garamantes: Souvenirs d'un saharien 1984. *Leisure interest:* field natural history. *Address:* Muséum National d'Histoire Naturelle, 57 rue Cuvier, 75005 Paris; 14 quai d'Orléans, 75004 Paris, France (Home). *Telephone:* 43-31-40-10 (Office); 43-26-79-50 (Home).

MONORY, René Claude Aristide; French administrator and politician; b. 6 June 1923, Loudun; s. of Aristide and Marguerite (Devergne) Monory; m. Suzanne Cottet 1945; one d.; ed. Ecole primaire supérieure de Thouars; dealer in vehicles and agricultural machinery 1952; Chair. agricultural machinery and oil cos.; Mayor of Loudun 1959–; Pres. Mayors' Assen. of Vienne; Councillor, Canton of Loudun 1961–; municipal judge; Senator for Vienne 1968–77, 1981–, Rapporteur, Senate Finance Comm. 1976–77; Minister of Industry and Trade 1977–78, of the Economy 1978–81, of Educ. 1986–88; Pres. Conseil général de la Vienne 1979–; Chair. Interim Cttee. of Bd. of Govs., IMF 1981; Pres. Assen. de l'union républicaine des présidents de conseils généraux 1983–; mem. Centre des démocrates sociaux (fmr. nat. sec.), First Vice-Pres. 1984–; mem. Union pour la démocratie française; Pres. Conseil régional Poiton-Charentes 1985–; Senator for Vienni Sept. 1988. *Publication:* Combat pour le bon sens 1983.

Address: Palais de Luxembourg, 75291 Paris Cedex 06, France; Beaurepaire, 86200 Loudun, France (Home).

MONREAL LUQUE, Alberto, DR.ECON.SC.; Spanish politician and economist; b. 18 Nov. 1926, Madrid; m.; three c.; ed. Univ. de Madrid; mem. Cuerpo de Economistas del Estado 1957–; Prof. Faculty of Econ. Sciences, Univ. de Madrid 1957–68; Tech. Sec. Ministry of Public Works 1965–68; Sec. of State, Ministry of Educ. and Science 1968–69; Minister of Finance 1969–73; Pres. Tabacalera (Tobacco Monopoly Co.) 1974–82; Econ. Consultant, Superior Council of Commerce, Ministry of the Economy. *Address:* Zurbaran 10, Madrid 28010, Spain.

MONRO, David Hector, M.A., F.A.H.A., F.A.S.S.A.; New Zealand professor of philosophy; b. 21 Oct. 1911, Whangarei; s. of the late Alexander Monro and of Davidina Monro; m. Joyce Estelle Grey 1938; two s.; ed. Auckland Grammar School and Auckland Univ. Coll.; lecturer in Philosophy Otago Univ. 1946–53; Sr. Lecturer Sydney Univ. 1953–61; Foundation Prof. Monash Univ., Melbourne 1961–76, Emer. Prof. 1977–; Nuffield Fellow, Oxford 1952–53; Commonwealth Fellow St. John's Coll., Cambridge 1965; Canadian Commonwealth Fellow Victoria Univ., B.C. 1972–73. *Publications:* Argument of Laughter 1951, Godwin's Moral Philosophy 1953, Empiricism and Ethics 1967, The Ambivalence of Bernard Mandeville 1975, The Sonneteer's History of Philosophy 1981, Ethics and the Environment 1984, Don Juan in Australia 1986. *Leisure interests:* reading, walking, travel and writing light verse. *Address:* Department of Philosophy, Monash University, Clayton, Vic. 3168; 55 Torwood Avenue, Glen Waverley, Vic., Australia 3150 (Home). *Telephone:* (03) 565-2198 (Office); (03) 561-4131 (Home).

MONS, Jean; French civil servant; b. 25 Feb. 1906; s. of Antonie and Mme. Mons (née Martinie); m. Françoise Delval (deceased); one d.; ed. Ecole profesionnelle, Ussel, Ecole des industries agricoles, Douai; teacher 1924–26; Chief Controller of Indirect Contributions 1926; served French Army 1939–40; Prefect, Sec.-Gen. of the Seine 1944; Dir. Office of Prés. du Conseil 1946; placed at disposal of Ministry of Foreign Affairs; Resident Gen. in Tunis 1947–50; Perm. Sec.-Gen. for Nat. Defence 1950–56; Conseiller Maître à la Cour des Comptes 1956; mem. Cttee. of Enquiry into Public Costs 1960, Nat. Conciliation Cttee. for Nat. Educ. 1961–; Prés. de Chambre à la Cour des Comptes 1970–76; Prés. Comm. Marchés de Gaz de France 1975–; Grand Master, Grande Loge Nat. 1980–88; Commdr. Légion d'honneur, Grand Officier, Ordre nat. du Mérite, Croix de guerre, Rosette de la Résistance, etc. *Publication:* Sur les chemins de l'histoire (biography). *Address:* 63 rue de Prony, 75017 Paris, France. *Telephone:* 47.63.31.57.

MONSON, Sir William Bonnar Leslie, K.C.M.G., C.B.; British diplomatist (retd.); b. 28 May 1912, Edinburgh; s. of John William and Selina Leslie Monson; m. Helen Isobel Browne 1948; ed. Edinburgh Acad. and Hertford Coll., Oxford; Dominions Office 1935–39; Colonial Office 1939–64; Chief Sec., W. African Council 1947–51; Asst. Under-Sec. of State, Colonial Office 1952–64; High Commr. in Zambia 1964–66; Asst. Under-Sec. of State, Commonwealth Office 1966–67, Deputy Under-Sec. of State 1967–68; Deputy Under-Sec. of State, FCO 1968–72; Dir. Overseas Relations, St. John Ambulance HQ 1975–81. *Address:* Golf House, Goffers Road, London, S.E.3, England. *Telephone:* 01-852 7257.

MONTAGNE SÁNCHEZ, Gen. Ernesto; Peruvian army officer and politician; b. 18 Aug. 1916, Barranco, Lima; s. of Gen. Ernesto Montagne Markholtz and Raquel de Montagne; m. Isabel Landázuri de Montagne; one s. one d.; ed. Military School of Chorrillos; Capt. 1944, Lieut.-Col. 1953, Col. 1958, Brig.-Gen. 1963, Gen. of Div. 1968; taught at various mil. schools; several posts as Div. Chief of Staff; Dir. Chorrillos Mil. School; Dir. Escuela Superior de Guerra; Prefect of Lima; Gen. Commdr. 3rd Mil. Zone; Minister of State for Educ.; Dir. of Personnel; Deputy Chief of Staff of Army; Gen. Commdr. 1st Mil. Zone and Insp. Gen. of Army; Gen. Commdr. of Army, Pres. of Council of Ministers and Minister of War 1968–72; Orden Militar de Ayacucho, Cruz Peruana al Mérito Militar, Orden del Sol, Orden de San Gregorio Magno, and numerous other foreign awards. *Leisure interest:* sailing. *Address:* Lima, Peru.

MONTAGNIER, Luc, L. ÈS SC., D.MED.; French research scientist; b. 18 Aug. 1932, Chabris; s. of Antoine Montagnier and Marianne Rousselet; m. Dorothea Ackermann 1961; one s. two d.; ed. Univs. of Poitiers and Paris; Asst. in Faculty of Science, Paris 1955–60, Attaché 1960, Head 1963, Head of Research 1967; Dir. of Research C.N.R.S. 1974–; Head of Lab. Inst. of Radium 1965–71; Head of Viral Oncology Unit, Pasteur Inst. 1972–, Prof. Pasteur Inst. 1985–; Chevalier, Légion d'Honneur, Commdr. Ordre nat. du Mérite; Lauréat du C.N.R.S. 1964, 1973, Prix Rosen de Cancérologie 1971, Prix Galien 1985, Prix de la Fondation Louis-Jeantet 1986, Prix Lasker 1986. *Publications:* Vaincre le Sida 1986, numerous scientific papers. *Leisure interests:* piano playing, swimming. *Address:* Institut Pasteur, 25 rue du Docteur-Roux, 75015 Paris, France (Office).

MONTAGU, Hon. David Charles Samuel; British banker; b. 6 Aug. 1928, London; s. of the 3rd Baron Swaythling and Mary Levy; m. Christiane F. Dreyfus; one s. two d. (one deceased); ed. Eton Coll. and Trinity Coll., Cambridge; joined Samuel Montagu & Co. Ltd. 1948, Dir. 1954, Chair. 1970–73; Chair. and Chief Exec. Orion Bank Ltd. 1974–79; Exec. Chair. Rothmans International PLC 1988–; Dir. J. Rothschild Holdings PLC, The Daily Telegraph PLC, Anglo Leasing PLC; mem. Horserace Totalisator

Bd. 1981–. *Leisure interests:* racing, shooting, theatre. *Address:* 15 Hill Street, London, W1X 7FB (Office); 14 Craven Hill Mews, Devonshire Terrace, London, W2 3DY, England (Home). *Telephone:* 01-491 4366 (Office); 01-724 7860 (Home).

MONTAGUE, Diana, A.R.C.M.; British mezzo-soprano opera and concert singer; b. 8 April 1953, Winchester; d. of Mr and Mrs N. H. Montague; m. Philip Doghan 1978; one s.; ed. Testwood School, Totton, Hants., Winchester School of Art and Royal Manchester Coll. of Music; professional début at Glyndebourne 1977; principal mezzo-soprano, Royal Opera House, Covent Garden 1978; freelance artist 1984–; has toured throughout Europe and U.S.A. appearing at Metropolitan Opera and Bayreuth, Aix-en-Provence, Salzburg and Glyndebourne festivals etc. *Leisure interests:* horse riding, country life in general. *Address:* 17 Sheridan Gardens, Testbourne Farm, Hants.; 28, 91 St. Martin's Lane, London, W.C.2., England. *Telephone:* (070386) 0457 (Hants.); 01-836 3770 (London).

MONTALENTI, Giuseppe, D.SC.; Italian professor of genetics; b. 13 Dec. 1904, Asti; s. of Paolo Montalenti and Ida Bertola; m. Luciana Fratini 1964 (died 1980); ed. Univ. of Rome; Asst. Prof. of Zoology, Univ. of Rome 1927, Univ. of Bologna 1937; Chief, Dept. of Zoology, Zoological Station, Aquarium, Naples 1939; Prof. of Genetics, Univ. of Naples 1944, Univ. of Rome 1961, now Prof. Emer.; Pres. Accademia Nazionale dei Lincei. 1981–85. *Publications:* L'Evoluzione 1958, Storia della Biologia e della Medicina 1962, Introduzione alla Genetica 1972. *Address:* Accademia Nazionale dei Lincei, via della Lungara 10, 00165 Rome; via Asmara 25, 00199 Rome, Italy (Home). *Telephone:* (06)6861159(Office);(06)8314525(Home).

MONTAND, Yves (pseudonym of Yves Livi); French actor and singer; b. 13 Oct. 1921, Monsummano, Italy; s. of Giovanni Livi and Joséphine Simoni; m. 2nd Simone Signoret 1951 (died 1985); one c.; ed. primary school, Marseilles; singer, numerous famous songs; stage performances in straight plays and variety. *Films include:* Les portes de la nuit 1946, Le salaire de la peur, Les héros sont fatigués, Marguerite de la nuit 1955, Hommes et loups, Les sorcières de Salem, Premier mai, La loi, Temps d'aujourd'hui, Napoléon, Un dénommé Squarcio, Aimez-vous Brahms 1961, Ma Geisha, La guerre est finie, Vivre pour vivre, Un soir un train, Z, Le Diable par la queue, L'aveu, On a Clear Day You Can See Forever, Le cercle rouge, Tout va bien 1972, César et Rosalie 1972, Etat de Siège, Le fils 1973, Le hasard et la violence, Vincent, François, Paul et les autres 1974, Le grand escogriffe 1976, I comme Icare 1979, Clair de femme 1979, Le choix des armes 1981, Tout feu tout flamme 1981, Garçon! 1983, Jean de Florette 1986, Manon des sources 1987, 3 Places pour le 26 1988, Heidi 1989. *Publication:* Du soleil plein la tête (memoirs) 1955. *Address:* 15 place Dauphine, 75001 Paris, France.

MONTANELLI, Indro; Italian journalist and writer; b. 22 April 1909; s. of Sestilio Montanelli; m. Colette Rosselli; ed. Univ. degli Studi, Florence and Univ. de Paris à la Sorbonne; Special Corresp. Corriere della Sera 1939–73; War Corresp. in Finland, Norway, Spain, Albania and Greece; Founder, Man. Ed. Il Giornale, Milan 1974–, now Man. Dir., Ed.-in-Chief; has won Bagutta and Marzotto Prizes. *Publications:* Storia di Roma 1957, Storia dei Greci 1958, Incontri 1961, Garibaldi 1962, Gente qualunque 1963, Dante e il suo secolo 1964, Italia dei secoli bui 1965; *Plays:* I sogni muoiono all'alba (also film), Il Generale della Rovere (also film), Kibbutz. *Address:* c/o Il Giornale Nuovo, Via Gaetano Negri 4, 1-20123 Milan, Italy.

MONTAZERI, Ayatollah Hussein Ali; Iranian religious leader; b. c. 1923, Najafabad, Isfahan; ed. Isfahan Theological School; teacher of science and philosophy, Theological School, Qom; arrested after riots over Shah's land reform 1963; visited Ayatollah Khomeini in Iraq 1964; arrested several times and exiled to rural parts of Iran 1964–74; imprisoned 1974–78; Leading Ayatollah of Teheran 1979–80; returned to Qom Feb. 1980; named Grand Ayatollah 1984; resigned as successor to Ayatollah Khomeini March 1989. *Address:* Madresseh Faizieh, Qom, Iran.

MONTEFIORE, Rt. Rev. Hugh William, M.A., B.D.; British ecclesiastic; b. 12 May 1920, London; s. of Charles Edward Sebag-Montefiore O.B.E. and Muriel Alice Ruth de Pass; m. Elisabeth Mary Macdonald Paton 1945; three d.; ed. Rugby School, St. John's Coll., Oxford and Westcott House, Cambridge; Chaplain and Tutor, Westcott House 1951–53, Vice-Prin. 1953–54; Fellow and Dean, Gonville and Caius Coll., Cambridge 1954–63; Vicar of Great St. Mary's, Cambridge 1963–70; Bishop of Kingston-upon-Thames 1970–78; Bishop of Birmingham 1978–87; Asst. Bishop, Diocese of Southwark 1987–; Hon. D.D. (Aberdeen) 1976, Birmingham 1985. *Publications include:* Commentary on the Epistle to the Hebrews 1964, The Question Mark 1969, The Probability of God 1985, So Near and Yet So Far 1986, Communicating the Gospel in a Scientific Age 1988. *Address:* White Lodge, 23 Bellevue Road, Wandsworth Common, London, SW17 7EB, England.

MONTEGRIFFO, Peter Cecil Patrick, LL.B.; British barrister; b. 28 Aug. 1960, Gibraltar; s. of Dr. Cecil Montegriffo and Lily Zammitt; m. Josephine Perera 1985; one s.; ed. Bayside Comprehensive School, Univ. of Leeds and Lincoln's Inn/Council of Legal Educ.; called to the Bar 1982; practitioner in law firm J. H. Hassan & Partner 1987–88, partner 1988–; Exec. mem. of Gibraltar Labour Party/Asscn. for Advancement of Civil Rights (GLP/AACR) 1982–88, Deputy Leader April 1988–; actively involved in GLP/AACR Constitutional Cttee. pursuing proposals for decolonization of

Gibraltar 1984-. *Leisure interests:* literature (especially political science), economics, music. *Address:* J. A. Hassan & Partner, 3 Library Ramp, Gibraltar (Office); 4 Hospital Hill, Gibraltar (Home). *Telephone:* 79000 (Office); 79912 (Home).

MONTFORT, Norbert; German diplomatist; b. 6 May 1925, Cologne; s. of Rudolf Montfort and Charlotte Montfort; m. Elisabeth Spelmeyer 1961; two d.; ed. Univ. of Cologne; joined foreign service 1955, attaché, Cairo Embassy 1956-57, Alexandria Consulate 1957, at Ministry of Foreign Affairs 1957-59; subsequently Third and Second Sec., Beirut Embassy 1959-61, Second Sec., Baghdad Embassy 1961-62, Chargé d'affaires, Taiz Embassy, Yemen 1962-63; at Ministry of Foreign Affairs 1964-66, 1976-84, Consul, Kuwait 1966-71; Amb. to Mauritania 1971-74, to Saudia Arabia 1974-76, to Morocco 1984-; at Ministry of Foreign Affairs, Head of Section 1976-79, subsequently Asst. Under-Sec. to Dir. N. Africa and Middle East 1979-84. *Leisure interest:* ornithology. *Address:* Embassy of Federal Republic of Germany, 7 Zankat Madnine, B.P. 235, Rabat, Morocco.

MONTGOMERY, (Charles) John, C.B.E., F.I.B.; British banker (retd.); b. 18 Feb. 1917, Llandudno; s. of the late Rev. Charles James Montgomery; m. Gwenneth Mary McKendrick 1950; two d.; ed. Colwyn Bay Grammar School; served with R.N. 1940-46; joined Lloyds Bank Ltd. 1935, Joint Gen. Man. 1968, Asst. Chief Gen. Man. 1970, Deputy Chief Gen. Man. 1973, Dir. 1972-83, Chief Gen. Man. 1973-78, Vice-Chair. 1978-83; Dir. Lloyds Bank Int. 1978-84, Yorkshire Bank 1979-84; Deputy Chair. Chartered Inst. of Bankers 1975-76, Pres. 1976-77, Vice-Pres. 1977-; Chair. C.E.O.'s Cttee. of The Cttee. of London Clearing Bankers 1976-78. *Leisure interests:* walking, photography. *Address:* High Cedar, 6 Cedar Copse, Bickley, Kent, England. *Telephone:* 01-467 2410.

MONTGOMERY, David; American photographer; b. 8 Feb. 1937, Brooklyn, New York; m. 2nd Martine King 1983; three d.; ed. Midwood High School; studied photography with Lester Bookbinder; toured U.S.A. as musician; freelance photographer/dir. 1960-; regular contrib. to Sunday Times Colour Magazine, Vogue, Tatler, Rolling Stone, Esquire, Fortune, New York Sunday Times, House and Garden magazines; has photographed H.M. Queen Elizabeth II, H.M. Queen Elizabeth the Queen Mother, Rt. Hon. Margaret Thatcher, Rt. Hon. Pierre Trudeau, Mick Jagger, Clint Eastwood, Lord Mountbatten, Lord Home, H.M. King Hussein, H.R.H. Queen Noor, Rt. Hon. Edward Heath, Rt. Hon. James Callaghan, Baron Thyssen-Bornemisza, Prince and Princess Thurn und Taxis, H.E. Cardinal Basil Hume; numerous other famous persons; numerous awards for photography. *Leisure interests:* gardening, photography, day-dreaming. *Address:* Studio B, 11 Edith Grove, London, S.W.10, England. *Telephone:* 01-352 6667/8.

MONTGOMERY, Deane, PH.D.; American mathematician; b. 2 Sept. 1909, Weaver, Minn.; s. of Richard and Florence (Hitchcock) Montgomery; m. Katherine Fulton 1933; one s. one d.; ed. Hamline Univ. and Univ. of Iowa; Asst. Prof. of Maths. Smith Coll. 1935-38, Assoc. Prof. 1938-42, Prof. 1942-46; Assoc. Prof. Yale Univ. 1946-48; Perm. mem. Inst. of Advanced Study, Princeton 1948-51, Prof. of Maths. 1951-; Adjunct Prof. of Math., Univ. of N.C. at Chapel Hill 1989-; Vice-Pres. Int. Mathematical Union 1967-72, Pres. 1975-78; Hon. Dr. (Hamline, Yeshiva Illinois, Tulane and Mich. Univs.). *Publication:* (with Leo Zippin) Topological Transformation Groups 1955. *Address:* Carolina Meadows, Apt. 1-207, Chapel Hill, N.C. 27514, U.S.A.

MONTGOMERY, John (see Montgomery, Charles John).

MONTGOMERY, John Warwick, B.L.S., M.A., B.D., S.T.M., PH.D., TH.D., LL.B., M.PHIL, F.R.S.A.; American professor of jurisprudence and theologian; b. 18 Oct. 1931, Warsaw, N.Y.; s. of Maurice Warwick Montgomery and Harriet (Smith) Montgomery; m. 1st Joyce Ann Bailer 1954; one s. two d.; m. 2nd Lanalee de Kant 1988; ed. Cornell Univ., Univ. of California at Berkeley, Wittenberg Univ., Ohio, Univ. of Chicago, Univ. of Strasbourg, France, LaSalle Extension Univ., Univ. of Essex, England; called to Bar Va. 1978, Calif. 1979, D.C. 1985, U.S. Supreme Court 1981, Middle Temple, England 1984; Librarian, Univ. of Calif. Library, Berkeley 1954-55; Instructor in Biblical Hebrew, Hellenistic Greek and Medieval Latin, Wittenberg Univ. and Hamma Divinity School, Springfield, Ohio 1956-59; ordained minister, Lutheran Church in America 1958; Head Librarian, Swift Library of Divinity and Philosophy and mem. Federated Theological Faculty, Univ. of Chicago 1959-60; Assoc. Prof., Chair. Dept. of History, Waterloo Lutheran (now Wilfrid Laurier) Univ., Waterloo, Ont. 1960-64; Prof. of Church History, Trinity Evangelical Divinity School, Deerfield, Ill. 1964-74; Prof. of Law and Theology, Int. School of Law, Washington, D.C. 1974-75; Theological Consultant to Christian Legal Soc. 1975-76; Dir. of Studies, Int. Inst. of Human Rights, Strasbourg 1979-81; Dean, Dir. of Library, of Jurisprudence, Simon Greenleaf School of Law, Anaheim, Calif. 1980-87; Prof. at Large, Inst. for Theology and Law, Irvine, Calif. and Strasbourg, France 1989-; John Warwick Montgomery MS collection established, Syracuse Univ. Library 1970; Fellow American Scientific Affiliation, Victoria Inst.; mem. Lincoln's Inn, Int. Bar Asscn., Int. Real Estate Fed., World Soc. of Law Profs., Union Internationale des Avocats, American Bar Assan., American Asscn. of Law Libraries, American Library Assan., American Theological Library Assan., American Historical Assan., Medical Library Assan., Evangelical Theological Soc., Soc. for Reformation Research, Creation Research Soc. *Publications:* The Shape

of the Past: An Introduction to Philosophical Historiography 1962, The "Is God Dead?" Controversy 1966, The Altizer-Montgomery Dialogue: A Chapter in the God Is Dead Controversy (with T. J. J. Altizer) 1967, Crisis in Lutheran Theology: The Validity and Relevance of Historic Lutheranism versus Its Contemporary Rivals 1967, Es confiable el Christianismo? 1968, Where Is History Going?: Essays in Support of the Historical Truth of the Christian Revelation 1969, Ecumenicity, Evangelicals and Rome 1969, History and Christianity 1970, The Suicide of Christian Theology 1970, In Defense of Martin Luther 1970, Damned Through the Church 1970, Computers, Cultural Change, and the Christ 1970, The Quest for Noah's Ark 1972, Debate on Situation Ethics (with J. Fletcher) 1972, La Mort de Dieu 1972, Principalities and Powers: The World of the Occult 1973, Cross and Crucible: Johann Valentin Andreae 1586-1654 1973, How Do We Know There Is a God? and Other Questions 1974, The Law Above the Law 1975, The Shaping of America 1976, Law and Gospel 1978, Faith Founded on Fact 1978, Slaughter of the Innocents 1981, The Marxist Approach to Human Rights 1983, Human Rights and Human Dignity 1987; Ed. and Translator of many books; Gen. Ed. of Evangelical Perspectives series 1970-72. *Leisure interests:* travel, music, gastronomy, vinology, antique Citroën cars, book collecting. *Address:* 1 rue de Palerme, Strasbourg 67000, France (May-Sept.); 3855 East La Palma Avenue, Anaheim, Calif. 92807, U.S.A.; Flat 9, 4 Crane Court, Fleet Street, London, E.C.4, England.

MONTI, Innocenzo; Italian banker; b. 3 Dec. 1909, Salerno; s. of Edoardo Monti and Maria Piera del Bo; m. Lalla Romano 1932; one s.; ed. Turin Univ.; joined Banca Commerciale Italiana, Cuneo Branch 1927; took part in preparations for post-war reconstitution of Bank's admin. 1944; joined Italian Banking Asscn. as mem. Tech. Comm. for Banking Admin. 1951; Adviser to Chair. of Banco de Credito del Perú, Lima 1953; Chief Accountant-Gen. Banca Commerciale Italiana 1966; invited by Bank of Italy to take part in Interbank Convention on Automation Problems (CIPA) 1968; supervised admin. aspects of establishment of branches in New York, London, Singapore, Tokyo, Los Angeles, Chicago, São Paulo 1968-74; Chair. Banca Commerciale Italiana 1976-81, S.I.A. (Interbanking Agency for Automation) 1977-; Chair. Mediobanca, Milan 1978-79, Dir. 1979-; Dir. Banca Commerciale Italiana 1981-; Dir. Associazione Amici di Brera e dei Musei milanesi 1980-, Fondazione G. Feltrinelli, Milan 1982-; Cavaliere di Gran Croce, Ordine al Merito della Repubblica Italiana. *Publications:* L'impiego degli elaborati elettronici nel lavoro bancario 1970, La banca di credito ordinario con filiali operanti in tutto il territorio nazionale 1970, Intervento finale al Convegno IRI "Inflation accounting" 1977. *Leisure interests:* literature, history, music, mountaineering. *Address:* Via Brera 17, 1-20121 Milan, Italy.

MONTREMY, Philipe Marie Waldruche de, L. ÈN D., L. ÈS L.; French business executive; b. 25 July 1913, Paris; m. Berthilde de Wendel 1945; two s. two d.; ed. Ecole Libre des Sciences Politiques; Insp. des Finances 1942; Deputy Dir. Direction des Prix 1947; Deputy Dir. Office of Minister of Finance and Econs. 1949; Dir. of Finance, Morocco 1955; Econ. and Financial Counsellor, French Embassy, Morocco 1956; Dir.-Gen. of Customs and Excise 1958-71; Insp. Gen. of Finance 1964-; Admin. Cie. Gén. Transatlantique 1962-74, Cie. des Messageries Maritimes 1964-74, Aéroport de Paris 1974-76; mem. Conseil d'Admin. Service d'Exploitation Industrielle des Tabacs et des Allumettes (SEITA) 1971, Pres. 1971-74; Pres. Banque Demachy 1976-77; Commdr. Légion d'honneur, Croix de guerre, Officier, Ordre nat. du Mérite. *Address:* 38 avenue Marceau, 75008 Paris, France. *Telephone:* (1) 47-23-95-17.

MONYAKE, Lengolo Bureng, M.SC., U.ED.; Lesotho politician; b. 1 April 1930, Lesotho; s. of Bureng L. Monyake and Leomile Monyake; m. Molulela Mapetla 1957; two s. one d.; ed. Fort Hare Univ. Coll., Univ. of Toronto, Carleton Univ., London School of Economics; headmaster, Jordan High School 1958-61; Dir. of Statistics, Govt. of Lesotho 1968-74, Perm. Sec. 1974-76, Deputy Sr. Perm. Sec. 1976-78; Amb. 1979-83; Man. Dir. Lesotho Nat. Devt. Corpn. 1984-86; Minister for Foreign Affairs 1986-88, of Works March 1988-. *Leisure interests:* tennis, table tennis, music, photography. *Address:* P.O. Box 526, Maseru 100, Lesotho. *Telephone:* 311710.

MONZEN, Mitsugi; Japanese business executive; b. 29 May 1918, Kogoshima; three s.; ed. Tokyo Azabu Veterinary Surgeon Speciality Coll.; Dir. Morinaga Milk Industry Co. Ltd. 1968, Man. Dir. 1976, Pres. 1979, Chair. 1985-; Official Commendation from Japan Milk Products Asscn. 1978. *Leisure interest:* reading. *Address:* 2-13-18 Tsukushino, Machida-si, Tokyo, Japan. *Telephone:* (0427) 95-5559.

MOODY, George Franklin; American banker; b. 28 July 1930, Riverside, Calif.; s. of William Clifford and Mildred E. (née Scott) Moody; m. Mary Jane Plank 1950; three s. one d.; ed. Riverside City Coll. and Pacific Coast Banking School; Business Officer, Univ. of Calif., Riverside 1950-52; joined Security Pacific Nat. Bank 1953, Vice-Pres. and Personnel Dir., Los Angeles 1970-71, Sr. Vice-Pres. (Inland Div. Admin.) 1971-73, Exec. Vice-Pres. 1973-78, Vice-Chair. 1978-81, Pres. and C.O.O. 1981-87, Chair. Exec. Cttee. (Security Pacific Corpn.) 1985-; Dir. Music Center Operating Co.; Los Angeles Chamber of Commerce (Chair. of Bd. and Dir.). *Address:* c/o Security Pacific Corporation, 333 South Hope Street, Los Angeles, Calif. 970071, U.S.A.

MOONEY, Harold Alfred, M.A., PH.D.; American professor of biology; b. 1 June 1932, Santa Rosa, Calif.; s. of Harold Walter Mooney and Sylvia A.

Stefany; m. Sherry L. Gulmon 1974; two d.; ed. Univ. of Calif., Santa Barbara and Duke Univ.; Instructor to Assoc. Prof. Univ. of Calif., L.A. 1960–68; Assoc. Prof. Stanford Univ. 1968–73, Prof. 1975–, Paul S. Achilles Prof. of Environmental Biology 1976–; Guggenheim Fellow 1974; mem. N.A.S., American Acad. of Arts and Sciences; Mercer Award (Ecology Soc. of America) 1961. *Publications:* 7 books. *Address:* Department of Biological Sciences, Stanford University, Stanford, Calif. 94305 (Office); 2625 Ramona Street, Palo Alto, Calif. 94306, U.S.A. (Home).

MOONS, Charles M. J. A., D.IUR.; Dutch jurist; b. 30 May 1917, Gemert; m. H. S. de Vriese 1949; three s. two d.; ed. Univ. of Nijmegen; Substitute Public Prosecutor 1940–56, Public Prosecutor 1956–58; Advocate-Gen. Court of Appeal 1958–61; Advocate-Gen. Hoge Raad der Nederlanden (Supreme Court) 1961–66, Judge 1966–76, Vice-Pres. 1976–81, Pres. 1981–87; Judge, Benelux Court 1976–79, Vice-Pres. 1979–83, Pres. 1983–; mem. Council of Govs., Leiden Univ. 1968–72; mem. Council of Govs., Royal Mil. Acad. 1970–; Appointing Authority Iran-U.S. Claims Tribunal 1983–; Ridder Orde Nederlande Leeuw; Commandeur Orde van Oranje-Nassau; Groot Officier Kroonorde van Belgie; Orde Nederlandse Leeuw; Grand Officier, Ordre Grand-Ducal de la Couronne de Chène. *Publication:* Conclusions Advocate-General Nederlandse Jurispendentie, 1961–67. *Leisure interest:* computer science. *Address:* Wassenaarseweg 81, 2596 CM, 's-Gravenhage, Netherlands. *Telephone:* 070-243571.

MOORBATH, Stephen Erwin, D.PHIL., D.SC., F.R.S.; British earth scientist; b. 9 May 1929, Magdeburg, Germany; s. of Heinz and Else Moosbach; m. Pauline Tessier-Varlêt 1962; one s. one d.; ed. Lincoln Coll., Oxford; Asst. Experimental Officer, Atomic Energy Research Est., Harwell 1948–51; Scientific Officer, A.E.R.E. 1954–56; Research Fellow, Univ. of Oxford 1956–61, Sr. Research Officer, 1962–78, Reader in Geology 1978–, Fellow Linacre Coll. 1970–; Research Fellow, M.I.T. 1961–62; several awards. *Publications:* numerous contributions to books and scientific journals. *Leisure interests:* music, philately, travel, linguistics. *Address:* Department of Earth Sciences, Oxford University, Parks Road, Oxford, OX1 3PR (Office); 53 Bagley Wood Road, Kennington, Oxford, OX1 5LY, England (Home). *Telephone:* (0865) 272035 (Office); (0865) 739507 (Home).

MOORE, Arch Alfred, Jr., LL.B.; American politician and lawyer; b. 16 April 1923, Moundsville, W. Va.; s. of Mr. and Mrs. Arch A. Moore; m. Shelley Riley 1949; one s. two d.; ed. Moundsville High School, West Virginia Univ.; served in Army, Second World War, as Combat Sergeant until severely injured and discharged with Bronze Star; entered Law School 1949; admitted to W. Va. State Bar 1951, joining family law partnership in the same year; elected Vice-Pres. W. Va. Bar Asscn.; elected to W. Va. House of Dels. 1952; elected to 85th–90th Congresses 1957–69; Gov. of West Virginia 1969–77, 1985–89; Chair. Nat. Govs. Asscn. 1971; Co-Chair. Appalachian Regional Comm. 1971, 1987; Pres. Educ. Comm. of U.S. 1974–76; Nat. Republican Govs.' Asscn. 1976, Interstate Mining Compact Comm. 1976; Purple Heart Medal; Commdr. and Grand Officer, Order of Merit (Italy); Republican. *Address:* 507 Jefferson Avenue, Glen Dale, W. Va. 26038, U.S.A. (Home).

MOORE, Bobby (see Moore, Robert).

MOORE, Brian, F.R.S.L.; Canadian novelist; b. 25 Aug. 1921, Belfast, N. Ireland; s. of the late James Bernard Moore and Eileen McFadden; m. Jean Denney 1967; one s.; Guggenheim Fellowship 1959; Canada Council Sr. Fellowships 1961, 1975; Authors Club of G.B. Novel Award 1956; Quebec Literary Prize 1958; Gov.-Gen. of Canada Fiction Award 1961, 1972; U.S. Nat. Inst. of Arts and Letters Award 1961; W. H. Smith Award (U.K.) 1973, James Tait Black Memorial Award 1975, Scottish Arts Council Nell Gunn Int. Fellowship 1983; Sunday Express Book of the Year Prize for The Colour of Blood 1988; Hon. D.Litt. (Queen's Univ. of Belfast) 1987. *Publications:* novels: The Lonely Passion of Judith Hearne 1956, The Feast of Lupercal 1958, The Luck of Ginger Coffey 1960, An Answer from Limbo 1963, The Emperor of Ice Cream 1965, I Am Mary Dunne 1968, Fergus 1971, Catholics 1972, The Great Victorian Collection 1975, The Doctor's Wife 1976, The Mangan Inheritance 1979, The Temptation of Eileen Hughes 1981, Cold Heaven 1983, Black Robe 1985, The Colour of Blood 1987; non-fiction: The Revolution Script 1971, Canada (with the Eds. of Life) 1963, 1967. *Address:* 33958 Pacific Coast Highway, Malibu, Calif. 90265, U.S.A.

MOORE, Carole Rinne, M.S.; Canadian librarian; b. 15 Aug. 1944, Berkeley, Calif., U.S.A.; d. of Clarence Rinne and Reola (née Johnson) Rinne; m. Thomas Moore; two s.; ed. Stanford and Columbia Univs.; Reference Librarian Columbia Univ. Libraries 1967-68, Univ. of Toronto Library 1968–73; Asst. Head Reference Dept., Univ. of Toronto Library 1973–74, Head 1974–80; Head Bibliographic Processing Dept., Univ. of Toronto Library 1980–86, Assoc. Librarian, Tech. Services 1986–87, Chief Librarian June 1987–; Columbian Univ. School of Library Service Centenary Distinguished Alumni Award 1987. *Publications:* Labour Relations and the Librarian (ed.) 1974, Canadian Essays and Collections Index 1972–73 1976. *Leisure interest:* gardening. *Address:* Robarts Library, 130 St. George Street, Toronto, Ont. M5S 1A5 (Office); 5 Albermarle Avenue, Toronto, Ont. M4K 1H6, Canada.

MOORE, Dudley Stuart John, B.A., B.MUS.; British actor, composer and musician; b. 19 April 1935; s. of John Moore and Ada Francis Huges; m.

1st Suzy Kendall (dissolved); m. 2nd Tuesday Weld (dissolved); one s.; m. 3rd Brogan Lane 1988; ed. County High School, Dagenham, Essex, and Magdalen Coll., Oxford. *Stage work:* composed incidental music for Royal Court Theatre productions; with Vic Lewis and John Dankworth jazz bands 1959-60; Beyond the Fringe, London 1960-62, Broadway, New York 1962-64; Play It Again Sam (Globe Theatre) 1970; Behind the Fridge (Cambridge Theatre) 1972–73; Good Evening, Broadway 1973–74; tour of U.S.A. 1975; Royal Command Performance; tours with own jazz piano trio. *TV work:* Not only . . . but also (series with Peter Cook, q.v.) 1964, 1966, 1970; Goodbye again (ITV); It's Lulu, not to mention Dudley Moore 1972; guest appearances with jazz trio. *Films:* The Wrong Box 1966, Thirty is a Dangerous Age Cynthia 1967, Bedazzled 1968, Monte Carlo or Bust 1969, The Bed-sitting Room 1969, Alice's Adventures in Wonderland 1972, The Hound of the Baskervilles, Foul Play, 10, Wholly Moses, Arthur (Golden Globe Award 1983), Six Weeks, Lovesick, Romantic Comedy, Unfaithfully Yours, Micki and Maude (Golden Globe Award 1985), Best Defense, Santa Claus, Like Father, Like Son, Arthur 2: On the Rocks; composed music for Bedazzled, Thirty is a Dangerous Age Cynthia, The Staircase, Six Weeks and various TV films. *Albums:* Beyond the Fringe and all that Jazz, The Other Side of Dudley Moore, Today, Dudley Moore Trio-Down Under, Dudley Moore and Cleo Laine—Smilin Through, The Music of Dudley Moore. *Publications:* Dud and Pete: the Dagenham Dialogues 1971, Dudley Moore—Offbeat 1986, The Complete "Beyond the Fringe" 1987, Voices of Survival 1988. *Leisure interests:* films, theatre, music. *Address:* 73 Market Street, Venice, Calif. 90291, U.S.A. *Telephone:* (213) 396-5937.

MOORE, Francis Daniels, M.D.; American surgeon; b. 17 Aug. 1913, Evanston, Ill.; s. of Philip Wyatt and Caroline (Daniels) Moore; m. Laura Benton Bartlett 1935; two s. three d.; ed. Harvard Coll. and Medical School; Intern and Resident, Mass. Gen. Hosp. 1939–43; Research Fellow, Nat. Research Council 1940–41; Tutor and Asst. Prof. in Surgery, Harvard Medical School 1944–48, Moseley Prof. of Surgery 1948–76, Elliott Carr Cutler Prof. of Surgery 1976–80; Surgeon-in-Chief, Peter Bent Brigham Hosp. 1948–76, Surgeon 1976–80, Surgeon-in-Chief Emer. 1980–; Sr. Consultant in Surgery, Sidney Farber Cancer Center 1976–; Moseley Prof. of Surgery (Emer.), Harvard Medical School 1980–; Pres. Mass. Health Data Consortium Inc. 1981–87; Consultant to Surgeon-Gen. of Navy 1981–; mem. Nat. Acad. of Sciences 1981–; Chair. Ed. Bd. Journal of Clinical Surgery 1981–82; Consultant, NASA 1966-69, 1986–; Ed. Staff New England Journal of Medicine 1981–; Silver Medal Award of Int. Soc. of Surgery 1959, Harvey Allen Award of American Burns Asscn. 1970, Gold Headed Cane of Univ. of Calif. 1970, Bigelow Medal of Boston Surgical Soc. 1974, Samuel D. Gross Medal of American Surgical Asscn. 1978, Lister Medal of Royal Coll. of Surgeons of England 1978; Hon. M.Ch. (Nat. Univ., Ireland) 1961, Hon. LL.D. (Glasgow) 1965, Hon. S.D. (Suffolk) 1966, Hon. M.D. (Edinburgh) 1975, (Paris) 1976, (Copenhagen) 1979, Hon. D.Sc. (Harvard) 1982. *Publications:* Metabolic Response to Surgery 1952, Metabolic Care of the Surgical Patient 1959, Give and Take, the Development of Tissue Transplantation 1964, Surgical Manpower in the United States 1975. *Leisure interests:* sailing, music. *Address:* 10 Shattuck Street, Boston, Mass. 02115; 66 Heath Street, Brookline, Mass. 02146, U.S.A. (Home). *Telephone:* (617) 734-0420 (Office); (617) 277-3552 (Home).

MOORE, Rt. Hon. John Edward Michael, M.P.; British politician; b. 26 Nov. 1937; s. of Edward O. Moore; m. Sheila S. Tillotson 1962; two s. one d.; ed. London School of Econs.; with Royal Sussex Regt. Korea 1955-57; Pres. Students' Union L.S.E. 1959-60; banking and stockbroking, Chicago 1962-65; Dir. Dean Witter Int. Ltd. 1968–79, Chair. 1975–79; underwriting mem. Lloyds 1978–; mem. Parl. for Croydon Cen. 1974–; Parl. Under-Sec. of State, Dept. of Energy 1979–83; Econ. Sec. to H.M. Treasury June–Oct. 1983, Financial Sec. to H.M. Treasury Oct. 1983–86; Sec. of State for Transport 1986–87, for Dept. of Health and Social Security 1987–88, for Social Security July 1988–; mem. Ct. of Govs. L.S.E. 1977; Conservative. *Address:* House of Commons, London, SW1A 0AA, England.

MOORE, John A(lexander), PH.D.; American biologist; b. 27 June 1915, Charles Town, W. Va.; s. of George Douglas and Louise Hammond Blume Moore; m. Anna Betty Clark 1938; one d.; ed. Columbia Coll. and Columbia Univ.; Tutor of biology Brooklyn Coll. 1939–41; instructor at Queens Coll. 1941–43; Asst. Prof. Zoology Barnard Coll. 1943–47, Assoc. Prof. 1947–50; Prof. 1950–68, Chair. Zoology Dept. 1948–52, 1953–54, 1960–66; Research Assoc. American Museum of Natural History 1942–; Asst. Zoology Dept., Columbia 1936–39, Chair. 1949–52, Prof. 1954–68; Prof. Biology Dept. Univ. of Calif. (Riverside) 1969–; mem. Nat. Research Council Comm. on Human Resources 1979–82; Fulbright Research Scholar, Australia 1952–53; Walker Ames Prof. Univ. of Washington 1966; Guggenheim Fellowship Award 1959; Biological Sciences Curriculum Study 1959; Commission on Science Educ. 1967–73, Chair. 1971–73; mem. Marine Biology Lab., A.A.A.S., Genetics Soc. of America, American Soc. of Zoologists, Pres. 1974, American Soc. of Naturalists, Pres. 1972, Soc. for Study Evolution, Pres. 1963, American Acad. Arts and Sciences, Nat. Acad. of Sciences. *Publications:* Principles of Zoology 1957, Heredity and Development 1963, 1972, A Guide Book to Washington 1963, Biological Science: An Inquiry into Life 1963, 1968, 1973 (Supervisor), Physiology of the Amphibia (Ed.) 1964, Ideas in Modern Biology (Ed.) 1965, Interaction of Man and the Biosphere (Co-author) 1970, 1975, 1979, Ideas in Evolution and Behavior (Ed.) 1970, Science for Society: A Bibliography 1970, 1971, Readings in Heredity and

Development 1972, Dobzhansky's Genetics of Natural Populations (Ed.) 1981, Science as a Way of Knowing—Evolutionary Biology 1984, Science as a Way of Knowing—Human Ecology 1985, Science as a Way of Knowing—Genetics 1986, Science as a Way of Knowing—Developmental Biology 1987. *Leisure interests:* photography, history of American science. *Address:* Department of Biology, University of California, Riverside, Calif. 92521; 11522 Tulane Avenue, Riverside, Calif. 92507, U.S.A. (Home).

MOORE, Capt. John Evelyn, R.N., F.R.G.S.; British editor, author and (retd.) naval officer; b. 1 Nov. 1921, Sant' Ilario, Italy; s. of William John Moore and Evelyn Elizabeth (née Hooper); m. 1st Joan Pardoe 1945, one s. two d.; m. 2nd Barbara Kerry; ed. Sherborne School, Dorset; entered R.N. 1939, specialised in hydrographic surveying, then submarines, commanded H.M. Submarines Totem, Alaric, Tradewind, Tactician, Telemachus; R.N. staff course 1950–51; Commdr. 1957; attached to Turkish Naval Staff 1958–60; subsequently Plans Div., Admiralty, 1st Submarine Squadron, then 7th Submarine Squadron in command; Capt. 1967; served as Chief of Staff, C.-in-C. Naval Home Command, Defence Intelligence Staff; retd. list at own request 1972; Ed. Jane's Fighting Ships 1972–; Ed. Forces Naval Review 1981–83; Ed. Jane's Naval Review 1982–. *Publications:* Jane's Major Warships 1973, The Soviet Navy Today 1975, Submarine Development 1976 Soviet War Machine (jtly.) 1976, Encyclopaedia of World's Warships 1978, World War 3 1978, Seapower and Politics 1979, Warships of the Royal Navy 1979, Warships of the Soviet Navy 1981, Submarine Warfare: Today and Tomorrow (jtly.) 1986. *Leisure interests:* gardening, swimming, archaeology. *Address:* Elmhurst, Rickney, Hailsham, Sussex, BN27 1SF, England. *Telephone:* (0323) 763294.

MOORE, Maj.-Gen. Sir (John) Jeremy, K.C.B., O.B.E., M.C.; British Royal Marines officer; b. 5 July 1928, Lichfield, Staffs.; s. of Lieut.-Col. C. P. Moore, M.C.; m. Veryan Acworth 1966; one s. two d.; ed. Cheltenham Coll.; with Royal Marines 1947–83; Staff Coll., Australia 1963–64; Chiefs of Staff Secr., London 1966–68; C.O. 42 Commando, Royal Marines 1972–73; Purveyor in Mil. Music to Royal Navy 1973–75; Royal Coll. of Defence Studies 1976; Commdr. 3rd Commando Brigade, Royal Marines 1977–79; Maj.-Gen. commanding commando forces, Royal Marines 1979–82 (Commdr. of British Land Forces in Falklands conflict 1982, accepted Argentine surrender 14 June 1982); Specialist Adviser Commons Select Cttee. on Defence 1984–; defence consultant; Dir.-Gen. Food Mfrs. Fed. 1984–85, Food and Drink Fed. 1984–85; Hon. Pres. British Biathlon team 1984–; mem. Parish Council, Bratton, Wilts. 1987–. *Leisure interests:* governor of two schools, music, sailing, hill walking. *Address:* c/o Lloyds Bank Ltd., Cox's & King's Branch, 6 Pall Mall, London, W.1, England.

MOORE, Michael Kenneth, M.P.; New Zealand politician; b. 1949, Whakatane; m.; fmr. social worker, printer etc.; M.P. for Eden 1972–75, Papanui, Christchurch 1978–84, Christchurch North 1984–; Minister of Overseas Trade and Marketing, also Minister of Tourism and Publicity, and of Recreation and Sport 1984–87; Minister of Overseas Trade and Marketing, and of Publicity 1987–88, of External Relations and Int. Trade Sept. 1988–; Labour. *Publications:* five books including A Pacific Parliament and Hard Labour. *Address:* House of Representatives, Wellington, New Zealand.

MOORE, Patrick, C.B.E.; British astronomer and author; b. 4 March 1923, Pinner, Middx.; s. of late Capt. Caldwell-Moore, M.C. and Gertrude Moore (née White); unmarried; ed. privately; Officer, Bomber Command, RAF 1940–45; BBC TV series, The Sky at Night 1957–, radio broadcasts; Ed. Year Book of Astronomy 1962–; Dir. Armagh Planetarium 1965–68; composed Perseus and Andromeda (opera) 1975, Theseus 1982; Pres. British Astronomical Asscn. 1982–84; Goodacre Medal (British Astronomical Asscn.) 1968; Jackson Gwilt Gold Medal (Royal Astronomical Soc.) 1977; Klumpke Medal (Astronomical Soc. of the Pacific) 1979; Hon. D.Sc. (Lancaster) 1974. *Publications:* numerous, including Guide to the Moon 1976, Atlas of the Universe 1980, History of Astronomy 1983, Guinness Book of Astronomy (revised edn.) 1983, The Story of the Earth (with Peter Cattermole) 1985, Halley's Comet (with Heather Couper) 1985, Patrick Moore's Armchair Astronomy 1985, Stargazing 1985, Exploring the Night Sky with Binoculars 1986, The A-Z of Astronomy 1986, Astronomy for the Under Tens 1987, Astronomers' Stars 1987, The Planet Uranus (jtly.) 1988, Space Travel for the Undertens 1988, The Planet Neptune 1989; Minor Planet No. 2602 is named in his honour. *Leisure interests:* music, cricket, tennis, chess. *Address:* Farthings, 39 West Street, Selsey, Sussex, England. *Telephone:* (0243) 603668.

MOORE, Robert F. (Bobby), O.B.E.; British professional footballer; b. 12 April 1941, Barking, Essex; s. of Robert E. and Doris Moore; m. Christina E. Moore 1962 (divorced 1986); one s. one d.; ed. Thomas Hood Tech. Coll., Leyton; played for West Ham Football Club 1958–74, Fulham F.C. 1974–78; Man. Oxford City F.C. 1979–81; Coach Eastern Athletic F.C., Hong Kong 1982–83; Dir. and C.E.O. Southend United F.C. 1983–86; Sports Ed. Sunday Sport 1986–; 18 England Youth Caps (record); many Under-23 Caps; 108 Full Int. Caps (record), 90 times as Captain; Winner's Medals in F.A. Cup Final 1964 (West Ham), European Cup Winners Cup Final 1965 (West Ham), World Cup Final 1966 (England); Runners-up Medal in F.A. Cup Final 1975 (Fulham); Footballer of the Year 1964; Player of Players in World Cup 1966; appeared in film Escape to Victory 1980.

Leisure interests: music, golf, different sports to relax. *Address:* c/o Sunday Sport, 50 Eagle Wharf Road, London, N.1., England.

MOORE, Robin James, M.A., PH.D., D.LIT., F.A.H.A.; Australian professor of history; b. 29 April 1934, Melbourne; s. of late F. E. Moore; m. 2nd Rosemary Sweetapple 1976; ed. Univs. of Melbourne and London; Exec. Containers Ltd. 1955–60, Western Mining Corpn. 1960–62; Sir Arthur Sims Travelling Scholar 1962–64; lecturer in Modern History S.O.A.S., London Univ. 1964–71; Prof. of History, Flinders Univ. of South Australia 1971–, mem. of Council 1986–, Dean of School of Social Sciences 1988–; Smuts Visiting Fellow in Commonwealth Studies, Cambridge Univ. 1974–75; Australian Vice-Chancellor's Cttee. Visiting Fellow, India 1979; Chapman Visiting Fellow Inst. of Commonwealth Studies, Univ. of London 1980–81; Gov. Adelaide Festival of Arts Inc. 1980–; Vice-Pres. Australian Historical Asscn. 1985–86, Pres. 1983–84; mem. Bd. Wakefield Press 1985–86; Visiting Prof. Univ. of Tulsa, Okla. 1987. *Publications:* Sir Charles Wood's Indian Policy 1853–1866 1966, Liberalism and Indian Politics 1872–1922 1966, The Crisis of Indian Unity 1917–40 1974, Churchill, Cripps and India 1939–45 1979, Escape from Empire 1983, Making the New Commonwealth 1987, Endgames of Empire 1988. *Leisure interests:* music, theatre, reading, walking. *Address:* 2 Palm Street, Medindie, S.A. 5081, Australia.

MOORE, Roger; British actor; b. 14 Oct. 1927, London; m. 1st Doorn van Steyn (divorced 1953); 2nd Dorothy Squires (divorced 1969); 3rd Luisa Mattioli; two s. one d.; ed. R.A.D.A.; *Films include:* Crossplot 1969, The Man With the Golden Gun 1974, That Lucky Touch 1975, Save Us From Our Friends 1975, Shout At The Devil 1975, Sherlock Holmes in New York 1976, The Spy Who Loved Me 1976, The Wild Geese 1977, Escape To Athena 1978, Moonraker 1978, Esther, Ruth and Jennifer 1979, The Sea Wolves, 1980, Sunday Lovers 1980, For Your Eyes Only 1980, Octopussy 1983, The Naked Face 1983, A View to a Kill 1985. *TV appearances include:* The Alaskans, The Saint 1962–69, The Persuaders. *Publication:* James Bond Diary 1973. *Address:* c/o London Management Ltd., 235 Regent Street, London, W.1, England.

MOORER, Admiral Thomas Hinman, D.S.M., D.F.C.; American naval officer (retd.); b. 9 Feb. 1912, Mount Willing, Ala.; s. of the late Richard Randolph Moorer and Hulda Hinson; m. Carrie Foy 1935; three s. one d.; ed. U.S. Naval Acad.; service in U.S. warships 1933–35, aviation squadrons 1936–43; Commdr. of bombing squadron 1943; Gunnery and Tactical Officer, Staff of Commdr., Naval Air Force, Atlantic 1944–45; Strategic Bombing Survey, Japan 1945–56; Naval Aviation Ordnance Test Station 1946–48; Exec. Officer aircraft carrier Midway 1948–49; Operations Officer on Staff of Commdr. Carrier Div. Four, Atlantic Fleet 1949–50; Naval Ordnance Test Station, Inyokern 1950–52; Capt. 1952; Staff of Commdr., Naval Air Force, Atlantic Fleet 1953–55; Aide to Asst. Sec. of Navy for Air 1955–56; Commdr. U.S.S. Salisbury Sound 1956–57; Special Asst., Strategic Plans Div., Office of Chief of Naval Operations, Navy Dept. 1957–58; Rear Adm. 1958; Asst. Chief of Naval Operations (War Gaming Matters) 1958–59; Commdr. Carrier Div. Six 1959–60; Dir. Long Range Plans 1960–62; Vice-Adm. 1962; Commdr. U.S. Seventh Fleet, W. Pacific 1962–64; Adm. 1964; C.-in-C. U.S. Pacific Fleet 1964–65; C.-in-C. U.S. Atlantic Fleet, C.-in-C. Atlantic and Supreme Allied Commdr. Atlantic (NATO Forces) 1965–67; Chief of Naval Operations, U.S. 1967–70; Chair. U.S. Joint Chiefs of Staff 1970–74; Vice-Chair. Blount Inc., Montgomery, Ala. 1974–; mem. Asscn. of Naval Aviation (Pres. 1974–); Silver Star Medal 1942, Legion of Merit 1945, Gray Eagle of U.S. Navy Award 1972, Defense Distinguished Service Medal 1973, included in Nat. Aviation Hall of Fame 1987, and many U.S. and foreign decorations. *Leisure interests:* golf, hunting, fishing. *Address:* 6901 Lupine Lane, McLean, Va. 22101, U.S.A.

MOORES, Hon. Frank Duff; Canadian politician; b. 18 Feb. 1933, Carbonear, Newfoundland; s. of Dorothy Duff and Silas Wilmot Moores; m. 2nd Janis Johnson 1973; m. 3rd Beth Champion 1982; two s. six d.; mem. Fed. House of Commons 1968–71, Newfoundland House of Ass. Oct. 1971–; Premier of Newfoundland 1972–79, also Minister of Fisheries 1972–73; mem. Progressive Conservative Party, Nat. Pres. 1969, Newfoundland Leader May 1970–79; Chair. Govt. Consultants Int.; Chair., C.E.O. Torngat Investments Inc.; SSF (Holdings) Inc.; Dir. several cos.; Hon. LL.D. (Memorial Univ. of Newfoundland) 1975. *Leisure interests:* golf, fishing, hunting. *Address:* Suite 1300, 50 O'Connor Street, Ottawa, Ont., K1P 6L2, Canada.

MOORES, Sir John, Kt., C.B.E.; British businessman; b. 25 Jan. 1896, Eccles, Lancs.; s. of John William Moores and Louisa Fethney; m. Ruby Knowles 1923; two s. two d.; ed. Higher Elementary School; joined P.O. at age of 14; wireless-telegraphist in R.N.; f. Littlewoods Pools 1924, Littlewoods Mail Order Stores 1932, Littlewoods Stores 1936, Chair. Littlewoods Org. 1924–77, 1980–82, Life Pres. 1982–; Hon. Freeman, City of Liverpool 1973; Hon. LL.B. (Liverpool Univ.) 1973; first winner Liverpool Gold Medal for Achievement 1978; estimated to be Britain's wealthiest man by Money Magazine 1988. *Leisure interests:* painting, languages, sport, travel. *Address:* c/o The Littlewoods Organisation PLC, JM Centre, Old Hall Street, Liverpool, L70 1AB, England. *Telephone:* 051-235 2222.

MOOREY, (Peter) Roger (Stuart), F.B.A., F.S.A., D.PHIL. (OXON.); British museum curator; b. 30 May 1937, Bush Hill Park, Middx.; s. of Stuart Moorey and Freda (née Harris) Moorey; ed. Mill Hill School, Corpus Christi

Coll., Oxford; Asst. Keeper, Ashmolean Museum, Oxford 1961-73, Sr. Asst. Keeper 1973-83, Keeper, Dept. of Antiquities 1983-; Fellow of Wolfson Coll., Oxford 1976-. *Publications:* Catalogue of the Ancient Persian Bronzes in the Ashmolean Museum 1971, Biblical Lands 1975, Kish Excavations 1923-33 1978, Cemeteries at Deve Hüyük 1980, Excavation in Palestine 1981, Materials and Manufacture in Ancient Mesopotamia 1985, The Bible and Recent Archaeology (with Kenyon) 1987, Ancient Near Eastern Seals in the Ashmolean Museum, vols. 2 and 3 (with Buchanan) 1984, 1988. *Leisure interests:* travelling, walking. *Address:* Ashmolean Museum, Oxford, OX1 2PH, England. *Telephone:* (0865) 278000.

MOORMAN van KAPPEN, Olav, LL.D.; Netherlands legal historian; b. 11 March 1937, The Hague; s. of Karel S. O. van Kappen and Johanna J. Moorman; m. Froukje A. Bosma 1963; one s. one d.; ed. Huygens Lyceum and Utrecht Univ.; Research Asst. Faculty of Law, Utrecht Univ. 1961-64, Jr. Lecturer 1965-68; Sr. Lecturer Faculty of Law, Amsterdam Univ. 1968-71; Asst. Prof. Faculty of Law, Leyden Univ. 1971-72; Prof. of Legal History, Nijmegen Univ. 1971-, Co. Dir. Gerard Noodt Inst. for Legal History 1972-; Visiting Prof. Munster Univ. 1982-83, Poitiers Univ. 1986; mem. Netherlands School for Archivists 1979-, Chair Bd. of Govs. 1981-; mem. Netherlands Council of Archives 1979-, Vice-Pres. 1986-; mem. editorial Bd., Legal History Review 1983; mem. Dutch Soc. of Sciences at Haarlem 1982, Royal Netherlands Acad. of Sciences 1986. *Publications:* several books and numerous articles on various aspects of legal history. *Address:* Institute of Legal Science of Nijmegen University, P.O. Box 9049, 6500 KK Nijmegen, Netherlands. *Telephone:* (080) 512186.

MOORTHY, Arambamoorthy Thedchana, B.A., BAR.-AT-LAW; Sri Lankan diplomatist (retd.); b. 10 Aug. 1928, Batticaloa; s. of S. Arambamoorthy and Nesammah Vairamuttu; m. Suseela Sri Skanda Rajah 1959; one s. two d.; ed. Univ. of Sri Lanka; entered Foreign Service 1953; Second Sec., Legation, Indonesia 1955-57; Second Sec., Embassy People's Repub. of China 1957-59; First Sec., High Comm., U.K. 1961-63; First Sec., Embassy, Fed. Repub. of Germany 1964-66; Chargé d'affaires a.i. to Thailand and Perm. Rep. to UN Econ. Comm. for Asia and the Far East 1969-70; Chargé d'affaires a.i. to Iraq 1970-74; Amb. to Pakistan 1978-81 (also to Iran 1980-81); High Commr. in U.K. 1981-84; private academic research and writing 1984-. *Address:* 19 Caverleigh Way, Worcester Park, Surrey, KT4 8DH, England.

MORAES, Dominic; Indian writer and poet; b. 19 July 1938; s. of late Frank Moraes; m. Leela Naidu 1970; ed. St. Mary's High School, Bombay, and Jesus Coll., Oxford; Consultant UN Fund for Population Activities 1973- (on loan to India); Man. Ed. The Asia Magazine Hong Kong 1972-; Hawthornden Prize for A Beginning 1957. *Publications include:* A Beginning 1957, Gone Away 1960, My Son's Father (autobiog.) 1968, The Tempest Within 1972-73, The People Time Forgot 1972, A Matter of People 1974, Voices for Life (essays) 1975, Mrs. Gandhi 1980, Bombay 1980, books of poems and travel books on India. *Address:* c/o United Nations Fund for Population Activities, 485 Lexington Avenue, 20th Floor, New York, N.Y. 10017, U.S.A.

MORAITIS, Georgios; Greek lawyer and politician; b. 1942, Vasilopoulo, Yannina; ed. Univ. of Athens; leader Centre Union youth org. until 1967; gaoled for political activities 1967-70; began legal practice 1970; founding mem. Pasok; Deputy to Parl. 1977-; Minister of Commerce July 1982-83, Minister of State 1985, Alt. Minister of Agric. 1985-86. *Address:* c/o Ministry of Agriculture, Odos-Aharnon 2-6, Athens, Greece. *Telephone:* 3291206.

MORALES, Armando; Nicaraguan artist; b. 15 Jan. 1927; ed. Inst. Pedagógico de Varones, Managua, Escuela de Bellas Artes, Managua and Pratt Graphic Art Center, New York; first one-man exhbn. Lima 1959, subsequently at Toronto, New York, Washington, D.C., Panama, Bogotá, Detroit, Caracas, Mexico City; Group exhbns. all over N. and S. America and in Europe; numerous awards for painting in the Americas including Carnegie Int. 1964, and award at Arte de América y España Exhbn., Madrid. *Address:* 32 West 82nd Street (3B), New York, N.Y. 10024, U.S.A.

MORALES BERMÚDEZ, Gen. Francisco: Peruvian army officer and politician; b. 4 Oct. 1921, Lima; grandson of the late Col. Remiro Morales (President of Peru, 1890-94); m. Rosa Pedraglio de Morales Bermúdez; four s. one d.; ed. Chorillos Mil. School; founder mem. Dept. of Research and Devt., Army Gen. Staff; taught at School of Eng. and at Army Acad. of War; Chief of Staff of First Light Div., Tumbes; Asst. Dir. of Logistics, Dir. of Econ., War Ministry; advanced courses at Superior Acad. of War, Argentina and Centre for Higher Mil. Studies, Peru; appointed to reorganize electoral registration system 1962; Minister of Econ. and Finance 1968-74; Chief of Army Gen. Staff 1974-75: Prime Minister, Minister of War and Commdr.-Gen. of Army Feb.-Aug. 1975; Pres. of Peru 1975-80. *Address:* c/o Oficina del Presidente, Lima, Peru.

MORALES BERMUDEZ PEDRAGLIO, Remigio, M.B.A., M.ECON.; Peruvian politician; b. 20 May 1947, Lima; ed. Univ. Nacional de Ingeniería, Inst. Americano de Economía, Univ. of Stanford; joined eng. firm DELCROSA 1970; Projects and Investment Div., Banco Industrial del Peru 1970-71; Legal Adviser, Corporación Financiera de Desarrollo 1971-76; Dir. Banco Popular 1976-77; Consultant and mem. various nat. and int. comms., including World Bank; Man. Dir., Gen. de Latinoamericana

de Radiodifusion (Channel 2) 1983-84; Minister of Agriculture 1986-88. *Address:* c/o Ministerio de Agricultura, S/N Avda. Salaverry, Edificio Ministerio de Trabajo, Lima, Peru. *Telephone:* 324040.

MORAN, 2nd Baron (cr. 1943), of Manton; **(Richard) John McMoran Wilson,** K.C.M.G.; British diplomatist (retd.); b. 22 Sept. 1924; s. of late Sir Charles McMoran Wilson, 1st Baron Moran; m. Shirley Rowntree Harris 1948; two s. one d.; ed. Eton, King's Coll., Cambridge; served in World War II; H.M.S. Belfast 1943, Sub-Lieut. R.N.V.R. in motor torpedo boats and H.M. Destroyer Oribi 1944-45; Foreign Office 1945; Third Sec., Ankara 1948, Tel-Aviv 1950; Second Sec., Rio de Janeiro 1953; First Sec., Foreign Office 1956; Washington, D.C. 1959; Foreign Office 1961; Counsellor, Pretoria 1965; Head of W. African Dept. of FCO 1968-73; Amb. to Chad 1970-73, to Hungary 1973-76, to Portugal 1976-81; High Commr. in Canada 1981-84; sits as independent peer, House of Lords; Vice-Chair. Atlantic Salmon Trust; Grand Cross of the Order of the Infante (Portugal) 1978. *Publications:* C.B., a Life of Sir Henry Campbell-Bannerman 1973 (Whitbread Award), Fairfax 1985. *Leisure interests:* fishing, fly-tying, bird watching. *Address:* c/o House of Lords, Westminster, London, S.W.1, England.

MORAN, Michael; Irish lawyer and politician; b. 25 Dec. 1912, Castlebar, Co. Mayo; s. of Brian Moran and Helen Rowland; m. Máiréad Ní Suibhne 1949; two s. one d.; ed. St. Gerald's Coll., Castlebar, and Univ. Coll., Dublin; admitted Solicitor 1933; mem. Mayo Co. Council 1938-57; Chair. Co. Mayo Cttee. of Agric. for number of years; T.D. South Mayo 1938-; Minister for the Gaeltacht 1957-59, 1961-68; Minister for Lands 1959-68; Minister of Justice 1968-70; Fianna Fáil. *Leisure interests:* shooting, hunting, fishing. *Address:* Ellison Street, Castlebar, Co. Mayo, Ireland. *Telephone:* Castlebar 42.

MORAN, Vincent, B.PHARM., M.D.; Maltese politician; b. 27 Jan. 1932; s. of John Moran and Carmela Debono; m. Margaret Debono 1963; ed. Lyceum, Univ. of Malta; mem. Malta Labour Party 1948-; M.P. for Third Dist. 1962-76, for Fourth Dist. 1976-; mem. Working Cttee. of Commonwealth Parl. Assen. 1967; Minister of Health and Environment 1981-87. *Address:* c/o Ministry of Health, Merchants Street, Valletta, Malta.

MORÁN LÓPEZ, Fernando; Spanish politician; b. 1926, Avilés; m. Maria Luz Calvo-Sotelo, one s. two d.; ed. Institut des Hautes Etudes Internationales, Paris, London School of Econs.; began diplomatic career 1954; Asst. Consul, Spanish Consulate-Gen., Buenos Aires 1956; Sec. Spanish Embassy, Pretoria; transferred to Ministry of Foreign Affairs 1963, specialized in African affairs, Asst. Dir.-Gen. for Africa, Near and Middle East, Political Dir. Dept. of Foreign Policy, later in charge of Africa, Near and Middle East 1971, Dir.-Gen. of African Affairs 1975-77; First Sec. Spanish Embassy, Lisbon; Consul-Gen. Spanish Embassy, London 1974; Partido Socialista Popular cand. for elections to Congress of Deputies 1977; elected Partido Socialista Obrero Español Senator for Asturias, socialist spokesman for Foreign Affairs in Senate; Minister of Foreign Affairs 1982-85; Perm. Rep. to the UN 1985-87; Légion d'honneur, Grand Cross of Carlos III, Grand Cross Order of Isabel la Católica 1985. *Publications:* include Una política exterior para España. *Address:* Juan XXIII 5, 28040 Madrid, Spain (Home).

MORAVIA, Alberto; Italian writer and journalist; b. 28 Nov. 1907; s. of Carlo and Teresa de Marsanich; m. 1st Elsa Morante 1941 (died 1985), m. 2nd Carmen Lelera 1986; Pres. Int. PEN 1959; Ed. Nuovi Argomenti; mem. European Parl. 1984-; Commdr., Légion d'honneur 1952. *Publications:* novels: Gli indifferenti 1929, Le Ambizioni Sbagliate 1935, La Mascherata 1941, Agostino 1944, La Romana 1947, La Disubbidienza 1948, L'Amore Coniugale 1949, Il Conformista 1951, Il disprezzo 1954, La Ciociara 1957, La noia 1961, L'Attenzione 1965; plays: Teatro 1958, Beatrice Cenci 1965, Il mondo è quello che è 1966, Il dio Kurt 1967, La Vita è Gioco 1970, La Vita Interiore 1978; short stories: La bella vita 1935, L'Imbroglio 1937, I Sogni del Pigro 1940, L'Amante infelice 1943, L'Epidemia 1945, Due Cortigiane 1945, Racconti Romani 1945, I Racconti 1954, Nuovi Racconti Romani 1959, L'Automa 1963, Una cosa è una cosa 1966, Il Paradiso 1970, Io e lui 1971, Un' altra Vita 1973, The Voice of the Sea 1978, The Voyeur 1986; essays: La speranza, L'Uomo come fine 1965, A quale tribù appartieni? 1974, Impegno Controvoglia 1980; travel: La rivoluzione culturale in Cina 1967, Passeggiate africane 1988. *Address:* Lungotevere della Vittoria 1, Rome, Italy. *Telephone:* 3603698.

MORAWSKI, Kazimierz, M.A.; Polish politician and journalist; b. 6 June 1929, Mała Wieś, Warsaw Voivodship; ed. Acad. of Political Sciences, Warsaw and Adam Mickiewicz Univ., Poznań; journalist of API Press Agency, later staff writer, daily Słowo Powszechne; co-founder, Christian Social Assen. 1956; Sub-Ed. Za i Przeciw 1956-62, corresp. Za i Przeciw, Vatican II Oecumenical Council 1962-65; mem., subsequently Gen. Sec. of Main Bd., Christian Social Assen. 1967-74, Pres. Main Bd. 1974-; Ed.-in-Chief Za i Przeciw 1978-83; Deputy to Seym 1976-, Vice-Chair. Seym Comm. of Culture and Art; mem. Council of State May 1982-; mem. Presidium of Provisional Nat. Council of Patriotic Movt. for Nat. Rebirth (PRON) 1982-83, mem. Presidium PRON 1983-; mem. Presidium Soc. for Connection with Poles Living Abroad (Polonia); took part in works of Int. man. of Christian Peace Conf.; Commdr.'s, Officer's and Kt.'s Cross of Order of Polonia Restituta, Order of Banner of Labour (2nd Class).

Address: Kancelaria Rady Państwa, ul. Wiejska 2/4/6, 00-902 Warsaw, Poland.

MORDKOVITCH, Lydia, PH.D.; Israeli violinist; b. 30 April 1944, Saratov, U.S.S.R.; d. of Mendel and Golda Sutimerman; m. 1st Leonid Mordkovitch 1962 (divorced), one d.; m. 2nd Malkia Chayoth 1977 (divorced 1983); ed. School for Talented Children, Kishinev, Stoliarski School, Odessa, Nejdanovh Conservatoire, Odessa, Tchaikovsky Conservatoire, Moscow and studied with David Oistrakh; Sr. Lecturer, Kishinev Inst. of Art 1970–73; Sr. Lecturer, Rubin Acad. of Music, Jerusalem 1974–80; Prof. of Violin, Royal Northern Coll. of Music, Manchester, England 1980-; soloist (violinist) in recitals, concerts, on radio and T.V., U.S.S.R., then Europe, U.S.A., S. and Cen. America 1974-; Prizewinner, Young Musicians Competition, Kiev 1967, Long-Thibaud Competition, Paris 1969; recordings: Franck and Ravel sonatas, Brahms concerto, Bartok, Prokofiev and Honegger sonatas, works by Bloch, Bruch, Ravel and Achron, Strauss and Fauré sonatas, Schumann sonatas. *Leisure interests:* theatre, literature, art. *Address:* 25B Belsize Avenue, London, N.W.3, England. *Telephone:* 01-794 2131.

MOREAU, Jeanne; French actress; b. 23 Jan. 1928, Paris; d. of Anatole-Désiré Moreau and Katherine Buckley; m. 1st Jean-Louis Richard 1949 (divorced), one s.; m. 2nd William Friedkin 1977 (divorced); ed. Collège Edgar-Quinet, Conservatoire national d'art dramatique; stage actress with Comédie Française 1948–52; Théâtre Nat. Populaire 1953; Pres. Cannes Film Festival July 1975; Paris Int. Film Festival 1975; Pres. Acad. des Arts et Techniques du Cinéma 1986–88; Chevalier, Légion d'honneur, Officier Ordre nat. du Mérite, Commdr. des Arts et Lettres, Moliere Award 1988; since 1954 has appeared on stage in L'heure éblouissante, La machine infernale, Pygmalion, La chatte sur un toit brûlant, La bonne soupe, La chevauchée sur le lac de Constance, Lulu, L'intoxe, Night of the Iguana, Le Récit de la Servante Zerline 1987, etc. *Films include:* Touchez pas au grisbi, Le salaire du péché, Ascenseur pour l'échafaud, Les amants, Moderato Cantabile, Les liaisons dangereuses, Dialogue des Carmélites, Jules et Jim, Eve, The Victors, La baie des anges, Peau de banane, Le train, Le journal d'une femme de chambre, Mata Hari—H21, The Yellow Rolls-Royce 1964, Viva Maria 1965, Mademoiselle 1965, Chimes at Midnight 1966, L'amour à travers les âges 1967, The Sailor from Gibraltar 1967, The Bride wore Black 1967, The Great Catherine 1968, Le corps de Diane 1970, Une histoire immortelle, Monte Walsh, L'humeur vagabonde, Comptes rebours 1971, Chère Louise 1972, Jeanne, la Française 1972, Nathalie Granger 1972, Je t'aime 1973, Les valseuses 1973, La race des seigneurs 1973, Pleurs 1974, Le jardin qui bascule 1974, Souvenirs d'en France, Lumière (also dir.) 1976, The Last Tycoon 1976, Mr. Klein 1976, Le Petit Théâtre de Jean Renoir 1976, L'adolescente 1978, Madame Rosa 1978, L'intoxe 1980, Plein Sud 1981, Mille milliards de dollars 1982, Au-delà de cette limite votre billet n'est plus valable 1982, Querelles 1982, La truite 1982, Le paltoquet 1986, Sauve-toi Lola 1986. *Leisure interest:* reading. *Address:* Georges Beaume, 4 rue de Ponthieu, 75008 Paris, France.

MOREIRA NEVES, H.E. Cardinal Lucas, O.P.; Brazilian ecclesiastic; b. 16 Sept. 1925, São João del Rei; ordained 1950, elected to the titular Church of Feradi Maggiore 1967, consecrated bishop 1967, Archbishop 1979, transferred to the titular Church of Vescovio 1987, then São Salvador da Bahia 1987; cr. Cardinal 1988. *Address:* Palácio de Sé, Praça da Sé 1, 40.000-Salvador, BA, Brazil. *Telephone:* (071) 247-7083.

MORELLI, Gaetano, LL.D.; Italian university professor and lawyer; b. 23 May 1900, Crotone; m. Giuseppina Sciacca 1964; ed. Univ. of Rome; Lecturer in Int. Law, Univ. of Urbino 1927–32; Prof. Univ. of Modena 1932–33, Univ. of Padua 1933–35, Univ. of Naples 1935–51, Univ. of Rome 1951–75, Prof. Emer. 1975-; Judge, Int. Court of Justice 1961–70; mem. Inst. de droit int. 1950-, First Vice-Pres. 1961–63, Pres. 1971–73, mem. Perm. Conciliation Comm. between Luxembourg and Switzerland 1950-, Higher Council of Public Educ. 1951–58, Perm. Court of Arbitration 1955-, Italian Nat. Comm. for UNESCO 1956–61. *Publications:* La sentenza internazionale 1931, Diritto processuale civile internazionale, La théorie générale du procès international 1937, Lezioni di diritto internazionale privato, Nozioni di diritto internazionale, Elementi di diritto internazionale privato italiano, Studi di diritto processuale civile internazionale 1961, Studi sul processo internazionale 1963, Nuovi studi sul processo internazionale 1972, etc. *Address:* Via Lucrezio Caro 67, Rome, Italy. *Telephone:* 3213573.

MORENO MARTÍNEZ, Alfonso, LL.D.; Dominican professor and diplomatist; b. 8 Dec. 1922, San Francisco de Macorís; m. Ligia Portalatin 1950; five c.; ed. Univ. de Santo Domingo; Founder and first Pres. Partido Revolucionario Social Cristiano 1961; Pres. Fifth Congress of Christian Dem. Org. of America (ODCA) 1969; Prof. of Sociology, Rural Sociology and Introduction to Social Sciences, Autonomous Univ. of Santo Domingo 1963–69; Prof. of Sociology and the History of Culture, Univ. of Pedro Henríquez Ureña 1974–75; Perm. Rep. to UN 1975–78; Sec.-Gen. Partido Revolucionario Social Cristiano (PRSC) 1979–80, Pres. 1980–84; Cand. for Presidency 1962, 1970. *Address:* Lorenzo Despradel 7, Los Prados, Santo Domingo 9, Dominican Republic. *Telephone:* 565-5018.

MORENO-SALCEDO, Luis, LL.B.; Philippines diplomatist; b. 5 Sept. 1918, Iloilo; m. Hermelinda Ycasiano; two s. two d.; ed. Royal and Pontifical Univ. of Santo Tomas, Manila; joined Ministry of Foreign Affairs 1946, Chief of Protocol 1948–54; Amb. to Argentina 1962–64, concurrently to Chile 1963–64, to Viet-Nam 1965–68, to France 1969–77, concurrently to Romania 1972–75, to Yugoslavia 1972–77, to Hungary 1975–77; Perm. Rep. to UNESCO, Paris 1969–77; Amb. to U.S.S.R. 1977–82, concurrently to Finland; Perm. Rep. to UN Comm. on Human Rights, Geneva 1980, 1982; Perm. Rep. to UN 1982–86; several honours and awards. *Publications:* A Guide to Protocol 1949, Selected Readings on Philippine Foreign Policy 1959. *Address:* c/o Ministry of Foreign Affairs, Padre Faura Street, Metro Manila, The Philippines.

MORF, Rudolf, PH.D.; Swiss chemist; b. 10 Nov. 1908, Kyburg, Canton Zürich; m. Irène Keller 1932; one s. three d.; ed. Univ. of Zürich and Oxford Univ.; research chemist, Nestlé Co., later Production Man. of a factory 1934–40; Pharmaceutical dept., Sandoz Ltd., Basel 1941–59; with F. Hoffmann-La Roche & Co. Ltd. 1959; Sec.-Gen. XIVth Int. Congress of Pure and Applied Chem. 1953–55; Sec.-Gen. of Int. Union of Pure and Applied Chem. (IUPAC) 1956; Sec.-Gen. Swiss Acad. of Sciences 1965–70. *Address:* Kyburg (Canton Zürich), Switzerland (Home).

MORGAN, James N. PH.D.; American economist; b. 1 March 1918, Corydon, Ind.; s. of John Jacob Brooke and Rose Ann Davis Morgan; m. Gladys Lucille Hassler 1945; three s. one d.; ed. Northwestern Univ. and Harvard; Asst. Prof. of Econs. Brown Univ. 1947–49; Carnegie Research Fellow Inst. for Social Research, Univ. of Mich. 1949–51, Fellow Center for Advanced Study in the Behavioral Sciences 1955–56, Program Dir. Survey Research Center, Inst. for Social Research 1956-, Prof. of Econs. 1957-; Fellow Wissenschaftskolleg zu Berlin 1983–84; mem. N.A.S.; Fellow American Statistical Asscn., American Acad. of Arts and Sciences, American Gerontological Assn. *Publications:* Income and Welfare in the United States 1962, Economic Behavior of the Affluent 1965, Economic Survey Methods 1971, Five Thousand American Families (Ed.) 10 Vols. 1972–84, Economics of Personal Choice 1980. *Leisure interests:* travel, photography. *Address:* Institute for Social Research, P.O. Box 1248, Ann Arbor, Mich. 48106 (Office); 1217 Bydding Road, Ann Arbor, Mich. 48103, U.S.A. (Home). *Telephone:* (313) 764-8388 (Office); (313) 668-8304 (Home).

MORGAN, Kenneth Owen, D.LITT., F.B.A., F.R.HIST.S.; British historian; b. 16 May 1934; s. of David James Morgan and Margaret Morgan; m. Jane Keeler 1973; one s. one d.; ed. University Coll. School, London, Oriel Coll., Univ. of Oxford; Lecturer History Dept. Univ. Coll., Swansea 1958–66, Sr. Lecturer 1965–66; Fellow and Praelector Modern History and Politics The Queen's Coll., Univ. of Oxford 1966–89; Prin., Univ. Coll. of Wales, Aberystwyth 1989-; Fellow American Council of Learned Socs. Columbia Univ. 1962–63, Visiting Prof. 1965; Prof. Univ. of Wales 1989; Hon. Fellow Univ. Coll. Swansea, 1985. *Publications:* Ed. Welsh History Review 1961-, Lloyd George: Family Letters 1973; Author Wales in British Politics 1963, David Lloyd George 1963, Freedom or Sacrilege? 1966, The Age of Lloyd George 1971, Lloyd George 1974, Keir Hardie: Radical and Socialist 1975, Consensus and Disunity 1979, Portrait of a Progressive (with Jane Morgan) 1980, Rebirth of a Nation: Wales 1880–1980 1981, Labour in Power 1945–51 1984, The Oxford Illustrated History of Britain (ed.) 1984, Labour People 1987, The Red Dragon and The Red Flag 1989. *Leisure interests:* music, sport, travel. *Address:* The Croft, 63 Millwood End, Long Hanborough, Oxon., OX7 2BP, England. *Telephone:* (0993) 881341.

MORGAN, Lee Laverne, B.S.; American business executive; b. 4 Jan. 1920, Aledo, Ill.; s. of Laverne and Gladys Hamilton Morgan; m. Mary Harrington 1942; ed. Univ. of Illinois; joined Caterpillar Tractor Co., various training, sales and advertising 1946–56, Man. Sales Devt. Dept. 1956–61, Vice-Pres. 1961–65, Dir. 1966, Exec. Vice-Pres. 1965–72, Pres. 1972–77, Chair. 1977–85, C.E.O. 1977–85; Dir. Boeing Co., Commercial Nat. Bank, Midwest Financial Group Inc., Minnesota Mining and Mfg. Co., Mobil Corpn., Proctor Community Hosp. of Peoria; Trustee, Monmouth Coll., Ill. *Address:* 100 NE Adams Street, Peoria, Ill. 61629, U.S.A. (Office). *Telephone:* (309) 675-4401.

MORGAN, Michèle (pseudonym of Simone Roussel); French actress; b. 29 Feb. 1920; d. of Louis Roussel; m. 1st Bill Marshall, one s.; m. 2nd Henri Vidal (deceased); studied with R. Simon (Paris); actress 1936-. *Films include:* Quai des brumes, Symphonie pastorale, Fabiola, Les sept péchés capitaux, Les orgueilleux, Obsession, Les grandes manoeuvres, Marguerite de la nuit, Marie Antoinette, Si Paris nous était conté, Le miroir à deux faces, Femmes d'un été, Pourquoi viens-tu si tard? Les scélérats, Fortunat, Le puits aux trois vérités, Les lions sont lâches, Rencontres, Le crime ne paie pas, Landru, Constance aux Enfers, Les yeux cernés, Dis-moi qui tuer Les centurions, Benjamin, Le chat et la souris 1975; has also appeared on television and in theatre; Cannes Festival Prize for Best Actress (in Symphonie pastorale) 1946; French "Victoire" for Best Actress 1946, 1948, 1950, 1952, 1955; Médaille de vermeil, Paris 1967; Officier, Légion d'honneur, Officier, Ordre nat. du Mérite. *Publication:* Mes yeux ont vu 1965. *Address:* 19 rue Eugène-Manuel, 75016 Paris, France.

MORGAN, Rev. Philip, B.A., D.D.; British minister of religion; b. 22 June 1930, Maryport; s. of David Lewis Morgan and Pamela Morgan; m. Greta Mary Hanson 1954; one s. one d.; ed. West Bridgford Grammar School, Overdale Coll., Selly Oak Colls., Birmingham Univ.; ordained to Ministry 1952; served in pastoral charge in S. Wales, London and Leicester 1952–66; Gen. Sec., Churches of Christ in G.B. 1966–80; Gen. Sec., British Council of Churches 1980–; Moderator of Gen. Ass., United Reformed Church in U.K. 1984–85. *Leisure interests:* hill walking, poetry, Celtic history. *Address:* Interchurch House, 35 Lower Marsh, London, SE1 7RH (Office); 8 Clivedon Place, London, SW1W 8LR, England (Home). *Telephone:* 01-620 4444 (Office); 01-730 3033 (Home).

MORGAN, Robert Burren, B.J., LL.D.; American lawyer and senator; b. 5 Oct. 1925, Lillington, N.C.; s. of James H. and Alice Morgan; m. Katie Owen 1960; one foster s. three d. (one deceased); ed. E. Carolina Univ. and Wake Forest Law School; mem. N.C. State Senate for five terms; Attorney-Gen. N.C. 1969–74; U.S. Senator from N. Carolina 1975–80; Dir. N.C. Bureau Investigation 1985–; Wyman Award 1974; Democrat. *Address:* 336 Keith Hills Road, Lillington, N.C. 27546, U.S.A.

MORGAN, Walter Thomas James, C.B.E., PH.D., D.SC., D.SC.TECH., C.CH-EM.F.R.S.C., F.R.S.; British biochemist; b. 5 Oct. 1900, London; s. of Walter Morgan and Annie E. James; m. Irene Price 1930; one s. two d.; ed. Univs. of London, Graz and Zürich; Grocers' Co. Research Student 1925–26; Beit Medical Research Fellow 1926–28; Biochemist and First Asst. to Serum Dept., Lister Inst., Elstree 1929–36; Rockefeller Research Fellow 1936–37; mem. of staff of Lister Inst., London 1928–68, Prof. of Biochem. 1951–68, Emer. Prof. 1968, Dir. Lister Inst. 1972–75; Hon. Sec. Biochemical Soc. 1940–45, Biological Council 1944–47; mem. Govt. Scientific Advisory Council 1955–59, mem. Medical Research Council 1966–70; Croonian Lecturer Royal Soc. 1959; Vice-Pres. Royal Soc. 1961–64; Hon. mem. Int. Soc. of Blood Transfusion; Hon. F.R.C.P. (London); M.D. h.c. (Basel), D.Sc. h.c. (Mich.); Conway Evans Prize (Royal Soc. and Royal Coll. Physicians) 1964, Karl Lansteiner Prize American Asscn. of Blood Banks 1967, Paul Ehrlich Prize 1968, Royal Medal (Royal Soc.) 1968. *Address:* 57 Woodbury Drive, Sutton, Surrey, England (Home). *Telephone:* 01-642 2319.

MORGAN, William Wilson, PH.D.; American astronomer; b. 3 Jan. 1906, Bethesda, Tenn.; s. of William T. and Mary W. Morgan; m. 1st Helen M. Barrett 1928 (deceased), 2nd Jean D. Eliot 1966; one s. one d.; ed. Washington and Lee Univ. and Univ. of Chicago; Man. Ed. The Astrophysical Journal 1947–52; Dir. of Yerkes and McDonald Observatories 1960–63; Chair. Dept. of Astronomy, Univ. of Chicago 1960–66, Bernard E. and Ellen C. Sunny Distinguished Prof. of Astronomy 1966–74, Prof. Emer. 1974–; mem. Nat. Acad. of Sciences, American Acad. of Arts and Sciences, Pontifical Acad. of Sciences, Royal Danish Acad. of Sciences and Letters, Soc. Royale des Sciences de Liège; Corresp. mem. Nat. Acad. of Sciences of Argentina; Ph.D. h.c. (Cordoba); Hon. D.Sc. (Yale Univ.) 1978; Bruce Gold Medal of Astronomical Soc. of the Pacific 1958, Henry Draper Medal, Nat. Acad. of Sciences 1980, Herschel Medal of Royal Astronomical Soc. 1983. *Publications:* An Atlas of Stellar Spectra (with P. C. Keenan and Edith Kellman) 1943, Revised MK Spectral Atlas for Stars Earlier than the Sun (with H. A. Abt and J. W. Tapscott) 1978; numerous research articles in professional journals. *Address:* Yerkes Observatory, Williams Bay, Wis. 53191, U.S.A. *Telephone:* (414) 245-5555 (Office); (414) 245-5839 (Home).

MORGENS, Howard J(oseph), A.B., M.B.A.; American businessman; b. 16 Oct. 1910; ed. Washington Univ. and Harvard Business School; with Procter and Gamble Co. 1933–, Advertising Man. 1946, Vice-Pres. (Advertising) 1948, Dir. 1950–, Exec. Vice-Pres. 1954, Pres. 1957–71, Chair. of Bd. 1971–74, Chair. Exec. Cttee. of Bd. of Dirs. 1974–77, Chair. Emer. 1977–; Dir. and fmr. Chair. Advertising Council; mem. Corporate Advisory Council Gen. Motors Corpn., Co. Dirs. Advisory Council Morgan Guaranty Trust Co.; Hon. LL.D. (Washington and Miami Univs. and Univ. of Cincinnati), Hon. Dr. of Humanities (Xavier Univ.). *Address:* c/o Procter and Gamble, Cincinnati, Ohio 45202, U.S.A.

MORGENTHAU, Robert Morris, LL.B.; American lawyer; b. 31 July 1919, New York; s. of Henry Morgenthau, Jr. and Elinor (née Fatman) Morgenthau; m. 1st Martha Pattridge (deceased); one s. four d.; m. 2nd Lucinda Franks 1977; ed. Deerfield Acad., Amherst Coll., Yale Univ.; barrister, New York 1949; Assoc. of Patterson, Belknap & Webb, New York 1948–53, Partner 1954–61; U.S. Attorney S. Dist. New York 1961–62, 1962–70; Dist. Attorney New York County 1975–; mem. New York Exec. Cttee. State of Israel Bonds; Democratic Candidate for Gov., New York 1962; mem. Bd. of Dirs. P.R. Legal Defense and Educ. Fund; Trustee Baron de Hirsch Fund, Fed. of Jewish Philanthropies; mem. Bar Asscn. City of New York; Hon. LL.D. (Amherst Coll.) 1966, (New York Law School) 1968. *Address:* Office of District Attorney, 155 Leonard Street, New York, N.Y. 10013, U.S.A.

MORI, Haruki; Japanese diplomatist; b. 1911; m. Tsutako Masaki 1941; four s.; ed. Univ. of Tokyo; Ministry of Foreign Affairs, served U.S.A. and Philippines 1935–41; Head of Econ. Section, Dept. of Political Affairs 1950–53; Counsellor Rome 1953–55; Counsellor Asian Affairs Bureau, Tokyo 1955–56; Pvt. Sec. to Prime Minister 1956–57; Deputy Dir.-Gen. Econ. Affairs Bureau 1957; Dir.-Gen. of American Affairs Bureau 1957–60; Minister to U.K. 1960–63, to France 1963–64; Amb. to OECD 1964–67; Deputy Vice-Minister for Foreign Affairs 1967–70, Vice-Minister 1970–72; Amb. to U.K. 1972–75; Adviser to Foreign Office 1975–. *Address:* Ministry of Foreign Affairs, Tokyo, Japan.

MORI, Hideo, B.A.; Japanese business executive; b. 1 April 1925, Osaka City; s. of Shigekazu Mori and Ikue Mori; m. Masako (née Okano) Mori;

two s.; ed. Kyoto Univ. 1947; joined Sumitomo Chemical Co. Ltd. 1947, Dir. 1977, Man. Dir. 1980, Sr. Man. Dir. 1982, Pres. March 1985–; Blue Ribbon Medal 1987. *Leisure interest:* golf. *Address:* Sumitomo Chemical Co. Ltd., 7-9, Nihonbashi 2-chome, Chuo-ku, Tokyo (Office); 13-16, Oyamadai 2-chome, Setagaya-ku, Tokyo, Japan (Home). *Telephone:* (03-278) 7005 (Office).

MORI, Taisuke: Japanese steel industry executive; b. 11 Nov. 1920, Tokyo, Japan; s. of the late Yoshitaro Mori and Chie Mori; m. Kikuko Sakashita 1959; two s. one d.; ed. Tokyo Univ. of Commerce and Industry (Hitotsubashi Univ.); Trade Corpn. of Japan (Govt. Agency for Foreign Trade) 1943–46; Ministry of Int. Trade and Industry 1946–50; Kinoshita & Co. Ltd. (Domestic and Int. Tradings) 1951–65; Kobe Steel Ltd. 1965–, Dir. of Bd., Gen. Man., Industrial Machinery Div. 1972–77, Sr. Man. Dir. Machinery Group 1977–79, Exec. Vice-Pres. Machinery Group and Marketing Activities 1979–83, Dir. 1983–, Exec. Vice-Chair. and Sr. Adviser 1983–87; Dir. Heninschfeger Industries Inc., Beloit Corpn., Syscon Corpn., Heninschfeger Corpn.; Chair. Steel Castings and Forgings Asscn. of Japan; Vice-Chair. Japan Industrial Machinery Mfrs.' Asscn.; Medal with Blue Ribbon (related to trade promotion and public services). *Publications:* many articles in magazines and newspapers. *Leisure interests:* golf, fishing, tourism. *Address:* 4-12-17 Shinoharakita-machi, 657 Nadu-ku, Kobe, Japan. *Telephone:*078-882-0600 (Home).

MORICE, André; French politician; b. 11 Oct. 1900, Nantes; s. of Emile Morice and Maria Dumec; m. Simone Rosaze 1944; three s. three d.; ed. Nantes Lycée and Univ. of Paris; in business 1931–39; served army 1939–44; Town Councillor for Nantes 1945, Asst. to Mayor 1945–47, Deputy for Loire-Atlantique 1945–58; Under-Sec. for Tech. Educ., Schuman Govt. 1947–48, Marie Govt. 1948; Sec. of State for Tech. Educ. and Sports in Queuille Govt. 1949, Bidault Govt. 1949–50, Pleven Govt. 1950–51, Queuille Govt. 1951; Minister of Nat. Educ., Queuille Govt. July 1951; Minister of the Merchant Marine, Pleven Govt. 1951–52, Faure Govt. 1952; Minister of Public Works, Travel and Tourism, Pinay Govt. 1952 and Mayer Govt. 1953; Dir. Eclair de l'Ouest 1954; Minister of Industry and Commerce, Faure Govt. 1955–56; Minister of Nat. Defence 1957–58; Mayor of Nantes 1965–77; Senator for Loire-Atlantique 1965–83; Pres. Asscn. Française pour la Promotion du Travail, Mouvement Libéral pour l'Europe Unie; Chevalier, Légion d'honneur, Croix de guerre, Médaille de l'Aéronautique, Commdr. du Mérite maritime, and several foreign decorations. *Address:* Les Hespérides Villiers Monceau, 66 avenue de Villiers, 75017, Paris, France.

MORIN, Jean, L. EN D.; French civil servant; b. 23 June 1916, Melun; m. Janine Lamouroux 1942; one s. two d.; ed. Ecole Libre des Sciences Politiques; Sec.-Gen. Inst. Scientifique des Recherches Economiques et Sociales 1939; Auditeur, Cour des Comptes 1941; Dir. of Personnel, Ministry of the Interior 1944, Prefect, Manche 1946; Deputy Dir. du Cabinet to Pres. of Provisional Govt. 1946, to Minister of Foreign Affairs 1947–48; Tech. Adviser, Minister of the Interior 1948–49; Prefect, Maine-et-Loire 1949; Conseiller Référendaire, Cour des Comptes 1949; Prefect, Haute-Garonne and Extraordinary Insp.-Gen. of Admin. (5th Region) 1958–60; Del.-Gen. in Algeria 1960–62; Sec.-Gen. of Merchant Navy 1962–68; Pres. Ass. de l'Org. Consultative Maritime Inter-Gouvernementale (IMCO) 1962–68; Pres. Société auxiliaire minière du Pacifique (Saumipac) 1968–72; Pres. Cie. française industrielle et minière du Pacifique 1969–72; Dir. Publicis S.A. 1970, Vice-Pres. 1972, Dir. Publicis Conseil, Pres. 1972–73; Pres. Communication et Publicité 1972, Intermarco 1974–84, Comité de surveillance Intermarco (Amsterdam); Chair. and Man. Dir. Régie-Presse 1974–83; Vice-Pres. Comité de surveillance Holding Farner (Zurich); mem. Conseil de Surveillance de Publicis S.A. 1987–; Grand Officier, Légion d'honneur, Croix de guerre, Médaille de la Résistance. *Leisure interest:* bridge. *Address:* 19 avenue du Maréchal-Franchet-d'Esperey, 75016 Paris, France.

MORIN, Roland Louis, L.EN D.; French public servant; b. 6 Sept. 1932, Taza, Morocco; s. Fernand and Emilienne (Carisio) Morin; m. Catherine Roussy 1961; one s. one d.; ed. Lycée Gouraud, Rabat, Faculty of Law and Humanities, Bordeaux and Ecole Nat. d'Administration; Auditor, Audit Office 1960; Asst. to Prime Minister and Chargé de Mission, Algeria 1960–61; Pvt. Recorder Comm. for Verification of Public Accounts, Asst. to Recorder-Gen. 1964; Tech. Counsellor Louis Joxe Cabinet (Minister of State for Admin. Reform) 1966–67, Edmond Michelet Cabinet (Minister of State for Public Office) 1967–68; Referandary Counsellor Audit Office 1967; Asst. to Prime Minister, Departmental Head for Econ. and Financial Programmes and Affairs 1968; Dir. of Financial Affairs, Gen. Del. for Scientific and Tech. Research 1969, Asst. to Del.-Gen. 1970, Asst. Del.-Gen. 1974, Dir. 1978; rejoined Audit Office 1980; Prof. Inst. d'Etudes Politiques de Paris; Chargé de Mission with Jean-Pierre Chevènement (Minister of State, Minister for Research and Tech.) 1981–82, Dir. Gen. Research and Technology, Ministry of Research and Industry 1982–86; Conseiller maître, Cour des comptes 1986; , Chevalier, Légion d'honneur, Ordre Nat. de Mérite, Palmes Académiques, Mérite Agricole. *Publications:* Les sociétés locales d'économie mixte et leur contrôle 1964, Théorie des grands problèmes économiques contemporains. *Leisure interest:* tennis. *Address:* Cour des comptes, 13 rue Cambon, 75001 Paris (Office); 24 Résidence des Gros-Chênes, 91370 Verrières-le-Buisson, France (Home).

MORINAGA, Teiichiro; Japanese financier and banker; b. 9 Sept. 1910, Miyazaki Prefecture; s. of Sadauemon Morinaga and Nobu Kishita; m.

Takako Tawara 1936; one s. one d.; ed. Tokyo Imperial Univ.; Ministry of Finance 1932–59, Deputy Vice-Minister of Finance 1949–53, Dir. Budget Bureau 1953–57, Admin. Vice-Minister of Finance 1957–59; Pres. Small Business Finance Corpn. 1961–62; Gov. The Export-Import Bank of Japan 1962–67; Pres. Tokyo Stock Exchange 1967–74; Gov. The Bank of Japan 1974–79. *Address:* 6-23-18 Honkomagome, Bunkyo-ku, Tokyo, Japan (Home).

MORINIGO, Gen. Higinio; Paraguayan officer and politician; b. 1897, Paraguarí; ed. Colegio Nacional and Escuela Militar, Asunción; 2nd Lieut. 1919, served Northern Operational Dept. and 2nd and 3rd Infantry Regts. to 1928; Capt. 1927; War Coll., apptd. Staff Maj. Battn. Commdt. Mil. School 1932; Dir. Reserve School; served Chaco War; fmr. Chief of Staff to C.-in-C., Ministry of War and Marine and Ministry of Interior; Gen. 1943; Pres. of Republic 1940–48; exiled in Argentina 1948–51, Brazil 1951–56; returned to Paraguay 1956, now living in Argentina; Cruz del Chaco, Cruz del Defensor and many other decorations; Dr. h.c. (Fordham and Brazil Univs.). *Address:* Calle General Urguiza 625-Acassuso, Buenos Aires, Argentina. *Telephone:* 792-4823.

MORISHIMA, Michio, M.A., F.B.A.; Japanese professor of economics; b. 18 July 1923, Osaka; s. of Kameji and Tatsuo Morishima; m. Yoko Tsuda 1954; two s. one d.; ed. Univ. of Kyoto; Asst. Prof. Univ. of Kyoto 1950–51; Asst. Prof. and Prof. Univ of Osaka 1951–69; Rockefeller Foundation Fellow, Oxford and Yale Univs. 1956–58; Visiting Sr. Fellow, All Souls Coll., Oxford 1963–64; Prof. of Econs. L.S.E. 1970–; mem. Econometric Soc., Pres. 1965; Hon. mem. American Econ. Asscn. 1976; Foreign Hon. mem. American Soc. of Arts and Sciences; Bunka Kunsho 1976. *Publications:* Equilibrium, Stability and Growth 1964, Theory of Economic Growth 1969, The Working of Econometric Models 1972, The Theory of Demand: Real and Monetary 1973, Marx's Economics 1973, The Economic Theory of Modern Society 1975, Walras' Economics 1977, Value, Exploitation and Growth 1978, Why has Japan "succeeded"? 1982, The Economics of Industrial Society 1984. *Address:* London School of Economics and Political Science, 10 Portugal Street, London WC2A 2HD (Office); Ker, 31 Greenway, Hutton Mount, Brentwood, Essex, CM13 2NP, England (Home). *Telephone:* 01-405 7686 (Office).

MORISHITA, Motoharu; Japanese politician; b. 12 April 1922, Tokushima Pref.; ed. Tokyo Univ. of Agric.; mem. House of Reps. 1963–; Parl. Vice-Minister of Agric., Forestry and Fisheries 1972, of Int. Trade and Industry 1973; Deputy Sec.-Gen. Liberal-Democratic Party 1977; Chair. Standing Cttee. on Social and Labour Affairs, House of Reps. 1978; Minister of Health and Welfare 1981–82. *Publication:* In a Whirling Current 1979. *Address:* c/o Liberal-Democratic Party, 7, 2-chome, Hirakawacho, Chiyoda-ku, Tokyo, Japan.

MORITA, Akio; Japanese business executive; b. 26 Jan. 1921, Nagoya; s. of S. Kyuzaemon and Shuko (Toda) Morita; m. Yoshiko Kamei 1950; two s. one d.; ed. Osaka Imperial Univ.; Co-Founder, SONY Corpn., Tokyo 1946, Exec. Man. Dir. 1958–59, Exec. Vice-Pres. 1959–71, Pres. 1971, Pres. and C.E.O. 1971–76, Chair. of Bd. and Chief Exec. Officer 1976–; Pres. SONY Corpn., America 1960–66, Chair. of Bd. 1966–74, Pres. 1968–71, Chair. of Finance Cttee. 1977–81; Chair. Exec. Cttee. SONY Corpn. of America 1974–77, 1981–; Dir. IBM World Trade Americas/Far East Corpn. 1972–77; Dir. Pan American World Airways Inc. 1980; Chair. Cttee. on Int. Investment and Tech. Change (IITEC), Keidanren (Fed. of Econ. Orgs.) 1981–; mem. Int. Council, Morgan Guaranty Trust Co.; Edwardo Rihan Award for Int. Marketing 1969; Albert Medal, Royal Soc. of Arts 1982. *Publications:* Gakureki Muyouron 1966, Shin Zitsuryoku Shugi 1969. *Leisure interests:* listening to music, playing golf. *Address:* SONY Corporation, 7-35, Kitashinagawa 6-chome, Shinagawa-ku, Tokyo 141, Japan. *Telephone:* 03-448-2600.

MORITS, Yunna Petrovna; Soviet poet; b. 2 June 1937, Kiev; ed. Gorky Literary Inst. 1961; began publishing poetry 1954. *Collections include:* Conversation on Happiness 1957, The Headland of Desire (Mys zhelaniya) 1961; Award of Merit 1987.

MORIYAMA, Raymond, O.C., M.ARCH, F.R.A.I.C., M.C.I.P., R.C.A., F.R.S.A.; Canadian architect and planner; b. 11 Oct. 1929, Vancouver; s. of John Michi and Nobuko Moriyama; m. Sachiko Miyauchi 1954; three s. two d.; ed. Univ. of Toronto, McGill Univ.; Raymond Moriyama Architects and Planners 1958–70; partner, Moriyama and Teshima Architects 1970–, Prin. 1980–; Design Tutor, Univ. of Toronto 1961–63; Chair. Ecological Research Ltd. 1970–; Chair. Mid-Canada Conf., Task Force on Environmental and Ecological Factors 1969–70; mem. Bd. and Life mem. Royal Canadian Inst.; Dir. Canadian Guild of Crafts 1973–75; mem. of Council, Ont. Coll. of Arts 1972–73; mem. Advisory Cttee., MBA Programme in Arts Admin., York Univ. 1982; founding mem. Asia Pacific Foundation of Canada 1982; mem. Bd., Multilingual TV; Civic Awards of Merit (Toronto and Scarborough), Governor General's Medal for Architecture (twice), and many other awards. *Leisure interest:* sailing. *Publications:* Great American Goose Egg Co. (Canada) Ltd., The Global Living System and Mid-Canada Task Force Committee on Ecological and Environmental Factors 1970, Can Your Life Become a Work of Art 1975, The Satisfactory City: The Survival of Urbanity 1975, Into God's Temple of Eternity, Drive a Nail of Gold, TANT—Time, Appropriateness, Nature and Transition 1982. *Leisure*

interests: fishing, sailing. *Address:* 32 Davenport Road, Toronto, Ont. M5R 1H3, Canada. *Telephone:* 416-925-4484.

MORIZET, Jacques, L. ES. L.; French diplomatist; b. 7 March 1921, Saint Mauré; m. Aline Reyss 1948; three s. one d.; ed. Lycée Voltaire, Paris, Sorbonne, Paris, Ecole Nat. d'Admin.; served UN Dept., Ministry of Foreign Affairs 1949–52, German Affairs High Comm. 1952–54, Secr.-Gen. of the Ministry 1954–56; First Sec., Bonn 1956, Second Counsellor 1959; Sec.-Gen.'s Chef du Cabinet 1960–61; Deputy Spokesman of Ministry 1961–62; Dir. of Information Office 1962–63; First Counsellor, Washington 1963–67; Deputy Dir. African Affairs 1967–69; Minister-Counsellor, Rome 1969–72; Embassy Minister, Bonn 1972–75; Amb. to Iraq 1975–80, to Morocco 1980–82, to Fed. Repub. of Germany 1982–86; Ambassadeur de France 1986–; Vice-Pres. State Cttee. on Nat. Defence; State Rep. on Bd. of Total/CFP; mem. Haut Conseil franco-allemand de la culture; Officier Légion d'honneur, Commandeur Ordre du Mérite, Croix de guerre 1939–45. *Publications:* articles and numerous lectures. *Address:* 4 rue Michel-Ange, 75016 Paris, France. *Telephone:* 42.88.31.85.

MORLEY, Malcolm, A.R.C.A.; British artist; b. 1931, London; ed. Royal Coll. of Art and Camberwell School of Arts and Crafts, London; one-man exhbns. in New York, Paris, Amsterdam, Cologne, Toronto, Zurich, London, etc.; numerous group exhbns. throughout U.S.A. and Europe; "Malcolm Morley", major retrospective exhbn. organized by Whitechapel Art Gallery, London, travelled to Kunsthalle, Basle, Museum Boymans-van Beuningen, Rotterdam, Whitechapel Art Gallery, London, Corcoran Gallery of Art, Washington D.C., Museum of Contemporary Art, Chicago and Brooklyn Museum, New York 1983–84; 1st Annual Turner Prize, The Tate Gallery, London 1984. *Address:* c/o Xavier Fourcade Inc., 36 East 75th Street, New York, N.Y. 10021, U.S.A. *Telephone:* (212) 535 3980.

MORLEY, Robert, C.B.E.; British actor and dramatist; b. 26 May 1908, Semley, Wilts.; s. of Maj. Robert and Gertrude Emily (née Fass) Morley; m. Joan Buckmaster (d. of the late Dame Gladys Cooper, D.B.E.) 1940; two s. one d.; ed. Wellington Coll.; stage debut at Margate, Kent 1928; London stage debut 1929; first appearance in New York 1938; appeared in provinces and established repertory company with Peter Bull at Perranporth, Cornwall; Hon. D.Litt. (Reading) 1979. *Plays include:* The Great Romancer 1937, Pygmalion 1937, The Man Who Came to Dinner 1941, The First Gentleman 1945, Edward My Son (also co-author with Noel Langley) 1947, The Little Hut 1950, Hippo Dancing 1954, A Likely Tale 1956, Fanny 1957, Hook, Line and Sinker 1958, A Majority of One 1960, A Time to Laugh 1962, Halfway Up the Tree 1968, How the Other Half Loves 1970, A Ghost on Tiptoe (also co-author with Rosemary Anne Sisson) 1974, Banana Ridge 1976, etc.: dir. The Tunnel of Love 1957, Once More with Feeling 1959. *Films since 1937 include:* Marie Antoinette 1938, Major Barbara 1940, The Young Mr. Pitt 1942, The Outcast of the Islands 1951, The African Queen 1952, Gilbert and Sullivan 1953, Beat the Devil 1953, Loser Takes All, Law and Disorder, The Journey, The Doctor's Dilemma 1959, Libel 1959, The Battle of the Sexes 1960, Oscar Wilde 1960, Murder at the Gallop 1963, Those Magnificent Men in their Flying Machines 1965, The Loved One 1965, The Alphabet Murders 1965, Hot Millions 1968, Sinful Davey 1969, Song of Norway 1970, Cromwell 1971, When Eight Bells Toll 1971, Theatre of Blood 1973, Great Expectations, The Blue Bird 1976, Too Many Cooks, The Human Factor, Little Dorrit, The Wind. *Publications:* Short Story 1935, Goodness How Sad 1937, Staff Dance 1944, Edward My Son (with Noel Langley) 1948, The Full Treatment (with Ronald Gow) 1952, Hippo Dancing 1954, Six Months Grace (with D. Hamilton) 1957, Robert Morley: Responsible Gentleman (with Sewell Stokes) 1966, A Musing Morley 1974, Morley Marvels 1976, More Morley 1978, Robert Morley's Book of Bricks 1978, Robert Morley's Book of Worries 1979, Morley Matters 1980, Robert Morley's Second Book of Bricks 1981, The Best of Robert Morley 1981, The Pleasures of Age 1988. *Leisure interests:* conversation, horse racing. *Address:* Fairmans, Wargrave, Berkshire, England.

MORLEY, Roger Hubert, M.B.A.; American business executive; b. 21 June 1931, Cleveland, Ohio; s. of Hubert and Ayleen (Mosier) Morley; m.; two d.; ed. Ohio Univ., Harvard Graduate School of Business; Controller, Commercial Products Div., Stromberg-Carlson, Rochester, N.Y. 1957–60; Pres. Parker-Kalon Div., Gen. American Transportation Corpn., Chicago, Ill. 1960–66, Gen. Man. Terminals Div. 1966–67; Vice-Pres. and Gen. Man. Burndy Corpn., Norwalk, Conn. 1967–68; Exec. Vice-Pres. and Dir. Gould Inc., Chicago, Ill. 1968–74; Exec. Vice-Pres. Financial Admin., American Express Co., New York 1974–75, Vice-Chair. 1975–77, Pres. 1977–79; Dir./Consultant, Winco NV, Rotterdam 1983–; Gov.-at-Large, Nat. Asscn. of Security Dealers 1975–78; Dir. Lincoln Center for Performing Arts Inc. 1976–81, Visiting Nurse Service of N.Y. 1974–81, McGraw-Hill Inc. 1975–79, Western Electric 1976–84, Allied-Signal Corpn. 1976–85, Converse Inc. 1982–86, John Laing (Strike Club Man.) Ltd. (London) 1986–, Schafer Value Trust, Inc. (New York) 1986; Invus Group Ltd. (New York) 1986–, R & R Inventions Ltd. (Birmingham, U.K.) 1986–, R.T. Holding (Nederland) N.V. 1987–; Trustee, Barnard Coll. 1976–80; Vice-Pres. Schiller Int. Univ. 1982–; Comité du Jumelage, Ville de Grasse 1985–88. *Leisure interest:* tennis. *Address:* L'Horizon, Clos Barnier, 06530 Spéracèdes, France (Home and Office). *Telephone:* (33) 93-60-56-24.

MORO, Peter, C.B.E., F.R.I.B.A., F.S.I.A.D.; British architect; b. 27 May 1911; s. of Ernst Moro and Greta Hönigswald; m. Anne Vanneck 1940 (divorced 1984); three d.; ed. Stuttgart, Berlin and Zürich; practice with Tecton 1937–39; mem. Exec. Cttee., Mars Group 1938; Lecturer, School of Architecture, Regent Street Polytechnic 1941–47; London Co. Council Associated Architect, Royal Festival Hall 1948–51; Peter Moro and Partners (architects) 1952–; Founder mem. Asscn. of British Theatre Technicians; Council mem. R.I.B.A. 1967–73; mem. Arts Council of Gt. Britain Housing the Arts Cttee. 1975–78; Gov. Ravensbourne Coll. of Art and Design 1976–87; Lecturer in U.K., Finland, Norway; Bronze Medal, R.I.B.A.; five Civic Trust Awards and Commendations; Concrete Award 1983. *Principal works:* Fairlawn School, London County Council 1957, Royal Opera House, Covent Garden (alterations) 1964, Birstall School, Leics. 1964, housing schemes, G.L.C. and Southwark 1967–80, theatre, Hull Univ., Gulbenkian Cen. 1970, Bristol Old Vic (additions and alterations) 1972, theatre, New Univ. of Ulster 1976, Theatre Royal, Plymouth 1982, Taliesin Theatre, Univ. Coll., Swansea 1984. *Publications:* contribs. to various technical journals in U.K., Germany, France, Italy, Portugal, Japan. *Address:* 13 Rathbone Street, London, W1P 1AF (Office); 20 Blackheath Park, London, SE3 9RP, England (Home). *Telephone:* 01-636 8101-3 (Office); 01-852 0250 (Home).

MORO, Vincenzo; Italian industrial executive; b. 26 Jan. 1922, Sartirana Lomellina, Pavia; s. of Paolo Moro and Carmelita Gei; m. Gianna Tagliabue 1948; one s. one d.; with Naclon Farmaceutici 1937; joined Filotecnica Salmoiraghi 1939, Sales Dir. 1954–59; Deputy Dir. Alfa Romeo S.p.A. 1959, Special Affairs Dir. 1960, Sales Dir. 1962, Deputy Gen. Man. 1969, Man. Dir. and Gen. Man. 1974–78; Chair. Alfa Romeo Int. S.A. 1978–80, Autodelta 1975–78, Termomeccanica S.p.A. 1978–83, Italgel S.p.A. 1979–80, Frendo Abex S.p.A., Aerimpianti S.p.A., Abex Rail S.A. 1989, Vice-Pres. Fiat Diesel do Brasil S.A. 1977–79, mem. Bd. Ducati Meccanica S.p.A. 1980–83, Aerospace Industries Asscn. of Italy 1953–74, Automotive Industries Asscn. of Italy 1968–78; Vice-Chair. E.E.C. Euroglaces Asscn. 1980; Chair. Fed. European Manufacturers of Friction Materials 1987. *Address:* Via delle Magnolie 2, Appiano Gentile (CO), Italy. *Telephone:* (031) 930830.

MOROCCO, King of (see Hassan II).

MOROSS, Manfred David, B.SC., M.B.A.; business executive; b. 30 Aug. 1931; s. of Dr. H. and A. Moross; m. Edna Fay Jacobson 1956; three s. one d.; ed. Witwatersrand and Harvard Univs.; Chair. A.I.M. Management Ltd., Houston; Dir. Park Street Holdings Ltd., Florida Nat. Banks of Florida Inc., Bradford Nat. Life Insurance Co., Lexington, Ky., Manhattan Inst. for Policy Research, New York. *Leisure interests:* tennis, reading. *Address:* The Park Street Group, 14 Cork Street, London, W1X 1PF (Office); 27, 7 Princes Gate, London, S.W.7, England (Home). *Telephone:* 01-491 2312 (Office); 01-589 9020 (Home).

MOROZOV, Platon Dmitriyevich, D.IUR.; Soviet lawyer and diplomatist; b. 1906, St. Petersburg (now Leningrad); ed. Leningrad Law Inst; practised as barrister and held high posts in office of Procurator of the U.S.S.R. until 1949; Diplomatic Service 1949–70, Deputy Chief, Treaty and Legal Dept. of Ministry of Foreign Affairs 1949–60; U.S.S.R. Rep. on UN Comm. for Human Rights and Del. to numerous Sessions of UN Gen. Assembly 1951–68; Deputy Rep. of U.S.S.R. on Security Council of UN and Deputy Perm. Rep. to UN 1960–68; Judge, Int. Court of Justice, The Hague 1970–86; mem. of U.S.S.R. Del. at Int. War Tribunal, Tokyo 1946; Rep. of U.S.S.R. on UN Special Cttee. for the Preparation of the Convention on Prevention and Punishment of the Crime of Genocide; numerous other UN missions. *Publications:* works and articles on legal questions. *Address:* c/o Ministry of Foreign Affairs, Moscow, U.S.S.R.

MOROZOV, Vladimir Mikhailovich; Soviet opera singer; b. 1933; ed. Leningrad Conservatory; soloist with Kirov Opera 1959–; mem. CPSU 1965–; Glinka Prize 1974; R.S.F.S.R. People's Artist 1976; U.S.S.R. People's Artist 1981. *Roles include:* Varlaam (Boris Godunov), Ivan the Terrible (The Women from Pskov), Grigory (Quiet Flows the Don), Peter the Great (Peter I). *Address:* c/o Kirov Opera Company, Kirov, U.S.S.R.

MORRICE, Norman Alexander; British choreographer; b. 10 Sept. 1931, Agua Dulce, Mexico; s. of Norman Morrice and Helen Vickers; ed. Rambert School of Ballet; joined Ballet Rambert as dancer 1952, Prin. Dancer 1958, Asst. Dir. 1966–70, Dir. 1970–74; freelance choreographer 1974–77; Dir. Royal Ballet Co. 1977–86; first success as choreographer with Two Brothers 1958; second ballet Hazaña (première, Sadler's Wells Theatre, London) 1958; ballet Hazard, Bath Festival 1967; 10 new ballets for Ballet Rambert by 1968; Elizabeth II Coronation Award for services to British ballet; *Ballets include:* 1-2-3, Them and Us, Pastorale Variée, Ladies, Ladies!, Spindrift. *Leisure interests:* literature, music, films. *Address:* c/o Royal Opera House, Covent Garden, London, W.C.2, England. *Telephone:* 01-240 1200.

MORRIS, Benjamin Stephen, B.SC., M.ED.; British educationist and psychologist; b. 25 May 1910, Sherborne, Dorset; s. of Rev. Benjamin Stephen and Annie McNicol (Duncan) Morris; m. Adeline Margaret Lamont 1938; two s. one d.; ed. Rothesay Acad., Isle of Bute, and Univ. of Glasgow; Asst. Master Glasgow schools 1936–38; Lecturer in Psychology, Logic and Ethics, Jordanhill Training Coll., Glasgow 1939–40, in Educ., Univ. of Glasgow 1940–46; Statistical and Intelligence Officer, Ministry of Food

1941–42; Research Psychologist, War Office Selection Bds. 1942–45, Sr. Psychologist (Lt.-Col.) 1945; Sr. Staff, Tavistock Inst. of Human Relations 1946–50 and Chair. Man. Cttee. 1947–48; Student, Inst. of Psychoanalysis, London 1946–50; Dir. Nat. Foundation for Educational Research in England and Wales 1950–56, Prof. of Educ., Univ. of Bristol 1956–75, Emer. Prof. 1975–, Dir. Inst. of Educ. 1956–68, Dir. Div. of Advanced Studies and Higher Degrees, Univ. of Bristol, School of Educ. 1968–75. *Publications:* Objectives and Perspectives in Education—Studies in Educational Theory 1972: Some Aspects of Professional Freedom of Teachers—an International Pilot Inquiry UNESCO 1977; numerous articles in professional journals. *Leisure interests:* music, theatre, living in the country. *Address:* 13 Park View, Leyburn, North Yorks., DL8 5HN, England. *Telephone:* (0969) 22603.

MORRIS, Desmond John, D.PHIL.; British zoologist; b. 24 Jan. 1928, Purton, Wilts.; s. of Capt. Harry Howe and Marjorie (née Hunt) Morris; m. Ramona Joy Baulch 1952; one s.; ed. Dauntsey's School, Wilts., Birmingham Univ. and Oxford Univ.; Head of Granada TV and Film Unit at Zoological Soc. of London 1956–59; Curator of Mammals at Zoological Soc. of London 1959–67; Dir. Inst. of Contemporary Arts, London 1967–68; Research Fellow at Wolfson Coll., Oxford 1973–81; now privately engaged in writing books on animal and human behaviour. *Television:* Zootime (Granada) 1956–67, Life in the Animal World (BBC) 1965–67, The Human Race (Thames TV) 1982, The Animal Roadshow (BBC) 1987–89. *Publications:* The Ten-spined Stickleback 1958, The Biology of Art 1962, The Mammals: A Guide to the Living Species 1965, Men and Snakes (with Ramona Morris) 1965, Men and Apes (with Ramona Morris) 1966, Men and Pandas (with Ramona Morris) 1966, Primate Ethology (Editor) 1967, The Naked Ape 1967, The Human Zoo 1969, Patterns of Reproductive Behaviour 1970, Intimate Behaviour 1971, Manwatching: A Field-Guide to Human Behaviour 1977, Gestures, Their Origins and Distribution 1979, Animal Days (autobiography) 1979, The Giant Panda 1981, The Soccer Tribe 1981, Inrock (fiction) 1983, The Book of Ages 1983, The Art of Ancient Cyprus 1985, Bodywatching 1985, The Illustrated Naked Ape 1986, Dogwatching 1986, Catwatching 1986, The Secret Surrealist 1987, Catlore 1987, The Animals Roadshow 1988, Horsewatching 1988. *Leisure interests:* painting and archaeology. *Address:* c/o Jonathan Cape, 32 Bedford Square, London, W.C.1, England.

MORRIS, James (Humphry) (see Morris, Jan).

MORRIS, Jan, F.R.S.L.; British writer; b. 2 Oct. 1926; editorial staff The Times 1951–56, editorial staff The Guardian 1957–62; Commonwealth Fellowship, U.S.A. 1954; George Polk Memorial Award for Journalism (U.S.A.) 1961; mem. Yr Academi Gymreig; Heinemann Award for Literature 1961. *Publications:* (as James Morris) Coast to Coast 1956, Sultan in Oman 1957, The Market of Seleukia 1957, Coronation Everest 1958, South African Winter 1958, The Hashemite Kings 1959, Venice 1960, The Upstairs Donkey (for children) 1962, The Road to Huddersfield 1963, Cities 1963, The Presence of Spain 1964, Oxford 1965, Pax Britannica 1968, The Great Port 1970, Places 1972, Heaven's Command 1973, Farewell the Trumpets 1978; (as Jan Morris) Conundrum 1974, Travels 1976, The Oxford Book of Oxford 1978, Spain 1979, Destinations, The Venetian Empire, My Favourite Stories of Wales, 1980, The Small Oxford Book of Wales, Wales The First Place, A Venetian Bestiary, Spectacle of Empire 1982, Stones of Empire 1983, Journeys 1984, The Matter of Wales 1984, Among the Cities 1985, Last Letters from Hav 1985, Stones of Empire: The Building of the Raj 1986, Manhattan, '45 1987, Hong Kong: Xianggang 1988. *Address:* Trefan Morys, Llanystumdwy, Cricieth, Gwynedd, Wales. *Telephone:* (0766) 522222.

MORRIS, Rt. Hon. John, P.C., Q.C., M.P., LL.D.; British barrister and politician; b. 5 Nov. 1931, Aberystwyth; s. of the late D. W. Morris; m. Margaret M. Morris J.P. 1959; three d.; ed. Ardwyn, Aberystwyth, Univ. Coll. of Wales, Aberystwyth, Gonville and Caius Coll., Cambridge, and Acad. of Int. Law, The Hague; commissioned Royal Welch Fusiliers and Welch Regt.; Called to Bar, Gray's Inn 1954, Bencher 1985; Labour M.P. for Aberavon Oct. 1959–; Parl. Sec. Ministry of Power 1964–66; Jt. Parl. Sec. Ministry of Transport 1966–68; Minister of Defence for Equipment 1968–70; Sec. of State for Wales 1974–79; Opposition Spokesman on Legal Affairs 1979; a Recorder, Crown Court 1982–; Opposition Spokesman on Legal Affairs and Shadow Attorney Gen. 1983–; fmr. Deputy Gen. Sec. and Legal Adviser, Farmers' Union of Wales; mem. U.K. Del., Consultative Assembly, Council of Europe and Western European Union 1963–64; Chair. Nat. Pneumoconiosis Jt. Cttee. 1964–66, Nat. Road Safety Advisory Council 1967–68, Jt. Review of Finances and Man. British Railways 1966–67; mem. N. Atlantic Assembly 1970–74; mem. Courts of Univ. Colls., Aberystwyth, Swansea and Cardiff. *Address:* House of Commons, London, S.W.1, England.

MORRIS, Peter Frederick; Australian politician; b. 29 July 1932, Sydney; m.; four s.; ed. Newcastle Boys' High School, Australian Nat. Univ., Canberra, Newcastle Tech. Coll.; Alderman, Newcastle City Council 1968–74; M.P. for Shortland, House of Reps. 1972–; Minister for Transport 1983–87, for Aviation 1984–87, for Resources 1987–88, for Industrial Relations and Minister Assisting the Prime Minister for Public Service Matters Dec. 1988–; mem. parl. dels. to China 1973, India, Pakistan and Iran 1974, Canada and Britain 1975; attended confs. in Europe at OECD,

Int. Maritime Org., European Conf. of Ministers of Transport 1984; Australian Labor Party. *Leisure interests:* lawn bowls, fishing. *Address:* Parliament House, Canberra, A.C.T. 2600; 5 Library Lane, Charlestown, N.S.W., 2290, Australia.

MORRIS, Peter John, M.B., B.S., PH.D., F.R.C.S., F.R.C.A.S.; Australian professor of surgery; b. 17 April 1934, Horsham, Vic.; s. of Stanley Henry Morris and Mary Lois (née Hennessy) Morris; m. Jocelyn Mary Gorman 1960; three s. two d.; ed. Univ. of Melbourne; Surgical Registrar, Southampton Gen. Hosp., U.K. 1963–64; Clinical Assoc. and Fellow, Mass. Gen. Hosp., Boston, U.S.A. 1964–66; Asst. Prof. of Surgery, Medical Coll., Richmond, Va., U.S.A. 1967; Dir. Tissue Transplantation Labs., Univ. of Melbourne, Australia 1968–74; Reader in Surgery 1971–74; Consultant Surgeon, Lymphona Clinic, Cancer Inst., Melbourne 1969–74; Nuffield Prof. of Surgery, Univ. of Oxford, U.K. 1974–; Pres. The Transplantation Soc. 1984–86; Vice-Chair. Clinical Medicine Bd., Univ. of Oxford 1982–84; Scientific mem. MRC, London 1983–87; Ed. Transplantation 1979–; Fellow, Balliol Coll., Univ. of Oxford 1974–; Selwyn Smith Prize (Australia). *Publications:* Kidney Transplantation 1979, Tissue Transplantation 1982, Transient Ischaemic Attacks 1982, Progress in Transplantation 1984. *Leisure interests:* golf, tennis. *Address:* Nuffield Department of Surgery, John Radcliffe Hospital, Headington, Oxford, OX3 9DU (Office); 19 Lucerne Road, Oxford, OX2 7QB, England (Home). *Telephone:* (0865) 817568 (Office); (0865) 58565 (Home).

MORRIS, Willie, M.A.; American editor and writer; b. 29 Nov. 1934, Jackson, Miss.; s. of Henry Rae and Marian Weaks Morris; m. Celia Buchan 1958; one s.; ed. Yazoo City High School, Miss., Univ. of Texas and New College, Oxford; Ed.-in-Chief The Texas Observer 1960–62; Exec. Ed. Harper's Magazine 1965–67, Ed.-in-Chief 1967–71; Writer-in-Residence Univ. of Miss. 1980–83; Rhodes Scholarship 1956; Fellow, Silliman Coll., Yale Univ.; Houghton-Miflin Literary Fellowship Award 1967; several hon. degrees. *Publications:* The South Today, 100 Years After Appomatox (Ed.) 1966, North Toward Home 1967, Yazoo: Integration in a Deep Southern Town 1971, The Last of the Southern Girls 1973, Good Old Boy 1973, James Jones: A Friendship 1978, The Ghosts of Ole Miss and Other Essays 1981, The Courting of Marcus Dupree, Always Stand in Against the Curve 1983.

MORRISON, William Lawrence, B.ECONS.; Australian politician (retd.) and diplomatist; b. 3 Nov. 1928; s. of Herbert Roy and Mary Morrison; m. Martha Elizabeth Hessell 1958; one s. two d.; ed. North Sydney Tech. High School, Univ. of Sydney, London School of Slavonic and East European Studies; joined Australian Diplomatic Service 1950; Australian Embassy, Moscow 1952–54; Econ. Relations Branch, Dept. of External Affairs 1954–57; Australian Embassy, Bangkok, concurrently Liaison Officer UN Econ. Comm. for Asia, Chair. SEATO Cttee. on Soviet Econ. Penetration in Asia and Far East 1957–59; Australian Embassy, Washington 1959–61, Moscow 1961–63; Head, Information and Cultural Relations Branch, Dept. of External Affairs 1963–66; Deputy High Commr. to Malaysia 1967–68; mem. Parl. for St. George, N.S.W. 1969–75, 1980–84; Amb. to Indonesia April 1985–; Deputy Chair. Jt. Parl. Foreign Affairs Cttee. 1969–72; mem. Exec. Council 1972; Minister for Science 1972–75, and External Territories 1972–73; Asst. Minister for Foreign Affairs 1973; Asst. Defence Minister 1974–75, Defence Minister June-Nov. 1975; Visiting Fellow Australian Nat. Univ. 1976; research fellow Univ. of N.S.W. 1979–80; Chair. Jt. Parl. Cttee. Foreign Affairs and Defence 1983–84. *Address:* Australian Embassy, Jl M.H. Thamrin 15, Jakarta, Indonesia; 20A Gipps Street, Arncliffe, N.S.W. 2205, Australia (Home). *Telephone:* 323109 (Indonesia); (02) 5972850 (Australia).

MORRISON-SCOTT, Sir Terence Charles Stuart, Kt., D.S.C., D.SC.; British museum director; b. 24 Oct. 1908, Paris; s. of the late R. C. S. Morrison-Scott, D.S.O. and Douairère Jhr. R. F. H. Quarles van Ufford; m. Rita Layton 1935; ed. Eton Coll., Christ Church, Oxford, and Royal Coll. of Science; Asst. Master, Eton Coll. 1935; joined staff British Museum (Natural History) 1936; served World War II; Dir. Science Museum 1956–60, British Museum (Natural History) 1960–68; Chair. Nat. Trust Nature Conservation Panel 1970–81, Architectural Panel 1973–81, Properties Cttee. 1968–83; mem. Standing Comm. on Museums and Galleries 1973–76; Treas. Zoological Soc. of London 1950–76; Deputy Lieut. W. Sussex 1982; Fellow, Linnean Soc. *Publications:* Checklist of Palaearctic and Indian Mammals (with J. R. Ellerman) 1951, Southern African Mammals: A Reclassification (with J. R. Ellerman and R. W. Hayman) 1953. *Address:* Upperfold House, Fernhurst, West Sussex, GU27 3JH, England.

MORROW, Sir Ian Thomas, C.A., F.C.M.A., J.DIP., M.A.; British chartered accountant; b. 8 June 1912, Manchester; s. of the late Thomas George Morrow and Jamesina Hunter; m. 1st Elizabeth Mary Thackray 1940 (dissolved 1967), one s. one d.; m. 2nd Sylvia Jane Taylor 1967, one d.; ed. Dollar Acad., Scotland; Chartered Accountant 1936; Asst. Accountant Brocklehurst-Whiston Amalgamated Ltd. 1937–40; Partner, Robson, Morrow & Co. Ltd. 1942–51; Financial Dir. The Brush Electrical Eng. Co. Ltd. (now The Brush Group Ltd.) 1951–52, Deputy Man. Dir. 1952–56, Jt. Man. Dir. 1956–57, Man. Dir. 1957–58; Jt. Man. Dir. H. Clarkson & Co. Ltd. 1961–72; Chair. Associated Fire Alarms Ltd. 1965–70, Rowe Bros. & Co. (Holdings) Ltd. 1960–70, Crane Fruehauf Trailers Ltd. 1969–71, MAI PLC (fmrly. J. H. Vavasseur Group Ltd.), Strong & Fisher Holdings PLC,

Efamol PLC, Argunex Ltd. 1985–, etc.; Dir. Hambros PLC, Deputy Chair. 1983–86; Dir. The Laird Group PLC (fmr. Chair.), Hambros Industrial Man. Ltd., Zeus Management Ltd., Psion PLC 1987–, C.E. Heath PLC 1988–, Harlow Ueda Savage (Holdings) Ltd. 1985–, and numerous other cos.; Council mem. Chartered Inst. of Man. Accountants 1952–70 (Pres. 1956–57; Gold Medallist 1961); Pres. Inst. of Chartered Accountants of Scotland 1981–82; mem. Press Council until 1981; Hon. D.Litt. (Heriot-Watt) 1982, Hon. D.Univ. (Stirling); Freeman, City of London; Liveryman, Worshipful Co. of Spectaclemakers. *Leisure interests:* reading, music, golf, skiing. *Address:* 2 Albert Terrace Mews, London, NW1 7TA, England. *Telephone:* 01-722 7110.

MORROW, Rev. John Watson, M.AGR., PH.D.; British ecclesiastic; b. 28 June 1931, Belfast; s. of late William Morrow and of Mary Morrow; m. Shirley H. E. Duncan 1959; three s. one d.; ed. Campbell Coll. Belfast, Queen's Univ. Belfast and Edinburgh Univ.; Minister (Presbyterian Church in Ireland), Kilmatree Church, Dunmurry 1960–67; Chaplain to Overseas Students, Glasgow 1967–71; Chaplain to Presbyterian Students, Dublin 1971–75; Chaplain, Queen's Univ. Belfast 1975–80; Leader Corrymeela Community (a community dedicated to reconciliation) 1980–. *Publications:* The Captivity of the Irish Churches, Laity under Pressure. *Leisure interests:* reading, music, walking, ecology. *Address:* Corrymeela House, 8 Upper Crescent, Belfast, BT7 1NT; 36 College Park Avenue, Belfast, BT7 1LR, Northern Ireland.

MORS, Dr. Walter B.; Brazilian chemist; b. 23 Nov. 1920, São Paulo; s. of Oscar G. and Ingeborg Flora Mors; m. Haydée Machado 1944; two s. one d.; ed. Univ. de São Paulo; Research Chemist, Northern Agricultural Inst., Belém 1943–46; Research Chemist, Inst. of Agricultural Chem., Rio de Janeiro 1947–62; Research Chemist, Inst. of Agricultural and Food Tech., Ministry of Agric. 1963–74, Dir. 1966–73; Prof. of Phytochem., Natural Products Research Center, Center of Health Sciences, Fed. Univ. of Rio de Janeiro, Dir. 1978–81, 1986–88; mem. Brazilian Acad. of Sciences, Sec.-Gen. 1965–69, 1978–79; Sec. Brazilian Chemical Assen. 1952–54, Pres. 1980–81; Pres. Fed. of Latin American Chemical Socs. 1984–86; mem. Ed. Bd. various scientific journals; Fellow, Linnean Soc. of London. *Publications include:* Useful Plants of Brazil (with Carlos Toledo Rizzini) 1966, Ed. Anais da Associacão Brasileira de Química. *Leisure interest:* botany. *Address:* Rua Geminiano Gois 1300/401, 227431 Rio de Janeiro, Brazil. *Telephone:* 392-5081.

MORSE, Bradford (see Morse, F. Bradford).

MORSE, Sir (Christopher) Jeremy, K.C.M.G.; British banker; b. 10 Dec. 1928, London; s. of late Francis J. and Kinbarra (née Armfield-Marrow) Morse; m. Belinda M. Mills 1955; three s. one d.; ed. Winchester and New Coll., Oxford; fmrly. with Glyn, Mills & Co., Dir. 1964; Dir. Legal and Gen. Assurance Society Ltd. 1963–64, 1975–; Exec. Dir. Bank of England 1965–72; Alt. Gov. IMF 1966–72; Chair. of Deputies of "Cttee. of Twenty", IMF 1972–74; Deputy Chair. Lloyds Bank Ltd. 1975–77, Chair. 1977–; Chair. Lloyds Merchant Bank Holdings 1985–; Chair. Cttee. of London Clearing Bankers 1980–82; Chair. City Communications Centre 1985–; Pres. Inst. Int. d'Études Bancaires 1982–83, British Bankers Assen. 1984–, Int. Monetary Conference 1985–86; Fellow, All Souls Coll., Oxford 1953–68, 1983–; Fellow, Winchester Coll. 1966–83; Chair. City Arts Trust 1977–79, Per Jacobsson Foundation 1987–; Chancellor Bristol Univ. 1988–; mem. NEDC 1977–81; Dir. (non-exec.) ICI Sept. 1981–; Legal and Gen. Assurance Soc. Ltd. *Leisure interests:* poetry, golf, problems and puzzles, coarse gardening. *Address:* c/o Lloyds Bank Ltd., 71 Lombard Street, London, EC3P 3BS; 102A Drayton Gardens, London, SW10 9RJ, England (Home). *Telephone:* 01-370 2265.

MORSE, David A., LITT.B., LL.B.; American lawyer; b. 31 May 1907; s. of Morris Morse and Sara Morse; m. Mildred Edna Hockstader 1937; ed. Rutgers Univ. and Harvard Law School; admitted to N.J. Bar (also mem. of Bar of N.Y. and Dist. of Columbia) 1932; U.S. Dept of Interior, Solicitor's Staff 1933–34; Chief Counsel, Petroleum Labor Policy Bd. 1934–35; Special Asst. to U.S. Attorney-Gen. 1934–35; Regional Attorney, Nat. Labor Relations Bd. 1935–38; Partner, Law Firm of Coult, Satz, Tomlinson & Morse, Newark, N.J. 1938–47; Lecturer on Labour Relations, Labour Law and Administrative Law, various colls. and law schools 1938–47; Dir. Labor Div., Allied Mil. Govt., Sicily and Italy 1943–44; Dir. Manpower Div., U.S. Group Control Council (Germany) 1944–45; Gen. Counsel Nat. Labor Relations Bd. Washington 1945–46; Asst. Sec. of Labor 1946–47; Under-Sec. of Labor 1947–48; Acting Sec. of Labor June-Aug. 1948; fmr. U.S. Govt. mem. of the Governing Body of the ILO, and Govt. Del. to Int. Labour Confs.; Dir.-Gen. ILO 1948–70; now Partner Jones, Day, Reavis and Pogue, New York, Washington, Paris, London, Riyadh, Hong Kong, Geneva; Sr. Consultant to UN Devt. Programme 1970–; Dir. Franklin D. Roosevelt Foundation, Gustav Pollak Lecturer on Research in Govt., Harvard Univ. 1955–56; mem. Bd. of Dirs. World Rehabilitation Fund; Charter Trustee, Rutgers Univ., N.J. 1972–78; Bd. of Trustees, American Arbitration Assen., Council Foreign Relations, Albert and Mary Lasker Foundation, UNA; Dir. E. W. Howell & Co., Selmer Corpn., Selmer, Inc.; Hon. LL.D. (Rutgers, Geneva, Strasbourg, Laval, Brandeis); numerous awards. *Leisure interests:* art collection, sports, literature. *Address:* 575 Park Avenue, New York, N.Y. 10021, U.S.A. (Home). *Telephone:* (212) 758-7868 (Home).

MORSE, F. Bradford, B.S., LL.B.; American politician, United Nations official and educator; b. 7 Aug. 1921, Lowell, Mass.; s. of Frank Young and Inez Rice (née Turnbull) Morse; m. 1st Vera Francesca Cassilly 1955 (divorced), one s. one d.; m. 2nd Josephine A. Neale 1981, one d.; ed. Lowell Public School and Boston Univ.; Service with U.S. Army 1942–46; admitted to Mass. Bar 1948; Law Clerk, Supreme Judicial Court, Mass. 1949; law practice, Lowell 1949–53; lecturer, Instructor School of Law, Boston Univ. 1949–53; City Councillor, Lowell, Mass. 1952–53; Special Counsel, U.S. Senate Cttee. on Armed Services 1953–54; Chief Asst. to Senator Leverett Saltonstall 1955–58; Deputy Admin. of Veterans Admin., Washington 1958–60; mem. U.S. House of Reps. 1960–72, mem. Foreign Affairs Cttee.; Under-Sec.-Gen. for Political and Gen. Assembly Affairs, UN 1972–76; Admin. of UNDP 1976–86, Pres. The Salzburg Seminar May 1986–; U.S. Observer Council of Europe, Latin American Parl.; Chair. Mems. of Congress for Peace Through Law 1968–70; mem. Nat. Acad. of Public Admin., Council on Foreign Relations, Bd. of Trustees, Boston Univ., Bd. of Visitors, School of Foreign Service, Georgetown Univ., Bd. of Dirs., Boston World Affairs Council, Pan-American Devt. Foundation; mem. Bd. Hunger Project Trust 1986–; Co-founder, Interaction Council of Fmr. Heads of Govt. 1983–; Presidential World Without Hunger Award 1985; Franklin D. Roosevelt Freedom Medal 1986; four hon. doctorates. *Address:* Salzburg Seminar, 30 John F. Kennedy Street, Cambridge, Mass. 02138 (Office); Apt. 18c, 411 East 53rd Street, New York, N.Y. 10022, U.S.A. (Home). *Telephone:* (617) 547-7070 (Ofice); (212) 688-6654 (Home).

MORSE, Sir Jeremy (see Morse, Sir Christopher Jeremy).

MORTIMER, Gerald James, C.B.E., B.SC., A.R.S.M., F.ENG., F.I.M.M.; British mining engineer (retd.); b. 2 Sept. 1918, Shepton Mallett; s. of late Rev. Fernley J. Mortimer; m. Connie Dodd 1942; two s. two d.; ed. Caterham School and Royal School of Mines, Imperial Coll., London Univ.; served with Royal Engineers 1939–46; joined Gold Fields Group 1946; various posts from trainee to Underground Man. in group's gold mines in South Africa; returned to London 1955, took leading part in establishing Group's operations in S.W. Africa, Australia, U.K.; Man. Gold Fields Group 1958, Exec. Dir. 1963, Deputy Chair. 1969–78, Group C.E.O. 1976–78, Consultant 1978–83; serves on various professional bodies; mem. Surrey Co. Council 1973–, Chair. Policy Cttee.; Pres. Inst. of Mining and Metallurgy 1977–78; Hon. Treas. Fellowship of Eng. 1981–84; Chair. Council of Eng. Insts. 1982–83; mem. Ct. Co. of Engineers 1983–. *Leisure interests:* County Council, party politics, school management. *Address:* 40 Harestone Valley Road, Caterham, Surrey, CR3 6HD, England (Home). *Telephone:* (0883) 44853 (Home).

MORTIMER, James Edward; British political administrator (retd.); b. 12 Jan. 1921; m.; two s. one d.; ed. Jr. Tech. School, Portsmouth, Ruskin Coll., Oxford, L.S.E.; worked in shipbuilding and eng. industries; T.U.C. Scholar, Oxford 1945–46; T.U.C. Econ. Dept. 1946–48; full-time trade union official, Draughtsmen's and Allied Technicians Assen. 1948–68; Dir. London Co-operative Soc. 1968–71; mem. Nat. Bd. for Prices and Incomes 1968–71; mem. London Transport Exec. 1971–74; Chair. A.C.A.S. (fmrly. Conciliation and Arbitration Service) 1974–81; Gen. Sec. Labour Party 1982–85; Wilberforce Cttee. of Inquiry into the Power Dispute 1970, Armed Forces Pay Review Body 1971–74, Econ. Devt. Cttee. for Chemical Industry 1973–74; Chair. Econ. Devt. Cttee. for Mechanical and Electrical Eng. Construction 1974–82; Visiting Fellow, Admin. Staff Coll., Henley 1976–82; Sr. Visiting Fellow, Bradford Univ. 1977–82; Visiting Prof., Imperial Coll. of Science and Tech., London Univ. 1981–83; Hon. D.Litt. (Bradford) 1982. *Publications:* A History of Engineering and Shipbuilding Draughtsmen 1960, British Trade Unions Today (with Clive Jenkins q.v.) 1965, The Kind of Laws the Unions Ought to Want 1968 (with Clive Jenkins), Industrial Relations 1968, Trade Unions and Technological Change 1971, History of the Boilermakers' Society, vol. I 1973, vol. II 1982, A Professional Union: the Evolution of the Institution of Professional Civil Servants (with Valerie Ellis) 1980. *Address:* 31 Charleston Street, London, SE17 1RL, England. *Telephone:* 01-708 4415.

MORTIMER, John Clifford, C.B.E., Q.C.; British barrister, author and playwright; b. 21 April 1923; s. of Clifford and Katherine (née Smith) Mortimer; m. 1st Penelope Fletcher 1949, one s. one d.; m. 2nd Penelope Gollop, two d.; ed. Harrow, Brasenose Coll., Oxford; called to the Bar 1948, Master of the Bench, Inner Temple 1975; mem. Bd. of Nat. Theatre 1968–; Chair. Council Royal Soc. of Literature 1989; British Acad. Writers' Award 1979, 1980; Dr. h.c. (Exeter) 1986; Hon. LL.D. (Susquehanna Univ.) 1985; Hon. D.Litt. (St. Andrews) 1987. *Plays include:* The Wrong Side of the Park 1960, Two Stars for Comfort 1962, The Judge 1967, A Voyage Round My Father 1970 (adapted for TV 1982, Int. Emmy Award), I, Claudius (adaptation from Robert Graves) 1972, Collaborators 1973, Mr. Luby's Fear of Heaven (radio) 1976, Heaven and Hell 1976, The Bells of Hell 1977, The Lady from Maxim's (trans. from Feydeau) 1977, TV adaptations of Rumpole of the Bailey (3 series), Brideshead Revisited 1981, Unity Mitford 1981, The Ebony Tower 1984, adaptation of Die Fledermaus 1989. *Publications:* novels: Charade 1947, Rumming Park 1948, Answer Yes or No 1950, Like Men Betrayed 1953, Three Winters 1956, Will Shakespeare 1977, Rumpole of the Bailey 1978, The Trials of Rumpole 1979, Rumpole's Return 1981, Rumpole and the Golden Thread 1983, Paradise Postponed 1985; Clinging to the Wreckage (autobiog.) 1982, In

Character 1983, Character Parts (interviews) 1986, Summer's Lease 1988, The Narrowing Stream; numerous articles in magazines. *Address:* c/o A. P. Peters Ltd., 10 Buckingham Street, Strand, London, W.C.2, England. *Telephone:* (049) 163237 (Home).

MORTIMER, Penelope Ruth, F.R.S.L.; British author; b. 19 Sept. 1918, Rhyl, N. Wales; d. of Rev. A. F. G. Fletcher and Caroline A. Fletcher (née Maggs); m. 1st Charles Dimont 1937 (dissolved 1949); m. 2nd John C. Mortimer (q.v.) 1949 (dissolved 1972); one s. five d.; ed. Univ. Coll., London; awarded Whitbread Prize for autobiography About Time 1979. *Publications:* A Villa in Summer 1954, The Bright Prison 1956, With Love & Lizards 1957, Daddy's Gone A-Hunting 1958, Saturday Lunch With The Brownings 1960, The Pumpkin Eater 1962, My Friend Says It's Bulletproof 1967, The Home 1971, Long Distance 1974, About Time 1979, The Handyman 1983, Queen Elizabeth 1986, Summer Story (screenplay) 1988. *Leisure interest:* gardening. *Address:* The Old Post Office, Chastleton, Moreton-in-Marsh, GL56 0AS, England. *Telephone:* Barton-on-Heath 242.

MORTON, Alastair (see Morton, R. A.).

MORTON, Sir Brian, Kt., F.R.I.C.S.; British chartered surveyor (retd.) and company executive; b. 24 Jan. 1912, Belfast; s. of Alfred Oscar Morton and Margaret Osborne Hennessy; m. Hilda Evelyn Elsie Hillis 1937; two s. (one deceased); ed. Campbell Coll., Belfast; Prin., Brian Morton & Co. (estate agents) 1936–64; Councillor (Ulster Unionist), Belfast Corpn. 1967–69; mem. Craigavon Devt. Comm. 1967–69; Chair. Londonderry Devt. Comm. 1969–73; Chair. Harland & Wolff Ltd. 1975–80; Dir. Bank of Ireland; Chair. Progressive Building Soc. 1981–; Hon. D. Sc. (Ulster) 1987. *Leisure interests:* golf, boating, gardening, landscape painting. *Address:* Rolly Island, Comber, Co. Down, BT23 6EL, Northern Ireland. *Telephone:* Killinchy 541472.

MORTON, David, M.A.; British business executive; b. 1929; ed. Pembroke Coll., Cambridge and Centre d'Etudes Industrielles, Geneva; joined Alcan, U.K. 1954; various man. and staff posts until 1974; Man. Dir. Alcan Booth Industries Ltd. 1974; Vice-Pres. Corporate Planning, Alcan Aluminium Ltd., Montreal 1977; Man. Dir. and C.E.O. Alcan Aluminium (U.K.) Ltd., London 1979; Vice-Pres. N. America and the Caribbean, Alcan Aluminium Ltd. and Pres. and C.E.O. Aluminium Co. of Canada Ltd. 1982; Exec. Vice-Pres. Alcan Aluminium Ltd. 1984, mem. Bd. of Dirs. 1985, Pres. and C.O.O. 1987–89, Chair. and C.E.O. July 1989–; Dir. Industrial Alliance Life Insurance Co., Bank of Nova Scotia, Conf. Bd. of Canada, IMI Foundation Bd., Geneva. *Address:* Alcan Aluminium Ltd., 1188 Sherbrooke Street West, Montreal H3A 3G2, Canada.

MORTON, Donald Charles, PH.D., F.A.A.; Canadian astronomer; b. 12 June 1933, Canada; s. of Charles O. Morton and Irene M. Wightman; m. Winifred Austin 1970; one s. one d.; ed. Univ. of Toronto and Princeton Univ.; astronomer, U.S. Naval Research Lab. 1959–61; from Research Assoc. to Sr. Research Astronomer (with rank of Prof.), Princeton Univ. 1961–76; Dir. Anglo-Australian Observatory (Epping and Coonabarabran, N.S.W.) 1976–86; Dir. Herzberg Inst. of Astrophysics, Nat. Research Council of Canada 1986–; Assoc. Royal Astronomical Soc. 1980. *Publications:* research papers in professional journals. *Leisure interests:* mountaineering, marathon running. *Address:* Herzberg Institute of Astrophysics, National Research Council of Canada, 100 Sussex Drive, Ottawa, Ont., K1A 0R6, Canada. *Telephone:* 613-990-0907.

MORTON, (Robert) Alastair, M.A.; British business executive; b. 11 Jan. 1938, Johannesburg, South Africa; s. of the late H. N. and E. M. V. Morton; m. Sara Stephens 1964; one s. one d.; ed. St. John's Coll., Johannesburg, Univ. of Witwatersrand, Johannesburg, Univ. of Oxford and M.I.T.; with Anglo-American Corpn. of South Africa (mining group), London and Cen. Africa 1959–63; World Bank Group, Washington, D.C. 1964–67; Industrial Reorganisation Corpn., London 1967–70; Exec. Dir. Investment Trust Group 1970–72; Chair. and CEO, Draymont Securities Ltd. 1972–76; (first) Man. Dir. British Nat. Oil Corpn. (BNOC) 1976–80; int. energy consultancy 1980–81; Chair. Thames Oil and Gas PLC 1981–83; Dir. Massey Ferguson Ltd. (Canada–now Varity Corpn.) and U.K. subsidiaries 1981; C.E.O. Guinness Peat Group PLC 1982–87, Chair. 1986–87; Chair. Guinness Mahon & Co. 1986–; Dir. New London Oil PLC 1986–, NOVA Corpn., Alta 1989–; Co-Chair. Eurotunnel 1987–; non-exec. mem. Royal Ordnance Factories Bd. 1974–76, British Steel Corpn. 1979–82. *Leisure interest:* yachting. *Address:* 32 St. Mary at Hill, London, EC3P 3AJ, England.

MORUZZI, Giuseppe, M.D.; Italian physiologist; b. 30 July 1910, Campagnola Emilia; s. of Giovanni Moruzzi and Bianca Carbonieri; m. Maria Vittoria Venturini 1941; two s.; ed. Univ. of Parma; Asst. Prof., Dept. of Physiology, Univ. of Parma 1933–36, Univ. of Bologna 1936–42; Acting Prof. of Physiology, Univ. of Siena 1942–43, Univ. of Parma 1945–47; Prof. of Physiology, Univ. of Ferrara 1947–48; Prof. of Physiology and Head of Inst. of Physiology, Univ. of Pisa 1948–80; Fellow, Rockefeller Foundation, Brussels 1937–38, Cambridge Univ. 1938–39; Visiting Prof., Northwestern Univ. 1948–49; Hon. mem. American Physiological Soc., American Acad. of Arts and Sciences, American Neurological Assen., E.E.G. Soc.; Foreign mem. American Philosophical Soc., Norske Videnskaps Akademi (Oslo), Kungl. Svenska Vetenskapsakademien (Stockholm); mem. Accad. Naz. dei Lincei, Pontifical Acad.; many hon. degrees. *Publications:* L'epilessia sperimentale 1946 (French 1950), Problems in Cerebellar Physiology 1950, The Physiology and Pathology of the Cerebellum (with R. S. Dow) 1958, Fisiologia della vita di relazione 1975, Fisiologia della vita vegetativa 1978. *Address:* Via S. Zeno 31, 56.100 Pisa, Italy. *Telephone:* 22218 (Home).

MOSAR, Nicolas, D. EN. D.; Luxembourg politician and lawyer; b. 25 Nov. 1927, Luxembourg; three c.; ed. Athénée Grand-Ducal and Faculté de Droit, Univ. of Paris, France; called to the Bar 1953; Town Councillor, Luxembourg 1959-70, Alderman 1970-75, Town Councillor 1975-85; Social Christian mem. of Parl. 1964-74, 1976-85; Chair. Social Christian Party Parl. Group 1979-85; Party Chair. 1972-74; EEC Commr. responsible for Energy, Euratom Supply Agency, Publs. Office 1985-. *Address:* Commission of the European Communities, 200 rue de la Loi, 1049 Brussels, Belgium.

MOSBACHER, Emil, Jr.; American business executive; b. 1 April 1922, Mt. Vernon, N.Y.; s. of Emil and Gertrude Mosbacher; m. Patricia Ryan 1950; three s.; ed. The Choate School and Dartmouth Coll.; Dir. Amax Inc., Amax Gold Inc., Avon Products Inc., Chemical Banking Corpn. and Chemical Bank, Chubb Corpn., Federal Insurance Co., Putnam Trust Co., Vigilant Insurance Co.; Chair. Operation Sail 1992; Hon. Life Trustee, Lenox Hill Hosp. New York, Univ. Club N.Y.; mem. Exec. Comm. Hoover Inst. on War, Revolution and Peace; Chief of Protocol of the U.S. 1969-72; fmr. Chair. N.Y. State Racing and Wagering Bd.; mem. Independent Petroleum Asscn.; Hon. M.A. (Dartmouth), Hon. LL.D. (Long Island). *Leisure interest:* yachting (successful defence of America's Cup 1962 and 1967). *Address:* Meridian Building, 170 Mason Street, Greenwich, Conn. 06830, U.S.A. *Telephone:* (203) 869-4100.

MOSBACHER, Robert Adam, B.SC.; American oil and gas executive and politician; b. 11 March 1927, New York; s. of Emil Mosbacher and Gertrude (née Schwartz) Mosbacher; m. Georgette Paulsin 1986; one s. three d.; ed. Washington and Lee Univs.; Ind. oil and gas producer 1948-; nominated Sec. of Commerce Dec. 1988; Chair., C.E.O. Mosbacher Energy Co., Houston; Dir. Texas Bankshares, Houston, New York Life Insurance Co.; Chair. Bd. Dirs., Choate School, Wallingford, Conn.; Dir. Aspen Inst. Centre for Strategic and Int. Studies; Chair. Nat. Finance, George Bush for Pres.; Pres. Ford Finance Cttee.; Co-Chair. Républican Finance Cttee.; Dir. Texas Heart Inst.; mem. Mid-Continent Oil and Gas Assen. (fmr. Chair.), American Petroleum Inst. (Dir., Exec. Cttee.), Nat. Petroleum Council (fmr Chair.), All American Wildcatters Assen. (fmr. Chair.), American Assen. Petroleum Landmen; Hon. LL.D. (Lee Univ.) 1984. *Address:* 14th Street between Constitution Avenue and East Street, N.W. Washington, D.C. 20230 (Office); 712, Main Street, Suite 2200, Houston, Texas 77002, U.S.A.

MOSBAKK, Kurt; Norwegian politican ; b. 21 Nov. 1934, Orkdal; m; ed. Norwegian Coll. Econs. and Business Admin.; Pvt. Sec. to Minister of Defence 1964-65; Minister of Trade and Shipping 1986-88; fmr. Deputy Mayor Lørenskog; Chair. Akershus Co. Labour Party 1969-74; Chief Co. Exec. Finnmark Co. 1976. *Address:* c/o Ministry of Trade and Shipping, Dep., Oslo 1, Norway.

MOSBY, Håkon, DR.PHIL.; Norwegian professor of geophysics; b. 10 July 1903, Kristiansand; s. of Salve Mosby and Mette Catharina Nodeland; m. Alfhild Heiberg Mowinckel 1930; two d.; ed. Univ. of Oslo; Asst. to Prof. Nansen, Univ. of Oslo 1923; Amanuensis, Geofysisk Inst., Bergen 1927; Prof. of Physical Oceanography, Bergen Museum 1947, Univ. of Bergen 1948-73; Dir. of Geophysical Inst. 1948-58, 1963-70; Dean of Faculty of Sciences, Univ. of Bergen 1954-59, Rector 1966-71; Pres. Int. Assen. of Physical Oceanography of the Int. Union of Geodesy and Geophysics 1954-60; Chair. Norwegian Geophysical Comm. 1948-58, 1963-70, Pres. NATO sub-cttee. on Oceanographic Research 1960-65; mem. NATO Science Cttee. 1965-69; mem. Acad. of Sciences Oslo, Bergen, Gothenburg, Helsinki, Commdr. Order of St. Olaf 1971. *Publications:* about 60 papers in Physical Oceanography and Meteorology partly concerning polar regions. *Leisure interest:* string quartet. *Address:* c/o Geofysisk Institutt, Universitetet i Bergen, Allégaten 70, N-5014, Bergen, Norway.

MOSCA, Ugo, D. EN D.; Italian diplomatist; b. 30 April 1914, Rome; s. of Michelle Mosca and Antonietta Dusc; m. Maria Caretti 1942 (divorced 1972); two d.; ed. Univs. of Milan and Florence; entered Diplomatic Service 1939; successively Vice-Consul, Tianjin, Second Sec., Bangkok; Third Sec. Belgrade 1947, Second Sec. 1949; Consul, La Plata 1950; various posts in Econ. Affairs Dept., Ministry of Foreign Affairs 1955, 1956, 1960; Minister-Counsellor, Deputy Perm. Rep. to EEC 1961; Dir.-Gen. of Finance and Econ. Affairs, Comm. of EEC May-Oct. 1967, Comm. of European Communities 1967-79; Special Adviser for monetary matters to EEC 1979-; mem. several econ. cttees. of Communities; Admin. European Investment Bank. *Publications:* Co-author Werner Report on European economic and monetary union; several publications on European economic and monetary problems. *Leisure interest:* sailing. *Address:* c/o Directorate-General of Economic and Financial Affairs, Commission of the European Communities, 200 rue de la Loi, 1040 Brussels, Belgium.

MOSCOSO DEL PRADO Y MUÑOZ, Javier; Spanish politician; b. 1934, Logroño; m.; two s. one d.; ed. Zaragoza Univ.; fmr. public prosecutor; set up legal practice, Pamplona 1978; elected mem. Congress of Deputies for Unión de Centro Democrática (UCD); Sec.-Gen. for Relations with the

Cortes; Sec.-Gen. for Relations with Judicial Admin., Ministry of Justice; left UCD for Partido de Acción Democrática; Special Minister in Prime Minister's Chancellery 1982-86; Deputy for Murcia 1986-. *Address:* Fernanflor 1, 28014 Madrid, Spain (Office).

MOSELEY, Harvey Sutherland Lewis, B.C.L., M.A.; Barbadian diplomatist and lawyer; b. 2 Feb. 1919; m. Sylvia Helen Gore; seven c.; ed. Univ. of Durham, Middle Temple, London, and Magdalen Coll., Oxford; Registrar, Supreme Court, Windward and Leeward Islands 1954-55; Magistrate, Barbados 1962-67; Sr. Crown Counsel, Barbados 1967-70; attorney-at-law, Barbados 1970-82; Perm. Rep. of Barbados to the UN 1982-86. *Address:* c/o Ministry of Foreign Affairs, Marine House, Bridgetown, Barbados.

MOSER, Sir Claus Adolf, K.C.B., C.B.E., F.B.A.; British statistician; b. 24 Nov. 1922, Berlin; s. of Dr. Ernest and Lotte Moser; m. Mary Oxlin 1949; one s. two d.; ed. Frensham Heights School, London School of Econs.; R.A.F. 1943-46; Asst. lecturer in Statistics, L.S.E. 1946-49, lecturer 1949-55, Reader in Social Statistics 1955-61, Prof. of Social Statistics 1961-70; Statistical Adviser Cttee. on Higher Educ. 1961-64; Dir. L.S.E. Higher Educ. Research Unit 1964-; Dir. Royal Opera House Covent Garden 1965-87, Chair. 1974-87; Dir. Cen. Statistical Office, Head of Govt. Statistical Service 1967-78; Visiting Fellow, Nuffield Coll. 1972-80; Vice-Chair. N.M. Rothschild and Sons 1978-84, Dir. 1978-; Dir. The Economist 1978-84, Chair. Economist Intelligence Unit 1978-84; Warden of Wadham Coll., Oxford July 1984-, Pres. 1989-(90); Dir. Equity & Law Life Assurance Soc. 1980-87, Int. Medical Statistics Inc. 1982-88, Octopus Publishing Group 1982-87, Property and Reversionary Investments 1986-87; Chancellor, Univ. of Keele 1986-; Hon. Fellow, R.A.M. 1970; mem. Gov. Body, Royal Ballet School 1974-87; Ordre national du Mérite 1976; Hon. Fellow, L.S.E. 1976; Hon. D.Sc. S. (Southampton) 1975, (Leeds, Surrey, Keele, York, Sussex, City Univs.) 1977, Hon. D.Tech. (Brunel) 1981; Commdr.'s Cross, Order of Merit (Fed. Repub. of Germany) 1986. *Publications:* Measurement of Levels of Living 1957, Survey Methods in Social Investigation 1958, Social Conditions in England and Wales (co-author) 1958, British Towns (co-author) 1961, and papers in statistical journals. *Leisure interest:* music. *Address:* Wadham College, Oxford; 3 Regents Park Terrace, London, NW1 7EE, England (Home). *Telephone:* (0865) 277904 (Oxford); 01-485 1619 (Home).

MOSER, Jürgen K.; American professor of mathematics; b. 4 July 1928, Königsberg, Germany (now Kaliningrad, U.S.S.R.); s. of Kurt Moser; m. Gertrude Moser 1955; two d.; ed. Univ. of Göttingen; Asst. Prof. New York Univ. 1956, M.I.T. 1957-60; Prof. of Math., New York Univ. 1960, Dir. Courant Inst. of Math. Sciences 1967-70; now with Eidgenössische Tech. Hochschule, Zürich; mem. N.A.S.; Sloan Fellow 1961, Guggenheim Fellow 1970-71; G. D. Birkhoff Prize; J. C. Watson Medal 1970. *Publications:* Lectures on Celestial Mechanics (with C. L. Siegel) 1971, Stable and Random Motions in Dynamical Systems 1973. *Address:* Eidgenössische Technische Hochschule, Rämistrasse 101, 8092 Zürich, Switzerland.

MOSES, Edwin, B.SC.; American athlete; b. 31 Aug. 1955, Dayton, Ohio; m. Myrella Bordt Moses 1982; ed. Fairview High School and Morehouse Coll., Atlanta, Ga.; won gold medal for 400 m. hurdles, Olympic Games, Montreal 1976, (in world record time), Los Angeles 1984; one of only three men to break 48 secs. for 400 m. hurdles; holds record for greatest number of wins consecutively in any event; winner 122 straight races 1977-87, lost to Danny Harris June 1987; holder of 10 fastest times ever recorded; mem. Jt. Olympic Cttee. Athletes Comm., Exec. Bd. of U.S.O.C., Bd. of Dirs. Jesse Owens Foundation; U.S. Rep. to Int. Amateur Athletic Fed. 1984-; dynamics engineer, Pomona, Calif. *Leisure interests:* aviation, scientific breakthroughs in athletics. *Address:* P.O. Box 9887, Newport Beach, Calif. 92660, U.S.A.

MOSES, Lincoln Ellsworth, PH.D.; American professor of statistics; b. 21 Dec. 1921, Kansas City; s. of Edward Walter Moses and Virginia (née Holmes) Moses; m. 1st Jean Runnels 1942, m. 2nd Mary Louise Coale 1968; two s. three d.; ed. Stanford Univ.; Asst. Prof. of Educ., Columbia Univ. 1950-52; Asst. Prof. of Statistics, Stanford Univ. and Stanford Medical School 1952-55, Assoc. Prof. 1955-59, Prof. 1959-, Assoc. Dean of Humanities and Sciences 1965-68, 1985-86, Dean of Graduate Studies 1969-75; (First) Admin. Energy Information Admin., U.S. Dept. of Energy 1978-80; Guggenheim Fellow, Fellow at Center for Advanced Study in Behavioral Sciences. *Publications:* (with Herman Chernoff) Elementary Decision Theory 1959, Biostatistics Casebook (Jt. Ed.) 1980, Think and Explain with Statistics 1986. *Leisure interests:* birds, chess. *Address:* Statistics Department, Sequoia Hall, Stanford, Calif. 94305, U.S.A. *Telephone:* 415-723 1886.

MOSEVICS, Mark; Israeli industrialist; b. 22 Aug. 1920; m. Blanka Griffin; one s.; ed. Dulwich Coll., London, Jesus Coll., Cambridge, England, Hebrew Univ., Jerusalem; Chair. Bd. of Dirs., Israel Export Inst. 1966-68; Chair. Bd. of Dirs., Israel Industrial Bank 1968-72, mem. Bd. of Dirs. 1972-; Chair. Bd. of Dirs., Elite Chocolate and Sweets Mfg. Co. Ltd., Coordinating Bureau of Econ. Orgs. 1968-; Pres. Mfrs. Assen. of Israel 1969-75; mem. Bd. of Dirs., Israel Corpn. Ltd. 1970-; Chair. Bd., First Int. Bank of Israel 1973; mem. Presidium, Prime Minister's 3rd Econ. Conf.; Hon. Pres. A'KIM (Appeal for Retarded Children) 1972-. *Address:*

Elite Chocolate and Sweets Manufacturing Co. Ltd., P.O. Box 19, Tel-Aviv (Office); 7 Wisotsky Street, Tel-Aviv, Israel.

MOSHOESHOE II, King, (Constantine Bereng Seeiso, LL.B.); King of Lesotho (Basutoland); b. 2 May 1938; s. of Seeiso Griffith, late Paramount Chief of Basutoland and 'Ma-Bereng; m. Princess Tabitha 'Masentle, d. of late Chief Lerotholi Mojela, 1962; ed. Roma Coll., Lesotho, Ampleforth Coll. and Corpus Christi Coll., Oxford; Paramount Chief of Basutoland 1960; King (since restoration of Lesotho's independence) 1966-; children: Prince Letsie David, Prin. Chief-designate of Matsieng and heir apparent to the throne, b. 17 July 1963; Prince Seeiso Simeone, b. 16 April 1966; Princess Constance Christina Sebueng, b. 24 Dec. 1969; exiled from Lesotho April-Dec. 1970; Chancellor, Nat. Univ. of Lesotho (fmrly. Univ. of Botswana, Lesotho and Swaziland) 1971. *Address:* The Royal Palace, P.O. Box 524, Maseru, Lesotho. *Telephone:* 22170.

MOSLER, Hermann, LL.D.; German international lawyer; b. 26 Dec. 1912, Hennef; s. of Karl and Marga (née Loenartz) Mosler; m. Anne Pipberger; five c.; ed. Bonn Univ.; Asst., later Research Fellow, Kaiser Wilhelm Inst. for Foreign Public Law and Public Int. Law 1937; Barrister-at-Law, Bonn 1946; Pvt. Dozent in Public Int. Law, Constitutional Law and Admin. Law, Univ. of Bonn 1946; Ordinary Prof. of Public Law, Univ. of Frankfurt 1949; Visiting Prof. of Int. Law, Georgetown Univ. 1950; Head of Legal Dept., Fed. Ministry of Foreign Affairs 1951-53: Ordinary Prof. Univ. of Heidelberg 1954; Dir. Max-Planck Inst. for Foreign Public Law and Public Int. Law, Heidelberg 1954, now Emer.; mem. Perm. Court of Arbitration 1954; Judge of European Court of Human Rights 1959-81; Lectures, Hague Acad. of Int. Law 1957, 1974; ad hoc Judge, Int. Court of Justice 1968-69; Judge 1976-85; mem. Heidelberg Acad. of Sciences 1975, Pres. 1982-86; Hon. Pres. German Soc. of Int. Law 1985; mem. Curatorium, Hague Acad. of Int. Law 1976, Inst. de Droit Int. 1977; Corresp. mem. Austrian Acad. of Sciences 1972; Dr. Iur. h.c. (Brussels) 1969, (Saarbrücken) 1982. *Publications:* in International Law, Comparative Public Law, European Law. *Address:* 6900 Heidelberg, Mühltalstr. 117a, Federal Republic of Germany.

MOSOEUNYANE, Col. Khethang Aloysius; Lesotho police officer and politician; b. 13 March 1942, Berea; ed. Sion Roman Catholic Mission, Civil Service Training Centre, Univ. of Botswana, Lesotho and Swaziland; also studied abroad; joined Police Mobile Unit (PMU) 1964 gaining rank of Col. 1980; controls Ministries of Works, Justice, Law, Constitutional and Parliamentary Affairs and Food Man. Unit 1986-; Medal for Meritorious Services 1977, Medal for Gallantry 1981. *Leisure interests:* soccer, athletics, music, reading. *Address:* The Military Council, Maseru, Lesotho.

MOSS, Stirling, O.B.E.; British racing driver; b. 17 Sept. 1929, London; s. of Nora Aileen and Alfred Moss; m. 1st Katherine Molson 1957 (dissolved 1963); m. 2nd Elaine Barbarino 1964 (dissolved 1968), one d.; m. 3rd Susie Paine 1980, one s.; ed. Haileybury and Imperial Service Coll.; bought his first racing car, a Cooper 500, with prize money from show-jumping 1947; British Champion 1951; built his own car, the Cooper-Alta 1953; drove in H.W.M. Formula II Grand Prix team 1950, 1951, Jaguar team 1950, 1951; leader of Maserati Grand Prix team 1954; mem. Mercedes team 1955; leader of Maserati Sports and Grand Prix teams 1956, Aston Martin team 1956; mem. Vanwall, Aston Martin, Maserati teams 1958; winner of Tourist Trophy (TT) race, U.K. 1950, 1951, 1955, 1958, Gold Coupe des Alpes (3 rallies without loss of marks) 1954, Italian Mille Miglia 1955, Sicilian Targa Florio 1955, 8 int. events including New Zealand, Monaco Grand Prix, Nurburgring 1,000 km. (Fed. Repub. of Germany) 1956, Argentine 1,000 km. U.K., Pescara (Italy), Moroccan Grand Prix 1957, 11 events incl. Argentine, Netherlands, Italian Grand Prix and Nurburgring 1,000 km. 1958, 19 events including New Zealand, Portuguese, U.S. Grand Prix 1959, 19 events including Cuban, Monaco, Austrian, S. African Grand Prix 1960, 27 events including Monaco, German, Pacific Grand Prix, Nassau Tourist Trophy 1961; competed in 492 events, finishing in 366, winning 222, during motor racing career 1947-62; retd. from racing after accident at Goodwood, U.K. April 1962, attempted comeback 1980; subsequently took part in many business ventures, consultancy work on vehicle evaluation, property conversion, design; Man. Dir. Stirling Moss Ltd.; Dir. 28 cos.; also journalism and lecturing; Pres. or Patron of 28 car clubs; Hon. F.I.E. 1959; Gold Star, British Racing Drivers' Club 10 times 1950-61, Driver of the Year (Guild of Motoring Writers) 1954; Sir Malcolm Campbell Memorial Award 1957. *Publications include:* Stirling Moss 1953, In the Track of Speed 1957, Le Mans '59 1959, Design and Behaviour of the Racing Car 1963, All But My Life 1963, How to Watch Motor Racing 1975, Motor Racing and All That 1980, My Cars, My Career 1987. *Leisure interests:* water and snow skiing, theatre and cinema, designing, model making, motor trials, swimming, interior decorating, woodwork, horse jumping and riding. *Address:* c/o Stirling Moss Ltd., 46 Shepherd Street, Mayfair, London, W1Y 8JN (Office); 44 Shepherd Street, London, W.1, England (Home). *Telephone:* 01-499 3272/7967 (Office).

MOSSAKOWSKI, Mirosław, M.D.; Polish neuropathologist; b. 23 Sept. 1929, Bereza Kartuska; s. of Thadeus Mossakowski and Janina Mossakowski; m. Biliana Mossakowska; one s.; ed. Medical Acad., Gdańsk; staff Medical Acad., Gdańsk 1950-54, Jr. Asst., Physiological Anatomy Research Centre 1950-53, Asst., Neurological Clinic 1953-54; postgrad. studies 1954-57, Sr. Asst. Research Centre on Histopathology of Nervous System,.

Polish Acad. of Sciences 1957-58; postgrad. fellow, Neurological Inst., Montreal 1959-60; researcher, Neuropathological Research Centre of Polish Acad. of Sciences 1961-66, Asst. Prof., Head, Research Unit on Nervous Tissue Culture; Visiting Prof., Nat. Inst. of Neurological Diseases and Blindness, N.I.H. Bethesda 1966-67; Staff Centre for Experimental and Clinical Medicine of Polish Acad. of Sciences, Warsaw 1967-, Extraordinary Prof. 1971-79, Ordinary Prof. 1979-, Head, Neuropathology Dept. 1967-, Deputy Dir. for Research 1967-68, Dir. 1975-; Corresp. mem. Polish Acad. of Sciences 1973-86, mem. 1986-; Deputy Sec., Medical Sciences Dept., Polish Acad. of Sciences 1968-80, Sec. 1981-, mem. Presidium of Polish Acad. of Sciences 1975-; Ed. Neuropatologia Polska (quarterly) 1969-72, 1978-; mem. numerous neurological and pathological Socs.; mem. Polish United Workers' Party (PZPR) 1953-; numerous Polish awards and decorations. *Publications:* numerous research works in Polish and foreign journals on pathomorphology and histochemistry of brain tumours and other disorders; Ed. Podstawy neuropatologii (Essentials of Neuropathology) 1981, Experimental and Clinical Neuropathology 1981. *Leisure interests:* mountaineering, 18th century Polish history, colour photography. *Address:* ul. Polna 54 m. 40, 00-644 Warsaw, Poland (Home). *Telephone:* 49-64-63 (Office), 25-29-86 (Home).

MÖSSBAUER, Rudolf, PH.D.; German physicist; b. 31 Jan. 1929, Munich; s. of Ludwig and Erna Mössbauer; m.; one s. two d.; ed. Tech. Hochschule, Munich; Research Asst. Max-Planck Inst., Heidelberg 1955-57; Research Fellow, Tech. Hochschule, Munich 1958-60; Research Fellow, Calif. Inst. of Tech. 1960, Sr. Research Fellow 1961, Prof. of Physics Dec. 1961; Prof. of Experimental Physics, Tech. Univ. of Munich 1964-72, 1977-; Dir. Inst. Max von Laue and of German-French-British High Flux Reactor, Grenoble, France 1972-77; Foreign mem. American Acad. of Arts and Sciences, Accad. Nazionale di Roma; mem. Deutsche Physische Gesellschaft, Deutsche Gesellschaft der Naturforscher, Leopoldina, American Physical Soc., European Physical Soc., Indian Acad. of Sciences, American Acad. of Sciences, Acad. of Sciences of the U.S.S.R., Pontifical Acad. of Sciences, Hungarian Acad. of Sciences; Hon. D.Sc. (Oxford) 1973, (Lille) 1973, (Leicester) 1975, Dr. h.c. (Grenoble) 1974; Grosses Bundesverdienstkreuz, Research Corpn. Award 1960, Röntgen Prize, Univ. of Giessen 1961, Elliot Cresson Medal of Franklin Inst., Philadelphia 1961, Nobel Prize for Physics 1961. *Publications:* Papers on Recoilless Nuclear Resonance Absorption. *Leisure interests:* piano, hiking, photography, languages. *Address:* c/o Technische Universität München, 8000 Munich, Arcissstrasse 21, Federal Republic of Germany.

MOSTELLER, Frederick, M.A., PH.D.; American professor of mathematical statistics; b. 24 Dec. 1916, Clarksburg, Va.; s. of William R. Mosteller and Helen (Kelley) Mosteller; m. Virginia Gilroy 1941; one s. one d.; ed. Carnegie Inst. of Tech. and Princeton Univ.; Instr. in Math. Princeton Univ. 1942-43, Research Mathematician 1944-45; Lecturer, Dept. of Social Relations Harvard Univ. 1946-48, Assoc. Prof. 1948-51, Prof. of Mathematical Statistics 1951-87, Emer. Prof. 1987-, Chair. Dept. of Statistics 1957-69, 1975-77, Chair. Dept. of Biostatistics, School of Public Health 1977-81, Chair. Dept. of Health Policy & Man. Harvard School of Public Health 1981-87, Roger I. Lee Prof. 1978-87, Dir. Tech. Assessment Program 1987-; mem. Faculty, Harvard Medical School 1977-; Miller Research Prof. Univ. of Calif. Berkeley 1974-75; Charles M. and Martha Hitchcock Prof. Univ. of Calif. Berkeley 1984-85; mem. American Acad. of Arts and Sciences, American Philosophical Soc., N.A.S., Royal Statistical Soc.; Myrdal Prize 1978, Lazarsfeld Prize 1979; S. S. Wilks Award 1986, R.A. Fisher Award 1987; four hon. degrees. *Address:* Department of Statistics, Harvard University, 1 Oxford Street, Cambridge, Mass. 02138, U.S.A. *Telephone:* 617-495-2583.

MOSTOW, George Daniel, M.A., PH.D.; American professor of mathematics; b. 4 July 1923, Boston, Mass.; s. of Isaac J. Mostow and Ida Rotman; m. Evelyn Davidoff 1947; three s. one d.; ed. Harvard Univ.; Instructor in Math. Princeton Univ. 1947-48; mem. Inst. for Advanced Study 1947-49, 1956-57, 1975, Trustee 1982-; Asst. Prof. Syracuse Univ. 1949-52; Asst. Prof. Johns Hopkins Univ. 1952-53, Assoc. Prof. 1954-56, Prof. 1957-61; Prof. of Math. Yale Univ. 1961-66, James E. English Prof. of Math. 1966-81, Henry Ford II Prof. of Math. 1981-, Chair. 1971-74; mem. Science Advisory Council, Math. Sciences Inst. Berkeley, Calif. 1988-; mem. Science Advisory Council, Weizman Inst. Rehovoth, Israel 1988-; Chair. U.S. Nat. Comm. for Math. 1971-73, 1983-85; Visiting Prof. at numerous univs. etc.; Fulbright scholar; Guggenheim Fellowship 1957-58; mem. N.A.S., American Acad. of Arts and Sciences, American Math. Soc., Int. Math. Union; many other professional affiliations and distinctions. *Address:* Yale University, New Haven, Conn. 06520 (Office); Beechwood Road, Woodbridge, Conn. 06525, U.S.A. (Home).

MOTESICZKY, Marie-Louise von; British painter; b. 24 Oct. 1906, Vienna, Austria; d. of Edmund von Motesiczky and Henriette von Lieben; started painting 1924. *Exhibitions:* Leger Gallery, London 1941; The Czechoslovak Inst., London 1944; Kunstzaal Van Lier, Amsterdam 1952; Kuntzaal Plaats, The Hague 1952, Städtische Galerie, Munich 1954 Kunstverein, Düsseldorf 1955; Beaux Arts Gallery, London 1960, Galerie der Wiener Secession, Vienna 1966, Wolfgang Gurlitt Museum, Linz 1966, Galerie Gunther Franke, Munich 1967, Kunsthalle, Bremen 1968, Kommunale Galerie, Frankfurt 1980; Goethe Inst., London 1985, The Fitzwilliam

Museum, Cambridge 1986; works in public collections in Amsterdam, Frankfurt, Vienna, Linz, London and Cambridge. *Leisure interests:* writing, walking, cultivating friends. *Address:* 6 Chesterford Gardens, London, N.W.3, England. *Telephone:* 01-435 1627.

MOTHERWELL, Robert, A.B., F.R.S.A.; American painter; b. 24 Jan. 1915, Aberdeen, Wash.; s. of Robert Burns Motherwell and Margaret Hogan; m. Renate Ponsold 1972; two d. by previous marriage; ed. Stanford, Harvard, Grenoble and Columbia Univs.; a founder in New York of Abstract Expressionism (Tachisme); first exhbn., Raymond Duncan Gallery Paris 1939; One-Man Shows Guggenheim Gallery 1944, 1985, Kootz Gallery 1946, 1948, 1949, 1952, Janis Gallery 1957, 1959, 1961, 1962, Museum of Modern Art 1965 (all New York), San Francisco Museum 1946, 1967, Chicago Arts Club 1946, Oberlin Coll. 1953, Bennington Coll. 1959, Berggruen Gallery, Paris 1961, Odyssia Gallery, Rome 1962, Der Spiegel Gallery, Cologne 1962, The Phillips Collection, Washington 1965; Minnesota Museum 1965, Witte Memorial Museum, Tex. 1966, Utah Museum 1966, Southern Florida Museum 1966, Contemporary Arts Museum, Houston 1966, Baltimore Museum 1966, Indiana Museum 1966, Virginia Museum of Art, Richmond 1969, Toledo Museum 1969, Museum of Fine Arts, Houston 1972, Boston Museum of Fine Arts 1973, Museo de Arte Moderna 1975, Stadtische Kunsthalle, Düsseldorf 1976, Kulturhuset, Stockholm 1976, Museum des 20 Jahrhunderts, Vienna 1977, Musée d'Art Moderne de la Ville de Paris 1977, Royal Scottish Acad., Edin. 1977, Royal Soc. of Arts, London 1978, Fundacio Juan March, Madrid 1980, San Francisco Museum of Modern Art 1984, Bavarian State Museum of Modern Art, Munich 1983, etc.; Retrospective Exhbn., Städtische Kunsthalle, Dusseldorf 1976, Kulturhuset, Stockholm, Museum des 20 Jahrhunderts, Vienna, Musée d'Art Moderne de la Ville de Paris, Royal Scottish Acad., Edinburgh, Royal Acad. of Arts, London 1976–77; work has been exhibited at Tate Gallery (London), New York, Paris and Madrid Museums of Modern Art and at Brussels, Moscow, Venice, São Paulo, Amsterdam, West Berlin, Kassel, Rome and elsewhere; works in U.S. Pavilion, Venice 1950, São Paulo 1953, Brussels 1958, Moscow 1959, São Paulo 1961; Gen. Ed. Documents of Modern Art 1944–52; Assoc. Prof. Hunter Coll. 1951–58, Distinguished Prof. 1972–73; Dir. Coll. Art Asscn. 1965–68; Art Adviser Partisan Review 1963–65; Educ. Adviser Guggenheim Foundation 1965–77; Counsellor Smithsonian Inst. 1966–68; Adviser Washington Univ. 1968–70, Tufts Univ. 1976–; Gen. Ed. Documents of XX Century Art 1968–80; Advisory Ed. The American Scholar 1969–73; mem. American Acad. Art and Letters, American Inst. of Arts and Letters, American Acad. of Arts and Sciences; Grand Medal, Paris 1977; Gold Medal, Philadelphia Acad. 1979, Skowhegan Award for Printmaking 1981; New York Mayor's Award 1981; Gold Medal of Honor, Nat. Arts Club, New York 1983, Macdowell Colony Medal of Honor 1985 and other awards. *Address:* c/o M. Knoedler and Co., 19 East 70th Street, New York, N.Y. 10021, U.S.A.

MOTION, Andrew, M.LITT.; British publisher and poet; b. 26 Oct. 1952; s. of Andrew R. Motion and Catherine G. Motion; m. 1st Joanna J. Powell 1973 (dissolved 1983); m. 2nd Janet Elisabeth Dalley 1985; one s.; ed. Radley Coll. and Univ. Coll., Oxford; Lecturer in English, Univ. of Hull 1977–81; Ed. Poetry Review 1981–83; Poetry Ed. Chatto & Windus 1983–, Editorial Dir. 1985–87; Rhys Memorial Prize for Dangerous Play 1984, Somerset Maugham Award for The Lamberts 1987. *Publications:* poetry: The Pleasure Steamers 1978, Independence 1981, The Penguin Book of Contemporary British Poetry (anthology) 1982, Secret Narratives 1983, Dangerous Play 1984, Natural Causes 1987; criticism: The Poetry of Edward Thomas 1981, Philip Larkin 1982; biography: The Lamberts 1986. *Leisure interest:* cinema. *Address:* 124 Becklow Road, London, W12 9HJ, England. *Telephone:* 01-743 2173.

MOTSUENYANE, Samuel Mokgethi, B.SC.(AGRIC.); South African business executive; b. 11 Feb. 1927, Potchefstroom; s. of the late Solomon P. and Christina D. Motsuenyane; m. Jocelyn Mashinini 1954; six s.; ed. N. Carolina State Univ., U.S.A., Jan Hofmeyr School of Social Work; Nat. Organizing Sec. African Nat. Soil Conservation Asscn. 1952–59; N.C. State Univ., U.S.A. 1960–62; Pres. NAFCOC 1968–; Chair. African Bank Ltd. 1975–88, African Devt. and Construction Co. Ltd. 1977–; mem. Bd. of Dirs. Barlow Rand Ltd. 1986–, Barclays Bank Ltd. 1986–; Chancellor, Univ. of the North (S.A.) 1984–; Pres. Boy Scouts of S. Africa 1976–81; serves on bds. of numerous cos. and orgs.; Harvard Business Award 1977; Dr. h.c. (Univ. of Witwatersrand) 1983; Hon. D.Econ.Sc. (Cape Town) 1986. *Leisure interests:* gardening, reading. *Publications:* numerous articles. *Address:* P.O. Box 189, Ga-Rankuwa 0208, South Africa. *Telephone:* Soshanguve 01214-2024 (Office); Mabopane 0146-23996 (Home).

MOTT, Sir Nevill Francis, Kt., D.SC., F.R.S.; British physicist; b. 30 Sept. 1905, Leeds; s. of C. F. Mott and Lilian Reynolds; m. Ruth Horder 1930; two d.; ed. Clifton Coll. and St. John's Coll., Cambridge; lecturer, Manchester Univ. 1929–30; Fellow and Lecturer, Gonville and Caius Coll., Cambridge 1930–33; Melville Wills Prof. of Theoretical Physics, Bristol Univ. 1933–48; Dir. H. H. Wills Physics Lab. and H. O. Wills Prof. of Physics, Bristol Univ. 1948–54; Cavendish Prof. of Experimental Physics, Univ. of Cambridge 1954–71; Chair. Bd. of Dirs., Taylor and Francis Ltd. 1970–75, Pres. 1976–; Chair. and Trustee Nat. Extension Coll. 1971–76; Pres. Int. Union of Physics 1951–57; Master, Gonville and Caius Coll., Cambridge 1959–66; Chevalier Ordre nationale du Mérite 1977; Hon. D.Sc.

(London, Paris, Oxford and others); shared Nobel Prize for Physics 1977. *Publications:* An Outline of Wave Mechanics 1930, The Theory of Atomic Collisions (with H. S. W. Massey) 1933, The Theory of the Properties of Metals and Alloys (with H. Jones) 1936, Electronic Processes in Ionic Crystals (with R. W. Gurney) 1940, Wave Mechanics and its Applications (with I. N. Sneddon) 1948, Elements of Wave Mechanics 1952, Atomic Structure and the Strength of Metals 1956, Electronic Processes in Non-Crystalline Materials (with E. A. Davis) 1971 (2nd Edn. 1979), Elementary Quantum Mechanics 1972, Metal-Insulator Transitions 1974, A Life in Science (autobiography) 1986, Conduction in Non-Crystalline Materials 1987, and papers on solid state physics and science education. *Leisure interest:* photography. *Address:* 63 Mount Pleasant, Aspley Guise, Milton Keynes, MK17 8JX, England. *Telephone:* (0908) 583257.

MOTULSKY, Arno Gunther, B.S., M.D.; American medical geneticist; b. 5 July 1923, Germany; s. of Herman and Rena (née Sass) Motulsky; m. Gretel Stern 1945; one s. two d.; ed. YMCA Coll., Chicago, Yale Univ., Univ. of Illinois Medical School; Intern, Fellow, Asst. and Sr. Resident (Internal Medicine) Michael Reese Hosp., Chicago 1947–51; Staff mem. in charge of Clinical Investigation, Dept. of Hematology, Army Medical Service Graduate School, Walter Reed Army Medical Center; Research Assoc. in Internal Medicine, George Washington Univ. School of Medicine, Washington 1952–53, Instructor 1953–55, Asst. Prof. 1955–58, Assoc. Prof. 1958–61, Prof. Dept. of Medicine 1961–, Prof. Dept. of Genetics 1961–, Dir. Medical Genetics Training Program 1961–, Dir. Center for Inherited Diseases 1972–; Pres. Int. Congress of Human Genetics 1986; Ed. American Journal of Human Genetics 1969–75, Human Genetics 1969–, Progress in Medical Genetics 1974–; Hon. D.Sc. (Illinois) 1982; mem. American Soc. of Human Genetics N.A.S., American Acad. of Arts and Sciences 1978; William Allan Memorial Award 1970, Alexander von Humboldt Award 1984. *Publications:* Human Genetics—Problems and Approaches (with F. Vogel) 1979, 1986 and others, more than 270 medical and scientific articles. *Leisure interests:* reading, hiking, collecting African art, antique maps. *Address:* Center for Inherited Diseases, RG-25, University of Washington, Seattle, Wash. 98195 (Office); 4347-53rd N.E., Seattle, Wash. 98105, U.S.A. (Home). *Telephone:* (206) 543-3593 (Office).

MOULAY HASSAN BEN EL MEHDI, H.R.H. Prince (cousin of King Hassan II); Moroccan diplomatist; b. 14 Aug. 1912, Fez; s. of Moulay El Mehdi Alaoui and Khnata Bent Mohamed Soussi; Caliph Northern Zone of Morocco 1925; Amb. to U.K. 1957–64, to Italy 1964–67; Gov. Banque du Maroc 1969–84; decorations include Ouissam Alaoui, Charles I Medal, Great Mil. Ouissam, Great Medal of Portugal, Great Dominican Medal, Great Naval Medal, Great Mahdaoui Medal, Great Houssni Medal. *Address:* c/o Banque du Maroc, P.O. Box 445, 277 avenue Mohammed V, Rabat, Morocco.

MOULAYE, Mohamed, D.SC.; Mauritanian public official and politician; b. 1 Oct. 1936, Ouagadougou, Burkina Faso; s. of El Hassan and Maimouna Moulaye; m. 1st Ginette Marcin 1962; m. 2nd Oumoulkheiry Mint Chérifoumar 1969; three s. five d.; Directeur des finances 1966; Contrôleur financier 1967–75; Minister of Finance 1975–77, 1979; mem. Nat. Ass. 1965–75; Parl. rapporteur to Comm. des Finances; fmr. mem. Interparl. Union; Dir. Office of Pres. of Mauritania 1979–80; Conseiller Econ. et Financier du Chef de l'Etat, Prés. de la Comm. Centrale des Marchés Publics; mem. Conseil général, Banque Centrale de Mauritanie 1980–; Dir. Personnel Air Afrique, Financial Dir. 1985–; Chevalier, Ordre nat. du mérite (France). *Address:* B.P. 289, Nouakchott, Mauritania; 06 B.P. 777, Abidjan 06, Côte d'Ivoire. *Telephone:* 52175 (Nouakchott); 441840 (Abidjan).

MOULE, Rev. Charles Francis Digby, C.B.E., F.B.A.; British ecclesiastic and university professor (retd.); b. 3 Dec. 1908, Hangchow, China; s. of Henry W. Moule and Laura C. Pope; unmarried; ed. Weymouth Coll., Dorset, Emmanuel Coll., Cambridge and Ridley Hall, Cambridge; ordained deacon 1933, priest 1934; Tutor, Ridley Hall 1933–34; Curate, St. Andrew's, Rugby 1934–36; Vice-Prin., Ridley Hall 1936–44; Fellow, Clare Coll., Cambridge 1944–, Dean 1944–51; Asst. Lecturer in Divinity, Univ. of Cambridge 1944–47, Lecturer 1947–51, Lady Margaret's Prof. 1951–76; Hon. Fellow, Emmanuel Coll., Cambridge; Collins Biennial Book Prize; Burkitt Medal (British Acad.); Hon. D.D. (St. Andrews, Cambridge). *Publications:* Idiom Book of New Testament Greek 1953, Commentary on Colossians and Philemon 1957, The Birth of the New Testament 1962, The Origin of Christology 1977, Essays in New Testament Interpretation 1982. *Address:* 1 King's Houses, Pevensey, East Sussex, BN24 5JR, England. *Telephone:* 0323-762436.

MOULINS, Max; French government official; b. 2 Jan. 1914, Saint-Brieuc; s. of Georges and Marguerite (Roques) Moulins; m. Lucie Coute 1937; two s. two d.; ed. Lycée de Lyon, Faculty of Arts, Lyon, Faculty of Law, Paris; successively Sec.-Gen. of Hérault, Deputy Prefect of Aix-en-Provence, later of Cherbourg, Prefect of Rennes, Albi and Niort; Dir. of La Sûreté Nationale; Prefect of Haut-Rhin 1955–58; Prefect, Regional Insp.-Gen. Algeria 1959–60, Sec.-Gen. Overseas Dept. 1961; Prefect Rhône-Alpes Region 1966–72; Pres. Cie. Nat. du Rhône 1972–79; fmr. Mayor of Toulaud; fmr. Mayor of Antibes; Commdr. Légion d'honneur, Grand Officier Ordre nat. du Mérite, Croix de guerre, Medal of Freedom. *Address:* Soledad, chemin des Maures, 06600 Antibes, France. *Telephone:* (93) 33-32.07.

MOULTON, Alexander Eric, C.B.E., R.D.I., M.A., F.ENG., F.I.MECH.E., F.P.R.I., F.R.S.A.; British engineer; b. 9 April 1920, Stratford-on-Avon; s. of John Coney and Beryl Latimer Moulton; ed. Marlborough Coll., King's Coll., Cambridge; worked in Engine Research Dept., Bristol Aeroplane Co. 1939–44, Personal Asst. to Sir Roy Fedden 1940–42; established Research Dept. of George Spencer, Moulton & Co. Ltd., originating work on rubber suspensions for vehicles and designing Flexitor, Works Man. then Tech. Dir. 1945–56; f. Moulton Devts. Ltd., devt. work on own designs of rubber suspensions including Hydrolastic and Hydragas 1956, Chair. and Man. Dir. 1956–67, Man. Dir. 1967–; designed Moulton Coach; f. Moulton Bicycles Ltd. to produce own design Moulton Bicycle 1962, Chair. and Man. Dir. 1962–67, Dir. 1967–; Dir. Alex Moulton Ltd.; Dir. S.W. Regional Bd., Nat. Westminster Bank 1982–87; Hon. Dr. R.C.A.; Hon. D.Sc. (Bath); Design Centre Award 1964, Amb. Award 1964, Bidlake Memorial Plaque 1964, Gold Medal Milan Triennale 1964, Queens Award to Industry for Tech. Innovation (Moulton Devts. Ltd.) 1967, Soc. of Industrial Artists and Designers (S.I.A.D.) Design Medal 1976, Council of the Inst. of Mechanical Engineers James Clayton Prize, Crompton Lanchester Medal (from Automobile Div.), Thomas Hawksley Gold Medal, 1979. *Publications:* various papers on vehicle suspension. *Leisure interests:* steamboating, canoeing, cycling, shooting. *Address:* The Hall, Bradford-on-Avon, Wiltshire, England. *Telephone:* (02216) 2991.

MOUMIN, Amini Ali, M.A.; Comoran diplomatist; b. 30 Aug. 1944, Mutsamudu Anjouan; m.; four c.; ed. King George Coll., Zanzibar, Univ. of Kuwait, Downing Coll., Cambridge, Paris Inst. of Int. Relations and Univ. of Paris-V; Accountant Ministry of Commerce and Industry, Zanzibar 1964–68; Adviser to Pres. of Comoros 1978–79; Chief Africa Dept. Ministry of Foreign Affairs and Co-operation 1979–82, Dir. Political Affairs 1982–86; Perm. Rep. of Comoros to UN 1986–. *Address:* Permanent Mission of the Comoros to the United Nations, 336 East 45th Street, New York, N.Y. 10017, U.S.A. *Telephone:* (212) 972-8010.

MOUNTCASTLE, Vernon Benjamin, Jr., M.D.; American neurophysiologist and educator; b. 15 July 1918, Shelbyville, Ky.; s. of Vernon B. Mountcastle and Anna-Francis Marguerite Waugh; m. Nancy Clayton Pierpont 1945; two s. one d.; ed. Roanoke Coll., Salem, Va., and Johns Hopkins Univ. School of Medicine; House Officer, Surgery, The Johns Hopkins Hosp. Baltimore, Md. 1943; with U.S.N. Amphibious Forces 1943–46; through jr. ranks, The Johns Hopkins Univ. School of Medicine 1948–59, Prof. of Physiology 1959–, Dir. of Dept. of Physiology 1964–80, Univ. Prof. of Neuroscience 1980–; Dir. Bard Labs. of Neurophysiology, Johns Hopkins Univ. 1981–; Pres. Neurosciences Research Foundation 1981–; Dir. Neuroscience Research Program 1981–84; Penfield Lecturer, American Univ., Beirut 1971; Sherrington Lecturer, Liverpool Univ. 1974; Sherrington Lecturer, Royal Soc. of Medicine, London, Mellon Lecturer, Univ. of Pittsburgh 1976, Visiting Prof. Collège de France, Paris 1980, and numerous other hon. lectureships; Nat. Pres. Soc. for Neuroscience 1971–72; mem. N.A.S., American Acad. of Arts and Sciences, American Phil. Soc.; Hon. Dr.Sc. (Pa.) 1976, (Roanoke) 1968, (Northwestern) 1985, Hon. M.D. (Zurich) 1983, (Siena) 1984; Lashley Prize, American Phil. Soc. 1974, F. O. Schmitt Prize and Medal, M.I.T. 1975, Gold Medal, Royal Soc. of Medicine 1976, Horwitz Prize, Columbia 1978, Gerard Prize, Soc. for Neuroscience 1980, Int. Prize, Fyssen Foundation Paris 1983, Lasker Award 1983, Nat. Medal of Sciences 1986. *Publications:* The Mindful Brain (with G. M. Edelman) 1978, Medical Physiology (two vols.) (Ed. and major contrib.) 14th edn. 1980 and more than 50 articles in scientific journals on the physiology of the central nervous system especially on the neuronal mechanisms in sensation and perception. *Leisure interests:* sailing, horsemanship. *Address:* Department of Physiology, The Johns Hopkins University School of Medicine, 725 North Wolfe Street, Baltimore, Md. 21205 (Office); 31 Warrenton Road, Baltimore, Md. 21210, U.S.A. (Home). *Telephone:* (301) 955-3635 (Office).

MOUNTER, Julian D'Arcy; British journalist and television producer and director; b. 2 Nov. 1944, Cornwall; s. of Francis Mounter and Elizabeth Moore; m. Patricia A. Kelsall-Spurr 1983; two s.; ed. Skinners Grammar School, Tunbridge Wells and Grenville Coll.; reporter, Cornish Guardian 1961–63, Western Morning News 1963–64; Chief Reporter, Bristol & West News Agency 1964–65; staff corresp., Wales and West Country, The Times 1965–68; various overseas, specialist and home assignments, The Times 1968–71; Weekend World, London Weekend TV 1971–73; Head of Current Affairs and Documentaries, Westward TV 1973–74; Reporter/Dir. Panorama and Midweek, BBC TV 1974–78; Ed., Inside Business, Thames TV 1978–79, Exec. Producer, Current Affairs 1979–81, Controller, Children's and Young Adults' Dept. 1981–84; Dir. Programmes and Production, Thorn–EMI Satellite and Cable 1984–86; Dir. Cosgrove Hall Ltd. 1981–84, JRA Ltd. 1980–85, Cameralink Ltd. 1980–85, Blackwell Videotec Ltd. 1980–85; Dir.-Gen. TV N.Z. 1985–; jt. winner, IPC Investigative Journalism award; various television awards. *Leisure interests:* ocean sailing, naval history, music. *Address:* Television New Zealand Ltd, Centrecourt, P.O. Box 3819, 100 Victoria Street, Auckland, New Zealand. *Telephone:* Auckland 770-630.

MOURANT, Arthur Ernest, D.PHIL., F.R.C.P., F.R.C.PATH., D.M., F.R.S.; British doctor of medicine; b. 11 April 1904, Jersey, C.I.; s. of Ernest Charles Mourant and Emily Gertrude Bray; m. Jean Elizabeth Cameron Shimell (née Dickson) 1978; one step-s., one step-d.; ed. Victoria Coll., Jersey,

Exeter Coll., Oxford Univ., St. Bartholomew's Hosp. Medical Coll.; engaged in geological survey of U.K. 1929–31; chemical pathologist, Jersey 1935–38; Nat. Blood Transfusion Service 1944–45; Galton Lab. Serum Unit, Cambridge 1945–46; Dir. Bloodgroup Reference Lab. (Ministry of Health and Medical Research Council) 1946–65 (incorporating WHO Int. Blood Group Reference Lab.); Dir. Serological Population Genetics Lab. (Medical Research Council) 1965–72; Visiting Prof. of Serology, Colombia Univ. 1953; Hon. Sr. Lecturer in Haematology, Medical Coll., St. Bartholomew's Hosp. 1965–78; Marett Memorial Lecture, Exeter Coll., Oxford 1978; Visiting Prof. of Anthropology, Coll. de France, Paris 1979; Pres. Section H (Anthropology) B.A.A.S. 1956; Foreign Corresp. mem. Acad. des Sciences, Inscriptions et Belles Lettres de Toulouse 1970; Hon. mem. Soc. Peruana de Patologia 1955, Soc. Jersiaise 1961, Int. Soc. of Blood Transfusion 1975, British Soc. for Haematology 1976, Soc. for the Study of Human Biology 1978, Human Biology Council (U.S.A.) 1987; Hon. Citizen of Toulouse 1985; Oliver Memorial Award 1953, Huxley Memorial Medal of the Royal Anthropological Inst. 1961, Landsteiner Memorial Award (American Asscn. of Blood Banks) 1973, Osler Memorial Medal, Oxford Univ. 1980, R. H. Worth Prize, Geological Soc. of London 1982. *Publications:* The Distribution of the Human Blood Groups 1954, 1976, The ABO Blood Groups (with others) 1958, Man and Cattle (jt. editor) 1963, Blood Groups and Diseases (with others) 1978, The Genetics of the Jews (with others) 1978, Blood Relations 1983. *Leisure interests:* geology, archaeology, photography, alpine gardening, reading in sciences other than his own, history of science, travel. *Address:* The Dower House, Maison de Haut, Longueville, St. Saviour, Jersey, Channel Islands. *Telephone:* (0534) 52280.

MOUREAUX, Philippe; Belgian politician; b. 12 April 1939, Etterbeek; m.; four c.; secondary school teacher 1961–62; Asst., subsequently Prof., Université Libre de Bruxelles 1967–; Adviser, Deputy Prime Minister's Office 1972–73, on staff Prime Minister's Office 1973–74, Chef de cabinet to Deputy Prime Minister 1977–80, Minister of the Interior and Institutional Reforms 1980, of Justice and Institutional Reforms 1980–81, Minister and Chair. Exec. of French Community, responsible for cultural affairs, budget and foreign affairs 1981–85, Feb.–May 1988, Deputy Prime Minister and Minister for the Brussels Region and Institutional Reforms May 1988–. *Address:* Ministry for the Brussels Region, 21-23 blvd du Régent, 1000 Brussels, Belgium. *Telephone:* (02) 513-82-00.

MOUSHOUTAS, Constantine, B.A., D.JUR.; Cypriot diplomatist; b. 15 Dec. 1928, Nicosia; m.; two c.; ed. Brooklyn Coll., City Univ. of New York and Brooklyn Coll. Law School; First Sec., Counsellor and Minister Plenipotentiary at Perm. Mission of Cyprus to UN and Del. at Gen. Ass. 1960–75, Perm. Rep. 1982–; fmr. Consul Gen. of Cyprus, New York; Acting Dir.-Gen. Ministry of Foreign Affairs 1976; High Commr. for Cyprus to Australia, N.Z., Papua New Guinea and Fiji 1976–82, to Trinidad and Tobago, Guyana, Barbados, Saint Lucia and Grenada 1982–; Amb. to China, Japan and the Philippines 1976–82, to Argentina, Cuba, Panama and Suriname 1982; Chair. Cttee. on Relations with the Host Country UN; Fourth Cttee. (Decolonisation) of Gen. Ass. 1987–. *Address:* Permanent Mission of Cyprus to the United Nations, 13 East 40th Street, New York, N.Y. 10016, U.S.A. *Telephone:* (212) 481-6023.

MOUSNIER, Roland Emile, D.ÉS.L.; French professor of history; b. 7 Sept. 1907, Paris; s. of Emile Mousnier and Zélie Mouviot; m. Jeanne Lecacheur 1934; ed. Ecole Primaire Publique, Lycée Janson de Sailly, Lycée Condorcet, Faculté des Lettres, Sorbonne, Ecole Pratique des Hautes Etudes; Prof. Lycées de Corneille, Rouen, and Janson de Sailly, Louis-le-Grand, Paris 1932–47; Prof. of Modern History, Faculty of Letters, Strasbourg Univ., and Political Insts., Strasbourg and Paris 1947–55; Prof. of Modern History, Sorbonne 1955–77, Prof. Emer. 1977–; Founder and Dir. Inst. de Recherches sur la Civilisation de l'Europe moderne 1958–77 and Inst. de Recherches sur les Civilisations de l'Occident moderne 1971–77; Pres. Comité Français des Sciences historiques 1970–75; Visiting Prof. Inst. for Research in the Humanities, Madison, Wis., U.S.A. 1963–64; mem. Inst. de France 1977–; Dr. h.c. (Stockholm, Bonn); Chevalier Légion d'honneur, Commdr. des Palmes académiques. *Publications include:* La vénalité des offices sous Henri IV et Louis XIII 1945, Le XVIIIe siècle: l'Epoque des Lumières 1953, Les XVIe et XVIIe siècles, La grande mutation intellectuelle de l'humanité. L'avènement de la science moderne et l'expansion de l'Europe 1954, L'assassinat d'Henri IV: le problème du tyrannicide et l'affermissement de la monarchie absolue 1964, Problèmes de stratification sociale: Actes du Colloque international de 1966, 1968, Les hiérarchies sociales de 1450 à nos jours 1969, La stratification sociale à Paris aux XVII et XVIII siècles (I) 1976, Paris capitale au temps de Richelieu et de Mazarin 1978, Les institutions de la France sous la monarchie absolue: I Société et Etat 1974, II Les organes de l'Etat et la société 1980; Histoire générale de l'Europe des origines à nos jours (ed.) 1980, La monarchie absolue en Europe du V siècle à nos jours 1982, L'Age d'or du Mécénat (ed.) 1985, Un nouveau Colbert (ed.) 1985, Richelieu et la culture (Ed.) 1987. *Leisure interests:* music, theatre, literature, walking, swimming, sailing. *Address:* 142 avenue de Versailles, 75016 Paris, France (Home). *Telephone:* 45 27 13 90 (Home).

MOUSSA, Pierre L.; French civil servant; b. 5 March 1922, Lyon, Rhône; m. Anne-Marie Trousseau 1957; ed. Ecole Normale Supérieure; Insp. of Finances 1946–50; Tech. Adviser to Sec. of State for Finance 1950–51,

Dept. of External Econ. Relations 1951–54, Dir. Econ. Affairs and Planning, Ministry for Overseas Territories 1954–59; Dir. of Civil Aviation, Ministry of Public Works and Transport 1959–62; Dir. Dept. of Operations for Africa, World Bank 1962–64; Pres. French Fed. of Assurance Cos. 1966–69; Pres. Banque de Paris et des Pays-Bas 1969–81, Chair. 1978–81; Chair. Finance and Devt. Inc. 1982–86, Pallas Group 1983–, Dillon, Read Ltd. 1984–87, France Développement (Frandev) 1986–; Dir. numerous cos.; Officier, Légion d'honneur 1976, Officier, Ordre national du Mérite. *Publications:* L'économie de la zone franc, Les chances économiques de la communauté Franco-Africaine, Les nations prolétaires, Les Etats-Unis et les nations prolétaires. *Address:* 14 Pelham Place, London, SW7 2NH, England. *Telephone:* 01-408 2123.

MOUSSAVI, Mir Hussein; Iranian politician; b. 1942, Iran; ed. Nat. Univ., Teheran; joined Islamic Soc. at univ. in Teheran and active in Islamic Socs. since; imprisoned briefly for opposition to the Shah 1973; a founder mem. Islamic Republican Party (IRP) 1979; appointed Chief Ed. IRP newspaper Islamic Republic 1979; Foreign Minister Aug.–Oct. 1981; elected Prime Minister by Majlis (consultative assembly) Oct. 1981–. *Address:* Office of the Prime Minister, Teheran, Iran.

MOUSTIERS, Pierre Jean (Rossi), L. EN D.; French author; b. 13 Aug. 1924, La Seyne (Var); unmarried; ed. Univs. of Aix-Marseilles and Neuchâtel; Attaché at the Office des Changes, French zone in Germany 1947–49; Chief, Information Services, Nat. Information and Protection Centre for Construction (C.N.I.P.) 1950–60; medical del., pharmaceutical lab. MERCK, Darmstadt 1961–, later regional insp.; literary critic Nice-Matin, Radio-Marseille; Hommes et Lectures prize 1962, Grand Prix de littérature sportive, Grand Prix du Roman, Acad. Française for La Paroi 1969, Prix des Maisons de la Presse for L'Hiver d'un Gentilhomme 1972, Grand Prix littéraire de Provence for Une place forte 1975, Prix Louis Philippe Kammans for Une place forte, Prix des libraires for Un crime de notre temps 1977, Grand Prix du Scénario for La ronde de nuit, Prix Acad. Balzac for TV adaptation of Curé de Tours 1980, Sept d'Or for L'Affaire Caillaux, Prix Jean Giano, Italy 1986; Chevalier des Arts et Lettres; Médaille des Combattants de la Résistance. *Publications:* Le journal d'un geôlier 1957, La mort du Pantin 1961, Le pharisien 1962, La paroi 1969, L'hiver d'un gentilhomme 1971, Une place forte 1974, Un Crime de Notre Temps 1976, Prima Donna 1978, Le Coeur du Voyage 1981, La grenade 1984, Un Aristocrate à La Lanterne 1986. *Essay:* Hervé Bazin ou le romancier en mouvement 1973. *TV:* L'hiver d'un gentilhomme 1973, La mort du Pantin 1975, Une place forte 1976, Un crime de notre temps 1977, La ronde de nuit 1978, Antoine et Julie 1981, Bel Ami 1983, L'Affaire Caillaux 1985, Le Coeur du Voyage 1986, L'Eté de la Revolution 1989. *Leisure interests:* mountaineering, reading, painting and drawing, taxidermy. *Address:* Campagne Sainte Anne, boulevard des Acacias, 83100 Toulon, France. *Telephone:* 41-09-36.

MOWAT, Farley McGill, O.C., B.A.; Canadian author; b. 12 May 1921, Belleville, Ont.; s. of Angus and Helen (née Thomson) Mowat; m. 1st Frances Mowat 1949; m. 2nd Claire Mowat 1961; two s.; ed. Toronto Univ.; served in the Canadian Army 1939–45; Arctic exploration 1947–49; full-time writer 1950–; Hon. D.Litt. (Laurentian Univ.) 1970, (Univ. of Victoria) 1982, (Lakehead Univ.) 1986; Hon. D. Laws (Lethbridge, Toronto, Prince Edward Island); Gov.-Gen.'s Award (twice), Canadian Centennial Medal, Leacock Medal for Humour, Hans Christian Anderson Award, Anisfield Wolf Award, Mark Twain Award, etc. *Publications:* People Of The Deer 1952, The Regiment 1955, Lost In The Barrens 1956, The Dog Who Wouldn't Be 1957, Coppermine Journey 1958, The Grey Seas Under 1958, The Desperate People 1959, Ordeal By Ice 1960, Owls in the Family 1961, The Serpent's Coil 1961, The Black Joke 1962, Never Cry Wolf 1963, Westviking 1965, The Curse of the Viking Grave 1966, Canada North 1967, The Polar Passion 1967, This Rock Within The Sea 1968, The Boat Who Wouldn't Float 1969, Sibir 1970, A Whale For The Killing 1972, Tundra 1973, Wake of the Great Sealers (with David Blackwood) 1973, The Snow Walker 1975, Canada North Now 1976, And No Birds Sang 1979, The World of Farley Mowat 1980, Sea of Slaughter 1984, My Discovery of America 1985, Virunga (Woman in the Mist, U.S.A.) 1987. *Leisure interests:* travel, all facets of nature. *Address:* c/o McClelland and Stewart, 481 University Avenue, Toronto, Ont., M5G 2E9, Canada.

MOXLEY, John Howard, III, M.D., F.A.C.P.; American physician and business executive; b. 10 Jan. 1935, Elizabeth, N.J.; s. of John Howard Moxley, Jr. and Cleopatra Mundy Moxley; m. Priscilla Lichty 1958; three s.; ed. Williams Coll. and Univ. of Colorado School of Medicine; hosp. posts 1961–63; Clinical Assoc. Nat. Cancer Inst., Solid Tumor Branch 1963–65; Sr. Resident Physician, Peter Bent Brigham Hosp. 1965–66; mem. Lymphoma Task Force Nat. Cancer Inst. 1965–77; Instructor in Medicine and Asst. to the Dean, Harvard Medical School 1966–69; Dean, Univ. of Md. School of Medicine and Assoc. Prof. of Medicine 1969–73; Vice-Chancellor for Health Sciences and Dean of School of Medicine, Univ. of Calif., San Diego, and Assoc. Prof. of Medicine 1973–80; Asst. Sec. of Defense for Health Affairs, Dept. of Defense, Washington, D.C. 1979–81; Sr. Vice-Pres., Corp. Planning and Alternative Services, American Medical Int. Inc. 1981–87; Pres. and C.E.O., MetaMedical Inc., Beverly Hills, Calif. 1987–88, Moxley Assocs. 1988–; Fellow American Fed. for Clinical Research; mem. Inst. of Medicine (N.A.S.), American Soc. of Clinical

Oncology, American Medical Assen.; Dir. Henry M. Jackson Foundation for the Advancement of Mil. Medicine 1983–; Sec. of Defense Medal for Distinguished Public Service and other awards. *Publications:* numerous papers in scientific journals. *Address:* 211 Culver Blvd., Suite L, Playa del Rey, Calif. 90293; 8180 Manitoba Street, 210 Playa del Rey, Calif. 90293, U.S.A. (Home). *Telephone:* (213) 821-0881 (Office).

MOXON, (Edward) Richard, M.B., B.CHIR., F.R.C.P.; British medical doctor; b. 16 July 1941, Leeds; s. of Gerald Richard Moxon and Margaret Forster Mohun; m. Marianne Graham 1973; two s. one d.; ed. Shrewsbury School, St. John's Coll., Cambridge and St. Thomas' Hosp. Medical School, London; with Hosp. for Sick Children, Great Ormond St., London 1969; Fellow in Infectious Diseases, Children's Hosp. Medical Center, Boston, Mass., U.S.A. 1971–74; Asst. Prof. of Pediatrics, Johns Hopkins Hosp., Baltimore, Md., U.S.A. 1974–80, Dir. Eudowood Pediatric Infectious Diseases Unit 1981–84; Prof. and Head of Dept. of Pediatrics, John Radcliffe Hosp., Oxford 1984–. *Publications:* (Contrib.) Barnett's Textbook of Pediatrics 1977, Mandell's Textbook on Principles and Practice of Infectious Diseases 1985, McKhann's Textbook on Diseases of the Nervous System 1986, Kennedy Textbook on Infections of the Nervous System 1987; articles in scientific journals. *Leisure interests:* music, literature, sports. *Address:* Department of Pediatrics, John Radcliffe Hospital, Headington, Oxford, OX3 9DU; 17 Moreton Road, Oxford, OX2 7AX, England (Home).

MOYA, (John) Hidalgo, C.B.E., R.I.B.A.; British architect; b. 5 May 1920, Los Gatos, Calif., U.S.A.; s. of Hidalgo Moya and Lilian Chattaway; m. Janiffer Innes Mary Hall 1947; one s. two d.; ed. Oundle School, Royal West of England Coll. of Art and Architectural Assen. School of Architecture; qualified 1944; in pvt. practice with Michael Powell and Philip Powell (q.v.) 1946–50, with Philip Powell 1950–61, with Philip Powell, Robert Henley and Peter Skinner 1961–76, with Philip Powell, Peter Skinner, John Cantwell and Bernard Throp (Powell, Moya and Partners) 1976–83; with Philip Powell, Peter Skinner, Bernard Throp, John Haworth and Roger Burr (Powell, Moya and Partners) 1983–; Pimlico Housing Scheme, Winning Design in Open Competition 1946, Vertical Feature Festival of Britain Winning Design 1950, R.I.B.A. London Architecture Bronze Medal 1950, Festival of Britain Award 1951, Mohlg Good Design in Housing Award 1953, 1954, R.I.B.A. (Bucks., Berks. and Oxon.) Bronze Medal 1958, 1961, Civic Trust Awards (Class I and II) 1961, Architectural Design Project Award 1965, R.I.B.A. Architectural Award 1967 (London and S.E. Regions), Royal Gold Medal for Architecture, R.I.B.A. 1974. *Major works include:* Churchill Gardens flats, Westminster 1948–62; "Skylon" for Festival of Britain 1951; Mayfield School Putney 1955; Brasenose Coll. and Corpus Christi Coll., Oxford, extensions 1961; Christ Church Oxford Picture Gallery and undergraduate rooms 1967; St. John's Coll., Cambridge, new bldgs. 1967; Wolfson Coll., Oxford 1974; Queen's Coll., Cambridge, new bldgs. 1978; Chichester Festival Theatre 1962; Public Swimming Baths, Putney 1967; Mental Hosp. extensions at Fairmile 1957 and Borocourt 1964; Plumstead Manor School, Woolwich 1970; dining rooms at Bath Acad. of Art 1970, Eton Coll. 1974; Gen. Hosps. at Swindon, Slough, High Wycombe, Woolwich, Wythenshawe and Maidstone; British Pavilion, Expo 70, Osaka, Japan; Museum of London 1977, Wolfson Coll., Oxford 1974; HQ London & Manchester, nr. Exeter 1978; Nat. Westminster Bank, Shaftesbury Ave., London 1982, New Bldgs. for Royal Holloway and Bedford New Coll., Egham 1986; Queen Elizabeth II Conf. Centre, Westminster 1986. *Address:* Powell, Moya and Partners, 21 Upper Cheyne Row, London, SW3 5JW, England (Office). *Telephone:* 01-351 3882 (Office).

MOYA PALENCIA, Lic. Mario; Mexican lawyer and politician; b. 14 June 1933, México, D.F.; s. of Mario Moya Iturriaga and Concepción Palencia de Moya; m. Marcela Ibáñez de Moya Palencia 1959; one s. one d.; ed. Univ. Nacional Autónoma de México; Public Relations Dept., Ferrocarriles Nacionales de México 1955–58; in Dept. of Nat. Property 1959–64; Dir. Gen. of Cinematography, Dept. of Interior 1964–68; Pres. of Bd. of Dirs. of Productora e Importadora de Papel, S.A. (PIPSA) 1968–69; Under-Sec., Dept. of Interior 1969; Sec. of Interior 1970–76; Prof. of Constitutional Law, Univ. Nacional Autónoma de México 1977–; Dir.-Gen. Organización Editorial Mexicana (OEM) 1977–79, Fondo Nacional de Fomento al Turismo (FONATUR) 1979–82, Banco Nacional de Turismo 1982; Exec. Pres. Ocean Garden Products Inc. 1983–; Gen. Man. Exportadores Assen. S.A. de C.V. 1983–; numerous foreign awards and decorations. *Publications:* La reforma Electoral 1964, Temas Constitucionales 1978, Democracia y Participación 1982. *Leisure interests:* reading, riding. *Address:* Insurgentes Sur Torre B, 4o. piso, C.P. 1000, México 20, D.F., Mexico. *Telephone:* 548-91-84.

MOYERS, Bill D.; American journalist; b. 5 June 1934, Hugo, Okla.; s. of Henry Moyers and Ruby Johnson; m. Judith Davidson 1954; two s. one d.; ed. Univ. of Texas, Edinburgh Univ. and Southwestern Baptist Theological Seminary; Exec. Asst. to Senator Lyndon Johnson 1959–60; Assoc. Dir. U.S. Peace Corps 1961–63, Deputy Dir. 1963; Special Asst. to Pres. Johnson 1963–66, Press Sec. to Pres. 1965–66; Publr. of Newsday, Long Island, N.Y. 1966–70; host of This Week, weekly current affairs TV programme 1970; Ed.-in-Chief Bill Moyers Journal, Public Broadcasting Service 1971–76, 1978–81; Contrib. Newsweek 1974–76; Chief Corresp. CBS Reports 1976–78, Sr. News Analyst, CBS News 1981–86; Exec. Ed. Public Affairs TV Inc. 1987–; Emmy award 1983, 1984, 1985. *Publications:*

Listening to America 1971, The Secret Government 1988, Joseph Campbell and the Power of Myth 1988. *Address:* 76 Fourth Street, Garden City, Long Island, New York, N.Y. 11530, U.S.A.

MOYERSOEN, Ludovic Marie Odilon; Belgian lawyer and politician; b. 1 Aug. 1904, Alost; s. of Baron Romain Moyersoen and Aline Liénart; m. Teresa Thuysbaert 1930; five s. six d.; ed. Coll. Saint Joseph, Alost, Coll. Notre Dame de la Paix, Namur and Univ. de Louvain; Sec. Union Catholique Belge 1935–38; Asst. Chef de Cabinet to Prime Minister 1944–45; Co-founder Social Christian Party 1945, mem. Nat. Cttee. 1945–47; Deputy for Alost 1946–68; Minister of Justice 1950–52, of Interior 1952–54; Vice-Pres. Chamber of Deputies 1958–64, First Vice-Pres. 1964; Sec. Comm. for Revision of Constitution 1965; Minister of Nat. Defence 1965–66; mem. Belgian Del. to UN 1948; Alt. mem. Council of Europe 1949–50, mem. 1960; mem. Western European Union 1960–63, Vice-Pres. 1963–65; Pres. ITECO (Int. Tech. Co-operation) and Nat. Cttee. for Voluntary Service Overseas 1958–68, Cttee. for Econ. Devt., Dist. of Alost 1959, Intercommunal "Land von Aalst" 1961–80, Damian Foundation 1977; mem. Centre d'études pour les réformes politiques 1978; numerous decorations. *Publications:* Prosper Poullet en de politiek van zijn tijd, Baron Romain Moyersoen en politieke problemen van zijn tijd. *Address:* Hof Villa "Ten Berg", Aelbrechtlaan, Aalst (Alost), Belgium (Home). *Telephone:* 053-211454.

MOYLE, Colin James, M.P.; New Zealand politician; b. 1929; m.; three c.; ed. Auckland Teachers' Coll. and Auckland Univ.; teacher and farmer; M.P. for Manakau 1963–69, Mangere 1969–77, Hunua 1981–84, Otara 1984–; Minister of Agric. and Fisheries, Forests and Science 1972–75; Minister of Agric. and Fisheries and Minister in Charge of the Rural Banking and Finance Corpn. 1984–87, of Agric. and Fisheries Aug. 1987–; mem. Parl. Select Cttee. on Lands and Agric.; Labour. *Leisure interests:* rugby, squash, tennis, golf, skin-diving, fishing, boating. *Address:* House of Representatives, Wellington, New Zealand.

MOYNE, 2nd Baron, cr. 1932, of Bury St. Edmunds; **Bryan Walter Guinness,** M.A., BAR. AT LAW, F.R.S.L.; British and Irish brewer (retd.) and writer; b. 27 Oct. 1905, London; s. of Walter Guinness, 1st Lord Moyne, and Lady Evelyn Erskine; m. 1st Diana Mitford 1929 (dissolved 1934), two s.; m. 2nd Elisabeth Nelson 1936, four s. (one deceased) five d.; ed. Eton and Christ Church, Oxford; fmr. Maj., Royal Sussex Regt.; fmr. Vice-Chair. Arthur Guinness, Son and Co.; Trustee Iveagh (Housing) Trust, Dublin, Guinness (Housing) Trust, London; a Gov., Nat. Gallery of Ireland 1955; mem. Irish Acad. of Letters; Hon. LL.D. (Trinity Coll., Dublin) 1958, (Nat. Univ. of Ireland) 1961. *Publications* (as Bryan Guinness): 23 Poems 1931, Singing out of Tune 1933, Landscape with Figures 1934, Under the Eyelid 1935, Johnny and Jemima 1936, A Week by the Sea 1936, Lady Crushwell's Companion 1938, The Children in the Desert 1947, Reflexions 1947, The Animal's Breakfast 1950, Story of a Nutcracker 1953, Collected Poems 1956, A Fugue of Cinderellas 1956, Catriona and the Grasshopper 1957, Priscilla and the Prawn 1960, Leo and Rosabelle 1961, The Giant's Eye 1964, The Rose in the Tree (verse) 1964, The Girl with the Flower (short stories) 1966, The Engagement 1969, The Clock 1973, Dairy Not Kept 1975, Hellenic Flirtation 1978, Potpouri (autobiographical essays) 1982, Personal Patchwork (letters) 1987. *Leisure interest:* travelling. *Address:* Biddesden House, Andover, Hants., England; Knockmaroon, Castleknock, Dublin, Ireland.

MOYNET, André; French politician and businessman; b. 19 July 1921, Saint-Mandé; s. of Gustave and Yvonne (née Laurent) Moynet; one s. (deceased) two d.; ed. Coll. Saint-Michel, Lycée Voltaire, Paris; with Free French Air Force, Cameroon, Gabon, Chad; with R.A.F., U.K.; with U.S.S.R. Air Force in Normandy; Commdr. Ecole des Moniteurs, Tours 1945–46; Deputy to Nat. Assembly 1946–67, Sec. of State to President's Council 1954–55; Pres. Nat. Assembly Cttee. of Nat. Defence and Armed Forces 1962–67; Test Pilot, Hurel-Dubois 32-01 and Caravelle 1966–70; Mayor of Biot 1971; builder of Moynet Jupiter aircraft, Moynet 860 motor boats, Moynet Sport Prototype racing cars; Dir.-Gen. Aérospatiale; Pres. Saint Chamond Granat; Grand Officier, Légion d'honneur, Médaille de l'Aéronautique, Compagnon de la Libération and several foreign decorations; Ind. Republican. *Publication:* Pilote de Combat. *Leisure interests:* golf, flying, yachting. *Address:* 32 boulevard de la Saussaye, 92200 Neuilly-sur-Seine; chemin de la Chèvre d'or, 06410 Biot, France. *Telephone:* 4722-1520 (Neuilly-sur-Seine); 93-650352 (Biot).

MOYNIHAN, Daniel Patrick, PH.D.; American university professor, diplomat and politician; b. 16 March 1927, Tulsa, Okla.; s. of John Henry and Margaret A. Phipps Moynihan; m. Elizabeth T. Brennan 1955; two s. one d.; ed. City Coll. of New York, Tufts Univ. and Fletcher School of Law and Diplomacy; Dir. of Public Relations, Int. Rescue Comm. 1954; successively Asst. to Sec., Asst. Sec., Acting Sec. to Gov. of N.Y. State 1955–58; mem. N.Y. Tenure Comm. 1959–60; Dir. N.Y. State Govt. Research Project, Syracuse Univ. 1959–61; Special Asst. to Sec. of Labor 1961–62, Exec. Asst. to Sec. 1962–63, Asst. Sec. of Labor 1963–65; Dir. Jt. Center Urban Studies M.I.T. and Harvard Univ. 1966–69; Prof. of Educ. and Urban Politics, Sr. mem., Kennedy School of Govt., Harvard 1966–69, 1971–; Asst. to Pres. of U.S.A. for Urban Affairs 1969, Counsellor to Pres. (with Cabinet rank) 1969–70; Amb. to India 1973–74; Perm. Rep. to UN 1975–76; Senator from New York 1977–; Chair. Bd. of Trustees Hirshborn

Museum; mem. American Philosophical Soc., American Acad. of Arts and Sciences; Hon. Fellow, L.S.E.; numerous hon. degrees; Democrat. *Publications:* Beyond the Melting Pot (co-author) 1963, Maximum Feasible Misunderstanding, Community Action in the War on Poverty 1969, The Politics of a Guaranteed Income 1973, Coping: Essays in the Practice of Government 1974, A Dangerous Place (with Suzanne Weaver) 1978; Ed.: Defenses of Freedom: The Public Papers of Arthur J. Goldberg 1966, On Understanding Poverty: Perspective from the Social Sciences 1969, Toward A National Urban Policy 1970, Counting Our Blessings: Reflections on the Future of America 1980, Loyalties 1984, Family and Nation 1986, Came the Revolution 1988; co-editor of several publs. *Address:* Senate Office Building, Washington, D.C. 20510, U.S.A. *Telephone:* (202) 224-4451.

MOYNIHAN, Rodrigo, C.B.E.; British artist; b. 17 Oct. 1910; s. of Herbert James Moynihan and Maria de la Puerta; m. 1st Elinor Bellingham Smith 1931, one s.; m. 2nd Anne Dunn 1960, one s.; ed. University Coll. School, various schools in U.S.A. and Slade School of Art; mem. London Group 1933; War Artist 1943–44; fmr. Prof. of Painting Royal Coll. of Art; shows include: Redfern Gallery 1940, 1958, 1961, Hanover Gallery 1963, 1967, Egan Gallery, New York 1966, Tibor de Nagy 1968, Fisher Fine Art 1973, Rodrigo Moynihan Retrospective, Royal Acad., London 1978, Claud Bernard Gallery Paris 1985, Robert Miller Gallery, New York 1980, 1983, 1986; pictures owned by Chantrey Bequest, Tate Gallery, Contemporary Art Soc., Imperial War Museum, Nat. Portrait Gallery, and numerous pvt. collectors; R.A. 1954–56; Hon. Dr. (Royal Coll. of Art) 1969; Fellow, Univ. Coll. London 1970–. *Publications:* Goya 1951, Art and Literature (a magazine, ed. with Anne Dunn) 1963–68. *Address:* c/o Royal Academy, Piccadilly, London, W1V 0DS, England; 70 avenue de Léman, Lausanne, Switzerland.

MOYOLA, Baron (Life Peer), cr. 1971, of Castledawson in the County of Londonderry; **Rt. Hon. Major James Dawson Chichester-Clark,** P.C.; British politician and farmer; b. 12 Feb. 1923, Castledawson; s. of James Jackson Chichester-Clark and Marion Caroline Chichester; m. Moyra Maud Haughton 1959; one step s. two d.; ed. Eton Coll.; entered Army 1942, Second Lieut. Irish Guards Dec. 1942; wounded Italy 1944; A.D.C. to Gov.-Gen. of Canada (Field-Marshal Earl Alexander of Tunis) 1947–49; attended Staff Coll., Camberley 1956; retd. from Army as Maj. 1960; M.P. for S. Derry, Parl. of N. Ireland 1960–73, Asst. Whip March 1963, Chief Whip 1963–67; Minister of Agric., N. Ireland 1967–69; Leader of Unionist Party and Prime Minister of N. Ireland 1969–71; Deputy Lieut. N. Ireland 1954; Vice-Lieut. Co. Derry 1972–. *Leisure interests:* fishing, shooting and skiing. *Address:* Moyola Park, Castledawson, Co. Derry, Northern Ireland (Home).

MOYSE, Alexis, D. ÈS SC.; French academic; b. 2 Oct. 1912, Arcueil; m. Hélène Mignon 1939 (died 1982); two d.; ed. Univ. of Paris; prisoner of war 1940–45; research scientist, CNRS 1945, founder Lab. of Photosynthesis 1953, Dir. of Research 1955; Maître de conferences, Univ. of Paris 1955, Prof. 1960, now Prof. Emer.; mem. Acad. d'Agric. de France, Acad. des Sciences (Inst. de France); Officier, Légion d'honneur, Ordre Nat. du Mérite. *Publications:* books and articles on plant physiology. *Leisure interests:* music, reading, alpinism. *Address:* Photosynthèse et Métabolisme, Bâtiment 430, Université de Paris-Sud F91405, Orsay; 11 rue du Docteur Roux, 92330 Sceaux, France. *Telephone:* 6941 7128.

MOZGOVOI, Ivan Alekseyevich; Soviet politician; b. 1927, Ukraine; ed. Kherson Agric. Inst.; mem. CPSU 1951–; agronomist at state farm 1948–53; Sec. of Kherson Dist. Cttee., Ukrainian Komsomol, First Sec. 1972–; Sec. Cen. Cttee. of Ukrainian Komosomol 1953–62; Second Sec. Trans-Carpathian Dist. Cttee. of Ukrainian CP 1962–66; First Sec. Rovno Dist. Cttee. of Ukrainian CP 1966–72; mem. Cen. Cttee. of Ukrainian CP 1966–; Deputy to U.S.S.R. Supreme Soviet 1966–; First Deputy Chair. Council of Ministers of Ukrainian S.S.R. 1979–; cand. mem., then mem. Politburo of Ukrainian S.S.R. 1980–; mem. CPSU Cen. Cttee. –1989. *Address:* Council of Ministers of Ukrainian S.S.R., Kiev, Ukrainian S.S.R., U.S.S.R.

MOZHAEV, Pavel Petrovich; Soviet politician; b. 1930; ed. Leningrad Tech. Inst. for Study of Cellulose and Paper Industry; engineer-technician 1953–59; mem. CPSU 1958–; party work 1959–61; Deputy Pres., Kirov District Exec. Cttee. 1961–62; Second Sec., First Sec. of Kirov CPSU Regional Cttee. 1962–70; Head of Section, Sec., Second Sec. of Leningrad District Cttee. 1970–86; work for CPSU Cen. Cttee. 1986–87; Cand. mem. of CPSU Cen. Cttee. 1986–; Amb. to Afghanistan 1986–88.

MOZHAYEV, Boris Andreyevich; Soviet author; b. 1 June 1923, Pitelino, Ryazan Dist.; ed. Higher Coll. of Eng., Leningrad; worked in Far East for many years; first works published 1953. *Publications:* Fairytales 1955, Sania 1959, The Earth Is Waiting 1961, In Soldatov, At Nikolai Lozovoi's 1961, Earth and Hands 1964, Experiments on Earth 1964, Excerpts From Fyodor Kuzkin's Life 1966, The Power of the Taiga 1959, Far Away on the Amur 1963, and many others.

MPHAHLELE, Es'kia (Ezekiel), M.A., PH.D., D.LITT.; South African author; b. 17 Dec. 1919, Marabastad; s. of Moses Mphahlele and Eva Mphahlele; m. Rebecca Nnana Mphahlele 1945; four s. one d.; ed. teacher training and private study; Teacher of English and Afrikaans, Orlando, Johannesburg until 1957; Fiction Ed. Drum magazine 1955; Lecturer in English Literature, Dept. of Extra-Mural Studies, Univ. Coll., Ibadan, Nigeria 1957; fmr.

Dir. African Programme for the Congress for Cultural Freedom, Paris; circuit schools inspector Lebowa 1978; Researcher African Studies Inst., Univ. of Witwatersrand 1979, Prof. of African Literature 1979-88, Head of African Literature 1983-88; fmr. lecturer Univ. of Nairobi, Univ. of Denver, Univ. of Penn., Dir. Council for Black Educ. *Publications include:* Man Must Live, The Living and the Dead (short stories), Down Second Avenue (autobiography), The Wanderers (novel) 1972, In Corner B (short stories), The African Image (essays), Voices in the Whirlwind (essays), Chirundu (novel) 1981, Afrika My Music (autobiog.) 1984, Father Come Home (novel) 1984, Creative Writing Guides: Let's Talk Writing, Prose and Let's Talk Writing, Poetry; The Story of African Literature 1986. *Leisure interests:* music, theatre. *Address:* 5444, Zone 5, Pimville, Johannesburg, South Africa. *Telephone:* (011) 933-2273.

MPINGA KASENDA, PH.D.; Zairian politician and university professor; b. 30 Aug. 1937, Tshilomba; ed. Elisabethville (now Lubumbashi) High School of Social Sciences, Catholic Univ. of Lovanium and Univ. of Bordeaux, France; Teacher, Tshilomba Secondary School 1957-59; studied at Lubumbashi and Lovanium Univ. 1959-65; Asst. lecturer, Lovanium Univ. 1965-66, Prof. 1966-70; Adviser to the Chancellor, Nat. Univ. of Zaire and to the Minister of Public Admin. 1971-72; mem. Political Bureau Mouvement Populaire de la Révolution (MPR) 1972, mem. Perm. Cttee. 1974-80; Deputy People's Commr. 1975, First State Commr. 1977-80; Dir. Makanda Kabobi Inst. (MPR school) 1974-; Commdr., Nat. Order of Zaire and Dem. People's Repub. of Korea, Grand Officier Ordre du Mérite national (Mauritania). *Publications:* Ville de Kinshasa, Organisation politique et administrative 1968, L'administration publique du Zaire 1973, Les reformes administratives au Zaire 1975. *Address:* Institut Makanda Kabobi, avenue de la Gombe, Kinshasa (Office); 384 Quartier Gombele, Kinshasa/Lemba, P.O.B. 850, Zaire (Home).

MPUCHANE, Samuel Akuna, M.SC.; Botswana government official; b. 15 Dec. 1943, Senyawe Village; m. Felicity Sisai 1972; two s. one d.; ed. Univ. of Botswana, Univ. of Southampton, England; Asst. Prin., Dept. of External Affairs, Gaborone 1969-70, Counsellor Sept.-Nov. 1974, Under-Sec. with responsibility for Admin., Political Affairs and Int. Orgs. 1974-75; First Sec. Botswana Mission to UN 1970-71; First Sec. Botswana Embassy, Washington 1971-74; Botswana High Commr. in Swaziland (non-resident) 1975-77; Deputy Perm. Sec. Ministry of Mineral Resources and Water Affairs 1977-78, Acting Perm. Sec. 1978-79; Admin. Sec. Office of the Pres. 1979-80; Perm. Sec. Ministry of Local Govt. and Lands 1980-82; High Commr. in U.K. 1982-85; Perm. Sec. for External Affairs 1986-. *Leisure interests:* watching and playing tennis and squash, watching soccer. *Address:* c/o Ministry of Foreign Affairs, Private Bag 1, Gaborone, Botswana.

MROUDJAE, Ali; Comoros politician; Minister of Foreign Affairs and Co-operation 1979-82; Prime Minister of the Comoros Feb. 1982-85; Minister of State for Internal and Social Affairs Jan.-Sept. 1985; and numerous other portfolios. *Address:* National Assembly, Moroni, Njazidja, République des Comores.

MROUWEH, Adnan; Lebanese politician; b. 21 March 1936, Nabatiya; s. of Mohamad Mrouweh; m. Randa Daouk 1968; two s. two d.; ed. Univ. of Calif.; obstetrician; Chair. Family Planning Soc.; Minister of Health, Labour and Social Affairs 1982-84; Clinical Prof. Obstetrics and Gynecology, American Univ. of Beirut 1983, Vice-Pres. for Health Affairs and Dean Faculty of Medicine 1987-. *Publications:* 52 articles and books. *Leisure interest:* reading. *Address:* c/o American University of Beirut, Beirut, Lebanon. *Telephone:* 371471 and 806622.

MROŻEK, Sławomir; Polish writer; b. 26 June 1930, Borzęcin; fmr. cartoonist and journalist. *Publications include:* Małeńkie lato 1956, The Elephant 1957, Wesele w Atomicach (Wedding in Atomice) 1959, The Rain 1962 (short stories), The Ugupu Bird (short stories) 1968, Dwa listy 1974, Małe listy 1981; Plays: The Police 1958, What a Lovely Dream, Indyk (Turkey), Kard, Let's Have Fun, The Death of the Lieutenant 1963, Striptease 1964, Tango 1964, On the High Seas Vatzlav 1970, Druga zmiana (Second Service) 1970, Testarium 1970, Blessed Event 1973, Rzeźnia (Butchery) 1973, Emigrants 1974, Garbus (Humpback) 1975, Utwory sceniczne nowe 1976, Wybór dramatów i opowiadań 1976, Krawiec (Tailor), Opowiadania o lisie (Fox Stories), Drugie danie (Second Dish), Amor 1979, Pieszo 1983, Moniza Clavier 1983; series of satirical drawings: Polska w obrazach (Poland in pictures) 1957, Postępowiec (Progressive man) 1960, Rysunki 1982. *Address:* Living in France.

MSUYA, Cleopa David, B.A.; Tanzanian civil servant and politician; b. 4 Jan. 1931, Chomvu Usangi, Mwanga Dist.; s. of David Kilenga and Maria Ngido; m. Rhoda Christopher 1959; four s. two d.; ed. Makerere Univ. Coll., Uganda; Civil Service, Community Devt. Officer 1956-61, Commr. for Community Devt. 1961-64, Prin. Sec. to Ministry of Community Devt. and Nat. Culture 1964, to Ministries of Land Settlement and Water Devt. 1965-67, to Ministry of Econ. Affairs and Devt. Planning 1967-70 and to Treas. 1970-72; Minister of Finance 1972-75, 1983-85, for Finance, Econ. Affairs and Planning 1985-; for Industries 1975-80; Prime Minister 1980-83; Gov. ADB, IMF; mem. Bd. of Dirs. of several public corpns. *Address:* Ministry of Finance, Economic Affairs and Planning, P.O. Box 9111, Dar es Salaam, Tanzania.

MTEI, Edwin Isaac Mbiliewi; Tanzanian public servant; b. 12 July 1932, Moshi; s. of Eliapenda N. Mtei and Ngianaeli N. Mtei; m. Johara N. Marealle 1960; two s., three d.; ed. Makerere Univ. Coll., Uganda; Man. Trainee, E. African Tobacco Co. 1957-59; entered govt. service 1959; responsible for Africanization and training in the Civil Service; worked with E. African Common Services Org. 1962-64; Prin. Sec. to Treasury 1964-65; Gov. Bank of Tanzania 1966-74; Sec.-Gen. E. African Community 1974-77; Minister of Finance and Planning 1977-79; farming, also management and financial consultant 1980-82; Alt. Exec. Dir. IMF 1982-84, Exec. Dir. 1984-86. *Address:* c/o Ministry of Foreign Affairs, P.O. Box 9000, Dar-es-Salaam, Tanzania.

MU QING; Chinese journalist, writer and government minister; b. 15 March 1921, Qi County, Henan Prov. (Hui nationality); s. of Mu Yunshan and Yang Wenfang; m. Xu Lei 1945; four s.; started journalistic career in 1940s; Deputy Dir.-Gen. Xinhua News Agency 1959; disappeared during Cultural Revolution 1966-72; resumed post as Deputy Dir.-Gen. and concurrently Ed.-in-Chief Xinhua News Agency, Pres. 1982-; Deputy for Tianjin Municipality to 5th NPC 1978; mem. 12th CCP Cen. Cttee. 1982-87; mem. Cen. Advisory Comm. of 13th CCP Cen. Cttee. 1987-; Vice-Chair. All-China Journalists' Assen. 1983-; Pres. China School of Journalism 1986-. *Publications:* Jiao Yulu (reportage) 1980, Sidelights of Italy (prose) 1981, Vienna Melodies (prose) 1983, Selected Essays on Journalism 1983, Selected Proses of Mu Qing 1984. *Leisure interest:* photography. *Address:* Xinhua News Agency, No. 57 Xuanwumen Xidajie, Beijing, People's Republic of China. *Telephone:* 668521.

MUALLA, H. H. Sheikh Rashid bin Ahmad Al; Ruler of Umm Al-Qaiwain; b. 1930; apptd. Deputy Ruler of Umm Al-Qaiwain, succeeded as Ruler on the death of his father Feb. 1981; Chair. Umm Al-Qaiwain Municipality 1967; constituted the Emirate's first municipal council 1975. *Address:* Rulers' Palace, Umm Al-Qaiwain, United Arab Emirates.

MUBAKO, Simbi Veke, B.A., B.C.L., LL.M., M.PHIL.; Zimbabwe politician and lawyer; b. 20 April 1936, Zaka; s. of Paul Vuta and Serudzai Mubako; m. Dr. Hazel Christie 1970; three s. two d.; ed. Univ. of South Africa, Univ. Coll., Dublin, L.S.E., Harvard Univ.; lecturer in Laws, Univ. of Zambia 1970-76, Univ. of Southampton 1977-79; Prof. and Dean of Law, Univ. of Lesotho 1979-80; Minister of Justice and Constitutional Affairs 1980-84, of Home Affairs 1984-85, of Nat. Supplies 1985-. *Leisure interests:* swimming, tennis, writing and reading novels. *Address:* c/o Ministry of National Supplies, Private Bag, Harare, Zimbabwe.

MUBARAK, Lt.-Gen. (Muhammad) Hosni; Egyptian air force officer and politician; b. 4 May 1928, Kafr El-Moseilha, Minuffya Governorate; ed. Mil. Acad., Air Acad.; joined Air Force 1950; Dir.-Gen. Air Acad. 1967-69; Air Force Chief of Staff 1969-72; C.-in-C. 1972-75; promoted to Lt.-Gen. 1973; Vice-Pres. of Egypt 1975-81; Vice-Chair. Nat. Democratic Party (NDP) 1976-81; mem. Higher Council for Nuclear Energy 1975-; Sec.-Gen. NDP and Political Bureau 1981-82, Chair. 1982-; Pres. of Egypt Oct. 1981- (Cand. of NDP); Prime Minister 1981-82; Order of Star of Sinai. *Address:* Presidential Palace, Abdeen, Cairo, Egypt.

MÜCKENBERGER, Erich; German politician; b. 8 June 1910, Chemnitz (now Karl-Marx-Stadt); fmr. locksmith, Chemnitz; mem. Social Dem. Party (SPD) 1927-46, Socialist Unity Party (SED) 1946-, SED Cen. Cttee. 1950-; cand. mem. SED Politburo 1950-54, mem. 1954-; Sec. for Agric. of SED Cen. Cttee. 1953-61; First Sec. of SED Frankfurt/Oder District 1961-71; Chair. Party Control Comm. 1971-; mem. Volkskammer (People's Chamber) 1950-, mem. Presidium; Chair. League of German-Soviet Friendship 1978-; Vaterländischer Verdienstorden in Gold, Karl-Marx-Orden and other decorations. *Address:* Volkskammer, Berlin F.1020, German Democratic Republic.

MUDD, Roger Harrison, M.A.; American news broadcaster; b. 9 Feb. 1928, Washington; s. of Kostka and Irma Iris (née Harrison) Mudd; m. Emma Jeanne Spears 1957; three s. one d.; ed. Washington and Lee Univ. and Univ of North Carolina; served with U.S. Army 1945-47; teacher Darlington School, Rome, Ga. 1951-52; Reporter Richmond (Va.) News Leader 1953; News Dir. Station WRNL, Richmond 1953-56; Reporter, radio and TV Station WTOP, Washington 1956-61; Corresp. CBS 1961-80; Chief Washington Corresp. NBC 1980-. *Address:* 4001 Nebraska Avenue, Washington, D.C. 20016, U.S.A. (Office).

MUDENDA, Elijah Haatukali Kaiba; Zambian agriculturist and politician; b. 6 June 1927; ed. Makerere Univ. Coll., Uganda, Fort Hare Univ. Coll., S. Africa, and Univ. of Cambridge; agricultural expert until 1962; mem. Legis. Assembly 1962-64; Parl. Sec. for Agric. 1962-64; mem. Zambian Parl. 1964-; Minister of Agric. 1964-67, of Finance 1967-68, of Foreign Affairs 1968-69, 1970-73, of Devt. and Finance 1969-70; Prime Minister 1975-77, also Minister of Nat. Guidance and Culture 1975-76; mem. Cen. Cttee. United Nat. Independence Party (UNIP), Chair. Political Sub-cttee. 1973-75, Rural Devt. Sub-cttee. 1977-78, Social and Cultural Sub-cttee. 1978-81, Econs. and Finance Sub-cttee. 1981-; Chair. Nat. Comm. for Devt. Planning April-July 1977. *Address:* United National Independence Party, Freedom House, P.O. Box 302, Lusaka, Zambia.

MUDENGE, Isack Stanislaus Gorerazvo, PH.D.; Zimbabwe diplomatist; b. 17 Dec. 1941; m.; four c.; ed. London and York Univs.; Lecturer, Univ.

of Sierra Leone 1971–73; various posts at Nat. Univ. of Lesotho 1973–80, Dir. Inst. of Southern African Studies 1979–80; Pres. Cen. African Historical Asscn. 1980–84; Perm. Sec. Ministry of Foreign Affairs of Zimbabwe 1980–85; Perm. Rep. to the UN 1985–. *Address:* Permanent Mission of the Republic of Zimbabwe to the United Nations, 19 East 47th Street, New York, N.Y. 10017, U.S.A. *Telephone:* 980-9511, 980-5084.

MUDGE, Dirk; Namibian (South West African) politician; Chair. of Turnhalle Constitutional Conf. 1977; Vice-Chair. of Nat. Party and mem. S.W. Africa Exec. Council Sept. 1977; formed Republican Party of S.W. Africa Oct. 1977; Chair. Democratic Turnhalle Alliance Nov. 1977–; mem. Constituent Ass. Nov. 1978–May 1979, Nat. Ass. 1979–83; Pres. Ministers' Council 1980–83, Minister for Finance and Governmental Affairs 1985–89. *Address:* c/o Private Bag 13289, PPS, Windhoek 9000, Namibia.

MUELLER, George E.; American electrical engineer and missile scientist; b. 16 July 1918, St. Louis, Mo.; s. of Edwin and Ella F. (Bosch) Mueller; m. 1st Maude Rosenbaum 1941 (divorced 1974), two d.; m. 2nd Darla Hix Schwartzman 1978; ed. Missouri School of Mines, Purdue Univ., Ohio State Univ.; Vice-Pres. for Research and Devt., Space Tech., Labs. Los Angeles until Aug. 1963; Assoc. Admin. for Manned Space Flight, Nat. Aeronautics and Space Admin. (NASA) 1963–69; Sr. Vice-Pres. Gen. Dynamics 1970–71; Chair., Pres. System Devt. Corpn. 1971–80, C.E.O. and Chair. 1981–83; Sr. Vice-Pres. Burroughs Corpn. 1981–83; Pres. George E. Mueller Corpn. 1984–; Fellow A.I.A.A., I.E.E.E., Royal Aeronautical Soc.; Pres. A.I.A.A. 1979; Pres. Int. Acad. of Astronomy 1982–; Vice-Pres. American Physical Soc.; mem. Nat. Acad. of Eng., New York Acad. of Sciences, American Geophysical Union; Hon. Fellow, British Interplanetary Soc., A.I.A.A.; NASA Distinguished Service Medal 1966, 1968, 1969, Eugen Sanger Medal 1970, Nat. Medal of Science 1971, Nat. Transportation Award 1979, Goddard Astronautics Award 1983. *Publications:* Communications Satellites (with E. Spangler), etc. *Address:* P.O. Box 5856, Santa Barbara, Calif. 93108, U.S.A.

MÜEZZINOĞLU, Ziya; Turkish civil servant and diplomatist; b. 5 May 1919; m.; one s. one d.; ed. Ankara Univ. and Germany and Switzerland; Insp. of Finance, Turkish Ministry of Finance 1942–53; Adviser to Treasury, Ministry of Finance 1953–59; Dir.-Gen. of Treasury 1959–60: Dir. Gen. of Treasury and Sec.-Gen. Org. for Int. Econ. Co-operation in Turkey 1960; mem. Constituent Ass. 1960; Chair. Interministerial Cttee. for Foreign Econ. Relations 1962; Sec. of State of State Planning Org. 1962–64; Amb. to Fed. Repub. of Germany 1964–67; Amb., Perm. Delegate of Turkey to the European Communities 1967–72; Minister of Finance 1972–73, 1978–79, of Trade June–July 1977; M.P. 1975–80; Republican People's Party (RPP). *Address:* Cankaya, Oran Sitesi 58/6, Ankara, Turkey.

MUGABE, Robert Gabriel, B.A., B.ADMIN., B.ED., M.SC.(ECON.), LL.M.; Zimbabwe politician and fmr. teacher; b. 21 Feb. 1924, Kutama; m. Sarah Mugabe; one c. (deceased); ed. Kutama and Empandeni Mission School, Fort Hare Univ. Coll., S. Africa, Univs. of S. Africa and London; teacher, at Drifontein Roman Catholic School, Umvuma 1952, Salisbury S. Primary School 1953, in Gwelo 1954, Chalimbana Teacher Training Coll. 1955, in Accra, Ghana 1958–60; entered politics 1960; Publicity Sec. of Nat. Dem. Party 1960–61; Publicity Sec. Zimbabwe African People's Union 1961; detained Sept.–Dec. 1962, March–April 1963; escaped to Tanzania April 1963; Co-founder of Zimbabwe African Nat. Union (ZANU) Aug. 1963; Sec.-Gen. Aug. 1963; in detention in Rhodesia 1964–74; Pres. ZANU; mem. Politburo ZANU 1984–; Jt. Leader of Patriotic Front (with Joshua Nkomo) 1976–79; contested Feb. 1980 elections as Leader of ZANU (PF) (name changed to ZANU 1984) Party; Prime Minister of Zimbabwe 1980–87; Pres. of Zimbabwe Jan. 1988–; Minister of Defence 1980–87, also fmrly. of Public Works, Industry and Tech.; attended Geneva Constitutional Conf. on Rhodesia 1976, Malta Conf., 1978, Lancaster House Conf. Sept.–Dec. 1979, Newsmaker of the Year Award (S. African Soc. of Journalists) 1980, Africa Prize 1988; Hon. Dr. (Ahmadu Bello Univ., Nigeria) 1980, (Edin. Univ.) 1984; Int. Human Rights Award (Howard Univ., Washington) 1981. *Address:* Office of the President, Harare, Zimbabwe.

MUGGERIDGE, Malcolm; British journalist; b. 24 March 1903; s. of the late H. T. Muggeridge; m. Katherine Dobbs; three s. (one deceased) one d.; ed. Selhurst Grammar School and Selwyn Coll., Cambridge; Lecturer, Egyptian Univ., Cairo 1927–30; editorial staff, Manchester Guardian 1930–32; Manchester Guardian corresp. in Moscow 1932–33; Asst. Ed. Calcutta Statesman 1934–35; editorial staff, Evening Standard 1935–36; served in E. and N. Africa, Italy and France, Maj., Intelligence Corps, in Second World War 1939–45; Daily Telegraph Washington corresp. 1946–47; Deputy Man. Ed. Daily Telegraph 1950–52; Ed. of Punch 1953–57; Rector of Edinburgh Univ. 1966–68; Légion d'honneur, Croix de guerre (with Palm), Médaille de la Résistance française. *Publications:* Three Flats (produced by Stage Society 1931), Autumnal Face 1931, Winter in Moscow 1933, The Earnest Atheist: A Life of Samuel Butler 1936, In a Valley of this Restless Mind 1938, The Thirties 1940; edited English edition of Ciano's Diary 1947, Ciano's Papers 1948; Affairs of the Heart 1949, Tread Softly for You Tread on My Jokes 1966, London à la Mode (with Paul Hogarth) 1966, Muggeridge Through the Microphone 1968, Jesus Rediscovered 1969, Something Beautiful for God 1971, Paul—Envoy Extraordinary (with Alec Vidler) 1972, Chronicles of Wasted Time: Vol. I The Green Stick 1972, Vol. II The Infernal Grove 1973, Jesus the Man who Lives 1976, A Third Testament

1977, A Twentieth Century Testimony 1978, Things Past 1978, Like It Was: Selections From the Diaries 1981, My Life in Pictures 1987, Conversion: A Spiritual Journey 1988. *Address:* Park Cottage, Robertsbridge, Sussex, England.

MUHAMMAD, Ali Nasser; Yemeni politician; b. 1939, Dathina Rural District; active mem. of Nat. Liberation Front (NLF) 1963–67; Gov. of the Islands 1967, of Second Province 1968; mem. Nat. Front Gen. Command March 1968; Minister of Local Govt. April 1969, of Defence 1969–77, of Educ. 1974–75; mem. Front Exec. Cttee. 1970; mem. Presidential Council of People's Democratic Repub. of Yemen 1971–78, Chair. June–Dec. 1978; Chair. Council of Ministers (Prime Minister) 1971–85; mem. Supreme People's Council (SPC) 1971, Chair. Presidium of SPC (Head of State) 1980–86 (overthrown in coup Jan. 1986); mem. Political Bureau of Nat. Front 1972–75, of United Political Org. Nat. Front 1975–78, of Yemen Socialist Party (YSP) 1978–86, Sec.-Gen. of YSP 1980–86.

MUHAMMADULLAH; Bangladesh lawyer and politician; b. 21 Nov. 1921, Saicha; m. Serajun Nahar Muhammadullah; three s. two d.; ed. Dacca and Calcutta Univs.; joined Dacca Bar 1950; Lawyer, High Court 1964; mem. Awami League 1950–; Sec. E. Pakistan Awami League 1952–72; mem. E. Pakistan Prov. Assembly 1970; Political Adviser to Acting Pres. Syed Nazrul Islam 1971; Deputy Speaker Bangladesh Constituent Assembly April–Nov. 1972, Speaker 1972–73; Speaker Bangladesh Parl. 1973–74: Acting Pres. of Bangladesh 1973–74, Pres. 1974–75; Minister of Land Admin. and Land Reforms Jan.–Aug. 1975; Vice-Pres. of Bangladesh Aug.–Nov. 1975.

MUHIEDDIN (see Mohieddin).

MUIR, (Isabella) Helen (Mary), C.B.E., M.A., D.PHIL., D.SC., F.R.S.; British biochemist; b. 20 Aug. 1920, Naini Tal, Uttar Pradesh, India; d. of the late Basil Fairlie Muir and Gwladys Helen Muir; ed. Somerville Coll., Univ. of Oxford; Research Fellow Univ. of Oxford 1947–48; Research Scientist Nat. Inst. for Medical Research 1948–54; at St. Mary's Hosp. 1954–66, Empire Rheumatism Council Fellow 1954–58, Pearl Research Fellow 1959–66; at Kennedy Inst. of Rheumatology 1966–, Head Div. Biochemistry 1966–, Dir. 1977–; Visiting Prof. of Biochemistry, Queen Elizabeth Coll. 1981–; Hon. Prof. of Biochemistry Charing Cross Hosp. Medical School 1978–; mem. Arthritis and Rheumatism Council Research Sub-Cttee. 1962–75, Editorial Bd. Biochemical Journal 1964–70, MRC Council 1973–77; Hon. Fellow Somerville Coll., Oxford; Hon. mem. American Soc. Biological Chemists; mem. Council Royal Soc. 1982–83, Council Chelsea Coll. 1982–85; Wellcome Trustee 1982–; numerous awards including Heberden Orator and Medallist 1976, Feldberg Prize 1977, Bunim Medal of American Arthritis Asscn. 1978; Co-Winner Basic Science Section Volvo Prize 1980; Neil Hamilton Fairley Medal 1981; CIBA Medal Biochemical Soc. 1981; Steindler Award Orthopaedic Research Soc., U.S.A. 1982. *Publications:* over 200 articles, mainly on biochemistry of connective tissues in relation to arthritis and inherited diseases; contrib. several specialist books. *Leisure interests:* gardening, music, horses, natural history, ballet. *Address:* The Kennedy Institute of Rheumatology, 6 Bute Gardens, Hammersmith, London, W6 7DW, England.

MUIR, Jean Elizabeth, C.B.E., F.R.S.A., F.C.S.D.; British couturier; d. of Cyril Muir and Phyllis Coy; m. Harry Leuckert 1955; ed. Dame Harper School, Bedford; designer, Jaeger Ltd. 1956–62, Jane & Jane; f. Jean Muir Ltd. 1966; mem. Business and Technician Education Council Bd. of Design 1977–78, the Council of the Design Centre (Dept. of Trade and Industry appointment) 1983, British Knitting and Clothing Export Council; trustee Victoria and Albert Museum 1983; Hon. D.R.C.A., Hon. D.Litt. (Newcastle upon Tyne) 1985, (Ulster) 1987; Dress of the Year award 1964, 1979; Ambassador award for achievement 1965; Harpers Bazaar trophy 1965; Maison Blanche Rex Int. Fashion Award (New Orleans) 1967, 1968, 1974; the Churchman's award 1970; Royal Designer for Industry 1972; Nelman Marcus award (Dallas) 1973; Hommage de la Mode (Fed. Française du Prêt-à-Porter Feminin) 1985, British Fashion Council award for services to Industry 1985; Chartered Soc. of Designers medal for outstanding achievement 1987; Textile Inst. Design medal 1987; Australian govt. bicentennial award 1988. *Address:* 59/61 Farringdon Road, London, EC1M 3HD, England. *Telephone:* (01) 831-0691 (Office).

MUIR, Kenneth (Arthur), M.A., F.B.A., F.R.S.L.; British university teacher and writer; b. 5 May 1907, London; s. of Robert D. Muir and Edith (née Barnes); m. Mary Ewen 1936; one s. one d.; ed. Epsom Coll. and St. Edmund Hall Oxford; Lecturer in English, St. John's Coll., York 1930–37; Lecturer in English Literature, Leeds Univ. 1937–51; King Alfred Prof. of English Literature, Liverpool Univ. 1951–74, Emer. Prof. and Hon. Research Fellow 1974–; Ed. Shakespeare Survey 1965–80; Chair. Int. Shakespeare Asscn. 1974–85; Dr. h.c. (Rouen, Dijon). *Publications include:* ed. Macbeth 1951, ed. King Lear 1952, Life and Letters of Sir Thomas Wyatt 1961, The Singularity of Shakespeare 1977, Four Comedies of Calderón (trans.) 1980, ed. Troilus and Cressida 1982, Shakespeare's Tragic Sequence 1972, Shakespeare's Comic Sequence 1979, Shakespeare's Sonnets 1979, Shakespeare's Didactic Art 1984, Shakespeare: Contrasts and Controversies 1985, King Lear: a Critical Study 1986, Antony and Cleopatra: a Critical Study 1986, Negative Capability and the Art of the Dramatist 1987. *Leisure interests:* theatre, writing and translating. *Address:* 6

Chetwynd Road, Oxton, Birkenhead, Merseyside, L43 2JJ, England. *Telephone:* (051) 652 3301.

MUIR WOOD, Sir Alan Marshall, Kt., M.A., F.ENG., F.R.S.; British consulting civil engineer; b. 8 Aug. 1921, London; s. of Edward Stephen Wood and Dorothy Wood (née Webb); m. Winifred Leyton Lanagan 1943; three s.; ed. Abbotsholme School, Derbyshire and Peterhouse, Cambridge; Engineer Officer, R.N. 1942-46; Asst. Engineer, British Rail 1946-50; Research Asst., Docks Exec. 1950-52; Engineer, Sir William Halcrow & Partners 1952-64, Consultant 1969-84, Partner, then Sr. Partner 1964-84; Fellow, Imperial Coll. London; Hon. Fellow, Peterhouse, Portsmouth Polytechnic; Hon. D.Sc. (City Univ.) 1978, (Southampton) 1986, Hon. LL.D. (Dundee); Telford Medal (ICE) 1976, Ewing Medal (ICE and Royal Soc.) 1984. *Publication:* Coastal Hydraulics 1969, 2nd edn. (ICE) 1976, with C. A. Fleming 1981. *Leisure interests:* music, arts and the countryside. *Address:* Franklands, Bere Court Road, Pangbourne, Berkshire, RG8 8JY, England.

MUIRSHIEL, 1st Viscount (cr. 1964), of Kilmacolm; **John Scott Maclay,** K.T., P.C., C.H., C.M.G.; British ship owner and politician; b. 26 Oct. 1905; s. of Joseph Paton, 1st Baron Maclay, and Martha Strang; m. Betty L'Estrange Astley 1930 (died 1974); ed. Winchester and Trinity Coll., Cambridge; M.P. for Montrose Burghs 1940-50, for Renfrewshire West 1950-64; Head British Merchant Shipping Mission to U.S.A. 1944; Parl. Sec. Ministry of Production 1945; Minister of Transport and Civil Aviation 1951-52; Minister of State for Colonial Affairs 1956-57; Sec. of State for Scotland 1957-62; Pres. Assembly Western European Union 1955-56; Pres. Nat. Liberal Council 1957-65; Chair. Jt. Exchequer Bd. (Northern Ireland) 1965-73; Dir. Clydesdale Bank 1970-82; Lord Lieut. of Renfrewshire 1968-81, D.L. 1981; Hon. LL.D. (Edinburgh) 1963, (Strathclyde) 1966, (Glasgow) 1970. *Address:* Knapps, Kilmacolm, Renfrewshire, Scotland. *Telephone:* (050 587) 2770.

MUKASHEV, Salamat; Soviet partyworker and politician; b. 1927, Kazakhstan; ed. All-Union High School of Professional Cadres; mem. CPSU 1950-; accountant at oil-works in Kazakhstan 1947-49; instructor with trade-union org. in the oil industry in Kazakhstan 1949-52; instructor of Gurev Dist. Cttee., Pres. of Gurev Dist. Soviet Trade Union 1952-61; First Sec. of regional cttee. in Kazakhstan 1961-65, First Sec. of regional cttee. in Gurev Dist., First Sec. of Gurev Dist. Cttee. 1965-77; Pres. of Kazakhstan Republican Trade-Union Movt. 1977-80; First Sec. of Mangyshlak regional cttee. 1980-85; Pres. of Presidium of Supreme Soviet of Kazakhstan S.S.R. 1985-; cand. mem. of Cen. Cttee. of CPSU 1986-89; Deputy Pres. of Supreme Soviet of U.S.S.R. 1985-. *Address:* U.S.S.R. Supreme Soviet, Kremlin, U.S.S.R.

MUKHA, Stepan Nesterovich; Soviet politician; Sec. Dnepropetrovsk City Cttee. Ukrainian Komsomol 1958; Deputy to Supreme Soviet of Ukrainian S.S.R. 1975-; First Deputy Chair. of Cttee. for State Security of Ukranian S.S.R. -1982, Chair. 1982-; cand. mem. of Politburo of Cen. Cttee. of Ukrainian CP 1982-. *Address:* Central Committee of the Ukrainian Communist Party, Kiev, Ukrainian S.S.R., U.S.S.R.

MUKHERJEE, Bharati; American (b. Indian) lecturer and author; b. 1950, India; m. Clark Blaise; two s.; ed. Univs. of Calcutta, Baroda and Iowa; Prof. of English, McGill Univ.; lecturer Skidmore Coll.; lecturer in literature and creative writing, Queen's Coll., New York. *Publications include:* The Tiger's Daughter 1971, The Tiger's Daughter and Wife 1975, Days and Night in Calcutta 1977, Darkness 1985, The Sorrow and the Terror (with Clark Blaise) 1987, The Middleman and Other Stories (Nat. Book Critics Circle Award for Fiction 1988) 1988.

MUKHERJEE, Pranab Kumar, M.A., LL.B.; Indian politician; b. 11 Dec. 1935, Mirati, Birbhum District, W. Bengal; s. of Mamada Kinkar; m.; two s. one d.; ed. Univ. of Calcutta; started career as lecturer; Ed. Palli-O-Panchayat Sambad (Bengali monthly); founder-Ed. Desher Dak (Bengali weekly) 1967-71; mem. Rajya Sabha 1969-, Leader 1980-88; Deputy Minister of Industrial Devt., Govt. of India 1973; Deputy Minister for Shipping and Transport Jan.-Oct. 1974; Minister of State, Ministry of Finance 1974-75; Minister for Revenue and Banking 1975-77; Minister of Commerce 1980-82, of Finance Jan.-Sept. 1982, of Finance 1982-85; f. Rashtriya Samajwadi Congress 1987-; mem. Exec. Cttee. Congress (I) Party 1972-73, All India Congress Cttee. 1986; Treas. Congress (I) Party, mem. Working Cttee., Deputy Leader in Rajya Sabha. *Publications:* Bangla Congress: An Aspect of Constitutional Problems in Bengal 1967, Mid-term Election 1969. *Address:* 2 Jantar Mantar Road, New Delhi 110001, India.

MUKHTAR, Mallam Abdul-Muhyi Mohammed; Nigerian business executive; b. 30 May 1944, Azare; s. of Mallam Mukhtar Abdallah and Hajia Asama'u Mukhtar; m. Hajia A. Mukhtar 1976; four s.; Admin. Man. MANSA Construction Co. Ltd.; Chair. SAA Group 1975-; Councillor Shira Local Govt. Council 1976-79; Dir. Fed. Mortgage Bank of Nigeria Ltd. 1980-83; Chair. Bauchi State Investment and Properties Devt. Co. Ltd. 1984-85; Daily Times Group 1984-86; W. Africa Magazine, London 1984-86; mem. Bd. of Dirs. Bauchi State Urban Utilities Bd. 1986-, Constitution Reviewing Cttee. 1987-88, Nigeria Tobacco Co. Ltd. Scholarship 1968. *Leisure interests:* tree planting and sports. *Address:* Badaluxus Business Complex, No. 19 Kano Road, P.O. Box 84, Azare, Bauchi State; SAA

House, No. 6 Zaria Road, P.O. Box 519, Kano, Kano State, Nigeria. *Telephone:* 064-622440/623220; 071-20595/20599.

MULAMBA NYUNYI WA KADIMA, Gen. (Léonard); Zairian army officer, politician and diplomatist; b. 1928, Luluabourg (now Kananga); s. of Kadima and Ngalula Mulamba; m. Adolphine N'galula 1956; six s. two d.; ed. Mil. School, Luluabourg; commissioned 1949; Maj. and Deputy Dir. of Cabinet, Ministry of Defence 1961-64; Lieut.-Col. 1962; Col., Chief of Staff and Commr. of Eastern Province (now Haut Zaïre) after re-occupation of Kivu Province 1964-65; Prime Minister 1965-66; Pres. Soc. nationale d'Assurances (SONAS) 1966; Amb. to India 1967-69; Amb. to Japan 1969-76, also accred. to Repub. of Korea 1971-76; Amb. to Brazil 1976-79; Gén. de Division, Gén. de Corps d'Armée 1979-; Mil. Medal, Cross of Bravery, Commdr. Ordre de la Couronne (Belgium), Grand Officier Ordre nat. du Léopard (Zaire), Ordre du Mérite (Cen. African Republic), Compagnon de la Révolution. *Leisure interests:* hunting, reading. *Address:* Chancellerie des Ordres Nationaux, B.P. 2014, Kinshasa, Zaire.

MULCAHY, Geoffrey John, B.SC., M.B.A.; British business executive; b. 7 Feb. 1942, Sunderland; s. of Maurice Mulcahy and Kathleen (née Blankinsop) Mulcahy; m. Valerie Elizabeth Mulcahy 1965; one s. one d.; ed. King's School, Worcester, Univ. of Manchester, Harvard Univ.; started career in labour relations, marketing and planning with Esso Corpn.; Finance Dir. Norton Abrasives' European Div., then for British Sugar; joined Woolworth Holdings 1983, firstly as Group Financial Dir., then Group Man. Dir. 1984-86, C.E.O. 1986-; non-exec. Dir. British Telecom. *Leisure interest:* sailing. *Address:* Woolworth Holdings PLC, North West House, 119 Marylebone Road, London, NW1 5PX, England. *Telephone:* 01-724 7749.

MULCAHY, Robert E., B.S.; American company executive; b. 2 March 1932, Cambridge, Mass.; s. of George Frances and Hazel (Douglass) Mulcahy; m. Ethel Walworth 1953; two s. two d.; ed. Lowell Textile Inst.; joined Allied Chemical Corpn. 1953, Nat. Aniline Div. 1953-63, Fibers Div. 1963-69, Corp. office 1969, Asst. to Group Vice-Pres., Fabricated Products Div. 1969-71, Vice-Pres. and Gen. Man. of Consumer Group 1969, Pres. 1969-71, Pres. Fibers Div. 1971-74, Group Vice-Pres. 1974-75, mem. Bd. of Dirs. 1975, Pres., Dir. 1975-79, Asst. to Chair. and Dir. 1979-80; Pres. Allied Chemical Corpn. 1975-79; Sr. Assoc., Corpn. Dir. Inc. 1980-83; Pres. Counsellors to Management, Inc. 1984-. *Address:* 42 Fairview Avenue, Verona, N.J. 07044, U.S.A.

MULDOON, Rt. Hon. Sir Robert David, P.C., G.C.M.G., C.H., M.P., F.C.A.N.Z., C.M.A.N.Z., F.C.I.S., A.I.A.N.Z.; New Zealand politician and public accountant; b. 25 Sept. 1921, Auckland; s. of James H. and Amie R. Muldoon; m. Thea Dale Flyger 1951; one s. two d.; ed. Mount Albert Grammar School; Sr. Partner, Kendon Mills Muldoon and Browne, Auckland; Lecturer in Auditing 1948-54; Pres. N.Z. Inst. of Cost Accountants 1956, Auckland Horticultural Council 1959-60; M.P. for Tamaki 1960-; Parl. Under-Sec. to Minister of Finance 1963-66; Minister of Tourism and Publicity 1967, of Finance 1967-72, 1975-84; Deputy Prime Minister Feb.-Dec. 1972; Deputy Leader of the Opposition 1973-74, Leader 1974-75, July-Nov. 1984; Prime Minister 1975-84; Shadow Minister of Foreign Affairs 1986; Chair. Global Econ. Action Inst. 1988-; mem. Select Cttee. on Fishing Industry 1963, Road Safety 1965, Parl. Procedure 1967; mem. Public Expenditure Cttee. 1961-66, Chair. 1963-66; Dominion Councillor, N.Z. Nat. Party 1960-; Chair. Bd. of Govs. IMF 1978-79; Fellow, N.Z. Inst. of Cost Accountants, N.Z. Soc. of Accountants, Inst. of Chartered Secs., Chartered Inst. of Man. Accountants, London, Royal Horticultural Soc.; Leverhulme Prize, Inst. of Cost and Works Accountants 1946, Maxwell Award, N.Z. Inst. of Cost Accountants 1956. *Publications:* Rise and Fall of a Young Turk 1974, Muldoon 1977, My Way 1981, The New Zealand Economy—A Personal View 1985, No 8 1986. *Leisure interest:* horticulture especially lilies. *Address:* 7 Homewood Place, Birkenhead, Auckland 10, New Zealand. *Telephone:* 4190343.

MULDOWNEY, Dominic John, B.PHIL.; British composer; b. 19 July 1952, Southampton; s. of William Muldowney and Barbara Muldowney (née Lavender); m. Diane Ellen Trevis 1986; ed. Taunton's Grammar School, Southampton and York Univ.; Composer-in-Residence to Southern Arts Asscn. 1974-76; Music Dir., Nat. Theatre 1976-82, Head of Music 1982-; has composed music for British and int. festivals, for many films and TV and over 50 scores for the theatre. *Publications:* Piano Concerto 1983, Saxophone Concerto 1984, Sinfonietta 1986, Ars Subtilior 1987, Lonely Hearts 1988. *Leisure interest:* France. *Address:* c/o Music Department, National Theatre, South Bank, London, SE1 1PX, England.

MULHOLLAND, William David, Jr., LL.D.; American banker; b. 16 June 1926, Albany, N.Y.; s. of William David and Helen Flack Mulholland; m. Nancy Louise Booth 1957; five s. four d.; ed. Christian Brothers Acad., Albany, Harvard Coll. and Harvard Graduate School of Business Admin.; served with U.S. Army, with service in Philippines as Co. Commdr. 1944-46; joined Morgan Stanley & Co. (investment bankers) New York 1952, Partner 1962-69, resgnd.; Pres. and C.E.O. Churchill Falls (Labrador) Corpn. Ltd. 1969-74, Brinco Ltd. 1969-75; Pres. Bank of Montreal 1975-81, C.E.O. 1979-, Chair. July 1981-. *Leisure interests:* fishing, shooting, hunting. *Address:* Bank of Montreal, 129 St. James Street, P.O. Box 6002, Montreal, Quebec H3G 2KI, Canada.

MÜLLER, Charles; Swiss diplomatist and international official; b. 4 July 1922, Zürich; s. of Hans Martin and Clara (née Meyer) Müller; m. Marlise

Brügger 1950; ed. Univs. of Zürich and Geneva and Graduate Inst. of Int. Studies, Geneva; Ministry of Foreign Affairs 1946-50; Embassy, Cairo 1950-55, Moscow 1955-58; Ministry of Foreign Affairs 1958-60; Head of Gen. and Legal Dept., European Free Trade Assn. (EFTA) 1960-61, Asst. Sec.-Gen. 1961-65, Deputy Sec.-Gen. 1965-66; Deputy Head of Mission, Washington, D.C. 1967-70; Amb. to Indonesia, Khmer Repub. and Repub. of Viet-Nam 1970-73; Head, Europe-N. America Div., Ministry of Foreign Affairs 1973-75; Sec.-Gen. EFTA 1976-81. *Leisure interests:* skiing, golf, painting.

MÜLLER, Claus, DR. RER. NAT.; German university professor and consultant; b. 20 Feb. 1920, Solingen; s. of Michael Müller and Grete (née Porfen) Müller; m. Irmgard Döring 1947; two s. one d.; ed. Univs. of Bonn and Munich; Asst. Prof. Göttingen Univ. 1945-46; service in German army and navy 1941-45; lecturer Bonn Univ. 1947-55; Prof. and Dir. Inst. of Math. Sciences, Tech. Univ. of Aachen 1955-85, Prof. Emer. 1985-; Fellow Peterhouse, Cambridge 1948; lecturer, Univ. Coll. Hull 1949; Visiting Prof. and Consultant Corant Inst., New York, Math. Residential Center Madison 1955-65. *Publications:* Foundations of the Mathematical Theory of Electromagnetic Waves, Spherical Harmonics; specialist articles in math. *Leisure interest:* music. *Address:* Horbacher Strasse 33, D-5100 Aachen, Federal Republic of Germany. *Telephone:* (10241) 12661.

MÜLLER, Gebhard, D.JUR.; German lawyer; b. 17 April 1900, Füramoos, Biberach; s. of Johannes and Josefa Müller; m. Marianne Lutz 1940; three s.; ed. Univs. of Tübingen and Berlin; held several legal positions in Württemberg Courts 1929-45; engaged in reconstruction of judicial system in Württemberg-Hohenzollern 1945; Ministerial Dir. in Provincial Ministry of Justice Dec. 1946; Provincial Pres. of CDU 1947-57; Pres. of State, Minister of Finance and of Justice of Württemberg-Hohenzollern 1948-52, Prime Minister of Baden-Württemberg 1953-58; mem. Bundesrat 1949-52, 1953-58; Pres. Constitutional Court, Karlsruhe 1959-71; Hon. Senator Univ. of Tübingen; Grosskreuzverdienstorden 1953, Grosskreuz päpstliches Piusorden 1972. *Leisure interests:* modern history, 18th and 19th century French literature. *Address:* Friedrich-Ebert-Strasse 112, 7000 Stuttgart 1, Federal Republic of Germany. *Telephone:* 25-15-83.

MÜLLER, Gerhard, DR.THEOL.; German ecclesiastic; b. 10 May 1929, Marburg/Lahn; s. of Karl Müller and Elisabeth Landau; m. Ursula Herboth 1957; two s.; ed. Marburg, Göttingen and Tübingen; priest in Hanau/Main 1956-57; Deutsche Forschungsgemeinschaft scholarship, Italy 1957-59; Asst., Ecumenical Seminar, Univ. of Marburg 1959-61, Docent, Faculty of Theology 1961-66; guest lecturer, German Historical Inst., Rome 1966-67; Prof. of Historical Theology (Modern Church History), Univ. of Erlangen 1967-82; Evangelical-Lutheran Bishop of Brunswick Oct. 1982-; mem. Mainz and Netherlands Acads.; Dr.theol. h.c. (St. Andrews). *Publications:* Franz Lambert von Avignon und die Reformation in Hessen 1958, Nuntiaturberichte aus Deutschland 1530-1532 (2 vols.) 1963, 1969, Die römische Kurie und die Reformation 1523-1534 1969, Die Rechtfertigungslehre 1977, Reformation und Stadt 1981, Zwischen Reformation und Gegenwart 1983, Zwischen Reformation und Gegenwart II 1988; ed. works of Andreas Osiander and a 17-vol. theological encyclopaedia. *Address:* 3340 Wolfenbüttel, Salzdahlumer Strasse 43; 3340, Wolfenbüttel, Neuer Weg 88-90, Federal Republic of Germany. *Telephone:* 05331/802333; 05331/802100.

MÜLLER, K. Alex, PH.D.; Swiss physicist; b. 20 April 1927; ed. Swiss Fed. Inst. of Tech.; with IBM Research Lab. Rüschlikon 1963-; Nobel Prize for Physics (with G. Bednorz) for discovery of new superconducting materials 1987. *Address:* IBM Zürich Research Laboratory, Säumerstrasse 4, CH-8803 Rüschlikon, Switzerland. *Telephone:* 41-1-72 48 111.

MÜLLER, Margarete; German politician and agronomist; b. 18 Feb. 1931, Neustadt, Upper Silesia; ed. Leningrad Univ., U.S.S.R.; joined Sozialistische Einheitspartei Deutschlands (SED) 1951; Chair. of an agricultural production co-operative 1958-; mem. SED Cen. Cttee., Volkskammer and cand. mem. Politburo 1963-; mem. Council of State 1971-; Vaterländischer Verdienstorden in Silber, Banner der Arbeit and other decorations. *Address:* 102 Berlin, Am-Marx-Engels Platz 2, German Democratic Republic.

MULLER, Steven, PH.D.; American (b. German) university and hospital president; b. 22 Nov. 1927, Hamburg, Germany; s. of Werner A. and Marianne (Hartstein) Muller; m. Margie Hellman 1951; two d.; ed. Hollywood High School, Los Angeles, Univ. of Calif., Los Angeles, Oxford Univ., Cornell Univ.; Instructor in Political Science, Wells Coll. 1953; U.S. Army 1954-55; Research Fellow in Social Science, Cornell Univ. 1955-56; Asst. Prof. of Political Science, Haverford Coll. 1956-58; Asst. Prof. of Govt., Cornell Univ. 1958-61, Assoc. Prof. and Dir. Center for Int. Studies 1961-66, Vice-Pres. for Public Affairs 1966-71; Provost, Johns Hopkins Univ. 1971-72, Pres. 1972-; Pres. Johns Hopkins Hosp. 1972-83; mem. Bd. of Dirs., CSX Corpn., German Marshall Fund of the U.S., Millipore Corpn., Beneficial Corpn., Alex. Brown & Sons Inc., Maryland Acad. of Sciences; mem. American Acad. Arts and Sciences, Council Foreign Relations, American Political Science Assen., Int. Inst. Strategic Studies; Commander's Cross of the Order of Merit (Fed. Repub. of Germany). *Publications:* Documents on European Government 1963; articles in learned journals. *Address:* The Johns Hopkins University, 34th and Charles Streets, Balti-

more, Md. 21218 (Office); 928½ Fell Street, Baltimore, Md. 21231, U.S.A. (Home). *Telephone:* (301) 338-8068 (Office); (301) 522-7857 (Home).

MULLER, Thomas Frederik; South African businessman; b. 12 Dec. 1916; s. of late Cornelius Johannes and Martha Aletta (née Dreyer) Muller; m. 1st Susanna Elizabeth Jordaan 1942 (died 1968), two d.; m. 2nd Nicolette van Schalkwyk 1970, one s. one step-s. one step-d.; ed. Ermelo High School, Univ. of the Witwatersrand and Birmingham Univ., England; employed by Rand Leases Mine of Anglo-Transvaal group of cos. 1937-49; Mine Man., Virginia Mine 1949-55; Asst. Consulting Engineer, Head Office 1955-57; Tech. Man., Federale Mynbou Beperk Feb. 1957-58, Gen. Man. 1958-61, Man. Dir. 1961-71; Man. Dir. Gen. Mining and Finance Corpn. Ltd. 1963-71; Chair. S. African Iron and Steel Industrial Corpn. Ltd. (ISCOR) 1971-83; Chair. Mercedes-Benz (S.A.) Ltd. and other cos.; fmr. Chancellor Univ. of Zululand; fmr. Pres. Chamber of Mines of S. Africa, Afrikaanse Handelsinstituut; mem. Prime Minister's Econ. Advisory Council; Hon. D.Comm. (Potchefstroom). *Publications:* several papers on mining matters, especially on shaft-sinking at Virginia and Merriespruit Mines. *Leisure interests:* farming, golf and angling. *Address:* 17 Molesey Avenue, Auckland Park, Johannesburg 2092, South Africa (Home). *Telephone:* 726-3445 (Home).

MÜLLER-SEIDEL. Walter, DR. PHIL.; German professor of modern literature; b. 1 July 1918, Schöna; s. of Martin Müller-Seidel and Rosa (née Seidel) Müller; m. Ilse Peters 1950; one s.; ed. Univs. of Leipzig and Heidelberg; lecturer Univ. of Cologne 1958, Privat-dozent 1958-59; Prof. Univ. of Munich 1960-65; Ordinary Prof. 1965, now Emer.; mem. Bayerischen Akademie der Wissenschaften 1974. *Publications:* Versehen und Erkennen: Eine Studie über Heinrich von Kleist 1961, Probleme der literarischen Wertung 1965, Theodor Fontane: Soziale Romankunst in Deutschland 1975, Die Geschichtlichkeit der deutscher Klassik 1983, Die Deportation des Menschen, Kafkas Erzählung 'In der Strafkolonie' im europäischen Kontext 1986. *Address:* Pienzenauerstrasse 164, 8000 Munich 81, Federal Republic of Germany. *Telephone:* 988250.

MÜLLER-WARMUTH, Werner; German professor of physical chemistry; b. 1 Oct. 1929, Hamburg; s. of Viktor and Luise Müller-Warmuth; m. Inge Schmidtke 1955; two s.; ed. Univs. of Frankfurt and Mainz; with Max Planck Inst. für Chemie, Mainz 1955-65; Euratom Research Center, Ispra, Italy 1965-73; Prof. and Dir. Inst. für Physikalische Chemie, Univ. of Münster 1973-, Rector 1978-82; Pres. Conf. of Univ. Rectors of Nordrhein-Westfalen 1981-83; Hon. Prof., Univ. of Lima. *Publications:* more than 150 scientific publications on physical chem., spectroscopy, materials, etc. *Address:* Institut für Physikalische Chemie, Schlossplatz 4/7, D-4400 Münster (Office); Julius-Hart-Strasse 6, D-4400 Münster, Federal Republic of Germany (Home). *Telephone:* 0251/833421 (Office); 0251/22104 (Home).

MULLEY, Baron (Life Peer) cr. 1983, of Manor Park in the City of Sheffield; **Frederick William Mulley,** P.C.; British barrister, economist and politician; b. 3 July 1918, Leamington Spa, Warwicks.; m. Joan Phillips 1948; two d.; ed. Warwick School and Christ Church, Oxford; fmr. clerk, Nat. Health Insurance Cttee., Warwicks.; Army Service 1939-45, Prisoner-of-War 1940-45; Adult Scholar, Christ Church, Oxford 1945-47; Research Studentship, Nuffield Coll., Oxford 1947-48; Fellow of St. Catharine's Coll., Cambridge 1948-50; M.P. 1950-83; Parl. Pvt. Sec. to Minister of Works 1951; called to Bar, Inner Temple 1954; mem. Nat. Exec. Cttee. Labour Party 1957-58, 1960-80; Deputy Sec. of State for Defence and Minister of Defence for the Army 1964-65; Minister of Aviation 1965-67; Minister of State for Foreign Affairs 1967-69; Minister of Transport 1969-70, 1974-75; Chair. Labour Party 1974-75; Sec. of State for Educ. and Science 1975-76, for Defence 1976-79, Pres. Parl. Assembly of WEU 1980-83; Deputy Chair. Sheffield Devt. Corpn. 1988-; Dir. Brassey's Defence Publs. 1983-; mem. Council of Europe 1980-83. *Publication:* The Politics of Western Defence 1962. *Address:* House of Lords, London, S.W.1, England.

MULLOVA, Viktoria; Soviet violinist; b. 27 Nov. 1959, Moscow; d. of Raisa Mullov and Juri Mullov; studied in Moscow at Cen. Music School and Moscow Conservatory under Leonid Kogan; first prize at Sibelius Competition, Helsinki 1981, Gold Medal, Tchaikovsky Competition, Moscow 1983; left U.S.S.R. 1983; has appeared with Berlin Philharmonic, Royal Philharmonic, Cleveland, Pittsburgh, Israel Philharmonic and many others. *Recordings include:* Tchaikovsky and Sibelius Violin Concertos with Boston Symphony under Seiji Ozawa (Grand Prix du disque). *Leisure interests:* reading, cinema, skiing, tennis, mountain climbing. *Address:* c/o Harold Holt Ltd., 31 Sinclair Rd., London, W14 0NS, England. *Telephone:* 01-603 4600.

MULRONEY, (Martin) Brian, M.P., LL.L.; Canadian politician and former business executive; b. 20 March 1939, Baie Comeau, Que.; s. of Benedict and Irene (O'Shea) Mulroney; m. Mila Pivnicki 1973; three s. one d.; ed. St. Francis Xavier Univ. and Univ. Laval; called to Bar of Quebec 1965; Partner, Ogilvy, Cope, Porteous, Montgomery, Renault, Clarke & Kirkpatrick, Montreal 1965-76; Exec. Vice-Pres. (Corp. Affairs), Iron Ore Co. of Canada 1976-77, Pres. and Dir. 1977-83; elected Leader, Progressive Party of Canada 1983; mem. Parl. 1983-; Prime Minister of Canada Sept. 1984-; Hon. LL.D. (Memorial and St. Francis Xavier Univs.). *Publication:* Where I Stand 1983. *Leisure interests:* tennis, swimming. *Address:* Office of the Prime Minister, Langevin Block, 80 Wellington Street, Ottawa, K1A 0A2, Canada.

MUMFORD, David Bryant, PH.D.; American professor of mathematics; b. 11 June 1937, Sussex, England; s. of William Bryant Mumford and Grace Schiott; m. Erika Jentsch 1959; three s. one d.; ed. Harvard Univ.; Higgins Prof. of Maths. Harvard Univ. 1967–, MacArthur Fellow 1987–(92); mem. N.A.S.; Hon. D. Sc. (Warwick) 1983; Fields Medal 1974. *Publications:* Geometric Invariant Theory 1965, Abelian Varieties 1970, Algebraic Geometry I 1976. *Leisure interest:* sailing. *Address:* 26 Gray Street, Cambridge, Mass. 02138, U.S.A. *Telephone:* (617) 547-2639.

MUMFORD, Lewis; American writer; b. 19 Oct. 1895; Flushing, N.Y.; s. of Lewis Mack and Elvina Baron Mumford; m. Sophia Wittenberg 1921; one s. (killed 1944) one d.; ed New York City Coll., New York Univ., Columbia Univ.; Assoc. Ed. The Dial 1919; Acting Ed. Sociological Review, London 1920; Lecturer, Geneva School of Int. Studies 1925 and 1929; Guernsey Centre Moore Foundation Lecturer, Dartmouth Coll. 1929; Earle Lecturer, Pacific School of Religion 1931; Bampton Lecturer, Columbia Univ. 1951; co-Ed. The American Caravan 1926–36; mem. Bd. of Higher Educ., City of New York 1935–37; mem. Comm. on Teacher Educ., American Council on Educ. 1938–44; Consultant on Planning, City and County Park Bd., Honolulu 1938; Prof. of Humanities, Stanford Univ. 1942–44; Prof. Univ. Pennsylvania 1952–61, Hon. Fellow R.I.B.A. 1942; Hon. mem. Town Planning Inst. (U.K.) 1946; Hon. Vice-Pres. Int. Housing and Town Planning Fed. 1947; Bemis Prof. M.I.T. 1957–60, Visiting Abrams Prof. 1975; Hon. Fellow Stanford Univ. 1941; Fellow American Acad. of Arts and Sciences; mem. American Philosophical Soc.; mem. Nat. Inst. of Arts and Letters, Pres. American Acad. of Arts and Letters 1963–65; Consultant on Planning, Christ Church, Oxford, England; hon. mem. A.I.A., American Inst. of Planners; Co-Chair. Wenner-Gren Conf. on Man's Role in shaping the Face of the Earth 1955; Guggenheim Fellow 1932, 1938, 1956; Ford Research Prof. Univ. of Pa. 1959–61, Univ. of Calif. 1961–62; Saposnekow lecturer, City Coll. of New York 1962, Hon. LL.D. (Edinburgh), Hon. D.Arch. (Rome) and numerous honorary doctorates from American univs.; numerous medals and awards incl. Royal Gold Medal, R.I.B.A. 1961, Nat. Medal for Literature 1972, for Arts 1986, Prix Mondial del Duca 1976, Benjamin Franklin Medal 1983. *Publications:* Story of Utopias 1922, Sticks and Stones 1924, The Golden Day 1926, Herman Melville 1929, The Brown Decades 1931, Technics and Civilisation 1934, The Culture of Cities 1938, Whither Honolulu? 1938, Men Must Act 1939, Faith for Living 1940, The South in Architecture 1941, The Condition of Man 1944, City Development 1945, Values for Survival 1946, Green Memories—The Story of Geddes Mumford 1947, The Conduct of Life 1951, Art and Technics 1952, In the Name of Sanity 1954, The Transformations of Man 1956, The City in History 1961, The Highway and the City 1963, Technics and Human Development 1967, The Urban Prospect 1968, The Pentagon of Power 1970, Interpretations and Forecasts 1922–1972 1972, Findings and Keepings 1914–1936—Analects for an Autobiography 1975, My Works and Days: A Personal Chronicle 1895-1975 1979, Sketches From Life 1982. *Leisure interest:* gardening. *Address:* Amenia, N.Y. 12501, U.S.A. *Telephone:* (914) 373-8579.

MUMFORD, Milton Christopher, A.B.; American businessman; b. 14 April 1913, Marissa, Ill.; s. of Manly J. Mumford and Emily Stearns; m. Dorothea Louise Green 1942; one s. two d.; ed. Univ. of Illinois; joined Marshall Field and Co., Chicago 1935, Vice-Pres. 1948–54, Gen. Man. Fieldcrest Mills Div. 1950–53; Pres. Fieldcrest Mills Inc. 1953–54; Vice-Pres. Lever Bros. Co. 1954–55, Exec. Vice-Pres. 1955–59, Pres. and C.E.O. 1959–65, Chair. of Bd. 1964–72; Dir. Equitable Life Assurance Soc. of U.S. 1962–; Chair. Educational Facilities Labs. Inc. (Ford Foundation) 1959–72; Trustee, Consolidated Edison Co. of New York 1964–; Dir. Stamford Hosp., Stamford, Conn. 1964–, Crown Zellerbach Corpn. 1965–, Nat. Educational TV 1965–69, Unilever subsidiaries 1965–, Fed. Reserve Bank of New York 1966–72; Nat. Volunteer Chair., United Community Campaigns of America 1966; mem. Nat. Industrial Conf. Bd. 1959–72; Dir. Nat. Merit Scholar Scholarship Corpn. 1965–71; Trustee, Presbyterian Hosp. (New York) 1967–; mem. Nat. Council Foreign Policy Assen. 1967–, Emergency Cttee. for American Trade 1968–72, Nat. Ind. Pollution Control Council 1970–72, Nat. Advisory Cttee. of "Jobs for Veterans" 1970; Dir. Int. Executives Service Corps. 1968–72; Hon. LL.D. (Long Island); Legion of Merit, U.S.N. 1945; Alumni Achievement Award (Univ. of Illinois) 1971. *Address:* Lever Brothers Co., 390 Park Avenue, New York, N.Y. 10022 (Office); P.O. Box 1379, Pebble Beach, Calif. 93953, U.S.A. (Home). *Telephone:* (212) 688-6000 (Office).

MUNA, Solomon Tandeng; Cameroonian politician; b. 1912, Ngyn-Mbo, Momo Division; s. of Muna Tayim and Ama Keng Muna; m. Elizabeth Fri Muna 1937; seven s. one d.; ed. Teacher Training Coll., Kumba and Univ. of London Inst. of Educ.; M.P. for Bamenda Dist. 1951; Eastern Nigeria Minister for Public Works 1951; Minister of Works, subsequently Minister of Commerce and Industries, Minister of Finance, Southern Cameroon Region; Fed. Minister of Transport, Mines, Posts and Telecommunications of Cameroon 1961–68; Prime Minister of W. Cameroon 1968–72, also Vice-Pres. Fed. Repub. of Cameroon 1970–72; Minister of State 1972–73; Pres. Nat. Assembly 1973–; Co-Pres. ACP-EEC States Consultative Assembly 1978–82; fmrly. Chair. Bd. of Dirs. Cameroon Railways, Chair. Higher

Cttee. on Cameroon Ports; has represented Cameroon at various int. confs.; mem. Bureau of the Cameroon People's Democratic Movt. (CPDM); Chief Scout of Cameroon 1970–77; Chair. African Scout Cttee. 1973–77, mem. World Bureau of Scouts 1975, Vice-Chair. World Scout Cttee. 1977–81; Commdr., Ordre de la Valeur du Cameroun, Officier, Légion d'honneur and numerous other foreign decorations. *Leisure interests:* horseback riding, stamp collecting, scouting, gardening, inland fish-farming. *Address:* c/o National Assembly, Yaoundé, Republic of Cameroon. *Telephone:* Yaoundé 22-20-44 (Office); 22-43-44 (Home).

MÜNCHINGER, Karl; German musician; b. 29 May 1915, Stuttgart; s. of Karl and Emilie Münchinger; m. Olga Rockenhäuser 1948; ed. Staatliche Musikhochschule, Stuttgart and Konservatorium Leipzig; church organist in Stuttgart 1937–41; Conductor Niedersachsenorchester Hanover 1941–43; founded Stuttgart Chamber Orchestra 1945, Conductor 1945–, Klassische Philharmonie Stuttgart 1966, Conductor 1966–; guest conductor of various symphony orchestras; Grosses Verdienstkreuz mit Stern and Schulterband 1985; Commdr. des Arts et des Lettres, Officier des Arts et des Lettres; Hon. Citizen of Menton; Württemberg-Badisches Verdienstkreuz, Stuttgart Hon. Citizen's Medal; Strasbourg Gold Medal for services to culture 1985, Officier, Légion d'honneur 1986; Officer of the Order of the Crown (Belgium); Hon. Prof. Kulturministerium Baden-Württemberg. *Leisure interests:* collecting antiques and books. *Address:* Haus am Rebenhang, 7000 Stuttgart-Rotenberg, Federal Republic of Germany. *Telephone:* Stuttgart 6 19 21-21.

MÜNCHMEYER, Alwin; German banker; b. 19 March 1908, Hamburg; s. of Hermann and Elisabeth Münchmeyer; m. Gertrud Nolte 1934; one s. four d.; ed. High School; Hon. Chair. Pres. Philips GmbH, Hamburg AG; fmr. Pres. Deutscher Industrie- und Handelstag, Assen. of German Banks; Hon. mem. Bds. and Advisory Bds. of other companies. *Leisure interests:* riding, tennis, hiking, icons. *Address:* Neuer Wall 84, 2000 Hamburg 36, Federal Republic of Germany (Office). *Telephone:* 36 30 46.

MUNDEBO, (Kurt Allan) Ingemar, FIL.LIC.; Swedish auditor-general, fmr. politician and university teacher; b. 15 Oct. 1930, Långasjö; s. of Magni and Hildegard Gustavsson; m. Lillemor Ericsson 1973; one s. one d.; Asst. in Nat. and Communal Admin. 1950–56; teacher in secondary school 1956–60; Lector in School of Social Studies 1960–64; Head of Dept., Univ. of Stockholm 1964–76; mem. Riksdag (Parl.) 1965–80, Nordic Council 1969–76; Minister of the Budget 1976–80 and Econ. Affairs 1978–79; Gov. Province of Uppsala 1980–86; Dir.-Gen., Swedish Nat. Audit Bureau 1986–; mem. Folkpartiet (Liberal Party); Kt., Order of North Star; Grand Cross, Icelandic Order of the Falcon, Kt. Commdr. Order of Dannebrog. *Publications:* Ny kris i befolkningsfrågan? 1962, Social Administration 1963, Socialkunskap 1968, Förvaltningskunskap 1970, Våra villkor 1975. *Leisure interest:* Rotarians. *Address:* Valhallavägen 133, 115 31 Stockholm, Sweden (Home). *Telephone:* 08-664 4345 (Home).

MUNGAI, Joseph James, M.P.A.; Tanzanian politician; b. 24 Oct. 1943, Iringa; s. of late James Mungai and late Marigeritta Semalangalita; m. Mary Chawe 1965; three s. two d.; ed. Mkwana High School, Tanzania, Colorado and Harvard Univs., U.S.A.; various posts with Singer Co. 1965–69; M.P. for Mufindi Dist. 1970–; Gen. Man. Tanzania Elimu (Educational) Supplies Ltd. 1970–72, Sugar Devt. Corpn. 1976–80; Minister for Agric. 1972–75, 1980–82; Chair. Nat. Sports Council 1976–80, 1982–; founder mem. Chama Cha Mapinduzi (CCM) (fmrly. Tanganyika African Nat. Union (TANU)); fmr. TANU br. Chair. Tanzania Elimu Supplies Branch. *Leisure interests:* sports, reading. *Address:* National Assembly, P.O. Box 9133, Dar es Salaam; P.O. Box 24, Mafinga, Mufindi District, Tanzania (Home).

MUNGAI, Njoroge, M.D.; Kenyan politician and doctor; b. 1926, Dagoretti, Kikuyu; ed. Presbyterian Church Elementary School, Kikuyu, Alliance High School, Fort Hare Univ. (S. Africa), Stanford Univ., Calif., and Columbia Univ. Presbyterian Medical Center, N.Y.; E. African Airways Ground Officer 1946–47; bus driver 1947–48; Intern King's County Hosp., N.Y. 1958; returned to Kenya and practised medicine at pvt. clinics in Thika, Riruta and Embu and ran mobile clinic; mem. Nat. Exec. KANU, Chair. Thika branch of KANU; mem. House of Reps. 1963–74; Minister for Health and Housing 1963–65; Minister of Defence 1965–69; Minister of Foreign Affairs 1969–74; mem. Kenya Educ. Fund Cttee., Nat. Nutritional Council; fmr. Pres. Kenya Medical Assen.; personal physician to late Pres. Jomo Kenyatta. *Leisure interest:* golf. *Address:* c/o Ministry of Foreign Affairs, P.O. Box 30551 Nairobi, Kenya.

MUNG'OMBA, Wila D'Israeli, B.A.; Zambian barrister and international official; b. 18 Oct. 1939, Mbereshi; s. of Duncan Israel and late Marjory Chitupa Mung'omba; m. Linda Eleanor Jordan 1967; two d.; ed. Munali Secondary School, Makerere Coll., Uganda, and Inner Temple, London; Solicitor, City Council of Lusaka 1968; legal and political adviser/First Sec. of Ministry of Foreign Affairs, to Zambia Perm. Mission to UN 1969–70; legal practitioner 1971–76; mem. Nat. Assembly 1971–78; Exec. Dir. IMF 1976–78; Sr. Exec. Officer, Standard Bank Zambia Ltd. 1979–80; Minister Counsellor (Econ.), Embassy of Zambia to U.S.A. 1977–79; Exec. Pres. and Chair. of ADB and ADF 1980–85; Chair. Law Assen. of Zambia; Sec.-Gen. Alumni Assen. of American and Int. Law, South Western Legal Foundation, Tex., U.S.A.; Officier Ordre nat. de la Côte d'Ivoire, Officier Ordre de la Valeur du Cameroun, Commdr. Ordre nat. Tunisien. *Leisure* *interests:* reading, music, swimming, gardening. *Address:* c/o African Development Bank, B.P. 1387, Abidjan 01, Ivory Coast. *Telephone:* 32 26 20 (Abidjan).

MUNIM, Mohammad Abdul, M. SC. ENG.; Bangladesh government official; b. 1 Jan. 1935, Bogra; s. of Emdad Ali and Sufia Khatum Munim; m. Dr. Ayesha Akhter 1961; four d.; ed. Imperial Coll. of Science and Tech., London; Directing Staff, Electrical and Mechanical Engineers Corps, Pakistan Army 1956–71, Bangladesh Army 1974–86, Dir. of Corps, Maj.-Gen.; Gen. Man. GEM Plant 1974–76; Chair. PDB 1979–83; mem. Council of Ministers 1983–, Minister for Works 1983–85, for Agric. 1985–86, for Commerce 1986–87, of Finance 1987–88, of Health and Family Planning 1988–. *Leisure interests:* reading, listening to Tagore songs. *Address:* Ministry of Health and Family Planning, Bangladesh Secretariat, Main Bldg., 3rd Floor, Dhaka; 33 Dhanmondi R.A. Road 7, Dhaka-1205, Bangladesh. *Telephone:* Dhaka 316270 (Home).

MUÑIZ, Carlos Manuel, LL.D.; Argentine diplomatist and university professor; b. 2 Feb. 1922, Buenos Aires; unmarried; ed. Univ. de Buenos Aires; Under-Sec. of Interior and Justice 1955, of Interior 1955–56; Amb. to Bolivia 1956–59, to Brazil 1959–62, to U.S.A. 1971–73; Minister of Foreign Affairs and Worship 1962–63; Prof. of Int. Public Law, Univ. de La Plata 1963–73, also Dir. Int. Law Inst.; Prof. of Constitutional Law, Univ. de Buenos Aires; fmr. Prof. of Int. Law and Int. Relations, Univ. Católica de La Plata; Perm. Rep. to UN 1982–86; Pres. Argentine Council on Foreign Relations; decorations from govts. of Bolivia, Brazil, Japan, Peru, Paraguay. *Publications:* National Basis for an International Policy 1969, Relations between Argentina and Brazil 1979, Diplomacy and Diplomats 1979 and others. *Address:* c/o Ministerio des Asuntos Exteriores, Arenales 761, 1061 Buenos Aires, Argentina.

MUNK, Frank; American (fmr. Czechoslovak) economist and political scientist; b. 26 May 1901, Kutna Hora, Czechoslovakia; s. of Alfred and Marie (Mautnerová) Munk; m. Naděžda Prasilová 1925; one s. one d.; ed. Prague, Columbia and Harvard Univs.; student and youth leader Czechoslovakia; Fellow Rockefeller Foundation U.S. 1931–33; Chair. Prague Univ. L.N. Fed. 1934–36, Masaryk Acad. 1931–38; with Social Inst., Ministry of Welfare, Prague 1931–39; Lecturer Reed Coll., Portland, Ore. 1939–41; Lecturer in Econs., Univ. of Calif., Berkeley, to 1944; Dir. UNRRA Training Centre, Univ. of Md. 1944–45; Chief Econ. Adviser UNRRA 1946; Prof. Reed Coll., Portland, Oregon 1946–65; Dean Northwest Inst. of Int. Relations 1947–56; Visiting Prof. Univ. of Washington 1952; Public mem. Regional Wage Stabilisation Bd. 1951–52; mem. Exec. Council, Pacific North-west Political Science Asscn. 1952–55, Pres. 1968–69; Adviser on Intellectual Co-operation to the European Dir., Radio Free Europe, Munich 1958–60; Research Fellow, Atlantic Inst. (Paris) 1961–62; Visiting Prof. Political Science, Coll. of Europe (Brussels) 1961–62; Research Consultant, Foreign Policy Research Inst., Univ. of Pa. 1963–65; Prof. of Political Science and Assoc. Dir. Cen. European Studies Center, Portland State Coll. 1965–; Emer. Prof. Political Science, Portland State Univ. 1983–; Exec. Council Western Slavic Assen. 1970–72; Pres. World Affairs Council of Oregon 1972–73, mem. Bd. 1985–87, mem. Bd. of Overseers 1985–; Chair. Portland Cttee. on Foreign Relations 1985–88; World Affairs Commentator, Public T.V. Oregon 1975–. *Publications include:* The Legacy of Nazism 1943, Atlantic Dilemma 1963. *Leisure interests:* hiking, swimming, photography. *Address:* 3808 S.W., Mt. Adams Drive, Portland, Oregon 97201, U.S.A.

MUNK, Walter Heinrich, PH.D.; American professor of geophysics; b. 19 Oct. 1917, Vienna, Austria; s. of Hans and Rega (Brunner) Munk; m. Judith Horton 1953; two d.; ed. Calif. Inst. of Tech. and Scripps Inst. of Oceanography; Asst. Prof. of Geophysics, Univ. of Calif. at San Diego 1947–49, Assoc. Prof. 1949–54, Prof. Inst. of Geophysics and Scripps Inst. 1954–; Assoc. Dir. Inst. of Geophysics and Planetary Physics (Systemwide), Univ. of Calif. 1959–; Guggenheim Fellow, Oslo Univ. 1948, Cambridge Univ. 1955, 1962, Josiah Willard Gibbs Lecturer, American Mathematical Soc. 1970; Sr. Queen's Fellow, Aust. 1978; Fellow, American Meteorological Soc., A.A.A.S.; mem. American Geological Soc., N.A.S. (Chair. Geophysics Section 1975–78), American Acad. of Arts and Sciences, American Philosophical Soc., Deutsche Akademie der Naturforscher Leopoldina, Acoustical Soc. of America; Foreign mem. Royal Soc., London; D.Phil. h.c. (Bergen) 1975, Hon. D.Sc. (Cambridge) 1986; Arthur L. Day Medal of Geological Soc. of America 1965, Sverdrup Gold Medal of American Meterological Soc. 1966, Alumni Distinguished Service Award of Calif. Inst. of Tech. 1966, Gold Medal of Royal Astronomical Soc. 1968, Calif. Scientist of the Year Award of Calif. Museum of Science and Industry 1969, Maurice Ewing Medal, American Geophysical Union, U.S. Navy 1976, Agassiz Medal Nat. Acad. of Science 1976, Capt. Robert Dexter Conrad Award, Dept. of the Navy 1978. *Publications:* Co-author The Rotation of the Earth: A Geophysical Discussion 1960, Sound Transmission through a Fluctuating Ocean 1979, and numerous scientific articles 1945–. *Leisure interests:* skiing, swimming. *Address:* IGPP Mail Code AO25, University of California at San Diego, La Jolla, Calif. 92093 (Office); 9530 La Jolla Shores Drive, La Jolla, Calif. 92037, U.S.A. (Home). *Telephone:* (619) 452-2877 (Office); (619) 453-2452 (Home).

MUNK ANDERSEN, Jens; Danish businessman; b. 21 Dec. 1928, nr. Vorupoer; one s. one d.; ed. Birkeroed, Univ. of Århus; joined Dansk Esso

AS 1956, Analyst, Economist 1956–64, Supply Man., Refinery Man., mem. Excom and Bd. of Dirs. 1964–75, Chair. of Bd. and Chief Exec. 1978–86; joined Esso Int., London 1963, Analyst, Supply 1963–64; joined Esso N. Europe AS, Copenhagen, PPD Dir. 1983–85, Pres. 1985–86; Exec. Asst. to Chair. Exxon Corpn., New York 1975–78; Pres. Statoil A/S (fmrly. Dansk Esso A/S) 1986–. *Address:* 13 Sankt Annae Plads, DK-1298 Copenhagen K (Office); 6A Skjoldhoj Allé, DK-2920 Charlottenlund, Denmark (Home). *Telephone:* 01-14-28-90 (Office); 01-64-06-29 (Home).

MUNK OLSEN, Birger, D.LITT.; Danish professor of medieval culture and philology; b. 26 June 1935, Copenhagen; m. Annalise Bliddal 1964 (divorced 1988); two d.; ed. Ecole Normale Superieure, the Sorbonne, Paris and Pontificia Univ. Gregoriana, Rome; Assoc. Prof. of Romance Philology, Univ. of Copenhagen 1961–68; lecturer Univ. Paris-Sorbonne 1968–74; Prof. of Romance Philology, Univ. of Copenhagen 1974–83, Prof. of Medieval Culture and Philology 1983–; Chair. Danish Nat. Research Council for the Humanities 1987–; Danish Rep. Standing Cttee. for the Humanities, European Science Foundation 1988–; mem. Royal Danish Acad. 1985–, Danish Council for Research Planning and Policy 1987–, Acad. Europaea 1988–; Kt. Order of Dannebrog, Officier Ordre Nat. du Merite; Prix Brunet 1984. *Publications:* Les "Dits" de Jahan de Saint-Quentin 1978, L'étude des auteurs classiques latins aux XIᵉ et XIIᵉ siecles, Vols. I-IV 1982–89. *Address:* Godthaabsvej 127, 2000 Frederiksberg, Denmark; 51 rue de Tolbiac, 75013 Paris, France. *Telephone:* (1) 873077; (1) 45 84 27 18.

MUNNIK, Lourens Albertus Petrus Anderson, M.B., CH.B.; South African doctor, farmer and fmr. politician; b. 3 Aug. 1925, Cape Town; m. Annes Turck 1953; one s. four d.; ed. Univ. of Cape Town; medical practice, Dordrecht 1951–63; mem. Provincial Council 1962, mem. Exec. Cttee. in charge of hosp. services 1966; mem. Nat. Assembly 1972, 1979–86; Admin. of Cape Prov. 1975; Minister of Health, Social Welfare and Pensions 1979–82, of Posts and Telecommunications 1982–84, of Communications and Public Works 1984–86; Decoration for Meritorious Service 1983, Order of Brilliant Star with Grand Cordon (Taiwan) 1984; National Party. *Address:* House of Assembly, Cape Town 8000, South Africa. *Telephone:* (021) 457240.

MUÑOZ LEDO, Porfirio; Mexican politician and university professor; b. 1933; ed. Univ. Nacional Autónoma de México; Prof. of Political Science, Univ. Nacional Autónoma de México and El Colegio de México 1958–69; Gen. Sec. Inst. Mexicano del Seguro Social 1966–70; worked for election campaign of Pres. Echeverría (q.v.) 1969; Pvt. Sec. to Pres. Echeverría 1970–72; Sec. for Labour and Social Security 1972–75, for Educ. 1976–77; Perm. Rep. of Mexico to UN 1979–81, 1982–85; Pres. Partido Revolucionario Institutional 1975–77. *Address:* c/o Ministry of Foreign Affairs, Mexico City, D.F., Mexico.

MUÑOZ VEGA, H.E. Cardinal Paolo, S.J., D.PHIL., D.THEOL.; Ecuadorean ecclesiastic; b. 23 May 1903, Mira; s. of Antonio Muñoz and Josefa Vega; ordained 1933; Prof. of Phil., Gregorian Univ. 1938–45, Prof. Theol. 1945–50; Rector, Pontificio Colegio Pio-Latino-Americano 1955–57; Rector, Pontifical Gregorian Univ., Rome 1957–64; Titular Bishop of Ceramo 1964–67; Archbishop of Quito 1967–86; cr. Cardinal 1969; mem. Sacred Congregation of Catholic Educ.; fmr. mem. Sacred Congregation of Religious Life. *Publications:* Introducción a la síntesis de San Agustín 1945, Causalidad filosófica y determinismo científico 1946, El estudio del hombre como introducción al problema de lo sobrenatural 1948, Los Problemas de la experiencia mística a la luz del pensamiento agustiniano en Augustinus Magister 1954, Fe e inteligencia en los origines de la ciencia moderna 1965, Fe y politica 1986. *Address:* Palacio Arzobispado, Apartado 106, Quito, Ecuador. *Telephone:* 210-703.

MUNRO, Dana G.; American diplomatist and historian; b. 18 July 1892, Providence, R.I.; s. of Dana Carlton and Alice (Beecher) Munro; m. Margaret Bennett Wiley 1920; one s., two d.; ed. Wisconsin, Pennsylvania and Brown Univs.; Regional Economist Dept. of State 1919–20; Economic Consul at Valparaiso 1920–21; mem. Latin-American Div. of State Dept. 1921–25; 1st Sec. Panama 1925–27 and Nicaragua 1927–29; Chief Latin-American Affairs Div. of State Dept. 1929–30; Minister to Haiti 1930–32; Prof. of Latin-American History and Affairs Princeton Univ. 1932–; Vice-Pres. Foreign Bondholders' Protective Council, New York 1938–58, Pres. 1958–67, Chair. Exec. Cttee. 1967–69; Dir. Woodrow Wilson School of Public and Int. Affairs, Princeton Univ. 1939–58; mem. Nat. Advisory Cttee. on Inter-American Affairs 1959–61. *Publications:* The Five Republics of Central America 1918, The United States and the Caribbean Area 1934, The Latin American Republics: A History 1942, Intervention and Dollar Diplomacy in The Caribbean 1900-21 1964, The United States and the Caribbean Republics 1921-33 1974, A Student in Central America 1914-1916 1983. *Leisure interests:* sailing, gardening. *Address:* Department of History, Princeton University, N.J. 08544; 345 Harrison Street, Princeton, N.J. 08540, U.S.A. (Home). *Telephone:* (609) 924-1238 (Home).

MUNRO, Hamish Nisbet, M.D., D.SC., F.R.S.E.; American (b. British) biochemist; b. 3 July 1915, Edinburgh, Scotland; s. of Donald Munro and Margaret (Nisbet) Munro; m. Edith Ekron Little 1946 (died 1987); three s. one d.; ed. Univ. of Glasgow, Scotland; Physician, Pathologist, Victoria Infirmary, Glasgow 1939–45; Lecturer in Physiology, Univ. of Glasgow 1946–47, Sr. Lecturer, Reader in Biochemistry 1948–63, Prof. of Biochemistry 1964–66; Prof. of Physiological Chem., M.I.T., Cambridge, U.S.A. 1966–; Dir. Human

Nutrition Center on Aging, Tufts Univ., Boston 1979–84, Prof. of Medicine 1984–; Ed. Mammalian Protein Metabolism vols. 1–4 1964–70; mem. N.A.S., American Soc. of Biological Chemists, American Inst. of Nutrition (Pres. 1978–79), British Biochemistry Soc. Dr. h.c. (Nancy) 1982; Osborn Mendel Award, American Inst. of Nutrition 1968; Borden Award 1978; Bristol-Myers Award 1981; Rank Prize for significant advances in nutrition 1982. *Address:* Human Nutrition Center, 711 Washington Street, Boston, Mass. 02111; 159 Concord Avenue, Cambridge, Mass. 02138, U.S.A. (Home).

MUNRO, Hon. John Carr; Canadian lawyer and politician; b. 16 March 1931; Hamilton, Ont; s. of John Anderson Munro, Q.C. and Katherine Alexander Carr; m. 1st Marguerite Harriet Clay 1956 (divorced 1978), two d.; m. 2nd Dr. Lily Oddie 1978, one s.; ed. Cen. Public School, Westdale Composite School, Univ. of Western Ontario, and Osgoode Hall Law School, Toronto; mem. Hamilton City Council 1955; Liberal mem. for Hamilton E.; Parl. Sec. to Minister of Citizenship and Immigration 1963, later Parl. Sec. to Ministers of Nat. Health and Welfare, Trade and Commerce, and Manpower and Immigration; Minister without Portfolio April-June 1968; Minister of Nat. Health and Welfare 1968–72, of Labour 1972–78, of Indian Affairs and Northern Devt. 1980–84; Commr., Canadian Transport Comm. 1984–; mem. Canadian Inst. of Int. Affairs. *Leisure interests:* reading, spectator sports, swimming. *Address:* 1051 Main Street East, Hamilton, Ont. L8M 1W5, Canada.

MUNS ALBUIXECH, Joaquín, PH.D.; Spanish university professor and international civil servant; b. 25 June 1935, Barcelona; m. Gloria Rubiol 1967; one s.; ed. Univ. of Barcelona and London School of Econs.; Economist, Nat. Studies Div. of OECD 1962–63; Asst. Prof. of Econs. Univ. of Barcelona 1963–65; Economist, Western Hemisphere Dept. of IMF 1965–68; Econ. Adviser to Barcelona City Council 1968–73; Prof. of Econs. Univ. of Barcelona 1968–73, and Senior Prof. of Int. Econ. Org. 1973–78; Econ. Adviser to Govt. of Spain and to various public and pvt. insts. 1973–78; Exec. Dir. IMF 1978–80; Exec. Dir. IBRD 1980–82; Adjunct Prof. SIS American Univ. 1982; Sr. Prof. of Int. Econ. Org., Univ. of Barcelona 1982–; mem. European Parl. (Liberal Group) 1987–; mem. Vatican Council of Econ. Advisers 1988–. *Publications:* (in English): Adjustment, Conditionality and International Financing (ed.) 1984; (in Spanish): Industrialization and Growth in the Developing Countries 1972, The European Option for the Spanish Economy 1973, The International Economic Crisis: Thoughts and Proposals 1975, Crisis and Reform of the International Monetary System 1978, History of the Relations between Spain and the IMF 1958–82, Twenty-five Years of the Spanish Economy 1986, over 30 essays and articles, with special reference to problems of the int. econ. orgs. *Address:* C. Muntaner, 268, 08021 Barcelona, Spain. *Telephone:* (93) 209 45 34.

MUNTYAN, Mikhail Ivanovich; Soviet opera singer (tenor); b. 1943; ed. Kishinev Inst. of Arts; mem. CPSU 1966–; soloist with Moldavian State Acad. Theatre of Opera and Ballet; U.S.S.R. People's Artist, 1986. *Roles include:* Lensky (Eugene Onegin); Richard (Ballo in Mascheva); Cavaradossi, Calaf (Tosca, Turandot) etc.

MUNU, Momodu; B.A. (ECONS); Sierra Leone international administrator; b. 13 Dec. 1938, Mateboi; s. of Paramount Chief Alhaji Bai Lama and Haja Yebu Kamara; m. Haja Kadе Konteh 1965; six d.; ed. Fourah Bay Coll., Freetown; joined Sierra Leone civil service 1964, served in Ministries of Devt., Information, the Interior and Social Welfare; Recruitment Attaché and Training Officer, Sierra Leone High Comm., London 1967–73; called to the Bar, London; Clerk of Parl., Freetown 1973–76, Establishment Sec. 1976–84; Exec. Sec., Econ. Community of W. African States (ECOWAS) 1985–89; Vice-Pres. of the Ass. of African Public Admin. 1984. *Leisure interests:* reading, walking. *Address:* c/o ECOWAS, 6 King George V Road, Lagos, Nigeria.

MURAKHOVSKY, Vsevolod Serafimovich; Soviet politician; b. 20 Oct. 1926, Ukraine; served in Red Army 1944–50; mem. CPSU 1946–; teacher in Stavropol dist. 1950–54; First Sec., Stavropol City Cttee. of All-Union Komsomol 1954–56; party posts in Stavropol Dist. 1956–59; Sec. of Stavropol City Cttee. CPSU 1959–61; Head of Dept. of Stavropol Dist. Cttee. CPSU 1961–63; Deputy Chair. of Exec. Cttee. of Stavropol Dist. Workers' Soviet 1963–64; First Sec. Kislovodsk City Cttee. CPSU 1965–70; First Sec. Stavropol City Cttee. CPSU 1970–74; Deputy to R.S.F.S.R. Supreme Soviet 1971–75; Sec. of Stavropol Dist. Cttee. CPSU 1974–75; First Sec. of Karachaevo-Cherkessk Autonomous Dist. Cttee. CPSU 1975–78; First Sec. of Stavropol Dist. Cttee. CPSU and mem. Mil. Council, North Caucasian Mil. Dist. 1978–85; Deputy to Council of the Union, U.S.S.R. Supreme Soviet 1979–; mem. Cen. Cttee. CPSU 1981–; Deputy Chair. of Mandate Comm. 1984–85; First Deputy Chair. of U.S.S.R. Council of Ministers, Chair. of U.S.S.R. State Agro-industrial Cttee. (Gosagroprom, encompassing functions of five ministries); First Deputy Prime Minister of U.S.S.R. 1986–; Order of October Revolution 1976, Order of Lenin 1982, Hero of Socialist Labour 1982. *Address:* The Kremlin, Moscow, U.S.S.R.

MURAŃSKI, Zygmunt; Polish politician; b. 11 March 1952, Czernica, Katowice Voivodship; ed. school of mining and mining tech. school for employees; miner, Rydułtowy Colliery, Wodzisław Śląski 1969–, Section foreman; mem. Polish Socialist Youth Union (ZSMP), fmr. Chair. ZSMP Town Board, Wodzisław Śląski; mem. Polish United Workers' Party (PZPR) 1971–; fmr. Instructor of PZPR Town Cttee., Wodzisław Śląski;

Sec. PZPR Basal Party Org. and mem. Exec. of PZPR Plant Cttee., Rydułtowy Colliery; mem. PZPR Cent. Cttee. 1986–, mem. Political Bureau 1986–88, Head, Comm. of Mining, Raw Materials and Power 1986–. *Address:* Komitet Centralny PZPR, ul. Nowy Świat 6, 00–497 Warsaw, Poland.

MURAOKA, Sadakatsu, B.ENG.; Japanese business executive; b. 2 Jan. 1910, Kyoto; s. of Yukichi and Masu Muraoka; m. Fuji Hirose 1937; two s. one d.; ed. Kyoto Imperial Univ.; Dir. Nippon Mining Co. Ltd. 1960, Sr. Man. Dir. 1969, Exec. Vice-Pres., Gen. Man. Research and Devt. Div., Corporate Co-ordination and 1st Control Div., Environmental Measures Promotion Centre 1971–; Dir. Koyo Iron Works and Construction Co. Ltd. 1965–, Nissho Shipping Co. Ltd. 1967–; Pres. Bio Research Center Co. Ltd. 1972–; Chair. Orient Catalyst Co. Ltd. 1973–, Toho Titanium Co. Ltd. 1973–; Medal with Blue Ribbon 1970. *Leisure interest:* golf. *Address:* Nippon Mining Co. Ltd., 3 Akasaka Aoi cho, Maitno-ku, Tokyo (Office); 1163-2, Ichigao-cho, Midori-ku, Yokohama, Kanagawa Prefecture, Japan (Home). *Telephone:* 03-582-2111 (Office).

MURAOKA, Takamitsu, PH.D., F.A.H.A.; Japanese academic; b. 9 Feb. 1938, Hiroshima; m. Keiko Kageyama 1965; two s. one d.; ed. Tokyo Kyoiku, The Hebrew Univ., Jerusalem; lecturer in Semitic Languages, Dept. of Near Eastern Studies, Univ. of Manchester, U.K. 1970–80; Prof. of Middle Eastern Studies, Chair. Dept., Melbourne Univ. 1980–; Ed. Abr-Nahrain (Leiden) 1980–; Academic Assoc., The Oxford Centre for Postgraduate Hebrew Studies. *Publications:* A Greek-Hebrew/Aramaic Index to I Esdras 1982, Emphatic Words and Structures in Biblical Hebrew 1985, Classical Syriac for Hebraists 1987. *Leisure interest:* angling. *Address:* 55 Longview Road, Balwyn North, Vic. 3104, Australia. *Telephone:* (03) 859-6088.

MURATA, Keijiro; Japanese politican; b. 12 Feb. 1924; ed. Kyoto Univ.; joined Home Affairs Agency; mem. House of Reps. 1969–; Parl. Vice-Minister for Construction 1975–76; Chair. of House of Reps. Construction Cttee.; Minister of Int. Trade and Industry 1984–85; Liberal Democratic Party. *Leisure interests:* go playing, music, photography. *Address:* c/o Ministry of International Trade and Industry, 1–3, Kasumigaseki, Chiyoda-ku, Tokyo 100, Japan. *Telephone:* 3-501-1511.

MURATA, Kiyoaki, M.A.; Japanese journalist, educator and author; b. 19 Nov. 1922, Ono, Hyogo; s. of the late Itsuji Murata and of Kazue Murata; m. 1st Minako Iesaka 1960 (divorced 1981); two s. one d.; m. 2nd Kayoko Matsukura 1987; ed. Carleton Coll., Minnesota and Univ. of Chicago; visiting lecturer, Kansei Gakuin Univ. 1949, Meiji Gakuin Univ. 1950, Aoyama Gakuin Univ. 1959–63, Univ. of Tokyo 1960–62; editorial writer, The Japan Times 1957–66, Man. Ed. 1971–76, Exec. Ed. 1976–77, Man. Dir. 1974–83, Ed.-in-Chief 1977–83; Prof. of Int. Communication, Yachiyo Int. Univ. 1988–; Dir. Japan Graphic Inc. 1977–; special adviser, Japanese del. to UN 1978, 1979; perm. adviser Simul Acad. 1983–; Hon. LL.D. (Carleton College); Vaughn Prize (Japan Newspaper Eds. and Publrs. Asscn.) 1957. *Publications:* Japan's New Buddhism—An Objective Account of Soka Gakkai 1969, Japan—The State of the Nation 1979, Saigo no Ryugakusei (memoirs) 1981, Kokuren Nikki—Suppon Wan no Kaiso (UN Diary—Recollections of Turtle Bay) 1985. *Leisure interests:* aikido, kendo. *Address:* 19-12 Hiroo 2-chome, Shibuya-ku, Tokyo 150, Japan. *Telephone:* 03-400-5362.

MURATA, Masachika; Japanese architect; b. 6 Sept. 1906, Yokkaichi Mie Pref.; s. of Masaichi and Hisa Murata; m. Yuri Kagitomi 1935; two s.; ed. Tokyo Acad. of Fine Arts; Designer, Shinichiro Okada Architect Office, Tokyo 1929–30, Bldg. Dept. of Ministry of Imperial Household, Tokyo 1931–36; Researcher of facilities of Museums of Europe and America at request of Ministry of Educ. 1937–39; Architect, Kameki Tuchiura Architect Office 1940–46; Vice-Chief of Architectural Div., Conf. of Devt. of Kainantow (Hainan Island, China) 1943; Pres. Masachika Murata Architect Office 1946–84, Consultant 1984–; Dir. Bd., Japan Architects Assn. 1954–74; Dir. Sports and Recreation Facilities, Union of Int. Architects 1959–74; Award of Ministry of Construction 1970; Nat. Medal for Merit 1973. *Works include:* Yokohama offices of Yokohama Trading Building Co. Ltd. (Kanagawa Pref. Architectural Prize) 1951; Tokyo Metropolitan Indoor Pool 1957; Exhbn. Halls of Tokyo Int. Trading Center 1959; Miyazaki Kanko Hotel, Miyazaki Pref. 1961; Ochiai Sewage Treatment Plant, Tokyo, 1961; Tokyo Olympic Komazawa Stadium (Special Prize of Architectural Inst. of Japan and Building Contractors' Soc. of Japan) 1962; Morigasaki Sewage Treatment Plant, Tokyo, 1962; Italian Embassy, Tokyo 1963; Kyodo News Service Building, Tokyo 1964; Y.M.C.A. Int. Youth Center, Shizuoka Pref. 1964; Hotel Matsukura, Nagasaki Pref. 1964; Hotel Hodaka, Nagano Pref. 1964; Residence of Consul Gen. of S. Africa, Tokyo 1965; Educ. Center I.B.M. Japan 1966; Police HQ, Aichi Pref. 1968; Mt. Tateyama Int. Hotel and Bus Terminal, Toyama Pref. 1968; Dentsu Advertising Office, Kyoto 1969; Netherlands Pavilion, Expo 1970; Matsuzakaya Dept. Store, Shizuoka 1970, new Exhbn. Hall of Tokyo Int. Trading Centre 1971; Yamagata Civic Centre 1971; Itabashi Cent. Library, Tokyo 1971; Yotsuya Civic Centre, Tokyo 1972; Ryoyu Club, Tokyo 1972; Yokkaichi Cen. Library Architectural Prize of Middle Part of Japan 1972; Tamagawa Sewage Treatment Plant, Tokyo 1973; Recreational facilities for Shinjuku-ku people, Hakone Nat. Park 1974; Nagano Municipal Stadium 1975; Shinjuku-ku Public Hall, Tokyo 1976; Dentsu Advertising Headquarters Office, Tokyo 1977 (annexes 1977, 1983); Club House of the Nippon Bank, Tokyo 1977; Indoor Pool and

Gymnasium Tsukuba Univ. 1978; Gymnasium and Athletic Field Tamagawa Univ. 1984; Youth Hostel, Itabashi-ku, Nagano Pref. 1982. *Leisure interests:* golf, skiing, painting. *Address:* Jingugaien Building, 2-7-25 Kita Aoyama, Minato-ku, Tokyo 107 (Office); 2-14-4-4 Moto-Azabu, Minato-ku, Tokyo 106, Japan (Home).

MURAYAMA, Tatsuo; Japanese politician; served in Finance Ministry; Chief, Accounts Bureau, Liberal-Dem. Party; mem. House of Reps. for Niigata Prefecture; Minister of Finance 1977-78, of Health 1978-81, of Finance Dec. 1988-. *Address:* c/o Liberal-Democratic Party, 7, 2-chome, Hirakawacho, Chiyoda-ku, Tokyo Japan.

MURDHANI, Gen. Benny; Indonesian army officer; served under Gen. Suharto in mil. campaign to take Dutch New Guinea (now Irian Jaya) from Netherlands 1962; played key role in restoring diplomatic relations with Malaysia following Pres. Sukarno's armed conflict over Sabah and Sarawak 1963-66; Head of Ministry of Defence intelligence staff and Deputy Chief of Bakin (overseas state intelligence body) 1976-88; Head of Nat. Strategic Intelligence Centre 1979-88; Commdr. of the Armed Forces and Head of Konkamtib (nat. security agency) 1983-88; Minister of Defence and Security March 1988-. *Address:* c/o Ministry of Defence and Security, Jalan Merdeka, Barat 13, Jakarta Pesat, Indonesia.

MURDOCH, Dame (Jean) Iris, D.B.E.; British writer and philosopher; b. 15 July 1919, Dublin, Ireland; d. of Wills John Hughes and Irene Alice (née Richardson) Murdoch; m. John O. Bayley; ed. Froebel Educational Inst. (London), Badminton School (Bristol) and Somerville Coll., Oxford; worked at the Treasury 1942-44, with UNRRA 1944-46; Phil. Studentship Newnham Coll., Cambridge 1947-48; Hon. Litt.D. (Univs. of Sheffield, Leicester, Washington, St. Louis, Hong Kong, Bristol, Warwick, Queen's, Belfast, Norwich, Caen, London, Oxford); C.Lit. (R.S.L.) 1987; Dr. h.c. (Buckingham) 1988; Fellow, St. Anne's Coll., Oxford 1948-63, Hon. Fellow 1963; Hon. Fellow Newnham Coll., Cambridge 1986; mem. Irish Acad. of Letters, American Acad. of Arts and Sciences 1981 (Hon. mem. 1975), Nat. Inst. of Arts and Letters 1975; Gifford Lecture, Univ. of Edinburgh 1982; James Tait Black Prize for Fiction (for The Black Prince) 1974, Whitbread Literary Award for Fiction (for The Sacred and Profane Love Machine) 1974, Booker Prize for Fiction (for The Sea, the Sea) 1978. *Publications:* Sartre: Romantic Rationalist 1953, Under the Net 1954, The Flight from the Enchanter 1955, The Sandcastle 1957, The Bell 1958, A Severed Head 1961 (play 1963), An Unofficial Rose 1962, The Unicorn 1963, The Italian Girl 1964 (play 1967), The Red and the Green 1965, The Time of the Angels 1966, The Nice and the Good 1968, Bruno's Dream 1969, A Fairly Honourable Defeat 1970, The Sovereignty of Good 1970, The Servants and the Snow (play) 1970, An Accidental Man 1971, The Three Arrows (play) 1972, The Black Prince 1973, The Sacred and Profane Love Machine 1974, A Word Child 1975, Henry and Cato 1976, The Sea, the Sea 1978, The Fire and the Sun 1978, Nuns and Soldiers 1980, Art and Eros (play) 1980, The Philosopher's Pupil 1983, The Good Apprentice 1985, Acastos (Platonic dialogues) 1986, The Book and the Brotherhood 1987, The Message to the Planet 1989. *Address:* St. Anne's College, Oxford, England.

MURDOCH, (Keith) Rupert, A.C.; American (b. Australian) newspaper publisher; b. 11 March 1931, Melbourne, Victoria; s. of the late Sir Keith Murdoch and of Dame Elisabeth Murdoch; m. Anna Maria Torv 1967; two s. two d.; ed. Geelong Grammar School, Victoria, and Worcester Coll., Oxford; inherited Adelaide News 1952; has since built up Cruden Investments, a Murdoch family co. which owns 43 per cent of News Corpn.; has acquired newspapers, magazines and other interests in Australia, U.K., U.S.A. and Hong Kong, including: Australia—newspapers: The Australian (national), Daily Telegraph, Sunday Telegraph, Daily Mirror (Sydney), Sunday Sun (Brisbane), The News and Sunday Mail (Adelaide), The Sunday Times (Perth); U.S.A.—The Chicago Sun-Times, New York Post, Boston Herald, Mirror Newspapers Ltd., Nationwide News Pty. Ltd., Southdown Press Ltd., Cumberland Newspapers Ltd., (C.E.O. and fmr. Man. Dir. News Ltd. Group and associated cos. as above); magazines: TV Week, New Idea; television: Channel 10 (Sydney), Channel 10 (Melbourne, 50 per cent interest through Ansett Transport); other interests: Bay Books, Santos (energy), C.E.O. Ansett Transport Industries. U.K.—newspapers: Sun, News of the World (national, acquired 1969), Berrows Org. (regional newspapers), Chair. News Int. Group Ltd., acquired Times Newspapers Ltd. Feb. 1981, group includes The Times, The Sunday Times, The Times Literary Supplement, The Times Educational Supplement, The Times Higher Education Supplement; Vice-Pres. Times Newspapers Holdings 1981-, Chair. Jan. 1982-; magazines: City Magazines (Antique Collector's Guide, The Trader, Licensed Bookmaker); television: News Group Productions (U.S.A.), Skyband (U.S.A.), Satellite Television PLC (U.K.), 11.8 per cent stake in London Weekend Television; C.E.O. Sky Television Jan. 1989-; other interests: Townsend Hook (paper), Bemrose (printing), Convoys (transport). U.S.A.—newspapers: New York Post, others in San Antonio and Houston, Chair. News America Publishing Inc., City Post Publishing Corpn.; acquired Triangle Push Inc. 1988, Premiere 1988, William Collins 1989; magazines: Star, New York Magazine (including Cue and Village Voice); Today newspaper acquired 1987; Dir. United Technologies (U.S.) 1984; Dir. (non-exec.) Reuters Holdings PLC 1984-; other interests: New York State Lotto; Commdr. of the White Rose (First Class) 1985. *Address:* c/o New York Post, 210 South Street, New York, N.Y. 10002, U.S.A.

MURENA, H. A.; Argentine writer; b. 14 Feb. 1923, Buenos Aires; lecturer in Phil., Univ. de Buenos Aires 1968-. *Publications:* Primer testamento (story) 1946, La vida nueva (poetry) 1951, El juez (play) 1953, El pecado original de América (essay) 1954, La fatalidad de los cuerpos (novel) 1955, El centro del infierno (short stories) 1956, El círculo de los paraísos (poetry) 1958, Las leyes de la noche (novel) 1958, El escándalo y el fuego 1959, Homo atomicus 1961, Relámpago de la duración 1962, Ensayos sobre subversión 1962, El demonio de la armonía 1964, Los herederos de la promesa 1965, El nombre secreto (essays) 1969, Epitalámica (novel) 1969, Nímas Nímenos (novel) 1969, La cárcel de la mente (essays) 1970, El coronel de caballería (short stories) 1970, Caina muerte (novel) 1971, F.G. un bárbaro entre la belleza (poetry) 1972. *Address:* San José 910, Buenos Aires, Argentina.

MURERWA, Herbert Muchemwa, ED.D.; Zimbabwean civil servant and diplomatist; b. 31 May 1941, Salisbury (now Harare); m. Ruth Dhliwayo 1967; one s. four d.; ed. George Williams Coll., Ill., U.S.A. and Harvard Univ.; Econ. Affairs Officer, UN ECA, Addis Ababa, Ethiopia 1979-80; Perm. Sec., Ministry of Manpower Planning and Devt. 1980-82, Ministry of Labour 1982-84; High Commr. in U.K. 1984-. *Leisure interest:* reading. *Address:* Zimbabwe House, 429 Strand, London, WC2 0SA, England.

MURGESCU, Costin, PH.D.; Romanian economist; b. 27 Oct. 1919, Rîmnicu Sărat; s. of C. Ion Murgescu and Erato Murgescu; m. Ecaterina Oproiu 1948; one d.; ed. Faculty of Law, Bucharest Univ.; Deputy Ed.-in-Chief România libera (newspaper) 1944-52; Deputy Dir. 1956-65 and Dir. of Inst. of Econs. 1965-68; Ed.-in-Chief. of Viaţa economică magazine 1963-68; Dir. of the Inst. for World Economy 1980-; Prof. of Econs.; Counsellor to the Romanian Council of Ministers 1968-74; Amb. at Large to UN econ. bodies 1965-70; First Vice-Pres. of ECOSOC, UN 1965-67; Romanian Acad. Prize 1968; corresp. mem. Romanian Acad. of Sciences; Pres. of the Econ. Dept. of the Acad. of Social and Political Sciences of Romania. *Works:* The Heavy Industry, Pivot of Romania's Reconstruction 1946, 1945 Agrarian Reform 1956, The Management Team of Economic Units 1970, David Ricardo in the England of Industrial Revolution 1972, Japan in the World Economy 1980. *Address:* Republicii Bd. 12, Bucharest 70348 (Office); Gheorghe Gheorghiu-Dej Bd. 44, Bucharest (Home).

MURGULESCU, Ilie, D.SC.; Romanian chemist and politician; b. 27 Jan. 1902, Cornu, Dolj County; s. of G. D. and Floarea Murgulescu; m. Elena Sălăgeanu 1934; ed. Charles 1 High School, Craiova, and Univs. of Cluj and Leipzig; Dir. of Studies and Prof. of Analytical and Physical Chem., Timişoara Polytechnical Inst. 1934-49; Prof. of Physical Chem., Univ. of Bucharest 1949-72, Consulting Prof. 1972-; mem. Grand Nat. Ass. 1948-75, Vice-Pres. 1967-75; Deputy Minister of Educ. 1950-51, Minister 1951-56, 1960-63; mem. Romanian Acad. of Sciences 1948-, Pres. 1963-66; Dir. Centre of Physical Chem. 1963-; Vice-Pres. Romanian Council of State 1965-67; Foreign mem. U.S.S.R. Acad. of Sciences, Czechoslovak, Hungarian and Bulgarian Acads. of Sciences; Laureate, State Prize of Romania 1964; Gold Medal of 39th Int. Congress of Ind. Chem. 1970; Hero of Socialist Labour 1971. *Publications:* Introduction to Physical Chemistry, Vol. I 1.: Atoms; Molecules; Chemical Bond; Vol. I 2.: Structure and Properties of Molecules; Vol. I 3.: Atomic Nucleus, Nuclear Reactions, Elementary Particles; Vol. II 1.: The Molecular Kinetic Theory of Matter; Vol. II 2.: Chemical Kinetics and Catalysor; Vol. III: Chemical Thermodynamics; over 200 papers in analytical and physical chemistry in Romanian and foreign scientific journals. *Leisure interest:* philosophy. *Address:* Soseaua Kiseleff 22, Bucharest, Romania. *Telephone:* 180476.

MURKOWSKI, Frank Hughes, B.A.; American banker and politician; b. 28 March 1933, Seattle, Wash.; s. of Frank Michael and Helen (Hughes) Murkowski; m. Nancy R. Gore 1954; two s. four d.; ed. Santa Clara Univ., Seattle Univ.; with Pacific Nat. Bank of Seattle 1957-59, Nat. Bank of Alaska, Anchorage 1959-67, Vice-Pres. in Charge of Business Devt., Anchorage 1965-67; Commr., Dept. of Econ. Devt., Alaska State, Juneau 1967-70; Pres. Alaska Nat. Bank of the North 1971-80, Alaska State Chamber of Commerce 1977; Senator from Alaska 1981-; Vice-Pres. Bd. of Trade, B.C. (Canada) and Alaska; mem. American and Alaskan Bankers' Assens., Alaska Conservation Soc.; Republican. *Address:* Senate Office Building, Washington, D.C. 20510; 3 Mile Chena Pump Road, Fairbanks, Alaska 99701, U.S.A. (Home).

MURPHY, Eddie (Edward Regan); American film actor; b. 3 April, Brooklyn, New York; feature player in Saturday Night Live TV show 1980-84; film debut in 48 Hours 1982; recipient of numerous awards and nominations. *Films include:* 48 Hours, Trading Places 1983, Beverly Hills Cop 1984, The Golden Child 1986, Beverly Hills Cop II 1987, Coming to America 1988, Harlem Nights 1989; tours with own comedy show; comedy albums: Eddie Murphy 1982, Eddie Murphy: Comedian 1983; has also released three record albums of comedy and songs. *Address:* c/o Paramount Pictures, 555 Melrose Avenue, Los Angeles, Calif. 90038, U.S.A.

MURPHY, Franklin David, M.D.; American educator and publisher; b. 29 Jan. 1916, Kansas City, Mo.; s. of Franklin E. and Cordelia Brown Murphy; m. Judith Harris Murphy 1940; one s. three d.; ed. Univs. of Kansas and Göttingen and Univ. of Pennsylvania School of Medicine; Dean of School of Medicine and Assoc. Prof. of Internal Medicine, Univ. of Kansas 1948-51; Chancellor, Univ. of Kansas 1951-60; Chancellor, Univ. of Calif. at Los

Angeles 1960-68; Chair. Times Mirror Co. 1968-81, Chair. Exec. Cttee. 1981-86; Chair. Bd. Nat. Gallery, Washington 1985-86; Dir. Emer., The Times Mirror Co.; Chair. Kress Foundation; Trustee, J. Paul Getty Museum, L.A. County Museum of Art, Nat. Gallery of Art; Hon. LL.D., Hon. L.H.D., Hon. D.Sc. *Publications:* in field of chemotherapy, cardiovascular diseases, medical education and general education. *Address:* c/o Times-Mirror Co., Times Mirror Square, Los Angeles, Calif. 90053 (Office); 419 Robert Lane, Beverly Hills, Calif. 90210, U.S.A. (Home).

MURPHY, John A., B.SC., J.D.; American business executive; b. 15 Dec. 1929, New York; s. of John A. Murphy and Mary J. Touhey; m. Carole Ann Paul 1952; four s. two d.; ed. Villanova Univ. and Columbia Univ. Law School; mem. of New York law firm Conboy, Hewitt, O'Brien and Boardman, then joined Philip Morris Inc. as Asst. Gen. Counsel 1962, held various posts in the group, then apptd. Dir. 1971, Pres. and C.O.O. 1985-; Pres. and C.E.O. Miller Brewing Co. 1971-78, Chair. and C.E.O. 1978-84; mem. Bd. of Dirs. Nat. Westminster Bank, U.S.A.; mem. American and New York Bar Assens. and Business Cttee., Metropolitan Museum of Art; Roberto Clemente Award, Nat. Asscn. for Puerto Rican Civil Rights, Distinguished Public Service Award, Anti-Defamation League Appeal, Blackbook Humanitarian Award 1982, New York Boys' Club Harriman Award 1982. *Address:* Philip Morris Companies Inc., 120 Park Avenue, New York, N.Y. 10017, U.S.A. *Telephone:* (212) 880-5000.

MURPHY, Most Rev. John Aloysius; British ecclesiastic (retd.); b. 21 Dec. 1905, Birkenhead; s. of John and Elizabeth Murphy; ed. St. Francis Xavier School, Liverpool, English Coll., Lisbon, Portugal; ordained as a Roman Catholic priest 1931; Co-adjutor Bishop of Shrewsbury 1948, Bishop of Shrewsbury 1949-61; Archbishop of Cardiff 1961-83; Archbishop Emer. 1983-; Hon. D.D. *Address:* "Ty-Mair", St. Joseph's Nursing Home, Harding Avenue, Malpas, Newport, Gwent, NP9 6ZE, Wales.

MURPHY, John Michael; British artist; b. 7 Sept. 1945, St. Albans; s. of James and Maureen (née Tarrant) Murphy; ed. St. Michael's Coll., Hitchin, Luton and Chelsea Schools of Art; one-man exhbns. include Jack Wendler Gallery, London 1973, Museum of Modern Art, Oxford 1975, The New Gallery, ICA, London 1976, Barry Barker Gallery, London 1976, Galerie Arno Kohnen, Düsseldorf 1978, Piwna Warsawa 1980, Arts Council of Northern Ireland Gallery, Belfast 1981, Orchard Gallery, Derry 1982, Vereniging voor het Museum van Hedendaagse Kunt, Ghent 1983, Serpentine and Lisson Galleries, London 1984, Whitechapel Art Gallery, London 1987, Arnolfini, Bristol 1988; has participated in several group exhbns. in Britain, Europe and U.S.A.; Arts Council of G.B. Award 1980. *Address:* 30 Ockendon Road, London, N1 3NP, England. *Telephone:* 01-226 3924.

MURPHY, Sir Leslie Frederick, Kt., B.SC., F.B.I.M.; British business executive; b. 17 Nov. 1915, Southall, Middx.; s. of Frederick Charles and Lillian Annie (Bradshaw) Murphy; m. Marjorie Iris Cowell 1940; one s. one d.; ed. Southall Grammar School and Birkbeck Coll., London; Civil Service 1934-52, incl. Prin. Pvt. Sec. to the late Hugh Gaitskell (then Minister of Fuel and Power) and Asst. Sec. in Petroleum Div. of Ministry; Mobil Oil Co. Inc. 1952-59, Chair. Mobil Supply and Mobil Shipping 1955; Exec. Dir. (Finance and Commercial Divs.) Iraqi Petroleum Co. Group 1959-64; Dir. J. Henry Schroder Wagg & Co. Ltd. 1964-75, Deputy Chair. 1972-73; Dir. Schroders Ltd. 1970-75, 1980-, Deputy Chair. 1973-75; Consultant on Middle East affairs, Schroder Group 1975-; Dir. Unigate Ltd. 1968-75; Deputy Chair. Nat. Enterprise Bd. (NEB) 1975-77, Chair. NEB 1977-79; Chair. Petroleum Econs. Ltd. 1980-87, Dir. 1980-; Dir. Simon Eng. Ltd. 1980-85, Folksam Int. Insurance Co. (U.K.) Ltd. 1980-; Trustee SDP 1981-. *Leisure interests:* music, golf. *Address:* Schroders Ltd., 120 Cheapside, London, E.C.2 (Office); Hedgerley, Barton Common Road, Barton-on-Sea, Hants., England (Home). *Telephone:* 01-588 4000 (Office).

MURPHY, Richard William; American diplomatist; b. 29 July 1929, Boston; s. of John Deneen Murphy and Jane Keenan Diehl; m. Anne Herrick Cook 1955; one s. two d.; ed. Phillips Exeter Acad., Harvard Univ., Emmanuel Coll., Univ. of Cambridge; served with U.S. Army 1953-55; with Dept. of State 1955-, Consultant Admin. Officer, Salisbury, Southern Rhodesia 1955-58, Arabic Language studies, Beirut, Lebanon 1959-60, Econ. Officer, Aleppo, Syria 1960-63, Political Officer, Jeddah, Saudi Arabia 1963-66, Amman, Jordan 1966-68, Dir. Personnel Affairs; S. Asia Bureau 1968-70; Dir. Arab Peninsula Affairs 1970-71; Amb. to Mauritania, Nouakchott 1971-74, to Syria 1974-78, to Philippines 1978-81, to Saudi Arabia 1981-83, Asst. Sec. of State, Washington 1983-; Superior Honor Award (Dept. of State) 1969. *Leisure interests:* archaeology, tennis. *Address:* Department of State, 2201 C Street, N.W. Washington, D.C. 20520; 2607 O Street, N.W., Washington, D.C. 20007, U.S.A. (Home).

MURPHY, Thomas, D.SC., LL.D., M.D., F.R.C.P.I., F.R.C.S.I., M.R.I.A.; Irish medical practitioner and university president; b. 3 Dec. 1915, Co. Wexford; s. of late John and Mary Murphy; m. Rosaline Byrne 1944; four s.; ed. Clongowes Wood Coll. and Univ. Coll., Dublin; jr. hosp. appts. 1940-43; Medical Officer, Bord na Mona 1943-48; Asst. Medical Officer of Health, Co. Kildare 1948-51; medical staff, Dept. of Health 1951-55; Prof. of Social and Preventive Medicine, Univ. Coll., Dublin 1955-72, Dean, Faculty of Medicine 1962-65, Registrar 1965-72, President 1972-86. *Publications:* 20 articles in scientific journals. *Address:* 11 Crannagh Road, Rathfarnham, Dublin, Ireland. *Telephone:* 906664.

MURPHY, Thomas Aquinas; American motor executive (retd.); b. 10 Dec. 1915, Hornell, N.Y.; s. of John Joseph and Alma Murphy; m. Catherine Maquire 1941; one s. two d.; ed. Leo High School, Chicago and Univ. of Illinois; joined Gen. Motors Corpn. 1938, Asst. Treas. 1959, Comptroller 1967, Treas. 1968-70, Vice-Pres. 1970-72, Vice-Chair. 1972-74, Chair. and C.E.O. 1974-80, Dir. 1980-. *Address:* c/o General Motors Corporation, General Motors Building, 3044 West Grand Boulevard, Detroit, Mich. 48202, U.S.A.

MURPHY, William Beverly, B.S.; American business executive; b. 17 June 1907, Appleton, Wis.; s. of S. W. and Hilma (née Anderson) Murphy; m. Helen Brennan 1930; three s. one d.; ed. Univ. of Wisconsin; Exec. Vice-Pres. A. C. Nielsen Co. 1928-38; Campbell Soup Co. 1938-42; War Production Bd., Washington 1942-45; rejoined Campbell Soup Co. 1945, Dir. 1949-79, Pres. 1953-72; Dir. Merck & Co. Inc. 1958-80; Chair. Radio Free Europe 1960-61, Dir. American Telephone and Telegraph Co. 1961-78; Chair. the Nutrition Foundation 1964-65, Business Council 1965-66; Dir. Int. Paper Co. 1969-80; Chair. Business Roundtable 1972-73; Life mem. and Trustee, Wisconsin Alumni Research Foundation; Life mem. Exec. Cttee. M.I.T.; Trustee, Phila. Museum of Art; Life mem. Philadelphia Soc. for the Promotion of Agric., Pres. 1985-86; awarded Medal for Merit by Pres. Truman 1947. *Address:* 110 Maple Hill Road, Gladwyne, Pa. 19035, U.S.A.

MURPHY-O'CONNOR, Rt. Rev. Cormac, S.T.L.; British ecclesiastic; b. 24 Aug. 1932, Reading, Berks.; s. of Dr. Patrick George Murphy-O'Connor and Ellen Theresa Cuddigan; ed. Prior Park Coll., Bath, The Venerable English Coll., Rome and Gregorian Univ., Rome; ordained Priest 1956; Parish Priest, Portswood, Southampton 1970-71; Rector Venerable English Coll., Rome 1971-77; Bishop of Arundel and Brighton 1977-; First Chair. Bishops' Cttee. for Europe 1980-83; Co.-Chair. Anglo-R.C. Int. Comm. 1983-; Chair. TVS Religious Advisers Panel 1985-. *Publication:* The Family of the Church 1984. *Leisure interests:* music (keen pianist), walking and reading. *Address:* St. Joseph's Hall, Storrington, Pulborough, W. Sussex, RH20 4HE, England. *Telephone:* (090 66) 2172.

MURRAY, Dame A. Rosemary, D.B.E., D.PHIL., J.P.; British chemist and university administrator; b. 28 July 1913, Havant; d. of late Admiral A. J. L. Murray and Ellen Maxwell Spooner; ed. Downe House School, Newbury, and Lady Margaret Hall, Oxford; Lecturer in Chem., Royal Holloway Coll. 1938-41, Univ. of Sheffield 1941-42; W.R.N.S. 1942-46; Fellow and Tutor, Girton Coll., Cambridge 1946-54; Pres. New Hall, Cambridge 1954-81; Univ. Demonstrator in Chem. 1947-52, Vice-Chancellor Cambridge Univ. 1975-77; City Magistrate, Cambridge 1953-83; Pres. Nat. Inst. of Adult Educ. 1977-80; Dir. Midland Bank 1978-84, The Observer 1981-; D.L. (Cambridgeshire) 1982; Chair., mem. cttees. and councils in univs., colls. of educ., schools, Wages Councils, Armed Forces Pay Review Body and others; Hon. D.Sc. (Ulster) 1972, (Leeds) 1975, (Pa.) 1975, (Wellesley, S. Calif.) 1976; Hon. D.C.L. (Oxford) 1976; Hon. LL.D. (Sheffield) 1977, (Cambridge) 1988. *Leisure interests:* foreign travel, gardening, book binding, restoring. *Address:* 9 Grange Court, Cambridge, CB3 9BD, England.

MURRAY, Allen Edward, B.S.; American business executive; b. 5 March 1929, New York; s. of Allen Murray and Carla Jones; m. Patricia Ryan 1951; one s. four d.; ed. New York Univ.; trainee, Nat. Bank & Trust Co., New York 1948-49; accountant, Gulf Oil Corpn. 1949-52; various financial positions, Socony-Vacuum Overseas Supply Co. (Mobil) 1952-56; with Mobil Oil Corpn. 1956-, Vice-Pres. Planning, N. American Div. 1968-69, Vice-Pres. Planning, Supply and Transportation, N. American Div. 1969-74, Exec. Vice-Pres. N. American Div. 1974, Pres. U.S. Marketing and Refining Div., Exec. Vice-Pres. 1975-82; Pres. Worldwide Marketing and Refining 1979-82, Corporate Pres. 1983-84, C.O.O. 1984-86, C.E.O., C.O.O., Chair. Exec. Cttee. 1986, Chair. 1986-, also Dir. 1976-; Dir. Metropolitan Life Insurance Co., Nat. Foreign Trade Council, American Petroleum Inst.; mem. Council on Foreign Relations. *Address:* Mobil Corporation, 150 East 42nd Street, New York, N.Y. 10017, U.S.A.

MURRAY, Charles Henry, B.COMM.; Irish banker; b. 1917, Dublin; m. Margaret Ryan; one s. four d.; ed. Christian Bros. School, Dublin; entered Civil Service 1934; Asst. Sec., Dept. of Finance 1961, Sec. 1969-76; Dir. Central Bank of Ireland 1969-76, Gov. 1976-81; Chair. Cttee. of Govs. of EEC Cen. Banks 1977/78; Dir. Northern Bank 1982-; Chair. Northern Bank (Ireland) 1986-; Deputy Chair. Co-operation North 1982-86; Pres. Inst. of Public Admin. 1980-86; Hon. LL.D.; Kt. Officer Order of Merit (Italy). *Leisure interests:* theatre, golf. *Address:* 6 Washington Park, Dublin 14, Ireland.

MURRAY, Hon. Lowell, M.A.; Canadian politician; b. 26 Sept. 1936, New Waterford, Nova Scotia; s. of late Daniel Murray and Evelyn Yound; m. Colleen Elaine; two s.; ed. St. Francis Xavier Univ., Queen's Univ., Ont.; fmr. Chief of Staff to Minister of Justice and Minister of Public Works, also to two Senators; Progressive Conservative Nat. Campaign Chair. in Gen. Election 1979, 1981-83; Senator 1979-, Co-Chair. Jt. Senate-House of Commons Cttee. on Official Languages 1980-81; Chair. Standing Cttee. on Banking, Trade and Commerce 1984-; Leader of the Senate and Minister of State for Fed.-Provincial Relations July 1986-; Acting Minister of Communications 1988-89; mem. Bd. of Trustees, Inst. for Research on

Public Policy 1984–, Trilateral Cttee. 1985–, Bd. of Dirs. Parl. Int. Forum 1984–; Progressive Conservative. *Address:* The Senate, Ottawa, Canada.

MURRAY, Noreen Elizabeth, PH.D., F.R.S.; British university teacher of molecular biology; b. (as Noreen Parker) 26 Feb. 1935, Burnley, Lancs.; d. of John and Lilian G. Parker; m. Kenneth Murray, 1958; no c.; ed. Lancaster Girls' Grammar School, King's Coll., Univ. of London, Univ. of Birmingham; Research Assoc. Dept. of Biological Sciences, Stanford Univ., Calif. 1960–64; Research Fellow Botany School, Univ. of Cambridge 1964–67; at Dept. of Molecular Biology, Univ. of Edin., Lecturer, then Sr. Lecturer 1974–80, Reader 1982–88, Prof. of Molecular Genetics 1988–; mem. MRC Molecular Genetics Unit 1968–74; Group Leader, European Molecular Biology Lab., Heidelberg 1980–82. *Publications:* numerous articles in specialist publs. and journals. *Leisure interest:* gardening. *Address:* Department of Molecular Biology, University of Edinburgh, King's Buildings, Mayfield Road, Edin. EH9 3JR, Scotland. *Telephone:* (031) 667-1081, ext. 2729.

MURRAY, Dame Rosemary (see Murray, Dame A. R.).

MURRAY, Timothy Vincent, F.R.I.B.A., F.R.A.I.C., F.R.I.A.I., M.C.D.; Canadian-Irish architect; b. 6 May 1930, Dublin, Ireland; s. of T. J. Murray and M. T. Purcell; m. Juliet J. Taylor 1958; two s. one d.; ed. Rockwell Coll., Cashel, Ireland, Univ. Coll., Dublin and Liverpool Univ.; architect and planner, Lord Holford 1953–55, London Co. Council 1955–57, Fed. Govt. of Canada 1957–58; Prin. and Founding Partner, Murray and Murray Assocs., architects and planners, Ottawa, Toronto, Dublin, Cork, Africa 1959–; Visiting Lecturer/Critic, Carleton Univ., Ottawa, Nova Scotia School of Architecture, Univ. of Dublin, Ireland; Chair. Bd. of Govs., Ashbury Coll. 1985–87; Acting Chair. Design Cttee., Nat. Capital Comm., Fed. Govt. of Canada 1985–87; recipient of several architectural awards; Kt. of St. Gregory, Kt. of St. Lazarus of Jerusalem. *Publications:* articles in professional journals. *Address:* 444 Springfield Road, Ottawa, Ont. K1M 0K4, Canada. *Telephone:* (613) 741-2212.

MURRAY OF EPPING FOREST, Baron (Life Peer), cr. 1985, of Telford in the County of Shropshire; **Rt. Hon. Lionel (Len) Murray,** P.C., O.B.E.; British trade unionist; b. 2 Aug. 1922; m. Heather Woolf 1945; two s. two d.; ed. Wellington Grammar School, Univ. of London, New Coll., Oxford; with Econ. Dept., TUC 1947, Head of Dept. 1954–69; Asst. Gen. Sec. TUC 1969–73, Gen. Sec. 1973–84; mem. Social Science Research Council 1965–70, NEDC 1973–84; Vice-Pres. European Trade Union Confed. 1974–84, Int. Confed. Free Trade Unions 1973–84; mem. Cttee. to Review Functioning of Financial Insts. 1977–80; Bd. of Trustees, Anglo-German Foundation for the Study of Industrial Soc. 1977–; Gov. L.S.E. 1970; Visiting Fellow, Nuffield Coll., Oxford 1974–82; Hon. Fellow, New Coll., Oxford 1975, Sheffield City Polytechnic 1979, Queen Mary Coll., London; Hon. D.Sc. (Aston) 1977, (Salford) 1978; Hon LL.D (St. Andrews) 1979, (Leeds) 1985. *Address:* 29 The Crescent, Loughton, Essex, England. *Telephone:* 01-508 4425.

MURRAY OF NEWHAVEN, Baron (Life Peer) cr. 1964, of Newhaven; **Keith (Anderson Hope) Murray,** K.C.B., PH.D.; British university administrator; b. 28 July 1903, Edinburgh; s. of the late Rt. Hon. Lord Murray, C.M.G., K.C., LL.D.; ed. Edinburgh Acad., Edinburgh Univ., Cornell Univ., New York and Oxford Univ.; Ministry of Agric. 1925–26; Commonwealth Fund Fellow 1926–29; Agricultural Econs. Research Inst., Oxford 1929–32, Research Officer 1932–39; Ministry of Food 1939–40; R.A.F.V.R. 1941–42; Dir. of Food and Agric., Middle East Supply Centre 1942–45; Fellow and Bursar, Lincoln Coll., Oxford 1937–53, Rector 1944–53; Chair. Univ. Grants Cttee. 1953–63; Chancellor, Southampton Univ. 1964–74; Visitor, Loughborough Tech. Univ. 1968–78; Dir. Leverhulme Trust 1965–72; Trustee, Wellcome Trust 1965–73; Hon. Fellow, Oriel and Lincoln Colls., Oxford, Downing Coll., Cambridge, Birkbeck Coll., London, UMIST; Hon. LL.D., Hon. D.C.L., Hon. D.Litt., Hon. D.U. *Address:* 224 Ashley Gardens, London, SW1P 1PA, England. *Telephone:* 01-828 4113.

MURTA, Jack Burnett; Canadian politician and farmer; b. 13 May, Carman, Man.; m. Lynda Morris; one s. two d. ed. Univ. of Manitoba; farm owner at Graysville, Man.; M.P. for Lisgar-Man., fmr. Fed. Progressive Conservative Party spokesperson on multi-culturalism, fmr. Caucus spokesperson for Northern Devt., for Transport, fmr. Chair. Transportation Cttee., Agric. Cttee., Parl. Sec. to Pres. of Treasury Bd. 1979, Chair. Fed. Task Force on problems of grain transportation industry 1979, mem. Special sub-cttee. on Latin America and the Caribbean 1981, Bd. Dirs. Parl. Centre for Foreign Affairs and Foreign Trade 1982; Minister of State for Multiculturalism 1984–85, for Tourism 1985–86; Progressive Conservative Party. *Address:* Room 535-C, House of Commons, Ottawa, Ont., K1A 0A6, Canada.

MURUMBI, Joseph A.; Kenyan politician; b. 18 June 1911; s. of Peter Nicholas Zuzarte and Njambiak Ole Murumbi; m. 1966; one s.; ed. Bangalore and Bellary, S. India; Staff of Admin. of Somalia 1941–51; Asst. Sec. Movement for Colonial Freedom 1951–57; Press and Tourist Officer, Moroccan Embassy, London 1957–62; Treas. Kenyan African Nat. Union (KANU) 1962; mem. Kenya House of Reps. 1963–; Minister of State in Prime Minister's Office 1963–64; Minister of External Affairs 1964–66; Vice-Pres. of Kenya May-Dec. 1966; fmr. Chair. Rothmans of Pall Mall (Kenya) Ltd. and several Kenya cos. *Leisure interests:* gardening and

collecting stamps, art and Africana. *Address:* P.O. Box 41730, Nairobi (Office); Intona Ranch, P.O. Box 76, Kilgoris via Kisii; P.O. Box 18654, Nairobi, Kenya (Homes). *Telephone:* Nairobi 558533.

MUSABAYEV, Isak Kurbanovich; Soviet specialist in infectious diseases; b. 9 Oct. 1920, Naukent, Pergana Dist., Uzbekistan; ed. Samarkand Med. Inst.; mem. CPSU 1944–; Chair. Dept. of Infectious Diseases Samarkand Med. Inst. 1949–51, of Tashkent Inst. for the Advanced Training of Physicians 1951–62; Deputy Dir. of Science, Tashkent Inst. of Epidemiology 1962–70; corresp. mem. U.S.S.R. Acad. of Sciences 1961, mem. Acad. of Sciences of Uzbek S.S.R. 1966; Order of Lenin, many other decorations. *Publications include:* Q Fever 1958, Infectious Hepatitis 1961, Diphtheria 1967, Cholera: Clinical Study, Treatment and Hygiene 1967. *Address:* Academy of Sciences, Tashkent, Uzbek S.S.R., U.S.S.R.

MUSCHG, Adolf, PH.D.; Swiss author and professor of German literature; b. 13 May 1934, Zürich; s. of Adolf Muschg and Frieda Muschg-Ernst; m. Hanna Johansen 1967; three s.; ed. Zürich and Cambridge, U.K.; teacher, Kant. Gymnasium, Zürich 1959–62; Lektor, Int. Christina Univ. Tokyo 1962–64; Asst. Seminar für deutsche Philologie, Univ. of Göttingen 1964–67; Asst. Prof. Cornell Univ. 1967–69; in charge of research, Univ. of Geneva 1969–70; Prof. of German Language and Literature, Eidgenössische Technische Hochschule, Zürich 1970–; Fellow, Wissenschaftskolleg, Berlin 1987–88; mem. Berlin, Mainz and Darmstadt Acads.; various literary prizes. *Publications:* novels: Im Sommer des Hasen 1965, Albissers Grund 1974, Baiyun 1980, Das Licht und der Schlüssel 1984; Liebesgeschichten 1972, Der Turmhahn 1987; monograph: Gottfried Keller; criticism: Literatur als Therapie? 1981. *Leisure interest:* writing. *Address:* Vorbühlstrasse 7, CH-8802 Kilchberg, Switzerland. *Telephone:* 01-715 55 61.

MUSEVENI, Yoweri Kaguta; Ugandan head of state; b. 1944; m.; four c.; ed. Univ. Coll. of Dar es Salaam; Research Asst. Office of fmr. Pres. Milton Obote (q.v.) 1970–71; in Tanzania planning overthrow of regime of Idi Amin (q.v.) 1971–79; participated in Tanzanian invasion of Uganda 1979; Defence Minister in interim Govt. following overthrow of Amin 1980; following election of Dr. Obote, amid allegations of ballot-rigging, in 1980, spent five years as leader of National Resistance Army (NRA) waging a guerrilla war 1980–86; President of Uganda (following overthrow of Govt. by NRA forces) and Minister of Defence Feb. 1986–. *Address:* Office of the President, Kampala, Uganda.

MUSGRAVE, Thea, MUS.DOC.; British composer; b. 27 May 1928, Edinburgh; d. of James and Joan (née Hacking) Musgrave; m. Peter Mark 1971; ed. Edinburgh Univ. and Paris Conservatoire (under Nadia Boulanger); Lecturer, Extra-Mural Dept., London Univ. 1958–65; Visiting Prof. Univ. of Calif., Santa Barbara 1970; Distinguished Prof., Queen's Coll., City Univ. of New York 1987; Koussevitzky Award 1972; Guggenheim Fellow 1974–75, 1982–83; Hon. D.Mus. (Council for Nat. Academic Awards, Smith Coll. and Old Dominion Univ.). *Works include:* Chamber Concerto 1, 2 & 3 1966, Concerto for Orchestra 1967, Clarinet Concerto 1968, Beauty and the Beast (ballet) 1969, Night Music 1969, Horn Concerto 1971, The Voice of Ariadne (chamber opera) 1972–73, Viola Concerto 1973, Space Play 1974, Mary, Queen of Scots (opera) 1976–77, A Christmas Carol (opera) 1978–79, An Occurrence at Owl Creek Bridge (radio opera) 1981, Harriet, A Woman Called Moses 1980–84; chamber music, songs, choral music, orchestral music. *Leisure interests:* cooking, cinema, reading. *Address:* c/o Novello and Co. Ltd., 8 Lower James Street, London, W1R 4DN, England.

MUSHKETIK, Yuri Mikhailovich; Soviet author; b. 21 March 1929, Verkiivka, Chernigiv Region; m.; two d.; ed. Kiev Univ.; mem. CPSU 1951–; first works published 1952; U.S.S.R. State Prize 1987. *Publications include:* Fires in the Middle of the Night 1959, Black Bread 1960, The Heart and the Stone 1961, Drop of Blood 1964, Ya Sa (novel) 1987. *Address:* U.S.S.R. Union of Writers, Ul. Vorovskogo 52, Moscow, U.S.S.R.

MUSIKER, Reuben, M.A.; South African university librarian; b. 12 Jan. 1931, Johannesburg; s. of Judel Musiker and Sarah Musiker; m. Naomi Measroch 1961; one s. two d.; ed. Univs. of Pretoria, the Witwatersrand and Cape Town; Fellow, S. African Inst. for Librarianship and Information Science; Deputy Univ. Librarian, Rhodes Univ., Grahamstown 1962–72; Dir. of Library Services, Univ. of the Witwatersrand 1973–74; Univ. Librarian and Head, Dept. of Librarianship and Information Science, Univ. of the Witwatersrand 1975–; Ad Hominem Prof. Univ. of the Witwatersrand. *Publications:* five books and numerous articles in periodicals, etc. *Leisure interest:* music. *Address:* c/o Library, University of the Witwatersrand, Private Bag X1, Wits. 2050, South Africa. *Telephone:* (011) 716-2400.

MUSIN, Dmitri Petrovich; Soviet diplomatist; Amb. to Australia 1972–75, to Fiji 1974–75, to Jamaica 1978–87, to Grenada 1980–82. *Address:* c/o Ministry of Foreign Affairs, Moscow, U.S.S.R.

MUSKIE, Edmund Sixtus, A.B., LL.B.; American lawyer and politician; b. 28 March 1914, Rumford, Maine; m. Jane Gray 1948; two s. three d.; ed. Bates Coll., Maine and Cornell Law School, Ithaca, N.Y.; admitted to Mass. Bar 1939, Maine Bar 1940, Fed. District Court 1941; practised as lawyer, Waterville, Maine 1940–; served U.S. Navy 1942–45; mem. Maine House of Reps. 1947–51; Dem. Floor leader 1949–51; Dist. Dir. for Maine, Office of Price Stabilization 1951–52; City Solicitor Waterville, Maine

1954–55; Gov. of the State of Maine 1955–59; U.S. Senator from Maine 1959–80; Senate Asst. Majority Whip 1966–80; fmr. Chair. Senate Sub-Cttees. on Environmental Pollution, Intergovt. Relations; Chair. Dem. Senatorial Campaign Cttee. 1967–69; Cand. for Vice-presidency of U.S.A. 1968; Chair. Senate Budget Cttee. 1974–80; Sec. of State 1980–81; Sr. Partner in law firm Chadbourne, Parke, Whiteside & Wolff 1981–; mem. Cttee. of Enquiry into Nat. Security Council 1986–87; mem. American Acad. of Arts and Sciences, Roosevelt Campobello Int. Park Comm.; Hon. LL.D. (Bates, Lafayette, Bowdoin and Colby Colls., Maine, Portland and Suffolk Univs.); Laetare Medal (Notre Dame) 1981; Presidential Medal of Freedom 1981; Democrat. *Publication:* Journeys 1972. *Leisure interests:* photography, golf, gardening. *Address:* 1101 Vermont Avenue, N.W., Suite 900, Washington, D.C. 20005, U.S.A.

MUSOKOTWANE, Rt. Hon. Kebby Sililo Kambulu; Zambian politician and educationist; b. 5 May 1946, Musokotwane; m. Muzya Regina Bulowa 1967; four s. two d.; ed. Monze Secondary School, David Livingstone Teachers' Training Coll., Univ. of Zambia; primary school teacher 1965, Demonstration Teacher 1965–71, Deputy Head Teacher 1968–69, Head Teacher 1970, Lecturer 1972–73; M.P. 1973–; Minister of Water and Natural Resources 1977–78, of Youth and Sport 1979, of Finance and Tech. Co-operation 1979–83, of Gen. Educ. and Culture 1983–85, of Educ., Sport and Culture March 1989–; Prime Minister 1985–89. *Address:* Ministry of Education and Culture, P.O. Box RW50093, Lusaka, Zambia. *Telephone:* Lusaka 211100.

MUSTAPHA BIN DATU HARUN, Tun Datu, S.M.N., S.P.D.K., S.I.M.P., P.N.B.S., S.P.M.J., S.P.M.P., S.P.C.M., K.R.C.L., K.V.O., O.B.E.; Sabah (Malaysian) administrator; b. 31 Aug. 1918; m. Helen Moore 1974; mem. Legis. Council of N. Borneo 1956–63; Chair. Sabah (N. Borneo) Nat. Council; Chair. and Leader United Sabah Nat. Org. (USNO) –1976, Pres. 1981–86; Yang di-Pertua Negara (Head of State) of Sabah 1963–67, Chief Minister 1967–76; mem. Royal Commonwealth Soc., Nat. Unity Council. *Address:* United Sabah National Organization, Kota Kinabalu, Sabah, Malaysia.

MUSY, Jean Edouard; French professor; b. 12 Aug. 1938, Montauban; s. of René and Susanne (née Rouffy) Musy; unmarried; ed. Lycée Charlemagne, Paris and Sorbonne, Paris; Prof. Lycée Pierre d'Ailly, Compiègne 1965–67; Fondation Thiers 1967–69; Asst. Prof., Sorbonne 1969–73; Counsellor, Office of Minister of Culture 1973–75; Del.-Gen. for Formation and Educ., Ministry of Educ. 1975–78; Dir. Ecole Nat. Supérieure des Beaux Arts, Paris 1978–82; Cultural Counsellor, Office of M. Jacques Chirac, Mayor of Paris 1982–84; Dir. Vidéothèque de Paris 1983–85; Dir. Affaires culturelles de la Ville de Paris 1985–; Columnist for Le Figaro 1983–; Officier, Ordre nationale du Mérite, Ordre des Palmes académiques; Commdr. des Arts et Lettres. *Publications:* Hérésie et mouvements populaires en France au XIe siècle 1975; numerous articles on history and politics of art. *Leisure interest:* music. *Address:* Hôtel de Ville, 75004 Paris; 31 rue Bonaparte, 75006 Paris, France. *Telephone:* 274 22 02.

MUTALLAB, Alhaji Umaru Abdul; Nigerian accountant and government official; b. 15 Dec. 1939, Katsina, Kaduna State; m.; three d.; ed. Barewa Coll., Zaria, Achimota Coll. of Admin., Ghana, S.W. London Coll., U.K.; mem. of Assen. of Certified Accountants 1965–; Man. Accountant, Fuller, Jenks, Beecroft Co. Ltd., London 1965–67; Chief Accountant, Defence Industries Corpn. of Nigeria, Kaduna 1967–71; Financial Controller, New Nigeria Devt. Co. 1971–74, Gen. Man. 1974–75; Fed. Commr. for Econ. Devt. 1975–76, for Co-operatives and Supply 1976–78; in banking in pvt. sector July 1978–. *Address:* c/o Federal Executive Council, Lagos, Nigeria.

MUTI, Riccardo; Italian conductor; b. 28 July 1941; Naples; s. of Domenico Muti and Gilda Sellitto; m. Cristina Mazzavillani 1969; two s. one d.; ed. Naples and Milan Conservatories of Music; Prin. Conductor, Maggio Musicale, Florence 1969–, Philharmonia Orchestra, London 1973–82, Music Dir. 1979–82, Conductor Laureate 1982–; Prin. Guest Conductor Philadelphia Orchestra 1977–80, Prin. Conductor and Music Dir. 1980–; Music Dir. La Scala (Milan) 1986–; concert tours in U.S.A. with Boston, Chicago and Phila. Orchestras; concerts at Salzburg, Edinburgh, Lucerne, Flanders and Vienna festivals; also conducted Berlin Philharmonic, Vienna Philharmonic and Concertgebouw Amsterdam; opera: Florence, Munich, Covent Garden, La Scala, Vienna; Accad. di Santa Cecilia, Rome; Accademico Dell'Accademia Cherubini, Florence; Ufficiale al merito Repubblica Tedesca; Diapason d'Oro; Premio Critica Discografia Italiana; Prix Academie nat. du disque 1977; Deutscher Schallplatten Preis; Grand Prix du disque for La Traviata (Verdi), Requiem in C minor (Cherubini) 1982. *Address:* Via Corti alle Mura 25, Ravenna, Italy. *Telephone:* 38428.

MUTO, Kabun; Japanese politician; b. 18 Nov 1926; s. of Kaichi Muto; m. Hisako Koketsu 1951; two s.; ed. Kyoto Univ.; worked in family brewing business; mem. House of Reps. 1967–; Parl. Vice-Minister of Home Affairs 1972–73, Minister of Agric., Forestry and Fisheries 1979–80; Chair. Liberal-Democratic Party (LDP) Commerce and Industry Div. 1974–76; Deputy Sec.-Gen. LDP 1978–79; mem. Standing Cttee. on Budget, House of Reps., LDP Finance Cttee.; Vice-Pres. LDP Cttee. on small and medium enterprises, LDP Tax Policy Cttee. etc. *Publications:* Kusa-no-Ne Minshushugi (Grassroots Democracy), Jiminto Saisei no Teigen, Nihon no Sentaku (Japan's Choice) etc. *Address:* 10-18, Daikanyama-cho, Shibuya-ku, Tokyo, Japan.

MUTTER, Anne-Sophie; German violinist; b. 29 June 1963, Rheinfelden; d. of Karl-Wilhelm Mutter and Gerlinde (née Winter) Mutter; ed. Studium am Konservatorium Winterthur, Switzerland; began musical career playing piano and violin 1969; won the Jugend musiziert Prize (Fed. Repub. of Germany) for violin 1970, for piano 1970, for violin 1974; played in the Int. Music Festival, Lucerne 1976; début with Berlin Philharmonic Orchestra at Pfingstfestspiele Salzburg 1977; played violin in chamber music ensemble throughout world 1977–; Guest teacher Royal Acad. of Music, London 1985; awards include Künstler des Jahres 'Deutscher Schallplattenpreis', Grand Prix Int. du Disque, Record Acad. Prize, Tokyo 1982, Hon. Pres. Mozart Soc., Univ. of Oxford 1983. *Leisure interests:* graphic arts, sport. *Address:* Rychenbergstrasse 199 d, CH-8400 Winterthur, Switzerland.

MUWAMBA, Jake Thomson, M.A., F.B.I.M.; Malawi diplomatist and business consultant; b. 14 Oct. 1925, Ndola, Zambia; s. of late Ernest Alexander Muwamba and Alice Nyawadama Muwamba; m. Vuyelwa Gladys Muwamba 1962; three s. one d.; ed. High School in S. Africa, Swansea Univ. Coll., S. Wales, Graduate School of Man. and Urban Professions, New School for Social Research, New York; Welfare Officer, later Asst. Personnel Officer, Anglo-American Group of Mines 1954–62; Head of Dept. of Social Welfare, Govt. of Malawi 1962–69; formed Dept. of Tourism 1969, Dir. of Tourism 1971–75; Perm. Rep. to UN 1975–81; High Commr. to Canada (non-resident) 1975–78; also served as first interim Dir. of Sports and Culture, Man. Dir. Int. Marketing and Promotion Services Ltd.; Dir. Blantyre Hotels Ltd., Smallholder Tea Authority, Marketing Services Malawi Ltd., Wills Faber Syfrets Advisory Services (Pvt.) Ltd., B.P. and P. Industries PLC (MW.) Ltd., Lake Shore Hotel (Salima) Ltd.; Chair. Designated Schools Bd., Monuments Advisory Council, Super Freeze Ltd.; Amb. to U.S.A. 1975–81. *Leisure interests:* sports, reading, music, gardening, service club activities. *Address:* International Marketing and Promotion Services Ltd., Dossani House, Glyn Jones Road, P.O. Box 631, Blantyre, Malawi.

MUWANGA, Paulo; Ugandan politician; mem. Uganda Nat. Congress in 1950s, mem. Cen. Exec.; with Foreign Ministry of Dr. Obote's govt. 1962, Chief of Protocol 1969–71; Amb. to Paris 1971–73; in exile, Dar es Salaam 1973–75, London 1975–77 (ran fish and chip shop in Caterham); mem. Exec. Cttee. Uganda Nat. Liberation Front (UNLF) 1979–80; Internal Affairs Minister in fmr. Pres. Lule's govt. and subsequently in Pres. Binaisa's govt. 1979–80, Minister of Labour 1980; Chair. Mil. Comm. UNLF May–Dec. 1980; Minister of Defence and Vice-Pres. of Uganda 1980–85, Prime Minister of Uganda Aug. 1985; under house arrest July 1986; on trial for treason Oct. 1986 and for kidnapping Nov. 1986; treason charges dropped Feb. 1987.

MUZENDA, Simon Vengai; Zimbabwean politician; b. 28 Oct. 1922; m. Mandy Muzenda 1950; three s. five d. (one deceased); returned to S. Rhodesia (now Zimbabwe) 1950; Sec.-Gen. Voice Assen. 1953; Chair. Umvuma Branch, Nat. Democratic Party, later Organizing Sec. Victoria Prov. 1960–61; founder mem. Zimbabwe African People's Union (ZAPU) and Admin. Sec. Victoria Prov. 1961–62; imprisoned 1962–64; founder mem. Zimbabwe African Nat. Union (ZANU) 1963, mem. Cen. Cttee. 1964; activity restricted 1964–71; mem. Exec., African Nat. Council, and Sec. of Law and Order 1971; Deputy Admin. Sec. Zambia 1975–76; co-ordinated activities of ZANU from Zambia and formed Zimbabwe People's Army (ZIPA) in conjunction with ZAPU leadership; Deputy Leader of ZANU 1976, Deputy Pres. 1977–, mem. Politburo; Deputy Prime Minister 1980–88, Vice-Pres. of Zimbabwe Jan. 1988–; Minister of Foreign Affairs 1980–81, of Energy and Water Resources 1984–85. *Leisure interests:* wrestling, music, traditional music. *Address:* Office of the Vice-President, Harare, Zimbabwe.

MUZOREWA, Abel Tendekayi, M.A.; Zimbabwean ecclesiastic; b. 14 April 1925, Old Umtali; m. Margaret Muzorewa; ed. Old Umtali Secondary School, Nyadiri United Methodist Mission, Cen. Methodist Coll., Fayette, Mo., Scarritt Coll., Nashville, Tenn., U.S.A.; Pastor, Chiduku N. Circuit 1955–57; studied in U.S.A. 1958–63; Pastor, Old Umtali Mission 1963; Dir. of Youth Work, Rhodesia Annual Conf. 1965; Joint Dir. of Youth Work, Rhodesia Christian-Council 1965; Travelling Sec. Student Christian Movt. 1965; Resident Bishop, United Methodist Church (Rhodesia Area) 1968–; Pres. African Nat. Council (ANC) 1971–85, All-Africa Conf. of Churches; Rep. of ANC at Geneva Conf. on Rhodesia 1976; mem. Transitional Exec. Council to prepare transfer to majority rule in Rhodesia 1978–79, Prime Minister of Zimbabwe Rhodesia, Minister of Defence and Combined Operations June–Dec. 1979; attended Lancaster House Conf. 1979; contested March 1980 election as Leader of ANC; detained Nov. 1983–Sept. 1984; fled to U.S.A. 1985, returned to Zimbabwe Nov. 1986; Hon. D.D. (Cen. Methodist Coll., Mo.) 1960; UN Prize for Outstanding Achievement in Human Rights 1973. *Publications:* Manifesto for African National Council 1972, Rise Up and Walk (autobiog.) 1978. *Address:* c/o United African National Council, 40 Charter Road, Harare, Zimbabwe.

MVENG, Engelbert, L. EN PHIL., L. EN THEOL., DR. D'ETAT; Cameroon Jesuit priest and professor of history; b. 9 May 1930, Enam-Ngal; ed. Univs. of Dakar, Lyons and Paris-Sorbonne; Prof. Coll. Libermann, Douala 1957–60, Univ. of Yaoundé 1965–; Pres. Art Comm. Société Africaine de Culture 1963–; consultant UNESCO 1963–66; Head, Dept. of Cultural Affairs, Ministry of Educ. and Culture 1966–74; Sec.-Gen. Ecumenical Assen. of

African Theologians 1980-, Pan-African Movt. of Christian Intellectuals; Pan-African co-ordinator, Ecumenical Asscn. of Third World Theologians 1981-86; Co-Pres. World Conf. on Religion and Peace, Africa chapter 1983-; mem. Acad. Française, Acad. des Sciences d'Outre-Mer; Gold Medal for Culture (Zaïre). *Publications:* L'Art d'Afrique Noire 1964, Art nègre, Art chrétien? 1969, Les Sources Grècques de l'Histoire négro-africaine 1972, L'Art et l'artisanat africain 1981, Histoire du Caméroun, 2 vols. 1985, L'Afrique dans l'Eglise 1985, Spiritualité et Libération en Afrique 1986. *Leisure interests:* drawing, painting, decoration. *Address:* P.O. Box 1539, Yaoundé, Cameroon. *Telephone:* 22-09-56.

MWAANGA, Vernon Johnson; Zambian diplomatist and businessman; b. 1939; ed. Hodgson Tech. Coll., Lusaka, Stanford Univ., U.S.A. and Oxford Univ., U.K.; joined Zambian independence movement 1960; mem. United Nat. Independence Party 1961-, later Regional Party Sec., Monze and Choma Areas; Deputy High Commr. for Zambia in U.K. 1964-65; Amb. to U.S.S.R. 1965-68; Perm. Rep. to UN 1968-72; Ed.-in-Chief Times of Zambia 1972-73; Minister of Foreign Affairs 1973-75; mem. UNIP Cen. Cttee. 1975; Sr. Business Exec. 1975-; reported detained Sept. 1985; Chair. Curray Ltd., Bank of Credit and Commerce (Zambia) Ltd., Zambia Safaris Ltd.; mem. Int. Public Relations Asscn.; Fellow, London Inst. of Dirs. *Address:* P.O. Box 30661, Lusaka, Zambia.

MWACHUKWU, Maj.-Gen. Ike; Nigerian politician; m.; four c.; Commandant Army School of Infantry 1979; Provost Marshal 1979-84; Mil. Gov. of Imo State 1984-85; Adjutant-Gen. 1985-86; Minister of Employment, Labour and Productivity 1986-87, of External Affairs 1988-; mem. Commonwealth Cttee. of Foreign Ministers, Lusaka Feb. 1988; mem. Governing Council Univ. of Sokoto. *Address:* Ministry of External Affairs, NTA Building, Awolowo Road, Ikoyi Island, Lagos, Nigeria.

MWAKAWAGO, Daudi Ngelautwa; Tanzanian politician; b. Sept. 1939; ed. Makerere Univ., Uganda, Victoria Univ. of Manchester, England; Tutor at Kivukoni Coll., Dar es Salaam 1965-72, Vice-Principal 1970, Principal 1971, 1977; Nat. M.P. 1970-75; Minister for Information and Broadcasting 1972-77; Constituent M.P. 1975-; mem. Party of Constitution Comm. 1976; mem. Constituent Ass. 1977, Cen. Cttee. Chama cha Mapinduzi 1977-; Minister of Information and Culture 1982-84, of Labour and Manpower Devt. 1984-86, of Industries and Trade 1986-88; fmr. mem. Historical Asscn. of Tanzania, Nat. Adult Educ. Asscn. of Tanzania, African Adult Educ. Asscn., Income Tax Local Cttee., Bd. of Inst. of Adult Educ., Nat. Advisory Council on Educ.; fmr. dir. Nat. Devt. Corpn., Nat. Museum; Chair. Wildlife Corpn. 1979-; Vice-Chair. Co-operative Coll., Moshi; mem. TIRDO. *Address:* c/o Ministry of Industries and Trade, P.O. Box 9503, Dar es Salaam, Tanzania.

MWALE, Siteke Gibson, DIP. SOC. SC., M.A., LL.D.; Zambian diplomatist, politician and administrator; b. 22 Oct. 1929, Nyimba; s. of Isaac P. Mwale and Esnati Aliness Sakaka; m. Mbangose Shawa 1948; four s. two d.; ed. Munali School, Lusaka, Univs. of London and Manchester, U.K., Temple Univ. and Univ. of Calif., U.S.A.; Sr. Social Welfare Officer, Ndola 1956-60; Asst. Sec., Ministry of Labour and Social Devt. 1965-66, Ministry of Natural Resources and Tourism 1966-67; Under-Sec., Ministry of Foreign Affairs 1967-68, Perm. Sec. of Foreign Service 1969; seconded as Head of Admin., OAU 1968-70; Amb. to Ivory Coast, Liberia, Guinea, Senegal, Mauritania 1970-74; High Commr. in Ghana, Gambia, Sierra Leone 1970-74; Amb. to U.S.A., Brazil, Argentina, Peru 1974-76; mem. Nat. Assembly 1976-78; Minister of Foreign Affairs 1976-78; Special Asst. to Pres. (Commonwealth Affairs) 1979, (Econ. and Tech. Co-operation) 1979-86; Prin. Adviser to Govt. on Regional, Econ. and Tech. Co-operation 1986-; Nat. Order of Ivory Coast, Nat. Order of Merit of Mauritania, Hon. Paramount Chief of Panta Chiefdom, Liberia, Kt. of Mark Twain (U.S.A.), Nat. Order of Rwanda, Nat. Order of Korea and several other decorations. *Publications:* many articles on regional econ. and tech. co-operation. *Address:* State House, P.O. Box 30135, Lusaka, Zambia.

MWANAKATWE, John Mupanga; Zambian politician (retd.); b. 1 Nov. 1926, Chinsali; s. of late Timothy and Maggie Mwanakatwe; m. Margaret Chipawpata 1952; three s. two d.; fmr. school teacher; Headmaster of secondary school, later Educ. Officer; Parl. Sec., Ministry of Lands and Mines, N. Rhodesia (now Zambia) 1963-64; Minister of Educ., N. Rhodesia Jan.-Oct. 1964, Zambia 1964-67; Minister of Lands and Mines 1967-69; Sec.-Gen. to the Govt. 1969-70; Minister of Finance 1970-73, 1976-78; mem. Nat. Ass. 1973-78; private law practice 1973-74; Chair. Salaries Comm. 1974-75; business consultant; Chair. Bd. of Int. Computers (Zambia) Ltd. *Publication:* The Growth of Education in Zambia since Independence. *Leisure interests:* reading, writing, golf, walking. *Address:* P.O. Box 8049, Woodlands, Lusaka, Zambia (Home).

MWINYI, Ali Hassan; Tanzanian teacher, politician and diplomatist; b. 8 May 1925, Kivure, Tanganyika; moved to Zanzibar as a child; schoolteacher, later Prin. Zanzibar teacher-training Coll.; Prin. Perm. Sec. of Educ. Zanzibar 1963-64; Asst. Gen. Man. Zanzibar State Trading Corpn. 1964-70; Minister of State, Office of Pres., Tanzania 1970; later Minister of Health and Home Affairs; Minister of Natural Resources and Tourism 1982-83, of State in Vice-Pres.'s Office 1983-84; interim Pres. of Zanzibar Feb.-April 1984, Pres. April 1984-; Vice-Pres. of Tanzania 1984-85, Pres. Aug. 1985-; C.-in-C. of Armed Forces; mem. Chama Cha Mapudinzi (CCM or Revolu-

tionary Party). *Address:* c/o Office of the President, Dar es Salaam, United Republic of Tanzania.

MYBURGH, Albert Tertius; South African newspaper editor; b. 26 Dec. 1934, Cape Prov.; s. of Albert Lambertus Myburgh; m. Wilhemina Magdalena Loubser 1958; one s. two d.; ed. Dale Coll., Univ. of Cape Town and Harvard Univ.; with London Bureau of Argus S.A. newspapers 1958-60; Political Corresp. of The Star, Johannesburg 1963; Assoc. Nieman Fellow 1965-66; Asst. Ed. The Daily News, Durban 1967; Ed. Pretoria News 1971-75; Ed. Sunday Times 1975-. *Leisure interests:* mountaineering. *Address:* P.O. Box 1090 Johannesburg, Tvl., South Africa.

MYERS, Barton, M.ARCH., F.R.A.I.C., A.I.A.; American and Canadian architect and planner; b. 6 Nov. 1934, Norfolk, Va.; s. of Barton and Meeta (Burrage) Myers; m. Victoria George 1959; one d.; ed. Norfolk Acad., U.S. Naval Acad. and Univ. of Pennsylvania; Partner, A. J. Diamond & Barton Myers, Toronto 1968-75; Founder and Prin. Barton Myers Asscs., Toronto 1975-; Asst. Prof. of Architecture Univ. of Toronto 1968-70; mem. Advisory Cttee. Nat. Capital Comm., Ottawa 1968-74; Founder and Pres. Bd. of Dirs., Trace Magazine 1980-82; Visiting Prof. Harvard Grad. School of Design 1981; Prof. of Architecture Univ. of Calif. (Los Angeles) School of Architecture 1981-; other lectureships and professional appointments; mem. Royal Canadian Acad. of Arts; recipient of numerous design awards. *Major Works by Diamond & Myers Asscs. include:* York Square, Toronto; Ont. Medical Asscn., Toronto; Myers & Wolf Residences, Toronto; Housing Union Bldg., Univ. of Alberta Citadel Theatre, Edmonton; Dundas-Sherbourne Housing, Toronto. *Major works by Barton Myers Asscs. include:* Seagram Museum, Waterloo, Ont.; Library, Unionville; Howard Hughes Center, L.A.; Wang Tower, L.A.; Performing Arts Center, Portland, Ore.; Hasbro Inc. Corp. HQ, R.I.; Phoenix Municipal Center, Ariz.; plans for Bunker Hill, L.A., Pasadena City Centre; Music Center Expansion, L.A., CBC Network HQ, Toronto, Cerritos Community Arts Center, N.W. Campus Housing, U.C.L.A., Art Gallery of Ont. expansion (competition winner), York Univ. Fine Arts Bldg. expansion, Toronto. *Leisure interests:* travel, reading, tennis. *Address:* Barton Myer Architect Inc., 322 King Street, Toronto, Ont., M5V 1J2, Canada; Barton Myers Associates, 6834 Hollywood Boulevard, Los Angeles, Calif. 90028, U.S.A. *Telephone:* (416) 977-5101 (Canada); (213) 466-4051 (U.S.A.).

MYERS, Dale Dehaven, B.S.A.E.; American engineer; b. 8 Jan. 1922, Kansas City, Mo.; s. of Wilson A. and Ruth Hall Myers; m. Marjorie Williams 1943; two d.; ed. Univ. of Washington, Seattle; Aerophysics Dept., N. American 1946, Chief Engineer Missile Div. 1954, Vice-Pres. and Program Man. Hound Dog Program 1960; Vice-Pres. and Program Man., Apollo CSM, N. American 1964, Vice-Pres. and Gen. Man. Space Shuttle Program 1969; Assoc. Admin. for Manned Space Flight, NASA Headquarters 1970-74; Pres. N. American Aircraft Operations, Rockwell Int. Corpn. 1974-77, Corporate Vice-Pres. 1974-77; Under-Sec., Dept of Energy, Washington 1977-79; Pres. and C.O.O. Jacobs Eng. Group Inc., Pasadena 1979-84; Pres. Dale Myers and Asscs., Leucadia, 1984-86, 1989-; Deputy Admin., NASA 1986-89; Fellow, American Astronautical Soc., American Inst. of Aeronautics and Astronautics; Hon. Ph.D. (Whitworth Coll.) NASA Certificate of Appreciation 1969, NASA Public Service Award for contributions to success of Apollo XI 1969, NASA Distinguished Service Medal for contributions to continuing success of Apollo program 1971, 1974; mem. Nat Acad. of Engineers 1974; D.S.M. (Dept. of Energy) 1979. *Address:* 1112 Neptune Avenue, Leucadia, California 92024, U.S.A.

MYERS, Jacke Duane, M.D.; American professor of medicine; b. 24 May 1913, New Brighton, Pa.; s. of Louis A. Myers and Esther Fern McCabe; m. Jessica Helen Lewis 1946; one s. four d. (one deceased); ed. Stanford Univ. School of Medicine, California; Research Fellow in Medicine, Harvard Medical School, Boston, Mass. 1938-39; Asst. Resident in Medicine, Peter Bent Brigham Hosp., Boston 1939-40, Resident 1940-42; Research Fellow in Medicine, Thorndike Memorial Lab., Boston City Hosp. and Harvard Medical School 1946; Assoc. in Medicine, Emory Univ. School of Medicine, Atlanta, Ga. 1946-47; Instructor in Medicine, Duke Univ. School of Medicine, Durham, N.C. 1947-48, Assoc. in Medicine 1948, Asst. Prof. 1948-51, Assoc. Prof. 1951-55; Prof. of Medicine and Chair. Dept. of Medicine, Univ. of Pittsburgh, Pa. 1955-70, Univ. Prof. of Medicine 1970-85, Prof. Emer. 1985-; mem. American Coll. Physicians (Regent 1971-78, Pres. 1976-77), Asscn. of American Physicians, American Soc. for Clinical Investigation (Sec. 1955-57), American Physiological Soc., American Fed. for Clinical Research, Asscn. of Profs. of Medicine (Sec. 1963-64, Pres. 1965), Inst. of Medicine, N.A.S.; Alfred Stengel Memorial Award, American Coll. of Physicians 1981, The Distinguished Teacher Award 1981. *Publications:* numerous articles in scientific journals. *Address:* University of Pittsburgh, 1291 Scaife Hall, Pittsburgh, Pa. 15261; 220 N. Dithridge Street, Dithridge House No. 900, Pittsburgh, Pa. 15213, U.S.A. *Telephone:* (412) 648-9933 (Office); (412) 687-8787 (Home).

MYERSON, Jacob M., M.A.; American economist; b. 11 June 1926, Rock Hill, S.C.; s. of Solomon and Lena (née Clein) Myerson; m. 1st Nicole Neuray 1965 (died 1968); one d.; m. 2nd Helen Hayashi 1974; ed. Washington, D.C., Pennsylvania State Coll., George Washington Univ.; entered U.S. Foreign Service 1950; Economic Analyst for the Office of the U.S. High Commr., Berlin 1950-52, mem. U.S. Regional Mission for the OEEC and Marshall Plan, Paris 1953–56; State Dept. Desk Officer for EEC and European Free Trade Area Affairs 1956–60; Chief of Political Section of U.S. Mission to the European Communities, Brussels 1960; Special Asst. to the Under-Sec. of State, Officer in charge of NATO Political Affairs, State Dept., then Deputy Political Adviser and Counsellor to the U.S. Mission to NATO, Brussels 1965–68, Adviser to the U.S. del. at several ministerial sessions of the N. Atlantic Council 1966–70; Econ. Counsellor U.S. Mission to the European Communities, Brussels, then Deputy Chief and Minister Counsellor 1970–75; Amb. to UN Econ. and Social Council, New York 1975–77; Minister Counsellor for Econ. and Commercial Affairs, U.S. Embassy, Paris 1977–80; Deputy Sec.-Gen. of the OECD 1980–88. *Leisure interest:* collecting twentieth century art. *Address:* 2 rue Lucien-Gaulard, 75018 Paris, France. *Telephone:* 4257-9503.

MYINT MAUNG, U; Burmese diplomatist and administrator; b. 10 March 1921, Magwe; m.; three c.; ed. Univ. of Rangoon; joined Army 1942; has held the following positions: Head of Co-operative Dept.; Chief of Admin. Div. of Burma Socialist Programme Party, also mem. Party Inspection Cttee.; mem. Pyithu Hluttaw (People's Congress) for Magwe Constituency; mem. Bd. of Dirs. of People's Bank of the Union of Burma, Exec. Cttee. of Burma Sports and Physical Fitness Cttee., Cen. Cttee. of Burma Red Cross Soc.; Chair. Resettlement Cttee. of Cen. Security and Admin. Cttee., Independence Award Cttee.; Perm. Rep. to UN 1975–77; Minister of Foreign Affairs 1977–79; mem. State Council and Attorney-Gen. 1988. *Address:* c/o Ministry of Foreign Affairs, Rangoon, Burma.

MYNORS, Sir Humphrey (Charles Baskerville), Bt.; British banker (retd.); b. 28 July 1903, Langley Burrell, Wiltshire; s. of Rev. A. B. Mynors; twin brother of Sir Roger (Aubrey Baskerville) Mynors (q.v.); m. Lydia M. Minns 1939; one s. four d.; ed. Marlborough and Corpus Christi Coll., Cambridge; Fellow Corpus Christi Coll., Cambridge 1926–33; with Bank of England 1933–64, Dir. 1949–54, Deputy Gov. 1954–64; Chair. Finance Corpn. for Industry Ltd. 1964–73. *Address:* Treago, St. Weonards, Hereford, England.

MYNORS, Sir Roger (Aubrey Baskerville), Kt., M.A.; British university professor; b. 28 July 1903, Langley Burrell, Wiltshire; s. of Rev. A. B. Mynors; twin brother of Sir Humphrey (Charles Baskerville) Mynors (q.v.); m. Lavinia Alington; ed. Eton Coll. and Balliol Coll. Oxford; Fellow Balliol Coll., Oxford 1926–44 (now Hon. Fellow); Prof. of Latin and Fellow of Pembroke Coll., Cambridge 1944–53; Prof. of Latin and Fellow of Corpus Christi Coll., Oxford 1953–70; Longman Fellow, Inst. of Bibliography and Textual Criticism, Leeds 1974–75; Fellow British Acad. 1944; Hon. D.Litt. (Cambridge, Edinburgh, Sheffield and Durham), Hon. LL.D. (Toronto); Hon. mem. American Acad. of Arts and Sciences, American Philosophical Soc.; fmr. Pres. Union Acad. Int. *Publications:* Cassiodorus 1937, Durham MSS 1939, Catullus 1960, Pliny's Letters 1963, Balliol MSS 1963, Panegyrici 1964, Virgil 1969. *Address:* Treago, St. Weonards, Hereford, England.

MYRDAL, Jan; Swedish writer; b. 19 July 1927, Stockholm; s. of the late Gunnar Myrdal and Alva Reimer; m. 1st Nadja Wiking 1948, 2nd Maj Liedberg 1953, 3rd Gun Kessle 1956; one s. one d.; Sunday Columnist (politics, culture) Stockholms-Tidningen 1963–66, Aftonbladet 1966–72; Chair. and Publr. Folket i Bild/Kulturfront 1971–72, columnist 1972–; Hon. D.Lit. (Upsala Coll., N.J.) 1980. *Works include:* films: Myglaren 1966, Hjalparen 1968, Balzac or the triumphs of realism 1975; TV documentaries: Democratic Kampuchea 1978–79, Guerilla Base Area of Democratic Kampuchea 1979, China 1979, 20 films on history of political caricature and posters 1975–87. *Publications:* (in Swedish) novels: Hemkomst 1954, Jubelvår 1955, Att bli och vara 1956, Badrumskranen 1957, Karriär 1975, Barndom 1982, En annan värld 1984; drama: Folkets Hus 1953, Moraliteter 1967, Garderingar 1969, B. Olsen 1972; travel: Resa i Afghanistan 1960, Bortom berg och öknar 1962, Turkmenistan 1966, En världsbild (co-author) 1977, Sidenvägen 1977, Indien väntar 1980; politics: Kina: Revolutionen går vidare 1970, Albansk utmaning 1970, Ett 50-tal 1972, lag utan ordning, Kinesiska frågor, Tyska frågor 1976, Kina efter Mao Tse-tung 1977, Kampuchea och kriget 1978, Kampuchea hösten 1979, Den albanska utmaningen 1968–86, 1987; art: Bartom Bergen 1983; essays: Söndagsmorgon 1965, Skriftställning 1968, Skriftställning II 1969, Skriftställning III 1970, Skriftställning IV 1973, V 1975, Klartexter 1978, Skriftställning X 1978, Balzac und der Realismus (in German) 1978, Strindberg och Balzac 1981,

Ord och Avsikt 1986; autobiography: Rescontra 1962, Samtida bekännelser 1964; art: Ansikte av sten, Angkor 1968, Ondskan tar form 1976; Dussinet fullt 1981, Den trettonde 1983; (in English) Report from a Chinese Village 1965, Chinese Journey 1965, Confessions of a Disloyal European 1968, Angkor: an essay on art and imperialism 1970, China: the Revolution Continued 1971, Gates to Asia 1971, Albania Defiant 1976, The Silk Road 1979, China Notebook 1975–78 1979, Return to a Chinese Village 1984, India Waits 1984. *Leisure interests:* collecting meccano, computing for fun. *Address:* Fagervik, S-150 30 Mariefred, Sweden. *Telephone:* Mariefred 108-38.

MYRES, John Nowell Linton, C.B.E., M.A., F.B.A., F.S.A.; British librarian; b. 27 Dec. 1902, Oxford; s. of late Prof. Sir John L. Myres; m. Joan Stevens 1929; two s.; ed. Winchester Coll., New Coll., Oxford; Lecturer, Tutor, Christ Church, Oxford 1928–48, Librarian 1938–48; Ministry of Food 1940–45; Librarian, Bodleian Library, Oxford Univ. 1948–65; Pres. Council for British Archaeology 1958–61; Vice-Pres. Soc. of Antiquaries 1959–63, Dir. 1966–70, Pres. 1970–75; Chair. Standing Conf. of Nat. and Univ. Libraries 1959–61; Ford's Lecturer, Oxford 1958–59; Pres. Library Assen. 1963; Pres. Soc. for Medieval Archaeology 1963–66; mem. Ancient Monuments Bd. 1959–76, Royal Comm. on Historical Monuments, England 1969–75; Fellow, Winchester Coll. 1951–77; Hon. Student Christ Church, Oxford 1971–; Hon. Fellow, New College, Oxford 1973–; Hon. LL.D. (Toronto), Hon. D.Litt. (Reading, Belfast, Durham); Gold Medal, Soc. of Antiquaries 1976. *Publications:* St. Catharine's Hill, Winchester (with others) 1930, Roman Britain and the English Settlements 1936, Anglo-Saxon Pottery and the Settlement of England 1969, A Corpus of Anglo-Saxon Pottery 1977, The English Settlements 1986. *Leisure interest:* British archaeology. *Address:* Manor House, Kennington, Oxford, OX1 5PH, England. *Telephone:* (0865) 735353.

MYRVOLL, Ole; Norwegian economist and politician; b. 18 May 1911, Kragerø; s. of Kristian and Marie Jensen; m. Ebba Tangen 1938; three d.; ed. Univ. of Oslo, School of Banking, and Univ. of Virginia, U.S.A.; Teacher, Norwegian School of Econs. and Business Admin., Bergen 1942, Prof. of Theoretical Social Econs. 1957–; Visiting Prof. Colgate Univ., U.S.A. 1958–59; Visiting Tallman Prof., Bowdoin Coll., Maine 1962; mem. State Banks Comm. 1955, Monetary and Credit Political Comm. 1960–63; mem. Bergen City Council 1948–55, 1972; Deputy mem. Storting 1965–73, mem. 1973–77; Minister of Wages and Prices 1963; Minister of Finance 1965–71; Mayor of Bergen 1971–72; Vice-Chair. Bd. of Dirs. Norwegian State Oil Co. (Statoil) 1974–; Chair. Norwegian Agency for Int. Devt. 1977–; Liberal. *Publication:* Studier i arbeidslönnsteorien 1956. *Address:* Starevossveien 40, N-5000 Bergen, Norway.

MZALI, Mohamed, LIC.EN.PHIL.; Tunisian politician; b. 23 Dec. 1925, Monastir; m.; six c.; ed. Sadiky School, Tunis, Univ. of Paris; Teacher at Sadiky School, Lycée Alaoui and Univ. of Zitouna 1950–56; Chef de Cabinet, Ministry of Education 1956–58; mem. Nat. Assembly 1959–; Dir. of Youth and Sports, President's Secr. 1959–64; Dir.-Gen. Radiodiffusion Télévision Tunisienne (RTT) 1964–67; Sec. of State for Nat. Defence 1968–69; Minister of Youth and Sports 1969–70, of Educ. 1969–70, 1971–73, 1976–80, of Health 1973–76; Co-ordinator of Govt. Activities, Dept. of the Pres. March-April 1980; Prime Minister 1980–84, Prime Minister and Minister of the Interior 1984–86; mem. Neo-Destour Party (now Parti Socialiste Destourien) 1947–, mem. Cen. Cttee. 1971–, Sec.-Gen. 1980–86; mem. Int. Olympic Cttee. 1981–; Municipal Councillor, Tunis 1960, 1963; First Vice-Pres. Tunis Town Council 1960–63, Pres. Culture, Youth and Sports Comm. 1960–66; Pres. Ariana Town Council 1959–72; Founder El Fikr (monthly cultural review) 1955; Pres., Tunisian Olympic Cttee. 1962–, Union des Ecrivains Tunisiens 1970–; First Vice-Pres. Int. Olympic Cttee. 1976–80; Pres. Int. Cttee. Jeux Méditerranéens 1979–; mem. Arab Language Acad., Cairo 1976–, Baghdad 1978–, Damascus 1980–, Jordan 1980–; mem. French Sports Acad. 1978–; Grand Cordon, Ordre de l'Indépendance, Ordre de la République, Grand Officier Légion d'honneur and numerous foreign decorations. *Publications:* La Démocratie 1955, Recueil d'Editoriaux d'El Fikr 1969, Prises de positions 1973, Etudes 1975, Points de Vue 1975, Les Chemins de la Pensée 1979, The Word of the Action 1984, The Olympism Today 1984. Living in France in self-imposed exile; fined and sentenced to 15 years forced labour after *in absentia* conviction for corruption 1987.

N

NA RENHUA; Chinese film actress; b. 1962; ed. Beijing Film Acad. *Roles include:* Let Women Stay Away from War. *Address:* Beijing Film Institute, Beijing, People's Republic of China.

NÄÄTÄNEN, Risto Kalervo, PH.D.; Finnish professor of psychology; b. 14 June 1939, Helsinki; s. of Prof. Esko K. Näätänen and Rauni (née Raudanjoki) Näätänen; m. Marjatta (née Kerola) Näätänen 1960; three s.; ed. Univ. of Helsinki; Research Asst. Dept. of Psychology, Univ. of Helsinki 1965–69, Prof. of Psychology 1975–; Researcher Acad. of Finland 1969–75, Research Prof. 1983–(93); mem. Finnish Acad. of Science and Letters 1980–; Purkinje Metal (Prague) 1988. *Leisure interests:* sports, the Green Movement, traffic safety. *Address:* The Department of Psychology, University of Helsinki, Ritarik. 5, 00170 Helsinki 17 (Univ.); Mäkipellontie 12 D, 00320 Helsinki 32, Finland (Home). *Telephone:* (3580) 191 4445 (Univ.); (3580) 576121 (Home).

NABARRO, Frank Reginald Nunes, M.B.E., D.SC., F.R.S., F.R.S.S.A.; British physicist; b. 7 March 1916, London; s. of Stanley Nunes Nabarro and Leah (née Cohen) Nabarro; m. Margaret Constance Dalziel 1948; ed. Nottingham High School, New Coll. Oxford, Univ. of Bristol; Sr. Experimental Officer Ministry of Supply 1941–45; Royal Soc. Warren Research Fellow, Univ. of Bristol 1944–49; lecturer in Metallurgy, Univ. of Birmingham 1949–53; Prof. of Physics, Univ. of the Witwatersrand, Johannesburg 1953–84, Emer. Prof. 1985–; Consultant Council for Scientific and Industrial Research 1985–; Beilby Memorial Award, South African Medal (S.A. Asscn. for the Advancement of Science) 1972, De Beers Gold Medal 1980, Claude Harris Leon Foundation Award of Merit 1983. *Publications:* Theory of Crystal Dislocations 1967, ed. Dislocations in Solids (7 vols.) 1979–86. *Leisure interests:* gardening, music. *Address:* 32 Cookham Road, Auckland Park, Johannesburg 2092, South Africa. *Telephone:* (011) 716-2175 (Office); (011) 726-7745 (Home).

NABI, Mohamed; Algerian politician; b. 15 May 1935, Algiers; m.; three c.; former prisoner during independence struggle; Dir. Ministry of Labour, Ministry of Agric.; Deputy, Nat. People's Assembly; Vice-Pres., Economic Comm. of the Nat. People's Ass.; Sec. of State for Educ. and Training; Minister of Labour and Educ. and Training, Public Health; Minister of Labour and Social Affairs 1988–. *Address:* rue Farid Zouieoueche, Kouba, Algiers, Algeria. *Telephone:* (2) 77-91-33.

NABIEV, Rakhman; Soviet official; b. 1930, Tadzhikistan; ed. Tashkent Inst. of Irrigation and Agricultural Mechanization; chief engineer with same inst. 1954–55, 1956–58; Dir. of tech. plant 1959–60; mem. CPSU 1960–; Head of Dept. of Agric. of Tadzhik S.S.R. 1960–61; party work at Cen. Cttee. Tadzhik CP 1961–63, 1964–71; Minister of Agric. Tadzhik S.S.R. 1971–73; Chair. Council of Ministers and Minister of Foreign Affairs of Tadzhik S.S.R. 1973–83, First Sec. of Cen. Cttee. –1985; mem. Cen. Auditing Comm. CPSU 1976–; mem. Politburo of Cen. Cttee. of Tadzhik CP; Deputy to U.S.S.R. Supreme Soviet. *Address:* c/o Council of Ministers, Dushanbe, Tadzhik S.S.R., U.S.S.R.

NABSETH, Lars, D.ECON.; Swedish industrial executive; b. 25 June 1928, Stockholm; s. of Arne and Annie (Westling) Nabseth; m. Birgitta Bygdeman 1956; one s. one d.; ed. Univ. of Stockholm and Stockholm School of Econs.; Research Asst., Industrial Inst. for Econ. and Social Research (IUI) 1952–60, Man. Dir. 1966–72; Dir. of Econ. Dept., Fed. of Swedish Industries 1961–65, First Vice-Pres. 1976–77, Dir.-Gen. 1977–; Man. Dir. Ironmasters' Assen. 1973–75; part-time Prof. of Econs., Stockholm Univ. 1973–75; oneman investigator of Swedish ordinary steel industry, appointed by Ministry of Industry 1976; mem. Bd., Mo & Domsjoe AB, Bd., Flaekt AB, Marabou AB; mem. Royal Swedish Acad. of Eng. Sciences. *Publications:* Swedish Industry during the 1970s 1970, The Diffusion of New Industrial Processes (Co-Ed. with G. Ray) 1974. *Leisure interests:* tennis, skiing, reading. *Address:* Industriförbundet, Storgatan 19, P.O. Box 5501, 11485 Stockholm (Office); Örnbogatan 27, 16139 Bromma, Sweden (Home). *Telephone:* 08-7838001 (Office); 08-80-17-78 (Home).

NABULSI, Mohammed Said, PH.D.; Jordanian banker, politician and administrator; b. 1928, Palestine; s. of Hamdi Nabulsi; m.; one s. two d.; ed. Univ. of Damascus, Syria, Univ. of Calif. at Berkeley, Georgetown Univ., Washington, D.C.; m. 1957; one s. two d.; Sec.-Gen., Cen. Bank of Syria 1964–67; Head of Research, Cen. Bank of Jordan 1968–71, Gov. and Chair. of Bd. 1973–86; Minister of Nat. Econ. 1971–73; Gov. IMF, Arab Monetary Fund; Exec. Sec. Econ. and Social Comm. for Western Asia (ESCWA) 1985–; Chair. Bd. of the Banking Inst. of Jordan 1973–85; mem. Bd. of Trustees, Univ. of Jordan, Yarmouk Univ. *Publications:* numerous articles, research papers in economic journals. *Address:* c/o Central Bank of Jordan, P.O. Box 37, Amman (Office); Shmeisani, Amman, Jordan (Home).

NABULSI, Omar N., LL.M.; Jordanian lawyer and politician; b. 1 April 1936, Nablus; s. of Hajj Nimre Nabulsi and Safia Ali; m. Haifa Hatough 1966; two s.; ed. Cairo, Ain Shams and London Univs.; Legal Adviser, Sasco Petroleum Co., Libya 1959–61; Legal and Political Attaché, League

of Arab States 1961–69; Asst. Dir. Royal Court of Jordan 1970–; Minister of Nat. Economy 1970–72; Amb. at the Foreign Ministry, Amman 1972; Amb. to the U.K. (and concurrently to the Netherlands and Portugal) 1972–73; Minister of Agric. June–Nov. 1973, of Nat. Economy 1973–75; Legal and Econ. Adviser to Arab Fund for Econ. and Social Devt. 1975–77; Lawyer and Consultant in Corporate and Business Legal Affairs 1977–; Minister of Reconstruction, Devt. and Labour 1977–80; pvt. law practice 1980–; mem. Nat. Consultative Council of Jordan; Order of Al-Kawkab of Jordan (1st class). *Leisure interests:* reading, cricket, squash, music, theatre. *Address:* P.O.B. 35116, Amman, Jordan. *Telephone:* 664724, 675724 (Office); 819030 (Home).

NACHTIGALL, Dieter, DR. RER. NAT.; German professor of didactic physics; b. 4 Feb. 1927, Berge; s. of Walter Nachtigall and Emma (née Eisermann) Nachtigall; m. Else (née Herre) Nachtigall 1959; two s. one d.; ed. Humboldt Univ., Berlin; schoolteacher, G.D.R. 1946–49, lecturer Teacher's Coll. 1949–50; Scientific Asst. and Lecturer, Tech. Univ. of Dresden 1956–59; Research Group Leader Nuclear Research Establishment, F.R.G. 1959–65; Research Assoc. CERN, Geneva 1965–66; Group Leader EURATOM BCNM, Geel 1966–71; Prof. of Didactics Physics, Univ. of Dortmund 1971–; Hon. Prof. Xian Highway Inst. 1988–. *Publications:* Physikalische Grundlagen für Dusimetrie und Strahlenschutz Thiemig 1971, Skizzen zur Physik Didaktik Lang 1986, Neues Physiklernen-Das Teilchen-Konzept Lang 1988. *Address:* Auf'm Hilmkamp 15, 5757 Wickede-Wiehagen, Federal Republic of Germany. *Telephone:* 02377-3548.

NADER, Ralph; American lawyer, author and consumer advocate; b. 27 Feb. 1934, Winsted, Conn.; s. of Nadra Nader and Rose Bouziane; ed. Princeton and Harvard Univs.; admitted to Conn. Bar 1958, Mass. Bar 1959, also U.S. Supreme Court; U.S. Army 1959; law practice in Hartford, Conn. 1959–; Lecturer in History and Govt., Univ. of Hartford 1961–63; fmr. Head of Public Citizen Inc. 1980; Lecturer, Princeton Univ. 1967–68; mem. American Bar Assen.; has advanced cause of consumer protection, particularly with regard to car safety in U.S.A.; Woodrow Wilson Award (Princeton Univ.) 1972. *Publications:* Unsafe at Any Speed 1965, Who Runs Congress? 1972, Ed. The Consumer and Corporate Accountability 1974, Taming the Giant Corporation (co-author) 1976, The Menace of Atomic Energy (with John Abbotts) 1979, The Lemon Book 1980, Who's Poisoning America? 1981, The Big Boys 1986; Contrib. Ed. Ladies Home Journal 1973–, syndicated columnist 1972–. *Address:* P.O. Box 19367, Washington, D.C. 20036; 2000 P Street, N.W., Washington, D.C. 20036, U.S.A.

NAFFAH, Fouad Georges, LIC.EN DROIT; Lebanese lawyer and politician; b. 1 March 1925, Zouk Mikhaël; s. of Georges Naffah and Malvina Takla; m. Zbeide Sfeir; three s. one d.; ed. Coll. des Frères Maristes, Coll. d'Antoura, Univ. St. Joseph, Beirut; elected Deputy for Kesrouan 1960, 1972; Lecturer in Constitutional Law and Lebanese Constitution, Coll. de la Sagesse and Univ. Libanaise; Minister of Agric. March-May 1972, of Finance 1972–73, of Foreign Affairs 1973–74, Centre Bloc. *Address:* P.O.B. 4504, Raouché, Beirut, Lebanon (Home). *Telephone:* 391840, 810385/6.

NAGAI, Michio, PH.D.; Japanese educator; b. 4 March 1923; s. of Rutaro and Tsuguyo Nagai; m. 1959; one s. two d.; ed. Kyoto Univ., Ohio State Univ.; Asst. Prof. Kyoto Univ.; later taught at Tokyo Inst. of Tech.; Dir. Communications Inst. of East-West Center, Hawaii 1972–73; Minister of Educ. 1974–76; Ed. Writer Asahi Shimbun 1976–; Sr. Adviser to Rector of UN Univ. *Leisure interests:* travel and reading. *Address:* c/o United Nations University, Shibuya, Tokyo, Japan. *Telephone:* 03-499-2811.

NAGAKURA, Saburo, DR.SC.; Japanese scientist; b. 3 Oct. 1920, Shizuoka Pref.; m. Midori Murayama 1953; one s.; ed. Shizuoka High School and Tokyo Imperial Univ.; Assoc. Prof., Univ. of Tokyo 1949–59, Prof. 1959–81; Head of Physical Organic Chem. Lab., Inst. of Physical and Chem. Research 1961–81; mem. Science Council of Japan 1972–75; mem. Science Council, Ministry of Educ., Science and Culture 1974–86; Dir.-Gen. Inst. for Molecular Science 1981–87; Pres. Int. Union of Pure and Applied Chem. 1981–83; Pres. Chem. Soc. of Japan 1984–85, Okazaki Nat. Research Insts. 1985–87; Pres. Grad. Univ. for Advanced Studies; mem. Japan Acad., Int. Acad. of Quantum Molecular Science, Deutsche Akademie der Naturforscher; Chem. Soc. of Japan Prize 1966; Asahi Prize 1971; Japan Acad. Prize 1978; Person of Cultural Merit, Japan 1985. *Publications:* Electronic Theory for Organic Chemistry 1966 and many publs. on electronic structure and dynamic behaviour of excited molecules. *Leisure interest:* appreciation of Japanese paintings. *Address:* 2-7-13 Higashi-cho, Kichijoji, Musashino, Tokyo 108, Japan.

NAGATA, Takao; Japanese business executive; b. 1 Sept. 1911, Kumamoto; ed. Nagasaki College of Commerce; with Hitachi Shipbuilding and Eng. Co. 1934–, Dir. 1951–60, Vice-Pres. 1960–62, Pres. 1962–, Chair. 1979–; Chair. Nippon Admin. Man. Assen.; Adviser, Japan Fed. of Employers' Assen.; Pres. Japan Overseas Enterprises Assen.; Vice-Pres. ILO Assen. of Japan; Man. Dir. Fed. of Econ. Orgs. (Keidanren); Dir. Hitachi

Ltd., Toyo Unpanki Co. Ltd., All Nippon Airways Co. Ltd.; standing mem., Industry and Labour Council of Ministry of Labour. *Address:* Hitachi Shipbuilding and Engineering Co. Ltd., 47, Edobori, 1-chome, Nishi-ku, Osaka, Japan (Office).

NAGATA, Takesi; Japanese geophysicist; b. 24 June 1913, Tokyo; Dir. Nat. Inst. of Polar Research; Prof. Emer. Tokyo Univ.; recipient of lunar samples from U.S. Apollo missions; Foreign mem. N.A.S. (U.S.A.); Gold Medal (Royal Astronomical Soc.) 1987. *Address:* National Institute of Polar Research, 9-10, Kaga-1, Itabashi-ku, Tokyo 173, Japan.

NAGEL, Günter; German landscape architect; b. 2 Feb. 1936, Dresden; s. of Heinrich Nagel and Erna (née Hempel) Nagel; m. Helga Jähnig 1962; one c. ed. Dresden, Humboldt Univ., Berlin and Berlin Tech. Univ.; Scientific Asst. Garden and Landscape Design, Berlin Tech. Univ. 1962-70, lectureship in Design, Garden and Lanscape; Freelance landscape architect; lectureships at Fine Arts Univ., Berlin (Prof. 1974) and Tech. Univ. Brunswick 1970-74; Prof. and Dir. Inst. for Park Planning and Garden Architecture, Univ. of Hannover 1977-; mem. German Soc. for Garden Design and Preservation of Natural Resources; Deutscher Werkbund; mem. Bd. of Trustees, Fritz Schumacher Foundation and Karl Foerster Foundation mem. Acad. of Arts, Berlin, German Acad. of Town and Country Planning; exhbn. "Wohnen in den Stadten?" (with H. Luz and F. Spengeli) 1984. *Publications:* Gärten in Cornwall 1975; Freiräume in der Stadtentwicklung 1978; Erholungsraum Stadtlandschaft 1980; Stadtumbau Grunfunktionen im Hamburger Hafen 1983; Gestaltung und Nutzung des Freiraums Strasse 1985, Verbesserung des Wohnumfeldes 1985; Qualität öffentlicher Freiräume 1986. *Address:* Institut Für Grünplanung und Gartenarchitektur, Universität Hannover, Herrenhäuser Strasse 2, 3000 Hannover 21, Federal Republic of Germany. *Telephone:* (0511) 762-26-94.

NAGEL, Louis; French publisher; b. 1 June 1908, Iglo, Hungary; s. of Ignace and Thérèse (née Kugel) Nagel; m. Josiane Champart 1942; ed. Univs. of Vienna, Prague and Geneva; founder of Nagel Publs., Paris 1930; publr. of Nagel Travel Guides 1949-; Ed. Who's Who in Switzerland 1960-; Dir. Les archives diplomatiques et consulaires 1963-; Pres. of Int. Acad. of Tourism 1966-70; mem. of PEN Club, Chancellor 1972-; Consul Gen. of Cyprus in Switzerland; Vice-Pres. Robert Schumann Asscn. for Europe; Gold Medal of City of Rome, Silver Medal of City of Rome, Silver Medal of Paris, Officer of Order of the Phoenix (Greece), Hon. G.C.M.G., Grand Officer of Order of Malta, Commdr. Ordine al Merito della Repubblica Italiana, Diploma "Prestige de la France", Ordre de la Couronne (Iran), Meridue Culturii of Romania (1st class). *Publications:* Works on philosophy, including La paix éternelle est-elle une utopie? 1946. *Address:* 7 rue de Savoie, 75006 Paris, France; and 5 rue de l'Orangerie, Geneva, Switzerland.

NAGIBIN, Yuriy Markovich; Soviet short-story writer; b. 3 April 1920, Moscow; ed. Inst. of Cinema, Moscow; began publishing 1940; war service 1941-45; two Orders of Merit, Order of October Revolution 1980. *Publications:* A Man from the Front (stories) 1943, Two Forces 1944, A Good Heart 1944, Guardsmen on the Dnieper 1944, English trans. Short Stories of the Red Army (London) 1945, The Seed of Life 1948, The Winter Oak 1955, In Early Spring 1961, My Friends, People 1961, Before the Holiday 1960, Clean Ponds 1962, The Placid Lake & Other Stories 1966, The Green Bird with a Red Crest 1966, The Heart of Another 1969, Stories 1970, The Back Streets of My Childhood 1971, My Africa (travel notes) 1973, Selected Works (2 vols.) 1973, You Will Live 1974, In April's Woods 1974, The Berendeevs 1978, Collected Works (4 Vols.) 1979, Morning at Tsarskoe Selo 1979, The Patroness (play) 1980.

NÁGR, Josef, C.SC.; Czechoslovak government official; b. 31 Dec. 1918, Trnová, N. Pilsen District; m. Jarmila Nágr 1946; one d.; ed. Univ. of Agric. and Forestry, Prague; Head of various agric. enterprises and orgs. in Karlovy Vary District 1946-59; Chief Agronomist, Head of Crop Production Dept., Ministry of Agric. 1959-62; Deputy Minister of Agric. 1962-64; First Deputy Minister of Agric., Forestry and Water Man. 1964-67; Man. Dir. of breeding and seed production enterprises, Prague 1967-70; First Deputy Minister of Agric. and Food of Czech Socialist Repub. 1970-71, Minister 1971-76; Minister of Agric. and Food, Czechoslovak Socialist Repub. Sept. 1976-83; mem. Agric. Comm. of Cen. Cttee. of CP of Czechoslovakia 1962; Deputy Fed. Ass. (Parl.) 1976-81; Decoration for Merit in Building, Order of Labour 1968, Order of the Republic 1978. *Publications:* a number of studies and papers on org. and man. of agric. production and devt. of crop production. *Leisure interests:* fishing and hunting. *Address:* Federální ministerstvo zemědělství a výživy, Těšnov 65, Prague 1, Czechoslovakia.

NAGY, János; Hungarian diplomatist; b. 23 Sept. 1928, Ujcsalános; s. of István Nagy and Julianna Pankucsi; m. Éva Peredi 1950; one d.; ed. Budapest Univ. and Acad. of Diplomacy; entered Diplomatic Service 1948; Asst. Attaché, Hungarian Legation, London 1949-51; Officer, Ministry of Foreign Affairs 1951-53, Sr. Officer 1960, Chief of Dept. 1967; posts in Washington 1955-56, Jakarta 1957-60; Amb. to India 1963-67, to U.S.A. 1968-71; Deputy Minister for Foreign Affairs 1971-80; Sec. of State for Foreign Affairs 1980-; Amb. to Austria 1985-. *Leisure interests:* reading and listening to music. *Address:* Embassy of the Hungarian People's Republic, Vienna, I, Bankgasse 416, Austria.

NAIPAUL, V. S., B.A.; Trinidad-born writer; b. 17 Aug. 1932; m. 1955; ed. Queen's Royal Coll., Port-of-Spain and Univ. Coll. Oxford; for two years freelance broadcaster with the BBC, producing programmes for the Caribbean area; fiction reviewer on New Statesman 1958-61; grant from Trinidad Govt. to travel in Caribbean 1961; in India 1962-63, in Uganda 1965-66, in U.S. 1969, in Argentina 1972, in Venezuela 1977, in U.S.A. 1978-79, in Iran, Pakistan, Malaysia and Indonesia 1979-80, in U.S.A. 1987-88; Hon. D.Litt. (St. Andrews) 1979, (Columbia) 1981, (Cambridge) 1983, (London) 1988; John Llewelyn Rhys Memorial Prize 1958, Somerset Maugham Award 1961, Phoenix Trust Award 1962, Hawthornden Prize 1964, W. H. Smith Award 1968, Booker Prize 1971, Jerusalem Prize 1983, Ingersoll Prize 1986. *Publications:* The Mystic Masseur 1957, The Suffrage of Elvira 1958, Miguel Street 1959, A House for Mr. Biswas 1961, The Middle Passage 1962, Mr. Stone and the Knights Companion 1963, An Area of Darkness 1964, The Mimic Men 1967, A Flag on the Island 1967 (collection of short stories), The Loss of El Dorado 1969, In a Free State 1971, The Overcrowded Barracoon 1972, Guerrillas 1975, India: A Wounded Civilization 1977, A Bend in the River 1979, The Return of Eva Perón 1980, Among the Believers 1981, Finding the Centre 1984, The Enigma of Arrival 1987, A Turn In The South 1989. *Address:* c/o Aitken & Stone Ltd., 29 Fernshaw Road, London, S.W.10 0TG, England.

NAIR, C. V. Devan (see Devan Nair, C. V.).

NAIRNE, Rt. Hon. Sir Patrick Dalmahoy, P.C., G.C.B., M.C., M.A.; British civil servant and university administrator; b. 15 Aug. 1921, London; s. of late C. S. Nairne and E. D. Nairne; m. Penelope Chauncy Bridges 1948; three s. three d.; ed. Radley Coll., Univ. Coll., Oxford; entered civil service 1947; Pvt. Sec. First Lord of Admiralty 1958-60; Defence Sec. 1965-67; Deputy Sec. Ministry of Defence 1970-73; Second Perm. Sec. Cabinet Office 1973-75; Perm. Sec. Dept. of Health and Social Security 1975-81; Master, St. Catherine's Coll., Oxford 1981-88, Chancellor of Essex Univ. 1983-; Dir. Cen. Independent Television 1982-; Deputy Chair., W. Midlands Bd. 1986-; Trustee Nat. Maritime Museum, Rowntree Memorial Trust 1982-; mem. Civil Service Security Appeals Panel 1982, Cttee. of Inquiry into the events leading to Argentine invasion of the Falklands 1982; U.K. Monitor, Anglo-Chinese Agreement on Hong Kong 1984; one-man painting exhbns., London 1971-83; Hon. LL.D. (Leicester) 1980, (St. Andrews) 1984; Dr. h.c. (Essex) 1983. *Leisure interests:* water-colour painting, calligraphy. *Address:* (from 1 Oct. 1988) Yew Tree, Chilson, Nr. Charlbury, Oxon, England. *Telephone:* Chadlington 456.

NAJARIAN, John Sarkis, M.D.; American surgeon; b. 22 Dec. 1927, Oakland, Calif.; s. of Garabed L. and Siranoush (Dimirjian) Najarian; m. Arlys Viola Mignette Anderson 1952; four s.; ed. Univ. of Calif., Berkeley and Univ. of Calif. Medical School, San Francisco; Internship (surgical) Univ. of Calif., San Francisco 1952-53, Residency (surgical) 1955-60; Special Research Fellow (Nat. Insts. of Health) Univ. of Pittsburgh 1960-61; Sr. Fellow and Assoc. (NIH) Scripps Clinic and Research Foundation, La Jolla, Calif. 1961-63; Asst. Prof. of Surgery, Dir. of Surgical Research Labs. and Chief, Transplantation Service, Univ. Calif., San Francisco 1963-66, Prof. and Vice-Chair. Dept. of Surgery 1966-67; Regents' Prof. and Chair. Dept. of Surgery, Univ. of Minn. Hosps. 1967-; Jay Phillips Prof. and Chair. Dept. of Surgery, Univ. of Minn. 1986-; several visiting professorships; mem. many editorial boards and professional groups; Hon. F.R.C.S. (England); numerous honours. *Publications:* several hundred articles and chapters, co-author several books. *Address:* Surgery Department, University of Minnesota Hospitals, Box 195 Mayo, Minneapolis, Minn. 55455, U.S.A. *Telephone:* (612) 373-8808.

NAJIBULLAH, Maj.-Gen.; Afghan politician; b. 1947, Paktia Prov.; m. Fatana Najibullah; one d.; ed. Habibia Lycee, Kabul Univ.; mem. People's Democratic Party of Afghanistan (PDPA) 1965; twice imprisoned for political activities; engaged in diplomatic duties 1978-79; head of the State Information Service (KHAD) 1979-80; mem. PDPA Cen. Cttee. 1977-78, mem. Politburo 1981-82; Pres. of Afghanistan Oct. 1987-; mem. DRA Revolutionary Council; Gen. Sec. PDPA Cen. Cttee. 1986-; several awards and state medals. *Address:* People's Democratic Party of Afghanistan, Kabul, Afghanistan.

NAKAE, Toshitada; Japanese journalist; b. 4 Oct. 1929, Chiba City; m. Yohko Nakae 1959; three s.; ed. Tokyo Univ.; local reporter Asahi Shimbun 1953-58, econ. reporter 1958-74, Econ. Ed. 1974-76, Asst. Man. Ed. 1976-78, Man. Ed. 1978-. *Publications:* (in English trans.) Cities 1966, The Pulitzer Story 1970, The News Media 1971, The Economy of Cities 1971. *Leisure interests:* driving, listening to music. *Address:* 4-8-5 Narita-nishi, Suginami-ku, Tokyo, Japan. *Telephone:* 03-392-5472.

NAKAE, Yosuke; Japanese diplomatist; b. 30 Dec. 1922, Osaka; s. of Yasuzo Nakae and Itsu (Kawase); m. Yasuko Takakura 1959; one s. one d.; ed. Kyoto Univ.; Dir.-Gen. of Asian Affairs Bureau, Ministry of Foreign Affairs 1975; Amb. to Yugoslavia 1978, to Egypt 1982, to People's Repub. of China 1984-87. *Publications:* ballet scenarios Creature 1975, Mobile et Immobile—Mirage à l'Abu-Simbel 1983, Friendship across the Water 1986. *Leisure interest:* writing scenarios for ballet. *Address:* 3-21-5, Eifuku, Suginami, Tokyo, Japan (168).

NAKAHARA, Nobuyuki, M.A.; Japanese business executive; b. 11 Dec. 1934, Tokyo; m. Kazuko Yamamoto; three s.; ed. Tokyo Univ. and Harvard

Univ., U.S.A.; Standing Auditor, Tonen Corpn. 1966–70, Dir. 1970–74, Man. Dir. 1974–84, Exec. Vice-Pres. 1984–86, Pres. 1986–; Pres. Japan Karate Asscn. 1986–. *Publications:* A New Approach to Petroleum Economics 1967, The Japanese Management 1975, Japan's Overall Diagnosis (co-author) 1982. *Leisure interests:* Japanese chess, 5th dan Karate. *Address:* 19-7 Oyamadai 2-chome, Setagaya-ku, Tokyo, Japan. *Telephone:* 702-5577.

NAKAJIMA, Fumio, D.LITT.; Japanese professor; b. 11 Nov. 1904, Tokyo; m. Chizu Takaba 1935; ed. First Prefectural School, First Nat. Coll. and Univ. of Tokyo; Asst. Prof., Univ. of Keijo, Seoul 1928, Assoc. Prof. 1933, Prof. of English Philology 1939; Prof. of English Philology, Univ. of Tokyo 1947–65, Prof. Emer. 1965–; Prof. Tsuda-juku Coll. 1965–73, Pres. 1973–80; Pres. English Literary Soc. of Japan 1952–64, Shakespeare Soc. of Japan 1964–75; mem. Japan Acad. 1974–; Order of the Sacred Treasure (2nd Class) 1975. *Publications:* Imiron 1939, Eigo-no-Joshiki 1944, Bunpo-no-Genri 1949, Eibunpo-no-taikei 1961, Eigo-no-Kozo 1980, Nihongo-no-Kozo 1985. *Address:* 2-24-10, Nishi-koigakubo, Kokubunji, Tokyo 185, Japan. *Telephone:* (0423) 24 5580.

NAKAJIMA, Gentaro; Japanese politician; b. Feb. 1929, Gunma Pref.; m. Taneko Nakajima; two s. one d.; ed. Keio Univ.; mem. House of Reps.; fmr. Parl. Vice-Minister of Int. Trade and Industry; Parl. Vice-Minister for Econ. Planning; Minister of Educ. 1987–88; Chair. Standing Cttee. on Foreign Affairs, House of Reps.; Liberal-Democratic Party (LDP). *Leisure interest:* paintings. *Address:* 3-12-34 Komaba, Meguro-ku, Tokyo, Japan.

NAKAJIMA, Hiroshi, M.D., PH.D.; Japanese international civil servant; b. 16 May 1928, Chiba City; m. Martha (née Dewitt) Nakajima; two s.; ed. Tokyo Medical Coll. and Univ. of Paris; Dir. of Research and Admin., Nippon Roche Research Centre, Tokyo 1967–73; Scientist, Evaluation and Control of Drugs 1973–76; Chief Drug Policies and Man., WHO HQ, Geneva 1976–79; Dir. WHO Regional Office for the Western Pacific, Manila 1979–88; Dir.-Gen. WHO July 1988–; Kojima Award 1984. *Publications:* more than 60 articles and reviews in the field of medical and pharmaceutical sciences. *Address:* c/o World Health Organization, 20 avenue Appia, 1211 Geneva 27, Switzerland. *Telephone:* 91 21 11.

NAKAJIMA, Takeshi; Japanese banker; b. 17 Jan. 1924, Tokyo; s. of Shinobu Nakajima and Kaneko Nakajima; m. Mihoko Hirano 1952; one s. one d.; ed. Tokyo Teikoku Univ.; joined Mitsui Trust 1946, Dir. 1973, Dir. and Gen. Man. Nagoya br. 1974, Man. Dir. and Gen. Man. Osaka br. 1977, Man. Dir. 1979, Sr. Man. Dir. 1979, Deputy Pres. 1982, Pres. 1987–. *Leisure interests:* reading, golf. *Address:* 5-24-4 Arai, Nakano-ku, Tokyo 164, Japan. *Telephone:* (03) 385-0357.

NAKAMURA, Hajime, D.LITT.; Japanese professor of philosophy; b. 28 Nov., 1912, Matsue City; s. of Kiyoji Nakamura and Tomo Nakamura; m. Rakuko Nakamura 1944; two d.; ed. Univ. of Tokyo; Prof. of Indian and Buddhist Philosophy, Univ. of Tokyo 1943–73; f. and Dir. Eastern Inst. 1973–; mem. Japan Acad. of Sciences 1984–; Hon. Fellow Royal Asiatic Soc. of Great Britain; Imperial Prize (Japan Acad. of Sciences); Order of Merit. *Publications:* A Comparative History of Ideas 1986, Ways of Thinking of Eastern Peoples. *Address:* Kugayama 4-37-15, Suginami-ku, Tokyo, Japan.

NAKAMURA, Hisao; Japanese business executive; b. 11 Nov. 1923, Kyoto Pref.; s. of Kinjiro Nakamura and Masao Nakamura; m. Fusako Nagai 1955; one s. one d.; ed. Kyoto Univ.; joined Kuraray Co. Ltd. 1950, Dir. 1972, Man. Dir. 1976, Exec. Vice-Pres. 1981, Pres. 1985–; Chair. Kurray Trading Co. Ltd. 1984–; Pres. Kyowa Gas Chemical Industries Co. Ltd. 1985–. *Leisure interests:* golf, car-driving, reading. *Address:* 52 Nigawadai, Takarazuka, Hyogo 665, Japan.

NAKAMURA, Ichiro, B.ECONS.; Japanese banker; b. 3 Feb. 1926; ed. Tokyo Univ.; joined The Nippon Kangyo Bank 1964, Gen. Man. Tokuyama Branch, Yamaguchi 1965–67, Gen. Man. Kamata Branch, Tokyo 1967–68, Deputy Gen. Man. Osaka Branch 1968–70, Sec. of Secretariat 1970–71; Sec. and Head Secretariat merged Dai-Ichi Kangyo Bank 1971–74, Gen. Man. Fund Operations Div. 1974–75, Dir. and Gen. Man. Admin. and Co-ordination Div. IV, Branch Admin. and Business Devt. Group 1975, Dir. and Gen. Man. Personnel Div. II 1976–79, Man. Dir. 1979–80, Man. Dir. and Gen. Man. Osaka Branch 1980–81, Man. Dir. and Head Branch Admin. and Business Devt. Group 1982, Sr. Man. Dir. 1982, also Head of Corporate Banking HQ 1983, Deputy Pres. 1983, Chair. Bd. of Dirs. June 1988–. *Address:* The Dai-Ichi Kangyo Bank, Ltd., 5-9 Sakuragaoka 1-chome, Tama City, Tokyo, Japan.

NAKAMURA, Kaneo, LL.B.; Japanese banker; b. 26 Oct. 1922; m. Kazuko Nakamura 1950; two s.; ed. Imperial Univ. of Tokyo; joined Industrial Bank of Japan Ltd. 1947; Chief Rep., New York Rep. Office 1969–72, Gen. Man. Loan Dept. No. 3 Feb.-Nov. 1972, Dir. 1972–75; Man. Dir. 1975–82, Deputy Pres. 1982–84, Pres. 1984–. *Leisure interests:* golf, driving. *Address:* The Industrial Bank of Japan Ltd., 1-3-3, Marunouchi, Chiyoda-ku, Tokyo 100, Japan.

NAKAMURA, Taro; Japanese politician; b. Dec. 1920, Ehime Pref.; m.; one s. three d.; ed. Waseda Univ.; elected to House of Councillors 1974; Parl. Vice-Minister of Finance 1978; Deputy Sec.-Gen. Liberal-Democratic Party (LDP) 1981; Minister of Labour 1987–88; Exec. mem. House of

Councillors Social Cttee. on Traffic Safety; Chair. House of Councillors LDP Standing Cttee. on Diet Policy; Pres. Kyoto Freight Trucks Ltd.; Chair. Yamanashi Transport Co. Ltd. *Leisure interests:* sea-fishery, cookery, reading. *Address:* Shukusha, 6-31-7 Jingumae, Shibuya-ku, Tokyo 159, Japan.

NAKAO, Eiichi; Japanese politician; b. Jan. 1930, Yamanashi Pref.; m.; one s. one d.; ed. Aoyama Gakuin Univ. and Waseda Univ.; mem. House of Reps. 1967–; Chair. Nippon Network Services Co., Ltd. 1970; Parl. Vice-Minister for Agric. and Forestry 1972; Chair. Exec. Council, Liberal-Democratic Party (LDP) 1978; Chair. LDP Nat. Org. Cttee. 1982; Minister of State, Dir.-Gen. Econ. Planning Agency 1987–88. *Leisure interests:* shigin (recitation of classical Chinese poetry), listening to music. *Address:* 708 Nissho-Iwai Otowa Mansions, 2-4-8 Otsuka, Bunkyo-ku, Tokyo 112, Japan.

NAKASONE, Yasuhiro; Japanese politician; b. 27 May 1917, Takasaki, Gumma Prov.; s. of Matsugoroh and Uhku Nakasone; m. Tsutako Kobayashi 1945; one s. two d.; ed. Tokyo Imperial Univ.; mem. House of Reps.; fmr. Minister of State, Dir.-Gen. of Science & Tech. Agency; Chair. Nat. Org. Liberal-Dem. Party, Jt. Cttee. on Atomic Energy, Special Cttee. on Scientific Tech.; Minister of Transport 1967–68; Minister of State and Dir.-Gen. Defence Agency Jan. 1970–71; Chair. Exec. Council Liberal-Dem. Party 1971–72; Minister of Int. Trade and Industry 1972–74; Sec.-Gen. Liberal-Dem. Party 1974–76, Chair. 1977–80; Minister of State and Dir.-Gen. of Admin. Man. Agency 1980–82; Prime Minister of Japan 1982–87; Chair. and Pres. Int. Inst. for Global Peace 1988–. *Publications:* Ideal of Youth, Frontier in Japan, The New Conservatism. *Leisure interests:* golf, swimming, painting. *Address:* 3-22-7, Kamikitazawa, Setagaya-ku, Tokyo, Japan (Home). *Telephone:* 304-7000 (Home).

NAKAYAMA, Komei; Japanese surgeon; b. 25 Sept. 1910, Tokyo; m. Yoshiye Nakayama; one s. one d.; ed. Chiba Univ.; Asst. Prof. of Surgery, Chiba Univ. 1941–47, Prof. of Surgery 1947–63; Prof. of Surgery, Tokyo Women's Medical Coll. 1964–, Pres. of Inst. of Gastroenterology; Visiting Prof. St. Vincent Hospital, Sydney, Australia 1961; Vice-Pres. Medical Div., Japanese Science Council; fmr. Pres. Int. Coll. of Surgeons; numerous Japanese and foreign awards. *Leisure interest:* fishing. *Address:* 2-3-18-704 Hirakawa-cho, Chiyoda-ku, Tokyo, Japan. *Telephone:* 261-0661.

NAKAYAMA, Masaaki; Japanese politician; b. 1932; ed. Chuo private Univ.; fmr. mem. Osaka City Ass.; now mem. House of Reps. for 2nd Constituency Osaka Prefecture; fmr. Parl. Vice-Minister of Labour, of Health and Welfare; fmr. Dir. Liberal Democratic Party Youth Dept, Regional Org. Dept; Chair. Special Cttee. on Northern Territories 1981; Chair. Nat. Campaign HQ Oct. 1984–; Liberal Democratic Party. *Address:* House of Representatives, Tokyo, Japan.

NAKAYAMA, Taro, M.D.; Japanese politician; b. 27 Aug. 1924, Osaka; ed. Osaka Medical Coll.; mem. Osaka Pref. Assembly 1955, Parl. Vice-Minister of Labour, Vice-Chair. of Liberal-Democratic Party (LDP) Diet Policy Cttee.; mem. House of Councillors 1968–, Chair. Cabinet Cttee., Steering Cttee.; Minister of State, Dir.-Gen. Prime Minister's Office and Okinawa Devt. Agency 1980–81. *Publications:* five books including Scientific Strategy for the Post-Oil Age 1979. *Address:* c/o Liberal-Democratic Party, 7, 2-chome, Harakawacho, Chiyoda-ku, Tokyo, Japan.

NAKAYAMA, Yoshihiro; Japanese diplomatist; b. 30 Jan. 1914, Onomichi, Hiroshima-Ken; s. of Ikutaro Nakayama; m. Chieko Ohmura 1942; two s. one d.; ed. Faculty of Law, Tokyo Imperial Univ.; entered Japanese Diplomatic Service 1938; served in France, N. Viet-Nam, U.K., Belgium and Ministry of Foreign Affairs 1938–63; Dir.-Gen. Econ. Affairs Bureau 1963–66; Amb. to Repub. of Viet-Nam 1966–67; Amb. to Int. Orgs., Geneva 1967–70, Vice-Chair. GATT, Geneva 1970; Amb. to France 1970–75; Special Envoy to Middle East 1975; Head of Suite of Honour for Visit of King Hussein of Jordan 1976, for Visit of Crown Prince of Japan to Jordan, Yugoslavia and U.K. 1976; Adviser Niigata Eng. Co. Ltd. 1976–; mem. Econ. Consultative Cttee. 1978–; Chair. Arab-Japanese Tech. Transfer Forum 1978; Chair. Cttee. of Reflection on Future of Japanese-French Relations (Wisemen Group) 1982; Prof., Aoyama Gakuin Univ. 1982–; Chair. Overseas Broadcast Programme Consultative Cttee., Nihon Hoso kyokai; Pres. Middle East Inst. of Japan; mem. Cttee. Inst. of Peace Affairs 1983; mem. Bd., Konishi Int. Exchange Fund 1983–; Pres. Japan-Syria Friendship Asscn. *Leisure interests:* skiing, literature. *Address:* Dorf Blumen 602, 4-8-29, Takanawa, Minato-ku, Tokyo, Japan. *Telephone:* 441-2852.

NAKIB, Ahmad Abdul Wahab al–; Kuwaiti diplomatist; b. 30 July 1933, Kuwait; m. Hannan Mohamed al-Bahar 1971; one s. one d.; ed. Adam State Coll., Colorado, U.S.A.; First Sec. Kuwait Embassy, London 1962–63; Counsellor first Perm. Mission of Kuwait to UN 1963–66; Consul-Gen., Kenya 1966–67; Amb. to Pakistan 1967–70, to U.K. and non-resident Amb. to Denmark, Norway and Sweden 1971–75; Amb. to Fed. Repub. of Germany 1976–86. *Address:* c/o Ministry of Foreign Affairs, P.O. Box 13001, Safat, Kuwait City, Kuwait.

NALBANDYAN, Dmitriy Arkadiyevich; Soviet painter; b. 1906, Armenia; ed. Tbilisi Acad. of Arts; mem. U.S.S.R. Acad. of Arts 1953–. *Awards include:* State U.S.S.R. Prize 1946, 1951, Merited Artist of the R.S.F.S.R.

1951, and of U.S.S.R. 1969, Hero of Socialist Labour 1976, Order of Lenin 1976, Gold Hammer and Sickle Medal 1977, Lenin Prize 1982.

NAŁĘCZ, Maciej, DR.; Polish scientist; b. 27 April 1922, Warsaw; s. of Aleksander and Stefania Nałęcz; m. Zofia Nałęcz 1952; one s.; ed. Warsaw Tech. Univ.; scholarship to Case Inst. of Tech., Cleveland, U.S.A. 1961–62; Assoc. Prof. 1962–72, Prof. 1972–; Corresp. mem. Polish Acad. of Sciences (PAN) 1967–73 (mem. 1974–), Presidium mem. and Sec. Tech. Sciences Section 1972–80, Deputy Gen. Sec. PAN 1981–83, Deputy to Seym (Parl.) 1985–, mem. Presidium 1983–; Dir. Inst. of Automatic Control 1962–72; Chair. Biomedical Eng. Cttee. of Section IV 1972–; Dir. Inst. of Biocybernetics and Biomedical Eng. 1975–; Chair. Nat. Cttee. for Pugwash Confs. 1972–, elected Chair. Pugwash Council 1974, 1977, 1982, 1987; Visiting Prof. Polytechnic Inst. of Brooklyn 1967–68; Distinguished Visiting Prof. Ohio State Univ. 1979–80, Campinas Univ., Brazil 1985, Cleveland Clinic Foundation 1985; mem. Int. Measurement Confed. (IMEKO), Cttee. on Data for Science and Tech. (CODATA) of ICSU; mem. Int. Fed. of Automatic Control, Chair. Exec. Cttee. 1972–; mem. Int. Soc. of Artificial Organs; Foreign mem. U.S.S.R. Acad. of Sciences 1976–; mem. Presidium, Polish Club of Int. Relations 1988–; Knight's, Officer's Cross and Commdr.'s with Star Cross of Order Polonia Restituta, Order Banner of Labour, 2nd Class 1972, 1st Class 1978, State Prize, 2nd Class 1972, Medal of 30th Anniversary of People's Poland 1974, Award med tack för värdefull insats (Sweden) 1957. *Publications:* Trends in Control Components (monograph), The Technology of Hall Generators and Their Use in Measurement and Conversion 1972, Control Aspects of Biomedical Engineering (Ed. and Contrib.) 1987, Computers in Medicine (Ed. and Contrib.) 1987. *Address:* Institute of Biocybernetics and Biomedical Engineering, ul. K.R.N. 55, 00-818 Warsaw, Poland. *Telephone:* 20-64-38.

NAM DUCK-WOO, PH.D.; Korean economist and government official; b. 10 Oct. 1924; s. of Sang Bom Nam and Cha Soon Yoo; m. Hye Sook Choi 1953; two s. one d.; ed. Kook Min. Coll., Seoul, Seoul Nat. Univ. Oklahoma State and Stanford Univs.; with Bank of Korea 1952–54; Asst. Prof., Assoc. Prof., Prof., Dean of Econ. Dept., Kook Min Coll. 1954–64; Prof. Sogang Univ. and Dir. Research Inst. for Econ. and Business 1964–69; Minister of Finance 1969; Gov. for Korea, IMF, IBRD, ADB 1969–72, Chair. Bd. of Govs. Asian Devt. Bank 1970; Deputy Prime Minister and Minister of Econ. Planning Bd. 1974–78; Special Asst. for Econ. Affairs to the Pres. Jan.-Dec. 1979; Prime Minister of Repub. of Korea 1980–82; mem. Advisory Cttee. on Evaluation of Econ. Devt. Plan, Nat. Mobilization Bd. 1964–69; Adviser to Korea Devt. Bank 1964–69; Assoc. mem. Econ. and Scientific Council 1967–69. *Publications:* History of Economic Theory 1958, Price Theory 1965, History of Economic Theory (co-author) 1962, The Determinants of Money Supply and Monetary Policy: in the case of Korea 1954–64 1966, Social Science Research and Population Policy (jt. author) 1980, Changes in the Pattern of Trade and Trade Policy in a Pacific Basin Community 1980. *Leisure interests:* reading, music appreciation. *Address:* 395-101 Soekyo-Dong, Mapo-ku, Seoul, Republic of Korea.

NAMALIU, Hon. Rabbie Langanai, C.M.G., M.A.; Papua New Guinea politician; b. 3 April 1947, Raluana, E. New Britain Prov.; m. Margaret Nakikus; two s.; ed. Keravat High School, Univ. of Papua New Guinea; fmrly. scholar and fellow Univ. of Papua New Guinea, Australian Nat. Univ., Univ. of Calif. (Santa Cruz); tutor and lecturer in History, Univ. of Papua New Guinea; Prin. Pvt. Sec. to Chief Minister 1974; fmr. Prov. Commr., East New Britain, and Chair. Public Services Comm.; held sr. positions in the Office of the Prime Minister and Leader of the Opposition under Mr. Somare; M.P. for Kokopo Open 1982–; Minister for Foreign Affairs and Trade 1982–84, Minister for Primary Industry 1984–85; Deputy Leader Pangu Pati 1985–88, Leader June 1988; Prime Minister July 1988–; Hon. LL.B. (Victoria, B.C.). *Address:* The Prime Minister's Office, Government Buildings, Port Moresby, Papua New Guinea.

NAMIAS, Jerome, M.S.; American meteorologist; b. 10 March 1910, Bridgeport, Conn.; s. of Joseph and Saydie (née Jacobs) Namias; m. Edith Paipert 1938; one d.; ed. Mass. Inst. of Technology, Univ. of Michigan, Clark Univ., Mass.; Meteorologist TWA 1934; Research Asst. Blue Hill Meteorological Observatory 1935–36; Research Assoc. M.I.T. 1936–41; Chief Extended Forecast Div. U.S. Weather Bureau, Washington, D.C. 1941–71; Research Meteorologist Scripps Inst. of Oceanography, Univ. of Calif. at San Diego, La Jolla, Calif. 1968–; Rossby Fellow Woods Hole Oceanographic Inst., Mass. 1972; Visiting Lecturer Univs. of Stockholm and Uppsala, Sweden 1949, Visiting Prof. Nat. Univ. of Mexico 1961, Distinguished Visiting Lecturer Pa. State Univ. 1962. Distinguished Visiting Scholar New York Univ. 1966, Visiting Scholar Rockefeller Study and Conference Center, Bellagio, Italy 1977; Meisinger Award for Aerological Research 1938, Award for Extraordinary Scientific Accomplishment 1955, Sverdrup Gold Medal 1981, American Meteorological Soc.; Citation from Navy Sec. 1943; Meritorious Service Award U.S. Dept. of Commerce 1950, Gold Medal 1965; Rockefeller Public Service Award 1955; San Diego Press Clubs Headliner Award 1978, Marine Tech. Soc. Compass Distinguished Achievement Award 1984, Univ. of Calif. at San Diego Chancellor Assoc.'s Award 1984; Hon. D.Sc. (Rhode Island) 1972; Hon. Sc.D. (Clark Univ.) 1984; mem. N.A.S.; Hon. mem. Royal Meteorological Soc. 1988; Fellow, American Acad. of Arts and Sciences. *Publication:* Short Periods of Climate Variations, Collected Works of J. Namias (3 vols.) 1934–74, 1975–82, 1983,

Namias Symposium Volume 1986. *Leisure interests:* music, fishing, current events. *Address:* University of California, San Diego, Scripps Institution of Oceanography, A-024, La Jolla, Calif. 92093 (Office); 240 Coast Boulevard, Apartment 2C, La Jolla, Calif 92093, U.S.A. (Home). *Telephone:* (619) 534-4509 (Office); (619) 459-6511 (Home).

NAMBOODIRIPAD, E. M. Sankaran; Indian politician; b. 14 June 1909, Elamkulam Village, Malappuram Dist.; s. of E. M. Parameswaran Namboodiripad and E. M. Vishnudatha Antherjanam; m. E. M. Arya Antherjanam 1937; two s. two d.; ed. Bd. High School, Perintalmanna, Victoria Coll., Palghat, St. Thomas Coll., Trichur; Chief Minister, Kerala 1957–59, 1967–69; Acting Gen. Sec., Indian CP 1962–63, then Sec.-Gen. 1978, now Sec.-Gen. Communist (Marxist) Party (CPM) of India. *Publications:* The Peasant Question in Kerala 1950, The National Question in Kerala 1952, Mahathma and the Ism 1958, Economics and Politics of India's Socialist Pattern 1966, India under Congress Rule 1967, Kerala-Yesterday, Today, Tomorrow 1967, Indian Planning in Crisis 1974, Conflicts and crisis: Political India 1974 1974. *Address:* 10, Shanthi Nagar, Press Road, Trivandrum, Kerala State, India.

NAMPHY, Lieut.-Gen. Henri; Haitian soldier and politician; fmr. Chief of Haitian Gen. Staff; Head of State and Pres. Nat. Governing Council (formed after overthrow of Jean-Claude Duvalier q.v. in coup) 1986–88; Vice-Chair. Legis. 1987–88; now living in exile in Dominica.

NAMSRAI, Tserendashiin; Mongolian politician, b. 19 Feb. 1939; ed. Leningrad State Univ., U.S.S.R.; Journalist, "Unen" editorial Bd.; "Unen" staff Corresp. in aimags (provs.), Unen and Montsame staff Corresp. in Moscow and Beijing; Instructor of the Mongolian People's Revolutionary Party Cen. Cttee.; Head of Dept. Mongolian People's Revolutionary Party (MPRP) Cen. Cttee. 1970–83; Sec. of MPRP Cen. Cttee. 1983–; mem. of Political Bureau, MPRP Cen. Cttee. 1984–; Deputy to the Great People's Hural; mem. of Pres. of Great People's Hural (Ass.) 1987–88, Deputy Chair. 1987–; awarded orders and medals of MPR. *Address:* Central Committee of the Mongolian People's Revolutionary Party, Ulan Bator, Mongolia.

NAN NGUEMA, Marc S., PH.D.; Gabonese international diplomatist; b. 13 April 1934, Lambaréné; s. of Edouard Nguema Nan and Abyale Oye; m. Eliane Nan Nguema 1967; two s. four d.; ed. Univ. of Paris; civil servant, Paris 1960; Dir. Econ. Affairs Dept., Libreville 1963; Econ. Affairs Adviser, UN Dept. of Econ. and Social Affairs (research and policies), New York 1964, transferred to UN Conf. on Trade and Devt. (UNCTAD) 1965; Amb. and Perm. Rep. of Gabon to UN, Geneva 1968; Econ. and Financial Exec., Elf Aquitaine, Paris 1970, Sec.-Gen. and Deputy Gen. Man. 1976–81; Adviser to Exec. Dir. of IMF 1972–75; rep. of Gabon to OPEC Econ. Comm. Bd. 1975–76; Sec.-Gen. of OPEC 1981–83. *Leisure interests:* windsurfing, reading, karate, swimming, Baroque music. *Address:* c/o Ministry of Foreign Affairs, Libreville, Gabon.

NANA OPOKU WARE II (see Otumfuo Nana Opoku Ware II).

NANA-SINKAM, Samuel, PH.D., M.B.A.; Cameroon international official; b. 20 Dec. 1942, Bafoussam; ed. Univ. of Grenoble, France, Inst. Nat. de Statistiques et d'Etudes Economiques, Paris, Inst. Africain de Développement Economique et de Plantification, Dakar, Senegal, Univ. of Poitiers, France, George Washington Univ., Washington, D.C.; Chief of Research, Programming and Planning Service, Ministry of Planning and Devt. 1966–67; Economist, FAO 1967–70; Economist, IMF 1970–71, Tech. Asst. 1971, Adviser to Exec. Dir. 1972, Alt. Exec. Dir. 1972–76, Exec. Dir. IMF 1976–82. *Publications:* Pays candidats au processus de développement, Monetary Intergration and Theory of Optimum Currency areas in Africa, Le nouveau système international de taux de change et les pays candidats au processus de développement, Paese di nuovo indipendenza e i rapporti imperialista, and numerous articles on economics and development planning in Africa. *Leisure interests:* tennis, soccer, judo, swimming, cycling. *Address:* 2707 Calkins Road, Herndon, Va. 22070, U.S.A. (Home). *Telephone:* (705) 860-3410 (Home).

NANNEN, Henri; German publisher and journalist; b. 25 Dec. 1913, Emden; s. of Klaas Nannen and Elise Buitenduif; m. Martha Kimm 1947; one s.; ed. Ludwig-Maximilians-Univ., Munich (art history); Art Ed. for Bruckmann Verlag, Munich 1937–39; served in Second World War; Publr. and Ed. Hannoversche Neueste Nachrichten 1946–47, Abendpost Hanover 1947–48; Founder and Publr. Stern (magazine), Hamburg, Ed.-in-Chief 1948–83; f. own publishing co. Verlag Henri Nannen GmbH, Hamburg 1969; Hon. Citizen of Volkach 1962; Stiftung Henri Nannen f. 1983; collection of expressionist and contemporary paintings and sculptures in Kunsthalle, Emden, named after him. *Publications:* Glanz von innen 1943, Kleines Musikbrevier 1943. *Leisure interest:* yachting. *Address:* Gruner und Jahr AG, Fontenay-Allee P2, 2000 Hamburg 36, Postfach 302040 (Office); Hamburg, Wellingsbütteler Weg 92, Federal Republic of Germany (Home).

NAPIER, R. Rev. Wilfrid Fox, B.PH., B.TH., M.A.; South African ecclesiastic; b. 8 March 1941, Matatiele; s. of Thomas D. Napier and Mary Davey; ed. Little Flower School, Ixopo, Natal, Univ. of Ireland, Galway and Catholic Univ., Louvain, Belgium; ordained priest 1970; Asst. Pastor, St. Anthony's Parish, Lusikisiki 1971; Parish Priest, St. Francis Parish, Tabankulu 1973;

Apostolic Administrator, Diocese of Kokstad 1978; Bishop of Kokstad 1980; Vice-Pres. S. African Catholic Bishops' Conf. 1984, Pres. 1987-. *Leisure interests:* gardening, tennis, golf, D.I.Y. mechanics, fishing. *Address:* 97 St. John's Street, P.O. Box 65, Kokstad, 4700 Natal, South Africa. *Telephone:* (0372) 2239.

NAPLEY, Sir David, Kt.; British solicitor; b. 25 July 1915; s. of late Joseph Napley and Raie Napley; m. Leah Rose Saturley 1940; two d.; ed. Burlington Coll.; solicitor 1937-; served with Queen's Royal (W. Surrey) Regt. 1940, commissioned 1942; Indian Army 1942, Capt. 1942; invalided 1945; stood for Parl. 1951 and 1955 as Conservative cand.; Pres. London (Criminal Courts) Solicitors Assen. 1960-63; Chair. Exec. Council, British Acad. of Forensic Sciences 1960-74, Pres. 1967, Dir. 1974-; mem. Council of Law Soc. 1962-86, Vice-Pres. 1975-76, Pres. 1976-77; Chair. Law Soc.'s Standing Cttee. on Criminal Law 1963-76, Contentious Business, Law Soc. 1972-75; Pres. City of Westminster Law Soc. 1967-68; mem. Editorial Bd. Criminal Law Review 1967-; Legal Aid Cttee. 1969-72; Home Office Law Revision Cttee. 1971-; mem. and Trustee Imperial Soc. of Kts. Bachelor 1981-; Chair. Mario & Franco Restaurants Ltd. 1968-77. *Publications:* Law on the Remuneration of Auctioneers and Estate Agents 1947, ed. Bateman's Law of Auctions 1954, The Law of Auctioneers and Estate Agents Commission 1957, Crime and Criminal Procedure 1963, Guide to Law and Practice Under the Criminal Justice Act 1967, The Technique of Persuasion 1970, Not Without Prejudice 1982, a section in Halsbury's Laws of England, contrib. to various legal and forensic scientific journals, press, radio, TV. *Leisure interests:* painting, reading, writing, music, eating. *Address:* 107-115 Long Acre, London, WC2E 9PT, England. *Telephone:* 01-240 2411.

NAPOLI, Jacopo; Italian composer; b. 26 Aug. 1911; ed. S. Pietro a Majella Conservatoire of Music, Naples; obtained diplomas in Composition, Organ and Piano; held Chair of Counterpoint and Fugue at Cagliari Conservatoire, and at Naples Conservatoire; Dir. S. Pietro a Majella Conservatoire of Music, Naples 1955, 1962; Dir. Giuseppe Verdi Conservatoire of Music, Milan -1972, then Dir. St. Cecilia Conservatory, Rome; Dir. Scarlatti Arts Soc. 1955-; works performed in Germany, Spain and on Italian radio. *Works:* (operas) Il Malato Immaginario 1939, Miseria e Nobiltà 1946, Un curioso accidente 1950, Masaniello 1953, I Pescatori 1954, Il Tesoro 1958, (oratorio) The Passion of Christ, Il Rosario 1962, Il Povero Diavolo 1963, Piccola Cantata del Venerdì Santo 1964, (orchestral works) Overture to Love's Labours Lost 1935, Preludio di Caccia 1935, La Festa di Anacapri 1940. *Address:* 55 Via Andrea da Isernia, I-80122, Naples, Italy.

NARAIN, Govind, M.SC.; Indian civil servant and business administrator; b. 5 May 1917, Mainpuri, Uttar Pradesh; s. of late Ram and Rajrani Narain; m. Chandra Lall 1939; three d.; ed. Allahabad Univ. and Balliol Coll., Oxford; Dist. Magistrate 1945-47; Home Sec. Uttar Pradesh 1948-51; Adviser-Sec. to King of Nepal 1951-54; Sec. to Uttar Pradesh Public Works Dept., Power and Information Depts. 1954-55; Devt. Commr. to Uttar Pradesh Govt.; Sec. Depts. of Planning, Econs., Statistics and Information 1955-58, Chief Sec. Uttar Pradesh Govt. 1958-61; Man. Dir. State Trading Corpn. of India Ltd. 1961-63, Chair. May-Sept. 1963; Chair. Minerals and Metals Trading Corpn. of India Ltd. Oct. 1963-66; Adviser to Gov. of Kerala 1965; Sec. Dept. of Family Planning, Govt. of India March-Dec. 1966; Sec. Ministry of Health and Family Planning, Govt. of India 1967-68; Sec. Defence Production, Ministry of Defence, Govt. of India 1968-70; Sec. Ministry of Home Affairs 1971-73, Ministry of Defence 1973-75; mem. Andhra Pradesh Admin. Tribunal 1976-77; Gov. of Karnataka 1977-83; Pres. Shankara Vidya Kendra, Vasant Vihar Welfare Assen.; Vice-Pres. Ma Anandamayee Sangha; mem. Governing Body, Common Cause, Fed. of Indo-German Assens. *Publications:* Memoirs of Old Mandarins of India, Governor: Sage or Saboteur?, and many articles. *Leisure interests:* photography, gardening. *Address:* C-4/2, Vasant Vihar, New Delhi 110057, India. *Telephone:* 673650.

NARASIMHA RAO, P. V., B.SC., LL.B.; Indian politician; b. 28 June 1921, Karimnagar, Andhra Pradesh; widower; three s. five d.; ed. Osmania, Bombay and Nagpur Univs.; mem. Andhra Pradesh Legis. Ass. 1957-77, Minister, Govt. of Andhra Pradesh 1962-71, Chief Minister 1971-73; Gen. Sec. All India Congress Cttee. 1975-76; mem. Lok Sabha (Congress (I) Party) 1977-; Minister of External Affairs, Govt. of India 1980-85, of Defence and Acting Minister of Planning 1985, of Human Resources Devt. and Health and Family Welfare 1985-88, of Human Resources Devt. Feb.-June 1988, of External Affairs June 1988-; Chair. Telugu Acad., Andhra Pradesh 1968-74; Vice.-Pres. Dakshin Bharat Hindi Prachar Sabha 1972. *Publications:* translations to Telugu and Hindi of several famous works; many articles in journals on political matters and allied subjects. *Leisure interests:* Indian Philosophy and culture, writing poems in Telugu and Hindi, music, theatre and cinema. *Address:*Lok Sabha, New Delhi, India.

NARASIMHAM, Maidavolu; Indian international bank official; b. 3 June 1927, Bangalore; s. of M. Seshachelapati; m. Shanthy Sundaresan; one s.; ed. Presidency Coll., Madras, and St. John's Coll., Cambridge; joined Reserve Bank of India, Bombay 1950; Chief of S. Asia Div., IMF 1960-63; Sec. Reserve Bank of India 1967, Gov. 1977; Additional Sec. Ministry of Finance 1972, Sec. Banking Dept. 1976-78; Exec. Dir. IBRD 1978-80; Vice-

Pres. Asian Devt. Bank 1985-88; Exec. Dir. of IMF for India, Bangladesh and Sri Lanka 1980-82; Sec. Ministry of Finance, Dept. of Econ. Affairs 1982; Finance Sec., Govt. of India 1983; Prin. Admin. Staff Coll. of India, Hyderabad 1983-85; Norton Prize (Madras Univ.). *Leisure interests:* reading, music. *Address:* "Sukruti", 8-2-681/7, Road No. 12, Banjara Hills, Hyderabad 500 034, India (Home).

NARAYAN, Rasipuram Krishnaswamy; Indian writer; b. 10 Oct. 1906; ed. Maharaja's Coll., Mysore; Hon. Litt. D. (Leeds) 1967; Hon. mem. American Acad. and Inst. of Arts and Letters 1982. *Publications:* (all in English), novels: Swami and Friends 1935, The Bachelor of Arts, The Dark Room, The English Teacher, Mr. Sampath, The Financial Expert, Waiting for the Mahatma, The Guide 1958, The Man-Eater of Malgudi 1961, Gods, Demons and Others 1964, The Sweet-Vendor 1967, The Painter of Signs 1977, A Tiger for Malgudi 1983, Under the Banyan Tree and other stories 1985, Talkative Man 1986; short stories: An Astrologer's Day, The Lawley Road, A Horse and Two Goats, Malgudi Days, The Ramayana (prose trans.) 1972; My Days (autobiog.) 1974. *Address:* Yadavagiri, Mysore 2, India; c/o Anthony Shiel Associates, 2-3 Maxwell Street, London, WC1B 3AR, England.

NARAYANAN, Kocheril Raman, M.A.; Indian diplomatist; b. 4 Feb. 1921, Ozhavoor, Kerala; s. of the late Raman Vaidyan; m. Usha Ma Tint Tint 1951; two d.; ed. Travancore Univ. and London School of Econs., Univ. of London; Lecturer in English Literature, Travancore Univ. 1943; worked in Editorial Dept. of Hindu newspaper, Madras 1944-45; Reporter, Times of India 1945; London Corresp. of Social Welfare (weekly), Bombay 1945-48; entered Foreign Service 1949; Joint Dir. of Orientation Centre for Foreign Technicians, Delhi School of Econs. 1954-55; served Rangoon, Tokyo, London and in Ministry of External Affairs 1949-60; Acting High Commr. in Australia 1961-62; Consul-Gen., Hanoi 1962-63; Dir. of China Div., Ministry of External Affairs 1963-67; Amb. to Thailand 1967-69; Joint Sec. for Policy Planning in Ministry 1969-70; Jawaharlal Nehru Fellow 1970-72; Hon. Prof., Jawaharlal Nehru Univ. 1970-72; Hon. Fellow, L.S.E. 1972-; Amb. to Turkey 1973-75; Additional Sec. for Policy Planning Div. of Ministry 1975-76; Sec. for the East, Ministry of External Affairs April-May 1976; Amb. to People's Repub. of China 1976-78, to U.S.A. 1980-83; mem. Lok Sabha for Ottapalath, Kerala 1984-; Minister of State for Planning, Govt. of India 1984-85, for External Affairs 1985-86, for Science and Tech., Atomic Energy, Space, Electronics and Ocean Devt. 1986-87; Vice-Pres. Council of Scientific and Industrial Research 1986-. Vice-Chancellor Jawaharlal Nehru University 1979-80; mem. Indian del. to UN Gen. Assembly 1979; Co-Chair. Indo-U.S. Sub-Comm. on Educ. and Culture 1980; mem. Indian Council for Social Science Research, New Delhi, Exec. Council, Children's Book Trust, Inst. of Defence Studies and Analysis, Indian Assen. of Social Science Inst. *Publications:* various on int. relations, Indian politics, literary subjects. *Leisure interest:* reading. *Address:* Kocheril House, Ozhavoor P.O., Kerala, India (Home).

NARAYANAN, Palayil Pathazapurayil; Malaysian trade unionist; b. 15 Feb. 1923, India; s. of Chettur Narayanan Nair; m. M. K. Dakshayani; three s. two d.; ed. Tech. Coll., Kuala Lumpur; mem. Fed. Legis. Council and Finance Cttee. 1948-53, 1955-59; mem. ILO Plantation Cttee. 1950, Dels. to ILO Conf. 1957, 1965, 1972, 1974, ILO Advisory Cttee. on Rural Devt. 1973-(78); mem. Exec. Council of Malayan (later Malaysian) TUC (MTUC) 1949-; Pres. MTUC 1950-52, 1954-55, 1975-76, now also Chair. Bldg., Educ. and Int. Cttees.; Gen. Sec. Nat. Union of Plantation Workers 1954-; Pres. ICFTU Asian Regional Org. (ICFTU-ARO) 1960-66, 1969-76, Chair. ICFTU-ARO Educ. Cttee. 1960-75; Chair. World Econ. Cttee. of ICFTU 1968-, Pres. ICFTU 1975-; mem. Court, Univ. of Malaya 1972-75; now Vice-Pres. Int. Fed. of Plantation, Agric. and Allied Workers; mem. Nat. Family Planning Bd., Nat. Unity Council, Nat. Joint Advisory Council, Nat. Electricity Bd.; Life mem. Commonwealth Parl. Assen., Tamil Journalists Union, Sri Aurobindo Soc.; Hon. LL.D. (Penang) 1974; Gold Medal, MTUC 1951, Ramon Magsaysay Award for Community Service 1962, Gold Medal of Railway's Union of Malaya 1966, Golden Key and Freedom of City of Osaka, Japan 1972, Commdr., Order of Merit (Luxembourg) 1987. *Publications:* short story collections: The Interview, Light in Darkness; various trade union publs.; poems in Malayalam. *Leisure interests:* trade unionism, creation of new employment opportunities, painting, sketching, writing short stories and poems. *Address:* ICFTU, 37-41 rue Montagne aux Herbes Potagères, 1000 Brussels, Belgium. *Telephone:* 217 80 85.

NARJES, Karl-Heinz; German politician and public servant; b. 30 Jan. 1924, Soltau; m.; two c.; ed. Hamburg Univ.; submarine commdr. during World War II; with Minstry of Foreign Affairs; Chef de Cabinet to Pres. of European Comm. 1963; Dir.-Gen. Press and Information Directorate of Comm. 1968-69; Minister of the Econ. and Transport, Schleswig-Holstein Province 1969-73; mem. Bundestag 1972-, Bundestag Foreign Affairs Comm. 1972-76, 1980-, Bundestag Econ. Affairs Comm. (Pres. 1972-76, 1980-); Commr. for Internal Market and Industrial Innovation, Customs Union, Environment and Consumer Protection and Nuclear Safety, Comm. of the European Communities 1981-84, for Economic Affairs and Employment 1985-86, for Industrial Affairs, Information Tech., Science and Research, Jt. Research Centre 1986-. *Address:* Commission of the European Communities, 200 rue de la Loi, 1049 Brussels, Belgium.

NARLIKAR, Jayant Vishnu, PH.D., SC.D.; Indian scientist; b. 19 July 1938, Kolhapur; s. of Prof. and Mrs. V. V. Narlikar; m. Mangala S. Rajwade 1966; three d.; ed. Banaras Hindu Univ. and Fitzwilliam Coll., Cambridge; Berry Ramsey Fellow, King's Coll., Cambridge 1963–69; Graduate Staff Mem., Inst. of Theoretical Astronomy, Cambridge 1966–72; Sr. Research Fellow, King's Coll. 1969–72; Jawaharlal Nehru Fellow 1973–75; mem. Science Advisory Council to the Prime Minister 1986–88; Sr. Prof., Tata Inst. of Fundamental Research; Fellow, Indian Nat. Science Acad., Assoc. Royal Astronomical Soc., London; awarded Padma Bhushan by the Indian Govt. 1965, S. S. Bhatnagar Award 1978, Rashtrabhushan Award of FIE Foundation 1981, Rathindra Award 1985. *Publications:* articles on cosmology, general relativity and gravitation, quantum theory, astrophysics etc. in the Proceedings of the Royal Soc., London, The Monthly Notices of the Royal Astronomical Soc., London, The Astrophysical Journal, Nature, Observatory and scientific articles in various magazines; Action at a distance in Physics and Cosmology (with Sir F. Hoyle (q.v.)) 1974, Structure of the Universe 1977, General Relativity and Cosmology 1978, The Physics Astronomy Frontier (with Sir F. Hoyle) 1980, Violent Phenomena in the Universe 1982, The Lighter Side of Gravity 1982, Introduction to Cosmology 1983, From Black Clouds to Black Holes 1985, Gravity Gauge Theories and Quantum Cosmology (with T. Padmanabhan) 1986. *Address:* Flat 701, Colaba Housing Colony, Homi Bhabha Road, Bombay, India (Home). *Telephone:* Bombay 495-2177.

NARR, Karl Josef, DR. PHIL.; German professor of prehistory and protohistory; b. 9 June 1921, Düsseldorf; s. of Otto Narr and Gertrud Busch; m. Theresia Pelzer 1952; one s. one d.; ed. Univ. of Bonn; part-time collaborator, State Museum, Bonn and grantee, German Research Council 1950–52; Asst. Seminary of Prehistory and Protohistory, Univ. of Göttingen 1953–59; lecturer, Assoc. Prof. Univ. of Göttingen 1959–65; Prof. of Prehistory and Protohistory, Univ. of Münster 1965–86, Prof. Emer. 1986–; Deputy Sec. Rheinisch-Westfälische Akad. der Wissenschaften 1978–79; Fellow, German Archaeological Inst. *Publications:* six books. *Address:* Universität Münster, Domplatz 20-22, D-4400 Münster/Westfalen; Nerzweg 48, 4400 Münster/Westfalen, Federal Republic of Germany (Home). *Telephone:* (0251) 834191; (0251) 248148 (Home).

NARUD, Odd, B.A.ECON.; Norwegian business executive; b. 3 Feb. 1919, Furnes; s. of Johannes and Martea Narud; m. Ruth Narud 1947; one s. one d.; ed. Norwegian Graduate School of Econs. and Business Admin.; with Norsk Hydro a.s., Rjukan Fabrikker 1943–58, Office Man. 1950–58; Office Man. Norsk Hydro a.s., Porsgrunn Fabrikker 1958–60; Vice-Pres. for Finance, Norsk Hydro 1960–75, Exec. Vice-Pres. 1975–77, Pres. 1977–83. *Leisure interests:* sports and outdoor life. *Address:* Myrhaugen 20, Oslo 7, Norway. *Telephone:* 50-33-22.

NASCIMENTO, Edson Arantes do (see Pelé).

NASCIMENTO, Lopo Fortunato Ferreira do; Angolan politician; b. 10 July 1940, Luanda; s. of Vaz I. do Nascimento and Arminda F. do Nascimento; m. Maria do Carmo Assis 1969; three c.; mem. Presidential Collegiate in transitional Govt. before independence from Portugal Jan.-Nov. 1975; Prime Minister of Angola 1975–78; Minister of Internal Trade 1977–78, of Foreign Trade 1979–82 and of Planning 1979–; Deputy Exec. Sec. UN ECA, Addis Ababa 1979; Head Fifth Mil. Region 1986–; Movimento Popular de Libertação de Angola (MPLA). *Address:* Ambufla Street 47, P.O. Box 136, Luanda, Angola. *Telephone:* 34.42.29.

NASH, Charles; Irish boxer; b. 10 May 1951, Londonderry, N. Ireland; s. of Alexander Nash and of late Bridget Nash; m. Elizabeth Nash; one s. one d.; ed. St. Joseph's Secondary School, Londonderry; five times Irish amateur lightweight champion; boxed for Ireland in Olympic Games and European championships; won Irish title in first professional contest Oct. 1975; won vacant British lightweight title v. Johnny Claydon Feb. 1978; won vacant European title v. Andre Holyk June 1979, retained it v. Ken Buchanan Dec. 1979; relinquished British and European titles Jan. 1980 to challenge, unsuccessfully, for world title v. Jim Watt, Glasgow March 1980; regained European title from Francisco Leon Dec. 1980; 25 fights, 23 wins. *Leisure interests:* football, snooker, table tennis, coaching amateur boxers.

NASH, David; British sculptor; b. 14 Nov. 1945, Surrey; s. of Lieut.-Col. W. C. E. Nash and Dora (née Vickery); m. Claire Langdown 1972; two s.; ed. Brighton Coll., Kingston Art School and Chelsea School of Art; has exhibited widely in Britain, Europe, U.S.A. and Japan; first exhbn. Briefly Cooked Apples, York Festival 1973; one-man shows include Loosely Held Grain, Arnolfini Gallery, Bristol 1976, 30 days 2 beech, Kroller Muller Museum, Netherlands 1982, Ki No Inoichi: Ni No Katachi, Japan 1984; major group exhbns. British Art Now, Guggenheim Museum, New York 1980, Aspects of British Art Today, Japan 1982; works in several public collections including Tate Gallery and Guggenheim Museum. *Leisure interests:* walking, thinking. *Address:* Rhiw Chapel, Blaenau Ffestiniog, Gwynedd, North Wales, United Kingdom.

NASHASHIBI, Nasser Eddin; Arab journalist, author and politician; b. 1924, Jerusalem; m. Ursula Nashashibi; one s. one d.; ed. American Univ. of Beirut; Chief Adviser, King Abdullah of Jordan 1950, Acting Chief Chamberlain 1951; fmr. Chief Controller and Dir. Hashemite Broadcasting; fmr. Head Press Dept., Foreign Office, Amman; Roving Ed. Akhbar El Yom, Cairo; Chief Ed. of daily Al-Goumhouria, Cairo 1959–64; Special Diplomatic Envoy of daily Al-Ahram in Europe; Roving Amb. of the Arab League 1965–67, Jordanian Independence Star (1st degree). *Publications include:* The Ink is Black 1971, No Camel No Sand 1976, I am the Middle East 1977, A Prayer in Jerusalem 1980, Who Killed King Abdullah? 1980, Jerusalem, My Love 1981, My Life in Journalism 1983. *Leisure interest:* travel. *Address:* 55 Av. Champel, Geneva, Switzerland; and 26 Lowndes Street, London, England. *Telephone:* 463763 (Geneva); 01-235 1427 (London).

NASI, Gicvanni, D.ING.; Italian industrialist; b. 24 Aug. 1918, Villarperosa, Turin; s. of Carlo Nasi and Aniceta Agnelli; grandson of Giovanni Agnelli, founder of FIAT; m. Marinella Wolf 1944; one s. one d.; ed. Politecnico di Torino; Vice-Chair. of FIAT (mfrs. of land, sea and air vehicles and engines) until 1972; Vice-Chair. IFI, Turin 1959–; Chair. Soc. Assicuratrice Industriale (SAI) 1972–76, UNICEM 1977–; Pres. Turin Agency for Int. Exhbns., Centre for Winter Road Transit; Commendatore della Repubblica Italiana. *Leisure interests:* golf, skiing. *Address:* Via Carlo Marenco 25, 10126, Turin, Italy. *Telephone:* 65-67.

NASIR, Agha, M.A.; Pakistani television executive; b. 9 Feb. 1937, Meerut, U.P., India; s. of Ali Ahmad Khan; m. Safia Sultana 1959; one s. two d.; Programmes Man. Pakistani TV 1967–68, Additional Gen. Man. 1967, Gen. Man. 1969–72, Dir. Programmes Admin. 1972–86, Deputy Man. Dir. 1986–87, Man. Dir. 1987–88; Man. Dir. Nat. Film Devt. Corpn. 1979; recipient of numerous awards for radio and TV plays. *Publications:* Saat Dramey (plays), Television Dramey (TV plays). *Leisure interest:* reading. *Address:* House No. 39, Street No. 3, Sector E-7, Islamabad, Pakistan (Home). *Telephone:* 821933 (Home).

NASIR, Amir Ibrahim; Maldivian politician; b. 2 Sept. 1926, Malé; s. of Ahmed Didi and Aishath Didi; m. 1st Aishath Zubair 1950; m. 2nd Mariyam Saeed 1953; m. 3rd Naseema Mohamed Kalegefaan 1969; four s. one d.; ed. Ceylon (now Sri Lanka); Under-Sec. of State to Minister of Finance and to Minister of Public Safety, Repub. of Maldives 1954; Minister of Public Safety 1956, of Home Affairs Aug. 1957; Prime Minister (1st term) Dec. 1957, Prime Minister (2nd term) and Minister of Home Affairs, Finance, Educ., Trade, External Affairs and Public Safety Aug. 1959, Prime Minister (3rd term) and Minister of Finance, Educ., External Affairs and Public Safety 1964; Pres. of the Repub. of Maldives 1968–78 (retd.); Award of Nishan Ghaazee ge Izzatheri Veriya, Ranna Bandeiri Kilegefaan; Hon. K.C.M.G. *Leisure interests:* fishing, yachting, gardening. *Address:* Velaanaage, Henvaru, Malé, Maldives (Home). *Telephone:* 822, 270 (Office); 546, 594 (Home).

NASON, John William, A.M.; American educator; b. 9 Feb. 1905, St. Paul, Minn.; s. of Albert J. Nason and Mary E. Eaton; m. 1st Bertha D. White 1935 (died 1955); m. 2nd Elizabeth M. Knapp 1957; two s. one step s. two step d.; ed. Chicago Latin School, Phillips Exeter Acad., Carleton Coll., Yale Divinity School, Harvard Graduate School, Oxford Univ.; Instructor in Phil. Swarthmore Coll. 1931–34, Asst. Prof. 1934–40, Pres. 1940–53; Pres. Foreign Policy Assen. 1953–62, mem. Bd. of Dirs. 1971–80; Pres Carleton Coll. 1962–70; Asst. to American Sec. Rhodes Trust 1934–40; Pres. UN Council Philadelphia 1942–45, Vice-Pres. 1945–47; Pres. World Affairs Council of Philadelphia 1949–51, 1952–53; Fellow and mem. Bd. of Dirs. Soc. for Religion in Higher Educ.; Trustee, Phillips Exeter Acad. 1946–50, 1952–62, Edward W. Hazen Foundation 1945–67, 1968–78, Vassar Coll. 1954–62, Eisenhower Exchange Fellowships 1953–65, Danforth Foundation 1961–68; mem. Educator's Advisory Comm. Esso Educ. Foundation 1964–68; mem. Visiting Comm. Harvard Graduate School of Educ. 1975–82; Dir. of Studies, Assen. of Governing Bds. of Univs. and Colls. 1973–75; Dir. of Study of Foundation Trustees for Council on Foundations 1975–77; Dir. of Study of Presidential Selection and Assessment, Assen. of Governing Bds. 1977–80; Educ. Consultant 1980–; Bd. of Dirs. Adirondack Conservancy Comm. 1977–, New York State Conservancy 1983–; Gov. Bruce L. Crary Foundation 1979–; Hon. LL.D. (Pennsylvania, Carleton, Swarthmore, Hamilton, Brandeis, Johns Hopkins); Litt.D. (Mühlenberg Coll., Hahnemann Medical School and Coll.); L.H.D. (Dropsie Coll., St. Olaf Coll. and Coll. of Wooster). *Publications:* American Higher Education in 1980—Some Basic Issues 1965, Crises of the University 1970, The Future of Trusteeship: The Role and Responsibilities of College and University Boards 1975, Trustees and the Future of Foundations 1977, Presidential Search: A Guide to the Process of Selecting and Appointing College and University Presidents 1979, Presidential Assessment: A Challenge to College and University Leadership 1980, The Nature of Trusteeship 1982, Foundation Trusteeship: Service in the Public Interest 1989. *Leisure interests:* tennis, skiing, mountain climbing, woodworking, reading. *Address:* Rocky Point, Keene, N.Y. 12942 (May–Oct.); Crosslands 12, Kennett Square, Pa. 19348, U.S.A. (Nov.–April). *Telephone:* (518) 576-4506 (N.Y.); (215) 388-1392 (Pa.).

NASRIDDINOVA, Yadgar Sadikovna; Soviet civil engineer and politician; b. 26 Dec. 1920; ed. Inst. of Railway Transport Eng., Tashkent; Works Supt. Great Ferghana Canal, and the Construction of the Railway Line at "Angrenugol" Coalmines; later Sec. for School affairs Cen. Cttee. Young Communist League of Uzbekistan 1942–50; mem. CPSU 1942–; Party work 1950–52; Minister of Bldg. Materials, Uzbek S.S.R. 1952–55, Vice-Chair. Council of Ministers Uzbek S.S.R. 1955–59; Deputy to U.S.S.R. Supreme

Soviet 1958–74; Chair. Presidium, Supreme Soviet of the Uzbek S.S.R. 1959–70; Vice-Chair. Presidium of Supreme Soviet of U.S.S.R. 1959–70; mem. Cen. Cttee. of CPSU 1956–76; mem. Cen. Cttee. of CP of Uzbekistan 1952–; Chair. Soviet of Nationalities, U.S.S.R. Supreme Soviet 1970–74; First Vice-Chair. Cttee. U.S.S.R. Parl. Group; Order of Lenin (four times), Order of October Revolution, and other decorations. *Address:* Presidium of U.S.S.R. Supreme Soviet, Moscow, U.S.S.R.

NASTASE, Ilie; Romanian lawn tennis player; b. 19 July 1946, Bucharest; m. 1st; one d.; m. 2nd Alexandra King 1984; nat. champion (13–14 age group) 1959, (15–16 age group) 1961, (17–18 age group) 1963, 1964; won the Masters Singles Event, Paris 1971, Barcelona 1972, Boston 1973, Stockholm 1975; winner of singles at Cannes 1967, Travemünde 1967, 1969, Gauhati 1968, Madras 1968, 1969, New Delhi 1968, 1969, Viareggio 1968, Barranquilla 1969, Coruna 1969, Budapest 1969, Denver 1969, Salisbury 1970, Rome 1970, 1973, Omaha 1971, 1972, Richmond 1971, Hampton 1971, Nice 1971, 1972, Monte Carlo 1971, 1972, Baastad 1971, Wembley 1971, Stockholm 1971, Istanbul 1971, Forest Hills 1972, Baltimore 1972, Madrid 1972, Toronto 1972, South Orange 1972, Seattle 1972, Roland Garros 1973; winner of doubles at Roland Garros (with Ion Ţiriac) 1970, Wimbledon (with Rosemary Casals) 1970, 1972, (with Jimmy Connors) 1975; winner of ILTF Grand Prix 1972, 1973; played 130 matches for the Romanian team in the Davis Cup; "Best Romanian sportsman of the year" 1969, 1970, 1971, 1973. *Publication:* Breakpoint 1986. *Address:* Clubul sportiv Steaua, Calea Plevnei 114, Bucharest, Romania.

NASUTION, Gen. Abdul Haris; Indonesian army officer; b. 3 Dec. 1918, Kotanopan (Tapanuli), N. Sumatra; s. of Hadji Abdul Halim Nasution and Hadji Sahara Lubis; m. Johana Sunarti Gondokusmo 1947; two d. (one deceased); ed. Netherlands Mil. Acad., Bandung; Sub-Lieut. Netherlands Indies Army 1941, Col. 1945, Commdr. Siliwangi Division 1946–48; Deputy C.-in-C. Armed Forces 1948; Commdr. of Java, planned and led guerrillas against Dutch 1948–49; Army Chief of Staff 1950–52, reappointed 1955–62; Chair. of Joint Chiefs of Staff and mem. Nat. Council 1957; Lieut.-Gen. 1958; planned campaign against rebellion in Sumatra and Sulawesi 1958; Minister of Defence and People's Security 1959–66; apptd. Gen. 1960; Deputy C.-in-C. West Irian (W. New Guinea) Liberation Command 1962; Chair. People's Consultative Congress 1966–72 (retd.); numerous awards from Indonesia and foreign countries. *Publications include:* Principles of Guerrilla Warfare, The Indonesian National Army, Notes on the Army Policy of the Republic of Indonesia, Truth and Justice, The Fight for Freedom, Rethinking New Order, Students and National Policies, From the 1965 Coup to the Congress Session in 1967, Leadership, Towards Harmony Among Religious Communities, To Bridge the Gap between Rich and Poor, Indonesian Struggle for Independence (11 vols.) 1979. *Address:* 40 Teuku Umar, Jakarta, Indonesia.

NASZKOWSKI, Marian, M.A.; Polish politician; b. 15 Aug. 1912, Lwów (now Lvov, U.S.S.R.); s. of Michał and Jadwiga Naszkowski; m.; two s. one d.; ed. Lwów Univ.; active in revolutionary youth movement and later in CP before Second World War; imprisoned for political activities 1938–39; during the war took part in formation of Polish army in U.S.S.R.; Chief Polish Mil. mission, Paris 1945–47; Amb. to U.S.S.R. 1947–50; Vice-Minister of Defence and Chief Gen. Political Bd. of Polish Army 1950–52; Vice-Minister of Foreign Affairs 1952–68; Deputy to Seym 1952–56; mem. Cen. Cttee. Polish United Workers' Party 1950–68, mem. Cen. Comm. of Party Control 1968–75; Chair. Polish Del. to Eighteen Nations Cttee. on Disarmament, Geneva 1962; Ed.-in-Chief Nowe Drogi 1968–72; Amb.-Rep. of Poland to ILO, Geneva 1972–77; Vice-Pres. Poland-Denmark Soc.; mem. Polish Cttee. of Peace; mem. World Peace Council; numerous decorations; Commdr. Cross of Polonia Restituta, Order of the Banner of Labour (1st Class), Légion d'honneur. *Publications:* Niespokojne dni (Unrestful Days), Lata próby (The Years of Trial) (memoirs), Zygmunt syn Łukasza (Zygmunt Son of Lukas) (novel), Paryż-Moskwa: wspomnienia dyplomaty (Paris-Moscow: The memoirs of a diplomat). *Address:* 00-759 Warszawa, ul. Parkowa 13/17 m. 143, Poland. *Telephone:* 41-47-47.

NATALI, Lorenzo; Italian lawyer and politician; b. 2 Oct. 1922; ed. Collegio d'Abruzzo dei Padri Gesuiti and Univ. di Firenze; Deputy to Parl.; Under-Sec. of State for the Press and Information 1955–57; Under-Sec. of State in Ministry of Finance 1957–59, in Ministry of Treasury 1960–64; Minister for the Merchant Marine Feb. 1966–68, of Public Works 1968, of Tourism and Entertainments 1968–69; Minister of Agric. 1970–73; Vice-Pres., Comm. of European Communities 1977–, with special responsibility for enlargement, environmental affairs, nuclear safety and Preparations for Direct Elections to the European Parl. 1977–81, for Mediterranean Policy, Enlargement and Information 1981–85; Commr. for Parl. July 1979–; Vice-Pres. responsible for enlargement negotiations with Portugal and Spain and for devt. co-operation and relations with ACP countries 1985–86, for Co-operation and Devt. Jan. 1986–; Christian Democrat. *Leisure interests:* education, sport. *Address:* Commission of the European Communities, 200 rue de la Loi, 1049 Brussels, Belgium (Office); Via Nibby 18, Rome, Italy (Home).

NATH, Dhurma Gian, M.A.; Mauritian diplomatist; b. 29 May 1934, Triolet; s. of Anmole Facknath and B. Facknath; m. Chitralekha Sud Chiranjilal 1961; two s. one d.; ed. Grammar School, Port Louis and Univ. of Delhi, India; Educ. Officer 1963–66; Head of Dept. of English, John Kennedy

Coll. 1965–66; Diplomatic Trainee, course in Int. Affairs, Postgraduate Inst. of Int. Affairs, New Delhi, India, practical training with Indian Ministry of External Affairs and British Foreign Office 1966–68; served High Comm., London 1968–82, Head of Chancery 1969–82; Counsellor, Mission to EEC, involved in negotiations for Mauritius' signature of Yaoundé Convention 1971–76, Deputy High Commr. 1976–82; Amb. Extraordinary and Plenipotentiary, Cairo 1982–83; High Commr., London and Amb. to Holy See 1983–87, to China 1988–; mem. 1977 Review Group on functions of Commonwealth Secr.; Sec. OAU Group in London 1973–82. *Leisure interests:* bridge, reading, history of World War II. *Address:* c/o Ministry of Foreign Affairs, Hôtel du Government, Port Louis, Mauritius.

NATHAN, Ove, D.PHIL.; Danish university administrator and professor; b. 12 Jan. 1926, Copenhagen; m. 1956; two d.; ed. Univ. of Copenhagen; Prof. of Physics, Univ. of Copenhagen 1970–, Rector 1982–; mem. Cttee. for European Devt. of Science and Tech., Comm. of the European Communities 1987–; Jens Rosenkjaer Prize 1974. *Publications:* books on science, articles in nuclear physics. *Address:* Svanevaenget 4, 2100 Copenhagen Ø, Denmark. *Telephone:* (01) 29 87 37.

NATHANS, Daniel, M.D.; American professor of molecular biology and genetics; b. 30 Oct. 1928, Wilmington, Del.; s. of Samuel and Sarah (Levitan) Nathans; m. Joanne Gomberg 1956; three s.; ed. Univ. of Delaware, Washington Univ. School of Medicine; Intern, Columbia-Presbyterian Medical Center, New York, N.Y. 1954–55, Resident 1957–59; Clinical Assoc., Nat. Cancer Inst. 1955–57; Guest Investigator, Rockefeller Univ., New York 1959–62; Asst. Prof. of Microbiology, Johns Hopkins Univ. School of Medicine, Baltimore, Md. 1962–65, Assoc. Prof. 1965–67, Prof. 1967–82, Dir. Dept. of Microbiology 1972–82, Prof. of Molecular Biology and Genetics 1982–; Sr. Investigator, Howard Hughes Medical Inst. 1982–; American Cancer Soc. Scholar in Genetics Dept. of Weizmann Inst. of Science, Rehovoth, Israel 1969; shared Nobel Prize for Physiology or Medicine 1978 with Prof. Werner Arber and Dr. Hamilton Smith (qq.v.) for the application of restriction enzymes to problems of genetics. *Address:* Department of Molecular Biology and Genetics, Johns Hopkins University School of Medicine, 725 North Wolfe Street, Baltimore, Md. 21205, U.S.A. *Telephone:* (301) 955-8445.

NATORF, Włodzimierz, M.ECON.; Polish politician; b. 12 Oct. 1931, Łódź; ed. Leningrad Univ.; with foreign service 1955–; participant sessions of UN econ. agencies, Chief Polish rep. on Econ. Cttee. at 18th and 19th UN Gen. Assembly Sessions, Second, later First Sec. of Polish Perm. Mission to UN, New York 1959–65; Vice-Dir. of Dept. at Ministry of Foreign Affairs 1966–69; Polish Perm. Rep., UN European Office, Geneva 1969–73; Vice-Dir. of Dept. at Ministry of Foreign Affairs 1973–81; Chair. Polish del. to Geneva Disarmament Cttee. 1981–82; Head of Foreign Dept. of Cen. Cttee. of Polish United Workers' Party (PZPR) 1981–82, 1985; Perm. Rep. to UN, New York 1982–84; Amb. to U.S.S.R. 1986–; mem. PZPR 1949–, mem. PZPR Cen. Cttee. 1986–; Officers and Kt.'s Cross of Order of Polonia Restituta, Gold Cross of Merit. *Address:* Embassy of the Polish People's Republic, ul. Klimashkina 4, Moscow, U.S.S.R. *Telephone:* 254-01-05.

NATTA, Alessandro; Italian politician; b. 1917, Sardinia; m.; fmr. teacher; mem. Partito Comunista Italiano (PCI) 1946–; M.P. 1948–; PCI Whip, Chamber of Deputies 1979–83; Gen. Sec. PCI 1985–88; fmr. Ed. Rinascita (PCI newspaper). *Address:* c/o Partito Comunista Italiano, Via delle Botteghe Oscure 4, 00186 Rome, Italy.

NAUDÉ, Rev. (Christiaan) Beyers; South African clergyman; b. 1915; f. multi-racial Christian Inst of S.A.; given seven-year Govt. banning order 1977; Gen. Sec. S.A. Council of Churches 1985–87. *Address:* c/o The South African Council of Churches, Khotso House, 42 De Villiers Street, P.O. Box 4921, Johannesburg 2000, South Africa.

NAUMANN, Konrad; German politician; b. 25 Nov. 1928, Leipzig; ed. Komsomol High School, Moscow; mem. of CP of Germany (KPD) 1945; mem. Socialist Unity Party (SED) 1946–; agricultural labourer 1945–46; Official of Freie Deutsche Jugend (FDJ) in Leipzig 1946–47, Chair. 1947–48; First Sec. FDJ, Bezirk Frankfurt/Oder 1952–57; mem. FDJ Cen. Council 1952–67, Second Sec. 1957–64; Cand. mem. SED Cen. Cttee. 1963–66, mem. 1966–; Cand. mem. Politburo 1973–76, mem. 1976–85; Second Sec. SED, Bezirk Berlin 1967–71, First Sec. 1971–85; mem. Volkskammer 1967–; mem. Council of State 1984–86; Vaterländischer Verdienstorden in Bronze and Silver and other decorations. *Address:* Sozialistische Einheitspartei Deutschlands, 102 Berlin, Am Marx-Engels-Platz 2, German Democratic Republic.

NAUMANN, Michael, D.PHIL.; German publisher; b. 12 Aug. 1941, Köthen; s. of Eduard Naumann and Ursula (née Schönfeld) Naumann; m. Christa Wessel 1969; one s. one d.; ed. Univ. of Munich and Queen's Coll., Oxford; Asst. Prof. Univ. of Bochum 1971–76; Florey Scholar Queen's Coll., Oxford 1976–78; Ed., Foreign Corresp. Die Zeit, Hamburg 1978–82; Sr. Foreign Ed. Der Spiegel, Hamburg 1982–84; Publr. Rowohlt Verlag, Reinbek 1984–. *Publications:* Der Abbau einer Verkehrten Welt 1969, Amerika liegt in Kalifornien 1983, Strukturwandel des Heroismus 1984. *Leisure interests:* books, motor-cycling. *Address:* Rowohlt Verlag, Hamburger Str. 17, 2057 Reinbek, Federal Republic of Germany (Office). *Telephone:* (040) 7272230 (Office).

NAUMANN, William L.; American business executive; b. 20 Nov. 1911, Desloge, Mo.; s. of Jules L. Naumann and Barbara Eichenlaub; m. Emma H. Bottin 1934; one s. one d.; joined Caterpillar Tractor Co. 1929, Man. Joliet Ill. Plant 1952, E. Peoria Plant Man. 1956, Vice-Pres. 1960, Admin. Dir. of Mfg., Purchasing, Quality and Traffic Gen. Offices 1963, Exec. Vice-Pres. 1966, Dir. 1967–84, Vice-Chair. 1972–75, Chair. 1975–77; Dir. Helmerich & Payne, Inc. *Address:* 2150 S. Ocean Boulevard, 6A Delray Beach, Fla. 33483, U.S.A.

NAUMOV, Vladimir Naumovich; Soviet film-maker; b. 1927, Leningrad; ed. Dept. of Directing, State Inst. of Cinematography (under I. A. Savchenko); began career at Dovzhenko studios as Savchenko's Asst. on film Taras Shevchenko (in collaboration with A. A. Alov); also in collaboration with Alov: Uneasy Youth 1955, Pavel Korchagin (based on Ostrovsky's novel How the Steel Was Tempered) 1957, Wind 1959, Peace to Him Who Enters (Prize at 22nd Venice Film Festival) 1961, Flight (based on M. Bulgakov's play) 1971; much work for Soviet TV, including series How the Steel Was Tempered 1974, Teheran-43 (First Prize at 12th Int. Film Festival, Moscow) 1981, The Shore (First Prize at 17th Int. Film Festival, Kiev) 1984. People's Artist of R.S.F.S.R. 1974, People's Artist of U.S.S.R. 1983.

NAUTA, Walle Jetze Harinx, M.D., D.SC.; American anatomist; b. 8 June 1916, Medan, Indonesia; s. of Haring Jelles and Janneke Bos; m. Ellie Plaat 1942; one s. two d.; ed. Univ. of Leiden; Lecturer, Univ. of Utrecht 1941–46; Assoc. Prof. Univ. of Leiden 1946–47; Assoc. Prof. Univ. of Zürich 1947–51; Neurophysiologist, Walter Reed Army Inst. of Research 1951–64; Prof. of Anatomy, Univ. of Md. 1955–64; Prof. of Neuroanatomy, M.I.T. 1964–73, Inst. Prof. 1973–86, Emer. 1986–; mem. Nat. Acad. of Sciences, American Acad. of Arts and Sciences, American Philosophical Soc.; Pres. Soc. for Neuroscience 1973. *Publications:* Hypothalamic Regulation of Sleep in Rats 1946, Silver Impregnation of Degenerating Axons 1954, Ascending Pathways in the Brain Stem Reticular Formation 1958, Hippocampal Projections 1958, Fiber Connections of the Hypothalamus 1969, The Problem of the Frontal Lobe 1971. *Address:* Department of Psychology, Massachusetts Institute of Technology, Cambridge, Mass. 02139, U.S.A.

NAVA-CARRILLO, Germán, DR.; Venezuelan diplomatist and politician; b. 21 Aug. 1930, Maracaibo; m.; two c.; ed. Universidad Central de Venezuela; joined Ministry of Foreign Affairs 1955; Minister Plenipotentiary, Chargé d'affaires, London; Asst. Dir.-Gen. of Int. Politics and Chief Div. of Inter-American Affairs, Ministry of Foreign Affairs; Minister-Counsellor, Perm. Mission at UN 1967–69; Amb. and Deputy Perm. Rep. to UN 1969–70; Amb. to Egypt, also accred. to Ethiopia 1970–72; Dir. of Protocol, Ministry of Foreign Affairs 1972–74; Amb. to Costa Rica 1974–75; Dir. of Int. Politics, Ministry of Foreign Affairs 1975–78, Gen. Dir. of Int. Politics and Vice-Minister 1978–79; Perm. Rep. to UN 1979–81; Vice-Minister, Ministry of Foreign Affairs 1984–88, Minister of Foreign Affairs Jan. 1988–; rep. of Venezuela to several UN and other int. confs.; Prof., Int. Studies School, Cen. Univ. of Venezuela 1981–. *Address:* Ministerio de Relaciones Exteriores, Casa Amarilla, Esq. Principal, Caracas, Venezuela.

NAVAJAS-MOGRO, Hugo, M.A.; Bolivian diplomatist; b. 1923; m.; two c.; ed. Univs. of Cochabamba and La Paz and Grad. School of Public Admin. and Public Service, New York Univ.; entered Foreign Service 1943; Head Int. Econ. Policy Dept., Foreign Ministry; Second Sec. Bolivian Embassy, Washington, D.C. 1946–49, First Sec. and Chargé d'Affairs Perm. Mission to UN 1951–52; Official Public Admin. Div., UN Secr. 1952; Head Programme for the Americas, UNDP 1961–63; Apptd. Deputy Resident Rep., UNDP, Argentina 1963; Political Adviser to Personal Rep. of the Sec.-Gen., Dominica 1965, UNDP Resident Rep. 1966; UNDP Resident Rep., Uruguay 1970–73, Argentina 1974–77, Venezuela 1977–80; Prin. Adviser Regional Bureau for Latin America 1973–74; Dir. Programme Policy, UNDP 1980–83; Asst. Admin. and Regional Dir., Latin America and the Caribbean, UDNP 1983–88; Perm. Rep. to UN Feb. 1988–. *Address:* Permanent Mission of Bolivia to the United Nations, 211 East 43rd St, 8th Floor (Room 802), New York, N.Y. 10017, U.S.A. *Telephone:* (212) 682-8132.

NAVARRE, Yves Henri Michel; French writer; b. 24 Sept. 1940, Condom; s. of René Navarre and Adrienne Bax; ed. Lycée Pasteur, Neuilly-sur-Seine, Ecole des Hautes Etudes Commerciales du Nord, Univ. of Lille; Publicity Ed. Havas agency 1965; Editorial Dir. Synergie 1966–67; Creative Head Publicis 1968–69; Creative Dir. B.B.D.O. advertising agency 1970; Chevalier, Ordre nat. du Mérite, des Arts et des Lettres, Prix Goncourt 1980 (for La guerre d'acclimatation). *Publications:* Novels: Lady Black 1971, Evolène 1972, Les Loukoums 1973, Le coeur qui cogne 1974, Killer 1975, Niagarak 1976, Le petit galopin de nos corps, Kurvenal, 1977, Je vis où je m'attache 1978, Portrait de Julien devant la fenêtre, Le temps voulu, 1979, Le jardin d'acclimatation 1980, Biographie 1981, Romances sans paroles 1982, Premières pages 1983 L'Espérance de beaux voyages 1984, Louise 1986, Une vie de chat 1986, Fêtes des Mères 1987, Romans, Un Roman 1988. *Plays:* Il pleut, si on tuait papa-maman, Dialogue des sourdes, Freaks Society, Champagne, Les valises, 1974, Histoire d'amour, La guerre des piscines, Lucienne de Carpentras, Les dernières clientes, 1976, Le Butoir, September Song, Happy End, Vue imprenable sur Paris 1982, Villa des Fleurs 1986. *Leisure interests:* piano-playing, collecting paintings. *Address:* 1 rue Pecquay, 75004, Paris, France.

NAVASKY, Victor Saul, A.B., LL.B.; American writer and editor; b. 5 July 1932, New York; s. of Macy Navasky and Esther Goldberg; m. Anne Landey Strongin 1966; one s. two d.; ed. Swarthmore Coll., Yale Univ.; Special Asst. to Gov. G. Mennen Williams, Mich. 1959–60; Ed. and Publisher, Monocle Magazine 1961–65; Ed. New York Times magazine 1970–72; Ed. The Nation magazine 1978–; American Book Award (for Naming Names) 1981. *Publications:* Kennedy Justice 1971, Naming Names 1980, The Experts Speak (Co-Ed. with C. Cerf) 1984. *Address:* The Nation, 72 Fifth Avenue, New York, N.Y. 10011, U.S.A.

NAVON, Itzhak; Israeli politician and Head of State; b. 9 April 1921, Jerusalem; s. of Yosef Navon and Miriam Ben-Atar; m. Ofira Reznikov-Erez; one s. one d.; ed. Hebrew Univ. of Jerusalem; Dir., Hagana Arabic Dept., Jerusalem 1946–49; Second Sec., Israel Legation in Uruguay and Argentina 1949–51; Political Sec. to Foreign Minister 1951–52; Head of Bureau of Prime Minister 1952–63; Head, Dept. of Culture, Ministry of Educ. and Culture 1963–65; mem. Knesset 1965–78; fmr. Deputy Speaker; fmr. Chair. Knesset Defence and Foreign Affairs Cttee.; Chair. World Zionist Council 1973–78; Pres. of Israel 1978–83; Vice-Premier and Minister of Educ. and Culture 1984–; mem. Mapai Party 1951–65, Rafi 1965–68, Israel Labour Party 1968–; Chair. Wolf Foundation. *Leisure interests:* theatre, folklore, cantorial music. *Address:* Ministry of Education and Culture, Jerusalem, Israel.

NAVRATILOVA, Martina; American (b. Czechoslovak) lawn tennis player; b. 18 Oct. 1956, Prague; d. of Miroslav Navratil and Jana Navratilova; professional since 1975, the year she defected to U.S.A.; Wimbledon singles Champion 1978, 1979, 1982, 1983, 1984, 1985, 1986, 1987; (doubles 1976, 1979, 1982, 1983, 1984, 1985); French Champion 1982, 1984; Australian Champion 1981, 1983, 1985; Avon Champion 1978, 1979, 1981; U.S. Open Champion 1983, 1984, 1987; 46 Grand Slam Titles (17 singles, 24 women's doubles, 4 mixed doubles) to 1987; set professional women's record for consecutive victories 1984; won 100th tournament of career 1985; Pres. Women's Tennis Asscn. 1979–80; World Champion 1980; Played Federation Cup for Czechoslovakia 1973, 1974, 1975. *Publication:* Being Myself (autobiog.) 1985. *Leisure interest:* golf. *Address:* International Management Group, 1 Erieview Plaza, Cleveland, Ohio 44199, U.S.A.

NAWAZ, S. Shah, M.A.; Pakistani diplomatist; b. 17 March 1917, Dehra Doon, India; s. of Sardar Shah Zaman Khan and Humaira Khanum; m. Maliha Nawaz 1959; ed. St. Stephen's Coll., Delhi; joined foreign service of Pakistan 1950; Deputy High Commr., U.K. 1964–66; Minister, Washington, D.C. 1966–68; Amb. to Iran 1968–72; Dir.-Gen. Ministry of Foreign Affairs 1972–74; Additional Foreign Sec. 1974–77, Foreign Sec. 1977–80, Sec.-Gen. for Foreign Affairs 1980–82; Perm. Rep. to UN 1982–. *Leisure interests:* hunting, painting. *Address:* Pakistan Mission to the United Nations, 8 East 65th Street, New York, N.Y. 10021, U.S.A. *Telephone:* (212) 879-8600.

NAWROCKI, Jerzy, D.ENG.; Polish university professor and politician; b. 20 Dec. 1926, Trzciana, Rzeszów Voivodship; s. of Wiktoria Machowska and Władysław Nawrocki; m. Teresa Belohlavek; one s.; ed. Silesian Tech. Univ., Gliwice; locksmith in Ironwork Plant, Cracow 1942–44; studied Silesian Tech. Univ., 1948–54, Asst. 1951–53; Asst. Foreman in "Rozbark" Coal-mine 1953–54; Sr. Designer in Mineral Processing Design Office 1956–59, Prof., Mineral Processing Inst. 1969, Vice-Pres. of Univ. 1970–74, Pres. 1974–81; Deputy to Seym (Parl.) 1972–, Chair. Parl. Comm. of Science and Tech. Progress 1974–81, Minister of Science, Higher Educ. and Tech. July–Dec. 1981; mem. Council of State 1985–; Chair. Scientific Council of Nonferrous Metals Inst. of Ministry of Metallurgy 1977–, Gen. Mining Inst. of Ministry of Mining and Energy 1982–, Group for Study of Columbian and Coal and Phosphate Utilization 1972, Group for Study of Balance of Fuel and Energy in Poland up to year 2000 1985; Chair-Co-ordinator Mineral Processing Scientific Investigation 1975–; Corresp. mem. Polish Acad. of Sciences 1979–; mem. Polish United Workers Party (PZPR) 1952–; Commdrs.' Cross of Order of Polonia Restituta, Nat. Educ. Comm. Medal, Meritorious Teacher of Polish People's Repub. and other decorations. *Publications:* Jiggs—Construction and Exploitation 1972, Effectiveness of Screening and Gravitational Separation 1974, Screening Machines Construction and Exploitation 1976, Gravitational Separators—Analytical and Graphical Evaluation 1976, Report on Coal Mining in the Forty Years of the Polish People's Republic; numerous papers, mainly on mineral processing tech. *Leisure interest:* gardening. *Address:* Kancelaria Rady Państwa, ul. Wiejska 4/6, 00-902 Warsaw (Office); ul. Kępowa 22d, 40-583 Katowice, Poland (Home).

NAYAR, Sushila, DR.P.H.; Indian doctor; b. 26 Dec. 1914, Kunjah District, Gujrat, Pakistan; d. of Brindaban and Taradevi Nayar; unmarried; ed. Lahore Coll. for Women, Lady Hardinge Medical Coll., Delhi, Johns Hopkins Univ., U.S.A.; Medical Attendant to Mahatma Gandhi and his Ashram; work for communal harmony in West Punjab, Noakhali; Dir. Mahatma Gandhi Inst. of Medical Sciences, Prof. of Preventive and Social Medicine 1969–; Pres. All-India Prohibition Council; mem. Lok Sabha 1957–71; fmr. Minister of Health, Rehabilitation and Transport, Delhi State; Speaker Delhi Legis. Ass. 1952–56; Minister of Health, Govt. of India 1962–67; Pres. S.P.C.A. 1952–62; Chair. Indian Red Cross; Pres. All-Indian Inst. of Medical Sciences, Tuberculosis Asscn. of India 1964–67, Kasturba Health Soc. 1964–; Dir. M. G. Inst. of Medical Sciences, Prof. of

Preventive and Social Medicine 1969-. *Publications:* Hamari Ba, Kasturba, Karavas ki Kahani, etc. *Leisure interests:* writing, painting, reading, bridge. *Address:* Kasturba Hospital, Sevragram, Wardha, A.2 Soami Nagar, New Delhi 17, India (Office). *Telephone:* 022-R33; 74147 (New Delhi).

NAYASHKOV, Ivan Semyonovich; Soviet scientist and politician; b. 1924; ed. Moscow Power Inst.; sr. research scientist, then head of dept., All-Union Lenin Electrical Eng. Inst. 1956-64; Dir. of the Inst. 1964-73; from 1973 Vice-Chair., then First Vice-Chair. of State Cttee. for Inventions and Discoveries, U.S.S.R. Council of Ministers; Chair. of U.S.S.R. State Cttee. for Inventions and Discoveries Jan. 1979-; mem. of CPSU 1961-; mem. of Cen. Auditing Comm. of CPSU 1981-. *Address:* The Kremlin, Moscow, U.S.S.R.

NAYEF IBN ABDUL AZIZ, H.R.H. Prince; Saudi Arabian politician; b. 1933; s. of the late King Abdul Aziz ibn Saud; brother of H.R.H. King Fahd (q.v.); fmr. Gov. of Riyadh; held several internal security posts; Minister of the Interior (also responsible for Special Security Forces) 1975-. *Address:* Ministry of the Interior, P.O. Box 2833, Airport Road, Riyadh, Saudi Arabia.

NAZARBAEV, Nursultan Abishevich; Soviet politician; b. 1940, Kazakhstan; ed. Higher Tech. Course at Karaganda Metallurgical Combine and Higher Party School of Cen. Cttee. CPSU; mem. CPSU 1962-; worked for Karaganda Metallurgical Combine 1960-64, 1965-69; First Sec. Temirtau City Cttee. of Kazakh CP 1969-71, Second Sec. 1971-73; sec. of party cttee. of Karaganda Metallurgical Combine 1973-77; Second, then First Sec. of Karaganda Dist. Cttee. of Kazakh CP 1977-79; Sec. of Cen. Cttee. of Kazakh CP 1979-84; Chair. of Council of Ministers of Cen. Cttee. of Kazakh CP 1984-; Deputy to U.S.S.R. Supreme Soviet; mem. CPSU Cen. Cttee. 1986-. *Address:* Council of Ministers, Kazakh Communist Party, Alma-Ata, Kazakh S.S.R., U.S.S.R.

NAZER, Hisham; Saudi Arabian politician; b. 1932; ed. Univ. of California; assisted in foundation of OPEC 1960; Deputy Minister of Petroleum 1962-68; with Ministry of Planning 1975-, Acting Minister of Planning 1986-; Minister of Petroleum and Mineral Resources 1986-; Pres. Cen. Org. for Planning 1968-; mem. Supreme Council for Petroleum and Minerals 1968-. *Address:* Ministry of Petroleum and Mineral Resources, P.O. Box 247, Riyadh 11191, Saudi Arabia.

NAZIR-ALI, Rt. Rev. Michael James, M.LITT., M.A., PH.D.; British/Pakistani ecclesiastic; b. 19 Aug. 1949, Karachi; s. of James Nazir-Ali and Patience Nazir-Ali; m. Valerie Cree 1972; two s.; ed. St. Paul's High School, Karachi, St. Patrick's Coll., Karachi, Univ. of Karachi, Fitzwilliam Coll., Cambridge, Ridley Hall, Cambridge, St. Edmund Hall, Oxford and Australian Coll. of Theology in asscn. with Centre for World Religions, Harvard; Tutorial Supervisor in Theology, Univ. of Cambridge 1974-76; Tutor then Sr. Tutor, Karachi Theological Coll. 1976-81; Assoc. Priest Holy Trinity Cathedral, Karachi 1976-79; Priest-in-Charge St. Andrew's Akhtar Colony, Karachi 1979-81; Provost Lahore Cathedral 1981-84; Bishop of Raiwind 1984-86; fmr. Visiting Lecturer, Centre for Study of Islam and Muslim-Christian Relations, Birmingham; Asst. to Archbishop of Canterbury; Co-ordinator of Studies for 1988 Lambeth Conf.; Pres. Horticultural Soc., Cambridge 1975; Dir.-in-Residence Oxford Centre for Mission Studies; Dir. Christian Aid; Trustee Traidcraft; Radio Pakistan Prize for English Language and Literature 1964; Burney Award (Cambridge) 1973, 1975; Oxford Soc. Award for Grads. 1973; Langham Scholarship 1974. *Publications:* Islam, a Christian Perspective 1982, Frontiers in Christian-Muslim Encounter 1985, numerous articles on Islam and Christianity. *Leisure interests:* cricket, hockey, table tennis and reading. *Address:* Anglican Consultative Council, 157 Waterloo Road, London, S.E.1, England (Office); St. Margaret's Vicarage, St. Margaret's Road, Oxford, OX2 6RX, England (Home). *Telephone:* 01-620 1110 (Office); 0865-52492 (Home).

NDAMASE, Tutor Nyangilizwe; South African (Transkei) politician; b. 11 Jan. 1921; m. 1st Jessie Tandiwe Ka Solomon Ka Dinizulu 1943 (died 1971), four c.; m. 2nd Ndileka Bikitsha 1975; ed. Healdtown Inst.; became Chief 1947; mem. United Transkeian Territories Gen. Council 1952; M.P. 1963; Paramount Chief of Pondoland (and nominated M.P.) 1974-; Pres. of Transkei Feb. 1986-. *Address:* Transkei, South Africa.

NDEGWA, Duncan Nderitu, M.A.; Kenyan public servant and business executive; b. 11 March 1925, Nyeri District; ed. Alliance High School, Kikuyu, Makerere Univ. Coll., Uganda and Univ. of St. Andrews, Scotland; Statistician, E. African High Comm. 1956-59; Asst. Sec. Kenya Treasury 1959-63, Deputy Perm. Sec. and Head of Civil Service 1963-66; Sec. to Cabinet 1963-67; Gov. Cen. Bank of Kenya and Alt. Gov. IMF 1967-82; Chair. Unga Group of Cos. 1983-; Chair. Comm. of Enquiry (Public Service Structure and Remuneration Comm.) 1970; Patron Kenya Golf Union 1975-85; Chief of the Burning Spear. *Address:* Keremara Chambers, P.O. Box 20423, Nairobi, Kenya. *Telephone:* 334621.

N'DIAYE, Babacar; Senegalese banker; b. 1937; joined African Devt. Bank 1965, subsequently Group Dir. of Finance, then Vice-Pres. for Finance, Pres. May 1985-; named Int. Banker of the Year by London-based Int. Financial Review 1984. *Address:* African Development Bank, 01 BP 1387, Abidjan 01, Ivory Coast. *Telephone:* 32-07-11.

N'DONG, Léon; Gabonese diplomatist; b. 15 Feb. 1935, Libreville; m. 1971; two s. one d.; ed. School of Law and Econ. Sciences, Rennes, France; Under-Sec. Gen. of Ministry of Foreign Affairs, later Sec.-Gen.; Teacher, Nat. School of Admin. 1969-72; Amb. to Cen. African Repub. and Sudan 1972-73, to Morocco 1973-74, to UN Office at Geneva 1974-76, to UN 1976-80, to U.K. 1980-86, to Fed. Repub. of Germany 1986-; Commdr. de l'Etoile Equatoriale, Grand Cordon of Order of the Brilliant Star (China), Commdr., Order of Devotion (Malta), Commdr. Nat. Order of Dahomey, Order of Nile (Sudan), Ordre nationale du Mérite (Gabon), Diplomatic Order of Repub. of Korea, Ordre de la Pléiade (France). *Leisure interests:* reading, music. *Address:* Embassy of Gabon, Kronprinzenstrasse 52, 5300 Bonn 2, Federal Republic of Germany.

NDUNGANE, Rev. Winston Njongo, M.TH., B.D., A.K.C., A.F.T.S.; South African ecclesiastic; b. 2 April 1941, Kokstad; s. of Foster Ndungane and Tingaza Ndungane; m. 1st Nosipo Ngcelwane 1972 (died 1986), 2nd Nomahlubi Vokwana 1987; one step-s. one step-d.; ed. Lovedale High School, Univ. of Cape Town, Fed. Theological Seminary and King's Coll. London; Rector, St. Nicholas Church, Matroosfontein, Cape Town 1980-81; Provincial Liaison Officer, Johannesburg 1982-84; Prin., St. Bede's Theological Coll. Umtata 1985-86; Exec. Officer, Church of the Prov. of S. Africa 1987-; Hon Provincial Canon. *Leisure interests:* music, walking. *Address:* Bishopscourt, Claremont 7700, Cape Town, South Africa. *Telephone:* (021) 71-7024.

NE WIN, U (Maung Shu Maung); Burmese politician and fmr. army officer; b. 24 May 1911; ed. Govt. High School, Prome and Rangoon Univ.; joined Allied Forces 1945; Vice-Chief of Gen. Staff and Major-Gen. 1948; Deputy Prime Minister 1949-50; Gen. 1956; Prime Minister and Minister of Defence 1958-60; Chief of Gen. Staff 1962-72; Prime Minister, Minister of Defence, Finance, and Revenue, Nat. Planning and Justice 1962-63; Prime Minister, Minister of Nat. Planning and Defence 1963; Prime Minister and Minister of Defence, also Chair. of Revolutionary Council 1965-74; Chair. Exec. Cttee. Burma Socialist Programme Party 1973-88; Chair. State Council and Pres. of Burma 1974-81; Legion of Merit (U.S.A.). *Address:* c/o Office of the President, Rangoon, Burma.

NEAGU, Paul; British sculptor, painter and fine art lecturer; b. 22 Feb. 1938, Bucharest, Romania; s. of Tudor Neagu and Rozalia Neagu; m. Sibyla Oarcea 1966 (divorced 1972); ed. Inst. of Belle Arts, Bucharest 1959-65; freelance artist 1965-; emigrated to England 1969; Lecturer in Fine Art, Hornsey School of Art 1972-; Visiting Lecturer and External Assessor throughout U.K. 1975-; Asst. Prof. Univ. of Montreal 1982-83; Part-time lecturer, Slade School of Art 1985, now part-time consultant lecturer; mem. Union of Visual Artists, Bucharest 1967-69; Tolly Cobbold Prize 1977; Westminster City Sculpture Prize 1987. *Publications:* Palpable Art Manifesto! 1969, Generative Art Group 1972, Hyphen 1975, Nine Catalytic Stations 1987. *Leisure interests:* poetry, philosophy, swimming. *Address:* 31c, Jackson Road, London N7 6ES. *Telephone:* (01) 607 7858.

NEAL, Sir Leonard Francis, Kt., M.A., C.B.E.; British industrial relations official; b. 27 Aug. 1913, London; s. of Arthur Henry Neal and Mary Cahill; m. Mary L. Puttock 1939; one s. one d.; ed. London School of Econs. and Trinity Coll., Cambridge; Deputy Employee Relations Adviser, Esso Petroleum Co. 1962-66; Labour Adviser, Esso Europe Inc. 1966; mem. for Personnel, British Railways Bd. 1967-71; Chair. Comm. on Industrial Relations 1971-74; Chair. MAT Int. Group 1975-84; Chair. Employment Conditions Abroad Ltd. 1977-84; Pres. Asscn. of Supervisory and Exec. Engineers 1974-80; non-exec. Dir. Pilkington Bros. Ltd. 1976-83; Adviser to Bd. of a number of private, commercial and industrial cos.; Chair. Trade Union Reform Cttee. Centre for Policy Studies 1978-85. *Publication:* A Manager's Guide to Industrial Relations (with A. Robertson). *Leisure interests:* gardening, reading. *Address:* Brightling, Sussex, England.

NEAL, Patricia; American actress; b. 20 Jan. 1926, Packard, Ky., U.S.A.; d. of William Burdette Neal and Eura Mildred Petrey; m. Roald Dahl (q.v.) 1953 (divorced 1983); one s. three d. (and one d. deeceased); ed. Northwestern Univ., Ill.; numerous TV appearances; public lectures in America and abroad. *Stage appearances include:* Another Part of the Forest 1946, The Children's Hour 1953, A Roomful of Roses 1954, Suddenly Last Summer 1958, The Miracle Worker 1959; Antoinette Perry Award (Tony) 1946; Academy Award (Oscar) for film Hud 1963. *Films:* John loves Mary 1949, The Hasty Heart 1949, The Fountainhead 1949, The Breaking Point 1950, Three Secrets 1950, Raton Pass 1951, The Day the Earth Stood Still 1951, Diplomatic Courier 1952, Something for the Birds 1953, A Face in the Crowd 1957, Breakfast at Tiffany's 1961, Hud 1963, The Third Secret 1964, In Harms Way 1965, The Subject was Roses 1968, The Road Builder 1970, The Night Digger 1970, The Boy 1972, Happy Mother's Day Love George 1973, Baxter 1973, Widow's Nest 1976, The Passage 1978, All Quiet on the Western Front 1979, Ghost Story 1981. *Publications:* As I Am (autobiog.) 1988, An Unremarkable Life 1989. *Leisure interests:* needlework, gardening, cooking. *Address:* 45 East End Avenue, New York, N.Y. 10028, U.S.A. *Telephone:* (212) 772-1268.

NEAME, Ronald; British film director; b. 23 April 1911, London; s. of Elwin Neame and Ivy Close; m. Beryl Heanly; one s.; messenger and tea boy, British Int. Film Studios 1925; became Dir. of Photography 1932. *Films photographed include:* Drake of England 1934, The Gaunt Stranger

1937, Four Just Men, Major Barbara 1940, One of Our Aircraft is Missing 1942; with Sir David Lean (q.v.) and Anthony Havelock-Allen, formed Cineguild and produced Great Expectations 1946, Oliver Twist 1947 and The Passionate Friends 1948, and photographed In Which We serve 1942, This Happy Breed 1943, Blithe Spirit 1945; film director 1950-. *Films directed include:* Take My Life 1947, The Golden Salamander 1950, The Card 1950, The Million Pound Note 1953, The Man Who Never Was 1956, Windom's Way 1958, The Horse's Mouth 1959, Tunes of Glory 1960, I Could Go On Singing 1962, The Chalk Garden 1964, Mr. Moses 1965, A Man Could Get Killed 1966, Gambit 1966, The Prime of Miss Jean Brodie 1968, Scrooge 1970, The Poseidon Adventure 1972, The Odessa File 1974, Meteor 1978, Hopscotch 1979, First Monday in October 1980, Foreign Body 1985. *Leisure interests:* photography, stereo and hi-fi equipment. *Address:* 2317 Kimridge Road, Beverly Hills, Calif. 90210, U.S.A.

NEARY, Martin Gerard James, M.A., F.R.C.O.; British organist; b. 28 March 1940; s. of Leonard W. Neary and Jeanne M. Thébault; m. Penelope J. Warren 1967; one s. two d.; ed. City of London School and Gonville & Caius Coll. Cambridge; Asst. Organist, St. Margaret's Westminster 1963-65, Organist and Master of Music 1965-71; Prof. of Organ, Trinity Coll. London 1963-72; Organist and Master of Music, Winchester Cathedral 1972-87; Organist and Master of Choristers, Westminster Abbey 1988-; founder and Conductor Martin Neary Singers 1972-; Conductor Waynflete Singers 1972-87; Pres. Cathedral Organists Assen. 1985-88; Pres. Royal Coll. of Organists 1988-; many organ recitals and broadcasts in U.K., U.S.A. and Canada; numerous recordings. *Publications:* editions of early organ music, contributions to organ journals. *Address:* 2 Little Cloister, Westminster Abbey, London, SW1P 3PL, England. *Telephone:* (01) 222-6923.

NEBBIA, Fernando, LIC.ECON.; Argentine international finance official; b. 1945; s. of Carlos and Livia de Nebbia; m. Elsa Breide 1974; one s. two d.; ed. Univ. of Buenos Aires; fmr. lecturer in Econs. and Statistics, Univ. of Buenos Aires; held various positions in Argentine Dept. of Commerce 1974-84, latterly Minister-Counsellor, External Econs. Service of Dept. of Commerce; del. to various int. confs.; Exec. Dir. IMF 1984-86. *Address:* c/o International Monetary Fund, 700 19th Street, N.W., Washington, D.C. 20431, U.S.A.

NECKERMANN, Josef Carl; German businessman and dressage rider; b. 5 June 1912, Würzburg; m. Annemarie Brückner 1934; two s. one d.; ed. grammar school, Würzburg; joined his father's business 1933; in charge of a Würzburg store 1934-38; owner and head of mail order house Berlin 1938; State Commr. for Clothing 1939-45; Head, Zentrallagergemeinschaft mbH., Berlin 1939-45; Founder textile wholesale business Frankfurt am Main 1948; fmr. Owner and Man. Neckermann Versand KGaA 1950, Mail Order Houses, Frankfurt am Main; founded Neckermann Eigenheim GmbH 1963, Neckura Neckermann Versicherungs-AG 1965, N.U.R. Neckermann und Reisen GmbH 1964; Pres. Stiftung Deutsche Sporthilfe 1967-89, Hon. Pres. 1989-; Hon. Consul of Kingdom of Denmark 1969-79; Pres. Stiftung Deutsche Sporthilfe; Dr. med. vet. h.c.; Bronze Medal, Olympic Games (1960), Gold Medal, Olympic Games (1964), World Championship of dressage (1966), Silver and Gold Medals, Olympic Games (1968), Silver and Bronze Medal, Olympic Games (1972); Grosses Bundesverdienstkreuz 1974, with Star 1982. *Address:* Geleitsstr. 25 D, 6000 Frankfurt 70, Federal Republic of Germany (Home).

NEEDHAM, James J.; American business consultant; b. 18 Aug. 1926, Woodhaven N.Y.; s. of James Joseph Needham (deceased) and Amelia Pasta Needham; m. Dolores A. Habick 1950; three s. two d.; ed. Cornell and St John's (Brooklyn) Univs.; with Price Waterhouse & Co., then Partner, Raymond T. Hyer & Co.; joined A. M. Pullen & Co. 1957, subsequently partner, in charge of New York office and mem. Exec. Cttee.; Commr. Securities and Exchange Comm. 1969-72; Chair. New York Stock Exchange 1972-76; Vice-Pres. Int. Fed. of Stock Exchanges 1973-75, Pres. 1976-86; Sr. Consultant Nomura Securities Int. Inc., New York 1986-; fmrly. Distinguished Prof., Graduate Dir., Coll. of Business Admin., St. John's Univ.; Commr. Gen. of U.S. Int. Exposition, Japan 1985; Hon. DLL. (St. John's Univ.) 1972. *Leisure interests:* golf, fishing. *Address:* Nomura Securities International Inc., 180 Maiden Lane, 38th Floor, New York, N.Y. 10038, U.S.A.

NEEDHAM, Joseph, PH.D., SC.D., F.R.S., F.B.A.; British biochemist, historian of science and orientalist; b. 1900, London; s. of the late Joseph and Alicia Needham; m. Dorothy Moyle 1924 (deceased); ed. Oundle School and Cambridge Univ.; Fellow, Caius Coll., Cambridge 1924-, Pres. 1959-66, Master 1966-76, Sr. Fellow 1976-; Univ. Demonstrator in Biochem., Cambridge 1928-33; Visiting Prof. of Biochem., Stanford Univ., Calif. 1929; Dunn Reader in Biochem., Cambridge 1933-66; Lecturer Yale Univ., Cornell Univ., Oberlin Coll. 1935; Oliver Sharpey Lecturer, Royal Coll. Physicians 1935-36, Herbert Spencer Lecturer, Oxford 1936-37; lectured Warsaw, Lwów, Cracow and Wilno Univs. 1937; Head of Sino-British Science Co-operation Office and Counsellor British Embassy, Chongqing 1942-46; Head of Div. of Natural Sciences UNESCO 1946-48; now Hon. Counsellor to UNESCO; Dir. E. Asian History of Science Library (Needham Research Inst.), Cambridge 1976-; Chair. Ceylon Govt. Comm. on Univ. Educ. 1958; Hitchcock Prof., Univ. of Calif., Noguchi Lecturer, Johns Hopkins Univ. 1950; Hobhouse Lecturer, London Univ. 1950; Visiting Prof.

Univ. of Lyon 1951; visiting lecturer at numerous European and Asian univs. 1956-; Visiting Prof. Coll. de France, Paris 1973, Univ. of British Columbia 1975, Northwestern Univ., Evanston, Ill. 1977; Danz Lecturer, Univ. of Washington, Seattle and Wickramasinghe Lecturer, Colombo 1978, Ch'ien Mu Prof., Chinese Univ. of Hong Kong and Huang Chan Lecturer, Univ. of Hong Kong 1979; Creighton Lecturer, Univ. of London 1979; First East Asian History of Science Foundation Lecturer, Univ. of Hong Kong 1983; Second Solomon Böchner Lecturer, Rice Univ. (Texas) 1983; foreign mem. Nat. Acad. of China (Academia Sinica), Royal Danish Acad. of Sciences; Pres. Int. Union of the History of Science 1972-75; mem. Int. Acads. of the History and the Philosophy of Science and the History of Medicine; Hon. F.R.C.P.; Hon. Fellow and Bernal Medallist, Science Policy Foundation, London; Phil. Dr. h.c. (Uppsala); Dr. h.c. (Beijing); Hon. D.Sc. (Brussels, E. Anglia); Hon. LL.D. (Toronto, St. Andrews); Hon. D.Litt. (Hong Kong, Salford, Cambridge, Peradeniya); Hon. Research Prof. Inst. History of Science, Academia Sinica (Beijing); Order of Brilliant Star (Third Class with Sash) (China); Sir William Jones Medallist, Asiatic Soc. of Bengal, George Sarton Medallist, History of Science Soc., Leonardo da Vinci Medallist, History of Technology Soc, Dexter Award for History of Chemistry, American Chem. Soc. Nat. Award (First Class), State Scientific and Technological Comm., Beijing, Wei-Kung Prize (with Wang Ling, q.v. and Lu Gwei-Djen), San Diego, Calif. 1988. *Publications:* Man a Machine 1927, The Sceptical Biologist 1929, Chemical Embryology (3 vols.) 1931, The Great Amphibium 1932, A History of Embryology 1935, Order and Life 1935, Adventures before Birth (trans.) 1935, Biochemistry and Morphogenesis 1942, Time, the Refreshing River 1942, History is on Our Side 1944, Chinese Science 1945, Science Outpost 1948, Science and Civilisation in China (7 vols.) 1954-, The Development of Iron and Steel Technology in China 1958, Heavenly Clockwork 1960, Time and Eastern Man 1965, Clerks and Craftsmen in China and the West 1970, The Grand Titration, Science and Society in East and West 1970, Within the Four Seas, the Dialogue of East and West 1970, Moulds of Understanding, a Pattern of Natural Philosophy 1977, Celestial Lancets: a history and rationale of Acupuncture and Moxa 1980, Science in Traditional China; a Historical Perspective 1981, Trans-Pacific Echoes and Resonances; Listening Once Again 1984, The Hall of Heavenly Records: Korean Astronomical Instruments and Clocks 1380-1780 1984; Editor: Science, Religion and Reality 1925, Christianity and the Social Revolution 1935, Perspectives in Biochemistry 1936, Background to Modern Science 1938, Science in the Soviet Union 1942, The Teacher of Nations 1942, Hopkins and Biochemistry 1949, The Chemistry of Life 1970. *Leisure interests:* theology, philosophy, archaeology, railway engineering. *Address:* East Asian History of Science Library, 8 Sylvester Road, Cambridge CB3 9AF (Office); 42 Grange Road, Cambridge CB3 9DG, England (Home). *Telephone:* (0223) 352183 and 311545; (0223) 332451 (College).

NEEL, James Van Gundia, PH.D., M.D.; American geneticist; b. 22 March 1915, Hamilton, Ohio; s. of Hiram A. Neel and Elizabeth Van Gundia; m. Priscilla Baxter 1943; one d. two s.; ed. Coll. of Wooster, Ohio, and Univ. of Rochester, New York.; Inst. of Zoology, Dartmouth 1939-41; Fellow in Zoology, Nat. Research Council 1941-42; Strong Memorial Hosp. 1944-46; Acting Dir. Field Studies, Atomic Bomb Casualty Comm., Nat. Research Council 1947-48; Assoc. Geneticist, Lab. of Vertebrate Biology, Asst. Prof. of Internal Medicine, Univ. of Mich. 1948-51; Geneticist, Inst. of Human Biology 1951-56; Chair. and Lee R. Dice Univ. Prof., Dept. of Human Genetics, Univ. of Mich. Medical School 1956-85, Prof. of Internal Medicine 1957-85, Prof. Emer. 1985-; Cutter Lecturer, Harvard Univ. 1956; Wilhemina Key Lecturer, American Genetics Assen. 1982; mem. N.A.S., American Phil. Soc., Assen. of American Physicians, American Soc. of Human Genetics (Vice-Pres. 1952-53, Pres. 1953-54, Bd. Dir. 1968-70), American Acad. of Arts and Sciences, Inst. of Medicine (Nat. Acad. of Sciences), Pres. 6th Int. Congress of Human Genetics 1981; Dir. Centre Royaumont pour une Science de l'Homme; Consultant Nat. Research Council, WHO, Pan American Health Org., etc.; Lasker Award 1950, Modern Medicine Award 1960, Allan Award, American Soc. of Human Genetics 1965, Russell Award, Univ. of Mich. 1966, Nat. Medal of Science 1974, Smithsonian Institution Medal 1981. *Publications:* Human Heredity (with W. J. Schull) 1954, A Clinical, Pathological and Genetic Study of Multiple Neurofibromatoses (with F. W. Crowe and W. J. Schull) 1956, Changing Perspectives on the Genetic Effects of Radiation 1963, Effects of Inbreeding on Japanese Children (with W. J. Schull) 1965; Ed. (with Crow) Proc. III Int. Congress Human Genetics. *Address:* University of Michigan, Department of Human Genetics, 1137 E. Catherine, Ann Arbor, Mich. 48104 (Office); 2235 Belmont, Ann Arbor, Mich. 48104, U.S.A. (Home). *Telephone:* (313) 764-5490.

NÉEL, Louis Eugène Félix; French scientist; b. 22 Nov. 1904, Lyon, Rhône; m. Hélène Hourticq 1931; one s. two d.; ed. Lycée du Parc, Lyons, Lycée Saint-Louis, Paris, and Ecole Normale Supérieure, Paris; Prof., Univ. of Strasbourg 1937-45, Grenoble 1945-76; Scientific Adviser to Navy 1952-; French Rep. to Scientific Cttee. of NATO 1960-83; Pres. French Physical Soc. 1957; Pres. Int. Union of Pure and Applied Physics 1963-65; Pres. Inst. Nat. Polytechnique, Grenoble 1971-76; Pres. Conseil Supérieur Sûreté Nucléaire 1981-86; mem. Acad. of Sciences (Paris); Foreign mem. U.S.S.R. Acad. of Sciences, Royal Netherlands Acad., German Leopoldina Acad., Romanian Acad. of Sciences, Royal Soc. (U.K.), American Acad. of

Arts and Sciences, Polish Acad. of Sciences; many hon. degrees; Prix Holweck 1952, Gold Medal (C.N.R.S.) 1965, Nobel Prize for Physics 1970; Croix de guerre 1940; Grand Croix, Légion d'honneur. *Publications:* over 200 works on various aspects of magnetism. *Leisure interests:* history, carpentry. *Address:* 15 rue Marcel Allégot, 92190 Meudon, France. *Telephone:* 45-34-36-51.

NE'EMAN, Yuval, DIP.ING., D.E.M., D.I.C., PH.D.; Israeli professor of physics; b. 14 May 1925, Tel-Aviv; s. of Gedalia and Zipora Ne'eman; m. Dvora Rubinstein 1951; one d. one s.; ed. Herzliya High School, Tel-Aviv, Israel Inst. of Tech., Haifa, and London Univ.; Hagana volunteer, taking part in activities against British rule in Palestine 1946–47; Hydrodynamical Design Engineer 1946–47; Capt., Israeli Defence Forces (Infantry) 1948, Maj. 1949, Lieut.-Col. 1950; Deputy Dir. Defence Intelligence Div. 1955–57; Defence Attaché, London 1958–60; resigned from Israeli Defence Forces active service May 1960; took part in six day war June 1967; Scientific Dir. Israel Atomic Energy Establishment 1961–63; Research Assoc. Calif. Inst. of Tech., Pasadena 1963–64, Visiting Prof. of Theoretical Physics 1964–65; Prof. of Physics and Head of Dept. Tel-Aviv Univ. 1965–73; Prof. of Physics and Dir. Centre for Particle Theory, Univ. of Texas (Austin) 1968–; Pollak Prof. of Theoretical Physics, Tel-Aviv Univ. 1968–76, Wolfson Prof. Extraordinary in Theoretical Physics 1977–; Vice-Pres. Tel-Aviv Univ. 1965–66, Pres. 1971–75; Dir. Sackler Inst. of Advanced Studies, Tel-Aviv Univ. 1979–; Adviser to Head of Mil. Intelligence 1973–74; Special Adviser to Israel Defence Ministry 1975–76; mem. Knesset 1981–; Minister of Science and Devt. 1982–84; Chair. Steering Cttee. Mediterranean-Dead Sea Conduit 1977–83; Chair. Israel Space Agency 1983–; mem. Israel Atomic Energy Cttee. 1966–84, Israel Nat. Acad. of Sciences 1966–; co-discoverer of Unitary Symmetry Theory; conceived basic field explaining compositeness of nuclear particles; Foreign Hon. mem. American Acad. Arts and Sciences, Hon. Life mem. New York Acad. of Sciences 1973–, Foreign Assoc. Nat. Acad. of Sciences; Hon. D.Sc. (Israel Inst. of Tech.) 1966, (Yeshiva Univ., New York) 1972; Weizmann Prize for Sciences 1966, Rothschild Prize 1968, Israel Prize for Sciences 1969, Albert Einstein Medal and Prize for Physics 1970, Wigner Medal 1982. *Publications:* The Eightfold Way (with M. Gell-Mann) 1964, Algebraic Theory of Particle Physics 1967, One Way to Unitary Symmetry, The Past Decade in Particle Theory (with E. C. G. Sudarshan) 1973, Symetries, Jauges et Variétés de Groupes 1979, Group Theoretical Methods in Physics (with L. P. Horwitz and A. Hilger) 1980, To Fulfil a Vision 1981, The Particle Hunters: The Search after the Fundamental Constituents of Matter (in Hebrew, with Y. Kirsch) 1983, Policy from a Sober Viewpoint 1984; about 250 articles on physics, astrophysics and philosophy of science. *Leisure interests:* music, history, linguistics. *Address:* Department of Physics and Astronomy, Tel-Aviv University, Ramat Aviv, Tel-Aviv 69978, Israel. *Telephone:* Tel-Aviv 410477.

NEFF, William Duwayne, PH.D.; American research scientist and teacher; b. 27 Oct. 1912. Lomax, Ill.; s. of Lyman Melvin Neff and Emma Mary (Jacobson) Neff; m. 1st Ernestine Anderson 1937 (divorced 1960); m. 2nd Florence Palmer Anderson 1961 (died 1978); one s. one d.; ed. Univ. of Illinois and Univ. of Rochester; Research Assoc., Swarthmore Coll. 1940–42, Columbia Univ. and Univ. of Calif. Divs. of War Research 1942–46; Asst., Assoc. and Full Prof. of Psychology, Univ. of Chicago 1946–61, Prof. of Psychology and Physiology 1959–61; Scientific Liaison Officer, London Branch Office, Office of Naval Research 1953–54; Dir. of Psychophysiology Lab., Bolt, Beranek and Newman Inc. 1961–63; Prof. of Psychology, Indiana Univ. 1963, Research Prof. 1963–83, Research Prof. Emer. 1983–, Dir. Center for Neural Sciences 1965–78; mem. N.A.S.; Award of Beltone Inst. for Hearing Research 1969. *Publications:* Articles in scientific journals. *Leisure interest:* golf. *Address:* Indiana University Center for Neurological Sciences, Bloomington, Ind. 47401 (Office); 3505 Bradley Street, Bloomington, Ind. 47401, U.S.A. (Home). *Telephone:* (812) 336-3489 (Home).

NEGAHBAN, Ezatollah, PH.D.; Iranian archaeologist; b. 1 March 1926; s. of Abdol Amir Negahban and Roghieh Dideban; m. Miriam Lois Miller 1955; five s.; ed. Teheran and Chicago Univs.; Assoc. Prof. Univ. of Teheran 1956–62, Prof. 1962, Founder and Dir. Univ. Inst. of Archaeology 1957, Head, Dept. Archaeology 1968–75, Dean Faculty of Letters and Humanities 1975–78; Prof. Univ. Chicago 1964; Tech. Dir. Iranian Archaeological Service 1960–65; Tech. Adviser to Ministry of Culture 1965–79; Visiting Curator Univ. Museum, Visiting Prof., Univ. of Pa. 1980–; Dir. Museum Iran Bastan 1966–68, Iranian Archaeological Assen. 1957–65; Sec.-Gen. Int. Congress, Iranian Art and Archaeology, Dir. 5th Congress; excavated at Mehranabad 1961, Marlik 1961–62, Haft Tepe 1966; Dir. Gazvin Plain Expedition (Zaghe, Qabrestan and Sagzabad) 1970; archaeological survey of N.E. Iran 1965, Mazandaran Highlands 1975; mem. German Archaeological Inst., Exec. Cttee. and Perm. Council, Congress of Pre- and Proto-History. *Publications:* The Buff Ware Sequence in Khuzistan 1954, Preliminary Report on the Marlik Excavation 1961–1962 1964, Archaeology of Iran 1973, Metal Vessels from Marlik 1983, Excavation of Haft Tepe; and numerous excavation reports and articles in journals. *Leisure interests:* Persian calligraphy. *Address:* 5226 Rexford Road, Philadelphia, Pa. 19131, U.S.A. *Telephone:* (215) 898-4057 (Office); (215) 877-1821 (Home).

NÈGRE, Louis-Pascal, L. EN D.; Mali banker and politician; b. 16 April 1928; ed. Univ. of Paris, Ecole Nat. d'Administration d'Outre-Mer; Tech.

Counsellor at the Presidency 1961–63; Gov. Bank of Mali 1964–68; Minister of Finance 1966–69, of Finance and Commerce 1969–70; Pres. Council of Ministers UDEAO 1968–70; Pres. African Group, World Bank and IMF 1968–70; Vice-Pres. African Devt. Bank 1970–78; Asst. Sec.-Gen., Office of Personnel Services, UN Secretariat 1982–86. *Address:* c/o African Development Bank, B.P. 1387, Abidjan, Ivory Coast.

NEGRI SEMBILAN, Yang di-Pertuan Besar, Tuanku Jaafar ibni Al-Marhum Tuanku Adbul Rahman: Malaysian Ruler; b. 19 July 1922; m. Tuanku Najihar binti Tuanku Besar Burhanuddin 1943; three s. three d.; ed. Malay School Sri Menanti, Malay Coll. and Nottingham Univ.; entered Malay Admin. Service 1944; Asst. Dist. Officer, Rembau 1946–47, Parti 1953–55; Chargé d'Affaires, Washington 1947; First Perm. Sec., Malayan Perm. Mission to the UN 1957–58; First Sec., Trade Counsellor, rising to Deputy High Commr., London 1962–63; Amb. to United Arab Repub. 1962; High Commr. concurrently to Nigeria, Lagos and then Ghana 1965–66; Timbalan Yang di-Pertuan Agong (Deputy Supreme Head of State) 1979–84, 1989–94. *Leisure interests:* well-planned housing schemes, sports. *Address:* Seremban, Malaysia.

NEHAMKIN, Lieut.-Col. Arieh; Israeli politician and farmer; b. 1925, Nahalal; m.; three c.; ed. secondary level; mil. service Israeli Defence Forces; mem. Tenth Knesset (Parl.); fmr. mem. Finance Cttee.; Minister of Agric. 1984–88; fmr. Sec. Moshav Movt.; Labour Party. *Address:* c/o Ministry of Agriculture, 13 Heleni Hamalka, Jerusalem, Israel.

NEHRU, Arun, B.A.; Indian politician; b. Allahabad; s. of the late Anand Kumar; m. Subhadra Nehru 1967; two d.; ed. La Martinere Coll., Govt. Christian Coll., Lucknow; fmrly. with Jenson & Nicholson, Pres. 1979–80; currently Controller, Intelligence Bureau; Head, Dept. of Internal Security 1985–87; fmr. mem. of Congress (1) Party. *Leisure interests:* music, table-tennis. *Address:* North Block, New Delhi 110011, India.

NEHRU, Braj Kumar, B.SC., B.SC.(ECON); Indian civil servant and barrister; b. 4 Sept. 1909, Allahabad; s. of Brijlal and Rameshwari Nehru; m. Magdalena Friedmann 1935; three s.; ed. Allahabad Univ., London School of Econs., Balliol Coll., Oxford, Inner Temple, London; joined Indian Civil Service 1934; Asst. Commr. 1934–39; Under-Sec. Dept. of Educ., Health and Lands, Govt. of India 1939; mem. Indian Legis. Ass. 1939; Officer on special duty, Reserve Bank of India, Under-Sec. Finance Dept., Govt. of India 1940, Joint Sec. 1947; rep. Reparations Conf. 1945, Commonwealth Finance Ministers Conf., UN Gen. Ass. 1949–52, 1960, FAO Confs. 1949–50, Sterling Balances Confs. 1947–49, Bandung Conf. 1955; deputed to enquire into Australian Fed. Finance 1946; mem. UN Advisory Cttee. on Admin. and Budgetary Questions 1951–53; Adviser to Sudan Govt. 1955; mem. UN Investments Cttee. 1962–, Chair. 1977–; Exec. Dir. IBRD (World Bank) 1949–54, 1958–62; Minister, Indian Embassy, Washington 1949–54; Sec. Dept. of Econ. Affairs, Ministry of Finance 1957–58, Commr.-Gen. for Econ. Affairs 1958–61; Amb. to U.S.A. 1961–68; Gov. of Assam and Nagaland 1968–73, of Manipur, Meghalaya and Tripura 1972–73, of Jammu and Kashmir 1981–84, of Gujarat 1984–86; Chair. North-Eastern Council 1972–73; High Commr. in U.K. 1973–77; Fellow, L.S.E.; Hon. LL.D. (Mo. Valley Coll.), Hon. Litt.D. (Jacksonville Univ.), Hon. D.Litt. (Punjab Univ.). *Publications:* Australian Federal Finance 1947, Speaking of India 1966, Thoughts on the Present Discontents 1986. *Leisure interests:* bridge, reading, conversation. *Address:* 1 Western Avenue, Maharani Bagh, New Delhi 110-065, India. *Telephone:* 637677.

NEIDLINGER, Gustav; German baritone singer; b. 21 March 1910; s. of Gustav Neidlinger and Margarete Wagner; m. Elisabeth Hartmann 1936; two c.; ed. Humanistisches Gymnasium, Mainz, and Opernschule, Frankfurt/Main; has performed at Stadttheater, Mainz, Stadttheater, Plauen, Staatsoper, Hamburg, Staatsoper, Stuttgart, Bayreuth Festival, Deutsche Oper, Berlin, La Scala, Milan, Covent Garden, London, Grand Opera, Paris, Teatro La Fenice, Venice, Rome Opera, Staatsoper, Vienna, Metropolitan Opera, New York, Chicago Opera, Theatro Colon, Buenos Aires and Opera San Carlo, Naples; currently with Staatsoper, Stuttgart; awarded Grosses Verdienstkreuz des Verdienstordens der Bundesrepublik Deutschland 1974, Ehrenmitglied der Staatsoper Stuttgart 1977, Gutenbergplakette der Stadt Mainz 1985. *Address:* Würtemberg Staatsoper, 7000 Stuttgart; 5427 Lahnstrasse 57, Bad Ems, Federal Republic of Germany.

NEIL, Andrew Ferguson, M.A.; British journalist; b. 21 May 1949, Scotland; s. of James Neil and Mary Ferguson; unmarried; ed. Paisley Grammer School, Univ. of Glasgow; with Conservative Party Research Dept. 1971–73; with The Economist 1973–83, Political then Industrial Corresp. for Ulster 1973–79, American Corresp. 1979–82, U.K. Ed. 1982–83; Ed. The Sunday Times 1983–; Exec. Chair. Sky Channel Nov. 1988–; regular anchorman and TV commentator. *Publication:* The Cable Revolution 1982. *Leisure interest:* New York. *Address:* The Sunday Times, 1 Pennington Street, London, E1 9XN, England. *Telephone:* 01-481 4100.

NEILD, Robert Ralph; British economist; b. 10 Sept. 1924, Peterborough; s. of Ralph and Josephine Neild; m. 1st Nora Clemens Sayre (dissolved 1961); 2nd Elizabeth W. Griffiths 1962 (dissolved 1986), one s. four d.; ed. Charterhouse, and Trinity Coll., Cambridge; R.A.F. 1943–44, Operational Research, R.A.F., 1944–47; Secr., UN Econ. Comm. for Europe, Geneva 1947–51; Econ. Section, Cabinet Office (later Treasury) 1951–56; Lecturer in Econs. and Fellow of Trinity Coll., Cambridge 1956–58; Nat. Inst. of

Econ. and Social Research 1958–64; Econ. Adviser to Treasury 1964–67; mem. Fulton Cttee. on the Civil Service 1966–68; Dir. Stockholm Int. Peace Research Inst. 1967–71, mem. Governing Bd. 1972–; mem. Governing Body Queen Elizabeth Coll., Oxford 1978–; Prof. of Econs., Cambridge Univ. 1971–84, Emer. 1984–; Fellow, Trinity Coll., Acorn Investment Trust 1988. *Publications:* Pricing and Employment in the Trade Cycle 1964, The Measurement and Reform of Budgetary Policy (with T. S. Ward) 1978, How to make up your mind about the Bomb 1981. *Address:* Trinity College, Cambridge, CB2 1TQ, England. *Telephone:* (0223) 338444.

NEILL, Rt. Hon. Sir Brian (Thomas) Neill, Kt., PC, Q.C., M.A.; British judge; b. 2 Aug. 1923; s. of Sir Thomas Neill and Lady (Annie Strachan) Neill (née Bishop); m. Sally Margaret Backus 1956; three s.; ed. Highgate School, Corpus Christi Coll., Oxford; served Rifle Brigade 1942–46; called to Bar, Inner Temple 1949, Bencher 1976; Q.C. 1968; a Recorder of the Crown Court 1972–78; a Judge of the High Court, Queen's Bench Div. 1978–84; a Lord Justice of Appeal 1985–; mem. Departmental Cttee. to examine operation of Section 2 of Official Secrets Act 1971; Chair. Advisory Cttee. on Rhodesia Travel Restrictions 1973–78; mem. Court of Assistants, 1972–, Master 1980–81. *Publications:* Defamation (with Colin Duncan) 1978. *Address:* c/o Royal Courts of Justice, Strand, London, W.C.2, England.

NEILL, Sir Francis Patrick, Kt., Q.C.; British lawyer; b. 8 Aug. 1926; s. of late Sir Thomas and Annie Strachan (née Bishop) Neill; m. Caroline Susan Debenham 1954; four s. two d.; ed. Highgate School and Magdalen Coll., Oxford; served with Rifle Brigade 1944–47; G.S.O. III (Training), British Troops Egypt 1947; called to the Bar, Gray's Inn 1951; Recorder of the Crown Court 1975–78; Judge of the Court of Appeal of Jersey and Guernsey 1977–; Fellow of All Souls Coll., Oxford 1950–77, Sub-Warden 1972–74, Warden 1977–; Vice-Chancellor Oxford Univ. 1985–87; Chair., Justice—All Souls Cttee. for Review of Admin. Law 1978, Press Council 1978–83, Council for Securities Industry 1978–85; Bencher, Gray's Inn 1971; mem. Bar Council 1967–71, Vice-Chair. 1973–74, Chair. 1974–75; Chair. Senate of the Inns of Court and the Bar 1974–75; Dir. Times Newspapers Holdings Ltd. 1988–; Hon. Fellow Magdalen Coll., Oxford 1988–; Hon. D.C.L. (Oxford) 1987. *Leisure interests:* music, forestry. *Address:* Warden's Lodgings, All Souls College, Oxford, OX1 4AL, England. *Telephone:* (0865) 722251.

NEILSON, Hon. William Arthur, A.C.; Australian politician (retd.); b. 27 Aug. 1925, Hobart; s. of Arthur Roland and Grace Maxwell (née Ramsay) Neilson; m. Jill Benjamin 1948; one s. three d.; ed. Ogilvie Commercial High School, Hobart; mem. Tasmanian House of Assembly 1946–77; Labor Party Whip 1946–55; Tasmania State Minister for Tourists and Immigration and for Forests 1956–58; Attorney-Gen. and Minister of Educ. 1958; Treas. and Minister of Educ. 1959; Minister of Educ. 1959–69, 1972–74; Attorney-Gen. 1974–75; Deputy Premier, Minister for the Environment, Minister administering Police Dept. and the Licensing Act 1974–75; Premier and Treas. 1975–77; Agent-Gen. for Tasmania in London 1978–81; Pres. Tasmanian Section of Australian Labor Party 1968–69; fmr. J.P. *Leisure interests:* writing, reading, theatre criticism. *Address:* 7 Amarina Court, Kingston Beach, Tasmania 7151, Australia.

NEÍZVESTNY, Ernst Iosifovich; Soviet artist and sculptor; b. 9 April 1925, Sverdlovsk; ed. V. I. Surikov State Inst. of Arts (M. G. Manizer's studio); Soviet Army 1942–45; sculptor at studios of U.S.S.R. Agricultural Exhbn. (now Econ. Achievements of U.S.S.R. Exhbn.) 1953–54; mem. Artists' Union of U.S.S.R. 1955–57; granted permission to emigrate to Israel 1976. *Main works:* Kremlin Builder, First Wings, The Youth, Mother, series: War—is ...; Robots and Semi-robots, Great Mistakes, etc.

NEKRICH, Aleksandr Moiseevich; DR. HIST.; Soviet historian; b. 1920; ed. Faculty of History, Moscow Univ., and U.S.S.R. Acad. of Sciences Inst. of History –1941; joined army 1941–67; published historical study 'June 22, 1941' containing criticism of Stalin 1967; expelled from CP and book removed from all libararies in U.S.S.R. 1967; *Publications include:* The Politics of English Imperialism in Europe 1955, 'June 22, 1941,' 1967, The Punished Peoples 1975, Cast Out Fear: Recollections of an Historian 1979, L'Utopie au pouvoir: Histoire de l'URSS de 1917 à nos jours, 1982.

NELDER, John Ashworth, M.A., D.SC., F.R.S.; British statistician; b. 8 Oct. 1924, Dulverton, Somerset; s. of Reginald Charles Nelder and Edith May Ashworth (née Briggs); m. Mary Hawkes 1955; one s. one d.; ed. Blundell's School, Tiverton, Sidney Sussex Coll., Cambridge Univ.; Head, Statistics Section, Nat. Vegetable Research Station, Wellesbourne 1950–68; Head, Statistics Dept., Rothamsted Experimental Station, Harpenden 1968–84; Sr. Research Fellow, London Business School 1984–87; Originator statistical computer programs Genstat and GLIM; Visiting Prof., Imperial Coll., London 1972–; sometime Pres., Int. Biometric Soc.; Pres. Royal Statistical Soc. 1985–86; Guy Medal (Silver) of Royal Statistical Soc. *Publications:* Generalized Linear Models (with P. McCullagh), Computers in Biology; more than 70 papers in scientific journals. *Leisure interests:* ornithology, music (especially playing piano). *Address:* Cumberland Cottage, 33 Crown Street, Redbourn, St. Albans, Herts., AL3 7JX, England. *Telephone:* (058285) 2907.

NELISSEN, Roelof J.; Netherlands banker; b. 4 April 1931, Hoofdplaat, Zeeland province; m.; three s. one d.; ed. grammar school at Dongen and Faculty of Law, Catholic Univ. of Nijmegen; various posts in employers' asscns., Amsterdam and The Hague 1956–; Sec.-Gen. Netherlands Catholic Employers' Asscn. June 1962, Fed. of Catholic and Protestant Employers' Asscns. Sept. 1968; mem. Second Chamber, States-Gen. (Parl.) 1963–70; Vice-Chair. Parliamentary Catholic People's Party; deputy mem. Council of Europe, Council of WEU; Minister of Econ. Affairs 1970–71; First Deputy Prime Minister, Minister of Finance 1971–73; mem. Bd. Man. Dirs. Amsterdam-Rotterdam Bank N.V. 1974–79, Vice-Chair. 1979–82, Chair. June 1983–. *Address:* Amro Bank, Foppingadreef 22, 1102 BS Amsterdam, Netherlands.

NELLEMOSE, Knud; Danish sculptor; b. 12 March 1908, Copenhagen; s. of Aage and Anna Nellemose; m. Pia Bendix 1950; three s.; ed. Royal Acad. of Art, Copenhagen; first exhbn. of sculpture 1928; mem. State Art Foundation 1958–64; Hon. mem. R.C.A. 1988; awarded Eckersberg Medal 1944, Kai Nielsen Bequest 1947, Carlsberg Travelling Scholarship 1947–48, Thorvaldson Medal 1968; Knight of the Order Dannebrog. *works include:* busts of Their Majesties King Frederik, Queen Ingrid and Queen Margrethe II of Denmark; Statues of Søren Kierkegaard, King Frederick IX; works represented in the State Gallery of Copenhagen and in other Danish Museums, Nat. Museums of Stockholm and Oslo, Auschwitz, Poland and include Group of Wrestlers and Young Man with Discus and a marble bust of Hans Andersen for his 150th anniversary celebrations; represented at Venice Biennale 1950, and other int. exhbns. *Address:* Christian IX's Gade 3, Copenhagen 1111, Denmark.

NELLIGAN, Kate; Canadian actress; b. 16 March 1951, London, Ontario; d. of Patrick Joseph and Alice (née Dier) Nelligan; ed. St. Martin's Catholic School, London, Ont., York Univ., Toronto, and Cen. School of Speech and Drama, London, England; professional stage début as Corrie in Barefoot in the Park, Little Theatre, Bristol 1972; other parts there and at Theatre Royal for Bristol Old Vic 1972–73 include: Hypatia in Misalliance, Stella Kowalski in A Streetcar Named Desire, Pegeen Mike in The Playboy of the Western World, Grace Harkaway in London Assurance, title role in Lulu, Sybil Chase in Private Lives; London début as Jenny in Knuckle, Comedy Theatre 1974; joined Nat. Theatre Co. at Old Vic to 1975 to play Ellie Dunn in Heartbreak House, also in Plenty and Moon for the Misbegotten 1984; As You Like It for R.S.C., Stratford; Serious Money, Broadway 1988, Spoils of War 1988; *films include:* The Count of Monte Cristo, The Romantic Englishwoman, Dracula 1979, Patman, Eye of the Needle 1980, Agent 1980, Without a Trace 1983, Eleni 1986; *TV includes:* The Onedin Line, The Lady of the Camellias, Licking Hitler, Measure for Measure, Thérèse Raquin 1980, Forgive our Foolish Ways 1980; Evening Standard Best Actress Award 1978. *Leisure interests:* reading, cooking. *Address:* c/o Larry Dalzell Associates, 3 Goodwin's Court, London, W.C.2, England.

NELSON, Gaylord Anton, LL.B.; American lawyer and politician; b. 4 June 1916, Clear Lake, Wis.; s. of Anton Nelson and Mary Bradt; m. Carrie Lee Dotson 1947; two s. one d.; ed. Clear Lake High School (Polk County, Wis.), San José State Coll., Calif., and Wisconsin Univ. Law School; army service 1942–46; admitted to Wis. Bar 1942; Practising Attorney, Madison, Wis. 1946–; Wisconsin State Senator 1949–58; Gov. of Wisconsin 1958–62; U.S. Senator from Wisconsin 1963–80; Chair. Wilderness Soc., Washington, D.C. 1981–; Democrat. *Address:* Wilderness Society, 1400 Eye Street, N.W., Washington, D.C. 20005 (Office); 3611 Calvend Lane, Kensington, Md. 20895, U.S.A. (Home).

NELSON, Ralph Alfred, M.D., PH.D., F.A.C.P.; American professor of medicine; b. 19 June 1927, Minneapolis; s. of Alfred Walter Nelson and Lydia (née Johnson) Nelson; m. Rosemarie Pokela 1954; three s. two d.; ed. Univ. of Minnesota; Pathology Residency, Univ. of Minnesota 1954–55; Fellowship in Physiology, Mayo Graduate School, Mayo Clinic, Rochester 1957–60, Resident Internal Medicine 1976–78; Asst. Prof. of Nutrition, Cornell Univ. 1961–62; Assoc. Prof. of Physiology, Assoc. Prof. of Nutrition, Mayo Medical School, Rochester 1967–78; Prof. of Nutrition, Dept. of Medicine, Univ. of Ill. 1979–, Prof. of Food Science, Prof. of Physiology, Univ. of Ill. 1979–, Diplomat, Internal Medicine 1981–, Head, Dept. of Internal Medicine, Univ. of Ill. Coll. of Medicine at Urbana-Champaign; Consultant for Nutritional Support Service, Danville Veterans Admin. Hosp.; Dir. of Research, Carle Foundation Hosp., Urbana; Mayo Clinic Alumni Award for Outstanding Research 1959. *Publications:* Mayo Clinic Renal Diet Cook Book 1974, numerous learned papers, including over 140 on the metabolism of bears. *Leisure interests:* walking, bicycling, canoeing, mountain hiking. *Address:* Carle Foundation Hospital, Department of Medical Research, 611 West Park Street, Urbana, Ill. 61801, U.S.A.

NELSON OF STAFFORD, Baron, succeeded to title 1962; **Henry George Nelson,** M.A., F.ENG., F.I.C.E., HON. F.IMECH.E., HON. F.I.E.E., F.R.AE.S.; British industrialist; b. 2 Jan. 1917, Manchester; s. of 1st Baron Nelson of Stafford and Florence M. Howe; m. Pamela R. Bird 1940; two s. two d.; ed. Oundle and King's Coll., Cambridge; with English Electric Co. Ltd. 1939–42; Man. Dir. D. Napier & Son Ltd. 1942–49; Exec. Dir. Marconi's Wireless Telegraph Co. Ltd. 1946–58; Deputy Man. Dir. English Electric Co. Ltd. 1949–56, Man. Dir. 1956–62, Chair. and Chief Exec. 1962–68; Chair. The Gen. Electric Co. Ltd. 1968–83, Dir. 1983–87; Dir. Int. Nickel of Canada 1966–88, Enserch Corpn. 1984–; London Bd. of Advice to Nat. Bank of Australasia 1950–81; Joint Chair. English Electric—Babcock & Wilcox & Taylor Woodrow Atomic Power Construction Co. Ltd.; Chair. Royal Worcester Ltd. 1978–83; Dir. Bank of England 1961–87; Joint Deputy

Chair. British Aircraft Corpn. 1960-77; mem. Minister of Technology's Advisory Council 1964-70; Pres. ORGALIME (Organisme des Liaison des Industries Métallique Européennes) 1966-70; Pres. Inst.E.E. 1970-71, Sino-British Trade Council 1973-83; mem. House of Lords Select Cttee. on Science and Tech., numerous other councils and cttees.; Fellow Inst. of Eng.; Hon. D.Sc (Aston, Cranfield and Keele), Hon. LL.D. (Strathclyde). *Leisure interests:* shooting, tennis, skiing. *Address:* 244 Cranmer Court, Sloane Avenue, London, S.W.3; 1 Stanhope Gate, London, W1A 1EH, England. *Telephone:* 01 493-8484 (Office).

NÉMEC, Jaroslav, DR.SC.; Czechoslovak engineer and metallurgist; b. 15 March 1921, Horažďovice, Klatovy District; s. of Karel Němec and Bohuslava Němcová; m. Zdenka Němcová 1944; ed. Eng. Faculty, Tech. Univ. of Prague (ČVUT); design engineer 1942-45; Dir. of Research and Devt., ČKD Sokolovo 1945-53; Prof., Coll. of Transport (VŠD), Dean 1953-55, Deputy Rector 1955-59; Prof., Head of Materials Dept. and Dept. of Specialization, Faculty of Nuclear and Physical Eng., ČVUT 1969-86, Deputy Dean 1967-74, Deputy Rector 1973-79; Corresp. mem. Czechoslovak Acad. of Sciences (ČSAV) 1972-75, mem. ČSAV 1975-; mem. Presidium and Chief of Dept. of Tech. Sciences, Czechoslovak Acad. of Sciences; Dir. Acad. Inst. of Theoretical and Applied Mech., Prague 1979-; mem. Czechoslovak Atomic Comm.; Expert Adviser, Skoda Works, ČKD and others; Hon. mem. Int. Conf. on Fracture; mem. various foreign scientific and eng. socs.; Kaplan Medal 1958, Klement Gottwald State Prize 1965, 1974, Felber Medal 1971, Křížík Medal 1976, Order of Labour 1981, Nat. Prize 1985, Kemensky Medal 1986 and many others. *Publications:* over 160 original papers on mechanics, elasticity and strength; books include: Strength of Pressure Vessels under Different Operational Conditions, Toughness and Strength of Steel Parts, Failure of Strength of Plastics (with Acad. Serensen, Moscow), Shape and Strength of Metal Bodies (with Prof. Puchner), New Methods of Calculations of Rigidity and Strength of Machines (with Prof. Valeuta), Fracture Dynamics, Dynamics and Reliability of Locomotive Parts, The Problem of Nuclear Equipment, with Special Reference to Reliability and Safety; founded a school of scientific work in the field of limit states of toughness and strength of bodies and in the field of general fracture techniques. *Leisure interest:* painting (12 exhbns. held). *Address:* Academy of Sciences, Karloba 2, 1 Prague 1000, Křemencova 10 (Office); Letohradská 60, 7 Prague 17000, Czechoslovakia (Home). *Telephone:* 372862 (Home).

NEMEIRY, Field Marshal Gaafar Mohammed al- (see Nemery, Field Marshal Gaafar Mohammed al-).

NEMEROV, Howard; American writer and teacher; b. 1 March 1920, New York; s. of David and Gertrude (Russek) Nemerov; m. Margaret Russell 1944; three s.; ed. Fieldston School and Harvard Coll.; Royal Canadian Air Force, U.S.A.F., attached R.A.F. Coastal Command 1941-45; Instructor in English, Hamilton Coll., Clinton, N.Y. 1946-48; mem. Faculty of Literature and Languages, Bennington Coll. 1948-66; Prof. of English, Brandeis Univ.; Visiting lecturer, Univ. of Minnesota 1958-59; Writer in residence, Hollins Coll. 1962-63; Consultant in Poetry, Library of Congress, Washington, D.C. 1963-64; Fannie Hurst Prof. Creative Literature Washington Univ., St. Louis 1969, Edward Mallinckrodt Distinguished Univ. Prof. 1976-; Chancellor, Acad. American Poets 1976-; U.S. Poet Laureate 1988; Fellow, American Acad. of Arts and Sciences; Guggenheim Fellow 1968, Wallace Stevens Poetry Fellow, Yale 1983; mem. American Acad. Arts and Letters, Nat. Inst. of Arts and Letters; Hon. degree (Lawrence Univ.) 1964, (Tufts Univ.) 1966, (Washington and Lee Univ.) 1976, (Univ. of Vermont) 1979, (Hamilton Coll.) 1980, (Cleveland State Univ.) 1980, (Univ. of Missouri, St. Louis) 1982, (Mt. St. Mary's Coll.) 1987; Pulitzer Prize for Poetry 1978, Nat. Award in Poetry 1978, Messing Award, St. Louis Univ. 1979, Bollingen Prize for Poetry (Yale) 1980/81, Wallace Stevens Award for Poetry, Yale Univ. 1983, Conrad Aiken/Taylor Prize, Sewanee Review (for poetry, first award) 1987, Nat. Medal of Arts 1987, and other awards. *Publications:* The Image and the Law 1947, The Melodramatists 1949, Guide to the Ruins 1950, Federigo 1954, The Salt Garden 1955, The Homecoming Game 1957, Mirrors and Windows 1958, A Commodity of Dreams and Other Stories 1959, New and Selected Poems 1960, The Next Room of the Dream 1962, Essays on Poetry and Fiction 1963, Journal of the Fictive Life 1965, The Blue Swallows (poems) 1967, Stories, Fables and Other Diversions 1971, Reflexions on Poetry and Poetics 1972, Gnomes and Occasions (poems) 1973, The Western Approaches, Poems 1973-75, Figures of Thought 1977 (essays), The Collected Poems of Howard Nemerov 1977, Sentences (poems) 1980, Inside the Onion (poems) 1984, New and Selected Essays 1984, The Oak in the Acorn: On Remembrance of Things Past and On Teaching Proust, Who Will Never Learn 1987, War Stories: Poems About Long Ago and Now 1987. *Address:* Washington University, St. Louis, Mo. (Office); 6970 Cornell Avenue, St. Louis, Mo. 63130, U.S.A. (Home).

NEMERY, Field Marshal Gaafar Mohammed al-; Sudanese army officer and political leader; b. 1 Jan. 1930, Omdurman; ed. Sudan Military Coll.; fmr. Commdr. Khartoum garrison; campaigns against rebels in Southern Sudan; placed under arrest on suspicion of plotting to overthrow the govt.; led successful mil. coup May 1969; promoted from Col. to Maj.-Gen. May 1969, to Field Marshal May 1979; Chair. Revolutionary Command Council (RCC) 1969-71, C.-in-C. of Armed Forces 1969-73, 1976-85; Minister of Defence May-June 1969, 1972-73, 1974-76, 1978-79; Prime Minister 1969-76, 1977-85; Minister of Foreign Affairs 1970-71, of Planning 1971-72, of Finance 1977-78, of Agric. and Irrigation 1982, of Defence 1983-85; Pres. of Sudan 1971-85 (overthrown in coup); Supreme Commdr. of Armed Forces 1985; stripped of rank of Field Marshal in absentia June 1985; Pres. Political Bureau Sudanese Socialist Union 1971-85, Sec.-Gen. 1971-76, 1979-82; Pres. of OAU 1978-79; in Egypt 1985-.

NEMES NAGY, Ágnes; Hungarian poetess, essayist and translator; b. 3 Jan. 1922, Budapest; m. Balázs Lengyel; ed. Budapest Univ.; teaching work 1945-58; Guest Lecturer Budapest University on Modern Domestic and World Literature; Baumgarten Prize 1948, Attila József Prize 1969, Kossuth Prize 1983. *Publications: volumes of verse:* Kettős világban (In a Double World) 1946, Szárazvillám (Summer lightning) 1957, Napforduló (Solstice) 1967, A lovak és az angyalok (The Horses and the Angels) 1969, Között (Between) 1981, A föld emlékei (Memories of the Globe) 1986. *essays:* 64 hattyu (Sixty-four Swans) 1975, Metszetek (Sections) 1982, A hegyi költő (Poet of the Mount) a study on M. Babits 1984. Translations cover verse and drama from antiquity to modern times, especially Corneille, Racine, Victor Hugo, Rilke, Saint-John Perse; *volume of translations:* Vándorévek (Years of Peregrination) 1965. *Address:* Budapest XII, Királyhágó utca 5B, Hungary. *Telephone:* 757-156.

NÉMETH, Károly; Hungarian politician; b. 14 Dec. 1922, Páka, County Zala; ed. Party Acad.; started as meat industry worker, joined CP 1945; studied Party Acad. 1952-54; First Sec. County Csongrád Party Cttee. 1954-59; Sec. Cen. Cttee., Head Party Cen. Cttee. Dept. of Agric. 1960-65; First Sec., Budapest Party Cttee., Hungarian Socialist Workers' Party 1965-74, Sec. Cen. Cttee. HSWP 1962-65, 1974-85; Deputy Sec. Gen. 1985-87; mem. Political Cttee., HSWP 1970-88, Head of Econ. Bd. attached to HSWP Cen. Cttee. 1974-78; Pres. of Presidential Council 1987-88; M.P. 1958-88; Labour Order of Merit 1955, 1959, Order of the Hungarian People's Repub. 1982. *Publications:* Tettekkel-felelősséggel (Acts-Responsibilities) 1974, A magasabb követelmények utján (On the Road of Higher Requirements) 1979, Párt, Társadalom, Politika (Party, Society, Politics) 1986. *Address:* Presidential Council, Kossuth Lajos tér 1, 1357 Budapest, Hungary. *Telephone:* 121-754.

NÉMETH, Miklós; Hungarian politician; b. 24 Jan. 1948, Monok; m.; two s.; ed. Karl Marx Univ.; lecturer Karl Marx Univ. of Political Economy, Budapest 1971-77; deputy section head Nat. Planning Office 1977-81; worked on staff, later as deputy leader, of HSWP Cen. Cttee. Dept. of Political Economy, Dept. Leader 1987-; mem. of Cen. Cttee., Sec. 1987-88; mem. Political Cttee. 1987-; Chair. Council of Ministers Nov. 1988-. *Address:* Office of the Chairman, 1055 Budapest, Kossuth Lajos tér 1, Hungary. *Telephone:* 123-500.

NEMITSAS, Takis; Cypriot politician; b. 2 June 1930, Limassol; m. 2nd Louki Noucaïdes; three c. from first marriage; fmr. Man. Nemitsas group of cos.; mem. House of Reps. 1976; fmr. Pres. Parl. Cttee. on Commerce and Industry; Minister of Commerce and Industry 1988-; fmr. mem. Bd. Cyprus Employers' and Industrialists' Fed., Chamber of Commerce and Industry, Bank of Cyprus and several cos.; fmr. Deputy Chair. Woolworth Cyprus. *Address:* Ministry of Commerce and Industry, Nicosia, Cyprus.

NENASHEV, Mikhail Fyodovovich, DR. HIST. SC.; Soviet politician and publishing official; b. 1929; ed. Magnitogorsk Pedagogical Inst.; mem. CPSU 1952-; research and teaching at inst. 1956-63; Second Sec., Magnitogorsk City Cttee. 1963-68; Sec. of Chelyabinsk District Cttee. 1968-75; Deputy Head of Section of CPSU Cen. Cttee. 1975-86; Pres. of U.S.S.R. State Cttee. for Publishing, Printing and Bookselling 1986-; Cand. mem. of CPSU Cen. Cttee. 1981-89, mem. April 1989-. *Address:* State Committee for Publishing, Printing and Bookselling, Strastnoy bul. 5, 101409 Moscow, U.S.S.R.

NERI, Aldo, DR.; Argentine medical practitioner; b. 19 Oct. 1930, Bahia Blanca; m. Mabel Beatriz Bianco; Prof. and Dir. of Public Health School, Univ. of Buenos Aires; consultant Pan-American Health Org., the World Bank and the Org. of American States; Minister of Public Health and Welfare 1983-86. *Publications:* books and articles on social medicine. *Address:* c/o Ministerio de Salud y Accion Social, Defensa 120 C.P. 1349, Buenos Aires, Argentina.

NERLICH, Graham Charles, M.A., B. PHIL., F.A.A.M.; Australian professor of philosophy; b. 23 Nov. 1929, Adelaide; ed. Oxford Univ.; lecturer, Univ. of Leicester 1958-61, Univ. of Sydney 1962-72; Prof. of Philosophy Univ. of Sydney 1972-73, Univ. of Adelaide 1974-. *Publication:* The Shape of Space 1976. *Address:* Department of Philosophy, University of Adelaide, S. Australia 5001.

NERLOVE, Marc L., PH.D.; American professor of economics; b. 12 Oct. 1933, Chicago; s. of Samuel Henry Nerlove and Evelyn (née Andelman) Nerlove; two d.; ed. Univ. of Chicago and Johns Hopkins Univ.; Analytical Statistician, U.S. Dept. of Agric., Washington, D.C. 1956-57; Assoc. Prof., Univ. of Minn., Minneapolis 1959-60; Prof., Stanford Univ. 1960-65, Yale Univ. 1965-69; Prof. of Econs., Univ. of Chicago 1969-74; F. W. Taussig Research Prof., Harvard Univ. 1967-68; Visiting Prof., Northwestern Univ., 1973-74, Cook Prof. 1974-82; Prof. of Econs., Univ. of Pa. 1982-86, Univ. Prof. 1986-; mem. N.A.S.; John Bates Clark Medal 1969; P. C. Mahalinobis Medal 1975. *Publications:* Dynamics of Supply 1958, Distributed Lags and Demand Analysis 1958, Estimation and Identification of Cobb-Douglas Production Functions 1965, Analysis of Economic Time Series: A Synthesis 1979, Household and Economy: Welfare Economics of Endogenous Fertility 1987; numerous articles. *Address:* Department of Economics, University of Pennsylvania, 3718 Locust Walk 6297, Philadelphia, Pa. 19104, U.S.A.

NESTERENKO, Aleksey Yefremovich; Soviet diplomatist; b. 1915; mem. diplomatic service 1949–; Counsellor for U.S.S.R. at UN 1960–61; Amb. to Pakistan 1961–65; Deputy UN Sec.-Gen. for Political Questions and World Security 1965–68; Head of Dept. of Int. Economic Orgs., Ministry of Foreign Affairs 1968–80; Amb. to Ireland 1980–86. *Address:* c/o Ministry of Foreign Affairs, Smolenskaya-Sennaya pl. 32/34, Moscow, U.S.S.R.

NESTERENKO, Yevgeniy Yevgeniyevich; Soviet singer (bass); b. 8 Jan. 1938, Moscow; m. Yekaterina Dmitrievna Alexeyeva; one s.; ed. Leningrad Eng. Inst. and Leningrad Conservatoire (V. Lukanin's class); soloist with Leningrad Maly Opera and Ballet Theatre 1963–67; soloist with Kirov Opera 1967–71; soloist with Bolshoi 1971–; mem. CPSU 1974–; Teacher of solo singing at Leningrad Conservatoire 1967–71; mem. staff, Moscow Musical Pedagogical Inst. 1972–74; Chair. of Singing at Moscow Conservatoire 1975–, Prof. 1981–; Pres. Opera Section, U.S.S.R. Musical Soc. 1987–; Grammy Award, American Acad. of Recording Artists 1979, Lenin Prize 1982; Hero of Labour. *Roles include:* Boris Godunov, Dosifey (Khovanshchina), Prince Igor, Mephistopheles (Gounod's Faust); Grigori (Dzerzhinsky's Quiet Flows the Don), Kutuzov (War and Peace). *Publication:* Thoughts on My Profession 1985. *Address:* Bolshoi Theatre, Marx Prospect 8/2, 103009 Moscow (Office); Fruzenskaya nab. 24/1-178, 119146 Moscow, U.S.S.R. (Home).

NESTERIKHIN, Yuri Efremovich; Soviet physicist; b. 1930, Ivanovo; ed. Moscow Univ.; mem. CPSU 1960–; with Inst. of Atomic Energy 1954–61, Inst. of Nuclear Physics 1961–67; Prof. 1970; Corresp. mem. of U.S.S.R. Acad. of Sciences 1970, mem. 1981–; Dir. of Inst. of Automation and Electrometrics, Siberian Branch of Acad. of Sciences 1967–; most important works on plasma physics and thermonuclear synthesis. *Address:* U.S.S.R. Academy of Sciences Institute of Automation and Electrometrics, Universitetsky Pr.1, Novosibirsk, U.S.S.R.

NESTOROWICZ, Tadeusz, M.ECON.; Polish economist and politician; b. 27 Oct. 1928, Bedlno; ed. Foreign Trade Faculty of Higher School of Econs., Szczecin; employee Customs Offices, Szczecin 1948–50 and Łódź 1950–51; official, head of section, CIECH Foreign Trade Enterprise 1951–56; Head of Czechoslovak and Hungarian Div. at Ministry of Foreign Trade 1956–58; Commercial Attaché in Commercial Counsellor's Office, Budapest 1958–62; Vice-Dir. Commodity Turnover Dept. at Ministry of Foreign Trade 1962–67; Commercial Counsellor of Embassy in Yugoslavia 1967–72; Dir. Commercial Policy Dept. at Ministry of Foreign Trade 1972–73; Under-Sec. of State in Ministry of Foreign Trade 1974–81, Ministry of Foreign Trade and Shipping 1973–81, First Deputy Minister Aug.–Nov. 1981, Minister of Foreign Trade 1981–85; Amb. to Fed. Repub. of Germany 1986–87; mem. Polish Youth Union 1946–56, Polish United Workers' Party (PZPR) 1962–; Officer and Kt.'s Cross of Order of Polonia Restituta. *Address:* c/o Ministry of Foreign Affairs, 00-918 Warsaw, al. I Armii WP 23, Poland.

NETANYAHU, Benjamin, M.A.; Israeli diplomatist; b. 21 Oct. 1949; m.; one c.; ed. M.I.T.; man. consultant, Boston Consulting Group 1976–78; Exec. Dir. Jonathan Inst. Jerusalem 1978–80; Sr. Man. Rim Industries, Jerusalem 1980–82; Deputy Chief of Mission, Israeli Embassy, Washington, D.C. 1982–84; Perm. Rep. to UN 1984–. *Address:* Permanent Mission of Israel to UN, 800 Second Avenue, United Nations, New York, N.Y. 10017, U.S.A.

NETHERLANDS, H.R.H. Prince of the (Bernhard Leopold Frederik Everhard Julius Coert Karel Godfried Pieter), Prince zur Lippe-Biesterfeld; b. 29 June 1911, Germany; s. of H.S.H. the late Prince Bernhard zur Lippe and Princess Armgard, Baroness von Sierstorpff-Cramm; m. Juliana Louise Emma Marie Wilhelmina, (q.v.), Queen of the Netherlands 1937–80; four d.; ed. Gymnasiums at Zuellichau and Berlin and Univs. of Lausanne, Munich and Berlin; assumed Netherlands nationality 1936; studied at Netherlands Staff Coll.; apptd. mem. State Council; after German invasion of Holland, May 1940, evacuated family to England and returned to Continent with army until fall of France; returned to England and qualified as pilot 1941; appointed Hon. Air Cdre. R.A.F.V.R. 1941; subsequently Chief Netherlands Liaison Officer with British Forces, Col. later Maj.-Gen. and Chief of Netherlands Mission to War Office; visited war fronts in N. Africa and Normandy; maintained liaison throughout the war between Netherlands Underground and the Allied Govts.; appointed Supreme Commdr. (Lieut.-Gen.) Netherlands Armed Forces 1944 and played important part in liberation of Netherlands; decorated for his services in this operation by H.M. Queen Wilhelmina (M.W.O.) and H.M. King George VI (G.B.E.); subsequently resigned from office of Supreme Commdr. 1945; mem. Council for Mil. Affairs of the Realm, and mem. Joint Defence, Army, Admiralty and Air Force Councils; Insp.-Gen. of Armed Forces; Adm., Gen. R. Netherlands A.F., Gen. (Army) 1954–76; Hon. Air Marshal R.A.F. 1964; Hon. Cdre. R.N.Z.A.F. 1973; mem. Bd. of the Netherlands Trade and Industries Fair; has greatly contributed to post-war expansion of Netherlands trade; founder and regent Prince Bernhard Fund for the Advance-

ment of Arts and Sciences in the Netherlands; Regent Praemium Erasmianum Foundation; Founder-Pres. World Wildlife Fund Int., Pres. W.W.F. Netherlands, Pres. Rhino Rescue Trust; Chair. Achievement Bd. ICBP; Hon. mem. Royal Aeronautical Soc., Royal Inst. Naval Architects, Aeromedical Soc., Royal Spanish Acad.; Hon. degrees (Utrecht) 1946, (Delft) 1951, (Montreal) 1958, (British Columbia) 1958, (Amsterdam) 1965, (Michigan) 1965, (Basel) 1971; many decorations. *Leisure interests:* golf, skiing, filming, photography, hunting. *Address:* Soestdijk Palace, Baarn, Netherlands.

NETTERSTROM, Henrik Munck; Danish diplomatist; b. 12 Feb. 1924; m.; ed. Univ. of Copenhagen; Ministry of Agric. 1949–67, serving also in Danish missions to OEEC, Paris, to the EEC, CECA and EURATOM, Brussels and UN and EFTA, Geneva; joined Ministry of Foreign Affairs 1967, Under-Sec. for int. econ. and trade policy matters 1980–86; Perm. Rep. to OECD 1986–. *Address:* Permanent Mission of Denmark, Organization for Economic Cooperation and Development, 2 rue André Pascal, 75775 Paris Cedex 16, France.

NEUBER, Friedel; German banker; b. 10 July 1935; Chair. Man. Bd., Westdeutsche Landesbank Girozentrale (WestLB), Düsseldorf/Münster 1981–; Chair. Supervisory Bd., Preussag AG, Hanover/Berlin, Deutsche Anlagen-Leasing 1984–; mem. Supervisory Bd. AEG Telefunken AG, Frankfurt, Co-op AG Frankfurt, Deutsche Solvay-Werke GmbH, Solingen, Krupp Industrietechnik GmbH, Duisburg, STEAG Essen, Thyssen Stahl AG, Duisburg, Vereinigte Industrie-Unternehmungen AG (VIAG) Bonn. *Address:* Friedrichstrasse 56, 4000 Düsseldorf, Federal Republic of Germany.

NEUBERGER, Albert, C.B.E., M.D., PH.D., F.R.C.P., F.R.C.PATH., F.R.S.; British emeritus professor of chemical pathology; b. 15 April 1908, Würzburg, Germany; s. of late Max Neuberger and Bertha Neuberger; m. Lilian Ida Dreyfus 1943; four s.; ed. Gymnasium, Würzburg, Univs. of Würzburg and London; Beit Memorial Research Fellow 1936–40; research at Biochem. Dept., Cambridge 1939–42; mem. Scientific staff, Medical Research Council 1943; Adviser to GHQ, Delhi (Medical Directorate) 1945; Head of Biochem. Dept., Nat. Inst. for Medical Research 1950–55; Prof., Chemical Pathology, Univ. of London 1955–73; Visiting Lecturer in Medicine, Harvard Univ. 1960; mem. Editorial Bd., Biochemical Journal 1947–55, Chair. 1952–55; Assoc. Man. Ed. Biochimica Biophysica Acta 1968–81; mem. Medical Research Council 1962–66; Chair. Biochemical Soc. 1967–69; mem. Agricultural Research Council 1969–79; Chair. Governing Body, Lister Inst. 1971–88; Chair. Jt. ARC/MRC Comm. on Food and Nutrition Research; mem. Independent Cttee. on Smoking and Health 1973–82; mem. Scientific Advisory Cttee., Rank Prize Funds 1974–86; William Julius Mickle Fellowship, Univ. of London 1946–47; Hon. Pres. British Nutrition Foundation 1982–86; Hon. LL.D. (Aberdeen) 1967, Hon. Ph.D. (Jerusalem) 1968, Hon. D.Sc. (Hull) 1981; Heberden Medal 1959, Frederick Gowland Hopkins Medal 1960, Kaplun Prize 1973. *Publications:* papers in Biochemical Journal, Proceedings of Royal Society and other learned journals. *Address:* 37 Eton Court, Eton Avenue, London NW3 3HJ, England.

NEUGARTEN, Bernice Levin, PH.D.; American social scientist; b. 11 Feb. 1916, Norfolk, Neb.; d. of David L. Levin and Sadie (née Segall) Levin; m. Fritz Neugarten 1940; one s. one d.; ed. Univ. of Chicago; Research Asst. Dept. of Educ. Univ. of Chicago 1937–39; Fellow, American Council on Educ. 1939–41; Instr. in Psychology, Englewood Coll, Chicago 1941–43; Research Assoc. Comm. on Human Devt., Univ. of Chicago 1948–50, Asst. Prof. 1951–60, Assoc. Prof. 1960–64, Prof. 1964–80, Prof. 1969–73; Prof. of Educ. and Sociology, Northwestern Univ. 1980–; mem. various advisory bodies; Fellow, A.A.A.S., American Psychological Asscn., American Sociology Asscn., American Acad. of Arts and Sciences; mem. Inst. of Medicine of N.A.S., Int. Asscn. of Gerontology; Hon. D.Sc. (Univ. of S. Calif.) 1980; Kleemier Award 1972, Brookdale Award 1980, Sandoz Int. Prize 1987 and other awards. *Publications:* co-author or ed.: American Indian and White Children: A Social-Psychological Investigation 1955, Society and Education 1957, Personality in Middle and Late Life 1964, Middle Age and Aging 1968, Adjustment to Retirement 1969, Social Status in the City 1971, Age or Need? Public Policies for Older People 1982 and numerous articles in professional journals. *Address:* 5801 Dorchester Avenue, Chicago, Ill. 60637, U.S.A.

NEUHARTH, Allen H.; American business executive; b. 22 March 1924, Eureka, S. Dakota; m. 1st Loretta F. Helgeland 1946 (divorced 1972), one s. one d.; m. 2nd Lori Wilson 1973 (divorced 1982); ed. Univ. of S. Dakota; reporter, The Associated Press, Sioux Falls, S. Dakota; launched weekly tabloid SoDak Sports 1952; reporter, rising to Asst. Man. Ed., Miami Herald 1954–60; Asst. Exec. Ed. Knight's Detroit (Mich.) Free Press 1960; joined Gannett (newspaper and communications group) 1963, Exec. Vice-Pres. 1966, Pres. and C.O.O. 1970, Pres. and Chief Exec. 1973, Chair., Pres. and C.E.O. 1979, Chair. and C.E.O. 1984–86, Chair. 1986–; f. and Chair. USA Today 1982–; Chair. and Pres. American Newspaper Publishers' Asscn. 1979, 1980; numerous awards and seven hon. degrees. *Address:* Gannett Co. Inc., P.O. Box 7858, Washington, D.C. 20044 (Office); 1100 Wilson Boulevard, Arlington, Va. 22209, U.S.A. (Home).

NEUHAUSER, Duncan vonBriesen, PH.D.; American professor of epidemiology and community health; b. 20 June 1939, Philadelphia, Pa.; s. of

Edward B. D. Neuhauser and Gernda von Briesen Neuhauser; m. Elinor Toaz Neuhauser 1965; one s. one d.; ed. Harvard Univ. and Univs. of Michigan and Chicago; Research Assoc. (Instructor), Center for Health Admin. Studies, Univ. of Chicago 1965–70; Asst. Prof., then Assoc. Prof., Harvard School of Public Health 1970–79; Assoc. Chair., Program for Health Systems Man., Harvard Business School 1972–79; Consultant in Medicine, Mass. Gen. Hosp. 1975–80; Prof. of Epidemiology and Community Health, Case Western Reserve Univ. 1979–, Prof. of Medicine 1981–, Keck Foundation Sr. Research Scholar 1982–, Adjunct Prof. of Organizational Behaviour 1979–; Consultant in Medicine, Cleveland Metropolitan Gen. Hosp. 1981–; Adjunct mem., Medical Staff, Cleveland Clinic Foundation 1984–; Ed. Medical Care 1983–, Health Matrix 1982–; mem. Inst. of Medicine (N.A.S.). *Publications:* (Co-author) Health Services in the U.S., The Efficient Organization 1977, Health Services Management, Health Services Management Case Studies, The Physician and Cost Control 1979, Clinical Decision Analysis 1980, Competition, Co-operation or Regulation 1981, The New Epidemiology 1982, Coming of Age 1984, and scientific papers. *Leisure interests:* sailing, curling. *Address:* Department of Epidemiology and Biostatistics, Medical School, Case Western Reserve University, Cleveland, Ohio 44106; 2655 North Park Boulevard, Cleveland Heights, Ohio 44106 (Home, winter); Parker Point Road, Blue Hill, Maine 04614, U.S.A. (Home, summer). *Telephone:* (216) 368-3725 (Office); (216) 321-1327 (Cleveland Heights); (207) 374-5325 (Blue Hill).

NEUMANN, Alfred; German politician; b. 15 Dec. 1909, Berlin; ed. elementary school; carpenter by trade; active mem. labour movement 1928–; mem. Communist Party (KPD) 1929; emigrated to U.S.S.R. 1934; mem. Int. Brigade in Spain 1938–39; returned to Germany 1941, imprisoned 1942–45; mem. KPD 1945–46, Socialist Unity Party (SED) 1946; First Sec. Greater Berlin District SED 1953–57; mem. SED Cen. Cttee. 1954–, cand. mem. Politburo 1954–58, mem. 1958–, Sec. of SED Cen. Cttee. 1957–61; Pres. Econ. Council 1961–65; Minister of Materials 1965–68, First Deputy Chair. Council of Ministers 1968–; mem. Volkskammer (People's Chamber) 1954; Vaterländischer Verdienstorden in Gold 1956, 1964, Karl-Marx-Orden (twice) and other decorations. *Address:* c/o Ministerrat, Berlin, German Democratic Republic.

NEUMANN, Bernhard Hermann, DR.PHIL., PH.D., D.SC., F.A.C.E., F.A.A., F.R.S.; British mathematician; b. 15 Oct. 1909, Berlin-Charlottenburg, Germany; s. of late Richard Neumann and Else Aronstein; m. 1st Hanna von Caemmerer 1938 (died 1971), three s. two d.; m. 2nd Dorothea F. A. Zeim 1973; ed. Berlin-Charlottenburg, Univs. of Freiburg, Berlin, Cambridge; Temp. Asst. Lecturer Univ. Coll. Cardiff 1937–40; Army Service 1940–45; Lecturer Univ. Coll. Hull 1946–48; Lecturer, Sr. Lecturer, Reader, Univ. of Manchester 1948–61; Prof., Head of Dept., Australian Nat. Univ. 1962–74, Emer. Prof., Hon. Fellow 1975–; Sr. Research Fellow, Div. of Math. and Statistics, CSIRO 1975–77, Hon. Research Fellow 1978–; Visiting Lecturer Australian Univs. 1959, Monash Univ. 1980; Visiting Prof. Tata Inst. Fundamental Research, Bombay 1959, Courant Inst. Math. Sciences, New York Univ. 1961–62, Univ. Wisconsin 1966–67, Vanderbilt Univ. 1969–70, Univ. of Cambridge 1970, Univ. Illinois Urbana-Champaign 1975; Visiting Scientist, Univ. of Manitoba 1979, Univ. of Bielefeld 1987; Visiting Fellow, Fitzwilliam Coll., Cambridge 1970; Matthew Flinders Lecturer of the Australian Acad. of Science 1984; Ed. Proceedings of London Mathematical Soc. 1959–61; Assoc. Ed. Pacific Journal of Mathematics 1964–; Foundation Ed. Bulletin of Australian Math. Soc. 1969–79, Hon. Ed. 1979–; mem. Editorial Bd. Zentralblatt Didaktik Math. 1969–84, Communications in Algebra 1972–84, Houston Journal of Math. 1974–, Math. Scientist 1975–85; Ed. and Publr. IMU Canberra Circular 1972–; Editorial Consultant, South-East Asian Math. Bulletin 1987–; Council London Math. Soc. 1954–61 (Vice-Pres. 1957–59); Council Australian Math. Soc. 1963–79 (Vice-Pres. 1963–64, 1966–68, 1971–73, Pres. 1964–66); Council Australian Acad. Science 1968–71, Vice-Pres. 1969–71; Foundation Pres. Australian Assen. Math. Teachers 1966–68, Vice-Pres. 1968–69; Foundation Pres. Canberra Math. Assen. 1963–65, Vice-Pres. 1965–66; Chair. Aust. Nat. Cttee. Math. 1966–75; Chair. Aust. Sub-Comm., Int. Comm. Math. Instruction 1968–75; mem.-at-large, Int. Comm. on Math. Instruction 1975–82, Exec. Cttee. 1979–82; mem. Exchange Comm., Int. Math. Union (IMU) 1975–79; mem. Acad. Advisory Council, Royal Aust. Naval Coll. 1978–87; Fellow (non-resident) Bruce Hall Australian Nat. Univ. 1963– (mem. Governing Body 1984–90); SERC Visitor, Univ. of Glasgow 1985; Hon. Life mem. Australian Assen. of Math. Teachers 1975–, Canberra Math. Assen. 1975–, New Zealand Math. Soc. 1975–, Australian Math. Soc. 1981–; Pres. Amateur Sinfonia of Canberra Inc. 1978–80, Vice-Pres. 1980–81, 1983–84, Hon. Life mem. 1984–; Vice-Pres. Friends of Canberra School of Music 1983–; mem. Governing Bd., Australian Math. Competition 1980–; Chair. Australian Mathematical Olympiad Cttee 1980–86; mem. Comm. for 1988 Int. Mathematical Olympiad 1984–88; Prize of Wiskundig Genootschap te Amsterdam 1949; Adams Prize (Cambridge Univ.) 1951–52; Hon. D.Sc. (Newcastle, N.S.W.) 1974, (Monash) 1982; Hon. D.Math. (Waterloo) 1986. *Publications:* Selected Works of B. H. Neumann and Hanna Neumann, 6 Vols., 1988; over 120 papers in mathematical journals. *Leisure interests:* chamber music, chess, cycling. *Address:* Department of Mathematics, Institute of Advanced Studies, Australian National University, G.P.O. Box 4, Canberra, A.C.T. 2601; CSIRO-DMS, G.P.O. Box 1965, Canberra, A.C.T. 2601 (Offices); 20 Talbot Street, Forrest, A.C.T. 2603, Australia (Home). *Telephone:* 818558 and 494504 (Office); 733447 (Home).

NEUMANN, Robert Gerhard, PH.D.; American diplomatist and educator; b. 2 Jan. 1916, Vienna, Austria; s. of Hugo and Stephanie Taussky; m. Marlen Eldredge 1941; two s.; ed. High School and Consular Acad., Vienna, Univ. of Rennes, Geneva School of Int. Studies, Amherst Coll., Mass., Univ. of Minnesota; Teacher of Political Science and Econs., State Teachers' Coll., Oshkosh, Wis. 1941–42; lecturer in Political Science, Univ. of Wisconsin 1946–47; Asst. Prof., Univ. of Calif., Los Angeles 1947–52, Assoc. Prof. 1952–58, Prof. of Political Science 1958–67, Dir. Inst. of Int. and Foreign Studies 1958–65; Chair. Atlantic and W. European Program 1965–66; Amb. to Afghanistan 1966–73, to Morocco 1973–76; Sr. Assoc. and Project Dir. Centre for Strategic and Int. Studies (CSIS), Georgetown Univ. 1976–79, Coordinator, Middle East Programs 1979–81, Vice-Chair. 1980–81, Dir. Middle East Studies; Sr. Adviser CSIS 1982–; Dir. State Dept. Transition Team 1980–81; Amb. to Saudi Arabia April–July 1981; Chair. Exec. Cttee. Moroccan-American Foundation 1982–; Vice-Chair. American-Saudi Business Round Table 1983–84, Chair. 1984–; Editorial Writer Los Angeles Times 1952–59; mem. Council, Johns Hopkins Centre, Bologna 1970–; mem. Bd. of Dirs. Americares for Afghans 1983–; Advisory Council, Cttee. for a Community of Democracies, U.S.A. 1984–; mem. Exec. Cttee. Islam and the West 1984–; mem. Int. Inst. for Strategic Studies 1984–; Chevalier, Légion d'honneur 1957, Order of the Star, 1st Class (Afghanistan) 1973, Commdr. Order of Merit (Fed. Repub. of Germany) 1974, Grand Officier, Order and Star of Ouissam Alami (Morocco) 1976, Hon. Medal Univ. of Brussels 1955. *Publications:* European and Comparative Government, The Government of Germany 1966, Toward a More Effective Executive-Legislative Relationship in the Conduct of American Foreign Policy 1977 and numerous articles in professional journals. *Leisure interests:* photography, hiking. *Address:* 4986 Sentinel Drive, No. 301, Bethesda, Md. 20816; and 11865 Lucile Street, Culver City, Calif. 90230, U.S.A. (Homes).

NEUMANN, Václav; Czechoslovak conductor; b. 29 Sept. 1920, Prague; ed. Prague Conservatoire; fmr. viola player, Smetana Quartet; mem. Czech Philharmonic Orchestra; deputised for Rafael Kubelík 1948; later conducted orchestras in Karlovy Vary and Brno; Conductor Prague Symphony Orchestra 1956–63, Czech Philharmonic 1963–64; Chief Conductor Komische Oper, Berlin 1957–60, conducted first performance of The Cunning Little Vixen (Janáček); Conductor Leipzig Gewandhaus Orchestra and Gen. Music Dir. Leipzig Opera House 1964–67; conductor Czech Philharmonic Orchestra 1967–68, Chief Conductor 1968–; Conductor Munich Opera Ensemble in Sweden 1969; Conductor Vienna Philharmonic 1987; toured Austria 1970, 1971, 1972, 1974, Romania 1951, 1971, 1973, Fed. Repub. of Germany 1962, 1965, 1967, 1971, 1973, 1974, 1975, Yugoslavia 1970, Bulgaria 1975, Belgium 1970, Switzerland 1970, 1975, Spain 1975, Finland 1975, U.K. 1983; Nat. Prize of German Dem. Repub. 1966, Honoured Artist 1967, Nat. Artist 1971, Order of Labour 1980. *Address:* Alsovo Nabrezi 12, 11001 Prague 1, Czechoslovakia.

NEUMEIER, John, B.A.; American ballet director and choreographer; b. 1942, Milwaukee, Wis.; ed. Marquette Univ., Milwaukee; dance training in Milwaukee, Chicago, Royal Ballet School, London and in Copenhagen with Vera Volkova; soloist, The Stuttgart Ballet 1963; Ballet Dir. Frankfurt 1969; Ballet Dir. and Chief Choreographer, The Hamburg Ballet 1973–; noted for his creation of new works and original interpretations of well-known ballets; founded a ballet training school in Hamburg 1978; appears as soloist, notably in The Chairs with Marcia Haydée, a ballet created for them by M. Béjart: *Works Choreographed Include:* A Midsummer Night's Dream (Mendelssohn/Ligeti), ballets to the Mahler symphonies, Le Sacré (Stravinsky), The Lady of the Camellias (Chopin), Bach's St. Matthew Passion, A Streetcar Named Desire (Prokofiev/Schnittke); Golden Camera Award for TV series of his Ballet Workshops 1978; Dance Magazine Award 1983; Deutscher Tanzpreis 1988; Bundesverdienstkreuz; Hon. D.F.A. (Marquette); Diaghilev Prize 1988. *Address:* Hamburg Ballet, Hamburgische Staatsoper, Grosse Theaterstrasse 34, 2000 Hamburg 36, Federal Republic of Germany.

NEURATH, Hans, PH.D.; American biochemist; b. 29 Oct. 1909, Vienna, Austria; s. of Rudolf and Hedda Samek Neurath; m. 1st Hilde Neurath 1936, 2nd Susi Neurath 1960; one s.; ed. Elementary and High School, Vienna, and Univ. of Vienna; Research Fellow, Univ. of London 1934–35; Instructor and George Fischer-Baker Fellow, Cornell Univ., N.Y. 1936–38; Asst. Prof., Assoc. Prof., Prof. of Physical Biochem., Duke Univ. 1938–50; Prof. of Biochem., Univ. of Washington, Seattle 1950–80, Prof. Emer. 1980–, Chair. Dept. of Biochem. 1950–75; Scientific Dir. Fred Hutchinson Cancer Research Center (Seattle) 1976–80; Dir. German Cancer Research Centre (Heidelberg) 1980–81; mem. N.A.S.; Foreign mem. Max-Planck Soc.; Hon. mem. Japanese Chemical Soc.; Fellow American Acad. of Arts and Sciences; specializes in biochem. of proteins and enzymes, relation of their structure and function; D.Sc. (Geneva) 1970, (Tokushima) 1977. *Publications:* Over 300 original publs. in biochemistry; Ed. Biochemistry, The Proteins. *Leisure interests:* music (piano), mountaineering, skiing. *Address:* University of Washington, Department of Biochemistry, Seattle, Washington WA 98195, U.S.A. *Telephone:* (206) 543-7893.

NEURRISSE, André, D. EN D., D. ÈS SC.ECON.; French banker; b. 21 April 1916, Pomarez; m. Louise Marie Verdier 1942; two d.; ed. Univs. of Bordeaux and Paris; civil servant, Ministry of Finance 1941–58, Treasurer-Paymaster Gen. 1958–82; Consultant to IMF, World Bank and UN 1982–;

Man. Dir. Société d'Etudes et des Participations (SEP) 1984–; Man. Dir. Banque Internationale de Financement et de Négociation (BIFEN) 1985–; Officier Légion d'honneur, Commandeur Mérite National. *Publications:* Précis de Droit Budgétaire 1961, La Comptabilité Économique Française 1963, Les Règlements Internationaux 1972, Histoire du Franc 1974, Les Jeux de Casino 1977, Histoire de l'Impôt 1978, L'Economie Sociale 1983, Le Trésorier-Payeur General 1986, Le Franc C.F.A. 1987. *Leisure interests:* swimming, cycling. *Address:* Banque BIFEN, 92 rue d'Ouffroy, 75017 Paris, France.

NEUSTADT, Richard Elliott, PH.D.; American politician and scientist; b. 26 June 1919, Philadelphia; s. of Richard Neustadt and Elizabeth Neufeld; m. 1st Bertha Cummings 1945; one s. one d.; m. 2nd Shirley Williams (q.v.) 1987; ed. Univ. of Calif. (Berkeley) and Harvard Univ.; Economist, Office of Price Admin. 1942; Staff mem., Bureau of Budget 1946–50, White House 1950–53; Prof. of Public Admin. Cornell Univ. 1953–54, of Govt., Columbia Univ. 1954–65, Harvard Univ. 1965–78; Lucius N. Littauer Prof. of Public Admin. John F. Kennedy School of Govt. 1978–86, Assoc. Dean 1965–75, Dir. Inst. of Politics 1966–71; Douglas Dillon Prof. of Govt., Harvard 1986–; mem. Inst. for Strategic Studies 1963–; Fellow, American Acad. of Arts and Sciences 1964–; Visitor, Nuffield Coll., Oxford 1961–62, Assoc. mem. 1965–67; Special Consultant, Sub-Cttee. on Nat. Policy Machinery, U.S. Senate 1959–61; mem. Advisory Bd. on Comm. on Money and Credit 1960–61; Special Consultant to Pres.-Elect Kennedy 1960–61, to Pres. Kennedy 1961–63, to Bureau of Budget 1961–70, to Dept. of State 1962–69; mem. Council on Foreign Relations 1963, American Political Science Assen., Nat. Acad. of Public Admin., American Philosophical Soc.; Consultant to Pres. Johnson 1964–66, to Rand Corpn. 1964–78; Trustee, Radcliffe Coll. 1977–80; Democrat. *Publications:* Presidential Power 1960 (revised 1980), Alliance Politics 1970, The Epidemic That Never Was (with Harvey Fineberg) 1983, Thinking in Time (with Ernest May) 1986. *Address:* Kennedy School of Government, Harvard University, Cambridge, Mass. 02138 (Office); 1010 Memorial Drive, Cambridge, Mass. 02138, U.S.A. (Home). *Telephone:* (617) 495 1196.

NEUVO, Yrjö A., PH.D.; Finnish research professor; b. 21 July 1943, Turku; s. of Olavi Neuvo and Aune (née Vaisala) Neuvo; m. Tuula Halsas 1968; two s. one d.; ed. Cornell Univ. and Helsinki Univ. of Tech.; Acting Prof. Helsinki Univ. of Tech. 1975–76; Prof. of Electronics, Tampere Univ. of Tech. 1976–; Sr. Research Fellow Acad. of Finland 1979–80, Research Prof. 1984–; Visiting Prof. Univ. of California 1981–82; I.E.E.E. Bicentennial Award 1986, Assen. in Finland Hon. Prize 1988. *Publications:* over 250 scientific publs. on computer eng. and new technologies. *Address:* Tampere University of Technology, P.O. Box 527, 33101 Tampere, Finland. *Telephone:* (358-31) 162 698.

NEUWIRTH, Lucien; French politician; b. 18 May 1924, Saint-Etienne; s. of René Neuwirth and Gabrielle Blanchon; m. Mariette Didier 1952; one d.; ed. Lycée Claude Fauriel, Saint-Etienne and Business School; mem. S.A.S.-Free French Forces 1942–46; town councillor, St.-Etienne (Gaullist Party) 1947–65; Man. French Nat. Broadcasting Network in Algeria 1958; Deputy of Loire 1958–81; Gen. Sec. Gaullist Group in Parl. 1959–62; Senator, Loire 1983; Gen. Councillor of Saint-Etienne 1967–; Pres. Co. Council of Loire 1979–; mem. Public Safety Cttee., Algeria 1958; Tech. Councillor Charles de Gaulle cabinet 1958; Officier Legion d'honneur; World War II War Cross, Officer Medal of Resistance, Medal of Freedom, and other French and foreign distinctions. *Publications:* The Fiscal Flail 1977, May Life Be 1979, My War at 16 1986. *Address:* Palais du Luxembourg, 75291 Paris, Cedex 06; 22 Rue du Général de Gaulle, 42000 Saint-Etienne, France. *Telephone:* (1) 42343079; (77) 33-42-45.

NEVANLINNA, Eero Olavi, DIP. ENG., DR. TECH.; Finnish professor of mathematics; b. 17 April 1948, Helsinki; m. Marja Lähdesmäki 1968; three s. one d.; ed. Helsinki Univ. of Technology; Asst. Math. Helsinki Univ. of Tech. 1971–74; Sr. Researcher Acad. of Finland 1975–77; Assoc. Prof. Applied Math. Oulu Univ. 1978–79; Prof. Math. Helsinki Univ. of Tech. 1980–; Research Prof. Acad. of Finland 1986–(92); Visiting Prof. Inst. for Math., Univ. of Minnesota 1986; Chair. Rolf Nevanlinna Inst. 1989–(90); mem. Finnish Acad. of Tech. Sciences 1984, Finnish Acad. of Sciences and Letters 1986, Ed. Bd. BIT, Nat. Cttee. in Math. 1984–. *Publications:* c. 60 scientific papers, esp. in numerical analysis. *Address:* Institute of Mathematics, Helsinki University of Technology, SF-02150 Espoo, Finland. *Telephone:* 358-0-4513034.

NEVILLE, John, O.B.E.; British actor and theatre director; b. 2 May 1925, Willesden, London; s. of Reginald D. Neville and Mabel L. Fry; m. Caroline Hooper 1948; three s. three d.; ed. Chiswick County Grammar School and Royal Acad. of Dramatic Art, London; with Bristol Old Vic Co., London 1953, played Othello, Iago, Hamlet, Aguecheek and Richard II; mem. Chichester Theatre Co. 1962; created part of Alfie (Alfie by Bill Naughton), London 1963; Dir. Nottingham Playhouse 1963–68, Newcastle Playhouse 1967; Hon. Prof. in Drama, Nottingham Univ. 1967–; Drama Adviser to Howard and Wyndham Ltd.; in musical Mr. & Mrs. 1968; series of TV plays 1968; presented four plays at Fortune Theatre, London with the Park Theatre Co.; appeared in the Apple Cart, Mermaid Theatre, London 1970, The Beggar's Opera, Chichester 1972, Happy Days, Nat. Theatre, London 1977; went to Canada 1973; staged The Rivals, Nat. Arts Theatre, Ottawa; Dir. opera Don Giovanni, Festival Canada, Ottawa; played Pro-

spero (The Tempest), Judge Brack (Hedda Gabler), Sir George Croft (Mrs. Warren's Profession), in Sherlock Holmes, New York 1975; Artistic Dir. of Citadel Theatre, Edmonton, Alberta, Canada 1973–78; Artistic Dir. Neptune Theatre, Halifax, Nova Scotia 1978–83; with Stratford Festival Theatre, Ont. 1983–89, Artistic Dir. 1985–89; Dir. Hamlet 1986, Mother Courage, Othello 1987; film (in title role) Adventures of Baron Munchausen 1987–88; Hon. Dr. Dramatic Arts (Lethbridge Univ., Alberta) 1979; Hon. D.F.A. (Nova Scotia Coll. of Art and Design) 1981. *Films acted in include:* Mr. Topaz, Oscar Wilde, Billy Budd, A Study in Terror, Adventures of Gerrard. *Leisure interests:* watching football, listening to music (all kinds), thinking about gardening. *Address:* c/o Larry Dalzell Associates Ltd., 3 Goodwin's Court, St. Martins Lane, London, W.C.2, England.

NEVIN, John Joseph, B.S., M.B.A.; American business executive; b. 13 Feb. 1927, Jersey City; s. of Edward Vincent Nevin and Anna (née Burns) Nevin; m. Anna Filice 1951; five s. one d.; ed. Univ. of Calif. 1950, Harvard Univ. 1952; served with U.S.N.R. 1945–46; various financial positions; product planning and marketing Ford Motor Co., Dearborn, Mich. 1954–71, Vice-Pres. Marketing 1969–71; Pres. Zenith Radio Corpn., Chicago 1971–76, Chair. 1976–79; Pres. Firestone Tire and Rubber Co., Akron, Ohio 1979–82, 1984–87, C.E.O. 1980–, Chair. 1981–; Gen. Chair. Summit County (AKRON) United Way 1983; Dir. American Natural Resources Co., First Chicago Corpn., First Nat. Bank Chicago; mem. Advisory Council J. L. Kellogg Graduate School of Man., Northwestern Univ.; mem. advisory bd. School of Business Admin., Berkeley, Univ. of Calif.; Chair. Bd. Council of Better Business Bureaus 1984–. *Address:* 205 North Michigan Avenue, Suite 3800, Chicago, Ill. 60601, U.S.A.

NEVO, Ruth, PH.D.; Israeli professor of humanities; b. 1924, Johannesburg, S.A.; d. of Benjamin Weinbren and Henrietta (née Goldsmith) Weinbren; m. Natan Nevo 1952; three s.; ed. Univ. of the Witwatersrand, Johannesburg and Hebrew Univ., Jerusalem; tutor Dept. of English, Hebrew Univ. 1952, Prof. 1973; Renee Lang Prof. of Humanities 1982–; mem. Israel Acad. 1985–. *Publications:* The Dial of Virtue 1963, Tragic Form in Shakespeare 1972, Comic Transformations in Shakespeare 1980, Shakespeare's Other Language 1987; trans. Selected Poems by Bialik 1981, Travels by Amiebai 1986. *Leisure interests:* riding, painting. *Address:* Hehalutz 22, Jerusalem; Department of English, Hebrew University, Mount Scopus, Jerusalem, Israel.

NEWBIGGING, David Kennedy, O.B.E.; British business executive; b. 19 Jan. 1934, Tientsin, China; s. of late D. L. and L. M. Newbigging; m. Carolyn S. Band 1968; one s. two d.; ed. Oundle School; joined Jardine, Matheson & Co., Ltd. 1954, Dir. 1967, Man. Dir. 1970, Chair. and Senior Man. Dir. 1975–83; Chair. Hongkong & Kowloon Wharf & Godown Co., Ltd. 1970–80; Chair. and Man. Dir. Hongkong Land Co., Ltd. 1975–83; Dir. Hongkong & Shanghai Banking Corpn. 1975–83; Dir. Hongkong Electric Holdings Ltd. 1975–83, Chair. 1982–83; Dir. Hongkong Telephone Co., Ltd. 1975–83; Chair. Jardine, Fleming & Co., Ltd. 1975–83; Dir. Rennies Consolidated Holdings Ltd. 1975–83; Dir. Safmarine and Rennies Holdings Ltd. 1984–85; Dir. Provincial Insurance PLC 1984–86, Deputy Chair. Provincial Group PLC 1985–; Dir. Rentokil Group PLC 1986– (Chair. 1987–), PACCAR (U.K.) Ltd. 1986–, Mason Best Int. Ltd. 1986– (Chair. 1987–), Int. Financial Markets Trading Ltd. 1986–, Ivory & Sime PLC 1987–, United Meridian Corpn. 1987–; Chair. Redfearn PLC 1988–; mem. Legis. Council of Hongkong 1978–82, mem. Exec. Council 1980–84; mem. Int. Council, Morgan Guaranty Trust Co. of New York 1977–85; mem. British Coal Corpn. (fmrly. Nat. Coal Bd.) 1984–87. *Leisure interests:* most outdoor sports, Chinese art. *Address:* 103 Mount Street, London, W1Y 5HE, England. *Telephone:* 01-499 7526.

NEWBIGIN, Rt. Rev. Lesslie, C.B.E., M.A., D.D.; British missionary; b. 8 Dec. 1909, Newcastle upon Tyne; s. of Edward R. Newbigin and Annie E. Affleck; m. Helen S. Henderson 1936; one s. three d.; ed. Leighton Park School, Queens' Coll., Cambridge, and Westminster Coll., Cambridge; Sec., Student Christian Movement, Glasgow 1931–33; ordained to Ministry, Church of Scotland 1936; with Mission, Madras, S. India 1936–39; Missionary in charge, Kancheepuram 1939–46; Bishop in Madura, Church of S. India 1947–59; Gen. Sec. Int. Missionary Council 1959–61; Assoc. Gen. Sec. World Council of Churches and Dir. Div. of World Mission and Evangelism 1961–65; Bishop in Madras 1965–74; Lecturer, Selly Oak Colls. 1974–79; Moderator, United Reformed Church of England and Wales 1978–79; Minister, Winson Green United Reformed Church 1980–88. *Publications:* Christian Freedom in the Modern World 1937, The Reunion of the Church 1948, South India Diary 1951, The Household of God 1953, Sin and Salvation 1955, One Body, One Gospel, One World 1958, A Faith for this One World? 1961, Trinitarian Faith for Today's Mission 1964, Honest Religion for Secular Man 1966, The Finality of Christ 1969, The Good Shepherd 1977, Christian Witness in a Plural Society 1977, The Open Secret 1979, The Light Has Come 1982, The Other Side of 1984 1983, Unfinished Agenda 1985, Foolishness to the Greeks 1986. *Leisure interests:* music, climbing mountains. *Address:* 15 Fox Hill, Birmingham, B29 4AG, England.

NEWBY, (Percy) Howard, C.B.E.; British author; b. 25 June 1918, Crowborough, Sussex; s. of Percy Newby and Isabel Clutsam (Bryant); m. Joan Thompson 1945; two d.; ed. St. Paul's Coll., Cheltenham; served in Army (R.A.M.C.) 1939–42; Lecturer in English Literature Fouad I Univ., Cairo 1942–46; mem. BBC Talks Dept. 1949–58, Controller Third Programme

1958-70, Controller Radio Three 1970-71; Dir. of Programmes, Radio 1971-75, Man. Dir. Radio 1976-78; Chair., English Stage Co. 1978-84; Atlantic Award for Literature 1946; Somerset Maugham Prize 1948, Yorkshire Post Fiction Award 1968, Booker Prize for Something to Answer For 1969. *Publications:* A Journey to the Interior 1945, Agents and Witnesses 1947, Mariner Dances 1948, The Snow Pasture 1949, Maria Edgeworth 1950, The Young May Moon 1950, The Novel 1945-50, A Season in England 1951, The Retreat 1953, The Picnic at Sakkara 1955, Revolution and Roses 1957, Ten Miles from Anywhere 1958, A Guest and his Going 1959, The Barbary Light 1962, One of the Founders 1965, Something to Answer For 1968, A Lot to Ask 1973, Kith 1977, The Egypt Story (photographs by Fred Maroon) 1979, Warrior Pharaohs 1980, Feelings Have Changed 1981, Saladin in His Time 1983, Leaning in the Wind 1986. *Leisure interests:* music and gardening. *Address:* Garsington House, Garsington, Oxford, OX9 9AB, England (Home). *Telephone:* (086 736) 420.

NEWCOMBE, John David O.B.E.; Australian professional tennis player; b. 23 May 1944, Sydney; s. of George Ernest and Lillian Newcombe; m. Angelika Pfannenberg 1966; one s. two d.; ed. Sydney Church of England Grammar School; winner of Wimbledon Singles Championship 1967, 1970, 1971, U.S.A. Singles Championship 1967, 1973, Australia Singles Championship 1973, 1975, World Championship Tennis Crown 1974, Wimbledon Doubles Championship 1965-66, 1968-70, 1974; played with Australian Davis Cup Team 1963-67, 1973-76; Pres. Assen. of Tennis Professionals 1976-78; Pres. Program Tennis Services, Texas Co., Nat. Australia Day Council; Chair. McDonald's Jr. Tennis Australia. *Publications:* The Family Tennis Book 1975, The Young Tennis Player 1981, Bedside Tennis 1983. *Leisure interests:* skiing, waterskiing, golf, fishing. *Address:* P.O. Box 1200, Crow's Nest, 2065 N.S.W., Australia.

NEWELL, Kenneth Wyatt, M.B., M.D., D.P.H.; New Zealand professor of tropical health; b. 7 Nov. 1925, Erode, India; s. of Herbert W. Newell and Mary I. Hare; m. Priscilla J. Newell 1977; four s.; ed. Wanganui Collegiate School, Univ. of Otago, London School of Hygiene and Tropical Medicine and Tulane Univ.; Lecturer in Social and Preventative Medicine, Queen's Univ. Belfast 1956-58; WHO epidemiologist, Indonesia 1958-60; W. H. Watkins Prof. of Epidemiology, Tulane Univ., U.S.A. 1960-67; Field Dir. Int. Center for Research and Training, Calif. Colombia 1960-67; Dir. Div. of Research, Epidemiology and Communications Science, WHO, Geneva 1967-72, Dir. Div. Strengthening Health Services 1972-77; Prof. of Community Health, Wellington Clinical School, N.Z. 1977-83; Middlemass Hunt Prof. of Tropical Community Health and Head of Dept. of Int. Community Health, Liverpool School of Tropical Medicine 1984-. *Publication:* Health by the People (Ed.) 1975. *Leisure interests:* gardening, opera, wine. *Address:* Department of International Community Health, Liverpool School of Tropical Medicine, Pembroke Place, Liverpool, L3 5QA (Office); Five Oaks, Street Hey Lane, Willaston, South Wirral, L64 1SS, England (Home). *Telephone:* 051-708 9393 (Office); 051-327 4057 (Home).

NEWELL, Norman Dennis, PH.D.; American palaeontologist and geologist; b. 27 Jan. 1909, Chicago, Ill.; s. of Virgil Bingham Newell and Nellie Clark; m. 1st Valerie Zirkle 1928 (died 1972); m. 2nd Gillian Wendy Wormall 1973; ed. Univ. of Kansas and Yale Univ.; Geologist, Kansas Geological Survey 1929-37; Faculty mem., Univ. of Kansas 1934-37; Assoc. Prof. of Geology Univ. of Wis. 1937-45; Prof. of Geology Columbia Univ. 1945-77, Prof. Emer. 1977-; Curator American Museum of Natural History, New York 1945-77, Curator Emer. 1977-; Consultant on Petroleum Geology, Govt. of Peru 1942-45; mem. N.A.S., American Acad. of Arts and Sciences, American Philosophical Soc., Geological Soc. of America, London Geological Soc., Paleontology Soc., Soc. for the Study of Evolution (Pres. 1960-61), Soc. of Systematic Zoology (Pres. 1972-73); awards include N.A.S. Mary Clarke Thompson Medal 1960, Yale Univ. Verrill Medal 1966, American Museum of Natural History Gold Medal for Achievement in Science 1978, Palaeontological Soc. Medal 1979 and A.A.A.S. Scientific Freedom and Responsibility Award 1987. *Publications:* Late Paleozoic Pelecypods 1937-42, Geology of the Lake Titicaca Region 1943, Upper Paleozoic of Peru 1953, Permian Reef Complex of the Guadalupe Mountains Region 1953, Geological Reconnaissance of Raroia Atoll 1956, Classification of the Bivalvia 1965, Revolutions in the History of Life 1967, Creation and Evolution: Myth or Reality? 1982, scientific and popular articles on evolution, extinction, etc. *Address:* Department of Invertebrates, American Museum of Natural History, CPW and 79 Street, New York, N.Y. 10024 (Office); 135 Knapp Terrace, Leonia, N.J. 07605, U.S.A. (Home). *Telephone:* (212) 873-1300 (Office); (201) 944-5596 (Home).

NEWMAN, Edwin Harold; American journalist; b. 25 Jan. 1919, New York; s. of Myron Newman and Rose Parker Newman; m. Rigel Grell 1944; one d.; ed. Univ. of Wisconsin, Louisiana State Univ.; Washington Bureau, Int. News Service 1941, United Press 1941-42, 1945-46; U.S. Navy 1942-45; CBS News, Washington, D.C. 1947-49; freelance, London 1949-52; NBC News, London Bureau 1952-57, Rome Bureau 1957-58, Paris Bureau 1958-61; Corresp. and Commentator, NBC News, New York 1961-83; Columnist, King Features Syndicate 1984-; freelance journalist and lecturer; Peabody, Overseas Press Club, Emmy, Univ. of Mo. School of Journalism Award and others. *Publications:* Strictly Speaking 1974, A Civil Tongue 1976, Sunday Punch 1979; articles for Punch, Esquire, Atlan-

tic, Harper's, New York Times, Saturday Review, Chicago Tribune, TV Guide, Sports Illustrated. *Leisure interests:* tennis, music, reading. *Address:* c/o Richard Fulton Inc., 101 W. 57th Street, New York, N.Y. 10019, U.S.A. *Telephone:* 582-4099.

NEWMAN, Sir Kenneth (Leslie), Kt., G.B.E.; British police officer; s. of John William and Florence Newman; m. Eileen Lilian Newman 1949; one s. one d.; ed. Univ. of London; with R.A.F. 1942-46; mem. Palestine Police 1946-48; with Metropolitan Police, London 1948-73, Commdr. New Scotland Yard 1972; with Royal Ulster Constabulary 1973-79, Sr. Deputy Chief Constable 1973, Chief Constable 1976-79; Commandant, Police Staff Coll. 1980-82; Insp. of Constabulary 1980-82; Commr. Metropolitan Police 1982-87; Prof. of Law, Bristol Univ. 1987-88; Dir. Control Risks 1987-; Chair. Disciplinary Cttee., Security Systems Inspectorate, British Security Industry Assen. 1987-; Vice-Pres. Defence Mfrs. Assen. 1987-; Companion of British Inst. of Man. 1977; Companion of the Order of St. John of Jerusalem 1984, Queen's Police Medal 1982. *Address:* University of Bristol, Bristol, BS8 1TH, England.

NEWMAN, Melvin Spencer, PH.D.; American professor of organic chemistry; b. 10 March 1908, New York; s. of Jacob K. Newman and Mae Polack; m. Beatrice Crystal 1933; two s. two d.; ed. Yale Univ.; Instructor, Ohio State Univ. 1936-40, Asst. Prof. of Organic Chem. 1940-44, Prof. 1944-78, Prof. Emer. 1978-, Regents' Prof. 1966; mem. N.A.S., American Chemical Soc., British Chemical Soc.; Guggenheim Fellow 1951; Hon. D.Sc. (New Orleans) 1975, (Bowling Green State Univ.) 1978, (Ohio State Univ.) 1979; American Chem. Soc. Award for Creative Work in Synthetic Organic Chem. 1961, Morley Medal, Cleveland Section American Chem. Soc. 1969, Wilbur Cross Medal, Yale Univ. 1970, Joseph Sullivant Medal, Ohio State Univ. 1976, Columbus Section Award of American Chem. Soc. 1976, Roger Adams Award, American Chem. Soc. 1979. *Publications:* Editor: Steric Effects in Organic Chemistry 1956, An Advanced Organic Laboratory Course 1972; over 360 publs. in scientific journals. *Leisure interests:* music, golf, billiards and pool, gardening. *Address:* 2239 Onandaga Drive, Columbus, Ohio 43221, U.S.A. (Home). *Telephone:* (614) 488-6441 (Home).

NEWMAN, Nanette; British actress and writer; b. Northampton; d. of Sidney and Ruby Newman; m. Bryan Forbes (q.v.) 1958; two d.; ed. Sternhold Coll., London, Italia Conti Stage School, Royal Acad. of Dramatic Art; *Film appearances include:* The L-Shaped Room 1962, The Wrong Arm of the Law 1962, Seance on a Wet Afternoon 1963, The Wrong Box 1965, The Whisperers 1966, The Madwoman of Chaillot 1968, The Raging Moon (Variety Club Best Actress Award) 1971, The Stepford Wives 1974, International Velvet 1978. *Television appearances include:* The Fun Food Factory, London Scene, Stay with me till Morning, Jessie, Let There Be Love, Late Expectations, The Endless Game 1988. *Publications:* God Bless Love 1972, Lots of Love 1973, All Our Love 1978, Fun Food Factory 1976, The Root Children 1978, Amy Rainbow 1980, That Dog 1980, Reflections 1981, Dog Lovers Coffee Table Book 1982, Cat Lovers Coffee Table Book 1983, My Granny was a Frightful Bore 1983, Christmas Cookbook 1984, Cat and Mouse Love Story 1984, The Best of Love 1985, Pigalev 1985, Archie 1986, The Summer Cookbook 1986, Small Beginnings 1987, Bad Baby 1988, Entertaining with Nanette Newman 1988. *Leisure interests:* needlepoint, china painting. *Address:* c/o John Redway & Associates Ltd., 16 Berners Street, London, W1P 3DD, England.

NEWMAN, Paul; American actor; b. 26 Jan. 1925, Cleveland; s. of Arthur Newman and Theresa Fetzer; m. 1st Jacqueline Witte 1949, one s. (died 1978) two d.; m. 2nd Joanne Woodward (q.v.) 1958, three d.; ed. Kenyon Coll. and Yale Univ. School of Drama; Mil. service 1943-46; Best Actor, Acad. of Motion Pictures, Arts and Sciences 1959, 1962, 1964, Hon. Acad. Award 1986, Head cos. Newman's Own, Salad King; Hon. D. Hum. Litt. (Yale) 1988. *Stage appearances include:* Picnic 1953-54, Desperate Hours 1955, Sweet Bird of Youth 1959, Baby Want a Kiss 1964. *Films include:* The Rack 1955, Somebody Up There Likes Me 1956, Cat on a Hot Tin Roof 1958, Rally Round the Flag, Boys 1958, The Young Philadelphians 1958, From the Terrace 1960, Exodus 1960, The Hustler 1962, Hud 1963, The Prize 1963, The Outrage 1964, What a Way to Go 1964, Lady L 1965, Torn Curtain 1966, Hombre 1967, Cool Hand Luke 1967, The Secret War of Harry Frigg 1968, Butch Cassidy and the Sundance Kid 1969, WUSA 1970, Pocket Money 1972, The Life and Times of Judge Roy Bean 1973, The Mackintosh Man 1973, The Sting 1973, The Towering Inferno 1974, The Drowning Pool 1975, Buffalo Bill and the Indians 1976, Silent Movie 1976, Slap Shot 1977, Absence of Malice 1981, The Verdict 1982, Harry and Son (Dir.) 1984, The Color of Money 1986, Fat Man and Little Boy. *Directed:* Rachel, Rachel 1968, The Effect of Gamma Rays on Man in the Moon Marigolds 1973, The Shadow Box 1980, When Time Ran Out 1980, Fort Apache: the Bronx 1981, The Glass Menagerie 1987. *Address:* c/o Rogers & Cowan Inc., 1000 Santa Monica Boulevard No. 400, Los Angeles, Calif. 90067-7007, U.S.A.

NEWMAN, Peter C., O.C.; Canadian journalist and author; b. 10 May 1929, Vienna; s. of Oscar and Wanda Newman; m. Camilla J. Turner 1978; two d.; ed. Upper Canada Coll., Toronto, Univ. of Toronto and McGill Univ.; Asst. Ed. The Financial Post 1951-55; Ottawa Ed. Maclean's 1955-64; Ottawa Ed. Toronto Daily Star 1964-69, Ed.-in-Chief 1969-71; Ed.-in-Chief, Maclean's 1971-82, Sr. Contributing Ed. 1982-; Dir. Maclean Hunter Ltd. 1972-83, Key Radio Ltd. 1983-; Prof. Creative Writing, Univ. of Victoria

1985; several honours and awards including Kt. Commdr. Order of St. Lazarus; Hon. LL.D. (Brock) 1974, (Wilfrid Laurier) 1983, (Royal Mil. Coll.) 1986, (Queens) 1986, Hon. D.Litt. (York) 1975. *Publications:* Flame of Power 1959, Renegade in Power 1963, The Distemper of our Times 1968, Home Country 1973, The Canadian Establishment: Vol. I 1975, Bronfman Dynasty 1978, The Acquisitors - The Canadian Establishment: Vol. II 1981, The Establishment Man 1982, True North - Not Strong and Free 1983, Debrett's Illustrated Guide to the Canadian Establishment 1983, Company of Adventurers 1985, Caesars of the Wilderness 1987, Sometimes A Great Nation 1988. *Leisure interest:* sailing. *Address:* Maclean Hunter Building, 777 Bay Street, Toronto, Ont. M5W 1A7 (Office); 4855 Major Road, Victoria, B.C., V8Y 2L8, Canada.

NEWSOM, David Dunlop, A.B., M.S.; American diplomatist; b. 6 Jan. 1918, Richmond, Ohio; s. of Fred Stoddard and Ivy Elizabeth (née Dunlop) Newsom; m. Jean Frances Craig 1942; three s. two d.; ed. Richmond Union High School and California and Columbia Univs.; Reporter, San Francisco Chronicle 1940-41; U.S. Navy 1941-45; Newspaper publr. 1945-47; Information Officer, U.S. Embassy, Karachi 1947-50; Consul, Oslo 1950-51; Public Affairs Officer, U.S. Embassy, Baghdad 1951-55; Dept. of State 1955-59; U.S. Nat. War Coll. 1959-60; First Sec. U.S. Embassy, London 1960-62; Dir. Office of Northern African Affairs, State Dept. 1962-65; Amb. to Libya 1965-69; Asst. Sec. of State for African Affairs 1969-73; Amb. to Indonesia 1974-77, to Philippines 1977-78; Under-Sec. of State for Political Affairs 1978-81, Assoc. Dean School of Foreign Service 1981-; Dir. Inst. for Study of Diplomacy, Georgetown Univ. 1981-; Dept. of State Meritorious Service Award 1958, Nat. Civil Service League Career Service Award 1971, Rockefeller Public Service Award 1973, Dept. of State Distinguished Honor Award 1981, John Adams Memorial Fellow in Int. Relations 1986. *Address:* Georgetown University School of Foreign Service Institute for the Study of Diplomacy, Washington, D.C. 20057 (Office); 3265 O Street, N.W., Washington, D.C. 20007, U.S.A. (Home).

NEWTON, (Charles) Wilfrid; British business executive; b. 11 Dec. 1928, Johannesburg, South Africa; s. of Gore M. and Catherine K. Newton; m. Felicity Mary Lynn Thomas 1954; two s. two d.; ed. Highlands North School, Johannesburg, Univ. of Witwatersrand; Territory Accounting and Finance Man., Vacuum Oil Co. of South Africa, Johannesburg 1955-58, Accounting and Finance Man., Head Office, Cape Town 1958-62; Controller, Mobil Sekiyu K.K., Tokyo 1962-63; Finance and Planning Man. and Deputy Gen. Man., Mobil Oil East Africa Ltd., Nairobi, then London 1963-65; Planning Dir., Mobil Sekiyu K.K., Tokyo 1966, Finance Dir. 1966-68; Finance Dir., Turner and Newall Ltd. 1968-74, Man. Dir., Group's Plastics and Industrial Materials, Chemicals and Asbestos Fibre Mining and Distribution Divs. 1974-78, Man. Dir. Worldwide Manufacturing Activities Jan.-Nov. 1979, Group Man. Dir. 1979-82, Chief Exec. 1982-; Chair. and C.E.O. Mass Transit Railway Corpn. Hong Kong 1983-89; Chair. Hong Kong Futures Exchange Ltd. 1987-89; Chair. and C.E.O. London Regional Transport March 1989-; Dir. Hong Kong and Shanghai Banking Corpn. 1980-. *Leisure interests:* sailing, reading, gardening. *Address:* 'Newtons Gate', Ramley Road, Pennington, Lymington, Hants., SO4 8GQ, England. *Telephone:* 01-222 5600 (Office); (0590) 79750 (Home).

NEWTON, Christopher, M.A.; Canadian actor, director and author; b. 11 June 1936, Deal, Kent; s. of Albert E. Newton and Gwladys M. née Emes; unmarried; ed. Sir Roger Manwood's School, Sandwich, Kent, Univs. of Leeds and Illinois and Purdue Univs.; actor, Stratford Festival, New York; founding Artistic Dir. Theatre Calgary, Calgary, Alberta 1968-71; Artistic Dir. Vancouver Playhouse and founder (with late Powys Thomas), The Playhouse Acting School 1973-79; Artistic Dir. The Shaw Festival, Niagara-on-the Lake 1979-; Hon. LL.D. (Brock Univ.). *Publications:* plays: You Two Stay Here, the Rest Come with Me, Slow Train to St. Ives, Trip, The Sound of Distant Thunder. *Leisure interest:* landscape architecture. ·*Address:* c/o Shaw Festival, Niagara-on-the-Lake, Ont. LOS 1JO (Office). *Telephone:* (416) 468-2153 (Office).

NEWTON, John Oswald, M.A., PH.D., F.A.A.; Australian/British professor of nuclear physics; b. 12 Feb. 1924, Birmingham; s. of O. J. Newton and R. K. Newton; m. Silva Dusan Sablich 1964; two s. one d.; ed. Bishop Vesey's Grammar School, Sutton Coldfield, St. Catharine's Coll., Cambridge, Cavendish Lab., Cambridge; Jr. Scientific Officer, Telecommunications Research Establishment, Great Malvern 1943-46; Harwell Fellow 1951-54; Prin. Scientific Officer, A.E.R.E. Harwell 1954-59; Sr. Lecturer, Univ. of Manchester 1959-67, Reader 1967-70; Prof. of Nuclear Physics 1970, Head of Dept. of Nuclear Physics, Inst. of Advanced Studies, A.N.U. 1970-88; Visiting Physicist, Lawrence Berkeley Lab. (several times since 1956); Visiting Prof. Univ. of Manchester 1985-86. *Publications:* more than 100 publs. in Nuclear Physics and several book chapters. *Leisure interests:* painting, chess, music, walking, tennis. *Address:* Department of Nuclear Physics, Australian National University, Canberra, A.C.T. 2601 (Office); 21 Ryrie Street, Campbell, A.C.T. 2601, Australia (Home). *Telephone:* (062) 492083 (Office); (062) 478167 (Home).

NEWTON, Sir (Leslie) Gordon, Kt., B.A.; British journalist; b. 16 Sept. 1907; m. Peggy Ellen Warren 1935; one s. (deceased); ed. Blundell's School and Sidney Sussex Coll., Cambridge; entered journalism 1935; Army Service 1939-45; joined Financial Times 1946, Features Editor, Leader Writer and Columnist 1946-50, Ed. 1950-72, Dir. 1967-72; Chair. J. H.

Vavasseur & Co. 1973-74; Chair. Lion Int. 1973; Chair. London Broadcasting Co. 1974-77; Deputy Chair. Mills and Allen 1974-81; Dir. Pearson-Longman 1972-76, Industrial and Trade Fairs Holdings 1968-75, Throgmorton Publs. 1968-75, Trust Houses Forte 1973-79, Mills and Allen Int. 1978-81; Int. Publ. Corpn. Hannen Swaffer Award as Journalist of the Year 1966-67; Granada TV special award 1970. *Address:* 51 Thames House, Phyllis Court Drive, Henley-on-Thames, Oxon RG9 2NA, England.

NEWTON-JOHN, Olivia, O.B.E.; British singer and actress; b. 26 Sept. 1948, Cambridge; d. of Brin Newton-John and Irene Born; m. Matt Lattanzi 1984; one d.; numerous awards. *Recordings (since 1971) include:* Let Me Be There, If You Love Me, Let Me Know, Clearly Love, Come On Over, Don't Stop Believin', Making a Good Thing Better, Totally Hot, Physical. *Film appearances include:* Grease 1978, Xanadu 1980, Two Of a Kind 1983. *TV appearances:* numerous, including It's Cliff Richard (BBC-TV series). *Leisure interests:* horse riding, song writing, cycling, astrology, conservation, animals. *Address:* c/o Triad Artists Inc., 10100 Santa Monica Boulevard, 16th Floor, Los Angeles, Calif. 91604, U.S.A.

NEY, Edward, PH.D.; American professor of physics; b. 28 Oct. 1920, Minneapolis, Minn.; s. of Otto F. and Jessamine Purdy Ney; m. June V. Felsing 1942; three s. one d.; ed. Univs. of Minnesota and Virginia; Research Asst., Univ. of Va. 1940-42, Research Assoc. 1943-46, Asst. Prof. 1946-47; Consultant Naval Research Lab. 1943-44; Asst. Prof. Univ. of Minn. 1947-50, Assoc. Prof. 1950-55, Prof. of Astrophysics 1955-, Regents Prof. 1974; mem. Nat. Acad. of Sciences, American Acad. of Arts and Sciences; NASA Exceptional Scientific Achievement Medal. *Publications:* over 100 articles in professional journals. *Address:* School of Physics and Astronomy, University of Minnesota, Minneapolis, Minn. 55455, U.S.A. *Telephone:* (612) 624-4392.

NEY, Edward Noonan, B.A.; American business executive; b. 26 May 1925, St. Paul, Minn.; s. of John and Marie Noonan Ney; m. 2nd Judith Ney 1974; one s. two d. (by previous marriage); ed. Amherst Coll.; Account Exec., Young & Rubicam Inc. 1951, Vice-Pres. 1959-63, Sr. Vice-Pres. 1963-67, Exec. Vice-Pres. 1967-68, Pres. Int. Div. 1968-70, Pres. and C.E.O. 1970-72, Pres., C.E.O. and Chair. 1972-83, Chair. and C.E.O. 1983-85, Chair. 1985-86, Chair. PaineWebber/Young Rubicam Ventures 1987-, Vice-Chair. PaineWebber 1987-; Vice-Chair. The Advertising Council 1984-87, Chair. 1987-88; mem. Bd. Int. Broadcasting 1984-, Bd. of Govs. Foreign Policy Asscn. 1980- (Vice-Chair. 1984-87); Trustee, Nat. Urban League 1974-, Amherst Coll. 1979-, New York Univ. Medical Center 1979-, Museum of Broadcasting 1982-; mem. Council on Foreign Relations 1974-, mem. Bd. of Dirs. Center for Communication 1986-; Advisory Council, Center for Strategic and Int. Studies 1986-. *Leisure interests:* tennis, paddle tennis, reading. *Address:* PaineWebber Incorporated, 1285 Avenue of the Americas, New York, N.Y. 10017, U.S.A.

NEY, Dr. Roman; Polish scientist and politician; b. 18 Feb. 1931, Pińsk; ed. Acad. of Mining and Metallurgy, Cracow; scientific worker, Acad. of Mining and Metallurgy, Cracow 1955-, Asst. Prof. 1968-72, Prof. 1972-, Pro-Rector 1969-72, Rector of Acad. 1972-74, 1979-81; Under-Sec. of State, Ministry of Science, Higher Educ. and Tech. 1974-78; Dir. Inst. of Energy Resources 1978-; corresp. mem. Polish Acad. of Sciences 1976-, Scientific Sec. Cracow Branch 1978-80, Sec. Section VII (Earth and Mining Sciences) 1984-; Sec.-Gen. Polish Acad. of Sciences 1988-; Head Econ. of Mineral Raw Materials 1986-; Chair. State Council for Energy Economy 1985-; fmr. mem. Polish Scouts' Asscn. and Polish Youth Union (ZMP); mem. PZPR 1961-; deputy mem. PZPR Cen. Cttee. Feb.-Oct. 1980, mem. Oct. 1980-81, deputy mem. Political Bureau 1980, Sec. 1980-81; Commdr.'s Cross, Order of Polonia Restituta, Meritorious Teacher of People's Poland and other decorations. *Publications:* numerous papers on geology of raw materials and regional geology of Poland. *Address:* ul. D. Chodowieckiego 5 m. 13, 30-065 Cracow, Poland. *Telephone:* 20-06-21 (Office); 37-30-68 (Home).

NEZERITIS, Andreas; Greek composer; b. 1897, Patras; m. Irena Skoufou 1939; ed. Conservatoire of Athens, and studies under Denis Lavrangas; Pres. League of Greek Composers 1957; awarded First Prize, Acad. of Athens 1952; Gold Cross, Order of King George 1965; Silver Medal and Prize, Acad. of Athens 1971; works performed in Greece, Germany, Netherlands, France, Italy, U.S.S.R., Czechoslovakia and U.S.A.; Fellow, Int. Inst. of Arts and Letters 1958-. *Works include:* two operas, The King Aniliagos and Hero and Leander; three symphonies, No. 1 in G minor, No. 2 in C minor and No. 3 in D minor; Concerto for Violin and Orchestra; Concerto for Violoncello and Orchestra; Concertino for Piano and Orchestra; Five Psalms of David for four Soloists, Mixed Chorus and Full Orchestra; Concerto for String Orchestra; two Greek Rhapsodies; five Symphonic dances; Greek Dance Suite on Cypriot Themes; also ballet and vocal music and piano music. *Leisure interest:* gardening.

NG CHENG KIAT, Encik, B.SC.; Malaysian barrister and politician; b. 16 Nov. 1941, Kelang, Selangor; m. Lim Siew Keok; ed. Chinese Univ. of Hong Kong and Lincoln's Inn, London; fmr. Deputy Minister of Finance; Minister of Housing and Local Govt. 1986-; Sec.-Gen. Malaysian Chinese Asscn. *Address:* Ministry of Housing and Local Government, Kuala Lumpur, Malaysia.

NGAKINAR, Col. Mamari Djime; Chad army officer and politician; Vice-Pres. of the Supreme Mil. Council 1975–78; Minister of the Interior and Security 1975–76; Minister of State 1976–78, of Defence 1978–79. *Address:* c/o Office du Vice-Président, Conseil Supérieur Militaire, N'Djamena, Chad.

NGAPO NGAWANG-JIGME (see Ngapoi Ngawang Jigmi).

NGAPOI NGAWANG JIGMI, Lieut.-Gen.; Chinese (Tibetan) politician; b. 1911, nr. Lhasa, Tibet; captured by Communist troops, Qamdo (Tibetan Mil. Region under his control) 1950; Vice-Chair. Qamdo Liberation Cttee. 1950; First Deputy Commdr. Tibet Mil. Region 1952–; Vice-Chair. and Sec. Gen. 1959; Deputy for Xizang, 1st NPC 1954; mem. Nat. Defence Council 1954–Cultural Revolution; Sec.-Gen. Preparatory Cttee. for Establishment of Xizang Autonomous Region (AR) 1956, Vice-Chair. 1959, Acting Chair. 1965; Vice-Chair. Standing Cttee., 3rd CPPCC 1959–64; Head, Cadre School, Lhasa 1961; Vice-Chair. Standing Cttee., 3rd NPC 1965–75, 4th NPC 1975–78, 5th NPC 1978–86; 6th NPC 1986–; Chair. Xizang AR 1965; Vice-Chair. Xizang AR Revolutionary Cttee. 1968–79; Chair. People's Congress, Xizang AR 1979; Exec. Chair. Presidium 6th NPC 1986–; Chair. Tibet Autonomous Regional 5th People's Congress Aug. 1988–; Chair. Nationalities Cttee., NPC, 1979–. *Publication:* Tibet (with others). *Address:* Office of the Governor, People's Government, Lhasa, Xizang Autonomous Region, People's Republic of China.

NGEI, Paul, B.SC.(ECON.); Kenyan politician; b. 1923, Machakos; grandson of Akamba Paramount Chief Masaku; ed. Makerere Coll., Kampala; Army Service, Second World War; founded Wasya wa Mukamba newspaper and Swahili magazine Uhuru wa Mwafrika 1950; Deputy Gen. Sec. Kenya African Union 1951–52; imprisoned and under restriction for connection with Mau-Mau 1953–61; Pres. Kenya African Farmers' and Traders' Union 1961; founded African Peoples' Party 1962; Chair. Maize Marketing Bd. 1963–64; Minister for Co-operatives and Marketing 1964–65, for Housing and Social Services 1965–66, for Housing 1966–74, of Local Govt. 1974–75, unseated by High Court ruling; M.P. for Kagunda Jan. 1976–; Minister of Co-operative Devt. 1976–79, of Works 1979–82, of Livestock Devt. 1982–83, of Lands and Settlement 1983–84, of Environment and Nat. Resources 1984–85, of Water Devt. 1985–87, of Livestock Devt. 1987–88, Minister of Culture and Social Services March 1988–; Man. Dir. Akamba Carving and Industrial Co. *Address:* Ministry of Culture and Social Services, Nairobi, Kenya.

NGO DINH NHU, Madame; Vietnamese politician; widow of Ngo Dinh Nhu, brother and Adviser to the late Pres. Ngo Dinh Diem; arrested by Viet Minh, later escaped 1946; organized first popular demonstration in support of Govt. of Prime Minister Ngo Dinh Diem 1954; Official Hostess for Pres. Ngo Dinh Diem 1955–63; fmr. Deputy, Nat. Assembly, author of "Family Bill"; f. programme of paramilitary service for women Oct. 1961; Founder-Pres. Vietnamese Women's Solidarity Movement.

NGONDA, Putteho Muketoi, B.SC.ECON.; Zambian diplomatist; b. 16 Aug. 1936, Mongu; s. of Sitali and Naluca Ngonda; m. Lungowe Mulale 1965; three s.; ed. Mongu and Mundi Secondary Schools, Univ. Coll. of Rhodesia and Nyasaland, Salisbury; District Officer 1963–64; Second Sec. Zambia Perm. Mission to UN 1964–65; First Sec. Zambian Embassy, Washington 1967–68; Asst. Sec. (Political), Ministry of Foreign Affairs 1968–70, Under-Sec. 1970–72; Amb. to Ethiopia 1972–74; High Commr. in U.K. 1974–75; Perm. Sec., Ministry of Foreign Affairs 1975–77; Amb. to U.S.A. (also accred. to Dominica, Peru, Brazil and Venezuela) 1977–87. *Leisure interest:* tennis. *Address:* c/o Ministry of Foreign Affairs, P.O.B. RW 50069, Lusaka, Zambia.

NGUEMA MBASOGO, Lieut.-Col. Teodoro Obiang (see Mbasogo, Lieut.-Col. Teodoro Obiang Nguema).

NGUGI, Wa Thiong'o (James); Kenyan novelist; b. 1938, Limuru; ed. Makerere Univ. Coll., Uganda and Leeds Univ., England; Lecturer in Literature, Univ. Nairobi 1967–69; Fellow in Creative Writing, Makerere Univ. 1969–70; Visiting Assoc. Prof. Northwestern Univ., U.S.A. 1970–71; fmr. Sr. Lecturer, then Assoc. Prof. and Chair. Literature Dept., Univ. Nairobi; arrested and detained Dec. 1977, released Dec. 1978. *Publications:* The Black Hermit (play) 1962, Weep Not Child 1964, The River Between 1965, A Grain of Wheat 1967, Homecoming (essays) 1972, Secret Lives (short stories) 1973, Petals of Blood (novel) 1977, The Trial of Dedan Kimathi (with Micere Mugo) 1977, Detained: A Writer's Prison Diary 1981, I'll Marry When I Want (with Ngugi wa Mirii) 1982, Devil on the Cross 1982, Writers in Politics (essays) 1982, Barrel of a Pen (essays) 1983, Decolonising the Mind (essays) 1986, Writing Against Neo-Colonialism 1986, Matigari ma Ngirũũngi (novel in Gĩkũyũ language) 1986. *Address:* c/o Heinemann Educational Books, 22 Bedford Square, London, W.C.1, England.

NGUYEN CAO KY, Air Vice-Marshal; Vietnamese air force officer and politician; b. 8 Sept. 1930; ed. High School, Hanoi, and Officers' Training School, Hanoi; Flight Training, Marrakesh until 1954; commanded Transport Squadron 1954, later commdr. Tan Son Nhât Air Force Base, Repub. of Viet-Nam; spent six months at U.S. Air Command and Staff Coll., Maxwell Field, Alabama, U.S.A.; later Commdr. Air Force, Repub. of Viet-Nam; Prime Minister 1965–67; Vice-Pres. Repub. of Viet-Nam 1967–

71; went to U.S.A. April 1975; owns liquor store. *Publication:* Twenty Years and Twenty Days 1977. *Address:* Huntington Beach, Los Angeles, Calif., U.S.A.

NGUYEN CO THACH; Vietnamese politician; served Embassy, Delhi 1956–60; took part peace talks, Geneva 1962; Chair. Cttee. to Investigate U.S. War Crimes 1966; Minister of Foreign Affairs Feb. 1980–; alt. mem. Politburo 1982–86, mem. 1986–; Vice-Premier State Council Feb. 1987–; Vice Chair. Council of Ministers. *Address:* Ministry of Foreign Affairs, Dien Bien Phu, Hanoi, Viet-Nam.

NGUYEN HUU THO; Vietnamese politician; b. 10 July 1910, Cholon; participated in liberation war against French colonialists; organized mass demonstration, Saigon-Cholon area March 1950 against U.S. interference; imprisoned 1950–52; campaigned for the implementation of the 1954 Geneva agreements on Indo-China; founded Saigon-Cholon Peace Movement; subsequently arrested, escaped 1961; Chair. Nat. Liberation Front Cen. Cttee. 1962–; Chair. Presidium of NLF Cen. Cttee. 1964–; Chair. Consultative Council, Provisional Revolutionary Govt. of Repub. of S. Viet-Nam 1969–76 (in Saigon 1975–76); Vice-Pres. Socialist Repub. of Viet-Nam 1976–80, Acting Pres. 1980–81, Vice-Pres. Council of State 1981–84, 1986–; Chair. Standing Cttee., Nat. Ass. 1981–; Order of Friendship among Nations (U.S.S.R.) 1980, Order of Friendship of the People (U.S.S.R.) 1980; Lenin Peace Prize 1985. *Address:* c/o Office of the President, Hanoi, Viet-Nam.

NGUYEN KHANH, Lieut.-Gen.; Vietnamese army officer and politician; b. 1927; ed. Viet-Nam Mil. Acad., Dalat, Army Staff Schools, Hanoi and France, and U.S. Command and Gen. Staff Coll., Fort Leavenworth; French Colonial Army 1954, Vietnamese Army 1954; Chief of Staff to Gen. Duong Van Minh 1955; took part in coup against Pres. Diem Nov. 1963; Prime Minister Jan.-Oct. 1964; Chair. Armed Forces Council 1964–65; led coup Jan. 1965; Roving Amb. 1965; mem. Secr. CP of Vietnam; Vice-Premier State Council Feb. 1987–; Minister, Gen. Sec. Council of Ministers Feb. 1987–. *Address:* 1 Hoang Van Thu, Hanoi, Vietnam.

NGUYEN PHU DUC, LL.D., DR.JUR.; Vietnamese diplomatist; b. 13 Nov. 1924, Son-Tay; m.; two s.; ed. Univ. of Hanoi, Harvard Law School; Perm. Observer to UN 1964–65; Special Asst. for Foreign Affairs to Pres. Thieu 1968; Envoy to Thailand, Khmer Repub., Laos, Indonesia, U.S.A. 1972; Minister of Foreign Affairs 1973; Amb. to Belgium 1974–75; has attended confs. on Viet-Nam 1966, 1967, 1968, 1969, 1973, active in negotiations leading to Paris Conf. 1968, and to Paris Agreement 1973.

NGUYEN THI BINH, Madame; Vietnamese politician; b. 1927; ed. Saigon; student political leader in Saigon; organized (with Nguyen Huu Tho, q.v.) first anti-American demonstration 1950; imprisoned by French authorities 1951–54; Vice-Pres. S. Vietnamese Cttee. for Solidarity with the American People; Vice-Pres. Union of Women for the Liberation of S. Viet-Nam; mem. Cen. Cttee. Nat. Liberation Front (NLF); appointed NLF spokesman to four-party peace talks, Paris Nov. 1968; Minister for Foreign Affairs, Provisional Revolutionary Govt. of S. Viet-Nam 1969–76 (in Saigon 1975–76); Minister of Educ., Socialist Repub. of Viet-Nam 1976–87; Vice-Pres. Vietnamese Women's Union, Hanoi 1976; Vice-Pres. OSPAA. *Address:* c/o Ministry of Education, 21 Le Thanh Tong, Hanoi, Viet-Nam.

NGUYEN VAN LINH; Vietnamese politician; b. 1913, North Viet-Nam; mem. Cen. Cttee. of Lao Dong Party for many years; fmr. Sec. Saigon (now Ho Chi Minh City) Cttee. of Lao Dong Party, second in command to Pham Hung (q.v.); now a party leader in Ho Chi Minh City; mem. Secr. and Politburo, CP of Viet-Nam 1976–81, 1985–, Perm. Sec. to Cen. Cttee. 1985–86, Sec.-Gen. CP of Vietnam Dec. 1986–; Pres. Viet-Nam Gen. Fed. of Trade Unions 1978–80. *Address:* Ho Chi Minh City Committee of the Communist Party of Viet-Nam, Ho Chi Minh City, Viet-Nam.

NGUYEN VAN LOC, LL.M.; Vietnamese lawyer, writer and politician; b. 24 Aug. 1922, Vinh-Long; s. of Nguyen Van Hanh and Tran Thi Ngo; m. Nguyen Thi Mong Hoa; two s.; ed. Univs. of Montpellier and Paris; Lawyer, Saigon Court of Appeal 1955; Lecturer, Nat. Inst. of Admin. 1965; Chair. People and Armed Forces Council 1966, People and Armed Forces Council Political Cttee. 1966; Vice-Chair. Constituent Assembly Electoral Law Preparation Cttee.; mem. Barristers Fraternity 1961–67; Del. in charge of campaigning, Cttee. for Aid to War Victims (Viet-Nam Red Cross); Counsellor, Viet-Nam Asscn. for Protection of Human and People's Rights; Sec.-Gen., Inter-Schools Asscn. 1965–67; Prime Minister of Repub. of Viet-Nam 1967–68; Prof. Univ. of Hóa-Hao 1970; Founder and Rector, Cao-Dai Univ. 1971–75; escaped to Singapore 1983. *Publications:* Uprising (novel) 1946, Rank 1948, New Recruits (novel) 1948, Poems on Liberation (collection) 1949, Recollections of the Green Years 1960, Free Tribune (collection) 1966, Poisonous Water (novel) 1971.

NGUYEN VAN THIEU, Lt.-Gen.; Vietnamese army officer and politician; b. 5 April 1923, Ninh Thlian; m. Nguyen Thi Mai Anh 1951; two s. one d.; ed. Catholic Pellerin School, Hué, and Nat. Mil. Acad., Hué; Viet-Nam Nat. Army 1948–54; Repub. of Viet-Nam Army 1954–75; Commdr. First Infantry Div. 1960–62, Fifth Infantry Div. 1962–63; Commdr. IV Corps and Armed Forces Chief of Staff 1963–64; Deputy Premier and Minister of Defence 1964–65; Chair. Nat. Leadership Cttee. and Head of State 1965–67; Pres. of Repub. of Viet-Nam 1967–75; f. Dan Chu Party 1973; went to Taiwan April 1975 and later to the U.K.; lives in Surrey.

NGUYEN VAN VY, Lt.-Gen.; Vietnamese politician; b. 16 Jan, 1916, Hanoi; ed. Univ., Tong Officers' School and School of Command and Staff, Paris; Chief Mil. Cabinet of Chief of State 1952; Commdr. Coastal Interzone 1954; Acting Chief, Gen. Staff, Vietnamese Army Oct. 1954; Insp. Gen. Dec. 1954; Asst. Chief of Staff for Training, R.V.N.A.F. Jan. 1964; Asst. to C.-in-C. Nov. 1964; Commdt. Quang Trung Training Centre Feb. 1965; Commdr. Training Command, R.V.N.A.F. June 1966; C.-of-S. Jt. Gen. Staff R.V.N.A.F. 1966-67; Minister of Defence 1968-72; Grand Officer Nat. Order of Viet-Nam; Army and Air Force Distinguished Service Orders; Officier, Légion d'honneur.

NGUZA KARL-I-BOND; Zairian diplomatist and politician; b. 1938, Musumba; m. N'Landu Kavidi; ed. Catholic schools, Elisabethville (now Lubumbashi), and Univ. of Louvain, Belgium; Announcer, Radio Lubumbashi 1957-60, Radio Kinshasa 1964; mem. of Prime Minister Tshombe's private cabinet 1964; Counsellor, Congolese Embassy, Brussels 1964-66; Govt. Commr. Union Minière 1965-66; Counsellor, Congolese Del. to UN, New York 1966-68; Deputy Perm. Rep. to UN 1968; Minister, later Amb., and Perm. Rep. at UN Office, Geneva 1970-72; State Commr. for Foreign Affairs 1972-74, 1976-77, 1979-80; First State Commr. 1980-81; mem. Political Bureau of the Mouvement populaire de la révolution 1972-77, 1979-81, Nat. Security Council 1979-81, Dir. 1974-77; Vice-Pres. Exec. Council, presiding over Political, Econ. and Finance Comm. Feb.-Aug. 1977; arrested Aug. 1977; accused of treason and sentenced to death, sentence commuted to life imprisonment Sept. 1977, reinstated March 1979; resgnd. posts while in Brussels April 1981; in exile 1982; returned to Zaire 1985; Amb. to U.S.A. 1986-88; State Commr. for Foreign Affairs and Int. Co-operation March 1988-. *Publications:* Mobutu ou l'Incarnation du Mal Zaïrois, Le Zaire de Demain 1984, Un Avenir pour le Zaire 1985. *Address:* Department of Foreign Affairs and International Co-operation, B.P. 7100, Kinshasa-Gombe, Zaire.

NHONGO MUGARI, Joice Teurai Ropa; Zimbabwean politician; b. 5 Feb. 1955, Mount Darwin; m. Rex Solomon Nhongo 1977; three d.; Minister of Youth, Sport and Recreation April-Dec. 1980, of Community Devt. and Women's Affairs Dec. 1980-. *Leisure interests:* political addresses, church services, women's meetings, knitting, sewing. *Address:* 7735 Causeway, Harare, Zimbabwe.

NHU, Madame (see Ngo Dinh Nhu, Madame).

NI CHIH-FU (see Ni Zhifu).

NI ZHENGYU, D.JUR.; Chinese international jurist; b. 28 July 1906, Wujiang, Jiangsu Province; m. Zhang Fengzhen 1930; one d.; ed. Dongwu Univ., Shanghai, Stanford Univ., Johns Hopkins Univ., U.S.A.; mem. Shanghai Bar Asscn. 1931-; Prosecutor, Int. Mil. Tribunal for the Far East 1946-48; attended many int. confs. as legal consultant to govt. del. of People's Repub. of China; legal adviser to Chinese Foreign Ministry; mem. UN Int. Law Comm. 1981-; Judge, Int. Court of Justice Feb. 1985-; Assoc. mem. l'Institut de Droit 1987-; LL.D. h.c. *Publications:* The Question of Judicial Jurisdiction in International Law, The Judicial Systems in the United States and the United Kingdom, The Theory and Practice Concerning Jurisdictional Immunities of States. *Address:* The International Court of Justice, Peace Palace, 2517 KJ The Hague, Netherlands.

NI ZHIFU; Chinese party official; b. 1933, Shanghai; errand boy for a Japanese oil company 1944; ed. elementary school 1945-48; apprentice, a Shanghai printing machine factory 1948; joined trades union 1950; mechanic, Yongding Machine Tool Factory 1953; joined CCP 1958; promoted engineer 1962; active participation in the criticism movt. during the Cultural Revolution; mem. 9th Cen. Cttee. CCP 1969; Chair. Municipal Trade Union Council, Beijing 1973; Second Sec. CCP Cttee., Beijing 1973-76; alt. mem. Politburo, 10th Cen. Cttee. CCP 1973; Vice-Chair. Municipal Revolutionary Cttee., Beijing 1974-78; Second Sec. CCP Cttee., Shanghai 1976-78; First Vice-Chair. Municipal Revolutionary Cttee., Shanghai 1976-78; mem. Politburo, 11th Cen. Cttee. CCP 1977; Second Sec. CCP Cttee., Beijing 1979; Deputy for Beijing, 5th NPC 1978; Pres. All-China Fed. of Trade Unions 1978-; mem. Politburo 12th Cen. Cttee. CCP 1982-87; Sec. Tianjin Municipal Cttee. of CCP 1984-87; mem. Presidium, 6th NPC 1986-; *Address:* 10 Fuxingmenwai Street, Beijing, People's Republic of China.

NIARCHOS, Stavros Spyros, LL.D.; Greek shipowner; b. 3 July 1909; m. 1st Melpomene Capparis 1939 (dissolved 1947); m. 2nd Eugenie Livanos 1947; three s. one d.; m. 3rd Charlotte Ford 1965 (dissolved 1967); one d.; m. 4th Mrs Athina Livanos 1971 (died 1974); ed. Athens Univ; joined family grain and shipping business; started ind. shipping concern 1939; served in R.H.N.V.R. 1941-45; Hon. Naval Attaché, Greek Legation, Washington 1944-48; returned to shipping business; pioneered supertankers; head of Niarchos group of cos.; Grand Cross, Order of the Phoenix, Commdr. of Order of George I, Commdr. Order of St. George and St. Constantine. *Address:* c/o Niarchos (London) Ltd., 41-43 Park Street, London, W.1, England.

NIARE, Seydou, B.L., B.ECONS.; Mali diplomatist; b. 22 Dec. 1933, Bamako; m.; six c.; Chief W. European and N. American Section Gen. Office for Int. Co-operation, Ministry of Foreign Affairs 1971-74; Co-ordinator of Rural Devt. Operations Ministry of Agric. 1974-79; Tech. Adviser to Ministry in Charge of State Cos. and Enterprises 1979-82, to Office of

Pres. 1982-84; Perm. Rep. to UN, New York 1984-88. *Address:* c/o Ministry of Foreign Affairs, Koulouba, Bamako, Mali.

NIASSE, Cheikh Moustapha; Senegalese politician; b. 4 Nov. 1939; ed. Lycée Faidherbe, Saint Louis, Univs. of Dakar and Paris, Nat. School of Admin., Dakar; Dir. for Information and Press Affairs, Ministry of Information 1968-69; Dir. de Cabinet at Presidency 1970-78; Minister of Town Planning, Housing and Environment March-Sept. 1978, of Foreign Affairs 1978-84; Minister of Foreign Affairs of the Confed. of Senegambia 1982-84; Political Sec. Union Progressiste Sénégalaise until 1984. *Address:* c/o Ministère des Affaires Etrangères, Place de l'Indépendance, Dakar, Senegal.

NIAZI, Maulana Kausar; Pakistani journalist and politician; b. 21 April 1934; ed. Punjab Univ; fmr. Ed. Tasneem (daily), Lahore and later Kausar, Lahore; f. Shahab (weekly) 1960; Information Sec. Pakistan People's Party 1970-78, Chair. breakaway Progressive People's Party 1978-; political imprisonment 1970; elected mem. Nat. Assembly while in prison 1970; Adviser to Pres. for Information and Religious Affairs 1971; Minister of Information and Broadcasting, Auqaf and Haj 1972-74, of Religious Affairs 1974-77, of Minority Affairs Overseas 1976-77; detained July 1977; mem. Senate March 1985-. *Publications:* several books on religious, historical and literary topics. *Address:* House 2, Street 59, F/7/4, Islam Ahad, Pakistan.

NICHOLAS, David, C.B.E.; British editor and television executive; b. 25 Jan. 1930, Tregaron; m. Juliet Nicholas (née Davies) 1952; one s. one d.; ed. Neath Grammar School, Univ. Coll. of Wales; Nat. Service 1951-53; journalist with Yorkshire Post, Daily Telegraph, Observer; joined ITN 1960, Deputy Ed. Ind. Television News 1963, Ed. and Chief Exec. 1977-, Chair. Jan. 1989-. *Leisure interests:* walking, sailing. *Address:* ITN, ITN House, 48 Wells Street, London, W1P 4DE, England. *Telephone:* 01-637-2424.

NICHOLAS, Herbert George, M.A., F.B.A., F.R.HIST.S.; British university teacher; b. 8 June 1911, Treharris; s. of Rev. W. D. Nicholas; ed. Mill Hill School, New Coll. Oxford and Yale Univ., U.S.A.; Lecturer, Exeter Coll. Oxford 1935-46, Fellow 1946-51; American Div., Ministry of Information, London and British Embassy, Washington, U.S.A. 1941-46; Faculty Fellow, Nuffield Coll. Oxford 1948-57; Fellow New Coll. Oxford 1951- (Hon. Fellow 1980-); Nuffield Reader in the Comparative Study of Insts. 1956-68; Rhodes Prof. of American History and Insts. 1969-78, Emer. 1978-; Hon. D.C.L. (Pittsburgh). *Publications:* The American Union 1948, The British General Election of 1950 1957, The United Nations as a Political Institution 1959, Tocqueville's Democratie en Amérique (Ed.) 1961, Britain and the U.S.A. 1963, The United States and Britain 1975, The Nature of American Politics 1980, Washington Despatches 1981. *Leisure interests:* gardening, music. *Address:* New College, Oxford, OX1 3BN; 3 William Orchard Close, Old Headington, Oxford, OX3 9DR, England (Home).

NICHOLAS, Sir Herbert Richard (Harry), Kt., O.B.E.; British political party executive; b. 13 March 1905, Bristol; s. of Richard Henry and Rosina Nicholas; m. Rosina Grace Brown 1932; ed. elementary school, Avonmouth, Bristol, and evening classes and correspondence courses; Clerk, Port of Bristol Authority 1919-36; District Officer, Transport and Gen. Workers' Union, Gloucester 1936-38, Regional Officer, Bristol 1938-40, Nat. Officer, London (Commercial Road Transport Group) 1940-42; Chemical Section, T.G.W.U. 1942-44, Metal and Eng. Group 1944-56, Asst. Gen. Sec. 1956-68 (Acting Gen. Sec. 1964-66); mem. Nat. Exec. Cttee., Labour Party 1956-64, 1967-68; mem. TUC Gen. Council 1964-66; Treas., Labour Party 1960-64; Gen. Sec. Labour Party 1968-72. *Leisure interests:* rugby football, fishing, reading, gardening. *Address:* 33 Madeira Road, Streatham, London, S.W.16, England.

NICHOLAS, (John Keiran) Barry (Moylan), M.A.; British academic lawyer; b. 6 July 1919, London; m. Hildegart Cloos 1948; one s. one d.; ed. Downside School and Brasenose Coll., Oxford; war service in Royal Signals (Major) 1939-45; Fellow Brasenose Coll., Oxford 1947-78, Tutor 1947-71, Prin. 1978-89; All Souls Reader in Roman Law, Oxford 1949-71, Prof. of Comparative Law 1971-78; Visiting Prof. Tulane Univ. 1960, Rome Univ. 1964, Fordham Univ. 1968, 1985; called to the Bar, Inner Temple 1950; Hon. Bencher of Inner Temple; Hon. Dr. (Paris V). *Publications:* Introduction to Roman Law 1962, Jolowicz's Historical Introduction to Roman Law (third edn.) 1972, The French Law of Contract 1982. *Address:* Brasenose College, Oxford, OX1 4AJ, England. *Telephone:* (0865) 277830.

NICHOLAS, Sir John William, K.C.V.O., C.M.G., B.A.; British diplomatist (retd.); b. 13 Dec. 1924, Worcester; m. Rita Jones 1947; two s.; ed. Birmingham Univ.; served in 7th Rajput Regt., Indian Army 1944-47; War Office 1949-57; Commonwealth Relations Office (now part of FCO) 1957-; First Sec. British High Comm., Malaysia 1957-61; Econ. Div., Commonwealth Relations Office 1961-63; Deputy High Commr., Malawi 1964-66, Sri Lanka 1970-71, Calcutta 1974-76; Diplomatic Service Insp. 1967-69; Dir. Establishments and Finance Div., Commonwealth Secr. 1971-73; Head of Pacific Dependent Territories Office, FCO 1973-74; Deputy High Commr., Calcutta 1974-76; Consul-Gen., Melbourne 1976-79; British High Commr. in Sri Lanka and to Maldives 1979-84. *Address:* Constant Spring, Whitmore Vale Road, Hindhead, Surrey, England.

NICHOLS, Mike; American entertainer, stage and film director; b. Michael Igor Peschowsky 6 Nov. 1931, Berlin, Germany (family name changed 1939); s. of Igor Nikolaievich Peschowsky and Brigitte Landauer; m. 1st Patricia Scott 1957 (divorced); m. 2nd Margot Callas 1974 (divorced); one d.; ed. private schools and Univ. of Chicago; started Playwrights Theatre Club, Chicago which became the Compass Players and later Second City; formed improvised nightclub double-act with Elaine May, touring for two years and recording television programmes and record albums; appeared in An Evening with Mike Nichols and Elaine May New York 1961-62; acted in Shaw's St. Joan and directed The Importance of Being Earnest, Vancouver. *Directed shows:* Barefoot in the Park, New York 1963, The Knack 1964, Luv 1964, The Odd Couple 1965, The Apple Tree 1966, The Little Foxes 1967, Plaza Suite 1968. *Directed films:* Who's Afraid of Virginia Woolf? 1966, The Graduate 1967, Catch-22 1969, Carnal Knowledge 1971, Prisoner of Second Avenue 1971, Day of the Dolphin 1973, The Fortune 1975, Streamers 1976, Gilda Live 1980, Silkwood 1983, Heartburn 1985, Biloxi Blues 1987, Working Girl 1988. *Directed plays:* Streamers 1976, Comedians 1976, The Gin Game 1978, Billy Bishop Goes to War, Lunch Hour 1980, Fools 1981, The Real Thing 1984, Hurlyburly 1984, Waiting for Godot 1988; producer Annie (New York) 1977; Antoinette Perry (Tony) awards for direction Barefoot in the Park, Luv, The Odd Couple, Plaza Suite, The Real Thing; Oscar for The Graduate; Emmy award for television programme Julie and Carol at Carnegie Hall; Nat Asscn. Theatre Owner's Achievement Award for direction for Who's Afraid of Virginia Woolf? *Leisure interest:* Arabian horse breeding. *Address:* c/o Sam Cohn International Creative Management, 40 W. 57th Street, New York, N.Y. 10019, U.S.A.

NICHOLS, Rt. Rev. Mgr. Vincent Gerard, S.T.L., PH.L., M.A., M.ED.; British ecclesiastic; b. 8 Nov. 1945, Crosby; s. of Henry Joseph Nichols and Mary Russell; ed. St. Mary's Coll., Crosby, Gregorian Univ., Rome, Manchester Univ. and Loyola Univ., Chicago; Chaplain St. John Rigby VI Form Coll., Wigan 1972-77; Priest in inner city of Liverpool 1978-81; Dir. Upholland Northern Inst., Lancs. 1981-84; Gen. Sec. Catholic Bishops' Conf. of England and Wales 1984-; Advisor to Cardinal Hume (q.v.) and Archbishop Worlock (q.v.) at the Int. Synods of Bishops 1980, 1983, 1985, 1987. *Address:* Bishops' Conference, 39 Eccleston Square, London, SW1V 1PD, England. *Telephone:* 01-630 8220.

NICHOLSON, Sir Bryan Hubert, Kt., M.A., F.R.S.A., C.B.I.M.; British business executive; b. 6 June 1932; s. of late Reginald H. Nicholson and Clara Nicholson; m. Mary E. Harrison 1956; one s. one d. (and one s. deceased); ed. Palmers School, Grays, and Oriel Coll. Oxford; Man. trainee, Unilever 1955-58; Dist. Man. Van den Berghs 1958-59; Sales Man. Three Hands/Jeyes Group 1960-64; joined Sperry Rand 1964, Sales Dir. U.K. Remington Div. 1964-66, Gen. Man. Australia, Remington Div. 1966-69, Man. Dir. U.K. and France, Remington Div. 1969-72; Dir. Operations, Rank Xerox (U.K.) 1972-76, Dir. Overseas Subsidiaries 1976, Exec. Dir. 1976-84, Chair. Rank Xerox (U.K.) and Rank Xerox G.m.b.H. 1979-84; Chair. Manpower Services Comm. 1984-87; Chair. The Post Office 1987-; Chair. Council for Nat. Academic Awards 1988-; mem. Nat. Econ. Devt. Council 1985-. *Leisure interests:* tennis, bridge, political history. *Address:* Point Piper, Lilley Drive, Kingswood, Surrey, KT20 6JA, England.

NICHOLSON, Jack; American actor and film maker; b. 22 April 1937, Neptune, N.J.; s. of John and Ethel May Nicholson; m. Sandra Knight 1961 (divorced 1966); one d. *Films include:* Cry-Baby Killer 1958, Studs Lonigan 1960, The Shooting (produced and acted), Ride the Whirlwind (wrote, produced and acted), Hell's Angels on Wheels 1967, The Trip (wrote screenplay) 1967, Head (co-scripted, co-produced) 1968, Psych-Out 1968, Easy Rider 1969 (Acad. Award for Best Supporting Actor), On a Clear Day You Can See Forever 1970, Five Easy Pieces 1971, Drive, He Said (directed) 1971, Carnal Knowledge 1971, The King of Marvin Gardens 1972, The Last Detail 1973, Chinatown 1974, The Passenger 1974, Tommy 1974, The Fortune 1975, The Missouri Breaks 1975, One Flew over the Cuckoo's Nest 1975 (Acad. Award for Best Actor 1976), The Last Tycoon 1976, Goin' South (actor, dir.) 1978, The Shining 1980, The Postman Always Rings Twice 1981, Reds 1981, The Border 1982, Terms of Endearment 1984 (Acad. Award for Best Supporting Actor), Prizzi's Honor 1984, Heartburn 1985, The Witches of Eastwick 1986, Ironweed 1987, Batman 1989, The Two Jakes 1989. *Address:* c/o Sandy Bresler Kelly and Assocs., 15760 Ventura Boulevard, Suite 1730 Encino, Beverly Hills, Calif. 91436, U.S.A.

NICHOLSON, Sir John (Norris), Bt., K.B.E., C.I.E., J.P.; British shipping executive (retd.); b. 19 Feb. 1911; s. of late Capt. George Crosfield Norris Nicholson and of Evelyn Izme Murray; m. Vittoria Vivien Trewhella 1938; two s. two d.; ed. Winchester Coll. and Trinity Coll., Cambridge; Capt. 4th Cheshires (T.A.) 1939-41; Ministry of War Transport, India and S.E. Asia 1942-46; Chair. Liverpool Port Employers' Asscn. 1957-61, Martins Bank Ltd. 1962-64 (Deputy Chair. 1959-62), Cttee. of European Nat. Shipowners' Asscns., Man. Cttee. H.M.S. Conway 1958-65, Ocean Steam Ship Co. Ltd. 1957-71; fmr. Dir. Barclays Bank Ltd., Royal Insurance Co. Ltd.; Dir. Ocean Steam Ship Co. Ltd., Martins Bank Ltd.; mem. Shipping Advisory Panel 1962-64; Pres. U.K. Chamber of Shipping 1970-71; Keeper of the Rolls, Isle of Wight 1974-86; Lord-Lieut. 1980-86; Chair. Isle of Wight Devt. Bd. 1986-88; mem. Econ. and Social Cttee., EEC 1973-74. *Address:* Mottistone Manor, Isle of Wight, England. *Telephone:* (0983) 740 322.

NICHOLSON, Sir Robin Buchanan, Kt., PH.D., F.ENG., F.R.S.; British metallurgist; b. 12 Aug. 1934, Sutton Coldfield; s. of Carroll and Nancy Nicholson; m. Elizabeth Mary Caffyn 1958; one s. two d.; ed. Oundle School and St. Catharine's Coll., Cambridge; Demonstrator in Metallurgy, Univ of Cambridge 1960-64, lecturer 1964-66, Fellow of Christ's Coll. 1962-66; Prof. of Metallurgy, Univ. of Manchester 1966-72; Dir. of Research Lab., Inco Europe Ltd. 1972-76, Dir. 1975-81, Man. Dir. 1976-81; Co.-Chair. Biogen N.V. 1979-81; Chief Scientist, Cen. Policy Review Staff 1981-83; Chief Scientific Adviser, Cabinet Office 1983-86; Chief. Exec., Chair. Electro-Optical Div., Pilkington PLC 1986-, Dir. Pilkington PLC 1986-; Dir. Rolls-Royce 1986-, BP PLC 1987-; Chair. Centre for Exploitation of Science and Tech. 1987-; mem. Council, Royal Soc. 1985-; Hon. D.Sc. (Cranfield, Aston) 1983, (Manchester) 1985, Hon. D.Met. (Sheffield) 1984, Hon. D.Eng. (Birmingham) 1986; Rosenhain Medal, Inst. of Metals 1971; Platinum Medal, Metals Soc. 1981. *Publications:* Precipitation Hardening (with A. Kelly) 1962, Electron Microscopy of Thin Crystals (with Sir P. Hirsch and others) 1965, Strengthening Methods in Crystals (ed. and contributor with A. Kelly) 1971. *Leisure interests:* family life, gardening, music. *Address:* Central Policy Review Staff, Cabinet Office, 70 Whitehall, London, SW1A 2AS; Whittington House, 8 Fisherwick Road, Whittington, nr. Lichfield, Staffs., WS14 9LH, England. *Telephone:* (0543) 432081.

NICKEL, Herman W., J.D.; American journalist and diplomatist; b. 23 Oct. 1928, Berlin; s. of the late Walter and Wilhelmine Nickel; m. Phyllis Fritchey 1958; one s.; ed. Arndt Gymnasium, Berlin, Union Coll., Schenectady, N.Y. and Syracuse Univ. Coll. of Law; political reporter, U.S. High Comm., Berlin 1951-53; Head of Research Unit, Foreign Policy Asscn., New York 1956-58; joined Time Inc. as corresp. in Washington, D.C. 1958, London corresp. 1958-61, Africa corresp., Johannesburg 1961-62, Bureau Chief, Bonn 1962-69, diplomatic corresp., Washington, D.C. 1969-71, Bureau Chief, Tokyo 1971-74, Bureau Chief, London 1974-77; mem. Bd. of Eds. Fortune Magazine, Washington, D.C. 1978-81; Amb. to South Africa 1982-86; Diplomat-in-Residence, Johns Hopkins Foreign Policy Inst., Washington, D.C. 1986-. *Publications:* numerous articles in Time, Life and Fortune. *Leisure interests:* art collecting, skiing. *Address:* 1619 Massachusetts Avenue, N.W., Washington, D.C. 20036, U.S.A. *Telephone:* (202) 663-5885.

NICKERSON, Albert Lindsay, B.SC.; American business executive; b. 17 Jan. 1911, Dedham, Mass.; s. of Albert L. Nickerson and Christine Atkinson; m. Elizabeth Perkins 1936; one s. three d.; ed. Harvard Univ.; began as service station attendant, Socony Mobil Oil Co. Inc. 1933; elected to Bd. of Dirs. Mobil Oil Co. Ltd., London 1945, Chair. 1946; Dir. Socony Mobil Oil Co. Inc. (now called Mobil Oil Corpn.) 1946-75, Vice-Pres., Dir. 1951, Pres. 1955, Chair. Exec. Cttee. and Chief Exec. Officer 1958-69, Chair. of the Bd. 1961-69; Dir. and Treas. American Petroleum Inst. 1965-66, Treas. 1966-68; Dir. Fed. Reserve Bank of New York 1961-66, Chair. of Bd. 1969-71; Trustee, Rockefeller Univ. 1957-86, Boston Symphony Orchestra 1974-85, Brigham and Women's Hospital, Boston 1977-; Fellow of Harvard Coll. 1965-75, Overseer of Univ. 1959-65; Chair. Balance of Payments Advisory Cttee. of U.S. Dept. of Commerce; Chair. The Business Council 1966-68; Dir. Metropolitan Life Insurance Co. 1965-81, Raytheon Co., Federal Street Fund Inc., State Street Investment Corpn, Harvard Man. Co. 1975-84, State Street Exchange Fund; mem. Corpn. Woods Hole Oceanographic Inst., The Business Council; Hon. LL.D. *Address:* 150 East 42nd Street, New York, N.Y. 10017 (Office); 3 Lexington Road (Box 346), Lincoln, Mass. 01773, U.S.A. (Home).

NICKLAUS, Jack William; American golfer; b. 21 Jan. 1940, Columbus, Ohio; s. of L. Charles Nicklaus and Helen (Schoener) Nicklaus; m. Barbara Bash 1960; four s. one d.; ed. Ohio State Univ.; professional golfer 1961-; won U.S. Amateur Championship 1959, 1961; U.S. Open Championship 1962, 1967, 1972, 1980, U.S. Masters 1963, 1965, 1966, 1972, 1975, 1986, U.S. P.G.A. Championship 1963, 1971, 1973, 1975, 1980, British Open Championship 1966, 1970, 1978; by 1980 had won more major titles (17 as professional, 2 as amateur) than any other player; Australian Open Champion six times, World Series winner five times, record three times individual winner World Cup, six times on winning team; rep. U.S.A. six Ryder Cup matches; 87 tournament wins total; 69 wins in U.S.A., 51 times second, 33 times third; total earnings over $3.5m.; has also designed golf courses in the U.S.A.; five times U.S. P.G.A. Player of the Year; U.S. Sportsman of the Year 1978; Athlete of the Decade Award 1970s; Hon. LL.D. (St. Andrews) 1984. *Publications:* numerous books about golf. *Address:* 11760 U.S. Highway 1, North Palm Beach, Fla. 33408, U.S.A. (Office).

NICKLES, Donald Lee; American politician and business executive; b. 6 Dec. 1948, Ponca City, Okla.; s. of Robert and Coeweene Nickles; m. Linda Morrison 1968; one s. three d.; mem. Nat. Guard 1971-76; mem. Okla. State Senate 1978-80, Republican Senator from Oklahoma, 1980-; Vice-Pres., Gen. Man. Nickles Machine Co. 1972-80; mem. Salvation Army Advisory Bd., and Dir. Ponca City Chamber of Commerce, Kay Co. Council for Retarded Children. *Address:* 713 Hart Senate Office Building, Washington, D.C. 20510 (Office); 1412 Meadowbrook, Ponca City, Okla. 74601, U.S.A. (Home).

NICKSON, Sir David Wigley, K.B.E.; British business executive; b. 27 Nov. 1929, Eton; s. of Geoffrey W. Nickson and Janet M. Nickson; m. Helen L. Cockraft 1952; three d.; ed. Eton and Royal Mil. Acad. Sandhurst; man.

trainee, Wm. Collins, Publrs. Glasgow 1954, Dir. 1961, Jt. Man. Dir. 1967, Vice-Chair. 1976, Vice-Chair. and Group Man. Dir. 1979–82, Non-exec. Dir. 1982–85; Non-exec. Dir. Scottish & Newcastle Breweries PLC 1981, Deputy Chair. 1982, Chair. 1983–; Chair. Atlantic Salmon Trust 1988–, Scottish Devt. Agency 1989–; Non-exec. Dir. Gen. Accident Fire & Life Assurance Corpn. PLC, Edinburgh Investment Trust PLC; Pres. Confed. of British Industry (CBI) 1986–88; Hon. D.L. *Leisure interests:* fishing, birdwatching, shooting, the countryside. *Address:* Scottish and Newcastle Breweries PLC, 111 Holyrood Road, Edinburgh, EH8 8YS (Office); Renagour, Aberfoyle, Stirling, FK8 3TF, Scotland (Home). *Telephone:* 031-556 2591 (Office); (08772) 275 (Home).

NICODIM, Ion; Romanian painter and engraver; b. 26 March 1932, Constanţa; ed. Nicolae Grigorescu Coll. of Fine Arts, Bucharest; mem. of the Romanian Artists' Union; exhbns. Bucharest, Cluj-Napoca, Rome, São Paulo, Cagnes-sur-Mer, Yugoslavia, Vienna, Warsaw, Prague; Prize of the Romanian Artists' Union 1964, 1977; Prize of the Romanian Acad. 1975. *Works:* frescoes, mosaics, tapestries including Praise to Man, at the UN headquarters in New York, painting, graphics, glass, furniture, design, engravings, monumental decorative designs. *Address:* Uniunea Artistilor Plastici, Str. Nicolae Iorga 42, Bucharest, Romania.

NICOL, Davidson Sylvester Hector Willoughby, C.M.G., M.D., PH.D.; Sierra Leonean diplomatist, scientist and educationist; b. 14 Sept 1924, Freetown of African parentage; m.; three s. two d.; ed. Prince of Wales School, Freetown, Cambridge Univ., London Hospital; medical and scientific research and teaching, London, Nigeria and Cambridge 1950–59; Senior Pathologist, Sierra Leone Govt. 1958–60, Hon. Consultant Pathologist 1960–; guest lecturer numerous American univs.; Principal, Fourah Bay Coll., The Univ. Coll. of Sierra Leone, Freetown 1960–68; Vice-Chancellor, Univ. Sierra Leone 1966–68; Chair. Conf. of Inter-Univ. Co-operation in W. Africa 1961, Needs and Priorities Cttee., Univ. of E. Africa 1963, Sierra Leone Nat. Library Board; attended WHO Annual Meetings 1959, 1960, UNESCO Conf. on Higher Educ. 1963, OAU Defence Comm. 1965, Commonwealth Prime Ministers Conf. 1965, 1968, 1971; Pres. Sierra Leone Nat. Red Cross Soc. 1963–65, W. African Science Assen. 1963–65; Vice-Pres. African Univs. Assen. 1965–68; Dir. Cen. Bank Sierra Leone 1963–68; Perm. Rep. to UN 1969–71, mem. Econ. and Social Council 1969–70, Security Council 1970–71 (Pres. 1970), Chair. Special Cttee. on Decolonization 1970–71; High Commr. to U.K. and Amb. to Denmark, Sweden, Finland, and Norway 1971–72; Under-Sec.-Gen. UN and Exec. Dir. UNITAR 1972–82, Hon. Sr. Fellow 1983; Pres. World Fed. of UN Assens. 1983–87, Hon. Pres. 1987; Commonwealth Lecturer (Cambridge) 1975; Chair. UN Interagency Humanitarian Mission to Angola 1976; Dir. Central Bank of Sierra Leone, Consolidated African Selection Trust Ltd. (London); Hon. Fellow, Christ's Coll., Cambridge; Fellow Royal Coll. of Pathologists, London, West African Coll. of Physicians, West African Coll. of Surgeons; Hon. D.Sc. (Newcastle upon Tyne, and Kalamazoo Coll. Mich.); Hon. LL.D. (Leeds and Univ. of West Indies); Hon. D.Litt. (Davis and Elkins Coll.); Hon. L.H.D. (Barat Coll., Illinois and Tuskegee Inst., Ala.); Margaret Wrong Prize for Literature in Africa 1952; Independence Medal (Sierra Leone); Grand Commdr. Order of Rokel (Sierra Leone); Grand Commdr. Star of Africa (Liberia); Companion of Order of St. Michael and St. George (U.K.), World Peace Gold Medal (Indian Fed. UNA). *Publications:* The Structure of Human Insulin 1960, Africa, A Subjective View 1964, African Self-Government 1865: The Dawn of Nationalism 1969, The Truly Married Woman and Other Stories (as Abioseh Nicol) 1965, New and Modern Role for the Commonwealth 1977, United Nations and Decision Making, The Role of Women 1978, Paths to Peace—the Presidency of the Security Council 1981, Regionalism and the new International Economic Order 1981, The United Nations Security Council—Towards Greater Effectiveness 1982, Creative Women in Changing Societies—A Quest for Alternatives 1983. *Leisure interests:* creative writing, travel. *Address:* c/o Christ's College, Cambridge, England. *Telephone:* (0223) 277351.

NICOL, Donald MacGillivray, PH.D., F.B.A., F.R.HIST.S.; British professor of Byzantine History; b. 4 Feb. 1923, Portsmouth; s. of George Manson Nicol and Mary Patterson (née MacGillivray); m. Joan Mary Campbell 1950; three s.; ed. King Edward VII School, Sheffield, St. Paul's School, London, Pembroke Coll. Cambridge and British School of Archaeology at Athens; Lecturer in Classics and Ancient History, Univ. Coll. Dublin 1952–64; Visiting Fellow, Dumbarton Oaks, Washington, D.C., U.S.A. 1964–65; Visiting Prof. of Byzantine History, Indiana Univ., U.S.A. 1965–66; Reader in Byzantine History, Univ. of Edin. 1966–70; Koraës Prof. of Modern Greek and Byzantine History, Language and Literature, King's Coll., Univ. of London 1970–88; Dir. Gennadius Library, Athens July 1989–; Fellow and fmr. Vice-Prin. King's Coll.; Birkbeck Lecturer, Cambridge 1976–77; Pres. Ecclesiastical History Soc. 1975–76; mem. Royal Irish Acad. *Publications:* The Despotate of Epiros 1957, Meteora: The Rock Monasteries of Thessaly 1963, The Byzantine Family of Kantakouzenos (Cantacuzenus) c. 1100–1460 1968, The Last Centuries of Byzantium 1972, Church and Society in the Last Centuries of Byzantium 1979, The Despotate of Epiros: a contribution to the history of Greece in the Middle Ages 1267–1479 1984, Studies in Late Byzantine History and Prosopography 1986, Byzantium and Venice. A Study in Diplomatic and Cultural Relations 1988. *Leisure interest:* bookbinding. *Address:* Gennadius Library, American

School of Classical Studies, Sonedias 54, GR-106 76 Athens, Greece; 16 Courtyards, Little Shelford, Cambridge, England (Home).

NICOL, Joseph Arthur Colin, D.PHIL., D.SC., F.R.S.; Canadian marine biologist; b. 5 Dec. 1915, Toronto; s. of George Nicol and Marie Noele Pitrie; m. Helen Wilhelmina Cameron 1941; one d.; ed. Montreal West High School, McGill, W. Ontario, Minnesota and Oxford Univs.; field work Quebec, Nova Scotia, Minn., Fisheries Research Bd., Canada 1938–40; rank of Capt. Canadian Army 1941–45; British Council Scholar Oxford 1945–47; Asst. Prof. Univ. of British Columbia 1947–49; Scientific Officer Marine Biological Assen. U.K. 1949–62; Guggenheim Fellow 1952; Prof. Univ. of Oregon 1966–67, Univ. of Texas 1967–81, Prof. Emer. 1982–; Fellow, Univ. of Christchurch, New Zealand 1976, Academia Sinica Taiwan 1981–82; on expedition RV Discovery II. *Publications:* Biology of Marine Animals 1968, numerous scientific articles. *Leisure interests:* gardening, natural history, literature. *Address:* Ribby, Lerryn, Lostwithiel, Cornwall, PL22 0PG, England. *Telephone:* (0208) 872319.

NICOL-COLE, Silvanus B., C.M.G., O.B.E.; Sierra Leonean banking executive; b. 8 Aug. 1920, Nigeria; s. of Joseph B. and Evelyn M. Cole (née Nicol); m. Rebecca Benjamin 1948; three d.; ed. Durham and Oxford Univs.; Part-time lecturer in Applied Econs., Fourah Bay Coll.; Asst. Sec., Deputy Perm. Sec. Ministry of Trade 1949–60; Asst. Sec. Ministry of Devt. 1960–62; Deputy Gov. Bank of Sierra Leone 1962–66, Gov. 1966–70; Alt. Gov. IMF 1966–70, Alt. Exec. Dir. 1970–72, Exec. Dir. 1972–74; Deputy Man. Dir. Barclays Bank of Sierra Leone Ltd. 1974–76, Chair. 1976–; Grand Commdr. Order of Rokel 1979. *Leisure interests:* swimming, hunting, gardening, fishing. *Address:* Barclays Bank of Sierra Leone Ltd., 25-27 Siaka Stevens Street, P.O. Box 12, Freetown, Sierra Leone.

NICOLAIDES, Maj.-Gen. Cristino; Argentine army officer; b. 2 Jan. 1925; ed. Mil. Acad.; Second Lieut., Corps of Engineers, Mil. Acad. 1947; Capt. 1954; Staff Officer army high command; Col. 1970; Dir. School for Combat Services 1974; Brig.-Gen. 1975; led mil. campaign against leftist guerrillas, Córdoba; Commdr. 1st Army Corps 1981–82; C.-in-C of the Army and mem. mil. junta 1982–83.

NICOLAZZI, Franco; Italian politician and teacher; b. 10 April 1924, Gattico, Novara; active in Resistance; fmr. Prov. Sec. Italian Social Democrat Party, Novara; fmr. mem. party Cen. Cttee., then of unified Italian Social Democrat and Italian Socialist parties; elected Mayor of Gattico, then Vice-Chair. Novara Prov. Authority 1956; M.P. for Turin-Novara-Vercelli 1963–; mem. Nat. Exec. Social Democrat party since split from Socialist Party 1969; fmr. Under-Sec. of State, Ministry of Interior; fmr. Minister of Industry, Trade and Crafts; Minister of Public Works 1979–87; Sec. Social Democrat Party 1987–88. *Address:* Camera dei Deputati, Rome, Italy.

NICOLET, Claude; French professor of Roman history; b. 15 Sept. 1930, Marseilles; s. of Edmond Nicolet and Suzanne Nicolet; m. 1st Michelle Brousset 1956 (divorced), 2nd Hélène Pierre 1963; four c.; ed. Ecole Normale Supérieure and Ecole Française de Rome; served in Cabinet of Minister of State Pierre Mendès-France 1956; Editorial Sec. Cahiers de la République 1956–57; mem. Ecole Française de Rome 1957–59; Maître de conférences, Univ. of Tunis 1959–61; Maître de conférences and Prof. Univ. of Caen 1961–69; Prof. of Roman History, Univ. of Paris/Sorbonne 1969–; Dir. of Studies, Ecole Pratique des Hautes Etudes (Section IV) 1969–; mem. Inst. for Advanced Studies, Princeton 1966–67, 1972; mem. Acad. des Inscriptions et Belles Lettres (Inst. de France); Corresp. Fellow British Acad. 1987; Chevalier, Légion d'honneur; Chevalier des Arts et des Lettres. *Publications:* ten books. *Address:* 2 rue de Paradis, 75010 Paris; L'huis, par Le Breuil, 51000 (Marne), France. *Telephone:* 47-70-02-91; 26-59-22-54.

NICOLIN, Curt René; Swedish company executive; b. 10 March 1921, Stockholm; s. of Felix and Anna-Lisa Nicolin; m. Ulla Sandén 1946; three s. two d.; ed. Royal Inst. of Tech., Stockholm; with STAL Finspong 1945–59, Vice-Pres. and Tech. Dir. 1953–55, Pres. 1955–59; Pres. Turbin AB de Laval Ljungström, Finspong 1959–61; Interim Pres. Scandinavian Airlines System (SAS) 1961–62, now Swedish Chair. SAS; Pres. ASEA AB, Västerås 1961–76, Chair. of Bd. 1976–; Chair. Swedish Employers' Fed. 1976–83; Chair. Swedish Match Co. 1985–88; Dr. Tech. h.c. 1974; Commdr., Order of Vasa, First Class 1974. *Publication:* Private Industry in a Public World 1973. *Leisure interests:* tennis, sailing. *Address:* ASEA, Box 7373, 103 91 Stockholm, Sweden. *Telephone:* 08-24-59-50.

NICOLSON, Sir David Lancaster, Kt., F.ENG.; British engineer and company executive; b. 20 Sept 1922, London; s. of Charles Tupper Nicolson and Margaret Lancaster Nicolson; m. Joan Eileen Griffiths 1945; one s. two d.; ed. Haileybury and Imperial Coll., London Univ.; Constructor-Lieut., Royal Corps of Naval Constructors 1942–45 (mentioned in despatches); Man. Consultant, Production Eng. Ltd. 1946–50, Man., later Dir. 1953–62; Production Man. Bucyrus-Erie Co., Milwaukee, U.S.A. 1950-52; Chair. P-E Consulting Group Ltd. 1963–68, BTR Ltd. 1969–84, British Airways 1971–75, Rothmans Int. PLC 1975–84, Selincourt PLC 1982–85; Dir. Delta Metal Co. Ltd. 1967–79, Bank of Montreal 1970–83, Richard Costain Ltd. 1970–78, Howden Group Ltd. 1971–72, MEPC Ltd. 1976–80, BTR Inc. 1976–81, Drayton Consolidated Trust Ltd. 1977–84, Carling O'Keefe Ltd. 1978–84; Chair. VSEL (Vickers Shipbldg. & Engineering)

1986–87, Northern Telecom PLC 1986–88, Dir. Northern Telecom Ltd., Canada 1987–; Chair. British Rail Eng. Ltd. 1986–, Union Group PLC 1987–, Farmer Stedall PLC 1982–87, Bulk Transport Ltd. 1984–, The German Securities & Investment Trust PLC 1985–, America European Community Assen. 1980–, The European Movt. 1985–; Dir. Todd Shipyards Corpn. 1976–, Confed. Life Insurance Co. 1981–88, BTR PLC 1967–84, Ciba-Geigy PLC 1978–, Guest Keen & Nettlefolds PLC 1984–, London & Scottish Marine Oil PLC 1983–, Sallingbury Casey 1987–; Dir. Dawnay Day Int. Ltd. 1988–; European Adviser to New York Stock Exchange 1985–; Pres. European Business Inst. 1984–, Britannia Arrow Holdings PLC 1987–, STC PLC 1987–; Pro-Chancellor Univ. of Surrey, mem. Council 1984–; Pres. Assen. of British Chambers of Commerce 1983–85; mem. European Parl. for London Cen. 1979–84: mem. Council, Inst. of Dirs. 1971–76, City & Guilds of London Inst. 1968–76; Gov. Imperial Coll. London Univ. 1966–77, B.I.M. 1964–69, Man. Consultants Assen. 1964, British Shipbldg. Mission to India 1957; Fellow Imperial Coll. London. *Publications:* contribs. to tech. journals, lectures and broadcasts on man. subjects in U.K., U.S.A., Australia and other countries. *Leisure interests:* sailing, collecting old books. *Address:* 3 Rembrandt Close, Graham Terrace, off Holbein Place, Sloane Square, London, SW1W 8HF (Office); Howicks, Dunsfold, Surrey, 10 Fordie House, 82 Sloane Street, London, S.W.1, England (Homes). *Telephone:* 01-823 4519 (Office); (048649) 296; 01-235 0053 (London Homes).

NICULESCU, Paul; Romanian politician; b. 25 Nov. 1923, Bucharest; ed. Acad. of Higher Commercial and Industrial Sciences, Bucharest; Prof. at Bucharest Univ., later at "Ştefan Gheorghiu" Acad. of Social and Political Sciences, Bucharest; mem. Romanian CP 1945–, Cen. Cttee. 1955–, Exec. Political Cttee. 1965– and Sec. of Cen. Cttee 1965–72; mem. Perm. Presidium of Cen. Cttee. 1966–74; mem. Standing Bureau 1978–81; Deputy to Grand Nat. Assembly 1957–; Chair. Standing Comm. for Culture and Educ. of Grand Nat. Assembly 1966–69; mem. Nat. Council of Socialist Democracy and Unity 1968–; mem. Defence Council 1969–74; Deputy Chair. Council of Ministers 1972–81, Minister of Educ. 1972–76, of Finance 1978–81; Chair. Council for the Co-ordination of Consumer Goods Production 1976–78, Cen. Union of Consumer Co-operatives 1981–; mem. Acad. of Social and Political Sciences 1970; Hero of Socialist Labour 1971. *Address:* c/o Centrocoop, Str. Brezoianu 31, Bucharest, Romania. *Telephone:* 14 48 00.

NICULESCU, Stefan; Romanian composer; b. 31 July 1927, Moreni Dîmboviţa; s. of Lazar Niculescu and Maria Niculescu; m. Colette Demetrescu 1952; ed. Academy of Music and Theatrical Art, Bucharest Coll. of Engineering, Bucharest, C. Porumbescu Conservatory of Music, Bucharest; studies in electronic music Munich 1966; researcher Inst. for Art History of the Romanian Acad., Bucharest 1960–63; prof. of Ciprian Porumbescu Conservatory, Bucharest 1963–; Guest, Deutscher Akademischer Austauschdienst, West Berlin 1971–72; Romanian Acad. Prize 1962; French Acad. Prize 1972; Prizes of the Romanian Composers' Union 1972, 1975, 1977, 1979, 1981, 1984, 1988; Festival Montreux Prize, Int. Record Critics Award 1985. *Works include:* symphonies, cantatas, chamber music; Aphorismes d'Héraclite, for mixed choir of 20 soloists 1969; Ricercare in uno, for synthesizer, clarinet and violin 1982; stage and film music. *Address:* Intr. Sublocotenent Stăniloiu 4, 73228 Bucharest, Romania (Home); Str. Constantin Esarcu 2, 70149 Bucharest (Office). *Telephone:* 424370 (Home).

NIE FENGZHI; Chinese military official; b. 1909, Shanxi; joined CCP 1934; took part in Long March 1934–35; Third sub-div. commdr. Shandong Mil. Region 1945; Supt. E. China Mil. and Admin. Acad. 1949–50; Commdr. 4th Army, E. China Air Force, Korean War 1950; commanded Chinese People's Volunteers air force battles 1952–53; Air Force Commdr. PLA E. China Mil. Region 1954; Deputy Commdr. PLA Nanjing Mil. Region 1955; Air Force Commdr. PLA Nanjing Mil. Region 1955; Air Force Commdr. Nanjing 1965–68; Deputy Commdr. PLA Nanjing Mil. Region 1975–77; Air Force commdr. PLA Nanjing Mil. Region 1975; Commdr. PLA Nanjing Mil. Region 1977–; mem. 11th Cen. Cttee. CCP 1977; Sec. CCP Cttee., PLA Nanjing Units 1979–, CCP Cen. Advisory Comm. 1987–. *Address:* People's Liberation Army Headquarters, Nanjing Military Unit, People's Republic of China.

NIE GONGCHENG; Chinese diplomatist; Amb. to Australia 1983–86; Dir. Dept. of Consular Affairs April 1988–. *Address:* Department of Consular Affairs, 225 Chaoyangmennei Street, Dongsi, Beijing, China.

NIE KUIJU; Chinese naval officer; commdr. of a unit under the South China Sea Fleet 1982; alt. mem. 12th CCP Cen. Cttee. 1982–87, mem. 13th Cen. Cttee. 1987–; Deputy Commdr. PLA Navy 1982; Commdr. E. China Sea Fleet 1985–; Deputy Commdr. Nanjing Mil. Area. Jan. 1988–. *Address:* People's Liberation Army Naval Headquarters, Beijing, People's Republic of China.

NIE RONGZHEN; Chinese politician; b. 1899, Jianglin, Sichuan; ed. Chingqing Middle School; joined CCP 1923; Sec. Political Dept., and Political Instructor Whampoa Mil. Acad., Canton 1925; Sec. Cen. Mil. Council 1926; Deputy Dir. General Political Dept., Red Army 1931; Political Commissar, First Army Corps 1932; Divisional Deputy Commdr., 8th Route Army 1937; Commdr., Shanxi-Chaha-Hebei Field Army 1937–48; Commdr., Red Shanxi-Suiyan Army 1943; mem. 7th Cen. Cttee. CCP 1945; Commdr. PLA N. China Mil. Region 1948; Commdr. Beijing-Tianjin

Garrison Force; Mayor Beijing, 1949–51; Deputy Chief of Gen. Staff, PLA 1949–54; Acting Chief of Gen. Staff, PLA 1949–54; Deputy to 1st NPC 1954; mem. Standing Cttee., 1st NPC 1954–57; Vice-Chair. Nat. Defence Council 1954–75; rank of Marshal, PLA 1955; mem. 8th Cen. Cttee. CCP 1956; Vice-Premier, State Council 1956–75; Chair. Scientific Planning Comm., State Council 1957–58; Deputy to 2nd NPC, 1958; Chair. Scientific and Tech. Comm., State Council 1958–66; Deputy to 3rd NPC 1964; Vice-Chair. CCP Mil. Comm. 1961–; mem. Politburo 8th Cen. Cttee. CCP 1967; Chair. Scientific and Technical Comm. for Nat. Defence 1968; mem. 9th Cen. Cttee. CCP 1969; mem. Cen. Cttee. CCP 1973; Deputy to 4th NPC 1975; Vice-Chair. Standing Cttee., 4th NPC 1975–78; mem. Politburo, 11th Cen. Cttee. CCP 1977; Deputy for PLA, 5th NPC 1978; Vice-Chair. Standing Cttee., 5th NPC 1978–80; mem. Constitution Revision Cttee. 1980–; mem. Politburo, 12th Cen. Cttee. CCP 1982–85; Vice-Chair. Cen. Mil. Comm. 1983–; Hon. Pres. China Inventors' Assen. 1985–; Hon. Chair. Nat. Cttee. on Ageing 1984–. *Address:* Central Military Commission, Beijing, People's Republic of China.

NIECKARZ, Stanisław, M.ECON.; Polish politician; b. 10 June 1941, Anówka; ed. Main School of Planning and Statistics, Warsaw; official, Ministry of Finance 1965–77, Dir. of Industry and Building Dept. 1973–77; Deputy Head, Econ. Planning and Analyses Dept. of Polish United Workers' Party (PZPR) Cen. Cttee. 1977–80; Deputy Chair. team of econ. advisers of Chair. of Council of Ministers 1980; Vice-Pres., First Deputy Pres. of Nat. Bank of Poland 1980–82; Minister of Finance 1982–86; mem. Presidium of Govt. 1985–86; mem. PZPR 1968–; Officer's and Kt.'s Cross of Polonia Restituta Order, Gold and Bronze Cross of Merit.

NIEH JUNG-CHEN, Marshal (see Nie Rongzhen).

NIEH K'UEI-CHU (see Nie Kuiju).

NIELSEN, Erik H., M.P., D.F.C.; Canadian politician; b. 1924, Regina; m. 1st Pamela Hall (died 1969), three c.; m. 2nd Shelley Coxford 1983; ed. Dalhousie Univ., Halifax; pilot in R.C.A.F.; called to Bar of Nova Scotia 1951; own legal practice Whitehorse, Yukon 1952; mem. House of Commons for Yukon 1957–; Minister of Public Works 1979–80, Deputy Prime Minister 1984–86, Pres. Queen's Privy Council for Canada 1984–85, Minister of Nat. Defence 1985–86; Deputy House Leader, House of Commons, House Leader; Interim leader, Progressive Conservative Party Feb.-June 1983, now Deputy Leader; mem. Canadian Bar Assen., Yukon Law Soc.; Hon. mem. Yukon Chamber of Commerce, House of Commons Protective Staff, Int. Union of Mine, Mill and Smelter Workers; Hon. Vice-Pres. Dawson City Museum and Historical Soc. *Leisure interests:* fishing, flying, hunting. *Address:* House of Commons, Ottawa, Ont. K1A 0A2, Canada.

NIELSEN, (Hans Karl) Helge; Danish politician; b. 12 Oct. 1918, Copenhagen; s. of late Johan G. and Sofie P. (née Poulson) Nielsen; m. Alice Larsen 1972; two s.; ed. primary school, Borups folk high school and workers' coll.; mem. of board, Glovers Assen. 1942–; Chair. Nordic Glovers' Union 1956–70; teacher, workers' coll. 1956–70; mem. Parl. 1960–77; Sec. to Parl. Group of Social Democratic Party 1965–71; mem. Nordic Council 1966–68; mem. Finance Cttee. 1968–70; Minister of Housing 1971–73, of Environmental Protection 1973–75, of Housing and Environmental Protection 1975–77; Man. Dir. Almennyttigt Saneringsselskab, s.m.b.a. 1977–85; mem. Bd. Dirs. Mortgage Credit Assen. 1977–, Chair. Bd. Dirs. 1983–. *Publications:* contributions to political magazines. *Leisure interest:* gardening. *Address:* Askeengen 40, 2740 Skovlunde, Denmark. *Telephone:* 02-849296.

NIELSEN, Sivert Andreas; Norwegian diplomatist; b. 24 Nov. 1916, Copenhagen; s. of Konrad Nielsen; m. Harriet Nielsen (née Eyde) 1945; one s. one d.; ed. Oslo Univ.; worked Bank of Norway 1940–41; political prisoner 1941–45; Deputy Attorney Oslo Police 1945–46; UN Secr. 1946–48; Sec. Norwegian Embassy, Washington 1948–50; Section Chief, Ministry of Defence 1950–51; Div. NATO Int. staff 1950–51; Div. Chief, Ministry of Defence 1952–55; Under-Sec. for Defence 1955–58; Permanent Del. to UN 1958–66; participated in preparatory work NATO· and ministerial confs. NATO 1949–58; rep. Advisory Cttee. to Sec.-Gen. UNEF 1958; Norwegian Rep. on UN Security Council 1963–64, Chair. or Vice-Chair. Norwegian Del. to 13th-21st Sessions of Gen. Assembly of UN; Gen. Man. Bergens Privatbank, Oslo 1966–76; Chair. Bd. Norwegian Agency for Int. Devt. 1969–75; Chair. Electrolux Norway 1979–; Dir. Finanzierungsgesellschaft Viking, Zürich, Deutsche Schiffahrtsbank, Bremen, Banque Scandinave en Suisse, Geneva 1968–76, AL-Norway and AL-Lab., U.S.A. 1976–, Fredriksstad Mek. Verksted Shipyard 1977–81. *Address:* c/o Lorentzen Chartering, Haakon VII's gt. 6, Oslo 1, Norway. *Telephone:* 41-10-10.

NIEMEYER, Gerhart, American political scientist; b. 1907; m. Lucie Lenzner 1931; four s. one d.; ed. Cambridge, Munich and Kiel Univs.; Lecturer, Law Faculty, Madrid Univ. 1933; Research Assoc., Inst. of Int. and Econ. Studies, Madrid 1934; Prof. Fed. Spanish Assens. Int. Studies 1934; Lecturer in Politics, Princeton Univ. 1937, Asst. Prof. 1940–44; Visiting Lecturer, Yale Univ. 1942; Prof. of Political Science, Oglethorpe Univ. 1944–50; Assoc. Prof. Yale Univ. Summer 1946; Visiting Prof. Columbia Univ. Summer 1952; U.S. Dept. of State 1950–53; Council on Foreign Relations 1953–55; Yale Univ. 1954–55; Univ. of Notre-Dame 1955–76, The Nat. War Coll. 1958–59; Fulbright Prof. Univ. of Munich 1962–63, Co-Dir. Inst. of Communism and Constitutional Democracy, Vanderbilt Univ. 1962-66, Foreign Policy Task Force, Republican Party 1965-68; Distinguished Visiting Prof., Hillsdale Coll. 1976-82; Special Consultant, U.S. Information Agency 1973; ordained Deacon, Episcopal Church 1973, Priest 1980 (Canon 1987); mem. bd. of Foreign Scholarships, U.S. Information Agency 1982-84, Chair. 1983. *Publications:* Einstweilige Verfügungen des Weltgerichtshofs 1932, Vom Wesen der gesellschaftlichen Sicherheit 1935, The Significance of Function in Legal Theory 1940, Law Without Force 1941, An Inquiry into Soviet Mentality 1956, Facts on Communism: 1, The Communist Ideology 1959; co-author The Second Chance 1944; Ed. Hermann Heller: Staatslehre 1934; co-editor Handbuch des Weltkommunismus 1958, Handbook on Communism 1962 (English Edn.), Hermann Heller: Gesammelte Schriften 1971, Communists in Coalition Governments 1963, Outline of Communism 1966, Deceitful Peace 1971, Between Nothingness and Paradise 1971, Aftersight and Foresight: Selected Essays 1988. *Leisure interest:* chamber music. *Address:* 806 East Angela Boulevard, South Bend, Ind. 46617, U.S.A. *Telephone:* 219-234-9949.

NIEMEYER, Oscar; Brazilian architect; b. 15 Dec. 1907, Rio de Janeiro; s. of Oscar Niemeyer Soares; m. Anita Niemeyer; one d.; ed. Escola Nacional de Belas Artes, Rio de Janeiro; in office of Lúcio Costa 1935; designed Ministry of Educ. and Health Bldg., Rio de Janeiro 1937-43, Brazilian Pavilion, New York World Fair 1939, with others designed UN bldg., New York 1947; Dir. of Architecture for new capital of Brasília and given a free hand in design of public and other bldgs. 1957-; Designer of Bienal Exhbn. Hall, São Paulo, urban area of Grasse (near Nice) 1966, French CP bldg., Paris 1966, Palace of Arches (for Foreign Ministry) Brasília; Lenin Peace Prize 1963, Prix Int. de l'Architecture d'aujourd'hui 1966, shared Pritzker Prize 1988. *Address:* 3940 avenida Atlàntica, Rio de Janeiro, RJ, Brazil.

NIEMI, Irmeli, DR.PHIL.; Finnish professor of comparative literature and drama; b. 3 Feb. 1931, Helsinki; s. of Taneli Kuusisto and Kyllikki Valtonen; m. Mikko Niemi 1953; one s. two d.; ed. Univ. of Helsinki; freelance translator, literature and theatre critic, ed. 1950-68; Jr. Research Fellow, Acad. of Finland 1968-69; Assoc. Prof. of Comparative Literature and Drama, Univ. of Turku 1970-78, Prof. 1978-81, 1984-; Sr. Teacher, Theatre Acad. Helsinki 1964-; Research Prof. Acad. of Finland 1981-84; Chair. Finnish Research Council for the Humanities 1986-88; mem. Science Policy Council of Finland 1986-. *Publications:* Maria Jotunin näytelmät 1964, Nykydraaman ihimiskuva 1969, Nykyteatterin juuret 1975, The Role of the Spectator 1984, Suomalainen alueteatteri 1978-82 1984. *Leisure interests:* modern music, forest walks, travel. *Address:* Department of Comparative Literature, Drama and Film, University of Turku, 20500 Turku (Office); Osmalahti, 21570 Sauvo, Finland (Home). *Telephone:* 358-21-645 270 (Office); 358-21-731 833 (Home).

NIEN TE-HSIANG (see Nian Dexiang).

NIER, Alfred O(tto) C(arl), M.S.E.E., PH.D.; American physicist; b. 28 May 1911; s. of August C. Nier and Anna J. Stoll; m. 1st Ruth E. Andersen 1937, 2nd Ardis L. Hovland 1969; one s. one d.; ed. Univ. of Minnesota; Nat. Research Fellow, Harvard Univ. 1936-38; Asst. Prof. Univ. of Minn. 1938-40, Assoc. Prof. 1940-44, Prof. of Physics 1944-66 (on leave for war work 1943-45), Regents' Prof. of Physics 1966-; activities include devt. of mass spectrometer and its application to problems in physics chem., etc.; first to separate rare isotope of uranium U-235, 1940; mem. N.A.S., A.A.A.S., American Geophysical Union, American Philosophical Soc., Max-Planck Inst. für Chemie, American Acad. of Arts and Sciences, Royal Swedish Acad. of Sciences. *Address:* University of Minnesota, Minneapolis, Minn. 55455; 2001 Aldine Street, St. Paul, Minn. 55113, U.S.A. *Telephone:* (612) 624-6804 (Univ.).

NIERENBERG, William Aaron, PH.D.; American physicist; b. 13 Feb. 1919, New York, N.Y.; s. of late Joseph Nierenberg and of Minnie Nierenberg (née Drucker); m. Edith Meyerson 1941; one s. one d.; ed. Townsend Harris Hall, New York, City Coll. of New York, Univ. of Paris and Columbia Univ.; Tutor, City Coll. of New York 1942; Physicist, Manhattan Project 1941-45; Instructor, Dept. of Physics, Columbia Univ. 1948; Asst. Prof. Dept. of Physics, Univ. of Mich. 1950; Asst. Prof. Univ. of Calif., Berkeley 1950-55; Hudson Labs., Dobbs Ferry, N.Y. 1951, Project Dir. 1954; Prof. Physics, Univ. of Calif., Berkeley 1955-65; Asst. Sec.-Gen. of NATO 1960-62; Prof. Associé, Univ. Paris 1960-62; Prof. Dept. of Physics, Univ. of Calif., San Diego 1965, Vice-Chancellor, Marine Sciences 1969-86, Vice-Chair./Dir. Emer. 1986-; Dir. Scripps Inst. of Oceanography, La Jolla, Calif. 1965-86; Special Consultant, Office of Science and Tech. Policy 1976-78; Adviser-at-Large, Dept. of State; mem. White House Task Force on Oceanography 1970; mem. Nat. Science Bd. 1972-78, 1982-; Chair. White House Office of Science and Tech. Policy Acid Rain Peer Review Panel June 1982-84; mem. Nat. Advisory Cttee. on Oceans and Atmosphere 1971-77, Chair. 1971-75; Chair. NASA Advisory Council 1978-81; Sr. Consultant to Pres.'s Science Adviser 1976; mem. MX Panel, Defense Dept. 1981; Pres. The Scientific Research Soc. 1981-82; Charles H. Davis Lecturer 1981; sometime consultant or adviser to various industrial corpns., govt. agencies, etc.; mem. N.A.S. (Council 1979-82), Nat. Acad. of Eng., American Acad. of Arts and Sciences, American Philosophical Soc., Joint U.S.-U.S.S.R. Cttee. for the U.S.S.R. Agreement for Co-operative Studies of the World Ocean; Nat. Research Council Fellowship, Gug-

genheim Fellowship, Fullbright Fellowship, Sloan Foundations Grant, NATO Sr. Science Fellowship, etc.; Hon. D.Sc. (Maryland) 1981; Proctor Prize, Sigma Xi, 1977; Officier, Ordre nat. du Mérite (France), Golden Dolphin Award (Asscn. Artistico Letteraria Internationale), Compass Award of the Marine Tech. Soc. 1975, NASA Distinguished Public Service Medal 1982, Delmer S. Fahrney Medal (The Franklin Inst.) 1987. *Publications:* over 130 articles in professional journals. *Leisure interests:* flying, hunting, travel. *Address:* Scripps Institution of Oceanography, University of California, La Jolla, Calif. 92038 (Office); P.O. Box 8949, La Jolla, Calif. 92038, U.S.A. (Home).

NIETO GALLO, Dr. Gratiniano; Spanish art official; b. 6 March 1917, La Aguilera, Burgos; s. of Francisco and Genoveva Nieto Gallo; m. María de Mergelina Cano-Manuel; one s. one d.; ed. Institución Teresiana, Instituto Ramiro de Maeztu and Univ. de Madrid; Prof., Univ. de Valladolid 1940-52; Dir. Colegio Mayor Santa Cruz de Valladolid 1943-52; Sec. School of Art and Archaeology, Univ. de Valladolid 1940-52; Dir. Colegio Mayor Nebrija, Univ. de Madrid 1952-56; Tech. Sec.-Gen. Directorate of Archives and Libraries 1956-61; attached to Univ. de Murcia 1959-61; Dir.-Gen. of Fine Arts 1961-68; Dir. Central Inst. for Conservation and Restoration of Works of Art 1968-; Prof. Univ. Madrid 1968-; Pres. Univ. Autónoma de Madrid 1973; decorations from Spain, Portugal, Malta, Fed. Repub. of Germany, Italy, France and Peru. *Publications:* La Necrópolis Ibérica del Cabecico del Tesoro 1940, 1944, 1947, Las tablas flamencas de la Igl. del Salvador de Valladolid 1941, Criterio de Reconstrucción de Objetos Arqueológicos 1941, El Oppidum de Iruña 1949, Guía Artistica de Valladolid 1954, Historia de los Monumentos de Lerma 1959, La cueva artificial del Bronco I de Alguazas 1959, Tendencias Actuales de la Arqueología 1959, Guía de la Exposición Conmemorativa de la Paz de los Pirineos 1963, Las Bellas Artes en España 1963, Conservación del Patrimonio Artistico 1968, Museos de Artes y Costumbres Populares 1968, Conservación de Objetos Arqueológicos 1969, Panorama de los Museos Españoles y cuestiones museológicas 1971, Reflexiones sobre la Universidad 1973. *Leisure interests:* swimming, rowing, mountaineering. *Address:* Universidad Autónoma de Madrid, Km. 15 Carretera de Colmenar Viejo, Canto Blanco, Madrid, Spain.

NIEWIADOMSKI, Józef, M.A.; Polish politician; b. 2 Jan. 1933, Łódź; m.; one s.; ed. Higher School of Social Sciences attached to Polish United Workers' Party (PZPR) Cen. Cttee., Warsaw; active leader in youth Orgs., mem. Polish Pathfinders' Union 1945-71, Rural Youth Union 1947-48, Polish Youth Union 1948-56; mem. PZPR 1951-; teacher in Weaving Industry Tech. School, Łódź 1954-55; Deputy Chair. Dist. Bd. of Polish Youth Union, Łódź-Centre 1955-56; Deputy Commdt. of Pathfinders' Org. of Łódź 1956-57; Deputy Commdt. of Łódź Troop of Polish Pathfinders' Union 1957-63, Commdt. 1968-70; Political Worker, PZPR Lodz Cttee. 1966-74; First Sec. PZPR District Cttee., Łódź-Centre 1974-77; Deputy Mayor of Łódź 1977-78; Mayor of Łódź 1978-85; alt. mem. PZPR Cen. Cttee. 1980-81; Minister of Bldg. and Spatial and Communal Economy 1985-86; First Sec. PZPR Voivodship Cttee., Łódź June 1986-; mem. PZPR Cen. Cttee. July 1986-; Commdr.'s and Knight's Cross of Order of Polonia Restituta, Gold Cross of Merit, Hon. Award of Łódź City and other decorations. *Publications:* articles on social and economic Devt. of Łódź and Łódź Voivodship. *Leisure interests:* hunting, angling, tinkering. *Address:* Komitet Łódzki PZPR, Al. Kościuszki 107/109, 90-441 Łódź, Poland. *Telephone:* 36-50-65 (Office).

NIGH, George; American politician; b. 9 June 1927, McAlester, Okla.; s. of Wilber and Irene (Crockett) Nigh; m. Donna Skinner Mashburn 1963; one s. one d.; ed. Eastern Oklahoma State Coll. and East Central Oklahoma State Univ.; teacher, History and Govt., McAlester High School; mem. Oklahoma House of Reps. 1951-59; Lieut.-Gov. of Oklahoma 1959-63, completed unexpired term as Gov. 1963; Lieut.-Gov. for three terms 1967-79, Gov. of Oklahoma 1979-87; Dir. J. C. Penney Co.; Democrat. *Leisure interests:* tennis, racketball, swimming, riding. *Address:* 621 North Robinson, Suite 500, Oklahoma City, Okla. 73105, U.S.A.

NIGHTINGALE, (William) Benedict (Herbert), B.A.; British author and theatre critic; b. 14 May 1939, London; s. of R. E. and Hon. Mrs. Nightingale (née Gardner); m. Anne B. Redmon 1964; two s. one d.; ed. Charterhouse School, Magdalene Coll., Cambridge and Univ. of Pennsylvania; general writer, The Guardian 1963-66; Literary Ed. New Society 1966-67; theatre critic, New Statesman 1968-86; Prof. of English, Theatre and Drama Univ. of Mich. 1986-; Sunday theatre critic, New York Times 1983-84. *Publications:* Charities 1972, Fifty British Plays 1982, Fifth Row Center 1986; numerous articles on cultural and theatrical matters in British and American journals. *Leisure interests:* music, literature, squash, jogging, watching soccer. *Address:* 40 Broomhouse Road, London, S.W.6, England. *Telephone:* 01-736 0158.

NIHAL SINGH, Surendra, B.A.; Indian journalist; b. 30 April 1929, Rawalpindi (now in Pakistan); s. of Gurmukh and Lachchmi Nihal Singh; m. Geertje Zuiderweg 1957; ed. Delhi Univ.; Sub-ed. The Times of India, Delhi 1951-53; Staff Reporter, Parl. Corresp., The Statesman, Calcutta 1954-61, Special Corresp. for S.E. Asia and Far East, Singapore 1962-67, Pakistan 1967, for U.S.S.R. and Eastern Europe, Moscow 1968-69, Political Corresp., Delhi 1969-71, Special Corresp., London 1971-74, Resident Ed., Delhi 1974-75, Ed. Calcutta 1975-80; Ed.-in-Chief, Indian Express 1981-82; Int. Ed. of the Year Award, Atlas World Press Service, New York 1978.

Publications: Malaysia—A Commentary 1971, From the Jhelum to the Volga 1972, Indira's India 1978, The Gang and 900 Million 1979, My India 1981. *Leisure interest:* reading, travel. *Address:* Indian Express, Bahadur Shah Zafar Marg, New Delhi 2 (Office); G-4, Maharani Bagh, New Delhi 110065, India (Home). *Telephone:* 276094 (Office); 637668 (Home).

NIILUS, Leopoldo Juan; Argentine lawyer; b. 19 Jan. 1930, Tallinn, Estonia; s. of Jaan Eduard Niilus and the late Meta Kiris; m. Malle Reet Veerus de Niilus 1961; one d.; ed. primary and secondary schools in Estonia, Faculty of Law, Univ. de Buenos Aires, Southern Methodist Univ., Dallas, Tex.; fmrly. practising lawyer, Buenos Aires; founding mem. Argentine Inst. of Science and Admin. and Inst. de Sociología Económica, Buenos Aires; fmr. mem. Exec. Cttee. and legal adviser, Iglesia Evangélica Luterana Unida (IELU) Buenos Aires; fmr. Chair. Argentine Student Christian Movement; mem. World Student Christian Fed. (WSCF) political comm.; mem. Christian Peace Conf. (CPC) working party and other orgs. dealing with socio-religious literature and research; has participated in numerous major ecumenical consultations; Dir. Argentine Dept. River Plate Centre of Christian Studies 1966–67; Gen. Sec. ISAL (Comm. for Church and Soc. in Latin America) 1968–69; Dir. Comm. of the Churches on Int. Affairs of WCC Geneva 1969–81; Dir. Middle East Council of Churches (MECC) Int. Project (Geneva) 1982–; participated in mediation for Sudan peace negotiations 1972; Order of Two Niles, 1st grade (Sudan). *Publications:* On Penal Law (essays); numerous articles and essays in ecumenical publications on peace, disarmament, North-South rels., Middle East. *Address:* MECC International Project, Ecumenical Centre, 150 route de Ferney, 1211 Geneva 20 (Office); 7 chemin Champ d'Anier, 1209 Geneva, Switzerland (Home). *Telephone:* 91-62-22 (Office); 98-32-59 (Home).

NIITAMO, Olavi Ensio, D.ECON.; Finnish economist; b. 23 Nov. 1926, Kotka; s. of Tenho Armas Niitamo and Alja Elisabet Väliaho; m. Helka Narinen 1953; three s. one d.; ed. Lyceum of Kotka and Univ. of Helsinki; Chief, Econ. Statistics Div., Central Statistical Office of Finland 1959–63, Chief, Nat. Income Statistics Div. 1963–71, Chief, Planning Div. 1971–78, Dir. 1979–, Dir.-Gen. 1982–; Docent of Econs., Univ. of Helsinki 1962–, Acting Prof. of Econs. 1964–65, Acting Prof. of Econometrics 1970–; Acting Prof. of Econs., Univ. of Tampere 1965–66; Visiting Fellow, Univ. of Calif. (Berkeley) and Harvard Univ. 1967–68; mem. Finnish Acad., Cen. Research Bd. 1971–; mem. UN Statistical Comm. 1981–; Kt., First Class of White Rose of Finland. *Publications:* several books and more than 150 articles in learned journals. *Leisure interests:* family life, car racing, cybernetics of human life. *Address:* Central Statistical Office of Finland, Annankatu 44, 00100 Helsinki 10 (Office); Riihitie 21 A 2, 00330 Helsinki 33, Finland (Home). *Telephone:* 17341 (Office); 487490 (Home).

NIJENHUIS, Emmie te, PH.D.; Netherlands ethnomusicologist; b. 11 Nov. 1931, Bussum; d. of Dirk te Nijenhuis and W. Margarete Küchenthal; m. Sytze Wiersma 1965; one s.; ed. Utrecht Conservatory and Utrecht Univ.; teacher of theory and history of Western Music, Zwolle Conservatory 1958–61; Reader Indian Musicology, Utrecht Univ. 1964–88; Visiting Lecturer Oxford and Basel Univs. 1978, 1984; mem. Royal Netherlands Acad. of Sciences 1978. *Publications:* Dattilam: Compendium of Ancient Indian Music 1970, Indian Music, History and Structure 1974, The Ragas of Somanatha, 2 Vols. 1976, Musicological Literature 1977, Sacred Songs of India: Muttusvami Diksitar's Cycle of Hymns to the Goddess Kamala, 2 Vols. 1987. *Address:* Verlengde Fortlaan 39, 1412 CW Naarden, The Netherlands. *Telephone:* 02159-49322.

NIJPELS, Eduardus Hermannes Theresia Maria, B.LL.; Netherlands politician; b. 1 April 1950, Den Helder; m. I. M. Pieters; ed. Utrecht Univ.; fmr. Nat. Chair. Young People's Org. of the JOVD; M.P. 1977–; Chair. Standing Cttee. on the Police, Parl. Party of VVD (People's Party for Freedom and Democracy) 1982–; mem. Cttee. Liberal Renascence Soc., AVRO Broadcasting Asscn.; Minister of Housing, Physical Planning and the Environment July 1986–; regular columnist for the Algemeen Dagblad newspaper; fmr. mem. Consultative Cttee. on Environmental Activities in the Belgian/Dutch border region (BENEGORA). *Address:* c/o Ministry of Welfare, Public Health and Culture, Steenvoordelaan 370, P.O.B. 5406, 2284 EH Rijswijk, Netherlands. *Telephone:* (070) 94-93-93.

NIKAIDO, Susumu; Japanese politician; b. 16 Oct. 1909; ed. Univ. of Southern Calif.; mem. House of Reps.; Deputy Sec.-Gen. Liberal Democratic Party; fmr. Dir.-Gen. Science and Tech. Agency; fmr. Dir.-Gen. Hokkaido Devt. Agency; Chief Cabinet Sec. 1972–74; Sec.-Gen. Liberal Democratic Party Nov.–Dec. 1974, 1981–83, Vice-Pres. 1983–87. *Address:* c/o Liberal Democratic Party, 7, 2-chome, Hirakawacho, Chiyoda-ku, Tokyo, Japan. *Telephone:* (03) 581-5111, Ext. 523.

NIKITIN, Sergey Konstantinovich; Soviet author; b. 1926, Kovrov, Vladimir Dist.; ed. Gorky Inst. of Literature 1948–52; mem. CPSU 1956–; first works published 1948. *Publications include:* The Return 1952, Seven Elephants 1954, One's Own House 1962, Private Life 1966, On a Spring Morning 1966. *Address:* U.S.S.R. Union of Writers, ul. Vorovoskogo 52, Moscow, U.S.S.R.

NIKOI, Amon, PH.D.; Ghanaian banker; b. 19 Jan. 1930, Labadi, Accra; m. Gloria Addae (q.v.) three c.; ed. Achimota Coll., Amherst Coll., U.S.A., Harvard Coll., U.S.A.; Trade and Econ. Section, Embassy of Ghana, Washington 1957–59; Perm. Mission of Ghana to the UN 1959–60; Alt.

Exec. Dir., IMF 1961–65, Exec. Dir. 1965–68; Prin. Sec. Minister of Finance and Planning 1969–73, Minister 1979–80; Econ. Adviser to Pres. 1980; Gov., Bank of Ghana 1973–77; Chair. Ashanti Goldfields Corpn. *Leisure interests:* farming, gardening, walking.

NIKOLAYEVA, Tatiana Petrovna; Soviet pianist and composer; b. 4 May 1924, Bezhitsa; m. Tarasevich Nikolayeva; ed. Moscow Conservatory (under A. Goldenweiser); first prize for playing Bach at Leipzig Music Festival 1950; Dean, Prof, at Moscow Conservatory; U.S.S.R. State Prize 1951. *Compositions include:* Symphony No. 1 1955, two concertos for piano, other works for piano. *Address:* Moscow Conservatory, № 13 Hertsen Street, Moscow, U.S.S.R.

NIKOLSKY, Sergey Ivanovich; Soviet physicist; b. 1923; ed. Moscow State Univ.; served in Soviet Army 1941–43; mem. of staff of Inst. of Physics, U.S.S.R. Acad. of Sciences 1948–, head of section 1970–73, Deputy Dir. 1973–; numerous publs. on space research 1947–80; elected to Congress of People's Deputies of the U.S.S.R. 1989; Lenin Prize 1982. *Address:* Institute of Physics, U.S.S.R. Academy of Sciences, Leninsky Prospekt 14, Moscow V-71, U.S.S.R.

NIKONOV, Viktor Petrovich; Soviet politician and civil servant; b. 1929; ed. Azovo-Chernomorsky Agricultural Inst.; mem. CPSU 1954–; Deputy Dir., Dir. of a machine and tractor station 1950–58; Head of Agricultural Dept. of Krasnoyarsk Regional CPSU Cttee. 1958–61; Second Sec. of Tartar A.S.S.R. Dist. CPSU Cttee. 1961–67; Deputy to U.S.S.R. Supreme Soviet 1962–; First Sec. of Mari A.S.S.R. Dist. CPSU Cttee. 1967–79; Cand. mem. 1971–76, mem. of Cen. Cttee. CPSU 1976–; Deputy Minister of Agric. 1979–; mem. Secr. Cen. Cttee. of CPSU 1985–; mem. Politburo June 1987–; Order of October Revolution. *Address:* Council of Ministers, The Kremlin, 1/11 Orlikov per., Moscow, U.S.S.R.

NILES, Thomas Michael Tolliver, M.A.; American diplomatist; b. 22 Sept. 1939, Lexington, Ky.; s. of John Jacob Niles and Rena (née Lipetz) Niles; m. Carroll C. Ehringhaus 1967; one s. one d.; ed. Harvard Univ. and Univ. of Kentucky; Foreign Service Officer, Dept. of State 1962; posts in Moscow, Belgrade and Brussels; Amb. to Canada 1985–89; Perm. Rep. to the EEC, Brussels April 1989–; Superior Honor Award, Dept. of State 1982, 1985. *Address:* Permanent Representative of the United States to the European Communities, 40 blvd du Regent, 1000 Brussels, Belgium. *Telephone:* (02) 513-44-50.

NILSSON, Birgit (Fru Bertil Niklasson); Swedish opera singer (soprano); b. 17 May 1918, Karup; m. Bertil Niklasson 1948; ed. Stockholm Royal Acad. of Music; with Stockholm Opera 1947–51; sang at Glyndebourne (England) 1951, Bayreuth 1954, 1957–70, Munich 1954–58, Hollywood Bowl, Buenos Aires and Florence 1956, London (Covent Garden) 1957, 1962, 1963, 1973, Milan (La Scala), Naples, Vienna, Chicago and San Francisco 1958, New York (Metropolitan) 1959, Moscow 1964; sang in Turandot, Paris 1968, Josen, New York 1968, Elektra, London 1969; particularly well known for her Wagnerian roles (Brünnhilde, Isolde, etc.); Royal Court singer 1954; retd. 1985; Austrian Kammersängerin, Bavarian Kammersängerin and Hon. mem. of the Vienna State Opera 1968; Commdr., Order of Vasa 1968, Medal Litteris et Artibus 1960, Medal for Promotion of Art of Music, Royal Acad. of Music, Stockholm 1968. *Address:* Box 527, Stockholm C, Sweden.

NILSSON, Gösta; Swedish engineer and business executive; b. 18 Feb. 1912, Jonstorp in Skåne; s. of Jöns and Hilda (Hansson) Nilsson; m. Ingeborg Nilsson 1939; one s. and three d.; High Tension and Lighting Research Inst., Uppsala 1936–37; Swedish State Power Bd. 1937–53 (Exec. Vice-Pres. 1948–53); Man. Dir. Scania Vabis 1953–69; Deputy Chair. Saab-Scania (mfrs. of trucks, buses, engines, cars, aircraft) 1969–80, Chair. 1980–83; Chair. Svenska Volkswagen 1969–83; Deputy Chair. Svenska Dagbladet 1965–82, SPP 1957–82; Dir. Swedish Wine Monopoly 1964–82, Swedish Tobacco Co. 1970–82, Suomen Autoteollisuus AB (mfrs. of trucks and buses in Finland) 1977–83. *Leisure interest:* golf. *Address:* Uddeboö Gård, 76100 Norrtälje, Sweden. *Telephone:* 0176-36064.

NILSSON, Robert, B.A.; Swedish administrator; b. 13 Feb. 1938, Trelleborg; s. of Harald Nilsson and Anna Nilsson; m. Margot Widlund 1965; one s. one d.; ed. Stockholm School of Econs.; Dir. Swedish Medical Asscn. 1962–67; Dir. S.P.R.I. (Planning Inst. of Social Sector) 1968–75; Dir. Swedish Farmers' Asscn. 1975–77; Under-Sec. of State, Govt. of Sweden 1978–82; Pres. Swedish State Co. 1982–83; Man. Dir. Södra Skogsägarna 1983, Volvo Dealers' Asscn. 1984–86, Hammenhögs 1987–. *Leisure interests:* sport, travelling. *Address:* Hammenhögs, 27050 Hammenhög, Sweden. *Telephone:* 0414-40400.

NIMATALLAH, Yusuf A., PH.D.(ECONS.); Saudi Arabian economist; b. 1936; ed. American Univ., Beirut and Univ. of Mass.; with Banque de l'Indochine 1952–57; Teaching Asst. in Econs., Univ. of Mass. 1963–65; Prof. Monetary and Int. Econs., Univ. of Riyadh (King Saud Univ. 1982–) 1965– (on leave 1973–); Adviser to Minister of Finance on Money and Banking, Oil Finance and Planning 1967–73; Adviser to Sultan of Oman on Oil, Finance, Money and Banking; Deputy Chair. and Pres. Central Bank of Oman 1975–78; Deputy Chair. UBAF Arab American Bank, New York 1976–78; Alt. Exec. Dir. IMF 1979–81, Exec. Dir. 1981–. *Address:*

International Monetary Fund, 700 19th Street, N.W., Washington, D.C. 20431, U.S.A.

NIMERI, Field-Marshal Gaafar Mohammed al- (see Nemery, Field-Marshal Gaafar Mohammed al-).

NIMR, Nabih Al-; Jordanian diplomatist; b. 26 Oct. 1931, Tubas; m. Rabab Al-Nimr 1961; one s. one d.; ed. Alexandria Univ.; Amb. to Syria 1974–78, to Fed. Rep. of Germany (also accred. to Sweden, Denmark, Norway and Luxembourg) 1978–81, to Tunisia and Perm. Rep. to the Arab League 1981–85, to U.K. 1985–87, (also accred. to Ireland 1986–87). *Address:* c/o Ministry of Foreign Affairs, P.O. Box 1577, Amman, Jordan.

NIN-CULMELL, Joaquín Maria; American musician; b. 5 Sept. 1908, Berlin, Germany; s. of Joaquín Nin and Rosa Culmell; ed. Schola Cantorum and Nat. Conservatoire, Paris; studied privately with Manuel de Falla; Instructor, Middlebury Coll., Vermont 1938, 1939, 1940, Williams Coll. 1940–50; Prof. of Music, Univ. of Calif. 1949–74, Emer. Prof. 1974–, Inst. of Creative Arts 1965–66; has appeared as pianist and conductor with the San Francisco Symphony and other orchestras in the U.S.A. and Europe; Corresp. mem. Royal Acad. of Fine Arts of San Fernando (Madrid 1962); mem. Int. Jury Maria Canals Int. Competition, Barcelona, Marguerite Long Int. Competition, Paris. *Compositions:* Piano Concerto, El burlador de Sevilla (ballet), Piano Quintet, Sonata Breve, Tonadas (piano), Twelve Cuban Dances (piano), Three Old Spanish Pieces (orchestra), Diferencias (orchestra), Concerto for cello and orchestra (after Padre Anselmo Viola), Mass in English (for mixed chorus and organ), La Celestina (opera), Cantata for voice and harpsichord or piano and strings (after Padre José Pradas), Le rêve de Cyrano (ballet), incidental music for Shakespeare's Cymbeline, Federico García Larca's Yerma, Six Sephardic Folksongs (for voice and piano), songs, choral pieces, organ variations, pieces for guitar, etc. For theatre: Cuban Evocations, commissioned by Spanish Repertory Theatre of New York 1985–86. *Publications:* Ed. Spanish Choral Tradition, Prefaces in English and French for the early diaries of Anaïs Nin (Vols. I–IV). *Leisure interests:* philosophy, detective stories, swimming. *Address:* 165 Hillcrest Road, Berkeley, Calif. 94705, U.S.A.

NINEHAM, Rev. Canon Dennis Eric, M.A., D.D.; British professor of theology and ecclesiastic (retd.); b. 27 Sept. 1921, Southampton; s. of Stanley Martin Nineham and Bessie Edith Gain; m. Ruth Corfield Miller 1946; two s. two d.; ed. King Edward VI School, Southampton, Queen's Coll., Oxford and Lincoln Theological Coll.; Chaplain Queen's Coll., Oxford 1944–54, Fellow 1946–54; Prof. of Biblical and Historical Theology London Univ. 1954–58, Prof. of Divinity 1958–64; Regius Prof. of Divinity Cambridge Univ. 1964–69; Fellow of Emmanuel Coll. 1964–69; Warden Keble Coll., Oxford 1969–79; Prof. of Theology Bristol Univ. 1980–86; Fellow King's Coll., London; Canon Emer. Bristol Cathedral; Hon. Fellow Keble Coll., Oxford; Hon. D.D. (Yale) 1965, (Birmingham) 1972. *Publications:* The Gospel of St. Mark 1963, The Use and Abuse of the Bible 1976, Explorations in Theology 1977. *Leisure interests:* walking and reading. *Address:* 4 Wootten Drive, Iffley Turn, Oxford, OX4 4DS, England (Home). *Telephone:* (0865) 715941.

NINN-HANSEN, Erik, LL.D.; Danish politician; b. 12 April 1922, Skørpinge, Western Zealand; s. of Christian Hansen; in pvt. law practice 1955–; mem. Folketing (Parl.) 1953–; Minister of Defence 1968–71, of Finance 1971, of Justice 1982–89; Pres. of the Folketing (Parl.) Jan. 1989–; Nat. Chair. Conservative Youth 1948–50. *Publication:* Syv år for VKR. *Address:* c/o Ministry of Justice, Slotsholmsgade 10, 1216 Copenhagen K, Denmark.

NIORDSON, Frithiof Igor Niord, PH.D.; Danish professor of engineering; b. 1 Aug. 1922, Johannesburg, South Africa; s. of Niord Gustafson and Helena de Makeeff; m. 1st Ann-Marie Odqvist 1954; m. 2nd Hanne Oerregaard 1975; two s. two d.; ed. Royal Inst. of Tech., Sweden, Brown Univ., Providence, R.I., U.S.A.; Consulting Eng. 1949–58; Prof. of Mechanical Eng., Tech. Univ. of Denmark 1958–, Dean 1975–; mem. NATO Advisory Group for Aerospace Research and Devt. 1963–86; Sec. Danish Cen. of Applied Math. and Mechanics 1968–; Sec.-Gen. Int. Union of Theoretical and Applied Mechanics 1968–74, Pres. 1974–80, Vice-Pres. 1980–84; Chair. Bd. of Dirs., Northern Europe Univ. Computing Cen. 1980; mem. Royal Acad. of Sciences (Sweden), Danish-Soviet Gov. Comm. for Scientific Cooperation 1982–, Polish Acad. of Sciences; hon. mem. American Asscn. of Mechanical Engs.; Kt. of the Dannebrog. *Publications:* several books and papers on shell-theory, stability and vibrations. *Leisure interests:* sailing, riding, skiing. *Address:* Department of Solid Mechanics, Technical University of Denmark, 2800 Lyngby (Office); Geelsvej 19, 2840 Holte, Denmark (Home).

NIRENBERG, Louis, PH.D.; American professor of mathematics; b. 28 Feb. 1925, Hamilton, Ont., Canada; s. of Zuzie Nirenberg and Bina Katz; m. Susan Blank 1948; one s. one d.; ed. McGill and New York Univs.; Instructor, New York Univ. 1949–51, Asst. Prof. 1951–54, Assoc. Prof. 1954–57, Prof. 1957–; Dir. Courant Inst. of Mathematical Sciences 1970–72; mem. N.A.S., American Acad. of Arts and Sciences, American Philosophical Soc., Accad. dei Lincei; Hon. Prof. Nankai Univ., Zhejian Univ.; Hon. D.Sc. (McGill Univ.); Bôcher Prize of American Mathematical Soc, Craoford Prize (Royal Swedish Acad. of Sciences) 1982. *Publications:* various papers in mathematical journals. *Leisure interests:* classical music, reading fiction, cinema, walking. *Address:* Courant Institute of Mathematical Sciences,

New York University, 251 Mercer Street, New York, N.Y. 10012 (Office); 221 W. 82nd Street, New York, New York, N.Y. 10024, U.S.A. (Home). *Telephone:* 212-998-3192 (Office).

NIRENBERG, Marshall Warren, PH.D.; American biochemist; b. 10 April 1927; s. of Harry Edward and Minerva (Bykowsky) Nirenberg; m. Perola Zaltzman 1961; ed. Univ. of Florida and Univ. of Michigan; Postdoctoral Fellow, American Cancer Soc., Nat. Insts. of Health (N.I.H.) 1957–59, U.S. Public Health Service, N.I.H. 1959–60; mem. staff, N.I.H. 1960–, research bio-chemist 1961–62; research biochemist, Head of Section for Biochemical Genetics, Nat. Heart Inst. 1962–66; Chief, Lab. of Biochemical Genetics, Nat. Heart, Lung and Blood Inst. 1966–; has researched on mechanism of protein synthesis, genetic code, nucleic acids, regulatory mechanism in synthetic macromolecules; mem. New York Acad. of Sciences, A.A.A.S., N.A.S., Pontifical Acad. of Sciences 1974, Deutsche Leopoldina Akad. der Naturforscher; hon. mem. Harvey Soc.; Molecular Biology Award, Nat. Acad. of Sciences 1962; Medal from Dept. of Health, Educ. and Welfare 1963, Modern Medicine Award 1964, Nat. Medal for Science, Pres. Johnson 1965, Nobel Prize for Medicine (with Holley and Khorana) for interpreting the genetic code and its function in protein synthesis 1968, Louisa Gross Horwitz Prize for Biochemistry 1968. *Address:* Laboratory of Biochemical Genetics, National Heart, Lung and Blood Institute, Bethesda, Md. 20205, U.S.A.

NISBET, Robin George Murdoch, M.A., F.B.A.; British classical scholar; b. 21 May 1925, Glasgow, Scotland; s. of Robert George Nisbet and Agnes Thomson Husband; m. Anne Wood 1969; ed. Glasgow Acad., Glasgow Univ. and Balliol Coll. Oxford; Fellow and Tutor in Classics, Corpus Christi Coll. Oxford 1952–70, Prof. of Latin 1970–. *Publications:* Commentary on Cicero, In Pisonem 1961, Horace, Odes I, II (with M. Hubbard) 1970, 1978. *Address:* Corpus Christi College, Oxford; 80 Abingdon Road, Cumnor, Oxford, England (Home). *Telephone:* Oxford 276700 (Coll.); Oxford 862482 (Home).

NISHIKAWA, Shojiro, B.ECON.; Japanese banker; b. 23 Sept. 1913, Tokyo; s. of Kihachi and Taki Nishikawa; m. Fumiko Hida 1941; one s. two d.; ed. Tokyo Imp. Univ.; Joined Nippon Kangyo Bank Ltd. 1936, Gen. Man. Nagoya branch 1961, Osaka branch 1962–63, Securities Div. 1965, Admin. Gen. Man. Branch Admin. and Business Devt. Group 1968–79, Dir. 1961–62, Man. Dir. 1963–68, Deputy Pres. 1969; Deputy Pres. Dai-Ichi Kangyo Bank Ltd. 1971–76, Chair. 1976–82, Dir. and Adviser 1982–85, Adviser 1985–; Medal with Blue Ribbon 1978, Order of the Rising Sun (Second Class) 1984. *Leisure interests:* reading, golf. *Address:* 48-16 Shakujii-cho 8-chome, Nerima-ku, Tokyo 177, Japan.

NISIBORI, Masahiro; Japanese diplomatist; b. 14 Nov. 1918, Hakodate; m. Chieko Kurita 1943; two s. one d.; ed. Hitotsubashi Univ., Tokyo, Brown Univ. and Harvard Univ., U.S.A.; entered Foreign Service 1941; Deputy Vice-Minister of Foreign Affairs for Admin. Affairs 1965; Consul-Gen., Geneva and concurrently Minister of Del. to Int. Orgs. 1966–69; Dir.-Gen. UN Bureau in Ministry of Foreign Affairs 1970–71; Amb. to Disarmament Cttee. in Geneva 1972–75, to Belgium, Luxembourg and EEC 1976–78, to UN 1979–83; Commr. Japan Atomic Energy Comm. 1983–86; Man. Dir. UN Asscn. of Japan 1987–. *Leisure interest:* golf. *Address:* 3-2-19, Kamiuma, Setagaya-ku, Tokyo, 154 Japan. *Telephone:* 03-410-2077.

NISSEL, Siegmund, O.B.E.; British musician; b. 3 Jan. 1922, Munich, Germany; s. of Isidor Nissel and Malvine Nissel; m. Muriel Nissel 1957; one s. one d.; ed. Mittelschule Vienna, London Univ. and private tuition with Prof. Max Weissgärber, Vienna and Prof. Max Rostal, London; Leader, London Int. Orchestra 1947; Founder mem. Second Violin, Amadeus Quartet 1948–; Prof. of Chamber Music, Musikhochschule, Cologne, Feb. Repub. of Germany 1978–, R.A.M., London 1986–; Hon. mem. R.A.M.; Hon. D.Mus. (York, London); Grosses Verdienstkreuz, Germany; Ehrenkreuz für Wissenschaft und Kunst, Austria. *Leisure interests:* opera and theatre. *Address:* 29 The Park, London, NW11 7ST, England.

NISSIM, Moshe, LL.D.; Israeli politician; b. 1935, Jerusalem; ed. Hebrew Univ. of Jerusalem; elected to Knesset 1959– (as rep. of Union of Gen. Zionists 1959, subsequently as rep. of Gahal faction of the Liberal Party, then of the Likud Bloc); has served on Defence, Foreign Affairs and Security, Constitution Law and Legislation, Labour and Housing Cttees. in the Knesset; Co-Chair. Likud group 1975–79; Chair. Exec. Cttee., Likud Feb. 1978–; Minister without Portfolio 1978–80, Dec. 1988–; Minister of Justice 1980–86, of Finance 1986–88. *Address:* c/o Ministry of Finance, Jerusalem, Israel.

NITISASTRO, Widjojo, PH.D.; Indonesian politician; b. 23 Sept. 1927, Malang; ed. Univ. of Indonesia and Univ. of Calif., Berkeley, U.S.A.; Dean, Faculty of Econs., Univ. of Indonesia 1965–67; seconded to UN as expert engaged in drawing up plan for 2nd UN Econ. Devt. Decade and mem. Gov. Council, UN Asian Inst. of Devt. and Planning 1967–71; Minister of State for Nat. Planning and Construction 1971–74, for Econ. Financial and Industrial Affairs 1974–83 (named Minister Co-ordinator 1978); Chair. Nat. Planning Bd. 1978–83. *Publications include:* Population Trends in Indonesia, The Relevance of Growth Models for Less Developed Economics, The Role of Research in a University, Public Policies, Land Tenure and Population Movements, Population Problems and Indonesia's Economic

Development. *Address:* c/o Ministry for Economic, Financial and Industrial Affairs, Jakarta, Indonesia.

NITZE, Paul Henry A.B.; American adviser; b. 16 Jan. 1907, Amherst, Mass.; s. of William A. and Anina (Hilken) Nitze; m. Phyllis Pratt 1932; two s. two d.; ed. Harvard Univ.; New York Investment Banker 1929–41; financial Dir. Office of Co-ordinator of Inter-American Affairs 1941–42; Chief, Metals and Minerals Branch, Bd. of Econ. Welfare, Dir. Foreign Procurement and Devt. 1942–43; Vice-Chair. Strategic Bombing Survey 1944–46; Deputy Dir. Office of Int. Trade Policy 1946–48; Deputy to Asst. Sec. of State for Econ. Affairs 1948–49; Dir. Policy Planning Staff, Dept. of State 1950–53; Pres. Foreign Service Educ. Foundation 1953–61; Asst. Sec. of Defense for Int. Security Affairs 1961–63; Sec. of the Navy 1963–67; Deputy Sec. of Defense 1967–69; mem. U.S. Del. to Strategic Arms Limitation Talks (SALT) 1969–74; Chair. Advisory Council, School of Advanced Int. Studies, Johns Hopkins Univ.; Consultant, System Planning Corpn. 1974–81; Head of U.S. Del. to the Intermediate Range Nuclear Forces Negotiations with U.S.S.R. 1981–83; Adviser to the Pres. and the Sec. of State 1984–89; Lecturer Johns Hopkins School of Advanced Int. Studies 1989–; Medal of Merit, Medal of Freedom, George C. Marshall, Kt. Commdr.'s Cross (badge and star) of Order of Merit, Fed. Repub. of Germany. *Publication:* U.S. Foreign Policy 1945-1954. *Leisure interests:* skiing, tennis. *Address:* Johns Hopkins School of Advanced International Studies, 1730 Massachusettes Avenue, Washington, D.C. 20036 (Office); 3120 Woodley Road, Washington, D.C. 20008, U.S.A. (Home).

NIU SHUCAI; Chinese state official (retd.); b. Aug. 1908, Quyang Co., Hebei Prov.; m. Zhang Wenxiu 1944; three s. three d.; ed. Baoding Industrial School; f. and Prin. Chengxiang Secondary School; Sec. CCP, Quyang Co., Hebei Prov.; Sec. CCP, S. Anhui Dist. Cttee. 1949; Political Commissar, S. Anhui Mil. Area 1949; Vice-Chair. Land Reform Cttee., E. China Mil. and Admin. Council 1950; Deputy Sec. CCP, N. Anhui Dist. Cttee. 1951; Deputy Sec. CCP Cttee., Anhui 1952; Second Deputy Political Commissar, Anhui Mil. Area 1952; Vice-Chair. Prov. People's Govt., Anhui 1952; Vice-Mayor Shanghai 1957; C.-in-C. Shanghai Flood Prevention Cttee. 1957, Deputy C.-in-C. 1959; Vice-Chair. Cttee. for Eng. Control of Dykes, Rivers and Ponds in Shanghai 1959; Vice-Gov. Hebei 1960; Vice-Chair. Prov. People's Political Consultative Conf., Hebei 1962, 1979; Vice-Chair. Standing Cttee., Prov. People's Congress, Hebei 1980, Acting Chair. 1982–83; Deputy Head, Preparatory Group of Advisory Cttee. CCP Cttee., Hebei Prov. 1983–85. *Address:* c/o General Office of the Standing Committee, People's Congress, Hebei Province, People's Republic of China.

NIWA, Hyosuke; Japanese politician; b. 1911; mem. Aichi Prefectural Assembly (Progressive Party) before joining Liberal-Democratic Party (LDP) and standing for House of Reps.; elected to House of Reps. nine times from Aichi Pref.; fmrly. Parl. Vice-Minister for Agric. and Forestry, Chair. Agric., Forestry and Fisheries Cttee., House of Reps., Head Agricultural Policy Council LDP; Dir.-Gen. Nat. Land Agency under Prime Minister Tanaka Nov. 1974; Minister of State, Dir.-Gen. Prime Minister's Office 1982–83; Minister of Labour Jan. 1989–. *Address:* Ministry of Labour, 2-2, Kasumigaseki 1-chome, Chiyoda-ku, Tokyo, Japan.

NIWANO, Nikkyō; Japanese religious leader; b. 15 Nov. 1906, Niigata Pref.; s. of Jukichi and Mii (Hosaka) Niwano; m. Sai Abè 1930; three s. three d.; ed. Ōike Primary School, Suganuma; Pres. Rissho Kosei-kai, a lay Buddhist asscn. with 6 million mems. 1938–; Chair. Shinshuren (Fed. of the New Religious Orgs. of Japan) 1965–; Pres. Japanese Cttee. for World Conf. on Religion and Peace 1972–; Pres. Int. Ass, cn. for Religious Freedom 1981–84; Pres. Niwano Peace Foundation 1978–; Chair. Asian Conf. on Religion and Peace 1977–; Hon. Pres. World Conf. on Religion and Peace 1979–; Trustee, Japan Religions League 1967–; Hon. LL.D. (Meadville/Lombard Theol. School) 1975; Imperial Household Agency Medal of Honour with Dark Navy Blue Ribbon 1958, Templeton Foundation Prize for Progress in Religion 1979, Artigiana derra Pace, United Nations Plaque 1983. *Leisure interests:* calligraphy, ink painting, golf. *Publications:* in English: Buddhism for Today: a Modern Interpretation of the Threefold Lotus Sutra 1976, A Buddhist Approach to Peace 1977; Lifetime Beginner (autobiog.) 1978; in Japanese: Buddhism for Today (5 vols.) 1959–60, A New Interpretation of the Threefold Lotus Sutra (10 vols.) 1964–68, A Guide to the Threefold Lotus Sutra 1975. *Address:* Rissho Kosei-kai, 2-11-1 Wada Suginami-ku, Tokyo 166, Japan. *Telephone:* (03) 383-1111.

NIXON, Sir Edwin Ronald, Kt., C.B.E., M.A.; British computer industry executive; b. 21 June 1925, Leicester; s. of William Archdale Nixon and Ethel (née Corrigan); m. Joan Lilian Hill 1952; one s. one d.; ed. Alderman Newton's School, Leicester, and Selwyn Coll., Cambridge; served R.A.F. 1946–50; Man. Accountant, Dexion Ltd. 1950–55; joined IBM as a data processing salesman 1955, various man. posts 1955–65, Man. Dir. 1965–; Chair. and Chief Exec. IBM United Kingdom Holdings Ltd. 1979–86, Chair. 1986–; Dir. Nat. Westminster Bank PLC 1975– (Deputy Chair. 1987–), Royal Insurance Co. Ltd. 1980–, Business in the Community, Amersham Int. PLC 1987– (Chair. 1988–); mem. Pres.'s Cttee. 1986–88, CBI, Advisory Council of Business Graduates Assccn., British Cttee. of Awards for Harkness Fellowships 1976–82, Council of Business in the Community; Council mem., Oxford Cen. for Man. Studies, Foundation for Man. Educ. 1973–83, Open Univ. 1986–; Gov. United World Coll. of the Atlantic 1977–; Pres. Nat. Asscn. of Gifted Children; Vice-Pres. Opportunit-

ies for the Disabled; Trustee Monteverdi Choir and Orchestra; Vice-Pres. and Fellow Inst. of Marketing; Hon. Dr. h.c. (Stirling) 1984, (Aston) 1985, (Brunel) 1986, (Manchester) 1987. *Leisure interests:* music, tennis, golf, sailing. *Address:* IBM United Kingdom Ltd., 76 Upper Ground, London, SE1 9PZ (Office); Starkes Heath, Rogate, Nr. Petersfield, Hants., England (Home). *Telephone:* 01-928 1777 (Office); (073080) 504 (Home).

NIXON, Peter James; Australian politician (retd.), farmer and grazier; b. 22 March 1928, Orbost, Victoria; s. of Percival C. and Grace Hunter Nixon; m. Jacqueline Thelma Sally Dahlsen 1954; two s. one d.; ed. Wesley Coll. Melbourne; elected to House of Reps. 1961; mem. Joint Cttee. Public Accounts 1964; mem. Joint Cttee. Foreign Affairs 1967; Minister for the Interior 1967–71, for Shipping and Transport 1971–72; Minister of Transport 1975–79, for Primary Industry Dec. 1979–83; Postmaster-Gen. Nov.-Dec. 1975; Chair. Techcom (Australia) 1983–, Southern Cross Communications 1983–, Agridata (Australia) 1983–; Chair. and Dir. Amalgamated Marketers Australia Co-op Ltd. (ACMAL) 1984–85; Dir. Assoc. Cont. Trans. Australia (ACTA) 1984– (Chair. 1987–), Emery Worldwide (Australia) 1984–; Chair. Gippsland & Northern 1985–; Chair. Tricom Corpn. 1986–; Dir. Lin Fox 1988–, Budget 1988–; Commr. Victoria Football League 1984–; Trustee Melbourne Cricket Ground 1986–; Nat. Country Party. *Leisure interests:* fly fishing, racing, shooting. *Address:* P.O. Box 262 Orbost, 3888 Victoria, Australia. *Telephone:* 03-209 2211 (Office); 051-541444 and 03-882 5453 (Home).

NIXON, Richard Milhous, A.B., LL.B.; American politician (retd.); b. 9 Jan. 1913, Yorba Linda, Calif.; s. of Francis A. and Hannah (Milhous) Nixon; m. Thelma Catherine ("Pat") Ryan 1940; two d.; ed. Whittier Coll. and Duke Univ. Law School; practised law in Whittier 1937–42; Attorney with Office of Emergency Man., Washington, D.C. 1942; served with U.S. Navy 1942–46; attained rank of Lieut.-Commdr.; mem. Congress for 12th Calif. District 1947–50; Senator from Calif. 1950–53; Vice-Pres. of U.S.A. 1953–61; Republican candidate for Presidency (ran against John F. Kennedy) 1960; affiliated with law firm Adams, Duque and Hazeltine 1961–63; Republican Candidate for Gov., Calif. 1962; mem. Mudge, Stern, Baldwin and Todd 1963–64; partner, Nixon, Mudge, Rose, Guthrie, Alexander & Mitchell 1964–68; 37th Pres. of U.S.A. 1969–74, resigned 10 Aug. 1974; granted Presidential Pardon by Pres. Ford, Sept. 1974, after Watergate investigations; responsible for Viet-Nam Peace Settlement Jan. 1973; first U.S. Pres. to make official visit to People's Repub. of China Feb. 1972, U.S.S.R. May 1972; revisited China Feb. 1976, Sept. 1982; Foreign Assoc. Acad. des Beaux-Arts. *Publications:* Six Crises 1962, RN: Memoirs 1978, The Real War 1980, Leaders 1982, Real Peace: a Strategy for the West 1984, No More Vietnams 1986, 1999: Victory Without War 1988. *Address:* 26 Federal Plaza, New York, N.Y. 10278, U.S.A.

NIYAZOV, Saparmurad Atayevich; Soviet party official and politician; b. 1940, Turkmenistan; ed. Leningrad Polytechnic Inst.; mem. CPSU 1962; instructor with Trade-Union Org. of mineral prospecting works in Turkmenistan 1959–67; instructor, then deputy head of section of Cen. Cttee. of Turkmen CP 1970–79; head of section and first sec. of Ashkhabad City Cttee. of Turkmen CP 1979–84; party-work with Cen. Cttee. of CPSU 1984–85; Pres. of Council of Ministers of Turkmen S.S.R. 1985; First Sec. of Cen. Cttee. of C.P. of Turkmen S.S.R. Dec. 1985–; mem. Cen. Cttee. of CPSU 1986–. *Address:* Central Committee of Turkmen Communist Party, Ashkhabad, U.S.S.R.

NIYUNGEKO, Jonathas, B.L.; Burundi diplomatist; b. 22 Dec. 1946, Gakonko; m.; three c.; ed. Bujumbura Univ.; Deputy Dir. Political Affairs, Ministry of Foreign Affairs 1974–76, Dir. 1976–78, Dir.-Gen. Political and Admin. Affairs and then Africa, Latin America, Asia and Oceania Affairs 1978–81; Amb. to Uganda 1981–85, to China 1985–87; Perm. Rep. of Burundi to UN 1987–. *Address:* Permanent Mission of Burundi to the United Nations, 201 East 42nd Street, 28th Floor, New York, N.Y. 10017, U.S.A. *Telephone:* (212) 687-1180.

NJOKU, Eni, PH.D.; Nigerian university teacher and administrator; b. 6 Nov. 1917, Ebem Ohafia; s. of Njoku Eni and Obo Uche; m. Winifred Oliver Beardsall; one s. three d.; ed. Ebem Ohafia primary school, Hope Waddell Coll., Calabar, Yaba Higher Coll. and Univ. of Manchester, England; teacher, Hope-Waddell Secondary School 1940–42, Clerk (Army) Training School 1942–44; studied in Manchester 1944–48; lecturer, Univ. of Ibadan 1948–52; Minister for Mines and Power, Govt. of Nigeria 1952–53; Sr. lecturer, Prof. of Botany, Univ. of Ibadan 1953–62; Vice-Chancellor and Prof. of Botany, Univ. of Lagos 1962–65; Visiting Prof. of Botany, Mich. State Univ. 1965–66; Vice-Chancellor, Univ. of Nigeria 1966–70; Prof. of Botany, Univ. of Nigeria 1966–74; mem. House of Reps. 1952–53, Senate 1960–62; Chair. Electricity Corpn. of Nigeria 1956–62; Pres. Science Asscn. of Nigeria 1959–60; mem. Commonwealth Scientific Cttee. 1961–66; mem. UN Cttee. on Application of Science and Tech. to Devt. 1964–69; mem. Provisional Council of Univ. of Zambia 1964–65; mem. Superior Academic Council of Univ. of Lovanium (Kinshasa) 1963–66; Hon. D.Sc. (Nigeria and Lagos), Hon. LL.D. (Mich. State Univ.). *Publications:* Plant Life in a Tropical Environment 1954 and numerous research articles in botanical journals. *Address:* Ebem Ohafia, East Central State, Nigeria.

NJONJO, Charles E. G. H., B.A., BARR.-AT-LAW, M.P.L.; Kenyan lawyer; b. 23 Jan. 1920, Kabete; s. of ex-Senior Chief Josiah Njonjo of Kiambu and

Elizabeth Njonjo; m. Margaret Bryson 1972; one s. two d.; ed. Fort Hare Univ. (South Africa), Univ. Coll., Exeter (U.K.), London School of Econs., Gray's Inn; Asst. Registrar-Gen., Kenya 1955-60; Crown Counsel 1960-61; Senior Crown Counsel 1961-62; Deputy Public Prosecutor 1962-63; Attorney-Gen. 1963-80; M.P. for Kikuyu 1980-83; Minister of Home and Constitutional Affairs June 1980-82, of Constitutional Affairs 1982-83. *Leisure interests:* farming, dogs, music. *Address:* c/o Ministry of Constitutional Affairs, Nairobi, Kenya.

NJOROGE, Ng'ethe, M.SC.; Kenyan diplomatist, farmer and business executive; b. Kikuyu; s. of George and Leah Njoroge; m. Florence Njeri 1972; three s.; ed. Alliance High School, Kenya, Busoga Coll., Uganda Central State Univ., Wilberforce, Ohio, and Boston Univ.; Asst. Sec. Ministry of Lands and Settlement 1963-64; Senior Asst. Sec. Ministry of Foreign Affairs 1964, later Head, Africa and Middle East Division; Counsellor, Bonn 1968-70; High Commr. in U.K. 1970-79, concurrently Amb. to Italy and Switzerland 1974-79; Chair. Mitchell Cotts (Kenya) Ltd. 1979-83; tea and dairy cattle farmer 1983-; mem. Kenya Del. to OAU; mem. Kenya Del. to UN Gen. Ass. 1964, 1965, 1966, Commonwealth Heads of Govt. Meetings 1964, 1966, 1971, 1973, 1975, 1977. *Address:* P.O.B. 30384, Nairobi, Kenya. *Telephone:* 339387.

NKALA, Enos; Zimbabwe politician; b. *c.* 1933; founder mem. and Treasurer Zimbabwe African Nat. Union (ZANU) 1963-; mem. Cen. Cttee. ZANU; spent more than 15 years in detention, released Nov. 1979; Senator 1980-85; M.P. for Kariba Aug. 1985-; Minister of Finance 1980-82, of Nat. Supply 1982-85, of Home Affairs 1985-87, of Defence 1988-89; Gov. IMF 1981-82; mem. Politburo (ZANU) 1984-89. *Address:* c/o Ministry of Defence, Munhumutapa Building, Samora Machel Avenue, Private Bag 7713, Causeway, Harare, Zimbabwe.

NKOMO, Joshua; Zimbabwean politician; b. 19 June 1917; ed. Adam's Coll., Natal, Univ. of S. Africa, Johannesburg; Welfare Officer, Rhodesia Railways, Bulawayo, then Organizing Sec., Rhodesian African Railway Workers' Union 1945-50; Pres. African Congress; employed in insurance and real estate; Pres.-Gen. African Nat. Congress 1957; lived abroad when African Nat. Congress banned 1959; elected Pres. Nat. Dem. Party Aug. 1960; returned to S. Rhodesia; Pres. Zimbabwe African People's Union (ZAPU) 1961-87, amalgamated in African Nat. Council (ANC) 1974-76; imprisoned 1963-64; banished to Nuanetsi area April 1964, to Gonakudzingula Restriction Camp Nov. 1964 and for a further five years Dec. 1968, released Dec. 1974; mem. ANC Exec. 1974-76; involved in constitutional negotiations with Prime Minister Ian Smith 1976; Leader ANC del. at Geneva Conf. on Rhodesia; Joint Leader (with Robert Mugabe, q.v.) of Patriotic Front 1976-80; attended Lancaster House Conf. 1979; contested Feb. 1980 elections as Leader of Patriotic Front; Minister of Home Affairs 1980-81, without Portfolio 1981-82; Sr. Minister in the Pres.'s Office Jan. 1988-; Interim Second Vice-Pres. ZANU April 1988; fmr. mem. Cabinet Cttee. on Public Security; Hon. LL.D. (Atlanta) 1979. *Publication:* The Story of My Life 1984.

NOAH, Harold Julius, M.A., PH.D.; British academic; b. 21 Jan. 1925, London; s. of Abraham Noah and Sophia Cohen; m. 1st Norma Mestel 1945 (divorced 1966), 2nd Helen Claire Chisnall 1966; two s. two d.; ed. Stratford Grammar School, L.S.E., King's Coll., London, Teachers Coll. Columbia Univ., New York; Asst. Master then Head of Econs., Henry Thornton School, London 1949-60; Asst., Assoc. and full Prof. of Econs. and Educ. Teachers Coll., Columbia Univ., New York 1964-87, Dean 1976-81; Prof. of Educ., State Univ. of New York, Buffalo 1987-; has received numerous academic honours and awards. *Publications include:* Educational Financing and Policy Goals for Primary Schools: General Report (with Joel Sherman) 1979, The National Case Study: An Empirical Comparative Study of Twenty-one Educational Systems (with Harry Passow and others) 1976, Canada: Review of National Policies for Education 1976, International Study of Business/Industry Involvement in Education 1987. *Address:* 468 Baldy Hall, State University of New York, Buffalo, N.Y. 14260, U.S.A. *Telephone:* (716) 636-2487.

NOAKES, Most Rev. George, B.A.; British (Welsh) ecclesiastic; b. 13 Sept. 1924, Bwlchllan, Dyfed; s. of David John Noakes and Elizabeth Mary Noakes; m. Jane Margretta Davies 1957; no. c.; ed. Tregaron Co. School, Univ. Coll. of Wales and Wycliffe Hall, Oxford; Curate of Lampeter 1950-56; Vicar, Eglwyswrw w. Meline 1956-59, Tregaron 1959-67, Dewi Sant 1967-76; Rector, Aberystwyth 1976-80; Canon, St. Davids Cathedral 1977-79; Archdeacon, Cardigan 1979-82; Vicar of Llanychaearn w. Llanddeiniol 1980-82; Bishop of St. Davids 1982; Archbishop of Wales 1987. *Leisure interest:* angling. Address: Llys Esgob, Abergwili, Carmarthen, Dyfed, SA31 2JG, Wales. *Telephone:* (0267) 236597.

NOAKES, Michael; British portrait and landscape painter; b. 28 Oct. 1933, Brighton, Sussex; s. of Basil Noakes and Mary Noakes; m. Vivien Langley 1960; two s. one d.; ed. Downside, Reigate School of Art, The Royal Acad. Schools; comm. nat. service 1954-56; has painted numerous portraits of mems. of royal family including H.M. Queen Elizabeth II, H.M. Queen Elizabeth, The Queen Mother, H.R.H. Prince of Wales, H.R.H. Prince Philip, H.R.H. the Duke and H.R.H. Duchess of York, H.R.H. the Princess Royal, H.R.H. Princess Margaret, H.R.H. Princess Alice Countess of Athlone, Earl Mountbatten, Earl of Snowdon, and of other leading

figures, including Duke of Norfolk, Cardinal Hume, Lord Aberconway, Princess Ashraf of Iran, Lord Denning, Sir Alec Guinness, Haham Dr. Solomon Gaon, Gen. Sir John Hackett, Robert Hardy, Cliff Michelmore, Robert Morley, Malcolm Muggeridge, Airey Neave, Valerie Hobson Profumo, Sir Ralph Richardson, the Archbishop of Canterbury Dr. Runcie, Dame Margaret Rutherford, Dennis Wheatley, Sir Mortimer Wheeler, etc.; exhbns. internationally, including Royal Acad., Royal Inst. of Oil Painters, Royal Soc. of British Artists, of Marine Artists, of Portrait Painters, Nat. Soc. etc.; represented in perm. collections, The British Museum, Nat. Gallery, Nat. Portrait Gallery, House of Commons, H.R.H. The Prince of Wales, Frank Sinatra, etc.; mem. Royal Inst. of Oil Painters 1964, Vice-Pres. 1968-72, Pres. 1972-78, Hon. mem. Council 1978-; mem. Royal Soc. of Portrait Painters 1967-, served Council, 1969-71, 1972-74, 1978-80; Gov. Fed. of British Artists 1972-83, Dir. 1981-83; Hon. mem. numerous socs. including Nat. Soc., United Soc.; fmr. Chair. Contemporary Portrait Soc.; Platinum Disc Award for record sleeve, Portrait of Sinatra 1977. *Publications:* A Professional Approach to Oil Painting 1968, numerous contribs. to art journals and books on art; has broadcast widely in U.K. and U.S.A. on art subjects. *Leisure interest:* idling. *Address:* 146 Hamilton Terrace, St. John's Wood, London, NW8 9UX, England. *Telephone:* 01-328 6754.

NOBLE, Denis, PH.D., F.R.S.; British professor of physiology; b. 16 Nov. 1936, London; s. of George Noble and Ethel Rutherford; m. Susan Jennifer Barfield 1965; one s. (adopted) one d.; ed. Emanuel School and Univ. Coll. London; Asst. Lecturer Univ. Coll. London 1961-63; Fellow, Lecturer and Tutor in Physiology Balliol Coll., Oxford 1963-, Praefectus Balliol Graduate Centre 1971-89, Burdon Sanderson Prof. of Cardiovascular Physiology, Oxford 1984-; Visiting Prof., Alberta 1969-70; Ed. Progress in Biophysics 1967-; Chair. Jt. Dental Cttee. 1984-; Hon. Sec. Physiological Soc. 1974-80, Foreign Sec. 1986-; Darwin Lecturer British Asscn. 1966; Nahum Lecturer Yale Univ. 1977; Scientific Medal, Zoological Soc. 1970, British Heart Foundation Gold Medal and Prize 1985; Corresp. mem. Acad. de Medécine de Belgique; Fellow of University Coll., London 1986; Lloyd Roberts Lecturer 1987; Bowden Lecturer, Alderdale Wyld Lecturer 1988; Hon. mem. Royal Coll. of Physicians. *Publications:* Initiation of the Heartbeat 1975, Electric Current Flow in Excitable Cells 1975; scientific papers mostly in Journal of Physiology. *Leisure interests:* Occitan language and music, Indian and French cooking. *Address:* Holywell Manor, Manor Road, Oxford, OX1 3UH, England. *Telephone:* (0865) 271502 (Office); (0865) 271509 (Home).

NOBLE, Robert Laing, M.D., PH.D., D.SC., F.R.S.C.; Canadian university professor; b. 3 Feb. 1910, Toronto; s. of late Dr. Robert Thomas Noble and Susannah Harriett (née Hodgetts) Noble; m. Eileen A. Dillon 1934; four s.; ed. Univs. of Toronto and Aberdeen; Asst. Ed. Journal of Endocrinology, London 1938; Sec. of Canadian Physiological Soc. 1945-49; fmr. Prof. and Assoc. Dir. The Collip Medical Research Lab., Univ. of Western Ont.; Ellen Mickle Fellowship 1934; Leverhulme Fellowship of Coll. of Physicians 1935-37; Pres. Canadian Physiological Soc. 1959; Dir. B.C. Cancer Research Centre, Univ. of B.C., and Prof. of Physiology 1960-75, Prof. Emer. 1977-; Sr. Scientist, Dept. of Cancer Endocrinology, Cancer Control Agency of B.C., Vancouver; mem. numerous nat. and int. socs.; Hon. D.Sc., Univ. of Western Ont.; Comfort Cruickshank Award for Cancer Research, Middx. Hosp. 1964, Canada Centennial Medal 1967, Canada Discoveries Award 1970, Queen's Silver Jubilee Medal 1977, Robert M. Taylor Medal, Canada Cancer Soc. 1980. *Publications:* over 200 written works, especially on endocrinology, hormones and tumours, discovery of vinca alkaloids for cancer treatment and development of Nb strain of rats and unique tumour models. *Leisure interests:* fishing, hunting. *Address:* Department of Cancer Endocrinology, Cancer Control Agency, Vancouver, B.C., Canada.

NOCKOLDS, Stephen Robert, PH.D., F.R.S.; British academic scientist; b. 10 May 1909, St. Columb Major; s. of Dr. and Mrs Stephen Nockolds; m. 1st Hilda Jackson 1932 (died 1976), 2nd Patricia Horsley 1978; one step.-s. two step.-d.; ed. Felsted School, Univs. of Manchester and Cambridge; Asst. lecturer in Geology, Univ. of Manchester 1932-37; Demonstrator in Petrology, Cambridge 1937-45, Lecturer in Petrology 1945-57, Reader in Geochemistry 1957-72, Reader Emer. 1972-; Fellow of Trinity Coll., Cambridge 1950-; Ed. Geological Magazine 1950-74, Assoc. Ed. 1975-79; fmr. Ed. for Journal of Petrology and Geochimica Acta; Murchison Medal, Geological Soc. 1972, Hon. Fellow Geological Soc. of India. *Publications:* Petrology for Students (co-author), papers in various geological petrological and geochemical journals. *Leisure interests:* gardening, reading, boating. *Address:* Elm Lodge, Station Road, Keyingham, North Humberside, HU12 9TB, England.

NOEL, Emile; French international civil servant; b. 17 Nov. 1922, Constantinople (now Istanbul); s. of Fernand Noel and France Giraud; m. Lise Durand 1946 (died 1985); two d.; ed. Ecole normale supérieure, Paris; with Int. Secr., European Movt., Paris 1949; Sec. of Gen. Affairs Comm., Consultative Assembly, Council of Europe 1949-52; Dir. of Constitutional Comm. of Assembly, to look at the possibilities of a European Political Community 1952-54; Chef de Cabinet to Pres. Consultative Assembly, Council of Europe 1954-56; Chef de Cabinet, then Deputy Dir. de Cabinet of Pres. of the Council of Ministers, Paris 1956-57; Exec. Sec. Comm. of EEC, Brussels 1958-67; Sec.-Gen. Comm. of European Communities 1968-87; Pres. European Univ. Inst. 1987-; Hon. Prof. Fudan and Sichuan

Univs. 1988; Dr. h.c. (Ireland) 1981, (Edinburgh) 1982, (Urbino) 1987, (Marmara, Turkey) 1988. *Publications:* Le comité des représentants permanents 1966, Les rouages de l'Europe 1979, Les Institutions des Communautés européennes 1988. *Address:* Institut Universitaire Européen, Badia Fiesolana, 50016 San Domenico di Fiesole, Florence, Italy. *Telephone:* (55) 509-23-10.

NOELLE-NEUMANN, Elisabeth, DR.PHIL.; German professor of communication research; b. 19 Dec. 1916, Berlin; d. of Dr. Ernst Noelle and Eva Schaper; m. 1st Erich P. Neumann 1946 (died 1973), 2nd Heinz Maier-Leibnitz 1979; ed. Univ. of Berlin; journalist 1940-43, anonymous work as journalist 1943-45; f. and Dir. Inst. für Demoskopie Allensbach (first German survey research inst.) 1947-; Lecturer in Communication Research, Free Univ. of Berlin 1961-64; Prof. of Communication Research, Univ. of Mainz 1964-, also Dir. Inst. für Publizistik (until 1983); Visiting Prof., Dept. of Political Science, Univ. of Chicago 1978-; Grosses Bundesverdienstkreuz; Dr.oec. h.c. (St. Gallen). *Publications:* Umfragen in der Massengesellschaft: Einführung in die Methoden der Demoskopie 1963, Die Schweigespirale: Öffentliche Meinung—unsere soziale Haut 1980 (English trans. The Spiral of Silence: Public Opinion—Our Social Skin 1984), Macht Arbeit krank? Macht Arbeit glücklich? 1984, Die verletzte Nation 1987, and ed. of several vols. *Address:* Seeweg 14, 7753 Allensbach am Bodensee, Federal Republic of Germany. *Telephone:* 07533/777.

NOELTE, Rudolf; German producer; b. 20 March 1921, Berlin; two s.; productions in Berlin, Hamburg, Düsseldorf, Cologne, Frankfurt, Munich, Stuttgart, Vienna, Salzburg, Cardiff and London of works by Sophocles, Shakespeare, Schiller, Goethe, Dürrenmatt, Kafka, Ibsen etc. since 1948; TV producer 1956-; film producer 1968-; opera producer (including works by Mozart, Tchaikovsky, Weber, Smetana and Berg) 1970-; Preis des Verbandes der deutschen Kritiker, Kunstpreis der Stadt Berlin; Bayerischer Maximiliansorden für Wissenschaft und Kunst; Bundesverdienstkreuz. *Address:* 8137 Berg 3, Federal Republic of Germany.

NOFAL, Sayed, DR. ARTS; Egyptian international civil servant; b. 16 March 1910, Al Mansoura; s. of Mohamed Ali Nofal and Fatima Al Sayed Amer; m. 1940; three s.; ed. Cairo Univ.; Head of Literary Dept. Al Siyassa 1935-38; teacher, Cairo Univ. 1938; later Dir. of Tech. Secr., Ministry of Educ. and Ministry of Social Affairs; later Dir. of Legis. Dept., Upper House of Egyptian Parl.; later Dir. Political Dept., Arab League 1960-79, Sec.-Gen. 1980; Chair. Arab Foreign Affairs and Nat. Security Cttee. Nov. 1980-; mem. Shura Council 1980-. *Publications include:* History of Arabic Rhetoric 1940, Poetry of Nature in Arabic and Western Literature 1944, Egypt in the United Nations 1947, The Egyptian Parliament in a Quarter of a Century 1951, The Political Status of the Emirates of the Arab Gulf and Southern Arabia 1959, The Arab-Israeli Conflict 1962, Arab Unity 1964, Arab Nationalism 1965, Arab Socialism 1966, The Record of Israel 1966, Joint Arab Action Book I 1968, Book II 1971, The Arab Gulf 1969, An Introduction to Israeli Foreign Policy 1972, The Relationship between the United Nations and the Arab League 1975, The International Function of the Arab League 1975, The Future of Joint Arab Action 1977. *Address:* 9 Khan Younis Street, Madinat Al-Mohandiseen, Dokki, Cairo, Egypt. *Telephone:* 807999.

NOGAWA, Shoji; Japanese business executive; b. 6 March 1927; m. Kumiko Nogawa; two s.; ed. Univ. of Tokyo; entered Komatsu Ltd. 1951, Dir. 1973-78, Man. Dir. 1978-82, Exec. Man. Dir. 1982-, Pres 1982. *Leisure interests:* golf, growing Bonsai. *Address:* 3-6 Akasaka, Minato-ku, Tokyo 107, Japan.

NOGUCHI, Teruo, D.S.; Japanese businessman; b. 5 Nov. 1917, Tokyo; s. of Eizaburo and Yae Noguchi; m. Michiko Kohama 1948; two s.; ed. Osaka Univ.; Lecturer in Physical Science, Osaka Univ. 1944-57; employed by Koa Oil Co. Ltd. 1944, Dir. 1961-64, Man. Dir. 1964-67, Chief Man. Dir. 1967-73, Pres. 1973-; Dir. Mitsui Petro-chemical Industries Ltd. 1973-, Tokyo Tanker Co. Ltd. 1974-, Nippon Oil Staging Terminal Co. Ltd. 1977-; Chair. Research Asscn. for Residual Oil Processing 1979, Research Asscn. for Petroleum Alternative Devt. 1980-, Japan Co-operation Centre for Petroleum Industry Devt. 1981-, Research Asscn. for Utilization of Light Oil 1983-; mem. Keidanren, Japan Petroleum Inst., Tokyo Chamber of Commerce, Petroleum Asscn., Japan; Order of Blue Ribbon 1982. *Leisure interests:* photography, music. *Address:* 2-6-2 Ohtemachi, Chiyoda-ku, Tokyo 100 (Office); 30 Minami-cho, Shinjuku-ku, Tokyo 162, Japan (Home).

NOGUEIRA, Albano Pires Fernandes; Portuguese diplomatist, writer and literary critic; b. 8 Nov. 1911, Arganil; s. of Albano P. D. Nogueira and Albertina F. Nogueira; m. Alda Xavier da Cunha 1937; ed. Coimbra Univ.; entered Diplomatic Service 1941; posts in embassy in Washington, and legations in Pretoria and Tokyo 1944-49; Chargé d'Affaires and Rep. to Allied High Comm. in Japan 1950-52, Rep. of Portuguese Govt. to Japanese Govt. 1952; Counsellor, London 1952; Consul-Gen., Bombay 1955, New York 1955; mem. Perm. Mission of Portugal at UN 1955-59; Amb. to EEC 1964; Perm. Rep. to North Atlantic Council 1970-74; Amb. to U.K. 1974-76; Sec.-Gen. Ministry of Foreign Affairs 1977-78; Visiting Prof. Univ. of Minho 1979-80; mem. Int. Asscn. of Literary Critics 1981-. *Publications:* a novel, two books of essays, contribs. to books on NATO, book reviews. *Leisure interests:* writing, reading. *Address:* Avenida Gaspar

Corte Real 18, Apt. 4D, 2750 Cascais; Rua Alberto de Oliveira, 5-3, 3000 Coímbra, Portugal. *Telephone:* Cascais 2868264; Coímbra 715035.

NOGUEIRA, Alberto Franco; Portuguese diplomatist and politician; b. 1918; ed. Lisbon Univ.; Third Sec., Ministry of Foreign Affairs 1943-45, Second Sec. 1945-51; Second Sec. and Chargé d'Affaires, Portuguese Embassy, Tokyo 1946-50; First Sec., Ministry of Foreign Affairs 1951-54; Head of Political Affairs 1954; Consul-Gen., London 1955-58; Portuguese Rep., C.C.T.A. 1955-60; Dir.-Gen. Political Affairs 1960-61; Minister of Foreign Affairs 1961-69. *Publications:* Journal of Literary Critic 1953, Struggle for the East 1957, United Nations and Portugal 1963, The Third World 1967. *Address:* c/o Ministry of Foreign Affairs, Lisbon, Portugal.

NOGUEIRA, Dênio Chagas; Brazilian economist; b. 12 Dec. 1920, Rio de Janeiro; s. of Outubrino Nogueira and Anna Cândida Nogueira: m. Orsina de Fonseca 1956; one s. one d.; ed. Universidade do Brasil and Univ. of Michigan; Head, Finance Dept. Nat. Econ. Council 1951-64; Ed.-in-Chief Conjuntura Econômica 1953; Econ. Consultant to Econ. Comm. for Latin America and OAS on Foreign Investments in Latin American Free Trade Assen. 1960, to OAS on the Treaty of Montevideo (LAFTA) 1961; Exec. Dir. Superintendency of Money and Credit, Brazil (SUMOC) 1964-65; fmr. Pres. Banco Central do Brasil; Pres. Banco Geral do Brasil. *Publications:* Joint International Business Ventures in Brazil 1959, Foreign Private Investments in LAFTA 1960, Reforma Agraria: Problemas e Soluções 1964. *Leisure interests:* tennis, yachting. *Address:* Banco Geral do Brasil, S.A., Belém, Brazil.

NOGUEIRA-BATISTA, Paulo, M.A.; Brazilian diplomatist; b. 4 Oct. 1929, Recife; m.; four c.; ed. Univ. of Rio de Janeiro and Carleton Univ.; entered Foreign Service 1952; First Sec. Brazilian Embassy, Ottawa 1964-66; Minister-Counsellor, Bonn 1969-70; Head Brazilian Del. to Preparatory Cttee., Tokyo Round of Trade Negotiations, Geneva 1973; Chief Negotiator Tripartite Agreement on Safeguards for the Peaceful Uses of Nuclear Energy between Brazil, the Fed. Repub. of Germany and the IAEA, Vienna 1985; Head. Brazilian Del. ECOSOC, Geneva and UNCTAD 1983-86; Chair. Negotiating Cttee., Gen. System of Trade Preferences among Developing Countries, Geneva March-Oct. 1986; Amb. to UN Office, Geneva 1983-87; Perm. Rep. to UN Sept. 1987-; Pres. and Chair. Bd. of the Brazilian State Corpn. for Nuclear Activities (NUCLEBRAS) 1975-82. *Address:* Permanent Mission of Brazil to the United Nations, 747 Third Avenue, 9th Floor, New York, N.Y. 10017, U.S.A *Telephone:* (212) 832-6868.

NOGUÈRES, Henri, LIC. EN DROIT; French journalist, lawyer and author; b. 13 Nov. 1916, Bages; s. of Louis Noguères; m. Jacqueline Profichet 1939; one d.; ed. Janson-de-Sailly High School, Paris; worked for journal Populaire de Paris 1936-, Man. Ed. 1946-49; lawyer in Paris court 1942-46, 1977-; Dir. and Ed.-in-Chief, Cen. Press Agency, Paris 1949-59; has written for radio and television, also produced and directed several plays and reviews; Admin. Dir. Editions Robert Laffont 1962-66; Sec.-Gen. Editions Flammarion 1966-76; Pres. Assen. of Journalists 1960-74; Pres. League of Rights of Man 1975-84; Commandeur, Légion d'honneur, Military Medal, Croix de guerre 1939-45, Rosette de la Résistance. *Publications:* many historical works, including Le Saint-Barthélemy 1960, Munich ou la drôle de paix 1963, Histoire de la Résistance en France (5 vols.) 1967-72, La vie quotidienne en France au temps du Front populaire 1977, La vie quotidienne des résistants de l'armistice à la liberation 1983, La vérité aura le dernier mot. *Address:* 70 avenue Marceau, 75008 Paris, France. *Telephone:* (1) 47.20.08.21.

NØJGAARD, Morten, D.PHIL.; Danish professor of romance philology; b. 28 July 1934, Holbaek; s. of Niels Nøjgaard and Annie (née Bay) Nøjgaard; m. Stina Lund 1962; two s. two d.; secondary school teacher Roedovre Statskole 1960-63; research scholar Univ. of Copenhagen 1963-65; Prof. of Romance Philology, Univ. of Odense 1966-; Chief Ed. Orbis Litterarum 1968-; Pres. Assen. of French Prof. 1962-63, Alliance Française, Odense 1970-; mem. Royal Danish Acad. of Science 1982; Fnske Bladfond Research Award 1975, Ordre du Mérite 1980. *Publications:* La Fable Antique, (vols I–II) 1964-67, Elévation et Expansion. Les deux Dimensions de Baudelaire 1973, An Introduction to Literary Analysis 1975, Romainary-Emile Adar, Momo Duplex 1986, numerous scientific articles. *Address:* Aløkken 48, 5250 Odense SV, Denmark. *Telephone:* (09) 96 18 06.

NOKIN, Max; Belgian businessman; b. 10 Dec. 1907; m. Denise Malfeson; two s. three d.; ed. Liège Univ.; Dir. Soc. Générale de Belgique 1949-61, Gov. 1962-75, Hon. Gov. 1976-; Hon. Chair. Usines de la Vieille Montagne, S.I.D.M.A.R.; Croix de guerre avec palme, Grand Officier Ordre Léopold II, Commdr. Ordre de Léopold, Officier Ordre de la Couronne, Hon. K.B.E., Commdr. Ordre du Chêne (Luxembourg), Grand Officier, Ordre du Mérite Civil et Militaire d'Adolphe de Nassau (Luxembourg). *Leisure interests:* golf, astronomy. *Address:* rue Royale 30, 1000 Brussels, Belgium.

NOLAN, Sir Sidney Robert, Kt., O.M., C.B.E.; Australian artist; b. 22 April 1917, Melbourne; s. of late Sidney Henry Nolan; m. 1st Elizabeth Patterson 1939 (divorced 1942); m. 2nd Cynthia Hansen 1948 (died 1974); m. 3rd Mary Elizabeth à Beckett Perceval 1977; ed. Melbourne State and Tech. schools, Melbourne Nat. Gallery; one-man shows Paris, London, New York, Rome, Venice and capital cities of Australia; Arts Council Travelling Exhbn., Great Britain; also exhibited at Pittsburgh Int. Exhbn. 1953, 1954,

1955, 1964, 1967, 1970, 1971, New Delhi Int. Exhbn. 1953, Pacific Loan Exhbn. Australia and U.S.A. 1956, Brussels Int. Exhbn. 1958, Documenta II, Kassel 1959, Dunn Int. Exhbn., London 1963, Edinburgh Festival 1964, Aldeburgh Festival 1964, 1968, 1971; Retrospective Exhbn. New South Wales 1967, Darmstadt, Edinburgh 1971, Dublin 1973; set designs for Icare, Colonel de Basil's Ballet Russe 1940, The Rite of Spring, Covent Garden 1962, The Display, Canberra 1965; illustrated Children's Crusade by Benjamin Britten 1973, Samson et Delilah, Covent Garden 1981, Il Trovatore, Sydney 1983; Commr. for Australia and Del. for Australian Documentary Films, Venice Biennale 1954; Italian Govt. Scholarship 1956; Commonwealth Fund Fellowship for Travel in U.S.A. 1959-61; Nat. Univ., Canberra Fellowship 1965; Fellow Bavarian Acad. 1971; Hon. Fellow York Univ. 1971; Hon LL.D. (Nat. Univ. Australia) 1968, Hon. D.Litt. (London) 1971; Britannica Award (Australia) 1969. *Principal works:* in Tate Gallery (London), Museum of Modern Art (New York), Nat. Galleries of Australia, Tom Collins Memorial (Perth Univ.), Contemporary Art Soc. and Arts Council of Great Britain (London). *Publications:* Ned Kelly 1963, Sidney Nolan: Myth and Imagery 1967, Open Negative 1967, Paradise Gardens 1971. *Address:* c/o Marlborough Fine Art Ltd., 6 Albemarle Street, London, W.1, England.

NOLAN, Thomas Brennan, PH.B., PH.D.; American geologist; b. 21 May 1901, Greenfield, Mass.; s. of Frank Wesley and Anna (née Brennan); m. Mabelle Orleman 1927; one s.; ed. Yale Univ.; Geologist, U.S. Geol. Survey 1924-44, Asst. Dir. 1944-56, Dir. 1956-65, Research Geologist 1965-; mem. American Philosophical Soc., American Acad. of Arts and Sciences; mem. Emer. Nat. Acad. of Sciences; Pres. Soc. of Econ. Geologists 1950, Geological Soc. of America 1961; Vice-Pres. Int. Union of Geological Sciences 1964; Hon. Fellow, Royal Soc. of Edinburgh; Foreign mem. Geological Soc. of London; Hon. LL.D. (St. Andrews) 1962; Spendiaroff Prize, Int. Geol. Congress 1933, K.C. Li Medal and Prize, Columbia Univ. 1954, Rockefeller Public Service Awards, Princeton Univ. 1961, Silver Medal, Tokyo Geog. Soc. 1965, Wilbur Cross Medal, Yale Univ. 1987. *Publications:* Geological articles in scientific journals. *Address:* U.S. Geological Survey, Reston, Virginia 22092 (Office); 2219 California Street, N.W., Washington, D.C. 20008, U.S.A. (Home). *Telephone:* (703) 648-6605 (Office); (202) 462-2040 (Home).

NOLAND, Kenneth Clifton; American artist; b. 10 April 1927, Asheville, N.C.; s. of Harry C. and Bessie (Elkins) Noland; m. 1st Cornelia Langel (divorced), 2nd Stephanie Gordon 1967; three c.; ed. Black Mountain Coll., North Carolina and Paris; Teacher Inst. of Contemporary Arts 1950-52, Catholic Univ. 1951-60, Bennington Coll. 1968; one-man shows: Galerie Creuze, Paris 1949, Tibor de Nagy, New York 1957, 1958, French and Co., New York 1959, André Emmerich Gallery, New York 1967, 1973, 1975, 1977-78 1980-83, André Emmerich Gallery, Zurich 1973, 1976, 1979, 1982, Nicholas Wilder Gallery, Los Angeles 1967, also Milan, Paris, London; work in permanent collections in Museum of Modern Art, Guggenheim Museum, Whitney Museum, Tate Gallery, Stedelijk Museum (Amsterdam), Zürich Kunsthaus and others. *Address:* Box 125, South Salem, N.Y. 10590, U.S.A.

NOLTING, Frederick Ernest, Jr., PH.D.; American diplomatist, banker and university professor; b. 24 Aug. 1911, Richmond, Va.; s. of Frederick E. Nolting and Mary Buford; m. Olivia Lindsay Crumpler 1940; four d.; ed. St. Christopher's School, Richmond, Virginia, Univ. of Virginia and Harvard Univ.; Investment Firm, Richmond 1934-39; Lecturing Fellowship in Philosophy, Univ. of Va. 1941-42; U.S. Navy 1942-46; Dept. of State 1946-64, Asst. to Deputy Under-Sec. of State 1950-53, Special Asst. to Sec. of State for Mutual Security Affairs 1953-55; Dir. Office of Political Affairs, U.S. Del. to NATO 1955-57; Deputy Chief of Mission, U.S. Del. to NATO and European Regional Orgs. (USRO), Alt. U.S. Rep. on North Atlantic Council 1957-61; Amb. to Viet-Nam 1961-63; Vice-Pres. European Offices Morgan Guaranty Trust Co. of New York 1964-69, Asst. Chair. 1969-73, Consultant 1973-76; Diplomat-in-Residence, Univ. of Va. 1971-73; Olsson Prof. of Business Admin., Grad. School of Business, Univ. of Va. 1973-76; Dir. Miller Center of Public Affairs, Univ. of Va. 1975-78; Prof. Univ. of Va. 1978-82, Dir. Fed. Execs. Program 1979-82; Prof. Emer. 1982-; mem. Bd. of Trustees, Thomas Jefferson Memorial Foundation, Va. *Publication:* From Trust to Tragedy 1988. *Leisure interests:* sport, music. *Address:* Route 7, Box 168, Charlottesville, Va. 22901, U.S.A. (Home). *Telephone:* (804) 293-9013 (Office); (804) 295-3869 (Home).

NOMURA, Masayasu, PH.D.; Japanese molecular biologist and academic; b. 27 April 1927, Hyogo-ken; s. of Hiromichi Nomura and Yaeko Nomura; m. Junko Hamashima 1957; one s. one d.; ed. Univ. of Tokyo; Research Assoc., Prof. S. Spiegelman's Lab., Univ. of Ill. and Prof. J. D. Watson's Lab., Harvard Univ., U.S.A. 1957-59, Prof. S. Benzer's Lab., Purdue Univ. 1959-60; Asst. Prof., Inst. for Protein Research, Osaka Univ. 1960-63; Assoc. Prof., Dept. of Genetics, Univ. of Wis., U.S.A. 1963-66, Prof. 1966-70, Elvehjem Prof. of Life Sciences, Inst. for Enzyme Research, with jt. appts. in Depts. of Genetics and Biochemistry 1970-84, Grace Bell Prof. of Biol. Chem., Univ. of Calif., Irvine 1984-; Fellow A.A.A.S.; mem. American Acad. of Arts and Sciences, N.A.S.; Foreign mem. Royal Danish Acad. of Sciences and Letters; U.S. Steel Award in Molecular Biology (N.A.S.), Japan Acad. Award 1972, Y. D. Mattia Award (Roche Ints.). *Leisure interests:* hiking, reading. *Address:* University of California,

Department of Biological Chemistry, Med. Sci. I, D240, Irvine, Calif. 92717; 26 Starlight, Irvine, Calif. 92715, U.S.A. (Home). *Telephone:* (714) 856-4564 (Office); (714) 854-3482 (Home).

NOMURA, Yoshihiro; Japanese professor of law; b. 3 Jan. 1941, Nagoya; m. 1966; three s. one d.; ed. Univ. of Tokyo; Asst. Lecturer in Law, Univ. of Tokyo 1963; lecturer Tokyo Metropolitan Univ. 1966, Assoc. Prof. 1967, Prof. of Law 1977-. *Publication:* Automobile Accident Damages 1988. *Leisure interests:* dogs, driving. *Address:* 7-19 Mitakedai, Midori-ku, Yokohama, Japan. *Telephone:* (045) 973-2612.

NONO, Luigi; Italian composer; b. 29 Jan. 1924; s. of Mario and Maria Manetti Nono; m. Nuria Schoenberg 1955; two d.; studied with Bruno Maderna and Hermann Scherchen; teacher New Music Summer School, Kranichsteiner Musikinstitut, Darmstadt 1957-, Dartington Hall Music Summer School, Devon (England) 1959, 1960; *Compositions:* Variazioni canoniche sulla serie dell' op. 41 di A. Schoenberg 1950, Polifonica-Monodia-Ritmica 1951, Composizione per Orchestra, I Epitafio per F. García-Lorca, II Epitafio per F. García-Lorca 1952, III Epitafio per F. García-Lorca, Due Espressioni per Orchestra 1953, La victoire de Guernica (poem by P. Eluard), Liebeslied, Der Rote Mantel (ballet) 1954, Canti per 13, Incontri 1955, Il Canto Sospeso 1956, Varianti 1957, La Terra e la Campagna (Words by C. Pavese), Cori di Didone (words by G. Ungaretti) 1958, Composizione per Orchestra N. 2—Diario Polacco '58 1959, Ha Venido (words by A. Machado) 1960, Sarà dolce tacere (words by C. Pavese) 1960, Omaggio a Emilio Vedova (electronic music) 1960, Intolleranza 1960 1961 (words by A. M. Ripellino, V. Mayakovsky, P. Eluard, H. Alleg, J.-P. Sartre, B. Brecht, I. Fucik), Sul Ponte di Hiroshima 1962 (words by G. Anders. J. L. Pacheco and C. Pavese), Canciones A Guiomar 1963 (words by A. Machado), Dal Diario Italiano 1964, A Floresta é Jorem e Cheia de vida 1966, La Fabrica illuminata (words by G. Scabia) 1966, Ricorda Cosa ti Hanno Fatto in Auschwitz 1966, Per bastiana tai-yangcheng 1967, Contrappunto dialettico alla mente (words by S. Sanchez, N. Balestrini; for tape) 1968, Musica manifesto N.1: Un volto, del mare (words by C. Pavese; for voice and tape) 1968-69, Y entonces comprendió (Words by C. Franqui; for tape, 6 women's voices and chorus) 1969-70, Ein Gespenst geht um in der Welt (words by K. Marx, C. Sanchez, H. Santamaria; for solo soprano, chorus and orchestra) 1971, Como una ola de fuerza y luz (words by J. Huasi; for soprano, piano, orchestra, tape) 1971-72, Al gran sole carico d'amore (words by E. Guevara, A. Rimbaud, Louise Michel, T. Bunke, B. Brecht, K. Marx, Lenin, C. Pavese, C. Sanchez, H. Santamaria, etc.; scenic action in two acts) 1972-75, Canto per il Vietnam (mixed chorus) 1973, Für Paul Dessau (for tape) 1974, ... sofferte onde serene ... (for piano and tape) 1976. *Address:* Giudecca 882, 30123 Venice, Italy. *Telephone:* Venice 28368.

NOONAN, Michael, B.A., T.D.; Irish politician; b. May 1943, Foynes, Co. Limerick; m. Florence Knightly; two s. two d.; ed. St. Patrick's Glin, Co. Limerick, St. Patrick's Coll., Drumcondra, Dublin and Univ. Coll., Dublin; fmr. teacher of English, Crescent Coll., Limerick; mem. Limerick County Council 1974-; mem. Dail Eireann 1981-; Minister for Justice 1982-86, for the Environment 1986-87, for Defence March 1987-; fmr. mem. Nat. Council and Nat. Exec. of Fine Gael, now mem. of Fianna Fáil. *Address:* Department of Defence, Parkgate, Dublin 8, Ireland. *Telephone:* 771881.

NOORBAKHSH, Mohsen, PH.D.; Iranian banker; b. 18 May 1948, Isfahan; m. Moazam Karbasizadeh; two s. one d.; fmr. Gov. Bank Markazi. *Address:* c/o Bank Markazi Iran, Ferdowsi Avenue, Teheran, Iran.

NORA, Simon, L. EN D.; French government official; b. 21 Feb. 1921, Paris; s. of Gaston Nora and Julie Lehman; m. 1st Marie-Pierre de Cosse-Brissac (divorced), one s. one d.; m. 2nd Léone Georges-Picot, one s. two d.; ed. Lycée Janson-de-Sailly, Paris, Facultés de droit et des lettres, Grenoble and Paris, and Ecole nat. d'Admin.; Insp. of Finance 1949, Insp. Gen. 1971; held various posts in Ministry of Finance 1951-60, 1963-71; Dir-Gen. econ. and energy service, European Coal and Steel Community 1960-63; inter-ministerial del. for colour TV 1967-71; mem. supervisory council, Entreprise minière et chimique 1967-71; in office of PM Jacques Chaban-Delmas 1969-71; Dir.-Gen. Librairie Hachette 1971-74; Dir. Soc. d'études de télévision (Télétudes) 1971-74; Cie. luxembourgeoise de télédiffusion 1972-75; Dir. Ecole nat. d'Admin. 1982-85; Sr. Adviser, Shearson Lehman Brothers Int. 1986-; Commdr., Légion d'honneur, des Palmes académiques; Croix de guerre; Commdr. Order of Merit (Italy). *Publications:* Rapport sur les entreprises publiques 1967, l'Amélioration de l'habitat ancien (in collab.) 1976, Informatisation de la société (in collab.) 1978. *Address:* Shearson Lehman Brothers International, 9 Devonshire Square, London, EC2M 4YL, England, and 12/14 Rond Point des Champs Elysées, 75008 Paris, France. *Telephone:* 01-626 2525 (London); (1) 42.25.15.16 (Paris).

NORBERG, Dag, D.PH.; Swedish classical scholar; b. 31 July 1909, Strängnäs; s. of Otto Norberg and Gunhild Rappe; m. Brita von Otter 1939; four s.; ed. Uppsala Univ.; Docent, Uppsala Univ. 1937-48; Prof. of Latin Language and Literature, Stockholm Univ. 1948-75, Dean, Faculty of Humanities, 1960-63; Pres. (Rector), Stockholm Univ. 1966-74; mem. Human Vetenskapssamfundet i Uppsala 1946, Vitterhetsakademien 1955, Danske Videnskabernes Selskab 1964, Vetenskapsakademien 1965, Acad. Inscriptions et Belles-Lettres 1984; Pres. Int. Fed. of Socs. of Classical Studies 1964-69. *Publications:* In Registrum Gregorii Magni studia I-II,

1937–39, Syntaktische Forschungen 1943, Beiträge zur spätl. Syntax 1944, Horatius sista lyriska diktning 1945, La poésie latine rythmique du haut moyen âge 1953, Introduction à l'étude de la versification latine médiévale 1958, Den romerska litteraturen in Bonniers allmänna litteraturhistoria 1959, Epistulae s. Desiderii Cadurcensis 1961, Processen mot Caelius och Ciceros försvarstal 1965, Manuel pratique de latin médiéval 1968, Au seuil du Moyen Age 1974, Notes critiques sur l'Hymnarius Severinianus 1977, L'œuvre poétique de Paulin d'Aquilée 1979, S. Gregorii Magni Registrum Epistularum 1982, L'accentuation des mots dans le vers latin du Moyen Age 1985, Les vers latins iambiques et trochaïques au Moyen Age et leurs répliques rythmiques 1987. *Address:* Västmannagatan 32, S-11325, Stockholm, Sweden.

NORBOM, Jon Ola; Norwegian economist and politician; b. 15 Dec. 1923, Baerum; m. Ellen Ann Hook 1954; two d.; ed. Oslo Univ.; Sec., Ministry of Industry 1950–54; Asst. Research Economist, Nat. Bureau of Econ. Research, N.Y. 1954; Statistician UN Office, N.Y. 1955; Research Econ. and later Expert on Commercial Policy, GATT, Geneva 1959–67; Under-Sec. of State, Ministry of Finance 1967–69; Dir. Int. Trade Centre, UNCTAD/GATT, Geneva 1971–72, 1973–83; Minister of Finance and Customs 1972–73; Perm. Sec., Ministry of Social Affairs 1984–; mem. UN Comm. on Social Devt. 1987–; Chair. Norwegian Young Liberals 1950–52; mem. Nat. Exec. Liberal Party. *Address:* Ministry of Social Affairs, Oslo, Norway.

NORD, Hans Robert, D.IUR.; Netherlands lawyer and politician; b. 11 Oct. 1919, The Hague; s. of Charles F. L. Nord and Philippina C. Elshout; m. Margaret Ena Bevan 1951; two s.; ed. Gymnasium, The Hague, and Leiden Univ.; Barrister, The Hague 1943–45; Legal Adviser 1945–61; Pres. European Movement in the Netherlands 1958–61; Chair. Netherlands Atlantic Cttee. 1954–61; Sec.-Gen. European Parl. 1961–79, mem. 1979–, Vice-Pres. 1984–87; Commdr. Order of Orange-Nassau, Commdr. Order of Merit of Italy, Commdr. Order of San Carlos, Colombia, Commdr. Nat. Order, Ivory Coast, Grand Officier, Ordre de la Couronne de Chênt, Luxembourg, Grand Officier, Ordre de la Couronne (Belgium), Grand Officier, Ordre de l'Aigle Aztèque (Mexico), Commdr., Croix de Mérite (Fed. Repub. of Germany). *Publications:* The Idea of Representation in Constitutional Law 1945, Problems of International Government 1948, International and Supra-National Co-operation 1952, In Search of a Political Framework for a United Europe 1956, NATO 1961. *Leisure interests:* music, literature, travel. *Address:* European Parliament, Rue Belliard, 97–113, B-1040 Brussels, Belgium; 15 rue des Astronomes, 1180 Brussels, Belgium (Home). *Telephone:* 379 7781 (Home).

NORDAL, Jóhannes, PH.D.; Icelandic economist and banker; b. 11 May 1924, Reykjavík; s. of Prof. Sigurdur Nordal and Olöf Jónsdóttir; m. Dóra Gudjónsdóttir 1953; one s. five d.; ed. Reykjavík Grammar School and L.S.E., London; Chief Economist, Nat. Bank of Iceland 1954–59, Gen. Man. 1959–61; Gov., Central Bank of Iceland (Sedlabanki Islands) 1961–, (Chair. Bd. of Governors 1964–); Chair. of Bd. Nat. Power Co. (Landsvirkjun) 1965–; Gov. IMF for Iceland 1965–; Chair. Humanities Div. of Science Fund for Iceland 1958–; mem. Soc. Scientiarum Islandica 1959–; Grand Kt. Order of Falcon 1966. *Publications:* Iceland 1966, 1974, 1986; Ed. Fjármálatíáindi (Financial Review) 1954–; Co. Ed. Nýtt Helgafell (literary periodical) 1955–59. *Address:* Sedlabanki Islands, Kalkofnsvegur 1, 150 Reykjavík (Office); Laugarásvegur 11, Reykjavík, Iceland (Home). *Telephone:* 699600 (Office); 33350 (Home).

NORDENFALK, Carl (Adam Johan), FIL.DR.; Swedish museum official and university professor; b. 13 Dec. 1907; ed. Univs. of Uppsala, Stockholm, Gothenburg; Asst. Curator, Gothenburg Art Museum 1935–44; Curator, Nat. Museum of Arts, Stockholm 1944–58, Dir.-Gen. 1958–69; Mellon Prof., Univ. of Pittsburgh 1971–72, 1973–; Slade Prof. Univ. of Cambridge 1972–73; Kress Prof. Nat. Gallery, Washington 1973–; mem. Royal Soc. of Sciences (Uppsala), Royal Swedish Acad. of Letters; Visiting mem. Inst. for Advanced Study, Princeton 1949–50, 1957, 1967–70; Corresp. Fellow British Acad. 1967–, Bavarian Acad. of Sciences (Munich), German Archaeological Inst. etc.; Hon. mem. Swedish Royal Acad. of Fine Arts, Real Acad. de Bellas Artes de San Fernando (Madrid), American Philosophical Soc. *Publications:* Die spätantiken Kanontafeln 1938, Vincent van Gogh 1943, Kung Praktiks och Drottning Teoris jaktbok 1955, Die spätantiken Zierbuchstaben 1970, Codex Caesareus Upsaliensis 1971; also co-author of several books: (with A. Grabar) Le Haut Moyen-Age 1957, La peinture romaine 1958, Treasures of Swedish Art 1965, Medieval and Renaissance Miniatures from the Lessing J. Rosenwald collection 1975, Vergilius Augusteus 1976. *Address:* c/o National museum, S-10324 Stockholm, Sweden.

NORDLI, Odvar; Norwegian politician; b. 3 Nov. 1927, Stange, Hedmark; ed. in business administration; Asst. Baerum Municipal Auditor's Office 1948–49; Chief Clerk, Hedmark County Auditor's Office 1949–57; District Auditor, Vang and Löten 1957–61; mem. Storting (Parl.) 1961; mem. and Deputy Chair. Stange Municipal Council 1952; Chair. Municipal Cttee. of Hedmark Labour Party 1960–; Deputy mem. Central Cttee. of Labour Party 1965, Chair. Hedmark Labour Party 1968; Chair. Trade Union and Labour Party Tax Cttee. 1967–68; Vice-Chair. Parl. Municipal Cttee. 1965–69; Chair. Parl. Social Welfare Cttee. 1969–71; Minister of Labour and Municipal Affairs 1971–72; Chair. Comm. of Defence 1974–75; Prime

Minister 1976–81; Vice-Pres. Parl. 1981; Leader Parl. Labour Party 1973–76.

NORDSTRÖM, Torkel, LL.D.; Swedish fmr. judge; b. 12 March 1910, Halmstad; s. of Thorsten Nordström and Tora Afzelius; m. Vera Starfelt 1937; three d.; ed. Univ. of Lund; Assoc. Judge, Svea Court of Appeal 1946–53, Ordinary Judge 1953–55; Justice of the Supreme Court 1955–77, Chief Justice 1976–77; mem. Drafts Legislation Cttee. 1951–55; Hon. LL.D. (Lund) 1973; Commdr. Grand Cross Order of North Star (Sweden), Icelandic Falcon, Kt. Order of Dannebrog (Denmark), White Rose of Finland, King's Medal. *Publications:* Commentaries on the Citizenship Act 1952 and the Hire Purchase Act 1957; Ed. Swedish Statute Book (annual) 1974–. *Leisure interests:* gardening, genealogy. *Address:* Åsbacken 25, S-16139 Bromma, Sweden. *Telephone:* 08/26-06-34.

NORFOLK, 17th Duke of, cr. 1483; **Miles Francis Stapleton Fitzalan-Howard,** K.G., G.C.V.O., C.B., C.B.E., M.C., D.L.; Earl of Arundel, Baron Beaumont, Baron Maltravers, Earl of Surrey, Baron FitzAlan, Clun, and Oswaldestre, Earl of Norfolk, Baron Howard of Glossop, Earl Marshal and Hereditary Marshal and Chief Butler of England; Premier Duke and Earl; British landowner and fmr. army officer; b. 21 July 1915, London; s. of 3rd Baron Howard of Glossop, M.B.E., and Baroness Beaumont (11th in line), O.B.E.; m. Anne Mary Teresa Constable Maxwell 1949; two s. three d.; ed. Ampleforth Coll., Christ Church, Oxford; 2nd Lieut. Grenadier Guards 1937; served World War II, France, N. Africa, Sicily, Italy, N.W. Europe; Head of British Mil. Mission to Soviet forces, Germany 1957; Commdr. 70 Brigade, King's African Rifles 1961–63; GOC (Maj.-Gen.) 1 Div. 1963–65; Dir. Man. and Support Intelligence, Ministry of Defence 1965-66, Service Intelligence 1966–67; retd. 1967; Chair. Arundel Castle Trustees Ltd. 1976–; D.L. West Sussex 1977–; Dir. Robert Fleming Holdings Ltd. 1969–85; Pres. Building Socs. Asscn. 1982–86; Hon. Master of the Bench of the Inner Temple 1984–; Prime Warden, Fishmongers' Co. 1985–86; Kt. of Sovereign Order of Malta. *Address:* Arundel Castle, West Sussex, BN18 9AB; Carlton Towers, Goole, North Humberside, DN14 9LZ; Bacres House, Hambleden, Henley-on-Thames, Oxon., RG9 6RY, England. *Telephone:* (0903) 882173; (0405) 860243; (0491) 571-350.

NØRGAARD, Carl Aage, DR. JUR.; Danish professor of law; b. 15 Sept. 1924, Denmark; s. of Edvard Nørgaard and Jensine Kristine Kristensen; m. Hedvig Hauberg 1951; one d.; ed. Univs. of Aarhus, Cambridge and Geneva; Asst. Faculty of Law, Univ. of Aarhus 1955–58, Lecturer 1958–64, Prof. 1964–, Head of Inst. of Public Law 1964–86; Rockefeller Fellowship, Univ. of Geneva 1959–60; mem. European Comm. of Human Rights 1973–, Second Vice-Pres. 1976–81, Pres. 1981–. *Publications:* The Position of the Individual in International Law 1962, Forvaltningsret-Sagsbehandling 1972, Administration og Borger (with Claus Haagen Jensen) 1972, 1984, 1988; articles in legal periodicals. *Leisure interests:* rowing, gardening. *Address:* Hójlygaard, Skórring, 8464 Galten, Denmark. *Telephone:* 06-130111 (Office); 06-944047 (Home).

NØRGAARD, Ivar, MA. (ECON.); Danish politician; b. 26 July 1922, Kongens Lyngby; s. of Ingvar and of the late Olga Nørgaard; m. 1st Inge Gothenborg 1947 (died 1972), two d.; m. 2nd Sonja Nørgaard 1974; ed. Copenhagen Univ.; Sec., Customs Dept., Ministry of Finance 1947; Sec., Econ. Council, Labour Movement 1948–55; Dir. Workers' High School, Esbjerg 1955; Political Editor-in-Chief Aktuelt 1961–64, Man. Ed. 1964–65; Minister of Econ. Affairs 1965–68, also Minister for European Market Relations 1967–68; mem. Parl. 1966–; taught at Danish High School of Admin. 1969; Minister for Foreign Econ. Affairs and Nordic Relations 1971–73, 1975–77, for Trade, Industry and Shipping 1977–78; Minister for the Environment 1978–80, for Econ. Affairs 1979–82; Dir. Workers' Educ. Assn. 1964–65; mem. Bd. of Danish Nat. Bank 1968, Lyngby-Taarbaek Municipality 1954-55, Atomic Energy Comm. 1956–65, Nat. Wage Bd. 1968–71; co-founder and fmr. Vice-Pres. of Social Dem. students org. Free Forum; mem. Nordic Ministerial Council; mem. and Vice-Pres. European Parl. 1974–75; Pres. Danish System Export 1986, Politico-Econ. Cttee. and Vice-Pres. European Market Cttee. of Danish Parl.; Pres. Danish IPU Del. *Publications:* Lœrebog i Nationaløkonomi (Textbook on National Economy) 1949, Focus på Nationaløkonomien (Focus on the National Economy), Din løn og Samfundets økonomi (Your Wage and the National Economy); Ed. and Co-author Din økonomi og Samfundets (Your Own and the Community's Economy) 1960; Co-editor and Co-author Arbejderhåndbog for Samarbejdsudvalg (Workers' Manual on Industrial Council Work) 1954. *Address:* Nydamsvej 15, 2880 Bagsvaerd, Denmark. *Telephone:* 01-11-66-00.

NORIEGA, Gen. Antonio; Panamanian army officer; b. 11 Feb. 1940, Panama City; m. Felicidad Sieiro; 3 c.; ed. Univ. of Panama, Mil. Acad., Peru; First Lieut. Panama Nat. Guard 1962; Head Panama Intelligence Services 1970; mem. Jt. Chiefs of Staff, Guardia Nacional 1970–81, Chief 1982–83; C.-in-C. Panama Defence Forces 1983–; numerous medals *Publication:* Immortal Ayacucho 1952. *Address:* Panamanian Armed Forces, Avenida B, Panama 3434 Zona 1, Panama.

NORLING, Bengt Olov; Swedish politician; b. 12 Jan. 1925; Malmö; s. of David Norling and Margareta Thorsén; m. Elisabeth Stöfling 1946; one s.; ed. privately; railway worker until 1956; Ombudsman, Swedish Railwaymen's Union 1956–65; Ombudsman, Swedish Confed. of Trade Unions 1965–68, Sec. 1969; Minister of Transport and Communications 1969–76;

M.P. (Social Dem. Party) 1971-; Gov. of Värmlands 1977-. *Leisure interest:* music. *Address:* Länsstyrelsen, Värmlands-län, 65186 Karlstad, Sweden.

NORMAN, Sir Arthur Gordon, K.B.E., D.F.C.; British business executive; b. 18 Feb. 1917, North Pertherton, Somerset; s. of Christopher William Norman and Mary Christine Milton; m. Margaret Doreen Harrington 1944 (died 1982); three s. two d.; ed. Blundell's School; Thomas De La Rue and Co. 1934-87, Asst. Gen. Man. 1947, Dir. 1951, Man. Dir. 1953; Chair. The De La Rue Co. PLC 1964-77, non-exec. Chair. 1977-87; Dir. Kleinwort, Benson, Lonsdale PLC; R.A.F. 1941-46; Pres. CBI 1968-70; Chair. U.K. Centre for Econ. and Environmental Devt. 1984-; Vice-Chair. Sun Life Assurance Soc. 1984-87; Dir. SKF (U.K.) Ltd. 1970-87, Kleinwort, Benson, Lonsdale PLC 1985-; Chair. of Trustees, World Wildlife Fund (U.K.) 1977-84; Treasurer Int. Inst. for Environment and Devt.; mem. Nature Conservancy Council 1980-86. *Leisure interests:* tennis, golf, country life. *Address:* Fir Tree Cottage, Hammoon, Sturminster Newton, Dorset, DT10 2DB, England.

NORMAN, Barry Leslie; British writer and broadcaster; b. 21 Aug. 1933, London; s. of Leslie Norman and Elizabeth Norman; m. Diana Narracott 1957; two d.; ed. Highgate School, London; Entertainments Ed. Daily Mail, London 1969-71; weekly columnist The Guardian 1971-80; Writer and Presenter of BBC 1 Film 1973-81, 1983-89, The Hollywood Greats 1977-79, 1984, The British Greats 1980, Omnibus 1982, Film Greats 1985, Talking Pictures 1988; Radio 4 Today 1974-76, Going Places 1977-81, Breakaway 1979-80; Richard Dimbleby Award, BAFTA award 1981. *Publications:* Novels: The Matter of Mandrake 1967, The Hounds of Sparta 1968, End Product 1975, A Series of Defeats 1977, To Nick a Good Body 1978, Have a Nice Day 1981, Sticky Wicket 1984; non-fiction: Tales of the Redundance Kid 1975, The Hollywood Greats 1979, The Movie Greats 1981, Talking Pictures 1987. *Leisure interest:* cricket. *Address:* c/o Curtis Brown, 162-168 Regent Street, London, W1R 5TA, England. *Telephone:* 437 9700.

NORMAN, Dennis; Zimbabwe farmer and politician; b. 1931, Oxfordshire, U.K.; settled in Rhodesia as farm asst. 1953; Chair. various agricultural cttees.; Pres. Commercial Farmers' Union 1978-80; Minister of Agric. 1980-85; mem. Parl. 1987-; Chair. Int. Red Locust Control Org. for Cen. and Southern Africa 1985-. *Address:* c/o Ministry of Agriculture, Harare, Zimbabwe.

NORMAN, Jessye, M.MUS.; American concert and opera singer; b. 15 Sept. 1945, Augusta, Ga.; d. of Silas and Janie (King) Norman; ed. Howard Univ., Washington, D.C., Peabody Conservatory, Univ. of Michigan; Vocal Winner, Int. Musikwettbewerb, Bayerischer Rundfunk, Munich, Fed. Repub. of Germany 1968; operatic début Deutsche Oper Berlin 1969; début La Scala, Milan 1972, Royal Opera House, Covent Garden 1972; American operatic début, Hollywood Bowl 1972; tours in N. and S. America, Europe, Middle East, Australia; int. festivals incl. Aix-en-Provence, Aldeburgh, Berliner Festwochen, Edinburgh, Flanders, Helsinki, Lucerne, Salzburg, Tanglewood, Spoleto, Hollywood Bowl, Ravinia; with leading orchestras from U.S.A., U.K., Israel, Australia; Hon. Mus.Doc. (Howard) 1982, (Univ. of the South, Sewance) 1984, (Univ. of Mich.) 1987, (Edinburgh) 1989; Hon. D.Sc. (Cambridge) 1989; Grand Prix du Disque (Acad. du Disque Français) 1973, 1976, 1977, 1982; Deutsche Schallplatten Preis für Euryanthe 1975; Cigale d'Or (Aix-en-Provence Festival) 1977; Grammy Award 1980, 1982, 1985, Musician of the Year (Musical America) 1982, IRCAM record award 1982, Alumna Award (Univ. of Michigan) 1982; Commdr., Ordre des Arts et des Lettres 1984. *Leisure interests:* reading, cooking, houseplant growing, fashion designing. *Address:* c/o Shaw Concerts, 1900 Broadway, New York, N.Y. 10023, U.S.A.

NORMAN, Sir Richard Oswald Chandler, K.B.E., D.SC., F.R.S.; British scientific adviser; b. 27 April 1932, London; s. of Oswald G. Norman and Violet M. Chandler; m. Jennifer M. Tope 1982; ed. St. Paul's School, London and Balliol Coll., Oxford; Junior Research Fellow, Merton Coll., Oxford 1956-58, Fellow and Tutor 1958-65, Univ. Lecturer in Chem. 1958-65; Prof. of Chem., Univ. of York 1965-83; Chief Scientific Adviser, Ministry of Defence 1983-88, Dept. of Energy 1988-; Rector Exeter Coll., Oxford 1987-; Pres. Royal Inst. of Chem. 1978-80; Pres. Royal Soc. of Chemistry 1984-86; Dir. Salters' Inst. of Industrial Chem. 1975-; mem. Science Eng. Research Council 1983-88; Meldola Medal 1962; Corday Morgan Medal 1968. *Publications:* Principles of Organic Synthesis 1968, Modern Organic Chemistry (with D. J. Waddington) 1972; papers in Journal of Chem. Soc. *Leisure interests:* cricket, music, gardening. *Address:* The Rector's Lodgings, Exeter College, Oxford, England. *Telephone:* (0865) 279644.

NORMAN, Willoughby Rollo; British business executive; b. 12 Oct. 1909, Hindhead; s. of Sir Henry Norman and The Hon. Lady Florence Priscilla McLaren; m. 1st The Hon. Barbara Jacqueline Boot 1934, one s. two d.; m. 2nd Caroline Haskard 1973; ed. Eton Coll. and Magdalen Coll., Oxford; Army Service 1939-45; Vice-Chair. Boots Pure Drug Co. Ltd. 1954-61, Chair. 1961-72, Hon. Pres. 1972-; Deputy Chair., English China Clays Ltd.; High Sheriff of Leics. 1960; fmr. Dir. Nat. Westminster Bank Ltd., Guardian Royal Exchange Assurance, Sheepbridge Eng. Ltd., and fmr. Chair. Eastern Region. *Leisure interests:* shooting, fishing, gardening. *Address:* The Grange, South Harting, Petersfield, Hants.; 28 Ranelagh House, Elystan Place, London, S.W.3, England. *Telephone:* 01-584 9410.

NORMANT, Henri, D. ÈS SC.; French scientist; b. 25 June 1907, Plozévet; s. of Jean Normant and Anne Gentric; m. Madeleine Sosson 1932; two s. three d.; ed. Collège Saint Louis, Brest, and Univ. de Caen; Prof. of Organic Synthesis, Faculty of Sciences, Paris 1952-; Pres. Second Section, Ecole Pratique des Hautes Etudes 1969-; mem. Centre Nat. de la Recherche Scientifique; mem. Conseil Nat. de l'Enseignement Supérieur et de la Recherche; mem. Acad. des Sciences 1966, Deutsche Akademie Leopoldina, Comité Consultatif des Univs.; Lauréat de la Soc. Chimique de France et l'Acad. des Sciences; Pres. Soc. Chimique de France 1971; Hon. Pres. Soc. Encouragement pour l'Industrie Nat.; Officier, Légion d'honneur; Officier de l'Instruction Publique. *Publications:* Chimie Organique (2nd edition) 1968, Recherches sur les Hétérocycles Oxygénés, sur les Organo-Métalliques (Magnésiens Vinyliques) et sur les Solvants. *Leisure interests:* hunting and fishing. *Address:* 40 bis rue Violet, 75015 Paris, France. *Telephone:* 45.79.99.99.

NORO, Kyoichi; Japanese politician; b. 30 Nov. 1919; ed. Tokyo Univ. of Educ.; mem. Mie Prefectural Ass. 1947, then Chair.; mem. House of Reps. 1963-; Parl. Vice Dir.-Gen. Defence Agency 1971-72; Parl. Vice-Minister of Justice 1972-73; Deputy Sec.-Gen. Liberal-Democratic Party 1974-76; Minister of Health and Welfare 1979-80; Chair. Standing Cttee. on Commerce and Industry 1976-78; Vice-Chair. Policy Affairs Research Council 1978-79. *Publications:* Ongyu wa Rinri, Kyosai wa Rentai 1978. *Address:* c/o House of Representatives, Tokyo, Japan.

NORODOM SIHANOUK, Prince Samdech Preah; former King of Cambodia (Kampuchea); b. 31 Oct. 1922; s. of late King Norodom Suramarit and Queen Kossamak Nearireath; m. Princess Monique; fourteen c. (six deceased); ed. in Saigon (now Ho Chi Minh City), Viet-Nam, and Paris; mil. training in Saumur, France; elected King April 1941, abdicated March 1955; Prime Minister and Minister of Foreign Affairs Oct. 1955, March 1956, Sept. 1956, April 1957; Perm. Rep. to UN Feb.-Sept. 1956; elected Head of State after death of his father 1960, took oath of fidelity to vacant throne 1960, deposed by forces of Lon Nol (q.v.) March 1970; resided in Peking (now Beijing), People's Repub. of China; est. Royal Govt. of Nat. Union of Cambodia (GRUNC) May 1970; restored as Head of State when GRUNC forces overthrew Khmer Repub. April 1975, resigned April 1976; Special Envoy of Khmer Rouge to UN 1979; f. Nat. United Front for an Independent Neutral, Peaceful Co-operative Kampuchea 1981-; Head of the Popular Socialist Community 1955-70; Head of State in exile of Govt. of Democratic Kampuchea 1982-88, Feb. 1989-; musician and composer; producer of films including Le Petit Prince. *Publications:* L'Indochine vu de Pékin (with Jean Lacouture) 1972, My War With the C.I.A. (with Wilfred Burchett) 1973, War and Hope: The Case for Cambodia 1980, Souvenirs doux et amers 1981, Prisonnier des Khmers Rouges 1986, Charisme et Leadership 1989. *Leisure interests:* badminton, film making in DPR Korea, French style cooking in Peking. *Address:* Pyongyang, Democratic People's Republic of Korea; Beijing, People's Republic of China.

NORRBACK, Johan Ole; Finnish politician; b. 18 March 1941, Overmark; m. Vivi-Ann Lindqvist 1959; teacher 1966-67; Dist. Sec. Swedish People's Party in Ostrobothnia 1967-71; Exec. Man. Provincial Union of Swedish Ostrobothnia 1971-; Political Sec. to Minister of Communications 1976-77; mem. Parl. 1979-87; mem. Exec. Cttee. Swedish People's Party 1983-; Minister of Defence 1987-. *Address:* Ministry of Defence, Et. Makasiinikatu 8A, 00130 Helsinki, Finland. *Telephone:* (90) 625801.

NORRINGTON, Roger Arthur Carver, O.B.E.; British conductor; b. 16 March 1934; s. of Sir Arthur Norrington and Edith Joyce Carver; m. Susan Elizabeth McLean May 1964 (divorced 1982); one s. one d.; ed. Dragon School, Oxford, Westminster School, Clare Coll., Cambridge, Royal Coll. of Music; freelance singer 1962-72; Prin. Conductor, Kent Opera 1966-84; Guest Conductor many British and European orchestras, appearances BBC Promenade Concerts, and City of London, Bath, Aldeburgh, Edin. and Harrogate festivals; regular broadcasts U.K., Europe, U.S.A.; Prin. Conductor Bournemouth Sinfonietta 1985-89; Musical Dir. London Classical Players 1978-, London Baroque Players 1975-, Schütz Choir of London 1962-; many gramophone recordings; Cavaliere, Ordine al Merito della Repubblica Italiana. *Leisure interests:* reading, walking, sailing.

NORRIS, Sir Eric George, K.C.M.G.; British diplomatist (retd.); b. 14 March 1918, Hertford; s. of late Henry F. Norris and of Ruth Norris; m. Pamela Crane 1941; three d.; ed. Hertford Grammar School and St. Catharine's Coll., Cambridge; mil. service 1940-46; Dominions Office 1946; First Sec., Dublin 1948-50, Pakistan 1952-55; Counsellor, Delhi 1955-57; Deputy High Commr., Bombay 1957-60, Calcutta 1962-65; Asst. Under Sec. of State, Commonwealth Office 1966-68; High Commr. to Kenya 1968-72; Deputy Under Sec. of State, Foreign and Commonwealth Office 1972-73; High Commr. in Malaysia 1974-77; Dir. Inchcape (Deputy Chair. 1981-86), London Sumatra Plantations Ltd., Gray Mackenzie & Co. Ltd.; Chair. Royal Commonwealth Soc. 1980-84. *Address:* The Old Homestead, Great Amwell, Ware, Herts., England. *Telephone:* (0920) 870739.

NORTH, Alastair Macarthur, PH.D.; British professor of chemistry; b. 2 Aug. 1932, Aberdeen, Scotland; s. of Norman North and Anne North; m. Charlotte Muriel Begg 1957; two s. two d.; ed. Univs. of Aberdeen and Birmingham; Lecturer, Dept. of Inorganic, Physical and Industrial Chem.,

Univ. of Liverpool; apptd. to Burmah Chair of Physical Chem., Univ. of Strathclyde, Scotland 1967, subsequently Dean of School of Chemical and Materials Science, then Vice-Prin. of the Univ.; Pres. Asian Inst. of Tech. 1983–; mem. several nat. cttees. on formation of science educ. policy and support of univ. research; D.Sc. (Aberdeen) and Sc.D. h.c. (Politechnika Lodzka) for research in polymer and materials science. *Leisure interests:* golf, scuba diving. *Address:* Asian Institute of Technology, P.O. Box 2754, Bangkok 10501, Thailand. *Telephone:* Bangkok 529-1117.

NORTH, Alex; American composer; b. 4 Dec. 1910, Chester, Pa.; s. of Jesse North and Bela North; m. Annemarie Hoellger 1972; two s. one d.; ed. Juilliard School of Music, New York, Moscow Conservatory of Music and under composers Aaron Copland and Ernst Toch; wrote ballets for Martha Graham and Anna Sokolov in 1930s; composer of opera Hither and Thither of Danny Dither and of several concert and symphonic works including Revue for Clarinet and Orchestra 1946; composed music for stage production of Death of a Salesman; composer of 55 film scores including A Streetcar Named Desire, The Member of the Wedding, Spartacus, Cleopatra, Daddy Longlegs, Cheyenne Autumn, The Agony and the Ecstasy, Bite the Bullet, Under the Volcano, Prizzi's Honour, Who's Afraid of Virginia Woolf, Revue for Benny Goodman, Viva Zapata, The Dead, The Penitent, Good Morning Vietnam; Guggenheim Fellow; numerous awards including Emmy Award for television mini-series Rich Man Poor Man, five Laurel Awards, Golden Globe Award 1969, Hon. Acad. Award (Oscar) 1986, American Soc. of Composers, Authors and Publishers Award 1986. *Address:* 630 Resolano Drive, Pacific Palisades, Calif. 90272, U.S.A.

NORTH, John David, M.A. D.PHIL.; British professor of the history of philosophy and the exact sciences; b. 19 May 1934, Cheltenham; s. of J. E. North and G. A. North; m. Marion J. Pizzey; one s. two d.; ed. Merton Coll., Oxford and Univ. of London; Nuffield Foundation Research Fellow Univ. of Oxford 1963–68, Museum of History of Science, Univ. of Oxford 1968–77; Visiting Prof. of History of Science, Aarhus Univ. 1974, Prof. of the History of Philosophy and the Exact Sciences, Univ. of Groningen, 1977–; Dean of the Cen. Interfaculty 1981–84; Sec. Perpétuel, Acad. int. d'histoire des sciences, Paris 1983–; mem. Royal Netherlands Acad.; Foreign mem. Royal Danish Acad. *Publications:* The Measure of the Universe 1965, Richard of Wallingford, (3 vols) 1976, The Light of Nature (Ed.) 1985, Horoscopes and History 1986, Chaucer's Universe 1988, Stars, Minds, and Fate 1988, The Universal Frame 1988. *Leisure interest:* travel. *Address:* Kamperfoelieweg 25, 9765 HJ Paterswolde, The Netherlands; 28 Chalfont Road, Oxford, OX2 6TH, England.

NORTH, Oliver L.; American marine officer; b. 7 Oct. 1943, San Antonio, Texas; s. of Oliver Clay North and Ann North; m.; c.; ed. U.S. Naval Coll., Annapolis; joined marines, platoon commdr. Vietnam; marine instructor 1969; leader marine mission, Turkey 1980; mem. Nat. Security Council as Deputy Dir. for Political Mil. Affairs 1981–86; dismissed Nov. 1986 because of involvement with secret operation to sell arms to Iran and the diversion of proceeds from the sales to aid anti-govt. "Contra" guerrillas in Nicaragua; rank of Lieut.-Col. 1983, retd. from Marines 1988; on trial Feb. 1989, found guilty on three counts May 1989; Dr. h.c. (Liberty Univ.) 1988. *Address:* c/o The Pentagon, Washington, D.C. 20301, U.S.A.

NORTHARD, John Henry, O.B.E., F.ENG., C.B.I.M., F.R.S.A.; British industrialist; b. 23 Dec. 1926, Pudsey; s. of William Henry Northard and Nellie Northard; m. Marian Josephine Lay 1952; two s. two d.; ed. St. Bede's Grammar School, Bradford, Yorks, Barnsley Mining and Technical Coll.; Colliery Man., Yorkshire 1955–57, Leicestershire 1957–63; Group Man., Leicestershire Colleries 1963–65; Deputy Chief Mining Engineer, Staffordshire Colleries 1965–70; Area Deputy Dir. (Mining), N. Derbyshire 1970–73, Area Dir. 1973–81; Area Dir., Western Area 1981–85; Pres. Inst. of Mining Engineers 1982; Operations Dir. British Coal Corp. 1985, Deputy Chair. 1988–; Serving Brother Order of St. John 1981. *Publications:* numerous papers in various mining eng. insts. and tech. journals. *Address:* British Coal Corporation, Hobart House, Grosvenor Place, London, SW1X 7AE, England. *Telephone:* (01) 235-2020.

NORTHCOTE, Donald Henry, D.S., F.R.S.; British plant biochemist; b. 27 Dec. 1921, Plymouth; s. of F. Northcote and F. Corbin; m. Eva Marjorie Mayo 1948; two d.; ed. Univs. of London and Cambridge; Demonstrator in Biochemistry, Univ. of Cambridge 1948, Prof. of Plant Biochemistry 1972–, Master of Sidney Sussex Coll. 1976–; Fellow, St. John's Coll. Cambridge 1960; Hon. Fellow, Downing Coll. Cambridge 1979. *Publications:* 200 papers on plant cell growth and differentiation 1948–84. *Leisure interest:* sailing. *Address:* The Master's Lodge, Sidney Sussex College, Cambridge, CB2 3HU, England. *Telephone:* (0223) 338800.

NORTON, Robert Anthony, M.A.; South African stock exchange executive; b. 1 Feb. 1939, Johannesburg; s. of W. O. Norton and M. C. Norton; m. Peta-Ann Sammell 1962; three s.; ed. Durban High School, Natal and Oxford Univs.; merchant banking 1966–77; industrial appts. 1977–85, latterly Dir. Barlow Rand; Pres. Johannesburg Stock Exchange 1985–; Rhodes Scholar 1959. *Leisure interests:* music, sport of all kinds. *Address:* P.O. Box 1174, Johannesburg 2000, South Africa. *Telephone:* (011) 833-6580.

NOSIGLIA, Enrique; Argentinian politician; b. 28 May 1949, Posadas; m. Nina Ciarlotti; four c.; ed. Universidad Nacional de Buenos Aires; joined

Unión Cívica Radical 1972; mem. Nat. Exec. Movimiento de Renovación y Cambio 1975–80; Sec. Comité de la Capital (Wealth) 1983–87, Pres. 1987; Under-Sec. for Health and Social Affairs, Ministry of Health and Social Affairs 1983–85; Sec. Exec. Comm. Programa Alimentario Nacional (PAN) 1983–85; mem. Consejo para la Consolidación de la Democracie 1986; Minister of the Interior 1987–. *Address:* Ministerio del Interior, Buenos Aires, Argentina.

NOSOV, Yevgeny Ivanovich; Soviet author; b. 15 Jan 1925, Kursk; ed. Gorky Inst., Moscow, grad. 1962; Writer 1947–. *Publications include:* stories: Where the Sun Awakes 1965, Lunar Eclipse & Others 1966, The Red Wine of Victory & Other Tales (English trans.) 1974, Way Beyond the Hamlet, Country Stories 1974, Oats in the Meadow, Stories 1977, Usvyatskiye shlemonostsy. A Story 1977. *Address:* USSR Union of Writers, Ulitsa Vorovskogo 52, Moscow, U.S.S.R.

NOSS, John Bramble; British diplomatist; b. 20 Dec. 1935, Portsmouth; s. of John Noss and Vera E. Mattingly; m. Shirley M. Andrews 1957; two s. one d.; ed. Portsmouth Grammar School; entered Foreign Office 1954; R.A.F. 1955–57; served Beirut 1957–59, Copenhagen 1960–63, Moscow 1965–68, Santiago 1968–70; First Sec. (Econ.) Pretoria 1974–77; First Sec. (Commercial), Moscow 1977–78; Consul (Inward Investment), British Consulate-Gen., New York 1981–85; High Commr. in Solomon Islands 1986–88; Counsellor (Commercial and Econ.) British Embassy Helsinki 1988–. *Leisure interests:* golf, photography, reading. *Address:* c/o Foreign and Commonwealth Office (Helsinki), King Charles Street, London, SW1A 2AH, England.

NOSSAL, Sir Gustav Joseph Victor, Kt., C.B.E., M.B., B.S., PH.D., F.R.C.P., F.R.C.P.A., F.A.C.M.A., F.R.S.E., F.T.S., F.A.A., F.R.S.; Australian medical research scientist; b. 6 June 1931, Bad Ischl, Austria; m. Lyn B. Dunnicliff 1955; two s. two d.; ed. St Aloysius Coll., Sydney, Univs. of Sydney and Melbourne; jr. and sr. resident officer, Royal Prince Alfred Hosp., Sydney 1955–56; Research Fellow, The Walter and Eliza Hall Inst. of Medical Research, Melbourne 1957–59; Asst. Prof., Dept. of Genetics, Stanford Univ. School of Medicine, Calif. 1959–61; Deputy Dir. (Immunology), The Walter and Eliza Hall Inst. of Medical Research 1961–65, Dir. and Prof. of Medical Biol. 1965–; Dir., CRI Foundation 1977–; Foreign Assoc. N.A.S.; Foreign hon mem. American Acad. of Arts and Sciences and many other nat. and foreign acads. and learned socs.; Ciba Foundation Gold Medal 1978; ANZAAS Medal 1982 and many other awards and prizes; Hon. M.D. (Mainz), (Leeds) 1989. *Publications:* Antibodies and Immunity 1968, Antigens, Lymphoid Cells and Immune Response 1971, Medical Science and Human Goals 1975, Nature's Defences (1978 Boyer Lectures), Reshaping Life: Key issues in genetic engineering 1984; 300 publications on immunity. *Leisure interests:* golf, literature. *Address:* The Walter and Eliza Hall Institute of Medical Research, Post Office, Royal Melbourne Hospital, Vic., 3050; 46 Fellows Street, Kew, Vic. 3101, Australia (Home). *Telephone:* (03) 347-1511 (Office); (03) 861-8256 (Home).

NOTERDAEME, Paul M. J., D.IUR.; Belgian diplomatist; b. 14 Oct. 1929, Bruges; m.; four c.; Sec. Perm. Mission of Belgium to the EEC 1962–65; Sec., later First Sec. Belgian Embassy, London 1965–68; Deputy Prin. Pvt. Sec. to the Foreign Minister 1968–69, Prin. Pvt. Sec. 1969–74; Amb. and Perm. Rep. to UN Office, Geneva 1974–79, to the EEC, Brussels 1979–87; Perm. Rep. to UN Nov. 1987–. *Address:* Permanent Mission of Belgium to the United Nations, 809 United Nations Plaza, 2nd Floor, New York, N.Y. 10017, U.S.A. *Telephone:* (212) 599-5250.

NOTHOMB, Charles Ferdinand, D. EN D.; Belgian politician; b. 3 May 1936, Brussels; s. of Pierre Nothomb and Ghislaine Montens; m. Michèle Pouppez de Kettenis 1963; two s. one d.; ed. Catholic Univ., Louvain; civil servant 1959–68; M.P. for Luxembourg Prov. 1968–; mem. Consultative Ass., Council of Europe 1968–73, European Parl. 1979–80; Chair. Parti Social Chrétien (Christelijke Volkspartij) 1972–79; Speaker House of Reps. 1979–80; Minister of Foreign Affairs 1980–81; Deputy Prime Minister and Minister of the Interior, and of the Civil Service 1981–86. *Leisure interests:* walking, tennis. *Address:* 1 rue du Paradis, 6720 Habay or 17 avenue Mesens, 1040 Brussels, Belgium. *Telephone:* 063-422320 (Habay).

NOTOSUSANTO, Nugroho, PH.D.; Indonesian historian and politician; b. 15 June 1931, Rembang, Cen. Java; ed. Univ. of Indonesia, Jakarta and Univ. of London; Lecturer, Faculty of Letters, Univ. of Indonesia 1960–, Rector 1982; Lecturer, Inst. of Nat. Defence 1967–; has participated in numerous int. congresses and seminars, etc.; Minister of Educ. and Culture 1983–85. *Address:* c/o Ministry of Education and Culture, Jln. Jend Sudirman, Jakarta Selatan, Indonesia.

NOTT, Rt. Hon. Sir John William Frederic, K.C.B., P.C., B.A.; British business executive and fmr. politician; b. 1 Feb. 1932; s. of Richard Nott and Phyllis Francis; m. Miloska Sekol 1959; two s. one d.; ed. Bradfield Coll. and Trinity Coll., Cambridge; Lieut. with 2nd Gurkha Rifles, (regular officer) 1952–56; called to the Bar, Inner Temple 1959; M.P. for St. Ives, Cornwall 1966–83; Minister of State at Treasury 1972–74; Sec. of State for Trade 1979–81, for Defence 1981–83; Man. Dir. Lazard Brothers April 1983–, Chair. and Chief Exec. 1985–; Deputy Chair. Royal Insurance PLC 1986–89; Pres. Cambridge Union 1959. *Address:* 21 Moorfields, London, EC2P 2HT, England.

NOTT, Rt. Rev. Peter John, M.A.; British ecclesiastic; b. 30 Dec. 1933, Belfast, Northern Ireland; s. of Cecil Frederick Wilder Nott and Rosina

Mabel Nott; m. Elizabeth May Maingot 1961; one s. three d.; ed. Bristol Grammar School, Dulwich Coll., London, R.M.A. Sandhurst and Fitzwilliam House and Westcott House, Cambridge; served in regular army, commissioned R.A. 1951-55; Curate of Harpenden 1961-64; Chaplain and Fellow of Fitzwilliam Coll. Cambridge 1966-69; Chaplain of New Hall, Cambridge 1966-69; Rector of Beaconsfield 1969-77; Bishop of Taunton 1977-85; Bishop of Norwich 1985-; Archbishop's Adviser to H.M.C. 1980-85; Vice-Chair. Archbishops' Comm. on Rural Areas 1988-; Pres. SW Region of Mencap 1978-84, Somerset Rural Music School 1981-85. *Address:* Bishop's House, Norwich, NR3 1SB, England. *Telephone:* (0603) 629001.

NOUEL, Philippe, D. EN D.; French lawyer; b. 21 July 1926, Maisons-Laffitte; s. of Jacques Nouel and Jacqueline Vallet; m. Nicole Danet 1955; two s. two d.; ed. Lycée Carnot and Faculté de Droit, Paris; lawyer at English Bar 1952-, Paris Court 1954-; Assoc. Gide Loyrette Nouel 1956-; fmr. mem. Council, Ordre des Avocats; Chevalier, Légion d'honneur. *Address:* Gide Loyrette Nouel, 26 cours Albert ler, 75008 Paris (Office); 9 boulevard Raspail, 75007 Paris, France (Home). *Telephone:* 40 75 60 00 (Office).

NOUIRA, Hedi; Tunisian politician; b. 6 April 1911, Monastir; ed. High School, Sousse, and Paris; Sec. of Gen. Confed. of Tunisian Workers 1938; in detention 1938-43; Sec.-Gen. of Neo-Destour Party 1942-54, 1969-80; Minister of Commerce 1954-55, of Finance 1955-58; Dir. of Central Bank of Tunisia 1958-70; Minister of State in Charge of the Economy June-Oct. 1970; Prime Minister 1970-80; Chair. IMF-IBRD Annual Meetings, Copenhagen 1970; mem. Interaction Council UNDP; Enrico Mattei Prize for Economy 1987. *Address:* c/o Office of the Secretary-General, Parti Socialiste Destourien, boulevard 9 avril 1938, Tunis, Tunisia.

NOUMAZALAY, Ambroise; Congolese politician; b. 23 Sept. 1933, Brazzaville; ed. Mathematics Faculty Univ. of Toulouse, France; First Sec. Nat. Revolutionary Movement (MNR); Dir. of Econ. Affairs 1964-66; mem. Nat. Revolutionary Council (CNR) and Sec. Org. Cttee. of the CNR Aug.-Oct. 1968; Prime Minister and Minister of Planning 1966-68; Minister of State in charge of Planning Aug.-Dec. 1968, for Agric., Water Resources and Forests 1968-69; Second Sec. responsible for the Execution of the Plan 1970-71; sentenced to life imprisonment March 1972; amnestied Oct. 1973; Minister of Industry and Manufacturing 1984-85, of Industry and Fisheries 1985-88, of Crafts 1986-88, of Forestry 1988-. *Address:* Palais du Peuple, Brazzaville, The Congo.

NOURISSIER, François; French writer and journalist; b. 18 May 1927, Paris; s. of Paul E. E. Nourissier and Renée Heens; m. 1st Marie-Thérèse Sobesky 1949, two s.; m. 2nd Cécile Muhlstein 1962, one d.; ed. Lycée Saint Louis, Lycée Louis-le-Grand, Paris, Ecole libre des Sciences politiques, Paris, and Faculté de Droit, Paris; on staff of Secours Catholique Int., and work with Int. Refugee Org. 1949-51; Dir. Chalet Int. des Etudiants, Combloux (World Univ. Service) 1951-52; Sec.-Gen. Editions Denoël 1952-56; Editor-in-Chief La Parisienne (review) 1956-58; Literary Adviser to Editions Grasset 1958-; Literary Dir. Vogue (French) 1964-66, Contributing Ed. Vogue (American) 1964-; Literary Critic Les Nouvelles littéraires 1963-72; Cinema Critic L'Express 1970-72; Literary Critic Le Point 1972-, Le Figaro 1975-, Figaro-Magazine 1978-; mem. l'Acad. Goncourt 1977, Sec.-Gen. 1983-; Prix Félix Fénéon 1952, Grand Prix de la Guilde du Livre 1965 (Swiss), Grand Prix du Roman de l'Acad. française 1966, Prix Fémina 1970, Prix Prince Pierre de Monaco 1975; Grand Prix de la Ville de Paris 1987, Officier Légion d'honneur, Commdr., Ordre nat. du Mérite, des Arts et des Lettres. *Publications:* L'eau grise (novel) 1951, Lorca (essay) 1955, Les orphelins d'Auteuil (novel) 1956, Le corps de Diane (novel) 1957, Portrait d'un indifférent 1957, Bleu comme la nuit 1958, Un petit bourgeois 1964, Une histoire française 1966, Les Français (essay) 1967, Le maître de maison 1968, The French (trans. of Les Français) 1970, Cartier-Bresson's France 1971, La crève (novel) 1970, Allemande (novel) 1973, Lettre à mon chien (essay) 1975, Lettre ouverte à Jacques Chirac (essay) 1977, Le musée de l'homme (essay) 1979, L'empire des nuages (novel) 1981, La fête des pères (novel) 1986, En avant, calme et droit (novel) 1987. *Leisure interests:* tennis, ski-ing. *Address:* 23 rue Henri Heine, 75016 Paris, France; En Cerniaz, 1824 Caux (Vaud), Switzerland.

NOVÁK, Josef, PROF. RNDR.; Czechoslovak mathematician; b. 19 April 1905, Třebětín, Letovice; s. of Alois Novák and Františka Loubalová; m. Vladimíra Plocková 1936; one s. one d.; Asst. Univ. of Brno 1935-45, Prof. Mathematics, Univ. of Brno 1945-48; Czech Technical Univ., Prague 1948-51; Charles Univ. Prague 1952-; Mathematics Inst. of the Czechoslovak Acad. of Sciences 1952-; Academician, Czechoslovak Acad. of Sciences 1952-; Chair. of Mathematics and Physics Section of the Czechoslovak Acad. of Sciences 1955-61; Chair. Bd. of Mathematics, Czechoslovak Acad. of Sciences 1966-82; Dir. Mathematical Inst. of the Czechoslovak Acad. of Sciences 1972-76; Chair. Asscn. of Czechoslovak Mathematicians and Physicists; mem. Advisory Cttee. for Science and Tech., ECOSOC; mem. Scientific Bd. of Int. Mathematical S. Banach Center 1972-82; Order of Labour 1965, 1982, Gold Medal of Bernard Bolzano 1970, of Palacký Univ., Olomouc 1971, Gold Felber Medal, Czech Tech. Univ. 1975, Gold Medal of Brno Univ. 1976. *Leisure interests:* genetics, music, gardening. *Address:* Žitná 25, 115 67 Prague I, Czechoslovakia. *Telephone:* 226601-03.

NOVAK, Michael, B.T., M.A.; American theologian; b. 9 Sept. 1933, Johnstown, Pa.; s. of Michael J. Novak and Irene Sakmar; m. Karen R. Laub

1963; one s. two d.; ed. Stonehill Coll., North Easton, Mass. and Gregorian Univ., Rome; Teaching Fellow, Harvard Univ. 1961-63; Asst. Prof. of Humanities, Stanford Univ. 1965-68; Assoc. Prof. of Philosophy and Religious Studies, State Univ. of N.Y., Old Westbury 1969-71; Assoc. Dir. Humanities, Rockefeller Foundation 1973-75; Ledden-Watson Distinguished Prof. of Religion, Syracuse Univ. 1976-79; George Frederick Jewett Prof. in Religion and Public Policy, American Enterprise Inst. 1988-; Visiting Prof. Univ. of Notre Dame 1987-88; columnist, The Nat. Review 1979-86; Judge, Nat. Book Awards, DuPont Awards in Broadcast Journalism; Head, U.S. Del. to UN Human Rights Comm., Geneva 1981, 1982; other public appts.; numerous awards and hon. degrees. *Publications include:* Choosing Our King 1974, Moral Clarity in the Nuclear Age 1983, Freedom with Justice: Catholic Social Thought and Liberal Institutions 1984, Taking Glasnost Seriously 1988, and numerous articles in journals. *Address:* American Enterprise Institute, 1150 17th Street, Washington, D.C. 20036, U.S.A. *Telephone:* 202-862-5838.

NOVARINA, Maurice Paul Joseph; French architect and planner; b. 28 June 1907, Thonon les Bains, Haute Savoie; s. of Joseph Novarina and Anaïs Detruche; m. Manon Trolliet 1937; two s.; ed. Ecole Speciale des Travaux Publics and Ecole Nat. Supérieure des Beaux Arts, Paris; Chief Architect of Public Bldgs. and Nat. Palaces; Chief Architect, Reconstruction of the Eure 1947-55; fmr. Prof. Ecole Speciale d'Architecture, Ecole Nat. des Beaux Arts; works include churches, cultural bldgs., schools, hosps., hotels, commercial bldgs. etc.; mem. Acad. des Beaux Arts (Inst. de France); Commdr., Légion d'honneur, Officier, Ordre Nat. du Mérite, Ordre des Arts et Lettres; several awards and prizes. *Address:* Atelier d'Urbanisme et d'Architecture Novarina, 3 Square Pétrarque, 75116 Paris (Office); 23 boulevarde de la Corniche, 74200 Thonon les Bains, France.

NOVE, Alexander, F.B.A., F.R.S.E.; British professor of economics (retd.); b. 24 Nov. 1915, Leningrad; s. of Jacob and Rachel Novakovsky; m. Irene MacPherson 1951; three s.; ed. King Alfred School, London and L.S.E.; served British army 1939-46; civil servant, London 1946-58; Reader, Univ. of London 1958-63; Prof. of Econs., Univ. of Glasgow 1963-82, Prof. Emer. 1982-; Hon. Sr. Research Fellow, Glasgow Univ. 1982-; Hon. Fellow L.S.E.; Dr. h.c. (Giessen). *Publications:* Soviet Economy 1961, Was Stalin Really Necessary? 1963, Efficiency Criteria for Nationalized Industries 1971, Economic History of U.S.S.R. 1969, Stalinism and After 1972, Political Economy and Soviet Socialism 1979, The Soviet Economic System 1977, Economics of Feasible Socialism 1983, Socialism, Economics and Development 1986. *Leisure interests:* music, travel, good eating. *Address:* 55 Hamilton Drive, Glasgow, G12 8DP, Scotland. *Telephone:* 041-339 1053.

NOVIKOV, Sergey Petrovich; Soviet mathematician; b. 1938, Gorky; ed. Moscow Univ.; Prof. 1967; Corresp. mem. of U.S.S.R. Acad. of Sciences 1967, mem. 1981; on staff of Steklov Mathematical Inst. 1963- (post-grad., jr. and sr. research fellow); Prof. at Moscow Univ. 1966-; Lenin Prize 1967, Prize of Int. Mathematical Soc. 1970. *Address:* U.S.S.R. Academy of Sciences, Steklov Institute of Mathematics, Ul. Vavilova 42, Moscow 117 333, U.S.S.R.

NOWAK, Tadeusz; Polish writer and poet; b. 11 Nov. 1930, Sikorzyce, near Dąbrowa Tarnowska; m.; ed. Jagiellonian Univ., Cracow; work first published 1948; mem. Polish United Worker's Party 1954-; Polish Writers' Asscn. 1952-83, mem. Gen. Bd. 1978-83; Ed. poetry section in Tygodnik Kulturalny, Warsaw 1965-81; Prize of City of Cracow 1966; Gold Cross of Merit 1967; St. Piętrzak Prize 1969; Prize of Minister of Culture and Arts, 1st Class 1971, State Prize, 2nd Class, 1974, Knight's Cross of Polonia Restituta 1975, Prize of weekly Kultura 1978, Literary Prize of Cen. Council of Trade Unions 1978. *Publications:* poetry: Uczę się mówić 1953, Porównania 1954, Prorocy już odchodzą 1956, Ślepe koła wyobraźni 1958, Kolędy streczyciela 1962, Psalmy 1971, Bielsze nad śnieg 1973, Wybór wierszy (selected poems) 1973, Nowe psalmy 1978, Psalmy wszystkie 1980, Wniebogłosy 1982, Zapisane na Dunajcu 1987, Pacierze i paciarki 1988; novels: Obcoplemienna ballada 1963, A jak królem, a jak katem będziesz 1968, Diabły 1971, Takie większe wesele 1966, 1973, Dwunastu 1974, Prorok 1977; short stories: Przebudzenia 1962, Wybór opowiadań (selected short stories) 1969, Półbaśnie 1976. *Leisure interests:* excursions in forests, travel. *Address:* Ul. Wiolinowa 2 m. 45, 02-789 Warsaw, Poland.

NOWORYTA, Eugeniusz, D.JUR.; Polish diplomatist; b. 25 Dec. 1935, Cracow; s. of Marian Noworyta and Anna Noworyta; m.; one d.; ed. Cen. School of Foreign Service and Warsaw Univ.; entered Polish Ministry for Foreign Affairs 1958, attaché Second Sec. of Embassy in Havana; Amb. to Chile 1971-73, to Spain 1977-81; Deputy Dir. of Policy Planning Dept. 1973-77, Head, West European Dept. 1981-85; mem. Polish del. to UN Gen. Ass. 1974-76, 1985-87; Perm. Rep. to UN 1985-; Vice-Pres. Disarmament Comm. 1986; Vice-Pres. ECOSOC 1986, Pres. 1987; mem. of Bd. of Polish Inst. of Int. Affairs, of the Inst. of Political Science and of the Inst. of Journalism; Kt's Cross of Polonia Restituta Order, numerous other decorations. *Publications:* several articles on int. issues. *Leisure interests:* sport, sociology, history. *Address:* Permanent Mission of Poland to the United Nations, 9 East 66th Street, New York, N.Y. 10021, U.S.A.; ul. Korotynskiego 19m. 3, 02-121 Warsaw, Poland. *Telephone:* 744-2506.

NOWOTNIK, Adam, M.ECON.SCI.; Polish politician; b. 20 Aug. 1933, Wólka Maziarska, Radom Voivodship; s. of Tomasz Nowotnik and Marianna

Nowotnik; m. Barbara Nowotnik 1959; two s.; ed. Higher School of Econs., Sopot; worked in port admin. as a store-keeper, subsequently head of warehouse, and other tasks, Gdańsk 1956-69; Head of Maritime Dept. of Polish United Workers' Party (PZPR) Voivodship Cttee., Gdańsk 1969-72, Econ. Sec. of PZPR Voivodship Cttee., Gdańsk 1973-77; Chair. Municipal Nat. Council, Gdańsk 1973-77; Commerce Counsellor for Maritime Econ. Matters, Embassy, Moscow 1977-82; Gen. Dir. of Merchant Seaport, Gdańsk 1982-85; Minister of Maritime Economy Office Nov. 1985-87; Under-Sec., Ministry of Transport, Shipping and Communications Oct. 1987-; Kt.'s Cross Order of Polonia Restituta, Meritorious Longshoreman of Polish People's Repub. and other decorations. *Address:* Ministerstwo Transportu Zeglugi 1, Lacznosci, ul. Chalubińskiego 4/6, 00-098 Warszawa, Poland.

NOYCE, Robert Norton, PH.D.; American businessman; b. 12 Dec. 1927, Burlington; s. of Ralph B. and Harriett Norton Noyce; m. Ann S. Bowers 1975; one s. three d.; ed. Grinnell Coll., Iowa, Mass. Inst. of Tech.; mem. research staff Philco Corpn. 1953-56; mem. research staff Shockley Semiconductor Corpn. 1956-57; founder and Research Dir. Fairchild Semiconductor Corpn. 1957-58, Vice-Pres. Gen. Man. 1958-63, Group Vice-Pres. Fairchild Camera and Instrument Corpn. 1963-68; founder and Pres. Intel Corpn. 1968-75, Chair. 1975-79, Vice-Chair. 1979-; Inst. of Electrical and Electronic Engineers Medal of Honor, I.E.E. Faraday Medal, Nat. Medal Science, mem. N.A.S., Nat. Acad. Eng. *Leisure interests:* skiing, flying. *Address:* Intel Corpn., 3200 Lakeside Drive, Mail Stop SC6-30, Santa Clara, Calif. 95051, U.S.A. *Telephone:* (408) 987-8165.

NOYER-WEIDNER, Alfred, DR. PHIL.; German university professor; b. 31 Aug. 1921, Schönwald; Prof. Univ. of Saarbrücken 1959, Univ. of Vienna 1962, Univ. of Munich (Inst. of Italian Philology) 1964; mem. Bayerische Akad. der Wissenschaften; Dr. Ludwig Gebhard Prize 1957. *Publications:* books and articles in professional journals. *Address:* Institut für Italienische Philologie der Universität München, 8000 Munich 22, Ludwigstrasse 25, Federal Republic of Germany. *Telephone:* (089) 21 80-23 66.

NOYES, Richard Macy, PH.D.; American professor of chemistry; b. 6 April 1919, Champaign, Ill.; s. of William Albert Noyes and Katharine Haworth Macy; m. 1st Winninette Arnold 1946 (died 1972); m. 2nd Patricia Harris 1973; ed. Harvard Coll. and Calif. Inst. of Tech.; Research Assoc. Calif. Inst. of Tech. 1942-46; Instructor Columbia Univ. 1946-49, Asst. Prof. 1949-54, Assoc. Prof. 1954-58; Prof. of Chem. Univ. of Ore. 1958-, Acting Head or Head of Dept. of Chem. 1960-61, 1963-64, 1966-68, 1975-78; Guggenheim Fellow Univ. of Leeds 1955-56; Fulbright Fellow, Vic. Univ. of Wellington 1964; Nat. Science Foundation Sr. Postdoctoral Fellow Max-Planck-Inst. of Physical Chem, Göttingen 1965; Visiting Prof. Oxford 1971-72, Max-Planck-Inst. of Biophysical Chem. 1982-83; mem. N.A.S.; Alexander von Humboldt Sr. American Scientist Award 1978-79. *Publications:* over 180 articles in chemical journals. *Leisure interest:* trying to influence land use decisions regarding forestry and wilderness areas. *Address:* Department of Chemistry, University of Oregon, Eugene, Ore. 97403 (Office); 2014 Elk Drive, Eugene, Ore. 97403, U.S.A. (Home). *Telephone:* (503) 686-4611 (Office); (503) 344-0639 (Home).

NOZIERES, Philippe Pierre Gaston François; French physicist; b. 12 April 1932, Paris; s. of Henri Nozieres and Alice Noel; m. Catherine Michel 1982; one d. and one s. one d. by previous m.; ed. Ecole Normale Supérieure and Princeton Univ.; Prof. of Physics, Univ. of Paris 1961-72; Physicist, Laue-Langevin Inst. 1972-76; Prof. of Physics, Grenoble Univ. 1976-83; Prof. of Statistical Physics, Coll. de France 1983-; mem. Acad. des Sciences (Inst. de France); Holweck Prize 1976; Prix du CEA (Acad. des Sciences) 1979; Wolf Prize 1985. *Publications:* papers on theoretical physics and statistical physics. *Address:* I.L.L., B.P. 156, 38042 Grenoble, Cedex (Office); 15 route de Saint Nizier, 38180 Seyssins, France (Home).

NSEKELA, Amon James, M.A., DIP.ED., F.I.B.A.; Tanzanian diplomatist; b. 4 Jan. 1930, Lupepo, Rungwe; s. of late Ngonile Reuben Nsekela and of Anyambilile Nsekela (née Kalinga); m. Christina Matilda Kyusa 1957; two s.; ed. Rungwe District School, Malangali Secondary School, Tabora Govt. Sr. Secondary School, Makerere Univ. Coll., and Univ. of the Pacific, Calif., U.S.A.; Dist. Officer 1960-61; Clerk to the Cabinet 1961-63; Perm. Sec. Ministry of External Affairs and Defence 1963-64; Principal Sec. Ministry of Commerce and Industries 1964-66; Principal Sec. to Treasury 1966-67; mem. E. African Legis. Assembly 1967-70; mem. and Sec. of Presidential Comm. on the Establishment of a Democratic One-Party State, mem. Pratt Cttee. on Decentralization of Govt.; mem. Parl. 1973-74; High Commr. in U.K. 1974-81; Chair. and Man. Dir. Nat. Bank of Commerce 1967-74, 1981-, Tanzania Investment Bank 1982-, Nat. Insurance Corpn. of Tanzania 1967-72, Council of the Inst. of Finance Man. 1970-72; Dir. Tanzania Zambia Railway Authority 1982-; Chair. Inst. of Devt. Man., Mzumbe, Morogoro, Tanzania 1982-; mem. Council Sokoine Univ. of Agric. 1984-, Vice-Chair. 1985-; mem. Council of Finance Management, Dar es Salaam 1982-; Pres. Tanzania Soc. for Int. Devt. 1984-; Chair. Britain-Tanzania Soc. 1982-; Chair. Public Service Salaries Review Comm. 1985-86; mem. Int. Council of Trustees of Int. Defence and Aid Fund for Southern Africa 1985-; Dir. African Medical and Research Fund 1986-; African Insurance Org. Award 1982; Order of the United Republic of Tanzania. *Publications:* Minara ya Historia ya Tanganyika: Tanganyika hadi Tanzania, Demokrasi Tanzania, Socialism and Social Accountability in a Developing Nation, The Development of Health Services in Mainland Tanzania.

Tumetoka Mbali (with Dr. A. L. Nhonoli). *Leisure interests:* swimming, darts, reading and writing. *Address:* P.O. Box 1863, Dar es Salaam (Office); 9 Lupa Way, P.O. Box 722, Mbeya, Tanzania (Home). *Telephone:* 20962 (Office); 2541 (Home).

N'SINGA UDJUU ONGWABEKI UNTUBE; Zairian politician; b. (as Joseph N'Singa) 29 Oct. 1934, Bandundu; s. of Nshue O. Nsinga and Monkaju Medji; m. Mbu Modiri; four s. five d.; Minister of Justice 1966-69; Minister of State for Home Affairs March-Aug. 1969; Minister of the Interior 1969-70; Minister of State at the Presidency Sept. 1970, dismissed Sept. 1970; mem. Cen. Cttee., Mouvement populaire de la révolution (MPR) 1980-83 (Exec. Sec. 1981-83), First Vice-Chair. 1980-83; First State Commr. 1981-82; State Commr. for Justice Oct. 1986-; Pres. Judiciary Council 1986-; mem. Sacred Congregation for the Evangelization of Peoples. *Address:* c/o Office of the State Commissioner for Justice, B.P. 3137, Kinshasa (Office); B.P. 3559, Kinshasa/Gombe, Zaire (Home).

NSUBUGA, H.E. Cardinal Emmanuel; Ugandan ecclesiastic; b. 5 Nov. 1914, Kisule; ed. seminaries in Buganda; Ordained priest 1946; Vicar-Gen. Rubaga Archdiocese 1961, later Vicar Capitular; Archbishop of Kampala; created Cardinal 1976. *Address:* Archdiocese of Kampala, P.O. Box 14125, Mengo, Kampala, Uganda.

NU, U (formerly **Thakin Nu**), B.A.; Burmese politician and writer; b. 1907; ed. Rangoon Univ.; for some years headmaster Nat. High School, Pantanaw; joined Dobhama Asiayone (Our Burma) Org.; sentenced to term of imprisonment at outbreak of Second World War; released after Japanese occupation; organized Dobhama Asiayone and later joined wartime Govt. as Minister of Foreign Affairs in Dr. Ba Maw's Cabinet 1943-44; Minister for Publicity and Propaganda 1944-45; elected Vice-Pres. Anti-Fascist People's Freedom League (Nationalist Coalition) after Allied re-occupation; elected Speaker Constituent Assembly 1947; Deputy Chair. Gov.'s Exec. Council July 1947; signatory Anglo-Burmese Treaty, London, preliminary to Burmese Independence and first Prime Minister of Burmese Republic 1948-56; resigned to devote himself to the reorganization of Anti-Fascist People's Freedom League; Prime Minister 1957-58; Prime Minister, Minister of Home Affairs, Relief and Resettlement, Democratization of Local Admin., Information, Transport, Posts and Telegraphs, Shipping and Aviation, Housing and Rehabilitation 1960-62; in custody 1962-66; left Burma 1969 to organize opposition movement to Burmese regime; living in Thailand 1969-70; returned to Burma to lead revolutionary movement opposing Government of Gen. Ne Win Oct. 1970, living in Thailand, then in India until 1980; returned to Burma July 1980 requested foreign support for his formation of an alternative govt. Sept. 1988, rebuffed; State Medal (1st class), Burma 1981. *Publications:* plays and stories.

NUJOMA, Sam Daniel; Namibian nationalist leader; b. 12 May 1929, Ongandjera; ed. Finnish Protestant Mission School, St. Barnabas School, Windhoek; with State Railways until 1957; Municipal Clerk, Windhoek 1957; Clerk in wholesale store 1957-59; Founder, with Herman Toivo ja Toivo (q.v.), and Pres. SWAPO (S.W. Africa People's Org.) April 1959-; arrested Dec. 1959; went into exile 1960; appeared before UN Cttee. on S.W. Africa June 1960; set up SWAPO provisional HQ in Dar es Salaam, Tanzania March 1961; arrested on return to Windhoek and formally ordered out of the country March 1966; turned to armed struggle after rejection by Int. Court of Justice of SWAPO complaint against S. Africa Aug. 1966; gave evidence at UN Security Council Oct. 1971. *Address:* c/o SWAPO Headquarters, P.O. Box 2603, Dar es Salaam, Tanzania; and, Box 577, Lusaka, Zambia.

NUMAIRI, Field-Marshal Gaafar al- (see Nemery).

NUMAN, Yasin Said; Yemeni politician; fmr. Deputy Prime Minister and Minister of Fisheries; Prime Minister of Democratic Republic of Yemen Feb. 1986-, Minister of Labour and Civil Service 1986. *Address:* Office of the Prime Minister, Aden, People's Democratic Republic of Yemen.

NUNES, Manuel Jacinto, PH.D.; Portuguese economist and politician; b. 27 Jan. 1926, Lisbon; of José and Lourença da Conceição Nunes; m. Lutgarda da Silva Rodrigues Nunes 1950; one d.; Prof., Inst. for Advanced Mil. Studies 1953-74; Sec. of State for Finance 1955-59; Vice-Gov. Banco de Portugal 1960-74, Gov. 1974-75, 1980-85; Pres. Caixa Geral de Depositos 1976-80; Deputy Prime Minister and Minister of Finance and the Plan 1978-79; Econ. Adviser 1985-; Pres. Lisbon Acad. of Sciences 1980-88; Vice-Pres. Nat. Geographic Soc. 1974-79; Grand Officer of the Order of Christ, Grand Officer of the Order of the Southern Cross, Grand Cross of the Viscount of Rio, Distinguished Service Silver Medal; Officier, Légion d'honneur (France). *Publications:* Structure of the Portuguese Economy 1954, National Income and Budgetary Balance 1957, Economic Growth and Budget Policy 1961, Economic Development and Planning, The Monetary Controversy. *Leisure interests:* literature, history, swimming. *Address:* Caixa Geral de Depositos, R St. Catarina 1, 1200 Lisbon; Academia das Ciências de Lisboa, Rua da Academia das Ciências 19, 1200 Lisbon, Portugal.

NUNGESSER, Roland, L. EN D.; French politician; b. 9 Oct. 1925, Nogent-sur-Marne; m. 1st Michèle Jeanne Elizabeth Selignac 1957 (divorced 1981), three d.; m. 2nd Marie-Christine Ventrillou 1981; ed. Ecole Libre des Sciences Politiques; Commissaire-général du Salon Nautique Int. 1957-;

Vice-Pres. Chambre Syndicale des Industries Nautiques; Pres. Conseil Nat. de la Navigation de Plaisance 1961-67; Regional Adviser 1962; Mayor of Nogent-sur-Marne 1959-; mem. Nat. Ass. 1958-; Sec. of State for Housing 1966-67; Sec. of State at Ministry of Economy and Finance 1967-68; Minister of Youth and Sports May-July 1968; Pres. Franco-Soviet Chamber of Commerce 1969-, Liaison Cttee. for Local Councillors 1971-, Union of Partisan Region Mayors 1983-, Soc. for Protection of Animals (SPA) 1984-; Vice-Pres. Nat. Ass. 1969-74; Pres. Conseil Général du Val de Marne 1970-76; Pres. and Founder of Consortium Fluviae Seiniasnor 1969-, Cttee. Seine-Est-Nord 1976; mem. Rassemblement pour la République (fmrly. U.D.R.); mem. various socs. and asscns. *Leisure interests:* motor yachting, athletics, tennis. *Address:* Assemblée Nationale, 75355 Paris; 18 avenue Duvelleroy, 94130 Nogent-sur-Marne, France. *Telephone:* 871-16-53.

NUNN, John Francis, M.D., PH.D., F.R.C.S.; British anaesthetist; b. 7 Nov. 1925; s. of Francis Nunn and Lilian née Davies; m. Sheila Doubleday 1949; one s. two d.; ed. Wrekin Coll. and Birmingham Univ.; Malayan Medical Service 1949-53; Resident Anaesthetist, Birmingham 1953-56; Leverhulme Research Fellow, Royal Coll. of Surgeons 1957-64; Prof. of Anaesthesia, Univ. of Leeds 1964-68; Head of Div. of Anaesthesia, Clinical Research Centre, and Hon. Consultant Anaesthetist 1968-; Dean Faculty of Anaesthetics, Royal Coll. of Surgeons 1979-82; Pres. Section of Anaesthetics, Royal Soc. of Medicine 1984-85. *Publications:* Applied Respiratory Physiology, General Anaesthesia (Gen. Ed.); 180 publs. in scientific journals. *Leisure interests:* Egyptology, model eng., music, skiing. *Address:* Division of Anaesthesia, Clinical Research Centre, Watford Road, Harrow, Middx. HA1 3UJ, England. *Telephone:* 01-864 5311.

NUNN, Sam, LL.B.; American politician and lawyer; b. 8 Sept. 1938, Perry, Ga.; s. of Samuel Augustus Nunn and Elizabeth Canon; ed. Georgia Tech. Coll. and Emory Univ.; m. Colleen O'Brien 1964; one s. one d.; ed. Emory Univ. and Emory Univ. Law School, Atlanta; State Rep. to Ga. Ass. 1968-72; U.S. Senator from Georgia 1973-; Chair. Armed Services Cttee. 1986-; Democrat. *Leisure interest:* golf. *Address:* 303 Dirksen Senate Office Building, Washington, D.C. 20510, U.S.A. *Telephone:* (202) 224-3521.

NUNN, Trevor Robert, C.B.E.; British theatre director; b. 14 Jan. 1940, Ipswich; s. of Robert Alexander Nunn and Dorothy May (née Piper); m. 1st Janet Suzman (q.v.) 1969 (divorced 1986); one s.; m. 2nd Sharon Lee Hill 1986; one d.; ed. Northgate Grammar School, Ipswich and Downing Coll., Cambridge; Trainee Dir. Belgrade Theatre, Coventry; Assoc. Dir. Royal Shakespeare Co. 1964, 1987-, Artistic Dir. 1968-78, Chief. Exec. 1968-86, Jt. Artistic Dir. 1978-87, now also Deputy Chief Exec.; toured U.S.A., Australia with own version of Hedda Gabler 1975; Hon. Litt.D. (Warwick) 1982; Hon. M.A. (Newcastle upon Tyne) 1982, London Theatre Critics' Best Dir. Award for The Revenger's Tragedy and The Winter's Tale 1969, Soc. of Film and TV Arts Award for Antony and Cleopatra 1975, Ivor Novello Award for Best British Musical of 1976 for The Comedy of Errors (Lyrics), Soc. of West End Theatre Awards, Best Musical of the Year, for The Comedy of Errors 1977, Plays and Players Award 1978, 1979 for Best Production (Dir.) and Sydney Edwards Award for Best Director in Evening Standard Drama Awards 1978, 1979, both for Once in a Lifetime, Soc. of West End Theatres Awards, incl. Best Dir., Best New Play, Evening Standard Award, Best Dir., Drama Award for Best Dir. (all for The Life and Adventures of Nicholas Nickleby). *Productions:* Tango 1965, The Revenger's Tragedy 1965, 1969, The Taming of the Shrew, The Relapse, The Winter's Tale 1969, Hamlet 1970, Henry VIII 1970; Roman Season: Antony and Cleopatra, Coriolanus, Julius Caesar, Titus Andronicus 1970; Macbeth 1974, 1976, Hedda Gabler (own version) 1975, Romeo and Juliet 1976, Comedy of Errors 1976, Winter's Tale (co-dir.) 1976, King Lear (co-dir.) 1976, Macbeth 1976, The Alchemist 1977, As You Like It 1977, Every Good Boy Deserves Favour 1977, Three Sisters 1978, The Merry Wives of Windsor 1979, Once in a Lifetime 1979, Juno and the Paycock 1980, The Life and Adventures of Nicholas Nickleby 1980 (New York 1981), Cats 1981, All's Well That Ends Well 1981, Henry IV (parts I & II) 1981, 1982, Starlight Express 1984, Les Miserables (with John Caird) 1985, Chess 1986, The Fair Maid of the West 1986, Aspects of Love 1989. *TV:* Antony and Cleopatra 1975, Comedy of Errors 1976, Every Good Boy Deserves Favour 1978, Macbeth 1978, Shakespeare Workshops Word of Mouth (written and directed by T. Nunn) 1979, The Three Sisters, Peter Pan (with John Caird) 1982. *Film:* Hedda (own scripted version), Lady Jane 1985. *Address:* c/o Campbell, Hooper, Wright & Supperstone, 35 Old Queen Street, London, SW1Y 9JD; Homevale Ltd., 28/29 Southampton Street, London, WC2E 7JA, , England.

NUORVALA, Aarne Johannes; Finnish judge; b. 18 April 1912, Viipuri; s. of Karl Elias Nylenius and Aino Tyyne Ranta; m. Hellin Helena Hintikka 1945; one s. three d.; ed. Helsinki Secondary School and Univ. of Helsinki; Civil Servant, Ministry of Finance 1944; Junior Cabinet Sec. 1945, Junior 1946-50; Junior mem. Comm. for Drafting Legislation 1950-55, Senior mem. 1955; Extra Justice of Supreme Admin. Court 1955-57, Justice 1957-63; Sec.-Gen. Deputy Prime Minister and mem. Cabinet 1963-64; Chancellor of Justice 1964, Pres. Supreme Admin. Court 1965-82; mem. High Court of Impeachment 1965-82; Chair. Supreme Court of Office 1966-81; Hon. LL.D. *Address:* c/o Korkeavuorenkatu 13A, 00130 Helsinki 13, Finland. *Telephone:* 62-66-38.

NUR KHAN, Air Marshal M.; Pakistani air force officer and airline executive; b. 1923, Tamman, Punjab; m.; one s. three d.; ed. Col. Brown's Cambridge School and Prince of Wales Royal Indian Mil. Coll., Dehra Dun.; commissioned Royal Indian Air Force 1941; Man. Dir. Pakistan Int. Airlines (PIA) 1959-65; C.-in-C. Pakistan Air Force 1965-69; Gov. W. Pakistan 1969; Chair. PIA 1973-79; Head, PIA Investments Ltd. 1981-; Pres. Pakistan Hockey Fed. 1967-69, 1977-; Hilal-e-Jurat 1965. *Leisure interests:* boxing, football, hockey, swimming, squash. *Address:* c/o Pakistan International Airlines Corporation, PIA Building, Karachi Airport, Pakistan. *Telephone:* 412011-96, Ext. 2666.

NUREYEV, Rudolf (Hametovich); ballet dancer (b. U.S.S.R.); b. 17 March 1938, Razdolnaia; ed. Ufa and Leningrad Choreographic School; Winner Moscow Nat. Students Competition; joined Kirov Ballet, Leningrad as soloist 1958; sought political asylum in the West during tour in Paris 1961; joined Grand Ballet du Marquis de Cuevas 1961; London début Charity Gala 1961; appeared with Dame Margot Fonteyn and the Royal Ballet, London 1962, and became her principal partner; has since danced all over the world in over 80 ballets, including all the nineteenth century classics as well as contemporary roles in both classical and modern style; took Austrian citizenship 1982; Guest artist in 25 companies; Artistic Dir. Paris Opera Ballet Sept. 1983-, Palais Garnier Dec. 1988-; Chevalier, Légion d'honneur; Choreographer Tancredi 1966, The Nutcracker 1967, Romeo and Juliet 1977, Manfred 1979, The Tempest 1982, Washington Square 1985, Cinderella 1986; revised and directed La Bayadère, Act III 1963, Raymonda 1964, Swan Lake 1964, The Sleeping Beauty 1966, Don Quixote 1970; Nutcracker; Raymonda (Dir.) 1983. *Films include:* An Evening with the Royal Ballet 1963, Romeo and Juliet 1966 and 1982, Swan Lake 1966, Le Jeune Homme et la Mort 1966, I am a Dancer 1972, Don Quixote 1972, Valentino 1977, Exposed 1982, Cinderella 1986. *Publication:* Nureyev, an autobiography. *Address:* c/o S. A. Gorlinsky Ltd., 33 Dover Street, London, W1X 4NJ, England.

NURIYEV, Ziya Nuriyevich; Soviet politician; b. 21 March 1915, Bashkir; ed. CPSU High School; in educ. system 1933-38, 1940-42; Soviet Army 1938-40; Party work 1942-52; Second Sec. Bashkir Regional Party Cttee. 1952-57, First Sec. 1957-69; mem. U.S.S.R. Supreme Soviet 1954-, Deputy mem. Presidium 1954-59; mem. U.S.S.R. Council of Collective Farms; Minister of Agricultural Procurements of U.S.S.R. 1969-73; Vice-Chair. Council of Ministers 1973; Chair. Comm. for Agro-industrial Complex 1982-; mem. Cen. Cttee. of CPSU 1961-; Order of Lenin (twice), Order of Red Banner and other decorations.

NURJADIN, Air Chief Marshal Roesmin; Indonesian diplomatist and politician; b. 31 May 1930, Malang; m. Surjati Subali 1962; ed. primary and high schools, and Gajah Mada Univ.; Squadron Commdr. 1953-60; Commdr.-in-Chief, Operational Command 1962-64; Air Attaché, Bangkok and Moscow 1964-66; Minister, Commdr.-in-Chief, Chief of Staff, Air Force 1966-70; Amb. to U.K. 1970-74, to U.S.A. 1974-77, Minister of Transport, Communications and Tourism 1978-83, of Communications 1983-88; various mil. and foreign decorations. *Leisure interests:* golf, sport, reading. *Address:* c/o Ministry of Communications, Jakarta, Indonesia.

NUROWSKI, Marcin, M.A.; Polish politician; b. 7 Sept. 1934, Lublin; m.; two d.; ed. Warsaw Univ.; mem. Democratic Party (SD) 1957-, political worker of SD Cen. Cttee. 1957-, managerial posts in SD Cen. Cttee. 1977-, including Head of SD Centre for Personnel Training, Warsaw 1979-81; Deputy Dir. of Dept., Small Industries Cttee. 1965-72; Chief Specialist (in charge of preparing legal basis for promotion of handicraft, private trade and small industries) at Ministry of Internal Trade and Services 1972-81, Deputy Dir. of Dept. 1981, Under-Sec. of State 1981-87; Deputy Mayor of Warsaw 1988; Minister of Internal Market 1988-; mem. Econ. Cttee. of Council of Ministers 1988-; Knight's Cross of Polonia Restituta Order and other decorations. *Publications:* numerous works on trade, small industries and handicraft. *Leisure interests:* walking at the waterside, Poland's history between the Wars, photography, watching Lech Posnań football club. *Address:* Ministerstwo Rynku Wewnętrznego, Pl. Powstańców Warszawy 1, 00-950 Warsaw, Poland. *Telephone:* 27 35 34 (Office).

NUSEIBEH, Dr. Hazem, M.A., PH.D.; Jordanian politician and diplomatist; Deputy Chair. of Devt. Bd. 1958-60; Under-Sec. Ministry of Nat. Economy 1959-60; Sec.-Gen. of Devt. Bd. 1961-62; Minister of Foreign Affairs 1962-63, 1965-66; Minister of Reconstruction and Devt. 1967-68; Amb. to Egypt 1969-71, to Turkey 1971-73, to Italy 1973-76; Perm. Rep. to UN 1976-83. *Publication:* Ideas of Arab Nationalism 1956. *Address:* c/o Ministry of Foreign Affairs, Amman, Jordan.

NUTMAN, Phillip Sadler, PH.D., A.R.C.S., D.I.C., F.R.S.; British agricultural scientist (retd.); b. 10 Oct. 1914, Lea, Malmesbury; s. of William J. and Elizabeth H. Nutman; m. Mary M. Stanbury 1940; two s. one d.; ed. Teignmouth Grammar School, Univ. Coll., Exeter and Imperial Coll., London; Inst. of Plant Physiology, Imperial Coll. 1937-40; Research Asst. Rothamsted Experimental Station, 1940; Sr. Research Fellow, CSIRO, Canberra 1953-56; Head, Soil Microbiology Dept., Rothamsted Experimental Station 1957-79; Hannaford Research Fellow, Waite Inst., Adelaide 1980; mem. several learned socs.; Huxley Research Medal. *Publications:* 80 research papers. *Leisure interests:* music (piano and organ), carpentry, gardening, travel. *Address:* Great Hackworthy Cottage, Tedburn St. Mary, Exeter, EX6 6DW, England. *Telephone:* (0647) 61364.

NUTTER, Most Rev. Harold Lee, M.A., M.S.LITT.; Canadian ecclesiastic; b. 29 Dec. 1923, Welsford, N.B.; s. of William L. Nutter and Lillian A. Joyce; m. Edith M. Carew 1947; one s. one d.; ed. Mount Allison Univ., Dalhousie Univ., Univ. of King's Coll., Halifax; ordained Deacon, Anglican Church of Canada 1946; ordained Priest 1947; Rector, Parish of Simonds and Upham 1947-51; Rector, Parish of Woodstock 1951-57; Rector, Parish of St. Mark, Saint John, N.B. 1957-60; Dean of Fredericton 1960-71, Bishop 1971-, Archbishop of Fredericton and Metropolitan of the Ecclesiastical Prov. of Canada 1980-; Examining Chaplain to Bishop of Fredericton 1960-71; Co-Chair. New Brunswick Task Force on Social Devt. 1970-71; Vice-Chair. New Brunswick Police Comm. 1988; Hon. D.D. (King's Coll., Halifax, Montreal Diocesan Coll., Wycliffe Coll., Toronto, Trinity Coll., Toronto), Hon. LL.D. (Mount Allison Univ.). *Publication:* New Brunswick Report on Social Development 1971 (Co-author). *Leisure interests:* gardening, skiing. *Address:* 791 Brunswick Street, Fredericton, N.B. E3B 1H8, Canada.

NUTTING, Rt. Hon. Sir (Harold) Anthony, Bt., P.C.; British politician and writer; b. 11 Jan. 1920; s. of Sir Harold Stansmore Nutting and Enid Hester Nina; m. 1st Gillian Leonora Strutt 1941 (divorced 1959), two s. one d.; m. 2nd Anne Gunning Parker 1961; ed. Eton and Trinity Coll., Cambridge; in British Foreign Service 1940-45; M.P. 1945-56; Chair. Young Conservative and Unionist Movement 1946, Nat. Union of Conservative and Unionist Assens. 1950, Conservative Nat. Exec. Cttee. 1951; Parl. Under-Sec. of State for Foreign Affairs 1951-54; Minister of State for Foreign Affairs 1954-56 (resigned over British Suez policy); Leader, U.K. Del. to UN Gen. Assembly and UN Disarmament Comm. 1954-56; Privy Counsellor 1954; Special Corresp., New York Herald Tribune 1957-59. *Publications:* I Saw for Myself 1958, Disarmament 1959, Europe Will Not Wait 1960, Lawrence of Arabia 1961, The Arabs 1964, Gordon, Martyr and Misfit 1966, No End of a Lesson 1967, Scramble for Africa 1970, Nasser 1972. *Leisure interest:* fishing. *Address:* 2 Douro Place, London, W.8, England.

NWAPA, Flora; Nigerian writer; b. Oguta, Eastern Nigeria; After Civil War, worked in local govt.; became Commr. for Lands, Survey and Urban Devt., Oguta; then set up own publishing co. and printing press Nwamife Publrs.; is first published African woman novelist. *Publications:* Efuru, Idu, This is Lagos and other stories, Emeka—Driver's Guard, Never Again 1981.

NYAGAH, Jeremiah Joseph Mwaniki; Kenyan politician; b. 24 Nov. 1920, Kigare, Embu; s. of Joseph Nthiga Mwonge and Mary Mbiro; m. Eunice Wambere 1947; five. s. two d.; ed. Alliance High School, Makerere Coll. and Oxford Univ.; teacher, Intermediate Schools and Teacher Training Coll.; Secondary schools and Teacher Training Coll. teacher 1954-56; Asst. Educ. Officer; mem. Legis. Council 1958-60, 1961-63; Deputy Speaker 1960; mem. House of Reps. 1963-; Jr. Minister, Ministry of Works, Communications and Power 1963-64; Jr. Minister, Ministry of Home Affairs 1964-66; Vice-Pres. for Kenya African Nat. Union (KANU) E. Region March 1966-; Minister of Educ. 1966-68; Chair. Nat. Library Service Bd. April 1966-; Minister of Natural Resources 1968-69, of Information 1969-70, of Agric. and Animal Husbandry 1970-79, of Livestock Devt. 1979-80, for Culture and Social Services 1980-82, of Water Devt. 1982-85, of Environment and National Resources 1985-; Pres. Inter-African Coffee Org.; Chair. Int. Red Locust Control Org. for Cen. and Southern Africa 1980-; mem. Boards of Govs. of many schools, Univ. Coll. Council, Nairobi, E. African Univ. Council, Boy Scouts' Training Team; Elder of the Golden Heart (Kenya), Africa Star Medal (Liberia). *Leisure interests:* sport, athletics. *Address:* Ministry of Environment and Natural Resources, Kencom House, P.O. Box 30126, Nairobi, Kenya.

NYAKYI, Anthony Balthazar, B.A.; Tanzanian diplomatist; b. 8 June 1936, Moshi; m. Margaret Mariki 1969; two s. two d.; ed. Umbwe Secondary School, Moshi, Holy Ghost Secondary School, Pugu, Makerere Univ. Coll., Kampala, Uganda; Dir. Political Div., Ministry of Foreign Affairs 1966-68; Amb. to Netherlands 1968-70, to Fed. Repub. of Germany (also accred. to the Holy See 1970 and Romania 1972) 1970-72; Prin. Sec. Ministry of Foreign Affairs 1972-78, Ministry of Defence and Nat. Service 1978-80; High Commr. in Zimbabwe 1980-81, in U.K. Nov. 1981-. *Address:* Tanzanian High Commission, 43 Hertford Street, London, W1Y 7TF, England.

NYAMDOO, Gendengiyin, PH.D.; Mongolian diplomatist; b. 1 April 1934; m.; three c.; ed. Inst. of Int. Relations, Moscow; served in Mongolian Dept. of Legal Affairs and Dept. of Int. Orgs., Ministry of Foreign Affairs 1962-68, Chief of Section of Legal Affairs 1969-72, Dir. of Dept. of Treaties and Legal Affairs 1972-76, 1980-84; Counsellor of Mongolian Mission to the UN 1976-78, Perm. Rep. to UN 1984-88. *Address:* c/o Ministry of Foreign Affairs, Ulaanbaatar, Mongolian People's Republic.

NYAMOYA, Albin; Burundian politician; b. 1924, Ngozi Province; ed. Ecole Supérieure, Astrida (now Butare, Rwanda); qualified as veterinary surgeon; held various posts at the Ministry of Agric. and Stockbreeding, Ruanda-Urundi 1945-61, Minister of Agric. and Stockbreeding 1961-62; Minister of Interior and Information, Burundi 1962-63; Prime Minister and Minister of State 1964-65; Minister of State 1965-66; Deputy to Nat.

Assembly 1963-66; various posts in Ministry of Agric. and Stockbreeding 1966-72, Dir.-Gen. 1970-71, Minister 1971-72; Prime Minister and Minister of the Interior 1972-73; Nat. Exec. Sec., mem. Cen. Cttee., Political Bureau, Unity and Nat. Progress Party until 1973. *Address:* P.O. Box 1017, Bujumbura, Burundi.

NYAMWEYA, James, LL.B.; Kenyan politician; b. 28 Dec. 1927, Kisii; m. Tabitha Moige 1948; four s. four d.; ed. King's Coll., London and Lincoln's Inn, London; Legal Asst. in Ministry of Legal Affairs, Kenya 1958-59; Advocate, Private Legal Practitioner, Supreme Court of Kenya 1959-63; Founder-mem. and mem. Central Exec. Cttee. Kenya African Nat. Union (KANU) 1959-63, Chair. Kisii 1962-64; Parl. Sec. to Ministry of Justice and Constitutional Affairs 1963, and in the Office of the Prime Minister 1964-65; Minister of State, Provincial Admin. Civil Service, Office of the Pres. 1965-66; Leader of Govt. Business in the House of Reps. May-Dec. 1966; Minister of State, Foreign Affairs, Office of the Pres. and Leader of Govt. Business in Nat. Assembly Jan. 1967, Minister of Power and Communications until Dec. 1969, Minister of Works 1969-74, of Labour 1974-79; Chair. of Electoral Comm. of Kenya; Hon. LL.D. (U.S.A.). *Address:* c/o Nyamweya Osoro & Nyamweya, Advocates, International House, P.O. Box 14339, Nairobi, Kenya.

NYANJA, Rt. Rev. Peter Nathaniel; Malawi ecclesiastic; b. 10 June 1940, Malawi; m. Irene Matrida Kayamba 1964; seven s. one d.; ed. secondary school; primary school teacher 1963-67; parish priest 1972-77; Diocesan Bishop, Diocese of Lake Malawi 1978-. *Leisure interest:* gardening. *Address:* Diocese of Lake Malawi, P.O. Box 30349, Capital City, Lilongwe 3, Malawi. *Telephone:* 731966 (Office); 722670 (Home).

NYE, John Frederick, M.A., PH.D., F.R.S.; British professor of physics; b. 26 Feb. 1923, Hove; s. of Haydn Percival and Jessie Mary (née Hague) Nye; m. Georgiana Wiebenson 1953; one s. two d.; ed. Stowe School, King's Coll., Cambridge; University Demonstrator, Dept. of Mineralogy and Petrology, Cambridge 1949-51; mem. of Tech. Staff, Bell Telephone Labs., N.J. 1952-53; lecturer in Physics, Bristol Univ. 1953-65, Reader 1965-69, Prof. 1969-; Foreign mem. Royal Swedish Acad. of Sciences 1977. *Publications:* Physical Properties of Crystals, numerous papers in scientific journals on glaciers, physics of ice, waves and mathematical catastrophes. *Leisure interest:* gardening. *Address:* H. H. Wills Physics Laboratory, Tyndall Avenue, Bristol, BS8 ITL (Office); 45 Canynge Road, Bristol, BS8 3LH, England (Home). *Telephone:* (0272) 303030 (Office); (0272) 733769 (Home).

NYE, Peter Hague, B.SC., M.A., F.R.S.; British reader in soil science; b. 16 Sept. 1921; s. of Haydn P. Nye and Jessie M. Hague; m. Phyllis M. Quenault 1953; one s. two d.; ed. Charterhouse, Balliol Coll. Oxford and Christ's Coll. Cambridge; agricultural chemist, Gold Coast 1947-50; lecturer in Soil Science, Univ. Coll. of Ibadan, Nigeria 1950-52; Sr. Lecturer in Soil Science, Univ. of Ghana 1952-60; Research Officer, I.A.E.A. Vienna 1960-61; Reader in Soil Science, Univ. of Oxford 1961-; Professorial Fellow, St. Cross Coll. Oxford 1966- (Sr. Fellow 1982-83); Pres. British Soc. of Soil Science 1968-69; mem. Council, Int. Soc. of Soil Science 1968-74; Gov. Nat. Vegetable Research Station 1972-88; Visiting Prof. Cornell Univ. 1974, 1981, Univ. of W. Australia 1979; IMPHOS Award 1982; *Publications:* The Soil Under Shifting Cultivation 1961, Solute Movement in the Soil-Root System 1977. *Address:* Hewel Barn, Common Road, Beckley, Oxon., OX3 9UR, England.

NYEMBO SHABANI, D.SC.(ECON.); Zairian professor of economics and politician; b. 5 Aug. 1937, Kayanza; ed. Inst. Saint Boniface, Elisabethville (now Lubumbashi), and Univ. Catholique de Louvain, Belgium; Dir., Bureau of Econ. Co-operation attached to the Prime Minister's Office 1964-65; Research in Econs. Univ. Catholique de Louvain 1967-76; Prof. Faculty of Econ. Science, Nat. Univ. of Zaire Oct. 1976-; State Commr. for Nat. Econ. and Industry Feb.-Aug. 1977, for Nat. Econ. 1977-78, for the State Portfolio (Investments) 1978-80, for Agric. and Rural Devt. 1980-81, 1983-84, for Econ., Industry and Foreign Trade 1982-83, for Finance and Budget 1986-88, for Agric. March 1988-; Pres. Gécamines Holdings April 1985-. *Publications:* L'industrie du cuivre dans le monde, Le progrès économique du Copperbelt Africain, Bruxelles, la Renaissance du Livre 1975. *Address:* Department of Agriculture and Rural Devt., BP 8722, Kinshasa-Gombe; B.P. 3. 824, Kinshasa 1, Zaire (Home).

NYERERE, Dr. Julius Kambarage, M.A.; Tanzanian politician; b. April 1922, Butiama-Musoma, Lake Victoria; s. of Chief Nyerere Burito; m. Maria Magige 1953; five s. two d.; ed. Musoma Native Authority Primary School, Tabora Govt. Senior Secondary School, Makerere Coll., Uganda and Edinburgh Univ.; teacher, St. Mary's R.C. School, Tabora 1946-49; student at Edinburgh Univ. 1949-52; teacher, St. Francis' R.C. Coll. 1953-55; Founder-Pres. Tanganyika African Nat. Union (TANU) 1954-77; Founder-Chair. Chama Cha Mapinduzi Feb. 1977-; elected mem. Tanganyika Legis. Council 1958, leader Elected Members Org. 1958-60; Chief Minister 1960-61; Prime Minister 1961-62; Pres. of Tanganyika 1962-64, of Tanzania 1964-85; Chair. Defence and Security Cttee. of Tanzania; Minister of External Affairs 1962-63, 1965-72; Commdr.-in-Chief of the Armed Forces 1973-85; Chancellor, Univ. of East Africa 1963-70, Univ. of Dar es Salaam 1970-85; Chair. OAU 1984; Third World Award 1981, Distinguished Son of Africa Award 1988. *Publications:* Freedom and

Unity—Uhuru na Umoja 1967, Freedom and Socialism—Uhuru na Ujamaa 1968, Ujamaa: Essays on Socialism 1969, Freedom and Development—Uhuru na Maendelo 1973, Crusade for Liberation; Swahili trans. of Julius Caesar and The Merchant of Venice 1969. *Leisure interest:* reading. *Address:* P.O. Box 9120, Dar es Salaam, Tanzania.

NYERS, Rezsö; Hungarian economist and politician; b. 21 March 1923, Budapest; m. Ilona Witz 1946; one s.; printer until 1945; mem. Parl. 1958–; Vice-Pres. Nat. Asscn. of Co-operatives 1954–56; Minister of Food Industry 1956–57; Pres. Nat. Asscn. of Co-operatives 1957–60; Minister of Finance 1960–62; Sec. Cen. Cttee. HSWP 1962–74; mem. Political Cttee. HSWP 1966–75, 1988–; Dir. Inst. of Econs., Hungarian Acad. of Sciences 1974–82; Vice-Pres. Hungarian Soc. of Economists 1982–; Minister of State 1988–. *Publications:* The Co-operative Movement in Hungary 1963, Gazdaságpolitikánk és a gazdasági mechanizmus reformja (Economic Policy and Reform of Economic Management) 1968, A magyar népgazdaság a szocializmus építésének útján (Hungary's National Economy on the Road towards Socialism) 1973. *Leisure interests:* reading, theatre, tennis, riding, philately. *Address:* Hungarian Socialist Workers Party Headquarters, 1358 Budapest, Széchenyi rakpart 19, Hungary. *Telephone:* 111-400.

NYKVIST, Sven; Swedish cinematographer; b. 1924, Moheda; ed. Stockholm Municipal School for Photographers; asst. photographer, Sandew movie studios 1941–59; photographer, Cinecitta, Rome; filmed nearly 40 feature-length films and several documentaries in Africa including Vördnad för Livet (Albert Schweitzer); Dir. of photography for Ingmar Bergman (q.v.) from 1960; has worked with many other famous directors including John Huston, Caspar Wrede, Richard Fleischer, Roman Polanski, Louis Malle, Alan J. Pakula and Andrei Tarkovsky; numerous Swedish and int. honours and awards inc. Acad. Award for photography in Bergman's Cries and Whispers 1973. *Films include:* with Bergman: The Virgin Spring 1960, Through a Glass Darkly 1960, Winter Light 1963, The Silence 1963, All these Women 1964, Persona 1966, Hour of the Wolf 1968, A Passion 1969, The Touch 1971, Cries and Whispers 1973, Scenes from a Marriage 1973, The Magic Flute 1975, Face to Face 1976, The Serpent's Egg 1977, The Autumn Sonata 1978; other recent films include: The Postman Always Rings Twice 1980, Star 80 1982, The Tragedy of Carmen 1983, Swann in Love 1985, The Sacrifice, Agnes of God 1987, The Unbearable Lightness of Being 1987. *Publications:* three books. *Address:* c/o Svenska Filminstitutet, Filmhuset Borgvagen 1–5, Box 27126, S-10252 Stockholm 27, Sweden. *Telephone:* (08) 665 1100.

NZAMBIMANA, Lieut.-Col. Edouard; Burundian army officer and politician; Minister of Public Works, Transport and Equipment 1974–76; participated in coup which overthrew Pres. Micombero Nov. 1976; Prime Minister 1976–78 and Minister of Planning 1976–78, of Agric., Livestock and Rural Devt. 1978, of Foreign Affairs and Co-operation 1978–82; Chair. Union Commerciale d'Assurances et de Réassurance (U.C.A.R.). *Address:* B.P. 3012, Bujumbura, Burundi.

O

OAKES, John Bertram, A.M., LL.D.; American journalist; b. 23 April 1913, Elkins Park, Pa.; s. of George W. Ochs Oakes and Bertie Gans Ochs; m. Margery C. Hartman 1945; one s. three d.; ed. Princeton Univ., and The Queen's Coll., Oxford (Rhodes Scholar); Reporter Trenton Times 1936–37; Political Reporter Washington Post 1937–41; served U.S. Army 1941–46; Editor, Review of the Week, Sunday New York Times 1946–49, mem. Editorial Bd. 1949–61, Editorial Page Ed. 1961–76, Sr. Ed. 1977–78, Contributing Columnist 1977–; Carnegie Foundation Travel Award 1959, Columbia Catherwood Award (for int. journalism) 1961, George Polk Memorial Award 1966 (as editor), Jefferson Award of Unitarians 1968 (service in cause of religious liberty), Dept. of Interior of U.S. Conservation Award 1962, Silurian Soc. Award 1969, Garden Club of America Award 1969, Woodrow Wilson Prize (Princeton Univ.) 1970,.John Muir Award, Sierra Club 1974, Audubon Medal, Nat. Audubon Soc. 1976, Environment Award, Natural Resources Defense Council 1977, UN Environment Programme Award 1982; Bronze Star (U.S.); Hon. M.B.E.; Croix de guerre, Médaille de Reconnaissance (France). *Publications:* The Edge of Freedom 1961; contributions to Essays Today 1955, Foundations of Freedom 1958; Tomorrow's American 1977, On the Vineyard 1980, Goodbye History, Hello Hamburger 1986. *Address:* 229 West 43rd Street, New York, N.Y., 10036 (Office); 1120 Fifth Avenue, New York, N.Y., U.S.A. (Home).

OAKESHOTT, Michael Joseph, M.A., F.B.A.; British political scientist; b. 11 Dec. 1901; s. of Joseph Francis Oakeshott and Frances Maude Hellicar; ed. Caius Coll., Cambridge; Fellow of Gonville and Caius Coll. 1925–; Univ. lecturer in History, Cambridge 1929–49; Fellow of Nuffield Coll., Oxford 1949–50; Prof. of Political Science, Univ. of London (L.S.E.) 1950–69, Prof. Emer. 1969–; Muirhead Lecturer, Birmingham Univ. 1953; Ludwig Mond Lecturer, Univ. of Manchester 1959. *Publications:* Experience and its Modes 1933, 1966, A Guide to the Classics 1936, Social and Political Doctrines of Contemporary Europe 1937, Hobbe's Leviathan (editor) 1946, The Voice of Poetry in the Conversation of Mankind 1959, Rationalism and Politics 1962, On Human Conduct 1975, Hobbes on Civil Association 1975, On History 1983, Essays on Learning and Teaching 1989. *Address:* Victoria Cottage, Acton, Langton Matravers, Swanage, Dorset, England.

OAKLEY, Brian Wynne, C.B.E., M.A.; British civil servant; b. 10 Oct. 1927, London; s. of Bernard Oakley and Edna Oakley; m. Marian Elizabeth Wooley 1953; one s. three d.; ed. Sutton Valance and Exeter Coll., Oxford; at T.R.E. (now R.S.R.E.) 1950–53, 1956–69; Scientific Adviser Air Ministry 1953–56; Computer Div., Mintech 1969–73; Requirements Div., Dept. of Industry 1973–78; Sec. Science and Eng. Research Council 1978–83; Deputy Sec. and Dir. Alvey Programme Dept. of Trade and Industry 1983–87; Chair. Logica (Cambridge) Ltd. *Publication:* The Alvey Experiment 1989. *Leisure interests:* theatre, opera, sailing. *Address:* 120 Reigate Road, Ewell, Epsom, Surrey, England. *Telephone:* 01-393 4096.

OATES, Joyce Carol, M.A.; American author; b. 16 June 1938, Lockport, N.Y.; s. of Frederic J. Oates and Caroline Bush; m. Raymond J. Smith 1961; ed. Syracuse Univ. and Univ. of Wisconsin; Prof. of English, Univ. of Detroit 1961–67, Univ. of Windsor, Ont. 1967–87; Writer-in-residence, Princeton Univ. 1978–81, Prof. 1987–; mem. American Acad., Inst. of Arts and Letters; Guggenheim Fellow 1967–68. *Publications:* novels: With Shuddering Fall 1965, A Garden of Earthly Delights 1967, Wonderland 1971, Do With Me What You Will 1973, The Assassins 1975, Childwold 1976, The Triumph of the Spider Monkey 1977, Son of the Morning 1978, Unholy Loves 1979, Cybele 1979, Bellefleur 1980, A Sentimental Education 1981, Angel of Light 1982, A Bloodsmoor Romance 1982, Mysteries of Winterthurn 1984, Solstice 1985, Wild Nights 1985, The Lives of the Twins 1987; several volumes of poems including Them 1969 (Nat. Book Award 1970); plays, stories, essays; fiction in nat. magazines. *Address:* Department of English, Princeton University N.J. 08544, U.S.A.

OATLEY, Sir Charles (William), Kt., O.B.E., M.A., F.I.E.E., F.ENG., F.I.E.E.E., F.R.S.; British professor of electrical engineering; b. 14 Feb. 1904, Frome, Somerset; s. of William and Ada M. (née Dorrington) Oatley; m. Dorothy E. West 1930; two s.; ed. Bedford Modern School and St. John's Coll., Cambridge; Lecturer, Univ. of London 1935–39; Radar Research and Devt. Establishment 1939–45, Acting Supt. in charge of scientific work 1944–45; Fellow Trinity Coll., Cambridge 1945–; Lecturer, later Reader, Dept. of Eng., Cambridge Univ. 1945–60, Prof. of Electrical Eng. 1960–71, Emer. Prof. 1971–; Dir. English Electric Valve Co. Ltd. 1966–85; mem. Council of Royal Soc. 1970–72; Fellow, King's Coll., London 1976–; Hon. Fellow, Royal Microscopical Soc. 1970; Foreign Assoc. Nat. Acad. of Eng. 1979; Hon. D.Sc. (Heriot-Watt) 1974, (Bath) 1977; Achievement Award, Worshipful Co. of Scientific Instrument Makers 1966; Royal Medal, Royal Soc. 1969; Duddell Medal Inst. of Physics and Physical Soc. 1969; Faraday Medal, Inst. of Electrical Engineers 1970; Mullard Award, Royal Soc. 1973; James Alfred Ewing Medal, Inst. of Civil Eng. 1981; Distinguished Scientist Award, Electron Microscopy Soc. of America 1984. *Publications:* The Scanning Electron Microscope Vol. I 1972, Electric and Magnetic Fields: An Introduction 1976; miscellaneous papers in scientific and technical

journals. *Leisure interest:* gardening. *Address:* 16 Porson Road, Cambridge, England. *Telephone:* (0223) 356194.

OBAID, Fikri Makram, M.A.; Egyptian politician; b. 29 Feb. 1916, Hermidat, nr. Qenna; ed. Univ. of Cairo Law School; Law School Rep. on Higher Cttee., Cairo Univ. Student Union 1932; joined private law firm 1937–50; Lawyer, Court of Cassation, and own law practice 1950–; Sec.-Gen. Heliopolis Branch, Liberation Rally 1953; mem. nat. congress, Nat. Union 1956; appointed to People's Assembly Oct. 1976; joined Socialist Liberal Party 1976, then Vice-Chair.; appointed Sec.-Gen. at foundation of Nat. Democratic Party July 1978; mem. Political Bureau, Nat. Democratic Party; Deputy Prime Minister in charge of People's Ass. Affairs 1978–83, also of Consultative Council Affairs 1980–83; mem. People's Assembly 1979–84. *Address:* c/o Office of the Deputy Prime Minister, People's Assembly Building, Cairo, Egypt.

OBAIDI, Mahdi M. Al-; Iraqi government official; b. 14 Nov. 1928, Baghdad; m. Afifa F. Hussain; four c.; ed. Univ. of California (Berkeley); served in Iraqi Ministries of Economy and Trade 1954–83; Dir.-Gen. of Foreign Econ. Relations 1969–72; Deputy Minister for Foreign Trade 1972–83; now Sec.-Gen. Council of Arab Econ. Unity; Hon. Medal of Italian Govt. 1964. *Publication:* Lectures in Agricultural Co-operation 1961. *Leisure interests:* travel, reading. *Address:* Council of Arab Economic Unity, P.O.B. 925100, Amman, Jordan; 35/5/1 Marifa District, Saydia, Dora, Baghdad, Iraq.

OBANDO BRAVO, H.E. Cardinal Miguel; Nicaraguan ecclesiastic; b. 2 Feb. 1926, La Libertad (Chontales), Juigalpa; ordained 1958; consecrated Bishop (Titular Church of Puzia di Bizacena) 1968, Archbishop 1970; cr. Cardinal 1985; Chair. Nat. Reconciliation Comm. for Nicaragua 1987. *Address:* Arzobispado, Apartado 3058, Managua, Nicaragua. *Telephone:* 71.754.

OBASANJO, Gen. Olusegun; Nigerian army officer and political administrator (retd.); b. 5 March 1937, Abeokuta, Ogun State; m. (wife deceased); two s. three d.; ed. Abeokuta Baptist High School and Mons Officers' Cadet School, U.K.; joined Nigerian Army 1958, commissioned 1959; served in Congo (now Zaire) 1960; promoted Capt. 1963, Major 1965, Lt.-Col. 1967, Col. 1969, Brig. 1972, Gen. 1979; Commdr. Eng. Corps 1963, later Commdr. 2nd Div. (Rear), Ibadan; G.O.C. 3rd Infantry Div. 1969; Commdr. 3rd Marine Commando Div. during Nigerian Civil War, accepted surrender of Biafran forces Jan. 1970; Commdr. Eng. Corps 1970–75; Fed. Commr. for Works and Housing Jan-July 1975; Chief of Staff, Supreme HQ 1975–76; mem. Supreme Mil. Council 1975–79; promoted from Brig. to Lt.-Gen. Jan. 1976; Head of Fed. Mil. Govt. and C.-in-C. of Armed Forces 1976–79; mem. Advisory Council of State 1979; farmer 1979–; Fellow, Univ. of Ibadan 1979–81; mem. Ind. Comm. on Disarmament and Security 1980; Hon. D. Hum. Litt (Howard); mem. Eminent Persons Group on S. Africa (EPG) 1985; Hon. LL.D. (Maiduguri) 1980; Hon. D.Hum.Litt. (Howard); Grand Commdr. Fed. Repub. of Nigeria 1980. *Publications:* My Command 1980, Africa in Perspective 'Myths and Realities' 1987. *Leisure interests:* table tennis, billiards, snooker, squash. *Address:* P.O. Box 2286, Abeokuta, Ogun State, Nigeria.

OBEID, Atef, M.A., PH.D.; Egyptian politician; m.; two c.; ed. Faculty of Commerce, Cairo Univ. and Univ. of Illinois; mem. Arab League Media Policy Co-ordinating Cttee. 1970; fmr. Prof. of Business Admin. Faculty of Commerce, Cairo Univ. and Pres. Int. Man. Centre; Minister of Cabinet Affairs and Minister of State for Admin. Devt. 1985–. *Address:* c/o Council of Ministers, Cairo, Egypt.

OBEIDAT, Ahmad Abdul-Majeed; Jordanian politician; b. 1938, Hartha, Irbid; m.; five c.; ed. Salahiyah School and Univ. of Baghdad; Teacher, Min. of Educ. 1957; Customs Officer 1961; First Lieut. Gen. Security Service 1962–64; Asst. Dir. Gen. Intelligence Service 1964–74, Dir. 1974–82; Minister of the Interior 1982–84; Prime Minister of Jordan and Minister of Defence 1984–85; partner Law and Arbitration Centre 1985–. *Address:* Law and Arbitration Centre, P.O. Box 926544, Amman, Jordan. *Telephone:* 672222.

OBERLE, Hon. Frank, P.C.; Canadian businessman and politician; b. 24 March 1932, Forchheim, Germany; s. of Adolf Oberle and Rosa Leibold; m. Joan Instner 1952; two s. two d.; ed. Forchheim, Germany; Alderman of Chetwynd 1963–64, Mayor 1968–72; Chair. Chetwynd and Dist. Hosp. Soc. 1966–72; mem. Chamber of Commerce; M.P. 1972–; fmr. Chair. Industrial Affairs Cttee.; Critic for Mines and Forestry 1980; Sec. to Minister of State (Mines); Minister of State for Science and Tech. 1985–89, for Forestry Jan. 1989–; Progressive Conservative. *Address:* Department of Science and Technology, C. D. Howe Building, 235 Queen Street, Ottawa, K1A 1A1, Canada.

OBERLIN, David W.; American administrator; b. 6 Jan. 1920, Atchison, Kan.; s. of William C. and Dorothy A. Wright Oberlin; m. Alida Elinor Houston 1944; two s. two d.; ed. Navy schools and Univs. of Michigan and

Kansas; Asst. Sec. and Fiscal Officer, Toledo-Lucas County Port Authority 1956–67; Port Dir., Seaway Port Authority of Duluth 1967–69; Admin. St. Lawrence Seaway Devt. Corpn. June 1969–; acting Dir. Office Deepwater Ports, Office Sec. of Transport 1975–76; fmr. Dir. American Asscn. of Port Authorities and Int. Asscn. of Port Authorities, Defence Exec. Reserve, Upper Midwest Regional Export Expansion Council, Water Transportation Sub-Cttee. for Upper Great Lakes Regional Comm.; Dept. of Transportation Commr. Great Lakes Basin Comm.; U.S. Commr. Perm. Int. Asscn. of Navigation Congresses (American Section); Silver Star Medal; Dept. of Transportation's Outstanding Achievement Award with Gold Medal. *Leisure interests:* golf, boating. *Address:* 800 Independence Avenue, S.W., Room 814, Washington, D.C. 20591, U.S.A. (Office).

OBI, Onyeabo C., L.L.B.; Nigerian international business lawyer; b. 20 Nov. 1938, Ogidi; s. of Chief Z.C. Obi; m. Evelyn Nnenna Obioha 1967; two s. three d.; ed. London School of Economics, London Univ.; admitted to Bar (Gray's Inn) 1962; in pvt. practice as barrister and solicitor of Supreme Court of Nigeria 1963–; Dir. Nigerian Rubber Bd. 1977–79; Senator of Fed. Repub. of Nigeria 1979–83; mem. of Council (and Vice-Chair. Cttee. on Procedures for Settling Disputes), Section on Business Law, Int. Bar Asscn. 1986–; mem. Advisory Cttee. on Rules of the Supreme Court of Nigeria (by appt. of Hon. Chief Justice) 1986–. *Leisure interest:* lawn tennis. *Address:* Western House (13th Floor), 8-10 Broad Street, P.O. Box 4040, Lagos, Nigeria. *Telephone:* (01) 634604 and 630843.

OBODOWSKI, Janusz, DR.ECON.SC.; Polish politician and economist; b. 2 Jan. 1930, Siedlce; s. of Antoni Obodowski and Stanisława Obodowska; m. Grażyna Prawdzic-Rudzka 1954; one d.; ed. Main School of Planning and Statistics, Warsaw and Warsaw Tech. Univ.; Head of Section for Manpower Balance, Employment Dept. of State Comm. of Econ. Planning, Warsaw 1954–57; Deputy Dir., Employment Dept. in Ministry of Labour and Social Welfare 1957–60; Deputy Dir., then Dir., Team of Comprehensive Econ. Analysis, Labour and Wages Cttee. 1960–68; Ed. Labour and Social Security monthly 1961–74; Dir. Team of Employment, Wages and Qualified Personnel in Planning Comm. of the Council of Ministers 1968–72; Lecturer at School of Planning and Statistics, Warsaw 1974–77; Under-Sec. of State, Ministry of Labour, Wages and Social Affairs 1972–80, Minister 1980–81; Vice-Prime Minister 1981–85; Chair. Econ. Cttee. of the Council of Ministers 1981–82, Chair. Planning Comm. 1982–83; Chair. Co-ordinating Comm. for Econ., Scientific and Tech. Co-operation with Foreign Countries 1983–85; Perm. Polish Rep. to COMECON 1983–85, Chair. Exec. Cttee. COMECON 1984–85; Amb. to G.D.R. Feb. 1986–; mem. PZPR 1948–; mem. Demographic Cttee. Polish Academy of Sciences, Labour and Social Policy Cttee. 1975–80; Commdr.'s, Officer's and Knight's Cross of Order of Polonia Restituta, Order of Banner of Labour and other Polish and foreign decorations. *Publications:* Walk on Earth (essays on economy) 1987, over 150 articles on social policy, employment, etc. *Leisure interests:* general history, jazz. *Address:* c/o Embassy of Poland, Unter den Linden, 1080 Berlin, German Democratic Republic. *Telephone:* 229 17 29.

OBOLENSKY, Sir Dimitri, KT., PH.D., D.LITT., F.B.A., F.R.HIST.S.; British professor of history; b. 1 April 1918, Petrograd, Russia; s. of late Prince Dimitri Obolensky and Countess Mary Shuvalov; m. Elizabeth Lopukhin 1947; ed. Lycée Pasteur, Paris and Trinity Coll. Cambridge; came to Britain 1937, naturalized 1948; Lecturer, Trinity Coll. Cambridge; Univ. Lecturer in Slavonic Studies 1946; Fellow, Trinity Coll. Cambridge 1942–48; Reader in Russian and Balkan Medieval History, Univ. of Oxford 1949–61, Prof. of Russian and Balkan History 1961–85, Prof. Emer. 1985–; Student of Christ Church, Oxford 1950–85; Visiting Scholar (Fellow), Dumbarton Oaks Center for Byzantine Studies, Harvard Univ. 1952, 1964, 1977, 1981–82; Visiting Prof. at other U.S. univs. etc.; Fellow, Soc. of Antiquaries; corresp. mem. Acad. of Athens; Dr. h.c. (Sorbonne, Paris); Hon. D.Litt. (Birmingham). *Publications:* The Bogomils: A Study in Balkan Neo-Manichaeism 1948, The Penguin Book of Russian Verse (Ed.) 1962, The Christian Centuries, Vol. II (jtly.) 1969, Byzantium and the Slavs 1971, The Byzantine Commonwealth 1971, Companion to Russian Studies (Ed. jtly.), 3 Vols. 1976–80, The Byzantine Inheritance of Eastern Europe 1982, Six Byzantine Portraits 1988. *Address:* 29 Belsyre Court, Woodstock Road, Oxford, England. *Telephone:* (0865) 56496.

OBOTE, Dr. (Apolo) Milton; Ugandan politician; b. 1924; s. of the late Stanley Opeto; labourer, clerk, salesman, Kenya 1950–55; founder-mem. Kenya African Union; mem. Uganda Nat. Congress 1952–60; mem. Uganda Legis. Council 1957–71; formed and mem. of Uganda People's Congress 1960–71, now Leader; Leader of the Opposition 1961–62; Prime Minister 1962–66; Minister of Defence and Foreign Affairs 1963–65; assumed full powers of Govt. Feb. 1966; Pres. of Uganda 1966–71 (deposed by mil. coup); in exile in Tanzania 1971–80; returned to Uganda May 1980, re-elected Pres. 1980–85, Minister of Foreign Affairs and Finance 1980–85; resident in Zambia 1985–. *Address:* c/o Uganda People's Congress, P.O. Box 1951, Kampala, Uganda.

OBOUKHOV, Alexei; Soviet diplomatist; b. 1938; ed. Moscow Inst. of Int. Relations; joined Ministry of Foreign Affairs 1965; served in Embassy in Thailand; took part in Strategic Arms Limitation Talks (SALT) I and Strategic Arms Reduction Talks (START) II; Deputy Dir. U.S. Dept., Ministry of Foreign Affairs; mem. Soviet negotiating team in arms control talks, responsible for negotiations on long-range strategic weapons, subse-

quently for negotiations on medium-range nuclear weapons, Geneva 1985; Head Soviet Del., Nuclear and Space Talks Jan. 1988. *Address:* The Kremlin, Moscow, U.S.S.R.

OBRAZTSOV, Ivan Filoppovich; Soviet politician; b. 1920; ed. Moscow Aviation Inst.; active service with Soviet Army; mem. CPSU 1944–; teaching 1944–58; Rector of Moscow Aviation Inst. 1958–72; R.S.F.S.R. Minister of Higher and Intermediate Special Educ. 1972–; mem. of U.S.S.R. Acad. of Sciences 1974; cand. mem. of CPSU Cen. Cttee. 1981–; State Prize 1976. *Address:* The Kremlin, Moscow, U.S.S.R.

OBRAZTSOVA, Yelena Vasiliyevna; Soviet mezzo-soprano; b. 7 July 1937, Leningrad; m. M. Makarov; ed. Leningrad Conservatoire (under tuition of Prof. Grigoriye); attached to Staff, Moscow Conservatoire; Glinka Prize 1963; Tchaikovsky Int. Competition, Moscow 1970; prizewinner at Francisco Viñas Int. Competition, Barcelona 1970; People's Artist of R.S.F.S.R. 1973; Lenin Prize 1976; début as Marina (Mussorgsky's Boris Godunov) with Bolshoi 1964–65 and thereafter became soloist with the co.; many int. appearances including: Sofia, Brno, Prague (Nat. and Smetana), Marseilles, Paris, Wiesbaden, Berlin (Komische Oper and Staatsoper), Budapest, Milan (La Scala) 1976, Rome (Caracalla), Monte Carlo, Bucharest, Majorca, Barcelona, Kiev, Leningrad, Moscow (Bolshoi and Stanislavsky), Tbilisi, San Francisco, Metropolitan 1975, London. *Roles include:* Azucena, Carmen, Léonore (Donizetti's Favorite), Charlotte (Massenet's Werther), Cherubino, Marina (Boris Godunov), Marfa (Khovanshchina), Hélène (Prokofiev's War and Peace), Dalila, Jocasta (Stravinsky's Oedipus Rex); Comtesse (Tchaikovsky's Queen of Spades), Amneris, Ulrica (A Masked Ball), Eboli (Don Carlo), Konchakovna (Prince Igor), Lyubashka (Rimsky-Korsakov's The Tsar's Bride), Oberon (Britten's A Midsummer Night's Dream; also song-cycles by Glinka, Tchaikovsky, Rachmaninov and Schumann, and oratorios by Bach and Handel. *Address:* Bolshaya Doroga, Milovskaya 21, Moscow, U.S.S.R.

OBREGÓN, Alejandro; Colombian painter; b. 4 June 1920; s. of Pedro and Carmen Obregón; three s. one d.; ed. Stonyhurst Coll., England, Middlesex School, Concord, and Museum School of Fine Arts, Boston, U.S.A.; Dir. School of Fine Arts, Bogotá 1949–51, Barranquilla 1956–57; one-man exhbns. Bogotá, Barranquilla, Cali, Paris, Milan, Washington, New York, Lima, Madrid, Barcelona, Munich, São Paulo and Rio de Janeiro; numerous prizes include 1st Nat. Prize Guggenheim Int. 1959; Prize at São Paulo Biennial 1967; represented in numerous galleries including: Museum of Modern Art and Guggenheim Museum, New York, Phillips Gallery, Washington, Museo Nacional, Bogotá, Inst. de Arte Contemporáneo, Lima, Museo de Arte Moderno, Bogotá, Museo Nacional, La Paz, Galerie Creuze, Paris, Galerie Buchholz, Munich, The Vatican Museum, Rome, Galeria Profili, Milan and Inst. Cultura Hispánica, Madrid. *Address:* Apartado Aereo 37, Barranquilla, Colombia.

O'BRIEN, Albert James, M.A., LL.B.; American business executive; b. 30 Oct. 1914, St. Louis, Mo.; s. of James Daniel O'Brien and Lydia Helena Dreher; m. Ruth Virginia Foster 1938; three s.; ed. Washington Univ. and Missouri Inst. of Accountancy and Law; Econ. Research and Investment Analysis, First Nat. Bank of St. Louis 1935–42; Special Asst. to Gen. Man. Atlas Powder Co., Weldon Springs, Mo. 1942–44; Personnel Man. Production and Production Staff Man., Production Ralston Purina Co. 1944–57, Sec. 1957–59, Vice-Pres., Sec. and Chief Finance Officer 1959–61, Exec. Vice-Pres. (Chow Marketing & Finance) 1961–64, Exec. Vice-Pres. (Admin.) 1964–68, Pres. 1968–69, Vice-Chair. 1969–71, Dir. 1961–72; Chair. Exec. Cttee. R. Rowland & Co. 1972–74; business man. consultant 1974–; Silver Beaver Award, Boy Scouts of America 1967. *Leisure interests:* tennis, golf, bicycling, stereo music. *Address:* 5 Doubletree Lane, St. Louis, Mo. 63131, U.S.A. (Home).

O'BRIEN, Brian, PH.B., PH.D.; American physicist; b. 2 Jan. 1898, Denver, Colo.; s. of Michael Philip O'Brien and Lina Prime O'Brien; m. 1st Ethel Dickerman 1922 (deceased), 2nd. Mary Nelson Firth 1956; one s.; ed. Yale Univ., M.I.T. and Harvard Univ.; Prof. of Physiological Optics, Univ. of Rochester, New York 1930–46, Research Prof. of Physics and Optics 1946–54, Dir. Inst. of Optics 1938–54; Vice-Pres. and Dir. of Research, American Optical Co., Mass. 1953–58; Consulting Physicist and Engineer 1958–; Pres. Optical Soc. of America 1951–53; Chair. Div. of Physical Sciences, Nat. Research Council 1953–61; mem. U.S.A.F. Scientific Advisory Bd. 1959–; Chair. Nat. Acad. of Sciences advisory Cttee. to Air Force Systems Command 1962–; Chair. Space Program Advisory Council, NASA 1970–73; mem. Nat. Acad. of Sciences, American Philosophical Soc., American Acad. of Arts and Sciences, Nat. Acad. of Eng.; U.S.A. Presidential Medal for Merit 1948, Frederick Ives Medal, Optical Soc. of America 1951, Sec. of Air Force Exceptional Civilian Service Medal 1969, 1973, Distinguished Public Service Medal, NASA 1972, Leader Medal, N.A.S. 1987. *Publications:* Approx. 60 scientific papers in physics of upper atmosphere, physical optics of metals, solar spectrum, silver halide emulsion reactions, photographic reciprocity, photographic photometry, reactions of the retina, resolution of the retina, binocular flicker phenomena, iris pulsations, etc. *Leisure interests:* fly fishing, deep sea fishing. *Address:* Box 166, Woodstock, Conn. 06281, U.S.A. *Telephone:* (203) 928-7295.

O'BRIEN, Conor Cruise, PH.D.; Irish writer and diplomatist; b. 3 Nov. 1917, Dublin; s. of Francis Cruise O'Brien and Katherine Shechy; m. 1st

Christine H. Foster 1939 (dissolved 1962), one s. two d.; m. 2nd Maire MacEntee 1962, one s. one d. (both adopted); ed. Sandford Park School, Dublin, Trinity Coll., Dublin; entered Dept. of External Affairs of Ireland 1944, Counsellor, Paris 1955–56, Head UN Section and mem. Irish Del. to UN 1956–60, Asst. Sec.-Gen., Dept. of External Affairs of Ireland 1960; Rep. of Sec.-Gen. of UN in Katanga, Congo (now Shaba, Zaire) May–Dec. 1961; Vice-Chancellor, Univ. of Ghana 1962–65; Regent's Prof. and Holder of Albert Schweitzer Chair in Humanities, New York Univ. 1965–69; mem. Dáil Eireann (House of Reps.) for Dublin (Labour) 1969–77; Minister for Posts and Telegraphs 1973–77; resgnd. from Labour Party; Senator for Dublin Univ. 1977–79; Ed.-in-Chief The Observer, London 1978–81, Consultant Ed. 1981; Contributing Ed. The Atlantic, Boston; Pro-Chancellor Univ. of Dublin 1973–; Visiting Fellow, Nuffield Coll., Oxford 1973–75; Fellow, St. Catherine's Coll., Oxford 1978; Visiting Prof. Dartmouth Coll., U.S.A. 1984–85; mem. Royal Irish Acad.; Hon. D.Litt. (Bradford) 1971, (Ghana) 1974, (Edinburgh) 1976, (Nice) 1978, (Liverpool) 1987; Valiant for Truth Media Award 1979. *Publications:* Maria Cross (under pseudonym Donat O'Donnell) 1952, Parnell and his Party 1957, The Shaping of Modern Ireland (ed.) 1959, To Katanga and Back 1962, Conflicting Concepts of the United Nations 1964, Writers and Politics 1965, The United Nations: Sacred Drama 1967, Murderous Angels (play) 1968, Power and Consciousness (ed.) 1969, Conor Cruise O'Brien Introduces Ireland 1969, Edmund Burke's Reflections on the Revolution in France (ed.) 1969, Camus 1969, A Concise History of Ireland (with Máire Cruise O'Brien) 1972, The Suspecting Glance 1972, States of Ireland 1972, Herod's Reflections on Political Violence 1978, Neighbours: Ewart-Biggs memorial lectures 1978–79 1980, The Siege: the Saga of Israel and Zionism 1986, Passion and Cunning 1988, God Land: reflections on religion and nationalism 1988. *Leisure interest:* travelling. *Address:* Whitewater, The Summit, Howth, Dublin, Ireland. *Telephone:* Dublin 322474.

O'BRIEN, Edna; Irish author; b. 15 Dec. 1936, Co. Clare; d. of Michael O'Brien and Lena Cleary; m. 1954 (divorced 1964); two s.; ed. convents, Pharmaceutical Coll. of Ireland; engaged in writing from an early age; Yorkshire Post Novel Award 1971, Kingsley Amis Award. *Publications:* The Country Girls 1960 (film 1983), The Lonely Girl 1962, Girls in Their Married Bliss 1963, August is a Wicked Month 1964, Casualties of Peace 1966, The Love Object 1968, A Pagan Place 1970 (play 1971), Night 1972, A Scandalous Woman (short stories) 1974, Mother Ireland 1976, Johnny I Hardly Knew You (novel) 1977, Arabian Days 1977, Mrs. Reinhardt and other stories 1978, The Wicked Lady (screenplay), Virginia (play) 1979, The Hard Way 1980 (TV play), Mrs. Reinhardt (adapted for TV) 1981, The Dazzle (children's book), Returning: A Collection of New Tales 1982, A Christmas Treat 1982, Home Sweet Home (play) 1984, Stories of Joan of Arc (film) 1984, A Fanatic Heart (Selected Stories) 1985, Flesh and Blood (play) 1987, Madame Bovary (play) 1987, Vanishing Ireland 1987, Tales for the Telling (children's book) 1987, The High Road (novel) 1988, On the Bone (poetry) 1989. *Leisure interests:* reading, walking, dreaming. *Address:* c/o Duncan Heath Associates, 162–170 Wardour Street, London, W1V 3AT, England.

O'BRIEN, Most Rev. Keith Michael Patrick, B.SC., DIP. ED.; British ecclesiastic; b. 17 March 1938, Ballycastle; s. of Mark Joseph O'Brien and Alice Mary Moriarty; ed. St. Patrick's High School, Dumbarton, Holy Cross Acad., Edinburgh, Univ. of Edinburgh, St. Andrew's Coll., Drygrange and Moray House Coll. of Educ.; ordained to priesthood 1965; Chaplain and teacher St. Columba's High School, Dunfermline 1966–71; Asst. Priest St. Patrick's, Kilsyth 1972–75, at St. Mary's, Bathgate 1975–78; Spiritual Dir. St. Andrew's Coll. 1978–80; Rector St. Mary's Coll., Blairs 1980–85; R.C. Archbishop of St. Andrews and Edin. 1985–. *Address:* 42 Greenhill Gardens, Edinburgh, EH10 4BJ, Scotland. *Telephone:* 031-447 3337.

O'BRIEN, Lawrence Francis, LL.D.; American government official; b. 7 July 1917, Springfield, Mass.; s. of Lawrence O'Brien Sr. and Myra Sweeney; m. Elva Lena Brassard 1944; one s.; ed. Cathedral Grade and High Schools, Springfield, Mass., Northeastern Univ.; U.S. Army 1943–45; O'Brien Realty Co. (family business), Springfield, Mass. 1942–52; Bd. Pres. and Business Man. Western Mass. Hotel and Restaurant Health Fund 1952–58; State Dir. of Org. for campaigns of John F. Kennedy for Senate of U.S., Mass. 1952, 1958; Public Relations work, Springfield 1958–60; Nat. Dir. of Org. for Dem. Nat. Cttee. and for Kennedy-Johnson campaign 1960; Special Asst. to Pres. of U.S. for Congressional Relations 1961–65; Postmaster-Gen. 1965–68; Dem. Party Campaign Man. for Presidential Election 1968; Chair. Dem. Nat. Cttee. 1968–69, 1970–72; Chair. Dem. Nat. Convention 1972; Pres. McDonnell & Co. (New York investment banking firm) 1969; Man. Consultant, Washington D.C. 1973–75; Commr. Nat. Basketball Asscn., New York 1975–84, Sr. Adviser 1984–87; Pres. Int. Basketball Hall of Fame 1985–87; Hon. LL.D. (Western New England Coll.) 1962, (Villanova) 1966, (Loyola) 1967, (Xavier) 1971; Hon. L.H.D. (St. Anselm's Coll.) 1966, (American Int. and Wheeling Colls.) 1971; Hon.D. Public Admin. (Northeastern Univ.) 1965, Hon.D. Public Affairs (Seton Hall) 1967, Hon. D.S. (Bryant Coll.) 1978, Hon. D.H. (Springfield Coll.) 1982; Brotherhood Award (Nat. Conf. of Christians and Jews) 1977, Prime Minister's Medal for distinguished service to democracy and freedom (Israel) 1978, named Man of Year, Basketball Weekly 1976, Sports Man of Year, Sporting News 1976, Nat. Basketball Asscn. World Championship Trophy (desig.) Larry O'Brien Trophy 1984, John W. Bunn Award for

outstanding contribs. to basketball and sports 1984. *Publications:* The O'Brien Campaign Manual 1960, 1964, 1968, 1972, No Final Victories 1974. *Leisure interests:* theatre, books. *Address:* 860 United Nations Plaza, New York, N.Y. 10017, U.S.A.

O'BRIEN, (Michael) Vincent; Irish racehorse trainer; b. 9 April 1917, Cork; s. of Daniel P. O'Brien and Kathleen (née Toomey); m. Jacqueline Wittenoom 1951; two s. three d.; ed. Mungret Coll., Limerick; started training in Co. Cork 1944, moved to Co. Tipperary 1951; Hon. LL.D. 1983; won all principal English and Irish steeplechases, including 3 consecutive Champion Hurdles, 3 consecutive Grand Nationals and 4 Gold Cups; has concentrated on flat racing 1959–; trained winners of 16 English classics, including 6 Derbys; trained Nijinsky, first Triple Crown winner since 1935, also winners of 25 Irish Classics (including 6 Irish Derbys), 1 French Derby, 3 Prix de l'Arc de Triomphe, 2 King George VI and Queen Elizabeth Diamond Stakes, Washington Int., etc. *Leisure interests:* golf, fishing. *Address:* Ballydoyle House, Cashel, Co. Tipperary, Ireland. *Telephone:* (062) 61222.

O'BRIEN, Terence John, C.M.G., M.C., M.A.; British diplomatist (retd.); b. 13 Oct. 1921, Ranchi, India; s. of Joseph O'Brien; m. 1st Phyllis Mitchell 1950 (died 1952), 2nd Rita Reynolds 1953; one s. two d.; ed. Gresham's School, Holt, Merton Coll., Oxford; Ayrshire Yeomanry, later Air Liaison Office with 83 Group R.A.F. 1942–45; Dominions Office 1947, Commonwealth Relations Office (CRO) 1947–49, 1952–54; Second Sec., British High Comm., Ceylon (now Sri Lanka) 1949–52; Principal, Treasury 1954–56; First Sec. (Financial), High Comm., Canberra 1956–58; Planning Officer, CRO 1958–60; First Sec. Kuala Lumpur 1960–62; Sec. to Inter-Governmental Cttee., Jesselton, North Borneo (now Kota Kinabalu, Sabah, Malaysia) 1962–63; Head of Chancery, New Delhi 1963–66; Imp. Defence Coll. 1967; Counsellor, Foreign Office, FCO 1968–70; Amb. to Nepal 1970–74, to Burma 1974–78, to Indonesia 1978–81. *Address:* Beaufort House, Woodcutts, Salisbury, Wiltshire, England (Home).

O'BRIEN, Vincent (see O'Brien, Michael Vincent).

O'BRIEN OF LOTHBURY, Baron (Life Peer) cr. 1973; **Leslie Kenneth O'Brien,** G.B.E., P.C., F.R.C.M.; British banker; b. 8 Feb. 1908, London; s. of Charles John Grimes O'Brien and Carrie Abbott; m. 1st Isabelle Gertrude Pickett 1932 (deceased 1987); one s.; m. 2nd Marjorie Violet Taylor 1989; entered Bank of England 1927, apptd. Deputy Chief Cashier 1951, Chief Cashier 1955–62, Dir. 1962–64, Deputy Gov. 1964–66, Gov. 1966–73; Pres. British Bankers' Asscn. 1973–80; Dir. Prudential Assurance Co. Ltd. 1973–80, Prudential Corpn. 1979–83, Rank Org. 1974–78; Consultant to J. P. Morgan and Co. 1973–79; Chair. Int. Advisory Council, Morgan Guaranty Trust Co. 1974–78, Advisory Bd. Unilever 1973–78, Int. Advisory Council, Morgan Grenfell Co. Ltd. 1974–87; Dir. Bank for Int. Settlements 1974–83, Vice-Pres. 1979–83; Dir. Saudi Int. Bank 1975–84, Chair. Audit Cttee. 1984–; Hon. Fellow, Chartered Inst. of Bankers; Vice-Chair. Banque Belge 1981–88; Dir. Belgian and Gen. Investments 1981–88; Hon. D.Sc. (City Univ.); Hon. LL.D. (Univ. of Wales); Kt. Grand Cross of the Order of Merit (Italy); Grand Officer of the Order of the Crown of Belgium.

O'BRIEN QUINN, Hon. Mr Justice James Aiden, B.A., LL.B.; Irish lawyer; b. 3 Jan. 1932, Tipperary; s. of the late William Patrick Quinn and Helen Mary Quinn (née Walshe); m. Christel Mary Tyner 1960; two s. one d.; ed. Presentation Coll., Bray, Univ. Coll. Dublin and King's Inns, Dublin; studied banking, Nat. City Bank, Dublin 1949–53; Crown Counsel and Acting Sr. Crown Counsel, Nyasaland (Malawi) 1960–64; Asst. Attorney-Gen. and Acting Attorney-Gen., West Cameroon 1964–66; Procureur-Général près la Cour Suprême Cameroun Occidental 1966–68; Avocat-Général près la Cour Fédérale de Justice, Cameroun 1966–68; Conseiller à la Cour Fédérale de Justice, Yaoundé, Cameroun 1968–72; Président du Tribunal Administratif du Cameroun Occidental 1968–72; Conseiller Technique (Harmonisation des Lois), Yaoundé, Cameroun 1968–72; Attorney-Gen. of Seychelles and British Indian Ocean Territory 1972–76; Chief Justice of Seychelles 1976–77; Acted as Deputy Gov. of Seychelles for a period during 1974; mem. Seychelles dels. on self-govt. and independence constitutions 1975, 1976; Chief Justice of Gilbert Islands (later Kiribati), Pacific Ocean 1977–81; Judge of High Court of Solomon Islands 1977–81; Chief Justice of Botswana 1981–87; Chair. of Judicial Service Comm., Botswana 1981; Third Place, Inst. of Bankers in Ireland 1950; Chevalier de l'Ordre National de la Valeur, Cameroun 1967; Q.C., Seychelles 1973; Kiribati Independence Medal 1979. *Publications:* Ed. W. Cameroon Law Reports 1961–68 and Gilbert Islands Law Reports, Kiribati Law Reports 1977–79; Magistrates' Courts' Handbook, W. Cameroon 1968, Magistrates' Courts' Handbook, Kiribati 1979. *Leisure interests:* swimming, reading, languages, travel. *Address:* 9 Lorane Court, Langley Road, Watford, Herts., England.

OBUCHI, Keizo; Japanese politician; b. 25 June 1937, Gunma Pref.; m.; ed. Waseda Univ.; mem. House of Reps. 1963–, Parl. Vice-Minister for Posts and Telecommunications 1970, for Construction 1972; Deputy Dir.-Gen. Prime Minister's Office 1973, then Dir.-Gen. and Minister of State 1979–80; State Minister and Chief Cabinet Sec. Nov. 1987–; Dir.-Gen. Okinawa Devt. Agency 1979–80; Chair. Standing Cttee. on Finance, House of Reps. 1976. *Leisure interests:* paintings, aikido. *Address:* 2-16-2 Ojihoncho, Kita-ku, Tokyo 114, Japan.

OBUKHOV, Aleksandr Mikhailovich, D.SC.; Soviet physicist; b. 5 May 1918, Saratov; ed. Moscow State Univ.; Research Assoc., Geophysical Inst., U.S.S.R. Acad of Sciences 1940-56; Dir. Inst. of Atmospheric Physics 1956-; lecturer, Moscow State Univ. 1946-49, Prof. 1949-; corresp. mem. U.S.S.R. Acad. of Sciences 1953-70, Acad. 1970-; various decorations. *Address:* Institute of Atmospheric Physics, 3 Pyzhevsky pereulok, Moscow, U.S.S.R.

OBZINA, Jaromír, PH.DR., DR.SC.; Czechoslovak politician and university lecturer; b. 28 May 1929, Brodek; s. of late František Obzina and Žofie Obzinová; m. Světla Obzinová; one s. one d.; ed. Přerov Secondary School, Central Cttee. of the CPSU Higher Educ. Coll., Moscow; Sec. Chrudim District Cttee., CP of Czechoslovakia, First Sec. Polička and Pardubice District Cttee., Instructor Pardubice Regional Cttee.; held positions on Main Political Bd. of Czechoslovak People's Army 1953-56; Commdr. Antonín Zápotocký Mil. Acad. Political Dept. 1956-64; Head of Division for Science, CP Central Cttee. Dept. of Educ. and Science 1965-68; Deputy Commdr., Czechoslovak People's Army Inst. for Scientific Affairs 1968-69; Head of Division for Science, Deputy Head (later Head) Dept. of Educ., Science and Culture 1969-73; Minister of Interior 1973-83; Deputy Premier Czechoslovak Govt. 1983-; Chair. State Comm. for Scientific-Tech. Devt. and Investments 1983-88; Perm. Rep. to CMEA 1988-; mem. House of the People of Fed. Assembly., mem. CP Central Cttee. March 1973-; many decorations incl. Medal For Outstanding Work, Medal for Distinction in Construction, Medal for Service in Favour of the Country, Medal for Distinction in Defence of the Country, Order of Labour 1979, Order of Friendship (Cuba) 1983. *Publications:* several scientific books and a number of articles. *Leisure interest:* sports. *Address:* Government Presidium of Czechoslovakia, nábř. Kpt. Jarose 4, Prague 1, Czechoslovakia.

O'CALLAGHAN, (Donal N.) Mike; American fmr. state governor; b. 10 Sept. 1929, La Crosse, Wis.; s. of Neil T. and Olive Berry O'Callaghan; m. Carolyn Randall; three s. two d.; ed. Cotter High School, Winona, Minn., Univs. of Idaho and Nevada, Colorado State and Georgetown Univs. and Claremont Graduate School; High School teacher 1956-61; Chief Probation Officer and Dir. of Court Services, Clark County, Nev. 1961-63; State Dir. of Health and Welfare 1963-64; Project Man. Dir., Job Corps Conservation Centres, Washington, D.C. 1964-66; Regional Dir. Office of Emergency Planning (OEP), San Francisco 1967-69; Gov. of Nevada 1971-79; Democrat. *Leisure interests:* falconry, hiking, camping. *Address:* c/o Office of the Governor, State Capitol, Carson City, Nev., U.S.A.

OCCHIUTO, Antonino, B.ECON. AND DIPL.; Italian central banker; b. 21 Dec. 1912, Naples; s. of late Stefano Occhiuto and Margherita Ruggiero; m. Valeria Marcucci 1952; one s. two d.; ed. Univ. of Naples; Head of Gen. Secr., Banca d'Italia 1961-64, Head of Personnel Dept 1965-67, Gen. Insp. 1967-69, Deputy Dir.-Gen. 1969-76, Hon. Dir.-Gen. Banca d'Italia 1976-; mem. Bd. of Dirs., BIS 1975-; Chair. Luigi Einaudi Inst. for Monetary, Banking and Financial Studies 1976-; Pres. Istituto Italiano di Credito Fondiario, Istituto di Credito per le Imprese di Pubblica Utilità (ICIPU) 1979-; Grande Ufficiale dell'Ordine al Merito della Repubblica Italiana. *Address:* Istituto di Credito Fondiario, via Piacenze 6, 00184 Rome (Office); Via Nomentana 293, Rome, Italy. *Telephone:* 4987/131 (Office).

OCHAB, Edward; Polish politician; b. 16 Aug. 1906, Cracow; ed. Cracow School of Commerce and Jagiellonian Univ.; joined Polish CP 1929; frequently imprisoned; co-organizer of Union of Polish Patriots and Polish Army in the U.S.S.R. 1942-45; Minister of Public Admin. 1944-45; Deputy to Seym 1947-69; Chair. Cen. Council of Trade Unions 1948-49; Vice-Minister of Nat. Defence 1949-50; Sec. Cen. Cttee. PZPR 1950-56, 1959-64, mem. Politburo 1954-68, First Sec. Cen. Cttee. 1956; Minister of Agriculture 1957-59; Vice-Pres. Council of State 1961-64, Pres. (Head of State) 1964-68; Chair. All-Polish Cttee. of Nat. Unity Front 1965-68; retd.; numerous decorations.
[*Died 1 May 1989.*]

OCHI, Ihei; Japanese politician; b. Dec. 1920, Ehime Pref.; m.; one s.; ed. Sagamihara Eng. School; mem. House of Reps. 1972-; Parl. Vice-Minister for the Environment 1975; Parl. Vice-Minister for Labour 1976; Chair. Liberal-Democratic Party (LDP) Exec. Council 1983; Deputy Sec.-Gen. LDP 1983; Chair. House of Reps. Standing Cttee. on Finance; Minister of Construction 1987-88. *Leisure interest:* Shorinji Kempo (a martial art). *Address:* Takanawa Shukusha, 3-13-57 Takanawa, Minato-ku, Tokyo 108, Japan.

OCHIAI, Eiichi, B.SC.; Japanese trade unionist; b. 15 Feb. 1916, Kuzumaki-Machi; s. of the late Eisaburo Ochiai and Mitori Ochiai; m. Eiko Ochiai 1945; one s. one d.; ed. Yokohama Nat. Univ.; Mitsui Metal Mine Co. Ltd. 1936-41, Toshiba Electric Co. 1943-46; Adviser, Japan Asscn. of Science and Tech. 1944-47; Pres. All-Japan Electric Industry Workers Unions 1946-48; mem. Exec. Bd. Congress of Industrial Labour Union 1946-49; mem. Exec. Bd. Japan Socialist Party 1948-49; Gen. Sec. Nat. Fed. of Industrial Orgs. 1949-64; mem. Labour Problems Cttee. 1961-64, Small and Medium Enterprise Retirement Counter-measure Cttee. 1960-64; Dir. Tokyo Office, Int. Confed. of Free Trade Unions (ICFTU) and Special Rep. in Japan 1964-77; Trustee, Japan ILO Asscn. 1962-, Inst. of Asian Social Problems 1977-81. *Publications:* Import of Foreign Capital and Production Struggle 1949, Directory of Trade Union Administration 1949,

Earth of North America and Blood of Great Britain 1959. *Leisure interests:* horse riding, rugby. *Address:* Keyakidai 38-302, Nishimachi-4, Kokubunji-shi, Tokyo 185, Japan. *Telephone:* 0425-36-8306.

OCHMAN, Wiesław; Polish singer; b. 6 Feb. 1937, Warsaw; s. of Jan Ochman and Bronisława Ochman; m. Krystyna Ochman 1963; one s. one d.; ed. Acad. of Mining and Metallurgy, Cracow 1960, studied with Prof. Gustaw Serafin, Cracow and under Prof. Maria Szłapak, Jerzy Gaczek and Sergiusz Nadgryzowski; début Silesian Opera, Bytom 1960; soloist: Silesian Opera, Bytom 1960-63, Opera in Cracow 1963-64, Great Theatre, Warsaw 1964-, Deutsche Staatsoper 1967, Hamburgische Staatsoper 1967-, Metropolitan Opera, New York 1975-, La Scala, Milan 1981; Festivals at Glyndebourne, Salzburg, Orange; Minister of Culture and Art Prize 1973, The City of Warsaw Prize 1976, Pres. of Radio and TV Cttee. Prize (1st Class) 1976, Prime Minister Prize (1st Class) 1979, Minister of Foreign Affairs Diploma 1977, Medal Maecenas of Art 1976, Kt.'s Cross Order of Polonia Restituta, The City of Cracow Gold Award.; Medal of Merit for Nat. Culture 1986; participation in TV films including Eugene Onegin, Czarevitch, Salome, Don Giovanni. *Leisure interests:* painting, collecting objects of art. *Address:* ul. Miączyńska 46B, 02-637 Warsaw, Poland. *Telephone:* 26-30-01 (Office).

OCHOA, Severo, M.D.; Spanish-born American biochemist; b. 24 Sept. 1905, Luarca, Spain; s. of Severo and Carmen (Albornoz) Ochoa; m. Carmen G. Cobian 1931; ed. Madrid, Glasgow, Berlin, Heidelberg and London Univs.; Lecturer Univs. of Madrid, Heidelberg, Plymouth and Oxford 1931-41; Instructor and Research Assoc. Washington Univ. St. Louis 1941-42; Research Assoc. New York Univ. 1942, Chair. Dept. of Biochemistry 1954-75; with Roche Inst. of Molecular Biology 1976-; U.S. citizen 1956-; Visiting Prof. Univ. of Calif. 1949, Univ. of Brazil 1956; Foreign mem. Royal Soc. (U.K.) 1965, Indian Nat. Science Acad., Acad. of Sciences of D.D.R.; Nobel Prize in Medicine (with Kornberg) 1959; Pres. Int. Union of Biochemistry 1961-67; mem. U.S. Nat. Acad. of Sciences, Acad. of Arts and Sciences, American Philosophical Soc., U.S.S.R. Acad. of Sciences, Polish Acad. of Sciences, Brazilian Acad. of Sciences, Pontifical Acad. of Sciences 1974, and many other academies; numerous hon. degrees and decorations. *Address:* Centro de Biología Molecular, Facultad de Ciencias, Universidad Autónoma, Campus de Cantoblanco, 28049 Madrid (Office); Miguel Angel 1 duplicado, 28010 Madrid, Spain (Home). *Telephone:* Madrid 734-9300 (Office); Madrid 410-0709 (Home).

OCKRENT, Christine; French radio and television journalist; b. 24 April 1944, Brussels, Belgium; d. of Roger Ockrent and Grett Bastenie; ed. Collège Sevigné, Paris, Cambridge Univ., England and Institut d'études politiques de Paris; journalist, Information Office, EEC 1965-66; Researcher, NBC News, U.S.A. 1967-68; Producer and Journalist, CBS News, U.S.A.1968-76, Correspondent 1976-77; Journalist and Producer, FR3, France 1976-80, several posts as journalist, editor and presenter on news programmes 1980-82; Presenter 8 p.m. news on Antenne 2 1982-85; Chief Ed. RTL 1985-86; Deputy Dir.-Gen. TFI 1986-87; Deputy News Controller Antenne 2 1988-. *Publication:* The Evil Empire (with Count de Marenches) 1988. *Address:* 4 rue Cruynemer, 75006 Paris, France.

Ó COFAIGH, Tomás F.; Irish banker; b. 7 Oct. 1921, Dublin; s. of James J. and Sarah (née Leahy) Coffey; m. Joan Kinsella 1953; three s. one d.; ed. O'Connell School, Dublin, Dublin Univ.; entered civil service 1939; Second Perm. Sec., Dept. of Finance 1974-77, Sec.-Gen. 1977-81; Dir. Cen. Bank of Ireland 1977-81, Gov. 1981-87; Alt. Gov. for Ireland, World Bank 1977-81; mem. Cttee. of Govs. of Cen. Banks of mem. States of EEC (Chair. 1984), Bd. of Govs., European Monetary Co-operation Fund (Chair. 1984); Alt. Gov. for Ireland, IMF 1981-89; mem. Nat. Econ. and Social Council (various periods), Council and Exec. Cttee. of Econ. and Social Research Inst. 1981-, Inst. of Public Admin., Irish Man. Inst. *Leisure interests:* music, hill walking, reading. *Address:* c/o Central Bank of Ireland, Dame Street, Dublin 2, Ireland. *Telephone:* (01) 716666 (Office).

O'CONNELL, Hon. Martin Patrick, P.C., PH.D., M.P.; Canadian politician; b. 1 Aug. 1916, Victoria, B.C.; s. of James and Mary (née Kyle) O'Connell; m. Helen Alice Dionne 1945; one s. one d.; lecturer in Political Economy, Univ. of Toronto 1948-56; mem. of investment firm 1958-68; mem. House of Commons 1968-79; Parl. Sec. to Minister of Regional Econ. Expansion 1969, Minister of State 1971, Minister of Labour 1972; Principal Sec. to Prime Minister 1972-74; Minister of Labour 1978-79; Chair. Canadian Parl. Helsinki Group 1976-78, Consultant 1979-82; Co-Chair. Special Joint Cttee. of the House of Commons and Senate on Immigration Policy 1975-76, Canada-U.S. Interparl. Cttee. 1976-78. *Address:* Ste. 719, 2 Carleton Street, Toronto, Ont. M5B 1J3, Canada.

O'CONNOR, Charmian Jocelyn, J.P., PH.D., C. CHEM., F.R.S.N.Z., F.R.S.C., F.N.Z.I.C.; New Zealand professor of chemistry; b. 4 Aug. 1937, Woodville; d. of Cecil J. O'Connor and Kathrene M. Bishop; m. Peter S. O'Connor 1963 (divorced 1970); one s. one d.; ed. Univ. of Auckland; Post-doctoral Fellow, Univ. Coll. London 1967, Univ. of Calif. Santa Barbara 1967-68; lecturer, Univ. of Auckland 1958-66, Sr. Lecturer 1967-71, Assoc. Prof. 1972-85, Prof. of Chemistry 1986-; Visiting Prof. Texas A & M Univ. 1972, Nagasaki Univ. 1982, 1986, 1987, Tokushima Univ. 1987; numerous awards and prizes. *Publications:* 150 articles in refereed journals and several book chapters. *Leisure interests:* swimming, knitting, watching television.

Address: Department of Chemistry, University of Auckland, Private Bag, Auckland, New Zealand. *Telephone:* 64 (9) 737999.

O'CONNOR, H.E. Cardinal John, PH.D.; American ecclesiastic and fmr. naval officer; b. 15 Jan. 1920, Philadelphia; s. of Thomas Joseph and Dorothy Magdalene (Gomple) O'Connor; ed. St. Charles Coll., Catholic Univ. of America, Georgetown Univ.; ordained R.C. Priest 1945, Msgr. 1966, consecrated Bishop 1979, Auxiliary Bishop, Vicar-Gen. (Mil. Vicariate) 1979–83; Bishop of Scranton 1983; Archbishop of New York 1984–; cr. Cardinal 1985; served in Chaplain Corps U.S. Navy 1952, rose to rank of Rear Adm., assigned to Atlantic and Pacific fleets, Okinawa and Vietnam. *Publications:* Principles and Problems of Naval Leadership 1958, A Chaplain Looks at Vietnam 1969, In Defense of Life 1981, His Eminence and Hizzoner (with Ed. Koch, q.v.) 1989. *Address:* Archdiocese of New York, 452 Madison Avenue, New York, N.Y. 10022, U.S.A.

O'CONNOR, Raymond James, M.L.A.; Australian politician; b. March 1926, Perth; ed. York, Narrogin and Perth; joined the army 1943; served Bougainville and New Britain; discharged 1946; in motor trade; mem. Western Australia Legis. Assembly 1959–; Hon. Minister assisting Minister for Railways and Transport 1965, later Minister for Transport (cabinet post); Minister for Transport and Railways 1967–71; Minister for Transport, Traffic and Police 1974, subsequently of Works, Water Supplies and Housing; Minister of Labour and Industry, Consumer Affairs, Immigration, Fisheries and Wildlife and Conservation and the Environment 1978; Deputy Leader Parl. Liberal Party 1980; Deputy Premier 1980–82; Premier of Western Australia 1982–83; Leader of Opposition Feb. 1983–; also Treas. and Minister Co-ordinating Econ. and Regional Devt. *Address:* Parliament House, Perth Harvest Terrace; Perth, Western Australia 6000, Australia. *Telephone:* Perth 322 1344.

O'CONNOR, Sandra Day; American judge; b. 26 March 1930, El Paso, Tex.; d. of Harry A. and Ada Mae (née Wilkey) Day; m. John Jay O'Connor III 1952; three s.; pvt. practice Phoenix, Ariz. 1959–65; served in Arizona Senate 1969–74, Majority Leader 1973–74; elected Superior Court Judge, Ariz. 1975, Judge of Appeals 1979–81; Judge (Assoc. Justice), U.S. Supreme Court Sept. 1981–; mem. Nat. Bd. Smithsonian Assocs. 1981–82. *Address:* Supreme Court Building, 1 First Street, N.E., Washington, D.C. 20543, U.S.A.

ODA, Shigeru, LL.M., J.S.D., LL.D.; Japanese lawyer; b. 22 Oct. 1924; s. of Toshio and Mioko Oda; m. Noriko Sugimura 1950; one s. one d.; ed. Univ. of Tokyo, Yale Univ.; Research Fellow, Univ. of Tokyo 1947–49; Lecturer Univ. of Tôhoku 1950–53, Asst. Prof. 1953–59, Prof. 1959–76; Prof. Emer. 1985–; Tech. Adviser, Atomic Energy Comm. 1961–64; Special Asst. to Minister for Foreign Affairs 1973–76; mem. Science Council of Ministry of Educ. 1969–76, of Council for Ocean Devt. in Prime Minister's Office 1971–76, Advisory Cttee. for Co-operation with UN Univ. 1971–76; Judge, Int. Court of Justice Feb. 1976–; del. to UN Confs. on Law of the Sea 1958, 1960, 1973–75; Rep. at 6th Gen. Conf. of Inter-Governmental Oceanographic Comm. 1969; consultative positions with bodies concerned with marine questions; Counsel for Fed. Repub. of Germany before Int. Court of Justice 1968; Editor-in-Chief, Japanese Annual of International Law 1973–77; Assoc. Inst. de Droit Int. 1969 (mem. 1979); Hon. mem. American Soc. of Int. Law 1975; Hon. D.Jur. (Bhopal Univ.) 1980, (New York Law School) 1981. *Publications:* in Japanese: International Law of the Sea 1956–85 (8 vols.), International Law and Maritime Resources 1971–75; Judicial Decisions relating to International Law before Japanese Courts 1978; in English: International Control of Sea Resources 1962, The International Law of Ocean Development (4 vols.) 1972–79, The Law of the Sea in Our Times (2 vols.) 1977, The Practice of Japan in International Law 1961–70 1982, The International Court of Justice 1987; various articles. *Address:* International Court of Justice, Peace Palace, The Hague 2517 KJ, The Netherlands (Office). *Telephone:* 070-92.44.41 (Office).

ODDI, H.E. Cardinal Silvio; Italian ecclesiastic; b. 14 Nov. 1910, Morfasso; ordained 1933; Titular Archbishop of Mesembria 1953; Apostolic Del. in Palestine, Jerusalem and Cyprus 1953–56; Apostolic Internuncio in Egypt and U.A.R. 1956–62; Apostolic Nuncio in Belgium and Luxembourg 1962–69; cr. Cardinal March 1969; Pres. of the Pontifical Comm. for the Sanctuaries of Loreto and Pompei; Pontifical Del. for the Basilica of Assisi; Prefect of the Sacred Congregation for the Clergy; Camerlengo of Coll. of Cardinals. *Address:* Piazza Pio XII, M3, Rome, Italy (Office); Via Pompeo Magno 21, 00192 Rome, Italy (Home). *Telephone:* 698 4031; 698 4136 (Office); 3568957 (Home).

ODEGAARD, Charles (Edwin), PH.D.; American university professor; b. 10 Jan. 1911, Chicago Heights, Ill.; s. of Charles A. and Mary C. Odegaard; m. Elizabeth Ketchum 1941; one d.; ed. Dartmouth Coll., and Harvard Univ.; Travelling Fellowship for study in France 1934–35; Asst. in History, Radcliffe Coll. 1935–37; Instructor to Prof. in History, Univ. of Ill. 1937–48, Asst. for Humanities to Dean of Graduate Coll. 1948; Exec. Dir. American Council of Learned Socs. 1948–52; Prof. of History, Dean of Coll. of Literature, Science and Arts, Univ. of Mich. 1952–58; Pres. Univ. of Washington, Seattle 1958–74, Prof. of Higher Educ. 1974–, Prof. Biomedical History 1975–; mem. U.S. Nat. Comm. UNESCO 1949–55; Pres. Int. Council of Phil. and Humanistic Studies 1959–65; U.S. Naval Reserve 1942–46; mem. American Council on Educ. (fmr. Chair.), American Historical Assocn., Inst. of Medicine, N.A.S. 1980–. *Publications:* Fideles and Vassi

in the Carolingian Empire 1945, Minorities in Medicine 1977, Area Health Education Centers 1979, Dear Doctor: A Personal Letter to a Physician 1986. *Leisure interest:* gardening. *Address:* College of Education, University of Washington, Seattle, Wash. 98195, U.S.A. *Telephone:* (206) 545-1800.

ODELOLA, Amos Oyetunji, B.SC., M.A.; Nigerian economist; b. 4 March 1927, Modakeke, Ife; s. of the late Mr. and Mrs. J. Odelola; m. Bola Odeloye 1953; one s. three d.; ed. Oduduwa Coll., Ife, Univ. of Hull, England, and Yale Univ., U.S.A.; Agricultural Asst., Dept. of Agriculture, Nigeria, then Statistical Asst., Dept. of Statistics; then Admin. Officer, W. Nigerian Govt.; Special Asst. to Sec.-Gen., Comm. for Tech. Cooperation in Africa (CCTA) 1963–64, Acting Sec.-Gen. 1964–65; Exec. Sec. Scientific, Tech. and Research Comm. of OAU (successor to CCTA) 1965–80. *Leisure interests:* lawn tennis, table tennis, numismatology. *Address:* P.M.B. 2359, Lagos, Nigeria.

ODGERS, Graeme David William, M.A., M.B.A.; British business executive; b. 10 March 1934, Johannesburg, S.A.; s. of William Arthur Odgers and Elizabeth Minty (née Rennie); m. Diana Patricia Berge 1957; one s. three d. (one deceased); ed. St. John's Coll., Johannesburg, Gonville and Caius Coll., Cambridge, Harvard Business School, U.S.A.; Investment Officer, IFC, Washington D.C. 1959–62; Man. Consultant, Urwick Orr & Partners Ltd. 1962–64; Investment Exec., Hambros Bank Ltd. 1964–65; Dir. Keith Shipton Ltd. 1965–72, C. T. Bowring (Insurance) Holdings Ltd. 1972–74; Chair. Odgers & Co. Ltd. (Man. Consultants) 1970–74; Dir. Industrial Devt. Unit, Dept. of Industry 1974–77; Assoc. Dir. (Finance) Gen. Electric Co. 1977–78; Group Finance Dir., Tarmac PLC, 1979–86, Group Man. Dir. 1983–86, Non-Exec. Dir. 1986–87; Non-Exec. Dir. Dalgety PLC 1987–; Part-time Bd. mem. British Telecommunications PLC 1983, Govt. Dir. 1984–86, Deputy Chair. and Chief Finance Officer 1986–87, Group Man. Dir. 1987–. *Leisure interests:* tennis, golf. *Address:* British Telecommunications PLC, British Telecom Centre, 81 Newgate Street, London, EC1A 7AJ, England.

ODINGA, A. Oginga; Kenyan politician; b. 1911; ed. Alliance High School, Kikuyu, and Makerere Coll.; fmr. teacher; mem. Central Nyanza African District Council, Sakwa Location Advisory Council 1947–49; mem. Legis. Council 1957; Vice-Pres. Kenya African Nat. Union (KANU) 1960–66, founded Kenya People's Union 1966 (party banned Oct. 1969); Minister for Home Affairs 1963–64; Vice-Pres. of Kenya 1964–66; arrested Oct. 1969, released March 1971; rejoined KANU Sept. 1971, membership withdrawn, rejoined 1980–; arrested, then released Dec. 1977, under house arrest 1982–83; Chair. Cotton, Seed and Lint Marketing Bd. 1979. *Publication:* Not Yet Uhuru 1967. *Address:* c/o KANU, P.O. Box 12394, Nairobi, Kenya.

O'DRISCOLL, Timothy Joseph, B.A.; Irish tourist official; b. 6 July 1908, Cork; s. of Michael O'Driscoll and Mary Hélena Walshe; m. Elizabeth McKay 1941; three d.; ed. Presentation Coll., Cork, and Trinity Coll., Dublin; Irish Civil Service 1928–56; Irish Rep. to Int. Civil Aviation Org. 1946–48, OEEC 1948–50; Chair. Irish Export Bd. 1951–55; Amb. to Netherlands 1955–56; Dir.-Gen. Irish Tourist Bd. 1956–71; mem. Bd. Irish Airlines; Pres. Int. Union of Official Tourist Orgs. 1961–63; Exec. Dir. European Travel Comm. 1971–86; Consultant on Tourism to UN 1967–68; Chair. OECD Tourism Cttee. 1964–66, Algemene Bank Nederland (Ireland) Ltd. 1972–80; mem. Exec. Advisory Bd. Gulf Oil (Ireland); mem. Council of Design; Consultant to Indian Inst. of Public Admin. 1969; Pres. An Taisce Irish Nat. Trust 1969–75; Adviser on Tourism to Bahamas, to Jordan, under UNDP to India 1970, to Iran 1971–; Pres. Marketing Inst. of Ireland 1973–80; Chair. Systems Devt. Programme TCD; Chair. Dublin Theatre Festival; Chair. Bd. of Trustees Edward de Bono Foundation 1984–; mem. Bd. Transportation Analysis Int. 1982–85; Hon. LL.D. (Dublin); First American Soc. of Travel Agents Hall of Fame 1973; Commdr. Order of George I (Greece), Order of Prince Henry the Navigator (Portugal); Royal Danish Tourist Medal; Commendatore of Italian Repub. *Leisure interests:* gardening, reading, photography. *Address:* Farm Lodge, Ballyboden, Dublin 16, Ireland. *Telephone:* Dublin 931265 (Home).

ODUBER, Nelson O.; Aruban politician; Leader Movimentu Electoral di Pueblo (People's Electoral Movt.); Prime Minister of Aruba Feb. 1989–. *Address:* Office of the Prime Minister, Oranjestad, Aruba.

ODUBER QUIRÓS, Daniel; Costa Rican politician and diplomatist; b. 25 Aug. 1921, San José; s. of Porfirio Oduber and Ana María Quirós; m. Marjorie Elliott Sypher 1950; one s.; ed. Univ. de Costa Rica, McGill Univ., Canada, and Univ. de Paris; Amb. to UN 1949; Head of Public Relations, Partido de Liberación Nacional (PLN) 1951–53, Sec.-Gen. 1956–58, Pres. 1970–77; Minister of Foreign Affairs 1962–64; Head various dels. to UN Gen. Assembly; co-ordinator at the meeting of Presidents of Central America U.S.A. and Panama 1963; PLN Presidential Cand. 1965; Pres. of Congress 1970–74; Pres. of Costa Rica 1974–78; Dr. h.c. (Yale) 1986; Grand Cross Order of Malta, Gran Cruz, Orden de Isabel la Católica (Spain), and numerous other foreign decorations. *Leisure interests:* sports, reading, travel. *Address:* c/o Casa Presidencial, San José, Costa Rica.

ODUM, Eugene P., PH.D.; American ecologist, educator, lecturer and writer; b. 17 Sept. 1913, Newport, N.H.; s. of the late Howard W. Odum and Anna Louise Kranz Odum; m. Martha Ann Huff 1939; one s.; ed. Univs. of North Carolina and Illinois; Instructor, then Asst. Prof., Assoc.

Prof., Prof., Univ. of Georgia 1940-57, Alumni Distinguished Prof. of Zoology 1957, Callaway Prof. of Ecology 1977, Dir. Inst. of Ecology 1960-84, Dir. Emer. and Prof. Emer. 1984-; Instructor-in-charge, Marine Ecology Training Program, Marine Biological Lab., Woods Hole, Mass. summers 1957-61; pioneer in field of ecosystem ecology as a new "integrative" science; research interests include ecological energetics, estuarine and wetland ecology, ornithology and resource econs.; Fellow A.A.A.S., American Acad. of Arts and Sciences, American Ornithologists' Union; mem. N.A.S., Ecological Soc. of America, American Soc. of Limnology and Oceanography, American Soc. of Mammalogists, American Inst. of Biological Sciences, Wildlife Soc., Soc. for Study of Evolution, American Naturalist Soc.; Institut de la Vie Prize, France 1957; Mercer Award, Ecological Soc. of America 1956, Eminent Ecologist's Award 1974; Conservationist of the Year, Nat. Wildlife Fed. 1976, Tyler Ecology Award 1977; Crafoord Prize, Royal Swedish Acad. 1987.. *Publications:* Fundamentals of Ecology 153, Ecology 163, Basic Ecology 1983 (all translated into several languages); more than 200 papers in scientific journals. *Leisure interests:* natural history, tennis. *Address:* Institute of Ecology, University of Georgia, Athens, Ga. 30602; Beech Creek Road, Athens, Ga. 30606, U.S.A. (Home). *Telephone:* (404) 542-2968 (Office); (404) 543-2290 (Home).

OË, Kenzaburo: Japanese author; b. 1935; m.; two c.; first stories published 1957; Akutagawa prize for novella The Catch 1958; first full-length novel Pluck The Flowers, Gun The Kids 1958; represented young Japanese writers at Peking (now Beijing) 1960; travelled to Russia and Western Europe writing a series of essays on Youth in the West 1961; Shinchosha Literary Prize 1964; Tanizaka Prize 1967. *Publications:* The Catch 1958, Pluck The Flowers, Gun The Kids 1958, Our Age 1959, Screams 1962, The Perverts 1963, Hiroshima Notes 1963, Adventures in Daily Life 1964, A Personal Matter 1964 (English 1969), Football in The First Year of Mannen 1967. *Address:* 585 Seijo-machi, Setagaya-Ku, Tokyo, Japan. *Telephone:* 482-7192.

OELMAN, Robert Schantz, A.B.; American business executive (retd.); b. 9 June 1909, Dayton, Ohio; s. of William Walter and Edith (Schantz) Oelman; m. Mary Coolidge 1936; two s. two d.; ed Dartmouth Coll., and Univ. of Vienna; with NCR Corpn., Dayton, Ohio 1933-, Asst. to Pres. 1942-45, Asst. Vice-Pres. 1945-46, Vice-Pres. 1946-50, Exec. Vice-Pres. 1950-57, Pres. 1957, Chair. and Pres. 1962, Chair. 1964-74, Chair. Exec. Cttee. 1974-80, Dir. 1948-80; Dir. Koppers Co. Inc., Winters Nat. Bank & Trust Co., Ford Motor Co., etc.; fmr. Pres. and Dir. Nat. Asscn. of Mfrs.; fmr. Pres. and Dir. Business Equipment Asscn.; fmr. Chair. Bd. of Trustees, Wright State Univ., Dayton; fmr. Trustee Dartmouth Coll., Nat. Safety Council, N.Y.; Hon. H.H.D. (Dayton), Hon. LL.D. (Miami Univ. and Wright State Univ.), Hon. M.A. (Dartmouth Coll.), Hon. L.H.D. (Wilmington Coll.). *Leisure interests:* reading, music, golf. *Address:* 5 Pine Lane, Village of Golf, Fla. 33436, U.S.A. (Home).

OENNERFORS, Alf, PH.D.; Swedish university professor; b. 30 Nov. 1925, Hovmantorp; s. of Carl-Oscar Önnerfors and Karin Widerström; m. 1st Ingrid Åhlén 1949, 2nd Ute Michaelis 1964; four s.; ed. Univ. of Uppsala; Lecturer, then Assoc. Prof., Univ. of Upsala 1957-62, Univ. of Lund 1962-63; Prof., Freie Universität Berlin, West Berlin 1963-70, Univ. of Cologne, Fed. Repub. of Germany 1970-; research into Latin language and literature; mem. Rheinisch-Westfälische Akademie der Wissenschaften. *Publications:* Pliniana (dissertation) 1956, In Medicinam Plinii studia philologica 1963, Die Hauptfassungen des Sigfrid-Offiziums 1968, Vaterporträts in der römischen Poesie 1974, Willem Jordaens, Conflictus virtutum et viciorum 1986; critical edns. of Cicero, Ad Atticum 13-16 1960, Medicina Plinii (Corpus Med. Lat.) 1964, C. de Bridia, Hystoria Tartarorum 1967, Tacitus, Germania (Teubner) 1983, W. Jordaens, Confluctus virtutum et viciorum 1986. *Leisure interests:* riding (military), chemistry, pharmacology. *Address:* Trebetastrasse 3, D-5500 Trier, Federal Republic of Germany; S-360 51 Hovmantorp, Sweden. *Telephone:* (0651) 305 84 (Germany); (0478) 190 39 (Sweden).

OERTER, Alfred A.; American athlete; b. 19 Sept. 1936, Astoria, N.Y.; s. of Alfred and Mary (Strup) Oerter; m. 1st Corinne Benedetto 1958 (divorced 1975), two d.; m. 2nd Cathy Carroll 1983; competed Olympic Games, winning gold medals at discus, Melbourne 1956, Rome 1960, Tokyo 1964, Mexico 1968; only athlete to win gold medals at four successive Olympic Games; held world records at discus and was first man to throw over 200 feet; current world record holder for Masters track and field; motivational speaker athletic and corporate promotions; mem. track and field Hall of Fame, Olympic Hall of Fame, Olympic Order 1982. *Address:* 135 West Islip Road, West Islip, N.Y. 11795; 5485 Avenida Pescadora, Ft. Myers Beach, Fla. 33931, U.S.A. *Telephone:* (813) 765-0112.

OESTREICHER, Rev. Canon Paul, M.A.; British and New Zealand (b. Germany) clergyman and journalist; b. 29 Sept. 1931, Meiningen, Germany; s. of Paul Oestreicher, M.D., and Emma (née Schnaus); m. Lore Feind 1958; two s. two d.; ed. Otago and Victoria Univs., N.Z., Bonn Univ., Fed. Repub. of Germany, Lincoln Theological Coll., U.K.; emigrated to New Zealand with parents 1939; Ed. Critic student newspaper, Otago Univ. 1952-53; Humboldt Research Fellow, Bonn Univ. 1955; studied industrial mission (Opel, Gen. Motors), Rüsselsheim 1958-59; ordained in Church of England 1959; freelance journalist and broadcaster in Fed. Repub. of Germany and U.K. 1959-; Curate in Dalston, London 1959-61; Programme

Producer, Religious Dept., BBC Radio 1961-64; Assoc. Sec., Dept. of Int. Affairs, British Council of Churches, with special responsibility for East-West relations 1964-69, Hon. Sec. East-West Relations Cttee. 1964-; Vicar, Church of the Ascension, Blackheath, London 1968-81; Dir. of Lay Training, Diocese of Southwark 1969-72; mem. Gen. Synod of Church of England 1970-86; mem. Exec. Council Amnesty Int. (U.K. Section) 1969-80, Chair. 1974-79; Founder and Trustee, Christian Inst. (of Southern Africa) Fund 1974-, Chair. Trustees 1983-; Hon. Chaplain to Bishop of Southwark 1975-80; mem. Council, Keston Coll. 1975-83; mem. Nat. Council, Campaign for Nuclear Disarmament 1980-82, Vice-Chair. 1983-; Hon. Canon of Southwark Cathedral 1978-83, Canon Emer. 1983-86; Dir. Int. Ministry of Coventry Cathedral 1986-, Canon Residentiary 1986-; Asst. Gen. Sec. and Div. Sec. for Int. Affairs, British Council of Churches 1981-86; Public Preacher, Diocese of Southwark 1981-86; mem. Soc. of Friends 1982-. *Publications:* Editor: Gollwitzer: The Demands of Freedom (English edn.) 1965, The Christian Marxist Dialogue 1969, (with J. Klugmann) What Kind of Revolution 1969, The Church and the Bomb (jtly.) 1983, The Double Cross 1986; trans. Schulz: Conversion to the World 1967; contributor to British Council of Churches working party reports on Eastern Europe and Southern Africa. *Leisure interests:* horse riding, sauna bathing, stamp collecting, Mozart. *Address:* 20 Styvechale Avenue, Coventry, CV5 6DX, England. *Telephone:* (0203) 73704.

OETKER, Rudolf-August; German industrialist and shipowner; b. 20 Sept. 1916, Bielefeld; s. of Rudolf Oetker; m. 3rd Maja von Malaisé 1963; Owner Dr. August Oetker, Bielefeld 1944-; holder of controlling interest of Bankhaus Hermann Lampe KG, Bielefeld; numerous other business interests. *Leisure interests:* art, tennis. *Address:* Lutterstrasse 14, 4800 Bielefeld, Federal Republic of Germany. *Telephone:* 0521/1550.

O'FAOLÁIN, Seán, M.A., A.M., D.LITT.; Irish writer; b. 1900; s. of Denis Whelan; m. Eileen Gould 1928; one s. one d.; ed. Nat. Univ. of Ireland and Harvard Univ.; Commonwealth Fellow 1926-28; John Harvard Fellow 1928-29; lecturer in English Boston Coll. 1929, St. Mary's Coll. Strawberry Hill 1929-33; Dir. Arts Council of Ireland 1957-59. *Publications:* Lyrics and Satires from Tom Moore 1929, Midsummer Night Madness 1932, Life Story of De Valera 1933, A Nest of Simple Folk 1933, Constance Markievicz: a Biography 1934, There's a Birdie in the Cage 1935, A Born Genius 1936, Bird Alone 1936, The Autobiography of Wolfe Tone 1937, A Purse of Coppers 1937, The Silver Branch (translations) 1937, King of the Beggars (biography) 1938, She Had to Do Something (play) 1938, An Irish Journey 1939, Come Back to Erin 1040, The Great O'Neill (biography) 1942, Story of Ireland 1943, Teresa 1947, The Irish 1948, The Short Story 1948, Summer in Italy 1949, Newman's Way (biography) 1952, South to Sicily 1953, The Vanishing Hero 1956, The Stories of Seán O'Faoláin 1958, I Remember, I Remember 1962, Vive Moi 1965, The Heat of the Sun (short stories) 1966, The Talking Trees 1970, Foreign Affairs (short stories) 1975, Selected Stories of Seán O'Faoláin 1978, And Again (novel) 1979, Collected Stories Vol. I 1980, Vol. II 1981, Vol. III 1982. *Leisure interests:* travel, gardening. *Address:* 17 Rosmeen Park, Dun Laoghaire, Dublin, Ireland.

O'FARRELL, Patrick James, PH.D.; New Zealand professor of history; b. 17 Sept. 1933, Greymouth; s. of P. V. O'Farrell; m. Deidre G. MacShane 1956; three s. two d.; ed. Marist Bros. High School, Greymouth, Univ. of Canterbury, Christchurch and Australian Nat. Univ. (A.N.U.), Canberra; Research Scholar A.N.U. 1956-59; lecturer, Sr. Lecturer, Assoc. Prof. Univ. of N.S.W. 1959-72, Prof. of History 1972-; Visiting Prof. Univ. Coll. and Trinity Coll., Dublin 1965-66, 1972-73; N.S.W. Premier's Literary Award 1987. *Publications:* Harry Holland: Militant Socialist 1964, The Catholic Church in Australia 1968, Documents in Australian Catholic History 1969, Ireland's English Question 1971, England and Ireland since 1800 1975, The Catholic Church and Community in Australia 1977, Letters from Irish Australia 1825-1929 1984, The Irish in Australia 1986. *Leisure interest:* reading thrillers. *Address:* School of History, University of New South Wales, P.O. Box 1, Kensington, N.S.W. 2033, Australia. *Telephone:* (02) 6972348.

OFFERGELD, Rainer; German politician; b. 26 Dec. 1937, Genoa, Italy; s. of Carlo O. and Erna (Buchter) Offergeld; m. Christel Hiller 1967; three d.; ed. Grammar School, Meersburg, and Frankfurt, Freiburg, Lyon and Zürich Univs.; Councillor, Fed. Law and Tax Admins.; Town Councillor and Administrator; Mayor, Lörrach 1984-; mem. Bundestag 1969-84; Sec. of State to Minister of Finance 1975-78; Minister for Econ. Co-operation 1978-82. *Leisure interest:* skiing. *Address:* Rathaus, 7850 Lörrach, Federal Republic of Germany.

OFFORD, Albert Cyril, D.SC., F.R.S., F.R.S.E.; British mathematician; b. 9 June 1906, London; s. of Albert Edwin and Hester Louise (née Sexton) Offord; m. Marguerite Yvonne Pickard 1945; one d.; ed. Hackney Downs School, Univs. of London and Cambridge; Fellow St. John's Coll., Cambridge 1937-40; Lecturer Univ. Coll., Bangor 1940-41, King's's Coll., Newcastle upon Tyne 1941-45, Prof. 1945-48; Prof. Birkbeck Coll., Univ. of London 1948-66; Prof. L.S.E. 1966-73, Prof. Emer. 1973-; Sr. Research Fellow Imperial Coll., London 1973-82; Fellow Univ. Coll. (London) 1969, Hon. Fellow L.S.E. 1976. *Publications:* numerous articles in mathematical journals. *Leisure interest:* early music. *Address:* West Cottage, 24A Norham Gardens, Oxford, OX2 6QD, England. *Telephone:* (0865) 513703.

OFFROY, Raymond, LL.D.; French diplomatist; b. 3 May 1909, Paris; s. of Georges Offroy; m. 1st Geneviève Saint-Fort-Paillard 1929, three d.; m. 2nd Countess de Scaffa 1965, three d. (one step-d.); Attaché Bucharest 1937, Sec. 1938; Sec. Athens 1940, Acting Consul-Gen. Salonika 1941; Head of Admin. Service Free French Foreign Office, French Nat. Cttee.'s rep. to Inter-Allied War Crimes Comm. 1941 and to Netherlands Govt. 1942; Acting Counsellor of Embassy 1942; Diplomatic Asst. to Gen. Catroux mission to Gen. Giraud, Algiers 1943; Deputy Sec. to French Provisional Govt., Gen. Sec. to Econ. Cttee. 1944; Head of Information and Press Section, Ministry of Foreign Affairs 1945–49; Consul-Gen. Milan 1949–52; Diplomatic Adviser to High Commr. in Indo-China 1951, Deputy Commr.-Gen. 1953; Asst. Del. to Geneva Conf. 1954; Amb. to Thailand 1954–57; French Rep to SEATO 1955–57; Dir. of Central Information Office, Paris 1957–59; Head, Franco-African Community Dept., Ministry of Foreign Affairs, Chair. Franco-African Community, Cttee. of Foreign Affairs 1959–60; Amb. to Nigeria 1960–61, to Mexico 1962–65; Député de la Seine Maritime 1967–68, 1968–78; Rep. for France to European Parl. 1969–73; Pres. French Parl. Fed. of Friendship Groups with Arab Countries 1973–78, European Parl. Asscn. for Euro-Arab Co-operation 1974–78, (Hon. Chair. 1978–), French Asscn. How to know the Arab World 1975; Vice-Pres. France-Iraq Asscn. 1979–; Officier légion d'honneur. *Publications:* Le problème de l'eau en Syrie 1934, Au service de l'ennemi 1941, La France combattante à l'étranger 1943, Quand le coeur a raison 1973, De Gaulle et le service de l'état 1977. *Address:* 18 avenue de Friedland, 75008 Paris, France. *Telephone:* 561-18-11.

Ó FIAICH, H.E. Cardinal Tomás, M.A.; Irish ecclesiastic; b. 3 Nov. 1923, Co. Armagh; s. of Patrick and Annie (Caraher) Fee; ed. St. Patrick's Coll. Armagh, St. Patrick's Coll. Maynooth, St. Peter's Coll. Wexford, Univ. Coll., Dublin, Catholic Univ. of Louvain; Lecturer in Modern History, St. Patrick's Coll. Maynooth 1953–59, Prof. 1959–74, Registrar 1968–70, Vice-Pres. 1970–74, Pres. 1974–77; ed. Seanchas Ardmhacha: Journal of the Armagh Historical Soc. 1953–77; Pres. of Irish-speaking Priests 1955–67; Chair. Govt. Comm. on Restoration of Irish Language 1959–63, Govt. Advisory Council on Irish Language 1965–68; Mem. Senate, Nat. Univ. of Ireland 1964–72, 1974–77, Higher Educ. Authority 1972–74; Archbishop of Armagh and Primate of All Ireland 1977–; Chair. Irish Episcopal Conf. 1977–; cr. Cardinal June 1979. *Publications:* Gaelscrínte i gCéin 1960, Irish Cultural Influence in Europe 1966, Imeacht na nIarlaí 1972, Má Nuad 1972, Art Mac Cooey and his Times 1973, Columbanus in his own Words 1974, Oliver Plunkett, Ireland's New Saint 1975, Aifreann Ceolta Tíre 1977, Art Mac Bionaid 1979, Gaelscrínte san Eoraip 1986, many articles in Irish historical and literary journals. *Leisure interests:* reading, travel, sport. *Address:* Ara Coeli, Armagh, N. Ireland. *Telephone:* (0861) 522 045.

O'FLYNN, Francis Duncan, B.A., LL.M., Q.C.; New Zealand politician; b. 1918, Greymouth; m.; four c.; ed. Victoria Univ., Wellington; barrister and Q.C. 1954–; M.P. for Kapiti 1972–75, Island Bay 1978–; Minister of State, and of Defence, Minister in Charge of War Pensions and Rehabilitation, Deputy Minister for Foreign Affairs, Assoc. Minister of Overseas Trade and Industry 1984–87; Chair. State Service Tribunals 1970–72; part-time Ed. N.Z. Law Reports 1977–78; mem. Wellington City Council 1977; mem. Parl. Select Cttees. on Foreign Affairs, Defence and Privileges; Labour. *Address:* House of Representatives, Wellington, New Zealand.

OFNER, Harald, DR.JUR.; Austrian politician; b. 25 Oct. 1932, Vienna; m.; three c.; ed. Univ. of Vienna; private legal practice 1965–; Chair. Lower Austrian FPÖ (Austrian Freedom Party) 1976; mem. Nationalrat 1979–; Fed. Minister of Justice 1983–87. *Leisure interests:* mountaineering, skiing, hiking, travel. *Address:* c/o Federal Ministry of Justice, Vienna, Austria.

OGARKOV, Marshal Nikolay Vasiliyevich; Soviet army officer; b. 30 Oct. 1917, Molokovo, Tver (now Kalinin) Region; ed. Acad. of Mil. Eng. and Gen. Staff Acad.; Sec. and book-keeper of trade union district cttee. while a student 1933–38; served army 1938–; regt., brig., div. engineer 1939–45; staff and other sr. posts including Commdr. of Motorized Infantry Div., Chief of Staff and First Deputy Commdr. of Byelorussian Mil. District, Commdr. of Volga Mil. District until 1968; Deputy to U.S.S.R. Supreme Soviet 1966–; First Deputy Chief of Gen. Staff 1968–77; Deputy Minister of Defence 1974–84, 1985–; Chief of Gen. Staff 1977–84; Head Acad. of Gen. Staff 1984–; mem. CPSU 1945–, Cand. mem. Cen. Cttee of CPSU 1966–71, mem. 1971–89; Order of Red Banner, Order of Great Fatherland War, Hero of Soviet Union and other decorations. *Publication:* Always Ready to Defend the Fatherland 1982, History Teaches 1985. *Address:* c/o Ministry of Defence, 34 Naberezhnaya M. Thoreza, Moscow, U.S.S.R.

OGAWA, Heiji; Japanese politician; b. 1910, Nagano Prefecture; s. of Heikichi Ogawa; elected 10 times to House of Reps. 1952–; fmr. Deputy Cabinet Sec.; Minister of Labour 1967–68, of Educ. 1981–82; Vice-Chair. Policy Affairs Research Council of Liberal Dem. Party (LDP), also Chair. LDP Research Comm. on the Tax System; assoc. of late Masayoshi Ohira; Minister of Home Affairs, Chair. Nat. Public Safety Comm., Dir.-Gen. of Hokkaido Devt. Agency 1976–77. *Address:* c/o Ministry of Education, Tokyo, Japan.

OGAWA, Heishiro, B.A.; Japanese diplomatist; b. 17 March 1916, Tokyo; s. of Heikichi and Kin Ogawa; m. Yoshiko Ito 1945; two d.; ed. Tokyo Univ. Laws Dept.; joined Ministry of Foreign Affairs 1938; Consul, Hong Kong 1952; Head China Div., Ministry of Foreign Affairs 1954–57; Counsellor, Japanese Embassy, Washington, D.C. 1957–60; Consul-Gen., Hong Kong 1960–63; Dir.-Gen. Asian Affairs Bureau 1966–68; Amb. to Denmark 1968–72; Pres. Foreign Service Inst. 1972–73; Amb. to People's Repub. of China 1973–77; Fellow Woodrow Wilson Center, Washington, D.C. 1977–78; Adviser Sumitomo Corpn., Tokyo 1978–85; Vice-Pres. Japan-China Soc., Tokyo 1980–; Pres. Japan-Denmark Soc., Tokyo 1985–. *Publications:* Four Years in Peking, China Revisited. *Leisure interests:* reading, golf, travelling. *Address:* Denenchofu 1-10-26-610, Otaku, Tokyo 145, Japan. *Telephone:* 03-722-4550.

OGAWA, Masaru, M.A.; Japanese journalist; b. 22 March 1915, Los Angeles, U.S.A.; s. of Kenji Ogawa and Mine Fuijioka; m. Ayame Fukuhara 1942; one s. two d.; ed. Univ. of California at Los Angeles, Tokyo Imperial, Columbia Univs.; Domei News Agency 1941–46; Kyodo News Service 1946–48; The Japan Times 1948–, Chief, political section 1949, Asst. Man. Ed. 1950, Chief Ed. 1952, Man. Ed. 1958–64, Dir. 1959–, Exec. Ed. 1964–68, Senior Ed. 1968–71, Chief Editorial Writer 1969–71, Ed. 1971–77, Adviser 1977–, weekly columnist; Chair. Bd. Asia-Pacific Magazine, Manila 1981–85; Lecturer, Tokyo Univ. 1954–58; mem. Yoshida Int. Educ. Foundation 1968–, Exec. Dir. 1972–; mem. Japan Broadcasting Corpn. Overseas Program Consultative Council 1974–84, Japan Editors' and Publishers' Asscn., Int. Press Inst., Editorial Bd. Media Magazine, Hong Kong 1974; Dir. Int. Motion Picture Co. 1970, American Studies Foundation 1980–, Yoshida Shigeru Memorial Foundation 1980–; Pres. Pacific News Agency 1973–; life mem. Foreign Corresp. Club of Japan 1973–; Exec. Dir. America-Japan Soc. 1981–, Tokyo-American Club 1980–; Hon D.Litt. (Lewis and Clark Coll., Portland, Oregon) 1979, Vaughn-Ueda Prize 1986. *Leisure interests:* reading, sport. *Address:* 2, 14-banchi, 5-chome, Mejiro, Toshima-ku, Tokyo, Japan. *Telephone:* 952-8822.

OGDON, John (Andrew Howard); British concert pianist; b. 27 Jan. 1937, Mansfield Woodhouse, Notts.; s. of late John Andrew Howard Ogdon and of Dorothy Louise (née Mutton); m. Brenda Mary Lucas 1960; one s. one d.; ed. Manchester Grammar School and Royal Manchester Coll. of Music; Concert appearances in U.S.A., Japan, Australasia, Europe; Liszt Prize, London 1961, First Prize Int. Tchaikovsky Piano Competition (jointly with Vladimir Ashkenazy, q.v.), Moscow 1962; Joint Dir. Cardiff Festival of Twentieth Century Music; Prof. of Music, Univ. of Indiana 1977–80. *Leisure interests:* history, literature. *Address:* c/o Basil Douglas Ltd., 8 St. George's Terrace, Regent's Park Road, London, NW1 8XJ, England. *Telephone:* (01) 722-7142.

OGILVIE THOMPSON, Julian, M.A.; South African business executive; b. 27 Jan. 1934, Cape Town; s. of the Hon. Newton and Eve Ogilvie Thompson; m. the Hon. Tessa M. Brand 1956; two s. two d.; ed. Diocesan Coll., Rondebosch and Worcester Coll., Oxford; Chair. De Beers Consolidated Mines Ltd., Mineral and Resources Corpn., Deputy Chair. Anglo-American Corpn. of S.A. Ltd. 1982–; Chair. Anglo-American Gold Investment Co. Ltd. 1976–; Vice-Chair. First Nat. Bank Ltd. 1977–; Dir. AECI Ltd., Anglo-American Coal Corpn., Charter Consolidated PLC, Consolidated Gold Fields PLC, Free State Consolidated Gold Mines Ltd., Highveld Steel and Vanadium Corpn. Ltd., The Urban Foundation, Zambian Copper Investments Ltd.; Rhodes Scholar 1953. *Leisure interests:* golf, fishing, shooting. *Address:* 44 Main Street, Johannesburg (Office); Froome, Froome Street, Athol Ext. 3, Sandton, Tvl., South Africa (Home). *Telephone:* 638.9111 (Office); 884.3925 (Home).

OGILVY, H.R.H. Princess Alexandra, the Hon. Mrs. Angus, G.C.V.O., C.D.; b. 25 Dec. 1936; d. of the late Duke of Kent (fourth s. of King George V) and Princess Marina (d. of late Prince Nicholas of Greece); m. Hon. Angus James Bruce Ogilvy (second s. of late 12th Earl of Airlie, K.T., G.C.V.O., M.C.) 1963; one s. one d.; ed. Heathfield School, Ascot; Chancellor, Univ. of Lancaster; Col.-in-Chief, 17th/21st Lancers, the King's Own Royal Border Regt., The Queen's Own Rifles of Canada and the Canadian Scottish Regt. (Princess Mary's); Deputy Col.-in-Chief, The Light Infantry; Deputy Hon. Col., The Royal Yeomanry (Territorial Army Voluntary Reserves); Hon. Commdt. Gen., The Royal Hong Kong Police Force and Royal Hong Kong Auxiliary Police Force; Hon. Commdt. Women's Royal Australian Naval Service; Patron and Air Chief Commdt., Princess Mary's Royal Air Force Nursing Service; Patron, Queen Alexandra's Royal Naval Nursing Service; Pres. or Patron of many charitable and social welfare orgs.; Hon. Fellow, Royal Coll. of Physicians & Surgeons of Glasgow, Faculty of Anaesthetists of the Royal Coll. of Surgeons of England, Royal Coll. of Obstetricians & Gynaecologists; Hon. Freedom, Worshipful Co. of Clothworkers, City of Lancaster; Hon. degrees (Queensland, Hong Kong, Mauritius, Liverpool); decorations from Mexico, Peru, Chile, Brazil, Japan, Finland, Luxembourg, the Netherlands; rep. H.M. Queen Elizabeth II at independence celebrations of Nigeria 1960 and St. Lucia 1979, 150th anniversary celebrations, Singapore 1969. *Leisure interests:* music, reading, tapestry, outdoor recreations incl. swimming, skiing, riding. *Address:* Thatched House Lodge, Richmond Park, Surrey; 22 Friary Court, St. James's Palace, London, SW1A 1BJ, England. *Telephone:* 01-930 1860.

OGILVY, David Mackenzie, C.B.E.; British advertising executive; b. 23 June 1911, West Horsley; s. of Francis J. L. and Dorothy (née Fairfield) Ogilvy; m. Herta Lans 1973; one s.; ed. Fettes Coll., Edinburgh, and Oxford Univ.; Assoc. Dir. Audience Research Inst., Princeton 1939–42;

with British Security Co-ordination 1942–44; Second Sec. British Embassy, Washington 1944–45; founder 1948, Pres., Ogilvy, Benson and Mather Int., New York 1965–75, Creative Dir. 1973–; Chair. Public Participation Cttee., Lincoln Center 1959, United Negro Coll. Fund 1968; Dir. New York Philharmonic 1957–67; Trustee Colby Coll. 1963–69; Trustee and mem. Exec. Council World Wildlife Fund Int. 1975–; mem. American Assen. of Advertising Agencies, Gov. Eastern Region 1959–61; Hon. Litt.D. (Adelphi) 1977; Parlin Award of American Marketing Assen. 1972, elected to Advertising Hall of Fame 1977. *Publications:* Confessions of an Advertising Man 1964, Blood, Brains and Beer (autobiog.) 1978, Ogilvy on Advertising 1983. *Leisure interest:* gardening. *Address:* Château de Touffou, 86300 Bonnes, France (Home).

O'GREEN, Frederick W., M.S.; American industrialist; b. 25 March 1921; m. Mildred Ludlow; two s. two d.; ed. Iowa State Univ. and Univ. of Maryland; Engineer, Naval Ordnance Lab. 1943–55; Dir. Lockheed's Agena-D project 1955–62; Vice-Pres. Litton Industries 1962–66, Senior Vice-Pres. 1966–67, Exec. Vice-Pres. 1967–72, fmr. Pres., C.E.O. and Chair. 1981–86, Chair. 1986–88; mem. American Inst. of Aeronautics and Astronautics; Hon. LL.D. (Pepperdine Univ.) 1977; Meritorious Civilian Service Award (U.S. Navy) 1954, Outstanding Achievement Award, Air Force Systems Command 1964, Distinguished Achievement Citation, Iowa State Univ. 1973, Energy Exec. of the Year Award (Assen. of Energy Engineers) 1980.

OGRIS, Werner, DR.IUR.; Austrian professor of law; b. 7 Sept. 1935, Vienna; s. of Alfred Ogris and Maria Erber; m. Eva Scolik 1963; two s.; ed. Univ. of Vienna; Asst. Inst. für Deutsches Recht, Vienna 1958–61; Prof. Freie Univ. Berlin 1962, Univ. of Vienna 1966–; mem. Austrian Acad. of Sciences; corresp. mem. Leipzig Acad.; Foreign mem. Royal Netherlands Acad.; Prize of Theodor-Körner-Stiftung 1961. *Publications:* Der mittelalterliche Leibrentenvertrag 1961, Die Entwicklungsgang der österreichischen Privat-rechtswissenschaft im 19. Jahrhundert 1968, Die Rechtsentwicklung in Österreich 1848–1918 1975, Personenstandsrecht 1977, Recht und Macht bei Maria Theresia 1980, Goethe—amtlich und politisch 1982, Jacob Grimm; Ein politisches Gelehrtenleben 1986, Friedrich der Grosse und das Recht 1987, Joseph von Sonnenfels als Rechtsreformer 1988. *Leisure interest:* tennis. *Address:* Institut für Österreichische und Deutsche Rechtsgeschichte, Schottenbastei 10–16, A-1010 Vienna (Office); Mariahilferstrasse 71, A-1060 Vienna, Austria (Home). *Telephone:* 4300-3269 (Office); 56-41-57 (Home).

OGSTON, Alexander George, D.PHIL., F.A.A., F.R.S.; British professor of biochemistry; b. 30 Jan. 1911, Bombay, India; s. of late Walter H. Ogston and Josephine E. Carter; m. Elizabeth Wicksteed 1934; one s. three d.; ed. Eton Coll. and Balliol Coll., Oxford; Demonstrator in Chemistry, Balliol Coll., Oxford 1933–35; Research Fellow, London Hosp. 1935–37; Fellow and Tutor, Balliol Coll. 1937–60; Reader in Biochemistry, Univ. of Oxford 1955; Prof. of Physical Biochem., John Curtin School of Medical Research, A.N.U. 1959–70, Prof. Emer. 1970–; Pres. Trinity Coll., Oxford 1970–78; Vice-Chair., Cen. Council, Selly Oak Colls. Birmingham 1976–80, Chair. 1980–84; Visiting Fellow Inst. for Cancer Research, Philadelphia 1978–79, 1981; Hon. mem. American Soc. of Biological Chemists 1965; Fellow, Australian Acad. of Science 1962, Hon. Fellow, Balliol Coll., Oxford 1969, Trinity Coll., Oxford 1978, Univ. of York 1980, Selly Oak Colls. 1984; Hon. D.Med. (Uppsala) 1977; Davy Medal 1986. *Publications:* scientific papers. *Address:* 6 Dewsbury Terrace, York, YO1 1HA, England.

OGURA, Takekazu; Japanese agriculturist; b. 2 Oct. 1910, Fukui Prefecture; s. of Reizô and Hisako Ogura; m. Chieko Ogura 1937; two s. one d.; ed. Tokyo Imperial Univ.; Posts with Ministry of Agriculture and Forestry 1934–56; lecturer, Faculty of Agriculture, Univ. of Tokyo 1947–61; Dir.-Gen. Food Agency 1956–58; Sec.-Gen. Agriculture, Forestry and Fisheries Research Council 1958–60; Vice-Minister of Agriculture and Forestry 1960–61; Chair. Agriculture, Forestry and Fisheries Research Council 1963–75; Chair. Food and Agric. Policy Research Cen. 1967–; Commissioner, Tax Comm., Prime Minister's Office 1963–69, Chair. 1969–71, 1974–; Pres. Inst. of Developing Economies 1967–72, Chair. 1972–75; Adviser 1975–; mem. Policy Board, The Bank of Japan 1975–83; Chair. Japan FAO Assen. 1975–80. *Publications:* Agricultural Policy of Japan 1965 (in Japanese), Agricultural Development in Modern Japan 1966, Agrarian Problems, Agricultural Policy in Japan 1967, Can Japanese Agriculture Survive? A Historical and Comparative Approach 1982, Toward Structural Reform of Japanese Agriculture 1983, Co-operation in World Agriculture (ed. with Th. Bergmann) 1985, Ed. and Trans. Les Industries Agro-dimentaires Françaises Recueil de documents et d'articles (in Japanese) 1986, Japanese Food Industry, Can Japanese Agriculture Survive?, For Whom the Food is Produced 1987; articles in English and Japanese. *Leisure interest:* reading. *Address:* Food and Agriculture Policy Research Centre, Norinchukin Yurakucho Building, 1-13-2, Yurakucho, Chiyodaku, Tokyo 100 (Office); 3-1-1006 Otsuka 2-chome, Bunkyo-ku, Tokyo 112, Japan (Home). *Telephone:* Tokyo 945-1805 (Home).

O'HALI, Abdulaziz A., PH.D.; Saudi Arabian business executive; b. 1937, Onayza; one s. three d.; ed. Univ. of Puget Sound, Tacoma, Wash. and Claremont Graduate School, Calif.; entered govt. service 1957, held various posts, including Mil. Advisory Dir., Prime Minister's Office, Acting Dir. of Planning and Budgeting, Dir. Cultural and Educ. Directorate, Ministry of

Defense and Aviation; retd. from Govt. Service 1979; founding shareholder United Saudi Commercial Bank, Nat. Industrialization Co. 1983; Chair. Saudi Investment Bank; Man. Dir. Gulf Center Man. Consultants; mem. Jt. Econ. and Tech. Comm. of Saudi Arabia and U.S.A., of Saudi Arabia and Fed. Repub. of Germany. *Address:* Saudi Investment Bank, P.O. Box 3533, Riyadh 11481; Gulf Center Management Consultants, P.O. Box 397, Riyadh 11411, Saudi Arabia. *Telephone:* 477 8433; 477 3247.

O'HANLON, Rory; Irish politician and doctor; b. 16 Feb. 1934, Dublin; m. Teresa Ward; four s. two d.; ed. Blackrock Coll. Dublin and Univ. Coll. Dublin; mem. Dail 1977–; mem. Monaghan County Council 1979–; Minister of State, Dept. of Health and Social Welfare Oct.–Dec. 1982; Minister of Health 1987–; Fellow Royal Acad. of Medicine; Fianna Fail. *Address:* Carrickmacross, Co. Monaghan, Ireland (Home). *Telephone:* (042) 61530.

Ó hEOCHA, Colm, PH.D.; Irish university administrator; b. 19 Sept. 1926, Dungarvan, Co. Waterford; s. of Seamas Ó hEocha and Máiréad Drohan; m. Daiden Fahy 1957; two s. four d.; ed. Univ. Coll., Galway and Univ. of Calif. (Los Angeles and La Jolla); teaching asst. UCLA 1950–51; Research Asst. Scripps Inst. of Oceanography, La Jolla 1952–55; Research Assoc. Univ. of Minn. Minneapolis 1961–62; lecturer in Chem. Univ. Coll., Galway 1955–63, Prof. of Biochem. 1963–75, Pres. 1975–; Chair. New Ireland Forum 1983–84, European Centre for Higher Educ. Arts Council (Ireland) 1989–; mem. Admin. Bd. Int. Assen. of Univs. 1986–; Chevalier, Légion d'honneur; Commendatore del-l'ordine Al merito della Repubblica Italiana; Hon. LL.D. (Queen's Univ., Belfast), (Univ. of Dublin). *Publications:* numerous papers on algal pigments, science and educ. policies. *Leisure interests:* gardening, drinking in good company. *Address:* Chestnut Lane, Bushy Park, Galway, Ireland. *Telephone:* 091.24436.

OHGA, Norio, B.MUS.; Japanese business executive; b. 29 Jan. 1930, Shizuoka; s. of Shoichi Ohga and Toshi Mizuno; m. Midori Matsubara 1957; ed. Tokyo Univ. of Art, Hochschule für Musik, Berlin; joined Tokyo Tsushin Kogyo K.K. (Tokyo Telecommunications Eng. Corpn.) as Consultant and Adviser 1953, co. name changed to Sony Corpn. 1958; Gen. Man. Tape Recorder Div. and Products Planning (also in charge of Industrial Design) 1959, Dir. 1964; Sr. Man. Dir. CBS/Sony Inc. 1968, Pres. 1970; Man. Dir. Sony Corpn. 1972, Sr. Man. Dir. 1974, Deputy Pres. 1976, Pres. and C.O.O. 1982–; Chair. CBS/Sony 1980–. *Leisure interests:* yachting and flying. *Address:* Sony Corporation, 6-7-35 Kita Shinagawa 6-chome, Shinagawa-ku, Tokyo 141, Japan. *Telephone:* (03) 448-2111.

OHKUCHI, Shunichi; Japanese business executive; b. 15 Jan. 1918, Tokyo; s. of Tatsuzo and Takae Ohkuchi; m. Kazuko Ohkuchi 1948; two s.; ed. Tokyo Imperial Univ.; Ministry of Agric. and Forestry 1941; mil. service 1942–48; Chief, Import Planning Div., Food Agency, Ministry of Agric. and Forestry; First Sec. Embassy, London 1956–59; Dir. Overseas Fishery Dept., Fishery Agency, Ministry of Agric. and Forestry 1961–64; Deputy Vice-Minister of Agric. and Forestry 1965, Vice-Minister 1968–69; Dir.-Gen. Food Agency, Ministry of Agric. and Forestry 1966–68; retd. from govt. service 1969; Adviser, Nippon Suisan Kaisha Ltd. 1970, Man. Dir., Sr. Man. Dir., then Vice-Pres. 1971–75, Exec. Vice-Pres. 1975–80, Pres. 1980–86, Chair. 1986–. *Leisure interests:* golf, audio (classical music), billiards. *Address:* Nippon Suisan Kaisha Ltd., 6-2, Ohtemachi 2-chome, Chiyoda-ku, Tokyo, Japan.

OHLSSON, Garrick; American pianist; b. 1948, White Plains, New York; ed. Westchester Conservatory of Music (with Thomas Lishman), Juilliard School of Music (with Sascha Gorodnitsky) and later with Olga Barabini and Rosina Lhevinne; winner Chopin Int. Piano Competition, Warsaw 1970; has since appeared with most of the maj. orchestras in Europe, U.S.A., S. America and New Zealand and performs regularly in Eastern Europe; recordings for EMI include Liszt and Chopin concertos. *Address:* c/o Harold Holt Ltd., 31 Sinclair Road, London, W14 0NS, England.

OHLY, Friedrich, DR.PHIL.; German professor of German language and literature; b. 10 Jan. 1914, Breidenbach; s. of Pfarrer Ludwig Ohly and Luise Keding; m. 1st Dr. Marga Barthel 1940 (died 1945), 2nd Dr. Marianne Steimer 1954; one s. three d.; ed. Univs. of Frankfurt and Berlin; P.O.W., U.S.S.R. 1944–53; Asst. Prof. Univ. of Frankfurt 1954–57; Visiting Prof. Univ. of Chicago 1956; Extraordinary Prof. Univ. of Mainz 1957–58; Prof. Univ. of Kiel 1958–64, Dean, Faculty of Philosophy 1962–63; Prof. Univ. of Münster 1964–82, Dean, Faculty of Philosophy 1966–67, Dir. Sonderforschungsbereich Mittelalterforschung 1973–79, Prof. Emer. 1982–; mem. Acads. of Vienna, Düsseldorf, Siena, Messina, Medieval Acad. of America; hon. mem. Language Assen. of America; Dr. phil. h.c. (Chicago) 1986. *Publications:* Sage und Legende in der Kaiserchronik 1940, Hohelied-Studien 1958, Vom geistigen Sinn des Wortes im Mittelalter 1966, Der Verfluchte und der Erwählte 1976, Diamant und Bocksblut 1976, Schriften zur mittelalterlichen Bedeutungsforschung 1977, Gesetz und Evangelium 1985, Geometria e Memoria: Lettera e allegoria 1985, Süsse Nägel der Passion 1988. *Address:* Goerdelerstrasse 54, 4400 Münster, Federal Republic of Germany. *Telephone:* 0251-73552.

OHNISHI, Minoru; Japanese business executive; b. 28 Oct. 1925, Hyogo Pref.; s. of Sokichi and Mitsu Ohnishi; m. Yaeko Yui 1951; two s.; ed. School of Econs., Tokyo Univ.; joined Fuji Photo Film Co. Ltd. 1948, Man. Tokyo Sales Dept. of Consumer Products Div. 1957–61, Sales Dept. of Industrial Products Div. 1961–62, Fukuoka Branch Office 1962–64, Exec.

Vice-Pres. Fuji Photo Film U.S.A. Inc. 1964–68, Man. Export Sales Div. Fuji Photo Film Co. Ltd. 1968–76, Dir. 1972–, Man. Dir. 1976–79, Sr. Man. Dir. 1979–80, Pres. May 1980–; Pres. Photo-Sensitized Materials Mfrs. Asscn. of Japan June 1980–. *Leisure interests:* golf, reading. *Address:* 15–12, Okusawa 3-Chome, Setagaya-ku, Tokyo 158, Japan. *Telephone:* 03-406-2111 (Office).

OHNO, Susumu, PH.D., D.SC.; Japanese research scientist; b. 1 Feb. 1928, Seoul, Korea; s. of Kenichi Ohno and Toshiko (Saito) Ohno; m. Midori Aoyama 1951; two s. one d.; ed. Tokyo Univ. of Agric. and Tech. and Hokkaido Univ., Sapporo; Research Staff, Pathology, Tokyo Univ. 1950–53; Research Assoc., City of Hope, Duarte, Calif., U.S.A. 1953–66, Chair. Biology 1966–81, Ben Horowitz Chair of Distinguished Scientist in Reproductive Genetics, Beckman Research Inst. of The City of Hope 1981–; Hon. D.Sc. (Pennsylvania); Amory Prize, American Acad. of Arts and Sciences; Kihara Prize, Japanese Soc. of Genetics. *Publications:* Sex Chromosomes and Sex-linked Genes 1967, Evolution by Gene Duplication 1970, Major Sex Determining Genes 1979. *Leisure interests:* horsemanship (dressage), fishing, history. *Address:* Beckman Research Institute of The City of Hope, 1450 E. Duarte Road, Duarte, Calif. 91010; 7329 Oak Drive, Glendora, Calif. 91740, U.S.A. (Home). *Telephone:* (818) 357-9711 (Office).

OHTANI, Ichiji; Japanese textile executive; b. 31 Aug. 1912, Kobe; s. of Kyosuke and Tama Ohtani; m. Atsuko Suzuki 1943; two s. one d.; ed. Kobe Univ.; Dir. Toyobo Co. Ltd. 1964–68, Man. Dir. 1968–72, Senior Man. Dir. 1972–74, Deputy Pres. 1974, Pres. 1974–78, Chair. 1978–83, Counsellor July 1983–; Dir. Toyobo Petcord Co. Ltd. 1969–83, Chair. Toyobo Co. Ltd. 1978–83, Counsellor 1983–; Vice-Pres. Industrias Unidas, S.A. 1973–79; Exec. Dir. Fed. of Econ. Orgs. 1976–; Chair. Japan Spinners' Asscn. 1976–79, Diafibres Co. Ltd. 1977–88; Vice-Pres. Japan Textile Fed. 1976–79; Junior Vice-Pres. Int. Textile Mfrs. Fed. 1976–78, Senior Vice-Pres. 1978–80, Pres. 1980–82, Hon. Life mem. 1982–; Blue Ribbon Medal 1979; Order of the Rising Sun (Second Class) 1984. *Leisure interests:* sports, especially soccer and golf. *Address:* Toyobo Co. Ltd., 2-8 Dojima Hama 2-chome, Kita-ku, Osaka 530 (Office); 7-18 Yamate-cho, Ashiya-shi 659, Japan (Home).

OHTANI, Monshu Koshin, M.A.; Japanese ecclesiastic; b. 12 Aug. 1945, Kyoto; s. of Kosho Ohtani and Yoshiko Ohtani; m. Noriko Tanaka 1974; two s. one d.; ed. Tokyo Univ. and Ryukoku Univ.; ordained Priest of Jodo Shinshu Hongwanji-ha Aug. 1960, Monshu (Ecclesiastic Patriarch) Apparent 1970–1977, Monshu April 1977–; Pres. Fed. Hongwanji Dharma Schools April 1969–, Fed. Hongwanji Young Buddhist Asscns. April 1970–, Hongwanji Scout Masters Assoc. April 1970–, All-Japanese Buddhist Fed. 1978–80, Feb. 1988–. *Leisure interests:* the study of literature, skiing. *Address:* Horikawa-dori, Hanayacho-sagaru, Hongwanji Monzen-cho 6, Shimogyo-ku, Kyoto 600, Japan. *Telephone:* (075) 371-5181.

OHUCHI, Teruyuki; Japanese businessman; b. 16 April 1929, Tokyo; m. Junko Ohmori 1959; one s. one d.; ed. Seijo High School, Tokyo, Tokyo Univ., Univ. of Michigan, Harvard Business School; worked in Accounting, Credit Analysis and Foreign Depts. Industrial Bank of Japan, Tokyo 1952–66, Deputy Gen. Man. Loan Dept. 1971–72, Deputy Gen. Man. Foreign Dept. 1972–74, Gen. Man. and Chief Agent, Chair. and C.E.O. Industrial Bank of Japan Trust Co., New York 1974–78, Dir. 1979–, Gen. Man. Foreign Dept. 1978–81, Dir. and Gen. Man. Loan Dept. 1981–82, Dir. Int. HQ 1982, Man. Dir. 1983; Loan Officer, Man., Deputy Dir. Operations Dept. Asian Development Bank, Manila 1966–71; Vice-Pres. Cofinancing, World Bank, Washington D.C. 1983–86. *Leisure interests:* golf, painting, carpentry, music. *Address:* c/o IBRD, 1818 H Street, N.W., Room F. 1220, Washington D.C. 20433, U.S.A.

ØIEN, Arne; Norwegian politician; b. 22 Dec. 1928, Oslo; m.; fmr. C.E.O. Cen. Bureau of Statistics, Asst. Deputy Dir. Gen.; Dir. Gen. Ministry of Finance 1970–80; State Sec. to Prime Minister 1981; Minister of Petroleum and Energy May 1986–. *Address:* Ministry of Petroleum and Energy, P.O. Box 8148, Dep., Oslo 1, Norway. *Telephone:* (2) 34-90-90.

OISTRAKH, Igor Davidovich; Soviet violinist; b. 27 April 1931, Odessa; s. of late David Oistrakh; ed. Music School and State Conservatoire, Moscow; Student State Conservatoire 1949–55; many foreign tours, several concerts with father David Oistrakh; 1st prize, Violin competition, Budapest 1952, Wieniawski competition, Poznań; Honoured Artist of R.S.F.S.R. *Address:* State Conservatoire, 13 Ulitsa Herzen, Moscow, U.S.S.R.

OIZERMAN, Teodor Ilyich; Soviet philosopher; b. 14 May 1914, Petroverovka; s. of Ilya Davidovich Oizerman and Yelizaveta Abramovna Nemirovskaya; m. Genrietta Kasavina; two s. one d.; ed. Moscow Inst. of History, Philosophy and Literature; Industrial worker 1930–33; Postgraduate 1938–41; Army service 1941–46; Asst. Prof., Moscow Inst. of Econs. 1946–47; Asst. Prof., Prof. Moscow Univ. 1952–, Head of Chair 1954–68; corresp. mem. U.S.S.R. Acad. of Sciences 1966–81, mem. 1981–; Foreign mem. Acad. of Sciences, GDR 1981–; mem. Int. Inst. of Philosophy 1982–; Head Dept. of History of Philosophy, Inst. of Philosophy of Acad. of Sciences 1971–; various decorations. *Publications:* (works have been translated into German, French and English); Razvitije Marxistskoi teorii na opite revolutzii 1848 goda (Development of Marxist theory in Experience of the Revolution of 1848) 1955, Philosophie Hegels 1959, Formirovanie filosofii Marxisma (Formation of the Philosophy of Marxism) 1962, 1974, Zur Geschichte der vormarxischen Philosophie (On the History of pre-

Marxist Philosophy) 1961, Die Entfremdung als historische Kategorie (Alienation as an Historical Category) 1965, Problemi istoriko-filosofskoi nauki (Problems of Historical-Philosophical Science) 1969, Glavnie filosofskie napravlenija (Principal Philosophical Trends) 1971, Krisis sovremennogo idealisma (Crisis of Contemporary Idealism) 1973, Problems of the History of Philosophy 1973, Filosofiya I. Kanta (Philosophy of Kant) 1974, Dialektitcheskij materialism i istorija philosophii (Dialectic Materialism and the History of Philosophy) 1979, Teorii istoriko-philosophskogo prozessa (Dialectic Materialism and the Historical-Philosophical Progress) 1983, The Main Trends in Philosophy 1988, and over 400 articles on philosophical problems. *Leisure interest:* walking. *Address:* Institute of Philosophy, U.S.S.R. Academy of Sciences, 14 Volchonka, Moscow (Office); Ap. 168, 1 Mendelev Street, Moscow 117234, U.S.S.R. (Home).

OJANEN, Risto Ensio, M.SC.; Finnish business executive; b. 12 Jan. 1927, Porvoo; s. of Yrjö and Tyyne (Lahti) Ojanen; m. Vappu Sinikka Nuora 1950; two c.; ed. Porvoon Yhteislvseo and The Helsinki School of Econs.; Export Man. Puutalo Oy 1949–61; Sales Man. Finnair (then called Aero Oy) 1961–66, Vice-Pres. Sales 1966–74, Vice-Pres. Marketing 1974–85, Pres. 1985–; mem. of numerous travel and aviation cos.; Commdr., Order of the Finnish Lion; Kt. of the Order of the White Rose of Finland; Finnish Olympic Cross of Merit. *Leisure interests:* music, sailing. *Address:* Airoranta 3B, 00830 Helsinki; Mannerheimintie 102, 00250 Helsinki, Finland. *Telephone:* 789 911 (Home); 81881 (Office).

OJEDA EISELEY, Jaime de; Spanish diplomatist; b. 5 Aug. 1933; ed. Int. Acad. of The Hague, Naval War Coll. of Madrid and Higher Center for Nat. Defence Studies (CESEDEN), Madrid; Prof. of Political Law, Complutense Univ. of Madrid 1958; joined diplomatic service 1958; served Washington, D.C. 1962–69; Minister-Counsellor, Beijing 1973–76; Consul-Gen. of Spain in Hong Kong and Macao 1976–79; Assoc. mem. Center for Int. Relations, Harvard Univ. 1979–80; Deputy Perm. Rep. to North Atlantic Council 1982–83, Perm. Rep. to NATO 1983–. *Address:* NATO, 1110 Brussels, Belgium.

OJEDA PAULLADA, Pedro; Mexican lawyer; b. 19 Jan. 1934, México, D.F.; s. of Manuel Ojeda Lacroix and Adela Paullada de Ojeda; m. Olga Cárdenas de Ojeda 1959; two s. three d.; ed. Univ. Nacional Autónoma de México; Head of Personnel and lawyer, Técnica y Fundación, S.A. de C.V. 1955, Sub-Man. 1955–57; Gen. Man. Industria Química de Plásticos S.A. 1957–58; Deputy Dir.-Gen. Juntas Federales de Mejoras Materiales 1959–65; Dir.-Gen. of Legal Affairs, SCT 1966–70; Sec.-Gen. Presidential Secr. 1970–71; Attorney-Gen. 1971–76; Sec. of Labour and Social Welfare 1976–81; Pres. Nat. Exec. Cttee. of Institutional Revolutionary Party (PRI) 1981; Minister of Fisheries 1982–88; Gen. Coordinator, Mexican Programme for Int. Women's Year 1975; Chair. World Conf. of Int. Women's Year 1975, 64th Int. Conf. of ILO 1978; Order of Merit (Italy), La Gran Cruz al Mérito (Italy), Order de Isabel la Católica (Spain). *Address:* Montaña 600, Villa Alvaro Obregón, México 20, D.F., Mexico. *Telephone:* 521-37-14.

OJUKWU, General Chukwuemeka Odumegwu, M.A.; Nigerian army officer and politician; b. 4 Nov. 1933; ed. C.M.S. Grammar School and King's Coll., Lagos, Epsom Coll., U.K., Lincoln Coll., Oxford, Eaton Hall Officer Cadet School, U.K. and Joint Services Staff Coll., U.K.; Admin. Officer, Nigerian Public Service 1956–57; joined Nigerian Army 1957; at Nigerian Army Depot, Zaria 1957; army training in U.K. 1957–58; joined 5th Battalion Nigerian Army 1958; Instructor, Royal West African Frontier Force Training School, Teshie 1958–61; returned to 5th Battalion Nigerian Army 1961; Maj. Army HQ 1961; Deputy Asst. Adjutant and Quartermaster-Gen. Kaduna Brigade HQ 1961; Congo Emergency Force 1962; Lieut.-Col. and Quartermaster-Gen. 1963–64; Commdr. 5th Battalion, Kano 1964–66; Mil. Gov. of E. Nigeria 1966–67; Head of State of Republic of Biafra (E. Region of Nigeria) 1967–70; sought political asylum in Ivory Coast 1970–82; returned to Nigeria 1982; joined Nat. Party of Nigeria 1983–84; imprisoned Jan.-Oct. 1984; now released and living in Nigeria.

OKASHA, Sarwat Mahmoud Fahmy, D. ÈS L.; Egyptian diplomatist and politician; b. 18 Feb. 1921, Cairo; s. of Mahmoud and Sameya Okasha; m. Islah Abdel Fattah Lotfi 1943; two s. one d.; ed. Military Coll. and Cairo Univ.; Cavalry Officer 1939; took part in Palestine war 1948–49: Mil. Attaché, Berne 1953–54, Paris 1954–56; Counsellor in Presidency of Repub. 1956–57; Egyptian Amb. to Italy 1957–58; U.A.R. Minister of Culture and Nat. Guidance 1958–62; Chair. and Man. Dir. Nat. Bank 1962–66; Deputy Prime Minister and Minister of Culture 1966–67; Minister of Culture 1967–71; Asst. to the Pres. 1971–72; Visiting Prof. Coll. de France 1973; Pres. of Supreme Council for Literature, Art and Social Sciences; Pres. Egypt-France Assn. 1965–; mem. Exec. Bd. UNESCO 1962–70 (masterminded int. campaign to save temples of Abu Simbel, etc. from the rising waters of the Aswan Dam); Corresp. Fellow British Acad.; numerous awards (including UNESCO Gold Medal 1970, State Award for the Arts 1988) and foreign decorations. *Publications:* Fifty works (including translations): Ovid's Metamorphoses and Ars Amatoria, Gibran, Khalil's works, Etienne Drioton's Le Théâtre Egyptien, studies of the works of Wagner, The Development of European Music (in Arabic), History of Art (13 vols.), The Muslim Painter and the Divine 1979. *Leisure interests:* horse-riding, golf, music. *Address:* Villa 34, Rue 14, Maadi, Cairo, Egypt. *Telephone:* 3505075.

OKAWARA, Yoshio, LL.B.; Japanese diplomatist (retd.); b. 5 Feb. 1919, Gunma; s. of Kingo Okawara and Sei Okawara; m. Mitsuko Terajima 1948; three s.; ed. Tokyo Univ.; Second, then First Sec. Embassy, London 1954-56; First Sec. Embassy, Manila 1956-58; First Sec. Washington, D.C. 1962, Counsellor 1963-65; Dir. Personnel Div., Ministry of Foreign Affairs 1965-67, Deputy Dir.-Gen. of American Affairs Bureau 1967-71, Dir.-Gen. 1972-74; Minister, Washington, D.C. 1971-72; Deputy Vice-Minister for Admin., Ministry of Foreign Affairs 1974-76; Amb. to Australia (also accred. to Nauru and Fiji) 1976-80, to U.S.A. 1980-85; Exec. Adviser KEIDANREN (Fed. of Econ. Orgs.); Fellow, Center for Int. Affairs, Harvard Univ. 1962. *Leisure interests:* golf, reading. *Address:* 1-22-20 Seijo, Setagaya-ku, Tokyo 157, Japan. *Telephone:* 03-416-7141.

ÖKÇÜN, Gündüz; Turkish university professor and politician; b. 1936; fmr. Dean, Faculty of Political Sciences, Univ. of Ankara; Minister for Foreign Affairs June-July 1977, 1978-79; Republican People's Party. *Address:* c/o Ministry of Foreign Affairs, Ankara, Turkey.

O'KENNEDY, Michael, M.A.; Irish politician; b. 21 Feb. 1936, Menagh, Co. Tipperary; s. of Éamonn and Helena (Slattery) O'Kennedy; m. Breda Heavey 1965; one s. two d.; ed. St. Flannan's Coll., Ennis, Univ. Coll. Dublin, King's Inns, Dublin; practised as barrister 1961-70, as Senior Counsel 1973-77, 1982-; mem. Senate 1965-69, Front Bench Spokesman on Educ. and Justice, Senate Statutory Instruments Cttee. on the Constitution until 1967; mem. Dáil for North Tipperary 1969-80, 1982-; Parl. Sec. to Minister of Educ. 1970-72, Minister without Portfolio 1972-73; Minister for Transport and Power 1973; Opposition Spokesman on Foreign Affairs 1973-77; Minister for Foreign Affairs 1977-79, of Finance 1979-80; mem. Comm. of European Communities 1980-82; Commr. for Personnel, Consumer Affairs, Environment 1981-82; Opposition Spokesman for Finance 1982-87, Minister of Agric. March 1987-; mem. All-Parties Cttee. on Irish Relations, Chair. 1973-80; mem. Informal Cttee. on Reform of Dáil Procedure until 1972, Dáil and Senate Joint Cttee. on Secondary Legislation of EEC 1973-80; mem. Inter-Parl. Union, mem. Exec. of Irish Council of European Movement; Pres. EEC Council of Ministers July-Dec. 1979; Pres. Re-negotiation EEC/ACP at 2nd Lomé Convention 1979; Nat. Trustee Fianna Fáil. *Leisure interests:* reading, philosophy, history, politics, drama, music, sports. *Address:* Department of Agriculture, Agriculture House, Kildare Street, Dublin 2; Gortlandroe, Nenagh, Co. Tipperary, Ireland. *Telephone:* (01) 789011 (Office); (067) 31366 (Home).

OKER-BLOM, Nils Christian Edgar, DR.MED.; Finnish professor of virology; b. 5 Aug. 1919, Helsinki; s. of Edgar Alexander Oker-Blom and Zea Margit Bergroth; m. Constance Victorine Nordenswan 1944; two s. one d.; ed. Univ. of Helsinki, State Serum Inst., Copenhagen, State Bacteriological Laboratory, Stockholm, Yale Univ.; lecturer in Microbiology, Univ. of Helsinki 1951-57, Prof. of Virology and Head of Virology Dept. 1957-83, Dean and Vice-Dean, Faculty of Medicine 1968-71, Vice-Rector 1973-78, Rector 1978-83, Chancellor 1983-88; Head of Municipal Bacteriological Lab., Helsinki 1951-57; Vice-Pres. European Asscn. of Poliomyelitis and Allied Diseases 1969-73; Sec. Int. Asscn. of Microbiological Socs., Virology Section 1970-74; Vice-Pres. Int. Union of Biological Sciences 1973-75, Pres. 1975-79, Past Pres. 1979-82; Chair. Joint Cttee. of the Nordic Research Councils 1977-80, Finnish Nominating Cttee. for NIH; Section Ed. (Immunology Section) Intervirology; mem. IUBS Comm. of Biological Educ., WHO Expert Advisory Panel (Virus Diseases) 1964-, Finnish Soc. of Science, New York Acad. of Science, Swedish Medical Soc., Advisory Cttee. of the European Centre for Higher Educ./UNESCO 1982-; Hon. mem. of several student and medical assens.; Per Dubb lecture, Univ. of Gothenburg 1969; Dr.Med. h.c. (Uppsala Univ) 1967; Hugo Standertskiöld Award for Cancer Research 1960; J. W. Runeberg Award and Medal 1981. *Publications:* various publications on virology and cancer research. *Leisure interest:* sculpture. *Address:* Department of Virology, University of Helsinki, Haartmaninkatu 3, SF-00290 Helsinki; Enåsvägen 22 H 51, 00200 Helsinki 20, Finland (Home). *Telephone:* 358-0-43461 (Office), 692 5967 (Home).

OKERO, Isaac Edwin Omolo; Kenyan politician; b. 1931, Ulumbi, Nyanza Province; s. of Ibrahim and Flora Arnolo Okero; m. Jane M. A. Okero 1964; four s. two d.; ed. Makerere Univ. Coll., Uganda, Univs. of Bombay and Leiden and Middle Temple, London; State Counsel, Kenya 1962-63, Deputy Public Prosecutor 1963-65; Commr.-Gen. of Customs and Excise, East African Community 1965-69; M.P. 1969-; Minister of Health 1969-73, of Power and Communications 1973-77, 1978-79, of Information and Broadcasting 1978-79; Chair. Kenya African National Union (KANU) 1978-79; mem. Communications Council 1971. *Leisure interests:* flying, music. *Address:* c/o KANU, P.O. Box 72394, Nairobi, Kenya.

OKEZIE, Dr. Josiah Onyebuchi Johnson, L.S.M., F.M.C.G.P.; Nigerian physician and politician; b. 26 Nov. 1924, Umuahia-Ibeku; s. of Chief Johnson Okezie and Esther Okezie; m. Rose Chioma Onwucheka 1966; four s. one d.; ed. Higher Coll., Yaba, Achimota Coll., Ghana, Yaba Coll. of Medicine, Univ. Coll., Ibadan and Royal Coll. of Surgeons, U.K.; Asst. Medical Officer, Nigerian Civil Service 1950-54; Founder and Medical Supt. Ibeku Central Hosp., Umuahia-Ibeku 1958-69; Sr. Medical Officer in charge of Queen Elizabeth Hosp., Umuahia-Ibeku 1970; Assoc. Editor, The Nigerian Scientist 1961-62; Sec. E. Nigerian Science Assen. 1961-63; mem. Nigerian Medical Council 1965-66; mem. E. Nigeria House of Assembly 1961-66;

Leader, Republican Party 1964-66; Rep. of E. Central State, Fed. Exec. Council 1970; Fed. Commr. for Health 1970-71, for Agric. and Natural Resources 1971-74; installed Chief Ezeomereoha of Bende 1974; Chair. Imo State Branch, Nigerian Medical Assen. 1976, Alvan Ikoku Coll. of Educ., Owerri 1980-82; Chair. Bd. of Dirs. African Continental Bank Ltd. 1982-84; Sec. Nigerian Medical Assen. (E. Region Branch) 1960-70; Life mem. Nigerian Bible Soc. 1972. *Publications:* The Evolution of Science 1959, Atomic Radiation 1961. *Leisure interests:* English literature, reading poetry, gardening. *Address:* P.O. Box 306, Umuahia-Ibeku, Imo State, Nigeria. *Telephone:* Umuahia 220673.

OKHOTNIKOV, Nikolai Petrovich; Soviet bass; b. 5 July 1937, Glubokoye, Kazakh Repub.; s. of P. Y. Okhotnikov and K. A. Okhotnikov; m. Larkina Tamara Georgievna 1973; two s.; ed. Leningrad Conservatoire (pupil of I. I. Pleshakov); mem. CPSU 1974-; soloist with Leningrad Concert Orchestra; with Maly Theatre, Leningrad 1967-71, with Kirov Opera 1971-; teacher of singing at Leningrad Conservatoire 1976-; Grand Prix, Barcelona 1972; People's Artist of U.S.S.R. 1983. *Major roles include:* Kochubey in Mazeppa, René in Iolanta, the Miller in Rusalka, Susanin, Dosifey in Mussorgsky's Khovanshchina, Kutuzov in Prokofiev's War and Peace, Philip II in Don Carlos, Heinrich in Lohengrin, Gremin in Eugene Onegin, Boris Godunov and Pimen in Boris Godunov. *Leisure interests:* fishing, photography. *Address:* The Kirov Theatre, Teatralnaya pl.1, Leningrad, U.S.S.R. *Telephone:* 216-47-54.

OKINDA, Jérôme; Gabonese politician; b. 1933, Omoy, Franceville District; ed. St. Jean Lower Seminary, Libreville, Grand Séminaire Libermann, Brazzaville and Univ. of Aix-en-Provence, France; Mil. service 1957-62; subsequently Sec. at Gabon Embassy, London, Chargé de Mission, Ministry of Justice; elected mem. Nat. Assembly 1964; Pres. First Comm. of Admin. Affairs 1964-65, of Finance Comm. 1965, subsequently mem. Higher Admin. Council, Pres. Admin. Council, Gabonese Office of Social Security; Minister of Justice and Keeper of the Seals Jan.-Feb. 1969; Minister of Public Health and Population 1969-70, of Nat. Educ. and Culture; Minister of Nat. Educ. and Scientific Research March-Oct. 1973, of Labour and Social Security 1973-75, of the Economy and Finance 1975-76; Minister of State for the Economy and Finance 1976-80, of State Participation 1976-78, 1978-80; Pres. Foundation for Higher Instruction in Cen. Africa (FESAC) 1970-71; Officer of Equatorial Star. *Address:* c/o Ministère de l'Economie et des Finances, Libreville, Gabon.

OKITA, Saburo, D.ECON.; Japanese economist; b. 3 Nov. 1914, Dairen, Manchuria; s. of Shuji and Hana Okita; m. Hisako Kajii 1942; three s. one d.; ed. Tokyo Univ.; joined Govt. service as engineer in Ministry of Posts 1937; Econ. Stabilization Board, Chief Research Section 1947; UN Econ. Comm. for Asia and the Far East 1952; Dir.-Gen. Planning Bureau 1957, Dir.-Gen. Devt. Bureau 1962-63; Pres. Japan Econ. Research Centre 1964-73, Chair. 1973-79; mem. Pearson Comm. on Int. Devt. 1969-70, OECD High-Level Expert Group on Science Policy in 1970s 1970-71, the Group of Experts on the Structure of the UN 1975, UN Cttee. on Devt. Planning 1965-80, Bd. of Govs. of Japan Broadcasting Corpn. 1975-77; Special Adviser Int. Devt. Centre of Japan 1973-79; Pres. Overseas Econ. Co-operation Fund 1973-77; Minister for Foreign Affairs 1979-80; Govt. Rep. for External Econ. Relations July 1980-81; Chair. Inst. for Domestic and Int. Policy Studies 1981-; Pres. and Chancellor Int. Univ. of Japan April 1982-; Chair. Japanese Br. World Wide Fund for Nature 1984-; mem. U.N. World Comm. on Environment and Devt. (Brundtland Comm.) 1984-87, Comm. on Health Research for Devt. (John Evans Comm.) 1987-; Chair. Panel for Role of Asian Devt. Bank in the 1990's 1989-; Ramon Magsaysay, Award for Int. Understanding 1971; Asia Soc. Award 1984; Britannica Award 1987; Hon. LL.D. (Univ. of Mich.) 1977, (ANU) 1982, (UBC) 1984, (Princeton) 1985. *Publications:* The Future of Japan's Economy 1960, Japan's Post-War Economic Policy 1961, Economic Planning 1962, Conditions for a Developed Nation 1965, Japanese Economy in the Asian Setting 1966, Future Vision for Japanese Economy 1968, Essays in Japan and World Economy (English) 1971, New Image of Japanese Economy 1971, Role of the Economist 1973, Resource-poor Japan and the World Economy 1975, Japan and the World Economy (English) 1975, Autobiography 1977, Economic Strategy for Vulnerability 1978, Developing Economies and Japan—Lessons in Growth (English) 1980, 252 Days of an Economist Foreign Minister 1980, Hurried Missions in Various Directions (autobiog.) 1981-, Japan's Challenging Years—Reflections on my Lifetime (English) 1983, and numerous articles. *Leisure interest:* golf. *Address:* 5-13-12 Koishikawa, Bunkyo-ku, Tokyo 112, Japan. *Telephone:* 03-811-0742.

OKOGIE, Mgr. Anthony Olubunmi, S.T.L., D.D.; Nigerian ecclesiastic; b. 16 June 1936, Lagos; s. of Prince Michael Okogie and Lucy Adumni Okogie; ed. St. Gregory's Coll., Lagos, St. Theresa Minor Seminary, Ibadan, St. Peter and St. Paul's Seminary, Ibadan, Urban Univ., Rome; ordained priest 1966; Act. Parish Priest, St. Patrick's Church, Idumagbo, Lagos; Asst. Priest, Holy Cross Cathedral, Lagos; Religious Instructor, King's Coll., Lagos; Dir. of Vocations, Archdiocese of Lagos; Man. Holy Cross Group of Schools, Lagos; Master of Ceremonies, Holy Cross Cathedral; Broadcaster of religious programmes, NBC/TV; Auxiliary Bishop of Oyo Diocese 1971-72; Auxiliary Bishop to the Apostolic Admin., Archdiocese of Lagos 1972-73; Archbishop of Lagos May 1973-; Vice-Pres. Catholic Bishops' Conf. of Nigeria 1985-88, Pres. 1988-; Nat. Pres. Christian Assen.

of Nigeria 1988-; mem. Prerogative of Mercy, Religious Advisory Council. *Leisure interests:* reading, watching films. *Address:* Archdiocese of Lagos, 19 Catholic Mission Street, P.O. Box 8, Lagos, Nigeria. *Telephone:* 633841, 635729.

OKONDO, Peter Habenga, B.COMM.; Kenyan accountant, business executive and politician; s. of Gaetano Okondo; m. Marialuisa Okondo 1958; one s. three d.; ed. St. Mary's, Yala, Kenya, St. Mary's, Kisubi, Uganda, Univ. of Cape Town, S.A.; Auditor-Gen. Kenya African Union 1951-52; Accountant, Kisumu 1951-52; arrested during Mau Mau Emergency 1952; escaped from detention 1953; Accountant, Uganda Civil Service 1954-59; Auditor, Shell Co., Tanzania 1960; mem. Kenya Legis. Council 1961-63; Asst. Minister of Finance, Kenya 1961-62, of Works 1963, of Co-operative Devt. 1984, Minister of Commerce and Industry 1984-86, of Labour 1986-; Head, African Transport Devt. Studies, UN/ECA, Addis Ababa 1963-64; Sec. Econ. Cttee., ECOSOC, UN Secr. New York 1965-67; returned to Kenya and started own business 1968; Chair. Habenga Trust Co. Ltd. 1968-; Menengai Investments Ltd. 1973-, Tysons Habenga Ltd. (Real Estate Agency) 1976-, Phoenix of East Africa Assurance Co. Ltd. 1980-; M.P. for Busia South June 1981-; dir. 18 cos. *Publication:* Portrait of Apartheid 1979. *Leisure interests:* golf, swimming, walking. *Address:* National Social Security House, P.O. Box 40326, Nairobi (Office); P.O. Box 30727, Nairobi (Home); Ruambwa, P.O. Box 18, Hakati, Busia District, Kenya (Country Residence). *Telephone:* Nairobi 729800 (Office); Nairobi 88-2638 (Home); Hakati 4 (Country).

ØKSNES, Oskar, M.SC.; Norwegian politician; b. 11 April 1921, Kvam, Nord-Trøndelag; s. of Egil and Borghild Øksnes; m. Ragnhild Barkhald 1950; one s. one d.; ed. Nat. Teachers' Training School for Smallhold Farming, Agricultural Univ. of Norway; Man. Agronomist, later Chief County Agricultural Officer for Agricultural Econs., Agricultural Cttee. of Nord-Trøndelag 1948-62; Special Assignment in Ministry of Agric. 1952-53; County Dir. of Agric., Møre og Romsdal 1963-75; Under-Sec. of State, Ministry of Agric. 1964-65; County Dir. of Agric., Nord-Trøndelag Aug. 1975-; Minister and Head of Ministry of Agric. 1976-81. *Leisure interest:* outdoor life. *Address:* Sophus Lies gt. 6 B, Oslo 2, Norway (Home).

OKUDZHAVA, Bulat Shalvovich; Soviet poet, singer and writer; b. 9 May 1924 (mixed Georgian and Armenian descent), Tbilisi, Georgian S.S.R.; ed. Tbilisi Inst.; War service 1941-45; began publishing 1953; mem. CPSU 1955-; taught in village schools -1956; Poetry editor of Moscow Literary Gazette 1956-64; visits to France, late 1960s, to U.K. 1977. *Publications:* Islands 1959, How are Things, School-Boy?, Published & Unpublished Verse (Frankfurt) 1964, The Merry Drummer 1964, A Ditty about Fools: A Collection of Verse (London) 1964, March Magnanimous 1967, Two Novels (Poor Avrosimov; Zhor's Photograph) (Frankfurt) 1970 (French trans. 1972), Gulp of Freedom. A Story about Pavel Pestel 1971, The Extraordinary Adventures of Secret Agent Shipov in Pursuit of Count Leo Tolstoy in the Year 1862 1973, Selected Prose 1979, A Journey of Dilettanti 1979, The Poems of Bulat Okudzhava 1984; Scenario: Zhenya Zhemechka and 'Katyusha' 1968; Records: Bulat Okhudzhava (Le Chant du Monde) and others; songs include: Prayer of François Villon, The Paper Soldier, A Georgian Song, We'll Pay Any Price, Good-bye lads, Song about Mozart etc.

OKUN, Daniel A., SC.D.; American professor of environmental engineering and consulting engineer; b. 19 June 1917, New York; m. Beth Griffin 1946; one s. one d.; ed. Cooper Union, New York, California Inst. of Tech., Pasadena and Harvard Univ.; Sanitary Engineer, U.S. Public Health Service 1940-42; served U.S. Army 1942-46; Assoc., Malcolm Pirnie Inc., Consulting Engineers 1948-52; Assoc. Prof., then Kenan Prof., Univ. of N.C. 1952-, Head, Dept. of Environmental Sciences and Eng. 1955-73, Dir. Inst. of Environmental Health Studies 1965-73, Dir. Int. Programmes, Dept. of Environmental Sciences and Eng. 1954-84, Chair. of Faculty, Univ. of N.C. 1970-73; Consultant to local, State and Nat. Govts., int. agencies and industry 1952-; mem. Nat. Acad. of Eng., Inst. of Medicine (N.A.S.); Eddy and Fair Medals, Water Pollution Control Fed.; Fair Award, American Acad. of Environmental Engineers; Billard Award, New York Acad. of Sciences; Freese Award, American Soc. of Civil Engineers; Friendship Medal, British Inst. of Water Engineers and Scientists, Best Paper Award, Educ. Div., American Waterworks Asscn. *Publications:* Water and Wastewater Engineering (with Fair and Geyer), Elements of Water Supply and Wastewater Disposal (with Fair and Geyer), Regionalization of Water Management, Community Wastewater Collection and Disposal (with George Ponghis), for WHO, Surface Water Treatment for Communities in Developing Countries (with Schulz). *Address:* Department of Environmental Sciences and Engineering, University of North Carolina, Chapel Hill, N.C. 27599 (Office); Route 7, Linden Road, Chapel Hill, N.C. 27514, U.S.A. (Home). *Telephone:* (919) 966-3751 (Office); (919) 933-7903 (Home).

OKUN, Lev Borisovich; Soviet theoretical physicist; b. 7 July 1929, Sukhinichi, Kaluga Dist.; s. of B. G. Okun and B. R. Ginzburg; m. Erica Gulyaeva 1954; one s. two d.; ed. Moscow Physics and Eng. Inst.; mem. of staff of Inst. of Experimental and Theoretical Physics 1954-; main work has been on the theory of elementary particles; Corresp. mem. of U.S.S.R. Acad. of Sciences 1966-. *Publications include:* The Weak Interaction of Elementary Particles 1963, Leptons and Quarks 1981, Particle Physics: The Quest for the Substance of Substance 1984, A-Z: A Primer in Particle

Physics 1987. *Address:* Institute of Theoretical and Experimental Physics, 117259 B. Cheremushkinskaya 25, Moscow, U.S.S.R. *Telephone:* 123-02-92.

OKUNIEWSKI, Józef, D.ECON.; Polish economist and politician; b. 5 May 1920, Lubotyń, Poznań Voivodship; s. of Józef and Małgorzata Okuniewski; m. Krystyna Okuniewski 1942; one s.; ed. Łódź Univ.; Agricultural instructor, Wieluń district; worked in timber firm, Warsaw during Occupation; later became headmaster of agricultural school at Tymianka and subsequently lecturer, Agricultural Teachers' Inst., Pszczelin; mem. PUWP 1950-, Deputy mem. Cen. Cttee. 1964-68, 1972-76; Dir. of Univ. Studies, Ministry of Higher Learning 1953-54; subsequently Deputy Prof. Warsaw Agric. Univ., then Asst. Prof. and Chair. Faculty of Political Econs. 1961, Extraordinary Prof. 1967-85, Ordinary Prof. 1985-; Under-Sec. of State Ministry of Agric. 1959-70; Minister of Agric. 1970-74; Amb. to Netherlands 1974-79; Prof. of Agric. Econs. in Agric., Univ. Warsaw 1979-86; Dir. Inst. of Rural and Agric. Devt., Polish Acad. of Science 1986-; Order of Banner of Labour (1st Class) 1969, Commdr. Cross with Star of Order Polonia Restituta 1974. *Leisure interests:* photography, tennis. *Address:* ul. Jazgarzewska 15, 00-730 Warsaw, Poland. *Telephone:* 41 20 68 (Home).

OKUNO, Seisuke; Japanese politician; b. 2 July 1913, Nara Pref.; s. of Teiji and Toki Okuno; m. 1942; two s.; ed. First High School, Univ. of Tokyo; Chief, Gen. Affairs Section, Yamanashi Pref. Govt. and Kagoshima Pref. Govt. 1938; Officer Dept. of Local Govt., Ministry of Home Affairs 1943; Head of Police Dept., Kochi Pref. Govt. 1947; Head, Finance and Research Divs., Local Autonomy Agency 1949; Dir. Bureau of Taxation, Ministry of Autonomy 1953, Bureau of Finance 1958; Perm. Vice-Minister, Ministry of Autonomy 1963; mem. House of Reps. 1963-; Minister of Educ. 1972-74, of Justice 1980-81, 1987-; Dir.-Gen. Nat. Land Agency 1987-88; Chair. Liberal-Democratic Party (LDP) Educ. System Research Council 1974-76; Pres. Foundation for the Welfare and Educ. of the Asian People 1976-; Dir. Gen. Man. and Co-ordination Agency 1987-88; Dir. LDP Nat. Campaign Headquarters 1980; Liberal-Democratic Party. *Publications:* Several articles on aspects of local government. *Leisure interests:* golf, tennis, go, bonsai. *Address:* 5-7-10 Jingumae, Shibuya-ku, Tokyo 150, Japan. *Telephone:* 03-407-3535.

OLANG', Most Rev. Festo Habakkuk; Kenyan ecclesiastic; b. 14 Nov. 1914, Maseno; m. Eseri Olang' 1937; four s. eight d.; ed. Alliance High School, St. Paul's Theological Coll., Wyclif Hall, Oxford; Teacher Maseno Secondary School 1936-39; on staff Butere Girls' School 1940-45; ordained Deacon 1945; consecrated Bishop 1955; Bishop of Maseno 1961-70; Archbishop of Kenya (Anglican Church) 1970-79. *Address:* P.O. Box 1, Maseno, Kenya. *Telephone:* Maseno 1.

OLAV V; King of Norway; b. 2 July 1903; ed. secondary school, Oslo, Norwegian Mil. Acad. and Balliol Coll., Oxford; studied economics and political science; married Princess Märtha of Sweden 1929 (died 1954); one s. two d.; Commdr.-in-Chief, Norwegian Forces, Second World War; succeeded his father, King Haakon VII, 21 Sept. 1957; Hon. K.G., K.T., G.C.B., G.C.V.O. *Address:* Royal Palace, Oslo, Norway.

OLCAY, Osman; Turkish diplomatist; b. 17 Jan. 1924, Istanbul; s. of Seyfi and Cezibe Olcay; m. Necla Baran 1946; ed. St. Joseph French Coll., Istanbul, and Faculty of Political Science, Univ. of Ankara; joined Ministry of Foreign Affairs, Turkey 1945; Lieut., Turkish Army 1946; Foreign Ministry 1947; Vice-Consul, London 1948-50, Second Sec., London 1950-52; Chief of Section, Dept. of Econ. Affairs, Ministry of Foreign Affairs 1952-54; First Sec. NATO, Paris 1954, Counsellor and Deputy Perm. Rep. 1958-59; Asst. Dir.-Gen. NATO Dept., Ministry of Foreign Affairs, Ankara 1959-60, Dir.-Gen. 1960-63, Deputy Sec.-Gen. 1963-64; Amb. to Finland 1964-66, to India and Ceylon 1966-68; Deputy Sec.-Gen. of NATO, Brussels 1969-71; Minister of Foreign Affairs March-Dec. 1971; Perm. Rep. to UN 1972-75, to NATO Aug. 1978-. *Address:* Turkish Delegation to NATO, Boulevard Léopold III, 1110 Brussels, Belgium.

OLDENBOURG, Zoé; French (born Russian) writer; b. 31 March 1916, Petrograd (now Leningrad); d. of Sergius Oldenbourg and Ada Starynkevitch; m. H. Idalie 1948; one s. one d.; ed. Lycée Molière and Sorbonne, Paris; in France 1925-, studied history and literature at the Sorbonne; studied theology, Great Britain 1938; mem. Jury of Prix Fémina 1961-; Prix Fémina for La pierre angulaire (The Cornerstone) 1953, Chevalier, Légion d'Honneur 1981, Commdr. de l'Ordre du Mérite des Arts et Lettres. *Publications:* Argile et cendres 1946, La pierre angulaire 1953, Bûcher de Montségur 1959, Les brûlés 1961, Les cités charnelles 1961, Les Croisades 1963, Catherine de Russie 1965, Saint Bernard 1969, La joie des pauvres 1970, L'épopée des cathédrales 1973, Que vous a donc fait Israël? 1974, Visages d'un autoportrait 1977, La joie-souffrance 1980, Le procès du rêve 1982, L'évêque et la vieille dame 1983, Que nous est Hécube? 1984, Les amours égarées 1987. *Address:* 4 rue de Montmorency, 92100 Boulogne-Billancourt, France.

OLDENBURG, Claes; American (naturalized) artist; b. 28 Jan. 1929, Stockholm, Sweden; s. of Gösta Oldenburg and Sigrid E. Lindfors; brother of Richard Oldenburg (q.v.); m. 1st Pat Muschinski 1960 (divorced 1970); m. 2nd Coosje van Bruggen 1977; ed. Yale Coll. and Art Inst. of Chicago; Apprentice reporter, City News Bureau, Chicago 1950-52; various odd jobs 1952-53; first group exhbn., Club St. Elmo, Chicago 1953; participated in other local shows, Chicago and Evanston 1953-56; moved to New York

1956; part-time job at Cooper Union Museum Library 1956-61; exhibited in group show, Red Grooms's City Gallery 1958-59; first public one-man show, Judson Gallery, New York 1959; two-man show with Jim Dine (q.v.), Judson Gallery Nov.-Dec. 1959; has since participated in numerous exhbns. of contemporary art throughout U.S.A. and Europe; several one-man shows at Sidney Janis Gallery, New York; works included in XXXII Biennale, Venice 1964; IX Bienal do Museu de Arte Moderno, São Paulo 1967; installed Giant Soft Fan in Buckminster Fuller's (q.v.) dome for U.S. Pavilion, Expo 67, Montreal 1967; travelling one-man exhbn. sponsored by Museum of Modern Art, New York shown at Tate Gallery, London and other European galleries 1970; Wilhelm Lehmbruck Sculpture Award 1981, Wolf Prize for the Arts 1989. *Publications:* Claes Oldenburg, Proposals for Monuments and Buildings 1965-69 1969, Claes Oldenburg, Drawings and Prints 1969, Notes in Hand 1971, Raw Notes 1973. *Address:* c/o Sidney Janis Gallery, 15 E 57th Street, New York, N.Y. 10022, U.S.A.

OLDENBURG, Richard Erik, A.B.; American museum director; b. 21 Sept. 1933, Stockholm, Sweden; s. of Gösta Oldenburg and Sigrid E. Lindfors; brother of Claes Oldenburg (q.v.); m. Harriet L. Turnure 1960; ed. Harvard Coll.; Man. Editor, The Macmillan Co. 1964-69; Dir. of Publications, Museum of Modern Art, New York 1969-71; Acting Dir. Museum of Modern Art Jan.-June 1972, Dir. June 1972-. *Leisure interest:* reading. *Address:* The Museum of Modern Art, 11 West 53rd Street, New York, N.Y. 10019 (Office); 447 East 57th Street, New York, N.Y. 10022, U.S.A. (Home). *Telephone:* 212-708-9773 (Office).

OLDFIELD, Bruce; British fashion designer; b. 14 July 1950; ed. Ripon Grammar School, Sheffield City Polytechnic, Ravensbourne Coll. of Art and St. Martin's Coll. of Art; grew up at Dr. Barnardo's, Ripon; established own fashion house, producing designer collections 1975; began making couture clothes for individual clients 1981; opened retail shop selling couture and ready-to-wear 1984; apptd. to Man. Bd., British Knitting and Clothing Export Council 1989; regular columnist for Welt Am Sonntag 1988-; designed for films Jackpot 1974, The Sentinel 1976; Hon. Fellow Sheffield Polytechnic 1987. *Publication:* Seasons 1987. *Leisure interests:* music, reading, driving, working. *Address:* 27 Beauchamp Place, London, S.W.3, England. *Telephone:* 01-584 1363.

O'LEARY, Michael; Irish politician; b. 8 May 1938, Cork; s. of John O'Leary and Margaret McCarthy; ed. Univ. Coll., Cork, Kings Inns Dublin; Deputy Pres. Nat. Students' Union 1960-61; Educ. Officer, Irish TUC 1962-65; T.D. for Dublin North Cen. 1965-; spokesman on Industry and Commerce, Labour, Foreign Affairs and Educ. 1965-73; Minister for Labour 1973-77; Deputy Prime Minister and Minister of Energy 1981-82; fmr. Leader, Labour Party (resgnd.); Pres. 2nd European Regional Conf., ILO 1974, Annual Conf. 1976, EEC Council of Ministers for Social Affairs Jan.-June 1975; mem. European Parl. 1979-81; resgnd. from Labour Party 1982 and joined Fine Gael Party; mem. Hon. Soc. of the Middle Temple. *Address:* Leinster House, Kildare Street, Dublin 2, Ireland.

O'LEARY, Terence Daniel, C.M.G., M.A.; British diplomatist (retd.); b. 18 Aug. 1928, London; s. of the late Daniel and Mary O'Leary; m. Janet Douglas Berney 1960; two s. one d.; ed. Dulwich Coll., St. John's Coll., Cambridge; commissioned officer Queen's Royal Regt. 1946-48; worked in industry 1951-53; Asst. Prin. Commonwealth Relations Office (later FCO) 1953, subsequently served New Zealand, India, Tanganyika, Australia, South Africa, and in Cabinet Office and as Sr. Directing Staff, Nat. Defence Coll. 1978-81; High Commr. in Sierra Leone 1981-84, in New Zealand, and concurrently to W. Samoa, and Gov. of Pitcairn Island 1984-87. *Leisure interests:* cutting grass, walking, foreign travel. *Address:* The Old Rectory, Petworth, West Sussex, England.

OLECHOWSKI, Tadeusz, M.A.; Polish diplomatist and politician; b. 10 Jan. 1926, Vilnius; m.; one c.; ed. Faculty of Law, Jagiellonian Univ., Cracow and Acad. of Trade, Cracow; Chief of Polish Trade Mission, Rangoon 1955; Commercial attaché, Polish Embassy, Burma 1956; Deputy Dir. Metalexport; with Ministry of Foreign Trade 1958-61; Commercial Attaché, Rome 1961-64; Vice-Minister of Foreign Trade 1965-69; Amb. to France 1969-72, 1976-80; Minister of Foreign Trade 1972-74; Amb. to Egypt, Yemen and Sudan 1974-76; Under-Sec. of State, Ministry of Foreign Affairs 1980-83; Amb. to Federal Repub. of Germany 1983-86; Under-Sec. of State, Ministry of Foreign Affairs 1986-88; Minister of Foreign Affairs June 1988-; mem. PZPR; Commdr.'s and Knight's Cross of Polonia Restituta Order, Order of Banner of Labour, 2nd Class; other decorations. *Leisure interest:* gardening. *Address:* Ministerstwo Spraw Zagranicznych, Al. I Armii Wojska Polskiego 23, 00-580 Warsaw, Poland.

OLESEN, Aase, Danish politician; b. 24 Sept. 1934, Horsens; teacher 1956-58; housewife 1958-70; Co-owner Tormod Olesen's architectural practice 1970-; mem. Folketing (Parl.) 1974-77, 1979-; mem. Exec. Cttee and General Council, Radical Liberal Party 1986, Sec. to Parl. Group 1980-; Chair. Parl. Social Cttee. 1987-88; Minister of Social Affairs 1988-. *Address:* Ministry of Social Affairs, Slotsholmsgade 6, 1216 Copenhagen K, Denmark. *Telephone:* (01) 12-25-17.

OLESEN, Poul; Danish physicist; b. 28 April 1939, Aalborg; s. of Viktor Olesen and Herdis Olesen; m. Birgitte Sode-Mogensen 1984; no c.; ed. Univ. of Copenhagen; Research Assoc. Univ. of Rochester, New York 1967-69; Research Assoc. CERN, Geneva 1969-71, Visiting Fellow 1985;

Prof. of Theoretical Physics, The Niels Bohr Inst. Copenhagen 1971-; mem. Royal Danish Acad. *Publications:* articles in int. journals on particle physics. *Address:* The Niels Bohr Institute, Blegdamsvej 17, 2100 Copenhagen Ø (Office); Malmmosevej 1, 2840 Holte, Denmark (Home). *Telephone:* 01 42 16 16 (Office); 02 42 55 64 (Home).

OLESIAK, Kazimierz, D. AGRIC. SC.; Polish agriculture economist and politician; b. 22 Feb. 1937, Huta Drewniana, Piotrków Trybunalski Voivodship; m.; two d.; ed. Main School of Farming, Warsaw 1961; fmr. mem. youth orgs. Polish Youth Union (ZMP) 1953-56, Rural Youth Union (ZMW) 1957-59; mem. United Peasant's Party (ZSL) 1959-; scientific worker, Econ. Agric. Faculty of Main School of Farming, Warsaw, Asst. Prof. 1974; Adviser to Deputy Chair. of Council of Ministers for Agric. Economics and Policy Matters 1967-71; Deputy Head, Presidential Dept. of ZSL Chief Cttee. 1971-75; FAO Expert, Sri Lanka 1975-76; Dir. of Office of Deputy Chair. of Council of Ministers 1976-82; Under-Sec. of State, Ministry of Finance 1982-84; mem. Presidium of Revisional Comm. of ZSL Chief Cttee. 1976-80, alt. mem. 1981-82, mem. 1984-; ZSL Chief Cttee., mem. Presidium ZSL Chief Cttee. 1984-, Sec. ZSL Chief Cttee. 1984-88; Sec. Food Economy Council 1981-85; Deputy to Seym 1985-, Deputy Chair. Seym Comm. of Agric., Forestry and Food Economy 1985-; Deputy Chair. Council of Ministers 1988-, Minister of Agric., Forestry and Food Economy 1988-; mem. Presidium of Govt. 1988-; Deputy Chair. Econ. Cttee. of Council of Ministers 1988-; Knight's and Officer's Cross of Polonia Restituta Order, Gold Cross of Merit and other decorations. *Publications:* numerous articles on agric. policy, mainly on land policy, Obrót ziemią w gospodarstwach chłopskich w rejonach uprzemysławianych 1967, Obrót i gospodarka ziemią w Polsce Ludowej 1976. *Leisure interests:* gardening, books. *Address:* Urząd Rady Ministrów, Al. Ujazdowskie 1/3, 00-583 Warsaw, Poland.

ØLGAARD, Anders, DR.POLIT.; Danish professor of economics; b. 5 Sept. 1926, Aabenraa; s. of Axel Ølgaard and Anna Lebeck; m. Alice Christiansen 1951; three c.; ed. Univ. of Copenhagen; Civil servant, Econ. Secr. 1953-60; Prof. of Econs., Univ. of Copenhagen 1962-; Adviser in Malaysia, Harvard Univ. Devt. Advisory Service 1968-69; mem., Econ. Council 1966-68; Chair. 1970-76; Pres. Danish Econ. Asscn. 1983-88. *Publications:* Growth, Productivity and Relative Prices 1966, The Danish Economy, EEC Economic and Financial Series 1980. *Address:* Institute of Economics, University of Copenhagen, 6 Studiestraede, 1455 Copenhagen (Office); 12 Lerbaekvei, 2830 Virum, Denmark (Home). *Telephone:* 01-912166 (Office); 02-851239 (Home).

OLIART SAUSSOL, Alberto; Spanish politician; b. 29 July 1928, Mérida, Badajoz; m. Carmen Delgado de Torres; six c.; ed. Univ. of Barcelona; practised as Lawyer of State at Ministry of Finance 1949-58; Head of Tech. Bureau and Advisory Dept. of Directorate-Gen. of Budgets, Ministry of Finance 1963-68; Admin. and Financial Man., then Sec.-Gen. RENFE (Spanish Nat. Railways) 1965-68; Companies' Adviser, Supreme Court 1968-; mem. Bd. and Dir.-Gen. Banco Hispano Americano 1973-, mem. Bd. Banco Urquijo 1973-, mem. Bd. RENFE; Minister of Industry and Energy 1977-78, for Health and Social Security 1980-81, for Defence 1981-82. *Address:* c/o Ministerio de Defensa, Alcalasz, Madrid 14, Spain.

OLIPHANT, Sir Mark Laurence Elwin, A.C., K.B.E., F.R.S., F.A.A., F.T.S., M.A., PH.D.; British physicist and administrator; b. 8 Oct. 1901, Adelaide, Australia; s. of Harold George Oliphant and Beatrice Fanny Tucker; m. Rosa Louise Wildbraham 1925 (died 1987); one s. one d.; ed. Adelaide Univ., and Trinity Coll., Cambridge; Messel Research Fellow, Royal Soc. 1931; Lecturer and Fellow, St. John's Coll. 1934; Asst. Dir. Research, Cavendish Lab., Cambridge 1935; Prof. and Dir. of Dept. of Physics Birmingham Univ. 1937-50, Vice-Principal Sept. 1948-49; Dir. of post-graduate Research School of Physical Sciences, Australian Nat. Univ. 1950-63; Prof. of Particle Physics 1950-64; Pres. Australian Acad. of Sciences 1954-57; Gov. of S. Australia 1971-76; Hon. Fellow, St. John's Coll., Cambridge 1952, Australian Nat. Univ. 1968-71; Hon. LL.D. (St. Andrews), Hon. D.Sc. (Toronto, Flinders, Belfast, Melbourne, Birmingham, New South Wales, Australian Nat. Univ. and Adelaide); K.St.J. *Publications:* Rutherford: Recollections of the Cambridge Days 1972, and various technical and scientific papers. *Leisure interests:* music, gardening, carpentry. *Address:* 28 Carstensz Street, Griffith, A.C.T. 2603, Australia. *Telephone:* (062) 950417.

OLIPHANT, Patrick, D.HUM.LITT.; American political cartoonist, artist and sculptor; b. 24 July 1935, Adelaide, Australia; s. of Donald K. Oliphant and Grace L. Price; m. 1st Hendrika deVries 1958 (divorced 1978); one s. two d.; m. 2nd Mary A. Kuhn 1983; copyboy, press artist, Adelaide Advertiser 1953-55, cartoonist 1955-64; cartoonist, Denver Post 1964-75, Washington Star 1975-81; now independent cartoonist syndicated through Universal Press Syndicate; Hon. L.H.D. (Dartmouth Coll.) 1981; awards include Pulitzer Prize 1967, Nat. Cartoonist of Year Award 1968, 1972, Washington Journalism Review 'Best in the Business' Award 1985. *Publications:* The Oliphant Book 1969, Four More Years 1973, An Informal Gathering 1978, Oliphant, A Cartoon Collection 1980, The Jellybean Society 1981, Ban This Book 1982, But Seriously Folks 1983, The Year of Living Perilously 1984, Make My Day! 1985, Between Rock and a Hard Place 1986, Up to Here in Alligators 1987. *Leisure interests:* skeet and trap shooting, tennis, swimming, bicycling, reading. *Address:* c/o Universal Press Syndicate, 4400 Johnson Drive Fairway, Kan. 66205, U.S.A.

OLITSKI, Jules, M.A.; American (b. Russian) painter and sculptor; b. 27 March 1922, Snovsk, Russia; s. of late Jevel Demikovsky and of Anna Zarnitsky; m. 1st Gladys Katz 1944 (divorced 1951); one d.; m. 2nd Andrea Hill Pearce 1956 (divorced 1974); one d.; m. 3rd Kristina Gorby 1980; ed. Beaux Arts Inst., N.Y., New York Univ.; Assoc. Prof. of Art, State Univ. Coll., New Paltz 1954-55; Curator New York Univ. Art Educ. Gallery 1955-56; Art Instructor, Co-ordinator Fine Arts Dept., C. W. Post Coll., Long Island Univ. 1956-63; Art Teacher Bennington Coll., Vt. 1963-67; one-man exhbns. of paintings, drawings and sculpture in U.S.A. at Corcoran Gallery, Washington, D.C. 1967, 1974, 1975, Metropolitan Museum of Art, New York 1969, retrospective exhbn. at Museum of Fine Arts, Boston 1973, Galleria dell' Ariete, Milan 1974, Knoedler Contemporary Arts, New York 1974-77, Waddington Gallery, London 1975, Boston Museum of Fine Art 1977, Galeria Wentzel, Fed. Repub. of Germany 1975, 1977, Hirshhorn Museum, Washington 1977; exhbns. at Galerie Huit, Paris 1950, Kasmin Gallery, London 1964-75, David Mirvish Gallery, Toronto 1964-77, André Emmerich Gallery, New York 1966-77, Zürich 1973-74, one-man exhbn. Edmonton Art Gallery, Canada 1978; numerous group exhbns. in U.S.A., Canada, France, Fed. Repub. of Germany; chosen for Carnegie Int. 1961, 1967, for Venice Biennale 1966; Second Prize Carnegie Int. 1961, First Prize Corcoran Biennal 1967. *Publications:* The Courage of Conviction (essay) 1985, How I Got My First New York Show (essay) 1989. *Address:* 207 Fifth Avenue, Brooklyn, New York, N.Y. 11215, U.S.A. *Telephone:* (718) 636-9753.

OLIVE, David Ian, M.A., PH.D., F.R.S.; British professor of theoretical physics; b. 16 April 1937, Staines; m. Jenifer Tutton 1963; two d.; ed. Royal High School, Edinburgh and Univs. of Edinburgh and Cambridge; Fellow, Churchill Coll., Cambridge 1963-70; Asst. Lecturer, lecturer, Univ. of Cambridge 1965-71; staff mem. CERN Theory Div. 1971-77; lecturer, Reader, Blackett Lab. Imperial Coll., London 1977-84, Prof. of Theoretical Physics 1984-. *Publications:* The Analytic S-Matrix (with others) 1965; many scientific papers and articles on the theory of elementary particles and their symmetries. *Leisure interests:* golf, listening to music. *Address:* Blackett Laboratory, Imperial College, London, SW7 2BZ (Office); 54 The Avenue, Kew, Richmond, Surrey, TW9 2AH, England (Home). *Telephone:* 01-589 5111 Ext. 6974 (Office).

OLIVEIRA, Gen. Araken de; Brazilian army officer; ed. Escola Militar, Realengo, Command and Gen. Staff School and Catholic Univ.; Instructor, Escola Militar Realengo and Command and Gen. Staff School; Gunnery Officer, then Operations Officer, First Howitzer Battalion, Brazilian Expeditionary Force; with Command and Gen. Staff, Officer in War Minister's Office; promoted to rank of Gen.; Chief, President's Office, Nat. Oil Council, later Pres.; Pres. Petrobrás 1974-78; Commdr., Order of Merit and several other mil. honours. *Address:* c/o Petrobrás, Avenida República do Chile 65, C.P. 809, Rio de Janeiro, RJ, Brazil.

OLIVEIRA, Manoel de; Portuguese film director; b. 1908, Oporto. *Films include:* Douro, Faina Fluvial 1931, Aniki-Bóbó 1942, O Pinto e a Cidade 1956, O Pão 1959, O Acto da Primavera 1963, A Caca 1964, O Passado e Presente 1972, Benilde ou A Virgem Mae 1975, Amor de Perdição 1979, Francisca 1981.

OLIVER, Covey T., M.A., J.D., LL.M., JURIS SCI.DR.; American lawyer, diplomatist and legal scholar; b. 21 April 1913, Laredo, Texas; s. of Pheneas Noah Oliver and Jane Covey Thomas; m. Barbara Frances Hauer 1946; two s. three d.; ed. Univ. of Texas and Columbia Univ.; Prof. of Law, Univs. of Tex., Calif. (Berkeley) and Pa. 1936-41, 1949-64, 1966-67, 1969-; U.S. Govt. official (mainly in Dept. of State) 1942-49; Amb. to Colombia 1964-66; Asst. Sec. of State for Inter-American Affairs and U.S. Coordinator of Alliance for Progress 1967-69; U.S. Exec. Dir. IBRD 1969; Carnegie Endowment Lecturer, Hague Acad. of Int. Law 1955, 1974, Emer. 1981-; Hubbell Prof. of Law, Univ. of Pa. 1966-78, Emer. 1978-; Radoslav A. Tsanoff Prof. of Public Affairs, Rice Univ. Houston 1978-; Visiting Prof., Washington Coll. of Law, American Univ., Washington, D.C. 1982-85, Distinguished Prof. Southern Methodist Univ., Dallas, Texas 1984 and 1986; Special Adviser U.S. Del. to UN Law of the Sea Conf. 1976; Pres. American Soc. of Int. Law 1982-84; mem. Bd. of Eds. American Journal of Int. Law. *Publications:* The Restatement of the Foreign Relations Law of the United States (co-author), The Inter-American Security System and the Cuban Crisis, Law and Politics in the World Community (co-author), Cases and Materials on the International Legal System (co-author) 3rd Ed. 1988, The Regulation of International Trade, Direct Foreign Investment and Financial Transactions 1980; and monographs and articles in legal and foreign affairs periodicals. *Leisure interests:* boating, observance of nature, cultural anthropology. *Address:* R.F.D. 1, Box 194, Easton, Md. 21601; Inverness, Calif. 94937, U.S.A. *Telephone:* (301) 822-4498 and (415) 669-7580.

OLIVER, Roland, PH.D.; British Africanist; b. 30 March 1923, Srinagar, Kashmir; m. Caroline Linehan 1947; one d.; ed. Cambridge Univ.; Lecturer, SOAS., Univ. of London 1948-49, 1950-57, Reader 1958-63, Prof. of African History 1963-86; organized first confs. on history and archaeology of Africa, London Univ. 1953, 1957, 1961; founded and edited Journal of African History 1960-73; Pres. British Inst. in E. Africa 1981-; Chair. Minority Rights Group. *Publications:* The Missionary Factor in East Africa 1952, Sir Harry Johnston and the Scramble for East Africa 1957, The Dawn of African History 1961, Short History of Africa (with J. D. Fage)

1962, History of East Africa (with G. Mathew) 1963, Africa since 1800 (with A. Atmore) 1967, Africa in the Iron Age (with B. M. Fagan) 1975, The African Middle Ages 1400-1800 (with A. Atmore) 1980, general editor Cambridge History of Africa 8 vols. 1975-86. *Address:* Frilsham Woodhouse, near Newbury, Berkshire, RG16 9XB, England. *Telephone:* (0635) 201407.

OLIVER of AYLMERTON, Baron (Life Peer), cr. 1986, of Aylmerton in the County of Norfolk; **Peter Raymond Oliver,** Kt., P.C.; British lawyer; b. 7 March 1921; s. of David Thomas Oliver and Alice Maud Oliver; m. 1st Mary Chichester Rideal 1945 (died 1985), one s. one d.; m. 2nd Wendy Anne Oliver 1987; ed. The Leys, Cambridge, Trinity Hall, Cambridge; Mil. Service 1941-45; called to Bar, Lincoln's Inn 1948, Bencher 1973; Q.C. 1965; Judge of the High Court of Justice, Chancery Div. 1974-80; mem. Restrictive Practices Court 1976-80; Chair. Review Body on Chancery Div. of High Court 1979-81; Lord Justice of Appeal 1980-85; Lord of Appeal in Ordinary 1986-; Hon. Fellow, Trinity Hall, Cambridge 1980. *Leisure interests:* gardening, music. *Address:* House of Lords, London, S.W.1 (Office); 24 Westbourne Park Road, London, W.2, England (Home). *Telephone:* 01-229 1058 (Home).

OLIVIER, Baron (Life Peer), cr. 1970, of Brighton; **Laurence Kerr Olivier,** Kt., O.M.; British actor and director; b. 22 May 1907; s. of the late Rev. G. K. Olivier and Agnes Louise Crookenden; m. 1st Jill Esmond 1930 (divorced 1940), one s.; m. 2nd Vivien Leigh 1940 (divorced 1961); m. 3rd Joan Plowright (q.v.) 1961, one s. two d.; ed. St. Edward's School, Oxford; First appearance, The Taming of the Shrew, Stratford 1922; Birmingham Repertory Co. 1925-28; subsequent appearances in London, New York, Paris and Denmark; Old Vic Theatre Co. 1944-45, 1949, toured Australia and New Zealand 1948; Actor-Manager, St. James's Theatre, London 1950-51; Shakespeare Memorial Theatre, Stratford-on-Avon 1955; Dir. Chichester Festival Theatre 1962-65, The National Theatre 1962-73; mem. South Bank Theatre Bd. 1967-; Hon. D.Litt. (Oxon., Manchester, London, Sussex), Hon. LL.D. (Edin.), Hon. M.A. (Tuft's); Chevalier, Légion d'honneur; Commdr., Order of Dannebrog (Denmark) and Grand Officer, Ordine al Merito della Repubblica (Italy); Acad. Award 1948; Sonning Prize (Denmark) 1966; Gold Medallion, Swedish Acad. of Literature 1968; Order of Yugoslav Flag with Gold Wreath 1971, Albert Medal, R.S.A. 1976; Hon. Acad. Award 1979. *Stage appearances include:* many Shakespearian, classical and modern plays; produced and appeared in Venus Observed, Caesar and Cleopatra, The Broken Heart, Uncle Vanya, etc.; National Theatre appearances include Uncle Vanya, Othello, Master Builder, Love for Love, The Dance of Death, A Flea in Her Ear, The Merchant of Venice, Long Day's Journey into Night, Saturday Sunday Monday, The Party; Dir. Eden End 1974. *Films include:* Wuthering Heights, Rebecca, Pride and Prejudice, 49th Parallel, Carrie, Beggar's Opera, The Devil's Disciple, Spartacus, The Entertainer, Term of Trial, Khartoum, Othello, The Shoes of the Fisherman, The Dance of Death 1968, Battle of Britain, Oh! What a Lovely War, Three Sisters 1969, David Copperfield, Nicholas and Alexandra, Lady Caroline Lamb, Sleuth, Seven Per Cent Solution 1975, Marathon Man 1975, A Bridge Too Far 1976, Jesus of Nazareth 1976, The Betsy 1977, The Boys from Brazil 1978, A Little Romance 1978, Dracula 1978, Clash of the Titans 1979, Inchon 1979, The Jazz Singer 1980, Richard Wagner 1982, The Bounty 1984, Wild Geese II 1984, Peter the Great, War Requiem 1988; produced, directed and played in Henry V, Hamlet, Richard III and The Prince and the Showgirl. *Television appearances include:* John Gabriel Borkman, The Moon and Sixpence, The Power and the Glory, Long Day's Journey into Night, The Merchant of Venice, World at War (narrator) 1973, Love among the Ruins 1974, Jesus of Nazareth 1976, Brideshead Revisited (Emmy Award) 1978/80, A Voyage Round My Father 1982, King Lear 1982, Mr. Halpern and Mr. Johnson; television productions include The Best Play of the Year 19— (a series of plays) 1976, 1977, The Ebony Tower 1984. *Publications:* Confessions of an Actor 1982, On Acting 1986. *Leisure interests:* tennis, flying, gardening. *Address:* c/o Write on Cue, 10 Garrick Street, London, WC2A E9BH, England.

OLIVIER, Louis, D. EN D.; Belgian politician; b. 19 July 1923, Bastogne; m. Marie-José Leclerq 1946; one s. three d.; Local Councillor 1958-; Mayor of Bastogne 1965-; Provincial Councillor 1954-; Vice-Pres. Provincial Council of Luxembourg 1956; Vice-Pres. Soc. de Développement Economique du Luxembourg, Conseil Economique du Luxembourg, Asscn. Intercommunale du Luxembourg pour la Valorisation de l'Eau; mem. House of Reps. for Arlon-Marche-Bastogne 1965-, Intercommunale de Développement Economique du Luxembourg; Sec. of State for Inst. Reforms and Admin. (Wallonia) 1973-74; Minister of the Middle Classes 1973-76; Sec. of State for Forestry, Hunting and Fishing (Wallonia) 1974-79; Minister of Public Works 1976-77, 1981-88, and of the Middle Classes 1983, Vice-Pres. Chamber of Reps. 1980-81. *Leisure interest:* economic problems. *Address:* Place MacAuliffe 31, 6650 Bastogne, Belgium.

OLIWA, Gen. Włodzimierz; Polish politician; b. 17 Nov. 1924, Sułkowice; m.; one s. one d.; ed. Tadeusz Kościuszko Infantry Coll., Cracow, Acad. of Gen. Staff of Armed Forces of U.S.S.R., Moscow; mil. service in People's Polish Army 1945-; various commanding posts and posts in political apparatus of Polish Army, including Deputy Divisional Commdr. and Corps Commdr. 1947-59; Chief of Organizational Board of Gen. Political Board Polish Army 1960-65; Brig.-Gen. 1963; Chief of Bd., Gen. Staff 1965-71;

Commdr. Tadeusz Kościuszko I Mechanized Div. 1971–72; Commdr. Warsaw Mil. Dist. 1973–83; Divisional Gen. 1974; mem. Mil. Council for Nat. Salvation 1981–83; Minister of Admin. and Spatial Econ. 1983–85; Chief Quartermaster of Polish Army; Vice-Minister of Nat. Defence 1985–; Deputy to Seym 1976–85; Gen. of Arms 1986; mem. PZPR 1948–; Commdr.'s Cross with Star and Commdr.'s Cross Order of Polonia Restituta, Order of Banner of Labour (1st Class) and other distinctions. *Address:* Ministerstwo Obrony Narodowej, 00-909 Warsaw, Poland.

OLLILA, Esko Juhani, LL.M.; Finnish politician and bank executive; b. 14 July 1940, Rovaniemi; s. of Heikki Armas Ollila and Lempi Maria (née Häggman) Ollila; m. Riitta Leena, née Huhtala 1963; two s.; Credit Officer Skopbank 1964–65; Asst. and Notary Lapland Judicial Dist. 1965–66; Attorney, Rovaniemi Colonization Dist. 1966–67; Attorney-at-law 1967–71; Man. Dir. Rovaniemi Savings Bank 1971–75; Man. Dir. and Chair. Bd. Regional Devt. Fund of Finland 1975–79; mem. Bd. Skopbank 1979–83; Minister of Trade and Industry 1982–83; First Minister of Finance 1986–87; mem. Bd. Bank of Finland 1983–; Chair. Supervisory Bd. Enso-Gutzeit Oy 1983–; mem. Supervisory Bd. Tervakoski Oy 1983–86; mem. Bd. Mortgage Bank of Finland Ltd. 1983–86, Industrialization Fund of Finland Ltd. 1984–85, Chair. 1985–86. *Leisure interest:* literature. *Address:* c/o Bank of Finland, Snellmaninaukio, 00170 Helsinki 17, Finland.

OLLOQUI, Dr. José Juan de; Mexican banker and diplomatist; b. 5 Nov. 1931, México, D.F.; s. of Fernando de Olloqui and Margarita Labastida de Olloqui; m. Guillermina G. de Olloqui 1962; three s. one d.; ed. Nat. Autonomous Univ. of Mexico and George Washington Univ.; fmr. Prof. of Econs. at various Mexican Univs.; served in Banco de México; fmr. Head, Dept. of Banks, Currency and Investment, Secr. of Finance and Public Credit; fmr. Dir.-Gen. of Credit; fmr. mem. Bd. of Dirs. of several Mexican credit insts. and technical orgs.; Exec. Dir. for Mexico, Barbados, Dominican Repub., Jamaica and Panama, Inter-American Devt. Bank 1966–71; Dir. Nat. Stock Comm. 1971; Amb. to U.S.A. 1971–76 (also accred. to Barbados 1973–76), to U.K. 1979–82 (also accred. to Ireland 1980–82); Under-Sec. of Foreign Relations 1976–79; Dir. Gen. Banca Serfin, Mexico 1982–; fmr. Chair. Euro-Latinamerican Bank Ltd. (Eulabank) London; mem. Bd. Trustees Nat. Univ. of Mexico Feb. 1983–; Prof. of Int. Law Research, Nat. Univ. of Mexico April 1983–; D.Hum.Litt. h.c. (St. Mary's Coll.) 1975; Hon. Eminent Amb. 1982 and decorations from Spain, Fed. Repub. of Germany, Brazil, Hungary, Colombia, Bulgaria, France. *Publications:* México fuera de México (Mexico outside Mexico), translations and articles. *Leisure interests:* hunting, weight-lifting. *Address:* Banca Serfin S.A., 16 de Septiembre 38, 06000 México, D.F. (Office); Francisco Sosa No. 78, Coyoacan, 04000 México D.F., México (Home). *Telephone:* 521-9578; (Office); 554-0833 (Home).

OLMI, Ermanno; Italian film director; b. 1931, Bergamo; fmr. clerk, Edison-Volta electric plant; later dir. and produced sponsored documentary films; made first feature film 1959. *Films include:* Il Tempo si è Fermato 1959, Il Posto 1961, I Fidanzati 1963, E Venne un Uomo 1965, Un Certo Giorno 1969, I Recuperanti 1970, Durante l'Estate 1971, La Circostanza 1974, L'Albero degli Zoccoli (Palme d'Or, Cannes) 1978, Legend of a Holy Drinker 1988.

OLSEN, Olaf, PH.D.; Danish archaeologist, historian and museum director; b. 7 June 1928, Copenhagen; s. of the late Prof. Albert Olsen and of Agnete Bing; m. 1st Jean Catherine Dennistoun Sword, one s; m. 2nd Rikke Agnete Clausen 1971; ed. Copenhagen Univ.; Asst., Medieval Dept., Nat. Museum 1950–58, Asst. Keeper 1958–71, State Antiquary and Dir. Nat. Museum 1981–; Prof. of Medieval Archaeology, Aarhus Univ. 1971–81; Dir. Hielmstierne-Rosencrone Foundation 1979–; Vice-Pres. Det kgl. nordiske Oldskriftselskab 1981–, Royal Danish Acad. of Sciences and Letters 1983–; Dir. numerous archaeological excavations, mainly of Viking ships and fortresses and medieval churches and monasteries; Hon. Fellow, Soc. of Antiquaries; GEC Gad Foundation Prize 1966. *Publications:* numerous books and papers on history and medieval archaeology. *Address:* Nationalmuseet, Frederiksholms Kanal 12, DK-1220 København K (Office); Lille Mølle, Christianshavns Voldgade 50, DK-1424 København K, Denmark. *Telephone:* 01-134411 (Office); 01-575534 (Home).

OLSEN, Torkil, M.A.; Danish librarian; b. 31 March 1922, Copenhagen; s. of late L. M. and Ellen Olsen; ed. Copenhagen Univ.; Asst., Univ. Library, Copenhagen 1945, Asst. Librarian 1951; Leading Librarian, Atomic Energy Comm. Library, Risø 1957; Chief Librarian, Odense Univ. Library 1965; Chair. Bookcraft Soc. 1975–78; Nat. Librarian 1982–86, Consultant at the Office of the Nat. Librarian 1986–. *Address:* Godthåbsvej 74, 2', B.21, DK-2000, Copenhagen F, Denmark. *Telephone:* 01-87 36 90.

OLSON, Allen Ingvar, J.D.; American lawyer and politician; b. 5 Nov. 1938, Rolla, N.D.; s. of Elmer Martin and Olga (Sundin) Olson; m. Barbara Starr Benner 1964; one s. two d.; ed. Univ. of North Dakota; admitted to N.D. bar 1963, U.S. Supreme Court bar 1967; Asst. Dir. North Dakota Legis. Council 1967–69; partner Conmy, Rosenberg, Lucas and Olson, Bismarck, N.D. 1969–72; Attorney-Gen., State of N.D., Bismarck 1972–80; Gov. of North Dakota 1981–85; Dir. Bank of N.D.; Republican. *Address:* 400 East Oway, Bismarck, N.D. 58502, U.S.A.

OLSON, Everett C., PH.D.; American vertebrate paleobiologist; b. 6 Nov. 1910, Waupaca, Wis.; s. of Myron Claire Olson and Aimee Hicks; m. Lil

R. Baker 1939; one s. two d.; ed. Univ. of Chicago; Dept. of Geology Univ. of Chicago 1935–69, Assoc. Dean Physical Sciences 1942–58, Chair. Cttee. on Paleozoology 1948–68, Prof. of Geology 1958–62; Prof. of Zoology, Univ. of Calif., Los Angeles 1969–77, Chair. Dept. of Zoology 1971–73, Prof. Emer. 1977–; Ed. Evolution 1952–58, Journal of Geology 1962–67; Pres. Soc. for Study of Evolution, Soc. of Vertebrate Paleontology, Soc. of Systematic Zoology; mem. N.A.S.; Paleontological Medal (Soc. of Paleontology), Vertebrate Paleontology Medal (Soc. of Vertebrate Paleontology). *Publications:* Morphological Integration (with R. Miller), Concepts of Evolution (with J. Robinson), Vertebrate Paleozoology, Upper Permian Vertebrates U.S.A.-U.S.S.R., Zoology (with M. Gordon, J. O'Connor, G. Bartholomew), Community Evolution and the Origin of Mammals. *Leisure interests:* lepidoptery, piano. *Address:* Department of Zoology, University of California, Los Angeles, Calif. 90024, U.S.A. *Telephone:* (213) 825-6677.

OLSON, Horace Andrew (Bud), P.C.; Canadian farmer; b. 6 Oct. 1925, Iddesleigh, Alberta; s. of Carl J. Olson and Alta I. (née Perry); m. Lucille McLachlan; one s. three d.; ed. Iddesleigh and Medicine Hat, Alberta; mem. for Medicine Hat, Canadian House of Commons 1957–58, 1962–72; Minister of Agric. 1968–72, Minister of State for Econ. Devt. 1980–81, for Econ. and Regional Devt. 1981–82; Chair. Alberta Liberal Caucus 1973–74; mem. Senate April 1977–, House Leader Official Opposition 1979, Deputy Leader 1979, Leader 1982–84; Chair. Senate Cttee. on Northern Pipeline 1978; Minister responsible for Northern Pipeline Agency 1980–84; Minister of Economic Devt. 1980–82; mem. UN Gen. Assembly Oct.–Nov. 1966; mem. Commonwealth Parliamentary del. to Nigeria 1962, Canadian Parliamentary del. to U.S.S.R. and Czechoslovakia 1965, Econ. Council of Canada 1975–78, Inter-Parliamentary Union del. Bulgaria 1977; Hon. Col. South Alberta Light Horse Regt.; Centennial Medal 1967; Citation for Distinguished Citizenship, Medicine Hat College 1968, Queen's Silver Jubilee Medal 1977; Liberal. *Leisure interests:* hunting, fishing. *Address:* Iddesleigh, Alberta T0J 1T0, Canada (Home). *Telephone:* (613) 992-4297 (Office); (403) 898-2511 (Home).

OLSSON, Curt G., B.SC.ECON.; Swedish banker; b. 20 Aug. 1927, Mjällby; s. of N. E. and Anna (née Nilsson) Olsson; m. Asta Olsson 1954; two d.; Man. Dir. Swedish Bank Giro Centre 1959; Deputy Man. and Head of Marketing, Skandinaviska Banken, Stockholm 1964, Man. and Head of Central Management Group 1966, Man. Dir. (Stockholm Group) 1970; Man. Dir. Skandinaviska Enskilda Banken, Stockholm Group 1972; Man. Dir. and Chief Exec. Head Office, Stockholm 1976–82, 1st Deputy Chair. of Bd. 1982–84, Chair. March 1984–; Chair. of Bd., Esselte AB, Stockholm Chamber of Commerce, Svenska Dagbladets AB, Dir. Atlas Copco AB, Fastighets AB Hufvudstaden, Försäkrings AB Skandia, Swedish Bankers' Assen.; mem. Royal Swedish Acad. of Eng. Sciences, Inst. Int. d'Etudes Bancaires; Kt., Order of Vasa, H.M. King Carl XVI Gustaf's Gold Medal, Commdr. Royal Norwegian Order of Merit, Commdr. Order of the Lion of Finland. *Address:* Skandinaviska Enskilda Banken, S-106 40 Stockholm, Sweden. *Telephone:* 22 19 00.

OLSZEWSKI, Kazimierz; Polish politician (retd.); b. 9 Aug. 1917, Trześniowo, Lwów (now Lvov, U.S.S.R.); ed. Lwów Polytechnical Univ.; worked at State Artificial Fibres Factory, Jelenia Góra 1947, later at Design Office of Artificial Fibre Industry Łódź; Dir. of Dept., Ministry of Chemical Industry 1952–55, Vice-Minister of Chemical Industry 1955–59; del. to COMECON, Moscow 1959–61; First Vice-Chair. Cttee. on Econ. Co-operation with Foreign Countries, Council of Ministers 1962–70; Asst. Rep. of Polish Govt. at COMECON 1970–71, Perm. Rep. 1975–77, Chair. Exec. Cttee. 1976–77; Minister of Foreign Trade 1971–72; Vice-Pres., Council of Ministers 1972–77; Minister of Shipping 1973–74, of Foreign Trade and Maritime Econ. April-Nov. 1974; Amb. to U.S.S.R. 1978–82; mem. Cen. Cttee. PZPR 1971–81; Deputy to Seym 1976–80; Order of Banner of Labour (1st Class), Cross of Valour, Order of Builders of People's Poland 1974, etc.

OLSZOWSKI, Stefan, M.A.; Polish politician; b. 28 Aug. 1931, Toruń; m. 1st (divorced); m. 2nd Zofia Skowron 1988; one s.; ed. Łódź Univ.; fmr. mem. Polish Pathfinders' Org., Polish Students' Assen., Presidium of Polish Youth Union; mem. Central Bd. Polish Youth Union 1954–56; later Polish rep. at Int. Union of Students, Prague; Chair. Cen. Council, Polish Students' Assen. 1956–60; mem. Cen. Cttee. Socialist Youth Union 1956–60; Sec. Voivodship Cttee. Polish United Workers' Party (PZPR) in Poznań 1960–63; Head of Press Bureau, Cen. Cttee. of PZPR 1963–68, mem. Cen. Cttee. 1964–86, Sec. 1968–71, 1976–80, 1980–82; mem. Political Bureau 1970–80, 1980–86; Chair. Ideological Comm. of Cen. Cttee. 1981–86; Minister of Foreign Affairs 1971–76, 1982–85; Amb. to G.D.R. March-Oct. 1980; Deputy to Seym 1969–80; mem. Presidium All-Poland Cttee. of Nat. Unity Front 1981–83; Order of the Banner of Labour (1st and 2nd class), Officer's Cross of Order of Polonia Restituta and others. *Address:* Living in New York (1988).

OLUFOSOYE, Rt. Rev. Timothy Omotayo, D.D., S.T.H.; Nigerian ecclesiastic; b. 31 March 1918, Ondo; m. 1947; one s. three d.; ed. St. Andrew's Coll., Oyo and Univ. of British Columbia; Bishop of Gambia and Rio Pongas 1965–70; Bishop of Ibadan 1970; Archbishop of Nigeria 1979–88; Officer, Order of the Niger; Kt. Commdr. of African Redemption. *Publications:* Glossary of Ecclesiastical Terms, My Memoirs, The Beacon, The Rubric, Ibadan Ecclesia Anglicana. *Leisure interests:* poultry, reading, writing, travelling. *Address:* 12 Awosika Street, P.O. Box 1666, Bodija Estate, Ibadan, Oyo State, Nigeria. *Telephone:* 022 412580.

OLULEYE, Maj.-Gen. James Johnson; Nigerian army officer and politician; b. 14 Oct. 1937, Effon-Alaye, Ondo State; ed. St. Luke's Coll., Ibadan, Regular Officers' Special Training School, Ghana, Nigerian Mil. Training Coll., Kaduna, Defence Services Staff Coll., Wellington, India; worked as a teacher 1947–59; joined Nigerian Army as Officer Cadet 1959; promoted Second Lieut. 1960; with First Bn., Enugu 1961–63; Chief Mortar Instructor, Nigerian Mil. Training Coll. 1964–65, Commdt. 1966; served as Operations Officer, Nigerian Army HQ, during civil war, Gen. Officer Commanding Second Infantry Div. 1970–75; Fed. Commr. for Establishments 1975–77, for Finance 1977–79; mem. Supreme Mil. Council 1975–79; decorations from Senegal and Mauritania. *Address:* c/o Ministry of Finance, Lagos, Nigeria.

O'MALLEY, Desmond Joseph, B.C.L.; Irish politician and solicitor; b. 2 Feb. 1939, Limerick; s. of Desmond J. and Una O'Malley; m. Patricia McAleer 1965; two s. four d.; ed. Crescent Coll., Limerick, Nat. Univ. of Ireland; practised as solicitor 1962; mem. Dáil (House of Reps.) for Limerick East 1968–; mem. Limerick Corpn. 1974–77; Parl. Sec. to Taoiseach (Prime Minister) and to Minister for Defence 1969–70; Minister for Justice 1970–73; Opposition Spokesman on Health 1973–75, on Industry and Commerce 1975–77; Minister for Industry and Commerce 1977–81, for Energy 1977–80; Opposition Spokesman on Industry and Commerce 1981–82; Minister for Trade, Commerce and Tourism 1982; Opposition Spokesman on Energy 1983–84; fmrly. Fianna Fáil (expelled 1984); co-f. and Leader of Progressive Democrats Party 1985–. *Leisure interest:* golf. *Address:* c/o Leinster House, Kildare Street, Dublin 2, Ireland. *Telephone:* (01) 789911.

OMAN, Julia Trevelyan, C.B.E., R.D.I., F.C.S.D., DES.R.C.A.; British designer; b. 11 July 1930, London; d. of Charles Chichele Oman and Joan Trevelyan; m. Dr. (now Sir) Roy Strong (q.v.) 1971; ed. Royal Coll. of Art; Designer BBC Television 1955–67 (including TV film Alice in Wonderland 1966); designer for theatre: Brief Lives (London and New York) 1967, 1974, Country Dance 1967, Forty Years On 1968, The Merchant of Venice 1970, Othello 1971, Getting On 1971, The Importance of Being Earnest (Burgtheater, Wien) 1976; ballet: Enigma Variations (Royal Ballet, London) 1968; opera: Eugene Onegin (Covent Garden) 1971, Un Ballo in Maschera (Hamburg) 1973, La Bohème (Covent Garden) 1974, A Month in the Country (Royal Ballet, London) 1976, Die Fledermaus (Covent Garden) 1977, Le Papillon (Ashton, Pas-de-Deux) 1977; films: The Charge of the Light Brigade (art dir.) 1967, Laughter in the Dark (art dir.) 1968, Julius Caesar (production designer) 1969, Straw Dogs (design consultant) 1971; exhbns.: Samuel Pepys (Nat. Portrait Gallery) 1970, Hay Fever (Danish TV) 1979; Designer Mme Tussaud's Hall of Historical Tableaux 1979, Hay Fever (Lyric, Hammersmith) 1980, The Wild Duck (Lyric, Hammersmith) 1980, Sospiri (Ashton, Pas-de-Deux) 1980, The Bear's Quest for the Ragged Staff—A Spectacle, Warwick Castle 1981, Swan Lake, Boston Ballet 1981, The Shoemaker's Holiday, Nat. Theatre 1981, Die Csárdasfürstin, Kassel, Fed. Repub. of Germany 1982, Separate Tables 1982, Otello, Stockholm 1983, Arabella, Glyndebourne Opera 1984, Nutcracker, Royal Ballet Covent Garden 1984, The Consul, Edin. and U.S.A. 1985, Mr. & Mrs. Nobody 1986, A Man for All Seasons (Chichester Festival and Savoy, London) 1987; Dept. Educ. and Science Visiting Cttee., Royal Coll. of Art 1980; Dir. Oman Productions Ltd.; Hon. D. Litt. (Bristol) 1987; Silver Medal, Royal Coll. of Art; Royal Scholar, Royal Coll. of Art; elected, Royal Designer for Industry (R.D.I.), Designer, Royal Coll. of Art; Designer of the Year Award 1967, ACE Award for Best Art Dir., NCTA, U.S.A. 1983. *Publications:* Street Children (with B. S. Johnson) 1964, Elizabeth R. (with Roy Strong) 1971, Mary Queen of Scots (with Roy Strong) 1972, The English Year (with Roy Strong) 1982. *Address:* c/o Curtis Brown, 162–168 Regent Street, London, W1R 5TA, England; c/o Clifford Stevens, 888 Seventh Avenue, 18th Floor, New York, N.Y. 10019, U.S.A. *Telephone:* 01-437 9700 (London); (212) 246-1030 (New York).

OMAR, Dato Abu Hassan Bin Haj; Malaysian politician; b. 15 Sept. 1940, Bukit Belimbing, Kuala Selangor; m. Datin Wan Noor bint Haj Daud; five c.; ed. Univ. of Hull; fmr. Deputy State Sec. State of Selangor and Deputy Sec.-Gen. Ministry of Land and Fed. Devt.; mem. Parl. 1978–; Parl. Sec. Ministry of Commerce and Industry 1978–80; Deputy Minister of Defence 1980–81, of Transport 1981–84; Minister of Welfare Services 1984–86, of Fed. Territory 1986–87, of Foreign Affairs May 1987–; mem. UMNO Supreme Council 1978–; recipient of several awards. *Leisure interests:* gardening, photography. *Address:* Ministry of Foreign Affairs, Wisma Putra, Jalan Wisma Putra, 50602 Kuala Lumpur, Malaysia.

OMARI, Dunstan Alfred, M.B.E., B.A., DIP. ED.; Kenyan (naturalized 1972) business executive and former civil servant; b. 1922, Newala, Tanzania; s. of Rev. Alphege and Josephine Omari; m. Fidelia Shangali 1962; two s. one d.; ed. St. Joseph's Secondary School, Chidya, St. Andrew's Secondary School, Minaki, Makerere Univ. Coll. and Univ. of Wales (Aberystwyth); Educ. Officer (Broadcasting Duties) 1953–54; District Officer 1955–58; District Commr. 1958–61; Tanganyika High Commr. in the U.K. 1961–62; Perm. Sec., Prime Minister's Office, and Sec. to the Cabinet, Tanganyika 1962; Perm. Sec., President's Office, and Sec. to the Cabinet, Tanganyika 1962–63; Sec.-Gen. E. African Common Services Org. 1964–67, 1967–68 (since called E. African Community); Chair. E. African Currency Bd.

1964–72; mem. Presidential Comm. of Inquiry into the Structure and Remuneration of Public Service in Kenya 1970–71; Chair. E. African Railways Salaries Review Comm. 1971–72; Chair. Kenya Bd. of Standard Bank Ltd. 1974–. *Publication:* Talks on Citizenship 1954. *Address:* P.O. Box 25015, Nairobi, Kenya. *Telephone:* Nairobi 333731.

Ó MORÁIN, Dónall; Irish public official; b. 6 Sept. 1923; s. of Mícheál Ó Móráin and Eibhlín Ní Loingsigh; m. Maire Beaumont 1949; three s. two d.; ed. Coláiste Muire, Dublin, Univ. Coll., Dublin, and King's Inns, Dublin; called to the Bar 1946; Man. Ed. of Retail Food Trade Journal 1946–50; Gen. Man., printing and publishing firm 1951–63; Founder, Gael-Linn (voluntary nat. cultural and social asscn.) 1953, Chair. 1953–63, Dir.-Gen. 1963–; Chair. Convocation of Nat. Univ. of Ireland 1955–84; Chair. Inisfree Handknits Group 1965–; mem. Radio Telefis Eireann Authority 1965–70, Chair. 1970–72, 1973–76; mem. Language Consultative Council, Dept. of Finance 1965–75; Dir. Glens of Antrim Tweed Co. Ltd. 1967–79; mem. Irish Comm. for UNESCO 1966–, Irish Film Industry Comm. 1967–69; Chair. Consultative Council to Radio na Gaeltachta (first local radio service in Ireland) 1971–76; Hon. LL.D. (Nat. Univ. of Ireland) 1979; founder and Man. Dir. Anois, Sunday newspaper 1984–. *Leisure interests:* fowling, salmon fishing. *Address:* 32 Sydney Avenue, Blackrock, Dublin, Ireland. *Telephone:* Dublin 880541.

OMOROGBE, Oluyinka Osayame, LL.B.; Nigerian lecturer and legal practitioner; b. 21 Sept. 1957, Ibadan; d. of Samuel O. Ighodaro and Irene E. B. Ighodaro; m. Allan Omarogbe 1984; one s.; ed. Univ. of Ife and L.S.E.; Nat. Youth Service 1979–80; Pvt. Legal Practitioner 1980–81; lecturer Dept. of Jurisprudence and Int. Law, Univ. of Benin 1983–, Head of Dept. Oct. 1988–; mem. Exec. Cttee. Petroleum Energy and Mining Law Asscn. of Nigeria 1986–. *Publications:* numerous articles on petroleum and energy law in int. journals. *Leisure interests:* cooking, baking, handcrafts. *Address:* 4 Izoduwa Way, P.O. Box 4202, Benin City, Nigeria. *Telephone:* (052) 247704.

ONANA-AWANA, Charles; Cameroonian politician; b. 1923, Ngoulemekong; ed. Ecole Supérieure, Yaoundé and Ecole nat. de la France d'Outre-Mer, Paris; with the Ministry of Finance 1943–57; Head, Office of Deputy Prime Minister for the Interior 1957–58; Asst.-Dir. Office of Prime Minister Feb.-Oct. 1958; Perm. Sec. French Cameroons, Paris 1958–59; Minister of Finance 1960–61; Del. to the Presidency in charge of Finance, the Plan and Territorial Admin. 1961–65; Sec.-Gen. UDEAC 1965–70; Minister of Planning and Territorial Improvement 1970–72, of Finance 1972–75, Minister Del. to the State Inspectorate and Admin. Reform 1975–80; fmr. Dir. Banque Centrale de l'Afrique Equatoriale et du Cameroun; fmr. Gov. IMF; Officier Ordre de la Valeur, Cameroon, Commdr. Légion d'honneur, Ordre de la Rédemption Africaine (Liberia), Ordre Tchadien. *Address:* c/o State Inspectorate, Yaoundé, United Republic of Cameroon.

ONASSIS, Jacqueline Lee Bouvier; American editor and widow of former President Kennedy; b. 28 July 1929, Southampton, Long I., N.Y.; d. of John V. and Janet (Lee) Bouvier; m. 1st John F. Kennedy (Pres. of the U.S.A., 1961–63) 1953 (assassinated 1963); one s. one d. (and one s. deceased); m. 2nd Aristotle Onassis 1968 (died 1975); ed. Vassar Coll., George Washington Univ., U.S.A., and the Univ. of Paris; photographer Washington Times-Herald 1952; initiated and supervised historical reconstruction of décor of the White House 1961–63; Rep. of the late Pres. Kennedy on tour of India 1962; Consultant Viking Publs., New York 1975–77; Assoc. Ed. Doubleday and Co. 1978–82, Ed. 1982–. *Address:* Doubleday and Co., Inc., 245 Park Avenue, New York, N.Y. 10028; 1041 Fifth Avenue, New York, N.Y. 10028, U.S.A.

ONDAATJE, Michael; Canadian author; b. 12 Sept. 1943, Colombo, Sri Lanka; two s.; ed. Dulwich Coll. London and Univ. of Quebec; teacher; owner and man. of own small publishing house. *Publications include:* The Collected Works of Billy the Kid, Coming Through Slaughter, Running in the Family, In the Skin of a Lion. *Address:* c/o Secker & Warburg, 54 Poland Street, London, W.1, England.

ONDARTS, Raúl Agustín; Argentine business executive and politician; b. 28 Aug. 1915, Buenos Aires; s. of Juan Ondarts and Juana Ansolabehere; m. Norah Elsa Unia 1942; three s. two d.; ed. Univ. de Buenos Aires; private engineering practice 1938–75; Under-Sec. for Industry 1957; Del. Econ. Conf. OAS 1957; Pres., with rank of Amb., Argentine purchasing Comm. in European communist countries 1958; Sec. of State for Communications 1962; Under-Sec. for Economy and Labour 1967; Vice-Pres. and Pres. of Exec. Cttee. Hidronor 1968–70; Pres. Metallurgical Industries of San Martín (TAMET SA) 1970–75; Pres. Iron and Steel Industry's Centre 1971–77; Pres. Yacimientos Petrolíferos Fiscales Sociedad del Estado 1977–80; Pres. Centre of Engineers and Union of Engineers 1958–60; mem. Acad. de Ingeniería de Argentina. *Leisure interests:* sport, reading. *Publications:* La Ingeniería y los Ingenieros (essay), articles in technical periodicals published in Brazil, Italy, U.K. and Japan. *Address:* c/o Avda. Pres. Roque Sáenz Peña 777, Buenos Aires, Argentina. *Telephone:* 46-7271.

ONDŘICH, František; Czechoslovak politician; b. 26 Nov. 1929, Krásetín, Český Krumlov district; s. of Petr Ondřich and Terezie Ondřich; m. Marie Panniová 1951; one s.; ed. Coll. of Politics of Central Cttee. of CP of Czechoslovakia; electrical engineer 1945–49; active in Czechoslovak Union of Youth and later district Cttee. of CP of Czechoslovakia, Český Krumlov 1949–58; Official, political-organizational dept., Cen. Cttee. of CP of Czechoslovakia 1961–64, Head 1970–72; Head, Nat. Econ. Dept., Regional Cttee. of CP, České Budějovice 1964–66, Chief Sec. District Cttee. 1966–69; mem. Cen. Cttee. CP of Czechoslovakia 1970–76, Sec. and mem. Secr. 1971–76; Deputy to House of People, Fed. Assembly 1971–; mem. Presidium, Cen. Cttee. of Czechoslovak Nat. Front 1972–76; Minister-Chair. Czechoslovak People's Control Comm. 1976–; mem. Cen. Control and Auditing Comm., CP of Czechoslovakia 1976–; Order for Merit in Construction 1971, Order of Victorious February 1973, Order of Labour 1979. *Address:* Výbor lidové kontroly Č.S.S.R., Jankovcova 63, 170 04 Prague 7, Czechoslovakia.

O'NEAL, Ryan; American actor; b. 20 Apr. 1941, Los Angeles; s. of Charles and Patricia (Callaghan) O'Neal; m. 1st Joanna Moore 1963 (divorced 1967), one s. one d.; m. 2nd Leigh Taylor-Young 1967, one s.; one s. by Farrah Fawcett; father of Tatum O'Neal (q.v.). *TV appearances include:* Dobie Gillis, Two Faces West, Perry Mason, The Virginian, This is the Life, The Untouchables, My Three Sons, Bachelor Father, Empire, Peyton Place. *Films include:* The Big Bounce 1969, Love Story 1970, The Wild Rovers 1971, What's Up, Doc? 1972, The Thief Who Came to Dinner 1973, Paper Moon 1973, Oliver's Story 1978, The Main Event 1979, So Fine 1981, Partners 1982, Irreconcilable Differences 1983, Fever Pitch 1985, Tough Guys Don't Dance 1986. *Address:* c/o Creative Artist Agency Inc., 1888 Century Park East Suite 1400, Los Angeles, Calif. 90067, U.S.A.

O'NEAL, Tatum; American actress; b. 1963, Los Angeles; d. of Ryan O'Neal (q.v.) and Joanna Moore; m. John McEnroe (q.v.) 1986; one s. *Film appearances include:* Paper Moon 1973, The Bad News Bears 1976, Nickelodeon 1976, International Velvet 1978, Little Darlings 1980, Circle of Two 1980, Certain Fury 1985. *Address:* c/o Bill Treusch Assocs., 853 7th Avenue, Apt. 9A, New York, N.Y. 10019, U.S.A.

O'NEIL, Michael Gerald, A.B.; American business executive (retd.); b. 29 Jan. 1922, Akron, Ohio; s. of William O'Neil and Grace Agnes; brother of Thomas O'Neil (q.v.); m. Juliet P. Rudolph 1950 (divorced); four s. three d.; ed. Coll. of Holy Cross, and Harvard Univ.; Dir. Gencorp (fmrly. The Gen. Tire and Rubber Co.) 1950–, Asst. to Pres. 1951–57, Vice-Pres. and Exec. Asst. to Pres. 1957–60, Pres. 1960–82, Chief Exec. Officer 1977–87, Chair. 1981–87; served Second World War; official of numerous business and philanthropic orgs. *Address:* Gencorp Inc., 1 General Street, Akron, Ohio 44329, U.S.A.

O'NEIL, Thomas Francis, A.B.; American business executive; b. 18 April 1915, Kansas City, Mo.; s. of William O'Neil and Grace Agnes (Savage) O'Neil; m. Claire Miller McGahey 1946; five s. four d.; ed. Holy Cross Coll.; with Gencorp (fmrly. General Tire and Rubber Co.), Akron, Ohio 1937–41, Dir. 1946–, Vice-Pres. 1948, Vice-Chair. 1950–60, Chair. 1960–81; Vice-Pres. and Dir. The Yankee Network, Boston 1948–51; Pres. and Dir. RKO, New York 1955–66, Chair. RKO Gen. 1966–76; Dir. Frontier Airlines, Flintkote Co. *Address:* 1 General Street, Akron, Ohio 44329, U.S.A.

O'NEILL, Paul H., M.P.A.; American business executive; b. 4 Dec. 1935, St. Louis, Mo.; ed. Fresno State Coll., Indiana Univ., Claremont Grad. School and George Washington Univ.; computer systems analyst, U.S. Veterans Admin.; later engineer, Morris-Knudsen, Anchorage, Alaska; mem. staff, Office of Man. and Budget 1967–77, Deputy Dir. 1974–77; Vice-Pres. Planning, Int. Paper Co. 1977, Sr. Vice-Pres. Planning and Finance 1981, Sr. Vice-Pres. paperboard and packaging Div. 1983, Pres. 1985–87; Chair. Aluminum Co. of America (Alcoa) 1987–; Dir. Nat. Westminster Bank, Manpower Demonstration Research Group, Aluminum Co. of America; many other business and community affiliations. *Address:* 1501 Alcoa Building, Pittsburgh, Pa. 15219, U.S.A. (Office).

O'NEILL, Robert James, C.M.G., M.A.; British diplomatist; b. 17 June 1932, Chelmsford; s. of Robert O'Neill and Dorothy O'Neill; m. Helen Juniper 1958; one s. two d.; ed. King Edward VI School, Chelmsford and Trinity Coll., Cambridge; entered Diplomatic Service 1955; served in British Embassy, Ankara 1957–60, Dakar 1961–63, Bonn 1968–72; Pvt. Sec. to Chancellor of the Duchy of Lancaster and to Minister of State, Foreign Office 1966–68; Deputy Gov. Gibraltar 1978–81; Under-Sec. Cabinet Office 1981–84; Asst. Under-Sec. FCO 1984–86; Amb. to Austria and Head Del. to Negotiations on mutual reduction of forces in Europe 1986–. *Leisure interests:* hill walking, history. *Address:* British Embassy, Jauresgasse 12, 1030 Vienna, Austria; c/o Foreign and Commonwealth Office, King Charles Street, London, SW1A 2AH, England. *Telephone:* 713 15 75.

O'NEILL, Thomas Philip ("Tip"), Jr.; American politician; b. 9 Dec. 1912, Cambridge, Mass.; s. of Thomas P. and Rose Ann (Tolan) O'Neill; m. Mildred Ann Miller 1941; three s. two d.; ed. St. John's High School and Boston Coll.; employed in insurance co., Cambridge, Mass. 1935–36; mem. Mass. House of Reps. 1936–52, Minority Leader 1947–48, Speaker 1948–52; mem. U.S. House of Reps. from Mass. 11th, later 8th District 1953–87, fmr. mem. Rules Cttee., Majority Whip 1971–73, Majority Leader 1973–76, Speaker 1977–87; Partner O'Neill and Athy, Washington 1987–; Democrat. *Publication:* Man of the House: The life and political memoirs of Speaker Tip O'Neill 1988. *Address:* 1310 19th Street, N.W., Washington, D.C. 20036, U.S.A.

O'NEILL, William Atchison; American politician; b. 11 Aug. 1930, Hartford, Conn.; s. of the late Joseph O'Neill and of Frances O'Neill; m. Natalie Scott Damon 1962; ed. schools, East Hampton, Conn., New Britain Teacher's Coll., Conn., and Univ. of Hartford, Conn.; served with U.S.A.F. 1950–53; mem. East Hampton Democratic Town Cttee.; mem. House of Reps., Conn., from 52nd Assembly Dist. 1966–78, Asst. Majority Leader 1971–72, Asst. Minority Leader 1973–74, Majority Leader 1975–78; mem. Conn. Gov.'s Finance Advisory Cttee. 1968–74; Chair. House Cttee. on Exec. Nominations; State Chair. Ella Grasso for Gov. Cttee. 1974; Chair. Democratic State Cen. Cttee. 1975–78; Lieut.-Gov. of Conn. 1979–80, Gov. of Connecticut Dec. 1980–; mem. Nat. Gov.'s Asscn.; mem. American Legion; Hon. Alumnus Award, Univ. of Hartford 1981. *Address:* Office of the Governor, State Capitol, Room 202, Hartford, Conn. 06115; Governor's Residence, 990 Prospect Avenue, Hartford, Conn. 06115, U.S.A.

O'NEILL OF THE MAINE, Baron (Life Peer), cr. 1970, of Ahoghill in the County of Antrim; **Terence Marne O'Neill,** P.C.; British (N. Ireland) politician; b. 10 Sept. 1914, London; s. of Capt. Hon. Arthur O'Neill and Lady Annabel O'Neill; m. Katherine Jean Whitaker 1944; one s. one d.; ed. Eton Coll.; Irish Guards 1939–45; M.P. (N. Ireland) 1946–70; Parl. Sec. Ministry of Health 1948–53; Deputy Speaker and Chair. Ways and Means Cttee. 1953–55; Joint Parl. Sec. Home Affairs and Health 1955; Minister of Home Affairs April–Oct. 1956, of Finance Sept. 1956–63; Prime Minister (N. Ireland) 1963–69; mem. Comm. on Electoral Reform 1975–76; Dir. Phoenix Assurance 1969–84, Warburg Int. Holdings 1969–83; mem. Museum and Galleries Comm. 1987–; Unionist Party. *Publications:* Ulster at the Crossroads (speeches and writings) 1969, The Autobiography of Terence O'Neill 1972. *Address:* House of Lords, London, S.W.1; Lisle Court, Lymington, Hampshire, England. *Telephone:* Lymington 72010.

ONETTI, Juan Carlos; Uruguayan writer; b. 1 July 1909; ed. High School; Ed. Marcha (weekly newspaper), Montevideo 1939–42; Ed. Reuter Agency, Montevideo 1942–43, Buenos Aires 1943–46; Ed. Vea y Lea (magazine), Buenos Aires 1946–55; Man. of advertising firm in Montevideo 1955–57; Dir. of Municipal Libraries, Montevideo 1957; Nat. Literature Prize of Uruguay 1963. *Publications: novels:* Elpozo 1939, Tierra de nadie 1941, Para esta noche 1943, La vida breve 1950, Un sueño realizado y otros cuentos (stories) 1951, Una tumba sin nombre 1959, Los adioses 1954, La cara de la desgracia 1960, Jacob y el otro (story) 1961, El Astillero 1961, El infierno tan temido 1962, Tan triste como ella 1963, Juntacaddveres 1965. *Address:* Montevideo, Uruguay.

ONG, John Doyle, M.A., L.L.B.; American business executive; b. 29 Sept. 1933, Uhrichsville, Ohio; s. of Louis Brosee and Mary Ellen (née Liggett) Ong; m. Mary Lee Schupp 1957; two s. one d.; ed. Ohio State Univ., Harvard Univ.; admitted to Ohio Bar 1958; Asst. Counsel B. F. Goodrich Co., Akron 1961–66, Group Vice-Pres. 1972–73, Exec. Vice-Pres. 1973–74, Vice-Chair. 1974–75, Pres. 1975–84, Dir. 1975–, C.O.O. 1978–79, Chair. and C.E.O. 1979–; Asst. to Pres. Int. B. F. Goodrich Co., Akron 1966–69, Vice-Pres. 1969–70, Pres. 1970–72; Dir. Cooper Industries, The Kroger Co., Ameritech Corpn.; mem. Bd. Dirs. Nat. Alliance for Business; Pres. Bd. of Trustees, Western Reserve Acad., Hudson 1977–. *Leisure interests:* fishing, hunting. *Address:* 3925 Embassy Parkway, Akron, Ohio 44313 (Office); 230 Aurora Street, Hudson, Ohio 44236, U.S.A. (Home).

ONG, Tan Sri Haji Omar Yoke-Lin; Malaysian politician and diplomatist; b. 23 July 1917, Kuala Lumpur; m. Toh Puan Datin (Dr.) Hajjah Aishah 1974; three s. one d.; mem. Kuala Lumpur Municipal Council 1952–55; co-founder Alliance Party; mem. Fed. Legis. Council 1954–; Malayan Minster of Posts and Telecommunications 1955–56, of Transport 1956–57, of Labour and Social Welfare 1957–59, of Health and Social Welfare 1959–72; M.P. 1959–72; Vice-Pres. Commonwealth Parl. Asscn. 1961; Amb. to U.S.A. and UN 1962–64, to U.S.A. 1962–72, also accred. to Canada 1966–72 and Brazil 1967–72; Minister without Portfolio 1964–73; Pres. of the Senate 1973–80; Chair. Asian Int. Merchant Bankers Bhd., Malaysian Oxygen Bhd., Omariff Holdings Sdn. Bhd., Syarikat Ong Yoke Lin Sdn. Bhd., OYL Industries Sdn. Bhd., Raza Sdn. Bhd.; Dir. Esso Malaysia Berhad, Hume Industries (Malaysia) Berhad, Malayan Flour Mills Bhd., United Chemical Industries Bhd.; Pro-Chancellor Nat. Univ. of Malaysia 1987; Council mem. Inst. of Strategic Studies, Malaysia; Vice-Pres. UN Malaysia Asscn.; Hon. LL.D. (Hanyang Univ.) Seoul 1978, Hon. Ph.D. (Malaysia); S.S.M. 1979; Panglima Mangku Neyara (Malaysia) 1959; Order of First Homayon (Iran) 1969, Grand Cross (1st Class) Fed. Rep. of Germany; Order of Civil Merit (1st Class) Rep. of Korea, Commdr. Ordre nat. du Mérite. *Leisure interests:* golf, photography, swimming. *Address:* Asian International Merchant Bankers Ltd., UMBC Annexe 9-11 Floors, Jalem Salaiman, Kuala Lumpur (Office); 44 Pesiaran Duta, Kuala Lumpur, Malaysia (Home). *Telephone:* 03-274 9011 (Office); 03-254 6637/255 9731 (Home).

ONG, Romualdo Añover, B.SC.; Philippines diplomatist; b. 25 April 1939, Manila; s. of late Juan Salido Ong and of Adelaida Añover; m. Cecilia Hidalgo 1964; two s. two d.; ed. Ateneo de Manila and Univ. of the Philippines; joined Ministry of Foreign Affairs 1968; served Bonn 1972–75, Geneva 1975–79, Minister Counsellor, Beijing 1979–82; Special Asst. to Deputy Minister for Foreign Affairs 1983; Asst. Minister for ASEAN Affairs 1984–85; Sr. Econ. Consultant, Tech. Secr. for Int. Econ. Relations/Bd. of Overseas Econ. Promotion 1985; Amb. to Australia (also accred. to Vanuatu) 1986–. *Leisure interests:* reading, car driving, basketball, hiking, movies, listening to music. *Address:* Embassy of the Philippines, 1 Moonah Place, Yarralumla, A.C.T. 2600; P.O. Box 297, Manuka, A.C.T. 2603, Australia. *Telephone:* (062) 732-535.

ONG PANG BOON; Singapore politician; b. 28 March 1929, Kuala Lumpur, Malaysia; m. Chan Choy Siong 1961; one s. two d.; ed. Methodist Boys' School, Kuala Lumpur and Univ. of Malaya; mem. Parl. 1959–; Minister for Home Affairs 1959-63, for Educ. 1963-70, for Labour 1971-81, for Environment 1981-85. *Address:* c/o Ministry of the Environment, Singapore.

ONG TENG CHEONG, M.A.; Singapore architect and politician; b. 22 Jan. 1936, Singapore; m. Ling Siew May 1963; two s.; ed. Chinese High School and Univs. of Adelaide and Liverpool; joined Planning Dept., Ministry of Nat. Devt. 1967, later seconded to UNDP (Special Fund) assistance in Urban Renewal and Devt. Project; est. own architectural practice with wife 1971; mem. Parl. 1972–; Sr. Minister of State for Communications 1975, also Acting Minister for Culture 1977; Minister for Communications, concurrently Minister for Culture 1978; Minister for Communications and Labour 1981; Sec.-Gen. Nat. Trades Union Congress 1983–; Minister without Portfolio 1983-85; Second Deputy Prime Minister Jan. 1985–; Chair. PAP Cen. Exec. Cttee. 1981. *Address:* Parliament Buildings, Singapore.

ONGANÍA, Lt.-Gen. Juan Carlos; Argentine army officer and politician; b. 17 March 1914; ed. Escuela de Guerra; Army career in cavalry and armoured corps; C.-in-C. of Army 1963-65; Pres. of Argentina 1966-70. *Address:* Buenos Aires, Argentina.

O'NIONS, Robert Keith, M.A., PH.D., F.R.S.; British geochemist; b. 26 Sept. 1944, Birmingham; s. of William Henry O'Nions and Eva Stagg; m. Rita Bill 1967; three d.; ed. Univ. of Nottingham, Univ. of Alberta; Postdoctoral Fellow, Univ. of Alberta 1969-70; Unger Vetlesen Postdoctoral Fellow, Univ. of Oslo 1970-71; Demonstrator in Petrology, Univ. of Oxford 1971-72, Lecturer in Geochemistry 1972-75; Assoc. Prof. and Prof. of Geology, Columbia Univ. 1975-79; Royal Soc. Research Prof., Univ. of Cambridge 1979–; Fellow, American Geophysical Union 1979–; mem. Norwegian Acad. of Sciences; J. B. Macelwane Award 1979; Bigsby Medal 1983. *Publications:* numerous publications in scientific journals on the subject of geochemistry. *Address:* Department of Earth Sciences, University of Cambridge, Downing Street, Cambridge, CB2 3EQ, England.

ONITRI, Herbert M. Adebola, M.A, PH.D.; Nigerian economist; b. 20 April 1928, Lagos; s. of Thomas A. and Adepate Amoke Onitri; m. Agnes I. Osobase 1961; three s. two d.; ed. Ibadan Grammar Scool, L.S.E., Univ. of Calif. (Berkeley) and Yale Univ.; Lecturer and Sr. Lecturer in Econs., Univ. of Ibadan 1958-64; Research Prof. and Dir. Nigerian Inst. of Social and Econ. Research 1974-81. *Publications:* Reconstruction and Development in Nigeria (co-author), The Marketing Board System (co-author). *Leisure interests:* table tennis, lawn tennis. *Address:* c/o Nigerian Institute of Social and Economic Research, P.M.B. 5, University of Ibadan, Ibadan, Nigeria.

ONN, Datuk Hussein bin (see Hussein bin Onn).

ONO, Akira; Japanese politician; b. 1928; ed. Keio Univ.; elected to House of Reps. seven times from Gifu Pref.; fmr. Parl. Vice-Minister of Finance and of Labour, Deputy Sec.-Gen. Liberal-Democratic Party; Minister of Labour 1982-83. *Leisure interests:* shogi (Japanese chess), mahjong, baseball, composing haiku poetry. *Address:* Liberal-Democratic Party, 7, 2-chome, Hirakawacho, Chiyoda-ku, Tokyo, Japan.

ONOE, Morio, PH.D.; Japanese business executive; b. 28 March 1926, Tokyo; one s. two d.; ed. Univ. of Tokyo; Prof. Univ. of Tokyo 1962-86; Dir. Inst. of Industrial Science, Univ. of Tokyo 1983-86; Exec. Dir. Ricoh Co. Ltd. 1986-88, Exec. Vice-Pres. 1988–; C. B. Sawyer Award 1975. *Publications:* Digital Processing of Biomedical Images (edited with K. Preston, Jr.) 1976, Medical Image Processing (ed.) 1982, Handbook of Image Processing (ed.) 1987. *Leisure interests:* travel, books. *Address:* 4-9-7, Taishido, Setagaya, Tokyo 154, Japan. *Telephone:* (03) 422-1092.

ONOFRE JARPA REYES, Sergio; Chilean diplomatist and politician; b. 8 March 1921, Rengo; m. Silvia Moreno Anwandter; four c.; ed. Colegio Patrocino San José, Valparaiso and higher studies in electronics and agric. econs. in Valparaiso; Pres. Nat. Party 1967-73; Senator 1973; del. to UN 1974; Amb. to Colombia 1976-78, to Argentina 1978-83; Minister of the Interior 1983-85. *Address:* c/o Ministerio del Interior, Santiago, Chile.

ONSLOW, Cranley Gordon Douglas; British politician; b. 8 June 1926, Bexhill; s. of the late F.R.D. Onslow and M. Onslow; m. Lady June Hay 1955; one s. three d.; ed. Harrow School, Oriel Coll. Univ. of Oxford, Geneva Univ.; served R.A.C., Lieut. 7th Queen's Own Hussars 1944-48, Capt. 3rd/4th Co. of London Yeomanry 1948-52; joined Foreign Service 1951, Third Sec. Embassy, Rangoon 1953-55, Consul, Maymyo, N. Burma 1955-56, resgnd. 1960; served Dartford Rural Dist. Council 1960-62, Kent County Council 1961-64; M.P. for Woking 1964–; Parl. Under-Sec. of State for Aerospace and Shipping, Dept. of Trade and Industry 1972-74, Opposition Spokesman on Health and Social Security 1974-75, on Defence 1975-76; Minister of State, Foreign and Commonwealth Office 1982-83; mem. Exec. 1922 Cttee. 1968-72, 1981-82, 1983–, Chair. 1984–; U.K. del.

to Council of Europe and WEU 1977-81; Chair. Conservative Aviation Cttee. 1970-72, 1979-82, Select Cttee. on Defence 1981-82; Dir. Argyll Group PLC 1983–, Rediffusion 1985–, Rediffusion Radio Systems 1985–; mem. Council Nat. Rifle Asscn., Salmon and Trout Asscn., Anglers' Co-operative Asscn.; Conservative. *Publication:* Asian Economic Development (Ed.) 1965. *Leisure interests:* fishing, shooting, watching cricket. *Address:* Highbuilding, Fernhurst, West Sussex, England.

ONWUMECHILI, Cyril Agodi, PH.D.; Nigerian professor of physics and administrator; b. 20 Jan. 1932, Inyi; s. of Nwaime and Akuviro (née Orji) Onwumechili; m. Cecilia Bedeaka (née Anyadibe) 1958; two s. one d.; ed. King's Coll., Lagos, Univ. Coll., Ibadan and Univ. of London; Professor 1962–; Dir. of chain of observatories 1960-66; Dean, Faculty of Science, Univ. of Ibadan 1965-66; Prof. and Head of Dept. Univ. of Nigeria 1966-73, 1976-78, Dean, Faculty of Science 1970-71, Dean, Faculty of Physical Sciences 1973-76, 1978; Visiting Prof. of Geophysics, Univ. of Alaska 1971-72; Consultant, Inst. for Space Research, Nat. Research Council of Brazil 1972; Vice-Chancellor, Univ. of Ife, Ile-Ife 1979-82; Deputy Pres. Anambra State Univ. of Tech., Enugu 1983-84, Pres. 1984-85, Vice-Chancellor 1985-86; mem. Int. Scientific Programmes Cttee., Int. Symposia on Equatorial Aeronomy 1972–, American Geophysical Union, Soc. for Terrestrial Magnetism and Electricity of Japan, UN Advisory Cttee. on Science and Tech. for Devt. 1981-83, Fellow U.K. and Nigerian Inst. of Physics 1969; Foundation Fellow and Former Pres. Nigerian Acad. of Science; U.K. Chartered Physicist 1986; Fellow African Acad. of Sciences 1987; Foundation Fellow, Science Asscn. of Nigeria 1974; Vice Pres. Asscn. of African Univs. 1984-89; Consultant U.N. Econ. Comm. for Africa 1987, Commonwealth Science Council 1988; chair. or mem. of many nat. and int. bds. and councils; Hon. D.Sc. (Ife) 1977. *Publications:* numerous scientific articles. *Leisure interests:* swimming, table tennis, lawn tennis. *Address:* P.O. Box 9059, Uwani, Enugu, Nigeria.

ONYEAMA, Charles Dadi, LL.B.; Nigerian judge; b. 5 Aug. 1917, Eke, Enugu; s. of Chief Onyeama; m. 1st Susannah Ogwudu 1950, 2nd Florence Wilcox 1966; five s. two d.; ed. King's Coll., Lagos, Achimota Coll., Gold Coast, Univ. Coll., London and Brasenose Coll., Oxford; Cadet Admin. Officer, Nigeria 1944; mem. Legis. Council of Nigeria and Eastern House of Ass. 1946-51; mem. Nigerianization Comm. and mem. Gen. Conf. and Constitutional Drafting Cttee. 1948-50; Chief Magistrate, Nigeria 1952-56; Acting High Court Judge, W. Nigeria 1956-57; High Court Judge, Lagos 1957-64; Acting Chief Justice, Lagos High Court 1961 and 1963; Justice of Supreme Court of Nigeria 1964-66; Judge Int. Court of Justice, The Hague 1967-76; Chair. Cttee. on the Prerogative of Mercy, Nigeria 1976-79, Ife Univ. Teaching Hospitals Complex Bd. 1976-79, Orthopaedic Hospitals Man. Bd. 1979–; Judge, World Bank Admin. Tribunal 1982–; Hon. LL.D.; Commdr. of the Fed. Repub. of Nigeria. *Leisure interest:* reading. *Address:* 1 Church Road, P.O. Box 602, Enugu, Nigeria.

ONYONKA, Zachary, PH.D.; Kenyan politician; b. 28 Feb. 1939; s. of Godrico Deri and Kerobina (née Kebati) Onyonka; m. 1968; three s. three d.; ed. Mosocho School, Nyaburu School, St. Mary's School, Yala; Research Fellow, Univ. Coll., Nairobi 1967, Lecturer, Dept. of Econs. 1968-69; M.P. for Kisii 1969–; Minister of Econ. Planning and Devt. 1969-70, of Information and Broadcasting 1970-73, of Health 1973-74, of Educ. 1974-76, of Housing and Social Services 1976-78, for Economic Planning and Devt. 1979-83, of Foreign Affairs 1987-88, of Planning and Nat. Devt. March 1988–; mem. Nat. Exec. Cttee., Kenya African Nat. Union; Pres. African-Caribbean and Pacific Group of Countries 1981; Fellow, Int. Bankers' Asscn.; Hon. Dr. Public Service (Syracuse Univ.) 1981; Elder Golden Heart Medal. *Address:* P.O. Box 3005, Nairobi, Kenya. *Telephone:* Nairobi 338220.

OORT, Jan Hendrik; Netherlands astronomer; b. 28 April 1900, Franeker; s. of Abraham Hermanus and Ruth Hannah Faber; m. Johanna Maria Graadt van Roggen 1927; two s. one d.; ed. Univ. of Groningen; Asst. Astronomical Lab., Groningen 1921; Research Asst. Yale Univ. Observatory, U.S.A. 1922-24; Astronomer Leiden Observatory 1924; Prof. of Astronomy and Dir. of Observatory, Univ. of Leiden 1945-70; Gen. Sec. Int. Astronomical Union 1935-48, Pres. 1959-61; Foreign mem. of N.A.S. and various Acads. of Arts and Sciences; Vetlesen Prize, Columbia Univ. 1966, Balzan Prize, Milan 1984; Kyoto Prize 1987; Hon. Dr. Univs. of Copenhagen, Glasgow, Oxford, Louvain, Harvard, Brussels, Cambridge, Bordeaux, Canberra, Toruń. *Publications:* numerous contributions to learned journals. *Leisure interests:* reading, hiking, skating. *Address:* President Kennedylaan 169, 2343GZ Oegstgeest, Netherlands. *Telephone:* 071-176702.

OPEL, John Roberts, B.A., M.B.A.; American data processing company executive; b. 5 Jan. 1925, Kansas City, Mo.; s. of Norman J. Opel and Esther (Roberts) Opel; m. Julia Carole Stout 1953; two s. three d.; ed. Westminster Coll., Fulton, Mo. and Univ. of Chicago; joined Int. Business Machines Corpn. (IBM) 1949, Sales Rep. 1949, Vice-Pres. 1966, Sr. Vice-Pres. 1969, Dir. 1972–, Pres. 1974-83, and C.E.O. 1980-85, Chair. 1983-86, Chair. Exec. Cttee. 1986–; Vice-Chair. The Business Council 1983–; Dir. Fed. Res. Bank of New York Co. Inc. (Chair. 1987-89), Pfizer Inc., Prudential Insurance Co. of America, Time Inc.; Trustee, Westminster Coll., Univ. of Chicago, Inst. for Advanced Study; mem. Bd. of Govs. of Wilson Council, United Way of America, Task Force on Market Mechanisms 1987; Vice-Chair. Business Council; mem. Council on Foreign

Relations, Policy and Planning Cttees. of Business Round Table. *Address:* International Business Machines Corporation, Old Orchard Road, Armonk, N.Y. 10504, U.S.A.

OPIE, Julian Gilbert, B.A.; British artist; b. 12 Dec. 1958, London; s. of Roger G. Opie and Norma Opie; m. Lisa K. Milroy 1984; ed. Magdalen Coll. School, Oxford, Chelsea School of Art, London and Goldsmiths' School of Art, London; exhibited Young Blood, Riverside Studios, London 1983, Sculpture 1983, Rotterdam 1983, The Sculpture Show, Hayward Gallery, London 1983, Making Sculpture, Tate Gallery, London 1983, Perspective, Basle Art Fair, Basle 1984, Home and Abroad, Serpentine Gallery, London 1984, Myth and Symbol, Tokyo Museum of Modern Art 1984, The British Show touring Australia 1984, Paris Biennale, Paris 1985, Anniotanta, Ravenna 1985, British Sculpture Louisiana Museum, Denmark 1986, De Sculptura, Vienna 1986, Correspondence Europe, Stedelijk Museum, Amsterdam 1986, Prospect 86, Frankfurt 1986; one-person exhbns. at Lisson Gallery, London 1983, Kunstverein Köln, Cologne 1984 and Groningen Museum, Netherlands 1985, ICA, London 1985, Lisson Gallery 1985, 1986, Franco Toselli Gallery, Milan 1985; works in the collections of The British Council, The Contemporary Arts Soc., Tate Gallery, Cincinatti Museum of Modern Art, Documenta 8, Kassel 1987, Stedelijk Museum, Amsterdam. *Publications:* Julian Opie, Kunstverein Köln: Catalogue of Works 1984, Julian Opie Drawings, ICA, London, Julian Opie New Works, Lisson Gallery. *Leisure interests:* art, music, films, books, architecture, travel, a 1981 Chevrolet Caprice Classic, supermarkets, fast food restaurants, hotel lobbies, petrol stations. *Address:* Lisson Gallery, 66-68 Bell Street, London, NW1 6SP, England. *Telephone:* 01-262 1539.

OPIE, Lionel Henry, M.D., PH.D., M.R.C.P., F.A.C.C., F.R.S.S.A.; South African professor of medicine; b. 6 May 1933, Hanover, S.A.; s. of Prof. William Henry Opie and Marie Opie (née Le Roux); m. Carol June Sancroft Baker 1969; two d.; ed. Diocesan Coll., Rondebosch, Cape Town, Univ. of Cape Town, Oxford Univ., England; Intern, Groote Schuur Hosp. 1956; Sr. House Officer, Dept. of Neurology, Radcliffe Infirmary, Oxford, England 1957-59; House Physician (Endocrinology), Hammersmith Hosp., London 1959; Asst. in Medicine, Peter Bent Brigham Hosp., Boston, Mass., U.S.A., Samuel A. Levine Fellow in Cardiology, Harvard Medical School 1960-61; Asst. Resident in Medicine, Toronto Gen. Hosp., Canada 1961-62; Consultant Physician, Karl Bremer Hosp. and Univ. of Stellenbosch, S.A.; Out-Patient Asst. Physician, Radcliffe Infirmary, Wellcome Research Fellow, Dept. of Biochemistry, Oxford Univ. 1964-66; Part-Time Registrar, Hammersmith Hosp., London 1966-67; Research Fellow, Dept. of Biochemistry, Imperial Coll., London 1966-68; Sr. Registrar in Medicine (Cardiology), Hammersmith Hosp. 1967-69, Consultant in Medicine 1969; Sr. Specialist Physician, Groote Schuur Hosp. 1971; Assoc. Prof. of Medicine, Univ. of Cape Town 1975, Dir. MRC Research Unit for Ischaemic Heart Disease 1976, Personal Chair in Medicine, Prof. of Medicine 1980; Prin. Physician, Groote Schuur Hosp., Dir. Hypertension Clinic 1979; Pres. Southern Africa Cardiac Soc. 1980-82; Chair. Council on Cardiac Metabolism, Int. Soc. and Fed. of Cardiology 1980; Pres. Southern Africa Hypertension Soc. 1986; mem. Royal Soc. of Medicine, London, British Cardiac Soc., Physiological Soc. (U.K.), S.A. Socs. of Cardiology, Pharmacology, Biochemistry and Hypertension, Int. Hypertension Soc. *Publications:* over 300. *Address:* Heart Research Unit, Department of Medicine, University of Cape Town Medical School Observatory 7925; 66A Dean Street, Newlands 7700, South Africa (Home). *Telephone:* 47-1250 (ext. 358) (Univ.); 685-3855 (Home).

OPLE, Blas F.; Philippine politician; b. 3 Feb. 1927, Hagonoy, Bulacan; s. of Felix Ople and Segundina Fajardo; m. Susana Vasquez 1949; five s. two d.; ed. Philippine public and pvt. schools, Far Eastern Univ. and Manuel L. Quezon Univ., Manila; copy Ed. and columnist The Daily Mirror, Manila 1950-53; Asst. to Pres. Ramon Magsaysay on labour and agrarian affairs 1954-57; writer and labour leader 1958-64; Head, Propaganda Div., Ferdinand E. Marcos' presidential campaign 1965; Special Asst. to Pres. Marcos and Commr. Social Security System 1966; Sec. of Labour 1967-78, Minister of Labour and Employment 1978-86; f. Partido Nacionalista ng 'Pilipinas (PNP) 1986-; Chair. Nat. Manpower and Youth Council 1967-71; mem. Bd. of Trustees, Land Bank 1968; Chair. Govt. Group, Int. Labour Conf. 1969, Pres. Int. Labour Conf. 1975-76; Chair. Asian Labour Ministers' Conf. 1967; various govt. and civic awards. *Address:* 61 Visayas Avenue, Project 6, Quezon City, Philippines. *Telephone:* 98-20-56.

OPPENHEIM, Tan Sri Sir Alexander, S.M.N., Kt., O.B.E., PH.D., D.SC.; British mathematician (retd.); b. 4 Feb. 1903, Salford; s. of Harris Jacob Oppenheim and Fanny Ginsberg; m. Beatrice Templer Nesbit 1930 (divorced 1977); two s. one d.; ed. Manchester Grammar School, and Balliol Coll., Oxford; Commonwealth Fund Fellow Chicago 1927-30; Lecturer Edinburgh Univ. 1930-31; Prof. of Math. Raffles Coll. Singapore 1931-42, 1945-49, Deputy Prin. 1947 and 1949; Prof. of Math. Univ. of Malaya 1949-57, Dean Faculty of Arts 1949, 1951 and 1953, Acting Vice-Chancellor 1955, Vice-Chancellor 1957-65; Visiting Prof. of Math., Reading Univ. 1965-68, Univ. of Ghana 1968-73, Univ. of Benin, Nigeria 1973-77; prisoner of war in Singapore and Thailand 1942-45; Dean, Prisoner of War Univ. 1942; Pres. Malayan Mathematical Soc. 1951-55, 1957, Singapore Chess Club 1956, Oxford and Cambridge Soc. 1952, 1957; mem. Asscn. of Southeast Asian Insts. of Higher Learning 1959-61, Academic Advisory Cttee., Univ. of Cape Coast 1972; Pres. Mathematical Asscn. of Ghana 1969-70; Fellow, Royal Soc. of

Edinburgh, World Acad. of Art and Science; Alumni Medal, Chicago Univ. Alumni Asscn. 1977. *Leisure interests:* chess, bridge. *Address:* Matson House, Matson Drive, Henley-on-Thames, Oxon., RG9 3HB, England.

OPPENHEIM, Dennis A., M.F.A.; American artist; b. 6 Sept. 1938, Washington; s. of David Oppenheim and Katherine Belknap; m. (divorced); three c.; ed. Coll. of Arts and Crafts, Oakland, Calif., Stanford Univ.; Prof. of Art, Yale Univ. 1969, State Univ. of New York at Stony Brook 1969; Guggenheim Foundation Sculpture Grant 1972; Nat. Endowment for the Arts Sculpture Grant 1974; numerous individual and group exhbns. at galleries in U.S.A. and Europe since 1968; works in many public collections including Museum of Modern Art, New York, Tate Gallery, London, Stedelijk Museum, Amsterdam and Musée d'Art Moderne, Paris. *Publications:* Catalyst 1967-70, Indentations 1974; articles in journals. *Leisure interest:* computer programming. *Address:* 54 Franklin Street, New York, N.Y. 10013, U.S.A.

OPPENHEIM, Sir Duncan Morris, Kt.; British tobacco manufacturer and solicitor; b. 6 Aug. 1904; s. of Watkin and Helen Oppenheim (née McKechnie); m. 1st Joyce Mitcheson 1932 (deceased), 2nd Susan Macnaghten 1936 (deceased); one s. one d.; ed. Repton School; Asst. Solicitor Messrs. Linklaters & Paines, London 1929; Solicitor to and Dir. of China Assoc. Co. of British-American Tobacco Co. Ltd. 1934; Asst. Solicitor, British-American Tobacco Co. London 1935, Solicitor 1936-49, Dir. 1943-72, Deputy Chair. 1947-49, Vice-Chair. 1949-53, Chair. 1953-66, Pres. 1966-72; Chair. Tobacco Securities Trust Ltd. 1969-74; Deputy Chair. Commonwealth Devt. Finance Co. Ltd. 1968-74; Chair. Royal College of Art Council 1956-72, Pro-Provost 1967-72; Chair. Council of Industrial Design 1960-72; Dir. Lloyds Bank Ltd. 1956-75, Equity, Law Life Assurance Soc. Ltd. 1966-80; Chair. British Nat. Cttee. of Int. Chamber of Commerce 1963-74, Overseas Investment Cttee., CBI 1970-74, Court of Govs., Admin. Staff Coll., Henley 1963-71; Chair. Royal Inst. of Int. Affairs 1966-71; Gov. Repton School 1959-79; mem. Advisory Cttee. Victoria and Albert Museum, London 1966-79, Crafts Council 1971-83; Deputy Chair. 1977-83; Hon. Dr. and Sr. Fellow, Royal Coll. of Art; Hon. Fellow Chartered Soc. of Designers; Bicentenary Medal, Royal Soc. of Arts 1969. *Leisure interests:* painting, sailing. *Address:* 43 Edwardes Square, London, W.8, England.

OPPENHEIM-BARNES, Rt. Hon. Sally, cr. Life Peer 1989; P.C.; fmr. British politician; b. 26 July 1930; d. of Mark Viner and Jeanette Viner; m. 1st Henry M. Oppenheim; one s. two d.; m. 2nd John Barnes 1984; ed. Sheffield High School, Lowther Coll., N. Wales; fmr. Exec. Dir. Industrial & Investment Services Ltd.; fmr. Social Worker, School Care Dept. ILEA; M.P. for Gloucester 1970-87; Vice-Chair. Conservative Party Parl. Prices and Consumer Protection Cttee. 1971-73, Chair. 1973-74; Opposition Spokesman on Prices and Consumer Protection 1974-79; mem. Shadow Cabinet 1975-79; Minister of State (Consumer Affairs), Dept. of Trade 1979-82; Chair. Nat. Consumer Council 1987-; Conservative; fmr. Nat. Vice-Pres. Nat. Union of Townswomen's Guilds; Pres. Glos. Dist. Br. BRCS; fmr. Trustee Clergy Rest House Trust. *Leisure interests:* tennis, bridge. *Address:* Quietways, The Highlands, Painswick, Glos., England.

OPPENHEIMER, Harry Frederick, M.A.; South African industrialist (retd.); b. 28 Oct. 1908, Kimberley; s. of late Sir Ernest Oppenheimer and Lady Oppenheimer; m. Bridget Denison McCall 1943; one s. one d.; ed. Charterhouse and Christ Church, Oxford (Hon. student); Chair. Anglo-American Corpn. of S. Africa Ltd. -1983, Chair. De Beers Consolidated Mines Ltd. -1984, Chair. E. Oppenheimer and Son; M.P. 1947-58; Chancellor Cape Town Univ. 1967-; Hon. D.Econ. (Natal); Hon. LL.D. (Leeds, Witwatersrand and Rhodes); Hon. D.Litt. (Cape Town). *Leisure interests:* reading, photography. *Address:* P.O. Box 61631, Marshaltown 2107; Brenthurst, Federation Road, Parktown, Johannesburg, South Africa (Home) *Telephone:* 833-7912.

OPPENHEIMER, Nicholas Frank, M.A.; South African business executive; b. 8 June 1945, Johannesburg; s. of Harry F. Oppenheimer (q.v.); m. Orcillia M. L. Lasch 1968; one s.; ed. Harrow School and Christ Church, Oxford; Chair. De Beers Consolidated Mines Ltd. 1984-85; Chair. East Dagga and S.A. Land; Dir. Anglo-American Corpn. of S.A. Ltd., East Rand Gold &' Uranium, Afrikander Lease Ltd., Barclays Nat. Bank, Diamond Corpn. (Pty.) Ltd., Elandsrand Gold Mining Co. Ltd., Freddies Consolidated Mines Ltd., F.S. Geduld Mines Ltd., Anglo-American Properties Ltd., De Beers Holdings Ltd., De Beers Industrial Corpn. Ltd., E. Oppenheimer & Son. (Pty.) Ltd., Free State Saaiplaas G.M. Co. Ltd., Vaal Reefs Exploration and Mining Co. Ltd., African Eagle Life Assen. Soc. Ltd., Anglo-American Insurance Holdings, Guarantee Life Assurance Co., (Non-Exec.) Minorco. *Leisure interests:* squash, golf. *Address:* Little Brenthurst, Third Avenue, P.O. Box 61631, Parktown, Johannesburg, South Africa.

OPPENLÄNDER, Karl Heinrich, D.ECON.; German economist; b. 17 Jan. 1932, Dörzbach; ed. Univ. of Munich; entered IFO Inst. for Econ. Research 1958, Head of Dept. 1966, mem. Exec. Cttee. 1972, Pres. 1976-; Lecturer, Univ. of Tübingen 1975, Univ. of Munich 1979-, Univ. of Augsburg 1980-83. *Publications:* Die moderne Wachstumstheorie 1963, Der investitionsinduzierte technische Fortschritt 1976. *Address:* IFO Institut für Wirtschaftsforschung, Poschingerstrasse 5, 8000 Munich 80, Federal Republic of Germany. *Telephone:* 089-92-24-279.

OPREA, Gheorghe; Romanian politician; b. 15 April 1927, Ţintea-Băicoi, Prahova County; ed. Polytechnic Inst., Bucharest; Gen. Man., Ministry of Machine Building Industry 1957-62, Deputy Minister 1962-70; alt. mem. Cen. Cttee. Romanian CP 1965-72, mem. Cen. Cttee. 1972-, Counsellor Cen. Cttee. 1970-74, mem. Exec. Political Cttee. Nov. 1974-; mem. Standing Bureau 1974-; Vice-Chair. Supreme Council for Econ. and Social Devt. 1974-; Deputy Chair. Council of Ministers 1974-78, First Deputy Chair. 1978-; Vice-Pres. Bureau, Nat. Council of Working People 1981-; mem. Grand Nat. Ass. March 1975-, Nat. Council Front of Socialist Democracy and Unity 1980. *Address:* Central Committee, Partidul Comunist Român, Str. Academiei 34, Bucharest, Romania. *Telephone:* 15 02 00.

OPSAHL, Torkel; DR.IUR., M.C.L.; Norwegian lawyer; b. 17 March 1931, Stavanger; m. Ist Torgunn Fosse 1957 (divorced 1972), one s. one d.; m. 2nd Kirsten Hofseth 1974, one s. one d.; ed. Univs. of Oslo, Moscow and Columbia, N.Y.; Prof. of Law (constitutional, Int. and Human Rights) 1965-; Adviser, Nobel Peace Prize Cttee. 1959-74; Ed. Samtiden (monthly review, Oslo) 1969-78; mem., European Comm. of Human Rights 1970-84, Human Rights Cttee., UN 1976-86; Pres. Norwegian Inst. of Human Rights 1987-. *Publications:* author of and contributor to many books and articles in Norwegian and English on Constitutional and Int. Law and Human Rights. *Address:* Institute of Public Law, University of Oslo, Oslo 1, Norway. *Telephone:* (02) 11-10-52.

ORAMAS-OLIVA, Oscar; Cuban diplomatist; b. 12 Nov. 1936, Las Villas; m.; four c.; Attaché Embassy, France 1960-61; Chargé d'Affaires, Japan 1961; Dept. Chief, Directorate for W. Europe, Ministry of External Relations 1963-64, Dir. for Africa and Middle E. 1973-75, Dir. for Sub-Saharan Africa 1977-81, Vice-Minister for External Relations 1981-84; Chargé d'Affaires, Algeria 1965-66; Amb. to Guinea, Mali and Equatorial Guinea 1966-73, to Angola and São Tomé and Príncipe 1975-77; Perm. Rep. of Cuba to the UN 1984-. *Address:* Permanent Mission of Cuba to the United Nations, 315 Lexington Avenue and 38th Street, New York, N.Y. 10016, U.S.A. *Telephone:* (212) 689-7215.

ORAYEVSKY, Anatoli Nikolaevich, DR. PHY. SCI.; Soviet physicist; b. 1934; ed. Moscow Physio-Tech. Inst.; mem. U.S.S.R. Acad. of Sciences Inst. of Physics 1956-, head of dept. 1982-; Prof. 1969; mem. CPSU 1962-; Lenin Prize 1984 (for contribution to publication of Fundamental Research on Chemical Lasers and Chain Reactions 1963-78). *Address:* U.S.S.R. Academy of Sciences, Moscow V-71, Leninsky Pr. 14, U.S.S.R.

ORBELIAN, Konstantin Agaparonovich; Soviet composer; b. 29 July 1928, Armenia; m. Nellie Orbelian 1986; ed. Yerevan Conservatoire (Mirzoyan composition class); mem. CPSU 1961-; work with Armenian State Orchestra of Light Music 1946-, Artistic Dir. and Chief Conductor 1956-; sr. mem. of Armenian Musicians' Union; Deputy Pres. of Int. Jury at Golden Orpheus Festival in Bulgaria 1971-; People's Artist of Armenia 1974, People's Artist of U.S.S.R. 1979; composer of ballets, works for symphony and chamber orchestras, film music, etc., notably Immortality (ballet) 1975, Zangezur (symphonic poem) 1971, string quartet 1956, symphony 1962, choreographic symphony 1967. *Address:* Armenian Musicians' Union, Yerevan, Armenian S.S.R.

ORCHARD, Peter Francis, C.B.E., M.A., C.B.I.M.; British business executive; b. 25 March 1927, Bromley, Kent; s. of Edward Henslowe and Agnes Marjory Orchard (née Willett); m. Helen Sheridan 1955; two s. two d.; ed. Downside School, Bath, Magdalene Coll., Cambridge; joined De La Rue Company Ltd. 1950; Man. Dir. Thomas De La Rue S.A., Brazil 1959-61; Man. Dir. Thomas De La Rue Int. 1962-70; Dir. De La Rue Co. PLC 1963-; Dir. of Manpower, De La Rue Co. 1972-75, Exec. Dir. Security and Graphics Divs. 1975-77, Chief Exec. De La Rue Co. PLC 1977-87, Chair. 1987-; Dir. Delta Group PLC 1981-; Hon. Col. 71st (Yeomanry) Signal Regt. T.A. 1984-88. *Leisure interest:* Court of Assistants, The Drapers Co. *Address:* The De La Rue Company PLC, 5 Burlington Gardens, London, W1A 1DL, England (Office). *Telephone:* 01-734 8020.

OREFFICE, Paul F(austo); B.S.; American company executive; b. 29 Nov. 1927, Venice, Italy; s. of Max and Elena (Friedenberg) Oreffice; m. Franca Giuseppina Ruffini 1956; one s. one d.; ed. Purdue Univ.; joined Dow Chemical Int., Midland, Mich. 1953, Mediterranean Area Sales Man., Milan, Italy 1955-56, Man. Dow Quimica do Brazil, São Paulo 1956-63, Gen. Man. Dow. Int., Spain 1963-65, Gen. Man. Dow Chemical Latin America 1965-67, Pres. Dow Chemical Inter-American Ltd. 1967-69, Financial Vice-Pres. The Dow Chemical Co. 1969-75, Dir. Dow Chemical Co. 1971-, Pres. Dow Chemical U.S.A. 1975-78, Chair. Exec. Cttee. Dow Chemical Co. 1978-87, Pres. and C.E.O. 1978-87, Chair. May 1986-; Dir. Dow Corning Corpn. 1976-, Cigna Corpn., Northern Telecom Ltd. 1983, The Coca-Cola Company 1985; Trustee, American Enterprise Inst., the Conf. Bd.; mem. Policy Cttee., The Business Roundtable; mem. The Business Council; Encomienda del Merito Civil (Spain) 1966; Hon. D.Eng. (Purdue) 1976, Hon. Dr. Industrial Management (Lawrence Inst. of Tech.), Science (Saginaw Valley State Coll.), Business Admin. (Tri-State Univ.). *Leisure interests:* tennis, bridge, golf, various other sports. *Address:* 2030 Dow Center, Midland, Mich. 48674, U.S.A. (Office). *Telephone:* (517) 636-3115.

O'REGAN, (Andrew) Brendan; Irish business executive; b. 15 May 1917, Co. Clare; s. of James and Norah O'Regan; m.; two s. three d.; ed. Blackrock Coll., Dublin; Comptroller, Sales and Catering, Shannon Airport 1943-73; Chair. Bord Fáilte Eireann 1957-73, Shannon Free Airport Devt. Co. 1959-78, State Agencies Devt. Co-operation Org. (DEVCO) 1974-79, 1988-89, Co-operation N. 1979-82; Pres. Co-operation Ireland Inc. (N.Y.) 1982-; Chair. Irish Peace Inst. 1984-, Shannon Centre for Int. Co-operation 1987-; Fellow, Inst. of Engineers of Ireland 1977, Irish Hotel and Catering Inst. 1977; Hon. LL.D. (Nat. Univ. of Ireland) 1978; United Dominions Trust Endeavour Award for Tourism 1973; American Soc. of Travel Agents—Hall of Fame 1977; British Airways Tourism Endeavour Award 1980; Clare Person of the Year 1983; Rotary's Paul Harris Award. *Publications:* numerous speeches and articles on peace through managed co-operation. *Leisure interests:* reading, sailing, riding. *Address:* "Molne", Killaloe, Co. Clare, Ireland.

O'REILLY, Anthony J. F., B.C.L.; company executive; b. 1936, Dublin, Ireland; s. of John Patrick and Aileen (O'Connor) O'Reilly; m. Susan Cameron 1962; six c.; ed. Univ. Coll., Dublin; qualified as solicitor 1958; Demonstrator and Lecturer, Univ. Coll., Cork 1960-62; Personal Asst. to Chair., Suttons Ltd., Cork 1960-62; Dir. Robert McCowen & Sons Ltd., Tralee 1961-62; Gen. Man. Bord Bainne (Irish Dairy Bd.) 1962-66; Man. Dir. and C.E.O., Comhlucht Siuicre Eireann Teo. (Irish Sugar Co.) 1966-69; Jt. Man. Dir. Heinz-Erin Ltd. 1967-70, Man. Dir. H. J. Heinz Co. Ltd., U.K. 1969-71, Sr. Vice-Pres. N. America and Pacific H. J. Heinz Co. 1971-72, Exec. Vice-Pres. and C.O.O. 1972-73, Pres. and C.O.O. 1973-79, Pres. and C.E.O. 1979-, Chair. 1987-; Fellow B.I.M. *Publications:* Prospect 1962, Developing Creative Management 1970, The Conservative Consumer 1971, Food for Thought 1972. *Address:* P.O. Box 57, Pittsburgh, Pennsylvania, Pa. 15230, U.S.A.

O'REILLY, Edward, M.P.A.; Irish politician; b. 19 April 1948, Claremorris; s. of Philip O'Reilly and Margaret O'Reilly; m. Theresa Kilgallon 1986; ed. St. Colmans Coll., St. Patricks Coll., Univ. Colls. Galway and Dublin; English Teacher Vocational School, Ballina 1970-74; Prin. Ballaghadereen Vocational School 1979-83, Wexford Vocational School 1983-87; Gen. Sec. Fine Gael 1987-. *Publication:* COMECON and the EEC—the formal and informal relationship 1977. *Leisure interests:* music, tennis, golf. *Address:* 51 Upper Mount Street, Dublin 2 (Office); Newtown Road, Wexford, Ireland (Home). *Telephone:* 761573 (Office); (053) 23893 (Home).

OREJA AGUIRRE, Marcelino; Spanish diplomatist and government official; b. 13 Feb. 1935; entered diplomatic service 1958; Dir. Tech. Office of Minister of Foreign Affairs 1962; fmr. Asst. Dir., Prof. of Foreign Affairs at Escuela Diplomática; mem. Dels. to UN, IMF, IDB, OECD; mem. interministerial cttee. drafting bill for religious freedom; Dir. of Int. Relations, Banco de España 1971-74; Under-Sec. for Information and Tourism 1974, for Foreign Affairs Dec. 1975; Minister of Foreign Affairs 1976-80; elected Deputy for Guipuzcoa and Alava in 1979 and 1982; Govt. Rep. in Basque Country 1980-82; Sec. Gen. Council of Europe 1984-; Senator by royal appointment June 1977. *Address:* The Council of Europe, BP 431, R6-67006, Strasbourg Cedex, France.

OREK, Osman Nuri; Cypriot lawyer and politician; b. 26 Dec. 1925, Nicosia; s. of the late Ahmet Mustafa Orek and of Muride Ahmet; m. Neriman Orek 1958; one s. one d.; ed. Turkish Lycée, Nicosia, Univ. of Istanbul and Middle Temple, London; Founder-mem. Cyprus-Turkish Asscn., London, Chair. 1951-52; Sec. Nicosia Branch, Cyprus Turkish Nat. Union Party 1953-55, Sec.-Gen. 1955-60, Deputy Chair. July 1960-; Deputy Chair. High Council of Evcaf 1956-60; rep. Turkish Cypriot Community at London Conf. 1959 and subsequent Joint Cttee.; Minister of Defence 1959; mem. Exec. Council of Turkish Cypriot Provisional Admin. for Defence 1967-74, concurrently for Internal Affairs 1967-70, and External Affairs 1967-72; mem. Exec. Council of Autonomous Turkish Cypriot Admin. for Vice-Presidency and Defence 1974-75; Vice-Pres. "Turkish Federated State of Cyprus" "TFSC" 1975-76, Minister of Defence 1975-76; Pres. "TFSC" Legis. Ass. 1976-78; Prime Minister April-Dec. 1978; Leader of Nat. Unity Party 1978; M.P. "TFSC" 1979-81; mem. Constituent Ass. T.R.N.C. 1983-85; Chair. Bar Council of TRNC 1988-. *Leisure interests:* swimming, water-skiing, hunting. *Address:* Orek and Associates Law Office, Mufti Raci Street, Nicosia, Mersin 10, (Office); 10 Ismail Beyoglu Street, Lefkosa, Mersin 10, Turkey (Home).

ORFILA, Alejandro; Argentine diplomatist; b. 9 March 1925, Mendoza; ed. Univ. de Buenos Aires, Stanford and Tulane (New Orleans) Univs.; Sec. Ministry of Foreign Affairs 1946, Moscow 1946; Consul, Warsaw 1947-48, San Francisco 1948-49; Consul-Gen. New Orleans 1949-50; Sec. Washington D.C. 1951-52; Man. José Orfila, Ltda., Mendoza 1952, Dir. of Information, OAS 1953-58; Minister Plenipotenitary, Washington D.C. 1958-60; Amb. to Japan 1960-62; private consultant in int. financial and econ. affairs 1962-73; Amb. to U.S.A. 1973-75; Sec.-Gen. OAS 1975-84; Vice-Chair. Gray and Co. also Head of Int. Div. March 1984—. *Address:* c/o Organization of American States, General Secretariat, 17th Street and Constitution Avenue, N.W., Washington, D.C. 20006, U.S.A.

ORGAD, Ben Zion; Israeli composer; b. 1926, Germany; ed. Acad. of Music in Jerusalem and Brandeis Univ., U.S.A.; studied violin with Kinory and Bergman and composition with Paul Ben-Haim and Josef Tal; studied in U.S.A. under Aaron Copland (q.v.) and Irving Fine; Supervisor of Musical Educ., Israel Ministry of Educ. and Culture 1950-; Chair. Israel Composers' League; recipient of several awards for compositions. *Compo-*

sitions include: cantatas: The Story of the Spies (UNESCO Koussevitsky Prize 1952), Isaiah's Vision; orchestral: Building a King's Stage, Choreographic Sketches, Movements on 'A', Kaleidoscope, Music for Horn and Orchestra, Ballad for Orchestra, Dialogues on the First Scroll; Hatsvi Israel (baritone and orchestra), Suffering for Redemption (mezzo-soprano, choir and orchestra), Out of the Dust (for solo and instruments); Ballada (for violin), Taksim (for harp), Monologue (for viola); works for soloists and orchestra, songs, piano pieces, etc. *Address:* Ministry of Education and Culture, Hadar-Daphna Building, Tel-Aviv (Office); 14 Bloch Street, Tel-Aviv, Israel (Home). *Telephone:* 254122 (Office).

ORGAN, (Harold) Bryan; British artist; b. 31 Aug. 1935, Leicester; s. of Harold Victor and Helen Dorothy Organ; m. 2nd Sandra Mary Mills 1982; ed. Loughborough Coll. of Art; Royal Acad. Schools, London; Lecturer in Drawing and Painting, Loughborough 1959-65; One-man Exhbns.: Leicester Museum and Art Gallery 1959, Redfern Gallery, London 1967, 1969, 1971, 1973, 1975, 1978, 1980, Leicester 1973, 1976, New York 1976, Baukunst, Cologne 1977, Turin 1981; Represented: Kunsthalle, Darmstadt 1968, Mostra Mercatao d'Arte Contemporanea, Florence 1969, 3rd Int. Exhbns. of Drawing Germany 1970, São Paulo Museum of Art, Brazil; Works in private and public collections in England, France, Germany, Italy, Switzerland, U.S.A., Canada, Brazil, Hon. M.A. (Loughborough) 1974, Hon. D.Litt. (Leicester) 1985. *Portraits include:* Sir Michael Tippett 1966, David Hicks 1968; Mary Quant 1969, Princess Margaret 1970, Elton John 1973, Viscount Stockton 1980, The Prince of Wales 1980, The Princess of Wales 1981, Lord Denning 1982, Sir James Callaghan 1982, H.R.H. The Duke of Edinburgh 1983. *Leisure interest:* cricket. *Address:* c/o Redfern Gallery, 20 Cork Street, London, W.1, England. *Telephone:* 01-734 1732.

ORIEUX, Jean; French author; b. 20 May 1907, Duras, Lot-et-Garonne; ed. Ecole Normale Supérieure, Saint Cloud. *Publications:* novels include Fontagre 1940 (Grand prix) du roman, Acad. française), Kasbahs en plein ciel 1953 (Prix du Maroc), Petit Sérail 1952; *biographies:* Bussy-Rabutin 1958, Voltaire 1966, Talleyrand 1971 (Prix des Ambassadeurs), La Fontaine 1966, Catherine de Médicis 1986 (Prix Paul-Morand, Acad. française). *Address:* Flammarion et Cie, 26 rue Racine, 75278 Paris Cedex 06, France.

ORLANDI CONTUCCI, Corrado, D.IUR.; Italian diplomatist; b. 10 July 1914, Monte Colombo; s. of Antonio and Ginevra (dal Pero-Bertini) Orlandi Contucci; m. Eleonora Ponno 1950; three d.; ed. Univs. of Rome, Cambridge, Tours; entered Foreign Service 1939; joined Cavalry as Lieut. 1940; sent to open Italian Embassy in Washington, D.C. 1945, in Belgrade 1947; Vice-Dir. of Cabinet of Foreign Minister Sforza 1949-51; First Sec. in Del. to NATO 1951-54, Head of Eastern European Office in Political Affairs Dept. 1954-58; Minister Counsellor, Cairo 1958-60; Deputy Perm. Rep. to NATO 1960-67; Amb. to Luxembourg 1967-68; Chief of Protocol of Italian Republic 1968-76; Amb. to Fed. Repub. of Germany 1976-80; Diplomatic Adviser to Chair. ENI 1980-84; mem. Bd. Alitalia 1983-86; Chair. Italian Center of Studies for Int. Conciliation, Rome 1987-; Grand Cross of Italian Repub., Knight Grand Cross of Victorian Order (U.K.), Grand Cross of Honour (Fed. Repub. of Germany) Grand Officier, Légion d'honneur (France). *Publications:* numerous articles in Affari Esteri. *Address:* 24 Corso Vittorio Emanuele 11, Rome, Italy (Home).

ORLOV, Vladimir Pavlovich; Soviet politician; b. 1921; trained at a textile inst.; First Sec. Kuibyshev Regional Cttee. of the CPSU 1967-79; First Deputy Prime Minister of the R.S.F.S.R. 1979-85; Pres. Presidium of the Supreme Soviet of the R.S.F.S.R. 1985-88, a Vice-Chair. Presidium of the Supreme Soviet of the U.S.S.R. 1985-88; mem. CPSU Cen. Cttee. 1979. *Address:* Supreme Soviet of R.S.F.S.R., Moscow, U.S.S.R.

ORLOV, Yuri F.; Soviet physicist and human rights activist; b. 13 Aug 1924, Moscow; worked in a factory; served in army in World War II; ed. Moscow Univ.; mem. staff of Inst. of Theoretical and Experimental Physics until dismissed for political reasons 1956; subsequently worked in Yerevan, Armenian S.S.R.; obtained doctorate 1963, became an expert on particle acceleration; returned to Moscow 1972; dismissed from post after pleading on behalf of Andrei Sakharov 1973; co-founder and Chair. Helsinki Monitoring Group following signing of Helsinki Agreement 1975; arrested 1977, on trial 1978 and sentenced to seven years in strict-regime labour camp followed by five years' exile; wrote account of prison conditions, smuggled out and printed in Belgian newspaper 1979; released from labour camp and exiled to Kobyai, nr. Yakutsk, Siberia 1984; released Oct. 1986, living in U.S.A.

ORME, Rt. Hon. Stanley, P.C.; British politician; b. 5 April 1923, Sale, Cheshire; s. of Sherwood Orme; m. Irene Mary Harris 1951; ed. elementary and tech. schools, Nat. Council of Labour Colls. and Workers' Educ. Asscn. classes; Shop Steward, Amalgamated Union of Engineering Workers (AUEW) 1949-64; Councillor, Sale Borough Council 1957-65; M.P. for Salford W. 1964-83, for Salford E. 1983-; Minister of State, Northern Ireland Office 1974-76, Dept. of Health and Social Security April-Sept. 1976; Minister for Social Security 1976-79; Opposition Spokesman for Health and Social Security 1979-80, for Industry 1980-83, for Energy 1983-87; Chair. Parl. Labour Party 1987-; Chair. AUEW Parl. Group of Labour M.P.s 1977; Hon. Dr. Sc. (Salford) 1985. *Address:* House of Commons, Westminster, London, S.W.1; 8 Northwood Grove, Sale, Cheshire, England (Home).

ORMESSON, Comte Jean d'; French author, journalist and international official; b. 16 June 1925; s. of Marquis d'Ormesson; nephew of late Comte Wladimir d'Ormesson; m. Françoise Béghin 1962; one d.; ed. Ecole Normale Supérieure; Deputy Sec.-Gen. Int. Council for Philosophy and Humanistic studies (UNESCO) 1950-71, Sec.-Gen. 1971; staff of various govt. ministers 1958-66; Deputy Ed. Diogène (int. journal) 1952-72, mem. Man. Cttee. 1972-; mem. Council ORTF 1960-62, Programme Cttee. 1973; mem. Control Comm. of Cinema 1962-69; mem. Editorial Cttee. Editions Gallimard 1972-74; Ed.-in-Chief, Columnist, Le Figaro 1974-77, leader writer, columnist 1977-, Dir.-Gen. 1976-; mem. Acad. Française 1973; Pres., Soc. des amis de Jules Romains 1974-; Grand Prix du Roman (Acad. Française) for novel La gloire de l'empire 1971; Officier, Légion d'honneur. *Publications:* L'amour est un plaisir 1956, Du côté de chez Jean 1959, Un amour pour rien 1960, Au revoir et merci 1966, Les illusions de la mer 1968, La gloire de l'empire 1971, Au plaisir de Dieu 1974, Le vagabond qui passe sous une ombrelle trouée 1978, Dieu, sa vie, son oeuvre 1981, Mon dernier rève sera pour vous 1982, Jean qui grogne et Jean qui rit 1984, Le vent du soir 1985, Tous les hommes en sont fous 1985; numerous articles in Le Figaro, Le Monde, France-Soir, Paris Match, etc. *Address:* c/o Le Figaro, 37 rue du Louvre, Paris 75001 (Office); 10 avenue du Parc-Saint-James, 92200 Neuilly-sur-Seine, France (Home). *Telephone:* 577-16-10.

ORNANO, Comte Michel d'; French politician and administrator; b. 12 July 1924, Paris; s. of Comte Guillaume d'Ornano and Elisabeth de Michalska; m. Anne de Contades 1960; one s. one d.; ed. Lycée Carnot, Univ. of Paris; Mayor of Deauville 1962-77; mem. Council on Foreign Trade 1956-, mem. Directing Council 1963-; elected Deputy for Calvados, Nat. Ass. 1967, 1968, 1973, 1978, 1981; Conseiller gen., Trouville 1976-; Sec. Comm. of Foreign Affairs to Nat. Ass.; Sec.-Gen. Independent Republicans 1974, Vice-Pres. 1975-; Minister of Industry and Research 1974-77, of Culture and Environment 1977-78, of Environment and Equipment 1978-81; Pres. Conseil Général, Calvados 1979-, and of Conseil régional, Basse-Normandie 1983-86, Econ. and Finance Cttee. of Nat. Ass. *Publications:* Une certaine idél de Paris 1976, La manipulation des médias 1983. *Address:* 88 rue du Général-Leclerc, 14800 Deauville, France.

ORNAT, Andrzej, M.A.; Polish politician; b. 16 Sept. 1946, Garwolin; m.; one d.; ed. Warsaw Univ.; teacher, primary school, Zagórze 1964-67; instructor Garwolin Troop of Polish Pathfinders' Union 1967-68, Commandant 1968-71; Deputy Commandant Mazovian Troop 1971-74, Commandant 1974-75; Head, Organizational Dept. of Polish Pathfinders' Union Chief HQ 1975-79, mem. Chief HQ 1977-82, Deputy C.-in-C. 1979-80, C.-in-C. of Polish Pathfinders' Union 1980-82; mem. Council of Ministers, Sec. Cttee. of Council of Ministers for Youth Matters 1982-85; First Sec. PZPR Voivodship Cttee., Siedlce 1986-; mem. Polish United Workers' Party (PZPR) 1966-, mem. PZPR Cen. Cttee. 1981-86, Nat. Council of Culture 1983-; Councillor, City of Warsaw Nat. Council 1973-76; Knight's Cross of Polonia Restituta Order; Silver and Gold Cross of Merit, Nat. Educ. Comm. Medal, Silver Order of Peace and Friendship Star (G.D.R.). *Address:* Komitet Wojewódzki PZPR, ul. Buczka 2, 08-110 Siedlce, Poland. *Telephone:* 23-274 (Office).

ORNSTEIN, Donald Samuel, PH.D.; American mathematician; b. 30 July 1934; s. of Harry Ornstein and Rose (Wisner) Ornstein; m. Shari Richman 1964; two s. one d.; ed. Swarthmore Coll. and Univ. of Chicago; mem. Inst. for Advanced Study, Princeton 1956-58; Instructor, Univ. of Wisconsin 1958-60; Asst. Prof. Stanford Univ. 1960-63, Sloan Fellow and Assoc. Prof. 1963-65, Assoc. Prof. 1965-68, Prof. of Math. 1969-; Visiting Prof. Cornell Univ. and New York Univ. (Courant Inst.) 1967-68, Hebrew Univ. Jerusalem 1975-76, Mathematical Sciences Research Inst. Berkeley 1983-84; mem. N.A.S.; Bocher Prize, American Math. Soc. 1974. *Publications:* mathematical papers in many journals since 1959. *Address:* Department of Mathematics, Stanford University, Stanford, Calif. 94305 (Office); 857 Tolman Drive, Stanford, Calif. 94305, U.S.A. (Home).

O'ROURKE, Andrew; Irish diplomatist; b. 7 May 1931, Dublin; s. of Joseph O'Rourke and Elizabeth (née O'Farrell) O'Rourke; m. Hanne Stephensen 1962; one s. two d.; ed. Univ. of Dublin; served in Depts. of Finance and Educ. 1949-57; joined Dept. of Foreign Affairs 1957; served Berne and London; Counsellor, Perm. Mission of Ireland to EEC 1973, Deputy Perm. Rep. 1974-78; Sec. Dept. of Foreign Affairs 1978-81; Perm. Rep. to EEC 1981-86; Amb. to France and Perm. Rep. to OECD 1986-87, to U.K. 1987-. *Leisure interests:* walking, golf, reading. *Address:* Irish Embassy, 17 Grosvenor Place, London. S.W.1, England.

O'ROURKE, Mary; Irish politician; b. 31 May 1937, Athlone; d. of P. J. Lenihan; m. Enda O'Rourke; two s.; ed. St. Peter's Convent, Univ. Coll. Dublin and St. Patrick's Coll. Maynooth, Co. Kildare; fmr. secondary school teacher; mem. Westmeath County Council 1979-; mem. Dail 1982; Minister for Educ. 1987-; Fianna Fail. *Address:* Aisling, Arcadia, Athlone, Co. Westmeath, Ireland. *Telephone:* (0902) 75065.

OROWAN, Egon, M.A., DR.ING.; American professor emeritus of mechanical engineering; b. 2 Aug. 1902, Budapest, Hungary; s. of Berthold Orowan and Josephine Ságvári; m. Jolan Schonfeld 1941 (deceased 1986); one d.; ed. Univ. of Vienna and Technical Univ. of Berlin; Asst. Prof. Tech. Univ. of Berlin 1928-33; Research Assoc. Univ. of Birmingham, England 1937-39; Research Assoc. Univ. of Cambridge (Cavendish Lab.) 1939-45, Nuffield

Research Fellow 1945–47, Reader in Physics of Metals 1947–50; Prof. of Mechanical Eng., M.I.T., U.S.A. 1950–68, Sr. Lecturer 1968–73, Prof. Emer. 1973–; Fellow, Royal Soc. of London; mem. N.A.S., American Acad. of Arts and Sciences; Corresp. mem. Göttingen Acad. of Sciences; Dr.Ing. h.c. (Tech. Univ. Berlin); Thomas Hawksley Gold Medal of Inst. of Mechanical Engineers, London 1944, Eugene C. Bingham Medal of American Soc. of Rheology 1959, Carl Friedrich Gauss Medal, Braunschweiger Wissenschaftliche Gesellschaft 1968, Vincent Bendix Gold Medal 1971, Paul Bergsoe Medal, Danish Metal Soc. 1973, TMS-AIME Special Award 1984, Acta Metallurgica Medal 1985, Heyn Memorial Medal 1985. *Publications:* Papers in scientific journals and chapters in books. *Leisure interest:* getting acquainted with next field of professional interest. *Address:* 44 Payson Terrace, Belmont, Mass. 02178, U.S.A. (Home). *Telephone:* 617-484-8334 (Home).

ORR, Sir David Alexander, Kt., M.C., LL.D.; British business executive; b. 10 May 1922, Dublin, Ireland; s. of Canon A. W. F. Orr and Grace Robinson; m. Phoebe R. Davis; three d.; ed. High School and Trinity Coll., Dublin; with Unilever 1948–82; Marketing Dir., Hindustan Lever, Bombay 1955; mem. Overseas Cttee., Unilever 1960; Vice-Pres. Lever Brothers Co., New York 1963, Pres. 1965; Dir. Unilever PLC 1967–82, Vice-Chair. 1970–74, Chair. 1974–82; Vice-Chair. of Unilever NV 1974; Chair. British Council 1985–; Dir. Rio Tinto-Zinc Corpn. 1981–, Shell Transport and Trading Co. July 1982–; non-exec. Dir. Inchcape PLC Sept. 1982– (Chair. 1983–86, Deputy Chair. 1986–); Dir. Bank of Ireland 1986–; Vice-Pres. then Pres. Liverpool School of Tropical Medicine; Leverhulme Trust 1979–81, Chair. 1982–; Dir. Bank of Ireland; Fellow of Royal Soc. for the Encouragement of Arts, Manufactures and Commerce 1974; Council mem. L.S.E.; Hon. LL.D. (Trinity Coll. Dublin) 1978, Hon. D.Univ. (Surrey) 1982; Commdr. of Order of Oranje Nassau (Netherlands) 1979. *Leisure interests:* books, travel and sport. *Address:* Inchcape PLC, London; Home Farm House, Shackleford, Godalming, Surrey, GU8 6AH, England. *Telephone:* Guildford 810350 (Home).

ORR, Kay A.; American politician; b. 2 Jan. 1939, Burlington, Iowa; d. of Ralph Roger Skoglund and Sadie Lucille Skoglund; m. William Dayton Orr 1957; one s. one d.; ed. Iowa Univ.; Exec. Asst. to Gov. of Neb. 1979–81; Treasurer, State of Neb. 1981–87; Gov. of Nebraska Jan. 1987–; mem. Nat. Council on Rural Devt. (U.S.D.A.); Vice-Chair. Cttee. on Transportation, Commerce and Communications (Nat. Govs'. Asscn.); Chair. Nat. Repub. Platform Cttee. 1988; Republican. *Address:* State Capitol, Lincoln, Neb., U.S.A.

ORR, Robert Dunkerson, A.B.; American politician; b. 17 Nov. 1917, Ann Arbor, Mich.; s. of Samuel Lowry Orr and Louise (Dunkerson) Orr; m. Joanne Wallace 1944; one s. two d.; ed. Yale Univ. and Harvard Business School; army service 1942–46, rank of Maj.; Officer, Dir. Orr Iron Co., Ind. 1946–60, Sign Crafters Inc. 1957–74, Hahn Inc. 1957–69, Indian Industries Inc. 1962–73; Dir. Sterling Brewers, Ernie Investments 1965–71; mem. Ind. Senate 1968–72; Lieut.-Gov. of Indiana 1973–81, Gov. 1981–89; Amb. to Singapore 1989–; Leader Foreign Operations Admin. evaluation team, Viet-Nam 1954; Chair. Vanderburgh County Republican Party, Ind. 1965–71; hon. degrees (Indiana State Univ., Terre Haute) 1973, (Hanover Coll., Ind.) 1974, (Butler Univ., Indianapolis) 1977, (Univ. of Evansville) 1985, (Univ. of Ind.) 1985; Republican. *Leisure interests:* politics, tennis, skiing, golf. *Address:* American Embassy, 30 Hill Street, Singapore 0617.

ORR-EWING, Hamish; British company director; b. 17 Aug. 1924, London; s. of Hugh Eric Douglas Orr-Ewing and Esme Victoria (née Stewart); m. 1st Morar Margaret Kennedy 1947, one s. one d. (deceased); m. 2nd Ann Mary Teresa Terry 1954; ed. Eton; served as Capt., Black Watch, 2nd World War; Salesman, EMI 1950; joined Ford Motor Co. 1954; Ford Light Car Planning Man. 1959–63; Leyland Motor Corpn. Ltd. 1963–65; joined Rank Xerox 1965, apptd. to Bd. as Dir. of Product Planning 1968, Dir. of Personnel 1970; Man. Dir. Rank Xerox (U.K.) Ltd. 1971–; Registered Dir. for Rank Xerox Operations in U.K., France, Netherlands, Sweden and Belgium 1977; Dir. Tricentrol PLC 1975–; Chair. Jaguar PLC 1984–85; Chair. Rank Xerox Ltd. 1980–86; Chair. European Govt. Business Relations Council 1980–84, White Horse Holdings Ltd. 1987–; Manpower Services Commr. 1983–84; mem. Eng. Council 1984–87; Chair. Work and Soc. 1982–84; mem. Bd. CBI Educ. Foundation-UBI 1982; Chair. CBI Educ. and Training Cttee. 1985–87, Chair. Trustee Shaw Trust 1985–. *Leisure interests:* anything mechanical, country life, the Roman Empire. *Address:* Fox Mill, Purton, near Swindon, Wilts., SN5 9EF, England. *Telephone:* Swindon 770496.

ORREGO VICUÑA, Francisco, PH.D.; Chilean lawyer and diplomatist; b. 12 April 1942, Santiago; m. Soledad Bauza; three c.; ed. schools in Chile, Argentina, Spain and Egypt, Univ. of Chile and L.S.E.; fmr. Dir. Inst. of Int. Studies and Prof. at Univ. of Chile; fmr. Visiting Prof. Stanford Univ. and Univ. of Paris II Law School; participated in projects for Acad. of Int. Law, The Hague, UNITAR and various studies and projects undertaken by univs. in Europe, U.S.A., Asia and Latin America; fmr. legal adviser to OAS; fmr. Del. Law of Sea Conf.; fmr. int. ed., El Mercurio (daily newspaper); Amb. to U.K. 1983–85; Prof. of Int. Law, Inst. of Int. Studies, Univ. of Chile 1985–. *Publications:* Antarctic Resources Policy 1983, Antarctic Mineral Exploitation 1988, The Exclusive Economic Zone 1989, and other books and articles. *Address:* Institute of International Studies,

University of Chile, P.O. Box 14187 Suc. 21, Santiago 9, Chile. *Telephone:* (2) 740-730.

ORRICK, William Horsley, Jr.; American government official; b. 10 Oct. 1915; ed. Hotchkiss School, Yale and Univ. of California (Berkeley); admitted to Calif. Bar 1941; Partner, Orrick, Herrington, Rowley and Sutcliffe, San Francisco 1941–61, 1965–74; Asst. Attorney Gen. Dept. of Justice 1961–62; Deputy Under Sec. for Admin., Dept. of State 1962–63; Asst. Attorney Gen. Dept. of Justice 1963–65; Chair. U.S. Del. to OECD Cttee. on Restrictive Business Practices 1963; U.S. District Judge, Northern District of Calif. Aug. 1974–; Citation Award, Univ. of Calif. School of Law 1980. *Address:* 450 Golden Gate Avenue, P.O. Box 36060, San Francisco, Calif. 94102, U.S.A.

ORSETTI, Christian Ernest, L. EN D.; French diplomatist; b. 1 April 1923, Montpellier; s. of Antoine Orsetti and Marie-Louise Couffinhal; m. Marie-Antoinette Vincent 1946; three d.; ed. Univ. of Monpellier, Ecole Libre des Sciences Politiques; holder of numerous government posts since 1945, including: Sec.-Gen. for Haute-Marne 1952, Tarn-et-Garonne 1955, Fougères 1960; Cabinet Dir. for Minister of Agric. 1962–64, then Minister for Material Resources 1966–67; Auditor to Inst. des Hautes Etudes de Défense Nat. 1972–73; Prefect for Martinique 1973–75; with Ministry of Foreign Affairs 1977; Amb. of Monaco to France 1977–; Officier Légion d'honneur, Commdr. Ordre nat. du Mérite, Ordre du Mérite Agricole, Officier des Palmes Académiques, etc. *Address:* 12 avenue Georges-Mandel, 75116 Paris (Office); Ambassade de la Principauté de Monaco, 22 boulevard Suchet, 75016 Paris (Office); 8 rue de Champmotteux, Gironville-sur-Essonne, 91720 Maisse, France (Home).

ORTEGA SAAVEDRA, Daniel; Nicaraguan politician and fmr. resistance leader; b. 11 Nov. 1945, La Libertad, Chontales; s. of Daniel Ortega and Lidia Saavedra; m. Rosario Murillo; seven c.; ed. Univ. Centroamericano, Managua; active in various underground resistance movts. against regime of Anastasio Somoza from 1959 and was several times imprisoned and tortured for revolutionary activities; ed. El Estudiante, official publ. of Frente Estudiantil Revolucionaria and directed org. of Comités Civicos Populares in Managua 1965; mem. Nat. Directorate of FSLN (Sandinista Liberation Front) 1966–67; imprisoned 1967–74; resumed position with FSLN and with José Benito Escobar became involved in further revolutionary activities; fought on front in two-year mil. offensive which overthrew Somoza regime 1979; mem. Junta of Nat. Reconstruction Govt. 1979, Co-ordinator of Junta 1981–85, Pres. of Nicaragua Jan. 1985–. *Address:* Office of the President, Managua, Nicaragua.

ORTEZ COLINDRES, Enrique, LL.D.; Honduran diplomatist, banker and lawyer; b. 29 Oct. 1931, Juitcalpa; ed. Nat. Autonomous Univ. of Honduras, Univ. of Paris; First Sec. Honduran Embassy, France 1955–59, Chargé d'affaires 1959; Amb. special mission to the Govts. of Brazil, Trinidad and Tobago and Venezuela; mem. Honduras del. to 2nd special session of the UN Gen. Ass. on disarmament; Perm. Rep. of Honduras to the UN 1982–84; Sec. Honduras del. to Int. Court of Justice 1959; Dir. Dept. of Cultural and Educational Affairs, Org. of Cen. American States 1960–63; Dir. (later Vice-Pres.) Banco Centroamericano de Integración Económica 1964–68, Pres. 1968–75; f. Financiera Centro-Americana S.A. 1975, Credomatic de Honduras 1979; pvt. legal practice, Tegucigalpa 1978–; Prof. of Int. Law, Nat. Autonomous Univ. of Honduras 1979–81; f. La Tribuna (newspaper), Tegucigalpa 1980; Pres. Asscn. of Honduran Law Students 1953; mem. Comm. on Human Rights, Coll. of Lawyers of Honduras 1979–81. *Address:* c/o Ministerio de Asuntos Exteriores, Palacio de los Ministerios, Tegucigalpa, Honduras.

ORTIZ, Cristina; Brazilian concert pianist; b. 17 April 1950, Bahia, Brazil; d. of Silverio M. Ortiz and Moema F. Ortiz; m. Jasper W. Parrott 1974; two d.; ed. Conservatório Brasilieiro de Música, Rio de Janeiro, Acad. Int. de Piano (with Magda Tagliaferro), Paris and Curtis Inst. of Music, Philadelphia (with Rudolph Serkin); First Prize Van Cliburn Int. Competition, Texas 1969; has since appeared in concerts with the Vienna Philharmonic, the Concertgebouw, Chicago Symphony, N.Y. Philharmonic, Israeli Philharmonic, L.A. Philharmonic, all the leading British orchestras etc. and has undertaken many tours of North and South America, the Far East, N.Z. and Japan; has recorded extensively for EMI, Decca, Pantheon and Pickwick Records. *Leisure interests:* tennis, swimming, gardening, reading, hiking, holidaying. *Address:* c/o Harrison-Parrott Ltd., 12 Penzance Place, London, W11 4PA, England. *Telephone:* 01-229 9166.

ORTIZ, Frank Vincent, M.S.; American diplomatist; b. 14 March 1926, Santa Fé; s. of Frank V. Ortiz and Margaret Delgado Ortiz; m. Mary Dolores Duke 1953; three s. one d.; ed. Georgetown, George Washington, New Mexico, Madrid Univs.; diplomatic posts in Ethiopia and Mexico 1953–57; Special Asst. to Under-Sec. of State 1957–60, to Amb. to Mexico 1961–63; Country Dir. for Spain and Portugal 1963–67, for Argentina, Uruguay and Paraguay 1973–75; Head, Political Section and Chargé d'Affaires, Peru and Uruguay 1967–73; Deputy Exec. Sec. of State 1975–77; Amb. to Barbados, Grenada, St. Lucia and Dominica 1977–79, to Guatemala 1979–80, to Peru 1981–83, to Argentina 1983–86; Diplomat in Residence, Latin American Inst., New Mexico Univ. 1986–; Political Adviser, C.-in-C., Southern Command 1980–81; Hon. Dr. Iur. (New Mexico); Superior Service Award, Order of Civil Merit of Spain, Order of the Kts. of Malta;

Meritorious Honor Award, Presidential Chamizal Medal (Mexico), and others. *Leisure interests:* history, tennis. *Address:* 3843 Garrison Street S.W., Washington D.C. 20016, U.S.A. *Telephone:* (202) 362-4014.

ORTIZ, Rene Genaro; Ecuadorian chemical and industrial engineer; b. 31 Dec. 1941, Quito; s. of Genaro Ortiz and Anita de Ortiz; m. Maria Augusta de Ortiz 1970; two d.; ed. Nat. Polytechnic School, Quito, Univ. of Miami, Tufts Univ. and Harvard Univ.; Marketing Head of Ecuadorian State Petroleum Corpn. (CEPE) 1973–75, Asst. Consultant for CEPE Gen. Man. 1975–78; Chief Adviser to Minister of Natural and Energy Resources and Chief Co-ordinator of Petroleum Policy Advisory Bd., 1975–78; mem. OPEC Econ. Comm. Bd. 1975–78, of Bd. of Govs. 1975–78, Sec. Gen. of OPEC 1979–81; Head del. to Bd. of Latin American Energy Org. 1976–78; mem. Oxford Energy Club 1978–; Hon. Citizen, Cape Canaveral, of Brebad County, Fla.; Exec. of Year, Ecuador 1977. *Publications:* Programmed Instruction for Management Training Centre in Ecuador 1973, Project Management with PERT and CPM 1978. *Leisure interests:* music, tennis, swimming.

ORTIZ DE ROZAS, Carlos; Argentine diplomatist; b. 26 April 1926, Buenos Aires; s. of Alfredo Ortiz de Rozas and Susana del Valle; m. Carmen Sarobe 1952; ed. Univ. de Buenos Aires; entered foreign service 1948; Chargé d'Affaires, Bulgaria 1952–54; Sec. Greece 1954–56; mem. Cabinet, Argentine Ministry of Foreign Affairs 1958–59; Counsellor, Argentine Mission at UN 1959–61; subsequently Dir.-Gen. Policy Dept., Ministry of Foreign Affairs and later Minister at embassies in U.A.R. and U.K.; Amb. to Austria 1967–70; Chief Rep. to Conf. of Cttee. on Disarmament, Geneva 1969 (Chair. of Cttee. 1979); Perm. Rep. to UN 1970–77; Amb. to U.K. 1980–82, to France 1984–; Head of Argentine Special Mission to Holy See 1982–83; Pres. UN Security Council 1971, 1972; mem Advisory Bd. to Sec.-Gen. on Disarmament 1978–82; Chair. Del. of Conf. on Law of the Sea 1973, First (Political and Security) Cttee. of the 29th General Assembly 1974; has held several teaching posts including Prof. of Public Law and Int. Relations, Univ. del Salvador, Buenos Aires (now mem. Bd. of Dirs.); decorations from Italy, Chile, Brazil, Greece, Japan, Peru, Thailand, Egypt, Austria, Nicaragua, the Republic of Korea, Spain, Holy See and France. *Address:* Embassy of Argentina, 6 rue Cimarosa, 75116 Paris; 22 Avenue Foch, 75116 Paris, France (Residence). *Telephone:* 45-53-33-00 (Office); 45-00-70-87 (Residence).

ORTIZ MENA, Antonio, LL.L.; Mexican lawyer, politician and banker; b. 1912, Parral, Chihuahua; ed. Escuela Nacional de Jurisprudencia; leading legal positions, Dept. of Fed. District and office of Attorney-Gen.; Dir.-Gen. of Professions at the Secr. of Public Educ.; during Second World War, mem. of Cttee. for Political Defence of the American Continent and Adviser to Mexican Del. at the Chapultepec Conf.; on Editorial Comms. for the Fed. Law of Civil Procedure, to reform certain Articles of the Constitution; Deputy Dir. Banco Hipotecario Urbano y de Obras Públicas, S.A. 1948–52; Dir.-Gen. Inst. of Social Security 1952–58; Vice-Pres. Admin. Council, Int. Asscn. of Social Security 1955–59; Alt. Del. to Conf. of Ministers of Finance and Economy, Rio de Janeiro 1954, Inter-American Conf. of Insurance, Caracas 1955; Pres. Inter-American Perm. Cttee. of Social Security 1955; Sec. for the Treasury and Public Credit 1958–70; Pres. IDB 1971–87; Dir.-Gen. Banamex Dec. 1988–; numerous honours from Belgium, France, Germany, Yugoslavia, Brazil, Netherlands, Chile, Italy and U.A.R. *Publications:* El Desarrollo Estabilizador 1969, Finanzas Públicas de México 1969, Development in Latin America 1975.

ORTOLI, François-Xavier; French economist; b. 16 Feb. 1925, Ajaccio, Corsica; s. of Antoine Ortoli and Angèle Tessarech; m. Yvonne Calbairac 1946; one s. three d.; ed. Hanoi Faculty of Law, and Ecole Nat. d'Administration, Paris; Insp. of Finances 1948–51; Tech. Adviser to the Office of the Minister of Econ. Affairs and Information 1951–53; Technical Adviser, Office of the Minister of Finances 1954; Asst. Dir. to the Sec. of State for Econ. Affairs and Sec.-Gen. Franco-Italian Conf. of EEC 1955; Head, Commercial Politics Service of Sec. of State for Econ. Affairs 1957; Dir.-Gen. of the Internal Market Div. of EEC 1958; Sec.-Gen. Inter-Ministerial Cttee. for Questions of European Econ. Co-operation, Paris 1961; Dir. of Cabinet to Prime Minister 1962–66; Commr.-Gen. of the Plan 1966–67; Minister of Works 1967–68, of Educ. 1968, of Finance 1968–69, of Industrial and Scientific Devt. 1969–72; Pres. Comm. of European Communities 1973–76; Vice-Pres. for Econ. and Monetary Affairs 1977–84; Pres., Dir. Gen. TOTAL Compagnie française des pétroles 1984–; Advisory Dir. Unilever 1985–; mem. Supervisory Bd. Philips NV 1985; Admin. Cie Financière Paribas; Dr. h.c. (Oxford and Athens Univs.); Commdr. Légion d'honneur, Médaille militaire, Croix de guerre 1945, Médaille de la Résistance, etc. *Address:* 18 rue de Bourgogne, 75007 Paris, France.

ORTONA, Egidio; Italian diplomatist; b. 16 Sept. 1910, Casale, Monferrato; s. of Luigi Egidio and Maria Brizio; m. Giulia Rossi 1935; one s. two d.; ed. Univs. of Turin and Poitiers, LSE; entered diplomatic service 1932; mem. Italian Del. to World Econ. Conf., London 1933; Consul, Cairo and Johannesburg; Sec. of Embassy, London, Chief of Office of Minister of Foreign Affairs 1943; mem. Econ. Mission to U.S.A. 1944; Counsellor, later Minister, Italian Embassy, Washington 1945–58; Permanent Rep. of Italy to UN with Ambassador's rank 1958–61; Pres. UN Security Council 1959–60; Dir.-Gen. of Econ. Affairs, Italian Ministry of Foreign Affairs 1961–66; Sec.-Gen. Ministry of Foreign Affairs 1966–67; Amb. to U.S.A.

1967–75; Pres. XIV Ass. of ICAO 1962, European Conf. on Satellite Communication 1963–64; Hon. Pres. Bull-Italia, Italy, Aeritalia; Pres. of Confed. of Italian Shipowners, of Inst. of Studies of Int. Relations (I.S.P.I.). *Leisure interests:* riding, writing and music. *Address:* Via Carlo Dolci, 19 Rome, 00197, Italy. *Telephone:* 360 9421.

ORZECHOWSKI, Marian Odon, H.H.D.; Polish historian, political scientist and politician; b. 24 Oct. 1931, Radom; ed. State A. Zhdanow Univ., Leningrad; teacher Wrocław Univ. 1955–; Asst. 1955–61, Lecturer 1961–65, Asst. Prof. 1965–71, Extraordinary Prof. 1971–77, Dir. Inst. of Political Sciences 1969–72, Rector 1972–75, Ordinary Prof. 1977–; mem. Political Sciences Cttee. of Polish Acad. of Sciences 1977–; mem. Cen. Comm. for Acad. Appointments of Prime Minister 1976–79; mem. Youth Org. of Workers' Univ. Soc. 1947–48, Polish Youth Union 1948–57; mem. Polish United Workers' Party (PZPR) 1952–, mem. PZPR Cen. Cttee. 1981–, Sec. PZPR Cen. Cttee. 1981–83, Alt. mem. Political Bureau PZPR Cen. Cttee. 1983–86, mem. Political Bureau 1986–; Rector, Acad. of Social Sciences attached to Cen. Cttee. PZPR 1984–85; Sec.-Gen. Provisional Nat. Council of Patriotic Movt. for Nat. Rebirth PRON 1982–83, Sec. Gen. Nat. Council 1983–84, mem. Presidium of Nat. Council 1983–84; Minister of Foreign Affairs 1985–88; Sec. PZPR Cen. Cttee. 1988–, Chair. Ideology Comm., PZPR Cen. Cttee. 1988–; Kt.'s and Commdr.'s Cross of Order of Polonia Restituta, Medal of Nat. Educ. Comm. *Publications:* numerous works on contemporary history of Poland, Polish labour movement and history of political thought including Narodowa Demokracja na Górnym Śląsku do 1919 r. 1965, Wojciech Korfanty. Biografia polityczna 1975, Rewolucja. Socjalizm. Tradycje 1978, Maxa Webera teoria polityki 1982, Naród-państwo-ojczyzna w myśli politycznej J. Bruna-Bronowicza 1986. *Address:* Kamitet Centralny PZPR, ul. Nowy Świat 6, 00-497 Warsaw, Poland.

OSAFUNE, Hiroe, D.ENG.; Japanese engineer; b. 27 Jan. 1917; s. of Torao and Hideko Osafune; m. Akiko Fukuda 1944; one s. two d.; ed. Tokyo Univ.; Gen. Man. Semiconductor Div., Nippon Electric Co. 1971, Vice-Pres. Int. Business 1973, Adviser 1979–, Chair. Bd. Nippon Electric Co. Electron Inc. 1979–, Electronic Arrays Inc. 1979–, Nippon Electric Co. Micro-computers Inc. 1979–. *Publication:* Crystal Luminescense 1942. *Leisure interests:* golf, collecting oriental ceramics. *Address:* 1850 Willow Road, 4 Palo Alto, Calif. 94304, U.S.A. *Telephone:* (415) 327-6926.

OSBALDESTON, Gordon Francis, P.C., O.C., B.COMM., M.B.A., LL.D.; Canadian government official; b. 29 April 1930, Hamilton, Ont.; s. of John E. and Margaret (Hanley) Osbaldeston; m. Geraldine M. Keller 1953; three s. one d.; ed. St. Jerome's Coll., Kitchener, Ont. and Univs. of Toronto and Western Ontario; Sec. Treasury Bd. 1973–76; Deputy Minister, Dept. of Industry, Trade and Commerce 1976–78; Sec. Ministry of State for Econ. Devt. 1978–82; Under-Sec. of State for External Affairs 1982; Clerk of Privy Council and Sec. to Cabinet 1982–86; Sr. Fellow, School of Business Admin., Univ. of Western Ontario 1986–; mem. of Queen's Privy Council of Canada 1985. *Leisure interests:* golf, stamp collecting. *Address:* School of Business Administration, University of Western Ontario, London, Ont. N6A 3K7, Canada. *Telephone:* (519) 661-3280.

OSBORN, Eric Francis, PH.D., D.D.; Australian professor of New Testament and early church history; b. 9 Dec. 1922, Melbourne; s. of William F. Osborn and Hilda P. Osborn; m. Lorna G. Grierson 1946; two s.; ed. Wesley Coll. Melbourne, Queen's Coll., Univ. of Melbourne and Queen's Coll., Cambridge; army service 1942–44; Methodist Minister in country parishes 1948–51, 1954–57; research student, Cambridge 1952–54; Prof. of New Testament and Early Church History, Queen's Coll. Univ. of Melbourne 1958–87, Pres. United Faculty of Theology 1987; Guest Prof. Univ. of Strasbourg 1981–82. *Publications:* The Philosophy of Clement of Alexandria 1957, Justin Martyr 1973, Ethical Problems in Early Christian Thought 1976, The Beginning of Christian Philosophy 1981. *Leisure interests:* swimming, running. *Address:* Queen's College, University of Melbourne, Parkville, Vic. 3052; 2 Ocean Road, Point Lonsdale, Vic. 3225, Australia. *Telephone:* 052 522827 (Home).

OSBORNE, Denis Gordon, PH.D., F.INST.P.; British diplomatist; b. 17 Sept. 1932, London; s. of Alfred G. Osborne and Frances A. Osborne; m. Christine S. Shepherd 1970; two d.; ed. Dr. Challoner's Grammar School, Amersham and Univ. of Durham; lecturer in Physics, Univ. of Durham 1957; lecturer, Fourah Bay Coll. Sierra Leone 1957–58; lecturer, Sr. Lecturer, Univ. of Ghana 1958–64; Reader in Physics, Univ. of Dar es Salaam 1964–66; Prof 1966–71, Dean of Science 1968–70; IBRD consultant in Malaysia 1971; Research Fellow, Univ. Coll. London 1971–72; IBRD consultant in Ethiopia 1972; Prin., Overseas Devt. Admin. London 1972–80, Asst. Sec. 1980–87; High Commr. in Malawi 1987–. *Publications:* Way Out: Some Parables of Science and Faith 1977; research papers on geophysics, technology, education. *Leisure interests:* reading, writing, attempts at windsurfing. *Address:* c/o Foreign and Commonwealth Office, King Charles Street, London, SW1A 2AH, England.

OSBORNE, John James., F.R.S.A.; British playwright, actor and producer; b. 12 Dec. 1929, London; m. 1st Pamela Lane 1951 (divorced 1957); 2nd Mary Ure 1957 (divorced 1963); 3rd Penelope Gilliatt (q.v.) 1963 (divorced 1968); 4th Jill Bennett 1968 (divorced 1977); 5th Helen Dawson 1978; one d.; ed. state schools and privately; Journalist 1947–48; tour No Room at the Inn 1948–49; actor-manager, Ilfracombe 1951; repertory Leicester,

Camberwell, Kidderminster, Derby, Bridgewater, etc.; also appeared London; Dir. Woodfall Films; Dr. h.c. (R.C.A.). *Plays:* Look Back in Anger 1956, The Entertainer 1957, Epitaph for George Dillon (with Anthony Creighton) 1958, The World of Paul Slickey 1959, A Subject of Scandal and Concern 1960, Luther 1961, Plays for England 1962, Inadmissible Evidence 1964 (film 1969), A Patriot for Me 1964, A Bond Honoured (trans. of Lope de Vega's La Fianza Satisfecha) 1966, The Hotel in Amsterdam 1968, Time Present 1968, The Right Prospectus 1970, Very Like a Whale 1970, West of Suez 1971, A Sense of Detachment 1972, Hedda Gabler (adaptation) 1972, The Gift of Friendship 1972, A Place Calling Itself Rome 1973, The Picture of Dorian Gray (dramatization of Oscar Wilde story) 1973, The End of Me Old Cigar 1975, Watch It Come Down 1975, Almost a Vision 1976; screenplay for Tom Jones 1963 (Acad. Award); Ms or Jill and Jack (TV play) 1974, You're Not Watching Me Mummy 1978, Try a Little Tenderness 1978 (two plays for TV), God Rot Tunbridge Wells! (TV play) 1985. *Publication:* A Better Class of Person: an Autobiography 1929-1956 1981. *Film appearances:* First Love 1971, Tomorrow Never Comes 1978, Flash Gordon 1980. *Leisure interests:* music hall, opera, riding, critic, Yank and Aussie bashing. *Address:* c/o Fraser and Dunlop, 91 Regent Street, London, W.1, England.

OSBORNE, Richard de Jongh, A.B.; American business executive; b. 19 March 1934, Bronxville, New York; s. of Stanley De Jongh and Elizabeth Ide Osborne; m. Cheryl A. Archibald 1957; two s. two d.; ed. Milton M. Acad., and Princeton Univ.; Cuno Eng. Corpn. 1956-60; Planning and Marketing Exec., Finance, IBM 1960-69; Investment Adviser, Sherman M. Fairchild 1969-70; Exec. Vice-Pres. Fairchild Camera & Instrument Corpn. 1970-74; Vice-Pres. Finance, ASARCO Inc. 1975-77, Exec. Vice-Pres. 1977-81, Pres. 1981-85, Chair., Pres. and C.E.O. 1985-; Dir. Mexico Desarrollo Industrial Minero (SA), Southern Peru Copper Corpn., E. T. & H. K. Ide, Schering-Plough Corpn., Nat. Asscn. of Mfrs.; Chair. Int. Copper Research Asscn.; Dir., Council of the Americas; Trustee, Cttee. for Econ. Devt. *Address:* ASARCO Inc., 180 Maiden Lane, New York, N.Y. 10038, U.S.A.

OSCARSSON, Per Oscar Heinrich; Swedish actor; b. 28 Jan. 1927, Stockholm; s. of Ing. Einar Oscarsson and Theresia Küppers; m. Bärbel Krämer 1960; one s. two d.; ed. Royal Dramatic School; Royal Dramatic Theatre 1947-52, Gothenburg Town Theatre 1953-59, TV-Theatre 1966-67; now works mainly as free-lance film-actor; Best Actor Award, Cannes 1966; New York Critics Award for Best Actor 1968; Silver Hugo Best Actor Award, Chicago Int. Film Festival 1969; appeared on stage in Hamlet 1953, Candida 1961, Waiting for Godot 1963; films: The Doll 1962, My Sister My Love 1965, Hunger 1965, Ole Dole Doff 1967, It's Up to You 1968, Close to the Wind 1970, A Last Valley, Salem Comes to Supper 1971. *Leisure interests:* reading and riding. *Address:* Breviksvägen 194, 135 Ol Tyresö, Sweden.

OSHIMA, Nagisa; Japanese film director; b. 31 March 1932, Kyoto; m. Akiko Koyama 1960; two s.; ed. Kyoto Univ.; with Shochiku Co. 1954-59; formed own film company 1959; has also directed television films. *Films:* Ai To Kibo No Machi (A Town of Love and Hope) 1959, Seishun Zankoku Monogatari (Cruel Story of Youth) 1960, Taiyo No Hakaba (The Sun's Burial) 1960, Nihon No Yoru To Kiri (Night and Fog in Japan) 1960, Shiiku (The Catch) 1961, Amakusa Shiro Tokisada (The Rebel) 1962, Etsuraku (The Pleasures of the Flesh) 1965, Yunbogi No Nikki (Yunbogi's Diary) 1965, Hakuchu No Torima (Violence at Noon) 1966, Ninja Bugeicho (Band of Ninja) 1967, Nihon Shunka-ko (A Treatise on Japanese Bawdy Song) 1967, Muri Shinju Nihon No Natsu (Japanese Summer: Double Suicide) 1967, Koshikei (Death By Hanging) 1968, Kaettekita Yopparai (Three Resurrected Drunkards) 1968, Shinjuku Dorobo Nikki (Diary of a Shinjuku Thief) 1968, Shonen (Boy) 1969, Tokyo Senso Sengo Hiwa (He Died After the War, or The Man Who Left His Will on Film) 1970, Gishiki (The Ceremony) 1971, Natsu No Imooto (Dear Summer Sister) 1972, Ai no Corrida (In the Realm of the Senses) 1976, Ai no Borei (Empire of Passion) 1978, Merry Christmas, Mr. Lawrence 1982, Max, mon amour 1985. *Address:* Oshima Productions, 2-15-7 Akasaka, Minato-ku, Tokyo, Japan.

OSIPOV, Gen.-Col. Vladimir Vasilevich; Soviet military official; b. 1933; ed. GHQ Mil. Acad.; service in Soviet Army 1951-; mem. CPSU 1958-; command posts 1968-; First Deputy Commdr. 1983-; Commdr. of Armed Forces 1984; Gen.-Col. 1984-; mem. Cen. Cttee. CPSU April 1989-; Deputy to U.S.S.R. Supreme Soviet. *Address:* Ministry of Defence, Moscow, U.S.S.R.

OSIPYAN, Yuri Andreyevich; Soviet physicist; b. 1931; ed. Moscow Steel Inst.; mem. CPSU 1959-; on staff of Cen. Inst. of Metallo-Physics (sr. researcher) 1955-62; Deputy Dir. of U.S.S.R. Acad. of Sciences Inst. of Crystallography 1962-63; on staff of U.S.S.R. Acad. of Sciences Inst. of Solid State Physics (Deputy Dir., Dir. 1973-) 1963-, Prof. 1970-; Corresp. mem. of U.S.S.R. Acad. of Sciences 1972, mem. 1981-, Vice-Pres. 1988-; Dean, Prof. and head of Faculty of Moscow Inst. of Physics and Tech. 1963-. *Address:* U.S.S.R. Academy of Sciences Institute of Solid State Physics, Ul. Radio 23/29, Moscow, U.S.S.R.

OSISIOGU, (Isaac Udo) William, PH.D.; fmr. Nigerian government official and fmr. professor of pharmacy; b. 3 Nov. 1930, Old Umuahia, Imo State; m. Peggy Oyiya Green 1962; two s. one d.; ed. Okrika Grammar School, Yaba School of Pharmacy, London Univ. School of Pharmacy and Chelsea

Coll., London Univ.; Hospital Pharmacist, Bamenda, Cameroon 1953; Lecturer, Yaba School of Pharmacy 1954-55; Lecturer, Univ. of Nigeria at Nsukka 1963, Prof. 1974-79; Fed. Commr. for Water Resources 1975-77, for Aviation 1977-78, for Trade 1978-79; Exec. Dir. Ibafon Chemicals Ltd., Lagos 1979-; mem. Bd. of Dirs. Franco-Nigerian Chamber of Commerce; mem. Science Asscn. of Nigeria, Nigerian Soc. of Pharmacognosy (Pres. 1987-88); Patron, Old Umuahia Progressive Club; traditional title holder of Ogbuagu of Old Umuahia. *Publications:* research papers in chemistry and pharmacy, Hannah's Poems. *Address:* P.O. Box 60262, Ikoyi, Lagos, Nigeria.

OSMAN, Abdillahi Said, D.JUR.; Somali diplomatist; b. 1939; m.; three c.; ed. Hull, London and Cambridge Univs.; Sec. and Legal Counsellor, Prime Minister's Office 1964-65, Co-Chair. Consultative Comm. for Legislation and Dir. of Legal Dept., Ministry of Justice 1965-68, Dir. Ministry of Justice, Religious Affairs and Labour 1968-71, Gen. State Attorney and Sr. Legal Adviser to Pres. of Somalia 1971-76; Perm. Rep. to UN Office 1976-84; Perm. Rep. to UNIDO 1981-84; Perm. Rep. to UN 1984-; Pres. Plenipotentiary Conf. on Territorial Asylum 1977, Pres. 27th session of Trade and Devt. Bd. of UNCTAD 1983, Chair. Group of 77 at 6th UNCTAD session 1983; Judge of Arbitration Court of EEC and the Afro-Malagasy states 1971; Chair. Charter Review Cttee. Meeting of OAU 1980; leader of Somali del. to numerous int. confs. *Address:* Permanent Mission of the Somali Democratic Republic to the United Nations, 711 3rd Avenue, 12th Floor, New York 10017, U.S.A. *Telephone:* 687-9877-79.

OSMAN, Sir (Abdool) Raman (Mahomed), G.C.M.G., C.B.E.; Mauritian fmr. judge; b. 29 Aug. 1902; s. of the late Mahomed Osman; called to the Bar Middle Temple 1925; Senior Puisne Judge, Supreme Court Mauritius 1950-61; Acting Gov.-Gen. Mauritius Aug.-Oct. 1970, Dec. 1971-Feb. 1972, Gov.-Gen. 1972-1977 (retd.); Hon. D.C.L. (Mauritius) 1975. *Leisure interest:* horticulture. *Address:* Le Goulet Terrace, Tombeau Bay, Mauritius.

OSMAN, Ahmed, LL.B., LL.M.; Moroccan diplomatist and politician; b. 3 Jan. 1930, Oujda; m. H.R.H. Princess Lalla Nezha (sister of King Hassan II, q.v.) 1965; one s.; ed. Royal High School, Rabat, Univ. of Rabat and Univ. of Bordeaux, France; Head of the Legal Section, Royal Cabinet 1956; joined Ministry of Foreign Affairs 1957; Sec.-Gen. Ministry of Nat. Defence 1959-61; Amb. to Fed. Repub. of Germany 1961-62; Under Sec.-of-State for Industry and Mines 1963-64; Pres. and Gen. Man. Moroccan Navigation Co. 1964-67; Amb. to U.S.A., Canada and Mexico 1967-70; Minister of Admin. Affairs 1970-71; Dir. of Royal Cabinet 1971-72; Prime Minister 1972-79; Parl. Rep. for Oujda 1977-; Pres. Rassemblement Nat. des Indépendants 1978-; mem. Nat. Defence Council March 1979-; Leader Ind. Liberals Dec. 1980-; Minister of State 1983; Pres. Chamber of Reps. 1984-; participated in UN sessions 1957, 1958, 1960, 1961, 1968, Conf. on Maritime law 1958, Conf. of the League of Arab States 1961. *Leisure interests:* bridge, sports, reading. *Address:* National Defence Council, Rabat, Morocco.

OSMAN, Amal Abd ar-Rahim, PH.D.; Egyptian politician; m.; ed. Univs. of Cairo and Rome; perm. mem. of most political and social confs.; Minister of Social Insurance and Social Affairs 1978-. *Publications:* several works on criminal law. *Address:* Ministry of Social Insurance, 3 Sharia El Alfi, Cairo, Egypt. *Telephone:* 922717.

OSMAN, Osman Ahmed, B.SC.; Egyptian civil engineer (retd.); b. 1917, Ismailia; s. of Ahmed Mohamed Osman; m. Samia Ismail Wahbi 1947; four s. one d.; ed. Cairo Univ.; Chair. The Arab Contractors (Osman Ahmed Osman & Co) 1949-73, and of its assoc. companies, Saudi Enterprises, Kuwaiti Eng. Co., The Arab Contractors (Libya), The Libyan Co. for Contracting and Devt., The Osman Ahmed Osman & Co. (Abu Dhabi, Arabian Gulf); Minister of Reconstruction 1973-76, and of Housing 1975-76; Deputy Premier, responsible for Popular Devt. Jan.-May 1981; mem. People's Ass. 1976-; Chair. Syndicate of Engineers March 1979-; Hon. LL.D. (Ricker Coll. of North East) 1976; Repub. Medal (1st Class), Soviet Hero of Labour Medal, Nile Medal (1st Class) 1980; Chief works undertaken include: (in Egypt) Aswan High Dam, Suez Canal deepening and widening, Port Said Shipyard, Cairo Int. Airport, Salhia reclamation project, High Dam Electric Power Transmission Lines, Giza Bridge and Ramsis Bridge over the Nile; (in Saudi Arabia) Dhahran Airport, Riyadh Mil. Coll., Dammam Mil. Barracks; (in Kuwait) Municipality Centre, Kuwait sewer system, secondary schools, Sabahia roadsand drainage system; (in Libya) Benghazi drainage system, Stadium, and Highway; (in Iraq) Kirkuk Feeder Canal No. 2 and 3; (in Jordan) Khaled Ibn El-Walid Dam and Tunnels; (in Abu Dhabi) Zayed City, Ruler's Palace Kharj Mil. Base and City, Taif Mil. Base, numerous airports, hospitals and land reclamation. *Publication:* The High Dam (lecture) 1966, My Experience 1981. *Leisure interests:* fishing, football. *Address:* c/o People's Assembly, Cairo, Egypt.

OSMAŃCZYK, Edmund Jan, H.H.D.; Polish journalist and author; b. 10 Aug. 1913, Jagielno; s. of Ryszard Osmańczyk and Feliksa Szulc; m. Jolanta Klimowicz 1961; one d.; ed. in Warsaw, Berlin and Bordeaux; Ed. of Press Centre, Union of Poles in Germany 1932-39; War corresp. Radio Warsaw 1939; Warsaw underground 1939-44; War corresp. 1945; Corresp. Potsdam Conf., Nuremberg Trials; Perm. Corresp., Czytelnik in Berlin 1945-50; Corresp. Polish Radio Moscow 1956, 1959-60, Diplomatic Corresp. Polish

Press Agency (PAP) and Polish Radio, Washington 1957-58, Diplomatic Corresp. for Latin America 1961-68; Deputy to Seym 1952-61, 1969-85; mem. State Council 1979-80; Chair. Polish Cttee. for Solidarity with Chilean People 1973-; Pres. Polish Copyright Asscn. (ZAIKS) 1984-88; mem. Polish PEN Club; Hon. Dr. rer. pol. (Silesian Univ., Katowice) 1979; Officer's Cross of Polonia Restituta; Order of Builders of People's Poland 1972. *Publications:* Dictionary of the Polish Minority in Germany 1939, Walka jest zwycięska (The Struggle is Victorious) (verse) 1945, Sprawy Polaków (Polish Affairs) 1946, Dokumenty pruskie (Prussian Documents) 1947, Niemcy 1945-1950 (Germany 1945-1950) 1951, Współczesna Ameryka (The Contemporary America) 1960, Ciekawa Historia ONZ 1945-1965 (The Interesting History of UN 1945-1965) 1965, Był rok 1945 . . . (It was a year 1945 . . .) 1970, Nasza Europa (Our Europe) 1971, Polacy spod znaku Rodła (Poles of the Rodlo Sign) (with Helena Lehr) 1972, Encyklopedia spraw międzynarodowych i ONZ (Encyclopaedia of Int. Affairs and the UN) 1974 and 1986, Enciclopedia Mundial de Relaciones Internacionales y Naciones Unidas (Spanish: World Encyclopedia of Int. Relations and the UN) 1976, Rzeczpospolita Polaków (The Republic of the Poles) 1977, Encyklopedia ONZ (Encyclopedia of the UN) 1982, Kraj i Emigracja, Mowy Posła Ziemi Opolskiej (Poland and the Poles Abroad, Speeches of an M.P. for Opole region) 1983, Encyclopaedia of the United Nations and International Agreements 1985. *Leisure interests:* travelling, reading, music. *Address:* Stowarzyszenie Autor ów ZAIKS, ul. Hipoteczna 2, 00-092, Warsaw (Office); Plac Zamkowy 8 m. 5, 00-277 Warsaw, Poland. *Telephone:* 27-60-60 (Office); 31-57-97 (Home).

OSMOND, Charles Barry, F.R.S., F.A.A.S., PH.D.; Australian professor of biology; b. 20 Sept. 1939, Australia; s. of Edward Charles Osmond and Joyce Daphne (née Krauss) Osmond; m. 1st Suzanne Ward 1962 (divorced 1983), two s. one d.; m. 2nd Cornelia Gauhl 1983; ed. Wyong High School and Univs. of New England and Adelaide; Postdoctoral fellow, Univ. of Calif. at Los Angeles 1965-66, Univ. of Cambridge 1966-67; Research Fellow, Dept. of Environmental Biology, Research School of Biol. Sciences, A.N.U. 1967, subsequently Fellow, Sr. Research Fellow, Prof. of Biol. 1978-87; Exec. Dir. Biol. Science Center, Desert Research Inst., Univ. of Nevada 1982-86; Arts and Sciences Prof., Dept. of Botany, Duke Univ. 1988-; Sr. Fulbright Fellowship, Univ. of Calif. (Santa Cruz) 1973-74; Guest Prof., Technical Univ., Munich 1974; Overseas Fellow, Churchill Coll., Cambridge 1980; mem. Australian Nat. Comm. for UNESCO 1980-82; mem. Council, Australian Acad. of Sciences 1982-85. *Publications:* numerous publications in plant physiology. *Address:* Department of Botany, Duke University, Durham, N.C. 27706, U.S.A. *Telephone:* (919) 684-3715.

OSOGO, James Charles Nakhwanga, M.P.; Kenyan teacher and politician; b. 10 Oct. 1932, Bukani; m. Maria Nakhubal Obara 1959; seven s. one d.; ed. Port Victoria Primary School, St. Mary's High School, Yala, Railway Training School, Nairobi and Kagumo Teachers' Training Coll.; Teacher, Sigalame School 1955, Withur School 1956, Barding School 1957, Ndenga School 1958, Port Victoria School 1959; Headmaster Kibassanga School 1960, Nangina School 1961-62; Vice-Chair. Kenya Nat. Union of Teachers, Central Nyanza 1958-62; mem. Kenya House of Reps. 1963-81; Asst. Minister, Ministry of Agric. 1963-66; Minister for Information and Broadcasting 1966-69; Minister of Commerce and Industry 1969-73, also acting Minister of Agric. 1970; Minister for Local Govt. 1973-74, of Health 1974-79, of Agric. 1979-80, of Livestock Development 1980-82; Chair. Kenya Youth Hostels Asscn. 1964-70, Patron 1970-; Elder, Order of the Golden Heart (Kenya), Order of the Star of Africa (Liberia), Grand Cordon of the Star of Ethiopia, Grand Cross of the Yugoslav Flag. *Leisure interests:* volley ball, reading. *Address:* P.O. Box 1, Port Victoria, Kenya.

OSORIO GARCÍA, Alfonso, LIC. EN DER.; Spanish lawyer and politician; b. Dec. 1923, Madrid; s. Alfonso Osorio and María de Los Angeles; m. María Teresa Iturmerdi Gómez-Nales; two s. one d.; ed. Univ. of Oviedo and Gen. Acad. of Air Force; entered Air Force Legal Corps 1947; Legal Adviser, Cen. Air Force Region for 5 years, attaining rank of Capt.; worked in State Legal Service 1953-57, in provincial Finance Depts. of Cuenca and Toledo 1953-57; studied Admin. in U.S.A. 1957; Chair. Bd. of a group of companies 1957-64; rejoined Air Force Legal Corps. 1961, rank of Major 1962; Sec. Transport Comm. and Maritime Transport Sub-Comm. of Econ. Devt. Planning Org. 1962-64; rejoined State Legal Service 1964; Under-Sec. of Commerce 1965-68; Pres. RENFE (Nat. Railways System) 1968-70; mem. Cortes for Santander 1967-71, Council of the Realm 1969-; co-founder, Grupo Tácito 1973; took part in formation of Unión Democrática Espanola 1975; Minister for Presidential Affairs 1975-77, also Second Deputy Prime Minister 1976-77; Senator apptd. by King 1977; Deputy for Madrid 1979, 1982, for Cantabria 1986; Pres. Budget Comm. 1982-; Spanish mem. for Trilateral Comm.; Vice-Pres. Petróleos del Mediterraneo. *Publication:* Political Career of a Minister of the Crown 1980. *Address:* AP, Genova 18, 28004 4 Madrid, Spain. *Telephone:* (91) 4194008.

OSSWALD, Albert; German politician; b. 16 May 1919, Wieseck, nr. Giessen; m. Margarete Osswald; Town Councillor 1949-63; Mayor of Giessen 1954; Minister of Econs. and Transport, State Govt. of Hesse 1963, subsequently Minister of Finance; Minister-President of Hesse 1969-76; mem. Social Democratic Party, mem. Exec. Cttee. 1968; Chair. Admin. Bd., Hessische Landesbank-Girozentrale until 1974; Grosses Bundesverdienstkreuz 1975. *Leisure interests:* hiking, fishing, swimming, and games. *Address:* Inselweg 31, 63 Giessen, Federal Republic of Germany.

OSTERBROCK, Donald E., PH.D.; American astronomer; b. 13 July 1924, Cincinnati, Ohio; s. of William C. Osterbrock and Elsie W. Osterbrock; m. Irene Hansen 1952; one s. two d.; ed. Univ of Chicago; Instructor Princeton Univ. 1952-53; Instructor, then Asst. Prof. Calif. Inst. of Technology 1953-58; Asst. Prof., then Assoc. Prof., Univ. of Wis. 1958-61, Prof. of Astronomy 1961-73, Chair. Dept. of Astronomy 1967-68, 1969-72; Visiting Prof., Univ. of Chicago 1963-64; Letters Ed., Astrophysical Journal 1971-73; Prof. of Astronomy, Univ. of Calif., Santa Cruz 1972-; Dir. Lick Observatory 1972-81; Hill Family Prof., Univ. of Minn. 1977-78; Visiting Prof., Ohio State Univ. 1980, 1986; Hon. D.Sc. (Ohio State Univ.) 1986; Guggenheim Fellow 1960-61, 1982-83, Nat. Science Sr. Foundation Fellow 1968-69; Assoc., Royal Astronomical Soc. 1976; mem. Nat. Acad. of Sciences, American Acad. of Arts and Sciences, Wisconsin Acad. of Sciences, Arts and Letters; Univ. of Chicago Alumni Asscn. Professional Achievement Award 1982. *Publications:* Astrophysics of Gaseous Nebulae 1974, James E. Keeler, Pioneer American Astrophysicist and the Early Development of American Astrophysics 1984, Astrophysics of Gaseous Nebulae and Active Galactic Nuclei 1989, (with J. R. Gustafson and W. J. S. Unruh) Eye on the Sky: Lick Observatory's First Century 1988, numerous scientific papers in Astrophysical Journal and Publications of the Astronomical Society of the Pacific, etc. *Leisure interests:* drama, hiking, conservation. *Address:* Lick Observatory, University of California, Santa Cruz, Calif. 95064; 120 Woodside Avenue, Santa Cruz, Calif. 95060, U.S.A. (Home). *Telephone:* 408-429-2605 (Office).

OSTRIKER, Jeremiah (Paul), PH.D.; American professor of theoretical astrophysics; b. 13 April 1937, New York; s. of Martin Ostriker and Jeanne Sumpf; m. Alicia S. Suskin 1959; one s. two d.; ed. Harvard Univ. and Univ. of Chicago; Postdoctoral Fellow, Cambridge Univ., England 1964-65; Research Assoc. and Lecturer, Princeton Univ. 1965-66, Asst. Prof. 1966-68, Assoc. Prof. 1968-71, Prof. 1971-, Chair. Dept. of Astrophysical Sciences and Dir. Observatory 1979-, Charles A. Young Prof. of Astronomy 1982-; mem. Editorial Bd. and Trustee, Princeton Univ. Press 1982-84; Visiting Prof. Harvard Univ. and Regents Fellow Smithsonian Inst. 1984-85; mem. N.A.S., American Acad. of Arts and Sciences, American Astronomical Soc., Int. Astronomical Union; Nat. Science Foundation Fellowship 1960-65; Alfred P. Sloan Fellowship 1970-72; Sherman Fairchild Fellowship of CalTech 1977; Helen B. Warner Prize, American Astronomical Soc. 1972, Henry Norris Russell Prize, 1980. *Leisure interest:* squash. *Address:* Princeton University Observatory, Peyton Hall, Princeton, N.J. 08544 (Office); 33 Philip Drive, Princeton, N.J. 08540, U.S.A. (Home). *Telephone:* (609) 452-3800 (Office); (609) 924-5737 (Home).

OSTROWER, Fayga; Brazilian (b. Polish) painter and engraver; b. 14 Sept. 1920, Łódź, Poland; m. Heinz Ostrower 1941; one s. one d.; ed. Fundação Getúlio Vargas, Rio de Janeiro; Lecturer in Theory of Composition and Analysis, Museum of Modern Art, Rio de Janeiro 1954-70, Univ. Federal de Minas Gerais 1966-70; Post-graduate Prof., Univ. Rio de Janeiro 1982-; Vice-Pres. Brazilian Cttee., Int. Soc. of Educ. through Art, UNESCO 1983; John Hay Whitney Lecturer, Spelman Coll., Atlanta 1964; mem. Jury for Bienal of São Paulo and Nat. Show of Fine Arts, Rio de Janeiro; Vice-Pres. Brazilian Cttee., Int. Asscn. of Plastic Arts, Int. Council of ICIS (Int. Centre for Integrative Studies, New York); Pres. INSEA (Int. Soc. for Educ. through Art, Brazil); mem. Bd. Cultural Council, Museum of Modern Art, Rio de Janeiro, Escola de Artes Visuais Parque Lase, Rio de Janeiro; Counsellor, Instituto Cultural Brasil-Alemanha, Goethe Institut, Rio de Janeiro; elected mem. State Council for Culture, Rio de Janeiro; numerous one-man exhbns. and works in collections in the Americas and Europe; Hon. mem. Accad. delle Arti del Disegno, Florence; numerous prizes including awards at São Paulo Bienal in 1955, 1957, 1961, 1963, Venice Biennale 1958, 1962, Venezuela Biennale 1967, Rio de Janeiro City Award 1969, II Biennale Internazionale della Grafica, Florence 1970; Grand Int. Prize Venice; Chevalier Order of Rio Branco 1972; Hon. Citizenship of Rio de Janeiro 1985. *Publications:* Criatividade e Processos de Criação (Creativity and Creative Processes) 1977, Universos de Arte 1983. *Leisure interest:* art. *Address:* Avenida Rui Barbosa 532, apdo. 1001, Rio de Janeiro, RJ, Brazil. *Telephone:* 551.3015, 551.8916.

OSTROWSKI, Włodzimierz Stanisław, M.D.; Polish biochemist; b. 21 Oct. 1925, Sosnowiec; s. of Joseph and Maria Ostrowski; m. Alexandra Skwarczyńska 1951; two s.; ed. Faculty of Medicine, Jagiellonian Univ. and Medical Acad., Cracow; Doctor 1959-61, Docent 1961-69, Extraordinary Prof. 1969-79, Prof. 1979-; Corresp. mem. Polish Acad. of Sciences 1973-, mem. 1983-; mem. Presidium 1974-, Chair. Cttee. of Biochemistry and Biophysics, Polish Acad. of Sciences; Scientific Sec., Cracow Br. of Polish Acad. of Sciences; Dean, Faculty of Medicine, Medical Acad., Cracow 1969-72, Head, Dept. of Physiological Chem. 1963-72, Dir. Inst. of Medical Biochem. 1972-; Visiting Research Prof., Dept. of Biochem., State Univ. of New York 1966-67, 1972-73; expert of WHO 1978-; mem. Polish United Workers Party (PZPR) 1960-; mem. Editorial Staff Folia Biologica, Materia Medica Polona and Przegląd Lekarski (Medical Review); mem. Acta Biochim. Polon., Polish Chem. Soc., Polish Biochemical Soc., Polish Lab. Diagnostics Soc., A.A.A.S., New York Acad. of Science 1980; State Prize, 3rd Class 1957, 2nd Class 1958, Gold Cross of Merit 1969, Minister of Health and Social Welfare Prize 1968, 1984, 1st Class, Knight's, Officer's and Commdr.'s Cross of Order Polonia Restituta, Bronze Medal Nat. Acad. of Medical Sciences (France) 1978, Meritorious Teacher of People's Poland

1981 and others. *Publications:* Electrophoretic Methods in Biochemistry and Clinical Investigations 1970, Practical Manual for General and Physiological Chemistry 1973, Selected Methods in Clinical Chemistry 1974, Flavins and Flavoproteins, Physiochemical Properties and Function 1977, Exercises in General and Physiological Chemistry 1980 and numerous articles in Polish and foreign languages. *Address:* Ul. Jaracza 12 m. 6, 31-143 Cracow, Poland. *Telephone:* 22-31-73.

OSTRY, Sylvia, O.C., PH.D.; Canadian economist and goverment official; b. 3 June 1927, Winnipeg; d. of Morris J. and B. (Stoller) Knelman; m. Bernard Ostry; two s.; ed. McGill and Cambridge Univs.; Chief Statistician, Statistics Canada 1972–75; Deputy Minister of Consumer and Corpn. Affairs and Deputy Registrar Gen. 1975–78; Chair. Econ. Council of Canada 1978–79; Head, Econ. and Statistics Dept., OECD 1979–83; Deputy Minister (Int. Trade) and Co-ordinator for Int. Econ. Relations, Dept. of External Affairs 1984–85; Amb., Multilateral Trade Negotiations and Personal Rep. of the Prime Minister, Econ. Summit, Dept. of External Affairs 1985–; Per Jacobsson Foundation Lecture, Washington 1987; mem. several learned socs. and professional orgs.; seventeen hon. degrees; Outstanding Achievement Award, Govt. of Canada 1987. *Publications:* Labour Economics in Canada, International Economic Policy Co-ordination (co-author) 1986; articles on labour econs., demography, productivity, competition policy. *Leisure interests:* films, theatre, contemporary reading. *Address:* Lester B. Pearson Building, 125 Sussex Drive, Ottawa, Ont. K1A 0G2, Canada.

O'SULLIVAN, John B.A.; British editor and journalist; b. 25 April 1942, Liverpool; s. of Alfred M. O'Sullivan and Margaret (née Corner) O'Sullivan; ed. London Univ.; Jr Tutor Swinton Conservative Coll. 1965–67, Sr. Tutor 1967–69; Ed. Swinton Journal 1967–69; London Corresp. Irish Radio and TV 1970–72; Editorial Writer and Political Columnist Daily Telegraph 1972–79; Ed. Policy Review 1979–83; Asst. Ed. Daily Telegraph 1983–84; Columnist The Times 1984–86, Assoc. Ed. 1986–87; Editorial Page Ed. New York Post 1984–86; Ed. Nat. Review 1988–; Columnist Sunday Telegraph 1988–; Dir. of Studies Heritage Foundation 1979–83; Special Adviser to the Prime Minister 1987–88; Fellow Inst. of Politics, Harvard Univ. 1983. *Leisure interests:* reading, cinema, theatre, dining out. *Address:* National Review, 150 East 35th St., New York, N.Y. 10016, U.S.A. *Telephone:* (212) 679-7330.

OSUMI, Kenichiro, LL.D.; Japanese lawyer and academic; b. 2 Oct. 1904, Gamagori-shi; s. of Tsunetaro Osumi and Ura Osumi; m. Ayako Iwasa 1933; two s.; ed. Kyoto Univ.; Prof. Kyoto Univ. 1938–66, Prof. Emer. 1966–; Prof. Kobe Gakuin Univ. 1974–86, Prof. Emer. 1986–; Justice Supreme Court of Japan 1966–74; Auditor Toyota Motor Corpn. 1974–86; mem. Osaka Bar Asscn. 1974, Japan Acad. 1977; Order of the Sacred Treasure (1st Class) 1974, Person of Cultural Merits 1985. *Publications:* Studies on the Law of Group Enterprises 1935, Treatise on Corporation Law 1980, Development and Transformation of Stock Corporation Law 1987. *Leisure interest:* golf. *Address:* 8–15 Tonoyama-cho, Nishinomiya-shi 662, Japan. *Telephone:* (0798) 71-7787.

OSWALD, Adm. Sir John Julian Robertson, K.C.B.; British naval officer; b. 11 Aug. 1933, Selkirk, Scotland; s. of George Oswald and Margaret (née Robertson) Oswald; m. Veronica Thompson 1958; two s. three d.; ed. Beandesert Britannia Park, Minchinhampton; Britannia Royal Naval Coll., Royal Coll. of Defence Studies; joined R.N. 1947; served in H.M. ships Devonshire, Vanguard, Verulam, Newfoundland, Jewel, Victorious, Naiad; specialised in Gunnery 1960; Commdr. H.M.S. Yarnton 1962–63, H.M.S. Bacchante 1971–72, H.M.S. Newcastle 1977–79; Ministry of Defence 1972–75; R.N. Presentation Team 1979–80; Capt. Britannia, R.N. Coll. 1980–82; Asst. Chief of Defence Staff (Progs.) 1982–84, (Policy and Nuclear) 1985; Flag Officer, Third Flotilla, Commdr., Anti-Submarine Warfare, Striking Fleet 1985–87; C.-in-C., Fleet, Allied C.-in-C., Channel and C.-in-C., E. Atlantic Area 1987–89; First Sea Lord and Chief of Naval Staff May 1989–. *Leisure interests:* gliding, travel, stamp collecting, music, tennis. *Publications:* defence and strategy articles in specialised journals, book reviews. *Address:* c/o Ministry of Defence, Whitehall, London SW1A 2HB, England. *Telephone:* (01) 218-9000.

OTANI, Sachio, B.ARCH.; Japanese architect; b. 20 Feb. 1924, Tokyo; s. of Morisuke and Yuko Otani; m. Yoshiko Otani; one c.; ed. Univ. of Tokyo; Architectural designer under Dr. Kenzo Tange 1946–60; Lecturer in Architecture, Univ. of Tokyo 1955–64; Assoc. Prof. of Urban Eng., Univ. of Tokyo 1964–73, Prof. of Urban Design 1973; works include Kojimachi area (of Tokyo) redevt. plan 1960–64, Tokyo children's cultural centre 1961–63 and Kyoto Int. Conf. Hall 1963–66. *Address:* 15-22-3 Shoan, Suginami-ku, Tokyo, Japan (Home). *Telephone:* 333-6708.

OTCHAKOVSKY-LAURENS, Paul, L. EN D.; French publisher; b. 10 Oct. 1944, Valreas, Vaucluse; s. of Zelman Otchakovsky and Odette Labaume; adopted s. of Berthe Laurens; m. Monique Pierret 1970; one s. one d.; ed. Coll. and Lycée de Sablé sur Sarthe, Coll. Montalembert de Courbevoie, Coll. St. Croix de Neuilly and Faculté de Droit, Paris; Reader, Editions Christian Bourgois 1969–70; Dir. of Collection, Editions Flammarion 1970–77; Dir. of Collections, then Dir. of Dept. Editions Hachette 1978–82; Pres. Dir.-Gen. Editions P.O.L. 1983–; Officier des Arts et Lettres. *Address:* Editions P.O.L., 8 Villa d'Alesia, 75014 Paris (Office); 56 rue du Moulin

Vert, 75014 Paris, France (Home). *Telephone:* 45 42 77 21 (Office); 45 39 32 67 (Home).

OTEIBA, Mana Saeed al-, M.SC.; United Arab Emirates economist; b. 15 May 1946, Abu Dhabi; m.; five c.; ed. Univ. of Baghdad; Chair. of Bd., Abu Dhabi Nat. Oil Co.; mem. Abu Dhabi Planning Bd; Pres. Abu Dhabi Dept. of Petroleum; Chair. of Bd., Abu Dhabi Gas Liquefaction Co.; Minister of Petroleum and Mineral Resources 1973–; Pres. OPEC 1979, OAPEC 1980; mem. Bd. all seven oil cos. in Abu Dhabi; has travelled on State visits, etc. throughout Arab countries, Western Europe, U.S.A., Canada. *Publications:* The Abu Dhabi Planning Board, The Economy of Abu Dhabi, Organization of the Petroleum Exporting Countries, OPEC and the Petroleum Industry, Petroleum and the Economy of the United Arab Emirates. *Leisure interests:* poetry, hunting, fishing. *Address:* Ministry of Petroleum and Natural Resources, P.O. Box 59, Abu Dhabi, United Arab Emirates. *Telephone:* 62810, 61051.

OTERO, Alejandro; Venezuelan artist; b. 7 March 1921; ed. School of Fine Arts, Caracas; early portraits in expressionist impasto, then landscapes in yellow, ochre and blue until shared a studio with Pascual Navarro in Paris 1945–48; transition from figurative to abstract art through still lifes 1945–48; participated in exhbn. Les Mains Eblouies, Galerie Maeght 1947; returned to Venezuela and presented one-man exhbns. at Museum of Fine Arts, Caracas 1949; Ed. Los Disidentes after return to Paris 1950; turned to optical art and collages 1951; executed monumental comms. for Univ. City of Caracas 1952–55; series of abstract paintings Colour-Rhythms 1955–60; returned to Paris 1960–64; Vice-Pres. Inst. of Culture and Fine Arts, Caracas 1964–; collages from newspaper cuttings, in bright colours 1964–; Retrospective Exhbn. Signals, London, 1966; other one-man exhbns. in Washington, D.C., Caracas, Venezuela, and Klagenfurt, Austria; numerous awards and honours. *Address:* Institute of Culture and Fine Arts, Caracas, Venezuela.

OTHMAN BIN WOK; Singapore journalist, politician and diplomatist; b. 8 Oct. 1924, Singapore; m. Che Dah Mohd Noor 1949; one s. three d.; ed. Telok Saga Malay School, Raffles Inst. and London School of Journalism; worked on Utusan Melayu as reporter and Deputy Ed. 1946–63; mem. People's Action Party 1954–; M.P. for Pasir Panjang Constituency 1963–81; Minister for Social Affairs 1963–65; Minister for Culture and Social Affairs 1965–68; Minister for Social Affairs 1968–77; Amb. to Indonesia (also accred. to Papua New Guinea) July 1977–81; Dir. Overseas Investment Pte. Ltd. 1981; Sentosa Devt. Corpn. 1981–; mem. Singapore Tourist Promotion Bd. 1981–; Maj. People's Defence Force. *Address:* Singapore Tourist Promotion Board, Raffles City Tower, Singapore.

OTHMAN, Dato Abdul Manan bin, D.P.M.T., P.P.T.; Malaysian politician; b. 1935, Kampung Balik Bukit, Kuala Terengganu; ed. Sekolah Melayu Marang, Terengganu and Malay Coll., Kuala Kangsar; and legal studies in London; joined legal service, served in Alur Setar; later practised law in Kuala Lumpur; fmr. Sec. Port Klang Authority, Gen. Man. Terengganu State Econ. Devt. Corpn.; M.P. 1976–86; Deputy Minister of Public Enterprises 1977; Deputy Trade and Industry Minister 1978; Minister of Public Enterprises 1978–1980, of Agric. 1980–84; now in insurance and shipping. *Address:* c/o Room 202, 2nd Floor, Wisma S1A, Jalan Dang Wangi, 50100 Kuala Lumpur, Malaysia.

OTHMER, Donald Frederick, PH.D.; American chemical engineer and educator; b. 11 May 1904, Omaha, Neb.; s. of Frederick George and Fredericka Darling (Snyder) Othmer; m. Mildred Jane Topp 1950; ed. Ill. Inst. of Tech., Chicago, and Univs. of Nebraska and Michigan; Devt. Engineer Eastman Kodak Co. and Tennessee Eastman Corpn. 1927–32; Prof. Polytechnic Inst. of New York (now Polytechnic Univ., Brooklyn) 1932, Head Dept. of Chemical Eng. 1937–61, Sec. Graduate Faculty 1948–58, Distinguished Prof. 1961–; consulting chemical engineer to numerous companies and govt. depts. in U.S. and abroad incl. U.S. Army, Chemical and Ordnance Corps, and Scientific Advisory Board, U.S. Navy, Special Devices Div., Depts. of State and Interior, Office of Saline Water, Dept. of Energy, UN, WHO, UNIDO, U.S. Dept. of Health, Educ. and Welfare, Nat. Materials Advisory Board, Nat. Research Council, Delaware River Basin Comm., leading financial institutions, etc.; Adviser Congressional Cttee. on Energy 1984–; Fellow A.A.A.S., New York Acad. of Sciences (Chair. Eng. Section 1972–73), American Soc. Mechanical Eng., Chair. Process Industries Division 1949, American Inst. of Chemists, American Inst. of Chemical Engineers (Dir. 1956–59); mem. American Chemical Soc., Japan Soc. of Chemical Engineers, Nat. Panel of Arbitrators, American Arbitration Asscn., Soc. de Chimie Industrielle (Pres. American Section 1973–74), Soc. Chemical Industry, American Soc. of Eng. Educ., Newcomen Soc., etc.; Dir. Engineers Joint Council 1956–59, Chemurgic Council, Chemists' Club, Pres. 1973–76; inventor and licensor (over 150 U.S. and many foreign patents) of methods, processes and equipment in manufacture of chemicals, solvents, synthetic fibres, acetylene, wall-board, petroleum refining, fermentation, desalination of seawater, pollution abatement, solar energy utilization, pipeline heating, solvents, plastics, refrigeration, wood utilization, acetic acid, evaporation, heat transfer, petrochemicals, pigments, eng. equipment, salt, pharmaceuticals, distillation, sugar refining, coal desulphurization, methanol, pulping liquor recovery, extractive metallurgy of aluminium, titanium, zinc, etc.; regent and trustee of various hospitals and univs.; developed chemical industry programme for all Burma

1951–53; Lecturer in Argentina 1969, Canada 1950, 1971, 1981, Czechoslovakia 1962, 1969, 1987, France 1968, Germany, Hon. Del. Achema, Frankfurt 1958, 1961, 1964, 1967, 1970, 1973, 1976, 1979, 1982, 1985, 1988, Greece 1962, India 1952, 1971, Iran 1971, 1973, Iraq 1980, Japan 1955, Netherlands 1951, 1985, Romania 1970, Kuwait 1971, Poland 1964, 1967, 1969, 1973, Puerto Rico 1965, Switzerland 1948, Turkey 1969, U.A.E. 1975, 1976, Yugoslavia 1963, 1970, People's Republic of China 1983, 1985, U.S. Army War Coll. 1964, ASTM 1966, TAPPI 1966, New York Acad. of Sciences 1971; Hon. Prof. Concepción Univ., Chile 1951; Hon. Dr. Eng. Univ. of Nebraska 1962, Polytechnic Inst. of New York 1977, N.J. Inst. of Tech. 1978; Shri Ram Memorial Lecturer, New Delhi 1980, Waddell Memorial Lecture, Royal Mil. Coll. of Canada 1981; Barber-Coleman Award 1958, Tyler Award 1958, Honour Scroll AIC 1970; Hon. life mem. N.Y. Acad. of Sciences 1974, American Chemical Soc., Deutsche Gesellschaft für Chemisches Apparatewesen; Hon. Life Fellow, Inst. of Chem. Eng. (London) 1979, American Soc. Mech. Eng. 1980; 1st Distinguished Service Award, Asscn. of Chemists and Chemical Engineers 1975, Golden Jubilee Award, Ill. Inst. of Tech. 1975, Chemist's Pioneer Award AIC 1977, Perkin Medal, Soc. of Chemical Industries 1978, Murphree Award, American Chem. Soc. and Exxon Corpn. 1978, Professional Achievement Award, Ill. Inst. of Tech. 1978, Hall of Fame, Ill. Inst. of Tech. 1981, Citation for Distinguished Research, New York City Mayor's Award of Honour for Science and Tech. 1987. *Publications:* Over 350 articles in technical press; Ed. Fluidization 1956, Kirk-Othmer Encyclopaedia of Chemical Technology (Co-founder and Co-Ed. 1st edn., 17 vols. 1947–60; 16 Vols., Spanish edn. 1960–66; 24 Vols., 2nd edn. 1963–70; Vols. 1—26, 3rd edn. 1978–84), Co-author Fluidization and Fluid Particle Systems 1960, Adviser, Perry's Chemical Engineer's Handbook, Tech. Ed. UN Report, Technology of Water Desalination 1964, Editorial Bd. Desalination. *Leisure interests:* forestry, collecting old maps and books. *Address:* 333 Jay Street, Brooklyn, New York 11201 (Office); 140 Columbia Heights, Brooklyn, N.Y. 11201, U.S.A. (Home). *Telephone:* 718-625-1845 (Office); 718-875-8398 (Home).

OTMAN ASSED, Mohamed; Libyan politician; b. Oct. 1922; ed. Libyan religious and Arabic schools; Teacher 1942–43; in Liberation Movement; Head of Fezzan Del. in Legis. Ass. 1950–51; Rep. for Fezzan, UN Council for Libya 1951; Minister of Health, Fed. Govt. 1951–58, of Econ. Affairs Feb.-Oct. 1960; Prime Minister Oct. 1960–63; Deputy 1964; pvt. business 1964–; emigrated to Morocco 1969. *Address:* Villa Rissani, Route Oued Akrach, Souiss; Rabat, Morocco.

O'TOOLE, Peter Seamus; Irish actor; b. 2 Aug. 1932, Connemara, Co. Galway; s. of Patrick Joseph O'Toole; m. Siân Phillips (q.v.) 1960 (divorced 1979); one s. two d.; ed. Royal Acad. of Dramatic Art; office boy, later reporter for Yorkshire Evening News; Nat. Service as signalman, Royal Navy; joined Bristol Old Vic Theatre Co., playing 73 parts 1955–58; West End debut in musical play Oh, my Papa 1957; toured England in play The Holiday; appeared in The Long, the Short and the Tall 1959; Stratford season 1960, playing Shylock, Petruchio, and Thersites; stage appearances in Pictures in the Hallway 1962, Baal 1963, Ride a Cock Horse, Waiting for Godot 1971, Dead Eyed Dicks 1976, Present Laughter 1978; Bristol Old Vic Theatre Season 1973; inaugurated Britain's Nat. Theatre Co.; appeared with Abbey Theatre Co. in Waiting for Godot, Man and Superman 1976; fmr. Assoc. Dir. Old Vic Theatre Co.; Artistic Dir., North American Tour of Royal Alexandra Theatre Co. playing Present Laughter and Uncle Vanya 1978; Macbeth, Old Vic 1980; Man and Superman 1982–83, Pygmalion 1984, 1987, The Apple Cart 1986, Jeffrey Bernard is Unwell 1989. *Films include:* Kidnapped 1959, The Day they Robbed the Bank of England 1959, Lawrence of Arabia 1960, Becket 1963, Lord Jim 1964, The Bible 1966, What's New Pussycat? 1965, How to Steal a Million 1966, Night of the Generals 1967, Great Catherine 1967, The Lion in Winter 1968, Goodbye Mr. Chips 1969, Brotherly Love 1970, Country Dance 1970, Murphy's War 1971, Under Milk Wood 1972, The Ruling Class 1972, Man of La Mancha 1972, Rosebud 1974, Man Friday 1975, Foxtrot 1975, Rogue Male (TV) 1976, Caligula 1977, Power Play 1978, Stuntman 1978, Zulu Dawn 1978, Masada (TV) 1981, The Antagonists 1981, My Favourite Year 1981, Svengali (TV) 1982, Supergirl 1984, Banshee (TV) 1986, Club Paradise 1986, The Last Emperor 1986, High Spirits 1988, The Dark Angel (TV) 1989; Commdr. des Arts et des Lettres 1988. *Address:* Guyon House, Hampstead High Street, London, N.W.3, England.

OTT, Harry; German diplomatist and politician; b. 15 Oct. 1933, Karl-Marx Stadt (fmrly. Chemnitz); s. of Karl and Luise Ott; m. Anita Ott 1962; one s. one d.; ed. Karl Marx Univ., Leipzig, State Inst. for Int. Relations, Moscow; joined Ministry of Foreign Affairs of G.D.R. 1959; Amb. to U.S.S.R. 1974–81; Deputy Minister of Foreign Affairs 1981–; mem. of G.D.R. del. to 36th session of the UN Gen. Ass.; Perm. Rep. of G.D.R. to the UN 1982–88; Deputy Head of Int. Relations Dept., Cen. Cttee., Socialist Unity Party (SUP) of Germany; mem. Cen. Cttee., SUP 1976–. *Publications:* various works on int. relations and foreign policy. *Address:* c/o Ministry of Foreign Affairs, 1020 Berlin, Max-Engels-Platz 2, German Democratic Republic.

OTTEWILL, Ronald Harry, M.A., PH.D., F.R.S.; British professor of physical chemistry; b. 8 Feb. 1927, Southall, Middx.; s. of Harry A. and Violet D. (née Bucklee) Ottewill; m. Ingrid G. Roe 1952; one s. one d.; ed. Southall County School, Queen Mary Coll., London and Fitzwilliam Coll., Cam-

bridge; Asst. Lecturer, Queen Elizabeth Coll., London 1951–52; Nuffield Fellowship, Dept. of Colloid Science, Univ. of Cambridge 1952–55, Sr. Asst. in Research 1955–58, Asst. Dir. of Research 1958–63; Lecturer in Physical Chem., Univ. of Bristol 1964–66, Reader in Colloid Science 1966–71, Prof. of Colloid Science 1971–82, Leverhulme Prof. of Physical Chem. 1982–; Alexander Lecturer, Royal Australian Chem. Inst. 1982; Liversidge Lecturer, Royal Soc. of Chem. 1985–86; Chem. Soc. Medal 1974; Wolfgang Ostwald Prize, Kolloid Gesellschaft 1979. *Publications:* 180 papers in scientific journals. *Leisure interests:* gardening, walking, music. *Address:* School of Chemistry, University of Bristol, Bristol, BS8 1TS (Office); 17 St. Oswalds Road, Bristol, BS6 7HU, England (Home). *Telephone:* 0272-303680 (Office); 0272-736611 (Home).

OTTLIK, Géza; Hungarian novelist and essayist; b. 9 May 1912, Budapest; s. of Géza Ottlik and Erzsébet Cs. Szabó; m. Gyöngyi Debreczeni 1939 (died 1979); ed. Military Acad., Köszeg and Budapest Univ.; regular contrib. to literary periodical Nyugat (Occident) 1939–; staff mem. Hungarian Radio Literature Dept. 1945–46; Sec. Hungarian PEN 1945–57. *Publications:* Hajnali háztetők (Roofs at Dawn) short novel and stories 1958, Iskola a határon (School at the Frontier) novel 1959, Minden megvan (Nothing got Lost) short stories 1969; Próza (Prose) an essay-novel 1980, Garabó Gereben (fairy-tale adaptations, with G. Debreczeni) 1983, Hajónapló (The Logbook), Short novel 1987, Buda (novel) 1989; in co-authorship with Hugh Kelsey of Scotland: Adventures in Card Play, Gollancz, London 1979; has translated works by Keller, Dickens, Shaw, Waugh, Giraudoux, Hemingway, Osborne, O'Neill; Ed.: Hungarian anthology of modern American short stories, in two vols; film scripts: Hajnali háztetők (Roofs at Dawn, with J. Dömölky) 1987, A Valencia-rejtély (The Valencia Mystery) 1988. *Address:* 1013 Budapest, Attila ut 45, Hungary. *Telephone:* 757-942.

OTTO, Frei P(aul), DR.ING.; German architect; b. 31 May 1925, Siegmar; s. of Paul and Eleonore Otto; m. Ingrid Smolla 1952; one s. four d.; ed. Schadowschule, Technische Universität, Berlin, Univ. of Va., Charlottesville; Dir. Inst. für Leichte Flächentragwerke, Univ. of Stuttgart 1964–, Hon. Prof. 1978–; Visiting Prof. Washington Univ., St. Louis, Yale Univ., Univ. of Calif. (Berkeley), M.I.T., and Harvard Univ. 1958–62; f. research group Biologie und Bauen 1961; Hon. Prof. Univ. Frederico Villareal, Lima; mem. Akad. der Künste, Berlin; Hon. Fellow American Inst. of Architects, R.I.B.A.; Hon. Dr. Arts and Arch. (Washington Univ. of St. Louis), Hon. Dr. Sc. (Bath); Berlin Art Prize 1967, Prix Perret (Union Int. des Architectes) 1967, Bonatzpreis, Stuttgart 1971, Kölner Kunstpreis 1971, Thomas Jefferson Medal and Prize, Univ. of Va. 1974, Hugo-Häring Prize 1978, Deutscher Holzbaupreis 1979, Aga Khan Award for Architecture (Lahore) 1980, Grosser BDA-Preis, Biberach 1982. *Major works:* German Pavilion Expo, Montreal 1967, Conference Centre, Mecca, Saudi Arabia 1967, roof structure of Olympic Sports Stadium, Munich 1972, Multihalle Herzogenried, Mannheim 1975, Sports Hall, King Abdulaziz Univ., Jeddah 1981. *Publications:* Das hängende Dach 1954, Zugbeanspruchte Konstruktionen, Vol. 1 1962, Vol. 2 1966, Natürliche Konstruktionen 1982, Ed. of series IL1-29 on lightweight structures. *Leisure interest:* gardening. *Address:* 725 Leonberg 7 Warmbronn, Berghalde 19, Federal Republic of Germany. *Telephone:* 0711-7843599 (Office); 07152-41084 (Home).

OTTONE, Piero; Italian journalist; b. 3 Aug. 1924, Genoa; s. of Giovanni Battista and Vittoria Ottone; m. Hanne (Winslow) Ottone 1958; one s. one d.; ed. Univ. of Turin; Reporter, Corriere Ligure 1945; Reporter, Gazzetta del Popolo 1945–58, London corresp. 1948–50, Bonn corresp. 1950–53; London and Moscow corresp., Corriere della Sera 1953–61, Special Corresp. in Italy 1962, Ed.-in-Chief 1972–77; Ed. Secolo XIX 1968; Man. Dir. La Repubblica Nov. 1977; Gen. Man. Mondadori 1977; Palazzi Prize for Journalism 1973. *Publications:* Gli industriali si confessano 1965, Fanfani 1966, La nuova Russia 1967, De Gasperi 1968, Potere economico 1968, Intervista sul giornalismo italiano 1978, Come finirà 1979. *Address:* c/o Arnoldo Mondadori, Via Marconi 27, 20090 Segrate, Milan, Italy.

OTUMFUO NANA OPOKU WARE II; Ghanaian ruler (The Asantehene); b. 30 Nov. 1919, Kumasi, Ashanti; s. of Nana Kwabena Poku and Nana Akua Achiaa; m. Nana Akua Afriyie 1947; one s. three d.; successor and nephew of Sir Osei Agyeman Prempeh II; ed. Adisadel Coll., Cape Coast and Middle Temple, London; called to the Bar 1962; Commr. for Communications 1968–69; First Pres. African Civil Aviation Comm. 1969; named Amb. to Rome 1970; King of the Ashantis July 1970; Pres. Ghana Nat. House of Chiefs 1970–78, Ashanti Regional House of Chiefs, Kumasi Traditional Council; mem. Council of State 1971–72. *Leisure interests:* golf, farming. *Address:* Asantehene's Palace, Manhyia, Kumasi, Ashanti, Ghana. *Telephone:* 3680.

OTUNGA, H.E. Cardinal Maurice: Kenyan ecclesiastic; b. Jan. 1923, Chebukwa; ordained priest 1950; consecrated titular Bishop of Tacape 1957; Bishop of Kisii 1961; titular Archbishop of Bomarzo 1969; Archbishop of Nairobi 1971–; created Cardinal by Pope Paul VI 1973; Primate of Kenya 1983–; Dir. Castrense for Kenya. *Address:* Cardinal's Residence, P.O. Box 14231, Nairobi, Kenya.

OUATTARA, Alassane D., D.SC.; Côte d'Ivoire financial official; b. 1 Jan. 1942, Dimbokro; ed. Drexel Inst. of Tech., Phila. and Univ. of Pennsylvania; Economist, IMF 1968–73; Official Rep. Banque Centrale des Etats de l'Afrique de l'Ouest 1973-75, Special Adviser to the Gov. and Dir. of Studies 1975-82, Vice-Gov. 1983-84, Gov. Oct. 1988-; Dir. African Dept., IMF Nov. 1984-, Adviser to the Dir.-Gen. May 1987-; Pres. CNUCED 1979-80; mem. Bd. Dirs., Global Econ. Action Inst.; Expert Adviser Comm. sur les Corpns. Transnat.; Commandeur Ordre du Lion de Senegal, Ordre du Mono du Togo, Ordre National du Niger, Officier Ordre National de Côte d'Ivoire. *Address:* c/o Office of the Governor of Banque Centrale des Etats de l'Afrique de l'Ouest, avenue du Barachois, BP 3108 Dakar, Senegal. *Telephone:* (221) 21 16 15.

OUCHI, Tsutomu, D. ECON.; Japanese professor and politician; b. 19 June 1918, Tokyo; s. of Hyoe Ouchi; m. Setsuko Otsuka 1944; one s. one d.; ed. The Daiichi Kotogakko and Tokyo Imperial Univ.; researcher Japan Inst. of Agric. 1942-46; Assoc. Prof. Univ. of Tokyo 1947-60, Prof. 1960-79, Prof. Emer. 1979-; Prof. Emer. Shinshu Univ. 1979-, Prof. Daita Bunka Univ. 1987-; Dean Faculty of Econs., Univ. of Tokyo 1968-69; Vice-Pres. Univ. of Tokyo 1972-73; Chair. Central Cttee. for Security of Employment 1976-88, Employment Cttee., Ministry of Labour 1988-; mem. Japan Acad. 1981-; Mainichi Press Prize, Nasu Prize, Nihon Keizai Press Prize. *Publications:* Agricultural Crisis 1954, American Agriculture 1965, State Monopolistic Capitalism 1970, American Agriculture in the 1960's 1975, Japanese Agriculture 1978, Methodology of Economics 1980, Principles of Economics (2 vols) 1981-82, Imperialism, (2 vols.) 1984-85. *Leisure interests:* skiing, trekking. *Address:* 26-19 Hyakunin-cho II, Shinjuku-ku, Tokyo 169, Japan. *Telephone:* (03) 371-3760.

OUDOVENKO, Guennadi I., M.SC.; Soviet diplomatist; b. 22 June 1931, Ukraine; m.; one d.; ed. Kiev Univ.; Head, Personnel Div., Head, Div. of Int. Econ. Orgs., mem. of Ministerial Bd., Ukrainian Ministry of Foreign Affairs, Deputy Minister of Foreign Affairs for the Ukraine 1980-85; Sr. Recruitment Officer, UN Tech. Assistance Recruitment Service 1965-71; Dir. of Interpretation and Meetings Div., Dept. of Conf. Services, UN HQ 1977-80; Perm. Rep. of the Ukraine to the UN 1985-; Rep. of the Ukraine on Governing Body of ILO 1981-85; Rep. to UN Security Council 1985; Chair. Second Cttee. of 42nd Session UN Gen. Ass. *Publications:* several publs. on int. affairs. *Address:* Permanent Mission of the Ukrainian Soviet Socialist Republic to the United Nations, 136 East 67th Street, New York, N.Y. 10021, U.S.A. *Telephone:* 535-3418.

OUEDDEI, Goukouni; Chad politician; b. 1944, Zouar; formed the Second Army of the Front de Libération Nationale du Tchad (FROLINAT) 1972; head of Northern Armed Forces Command Council 1977-; Chair. Revolutionary Cttee., Popular Armed Forces of FROLINAT 1978-84; Chair. Provisional State Council of Chad after Kano peace agreement March-April 1979, in charge of Information; Minister of State for the Interior in Shawa Govt. April-Sept. 1979; Pres. of Chad and Head of State (Gouvernement d'union nationale de transition-GUNT) 1979-82 (deposed); Pres. GUNT forces in N. Chad 1982-86, Pres. Conseil suprême de la Révolution 1985-86. *Address:* c/o Conseil Suprême de la Révolution, Badai, Chad.

OUÉDRAOGO, Gérard Kango; Burkina Faso politician; b. 19 Sept. 1925, Ouahigouya; Rep. to French West African Fed. 1952; Deputy to French Nat. Assembly 1956-59; co-founder Mouvement Démocratique Voltaïque; mem. Parl. 1957-65; Amb. to U.K. 1961-66; Adviser, Ministry of Foreign Affairs; Pres. Union Démocratique Voltaïque 1970-74, now Commr.; Prime Minister 1971-74; Pres. Nat. Ass. 1978-80. *Address:* Union Démocratique Voltaïque, Ouagadougou, Burkina Faso.

OUELLET, Hon. André, P.C., B.A., LL.L.; Canadian lawyer and politician; b. 6 April 1939, St. Pascal, Quebec; s. of Dr. Albert Ouellet and Rita Turgeon; m. Edith Pagé 1965; two s. two d.; ed. Pensionnat St. Louis de Gonzague, Quebec Seminary, Ottawa and Sherbrooke Univs.; M.P. for Papineau 1967-; Parl. Sec. to Minister for External Affairs 1970, to Minister for Nat. Health and Welfare 1971; Postmaster Gen. 1972-74; Minister for Consumer and Corporate Affairs 1974-76, 1980-84, for Urban Affairs 1976-79, for Public Works 1978-79, for Canada Post Corpn. 1980-83, for Labour 1983, for Regional Econ. Devt. 1983-84; Pres. Privy Council 1984; Govt. Leader of Commons 1984; Opposition Transport Critic 1984, Opposition External Affairs Critic 1987; Liberal. *Leisure interests:* tennis, swimming, squash, skiing, reading and collecting works of art. *Address:* Room 484, Confederation Building, House of Commons, Parliament Buildings, Ottawa, Ont., K1A 0A6 (Office); 17 Chase Court, Ottawa, Ont. K1V 9Y6, Canada (Home). *Telephone:* 995-8872 (Office) 733-2310 (Home).

OUIMET, J. Alphonse, C.C., B.A., B.ENG.; Canadian communications executive and engineer; b. 12 June 1908, Montreal; s. of J. Alphonse Ouimet and Marie Blanche Geoffrion; m. Jeanne Prévost 1935; one d.; ed. St. Mary's Coll., Montreal and McGill Univ.; Research Engineer, Canadian Television Ltd. 1932-33, Research Engineer and Dir. Canadian Electronics Co. 1933-34; Research Engineer Canadian Broadcasting Corpn. (C.B.C.), Ottawa 1935-36, Operations Engineer, Montreal 1937-39, Gen. Supervisor of Eng. 1939-40, Asst. and later Chief Engineer 1941-51, Asst. Gen. Man. 1951-52, Gen. Man. 1953-58, Pres. 1958-68; Chair. Telesat Canada 1969-80, Dir. 1980-84; Fellow Inst. of Radio Engineers; mem. Eng. Inst. of Canada, Int. Television Cttee., Ministerial Advisory Cttee. on Telecommunications and Canada 1978-79; Chair. Communications Research Advisory Bd. 1975-80, Dir. 1980-; Fellow Canadian Acad. of Eng. 1987; Hon. Degrees from

Laval Univ. and Univs. of Montreal, Acadia, Saskatchewan, McGill, Ottawa and Sherbrooke, Royal Mil. Coll. of Canada, Int. Emmy Directorate Award 1977, Great Montrealer Award 1978, Int. Communications Soc. Public Service Award 1978, and several other awards. *Address:* 227 Lakeview Avenue, Pointe Claire, H95 4C8, P.Q., Canada. *Telephone:* 697-1922.

OUKO, Robert John; Kenyan administrator and politician; b. 31 March 1932, Kisumu; s. of Erasto and Susanah Seda; m. Christabel Akumu Odolla 1965; one s. four d.; ed. Ogada School, Kisumu, Nyangori School, Kakamega, Siriba Coll., Haile Sellassie I and Makerere Univs.; Teacher 1952-55; worked in Kisii District, Ministry of African Affairs 1955-58; Asst. Sec. Foreign Affairs Dept., Office of the Prime Minister 1962-63, Senior Asst. Sec. 1963; Perm. Sec. Ministry of Foreign Affairs 1963-64, Ministry of Works 1965-69; E. African Minister for Finance and Admin. 1969-70, for Common Market and Econ. Affairs 1970-77; Minister of Econ. Planning and Community Affairs 1978-79, of Foreign Affairs 1979-83, of Planning and Nat. Devt. 1985-87, of Industry 1987-88, of Foreign Affairs and Int. Co-operation March 1988-; Pres. African Asscn. for Public Admin. and Man. 1971-74; mem. E. African Legis. Ass.; mem. ILO 1983-; Fellow, Kenya Inst. of Man.; Hon. LL.D. (Pacific Lutheran Univ.) 1971. *Publications:* essays on admin. in professional journals; co-author of univ. textbook on managements. *Leisure interests:* reading, music, hunting. *Address:* P.O. Box 48935, Nairobi, Kenya (Home).

OULD HAMODY, Mohamed-Said; Mauritanian journalist and diplomatist; b. 23 May 1942, Atar; s. of Hamody Ould Mahmoud and Salka Bent Brahim Ould Ebdeba; m. Mariem Bent Ali Ould Salem 1965; one s. two d.; ed. Inst. de développement économique et social, Paris, Centre français du journalisme, Paris; journalist, Nat. Information Office 1968-70; Chief Exec. Nat. Broadcasting 1970-72; Counsellor, Embassy, Cairo 1972-76, Washington 1976-78; Sec.-Gen. Govt. of Mauritania 1978-80; Perm. Rep. to UN 1980-84; Political Adviser to Minister of Foreign Affairs and Co-operation 1985-; mem. City Council of Atar 1986-. *Leisure interests:* reading, writing, music. *Address:* c/o Ministry of Foreign Affairs, Nouakchott (Office); P.O. Box 311, RP, Nouakchott, Mauritania (Home). *Telephone:* 52682 (Office); 52324 (Home).

OUMAROU, Ide; Niger politician and civil servant; b. 1937, Niamey; ed. William Ponty School, Dakar, Senegal and Institut des Hautes Etudes d'Outre-mer, Paris; started as journalist in Ministry of Information, Niger 1960; Ed. Le Niger 1961-63; Dir. of Information 1963-70, Comm.-Gen. for Information 1970-72; Dir.-Gen. Office of Posts and Telecommunications 1972-74; Head of Cabinet of Pres. of Supreme Mil. Council 1974-79; Perm. Rep. UN New York 1979-83; Minister of Foreign Affairs 1983-85; Sec.-Gen. OAU 1985-. *Publications include:* Gros Plan (Grand Prix littéraire d'Afrique noire, Paris 1978), Le Représentant 1984. *Address:* Organisation of African Unity, P.O. Box 3243, Addis Ababa, Ethiopia.

OURISSON, Guy, DR.SC., PH.D.; French chemist; b. 26 March 1926, Boulogne-sur-Seine; s. of Jacques Ourisson and Colette (née de Bosredon); m. 1st Paula Baylis 1950 (deceased 1958), 2nd Nicole Heiligenstein 1959 (divorced); one s. two d.; ed. Ecole Normale Supérieure, Paris, Harvard Univ.; Maître de Conférences, Univ. Louis Pasteur, Strasbourg 1955-58, Prof. of Chem. 1958-, Pres. of Univ. Louis Pasteur 1971-75; Dir. of Univ. Studies, Ministry of Educ. Nat. 1981-82; Dir. Inst. of Chem. of Natural Products, C.N.R.S., Gif/Yvette; Chair. Scientific Council, Rhône-Poulenc; Pres. of many scientific cttees. in France; Chair. Publications Cttee., IUPAC 1973-77, Sec.-Gen. 1975-83; Regional Ed. Tetrahedron Letters 1965-; Officier, Légion d'honneur; Commdr., Ordre national du Mérite; Commdr. des Palmes académiques; mem. Acad. Leopoldina (Halle), Danish, Swedish, Indian and French Acads. of Sciences; awards from Chemical Socs. of France, Fed. Repub. of Germany, Belgium, U.K., U.S.A.; Hon. mem. Chemical Socs. of Belgium, U.K., Switzerland. *Publications:* over 300 on chem. and on ethics of science; several books on chem. of natural products. *Leisure interests:* nature, manual work, bonsai, reading, people. *Address:* Centre du Neurochimie, 5 rue Blaise Pascal, F67084 Strasbourg (Office); 5 rue du Petersgarten, F67000, Strasbourg, France (Home). *Telephone:* (88) 61-48-48; (88) 31-36-15 (Home).

OUSMANE, Sembene; Senegalese writer and film-maker; b. 1 Jan. 1923, Ziguinchor, Casamance region; plumber, bricklayer, apprentice mechanic; served in Europe in World War II; docker in Marseille; studied film production in U.S.S.R. under Marc Donski; Founder Ed. first Wolof language monthly, Kaddu; first prize for novelists at World Festival of Negro Arts, Dakar 1966; numerous int. awards. *Films:* Borom Sarret 1963, niaye 1964, La noire de ... 1966, Mandabi 1968, Taaw 1971, Emitai 1971, Xala 1974, Ceddo 1977. *Publications:* novels: Le docker noir 1956, O pays mon beau peuple 1957, Les bouts de bois de Dieu 1960, Voltaïque 1962, L'harmattan 1964, Vehi -Ciosane suivi du mandat 1966, Xala 1974, Fat Ndiay Diop 1976, Dernier de l'empire 1979. *Address:* P.O. Box 8087 YOFF, Dakar, Senegal.

OUVRIEU, Jean-Bernard; French diplomatist; b. 13 March 1939; m. Arabella Cruse 1968; three c.; ed. Ecole Nat. d'Administration; Head of Mission, Office of Prime Minister 1968-69; served Perm. Mission to European Communities, Brussels 1971-74, Baghdad 1975-77, Washington 1977-79; Deputy Dir., Office of Minister of Foreign Affairs 1979-80; Rep. to Governing Council of IAEA 1981-85; Amb. to Repub. of Korea 1985-87;

Dir. of Econ. and Financial Affairs, Ministry of Foreign Affairs 1987. *Address:* 23 Square des Peupliers, 75013 Paris, France.

OUYANG SHAN; Chinese author, party and cultural official; b. Ouyang Yangyi, Guangdong Prov.; active in Guangdong dialectical literary movt., studied under Lu Xun in Shanghai 1930s; active in Fed. of Literary and Art Circles, Yun'an 1940–; Deputy Dir. Cultural and Educ. Dept., Guangdong Prov. People's Congress, Chair S. China Fed. of Literary and Art Circles 1951–; Pres. S. China Inst. of People's Literature and Art 1952–; published self-criticism in Yangtze Literature and Art Feb. 1952; Chair Canton Br. of Union of Chinese Writers 1953–66; Council mem. China-Pakistan Friendship Assen. 1956–66; Standing Cttee. mem. Guangdong Prov. CPPCC Cttee. 1959–66; mem. 3rd NPC Sept. 1964; criticized 1964; purged 1966; rehabilitated 1978; Vice-Chair. Guangdong Prov. People's Congress 1979–81; mem. Cen. Advisory Cttee. of CCP Cen. Cttee. 1982–. *Publications:* Stranger in the Village, The Proud Lady, Three-Family Lane, Bitter Struggle. *Address:* Central Advisory Committee of the Central Committee of the Chinese Communist party, Zhongnanhai, Beijing, People's Republic of China.

ÓVÁRI, Miklós; Hungarian politician; b. 24 Aug. 1925, Budapest; ed. Budapest Univ. of Liberal Arts; Teacher, Party School 1949–58; Deputy Head of Agitation and Propaganda Dept., Hungarian Socialist Workers' Party (HSWP) Cen. Cttee. 1958–61; Deputy Head Dept. of Science, Culture and Public Educ. 1961–66, Head 1966–70; mem. Cen. Cttee., HSWP 1966–88, Sec. Cen. Cttee. 1970–88, mem. Political Cttee. 1975–88, Head Agitation and Propaganda Bd. attached to HWSP Cen. Cttee 1975–85; M.P. *Publication:* Történelem, ideológia, kultura (History, Ideology, Culture) 1980. *Address:* Hungarian Socialist Workers' Party, 1358 Budapest V, Széchenyi rakpart 19, Hungary. *Telephone:* 111-400.

OVCHINNIKOV, Lev Nikolayevich; Soviet geologist; b. 9 Oct. 1913, Perm; s. of Nicolai Alexanrovich Ovchinnikov and Marija Michailovna Ovchinnikova; m. Ludmila Ovchinnikova 1952; three s. one d.; ed. Uralsk Univ.; mem. CPSU 1944–; Head of Lab. for Mineralogy and Geochemistry, Inst. of Mining and Geology, Uralsk Br. U.S.S.R. Acad. of Sciences 1946–; Dir. Inst. of Geology 1962–; Dir. Inst. of Mineralogy, Geochemistry and Crystallochemistry 1966–, Head Div. of Metallogeny 1986–; Corresp. mem. U.S.S.R. Acad. of Sciences. *Publications:* numerous publs., mainly on geology of the Urals, ore deposits and geochemical methods in geological prospecting. *Leisure interests:* fishing, mycology. *Address:* Institute of Mineralogy, Geochemistry and Crystallochemistry of Rare Elements, Sadownicheskaja Embankment, 71, Moscow, U.S.S.R.

OVENDEN, Graham Stuart, M.A., A.R.C.A., A.R.C.M.; British artist, poet and art historian; b. 11 Feb. 1943, Alresford, Hants.; s. of Henry Ovenden and Gwendoline D. Hill; m. Ann. D. Gilmore 1969; one s. one d.; ed. Alresford Dames School, Itchen Grammar School, Southampton, Southampton Coll. of Art, Royal Coll. of Music and Royal Coll. of Art; corresp. and critic, Architecture Design Magazine. *Publications:* Illustrators of Alice 1971, Victorian Children 1972, Clementina, Lady Harwarden 1973, Pre-Raphaelite Photography 1972, Victorian Erotic Photography 1973, Aspects of Lolita 1975, A Victorian Album (with Lord David Cecil) 1976, Satirical Poems and Others 1983, The Marble Mirror (poems) 1984, Lewis Carroll Photographer 1984; photographs: Alphonse Mucha 1973, Hill & Adamson 1973; Graham Ovenden . . . A Monograph with essays by Laurie Lee, etc. 1987, contributions on art to numerous journals. *Leisure interests:* music (very seriously indeed), architecture, social science. *Address:* Barly Splatt, Panters Bridge, Mount, nr. Bodmin, Cornwall, England.

OVERBECK, Egon, DR. RER. POL.; German business executive; b. 11 Jan. 1918, Heide/Holstein; s. of Georg Hermann and Anna Luise Overbeck; m. Hannegret Wiechell 1948; three s. one d.; ed. Reform-Realgymnasium Rendsburg/Holstein, and Johann Wolfgang Goethe Universität, Frankfurt am Main; Army service, Lieut. 1938, Maj. on Gen. Staff 1944; univ. studies after Second World War; Deputy Dir. Metallgesellschaft A.G., Frankfurt/Main 1954; mem. Exec. Bd. Vereinigte Deutsche Metallgesellschaft A.G., Frankfurt/Main 1956; Chair. of Man. Bd., Mannesmann A.G., Düsseldorf 1962–83; mem. Advisory Bd. Siemens A.G., Munich, and numerous other firms; Chair. Advisory Bd. Victoria Vers A.G., Berlin Ruhrgas A.G., Essen, Voith GmbH., Heidenheim; Grosses Bundesverdienstkreuz and several foreign and war decorations. *Publications:* Possibilities of Maintaining and Increasing West German Lead-Zinc Production 1951. *Leisure interests:* shooting, tennis, historic literature. *Address:* Mannesmann A.G., Mannesmann-Ufer 4, D-4000 Düsseldorf, Federal Republic of Germany. *Telephone:* (0211) 820-2302.

OVERBEEK, Jan Theodoor Gerard, DRS.CHEM., PH.D.; Dutch professor of physical chemistry; b. 5 Jan. 1911, Groningen; s. of Dr. A. A. and J. C. (van Ryssel) Overbeek; m. Johanna Clasina Edie 1936; four d.; ed. Univ. of Utrecht; Asst. at Univ. of Ghent, Belgium 1935–36, Univ. of Utrecht 1936–41; Scientific Officer, N. V. Philips, Eindhoven 1941–46; Prof. of Physical Chem., Univ. of Utrecht 1946–81, Vice-Pres. of Univ. 1971–76; Visiting Prof., M.I.T., Cambridge, Mass. 1952–53, 1966–67, 1969–81, 1984–88, Columbia Univ., New York 1956, Univ. of Southern Calif., Los Angeles 1959–60; mem. Board, Verenigde Bedrijven Bredero, Utrecht 1963–83; mem. Royal Netherlands Acad. of Arts and Sciences 1953–, Royal Flemish Acad. of Sciences (Belgium), American Acad. of Arts and Sciences; Hon.

Fellow Royal Soc. of Chemistry (London) 1983; Hon. D.Sc. (Clarkson Coll. of Tech., Potsdam, N.Y.) 1967, Univ. of Bristol 1984. *Publications:* Theory of Stability of Lyophobic colloids (with E. J. W. Verwey) 1948, Colloid Science (with H. R. Kruyt) Vol. I 1949, Vol. II 1952, The Electrical Double Layer (with A. L. Loeb, P. H. Wiersema) 1960; An Introduction to Physical Chemistry (with H. R. Kruyt) 1960, Electrochemistry Vols. I, II & III 1981; numerous articles and study guides on colloid and surface science. *Leisure interests:* outdoor activities, hiking, photography. *Address:* Van't Hoff Laboratory, Padualaan 8, 3584 CH Utrecht (Office); Zweerslaan 35, 3723HN Bilthoven, Netherlands (Home). *Telephone:* 030-532391 (Office); 030-282882 (Home).

OVERHAUSER, Albert Warner, PH.D.; American physicist; b. 17 Aug. 1925, San Diego; s. of Clarence Albert Overhauser and Gertrude Irene (Pehrson) Overhauser; m. Margaret Mary Casey 1951; four s. four d.; ed. Univ. of California at Berkeley; service with USNR 1944–46; Research Assoc., Univ. of Ill. 1951–53; Asst. Prof. of Physics, Cornell Univ. 1953–56, Assoc. Prof. 1956–58; Supervisor, Solid State Physics, Ford Motor Co., Dearborn, Mich. 1958–62, Man. Theoretical Sciences 1962–69, Asst. Dir. of Physical Sciences 1969–72, Dir. 1972–73; Prof. of Physics Purdue Univ., W. Lafayette, Ind. 1973–74, Stuart Dist. Prof. of Physics 1974–; Oliver E. Buckley Solid State Physics Prize (American Physics Soc.) 1975; Alexander von Humboldt Sr. U.S. Scientist Award 1979; Fellow American Physics Soc., American Acad. of Arts and Sciences; mem. N.A.S.; Hon. D.Sc. (Chicago) 1979. *Address:* Department of Physics, Purdue University, West Lafayette, Ind. 47907; 236 Pawnee Drive West, Lafayette, Ind. 47906, U.S.A. (Home).

OVETT, Stephen Michael, M.B.E.; British athlete; b. 9 Oct. 1955, Brighton, Sussex; m. Rachel Waller 1981; ed. Brighton College of Art; competed Olympic Games, Montreal 1976, finished 5th in 800 m., reached semi-final of 1500 m.; Moscow 1980, won gold medal at 800 m. and bronze medal at 1500 m.; European Junior Champion at 800 m. 1973; European Champion at 1500 m. 1978 and silver medallist at 800 m. 1974 and 1978; world record holder at 1500 m., fmr. world record holder at mile; holder of record for greatest number of mile/1500 m. victories (45 to 1980); also winner of major titles at 5,000m. *Leisure interest:* art.

OVINNIKOV, Richard Sergeyevich; Soviet diplomatist; b. 29 Dec. 1930, Voronezh, R.S.F.S.R.; s. of Sergey Ovinnikov and Tatiana Bizulya; m. Liudmila Bulatova 1951; two d.; ed. Moscow State Inst. of Int. Relations; with Ministry of Foreign Affairs 1958–; Sec. to Perm. Mission of U.S.S.R. at UN, New York 1960–66; Counsellor at Ministry of Foreign Affairs, Moscow 1966–70; Minister with Perm. Mission of U.S.S.R. at UN, New York 1970–77; Head of Advisers to Minister of Foreign Affairs 1977–80; First Deputy Perm. Rep. to UN, Amb. Extraordinary and Plenipotentiary 1980–86. *Publications:* Behind the Screen of Non-Intervention 1959, The Bosses of British Foreign Policy 1966, Supermonopolies 1978, Wall Street and Foreign Policy 1980, From Nixon to Reagan 1985. *Leisure interest:* fishing. *Address:* c/o Ministry of Foreign Affairs, 32–34 Smolenskaya-Sennaya ploshchad, Moscow, U.S.S.R.

OWEN, Rt. Hon. David Anthony Llewellyn, P.C., M.A., M.B., B.CHIR.; British politician; b. 2 July 1938, Plymouth; s. of Dr. John William Morris Owen and Mary Llewellyn; m. Deborah Schabert 1968; two s. one d.; ed. Bradfield Coll., Sidney Sussex Coll., Cambridge, St. Thomas' Hosp.; house appointments, St. Thomas' Hosp. 1962–64, Neurological and Psychiatric Registrar 1964–66, Research Fellow, Medical Unit 1966–68; M.P. for Sutton Div. of Plymouth 1966–74, for Devonport Div. of Plymouth 1974–; Parl. Private Sec. to Minister of Defence, Admin. 1967; Parl. Under-Sec. of State for Defence, Royal Navy 1968–70; Opposition Defence Spokesman 1970–72, resigned over party policy on EEC 1972; Parl. Under-Sec. of State, Dept. of Health and Social Security (DHSS) March-July 1974; Minister of State, DHSS 1974–76, FCO 1976–77; Sec. of State for Foreign and Commonwealth Affairs 1977–79; Opposition Spokesman for Energy 1979–80; co-f. Social Democratic Party March 1981; Chair. Parl. Cttee. 1981–82; Deputy Leader S.D.P. 1982–83, Leader 1983–87, 1988–; Leader Campaign for Social Democracy 1987–88; Chair. Decision Tech. Int. 1970–72, Palme Comm. on Disarmament and Security Issues 1980–, Ind. Comm. on Int. Humanitarian Issues 1983–; Gov. Charing Cross Hosp. 1966–68; Patron, Disablement Income Group 1968–; Chair, South West Regional Sports Council 1967–71. *Publications:* Ed.: A Unified Health Service 1968; Contributor: Social Services for All 1968; Author: The Politics of Defence 1972, In Sickness and in Health—The Politics of Medicine 1976, Human Rights 1978, Face the Future 1981, A Future that Will Work 1984, A United Kingdom 1986, Personally Speaking to Kenneth Harris 1987; articles in Lancet, Neurology and Clinical Science. *Leisure interest:* sailing. *Address:* House of Commons, Westminster, London, S.W.1; 78 Narrow Street, Limehouse, London, E.14, England (Home). *Telephone:* 01-219 5531 (Home).

OWEN, Paul Robert, C.B.E., M.SC., D. ÉS SC., F.R.S., F.ENG., F.R.AE.S.; British university professor; b. 24 Jan. 1920, London; s. of late Joseph Owen and Deborah Owen; m. Margaret A. Baron 1958; two s. two d.; ed. Queen Mary Coll., Univ. of London; Head, Fluid Motion Section, Aerodynamics Dept., Royal Aircraft Establishment, Farnborough 1941–52; Prof. of the Mechanics of Fluids, Univ. of Manchester 1953–62; Zakharoff Prof. of Aviation, Imperial Coll., London 1963–84, Prof. Emer. and Sr. Research

Fellow 1984–; Visiting Prof. Univ. of Colorado at Boulder 1985–86; Chair. Aeronautical Research Council 1971–79; Fellow, Queen Mary Coll., London; Hon. Fellow, City and Guilds Inst.; Gold Medal, Royal Aeronautical Soc. *Publications:* articles in professional journals. *Leisure interests:* theatre, music. *Address:* Flat 1, Stanley Lodge, 25 Stanley Crescent, London, W11 2NA, England. *Telephone:* 01-229 5111 (Home).

OWEN, Ray David, PH.D., SC.D.; American biologist; b. 30 Oct. 1915, Genesee, Wis.; s. of Dave Owen and Ida Hoeft Owen; m. June Johanna Weissenberg 1939; one s.; ed. Carroll Coll., Wis., Univ. of Wisconsin; Research Fellow, Wisconsin 1941–43, Asst. Prof. of Genetics and Zoology 1943–47; Gosney Fellow, Calif. Inst. of Tech. 1946–47, Assoc. Prof. 1947–53, Prof. 1953–83, Chair. Div. of Biology 1961–68, Vice-Pres. for Student Affairs and Dean of Students 1975–80, Prof. Emer. 1983; Research Participant, Oak Ridge Nat. Lab. 1957–58; mem. Genetics Soc. of America (Treas. 1957–60, Vice-Pres. 1961, Pres. 1962), Nat. Acad. of Sciences, American Acad. of Arts and Sciences, American Philosophical Soc., Soc. for the Study of Evolution, American Asscn. of Immunologists; served on numerous scientific cttees. *Publications:* General Genetics (with Srb and Edgar) 1952, 1965; numerous research papers. *Address:* Division of Biology, 156-29, California Institute of Technology, Pasadena, Calif. 91125, U.S.A. (Office). *Telephone:* (818) 356-4960 (Office).

OWEN-JONES, Lindsay, B.A.; British business executive; b. 17 March 1946, Wallasey; s. of Hugh A. Owen-Jones and Esmee (Lindsay) Owen-Jones; m. Violaine de Dalmas 1984; ed. Univ. of Oxford and European Inst. of Business Admin. (INSEAD); Product Man. L'Oreal 1969, Head, Public Products Div., Belgium 1971–74, Man. SCAD (L'Oreal subsidiary), Paris 1974–76, Marketing Man. Public Products Div., Paris 1976–78, Gen. Man. SAIPO (L'Oreal subsidiary, Italy) 1978–81, Pres. COSMAIR Inc. (exclusive L'Oreal agent) U.S.A. 1981–83, Vice-Pres. L'Oreal Man. Cttee. Jan. 1984–, mem. Bd. of Dirs. 1984, Pres. and C.O.O. 1984–88, Chair. and C.E.O. Sept. 1988–. *Leisure interest:* private helicopter pilot. *Address:* L'Oreal, 41 rue Martre, 92117 Clichy Cedex, (Office); 36 Quai de Bethune, 75004 Paris, France (Home). *Telephone:* (1) 47-56-70-00 (Office).

OWREN, Paul A., M.D., F.A.C.P., F.A.C.C.P.; Norwegian professor of medicine; b. 27 Aug. 1905, Faaberg; s. of Peder A. Owren and Anna Nermo; m. 1st Marit V. E. Roedland 1935 (died 1964); 2nd Kathleen M. Thrane 1968; one d.; ed. Univ. of Oslo; Resident, Oslo City Hosps. and Rikshospitalet 1940–44; Sr. Resident Aker Hosp. 1945–47; Research Assoc. Lister Inst. of Preventive Medicine, London 1946; Sr. Resident Rikshospitalet 1948, Head of Medical Dept. 1949–70, Head Inst. for Thrombosis Research 1955–63, Researcher 1971–; Prof. of Medicine Univ. of Oslo 1949–70; mem. advisory panel for cardiovascular diseases, WHO 1962–; Chair. Norwegian Research Council for Science and Humanities 1958–61; mem. Acad. of Science and Letters (Oslo), Royal Norwegian Soc. of Science, Royal Soc. of Science (Sweden), Acad. Royale de Médecine, Belgium (foreign hon. mem. 1983), Int. Soc. on Thrombosis and Haemostasis (Pres. 1970), Int. Cttee. on Haemostasis and Thrombosis (Chair. 1967–68), Int. Soc. of Haematology (Vice-Pres. 1950–54), Int. Coll. of Angiology (Vice-Pres. 1965–73), American Coll. of Chest Physicians (Gov. 1968–74); Hon. Fellow, American Coll. of Physicians, other medical and haematological Socs.; Commdr. Order of St. Olav 1954, with Star 1970; Int. Award for Heart and Vascular Research, James M. Mitchell Foundation 1969; Medical Prize, Anders Jahre Foundation 1969; Gran Cruz da Ordem do Infante Dom Henrique 1978; Order of the Rising Sun (Third Class) 1983. *Publications:* The Coagulation of Blood: Investigations on a New Clotting Factor 1947; about 200 publications in the field. *Address:* Bjerkaasen 44, 1310 Blommenholm, Norway (Home). *Telephone:* 02-548633.

OWUSU, Victor; Ghanaian politician; b. 26 Dec. 1923, Agona-Ashanti; ed. Univs. of Nottingham and London; called to the Bar, Lincoln's Inn 1952; practising barrister 1952–67; M.P. for Agona-Kwabre 1956–61; Attorney-Gen. 1966–69; concurrently Minister of Justice 1967–69; Minister of External Affairs April 1969, 1969–71; Attorney-Gen. and Minister of Justice 1971–72; Leader fmr. Popular Front Party 1979– (political activity suspended by Flt.-Lieut. Jerry Rawlings Jun. 1982); Presidential Cand. 1979; has served on several govt. comms. and corpns.; fmr. mem. Council of Univ. of Ghana, Legon, Council of Univ. of Science and Technology, Kumasi and Cen. Legal Council of Ghana. *Address:* Popular Front Party, Accra, Ghana.

OXBURGH, Ernest Ronald, PH.D., F.R.S.; British geologist; b. 2 Nov. 1934, Liverpool; s. of Ernest Oxburgh and Violet Bugden; m. Ursula Mary Brown; one s. two d.; ed. Liverpool Inst., Univ. of Oxford and Univ. of Princeton, U.S.A.; Departmental Demonstrator, Univ. of Oxford 1960–61, Lecturer in Geology 1962–78, Fellow, St. Edmund Hall 1964–78, Emer. Fellow 1978–, Hon. Fellow 1985; Prof. of Mineralogy and Petrology, Univ. of Cambridge 1978–, Head of Dept. of Earth Sciences 1980–88; Chief Scientific Adviser, Ministry of Defence 1988–; Fellow, Trinity Hall Cambridge 1978–82, Hon. Fellow 1983–; Pres. Queens' Coll. Cambridge 1982–89; Sherman Fairchild Distinguished Scholar, Calif. Inst. of Tech. 1985–86; Hon. Fellow Univ. Coll., Oxford 1983; Pres. European Union of Geosciences 1985–87; Hon. mem. Geologists' Asscn.; Dr. h.c. (Paris) 1986; Bigsby Medal, Geological Soc. of London 1979. *Publications:* The Geology of the Eastern Alps (Ed. and Contrib.) 1968, Structural, Metamorphic and Geochronological Studies in the Eastern Alps 1971 and contribs. to Nature, Journal of Geophysical Research, Tectonophysics, Journal of the Geological Soc. of London and other learned journals. *Leisure interests:* reading, walking and various sports. *Address:* Department of Earth Sciences, University of Cambridge, Downing Street, Cambridge, CB2 3EQ; Queens' College, Cambridge, England. *Telephone:* Cambridge 333400 (Dept. of Earth Sciences); Cambridge 335511 (Queens' Coll.).

ØYANGEN, Gunhild; Norwegian politician; b. 31 Oct. 1947, Levanger; m.; Chair. Agdenes Labour Party, mem. Co. Council 1982–, mem. Nat. Bd. of Labour Party, Agricultural Cttee. 1985–; Minister of Agric. May 1986–. *Address:* Ministry of Agriculture, P.O. Box. 8007, Dep., Oslo 1, Norway. *Telephone:* (2) 11-90-90.

OYÉ-MBA, Casimir, D. EN D.; Gabonese banker; b. 20 April 1942, Libreville; m. Marie-Françoise Razafimbelo 1963; three c.; ed. Univs. of Rennes and Paris; trainee Banque Centrale, Libreville 1967–69, Asst. Dir. 1969–70, Dir. 1970–73; Nat. Dir. Banque pour le Gabon 1973–76; Asst. Dir.-Gen. Banque Cen. 1977–78; Gov. Banque des Etats de l'Afrique Cen. April 1978–; Acting Gov. IMF for Gabon 1969–76; Pres. Assen. des Banques Centrales Africaines 1987–(89); Gabon, Cameroon, Congo and Equatorial Guinea decorations. *Leisure interests:* football, tennis, cinema, reading. *Address:* B.E.A.C., BP 1917, Yaoundé, Cameroon (Office).

OYONO, Ferdinand Léopold; Cameroonian author and diplomatist; b. 14 Sept. 1929; ed. Lycée le Clerc, Yaoundé, Lycée de Provins, France, Faculty of Law and Econ. Science, Paris; fmr. Amb. to Liberia; Amb. to Belgium, also accred. to Luxembourg and the Netherlands Oct. 1969–Sept. 70; Amb. to France (also accred. to Italy) 1970–75; Perm. Rep. to the UN 1975–83; Chair. UNICEF Cen. Cttee. 1977–78; Amb. to U.K. 1984–86; Commdr., Légion d'honneur and other decorations. *Publications:* Une vie de boy 1956, Le vieux nègre et la médaille 1967, Le pandemonium, Chemin d'Europe. *Address:* c/o Ministry of Foreign Affairs, Yaoundé, Cameroon.

OYOUE, Jean-Félix; Gabonese diplomatist; b. 12 Oct. 1928, Libreville; m.; nine c.; ed Teachers' Training Coll., Mouyondzi; teacher, Owendo Vocational School, Libreville 1949–50; prin. Mitzic mil. school; head of Tchibanga school dist.; chief North Woleu-Ntem and South Ngounie school dists. 1950-66; joined diplomatic service as First Counsellor, Embassy, Washington D.C. 1966–67; Perm. Rep. to UNESCO 1967–76; Amb. to Canada 1976–79, to Ivory Coast 1979–83; Perm. Rep. to UN 1983–87. *Address:* c/o Ministère des Affaires Etrangères, B.P. 2245, Libreville, Gabon.

OZ, Amos, B.A.; Israeli author; b. 4 May 1939, Jerusalem; m. Nily Zuckermann 1960; three c.; ed. Hebrew Univ. Jerusalem; Kibbutz Hulda 1957–86; teacher of literature and philosophy, Hulda High School and Givat Brenner Regional High School 1963–86; Visiting Fellow, St. Cross Coll. Oxford; Writer-in-residence Hebrew Univ. Jerusalem 1975; Visiting Prof. Univ. of Calif. at Los Angeles (Berkeley); Writer-in-residence, and Prof. of Literature Colorado Coll., Colorado Springs 1984–85; Prof. of Hebrew Literature, Ben Gurion Univ. 1987–88; Visiting Prof. of Literature, Writer in Residence, Boston Univ. 1987; Holon Prize 1965, Brenner Prize 1976; Zeev Award for Children's Books 1978; Bernstein Prize 1983, Bialik Prize 1986; Officier des Arts et des Lettres (France). *Publications:* novels: Elsewhere, Perhaps 1966, My Michael 1968, Touch the Water, Touch the Wind 1973, A Perfect Peace 1982, Black Box 1987; novellas and short stories: Where the Jackals Howl 1965, Unto Death 1971, The Hill of Evil Counsel 1976; essays: Under this Blazing Light 1979, In the Land of Israel 1983, The Slopes of Lebanon 1987; Different People (selected anthology) 1974; Soumchi (children's story) 1978. *Address:* Arad 80700, Arad, Israel.

ÖZAL, Turgut; Turkish politician; b. 1927, Malatya; s. of Mehmet and Hafize Özal; m. Semra Özal 1954; two s. one d.; ed. Istanbul Tech. Univ.; Under-Sec. State Planning Org. 1967–71; with World Bank 1971; then Chief Exec. Sabanci Group; Under-Sec. Prime Minister's Office, Acting Under-Sec. State Planning Org. 1979–80; Deputy Prime Minister 1980–82, Prime Minister of Turkey Dec. 1983–; also responsible for State Planning Org., Treasury and Foreign Trade Undersecr. March 1989–; Chair. Motherland Party 1988–. *Leisure interests:* reading, computers. *Address:* Basbakanlık, Bakanlıklar, Ankara, Turkey.

OZAWA, Seiji; Japanese conductor; b. 1 Sept. 1935, Shenyang, China; m. 1st Kyoko Edo, 2nd Vera Ilyan; one s. one d.; ed. Toho School of Music, Tokyo (under Prof. Hideo Saito), Tanglewood, U.S.A., and in West Berlin under Herbert von Karajan (q.v.); Asst. Conductor (under Leonard Bernstein, q.v.), New York Philharmonic 1961–62 (including tour of Japan 1961); guest conductor, San Francisco Symphony, Detroit Symphony, Montreal, Minneapolis, Toronto and London Symphony Orchestras 1961–65; Music Dir. Ravinia Festival, Chicago 1964–68; Music Dir. Toronto Symphony Orchestra 1965–69; toured Europe conducting many of the major orchestras 1966–67; Salzburg Festival 1969; Music Dir. San Francisco Symphony Orchestra 1970–76; Music Dir. Boston Symphony 1973–; toured U.S.A., France, Fed. Repub. of Germany, China 1979, Austria, U.K. 1981, Japan 1981, 1986, toured England, Netherlands, France, Germany, Austria and Belgium 1988; now makes frequent guest appearances with most of the leading orchestras of America, Europe and Japan; has conducted opera at Salzburg, Covent Garden, La Scala, Vienna Staatsoper and Paris Opera; conducted world premiere, Messiaen's St. Francis of Assisi, Paris 1983; First Prize, Int. Competition of Orchestra Conductors, France 1959, Koussevitsky Prize for outstanding student conductor 1960, Laureate, Fondation du Japon 1988; many recordings; Hon. D.Mus. (Univ. of Mass., New England Conservatory, Wheaton Coll., Norton, Mass.). *Leisure interests:* golf, tennis, skiing. *Address:* c/o Ronald A. Wilford (Columbia Artists Management Inc., Conductors Division), 165 West 57th Street, New York, N.Y., U.S.A.; c/o Harold Holt Ltd., 31 Sinclair Road, London, W.14, England.

OZAWA, Tatsuo; Japanese politician; ed. Tokyo Univ.; Official, Ministry of Home Affairs; Head of Health Insurance Section, Ministry of Health and Welfare; mem. House of Reps.; Dir.-Gen. Affairs Bureau and Treasury Bureau, Liberal-Democratic Party; Minister of Construction Nov.-Dec. 1974; Minister of State and Dir.-Gen. Environment Agency 1974-76; Minister of Health and Welfare 1977-79, of Home Affairs 1985-86. *Address:* House of Representatives, Tokyo, Japan.

OZBEK, (Ibrahim Mehmet) Rifat, B.A.; Turkish/British couturier; b. 8 Nov. 1953, Istanbul; s. of Melike Osbek and Abdulazim Mehmet Ismet; ed. St. Martin's School of Art, London; worked with Walter Albini for Trell; designer Monsoon Co.; presented first collection 1984; Designer AEFFE S.p.A. 1988; British Fashion Council Designer of the Year 1988. *Address:* c/o OZBEK (London) Ltd., 18 Haunch of Venison Yard, London, W1Y 1AF, England. *Telephone:* 01-491 7033.

ÖZBEK, Dr. Sabahattin; Turkish agronomist and politician; b. 1915, Erzincan; ed. Secondary School, Istanbul, Faculty of Agric., Univ. of Ankara; lecturer, Faculty of Agric., Univ. of Ankara 1938, Asst. Prof. 1941, Prof. 1953, Dean 1955-57, 1965-68; Visiting Prof. Univs. of Michigan and Calif. 1950-51, 1957-58; Minister of Nat. Educ. 1972-73, of Communications 1973-74, 1974-75; founded Atatürk Univ., Erzurum, later Co-Founder Faculty of Agric., Adana; Chair. Agricultural Cttee. for the preparation of First Five-Year Devt. Plan; mem. Turkish Atomic Energy Comm.; Prize of Professional Honour, Union of Agricultural Engineers. *Publications:* 35 books in Turkish and foreign languages. *Address:* c/o Ministry of Communications, Ulaştirma Bakanliği, Hipodrom Caddesi, Ankara, Turkey.

ÖZDAŞ, Mehmet Nimet, DR.ING.; Turkish professor of mechanical engineering; b. 26 March 1921, Istanbul; s. of Izzet and Refia Özdaş; m. Suna Taki 1956; two s.; ed. Tech. Univ. of Istanbul, Imperial Coll., London and London Univ.; Dozent, Tech. Univ. of Istanbul 1952, Prof. 1961-73, Prof. of Automatic Control 1979-, Dir. Computation Centre 1962-64; Visiting Prof. Case Inst. of Tech. 1958-59; Sec.-Gen. Scientific and Tech. Research Council 1964-67, mem. Science Bd. 1968-71; Rep. to CENTO Science Council 1965, to NATO Science Cttee. 1966-73; Dir. Marmara Scientific and Industrial Research Inst. 1969-73; Asst. Sec.-Gen. for Scientific and Environmental Affairs, NATO Sept. 1973-79; Minister of State in charge of Scientific and Environmental Affairs Sept. 1980-83. *Publications:* about 20 articles in English in scientific periodicals, many articles in Turkish and five books. *Leisure interest:* sport. *Address:* Istanbul Technical University, Istanbul, Gümüşsuyu; Başbakanlık, Ankara, Turkey. *Telephone:* Ankara 189248.

OZDOWSKI, Jerzy, D.ECON.SC.; Polish economist and politician; b. 19 Sept. 1925, Pawłowice; s. of Seweryn and Czesława Ozdowski; m. Maria Ozdowska 1955; three s.; ed. Poznań Univ.; managerial posts in commerce and co-operative movt., Poznań 1949-67; scientific worker, Co-operative Research Inst., Warsaw 1967-79, Head Dept. of Co-operative Movt. Theory 1968-79, Asst. Prof. 1971-79; Prof. of Econ. Sciences 1979-; lecturer in Catholic schools; Head Dept. of Social Econ., Catholic Lublin Univ. 1973-; mem. Polish Econ. Soc., Scientific Soc. of Catholic Univ. of Lublin and Poznań Soc. of the Friends of Sciences; Pres. Catholic Intellectuals' Club, Poznań 1965-80; Deputy Chair. Social Council attached to Centre of Documentation and Social Studies, Warsaw 1965-80, Chair. 1980-; mem. Council of State April-Nov. 1980; Deputy Chair. Council of Ministers 1980-82; Chair. Council for Family Matters 1981-82; Deputy to Seym 1976-, Vice-Marshal 1982-; Vice-Chair. Provisional Nat. Council of Patriotic Movt. for Nat. Rebirth PRON 1982-83, mem. Nat. Council and Vice-Chair. Presidium Exec. Cttee. 1983-; Order of Banner of Labour (Second Class),

Kt.'s Cross, Order of Polonia Restituta, Gold Cross of Merit and other decorations. *Publications:* numerous books and about 200 articles on problems of econs. of trade and on social ethics. *Leisure interest:* sport. *Address:* Kancelaria Sejmu PRL, ul. Wiejska 4/6, 00-902 Warsaw, Poland. *Telephone:* 28-87-66.

OZENDA, Paul, DR. SC.; French professor of biology; b. 1920, Nice; s. of Gabriel Ozenda and Félicie Ozenda-Barrel; m. Denise Seguinaud 1951; two s.; ed. Univ. of Paris and Ecole Normale Supérieure; Prof. Univ. of Algiers 1949-54; Prof. and Dir. Plant Biology and Ecology Lab. Univ. of Grenoble 1954-; Scientific Counsellor, Nuclear Research Centre for Plant Radiobiology, Grenoble 1958-85; mem. Acad. des Sciences; Pres. Soc. Française d'Ecologie 1988-91; Co.-Dir. Handbook of Plant Anatomy 1962-; Assoc. mem. Royal Belgian Acad., Italian Acad. of Forestry; mem. Acad. Dauphiné, Pres. 1988-(90); Chevalier, Légion d'Honneur; Commdr. des Palmes Académiques; Dr. h.c. (Innsbrück). *Publications:* 12 books and 108 other publs. *Address:* University of Grenoble, Botany, Post Box 68, 38402 Saint-Martin d'Hères Cédex (Office); 5 avenue de la Foy, 38700 Corenc, France (Home). *Telephone:* 76 51 46 80 (Office); 76 90 11 94.

OZGA-MICHALSKI, Józef; Polish politician and writer; b. 8 March 1919, Bieliny, Kielce Voivodship; s. of Władysław and Józefa Ozga-Michalski; m. Stanisława Ozga-Michalski 1944; one s. two d.; during occupation, mem. of the leadership of the Peasant Battalions and editor of underground peasant periodicals 1940-44; Organizer of Peasant Party (SL) and co-organizer of the Voivodship People's Council (WRN), Kielce 1944; after the liberation, first Chair. of WRN Kielce 1945-47; Chair. Central Bd. of Peasant Self-Aid Union 1949-53; Chair. Central Union of Agricultural Circles 1959-62; Vice-Chair. Polish Cttee. of Peace Defenders 1950-58, All-Poland Peace Cttee. 1958-; mem. World Peace Council 1952-; mem. Cen. Bd. of the Lay Schools Soc. 1959-62, Chair. Polish-Italian Group of the Interparl. Union 1961-69; mem. Polish-Brazilian Friendship Soc. 1962-74, Chair. May 1974-; mem. S.L. 1944-49, United Peasant Party (ZSL) 1949-, Sec. of S.L. Cen. Cttee. 1949, and ZSL Central Cttee. 1949-55, Vice-Chair. ZSL Cen. Cttee. 1955-80; mem. Home Nat. Council (KRN) and Seym 1947-; Vice-Marshal of Seym 1952-56; mem. Council of State 1957-85, Vice-Chair. 1972-76; mem. Polish Writers' Union ZLP 1945-83, mem. Gen. Bd. newly-founded ZLP 1983-; Vice-Chair. Presidium of All Poland Cttee. of Nat. Unity Front 1971-81; Vice-Chair. Chief Council of Union of Fighters for Freedom and Democracy 1945-; Vice-Chair. Cen. Bd. of Polish-Soviet Friendship Soc. 1950-84; Commdr's. Cross with the Star of the Polonia Restituta Order 1964; Georgi Dymitrov Medal 1972; Order of Banner of Labour, 1st Class; Grunwald Cross, 3rd Class; Partisan Cross, Order of Builders of People's Poland 1979, Heroes of Warsaw Award 1986, and others. *Publications:* poetry including Poemat nowosielecki, Lutnia wiejska, Pełnia, Druga strona księżyca, Swiatowid, Polska, Czernek i Anna, Ta—bądź, Ściernisko, Walc karnawałowy, Poezje Wybrane 1975, Rajski oset 1977, Czary Miłosne 1984, Ciagi, wiry, zwory 1987; novels: Ludowy potok, Młodzik, Sklepienie niebieskie, Sowizdrzał świętokrzyski, Piołun i popiół, Powrót z Litwy, Dusze i Manekiny, Przygoda z Bibichamem, Ujawnienia 1988; stories: Krajobraz rodzinny, Smutne i wesołe, W kogo trafi grom 1978; has translated Kalevali into Polish. *Leisure interest:* writing. *Address:* Aleja 1 Armii Wojska Polskiego 16 m. 27, 00-582 Warsaw, Poland. *Telephone:* 28-18-60.

OZIM, Igor; Yugoslav violinist; b. 9 May 1931, Ljubljana; s. of Rudolf Ozim and Marija Kodric; m. Dr. Breda Volovsek 1963; one s. one d.; ed. Akad. za glasbo Ljubljana, R.C.M.; studied with Prof. Max Rostal; Prof. of Violin, Akad. za glasbo Ljubljana 1960-63, Staatliche Hochschule für Musik, Cologne 1963-, Berne Conservatoire 1985-; First Prize, Int. Carl-Flesch Competition, London 1951, Munich 1953. *Address:* D-5000 Cologne 41, Breibergstrasse 6, Federal Republic of Germany. *Telephone:* (221) 414707.

ÖZTEKIN, Mukadder; Turkish politician; b. 1919, Niğde Prov.; ed. Galatasaray Lycée, Istanbul, Ankara Univ.; joined Ministry of Interior 1944; Country Chief Officer in various districts, Insp.; Gov. of Adana 1960; Senator for Adana 1966; Minister of Public Works 1971-73, of the Interior 1973-74, 1974-75; Officier, Légion d'honneur; Independent. *Address:* c/o Ministry of the Interior, Ankara, Turkey.

P

PAAR, Jack; American television performer; b. 1 May 1918; Radio announcer, Indianapolis, Youngstown, Pittsburgh, Cleveland, Buffalo; appeared in films: Walk Softly Stranger 1950, Love Nest 1951, Down Among the Sheltering Palms 1953; TV programmes Up to Paar 1952, TV Morning Show 1955, Tonight Show 1957-58, Jack Paar Show 1958-62, The Jack Paar Program 1962-65, Jack Paar Tonite 1973. *Address:* c/o ABC-TV, 1330 Avenue of the Americas, New York, N.Y. 10019, U.S.A.

PACAVIRA, Manuel Pedro, M.SC.S.; Angolan diplomatist; b. 1939, Golungo Alto; f. Popular Movt. for the Liberation of the Angola-Worker's Party (MPLA-PT); arrested 1960, imprisoned for 14 years; subsequently mem. MPLA-PT Cen. Cttee. and Govt.; Head Angolan Ports and Railway Admin., Minister of Transport, Minister of Agric., Co-ordinator Dept. of Nat. Reconstruction 1976-77; mem. MPLA-PT Regulatory Cen. Cttee., Head Ideological and Disciplinary Control 1977-82; Sec. Cen. Cttee. for the Ideological Sphere 1980-81, for the Production of Econ. Sphere 1981-82; Amb. to Cuba, (also accred. to Nicaragua, Mexico and Guyana) 1985-88; Perm. Rep. to UN Feb. 1988-. *Address:* Permanent Mission of Angola to the United Nations, 747 Third Avenue, 18th Floor, New York, N.Y. 10017, U.S.A. *Telephone:* (212) 752-4612.

PACE, Stanley Carter, M.S.; American business executive; b. 14 Sept. 1921, Waterview, Ky.; s. of Stanley Dan Pace and Pearl Carter; m. Elaine Cutchall 1945; three s.; ed. Univ. of Kentucky, U.S. Mil. Acad. and California Inst. of Tech.; U.S.A.F. 1943-53, latterly Deputy Chief of Procurement Div. U.S.A.F. Air Material Command; Sales Man. and Div. Man. TRW Inc. 1954-55, Man. Jet Div., Cleveland 1955-58, Vice-Pres. and Gen. Man. Tapco Group (later renamed Equipment Group) 1958-65, Exec. Vice-Pres. and Dir. 1965, headed TRW Automotive Worldwide 1971-76, Asst. Pres. 1976-77, Pres. and Dir. TRW Inc. 1977-85, Vice-Chair. Jan.-May 1985; Vice-Chair. General Dynamics 1985, Chair. and C.E.O. Dec. 1985-; Dir. Consolidated Natural Gas Co.; Air Medal with two bronze oak leaf clusters, Purple Heart, European Campaign Medal with four bronze stars, World War II Victory Medal. *Address:* c/o General Dynamics Corporation, Pierre Laclede Center, St. Louis, Mo. 63105 (Office). *Telephone:* (314) 889-8295 (Office).

PACEA, Ion; Romanian painter; b. 7 Sept. 1924, Salonica; s. of Dumitru Pacea and Ecaterina Pacea (née Girtu); m. Lucrezia Hagi; one s. one d.; ed. The Fine Arts Acad. Bucharest; Sec. of the Romanian Fine Arts Union; Vice-Pres. of the Romanian Fine Arts Union; has held exhbns. in Romania and Sofia, Prague, Berlin, Dresden, Venice, Le Havre, Tokyo, Aachen, Munich, Rome, Turin, Edinburgh, Washington, Salzburg; Romanian Acad. Award 1963; The Great Prize of the Romanian Fine Arts Union "Trionfo 81" Rome, Italy. *Address:* 42 N. Iorga, Bucharest, sector 1, Romania.

PACH, Zsigmond Pál; Hungarian historian; b. 4 Oct. 1919; s. of Lipót Pach and Rózsa Weisz; m. Klára Edit Sós 1945; one s. one d.; ed. Budapest Univ. of Arts and Sciences; High School Teacher 1943-48; Reader, Budapest Univ. of Econs. 1948-52, Prof. for Econ. History 1952-63, Rector 1963-67; Deputy Dir. Hungarian Acad. of Sciences Inst. of History 1949-56, Dir. 1967-89; mem. Editorial Bd. Jahrbuch für Wirtschaftsgeschichte, Berlin 1960-, The Economic History Review 1966-75; Ed.-in-Chief Acta Historica, Hungarian Acad. of Science 1973-; mem. Hungarian Acad. of Science (Vice-Pres. 1976-85), Istituto Int. di Storia Economica, Exec. Cttee. Int. Econ. History Assen. (Pres. 1978-82, Hon. Pres. 1982-); Foreign mem. U.S.S.R. Acad. of Sciences 1982, Bulgarian Acad. of Sciences 1985; Hon. Dr. Tartu Univ. 1982; Kossuth Prize 1949, State Prize 1978. *Publications:* Gazdaságtörténet— a feudalizmus hanyatlásáig (Economic History up to the decline of Feudalism) 1947, Az eredeti tőkefelhalmozás Magyarországon (Previous accumulation of capital in Hungary) 1952, A földesuri gazdaság "porosz-utas" fejlődése Oroszországban a 19. sz. második felében (Development of the "Prussian type" manorial economy in Russia in the second part of the 19th century) 1958, Nyugateurópai és magyarországi agrárfejlődés a 15-17. sz.-ban (West-European and Hungarian development of agrarian relations in the 15th to 17th centuries) 1963, Die ungarische Agrarentwicklung im 16-17. Jahrhundert 1964, Problemi razvitiya vengerskoy marxistskoy istoricheskoy nauki 1966, A nemzetközi kereskedelmi utvonalak 15-17. sz.-i áthelyeződésének kérdéséhez (On the shifting of international trade routes in the 15th to 17th centuries) 1968, The Role of East Central Europe in International Trade: 16th and 17th Centuries 1970, Le commerce du Levant et la Hongrie au Moyen Age 1976, Történetszemlélet és történettudomány (History and its View) 1978, The Transylvanian Route of Levant Trade at the Turn of the 15th and 16th Centuries 1980, East Central Europe and World Trade at the Dawn of Modern Times 1982, Business Mentality and Hungarian National Character 1985, Történelem és nemzettudat (History and National Consciousness) 1987, Le Développement de l'Historiographie Hongroise après 1945, 1987, Von der Schlacht bei Mohács bis zur Rückeroberung Budas 1988. *Leisure interest:* history. *Address:* Németvölgyi ut 72/C, H-1124 Budapest, Hungary. *Telephone:* 558-133.

PACHACHI, Adnan Musahim al-, PH.D.; Iraqi diplomatist; b. 14 May 1923; ed. American Univ. of Beirut, Georgetown Univ., Washington, D.C.; joined Foreign Service 1944, served Washington, Alexandria; Dir.-Gen. Political Affairs, Council of Ministers 1957-58; Dir.-Gen. Ministry of Foreign Affairs 1958-59; Perm. Rep. to UN 1959-65, 1967-69; Minister of Foreign Affairs 1965-67; Minister of State, Abu Dhabi, United Arab Emirates 1971-74; mem. Abu Dhabi Exec. Council 1974-; Personal Rep. of Head of State of U.A.E. 1974-. *Address:* c/o Manhal Palace, Abu Dhabi, United Arab Emirates.

PACHARIYANGKUN, Upadit, DR.RER.POL; Thai diplomatist and government official; b. 10 Dec. 1920, Bangkok; s. of Taad and Kim Pachariyangkun; m. Aphira Hemachan 1951; one s. one d.; ed. Univs. of Berlin and Berne, Nat. Defence Coll.; joined Foreign Service and served at Legation, Berlin 1942; Chief of Div., UN Dept. 1954; First Sec., Legation in Buenos Aires 1957; Dir.-Gen. of Econ. Dept., Ministry of Foreign Affairs 1963; Amb. and acting Perm. Rep. to UN 1964; Amb. to Nigeria, Ivory Coast, Liberia 1966; Dir.-Gen. Econ. Dept., Secr.-Gen. of ASEAN 1970; Amb. to Switzerland, Yugoslavia, Vatican City and UN Office in Geneva 1972, to Fed. Repub. of Germany 1973, to U.S.A. Feb.-Oct. 1976; Minister of Foreign Affairs 1976-80; Knight Grand Cross, Order of the Crown; Grand Cordon, Order of the White Elephant. *Leisure interest:* reading. *Address:* c/o Ministry of Foreign Affairs, Saranrom Palace, Bangkok 10200; 1097 Nakorn Chaisri Road, Bangkok 10300, Thailand (Home). *Telephone:* 241-1212 and 241-3224 (Home).

PACHE, Bernard; French engineer and business executive; b. 13 Oct. 1934, Sallanches; s. of Joseph Pache and Sabine Pache (née Minjoz); m. Yvette Vitaly 1959; three c.; ed. Ecole Polytechnique de Paris and Ecole des Mines de Paris; mining engineer 1957-; Asst. to Dir. of Mines 1963-65; Tech. Adviser to Minister of Industry 1965-67; Chief Mining Engineer 1967; joined Compagnie Pechiney 1967, Asst. to Dir., Uranium and Nuclear Activity Dept., then Dir. of Mines Div., Nuclear Branch of Pechiney Ugine Kuhlmann 1969-73; Gen.-Man. Société des Electrodes et Refractaires Savoie (SERS) 1972-73; Chair. Compagnie Générale d'Electrolyse du Palais 1972-76; Gen.-Man. Société Cefilac 1973-74; Dir. and Gen. Man. Société Française d'Electrométallurgie 1974-79; Dir. of Industrial Policy, Pechiney Ugine Kuhlmann Group 1979-83, Deputy Dir. of Pechiney 1983-84, Chair. and C.E.O. 1985-86, Hon. Pres. 1986-; Dir.-Gen. Charbonnages de France 1986, Chair. and C.E.O. 1987; Chevalier Légion d'Honneur; Officier Ordre Nat. du Mérite. *Address:* Charbonnages de France, Tour Albert 1er, 65 avenue de Colmar, 92507 Rueil Malmaison Cedex (Office); 8 rue Bel Air, 92190 Meudon, France (Home). *Telephone:* 46-26-32-90 (Home).

PACHECHO, Rondon; Brazilian politician; b. 31 July 1919; m. Maria de Freitas Pachecho 1943; one s. (deceased) two d.; ed. Univ. de Minas Gerais; State deputy and in Secr. of Legis. Ass. of Minas Gerais 1946; Sec. to Min. of Interior; Deputy Leader of União Democrática Nacional in Chamber of Deputies; mem. Constitutional and Judicial Cttee., Chamber of Deputies; Deputy Leader of Castelo Branco Govt. and of the Majority in Chamber of Deputies; Gen. Sec., Aliança Renovadora Nacional; Minister in charge of Cabinet Affairs, Costa e Silva Govt.; Brazilian del. UN 20th Gen. Ass. 1965; Pres. of Nat. Directorate, Aliança Renovadora Nacional for 1970 elections; Gov. of State, Minas Gerais 1971-74; Grand Cross of the Order of Merit, Brazil 1967, Officer 1st Class Imperial Order of the Sacred Treasure of Japan 1967, numerous other decorations. *Address:* c/o Palácio do Govêrno, Estado de Minas Gerais, Brazil.

PACHECO ARECO, Jorge; Uruguayan journalist, politician and diplomatist; b. 9 April 1920, Montevideo; s. of Manuel Pacheco and Lilina Areco; ed. Facultad de Derechos y Ciencias Sociales; Asst. Ed. El Día (Montediveo daily) until 1961, Ed. 1961-65; Vice-Pres. of Uruguay 1967; Pres. of Uruguay 1967-72; Amb. to Spain 1972-79, to Switzerland 1979-80, to U.S.A. 1980-82, to Paraguay 1988-. *Address:* Uruguayan Embassy, Brasília esq. Rca de Siria, Asunción, Paraguay.

PACINO, Al (Alfredo James); American actor; b. 25 April 1940, New York; s. of Salvatore and Rosa Pacino; ed. High School for the Performing Arts, New York, The Actors Studio; worked as messenger and cinema usher; Co-artistic Dir., The Actors Studio, Inc., New York 1982-83; Broadway début in Does a Tiger Wear a Necktie? 1969; appeared with Lincoln Center Repertory Co. as Kilroy in Camino Real 1970; other New York appearances include The Connection, Hello Out There, Tiger at the Gates and The Basic Training of Pavlo Hummel 1977, American Buffalo 1981 (U.K. 1984), Julius Caesar 1988; appearances at Charles Playhouse, Boston, include: Richard III 1973 (repeated on Broadway 1979), Arturo Ui 1975, Rats (director) 1970; films include: Me, Natalie 1969, Panic in Needle Park 1971, The Godfather 1972, Scarecrow 1973, Serpico 1974, The Godfather Part II 1974, Dog Day Afternoon 1975, Bobby Deerfield 1977, And Justice For All 1979, Cruising 1980, Author! Author! 1982, Scarface 1983, Revolution 1985; Tony Award 1969; Nat. Soc. of Film Critics Award, The Godfather; British Film Award, The Godfather Part II. *Address:* c/o Actors Studio, 432 W. 44th Street, New York, N.Y. 10036, U.S.A.

PACKARD, David, A.B., F.I.E.E.E.; American business executive and fmr. government official; b. 7 Sept. 1912, Pueblo, Colo.; s. of Sperry Sidney and Ella Lorna (Graber) Packard; m. Lucile Salter 1938 (died 1987); one s. three d.; ed. Centennial High School, Pueblo, and Stanford Univ., Calif.; formed Hewlett-Packard Co. (to design and manufacture electronic measurement instrumentation) with William R. Hewlett 1939, Pres. 1947-64, Chair. of Bd., C.E.O. 1964-68, 1972-; U.S. Deputy Sec. of Defense 1969-71; Dir. Chevron Corpn. 1972-85, Caterpillar Tractor Co. 1972-83, Boeing Co. 1978-86; Chair. Bd. of Regents Uniformed Services, Univ. of the Health Sciences 1975-82, the Trilateral Comm. 1973-81, Advisory Cttee. Woodrow Wilson Int. Center for Scholars; Chair. U.S.-Japan Advisory Comm. 1983-85; Co-Chair. Cttee. on the Present Danger 1975-81, the Calif. Roundtable; mem. the Business Council (fmr. Chair. 1972-74), the Business Roundtable, U.S. and U.S.S.R. Trade and Econ. Council Cttee. on Science and Tech. 1975-82, Bd. Dirs. American Enterprise Inst. for Public Policy Research 1978-, Bd. Dirs. Genetech Inc. 1981-; Trustee Herbert Hoover Foundation 1972-, Colo. Coll. 1966-69, Stanford Univ. 1954-69, Ronald Reagan Presidential Foundation 1986-; Vice-Chair. Calif. Nature Conservancy 1983-; Chair. U.S.-Japan Advisory Comm.; Dir. Nat. Fish and Wildlife Foundation 1985-; Life mem. Instrument Soc. of America; mem. Nat. Acad. of Eng.; numerous awards; Hon. D.Sc. (Colorado Coll.) 1964, Hon. LL.D. (Calif.) 1966, (Catholic Univ.) 1970, (Pepperdine) 1972, D.Litt. (Southern Colo. State Coll.) 1973, D.Eng. (Notre Dame) 1974. *Address:* Hewlett-Packard Co., 1501 Page Mill Road, Palo Alto, Calif. 94304, U.S.A.

PACKARD, Vance, A.B., M.S.; American author and teacher; b. 22 May 1914, Granville Summit, Pa.; s. of Philip and Mabel Packard; m. Virginia Mathews 1938; two s. one d.; ed. Pennsylvania State Univ. and Columbia Univ.; Reporter for Boston Record 1937-38; Writer and Ed. Associated Press Feature Service 1938-42; Ed. and Staff Writer American Magazine 1942-56; Staff Writer Collier's Magazine 1956; mem. nat. bd. Nat. Book Cttee., Authors' Guild, American Acad. of Political and Social Sciences, American Sociology Asscn.; Distinguished Alumni Award, Pa. State Univ. 1961. *Publications:* The Hidden Persuaders 1957, The Status Seekers 1959, The Waste Makers 1960, The Pyramid Climbers 1962, The Naked Society 1964, The Sexual Wilderness 1968, A National of Strangers 1972, The People Shapers 1977, Our Endangered Children 1983, The Ultra Rich 1989. *Address:* 87 Mill Road, New Canaan, Conn. 06840, U.S.A.

PACKER, Kerry Francis Bullmore, A.C.; Australian business executive; b. 17 Dec. 1937, Sydney; s. of late Sir Frank and Lady Packer; m. Roslyn Weedon 1963; one s. one d.; ed. Cranbrook School, Geelong Church of England Grammar School; Chair. Consolidated Press Holdings Ltd., and Television Corpn. Ltd. (now Publishing and Broadcasting Ltd.) 1974-; Chair. Australian Consolidated Press Ltd. 1974-; promoted World Series Cricket, Australia 1978-79; came to agreement with Australian Cricket Bd. in organizing and televising Test Series, Australia 1979-80. *Leisure interests:* golf, cricket, tennis, shooting, polo. *Address:* Consolidated Press Holdings Ltd., 54 Park Street, Sydney, N.S.W. 2000, Australia. *Telephone:* (02) 282. 8000.

PACKWOOD, Bob, LL.B.; American lawyer and politician; b. 11 Sept. 1932, Portland, Ore.; m. Georgie Oberteuffer 1964; one s. one d.; ed. Williamette Univ., N.Y. Univ.; practised law in Portland 1958-68; mem. Oregon House of Reps. 1962-68; U.S. Senator from Oregon 1969-; Chair. Senate Commerce, Science and Transportation Cttee. 1981-85; mem. Senate Finance Cttee. (Chair. 1985-86); mem. Senate Small Business Cttee., Bd. Dirs. New York Univ.; Hon. LL.D. (Yeshiva Univ.) 1982, (Gallaudet Coll.) 1983; several awards. *Address:* 259 Russell Senate Office Building, Washington, D.C. 20510, U.S.A.

PAÇO D'ARCOS, Joaquim; Portuguese writer; b. 14 June 1908, Lisbon; s. of Henrique Corrêa da Silva (Conde de Paço d'Arcos) and Maria do Carmo Corrêa da Silva; m. 1st Maria Candida Magalhães Corrêa 1932 (died 1945), 2nd Maria da Graça Moura Braz 1949; three s.; novelist, playwright, essayist, poet; awarded many literary prizes; work translated into various language; mem. Acad. Brasileira de Leteras; Chair. Portuguese Soc. of Writers 1960-62, 1965-. *Publications:* The Last Hero, Ana Paulo, Diary of an Emigrant, Anxiety, Loves and Voyages of Pedro Manuel, Snow over the Sea, The Accomplice, The Absent, Pathology of Dignity, United States 1942, The Novel and the Novelist, The Road to Sin, Triple Mirror, Imperfect Poems, Churchill—The Statesman and the Writer, The Forest of Concrete—Lights and Shadows of the United States, The Captive Doe, Carnival and Other Tales, Memoirs of a Banknote, Cela 27, The Long Arm of Justice, Not Too Exemplary Tales, Memoirs of My Life and Times etc. *Address:* Avenida A.A. Aguiar 38, Lisbon, Portugal.

PADILLA ARANCIBIA, Gen. David; Bolivian army officer and politician; Career officer with regional commands; Pres. of Bolivia and C.-in-C. of the Armed Forces 1978-79. *Address:* c/o Oficina del Presidente, La Paz, Bolivia.

PADIYARA, H.E. Cardinal Anthony; Indian ecclesiastic; b. 11 Feb. 1921, Changanacherry; ordained 1945, elected to Ootacamund 1955, consecrated bishop 1955, prefect to Chaganacherry· dei Siro-Malabaresi 1970, transferred to Ernakulani 1985; cr. Cardinal 1988. *Address:* The Archdiocesan Curia, Post Bag No. 2580 Ernakulam, Cochin-682031, Kerala, India. *Telephone:* 352.629.

PADOA-SCHIOPPA, Tommaso, M.SC.ECON.; Italian economist and bank official; b. 23 July 1940, Belluno; s. of Fabio Padoa and Stella Schwarz; m. Fiorella Kostoris 1966; one s. two d.; ed. Italian Grammar School, Università Commerciale Luigi Bocconi, Milan, Massachusetts Inst. of Tech., U.S.A.; with insurance co., Bremen, Fed. Repub. of Germany 1959-60, C. & A. Brenninkmeyer 1966-68; Economist, Research Dept., Banca d'Italia, Rome 1970-79, Head, Money Market Dept. 1975-79, Direttore Centrale for Econ. Research 1983-84, Deputy Dir.-Gen. 1984-; Economic Adviser, the Treasury 1978-79; Dir.-Gen. Econ. and Financial Affairs, Comm. of European Communities 1979-83; mem. Group of Thirty; Vice-Pres. Banking Advisory Cttee., European Comm. *Publications include:* The Management of an Open Economy with One Hundred Per Cent Plus Wage Indexation (with F. Modigliani, in Essays in International Finance) 1978, Agenda e non Agenda (with Fiorella Padoa-Schioppa) 1984, Money, Economic Policy and Europe 1985. *Address:* Banca d'Italia, Via Nazionale 91, 00184 Rome, Italy. *Telephone:* (06) 47921.

PAE MYUNG-IN; Korean lawyer and politician; b. 8 Nov. 1932; ed. Coll. of Law, Seoul Nat. Univ.; Prosecutor, Chungju, Pusan, Seoul and Taegu Dist. Public Prosecutor's Office (PPO) 1959-68; Head Claims Div., Ministry of Justice, and Prosecutor, Seoul High PPO 1968; Sr. Prosecutor Songdong Branch Office, Seoul Dist. PPO 1971; Sr. Prosecutor Seoul Dist. PPO 1973, and 1st Dept. of Gen. Criminal Cases, Seoul Dist. PPO 1974; Dir. Songbuk Branch Office, Seoul Dist. PPO 1976; Deputy Head Taegu Dist. PPO 1978; Head Kwangju Dist. PPO 1979; Dir. Prosecutor's Bureau, Ministry of Justice, and Prosecutor Supreme PPO 1980; Deputy Prosecutor-Gen. Supreme PPO 1981; Head of Kwangju High PPO 1981; Dir. Legal Affairs Training Inst., Ministry of Justice 1982; Minister of Justice 1982-85. *Address:* c/o Ministry of Justice, Seoul, Republic of Korea.

PAFFORD, John Henry Pyle, M.A., D.LIT., F.S.A., F.L.A.; British librarian; b. 6 March 1900, Bradford-on-Avon, Wilts.; s. of John and Bessie Pyle Pafford; m. Elizabeth R. Ford 1941; one d.; ed. Trowbridge High School and Univ. Coll., London; Library Asst., Univ. Coll., London 1923-25; Librarian and Tutor, Selly Oak Colleges, Birmingham 1925-31; Sub-librarian, Nat. Central Library, London 1931-45; Lecturer, Univ. of London School of Librarianship 1937-61; War Office, Books and Libraries for Army Educ. 1944-45; Goldsmiths' Librarian, Univ. of London 1945-67; Library Adviser, Inter-Univ. Council for Higher Educ. Overseas 1960-68; Fellow, Univ. Coll. London; Hon. Fellow, Selly Oak Coll. *Publications:* Bale's King Johan 1931, Library Co-operation in Europe 1935, The Sodder'd Citizen (Malone Soc.) 1936, Books and Army Education 1946, American and Canadian Libraries 1949, W. P. Ker: A Bibliography 1950, The Winter's Tale (Arden Shakespeare) 1963, Isaac Watts: Divine Songs for Children 1971, L. Bryskett: Works 1972, Employer and Employed (with E. R. Pafford) 1974. *Leisure interests:* home, walking, book-hunting. *Address:* Hillside, Allington Park, Bridport, Dorset DT6 5DD, England. *Telephone:* (0308) 22829.

PAFFRATH, Hans-Georg; German art dealer; b. 12 April 1922, Düsseldorf; s. of Hans and Eleonore (née Theegarten) Paffrath; m. Helena née Baroness Åkerhielm 1958; two s. three d.; ed. Gymnasium; war service 1941-45; art dealer 1945-; Royal Swedish Consul-Gen. for North Rhine Westphalia. *Leisure interest:* riding. *Address:* Königsallee 46, Postfach 200604, D-4000 Düsseldorf 1, Federal Republic of Germany. *Telephone:* 326405; 324632; 323128.

PAGANELLI, Robert Peter, B.A.; American diplomatist (retd.); b. 3 Nov. 1931, New York; s. of Charles Paganelli and Mary Spalla; m. Donna Marie Smith 1957; two d.; ed. Hamilton Coll., Clinton and Harvard; Air Force 1951-54; joined Foreign Service 1958; Attaché, U.S. Embassy, Beirut 1960-61, Second Sec. 1963-65; Vice-Consul and Third Sec., Basra and Baghdad 1961-63; Second Sec. and Political Officer, Damascus 1965-67, Amman 1967-68; assigned to Washington, D.C. 1968-71; First Sec. and Political Officer, Rome 1971-74; Amb. to Qatar 1974-77; mem. Exec. Seminar on Nat. and Int. Affairs, Dept of State 1977-78; Dir. Office of Western European Affairs 1978-79; Minister-Counsellor and Deputy Chief of Mission, Rome 1979-81; Amb. to Syria 1981-84; Diplomat-in-Residence, Yale Univ. 1984-85; Exec. Dir. Young Pres'. Org. 1985-; Woodrow Wilson Fellow 1957-58; Meritorious Honor Award (Dept. of State) 1966, 1974. *Address:* 519 Manor Lane, Pelham, N.Y. 10803, U.S.A. *Telephone:* (212) 867-1900.

PAGANO, Gino; Italian industrialist; b. 2 Sept. 1921, Naples; ed. Naples Univ.; joined ANIC (Associazione Nazionale dell'Industria Chimica) 1951, Man. Dir. 1967-, Vice-Pres. 1970-72, Pres. 1972-76, 1980; co-ordinator, chemical and nuclear sector, ENI -1975; Pres. SIR Finanziaria S.p.A. 1980-; Consultant Bastogi S.p.A. 1978-80; Pres. SAPIR Porto Intermodale Ravenna S.p.A. 1974-76, 1980-; Vice-Pres. Associazione Italiano di Ingegneria Chimica 1973-; mem. Bd. Dirs. Hydrocarbons Int., Consultative Bd. Liquifar Agropecuaria do Brasil 1981-. *Address:* c/o ANIC, San Donato Milanese, Milan, Italy. *Telephone:* 02-53531.

PAGBALHA GELEG NAMGYAI; Chinese (Tibetan) administrator; b. 1940, Litang Co., Sichuan Prov., was confirmed by the Qangdin Lamasery as 11th incarnation of a living Buddha 1942; Vice-Chair. CPPCC 1959; mem. Presidium 4th NPC 1975-78; mem. Presidium 5th NPC 1978-82;

Vice-Chair. People's Govt. of Tibet Autonomous Region 1979–83; Exec. Chair. 6th CPPCC 1983–88; Acting Chair., Tibet Autonomous Region People's Congress 1983–; Vice-Chair, CPPCC 7th Nat. Cttee. 1988–. *Address:* Chinese People's Political Consultative Conference, Beijing, People's Republic of China.

PAGE, Sir Alexander Warren, Kt., M.B.E., M.A., F.I.MECH.E.; British business executive; b. 1 July 1914, Surbiton, Surrey; s. of Sydney and Phyllis Spencer Page; m. 1st Anne Lewis Hickman 1940 (dissolved), two s. one d.; m. 2nd Andrea Mary Wharton 1981; ed. Tonbridge School and Clare Coll., Cambridge; joined Metal Box Ltd. 1936; served in army 1940–45; Sales Dir. Metal Box Ltd. 1957, Man. Dir. 1966, Deputy Chair. 1969, Chair. 1970–79; Dir. Electrolux Ltd. 1977, Chair. 1978–82; Dir. C. Shippam Ltd. 1979–84; Chair. GT Pension Services Ltd. 1980–85, Paine & Co. Ltd. 1981–87, P.F.C. Int. Portfolio Fund 1985–. *Leisure interests:* golf, tennis, do-it-yourself. *Address:* 2 Montagu Square, London, W1H 1RA; Merton Place, Dunsfold, Nr. Godalming, Surrey, England. *Telephone:* 01-935 9894 (London); (0486-49) 211 (Surrey).

PAGE, Bruce; British journalist and publisher; b. 1 Dec. 1936, London; s. of Roger and Amy B. Page; m. 1st Anne Gillison 1964 (divorced 1969); m. 2nd Anne L. Darnborough 1969; one s. one d.; ed. Melbourne High School and Melbourne Univ.; trained as journalist, Melbourne Herald 1956–60; Evening Standard, London 1960–62; Daily Herald, London 1962–64; various exec. posts, Sunday Times, London 1964–76; Assoc. Ed. Daily Express 1977; Ed. New Statesman 1978–82; Man. Dir. Pagemakers Ltd. 1983–; various awards for journalism. *Publications:* co-author: Philby, the Spy who Betrayed a Generation, An American Melodrama, Do You Sincerely Want to be Rich?, Destination Disaster, Ulster (contrib.), The Yom Kippur War, The British Press. *Leisure interests:* reading, sailing, computers. *Address:* 35 Duncan Terrace, London, N1 8AL, England. *Telephone:* 01-359 1000.

PAGE, Geneviève (pseudonym of Geneviève Bonjean); French actress; b. 13 Dec. 1927, Paris; d. of Jacques Bonjean and Germaine Lipmann; m. Jean-Claude Bujard 1959; one s. one d.; ed. Lycée Racine, Paris, Sorbonne, Paris, Conservatoire nat. d'art dramatique; prin. actress in the Comédie Française and the Jean-Louis Barrault company; has appeared in many famous classical and tragic stage roles, including Les larmes amères de Petra von Kant (Critics' Prize for Best Actress 1980), La nuit des rois, L'aigle à deux têtes, Angelo, tyran de Padoue 1984. *Films include:* Ce siècle a cinquante ans, Pas de pitié pour les femmes, Fanfan la tulipe, Lettre ouverte, Plaisirs de Paris, Nuits andalouses, L'étrange désir de M. Bard, Cherchez la femme, L'homme sans passé, Foreign Intrigue, The Silken Affair, Michael Strogoff, Un amour de poche, Song Without End, Le bal des adieux, El Cid, Les égarements, Le jour et l'heure, L'honorable correspondence, Youngblood Hawke, Le majordome, Les corsaires, L'or et le plomb, Trois chambres à Manhattan, Grand Prix, Belle de jour, Mayerling, A Talent for Loving, The Private Life of Sherlock Holmes, Les Gémeaux, Décembre, Buffet Froid; *TV:* La Nuit des rois, La Chambre, La Chasse aux hommes, Athalie; Chevalier du Mérite sportif. *Address:* 52 rue de Vaugirard, 75006 Paris, France.

PAGE, Irvine Heinly, M.D., LL.D.; American physician; b. 7 Jan. 1901, Indianapolis; s. of Lafayette Page and Marian Heinly Page; m. Beatrice Allen 1930; two s.; ed. Cornell Univ. and Medical School; Intern, Presbyterian Hosp., New York 1926–28; Head, Chemistry Div., Kaiser Wilhelm Inst., Munich 1928–31; Assoc. Mem. Hosp. of Rockefeller Inst. for Medical Research 1931–37; Dir. Clinical Research Lab., Indianapolis City Hosp. 1937–44; Dir. Research Div., Cleveland Clinic Foundation 1945–66, Sr. Consultant 1966–68, Consultant Emer. 1968–; Chair. Governing Bd., Methods in Medical Research; several hon. doctorates; mem. of various socs. including N.A.S., American Acad. of Arts and Sciences, Inst. of Medicine and American Medical Assen; Gairdner Award 1963; Achievement Award, American Medical Assen. 1966, Sheen Award 1968; Stouffer Prize 1970. *Publications:* Chemistry of the Brain 1937, Hypertension 1943, Arterial Hypertension-Its Diagnosis and Treatment 1945, Experimental Renal Hypertension 1948, Strokes 1961, Renal Hypertension 1968, Arialotensin 1974; Co-author: Serotonin 1968, Speaking to the Doctor 1972, Hypertension Mechanisms 1987, Hypertension Research: A Memoir 1988; Chief Ed. Modern Medicine. *Address:* Box 516, Hyannis Port, Mass. 02647, U.S.A. *Telephone:* (617 775-5652).

PAGE, John Brangwyn, C.B.I.M., F.I.B., F.R.S.A.; British banking executive; b. 23 Aug. 1923, London; s. of Sidney J. and Doris M. Page; m. Gloria Vail 1948; two s. one d.; ed. Highgate School and King's Coll., Cambridge; served in R.A.F. 1942–46; with Bank of England 1948–82, Deputy Chief Cashier 1968–70, Chief Cashier 1970–80, Exec. Dir. 1980–82; Chair. Agricultural Mortgage Corpn. 1982–85; Dir. Nationwide Anglia (fmrly. Nationwide Bldg. Soc) 1982–, Standard Chartered Bank 1982–. *Leisure interests:* music, travel. *Address:* Nationwide Anglia, Chesterfield House, Bloomsbury Way, London, WC1V 6PW, England.

PAGE, Walter Hines, A.B.; American banker; b. 7 July 1915, Huntington, N.Y.; s. of Arthur W. and Mollie Hall Page; m. Jane N. Nichols 1942; two s. one d.; ed. Milton Acad. and Harvard Univ.; joined J. P. Morgan and Co. Inc. (merged with Guaranty Trust Co. of New York 1959) 1937; Vice-Pres. Morgan Guaranty Trust Co. 1959–64, Senior Vice-Pres. 1964–65,

Exec. Vice-Pres. 1965–68, Vice-Chair. 1968–71, Dir., Pres. Morgan Guaranty Trust Co. and J. P. Morgan and Co. Inc. 1971–77, Chair. of Bd. 1978–79; Chair. Cold Spring Harbor Laboratory 1979–86; Dir. U.S. Steel Corpn. 1979–86, Saudi Int. Bank 1981–86; *Leisure interest:* sailing. *Address:* Cold Spring Harbor, N.Y. 11724, U.S.A. (Home).

PAHANG, H.H. Sultan of, Sultan Haji Ahmad Shah Al-Mustain Billah ibni Al-Marhum Sultan Abu Bakar Ri'Ayatuddin Al-Muadzam Shah, D.K., S.P.C.M., S.P.M.J.; Malaysian Ruler; b. 24 Oct. 1930, Istana Mangga Tunggal, Pekan; m. Tengku Majjaj Afzan binti Tengku Muhammad 1954; ed. Malay Coll. Kuala Kangsar, Worcester Coll., Oxford, Univ. Coll., Exeter; Tengku Mahkota (Crown Prince) 1944; Capt. 4th Battalion, Royal Malay Regt. 1954; Commdr. of 12th Infantry Battalion of Territorial Army 1963–65, Lieut.-Col.; mem. State Council 1955; Regent 1956, 1959, 1965; succeeded as Sultan; Timbalan Yang di Pertuan Agong (Deputy Supreme Head of State of Malaysia) 1975–79, Yang di Pertuan Agong (Supreme Head of State) 1979–84. *Address:* Istana Abu Bakar, Pekan, Pahang, Malaysia.

PAHLAVI, Farah Diba; fmr. Empress of Iran; b. 14 Oct. 1938; d. of Sohrab and Farida Diba; ed. Jeanne d'Arc School and Razi School, Teheran, and Ecole Spéciale d'Architecture, Paris; married H.I.M. Shah Mohammed Reza Pahlavi 1959 (died 1980); two s. two d.; Foreign Assoc. mem. Fine Arts Acad., France 1974; fmr. Patron Farah Pahlavi Assen. (admin. of Social Educ. Assen.), Iran Cultural Foundation, and 34 other educational, health and cultural orgs.; left Iran Jan. 1979; living in Egypt June 1980.

PAHR, Willibald P., DR.IUR.; Austrian administrator and politician; b. 5 June 1930, Vienna; m. Ingeborg Varga 1961; one s. one d.; ed. Univ. of Vienna and Coll. of Europe, Bruges, Belgium; Asst. in Inst. of Int. Law and Int. Relations, Univ. of Vienna 1952–55; served Fed. Chancellery 1955–76, Head of Section 1968, Head of Dept. 1973, Dir.-Gen. 1975–76; Fed. Minister for Foreign Affairs 1976–83; Amb. to Fed. Repub. of Germany 1983–85, 1986–88; Sec.-Gen. World Tourism Org. 1985–86. *Publications:* Der österreichische Status der dauernden Neutralität 1967, several articles in Revue des Droits de l'Homme, numerous articles on current int. problems in various periodicals; co-editor Grundrechte, die Rechtsprechung in Europa (journal). *Address:* c/o Ministry of Foreign Affairs, 1014 Vienna, Ballhausplatz 2, Austria.

PAIGE, Hilliard Wegner, B.S.; American business executive; b. 2 Oct. 1919, Hartford, Conn.; s. of Commdr. Joseph W. Paige and Ruth Hill Paige; m. Dorothea Magner 1945; one s. two d.; ed. Worcester Polytechnic Inst.; joined General Electric Co. 1941, Gen. Man. Missile and Space Div. 1962, Vice-Pres. 1964, Aerospace Group Exec. 1967–69, Computer Group Exec. 1969–70, Sr. Vice-Pres. 1970–71; Pres. General Dynamics Corpn. 1971–73; Chair., Chief Exec., SBS Satellite Corpn. 1973–76, Vice-Chair. Int. Energy Assocs. Ltd., Washington 1977–85; Chair. H.A. Knott Ltd. 1984–; Dir. ERC Int., Computer Data Systems Inc. Greater Washington Investors Inc., Digilog-Inc., Electronic Assocs. Inc., The Atlantic Council of the U.S.; Trustee Worcester Polytechnic Inst.; mem. Defense Science Board, Nat. Acad. of Eng.; Fellow A.I.A.A.; NASA Public Service Award, Order of Merit (Italy). *Publications:* articles in professional journals, etc. *Leisure interests:* tennis, skiing, scuba diving. *Address:* 5163 Tilden Street, N.W., Washington, D.C., U.S.A. (Home). *Telephone:* (202) 966-6051.

PAIGE, Victor Grellier, C.B.E., C.I.P.M., F.C.I.T., C.B.I.M.; British administrative official; b. 5 June 1925; s. of Victor and Alice (née Grellier) Paige; m. Kathleen W. Harris 1948; one s. one d.; ed. East Ham Grammar School and Univ. of Nottingham; Roosevelt Scholar 1954; Deputy Personnel Man. Boots Pure Drug Co., Ltd. 1957–67; Controller of Personnel Services, CWS Ltd. 1967–70, Dir. Manpower Org. 1970–74; Exec. Vice-Chair. (Admin.) Nat. Freight Corpn. (later Nat. Freight Co.) 1974–77, Deputy Chair. 1977–82; Dir. and Deputy Chair. Nat. Freight Consortium 1982–85, non-exec. Dir. 1985–; Chair. Nat. Health Service Man. Bd. and 2nd Perm. Sec., Dept. of Health and Social Security Jan. 1985-July 1986; Pres. Inst. of Admin. Man. 1984–; other professional appointments; Commdr. Order of Orange Nassau. *Publications:* contribs. on management to technical press. *Leisure interests:* reading, sport (especially athletics). *Address:* Queen's Wood, Frithsden, Berkhamsted, Herts., England. *Telephone:* (04427) 5030.

PAINE, Thomas Otten, A.B., M.S., PH.D.; American scientist-executive; b. 9 Nov. 1921, Berkeley, Calif.; s. of Cdre. George Thomas Paine, U.S.N. and Ada Louise Otten Paine; m. Barbara Helen Taunton Pearse 1946; two s. two d.; ed. Brown Univ., Providence, R.I., and Stanford Univ., Calif.; Submarine Officer, U.S. Navy 1942–46; Man. Gen. Electric Meter and Instrument laboratory 1951–58; Man. Eng. Applications, Gen. Electric Research and Devt. Center 1958–63; Man. Gen. Electric Center for Advanced Studies 1963–68; Deputy Admin. NASA March-Oct. 1968, Admin. 1968–70; Vice-Pres. Gen. Electric Co. 1970–76; Pres. and C.O.O., Northrop, Nat. Comm. on Space 1985; Corpn. 1976–82; Chair. Thomas Paine Assocs. Los Angeles 1982–; Dir. Eastern Air Lines; mem. Bd. of Dirs., several cos.; Fellow A.I.A.A.; mem. Nat. Acad. Eng., N.A.S.; Distinguished Service Medal NASA 1970, John Fritz Medal 1976, Faraday Medal, Inst. Electrical Engs. 1976. *Publications:* numerous scientific papers. *Leisure interests:* sailing, beachcombing, skin diving, photography, book collecting and oil painting. *Address:* Thomas Paine Associates, 2401 Colorado Avenue, 178 Santa Monica, Calif. 90404 (Office); 765 Bonhill Road, Los Angeles, Calif. 90049, U.S.A. (Home).

PAINTAL, Autar Singh, M.D., PH.D., F.R.C.P., F.R.S., F.R.S.E.; Indian professor of physiology; b. 24 Sept. 1925; s. of Dr. Man Singh and Rajwans Kaur; one s. two d.; ed. Forman Christian Coll., Lahore, Lucknow and Edinburgh Univs.; lecturer, King George's Medical Coll. Lucknow Univ. 1949; Rockefeller Fellow 1950; lecturer, Univ. of Edinburgh 1951; Control Officer, Tech. Devt. Establishment Labs., Ministry of Defence, Kampur 1952–54; Prof. of Physiology, All India Inst. of Med. Sciences, Delhi 1958–64; Prof. of Physiology and Dir. Vallabhbhai Patel Chest Inst., Delhi Univ. 1964–; Dean Faculty of Med. Sciences, Delhi Univ. 1966–77; Fellow, Indian Acad. of Medical Sciences, Indian Nat. Science Acad. and other learned socs.; Pres. Nat. Coll. of Chest Physicians 1981–86, Indian Science Congress 1984–85; numerous awards and distinctions including R.D. Birla Award 1982, Nehru Science Award 1983, Acharya J. C. Bose Medal 1985; Hon. D.Sc. (Benares Hindu Univ.) 1982, (Delhi) 1984, (Aligarh Muslim Univ.) 1986. *Publications:* articles in professional journals. *Leisure interests:* swimming, rowing, bird watching. *Address:* Vallabhbhai Patel Chest Institute, Delhi University, P.O. Box 2101, Delhi 110007, India. *Telephone:* Delhi 2523856 and 231749.

PAIS, Abraham, B.SC., M.SC., PH.D.; American physicist; b. 19 May 1918, Amsterdam, Netherlands; s. of Isayah Pais and Kaatje van Kleef; m. Lila Atwill 1956 (divorced 1962), one s.; ed. Univs. of Amsterdam and Utrecht; Rask Oersted Fellow, Inst. of Theoretical Physics, Copenhagen 1946; Fellow, Inst. of Advanced Study, Princeton 1946–50, Prof. 1950–63; Prof. Rockefeller Univ. 1963–81, Detlev Bronk Prof. Rockefeller Univ. 1981–; Staff mem. Lawrence Radiation Lab., Berkeley, Calif. 1958–; Consultant Brookhaven Nat. Laboratory, Upton, N.Y.; Guggenheim Fellow 1960; Fellow American Physical Soc.; mem. N.A.S., American Acad. Arts and Sciences, American Philosophical Soc., Council for Foreign Relations; Corresp. mem. Royal Acad. of Sciences, Netherlands; Oppenheimer Prize 1979, American Book Award and American Inst. of Physics Award for Subtle is the Lord 1983. *Publications:* Subtle is the Lord (biography of Albert Einstein) 1983, Inward Bound 1987, contributions to Physical Review, Physical Review Letters, Physics Letters, Annals of Physics and other physics journals. *Leisure interests:* squash, swimming, mountaineering. *Address:* Rockefeller University, New York, N.Y. 10021 (Office); 450 East 63rd Street, New York, N.Y. 10021, U.S.A. (Home). *Telephone:* (212) 570-8833 (Office); (212) PL3-3083 (Home).

PAIS, Arie, PH.D.; Dutch economist, politician and financial executive; b. 16 April 1930, The Hague; m. Eegje Schoo; ed. Univ. of Amsterdam; admin. posts in Rijkspostspaarbank 1959–67, latterly Personal Adviser to Dir.-Gen. of PTT; Reader, later Prof. of Econs., Univ. of Amsterdam 1967–77; mem. Amsterdam City Council 1967–77; mem. Advisory Bd. Banque de Paris et des Pays-Bas 1975–77; mem. Econ. and Social Council 1975–77; M.P. 1977, 1981–82; Minister of Educ. and Science 1977–81; Vice-Pres. and Vice-Chair. Bd. of Dirs., European Investment Bank (EIB) 1982–88. *Publications:* Consumer Credit in the Netherlands 1975, various articles.

PAISLEY, Rev. Ian Richard Kyle, D.D., M.P., F.R.G.S.; British minister of religion and politician; b. 6 April 1926; s. of Rev. J. Kyle Paisley and Isabella Paisley; m. Eileen E. Cassells 1956; two s. (twins) three d.; ed. Ballymena Model School, Ballymena Tech. High School and S. Wales Bible Coll. and Reformed Presbyterian Theological Coll., Belfast; ordained 1946; Minister, Martyrs Memorial Free Presbyterian Church 1946–; Moderator, Free Presbyterian Church of Ulster 1951–; founded The Protestant Telegraph 1966; M.P. for N. Antrim 1970–; M.P. (Protestant Unionist) for Bannside, Co. Antrim, Parl. of N. Ireland (Stormont) 1970–72, Leader of the Opposition 1972, Chair. Public Accounts Cttee. 1972; mem. N. Ireland Ass. 1973–74, elected to Second N. Ireland Ass. 1982; mem. European Parl. 1979–; mem. Constitutional Convention 1975–76; Leader (co-founder) of Democratic Unionist Party 1971–; Chair. Agric. Cttee. and Cttee. of Privileges 1983; Pres. Whitefield Coll. of the Bible, Laurencetown, Co. Down 1980; Co-Chair. World Congress of Fundamentalists 1978; mem. Political Cttee. European Parlt.; mem. Int. Cultural Soc. of Korea 1977. *Publications:* History of the 1859 Revival 1959, Christian Foundations 1960, Ravenhill Pulpit Vol. I 1966, Vol. II 1967, Exposition of the Epistle to the Romans 1968, Billy Graham and the Church of Rome 1970, The Massacre of Saint Bartholomew 1972, Paisley, the Man and his Message 1976, America's Debt to Ulster 1976, Ulster—the facts 1981 (jtly.), No Pope Here 1982, Dr. Kidd 1982, Those Flaming Tennents 1983, Crown Rights of Jesus Christ 1985, Be Sure: 7 Rules for Public Speaking 1986, Paisley's Pocket Preacher 1986, Jonathan Edwards, The Theologian of Revival 1987. *Address:* The Parsonage, 17 Cyprus Avenue, Belfast, BT5 5NT, N. Ireland.

PAJESTKA, Józef, M.L., DR. ECON. SC.; Polish economist and politician; b. 9 March 1924, Milówka, Żywiec district; s. of Feliks Pajestka and Maria Szczotka; m. Irena Piotrowska 1949; one s. one d.; ed. Warsaw Univ.; worked at Cen. Planning Office, subsequently at State Comm. of Econ. Planning and Comm. of Planning attached to Council of Ministers 1948–56; Dir. Inst. for Econ. Research 1956–65; Dir. Inst. of Planning 1962–72; Extraordinary Prof. Univ. of Warsaw 1968–74, Prof. 1974–79; Vice-Chair. Planning Comm. attached to Council of Ministers 1968–79; Dir. Inst. of Econ. Sciences, Polish Acad. of Sciences 1981–; Pres. Cen. Bd. of Polish Econ. Soc. 1966–81, Chair. Main Council 1985–; Corresp. mem. Polish Acad.

of Sciences 1973–; mem. UN Planning Cttee., Exec. Cttee. of Int. Econ. Asscn. 1977–; mem. Cen. Cttee. Polish United Workers' Party 1968–81; mem. Club of Rome 1973–; Gold Cross of Merit 1956, Kt.'s Cross of Order Polonia Restituta 1964, Commdr. Cross 1969, Prize of UNO 1972, Order of Banner of Labour First Class 1980 and others. *Publications:* The State and Approach to Future Studies in Socialist Countries 1969, Social Dimensions of Development 1971, Problems, Prospects and Challenge: The Three Socio-Economic Systems towards the End of XXth Century 1972, Examinations of Policy Measures that Contribute to Equity and Social Justice Without Substantial Sacrifice of Economic Growth 1973, Need for Greater World-Wide Rationality 1973, Progress Determinants, Factors and Correlations of the Socio-Economic Progress of the Country 1975, Progress Determinants II, Manner of Functioning of Socialist Economy 1979, The Relevance of Economic Theories 1980, Formation of Development Process, Rationality and Wilderness of Policy 1983. *Leisure interest:* collecting and repairing antique clocks. *Address:* ul. Sulkiewicza 7 m. 20, 00-758 Warsaw, Poland (Home). *Telephone:* 410846.

PAKE, George Edward, PH.D.; American physicist and business executive; b. 1 April 1924, Jeffersonville, Ohio; s. of Edward Howe and Mary Mabel (Fry) Pake; m. Marjorie Elizabeth Semon 1947; three s. one d.; ed. Carnegie Inst. of Tech. and Harvard Univ.; Jr. Engineer, Westinghouse Research Labs., Pittsburgh 1945; Asst. Prof. of Physics, Wash. Univ., St. Louis, Mo. 1948–52, Assoc. Prof. and Chair. of Dept. 1952–53, Prof. and Chair. of Dept. 1953–56; Prof. of Physics, Stanford Univ. 1956–62; Provost and Prof. of Physics, Wash. Univ. 1962–67, Exec. Vice-Chancellor and Provost, and Prof. of Physics 1969–70, Edward Mallinckrodt Distinguished Univ. Prof. of Physics 1969–70; Vice-Pres. and Man., Xerox Palo Alto Research Center 1970–-73; Vice-Pres., Xerox Research and Devt. Staff 1973–74; Vice-Pres., Xerox Corpn., Man. Palo Alto Research Center 1974–78; Vice-Pres., Xerox Corpn., Corp. Research 1978–83, Group Vice-Pres. 1983–86; special field of research: magnetic resonance, solid state physics and magnetism; Dir. Inst. for Research on Learning 1987–; mem. Nat. Science Foundation Industrial Panel on Science and Tech. 1974–, Nat. Reasearch Council Comm. on Physical Sciences, Mathematics and Resources 1982–, N.A.S. Council of Govt.-Univ.-Industry Research Roundtable 1984–, Lockheed Missiles and Space Co. Inc., Lockheed Bd. of Advisers 1985–, and several other bodies; mem. N.A.S., American Acad. of Arts and Sciences, American Physical Soc., Inst. of Medicine, A.A.A.S.; Trustee Washington Univ. 1970–, Danforth Foundation 1971–, Univ. of Rochester 1982–; three hon. degrees; George E. Pake Prize, American Physical Soc. (created 1983). *Publications:* Quantum Theory of Angular Momentum (with Eugene Feenberg) 1953, Paramagnetic Resonance 1962, The Physical Principles of Electron Paramagnetic Resonance (with Thomas L. Estle) 1973; numerous papers in scientific journals. *Address:* Institute for Research on Learning, Palo Alto, Calif. 94304 (Office); 2 Yerba Buena Avenue, Los Altos, Calif. 94022, U.S.A. (Home). *Telephone:* (415) 496-7910 (Office); (415) 941-5043 (Home).

PAKULA, Alan J., B.A.; American film producer and director; b. 7 April 1928, New York; m. Hannah C. Boorstin 1973; ed. Yale Univ.; producer's apprentice MGM 1950; producer's asst. Paramount pictures 1951; producer 1955; f. own production co. Pakula-Milligan Productions, Los Angeles. *Films produced and/or directed include:* Fear Strikes Out 1957, To Kill a Mockingbird 1963, Love With the Proper Stranger 1964, Baby, the Rain Must Fall 1965, Inside Daisy Clover 1966, Up the Down Staircase 1967, The Stalking Moon 1969, Sterile Cuckoo 1969, Klute 1971, Love and Pain and the Whole Damned Thing 1973, The Parallax View 1974, All the President's Men 1976, Comes a Horseman 1978, Starting Over 1979, Rollover 1981, Sophie's Choice 1982, Orphans (with Susan Solt) 1987, See You In The Morning 1988. *Address:* Pakula Productions Inc., 330 West 58th Street, New York, N.Y. 10019, U.S.A.

PAL, Benjamin Peary, M.SC., PH.D., F.R.S.; Indian agricultural scientist; b. 26 May 1906, Mukandpur, Punjab; s. of Dr. R. R. and Mrs. I. D. Pal; ed. Rangoon and Cambridge Univs.; Second Econ. Botanist, Imperial Agricultural Research Inst. 1933–37, Imperial Econ. Botanist 1937–50; Designated as Head, Div. of Botany, Indian Agricultural Research Inst. then Dir. 1950–65; fmr. Dir.-Gen. Indian Council of Agricultural Research 1965–71, Scientist Emer. 1972–; fmr. Chair. Special Advisory Cttee. on Food and Agric., Dept. of Atomic Energy; Chair. Nat. Cttee. on Environmental Planning and Co-ordination 1977–81; fmr. Pres. many botanical and agricultural socs.; Gen. Pres. Indian Science Congress 1970–71; has served on Govt. Educ. Comm., heading its Task Force on Agricultural Educ.; fmr. Chair. All India Fine Arts and Crafts Soc.; helped to establish Postgraduate School at Indian Agricultural Research Inst.; research in wheat breeding and genetics; revision work on Int. Code of Nomenclature of Agricultural and Horticultural Plants; mem. Royal Nat. Rose Soc., Indian Botanical Soc.; Foreign mem. All Union Lenin Acad. of Agricultural Sciences 1967–; Hon. mem. Japan Acad., Acad. d'Agric. de France; Fellow, Indian Nat. Science Acad., (Pres. 1975–76), Linnean Soc. of London, Royal Soc., London; Awards include Padma Shri 1958, Rafi Ahmed Kidwai Memorial Prize of the Indian Council of Agricultural Research 1960, Srinivisa Ramanujan Medal, Nat. Inst. of Sciences of India 1964, Padma Bhushan 1968, Birbal, Sahni Medal of Indian Botanical Soc. 1962, Aryabhata Medal, Indian Nat. Science Acad. 1980; Hon. D.Sc. (Punjab, Sardar Patel, Uttar Pradesh, Haryana Univs.). *Publications:* Beautiful Climbers of India, Charophyta, The Rose in India, Wheat, Flowering Shrubs 1968, Bougainvilleas 1974; and over 200 scientific papers. *Leisure interests:* rose breeding, painting. *Address:* P-11, Hauz Khas Enclave, New Delhi 16, India. *Telephone:* 660245.

PÁL, Lénárd; Hungarian physicist; b. 7 Nov. 1925, Gyoma; s. of Imre Pál and Erzsébet Varga; m. Angela Danóci 1963; one d.; ed. Budapest and Moscow Univs.; Dept. Head, Cen. Research Inst. for Physics, Budapest 1953–56, Deputy Dir. 1956–69, Dir. 1970–74, Dir.-Gen 1974–78; Prof. of Nuclear Physics, Eötvös Lóránd Univ. Budapest 1961–77, 1989–; Pres. State Office for Tech. Devt. 1978–80, 1984–85, Nat. Atomic Energy Comm. 1978–80, 1984–85; mem. Science Policy Cttee., Council of Ministers 1978–85; Sec. Cen. Cttee. Hungarian Socialist Workers' Party 1985–88; Corresp. mem. Hungarian Acad. of Sciences 1961–73, mem. 1973–, Gen. Sec. 1980–84, Pres. Intercosmos Council 1980–84; Foreign mem. Acad. of Sciences of the U.S.S.R. 1976–, of G.D.R. 1982–, of Czechoslovakia 1983–; Gold Medal, Order of Labour 1956, 1968; Kossuth Prize 1962; Memorial Medal 25th Anniversary of the Liberation 1970; Kurtchatov Memory Medal (U.S.S.R.) 1970; Gold Medal of the Hungarian Acad. of Sciences 1975, Eötvös Lóránd Physical Soc. Medal 1976, Red Banner Order of Labour (U.S.S.R.) 1975, Red Banner of Work 1985. *Publications:* Science and Technical Development 1987, Science and Technology Policies in Finland and Hungary 1985; approximately 275 articles in Hungarian and foreign scientific journals. *Leisure interests:* hunting, angling. *Address:* Széher út 21/A, 1021 Budapest II, Hungary. *Telephone:* 767-890.

PALACIOS DE VIZZIO, Sergio, LL.D.; Bolivian international lawyer and diplomatist; b. 27 Sept. 1936, Cochabamba; s. of Dr. Alfredo Palacios Mendoza and Lucia de Vizzio de Palacios; m. Helga Weber 1976; ed. Univ. of San Francisco Xavier de Chuquisaca, Harvard Law School, Bolivian War Coll. and Inst. of Int. Law, The Hague; Dir.-Gen. of Latin-American Affairs, Ministry of Foreign Affairs 1966–67; Chargé d'affaires, Japan and Taiwan 1967–70; Sec.-Gen. of Co-ordination for Presidency of Repub. 1974; mem. Nat. Maritime Comm. 1974; Chief of Legal Dept., Banco Mercantil S.A. and self-employed attorney 1974–79; Prof. Inst. of Higher Studies on Nat. Issues; lecturer, War Coll. 1973–79; Pres. Center of War Coll. Graduates 1976–78; Adviser, Bolivian Nat. Security Council 1977–78; Amb. and Perm. Rep. to UN 1979–81; Rep. to UN Law of Sea Conf. 1974; mem. Inst. of Int. Law, American Soc. of Int. Law, Centre for Higher Nat. Studies; Orden Cruzeiro do Sul (Brazil), Order of the Rising Sun (Japan). *Leisure interests:* tennis, theatre, classical music. *Address:* c/o Ministerio des Asuntos Exteriores, La Paz, Bolivia.

PALADE, George Emil; American (Romanian-born) scientist; b. 19 Nov. 1912, Iași, Romania; s. of Emil Palade and Constanța Cantemir; m. 1st Irina Malaxa 1940 (died 1969); m. 2nd Marilyn Farquhar 1970; one s. one d.; ed. Hasdeu Lyceum, Buzău, Univ. of Bucharest; went to the U.S.A. 1946; naturalized U.S. citizen 1952; Instructor, Asst. Prof. of Anatomy, School of Medicine, Univ. of Bucharest 1935–45; Visiting Investigator, Asst., Assoc., Prof. of Cell Biology, Rockefeller Univ. 1946–73; Prof. of Cell Biology, Yale Univ. 1973–83, Sr. Research Scientist 1983–; Fellow American Acad. of Arts and Sciences; mem. N.A.S., Pontifical Acad. of Sciences; Foreign mem. Royal Soc.; Albert Lasker Basic Research Award 1966, Gairdner Special Award (Canada) 1968, Hurwitz Prize 1970, Nobel Prize for Medicine 1974, Nat. Medal of Science 1986. *Leisure interest:* history. *Address:* Department of Cell Biology, Yale University School of Medicine, 333 Cedar Street, P.O. Box 3333, New Haven, Conn. 06510, U.S.A. *Telephone:* (203) 785-4317.

PALAMENGHI-CRISPI, Francesco; Italian banking official; b. 28 Dec. 1917, Rome; m.; four c.; ed. Univ. of Rome; with Bank of Italy 1946–49, Dir. 1963; Sec., Somali Currency Bd. 1950–59, first Gen. Dir. 1959–60; Prof. of Politics and Financial Econ. Univ. of Mogadishu, Somalia 1959–66; first Man. Dir. and Deputy Pres. Somali Nat. Bank 1960–66; Alt. Gov. for Somalia for Int. Bank for Reconstruction and Devt. (IBRD)—World Bank 1961–66; mem. Gen. Banking Panel of Experts in Trinidad and Tobago, Int. Monetary Fund (IMF) 1966–67; Temp. Alt. Gov. IMF 1969, 1970, 1972, IBRD 1969; Exec. Dir. IMF for Italy (also Malta, Portugal and Spain) 1967–76; mem. Italian Econ. Del to Peace Conf., Paris 1946; Lecturer, Univ. of Rome 1946–56. *Address:* c/o Ministry of Foreign Affairs, Piazzale della Famesia 1, 00100 Rome, Italy.

PALAU, Luis; American (b. Argentinian) evangelist and writer; b. 27 Nov. 1934, Buenos Aires, Argentina; s. of Luis Palau Sr.; m. Patricia Marilyn Scofield 1961; four s.; ed. St. Alban's Coll., Buenos Aires, Multnomah School of the Bible, Portland, Ore., U.S.A.; mem. staff Bank of London, Buenos Aires and Cordoba 1952–59; moved to U.S.A. 1960; worked as interpreter for Billy Graham 1962; began Spanish radio broadcasts as missionary in Colombia 1967; began evangelistic ministry as part of Overseas Crusades 1968; made crusades broadcasts to all Latin America 1975; named Pres. Overseas Crusades 1976; f. Luis Palau Evangelistic Asscn. 1978; first major crusade in U.S.A., San Diego 1981; crusades on four continents 1982; launched 12-year crusade in India 1988; Dr. h.c. (Talbot Theological Seminary) 1977, (Wheaton Coll.) 1985. *Publications:* Heart After God 1978, My Response 1985, Time To Stop Pretending 1985, So You Want To Grow 1986; 17 books and booklets in Spanish; works have been transl. into 29 languages. *Leisure interest:* family. *Address:* P.O. Box 1173, Portland, Ore. 97207, U.S.A. *Telephone:* (503) 643-0777.

PALAZZINI, H.E. Cardinal Pietro, S.T.D., J.U.D.; Vatican ecclesiastic; b. 19 May 1912, Piobbico, Pesaro; s. of Giovanni Palazzini and Luigia Conti; ed. Lateran Univ.; ordained 6 Dec. 1934; advocate of the Sacred Roman Rota; fmr. Asst. Dir. Pontificio Seminario Maggiore; Prof. of Moral Theology, Lateran Univ. 1945–56; Under-Sec. Sacred Congregation for the Religious 1956–58; Sec. Sacred Congregation for the Clergy 1962; cr. Cardinal by Pope Paul VI 1973; Prefect Sacred Congregation for the Causes of Beatification and Canonization of Saints. *Publications:* Il Monoteismo dei Padri Apostolici 1946, Indissolubilità del Matrimonio 1952, Il Diritto Strumento di Riforma in S. Pier Damiani 1956, Theologia Moralis (with A. Lanza) 4 vols. 1953–63, Morale Cattolica e Morale Protestante 1961, La Coscienza 1963, Morale dell'Attualità 1963, S. Pier Damiani il Superfluo 1972, Vita Sacramentale (3 vols.) 1972–86, Dizionario dei concili 6 vols. 1963–67, Dictionarium morale et canonicum 4 vols. 1962–68 (Dir.); Vita e virtù cristiane 1975, Avviamento allo studio della morale Cristiana 1976, Pio IX nel primo centenario della morte 1978, Francesco Faà di Bruno, scienziato e prete 1980, La Santissima Vergine 1984. *Address:* Via Proba Petronia 83, 00136 Rome, Italy. *Telephone:* 06 3452 555.

PALEY, Grace; American writer and teacher; b. 11 Dec. 1922, The Bronx, New York, N.Y.; d. of Isaac Goodside and Manya Ridnik Goodside; m. 1st Jess Paley 1942, 2nd Robert Nichols 1972; one s. one d.; ed. Hunter Coll. and New York Univ.; teaching staff Sarah Lawrence Coll. 1966–, Columbia Univ., New York 1984–; mem. Inst. of American Writers; Guggenheim Fellow; Edith Wharton Award, New York State. *Publications:* The Little Disturbances of Man 1959, Enormous Changes at the Last Minute 1974, Later the Same Day 1984, Leaning Forward (poems) 1985. *Address:* Sarah Lawrence College, Bronxville, N.Y. 10708, U.S.A.

PALEY, William S., B.S.; American business executive; b. 28 Sept. 1901, Chicago; s. of Samuel and Goldie (Drell) Caley; m. 1st Dorothy Hart Hearst 1932, one s. one d.; m. 2nd Barbara Cushing Mortimer 1947, one s. one d.; ed. Univ. of Chicago, Univ. of Pennsylvania; Pres. CBS Inc. 1928–46, Chair. 1946–83, Sept. 1986–, Consultant April 1983–, to remain Dir. and Chair. Exec. Cttee., retd. as C.E.O. 1977; Founder, mem. Bd. of Dirs. Genetics Inst. 1980–, Thinking Machines Corpn. 1983–; Partner Whitcom Investment Co. 1982–; Pres. and Dir. William S. Paley Foundation Inc.; Co-Chair. and Trustee Emer. N. Shore Univ. Hosp. 1954–73, Dir. 1949–73; Hon. Dir. Resources for the Future Inc. 1969–; Trustee Museum of Modern Art 1937–, Pres. 1968–72, Chair. 1972–85, Chair. Emer. 1985–; Founder and Chair. Museum of Broadcasting 1976–; Co-Chair. Bd. Int. Herald Tribune 1983; Life Trustee, Fed. of Jewish Philanthropies, New York, Trustee Emer. Colombia Univ. 1973–; Hon. LL.D. (Adelphi Univ.) 1957, (Bates Coll.) 1963, (Univ. of Pa.) 1968, (Columbia, Brown Univs.) 1975, (Pratt Inst.) 1977, (Dartmouth Coll.) 1979; Hon. L.H.D. (Ithaca Coll.) 1978; Legion of Merit, Medal of Merit, Officer, Légion d'honneur, Croix de guerre avec palme, Order of Merit (Italy); numerous awards. *Address:* Columbia Broadcasting System Inc., 51 West 52nd Street, New York, N.Y. 10019, U.S.A.

PALKHIVALA, Nani Ardeshir; Indian diplomatist, lawyer and businessman; b. 16 Jan. 1920, Bombay; s. of Ardeshir Nanabhoy and Sheherbanoo A. Palkhivala; m. Nargesh H. Matbar 1945; ed. St. Xavier's Coll. and Govt. Law Coll., Bombay; Sr. advocate, Supreme Court of India; Amb. to U.S.A. 1977–79; Chair. Assoc. Cement Cos. Ltd., Tata Exports Ltd.; Vice-Chair. Tata Eng. and Locomotive Co., Assoc. Bearing Co.; Dir. Tata Sons Ltd., Tata Iron and Steel Co. Ltd., Nat. Organic Chemical Industries Ltd.; Prof. Law, Calcutta Univ.; Pres. Forum of Free Enterprise; Chair. Income-tax Appellate Tribunal Bar Asscn.; elected Hon. mem. Acad. of Political Science, New York 1975; Hon. LL.D. (Princeton) 1978, (Lawrence) 1979. *Publications:* The Law and Practice of Income-tax (co-author) 7th edn. 1976, 1982, Taxation in India 1960, Our Constitution Defaced and Defiled 1975, India's Priceless Heritage 1980, We, The People 1984. *Leisure interests:* motoring, history, literature. *Address:* "Commonwealth", 181 Backbay Reclamation, Bombay 400 020, India.

PALLAEV, Gaibnazar; Soviet politician; b. 1929, Tadzhikistan; mem. CPSU 1957–; political activities 1958; Deputy Minister of Agric. of Tadzhik SSR 1960; Chair. of Tadzhikselkhoztechnika Union 1973; First Sec. of Kurgan-Tube Regional Cttee. of Tadzhik CP 1977; Chair. of Presidium of Tadzhik Supreme Soviet and Deputy Chair. of the U.S.S.R. Supreme Soviet 1984–; mem. Cen. Auditing Comm. CPSU 1986–; Deputy to U.S.S.R. Supreme Soviet 1977. *Address:* The Kremlin, Moscow, U.S.S.R.

PALLISER, Rt. Hon. Sir (Arthur) Michael, P.C., G.C.M.G., M.A.; British diplomatist; b. 9 April 1922, Reigate, Surrey; s. of late Admiral Sir Arthur Palliser, K.C.B., D.S.C., and of Lady Palliser (née Margaret E. King-Salter); m. Marie M. Spaak (d. of late Paul-Henri Spaak) 1948; three s.; ed. Wellington Coll. and Merton Coll., Oxford; war service in Coldstream Guards (mentioned in despatches) 1942–46; entered diplomatic service 1947; Foreign Office 1947–49, 1951–56; posted to Athens 1949–51, Paris 1956–60; Head of Chancery, Dakar 1960–62; Counsellor and seconded to Imperial Defence Coll. 1963; Head of Planning Staff, Foreign Office 1964; a Pvt. Sec. to Prime Minister 1966–69; Minister, Paris 1969–71; Amb. and Head, U.K. Del. to EEC 1971–72; Amb. and U.K. Perm. Rep. to European Communities 1973–75; Perm. Under-Sec., Head of Diplomatic Service 1975–82; Chair. Council, Int. Inst. for Strategic Studies 1983–; Deputy Chair. Midland Bank PLC 1987–; Deputy Chair. Midland Montagu (Holdings) 1987–; Dir. Samuel Montagu and Co. Ltd. (Vice-Chair. 1983–84, Chair. 1984–85, 1986–), Arbor Acres Farm Inc., Booker PLC, BAT Industries PLC, Eagle Star (Holdings), Shell Transport and Trading Co. PLC; Deputy Chair. British Invisible Exports Council 1987–; mem. Exec. Cttee. David Davies Memorial Inst. of Int. Studies, Security Comm. 1983–; Assoc. Fellow Centre for Int. Affairs, Harvard Univ. 1982; Hon. Fellow Merton Coll., Oxford 1986; Chevalier, Order of Orange-Nassau, Légion d'honneur. *Address:* c/o Midland Bank PLC, Poultry, London EC2P 2BX, England.

PALLOTTINO, Massimo, D.LITT.; Italian university professor; b. 9 Nov. 1909, Rome; s. of Carlo Pallottino and Margherita Perotti; m. Maria Sechi 1936; one s. two d.; ed. Univ. of Rome; Insp., Dept. of Antiquities of Rome 1933; Dir. Museo Nazionale di Villa Giulia, Rome and excavations of Cerveteri 1937; Lecturer and later Acting Prof. Univ. of Rome 1938; Prof. of Classical Archaeology, Univ. of Cagliari 1940; Prof. of Etruscology and Italic Antiquities, Univ. of Rome 1945; Pres. Inst. of Etruscan Studies; Pres. Int. Asscn. for Classical Archaeology; mem. Accademia Nazionale dei Lincei, Pontificia Accademia di Archeologia, Acad. des Inscriptions et Belles Lettres (Inst. de France), Deutsches Archäologisches Institut, Soc. Antiquaries of London, Prehistoric Soc., London; Dir. Studi Etruschi, Archeologia Classica; Int. Prize Balzan for Sciences of Antiquity 1982, Prize Erasmus for Classical Archaeology. *Publications:* Elementi di Lingua Etrusca 1936, Tarquinia 1937, Etruscologia 1942, 1947, 1955, 1968, 1984, L'Arco degli Argentari 1946, L'Origine degli Etruschi 1947, La Civilisation Etrusque 1950, La Sardegna Nuragica 1950, Etruscan Painting 1952, Testimonia Linguae Etruscae 1954, 1968, The Etruscans 1956, Che cos' è l'Archeologia 1963, 1980, Civiltà Artistica Etrusco-Italica 1971, Genti e Culture dell'Italia Preromana 1981, Storia della prima Italia 1984. *Address:* 9 Via dei Redentoristi, 00186 Rome, Italy.

PALMAR, Sir Derek (James), Kt., F.C.A., C.B.I.M.; British business executive; b. 25 July 1919, Romford; s. of the late Lieut.-Col. F. J. Palmar and Hylda (née Smith) Palmar; m. Edith Brewster 1946; one s. one d.; ed. Dover Coll.; R.A. 1941–46; Staff Coll.; Lieut.-Col. 1945; with Peat, Marwick Mitchell & Co. 1937–57; Dir. Hill Samuel Group 1957–70; Industrial Adviser Dept. of Econ. Affairs 1965–67; Pres. Bass PLC 1987– (Dir. 1970–76, C.E.O. 1976–84, Chair. 1976–87); Chair. Rush & Tomkins Group PLC 1974–, Yorkshire TV 1982–, Baythorpe 1986–; Dir. United Newspapers, Centre for Policy Studies Ltd., CM Group Holdings Ltd., Consolidated Venture Trust PLC, Drayton Consolidated Trust PLC; Chair. Leeds University Foundation Trust, Zoological Society of London Development Trust; Accounting Standards Comm. 1982–84; World Wildlife Fund (U.K.) 1982–85; Trustee, Civic Trust; Vice-Pres. Brewers' Soc. (Chair. 1982–84, Vice-Chair. 1980–82); Chair. British Rail Southern Regional Advisory Bd. 1972–79; mem. British Railways Bd. 1969–72, Dover Harbour Bd. 1964–75; Dir. Grindlays Bank Ltd. 1973–85, Grindlays Holdings PLC 1979–85; mem. Alcohol Educ. and Research Council 1982–87, Ct. Brewers' Co. 1982–88; Freeman, City of London. *Leisure interests:* shooting, gardening. *Address:* 30 Portland Place, London, WC1N 3DF, England. *Telephone:* 01-637 5499.

PALMER, Arnold Daniel; American professional golfer and business executive; b. 10 Sept. 1929, Latrobe, Pa; s. of Milfred J. and Doris Palmer; m. Winifred Walzer 1954; two d.; ed. Wake Forest Univ., N.C.; U.S. Coast Guard 1950–52; U.S. Amateur Golf Champion 1954; professional golfer 1954–; winner of 91 professional titles, incl. British Open 1961, 1962, U.S. Open 1960, U.S. Masters 1958, 1960, 1962, 1964, Canadian P.G.A. 1980, U.S. Srs. Championship 1981, and more than $3 million in prize money; mem. U.S. Ryder Cup team 1961, 1963, 1965, 1967, 1971, 1973, Captain 1963, 1975; Pres. Arnold Palmer Enterprises, five automobile agencies, three aviation service cos. and one aviation charter operation, Latrobe Country Club, Bay Hill Club, Isleworth Club, Fla.; mem. Bd. of dirs. Progroup Inc., Tenn., Latrobe Area Hospital, Hon. Nat. Chair. Nat. Foundation March of Dimes 1971–; designer numerous golf courses; Hon. LL.D. (Wake Forest, Nat. Coll. of Educ.), Hon. D.H. (Thiel Coll.), Hon. D.H.L. (Fla. Southern Coll.); Athlete of Decade, Associated Press 1970; Sportsman of the Year, Sports Illustrated 1960; Hickok Belt, Athlete of Year 1960. *Publications:* My Game and Yours 1965, Situation Golf 1970, Go for Broke 1973, Arnold Palmer's Best 54 Golf Holes 1977, Arnold Palmer's Complete Book of Putting 1986, Play Great Golf 1987. *Leisure interests:* bridge, occasional hunting. *Address:* One Erieview Plaza, Suite 1300, Cleveland, Ohio 44114 (Office); P.O. Box 52, Youngstown, Pa. 15696, U.S.A. (Home and Personal Office). *Telephone:* (216) 522-1200 (Office); (412) 537-7751 (Home).

PALMER, Frank Robert, M.A. (Oxon.), F.B.A.; British professor of linguistics; b. 9 April 1922, Westerleigh, Glos.; s. of George Samuel Palmer and Gertrude Lilian (née Newman) Palmer; m. Jean Elisabeth Moore 1948; three s. two d.; ed. Bristol Grammar School, New College, Oxford, Merton College, Oxford; Lecturer in Linguistics, School of Oriental and African Studies (SOAS), Univ. of London 1950–60; Prof. of Linguistics, Univ. Coll. of North Wales, Bangor 1960–65; Prof. of Linguistic Science, Univ. of Reading 1965–87, Dean, Faculty of Letters and Social Sciences 1969–72; mem. Council of the Philological Soc.; Chair. Linguistics Asscn. (G.B.) 1965–68, Ed. Journal of Linguistics 1969–79, Linguistic Soc. of America Prof., Buffalo, U.S.A. 1971; Distinguished Visiting Prof. Univ. of Del., Newark, U.S.A. 1982. *Publications:* The Morphology of the Tigre Noun 1962, A Linguistic Study of the English Verb 1965, Ed. Selected Papers

of J. R. Firth (1951–58) 1968, Ed. Prosodic Analysis 1970, Grammar 1971, 1984, The English Verb 1974, 1987, Semantics 1976, 1981, Modality and the English Modals 1979, Mood and Modality 1986. *Leisure interests:* gardening, crosswords. *Address:* 'Whitethorns', Roundabout Lane, Winnersh, Wokingham, Berks., RG11 5AD, England. *Telephone:* (0734) 786214.

PALMER, Rt. Hon. Geoffrey Winston Russell, P.C., B.A., LL.B., J.D.; New Zealand politician; b. 21 April 1942, Nelson; s. of Leonard R. and Jessie P. Palmer; m. Margaret E. Hinchcliff 1963; one s. one d.; ed. Nelson Coll., Victoria Univ. of Wellington and Univ. of Chicago; solicitor, Wellington 1964–66; Lecturer in Political Science, Vic. Univ. 1968–69; Prof. of Law, Univ. of Ia. and Univ. of Va. 1969–73; Principal Asst. to Australian Nat. Comm. of Inquiry on Rehabilitation and Compensation 1973; Prof. of English and New Zealand Law, Victoria Univ. 1974–79; Visiting Fellow, Wolfson Coll., Oxford 1978; mem. Parl. for Christchurch Cen. 1979–; Deputy Leader N.Z. Labour Party 1983–; Deputy Prime Minister, Minister of Justice and Attorney-Gen. 1984–, for the Environment Aug. 1987–. *Publications:* Unbridled Power?—An Interpretation of New Zealand's Constitution and Government 1979, Compensation for Incapacity—A Study of Law and Social Change in Australia and New Zealand 1979. *Leisure interests:* cricket, golf, playing the trumpet. *Address:* 288 Bealey Avenue, Christchurch, New Zealand. *Telephone:* 892-584.

PALMER, Robie Marcus Hooker (Mark), B.A.; American diplomatist; b. 14 July 1941, Ann Arbor, Mich.; s. of Robie E. Palmer and Katherine Hooker; m. Sushma Palmer; ed. Yale Univ.; copy asst. New York Times 1963; asst. to producer, WNDT-TV, New York 1963–64; joined U.S. Foreign Service 1964; Third Sec., Embassy, Delhi 1964–66; Dept. of State 1966–68; Second Sec., Embassy, Moscow 1968–71; prin. speechwriter to Sec. of State 1971–75; Counsellor, Embassy, Belgrade 1975–78; Dept. of State 1978–86; Amb. to Hungary 1986–; mem. Council on Foreign Relations, American Foreign Service Asscn.; Superior Honor Award, Dept. of State 1980. *Leisure interest:* tennis. *Address:* U.S. Embassy, A.P.O., New York, N.Y. 09213, U.S.A.

PALOMINO ROEDEL, Jose; Peruvian politician and engineer; b. 23 Nov. 1937, Lima; ed. Universidad Nacional de Ingeniería; Project Evaluation Officer, Nat. Planning Inst. 1963, Dir.-Gen. of Macroeconomics 1967; mem. Organizing Comm., Ministry of Industry 1968; Head of Gen. Programming Dept., Cartagena Agreement Jt. Comm. 1970; Dir. of team which drafted devt. strategy for Andean Sub-region 1972; mem. of UNIDO Working Group on investment promotion policies in developing countries, Vienna 1976; Dir. of team which drafted Evaluation Report on First Decade of Andean Integration 1979; mem. of Govt. Cen. Planning Comm., Partido Aprista Peruano 1981; Minister of Fisheries 1985–86. *Address:* c/o Ministry of Fisheries, Avenida Javier Prado Este 2465, San Luis, Lima, Peru. *Telephone:* 362630.

PÁLSSON, Thorsteinn; Icelandic politician; b. 29 Oct. 1947; m. Ingibjörg Rafnar; three c.; ed. Commercial Coll., Reykjavík and Univ. of Iceland; Chair. Vaka (student's union) 1969–70; Ed. Vísir 1975; Dir. Confed. of Icelandic Employers 1979–; M.P. April 1983–; Chair. Independence Party Nov. 1983–; Minister of Finance 1985–87, Prime Minister of Iceland 1987–88. *Address:* c/o Prime Minister's Office, Stjórnarrádshúsidv/Laekjartorg, 150 Reykjavík, Iceland.

PALTRIDGE, Garth William, PH.D., F.A.A.; Australian research scientist; b. 24 April 1940, Brisbane; s. of T.B. Paltridge and A.T. Savage; m. Kay L. Petty 1965; one s. one d.; ed. Brisbane Boys' Coll., and Queensland and Melbourne Univs.; Postdoctoral Fellow, New Mexico Tech. 1965; Sr. Scientific Officer R.S.R.S., U.K. 1966; research scientist, CSIRO Div. of Meteorological Physics 1967; Exec. Dir. P.I.E.C.E. of Australian Inst. of Petroleum 1980; Chief Research Scientist, CSIRO Div. of Atmospheric Research 1981–; WMO Research Prize. *Publications:* Radiative Processes in Meteorology and Climatology; 100 research papers on environmental topics. *Leisure interests:* golf, history, furniture and cabinet making. *Address:* c/o CSIRO Division of Atmospheric Research, Private Bag No. 1, Mordialloc, Vic. (Office); 21 Wattle Avenue, Beaumaris, Vic., Australia (Home).

PALUMBO, Peter Garth, M.A.; British property developer; b. 20 July 1935, London; s. of Rudolph Palumbo and Elsie Palumbo; m. 1st Denia Wigram 1959 (divorced 1986), 2nd Hayat Morowa 1986; one s. two d.; ed. Eton Coll. and Worcester Coll., Oxford; Gov. London School of Econs. 1976–; Trustee, Mies van der Rohe Archive 1977–, The Tate Gallery 1978–85, Whitechapel Art Gallery Foundation 1981–87; Trustee and Hon. Treas. Writers and Scholars Educational Trust 1984–; Chair. The Tate Gallery Foundation 1986–87, Painshill Park Trust Appeal 1986–; Chair. The Arts Council of Great Britain April 1989–; Hon. F.R.I.B.A. *Leisure interests:* music, travel, gardening, reading. *Address:* Bagnor Manor, Bagnor, Newbury, Berks., RG16 8AG, England. *Telephone:* Newbury 40930.

PAN HE; Chinese sculptor; b. 1926, Nanhai Co., Guangdong; exponent of socialist realism in art; currently teaches at Guangzhou Inst. of Fine Arts. *Address:* Guangzhou Institute, Guangzhou Province, People's Republic of China.

PAN HONG; Chinese film actress; b. 4 Nov. 1954, Shanghai; m. Mi Jingshan; ed. Shanghai Drama Acad. 1973–76; actress, Shanghai Film Studio, Shanghai 1977–80, Omei Film Studio, Chengdu 1980–; 3rd Golden Rooster Best Actress Award for A Middle-aged Women 1983; 8th Golden Rooster Best Actress for Well 1988. *Address:* Omei Film Studio, Tonghui Menwai, Chengdu City, Sichuan Province, People's Republic of China. *Telephone:* 22991 (Chengdu).

PAN RONGWEN; Chinese physician; alt. mem. 12th CCP Cen. Cttee. 1982; Physician-in-Charge, Changzheng Mil. Hosp. 1982. *Address:* Changzheng Military Hospital, Changzheng, People's Republic of China.

PANĂ, Gheorghe; Romanian politician; b. 9 April 1927, Gherghiṭa, Prahova County; m. Antoneta Pană; one d.; ed. Acad. of Econ. Studies, Bucharest; joined Communist Youth Union 1944, Romanian Communist Party (RCP) 1947; Sec. Bucharest RCP Cttee. 1959–64; First Sec. Brașov Regional RCP Cttee. 1966–68, Brașov County Cttee. of RCP 1968–69; mem. Exec. Cttee. of the Cen. Cttee. of RCP 1969–, Perm. Presidium of Cen. Cttee. 1969–74; Sec. Central Cttee. of RCP 1969–75; mem. Grand Nat. Ass. 1969–, Nat. Council of Front of Socialist Democracy and Unity 1968–, State Council 1969–75, 1979–86; Chair. Gen. Trade Union Confed. 1975–79; Minister of Labour 1978–79, of Food Industry and Agricultural Products Acquisition 1985–87; Chair. Cttee. for the People's Council's Problems 1987–; Mayor of Bucharest 1979–85; First Sec. of RCP Cttee. Bucharest Municipality 1979–85; Hero of Socialist Labour 1971. *Address:* Bd. Gh. Gheorghiu-Dej 27, Bucharest, Romania.

PANARD, Pierre Marie Maurice; French public servant (retd.); b. 1 Nov. 1916, Dun le Palestel; m. Monique de Rigaud de Vaudreuil; ed. Univ. de Paris Faculté de Droit and Ecole Libre des Sciences Politiques; Clerk, Ministry of Finance 1941–46, Civil Admin. 1946–47; transferred to Finance Comm. of Nat. Ass. 1947–49, Chief, Tech. Services 1961–62; Chief, Office Sec. of State for Marine 1949–50; Financial Comptroller 1956–61; Dir. Office, Minister of Public Works and Transport 1962–64; Chief, Cen. Bureau of Finance 1964; Dir.-Gen. Cie. Générale Transatlantique 1964–74; Vice-Chair. Nat. Fed. of Breeders of Saddle Horses 1974–84; Officier, Légion d'honneur, Commdr. Ordre nat. du Mérite, Croix de guerre. *Leisure interest:* horse breeding. *Address:* 3 rue Agrippa d'Aubigné, 75004 Paris, France.

PANAS, Eustace G., PH.D.; Greek professor of economics; b. Nov. 1924, Athens; s. of George and Helen Panas; m. Athena Kossifakis 1958; one d.; ed. Nat. Univ. of Athens and Harvard Univ.; joined Ministry of Co-ordination 1950, Nat. Accounts Div. 1951–61, Dir. Fiscal and Monetary Matters Div. 1961–69; Sec., Ministerial Econ. Cttee. 1962–63; Sec., Nat. Council of Econ. Policy 1967–69; Statistician, UN Statistical Office, Nat. Accounts Branch 1956, 1957, 1958–59; mem. Greek Nat. Tobacco Bd., Prices and Incomes Comm., Cen. Planning Cttee.; Assoc. Prof. Econs., Graduate School of Industrial Studies 1968–72; Chair. Capital Market Cttee., 1967–74; Alt. Gov., IMF 1969–74; Chair. Export Credit Guaranty Council 1969–74; Deputy Gov. Bank of Greece 1969–74; Prof. of Econs., Graduate School of Econ. and Business Science 1972–75; IMF Research Advisor to Cen. Bank of Mauritania 1975–77, to Cen. Bank of Kuwait 1979–83; Prin. Man. Banque du Zaire 1984–; mem. American Econ. Asscn., American Statistical Asscn., Royal Econ. Soc., Greek Econ. Soc., Int. Asscn. for Research in Income and Wealth. *Publications:* articles and papers in Greek and English on economic topics. *Address:* 6 Naiadon Street, Athens 116-34, Greece. *Telephone:* 7217-177 (Home).

PANAYIDES CHRISTOU, Tasos, M.A., M.P.A.; Cypriot diplomatist; b. 9 April 1934, Ktima-Paphos; s. of Christos Panayi and Efrosini Savva; m. Pandora Constantinides 1969; two s. one d.; ed. Paphos Gymnasium, Cyprus Teacher's Training Coll., Univ. of London, and Univ. of Indiana; Teacher, Cyprus 1954–59; First Sec. to Pres. (Archbishop Makarios), then Dir. President's Office 1960–69; Amb. to Fed. Repub. of Germany (also to Austria and Switzerland) 1969–79; Sec. and Dean, Commonwealth Group, Bonn 1976–79; High Commr. in U.K. (also Amb. to Denmark, Iceland, Norway and Sweden) 1979–; Doyen Diplomatic Corps in London and Sr. High Commr. Feb. 1988–; Chair. Commonwealth Foundation Grants Cttee. 1985–88, Commonwealth Fund for Tech. Co-operation (C.F.T.C.) 1986–89, Finance Cttee. of Commonwealth Secr. 1988–; Rep. to IAEA 1976–; Fellow, Ealing Coll.; Grand Cross (with Star and Sash) of Fed. Repub. of Germany, Grand Cross (with Star and Sash) of Austria, Thyateira Archbishopric Grand Cross (in Gold), Grand Cross (in Gold) of the Patriarchate of Antioch 1984, Freeman of City of London 1984. *Leisure interests:* history, swimming, reading. *Address:* Cyprus High Commission, 93 Park Street, London, W1Y 4ET (Office); 5 Cheyne Walk, London, S.W.3, England (Residence). *Telephone:* 01-499 2810 (Office); 01-351 3989 (Residence).

PANAYOTACOS, Constantine P., LL.D.; Greek diplomatist; b. 1918, Zürich, Switzerland; s. of late Panayotis Panayotacos; m. Irene Arvanitis 1957; one s.; ed. Univ. of Athens; Prof. of Int. Law, Univ. of Athens 1948; joined Diplomatic Service, held several diplomatic posts 1950–67, including Sec., Greek Embassy, Washington, D.C. 1959–61, Counsellor, Perm. Mission to UN 1965, Counsellor, Washington, D.C. 1965; Amb. to India, concurrently accred. to Nepal, Ceylon, Thailand, Burma, Singapore, Malaysia, Indonesia, Repub. of Viet-Nam 1968; Perm. Rep. to Council of Europe 1969–70; Amb. to Cyprus 1971; Under-Sec. of State for Foreign Affairs 1972; Perm. Rep.

to UN 1973–74; Amb to U.S.A. 1974; Grand Officer Order of George I, Order of the Phoenix; Officer Order of the Crown (Belgium), Order of the Oak (Luxembourg); Grand Cross Order of Holy Sepulchre and several others. *Publications:* In the First Line of Defence (3rd Edn. 1980) (in Greek), Diplomatic Memoirs covering the period 1967–74 (in Greek). *Leisure interests:* reading, fishing, music. *Address:* c/o Ministry of Foreign Affairs, Athens, Greece. *Telephone:* 9842805.

PANCIROLI, Most Rev. Romeo; Vatican ecclesiastic; b. 21 Nov. 1923, Italy; s. of Anthony Panciroli and Celestine Cavazzoni; ordained Priest 1949; teacher of natural ethics and sociology 1951–59; Vatican Secr. of State 1960; Attaché to Apostolic Nunciature, Nigeria 1961–64; Sec. to Pontifical Comm. for Social Communications 1965–76; Dir. Vatican Press Office and Spokesman of Holy See 1976–84; Information Officer and mem. Papal Suite with Pope John Paul II in His journeys to 54 countries 1978–84; Archbishop Nov. 1984–, Pro-Nuncio to Liberia, Guinea, The Gambia Nov. 1984–, Apostolic Del. to Sierra Leone Nov. 1984–. *Address:* Apostolic Nunciature, P.O. Box 4211, Monrovia, Liberia. *Telephone:* 26 29 48.

PANDAY, Kedar, LL.B., M.SC.; Indian agriculturalist and politician; b. 14 June 1920, Taulaha, W. Champaran, Bihar; s. of late Pandit Ramphal Panday; m. Kamla Panday 1948; two s. two d.; ed. Banaras Hindu Univ.; practised in Dist. Court of Motihari and Betiah 1945–48; advocate, Patna High Court 1949; participated in trade union management 1946–57; Deputy Minister with various portfolios, Bihar 1957–62, Minister 1970–71, Chief Minister 1972–73; Pres. Bihar Pradesh Congress Cttee. (I) 1977–; mem. Lok Sabha 1980–; Minister for Irrigation June-Nov. 1980, 1982–83, for Railways 1980–82; mem. A.I.C.C. for 25 years. *Address:* 5 Safdarjung Road, New Delhi 110003, India. *Telephone:* 376293, 376363 (Home).

PANDIT, Jasraj, D.MUS.; Indian musician; b. 28 Jan. 1930, Hissar, Haryana; s. of Motiram Pandit; m. Madhura Pandit 1962; one s. one d.; studied under elder brother Maniram Pandit; belongs to Mewati Gharana (school of music); has conducted extensive research in Haveli Sangeet and successfully presented the original Pure Haveli Sangeet with its devotional content intact; has established an Ashram Motiram Sangeet Natale Acad. with main object of propagating Indian classical music by teaching bright students free of charge; mem. advisory bd. of radio and TV. *Works include:* compositions for opera, ballet and short films etc. including Kan Khani Sunyo Kare, Geet Govindam, Sur, Laya Aur Chhanda. *Publication:* Sangeet Saurabh. *Leisure interests:* teaching, travel, sport. *Address:* Rajkamal Building, 138 Shivaji Park, Bombay 400016, India. *Telephone:* 456281.

PANDIT, Vijaya Lakshmi; Indian politician and diplomatist; b. 18 Aug. 1900, Allahabad; d. of Motilal and Sarup Rani Nehru; sister of the late Pandit Jawaharlal Nehru (Prime Minister of India, 1947–64); m. Ranjit S. Pandit 1921; three d.; ed. privately; joined Non-Co-operative Movement, imprisoned for one year 1931; mem. Allahabad Municipal Bd. 1936, Chair. Educ. Cttee. Municipal Bd.; Minister of Local Self-Govt. and Public Health, Uttar Pradesh Govt. 1937–39, 1946–47 (1st woman Minister); joined Congress Party; sentenced to three terms of imprisonment 1932, 1941 and 1942; detained 1942–43; Leader of Indian Del. to UN 1946–51, 1963; Amb. to U.S.S.R. 1947–49, to U.S.A. and Mexico 1949–51; Pres. UN Gen. Ass. 1953–54; High Commr. in U.K. and Amb. to Ireland 1955–61, concurrently Amb. to Spain 1958–61; Gov. of Maharashtra 1962–64; Indian Rep. Human Rights Comm. 1978; mem. Lok Sabha 1952–54, 1964–68; left Congress Party to join Congress for Democracy (merged with Janata Party 1977) 1977, mem. 1977–; Indian Rep. Human Rights Comm. 1978; Trustee, Mountbatten Memorial Trust 1980–; Hon. D.C.L. (Oxford) and numerous other hon. degrees. *Publications:* The Evolution of India 1958, The Scope of Happiness (memoirs) 1979. *Leisure interests:* cooking, reading. *Address:* 181-B Rajpur Road, Dehra Dun, Uttar Pradesh, India.

PANDOLFI, Filippo Maria, PH.D.; Italian politician; b. 1 Nov. 1927, Bergamo; fmr. company dir.; mem. Chamber of Deputies for Brescia-Bergamo 1968–; mem. Comm. on Finance and the Treasury; fmr. Under-Sec. of State in Ministry of the Budget; Minister of Finance 1976–78, of the Treasury 1978–80, of Industry 1980–81, 1982–83, of Agric. 1983–88; EEC Commr. for Science, Research, Telecommunications and Information Tech. Jan. 1989–; Christian Democrat. *Address:* Commission of the European Communities, 200 rue de la Loi, 1049 Brussels, Belgium.

PANFILOV, Gleb; Soviet film director; b. 1933, Sverdlovsk; grad. Sverdlovsk Polytechnic Inst. as chemical engineer and Mosfilm Studios (course in directing); No Ford in the Fire (Lenfilm) (scenario: Yevgeniy Gabrilovich) 1968 (Grand Prix Locarno 1969), Début 1970, both starring Inna Churikova, The Theme 1981. *Address:* Lenfilm, Kirovsky prospekt, Leningrad, U.S.S.R.

PANGALOS, Theodoros, PH.D.; Greek politician; b. 1938; ed. Athens and Sorbonne Univs.; a founder of the Grigoris Lambrakis Youth Movt.; stood as EDA candidate in 1964 election; active in dissident movement during mil. dictatorship; deprived of Greek citizenship by junta 1968; Lecturer and Researcher specializing in Econ. Devt., Programming and Town and Country Planning, Sorbonne, Paris, and Head of Econ. Devt. Inst. 1969–78; practises as lawyer in Athens; Legal Adviser to trade unions in Megarida; active in movt. to protect environment, a founder mem. of Citizens Against Pollution: Alt. Minister of Foreign Affairs 1986–87; Minister of State for EEC Affairs 1987–88; an Ed. of newspaper The Thriasio and the Megenda, and periodical ANTI. *Publications:* several works on economics, sociology and philosophy. *Address:* c/o Ministry of Foreign Affairs, Odos Zalokosta 2, Athens, Greece.

PANGO VILDOSO, Grover; Peruvian politician and teacher; b. 19 July 1947, Tacna; ed. Universidad Nacional de Educación "Enrique Guzmán y Valle", La Cantuta; secondary school teacher of history, geography and literature; Sec. Gen. Tacna branch of Partido Aprista Peruano 1981–83; Prov. Mayor of Tacna 1984–86; elected Deputy for Tacna 1985; Minister of Educ. 1985–87. *Address:* c/o Ministry of Education, Parque Universitario s/n, Lima, Peru.

PANGGABEAN, Gen. Maraden Saur Halomoan; Indonesian politician and army officer; b. 29 June 1922, Tarutung, N. Sumatra; s. of M. Patuan Natoras and Katharina Panjaitan; m. Meida Seimina Matiur Tambunan; one s. three d.; studied mil. affairs in various mil. acads. including the Advanced Infantry Officer Course, U.S.A.; mil. posts include C.-in-C. of the Army 1968, Vice-Commdr. Armed Forces 1969–73, C.-in-C. 1973–78; Deputy Commdr. for Restoration of Security and Order 1968, Commdr. 1969–73, Exec. Officer Command 1973–78; Minister of State for Defense and Security 1969–73, Minister 1973–78; Acting Minister of Home Affairs 1973; Minister Co-ordinator for Political and Security Affairs 1978–83; Acting Foreign Minister 1978–83; Chair. Bd. of Guidance, GOLKAR 1973–78, Vice-Chair. 1978–83; Chair. Exec. Presidium, Bd. of Guidance, GOLKAR 1978–83; mem. People's Consultative Ass. 1973–78, 1978–83, 1983–; War of Independence Medal, Service Award Medal, Best Son of the Nation Medal, Rep. of Indonesia Medal and numerous other medals and awards. *Leisure interests:* golf, jogging, gymnastics, hunting, reading. *Address:* Jalan Teuku Umar 21, Jakarta, Indonesia. *Telephone:* 378012.

PANHOFER, Walter; Austrian concert pianist; b. 3 Jan. 1910, Vienna; s. of Josef and Maria Panhofer; m. Gertraut Schmied 1956; two s.; ed. Akademie für Musik und darstellende Kunst, Hochschule für Musik und darstellende Kunst, Vienna; concerts in Austria, Germany, England, Switzerland, Italy and Yugoslavia; performed with Vienna Philharmonic and Vienna Symphony Orchestras and Royal Philharmonic and London Chamber Orchestras, England; has toured with, and made records with Vienna Octet; master classes in Brussels, Vienna and in Italy; has adjudicated many times at Int. Beethoven piano competition, Vienna; Ehrenkreuz für Wissenschaft und Kunst. *Leisure interests:* mountains, skiing, books. *Address:* Erdbergstrasse 35/9, A-1030 Vienna, Austria. *Telephone:* 757902.

PANICHAS, George Andrew, F.R.S.A., M.A., PH.D., LITT.D.; American university professor and writer; b. 21 May 1930, Springfield, Mass.; s. of Andrew and Fannie Dracouli Panichas; ed. Springfield Classical High School, American Int. Coll., Trinity Coll. and Nottingham Univ., England; Instructor in English, Univ. of Maryland 1962, Asst. Prof. 1963, Assoc. Prof. 1966, Prof. 1968–; Co-Dir. of Conf. "Irving Babbitt: Fifty Years Later" 1983; mem. Richard M. Weaver Fellowship Awards Cttee. 1983–; Academic Bd. Nat. Humanities Inst. 1985–, Ingersoll Prizes Jury Panel 1986; Earhart Foundation Award 1982; lectures on the modern novel, the British novel between the two world wars and writes in the area of comparative literature and on inter-disciplinary subjects (politics, history, philosophy and religion). *Publications:* Adventure in Consciousness: The Meaning of D. H. Lawrence's Religious Quest 1964, Renaissance and Modern Essays: Presented to Vivian de Sola Pinto in Celebration of his Seventieth Birthday (Ed. with G. R. Hibbard and A. Rodway) 1966, Epicurus 1967, Mansions of the Spirit: Essays in Literature and Religion (Ed.) 1967, Promise of Greatness: The War of 1914–1918 (Ed.) 1968, The Politics of Twentieth-Century Novelists (Ed.) 1971, The Reverent Discipline: Essays in Literary Criticism and Culture 1974, The Burden of Vision: Dostoevsky's Spiritual Art 1977, The Simone Weil Reader (Ed.) 1977, Irving Babbitt: Representative Writings (Ed.) 1981, The Courage of Judgment: Essays in Criticism, Culture and Society 1982, Irving Babbitt in Our Time (Ed. with C. G. Ryn) 1986, Modern Age: The First Twenty-Five Years. A Selection (Ed.) 1988; also numerous articles, translations and reviews for books and journals published in U.S. and Europe; Editorial Adviser, Modern Age: A Quarterly Review 1972–77, Assoc. Ed. 1978–83, Ed. 1984–; mem. advisory Bd. Continuity: A Journal of History 1984. *Leisure interests:* hiking, playing racquetball, keeping physically fit, listening to music. *Address:* Department of English, University of Maryland, College Park, Maryland 20742 (Office); 4313 Knox Road, Apartment 402, College Park, Maryland 20740, U.S.A. (Home). *Telephone:* (301) 454-6961 (Office); (301) 779-1436 (Home).

PANIGRAHI, Sanjukta; Indian dancer and choreographer; b. 24 Aug. 1944, Berhampur; m. 1960; two s.; first performance aged four; has toured extensively in Europe giving lecture demonstrations and performances in Odyssi style; has appeared at int. festivals of music, dance and drama in India, U.S.S.R., Australia, Japan, Indonesia, U.K. etc.; conducts regular workshops at cultural and educ. insts. abroad; Life Pres. Kalinga Kala Kshetra and the Natyotkala; mem. Gen. Council Orissa Sangeet Natak Acad.; mem. Gov. Bd. Utkal Sangeet Mahavidyalaya, Bhubaneswar; mem. various social and cultural orgs.; several awards including Padmashree (Govt. of India) 1978. *Publications:* articles in journals in India and abroad. *Address:* Plot No. 4114/A, Ashok Nagar East, Unit II, Bhubaneswar 751009, Orissa, India.

PANIKKAR, Raimon, PH.D., TH.D.; Indian academic and author; b. 3 Nov. 1918, Barcelona, Spain; s. of Ramuni Panikkar and Carme Panikkar; ed.

Univs. of Barcelona, Madrid, Bonn, Rome (Lateran), Mysore and Varanasi; Prof. of Indian Culture and Comparative Cultures, Theological Seminary Madrid 1946–51; Prof. of Religious Sociology, Inst. of Social Science Leon XIII, Madrid 1950–51; Prof. of Philosophy of History, Univ. of Madrid 1952–53; Prof. of Religious Sociology, Int. Univ. for Social Studies, Rome 1962–63; Visiting Prof. Harvard Univ. 1967–71, Univ. of Montreal 1968, Union Theological Seminary, New York 1970; Hon. Prof. United Theological Coll. Bangalore 1970; Prof. of Comparative Philosophy of Religion, Univ. of Calif. Santa Barbara 1971–86, now Prof. Emer.; Premio Español de Literatura 1961. *Publications:* author of 31 books. *Leisure interests:* reading, walking. *Address:* 900 Hot Springs Road, Santa Barbara, Calif. 93108-1111, U.S.A. *Telephone:* 805-969-0090.

PANNENBERG, Wolfhart Ulrich, DR. THEOL.; German professor of systematic theology; b. 2 Oct. 1928, Stettin; s. of Kurt B. S. Pannenberg and Irmgard Pannenberg; m. Hilke S. Schütte 1935; ordained as Lutheran Minister 1955; Privatdozent, Heidelberg 1955; Prof. of Systematic Theology, Wüppertal 1958, Univ. of Mainz 1961, Univ. of Munich 1967–; Head, Inst. of Ecumenical Theology, Munich; mem. Bavarian Acad. of Sciences; Hon. D.D. (Glasgow, Manchester, Trinity Coll. Dublin). *Publications:* What is Man? 1962, Jesus: God and Man 1968, Revelation as History 1969, Theology and the Kingdom of God 1969, Basic Questions in Theology (Vol. I) 1970, (Vol. II) 1971, The Apostle's Creed 1972, Theology and the Philosophy of Science 1976, Human Nature, Election and History 1977, Anthropology in Theological Perspective 1985. *Leisure interests:* history, music, philosophy. *Address:* Sudetenstrasse 8, 8032 Gräfeling, Federal Republic of Germany. *Telephone:* (089) 85 50 15.

PANNI, Marcello; Italian composer and conductor; b. 24 Jan. 1940, Rome; s. of Arnaldo and Adriana Cortini; m. Jane Colombier 1970; one d.; ed. Accademia di Santa Cecilia, Rome under Goffredo Petrassi and Conservatoire Nat. Superieur, Paris; conducting debut, Festival of Contemporary Music, Venice 1969; has since achieved renown in field of avant-garde music conducting first performances of works by Berio, Bussotti, Cage, Feldman, Donatoni, Clementi, Sciarrino, Pennisi, Vandor, Ferrero and others at all major European festivals and for Italian Radio; regular guest conductor for Accademia di Santa Cecilia, the four Italian radio orchestras and other Italian Orchestras performing full range of baroque, classical and modern works; opera debut with The Barber of Seville, Hamburg 1977 and has since conducted opera in all the principal opera houses in Europe; American debut with Elisir d'amore, Metropolitan Opera, New York 1988; conducted world premiere of Bussotti's Cristallo di Rocca (opera) at La Scala 1983; Milhaud Prof. of Composition and Conducting, Mills Coll., Oakland, Calif. *Works include* symphonic and chamber music and music for experimental theatrical works. *Leisure interests:* arts, sport. *Address:* 3 Piazza Borghese, 00186 Rome, Italy. *Telephone:* 06/6873617

PANOFSKY, Wolfgang Kurt Hermann, A.B., PH.D.; American scientist; b. 24 April 1919, Berlin, Germany; s. of Erwin Panofsky and Dorothea Mosse Panofsky; m. Adele Dumond 1942; three s. two d.; ed. Princeton Univ. and California Inst. of Tech.; in U.S.A. 1934–; mem. of staff Radiation Laboratory, Calif. Univ. 1945–51; Asst. Prof. 1947–48, Assoc. Prof. 1948–51; Prof. Stanford Univ. 1951–, Dir. High Energy Physics Laboratory 1953–61, Dir. Linear Accelerator Center 1962–84, Dir. Emer. 1984–; Consultant Office of Science and Tech., Exec. Office of Pres. 1965–; Consultant, Arms Control and Disarmament Agency 1968–81; mem. President's Science Advisory Cttee. 1960–64; mem. Panel Office of Science and Tech. Policy 1977–; mem. N.A.S., American Physical Soc. (Vice-Pres. 1974), American Acad. of Arts and Sciences; Hon. D.Sc. (Case Inst. of Tech., Univ. of Saskatchewan, Columbia Univ.); Dr. h.c. (Univ. of Princeton) 1983; Officier, Légion d'honneur; Lawrence Prize, U.S. Atomic Energy Comm. 1961; Calif. Scientist of Year Award 1967; Nat. Medal of Science 1969, Franklin Medal 1970; Enrico Fermi Award, Dept. of Energy 1979; Shoong Foundation Award for Science 1983. *Leisure interest:* music. *Address:* Stanford Linear Accelerator Center, Stanford University, P.O. Box 4349, Stanford, Calif. 94305 (Office); 25671 Chapin Avenue, Los Altos Hills, Calif. 94022, U.S.A. (Home). *Telephone:* 854-3300.

PANSA CEDRONIO, Paolo, LL.D., LIC.POL.SC.; Italian diplomatist; b. 15 Nov. 1915, Naples; s. of Ciro Pansa Cedronio and Elina Stammelluti; ed. Univs. of Naples and Florence; entered Italian diplomatic service 1940; Sec., Italian Embassy, Washington 1945–49; Sec., Italian Del. to NATO, London and Paris 1951–55; Head of Service, Ministry of Foreign Affairs, Rome 1955–61; Minister, Italian Embassy, London 1961–66; Amb. to Chile 1966–70, to Canada 1970–71; Deputy Sec.-Gen. NATO 1971–78; Amb. to U.S.A. 1978–81; Vice-Pres. and mem. Cttee. of Patrons, Atlantic Treaty Assen., Paris; alt. Pres. NATO Appeals Bd., Brussels; mem. Consiglio del Contenzioso Diplomatico, Ministry of Foreign Affairs, Rome; Circolo Studi Diplomatici, Rome; Croce di Guerra, Cavaliere di Gran Croce al Merito della Repubblica Italiana, Gran-Cruz Orden al Mérito de Chile, Officier, Légion d'honneur, etc. *Address:* Palazzo Borghese, Largo Fontanella Borghese, Rome 00186, Italy.

PANT, Apasaheb Balasaheb; Indian politician and diplomatist (retd.); b. 11 Sept. 1912, Aundh, Satara District, Maharashtra; s. of Balasaheb Pant (Raja of Aundh) and Mainabai Pant Pratinidhi; m. Nalini Natesh Dravi 1942; two s. one d.; ed. Univs. of Bombay and Oxford, and Lincoln's Inn, London; fmr. Minister of Educ., Aundh State, Prime Minister 1938–44,

Minister 1944-48; mem. All-India Congress Cttee. 1948; Commr. for Govt. of India, British E. Africa 1948-54, concurrently Consul-Gen. in Belgian Congo and Ruanda Urundi 1948-54, concurrently Commr. in Cen. Africa and Nyasaland 1950-54; Officer on Special Duty, Ministry of External Affairs, New Delhi 1954-55; Political Officer, Sikkim and Bhutan, with control over Indian missions in Tibet 1955-61; Amb. to Indonesia 1961-64, to Norway 1964-66, to U.A.R. 1966-69; High Commr. in U.K. 1969-72; Amb. to Italy and High Commr. in Malta 1972-76; Del. to UN Gen. Ass. 1951, 1952, 1965; Padma Shri 1954; Fellow Indian Inst. of Advanced Studies. *Publications include:* Tensions and Tolerance 1965, Aggression and Violence: Ghandian Experiments to Fight Them 1968, Yoga 1968, Surya Namaskar 1969, A Moment in Time 1973, Mandala—An Awakening 1976, Survival of the Individual 1978, A Different Kind of King 1985, Un-Diplomatic Incidents, Story of the Pants 1985, Energy, Intelligence, Love 1986, An Unusual Raja and the Mahatma 1987. *Leisure interests:* photography, yoga, tennis, skiing, riding, archaeology, music. *Address:* Pant Niwas, Bhandarkar Road, Deccan Gymkhana, Poona 4, India. *Telephone:* 58615.

PANT, Krishna Chandra; M.SC.; Indian politician; b. 10 Aug. 1931, Bhowali, Nainital Dist.; s. of late Pandit Govind Ballabh Pant; m. Ila Pant 1957; two s.; ed. St. Joseph's Coll., Nainital, Univ. of Lucknow; Mem. Lok Sabha for Nainital 1962-77, re-elected 1978-; Minister of Finance 1967-69, of Steel and Heavy Eng. 1969-70, of Home Affairs and Head, Depts. of Science, Electronics and Atomic Energy 1970-73; Minister of Irrigation and Power 1973-74, of Energy 1974-77, 1979-80, of Educ. Jan.-Sept. 1985, of Steel and Mines 1985-87, of Defence April 1987-; First Vice-Pres. Human Rights Comm. 1966; Leader del. to Int. Conf. on Human Rights, Teheran 1968; del. to various other int. confs.; Hon. Fellow Inst. of Engineers; Hon. D.Sc. (Udaipur). *Leisure interests:* welfare work, reading, travelling, sports. *Address:* Ministry of Defence, South Block, New Delhi 110001, India.

PANT, Sumitranandan; Indian poet; b. 1900, Kausani; s. of G. Pant; Fellow of Sahitya Acad.; Padma Bhushan 1961; Jnan Pith Award 1969. *Publications:* Vina Granthi 1919, Jyotsna (drama) 1922, Pallav 1926, Vina-Gramthi 1930, Gunjan 1931, Birth of Poetry, Jyotsna (drama) 1934, Panch Kahaniyan (short stories) 1936, Uygvani-Gramya 1938, Swarana Kiran 1946, Uttara 1948, Gradya Path (essays) 1953, Atima 1955, Vani 1957, Chidambara (poetry) 1958, Kala Aur Boodhachand (Acad. Award Winner) 1959, Lokayatan (epic, Soviet Nehru Award Winner) etc. *Address:* 18/B.7, K. G. Marg, Allahabad, Uttar Pradesh, India. *Telephone:* Allahabad 3540.

PANTON, Verner; Danish architect and designer; b. 13 Feb. 1926, Gamtofte; s. of Henry and Ellen Panton; m. Marianne Pherson 1964; one d.; ed. Odense Technical School, Copenhagen Royal Acad. of Fine Arts; study in various European countries 1953-55; independent designer and architect 1955-; Visiting Prof. Industrial Design, Hochschule für Gestaltung Offenbach 1984; has designed furniture, lamps, carpets, curtains, upholstery fabrics, wall decorations etc.; buildings include cardboard house 1957, inn at Fyn (Denmark) 1958, spherical house 1960, plastic house 1960; exhbns. include Dansk Köbestaevne Exhbn. 1958, Bayer exposition ships Visiona I & II, Cologne 1968, 1970, Musée des Arts Décoratifs, Louvre 1969; interiors include hotel at Trondheim (Norway) 1960, Spiegel Publ. House, Hamburg 1969, Varna Restaurant, Aarhus 1971, Junior Casino, Goslar, Germany 1973, Gruner and Jahr Publ. House, Hamburg 1974, Circus Building, Copenhagen 1984; mem. Medlem Akademisk Arkitektforening (Denmark), Danske Arkitekters Landsforbund, Industrial Designers (Denmark), Schweizerischer Werkbund; F.R.S.A.; awards include PH Prize, Copenhagen 1967; Rosenthal Studio Prize, Germany 1967; Int. Design Award, U.S.A. 1963, 1968, 1981; Eurodomus 2, Italy 1968, Medal of Österreichisches Bauzentrum 1968, Ehrenpreis, Fourth Vienna Int. Furnishing Salon 1969, 3 Bundespreise "Gute Form", Fed. Repub. of Germany 1972, Möbelprisen 1978 (Denmark), Deutsche Auswahl 1981, 1982 (twice), 1984 (Fed. Repub. of Germany), Bundespreis "Gute Form", Fed. Repub. of Germany 1986, Sadolin Colour Prize, Denmark 1986. *Address:* Kohlenberggasse 21, 4051 Basle, Switzerland. *Telephone:* 061-23 50 70.

PANUFNIK, Andrzej; British composer and conductor; b. 24 Sept. 1914, Warsaw, Poland; s. of Tomasz Panufnik and Matylda Thonnes Panufnik; m. Camilla Jessel 1963; one s. one d.; ed. Warsaw State Conservatoire and the State Acad. of Music (with Felix Weingartner), Vienna; Conductor Cracow Philharmonic Orchestra 1945-46; Dir. Warsaw Philharmonic Orchestra 1946-47; Vice-Pres. Polish Composers' Union 1948-54; Vice-Chair. Int. Music Council of UNESCO 1950-53; settled in England 1954, naturalized British citizen 1961; Musical Dir. City of Birmingham Symphony Orchestra 1957-59; visiting conductor leading European and S. American orchestras 1947-; mainly composer since 1959; First Prize Chopin Competition 1949; Banner of Labour 1st Class 1949; State Prizewinner 1951 and 1952; Pre-Olympic Competition First Prize 1952; First Prize for Musical Composition, Prince Rainier III of Monaco 1963, Sibelius Centenary Medal 1965; Knight of Mark Twain (U.S.A.) 1966, Prix de Prince Pierre de Monaco 1983, hon. mem. R.A.M. *Compositions:* Piano Trio 1934, Five Polish Peasant Songs 1940, Tragic Overture 1942, Nocturne 1947, Lullaby 1947, Twelve Miniature Studies 1947, Sinfonia Rustica 1948, Hommage à Chopin 1949, Old Polish Suite 1950, Concerto in Modo Antico 1951, Heroic Overture 1952, Rhapsody 1956, Sinfonia Elegiaca 1957, Polonia—Suite 1959, Concerto for Piano and Orchestra 1962, Landscape

1962, Sinfonia Sacra 1963, Two Lyric Pieces 1963, Song to the Virgin Mary 1964, Autumn Music 1965, Katyń Epitaph 1966, Jagiellonian Triptych 1966, Reflections for Piano 1968, The Universal Prayer 1968-69, Thames Pageant 1969, Concerto for Violin and Strings 1971, Triangles 1972, Winter Solstice 1972, Sinfonia Concertante 1973, Sinfonia di Sfere 1974-75, String Quartet 1976, Dreamscape 1976, Sinfonia Mistica 1977, Metasinfonia 1978, Concerto Festivo 1979, Concertino 1980, String Quartet No. 2 1980, Paean for Queen Elizabeth 1980, Sinfonia Votiva 1981, A Procession for Peace 1982, Arbor Cosmica 1983, Pentasonata 1984, Bassoon Concerto 1985, Symphony No. 9 1986; Ballet Music: Elegy (N.Y. 1967), Cain and Abel (Berlin 1968), Miss Julie (Stuttgart 1970), Homage to Chopin (London 1980), Adieu (London 1980), Polonia (London 1980), String Sextet 1987, Symphony No. 10 1988. *Publication:* Composing Myself (autobiography) 1987. *Leisure interests:* travel, all arts. *Address:* Riverside House, Twickenham, Middlesex, TW1 3DJ, England. *Telephone:* 01-892 1470.

PANYARACHUN, Anand; Thai diplomatist; b. 9 Aug. 1932; s. of Phya and Khunying Prichanusat; m. M. R. Sodsee Panyarachun Chakrabandh 1956; two d.; ed. Bangkok Christian Coll., Dulwich Coll., London, and Univ. of Cambridge; joined Ministry of Foreign Affairs 1955; Sec. to Foreign Minister 1959; First Sec. Perm. Mission to UN 1964, Counsellor 1966, Acting Perm. Rep. 1967-72, concurrently Amb. to Canada; Amb. to U.S.A. concurrently Perm. Rep. to UN 1972-75, Amb. to Fed. Repub. of Germany 1977; Perm. Under-Sec. of State for Foreign Affairs 1975-76; del. to several sessions of UN Gen. Ass. and SEATO Council; Chair. Group of 77 on Law of Sea 1973; Rep. to UN Econ. and Social Council 1974-75; Chair. Thai Del. to 7th Special Session of UN Gen. Ass., Vice-Chair. Ad Hoc Cttee. 7th Special Session, Sept. 1975; Chair. Textport Int. Corpn. Ltd.; Pres. ASEAN-CCI Council 1980; Vice-Chair. Saha-Union Corpn. Ltd. 1979-; Vice-Pres. Asscn. Thai Industries; Vice-Chair. ASEAN-U.S. Business Council 1980; Dir. Sime Darby 1982-. *Leisure interests:* tennis, squash, reading. *Address:* Texport International Corporation Ltd., 32/3 Lardprao 80, Bangkapi, Bangkok, Thailand. *Telephone:* 514-0540.

PAO, Sir Yue-Kong, Kt., C.B.E., LL.D., J.P.; Hong Kong shipowner; b. 1918, Chekiang, China; s. of the late Pao Sui-Loong and Pao Chung Sau-Gin; m. Huang Sue-Ing; four d.; ed. Shanghai; Banking 1939-49; Chair. Supervisory Bd., World-Wide Shipping Group, China Capital Partners Ltd.; Chair. World-Wide Marine and Fire Insurance Co. Ltd., Hong Kong Dragon Airlines Ltd.; Dir. Hang Seng Bank Ltd., Inchcape Far East Ltd.; Adviser, The Industrial Bank of Japan Ltd.; life mem. Court, Univ. of Hong Kong; mem. Advisory Council, Nippon Kaiji Kyokai of Japan, Hon. Chair. The Wharf (Holdings) Ltd. World Int. (Holdings) Ltd.; Group Deputy Chair. Standard Chartered Bank PLC, London 1986-88; Hon. Vice-Pres. Maritime Trust of U.K.; specially elected Gen. Cttee. mem. Lloyd's, Register of Shipping; mem. Bd. of Mans. of American Bureau of Shipping, Int. Advisory Cttee., Chase Manhattan Bank, Asia-Pacific Advisory Council American Telephone and Telegraph Int., Rockefeller Univ. Council, New York; Trustee Westminster Abbey Trust, U.K.; Commdr., Nat. Order of Cruzeiro do Sul (Brazil) 1977, Order of the Sacred Treasure (Japan) 1981, Commdr., Order of the Crown (Belgium) 1982, Vasquo Nunez de Balboa (Panama) 1982. *Leisure interests:* swimming, golf. *Address:* World-Wide Shipping Group, 6th Floor, Wheelock House, 20 Pedder Street, Hong Kong. *Telephone:* 5-8423888.

PAOLETTI, Claude, PHARM.D., D.ES.SC.; French scientist; b. 26 March 1928, Paris; ed. Ecole de Santé Navale, Bordeaux; lecturer in Biochemical Toxicology, Univ. of Paris 1958; Prof. of Biochemistry and Molecular Biology, Châtenay-Malabry 1972; Dir. Pharmacology and Toxology Lab., C.N.R.S., Scientific Dir. Dept. of Life Sciences, 1988-. *Address:* Département des Sciences de la Vie, Centre National de la Recherche Scientifique, 15 quai Anatole France, 75700 Paris, France.

PAOLOZZI, Eduardo Luigi, C.B.E., R.A.; British sculptor; b. 7 March 1924, Leigh, Scotland; s. of Rudolfo and Carmella Paolozzi; m. Freda Elliot 1951; three d.; ed. Edinburgh Coll. of Art and Slade School of Fine Art, Oxford and London; first exhibitions, Mayor Gallery, London 1947, 1948, 1949; teacher of textile design, Cen. School of Art and Design 1949-55; Lecturer in sculpture, St. Martin's School of Art 1955-58; Visiting Prof. Hochschule für Bildende Künste, Hamburg 1960-62; Visiting Lecturer, Univ. of Calif., Berkeley 1968; Lecturer in Ceramics, Royal Coll. of Art 1968-; Prof. in Ceramics, Fachhochschule, Cologne 1976-81, Prof. of Sculpture at Akad. der Bildenen Künste, Munich 1981-; Prof. Master Class, Int. Summer Acad., Salzburg 1982; one-man exhbns. have included Hanover Gallery, London 1958, 1967, Betty Parsons Gallery, N.Y. 1960, 1962, Robert Fraser Gallery, London 1964, 1966, Museum of Modern Art, N.Y. 1964, Pace Gallery, N.Y. 1966, 1967, Stedelijk Museum, Amsterdam 1968, Tate Gallery, London 1971, Victoria and Albert Museum 1977, Nationalgalerie, Berlin retrospective 1975, Crawford Centre, Edinburgh 1979, Kölnischer Kunstverein, Cologne 1979, Westfaliser Kunstverein 1980, Museum für Kunst und Gewerbe, Hamburg 1982, Aedes Gallery, Berlin, Royal Scottish Acad. 1984, Lenbachhaus, Munich 1984, Museum Ludwig, Cologne 1985, Museum of Mankind, London 1986, Royal Acad., London and other galleries in U.K., U.S.A., Canada, Netherlands, Germany; has participated in numerous group exhbns. including Venice Biennale 1952, 1960, São Paulo Biennale 1957, 1963, New Images of Man, Museum of Modern Art, N.Y. 1959, 2nd 3rd and 4th Int. Biennial Exhbns. of Prints, Museum of Modern Art,

Tokyo 1960, 1962, 1964, British Art Today (travelling exhbn., tour of U.S.A.) 1962, 7th Int. Art Exhbn., Tokyo 1963, Neue Realisten und Pop Art, Akad. der Künste, Berlin 1964, Premier Bienniale Exhbn., Cracow 1966, Sculpture from Twenty Nations, Guggenheim Museum, N.Y. 1967, Pop Art Redefined, Hayward Gallery, London 1969, Expo 70, Osaka 1970, Hayward Annual Arts Council Exhbn. 1977, Jubilee Exhbn. of British Sculpture, Dovecot Studios -1980, Nat. Gallery of Scotland 1980, 20th Century British Sculpture, London 1981, West-Kunst, Cologne 1981, Innovations in Contemporary Printmaking, Oxford 1982, English Painters 1900–82, Museo Municipal of Madrid 1983, Drawing in Air—Sculptors' Drawings, Sunderland Arts Centre 1983; designed mosaics for Tottenham Court Road underground station, London; set designer for film, Herschel and the Music of the Stars 1985; Fellow, Univ. Coll. London 1986; apptd. Her Majesty's Sculptor-in-Ordinary for Scotland 1986; Hon. mem. Architectural Asscn., London; Dr. h.c. R.C.A., London; Hon. D.Litt. (Univ. of Glasgow) 1980, (Heriot-Watt Univ., Edin.) 1987, (London) 1987; British Critics' Prize 1953, Copley Foundation Award 1956, Bright Foundation Award 1960, Blair Prize, 64th Annual American Exhbn., Chicago 1961, 1st Prize for Sculpture, Carnegie Int. Exhbn., Pittsburgh 1967, Saltire Soc. Award 1981, Grand Prix d'Honneur, 15th Int. Print Biennale, Ljubljana 1983; Invited Artist, Cleveland Sixth Int. Drawing Biennale 1983. *Address:* 107 Dovehouse Street, London, S.W.3, England; Akademie der Bildenden Kunste, Akademiestrasse 2, 8000 Munich 2, Federal Republic of Germany.

PAPACONSTANTINOU, Theophylactos; Greek author and journalist; b. 1905, Monastir, Serbia; s. of Prof. Philotheos Papaconstantinou and Paraskevi Kyriakou; m. Irene Oeconomopoulou 1932; one d.; ed. Univ. of Athens; Ed. and Contrib. Great Hellenic Encyclopaedia 1928–34; Ed. and Leader-writer Mahomeni Hellas (Underground) 1942–43; Contrib. to newspapers, Anexartitos 1933–36, Proïa 1936–43, Eleftheria 1945–63, Makedonia 1958–59, Messimvrini 1963–67; Press Dir. Hellenic Information Service, Cairo 1943–44; Radio Commentator N.B.I. Athens, 1950–53, 1959–64; Under-Sec. to Prime Minister's Office 1967; Minister of Educ. 1967–69; mem. Union of Athens Daily Newspaper Journalists, Fed. Int. Journalists, Hellenic Soc. for Humanistic Studies; Athens Acad. Prize for Anatomy of the Revolution; Commdr. Royal Order of Phoenix, Kt. Commdr. of Royal Order of George I, Gold Medal of City of Athens. *Publications:* Castoria 1930, Falsifications of Marxism in Greece 1931, Introduction to Dialectics 1933, The Prussians of the Balkans 1944, Against the Current 1949, Anatomy of the Revolution 1952, Manual of the Free Citizen 1955, The New Line of Communism 1956, Ion Dragoumis and the Political Prose 1957, Anatomy of Fellow-travel 1960, Problems of Our Era 1960, Greek Philosophy 1964, The Battle of Greece 1966, 1971, Political Education 1970, The Pathology of Democracy 1981, The Great Adventure 1987, and Greek trans. of Karl Marx, Sigmund Freud, Charles Gide and Sidney Hook. *Leisure interests:* gardening, swimming. *Address:* Agias Philotheis 23, 152.37 Philothei, Athens, Greece. *Telephone:* 6810751.

PAPACOSTEA, Serban, D.HIST.; Romanian historian; b. 25 June 1928, Bucharest; s. of Petre G. Papacostea and Josefina Papacostea; ed. Univ. of Bucharest; scientific researcher and head of dept., "Nicolae Iorga" Inst. of History, Bucharest; mem. editorial bd. Revue Roumaine d'Histoire, Studii si materiale de istorie medie (Studies and Materials of Medieval History); Prize of the Roman Acad. 1971. *Publications:* Istoria României (The History of Romania), vol. III 1964 (in collaboration), Istoria poporului român (History of the Romanian People) 1970 (in collaboration), Nochmals Wittenberg und Byzanz: die Moldau im Zeitalter der Reformation 1970, Oltenia sub stăpînirea austriacă, 1718–1739 (Oltenia under Austrian Rule, 1718–1739) 1971, Venise et les Pays Roumains au Moyen Age, in Venezia e il Levante fino al secolo XV, 1973; Stephan der Grosse, Fürst der Moldau 1975; Kilia et la politique orientale de Sigismond de Luxembourg 1976, Die politischen Voraussetzungen für die wirtschaftliche Vorherrschaft des Osmanischen Reiches im Schwarzmeergebiet 1453–1484 1978; La fondation de la Valachie et de la Moldavie et les Roumains de Transylvanie 1978, "Quod non iretur ad Tanam": Un aspect fondamental de la politique génoise dans la Mer Noire au XIV-e siècle 1979, Inceputurile politicii comerciale al Tării Românești și Moldovei (The Beginnings of Trade Policy in Wallachia and Moldavia) 1983, La fin de la domination génoise à Licostomo 1985, La Valachie et la crise de structure de l'Empire Ottoman (1402-1413) 1986, La Mer Noire: du monopole byzantin à la domination des Latins aux Détroits 1988, La première crise des rapports byzantino-génois après Nymphaion: le complot de Guglielmo Guercio (1264) 1988. *Address:* Institutul de Istorie "Nicolae Iorga", Bd. Aviatorilor 1, Bucharest (Office); Caragea Vodă 19, 71149 Bucharest, Romania (Home). *Telephone:* 507391 (Office); 104455 (Home).

PAPADIMITRIOU, Yiorghos D.; Greek politician; b. 23 April, 1916, Babini, Xeromeri; active in student politics; served in Albania in second world war, wounded and decorated; with Resistance during Axis occupation, imprisoned; after war, civil servant in Ministry of Social Welfare; founder mem. Civil Servants' Supreme Exec. Cttee.; arrested and detained during mil. dictatorship; a founder mem. of PASOK; M.P., Centre Union 1963–64, PASOK 1974–77, 1981–; Minister of Transport and Communications 1986–87; Nat. Resistance Medal. *Address:* c/o Ministry of Transport and Communications, Leoforos Syngrou 49, Athens, Greece.

PAPADONGONAS, Alexandros; Greek naval officer and politician; b. 11 July 1931, Tripolis; s. of Dionisios and Vasiliki Papadongonas; m. Niki

Maidonis 1976; one s. one d.; ed. Greek Naval Acad., Naval War Coll., U.S. Naval Schools, NATO Defence Coll.; has served on Greek fleet vessels and submarines and has held staff positions; organized with other Navy officers movt. of Navy against the dictatorship; arrested May 1973 and removed from service; returned to Navy July-Nov. 1974; M.P. 1974–; Minister of Merchant Shipping 1974–77, of Communications 1977–80; mem. Council of Europe 1982; Medal of Mil. Valour, Commdr. Order of the Phoenix, Officer Order of George I; New Democracy Party. *Leisure interests:* sailing, scuba diving, underwater archaeology. *Address:* 33 Nikis Street, Athens 105 57, Greece. *Telephone:* 3255150.

PAPADOPOULOS, Achilles Symeon, C.M.G., L.V.O., M.B.E.; British diplomatist (retd.); b. 16 Aug. 1923, Palekhori, Cyprus; s. of the late Symeon Papadopoulos and Polyxene Papadopoulos; m. Joyce Martin (née Stark) 1954; one s. two d.; ed. The English School, Nicosia, Cyprus; British Mil. Admin., Eritrea 1943; with Overseas Civil Service, Cyprus 1953–59, Tanganyika 1959–61, Malta 1961–65; with British Diplomatic Service, Malta 1965, Kenya 1965; Asst. Head, UN Political Dept., FCO 1968–71; served Colombo 1971–74, Washington, D.C. 1974, Havana 1974; Amb. to El Salvador 1977–79, to Mozambique 1979–80; U.K. Mission to UN 1980; High Commr. in Bahamas 1981–83. *Leisure interests:* golf, bridge. *Address:* 14 Mill Close, Great Bookham, Surrey, KT23 3JX, England.

PAPADOPOULOS, Georgios; Greek army officer (retd.) and politician; b. 5 May 1919, Eleochorion, Achaia; brother of Konstantinos Papadopoulos (q.v.); m. Nekee Vassiliadis 1941; two c.; ed. War Acad., Artillery School, and Officers' Training School in Middle East; Second Lieut. 1940, Lieut. 1943, Capt. 1946, Maj. 1949, Lieut.-Col. 1956, Col. 1960, Brig. and retd. Dec. 1967; served on Albanian front in Greek-Italian war 1940; joined nat. resistance units during German occupation; Staff Officer 1944–45, Intelligence Officer 1945–46; Commdr. Artillery Battery 1946; Training Officer, Artillery School 1946–48; Commdr. 131st Mountain Artillery Unit 1948, 144th Mountain Artillery Unit 1948–49; then Artillery Instructor and Unit Commdr. 1949–54; Intelligence Bureau, Army Gen. Staff 1954; Chief of Staff, Artillery Div. 1955–57; Cen. Intelligence Service 1959–64; Commdr. 117th Field Artillery Unit 1964–65, First Army Force 1965–66; at Third Staff Bureau, Army Gen. Staff 1966–67; led mil. coup to overthrow govt. April 1967, Minister to Prime Minister's Office April-Dec. 1967; Prime Minister, Minister of Defence and Minister to Prime Minister's Office 1967–73, also Minister of Educ. 1969–70, of Foreign Affairs 1970–73, Regent 1972–73; Pres. of Repub. of Greece June-Nov. 1973, arrested Oct. 1974, sentenced to death for high treason and insurrection Aug. 1975 (sentence commuted to life imprisonment); Leader Nat. Political Society (EPEN) 1984–; Commdr. Royal Order of Phoenix; Medal of Mil. Merit, and numerous other medals. *Publication:* To Pistero Mas (Credo) 1968. *Leisure interests:* ancient Greek authors, book collecting, hunting, the countryside. *Address:* Kordallous Prison, near Piraeus, Greece.

PAPADOPOULOS, Konstantinos; Greek army officer and politician; b. 1921, Achaïa; brother of Georgios Papadopoulos (q.v.); ed. Army Cadet School and Higher School of Welfare; commissioned 1943, Col. 1968; Sec.-Gen. Office of Prime Minister 1968; Under-Sec. of State and Regional Gov. of Attica and the Islands 1971; Minister at Prime Minister's Office responsible for Planning 1972–73; arrested Feb. 1975, sentenced to life imprisonment for high treason and 10 years' imprisonment for insurrection Aug. 1975; Medal for Exceptional Bravery and many Greek and foreign decorations.

PAPADOPOULOS, Tassos; Cypriot politician and lawyer; b. 1934, Nicosia; m.; ed. Pancyprian Gymnasium, Nicosia, King's Coll., Univ. of London, U.K.; called to Bar at Gray's Inn 1955; practised law, Nicosia 1955–59; leading mem. EOKA during guerrilla struggle against British colonial rule; mem. del. to London Conf. negotiating Independence of Cyprus, del. to Constitutional Comm. 1959–60; interim Minister of Interior 1959–60; Minister of Labour and Social Insurance 1960–70, of Agric. and Natural Resources 1964–67, of Health 1967–70; rep. of Cyprus at several int. confs. including ILO Annual Confs., Geneva and Council of Europe meetings, Strasbourg and Paris; Parl. Leader and Spokesman of Unified Party, Deputy Pres. of House of Reps. 1970–75, Pres. of House 1976, elected only independent mem. House of Reps., for Nicosia 1976; mem. House Foreign Affairs Cttee., Chair. Standing Cttee. on Financial and Budgetary Affairs; Greek-Cypriot Rep.-Negotiator, intercommunal talks on Cyprus, and fmr. Head Greek-Cypriot Del. to meetings under UN auspices; Pres. Centre Union party. *Address:* Centre Union, 12 Diagorou Street, Nicosia, Cyprus.

PAPADOPOULOS, Yiannis; Greek politician; b. 1924, Samothrace; ed. Univ. of Athens and U.K.; active in Resistance during German occupation; practised plastic surgery, Athens 1961–64; worked in Cyprus 1964–67; joined Democratic Defence 1967, apptd. mem. Admin. Cttee., arrested, tortured and imprisoned by mil. junta 1969; after end of mil. dictatorship became a founder mem. of New Forces; elected Centre Union/New Forces M.P. 1974; unsuccessful candidate elections 1977; joined PASOK 1979, elected M.P. for Evros 1981; Minister of Northern Greece 1986–87. *Address:* c/o Ministry of Northern Greece, Odos El. Venizelou 48, Salonika, Greece.

PAPAGEORGHIOU, Panikkos; Cypriot physician and politician; b. 1946, Peya, Paphos; m. Astero Neocleous; three c.; ed. Paphos Gymnasium,

Athens Univ., Greece; specialized in cardiology, Leeds Univ. Hosp., 1970–76; pvt. practice 1979–; Minister of Health 1988–; Chair. Paphos Medical Asscn. 1982–88. *Address:* Ministry of Health, Nicosia, Cyprus.

PAPAIOANNOU, Ezekias; Cypriot politician; b. 1908, Kellaki, Limassol Dist.; ed. American Acad., Larnaca; worked in mines in Cyprus, then Greece and U.K. in labouring and driving jobs; fought with Int. Brigade, Spanish Civil War; mem. London Air Raid Precautions Service, Second World War; was Sec. Cttee. for Cyprus Affairs, London; returned Cyprus 1946; Ed. Anorthotiko Komma Ergazomenou Laou (AKEL) newspaper Demokratis, then Organizing Sec. Cen. Cttee. of AKEL; Sec.-Gen. AKEL 1949–; held in detention by British colonial authorities 1955–56; elected mem. House of Reps. for Nicosia, 1960, for Limassol 1970, 1976; AKEL Party Spokesman in House of Reps. 1960–; Chair. several parl. cttees.; mem. Nat. Council. *Address:* AKEL, 8 Akamas Street, Nicosia (Office); 8 Doiranis Street, Nicosia, Cyprus. *Telephone:* 41121, 41122 (Office); 64912 (Home).

PAPAJORGJI, Justin: Albanian diplomatist; b. 13 June 1939, Vlora; m.; two c.; with Foreign Ministry 1963–, served embassies in Cuba, Greece, and in Del. to UN Gen. Ass.; Perm. Rep. to UN 1983–86. *Address:* c/o Ministria e Punëvet të Jashtme, Tirana, Albania.

PAPALIGOURAS, Panayotis; Greek politician; b. 1917, Kerkyra; m. Andromache Koryzis; one s. one d.; ed. Univs. of Athens and Geneva; Asst. Prof. Univ. of Geneva 1941; Reserve Officer, Greek Forces, World War II; Sec.-Gen., Ministry of Supply 1945; Under-Sec. for Supply 1945; Unity Party M.P. 1946, Greek Rally M.P. 1951, 1952, Nat. Radical Union M.P. 1956, Populist Party M.P. 1958, Nat. Radical Union M.P. 1961, 1963, 1964, New Democracy Party M.P. 1974; Under-Sec. of Commerce 1952–53; Minister of Commerce 1953–54, of Co-ordination 1954–55, of Commerce and Industry 1956–58, of Co-ordination 1961–63; Gov. Bank of Greece 1974; Minister of Co-ordination and Planning 1974–77, of Foreign Affairs 1977–78; Kt. Commdr. Order of the Phoenix, Gold Cross Order of King George I, Grand Crosses of Fed. Repub. of Germany, Ethiopia, Yugoslavia, Italy, Commdr., Légion d'honneur. *Publications:* Théorie de la Société Internationale 1941. *Leisure interests:* mathematics, arts. *Address:* Karneadou 28, Athens, Greece.

PAPANDREOU, Andreas George, PH.D.; Greek educationist and politician; b. 5 Feb. 1919, Chios; s. of the late George Papandreou (fmr. Prime Minister of Greece) and Sophia (née Mineiko); m. 2nd Margaret Chant 1951 (divorced 1989); three s. one d.; ed. Athens Univ. Law School and Harvard Univ., U.S.A.; Assoc. Prof., Univ. of Minnesota 1947–50, Northwestern Univ. 1950–51; Prof. Univ. of Minnesota 1951–55; Prof., Chair. Econ. Dept., Univ. of Calif. 1955–63; Dir. Centre of Econ. Research, Athens, Greece 1961–64; Econ. Adviser, Bank of Greece 1961–62; Minister to Prime Minister, Greece Feb.-Nov. 1964; Minister of Econ. Co-ordination 1965; Deputy from Ahaia 1965–67; in prison April-Dec. 1967; Founder and Chair. Pan-Hellenic Liberation Movement 1968–74; Prof. Univ. of Stockholm 1968–69; Prof. of Econ. York Univ., Canada 1969–74; returned to Greece Aug. 1974; Founder and Pres. Panhellenic Socialist Movement 1974–; Leader of Opposition in Parl. 1977–81; Prime Minister of Greece Oct. 1981–; Minister of Defence 1981–86. *Publications:* Economics as a Science 1958, A Strategy for Greek Economic Development 1962, Fundamentals of Model Construction in Macroeconomics 1962, The Greek Front 1970, Man's Freedom 1970, Democracy at Gunpoint 1971, Paternalistic Capitalism 1972, Project Selection for National Plans 1974, Socialist Transformation 1977. *Address:* Office of the Prime Minister, Odos Zalokosta 3, Athens, Greece. *Telephone:* (21) 3231506.

PAPANDREOU, Vasso, PH.D.; Greek politician; b. 1944; ed. London and Reading Univs.; lecturer Exeter and Oxford Univs.; worked in Office for Small and Medium-sized Businesses, Athens; mem. Admin. Council, Greek Commercial Bank; fmr. Minister for Industry, Energy and Tech., fmr. Minister for Commerce; founder mem. Greek Socialist Party 1984, mem. Cen. Cttee.; Commr. for Educ., Comm. of European Communities Jan. 1989–. *Address:* Commission of the European Communities, 200 rue de la Loi, 1049 Brussels, Belgium.

PAPATHANASSIOU, Aspassia; Greek actress; b. Amphissa; m. Costas Mavromatis 1944; ed. Dramatic Art School of National Theatre of Greece; played a variety of leading roles with various Greek theatrical groups; founder-mem. Piraikon Theatre; has toured extensively in Europe and N. and S. America; appeared at Int. Festivals in Berlin, Paris, Florence and Vienna; has given over 450 performances of ancient tragedy; appeared on T.V. in England, U.S.S.R., U.S.A. and several other countries; Paris Théâtre des Nations 1st Prize; Gold Medal of City of Athens 1962; Silver Palladium Medal for best European actress 1963.

PAPIERNIK-BERKHAUER, Emile, D. EN MED., F.R.C.O.G.; French obstetrician and gynaecologist; b. 14 Feb. 1936, Paris; m. Martine Czermichow 1961; two s. one d.; ed. Univ. of Paris; Asst. Prof. Faculté de Médicine René Descartes, Paris and Maternité de Port-Royal, Paris 1966–72; Prof. of Obstetrics and Gynaecology, Univ. of Paris-Orsay and Chair. Dept. of Obstetrics and Gynaecology, Hôpital Béclère, Clamart 1972–; Dir. Research Unit 187, Inst. de la santé et de la recherche médicale (INSERM) (Physiology and Psychology of Human Reproduction) 1979–; Fellow, American Acad. of Pediatrics; Chevalier, Légion d'Honneur. *Leisure interest:* collec-

tor of contemporary painting. *Address:* Hôpital Antoine Béclère, 157 avenue de la Porte de Trivaux, 92141 Clamart, France.

PAPON, Maurice Arthur Jean, L. EN D.; French politician; b. 3 Sept. 1910, Gretz-Armainvilliers (Seine-et-Marne); s. of Arthur Papon and Marie Dussiau; m. Paulette Asso 1932; one s. two d.; ed. Lycée Louis-le-Grand, and Facultés de Droit et de Lettres, Paris; Ed., Ministry of Interior 1935–36; Attachée, Cabinet of the Under-Sec. of State 1936, Foreign Affairs 1937–39; Sec.-Gen. Gironde 1942–44; Prefect and Dir. of Cabinet of the Comm. of the Repub. of France 1944–45; Deputy Dir. for Algeria at Ministry of Interior 1946–47; Prefect of Corsica 1947–49, Constantine, Algeria 1949–51; Sec.-Gen., Prefecture of Police 1951–54, Protectorate of Morocco 1954–55; Tech. Adviser, Cabinet of Sec. of State for Interior 1956; Insp.-Gen. for Admin., E. Algeria 1956–58; Prefect of Police, Paris 1958–66; Pres., Dir.-Gen. Sud-Aviation 1967–68; elected Deputy for Cher, Nat. Ass. 1968, 1973, 1978; Pres. Ass. Finance Comm. 1972–73, Rapporteur 1973–78; Minister of the Budget 1978–81; Mayor of Saint-Amand-Montrond 1971–82; Chair. and Man. Dir. Verreries champenoises, Rheims; Hon. Prefect of Police 1972; Commdr., Légion d'honneur, Commdr., Ordre du Mérite Civil and mil. awards. *Publications:* L'ère des responsables 1954, Vers un nouveau discours de la méthode 1965, Le Gaullisme ou la loi de l'effort 1973. *Address:* Gretz-Armainvilliers, 77220 Tournan-en-Brie, France.

PAPOULIAS, Karolos; Greek politician; b. June 1929, Ioannina; m.; three d.; ed. Univs. of Athens, Munich and Cologne; mem. Cen. Cttee., PASOK 1974–, Sec. Int. Relations Cttee. 1975–; Alt. Minister of Foreign Affairs 1981–85, Minister of Foreign Affairs 1985–; Sec.-Gen. Inst. for Mediterranean Studies; Scientific Collaborator Inst. of S.E. Europe, Munich Univ., Fed. Repub. of Germany. *Publications:* a book on Greek Resistance and several articles in foreign newspapers and magazines. *Address:* Ministry of Foreign Affairs, Odos Zalokosta 2, Athens, Greece. *Telephone:* (21) 361 0581.

PAPP, Joseph; American theatre producer and director; b. 22 June 1921, Brooklyn, New York; s. of Samuel and Yetta (Miritch) Papirofsky; m. 3rd Gail Bovard Merrifield 1976; two s. three d. (from previous m.); ed. Eastern District High School, Brooklyn, Actors' Laboratory, Hollywood, Calif.; Founder Shakespeare Workshop (renamed New York Shakespeare Festival, including Delacorte Theater, Mobile Theater, Public Theater complex, with productions on Broadway and TV); Theater Constituent, Lincoln Cen. 1973–77; 114 Shakespeare productions; *other productions include:* Delacorte Theater: Electra, Threepenny Opera, The Pirates of Penzance; Mobile Theater: An Evening at New Rican Village, The Mighty Gents, Under Fire; Public Theater complex: over 250 new works, including premiere productions: Hair, No Place To Be Somebody, The Basic Training of Pavlo Hummel, Short Eyes, A Chorus Line, For Colored Girls Who Have Considered Suicide/When The Rainbow Is Enuf, Curse of the Starving Class, I'm Getting My Act Together and Taking It On The Road, A Prayer For My Daughter, The Art of Dining, Sorrows of Stephen, The Normal Heart, Cuba and his Teddy Bear; Beaumont and Newhouse Theaters (Lincoln Center): Boom Boom Room, The Taking of Miss Janie, Threepenny Opera, Streamers, The Cherry Orchard, Measure for Measure, The Colored Museum, New York 1987; *Broadway productions include:* Two Gentlemen of Verona, Sticks and Bones, That Championship Season, Much Ado About Nothing, A Chorus Line, For Coloured Girls Who Have Considered Suicide/When The Rainbow is Enuf, Runaways, The Pirates of Penzance, Plenty, The Human Comedy 1984, The Mystery of Edwin Drood, 1985, Julius Caesar 1988, Cuba and his Teddy Bear, Serious Money; *film, TV and cable productions include:* Much Ado About Nothing, Sticks and Bones, Wedding Band, Kiss Me Petruchio, The Haggadah, Alice at the Palace, The Pirates of Penzance, The Dance and the Railroad, Swan Lake Minnesota, A Midsummer Night's Dream, Rehearsing Hamlet, Plenty; mem. Nat. Screening Cttee. Fulbright-Hays Awards 1962–67, Advisory Cttee. New York Educ. Task Force on Performing Arts Centers 1962, Playwrights Nominating Cttee. Rockefeller Foundation 1971, Advisory Council on Theatre, Princeton Univ. 1977, American Theater Planning Bd. 1977, ANTA (Pres. 1969, Dir. annual award 1965), Dirs. Guild of America, Int. Theater Inst., Actors Equity Asscn., Nat. Acad. for TV Arts and Sciences; Hon. D.F.A. (Columbia Coll.) 1971, (Northwestern Univ.) 1972, (City Univ. of New York) 1974, (Villanova Univ.) 1976, (Kalamazoo Coll.) 1977, (New York and Carnegie-Mellon Univs.) 1978, (Princeton Univ.) 1979; three Pulitzer Prizes, eight Tony Awards, three New York Drama Critics' Circle Awards, three Drama Desk/Vernon Rice Awards, eight Obie Awards, the American Acad. and Inst. of Arts and Letters Gold Medal Award for Distinguished Service to the Arts 1981, numerous other awards. *Leisure interests:* music, carpentry, mowing. *Address:* New York Shakespeare Festival, 425 Lafayette Street, New York, N.Y. 10003, U.S.A.

PAPP, László; Hungarian boxer; b. 25 March 1926; s. of Imre Papp and Erzsébet Burgus; m. Erzsébet Kovács 1950; one s.; original profession mechanic; three times Olympic Champion and twice European champion; professional boxer 1956–64 and professional European Champion 1962–64; official coach with the Hungarian amateur boxing fed. 1968–; Labour Order of Merit, Sport Order of Merit, Olympic Silver Order of Merit. *Leisure interest:* angling. *Address:* Ora-utca 6, 1125 Budapest, Hungary. *Telephone:* 556-805.

PAPPALARDO, H.E. Cardinal Salvatore, D.S.T.; Italian ecclesiastic; b. 23 Sept. 1918, Villafranca; s. of the late Alfio Pappalardo and Gaetana Coco; ed. Pontifical Univ. Lateranensis; ordained Priest 1941; Counsellor, Vatican Secr. of State 1947–65; Apostolic Pronuncio, Indonesia 1965–69; Pres. Pontifical Ecclesiastical Acad., Rome 1969–70; Archbishop of Palermo 1970–; cr. Cardinal by Pope Paul VI 1973. *Address:* Arcivescovado, Via Matteo Bonello 2, 90134 Palermo, Italy. *Telephone:* 58-34-42.

PAPPENHEIMER, Alwin M., Jr., PH.D.; American biomedical research scientist; b. 25 Nov. 1908, New York; s. of Alwin M. Pappenheimer and Beatrice Leo; m. Pauline Forbes 1938; one s. two d.; ed. Harvard Coll. and Harvard Univ.; Nat. Research Council Fellow in Medicine 1933–35; Instructor in Applied Immunology, Harvard School of Public Health 1935–39; Sr. Chemist, Mass. Antitoxin Labs. 1936–39; Asst. Prof. of Biochemistry Univ. of Pa. 1939–41; Asst. Prof., Assoc. Prof., then Prof. and Chair. of Dept. of Microbiology, New York Univ. Coll. of Medicine 1941–58; Prof. of Biology, Harvard Univ. 1958–79, Emer. Prof. of Biology 1979–, Master of Dunster House 1961–70; Eli Lilly Award in Bacteriology 1942, Guggenheim Fellow 1966–67; mem. N.A.S., American Acad. of Arts and Sciences, New York Acad. of Medicine; Pres. American Asscn. of Immunologists 1954–57. *Publications:* about 150 papers and reviews in scientific journals and books. *Leisure interest:* chamber music (viola, clarinet). *Address:* The Biological Laboratories, Harvard University, 16 Divinity Avenue, Cambridge, Mass. 02138, U.S.A. *Telephone:* (617) 495-2322.

PAPPENHEIMER, John Richard, PH.D.; American professor of physiology; b. 25 Oct. 1915, New York, N.Y.; s. of Alwin M. and Beatrice L. Pappenheimer; m. Helena F. Palmer 1949; three s. one d.; ed. Harvard Coll. and Cambridge Univ., England; Demonstrator in Pharmacology, University Coll., London 1939–40; Instructor in Physiology, Coll. of Physicians and Surgeons, New York 1940–42; Fellow in Biophysics, Johnson Foundation, Univ. of Pennsylvania 1942–45; Asst. Prof. Harvard Univ. Medical School 1946–53, George Higginson Prof. of Physiology 1969–82, Prof. Emer. 1982–; Career Investigator, American Heart Asscn. 1953–; Ed. Physiological Reviews and other scientific journals; Pres. American Physiological Soc. 1964–65; Council Int. Union of Physiological Sciences 1974–; mem. American Acad. of Arts and Sciences, N.A.S.; Overseas Fellow Churchill Coll., Cambridge 1971–72; George Eastman Visiting Prof., Oxford 1975–76. *Publications:* Technical articles and reviews in physiological journals. *Leisure interest:* violoncello. *Address:* Department of Physiology, Harvard Medical School, 25 Shattuck Street, Boston, Mass. 02115, U.S.A.

PARADZHYANOV, Sergey Iosifovich; Soviet film director; b. 18 March 1924, Tbilisi; ed. Tiflis Conservatory, U.S.S.R. State Inst. of Cinematography; Dir. at Kiev Dovzhenko Studios 1952; student of Savchenko and Kuleshov; joined Aremenfilm Studios 1968; arrested 1974, sentenced to five years in labour camp, released 1978; Mar del Plata Film Festival Award, Argentina, for Shades of Forgotten Ancestors 1965. *Films include:* Andreish 1954, First Lad 1956, Ukrainian Rhapsody 1958, Flower on the Stone 1959, Shades of Forgotten Ancestors 1964, The Colour of Pomegranates 1969, The Legend of the Suram Fortress 1984.

PARAENSE, Wladimir Lobato, M.D.; Brazilian scientist; b. 16 Nov. 1914, Pará; s. of Raymundo Horminho Paraense and Maria da Costa Paraense; m. Lygia dos Reis Corrêa 1972; one d.; ed. Colégio Estadual País de Carvalho, Pará, and Univ. do Recife; Scientific Investigator, Ministry of Health, Brazil 1940–; Prof. of Protozoology, Instituto Oswaldo Cruz 1951, Inst. Nacional de Endemias Rurais 1960; Research Assoc., Serviço Especial de Saúde Pública 1954–56; mem. Pan American Health Org./WHO Working Group for Devt. of Guidance for Identification of American Planorbidae 1961–; Dir. Inst. Nacional de Endemias Rurais 1961–63; Active mem. Inst. of Malacology, Mich., U.S.A. 1963–; mem. WHO Bd. of Experts in Parasitic Diseases 1964–; Chief, Schistosomiasis Snail Identification Center for the Americas, Pan American Health Org. and Ministry of Health of Brazil 1964–; Councillor, Nat. Research Council 1968–74; Dir. Inst. of Biology, Univ. de Brasília 1968–72; Vice-Pres. (Research) Oswaldo Cruz Foundation 1976–78; mem. Soc. de Biologia do Rio do Janeiro, Soc. Brasileira para o Progresso da Ciência (Councillor 1959–), American Asscn. for Advancement of Science, Royal Soc. of Tropical Medicine and Hygiene (U.K.), Academia Brasileira de Ciências and other Brazilian socs., Soc. of Protozoologists, U.S.A., Int. Acad. of Zoology, India, Conchological Soc. of G.B. and Ireland, New York Acad. of Sciences, American Microscopical Soc.; American Malacological Union, Golfinho de Ouro, Oswaldo Cruz prizes for Scientific Achievement and several medals. *Publications:* over 130 papers on zoological, parasitological and pathological aspects of tropical medicine, chiefly malaria, piroplamosis, leishmaniasis and bilharziasis (especially molluscan intermediate hosts). *Leisure interests:* music, literature, history. *Address:* Instituto Oswaldo Cruz, Caixa Postal 926, Rio de Janeiro, Brazil. *Telephone:* (021) 280-5840.

PARAYRE, Jean-Paul-Christophe; French building and civil engineering executive; b. 5 July 1937, Lorient; s. of Louis and Jeanne (Malarde) Parayre; m. Marie-Françoise Chaufour 1962; two s. two d.; ed. Lycées in Casablanca (Morocco) and Versailles, Ecole Polytechnique, Paris, Ecole Nat. des Ponts et Chaussées; Engineer, Dept. of Highways 1963–67; Tech. Adviser, Ministry of Social Affairs 1967, Ministry of Econ. and Finance 1968; Dir. of Mech. Industries at Ministry of Industry and Research

1970–74; Chief Adviser to Pres. and Gen. Man. Banque Vernes et Commerciale 1974; Man. of Planning, Automobile Div. of Peugeot 1975; Man. Automobile Div. of Peugeot-Citroën 1976, Chair. Bd. of Dirs. Peugeot S.A. 1977–84, mem. Supervisory Bd. 1984–; mem. Supervisory Bd. Soc. Dumez 1977–84 (Dir.-Gen. 1984–, Chair. 1988–), mem. Bd. of Dirs. Crédit National 1978–, Compagnie Générale d'Electricité 1986–, Eurotunnel 1986–, Framatome 1985–, LV MH Moët Hennessy-Louis Vuitton 1987–, Valeo 1986–, Scoa 1985–; Chevalier, Légion d'Honneur, Officier Ordre nat. du Mérite. *Leisure interests:* golf, tennis. *Address:* Dumez, 345 avenue Georges Clemenceau, 92000 Nanterre (Office); 3 Rond-Point, Saint-James, 92200 Neuilly-sur-Seine, France (Home).

PARBO, Sir Arvi Hillar, Kt., B.ENG.; Australian mining engineer; b. 10 Feb. 1926, Tallinn, Estonia (now part of U.S.S.R.); s. of Aado Parbo and Hilda Rass; m. Saima Soots 1953; two s. one d., ed. Estonia, Germany and Univ. of Adelaide; joined Western Mining Corpn. Ltd. 1956, Mining Eng. 1956, Underground Man. Nevoria Mine 1958, Tech. Asst. to Man. Dir. Western Mining Corpn. 1960, Deputy Gen. Supt. W. Australia 1964, Gen. Man. Western Mining Corpn. Ltd. 1968, Deputy Man. Dir. 1970, Man. Dir. 1971–86, Vice-Chair. 1973, Chair. 1974–86, Exec. Chair. 1986–; Chair. Alcoa of Australia Ltd. 1978–; Dir. Aluminium Co. of America 1980–, Chase AMP Ltd. 1985–, Zurich Australia Insurance Group 1985–, Broken Hill Proprietary Co. 1987–; Pres. Australia-Japan Business Co-operation Cttee. 1985–; mem. Chase Manhattan Int. Advisory Cttee. 1983–. *Leisure interests:* reading, carpentry. *Address:* Western Mining Corporation Ltd., 360 Collins Street, Melbourne, Vic. 3001 (Office); Longwood, 737 Highbury Road, Vermont South, Vic. 3133, Australia (Home). *Telephone:* 602 0300 (Office); 232-8264 (Home).

PARDEE, Arthur Beck, PH.D.; American biochemist; b. 13 July 1921, Chicago, Ill.; s. of Charles A. and Elizabeth Beck; m. Ruth Sager; three s. one d.; ed. Univ. of California (Berkeley) and California Inst. of Tech.; Postdoctoral Fellow, Univ. of Wisconsin 1947–49; Instructor, Asst. and Assoc. Prof. Univ. of Calif. (Berkeley) 1949–61; Sr. Postdoctoral Fellow, Pasteur Inst. 1957–58; Prof. and Chair. Biochemical Sciences, Princeton Univ. 1961–67, Prof. of Biology 1967–75; Prof. of Biological Chem. and Molecular Pharmacology, Harvard Medical School 1975–; Chief, Cell Growth and Regulation, Dana Farber Cancer Inst. 1975–, Dir. for Tumor Biology 1977–78; Dir. American Asscn. for Cancer Research 1983–85, Pres. 1985–86; mem. Editorial Bd. Biochimica Biophysica Acta 1962–69, Proceedings of the N.A.S. 1971–74; mem. Advisory Council, American Cancer Soc., Cttee. on Science and Public Policy; Pres. Scientific Cttee. Ludwig Inst. for Cancer Research 1988–; Trustee Cold Spring Harbour Lab. 1963–69; mem. N.A.S. 1968–, American Acad. of Arts and Sciences 1963–, Councillor 1977–81; Pres. American Soc. of Biological Chemists 1980–81; Paul Lewis Award, American Chemical Soc. 1960, Krebs Medal, European Biochemical Soc. 1973, Rosenstiel Award, Brandeis Univ. 1975, 3 M Award (Experimental Biology) 1980. *Publications:* articles on bacterial physiology and enzymology in synchronous cultures, cell division cycle events, growth regulation in cancer and normal cells, enzymology of DNA synthesis, repair of damaged DNA; Experiments in Biochemical Research Techniques 1957. *Leisure interests:* music, tennis, travel, art. *Address:* Dana Farber Cancer Institute, 44 Binney Street, Boston, Mass. 02115 (Office); 30 Codman Road, Brookline Mass. 02146, U.S.A. (Home). *Telephone:* (617) 732-3372 (Office).

PÁRDI, Imre; Hungarian politician; b. 16 April 1922, Tatabánya; s. of Mátyás Párdi and Mária Miatton; m. Mária Kisfaludi 1945; one s. two d.; fmr. machine fitter; worked as Party official 1945–, fmr. Sec. Tatabánya Town, Komárom County and Veszprém County Cttees., Hungarian Socialist Workers' Party; mem. Cen. Cttee. Hungarian Socialist Workers' Party 1962–88; Chair. Nat. Planning Office 1967–73; Head Econ. Policy Dept., Cen. Cttee. of Hungarian Socialist Workers' Party 1973–75, mem. 1975–78; Labour Order of Merit, Golden Degree 1970. *Leisure interests:* reading, music. *Address:* c/o Hungarian Socialist Workers' Party, H-1387 Budapest, Széchenyi rakpart 19, Hungary.

PARDO, Arvid; Maltese diplomatist; b. 12 Feb. 1914, Rome; s. of Guido Pardo and Dagmar Julin; m. Margit Claeson 1947; two s. one d.; ed. Univ. degli Studi, Rome, and Univ. de Tours; Officer-in-Charge, UN Archives 1945–46; Dept. of Trusteeship and Information for Non-Self-Governing Territories, UN 1946–60; Secr., Tech. Assistance Bd., UN, later Deputy Resident Rep. in Nigeria and Ecuador 1960–64; Perm. Rep. of Malta to the UN 1965–71, concurrently Amb. to U.S.A. and U.S.S.R., and High Commr. to Canada; Co-ordinator Marine Programme, Woodrow Wilson Int. Centre for Scholars, concurrently Maltese Rep. to UN for Ocean Affairs, Prof. of Political Science, Univ. of S. Calif. 1975–81, of Int. Relations 1981–, Sr. Fellow Inst. of Coastal Marine Studies 1975–; Hon. D.Sc. (Univ. of Malta) 1987; Paul Hoffman Award 1982; Third World Prize 1983, Compass Int. Award, Maine Tech. Soc. (U.S.A.) 1988. *Publications:* The Common Heritage 1975, The New International Economic Order and the Law of the Sea (2nd edn. with Mrs. E. Borgese) 1977. *Leisure interests:* chess, reading. *Address:* University of Southern California, Institute of Marine Coastal Studies, University Park, Los Angeles, Calif. (Office); 900 Euclid Street, Apt. 111, Santa Monica, Calif. 90403, U.S.A. (Home).

PARDO, Luis María de Pablo; Argentine professor of law and politician; b. 15 Aug. 1914, Buenos Aires; s. of Augusto de Pablo Pardo and Luisa

Gosset; m. Aida Quinteros Sánchez de Bustamente; one s. two d.; ed. Law Faculty, Univ. de Buenos Aires, postgraduate Univ. of Georgetown (Washington, D.C.); Dir. of Courses, Law and Social Sciences Faculty, Univ. de Buenos Aires, Prof. adjunct of Int. Public Law, Faculty of Econ. Sciences 1947-51; Prof. titular of Int. Public Law, Univ. Católica, Argentina, then Prof. titular of Int. Relations 1961-; also Prof. of Int. Public Law and Int. Policy, Naval War School, and lecturer at Aeronautical Staff's Officers School 1966-; imprisoned 1951, 1952, and 1953 for anti-Peronist activities, exiled to Brazil until 1955; Minister of the Interior designate 1955; Legal Adviser to Ministry for Foreign Relations and Worship 1958-61; Rep. UN 2nd Sea Law Conf. 1960; Tech. Adviser at 5th, 6th and 7th "Reunión de Consulta" of American Foreign Ministers; Amb. to Chile 1961; Legal Adviser of Chancellery at the "Rio Encuentro" Affair; Legal Adviser of the "Tech. Argentine-Uruguayan Mixed Comm. for the Salto Grande"; Minister for Foreign Relations and Worship 1970-72; Judge adjunct of Supreme Court; Grand Cross of Orders Cruzeiro del Sur, Rio Branco (Brazil), Bernardo O'Higgins (Chile), Del Sol (Peru), Al Mérito (Ecuador), and many other decorations, incl. from German and Japanese Govts. *Publications:* manual of International Public Law for use of Navy Officers, The Geographic Position of Argentina as a Factor of its Foreign Policy 1947, The Tendency towards Federation within Interamerican Relations 1947, Dominant Economics within the International Order, Foreign Policy 1952, The Contemporary International System and Argentine International Policy 1973. *Address:* Paraná 976, Buenos Aires (Office); Avenida Quintane 325, 1014 Buenos Aires, Argentina (Home). *Telephone:* 44-43-50/42-29-80 (Office); 44-27-34 (Home).

PAREDES, Gen. Rubén Darío; Panamanian army officer (retd.); b. 1931; ed. Mil. Acad., Nicaragua; Commdr. Colon mil. zone at time of coup 1968; Minister of Agric. Devt. 1975-78; Commdr. Nat. Guard 1982-83; f. Partido Nacionalista Popular (PNP) 1983; Pres. cand. 1984. *Address:* Panama City, Panama.

PAREKH, Hasmukh, B.A., B.SC.; Indian investment broker; b. 10 March 1911, Surat; ed. Bombay Univ. and London School of Econs.; worked as stockbroker with leading Bombay firm 1936-56; Deputy Gen. Man. Industrial Credit and Investment Corpn. of India 1958-68, Deputy Chair., Man. Dir. 1968-71, Chair., Man. Dir. 1972-73, Exec. Chair. 1973-78; Chair. Housing Devt. Finance Corpn. Oct. 1977-; Chair. Thomas Cook (India) Ltd.; Vice-Chair. Hindustan Oil Exploration Co. Ltd. *Publications:* The Bombay Money Market 1953, The Future of Joint Stock Enterprise in India 1958, India and Regional Development 1969, Management of Industry in India. *Leisure interests:* reading, light music. *Address:* Housing Development Finance Corporation, 169 Backbay Reclamation, Bombay 400 020 (Office); Rasik Nivas No. 1, French Road, Chowpatty, Bombay 400 007, India (Home). *Telephone:* 223725 (Office); 8110149 (Home).

PARGETER, Edith, B.E.M.; British author; b. 28 Sept. 1913, Hordley, Horsehay Shrop.; d. of Edmund Pargeter and Edith Pargeter; unmarried; ed. Church of England Primary School, Dawley, Coalbrookdale High School for Girls; Chemist's Asst. and dispenser; began writing novels 1936; Edgar Award (Mystery Writers of America) 1962, Silver Dagger of Crime Writers Asscn. 1980. *Publications:* Hortensius, Friend of Nero 1936, Iron-Bound 1936, The City Lies Foursquare 1939, Ordinary People 1941, She Goes to War 1942, The Eighth Champion of Christendom 1945, Reluctant Odyssey 1946, Warfare Accomplished 1957, By Firelight 1948, The Fair Young Phoenix 1948, The Coast of Bohemia 1950, Lost Children 1951, Fallen into the Pit 1951, Holiday with Violence 1952, This Rough Magic 1953, Most Loving Mere Folly 1953, The Soldier at the Door 1954, A Means of Grace 1956, The Assize of Dying (short stories) 1958, The Heaven Tree 1960, The Green Branch 1962, The Scarlet Seed 1963, The Lily Hand (short stories) 1965, A Bloody Field by Shrewsbury 1972, Sunrise in the West 1974, The Dragon at Noonday 1975, The Hounds of Sunset 1976, Afterglow and Nightfall 1977, The Marriage of Meggotta 1979; mystery novels under *pseudonym* Ellis Peters: Death Mask 1959, The Will and the Deed 1960, Death and the Joyful Woman 1961, Funeral of Figaro 1962, Flight of a Witch 1964, A Nice Derangement of Epitaphs 1965, The Piper on the Mountain 1966, Black is Widow's Tale 1968, The House of Green Turf 1969, Mourning Raga 1969, The Knocker on Death's Door 1970, Death to the Landlords 1972, City of Gold and Shadows 1973, The Horn of Roland 1974, Never Pick Up Hitch-Hikers! 1976, A Morbid Taste for Bones 1977, Rainbow's End 1978, One Corpse Too Many 1979, Monk's Hood 1980, Saint Peter's Fair 1981, The Leper of Saint Giles 1981, The Virgin in the Ice 1982, The Sanctuary Sparrow 1983, The Devil's Novice 1983, Dead Man's Ransom 1984, The Pilgrim of Hate 1984, An Excellent Mystery 1985, The Raven in the Foregate 1986, The Rose Rent 1986; numerous trans. of works by Czech authors. *Leisure interests:* literature, music (especially voice and all early music, sacred and secular). *Address:* Parkville, Park Lane, Madeley, Telford, Salop, TF7 5HF, England.

PARK, Charles Rawlinson, A.B., M.D.; American professor of physiology; b. 1916, Baltimore, Md.; s. of Edwards A. Park and Agnes Bevan Park; m. Jane Harting 1953; one s.; ed. Harvard Coll. and Johns Hopkins School of Medicine; Intern in Medicine, Johns Hopkins 1942; Asst. Resident then Chief Resident, Harvard 1943-44; U.S. army 1944-47; Welch Fellow in Biochemistry, Wash. Univ. 1947-52; Prof. of Physiology and Chair. of Dept., Vanderbilt School of Medicine 1952-84, Prof. of Molecular Physiology

and Biophysics, Emer. 1984-; mem. Bd., Life Insurance Fund, Howard Hughes Medical Inst. 1964-84, Juvenile Diabetes Foundation, Int. Inst of Cellular and Molecular Pathology, Nat. Inst. of Heart, Lung and Blood (Nat. Insts. of Health); mem. Editorial Bd., Journal of Biological Chem.; mem. American Physiological Soc., American Soc. of Biological Chemists, American Soc. of Clinical Investigation (Vice-Pres. 1961), Asscn. of American Physicians, N.A.S.; Banting Medal for Research, American Diabetes Asscn. *Publications:* approx. 120 scientific papers in journals of biochemistry and physiology 1942-; major topics concern action of hormones, diabetes, metabolic regulation, sugar and fat transport into mammalian cells. *Leisure interests:* music, reading, outdoor sports. *Address:* Department of Molecular Physiology and Biophysics, Vanderbilt School of Medicine, Nashville, Tenn. 37232; 5325 Stanford Drive, Nashville, Tenn. 37215, U.S.A. (Home). *Telephone:* (615) 322-7000 (Office); (615) 385-1237 (Home).

PARK, Dame Merle Florence, D.B.E.; British ballerina; b. 8 Oct. 1937, Salisbury, Rhodesia (now Harare, Zimbabwe); m. 1st James Monahan, C.B.E. 1965 (divorced 1970; died 1985); one s.; m. 2nd Sidney Bloch 1971; one s.; ed. Elmhurst Ballet School and Royal Ballet School; joined Royal Ballet 1954; first solo role 1955; opened own ballet school 1977; Dir. Royal Ballet School Sept. 1983-; Prin. Royal Ballet; repertoire includes Façade, Coppelia, Sleeping Beauty, La Fille Mal Gardée, Giselle, Les Sylphides, The Dream, Romeo and Juliet, Triad, The Nutcracker, La Bayadère, Cinderella, Shadow Play, Anastasia, Pineapple Poll, Swan Lake, The Firebird, Walk to the Paradise Garden, Dances at a Gathering, Shadow, Don Quixote, Deux Pigeons, Serenade, Scène de Ballet, Wedding Bouquet, Les Rendezvous, Mirror Walkers, Symphonic Variations, Daphnis and Chloë, Serenade, In the Night, Laurentia, Mamzelle Angot, Manon, Apollo, Flower Festival, Le Corsaire, The Moor's Pavane, Aureole, Elite Syncopations, Lulu, The Taming of the Shrew, Mayerling, Birthday Offering, La Fin du Jour, Adieu, Isadora, etc.; Adelaine Genée Medal, Queen Elizabeth Award, Royal Acad. of Dancing 1982 and many other certificates and medals. *Leisure interests:* travel, lying in the sun, listening to music. *Address:* c/o Royal Ballet School, 144 Talgarth Road, London, W.14, England.

PARK CHOONG-HOON, Maj.-Gen.; Korean air force officer and politician; b. 19 Jan. 1919, Cheju-Do Prov.; s. of Park Chong-Sil; m. Chung Kyungsook 1943; two s. four d.; ed. Doshisha Commercial Coll., Japan; Trade Affairs Dir. of Minister of Commerce and Industry, Repub. of Korea 1948; retired as Air Force Maj. Gen. 1961; Vice-Minister of Commerce and Industry 1961, Minister of Commerce and Industry 1963; Deputy Premier and Minister of Econ. Planning 1967-69; Prime Minister May-Sept. 1980, Acting Pres. Aug.-Sept. 1980; Standing mem. Econ. and Scientific Council 1970-71; Chair. AIRC 1971-73, Korean Traders' Asscn., Naeoe Business Journal (daily), Korea Industrial Devt. Research Inst. 1980-; Pres. Trade Press 1973-; Chair. Korea-Saudi Arabia Econ. Co-operation Cttee. 1974-, Korea-U.S. Econ. Council 1974-80; mem. Advisory Council of State Affairs Jan. 1981-. *Leisure interest:* golf. *Address:* 1-36, Seongbuk-dong, Seongbuk-ku, Seoul, Republic of Korea. *Telephone:* 762-2750.

PARK KYUNG WON, M.A.; Korean civil servant; b. 3 Jan. 1923, Julanam-Do; s. of Park Young Chlin and Chung Dong Rae; m. Ko Kum Ok 1946; two s.; ed. U.S. Army Artillery School, Republic of Korea Command and Gen. Staff Coll., Nat. Defence Coll. and Dankuk Univ.; Minister of Home Affairs 1962-63, 1968-71, 1974-76; Dir. of Joint Staff, Rep. of Korea 1963-65, Commdg. Gen. 2nd Army 1965-66; Minister of Communication 1966-67, of Transport 1967-68; Sec.-Gen. People's Council for Nat. Unification 1972-74; Congress rep. for Yong San and Mapoku 1978-80; Chair. of Korean Coal Mines 1972; various mil. and civil awards. *Leisure interests:* golf, judo, Igo. *Address:* 11-347 Han Nam Dong, Yong San Ku, Seoul, Republic of Korea. *Telephone:* 793-0010, 793-0100.

PARK SUNG SANG, M.A.; Korean economist; b. 12 Oct. 1923, Kyungsang-bukdo; s. of late Soon Young Park and Nan Kyo Chung; m. Chang Sook Kim 1947; one s. two d.; ed. Kukmin Univ. and American Univ. Grad. School; Asst. Gov. Bank of Korea 1972-76; Deputy Pres. Small and Medium Industry Bank 1976-80, Pres. 1980-81; Pres. Korea Int. Econ. Inst. Oct.-Nov. 1981, Korea Scientific and Technological Information Center 1981-82, Korea Inst. for Industrial Econs. and Tech. 1982-83; Chair. and Pres. Export-Import Bank of Korea 1983-86; Gov. Bank of Korea 1986-88; Pres. Korea Inst. for Industrial Econs. and Tech. July 1988-. *Publication:* Growth and Development 1985. *Leisure interest:* golf. *Address:* Korea Institute for Industrial Economics and Technology, 206-9, Cheonryangri-dong, Dongdaemun-ku, Seoul (Office); No. 1-103 Hanshinbang-bae Villa, Socho-ku, Seoul, Republic of Korea (Home). *Telephone:* 966-6501 (Office); 533-1477 (Home).

PARKER, Alan William; British film director and writer; b. 14 Feb. 1944, London; s. of William Parker and Elsie Parker; m. Annie Inglis 1966; three s. one d.; ed. Owen's School, Islington, London; Advertising Copywriter 1965-67; TV Commercials Dir. 1968-78; wrote screenplay Melody 1969; *wrote and directed:* No Hard Feelings 1972, Our Cissy 1973, Footsteps 1973, Bugsy Malone 1975; *directed:* The Evacuees 1974, Midnight Express 1977, Fame 1979, Shoot the Moon 1981, The Wall 1982, Birdy 1984, A Turnip Head's Guide to the British Cinema 1985, Angel Heart 1987, Mississippi Burning 1988, Les Misérables 1989; Vice-Chair. Dirs.' Guild of G.B. 1982-; mem. British Screen Advisory Council 1985-; British

Acad. of Film and TV Arts Michael Balcon Award for Outstanding Contrib. to British Film, Nat. Review Bd. Best Dir. Award for Mississippi Burning 1988. *Publications:* (novels) Bugsy Malone 1976, Puddles in the Lane 1977; (cartoon) Hares in the Gate 1983. *Leisure interest:* cartooning. *Address:* Judy Scott-Fox, William Morris Agency, 151 El Camino Drive, Beverly Hills, Calif. 90212, U.S.A.

PARKER, Eric Wilson, F.C.A., F.R.S.A.; British business executive; b. 8 June 1933; s. of Wilson Parker and Edith Gladys Wellings; m. Marlene Teresa Neale 1955; two s. two d.; ed. The Priory Grammar School for Boys, Shrewsbury; articled clerk with Wheeler, Whittingham & Kent, Shrewsbury 1950–55; nat. service, Pay Corps 1956–58; Taylor Woodrow Group 1958–64; joined Trafalgar House Group 1965, Finance/Admin. Dir. 1969, Deputy Man. Dir. 1973, Group Man. Dir. 1977, Dir. Associated Container Transportation (Australia) 1983–, Group Chief Exec. 1983–; Non-Exec. Dir. Sealink UK Ltd. 1979–81, British Rail Investments Ltd. 1980–84, Evening Standard Co. Ltd. 1982–85, Touche Remnant Holdings Ltd. 1985–, European Assets Trust NV 1972–85, Metal Box PLC 1985–, Automobile Proprietary Ltd. 1986–. *Leisure interests:* golf, horse racing, wines. *Address:* Trafalgar House, 1 Berkeley Street, London, W1A 1BY (Office); Nower Hayes, The Drive, Tyrrell's Wood, Leatherhead, Surrey, KT22 8QW, England (Home).

PARKER, Eugene N., PH.D.; American physicist; b. 10 June 1927, Houghton, Mich.; s. of Glenn H. Parker and Helen M. Parker; m. Niesje Meuter 1954; one s. one d.; ed. Mich. State Univ. and Calif. Inst. of Tech.; Instructor, Dept. of Mathematics and Astronomy, Univ. of Utah 1951–53, Asst. Prof., Dept. of Physics 1953–55; at Univ. of Chicago 1955–, Prof. Dept. of Physics 1962–, Prof. Dept. of Astronomy 1967–; mem. N.A.S. 1967–, Norwegian Acad. of Sciences 1988–; Hon. D.Sc. (Michigan State Univ.) 1975; Dr. h.c. (Utrecht) 1986; Space Science Award, American Inst. of Aeronautics and Astronautics 1964, John Adam Fleming Award, American Geophysical Union 1968, Henryk Arctowski Medal, Nat. Acad. of Sciences 1969, Henry Norris Russell Lecture, American Astronomical Soc. 1969, George Ellery Hale Award, Solar Physics Div. American Astronomical Soc. 1978, Sydney Chapman Medal, Royal Astronomical Soc. 1979, Distinguished Alumnus Award, Calif. Inst. of Tech. 1980, James Arthur Prize Lecture, Harvard Smithsonian Center for Astrophysics 1986. *Publications:* Interplanetary Dynamical Processes 1963, Cosmical Magnetic Fields 1979. *Leisure interests:* hiking, history, wood-carving. *Address:* Laboratory for Astrophysics and Space Research, University of Chicago, 933 East 56th Street, Chicago, Ill. 60637 (Office); 1323 Evergreen Road, Homewood, Ill. 60430, U.S.A. (Home). *Telephone:* (312) 798-3497 (Home).

PARKER, Franklin, B.A., M.S., ED.D.; American writer and educationalist; b. 2 June 1921, New York; m. Betty June Parker 1950; ed. Berea Coll., Ky., Univ. of Illinois, Peabody Coll. Vanderbilt Univ., Nashville, Tenn.; Librarian and Speech Teacher, Ferrum Jr. Coll., Va. 1950–52; Belmont Coll., Nashville, Tenn. 1952–54, Peabody Coll. Vanderbilt Univ. 1955–56; Assoc. Prof. of Educ., State Univ. Coll., New Paltz, N.Y. 1956–57, Univ. of Tex. 1957–64; Prof., Univ. of Okla. 1964–68; Benedum Prof. of Educ., West Va. Univ., Morgantown 1968–86; Distinguished Prof., Center for Excellence in Educ. 1986–; several visiting professorships; Sr. Fulbright Research Scholar, Zambia 1961–62; Distinguished Alumnus Award, Peabody Coll., Vanderbilt Univ. 1970. *Publications include:* African Development and Education in Southern Rhodesia 1960, Government Policy and International Education 1965, Church and State in Education 1966, Strategies for Curriculum Change: Cases from 13 Nations 1968, International Education: Understandings and Misunderstandings 1969, George Peabody, A Biography 1971, American Dissertations on Foreign Education: Abstracts of Doctoral Dissertations (19 vols.) 1971–85, What We Can Learn From China's Schools 1977, Education in Puerto Rico and of Puerto Ricans in the U.S.A. Vol. 1 1978, Vol. 2 1984, British Schools and Ours 1979, Women's Education (2 vols.) 1979–81, U.S. Higher Education: Guide to Information Sources 1980, Education in the People's Republic of China, Past and Present: Annotated Bibliography 1986, Education in England and Wales, Past and Present: Annotated Bibliography 1989, many articles, contributions to encyclopedias. *Address:* College of Education and Psychology, Western Carolina University, Cullowhee, N.C. 28723, U.S.A. *Telephone:* (704) 227-7311.

PARKER, Jack Steele; American business executive; b. 6 July 1918, Palo Alto, Calif.; s. of William L. and Mary I. (Steele) Parker; m. Elaine Simons; one d.; ed. Stanford Univ.; fmrly. associated with Western Pipe and Steel Co. of Calif. and Todd Shipyards; Asst. Chief Engineer American Potash and Chemical Co. 1946–50; joined Gen. Electric Co. 1950; Gen. Man. Aircraft Gas Turbine Div. 1955; Vice-Pres. 1956, in charge of Relations Services 1957; Vice-Pres. and Group Exec., Aerospace and Defense Group 1961; Exec. Vice-Pres. and mem. Pres.'s Office Jan. 1968; Dir., Vice-Chair. of Bd. and Exec. Officer, Gen. Electric Co. 1968–80; Dir. Southern Pacific Co., Continental Group, J. G. Boswell Co., Utah International Inc., TRW Inc., Trans World Airways; Assoc. Fellow, Royal Aeronautical Soc.; Fellow, A.I.A.A., American Soc. of Mechanical Engineers; mem. Bd. of Govs. and Exec. Cttee., Aerospace Industries Assen.; Trustee, Rensselaer Polytechnic Inst., Grand Cen. Art Galleries, African Wildlife Leadership Foundation; Chair. Wildlife Man. Inst.; mem. Advisory Council, Stanford Univ.

Grad. School of Business, Bd. of Overseers Hoover Inst. on War; Fellow, Inst. of Judicial Admin.; Life Councillor Conf. Bd. *Address:* 3135 Easton Turnpike, Fairfield, Conn. 06431 (Office); Round Hill Club Road, Greenwich, Conn. 06830, U.S.A.

PARKER, John Havelock, O.C., B.SC.; Canadian government official; b. 2 Feb. 1929, Didsbury, Alberta; s. of late Bruce T. and Rose H. Parker; m. Helen A. Panabaker 1955; one s. one d.; ed. Didsbury High School and Univ. of Alberta; Geologist and Man. Eng. Norman W. Byrne, Consulting Engineer, Uranium City, Sask. 1951–54; Geological Eng. and Man. Rayrock Mine, Yellowknife, Northwest Territories 1954–56; Chief Eng. Norman W. Byrne Ltd., Yellowknife 1956–64; Pres. Precambrian Mining Services Ltd., Yellowknife 1964–67; Deputy Commr. of Northwest Territories 1967–79, Commr. 1979–; mem. Canadian Inst. of Mining and Metallurgy, Professional Engs. of Alberta; Vice-Chair. Alberta/N.W.T. Bd., Duke of Edin.'s Award in Canada; mem. Senate, Univ. of Alberta; Patron, Tree of Peace, Yellowknife; Vice-Prior St. John Ambulance for N.W.T.; Kt. Order of St. John. *Leisure interests:* gardening, boating, cross country skiing, collecting northern art and sculpture. *Address:* Executive Offices, Government of the Northwest Territories, Yellowknife, N.W.T. X1A 2L9 (Office); 4912 52 Street, Box 878, Yellowknife, N.W.T. X1A 2N6, Canada (Home). *Telephone:* (403) 873 7400 (Office); (403) 873 4879 (Home).

PARKER, Sir Karl Theodore, Kt., C.B.E., M.A., PH.D., F.B.A.; British art historian; b. 1895; s. of the late R. W. Parker and Marie Luling; m. Audrey James (died 1976); two d.; ed. Bedford, Paris, Zürich; studied Continental art centres and British Museum; Ed. Old Master Drawings since inception 1926; fmr. Asst. Keeper Dept. of Prints and Drawings, British Museum; Keeper Dept. of Fine Art, Ashmolean Museum, Oxford 1934–35; Keeper of the Ashmolean Museum 1945–62 (retd.); Trustee, Nat. Gallery 1962–69; Hon. Antiquary to the Royal Acad.; Hon. Fellow Oriel Coll., Oxford; Hon. D.Litt. (Oxford) 1972. *Publications:* North Italian Drawings of the Quattrocento, Drawings of the Early German Schools, Alsatian Drawings of the XV and XVI Centuries, Drawings of Antoine Watteau, Catalogue of Drawings in the Ashmolean Museums (Vol. I 1938, Vol. II 1956), Holbein's Drawings at Windsor Castle 1945, The Drawings of Antonio Canaletto in Windsor Castle 1948, Antoine Watteau: Catalogue Complet de son Oeuvre dessiné Vol. I (with J. Mathey) 1957, Vol. II 1958. *Address:* 4 Saffrons Court, Compton Place Road, Eastbourne, Sussex, England.

PARKER, Maynard Michael, M.S.; American journalist; b. 28 July 1940, Los Angeles; s. of Clarence N. and Virginia E. Parker; m. 1st Judith K. Seaborg 1965 (divorced), one d.; m. 2nd Susan Fraker 1985, one s.; ed. Burbank High School, Stanford Univ. and Columbia Graduate School of Journalism; public affairs reporter, Life magazine, New York 1963–64; Lieut., U.S. Army 1964–66; corresp., Life magazine, Hong Kong 1966–67; Saigon Bureau Chief, Newsweek 1969–70, Hong Kong Bureau Chief 1970–73; Man. Ed. Newsweek Int. 1973–75; Senior Ed., Nat. Affairs, Newsweek 1975–77, Asst. Man. Ed. 1977–80, Exec. Ed. 1980–82, Ed. 1982–; mem. Council on Foreign Relations. *Publications:* articles in journals. *Leisure interests:* reading, tennis, fly-fishing, playing with daughter and son. *Address:* Newsweek, 444 Madison Avenue, New York, N.Y. 10022, U.S.A. *Telephone:* (212) 350-4470.

PARKER, Sir Peter, Kt., L.V.O., M.A.; British business executive; b. 30 Aug. 1924, Malo-les-Bains, France; s. of late Tom Parker and of Dorothy Mackinlay Parker; m. Gillian Rowe-Dutton 1951; three s. one d.; ed. in France and China, Bedford School, London Univ., Lincoln Coll., Oxford, Cornell and Harvard Univs.; worked for Philips Electrical 1951–53; Head, Overseas Dept., Industrial Soc. 1953–54; Sec., Duke of Edinburgh Study Conf. 1954–56; Chair. Eng. Group, Booker McConnell 1957–70; mem. Org. Cttee., later of Main Board, British Steel Corpn. 1966–67; mem. Mech. Eng. EDC 1966–70; Chair. British Pump Mfrs. Assen. 1966–69; mem., later Deputy Chair. Court of London Univ. 1964–; Chair. Dillons Univ. Bookshop 1967–75, London Univ. Computing Services 1969–76, Mitsubishi Electric (UK) Ltd. 1983–; mem. British Tourist Authority 1969–75; Chair. Rockware Group Ltd. 1971–76, 1983–; Chair. Westfield Coll., London Univ. 1970–76, Econ. Devt. Cttee. for the Clothing Industry 1971–78, Landel Insurance Holdings Ltd. 1971–75, Victoria Deepwater Terminal Ltd. 1971–76, H. Clarkson (Holdings) Ltd. –1976, subsequently Vice-Chair. 1984–, Whitehead Mann Group PLC 1984, Target Group PLC 1984–87, B.I.M. 1984–86; mem. Bd. British Airways 1971–81; Dir. Int. Research and Devt. Co. Ltd. 1970–75, Renold Ltd. 1971–76, Shipping Industrial Holdings Ltd. 1971 (Chair. 1972–75), Fullemploy Ltd. 1973–76, Group 4 Securitas Ltd.; Chair. Dawnay Day Group Ltd. 1971–76, British Railways Bd. 1976–83, Oakland Devt. Capital Fund Ltd. 1985–, Parkdale Holdings PLC 1988–, Group 4 Total Security Ltd. 1988, Whitehead Rice Ltd. 1988–, Horace, Holman Group Ltd. 1988–, Art Advisers Ltd. 1988–; Chair. (non-Exec.) Evered July 1989–; Pres. British Assen. of Industrial Editors 1971–74, British Mechanical Eng. Confed. 1972–74, British Graduates Assen. Advisory Council 1972, Design and Industry Assen.; Chair. Nat. Theatre Devt. Council 1985–, Court of Govs. of L.S.E. 1988–, The Japan Festival 1991 1987–; Dimbleby Lecture (BBC TV) 1983; mem. Inst. for Social Work Training 1970–76, York and Humberside Devt. Assen. Ltd. –1976, Foundation for Man. Educ., Nat. Theatre Bd. 1986–; Trustee, British Architectural Library Trust 1984; Council mem. Museum of Modern Art, Oxford 1987–; Dir. Metropolitan Radio 1983–; Vice-Chair. Friends of the Earth

Trust Ltd. 1988, Trustees of H.R.H. The Duke of Edinburgh's Commonwealth Study Conf. (U.K. Fund); Dir. The U.K.-Japan 2000 Group; Companion and mem. Council, British Inst. of Man.; Visiting Fellow, Nuffield Coll., Oxford 1980 (Hon. Fellow); Hon. Fellow, Westfield Coll., Manchester Polytechnic, Lincoln Coll., Oxford, Soc. of Industrial Artists and Designers; Hon. LL.D. (London Univ., Bath) 1982; Hon. Dr. (Open Univ.). *Leisure interests:* rugby, swimming, theatre, browsing. *Address:* 5 Chandos Street, London, W1M 9DG, England. *Telephone:* 01-6370369.

PARKER, (Thomas) John, D.SC.(ENG.), SC.D., F.ENG.; British business executive; b. 8 April 1942, Downpatrick, Northern Ireland; s. of Robert Parker and Margaret Elizabeth Parker (née Bell); m. Emma Elizabeth Blair 1967; one s. one d.; ed. Belfast Coll. of Tech.; Ship Design Staff, Harland and Wolff PLC 1963-69, Ship Production Man. 1969-71, Production Drawing Office Man. 1971-72, Sales and Projects Dept. Gen. Man. 1972-74; Man. Dir. Austin & Pickersgill 1974-78; Bd. mem. for Shipbuilding (Marketing and Operations), British Shipbuilders 1978-80, Corpn. Deputy Chief Exec. 1980-83; Chair. and C.E.O. Harland and Wolff 1983-; Chair. Harland-MAN Engines 1983-; Bd. mem. Industrial Devt. Bd. for Northern Ireland 1983-87; Bd. mem. QUBIS 1984-; British Coal Bd. mem. 1986; Vice-Pres. Royal Inst. of Naval Architects 1985-. *Publications:* A Profile of British Shipbuilders 1979, British Shipbuilders—A Period of Constructive Change (Marintec Conf., Shanghai) 1981, The Challenge of Change in Shipbuilding Today (ICCAS '85 Conf., Trieste) 1985. *Leisure interests:* reading, music, family pursuits, ships, sailing. *Address:* Harland and Wolff PLC, Queen's Island, Belfast, BT3 9DU, Northern Ireland. *Telephone:* (0232) 458456.

PARKES, Sir Alan Sterling, Kt., C.B.E., PH.D., SC.D., F.R.S.; British biologist; b. 10 Sept. 1900, Rochdale, Lancs.; s. of E. T. Parkes; m. Ruth Deanesly 1933; one s. two d.; ed. Willaston School and Christ's Coll., Cambridge; mem. scientific staff of Medical Research Council 1932-61; Mary Marshall Prof. of the Physiology of Reproduction, Univ. of Cambridge 1961-67, Prof. Emer 1968-; Fellow, Christ's Coll., Cambridge 1961-69, Hon. Fellow 1970; Fellow, Univ. Coll., London; Chair. The Galton Foundation 1969-; Exec. Ed. Journal of Biosocial Science 1969-78, Consultant 1978-; Consultant Cayman Turtle Farm Ltd., Grand Cayman 1973-80. *Publications:* The Internal Secretions of the Ovary 1929, Marshall's Physiology of Reproduction (Editor), 4 vols. 1952-66, Sex, Science and Society 1966, Patterns of Sexuality and Reproduction 1976, Off-beat Biologist 1985, Biologist at Large 1988. *Address:* 1 The Bramleys, Shepreth, Royston, Herts., SG8 6PY, England. *Telephone:* (0763) 60159.

PARKES, Ed.; American business executive; b. 22 Nov. 1904, Bessemer, Ala.; s. of William Jay and Myra (Huey) Parkes; m. Julia Alice Washburn 1930; two d.; ed. Univ. of Arkansas; Design Engineer Ark. Power & Light Co. 1926-28; Engineer United Gas Pipe Line Co. 1928-29, Dist. Supt. 1929-30, Asst. Gen. Supt. 1930-37, Gen. Supt. Field Lines 1937-47, Vice-Pres. 1947-56, Dir. 1946-67, Pres. 1956-67; Exec. Vice-Pres. United Gas Corpn. 1955-58, Dir. 1955-68, Pres. 1958-67, Chair. of Exec. Cttee. 1967-68; Dir. American Gas Asscn. 1955-65, mem. Exec. Cttee. 1959-65; Pres. 1964; Chair. Natural Gas Reserves Cttee. 1957-69; Dir. American Petroleum Inst. 1956-63, mem. Exec. Cttee. 1963-68, Hon. Life mem. of Bd.; Dir., Chair. Exec. Cttee. Pennzoil United Inc. 1967-72; Advisory Dir. Pennzoil Co. 1972-76, Dir. Emer. 1976-; Trustee, Southwest Research Inst. 1961-70; United Fund Medallion 1966. *Leisure interest:* lapidary. *Address:* 5815 Creswell Road, Shreveport, La. 71106, U.S.A. *Telephone:* (318) 868-1370.

PARKINSON, Rt. Hon. Cecil Edward, P.C., M.A., M.P.; British chartered accountant and politician; b. 1 Sept. 1931; s. of Sidney Parkinson; m. Ann Mary Jarvis 1957; three d.; ed. Royal Lancaster Grammar School and Emmanuel Coll., Cambridge; joined Metal Box Co. as man. trainee; joined West, Wake, Price & Co. (chartered accountants) as articled clerk 1956, Partner 1961-71; f. Parkinson Hart Securities Ltd. 1967, Chair. 1967-79, Dir. 1967-79, 1984-; Dir. several other cos. 1967-79; Branch Treas. Hemel Hempstead Conservative Asscn. 1961-64, Constituency Chair. 1965-66, Chair. and ex officio mem. all cttees. 1966-69; Chair. Herts. 100 Club 1968-69; Pres. Hemel Hempstead Young Conservatives 1968-71, Northampton Young Conservatives 1969-71; contested Northampton, Gen. Election 1970; M.P. for Enfield West 1970-74, for Hertfordshire South 1974-83, for Hertsmere 1983-; Sec. Conservative Backbench Finance Cttee. 1971-72; Parl. Pvt. Sec. to Minister for Aerospace and Shipping 1972-74; Asst. Govt. Whip 1974, Opposition Whip 1974-76; Opposition Spokesman on Trade 1976-79; Minister of State for Trade 1979-81; Paymaster-Gen. 1981-83; Chair. Conservative Party 1981-83, Sec. of State for Trade and Industry June-Oct. 1983, for Energy June 1987-; Chancellor of the Duchy of Lancaster 1982-83; Leader, Inst. of Dirs. Parl. Panel 1972-79; Sec. Anglo-Swiss Parl. Group 1972-79, Chair. 1979-82; Chair. Anglo-Polish Conservative Soc. 1986-, Chemical Dependency Centre Ltd. 1986-; Dir. Babcock Int. 1984-, Jarvis (Harpenden) Holdings, Sports Aid Foundation, Counter Products Marketing, Aldenham School, Save and Prosper July 1984-, Tarmac 1984-, Sears PLC 1984-. *Leisure interests:* skiing, reading, golf. *Address:* House of Commons, London, S.W.1, England.

PARKINSON, C(yril) Northcote, M.A., PH.D., F.R.HIST.S.; British historian and author; b. 30 July 1909, Barnard Castle, Co. Durham; s. of William Edward Parkinson, A.R.C.A., and Rose Mary Emily (née Curlow) Parkinson; m. 1st Ethelwyn Edith Graves 1943 (dissolved 1949); one s. one d.; m. 2nd Elizabeth Ann Fry 1952 (died 1983), two s. one d.; m. 3rd Iris Hilda Waters 1985; ed. St. Peter's School, York, Emmanuel Coll., Cambridge, and King's Coll., London; following a period of research in London, was elected Fellow of Emmanuel Coll., Cambridge; Sr. History Master, Blundell's School, Tiverton, Devon 1937-39; Master, Royal Naval Coll., Dartmouth 1939-40; commissioned in Queen's Royal Regt. 1940 and served as O.C.T.U. instructor, instructor and staff officer attached to R.A.F. and on Gen. Staff; lecturer, Liverpool Univ. 1946; Raffles Prof. of History, Univ. of Malaya 1950-58; Visiting Prof., Illinois Univ. 1959, Visiting Prof. Univ. of Calif. 1960; Emer. fmr. Prof. Troy State Univ. of Ala.; Chair. Leviathan House (Publrs.) 1972-; Fellow of the Royal Historical Soc.; Hon. D.Litt. (Troy State); Hon. LL.D. (Maryland); Julian Corbett Prize, London Univ. *Publications:* Edward Pellew, Viscount Exmouth 1934, Trade in the Eastern Seas 1793-1813 1937, Always a Fusilier 1949, War in the Eastern Seas 1793-1815 1954, Parkinson's Law: The Pursuit of Progress 1957, The Evolution of Political Thought 1958, The Law and the Profits 1960, British Intervention in Malaya 1867-77 1960, In-laws and Outlaws 1962, East and West 1964, Ponies Plot 1965, A Law unto Themselves 1966, Left Luggage 1967, Mrs. Parkinson's Law 1968, The Law of Delay 1970, The Life and Times of Horatio Hornblower 1970, Devil to Pay 1973 (novel), Industrial Disruption (editor) 1973, Big Business 1974, The Fireship 1975 (novel), Gunpowder, Treason and Plot 1976, The Rise of Big Business 1976, Communicate (with Nigel Rowe) 1977, Touch and Go 1977 (novel), Britannia Rules 1977, Dead Reckoning 1977 (novel), Jeeves, A Gentleman's Personal Gentleman 1979, The Law, Still in Pursuit 1979, The Law of Longer Life 1980, So Near So Far 1981, The Guernseyman 1982. *Leisure interests:* painting, architecture, travel. *Address:* 36 Harkness Drive, Canterbury, Kent, CT2 7RW, England. *Telephone:* (0227) 452742.

PARKINSON, Michael; British television presenter and writer; b. 28 March 1935, Yorks.; m. Mary Heneghan; three s.; ed. Barnsley Grammar School; began career as journalist with local paper, then worked on The Guardian, Daily Express, Sunday Times, Punch, The Listener etc.; joined Granada TV as interviewer/reporter 1965; joined 24 Hours (BBC) as reporter; Exec. Producer and Presenter, London Weekend TV 1968; Presenter Cinema 1969-70, Tea Break, Where in the World 1971; hosted own chat show "Parkinson" 1972-82; Presenter TV-AM 1983-84, Give Us a Clue 1984-, All Star Secrets 1985, The Skag Kids 1985, Desert Island Discs 1986-88; columnist for Daily Mirror 1986-; Parkinson One-to-One 1987-; has worked extensively on Australian TV; f. and Dir. Pavilion Books 1980-. *Publications:* Football Daft 1968, Cricket Mad 1969, Sporting Fever 1974, George Best: An Intimate Biography 1975, A-Z of Soccer (jt. author) 1975, Bats in the Pavilion 1977, The Woofits 1980, Parkinson's Lore 1981, The Best of Parkinson 1982. *Address:* c/o I.H.G., The Pier House, Strand on the Green, London, W4 3NN, England. *Telephone:* 01-994 1444.

PARKINSON, Norman, C.B.E.; British photographer; b. 21 April 1913; m. Wenda Rogerson 1945 (died 1987); one s.; ed. Westminster School; photographer of people of all ages, horses, birds, still-life, active life, fashion, reportage and travel; has taken many official photographs of members of the Royal Family; retrospective exhbn. Nat. Portrait Gallery 1981; exhbn. of photographs, Sotheby Parke Bernet Gallery, New York 1983; retrospective exhbn. Nat. Acad. of Design, New York 1987-88, then Bradford, England, 1988; Hon. F.R.P.S.; Hon. Fellow Int. Inst. of Photography. *Publications:* Sisters Under the Skin 1978, Photographs by Norman Parkinson 1981, Fifty Years of Style & Fashion (U.S.A.), Lifework (U.K.) 1983, Would You Let Your Daughter . . . ? 1985; has contributed photographs to most of the world's leading periodicals including Vogue, Life, Look and Town & Country magazines. *Leisure interests:* pig-farming, sun-worshipping, bird-watching, breeding Creole racehorses. *Address:* Tobago, West Indies; c/o Hamilton Gallery, 13 Carlos Place, London, W.1, England.

PARNAS, Joseph, DR. MED. VET.; Danish microbiologist; b. 14 June 1909, Przemysl, Poland; s. of Leon and Etylda Parnas; m. Sophie Parnas 1937; two s.; ed. Lvov Univ.; fmr. Asst. Prof. of Scientific Inst., Pulawy; served World War II; fmr. Prof. Acad. of Medicine, Lublin; Chief, Dept. of Microbiology; Founder, Chodźko Inst. of Rural Medicine; fmr. Rector, Marie Curie Univ., Lublin; Hon. Pres. Int. Asscn. of Rural Medicine, France, Polish Soc. for Microbiology, Lublin; Fellow of Royal Soc. of Medicine, Royal Soc. of Tropical Medicine and Hygiene, London; Sec. Cttee. of Veterinary Medicine Polish Acad. of Sciences; mem. American Soc. for Microbiology, Soc. of Tropical Medicine in Antwerp, Danish Soc. for Pathology, Purkyně Medical Soc., Prague, Argentine Medical Soc., Brucellosis Cttee., Int. Asscn. of Microbiological Socs., Nature Int. Acad., Rome; Hon. mem. Danish Acad. of Postgraduate Medical Studies; adviser to the WHO; Prof. at Polish Univ. of London; Visiting Prof. Copenhagen Univ.; Prof. in State Veterinary Serum Inst. Copenhagen 1971-; lecturer, FAO Veterinary Faculty for Africans and Asians, Copenhagen; Chief Ed. Historia Medicinae Veterinariae (int.), Copenhagen; Fellow The Explorers Club, New York; Dr.med. h.c. (Purkyně Univ.), Dr.med.vet. h.c. (Brno); Charles Darwin Medal, U.S.S.R. Acad. of Sciences. W. Bieganski Medal for popularization of science, Golden Medal of Honour (Univ. N.C.); Order of Polonia Restituta, Order of Military Courage, Bundesverdienstkreuz First Class (Fed. Repub. of Germany). *Publications:* 4 books, 5 monographs and over 300 other items, including Anthropozoonoses, Brucellosis, Rural

Medicine and Hygiene, Leptospirosis, Tularemia, Contrib. to Theory of Anthropozoonoses, Colibacillosis of Newborns. *Leisure interests:* music, sport. *Address:* 27 Bülowsvej, DK-1870 Copenhagen, Denmark. *Telephone:* 95-36-32.

PARODI, Anton Gaetano; Italian journalist and playwright; b. 19 May 1923, Castanzaro Lido (Calabria); s. of Luigi Parodi and Grazia Scicchitano; m. Piera Somino 1952; two c.; ed. Università degli Studi, Turin and Genoa; journalist 1945–; professional journalist 1947–; Corresp. of Unità, Budapest 1964–; Premio nazionale di teatro Riccione 1959, 1965, Premio nazionale di teatro dei giovani 1947 and numerous other prizes. *Plays include:* Il gatto, Il nostro scandalo quotidiano, L'ex-maggiore Hermann Grotz, Adolfo o della nagia, Filippo l'Impostore, Una corda per il figlio di Abele, Quel pomeriggio di domenica, Dialoghi intorno ad un'uovo, Una storia della notte, Pioggia d'estate, Cielo di pietra. I giorni dell'Arca, Quello che dicono. *Address:* Via Benvenuto Cellini 34/7, Genoa, Italy.

PARR, Albert Eide, D.SC.; American (b. Norwegian) oceanographer and environmentalist; b. 15 Aug. 1900, Bergen, Norway; s. of Dr. Thomas Parr and Helga Eide; m. Ella Hage Hanssen 1925; two s. two d.; ed. Royal Univ., Oslo and Bergen; Asst. in Zoology, Bergen Museum 1918-19; Asst. Norwegian Bureau of Fisheries 1924-26; Asst. N.Y. Aquarium 1926; Curator Bingham Oceanographic Collection, Yale Univ. 1927-42, Asst. Prof. of Zoology 1931-37, Assoc. Prof. 1937-38, Prof. of Oceanography 1938-42; Dir. Marine Research 1937-42, Dir. Peabody Museum 1938-42; Dir. American Museum of Natural History 1942-59, Sr. Scientist 1959-68, Dir. Emer. 1968–; Trustee Woods Hole Oceanographic Inst. 1938–; Hon. Curator Peabody Museum 1975–. *Publications:* Mostly about Museums 1959, 194 articles on oceanography, biology, museums, urban environment. *Leisure interest:* the study of cities. *Address:* P.O. Box 508, Wilder, Vt. 05088, U.S.A. (Home). *Telephone:* (802) 295-6547.

PARR, Robert Ghormley, PH.D., A.B.; American educator and physical chemist; b. 22 Sept. 1921, Chicago, Ill.; s. of Leland Wilbur Parr and Grace Ghormley; m. Jane Bolstad 1944; one s. two d.; ed. Western High School, Washington, D.C., Brown Univ., Univ. of Minnesota; Asst. Prof. of Chem., Univ. of Minn. 1947-48; Asst. Prof. to Prof. of Chem., Carnegie Inst. of Tech. 1948-62, Chair. of Gen. Faculty 1960-61; Prof. of Chem. Johns Hopkins Univ. 1962-74, Chair. of Dept. of Chem. 1969-72; William R. Kenan, Jr. Prof. of Theoretical Chem. Univ. of N.C. 1974–; Guggenheim Fellow and Fulbright Scholar Univ. of Cambridge 1953-54; Sloan Fellow 1956-60; Visiting Prof. at Univ. of Ill. 1962, State Univ. of New York at Buffalo and Pa. State Univ. 1967, Japan Soc. for Promotion of Sciences 1968, 1979; Firth Prof. Univ. of Sheffield 1976; Visiting Prof. Univ. of Berlin 1977; Fellow Univ. of Chicago 1949, Research Assoc. 1957; Nat. Science Foundation Sr. Postdoctoral Fellow, Univ. of Oxford and CSIRO, Melbourne 1967-68; mem. of numerous academic and scientific socs., including A.A.A.S., American Physical Soc., American Chemical Soc., N.A.S., American Acad. of Arts and Sciences; mem. Int. Acad. of Quantum Molecular Science, Vice-Pres. 1973-79, Hon. Pres. 1979–; N.C. Inst. of Chemists Distinguished Chemists Award 1982; Dr. h.c. (Louvain) 1986. *Publications:* The Quantum Theory of Molecular Electronic Structure 1963; Density—functional theory of Atoms and Molecules 1989; more than 200 scientific articles in specialist publs., fmr. mem. Editorial Bd. numerous specialist magazines and reviews. *Address:* Department of Chemistry, University of North Carolina, Chapel Hill, N.C. 27599 (Office); 701 Kenmore Road, Chapel Hill, N.C. 27154, U.S.A. (Home). *Telephone:* (919) 929-2609 (Home).

PARRA, Nicanor; Chilean poet; b. 5 Sept. 1914, San Fabián; s. of Nicanor P. Parra and Clara S. Navarrete; m. 1st Ana Troncoso 1948; m. 2nd Inga Palmen; seven c.; ed. Univ. de Chile, Brown Univ., U.S.A., and Oxford; Prof. of Theoretical Mechanics, Univ. de Chile 1964–; has given poetry readings in Los Angeles, Moscow, Leningrad, Havana, Lima, Ayacucho, Cuzco; Premio Municipal de Poesía, Santiago 1937, 1954; Premio Nacional de Literatura 1969. *Publications:* Poetry: Cancionero sin nombre 1937, Poemas y antipoemas 1954, La cueca larga 1958, Antipoems 1958, Versos de salón 1962, Discursos (with Pablo Neruda) 1962, Deux Poèmes (bilingual) 1964, Antología (also in Russian) 1965, Antología de la Poesía Soviética Rusa (bi-lingual) 1965, Canciones Rusas 1967, Defensa de Violeta Parra 1967; Scientific Works: La Evolución del Concepto de Masa 1958, Fundamentos de la Física (trans. of Foundation of Physics by Profs. Lindsay and Margenau) 1967, Obra Gruesa 1969. *Address:* Julia Bernstein, Parcela 272, Lareina, Santiago, Chile.

PARRA HERRERA, Gen. German; Peruvian army officer and politician; ed. Escuela Superior de Guerra del Ejército del Perú; Dir. Escuela de Transmisiones del Ejército; Head of Army Communications; Dir.-Gen. for Communications, Ministry of Transport and Communications 1972-74; Dir. Cía. Peruana de Teléfonos for 5 years; Pres. Council of Admin. INICIEL, Co-operative Abraham Lincoln; Gen. Man. Indumil Peru 1982-85, Cía. Peruana de Teléfonos 1985-87; Pres. Comm. for Army History 1980-85; Minister of State for Transport and Communications 1987-89. *Address:* c/o Ministerio de Transportes y Comunicaciones, 800 Avda. 28 Julio, Lima, Peru.

PARRATT, James Roy, D.SC., PH.D., M.R.C.PATH., F.P.S., F.R.S.E.; British professor of cardiovascular pharmacology; b. 19 Aug. 1933, London; s. of James J. Parratt and Eunice E. King; m. Pamela J. Lyndon 1957; two s.

one d.; ed. St. Clement Danes Holborn Estate Grammar School, London and Univ. of London; Nigerian School of Pharmacy 1958-61; Dept. of Physiology, Univ. Coll. Ibadan, Nigeria 1961-67; Univ. of Strathclyde, Glasgow 1967–, Reader 1970, Personal Prof. 1975, Prof. of Cardiovascular Pharmacology 1983–, Head, Dept. of Physiology and Pharmacology 1986–; Gold Medal, Univ. of Szeged, Hungary. *Leisure interest:* active within Baptist denomination in Scotland and involved in Christian work among students and in Christian mission. *Address:* 16 Russell Drive, Bearsden, Glasgow, G61 3BD, Scotland. *Telephone:* 041-942 7164.

PARRAVICINI, Giannino; Italian economist and financial official; b. 3 July 1910, Castellanza (Varese); s. of Renzo and Edvige Parravicini; m. Carla Benini; two c.; ed. Univs. of Pavia, Vienna, Berlin, Paris and London; with Banca d'Italia 1935-60, latterly Chief Exec.; Chair. Bd. of Dirs. Istituto Centrale per il Credito a Medio Termino 1962-78; mem. Bd. of Dirs. EFIM and Finsider until 1975; Chair. Consiglio Tecnico Scientifico of Econ. Planning; Chair. Banco di Sicilia Jan. 1979–; teacher of financial science, Univs. of Pavia, Florence and Milan 1954-72; Prof. of Monetary and Financial Economy, Rome Univ. 1972-85, Prof. Emer. 1985–; has participated in numerous official cttees. and was charged with formation of monetary and currency system in Somalia; fmr. Head, UN Financial Office, Léopoldville (now Kinshasa, Zaire); Knight Grand Cross and Cavaliere del Lavoro. *Leisure interests:* historical and political works. *Address:* 10 Piazza Cavour, 10-00193 Rome, Italy. *Telephone:* 6569955.

PARRIS, Matthew; British politician, writer and broadcaster; b. 7 Aug. 1949, Johannesburg, S. Africa; s. of Leslie F. Parris and Theresa E. (née Littler) Parris; ed. Waterford School, Swaziland, Clare Coll., Cambridge and Yale Univ.; FCO 1974-76; with Conservative Research Dept. 1976-79; mem. Parl. (Conservative) for W. Derbyshire 1979-86; Presenter Weekend World 1986-88. *Leisure interest:* running. *Address:* The Spout, Gratton, Bakewell, Derbyshire, DE4 1LN, England.

PARROTT, Andrew Haden, B.A.; British conductor and scholar; b. 10 March 1947, Walsall; s. of R. C. and E. D. Parrott; m. 1st Emma Kirkby 1971, 2nd Emily Van Evera 1986; ed. Queen Mary's Grammar School, Walsall, Merton Coll., Oxford; Conductor, Schola Cantorum, Oxford 1968-71; Dir. of Music Merton Coll., Oxford 1969-71; Conductor, Musica Reservata 1973-76; Founder, Conductor and Dir., Taverner Choir, Taverner Consort and Taverner Players 1973–; BBC Promenade Concerts début 1977; fmr. musical Asst. to Sir Michael Tippett; freelance orchestral conductor; occasional writer, broadcaster, lecturer, continuo-player and singer; Open Post-Mastership, Merton Coll. 1966-69; Leverhulme Fellowship 1984-85. *Publications include:* Transposition in Monteverdi's Vespers of 1610 (Early Music, Nov. 1984). *Recordings include:* Bach: Mass in B Minor 1985, Handel: Carmelite Vespers 1989, Monteverdi: Vespers of 1610 1984, Purcell: Dido and Aeneas 1981. *Address:* c/o Norman McCann International Artists Ltd., The Coach House, 56 Lawrie Park Gardens, London, SE26 6XJ, England. *Telephone:* 01-659 5955.

PARRY, Charles William, B.S.; American business executive; b. 31 July 1924, Pittsburgh, Pa.; s. of Elmer J. Parry and Florence E. Satler; m. Margery Brahmer 1948; four c.; ed. Univ. of Pittsburgh; operating and financial positions, Aluminium Co. of America, Pittsburgh 1952; Financial Dir. Alcoa of Australia, Melbourne 1962; Vice-Pres. Corporate Planning, Aluminium Co. of America 1974, Pres. 1981, Chair. and C.E.O. 1983-87; Chair. American Australian Bicentennial Foundation; Dir. First Interstate Bancorpn., Int. Primary Aluminium Inst., Regional Industrial Devt. Soc., NALCO Chemical Co.; Trustee, Cttee. for Econ. Devt., Tax Foundation, American Enterprise Inst., Penn's Southwest Asscn.; Trustee and Sr. mem. Conf. Bd. *Leisure interests:* tennis, gourmet cooking. *Address:* c/o Aluminium Company of America, 1501 Alcoa Building, Pittsburgh, Pa. 15219, U.S.A.

PARSHIN, Aleksandr Yakovlevich, DR. PHYS.-MATH. SC.; Soviet physicist; b. 1939; ed. Moscow Phys.-Tech. Inst.; sr. laboratory asst., U.S.S.R. Acad. of Sciences Inst. of Physics 1962-70; sr. engineer, Kurchatov Inst. of Atomic Energy 1970-75; jr. then sr. researcher with Acad. of Sciences Inst. of Crystallography 1975-86; leading scientific worker at Inst. of Physics 1986–; mem. CPSU 1986–; deputy Ed.-in-Chief of Journal of Experimental and Theoretical Physics; Lenin Prize 1986. *Address:* U.S.S.R. Academy of Sciences Institute of Physics, Moscow, U.S.S.R.

PARSONS, Sir Anthony Derrick, G.C.M.G., L.V.O., M.C., M.A. (OXON.); British diplomatist (retd.); b. 9 Sept. 1922, London; s. of late Col. H. A. J. Parsons; m. Sheila Emily Baird 1948; two s. two d.; ed. King's School, Canterbury, Balliol Coll., Oxford; Army service 1940-54; Asst. Mil. Attaché, Baghdad 1952-54; Foreign Office 1954-55; at British Embassy, Ankara 1955-59, Amman 1959-60, Cairo 1960-61; Foreign Office 1961-64; British Embassy, Khartoum 1964-65; British Political Agent, Bahrain 1965-69; with U.K. Mission to UN 1969-71; FCO 1971-74; Amb. to Iran 1974-79; Deputy to Perm. Under-Sec., FCO 1979; Perm. Rep. to UN 1979-82; Foreign Affairs Adviser to Prime Minister 1982-83, Lecturer, Dept. of Arabic and Islamic Studies and Research Fellow, Centre for Arab Gulf Studies, Exeter Univ. 1984-87. *Publication:* The Pride and the Fall: Iran 1974-1979 1984, They Say the Lion 1986. *Address:* Highgrove, Ashburton, South Devon, England.

PARSONS, Geoffrey, O.B.E.; Australian pianist; b. 15 June 1929, Sydney; s. of Francis Hedley Parsons and Edith Vera Buckland; ed. Canterbury

High School, Sydney, N.S.W. State Conservatorium of Music (with Winifred Burston), Sydney; won ABC Concerto Competition 1947; Australian tour 1948; went to U.K. 1950; has accompanied many of world's leading singers, including Elisabeth Schwarzkopf, Victoria de los Angeles, Janet Baker, Jessye Norman, Margaret Price in 40 countries; master classes London 1977, 1978, Sweden 1984, 1985, Austria 1985; 25th Australian tour 1983; int. song recital series, Geoffrey Parsons and Friends, Barbican Concert Hall, London 1982–; Harriet Cohen Int. Music Award 1968; Hon. R.A.M., Hon. G.S.M. *Address:* 176 Iverson Road, London, NW6 2HL, England. *Telephone:* 01-624 0957.

PARSONS, Peter John, M.A., F.B.A.; British academic; b. 24 Sept. 1936, Surbiton, Surrey; s. of Robert John Parsons and Ethel Ada (née Frary); ed. Raynes Park County Grammar School and Christ Church, Oxford; Lecturer in Documentary Papyrology, Oxford Univ. 1960–65, Lecturer in Papyrology 1965–; Student (Fellow) Christ Church Oxford 1964–; J. H. Gray Lecturer, Cambridge Univ. 1982; Hon. Ph.D. (Berne) 1985. *Publications:* The Oxyrhynchus Papyri (jtly.) vols. XXXI 1966, XXXIII and XXXIV 1968, (solely) vol. XLII 1973, Supplementum Hellenisticum (with H. Lloyd-Jones) 1983; articles in learned journals. *Leisure interests:* music, cinema, cooking, eating. *Address:* Christ Church, Oxford, OX1 1DP, England. *Telephone:* (0865) 276223.

PARSONS, Sir Richard Edmund Clement Fownes, K.C.M.G.; British diplomatist; b. 14 March 1928; s. of Dr R. A. Parsons; m. Jennifer J. Matthews 1960 (died 1981); three s.; ed. Bembridge School and Brasenose Coll., Oxford; joined Foreign Office 1951; served Washington 1953–56, Vientiane 1956–58, Buenos Aires 1960–63, Ankara 1965–67, Lagos 1969–72; Amb. to Hungary 1976–79, to Spain 1980–84, to Sweden 1984–87. *Leisure interests:* reading, writing, music, travel. *Address:* c/o Foreign and Commonwealth Office, King Charles Street, London, SW1A 2AH, England.

PARSONS, Roger, D.SC., PH.D., F.R.S.; British professor of chemistry; b. 31 Oct. 1926, London; s. of Robert H. A. Parsons and Ethel Fenton; m. Ruby M. Turner 1953; three s. one d.; ed. King Alfred School, London, Strathcona High School, Edmonton, Alberta and Imperial Coll., London; Asst. Lecturer, Imperial Coll. 1948–51; Deedes Fellow, Univ. Coll., Dundee 1951–54; Lecturer, Univ. of Bristol 1954–63, Reader 1963–79; Dir. Lab. d'Electrochimie Interfaciale du CNRS, Meudon, France 1977–84; Prof. of Chem. Univ. of Southampton 1985–; Prix Pascal, Palladium Medal, Breyer Medal, Galvani Medal. *Publications:* Electrochemical Data 1956, Electrical Properties of Interfaces (with J. Lyklema); Co-Ed. Standard Potentials in Aqueous Solution 1985, Electrochemistry in Research and Development 1985; over 150 scientific papers. *Leisure interests:* listening to music, going to the opera. *Address:* Department of Chemistry, Southampton University, Southampton, SO9 5NH, England. *Telephone:* (0703) 559122.

PART, Sir Antony Alexander, G.C.B., M.B.E., C.B.I.M.; British business executive and fmr. civil servant; b. 28 June 1916, London; s. of late Alexander Francis Part and Una Margaret Reynolds (née Snowdon); m. Isabella Bennett 1940; ed. Harrow School and Trinity Coll., Cambridge; Asst. Prin., Bd. of Educ. 1937–39; Asst. Private Sec. to successive Ministers of Supply 1939–40; Army 1940–44; Pvt. Sec. to successive Ministers of Educ. 1945–46; Head of Bldg. Branch, Ministry of Educ. 1946–52; Commonwealth Fund Fellowship, U.S.A. 1950–51; Under-Sec., Ministry of Educ. 1954–60, Deputy Sec. 1960–63; Deputy Sec., Ministry of Public Bldg. and Works 1963–65, Perm. Sec. 1965–68; Perm. Sec. Bd. of Trade 1968–70, Dept. of Trade and Industry 1970–74, Dept. of Industry 1974–76; Chair. The Orion Insurance Co. 1976–87; Dir. of numerous other cos.; Gov. L.S.E. 1968–, Vice-Chair. 1979–84, Hon. Fellow 1983; Gov. Henley Man. Coll. 1968–88; Chair. Cttee. on Taxation of N. Sea Oil 1981, Govt. Panel on Direct Broadcasting by Satellite 1982; Hon. D.Tech. (Brunel) 1966, (Cranfield) 1976; Hon. D.Sc. (Aston) 1974. *Leisure interest:* travel. *Address:* Flat 5, 71 Elm Park Gardens, London, S.W.10, England. *Telephone:* 01-352 2950.

PARTELI, Most Rev. Carlos; Uruguayan ecclesiastic; b. 8 March 1910, Rivera; s. of Francisco and Maria (née Keller) Parteli; ordained priest, Rome 1933; Bishop of Tacuarembo 1960; Coadjutor Archbishop, Apostolic Admin. Sede Plena of Montevideo 1966; Archbishop of Montevideo 1976–85, Archbishop Emer. 1985–. *Address:* Arzobispado, Calle Treinta y Tres 1368, Montevideo, Uruguay. *Telephone:* 95 8127; 95 8926; 95 8879.

PARTON, Dolly Rebecca; American singer, composer; b. 19 Jan. 1946, Sevier County, Tenn.; d. of Robert Lee and Avie Lee (née Owens) Parton; m. Carl Dean 1966; radio appearances include Grand Ole Opry; appeared in films Nine to Five, The Best Little Whorehouse in Texas 1982, Rhinestone 1984; *albums include:* Dumb Blonde, Something Fishy, I Couldn't Wait Forever, Daddy Was An Old Time Preacher Man, Joshua, Jolene, Coat of Many Colors, I Will Always Love You, Love is Like a Butterfly, The Bargain Store, The Seeker, We Used To , All I Can Do, 9 to 5, Odd Jobs; *composed songs including:* Dumb Blonde, Something Fishy; Vocal Group of the Year 1968, Vocal Duo of the Year, All Country Music Asscn. 1970, 1971; Nashville Metronome Award 1979; Female Vocalist of the Year 1975, 1976; Country Star of the Year 1978; People's Choice 1980; Female Vocalist of the Year, Academy of Country Music 1980. *Address:* c/o Creative Artists Agency Inc., 1888 Century Park, E. Suite, 1400 Los Angeles, Calif. 90067, U.S.A.

PARTRIDGE, Derek William, C.M.G.; British diplomatist; b. 15 May 1931, London; s. of late Ernest Partridge and Ethel E. Buckingham; unmarried; ed. Preston Manor Co. Grammar School, Wembley, Middx.; entered Foreign Office 1949; R.A.F. 1949–51; served Oslo 1954–56, Jeddah 1956, Khartoum 1957–60, Sofia 1960–62, Manila 1962–65, Djakarta 1965–67, Brisbane 1972–74, Colombo 1974–77; FCO 1977–86; High Commr. in Sierra Leone 1986–. *Address:* c/o Foreign and Commonwealth Office, King Charles Street, London, SW1A 2AH, England.

PARTRIDGE, John Albert, C.B.E., R.A., F.R.I.B.A.; British architect; b. 26 Aug. 1924, London; s. of George and Gladys Partridge; m. Doris Foreman 1953; one s. one d.; ed. Shooter's Hill Grammar School, Woolwich, and Polytechnic School of Architecture, London; London County Council Housing Architects' Dept. 1951–59; Sr. and Founding Partner, Howell, Killick, Partridge & Amis (HKPA) 1959–; Vice-Pres. R.I.B.A. 1977–79, Concrete Soc. 1979–81; R.I.B.A. Hon. Librarian 1977–81; Chair. R.I.B.A. Architectural Research Steering Cttee. 1978–84; Gov. Building Centre, London 1981–; Chair. Assen. of Consultant Architects 1983–85; mem. NEDO Construction Research Strategy Cttee. 1983–86; Architect mem. FCO Advisory Bd. on the Diplomatic Estate 1985–; External Examiner in Architecture, Univ. of Bath 1975–78, Thames Polytechnic 1978–86, Univ. of Cambridge 1979–81, Univ. of Manchester 1982–, South Bank Polytechnic (London) 1981–86, Brighton Polytechnic 1987–. *Major works include:* Wolfson Rayne and Gatehouse Bldg., St. Anne's Coll., Oxford, New Hall and Common Room, St. Antony's Coll., Oxford, Wells Hall, Univ. of Reading, Middlesex Polytechnic Coll. of Art, Cat Hill, Medway Magistrates Court, The Albany, Deptford, Hall of Justice, Trinidad & Tobago, in asscn. with ACLP, Trinidad; Warrington Crown Courthouse, Basildon Courthouse, Fawley B Power Station, Haywards Heath Magistrates Courthouse; exhbns. of HKPA work at Heinz Gallery, London 1983, Puck Bldg., New York 1983; 25 Nat. Design Awards for HKPA 1965–. *Publications:* articles in the tech. press and architectural papers to conferences. *Leisure interests:* looking at buildings, travel, sketching, taking photographs, listening to music. *Address:* Cudham Court, Cudham, Nr. Sevenoaks, Kent (Home); 20 Old Pye Street, Westminster, London, S.W.1, England (Office). *Telephone:* Biggin Hill 71294 (Home); 01-222 0606 (Office).

PARTRIDGE, Mark Henry Heathcote; Zimbabwean chartered accountant and politician; b. 23 Nov. 1922, East Rand, Transvaal; s. of Samuel Cherrington and L'Amie (née Heathcote) Partridge; m. Barbara Hamilton Black 1950; one s. three d.; ed. St. George's Coll., Salisbury; served in King's Royal Rifle Corps, Middle East, Italy, Greece 1940–45; with own accountancy firm, Rocke, Partridge & Adair, Salisbury; M.P. for Greendale 1962; Minister of Local Govt. and Housing 1966–73, of Lands and Natural Resources and of Water Devt. 1973–77, of Defence March-Sept. 1977, of Agric. 1977–79 (Co-Minister 1978–79); Senator 1980–85, M.P. for Mazowe/Mutoko 1985–87; Acting Leader Conservative Alliance 1987–88; Independence Commemorative Decoration, Grand Officer of Legion of Merit. *Leisure interests:* tennis, fishing, farming. *Address:* Box 1435, Harare, Zimbabwe. *Telephone:* 47095 (Home).

PARTRIDGE, Stanley Miles, PH.D., F.R.S.; British biochemist (retd.); b. 2 Aug. 1913, Whangarei, New Zealand; s. of Ernest J. Partridge and Eve Miles (later McCarthy); m. Ruth Dowling 1940; four d.; ed. Harrow County School, Roundhay School, Leeds, Battersea Coll. of Tech. and Univ. of Cambridge; Beit Memorial Fellow, Lister Inst. of Preventive Medicine 1940; Dept. of Scientific and Industrial Research, Low Temperature Station, Cambridge 1942; Tech. Adviser, Govt. of India 1944; returned to Low Temp. Stn. 1946; Principal Scientific Officer, Agricultural Research Council 1952, Deputy Chief Scientific Officer 1964–78; mem. Nuffield Foundation Rheumatism Cttee. 1965–73; Hon. Prof. of Biochem. Univ. of Bristol 1976; Hon. D.Sc. (Reading) 1984, D.Med. (Laurea ad honorem, Padua) 1986. *Publications:* many papers in scientific journals. *Leisure interests:* travel, gardening. *Address:* Millstream House, St. Andrew's Road, Cheddar, Somerset, BS27 3NG, England. *Telephone:* (0934) 742130.

PASCAL, Jean-Baptiste Lucien, L. EN D., DIPL.; French banker; b. 26 Nov. 1930, Bordeaux; s. of Ernest Pascal and Paule de Battisti; m. Christiane Gardelle 1962; three s. (one deceased); ed. Univ. of Paris; attached to Banque Nat. pour le Commerce et l'Industrie 1954; Head of Supplies Mission for the Devt. of Algeria and Jt. Govt. Commr. for Crédit Populaire de France in Algeria 1959; Head of Bureau for Financial Co-operation to Sec. of State for Algerian Affairs 1963; mem. Crédit Commercial de France (CCF) 1965, Deputy Dir. Cen. Admin. CCF 1967, Dir.-Gen. d'Interbail 1971, Dir. Cen. Admin. 1973–, Admin. Dir.-Gen. 1974–, Vice-Pres. Dir.-Gen. d'Interbail 1976–; Dir. Crédit Commercial de France 1977; Pres. Dir.-Gen. Banque Hervet 1986–. *Publication:* La Décolonisation de l'Europe—Querelle des Continents 1964. *Leisure interests:* alpinism, hunting. *Address:* Banque Hervet, 127 av. Charles de Gaulle, 92201 Neuilly-sur-Seine (Office); 24 rue Jules Claretie, 75116 Paris, France (Home).

PASCHKE, Fritz, DR.TECH.SC.; Austrian electrical engineer; b. 2 March 1929, Graz/Goesting; s. of late Eduard Paschke and Stefanie Mittellehner; m. Gertrud P. Kutschera 1955; two d.; ed. Tech. Univs. of Graz and Vienna; Asst. Tech. Univ. Vienna 1953–55; consultant, New York 1955–56; mem. tech. staff, RCA David Sarnoff Research Center 1956–61; Components Div. Siemens AG, Munich 1961–66; Prof. of Electrical Eng. Tech. Univ. Vienna 1965–, Dean, School of Electrical Eng. 1970–71, Rector/Pro-

Rector 1971-76, Head, Inst. für Allgemeine Elektrotechnik und Elektronik 1980-; Vice-Pres. Austrian Nat. Science Foundation 1974-82; Ludwig Boltzmann Award 1977, Cardinal Innitzer Award 1984, Erwin Schrödinger Award (Austrian Acad.) 1988, Award of City of Vienna for Science and Tech. 1988 etc.; Dr. h.c. (Budapest) 1974. *Publications:* articles in professional journals. *Leisure interests:* art, hiking, swimming. *Address:* Technical University of Vienna, Gusshaus-Strasse 27-29, A-1040 Vienna, Austria. *Telephone:* 0222-58801-3836.

PASCO, Richard Edward, C.B.E.; British actor; b. 18 July 1926, Barnes; s. of Cecil George and Phyllis (née Widdison) Pasco; m. 1st Greta Watson 1956 (dissolved 1964); m. 2nd Barbara Leigh-Hunt 1967; one s.; ed. Colet Court and King's Coll. School, Wimbledon, Cen. School of Speech and Drama; first appearance on stage, Q Theatre 1943; served in H.M. forces 1944-48; Old Vic Co. 1950-52; Birmingham Repertory Co. 1952-55; played Fortinbras in Hamlet (Moscow and London) 1955; English Stage Co. 1957, played in The Member of the Wedding, Look Back in Anger, The Entertainer, Man from Bellac and The Chairs. *Roles include:* The Entertainer (New York) 1958, Moscow Youth Festival in Look Back in Anger 1959, Teresa of Avila (Dublin Theatre Festival and Vaudeville) 1961, Henry V, Love's Labour's Lost (Bristol Old Vic, Old Vic and tour to Europe) 1964; Hamlet, Bristol Old Vic, 1965, Measure for Measure, Peer Gynt, Man and Superman, Hamlet 1966; toured U.S.A. and Europe 1967; joined R.S.C. 1969; *roles include:* Polixenes in The Winter's Tale, Proteus in The Two Gentlemen of Verona, Buckingham in Henry VIII 1969, Major Barbara, Richard II, Duchess of Malfi 1971, Becket in Murder in the Catherdral, Medraut in the Island of the Mighty 1972, Richard and Bolingbroke in Richard II 1973-74; The Marrying of Ann Leete 1975, Jack Tanner in Man and Superman 1977, Trigorin in The Seagull 1978, Timon in Timon of Athens 1980, Clarence in Richard III 1980, in The Forest 1981, La Ronde 1982, joined Nat. Theatre 1987: *roles:* Father in Six Characters in Search of an Author 1987, Pavel in Fathers and Sons 1987; tours with R.S.C. to Japan, Australia 1970, Japan 1972; Assoc. Artist of R.S.C. 1972-, has made broadcastings and recordings of plays and verse, including complete sonnets of Shakespeare. *TV appearances include:* Henry Irving, The Three Musketeers, Savages, As You Like It, Julius Caesar, British in Love, Trouble with Gregory, Philby, The House Boy, Number 10—Disraeli, The Plot to Murder Lloyd George, Let's Run Away to Africa, Sorrell and Son, Drummonds, etc. *Films include:* Room at the Top, Yesterday's Enemy, The Gorgon, Rasputin, Watcher in the Woods, Wagner, Arch of Triumph, etc. *Leisure interests:* music, gardening, preservation of rural England. *Address:* c/o Michael Whitehall Ltd., 125 Gloucester Road, London, SW1 4TE, England.

PASETTI, Peter; German actor; b. 8 July 1916, Munich; s. of Prof. Leo and Inge (née Hartmann) Pasetti; m. 3rd Marianne Swoboda 1968; ed. Munich Drama Acad.; performances at various theatres in Germany, Switzerland and Austria; film and TV roles in Germany and abroad; Staatsschauspiel and Kammerspiele, Munich; Fed. Cross of Merit, Schwabinger Kunstpreis 1976, Filmband in Gold 1986. *Leisure interests:* music, amateur films. *Address:* Feilitzschstrasse 34, D 8000 Munich 40, Federal Republic of Germany. *Telephone:* 089 346 281 and 08807 5505.

PASHLEY, Donald William, PH.D., A.R.C.S., D.I.C., F.INST.P, F.I.M., F.R.S.; British university professor; b. 21 April 1927, London; s. of Harold William Pashley and Louise Pashley; m. Glenys Margaret Ball 1954; one s. one d.; ed. Imperial Coll., London; Demonstrator in Physics, Imperial Coll., London 1948-51, DSIR Research Fellow 1951-53, ICI Research Fellow 1953-56, Prof. of Materials and Head of Dept. of Materials 1979-, Dean, Royal School of Mines 1986-; Sr. Research Scientist, TI Research Labs., Cambridge 1956-61, Group Leader 1961-63, Head, Metal Science Div. 1963-67, Asst. Dir. 1967-68, Dir. of Labs 1968-79, Research Dir., TI Group 1976-79; Rosenham Medal, Inst. of Metals 1968. *Publications:* Co-author; Electron Microscopy of Thin Crystals; numerous scientific papers. *Address:* 50 Exeter House, Putney Heath, London, SW15 3SX, England. *Telephone:* 01-788 4800.

PASINETTI, Luigi Lodovico, M.A., PH.D.; Italian professor of economics; b. 12 Sept. 1930, Bergamo; s. of Giovanni and Romilda Arzuffi; m. Carmela Colombo 1966; one s.; ed. secondary schools, Bergamo, Univ. Cattolica del Sacro Cuore, Milan, Univ. of Cambridge, Harvard Univ.; Research Fellow, Nuffield Coll., Oxford 1960-61; Fellow and Lecturer in Econs., King's Coll., Cambridge 1961-73; Lecturer, then Reader in Econs., Univ. of Cambridge 1961-76; Prof. Faculty of Econs., Univ. Cattolica del Sacro Cuoro 1980-, Chair. 1980-87; Wesley Clair Mitchell Visiting Research Prof. of Econs., Columbia Univ., New York 1971, 1975; Visiting Research Prof., Indian Statistical Inst., Calcutta and New Delhi Feb.-March 1979; Visiting Prof. of Econs., Univ. of Ottawa, Carleton Univ. 1981; mem. Council and Exec. Cttee. Int. Econ. Asscn. 1980-; Fellow Econometric Soc. 1978-; St. Vincent Prize for Econs. 1979; Gold Medal (First Class) for Educ., Culture and Arts 1982; mem. Accademia Lincei, Rome 1986-. *Publications:* Growth and Income Distribution 1974, Lectures on the Theory of Production 1977, Structural Change and Economic Growth 1981; numerous articles on income distribution, capital theory and economic growth. *Leisure interests:* tennis, climbing, music. *Address:* c/o Faculty of Economics, Università Cattolica del Sacro Cuore, Largo A. Gemelli 1, 20123 Milan, Italy.

PASKAI, H.E. Cardinal Dr. László; Hungarian ecclesiastic; b. 8 May 1927, Szeged; ed. high-school, Szeged; joined Franciscan Order, professed his vows 1949; assumed diocesan service 1950; ordained priest 1951; Episcopal liturgist 1952-55, Szeged; Prof. of Philosophy, Theological Acad., Szeged 1955-65, simultaneously Apostolic Prefect 1955-62, Spiritual 1962-65; Spiritual Prefect, Central Seminary of Budapest 1965-69; commissioned lecturer 1965-67, leading Prof. of Philosophy, Theological Academy, Budapest 1967-78; Rector of Seminary 1973-78; appointed titular Bishop of Bavagaliana and Apostolic Gov. of Veszprém 1978; Diocesan Bishop of Veszprém 1979, coadjutor with right of succession to Archbishop of Kalocsa 1982; Archbishop of Esztergom and Primate of Hungary 1987-; Created Cardinal 1988; mem. Hungarian Parliament; Chair. Hungarian Catholic Bench of Bishops 1986-. *Address:* Berényi Zsigmond utca 2, 2500 Esztergom, Hungary. *Telephone:* Esztergom 1.

PASMORE, (Edwin John) Victor, C.H., C.B.E., M.A.; British artist; b. 3 Dec. 1908, Chelsham, Surrey; s. of late E. S. Pasmore; m. Wendy Blood 1940; one s. one d.; ed. Harrow School and L.C.C. Central School of Arts and Crafts (evening classes); Local Govt. service, L.C.C. County Hall 1927-37; associated with "Euston Road" school of painting 1937-39; Visiting teacher Camberwell School of Art 1945-49, Cen. School of Arts and Crafts 1949-53; Master of Painting, Durham Univ. 1954-61; Consultant Architectural Designer Peterlee New Town 1955-77; retrospective exhbns. Venice Biennale 1960, Musée des Arts Décoratifs, Paris 1961, Stedelijk Museum, Amsterdam 1961, Palais des Beaux Arts, Brussels 1961, Louisiana Museum, Copenhagen 1962, Kestner Gesellschaft, Hanover 1962, Kunsthalle, Bern 1963, Tate Gallery, London 1965, São Paulo Biennale 1965, Marlborough Gallery, London 1966, 1969, 1972, Cartwright Hall, Bradford 1980, Royal Acad. 1980, Musée des Beaux Arts, Calais 1985; mem. ICA (London); Trustee, Tate Gallery; Hon. degrees from (Newcastle-upon-Tyne) 1967, (Surrey) 1969, (Warwick) 1985; Carnegie Prize for Painting 1964, Grand Prix d'honneur, Int. Graphics Biennale 1977, Charles Wollaston Award 1983. *Principal works include:* The Gardens of Hammersmith (Nat. Gallery of Canada), The Thames at Chiswick (Melbourne Nat. Gallery), The Snow Storm (Arts Council of Great Britain), The Inland Sea, Abstract Relief (Tate Gallery), Abstract Mural Painting (Barnsbury School, London). *Publication:* Monograph and Catalogue Raisonnée 1980. *Address:* Dar Gamri, Gudja, Malta; 12 St. German's Place, Blackheath, London, S.E.3, England. *Telephone:* 01-858 0369 (London).

PASQUA, Charles Victor; French politician; b. 18 April 1927, Grasse; s. of André Pasqua and Françoise Rinaldi; m. Jeanne Joly 1947; one s.; ed. College de Grasse, Inst. d'Etudes Juridiques, Nice and Faculté de Droit, Aix-en-Provence; Rep. Société Ricard 1952, Insp. 1955, Regional Dir. 1960, Dir. French Sales 1962, Dir.-Gen. French Sales and Export 1963; Pres.-Dir.-Gen. Société Euralim 1967-71; Commercial Consultant 1972-; Deputy to Nat. Ass. (UDR) 1968-73; Sec.-Gen. UDR 1974-76; Senator, Hauts de Seine 1977-86; Pres. RPR Group in Senate 1981-86; Minister of the Interior 1986-88; Chevalier, Légion d'Honneur. *Address:* c/o RPR, 123 rue de Lille, 75007 Paris, France.

PASSARINHO, Jarbas Gonçalves; Brazilian politician; b. 11 Jan. 1920, Xapuri, Acre; s. of Inácio Loyola Passarinho and Júlia Gonçalves Passarinho; m. Ruth de Castro Passarinho 1945; two s. three d.; ed. Escola Militar do Realengo, Escola de Comando and Estado-Major de Exército; Gov., State of Pará 1964-66; Pres. ARENA, Pará; Senator, State of Pará 1967-74, 1975-83, 1987-; Minister of Labour and Social Welfare 1967-69, of Educ. and Culture 1969-74, of Social Welfare 1983-85; Pres. Brazilian Del. to Int. Cong. UNESCO 1970-71; Chief of Brazilian Del., Inter-American Council for Educ., Science and Culture, Perm. Exec. Cttee. 1972; Majority Leader Fed. Senate 1979-80, Pres. 1981-82; Counsellor, Bank Sul Brasileiro, D.F.; numerous awards. *Publications:* Terra Encharcada (Samuel MacDowell Prize), Roteiro 1964, Amazonia—The Challenge of the Tropics 1971. *Leisure interest:* sports. *Address:* QI 02 Conjunto 06, Casa 16, SHIN, 71-500, Brasília, D.F., Brazil. *Telephone:* (061) 577-4668.

PASSICOT CALLIER, Andrés; Chilean economist and politician; b. 21 Nov. 1937, Concepción; m. María Cloria Guzmán Fredes; ed. Colegio La Salle, Temuco and Univ. of Chile; Asst. lecturer, later Prof. of Statistics, Univ. of Chile 1968, Head, Econ. Dept. 1980; Head, Nat. Accounts, Nat. Org. of Planning; Dir. Chilean Nat. Electricity Co., Nat. Inst. of Statistics; Minister of Economy 1983-84; Vice-Chair. Banco del Estado de Chile 1984-. *Address:* Banco del Estado de Chile, Avda. B. O'Higgins 1111, Casilla 24, Santiago, Chile.

PASSMORE, John Arthur, M.A., F.A.H.A., F.A.S.S.A.; Australian professor of philosophy; b. 9 Sept. 1914, Manly; s. of F. M. Passmore and Ruby Moule; m. Annie D. Sumner 1936; two d.; ed. Sydney Boys' High School and Sydney Univ.; Tutor, Lecturer and Sr. Lecturer in Philosophy, Sydney Univ. 1935-49; Prof. of Philosophy, Otago Univ., Dunedin, N.Z. 1950-54; Reader in Philosophy, Inst. of Advanced Studies, A.N.U. 1955-58, Prof. 1959-79, now Prof. Emer.; Univ. Fellow, History of Ideas, A.N.U. 1981-82, Visiting Fellow in History of Ideas 1983-; Visiting Distinguished Prof. in Russell Studies and Gen. Ed. Russell Project, McMaster Univ., Canada 1984-; Visiting Prof. Brandeis Univ. 1960; Visiting Fellow, All Souls, Oxford 1970, 1978, Clare Hall, Cambridge 1973; Pres. Australian Acad. of Humanities 1974-77; Corresp. Fellow, British Acad.; Foreign Fellow, American Acad. of Arts and Sciences, Royal Danish Acad. of Arts and

Letters; Hon. D. Litt. (Sydney, McMaster). *Publications:* Ralph Cudworth 1950, Hume's Intentions 1952, A Hundred Years of Philosophy 1957, Philosophical Reasoning 1961, The Perfectibility of Man 1970, Man's Responsibility for Nature 1974, Science and its Critics 1978, The Philosophy of Teaching 1980, The Limits of Government 1981, Recent Philosophers 1985. *Leisure interests:* theatre, film, travel, walking. *Address:* Australian National University, Canberra, A.C.T.; 6 Jansz Crescent, Manuka, A.C.T. 2603, Australia. *Telephone:* 493290; 957745.

PASTINEN, Ilkka Olavi, M.POL.SC.; Finnish diplomatist; b. 17 March 1928, Turku; s. of Martti Mikael and Ilmi Saga Karlström Pastinen; m. Eeva Marja Viitanen 1950; two d.; ed. Åbo (Turku) Akad., Inst. d'Etudes Politiques, Paris, Inst. Int. des Sciences et Recherches Diplomatiques; entered Foreign Service 1952; served Stockholm 1955–57, Mission to UN 1957–59; Deputy Chief of Mission, Beijing 1962–64; Deputy Chief of Mission, London 1966–69; Amb., Deputy Perm. Rep. to UN and Deputy Rep. to Security Council 1969–70; Asst. Sec.-Gen. UN and Special Rep. of Sec.-Gen. of UN to Cttee. for Disarmament 1971–75; Amb., Perm. Rep. to UN 1977–82; Amb. to U.K. 1983–. *Leisure interests:* golf, music, bridge. *Address:* Embassy of Finland, 38 Chesham Place, London, SW1X 8HW, England.

PASTOR DE LA TORRE, Celso, LL.B.; Peruvian diplomatist; b. 20 Dec. 1914; m. (wife deceased); four c.; ed. Bogotá, Berlin, Catholic Univ. of Peru; Amb. to U.S.A. and Rep. to IBRD and IMF 1963–68; Perm. Rep. to UN 1983–84; Consultant to various int. cos., Chair. Int. Insurance Co. –1983; f. and fmr. Sec.-Gen. of Acción Popular Party 1956; promoter of numerous exhbns. of Peruvian Culture in U.S.A. *Publications:* Escuela Pictórica del Cuzco. *Address:* c/o Ministerio des Asuntos Exteriores, Lima, Peru.

PASTORINO VISCARDI, Enrique Juan; Uruguayan trade union official; b. 6 March 1918, Montevideo; s. of Antonio and Catalina Pastorino Viscardi; m. Alba Chasate; two s. one d.; ed. primary schools; Sec. Union of Workers of the Leather Industry 1940; Sec. Gen. Union of Workers of Uruguay 1950; Sec. Cen. Council of Workers of Uruguay 1960; Sec. Nat. Convention of Workers of Uruguay 1966; Pres. World Fed. of Trade Unions (WFTU) 1969–78, Gen.-Sec. 1978–82; Lenin Peace Prize 1973. *Leisure interest:* studies on social questions. *Address:* Calle Ganaderos, 4306, Montevideo, Uruguay (Home).

PASTRANA BORRERO, Misael, LL.D.; Colombian politician and diplomatist; b. 14 Nov. 1923, Neiva; s. of Misael Pastrana Pastrana and Elisa Borrero de Pastrana; m. Cristina Arango Vega; three s. one d.; ed. Pontificia Univ. Javeriana, Bogotá; Founder and ed. El Porvenir and Civil Law Circuit Judge 1945; Sec. Colombian Embassy, The Vatican 1947–49; Pvt. Sec. to Pres. Ospina Pérez 1949–50; Counsellor, Colombian Embassy, Washington, D.C. 1950–52; Sec. Ministry of Foreign Affairs 1953; alt. rep. at UN 1954–56; Founder and Vice-Pres. Corpn. Financiera Colombiana 1957; Minister of Devt. 1960, of Public Works and Finance 1961; in private business 1961–65; Minister of the Interior 1966–68; Amb. to U.S.A. 1968–69; Pres. of Colombia 1970–74; Ed. GUION 1975–84; mem. Nat. Comm. on Foreign Affairs 1974–, Exec. Cttee. InterAction; Vice-Chair. Int. Democratic Union; Chair. UN Int. Environment Cttee.; Leader Partido Conservador. *Address:* Carrera 4, 92-10, Bogotá, D.E., Colombia. *Telephone:* 2-36-19-04.

PASTUKHOV, Boris Nikolayevich; Soviet politician; b. 1933; ed. Bauman Coll., Moscow; mem. CPSU 1959; First Sec. Bauman Regional Komsomol Cttee., Moscow 1959–61; Second Sec. Moscow City Komsomol Cttee. 1961–62, First Sec. 1962–64; Second Sec. All-Union Komsomol Cttee. 1964–77; mem. U.S.S.R. Trade and Public Services Comm., Soviet of Nationalities, U.S.S.R. Supreme Soviet 1966–68; mem. Comm. of Youth Affairs, Soviet of Nationalities 1968–83; First Sec. All-Union Young Communist League Komsomol 1977–82; Chair. U.S.S.R. State Cttee. for Publishing, Printing and Bookselling, U.S.S.R. Goskomizdat 1982–86; mem. Presidium, Supreme Soviet of the U.S.S.R. 1978–83. *Address:* c/o State Committee for Publishing, Printing and Bookselling, Strastnoi bul. 5, Moscow, U.S.S.R.

PĂTAN, Ion; Romanian economist and politician; b. 1 Dec. 1926, Daia, Alba County; ed. Economic Studies Acad., Bucharest; several posts in the Ministry of Light Industry 1956–62, Gen. Sec. 1962–64; Deputy Minister of Light Industry 1964–65; Alt. mem. Cen. Cttee. of R.C.P. 1965–69, mem. 1969–; Head of Section, Cen. Cttee. R.C.P. 1965–68; mem. Grand Nat. Ass. 1969–; Alt. mem. Exec. Political Cttee. 1972–74; mem. 1974–89; mem. Standing Bureau 1974–; Minister of Home Trade 1968–69; Vice-Chair. Council of Ministers 1969–86; Minister of Foreign Trade 1972–78; Chair. Govt. Comm. on Econ. and Tech. Cooperation 1974–78; Minister for Tech. Material Supply and Fixed Assets Man. Control 1978–84, of Light Industry 1984–86, of Finance March 1989–; Amb. to Czechoslovakia 1987–89; Perm. Rep. to Council for Mutual Economic Assistance 1978–79. *Address:* Ministry of Finance, Bucharest, Str. Vatter Mărăcineanu 1-3, Romania.

PATANÉ, Giuseppe; Italian conductor, violinist and pianist; b. 1 Jan. 1931, Naples; m. Rita Saponaro 1956 (divorced); two d.; ed. Conservatorio di Napoli and privately with Cilea, Longo and Gargiulo; aged seven played bells in a performance of Cavalleria Rusticana conducted by Mascagni; conducting debut, La Traviata, Teatro Mercadante di Napoli 1950; now

conducts regularly at all the maj. opera houses of Europe and the USA and conducts symphony concerts with all the leading orchestras; Permanent Dir. Landestheater Linz 1961–62, Deutsche Oper Berlin 1962–72; numerous opera and orchestral recordings; Targa d'Oro, Brescia 1970; Bacchetta d'Oro, Parma 1973; Grand Prix de Disque, Paris; Gold Medal for Falstaff, Budapest 1985. *Leisure interests:* collecting records and partiturs for study, table tennis, Italian cooking. *Address:* 8000 Munich 80, Holbeinstrasse 6, Federal Republic of Germany; Immeuble Michelangelo, 7 avenue de Papalins, Monte Carlo, Monaco. *Telephone:* 0033-93-256952 (Monte Carlo).

PATASSE, Ange; Central African Republic politician; b. 25 Jan. 1937; ed. French Equatorial Coll.; Agricultural inspector 1959–65; Dir. of Agric. 1965; Minister of Devt. 1965; Minister of State for Transport and Power 1969–70, concurrently Minister of State for Devt. and Tourism 1969–70; Minister of State for Agric., Stock-breeding, Waters and Forests, Hunting, Tourism, Transport and Power Feb.-June 1970; Minister of State for Devt. June-Aug. 1970; Minister of State for Transport and Commerce 1970–72, for Rural Devt. 1972–73, of Health and Social Affairs 1973–74; Minister of State for Tourism, Waters, Fishing and Hunting 1974–76, Prime Minister 1976–78, also Keeper of the Seals Sept.-Dec. 1976; Vice-Pres. Council of the Cen. African Revolution Sept.-Dec. 1976; Leader Mouvement pour la libération du peuple centrafricain; under house arrest Oct. 1979, escaped, recaptured and detained Nov. 1979; Cand. in Pres. Election March 1981; took refuge in French Embassy March 1982, fled to Togo April 1982; now living in France.

PATE, John Stewart, PH.D., F.A.A., F.R.S.; British professor of botany; b. 15 Jan. 1932; s. of H. S. Pate and M. M. Pate; m. Elizabeth L. Sloan 1959; three s.; ed. Campbell Coll. Belfast and Queen's Univ. Belfast; lecturer in Botany, Univ. of Sydney 1957–60; lecturer in Botany, Queen's Univ. Belfast 1960–65, then Reader, Personal Chair. in Plant Physiology 1970–83; Prof. of Botany, Univ. of W. Australia 1974–. *Publications:* books, research articles, reviews, chapters for textbooks and conf. proceedings. *Leisure interests:* music, reading, nature study, committee Christian. *Address:* 83 Circe Circle, Dalkeith, Western Australia 6009. *Telephone:* 3866070.

PATEL, Hirubhai, C.I.E., B.A., B.COM.; Indian politician; b. 26 Aug. 1904, Bombay; s. of Muljibhai and Hiraben Patel; m. Savitaben Patel 1928; ed. Oxford and London Univs.; Separation Officer, Sing 1935; Finance Dept., Bombay 1936; Sec. to Stock Exchange Cttee. 1936–37; Trade Commr., for N. Europe, Hamburg 1937–39; Deputy Trade Commr., London 1939–40; Deputy Sec. Eastern Group Supply Council 1941–42; Deputy Dir. Gen., Supply Dept. 1942–43; Jt. Sec. and Sec., Industries and Civil Supplies Dept. 1943–46, Cabinet Secr. 1946–47; Defence and Partition Sec. 1947–53; Sec. Food and Agric. 1953–54, Dept. of Econ. Affairs, Ministry of Finance 1957; Prin. Finance Sec. 1957–59; Chair. Life Insurance Corpn. of India 1956–57; Chair Gujarat Electricity Bd. 1960–66; mem. Gujarat Legis. Assembly 1967–71; Chair. Charutar Vidyamandal, Vallal Vidyanagar 1959–; Pres. Gujarat Swatantra Party 1967–72, All India Swatantra Party 1971–72; Minister of Finance 1977–79, of Home Affairs 1979; Gov. IMF 1977–79; mem. Lok Sabha 1971–80; mem. Cttee. of Janata Party Jan. 1977–; Hon. LL.D. (Sardar Patel Univ.); Albert Schweitzer Medal of Animal Welfare Inst., U.S.A. 1980. *Address:* Charutar Vidyamandal, Vallabh Vidyanagar, W. Railway, India.

PATEL, Indraprasad Gordhanbhai, PH.D.; Indian economist; b. 11 Nov. 1924, Baroda; s. of Gordhanbhai Patel and Kashiben Patel; m. Alaknanda Dasgupta 1958; one d.; ed. Baroda Coll., Bombay Univ., King's Coll., Cambridge and Harvard Univ.; Prof. of Econs. and Principal Baroda Coll., Maharaja Sayajirao Univ., Baroda 1949–50; Economist and Asst. Chief, Financial Problems and Policies Div., IMF 1950–54; Deputy Econ. Adviser, Indian Ministry of Finance 1954–58; Alt. Exec. Dir. for India, IMF 1958–61; Chief Econ. Adviser, Ministry of Finance, India 1961–63, 1965–67, Econ. Adviser Planning Comm. 1961–63; Special Sec. Ministry of Finance 1968–69, Sec. 1970–72; Deputy Admin., UN Devt. Programme 1972–77; Gov. Reserve Bank of India 1977–82; Dir. Indian Inst. of Man., Ahmedabad, India 1982–84; Dir. L.S.E. Oct. 1984–; Visiting Prof., Delhi School of Econs., Delhi Univ. 1964; Hon. Fellow King's Coll., Cambridge 1986. *Publications:* On the Economics of Development 1986, Essays in Economic Policy and Economic Growth 1986 and articles on inflation and econ. devt., monetary and credit policy, etc. *Leisure interests:* reading, music. *Address:* Office of the Director, London School of Economics and Political Science, Houghton Street, London, WC2A 2AE, England. *Telephone:* 01-405 7686.

PATEL, Jeram; Indian painter and graphic designer; b. 20 June 1930; ed. Sir J. J. School of Art, Bombay, Central School of Arts and Crafts, London; Reader in Applied Arts, M.S. Univ., Baroda (now Vadodara) 1960–61, 1966–; Reader in Visual Design, School of Architecture, Ahmedabad 1961–62; Deputy Dir. All India Handloom Bd. 1963–66; mem. Group 1890 (avant-garde group of Indian artists), Lalit Kala Akademi; one-man exhbns. in London 1959, New Delhi 1960, 1962–65, in Calcutta 1966; in Tokyo Biennale 1957–63, São Paulo Biennale 1963; represented in Nat. Gallery of Modern Art, New Delhi, Art Soc. of India, Bombay, Sir J. J. Inst. of Applied Art, Bombay, and in private collections in U.S.A., London, Paris and Tokyo; Lalit Kala Akademi Nat. Awards 1957, 1964; Bombay State Award 1957; Silver Medal, Bombay Art Soc. 1961; Gold Medal Rajkot Exhbn. *Address:* Faculty of Fine Arts, M.S. University, Vadodara 2, India.

PATEL, Praful Raojibhai Chaturbhai; British race relations adviser and company director; b. 7 March 1939, Jinja, Uganda; s. of Raojibhai Chaturbhai Patel and Maniben Jivabhai Lalaji Patel; unmarried; ed. Govt. Secondary School and London Inst. of World Affairs (Extra-Mural Dept., Univ. Coll., London); Sec. Uganda Students' Union 1956-58; del. to Int. Youth Assembly, New Delhi 1958; studied and lectured on politics and econs. in Africa and Middle East before arrival in Britain as student 1958, where developed commercial activities 1962; spokesman for Asians in U.K. following Commonwealth Immigrants Act 1968; Hon. Sec. All Party Parl. Cttee. on U.K. Citizenship 1968-; mem. Council, U.K. Immigrants Advisory Service 1970-; mem. Uganda Resettlement Bd. 1972-74, Hon. Sec. Uganda Evacuees Resettlement Advisory Trust 1974-; Pres. Nava Kala India Socio-Cultural Centre, London 1962-75; Chair. Bd. of Trustees, Swaminarayan Hindu Mission, U.K. 1970-76; Jt. Convenor, Asian Action Cttee. 1976; Convener Manava Trust 1979-; frequent appearances on radio and television programmes concerned with immigration and race relations. *Publications:* many articles in newspapers and journals on race relations and immigration. *Leisure interests:* cricket, campaigning and lobbying, current affairs, inter-faith co-operation. *Address:* 60 Bedford Court Mansions, Bedford Avenue, London, WC1B 3AD, England. *Telephone:* 01-580 0897.

PATEMAN, John Arthur, F.R.S., F.R.S.E., F.R.S.A.; Australian geneticist; b. 18 May 1926, London, England; s. of John and Isobel May (née Kirk) Pateman; m. Mary D. F. Phelps 1952; one s. two d.; ed. Clacton County High School, Univ. Coll., Leicester; lecturer in Genetics, Univ. of Sheffield 1954-57; Sr. Lecturer in Botany, Univ. of Melbourne 1957-60; Lecturer in Genetics, Cambridge Univ. 1960-67; Prof. of Biology, Flinders Univ., S. Australia 1967-70; Prof. of Genetics, Univ. of Glasgow 1970-79; Prof. and Head, Dept. of Genetics, A.N.U. 1979-, Exec. Dir., Centre for Recombinant DNA Research 1982-. *Publications:* numerous articles in scientific journals. *Leisure interests:* reading, music, walking. *Address:* Department of Genetics, Research School of Biological Sciences, Australian National University, Canberra, A.C.T. 2601 (Office); 46 Amaroo Street, Reid, Canberra, A.C.T. 2601, Australia (Home). *Telephone:* 062 494011 (Office); 062 488327 (Home).

PATERNOTTE de la VAILLÉE, Baron Alexandre E. M. L. G. C.; Belgian diplomatist; b. 6 May 1923, Berne, Switzerland; s. of Baron Paternotte de la Vaillée and Ann Cruger; m. Eliana, Countess Orsolini Cencelli 1946; three c.; entered Foreign Ministry 1945; Sec., Embassy in Washington, D.C. 1946-49, Paris 1952-57; Counsellor, Rio de Janeiro 1957-62; Dir. of Scientific Policy, Brussels 1962-66; Chair. European Launcher Devt. Org. 1966-67; Amb. to Lebanon, Jordan, Cyprus and Kuwait 1967-69, to Brazil 1970-74; Dir. for Middle East and N. Africa Affairs 1974-79; Amb. to France 1979-84, to the Holy See 1985-88; mem. Acad. of Fine Arts of Brazil; LL.D. (Brussels), LL.L. (Lyon); Grand Officer, Orders of Léopold, Léopold II and Crown; Kt., Order of Malta; Commdr., Légion d'honneur; Croix de guerre (Belgium and France). *Leisure interests:* art, literature, history, riding, shooting, water skiing. *Publications:* Benjamin Mary 1974, L'Hôtel de La Marck 1980.

PATERSON, Sir Dennis Craig, Kt., B.S., M.D., F.R.C.S., F.R.A.C.S.; Australian orthopaedic surgeon; b. 14 Oct. 1930, Adelaide; s. of Gilbert Charles Paterson and Thelma Drysdale Paterson; m. Mary Mansell Hardy 1955; one s. three d.; ed. Collegiate School of St. Peter, Adelaide, Univ. of Adelaide; Resident Medical Officer, Royal Adelaide Hosp. 1954, Adelaide Children's Hosp. 1956; Registrar, Robert Jones and Agnes Hunt Orthopaedic Hosp., Oswestry, Shropshire, England 1958-60; Sr. Registrar, Royal Adelaide Hosp. 1960-62; Consultant Orthopaedic Surgeon, Repatriation Gen. Hosp., Adelaide 1962-70; Asst. Hon. Orthopaedic Surgeon, Adelaide Children's Hosp. 1964-66, Sr. Hon. Orthopaedic Surgeon 1966-70, Dir. and Chief Orthopaedic Surgeon 1970-, mem. Bd. of Man., Chair. Medical Advisory Cttee., Medical Staff Cttee. 1976-84; Sr. Hon. Orthopaedic Surgeon, Queen Victoria and Modbury Hosps., Adelaide 1970; Sr. Visiting Consultant Orthopaedic Surgeon, Royal Adelaide Hosp.; mem. Bd. of Orthopaedic Surgery, R.A.C.S. 1974-82, 1984-87, Chair. 1977-82, mem. Court of Examiners 1974-84; Censor-in-Chief, Australian Orthopaedic Assen. 1976-80, Dir. Continuing Educ. 1982-86; Pres. Crippled Children's Assen. of S. Australia 1970-84; Pres. Int. Soc. of Orthopaedic Surgery and Traumatology (SICOT) 1987-; Queen's Jubilee Medal 1977; L.O. Betts Medal in Orthopaedic Surgery 1980. *Publications:* Electrical Stimulation and Osteogenesis (Thesis) 1982; over 60 articles in scientific journals. *Leisure interests:* golf, gardening. *Address:* Department of Orthopaedic Surgery, Adelaide Children's Hospital, 72 King William Road, North Adelaide, South Australia 5006; 31 Myall Avenue, Kensington Gardens, South Australia 5069, Australia (Home). *Telephone:* (08) 267 7223 (Office); (08) 332 3364 (Home).

PATERSON, Mervyn Silas, F.A.A., PH.D.; Australian geophysicist; b. 7 March 1925, South Australia; s. of Charles Paterson and Edith M. Michael; m. Katalin Sarosy 1952; one s. one d.; ed. Adelaide Technical High School, Univs. of Adelaide and Cambridge; research, Aeronautical Research Labs. Melbourne 1945-53; A.N.U., Canberra 1953-, Prof. Research School of Earth Sciences 1987-; Fellow, American Mineralogical Soc., American Geophysical Union; Hon. Fellow, Geological Soc. of America. *Publications:* Experimental Rock Deformation: The Brittle Field 1978; about 90 research

papers in rock deformation and materials science. *Leisure interests:* walking, reading. *Address:* Research School of Earth Sciences, Australian National University, G.P.O. Box 4, Canberra 2601, Australia. *Telephone:* 062-492497 (Office).

PATIASHVILI, Dzhumber Ilyich; Soviet politician; b. 1939 Georgia; ed. Georgian Agric. Inst., Tbilisi; mem. CPSU 1962-; Deputy Sec., Sec. of Komsomol Cttee., postgraduate and scientific worker at Georgian Agric. Inst. 1962-65; komsomol work in Georgia, Head of Dept. of Georgian Komsomol Rural Youth 1965-69; Deputy to Georgian S.S.R. Supreme Soviet 1967-; Second Sec. Cen. Cttee. Georgian Komsomol 1969-70, mem. 1969-74; mem. Cen. Cttee. Georgian CP 1971-89; cand. mem. of Politburo of Cen. Cttee. Georgian CP 1971-73, mem. 1974-89; mem. Presidium of Georgian S.S.R. Supreme Soviet 1971-73; First Sec. of Gori Regional Cttee. Georgian CP 1973-74; Sec. (responsible for agric.) of Cen. Cttee. Georgian CP; First Sec. Cen. Cttee Georgian CP 1985-89; mem. Presidium of Georgian S.S.R. Supreme Soviet 1985-89; mem. of Mil. Council, Transcaucasian Mil. Dist. 1985-89; mem. Cen. Cttee. CPSU 1986-; Order of Lenin, Order of October Revolution, Order of Red Banner (twice), numerous medals. *Address:* The Kremlin, Moscow, U.S.S.R.

PATIL, Veerendra, B.A., LL.B.; Indian politician and lawyer; b. 28 Feb. 1924, Chincholi, Gulbarga District; s. of Bascappa and Chinnamma Patil; m. Saradabai (Patil) 1944; one s. two d.; ed. Osmania Univ., Hyderabad; practised law 1947, 1950-55; mem. Hyderabad State Ass. 1952-55; Gen. Sec. Hyderabad Prov. Congress Cttee. 1955-56; mem. Exec. Cttee. Mysore Congress Party 1957; mem. All India Congress Cttee.; mem. Karnataka State Ass. 1956-71, Deputy Minister 1957-58, Minister 1961-68, Chief Minister of Karnataka 1968-71; Chief Minister of Mysore 1968-72; Minister of Petroleum and Chemicals, Govt. of India Jan.-Oct. 1980, of Shipping and Transport 1980-82, of Labour and Rehabilitation 1982, of Shipping and Transport 1984-85, of Chemicals and Fertilizers Jan. 1985; mem. Rajya Sabha 1972-78; Pres. Karnataka Janata Party; mem. Del. to U.S.S.R. 1965, to Japan and S.E. Asia 1970, to Australia 1972, to U.K. and Europe 1973; Janata Party. *Leisure interests:* golf, tennis. *Address:* 174-49, 9th Main Road, II Cross, Rajamahal Vilas Extension, Bangalore 560 006, India. *Telephone:* 30998.

PATINKIN, Don, PH.D.; Israeli professor of economics; b. 8 Jan. 1922, Chicago, Ill., U.S.A.; s. of Albert and Sadie Brezinsky Patinkin; m. Deborah Trossman 1945; one s. three d.; ed. John Marshall High School, Chicago, Chicago Yeshiva, Univ. of Chicago; Research Asst. Cowles Comm. for Econ. Research 1946-47, Research Assoc. 1947-48; Asst. Prof. of Econs., Univ. of Chicago 1947-48; Assoc. Prof. of Econs., Univ. of Ill. 1948-49; Lecturer in Econs., Hebrew Univ. of Jerusalem 1949, Assoc. Prof. 1952, Prof. 1957-, Rector 1982-85, Pres. 1983-86; Dir. of Research, Maurice Falk Inst. for Econ. Research in Israel 1956-72; Pres. Econometric Soc. 1974, Israel Econ. Assen. 1976; mem. Israel Acad. of Sciences and Humanities 1963; Hon. mem. American Econ. Assen.; Foreign Hon. mem. American Acad. of Arts and Sciences; Corresp. Fellow, British Acad.; Hon. D. Hum. Litt. (Univ. of Chicago) 1976, Hon. LL.D. (Univ. of W. Ontario) 1983; Rothschild Prize 1959, Israel Prize 1970. *Publications:* Money, Interest, and Prices: An Integration of Monetary and Value Theory 1956, 1965, The Israel Economy: the First Decade 1959, Studies in Monetary Economics 1972, Keynes' Monetary Thought: A Study of Its Development 1976, Keynes, Cambridge and the General Theory: The Process of Criticism and Discussion Connected with the Development of the General Theory (ed. with J. C. Leith) 1977, Essays On and In the Chicago Tradition 1981, Anticipations of the General Theory? and other essays on Keynes 1982. *Leisure interests:* hiking, swimming, archaeology. *Address:* Israel Academy of Sciences and Humanities, P.O. Box 4040, Jerusalem 91040, Israel. *Telephone:* 636211; 631076.

PATNAIK, Bijoyanananda (Biju); Indian politician; b. 5 March 1916, Cuttack; s. of Lakhminarayan Patnaik and Ashalata Devi; m. 1939; two s. one d.; ed. Ravenshaw Coll., Cuttack; joined Indian Nat. Airways; f. Kalinga Airways; participated in Quit India Movement 1942; elected to Orissa Legis. Ass. 1952, leader Pragati Party legis. group until 1973; Chief Minister of Orissa 1961-63; resgnd. to work in party org.; mem. Rajya Sabha 1972; Chair. Orissa Planning Bd. 1963-67, 1972; f. Kalinga Foundation Trust awarding Kalinga Prize for promotion and popularization of science; mem. Janata Party 1977-80, Lok Sabha 1980-84; Minister for Steel and Mines 1977-80, mem. Orissa Legis. Ass. 1985-, Leader of Opposition, Chair. Public Accounts Cttee. *Leisure interests:* reading, music, sports, science, cultural affairs. *Address:* Naveen Nivas, Aerodrome Gate, Bhubaneswar 751009, India. *Telephone:* 53260 (Office); 50006 (Home).

PATNAIK, Janaki Ballav, M.A.; Indian politican; b. 3 Jan. 1927, Rameswar, Puri District, Orissa; s. of Gokulanand and Rambha Devi; m. Jayanti Patnaik; one s. two d.; ed. Banaras Univ.; Sub-Ed. Eastern Times 1949, Jt. Ed. 1950, Ed. (also for Prajatantra) 1952-67; Ed. Paurusha; led tenants' agitation in Madhupur, Cuttack District 1953; mem. Sahitya Akademi, Orissa 1956-57, Lok Sabha 1971-77, 1980-; Minister of State for Defence, Govt. of India 1973-77; Minister of Tourism, Civil Aviation and Labour Jan.-Dec. 1980; Chief Minister of Orissa State 1980-. *Address:* Office of the Chief Minister, State Government, Bhubaneswar, India.

PATON, Sir Angus (see Paton, Sir Thomas Angus Lyall).

PATON, Boris Yevgeniyevich; Soviet metallurgist; b. 27 Nov. 1918, Kiev; m. Olga Borisovna Milovanova 1948; one d.; ed. Kiev Polytechnic Inst.; Dir. E. O. Paton Electric Welding Institute of Ukrainian S.S.R. Acad. of Sciences 1953–; corresp. mem. Ukrainian S.S.R. Acad. of Sciences 1951–58, mem. 1958–, Pres. 1962–; mem. U.S.S.R. Acad. of Sciences 1962, mem. Presidium 1963–; Chair. of Co-ordination Council on Welding in U.S.S.R. 1958–; Chair. of Scientific Council of U.S.S.R. Acad. of Sciences "New processes of production and treatment of metallic materials" 1964–; Chair. of Co-ordination Bd. of CMEA on joint works in the field of welding 1972–; Chair. of U.S.S.R. Nat. Cttee. on Welding 1976–; mem. of editorial bd. and ed.-in-chief of a number of scientific and tech. journals; author of 19 books, 960 articles and numerous inventions; Honoured Scientist of Ukrainian S.S.R. 1968; Honoured Inventor of U.S.S.R. 1983; Foreign mem. of Acad. of Sciences of Bulgaria 1969, Czechoslovakia 1973, Bosnia and Herzegovina 1975, G.D.R. 1980; mem. CPSU 1952–, cand. mem. Cen. Cttee. of CPSU 1961–1966, mem. 1966–; mem. Central Cttee. of CP of Ukraine 1960–; Deputy to U.S.S.R. Supreme Soviet 1962–; Vice-Chair. Soviet of the Union U.S.S.R. Supreme Soviet 1966; Deputy to Ukrainian S.S.R. Supreme Soviet 1959–, mem. of Pres. 1963–80; elected to Congress of People's Deputies of the U.S.S.R. 1989–; State Prize 1950, Lenin Prize 1957, numerous Gold Medals, Gold Medal "Hammer and Sickle" of Hero of Socialist Labour 1969, 1978; Order of Lenin (four times), Order of October Revolution 1984; Order of Red Banner of Labour 1943 and other awards. *Address:* E. O. Paton Electric Welding Institute, 11 Bozhenko Street, Kiev-5, U.S.S.R. *Telephone:* 227 31 83.

PATON, Sir (Thomas) Angus (Lyall), Kt., C.M.G., F.R.S.; British civil engineer; b. 10 May 1905, Jersey, C.I.; s. of Thomas Lyall Paton and Janet Gibb; m. Eleanor Joan Delmé-Murray (died 1964); two s. two d.; ed. Cheltenham Coll. and Univ. Coll. London; joined Sir Alexander Gibb and Partners 1925, Partner 1938, Sr. Partner 1955–77, Sr. Consultant 1977–84; work in U.K., Canada, Burma and Turkey on harbour works, hydroelectric schemes and industrial projects; responsible for design and supervision of many projects, including Owen Falls and Kariba hydroelectric schemes and Indus Basin project, W. Pakistan; Pres. Inst. of Civil Engineers 1970–71; Chair. Council of Eng. Insts. 1973; Vice-Pres. Royal Soc. 1976–78; Founder Fellow Fellowship of Eng. (U.K.) 1976; Fellow Univ. Coll. London 1952, Imperial Coll., London 1978; Foreign Assoc. Nat. Acad. of Eng. U.S.A. 1979; Hon. D.Sc.(Eng.) (London) 1977, (Bristol) 1981. *Publications:* numerous technical papers and articles on civil engineering; Power from Water 1960. *Leisure interests:* walking, do-it-yourself. *Address:* L'Epervier, Route Orange, St. Brelade, Jersey. *Telephone:* 0534 45619.

PATON, Sir William Drummond Macdonald, Kt., C.B.E., F.R.S., M.A., D.M., F.R.C.P.; British pharmacologist (retd.); b. 5 May 1917, Hendon, London; s. of Rev. William Paton and Grace Mackenzie Macdonald; m. Phoebe Margaret Rooke 1942; ed. Winchester House School, Repton School, Oxford Univ. and University Coll. Hospital Medical School; House Physician, Univ. Coll. Hospital (U.C.H.) 1942; Pathologist, Midhurst Sanatorium 1943; mem. staff Nat. Inst. for Med. Research 1944–52; Reader, Applied Pharmacology, U.C.H. 1952–54; Prof. of Pharmacology, Royal Coll. of Surgeons, London 1954–59; Prof. of Pharmacology, Oxford Univ., and Fellow Balliol Coll. 1959–84; Hon. Dir. Wellcome Inst. for History of Medicine 1983–87; Sec. Physiological Soc. 1951–57; Medical Research Council 1963–67; Council of Royal Soc. 1967–69; Jt. Ed. Notes and Records of the Royal Soc. 1971–89; Chair. Research Defence Soc. 1972–77, Smithkline Foundation 1983–87; Trustee, Rhodes Trust 1968–87 (Chair. 1978–82), Wellcome Trust 1978–87; Hon. F.F.A.R.C.S. 1975; Hon. D.Sc. (London) 1985, (Edinburgh) 1987; Cameron Prize (with E. J. Zaimis) 1956; Gairdner Award (with E. J. Zaimis) 1959; Gold Medal Soc. of Apothecaries 1976; Clover Lecturer 1958; Paget Lecturer 1978; Bertram Louis Abraham Lecturer (R.C.P.) 1962; Osler Oration (R.C.P.) 1978; Baly Medal (R.C.P.) 1983, Osler Memorial Medal, Univ. of Oxford 1986, Boyd Medal (R.D.S.) 1987. *Publications:* Pharmacological Principles and Practice (with J. P. Payne) 1968, Man and Mouse: Animals in Medical Research 1984 and papers in scientific journals on diving and high-pressure biology, histamine, synaptic transmission, drug action and drug addiction. *Leisure interests:* music and old books. *Address:* 13 Staverton Road, Oxford, England (Home). *Telephone:* 58355 (Home).

PATORSKI, Janusz, M.ENG.; Polish politician; b. 26 July 1946, Lębork, Słupsk Voivodship; m.; one c.; ed. Warsaw Technical Univ.; fmr. active leader of Polish Students' Asscn. (ZSP), including Sec. ZSP Acad. Council of Warsaw Tech. Univ. 1969; Sec. ZSP District Council, Warsaw 1970–72, Chair. ZSP District Revisional Comm., Warsaw 1972–73; mem. Polish United Workers' Party (PZPR) 1969–; Constructor, Polish Optics Works, Warsaw 1972; political worker in party apparatus 1972–81 including Sec. 1976–81 and First Sec. 1981–84 of PZPR District Cttee., Warsaw-Praga South; Sec. for Economic Reform, Industry, Foreign Trade, Workers' Self-government and Trade Unions Matters, PZPR Warsaw Cttee. 1984–88; mem. Nat. Governmental Comm. for Organizational Structures Inspection 1986–; mem. Comm. of Econ. Policy, Econ. Reform and Self-Govt. of PZPR Cen. Cttee. 1986–; mem. Experts' Team of Personnel Policy Dept. of PZPR Cen. Cttee. 1987–; Deputy Chair. Council of Ministers, mem. Presidium of Government 1988–; Deputy Chair. Council of Ministers 1988–; Knight's Cross of Polonia Restituta Order and other decorations. *Publications:* numerous works on social aspects of organization and management. *Leisure interests:* sport, car driving, relations with interesting people, experimentation. *Address:* Urząd Rady Ministrów, Al. Ujazdowskie 1/3, 00-583 Warsaw, Poland.

PATRÍCIO, Rui Manuel de Medeiros d'Espiney, LL.D.; Portuguese lawyer and politician; b. 17 Aug. 1932, Lisbon; s. of Emílio Patrício and Maria Augusta Medeiros d'Espiney; m. Maria Ignês Morais Sarmento; two s. two d.; ed. Faculty of Law, Univ. of Lisbon; Asst., Faculty of Law, Univ. of Lisbon 1958–64; fmr. Prof. Inst. de Estudos Sociais; Del. to Congress of Int. Chamber of Commerce 1961, World Oil Congress 1963; Under-Sec. of State for Overseas Devt. 1965–69; Under-Sec. of State for Foreign Affairs 1969–70; Minister of Foreign Affairs 1970–74; Grand Cross of the Order of the Crown of Oak of Luxembourg; Grand Officier, Légion d'honneur; Grand Officer of Order of Merit (Fed. Repub. Germany) and numerous other awards. *Address:* c/o Ministério dos Negócios Estrangeiros, Lisbon, Portugal.

PATRICK, Alison Mary Houston, B.A., PH.D., F.A.H.A.; Australian historian; b. 24 March 1921, Melbourne; d. of Hubert Ralph Hamer and Elizabeth Anne (née McLuckie) Patrick; m. James Finley Patrick 1944; two s. two d.; ed. St. Catherine's School, Univ. of Melbourne; tutor (part-time) Univ. of Melbourne 1946, lecturer (part-time) 1950, (full time) 1963, Sr. Lecturer 1970, Reader 1981–86; Chair. Dept. of History 1977–80, Sr. Assoc. 1987–; Chair. Dept. of Italian 1983–84; Assoc. Dean, Faculty of Arts 1983–86; mem. univ. and faculty cttees.; Council at Trinity Coll., Univ. of Melbourne 1978–86; Dwight's Prize and R.G. Wilson Scholarship in History 1941. *Publications:* The Men at The First French Republic 1972; articles in historical journals, documents for schools. *Leisure interests:* reading, writing, seeing new places. *Address:* 10 Gwenda Avenue, Canterbury 3126, Vic., Australia. *Telephone:* (03) 830-5257.

PATRICK, John; American dramatist; b. 17 May 1905, Louisville; s. of John Francis and Myrtle (Osborne) Goggan Patrick; ed. Holy Cross Coll., Harvard and Columbia Univs.; radio writer, San Francisco 1932–35, film writer, Hollywood 1936–37, free-lance dramatist, London and New York 1940–; served American Field Service 1942–44; Pulitzer Prize 1954, Drama Critics Circle Award, Tony Award and Donelson Award 1954, Screen Writers' Guild Award 1957, Foreign Corresp. Award 1957, Hon. D.F.A. (Baldwin-Wallace Coll.) 1972. *Publications:* plays: The Willow and I 1942, The Hasty Heart 1945, The Story of Mary Surratt 1947, The Curious Savage 1950, Lo and Behold 1951, The Teahouse of the August Moon 1953, Good as Gold 1957, Everybody Loves Opal 1962, It's Been Wonderful 1965, Everybody's Girl 1966, Scandal Point 1967, Love is a Time of Day 1969, A Barrel Full of Pennies 1970, Opal is a Diamond 1971, Macbeth Did It 1971, The Dancing Mice 1971, Lovely Ladies, Kind Gentlemen (Musical) 1971, The Small Miracle (TV) 1972, Hallmark Hall of Fame (TV Script) 1972, Anybody Out There? 1972, The Savage Dilemma 1972, Opal's Baby 1974, The Enigma 1974, Opal's Husband 1975, A Bad Year For Tomatoes 1975, Divorce, Anyone? 1976, Suicide, Anyone? 1976, Noah's Animals (Musical) 1976, Love Nest for Three, Sex on the Sixth Floor 1977, Girls of the Garden Club, That's Not My Father 1978, People! 1979, That's Not My Mother, Opal's Million Dollar Duck, The Indictment 1980, Cheating Cheaters 1985, The Reluctant Rogue 1986, The Gay Deceiver 1987, The Green Monkey 1987; films: Enchantment 1948, The President's Lady 1952, Three Coins in the Fountain 1954, Mister Roberts 1954, A Many Splendoured Thing 1955, High Society 1956, Les Girls 1957, Some Came Running 1958, The World of Suzie Wong 1960, Gigot 1961, Main Attraction 1963, Shoes of the Fisherman 1968. *Address:* c/o The Dramatists' Guild, 234 West 44th Street, New York, N.Y. 10036; Fortuna Mill Estate, Box 2386, St. Thomas, U.S. Virgin Islands 00801, U.S.A. (Home).

PATRICK, Ruth, PH.D.; American limnologist; b. 26 Nov. 1907, Topeka, Kan.; d. of Frank and Myrtle Jetmore Patrick; m. Charles Hodge IV 1931; one s.; ed. Coker Coll. and Univ. of Virginia; Curator, Leidy Microscopical Soc. 1937–47; Asst. Curator, Microscopy Dept., Acad. of Natural Sciences of Philadelphia 1939–47, Curator Dept. of Limnology 1947–, Chair. 1947–73, Francis Boyer Chair. 1973–, Chair. Bd. of Trustees 1973–76, Hon. Chair. 1976–; Lecturer in Botany, Univ. of Pa. 1950–70, Prof. of Biology 1970–; Lecturer in Algae Course, Marine Biological Lab., Woods Hole, Mass. 1951–55; mem. limnological expedition to Mexico (sponsored by American Philosophical Soc.) 1947; leader of expedition to Peru and Brazil (sponsored by Catherwood Foundation) 1955; Chair. panel of Cttee. on Pollution, N.A.S. 1966; mem. many other cttees. concerned with water pollution, environmental resources and control; mem. N.A.S., A.A.A.S., Ecological Soc. of America, American Soc. of Naturalists (Pres. 1975), Int. Asscn. of Limnology, American Philosophical Soc., American Acad. of Arts and Sciences; Hon. mem. S. Carolina Acad. of Sciences; Richard Hopper Day Memorial Medal, Acad. of Nat. Sciences 1969, YWCA Gold Medal 1970, Gold Medal, Phila. Soc. for Promoting Agric. 1975, Frances K. Hutchinson Medal 1977; Lewis L. Dollinger Pure Environment Award, Franklin Inst. 1970, 1970 Pa. Award for Excellence in Science and Tech., Botanical Soc. of America Merit Award 1971, Eminent Ecologist Award, Ecological Soc. of America 1972, Phila. Award 1973, Second Annual Tyler Int. Ecology Award 1975, Dept. of Interior Public Service Award 1975, Iben Award 1976, Hugo Black Award (Univ. of Ala.) 1979; Hon. D.Sc. from numerous univs. and colls.; Hon. LL.D. (Coker Coll.); Hon. L.H.D. (Chesnut Hill Coll.); Gold Medal (Royal Zoological Soc. of Antwerp) 1978; Hutchinson Award (Garden Club of America) 1977, Green World Award in Science

(N.Y. Botanical Gardens) 1979. *Publications:* numerous articles in professional journals. *Address:* Department of Limnology, Academy of Natural Sciences of Philadelphia, 19th and The Parkway, Philadelphia, Pa. 19103, U.S.A. *Telephone:* (215) 299-1097.

PATSALIDES, Andreas, B.SC.ECONS.; Cypriot politician; b. 1922, Tseri, Nicosia; m.; two c.; ed. Greek Gymnasium, Limmassol, School of Econs. and Political Science, London, and Harvard Univ., Mass.; various posts in public service; Gen. Dir. Planning Bureau 1962-68; Minister of Finance 1968-79; Gov. Bank of Cyprus 1979-, C.E.O. 1989-. *Address:* Bank of Cyprus Ltd., P.O. Box 1472, 86-90 Phaneromeni Street, Nicosia, Cyprus. *Telephone:* (02) 464540.

PATTAKOS, Stylianos; Greek politician; b. 8 Nov. 1912, Crete; s. of George and Maria Pattakos; m. Dimitra Nickolaidou 1940; two d.; ed. high school, cadet school, War Coll. and Nat. Defence Acad.; commissioned 1937, promoted Maj.-Gen. Dec. 1967, retd.; Minister of the Interior 1967-73, Deputy Premier Dec. 1967; First Deputy Premier 1971-73; arrested Oct. 1974, sentenced to death for high treason and insurrection Aug. 1975 (sentence commuted to life imprisonment).

PATTERSON, Right Rev. Cecil John, C.M.G., C.B.E., D.D., M.A.; British ecclesiastic; b. 9 Jan. 1908, London; s. of James Bruce and Alice Maud Patterson; ed. St. Paul's School and St. Catharine's Coll., Cambridge; Deacon 1931, Priest 1932; London curacy 1931-34; Missionary, Nigeria 1934-69; Asst. Bishop 1942-45, Bishop on the Niger 1945-69, Archbishop of W. Africa 1961-69; Rep. for Archbishops of Canterbury and York for Community Relations 1970-72; Hon. Asst. Bishop of London 1970-76; Hon. D.D. (Univ. of Nigeria) 1963, Hon. D.D. (Lambeth) 1963; Commdr. Fed. Repub. of Nigeria 1965. *Address:* 6 High Park Road, Kew, Richmond, Surrey, TW9 4BH, England. *Telephone:* 01-876 1697.

PATTERSON, Ellmore Clark, B.S.; American banker; b. 29 Nov. 1913, Western Springs, Ill.; s. of Ellmore Clark Patterson and Harriet Emma (Wales) Patterson; m. Anne Hyde Choate 1940; five s.; ed. Lyons Township High School, Lake Forest Acad. and Univ. of Chicago; with J. P. Morgan & Co. 1935-41, 1946-59 (Vice-Pres. 1951-59); following merger of J. P. Morgan & Co. and Guaranty Trust Co., became Exec. Vice-Pres. Morgan Guaranty Trust Co. of New York 1959-65. Dir. and Vice-Chair. of Bd. 1965-67, Chair. Exec. Cttee. 1967-68, 1977-78, Pres. 1969-71, Chair. 1971-77; Dir. Bethlehem Steel Corpn., Nabisco Brands, Inc., Commercial Union Corpn. 1982-, Santa Fe Southern Pacific Corpn. *Address:* 23 Wall Street, New York, N.Y. 10015 (Office); 112 Narrows Road, Bedford Hills, New York 10507, U.S.A. (Home). *Telephone:* (212) 483-2323.

PATTERSON, Gardner, M.A., PH.D.; American economist; b. 13 May 1916, Burt, Ia.; s. of Charles W. and Trella Gardner Patterson; m. Evelyn R. Roelofs 1942; one d.; ed. Univ. of Michigan and Harvard Univ.; U.S. Treasury Rep. Africa and Middle East 1941-44; U.S. Navy 1944-46; U.S. mem. Greek Currency Cttee., Athens 1946-48; Asst. Prof. of Econs. Univ. of Michigan 1948-49; Prof. of Econs. and Dir. of Int. Finance Section, Princeton Univ. 1949-57; Prof. of Econs. and Dir. of Woodrow Wilson School of Public and Int. Affairs, Princeton Univ. 1957-64, Prof. of Econs. and Acting Chair. Dept. of Econs. 1965-66; Asst. Dir.-Gen. GATT 1966-67, 1969-73, Deputy Dir. Gen. 1973-81; Visiting Prof., Yale Univ. 1983; Consultant 1984-; Econ. Adviser, U.S. Embassy, Israel 1953-54, U.S. Embassy, Ankara 1955-56; Head, U.S. Econ. Survey Mission to Tunisia 1961; Ford Foundation Research Fellow, Geneva 1963-64; Dir. Foreign Bondholders Protective Council (U.S.A.) 1963-64, 1968-69. *Publications:* Survey of United States International Finance 1949-54 1950-55, Discrimination in International Trade, The Policy Issues 1966. *Address:* 1517 Vermont Avenue, N.W., Washington, D.C. 20005, U.S.A.

PATTERSON, Harry (pseudonym Jack Higgins); British-Irish novelist; b. 27 July 1929; s. of Henry Patterson and Rita Higgins Bell; m. Amy Margaret Hewitt 1958; one s. three d.; ed. Roundhay School, Leeds, Beckett Park Coll. for Teachers, London School of Econs.; N.C.O., The Blues 1947-50, tried numerous jobs including clerk and circus tent hand 1950-58; schoolmaster, lecturer in liberal studies, Leeds Polytechnic, Sr. Lecturer in Educ., James Graham Coll. and Tutor in School Practice, Leeds Univ. 1958-72; full-time writer since age of 41. *Publications include:* (as Jack Higgins) Prayer for the Dying 1973 (filmed 1985), The Eagle has Landed 1975, Storm Warning 1976, Day of Judgement 1978, Solo 1980, Luciano's Luck 1981, Touch the Devil 1982, Exocet 1983, Confessional 1985 (filmed 1985), Night of the Fox 1986, A Season Hell 1989, Memoirs of a Dancehall Romeo 1989, The Dark Side of the Island 1989; (as Harry Patterson) The Valhalla Exchange 1978, To Catch a King 1979 (filmed 1983), Dillinger 1983, Walking Wounded (play) 1987; others under pseudonyms Martin Fallon, Hugh Marlowe, Henry Patterson. *Leisure interests:* tennis, old movies. *Address:* c/o Higham Associates Ltd., 5/8 Lower John Street, Golden Square, London, W1R 4HA, England.

PATTERSON, Rex Alan, PH.D.; Australian politician; b. 8 Jan. 1927, Bundaberg, Queensland; m. Eileen Nelson 1954; one d.; ed. Univ. of Queensland, Australian Nat. Univ., Univs. of Illinois and Chicago, U.S.A.; with R.A.A.F. Feb.-Sept. 1945; mem. Research Staff, Bureau of Agricultural Econs. 1949, Deputy Dir. 1960-64; Dir. Northern Devt. Div., Dept. of Nat. Devt. until 1966; mem. House of Reps. for Dawson, Queensland 1966-75; Minister for Northern Devt. 1972-75, for the Northern Territory

1973-75, for N. Australia June-Nov. 1975, for Agric. 1975; Leader, Australian Sugar Del., Int. Sugar Agreement Conf., Geneva 1973, Japan, S. Korea, Malaysia 1974, London 1975; mem. Ministerial Del., China 1974; Financial and Econ. Consultant to Int. Corpns. on sugar 1976-80; Labor Party. *Address:* Mackay, North Queensland 4740, Australia.

PATTINSON, John Mellor, C.B.E., M.A.; British oil executive; b. 21 April 1899, Knutsford, Cheshire; s. of late James Pearson Pattinson; m. Wilhelmina Newth 1927 (died 1983); two s.; ed. Rugby School, Cambridge Univ. and Royal Mil. Acad., Woolwich; Royal Field Artillery 1918-19; Anglo-Iranian Oil Co., Iran 1922-45, Gen. Man. 1937-45; Man. Dir. British Petroleum Co. Ltd. 1952-65, Deputy Chair. 1960-65; Dir. other oil and chemical cos.; Dir. Chartered Bank 1965-73; mem. Supervisory Bd. Erdölchemie GmbH, Cologne. *Leisure interest:* gardening. *Address:* Oakhurst, Oakcroft Road, West Byfleet, Surrey, England. *Telephone:* (09323) 42813.

PATTINSON, (William) Derek, M.A.; British administrator; b. 31 March 1930, Barrow-in-Furness; s. of late Thomas William Pattinson and Elizabeth Pattinson; ed. Whitehaven Grammar School, The Queen's Coll., Oxford; Home Civil Service 1952-70; Asst. Prin., Inland Revenue Dept. 1952, Pvt. Sec. to Chair. of Bd. 1955-58, Prin. 1957; Prin., H.M. Treasury 1962-65; Asst. Sec., Inland Revenue 1965-68; Asst. Sec., H.M. Treasury 1968-70; Assoc. Sec.-Gen., Gen. Synod of Church of England 1970-72, Sec.-Gen. 1972-(90); Presiding Officer Crown Appointments Comm. 1987-; Stanhope Historical Essay Prize, Oxford 1957, Chair. Govs. of Liddon House 1972-; Master, Worshipful Co. of Parish Clerks, Vice-Pres. SPCK. *Address:* 4 Strutton Court, Great Peter Street, London, SW1P 2HH, England.

PATZAICHIN, Ivan; Romanian canoeist; b. 26 Nov. 1949, Mila, Tulcea Co.; m.; one d.; ed. Coll. for Physical Educ. and Sport, Bucharest; World champion: simple canoe 1000m. (Tampere 1973, Sofia 1977) and 10000m. (Belgrade 1978, 1982); double canoe 500m. (Duisburg 1979) and 1000m. (Copenhagen 1970, Nottingham 1981, Tampere 1983); Olympic champion simple canoe 500m. (Munich 1972) and double canoe 1000m. (Ciudad de Mexico 1968, Moscow 1980, Los Angeles 1984); numerous silver and bronze medals at World and Olympic Championships; 25 times nat. champion of Romania. *Address:* Clubul Sportiv Dinamo, Soseaua Stefan cel Mare nr. 9, Bucharest, Romania.

PATZIG, Guenther, DR.PHIL.; German professor of philosophy; b. 28 Sept. 1926, Kiel; s. of Admiral Conrad Patzig; m. Christiane Koehn; one s. one d.; ed. Gymnasiums in Kiel and Berlin-Steglitz, Univs. of Göttingen and Hamburg; Asst. Philosophisches Seminar, Göttingen 1953-60, Privatdozent 1958-60, Prof. of Philosophy 1963-; Prof. of Philosophy, Univ. of Hamburg 1960-63; UNESCO Fellowship in Philosophy 1951-52; Howison Memorial Lecturer, Berkeley 1971; mem. Göttingen Acad. of Sciences, Wissenschaftskolleg, Berlin 1984; Pres. Acad. of Sciences Göttingen 1988-; Lower Saxony Prize for Science 1983. *Publications:* Die aristotelische Syllogistik 1959, Sprache und Logik 1970, Ethik ohne Metaphysik 1971, Tatsachen, Normen, Sätze 1980, Aristoteles Metaphysik Z: Text, Übersetzung, Kommentar (with M. Frede) 1988. *Address:* Philosophisches Seminar, Universität Göttingen, Platz d. Göttinger Sieben 5, D-3400 Göttingen, Federal Republic of Germany.

PAUK, György; British (b. Hungarian) violinist; b. 26 Oct. 1936, Budapest, Hungary; m. Susan Mautner 1959; one s. one d.; ed. Franz Liszt Acad. of Music, Budapest under Zathureczky, Leo Weiner and Zoltán Kodály; concerts all over East Europe 1952-58, and over the rest of the world; settled in Western Europe 1958, Holland 1958-61, England 1961-; Prof. of Violin, Royal Acad. of Music 1987-; has recorded numerous concertos, and the complete violin/piano music of Mozart and Schubert and all Handel's sonatas; First performances of Penderecki's violin concerto, U.K., Japan, Sir Michael Tippett's Triple Concerto, London 1980, Lutoslawski's Chain 2, U.K., Netherlands, Hungary, with composer conducting; Hon. mem. and Prof. Guildhall School of Music and Drama, London; Paganini Prize 1956, Sonata Competition Prize, Munich 1957, Jacques Thibaud Prize 1959, Grand Prix for Bartók Records (Ovation Magazine, U.S.A.) 1982, Best Record of 1983 (Gramophone Magazine). *Leisure interests:* football, tennis, theatre, reading, swimming, my family. *Address:* 27 Armitage Road, London, N.W.11, England. *Telephone:* 01-455 5042.

PAUL, Sir John Warburton, G.C.M.G., O.B.E., M.C., M.A., K.ST.J.; British overseas administrator; b. 29 March 1916, Weymouth; s. of W. G. Paul and Elizabeth Bull; m. Kathleen Audrey Weeden 1946; three d.; ed. Weymouth Coll., and Selwyn Coll., Cambridge; Royal Tank Regt. 1937-45; Colonial Service, Sierra Leone 1945-62, called to the Bar (Inner Temple) 1947; Dist. Commr. 1952-56; Perm. Sec. 1956-59; Prov. Commr. 1959-60; Sec. to the Cabinet 1960-62; Gov. of The Gambia 1962-65, Gov.-Gen. 1965-66; Gov. of British Honduras 1966-72; Gov. of the Bahamas 1972-73, Gov.-Gen. July-Oct. 1973; Lieut.-Gov. Isle of Man 1973-80; Chair. St. Christopher M.S.A. Ltd. 1980-; Dir. Overseas Relations St. John's Ambulance 1981-; mem. Bd. of Govs. Pangbourne Coll. 1981-86; Hon. Fellow, Selwyn Coll., Cambridge 1982. *Leisure interest:* painting. *Address:* Sherrens Mead, Sherfield-on-Loddon, Hants., England.

PAUL, Robert Cameron, M.A., C.ENG., F.I.CHEM.E., F.R.S.A., C.B.I.M.; British chemical engineer; b. 7 July 1935, Uxbridge; s. of Dr. F.W. Paul; m. Diana Kathleen Bruce 1965; two d.; ed. Rugby School and Corpus Christi Coll., Cambridge; Nat. Service (2nd Lieut. in Royal Engineers) 1953-55; Imperial

Chemical Industries (ICI) 1959–86; Dir. ICI Fibres 1976–79, Deputy Chair. ICI Mond Div. 1979–86; Deputy Chair. and Man. Dir. Albright and Wilson Nov. 1986–. *Leisure interests:* music (piano) and golf. *Address:* Albright and Wilson Ltd., 1 Knightsbridge Green, London, SW1X 7QD, England (Office). *Telephone:* 01-589 6393 (Office).

PAULINELLI, Allysson; Brazilian agronomist; b. 1936, Minas Gerais; Lecturer, later Dir. Agricultural High Inst., Minas Gerais; Sec. of Agric., Minas Gerais 1971; Minster of Agric. 1974–78. *Address:* c/o Ministério da Agricultura, Esplanada dos Ministérios, Bloco 8, Brasília, D.F., Brazil.

PAULING, Linus Carl, PH.D., SC.D., L.H.D., U.J.D., D.H.C.; American university professor; b. 28 Feb. 1901; m. Ava Pauling (died 1981); ed. Oregon State Coll., Calif. Inst. of Tech. and Univs. of Munich, Copenhagen and Zürich; full-time Asst. in Quantitative Analysis, Oregon State Coll. 1919–20; part-time Asst. Chem., Mechanics and Materials, Oregon State Coll. 1920–22; Graduate Asst., Calif. Inst. of Tech. 1922–23, Teaching Fellow 1923–25, Research Assoc. 1925–26, Nat. Research Fellow, Chem. 1925–26; Fellow, John Simon Guggenheim Memorial Foundation 1926–27; Asst. Prof. of Chem., Calif. Inst. of Tech. 1927–29, Assoc. Prof. 1929–31, Prof. 1931–64; Prof. of Chem., Univ. of Calif., at San Diego 1967–69, Stanford Univ. 1969–74, Prof. Emer. 1974–; Pres. Linus Pauling Inst. of Science and Medicine 1973–75, Research Prof. 1973–; Chair. Div. of Chem. and Chemical Eng., Calif. Inst. of Tech., Dir. of the Gates and Crellin Laboratories 1936–58; George Fisher Baker Lecturer in Chem., Cornell Univ. 1937–38; Eastman Prof. Oxford Univ. 1948; Research Prof. Center for Study of Dem. Insts. 1963–67; mem. N.A.S., American Acad. of Arts and Sciences, Deutsche Akad. der Naturforscher Leopoldina; Hon. mem. or Fellow Chemical Soc. of London, Acad. of Sciences of Liège, Royal Inst., Swiss Chemical Soc., Chemical Soc. of Japan, Nat. Inst. Sciences India, Royal Norwegian Scientific Soc., Trondheim; foreign mem. Royal Soc., Norwegian Acad. Science and Letters; Acad. of Sciences U.S.S.R.; corresp. foreign mem. Accad. delle Scienze, Lisbon Acad. Science; Foreign Assoc. Acad. des Sciences (France); Hon. Fellow, Indian Acad. Sciences, Austrian Acad. of Science, European Soc. of Haematology, etc.; hon. degrees from numerous univs., awards include: Langmuir Prize 1931, William H. Nichols Medal 1941, Willard Gibbs Medal 1946, Theodore William Richards Medal 1947, Davy Medal 1947, Medal for Merit 1948, Gilbert Newton Lewis Medal 1951, Nobel Prize for Chem. 1954, for Peace 1962, Thomas Addis Medal 1955, John Phillips Memorial Award, Avogadro Medal 1956, Pierre Fermat Medal, Paul Sabatier Medal 1957 Lenin Prize 1970, Martin Luther King, Jr. Medical Award 1972, U.S. Nat. Medal of Science 1974, Lomonosov Gold Medal 1978, N.A.S. Award in Chemical Sciences 1979, Gold Medal of the Nat. Inst. of Social Sciences 1979, Priestley Medal 1984, American Chemical Soc. Award in Chemical Educ. 1987. *Publications:* The Structure of Line Spectra (with S. Goudsmit) 1930, Introduction to Quantum Mechanics, with Applications to Chemistry (with E. Bright Wilson, Jr.) 1935, The Nature of the Chemical Bond 1939, General Chemistry 1947, College Chemistry 1950, No More War! 1958, 1962, The Architecture of Molecules (with R. Hayward) 1965, The Chemical Bond 1967, Vitamin C and the Common Cold 1971, Vitamin C, the Common Cold and the Flu, Cancer and Vitamin C (with Ewan Cameron) 1979, How to Live Longer and Feel Better 1986. *Address:* Linus Pauling Institute of Science and Medicine, 440 Page Mill Road, Palo Alto, Calif. 94306; Salmon Creek 15, Big Sur, Calif. 93920, U.S.A.

PAULS, Dr. Rolf Friedemann; German diplomatist; b. 26 Aug. 1915, Eckartsberga; s. of Bodo Pauls and Alma Pauls (née Wilkens); m. Lilo Serlo 1951; three s.; ed. Naumburg Domgymnasium and Univ. of Hamburg; Maj. in German Army 1936–45; Sec. to Parl. Council, Bonn 1948–49; Foreign Service 1950–; Personal Asst. to Sec. of State for Foreign Affairs (Prof. Hallstein) 1952–58; Counsellor for Political Affairs, Washington 1956–60; Counsellor and Deputy Amb., Athens 1960–63; Deputy Dir.-Gen. of Dept. for Econ. Affairs, Foreign Office, Bonn 1963–65; Amb. to Israel 1965–68, to U.S.A. 1969–73, to People's Repub. of China 1973–76; Amb. and Perm. Rep. of the Fed. Repub. of Germany to NATO 1976–80. *Leisure interests:* reading, riding. *Publications:* Deutschlands Standort in der Welt 1984; works on foreign policy and security. *Address:* 5300 Bonn 3, Kohlbergstrasse 11, Federal Republic of Germany. *Telephone:* 0228-481357.

PAUN, Radu, M.D., D.SC.; Romanian professor of medicine (retd.); b. 26 May 1915, Iasi; m. Florica Popa 1942; ed. Faculty of Medicine, Iasi Univ.; Asst. Prof., Inst. of Medicine, Iasi and Bucharest 1943–51, Assoc. Prof., Inst. of Medicine and Pharmacy, Bucharest 1962–65, Prof. 1965–79; Head of Lab., Romanian Acad. Inst. of Therapeutics 1953–54; Dir. State Medical Printing House 1954–59; Head of Medical Div., Colentina Hosp., Bucharest 1954–65, Cantacuzino Hosp., Bucharest 1965–77; Chair. Internal Medicine Soc. 1959–63; Vice-Chair. Union of Medical Science Socs. of Romania 1969–; Vice-Pres. Acad. of Medical Sciences 1969–, Acting Pres. 1975–81; Chair. Allergy Soc. 1963–67; Minister of Health 1975–76; Chair. Immunology Soc. 1975–83; Physician Emer. of Romania; mem. Acad. of Medical Sciences 1969–; Dr. Gheorghe Marinescu Award 1974; Steaua Romaniei. *Publications:* Structure Fonctionnelle de la Dure Mère chez les Vertèbres 1940, Terapia Imuno-supresivă 1972, Astmul Bronsic 1974, Boli Alergice 1977; Ed. and Co-author: Terapeutica Medicată 1982, Tratat de Medicină Internă 1983, 1986, 1987, 1988, 1989; over 150 scientific papers. *Leisure interest:* piano playing. *Address:* 29 Maria Rosetti Street, Bucharest 70232, Romania. *Telephone:* 111703.

PAUNIO, Jouko Juhani Kyösti, D.SC.S.; Finnish economist and international official; b. 18 May 1928, Helsinki; s. of Tauno Erhard Paunio and Saara Elina Paunio; m. 1st Terttu Jääskeläinen 1949 (divorced 1978), three s.; m. 2nd Riitta-Leena Heiskanen 1979, one d.; ed. Univ. of Helsinki; Head Research Dept., Bank of Finland 1959–66; Prof. of Econs., Univ. of Helsinki 1966–; Research Prof., Acad. of Finland 1972–75; Assoc. Dean, Faculty of Social Sciences, Univ. of Helsinki 1969, 1976–77, 1978, 1980; Dir. of Gen Econ. Analysis Div., UN Econ. Comm. for Europe 1981–86; Research Assoc., Univ. of Calif. at Berkeley 1962–63; Scientific Adviser to Bank of Finland 1966–76; Ford Foundation Research Fellow, Harvard Univ. 1969–70; mem. Exec. Cttee. Int. Econ. Assen. 1974–80; Chair. Nordic Econ. Research Council 1986–; Dr. h.c. (Åbo Acad.) 1988, (Turkish School of Econs.) 1988; Commdr. Order of the Finnish Lion 1983; Special Prize, Finnish Cultural Foundation 1976. *Publications:* A Study in Theory of Open Inflation 1959, A Theoretical Analysis of Growth and Cycles 1969 and numerous articles on macroeconomic theory and application. *Leisure interests:* long distance running, literature. *Address:* University of Helsinki, Aleksanterink 7, 00100 Helsinki, Finland. *Telephone:* 1912524.

PAUPINI, H.E. Cardinal Giuseppe; Italian ecclesiastic; b. 25 Feb. 1907, Mondario, Fano; ordained 1930; Titular Archbishop of Sebastopolis in Abasgia 1956; Apostolic Nuncio in Colombia 1959; cr. Cardinal 1969; Grand Penitentiary 1973–84. *Address:* Via Rusticucci 13, 00193 Rome, Italy.

PAUWELS, Louis; French author and journalist; b. 1920, Paris; m. 1st Suzanne Bregeon 1941, one s. one d.; m. 2nd Elina Labourdette 1956, one d.; Ed.-in-chief, Combat 1945, Arts (review) 1952, Marie-France (weekly magazine) 1956; founder Planète (review) 1961–71; Dir. Figaro Magazine 1978–, Madame Figaro 1978–, TV-France-Soir 1986–; mem. Acad. des Beaux Arts (Inst. de France); Chevalier, Légion d'honneur; Officier des Arts et Lettres, Ordre Nat. du Mérite. *Publications include:* Les voies de petite communication 1949, Le château du dessous 1952, L'amour monstre 1955, Saint Quelqu'un 1956, Matin des Magiciens (with J. Bergier) 1961, L'homme éternel (with J. Bergier) 1970, Ce que je crois 1974, Blumroch l'admirable ou le déjeuner du surhomme 1976, L'apprentissage de la sérénité 1977, Comment devient-on ce que l'on est? 1978, le Droit de parler 1981, La liberté guide mes pas 1984; essays, portraits, adaptations for stage and TV. *Address:* Le Bungalow, Mesnil-le-Roi, 78600 Maisons-Laffitte, France.

PAVAN, H. E. Pietro; Italian ecclesiastic; b. 30 Aug. 1903, Treviso; ordained 1928; cr. Cardinal 1985; Deacon of San Francesco da Paola ai Monti. *Address:* Via della Magliana 1240, Ponte Galeria, 00050 Rome, Italy. *Telephone:* (06) 647.00.69.

PAVAROTTI, Luciano, D.MUS.; Italian opera singer; b. 12 Oct. 1935, Modena; s. of Fernando and Adele (Venturi) Pavarotti; m. Adua Veroni 1961; three d.; ed. Istituto Magistrale; tenor range; début as Rodolfo in La Bohème at Reggio nell'Emilia 1961, Staatsoper Vienna, Royal Opera House of London 1963, La Scala 1965, Metropolitan Opera House, New York 1968, Paris Opera and Lyric Opera of Chicago 1973; début as Edgardo in Lucia di Lammermoor in U.S.A. (Miami) 1965; La Scala tour of Europe 1963–64; recitals and concerts abroad including the U.S.A. and Europe 1973–; about 30 albums 1964–79; appeared in MGM film Yes, Giorgio 1981; hon. degree (Pa.) 1979; Grand Officer, Italian Repub., Noce d'Oro Nat. Prize, Luigi Illica int. prize, first prize Gold Orfeo (Acad. du Disque Lyrique de France), Grammy Award for best classical vocal soloist 1981 and many other prizes. *Publications:* Pavarotti: My Own Story (with William Wright), Grandissimo Pavarotti 1986. *Leisure interests:* tennis, painting, equitation. *Address:* c/o Herbert Breslin, 119 West 57th Street, New York, N.Y. 10019, U.S.A. (Office); Via Giardini 941, 41040 Saliceta, Modena, Italy (Home).

PAVITT, Edward, M.C., B.SC.(ENG.); South African mining engineer and executive; b. 14 July 1918, Vryburg, N. Cape; s. of Edward P. R. and Gertrude Pavitt (née Hornby); m. Elizabeth Saunders 1942; three d.; ed. Kingswood Coll., Grahamstown and Witwatersrand Univ., Johannesburg; active mil. service 1939–45, Maj. 11th Field Cos., S.A. Eng. Corps 1944–45; Mining Engineer, Union Corpn. Ltd. 1946–62, Gen. Man. Leslie Gold Mines Ltd. 1962–64, Consulting Engineer 1964–67, Chief Consulting Engineer 1967–69, Dir. Union Corpn. Ltd. 1969–71, Asst. Man. Dir. 1971–72, Man. Dir. 1972–83, Chair. 1974–83, Chair. (non-exec.) 1983–86; Deputy Chair. Gen. Mining Union Corpn. Ltd. 1980–82, Exec. Chair. 1982–86; Dir. many mining, industrial and banking cos. *Address:* 31 Fricker Road, Illovo, Johannesburg 2196, South Africa (Home). *Telephone:* 442-7636 (Home).

PAVLOV, Sergey Pavlovich; Soviet politician; b. 19 Jan. 1929, Kalinin; s. of Pavel Petrovitch Pavlov and Valentina Nikolaevna Pavlova; m. Evguenia Mikhailovna; one s. one d.; ed. Technical Inst. and Moscow Inst. of Physical Culture; Komsomol work 1952–56; mem. CPSU 1954–; Sec., Second Sec., First Sec., Moscow City Cttee., Komsomol 1956–58; Sec. Cen. Cttee., Komsomol 1958–59, First Sec. 1959–68; Chair. Cen. Council of Sports Socs. June 1968, U.S.S.R. Cttee. for Sports and Physical Culture 1968–83; Amb. to Mongolia 1983–85, to Burma 1985–; mem. Cen. Cttee. CPSU 1961–71; mem. CPSU Cen. Auditing Comm. 1971–86; Deputy to U.S.S.R. Supreme Soviet 1962–70; received several decorations. *Leisure interest:* music. *Address:* Embassy of the U.S.S.R., 38 Newlyn Road, Rangoon, Burma.

PAVLOV, Vladimir Yakovlevich; Soviet politician and diplomatist; b. 26 Oct. 1923, Mosalsk, Kaluga oblast'; ed. Moscow Railway Eng. Inst.; mem.

CPSU 1948-, mem. Cen. Cttee. 1966-; railway engineer 1941-49; party and Komsomol work 1949-56; First Sec. Moscow Dist. Cttee., CPSU 1956-62; Sec. Moscow City, CPSU 1962-65, Second Sec. 1965-71; Amb. to Hungary 1971-81, to Japan 1982-85; Deputy to U.S.S.R. Supreme Soviet 1966-; Vice-Chair. Comm. for Transport and Communications of U.S.S.R.; mem. Cen. Cttee. of CPSU; Order of October Revolution and other decorations. *Address:* c/o Ministry of Foreign Affairs, Moscow, U.S.S.R.

PAWAR, Sharadchandra Govindrao, B.COM.; Indian politician; b. 12 Dec. 1940, Katychiwadi, Poona; s. of Govindrao Jijaba Pawar; m.; one d.; Head State Level Youth Congress; Gen. Sec. Maharashtra Pradesh Congress Cttee.; elected to State Legis. 1967, held Portfolios of Home and Publicity, and Rehabilitation; Minister of State and Educ. and Youth Welfare, Home, Agric. and Industries and Labour; Chief Minister of Maharashtra 1978-80, 1988-; Pres. Nat. Congress (opposition) 1981-86; rejoined Congress (I) 1986; fmr. Pres. Congress Forum for Socialistic Action; Sec. Defence Cttee. *Address:* 3 Raisina Road, New Delhi 110001, India.

PAWEŁKIEWICZ, Jerzy, D.SC.; Polish biochemist; b. 16 Oct. 1922, Częstochowa; ed. Poznań Univ.; Doctor 1951-54, Docent 1954-60, Assoc. Prof. 1960-67, Prof. 1967-; Corresp. mem. Polish Acad. of Sciences 1967-77, mem. 1977-; mem. Biochemical and Biophysical Cttee. 1969-, now also mem. Scientific Councils of Inst. of Biochem. and Biophysics and of Dept. of Dendrology, Chair. Scientific Council of Plant Genetics Dept.; Head of Biochem. Inst., Poznań Acad. of Agric. 1972-; mem. Polish Biochemical Soc.; worked on Vitamin B12, biosynthesis of proteins and plant ribonucleic acids; Gold Cross of Merit 1959, Medal of 10th Anniversary of People's Poland 1955, State Prize, 1st Class 1974, Minister of Science, Technics and Higher Educ. Prize 1975, Kt.'s Cross of Order of Polonia Restituta. *Publications:* Fizyko-chemiczne metody w analizie żywnościowej (Physico-Chemical Methods in Food Analysis) 1954, co-author Chromatografia 1957; numerous articles in Polish and other languages. *Address:* Ul. Kniewskiego 1 m. 7, 60-743 Poznań, Poland. *Telephone:* 22-45-81.

PAWŁOWSKI, Janusz, M.A.; Polish politician and economist; b. 1932, Kasina Wielka, Nowy Sącz Voivodship; m.; three s.; ed. Wrocław Econ. Acad.; employed in Horticulture Head Office, Cracow 1950-51; Deputy Man. of Production in Fruit-Vegetable Industry Plants, Tymbark 1952-64; Sr. Instructor for Labour Org. Matters, Mazovian Fruit-Vegetable Industry Plants 1964-65; Head, Dept. for Employees' Matters, Union of Fruit-Vegetable Industry, Warsaw 1965-77; Head, Dept. for Employees' Matters and Chief of Trade Centre for Labour Org. and Standardization in Meat Industry Union, Warsaw 1977-80; Deputy Dir., subsequently Dir. of Dept. of Wages in Production Sphere in Ministry of Labour, Wages and Social Services 1980-84; Deputy Minister of Labour, Wages and Social Services 1984-87, Minister April-Oct. 1987; Minister of Labour and Social Policy 1987-88; mem. Polish United Workers' Party (PZPR); Kt.'s Cross of Polonia Restituta Order and other decorations. *Address:* c/o Ministerstwo Pracy i Polityki Socjalnej, ul. Nowogrodzka 1/3/5, 00-513 Warsaw, Poland.

PAYAN, Jean-Jacques, D. ÈS SC.; French professor of education; b. 3 May 1935, Grenoble; s. of Edmond Payan and Madeleine Roche; m. Ghislaine Vallaeys 1958; one s. four d.; ed. Ecole Normale Supérieure; Asst. and Dir. of Studies, Univ. of Paris-Sud 1959-62; Maître de conferences, Faculty of Sciences, Grenoble 1964-67; Prof. Univ. of Grenoble I 1968-69, 1970-72, 1986-; Prof. Univ. of Tunis 1969-70; Dir. Centre Interuniversitaire de Calcul, Grenoble 1978-81; Pres. Univ. of Grenoble I 1981-82, 1987-; Dir.-Gen. C.N.R.S. 1981-82; Dir.-Gen. of Further Educ. and Research, Ministry of Educ. 1982-86; Resident Prof., Univ. Concordia, Montreal, Canada 1987; Commdr. des Palmes académiques (and mem. Council). *Leisure interests:* excursions, tennis, collecting stamps, reading. *Address:* Institut Fourier, Université de Grenoble, B.P. 116, 38402 St. Martin d'Heres, France.

PAYE, Jean-Claude; French diplomatist; b. 26 Aug. 1934; ed. Inst. d'Etudes Politiques and Ecole Nat. d'Admin.; Head, private office of Mayor of Constantine 1961-62; Sec. of Embassy , Algiers 1962-63; Ministry of Foreign Affairs 1963-65; special adviser, Office of Sec. of State for Scientific Research 1965, Office of Minister for Social Affairs 1966; Head of private office of M Barre (Vice-Pres. of Comm. of European Communities) 1967-73; Counsellor, Bonn 1973-74; Deputy Head, Office of Minister for Foreign Affairs 1974-76; Counsellor to Prime Minister Raymond Barre 1976-79; Sec.-Gen. Interministerial Cttee. for European Econ. Co-operation questions 1977-79; Dir. Econ. and Financial Affairs, Ministry for External Relations 1979-84; Sec.-Gen. OECD 1984-. *Address:* c/o Organization for Economic Co-operation and Development, 2 rue André Pascal, 75775 Paris, Cedex 16, France. *Telephone:* 45-24-82-00.

PAYNE, Anthony Edward, B.A.; British composer; b. 2 Aug. 1936, London; s. of Edward Alexander Payne and (Muriel) Margaret Payne; m. Jane Manning (q.v.); ed. Dulwich Coll., London and Durham Univ.; freelance musical journalist, musicologist, lecturer, etc. with various publs. and BBC Radio, active in promoting "new music", serving on cttee. of Macnaghten Concerts (Chair. 1967) and Soc. for the Promotion of New Music (Chair. 1969-71), composed part-time 1962-73; full-time composer 1973-; Prof. of Composition, London Coll. of Music 1983-; Milhaud Prof., Mills Coll., Oakland, Calif. 1983. *Compositions:* Concerto for Orchestra 1976, Phoenix Mass 1974, The World's Winter 1976, String Quartet 1978, The Stones and Lonely Places Sing 1979, Song of the Cloud 1980, A Day in the Life

of a Mayfly 1981, Evening Land 1981, Spring's Shining Wake 1981, The Spirit's Harvest 1985, The Song Streams in the Firmament 1986, Fanfares and Processional 1986; mem. Cttee. Asscn. of Professional Composers; Radcliffe Award 1975; Int. Jury Choice for Int. Soc. for Contemporary Music Festival 1976 (Concerto for Orchestra); Gramophone Critics' Choice 1977 (The Music of Anthony Payne). *Publications:* Schoenberg 1968, The Music of Frank Bridge 1984. *Leisure interests:* English countryside, cinema. *Address:* 2 Wilton Square, London, N1 3DL and c/o J. & W. Chester, 7-9 Eagle Court, London, EC1M 5QD, England.

PAYNE, Sir Norman John, Kt., C.B.E., F.ENG.; British nationalized industry executive; b. 9 Oct. 1921, London; s. of the late F. Payne; m. Pamela V. Wallis 1946; four s. one d.; ed. Lyon School, Harrow and Imperial Coll. of Science and Technology; joined Sir Frederick Snow and Partners 1949, Partner 1955; Eng. Dir. British Airports Authority 1965, Planning Dir. 1969, mem. Bd. 1971, Chief Exec. 1972, Chair. 1977-86, Chair. BAA PLC 1986-; several other professional appts.; Hon. D. Tech. (Loughborough) 1985. *Publications:* various papers on airports and air transport. *Leisure interests:* gardening, photography. *Address:* BAA PLC, 130 Wilton Road, London, SW1V 1LQ; 44 Catherine Place, London, SW1E 6HL, England.

PAZ, Octavio; Mexican writer and diplomatist; b. 31 March 1914, Mexico City; s. of Octavio Paz Sr. and Josefina Lozano; m. Marie José Tramini; one d.; ed. Univ. of Mexico; Founder, Dir. or Ed. several Mexican literary reviews, including Barandal 1931, Taller 1939, El Hijo Pródigo 1943; Guggenheim Fellowship (U.S.A.) 1944; fmr. Sec. Mexican Embassy, Paris; Chargé d'affaires a.i., to Japan 1951; posted to Secr. for External Affairs; Amb. to India 1962-68; Simón Bolívar Prof. of Latin-American Studies and Fellow, Churchill Coll., Cambridge 1970-71; Charles Eliot Norton Prof. of Poetry, Harvard Univ. 1971-72; Hon. mem. American Acad. of Arts and Letters 1972; Int. Poetry Grand Prix 1963, Jerusalem Prize 1977, Grand Golden Eagle of the Int. Festival, Paris 1979, Peace Prize (Fed. German Book Trade) 1984, Gran Cruz de Alfonso X el Sabrio 1986, Ingersoll Prize (shared) 1987, T. S. Eliot Prize, Ingersoll Foundation 1987, De Tocqueville Prize. *Publications:* poetry: Luna Silvestre 1933, Raíz del Hombre 1937, Entre la Piedra y la Flor 1940, A la Orilla del Mundo 1942, Libertad bajo Palabra 1949, Piedra de Sol 1957, La Estación Violenta 1958, Ladera este 1970, La Centena 1970, Topoemas 1971, Renga 1971, Pasado en Claro 1975, Vuelta 1976, Poemas 1935-75 1979, Arbol adentro 1987, also writes poetry in English; prose: El Laberinto de la Soledad 1950 (Labyrinth of Solitude 1961), Aguila o Solé 1951, El Arco y la Lira 1956, Las Peras del Olmo 1957, Conjunciones y disyunciones (essays) 1970, Posdata 1971, Claude Lévi-Strauss: An Introduction 1972, Alternating Current (essays) 1973, The Siren and the Seashell 1976, Marcel Duchamp: Appearance Stripped Bare, 1981, One Earth, Four or Five Worlds 1985, Convergences 1987, Sor Juana: Her life and her world 1988, Collected Poems 1957-87 1989. *Address:* c/o Revista Vuelta, Leonardo da Vinci 17, México 03910 D.F., Mexico.

PAZ ESTENSSORO, Víctor; Bolivian politician; b. 2 Oct. 1907; s. of Domingo Paz Rojas and Carlos Estenssoro de Paz; m. 1st Carmela Cerruto Calderón 1936, one s. one d.; m. 2nd Teresa Cortez Velasco, three d.; ed. Univ. Mayor de San Andrés; Finance official 1932-33; Deputy Tarija 1938-39 and 1940-41; Pres. Banco Minero 1939; Prof. Econ. History, Univ. of La Paz 1939-41; Minister of Finance 1941-44; Pres. of Bolivia 1952-56, 1960-64, Aug. 1985-; Amb. to the U.K. 1956-59; Prof. Econ. Devt. Theory, Planning Inst. Nat. Eng. Univ. de Lima 1966; Leader of Movimiento Nacional Revolucionario; presidential candidate in inconclusive elections 1979, 1980. *Publications:* Esquema de la Organización Política y Administrativa de Bolivia, Aspecto de la Economía Boliviana, Revolución y Contrarrevolución, Proceso y Sentencia de la Oligarquía Boliviana, La Revolución Boliviana, Discursos Parlamentarios, Discursos y Mensajes, Contra la Restauración por la Revolución Nacional, La Obra, Maestra de los Restauradores, El Imperativo Nacional, Presencia de la Revolución Nacional. *Leisure interest:* photography. *Address:* Palacio de Gobierno, Plaza Murillo, La Paz, Bolivia. *Telephone:* (02) 374030.

PEACOCK, Sir Alan, Kt., D.S.C., M.A., F.B.A.; British economist; b. 26 June 1922, Ryton-on-Tyne; s. of Alexander D. and Clara M. Peacock; m. Margaret Martha Astell-Burt 1944; two s. one d.; ed. Dundee High School, Univ. of St. Andrews; Lecturer in Econs., Univ. of St. Andrews 1947-48; Lecturer in Econs., L.S.E. 1948-51, Reader in Public Finance 1951-56; Prof. of Econ. Science, Univ. of Edinburgh 1956-62; Prof. of Econs., Univ. of York 1962-78; Prof. of Econs. and Prin. Univ. Coll. at Buckingham 1980-83, Vice-Chancellor 1983-84, Prof. Emer. 1984-; Research Prof. in Public Finance, Heriot-Watt Univ. 1985-; Chief Econ. Adviser, Dept. of Trade and Industry 1973-76; Pres. Int. Inst. of Public Finance 1966-69, Hon. Pres. 1975-; mem. Royal Comm. on Constitution 1970-73, Social Science Research Council 1971-72; mem. Council, Inst. of Econ. Affairs, Council, London Philharmonic Orchestra 1975-79; Chair. Arts Council Enquiry into Orchestral Resources 1969-70, Scottish Arts Council 1986-; mem. Bd. of Dirs. English Music Theatre Ltd. 1975-77; mem. Council of Man., Nat. Inst. of Econ. and Social Research 1977-86; non-exec. Dir. Economist Intelligence Unit 1977-84; Exec. Dir. David Hume Inst. 1987-; Chair. Cttee. on Financing the BBC 1985-86; Fellow British Acad. 1979-; Hon. Pres. Atlantic Econ. Soc. 1981-82; Hon. Fellow L.S.E. 1980-; Dr. h.c. (Univ. of Stirling) 1974; Hon. Dr. Econ. (Zürich) 1984, Hon. D.Sc. (Univ.

of Buckingham) 1986. *Publications:* Economics of National Insurance 1952, Growth of Public Expenditure in United Kingdom (with J. Wiseman) 1961, Economic Theory of Fiscal Policy (with G. K. Shaw) 1971, The Composer in the Market Place (with R. Weir) 1975, Welfare Economics: A Liberal Reinterpretation (with Charles Rowley), The Credibility of Liberal Economics 1977, The Economic Analysis of Government 1979, The Political Economy of Taxation (ed. with Francesco Forte) 1980, The Regulation Game (Ed.) 1984, Public Expenditure and Government Growth (Ed. with F. Forte) 1985, and numerous articles in professional journals on economics, public finance, social policy. *Leisure interest:* music. *Address:* David Hume Institute, 16 Hope Street, Edinburgh, EH2 4DD, Scotland. *Telephone:* (031) 225-6298.

PEACOCK, Hon. Andrew Sharp, LL.B., M.P.; Australian politician; b. 13 Feb. 1939, Melbourne; s. of the late A. S. Peacock and Iris Peacock; m. 2nd Margaret St. George 1983; three d. from previous marriage; ed. Scotch Coll., Univ. of Melbourne; Pres., Victorian Liberal Party 1965-66; mem. House of Reps. for Kooyong, Vic. 1966-; fmr. partner Rigby and Fielding, solicitors; fmr. Chair. Peacock & Smith Pty. Ltd., engineers; Minister for the Army and Minister Assisting the Prime Minister 1969-71, Assisting the Treasurer 1971-72; Minister for External Territories 1972; mem. Opposition Exec. 1973-75, Spokesman on Foreign Affairs 1973-75; Minister for Foreign Affairs 1975-80, for the Environment Nov.-Dec. 1975, for Industrial Relations 1980-81, for Industry and Commerce 1982-83; Leader Parl. Liberal Party 1983-85, Deputy Leader 1987-89, Leader May 1989-; Opposition Spokesman on Foreign Affairs 1985-87; Deputy Leader of the Opposition and Shadow Treas. 1987-. *Leisure interests:* horse racing, Australian Rules Football, surfing, reading. *Address:* 48 Berry Street, East Melbourne, Vic. 3002, Australia.

PEACOCK, Ronald, M.A., D.PHIL., LITT.D.; British university professor; b. 22 Nov. 1907, Leeds, Yorks.; s. of Arthur L. Peacock and Elizabeth Peacock (née Agar); m. Ilse G. E. Freiwald 1933; ed. Leeds Modern School, Univs. of Leeds, Berlin, Innsbruck and Marburg; Asst. Lecturer in German, Univ. of Leeds 1931-38, Lecturer 1938-39, Prof. 1939-45; Prof. of German Language and Literature, Univ. of Manchester 1945-62, Pro-Vice-Chancellor 1958-62; Visiting Prof. of German Literature, Cornell Univ. 1949; Visiting Prof. Univ. of Heidelberg 1960-61; Prof. German, Bedford Coll., Univ. of London 1962-75, Prof. Emer. 1975-; Prof. Univ. of Freiburg 1965, 1967-68; Fellow Bedford Coll. 1980-; Pres. Modern Humanities Research Assen. 1983; Hon. D.Litt. (Manchester); Goethe Medaille (Munich). *Publications:* The Great War in German Lyrical Poetry 1934, Das Leitmotiv bei Thomas Mann 1934, Hölderlin 1938, The Poet in the Theatre 1946, The Art of Drama 1957, Goethe's Major Plays 1959, Criticism and Personal Taste 1972, many contributions to periodicals. *Leisure interests:* music, theatre. *Address:* Greenshade, Woodhill Avenue, Gerrard's Cross, Bucks., England. *Telephone:* (0753) 884886.

PEACOCK, William James, PH.D., F.R.S., F.A.A.; Australian research scientist; b. 14 Dec. 1937, Leura, N.S.W.; s. of William Edward and Evelyn Alison Peacock; m. Margaret Constance Woodward 1961; one s. two d.; ed. Univ. of Sydney; Visiting Research Scientist, Genetics, CSIRO, Canberra 1963; Fellow, Dept. of Biology, Univ. of Oregon 1963-64, Visiting Assoc. Prof. 1964-65; Research Consultant, Biology Div., Oak Ridge Nat. Lab., U.S.A. 1965; Sr. Research Scientist, Div. of Plant Industry, CSIRO, Canberra 1965-69, Prin. Research Scientist 1969-73, Sr. Prin. Research Scientist 1973-77, Chief Research Scientist 1977-78, Chief 1978-; Adjunct Prof. of Biology, Univ. of Calif., San Diego 1969-70; Visiting Prof. of Biochem., Stanford Univ. 1970-71; Visiting Distinguished Prof. of Molecular Biology, Univ. of Calif., Los Angeles 1977; Chair. Bd. of Trustees, Int. Bd. of Plant Genetic Resources; Dir. Bioplantech Ltd., Melbourne; Scientific Adviser, Australian Genetic Eng. Ltd.; Edgeworth David Medal, Royal Soc. of N.S.W. 1967; Lemberg Medal, Australian Biochemical Soc. 1978. *Publications:* about 150 research papers on molecular biology, cytogenetics and evolution; ed. of six books. *Leisure interests:* squash, bushwalking, skiing. *Address:* CSIRO, Division of Plant Industry, G.P.O. Box 1600, Canberra, A.C.T. 2601 (Office); 16 Brassey Street, Deakin, A.C.T. 2601, Australia (Home). *Telephone:* 062-465250 (Office); 062-814485 (Home).

PEARCE, Baron (Life Peer), cr. 1962, of Sweethaws; **Edward Holroyd Pearce,** P.C., Kt., M.A., R.B.A.; British judge; b. 9 Feb. 1901, Sidcup, Kent; s. of late John W. E. Pearce, F.S.A. and Irene Pearce; m. Erica Priestman 1927 (died 1985); two s.; ed. Merton Court School, Charterhouse and Corpus Christi Coll., Oxford; called to the bar 1925; Q.C. 1945; Judge of Probate, Divorce and Admiralty Court 1948-54; Judge of Queen's Bench Div. 1954-57; Lord Justice of Appeal 1957-62; Lord of Appeal in Ordinary 1962-69; Treas. of Lincoln's Inn 1966; Chair. of Press Council 1969-74; Chair. British Comm. on Rhodesian Opinion 1972; fmr. Chair. Appeals Cttee. Takeover Panel 1969-76; Ind. Chair. Press discussions on Charter of Press Freedom 1976-77; retd. 1976; Pres. Artists League of Great Britain 1950-74; Prof. of Law, Royal Acad. of Arts 1971-; Hon. Fellow, Corpus Christi Coll., Oxford 1950-. *Leisure interest:* painting. *Address:* Sweethaws, Crowborough, Sussex, England. *Telephone:* (08926) 61520.

PEARCE, Sir Austin William, Kt., C.B.E., D.SC., PH.D.; British business executive; b. 1 Sept. 1921, Plymouth; s. of late William T. Pearce and of Florence Pearce; m. 1st Maglona Winifred Twinn 1947 (died 1975), 2nd Florence Patricia Grice 1979; three d. and two step-d.; ed. Devonport High

School for Boys, Birmingham Univ. and Harvard Business School; joined Esso Petroleum Co. 1945, Dir. 1963-80, Man. Dir. 1968-71, Chair. 1972-80, Dir. Esso Europe Inc. 1972-80; Chair. Irish Refining Co. Ltd. 1965-71, U.K. Petroleum Industry Advisory Cttee. 1977-80; Pres. Inst. of Petroleum 1968-70; Pres. Pipeline Industries Guild 1973-75; Pres. Oil Industries Club 1975-76; Pres. U.K. Petroleum Industry Assen. 1979-80; Vice-Pres. Soc. of British Aerospace Cos. 1981-82, Pres. 1982-83; Vice-Pres. Eng. Employers' Group 1983-87; Dir. Williams and Glyn's Bank Ltd. 1974-85, Deputy Chair. 1980-83, Chair. 1983-85; Dir. Royal Bank of Scotland Group 1978-, Vice-Chair. 1985-; Dir. British Aerospace 1977-, Chair. 1980-87; Chair. Oxford Instruments 1987-; Dir. Pearl Assurance PLC 1985-, Jaguar PLC 1986-, Smiths Industries 1987-; Chair. CBI Industrial Policy Cttee. 1982-85; mem. Advisory Council on Energy Conservation 1974-80, Energy Comm. 1977-79; mem. Bd., English-Speaking Union 1974-80; mem. Comm. on Energy and the Environment 1978-81; Trustee and Chair. Science Museum, London 1986-; Pro-Chancellor Univ. of Surrey 1985-; mem. Takeover Panel 1987-; Patron Nat. Training Awards 1988; Hon. D.Sc. (Exeter, Southampton) 1985, (Birmingham) 1986, (Salford Cranfield) 1987. *Leisure interests:* golf, general handicrafts. *Address:* 25 Caroline Terrace, Belgravia, London, SW1W 8JT, England.

PEARS, David Francis, M.A., F.B.A.; British university professor; b. 8 Aug. 1921, London; s. of Robert Pears and Gladys Meyers; m. Anne Drew 1963; one s. one d.; ed. Westminster School and Balliol Coll., Oxford; Research Lecturer, Christ Church, Oxford 1948-50, Student 1959-88; Fellow and Tutor, Corpus Christi Coll., Oxford 1950-59; Prof. of Philosophy, Oxford Univ. 1985-88; mem. L'Institut Internationale de Philosophie. *Publications:* Bertrand Russell and the British Tradition in Philosophy 1967, Ludwig Wittgenstein 1971, Some Questions in the Philosophy of Mind 1975, Motivated Irrationality 1983, The False Prison: A Study of the Development of Wittgenstein's Philosophy, (Vol. 1) 1987, (Vol. 2) 1988. *Leisure interests:* entomology, visual art. *Address:* 7 Sandford Road, Littlemore, Oxford, OX4 4P0, England.

PEARSE, Anthony Guy Everson, M.D., F.R.C.P.; British professor of histochemistry; b. 9 Aug. 1916, Birchington, Thanet; s. of Capt. R.G. Pearse and Constance Evelyn Steels; m. Elizabeth Himmelhoch 1947; one s. three d.; ed. Trinity Coll., Cambridge; House Physician, St. Bartholomew's Hosp., London 1940; Surgeon-Lieut., R.N.V.R. 1941-46; Lecturer in Pathology, Royal Postgraduate Medical School, London 1947-57; Consultant Pathologist, Hammersmith Hosp., London 1951-; Reader and Prof. of Histochemistry, London Univ. 1965-81, Prof. Emer. 1981-; Fulbright Fellow and Visiting Prof. of Pathology, Alabama Univ. 1953-54; Pres., Royal Microscopical Soc. 1972-74; Hon. mem. Mark Twain Soc. 1977; mem. Deutsche Akad. der Naturforscher Leopoldina (Schleiden Medal 1988); Hon. M.D. (Basel) 1960, (Krakow) 1978; Horton Smith Prize, Cambridge Univ. 1950; John Hunter Prize, Royal Coll. of Surgeons 1978; Ernst Jung Prize for Medicine 1979, Fred W. Stewart Prize in Oncology 1979, Jan Swammerdam Medal, Dutch Soc. for Advancement of Natural Sciences 1988. *Publication:* Histochemistry, Theoretical and Applied 1953. *Leisure interests:* horticulture, farming, sailing, ship modelling. *Address:* Gorwyn House, Cheriton Bishop, Exeter, Devon, England. *Telephone:* 064 724 231.

PEARSON, Andrall E.; American business executive; b. 3 June 1925; s. of Andrall E. Pearson and Dorothy MacDonald; m. Joanne Pope 1951; one d.; ed. Univ. of Southern Calif. and Harvard Business School; fmr. Dir. McKinsey & Co. (int. man. consultants); Exec. Vice-Pres. PepsiCo Inc. 1969-71, Pres. 1971-84, Dir. and C.O.O.; mem. Bd. of Dirs. Grocery Mfrs. of America Inc., Consumer Research Inst., TWA and TWC; mem. of Exec. Cttee. TWA; William H. Albers Award; Univ. of S. Calif. Outstanding Alumnus 1973. *Publications:* A Blueprint for Long Range Planning, An Approach to Successful Marketing Planning. *Address:* c/o PepsiCo Inc., Purchase, N.Y. 10577, U.S.A.

PEARSON, Ralph Gottfried, PH.D.; American professor of chemistry; b. 12 Jan. 1919, Chicago, Ill.; s. of Gottfried Pearson and Kerstin Pearson (née Larson); m. Lenore Johnson 1941 (died 1982); two s. one d.; ed. Lewis Inst., Northwestern Univ.; First Lieut. U.S.A.F. 1944-46; Asst. Prof. Chem. Dept., Northwestern Univ. 1946-52, Assoc. Prof. 1952-57, Prof. 1957-76; Prof. of Chem. Univ. of Calif., Santa Barbara 1976-; mem. N.A.S.; fmr. Guggenheim Fellow; Inorganic Award, American Chemical Soc. *Publications:* Kinetics and Mechanism 1953, Mechanisms of Inorganic Reactions 1958, Hard and Soft Acids and Bases 1974, Symmetry Rules for Chemical Reactions 1976. *Leisure interests:* classical music, hiking. *Address:* Chemistry Department, University of California, Santa Barbara, Calif. 93106 (Office); 715 Grove Lane, Santa Barbara, Calif. 93105, U.S.A. (Home). *Telephone:* (805) 961-3745 (Office); (805) 687-7890 (Home).

PEART, Sir (William) Stanley, Kt., M.B., B.S., M.D., F.R.C.P., F.R.S.; British professor of medicine; b. 31 March 1922, South Shields; s. of J. G. and M. Peart; m. Peggy Parkes 1947; one s. one d.; ed. King's Coll. School, Wimbledon, and St. Mary's Hospital Medical School, London; Lecturer in Medicine, St. Mary's Hospital, London 1950-56, Prof. of Medicine 1956-87, Prof. Emer. 1987-; Master, Hunterian Inst. Royal Coll. of Surgeons 1988-; Chair. Medical Research Soc. 1968, Beit Trust Advisory Bd. 1980; mem. Medical Research Council 1969; mem. Advisory Bd. for the Research Councils 1973; Trustee, Wellcome Trust 1975-; Councillor, Royal Coll. of Physicians 1977; Stouffer Prize 1968. *Publications:* articles in The Biochemical Journal, Journal of Physiology, The Lancet; chapters in textbooks on renal disease and high blood pressure. *Leisure interests:* reading and tennis. *Address:* 17 Highgate Close, London, N6 4SD, England. *Telephone:* 01-341 3111.

PEASE, Rendel Sebastian, M.A., SC.D., F.R.S.; British physicist; b. 2 Nov. 1922, Cambridge; s. of Michael Stewart Pease and Helen Bowen (née Wedgwood); m. Susan Spickernell 1952; two s. three d.; ed. Bedales School and Trinity Coll., Cambridge; Scientific Officer, Ministry of Aircraft Production at Operational Research Unit, HQ, R.A.F. Bomber Command 1942-46; Research at A.E.R.E., Harwell 1947-61; Div. Head, Culham Lab. for Plasma Physics and Nuclear Fusion, U.K. Atomic Energy Authority (U.K.A.E.A.) 1961-67, Dir. of Culham Lab. 1968-81, Programme Dir. of Fusion 1981-87; Gordon-Godfrey Prof. of Theoretical Physics, Univ. of N.S.W. 1984; Visiting Scientist, Princeton Univ. 1964-65; Asst. Dir. U.K.A.E.A. Research Group 1967; Vice-Pres. Inst. Physics 1973-77, Royal Soc. 1986-87; Chair. Int. Fusion Research Council 1976-84, Plasma Physics Comm., I.U.P.A.P. 1976-78; Pres. Inst. of Physics 1978-80; Hon. D.Univ. (Surrey) 1973; Hon. D.Sc. (Aston) 1981, (City) 1987. *Leisure interest:* music. *Address:* The Poplars, West Ilsley, Newbury, Berks., England.

PÉBEREAU, Georges Alexandre; French engineer and business executive; b. 20 July 1931, Digne, Basses-Alpes; s. of Alexandre Pébereau and Yvonne Raybaud; m. Bernadette Potier 1954; one s. two d.; ed. Lycées Buffon, Saint-Louis, Paris; engineer roads and bridges in various wards 1955-64; Pres. Assen. des ingénieurs des ponts et chaussées 1964; teacher of Urban Man. École nat. des ponts et chaussées 1964; Chief-Eng., Dept. Seine-St.-Denis 1966, Tech. Counsellor to Ministry of Equipment 1966, Dir. Office Ministry of Equipment and Housing 1967-68; Dir. Land and Urban Man. 1966-68; Vice-Pres. Cttee. action concertée Urbanisation 1967-68; at Cie. industrielle des télécommunications (Cit) 1968-70, Jt. Dir.-Gen. 1968-69, Dir.-Gen. 1969-70; at Cie. industrielle des télécommunications (Cit-Alcatel) 1970-, Admin.-Dir.-Gen. 1970-83, Pres., Dir.-Gen. 1983-; at Cie. Gén d'électricité 1970-86, Dir. then Jt. Dir.-Gen. 1970-72, Admin. 1971, Dir.-Gen. 1972, then Chair., Pres. and C.E.O. Admin., Dir. -1986; Co-owner Cie. Privée de Banque 1987-; Dir. numerous eng. cos.; mem. Cttee. de direction et de conseil d'admin. 1970-; Officier Légion d'honneur, Commdr., Ordre nat. du Mérite. *Address:* 54 rue La Boétie. 75008 Paris (Office); 28 rue des Tournelles, 75004 Paris, France (Home).

PECK, Sir Edward Heywood, G.C.M.G.; British diplomatist (retd.); b. 5 Oct. 1915, Hove, Sussex; s. of Lt.-Col. E. S. Peck and Doris Heywood; m. Alison Mary MacInnes 1948; one s. two d.; ed. Clifton Coll. and Queen's Coll., Oxford; Probationer Vice-Consul, Barcelona 1938-39; Foreign Office 1939-40; Consulate, Sofia 1940, Ankara 1940-44; Consul, Adana 1944, Iskenderun 1944-45; Consulate-Gen., Salonica 1946; with U.K. Del. to UN Special Comm. on the Balkans 1947; transferred to Foreign Office 1947; seconded to C.R.O. for service at New Delhi 1950-52; Counsellor, Foreign Office 1952-54, Berlin 1955-58, Singapore 1959-60; Asst. Under-Sec. of State for Far Eastern and S.E. Asian Affairs, Foreign Office 1961-66; High Commr. of U.K. in Kenya 1966-68; Deputy Under-Sec. of State, FCO 1968-70; Perm. Rep. of U.K. to North Atlantic Council 1970-75; Hon. Visiting Fellow in Defence Studies, Aberdeen Univ. 1976-85; mem. Council Nat. Trust of Scotland 1982-87. *Publications:* North-East Scotland (Bartholomew's Regional Guides) 1981, Avonside Explored. *Leisure interests:* skiing, mountaineering, reading history. *Address:* Easter Torrans, Tomintoul, Banffshire, Scotland.

PECK, Gregory, B.A.; American actor; b. 5 April 1916, La Jolla, Calif.; m. 1st Greta Konen Rice 1942 (divorced 1954), two s. (one s. deceased); m. 2nd Veronique Passani 1955, one s. one d.; ed. California Univ.; mem. Nat. Council on Arts 1965-67, reappointed 1968; Pres. Acad. of Motion Picture Arts and Sciences 1967-70; Medal of Freedom Award 1969; Acad. Award (Oscar) best actor 1962; Screen Actors' Guild Annual Award for Outstanding Achievement 1970; Acad. of Motion Picture Arts and Sciences Jean Hersholt Humanitarian Award 1968, Life Achievement Award 1988; Commdr., Ordre des Arts et des Lettres (France). *Appeared in plays including:* The Doctor's Dilemma, The Male Animal, Once in a Lifetime, The Play's the Thing, You Can't Take it With You, The Morning Star, The Willow and I, Sons and Soldiers. *Films include:* Days of Glory 1943, Keys of the Kingdom 1944, Spellbound 1945, The Valley of Decision 1945, Duel in the Sun 1946, The Macomber Affair 1947, Gentleman's Agreement 1947, The Paradine Case 1948, Yellow Sky 1949, Twelve O'Clock High 1949, The Great Sinner 1949, Captain Horatio Hornblower 1951, David and Bathsheba 1951, The Snows of Kilimanjaro 1952, Roman Holiday 1953, The Purple Plain 1954, The Man in the Grey Flannel Suit 1956, Moby Dick 1956, Designing Woman 1957, The Big Country, The Bravados 1958, Pork Chop Hill 1959, On the Beach 1959, Beloved Infidel 1959, Guns of Navarone 1961, Cape Fear 1962, To Kill a Mocking Bird 1962, How the West Was Won 1963, Captain Newman, M.D. 1963, Behold a Pale Horse 1964, Mirage 1964, Arabesque 1965, The Stalking Moon 1968, Mackenna's Gold 1969, The Chairman 1969, Marooned 1969, I Walk the Line 1970, Shoot Out 1971, Billy Two-Hats 1972, The Omen 1976, MacArthur 1977, The Boys from Brazil 1978, The Sea Wolves 1980, The Blue and the Gray 1981 (TV), The Scarlet and the Black 1983 (TV), Amazing Grace and Chuck 1987, The Old Gringo 1988; producer The Dove 1974. *Address:* P.O. Box 837, Beverly Hills, Calif. 90213, U.S.A.

PECK, Sir John Howard, K.C.M.G.; British diplomatist (retd.); b. 16 Feb. 1913, Kuala Lumpur, Malaysia; s. of Howard C. B. and Dorothea Peck; m. 1st Mariska Caroline Somló 1939 (died 1979); two s.; m. 2nd Catherine McLaren 1987; ed. Wellington Coll. and Corpus Christi, Oxford; Asst. Private Sec. to First Lord of Admiralty 1937-39, to Minister for Co-ordination of Defence 1939-40, to Prime Minister 1940-46; transferred to Foreign Service 1946, served UN Dept. 1946-47, The Hague 1947-50; Counsellor and Head of Information Research Dept. 1951-54; Counsellor (Defence Liaison) and Head of Political Div., British Middle East Office 1954-56; Dir.-Gen. British Information Services, New York 1956-59; Perm. Rep. to Council of Europe, and Consul-Gen., Strasbourg 1959-62; Amb. to Senegal 1962-66, and Mauritania 1962-65; Asst. Under-Sec. of State, Foreign Office, later FCO 1966-70; Amb. to Ireland 1970-73. *Publication:* Dublin from Downing Street 1978. *Leisure interests:* writing, photography, gardening, electronics, do-it-yourself. *Address:* Stratford, Saval Park Road, Dalkey, Co. Dublin, Ireland. *Telephone:* 852000.

PECKER, Jean-Claude; French astronomer; b. 10 May 1923, Reims; s. of Victor-Noel Pecker and Nelly Catherine Herrmann; m. 2nd Annie A. Vormser 1974; one s. two d. (by previous marriage); ed. Lycée de Bordeaux, Univ. of Grenoble and Paris (Sorbonne) and Ecole Normale Supérieure; Research Asst. Centre Nat. de la Recherche Scientifique (C.N.R.S.) 1946-52; Assoc. Prof. Univ. of Clermont-Ferrand 1952-55; Assoc. Astronomer, Paris Observatory 1955-62, Astronomer 1962-65; Dir. Nice Observatory 1962-69; Prof. Coll. de France 1963-88, Hon. Prof. 1989-; Asst. Gen. Sec. Int. Astronomical Union 1961-63, Gen. Sec. 1964-67; Pres. Comité Nat. Français d'Astronomie 1970-73; Dir. Inst. Astrophysique, Paris 1971-78; Pres. Soc. Astronomique de France 1973-76; Pres. French Assen. for Advancement of Science 1978; Chair. Orientation Cttee., Sciences-Industries Museum, La Villette 1983-85; Chair. Nat. Cttee. Scientific and Tech. Culture 1985-87; Assoc. Royal Soc. of Science, Liège 1967; Corresp. Bureau des Longitudes 1968; Assoc. Royal Astronomical Soc. 1968; Corresp mem. Acad. des Sciences, France 1969, mem. 1977; mem. Acad. Nat. Bordeaux 1977, Acad. Royale Belgique 1979, European Acad. 1982, Int. Acad. of Humanism 1983, Acad. Europaeia 1988 (Council mem.); Commdr., Palmes académiques, Officer, Légion d'honneur, Officier, Ordre nat. du Mérite; Prix Forthuny, Inst. de France, Prix Stroobant Acad. des Sciences de Belgique 1965, Prix Manley-Bendall de l'Acad. de Bordeaux 1966, Prix des Trois Physiciens 1969; Janssen Medal Astronomical Soc., France 1967, Prix Jean Perrin, Soc. Française de Physique 1973, Medal Univ. de Nice 1972, Adion Medal 1981, Prix Union Rationaliste 1983, Personnalité de l'année 1984. *Publications include:* L'astronomie au jour le jour (with P. Couderc and E. Schatzman) 1954, Astrophysique générale (with E. Schatzman) 1959, Le ciel 1959, L'astronomie expérimentale 1969, Les laboratoires spatiaux 1969, Papa, dis-moi: L'astronomie, qu'est-ce que c'est? 1971; Ed. L'astronomie nouvelle 1971, Clefs pour l'Astronomie 1981, Sous l'étoile soleil 1984, Astronomie Flammarion 1985. *Leisure interest:* painting. *Address:* Pusat-Tasek, Les Corbeaux, 85350, Ile d'Yeu, France.

PECKFORD, (Alfred) Brian, P.C.; Canadian politician; b. 27 Aug. 1942, Whitbourne, Newfoundland; s. of Ewart and Allison (Young) Peckford; m. 1st Marina Dicks 1969, two s.; m. 2nd Carol Ellsworth 1986, one s.; ed. Lewisporte High School and Memorial Univ. of Newfoundland; teacher, Lewisporte 1962-63, Grant Collegiate, Springdale 1966-72; mem. Newfoundland House of Ass. 1972-; Special Asst. to Premier of Newfoundland 1973; Minister, Dept. of Municipal Affairs and Housing, Govt. of Newfoundland and Labrador 1974, of Mines and Energy 1976, of Rural Devt. 1978; Leader, Progressive Conservative Party of Newfoundland 1979-89; Premier of Newfoundland and Labrador 1979-89; Progressive Conservative; Hon. LL.D. 1986; Vanier Award 1980. *Leisure interests:* reading, sports, swimming.

PECQUEUR, Michel André Fernand; French mining engineer and administrative official; b. 18 Aug. 1931, Paris; s. of Fernand and Marguerite (née Grat) Pecqueur; m. Marguerite Veyriès 1955; one d.; ed. Lycée Marcelin-Berthelot, Lycée Charlemagne, Paris, Ecole Nat. Supérieure des Mines, Paris, and Ecole Polytechnique; engineer, Commissariat à l'Energie Atomique (CEA) in charge of Pierrelatte plant process 1958-64; Tech. Counsellor to Gen. Admin., CEA 1964-66; Asst. to Dir. of Production, CEA 1966-70; Dir. CEA and Del. for nuclear industrial applications 1970-74, Deputy Gen. Admin. 1974-78, Gen. Admin. 1978-83; Chair. Société Française d'Energie Nucléaire 1977-78; mem. Bd. Framatome 1975-81; Cie. Générale des Matières Premières (COGEMA) 1976-82, Pres. 1982-84, Hon. Pres. 1984; mem. Bd. Electricité de France 1978-83; Pres. Soc. Nat. ELF Aquitaine 1983-89, Chair. 1985-; mem. Bd. Gaz de France 1984-, Soc. Générale 1984-, Cie. financière Paribas 1986-; mem. Conseil général des mines 1980-; Officier, Légion d'honneur, Ordre nat. du Mérite. *Leisure interests:* riding, skin-diving. *Address:* Tour ELF, 2 place de la Coupole, 92078 Paris La Defense, France. *Telephone:* (1) 47.44.45.46.

PEDERSEN, Arne Fog, B.D.; Danish ecclesiastic and politician; b. 25 Aug. 1911, Hinnerup; s. of A. J. Pedersen and E. Fog; m. Mette Høyer 1939; one s. two d.; Teacher, Rødding Folk High School 1939-50, Prin. 1953-68, 1971-76; Head of Denmark Radio's Lectures Dept. 1950-53; Minister of Ecclesiastical Affairs 1968-71; Chair. Liberal Educ. Assen. 1954; mem., Nat. Comm. for UNESCO 1955-, Gen. Council of Norden Assen. 1956-, Govt. Cttee. to promote Danish Language and Culture Abroad 1957-; Del.

to UN 1972; Consul-Gen., Flensburg 1976–; Chair. Grœnse-foreningen 1972–76, Filadelfia 1974; Liberal. *Publications:* Danmarks første Højskole (Denmark's First Folk High School) 1944, Ed. of Fyraften (Knocking-Off Time) 1953, Contrib. to Højskolens ungdomstid i breve (Early Years of the Folk High School Movement as Reflected in Contemporary Letters) Vol. 1; articles, mostly on history, North Slesvig and foreign policy. *Address:* Royal Danish Consulate, Hafendamm 41, Flensburg, Federal Republic of Germany. *Telephone:* Flensburg 23952.

PEDERSEN, Gert K., M.SC., DR.PHIL.; Danish mathematician; b. 13 April 1940, Copenhagen; m. Dorte Olesen 1971; two s. one d.; ed. Univ. of Copenhagen; lecturer, Univ. of Copenhagen 1968–75, Prof. of Math. 1975–; Chair. Danish Math. Soc. 1974–78; mem. Royal Danish Acad.; awarded Knud Sand Domicile 1988. *Publications:* C*-algebras and their automorphism groups 1979, Analysis Now 1988; numerous articles on operator algebra in scientific journals. *Leisure interest:* music. *Address:* Mathematical Institute, Universitetsparken 5, 2100 Copenhagen Ø (Office); Kildeskovsvej 81, 2820 Gentofte, Denmark (Home). *Telephone:* 01353133 (Office); 01681744 (Home).

PEDERSEN, Helga, CAND.JUR.; Danish judge; b. 24 June 1911, Taarnborg; d. of J. P. Pedersen and Vilhelmine Pedersen (née Kolding); ed. Copenhagen Univ. and Columbia Univ., New York; Dept. of Justice 1936–46; Judge, District Court of Copenhagen 1948–50, 1953–56; Minister of Justice 1950–53; Judge, Court of Appeal, Copenhagen 1956–64; Justice of Supreme Court, Copenhagen 1964–80; mem. Danish Parl. (Liberal Party) 1953–64; Del. to UN and UNESCO conferences on several occasions 1949–74; Judge, European Court of Human Rights 1971–81; Chair. Nat. Comm. of UNESCO 1974; mem. Danish Council for Planning of Higher Educ. 1968–73, Danish Council on Copyright 1962–73, Special Parole Bd. of Danish Prison Admin. 1968–73; Head Bd. of Danish Red Cross 1969–76; Chair. Reps. of Danish State Art Foundation 1965–73; Vice-Pres. Danish Welfare Assen. 1967–73; mem. Advisory Council on Prevention of Crime 1971–74; Vice-Pres. Revisionary Criminal Court; Chair. Danish Press Bd. 1971 and Controlling Bd. of Danish Press Financing Inst. 1973; Pres. of the Trustees, Foundation for Trees and Environment 1974–79; Extraordinary mem. Acad. of Fine Arts 1974; mem. Prize Cttee. Int. Balzan Foundation 1978–; Commdr. 1st Class, Order of Dannebrog (Denmark); Grand Cross Order of Orange-Nassau (Netherlands); Medal of Merit 1st Class, Danish Red Cross, Gold Medal (Assen. for World Peace through Law). *Publications:* Céline and Denmark 1975 and articles on legal and political subjects. *Leisure interests:* farming, travelling, art.

PEDERSEN, Olaf, DR.SC.; Danish professor of history of science; b. 8 April 1920, Egtved; s. of late Hans H. Pedersen and Jensine Pedersen; m. Anne S. Madsen 1945; one d.; ed. Queen Dorothy's School, Kolding, Univ. of Copenhagen, Coll. de France and Ecole des Hautes Etudes, Paris; science master, Randers Statsskole 1944–56; Reader in Physics, Aarhus Univ. 1956–67, Prof. of History of Science 1967–; founded Inst. of History of Science, Aarhus Univ. 1965; Visiting Prof. Kiel 1971, Cambridge 1975, 1988; mem. Danish UNESCO del. 1972–76; Fellow, Royal Danish Acad., Royal Astronomical Soc. (U.K.); mem. Acad. Int. d'Histoire des Sciences (Pres. 1985), Int. Union of History and Philosophy of Science (Vice-Pres. 1981–85); Pres. Historical Cttee. Int. Astronomical Union 1981–85; has served on various other professional bodies; Polish Order of Merit; Filtenborg Prize 1980; several academic medals and honours. *Publications:* From Kierkegaard to Sartre 1947, Man and Technology 1950, Peter Abelard 1953, Nicole Oresme 1956, The Universe of the Middle Ages 1962, Historical Introduction to Classical Physics 1963, Mechanics I-III (with O. Knudsen) 1967–69, Early Physics and Astronomy 1974, Mathematics and the Description of Nature in Antiquity 1975, A Survey of the Almagest 1975, Studium Generale 1979; papers and contribs. to books on history of science and science and theology. *Address:* Institute of History of Science, Aarhus University, Ny Munkegade, 8000 Aarhus C (Office); 16 Elbakvej, 8240 Risskov, Denmark (Home). *Telephone:* 06 12 71 88 (Office); 06 17 85 91 (Home).

PEDERSEN, Richard Foote, PH.D.; American university administrator and fmr. diplomatist; b. 21 Feb. 1925, Miami, Ariz.; s. of Ralph M. and Gertrude M. Pedersen; m. Nelda Newell Napier 1953; one s. two d.; ed. Univ. of the Pacific, Stanford and Harvard Univs.; Foreign Affairs Officer, UN Econ. and Social Affairs, Dept. of State 1950–53; Econ. and Social Affairs Adviser, Perm. Mission to UN 1953, held successive posts of Adviser on Political and Security Affairs, Sr. Adviser and Chief of Political Section, Counsellor, Sr. Adviser to Perm. Rep. to UN, with rank of Amb.; Deputy U.S. Rep. in UN Security Council 1967–69; Counsellor, Dept. of State 1969–73; Amb. to Hungary 1973–75; Sr. Foreign Service. United States Trust Co. 1975–78; Pres. American Univ. in Cairo 1978–; Hon. LL.D. (George Williams Coll.) 1964, (Univ. of the Pacific) 1965. *Leisure interests:* swimming, YMCA, Egyptology. *Address:* The American University in Cairo, 113 Sharia Kasr al-Aini, Cairo, Egypt (Office); Twilight Park, Haines Falls, N.Y. 12436, U.S.A.

PEDERSEN, Thor; Danish politician; b. 14 June 1945, Søllerød; s. of Laurits Pedersen; ed. Copenhagen Univ.; fmr. mem. staff, Assessments Div.; fmr. Man. Dir. of a construction co., North Zealand; mem. Folketing (Parl.) 1985–; Minister of Housing 1986–87, of the Interior 1987–, also of

Nordic Affairs 1988–. *Address:* Ministry of the Interior, Christiansborg Slotsplads 1, 1218 Copenhagen K, Denmark. *Telephone:* (01) 92-33-80.

PEDERSON, Donald Oscar, PH.D.; American professor of electrical engineering and computer science; b. 30 Sept. 1925, Hallock, Minn.; s. of Oscar Jorgan Pederson and Beda Emelia (Dahlof) Pederson; m.; one s. three d.; ed. Iowa State and Stanford Univs., Katholieke Univ., Leuven, Belgium; Research Assoc., Stanford Univ. 1951–53; mem. Tech. Staff, Bell Telephone Labs., Murray Hill, N.J. 1953–55; mem. Faculty, Univ. of Calif., Berkeley 1955–, Dir. Electronics Research Lab. 1960–64, now Prof. of Electrical Eng. and Computer Science, Chair. Dept. 1983–85; Guggenheim Fellow; mem. N.A.S., Nat. Acad. of Eng. *Publications:* Principles of Circuit Synthesis 1959, Elementary Circuit Properties of Transistors 1964, Multistage Transistor Circuits 1965, Electronic Circuits 1965, Introduction to Electronic Devices, Circuits and Systems 1966; contribs. to numerous engineering publs. *Address:* Department of Electrical Engineering and Computer Science, 516 Cory Hall, University of California, Berekeley, Calif. 94720; 1436 Via Loma, Walnut Creek, Calif. 94598, U.S.A. (Home).

PEERS, Most Rev. Michael Geoffrey, B.A. (HONS.), L.TH.; Canadian ecclesiastic; b. 31 July 1934; s. of Geoffrey H. Peers and Dorothy E. Mantle; m. Dorothy E. Bradley 1963; two s. one d.; ed. Univs. of British Columbia and Heidelberg and Trinity Coll. Toronto; ordained priest 1960; Curate, Ottawa 1959–65; Univ. Chaplain, Diocese of Ottawa 1961–66; Rector, St. Bede's, Winnipeg 1966–72, St. Martin's, Winnipeg with St. Paul's Middlechurch 1972–74; Archdeacon of Winnipeg 1969–74; Rector, St. Paul's Cathedral, Regina 1974–77; Dean of Qu'Appelle 1974–77; Bishop of Qu'Appelle 1977–82; Archbishop of Qu'Appelle and Metropolitan of Rupert's Land 1982–86; Primate, Anglican Church of Canada 1986–; Hon. D.D. (Trinity Coll. Toronto) 1978, (St. John's Coll. Winnipeg) 1981, (Kent Univ.) 1988. *Address:* 600 Jarvis Street, Toronto, Ont., M4Y 2JS, Canada. *Telephone:* (416) 924-9192.

PEERTHUM, Satteeanund; Mauritian diplomatist; b. 15 March 1941; m.; three s.; ed. People's Friendship Univ., Moscow; Sr. Research Fellow Inst. of Oriental Studies, Moscow 1973–74; Head History Dept., Bhojoharry Coll., Mauritius several times between 1975 and 1987; Sr. Research Fellow School of Mauritian Asian and African Studies, Mahatma Gandhi Inst. 1985–87; founding mem. Mouvement Socialiste Militant; mem. Mauritian Parl. and Minister of Labour and Industrial Relations 1982–83; Chair. Sugar Industry Devt. Fund Boards of Mauritius 1984–87; Perm. Rep. to UN Dec. 1987–; Chair. Nat. Steering Cttee. for the Teaching of Mauritian History; mem. Advisory Cttee. African Cultural Centre of Mauritius 1986–87; fmr. mem. Court Nat. Univ. of Mauritius. *Address:* Permanent Mission of Mauritius to the United Nations, 211 East 43rd Street, New York, N.Y. 10017, U.S.A. *Telephone:* (212) 949-0190.

PEI IEOH MING, M.ARCH., F.A.I.A., R.I.B.A.; American architect; b. 26 April 1917, Canton, China; s. of Tsu Yee Pei and Lien Kwun Chwong; m. Eileen Loo 1942; three s. one d.; ed. Shanghai, Massachusetts Inst. of Tech. and Harvard Univ.; in U.S.A. 1935–; naturalized citizen 1954; architectural practice 1939–, Webb and Knapp Inc. 1948–55, I. M. Pei & Partners 1955–; Asst. Prof. Harvard Graduate School of Design 1945–48; Wheelwright Traveling Fellowship, Harvard Univ. 1951; M.I.T. Traveling Fellowship 1940; Fellow A.I.A.; mem. Nat. Council on the Humanities 1966–70, American Acad. of Arts and Sciences, Nat. Acad. of Design, American Acad. of Arts and Letters (Chancellor 1978–80), Nat. Council on the Arts 1981–84, R.I.B.A., Urban Design Council (New York), Corpn. of M.I.T. 1972–77, 1978–83, American Philosophical Soc., Institut de France (Foreign Assoc.); Hon. D.F.A. (Pennsylvania) 1970, (Rensselaer Polytechnic Inst.) 1978, (Northeastern Univ.) 1979, (Univs. of Mass., Rochester, Brown) 1982, (New York Univ.) 1983; Hon. LL.D. (Chinese Univ. of Hong Kong) 1970, Hon. D.H.L. (Columbia Univ., Univs. of Colorado, Rochester); Hon. Prof. Tonji Univ., Shanghai 1985; Brunner Award, Nat. Inst. of Arts and Letters 1961; Medal of Honor N.Y. Chapter A.I.A. 1963, The Thomas Jefferson Memorial Medal for Architecture 1976, Gold Medal (American Acad. of Arts and Letters) 1979, Gold Medal (American Inst. of Architects) 1979, La Grande Medaille d'Or (Academie d'Architecture) 1981, Pritzker Architecture Prize 1983, Asia Soc. Award 1984, Medal of Liberty 1986, Nat. Medal of Arts 1988; Commdr., Ordre des Arts et des Lettres; Officier, Légion d'honneur 1988. *Projects include:* Mile High Center (Denver); M.I.T. Earth Science Bldg. (Cambridge, Mass.); U.S. Embassy Bldg. (Montevideo); East-West Center, Univ. of Hawaii; redevt. projects in New York, Philadelphia, Washington, Chicago, Pittsburgh and Singapore; Nat. Center for Atmospheric Research (Boulder, Colorado); Grave of Robert F. Kennedy; Nat. Airlines Terminal (Kennedy Int. Airport); Washington Sq. East (Philadelphia); Everson Museum of Art (Syracuse N.Y.); Nat. Gallery of Art East Bldg. (Washington, D.C.); Wilmington Tower (Wilmington, Del.); John Fitzgerald Kennedy Library Complex (Boston, Mass.); Canadian Imperial Bd. of Commerce Complex (Toronto); Des Moines Art Center Addition (Des Moines, Iowa); Cleo Rogers Memorial County Library (Columbus, Ind.); planning projects in Boston, Oklahoma City and New York; Master Plan Columbia Univ. (N.Y.) 1970; Dallas Municipal Bldg. (Dallas); Raffles City (Singapore); Overseas-Chinese Banking Corpn. Centre (Singapore); Herbert F. Johnson Museum of Art (Ithaca, N.Y.); New West Wing, Museum of Fine Arts (Boston, Mass.); Mellon Art Center, The Choate School (Wallingford, Conn.), Sunning Plaza (Hong Kong), Fragrant

Hills Hotel (Beijing), Javits Convention Center, Texas Commerce Tower (Houston), Meyerson Symphony Center, IBM (Purchase, N.Y.), Le Grand Louvre (Paris), Bank of China (Hong Kong), Luce Chapel (Taiwan). *Address:* 600 Madison Avenue, New York, N.Y. 10022 (Office); 11 Sutton Place, New York, N.Y. 10022, U.S.A. (Home). *Telephone:* (212) 751-3122 (Office).

PEI JIANZHANG; Chinese diplomatist; b. 1927, Shandong; Second Sec., then First Sec. at Chinese Embassy, Burma 1960-69; Counsellor Chinese Embassy, U.K. (London) 1970-73; Amb. to New Zealand 1973-79, to Papua New Guinea 1977-79, to Libya 1979-84; Dir. Editors' Office of The History of Diplomacy of The People's Republic of China, Ministry of Foreign Affairs 1986-. *Address:* c/o Ministry of Foreign Affairs, Beijing, People's Republic of China.

PEI SHENGJI; Chinese ethnobiologist; ed. Chengdu Agric. School, Sichuan Prov.; fmr. Dir. Yunnan Inst. of Tropical Botany; Deputy Dir. Kunming Inst. of Botany, Chinese Acad. of Sciences 1987-. *Address:* Kunming Institute of Botany, Kunming, Yunnan Province, People's Republic of China.

PEIERLS, Sir Rudolf Ernst, Kt., C.B.E., PH.D., M.A., D.SC., F.R.S.; British scientist; b. 5 June 1907, Berlin, Germany; s. of Heinrich Peierls and Elisabeth (née Weigert); m. Eugenia Kannegiser 1931; one s. three d.; ed. Berlin, Munich and Leipzig Univs. and Fed. Inst. of Tech., Zürich; Asst. Fed. Inst. Tech., Zürich 1929; Rockefeller Fellow 1932; Hon. Research Fellow, Manchester Univ. 1933-35; Research Asst. Royal Soc. Mond Laboratory, Cambridge Univ. 1935-37; Prof. of Applied Mathematics, Birmingham Univ. 1937-46; work on atomic energy, Birmingham, New York, Los Alamos 1940-45; Prof. of Mathematical Physics, Birmingham Univ. 1946-63; Wykeham Prof. Univ. of Oxford 1963-74; part-time Prof. of Physics, Univ. of Washington, Seattle 1974-77; Foreign Hon. mem. American Acad. of Arts and Sciences 1962; Foreign Assoc. U.S. N.A.S. 1970-, French Acad. of Sciences 1984; Foreign mem. Royal Danish Acad. 1980-; Hon. mem. French Physical Soc. 1979-; Corresp. mem. Yugoslav Acad. of Arts and Sciences 1983; Foreign mem. U.S.S.R. Acad. of Sciences 1988; Foreign Corresp. mem. Lisbon Acad. of Sciences; Fellow, New Coll., Oxford 1963-74; Emer. Fellow 1974-80, Hon. Fellow 1980-; Hon. Fellow, Inst. of Physics 1974; Hon. D.Sc. (Liverpool, Birmingham, Edinburgh, Sussex, Chicago, Coimbra); Council of Royal Soc., London 1958; Royal Medal of Royal Soc. 1959; Lorentz Medal, Royal Netherlands Acad. of Sciences 1962; Max Planck Medal, Assen. of German Physical Socs. 1963; Guthrie Medal, Inst. of Physics and Physical Soc. 1968; Enrico Fermi Award, U.S. Dept. of Energy 1980; Matteuci Medal, Italian Nat. Acad. of Science 1982; Copley Medal, Royal Soc. 1986. *Publications:* Quantum Theory of Solids, The Laws of Nature 1955, Surprises in Theoretical Physics 1979, Bird of Passage 1985. *Leisure interests:* travelling, photography. *Address:* 2B Northmoor Road, Oxford, OX2 6UP, England. *Telephone:* (0865) 56497.

PEINEMANN, Edith; German concert violinist; b. 3 March 1939, Mainz; d. of Robert Peinemann and Hildegard (née Rohde) Peinemann; studied under her father and later with Heinz Stauske and Max Rostal at the Guildhall School of Music, London; First Prize, ARD competition, Munich 1956; since then has performed with leading orchestras and conductors worldwide; Prof. of Music, Frankfurt. *Leisure interests:* art, hiking, cooking, cross-county skiing.

PEIRIS, Gamini Lakshman, D.PHIL., PH.D.; Sri Lankan university vice-chancellor; b. 13 Aug. 1946, Colombo; s. of Glanville S. Peiris and Lakshmi C. Salgado; m. Savitri N. Amarasuriya 1971; one d.; ed. St. Thomas' Coll. Mount Lavinia, Univ. of Ceylon and New Coll. Oxford; Prof. of Law, Univ. of Colombo 1979-, Dean, Faculty of Law 1982-88; Vice-Chancellor, Univ. of Colombo; Dir. Nat. Film Corpn. of Sri Lanka 1973-; Commr. Law Comm. of Sri Lanka 1986-; mem. Inc. Soc. of Legal Educ. 1986-; Visiting Fellow, All Souls Coll. Oxford 1980-81; Butterworths Visiting Fellow, Inst. of Advanced Legal Studies, Univ. of London 1984; Distinguished Visiting Fellow, Christ's Coll. Cambridge 1985-86; Smuts Visiting Fellow in Commonwealth Studies, Univ. of Cambridge 1985-86; mem. Securities Council of Sri Lanka 1987-; assoc. mem. Int. Acad. of Comparative Law; Presidential Award 1987. *Publications:* Law of Unjust Enrichment in South Africa and Ceylon 1971, General Principles of Criminal Liability in Ceylon 1972, Offences under the Penal Code of Sri Lanka 1973, The Law of Evidence in Sri Lanka 1974, Criminal Procedure in Sri Lanka 1975, The Law of Property in Sri Lanka 1976, Landlord and Tenant in Sri Lanka 1977. *Leisure interest:* walking. *Address:* 37 Kirula Place, Colombo 5, Sri Lanka. *Telephone:* 582488.

PEISACH, Max, PH.D., F.R.S.S.A.; South African nuclear analytical chemist; b. 3 Aug. 1926, Birzai, Lithuania; s. of Hyman Peisach and Sonia Kantor; m. Eunice Sheila Glick 1950; one s. three d.; ed. Boys' High School, Worcester, S.A., Univ. of Cape Town; demonstrator, Univ. of Cape Town 1948-49, Jr. lecturer 1949-50, lecturer 1950-53; Research Officer, Nat. Chemical Research Lab., S. African Council for Scientific and Industrial Research 1953-57, Sr. Research Officer 1957-60; Head, Isotope Production, Israel Atomic Energy Comm. 1960-63; Head Chem. Div., Southern Univs. Nuclear Inst. 1963-83; Head Nuclear Analytical Chem. Div., Nat. Accelerator Centre 1983-; mem. Int. Cttee. on Modern Trends in Activation

Analysis 1969-; Nat. Rep., IUPAC Comm. on Radiochemistry 1985-; Fellow Royal Philatelic Soc. London; AE & CI Gold Medal, S. African Chemical Inst. 1965, Inst. Gold Medal 1986; Int. Hevesy Medal 1981; Order of the Postal Stone (S.A.) 1988. *Publications:* many scientific papers; research papers on nuclear analytical chem.; book chapters on specialized analytical topics. *Leisure interest:* philately. *Address:* 11 Stuart Road, Rondebosch, 7700, South Africa. *Telephone:* (021) 689-1243 (Home); (024) 4-3820, Ext. 2163 (Office).

PEJIC, Dragoslav; Yugoslav diplomatist; b. 1929; m.; two d.; entered Foreign Service 1957; Press and Cultural Attaché Yugoslav Embassy, Baghdad 1958-61; Sec. Perm. Mission of Yugoslavia to UN 1965-69, Perm. Rep. 1986-; Deputy Dir. UN Dept. Fed. Secr. for Foreign Affairs 1969-72, Dir. 1976-79, Asst. Fed. Sec. for Foreign Affairs 1985-86; Minister-Counsellor Yugoslav Embassy, New Delhi 1972-76; Adviser on Foreign Policy to Pres. of Yugoslavia 1980-83; Amb. to Lebanon 1983-85; mem. Yugoslav del. to Eighth Conf. of Heads of State or Govt. of Non-Aligned Countries, Harare 1986, and several sessions UN Gen. Ass. *Address:* Permanent Mission of Yugoslavia to the United Nations, 854 Fifth Avenue, New York, N.Y. 10021, U.S.A. *Telephone:* (212) 879-8700.

PEKERIS, Chaim L., D.SC.; Israeli applied mathematician, geophysicist and educator; b. 15 June 1908, Alytus, Lithuania; s. of Samuel Pekeris and Chaya Rivel; m. Leah Kaplan 1933 (died 1973); ed. Massachusetts Inst. of Tech.; Rockefeller Fellow 1934-35; Research at Cambridge Univ., England 1935-36; Lecturer in Geophysics, M.I.T. 1936-40; mem. War Research Dept., Columbia Univ. 1940-45, Dir. Math. Physics Group 1945-47; mem. Inst. for Advanced Study, Princeton 1947-48; Prof. and Head, Dept. of Applied Mathematics, Weizmann Inst. of Science, Rehovot, Israel 1948-73, Distinguished Inst. Prof. 1973-; mem. Israel Acad. of Sciences and Humanities, Nat. Acad. of Sciences, N.A.S., U.S.A.; Foreign mem. Accademia Nazionale dei Lincei, American Acad. of Arts and Sciences, American Philosophical Soc.; Foreign Assoc. Royal Astronomical Soc., England; D.Phil. h.c. (Hebrew Univ., Jerusalem) 1979; Rothschild Prize in Mathematics 1966, Vetlesen Prize in Geophysics 1974, Gold Medal of Royal Astronomical Soc. 1980. *Publications:* papers in applied mathematics and geophysics. *Address:* Weizmann Institute of Science, Rehovot, Israel. *Telephone:* (054) 82-111.

PEKKALA, Ahti Antti Johannes; Finnish politician; b. 20 Dec. 1924, Haapavesi; s. of Antti and Alina (née Haavisto) Pekkala; m. Liisa Halmetoja 1959; seven c.; Bank Dir. Haapaveden osuuspankki 1952-; Presidential Elector, 1956, 1978 and 1982; M.P. 1970-; Vice-Chair. Cen. Party 1971-; Bank Supervisor, Parl. 1975-78; First Vice-Speaker, Parl. 1976-77, Speaker 1978-79; Minister of Finance 1979-86; mem. Supervisory Bd., Cen. Union of Co-operative Banks, Land and Industrial Mortgage Bank Ltd., Rautaruukki Oy, Aura Life Mutual Assurance Co.; mem. Bd. of Dirs. Oy Pohjolan Liikenne, Liitto Oy, Cen. Union of Co-operative Banks. *Leisure interest:* hunting. *Address:* c/o Ministry of Finance, Snellmaninkatu 1, 00170 Helsinki 17, Finland. *Telephone:* Haapavesi 86600 (Home).

PELÉ (Edson Arantes do Nascimento); Brazilian football player and author; b. 23 Oct. 1940, Três Corações, Minas Gerais State; s. of João Ramos do Nascimento and Celeste Arantes; m. Rosemeri Cholbi 1966 (divorced 1978); one s. two d.; ed. Santos Univ.; first played football at Baurú, São Paulo; Baurú Atlético Clube; joined Santos F.C. 1955; first int. game v. Argentina; played in World Cup 1958, 1962, 1966, 1970; finished career with New York Cosmos; Chair. Pelé Soccer Camps 1978-; Dir. Soccer Clinics; three World Cup winners' medals; two World Club Championship medals; 110 int. caps, 97 goals for Brazil; 1,114 appearances for Santos, 1,088 goals; career total 1,282 goals in 1,364 games, 9 league championship medals, 4 Brazil cup medals; most goals in season 53 (1958); has appeared in several films, including Escape to Victory 1981, A Minor Miracle 1983, Hot Shot 1986; has composed numerous songs in Samba style; Int. Peace Award 1978. *Publications:* Eu Sou Pelé 1962, Jogando com Pelé 1974, My Life and the Beautiful Game 1977, Pelé Soccer Training Program 1982, The World Cup Murders (novel) 1988. *Address:* 75 Rockefeller Plaza, New York, N.Y. 10019, U.S.A.

PELED, Natan; Israeli politician; b. 3 June 1913, Odessa; s. of Yosef and Lea Peled; m. Mania Peled 1936; two d.; ed. secondary school; immigrated to Palestine 1933; agricultural labourer in Kibbutz; Sec.-Gen. of Kibbutz Fed 'Hashomer Hatzair' 1950-55, 1975-79; Political Sec., Mapam Party 1956-58; Minister to Bulgaria 1958-60; Amb. to Austria 1960-63; mem. Knesset 1965-69; Minister of Immigrant Absorption 1970-74; Dir. Givat Haviva, Inst. for Advanced Studies. *Address:* Kibbutz Sarid, Israel.

PELEG, David; Israeli lawyer and civil servant; b. 1923; m. Judith Peleg 1953; one s. one d.; ed. Tel Aviv Univ.; Asst. Mil., Naval and Air Attaché, Israeli Embassy, Washington, D.C. 1950-52; Lieut. Col. Air Force 1952-53; Counsellor Scientific Affairs, Embassy, Paris 1959-63; Dir. Soreq Nuclear Research Centre 1964-65; Dir. Admin. Israel Atomic Energy Comm. (A.E.C.) 1971-75, Deputy Dir.-Gen. 1976-85, Acting Dir.-Gen. 1985-87, Deputy Dir.-Gen. 1987-; mem. Atomic Energy Comm. 1971-. *Address:* P.O. Box 7061, Tel Aviv 61070, Israel.

PELISSIER, Jacques Daniel Paul; French civil servant and railway administrator; b. 4 Feb. 1917, Versailles; s. of Jean Pelissier and Camille Bertrand; m. Jeanine Picard 1946; one s.; ed. Lycée Pasteur, Lycée Hoche,

Lycée Chaptal, Inst. Nat. Agronomique; engineer, external service of Ministry of Agric. 1938-44; Sec.-Gen. Landes 1944, Ardennes 1945; Sous-préfet hors cadre, Chef du Cabinet to Minister of Agric. 1946; Asst. Chef du Cabinet, Minister of Industry and Commerce 1948; Sec.-Gen. Indre-et-Loire 1950; Sous-préfet, Saumur 1954; Dir. for Gen. Govt. of Algeria, in Ministry for Algeria and in Gen. Del. of Govt. in Algeria 1956-60; Préfet hors cadre 1957; Préfet, Aude 1960, Hérault and Region of Languedoc-Roussillon 1964, Ille-et-Vilaine and Region of Brittany 1967, Rhône and Region of Rhône-Alpes 1972; Préfet hors cadre, Dir.-Gen. of Admin., Ministry of the Interior April 1974; Dir. du Cabinet for Prime Minister May 1974; Chair. Bd. of Dirs. Soc. Nat. des Chemins de Fer Français 1975-81; Pres. Office de Tourisme de Paris 1983-; Adviser to Prime Minister 1986-88; Hon. Préfet, Admin. de la Cie. Int. des Wagons-Lits et du Tourisme; Commdr., Légion d'honneur, Grand Officier, Ordre nat. du Mérite, Croix de guerre, Médaille de la Résistance. *Address:* 14 rue des Barres, 75004 Paris, France.

PELIZA, Major Robert John, O.B.E.; Gibraltar politician; b. 16 Nov. 1920, Gibraltar; s. of Robert Peliza and Emily Victory; m. Irma Risso 1950; three s. four d.; ed. Christian Brothers' Coll., Gibraltar; served in Gibraltar Reg. 1939-61; co. dir. 1962-; Leader, Integration with Britain Party 1967; elected mem. House of Ass. 1969-84; Chief Minister of Gibraltar 1969-1972; Leader of the Opposition 1972. *Leisure interests:* painting, writing, swimming, walking and sports in general. *Address:* 203 Water Gardens, Gibraltar. *Telephone:* 78387.

PELJEE, Myatavyn: Mongolian politician; b. 1927; ed. Mongolian State Univ. and Acad. of Social Sciences of CPSU Central Cttee., Moscow; Official of the Mongolian People's Revolutionary Party (MPRP) Cen. Cttee. 1950-56; Head of a Dept. of MPRP Cen. Cttee. 1960-66; Minister of Geology 1966-68, of Fuel, Power and Geology 1968-76, of Geology and Mining Industry April-June 1976; Vice-Chair. Council of Ministers 1976-; Chair. Comm. for CMEA (Comecon) Affairs 1977-; mem. MPRP Cen. Cttee. 1961-; Deputy to People's Great Hural (Assembly) 1963-; Order of the Red Banner of Labour, Order of the Pole Star. *Address:* Government Palace, Ulan Bator, Mongolia.

PELL, Claiborne de Borda, A.M.; American politician; b. 22 Nov. 1918, New York City; s. of Herbert Claiborne and Matilda (née Bigelow) Pell; m. Nuala O'Donnell 1944; two s. two d.; ed. Princeton and Columbia Univs.; Limited Partner, Auchinloss, Parker and Redpath; U.S. Coastguard 1941-45; Capt. U.S.C.G.R. (retd.); U.S. Foreign Service Officer; nstructor and Lecturer, Naval and Mil. Govt. Schools 1944-45; served State Dept., Czechoslovakia, Italy, Washington 1945-52; Co.-dir. and trustee 1952-60; Consultant, Dem. Nat. Cttee. 1953-60; U.S. Del. to Inter-Govtl. Maritime Consultative Org. (IMCO) London 1959; Senator from Rhode Island 1961-; Chair. Foreign Relations Cttee. Jan. 1987-; 33 hon. degrees; Légion d'honneur, Crown of Italy, six Grand Crosses, etc.; Democrat. *Publications:* Rochambeau and Rhode Island 1954, Megalopolis Unbound 1966, Challenge of the Seven Seas (with Harold L. Goodwin) 1966, Power and Policy 1972. *Address:* 335 Senate Office Building, Washington, D.C. 20510; Ledge Road, Newport, R.I. 02840, U.S.A.

PELLAT, Charles Lucien Paul, D. ÈS L.; French academic; b. 28 Sept. 1914, Souk-Ahras; s. of Paul Pellat and Denise Gayon; m. Andrée Chabalier 1937; one d.; ed. Lycée Lyautey, Casablanca, and Facultés des Lettres of Bordeaux and Algiers; Prof. Coll. de Marrakech, Morocco 1934-35; mil. service 1935-47; Prof. Lycée Louis-le-Grand, Paris 1947-51, Ecole des Langues Orientales, Paris 1951-56, Sorbonne, Paris 1956-78; mem. Editorial and Exec. Cttees. Encyclopaedia of Islam, Advisory Cttees. of Hamdard Islamicus (Karachi) and al-Karmil (Haifa); mem. Acad. des Sciences d'Outre-Mer, Acad. des Inscriptions et Belles-Lettres; corresp. mem. Indian Acad. of Arabic; Prix Bordin 1953, Prix du Budget 1983. *Publications include:* L'Arabe vivant 1951, Les avares de Jâhiz 1951, Le milieu basrien 1953, Dîwân d'Ibn Shuhayd 1963, Vie et oeuvre d'Ibn Shuhayd (in Arabic) 1965. *Leisure interest:* bridge. *Address:* 21 rue Ferdinand Jamin, 92430 Bourg-la-Reine, France. *Telephone:* 46 65 39 78.

PELLEGRINO, Edmund Daniel, M.D.; American professor of medicine; b. 22 June 1920, Newark, N.J.; m. Clementine Coakley; four s. three d.; ed. Xavier High School, New York, St. John's Univ., Jamaica and New York; Prof. and Chair. Dept. of Medicine, Univ. of Medical Center 1959-66; Vice-Pres. for Health Sciences, Dean of School of Medicine, Dir. of Health Services Center and Prof. of Medicine, State Univ. of New York 1966-73; Chancellor and Vice-Pres. for Health Affairs, Univ. of Tenn. and Prof. of Medicine and Medical Humanities, Univ. of Tenn. Center for Health Sciences 1973-75; Pres. and Chair. Bd. of Dirs. Yale-New Haven Medical Center and Prof. of Medicine, Yale Univ. 1975-78; Pres. and Prof. of Philosophy and Biology, Catholic Univ. of America, Washington, D.C., concurrently Prof. of Clinical Medicine and Community Medicine, Georgetown Univ. Medical School 1978-82; John Carroll Prof. of Medicine and Medical Humanities, Georgetown Univ. Medical Center 1982-; Dir. Kennedy Inst. of Ethics, Georgetown Univ. 1983-; Ed. Journal of Medicine and Philosophy 1983-; Fellow or mem. of 20 scientific, professional and honorary socs. including Inst. of Medicine of N.A.S.; mem. numerous nat. cttees. and bds.; recipient of numerous awards and 32 hon. degrees. *Publications:* two books and some 350 research papers in learned journals. *Leisure interests:* music, cooking, reading. *Address:* Kennedy Institute

of Ethics, Georgetown University, Washington, D.C. 20057 (Office); 6 Chalfont Court, Bethesda, Md. 20816, U.S.A. (Home). *Telephone:* (202) 687-6729.

PELLETIER, Hon. Gérard, P.C., B.A.; Canadian journalist and politician; b. 21 June 1919, Victoriaville, PQ.; s. of Achille Pelletier and Léda Dufresne; m. Alexandrine Leduc 1943; one s. three d.; ed. Nicolet and Mont-Laurier Colls., Univ. of Montreal; Sec-Gen. Jeunesse étudiante catholique 1939-43; Field Sec. World Student Relief, Geneva 1945-47; Reporter, Le Devoir 1947-50; Dir. of Le Travail, official paper of Confed. of Nat. Trade Unions 1950-61; Ed. of La Presse 1961-65; Special Columnist for Le Devoir and group of English language dailies 1965; M.P. for Hochelaga 1965; Parl. Sec. to Sec. of State for External Affairs 1967-68; Minister without Portfolio 1968; Sec. of State 1968-72; Minister of Communications 1972-75; Amb. to France 1975-81; Amb. and Perm. Rep. to UN 1981-84; Chair. Bd. of Trustees, Nat. Museums of Canada 1984-87; Pres. Montreal Council on Foreign Relations, Canadian Center for Int. Studies and Co-operation; Liberal. *Publications:* La Crise d'Octobre 1971, Les années d'impatience 1983, Le temps des choix 1986. *Leisure interests:* reading, music, boating, swimming. *Address:* 180 St. Catherine Street East, Montreal, Quebec, H2X 1K9, Canada.

PELLETIER, Pierre; French diplomatist and administrator; b. 11 Aug. 1919, Nogent-le-Rotrou; s. of Fernand and Berthe Pelletier, m.; two s. one d.; ed. Ecole Nat. d'Admin.; arts teacher 1939-46; admin. Ministry of Foreign Affairs 1950, Sec. for Foreign Affairs 1971, Sec., then Counsellor, French Embassy, Washington 1952-57, Diplomatic Adviser to Prime Minister 1957-58, Cabinet Sec. Ministry of Foreign Affairs 1958-61; Dir. du Cabinet, Ministry of Nat. Educ. and Research 1966-68, Minister and Dir. of Dept. 1968; with Commissariat à l'énergie atomique (CEA) 1961-, Sec.-Gen. 1972-84; Vice-Pres. Editions Moreux 1984; Officier, Légion d'honneur, Commdr., Ordre nat. du Mérite. *Publication:* Les affaires étrangères 1960. *Leisure interests:* agriculture, hunting, tennis. *Address:* 17 bis Place St. Germain des Longs Prés, 92100 Boulogne-Billancourt, France. *Telephone:* 620 39 44.

PELLETIER, Raymond; French business executive; b. 12 Oct. 1910, Lyon; m. Madeleine Bastide 1933; three s. three d.; ed. Ecole Polytechnique, Paris; joined Cie. Générale d'Electricité 1932, Deputy Dir.-Gen. 1955-63, Dir.-Gen. 1963-76, Vice-Pres. 1976-82; Hon. Chair. SAFT, Les Câbles de Lyon 1972; Dir. many other companies; Officier, Légion d'honneur; Croix de guerre. *Address:* 13 rue des Marronniers, 75016 Paris, France. *Telephone:* 527-33-66.

PELLETREAU, Robert Halsey, Jr., LL.B.; American diplomatist; b. 9 July 1935, Patchogue; s. of Robert Halsey Pelletreau and Mary (née Pigeon) Pelletreau; m. Pamela Day 1966; three d.; ed. Yale and Harvard Univs.; Assoc. Chadbourne, Parke, Whiteside & Wolfe 1961-62; joined Foreign Service 1962; served in Morocco, Mauritania, Lebanon, Algeria, Jordan and Syria; Amb. to Bahrain 1979-80, to Tunisia 1987-89; Deputy Asst. Sec. of Defence 1980-81, 1985-87, of State 1983-85; Asst. Sec. of State for Near Eastern and South Asian Affairs 1989-; mem. American Foreign Service Assen., Middle East Inst. *Address:* Department of State, Washington, D.C. 20520-6360, U.S.A. (Office).

PELLI, César, M.ARCH.; Argentinian architect; b. 10 Dec. 1926, Tucumán; s. of Victor Vicente Pelli and Teresa S. Pelli (née Suppa); m. Diana Balmori 1950; two s.; ed. Univ. of Tucumán, Illinois at Urbana Champaign; Project Designer Eero Saarinen Offices, Mich., Conn. 1954-64; Dir. of Design Daniel, Mann, Johnson and Medenhall (DMJM) 1964-68; Partner in Charge of Design Gruen Assocs 1968-77; Prof. of Architecture 1977-, Dean Yale School of Architecture 1977-84; Prin. César Pelli and Assocs. 1977-; numerous awards and prizes including UN City Competition First Prize, Vienna 1969, Arnold W. Brunner Prize Nat. Inst. Arts and Letters 1978, American Inst. for Architects Honor Award for Fed. Office Bldg., Lawndale and San Bernadino City Hall, Calif. *Buildings* include: Pacific Design Centre, Los Angeles, Calif. 1973, U.S. Embassy, Tokyo, Japan 1975, Museum of Modern Art, New York 1984, World Financial Centre, New York 1985-87; *Publications:* various articles in specialist journals. *Address:* César Pelli and Associates, 1056 Chapel Street, New Haven, Conn. 06510, U.S.A.

PELLY, Derek ("Derk") Roland, M.A., A.I.B.; British banker; b. 12 June 1929, Welwyn Garden City; s. of the late Arthur Roland Pelly and Phyllis Elsie Henderson; m. Susan Roberts 1953; one s. two d.; ed. Marlborough Coll. and Trinity Coll., Cambridge; joined Barclays Bank Ltd. (various positions) 1952, Local Dir., Chelmsford 1959, Sr Local Dir., Luton 1969; Vice-Chair. Barclays Bank Int. Ltd. 1977, full-time Vice-Chair. 1979; Group Vice-Chair. Barclays Bank PLC 1985, Group Deputy Chair. and Chair. Barclays Int. Ltd. 1986-88; Gov. London House for Overseas Graduates 1985-. *Leisure interest:* painting. *Address:* 11 Wallside, Monkwell Square, London, EC2Y 8BH, England. *Telephone:* 01-588 0454.

PELTSER, Tatiana Ivanovna; Soviet stage and film actress; b. 6 June 1904; on stage since 1920; mem. CPSU 1956-; work with Moscow Satire Theatre 1947-77; with Moscow Lenin Komsomol Theatre 1977-; U.S.S.R. People's Artist 1972; U.S.S.R. State Prize 1951. *Films include:* Simple Folk 1945 (released 1956), Wedding with a Dowry 1953, Ivan Brovkin, The Soldier 1955, The Tiger Tamer 1955, The Two Captains 1956, Honeymoon

1956, The Newly-weds 1960, The Country Detective 1969, The Adventures of a Yellow Suitcase 1971, The Crank from the Fifth 'B' 1972, You Didn't Dream it Either 1981, Quarantine 1983.

PEN SOVAN; Kampuchean soldier and politician; b. 1930, Takeo Prov.; joined armed unit of CP of Cambodia 1950; served in various units in eastern region, becoming Deputy to Div. Commdr. 1970; mem. Editorial Bd. Kampuchean United Front Radio 1970-75; C.-in-C. Kampuchean Armed Forces 1979-81; Vice-Pres. of People's Revolutionary Council of Kampuchea and Minister of Nat. Defence 1979-81; Sec. Gen. People's Revolutionary Party of Kampuchea May-Dec. 1981; mem. Politburo and Secr., Cen. Cttee. 1981. *Address:* c/o People's Revolutionary Council of Kampuchea, Phnom-Penh, Kampuchea.

PEÑA, Paco; Spanish flamenco guitarist; b. 1 June 1942, Cordoba; s. of Antonio Peña and Rosario Perez; m. Karin Vaessen 1982; two d.; int. concert artist since 1968; f. Paco Peña Flamenco Co. 1970; f. Centro Flamenco Paco Peña, Cordoba 1981; Prof. of Flamenco, Rotterdam Conservatory, Netherlands 1985-; Ramón Montoya Prize 1983. *Address:* c/o Hetherington Seelig, 28 Museum Street, London, WC1A 1LH, England. *Telephone:* 01-637 5661.

PEÑAHERRERA PADILLA, Blasco; Ecuadorian politician; b. 22 Feb. 1934, Quito; s. of Rafael Modesto Peñaherrera Peñaherrera and Rosa Elena Padilla; m. Zeyneb Solah Coronel; three c.; ed. Universidad Cen. del Ecuador, on editorial staff of Vistazo; TV dir. and producer; Chair. Compañía Consultrín; Prof., Cen. Univ. of Ecuador and Catholic Univ. of Quito; public appts. have included Under-Sec. for Educ., Chair. Nat. Educ. Council, Exec. Sec., Integration Secr. of Andean Pact, Dir. of Promotion, Andean Devt. Corpn.; active in Partido Liberal Radical Ecuatoriano since 1954, now Nat. Dir.; Vice-Pres. of Ecuador 1984. *Address:* c/o Oficina del Presidente, Quito, Ecuador.

PEÑALOSA, Enrique; Colombian economist; b. 31 Aug. 1930, Soacha; s. of Vicente Peñalosa and Abby Camargo; m. Pamela Gibson; four s. one d.; Econ. Ed. Semana weekly review 1952; Asst. in Nat. Planning Office 1952-53; IBRD Training Course 1954, missions in Colombia 1955; private econ. consultant 1956-61; mem. Comisión Paritaria Económica 1957, City Council, Bogotá 1958-62, Nat. Council for Petroleum Affairs 1958, Advisory Cttee. of Partido Liberal 1959; First Exec. Dir. Corpn. Autónoma Regional de la Sabana de Bogotá 1961; First Gen. Man. Colombia Inst. Colombiana de Reforma Agraria 1961-68; Minister of Agric. 1968-69; Alt. Exec. Dir. Inter-American Devt. Bank 1970-71, Admin. Man. 1971-74; Sec.-Gen. UN Conf. on Human Settlements (Habitat) 1974-76; Amb. to UN 1987-; Fellow, Adlai Stevenson Inst. of Int. Affairs 1972-74; Order of Orange-Nassau (Netherlands); Legion of Agricultural Merit (Peru). *Address:* P.O. Box 5214, G.C.O., New York, N.Y. 10163 (Office); 14 East 76th Street, New York, N.Y. 10021, U.S.A. (Home).

PENCHAS, Shmuel, M.D., D.I.C.; Israeli professor of internal medicine; b. 12 Feb. 1939, Romania; s. of Nathan Penchas and Luba Penchas; m. Mia Yael 1987; four s.; ed. Hebrew Univ. Hadassah Medical School, Haifa Technion Grad. School, Imperial Coll. London and Univ. Coll. London; physician, Hadassah Univ. Hosp., Jerusalem 1967-76, Dir. of Computing 1977-78; Deputy Dir.-Gen. Hadassah Medical Org. 1978, Dir.-Gen. 1981-; Chair. Israel Asscn. of Hosp. Dirs. *Publications:* articles in professional journals. *Address:* Hadassah Medical Center, Kiryat Hadassah, P.O.B. 12000, Jerusalem 91120, Israel. *Telephone:* (02) 446060.

PENCK, A. R.; German artist; b. (as Ralf Winkler) 5 Oct. 1939, Dresden; s. of Clemens and Elfriede Winkler; m.; two s. one d.; first exhbn. in West, Galerie Michael Werner, Cologne 1969; first museum show, Museum Haus Lange, Krefeld, Federal Repub. of Germany 1971; moved to Federal Repub. of Germany 1980; Will Grohmann Prize, Rembrandt Prize, Aachen. *Publications:* Standart Making 1970, Was ist Standart 1970, Ich-Standart Literatur 1971, Zeichen als Verständigung 1971, Europäische Sonette 1974, Ich bin ein Buch kaufe mich jetzt 1976, Sanfte Theorie über Arsch, Asche und Vegetation 1979, Ende im Ostem 1981. *Leisure interests:* music, painting, sculpture. *Address:* Galerie Michael Werner, Gertrudenstrasse 24-28, 5000 Cologne 1, Federal Republic of Germany; 55 Upper Leeson Street, Dublin, Ireland.

PENDERECKI, Krzysztof; Polish composer and conductor; b. 23 Nov. 1933, Dębica, Cracow District; s. of Tadeusz and Zofia Penderecki; m. Elzbieta Solecka 1965; two c.; ed. Jagellonian Univ., Cracow and State Higher Music School, Cracow; studied composition first with Skołyszewski, later with Malawski and Wiechowicz, Cracow; graduated from State Higher Music School, Cracow 1958; Lecturer in Composition, State Higher Music School (now Music Acad.), Cracow 1958-66, Prof. Extraordinary 1972-75, Prof. 1975-, Rector 1972-87; Prof. of Composition, Folkwang Hochschule für Musik, Essen 1966-68; Musical Adviser, Vienna Radio 1970-71; Prof. of Composition, Yale Univ., U.S.A. 1973-78; Hon. mem. R.A.M., London 1974; Corresp. mem. Arts Acad. of G.D.R., Berlin 1975; Extraordinary mem. Arts Acad. of W. Berlin 1975; mem. Royal Acad. of Music, Stockholm 1975; Hon. mem. Acad. Nazionale di Santa Cecilia, Italy 1976; Corresp. mem. Academia Nacional de Bellas Artes, Buenos Aires 1982; Dr. h.c. (Univ. of Rochester, N.Y.) 1972, (St. Olaf Coll., Northfield, Minn.) 1977, (Katholieke Univ., Leuven) 1977, (Univ. of Bordeaux) 1979, (Georgetown Univ., Washington, D.C.) 1984, (Belgrade) 1985, (Madrid) 1986; Fitelberg

Prize for Threnody for the Victims of Hiroshima 1960, also UNESCO award 1961, Polish Minister of Culture and Art Prize 1961, (First Class) 1981; Cracow Composition Prize for Canon 1962; North Rhine-Westphalia Grand Prize for St. Luke Passion 1966, also Pax Prize (Poland) 1966; Alfred Jurzykowski Foundation Award, Polish Inst. of Arts and Sciences 1966; Prix Italia 1967/68; State Prize (1st Class) 1968; Gustav Charpentier Prize 1971; Gottfried von Herder Prize 1977, Arthur Honegger Music Award for Magnificat 1977, Grand Medal of Paris 1982, Sibelius Prize (Wihouri Foundation, Finland) 1983, Order of Banner of Labour (1st Class) 1983, Premio Lorenzo il Magnifico (Italy) 1985, Wolf Foundation Prize 1987, Gamma Prize of Acad. of Recording Arts and Sciences for the best contemporary composition 1988. *Works include:* Psalms of David (for choir and percussion) 1958, Emanations (for 2 String Orchestras) 1959, Strophes (for soprano, speaker and ten instruments) 1959, Anaklasis (for strings and percussion) 1960, Dimensions of time and silence (for 40-part mixed choir and chamber ensemble) 1960, String Quartet 1960, Threnody for the Victims of Hiroshima (for 52 strings) 1960, Polymorphia (for 48 strings) 1961, Psalms for Tape 1961, Fluorescences (for large orchestra) 1962, Sonata for cello and orchestra 1964, Passio et mors domini nostri Jesu Christi secundum Lucam (for soprano, baritone, bass, speaker, boys' choir, mixed chorus and large orchestra) 1965-66, Capriccio per oboe e 11 archi 1965, De natura sonoris (for large orchestra) 1966, Dies irae (for soprano, tenor, bass, chorus and large orchestra) 1967, Quartetto per archi II 1968, The Devils of Loudun (opera) 1968, Cosmogony 1970, De Natura Sonoris II (for wind instruments, percussion and strings) 1970, Russian Mass Utrenja 1971, Partita (for harpsichord, guitars, harp, double bass and chamber orchestra) 1972, First Symphony 1973, Canticum Canticorum Salomonis (for 16 voices and chamber orchestra) 1973, Magnificat (for bass solo, voice ensemble, double choir, boys' voices and orchestra) 1974, When Jacob Awoke (for orchestra) 1974, Violin Concerto 1977, Paradise Lost (Opera) 1978, (Christmas) Symphony No. 2 1980, Te Deum 1979-80, Lacrimosa 1980, Cello Concerto 1982, Viola Concerto 1983, Polish Requiem 1983-84, The Black Mask (opera) 1986. *Address:* Państwowa Wyższa Szkoła Muzyczna, ul. Bohaterow Stalingradu 3, 31-038 Cracow; Home: ul. Cisowa 22, 30-229 Cracow, Poland; 324 Livingston Street, New Haven, Conn. 06511, U.S.A. *Telephone:* 2257-60 (Home); 203-789 0354 (U.S.A.).

PENG CHONG; Chinese politician; b. 1909, Zhangzhou, Fujian; joined CCP 1933; Political Commissar, regt. of New 4th Army 1938; Deputy Sec.-Gen. prov. People's Govt., Fujian 1950; Mayor of Nanjing 1955-59; First Sec. Municipal CCP Cttee., Nanjing 1955-60; Deputy for Jiangsu, 2nd NPC 1958; alt. Second Sec. CCP Cttee., Jiangsu 1960; Political Commissar Nanjing militia 1960; First Sec. Municipal CCP Cttee., Nanjing 1962-68; Second Sec. CCP Cttee., Jiangsu 1965-68; Vice-Chair. Prov. Revolutionary Cttee., Jiangsu 1968-74; alt. mem. 9th Cen. Cttee. CCP 1969; Sec. CCP Cttee., Jiangsu 1970-74; alt. mem. 10th Cen. Cttee. CCP 1973; Chair. Prov. Revolutionary Cttee., Jiangsu 1974-76; Second Political Commissar, PLA Nanjing Mil. Region 1975-80; Third Sec. CCP Cttee., Shanghai 1976-79; Second Vice-Chair. Municipal Revolutionary Cttee., Shanghai 1976-79; Chair. Municipal CPPCC Cttee., Shanghai 1977-79; mem. 11th Cen. Cttee. CCP 1977; Head, Group in Charge of Snail Fever Prevention, Cen. Cttee. CCP 1978-; Deputy for Shanghai, 5th NPC 1978; Vice-Chair. Nat. Cttee., 5th CPPCC 1978-80; First Sec. CCP Cttee., Shanghai 1979-80; Chair. Municipal Revolutionary Cttee., Shanghai 1979-80; Mayor of Shanghai 1980; Sec. 11th Cen. Cttee. CCP 1980-82; Vice-Chair. Standing Cttee., 5th NPC 1980-83; mem. 12th Cen. Cttee. CCP 1982-; Vice-Chair. Standing Cttee., 6th NPC 1983-; mem. Presidium 6th NPC 1986-; Chair. Law Cttee., NPC 1983-; Pres. China Int. Cultural Exchange Centre 1984-; Exec. mem. China Welfare Inst. 1978-; Hon. Pres. Gymnastics Asscn. 1983-. *Address:* Beijing, People's Republic of China.

PENG DEQING, Rear Adm.; Chinese naval officer and politician; b. 1915, Jiangxi Prov.; Deputy Commdr. 22nd Army, 3rd Field Army 1951; Commdr. 27th Army, 3rd Field Army 1954; Deputy Commdr. E. China Sea Fleet 1956; Commdr. Xiamen Naval Base, Fujian 1959; Commdr. Navy Unit 1072 1960; Vice-Minister of Communications 1965-67, 1975-81, Minister 1981-82, Adviser 1983-; mem. Cen. Advisory Comm. 1983-; Pres. Marine Navigation Soc. 1981-. *Address:* c/o State Council, Beijing, People's Republic of China.

PENG JIAQING; Chinese Soldier and party official; b. 1909, Ji'an Co., Jiangxi Prov.; joined CCP 1930; mem. Political Cttee. 4th Column N.E. PLA 1947; Council mem. Jiangxi Prov. People's Govt. 1950-54; Chair. Jiangxi Prov. CCP Control Cttee. 1950-; mem. Shandong Prov. People's Congress and Prov. People's Govt. 1954; Lieut.-Gen. Jinan Prov. PLA 1957-; Deputy PLA Political Cttee, Gen. Logistics Dept. 1966-; Adviser, Canton Mil. Region 1981; mem. Cen. Advisory Cttee. of CCP Cen. Cttee. 1987-. *Address:* Central Advisory Committee of the Central Committee of the Chinese Communist Party, Zhongnanhai, Beijing, People's Republic of China.

PENG SHILU; Chinese physicist and state official; b. 1925, Haifeng Co., Guangdong Prov.; s. of Peng Pai and Cai Suping; m. Ma Shuying 1958; two c.; ed. St. Joseph's English Inst., Hong Kong, Yan'an Inst. of Natural Science, Harbin Polytechnical Univ., Dalian Coll. of Eng., Kazan Inst. of Chem. Eng., Moscow Inst. of Power Eng.; joined E. River Column of Red Army 1939; joined CCP 1945; Deputy Dir. Nuclear Power Lab., Inst. of

Atomic Energy 1958–64; Assoc. Prof. of Physics, Chinese Univ. of Science and Tech. 1962–65; Chief Engineer and Deputy Dir. of Inst. of Nuclear Power 1964–73; Vice-Pres. Acad. of Marine Architecture 1974–79; Vice-Minister, 6th Ministry of Machine Building 1979–82; alt. mem. 12th CCP Cen. Cttee. 1982; mem. Standing Cttee. of CCP, Guangdong Prov. 1983–84; Vice-Minister of Water Resources and Electric Power 1983–85; Chair. and Chief Engineer, Science and Tech. Cttee., Ministry of Nuclear Industry 1986–; Vice-Pres. Chinese Nuclear Soc.; Pres. Chinese Nuclear Power Soc. 1984–; Prizewinner, Conf. of State Science 1978, Special Grade Prize of State Science and Tech. 1986. *Address:* P.O. Box 2102, Beijing, People's Republic of China. *Telephone:* 8012211.

PENG ZHEN; Chinese politician; b. 1902, Shanxi Prov.; joined CCP 1923; elected mem. 7th and 8th Cen. Cttees. CCP and mem. Political Bureau of CCP 1945, 1956; mem. Secr. CCP Cen. Cttee. 1956–66; Vice-Chair. Standing Cttee. of 1st, 2nd and 3rd NPC and Vice-Chair. 2nd, 3rd and 4th Nat. Cttees. CPPCC 1954, 1959, 1965; First Sec. Beijing Municipal Party Cttee. 1949; Mayor of Beijing 1951–66; criticized during Cultural Revolution, removed from all party and govt. posts; apptd. Chair. NPC Comm. of Legislative Affairs 1979; Vice-Chair. Standing Cttee. 5th NPC 1979–; mem. 11th Cen. Cttee. of CCP and mem. Political Bureau 1979–; mem. 12th Cen. Cttee. of CCP and mem. Political Bureau 1982–87; Sec. Cttee. on Political and Legal Affairs of CCP Cen. Cttee. 1980–84; Vice-Chair. Cttee. for Revision of Constitution 1980; Chair, NPC Standing Cttee. 1983–. *Address:* Standing Committee, Quanguo Renmin Diabiao Dahui, Beijing, People's Republic of China.

PENJORE, Lyonpo Sangye; Bhutanese diplomatist; b. 13 Feb. 1928, Bamthang; m.; two s. two d.; ed. local school; entered govt. service 1945; Officer-in-charge of Royal Household of Tashichholing; Chief Dist. Officer, Bamthang Dist., Deputy Chief Sec. 1960; fmr. Minister for Communications; Perm. Rep. to UN 1971–75; Amb. to India 1975–81 (also accred. to Bangladesh). *Address:* c/o Ministry of Foreign Affairs, Thimphu, Bhutan.

PENN, Arthur; American theatre and film director; b. 27 Sept. 1922, Philadelphia; m. Peggy Maurer 1955; one s. one d.; joined Army theatre company during World War II; worked in television 1951–53; taught at Actors' Studio mid-1970s; produced plays for Broadway theatre including The Miracle Worker, All the Way Home, Toys in the Attic, Two for the Seesaw, In the Council House, Wait Until Dark, Sly Fox, Monday after the Miracle. *Films:* The Left-Handed Gun 1957, The Miracle Worker 1962, Mickey One 1964, The Chase 1965, Bonnie and Clyde 1967, Alice's Restaurant 1969, Little Big Man 1971, Night Moves 1975, The Missouri Breaks 1976, Four Friends 1981, Target 1985, Dead of Winter 1987; Co-Dir. Visions of Eight 1973. *Address:* 1860 Broadway, New York, N.Y. 10023, U.S.A.

PENNEY, Baron (Life Peer), cr. 1967, of East Hendred; **William George Penney,** O.M., K.B.E., PH.D., D.SC., F.R.S.; British scientist; b. 24 June 1909, Gibraltar; s. of W. A. Penney; m. 1st Adele Minnie Elms (deceased); m. 2nd Eleanor Joan Quenell; two s.; ed. Sheerness Tech. School and Royal Coll. of Science, London Univ.; Commonwealth Fund Fellow, Univ. of Wis., U.S.A.; Sr. Student of 1851 Exhbn., Trinity Coll., Cambridge 1933–36; Asst. Prof. Mathematics, Imperial Coll., London Univ. 1936–45; Prin. Scientific Officer, Dept. Scientific and Industrial Research 1944–45; Chief Supt. Armaments Research, Ministry of Supply 1946–52; Dir. Atomic Weapons Research Establishment, Aldermaston 1953–59; mem. for Weapons Research and Devt., UKAEA 1954–59, for Research 1959–61, Deputy Chair. 1961–64, Chair 1964–67; Rector Imperial Coll. of Science and Tech. 1967–73; Dir. Tube Investments 1968–79, Standard Telephones and Cables 1971–83; Treas. Royal Soc. 1956–60; Rumford Medal, Royal Soc. 1966; Glazebrook Medal and Prize 1969; Kelvin Gold Medal 1971; Foreign Assoc. N.A.S. 1962; Hon. D.Sc. (Oxford, Durham and Bath Univ. of Tech.); Hon. LL.D. (Melbourne). *Address:* Orchard House, Cat Street, East Hendred, Wantage, Oxon., OX12 8JT, England.

PENNIE, Michael William, A.R.C.A.; British sculptor; b. 23 Oct. 1936, Wallasey, Cheshire; s. of George A. Pennie and Isabel Duff; m. 1st Norah Kimmit 1959 (divorced 1977); m. 2nd Marlene Stride 1985; two s. one d.; ed. Bede Collegiate for Boys, Sunderland, Sunderland Coll. of Art and Royal Coll. of Art; Visiting Lecturer, Bath Acad. of Art, Winchester and Wimbledon Schools of Art, Norwich Coll. of Art and Brighton Polytechnic 1962–82; Sen. Lecturer, Bath Coll. 1985–; Co-Organizer, Sculpture in the City, Bath 1986; one-man shows include ICA Gallery, London 1965, Welsh Arts Council Gallery, Cardiff 1971, Angela Flowers Gallery, London 1971, 1973, 1976, 1981, Ensembles Artsite, Bath 1988; numerous group shows 1961–; participant, Forma Viva, Yugoslavia 1980, Making Sculpture Tate Gallery, London 1983; works in various public collections including Victoria and Albert Museum and Arts Council of G.B.; Curator of touring exhbn. 'African' 1988. *Publications:* Trips to the Sculpture-making Tribes of West Africa 1987 and 1988, Where Shall We Put This One? 1988, Smoke of the Savannah 1989. *Leisure interest:* collecting tribal art. *Address:* 117 Bradford Road, Atworth, Melksham, Wilts., SN12 8HY, England. *Telephone:* (0225) 705409.

PENNOCK, Baron (Life Peer), cr. 1982, of Norton in the County of Cleveland; **Raymond Pennock,** Kt., M.A.; British business executive; b. 16 June 1920, Redcar, Yorks.; s. of Frederick Henry and Harriet Ann Pennock

(née Mathison); m. Lorna Pearse 1943; one s. two d.; ed. Coatham School, Redcar, Yorks., and Merton Coll., Oxford; Capt., Royal Artillery 1941–46; with ICI Ltd. 1947–80 (Deputy Chair. 1975–79); mem. Bd. Plessey Co. 1978–, Deputy Chair. 1985–; Chair. BICC PLC 1980–84; Pres. of CBI 1980–82; Dir. Morgan Grenfell Group PLC 1983–, Standard Chartered PLC 1982–, Willis Faber PLC 1985–; Pres. UNICE 1984–86, Vice-Pres. 1986–; Dir. Channel Tunnel Group Feb. 1986–; Dir. Eurotunnel PLC 1986–; Hon. Pres. Copper Devt. Ascn. *Leisure interests:* opera, ballet, music, tennis. *Address:* Morgan Grenfell Group PLC, 23 Great Winchester Street, London, EC2P 2AX, England.

PENROSE, Edith Tilton, M.A., PH.D.; British economist; b. 29 Nov. 1914, Los Angeles, Calif.; d. of George A. Tilton and Hazel D. Sparling; m. 1st David B. Denhardt 1934 (died 1938), 2nd Ernest F. Penrose 1944 (deceased); three s.; ed. Univ. of California (Berkeley) and Johns Hopkins Univ., Baltimore, Md.; research with Int. Labour Office, Geneva and Montreal 1939–41; special asst. to U.S. Amb., London 1941–46; mem. staff, U.S. del. to UN, New York 1946–47; lecturer and research assoc., Dept. of Econs., Johns Hopkins Univ. 1951–60; Visiting Fellow, Australian Nat. Univ., Canberra 1955; Assoc. Prof. Univ. of Baghdad 1957–59; Reader, L.S.E. and S.O.A.S., London 1960–64; Prof. of Econs. S.O.A.S. 1964–78, Prof. Emer. 1978–; Research Prof., Univ. of Dar es Salaam 1972; Dir. Commonwealth Devt. Corpn. 1975–78; mem. U.K. Medicines Comm. 1975–77; Chair. Econs. Cttee., Social Science Research Council, U.K. 1974–76; Prof. of Political Economy, European Inst. of Business Admin. (INSEAD), Fontainebleau, France 1977–84, Assoc. Dean of Research and Devt. 1982–84, Prof. Emer. 1984–, Econ. Consultant 1984–; Guggenheim Fellow 1955–56; Thomas Newcomen Award in Business History 1961; mem. Council Royal Econ. Soc. 1975–; Dr. h.c. (Uppsala) 1984; Award from Int. Ascn. of Energy Economists 1987. *Publications:* Economics of the International Patent System 1951, The Theory of the Growth of the Firm 1959, The Large International Firm in Developing Countries: The International Petroleum Industry 1968, The Growth of the Firm, Middle East Oil and Other Essays 1971, The Economic and Political Development of Iraq (with E. F. Penrose) 1978. *Leisure interests:* travel, theatre, walking. *Address:* The Barn, 30A Station Road, Waterbeach, Cambridge, CB5 9HT, England. *Telephone:* (0223) 861618.

PENROSE, Oliver, PH.D., F.R.S.; British professor of mathematics; b. 6 June 1929, London; s. of Lionel S. Penrose and Margaret Leathes; m. Joan L. Dilley 1953; three s. (one deceased) one d.; ed. Central Collegiate Inst. London, Canada, Univ. Coll. London and King's Coll. Cambridge; Mathematical Physicist, English Electric Co. Luton 1952–55; Research Asst. Yale Univ. 1955–56; lecturer, Reader, Imperial Coll. London 1956–69; Prof. of Math. Open Univ. 1969–86, Heriot Watt Univ. 1986–. *Publications:* Foundations of Statistical Mechanics 1969; about 50 papers in scientific journals. *Leisure interests:* music, chess. *Address:* 29 Frederick Street, Edinburgh, EH2 2ND, Scotland. *Telephone:* (031) 225 5879.

PENZIAS, Arno Allan, PH.D.; American astrophysicist; b. 26 April 1933, Munich, Germany; s. of Karl and Justine Penzias; m. Anne Barras Penzias 1954; one s. two d.; ed. City Coll. of New York, Columbia Univ.; mem. tech. staff Bell Laboratories, Holmdel, N.J. 1961–72, Head Radiophysics Research Dept. 1972–76, Dir. Radio Research Lab. 1976–79, Exec. Dir. Research, Communications Sciences Div. 1979–81, Vice-Pres. Research, Bell Labs., Murray Hill, N.J. 1981–; Lecturer, Princeton Univ. 1967–72, Visiting Prof. Astrophysical Sciences Dept. 1972–85; Assoc. Ed., Astrophysical Journal 1978–82; mem. Editorial Bd. Annual Review of Astronomy and Astrophysics 1974–78; mem. Bd. of Trustees of Trenton State Coll. 1977–79, Visiting Cttee. of Calif. Inst. of Tech. 1977–79; mem. Astronomy Advisory Panel of Nat. Science Foundation 1978–79, Bd. of Overseers, School of Eng. and Applied Science Univ. of Pa. 1983–86; mem. Fachbeirat 1978–85 (Chair. 1981–83); Dir. Grad. Faculties Alumni, Colombia Univ. 1987–; mem. N.A.S., American Astronomical Soc., Int. Astronomical Union; Vice-Chair. Cttee. Concerned Scientists; Fellow American Acad. of Arts and Sciences, American Physical Soc.; Nobel Prize for Physics 1978; Dr. h.c. Paris Observatory 1976; Henry Draper Medal, N.A.S. 1977; Herschel Medal, Royal Astronomical Soc. 1977. *Publications:* over 80 scientific papers in various journals; discovered cosmic microwave background radiation 1965. *Leisure interests:* swimming, jogging, skiing. *Address:* AT & T Bell Laboratories, 600 Mountain Avenue, Murray Hill, N.J. 07974, U.S.A. *Telephone:* (201) 582-3361.

PEPIN, Hon. Jean-Luc, P.C., C.C., B.A., L.PH., LL.L.; Canadian politician; b. 1 Nov. 1924; s. of Victor and Antoinette (née Morel) Pepin; m. Mary Brock-Smith 1952; one s. one d.; ed. Univ. of Ottawa and Inst. d'Etudes politiques, Paris; Prof. Univ. of Ottawa 1951–56, 1958–63; Rep., Nat. Film Bd., London (U.K.) 1956–58; M.P. for Drummond 1963–72, for Ottawa-Carleton 1979–84; Parl. Sec. to Minister of Trade and Commerce 1963; Minister without Portfolio 1965; Minister of Mines and Tech. Surveys (later Minister of Energy, Mines and Resources) 1965–68, of Industry, Trade and Commerce 1968–72, of Transport 1980–83, Minister of External Relations 1983–84; Pres. Interimco Ltd. 1973–75; Chair. Anti-Inflation Bd. 1975–77; Co-Chair. Task Force on Canadian Unity 1977–79; Prof. of Social Sciences, Univ. of Ottawa; Fellow-in-Residence, Inst. for Research on Public Policy, Ottawa; Hon. Dr. (Bishop's, Univ. of Ottawa, Carleton Univ.) 1977; Hon. Dr. Public Admin. (Sherbrooke, Laval). *Address:* Institute for Research on Public

Policy, 275 rue Slater, 5th Floor, Ottawa, Ont. K1P 5H9 (Office); 16 Rothwell Drive, Ottawa, Ont. K1J 7G4, Canada (Home). *Telephone:* (613) 231-4986 (Office); (613) 746-0845 (Home).

PÉPIN, Lucie; Canadian nurse; b. 7 Sept. 1936, St.-Jean d'Iberville, Que.; d. of Jean and Thérèse (Bessette) Pépin; two d.; ed Univ. of Montreal School of Fine Arts and McGill Univ.; Head Nurse, Gynaecology Dept., Notre-Dame Hosp., Montreal 1960-61, Family Planning Clinic, Faculty of Medicine, Univ. of Montreal 1966-70; Canadian Rep. WHO 1972-74; Instructor, Contraception, Dept. of Nursing, Dept. of Medicine, Univ. of Montreal 1972-77, Instructor Contraception and Sexuality 1976-78; Nat. Co-ordinator, Canadian Comm. for Fertility Research 1972-79; Co-ordinator, Fed. Badgeley Report, Justice Canada 1975; Co-ordinator, Int. Symposium on Family Planning, Int. Centre for Contraception Research, Nat. Symposium, Canadian Fertility Soc. 1979; Vice-Pres. Canadian Advisory Council on Status of Women 1979-81, Pres. 1981-. *Leisure interests:* tennis, sailing, painting, horseback riding. *Address:* 66 Slater Street, C.P. Box 1541, Succ./Station B, Ottawa, Ont. K1P 5R5, Canada (Office).

PEPPER, Michael, SC.D., F.R.S.; British physicist; b. 10 Aug. 1942, London; s. of Morris and Ruby Pepper; m. Dr. Jeannette D. Josse 1973; two d.; St. Marylebone Grammar School, London and Reading Univ.; Physicist, Mullard Research Lab. 1967-69; physicist engaged in solid state device research, Allen Clark Research Centre, Plessey Co. 1969-73; research at Cavendish Lab., Cambridge 1973-, Prof. of Physics, Univ. of Cambridge 1987-; Warren Research Fellow of Royal Soc. 1978-86; Fellow, Trinity Coll., Cambridge 1982-; Sr. Research Fellow, GEC Hirst Research Centre 1982-87; Visiting Prof. Bar-Ilan Univ., Israel 1984; Guthrie Prize and Medal, Inst. of Physics 1985; Hewlett-Packard Prize, European Physical Soc. 1985, Hughes Medal of the Royal Soc. 1987. *Publications:* numerous papers on solid state physics and semiconductors in scientific journals. *Leisure interests:* travel, music, whisky tasting. *Address:* Cavendish Laboratory, Cambridge, CB3 0HE, England. *Telephone:* (0223) 337330.

PERAHIA, Murray; American pianist and conductor; b. 19 April 1947, New York; s. of David Perahia and Flora Perahia; m. Naomi (Ninette) Shohet 1980; two s.; ed. High School of Performing Arts, Mannes Coll. of Music; studied with Jeanette Haien, Arthur Balsam, Mieczyslaw Horszowski; début, Carnegie Hall 1968; won Leeds Int. Pianoforte Competition 1972, Avery Fisher Award 1975; Kosciusko Chopin Prize; has appeared with many of world's leading orchestras and with Amadeus, Budapest, Guarneri and Galimir string quartets; regular recital tours N. America, Europe, Japan; Co-Artistic Dir. Aldeburgh Festival 1983-; numerous recordings including complete Mozart Piano Concertos. *Address:* c/o Frank Salomon Associates, 201 West 54th Street, Suite 4C, New York, N.Y. 10019, U.S.A.; c/o Harold Holt Ltd., 31 Sinclair Road, W14 0NS, England. *Telephone:* 01-603 4600 (London).

PERAK, H.H. Sultan of, Sultan Azlan Muhibbuddin Shah ibni Al-Marhum Sultan Yussuf Ghafarullahu—Lahu Shah; Malaysian ruler; b. 19 April 1928, Batu Gajah; m. Tuanku Bainun Mohamed Ali 1954; two s. three d.; ed. Govt. English School (now Sultan Yussuf School), Malay Coll. and Univ. of Nottingham; called to Bar, Lincoln's Inn; Magistrate, Kuala Lumpur; Asst. State Sec., Perak; Deputy Public Prosecutor; Pres. Sessions Court, Seremban and Taiping; State Legal Adviser, Pahang and Johore; Fed. Court Judge 1973; Chief Justice of Malaysia 1979; Lord Pres. 1982-83; Raja Kechil Bongsu (sixth-in-line) 1962, Raja Muda (second-in-line to the throne) 1983; Sultan of Perak Jan. 1984-; Yang di-Pertuan Agong (Supreme Head of State) 1989-(94); Pro-Chancellor Univ. Saina Malaysia 1971-, Chancellor Univ. of Malaya 1986-; Hon. Col.-in-Chief Malaysian Armed Forces' Engineers Corps.; Man. Malaysian Hockey Team 1972; Pres. Malaysian Hockey Fed., Asian Hockey Fed.; Vice-Pres. Int. Hockey Fed., Olympic Council of Malaysia.

PERALTA AZURDIA, Col. Enrique; Guatemalan army officer and politician; b. 11 June 1908, Guatemala City; s. of Juan Peralta and Ana Azurdia; m. Carmen Carrasco; two s.; ed. Polytechnic School, Guatemala City; Guatemalan army 1926, rose from Lieut. to Col.; fmr. Dir. Polytechnic School; Mil. Attaché, Mexico, Chile, Costa Rica, El Salvador and U.S.A.; fmr. Amb. to Cuba, El Salvador and Costa Rica; Dir.-Gen. Agrarian Affairs 1958-59, Minister of Agric. 1959-60, of Defence 1961-63, Chief of State and Minister of Defence 1963-66; unsuccessful cand. for Pres. elections 1978. *Leisure interests:* travelling, chess. *Address:* 5A Avenida 1-47, Zona 9, Guatemala City, Guatemala.

PERCEVAL, John de Burgh; Australian artist; b. 1 Feb. 1923, Bruce Rock, W. Australia; m. 1944 (dissolved); one s. three d.; ed. Trinity Grammar School; began painting at age 13 (self-taught); mem. and former Sec. Contemporary Artists' Soc.; represented in major Australian art galleries, including Melbourne, Monash and Canberra, Nat. Gallery of Australia; Zwemmer Galleries, London; Toronto Art Gallery; Mona McCaughey Prize 1957, shared Wynne Prize 1961; Fellow in Creative Arts, Australian Nat. Univ., Canberra 1965. *Address:* 1/53 Princess Street, Kew 3101, Australia.

PERCOVICH ROCA, Luis; Peruvian politician; Pres. Chamber of Deputies 1981-83; Minister of Fisheries Jan.-April 1983, Minister of the Interior 1983-84; Prime Minister of Peru and Minister of Foreign Affairs 1984-85; mem. Acción Popular (AP). *Address:* c/o Oficina del Prime Ministro, Ucayali 363, Lima, Peru.

PERCY, Charles Harting; American business executive and politician; b. 27 Sept. 1919, Pensacola, Fla.; s. of Edward H. and Elisabeth (née Harting) Percy; m. Jeanne Valerie Dickerson 1943 (deceased), one s. two d. (one deceased); m. 2nd Loraine Diane Guyer 1950, one s. one d.; ed. Univ. of Chicago; sales trainee, apprentice, Bell & Howell 1938, Man., War Co-ordinating Dept. 1941-43, Asst. Sec. 1943-46, Corpn. Sec. 1948-49, Pres. 1949-61, C.E.O. 1961-63, Chair. Bd. 1961-66; Senator from Illinois 1967-85; Head Charles H. Percy and Assocs. 1985-; Chair. Foreign Relations Cttee. 1981-85; Chair. Inst. of Int. Educ. 1985-; Chair. and Pres. Hariri Foundation 1985-; Officer U.S.N. 1943-45; Republican. *Publications:* Growing Old In the Country of the Young 1974, I Want To Know about the United States Senate 1976. *Address:* Charles H. Percy and Associates Inc., 1660 L Street, N.W., Suite 907, Washington, D.C. 20036; Wilmette, Ill. 60091, U.S.A.

PERDIGÃO, José de Azeredo, LL.D.; Portuguese lawyer and foundation official; b. 19 Sept. 1896, Viseu; s. of José Perdigão and Rachel Azeredo Perdigão; m. Dr. Maria Madalena Biscaia de Azeredo Perdigão 1960; two s. one d.; ed. Lisbon and Coimbra Univ.; Lawyer, Lisbon 1919-26; Keeper of Registered Bldgs. Dept., Lisbon 1926-58; Chair. Bd. of Admins. Calouste Gulbenkian Foundation 1956-; fmr. Pres. Conf. of Inst. of Portuguese Lawyers; fmr. Dir. Nat. Overseas Bank; nine hon. doctorates in Law, Science, Arts and Letters; Hon. mem. Brazilian Acad. Fine Arts; Corresp. mem. Acad. des Beaux Arts, Inst. de France 1969, Lisbon Acad. of Science, Portuguese Acad. of History; Hon. mem. Portuguese Acad. of Fine Arts; Pres. Bd. of Auditors of Bank of Portugal 1978-; 50 Portuguese and foreign decorations. *Publications:* Calouste Gulbenkian Collector and other titles. *Leisure interests:* cultural and artistic. *Address:* Rua Marquês de Fronteira, 8, 2°Dto., Lisbon, Portugal. *Telephone:* 536355.

PEREIRA, Aristides Maria; Cape Verde politician; b. 17 Nov. 1923, Boa Vista; s. of Porfírio Pereira Tavares and Maria das Neves da Cruz Silva; m. Carlina Fortes; one s. two d.; ed. Lycée du Cap-Vert; began career as radio-telegraphist; Head, Telecommunications Services, Bissau, Portuguese Guinea (now Guinea-Bissau); founded Partido Africano da Independência da Guiné e Cabo Verde (PAIGC) with the late Amílcar Cabral 1956; mem. Political Bureau, Cen. Cttee., PAIGC 1956-70; fled to Repub. of Guinea 1960; Asst. Sec.-Gen. PAIGC 1964-73, Sec.-Gen. 1973-81; Sec.-Gen. Partido Africano da Independência de Cabo Verde (PAICV) Jan. 1981-; mem. Perm. Comm. of Exec. Cttee. for Struggle in charge of Security, Control and Foreign Affairs 1970-; Pres. Repub. of Cape Verde July 1975-; Médaille, Ordre du Lyon (Senegal), Médaille Amílcar Cabral (Guinea-Bissau), Médaille de Fidélité au Peuple (Repub. of Guinea). *Leisure interests:* swimming, tennis, music. *Address:* Presidência da República, Cidade de Praia, São Tiago, Cape Verde. *Telephone:* 260.

PEREIRA, Helio Gelli, F.R.S., M.D.; British scientist; b. 23 Sept. 1918, Petropolis, Rio de Janeiro, Brazil; s. of R. and M. G. Pereira; m. Margurette Scott 1946 (died 1987); one s. two d. (one deceased); ed. British American School, Rio de Janeiro and Faculdade Fluminense de Medicina, Niteroi and Inst. Oswaldo Cruz, Rio de Janeiro; Asst. lecturer in microbiology, Faculdade Fluminense de Medicina 1942-45; British Council Scholarship, Univ. of Manchester and Nat. Inst. for Medical Research, London, 1945-47; worked on rickettsial diseases and on quantitative aspects of serological reactions, Inst. Oswaldo Cruz 1947-52; with Medical Research Council, Common Cold Unit, Salisbury (U.K.) 1952-57; with Nat. Inst. for Medical Research 1957-73, Dir. World Influenza Centre 1961-69, Head, Div. of Virology 1964-73; Head, Div. Epidemiology, Animal Virus Research Inst. 1973-79; Consultant, Dept. of Virology, Fundação Oswaldo Cruz, Rio de Janeiro 1979-; Carlos Findlay Prize (UNESCO) 1987. *Publication:* Viruses of Vertebrates 1972. *Leisure interest:* music. *Address:* Fundação Oswaldo Cruz, Caixa Postal 926, 21040 Rio de Janeiro, Brazil.

PEREIRA, Sir (Herbert) Charles, Kt., PH.D., D.SC., F.R.S.; British agricultural scientist; b. 12 May 1913, London; s. of Mr. and Mrs. H. J. Pereira; m. Irene Beatrice Sloan 1941; three s. one d.; ed. Prince Albert Coll., Sask., Canada, St. Alban's School, Herts., England, London Univ. and Rothamsted Experimental Station, Herts.; war service with Royal Engineers in Western Desert, Italy and Germany; Soil Scientist Coffee Research Team Kenya 1946-52; Head of Physics Div., E. African Agricultural and Forestry Research Org. 1952-55, Deputy Dir. 1955-61; Dir. Agricultural Research Council of Cen. Africa 1961-67; Consultant in Land Use Hydrology (I.H.D. Programme) FAO 1968-69; Dir. E. Malling Research Station, Kent, England 1969-72; Chief Scientist, Ministry of Agric., Fisheries and Food 1972-77; Consultant in Tropical Agricultural Research 1978-; mem. World Bank Tech. Advisory Cttee. to C.G.I.A.R. 1971-76; mem. Bd. of Trustees, Royal Botanical Gardens, Kew 1983-86; Hon. Fellow, Royal Agricultural Soc. of England 1976; Hon. D.Sc. (Cranfield) 1977; Haile Sellassie Prize for Research in Africa 1966. *Publications:* Land Use and Water Resources 1973, Policy and Practice in Watershed Management 1988, scientific papers on tillage and weed competition, soil fertility and water relations, catchment area research, tropical soil structure. *Address:* Peartrees, Teston, Maidstone, Kent, ME18 5AD, England. *Telephone:* (0622) 813333.

PEREIRA DOS SANTOS, Gen. Adalberto; Brazilian army officer; b. 11 April 1905, Taquara, Rio Grande do Sul; s. of Urbano Alves dos Santos and Otília Pereira dos Santos; m. Julieta Campos Pereira dos Santos (deceased); ed. Colégio Militar de Porto Alegre, Escola Militar do Realengo; rank of Brig.-Gen. 1958, Div. Gen. 1963, Gen. 1965; Adjutant, Mil. Gov. of São Paulo; Officer 1st Armoured Div., U.S. Army during Italian campaign 1945; Chief of Staff, Armoured Div.; Commdr. School of War Equipment; 2nd Army Sub-Chief of Staff; Army Chief of Staff; Amb., Special Mission to Chile 1964; Amb., Head of Special Mission to Paraguay 1968; Pres. Eighth Conf. of American Armies 1968; Minister of High Mil. Tribunal, then Pres.; Vice-Pres. of Brazil 1974–79; numerous decorations. *Leisure interests:* fencing, horse-riding. *Address:* c/o Office of the Vice-President of Brazil, Brasília, D.F., Brazil.

PEREIRA LIRA, Paulo H.; Brazilian economist; b. 30 Jan 1930, Rio de Janeiro; s. of José Pereira Lira and Beatriz de Almeida Pereira Lira; m. Laís Myriam Pereira Lira 1953; one s. one d.; ed. Univ. do Brasil, Rio de Janeiro, Harvard Univ.; Prof. of Micro-econs., Nat. Faculty of Econs., Univ. Brasil 1955–64; Prof. of Monetary Theory, Nat. Council of Econs. 1958–61; Prof. of Advanced Courses, Getúlio Vargas Foundation 1961; Pres. Banco Central do Brasil March 1974–78; mem. Monetary Council; mem. Tech. Council of Inst. of Econ. and Applied Social Research; mem. Nat. Foreign Trade Council; Alt. Gov. IMF, African Devt. Fund; Commdr., Order of Rio Branco; Order of Merit Tamandaré; Order of Merit Mauá. *Leisure interest:* golf. *Address:* c/o Edifício Sede do Banco do Brasil, 6°, 70.000 Brasília, D.F., Brazil. *Telephone:* (0612) 24-1503, 24-7753.

PEREK, Luboš, RN.DR., DR.SC.; Czechoslovak astronomer; b. 26 July 1919, Prague; s. of Zdeněk and Vilemina (née Trapp) Perek; m. Vlasta Straková 1945; ed. Masaryk Univ., Brno, and Charles Univ., Prague; Asst. Astronomical Inst., Masaryk Univ., Brno 1946, Head 1953; Head, Stellar Dept., Astronomical Inst. of Czechoslovak Acad. of Sciences, Prague 1956, Dir. Astronomical Inst. 1968–75; Vice-Pres. Comm. of the Galactic Structure and Dynamics, Int. Astronomical Union 1961–64, Asst. Gen. Sec., Int. Astronomical Union 1964–67, Gen. Sec. 1967–70; Chief, Outer Space Affairs Division, UN Secr. 1975–80; Visiting Prof., Dearborn Observatory, Evanston, Ill. 1964; Corresp. mem. Czechoslovak Acad. of Sciences 1965–; mem. Czechoslovak Astronomical Soc., Exec. Cttee. Int. Council of Scientific Unions 1967–70, Vice-Pres. 1968–70; Chair. Int. Astronomical Fed. 1980–82; mem. Leopoldina Acad., Int. Acad. of Astronautics, Int. Inst. of Space Law, Nat. Acad. of the Air and Space, Toulouse; Assoc. mem. Royal Astronomical Soc. silver plaque for services to science 1969. *Publications include:* Catalogue of Galactic Planetary Nebulae (with L. Kohoutek) 1967. *Leisure interest:* collecting seashells. *Address:* c/o Astronomical Institute of Czechoslovak Academy of Sciences, Budečská 6, 120 23 Prague 2, Czechoslovakia. *Telephone:* 258757 (Prague).

PERÉNYI, Miklós; Hungarian violoncellist and composer; b. 5 Jan. 1948, Budapest; s. of László Perényi and Erzsébet Seeger; m. Tünde Angermayer; one s.; started playing cello at age 6, first public recital at age 9, Budapest; ed. Music Acad. of Budapest; Prof. of Violoncello Liszt Ferenc Acad. of Music, Budapest 1974–; numerous int. appearances; holder of Liszt Prize 1970, Kossuth Prize 1980, Eminent Artist title. *Leisure interests:* swimming, cycling. *Address:* 1037 Budapest, Erdőalja ut 1/b, Hungary.

PERERA, Liyanagé Henry Horace, B.A.; Ceylonese international official; b. 9 May 1915, Yatiyantota, Ceylon; s. of L. H. Perera and Maud Mildred Sirimane; m. Sita Trixie Senarat 1942; one s. three d.; ed. St. Benedict's Coll., Colombo, Univ. Coll., London, Univ. of Ceylon; Sr. Master in Govt. and History, Ceylon 1936–59; Asst. Registrar, Aquinas Univ. Coll., Colombo 1960–61; Educ. Dir. World Fed. of UN Asscns. 1961–63, Deputy Sec.-Gen. and Educ. Dir. 1963–66, Sec.-Gen. 1966–76; Special Asst. for Asia and the S. Pacific, World Confed. of Orgs. of the Teaching Profession 1976–84; Consultant to World Fed. UN Asscns. 1985–; Sec. Masaryk Study Centre for UN Studies, Geneva; mem. Int. Cttee. Adult Educ. (UNESCO) 1963; Pres. non-Governmental orgs. in Consultative status with UN Econ. and Social Council 1969–72, Co-ordinator for Int. Year of the Child; Sec. Strategic Planning Cttee. WFUNA (World Fed. of UN Asscns.); lectures regularly in Asia and the S. Pacific on human rights; has organized and conducted nine seminars on educ. about the UN and 15 summer courses on the UN and its agencies, and numerous other confs., seminars and courses, and given keynote addresses at int. confs. on educ. and soc., educ. and work, educ. for a technological age, the elimination of all forms of discrimination against women; Hon. Pres. World Fed. of UN Asscns.; William Russel Award 1974, Int. Asscn. of Educators for World Peace Award; Gold Medal (Czechoslovak Soc. for Int. Relations). *Publications:* Ceylon and Indian History, Groundwork of Ceylon and World History, Ceylon Under Western Rule, Guides to the Study of the Status and Working Conditions of the Teacher, ILO Conventions and Trade Unionism, Ed. Human Rights in Hinduism, Buddhism, Christianity and Islam 1988, NGO Action for the Elimination of Apartheid. *Leisure interests:* swimming, tennis, photography, stamp collecting and reading. *Address:* 22 avenue Luserna, 1203 Geneva, Switzerland. *Telephone:* 44-07-37.

PERERA, Wahalatantrige D.R.; Sri Lankan attorney and diplomatist; b. 4 Aug. 1928; m.; two c.; ed. Royal Coll. of Sri Lanka and Sri Lanka Law Coll.; advocate Supreme Court of Sri Lanka 1954; apptd. Crown Counsel, Criminal Br. Attorney-Gen.'s Dept. 1956–64, 1966–70; Head Legal Branch, Sri Lanka Army HQ, Colombo 1964–66; entered Pvt. Practice 1970; Del. Law Asia Conf., Seoul, apptd. Vice-Chair. Standing Cttee. on Law and Drugs 1981; Rep. Asian Lawyers Legal Inquiry, Bangkok, Vice-Pres. All Asia Bar Asscn. 1981; apptd. Pres.'s Counsel 1981; Perm. Rep. to UN Feb. 1988–; Vice-Pres. Medico Legal Soc. of Sri Lanka 1983–86, Pres. 1987–. *Address:* Permanent Mission of Sri Lanka to the United Nations, 630 Third Avenue, 20th Floor, New York, N.Y. 10017, U.S.A. *Telephone:* (212) 986-7040.

PERES, Shimon; Israeli politician; b. 1923, Poland; s. of Isaac and Sara Persky; m. Sonia Gelman; two s. one d.; ed. New York Univ., Harvard Univ.; immigrated to Palestine 1934; fmr. Sec. Hano'ar Ha'oved Movt.; mem. Haganah Movt. 1947; Head of Israel Naval Service, Ministry of Defence 1948; Head of Defence Mission in U.S.A.; Deputy Dir.-Gen. of Ministry of Defence 1952–53, Dir.-Gen. 1953–59, Deputy Minister of Defence 1959–65; mem. Knesset 1959–; mem. Mapai Party 1959–65, founder mem. and Sec.-Gen. Rafi Party 1965, mem. Labour Party after merger 1968, Chair. April 1977–; Minister for Econ. Devt. in the Administered Areas and for Immigrant Absorption 1969–70, of Transport and Communications 1970–74, of Information March–June 1974, of Defence 1974–77; Acting Prime Minister April–May 1977; Leader of the Opposition 1977–84; Prime Minister of Israel Sept. 1984–86; Minister of the Interior and of Religious Affairs 1984–85; Vice-Premier and Minister of Foreign Affairs 1986–88, Vice-Premier and Finance Minister Dec. 1988–. *Publications:* The Next Step 1965, David's Sling 1970, Tomorrow is Now 1978, From These Men 1979 and numerous political articles in Israeli and foreign publications. *Address:* Ministry of Foreign Affairs, Jerusalem, Israel.

PERESYPKIN, Oleg Gerasimovich; Soviet diplomatist; Counsellor, Embassy, Yemen Arab Repub. 1971–76; Adviser, Near Eastern Countries Dept., U.S.S.R. Ministry of Foreign Affairs 1976–80; Amb. to Yemen Arab Repub. 1980–85. *Address:* The Kremlin, Moscow, U.S.S.R.

PÉREZ DE CUELLAR, Javier; Peruvian diplomatist; b. 19 Jan. 1920, Lima; m. Marcela Temple; two c.; ed. Catholic Univ., Lima; joined Foreign Ministry 1940, diplomatic service 1944; served as Sec. in embassies in France, U.K., Bolivia, Brazil (later Counsellor); Dir. Legal and Personnel Dept., Dir. of Admin., of Protocol and of Political Affairs, Ministry of External Relations 1961–63; Amb. to Switzerland 1964–66; Perm. Under Sec. and Sec.-Gen. Foreign Office 1966–69, Amb. to U.S.S.R. (concurrently to Poland) 1969–71, to Venezuela 1978; Perm. Rep. to UN 1971–75; mem. UN Security Council 1973–74, Pres. 1974; Special Rep. of UN Sec.-Gen. in Cyprus 1975–77; UN Under-Sec.-Gen. for Special Political Affairs 1979–81; UN Sec.-Gen. 1982–; fmr. Prof. of Diplomatic Law, Acad. Diplomática del Perú and Prof. of Int. Relations, Acad. de Guerra Aérea del Perú; del. to First UN Gen. Assembly 1946–47 and other int. confs.; Montague Burton Visiting Prof. of Int. Relations, Univ. of Edinburgh 1985; mem. Acad. Mexicana de Derecho Int. 1988–; Olaf Palme Prize for Public Service 1989; Hon. Dr. (Univ. of Nice) 1983, (Jagiellonian, Charles and Sofia Univs., Univ. of San Marcos and Vrije Univ., Brussels) 1984, (Carleton Univ., Ottawa, Sorbonne Univ., Paris) 1985, (Osnabruck) 1986, (Univs. of Mich., Coimbra, Mongolian State, Humbolt, Moscow State) 1987, (Univ. of Leiden) 1988, (Cambridge) 1989; Prince of Asturias Prize for Ibero-American Co-operation. *Publication:* Manual de Derecho Diplomático 1964. *Address:* c/o Office of the Secretary-General, United Nations, New York, N.Y. 10017, U.S.A. *Telephone:* (212) 754-5012.

PÉREZ ESQUIVEL, Adolfo; Argentine architect, sculptor and human rights leader; b. 26 Nov. 1931, Buenos Aires; m. Amanda Pérez 1956; three s.; ed. Nat. School of Fine Arts, Buenos Aires; trained as architect and sculptor; Prof. of Art, Manuel Belgrano Nat. School of Fine Arts, Buenos Aires 1956–71; Prof. Faculty of Architecture and Urban Studies; Univ. Nacional de la Plata; gave up teaching to concentrate on non-violent human rights movement; f. Servicio Paz y Justicia, Buenos Aires 1973, Sec.-Gen. 1974–; co-founder Ecumenical Movement for Human Rights, Argentina; Pres. Perm. Ass. for Human Rights; arrested 1977, released May 1978; visited Europe 1980; Pres. Int. League for the Rights and Liberation of Peoples 1987; Nobel Prize for Peace 1980; Hon. Citizen of Assisi 1982. *Address:* Servicio de Paz y Justicia, Calle México 479, Buenos Aires, Argentina.

PÉREZ FERNANDEZ, Pedro, LIC.ECON.; Spanish international finance official; b. 1949; ed. Univ. of Madrid; Adviser to Minister, Ministry of Planning 1975–76, Div. Dir. 1976–77; Deputy Dir.-Gen. of Econ. Research, Ministry of Economy and Chair. Bd. of Prices, Ministry of Economy and Finance 1982–84; concurrently lectured in econs. at Univ. of Madrid; fmr. mem. bd. of dirs. of several govt. agencies; Exec. Dir. IMF 1984–86. *Publications:* co-author of book on Spanish econ. policy; several articles on budgetary policy, prices and econ. issues. *Address:* c/o Ministerio de Economiá, Hacienda y Comercio, Alcalá 9, Madrid 14, Spain.

PÉREZ GODOY, Gen. Ricardo Pío; Peruvian army officer and politician; b. 9 June 1905; ed. Colegio Santo Tomás de Aquino and Escuela de Oficiales del Ejército; Dir.-Gen. of Training, Peruvian Army 1956–57; Controller-Gen. of Army 1958–59; Chief of Staff of Jt. Command of Armed Forces 1960–62; Prefect of Dept. of Arequipa 1952–53, 1955–56; Pres. of Mil. Junta of Govt. of Peru 1962–63; mem. Centro de Altos Estudios Históricos del Perú; now Gen. of a Division; numerous decorations. *Publications:* include

Teoría de la Guerra y Doctrina de Guerra, La Maniobra y la Batalla. *Address:* Blasco Nuñez de Balboa 225, Miraflores, Lima, Peru.

PÉREZ JIMÉNEZ, Col. Marcos; Venezuelan officer and politician; b. 1914; ed. Caracas Mil. School and Lima War Coll.; Army Chief of Staff in Acción Democrática Govt.; mem. of subsequent three-man Junta and Minister of Defence; Pres. of Venezuela 1952-58; extradited from U.S.A. to Venezuela Aug. 1963; imprisoned in Venezuela 1963-68; went to Madrid.

PÉREZ-LLORCA, José Pedro; Spanish lawyer and politician; b. 30 Nov. 1940, Cadiz; s. of José and Carmen Pérez-Llorca; m. Carmen Zamora Bonilla 1965; one s. one d.; ed. Madrid Central (Complutense) Univ., Univs. of Freiburg and Munich; entered diplomatic service 1964; adviser Spanish Del. to 21st and 22nd Gen. Assembly of UN and 5th extraordinary emergency session; Legal Advisor to Parl. 1968; Higher Council for Foreign Affairs 1970; practised law, Madrid 1970-; mem. Cortes 1977-82; parl. leader Unión de Centro Democrático (UCD); mem. Comm. for drawing up Constitution 1978; Minister of the Presidency 1979-80, Minister for Relations with Parl. Jan.-May 1980, Minister for Territorial Admin. May-Oct. 1980, Minister for Foreign Affairs 1980-82; pvt. law practice 1983-; Chair. AEG-Iberica SA, Urquiso Leasing SA; Dir. Robert Bosch Española SA; Prof. of Constitutional Law, School of Diplomacy. *Address:* Paseo de Recoletos 27, 28004 Madrid, Spain. *Telephone:* (91) 4196500.

PÉREZ RODRIGUEZ, Carlos Andrés; Venezuelan politician; b. 27 Oct. 1922, Rubio; m. Blanca Rodríguez de Pérez; one s. five d.; ed. Univ. Central de Venezuela; Pvt. Sec. to Pres. Rómulo Betancourt 1945; mem. Chamber of Deputies 1947-48, 1958-74; in exile 1949-58; Chief Ed. La República, San José 1953-58; Minister of the Interior 1963-64; Sec.-Gen. Acción Democrática 1968; Pres. of Venezuela 1974-79, 1989-. *Address:* c/o Oficina del Presidente, Palacio de Miraflores, Caracas, Venezuela.

PERI FAGERSTROM, Gen. René Alberto; Chilean police officer, politician and writer; b. 21 Dec. 1926; m. Graciela Mundaca; two s. one d.; ed. Carabineros Escuela de Instituto Superior de Carabineros, Academia de Seguridad Nacional; civil servant; journalist; Head First Carabineros Inspection Zone, Antofagasta 1976-77; Head Higher Carabineros Council of Assessors 1978-79; Minister of Land and Settlement (now Nat. Property) 1979; several literary prizes. *Publications:* (short stories): Mundo Aparte 1958, Ronda Rondando 1962, Caranchos 1968, Dioses Difuntos 1969, Orilla Adentro 1970, Caer en Desgracia 1972, Los Genocidas 1975, Los Barbados 1976, Cuentos de Niños y Pajaros. novels: Las Hermanas Gonzalez 1967, Dos Mujeres 1974. poems: Turnos 1963, Sol Mayor 1976, Uranidas Go Home (science fiction) 1966. essays: Bajo Dos Carabinas 1977, Paja Brava 1978, Los Batallones Bulnes y Valparaiso 1980. *Address:* c/o Ministry of National Property, Avenida Libertador B. O'Higgins 280, Santiago, Chile.

PÉRIER, François (pseudonym of François Pillu); French actor; b. 10 Nov. 1919, Paris; m. 1st Jacqueline Porel 1941, two s. (one decd.) one d.; m. 2nd Marie Daems 1949; m. 3rd Colette Boutouland 1961; ed. Conservatoire Nat. d'Art Dramatique, Paris; Co-Dir. Théâtre de la Michodière, Paris 1951-65; has appeared in numerous plays including Les jours heureux, Les J 3, Les mains sales, Bobosse, Le ciel de lit, Gog et Magog, La preuve par quatre, Le Diable et le Bon Dieu, Ne réveillez pas Madame, Le tube, Equus, Coup de chapeau, Amadeus, Tartuffe. *Films include:* Premier bal 1941, Lettres d'amour 1942, Un revenant, Le silence est d'or 1946, Orphée 1949, Les évadés 1954, Gervaise 1955, Le Notti di Cabiria 1956, Bobosse 1958, Le testament d'Orphée 1960, L'amant de cinq jours 1961, La visita 1963, Les enfants du palais (TV) 1967, Z 1968, Le cercle rouge 1970, Max et les ferrailleurs 1971, Juste avant la nuit 1971, L'attentat 1972, Antoine et Sébastien 1973, Stavisky, Sarah (TV) 1974, Dr. Françoise Gailland 1975, Police Python 357 1976, Mazarin (TV) 1978, La raison d'etat 1978, La guerre des polices 1979, Le bar du téléphone 1980, Le battant 1983, Le Tartuffe 1984; has also appeared on TV; British Film Acad. Award 1956, Victoria du Cinéma Français 1957, Médaille George Méliès 1976, Grand Prix nat. du Théâtre 1977; Commdr., Ordre des Arts et des Lettres. *Address:* c/o Artmedia, 10 avenue Georges V, Paris 75008, France.

PERIGOT, François; French business executive; b. 12 May 1926, Lyons; s. of Jean-Paul Perigot and Marguerite de la Tour; m. Gisèle Levainville 1954; one s. one d.; ed. Lycée de Bastia, Faculté de Droit, Paris and Inst. d'Etudes Politiques, Paris; joined Unilever group (France) 1955, Head of Personnel 1966; Pres.-Dir.-Gen. Thibaud Gibbs et Cie. 1968-70; Dir. Unilever (Spain) 1971-75; Pres.-Dir.-Gen. Unilever (France) 1976-86; mem. Exec. Council, Conseil Nat. du Patronat Français (CNPF) 1981-86; Pres. 1986-; Chevalier, Légion d'honneur. *Leisure interests:* yachting, riding. *Address:* Conseil national du patronat français, 31 avenue Pierre ler de Serbie, 75016 Paris, France.

PERIN, François; Belgian politician and professor of law; b. 31 Jan. 1921, Liège; ed. Univ. of Liège; mem. of Socialist Party 1943-64; Asst. Chef de Cabinet to Minister of Interior 1954-57; Asst. to Prof. of Public Law 1954-58; Dir. of Studies, Faculty of Law, Univ. of Liège 1958, Prof. of Constitutional Law 1967; Deputy to Nat. Ass. 1965-; Pres. Rassemblement Wallon 1968-74; Minister of Institutional Reforms 1974-76; mem. co-founders Parti Réformateur Libéral (PRL) 1976-. *Publications:* La démocratie enrayée—essai sur le régime parlementaire belge de 1918 à 1958 1960, La Belgique au défi: Flamands Wallons à la recherche d'un état 1962, La décision politique en Belgique (co-author) 1965, Le régionalisme

dans l'intégration européenne 1969, Germes et bois morts dans la société politique contemporaine 1981, Histoire d'une Nation Introuvable 1988. *Leisure interests:* music, concerts, history of religions, philosophy and science. *Address:* 10 rue Chevaufosse, 4000 Liège, Belgium. *Telephone:* 041-236782.

PERINAT, Luis Guillermo, Marqués de; Spanish diplomatist; b. 27 Oct. 1923, Madrid; s. of Luis Perinat and Ana Maria, Marquesa de Campo Real; m. Blanca Escriva de Romani, Marquesa de Alginet; two s. one d.; ed. Univs. of Salamanca and Valladolid; Sec., Embassy in Cairo 1949-51; Deputy Consul-Gen., New York 1954-56; Counsellor, Paris 1962-65; Perm. Sec. Spanish-American Joint Defence Cttee. 1965-70; Dir.-Gen. of N. American and Far Eastern Affairs in Ministry of Foreign Affairs 1973-76; Amb. to U.K. 1976-81, to U.S.S.R. 1981-83; mem. Senate 1983-87; mem. European Parl. 1986-, a Vice-Pres. 1987-; Grand Cross, Order of Civil Merit, Grand Cross, Order of Military Merit, Kt. Commdr. Order of Isabel La Católica, Kt. Commdr. Order of Mérito Aeronáutico, Commdr. Order of George I (Greece), Officer, Order of Leopold (Belgium), Kt., Order of the Nile (Egypt). *Address:* Calle de Prado 26, Madrid, Spain.

PERISIC, Zoran; Yugoslav film director, writer and producer; b. 16 March 1940, Yugoslavia; Man. Dir. Courier Films Ltd.; special optical effects rostrum cameraman, 2001—A Space Odyssey; writer and dir. of more than 5,000 television commercials, short films and documentaries; writer and dir. of TV series Captain Cook's Travels; inventor of ZOPTIC (special effects front projection system); flying unit dir. Superman II 1981; Dir. Sky Bandits 1986; several awards including Acad. Award (Oscar) for outstanding visual effects in Superman. *Address:* c/o Eric L'Epine Smith Ltd., 10 Wyndham Place, London, W1H 1AS, England.

PERISIN, Ivo, D.ECON.; Yugoslav economist and banker; b. 4 July 1925, Split; s. of Duje and Filomena Tadin Perišin; m. Magda Martinič 1949; one s. one d.; ed. Zagreb Univ.; Prof. of Econ., Zagreb Univ.; Under-Sec., Fed. Secr. for Finance; Gov. Nat. Bank of Yugoslavia (Narodna Banka Jugoslavije) 1969-72; Pres. Exec. Council, Socialist Repub. of Croatia 1972-74; Pres. Parl. 1974-78; Pres. Fed. Council for Devt. and Econ. Policy 1978-; mem. Yugoslav Acad. of Science; Partisan Memorial Award, Order of People's Merit, Order of the Repub., Medal for Valour. *Publications:* Money and Credit Policy 1964, Money and Economic Development 1961, Economics of Yugoslavia, Inflation 1965, Financial Dictionary 1967, Money, Credit and Banking 1975, Transformation of Monetary System 1975, Money, Monetary System and Associated Work 1978, Essays on the Reform of the Monetary System 1979, Interest Rates and Savings 1980, Inflation 1985, International Banking and Financial Markets, World Financial Whirlpool (a contrib. to Studies of Modern Banking and Financial Markets) 1988. *Address:* Moše Pijade 131, Zagreb, Yugoslavia. *Telephone:* 430-476.

PERKINS, David D(exter), PH.D.; American biologist and geneticist; b. 2 May 1919, Watertown, New York; s. of Dexter M. and Loretta F. (Gardiner) Perkins; m. Dorothy L. Newmeyer 1952; one d.; ed. Univ. of Rochester and Columbia Univ.; mem. Faculty, Stanford Univ. 1949-, Prof. of Biology 1961-; Research Fellow, Univ. of Glasgow, Scotland 1954-55, Columbia Univ. 1962-63, A.N.U., Canberra 1968-69; mem. India-U.S. Exchange Scientists' Program 1974; Ed. Genetics 1963-67; U.S. Public Health Service Research Career Award 1964; mem. Int. Genetics Fed. Exec. Bd. 1978-83, Genetics Soc. of America (Pres. 1977), N.A.S. *Publications:* The cytogenetics of Neurospora (with E. G. Barry) 1977, Chromosomal loci of Neurospora crassa (with others) 1982. *Address:* Department of Biological Sciences, Stanford University, Stanford, Calif. 94305; 345 Vine Street, Menlo Park, Calif. 94025, U.S.A. (Home).

PERKINS, Donald H., M.A., PH.D., F.R.S.; British professor of physics; b. 15 Oct. 1925, Hull; s. of G. W. Perkins and G. Perkins; m. Dorothy M. Maloney 1955; two d.; ed. Imperial Coll. London; Sr. 1851 Scholar, Univ. of Bristol 1949-52, G. A. Wills Research Assoc. 1952-55; Visiting Scientist, Univ. of Calif. 1955-56; Lecturer, then Reader in Physics, Univ. of Bristol 1956-65; Prof. of Elementary Particle Physics, Univ. of Oxford 1965-; Guthrie Medal, Inst. of Physics 1979; Hon. D. Sc. (Sheffield) 1982. *Publications:* Study of Elementary Particles by the Photographic Method (with C. F. Powell and P. H. Fowler) 1959, Introduction to High Energy Physics 1972. *Leisure interests:* squash, skiing, lepidoptera. *Address:* Department of Nuclear Physics, Keble Road, Oxford, OX1 3RH (Office); Birchwood, Bedwells Heath, Boars Hill, Oxford, OX1 5JE, England (Home). *Telephone:* (0865) 513354 (Office); (0865) 739308 (Home).

PERKINS, Edward J., D.P.A.; American diplomatist; b. 8 June 1928, Sterlington, La.; m. Lucy Liu; two c.; ed. Univ. of Calif., Lewis, Clark Coll., Univ. of Maryland and Univ. of S. Calif.; Chief of Personnel, Army and Air Force Exchange Service, Taiwan 1958-62; Deputy Chief, Okinawa, Japan 1962-64, Chief of Personnel and Admin. 1964-66; Asst. Gen. Services Officer, Far East Bureau, AID 1967-69, Man. Analyst 1969-70; Asst. Dir. Foreign Man. U.S. Operations, Mission to Thailand 1970-72; Staff Asst. Office of Dir.-Gen. of Foreign Service 1972; Personnel Officer 1972-74; Admin. Officer, Bureau of Near Eastern and South Asian Affairs 1974-75; Man. Analysis Officer, Office of Man. Operations, Dept. of State 1975-78; Counsellor for Political Affairs, Accra 1981-83; Deputy Chief of Mission, Monrovia 1983-85; Dir. Office of West African Affairs, Dept. of State 1985;

Amb. to Liberia 1985–86, to South Africa 1986–89; Dir.-Gen. Foreign Service, Washington 1989–. *Address:* Room 6218, Department of State, 2201 c Street, N.W., Washington, D.C. 20520, U.S.A.

PERKINS, James Alfred, PH.D.; American educationist; b. 11 Oct. 1911, Philadelphia, Pa.; s. of late H. Norman Perkins and Emily Taylor; m. 1st Jean E. Bredin 1938 (died 1970), two s. three d.; m. 2nd Ruth B. Aall, four step-c.; ed. Swarthmore Coll. and Princeton Univ.; Instructor in political science, Princeton Univ. 1937–39, Asst. Dir. School of Public and Int. Affairs 1939–41; Dir. Pulp and Paper Div., O.P.A. 1941–43; Asst. to Admin., Foreign Econ. Admin. 1943–45; Vice-Pres. Swarthmore Coll. 1945–50; Exec. Assoc., Carnegie Corpn. 1950–51, Vice-Pres. 1951–63; Sec. Carnegie Foundation for Advancement of Teaching 1954–55, Vice-Pres. 1955–63; Pres. Cornell Univ. 1963–69; Deputy Chair. Research and Devt. Board, Dept. of Defense 1951–52; consultant Rand Corpn. 1958–62, Trustee 1961–71; Chair. Bd. of Trustees, United Negro Coll. Fund 1965–68; Chair. Pres. Johnson's Gen. Advice Comm. on Foreign Assistance Programme 1965–69; Co-Chair. Int. Conf. on World Crisis in Educ. 1967; mem. various cttees. including Carnegie Comm. on Higher Educ. 1967–73, Carnegie Council on Policy Studies in Higher Educ. 1974–79, American Council for United Nations Univ., UNESCO's European Centre for Higher Educ.; founder and Chair. Centre for Educational Enquiry 1969: Chair. Bd. and C.E.O. Int. Council for Educ. Devt. 1970–; Chair. Presidential Comm. on Foreign Language and Int. Studies 1978–79, Ajijic Inst. for Int. Educ. 1978–; Vice-Chair. Nat. Council on Foreign Language and Int. Studies 1980–; Dir. Center for Inter-American Relations, Inst. of Int. Educ.; Overseas Devt. Council, Acad. for Educational Devt.; Dir. Emer. Council on Foreign Relations; Trustee, Aspen Inst. for Humanistic Studies, Inst. of Int. Educ., Change Magazine; Editorial Bd. Higher Education; Hon. LL.D., L.H.D. and numerous other hon. degrees; Gold Medal of Nat. Inst. of Social Sciences 1965. *Publications:* The University in Transition (Stafford Little Lectures) 1966, editor and contributor to Higher Education: From Autonomy to Systems 1972, The University in a Restless Decade 1972, Ed. and co-author of The University as an Organization 1973, Is the University an Agent for Social Reform? (trans. in several languages) 1973; and articles for various journals. *Leisure interests:* music, tennis, photography. *Address:* International Council for Educational Development, 20 Nassau Street, Princeton, N.J. 08540 (Office); 94 North Road, Princeton, N.J. 08540, U.S.A. (Home). *Telephone:* (609) 921-2440 (Office).

PERKINS, John H.; American banker; b. 28 Aug. 1921, Chicago; s. of Harold and Roschen Perkins; m. Len Welborn 1944; three s.; ed. North-western Univ., Graduate School of Banking, Univ. of Wisconsin; joined Continental Illinois Nat. Bank 1946, Asst. Cashier, Metropolitan Div. 1949, Second Vice-Pres. Bond Dept. 1952, Vice-Pres. 1956, Sr. Vice-Pres. 1965, Dir. 1968–71, Exec. Vice-Pres. and Dir. 1968–71, Vice-Chair. 1971–73, Pres. Continental Illinois Corpn. and Continental Bank 1973–84; Public advisor, Midwest Stock Exchange 1969–, Gov. 1972; Dir. The Pillsbury Co. 1969–; Chair., nominating cttee., Private Export Funding Corpn. (PEFCO) 1976–; Trustee, Underwriters' Laboratories Inc. *Address:* c/o Continental Illinois National Bank and Trust Co. of Chicago, 231 South LaSalle Street, Chicago, Ill. 60697, U.S.A. *Telephone:* (312) 923-5167 (Office).

PERKINSON, Jesse Dean, B.S., M.S., PH.D.; American science administrator and biochemist; b. 24 Oct. 1914, Etowah, Tenn.; s. of Jesse Dean Perkinson Sr. and Clara Bedell Perkinson; m. Dorothy Brumby 1943; three d.; ed. Univ. of Tennessee and Univ. of Rochester; Fellow, Univ. of Rochester 1939–43; U.S. Navy Reserve 1944–46; Research Assoc., Univ. of Ga. 1946–49; Sr. Scientist, Oak Ridge Inst. of Nuclear Studies 1949–52; Assoc. Prof. of Biochem., Univ. of Tenn. 1952–57; Chief of Training and Educ. U.S. Atomic Energy Comm. 1957–58; Exec. Sec. Inter-American Nuclear Energy Comm. (IANEC) 1958–77; Dir. Dept. of Scientific Affairs, OAS 1958–73, Special Adviser to Sec.-Gen. 1973–77; mem. U.S. Dept. of Commerce, Panel on Transfer of Tech.; mem. Advisory Bd. Pan American Devt. Foundation 1969–, Population Crisis Comm. 1967–; mem. American Chemical Soc., Radiation Research Soc.; Fellow Inst. of Chemists, Royal Soc. of Arts, A.A.A.S. *Address:* RFD 2, Box 127B, Saluda, Berryville, Va. 22611, U.S.A.

PERKOFF, Gerald Thomas, M.D.; American physician; b. 22 Sept. 1926, St. Louis; s. of Nat Perkoff and Ann Schwartz; m. Marion Helen Maizner 1947; one s. two d.; ed. Washington Univ.; Intern, Salt Lake City Gen. Hosp. 1948–49, Resident 1950–52; Instructor, then Assoc. Prof. of Medicine, Utah Univ. 1954–63; Chief, Medical Service of Salt Lake Va. Hosp. 1961–63; Assoc. Prof. then Prof. of Medicine, Wash. Univ. School of Medicine, St. Louis 1963–79; Chief of Medical Service, St. Louis City Hosp. 1963–68; Prof. of Medicine, Univ. of Mo. 1979–; Carrer Research Prof. of Neuromuscular Diseases, Nat. Foundation of Neuromuscular Diseases 1961; Founder, Dir., Medical Care Group of Wash. Univ. 1968–78; Henry J. Kaiser Sr. Fellow of the Center for Advanced Study in the Behavioral Sciences, Stanford, Calif. 1976–77, 1985–86. *Publications:* one book and over 100 scientific papers. *Leisure interests:* music, photography, books. *Address:* 109 Defoe Court, Columbia, Mo. 65203, U.S.A. *Telephone:* (314) 445 6359.

PERL, Martin Lewis, PH.D.; American research physicist and educator; b. 24 June 1927, New York; m. Teri Hoch 1948; three s. one d.; ed. Polytechnic Inst. of New York and Columbia Univ.; Chemical Engineer, General Electric Co. 1948–50; Asst., then Assoc. Prof. of Physics, Univ. of

Mich. 1955–63; Prof. of Physics, Stanford Linear Accelerator Center, Stanford Univ. 1963–; research in experimental elementary particle physics 1955–; discovered the elementary particle tau lepton 1975–78; mem. N.A.S.; Wolf Prize in Physics 1982. *Publications:* High Energy Hadron Physics 1974, articles on science and soc. issues and on physics educ. *Leisure interests:* classic automobiles, mechanical antiques, carpentry. *Address:* Stanford Linear Accelerator Center, Stanford University, Stanford, Calif. 94305, U.S.A. *Telephone:* (415) 854-3300, Ext. 2652.

PERLEMUTER, Vlado; French (b. Lithuanian) pianist; b. 26 May 1904, Kaunas; m. Jacqueline Deleveau 1937; ed. Conservatoire nat. supérieur de musique, Paris; studied with Moszkowski and Cortot; specialist in Ravel and Chopin; Prof. of Pianoforte, Paris Conservatoire 1951–; has appeared in concerts and recitals in Europe, N. Africa, N. America and Far East; Hon. R.A.M., London; Officier, Légion d'honneur, Commandeur des Arts et des Lettres. *Address:* 21 rue Ampère, 75017 Paris, France.

PERLIS, H.R.H. The Raja of; Tuanku Syed Putra ibni al-Marhum Syed Hassan Jamalullail, D.K., S.P.M.P., D.K.(M.), D.M.N., S.M.N., D.K.(SEL), D.K.(KE-LANTAN), D.K.(KEDAH), D.K.(PAHANG), D.K.(BRUNEI), S.P.D.K., D.P., K.C.M.G.; Malaysian ruler; b. 16 Oct. 1920, Arau, Perlis; s. of Syed Hassan Bin Syed Mahmud Jamalullail and Cik Wan Teh Binti Edut; m. H.R.H. Tengku Budriah Binti al-Marhum Tengku Ismail, D.K., D.M.N., S.M.N. 1940; eight s. six d.; appointed Bakal Raja (Heir-Presumptive) of Perlis April 1938; attached to Courts in Kangar 1940; worked for a year in the Land Office, Kuala Lumpur, and for a year in the Magistrates' Court, Kuala Lumpur; in private business during Japanese occupation; Timbalan Yang di-Pertuan Agung (Deputy Paramount Ruler) of Malaya April-Sept 1960, Yang di-Pertuan Agung (H.M. the Paramount Ruler) 1960–63, of Malaysia 1963–65. *Leisure interests:* golf, tennis, fishing and shooting. *Address:* Istana Arau, Perlis; and Istana Kenangan Indah, Perlis, Malaysia. *Telephone:* 752212.

PERLMAN, Isadore, PH.D.; American professor of chemistry; b. 12 April 1915, Milwaukee, Wisconsin; s. of Harry Perlman and Bella Karpman; m. Lee Grimblat 1937; three d.; ed. Univ. of California (Berkeley); Research Assoc. Manhattan project 1942–45; Assoc. Prof. Univ. of Calif. 1945–49; Prof. of Chem., Univ. of Calif. 1949; Assoc. Dir. Lawrence Radiation Lab. 1958–; Head, Nuclear Chem. Div., Lawrence Radiation Lab. 1958–; mem. American Chemical Asscn., American Physical Soc.; Calif. Section Award, American Chemical Soc. 1952; Guggenheim Fellow, Copenhagen, Denmark 1955, 1963; E. O. Lawrence Award, Atomic Energy Comm. 1960. *Publications:* numerous research papers and articles in scientific journals, especially Physical Review, Journal of Biological Chemistry, Journal of the American Chemical Soc. *Address:* 14th-29th November Street, Jerusalem, Israel.

PERLMAN, Itzhak; Israeli violinist; b. 31 Aug. 1945, Tel-Aviv; s. of Chaim Perlman and Shoshana Perlman; m. Toby Lynn Friedlander 1967; two s. three d.; ed. Tel-Aviv Acad. of Music, Juilliard School, U.S.A.; gave recitals on radio at the age of 10; went to U.S.A. 1958; studied with Ivan Galamian and Dorothy De Lay; first recital at Carnegie Hall 1963; has played with major American orchestras 1964–; has toured Europe regularly and played with major European orchestras 1966–; debut in U.K. with London Symphony Orchestra 1968; appearances at Israel Festival and most European Festivals; numerous recordings; Hon. Mus.D. (Univ. of S. Carolina) 1982; Medal of Liberty 1986. *Address:* c/o IMG Artists, 22 East 71st Street, New York, N.Y. 10021, U.S.A.

PERLOT, Enzo; Italian diplomatist; b. 17 Nov. 1933, Mezzolombardo; s. of the late Augusto and Ida (Paoli) Perlot; m. Ulla Segerstrale 1970; two c.; ed. Univ. of Rome; entered Foreign Ministry 1959; served at Presidency of the Repub. 1965–68; Consul in Munich and Counsellor in Embassy in Vienna 1968–70; served in Office of Prime Minister 1970–72; Spokesman and Dir.-Gen. of Information of EEC Comm. 1978–80; Amb. to Portugal 1984–. *Address:* Italian Embassy, Largo Conde de Pombeiro 6, Lisbon, Portugal. *Telephone:* 546144.

PERNOW, Bengt, PH.D.; Swedish professor of clinical physiology; b. 8 Nov. 1924, Stockholm; m. Ulla Ekström 1955; two c.; ed. Karolinska Inst., Stockholm; Assoc. Prof., Dept. of Physiology, Karolinska Inst. 1951–59, Prof. of Clinical Physiology 1959–, Medical Dir. 1974–77, Rector 1977–83, Chair. the Nobel Cttee. 1979–81, Chair. the Nobel Ass. 1986–, Chair. Dept. of Clinical Physiology 1973–; Chair. Dept. of Clinical Physiology, Seraphimer Hosp., Stockholm 1959–72, Huddinge Hosp., Stockholm 1972–73; Chair., the Swedish Soc. of Medicine 1986–. *Publications:* Ed. Muscle Metabolism during Exercise 1971, Substance P 1976, Peripheral Circulation 1978, Metabolic Risk Factors in Ischaemic Cardiovascular Disease 1982, Alcohol and the Developing Brain 1985, Coexistence of Neuronal Messengers: A New Principle in Chemical Transmission 1986; over 200 scientific papers. *Leisure interests:* physical exercise, tennis. *Address:* Karolinska Hospital, S-104 01 Stockholm; Norrtullsgatan 28, S-113 45 Stockholm, Sweden (Home). *Telephone:* 08-32 90 22 (Office).

PEROL, Gilbert; French diplomatist; b. 31 May 1926, Tunis, Tunisia; s. of René Pérol and Jeanne Garcin; m. Huguette Cuchet-Cheruzel 1949; three s.; ed. Univ. of Paris, Ecole Nat. d'Admin.; with Ministry of Foreign Affairs, diplomatic posts in Paris, Morocco, Ethiopia, Algeria 1953–62; with Office of Pres. de Gaulle 1963–67; Sec.-Gen. Air France 1967–74, Man. Dir.

1974–82; Dir. France Cables et Radio 1972–, Inst. of Air Transport 1975–; with Ministry of External Relations 1982–; Amb. to Tunisia 1983–85, to Japan 1985–87; Sec. Gen. Ministry of External Relations 1987–88; Amb. to Italy 1988–; Officer, Légion d'honneur, Commdr., Ordre du Mérite. *Leisure interest:* chess. *Address:* Ministry of External Relations, 37 quai d'Orsay, 75700 Paris; 54 rue de Rome, 75008 Paris, France (Home).

PERÓN, María Estela (Isabelita) (see Martínez de Perón).

PERONNET, Gabriel André; French politician and international consultant; b. 31 Oct. 1919, Le Vernet; s. of Antoine Peronnet and Jeanne Rousset; m. Noëlle Chabrier 1945; ed. Cusset High School, Nat. Veterinary Coll., Lyon Univ., qualified veterinary surgeon 1943; veterinary practice in Cusset 1949–62; Councillor 1952–79; mem. Nat. Ass. for L'Allier 1962–81, mem. Ass. Foreign Affairs Comm. 1962–81; Sec.-Gen. Parti radical socialiste 1973, Pres. 1975–77, Hon. Pres. 1977–; Rep. of France, Council of Europe 1967–74, 1976–81; Pres. Franco-Thai Asscn., Franco-Mexican Assn. and Franco-Moroccan Assn.; Sec. of State for the Environment June–Oct. 1974; Sec. of State for the Civil Service 1974–76; mem. Consultative Comm. on Int. Commerce 1982; Pres. French Assn. for the UN 1983–; Del. to UN 1983–; Chevalier Légion d'honneur, du mérite militaire, du mérite social, du mérite sportif, de l'ordre national malgache, Commdr. des Palmes académiques, Officier du mérite agricole, Officier de l'Ordre Nat. du Mérite, Officier de l'Ordre du Lion du Sénégal, Commdr. Order of White Elephant, Thailand. *Leisure interests:* horse-riding, hunting. *Address:* 6 square de l'avenue Foch, 75116 Paris; 9 rue Jean-Baptiste Bru, 03300 Cusset, France. *Telephone:* 500 14 55 and (70) 98 37 24.

PEROT, (Henry) Ross; American industrialist and philanthropist; b. 27 June 1930, Texarkana, Tex.; s. of Mr. and Mrs. Gabriel Ross Perot; m. Margot Birmingham 1956; one s. four d.; ed. U.S. Naval Acad.; U.S. Navy 1953–57; with IBM Corpn. 1957–62; formed Electronic Data Systems Corpn. 1962, Chair. of Bd. and C.E.O. 1982–86; Dir. Perot Group, Dallas 1986–; Chair. Bd. of Visitors U.S. Naval Acad. 1970–; numerous awards and citations. *Leisure interest:* horses. *Address:* The Perot Group, 12377 Merit Drive, Dallas, Tex. 75251, U.S.A.

PEROWNE, Stewart Henry, O.B.E., K.ST.J., M.A., F.S.A., F.R.S.A.; British historian and orientalist; b. 17 June 1901, Worcs.; s. of Arthur William Thomson Perowne and Helena Frances Oldnall-Russell; ed. Haileybury Coll., Corpus Christi Coll., Cambridge (Hon. Fellow 1981), Harvard Univ.; English Lecturer, Govt. Arab Coll., Jerusalem 1927–30; Asst. Sec. Palestine Govt. 1930–32, Asst. District Commr. 1932–34; Asst. Sec., Malta 1934–37; Political Officer, Aden 1937; Arabic Programme Organizer, BBC 1938; Information Officer, Aden 1939–41; Public Relations Attaché, British Embassy, Baghdad 1941–44; Oriental Counsellor 1944–47; Colonial Sec. Barbados 1947–49; Acting Gov. Mar.–Oct. 1949; Adviser, Ministry of Interior, Cyrenaica 1950–51; Adviser on Arab Affairs, U.K. Del. UN Gen. Assembly; discovered ancient Aziris 1951; Hon. Asst. Jerusalem Diocesan Refugee Org. 1952; designed and supervised building of seven Arab refugee villages 1952–56; mem. Church of England Council on Foreign Relations. 1965; Hon. Fellow, Corpus Christi Coll., Cambridge 1981. *Publications:* The One Remains 1954, Herod the Great 1956, The Later Herods 1958, Hadrian 1960, Caesars and Saints 1962, The Pilgrim's Companion in Jerusalem and Bethlehem 1964, The Pilgrim's Companion in Roman Rome 1964, The Pilgrim's Companion in Athens 1964, The Death of the Roman Republic 1964, Jerusalem (Famous Cities Series) 1965, The End of the Roman World 1966, The Siege Within the Walls—Malta 1940–43 1969, Rome 1971, The Journeys of Saint Paul 1973, The Caesars' Wives, Above Suspicion? 1974, The Archaeology of Greece and The Aegean 1974, Holy Places of Christendom 1976. *Leisure interests:* archaeology and the arts. *Address:* Vicarage Gate House, Vicarage Gate, London, W8 4AQ, England. *Telephone:* 01-229 1907.

PERPICH, Rudy, D.D.S.; American dentist and politician; b. 27 June 1928, Carson Lake, Minn.; s. of Anton and Mary Perpich; m. Delores (Lola) Simic 1954; one s. one d.; ed. Hibbing Junior Coll. and Marquette Univ.; served in U.S. Army 1946–48; Dental Surgeon 1954–; mem. Hibbing, Minnesota School Bd. 1956–62; mem. Minnesota State Senate 1962–70; Lieut.-Gov. of Minnesota 1970–76, Gov. of Minnesota 1976–79, Jan. 1983–; Vice-Pres., Exec. Consultant Control Data Worldtech Inc., Minneapolis. *Leisure interests:* bocce ball, fishing, cross-country skiing. *Address:* Office of the Governor, Capitol Building, Aurora Avenue, St. Paul, Minn. 55155, U.S.A.

PERRAULT, Hon. Raymond Joseph, P.C.; Canadian politician; b. 6 Feb. 1926, Vancouver, B.C.; s. of late Ernest Alphonse Perrault and of Florence Riebel; m. Barbara Joan Walker 1963; two s. one d.; ed. Univ. of British Columbia; Leader of Liberal Party, B.C. 1959–68; mem. B.C. Legis. Ass. 1960; mem. House of Commons 1968–73, 1980–; Del. to UN Session 1969; Parl. Sec. to Minister of Labour 1970; Parl. Sec. to Minister of Manpower and Immigration 1971–73; Asst. to Minister of Industry, Trade and Commerce in trade negotiations, Peking 1971; Rep. to ILO Convention, Geneva 1972; mem. Senate 1973–; Govt. Leader in Senate 1974–79, 1980–82; Minister of State for Fitness and Amateur Sport 1982–83. *Address:* The Senate, Parliament Buildings, Ottawa, Ont.; 437 Somerset Street, North Vancouver, B.C. V7N 1G4, Canada.

PERREAULT, Germain; Canadian banker; b. 23 May 1916, Montreal; s. of Lucien and Maria Dufault Perreault; ed. Montreal; with Montreal Stock Exchange 1936; Garneau, Ostiguy, and Co. (stockbrokers) 1937–39; joined Banque Canadienne Nat., Head Office 1939, Asst. Man., Investment Dept. 1947, Asst. Gen. Man. 1964–68, Gen. Man. 1968–71, Chief Gen. Man. 1971–72, Vice-Pres. and Chief Gen. Man. 1972–74, Exec. Vice-Pres. and Chief Gen. Man. 1974, Pres. 1974–82, C.E.O. 1976–82, Chair. 1978–82; Soc. de la Caisse de Retraite de la Banque Canadienne Nat.; Dir. Cie. Immobilière BCN Limitée, RoyNat Ltd., Domco Industries Ltd., Laurentia Mutual Assurance Co., Commerce Gen. Insurance Co., Corpn. d'Expansion Financière, Les Ensembles Urbains Limitée, Les Nouveaux Ensembles Urbains Limitée, Banque Canadienne Nat. (Europe), Banque Canadienne Nat. (Europe), York Lambton Corpn. Ltd., Sidbec Limitée Sidbec-Dosco Limitée, Régie de la Place des Arts, Montreal Museum of Fine Arts, Montreal Symphony Orch.; Gov., Thee Conference Bd. in Canada; Gov., Dir., mem. Exec. Cttee. Quebec Hosp. Service Assn. (Blue Cross); Gov. Old Exchange Arts Foundation; Chair. and Dir. Quebec Div. Canadian Arthritis and Rheumatism Soc.; mem. Montreal Bd. of Trade, Canadian Chamber of Commerce, Chambre de Commerce du district de Montréal, St.-Denis Club (Dir., mem. Exec. Cttee), Mount Royal (Montreal), Laval-sur-le-lac (Laval, Quebec). *Leisure interests:* golf, music, reading. *Address:* c/o Banque Canadienne Nationale, 500 Place d'Armes, Montreal, Quebec H2Y 2W3, Canada. *Telephone:* (514) 281-6576.

PERREIN, Michèle Marie-Claude; French writer; b. 30 Oct. 1929, La Réole; d. of Roger Barbe and Anne-Blanche Perrein; m. Jacques Laurent (divorced); ed. Univ. of Bordeaux, Centre de Formation des Journalistes; literary ed. and contrib. to periodicals Arts-Spectacles, la Parisienne, Marie-Claire, La Vie Judiciaire, Votre Beauté, Le Point, F. Magazine, Les Nouvelles Littéraires. *Publications:* La Sensitive 1956, Le Soleil dans l'oeil 1957, Barbastre 1960, La Flemme 1961, Le Cercle 1962, Le Petit Jules 1965, M'oiselle S, la Chineuse 1970, La Partie de plaisir 1971, Le Buveur de Garonne 1973, Le Mâle aimant 1975, Gemma Lapidaire 1976, Entre Chienne et louve 1978, Comme une fourmi cavalière 1980, Ave Caesar 1982, Les Cotonniers de Bassalane 1984; *plays:* l'Hôtel Racine 1966, a+b+c = la Clinique d'anticipation, 1971, l'Alter-Auto 1971; film collaborator La Vérité 1959. *Leisure interests:* tapestry, swimming, skating. *Address:* 11 bis rue Chomel, 75007 Paris, France (Home).

PERRIN, Francis Henri Jean Siegfried, D. ÈS SC.; French scientist; b. 17 Aug. 1901, Paris; s. of Jean Perrin (Nobel prize winner for Physics 1926); m. Colette Auger 1926; two s. one d.; ed. Lycée Henri IV, Paris, Ecole Normale Supérieure, Univ. of Paris; Asst., Univ. of Paris 1923, lecturer 1933, Prof. 1935–; Visiting Prof. Columbia Univ., New York 1941–44; Rep. to Consultative Ass., Algiers, later Paris 1944–45; Titular Prof. of Atomic Physics, Coll. de France 1946–72; High Commr. for Atomic Energy 1951–70; mem. Inst. de France (Acad. des Sciences) 1953–, Acad. d'Agric. 1958–; Dr. h.c. (Uppsala Univ.) 1952, (Columbia, New York) 1977; Grand Croix Légion d'honneur, Grand Croix Mérite national, Commdr. des Palmes académiques, Economie Nationale. *Leisure interests:* sailing, skiing. *Address:* 4 rue Froidevaux, 75014 Paris, France (Home). *Telephone:* 43.35.35.58.

PERRONE, João Consani, B.SC., M.A., D.CHEM.; Brazilian protein chemist; b. 22 Jan. 1922, Passa Quatro, Minas Gerais; s. of Raphael Perrone and Adelaide Consani Peronne; m. Moema Cruz Perrone 1952; three d.; ed. Universidade do Brasil, Rio de Janeiro, and Univ. of California (Berkeley); Head of Research, Nat. Council of Research 1952–60; Assoc. Prof. of Organic and Biological Chem., Univ. of Brazil 1951; Head, Laboratory of Protein Chem., Instituto Nacional de Tecnologia 1952; Prof. of Protein Chemistry and Gen. Enzymology, Inst. de Química 1962, Chair. Dept. of Biochem. 1968–72; Pres. Soc. Brasileira de Bioquímica 1972–74; mem. Brazilian Acad. of Sciences. *Leisure interests:* hunting, fishing. *Address:* Rua Senador Vergueiro, 99 Cobertura, Flamengo, Rio de Janeiro, RJ, Brazil. *Telephone:* 225-1617.

PERRY, Baron (Life Peer), cr. 1979, of Walton in Bucks.; **Walter Laing Macdonald Perry,** Kt., O.B.E., F.R.S.; British university professor; b. 16 June 1921, Dundee; s. of Fletcher Smith Perry and Flora Macdonald Macdonald; m. 1st Anne Grant 1946; three s.; m. 2nd Catherine Crawley 1971; two s. one d.; ed. Dundee High School and St. Andrews Univ.; Medical Officer in Colonial Service, Nigeria 1944–46, in the R.A.F. 1946–47; Medical Research Council 1947–52; Dir. Dept. of Biological Standards, Nat. Inst. for Medical Research 1952–58; Prof. of Pharmacology, Edin. Univ. 1958–68, Vice-Prin. 1967–68; Vice-Chancellor, Open Univ. 1968–81; Exec. Chair., Living Tapes Ltd. 1981; Consultant to UN Univ. 1981; Chair. Bd. of Govs. Int. Technological Univ. 1987; Hon. Dir., UN Univ. Int. Centre for Distance Learning 1983; Chair. Continuing Educ. Standing Cttee. 1985; Hon. D. Sc. 1974, Hon. LL.D. 1975, Hon. D. Litt 1981, D. Hum. Litt. 1982. *Publications:* Open University 1976; several chapters in other books. *Leisure interests:* golf, music. *Address:* The Open University in Scotland, 60 Melville Street, Edinburgh EH3 7HF; Glenholm, 2 Cramond Road South, Davidson's Mains, Edinburgh, EH4 6AD. Scotland (Home). *Telephone:* (031) 226 3851 (Office); (031) 336 3666 (Home).

PERRY, Fred(erick) John; former British tennis player (now a U.S. citizen), television and radio commentator; b. 18 May 1909, Stockport; ed. Ealing County School; won World Table Tennis Championship 1929; World professional tennis champion 1937, 1941; Wimbledon champion 1934, 1935, 1936; U.S.A. Champion 1933, 1934, 1936; Australian Champion 1934; French Champion 1935; played Davis Cup for G.B. 1931, 1932, 1933, 1934, 1935, 1936; Professional from 1936; f. Fred Perry Sportswear Co. *Publications:* My Story, Perry on Tennis, Fred Perry: An Autobiography 1984. *Address:* c/o The All England Club, Church Road, Wimbledon, London, S.W.19, England.

PERRY, Robert Palese, PH.D.; American molecular biologist; b. 10 Jan. 1931, Chicago; s. of Robert P. Perry, Sr. and Gertrude Hyman; m. Zoila Figueroa 1957; one s. two d.; ed. Univ. of Chicago and Northwestern Univ.; Postdoctoral Fellow Oak Ridge Nat. Lab. 1956–57, Univ. of Pa. 1957–59, Univ. of Brussels 1959–60; Staff mem. Inst. for Cancer Research, Fox Chase Cancer Center 1960–, now Sr. mem.; Prof. of Biophysics, Univ. of Pa.; UNESCO Tech. Asst. Expert Univ. of Belgrade 1965; Guggenheim Fellow Univ. of Paris 1974–75; Chair. Exec. Cttee. Int. Cell Research Org. (UNESCO) 1982–85; mem. N.A.S.; Dr. h.c. (Univ. of Paris VII). *Publications:* more than 100 articles in int. scientific journals. *Address:* Institute for Cancer Research, Fox Chase Cancer Center, 7701 Burholme Avenue, Philadelphia, Pa. 19111 (Office); 1808 Bustleton Pike, Churchville, Pa. 18966, U.S.A. (Home).

PERRY, Seymour Monroe, B.A., M.D., F.A.C.P.; American physician; b. 26 May 1921, New York; m. Judith Carol Kaplan 1951; two s. one d.; ed. Univs. of California and Southern California, Los Angeles; numerous positions in hosps. and public health orgs. 1951–83, including Assoc. Scientific Dir. for Clinical Trials, Chemotherapy, Nat. Cancer Inst., 1966–71, Assoc. Dir. for Program Planning, Div. of Cancer Treatment 1971–74, Deputy Dir. 1973–74, Assoc. Dir. for Medical Applications of Research, Nat. Insts. of Health 1978–80; Dir. Nat. Center for Health Care Tech., U.S. Dept. of Health and Human Services 1980–82; Asst. Surgeon Gen., U.S. Public Health Service 1980–82; Sr. Fellow and Deputy Dir. Inst. for Health Policy Analysis 1983–; Prof. of Medicine and Prof. of Community and Family Medicine, Georgetown Univ. Medical Center 1983–; Pres. Int. Soc. of Tech. Assessment in Health Care 1985–87; Fellow, American Coll. of Physicians, American Public Health Assen.; mem. Inst. of Medicine, N.A.S., and many other professional assens.; numerous awards. *Publications:* numerous articles on studies of tumour cell growth and biochemistry and on medical tech. assessment and health public policy. *Leisure interests:* gardening, photography, squash. *Address:* Institute of Health Policy Analysis, 2121 Wisconsin Avenue, N.W., Suite 220, Washington, D.C. 20007, U.S.A. *Telephone:* (202) 965-0025.

PERUTZ, Max Ferdinand, O.M., C.H., PH.D., F.R.S.; British biochemist and crystallographer; b. 19 May 1914, Vienna, Austria; s. of Hugo and Adele Perutz; m. Gisela Peiser 1942; one s. one d.; ed. Theresianum, Vienna, and Univs. of Vienna and Cambridge; Dir. Medical Research Council Unit for Molecular Biology, Cavendish Laboratory, Univ. of Cambridge 1947–62; Chair. Medical Research Council Laboratory of Molecular Biology, Univ. Postgraduate Medical School, Cambridge 1962–79, mem. scientific staff 1979–; Reader Davy Faraday Research Laboratory, Royal Inst. 1954–68; Chair. European Molecular Biology Org. 1963–69; Fullerian Prof. Physiology at Royal Inst. 1974–79; Hon. Dr. Phil (Vienna, Edinburgh, Aarhus, Norwich, Saltzburg); Hon. Sc.D. (Cambridge) 1981; Foreign Assoc. N.A.S. 1970–; Foreign mem. Acad. des Sciences 1976, Accad. dei Lincei, Rome 1984; shared Nobel·Prize for Chem. with Dr. (later Sir) John Kendrew (q.v.) for researches into blood chem. 1962; Royal Medal, Royal Soc. 1971, Copley Medal, Royal Soc. 1979. *Publications:* Proteins and Nucleic Acids: Structure and Function 1962, Atlas of Haemoglobin and Myoglobin (with G. Fermi) 1981, Ging's ohne Forschung besser 1983, various papers on the structure of proteins. *Leisure interests:* skiing, mountaineering. *Address:* MRC Laboratory of Molecular Biology, Hills Road, Cambridge; 42 Sedley Taylor Road, Cambridge, England. *Telephone:* (0223) 248011 (Office).

PERVYSHIN, Erlen Kirikovich; Soviet politician; b. 1932; ed. Moscow Electrotechnical Inst. of Communications; Cand. of Tech.; mem. CPSU 1959–; engineer 1955–, then Head of Ass. Section, Deputy Chief Engineer, Head of Admin., Manager of Design and Ass. Trust, Dir. Gen. All-Union Scientific production assen.; Deputy U.S.S.R. Minister of Radio and Communications Industry 1971–74, Minister 1974–80; cand. mem. of Cen. Cttee. of CPSU 1976–86, mem. 1986–; Minister of Communications Equipment Manufacturing 1980–; Deputy to U.S.S.R. Supreme Soviet, 9th Convocation. *Address:* The Kremlin, Moscow, U.S.S.R.

PESCATORE, Pierre, D.IUR.; Luxembourg diplomatist and professor of law; b. 20 Nov. 1919, Luxembourg; s. of Ferdinand Pescatore and Cunégonde Heuertz; m. Rosalie Margue 1948; three s. one d.; Ministry of Foreign Affairs 1946–67, Sec., later mem., Del. to UN Gen. Ass. 1946–52; Legal Adviser, Min. of Foreign Affairs 1950–58; Dir. for Political Affairs, Min. of Foreign Affairs 1958–64; Minister Plenipotentiary 1959; Sec.-Gen. Ministry of Foreign Affairs 1964–67; Judge, Court of Justice of the European Communities 1967–86; Prof. Law Faculty and Inst. for European Legal Studies, Univ. of Liège; Lectured Hague Acad. of Int. Law 1961; mem. Inst. de Droit International 1965–; Dr. h.c. (Nancy, Geneva and Tübingen Univs.). *Publications:* Essai sur la notion de la loi 1957, co-author Aspects juridiques du Marché commun 1958, Relations extérieures des Communautés européennes 1962, Conclusion et effet des traités internationaux selon le droit constitutionnel du G.-D. de Luxembourg 1964, La

fusion des communautés européennes 1965, L'union économique belgo-luxembourgeoise 1965, La fusion des communautés européenes au lendemain des Accords de Luxembourg 1967, Distribución de competencias y de poderes entre los Estados miembros y las Communidas Europeas 1968, Les droits de l'homme et l'intégration européenne 1968, Personnalité internationale et politique commerciale des communautés européennes 1969; co-author Les relations extérieures de la communauté européenne unifiée 1969, L'ordre juridique des communautés européennes 1973, The Law of Integration 1974, Introduction à la science du droit 1978, Cours d'institutions internationales 1978. *Address:* 16 rue de la Fontaine, Luxembourg. *Telephone:* Luxembourg 240-44 (Home).

PESENTI, Antonio; Italian economist and politician; b. 15 Oct. 1910, Verona; s. of Romeo Pesenti and Amalia Bisoffi; m. Ghiadistri Adriana 1947; ed. Univs. of Pavia, Vienna, Berne, Paris, London School of Econs.; lecturer Sassari Univ. 1935; active in underground anti-Fascist movement 1930–35; took part in Italian anti-Fascist Congress in Brussels 1935; arrested and sentenced to 24 years' imprisonment by special tribunal; released Sept. 1943; Under-Sec., later Minister of Finance 1944–45; lecturer on Finance, Univ. of Rome 1945; Prof. Univ. of Parma 1948, of Pisa 1960–71, of Rome 1971; Ed. Critica Economica; mem. Italian Constituent Ass.; Pres. Econ. Centre for Reconstruction; M.P. 1948, mem. Senate 1953–; Communist. *Publications:* Politica finanziaria e monetaria dell' Inghilterra 1934, La politica monetaria delle Devisenverordnungen 1933, I soggetti passivi dell'obbligazione doganale 1934, Ricostruire dalle rovine 1945, Scienza delle Finanze e diritto finanziario 1961, Manuale d'Economia Politica, 2 vols. 1970. *Leisure interests:* chess, mountaineering, rowing. *Address:* Via Nomentana 372, Rome; and 41 Via Nomentana, Istituto di Economia, Rome, Italy. *Telephone:* Rome 897530.

PESMAZOGLU, John Stevens, PH.D.; Greek economist, university professor, central banker and politician; b. 1 March 1918, Chios; s. of Stephanos G. Pesmazoglu and Angela Lorenzou; m. Miranda Economou 1945; two s.; ed. Varvakion High School, Athens, Univ. of Athens, and St. John's Coll., Cambridge; served in Greek Albanian campaign 1940–41 and in liberation of Greece 1944–45; research student, Cambridge 1945–49; Lecturer in Political Economy, Univ. of Athens 1950–67, Prof. 1967–70; Dir.-Gen. Greek Ministry of Co-ordination in charge of econ. devt. and external financial relations 1951–55; Econ. Adviser Bank of Greece 1955–60; Alt. Gov. for Greece, IMF 1955–67; Deputy Gov. Bank of Greece 1960–67; Leader of Greek mission to negotiations for European Free Trade Area and assen. of Greece with Common Market 1957–61; Chair. Interdepartmental Cttee. for European Co-operation 1962–65; Trustee Royal Hellenic Research Foundation 1959–68; Pres. Soc. for the Study of Greek Problems 1971–72; exiled by mil. govt. May–Dec. 1972; in prison April–Aug. 1973; Minister of Finance July–Oct. 1974; M.P. 1974–81, 1985–; mem. European Parl. 1981–84; Co-Pres. Jt. Parl. Comm. Greece-European Communities 1975–79; Pres. Party of Democratic Socialism 1979–84; Grand Commdr. Royal Order of George I, Commdr. Légion d'honneur, Grand Commdr. of the Yugoslav Standard with Gold Crown; Grand Commdr. German Order of Merit. *Publications:* Studies and articles on the int. trade cycle, economic devt. and monetary policies and on European integration with special reference to Greece's participation in the European Community. *Leisure interest:* painting. *Address:* 6 Neophytou Vamva Street, 10674 Athens, Greece. *Telephone:* 7212458.

PESOLA, Anja Helena, M.SOC.SC.; Finnish politician; b. 2 July 1947, Kuopio; m. Tapio Pesola 1971; Public Relations and Information Chief, Chamber of Commerce of Cen. Finland and information Chief of the Jvyäskylä Fair 1971–73; Acting Financial Man. Social Welfare Office of the City of Jyväskylä 1978–79; mem. Parl. 1979–; Minister of Social Affairs and Health 1987–; Nat. Coalition Party. *Address:* Ministry of Social Affairs and Health, Snellmaninkatu 4-6, 00170 Helsinki, Finland. *Telephone:* (90) 1601.

PETCH, Norman James, D.MET., F.R.S., F.ENG.; British professor of metallurgy (retd.); b. 13 Feb. 1917, Bearsden; s. of George and Jane Petch; m. 1st Marion Blight 1942 (divorced); m. 2nd Eileen Allen 1949 (died 1975), two d.; m. 3rd Marjorie Jackson 1976; ed. Queen Mary Coll., Univ. of London, and Sheffield Univ.; Research Asst., Cavendish Lab., Cambridge 1939–42; Scientific Officer, Royal Aircraft Research Establishment 1942–46; Sr. Scientific Officer, British Iron and Steel Research Assen., at Cavendish Lab. 1946–48, at Sheffield 1948–49; Reader in Metallurgy, Leeds Univ. 1949–56, Prof. 1956–59; Cochrane Prof. of Metallurgy, Newcastle Univ. 1959–73, Prof. Univ. of Strathclyde 1973–82; Rosenhain Medal, Metals Soc.; numerous scientific articles. *Leisure interest:* admiring Scotland. *Address:* Findon Cottage, Culbokie, Cononbridge, Ross-shire, 1V7 8JJ, Scotland. *Telephone:* (034987) 259.

PETER, Friedrich; Austrian politician; b. 13 July 1921, Attnang/Puchheim; s. of Friedrich and Alosia Peter; m. Anna Liselotte 1943; two d.; fmr. school teacher; founding mem. Freiheitliche Partei Österreichs (FPÖ); mem. Upper Austrian Diet 1955–66; Chair. Upper Austrian branch of FPÖ 1956–72, Chair. Nat. Exec. 1958–79; mem. Nationalrat 1966–; Leader FPÖ Parl. Group 1970; Grosses Goldenes Ehrenzeichen, Grosses Verdienstkreuz mit Stern (Fed. Repub. of Germany). *Leisure interest:* historical-political studies. *Address:* Klub der Freiheitliche Partei Österreichs, 1017 Vienna, Austria. *Telephone:* 42.15.25, Ext. 486.

PÉTER, János; Hungarian ecclesiastic and politician; b. 1910; ed. Budapest, Protestant Theological Faculty, Paris and Trinity Coll., Glasgow; Bishop Transtibiscan Synod of the Reformed Church 1949-56; Pres. Inst. of Cultural Relations 1957-58; mem. of Nat. Ass. 1953-, Deputy Speaker Dec. 1973-; First Deputy Minister for Foreign Affairs 1958-61, Minister 1961-73; mem. Cen. Cttee. Hungarian Socialist Workers' Party 1966-88; Banner Order 1st degree of the Hungarian People's Repub. 1970, Red Banner of Labour Order of Merit, State Prize 1985. *Publication:* History of Hungarian Soviet Diplomatic Relations 1939-1941 1980. *Address:* Országgyűlés, H-1357 Budapest, Kossuth Lajos tér, Hungary.

PETERS, Jonathan C., B.SC., M.B.A.; St. Vincent and the Grenadines diplomatist; b. 18 Jan. 1946, Georgetown; m. (divorced); four c.; ed. Hunter Coll., New York, Fairleigh Dickinson Univ., Rutherford, N.J. and Pupil Teachers' Training Centre, St. Vincent; Asst. Teacher Ministry of Educ. 1962-67; Sr. Instructor Ministry of Agric. 1967-72; Asst. Man. Schaefer Brewing Co., New York 1972-75; employee Merrill Lynch Futures, New York 1975-86; Perm. Rep. to UN 1986-. *Address:* Permanent Mission of St. Vincent and the Grenadines to the United Nations, 801 Second Avenue, 21st Floor, New York, N.Y. 10017, U.S.A. *Telephone:* (212) 687-4490.

PETERS, Wallace, M.D., D.S.C., .F.R.C.P.; British professor of parasitology; b. 1 April 1924, London; s. of Henry Peters and Fanny Peters; m. Ruth Scheidegger-Frehner 1954; ed. Haberdashers Aske's Hampstead School, St. Bartholomew's Hosp. Medical Coll., Univ. of London; Physician West and East Africa, including R.A.M.C. 1947-53; Scientist-Entomologist and Malariologist, WHO, in Liberia and Nepal 1953-55; Malariologist, Territory of Papua and New Guinea 1956-61; Research Assoc., CIBA Pharmaceutical Co., Basle 1961-66; Prof. of Parasitology, Liverpool School of Tropical Medicine 1966-79, Dean 1975-78; Prof. of Medical Protozoology, London School of Hygiene and Tropical Medicine 1979-; Hon. Consultant in Parasitology, Camden Area Health Authority 1978-, on malariology, to Army 1986-; Jt. Dir. Public Health Lab. Service Malaria Reference Centre 1979-; Pres. Royal Soc. of Tropical Medicine and Hygiene 1987- (Vice-Pres. 1982-83, 1985-87); mem. Expert Advisory Panel on Malaria of WHO 1967-; King Faisal Int. Prize, Medicine 1983, Rudolf Leuckart Medallist, German Soc. of Parasitology 1980. *Publications:* Checklist of Ethiopian Butterflies 1952, Chemotherapy and Drug Resistance in Malaria 1970, Rodent Malaria (co-ed.) 1978, Atlas of Tropical Medicine and Parasitology (with H. M. Gilles) 1977, Pharmacology of Antimalarials (2 vols.) (co-ed.) 1984, Leishmaniases in Biology and Medicine (co-ed.) 1987. *Leisure interests:* photography, entomology, writing. *Address:* London School of Hygiene and Tropical Medicine, Keppel Street, London, WC1E 7HT, England.

PETERSDORF, Robert George, M.D.; American physician and medical educator; b. 14 Feb. 1926, Berlin, Germany; s. of Hans H. Petersdorf and Sonja Petersdorf; m. Patricia Horton Qua 1951; two s.; ed. Brown and Yale Univs.; Instructor in Medicine, Yale Univ. 1957-58; Asst. Prof. of Medicine, Johns Hopkins Univ. 1958-59; Assoc. Prof. of Medicine, Univ. of Washington School of Medicine 1960-62, Prof. 1962-79, Chair. Dept. of Medicine 1964-79; Prof. of Medicine, Harvard Medical School 1979-81; Pres. Brigham and Women's Hosp., Boston 1979-81; Vice-Chancellor for Health Sciences and Dean, School of Medicine, Univ. of Calif., San Diego 1981-86; Pres. Asscn. of American Medical Colls. 1986-; Ed. Harrison's Principles of Internal Medicine 1968-; mem. editorial bds. of several scientific journals; Fellow American Coll. of Physicians, Royal Soc. of Medicine, Royal Coll. of Physicians, London, American Acad. of Arts and Sciences, A.A.A.S.; mem. Inst. of Medicine of N.A.S. and numerous professional orgs.; numerous hon. degrees and prizes. *Publications:* over 300 papers in professional and scientific journals. *Address:* Association of American Medical Colleges, One Dupont Circle, Suite 200, Washington, D.C. 20036 (Office); 1827 Phelps Place, N.W., Washington, D.C. 20008, U.S.A. (Home). *Telephone:* (202) 828-0460 (Office).

PETERSEN, Donald Eugene: American business executive; b. 4 Sept. 1926, Pipestone, Minn.; s. of William L. Petersen and Mae Pederson; m. Jo Anne Leonard 1948; one s. one d.; ed. Univ. of Washington, Stanford Univ.; served U.S. Marine Corps Reserve 1946-47, 1951-52; with Ford Motor Co. 1949-, Asst. to Vice-Pres. Car and Truck Group 1965-66, Car Product Planning Man. 1966-69, Exec. Dir., Admin. Eng. and Industrial Design 1969, Vice-Pres. Car Planning and Research 1969-71, Vice-Pres. Truck Operations 1971-73, and Recreation Products Operations 1973-75, Dir. 1977, Pres. 1980, Chair. Feb. 1985-, C.E.O. 1985-; mem. Soc. Automotive Engs., Eng. Soc., Detroit, The Business Council, Business Roundtable Cttee., Advisory Bd. Univ. of Washington Graduate School of Business Admin., Business Roundtable Policy Cttee., Business Council, U.S.—Japan Business Council, Emergency Cttee. for American Trade, etc.; Hon. D.Sc. (Detroit) 1986, Hon. D. Hum. Litt. (Art Center Coll. of Design, Pasadena, Calif.) 1986; numerous awards and prizes including American Achievement Award 1986, Business Statesman Award 1986, Nat. Humanitarian Award (Nat. Jewish Center) 1987, Top C.E.O., Fortune Magazine 1988. *Address:* Ford Motor Co., American Road, Dearborn, Mich. 48121, U.S.A.

PETERSEN, George Bouet, M.SC., M.A., D.PHIL., F.N.Z.I.C., F.R.S.N.Z.; British/New Zealand professor of biochemistry; b. 5 Sept. 1933, Palmerston North, N.Z.; s. of George C. Petersen and Elizabeth S, Petersen; m. Patricia J.E. Caughey 1960; four d.; ed. Univs. of Otago and Oxford; scientist, DSIR Plant Chemistry Div. Palmerston North 1959-60, 1963-67;

Departmental Demonstrator in Biochemistry, Univ. of Oxford 1961-63; Prof. of Biochemistry, Univ. of Otago 1968-; Visiting Research Fellow, Harvard Univ. 1964; Royal Soc. Commonwealth Bursar, MRC Lab. of Molecular Biology, Cambridge 1973-74, 1981; Carnegie Corpn. of New York Travel Grantee 1964. *Publications:* numerous papers on aspects of nucleic acid chemistry and biochemistry in various scientific journals. *Leisure interests:* music, literature, book collecting. *Address:* 47 Maori Road, Dunedin, New Zealand. *Telephone:* (024) 770784.

PETERSEN, Howard C., B.A., J.D., LL.D.; American lawyer and banker; b. 7 May 1910, East Chicago, Ind.; s. of Hans C. and Silvia Charles Petersen; m. Elizabeth Anna Watts 1936; one s. (deceased) one d.; ed. De-Pauw Univ., Univ. of Michigan Law School; admitted to N.Y. Bar 1935; Assoc. of law firm, Cravath, de Gersdorff, Swaine & Wood (now Cravath, Swaine and Moore) 1933-41; mem. of Nat. Emergency Cttee. of Mil. Training Camps Assen. and one of principal drafters of Burke-Wadsworth Bill, which became the Selective Service Act 1940; Counsel, Cttee. for drafting regulations under Selective Service Act 1940; Special Asst. and Exec. Asst. to Under-Sec. of War 1941-45, Special Asst. to Sec. of War Sept. 1945, Asst. Sec of War Dec. 1945-47; Exec. Vice-Pres. and Dir. Fidelity-Philadelphia Trust Co. Pa. (now The Fidelity Bank) 1947-50, C.E.O. 1950-75, Pres. 1950-66, Chair. 1966-79; Nat. Finance Chair. for Eisenhower pre-convention campaign 1952; mem. President's Cttee. on Educ. Beyond the High School 1957; Special Asst. to Pres. for Trade Policy 1961-62; engaged in formulation and promotion of Trade Expansion Act 1962; negotiated conclusion of GATT tariff negotiations with EEC 1960-62; Rep. on Fed. Advisory Council 1960-63; Pres. Pa. Bankers' Assen. 1963-64; Dir. Fed. Reserve Bank of Philadelphia 1965-68; fmr. mem. Advisory Cttee., Export-Import Bank of the U.S., Chair. 1965-67; mem. Harvard Overseers Visiting Cttee. to Econs. Dept. 1967-73, Advisory Cttee. on Int. Monetary Reform, Int. Monetary Conf. (Pres. 1973), Exec. Cttee., Cttee. for Econ. Devt.; fmr. Pres. World Affairs Council of Philadelphia; mem. Council on Foreign Relations, Philadelphia Cttee. on Foreign Relations, Chair.; Chair. Nat. Policy Panel of United Nat. Assen. on Organization of the U.S. Govt. for Effective Participation in Int. Org. 1973; Chair. Bd. of Mans., Univ. Museum (Pa.) 1964-80; Dir. Panama Canal Co. 1952-68, Insurance Co. of N. America, Rohm and Haas Co. 1967-76, Greater Philadelphia Movement (Co-Chair. 1965-67), American Acad. Political and Social Science, Adela Investment Co., S.A. (Chair. 1969-71); mem. Assen. of Bar of N.Y., Reserve City Bankers, American Bankers Assen., American Philosophical Soc., Chair. Bd. of Trustees, Inst. for Advanced Study, Princeton; Trustee, Carnegie Endowment for Int. Peace 1957-80, Eisenhower Exchange Fellowships, George C. Marshall Research Foundation; Hon. LL.D. (St. Joseph's Coll.) 1962; D.Sc. (Drexel Inst.) 1962; hon. degrees also from DePauw Univ. 1953, Swathmore 1968, Univ. of Pennsylvania 1974; Medal for Merit, Exceptional Civilian Service Award and Selective Service Medal 1945. *Leisure interests:* bridge, reading. *Address:* Radnor, Pa. 19087; c/o The Fidelity Bank, Broad and Walnut Sts., Philadelphia, Pa. 19109, U.S.A.

PETERSEN, Sir Jeffrey Charles, K.C.M.G.; British diplomatist (retd.); b. 20 July 1920, London; s. of late Charles Petersen and of Mrs. R. M. Petersen; m. Karin Kristina Petersen 1962; one s. three d.; ed. Westcliff High School and London School of Econs., London Univ.; served R.N. 1939-46; joined Diplomatic Service 1948; Second Sec., Madrid 1949-50; Second Sec., later First Sec., Ankara 1951-52; First Sec., Brussels 1953-56; NATO Defence Coll. 1956-57; Foreign Office 1957-62; First Sec., Jakarta 1962-64; Counsellor, Athens 1964-68; Minister, Rio de Janeiro 1968-71; Amb. to Repub. of Korea 1971-74, to Romania 1975-76, to Sweden 1977-80; Chair. British Materials Handling Bd. 1982-, Anglo-Korean Soc.; Non-Exec. Chair. North Sea Assets Jan. 1989-; Pres. Anglo-Swedish Soc.; Vice-Pres. Swedish Chamber of Commerce for the U.K. *Leisure interests:* painting, making things, totting. *Address:* 32 Longmoore Street, London, S.W.1; Crofts Wood, Petham, near Canterbury, Kent, England (Home). *Telephone:* 01-834 8262; (022770) 537.

PETERSEN, Jens, DR. JUR.; German diplomatist (retd.); b. 10 Oct. 1923, Hamburg; s. of Friedrich Ernest and Elli (née Kortenhaus) Petersen; m. Viola Petersen 1973; ed. Kiel Univ.; Foreign Office, Bonn 1955; Vice-Consul, Montreal 1957; Amb. to Trinidad and Tobago 1963, to Cyprus 1966, to Iran 1981-85, to Switzerland 1985-88; Perm. Del. to UNESCO 1970-77; mem. Exec. Bd. of UNESCO 1976-78; Dir. for Asian Affairs, Ministry of Foreign Affairs, Bonn 1977-81. *Address:* Am Hang 6, 5300 Bonn 3, Federal Republic of Germany.

PETERSEN, Niels Helveg, LL.D.; Danish politician; b. 17 Jan. 1939, Odense; ed. Copenhagen Univ. and Stanford Univ., Calif., U.S.A.; mem. Folketing (Parl.) 1966-74, 1977-; Chef de Cabinet to Danish Commr. for the European Communities 1974-77; mem. Radical Liberal Party's Foreign Affairs Cttee. 1968-74, Party Spokesman on Political Affairs 1968-74, 1977-78, Chair. Parl. Group 1977-; Parl. Politico-Econ. Cttee. 1982-84; Minister for Econ. Affairs 1988-. *Address:* Ministry of Economic Affairs, Slotsholmsgade 12, 1216 Copenhagen K, Denmark. *Telephone:* (01) 11-62-11.

PETERSON, David, B.A., B.L., Q.C.; Canadian politician; b. 28 Dec. 1943, Toronto; s. of Clarence Peterson; m. Shelley Matthews; two s. one d.; ed. Univ. of Western Ont., Univ. of Toronto; called to the Bar 1969; M.P. for

London Centre 1975, re-elected 1977, 1981; elected Leader Ont. Liberal Party 1982, won election for Liberal Party 1985; Premier of Ont. June 1985–; mem. Chamber of Commerce, Young Pres.' Org., Kidney Foundation of Canada (Ont. Branch), Cystic Fibrosis Foundation, YMCA; Fellow, McLaughlin Coll.; Hon. Patron of 1984 Free Olympiad; Pres. London Canadian Club; Liberal. *Address:* Office of the Premier, Queen's Park, Toronto M7A 1A1, Canada. *Telephone:* (416) 965-1931 (Office); (416) 965-1941 (Home).

PETERSON, Martha, PH.D.; American academic; b. 22 June 1916, Jamestown, Kan.; d. of Anton R. and Gail (French) Peterson; ed. Univ. of Kansas, Northwestern and Columbia Univs.; Instructor in Math, Univ. of Kansas 1942–46, Asst. Dean of Women 1946–52, Dean of Women 1952–56; Special Asst. to Pres., Univ. of Wisconsin 1956–63, Univ. Dean for Student Affairs 1963–67; Pres. Barnard Coll. and Dean Columbia Univ. 1967–75; mem. Exec. Bd. Nat. Asscn. of Women Deans and Counsellors 1959–61, Pres. 1965–67; Trustee, Chatham Coll. 1965–; Chair. Exec. Cttee. American Council on Educ. 1971–; Pres. Beloit Coll. 1975–81, Pres. Emer. 1981–; mem. American Asscn. of Univ. Administrators; mem. many other educational cttees. etc.; holds various educational and commercial directorships; several hon. degrees. *Address:* c/o Beloit College, Beloit, Wisconsin 53511, U.S.A.

PETERSON, Oscar Emmanuel, C.C.; Canadian jazz pianist; b. 15 Aug. 1925; s. of Daniel Peterson and Kathleen Peterson; m. 1st Lillian Alice Ann Peterson 1947, two s. three d.; m. 2nd Sandra Cythia King 1966; m. 3rd Charlotte Peterson, one s.; ed. Montreal High School and with private music tutors; 1st prize, amateur show 1940; Carnegie Hall début 1950; numerous concert tours in U.S.A., Canada, Europe, U.K. and Japan; has also performed in S. America, Mexico, West Indies, New Zealand and U.S.S.R.; composer and arranger of numerous pieces; many TV appearances; has won many jazz awards; Hon. LL.D. (Carleton Univ.) 1973, (Queen's Univ., Kingston, Jamaica) 1976; Civic Award of Merit, Toronto 1972; Diplôme d'Honneur, Canadian Conf. of the Arts 1974; named Best Jazz Pianist (13th time), Downbeat Magazine. *Publications:* Oscar Peterson New Piano Solos 1965, Jazz Exercises and Pieces 1965. *Leisure interests:* audio, photography, ham radio, sports. *Address:* 2421 Hammond Road, Mississauga, Ont. L5K 1T3, Canada. *Telephone:* 416/255 5651.

PETERSON, Paul E., PH.D.; American political scientist; b. 16 Sept. 1940, Montevideo, Minn.; s. of Alvin C. Peterson and Josephine M. Telkamp; m. Carol D. Schnell 1963; two s. one d.; ed. Concordia Coll., Moorhead, Minn. and Univ. of Chicago; Asst. Prof., then Assoc. Prof. and Prof., Depts. of Political Science and Educ., Univ. of Chicago 1967–83, Chair. Cttee. on Public Policy Studies 1981–83; Dir. Governmental Studies, The Brookings Inst., Washington, D.C. 1983–87; Benjamin H. Griswold III Prof. of Public Policy, Dept. of Political Science, Johns Hopkins Univ. 1987–; Research Assoc. Nat. Opinion Research Center 1978–83; Acad. Visitor, Dept. of Govt., L.S.E., England 1977–78; John Simon Guggenheim Fellowship, German Marshall Fund of the U.S. Fellowship 1977–78; mem. Nat. Acad. of Educ.; Gladys Kammerer Award for best book publ. 1976 on U.S. nat. policy (for School Politics Chicago Style), Woodrow Wilson Foundation Award for best book publ. 1981 (for City Limits), both from American Political Science Assscn. *Publications:* Urban Politics and Public Policy (with S. David) 1973, Race and Authority in Urban Politics (with J. D. Greenstone) 1973, School Politics Chicago Style 1976, City Limits 1981, The Politics of School Reform, 1870–1940 1985, The New Urban Reality (Ed.) 1985, The New Direction in American Politics (Ed. with J. Chubb) 1985, When Federalism Works (with B. Rabe and K. Wong) 1987. *Leisure interests:* tennis, piano. *Address:* Johns Hopkins University, Baltimore, Md. 21218 (Office); 3411 Ashley Terrace, N.W., Washington, D.C. 20008, U.S.A. (Home).

PETERSON, Peter G., M.B.A.; American business executive and government official; b. 5 June 1926, Kearney, Neb.; s. of George and Venetia (née Paul) Peterson; m. Sally Hornbogen 1953; four s. one d.; ed. Nebraska State Teachers Coll., M.I.T., Northwestern Univ. and Univ. of Chicago; Market Analyst, Market Facts Inc., Chicago 1947–49, Assoc. Dir. 1949–51, Exec. Vice-Pres. 1951–53; Dir. of Marketing Services, McCann-Erickson (advertising firm) 1953, Vice-Pres. 1954–58, Gen. Man. Chicago Office 1955–57, Dir., Asst. to Pres. co-ordinating services regional offices 1957–58; Exec. Vice-Pres. and Dir. Bell & Howell 1958–61, Pres., C.E.O. 1963–71, Chair. of Bd. 1968–71; Asst. to Pres. of U.S.A. for Int. Econ. Affairs 1971–72, also Exec. Dir. Council on Int. Econ. Policy; Sec. of Commerce 1972–73; Chair. Bd. Lehman Bros. Kuhn Loeb Inc. (fmrly. Lehman Bros. Inc.), New York 1973–83; mem. Ind. Comm. on Int. Devt. Issues, Trilateral Comm.; fmr. Dir. First Nat. Bank of Chicago, American Express Co., Illinois Bell Telephone Co.; Dir. Minnesota Mining and Mfg. Co., Federated Dept. Stores, Gen. Foods Corpn., Lehman Corpn., Black and Decker Mfg. Co., Nat. Bureau of Econ. Research, Cities Service Co., RCA Corpn.; Chair. Planning Comm. Illinois, U.S. Council of Int. Chamber of Commerce; Trustee, Council on Foreign Relations, Univ. of Chicago and Museum of Modern Art, New York; Per Jacobsson Lecture 1984. *Address:* 435 E. 52 Street, New York, N.Y., U.S.A.

PETERSON, Roger Tory; American ornithologist; b. 28 Aug. 1908, Jamestown, N.Y.; s. of Charles Gustav Peterson and Henrietta Bader; m. 1st Mildred Washington 1936; m. 2nd Barbara Coulter 1943; two s.; m. 3rd Virginia Westervelt 1976; ed. Nat. Acad. of Design; Art Students' League; decorative artist 1926; Science and Art Instructor, Brookline, Mass. 1931–34; engaged in bird painting and illustration of bird books 1934–; on admin. staff of Nat. Audubon Soc., Sec. 1960–; U.S. Army 1943–45; Ed. Houghton Mifflin Co. Field Guide Series 1946–, Naturalist Series 1965–; f. Roger Tory Peterson Inst. for Study of Natural History 1986–; Art Dir. Nat. Wildlife Fed.; Hon. D.Sc. (Franklin and Marshall Coll., Ohio State Univ., Fairfield Univ., Allegheny Coll., Wesleyan Univ. 1970, Colby Coll. 1974, Gustavus Adolphus Coll. 1978); Hon. D.H. (Hamilton Coll.) 1976; Hon. D.L. (Amherst Coll.) 1977; Hon. D.F.A. (Hartford) 1981, (New York) 1986, (Middlebury Coll.) 1986; numerous medals and awards including Linné Gold Medal of Royal Swedish Acad. of Science 1978, Geoffrey St. Hillaire Gold Medal of French Nat. History Soc. 1958, Officer of Order of the Golden Ark (Netherlands) 1978, Medal of Freedom 1980, Bradford Washburn Awards 1981, Great Swedish Heritage Award 1982 etc. *Publications:* Field Guide to the Birds 1934, Junior Book of Birds 1939, A Field Guide to Western Birds 1941, Birds over America 1948, How to Know the Birds 1949, Wildlife in Color 1951, A Field Guide to the Birds of Britain and Europe (with Guy Mountfort and P. A. D. Hollom) 1954, Wild America (with James Fisher) 1955, The Bird Watcher's Anthology 1957, Field Guide to Birds of Texas 1960, The Wonderful World of Birds (with James Fisher) 1964, Penguins 1979; co-author The Birds 1963, Field Guide to Wildflowers 1968, The Audubon Guide to Attracting Birds, Field Guide to Birds of Mexico 1973; Illustrator: Birds of South Carolina, Birds of Newfoundland, Arizona and its Birdlife, Birds of Nova Scotia, Birds of Colorado, Birds of New York State 1973; Ed.: Field Guide to Edible Wild Plants 1978, Field Guide to the Atmosphere 1981, Field Guide to the Coral Reefs of the Caribbean and Florida 1982. *Leisure interests:* photography (still and motion pictures), travel. *Address:* c/o Houghton-Mifflin Company, 2 Park Street, Boston, Mass. 02108; The Cedars, Neck Road, Old Lyme, Conn. 06371, U.S.A. *Telephone:* 434-7800.

PETERSON, Rudolph A.; American (b. Swedish) banker; b. 6 Dec. 1904, Svenljunga, Sweden; s. of Aaron and Anna (Johannson) Peterson; m. 1st Patricia Price 1927 (deceased), 2nd Barbara Welser Lindsay 1962; one s. one d. four step-c.; ed. Univ. of Calif. (Berkeley) Coll. of Commerce; Field Rep., successively Vice-Pres. and Gen. Man. Mexico City, Div. Operations Man., Chicago, Commercial Credit Co. 1925–36; Dist. Man. Fresno, later Vice-Pres. San Francisco, Bank of America Nat. Trust and Savings Asscn. 1936–46, Vice-Chair. of Bd. of Dirs. 1961–63, Pres. 1963–70, Chair. Exec. Cttee. 1970–75, Hon. Dir. 1975–; Pres. Allied Building Credits 1946–52; Vice-Pres. Transamerica Corpn. 1952–55; Pres. Man. Exec. Officer, Bank of Hawaii, Honolulu 1956–61; Pres. Bank of America Corpn. 1963–70, Chair. Exec. Cttee. 1970–76, Dir. –1981, Hon. Dir. 1981–; Chair. The Asia Foundation 1980, Calif. Acad. of Sciences 1980–, Exec. Comm. Euro-Canadian Bank 1982–; Dir. Alza Corpn., 1969–, Di Giorgio Corpn. 1969–, etc.; Administrator UN Devt. Programme (UNDP) 1972–76; Hon. D.Hum.-Litt. (Univ. of Redlands) 1967, Hon. LL.D. (Univ. of Calif.) 1968, Commdr. Royal Order of Vasa (Sweden) 1964, Grand Cross of Civil Merit of Spain 1965, Order of Merit of Italian Repub. 1967. *Leisure interests:* gardening, fly fishing, historical reading. *Address:* Bank of America Center, San Francisco, Calif. 94137 (Office); 86 Sea View, Piedmont, Calif. 94611, U.S.A. (Home). *Telephone:* (415) 622-6011 (Office); (415)-547-5461 (Home).

PETERSON, Russell Wilbur, PH.D.; American politician and chemist; b. 3 Oct. 1916, Portage, Wis.; s. of John Anton Peterson and Emma Marie Anthony; m. Eva Lillian Turner 1937; two s. two d.; ed. Portage High School and Univ. of Wisconsin; with Du Pont Company for 26 years, various research, sales and man. assignments to Dir. Research and Devt. Div. of Devt. Dept. 1968; Vice-Pres. Nat. Municipal League 1968–78; Gov. of Del. 1969–73; Chair. Cttee. on Law Enforcement, Justice and Public Safety, Nat. Govs. Conf. 1971, Mid-Atlantic Govs. Conf. 1971; Vice-Chair. Council of State Govts. 1971; Chair. President's Nat. Advisory Comm. on Criminal Justice Standards and Goals 1971–72; Chair. of Bd., Textile Inst.; Chair. Exec. Cttee., Comm. on Critical Choices for Americans 1973; Chair. Council on Environmental Quality 1973–76; Pres. and C.E.O. of New Directions, citizens' action org. focused on global problems 1976–77; Special Adviser to Aspen Inst. for Humanistic Studies 1976–77; Dir. A.A.A.S. 1977–82, U.S. Asscn. of Club of Rome 1975–80, Population Crisis Cttee. 1976–, World Wildlife Fund 1976–82, Office of Tech. Assessment, U.S. Congress 1978–79; Pres. Nat. Audubon Soc. 1979–85, Better World Soc. 1985–87; Chair. Advisory Bd. Solar Energy Research Inst. 1979–81; mem. President's Three Mile Island Comm. 1979; Regional Councillor, Int. Union for the Conservation of Nature (IUCN) 1981–85, Vice-Pres. and Regional Councillor 1985–88; Pres. Int. Council for Bird Preservation 1982–; Visiting Prof. Dartmouth Coll. 1985, Carleton Coll. 1986, Univ. of Wisconsin-Madison 1987; mem. Linnaean Soc., American Ornithologists' Union; Hon. D.Sc. (Williams Coll., Butler Univ., Alma Coll., Fairleigh Dickinson) 1976, Hon. Dr. Humanics (Springfield Coll.), Hon. D.Eng. (Stevens Inst. of Tech.), Hon. LL.D. (Gettysburg Coll.), Hon. L.H.D. (Ohio State Univ., Northland Coll.); Vrooman Award 1964, Nat. Conf. of Christians and Jews 1966 Citizenship and Brotherhood Award, Josiah Marvel Cup for Humanitarian and Civic Work, Commercial Devt. Asscn. Honor Award 1971, Gold Medal Award World Wildlife Fund 1971, Golden Plate Award American Acad. of Achievement 1971, Conservationist of the Year, Nat. Wildlife Fed. 1971, Parsons Award, American Chemical Soc. 1974, Proctor

Prize, Swedish American of the Year 1982; Republican. *Publications:* various articles on autoxidation, new product developments, crime reduction, environmental quality, conservation and population. *Leisure interest:* nature study. *Address:* 1613 North Broom, Wilmington, Del. 19806, U.S.A. *Telephone:* (302) 428-0736.

PETERSON, Thage G.; Swedish politician; b. 1933, Berg, Kronoberg; ed. Inst. of Social Studies, Lund 1955–57; Municipal Treas. Community Centre Assen. 1957–59, head 1967–70; Sec. and Vice-Chair. Social Democratic Youth Union 1964; elected to Parl. 1970; Under-Sec. of State to Cabinet 1971–75; Chair. Stockholm County br. of Socialdemokratiska Arbetarepartiet (Social Democratic Labour Party—SDLP) 1974–; mem. SDLP Exec. Cttee. 1975–; Minister without Portfolio 1975; SDLP spokesman for Industrial Policy 1976–82; mem. SDLP Parl. Group Exec. and head of Research Div.; Minister of Industry 1982–88, of Justice 1988; Speaker of Parl. Oct. 1988–. *Address:* The Swedish Parliament, Fack, S-100 12 Stockholm, Sweden.

PETERSON, Walter; American politician, educationist and real estate executive; b. 19 Sept. 1922, Nashua, New Hampshire; s. of Walter and Helen Reed Peterson; m. Dorothy Donovan 1949; one s. one d.; ed. New Hampton School, Coll. of William and Mary, Univ. of New Hampshire, Dartmouth; formed real estate firm 'The Petersons' with father and brother 1948, now Realtor and Treas.; elected to New Hampshire House of Reps. 1961, Majority Leader 1963, Speaker of the House 1965–68; Gov. of New Hampshire 1969–73; Partner Petersons Inc. 1973–; Pres. Franklin Pierce Coll., New Hampshire 1976–; Chair. N.H. Post Secondary Educ. Comm.; Vice-Chair. N.H. Coll. and Univ. Council; Pres. Finlay Hosp. Bd. 1983–84; Dir. Nat. Assen. of Ind. Colls. and Univs.; Dir. Monadnock Bank, Jaffrey, N.H.; Republican. *Address:* Franklin Pierce College, Rindge, New Hampshire 03461 (Office); East Mountain Road, Peterborough, N.H. 03458, U.S.A. (Home). *Telephone:* 603-924-3259.

PETHRICK, Richard Arthur, PH.D., F.R.S.C., F.R.S.E., C. CHEM.; British professor of chemistry; b. 26 Oct. 1942, Yate; s. of Arthur T. A. Pethrick and Lavinia M. Pethrick; m. Joan Knowles Hume 1975; one s.; ed. Univs. of London and Salford; Lecturer, Dept. of Pure and Applied Chem. Univ. of Strathclyde 1970, Sr. Lecturer 1978, Reader 1981, Prof. of Chem. 1983–; mem. Editorial Bd. British Polymer Journal 1979–; Ed. Polymer Yearbook 1983–; Visiting Prof. Univ. of Punjab 1979; British Council Visiting Lecturer, Australia 1985, 1989; mem. Int. Swedish Tech. Review Cttee. for Polymer Science 1988. *Publications:* Molecular Motion in High Polymers 1979; over 200 scientific papers and numerous book chapters and review articles. *Leisure interests:* Scottish country dancing, walking. *Address:* 40 Langside Drive, Newlands, Glasgow, G43 2QQ, Scotland. *Telephone:* 041-552 4400 Ext. 2260/2795 (Office); 041-637 5134 (Home).

PETIT, Eugène Pierre (see Claudius-Petit, Eugène Pierre).

PETIT, Pierre, L. ÈS L.; French composer; b. 21 April 1922, Poitiers; s. of Roger and Yvonne (née Bouchet) Petit; m. 3rd Liliane Fiaux 1974; four s. one d. from previous marriages; ed. Lycée Louis-le-Grand, Université de Paris à la Sorbonne and Conservatoire de Paris; Head of Course, Conservatoire de Paris 1951–; Dir. of Light Music, Office de Radiodiffusion et Télévision Française (ORTF) 1960–64, Dir. of Musical Productions, ORTF 1964–70, Chamber Music 1970–; Producer, Radio-Télévision luxembourgeoise (R.T.L.) 1980; Dir.-Gen. Ecole Normale de Musique de Paris 1963–; Pres. Jury Concours Int. Marguerite Long 1981–; Music Critic, Figaro; mem. Gov. Council Conservatoire de Paris; Vice-Pres. soc. des auteurs et compositeurs dramatiques 1985–; Chevalier, Légion d'honneur, Officier des Arts et Lettres, Ordre nationale du Mérite, Officier de l'Ordre du Cèdre du Liban; Premier Grand Prix de Rome 1946. *Compositions include:* Suite for four 'cellos 1945, Zadig (ballet) 1948, Ciné-Bijou (ballet) 1952, Feu rouge, feu vert 1954, Concerto for piano and orchestra 1956, Concerto for organ and orchestra 1960, Furia Italiana 1960, Concerto for two guitars and orchestra 1965. *Publications:* Verdi 1957, Ravel 1970. *Address:* 114 bis boulevard Malesherbes, 75017 Paris (Office); 16 avenue de Villiers, 75017 Paris, France (Home).

PETIT, Roland; French dancer and choreographer; b. 13 Jan. 1924, Villemomble; s. of Edmond and Victoria (née Repetto) Petit; m. Zizi Jeanmaire (q.v.) 1954; one s.; ed. Paris Opera Ballet School; Premier Danseur Paris Opera 1940–44; founded Les Vendredis de la Danse 1944, Les Ballets de Champs-Elysées 1945, Les Ballets de Paris 1948; Dir. Paris Opera Ballet 1970; founded Les Ballets de Marseilles; Chevalier, Légion d'honneur, Chevalier des Arts et des Lettres. *Works include:* Le rossignol et la rose, Le jeune homme et la mort, Les demoiselles de la nuit, Deuil en vingtquatre heures, Le loup, Cyrano de Bergerac, Carmen, Les forains, La belle au bois dormant, Hans Christian Andersen, Folies Bergères, L'éloge de la folie, Paradise Lost, Pelléas et Mélisande, Les intermittences du coeur 1975, La symphonie fantastique 1975, Die Fledermaus 1980, Soirée Debussy, Le mariage du ciel et de l'enfer 1985. *Address:* Ballet National de Marseille, 1 place Auguste-Carli, 13001 Marseille, France.

PETITMENGIN, Jacques; French engineer; b. 19 Jan. 1928, Paris; s. of Georges Petitmengin and Louise Diény; m. Magali Noyer 1952; three s. one d.; ed. Charlemagne and Saint Louis Schools, Ecole Polytechnique and Ecole Nat. Supérieure des Mines de Paris; Tech. Consultant Bureau of Oil Exploration 1952–58, Gen. Attaché S.N. Repal 1958–62, Industrial and

Commercial Dir. 1962–67; Dir. for Chem., Charbonnages de France (CdF) 1965–67, Chair. Bd. of Dirs. CdF, Chimie, Chem. Soc. of Collieries 1967–80, Pres. Supervisory Bd. CdF Chimie 1980–82, Dir.-Gen. CdF 1980–82, Chief Exec. 1982–; Chair. Gazocéan 1983–; Vice-Pres. Union of Chemical Industries 1977–80; Pres. Admin. Bd. Ecole nat. supérieure de chimie de Lille 1974–77; Chevalier, Légion d'honneur, Chevalier des Palmes académiques, Officier, Ordre nat. du Mérite, Officier, Ordre de la Couronne (Belgium). *Address:* 39 rue Saint-Charles, 78000 Versailles, France.

PETRASSI, Goffredo; Italian composer; b. 16 July 1904, Zagarolo; s. of Eliseo Petrassi and Erminia Calzoletti; m. Rosetta Acerbi 1962; one d.; ed. Conservatorio S. Cecilia, Rome; Supt. Teatro Fenice, Venice 1937–40; Pres. Int. Soc. for Contemporary Music 1954–56; now Prof. of Composition, Accad. S. Cecilia. *Works include:* orchestral: Partita 1932, First Concerto 1933, Second Concerto 1951, Récréation Concertante (Third Concerto) 1953, Fourth Concerto 1954, Fifth Concerto 1955, Invenzione Concertata 1957, Quartet 1957; operas and ballets: Follia di Orlando 1943, Ritratto di don Chisciotte 1945, Il Cordovano 1948, Morte dell'Aria 1950; choral works: Salmo IX 1936, Magnificat 1940, Coro di Morti 1941, Noche Oscura 1951, Mottetti 1965; voice and orchestra Quattro Inni Sacre 1942; chamber music: Serenata 1958, Trio 1959, Suoni Notturni 1959, Propos d'Alain 1960, Concerto Flauto 1960, Seconda Serenata-Trio 1962, Settimo Concerto 1964, Estri 1966–67, Beatitudines 1968, Ottetto di Ottori 1968, Souffle 1969, Ottavo Concerto 1970–72, Elogio 1971, Nunc 1971, Ala 1972, Orationes Christi 1975, Alias 1977, Grand Septuor 1978, Violasola 1978, Flou 1980, Romanzetta 1980, Poema 1977–80, Sestina d'Autunno 1981–82, Laudes Creaturarum 1982. *Address:* Via Ferdinando di Savoia 3, 00196 Rome, Italy. *Telephone:* 3601056.

PETRI, Carl Axel Henrik; Swedish lawyer and politician; b. 12 Aug. 1929, Ronneby; s. of Carl and Maud Petri; m. Brita Thulin 1953; one s. one d.; ed. Univ. of Lund; Asst. Judge 1963; Judge, Nat. Social Insurance Court 1964–72; Deputy Pres. Administrative Court of Appeal, Stockholm 1972–76, Pres. Court of Appeal Jönköping 1976–79; Minister of Energy 1979–81, of Justice 1981–82. *Address:* Riksdaghuset, 10012 Stockholm 46, Sweden.

PETRI, Michala; Danish musician; b. 7 July 1958, Copenhagen; d. of Kanny Sambleben and Hanne Petri; ed. Staatliche Hochschule für Musik und Theater, Hanover; recorder player; first appearance in Danish Radi 1963; first concert as soloist in Tivoli 1969; since 1969 has toured extensively all over the world; several prizes. *Publications:* ed. of several works for Wilhelm Hansen. *Leisure interests:* walking in the forest with the dog, reading. *Address:* Nöddehegnet 30, Nödebo, 3480 Fredensborg, Denmark. *Telephone:* 02 28 19 58.

PETRICIOLI, Gustavo, M. PHIL.; Mexican politician; b. 19 Aug. 1928, Mexico City; s. of Carlos Petricioli Alarcon and Ada Iturbide Preciat; m. Maria Luisa Castellon Cervantes; two s. two d.; ed. Autonomous Technology Inst. of Mexico and Yale Univ.; Prof. and Dean, Autonomous Technology Inst. of Mexico 1952–70; various appts. Bank of Mexico 1948–67; Dir. of Finance Studies, Secr. of Treasury and Public Finance 1967–70, Under-Sec. of Revenue 1970–74; Pres. Nat. Comm. of Stocks 1976–82; Gen. Dir. Multibanco Comermex 1982; Gen. Co-ordinator, Mexican Bank Assen. 1982; Gen. Dir. Nacional Financiera (NAFINSA) 1982–86; Sec. of Treasury and Public Finance 1986; Sec. of Finance and Public Credit June 1986–88; Amb. to U.S.A. Dec. 1988–; decorations from Japan, Chile, Brazil and U.S.A. *Address:* Mexican Embassy, 2829 16th Street, N.W., Washington, D.C. 20009, U.S.A.

PETRIE, Sir Peter, BT., C.M.G.; British diplomatist; b. 7 March 1932, London; s. of Sir Charles Petrie, Bt., C.B.E. and Lady Petrie; m. Countess Lydwine von Oberndorff 1958; two s. one d.; ed. Westminster School and Christ Church, Oxford; Second Sec. U.K. del to NATO 1958–62; First Sec. New Delhi 1961–63; Chargé d'affaires, Kathmandu 1963–64; Cabinet Office, London 1965–67; FCO 1967–69; First Sec. later Counsellor, U.K. Perm. Mission at UN, New York 1969–73; Counsellor, Bonn 1973–76; FCO 1976–79; Minister, Paris 1979–85; Amb. to Belgium 1985–. *Leisure interests:* gardening, golf. *Address:* 40 rue Lauriston, 75116 Paris, France; 16a Cambridge Street, London, SW1V 4QH, England.

PETRIGNANI, Rinaldo; Italian diplomatist; b. 18 Dec. 1927; m.; two c.; ed. Univ. of Rome; joined Ministry of Foreign Affairs 1949; Deputy Perm Rep. to Council of Europe 1953; served at Consulate-Gen., New York, subsequently at Embassy, Washington 1957–68; Head, Bureau of Disarmament and Nuclear Affairs, Asst. Dir.-Gen. of Political Affairs, Diplomatic Counsellor to Pres. of Council of Ministers, Dir. Cabinet of Ministers of Foreign Affairs 1968–76; Head, Italian Perm. Mission to Int. Orgs. in Geneva 1976; Deputy Sec.-Gen. NATO 1978; Amb. to U.S.A. July 1981–. *Address:* Embassy of Italy, 1601 Fuller Street, N.W., Washington, D.C. 20009, U.S.A.

PETRILLI, Giuseppe; Italian administrator; b. 24 March 1913, Naples; s. of Michele Petrilli and Anna Pellegrino; m. Angela Robèrti 1939; one s. two d.; ed. Univ. of Rome; Pres. Inst. Nat. d'Assurances contre les maladies 1950–58; mem. Council of Economy and Work; mem. EEC Comm., Pres. Social Affairs Section 1958–60; Pres. Inst. for Industrial Reconstruction (IRI) 1960–79; Sec.-Gen. of the European Christian Democratic Union (UEDC) 1978–82; Pres. Int. Council of European Movement 1981–85;

Senator of the Republic 1979-87; Cavaliere del Lavoro 1965. *Address:* Via T. Salvini 55, 00197 Rome, Italy.

PETRISHCHEV, Alexei Georgiyevich; Soviet politician; b. 2 April 1924, Dniepropetrovsk; m.; three c.; ed. Dniepropetrovsk Chemico-technological Inst.; mem. CPSU 1951-; foreman, technician at workshop, Deputy Chief Technician and Chief Technician of a plant; Sec. Plant Party Cttee. 1959-62; Dir. M. I. Kalinin chemical complex, Chernorechensk 1962; Head Soyuzazot Co.; Vice-Chair. State Cttee. on Material and Tech. Deliveries 1977-80; Minister of Fertilizer Production 1980-86; Cand. mem. CPSU Cen. Cttee. 1986-; Deputy to U.S.S.R. Supreme Soviet, 7th and 8th convocations; Hero of Socialist Labour 1971, Order of Lenin 1984. *Address:* c/o Ministry of Fertilizer Production, ulitsa Gritsebets 2/16, Moscow, U.S.S.R.

PETROSIAN, Suren Martirosovich; Soviet worker and politician; b. 23 May 1925, Sevan Tsovagyugh; s. of Martiros Aleksandrovich Petrosian and Anahit Markarovna Varakian; m. Emma Oganesovna Shakhverdian 1950; one s. one d.; ed. secondary school; worker at S. M. Kirov plant, Yerevan 1940-43, foreman 1948-; Soviet Army service 1943-48; mem. CPSU 1951-; mem. Cen. Cttee. of Armenian CP; Deputy to U.S.S.R. Supreme Soviet (Soviet of Nationalities) 1962-70; Vice-Chair. of Soviet of Nationalities 1966-70; Hero of Socialist Labour, Order of Lenin, Hammer and Sickle Gold Medal etc. *Leisure interest:* fiction. *Address:* S. M. Kirov Plant, Yerevan, Armenian S.S.R., U.S.S.R.

PETROV, Boris Nikolayevich; Soviet composer; b. 1930; ed. Leningrad Conservatory; mem. CPSU 1957-; State Prize 1967, 1976, U.S.S.R. People's Artist 1980; *Compositions include:* Radda and Loiko (Symphonic poem), The Postmaster (after Pushkin), Shore of Hope, The Creation of the World (ballets), Peter the Great (opera), Pushkin (choral work); also operettas, songs, film music.

PETROV, Rem Viktorovich; DR.MED.SC.; Soviet immunologist; b. 1930; ed. Voronezh Medical Inst.; mem. CPSU 1956-; research work at various grades in U.S.S.R. Ministry of Health Inst. of Bio-Physics 1959-83, Head of Lab. 1983-; Dir. of U.S.S.R. Ministry of Health Inst. of Immunology 1983-; mem. of Acad. of Medical Sciences 1978-; concurrently Head of Dept. of Immunology of Second Moscow Inst. of Immunology 1974-; mem. U.S.S.R. Acad. of Sciences 1984-, Vice-Pres. 1988-. *Address:* c/o U.S.S.R. Academy of Sciences, Moscow V-71, Leninsky Pr. 14, U.S.S.R.

PETROV, Marshal Vasiliy Ivanovich; Soviet army officer; b. 2 Jan. 1917, Chernolesskoye, Stavropol; ed. Frunze Mil. Acad. and Gen. Staff Mil. Acad. served in Soviet Army 1939-; mem. CPSU 1944-; command posts on Southern , Crimean, North Caucasian, Trans-Caucasian, Steppes, Voronezh, First and Second Ukrainian Fronts 1941-45; Chief of Staff and First Deputy Commdr. 1966-72; rank of Gen. 1969; Commdr. of Soviet Troops in Far East Dist. 1972-; mem. Cen. Cttee. CPSU 1976-89; C.-in-C. of Soviet Ground Forces 1980-; First Deputy Minister of Defence 1985-86; U.S.S.R. Gen. Inspectorate, Ministry of Defence 1986-; Marshal of U.S.S.R. 1983; Hero of Socialist Labour 1982. *Address:* The Kremlin, Moscow, U.S.S.R.

PETROV, Marshal Vladimir Mikhailovich; Soviet trade corporation official; b. 20 July 1922; ed. Industrial Inst. of the Urals and Acad. of Foreign Trade; Soviet Baltic Fleet 1939-42; foundry worker 1940-42; Asst. Dir., later Dir., Electrical Eng. Office, Mashinoimport (mining, electrical, railway goods, etc.) 1949-51; other posts, Mashinoimport, then Mashinoexport 1951-55; Asst. Soviet Trade Rep. in Yugoslavia 1956-59; Soviet Trade Rep. in Iraq 1959-61; fmr. Chair. Autoexport (automobiles); mem. CPSU; rank of Marshal 1983; several decorations. *Address:* c/o Autoexport, Ministry of Foreign Trade, 32-34 Smolenskaya-Sennaya ploshchad, Moscow, U.S.S.R.

PETROVICHEV, Nikolai Alexandrovich; Soviet politician; b. 1918; ed. Moscow Regional Teachers Training Inst.; mem. CPSU 1939; from 1932 fitter's apprentice, Kirov Works Training School, Leningrad, fitters' team leader 1934-37; Deputy Sec. of YCL Cttee 1937-, then Asst. Dir. of the plant's training school for political work; military-political work in Soviet Army 1938-46; Instructor, Tushino City Cttee. of CPSU 1947; Instructor, Head of Sector, Sec. of Party Cttee., of Moscow Regional Cttee., CPSU 1950; First Sec. of Krasnogorsk City Cttee. of CPSU 1954; Head of Dept. of Agitation and Propaganda 1958, then Head of Party Bodies Dept. of Moscow Regional Cttee of CPSU; Head of Sector, Deputy Head of Dept. for Party Bodies of CPSU Cen. Cttee. for R.S.F.S.R. 1961-65; Deputy Head of Dept. of Organizational-Party Work, CPSU Cen. Cttee. 1966-68; First Deputy Head of Dept. of Organizational-Party Work, CPSU Cen. Cttee. 1968-; mem. of Comm. for Foreign Affairs, Soviet of Nationalities; cand. mem. of CPSU Cen. Cttee. 1971-81, mem. 1981-; Deputy to U.S.S.R. Supreme Soviet (10th Convocation); Deputy to Soviet of Nationalities from Odessa Constituency No. 53, Ukrainian S.S.R.; Chair. of U.S.S.R. State Cttee. for Vocational Tech. Educ. 1983-. *Address:* Sadovaya-Sukharevskaya ulitsa 16, Moscow, U.S.S.R.

PETROVICS, Emil; Hungarian composer; b. 9 Feb. 1930, Nagybecskerek (now Zrenjanin, Yugoslavia); s. of Jovan Petrovics and Erzsébet Weninger; m. Eva Brunovszky; one d.; studied at Conservatory, graduated at Music Acad. of Budapest; Musical dir. Petőfi Theatre 1960-64; lecturer Coll. of Dramatic and Cinematographic Arts 1964-; Prof. of Composition Music

Acad., Budapest; Dir. Hungarian State Opera 1986-; mem. of Hungarian Parl. 1967-85; Erkel Prize 1960, 1963, Kossuth Prize 1966, holder of titles Merited Artist 1975, Eminent Artist 1982. *Compositions for musical stage:* C'est la guerre (single act) 1961, Crime and Punishment 1969; Book of Jonah (oratorio) 1965; Lysistrate (comic opera for concert performance) 1962 (all performed in Czechoslovakia, Finland, France, Fed. Repub. of Germany, Hungary and Yugoslavia); Salome (ballet) 1984; 2nd to 5th Cantatas: There Let Me Die 1972, Fanny's Posthumous Papers 1978, We All Must Go 1980, Letters from Turkey 1981, 6th Cantata: We Take a Rest. *Instrumental music:* Concerto for Flute 1957, String Quartet 1958, Symphony for Strings 1964, Quintet for Winds 1966; other works for chorus, incidental film and stage music. *Publication:* Ravel 1959. *Leisure interest:* child raising. *Address:* Dutka Ákos utca 30, H-1029 Budapest, Hungary. *Telephone:* 167-864.

PETROVSKY, Boris Vasiliyevich; Soviet surgeon; b. 27 June 1908, Essentuki; s. of Vasiliy and Lydia Petrovsky; m. Ekaterina Timofeeva; one d.; ed. First Moscow Univ.; physician at various hospitals 1930-50; mem. CPSU 1942-; Head of Chair of Surgery, Second Moscow Inst. of Medicine 1951-56; Head of Chair of Hospital Surgery, First Moscow Medical Inst., and Dir. Inst. of Clinical and Experimental Surgery 1956-; Minister of Health of U.S.S.R. 1965-80; Deputy to U.S.S.R. Supreme Soviet 1962-; Cand. mem. Cen. Cttee. of CPSU 1966-; mem. U.S.S.R. Acad. of Medical Sciences 1957-; mem. U.S.S.R. Acad. of Sciences 1966-; Honoured Scientific Worker of R.S.F.S.R., Lenin Prize, Hero of Socialist Labour 1968, Order of Lenin (four times), Order of October Revolution, "Hammer and Sickle" Gold Medal and other awards. Main works: has studied problems of blood transfusion, oncology, surgery of vessels and organs of thoracic cavity, surgical treatment of congenital and acquired heart diseases, kidney transplant. *Publications:* Drip Transfusion of Blood and Blood-Substitute Compounds 1948, Surgical Treatment of Vascular Wounds 1949, Surgical Treatment of Carcinoma of the Oesophagus and Cardia 1950, Blood Transfusion in Surgery 1954, Surgery of Mediastinum 1960, Surgery of patent arterial duct 1963, Cardiac aneurysms 1965, Resection & plastic repair of bronchi 1966, Prosthetic replacement of heart valves 1966, Surgery of diaphragm 1966, Oesophageal diverticuli 1968, Surgery for renovascular hypertension 1968, Selected lectures in clinical surgery 1968, Kidney transplantation 1969, Surgery of aortic arch branches 1970, Surgery of peripheral vessels 1970, Atlas of thoracic surgery 1973-74, Surgical hepatology 1972, Microsurgery 1976, Basics of Hyperbaric Medicine 1976, Tracheo-Bronchial Surgery 1978, Surgical Treatment of Chronic Ischemic Heart Diseases 1978, Surgical Diseases 1980, Reconstructive Surgery for extrabiliary Duct Disorders 1980, Emergency Cardiovascular Surgery 1980. *Leisure interests:* book collection and gardening. *Address:* c/o National Research Centre for Surgery, Abrikosovskyi 2, Moscow 119874, U.S.S.R.

PETRUSHEVSKAYA, Lyudmila; Soviet playwright; b. 1938, Moscow; ed. Moscow Univ.; journalist 1960-71; started writing 1963; one act plays performed in Moscow 1987. *Publicaions include:* Cinzano 1978, Smirnova's Birthday 1978, Love 1979, Music Lessons 1979, Three Girls in Blue 1985.

PETRY, Heinz, DIPL. ING; German industrial executive; b. 12 Jan. 1919, Rheinhausen; s. of Heinrich Petry and Elise Petry (née Maas); m. Liselotte Petry (née Gebauer) 1945; two s. one d.; ed. Berlin Tech. Coll., Stuttgart Univ.; construction engineer in dredger mfg., Krupp Industrie- und Stahlbau, Rheinhausen 1946, Deputy Head of Dept. 1950, given proxy of firm 1961, Head of Dept. 1962, Deputy mem. of Man. Bd. 1965, mem. 1966, Spokesman 1973; mem. Man. Bd., Friedrich Krupp GmbH, Essen 1974-, Deputy Chair. 1975-76, Chair. 1976-80; mem. Supervisory Bd. AG Weser, Bremen, Krupp-Koppers GmbH, Essen. *Leisure interests:* hunting, golf, films. *Address:* Krupp-Koppers GmbH, Limbecker Platz 1, 4300 Essen 1, Federal Republic of Germany. *Telephone:* (0201) 188-2100.

PETTENGILL, Gordon Hemenway, PH.D.; American professor of planetary physics; b. 10 Feb. 1926, Providence, R.I.; s. of Rodney G. Pettengill and Frances (Hemenway) Pettengill; m. Pamela Wolfenden 1967; one s. one d.; ed. M.I.T. and Univ. of California at Berkeley; staff mem., M.I.T. Lincoln Lab. 1954-68, Assoc. Leader, Haystack Observatory 1965-68; Dir. Arecibo Observatory, Puerto Rico (operated by Cornell Univ.) 1968-70; Prof. of Planetary Physics, Dept. of Earth and Planetary Sciences, M.I.T. 1970-; Dir. M.I.T. Center for Space Research 1984-; involved in the study of the solar system using radar and radio techniques; discovered 3/2 spin-orbit resonance of Mercury 1965; pioneered delay-doppler radar mapping of planets; prin. investigator of Pioneer Venus Radar Mapper 1978-81; mem. N.A.S., American Acad. of Arts and Sciences, A.A.A.S., American Physical Soc., American Astronomical Soc., Int. Radio Science Union; Guggenheim Fellow 1980/81. *Leisure interests:* ornithology, sailing. *Address:* Center for Space Research, 37-241, Massachusetts Institute of Technology, Cambridge, Mass. 02139, U.S.A. *Telephone:* (617) 253-7501.

PETTERSON, Donald K., M.A.; American diplomatist; b. 17 Nov. 1930, Huntington Park, Calif.; s. of Walter H. Petterson and Muriel F. (née McIntyre) Petterson; m. Julietta Rovirosa Argudín 1961; two s. two d.; ed. Univ. of Calif., Santa Barbara, Univ. Coll. L.A. and Stanford Univ.; analyst, State of Calif. Personnel Bd. 1958-59; Teaching Asst., Univ. Coll. L.A. 1959-60; Foreign Service Officer, Dept. of State 1960, Personnel Officer 1968-70; Vice-Consul, Mexico City 1961-62; Vice-Consul, Consul,

Prin. Officer, Zanzibar 1963–65; Personnel Officer, Dept. of State 1968–70; Political Office, Lagos 1966–67; Deputy Chief of Mission, Freetown 1970–72; Political Adviser, Pretoria 1972–75; mem., Policy Planning Dept. of State 1975–77; Dir., Office of S. African Affairs 1977–78; Deputy Asst. Sec. of State for African Affairs 1978; Amb. to Somalia 1978–82, to Tanzania 1986–; Visiting Distinguished Scholar, Univ. Coll. L.A. 1983–84; Deputy Dir., Office of Man. Operations, Dept. of State 1984–86; Superior Honour award 1964, 1972. *Publications:* articles in learned journals. *Leisure interests:* reading, running, tennis. *Address:* Department of State, Washington D.C. 20520, U.S.A.

PETTITI, Louis Edmond; French barrister; b. 14 Jan. 1916, Asnières; s. of Louis Pettiti and Clothile Mussino; m. Zina Cyrin 1952; two s.; ed. Park Univ.; joined the Bar, Paris 1935, Pres. 1978–79; Judge European Court of Human Rights 1980–; Vice-Pres. Soc. de législation comparée 1977; Pres. Soc. des Prisons 1985–88; mem. Nat. Cttee. of Human Rights 1985–89, French Branch, UNESCO 1985–89, Bicentenary Mission 1987–89; UNESCO Prize 1978; Commdr., Ordre nat. du Mérite, Officer, Légion d'honneur. *Publications:* le procès Charansky 1979, Mission en Iran 1982, Audio Visuel (with others), Liberté religion. *Address:* 4 square La Bruyère, 75009 Paris, France.

PEUGEOT, Roland; French motor-car executive; b. 20 March 1926, Valentigney; s. of Jean-Pierre and Colette (née Boillat-Japy) Peugeot; m. Colette Mayesky 1949; two s.; ed. Lycées Janson-de-Sailly and Saint-Louis, Paris, and Harvard Business School, Mass., U.S.A.; Pres. Etablissements Peugeot Frères 1959–; Pres. du Conseil de Surveillance de Peugeot S.A. 1972–; mem. Bd. Automobiles Peugeot 1982–; Dir. of subsidiaries and other cos.; Officier, Légion d'honneur, Officier des Arts et des Lettres. *Address:* 75 avenue de la Grande Armée, 75116 Paris (Office); 170 avenue Victor-Hugo, 75116 Paris, France (Home).

PEYNAUD, Emile Jean Pierre, PH.D.; French oenologist and engineer; b. 29 June 1912, Bordeaux; s. of Antoine Peynaud and Alexine (née Ferrier) Peynaud; m. Yvonne Jameau 1938; one s. one d.; ed. Bordeaux Faculty of Science; Oenologist for Calvet, Bordeaux 1928–49; Head of Research, Bordeaux Centre of Oenology and Head of Educ., Bordeaux Inst. of Oenology 1949–77; Tech. Adviser on Oenology, France and abroad; mem. French Soc. and Soc. of Expert Chemsits; Chevalier, Légion d'honneur; Officier des Palmes Académiques et du Mérite Agricole. *Publications:* Traité d'Oenologie, 1947, Knowing and Making Wine 1986, The Taste of wine 1987, Le Vin et Les Jours 1988; 300 articles and scientific papers. *Address:* 26, Avenue Maréchal-de-Lattre-de-Tassigny, 33400 Talence, France.

PEYREFITTE, Alain; French diplomatist, politician and writer; b. 26 Aug. 1925, Najac, Aveyron; s. of Jean and Augustine (Roux) Peyrefitte; m. Monique Luton 1948; one s. four d.; ed. Lycée de Montpellier, Univ. of Montpellier, Paris (Sorbonne), Ecole Normale Supérieure, Ecole Nationale d'Administration; Sec. Bonn 1949–52; Chargé, quai d'Orsay and Lecturer, Ecole Nat. d'Admin. 1952–54; Consul-Gen., Cracow 1954–56; Deputy Dir. of European Orgs. 1956–58; Counsellor of Foreign Affairs 1958; elected Deputy for Seine-et-Marne, Nat. Ass. 1958, 1962, 1967, 1968, 1973, 1978, defeated 1981 but won by-election 1982, elected 1986, 1988; Mayor of Provins 1965–; Rep. European Parl. and UN Gen. Ass. 1959–62; Sec. of State to Prime Minister (Information) April 1962, Minister for Repatriates Sept. 1962; Minister for Information 1962–66; Minister for Scientific Research and Atomic Questions 1966–67; Minister of Educ. 1967–68; Chair. Comm. of Cultural Educ. and Social Affairs, Nat. Ass. 1968–72; Rep. at UN Gen. Ass. 1969–71; Sec.-Gen. UDR (Gaullist Party) 1972–73; Minister of Admin. Reform and Planning 1973–74, of Culture and the Environment March-May 1974, of Justice 1977–81; mem. Acad. Française 1977–, Acad. of Moral and Political Sciences 1987–; Ed.-in-Chief Le Figaro 1983–; Chevalier Légion d'honneur, Commdr. des Palmes académiques, des Arts et Lettres. *Publications:* Rue d'Ulm, Le sentiment de confiance, Les roseaux froissés, Le mythe de Pénélope, Faut-il partager l'Algérie?, Quand la Chine s'éveillera, Le mal français, Réponses à la violence, Les chevaux du lac Ladoga (La Justice entre les extrêmes), Quand la rose se fanera, Chine immuable et changeante, Encore un effort, M. le Président, L'aventure du XXᵉ siècle, L'Empire immobile. *Leisure interests:* skiing, water skiing, riding. *Address:* 111 Rue du Ranelagh, Paris 16e., France.

PEYREFITTE, (Pierre) Roger, B.A.; French author; b. 17 Aug. 1907, Castres (Tarn); s. of Jean Peyrefitte and Eugénie Jamme; unmarried; ed. Coll. d'Ardouane (Hérault), du Caousou (Toulouse), Lycée (Foix), Toulouse Univ., Ecole des Sciences Politiques, Paris; joined Diplomatic Service 1931; Attaché, Ministry of Foreign Affairs 1931–33, 1938–40; Sec. Athens 1933–38; resigned 1940; re-instated 1943, mem. Del. of French Govt. in occupied France 1943–44; dismissed 1945; re-instated by judgement of Council of State 1962; judgement cancelled 1978. *Publications:* Les amitiés particulières (Prix Théophraste Renaudot) 1944–45, Mademoiselle de Murville 1946, Le prince des neiges 1947, L'oracle 1948, Les amours singulières 1949, La mort d'une mère 1950, Les ambassades 1951, Du Vésuve à l'Etna 1952, La fin des ambassades 1953, Les clés de St. Pierre 1955, Jeunes proies 1956, Chevaliers de Malte 1957, L'exilé de Capri 1959, Le spectateur nocturne 1960, Les fils de la lumière 1961, La nature du prince 1963, Les Juifs 1965, Notre amour 1967, Les Américains 1968, Des Français 1970, La Coloquinte 1971, Manouche 1972, La muse garçonnière 1973, Tableaux

de chasse ou la vie extraordinaire de Fernand Legros 1976, Propos secrets 1977, La jeunesse d'Alexandre 1977, L'enfant de coeur 1978, Roy 1979, Les conquêtes d'Alexandre 1979, Propos Secrets II 1980, Alexandre le Grand 1981, L'Illustre écrivain 1982, La soutane rouge 1983, Voltaire, sa Jeunesse et son Temps 1985, L'innominato, nouveaux propos secrets 1989. *Leisure interests:* walking, collection of antiques. *Address:* 9 avenue du Maréchal Maunoury, 75016 Paris, France.

PEYRELEVADE, Jean; French business executive; b. 1939; fmr. armaments and aviation engineer; Dir. Dept. of Foreign Business, Crédit Lyonnais 1973–82; Asst. Dir. Cabinet of M Pierre Mauroy 1982; Pres. Cie. Financière de Suez 1983–86; Pres. Banque Stern 1986–88; Chair. Union des Assurances de Paris 1988–. *Address:* Union des Assurances de Paris, Tour Assur, Cedex 14, 92083 Paris La Défense, France.

PEYTON OF YEOVIL, Baron (Life Peer), cr. 1983, of Yeovil in the County of Somerset; **John Wynne William Peyton,** P.C.; British politician; b. 13 Feb. 1919, London; m. Mary Constance Wyndham 1966; one s. one d.; ed. Eton Coll. and Trinity Coll. Oxford; called to the Bar 1945; Conservative M.P. for Yeovil 1951–83; Parl. Sec., Ministry of Power 1962–64; Minister for Transport Industries 1970–74; Shadow Leader of Commons 1974–76; Opposition Spokesman for Agric. 1976–79; Chair. Texas Instruments Ltd. 1974–; Chair. British Alcan Aluminium PLC 1987–; Dir. Alcan Aluminium Ltd., London and Manchester Group PLC; Chair. Zoo Operations Ltd. 1988–. *Address:* 6 Temple West Mews, London, S.E.11, also The Old Malt House, Hinton St. George, Somerset, England (Homes).

PFAFF, Judy; American artist; b. 22 Sept. 1946, London, England; ed. Wayne State Univ., Detroit, S. Illinois Univ., Univ. of Washington and Yale Univ.; numerous solo exhbns. including Webb & Parsons Gallery, New York 1974 and Daniel Weinberg Gallery, Los Angeles 1984; numerous group exhbns. including Razor Gallery, New York 1973 and Holly Solomon Gallery, New York 1984, Whitney Museum of American Art, Contemporary Art Museum, Houston, Tex., Wacoal Art Center, Tokyo, Japan, Brooklyn Museum, Venice Biennale, Museum of Modern Art, New York; Guggenheim Fellowship for Sculpture. *Address:* c/o Holly Solomon Gallery Inc., 724 Fifth Avenue, New York, N.Y. 10019, U.S.A. *Telephone:* 757-7777.

PFAFFMANN, Carl, M.SC., PH.D., D.SC.; American physiological psychologist; b. 27 May 1913, New York City; s. of Charles Pfaffmann and Anna Haaker Pfaffmann; m. Louise Brooks Pfaffmann; two s. (one deceased) one d.; ed. Brown, Oxford and Cambridge Univs.; Research Assoc., Johnson Foundation, Univ. of Pennsylvania 1939–40; Lieut. to Commdr., Aviation Psychologist, U.S. N.R. 1942–45; Asst. Prof. to Prof., Brown Univ., Providence, R.I. 1945–65; Vice-Pres. Rockefeller Univ. 1965–78, Prof. 1965–80, Vincent and Brooke Astor Prof. 1980–83, Prof. Emer. 1983–; Visiting Prof., Psychology, Yale Univ., Visiting Prof., Harvard Univ. 1962–63; Fellow American Psychological Assocn.; Emer. mem. American Physiological Soc., Soc. of Experimental Psychology, N.A.S., American Philosophical Soc., etc.; Emer. mem. Bd. of Fellows, Brown Univ.; Howard Crosby Warren Medal of Soc. of Experimental Psychologists 1960, Distinguished Scientific Contribution Award of American Psychological Assocn. 1963, Kenneth Craik Research Award of St. John's Coll., Cambridge. *Publications:* Gustatory Afferent Impulses 1941, Taste and Smell, Handbook of Experimental Psychology 1951, The Afferent Code for Sensory Quality (in American Psychologist) 1959, The Sense of Taste (in Handbook of Physiology Vol. 1) 1959, The Pleasures of Sensation (in Psychological Review) 1960, De Gustibus (in American Psychologist) 1965, Behavioral Sciences in Basic Research and National Goals (A Report to the Cttee. on Science Astronautics, U.S. House of Representatives) 1965, Olfaction and Taste 3rd Int. Symposium 1969, The Vertebrate Phylogeny, Neural Code and Integrative Processes of Taste (Handbook of Perception) 1978, Taste: A Model of Incentive Motivation (in The Physiological Mechanisms of Motivation) 1982. *Leisure interests:* skiing, sailing. *Address:* The Rockefeller University, New York, N.Y. 10021 (Office); 1 Gracie Terrace, Apt. 6-B, New York, N.Y. 10028; and Pond Meadow Road, Box 142, Killingworth, Conn., U.S.A. (Homes). *Telephone:* 212-570-8664 (Office); 212-744-8270 (N.Y.); 203-663-1154 (Conn.).

PFEIFFER, Ernst Friedrich, DR.MED.; German professor of internal medicine; b. 10 April 1922, Frankfurt am Main; s. of Fritz and Elisabeth (née Schmidt) Pfeiffer; m. Dr. Margret Heudorfer; one s. one d.; ed. Goethe Gymnasium, Frankfurt and Univs of Frankfurt, Munich and Heidelberg; Asst. Dept. of Internal Medicine, Univ. of Frankfurt 1848, Specialist 1954, Asst. Prof. 1956, Assoc. Prof. 1961; Prof. of Clinical and Experimental Medicine, New York Medical Coll. 1962; Prof. of Clinical Endocrinology, Univ. of Frankfurt 1963; Prof. of Internal Medicine, Head , Dept. of Internal Medicine and Chair. Center of Internal Medicine and Paediatrics, Univ. of Ulm 1967–, Rector 1975–79; Pres. German Soc. for Diabetes 1969, German Soc. for Endocrinology 1978, Study Group for Artificial Pancreas Transplantation of the EASD 1981–84, German Soc. for Internal Medicine 1986–87; Vice-Pres. Int. Diabetes Fed. 1982–; Fellow, Royal Soc. of Medicine, New York Acad. of Sciences; Hon. mem. Royal Acad. of Medicine of Belgium 1983; mem. of many other nat. and int. socs. and acads.; Hon. Prof. Univ. Nacional Mayor de San Marcos, Lima, Peru 1977; Dr. med. h.c. (Athens) 1979, (Cairo) 1981; Paul Langehaus Memorial Lecture and Award 1973, Claude Bernard Lecture, Medal and Award, Madrid 1985.

Publications: over 300 original papers in various German and international journals. *Leisure interests:* sailing, fishing, skiing, history. *Address:* Center for Internal Medicine, University of Ulm, Steinhövelstrasse 9, 7900 Ulm, (Office); Hasslerstr. 52, 7900 Ulm, Federal Republic of Germany (Home). *Telephone:* 0731/30728 (Home).

PFEIFFER, Michelle; American actress; b. Orange Co., Calif. *Films include:* Grease 2, Into the Night, The Witches of Eastwick, Sweet Liberty, Married to the Mob, Tequila Sunrise 1989, Dangerous Liaisons 1989.

PFLEIDERER, Otto, DR.SC.POL.; German banker; b. 17 Jan. 1904, Ulm; s. of Dr. Alfred Pfleiderer and Angelika Henning; m. Dr. Hildegard Hoffmann 1937 (died 1970); ed. Univs. of Tübingen, Hamburg and Kiel; Ministry of Finance, Württemberg-Baden 1945-48, Pres. Landeszentralbank von Württemberg-Baden 1948-52, von Baden-Württemberg 1953-57, in Baden-Württemberg, Stuttgart 1957-72; mem. Bd. of Dirs. Bank deutscher Länder 1948-57, Deutsche Bundesbank 1957-72; lecturer, Univ. of Heidelberg 1947-61, Hon. Prof. 1961-; Alt. mem. Man. Bd. European Payments Union, Paris 1950-51; mem. Scientific Advisory Bd., Fed. Ministry of Econs., Bonn 1965-; Exec. Dir. IMF, Washington 1952-53. *Publications:* Die Staatswirtschaft und das Sozialprodukt 1930, Pfund, Yen und Dollar in der Weltwirtschaftskrise 1937, Währungsordnung und europäische Integration 1964, Betrachtungen zur Stabilitätspolitik 1980. *Address:* Rosengartenstrasse 88, D-7 Stuttgart 1, Federal Republic of Germany. *Telephone:* (0711) 42-52-33.

PFLIMLIN, Pierre, DR. EN D.; French politician; b. 5 Feb. 1907, Roubaix; s. of Jules and Léonie (née Schwartz) Pflimlin; m. Marie-Odile Heinrich 1939; one s. two d.; ed. Lycée de Mulhouse, Institut Catholique, Paris, and Strasbourg Univ.; mem. of Bar, Strasbourg 1933-64; served French Army 1939-40; elected Deputy for Bas-Rhin, Nat. Ass. 1946, 1951, 1956, 1958; Under-Sec. for Nat. Economy 1946; Minister of Agric. 1947-49, 1950-51, for Foreign Econ. Relations 1951-52, for Overseas Territories 1952-53, of Finance 1955-56 and 1957-58; Prime Minister May 1958; Minister of State, de Gaulle Cabinet, 1958-59; Pres. Mouvement Républicain Populaire 1956-59; Co-Pres. "Centre Démocratique" Group, Nat. Ass. 1962-63; Mayor of Strasbourg 1959-83; Minister of Co-operation, April-May 1962; Pres. of Ass. of Council of Europe 1963-66; mem. European Parl. 1979-, Pres. 1984-87; Pres. Consortium of Rhine Navigation 1971-81; Croix de guerre. *Publications:* Perspectives sur notre économie, L'industrie de Mulhouse (with H. Laufenburger), La structure économique du IIIe Reich (with H. Laufenburger), L'Alsace—Destin et volonté (with René Uhrich), L'Europe communautaire (with Raymond Legrand-Lane). *Address:* 24 avenue de la Paix, 67000 Strasbourg, France.

PFLUG, Günther; German librarian (retd.); b. 20 April 1923, Oberhausen; s. of Richard and Annemarie (Winzer) Pflug; m. Dr. Irmgard Höfken 1953; ed. Univs. of Cologne, Bonn, Paris; Asst. Librarian, Univ. Library, Cologne 1953-62, Dir. Univ. Library Centre, 1974-76; Librarian, Ruhr Univ., Bochum 1963-74; Dir. Gen. Deutsche Bibliothek (Gen. German Library), Frankfurt am Main 1976-88; Hon. Prof. of Philosophy, (Bochum) 1965, (Frankfurt) 1977; Hon. mem. Int. Fed. of Library Assens. *Publications:* Henri Bergson 1959, The Development of Historical Method in the 18th Century 1971, Die Bibliotheken und die wissenschaftliche Literatur 1979, Albert Einstein als Publizist 1981, Die Bibliothek im Umbruch 1984. *Leisure interest:* opera. *Address:* Myliusstrasse 27, 6000 Frankfurt am Main, Federal Republic of Germany. *Telephone:* (069) 724874.

PHAM VAN DONG; Vietnamese politician; b. 1 March 1906, Quang Nam Province (S. Viet-Nam); close collaborator of Ho Chi Minh; underground communist worker from 1925; imprisoned by French authorities for seven years; upon release in 1936, resumed revolutionary activities; a founder of the Revolutionary League for the Independence of Viet-Nam (the Viet-Minh) 1941; mem. Lao Dong (Viet-Nam Workers') Party (now CP of Viet-Nam) 1951-; Minister for Foreign Affairs, Democratic Repub. of Viet-Nam 1954-61, Prime Minister 1955-76; Prime Minister, Socialist Repub. of Viet-Nam 1981-86 (called Chair. Council of Ministers 1981-86), Advisor Dec. 1986-; Vice-Chair. Nat. Defence Council July 1976. *Address:* Office of the Chairman, Council of Ministers, Hanoi, Viet-Nam.

PHAM VAN KY; Vietnamese writer; b. 1916; ed. Secondary School, Hanoi, and Univ. of Paris; went to France 1939; prepared thesis on religion for the Institut des Hautes Etudes Chinoises; Grand Prix du Roman, Académie Française 1961. *Publications:* Fleurs de jade (poems), L'homme de nulle part (short stories) 1946, Frères de sang (novel) 1947, Celui qui régnera (novel) 1954, Les yeux courroucés (novel) 1958, Les contemporains (novel) 1959, Perdre la demeure (novel) 1961, Poème sur soie (poems) 1961, Des femmes assises çà et là (novel) 1964, Mémoires d'un eunuque (novel) 1966, Le rideau de pluie (play) 1974. *Address:* 62/2 avenue du Général de Gaulle, Maisons-Alfort 94700, France. *Telephone:* 368-22-94.

PHANOS, Titos; Cypriot politician; b. 23 Jan. 1929, Nicosia, Cyprus; s. of Phanos Ioannides and Maria Georgallidou; m. Maro Phierou 1958; one s. two d.; ed. Pancyprian Gymnasium, Nicosia, Middle Temple, London; called to Bar 1951; practised law 1952-66; mem. EOKA fighters union during Cyprus independence campaign; mem. of Cttee. of Human Rights of the Nicosia Bar Assen.; arrested by British admin. and served 16 months as political detainee 1956-58; mem. Consultative Body to Archbishop Makarios 1959-60; mem. House of Reps. for Nicosia 1960-66; Parl. Spokesman (Floor Leader) of pro-govt. Patriotic Front 1963-66; mem. Consultative Assembly of Council of Europe 1963-65; Minister of Communications and Works 1966-70; Amb. to Belgium, Head of Cypriot Mission to European Communities 1971-78, concurrently Amb. to Luxembourg and the Netherlands 1973-78; Chair. Public Service Comm. of Cyprus 1979-; Vice-Chair. Supreme Sports Judicial Cttee. of Cyprus 1979-; Grand Cross of the Order of Merit of the Grand-Duchy of Luxembourg 1978. *Leisure interests:* music, chess, sports. *Address:* Public Service Commission, Nicosia, Cyprus.

PHANTOG; Chinese mountaineer; b. Aug. 1939, Xigaza, Tibet; d. of Cirhen Phantog and Cijiu Phantog; m. Mr. Jia-shang Deng 1963; one s. two d.; ed. Cen. Coll. of Nationalities; first Chinese woman to climb Everest 1975; Deputy Dir. Wuxi Sports and Physical Culture Comm. 1981-. *Leisure interests:* table tennis, badminton. *Address:* Wuxi Sports and Physical Culture Commission, Jiangsu, People's Republic of China. *Telephone:* 225810.

PHARAND, Donat, Q.C., LL.M., LL.D., S.J.D., F.R.S.C.; Canadian professor of international law; b. 7 Dec. 1922, Hanmer, Ont.; s. of Alphonse Pharand and Georgina Henri; m. Yolaine Michaud; three s. one d.; ed. Dalhousie Univ., Université de Paris, Hague Acad. of Int. Law and Univ. of Michigan; law practice 1956-59; Prof. of Law, Common Law Section, Univ. of Ottawa 1959-65, Chair. Dept. of Political Science 1965-67, Prof. of Int. Law, Civil Law Section 1968-, on leave as Academic in Residence, Dept. of External Affairs 1977-78, Dir. Grad. Studies, Faculty of Law 1979-82; Visiting Prof. and Lecturer, McGill Univ. 1970, Univ. of N.S.W. 1976, Louvain 1976, Thessalonica 1977, Toulouse 1980, Nantes 1980, Dalhousie 1983, Los Andes, Bogota 1985; Pres. Canadian Council on Int. Law 1976-78. *Publications:* The Law of the Sea of the Arctic, with special reference to Canada 1973, The Northwest Passage: Arctic Straits 1984, Canada's Arctic Waters in International Law 1988. *Leisure interests:* travelling, reading, cottaging. *Address:* 85 Marlborough Avenue, Ottawa, Ont., K1N 8E8, Canada.

PHARAON, Ghaith Rashad, PH.D., M.B.A.; Saudi Arabian business executive; b. 7 Sept. 1940, Riyadh; ed. Stanford Univ., Harvard Univ.; Founder Saudi Arabia Research and Devt. Corpn. (Redec) 1965, now Chair. of Bd. and Dir.-Gen.; Chair. Bd. Saudi Arabian Parsons Ltd., Saudi Automotive Industries Ltd., Redec Daelim Ltd., Interstal, Saudi Chemical Processors Ltd., Arabian Maritime Co., Saudi Inland Transport, etc.; Vice-Chair. Jezirah Bank Ltd., Saudi Light Industries Ltd., Arabian Chemical Industries Ltd.; mem. Bd. Okaz Publications, Tihama; Commendatore (Italy); King Abdul Aziz Award. *Address:* P.O. Box 1935, Jeddah (Office); Ghaith Pharaon Residence, Ruwais, Jeddah, Saudi Arabia (Home).

PHELAN, John Joseph, Jr., B.B.A.; American stock exchange executive; b. 7 May 1931, New York; s. of John Joseph Phelan and Edna K. Phelan; m. Joyce Catherine Campbell 1955; three s.; ed. Adelphi Univ., New York; with Nash and Co. stockbrokers, New York 1955-62, partner 1957-62; Man. partner Phelan and Co., New York 1962-72; Sr. partner Phelan Silver Vesce Barry and Co., New York 1972-84; Pres. New York Stock Exchange 1980-84, Chair. and C.E.O. 1984-; Chair. New York Futures Exchange 1979-85; Dir. Adelphi Univ.; mem. Bd. Dirs. Mercy Hosp. Heart Fund, Cardinal's Comm. of Laity, Bd. of Admin., Tulane Univ., Bd. of Trustees New York Medical Coll., Bd. of Advisers Center for Banking Law Studies, Boston Univ., Nat. Market Assen. (Chair. Operations Cttee. 1976-77); founder mem. Securities Industries Assen. (mem. Governing Bd. 1978-79, Exec. Cttee. 1979-80); Kt. Sovereign Mil. Order of Malta; Kt. Holy Sepulchre, Jerusalem. *Address:* New York Stock Exchange, 11 Wall Street, New York, N.Y. 10005 (Office); 88 Feeks Lane, Locust Valley, New York, N.Y. 10005, U.S.A. (Home).

PHELPS, Edmund Strother, PH.D.; American economist; b. 26 July 1933, Evanston, Ill.; s. of Edmund S. Phelps and Florence Stone Phelps; m. Viviana Montdor 1974; ed. Amherst Coll. and Yale Univ.; Research Economist, RAND Corpn. 1959-60; taught Yale Univ. 1960-66; Prof., Univ. of Pa. 1966-71; Columbia Univ. 1971-77, New York Univ. 1977-78, Columbia Univ. 1978-81, McVickar Prof. of Political Econ., Columbia Univ. 1981-; mem. N.A.S.; Hon. D. H. (Amherst Coll.). *Publications:* Golden Rules of Economic Growth 1966, Microeconomic Foundations of Employment and Inflation Theory (Ed.) 1970, Studies in Macroeconomic Theory: vol. 1, 2 1979, 1980, Political Economy: an Introductory Text 1985. *Leisure interest:* music. *Address:* 45 East 89th Street, New York, N.Y. 10128, U.S.A. *Telephone:* (212) 289-6311; (212) 854-2060.

PHILARET (Kyril Varfolomeyevich Vakhromeyev); Soviet ecclesiastic; b. 21 March 1935, Moscow; s. of Varfolomey and Aleksandra V. Vakhromeyev; ed. Moscow Theological Seminary and Moscow Theological Acad.; became monk 1959, ordained as a priest 1961; lecturer, Asst. Prof., Moscow Theological Acad. 1961-65, Rector 1966-73; Bishop of Tikhvin 1965, of Dmitrov 1966; Vice-Chair. Dept. of External Church Relations, Moscow Patriarchate 1968-71, Chair. April 1981-; Archbishop 1971; Archbishop of Berlin and Middle Europe 1973-78; Metropolitan 1975, of Minsk and Byelorussia 1978; Perm. mem. Holy Synod of Russian Orthodox Church April 1981-; Order of St. Vladimir, Order of St. Sergey of Radonezh, Order of Friendship of the Peoples. *Publications:* Russian Orthodox Church Relations to Western Non-Orthodox Churches, St. Cyril and Methodius' Works in the Territory of The Russian State in Russian

Historical Literature, Patriotic Character of Patriarch Aleksey, etc. *Address:* Danilov Monastery, Danilovsky Val 22, Moscow, U.S.S.R.

PHILIP, John Robert, B.C.E., D.SC., F.A.A., F.R.S.; Australian physicist and mathematician; b. 18 Jan. 1927, Ballarat, Victoria; s. of Percival N. and the late Ruth (née Osborne) Philip; m. Frances J. Long 1949; two s. one d.; ed. Scotch Coll., Melbourne and Queen's Coll., Melbourne Univ.; Research Asst. Melbourne Univ. 1947-48; Engineer Queensland Irrigation Comm. 1948-51; joined research staff at CSIRO 1951, Sr. Principal Research Scientist 1961-63, Chief Research Scientist and Asst. Chief, Div. of Plant Industry 1963-71, Chief, Centre for Environmental Mechanics 1971-80, 1983-, Assoc. mem. CSIRO Exec. 1978; First Dir. Inst. of Physical Sciences 1980-83; numerous visiting appointments at univs. in U.K. and U.S.A.; numerous honours and awards. *Publications:* some 240 papers in scientific journals on soil and porous medium physics, fluid mechanics, hydrology, micrometeorology, physical chem., mathematical and physical aspects of physiology and ecology. *Leisure interests:* reading, writing, architecture. *Address:* CSIRO Centre for Environmental Mechanics, GPO Box 821, Canberra, A.C.T. 2601 (Office); 42 Vasey Crescent, Campbell, A.C.T. 2601, Australia (Home). *Telephone:* (062) 46-5645 (Office); (062) 47-8958 (Home).

PHILIP, Kjeld, DR.ECON.; Danish economist and politician; b. 3 April 1912, Copenhagen; s. of Louis and Carli Sörine Philip; m. Inger Margrethe Nygaard, M.P., 1938; two d.; ed. Copenhagen Univ.; Instructor Aarhus Univ. 1937-43 and Prof. of Social Politics and Public Finance 1943-49, Prof. of Econs. and Social Politics, Stockholm Univ. 1949-51; Prof. of Econs., Univ. of Copenhagen 1951-57, 1964, 1966-69; Minister of Commerce 1957-60, of Finance 1960-61, of Econ. Affairs 1961-64; Chair. Co-ordination Cttee. 1955; Dir. Inst. of History and Econs. 1956-60; UN Sr. Econ. Adviser to Prime Minister of Somalia 1965; Chair. Comm. on East African Co-operation 1965-67, Danish Bd. for Co-operation with developing countries 1968-73, mem. 1975-83; Industrialization Fund for Developing Countries 1968-85; mem. Bd. of Dirs. Den Danske Bank 1975-82; Adviser to ILO 1969-71, UNECA 1972. *Publications:* En fremstilling og analyse af Den danske Kriselovgivning 1931-38, 1939, Bidrag til Laeren om Forbindelsen mellem det offentliges Finanspolitik og den økonomiske Aktivitet 1942, Staten og Fattigdommen 1947, La Política Financiera y la Actividad Económica, Madrid 1949, Intergovernmental Fiscal Relations 1953, Skattepolitik 1955, Kenya 1974, Dengang 1 Pilestraede 1985. *Address:* Rungstedvej 95, DK-2960 Rungsted Kyst; (summer address) Horsemose, DK-6973 Örnhöj, Denmark. *Telephone:* (02) 863848.

PHILIPPE, André, DR. EN D.; Luxembourg diplomatist; b. 28 June 1926, Luxembourg; Barrister Luxembourg 1951-52; joined Diplomatic Service 1952; Deputy Dir. of Political Affairs, Ministry of Foreign Affairs 1952-54; Deputy Perm. Rep. of Luxembourg to NATO 1954-61, to OECD 1959-61; Dir. of Protocol and Legal Adviser, Ministry of Foreign Affairs 1961-68; Amb. and Perm. Rep. to UN and Consul-Gen., New York 1968-72; Amb. to U.K. and Perm. Rep. to Council of WEU (concurrently Amb. to Ireland and Iceland) 1972-78, to France 1978-84, also accredited to OECD 1978-84; Perm. Rep. to the UN 1984-87; Amb. to the U.S.A. 1987-; Commdr. Order of Adolphe Nassau (Luxembourg), Order of the Oak Crown (Luxembourg), also holds numerous foreign decorations including Commdr., Légion d'honneur (France) and Hon. G.C.V.O. 1972. *Address:* Luxembourg Embassy, 2200 Massachusetts Avenue, N.W., Washington, D.C. 20008, U.S.A.

PHILIPPOU, Andreas N., PH.D.; Cypriot politician and fmr. university professor; b. 1944, Katokopia; m. Athina Roustani; one d.; ed. Pancyprian Gymnasium Athens Univ., Greece, Univ. of Wisconsin, U.S.A.; Teaching Researcher and Asst., Univ. of Wis., Asst. Prof. of Math., Univ. of Tex., El Paso, Asst. then Assoc. Prof. of Math., American Univ. of Beirut, Lebanon, Prof. of Business Admin., Beirut Univ. Coll., Prof. of Math., subsequently Pres. of Math. Dept., and Vice-Rector, Univ. of Patras, Greece; Minister of Educ. 1988-; fmr. Vice-Pres. Hellenic Aerospace Industry. *Publications:* two books, 60 research papers. *Address:* Ministry of Education, Nicosia, Cyprus.

PHILIPS, Sir Cyril Henry, Kt., M.A., PH.D., D.LITT., LL.D.; British professor of oriental history; b. 27 Dec. 1912, Worcester; s. of William H. and Mary E. Philips; m. 1st Dorcas Rose 1939 (deceased), one s. (deceased) one d.; m. 2nd Joan Rosemary Marshall 1975; ed. Rock Ferry High School and Univs. of Liverpool and London; Asst. Lecturer in Indian History, School of Oriental and African Studies 1936, Lecturer 1939, Sr. Lecturer 1945; war service 1940-46; Prof. of Oriental History and Head Dept. of History, S.O.A.S. 1946-80, Dir. S.O.A.S. 1957-76; Vice-Chancellor, Univ. of London 1972-76; Chair. Royal Comm. on Criminal Procedure 1978-80, India Cttee. of Inter-Univ. Council and British Council 1972, Police Complaints Bd. 1980-85; Adviser to Sec. of State for Home Affairs 1985-87; Pres. Royal Asiatic Soc. 1979-88; mem. Council, Chinese Univ. of Hong Kong 1965-78, Inter-University Council for Higher Educ. Overseas 1967-78; Chair. Council on Tribunals 1986-; Hon. D.Litt. (Warwick) 1967, LL.D. (Hong Kong Univ.) 1971; Hon. D.Litt. (Bristol) 1983, (Sri Lanka); Bishop Chavasse Prize, Gladstone Memorial Fellow, Frewen Lord Prize (Royal Empire Soc.), Alexander Prize (Royal Historical Soc.), Sir Percy Sykes Memorial Medal, James Smart Police Medal 1979, Bengal Asiatic Soc. Gold Medal 1984. *Publications:* The East India Company 1940, 1961, Handbook of Oriental History 1951, 1960, Correspondence of David Scott 1951, His-

torians of India, Pakistan and Ceylon 1961, The Evolution of India and Pakistan 1962, Politics and Society in India 1963, Fort William India House Correspondence 1964, History of the School of Oriental and African Studies 1917-1967 1967, The Partition of India 1970, The Correspondence of Lord William Bentinck 1828-35 1977, The Police in Politics 1982, Reform of the Police Complaints System 1984. *Address:* c/o School of Oriental and African Studies, Malet Street, London, WC1E 7HP, England.

PHILIPS, Frederick Jacques; Netherlands engineer, businessman and welfare worker; b. 16 April 1905, Eindhoven; s. of Dr. A. F. Philips and A. H. E. M. Philips-de Jongh; m. Sylvia van Lennep 1929; three s. four d.; ed. Technological Univ. of Delft; joined N. V. Philips' Gloeilampenfabrieken as Works Engineer 1930; Man. 1931, in control of mechanical workshops, Deputy Dir. 1936 and Dir. 1939, Vice-Pres. of the Bd. of Man. 1946-61, Pres. 1961-71, Chair. Supervisory Bd. 1971-77; Bd. mem. Stirling Thermal Motors, Ann Arbor, U.S.A.; Dr. h.c. (Louvain and Chinese Acad., Taiwan); Grand Officer, Order of Oranje-Nassau, Companion of the Order of the Dutch Lion, Commdr. of the Order of Saint Gregory the Great, Grand Cross Order of Merit (Italy and Spain), Grand Officier in the Order of Leopold II of Belgium, Officer Cross, Légion d'honneur, Order of the Rising Sun, Japan (3rd class) and numerous honours from other countries. *Publication:* Forty-five Years with Philips 1978. *Leisure interests:* tennis, sailing, skiing, golf, travelling, flying. *Address:* De Wielewaal, Eindhoven, Netherlands. *Telephone:* 512780 (Home).

PHILIPSON, Sir Robert James ("Robin"), Kt., F.R.S.E., R.A.; British artist; b. 17 Dec. 1916; s. of James Philipson; m. 1st Brenda Mark 1949; m. 2nd Thora Clyne 1962 (divorced 1975); m. 3rd Diana Mary Pollock 1976; one adopted s.; ed. Whitehaven Secondary School, Dumfries Acad., Edinburgh Coll. of Art; served in King's Own Scottish Borderers, India and Burma 1942-46, mem. teaching staff, Edin. Coll. of Art 1947, Head of School of Drawing and Painting 1960-82; works exhibited Browse & Darby Ltd. and Scottish Gallery, Edin.; Sec. Royal Scottish Acad. 1969-73, Pres. 1973-83; mem. Royal Fine Art Comm. for Scotland 1965-80, Royal Scottish Soc. of Painters in Watercolours; Hon. mem. R.C.A.; Commdr., Ordre du Mérite de la République Français; Hon. D.Univ. (Stirling) 1976, (Heriot-Watt) 1985, Hon. LL.D. (Aberdeen) 1977. *Address:* 23 Crawfurd Road, Edin., EH16 5PQ, Scotland. *Telephone:* (031) 667 2373.

PHILIPSON, William Raymond, PH.D., F.R.S.N.Z.; British professor of botany (retd.); b. 6 Dec. 1911, Newcastle-on-Tyne; s. of James Metcalf Philipson and Emily (née Moss) Philipson; m. Melva Noeline Crozier 1953; one s. three d.; ed. Dame Allens School, Downing Coll., Cambridge and Birkbeck Coll., London; Prin. Scientific Officer British Museum (Natural History) 1935-51; Prof. of Botany, Head of Botany Dept., Dean of Science, Univ. of Canterbury, N.Z. 1951-76, Emer. Prof. 1976-; Corresp. mem. Botanical Soc. of America; Hutton Medal. *Publications:* Birds of a Valley 1948, The Immaculate Forest 1952, Rock Garden Plants of the Southern Alps 1962, The Vascular Cambium 1971, numerous papers in journals. *Leisure interest:* walking among mountains. *Address:* 837 Cashmere Road, Christchurch 3, New Zealand.

PHILLIPS, Alfredo; Mexican international finance official; b. 2 Sept. 1935, Mexico; s. of Howard S. Phillips and Dolores Olmedo; m. Maureen Greene 1960; two s. one d.; ed. Univs. of Mexico and London and American Univ.; Deputy Chief of Dept. of Banks and Chief, Dept. of Econ. and Fiscal Planning, Secr. of Finance and Public Credit, Mexico 1960-65; Sr. Loan Officer, Inter-American Devt. Bank, 1965-66; Alt. Exec. Dir., IMF 1966-68, Exec. Dir. 1968-70; Prof. of Trade Cycles, School of Business Admin., Univ. Iberoamericana Mexico 1961-63; Sec., Group of Latin American Govs. to the IMF and IBRD 1968-70; Man. Banco de México 1971-75, Deputy Dir. 1975-; Treas. Bd. of Dirs. of Latin-American Bank for Foreign Trade 1978-, Vice-Chair. Deputies of Group of 24 1978-79, Chair. Deputies Intergovernmental Group of 24 on Int. Monetary Affairs 1979-. *Leisure interests:* golf, swimming. *Address:* Banco de México, S.A., Avenida 5 de Mayo 2, Apdo. 98 bis, México 1, D.F., Mexico. *Telephone:* 512-47-38 (Office).

PHILLIPS, David, PH.D., F.R.S.C.; British professor of natural philosophy; b. 3 Dec 1939, Kendal, Westmorland (now Cumbria); s. of Stanley Phillips and Daphne Ivy Phillips (née Harris); m. Caroline L. Scoble 1970; one d.; ed. South Shields Grammar Technical School and Univ. of Birmingham; Postdoctoral Fellow and Fulbright Scholar, Univ. of Texas 1964-66; Visiting Scientist, Acad. of Sciences of U.S.S.R. 1966-67; Lecturer, Dept. of Chemistry, Univ. of Southampton 1967-73, Sr. Lecturer 1973-76, Reader 1976-80; Wolfson Prof. of Natural Philosophy, The Royal Inst. of G.B. 1980-, Acting Dir. 1986, Deputy Dir. 1986-; Spinks Lecturer, Univ. of Sask. 1979; Wilsmore Fellow, Univ. of Melbourne 1983; Vice-Pres. and Gen. Sec. British Asscn. for the Advancement of Science; Hon. D. Sc. (Birmingham) 1987. *Publications:* Time-correlated single-photon counting 1984, Polymer Photophysics 1985, Time-Resolved Laser Raman Spectroscopy 1987. *Leisure interests:* music, theatre, popularization of science. *Address:* The Royal Institution of Great Britain, 21 Albermarle Street, London, W1X 4BS (Office); 195 Barnett Wood Lane, Ashtead, Surrey, KT21 2LP, England. (Home). *Telephone:* 01-409 2992 (Office); (03722) 74385 (Home).

PHILLIPS, Sir David (Chilton), K.B.E., PH.D., F.R.S.; British university professor; b. 7 March 1924, Ellesmere, Shropshire; only s. of late Charles

Harry Phillips and Edith Harriet Phillips; m. Diana Kathleen Hutchinson 1960; one d.; ed. Ellesmere primary schools, Oswestry High School for Boys, and Univ. Coll. Cardiff (Univ. of Wales); Sub-Lieut., R.N.V.R. 1944–47; Post-Doctoral Fellow, Nat. Research Labs., Ottawa, Canada 1951–53, Research Officer 1953–55; Research Worker, Davy Faraday Research Lab., Royal Institution, London 1956–66; Prof. of Molecular Biophysics, Univ. of Oxford 1966–; Fellow of Corpus Christi Coll. Oxford 1966–; Vice-Pres. Royal Soc. 1972–73, 1976–83, Biological Sec. Royal Soc. 1976–83; Chair. Advisory Bd. for the Research Councils 1983–; Dir. Celltech Ltd. 1982–; mem. Council European Molecular Biology Org. 1972–78, Medical Research Council 1974–78, Exec. Council Ciba Foundation 1973–; Visiting Fullerian Prof. of Physiology, Royal Inst. 1979–85, Christmas Lectures 1980; Foreign Hon. mem. American Acad. of Arts and Sciences 1968; Foreign Assoc. U.S. Nat. Acad. of Sciences 1985; Hon. D.Sc. (Leicester) 1974, (Wales) 1975, (Chicago) 1977, (Exeter) 1982, (Warwick) 1982, (Birmingham) 1987; Hon. D.Univ. (Essex) 1983; Feldberg Prize 1968, C. L. Mayer Prize of French Acad. of Sciences 1979; CIBA Medal 1971, Royal Medal (Royal Soc.) 1975, Wolf Prize 1987. *Publications:* scientific papers and review articles in various journals: Probability Distribution of X-Ray Intensities 1950, Crystal Structures of Ephedrine and Acridine 1950, Estimation of X-Ray Intensities 1954, Myoglobin Structure 1958, 1961, Effects of X-Irradiation 1962, Structure of Lysozyme 1965, Activity of Lysozyme 1966, Protein Crystal Chemistry 1968, Crystalline Proteins 1969, Vertebrate Lysozymes 1972, Structure of Triose Phosphate Isomerase 1975, Protein Mobility 1979. *Leisure interests:* reading history and talking to children. *Address:* Laboratory of Molecular Biophysics, Department of Zoology, The Rex Richards Building, South Parks Road, Oxford, OX1 3QU; 3 Fairlawn End, Upper Wolvercote, Oxford, OX2 8AR, England (Home). *Telephone:* (0865) 275365 (Laboratory); (0865) 55828 (Home).

PHILLIPS, Donald John, B.SC.; British-Canadian business executive; b. 8 Jan. 1930, Ebbw Vale, Wales; s. of Archibald Thomas Phillips and Ruth Emma (née Thorne) Phillips; m. 1st Wendy Leonora Billsborough 1976 (died 1984), one s. one d.; m. 2nd Susan Elizabeth Haire 1986; ed. Ebbw Vale Grammar School, Univ. of Wales; Chemistry Lecturer, Portsmouth Univ. 1954–56; Tech. Officer, The Int. Nickel Co. of Canada, London 1956–67, Sales Man. 1967–69, Gen. Marketing Man. 1969–70, Asst. Man. Dir. 1970–71, Man. Dir. 1971–72, Chair. and C.E.O. 1972–77; Pres. Inco Metals Co., Toronto 1977–79, Pres. and C.E.O. 1979–80; Pres. Inco Ltd. 1980–82, Pres. and C.O.O. 1982–87, C.E.O., Chair., Pres., April–Oct. 1987; Dir. American Standard Inc., The Toronto-Dominion Bank. *Leisure interests:* tennis, squash, golf. *Address:* Toronto Dominion Centre, Suite 2200, P.O. Box 44, Toronto, M5K 1N4; 65 Harbour Square, Apt. 401, Toronto, Ont., M5J 2L4, Canada (Home).

PHILLIPS, Sir Horace, K.C.M.G.; British diplomatist (retd.); b. 31 May 1917, Glasgow, Scotland; s. of Samuel and Polly Phillips; m. Idina Morgan 1944; one s. one d.; ed. Hillhead High School, Glasgow; Inland Revenue Dept., London 1935–39; Indian Army 1940–47; Consul, Persia and Afghanistan 1947–50; Foreign Office 1951–53; Chargé d'affaires, Saudi Arabia 1953–56; Aden Protectorate Sec. 1956–60; Counsellor, Teheran 1960–64; Deputy Political Resident, Persian Gulf 1964–66; Amb. to Indonesia 1966–68; British High Commr. in Tanzania 1968–72; Amb. to Turkey 1973–77; Resident Rep. of Taylor Woodrow Int. in Iran 1978–79, in Hong Kong 1979–83, in Bahrain 1984–85, Beijing 1985–87; Asst. Lecturer, Bilkent Univ., Ankara, Turkey 1988–; Hon. LL.D. (Glasgow); Order of the Taj (Iran). *Leisure interests:* languages, long-distance driving (especially in the Near and Middle East). *Address:* 34A Sheridan Road, Merton Park, London, SW19 3HP, England. *Telephone:* 01-542 3836/1780.

PHILLIPS, Leon Francis, PH.D.; New Zealand professor of chemistry; b. 14 July 1935; m. Pamela A. Johnstone 1959; two s.; ed. Westport Tech. Coll., Christchurch Boys' High School, Univs. of Canterbury (N.Z.) and Cambridge; Upper Atmosphere Chem. Group, McGill Univ. 1961; lecturer, Univ. of Canterbury 1962, Prof. of Chem. 1966–; Visiting Prof. Univ. of Washington 1968, Monash Univ. 1969; Visiting Fellow, Balliol Coll. Oxford 1975, Japan Soc. for Promotion of Science 1984; Visiting Scholar, Rice Univ., Houston 1987; Harkness Fellow 1968; Fulbright Award 1980; Corday-Morgan Medal (Royal Soc. of Chem.), Hector Medal, (Royal Soc. of N.Z.), Easterfield and ICI prizes (N.Z. Inst. of Chem.). *Publications:* Basic Quantum Chemistry, Electronics for Experimenters, Chemistry of the Atmosphere (with M. J. McEwan), First Year Chemistry (with J. M. Coxon and J. E. Fergusson), three novels, over 150 scientific papers. *Leisure interests:* sailing, skiing, reading, writing. *Address:* 12 Maidstone Road, Christchurch 4, New Zealand.

PHILLIPS, Owen Martin, PH.D., F.R.S.; American professor of science and engineering; b. 30 Dec. 1930, Parramatta, N.S.W., Australia; s. of Richard Keith Phillips and Madeline Constance (Lofts); m. Merle Winifred Simons 1953; two s. two d.; ed. Univ. of Sydney, Australia and Univ. of Cambridge; ICI Fellow, Univ. of Cambridge 1955–57, Fellow, St. John's Coll. 1957–60; Assoc. Prof., Johns Hopkins Univ., Baltimore, Md., U.S.A. 1960–63; Asst. Dir. of Research, Cambridge Univ. 1961–64; Prof. of Geophysical Mechanics and Geophysics, Johns Hopkins Univ. 1963–75, Chair. Dept. of Earth and Planetary Sciences 1968–78, Decker Prof. of Science and Eng. 1978–; Assoc. Ed., Journal of Fluid Mechanics 1964–; Adams Prize, Cambridge Univ. 1965; Sverdrup Gold Medal, American Meteorological Soc. 1974. *Publi-*

cations: The Dynamics of the Upper Ocean 1966 (Russian edns. 1969, 1979), The Heart of the Earth 1968, The Last Chance Energy Book 1979, Wave Dynamics and Radio Probing of the Ocean Surface (Ed.) 1985; many research publs. in the tech. literature. *Leisure interest:* sailing. *Address:* The Johns Hopkins University, Baltimore, Md. 21218, U.S.A. *Telephone:* (301) 338-7036.

PHILLIPS, Siân, B.A.; British actress; b. Bettws, Wales; d. of D. Phillips and Sally Phillips; m. 1st Peter O'Toole (q.v.) 1960 (divorced 1979), two d.; m. 2nd Robin Sachs 1979; ed. Pontardawe Grammar School, Univ. of Wales (Cardiff Coll.), RADA; BBC Radio Wales mid-1940s– and BBC TV Wales early 1950s–; newsreader and announcer and mem. BBC repertory co. 1953–55; toured for Welsh Arts Council with Nat. Theatre Co. 1953–55; Arts Council Bursary to study drama outside Wales 1955; 1978 Chichester Festival Season; Fellow, Cardiff Coll. (Univ. of Wales) 1982; Hon. Fellow Polytechnic Wales 1988; mem. Gorsedd of Bards (for services to drama in Wales) 1960; Hon. D.Litt. (Wales) 1984. *London stage appearances:* Hedda Gabler 1959, Ondine and The Duchess of Malfi 1960–61 (first RSC season at Aldwych), The Lizard on the Rock 1961, Gentle Jack, Maxibules and the Night of the Iguana 1964, Ride a Cock Horse 1965, Man and Superman and Man of Destiny 1966, The Burglar 1967, Epitaph for George Dillon 1972, A Nightingale in Bloomsbury Square 1973, The Gay Lord Quex 1975, Spinechiller 1978, You Never Can Tell, Lyric, Hammersmith 1979, Pal Joey, Half Moon and Albery Theatres 1980 and 1981, Dear Liar 1982, Major Barbara, Nat. Theatre 1982, Peg (musical) 1984, Love Affair 1984, Gigi 1986, Thursday's Ladies 1987, Brel (musical) 1987–88. *Films include:* Becket 1963, Goodbye Mr. Chips (Critics' Circle Award, New York Critics' Award and Famous Seven Critics' Award 1969), Laughter in the Dark 1968, Murphy's War 1970, Under Milk Wood 1971, The Clash of the Titans 1979, Dune 1983, Ewok II, The Two Mrs Grenvilles, Cineclaire, Valmont 1988. *TV appearances include:* Shoulder to Shoulder 1974, How Green was my Valley (BAFTA Award) 1975, I, Claudius (Royal Television Soc. Award and BAFTA Award 1978) 1976, Boudicca, Off to Philadelphia in the Morning 1977, The Oresteia of Aeschylus 1978, Crime and Punishment 1979, Tinker, Tailor, Soldier, Spy 1979, Sean O'Casey (RTE) 1980, Churchill: The Wilderness Years 1981, How Many Miles to Babylon 1982, Smiley's People 1982, George Borrow 1983, A Painful Case (RTE), Beyond All Reason, Murder on the Exchange, The Shadow of the Noose (BBC series) 1988, Snow Spider (HTV serial) 1988. *Recordings include:* Bewitched, Bothered and Bewildered, Pal Joey, Peg, I Remember Mama, Gigi. *Publication:* Siân Phillips' Needlepoint 1987. *Leisure interests:* canvas embroidery, gardening. *Address:* c/o Saraband Ltd., 265 Liverpool Road, London, N.1, England.

PHILLIPS, Thomas L.; American business executive; b. 2 May 1924; ed. Boston Public Latin School and Virginia Polytechnic Inst.; joined Raytheon Co. 1948, Vice-Pres. and Gen. Man. Missile and Space Div. 1960, Exec. Vice-Pres. 1961–64, Dir. 1961–, Pres., C.O.O. 1964–68, C.E.O. 1968–, Chair. 1975–; Dir. John Hancock Mutual Life Insurance Co., State Street Investment Corpn.; mem. Nat. Acad. of Eng., Business Council, The Business Roundtable; Vice-Pres. and mem. of the Corpn. of Joslin Diabetes Foundation Inc.; Trustee of Gordon Coll. and Northeastern Univ.; mem. Corpn. of The Museum of Science; hon. degrees from Northeastern Univ., Boston, Stonehill, Babson and Gordon Colls., and Univ. of Lowell; U.S.N. Meritorious Public Service Award 1958. *Address:* Raytheon Company, 141 Spring Street, Lexington, Mass. 02173, U.S.A.

PHILLIPS, Tom, M.A., N.D.D., A.R.A.; British artist, writer and composer; b. 24 May 1937, London; s. of David John Phillips and Margaret Agnes Arnold; m. Jill Purdy 1961 (divorced 1988); one s. one d.; ed. St. Catherine's Coll., Oxford and Camberwell School of Art; one-man exhbns. AIA Galleries, Angela Flowers Gallery, Marlborough Fine Art and Waddingtons, London and Galerie Ba Ma, Paris; several int. group exhbns.; touring retrospective exhbn. London, The Hague, Basel, Paris etc. 1975; 50 years of Tom Phillips, Angela Flowers Gallery 1987; first performance opera IRMA, York Univ. 1973, revival ICA, London 1983; collaborations with Jean-Ives Bosseut and John Tilbury on music works/performances 1970–84; working with Peter Greenaway on TV version of Dante's Inferno, as published, translated and illustrated by the artist; Vice-Chair. Copyright Council 1985–; John Moores Prize 1969; Frances Williams Memorial Prize V&A 1983. *Publications:* Trailer 1971, A Humument 1973, Works and Texts to 1974 1975, Dante's Inferno 1983, Heart of a Humument 1985, IRMA (an opera) 1975, music scores 1965–85. *Leisure interests:* collecting Ashanti gold weights, travel. *Address:* 57 Talfourd Road, London, S.E.15, England. *Telephone:* 01-701 3978.

PHILLIPS, Warren Henry, A.B.; American newspaper executive; b. 28 June 1926, New York City; s. of Abraham and Juliette Phillips; m. Barbara Anne Thomas 1951; three d.; ed. Queens Coll.; Copyreader Wall Street Journal 1947–48, Foreign Corresp., Germany 1949–50, Chief, London Bureau 1950–51, Foreign Ed. 1952–53, News Ed. 1953–54, Man. Ed. Midwest Edition 1954–57, Man. Ed. Wall Street Journal 1957–65; Exec. Ed. Dow Jones Publs.; Vice-Pres. and Gen. Man. Dow Jones Co. Inc. 1970–71; Editorial Dir. 1971–, Exec. Vice-Pres. 1972, Pres. 1972–79, C.E.O. 1975–, Chair. 1978–; Pres. American Council on Educ. for Journalism 1971–73; Pres. American Soc. of Newspaper Eds. 1975–76; mem. Pulitzer Prizes Bd. 1976–87; Trustee, Colombia Univ. 1980–. *Publication:* China:

Behind the Mask (with Robert Keatley) 1973. *Address:* World Finance Centre, 200 Liberty Street, New York, N.Y. 10281 (Office); 22 North Cortlandt Street, New York, N.Y. 10007, U.S.A. (Home).

PHILLIPS, William, M.A.; American educationalist and author; b. New York; s. of Edward Phillips and Marie (née Berman) Phillips; m. Edna M. Greenblatt; ed. New York Univ., Columbia Univ.; Ed. Partisan Review 1934–; fmr. ed. Dial Press, Criterion Books, Random House, Chilmark Press; Assoc. Prof. New York Univ. 1960–63; Prof. English Rutgers Univ. 1963–78, Boston Univ. 1978–; Grantee Rockefeller Foundation 1977–78; mem. Co-ordinating Council Literary Magazines of America, Chair. 1967–75, Hon. Pres. and Chair. 1975; mem. Authors League. *Publications:* A Sense of the Present 1967, A Partisan View: Five Decades of the Literary Life 1983, Ed. Short Stories of Dostoyevsky, Great American Short Novels. *Address:* 236 Bay State Road, Boston, Mass. 02215 (Office); 101 W. 12th Street, New York, N.Y. 10011, U.S.A. (Home).

PHOMVIHANE, Kaysone; Laotian politician; b. 1920, Savannakhet-Province; m. Thongvin; ed. Univ. of Hanoi; helped anti-French forces in Viet-Nam after 1945; joined Free Lao Front (Neo Lao Issara) nationalist movement in exile in Bangkok 1945; attended first resistance congress; Minister of Defence in Free Lao Front resistance Govt. 1950; C.-in-C. of Pathet Lao forces 1954–57; mem. People's Party of Laos 1955; mem. Lao Patriotic Front (Neo Lao Hak Sat) 1956, Vice-Chair. 1959, Vice-Chair. of Cen. Cttee. 1964; Prime Minister of Laos Dec. 1975–; Gen. Sec. Cen. Cttee. Lao People's Revolutionary Party; Order of Lenin. *Publication:* To Build a Peaceful, Independent and Socialist Laos 1978. *Address:* Office of the Prime Minister, Vientiane, Laos.

PHORORO, Daniel Rakoro, M.R.C.V.S., B.V.M.S.; Lesotho veterinarian and politician; b. 26 July 1934, Likhutlong, Butha-Buthe; ed. Lesotho High School; veterinary training in U.K. and Italy; employed by FAO 1979–; Country Projects Officer, Tanzania, Zimbabwe; Deputy Dir. Veterinary and Livestock Services; Veterinary Officer Ministry of Agric. 1964–86; Minister of Agric., Co-operatives and Marketing 1986–. *Publications:* 8 articles on Lesotho and Southern Africa, ranging from mohair industry, crop farming, soil conservation and pasture utilization. *Address:* c/o The Military Council, Maseru, Lesotho.

PHOUNSAVANH, Nouhak; Laotian politician; ed. primary school; owner of bus and truck business; visited Peking (now Beijing) in a Viet-Minh del. for Conf. of Asian and Pacific Region 1952; rep. of Pathet Lao at Geneva Conf. on Indochina with Viet-Minh del. 1954; became Minister of Foreign Affairs in Free Lao Front (Neo Lao Issara) resistance Govt.; Deputy for Sam Neua to Nat. Assembly 1957; arrested 1959, escaped 1960; led Lao Patriotic Front (Neo Lao Hak Sat) del. to Ban Namone peace talks 1961; mem. People's Party of Laos 1955; mem. Lao Patriotic Front, mem. Standing Cttee. 1964, of Cen. Cttee.; Vice-Chair. Council of Ministers and Minister of Finance 1975–82, Vice-Chair. Council of Ministers Dec. 1975–, now First Vice Chair; Deputy Gen. Sec. Lao People's Revolutionary Party. *Address:* Council of Ministers, Vientiane, Laos.

PIATIER, André (Sylvain); French economist and sociologist; b. 25 June 1914, Orne; s. of Maurice Piatier and Juliette Grenier; m. Caroline Werling 1940 (died 1976); m. 2nd Claude Arnulf 1983; one d.; ed. Univ. of Paris, London School of Econs., Inst. für Konjunkturforschung, Berlin, Hague Acad., etc.; Rockefeller Fellow and Asst., Faculté de Droit, Paris, and Sec. Inst. Int. de Finances Publiques 1936–39; war and resistance, lecturer Univ. of Strasbourg, Centre d'Etudes Economiques de la Marine 1939–45; Dir. Econ. Studies and Research, Inst. Nat. de la Statistique, Paris 1946–56; Prof. of Econ. Sciences, Cairo 1955–56, Teheran 1965–67; Pres. of Experts, Int. Travel Inst. 1948–57; UNESCO Expert, Econ. Devt., Athens 1959, Social Devt. Paris 1963, Bangkok 1973; UNO Expert, Population and Environment, Cairo 1973–75; Prof. Ecole Nat. d'Admin., Ecole d'Application de la Statistique, Inst. d'Etudes de Développement Economique et Social, Paris, etc.; Pres. Cttee. for Econ. Science and Devt. 1960–66, Délégation gén. à la Recherche Scientifique; Pres. Centre for Study and Research in Biology and Medical Oceanography 1984–; Pres. AREPIT 1985–, Int. Observatory for Regional Forecast 1988–; Prof. Ecole des Hautes Etudes Scientifiques Sociales, Inst. d'Etudes Politiques; Special Adviser for Scientific Information, EEC 1976–; Dir. Centre d'Etude des Techniques Economiques Modernes (CETEM) 1960–; past mem. of various int. consultative bds.; Officier, Légion d'honneur, Médaille de la Résistance, Commdr., Ordre nat. du Mérite. *Publications:* Barriers to Innovation 1984; studies on industrial innovation, long waves and growth, several works in field of economics, statistics and business studies; Dir. of collections Observation Economique, Développement Economique, Techniques Economiques Modernes, Rythmes Economiques, etc. *Leisure interests:* painting, music. *Address:* 5 place Garibaldi, 06300 Nice, France. *Telephone:* 93.85.87.60.

PIBULSONGGRAM, Nitya, M.A.; Thai diplomatist; b. 1941; m.; ed. Dartmouth Coll. and Brown Univ.; entered Foreign Service as Third Sec. Foreign News Div. Information Dept. June 1968; served in former SEATO Div., Thailand's Int. Org. Dept. 1969–72; Office of Sec. to Minister of Foreign Affairs 1973, Office of Under-Sec. of State, Policy Planning Div. 1974; Head Southeast Asia Div., Political Dept. 1975; First Sec. Perm. Mission to UN 1976–79, Deputy Perm. Rep. 1979–80, Perm. Rep. Feb.

1988–; Deputy Dir-Gen. Information Dept., Foreign Ministry 1980, Political Dept. 1981; Amb.-at-Large 1982; Dir.-Gen. Dept. of Int. Org. 1983–88. *Address:* Permanent Mission of Thailand to the United Nations, 628 Second Avenue, New York, N.Y. 10016, U.S.A. *Telephone:* (212) 689-1004.

PICACHY, H.E. Cardinal Lawrence Trevor, D.D.; Indian ecclesiastic; b. 7 Aug. 1916, Darjeeling; s. of the late Edwin Picachy and May McCue; ed. St. Joseph's Coll., Darjeeling; joined Soc. of Jesus 1934; ordained Roman Catholic priest 1947; Headmaster, St. Xavier's School, Calcutta 1954–60; Prin. St. Xavier's Coll., Calcutta 1954–58, Rector 1954–60; Parish Priest, Basanti village, W. Bengal 1960–62; First Bishop of Jamshedpur 1962–69; attended four sessions of II Vatican Council 1962–65; Chair. Social Communications (Mass Media) Comm., Catholic Bishop's Conf. of India 1966; world tour studying Mass Media 1968; Archbishop of Calcutta 1969–87; Vice-Pres. Catholic Bishops' Conf. of India 1972–76, Pres. 1976–81; cr. Cardinal May 1976; mem. Rotary Club of Calcutta 1971. *Address:* c/o Archbishop's House, 32 Park Street, Calcutta 700016, India. *Telephone:* 444-666.

PICASSO, Paloma; French couturier; b. 19 April 1949, Paris; d. of Pablo Picasso and Françoise Gilot; m. Rafael Lopez-Sanchez; studied jewelry design and fabrication; Fashion Jewelry designer for Yves St. Laurent 1969; first jewelry collection for Tiffany 1980; Designer for Jacques Kaplan and Zolotas; currently designs china and crystal for Villeroy and Boch; launched perfume 'Paloma' 1984; appeared in film Immoral Tales 1974. *Address:* c/o Tiffany and Co., 727 5th Avenue, New York City, N.Y. 10022, U.S.A.

PICCARD, Jacques Ernest Jean; Swiss scientist; b. 28 July 1922, Brussels, Belgium; s. of Auguste Piccard and Marianne (Denis) Piccard; m. Marie-Claude Maillard 1953; two s. one d.; ed. Univ. of Geneva and Inst. Universitaire de Hautes Etudes Internationales, Geneva; Asst. Prof. of Econs., Geneva 1946–48; consultant scientist to several American orgs. for deep sea research; collaborated with father, Prof. Auguste Piccard, in construction of bathyscaph Trieste; built first mesoscaph Auguste Piccard; has made more than 100 dives in Mediterranean and Pacific, one to 35,800 feet (deepest ever dive) in Jan. 1960 and approx. 700 dives in European lakes with submersible F.A.-FOREL; Chief Scientist, research submarine Ben Franklin for the Grumman-Piccard Gulf Stream Drift Mission, Summer 1969; Founder and Pres. Foundation for the Study and Preservation of Seas and Lakes; built research submersible F.A.-FOREL 1978; Visiting Prof. of Oceanic Eng. at Stevens Inst. of Tech., Hoboken, New Jersey; Hon. D.Sc. (American Int. Coll. and Hofstra Univ.); Croix de guerre (France), U.S. Distinguished Public Service award 1960, Officier, Ordre de Léopold (Belgium). *Publications:* The Sun beneath the Sea 1971, several technical papers. *Leisure interests:* reading, walking, swimming, diving. *Address:* 19 avenue de l'Avenir, 1012 Lausanne, Switzerland. *Telephone:* 021-28-80-83; 021-99-25-65 (Office).

PICCOLI, Michel; French actor; b. 27 Dec. 1925, Paris; s. of Henri Piccoli; m. 1st Juliette Greco 1966; m. 3rd Ludivine Clerc 1978; one s. from first marriage; ed. Collège d'Annel, Collège Ste. Barbe, Paris; Man. of the Théâtre de Babylone for two years before joining the Madeleine Renaud and Jean-Louis Barrault Theatre Co.; appeared in Phèdre at the Théâtre Nationale Populaire; Best Actor, Cannes 1980 (for Salto nel Vuoto). *Films include:* Le point du jour 1946, Parfum de la dame en noire 1949, French Cancan 1955, The Witches of Salem 1956, Le mépris 1963, Diary of a Chambermaid 1964, De l'amour 1965, Lady L 1965, La curée 1965, Les demoiselles de Rochefort 1967, Un homme de trop 1967, Belle de jour 1967, Dillinger is Dead 1968, The Milky Way 1969, Topaz 1969, The Discreet Charm of the Bourgeoisie 1972, Themroc 1972, Blowout 1973, The Infernal Trio 1974, Le fantôme de la liberté 1974, La faille 1975, Léonar 1975, Sept morts sur ordonnance 1976, La dernière femme 1976, Savage State 1978, Le divorcement 1979, Le saut dans le vide 1979, Le mors aux dents 1979, La città delle donne 1980, Salto nel Vuoto 1980, La passante du sans-souci 1982, Adieu Bonaparte 1985, The Night is Young 1986. *Publication:* Dialogues égoistes 1976. *Address:* 5 avenue MacMahon 75017 Paris, France.

PICKARD, Sir Cyril Stanley, K.C.M.G.; British diplomatist (retd.); b. 18 Sept. 1917, London; s. of late G. W. Pickard and Edith Pickard; m. 1st Helen Strawson 1941 (died 1982), three s. one d.; m. 2nd Mary Cecilia Rosser 1983; ed. Alleyn's School, Dulwich and New Coll., Oxford; Ministry of Home Security 1939; R.A. 1940–41; Office of Minister of State, Cairo 1941–45; UNRRA Balkan Mission 1944, later with UNRRA in Germany; Home Office 1945–48; Commonwealth Relations Office (C.R.O.) 1948–; Office of U.K. High Commr. in India 1950–52; Official Sec. to Office of U.K. High Commr. in Australia 1952–55; Head, S. Asia and Middle East Dept., C.R.O. 1955–58; Deputy High Commr. in New Zealand 1958–61; Asst. Under Sec. of State, C.R.O. 1962–66; Acting High Commr., Cyprus 1964; High Commr. in Pakistan 1966–71, in Nigeria 1971–74; Deputy Chair. Cen. Council, Royal Commonwealth Soc. 1976, Vice-Pres. 1979–. *Address:* 37A Brodrick Road, London, S.W.17; 3 Orwell Road, Norwich, Norfolk, England. *Telephone:* 01-672 6850.

PICKAVANCE, Thomas Gerald, C.B.E., PH.D., F.R.S.; British physicist; b. 19 Oct 1915, St Helens, Lancs.; s. of late William Pickavance and Ethel Pickavance; m. Alice Isobel Boulton 1943; two s. one d.; ed. Univ. of

Liverpool; Research on Atomic Bomb Project, Directorate of Tube Alloys, Liverpool 1940–46; Lecturer in Physics, Liverpool Univ. 1942–46; Head of Cyclotron Group A.E.R.E., Harwell 1946; Prin. Scientific Officer 1947 and Sr. Prin. Scientific Officer 1950; Deputy Head of Gen. Physics Div. A.E.R.E. 1955; Dir. Rutherford High Energy Lab., Nat. Inst. for Research in Nuclear Science 1957–65, Science Research Council 1965–69, Nuclear Physics Science Research Council 1969–71; Fellow St. Cross Coll., Oxford 1968–84, Emer. Fellow 1984–; Hon. D.Sc. (City Univ. London) 1969. *Leisure interests:* motoring, travel, photography. *Address:* 3 Kingston Close, Abingdon, Oxon., OX14 1ES, England. *Telephone:* Abingdon 23934.

PICKERING, Sir Edward Davies, Kt.; British journalist; b. 4 May 1912; ed. Middlesbrough High School; Chief Sub-Ed. Daily Mail 1939; R.A. 1940–44; Staff of Supreme HQ Allied Expeditionary Force 1944–45; Man. Ed. Daily Mail 1947–49, Daily Express 1951–57, Ed. Daily Express 1957–62; Dir. Beaverbrook Newspapers 1956–63; Man. Dir. Beaverbrook Publications 1962–63; Editorial Dir. and Dir. The Daily Mirror Newspapers Ltd. 1964–68; Editorial Dir. Int. Publishing Corpn., Chair. I.P.C. Newspaper Div. and Chair. Daily Mirror Newspapers Ltd. 1968–70; Chair. I.P.C. Magazines Ltd. 1970–74; Chair. Mirror Group Newspapers Ltd. 1974–77; mem. Press Council 1964–69, 1970–82, Vice-Chair. 1977–82; Chair. Commonwealth Press Union 1977–86; Exec. Vice-Chair. Times Newspapers Ltd. 1982–; Dir. Reed Publishing Holdings 1977–81, Times Newspapers Holdings 1981–, William Collins 1981–; Treas. Int. Fed. of the Periodical Press 1971–75; Vice-Pres. Periodical Publrs. Asscn. 1971–; Hon. D.Litt. (City Univ., London) 1986. *Address:* Chatley House, Norton St., Philip, Somerset, England.

PICKERING, Thomas Reeve, M.A.; American diplomatist; b. 5 Nov. 1931, Orange, N.J.; s. of Hamilton Reeve Pickering and Sara P. Chasteney; m. Alice Jean Stover 1955; one s. one d.; ed. Bowdoin Coll., Brunswick, Me., Fletcher School of Law and Diplomacy, Medford, Mass., Univ. of Melbourne, Australia; Lieut. U.S.N. 1956–59; joined Dept of State 1959, Intelligence Research Specialist 1960, Foreign Affairs Officer 1961, Arms Control and Disarmament Agency 1961–62; mem. U.S. Del. to Disarmament Conf., Geneva 1962–64; Prin. Officer, Zanzibar 1965–67; Deputy Chief of Mission, Dar es Salaam 1967–69; Deputy Dir. Bureau of Politico-Mil. Affairs 1969–73; Exec. Sec. Dept. of State, Special Asst. to Sec. of State 1973–74; Amb. to Jordan 1974–78; Asst. Sec. of State, Bureau of Oceans, Environment and Science 1978–81; Amb. to Nigeria 1981–83; Amb. to El Salvador 1983–85, to Israel 1985–88; Perm. Rep. to UN 1989–. *Address:* Permanent Mission of the United States to the United Nations, 799 United Nations Plaza, New York, N.Y. 10017, U.S.A.

PICKERING, William Hayward, M.S., PH.D.; American scientist; b. 24 Dec. 1910, Wellington, N.Z.; s. of Albert William and Elizabeth Hayward Pickering; m. Muriel Bowler 1932; one s. one d.; ed. Calif. Inst. of Tech.; Calif. Inst. of Tech. 1936–, Prof. of Electrical Eng. 1946–, Dir. Jet Propulsion Laboratory 1954–76, Prof. Emer. 1980–; mem. Scientific Advisory Bd. U.S.A.F. 1945–48; Chair. Panel on Test Range Instrumentation Research and Devt. Bd. 1948–49; directed devt. of Army Corporal and Sergeant missiles 1950–55, and many spacecraft, including Explorer I, Ranger, the first U.S. spacecraft to photograph the moon, Mariner II, first spacecraft to return scientific data from the vicinity of a planet (Venus), Mariner IV, first spacecraft to photograph Mars, Surveyor, first U.S. spacecraft to soft-land on the moon and return scientific data; mem. Advisory Cttee. Dept. of Aeronautics and Astronautics, Univ. of Wash., U.S. Tech. Panel on Earth Satellite Programs IGY 1956–58, Army Scientific Advisory Panel 1963–65; Pres. A.I.A.A. 1963; Fellow I.E.E.E.; Hon. Fellow A.I.A.A.; mem. N.A.S., American Asscn. Univ. Profs., American Geophysical Union, Nat. Acad. of Eng., A.A.A.S., Royal Soc. of New Zealand, Int. Acad. of Astronautics; mem. Int. Astronautics Fed., Pres. 1965–66; Dir. Research Inst., Univ. of Petroleum and Minerals, Saudi Arabia 1976–78; Pres. Pickering Research Corpn., Pasadena, Calif.; hon. mem. New Zealand Inst. of Eng., and Aerospace Medical Asscn.; Fellow, American Acad. of Arts and Sciences; Hon. D.Sc. (Occidental Coll., Clark Univ., Univ. of Bologna) 1974; Hon. K.B.E., Meritorious Civilian Service Award U.S. Army 1945, Distinguished Civilian Service Award U.S. Army 1959, Columbus Gold Medal 1964, Prix Galabert Award 1965, Robert H. Goddard Memorial Trophy 1965, Crozier Gold Medal 1965, Spirit of Saint Louis Medal 1965, Distinguished Service Medal NASA 1965, Italian Order of Merit 1966, Louis W. Hill Award 1968, Edison Medal (Inst. of Electrical and Electronics Engineers) 1972, Nat. Medal of Science 1975, Herman Oberth Engineering Award (Fed. Repub. of Germany) 1978, and many other awards. *Leisure interests:* swimming, fishing, hiking, gardening. *Address:* 292 St. Katherine Drive, Flintridge, Calif. 91011, U.S.A. (Home). *Telephone:* 213-795-7557 (Office).

PIDDINGTON, Jack Hobart, B.E., PH.D., F.A.A.; Australian research scientist (retd.); b. 6 Nov. 1910, Wagga, N.S.W.; s. of Frederic C. Piddington and Leonie M. Millenet; m. 1st Catherine Wynne-Dyke 1936 (deceased), one s.; m. 2nd Nancy Macdougall 1948 (deceased), two d.; m. 3rd Patricia Devereaux 1965; ed. Univs. of Sydney and Cambridge; Walter and Eliza Hall Fellow 1936–38; research scientist, CSIRO 1939, Sr. Prin. Research Scientist 1946, Chief Research Scientist 1968–85; Radar Adviser, British Army, Malaya, Hong Kong, Burma 1941; Air Ministry, U.K. 1944; Visiting Research Prof. Univ. of Md. 1960, Univ. of Ia. 1967; Consultant Astron-

omer, Kitt Peak Nat. Observatory 1974; Syme Medal, Univ. of Melbourne 1958; Sidey Medal, Royal Soc. of N.Z. 1959. *Publications:* Radio Astronomy 1961, Cosmic Electrodynamics 1969; 132 scientific papers. *Leisure interests:* lawn tennis, bowls. *Address:* Town House 4, Imoruben Road, Mosman, N.S.W. 2088, Australia.

PIEL, Gerard, A.B.; American editor and publisher; b. 1 March 1915, New York; s. of William Piel and Loretto (Scott) Piel; m. 1st Mary Tapp Bird 1938 (divorced 1955), two s. (one deceased); m. 2nd Eleanor Virden Jackson 1955, one d.; ed. Phillips Acad., Andover, Mass. and Harvard Coll.; Editorial Assoc., Science Ed., Life 1938–45; Asst. to Pres., Henry J. Kaiser Co. and associated enterprises 1945–46; Organizer, Pres. Scientific American Inc., Publr. Scientific American 1947–84, Chair of Bd. 1984–87, Chair. Emer. 1988–; Chair. Comm. Delivery Personal Health Services, New York 1966–68, Trustees, Foundation for Child Devt.; mem. Bd. Overseers Harvard Univ. 1966–68, 1973–79; Trustee American Museum of Natural History, Radcliffe Coll. 1962–80, Phillips Acad., New York Botanical Garden, Henry J. Kaiser Family Foundation, Mayo Foundation, American Bd. of Medical Specialities, René Dubos Center for Human Environment; mem. Council on Foreign Relations, American Philosophical Soc., Inst. of Medicine; Fellow American Acad. of Arts and Sciences, A.A.A.S. (Pres. 1985, Chair. 1986); George Polk Award 1961, Kalinga Prize 1962, Bradford Washburn Award 1966, Arches of Science Award 1969, Rosenberger Medal, Univ. of Chicago 1973, A. I. Djavakhishvili Medal (Univ. of Tbilisi), Publr. of the Year, Magazine Publrs. Asscn. 1980. *Publications:* Science in the Cause of Man 1962, The Acceleration of History 1972. *Address:* 41 Madison Avenue, New York, N.Y. 10010 (Office); 1115 Fifth Avenue, New York, N.Y. 10128 (Home); Lakeville, Conn. 06039, U.S.A. (Home).

PIENAAR, Louis Alexander, B.A., LL.B.; South African lawyer and diplomatist; b. 23 June 1926, Stellenbosch; s. of Jacobus Alexander Pienaar and Eleanore Angelique Pienaar (née Stiglingh); m. Isabel Maud van Niekerk 1954; two s. one d.; ed. Univ. of Stellenbosch and Univ. of South Africa; joined legal practice in Bellville 1953; mem. Prov. Council for Bellville Constituency 1966–70, M.P. for Belville Constituency 1970–75; Amb. to France 1975–79; Advocate at the Cape Town Bar 1979–85; Admin.-Gen. Admin. of Namibia (South West Africa) 1985–. *Leisure interests:* squash, theatre. *Address:* Private Bag 13278, Windhoek 9000, Namibia (Office) *Telephone:* Windhoek 32329.

PIENE, Otto; German artist and educator; b. 18 April 1928, Laasphe, Westphalia; s. of Otto and Anne (Niemeyer) Piene; one s. three d.; ed. Acad. of Fine Arts, Munich and Düsseldorf and Univ. of Cologne; Visiting Prof., Graduate School of Art, Univ. of Pa. 1964; Prof. of Environmental Art, School of Arch., M.I.T. 1972–; Dir. Center for Advanced Visual Studies, M.I.T. 1974–; one-man exhbns. include: Galerie Heseler, Munich 1971, 1972, 1975, 1977–79, 1981, 1983, Galerie Heimeshoff, Essen 1974, 1977, 1983, 1988, Galerie Schoeller, Düsseldorf 1976, 1977, 1980, 1984, 1987; retrospective exhbn. Hayden Gallery, M.I.T. 1975; group exhbns. include Tate Gallery 1964, Düsseldorf 1973, Antwerp 1979, Paris 1983; performed works include Olympic Rainbow 1972, Sky Events, SAC 1981, 1982, 1983, 1986, Sky Dance, Guggenheim 1984; recipient of several awards and prizes. *Publications:* More Sky 1973; author and ed., Zero 1973, Art Transition 1975–76, Centerbeam 1980, Sky Art Conference Catalog 1981, 1982, 1983, 1986. *Address:* Center for Advanced Visual Studies, Massachussetts Institute of Technology, W11, 40 Massachussetts Avenue, Cambridge, Mass. 02139 (Office); 383 Old Ayer Road, Groton, Mass. 01450, U.S.A. (Home). *Telephone:* (617) 253-4415 (Office).

PIENIĄZEK, Szczepan Aleksander, M.PH., M.S., PH.D.; Polish pomologist; b. 27 Dec. 1913, Słup, near Garwolin; s. of Józef and Zofia Pieniążek; m. Janina Praska 1939; one s. one d.; ed. Warsaw Univ., Cornell Univ., Ithaca, N.Y., U.S.A.; Instructor Rhode Island Univ. 1942–45, Asst. Res. Prof. 1945–46; Assoc. Prof., Warsaw Agric. Univ. 1946–54, Prof. 1954–, Chair. Dept. Pomology 1946–68; Corresp. mem. Polish Acad. of Sciences 1952–64, mem. 1964–; mem. Presidium 1960–, Vice-Pres. 1975–80; Dir. Res., Inst. of Pomology, Skierniewice 1951–83; mem. Polish Botanical Soc. 1936–, Hon. mem. 1980–; mem. American Soc. for Horticultural Science 1938–, Fellow 1974–; mem. Int. Soc. for Horticultural Science 1958–, Vice-Pres. 1966–70, Pres. 1970–74, Hon. Life mem. 1976–, Chair. Fruit-Growing Section 1962–66; Foreign mem. Bulgarian Acad. of Agric. Science 1968, G.D.R. Acad. of Agric. Science 1968, V.I. Lenin All-Union Acad. of Agric. Science 1970; Corresp. mem. Agric. Acad. of France 1976–79, mem. 1979–; Dr. h.c. (Cracow Agric. Acad.) 1973, (Bonn Univ.) 1983, (Warsaw Agric. Acad.) 1983, (Szczecin Agric. Acad.) 1984, (Agric. Acad., Poznań) 1985; Officer's Cross, Order of Polonia Resituta 1954, Commdr.'s Cross 1973; Order of Banner of Labour, 2nd Class 1959; State Prize, 2nd Class 1950, State Prize (1st Class) 1978, Order of the Builders of People's Poland 1977, Grand Officier, Order de l'Encouragement Public (France) 1981, Meritorious Agronomist of People's Poland 1985, and other decorations. *Publications:* Dookoła Sadowniczego Świata (Round the Fruit-Growing World) 1965, Gdy Zakwitną Jabłonie (When the Apple Trees Bloom) 1971, Sadownictwo (Textbook of Pomology) 1976. *Leisure interest:* growing tropical fruit plants in pots. *Address:* Ul. Niemodlińska 65, 04-635 Warszawa-Anin, Poland (Home). *Telephone:* 153649 (Home).

PIEPER, Ernst; German business executive; b. 20 Dec. 1928, Gerolstein, Eifel; s. of Wilhelm and Anne Pieper; m. Marianne Hansen 1954; one s.

one d.; ed. studies in industrial man. in Cologne and Bonn; with Klöckner-Werke AG 1954-61; Fed. Office for Trade and Industry 1962-64; Ministry of the Economy 1964-73; Ministry of Finance 1974-77; Vice-Chair. Exec. Bd. Salzgitter AG 1977-79, Chair. 1979-; Chair. Supervisory Bd. Stahlwerke Peine-Salzgitter AG, Howaldtswerke-Deutsche Werft AG; Deutsche Schachtbau und Tiefbohrgesellschaft mbH, Salzgitter Industriebau GmbH; mem. Supervisory Bd. Continental Gummi-Werke AG, Rhenus WTAG Westfälische Transport AG, WTB Bauaktiengesellschaft, VTG Vereinigte Tanklager und Transportmittel GmbH; Consultant Hermes Kreditversicherung AG, Landesbank Rheinland-Pfalz, Ruhrgas AG; Ingersoll Prize for Scholarly Letters 1987, Stoatspreis des Landes Nordrhein-Westfalen 1987. *Leisure interests:* sailing, skiing. *Address:* Malmedyweg 10, 4400 Münster-Westfalen, Federal Republic of Germany.

PIERCE, John Robinson, B.S., M.S., PH.D.; American electrical engineer; b. 27 March 1910, Des Moines, Ia.; s. of the late John S. and Harriett A. Robinson Pierce; m. 1st Martha Peacock 1938 (divorced 1964); m. 2nd Ellen Richter 1964 (died 1986); one s. one d.; m. 3rd Brenda Woodard 1987; ed. Calif. Inst. of Tech.; Bell Telephone Laboratories 1936-71, Dir. of Electronics Research 1952-55, Dir. of Research, Electrical Communications 1955-58, Communications Principles 1958-61; Exec. Dir. Research-Communications Principles and Systems Div. 1961-65, Research-Communications Sciences Div. 1965-71; Prof. of Eng., Calif. Inst. of Tech. 1971-80, Emer. 1980-, Chief Technician, Jet Propulsion Lab. 1979-82; Visiting Prof. of Music, Stanford Univ., Prof. Emer. 1983-; mem. N.A.S., Nat. Acad. of Eng. (Founders Award 1977), American Philosophical Soc., Royal Acad. of Sciences (Sweden); Fellow, Acoustical Soc. of America, American Physical Soc., Inst. of Electrical and Electronics Engineers, American Acad. of Arts and Sciences; Valdemar Poulsen Medal 1963, President's Nat. Medal of Science 1963, Marconi Int. Fellowship 1979, Japan Prize 1985 and many other medals and trophies. *Publications:* Theory and Design of Electron Beams 1954, Traveling Wave Tubes 1950, Electrons, Waves and Messages 1956, Man's World of Sound 1958, Symbols, Signals and Noise 1961, The Research State: A History of Science in New Jersey 1964, Electrons and Waves 1964, Quantum Electronics 1966, Waves and Messages 1967, Science, Art and Communication 1968, Almost All About Waves 1973, Introduction to Communication Sciences and Systems 1980, Signals, the Telephone and Beyond 1981, The Science of Musical Sound 1983, Information Technology and Civilization (with Hiroshi Inose) 1984. *Leisure interests:* writing, science fiction, music. *Address:* Stanford University, Department of Music, Stanford, Calif. 94305; 7 Peter Coutts Circle, Stanford, Calif. 94305, U.S.A. *Telephone:* (415) 725-3570 (Office); (415) 493-5197 (Home).

PIERCE, Samuel Riley, Jr., A.B, J.D., LL.M., LL.D., L.H.D., D.C.L.; American lawyer and public official; b. 8 Sept. 1922, Glen Cove, Long Island, N.Y.; s. of Samuel R. and Hettie E. (Armstrong) Pierce; m. Barbara Penn Wright 1948; one d.; ed. Cornell Univ., Yale Univ. Law School and New York Univ.; admitted to New York bar 1949, Supreme Court bar 1956; Asst. Dist. Attorney, County of New York 1949-53; Asst. U.S. Attorney, Southern Dist., N.Y. 1953-55; Asst. to Under-Sec., Dept. of Labor, Washington, D.C. 1955-56; Assoc. Counsel, Counsel Judiciary Sub-Cttee. on Antitrust, House of Reps. 1956-57; pvt. law practice 1957-59, 1961-70, 1973-81; on faculty New York Univ. School of Law 1958-70; Judge, N.Y. Court Gen. Sessions 1959-61; Gen. Counsel, Head of Legal Div., U.S. Treasury, Washington 1970-73; Gov. American Stock Exchange 1977-80; U.S. Sec. of Housing and Urban Devt. 1981-89; mem. Nat. Wiretapping Comm. 1973-76; Advisory Group Commr. Internal Revenue Service 1974-76; mem. Nat. Advisory Cttee., Comptroller of Currency 1975-80; dir. numerous cos; Republican. *Publications:* articles in professional journals. *Address:* 16 West 77th Street, New York, N.Y. 10024, U.S.A. (Home).

PIERRE, Abbé (see Groués, Henri).

PIERRE, Andrew J., DR.RER.POL.; American political scientist; b. 13 June 1934; ed. Amherst Coll., Inst. of Political Studies, Paris, Columbia Univ.; Adjunct Prof., Columbia Univ. 1962-64; worked for Dept. of State, Washington as specialist in UN affairs and for U.S. Embassy, London as specialist in political and mil. affairs; Dir.-Gen. Atlantic Inst. for Int. Affairs 1987-88. *Publications:* The Global Politics of Arm Sales and other books.

PIERRE-BROSSOLETTE, Claude, L. EN D.; French civil servant; b. 5 March 1928, Paris; s. of Pierre Brossolette and Gilberte (née Bruel); m. Sabine Goldet 1953; two d.; ed. Lycée Henri-IV, Faculty of Law of Paris Univ., Ecole nat. d'admin.; Inspecteur adjoint des Finances 1952, Insp. 1955; served under two successive Ministers in Office of Minister of Econ. and Financial Affairs 1956; Asst. to Financial Adviser, Embassy in U.S.A. 1957; served Direction des Finances Extérieures 1958; Tech. Adviser, Office of Minister of Finance 1960-62, Asst. Dir. of Office 1962, Deputy Dir. 1963; Asst. Dir. of External Financial Affairs in Direction du Trésor 1964, later Chef de Service 1966; Sec.-Gen. Conseil nat. du Crédit 1967-71; served in office of Valéry Giscard d'Estaing, Minister of Econ. and Financial Affairs 1969-71; Dir. du Trésor, Ministry of Econ. and Financial Affairs 1971; Censeur, Banque de France, Crédit nat. 1971; Vice-Chair. Caisse nat. des Télécommunications 1971-74; Dir. SNCF (Nat. Railways Bd.) 1971-74, Air France 1971-74; Sec.-Gen. of Presidency of the Repub. 1974-76; Chair. Crédit Lyonnais 1976-82, Omnium financier pour l'Industrie nat. (OFINA) Sept. 1976-, Europartners Securities Corpn., Banque

Stern 1982-86, Vice-Chair. 1986-; Assoc. Man. Worms et Cie 1986-; Admin. Crédit Nat. 1976-81; mem. Conseil nat. du Crédit 1976-81, Conseil de Surveillance de la Cie. Bancaire Oct. 1976-, Administrateur de la Société Air-liquide, du Crédit Foncier de France 1978-82, de la Générale Occidentale 1979-82, de Péchiney Ugine Kuhlmann 1980-82, de la Lyonnaise des Eaux 1980, de B.S.N. 1981; Chevalier, Légion d'honneur, Officier de l'Ordre nat. du Mérite, Chevalier de l'Ordre des Palmes académiques, Médaille de la Résistance. *Address:* Worms et Cie, 45 boulevard Haussmann, 75008 Paris (Office); 37 avenue d'Iéna, 75116 Paris, France (Home). *Telephone:* (031) 245371 (Israel); 54201644 (France).

PIERRET, Alain Marie, B.A.; French diplomatist; b. 16 July 1930, Mourmelon; s. of Henri Pierret and Yvonne Delhumeau; m. Jacqueline Nanta 1958; three d. (one deceased); ed. Faculties of Arts (Sorbonne) and Law, Paris and Ecole Nat. de la France d'Outre-Mer; reserve officer (navy) 1953-55; District Commr. Togo 1955-59, Sahara (S. Algeria) 1959-61; Sec. of Embassy, Sierra Leone 1961-63, South Africa 1963-66; Africa Div. Ministry of Foreign Affairs 1966-69; Counsellor, Moscow 1969-72; Head, Soviet Affairs Bureau, Ministry of Foreign Affairs 1972; mem. French Del. to Conf. on Security and Co-operation in Europe Helsinki 1972-75; Counsellor, Belgrade 1975-80; Amb. to Niger 1980-82; Asst. Sec. of State for UN Affairs and Int. Orgs. 1983-86; Amb. to Israel 1986-; Légion d'Honneur, Croix de Guerre (Vietnam). *Address:* 112 Herbert Samuel Promenade, Tel Aviv, Israel; Toisy, 41330 La Chapelle-Vendômoise, France.

PIESKE, Eckard, M.A., DR.RER.POL.; German economist; b. 31 May 1928, Brieg, near Breslau (now in Poland); s. of Dr. Erich Pieske and Beda-Johanna Pieske; m. Doris Ritter 1957 (died 1985); one s.; ed. Univ. of Tübingen and Western Reserve Univ., Cleveland, U.S.A.; Economist, Bank Deutscher Länder, Frankfurt 1953; Investment Analyst, Allianz-Lebensversicherung-AG, Stuttgart 1956; official of Fed. Ministries of Econ. Affairs and Finance 1958; Exec. Dir. IMF 1975-79; Ministerial Dirigent, Fed. Ministry of Finance. *Publications:* Gold, Devisen, Sonderziehungsrechte (3rd edn.) 1972. *Leisure interests:* gardening, hiking. *Address:* Bundesministerium der Finanzen, 53 Bonn; Zedernweg 7, 53 Bonn 1, Federal Republic of Germany (Home). *Telephone:* (0228) 6821 (Office).

PIETILÄ, Reima Frans Ilmari; Finnish architect; b. 25 Aug. 1923, Turku; s. of Frans Viktor Pietilä and Ida Maria Lehtinen; m. Raili Inkeri Marjatta Paatelainen 1961; one c.; ed. Inst of Tech.; State Prof. of Arts 1971-74; Prof. of Architecture Univ. of Oulu 1973-78; Partner, Reima Pietilä & Raili Paatelainen, Architects 1974-; Vice-Chair. Asscn. of Finnish Architects 1959-60, mem. Gov. Body 1969-70; Foreign mem. Royal Acad. for Liberal Arts, Sweden 1969-; Hon. mem. A.I.A.; Chevalier Ordre de la Couronne (Belgium) 1958; Kt. Order of the Finnish Lion 1967; Tapiola Medal for Town Planning Services 1981, Prince Eugene Medal (Sweden) 1981, U.I.A. Gold Medal (Brighton) 1987. *Major works:* Finnish Pavilion at Brussels World Fair 1958, Kaleva Church, Tampere 1966, Students' Activity Centre, Dipoli, Congress Centre, Otaniemi 1966, Hervanta Cultural Centre, Tampere 1979, Sief Palace Area Bldgs., Kuwait 1981, Suvituuli Housing, Tapiola 1981-82, Council of Ministers 1982, Ministry of Foreign Affairs 1982, Lieksa Church, E. Finland 1982, Tampere Main Library 1983, Finnish Embassy, New Delhi 1983. *Leisure interest:* pragmatic problems in architectural Hermeneutics. *Address:* Laivurinrinne 1A5, 00120 Helsinki 12, Finland. *Telephone:* 634602 (Helsinki).

PIETRUSKI, John Michael, Jr., B.S.; American business executive; b. 12 March 1933, Sayreville, N.J.; s. of John M. Pietruski, Sr. and of the late Lillian Christensen Pietruski; m. Roberta Jeanne Talbot 1954; two s. one d.; ed. Sayreville High School and Rutgers Univ.; First Lieut. U.S. Army 1955-57; Manufacturing Man., Industrial Eng. Man., Procter & Gamble Co. 1954-63; Pres. Hosp. Div., Manufacturing Div. and Medical Products Div., C. R. Bard Inc. 1963-77; Pres. Pharmaceutical Group. Sterling Drug Inc. 1977-81, Corp. Exec. Vice-Pres. 1981-83, Pres. and C.O.O. 1983-85, Chair. and C.E.O. 1985-88, mem. Bd. of Dirs. 1978-; mem. Bd. of Dirs. Council of Better Business Bureaus 1983-, Pharmaceutical Manufacturers Asscn. 1985-, Irving Bank Corpn. 1985-, Associated Dry Goods Corpn. 1985-. *Leisure interests:* boating, fishing, travelling, athletics. *Address:* Sterling Drug Inc., 90 Park Avenue, New York, N.Y. 10016 (Office); 3 Bruce Court, Edison, N.J. 08820, U.S.A. (Home). *Telephone:* (212) 907-3000 (Office).

PIETTRE, André, D. ÈS SC. ECON.; French academic; b. 3 May 1906, Caudry (North); m. 1934; six s. one d.; ed. Univ. of Paris; Prof. Univ. of Strasbourg 1936-40, 1945-52, Dean, Faculty of Law and Econ. Sciences 1951-53; Prof. Faculty of Law and Econ. Sciences, Paris 1953-77; mem. Inst. de France; Commdr. Légion d'Honneur, Officier des Arts et Lettres. *Publications:* Les Trois Âges de l'Economie 1967, La culture en question 1969, Marx et marxisme 1973, Eglise missionaire? 1978, Esthétique d'abord 1983, Histoire de la pensée économique 1985. *Address:* 82 avenue des 4 Chemins, 92290 Châtenay-Malabry, France. *Telephone:* (1) 47 02 39 35.

PIEYRE DE MANDIARGUES, André; French writer; b. 14 March 1909, Paris; s. of David Pieyre de Mandiargues and Lucie Bérard; m. Bona Tibertelli 1950 (divorced; remarried 1987); one d.; Prix des Critiques for Soleil des loups 1951; Prix Goncourt for La Marge 1967 (poetry), Grand Prix, Académie Française 1979. *Publications:* Dans les années sordides (poems and prose) 1943, Hedera ou la persistance de l'amour pendant une rêverie (poem) 1945, L'étudiante 1946, Le musée noir 1946, Les incongruités monumentales 1948, Les sept périls spectraux 1950, Les masques de Léonor Fini 1951, Soleil des loups 1951, Marbre 1953, Astyanax 1956, Les monstres de Bomarzo (essays) 1957, Le belvédère (essays) 1958, Feu de braise 1959, La marée 1959, Cartolines et dédicaces 1960, Sugai 1960, L'âge de craie 1961, Deuxième belvédère 1962, La motocyclette (novel) 1963, Saint-John Perse, A l'honneur de la chair 1963, Sabine 1964, Le point où j'en suis 1964, Beylamour 1965, Les corps illuminés 1965, Larmes de généraux 1965, Porte dévergondée 1965, La marge (novel) 1967, Ruisseau des solitudes 1968, Le marronnier 1968, Troisième belvédère 1971, Mascarets 1971, Bona l'amour et la peinture 1971, Le cadran lunaire 1972, Isabella Morra 1974, Chagall 1975, Le désordre de la mémoire 1975, Sous la lame 1976, Arcimboldo le merveilleux 1977, L'ivre oeil 1979, La nuit séculaire 1979, Le trésor cruel de Hans Bellmer 1979, L'Anglais décrit dans le château fermé 1979, Arsène et Cléopâtre 1981, Un Saturne gai 1982, Le deuil des roses, Tout disparaîtra 1987. *Address:* 36 rue de Sévigné, 75003 Paris, France. *Telephone:* 887 9889.

PIFER, Alan (Jay Parrish); American foundation executive; b. 4 May 1921, Boston; s. of Claude Albert and Elizabeth (Parrish) Pifer; m. Erica Pringle 1953; three s.; ed. Groton School, Harvard Univ., Emmanuel Coll., Cambridge; Executive Sec. U.S. Educ. Comm in U.K. 1948–53; joined Carnegie Corpn. 1953, Vice-Pres. 1963–65, Acting Pres. 1965–67, Pres. 1967–82, Pres. Emer. and Sr. Consultant 1982–, Vice-Pres. Carnegie Foundation for the Advancement of Teaching 1963–65, Acting Pres. 1965–67, Pres. 1967–79; Chair. Bd. Consortium for the Advancement of Pvt. Higher Educ. 1983–, Univ. of Cape Town Fund 1984–; mem. Man. Cttee. U.S.-S. Africa Leader Exchange Program 1957–; Dir. N.Y. Urban Coalition 1967–71, Fed. Reserve Bank 1971–76, Council on Foreign Relations, Comm. on Pvt. Philanthropy and Public Needs 1973–76, McGraw-Hill Inc. 1977–, American Asscn. for Higher Educ. 1982–, Technoserve, Inc. 1983–, Business Council for Effective Literacy 1984–; Co-Chair. Nutrition Watch Cttee. 1981–82; mem. Pres.'s Comm on White House Fellowships; Trustee, African-American Inst. 1952–72; Trustee, Foundation Library Center 1967–70, Chair. 1968–70; Trustee, Bd. of Overseers, Harvard Univ. 1969–75, Univ. of Bridgeport (Conn.) 1973–, American Ditchley Foundation 1973–82; Chair. Carnegie Corpn. Aging Soc. Project 1983–86, Nat. Conf. on Social Welfare Project on Fed. Social Role 1983–; Fellow, African Studies Asscn., U.S. Acad. of Arts and Sciences; Hon. LL.D.(Mich. State Univ.) 1971, (Hofstra Univ.) 1974, (Univ. of Notre Dame) 1975, (Millsaps Coll., Miss.) 1986; Hon. Dr. Univ. (Open Univ.) 1974; Hon. D.H.L. (Marymount Coll.) 1983; Hon. D.Educ. (Univ. of Cape Town) 1984; Barnard Coll. Medal of Distinction, Atlanta Univ. 1980, Teachers Coll., Columbia Univ. Cleveland E. Dodge Medal for Distinguished Service 1982. *Address:* 437 Madison Avenue, New York, N.Y. 10022; 311 Greens Farms Road, Greens Farms, Conn. 06436, U.S.A. (Home).

PIGEAT, Henri Michel; French administrator; b. 13 Nov. 1939, Montluçon; s. of Eugène Pigeat and Odette Micard; m. Passerose Cyprienne Rueff 1976; one d.; ed. Inst. des Sciences Politiques, Paris, and Ecole Nat. d'Admin.; Civil Servant Office of Gen. Admin. and Public Service 1965–69; Head Office of Sec. of State for Public Service 1969–71, Tech. Adviser 1971–72; Head of Information Services, Office of Sec. of State for Public Service and Information 1973; Sec.-Gen. Interministerial Cttee. for Information 1973–74; Asst. Gen. Dir. Information, Gen. Office of Information 1974, Dir. 1975–76; Dir. Information and Broadcasting Service 1976–; Deputy Man. Dir. Agence France-Presse 1976–79, Chair. and Man. Dir. 1979–86; Chair. and Gen. Man. Burson-Marsteller France; Chair. CEDICOM S.A.; Prof. Inst. d'Etudes Politiques de Paris; Dir. Soc. nat. des entreprises de presse 1974–76; Dir. Soc. financière de radiodiffusion (Sofirad) 1972–76; fmr. Dir. E1, R.M.C., Sud Radio, S.N.E.P., T.D.F., Europe 1, Radio Monte Carlo; Maître de confs. Inst. d'études politiques, Paris 1966–73, Ecole nat. d'admin. 1967–69, Inst. int. d'admin. publique 1966–73; mem. Exec. Cttee. Int. Inst. of Communications, London, Pres. of French section; mem. Int. Press. Inst.; Chevalier, Ordre nat. du Mérite; Commdr. Nat. Order of Fed. Repub. of Germany. *Publications:* La France contemporaine, L'Europe contemporaine (both jointly) 1966–70, Saint Ecran ou la Télévision par câbles 1974, Du Téléphone à la Télématique, La télévision par cable commence demain 1983, Le nouveau desordre mondiac de l'information 1987. *Address:* 23 quai Anatole France, 75007 Paris, France (Home). *Telephone:* 40.74.07.08 (Office); 45.51.70.01 (Home).

PIGGOTT, Lester Keith; British fmr. jockey, now trainer; b. 5 Nov. 1935; s. of Keith Piggott and Iris Rickaby; m. Susan Armstrong 1960; two d.; rode over 100 winners per year in U.K. alone in several seasons since 1955; rode 3,000th winner in U.K. 27 July 1974; Champion Jockey nine times (1960, 1964–71); frequently rides in France; equalled record of 21 classic victories 1975; won 29 English classic victories by Oct. 1985; 4,349 winners by Oct. 1985; retd. Oct. 1985; races won include: the Derby (9 times): 1954 (on Never Say Die), 1957 (on Crepello), 1960 (on St. Paddy), 1968 (on Sir Ivor), 1970 (on Nijinsky), 1972 (on Roberto), 1976 (on Empery), 1977 (on The Minstrel), 1983 (on Teenoso); St. Leger (8 times); Prix de l'Arc de Triomphe (3 times): 1973 (on Rheingold), 1977 and 1978 (on Alleged); Washington, D.C. Int. 1968 (on Sir Ivor, first time since 1922 an English Derby winner raced in U.S.A.), 1969 (on Karabas), 1980 (on Argument); sentenced to 3 years imprisonment for tax fraud Oct. 1987;

stripped of O.B.E. June 1988; released after 18 months for good behaviour. *Leisure interests:* swimming, water skiing, golf. *Address:* Florizel, Newmarket, Suffolk, England. *Telephone:* Newmarket 662584.

PIGGOTT, Stuart, C.B.E., D.LITT., F.B.A., F.S.A.; British university professor (retd.); b. 28 May 1910, Petersfield, Hants.; s. of G. H. O. Piggott and G. A. Phillips; ed. Churchers' Coll., Petersfield, and St. John's Coll., Oxford; Investigator, Royal Comm. on Ancient Monuments (Wales) 1928–33; Asst. Dir. Avebury Excavations (Wilts.) 1934–38; war service, Lieut.-Col., Intelligence Corps 1939–45; Abercromby Prof. of Prehistoric Archaeology, Univ. of Edinburgh 1946–77; Commdr. Royal Comm. on Ancient Monuments Scotland 1946; Trustee, British Museum 1969–74; mem. German Archaeological Inst. 1953; foreign hon. mem. American Acad. of Arts and Sciences 1960; Hon. Fellow, St. John's Coll., Oxford 1979; Fellow Univ. Coll. London 1985; Hon. D.Litt. Hum. (Columbia Univ.), Hon. D.Litt. (Edinburgh) 1984. *Publications:* Fire Among the Ruins (poems) 1948, British Prehistory 1949, Prehistoric India 1950, William Stukeley 1950, Neolithic Cultures of the British Isles 1954, Scotland Before History 1958, Approach to Archaeology 1959, Ancient Europe 1965, Prehistoric Societies (with J. G. D. Clark) 1965, The Druids 1968, Introduction to Camden's Britannia of 1695 1971, Ruins in a Landscape 1976, Antiquity Depicted 1978, The Earliest Wheeled Transport 1983; Ed. The Dawn of Civilization 1961. *Leisure interests:* reading, eating and drinking, talking. *Address:* The Cottage, West Challow, Wantage, Oxon., England. *Telephone:* Wantage 3478.

PIGOTT-SMITH, Tim; British actor; b. 1946, Stratford-upon-Avon; m. Pamela Miles; one s.; ed. Bristol Univ.; began stage career at Bristol Old Vic; mem. R.S.C. 1972–75. *Stage appearances include:* As You Like it, Major Barbara, Bengal Lancer 1985, Antony and Cleopatra, Coming into Land 1987, Cymbeline 1988. *TV appearances include:* Hamlet, Antony and Cleopatra, Glittering Prizes, North and South, Wings, Eustace and Hilda, Lost Boys, Measure for Measure, Fame is the Spur, The Hunchback of Notre Dame, The Jewel in the Crown, Chain Reaction, Dead Man's Folly, Double Helix. *Film appearances include:* Aces High 1975, Joseph Andrews 1977, Sweet William 1978, The Day Christ Died 1979, Clash of the Titans 1981, Escape to Victory, Richard's Things, State of Emergency. *Publication:* Out of India 1986. *Address:* c/o Michael Whitehall, 125 Gloucester Road, London. S.W.7, England.

PIGNON, Edouard; French painter; b. 12 Feb. 1905, Bully-les-Mines (Pas de Calais); s. of Lucien and Stella (née Allart) Pignon; m. 3rd Hélène Parmelin 1950; two s. one d.; miner, stonemason, metallurgist, etc. 1922–39; pupil of the painter Auclair 1928, of the sculptors Wlerick and Arnold 1930–34; devoted himself exclusively to painting 1940–; Salon des Indépendants 1932–38, des Surindépendants 1938, des Tuileries and d'Automne 1943, de Mai (founding mem.) 1944–; rep. at Paris Exhbns. 1941, 1942, 1943, 1954, 1955, 1956, 1957; one-man shows Paris 1946, 1949, 1952–56, 1958, 1959; Retrospective Exhbn., Musée d'Art Moderne, Paris 1966; many foreign exhibitions; costumes and décor for Scheherazade 1948, Mère courage (Théâtre Nat. Populaire) 1952, Mandragore 1953, Ce fou de Platonov, Le malade imaginaire 1956, On ne badine pas avec l'amour (Théâtre Nat. Populaire) 1959; retrospective exhbns. Bucharest, Budapest, Warsaw, Bologne, Luxembourg 1973–75; exhbn. of 50 nudes Musée d'Art Moderne, Paris 1976; works in museums at Paris (Art Moderne), Amsterdam, Brussels, Liège, London (Tate Gallery), New York (Modern Art), São Paulo, Stockholm, Gothenburg; exhbn. Grand Palais, Paris 1985; principal series: Les maternités 1942–43, Les poissons, femmes assises 1944, Les Catalanes 1945–46, Le port d'Ostende 1947, Les mineurs 1949, Les oliviers 1950, Les vendanges, Cueillettes de jasmins 1953, Les électriciens 1955, Les Paysages de bandol 1958, Les combats de coqs 1959–60, Pousseurs de blé 1961–62, Batailles 1963–64, Plongeurs 1964–67, Têtes de guerriers 1968, Céramique-sculpture, Maison de la Culture, Argenteuil 1970; Officier, Légion d'honneur, Officier des Arts et des Lettres. *Publications:* Illustrations for Les blasons (poem by Maurice Scève), Arbres et voiles (Verdet), Dialogue de l'arbre (Valéry) 1957, Jacques le fataliste (Diderot); La quête de la réalité, Contre-courant 1974. *Address:* Galerie Beaubourg, 23 rue du Renard, 75004 Paris; 26 rue des Plantes, 75014 Paris, France (Home). *Telephone:* 540-77-21 (Home).

PIHLAJAMÄKI, Veikko Jaako Uolevi, M.SC.; Finnish politician; b. 1922, Kauhava; surveyor, Vaasa Prov. 1952–72; mem. Kauhava City Council 1961–, Chair. 1965–; M.P. 1972–; Second Deputy Chair. of Parl. 1983; Minister of Defence 1983–87; Centre Party. *Address:* c/o Ministry of Defence, Et. Makasiinikatu 8, 00130 Helsinki 13, Finland.

PIIPARI, (KASURINEN) Anna-Liisa; Finnish politician; b. 8 May 1940, Kivijärvi; psychiatric nurse, Pitkaniemi Mental Hosp. 1964–66; nurse, Kotka Cen. Hosp. 1968–; mem. Parl. 1979–; Vice-Chair. Social Democratic Party (SDP) Parl. Group. 1986–87; Minister for Cultural Affairs, Ministry of Educ. 1987–. *Address:* Ministry of Education, Meritullinkatu 10, 00170 Helsinki, Finland. *Telephone:* (90) 134171.

PIKAIZEN, Viktor Aleksandrovich; Soviet violinist; b. 15 Feb. 1933, Kiev; ed. Moscow Conservatory (pupil of David Oistrakh); Second Prize, Int. Kubelik Violinists' Competition, Prague 1949; G. Thibault Competition, Paris 1957, First Prize, Paganini Competition, Genoa 1965; numerous recordings.

PIKE, Sir Philip, Kt., Q.C.; British judge; b. 6 March 1914, Jamaica; s. of Ernest B. and Dora C. (née Lillie) Pike; m. 1st Phyllis Kelvin Calder 1943, one s. one d.; m. 2nd Millicent Locke Staples 1959; ed. De Carteret School and Munro Coll., Jamaica, and Middle Temple, London; Crown Counsel Jamaica 1947–49; Legal Draftsman Kenya 1949–52; Solicitor-Gen., Uganda 1952–58; Attorney-Gen., Sarawak 1958–65; Chief Justice High Court, Borneo 1965–68; Judge and Acting Chief Justice, Malawi 1969–70; Chief Justice, Swaziland 1970–72; Coronation Medal; decorations from Malaysia and Sarawak. *Leisure interests:* golf, gardening. *Address:* 3 Earlewood Court, Penhaligon Way, Robina Waters, Queensland 4226, Australia.

PILARCZYK, Rev. Daniel Edward, M.A., PH.D., S.T.D.; American ecclesiastic; b. 12 Aug. 1934, Dayton, Ohio; s. of Daniel J. Pilarczyk and Frieda S. Hilgefort; ed. St. Gregory Seminary, Ohio, Pontifical Urban Univ. Rome, Xavier Univ. Cincinnati and Univ. of Cincinnati; ordained Roman Catholic priest 1959; Asst. Chancellor, Archdiocese of Cincinnati 1961–63; Faculty, Athenaeum of Ohio (St. Gregory Seminary) 1963–74, Vice-Pres. 1968–74, Trustee 1974–; Rector, St. Gregory Seminary 1968–74; Synodal Judge, Archdiocesan Tribunal 1971–82; Dir. of Archdiocesan Educ. Services 1974–82; Auxiliary Bishop of Cincinnati 1974–82, Archbishop 1982–; Vice-Pres. Nat. Conf. of Catholic Bishops 1986–; numerous professional appts.; Hon. LL.D. (Xavier Univ.) 1975, (Calumet Coll.) 1982. *Publications:* articles in newspapers and journals. *Address:* 100 East Eighth Street, Cincinnati, Ohio 45202 (Office); 29 East Eighth Street, Cincinnati, Ohio 45202 U.S.A. (Home). *Telephone:* 421-3131.

PILCHER, Sir John (Arthur), G.C.M.G.; former British diplomatist; b. 16 May 1912; s. of Col A. J. Pilcher and Edith Blair; m. Delia Margaret Taylor 1942; one d.; ed. Shrewsbury and Clare Coll., Cambridge; served Japan 1936–39, China 1939–41; Ministry of Information and Foreign Office 1941–48; Press Attaché, Rome 1948–51; Foreign Office 1951–54; Counsellor, Madrid 1954–59; Amb. to Philippines 1959–63; Asst. Under-Sec. of State, Foreign Office 1963–65; Amb. to Austria 1965–67, to Japan 1967–72; mem. Comm. on Museums and Galleries 1973–83; Dir. Foreign and Colonial Investment Trust 1973–82; Adviser to Robert Fleming and Co. 1973–85; Grand Cross, Austrian Order of Merit 1966; Order of the Rising Sun, First Class (Japan) 1971; Grand Officer Order of Merit, Italy 1977. *Leisure interests:* music, literature, the arts, history, gardening. *Address:* 33 The Terrace, London, S.W.13, England. *Telephone:* 01-876 9710.

PILE, Sir William Dennis, G.C.B., M.B.E.; British civil servant (retd.); b. 1 Dec. 1919, Whitley Bay, Northumberland; s. of James Edward and Jean Elizabeth Pile; m. Joan Marguerite Crafter 1948; one s. two d.; ed. Royal Masonic School and St. Catherine's Coll., Cambridge; entered Ministry of Educ. 1946; Cabinet Office 1951; returned to Ministry of Educ. 1952; Asst. Sec. 1955, Under-Sec. 1962; Ministry of Health 1966; Deputy Sec. Home Office Dir.-Gen. of H.M. Prison Service 1967; Perm. Sec. Dept. of Educ. and Science 1970–76; Chair. Bd. of Inland Revenue 1976–79; Dir. Nationwide Building Soc. 1980–87, Distillers Co. Ltd. 1980–87. *Address:* The Manor House, Riverhead, Near Sevenoaks, Kent, England (Home). *Telephone:* (0732) 54498.

PILKINGTON, Sir Lionel Alexander Bethune (known as Sir Alastair), Kt., M.A., F.R.S., F.B.I.M.; British glassmaker; b. 7 Jan. 1920, Calcutta, India; s. of late Col. L. G. Pilkington and Mrs Pilkington; m. 1st Patricia N. Elliot 1945 (died 1977); one s. one d.; m. 2nd Kathleen Haynes 1978; ed. Sherborne School and Trinity Coll., Cambridge; joined Pilkington Brothers Ltd. (now Pilkington PLC) 1947, Dir. 1955–80, Deputy Chair. 1971–73, Chair. 1973–80, non-exec. Dir. 1980–85, Pres. 1985–; inventor of the float glass process; Chair. Council for Nat. Academic Awards (C.N.A.A.) 1984–87; Dir. Bank of England 1974–84, British Petroleum 1976–, Business Int., Hambros Advanced Tech. Trust 1984–, Banque Nat. de Paris PLC 1985; non-exec. Chair. Chloride Group 1979–82, non-exec. Deputy Chair. 1982–87; non-exec. Dir. Wellcome Foundation 1984–; mem. Court of Govs., Admin. Staff Coll. Henley 1973–; Pro-Chancellor Lancaster Univ. 1980–; Fellow, Imperial Coll. of Science and Tech., London 1974; Hon. F. Eng.; Hon. Fellow UMIST 1969, Polytechnic of Wales 1988; Hon. D.Tech. (Loughborough) 1968; Hon. D.Eng. (Liverpool) 1971, (Birmingham) 1971; Hon. D.Tech. (C.N.A.A.) 1976; Hon. LL.D. (Bristol) 1979; Hon. D.Sc. (Univ. of E. Anglia) 1984; Toledo Glass and Ceramic Award 1964, Mullard Award (Royal Soc.) 1968, John Scott Award (City Trust, Philadelphia) 1969, Wilhelm Exner Medal (Austrian Trade Asscn.), Eleventh Annual Phoenix Award, Pittsburgh, Pa. 1980 (first Englishman to receive this award), Albert Gold Medal (R.S.A.). *Leisure interests:* music, walking, carpentry, gardening and skiing. *Address:* Pilkington PLC, St. Helens, Merseyside, (Office); Goldrill Cottage, Patterdale, Penrith, Cumbria, CA11 0NW (Home); 74 Eaton Place, London, SW1X 8AU, England. *Telephone:* (0744) 28882 (Office); 085-32-263 (Home); 01-235 5604.

PILLIOD, Charles J., Jr.; American business executive and diplomatist; b. 20 Oct. 1918, Cuyahoga Falls, Ohio; m. Marie Elizabeth Jacobs; three s. two d.; ed. Kent State Univ., Ohio; Production Trainee Goodyear 1941; Pilot U.S.A.F., World War II; Man. Dir. Goodyear-Panama 1947, Sales Man. Goodyear-Columbia 1954, Man. Dir. Goodyear, Brazil 1959, Man. Dir. Goodyear, U.K. 1964, Dir. of Operations, Goodyear Int. 1966, Vice-Pres. 1967, Pres. 1971; Vice-Pres. Goodyear Tire & Rubber Co. 1971, Exec. Vice-Pres., Dir. 1971, Pres. 1972–74, Chair. 1974–82, C.E.O. 1974–82, resgnd. from Bd. of Dirs. 1986; Amb. to Mexico 1986–; Dir. CPC Int.,

Mfrs. Hanover Corpn., Mfrs. Hanover Trust Co., Communications Satellite Corpn., Continental Group Inc., U.S. Chamber of Commerce; mem. The Business Council, Business Roundtable Policy Cttee., Chair. U.S. Section, Brazil-U.S. Business Council, Trustee Univ. of Akron, Mount Union Coll. of Alliance, Ohio, Muskingum Coll. of New Concorde, Ohio; Hon. C.B.E. 1972, Hon. Dr. of Laws (Kent State Univ.) 1974, (Eastern Kentucky Univ.) 1979, (Muskingum Coll.) 1980; Grand Officer, Order of Merit (Luxembourg) 1975, Order of Rio Branco (Brazil) 1977, Grand Officer of the Civilian and Military Order of Merit of Adolphe de Nassau (Luxembourg) 1980. *Address:* American Embassy, Paseo de la Reforma 305, Mexico City, Mexico.

PILLSBURY, Edmund Pennington, PH.D.; American museum director; b. 28 April 1943, San Francisco, Calif.; s. of Edmund P. Pillsbury and Priscilla K. (Giesen) Pillsbury; m. Mireille Marie-Christine Bernard 1969; one s. one d.; ed. Yale Univ. and Univ. of London; David E. Finley Fellow, Nat. Gallery of Art, Washington, D.C. 1967–70; Ford Foundation Fellow, Cleveland Museum of Art 1970–71; Curator, European Art, Yale Univ. Gallery and Lecturer, History of Art, Yale Univ. 1972–76; Dir. Yale Center, British Art and Adjunct Prof. of History of Art Yale Univ. 1976–80; C.E.O. Paul Mellon Centre, Studies in British Art, London 1976–80; Dir. Kimbell Art Museum and Vice-Pres. Kimbell Art Foundation 1980–; mem. Presidential Task Force on Arts and Humanities 1981–; Adjunct Prof. Tex. Christian Univ. 1985–; Chevalier, Ordre des Arts et des Lettres. *Publications:* Florence and the Arts 1971, David Hockney: Travels with Pen, Pencil and Ink 1977, The Graphic Art of Federico Barocci 1978. *Leisure interests:* skiing, running, reading. *Address:* Kimbell Art Museum, 3333 Camp Bowie Boulevard, Fort Worth, Tex. 76107 (Office); 4511 Ridgehaven Road, Fort Worth, Tex. 76116, U.S.A. (Home). *Telephone:* (817) 332-8451.

PILON, Jean-Guy, O.C., B.A., LL.L.; Canadian poet; b. 12 Nov. 1930, St. Polycarpe; s. of Arthur Pilon and Alida Besner; m. 2nd Denise Viens 1988; two s. by 1st marriage; ed. Univ. de Montréal; founded Liberté (review) 1959, Ed. 1959–79; Head of Cultural Programmes and Producer Radio-Canada 1970–88; Pres. Rencontre québecoise int. des écrivains; Acad. canadienne-française 1982–, mem. 1981–82; mem. Royal Soc. of Canada 1967–; Prix de Poésie du Québec 1956, Louise Labé 1969, France-Canada 1969, van Lerberghe (Paris) 1969, du Gouverneur gén. du Canada 1970, Athanase David 1984; Ordre Nat. du Québec. *Publications (poems):* La Fiancée du matin 1953, Les Cloîtres de l'été 1955, L'Homme et le jour 1957, La Mouette et le large 1960, Recours au pays 1961, Pour saluer une ville 1963, Comme eau retenue 1969 (enlarged edn. 1986), Saisons pour la continuelle 1969, Silences pour une souveraine 1972. *Address:* 5724 Côte St-Antoine, Montréal, P.Q., H4A 1R9, Canada.

PIMEN, Patriarch (Sergey Mikhailovich Isvekov); Soviet ecclesiastic; b. 23 July 1910, Bogorodsk, Moscow Region; became monk 1927; ordained priest 1932; Bishop of Balta 1957, Archbishop 1960; Metropolitan of Leningrad 1960–63; Metropolitan of Krutitsky and Kolomna 1963–71; Patriarch of Moscow and All Russia 1971–; Grand Cordon, Order of the Cedar of Lebanon 1972, Order of St. Sergius of Radonezh (U.S.S.R.) 1979, Order of Friendship of the Peoples 1980, Order of the Red Banner of Labour 1985. *Address:* Danilov Monastery, Danilovsky Val 22, Moscow, U.S.S.R.

PIMENTA, H.E. Cardinal Simon Ignatius; Indian ecclesiastic; b. 1 March 1920, Bombay; ordained 1949, elected to the titular Church of Bocconia 1971, consecrated bishop 1971, coadjutor bishop 1977, Bishop of Diocese 1978; cr. Cardinal 1988. *Address:* Archbishop's House, 21 Nathalal Parekh Marg, Bombay-400039, India. *Telephone:* (022) 202.10.93.

PIMENTEL, George Claude, A.B., PH.D.; American professor of chemistry; b. 2 May 1922, Rolinda, Calif.; s. of Emile Pimentel and Lorraine Reid; m. 1942; one s. four d.; ed. Univ. of Calif. at Berkeley. Instructor in Chem. Univ. of Calif. at Berkeley 1949–51, Asst. Prof. 1951–55, Assoc. Prof. 1955–59, Prof. of Chem. 1959–; Deputy Dir. Nat. Science Foundation, Washington 1977–80; Dir. Laboratory Chem. Biodynamics, LBL, Univ. of Calif., Berkeley 1980–; Fellow, American Acad. of Arts and Sciences; mem. N.A.S., American Chemical Soc. (Pres. 1985–87), American Physical Soc., American Optical Soc.; Hon. F.R.S.C. (U.K.) 1987; Hon. D.Sc. (Ariz.) 1986; Hon. Ph.D. (Colo. School of Mines) 1987, (Rochester) 1988; A.C.S. Petroleum Chem. Award 1959, Manufacturing Chemists College Teaching Award 1971, Joseph Priestley Award 1972, Pittsburgh Spectroscopy Award 1974, E. K. Plyler Prize in Molecular Spectroscopy 1979, E. R. Lippencott Medal 1980, A.C.S. Linus Pauling Medal 1982, Wolf Prize in Chem. 1982, Peter Debye Award in Physical Chem. A.C.S. 1983, A.C.S. Madison L. Marshall Award 1983, Franklin Medal 1985, William Proctor Prize 1985, Nat. Medal of Science Award 1985, Robert A. Welch Award in Chem., Challenges in Chem. Award 1986, American Inst. of Chem. Members' and Fellows' Lecture Award 1987, A.C.S. Joseph Priestley Medal 1989. *Publications:* Selected Values of Physical and Thermodynamic Properties of Hydrocarbons and Related Compounds (with Rossini and others) 1953, Introductory Quantitative Chemistry (with Olson and Koch) 1956, The Hydrogen Bond (with McClellan) 1960, Radical Formation and Trapping in the Solid Phase (in Formation and Trapping of Free Radicals, Edited by A. M. Bass and H. P. Broida) 1960, Chemistry: An Experimental Science 1963; Understanding Chemical Thermodynamics (with R. D. Spratley); Chemical Bonding Clarified through Quantum Mechanics (with R. D. Spratley), Understanding Chemistry (with R. D. Spratley), Opportunities in Chemistry 1985, Opportunities in Chemistry: Today and Tomorrow 1987; over 225 articles on molecular spectroscopy, chemical bonding, free radicals via matrix isolation, infra-red study of Mars, chemical lasers. *Leisure interests:* squash, photography. *Address:* Chemistry Department, University of California at Berkeley, Calif. 94720 (Office); 754 Coventry Road, Kensington, Calif. 94707, U.S.A. (Home).

PINARD, Rt. Hon. Yvon, B.A., LL.L.; Canadian lawyer and politician; b. 10 Oct. 1940, Drummondville, Quebec; s. of Jean-Jacques Pinard and Cécile Chassé; m. Renée Chaput 1964; two d.; ed. Immaculate Conception School, Drummondville, Nicolet Seminary, Sherbrooke Univ.; Pres. Sherbrooke Univ. Law Faculty 1963; admitted to Quebec Bar 1964; Pres. and f. Drummond Centre Chaise d'Entraide Economique; Pres. Drummond Co. Liberal Asscn. 1968–70; mem. Admin. Council Centre Communautaire d'Aide Juridique Mauricie-Bois-Francs region; mem. Commonwealth Parl. Asscn. and Canadian Del. Interparl. Union; mem. House of Commons 1974–84; Parl. Sec. to Pres. of Privy Council Oct. 1977; Pres. of H.M. the Queen's Privy Council for Canada 1980–84; Trial Div. Judge 1984–; Liberal. *Address:* Privy Council Office, 94 Ralph Street, Ottawa, Ont., K1S 5J4, Canada.

PINAY, Antoine; French industrialist and politician; b. 30 Dec. 1891, Saint-Symphorien-sur-Coise; s. of Claude and Marie (née Besson) Pinay; m. Marguerite Fouletier (deceased); one s. (deceased) two d.; served First World War 1914–18; engaged in leather industry; Dir. Tanneries Fouletier 1919–48; Mayor of Saint-Chamond 1929–77, Conseiller général, Canton of Saint-Chamond 1934–; Deputy for Loire, Nat. Ass. 1936–38, 1946–58, Senator from Loire 1938–40; elected to Constituent Ass. 1945; Pres. Conseil général de la Loire 1949–79; Sec. of State for Econ. Affairs, first Queuille Cabinet 1948–49; Minister of Public Works and Transport in first Pleven Cabinet and subsequent cabinets 1950–52; Prime Minister and Minister of Finance March–Dec. 1952; Minister of Foreign Affairs 1955–56; Minister of Finance and Econ. Affairs, de Gaulle Cabinet 1958–59, Debré Cabinet 1959–60; Pres. Cie. française pour la diffusion des techniques 1960–85; Adviser Soc. pour l'expansion industrielle française à l'étranger 1962–; Pres. of Regional Econ. Devt. for Rhône-Alpes 1964–73; Dir. Caisse d'aide à l'équipement des collectivités locales 1966–73; mem. Asscn. for Econ. and Social Recovery of the Rhône 1967–; first Ombudsman of France 1973–74; Médaille militaire, Croix de guerre, Commdr. du Mérite agricole; numerous foreign decorations. *Address:* 17 avenue de Tourville, 75007 Paris, France.

PINCOTT, Leslie Rundell, C.B.E., F.C.A., F.INST.M.S.M., C.B.I.M.; British company executive; b. 27 March 1923, London; s. of Hubert George and Gertrude Elizabeth (Rundell) Pincott; m. Mary Mae Tuffin 1944; two s. one d.; ed. Mercers School, Holborn, Harvard Business School; Lieut. in R.N.V.R. 1942–46; qualified as chartered accountant; joined Esso Petroleum Co. Ltd. 1950, Comptroller 1958–60, Asst. Gen. Man. (Marketing) 1961–65, Dir. and Gen. Man. Cleveland Petroleum Co. Ltd. 1966–68; seconded to Exxon Corpn. as Exec. Asst. to Pres. and then to Chair. 1968–70; Man. Dir. Esso Petroleum in U.K. 1970–78; Chair. Oxford Univ. Business School 1975–78; Vice-Chair. Remploy Ltd. 1979–87 (Dir. 1975–), Dir. British Railways Southern Bd. 1977–86, Chair. May 1986–; Pres. Dist. Heating Asscn. 1977–79; Chair. Canada Perm. Trust Co. 1978–80; Dir. George Wimpey & Co. Ltd. 1978–85; Deputy Chair., Chair. Price Comm. 1978–80; Chair. Stone-Platt Industries Ltd. 1980–82; Chair. Edman Communications Group PLC 1982–87; Chair. British Railways Southern Bd. 1986–; Chair. Printing Industries Econ. Devt. Cttee. 1982–; Dir. Brown & Root-Wimpey Highland Fabrication Ltd. 1984–; mem. Investment Cttee., London Devt. Capital Fund 1984–85, Chair. 1985–. *Leisure interests:* tennis, walking, travel, swimming. *Address:* Edman House, Maddox Street, London, W.1 (Office); 6 Lambourne Avenue, Wimbledon, London, SW19 7DW, England (Home). *Telephone:* 01-499 0477 (Office); 01-947 1305 (Home).

PINDBORG, Jens Jørgen, D.D.S.; Danish oral pathologist; b. 17 Aug. 1921, Copenhagen; s. of Marius and Sigrid Pindborg; m. Eva Hartz 1951; ed. Royal Dental Coll., Copenhagen, and Univ. of Illinois. Instructor Research Assoc. and Assoc. Prof., Royal Dental Coll., Copenhagen 1943–59, Prof. and Chair. Dept. of Oral Pathology 1959–; Head, Dental Dept., Univ. Hospital, Copenhagen 1953–; Consultant, Danish Nat. Health Service 1958–66; Chief, Dental Corps, Royal Danish Navy 1946–59; Perm. Guest Lecturer, Royal Dental Coll., Malmö, Sweden; Visiting Prof. Univ. of Ill. 1958, 1961, Hebrew Univ. Jerusalem 1969, WHO Visiting Prof. in India 1963–64; Dir. Indo-Danish Oral Cancer Control Project, Trivandrum 1969–78; Head, Collaborating Center under WHO Int. Reference Center for Oropharyngeal tumours, Agra, India 1964; Head Collaborating Center under WHO Int. Reference Center for Salivary Gland Tumours London 1966; Visiting Prof. Tata Inst. of Fundamental Research Bombay 1966; Consultant for Ministry of Health Uganda 1966; Research expert for WHO to New Guinea and Fiji 1966; Dir. WHO Int. Reference Centre on Odontogenic Tumours 1966; Consultant, WHO in Brazil and Colombia 1967; Dir. WHO Int. Reference Centre on Oral Precancerous Conditions 1967–; Consultant for WHO 1966; Ed. Danish Dental Journal 1961–; Scandinavian Journal of Dental Research 1970–, Int. Journal of Oral Surgery 1972–75; Pres. Asscn of Hospital Dentists 1954–66, Danish-Israeli Asscn. 1964–69; Consultant to WHO on classification of oral diseases; mem. Danish Medical Research Council 1972–77, Vice-Chair. 1974–76, Chair. 1976–77, 1985–87;

Ed.-in-Chief Community Dentistry & Oral Epidemiology 1973–; Hon. Fellow, American Acad. of Oral Pathology 1975, Royal Coll. of Surgeons of Ireland 1980; Dr. h.c. (Karolinska Inst., Stockholm) 1973, (Univ. of Lund) 1974, (Univ. of Oslo) 1976, (Witwatersrand Univ.) 1976, (Helsinki) 1981; Hon. Dr. of Laws (Glasgow) 1978, (Simmelweiss Univ., Budapest) 1985, (Göteborg) 1986; Hon. D.M. (Sheffield) 1988; Founding mem. Int. Acad. of Oral Pathology; Fellow, American Asscn. for Advancement of Science, Royal Coll. of Surgeons; Hon. Prof. Beijing Medical Coll.; Hon. Fellow, Dental Surgery, Royal Coll. of Pathology, American Acad. of Oral Pathology 1975; Hon. mem. Burmese Medical Asscn. 1976; Commemoration Lecture Odontological Section, Royal Soc. of Medicine 1972; K. H. Box Lecture, Toronto 1964; E. J. Goddard Oration, Brisbane 1970; Cordwainer's Lecturer, Univ. London 1974; Isaac Schour Memorial Award 1970; Elmer Best Award 1972; Robertson lecture Univ. of Sheffield 1975, Guest Lecturer, Chinese Univs. 1980. *Publications:* The Dentist in Art 1960, Syndromes of Head and Neck (with R. J. Gorlin) 1964, Atlas of Diseases of the Oral Mucosa 1968, Pathology of the Dental Hard Tissues 1970, Histological Typing of Odontogenic Tumours, Cysts and Allied Lesions (with I. R. H. Kramer and H. Torloni) 1972, Histology of the Human Tooth 1973, Atlas of Diseases of the Jaws (with E. Hjörting-Hansen) 1974, Oral Cancer and Precancer 1980, AIDS and the Dental Team (with D.S.J. Greenspan and M. Schiødt), and six books in Danish and 280 papers on oral pathology, oral medicine and cancer research. *Leisure interests:* archaeology, literature. *Address:* Brødhøj 2, 2820 Gentofte, Denmark.

PINDLING, Rt. Hon. Sir Lynden Oscar, Kt., P.C.; Bahamian politician; b. 22 March 1930; s. of Arnold Franklin and Viola Pindling; m. Marguerite McKenzie 1956; two s. two d.; ed. Govt. High School, Bahamas, and London Univ.; Lawyer 1952–67; Leader of Progressive Liberal Party; Premier of Bahamas 1967–69, Prime Minister 1969–; Minister of Econ. Affairs 1969–82, 1984–, Minister of Defence 1983–84. *Leisure interests:* swimming, boating, travel. *Address:* Office of the Prime Minister, Rawson Square, Nassau, Bahamas.

PINEAU, Christian; French politician; b. 14 Oct. 1904, Chaumont; m. 1st Nadine Desaunais de Guermarquer (divorced), four s.; m. 2nd Arlette Bonamour du Tartre (deceased), one s. (deceased) one d.; m. 3rd Blanche Bloys 1963, one d.; with Banque de France, Banque de Paris et des Pays-Bas 1931–38; Sec. Conf. Gen. du Travail 1934–36; founder, Dir. Banque et Bourse 1937; with Resistance, escaped to London, returned to France, arrested, again escaped to London, returned a second time, arrested and sent to Buchenwald; released 1945; Deputy to Constituent Assemblies 1945–46, for Sarthe, Nat. Ass. 1946–58; Minister of Food 1945, of Public Works 1948 and 1949, of Finance 1948, of Foreign Affairs 1956–58; Conseiller Général, canton de Grand-Luce 1955–79; Grand Officier, Légion d'honneur, Croix de guerre, Rosette de la Résistance, Compagnon de la Libération, C.B.E., G.C.M.G. *Publications:* Books for children include: Contes de je ne sais quand, Plume et le saumon, L'ourse aux pattons verts, Cornerouse le mystérieux, Histoires de la forêt de Bercé; Books for adults: La simple vérité (history of the French Resistance), Mon cher député, L'escalier des ombres, Suez 1956, Khroutchev. *Address:* 55 rue Vaneau, 75007 Paris, France. *Telephone:* 42.22.58.20.

PINEAU-VALENCIENNE, Didier; French company director; b. 21 March 1931, Paris; s. of Maurice and Madeleine (née Dubigeon) Pineau-Valencienne; m. Guillemette Rident 1964; one s. three d.; ed. Lycée Janson-de-Sailly, Paris, Dartmouth Univ. (U.S.A.) and Harvard Business School; Man. Asst. Banque Parisienne pour l'Industrie 1958, Prin. Man. Asst. 1962, Dir. 1964–67, Dir.-Gen. 1969 and Admin. 1971; Pres. and Dir.-Gen. Carbonisation et Charbons Actifs (CECA) 1972–74, Société Resogil 1975–76; Dir.-Gen. Société Celogil 1975–76; Admin. Isorel 1976–; Dir. of Admin. and Strategy and Planning Rhone-Poulenc S.A. 1976–77, Dir.-Gen. (Polymer Div.) 1978–; Admin. Quartz et Silice; Admin., Vice-Pres., Dir.-Gen. Schneider S.A. 1980–81, Pres. Dir.-Gen. 1981–; Asst. Admin. Société Electrorail S.A. 1980–; Admin. Merlin-Gérin 1981–; Chair. Empain-Schneider Group 1981–, Société Parisienne d'Etudes et de Participations 1982–; Chair. and Man. Dir. Creusot-Loire 1982–84; fmr. teacher Ecole des Hautes Etudes Commerciales; Chevalier, Légion d'honneur. *Leisure interests:* tennis, skiing, collecting books. *Address:* 12 rue des Pins, 92100 Boulogne-sur-Seine, France (Home).

PINGEL, Klaus G., DR.IUR.; German lawyer and civil servant (retd.); b. 29 April 1914, Grenzberg; s. of Paul and Else Pingel; m. Dorothea Arendt 1939; two c.; ed. Univs. of Berlin, Königsberg, Geneva and Kiel; Barrister-at-law; Supervisory Officer German/Danish Border, German Customs Admin. 1953; with Fed. Ministry of Finance; joined Comm. of European Communities 1959, Counsellor to Customs Directorate, Head of Negotiation Team of Community in GATT; Head Customs Valuation Div. 1963; Dir. Admin. of the Customs Union (fmrly. Customs Directorate) 1968–, Dir.-Gen. Customs Union Service 1978–79; lecturer Univ. of Int. Business and Econs., Beijing 1985; Kt's. Cross of Civil Merits, Italian Repub., Grosses Bundesverdienstkreuz, Fed. Repub. of Germany, Grosses Goldenes Ehrenzeichen mit Stern für Verdienste, Austria; Hon. Dir.-Gen. European Comm. *Leisure interests:* reading, writing, travel. *Address:* Birnauerstrasse 10, D-7750 Konstanz, Federal Republic of Germany.

PINGET, Robert, L. ÈS D.; French writer; b. 19 July 1919, Geneva, Switzerland; ed. legal studies Univ. of Geneva; fmr. barrister, later painter;

taught French in England; literary career 1951–; Prix des Critiques 1963, Prix Femina 1965, Grand Prix nat. 1987. *Publications:* Fantoine et Agapa 1951, Mahu et le matériau 1952, Le renard et la boussole 1955, Graal Flibuste 1956, Baga 1958, Le fiston 1959, Lettre morte (play) 1959, La manivelle (play) 1960, Clope au dossier 1961, Architruc (play) 1961, L'hypo-thèse (play) 1961, L'inquisitoire 1962, Quelqu'un 1965, Autour de Mortin (dialogue) 1965, Le libera 1968, La passacaille 1969, Fable 1971, Identité, Abel et Bela (play) 1971, Paralchimie 1973, Cette voix 1975, L'Apocryphe 1980, Monsieur Songe 1982, Le harnais 1984. *Address:* c/o Editions de Minuit, 7 rue Bernard-Palissy, 75006 Paris, France.

PINHEIRO FARINHA, João de Deus; Portuguese judge; b. 8 March 1919, Redondo; s. of Simão Martins Pereira and Isabel Gapete (Pinheiro) Farinha; m. Maria das Dores Pombinho 1947; ed. Liceu Nacional André da Gouveia and Univ. of Lisbon; Deputy Public Prosecutor 1943–50; Insp. of Prison Services 1944–49; Judge, Leiria Industrial Court 1950–51; Judge in lower courts 1951–66; Asst. Public Prosecutor 1957–58; Pres. Corregitor (3rd Civil Chamber) 1966–70; Judge, Coimbra and Lisbon Appeal Courts 1970–74; Attorney-Gen. 1974; Minister of Justice 1975–76; mem. Perm. Court of Arbitration 1975; Pres. Court of Accounts 1977–; Judge, European Court of Human Rights 1977–, Supreme Court of Justice 1978–; Vice-Pres. Int. Comm. on Civil Status 1977–79, Pres. 1980–; Gold Medal of Peniten-tiary Social Merit (Spain), Medal of Council of Europe. *Publications:* many legal publications. *Leisure interests:* travel, philosophy, religion. *Address:* Tribunal de Contas (Court of Accounts), Avenida Infante D. Henrique, 1194 Lisbon Codex; and Avenida de Paris no. 14-2° Esq., 1000 Lisbon; and Avenida Dr. Baraona 14, 7170 Lisbon, Portugal. *Telephone:* 365529 (Office); 888817 and 99197 (Home).

PINKER, George Douglas, C.V.O., F.R.C.S.ED., F.R.C.O.G.; British gynaecolo-gist and obstetrician; b. 6 Dec. 1924; s. of Ronald D. Pinker and Queenie E. Dix; m. Dorothy E. Russell; three s. one d.; ed. Reading School and St. Mary's Hosp., London; fmrly. consultant gynaecological surgeon, Bolingbroke Hosp. and resident officer, Nuffield Dept. of Obstetrics, Radcliffe Infirmary, Oxford; fmrly. consultant gynaecological surgeon, Queen Charlotte's Hosp., London; consulting gynaecological surgeon and obstetrician, St. Mary's Hosp. Paddington and Samaritan Hosp. 1958–; consulting gynaecological surgeon, Middx. and Soho Hosps. 1969–; consult-ant gynaecologist, King Edward VII Hosp. for Officers, London 1974–; Surgeon-Gynaecologist to H.M. Queen Elizabeth II 1973–. *Publications:* co-author of three books on obstetrics and gynaecology. *Leisure interests:* music, gardening, sailing, skiing, fell walking. *Address:* 96 Harley Street, London, W1N 1AF (Office); Medley, Kingston Hill, Kingston-on-Thames, Surrey, England (Home). *Telephone:* 01-935 2292 (Office).

PIŃKOWSKI, Józef; Polish politician; b. 17 April 1929, Siedlce; s. of Jan and Valeria Pińkowski; m. Daniela Pińkowski 1955; one d.; ed. Higher School of Econs., Poznań and Main School of Planning and Statistics, Warsaw; Officer Polish Army 1952–56; Dir. of Dept. Ministry of Purchase, then Ministry of Agricultural Products, later Chief Insp. of Corn, Ministry of Food Industry and Purchase 1956–58; Sec. Scientific Econ. Council, Voivodship Nat. Council, Warsaw 1958–60, Vice-Chair. of Presidium of Voivodship Nat. Council 1960–65, Chair. 1965–71; First Vice-Chair. Plan-ning Comm. attached to Council of Ministers 1971–74; Chair. Council of Ministers 1980–81; mem. Exec. Warsaw Voivodship Cttee., Polish United Workers' Party 1965–71, mem. Cen. Cttee. 1971–81, Sec. Cen. Cttee. 1974–80, Deputy mem. Political Bureau Feb.–Aug. 1980, mem. Political Bureau 1980–81; Deputy to Seym (Parl.) 1969–83, Chair. Seym Comm. of Econ. Planning, Budget and Finance 1974–83; mem. Seym Comm. for Foreign Affairs 1982; Order of Banner of Labour (1st and 2nd Class), Kt.'s Cross of Order of Polonia Restituta, Order of Builders of People's Poland 1979. *Leisure interests:* music, poetry. *Address:* Ul. Wiśniowa 61 m. 5, Warsaw, Poland. *Telephone:* 49-47-77.

PINNOCK, Trevor, A.R.C.M.; British harpsichordist and conductor; b. 16 Dec. 1946, Canterbury; s. of Kenneth and Joyce Pinnock; m. Pauline Heather Nobes 1988; ed. Canterbury Cathedral School, Royal Coll. of Music, London; Jt. F. Galliard Harpsichord Trio, début, London 1966, solo début, London 1968, Dir. The English Concert 1973; has toured Western Europe, U.S.A., Canada, Australia, Japan with the English Concert, as solo harpsichordist and as orchestral/opera conductor; début Metropolitan Opera, New York 1988. *Recordings* include Handel, J. S. Bach, C. P. E. Bach, Rameau, Vivaldi, Scarlatti, 16th-, 17th- and 18th-century harpsichord music, and most of the standard baroque orchestral/concerto/choral reper-toire. *Address:* c/o Basil Douglas Artists' Management, 8 St. George's Terrace, London, NW1 8XJ, England. *Telephone:* 01-722 7142.

PINOCHET UGARTE, Gen. Augusto; Chilean army officer; b. 25 Nov. 1915; m. María Lucía Hiriat Rodríguez; two s. three d.; ed. Mil. Acad., School of Infantry, Acad. of War, Acad. of Nat. Defence; Army career 1933–, Col. 1966, Brig.-Gen. 1969, Div. Gen. 1970, Gen. 1973; Instructor Acad. of War 1954, Deputy Dir. 1964; Asst. to Under-Sec. of War 1954; mem. Chilean mil. mission to U.S.A. 1956; Instructor Acad. of War, Ecuador 1956–59; C.-in-C. VI Army Div., Chief of Army Staff 1969; C.-in-C. of Armed Forces 1973–80; led coup to depose President Salvador Allende Sept. 1973; Pres. Gov. Council of Chile 1973–74; Pres. of Chile 1974–(90); Pres. Junta Militar; Mil. Star, Grand Mil. Merit Cross, High Command Hon. Officer (Ecuador), Abdón Calderón Parra Medal (Ecuador),

Order of Mil. Merit (Colombia), Grand Cross of Military Merit (Spain). *Publications:* Geopolítica—Diferentes Etapas para el Estudio Geopolítico de los Estados 1968, Geografía de Chile 1968, Geografía de Argentina, Perú y Bolivia 1972, Guerra del Pacífico 1879—Primeras Operaciones Terrestres 1972. *Address:* Palacio de la Moneda, Santiago, Chile.

PINTASILGO, Maria de Lourdes; Portuguese politician, engineer and diplomatist; b. 18 Jan. 1930, Abrantes; d. of Jaime de Matos Pintasilgo and Amélia Ruivo da Silva Pintasilgo; ed. Inst. Superior Técnico, Lisbon; mem. Research and Devt. Dept. Companhia União Fabril (CUF) 1954–60; Pres. Pax Romana 1956–58; Int. Vice-Pres. The Grail 1965–69; apptd. mem. women's ecumenical liaison group by Holy See 1966–70; Dept. of Politics and Gen. Admin., Corporative Chamber 1969–74; Chair. Nat. Comm. on Status of Women 1970–74; mem. Portuguese mission to UN 1971–72; Sec. of State for Social Security, First Provisional Govt. 1975; Minister of Social Affairs 1974–75; Amb. to UNESCO 1976–79, mem. Exec. Bd. UNESCO 1976–80; Prime Minister 1979–80; Adviser to Pres. of Repub. 1981–85; mem. World Policy Inst. 1982–, UN Univ. Council 1983–, Interaction Council of Fmr. Heads of Govt. 1983–, Club of Rome 1984–. *Publications:* Les nouveaux féminismes 1980, Dimensão da mudança 1985 and over a hundred articles on international affairs, development and the status of women. *Leisure interests:* poetry, piano. *Address:* Alameda Santo António dos Capuchos 4-5°, 1100 Lisbon, Portugal. *Telephone:* 57 82 70.

PINTER, Harold, C.B.E.; British playwright; b. 10 Oct. 1930, London; m. 1st Vivien Merchant 1956 (divorced 1980, died 1982), one s.; m. 2nd Lady Antonia Fraser (q.v.) 1980; ed. Hackney Downs Grammar School, London; actor mainly in English and Irish prov. repertory 1949–58; playwright 1957–; Assoc. Dir. Nat. Theatre 1973–83; Dir. United British Artists 1983–85; Jt. Ed. Publr. Greville Press 1988–; Bd. mem. Cricket World 1989–; Shakespeare Prize, Hamburg 1973, Austrian Prize for European Literature 1973; Pirandello Prize 1980, Commonwealth Award for Dramatic Arts, Washington, D.C. 1981, Donatello Prize 1982; Hon. D.Litt. (Reading) 1970, (Birmingham) 1971, (Glasgow) 1974, (East Anglia) 1974, (Stirling) 1979, (Brown) 1982, (Hull) 1986; Hon. Fellow (Queen Mary Coll.) 1987. *Plays:* The Room 1957, The Dumb Waiter 1957, The Birthday Party 1957, A Slight Ache 1958, The Hothouse 1958, The Caretaker 1959, A Night Out 1959, Night School 1960, The Dwarfs 1960, The Collection 1961, The Lover 1962, Tea Party (TV play) 1964, The Homecoming 1964, The Basement (TV play) 1966, Landscape 1967, Silence 1968, Night (one act play) 1969, Old Times 1970, Monologue (one act play) 1972, No Man's Land 1974, Betrayal 1978, Family Voices 1980, Other Places 1982, A Kind of Alaska 1982, Victoria Station 1982, Players 1983, One for the Road 1984, Mountain Language 1988; screen-play for The Caretaker 1962, The Servant 1962, The Pumpkin Eater 1963, The Quiller Memorandum 1965, Accident 1966, The Birthday Party 1967, The Go-Between 1969, Langrishe Go Down 1970, A la Recherche du Temps Perdu 1972, The Last Tycoon 1974, The French Lieutenant's Woman 1980, Betrayal 1981, Turtle Diary 1984, The Handmaid's Tale 1987, Reunion 1988, The Heat of the Day 1988; *other works:* Poems and prose 1949–77 1978, The Proust Screenplay (with Joseph Losey and Barbara Bray) 1978; Dir. The Man in the Glass Booth London 1967, N.Y. 1968, Exiles 1970, 1971, Butley 1971, (film) 1973, Next of Kin 1974, Otherwise Engaged 1975, The Rear Column 1978, Close of Play 1979, Quartermaine's Terms 1981, Incident at Tulse Hill 1982, The Trojan War Will Not Take Place 1983, The Common Pursuit 1984, Sweet Bird of Youth 1985, Circe and Bravo 1986, Collected Poems and Prose 1986, 100 Poems by 100 Poets (co-ed.) 1986. *Leisure interest:* cricket. *Address:* c/o Judy Daish Associates, 83 Eastbourne Mews, London, W2 6LQ, England.

PINTO BALSEMÃO, Dr. Francisco José Pereira; Portuguese lawyer, journalist and politician; b. 1 Sept. 1937, Lisbon; s. of Henrique Pinto Balsemão and Maria Adelaide C. P. Pereira; m. Mercedes Presas Pinto Balsemão 1975; two s. two d.; Ed.-in-Chief review Mais Alto 1961–63; Sec. to Man. Bd. Diário Popular, later Man. –1971; f. weekly Expresso 1973; mem. Nat. Assembly during Govt. of Dr. Marcello Caetano; f. Popular Democratic Party (PPD), later renamed Social Democratic Party (PSD), with late Dr. Sá Carneiro and Joaquim Magalhães Mota (q.v.) May 1974; Vice-Pres. Constituent Assembly 1975; Opposition Spokesman on Foreign Affairs 1977; mem. Assembly of the Repub. Dec. 1979–; Minister Without Portfolio and Deputy Prime Minister 1980; Prime Minister of Portugal 1981–83; Pres. Instituto Progresso Social e Democracia, Francisco dá Carneiro 1983–; Chair. Int. Relations Cttee. and mem. Political Cttee. PSD, party leader 1980–83. *Address:* Rua Duque de Palmela, 37-2° Dt°, 1296, Lisbon Codex, Portugal. *Telephone:* 526141.

PINTO BARBOSA, António Manuel; Portuguese economist and diploma-tist; b. 31 July 1917, Murtoza; s. of Manuel Maria Barbosa Junior and Mariana Vieira Pinto Barbosa; m. Maria das Dôres Soares; two s.; ed. Universidade Técnica de Lisboa; teacher 1941–50; Prof. Inst. of Higher Econ. and Financial Sciences 1951–; Pres. Comm. for Reorganization of Industrial Resources 1951–54; Under-Sec. of State at Treasury 1951–54; Minister of Finance and Econ. 1955–65; mem. Council of State; Gov. Bank of Portugal and Gov. IMF 1966–74; Chair. Higher Studies Inst., Acad. of Sciences; Grand Cross, Order of Christ, Order of Prince Henry and of Isabel la Católica (Spain). *Publications:* L'industrie des conserves au Portugal 1941, L'économie, aspects positifs et aspects théologiques 1943, L'économie du Café 1945, La crise des exportations métropolitaines pour l'étranger 1950, La tâche du Ministre des Finances 1955, Banco de Fomento Nacional 1959, L'activité du Ministre des Finances 1960, La défense de la stabilité financière 1962, Communication du Ministre des Finances sur le crédit extérieur 1962, La phase actuelle des finances portugaises 1964, La dévaluation de 1949 et le commerce extérieur portugais 1966, Portuguese Economic Development in the Presence of the Postwar Foreign Policies of the U.S. 1969, La reforme du systeme monétaire international et ses vicissitudes 1973, Keynes e o accordo de Bretton-Woods 1977, Problemas monetarios internacionais de actualidade 1983, A reabilitação do quantitativo na Economia 1984, Olado menos visivel do Plano Marshall: sua actualidade. *Address:* Rua António Saldanha 3, Barrio do Restelo, Lisbon, 1400, Portugal.

PIONTEK, Heinz; German writer; b. 15 Nov. 1925, Kreuzburg, Silesia; m. Gisela Dallmann 1951; ed. Theologisch-Philosophische Hochschule, Dillingen; Berlin Prize for Literature 1957, Andreas Gryphius Prize, Esslingen 1957; mem. Bavarian Acad. of Fine Arts 1960-, Central PEN of Fed. Repub. of Germany; Rom-Preis, Villa Massimo 1960, Münchner Literatur Preis 1967, Eichendorff-Preis 1971, Tukan-Preis 1971, Literatur Preis des Kulturkreises im BDI 1974, Georg-Büchner-Preis 1976, Werner-Egk-Preis 1981, Oberschlesischer Kulturpreis 1984; Bundesverdienstkreuz (1st Class) 1985. *Publications:* Die Furt (poems) 1952, Die Rauchfahne (poems) 1953, Vor Augen (stories) 1955, Wassermarken (poems) 1957, Buchstab-Zauberstab (essays) 1959, Aus meines Herzens Grunde (anthology) 1959, John Keats: Poems 1960, Weisser Panther (radio play) 1962, Mit einer Kranichfeder (poetry) 1962, Kastanien aus dem Feuer (stories) 1963, Windrichtungen (journey reports) 1963, Neue deutsche Erzählgedichte (anthology) 1964, Klartext (poetry) 1966, Die mittleren Jahre (novel) 1967, Liebeserklärungen (essays) 1969, Männer, die Gedichte machen 1970, Die Erzählungen 1971, Tot oder lebendig (poems) 1971, Deutsche Gedichte seit 1960 (editor) 1972, Helle Tage anderswo 1973, Gesammelte Gedichte 1974, Dichterleben (novel) 1976, Wintertage-Sommernächte (short stories) 1977, Juttas Neffe (novel) 1979, Was mich nicht loslässt (poetry) 1981, Die Münchner Romane 1981, Lieb', Leid und Zeit und Ewigkeit (anthology) 1981, Früh im September (collected poems) 1982, Werke in sechs Bänden (collected works) 1985, Helldunkel (poetry) 1987, Jeder Satz ein Menschengesicht (anthology) 1987. *Address:* Dülfer Strasse 97, 8000 München 50, Federal Republic of Germany.

PIORE, Emanuel Ruben, B.A., PH.D.; American physicist; b. 19 July 1908, Wilno, Poland (now Vilnius, U.S.S.R.); s. of Ruben and Olga Piore; m. Nora Kahn 1931; one s. two d.; ed. Univ. of Wisconsin; Chief Scientist U.S.N. Office of Naval Research 1951-55; Vice-Pres. for Research, Avco Corpn 1955-56; Dir. of Research, Int. Business Machines Corpn., York 1956-60, Vice-Pres. for Research and Eng. 1960-63, Vice-Pres. and Group Exec. 1963-65, Vice-Pres. and Chief Scientist 1965-, mem. Bd. of Dirs.; mem. Nat. Science Bd. 1961-; Adjunct Prof., Rockefeller Univ. 1974-; Fellow, American Physical Soc., Inst. of Electrical and Electronics Engineers, American Acad. of Arts and Sciences, A.A.A.S., Royal Soc. of Arts (U.K.); mem. Nat. Acad. of Sciences, Nat. Acad. of Eng., American Philosophical Soc.; consultant to President's Science Advisory Cttee.; mem. Bd. American Inst. of Physics, Stark Draper Lab., Nat. Information Bureau, SIAM, N.Y. State Foundation for Science, New York Bd. for Higher Educ. 1976-; visiting cttees. at M.I.T., Harvard, Johns Hopkins, Tulane, Michigan State Univ.; mem. several cttees. of Nat. Research Council; Treasurer of Nat. Cttee. of Research 1968-80; mem. Bd. Science Research Assocs., Health Advancement Inc., Paul Revere Investors, Guardian Mutual Fund; Hon. D.Sc. (Union and Wisconsin); Kaplun Int. Prize; Industrial Research Inst. Medal 1967. *Address:* International Business Machines Corporation, Armonk, N.Y. 10504; 115 Central Park West, New York, N.Y. 10023, U.S.A *Telephone:* 212-Endicott 2-1772 (Office).

PIOT, Peter, PH.D., M.D.; Belgian professor of microbiology; b. 17 Feb. 1949, Leuven; m. Greet Kimzeke 1975; two c.; ed. Univs. of Ghent, Antwerp and Washington; Asst. in Microbiology, Inst. of Tropical Medicine, Antwerp 1974-78, First Asst. 1979-82, Prof., Head Dept. of Microbiology 1986-; Sr. Fellow, Microbiology and Infectious Diseases, Washington Univ. 1978-79; Dir. WHO Collaborating Centre on AIDS, Antwerp; Head, Sexually Transmitted Diseases Clinic, Antwerp; Research into the epidemiology, clinical aspects and control of AIDS in Africa; Pres. Dutch Soc. for Study of Sexually Transmitted Diseases 1986; mem. WHO Expert Panel on Venereal Diseases and Treponematoses; NATO Fellow 1978-79; Onassis Int. Prize 1989. *Publications:* Gardnerella vaginalis and Gardnerella-associated vaginitis 1981, Sexueel Overdraagbare ziekten 1982, AIDS and HIV Infection in the Tropics (with J. M. Mann) 1988; Co-Author Human Chlamydial infections 1982-; articles on AIDS and other sexually transmitted diseases. *Leisure interests:* cooking, hiking, music, literature. *Address:* Institute of Tropical Medicine, Nationalestraat 155, B-2000 Antwerp, Belgium.

PIOTROVSKY, Boris Borisovich; Soviet historian; b. 1908; ed. Leningrad State Univ.; scientific worker, Head of Section State Acad. of Material Culture (now Inst. of Archaeology), U.S.S.R. Acad. of Sciences 1929-53; Dir. Leningrad Branch, Inst of Archaeology, U.S.S.R. Acad. of Sciences 1953-54; Scientific Collaborator, Scientific Dir. of Eastern Dept., and Deputy Dir. for Scientific Matters, State Hermitage Museum, Leningrad 1931-61, Dir. 1961-; Prof. 1968-; mem. CPSU 1945-; Corresp. mem. Armenian Acad. of Sciences; Honoured Art Worker of Armenia 1961;

Academician, U.S.S.R. Acad. of Sciences 1970- (mem. Presidium 1980-); Hon. mem. Prehistory and Protohistory Soc. of Florence; Corresp. mem. British Acad. 1967; Dr. h.c. (Delhi); State Prize, Red Banner of Labour (three times), Hero of Socialist Labour 1983, Order of the Hammer and Sickle 1983. *Main works:* History and archaeology of Ancient East and Caucasus; in charge of excavations at Urart Fortress, Erevan (Armenia) 1939-; directed U.S.S.R. Acad. of Sciences archaeological expedition in Nubia (Egypt) 1960-62; over 120 scientific works, incl. History and Culture of Urartu (State Prize) 1946. *Address:* State Hermitage, 34 Dvortsovaya naberezhnaya, Leningrad, U.S.S.R.

PIOTROWSKI, Lieut.-Gen. Czesław Wojciech, D.MIL.SC.; Polish politician; b. 23 April 1926, Huta Stepańska; s. of Stanisław and Paulina Libera; m.; two d.; ed Eng. Acad., U.S.S.R. and Acad. of Gen. Staff, Warsaw; during Word War II fought in partisan detachments; in Polish People's Army 1944-, Deputy Commdr. of Eng. Brigade, Chief of Engineers in Warsaw Mil. Dist.; Deputy Commdr. for tech. matters, subsequently Commdr. of Eng. Service at Ministry of Nat. Defence 1972-78; Brig.-Gen. 1971, Lieut.-Gen. 1978, Chief of Research and Devt. of Mil. Tech., Deputy Insp. for Tech. in Polish Army 1978-81; Minister of Mining and Power Industry 1981-86; Gen. Dir. of Mining; Gen. Dir. Energetics; Amb. to Yugoslavia 1986-; mem. Mil. Council of Nat. Salvation 1981-83; mem. Polish Workers' Party 1947-48, Polish United Workers' Party (PZPR) 1948-; State Prize 1972; Meritorious Miner of the Polish People's Repub., Meritorious Worker of Energy Industry of the Polish People's Repub. 1986; Order of Banner of Labour (1st and 2nd Class), Cross of Valour, Partisan Cross and other decorations. *Leisure interests:* fishing, tinkering. *Address:* Polish Embassy, Kneza Miloša 38, Belgrade, Yugoslavia.

PIOVANELLI, H.E. Cardinal Silvano; Italian ecclesiastic; b. 21 Feb. 1924; ordained 1947; consecrated Bishop (Titular Church of Tubune, Mauritania) 1982; Archbishop of Florence 1983-; cr. Cardinal 1985. *Address:* Arcivescovado, Piazza S. Giovanni 3, 50129 Florence, Italy. *Telephone:* (055) 29.88.13.

PIPER, Bright Harold (Peter), C.B.E., F.C.I.B.; British banker; b. 22 Sept. 1918, Guildford, Surrey; s. of Robert Harold Piper and Daisy Homewood; m. 1st Marjorie Joyce Arthur 1945 (dissolved 1979); one s. one d.; m. 2nd Leonie Mary Lane 1979; ed. Maidstone Grammar School; served in R.N. 1939-46; joined Lloyds Bank Ltd. 1935, Asst. Gen. Man 1963-65, Joint Gen. Man. 1965-68, Asst. Chief Gen. Man. 1968-70, Deputy Chief Gen. Man. 1970-73, Dir. 1970-84, Chief Gen. Man 1973, Group Chief Exec. Lloyds Bank Group 1973-78, Dir. Lewis' Bank 1969-75, Dir. Lloyds and Scottish 1970-75, Chair. Lloyds First Western (U.S.) 1973-78; Freeman of the City of London. *Leisure interest:* sailing. *Address:* Greenways, Hawks-hill Close, Esher, Surrey, England. *Telephone:* (0372) 64356.

PIPER, Carlyle Ashton; Dominican barrister; b. 1 Sept. 1925, Dominica; s. of Frederick Augustus Piper and Pearle (née Pemberton) Piper; m. Cecilia Ama Duncan 1955; five s. three d.; ed. Dominica Grammar School, Gray's Inn Law School and Univ. of New York; Judge High Court, Nigeria 1966-77; Chief Judge High Court, Bauchi Borno and Gongola States 1977-82; barrister and solicitor The Eastern Caribbean Associated States, Judge Supreme Court and Barrister at Law, England; Chair. Judicial Comm. of Inquiry into Elections 1966, into Affairs of Govt. Cos. 1977; Pres. Alliance Francaise D'Ibadan 1968-70; mem. Advisory Judicial Cttee. Fed. Govt. of Nigeria 1977-79, Judiciary Consultative Cttee., Fed. Govt. of Nigeria 1979-82, Mental Health Review Bd., Commonwealth of Dominica 1988-. *Leisure interests:* world events, sports, travel. *Address:* Chambers, 66 Queen Mary Street, Roseau, Dominica, The West Indies. *Telephone:* 83149.

PIPER, Sir David Towry, Kt., C.B.E., M.A., F.S.A.; British museum director and writer; b. 21 July 1918, London; s. of late Prof. S. H. Piper and Mary Piper; m. Anne Richmond 1945; one s. three d.; ed. Clifton Coll. and St. Catharine's Coll., Cambridge; served in Indian Army 1940-45, Japanese P.O.W. 1942-45; Asst. Keeper Nat. Portrait Gallery, London 1946-64, Dir. 1964-67; Slade Prof. of Fine Art, Oxford Univ. 1966-67; Dir. Fitzwilliam Museum, Cambridge 1967-73, Ashmolean Museum, Oxford 1973-85; Clark Lecturer, Cambridge Univ. 1977-78, Rede Lecturer 1983; Fellow Worcester Coll. Oxford 1973-85, now Emer.; mem. Royal Fine Art Comm. 1970-86; Hon. D.Litt. (Bristol) 1984. *Publications:* The English Face 1957, Catalogue of 17th Century Portraits in the National Portrait Gallery 1963, Companion Guide to London 1964, Enjoying Paintings (Editor) 1964, Painting in England, 1500-1880 1965, Shades 1970, London (World Cultural Guide series) 1971, The Genius of British Painting (Editor) 1975, The Treasures of Oxford 1977, Kings and Queens of England and Scotland 1980, Artists London 1982, The Image of the Poet 1983; novels (as Peter Towry) incl. It's Warm Inside 1953, Trial By Battle 1959. *Address:* Overford Farm, Wytham, Oxford, OX2 8QN, England. *Telephone:* (0865) 247736.

PIPER, John Anthony, M.A.; Australian diplomatist; b. 8 Nov. 1930, Shanghai; m. Ann (née Caro) Piper; one s. two d.; ed. Geelong Grammar School, Vic. and Brasenose Coll., Oxford; joined Dept. of External Affairs 1954-; posted to New Delhi, Rome, Karachi, Paris, Ottawa; Asst. Sec. UN Branch, Dept. of Foreign Affairs and Trade 1974-76, Head Econ. Org. Branch 1979-83; Amb. to Algeria and Tunisia 1976-78; Deputy Perm. Rep. to OECD 1983-86; High Commr. in Fiji and Tuvalu 1986-87; Visiting

Fellow, Dept. of Int. Relations, Research School of Pacific Studies, A.N.U. *Address:* c/o Department of Foreign Affairs and Trade, Canberra; 73 Wybalena Grove, Cook, A.C.T., Australia. *Telephone:* (062) 51 60 50.

PIPER, John Egerton Christmas, C.H.; British painter and author; b. 13 Dec. 1903; s. of late C. A. Piper; m. Mary Myfanwy Evans 1935; two s. two d.; ed. Epsom Coll. and Royal Coll. of Art; exhibited London 1925-; paintings bought by Tate Gallery, Victoria and Albert Museum, Contemporary Art Society, etc.; war artist, commissioned to paint ruins of House of Commons 1941, and two series of water-colours for H.M. The Queen 1942-43; Trustee of Tate Gallery 1946-53, 1954-61, 1968-74; mem. Royal Fine Art Comm. 1959-78; Trustee, Nat. Gallery 1967-74, 1975-78; designer of opera and ballet (London, Milan and Venice), of stained glass (Oundle Coll. Chapel, Coventry Cathedral, St. Andrew's, Plymouth, Eton Coll. Chapel, etc.); Retrospective Exhbn., Cologne 1965; mem. Oxford Diocesan Advisory Cttee. 1950-; Hon. D.Litt. (Oxford, Leicester, Sussex, Reading); Hon. A.R.C.A.; Hon. A.R.I.B.A.; Hon. F.R.I.B.A. *Publications:* Shell Guide to Oxfordshire 1938, Brighton Aquatints 1939, British Romantic Painters 1942, Buildings and Prospects; Romney Marsh (King Penguin series, with own water-colours); *and with John Betjeman:* Architectural Guide to Buckinghamshire, Architectural Guide to Berkshire; (illustrated) The Castles on the Ground by J. M. Richards 1973; Lincolnshire Churches (co-author) 1976, with Richard Ingrams: Piper's Places, John Piper in England and Wales 1983. *Address:* Fawley Bottom Farmhouse, nr. Henley-on-Thames, Oxon., England.

PIPER, Klaus; German publisher; b. 27 March 1911, Munich; s. of late Rheinhard Piper and Gertrud Engling; ed. Maximilians-Gymnasium, Munich; with R. Piper & Co., Munich (book publishers) 1932-, Partner 1941-53, sole Man. Dir. 1953-; mem. Finance Cttee. of German Booksellers Assen., Cen. PEN of Fed. Repub. of Germany 1955-, Rotary Club, Assen. of Literary Publishers, Max-Planck-Gesellschaft zur Förderung der Wissenschaften; Hon. D.Lit. (Washington, St. Louis) 1986; Golden Cultural Medal, Italian Ministry of Foreign Affairs 1963, Distinguished Service Cross (First Class), Fed. Repub. of Germany. *Publications:* Offener Horizont 1953, Nach 50 Jahren 1904-1954 1954, Stationen—Piper-Almanach 1904-1964 1964, Piper-Almanach 1964-74 1974; Ed.: Reinhard Piper Mein Leben als Verleger 1964, Erinnerungen an Karl Jaspers (co-editor). *Leisure interests:* music, art, literature. *Address:* R. Piper & Co. Verlag, Georgenstrasse 4, 8000 Munich 40 (Office); 81 Pienzenauerstrasse 63, 8000 Munich 40, Federal Republic of Germany (Home). *Telephone:* 39-70-71 (Office); 98-84-73 (Home).

PIPKIN, Charles Harry Broughton, C.B.E.; British company executive (retd.); b. 29 Nov. 1913, London; s. of late Charles Pipkin and of Charlotte Phyllis (née Viney) Pipkin; m. Viola Byatt 1941; one s. one d.; ed. Christ's Coll., Blackheath, and Faraday House; joined Callender's Cable and Construction Co., Erith, Kent 1935; served R.E.M.E. 1940-46, attaining rank of Maj.; personal asst. to a Dir. British Insulated Callender's Cables (now BICC) Ltd. 1946-48, Man. Special Business Arrangements 1948-52, Man. Home Sales 1952-58, Commercial Man. Home 1958-60, an Exec. Dir. 1960-68, Man. Dir. U.K. Cables Group 1968-73, Chief Exec. and a Deputy Chair. 1973-76, Chair. BICC Ltd. 1977-80; Pres. British Non-Ferrous Metals Fed. 1965-66, British Cable Makers' Confed. 1967-68, British Electrical and Allied Mfrs.' Assen. Ltd. 1975-76; Dir. Electrak Int. Ltd. 1982-85. *Leisure interests:* travel, reading, racing. *Address:* Pegler's Barn, Bledington, Oxon., OX7 6XQ, England. *Telephone:* (060871) 304.

PIPPARD, Sir (Alfred) Brian, Kt., M.A., PH.D., SC.D., F.R.S.; British professor of physics; b. 7 Sept. 1920, London; s. of Prof. A. J. S. Pippard, F.R.S. and Mrs. F. L. O. (Tucker) Pippard; m. Charlotte Frances Dyer 1955; three d.; ed. Clifton Coll., and Clare Coll., Cambridge; Scientific Officer Radar Research and Devt. Establishment 1941-45; Demonstrator in Physics, Cambridge Univ. 1946, Lecturer 1950, Reader 1959-60, J. H. Plummer Prof. of Physics 1960-71; Cavendish Prof. of Physics 1971-82; Pres. of Clare Hall, Cambridge 1966-73; Pres. Inst. of Physics 1974-76; Hughes Medal (Royal Soc.) 1959, Holweck Medal 1961, Dannie-Heineman Prize (Göttingen) 1969, Guthrie Medal (Inst. of Physics) 1970. *Publications:* Elements of Classical Thermodynamics 1957, Dynamics of Conduction Electrons 1962, Forces and Particles 1972, Physics of Vibration 1978, 1982, Response and Stability 1985, Magnetoresistance in Metals 1989; many papers in Proceedings of the Royal Society, etc. *Leisure interest:* music. *Address:* 30 Porson Road, Cambridge, CB2 2EU, England. *Telephone:* (0223) 358713.

PIRELLI, Leopoldo; Italian business executive; b. 27 Aug. 1925, Varese; s. of Alberto Pirelli and Ludovica Zambeletti; one s. one d.; ed. Politecnico, Milan; Chair. Pirelli S.p.A., Milan; Partner Pirelli and Co., Milan; Deputy Chair. Soc. Int. Pirelli, Basel; Dir. Mediobanca, Milan, Riunione Adriatica di Sicurtà, Milan, Generale Industrie Metallurgiche, Florence, Società Metallurgica Italiana, Florence, Banca Commerciale Italiana, Milan; Cavaliere del Lavoro della Repubblica. *Address:* Piazzale Cadorna 5, 20123 Milan, Italy. *Telephone:* (02) 85.351.

PIRES, Gen. Pedro Verona Rodrigues; Cape Verde politician; b. 29 April 1934, Sant' Ana, Fogo; s. of Luís Rodrigues Pires and Maria Fidalga Lopes Pires; m. Adélcia Maria da Luz Lima Barreto Pires 1975; two d.; ed. Licee Gil Eanes de São Vicente, Faculty of Science, Lisbon Univ., Portugal; left

Portugal to join Partido Africano da Independência da Guiné e Cabo Verde (PAIGC) 1961; mem. PAIGC dels. 1961-63; involved in preparation for liberation of Cape Verde 1963-65; mem. Cen. Cttee. of PAIGC 1965-, of Council of War, PAIGC 1967-; re-elected mem. of Commissáo Permanente do Comité Executivo da Luta (CEL) and of Council of War 1970; involved in admin. of liberated areas of southern Guinea-Bissau 1971-73; Pres. Nat. Comm. of PAIGC for Cape Verde 1973 (reaffirmed as mem. of Council of War and CEL), appointed an Asst. State Commr. in first govt. of Repub. of Guinea-Bissau 1973-74; negotiated independence agreements of Cape Verde and Guinea-Bissau 1974; Dir. PAIGC policies during transitional govt. before independence of Cape Verde 1975; elected Deputy in Nat. Popular Ass. of Cape Verde June 1975-, re-elected 1980; Prime Minister of Cape Verde July 1975-; elected Deputy Gen. Sec. Partido Africano da Independéncia de Cabo Verde (PAICV) Jan. 1981-; mem. Perm. Comm. of CEL 1977; Amilcar Cabral Medal 1976. *Leisure interests:* philosophy, sociology, politics. *Address:* Gabinete do Primeiro Ministro, Praça 12 de Setembro, Praia, Republic of Cape Verde. *Telephone:* 226-248-609.

PIRES DE MIRANDA, Pedro, M.ENG.; Portuguese business executive and diplomatist; b. 30 Nov. 1928, Leiria; s. of A. and A. Pires de Miranda; m. Maria Helena Pires de Miranda 1957; one s. two d.; ed. Lisbon Univ.; with William Halcrow & Partners, London; Sales Man. Companhia Portuguesa de Petróleos BP 1955-67, int. petroleum operations with BP, London 1967-70; Commercial Man. Petrosul 1972-73; Dir. Sonap 1973-75; Asst. Bd. of Dirs. for Marketing Affairs, Companhia Brasileira de Petróleos Ipiranga 1975-76; Dir. Petróleos de Portugal (Petrogal) 1976-, Pres. 1982-; Minister of Commerce and Tourism 1978; Pres. Comm. for Integration in EEC 1979; Amb. at large 1980-; Minister for Foreign Affairs 1985-87; Grand Officier de l'Ordre de Mérite Civil Français, Grand Officier de l'Ordre du Faucon Islandais; Grand Croix Ordem Nacional do Cruzeiro do Sul, Ordem do Rio Branco do Sul, Ordem da Aguia Azteca, Ordre Royal Suédois de l'Etoile Polaire; Gran Cordón de la Orden del Libertador. *Leisure interest:* sport. *Address:* Rua das Flores 7, 1200 Lisbon, Portugal. *Telephone:* 32 80 35; 370371.

PIRLOT DE CORBION, Edmond; French engineer; b. 1 June 1916, Bournemouth, England; s. of André and Louisa (née Meeus) Pirlot de Corbion; m. Irène Voruz de Vaux 1944; one s. two d.; ed. Ecole Saint-Louise-de-Gonzague, Lycée Janson-de-Sailly and Ecole Nat. Supérieure des Mines de Paris; worked for Cie. de Saint-Gobain 1943; Engineer, Chantereine Glassworks 1943-47, Franière Glassworks, Belgium 1947-50, Stolberg Glassworks, Germany 1950-53; Principal Engineer, Chantereine Glassworks 1953-56, Head Office, Cie. de Saint-Gobain 1956-59; Dir.-Gen. Saint-Gobain (America) 1960-64, Saint-Roch Glassworks, Belgium 1965-67; Admin. de Saint-Gobain 1967, Vice-Pres./Dir.-Gen. 1969, Vice-Pres./Div. Gen., Cie. de Saint-Gobain-Pont-à-Mousson 1970-; Pres. Saint-Gobain Industries 1970-75; Dir. Saint-Roch Glassworks, Cristaleria Española S.A., Pont-à-Mousson S.A.; Chevalier, Légion d'honneur. *Leisure interests:* tennis, walking, hunting. *Address:* 20-22 rue des Acacias, 75017 Paris, France (Home).

PIRONIO, H.E. Cardinal Eduardo; Argentine ecclesiastic; b. 3 Dec. 1920, Nueve de Julio; ordained priest 1943; Titular Bishop of Ceciri 1964-72; Bishop of Mar del Plata 1972-75; Titular Archbishop of Tiges 1975-; cr. Cardinal 1976; Prefect of the Sacred Congregation for Religious Orders and Secular Insts. 1976-84; Deacon of Ss. Cosma e Damiano; mem. Sacred Congregation for the Bishops, for the Eastern Churches, for the Sacraments and Divine Worship, for Catholic Educ.; Pres. Council for the Laity 1984-; Pres. Pontifical Comm. for Pastoral Care of Health Workers; mem. Pontifical Comm. for the Revision of Canon Law, for the Interpretation of the Decrees of the Second Vatican Council, for Latin America; mem. Council for the Public Affairs of the Church. *Address:* 00193 Roma, Piazza del S. Uffizio 11, Italy.

PIROŻYŃSKI, Jan, PH.D.; Polish historian and librarian; b. 7 March 1936, Tarnów; s. of Bolesław and Helena Jarosz; m. Czesława Ochał 1960; one d.; ed. Jagiellonian Univ., Cracow; Librarian, Jagiellonian Library 1957-58; Archivist, Nat. Archive of Cracow City and Dist. 1958-59; Keeper, Jagiellonian Library 1959-72, Head of Old Prints Dept. 1972-79, Deputy Dir. Jagiellonian Library 1979-81, Dir. 1981-; Awards of Minister of Science and Higher Educ., 3rd and 2nd Class. *Publications:* The Warsaw Parliament 1570 1971, The Printers in Old Poland, 15th-18th Centuries, Vol. I, Part I: 15th-16th Centuries (co-author) 1983, Sophia the Jagiellon, Duchess of Brunswick (1522-1575) and her library. A study of the History of Culture 1986; numerous articles on the history of culture and on 16th-18th century books. *Leisure interests:* literature, sport, tourism. *Address:* Biblioteka Jagiellońska, Al. Mickiewicza 22, 30-059 Kraków (Office); Ul. Na Błonie 9a m. 87, 30-147 Kraków, Poland (Home). *Telephone:* 37-40-53 (Home).

PIRUBHAKARAN, Vellupillai; Sri Lankan guerrilla leader; b. 26 Nov. 1954, Velvettithurai, Jaffna peninsula; m.; one s. one d.; joined Tamil movement 1970; f. Tamil New Tigers guerrilla movt. (Liberation Tigers of Tamil Eelam since 1976) 1972.

PIRZADA, Syed Sharifuddin, S.PK.; Pakistani lawyer and politician; b. 12 June 1923, Burhanpur; s. of S. Vilayat Ali Pirzada and Butul Begum; m. 1st Rafia Sultana (died 1960), m. 2nd Safiya Pirzada; two s. one d.; ed. Univ. of Bombay; Sec. Muslim Students Fed. 1943-45; Hon. Sec. to Quaid-i-Azam, Jinnah 1941–44; Sec. Bombay City Muslim League 1945–47; Prof., Sind Muslim Law Coll. 1947–54; Adviser to Constitution Comm. of Pakistan 1960–61; Chair. Co. Law Comm. 1962; Pres. Karachi High Court Bar Asscn., Pakistan Br. 1964–67; Attorney-Gen. of Pakistan 1965–66, 1968–72, 1977–; Minister of Foreign Affairs 1966–68; mem. or Pres. several asscns. and socs.; led Pakistan Del. to Session of UN Gen. Ass. 1966–67; on Panel of Perm. Court of Arbitration; mem. Int. Law Comm. 1981–86; elected Sec.-Gen. Org. of Islamic Conf. Dec. 1984, took office Jan. 1986. *Publications include:* Evolution of Pakistan 1962, Fundamental Rights and Constitutional Remedies in Pakistan 1966, Some Aspects of Quaid-i-Azam's Life 1978, Collected Works of Quaid-i-Azam Mohammad Ali Jinnah (vol. I) 1985, (vol. II) 1986. *Leisure interest:* bridge. *Address:* C-37, KDA Scheme No. 1, Drigh Road, Karachi, Pakistan; P.O. Box 178, Jeddah 21411, Saudi Arabia. *Telephone:* 215151 (Pakistan), 687-5848 (Saudi Arabia).

PISANI, Edgard, L.ÈS L.; French politician; b. 9 Oct. 1918, Tunis, Tunisia; s. of François and Zoë (née Nani) Pisani; m. Isola Chazereau (deceased); ed. in Tunis and Paris; Resistance during World War II; Sous-Préfet, Dir. de Cabinet of Chief Commr. of Police 1944–45; Dir. de Cabinet of Minister of the Interior 1946; Préfet, Haute-Loire 1946–47, Haute-Marne 1947–54; Senator, Haute-Marne 1954–61, 1974–81; Minister of Agric. 1961–66, of Equipment 1966–67; County councillor and Mayor of Montreuil-Bellay 1963–75; Deputy for Maine-et-Loire, Nat. Assembly 1967–68; mem. Ind. Comm. on Int. Devt. Issues; mem. Comm. for Foreign Affairs and Defence; mem. European Parl. Oct. 1979–; mem. Socialist Group; Commr. for Devt. Aid, Comm. of European Communities 1981–84; French High Commr. in New Caledonia 1984–85; Minister for New Caledonian Affairs May–Nov. 1985; Chargé de Mission, Cabinet du Président Nov. 1985–; Pres. Soc. for Int. Devt.; Pres. Institut du Monde Arabe 1988; Publr. quarterly review L'Evènement Européen 1987–; Prix 30 Jours d'Europe. *Publications:* La région: pour quoi faire?, Le général indivis, Utopie foncière, Socialiste de raison, Défi du monde—campagne d'Europe, La France dans le conflit économique mondial, La main et l'outil 1984, Pour l'Afrique 1988. *Address:* c/o Présidence de la République, Palais de l'Elysée, 55–57 rue du Faubourg St. Honoré, 75008 Paris (Office); 225 rue du Faubourg St. Honoré, 75008 Paris, France (Home). *Telephone:* 42.67.60.16 (Home).

PISCHINGER, Franz Felix, DR. TECH.; Austrian academic; b. 18 July 1930, Waidhofen; s. of Franz Pischinger and Karoline Pischinger; m. Elfriede Pischinger 1957; four s. one d.; ed. Technical Univ. Graz; technical asst. Technical Univ. Graz 1953–58; Head of Research Dept. Inst. of Internal Combustion Engines, Prof. List (AVL) 1958–62; leading positions in research and devt. Kloeckner-Humboldt-Deutz AG, Cologne, Fed. Germany 1962–70; Dir. Inst. for Applied Thermodynamics, Aachen Tech. Univ. 1970–; Pres. FEV Motorentechnik, Aachen 1978–; Vice-Pres. DFG (German Research Soc.) 1984–; Herbert Akroyd Stuart Award 1962; Oesterreichischer Ehrenring, Bundesverdienstkreuz. *Publications:* articles in professional journals. *Address:* Institute for Applied Thermodynamics, Aachen Technical University, Schinkelstrasse 8, 5100 Aachen (Office); Im Erkfeld 4, 5100 Aachen, Federal Republic of Germany (Home). *Telephone:* 241 80-6200 (Office); 241 12301 (Home).

PITARKA, Bashkim Pamiz, B.A.; Albanian diplomatist; b. 1942, Durres; m.; two c.; ed. Enver Hoxha Univ., Tirana; journalist with Radio Tirana 1965–68; Prof. of English, State Univ. of Tirana 1968–72; past Head, European and Latin American Dept. of Foreign Ministry, mem. Collegium of the Foreign Ministry; del. to several sessions of UN Gen. Ass.; Perm. Rep. to the UN Aug. 1986–. *Address:* Permanent Mission of Albania to the United Nations, 184 Lexington Avenue, New York, N.Y. 10016, U.S.A. *Telephone:* 889-9415.

PITBLADO, Sir David B., K.C.B., C.V.O.; British government official; b. 18 Aug. 1912, London; s. of Robert B. Pitblado and Mary (née Sear); m. Edith Mary Evans 1941 (died 1978); one s. one d.; ed. Strand School, London, Emmanuel Coll., Cambridge and Middle Temple; Dominions Office 1935–42, Asst. Pvt. Sec. to Sec. of State for Dominions Affairs 1937; N. American Secr. War Cabinet Office 1942; joined Treasury 1942; U.K. del. San Francisco Conf. 1945, and UN meetings 1946; Under-Sec. Econ. Planning Staff, Treasury 1949–51; Prin. Pvt. Sec. to Prime Minister (Lord Attlee, Sir Winston Churchill, Lord Avon) 1951–56; Financial Attaché, British Embassy, Wash.; Alt. Exec. Dir. IBRD 1956–58; Vice-Chair. Man. Bd. of European Payments Union and Monetary Agreement 1958–60; Third Sec. Treasury 1960; Exec. Dir. for U.K. of IBRD, and of IMF; Head of U.K. Treasury and Supply Del., and Econ. Minister, British Embassy, Washington 1961–63; Deputy-Sec., Ministry of Power 1965–66; Perm. Sec. Ministry of Power 1966–69; Perm. Sec. (Industry) Ministry of Tech. 1969–70; Second Perm. Sec. Civil Service Dept. 1970–71, Comptroller and Auditor-Gen. 1971–76; Jt. Ed. The Shetland Report 1978; Chair. Davies Educ. Services 1979–; Consultant Inst. of Dirs. 1977–81; Hon. Treas. Soldiers', Sailors' and Airmen's Family Asscn.; Cttee. Royal Postgraduate Medical School; Hon. Fellow, Emmanuel Coll., Cambridge. *Address:* 23 Cadogan Street, London, S.W.3, England. *Telephone:* 01-589 6765.

PITFIELD, Peter Michael, P.C., C.V.O., Q.C., D.E.S.D.; Canadian senator and lawyer; b. 18 June 1937, Montreal, P.Q.; s. of late Ward C. and Grace MacDougall Pitfield; m. Nancy E. Snow 1971; one s. two d.; ed. St. Lawrence Univ., Canton, N.Y., McGill Univ. and Univ. of Ottawa; Admin. Asst. to Minister of Justice and Attorney-Gen. of Canada 1959–60; Sec.

and Exec. Dir. Royal Comm. on Publications 1960–61; Attaché to Gov.-Gen. of Canada 1961–65; Sec. and Research Supervisor, Royal Comm. on Taxation 1962–65; Asst. Sec. to Cabinet 1966–69; Deputy Sec. 1969–71, Sr. Deputy Sec. and Deputy Clerk of Privy Council 1971–73; Deputy Minister of Consumer and Corpn. Affairs and Deputy Registrar-Gen. of Canada 1973–75; Sec. to Cabinet and Clerk of Privy Council 1975-79, 1980–82; Prof. Kennedy School of Govt. Harvard Univ. 1979–80; mem. Senate Dec. 1982–, Chair. Special Cttee. on Canadian Security Intelligence Service 1983; Canadian Rep. at UN Gen. Ass. 1983; Dir. Cadillac Fairview Corpn. & Power Financial Corpn. 1984; Trustee, Twentieth Century Fund 1983–; mem. Council Int. Inst. of Strategic Studies, London 1984–; Hon. D.Litt. (St. Lawrence) 1979. *Leisure interests:* squash, reading. *Address:* The Senate, Ottawa, Ont., K1A 0A4 (Office); 54 Belvedere Crescent, Ottawa, Ont. K1M 2G4, Canada (Home). *Telephone:* (613) 992-2784.

PITIŞ, Marcela Eugenia, M.D.; Romanian clinical endocrinologist; b. 12 June 1914, Ploieşti; d. of Adolph and Eugenia Pechert; m. Dr. I. Pitiş 1937 (deceased 1987); ed. Faculty of Medicine, Bucharest; Professor of Clinical Endocrinology at IMF Bucharest 1966–; Dir. Romanian Inst. of Endocrinology 1979–; researches on normal and pathological endocrine aspects of growth and aging, endocrine systems in various species related to environment and seasons, hypothalamo-hypophyseal dynamics influenced by endo and exogenous factors related to age and hypophyseal and suprarenal pathology; clinical-experimental studies on pineal and parathyroid glands; hirsutism, ovarian pathology, intersexuality etc. *Publications:* Contribuţiuni experimentale la studiul si terapeutica bătrîneţii (Experimental Contributions to the Study and Therapeutics of Old Age), Biologia vîrstelor (Biology of Ages), (ed. C.I. Parhon), Sistemul cardiovascular în patologia endocrină (Cardiovascular System in Endocrine Pathology) 1961, co-author Endocrinologie clinică (Clinical Endocrinology) 1975, ed. St. M. Milcu; Patologia vocală (Vocal Pathology) 1978 (co-author), Terapia medicală (Medical therapy) vol. III 1982 (ed. R. Păun), Clinical Endocrinology, 1985 (ed. M. Pitis). *Leisure interests:* classical music, archaeology, architecture, sculpture. *Address:* 25 C. A. Rosetti Str., Bucharest 2, Romania. *Telephone:* 33.06.02 (Office); 11.21.43 (Home).

PITMAN, Brian Ivor, F.I.B.; British banker; b. 13 Dec. 1931, Cheltenham; s. of Ronald Ivor Pitman and Doris Ivy (née Short); m. Barbara Mildred Ann Darby 1954; two s. one d.; ed. Cheltenham Grammar School; Asst. Gen. Man. Lloyds Bank PLC 1973–75, Jt. Gen. Man. 1975–76; Exec. Dir. (U.K. and Asia-Pacific Div.), Lloyds Bank Int. Ltd. 1976–78; Deputy Chief Exec. Lloyds Bank Int. Ltd. 1978–82; Deputy Group Chief Exec., Lloyds' Bank PLC 1982–83, Group Chief Exec. (now known as Chief Exec.) and Dir. 1983–. *Leisure interests:* golf, cricket, music. *Address:* Lloyds Bank PLC, 71 Lombard Street, London, EC3P 3BS, England.

PITRA, František, ING.; Czechoslovak politician; b. 13 Nov. 1932, Městec, Chrudim Dist.; ed. Coll. of Agric., Brno; agronomist, Prachatice 1955–58; with Secr. Regional Cttee. CP of Czechoslovakia, České Budějovice 1958–71, Sec. for party work in agric. 1971–77, First Sec. 1977–81; mem. Cen. Cttee. CP of Czechoslovakia (CPCz) 1977–, mem. Secr. and Sec. Cen. Cttee. 1981–88, Alt. mem. Presidium of Cen. Cttee. 1986–88, mem. 1988–; Deputy Prime Minister of Czechoslovak Socialist Repub. and Prime Minister Czech Govt. Oct. 1988–; Head CPCz Comm. for Food and Agric. 1981–88; Deputy to House of the People, Fed. Ass. 1978–; Distinction of Merit in Construction 1969, Order of the Repub. 1982. *Address:* Ústřední výbor Komunistické strany československa, nábřeží Ludvíka Svobody 12, Prague 1-Nové Město, Czechoslovakia.

PITT, Sir Harry Raymond, Kt., PH.D., F.R.S.; British mathematician and university administrator; b. 3 June 1914, West Bromwich; s. of Harry and Florence Pitt; m. Clemency C. Jacoby 1940; four s.; ed. King Edward's School, Stourbridge and Peterhouse, Cambridge; Bye-Fellow, Peterhouse, Cambridge 1936–39; Choate Memorial Fellow, Harvard Univ. 1937–38; Univ. of Aberdeen 1939–42; Air Ministry and Ministry of Aircraft Production 1942–45; Prof. of Math., Queen's Univ., Belfast 1945–50; Deputy Vice-Chancellor, Univ. of Nottingham 1950–64; Visiting Prof., Yale Univ. 1962–63; Vice-Chancellor, Univ. of Reading 1964–79; Chair. Univs' Cen. Comm. on Admissions, and Standing Conf. on Univ. Entrance Oct. 1975–79; Vice-Pres. Inst. of Mathematics 1980–84, Pres. 1984–85; Hon. LL.D. (Nottingham, Aberdeen); Hon. D.Sc. (Reading, Belfast). *Leisure interests:* walking, travel. *Publications:* Tauberian Theorems 1957, Measure, Integration and Probability 1963, Measure of Integration for Use 1985, papers in scientific journals. *Address:* 46 Shinfield Road, Reading, Berks., RG2 7BW, England. *Telephone:* 0734-872962.

PITTENDRIGH, Colin Stephenson, PH.D.; American professor of biology; b. 13 Oct. 1918, Whitley Bay, Northumberland, England; s. of Alexander Pittendrigh and Florence Hemy Stephenson; m. Margaret Eitelbach 1943; one s. one d.; ed. Univ. of Durham, England; at Int. Health Div. of Rockefeller Foundation 1942–45; at Princeton Univ. (posts included Prof. of Zoology and Dean of Graduate School) 1947–69; fmrly. Prof. of Biology Stanford Univ., Prof. of Human Biology 1970–76, Dir. Hopkins Marine Station and Harold A. Miller Prof. of Biology 1976–84, Emer. 1984–; Alexander von Humboldt Fellow, Max-Planck Institut für Verhaltensphysiologie 1984; mem. N.A.S., American Philosophical Soc.; Fellow, American Acad. of Arts and Sciences; Hon. D.Sc. (Newcastle upon Tyne) 1985. *Publications include:* Life (with George Gaylord Simpson and Lewis

Tiffany) 1957; and journal papers. *Leisure interest:* fly fishing. *Address:* Box 57, Sonoita, Ariz. 85637, U.S.A. *Telephone:* (602) 455-5891.

PITTER, Ruth, C.B.E.; British poet; b. 7 Nov. 1897, Ilford, Essex; d. of George Pitter and Louisa R. Murrell; ed. Coborn School, London; junior clerk War Office 1917-18; painter of furniture, etc. Suffolk and London 1918-30; own business in partnership with Kathleen O'Hara 1930-43; warwork at The Morgan Crucible Co., Battersea, London 1943-45; worked at home 1945-; Hawthornden Prize for A Trophy of Arms 1937; Heinemann Award 1954; Queen's Medal for Poetry 1955; C. Lit. 1974; Hon. F.R.S.L. *Publications:* First Poems 1920, First and Second Poems 1927, Persephone in Hades (privately printed) 1931, A Mad Lady's Garland 1934, A Trophy of Arms 1935, The Rude Potato 1941, The Bridge 1945, Pitter on Cats 1946, Urania 1951, The Ermine 1953, Still by Choice 1966, Poems 1926-1946 1968, End of Drought 1975. *Leisure interests:* gardening, cosmic curiosity, cooking. *Address:* The Hawthorns, 71 Chilton Road, Long Crendon, nr. Aylesbury, Bucks., England. *Telephone:* (0844) 208373.

PITTMAN, James A., Jr., M.D.; American professor of medicine; b. 12 April 1927, Orlando, Fla.; s. of James A. Pittman and Jean C. Garretson; m. Constance Ming Chung Shen 1955; two s.; ed. Davidson Coll. N.C., and Harvard Medical School; Clinical Assoc. Nat. Insts. of Health, Bethesda, Md. 1954-56; Instructor in Medicine, Univ. of Alabama 1956-59, Asst. Prof. 1959-62, Assoc. Prof. 1962-64, Prof. of Medicine 1964-, Prof. of Physiology 1967-, Dean, School of Medicine 1973-; Consultant, Children's Hosp. Birmingham, Ala. 1962-71; Prof. of Medicine, Georgetown Univ. School of Medicine, Washington, D.C. 1971-73; Hon. D.Sc. (Davidson Coll.) 1980, (Alabma) 1984. *Publications:* Diagnosis and Treatment of Thyroid Disease 1963; articles in professional journals. *Leisure interests:* flying, scuba diving, hunting, sailing. *Address:* Office of the Dean, University of Alabama School of Medicine, Birmingham, Ala. 35294 (Office); 5 Ridge Drive, Birmingham, Ala. 35213, U.S.A. (Home). *Telephone:* 205-934-1111 (Office); 205-871-9261 (Home).

PITZER, Kenneth Sanborn, PH.D.; American professor of chemistry; b. 6 Jan. 1914, Pomona, Calif.; s. of Russell and Flora S. Pitzer; m. Jean E. Mosher 1935; two s. one d.; ed. Calif. Inst. of Tech., Univ. of Calif.; Instructor, Univ. of Calif., later Prof. of Chem. 1937-61; Tech. Dir. Maryland Research Lab., Wash. 1943-44; Asst. Dean, Coll. of Letters and Science 1947-48; Dir. of Research, Atomic Energy Comm., Wash. 1949-51; Dean, Coll. of Chem. 1951-60; Pres. and Prof. of Chem., Rice Univ., Houston 1961-68; Pres. and Prof. of Chem., Stanford Univ., Calif. 1968-70; Prof. of Chem., Univ. of Calif., Berkeley 1971-; mem. Gen. Advisory Cttee. Atomic Energy Comm. 1958-65, Chair. 1960-62; Dir. Fed. Reserve Bank of Dallas 1965-68; Trustee RAND Corpn. 1962-72, Pitzer Coll. 1966-, Carnegie Fund for Advancement of Teaching 1966-71, Center for Advanced Materials 1983-84; mem. Bd. of Dirs. Owens-Illinois 1967-86, American Council on Educ. 1967-70, N.A.S. (mem. Council 1964-68, 1973-76), Comm. on Nat. Resources 1973-74; Hon. LL.D. (Univ. of Calif. and Mills Coll.), Hon. D.Sc. (Wesleyan Univ.); Priestley Medal, A.C.S. 1969, Nat. Medal of Science (U.S.A.) 1975, Robert A. Welch Award 1984, Rossini Lecture, Int. Union Pure and Applied Chem. 1988. *Publications:* Selected Values of Physical and Thermodynamic Properties of Hydrocarbons and Related Compounds 1947, Quantum Chemistry 1953, Thermodynamics (with L. Brewer) 1961. *Leisure interest:* sailing. *Address:* 12 Eagle Hill, Berkeley, Calif. 94707, U.S.A.

PIVOT, Bernard; French journalist; b. 5 May 1935, Lyons; s. of Charles Pivot and Marie-Louise Pivot (née Dumas); m. Monique Dupuis 1959; two d.; ed. Centre de formation des Journalistes; on staff of Figaro littéraire, then Literary Ed.; Figaro 1958-74; Chronique pour sourire, on Europe 1 1970-73; Columnist, Le Point 1974-77; producer and presenter of Ouvrez les guillemets 1973-74, Apostrophes, Channel 2 1975-; Ed. Lire 1975-; Dir. Sofica Créations 1986- Grand Prix de la Critique l'Académie française 1983. *Publications:* L'Amour en vogue (novel) 1959, La vie oh là là! 1966, Les critiques littéraires 1968, Beaujolaises 1978, Le Football en vert 1980. *Leisure interests:* tennis, football, gastronomy. *Address:* Antenne 2, 22 avenue Montaigne, 75387 Paris cedex 08 (Office); 7 avenue Niel, 75017 Paris, France (Home). *Telephone:* 299-42-42 (Office).

PIZA, Arthur Luiz de; Brazilian painter and printmaker; b. 1928; Painter and exhibitor 1943-; moved to Paris 1952; regular exhibitor at Bienal of São Paulo and of Ljubljana since 1951, at Triennali of Grenchen since 1958; one-man exhbns. in Brazil, Germany, Yugoslavia, U.S.A., France, Switzerland, Sweden, Spain, Belgium and Italy; works in many important museums and private collections; Purchase Prize 1953, and Nat. Prize for Prints São Paulo Biennale 1959, Prizes at biennales at Ljubljana 1961, Santiago 1966, Venice 1966, Grenchen Triennale 1961, biennales of Norway and Mexico 1980. *Address:* 16 rue Dauphine, 75006 Paris, France.

PLACE, John B. M.; American business executive; b. 21 Nov. 1925; s. of Hermann G. and Angela Toland Place (née Moore); m. Katharine Smart; one s. two d.; ed. St. Paul's School, Concord, N.H., The Citadel and New York Univ.; with Chase Manhattan Bank 1946-71, Asst. Treas. 1950, Second Vice-Pres. 1953, Vice-Pres. 1956, Sr. Vice-Pres. 1959, with Int. Dept. 1963, with Metropolitan Dept. 1965, Exec. Vice-Pres. 1965, Head U.S. Dept. 1967, Vice-Chair., mem. Exec. Office, Head of Domestic and Int. Banking 1969-71; with Anaconda Co. 1971, Pres., C.E.O. and Chair.

1971-77; Exec. Vice-Pres. Atlantic Richfield Inc. 1977-78; Dir. Anaconda Co., Chemical New York Corpn., Chemical Bank, Lever Bros. Co., Metropolitan Life Insurance Co., Union Pacific Corpn., Midland Bank 1981-, and others; Deputy Chair. Crocker Nat. Bank 1978-80, Chair. 1980-84; Vice-Pres. Int. Copper Research Assen. Inc.; Dir. American Mining Congress, Copper Devt. Assen.; mem. Council on Foreign Relations, New York Chamber of Commerce; Hon. D. Eng. (Colorado School of Mines) 1973; Grand Cross Order of Civil Merit (Spain) 1972, Man in Management Award, Pace Univ. 1975. *Address:* c/o Crocker National Bank, 1 Montgomery Street, San Francisco, Calif. 94138, U.S.A.

PLAJA, Eugenio, J.D.; Italian diplomatist (retd.); b. 26 April 1914, Rome; m.; three s.; Vice-Consul Chambéry and Cannes 1938-43; diplomatic posts in Buenos Aires 1946; First Sec., Santiago 1950; Head EEC and NATO Affairs, Dept. of Int. Co-operation, Ministry of Foreign Affairs 1952; Counsellor, later Minister Counsellor and Deputy Perm. Rep., Perm. Mission to UN 1955-61; Deputy Dir.-Gen. for Political Affairs, Ministry of Foreign Affairs 1962-63, Dir.-Gen. for Emigration 1963-67, Dir.-Gen. of Personnel and Admin. 1967-69; Amb. to Egypt 1969-73; Perm. Rep. to UN 1973-75, Dir.-Gen. for Political Affairs 1975-76; Perm. Rep. to European Communities 1976-80; pvt. consultant in int. econ. relations 1981-; mem. Diplomatic Judicial Advisory Council, Ministry of Foreign Affairs 1987-; Pres. Società Generale Immobiliare SOGENE, Rome 1983-85. *Address:* Via Archimede 181, 00197 Rome, Italy. *Telephone:* 06/802941.

PLANCHON, Roger; French theatrical director and playwright; b. 12 Sept. 1931, Saint-Chamond; s. of Emile and Augusta (née Nogier) Planchon; m. Colette Dompietrini 1958; one s. one d.; bank clerk 1947-49; Founder Théâtre de la Comédie, Lyon 1951; Dir. Théâtre de la Cité, Villeurbanne 1957-72; Co-Dir. Théâtre Nat. Populaire 1972-; aims to popularize the theatre by extending its units and recreating the classics within a modern social context; Prix Ibsen (for Le cochon noir) 1974; *acted in films:* Le grand frère 1982, Danton 1983, Un amour interdit, la septième cible 1984; *plays:* has directed and acted in over 60 plays by Shakespeare, Molière, Racine, Marivaux, Brecht, Adamov, Vinaver, Dubillard and himself, most recently: Ionesco 1983, L'avare 1986; Chevalier des Arts et des Lettres, Croix de guerre, Chevalier, Légion d'honneur. *Publications:* Plays: La remise 1961, Patte blanche 1965, Bleus, blancs, rouges ou les Libertins 1967, Dans le vent 1968, L'infâme 1969, La langue au chat 1972, Le cochon noir 1973, Gilles de Rais 1976, l'Avare 1986. *Address:* Théâtre National Populaire, 8 place Lazare Goujon, 69100 Villeurbanne; 8 rue Michel-Servet, 69100 Villeurbanne, France.

PŁANETA-MAŁECKA, Izabela, M.D.; Polish paediatrician and politician; b. 8 Dec. 1930, Lvov; m.; one d.; ed. Medical Acad., Łódź; Asst., Pharmacology Research Centre 1953-55, subsequently Gen. and Social Hygiene Research Centre 1955-58, Medical Acad., Łódź; Asst., Paediatric Ward Władysław Biegański Isolation Hospital, Łódź 1955-60; staff, Military Medical Acad., Łódź 1960-, Sr. Asst., Lecturer 1960-78, Asst. Prof. 1978-83 of Children's Diseases Dept., organizer and Head II Children's Diseases Dept., organizer and Head II Children's Diseases Clinic of Paediatric Dept. 1983-, Extraordinary Prof. 1985-; organizer, first gastroenterological dispensery in Poland for children, Łódź 1968; Deputy Dir. for paediatric matters, Health Centre of Mother-Pole, Łódź 1987-; Minister of Health and Social Welfare 1988-; mem. Polish Paediatric Soc. 1955-, Polish Gastroenterological Soc. 1978-; mem. Polish Women's League, Deputy Chair. Łódź Board 1982-; mem. Nat. Council of Patriotic Movement for Nat. Rebirth (PRON) 1983-, mem. PRON Executive Cttee.; mem. World Peace Council 1983-; non-party; Knight's Cross of Polonia Restituta Order, Gold Cross of Merit, Nat. Educ. Comm. Medal and other decorations. *Publications:* numerous articles, mainly on gastroenterology. *Leisure interests:* music, belle-lettres. *Address:* Ministerstwo Zdrowia i Opieki Społecznej, ul. Miodowa 15, 00-923 Warsaw, Poland.

PLANINC, Mrs. Milka; Yugoslav politician; b. 21 Nov. 1924, Drniš, Croatia; ed. Higher School of Administration; joined Communist Youth League 1941, Communist Party 1944; Yugoslav People's Liberation Army 1943; Co. Commissar 11th Dalmatian Shock Brigade and Dept. Head Divisional HQ; since 1947 Trešnjevka Communal Cttee. Sec., League of Communists of Croatia (LCC), Pres. Trešnjevka Communal Ass., Zagreb, Organizational Sec. Zagreb Municipal Cttee. LCC, Croatian Republican Sec. for Schooling and Educ., Chair. Cttee. for Educ., Science and Culture, Pres. Republican Chamber, Republican Ass. of Croatia; mem. Cen. Cttee. LCC 4th, 5th, 6th and 7th LCC Congresses; mem. LCC Presidency Cen. Cttee. 1964; mem. Exec. Cttee. LCC Cen. Cttee., 6th LCC Congress; Pres. Cen. Cttee. LCC 1971, re-elected 7th LCC Congress 1974; Pres. Fed. Exec. Council (Prime Minister) of Yugoslavia 1982-83; several decorations. *Address:* Federal Executive Council, Bul. Lenjina 2, 11075 Novi Beograd, Yugoslavia.

PLANTA, Louis von, DR. JUR.; Swiss pharmaceuticals executive; b. 15 March 1917, Basel; m. Anne-Marie Ehinger 1944; three s. one d.; ed. Univ. of Basel; Partner in Basel firm of lawyers 1946-; mem. Bd. J. R. Geigy S.A. 1965, Vice-Chair. 1967, Chair. 1968-70; Vice-Chair. of Bd., Chief Man. Dir. and Chair. Exec. Cttee. CIBA-GEIGY Ltd. 1970-72, Chair. of Bd. 1972-87; mem. Admin. Bd., Brown, Boveri and Co. (Vice-Chair. 1980-87), Swiss Bank Corpn.; Chair. Basel Chamber of Commerce 1969-76; Pres. Swiss Soc. of Chemical Industry 1975-76; mem. Bank Council and Bank

Cttee., Swiss Nat. Bank 1971–87; Pres. Swiss Fed. of Commerce and Industry, and Swiss Chamber of Commerce and Industry 1976–87; mem. Bd. Burlington Industries Inc. 1987–. *Address:* c/o CIBA-GEIGY Ltd., CH-4002 Basel, Switzerland.

PLANTEY, Alain Gilles; French government official; b. 19 July 1924, Mulhouse; m. Christiane Wioland 1955; four d.; ed. Univs. de Bordeaux and Paris à la Sorbonne; Staff of Council of State 1949; French Del. to UN 1951–52; Master of Requests Council of State 1956–; Legal Adviser OEEC 1956–57; Prof. Ecole Royale d'Administration, Cambodia, Faculté de Droit and Ecole Nationale d'Administration, Paris 1957–62; Gen. Sec. Agence France-Presse 1958; Asst. Sec.-Gen. for the Community and African and Malagasy Affairs at the Presidency 1961–66; Amb. in Madagascar 1966–72; Asst. Sec.-Gen. WEU 1972–82; Chair. Standing Armaments Cttee. 1972–82; Conseiller d'Etat 1974–; Chair. Int. Court of Arbitration, ICC; mem. Acad. of Moral and Political Sciences (Inst. of France), American Acad. of Social and Political Science; Chair. Int. Inst. of Law; Council mem. Radio-Télévision (R.F.O.); numerous decorations. *Publications:* La réforme de la justice marocaine 1949, La justice répressive et le droit pénal chérifien 1950, Au coeur du problème berbère 1952, Traité pratique de la fonction publique 1956, 1963 and 1971, La formation et le perfectionne-ment des fonctionnaires 1957, La communauté 1962, Indépendance et coopération 1964–77, Prospective de l'État 1975, Droit et pratique de la fonction publique internationale 1977, Réformes dans la fonction publique 1978, La négociation internationale 1980, International Civil Service: Law and Management 1981, Derecho y Práctica de la Función Pública Interna-cional y Europea 1982, De la politique entre les Etats: principes de diplomatie 1987. *Address:* International Chamber of Commerce, 38 cours Albert Iᵉʳ, Paris 75008 (Office); Conseil d'Etat, Palais Royal, 75001 Paris (Office); 6 avenue Sully-Prudhomme, Paris 75007, France (Home). *Telephone:* 49.53.28.21 (ICC); 40.20.80.00 (Conseil d'Etat); 4555-2649 (Home).

PLANTU (pseudonym of Plantureux, Jean Henri); French artist; b. 23 March 1951, Paris; s. of Henri Plantureux and Renée Seignardie; m. Chantal Meyer 1971; two s. one d.; ed. Lycée Henri IV, Paris; political cartoonist, Le Monde 1972–; caricaturist, Droit de réponse (TV show) 1981–; Grand Prix de l'humour noir Granville. *Publications:* Pauvres chéris 1978, La Démocratie? Parlons-en 1979, Les Cours de caoutchouc sont trop élastiques 1982, C'est le goulag 1983, Pas nette, la planète! 1984, Politic-look 1984, Bonne année pour tous 1985, Ça manque de femmes 1986, A la Soupe 1987, Wolfgang, tu feras informatique 1988, Ouverture en bémol 1988. *Address:* Le Monde, 7 rue des Italiens, 75009 Paris, France.

PLASTOW, Sir David Arnold Stuart, Kt., F.B.I.M., F.R.S.A.; British business executive; b. 9 May 1932, Grimsby, Lincs.; s. of James Stuart Plastow and Marie Plastow; m. Barbara Ann May 1954; one s. one d.; ed. Culford School, Bury St. Edmunds; apprenticed Vauxhall Motors Ltd. 1950; joined Rolls-Royce Ltd., Motor Car Div. Crewe 1958, Marketing Dir. Motor Car Div. 1967–71, Man. Dir. 1971–72; Man. Dir. Rolls-Royce Motors Ltd. 1972–74, Group Man. Dir. 1974–80; Regional Dir. Lloyds Bank 1974–76; Dir. Vickers Ltd. 1975–, Man. Dir. 1980–86, Chief. Exec. 1980–, Chair. 1987–; Dir. GKN Ltd. 1978–84; Dir. Legal & General 1985–87, Guinness PLC 1986–, Deputy Chair. 1987–; mem. Bd. Tenneco Inc. (Houston) 1985–; Pres. Soc. of Motor Mfrs. and Traders Ltd. 1976–78, Deputy Pres. 1978–80; Pres. Motor Industry Research Asscn. 1978–81; Vice-Pres. Inst. of Motor Industry 1974–82; Chair. Grand Council, Motor and Cycle Trades Benevol-ent Fund 1976–78; mem. Eng. Council 1981–83, Council CBI, Council, Manchester Business School, Court of Manchester Univ., Council, Regular Forces Employment Asscn., Council, Industrial Soc., Chair. 1983–, British Overseas Trade Bd. 1980–83, British North American Cttee.; Companion British Inst. of Man.; Patron, Coll. of Aeronautical and Automobile Eng. 1972–79; Chair. of Govs.; Culford School, Bury St. Edmunds; Hon. D.Sc. (Cranfield Inst. of Tech.) 1978; Young Businessman of the Year Award (The Guardian) 1976; Liveryman, Worshipful Co. of Coachmakers and Coach Harness Makers. *Leisure interests:* golf, music. *Address:* Vickers PLC, P.O.B. 177, Millbank Tower, London, SW1P 4RA, England. *Telephone:* 01-828 7777.

PLATEN, Baron Carl Henrik G:son von, B.A., M.POL.SC.; Swedish diploma-tist; b. 14 Dec. 1913, Malmö; s. of Baron Gösta von Platen ad Elsa Stina Hjorth; m. Mildred Ax:son Johnson 1950; one s. one d.; ed. Lunds Universitet, London School of Econs. and Université de Paris à la Sor-bonne; entered Foreign Service 1939, served Moscow, Rome, Ankara, Washington, Geneva, Paris; Envoy and Perm. Rep. to UN and other int. orgs., Geneva 1959, Amb. 1960–63; Amb. at Large and Negotiator, UN Disarmament Conf. 1963; Swedish Rep. to OECD, Paris 1964–72, to UNESCO 1965–72; Chair. OECD Industry Cttee. *Publications:* Diplomati och Politik 1966, The Uneasy Truce 1983 (enlarged version in Japanese 1986), Strängt förtroligt (Strictly Confidential) 1986. *Address:* Résidence Cologny Parc, 9D Plateau de Frontenex, 1208 Geneva, Switzerland.

PLATON, Dr. Nicolas; Greek archaeologist; b. Jan. 1909, Cephallonia; s. of Eleftherios and Angeliki Platon; m. Anastassia Logiadou 1952; one s. two d.; ed. Univ. of Athens and Ecole des Hautes pratiques supérieures, Paris; Asst. at Heraklion Museum, Crete 1930–35; Ephor of Antiquities in Beotia, etc. 1935–38; Ephor of Antiquities in Crete and Dir. Heraklion Museum 1938–62; Ephor of Antiquities and Dir. of Acropolis in Athens 1961–65; Gen. Ephor of Antiquities 1965; Prof. at Univ. of Salonika

1966–74, Univ. of Crete 1977–81; Hon. mem. German and Austrian Inst. Soc. for Promotion of Hellenic Studies; mem. Greek Archaeological Soc., Soc. of Cretan Historical Studies; Kt. Order of Phoenix, Greece; Commen-datore al Merito della Republica Italiana, Silver Medal of Acad. of Athens; Major works include: excavations in Crete, Beotia, Euboea, Skopelos and the great excavation of the Minoan Palace, Zakros, East Crete; reorganized Heraklion Museum. *Publications:* Crete in Archaeologia Mundi, Geneva 1966, Corpus Minoischer Siegel II, Vol. 1 1970, Vol. 2 1977, Zakros, Discovery of a Lost Palace on Ancient Crete 1971, Inscribed Tablets and Pithos of Linear A from Zakro (with Brice) 1975, la civilisation égéenne 1981 (2 vols.), and many scientific monographs. *Leisure interest:* music. *Address:* Léof. Alexandras 126, Athens 11471, Greece. *Telephone:* 6469092 (Athens).

PLATT, Kenneth Allan, M.D.; American physician; b. 14 Oct. 1923, Denver, Colo.; s. of Ralph B. Platt and Myrtle M. Platt; m. Margaret Elizabeth Platt 1947; one s. two d.; ed. Ohio State Univ. and Univ. of Colo.; Pres. Clear Creek Valley Medical Soc. 1965–66, Colo. State Medical Soc. 1971–72, Colo. Foundation for Medical Care 1971–73; Colo. Medical Soc. Del. to American Medical Assen. 1972–86; Medical Dir. Colo. Foundation for Medical Care 1973–; Pres. Dist. 50 Bd. of Educ. 1970–72; mem. Nat. PSRO Council 1977–80, N.A.S. 1980– (mem. Inst. of Medicine); Chair. Bd. St. Anthony's Hosp. Systems 1978–84; Chamber of Commerce Award, Anthon-ian Award. *Leisure interests:* archaeology, horse racing, hunting, fishing, travel. *Address:* 7401 N. Lowell Blvd., Westminster, Colo. 80030 (Office); 11435 Quivas Way, Westminster, Colo. 80234, U.S.A. *Telephone:* (303) 428-7449 (Office); (303) 469-7600 (Home).

PLATTNER, Karl; Italian painter; b. 13 Feb. 1919, Mals-Vinschgau; s. of Joseph and Anna (née Perwanger) Plattner; m. Marie-Josèphe Texier 1952; two d.; ed. Acad. of Florence, Brera Acad. Milan and Art Acad. Paris; one-man exhbns. at Merano, Bolzano, Verona, Innsbruck, Stuttgart, Munich, São Paulo, Rio de Janeiro, Chicago, Paris, Rome, Milan and Vienna 1951–81 and other European cities; Group shows in Germany, Italy, Brazil, France, Uruguay and Sicily, including Biennali at Venice and São Paulo; numerous prizes including Burda Preis für Malerei, Munich 1966, Verleihung des Ehrenzeichens für Wissenschaft und Kunst, Austria 1976, Verleihung des Walther von der Vogelweide Preises 1979. *Major Works:* Fresco for War Memorial, Naturno, Italy 1951; Fresco for Prov. Council Bldg., Bolzano 1954–55; Panel for Folhas Newspaper bldg. São Paulo and for Air France São Paulo 1955–56; Panel for new Festival Hall Salzburg 1960–61; Fresco for Europa Chapel, near Innsbruck 1963–64; Panel for Austria A.G. Bldg., Vienna 1965. *Leisure interest:* walking in the country. *Address:* La Bergerie des Combes, Cipières, 06620 le Bar sur Loup, France. *Telephone:* 599603.

PLAVINSKY, Dmitri; Soviet artist; b. 1937, Moscow; ed. secondary school specialising in art and Moscow Regional Art Coll.; painter and lithographer; exhbns. Moscow 1957–61, 1967, 1969–70, 1975, 1976; London (Grosvenor Gallery) 1964, Poland 1966, New York (Gallery of Modern Art), Rome 1967, Stuttgart 1969, Cologne, Geneva, Lugano, Zurich 1970, Copenhagen 1971, Bochum, Grenoble 1974, Vienna, Brunswick, Freiburg, West Berlin 1975, Konstanz, Mulhouse, Esslingen, St. Louis, U.S.A. 1976.

PLAYER, Gary (Jim); South African professional golfer; b. 1 Nov. 1935, Johannesburg; s. of Francis Harry Audley Player and late Muriel Marie Ferguson; m. Vivienne Verwey 1957; two s. four d.; first overseas player for 45 years to win U.S. Open Championship 1965; Winner, British Open Championship 1959, 1968, 1974; Piccadilly World Match Play Champion 1965, 1966, 1968, 1971, 1973; U.S. Open Champion 1965; U.S. Masters Champion 1961, 1974, 1978; U.S. Professional Golf Assen. Champion 1962, 1972; Winner, South African Open 13 times; South African P.G.A. Cham-pion 1959, 1960, 1969, 1979, 1982; Winner, Australian Open 7 times; Quadel Senior Classic Champion 1985; third player ever to win all four major World professional titles; holds world record for lowest 18-hole score in any Open Championship (59 in the Brazilian Open 1974). *Address:* c/o Mark McCormack Agency, 14 Fitzhardinge Street, London, W1H 9PL, England.

PLAYFAIR, Sir Edward Wilder, K.C.B.; British former government offi-cial; b. 17 May 1909, London; s. of Dr. E. Playfair; m. Dr. M. L. Rae 1941; three d.; ed. Eton and King's Coll., Cambridge; Inland Revenue 1931–34; Treasury 1934–46, 1947–56 (Control Office for Germany and Austria 1946–47); Perm. Under-Sec. of State for War 1956–59; Perm. Sec. Ministry of Defence 1960–61; Chair. Int. Computers and Tabulators Ltd. 1961–65; Trustee, Nat. Gallery 1967–74 (Chair. Bd. of Trustees 1972–74). *Address:* 62 Coniger Road, Fulham, London, SW6 3TA, England. *Telephone:* 01-736 3194.

PLEASENCE, Donald; British actor, producer and writer; b. 5 Oct. 1919, Worksop; s. of late Thomas Stanley Pleasence and of Alice Pleasence; m. 1st Miriam Raymond 1941, two d.; m. 2nd Josephine Crombie 1956, two d.; m. 3rd Meira Shore 1970, one d.; ed. Ecclesfield Grammar School, Yorkshire; made first stage appearance 1939; first London appearance in Twelfth Night at Arts Theatre 1942; R.A.F. 1942–46 (P.O.W. 1944–46); returned to stage in The Brothers Karamazov 1946, Peter Pan 1947; Perth Repertory Theatre 1947; Birmingham Repertory Theatre 1948–50; Bristol Old Vic Co. 1950–51; Right Side Up and Saints Day, London 1951; appeared in New York with Laurence Olivier's Co. 1951–52; Hobson's Choice Arts

Theatre 1952; played in own play Ebb Tide at Edinburgh Festival and Royal Court Theatre, London 1952; Stratford-on-Avon season 1953; Antony and Cleopatra, London 1953; The Rule of the Game 1955, The Lark 1955, Misalliance 1956, Restless Heart 1957, The Caretaker (London and New York) 1960, Poor Bitos (co-producer) 1964, The Man in the Glass Booth (co-producer) 1967, Tea Party, The Basement 1970, Wise Child (New York) 1972, Reflections (London) 1980; numerous film appearances include The Beachcomber, Manuela, Heart of a Child, The Caretaker, The Greatest Story Ever Told, Fantastic Voyage, The Hallelujah Trail, The Great Escape, Doctor Crippen, Cul-de-Sac, Will Penny, The Mad Woman of Chaillot, Arthur! Arthur?, Soldier Blue, Jerusalem File, Pied Piper, Outback, The Black Windmill, Wedding in White, The Rainbow Boys, Mutations, Henry VIII, Malachi's Cove, Escape to Witch Mountain, Journey into Fear, The Count of Monte Cristo, Doctor Jekyll and Mr. Hyde, Hearts of the West, I Don't Want to be Born, Trial by Combat, The Devil's People, The Eagle Has Landed, The Last Tycoon 1976, Telefon, Devil Cat, Sergeant Pepper's Lonely Hearts Club Band, Blood Relatives, Power Play, Halloween, Halloween 2, Centennial, A Breed Apart, Escape to New York, All Quiet on the Western Front, The French Atlantic Affair, The Monster Club, The Corsican Brothers, Black Arrow, Pleasure of the Amazon, Warrior of the Lost, A Breed Apart, Where is Parsifal; ; numerous television appearances in Britain and America including Dracula, Armchair Theatre, Call Me Daddy, Columbo, The Captain of Köpenick, Mrs. Columbo, It's Never Too Late, The Barchester Chronicles, Master of the Game, Arch of Triumph, The Falklands Factor 1983, Scoop 1987; Television Actor of the Year Award 1958; London Critics Best Stage Performance Award 1960; Variety Club Award; Stage Actor of 1967. *Publications:* Scouse the Mouse 1977, Scouse in New York 1978; recorded version of Scouse the Mouse 1977. *Address:* c/o Joy Jameson Limited, 7 West Eaton Place Mews, London, SW1X 8LY, England. *Telephone:* 01-245 9551.

PLESCOFF, Georges, L. ES L.; French administrator (retd.); b. 9 March 1918, Paris; m. Renée Voulot 1951; ed. Univ. of Paris, Ecole nat. d'admin.; Asst., Inspection générale des finances 1947; Adviser, Ministry of Econ. Affairs 1951–52; with UN Econ. Comm. for Europe 1952–54; assigned to the Treasury 1955; Dir. Caisse des dépôts et consignations 1957–67; Admin. IMF and World Bank, also Financial Adviser, French Embassy, Washington, D.C. 1967–70; Inspecteur général des Finances 1969–83; Chair. Assurances générales de France 1970–82, Cie. Financière de Suez 1982–83, Banque Indosuez 1982–83; Pres. Banque Eurofin 1984–; Grand Officier, Légion d'honneur, Grand Officier, Ordre nat. du Mérite, Croix de guerre, Chevalier de l'Economie nationale. *Address:* 41 rue Bienfaisance, 75008 Paris (Office); 13 avenue des Hauts Perreux, 94500 Champigny, France (Home). *Telephone:* 4562-77-87.

PLESSNER, Yakir, PH.D.; Israeli economist; b. 18 Jan. 1935, Haifa; s. of Martin Plessner and Eva Plessner; m. Ora Ester Frenkel 1959; one s. one d.; ed. Iowa State Univ. and Hebrew Univ. of Jerusalem; Visiting Lecturer, Pa. Univ. 1971–73; Research Consultant, The World Bank 1977–78; Econ. Advisor to Israel's Minister of Finance 1981–83; Deputy Gov. Bank of Israel 1982–85; mem. Israel's Securities Authority 1982–85; Joseph and Esther Foster Visiting Prof., Brandeis Univ. 1985–86; Sr. Lecturer, The Hebrew Univ. of Jerusalem 1973–; The Oded Levine Prize of the Operations Research Soc. of Israel. *Publications:* The Marketing of Israel's Citrus Fruit in Major European Markets 1976; several articles in learned society journals. *Leisure interests:* music, photography, tennis. *Address:* 7 Hahita Street, Rehovot 76352, Israel (Home). *Telephone:* (08) 468745 (Home); (08) 481233 (Office).

PLEVEN, René, D. EN D.; French politician; b. 15 April 1901, Rennes; s. of Jules and Andrée Pleven; m. Anne Bompard 1924 (died 1966); two d.; ed. Ecole des Sciences Politiques, Paris; Dir.-Gen. for Europe, Automatic Telephone Co. 1929–39; mem. Franco-British Co-ordination Cttee. 1940; Sec.-Gen. Govt. of French Equatorial Africa 1940; negotiated agreement for dispatch of war material to Free French, Washington 1941; Nat. Commr. for Economy, Finance and Colonies 1941–42, for Foreign Affairs and Colonies 1942–43, for Colonies 1943; Commr. for Colonies French Cttee. for Nat. Liberation 1943–44; Minister for Colonies, French Provisional Govt. Sept.-Nov. 1944, of Finance 1944–46, of Nat. Defence 1949–50, Prime Minister July 1950–March 1951, Aug. 1951–Jan. 1952; Minister of Nat. Defence 1952–54; Minister of Foreign Affairs 1958, of Justice 1969–73; Deputy (Côtes-du-Nord) 1945–73; Political Ed. Le petit bleu des Côtes-du-Nord 1945–; Pres. Conseil Général des Côtes du Nord 1948–76; Pres. Comm. for Regional Econ. Devt. of Brittany 1964–73; Pres. Conseil de la Région Bretagne 1974–76; mem. Acad. des Sciences d'Outre-mer 1948–; Hon. Dr. (Univ. of N.C.); Compagnon de la Libération, Commdr. du mérite maritime, Hon. M.B.E., and several foreign decorations. *Publication:* Avenir de la Bretagne 1962. *Leisure interest:* fishing. *Address:* Le petit bleu des Côtes-du-Nord, 7 rue d'Uzès, 75002 Paris (Office); 12 rue Chateaubriand, Dinan, Côtes-du-Nord, France.

PLIATZKY, Sir Leo, K.C.B., M.A.; British civil servant; b. 22 Aug. 1919, Salford; m. Marian Jean Elias 1948 (died 1979); ed. Manchester Grammar School, City of London School, Corpus Christi Coll., Oxford; Army service 1940–45, (mentioned in despatches); Research Sec., Fabian Soc. 1946–47; Ministry of Food 1947–50, Treasury 1950–77, Second Perm. Sec. in charge of Public Expenditure 1976–77; Perm. Sec., Dept. of Trade 1977–79;

retained on special duties for the Prime Minister Sept. 1979–Jan. 1980; Visiting Prof. City Univ. 1980–84; Non-exec. Dir. Assoc. Communications Corpn. 1980–82, Cen. Independent Television PLC June 1981–; Part-time mem. B.A. Bd. 1980–84, non-exec. Dir. British Airways PLC 1984–85; Treas. History of Parl. Trust 1982–; Dir. Ultramar Co. PLC Jan. 1980–; Assoc. Fellow, L.S.E. 1982–84, Visiting Fellow 1985–86; Hon. Fellow, Corpus Christi Coll., Oxford; Hon. D.Litt. (Salford) 1986. *Publications:* Getting and Spending: Public Expenditure, Employment and Inflation 1982, Paying and Choosing: The Intelligent Person's Guide to the Mixed Economy 1985, The Treasury under Mrs. Thatcher 1989. *Address:* 27 River Court, Upper Ground, London, SE1 9PE, England.

PLISETSKAYA, Maiya Mikhailovna; Soviet ballerina; b. 20 Nov. 1925, Moscow; ed. Moscow Bolshoi Theatre Ballet School; soloist Bolshoi Ballet 1943, now a Prin. Dancer; Artistic Dir. Nat. Ballet of Spain 1987–; Hon. mem. Portuguese Dance Centre; First Prize, Budapest Int. Competition 1949; People's Artist of the R.S.F.S.R. 1951; People's Artist of the U.S.S.R. 1959, Lenin Prize 1964, Hero of Socialist Labour 1985, and other decorations; Main ballet roles: Odette-Odile (Swan Lake, Tchaikovsky), Raimonda (Raimonda, Glazunov), Zaryema (The Fountain of Bakhchisarai, Asafiev), Kitri (Don Quixote, Minkus), Juliet (Romeo and Juliet, Prokofiev), Girl-Bird, Syunmbike (Shuralye, Yarullin), Laurencia (Laurencia, Krein), Yegina (Spartak, Khachaturian), Karmen (Karmen Suite Schedrin), Nina (The Seagull, by Schedrin) 1980; produced (with V. V. Smirnoviy-Golovanoviy and N. I. Ryzhenko) Anna Karenina 1972. *Address:* State Academic Bolshoi Theatre, 1 Ploshchad Sverdlova, Moscow, U.S.S.R.

PLÖCKINGER, Erwin, DIPL.ENG., PH.D.; Austrian metallurgist; b. 22 April 1914, Karwin; s. of Erwin and Auguste (Reimann) Plöckinger; m. Natalie von Günner 1939; two d.; ed. Tech. Univ. of Prague, Univ. of Mining and Metallurgy, Leoben; Man., melting shop (electric furnaces), Dept. of Metallurgy, Osterreichische-Alpine-Montan-Gesellschaft, Donawitz 1939–48; with Eisenholding GmbH 1949–50; Dept. of Quality and Production Control, Eisenwerk Breitenfeld GmbH 1950–53; Head of Metallurgical Dept., Röchlingsche Eisen-und Stahlwerke, Völklingen/Saar 1954–57; Chief Metallurgist, Friedrich Krupp, Essen 1958–60; Dir. of Research, Gebruder Böhler & Co. AG, Kapfenberg 1960–78; Univ. lecturer and Asst. Prof., Univ. for Mining and Metallurgy, Leoben 1960–; mem. Austrian Acad. of Sciences 1970–, Pres. 1982–86; Peter Tunner Medal 1968, Gold Medal of Honour 1969. *Publications:* Die Edelstahlerzeugung (with F. Leitner) 1950, Elektrostahlerzeugung (with F. Sommer) 1964; more than 80 papers on metallurgy of special steels and steel production. *Leisure interests:* genealogy and family history. *Address:* Sternwartestrasse 63, 1180 Vienna (Home); Austrian Academy of Sciences, Dr.-Ignaz-Seipel-Platz 2, 1010 Vienna, Austria (Office). *Telephone:* (0222) 3148122 (Home); (0222) 529681 (Office).

PLOIX, Hélène Marie Joseph, M.A., M.B.A.; French business executive; b. 25 Sept. 1944, Anould; d. of René Ploix; ed. Calif. and Paris Univs.; Man. Consultant McKinsey and Co., Paris 1968–78; Special Asst. to Cabinet of Sec. of State for Consumer Affairs 1977–78; Dir. Compagnie Européenne de Publication 1978–82; Pres. Man. Dir., Banque Industrielle et Mobilière Privée 1982–84; mem. of Bd. Comm. des Opérations de Bourse 1983–84; Advisor to P.M. for Econ. and Financial Affairs 1984–86; Exec. Dir. for France, I.M.F. and World Bank 1986–; Chevalier de l'Ordre National du Mérite. *Leisure interests:* golf, skiing. *Address:* International Monetary Fund, 700 19th Street, N.W., Washington, D.C. 20431, U.S.A.

PLOURDE, Most Rev. Joseph Aurèle; Canadian ecclesiastic; b. 12 Jan. 1915, St. François of Madawaska, N.B.; s. of Antoine Plourde and Suzanne Albert; ed. Bathurst Coll., Bourget Coll. of Rigau, St. Joseph's Univ. of Moncton, Holy Heart Seminary, Halifax, Inst. Catholique de Paris, Ottawa and Gregorian Univs.; ordained priest 1944; fmr. Prof. of Philosophy, St. Louis Coll. of Edmunston and diocesan dir. of social works; Pastor, St. Leonard of Madawaska 1955–59; consecrated Bishop 1964; Apostolic Admin. of Alexandria 1964; Archbishop of Ottawa 1967–; Pres. Canadian Conf. of Catholic Bishops 1969–71; Kt. of Malta, Kt. of Holy Sepulchre; Hon. Ph.D. (Moncton). *Address:* Archbishop's Residence, 145 Saint Patrick Street, Ottawa, Ont., K1N 5K1, Canada.

PLOWDEN, Baron, (Life Peer), cr. 1959; **Edwin Noel Plowden,** G.B.E., K.C.B.; British administrator; b. 6 Jan. 1907, Stachur, Argyll, Scotland; s. of the late Roger H. Plowden; m. Bridget Horatia Richmond, D.B.E., J.P. (Lady Plowden, q.v.), 1933; two s. two d.; ed. Switzerland and Pembroke Coll., Cambridge; temp. Civil Servant Ministry of Econ. Warfare 1939–40; Ministry of Aircraft Production 1940–46; mem. Aircraft Supply Council, Chief Exec. 1945–46; Chief Planning Officer and Chair. Econ. Planning Bd. in Cabinet Office and Treasury 1947–53; Vice-Chair. Temporary Council Cttee. of NATO 1951–52; Chair. Desig. U.K.A.E.A. 1953–54, Chair 1954–59; Chair. Cttee. of Enquiry into Control of Public Expenditure 1959–61, Cttee. of Enquiry into Org. of Representational Service Overseas 1963–64, Cttee. of Enquiry into Aircraft Industry 1964–65, Standing Advisory Cttee. on Pay of Higher Civil Service 1968–70, Cttee. of Enquiry into Structure of Electricity Supply Industry 1974–75, Enquiry into CBI's Aims and Organisation 1974–75; Deputy Chair. Cttee. of Enquiry into Police Pay and Related Matters 1977–79; mem. Top Salaries Review Body 1977–(Chair. 1981–89); Pres. AMDEA 1976–87; mem. Ford European Advisory Council 1976–83, mem. Int. Advisory Bd. Southeast Bank N.A. 1983–86;

Chair. Tube Investments Ltd. 1963-76, Pres. 1976-; Dir. Nat. Westminster Bank Ltd. 1960-77, Commercial Union Assurance Co. Ltd 1946-78; Pres. London Graduate School of Business Studies 1976-, Chair. Governing Body 1964-76; Chair. CBI Cos. Cttee. 1976-80, Vice-Chair. Pres.'s Cttee. 1977-80; Chair. Equity Capital for Industry Ltd. 1976-82, Police Complaints Bd. 1976-81, Police Negotiating Bd. 1979-82; Visiting Fellow, Nuffield Coll., Oxford 1956-64; Hon. Fellow, Pembroke Coll., Cambridge 1958; Hon. D.Sc. (Pennsylvania State) 1958, (Aston) 1972, Hon. D.Litt. (Loughborough) 1976. *Publication:* An Industrialist in the Treasury 1989. *Address:* Martels Manor, Dunmow, Essex; 11 Abingdon Gardens, Abingdon Villas, London, W8 6BY, England. *Telephone:* 01-937 4238 (London).

PLOWDEN, Lady (Bridget Horatia), D.B.E.; British administrator; b. 5 May 1910; d. of late Admiral Sir H. W. Richmond and Lady Richmond; m. Edwin Noel Plowden (Lord Plowden, q.v.) 1933; two s. two d.; ed. Downe House; Dir. Trust House Forte Ltd. 1961-72; J.P., Inner London Area Juvenile Panel 1962-71; Chair. Cen. Advisory Council for Educ. (England) 1963-66, Working Ladies Guild, Professional Classes Aid Council 1978-86, Advisory Cttee. for Educ. of Romany and other Travellers 1970-83 (Pres. 1983-), Metropolitan Architectural Consortium for Educ., Bd. of Govs. Philippa Fawcett Coll. of Educ. 1967-76, Robert Montefiore Comprehensive School 1968-79; co-opted mem. Educ. Cttee. Inner London Educ. Authority 1967-73, Vice-Chair. ILEA School Sub-Cttee. 1967-70; Vice-Chair. Gov. BBC 1970-75; Chair. IBA 1975-80, Manpower Services Comm. N. London Area Man. Bd. 1983-88; Pres. Pre-Schools Playgroups Asscn. 1972-82 (Vice-Pres. 1982-), Harding Housing Asscn.; mem. Nat. Theatre Bd. 1976-88; Pres. Nat. Inst. of Adult Continuing Educ. 1980-88, Nat. Marriage Guidance Council 1982-; Liveryman, Goldsmiths Co. 1979-; Fellow, Royal Television Soc. 1980-; Hon. Fellow, Coll. of Preceptors 1973, Vice-Pres. Inst. of Preceptors 1984, Pres. 1987; Hon. LL.D. (Leicester) 1968, (Reading) 1970, (Open Univ.) 1974, (London) 1976; Hon. D.Litt. (Loughborough) 1976. *Address:* 11 Abingdon Gardens, Abingdon Villas, London, W8 6BY; Martels Manor, Dunmow, Essex, England. *Telephone:* 01-937 4238 (London); (0371) 2141 (Essex).

PLOWRIGHT, David Ernest; British television executive; b. 11 Dec. 1930, Scunthorpe; s. of William E. Plowright and Daisy M. Plowright; m. Brenda M. Key 1953; one s. two d.; ed. Scunthorpe Grammar School; Reporter, Scunthorpe Star 1950; freelance correspondent and sports writer 1952; reporter, feature writer and briefly equestrial corresp., Yorkshire Post 1954; News Ed. Granada TV 1957, Producer, Current Affairs 1960, Exec. Producer, Scene at 6.30 1964, Exec. Producer, World in Action 1966, Head of Current Affairs 1968, Dir. 1968, Controller of Programmes 1969, Jt. Man. Dir. 1975-81, Man. Dir. 1981-87, Chair. Granada TV Ltd. 1987-; Dir. Granada Int. 1975-, Granada Group 1981-, Independent TV News 1981-, Superchannel 1986-, British Satellite Broadcasting 1987. *Leisure interests:* television, theatre, yachting. *Address:* Granada Television Ltd., Quay Street, Manchester, M60 9EA; Granada Television Ltd., 36 Golden Square, London, W.1, England. *Telephone:* 061-832 7211.

PLOWRIGHT, Joan Anne, C.B.E.; British actress; b. 28 Oct. 1929, Brigg, Lancashire; d. of William Plowright and Daisy (née Burton); m. 1st Roger Gage 1953 (divorced), 2nd Sir Laurence (now Lord) Olivier (q.v.) 1961; one s. two d.; ed. Scunthorpe Grammar School and Old Vic Theatre School; mem. Old Vic Company, toured South Africa 1952-53; first leading rôle in The Country Wife, London 1956; mem. English Stage Company 1956; at Nat. Theatre 1963-74; Best Actress (Tony) Award for A Taste of Honey, New York 1960; Best Actress (Evening Standard) Award for St. Joan 1964; Variety Club Award 1976 for The Bed Before Yesterday, Best Actress Soc. of West End Theatre (Filumena) 1978. *Plays and films acted in include:* The Chairs 1957, The Entertainer 1958, Major Barbara and Roots 1959, A Taste of Honey 1960, Uncle Vanya 1962, 1963, 1964, St. Joan 1963, Hobson's Choice 1964, The Master Builder 1965, Much Ado About Nothing 1967, Tartuffe 1967, Three Sisters 1967, 1969 (film 1969), The Advertisement 1968, 1969, Love's Labour's Lost 1968, 1969, The Merchant of Venice, 1970, 1971-72, Rules of the Game, Woman Killed with Kindness 1971-72, Taming of the Shrew, Doctor's Dilemma 1972, Merchant of Venice (TV film) 1973, Rosmersholm 1973, Saturday Sunday Monday 1973, Eden's End 1974, The Sea Gull 1975, The Bed Before Yesterday 1975, Equus (film) 1976, Daphne Laureola (TV film) 1977, Saturday Sunday Monday (TV film) 1977, Filumena 1977, Enjoy 1980, Who's Afraid of Virginia Woolf? 1981, Richard Wagner (film) 1982, Cavell 1982, Britannia Hospital (film) 1981, Brimstone and Treacle (film) 1982, The Cherry Orchard 1983, The Way of the World 1984, Mrs Warren's Profession 1985, Revolution 1985, The House of Bernarda Alba 1986, Drowning by Numbers (film) 1987, Uncle Vanga 1988, The Dressmaker (film) 1988, The Importance of Being Earnest (TV) 1988, Conquest of the South Pole 1989. *Address:* c/o LOP Ltd., 33-34 Chancery Lane, London, England.

PLOWRIGHT, Rosalind Anne, L.R.A.M.; British soprano; b. 21 May 1949; d. of Robert Arthur Plowright and Celia Adelaide Plowright; ed. Notre Dame High School, Wigan, Royal Northern Coll. of Music, Manchester; career began London Opera Centre 1973-75; Glyndebourne Chorus and Touring Co. 1974-77; debut with English Nat. Opera as Page in Salome 1975, Miss Jessel in Turn of the Screw 1979 (SWET award), at Covent Garden as Ortlinde in Die Walküre 1980; with Bern Opera 1980-81, Frankfurt and Munich Opera 1981; debuts in U.S.A. (Philadelphia and San

Diego), Paris, Madrid and Hamburg 1982; at La Scala, Milan, Edinburgh Festival, San Francisco and New York (Carnegie Hall) 1983; with Deutsche Oper, Berlin 1984; in Houston, Pittsburgh, Venice and Verona 1985. *Principal roles include:* Ariadne, Alceste, Médée, Norma; title rôle and Elizabeth I in Mary Stuart, Maddalena in Andrea Chénier, Antonia in The Tales of Hoffman, Donna Anna in Don Giovanni, Vitellia in La Clemenza di Tito, Madame Butterfly, Manon Lescaut, Suor Angelica, Giorgetta in Il Tabarro, Aida, Abigaille in Nabucco, Desdemona in Otello, Elena in I Vespri Siciliani, Leonora in Il Trovatore, Amelia in Un Ballo in Maschera, Leonora in La Forza del Destino, Violetta in La Traviata; has given recitals and concerts in U.K., Europe and U.S.A. and made opera recordings; First Prize 7th Int. Competition for Opera Singers, Sofia 1979, Prix Fondation Fanny Heldy, Acad. Nat. du Disque Lyrique 1985. *Leisure interests:* wind surfing, cliff climbing. *Address:* c/o Kaye Artists Management Ltd., Kingsmead House, 250 Kings Road, London, SW3 6NR, England. *Telephone:* 01-352 4494.

PLUG, Enrik C.H.A., LL.M.; Netherlands diplomatist; b. 22 March 1929, Rotterdam; m. Rozemarie Kerssemakers; three d.; ed. Univ. of Amsterdam; Third Sec., Madrid 1957-59, Wellington 1959-61; Second Sec., Guatemala 1961-63, Perm. Mission of the Netherlands at OECD, Paris 1963-64; First Sec., Canberra 1964-67; Consul, Hamburg 1967-70; Commercial Counsellor, later Minister Plenipotentiary, London 1970-76; Amb. to Cameroon 1979-83, to Australia 1983-86, to Spain 1986-. *Address:* Netherlands Embassy, Po. de la Castellana 178, 28036 Madrid (Office); Isla de Oza 24, 28035 Madrid, Spain (Home). *Telephone:* 091-458 21 00 (Office); 091-216 42 45 (Home).

PLUHAŘ, Zdeněk, Czechoslovak writer; b. 16 May 1913, Brno; s. of Dr. Ladislav Pluhař and Marie Hoffmeisterova; m. 1st Helena Špičková 1951; m. 2nd Marie Janir 1979; one d.; ed. Coll. of Tech. Brno 1931-36; engineer, works foreman, bldg. industry, Brno 1937-52; chief of design centre, n.p. Hydroprojekt, Brno 1952-56; mem. of Presidium, Czechoslovak Cttee. of Defenders of Peace 1952-56; writer by profession 1956-; Deputy Chair., Union of Czech Writers 1977-; mem. of Presidium, Union of Czech Writers 1977-; mem., World Peace Council; Klement Gottwald State Prize 1958, 1975, Award for Merit in Construction 1963, Artist of Merit 1974, Vít Nejedlý Prize 1974, National Artist 1982, Order of Labour 1983, Klement Gottwald State Prize 1984. *Works include:* novels: Kříže rostou k Pacifiku 1974, Mraky táhnou nad Savojskem 1949, Bronzová spirála 1953, Modré údolí 1954, Opustíš-li mne 1957, Ať hodí kamenem 1962, Úspěch 1965, Minutu ticha za mé lásky 1969, Konečná stanice 1971, Skleněná dáma 1971, Jeden stříbrný 1974, Devátá smrt 1977, V šest večer v Astorii 1982, Opona bez potlesku 1986; books for young people: Voda slouží člověku 1956, Vzpoura na Panteru 1967. *Address:* Svaz českých spisovatelaů, Národní tř. 11, Praha 1, Czechoslovakia.

PLUMB, Baron (Life Peer), cr. 1987, of Coleshill in the County of Warwickshire; **(Charles) Henry Plumb**, Kt., F.R.S.A.; British politician; b. 27 March 1925; s. of Charles Plumb and Louisa Plumb; m. Marjorie Dorothy Dunn 1947; one s. two d.; ed. King Edward VI School, Nuneaton; mem. Council Nat. Farmers Union 1959, Vice-Pres. 1964, 1965, Deputy-Pres. 1966-69, Pres. 1970-79; mem. Duke of Northumberland's Cttee. of Enquiry on Foot and Mouth Disease 1967-68; Chair. British Agricultural Council 1975-79; Pres. Nat. Fed. of Young Farmers' Clubs 1976-; Pres. Royal Agricultural Soc. of England 1977, Deputy Pres. 1978; Pres. Int. Fed. of Agricultural Producers 1979-82; mem. (Conservative) European Parl. 1979-, Chair. Agricultural Cttee. 1979-82, Chair. European Democratic Group (Conservative) 1982-87, Pres. European Parl. Jan. 1987-; Dir. United Biscuits Ltd., Lloyds Bank Ltd., Fisons Ltd.; Fellow Royal Agric. Soc.; Hon. D.Sc. (Cranfield) 1983; D. L. (Warwick); Order of Merit, Fed. Repub. of Germany. *Leisure interests:* fishing, shooting. *Address:* 2 Queen Anne's Gate, London, SW1H 9AA, England. *Telephone:* (0675) 63133 (Birmingham); 01-222 0411 (London).

PLUMB, Sir John Harold, Kt., PH.D., LITT.D., F.B.A.; British historian; b. 20 Aug. 1911; s. of late James Plumb; ed. Univ. Coll., Leicester, Christ's Coll., Cambridge; Ehrman Research Fellow King's Coll. Cambridge 1939-46; Foreign Office 1940-45; Fellow, Christ's Coll. 1946-, Steward 1948-50, Tutor 1950-59, Vice-Master 1964-68, Master 1978-82; Lecturer in History, Univ. of Cambridge 1946-62, Reader in Modern English History 1962-65, Prof. of Modern English History 1966-73; Trustee, Nat. Portrait Gallery 1961-82; Visiting Prof. Columbia Univ. 1960, Distinguished Visiting Prof. New York City Univ. 1971-72, 1976, Washington Univ. 1977; Ed. History of Human Society 1959-; European Advisory Ed. to Horizon 1959-; Historical Adviser, Penguin Books 1960-; Ed. Pelican Social History of Britain 1982-; mem. Council of British Acad. 1977-80; Hon. foreign mem. American Acad. of Arts and Sciences 1970; Hon. D.Litt. (Leicester) 1968, (East Anglia) 1973, (Bowdoin Coll., U.S.A.) 1974, (Univ. of Southern Calif.) 1978, (Westminster Coll., U.S.A.) 1983. *Publications:* England in the Eighteenth Century 1950, West African Explorers (with C. Howard) 1951, Chatham 1953, Sir Robert Walpole Vol. I 1956, Vol. II 1960, The First Four Georges 1956, The Renaissance 1961, Men and Places 1963, Crisis in the Humanities 1964, The Growth of Political Stability in England 1675-1725 1967, The Death of the Past 1969, In the Light of History 1972, The Commercialisation of Leisure 1974, Royal Heritage (with Sir Huw Wheldon) 1977; also televised version of Royal Heritage 1977, New Light on the Tyrant George

III 1978, Georgian Delights 1980, Royal Heritage: The Reign of Elizabeth II 1980, The Birth of a Consumer Society (with Neil McKendrick and John Brewer) 1982, The Making of an Historian: Collected Letters of J. H. Plumb 1988. *Address:* Christ's College, Cambridge; The Old Rectory, Westhorpe, Stowmarket, Suffolk, England. (Home). *Telephone:* (0223) 334900; (0449) 781235 (Home).

PLUMBRIDGE, Robin Allan, M.A.; South African business executive; b. 6 April 1935, Cape Town; s. of late C. O. Plumbridge and late M. A. Plumbridge; m. Celia Anne Millar 1959; two s. two d.; ed. St. Andrews Coll., Grahamstown, Univs. of Cape Town and Oxford; joined Gold Fields of South Africa Ltd. 1957, Asst. Man. 1962–65, Man. 1965–69, Exec. Dir. 1969–80, Deputy Chair. 1974–80, Chair. Dec. 1980–; Dir. Newmont Mining Corpn. 1983–. *Leisure interest:* squash. *Address:* 75 Fox Street, Johannesburg 2001, and P.O. Box 1167, Johannesburg 2000 (Offices); 17 Woolston Road, Westcliff, Johannesburg 2193, South Africa (Home). *Telephone:* 639.9111 (Office).

PLUMMER, (Arthur) Christopher (Orme), C.C.; Canadian actor; b. 13 Dec. 1929, Toronto; m. 1st Tammy Lee Grimes 1956; one d.; m. 2nd Patricia Audrey Lewis 1962 (divorced 1966); m. 3rd Elaine Regina Taylor 1970; public and pvt. schools in Montreal, P.Q.; professional debut as Faulkland in The Rivals, Ottawa Repertory Theatre; Broadway debut in Starcross Story 1951–52; Maple Leaf Award 1982; numerous appearances in theatres in U.S.A. have included: Mark Antony in Julius Caesar, Ferdinand in The Tempest, Earl of Warwick in Anouilh's The Lark, The Narrator in Stravinsky's L'Histoire du Soldat, The Devil in J.B., 1951–61, The Resistible Rise of Arturo Ui and The Royal Hunt of the Sun 1965–66, The God Doctor 1973, Iago in Othello 1981, Macbeth 1988; played many leading Shakespearian roles in productions by the Stratford Canadian Festival Co.; British debut in title role of Richard III, Stratford on Avon 1961 and then in London as Henry II in Anouilh's Becket; a leading actor in the Nat. Theatre Co. of Great Britain 1971–72; has appeared in Nat. Theatre productions of Amphytrion 38, Danton's Death 1971; many TV roles including Hamlet in BBC/Danish TV production, Hamlet in Elsinore, Jesus of Nazareth 1977. *Films include:* The Fall of the Roman Empire, The Sound of Music, Inside Daisy Clover, Triple Cross, Oedipus the King, Nobody Runs Forever, Lock Up Your Daughters, The Royal Hunt of the Sun, Battle of Britain, Waterloo, The Pyx, The Spiral Staircase, Conduct Unbecoming, The Return of the Pink Panther, The Man Who Would be King, Aces High 1976, The Disappearance 1977, International Velvet 1978, The Silent Partner 1978, Hanover Street 1979, Murder by Decree 1980, The Shadow Box 1980, The Disappearance 1981, The Janitor 1981, The Amateur 1982, Dreamscape 1984, Playing for Keeps 1985, Lily in Love 1985, Dragnet 1987, Souvenir 1988. *Leisure interests:* piano, skiing, tennis, old cars. *Address:* c/o Stanley, Gorrie, Whitson & Co., 9 Cavendish Square, London, W.1, England. *Telephone:* 01-580 6363.

PNIEWSKI, Jerzy, D.SC.; Polish physicist (retd.); b. 1 June 1913, Płock; s. of Henryk and Amelia Pniewski; m. Maria Chojnacka 1953; ed. Warsaw Univ.; Doctor 1951–54, Warsaw Univ., Assoc. Prof. 1954–63, Prof. 1963–; Dir. Inst. of Experimental Physics 1953–75, Dean Dept. of Physics 1975–81; specialist in high energy physics and co-founder of hyper-nucleus physics; Corresp. mem. Polish Acad. of Sciences (PAN) 1964–71, mem. 1971–; mem. Presidium of State Cttee. for Nuclear Physics 1960–80; Pres. Physics Cttee., PAN 1975–81; mem. IUPAP Comm. 1969–75, Polish Physical Soc., Società Italiana di Fisica, European Physical Soc.; Corresp. mem. Heidelberg Acad. of Sciences 1971–; Dr. h.c. (Lyons Univ.) 1975, (Heidelberg Univ.) 1980; Gold Cross of Merit 1952, Kt.'s Cross, Order of Polonia Restituta 1954, Commdr.'s Cross with Star 1974, Order of Banner of Labour, 1st Class 1964, State Prize 1955, 1966; Smoluchowski Medal of Polish Physical Soc. 1969, Copernicus Medal of Polish Acad. of Sciences 1983, Alfred Jurzykowski Foundation Award 1986. *Address:* Koszykowa 75 m-33, 00-662 Warsaw, Poland. *Telephone:* 28-47-43 (Home).

PODDAR, Prof. Ramendra Kumar, M.SC., PH.D.; Indian university professor and administrator; b. 9 Nov. 1930, Sagarkandi, Pabna, Bangladesh; s. of late Brojendra K. Poddar; m. Jharna Sarkar 1953; two s. one d.; Biophysicist, Univ. of California, Berkeley 1958–60; Research Fellow, Purdue Univ., U.S.A. 1960–61; Scientific Adviser, Int. Atomic Energy Authority, UN, Bamako, Mali, West Africa 1963; Assoc. Prof., Saha Inst. of Nuclear Physics 1968–73; Research Fellow, California Inst. of Tech. 1970; Prof. of Biophysics, Calcutta Univ. 1973–, Pro-Vice-Chancellor for Academic Affairs 1977–79, Vice-Chancellor 1979–83; mem. Rajya Sabha 1985–; research in molecular genetics, radiation and photo-biology; mem. Nat. Cttee. on Biophysics, Indian Nat. Science Acad. 1972–78, Indian Biophysical Soc.; Adviser West Bengal Pollution Control Bd.; Chair. Inst. of Wetland Man. and Ecological Design, Indian School of Social Sciences, Calcutta. *Publications:* over 25 articles in various scientific journals. *Leisure interests:* reading, and social commitment activity. *Address:* University of Calcutta, Calcutta 700 009 (Office); AA 10/7 Deshbandhu Nagar, Calcutta 700 059, India (Home). *Telephone:* 35-9186 (Office); 57-5260, 37-6572 (Home).

PODGAYEV, Grigoriy Yefimovich; Soviet politician; b. 1920; ed. Tomsk Industrial Inst. and Higher Party School; CPSU 1940–; Engineer 1940–42; with Soviet Army 1942–45; Instructor, Territorial Cttee. of CP then First Sec. Vyazma Dist. Cttee. of CP 1945–58; Chief of Section Khabarovsk Territorial Cttee. of CP, then First Sec. Khabarovsk City Cttee. of CP

1958–61; Chair. Exec. Cttee. Regional Soviet of Jewish Autonomous Region 1961–62; First Sec. Regional Cttee. of CP of Jewish Autonomous Region 1962–70; Chair. Exec. Cttee. Khabarovsk Territorial Soviet of Deputies Working People; Deputy to Supreme Soviet of U.S.S.R. 1966–; mem. Comm. for Industry, Soviet of Nationalities 1974–; mem. Legislative Proposals Cttee. 1974–. *Address:* Executive Committee, Territorial Soviet of Deputies of Working People, Khabarovsk, U.S.S.R.

PODHORETZ, Norman, M.A., B.H.L.; American author and editor; b. 16 Jan. 1930, Brooklyn; s. of Julius Podhoretz and Helen (née Woliner) Podhoretz; m. Midge R. Decter 1956; one s. three d.; ed. Columbia Univ., Jewish Theological Seminary and Univ. of Cambridge; Assoc. Ed. Commentary 1956–58, Ed.-in-Chief 1960–; Ed.-in-Chief, Looking Glass Library 1959–60; Chair. New Directions Advisory Comm. U.S. Information Agency 1981–87; mem. Council on Foreign Relations, Comm. on the Present Danger, Comm. for the Free World; Fulbright Fellow 1950–51; Hon. LL.D. (Jewish Theological Seminary); Hon. L.H.D. (Hamilton Coll.). *Publications:* Doings and Undoings, The Fifties and After in American Writing 1964, Making It 1968, Breaking Ranks 1979, The Present Danger 1980, Why We Were in Vietnam 1982, The Bloody Crossroads 1986. *Address:* 165 E 56th Street, New York, N.Y. 10022, U.S.A.

PODKOWIŃSKI, Marian Aleksander, M.A.; Polish journalist and writer; b. 19 April 1909, Vilnius; m.; one d.; ed. Warsaw Univ.; journalist with Kurier Poranny, Warsaw 1934; Ed.-in-Chief, Polska Informacja Literacka 1937–39; during Second World War served with Home Army, in Warsaw Uprising 1944; responsible to Ed. Polish Press Agency (PAP), Warsaw 1945–46; PAP Corresp. in Nuremberg 1946–47; Corresp. Robotnik and Express Wieczorny, Berlin 1947–48; Corresp. Trybuna Ludu, Berlin and Bonn 1948–56, 1960–68, Washington, D.C. 1956–60; Sr. staff writer for Świat 1968–69 and Perspektywy 1969–; Commentator govt. newspaper Rzeczpospolita 1982–; fmr. mem. Polish Journalists'; Pres. Int. Commentators' Club 1959, 1978; mem. Polish Writers' Union, Warsaw Bd. 1945–46, Foreign Comm. of Gen. Bd. 1978, ZAIKS Soc. of Authors, Main Bd. and Pres. Section of Journalists 1973, 1978; Pres. Polish Club of Int. Journalism 1983–; Deputy Chair. All-Poland Peace Cttee. 1982–; Hon. Chair. Journalists' Asscn. of Poland 1987; Award, Int. Commentators' Club of Polish Journalists' Asscn. 1972, 1986; Award Minister of Culture and Art 1974; Award Pres. of Prasa-Książka-Ruch Workers' Publishing Co-operative 1976; Bolesław Prus Award 1979; Julius Fučik Medal of Int. Journalists' Org. 1980; Golden Pen Award of Journalists' Union of G.D.R. 1985; Vorovsky Award, U.S.S.R. 1987; Gold Cross of Merit, Order of Banner of Labour (1st and 2nd Class), Commdr.'s Cross Order of Polonia Restituta, Order of Builders of People's Poland 1984, Kt.'s Cross Order of Iran, Gold Cross of Hon. Medal for Services to Austria and other decorations. *Publications:* IV Rzesza rośnie 1948, Spowiedź arcykłamcy 1948, Ameryka przez zwykłe okulary 1957, Czy zegary NRF chodzą szybciej? 1959, Czekanie na Straussa 1967, Niemcy i ja 1972, W kręgu Hitlera 1975, Dyliżansem po Warszawie 1975, Gdyby Polska nie była uparta 1977, Moje spotkania w NRD 1978, Między Renem a Łabą 1979, Po obu stronach Atlantyku 1984, Gdyby Hitler wygrał wojnę 1985. *Leisure interests:* Bach, historical biographies. *Address:* ul. Filtrowa 62 m. 51, 02-057 Warsaw, Poland. *Telephone:* 25 84 88 (Home); 26 15 51 (Office).

PODLENA, Frantisek; Czechoslovak politician; b. 1940, Zupanovice, Privan Dist.; mem. CP of Czechoslovakia (CPCZ) 1959–; political worker, Decin Dist. Party Cttee. 1971, later Sec.; Head, N. Bohemian Regional Party Cttee.'s dept. for Party work in industry; Deputy Chair. N. Bohemian Regional Nat. Cttee. 1983–85; Deputy Head of Dept. Cen. Cttee. of CPCZ 1985–88; Minister of Transport and Communications Oct. 1988–. *Address:* Ministry of Transport and Communications, Prague, Czechoslovakia.

POENSGEN, Gisbert; German diplomatist; b. 8 July 1923, Krefeld; s. of Helmuth Poensgen and Ursula von Ditfurth; m. Veronika Feine 1951; three s. one d.; ed. Univs. of Freiburg, Tübingen, Paris and Denver, Colorado; joined Foreign Service 1951; Amb. to Greece 1977–79; Amb. and Perm. Rep. to EEC 1979–85; Amb. to Portugal 1985–. *Address:* Embassy of the Federal Republic of Germany, Apt. 1046, 1001 Lisbon, Portugal.

PÖGGELER, Otto, D.PHIL.; German professor of philosophy; b. 12 Dec. 1928, Attendorn; ed. Bonn Univ.; Prof. of Philosophy, Bochum Univ. 1968–; Dir. Hegel Archives; mem. Rheinland-Westphalia Acad. of Sciences 1977–. *Publications:* Etudes hégéliennes 1985, Martin Heidegger's Path of Thinking 1987. *Address:* Hegel-Archiv der Ruhr-Universität, Postfach 10 21 48, 463 Bochum 1 (Office); Paracelsusweg 22, 4630 Bochum-Querenberg, Federal Republic of Germany (Home). *Telephone:* (0234) 700 2208 (Office); (0234) 701160 (Home).

POGORELICH, Ivo; Yugoslav concert pianist; b. 20 Oct. 1958, Belgrade; s. of I. and D. Pogorelich; m. Aliza Kezeradze 1980; ed. Moscow Cen. School of Music, Tchaikovsky Conservatoire of Moscow, then studied with Aliza Kezeradze; First Prize Casagrande Competition, Terni, Italy 1978; First Prize Montreal Int. Music Competition, Canada 1980; Special Prize, Int. Chopin Competition, Warsaw 1980; numerous recordings for Deutsche Grammophon, starting with a Chopin recital in 1981 and including works by Beethoven, Schumann, Ravel, Prokoviev and the Tchaikovsky Piano Concerto No. 1; has appeared in major concert halls throughout the world.

Address: c/o Anglo-Swiss Artists' Management Ltd., 16 Muswell Hill Road, London, N6 5UG, England.

POGORELOV, Dr. Aleksey Vasiliyevich; Soviet mathematician; b. 3 March 1919, Korocha (Belgorod Dist.); ed. Zhukovsky Air Force Acad.; Dr. of Physical mathematics 1949, Prof. 1951; Chair. Geometry Dept., Univ. of Kharkov 1947-59; Head of Dept. of Geometry, Research Inst. of Mathematics, Ukrainian Acad. of Sciences, Kiev 1959-60; Head of Dept. of Geometry at Physical-Technical Inst. of Low Temperatures at Ukrainian Acad. of Sciences, Kharkov, concurrently Prof., Univ. of Kharkov 1960-; Corresp. mem. U.S.S.R. Acad. of Sciences 1960-76, mem. 1976-; primarily concerned with problems of solid geometry; U.S.S.R. State Prize 1950, Lobachevsky Prize 1959; Lenin Prize 1962. *Publications:* more than 200 scientific papers. *Address:* Physical-Technical Institute of Low Temperatures at Ukrainian Academy of Sciences, Leninprospekt 47, Ukrainian S.S.R., U.S.S.R.

POGREBNYAK, Yakov Petrovich; Soviet politician; b. 1928, Ukraine; ed. Donetsk Industrial Inst.; mem. CPSU 1953-; Foreman, then Sr. Foreman in Mechanics Dept. of Machine Works 1954-57; Sec., then First Sec. Kramatorsk City Cttee. of Ukrainian CP, Second Sec. Donetsk Dist. Cttee. 1957-63; mem. Auditing Comm. 1961-66; mem. Cen. Cttee. of Ukrainian CP 1966; First Sec. for Industry in Poltava Dist. Cttee. 1963-64; Second Sec. Poltava Dist. Cttee. of Ukrainian CP 1964-66; First Sec. Ivano-Frankovsk Dist. Cttee. 1966-69, of Nikolayev Dist. Cttee. 1969-71; Deputy to U.S.S.R. Supreme Soviet 1966-; Sec., cand. mem. Politburo, Cen. Cttee. of Ukrainian CP 1971-; cand. mem. Cen. Cttee. of CPSU 1971-; First Sec. Lvov Dist. Cttee. 1987-; Order of Red Banner of Labour. *Address:* Central Committee of Ukrainian Communist Party, Kiev, Ukrainian S.S.R., U.S.S.R.

POGUTSE, Oleg Pavlovich, DR. PHY.MATH.SCI; Soviet theoretical physicist; b. 1936; ed. Moscow Inst. of Eng. and Physics; researcher at Kurchatov Inst. of Atomic Energy 1964-, Head of Lab. 1983-; Lenin Prize 1984 (for contribution to publication of The Theory of Thermodynamic Toroidal Plasma 1959-80. *Address:* c/o Institut Atomnoi Energii im. Kurchatova, Moscow, U.S.S.R.

POHER, Alain Emile Louis Marie; French politician; b. 17 April 1909, Ablon-sur-Seine (Val-de-Marne); s. of Ernest Poher and Louise (née Souriau); m. Henriette Tugler 1938; one d.; ed. Lycée Louis-le-Grand, Paris, Lycée Saint-Louis, Paris, and Faculty of Law, Univ. of Paris; Ministry of Finance 1935-46; Chef de Cabinet to Minister of Finance (R. Schuman) June-Nov. 1946; Senator for Seine-et-Oise 1946-48, 1952-68, for Val-de-Marne 1968-; Finance Comm. Conseil de la République 1946-48; Sec. of State for Finance 1948, for Budget 1948; Commr.-Gen. for German and Austrian Affairs 1948-50; French Del. to Int. Ruhr Authority 1950-52; Pres. Higher Trade Council 1953; Pres. Senate Group of Mouvement Républicain Populaire (M.R.P.) 1954-57, 1959-60; Pres. Transport Comm. of Coal and Steel Assembly 1954-55; Pres. of Common Market Comm. 1955-57; Pres. Franco-German Governmental Comm. for Canalisation of the Moselle 1955-56; Mayor of Ablon-sur-Seine 1945-; Asst. Sec.-Gen. Assen. of Mayors of France 1945-60, Pres. 1974-83, Hon. Pres. 1983; Sec. of State Armed Forces (Naval) 1957-58; Del. to European Parl. 1958-, Pres. Christian Democrat Group 1958-66, Pres. of European Parl. 1966-69; Pres. Euro-African Parl. Assembly 1967-68; Pres. of Senate 1968-; Acting Pres. of France April-June 1969, April-May 1974; Presidential Candidate June 1969; Pres. World Cttee. for the Salvation of the Jews of the Middle East; Prix Robert Schuman 1971, Prix Louise Weiss 1984; Chevalier, Légion d'honneur, Croix de guerre, Médaille de la Résistance. *Address:* 9 rue du Maréchal-Foch, 94480 Ablon-sur-Seine, France.

POHJALA, Toivo Topias; Finnish farmer, agronomist and politician; b. 27 July 1931, Harjavalta; m. Sinikka Linkomies 1983; farmer 1955-; mem. Harjavalta Mun. Council 1961-72, 1976-; mem. del. of Assen. of Union of Agricultural Producers 1965-, of Assen. of Forest and Agricultural Employers 1965-; mem. Parl. 1975-87; Minister of Agric. and Forestry 1987-; Nat. Coalition Party. *Address:* Ministry of Agriculture and Forestry, Hallituskatu 3A, 00170 Helsinki, Finland. *Telephone:* 125621.

PÖHL, Karl Otto; German economist; b. 1 Dec. 1929, Hanover; m. Dr. Ulrike Pesch; two s. two d.; ed. Univ. of Göttingen; Head of Dept. Ifo-Research Inst., Munich 1955-60; econ. journalist 1961-67; mem. Man. Bd. of the Federal Assen. of German Banks, Cologne 1968-69; Head of Dept. Fed. Ministry of Econ. Affairs 1970-71; Head of Econ. and Fiscal Policy Dept., Fed Chancellor's Office 1971-72; State Sec. Fed. Ministry of Finance 1972-77; Vice-Chair. Deutsche Bundesbank 1977-79, Pres. Jan. 1980-, Chair. Council Cen. Bank 1980-; German Gov. IMF, Washington and Bank of Int. Settlement, Basle; mem. Bd. of Dirs. Kreditanstalt für Wiederaufbau, Frankfurt am Main; Dr. h.c. (Georgetown, Ruhr Univ.) 1983, (Tel Aviv Univ.) 1986. *Address:* Deutsche Bundesbank, Wilhelm-Epstein-Strasse 14, 6000 Frankfurt am Main, Federal Republic of Germany.

POIGNANT, Raymond; French public servant; b. 26 Dec. 1917, Morainvilliers (S.-et-O.); s. of Jules Poignant and Marie Beaufourd; m. 1st Suzanne Auxionnaz 1939 (deceased), one s.; m. 2nd Gisele Berry 1983; ed. Ecole normale d'instituteurs de Versailles, Faculté des lettres de Paris and Ecole nat. d'admin. de Paris; Auditeur Council of State 1949; Tech. adviser in Cabinet of Minister of Educ. 1951-54, in Cabinet of Sec. d'Etat chargé de

la Fonction publique 1954-55 and in Cabinet of Minister of Educ. 1956-58; Maître des requêtes 1956; Rapporteur gén., School and Univ. Cttee. of Commissariat du Plan 1956-64; Sec.-Gen. of Interministerial Cttee. for Study of Medical Training Problems, Hosp. Structure and Health and Social Activities 1958-70; Sr. Staff mem., Int. Inst. for Educ. Planning, UNESCO 1963, Dir. 1969-74; Conseiller d'Etat 1974; Dir., Museum d'histoire naturelle 1985; mem. Nat. Cttee. to Assess Univs. 1986; Officier, Légion d'honneur, Commdr. de l'Ordre national du Mérite, Commdr. des Palmes Académiques, Chevalier des Arts et Lettres, Chevalier de la Santé publique. *Publications:* L'enseignement dans les pays du marché commun 1965, La planification de l'éducation en U.R.S.S. 1967, L'enseignement dans les pays industrialisés 1973. *Address:* Conseil d'Etat, place du Palais Royal, 75001 Paris (Office); 2 Chemin du Parterre, 78630 Morainvilliers, France (Home). *Telephone:* 975-86-75.

POINDEXTER, Rear-Admiral John Marlane; American government official; b. Washington, Ind.; m. Linda A. Goodwin; four s.; ed. U.S. Naval Acad. and Calif. Inst. of Tech.; fmrly. served on staff of several navy secs. and chief of naval operations; Deputy Chief of Naval Educ. and Training 1978-81; mem. staff, Nat. Security Council 1981, Deputy to Robert C. MacFarlane (Nat. Security Adviser) 1983-85; Nat. Security Adviser to Pres. of U.S.A. 1985-86 (resgnd); then on long range planning staff of Chief of Naval Operations 1986-87; retd. from Navy Dec. 1987.

POIRÉ, Jean Gustave (uses pseudonym **POIRET,** Jean); French actor; b. 17 Aug. 1926, Paris; s. of Georges and Anne-Marie (née Maistre) Poiré; m. Françoise Dorin (divorced); two c.; ed. Centre du Spectacle, Paris; Comedian with Les Chansonniers 1948-54; career in theatre and cinema 1955-; *theatre roles:* Monsieur Masure, l'Ami de la famille, la Coquine, Pour avoir Adrienne, le Train pour Venise, Vive de, Sacré Léonard, Fleur de cactus, Opération Lagrelèche 1967, le Vison voyageur, le Canard à l'orange 1971, la Cage aux folles 1973, Joyeuse Pâques 1980, les Clients 1986; *cinema roles:* Cette sacrée gamine, Clara et les méchants, le Naïf aux quarante enfants, Vous n'avez rien à déclarer, la Française et l'Amour (sketch), la Gamberge, les Parisiennes, les Vierges, la Foire aux cancres, Un drôle de paroissien, Jaloux comme un tigre, Candide, Trois hommes sur un cheval, le Dernier Métro 1980, Inspecteur Lavardin, Je hais les acteurs 1986, etc.; *television:* numerous variety roles; Chevalier de la Légion d'honneur; Prix des Humoristes 1973; Prix du théâtre de la Société des auteurs 1983. *Publications:* (with M. Serrault) Grosses Têtes 1969, Il était une fois l'opérette 1972, Douce amère 1970, l'Impromptu de Marigny 1974. *Address:* c/o Artmédia, 10 avenue George-V, 75008 Paris, France.

POIRET, Jean (see Poiré, Jean Gustave)

POIROT-DELPECH, Bertrand M.A.H.; French journalist and writer; b. 10 Feb. 1929, Paris; s. of Jean Poirot-Delpech and Jeanne Hauvette; one s. two d.; ed. Univ. of Paris; journalist 1951-; theatre critic for Le Monde 1959- and La Nouvelle Revue Française; literary critic Le Monde 1972-; Pres. Syndicat Professionel de la Critique Dramatique et Musicale 1967-71, Hon. Pres. 1986-; mem. Acad. Française; Chevalier Légion d'honneur; Prix Interallié 1958, Grand Prix du roman de l'Académie Française 1970. *Publications:* Le Grand dadais 1958, La Grasse Matinée 1960, l'Envers de l'eau 1963, Finie la comédie, Au Soir le Soir 1969, La Folle de Lituanie 1970, Les Grands de ce monde 1976, Saïd et moi 1980, Marie Duplessis la Dame aux Camélias 1981, La Légende du siècle 1981, Feuilleton (1972-1982) 1983, Le Couloir du dancing 1983, l'Eté 36 1984, Bonjour Sagan 1985. *Address:* 5 rue des Italiens, 75009 Paris (Office); 20 rue de l'Université, 75007 Paris, France (Home).

POITIER, Sidney; American actor; b. 20 Feb. 1924, Miami; s. of Reginald and Evelyn Poitier; m. 1st Juanito Hardy, four d.; m. 2nd Joanna Shimkus 1975, two d.; ed. Western Senior High School, Nassau, Governors High School, Nassau; army service 1941-45; acted with American Negro Theatre 1946; appeared in Anna Lucasta 1948, A Raisin in the Sun 1959; Silver Bear Award, Berlin Film Festival 1958; New York Film Critics Award 1958; Academy Award (Oscar) Best Actor of 1963 (for Lilies of the Field); Cecil B. De Mille Award 1982; Hon. K.B.E. 1974. *Appeared in the following films:* Cry the Beloved Country 1952, Red Ball Express 1952, Go, Man, Go 1954, Blackboard Jungle 1955, Goodbye My Lady 1956, Edge of the City 1957, Something of Value 1957, The Mark of the Hawk 1958, The Defiant Ones 1958, Porgy and Bess 1959, A Raisin in the Sun 1960, Paris Blues 1960, Lilies of the Field 1963, The Long Ships 1964, The Bedford Incident 1965, The Slender Thread 1966, A Patch of Blue 1966, Duel at Diablo 1966, To Sir with Love 1967, In the Heat of the Night 1967, Guess Who's Coming to Dinner 1968, For Love of Ivy 1968, The Lost Man 1970, They Call Me Mister Tibbs 1970, The Organization 1971, The Wilby Conspiracy 1975, Shoot to Kill 1988, Deadly Pursuit 1988; has appeared in and directed Buck and the Preacher 1972, Warm December 1973, Uptown Saturday Night 1974, Let's Do It Again 1975, A Piece of the Action 1977; directed Stir Crazy 1980, Hanky Panky 1982, Go for It 1984, Little Nikita 1987. *Publication:* This Life 1980. *Leisure interests:* football, tennis, gardening. *Address:* c/o Verdon Productions Ltd., 9350 Wiltshire Boulevard, Beverly Hills, Calif. 90212, U.S.A.

POL POT (also known as Saloth Sar, Tol Saut or Pol Porth), Kampuchean politician; b. 19 May 1928, Memot; worked on rubber plantation; joined anti-French resistance under Ho Chi Minh in 1940s; mem. Indo-Chinese

CP until 1946, Pracheachon (Cambodian CP) 1946-; mem. People's Representative Ass. representing rubber plantation workers 1976-79; Prime Minister 1976-79; overthrown after Vietnamese invasion of Kampuchea; charged with crimes of genocide; sentenced to death in absentia Aug. 1979; Commdr. of guerilla army after invasion 1979-85 ("retd."); Dir. "Higher Inst. for Nat. Defence" 1985-89.

POLAC, Michel; French journalist, writer and producer; b. 10 April 1930, Paris; s. of Claude Polac and Lilly (née Goldschmidt) Polac; one d.; ed. Lycée Janson-de-Sailly, Paris; Radio Producer ORTF 1953-71; journalist Arts 1953-64, L'Express 1962; Literary Critic L'Evènement du Jeudi 1987-; Prix Georges Sadoul 1970, Grand Prix du Festival du Film 1975. *Productions include:* Le masque et la plume (radio) 1953-71, Bibliothèque de poche 1966-70, Post-Scriptum 1970-71, Droit de réponse 1981-87, Libre et change 1987-88. *Publications:* La vie incertaine (novel) 1956, Maman pourquoi m'as tu laissé tomber de ton ventre? (novel) 1969, Le Grand Mégalo (essay) 1973, Hors de soi (aphorisms) 1985. *Films include:* Un fils unique 1970, Demain la fin du monde (TV) 1971, La chute d'un corps 1973, Monsieur Jadis (TV) 1976. *Address:* 11 rue de la Rosière, 75015 Paris, France.

POLAK, Jacques Jacobus, PH.D.; Netherlands economist and international official; b. 25 April 1914, Rotterdam; s. of James and Elisabeth F. Polak; m. Josephine Weening 1937; two s.; ed. Gymnasium Erasmianum, Rotterdam, and Univ. of Amsterdam; Economist League of Nations, Geneva, and Princeton, N.J. 1937-43; Economist, Netherlands Embassy, Washington, D.C. 1943-44; Asst. Financial Adviser, Econ. Advisor, UN Relief and Rehabilitation Admin., Washington, D.C. 1944-46; IMF, Washington, D.C. 1947-86, Chief, Statistics Div. 1947-48, Asst. Dir. Research Dept. 1948-52, Deputy Dir. Research Dept. 1952-58, Dir. 1958-79; Econ. Counsellor 1966-79, Adviser to Man. Dir. 1980, Exec. Dir. for Cyprus, Israel, Netherlands, Romania and Yugoslavia 1981-86; Sr. Adviser, OECD Devt. Centre 1986-; Pres. Per Jacobsson Foundation 1987-; Professorial Lecturer, Johns Hopkins Univ. 1949-50, 1987-; George Washington Univ. 1950-55; Fellow, Econometric Soc. *Publications include:* The Dynamics of Business Cycles (with Jan Tinbergen) 1950, An International Economic System 1952. *Address:* 3420 Porter Street, N.W., Washington, D.C. 20016, U.S.A. *Telephone:* (202) 966-6126 (Home).

POLANI, Paul Emanuel, M.D., F.R.C.P., F.R.C.O.G., F.R.C.PATH., F.R.S.; British doctor, geneticist and professor emeritus of pediatric research; b. 1 Jan. 1914, Trieste, Italy; s. of Enrico Polani and Elizabetta Zennaro; m. Nina E. Sullam 1944; ed. Univs. of Siena and Pisa; Evelina Children's Hosp., Southwark 1940-48; Nat. Birthday Trust Pediatric Research Fellow, Guy's Hosp., London 1948-50, Asst. Dir. Pediatric Dept. 1950-55, Research Physician on Cerebral Palsy 1955-58, Dir. Nat. Spastics Soc. Medical Research Unit. 1958-60, Prince Philip Prof. of Pediatric Research 1960-80, now Prof. Emer.; Geneticist, Guy's Hosp. and Pediatric Research Unit, Guy's Hospital Medical School, London 1961-; Consultant, Nat. Insts. of Health, Bethesda, Md. and WHO 1959-60; Visiting Prof. of Human Genetics and Devt. Univ. of Columbia 1977-86; Chair. EEC Cttee. on Medical Biology 1984-87; Int. Sanremo Prize for Genetic Research 1984; Baly Medal 1985. *Publications:* scientific papers and chapters in books on causes of cerebral palsy, causes of congenital heart disease, human sex chromosomes, anomalies, translocation Down Syndrome, experimental meiosis and other genetic matters. *Leisure interests:* riding, skiing, reading. *Address:* Pediatric Research Unit, Prince Philip Research Laboratories, Guy's Tower, Guy's Hospital Medical School, London, SE1 9RT (Office); Little Meadow, The Street, West Clandon, Guildford, Surrey, GU4 7TL, England (Home). *Telephone:* 01-407 7600, Ext. 2329 (Office); (0483) 222436.

POLAŃSKI, Roman; French (b. Polish) film director; b. 18 Aug. 1933, Paris; s. of Ryszard Polanski and Bule Katz-Przedborska; m. 1st Barbara Kwiatkowska-Lass, 2nd Sharon Tate 1968 (died 1969); ed. Polish Film School, Łódź; Dir. Two Men and a Wardrobe 1958, When Angels Fall, Le Gros et Le Maigre, Knife in the Water (prize at Venice Film Festival 1962), The Mammals (prize at Tours Film Festival 1963), Repulsion (prize at Berlin Film Festival 1965), Cul de Sac (prize at Berlin Film Festival 1966), The Vampire Killers 1967, Rosemary's Baby 1968, Macbeth 1971, What? 1972, Lulu (opera), Spoleto Festival 1974, Chinatown (Best Dir. Award. Soc. of Film and TV Arts 1974, Le Prix Raoul-Levy 1975) 1974, The Tenant 1976, Rigoletto (opera) 1976, Tess (Golden Globe Award) 1980, Vampires Ball 1980, Amadeus (play) 1981, Pirates 1986, Frantic 1988; has acted in: A Generation, The End of the Night, See You Tomorrow, The Innocent Sorcerers, Two Men and a Wardrobe, The Vampire Killers, What?, Chinatown, The Tenant, Pirates, Metamorphosis (play) 1988. *Publication:* Roman (autobiography) 1984. *Address:* c/o Bureau Georges Beaume, 3 Quai Malaquais, Paris 75006, France.

POLANYI, John Charles, C.C., PH.D., F.R.S., F.R.S.C.; Canadian professor of chemistry and physics; b. 23 Jan. 1929, Berlin, Germany; s. of Michael Polanyi and Magda Polanyi (née Kemeny); m. Anne Ferrar Davidson 1958; one s. one d.; ed. Manchester Grammar School and Manchester Univ., England; Postdoctoral Fellow, Nat. Research Council of Canada 1952-54; Research Assoc., Princeton Univ., U.S.A. 1954-56; Lecturer, Univ. of Toronto, Canada 1956-57, Asst. Prof. 1957-60, Assoc. Prof. 1960-62, Prof. of Chem. 1962, Univ. Prof. of Chem. and Physics 1974-; mem. Scientific Advisory Bd., Max Planck Inst. for Quantum Optics, Garching, Fed.

Repub. of Germany 1982-; hon. degrees from McMaster, Harvard and other univs.; shared Nobel Prize for Chemistry 1986; Hon. Foreign mem. American Acad. of Arts and Sciences; Foreign Assoc., N.A.S., U.S.A.; Marlow Medal, Faraday Soc. 1962; British Chemical Soc. Award 1971; Chemical Inst. of Canada Medal 1976; Henry Marshall Tory Medal, Royal Soc. of Canada 1977; Guggenheim Memorial Fellow 1979-80; Wolf Prize in Chem. (shared with G. Pimentel) 1982. *Publications:* Co-Ed.: The Dangers of Nuclear War 1979; author of over 150 scientific papers. *Address:* Department of Chemistry, University of Toronto, 80 St. George Street, Toronto, Ont., M5S 1A1; 142 Collier Street, Toronto, Ont., M4W 1M3, Canada (Home). *Telephone:* (416) 978-3580 (Univ.); (416) 961-6545 or 961-6548 (Home).

POLE, Jack Richon, PH.D., F.B.A., F.R.HIST.S.; British historian; b. 14 March 1922, London; s. of Joseph Pole and Phoebe Rickards; m. Marilyn Mitchell 1952; one s. two d.; ed. King Alfred School, London, King's Coll. London, Queen's Coll. Oxford and Princeton Univ., U.S.A.; served in army, rank of Capt. 1941-45; Instructor in History, Princeton Univ. 1952-53; Asst. Lecturer, then Lecturer in American History, Univ. Coll. London 1953-63; Reader in American History and Govt., Cambridge Univ. and Fellow of Churchill Coll. 1963-79, Vice-Master of Churchill Coll. 1975-78; Rhodes Prof. of American History and Insts., Oxford Univ. and Fellow of St. Catherine's Coll. 1979-. *Publications:* Political Representation in England and the Origins of the American Republic 1966, Foundations of American Independence 1972, The Pursuit of Equality in American History 1978, Paths to the American Past 1979, The Gift of Government: Political Responsibility from the English Restoration to American Independence 1983, Colonial British America (co.-ed.) 1984, The American Constitution: For and Against 1987. *Leisure interests:* cricket, painting. *Address:* St. Catherine's College, Oxford (Office); 20 Divinity Road, Oxford, OX4 1LJ England (Home). *Telephone:* (0865) 271744 (Office); (0865) 246950 (Home).

POLEDNÍK, Jindřich; Czechoslovak politician; b. 7 July 1937, Stonava, Karviná District; ed. Faculty of Natural Sciences, Palacky Univ., Olomouc; Sec. Cen. Cttee. of Czechoslovak Union of Youth 1967-68; Deputy Chair. of Council, Asscn. of Children's and Youth Orgs. of Czech Socialist Repub. 1969-70; Deputy Chair. Czech Cen. Cttee., Socialist Union of Youth (SSM) 1970-72, Chair. 1972-74, mem. Presidium and Secr. of (Fed.) Cen. Cttee., SSM 1972-74; Deputy Chair of (Fed.) Cen. Cttee. 1972-74, Chair. 1974-77; Deputy mem., later mem. Presidium of Czech Nat. Council 1971-76, mem. Presidium of Cen. Cttee., Czechoslovak Nat. Front 1974-; mem. Cen. Cttee. and Secr., CP of Czechoslovakia April 1976-; Deputy of House of Nations of Fed. Ass. 1976-; mem. Secr. Cen. Cttee. of CP of Czechoslovakia 1977-88; with Czechoslovak Union of Physical Training and Sport 1988-; Order of Labour 1977, Award of Outstanding Work 1983, Order of Repub. of Czechoslovakia 1987. *Address:* Central Committee of the Communist Party of Czechoslovakia, Prague, nábř. Ludvíka Svobody 12, Czechoslovakia.

POLETTI, H.E. Cardinal Ugo; Italian ecclesiastic; b. 19 April 1914, Omegna, Novara; ordained 1938; consecrated titular Bishop of Medeli 1958; promoted to Spoleto 1967; consecrated Archbishop of Cittanova 1969; cr. Cardinal by Pope Paul VI 1973; Vicar-Gen. of Rome 1973-; High Priest Patriarcale Arcabasilica Lateranese; Grand Chancellor, Pontifica Universitas Lateranensis; Pres. Acad. Liturgica. *Address:* Vicariato di Roma, Piazza S. Giovanni in Laterano 6, 00184 Rome, Italy.

POLILLO, Sergio; Italian businessman and publisher; b. 13 Oct. 1917, Fanano; m. Liliana Rusconi; one s.; army officer, World War II; father's legal office; Sec. to Founder, Arnoldo Mondadori Editore S.P.A. 1949, Gen. Man. 1964-, mem. Bd. 1974-, Man. Dir. July 1977-, Vice-Chair. Bd. 1982, Chair. Bd. April 1987-; Pres. Auguri di Mondadori; mem. Bd. of Dirs. Editoriale la Repubblica, Cartiera di Ascoli, Club degli Editori; Vice-Pres. Italian Publishers' Asscn. *Address:* Arnoldo Mondadori Editore S.P.A., Via Arnaldo Mondadori, 20090 Segrate (Milano), Italy. *Telephone:* (02) 7542-1.

POLIN, Raymond, D. ÈS L.; French academic; b. 7 July 1910, Briançon; s. of Marcel Polin and Jeanne Foulet; m. Marie-Thérèse Blahovcova 1934; two s.; ed. Lycée d'Evareux, Lycée Louis-le-Grand and Faculté des Lettres, Paris; Asst. Ecole Normale Supérieure 1935-38; Prof. Lycée de Laon 1938-39, Lycée de Chartres 1939-42, Lycée Marcelin Berthelot 1942-43, Lycée Rollin 1943-45, Lycée Condorcet 1945; Prof. Univ. of Paris/Sorbonne 1961-81, Pres. 1976-81, Prof. Emer. 1981-; Dir. Fondation Thiers 1981; Visiting Prof. Buffalo, Columbia, Harvard and Yale Univs.; mem. Admin. Council, ORTF 1972-74; mem. Acad. des sciences morales et politiques (Inst. de France); Officier, Légion d'Honneur. *Publications:* several books on political philosophy etc. *Address:* 26 boulevard Saint-Germain, 75005 Paris, France.

POLINSZKY, Dr. Károly; Hungarian chemical engineer and politician; b. 19 March 1922, Budapest; s. of Gyula Polinszky and Róza Morbitzer; m. Mária Magdolna Rézeky 1946; three s.; ed. Tech. Univ., Budapest; Asst. Lecturer Tech. Univ. 1944-49; Corresp. mem. Hungarian Acad. of Sciences 1964-76, mem. 1976-; Dean, later Rector Veszprém Univ. of Chemical Industry 1949-63; Dir. Research Inst. for Heavy Chemistry; Deputy Minister of Educ. 1963-74, Minister 1974-80; Vice-Pres. Hungarian Acad. of Sciences 1980-85; Prof. of Chemical Tech., Budapest Polytechnical Univ.

1980–; Rector, Tech. Univ. of Budapest 1981–87; Research Prof. Research Inst. for Tech. chem., Veszprem 1987–; Vice-Pres. Nat. Council of Patriotic People's Front 1981–; Corresp. mem. Acad. Sciences of Bologna 1982–, Corresp. mem. Acad. Sciences of Messina 1983–; Dr. h.c. (Lensoviet Technical Univ. of Leningrad) 1968; Kossuth Prize 1961; Order of Merit for Socialist Hungary. *Leisure interests:* literature, music. *Address:* Nagyajtai 4/6, 1026 Budapest, Hungary.

POLKINGHORNE, Rev. John Charlton, M.A., PH.D., SC.D., F.R.S.; British ecclesiastic and physicist; b. 16 Oct. 1930, Weston-super-Mare; s. of George B. Polkinghorne and Dorothy E. Charlton; m. Ruth I. Martin 1955; two s. one d.; ed. Perse School, Cambridge, Trinity Coll., Cambridge and Westcott House, Cambridge; Lecturer, Univ. of Edinburgh 1956–58; Lecturer, Univ. of Cambridge 1958–65, Reader 1965–68, Prof. of Mathematical Physics 1968–79; Fellow, Trinity Coll., Cambridge 1954–86; curate, St. Michael & All Angels, Bedminster 1982–84; Vicar of St. Cosmus and St. Damian in the Blean 1984–86; Hon. Prof. of Theoretical Physics, Univ. of Kent 1984–; Fellow and Dean, Trinity Hall, Cambridge 1986–. *Publications:* The Analytic S-Matrix (jointly) 1966, The Particle Play 1979, Models of High Energy Processes 1980, The Way the World Is 1983, The Quantum World 1984, One World 1986, Science and Creation 1988. *Leisure interest:* gardening. *Address:* Trinity Hall, Cambridge, CB2 1TJ, England. *Telephone:* (0223) 332525.

POLLACK, Ilana, B.A.; Israeli librarian; b. 13 Aug. 1946, Tel Aviv; d. of Mala First and Leon Pinsky; m. Joseph Pollack 1977; two s.; ed. Re'alit High School, Rishon Le Zion, Tel Aviv Univ. and Hebrew Univ. Jerusalem; served in Israeli Army 1964–66; joined Weizmann Inst. of Science, Rehovot as Librarian 1966, Librarian in charge of Physics Faculty Library 1975, Chief Librarian, Weizmann Inst. 1983–. *Address:* Wix Library, Weizmann Institute of Science, Rehovot 76100, Israel. *Telephone:* (08) 483583.

POLLACK, Sydney; American film director; b. 1 July 1934, Lafayette, Ind.; s. of David Pollack and Rebecca Miller; m. Claire Griswold 1958; one s. two d.; ed. Neighborhood Playhouse Theatre School, New York; Asst. to Sanford Meisner 1954, Acting Instructor 1954–57, 1959–60; Army service 1957–59; Exec. Dir. The Actors Studio (West Coast br.); appeared on Broadway in The Dark is Light Enough 1954, A Stone for Danny Fisher 1955; TV appearances include Aloa Presents; Dir. The Chrysler Theatre, Ben Casey 1962–63 (for TV); Acad. Award for Best Dir. and Best Picture 1986. *Films directed:* The Slender Thread 1965, This Property is Con-demned 1966, The Scalphunters 1967, Castle Keep 1968, They Shoot Horses, Don't They? 1969–70, Jeremiah Johnson 1971–72, The Way We Were 1972–73, The Yakuza 1974, Three Days of the Condor 1974–75, Bobby Deerfield 1976, The Electric Horseman 1978–79, Absence of Malice 1981, Tootsie 1982 (produced), Song Writer 1984, Out of Africa 1985 (produced); co-producer Bright Lights, Big City 1988. *Address:* c/o Mirage Productions, 100 Universal city Plaza, Bungalow 414, Universal City, Calif. 91608, U.S.A.

POLLEN, Arabella Rosalind Hungerford; British couturier and business executive; b. 22 June 1961, Oxford; d. of Peregrine Pollen and Patricia Pollen; m. Giacomo Dante Algranti 1985; one s.; ed. l'Ecole Français, New York, Nightingale Bamford, Hatherop Castle School, Glos., St. Swithins, Winchester and Queen's Coll., London; f. Arabella Pollen Ltd. in jt. venture with Namara Ltd. 1981; bought out Namara Ltd. and entered jt. partnership with Peregrine Marcus Pollen 1983–; Designer for other labels 1983–. *Leisure interests:* music/piano, literature. *Address:* Westbourne Terrace, London, W2; Norton Hall, Mickleton, Glos., England. *Telephone:* 01-724 8563; 0586-438 218.

POLLINI, Maurizio; Italian pianist; b. 5 Jan. 1942, Milan; has played with Berlin and Vienna Philharmonic Orchestras, Bayerischer Rundfunk Orchestra, London Symphony Orchestra, Boston, New York, Philadelphia, Los Angeles and San Francisco Orchestras; has played at Salzburg, Vienna, Berlin, Prague Festivals; recordings for Polydor Int.; First Prize Int. Chopin Competition, Warsaw 1960. *Address:* c/o Harrison/Parrott Ltd., 22 Hillgate Street, London W8 7SR, England.

POLLITT, John, M.D., F.R.C.P., F.R.C.PSYCH., D.P.M.; British consultant phys-ician in psychological medicine; b. 24 Aug. 1926, London; s. of Charles E. Pollitt and Sarah J. Pollitt; m. Erica E. Pollitt 1953; two d.; ed. City of London School, St. Thomas's Hosp. Medical School (Univ. of London) and Mass. Mental Health Center (Harvard Medical School); various posts, Dept. of Psychological Medicine, St. Thomas's Hosp.; Sr. Registrar, St. Andrew's Hosp. Northampton; Rockefeller Research Travelling Fellow, Mass. Mental Health Center 1959–60; Physician in Psychological Medicine, St. Thomas's Hosp. 1961–85, Physician in charge of Dept. of Psychological Medicine 1972–79, now Hon. Consulting Physician in Psychological Medicine; Regional Postgraduate Dean, S.E. Thames Region (Univ. of London) 1979–83; Medical Dir. Hayes Grove Priory Hosp. 1983–86, now Physician in Psychological Medicine, Dir. of Medical Educ. and Hon. Clinical Adviser; various other professional appts.; Planck Prize, Gaskell Gold Medal and Prize, Bronze Medal and Prize, Royal Medico-Psychological Assen. *Publi-cations:* Depression and its Treatment 1965, Psychological Medicine for Students 1973, Psychiatric Emergencies in Family Practice 1987; several chapters in textbooks and articles in professional journals. *Leisure inter-ests:* painting, printing, graphic arts, horology. *Address:* Hayes Grove

Priory Hospital, Prestons Road, Hayes, Kent, BR2 7AS; 144 Harley Street, London, W1N 1AH, England.

POLLOCK, Admiral of the Fleet Sir Michael (Patrick), G.C.B., L.V.O., D.S.C.; British naval officer; b. 19 Oct. 1916; m. 1st Margaret Steacy 1940 (died 1951); two s. one d.; m. 2nd Marjory Rees (née Bisset) Pollock 1954; one step-d.; ed. Royal Naval Coll., Dartmouth; entered Navy 1930, specialized in gunnery 1941; served in Warspite, Vanessa, Arethusa and Norfolk, Second World War; Capt. Plans Div. of Admiralty and Dir. of Surface Weapons; commanded H.M.S. Vigo and Portsmouth Squadron 1958–59, H.M.S. Ark Royal 1963–64; Asst. Chief of Naval Staff 1964–66; Flag Officer, Second-in-Command, Home Fleet 1966–67; Flag Officer, Submarines, and NATO Commdr., Submarines, E. Atlantic 1967–69; Con-troller of the Navy 1970–71; Chief of Naval Staff and First Sea Lord 1971–74; First and Prin. Naval Aide-de-Camp to the Queen 1972–74; Chair. Naval Insurance Trust 1975–85, Liddle-Hart Trustee 1976–81; Bath King of Arms 1976–85. *Address:* The Ivy House, Churchstoke, Montgomery, Powys, SY15 6DU, Wales. *Telephone:* (058 85) 426.

POLOTSKY, Hans Jacob, PH.D., D.HUM.LITT.; Israeli university professor; b. 13 Sept. 1905, Zürich, Switzerland; s. of Abraham Polotsky and Esther Rode; m. Yafa Kahansky 1936; one s.; ed. Berlin and Göttingen Univs.; Instructor in Egyptology, Hebrew Univ. of Jerusalem 1934–51, Prof. of Egyptian and Semitic Linguistics 1951–72, Emer. 1972–; Visiting Prof. at Chicago Univ. 1952, at Brown Univ. 1959–60, at Copenhagen Univ. 1967–68 and Visiting Lecturer at Yale Univ. 1985; founding mem. Israeli Acad. of Sciences and Humanities; corresp. mem. British, Danish and Netherlands Acads.; Lidzbarski Gold Medal; Rothschild Prize, Harvey Prize and Israel Prize. *Publications:* Collected Papers 1971, Les transpositions du verbe en égyptien classique 1976, Grundlagen des Koptischen Satzbaus 1988. *Leisure interest:* literature. *Address:* 4 Brenner Street, 92 150 Jerusalem, Israel. *Telephone:* (02) 63 44 34.

POLOZKOVA, Lidia Pavlovna; Soviet speed-skater; b. 8 March 1929, Zlatoust; d. of Pavel I. Skoblikov and Klavdia N. Skoblikova; m. Alexander G. Polozkov; one s.; title of Honoured Master of Sports 1960; six gold medals in Winter Olympic Games 1960 and 1964; all-round world champion 1963–64; won 40 gold medals for breaking records, 25 at world champion-ships and 15 in U.S.S.R.; mem. CPSU 1964–; Head Dept. of Physical Educ., Moscow Higher School of the All-Union Trade Union Movt. 1974–88; Sr. Vice-Pres. of All-Union Trade Unions Soc. for Physical Culture and Sports 1988–; two orders and various medals. *Publications:* numerous publs. on sport and physical culture. *Leisure interests:* reading, theatre, forest walking, sports, knitting. *Address:* Solianka Str. 14/2, Moscow 109240, U.S.S.R. *Telephone:* 9211392.

POŁTAWSKA, Wanda Wiktoria, M.D.; Polish neuropsychiatrist and pro-fessor of pastoral medicine; b. 2 Nov. 1921, Lublin; m. Andrzej Połtawski 1947; four d.; ed. Ursuline Sisters' High School, Lublin and Jagellonian Univ., Cracow; Polish Resistance 1939–41; interned in Nazi concentration camps 1941–45; teaching asst. Psychiatric Clinic, Medical Acad. Cracow 1957–69; Consultant, Educ. and Therapeutic Consulting Office of the Chair of Psychology, Jagellonian Univ. 1954–72; Prof. of Pastoral Medicine, Pontifical Inst. Giovanni Paolo II, Universita Lateranense, Rome 1981–84; Prof. of Pastoral Medicine, Pontifical Theological Acad. Cracow 1955–, Dir. Family Inst. 1967–; mem. Pontifical Council for the Family; Cross Pro Ecclesia et Pontifice. *Publications:* I boję się snòw 1961, Stare rachunki 1969; numerous articles. *Leisure interest:* mountain tourism. *Address:* Bracka 1/3, 31-005 Cracow, Poland. *Telephone:* (12) 22 68 98.

POLUNIN, Nicholas, C.B.E., M.S., M.A., D.PHIL., D.SC., F.L.S., F.R.G.S., F.R.H.S.; British environmentalist, author and editor; b. 26 June 1909, Checkendon, Oxon.; s. of late Vladimir Polunin and Elizabeth Violet (née Hart); m. 1st Helen Lovat Fraser 1939 (died 1973), one s.; m. 2nd Helen Eugenie Campbell 1948, two s. one d.; ed. Christ Church, Oxford, and Yale and Harvard Univs.; botanical etc. exploring expeditions Spitsbergen, Lapland, Greenland, Iceland, Labrador, Hudson Bay and Strait, Baffin, South-ampton, Devon and Ellesmere Islands 1930–38 (collections mainly in Nat. Museum of Canada, Gray Herbarium of Harvard Univ., British Museum, Fielding Herbarium Oxford); explorations in Canadian Northwest Territo-ries, Alaska, Ungava-Labrador, and Arctic Archipelago (where discovered in 1946 last major islands to be added to world map, named Prince Charles Island and Air Force Island in 1949) 1946–49; visited vicinity of magnetic North Pole 1947 and flew over geographical North Pole summer 1948 (demonstrating persistence of microbial life in the atmosphere there) and winter 1949; field work in Middle East 1956–59, and in West Africa 1962–65; U.S. Order of Polaris, Canadian Marie-Victorin Medal; Indian Ramdeo Medal 1986; Int. Sasekawa Environment Prize 1987; UN Sec.-Gen.'s illuminated certificate 'awarded to Nicholas Polunin in recognition of his most outstanding contribution in the Field of Environment'; Botanical Tutor various Oxford Colls. 1932–47; Henry Fellow, Yale Univ. 1933–34; Dept. of Scientific and Industrial Research, Sr. Research Award 1935–38; Research Assoc. Harvard Univ. 1936–37; Foreign Research Assoc. 1938–50, Research Fellow 1950–53; Fielding Curator and Keeper, Univ. Herbaria, Oxford, Univ. Demonstrator and Lecturer in Botany 1939–47; Univ. Moder-ator 1941–45; Lecturer (and latterly Sr. Research Fellow) New Coll., Oxford 1942–47; Haley Lecturer, Acadia Univ. 1950; Macdonald Prof. of Botany, McGill Univ., Montreal 1947–52; Guggenheim Memorial Fellow 1950–52; Lecturer in Plant Geography, Yale Univ. 1953–55 while Project

Dir. U.S.A.F.; Prof. of Plant Ecology and Taxonomy and Head Dept. of Botany, Dir. Univ. Herbarium, Faculty of Sciences, Baghdad 1955–59; Guest Prof. Univ. of Geneva 1959–61, 1975–76; Prof. of Botany and Head of Dept., Faculty of Science (which he established as first Dean) Univ. of Ife, Ibadan 1962–66; Founder and Sec.-Gen. Int. Confs. on Environmental Future 1971–; Pres. Foundation for Environmental Conservation 1974–, World Council for the Biosphere 1984–; Fellow, A.A.A.S., Arctic Inst. of North America, Indian Soc. of Naturalists, and mem. of other learned socs.; Life mem. Botanical Soc. of America, New England and Torrey Botanical Clubs, Asian Soc. for Environmental Protection, North American Assen. for Environmental Educ., Int. Soc. for Environmental Educ.; Founding Ed. Int. Industry 1943–46, World Crops Books 1954–74 and Plant Science Monographs 1954–78, Biological Conservation 1967–74, Environmental Conservation 1974–, Environmental Monographs and Symposia 1979–; Chair. Complementary Cambridge Studies in Environmental Policy 1984–; co-initiator of World Council For The Biosphere, Pres. 1984–. *Publications:* Russian Waters 1931, The Isle of Auks 1932, Botany of the Canadian Eastern Arctic (3 vols.) 1940–48, Arctic Unfolding 1949, Circumpolar Arctic Flora 1959, Introduction to Plant Geography and some related sciences 1960, Eléments de Géographie botanique 1967, The Environmental Future (ed.) 1972, Growth Without Ecodisasters? 1980, Ecosystem Theory and Application 1986; also responsible for numerous vols. in former and current series. *Leisure interests:* biological and environmental conservation, developing new ideas into plans (e.g. for World Campaign and its adopting Council For The Biosphere special conferences, series of books, new journals, etc.), world-wide correspondence and travel (including circumglobal tour in 1987 speaking on 'Our World Menaced'), international stock markets. *Address:* 7 Chemin Taverney, 1218 Grand-Saconnex, Geneva, Switzerland.

POLVINEN, Tuomo Ilmari, PH.D.; Finnish professor of history; b. 2 Dec. 1931, Helsinki; s. of Eino Ilmari Polvinen and Ilona Vihersalo; m. Eeva-Liisa Rommi 1965; two d.; ed. Univ. of Helsinki; Docent, Univ. of Helsinki 1965; Prof. of Modern History, Tampere Univ. 1968–70; Dir.-Gen. Nat. Archives of Finland 1970–74; Prof. of Modern History Univ. of Helsinki 1974–, on leave of absence 1979–; Research Prof. Acad. of Finland 1979–; Urho Kekkonen Prize 1981. *Publications:* Venäjän vallankumous ja Suomi 1917–1920, I–II 1967, 1971, Suomi kansainvälisessä politiikassa 1941–47, I–III 1979, 1980, 1981, Valtakunta ja rajamaa. N.I. Bobrikov Suomen kenraalikuvernöörinä 1898–1904 1984, Between East and West: Finland in International Politics 1944–47 1986. *Address:* Ruusulankatu 8 A 9, 00260 Helsinki, Finland. *Telephone:* 408 554.

POLWARTH, 10th Baron; Henry Alexander Hepburne Scott, T.D., D.L., M.A., LL.D., F.R.S.E., F.R.S.A.; British (Scottish) administrator and chartered accountant; b. 17 Nov. 1916, Edinburgh; s. of Hon. Walter Thomas Hepburne Scott and Elspeth Glencairn Campbell; m. 1st Caroline Margaret Hay 1943 (divorced 1969), one s. three d.; m. 2nd Jean Jauncey (née Cunninghame Graham); three step-c.; ed. Eton Coll. and King's Coll., Cambridge; Deputy-Gov. Bank of Scotland 1960–66, Gov. 1966–72, Dir. 1974–87; mem. Western Hemisphere Exports Council 1958–64; Partner Chiene and Tait, Edinburgh 1950–68; Chair. Gen. Accident, Fire and Life Assurance Co. 1968–72; Minister of State, Scottish Office 1972–74; given special responsibility for oil devt. in Scotland 1973–74; Chair. Oil Devt. Council for Scotland 1973–74; Dir. ICI 1969–72, 1974–81, Halliburton Co. 1974–87, Canadian Pacific Ltd. 1975–86, Sun Life Assurance Co. of Canada 1975–84, Brown and Root (U.K.) 1977; mem. Historic Bldgs. Council for Scotland 1953–66; Chancellor Univ. of Aberdeen 1966–86; Chair. Scottish Nat. Orchestra 1975–79; mem. British Section, Franco-British Council 1981–; mem. House of Lords Select Cttee. on Overseas Trade 1984–85; Hon. LL.D. (Univs. of St. Andrews, Aberdeen), Hon. D.Litt. (Heriot Watt), Hon. Dr. (Stirling). *Leisure interests:* managing family estate, country pursuits, travel, the arts. *Address:* Harden, Hawick, Roxburghshire, Scotland. *Telephone:* Hawick 72069 (Home).

POLYAKOV, Victor Nikolayevich; Soviet politician, b. 1915; ed. Moscow Automobile and Road Construction Inst.; from 1930 fitter's apprentice, fitter, technician, foreman, deputy shop superintendent at auto repair works in Moscow; with Soviet Army 1938–46; member of CPSU 1944; participant of Great Patriotic War; from 1946 test engineer, head of lab., shop superintendent, Deputy Chief Designer, Chief Engineer at Moscow Small-Displacement Car Plant; from 1958 Dir. of the Plant; First Vice-Chair., Chair. of Moscow City Council of Nat. Economy, Deputy Minister of Automobile Industry of U.S.S.R. 1963–65; Deputy Minister of Automobile Industry of U.S.S.R. 1966–74; Dir.-Gen. of Volga Assen. for Production of Cars; Minister of Automobile Industry of U.S.S.R. 1975–86; mem. of CPSU Cen. Cttee.–1989; Deputy to U.S.S.R. Supreme Soviet (9th, 10th convocations); Hero of Socialist Labour. *Address:* The Kremlin, Moscow, U.S.S.R.

POLYAKOV, Vladimir Porfiriyevich, PH.D.; Soviet diplomatist; b. March 1931, Smolensk; s. of Porfiriy and Yevdokia Polyakov; m. Nelly Polyakov 1953; one s.; ed. Inst. of Oriental Studies, Moscow; Diplomatic Service 1956–; Counsellor, Syria 1961–65; various posts in Ministry of Foreign Affairs 1965–67; Counsellor-Minister, Egypt 1968–71; Amb. to People's Democratic Repub. of Yemen 1972–74, to Egypt 1974–81 (expelled Sept. 1981). *Leisure interest:* politics. *Address:* c/o Ministry of Foreign Affairs, Moscow, U.S.S.R.

POLYANSKY, Anatoliy Trofimovich; Soviet architect; b. 29 Jan. 1928, Avdeyevko, Donetsk; ed. Moscow Inst. of Architecture; mem. CPSU 1953; Dir. of Cen. Scientific Research Inst. for Experimental Architectural Design 1958–; teacher at Moscow Inst. of Architecture 1955–60, and 1973–; First Sec. of Union of U.S.S.R. Architects 1983–; People's Architect 1980. *Buildings include:* U.S.S.R. Embassy in Athens 1978, Hotel Yalta, Crimea 1978, Issyk-kul Sanitorium 1979. *Address:* Union of U.S.S.R. Architects, Moscow, Ul. Shchuseva 3, U.S.S.R.

POLYANSKY, Dmitriy Stepanovich; Soviet politician; b. 7 Nov. 1917, Slavyanoserbskoe, Ukraine; s. of Stepan Lukich Polyansky and Praskoviya Tikhonovna Polyanskaya; m. Galina Danilovna Polyanskaya 1939; one s. two d.; ed. Kharkov Inst. of Agriculture and Higher Party School of Cen. Cttee. of CPSU; exec. work in Young Communist League, service in Soviet army and study at Higher Party School 1938–42; Party work in Siberia 1942–45; exec. in Cen. Cttee. of Party 1945–49; Second Sec. Crimea regional Cttee. of Party, and Chair. Exec. Cttee. Crimea regional Soviet of Working People's Deputies 1948–52; First Sec. Crimea regional Cttee. of Party 1953–55; First Sec. of Chkalov (now Orenburg) regional Cttee. 1955–57, First Sec. of Krasnodar territorial Party Cttee. 1957–58; Chair. Council of Ministers of R.S.F.S.R. 1958–62; Deputy Premier U.S.S.R. 1962–65, First Deputy Premier 1965–73; Deputy Supreme Soviet of the U.S.S.R. 1954–; mem. CPSU Cen. Cttee. 1956–81; cand. mem. Presidium of Cen. Cttee. of CPSU 1958–60, mem. 1960–66; mem. Political Bureau 1966–76; U.S.S.R. Minister of Agric. 1973–76; Amb. to Japan 1976–82, to Norway 1982–87; Order of Lenin (four times), Order of Peoples Friendship, and other awards. *Publications:* Pearl of Russia 1958, Great Plans for the Economic and Cultural Progress of the Russian Federation 1959. *Leisure interest:* winter hunting. *Address:* The Kremlin, Moscow, U.S.S.R.

POLZE, Werner, DR.RER.POL.; German banker; b. 26 March 1931; ed. School of Economics, Berlin, Akademie für Staat und Recht der DDR (studies in govt. and law); worked for Deutsche Notenbank, G.D.R. 1956–66; joined Deutsche Aussenhandelsbank AG 1966, Vice-Pres. 1969–78, Pres. Feb. 1978–; Vaterländischer Verdienstorden, Orden Banner der Arbeit, Stern der Völkerfremdschaft. *Address:* Deutsche Aussenhandelsbank, Unter den Linden 24/30, Berlin 1080, German Democratic Republic.

POMODORO, Arnaldo; Italian sculptor and theatrical designer; b. 23 June 1926, Morciano di Romagna; s. of Antonio Pomodoro and Beatrice Luzzi; has worked as jeweller and goldsmith 1950–; artist-in-residence, Stanford Univ. 1966–67; artist-in-residence, Univ. of Calif. (Berkeley) 1968; lecture course, Mills Coll., Oakland, Calif. 1979–; Premio Int. di Scultura alla Biennale di San Paolo (Brazil) 1963, Premio Nazionale di scultura alla Biennale de Venezia 1964, Premio Int. di Scultura (Carnegie Inst., Pittsburgh) 1967, Henry Moore Grand Prize (Hakone Open-Air Museum, Japan) 1981. *Exhibitions include:* Milan 1955, "New Work from Italy" at Bolles Galleries, San Francisco and N.Y. 1960–61, "Grande Sfera" at Montreal World Fair 1967 (now situated in Rome), works 1955–74 at Milan 1974, "Pietrarubbia's Work", Marlborough Gallery, N.Y. 1976, "Ecritures, Perforations d'objects", Musée d'art moderne de la Ville de Paris 1976, "Four Pillars", Copenhagen 1983–; Fort Belvedere, Florence 1984–. *Theatrical designs include:* "Agamemnon", Gibellina, Sicily 1983, "Semiramide", Opera House, Rome 1983. *Leisure interests:* photography, theatre, literature. *Address:* via Vigevano 3, 20144 Milan, Italy. *Telephone:* 02 8324131.

POMPEI, Gian Franco, DR.JUR.; Italian diplomatist; b. 31 Jan. 1915, Sète, France; s. of Raffaele Pompei (diplomat) and Countess Isabella Moroni Candelori; m. Ilde Scarpa 1939; one s. two d.; ed. Univ. of Turin; in Diplomatic Service 1939–, at Rome 1939–42; Vice-Consul Neuchâtel, Switzerland 1942–45; Sec., Berne 1945–47; Foreign Office, Rome 1947–50; Sec. then Counsellor, Paris Embassy 1950–63; Perm. Del. UNESCO 1953–63, elected mem. of Exec. Bd. 1962, 1966, 1980–85, Chair. of Exec. Bd. 1968–70, Pres. of Finance and Admin. Comm., of Italian Nat. Comm. for UNESCO 1981–86; Pres. of Interscience (Freiburg i. Breisgau); Diplomatic Adviser to Prime Minister, Rome 1963–68; Head of Cabinet, Ministry of Foreign Affairs 1968; Amb. to the Holy See 1969–77, to France 1977–81. *Leisure interests:* mountaineering, skiing, chess. *Address:* 1e Via Bertoloni, Rome, Italy; 62 Goethestrasse, Freiburg i. Breisgau, Federal Republic of Germany. *Telephone:* 805300 (Rome); 70395 (Freiburg i. Breisgau).

PONCE ENRILE, Juan, LL.M.; Philippine lawyer and public official; b. 14 Feb. 1924, Gonzaga, Cagayan; s. of Alfonso Ponce Enrile and Petra Furagganan; m. Cristina Castañer 1957; one s. one d.; ed. Ateneo de Manila, Univ. of the Philippines and Harvard Law School; practising corpn. lawyer and Prof. of Taxation 1955–66; Under-Sec. of Finance 1966–68; Acting Sec. of Finance; Acting Insurance Commr.; Acting Commr. of Customs; Sec. of Justice 1968–70; Sec. of Nat. Defence 1970–71 (resgnd.), 1972–78, Minister 1978–86 (reappointed under Aquino Govt. 1985); Chair. Cttee. on Nat. Security, Defense, Peace and Order; mem. Senate and Opposition Leader 1987–; mem. Finance, Appropriations and Steering Cttees.; Chair., Bds. of Dirs. Philippine Nat. Bank until 1978, Nat. Investment and Devt. Co., United Coconut Planters Bank, Nat. Disaster Control Center; Dir. Philippine Communications Satellite Corpn.; Trustee and Sec., Bd. of Trustees, Cultural Centre of the Philippines; Chair. Exec. Cttee., Nat. Security Council; mem. Bd., Nat. Econ. and Devt. Authority, Energy Devt., Philippine Nat. Oil Co., Nat. Environmental Protection Council,

Philippine Overseas Telecommunications Corpn., Philippine Crop Insurance Corpn.; mem. numerous law and commercial assens.; two hon. degrees; Mahaputra Adipranada Medal; Philippine Legion of Honor. *Publications:* A Proposal on Capital Gains Tax 1960, Income Tax Treatment of Corporate Merger and Consolidation Revisited 1962, Tax Treatment of Real Estate Transactions 1964; also various articles on law, the military and government. *Leisure interests:* reading, golf, tennis, swimming, water-skiing, fishing. *Address:* 2305 Morado Street, Dasmariñas Village, Makati, Metro Manila, Philippines (Home). *Telephone:* 78-97-26 and 79-03-90.

PONCELET, Christian; French politician; b. 24 March 1928, Blaise; s. of Raoul and Raymonde (née Chamillard) Poncelet; m. Yvette Miclot 1949; two d.; ed. Coll. Saint-Sulpice, Paris and Ecole Professionelle des Postes, Télégraphes et Télécommunications; Deputy to Nat. Assembly for the Vosges 1962-78; Deputy Sec.-Gen. U.D.R. 1971-76, responsible for social affairs; Sec. of State, Ministry of Social Affairs 1972-73, Ministry of Employment, Labour and Population 1973-74; Sec. of State for the Civil Service attached to Prime Minister March-May 1974; Sec. of State for the Budget, Ministry of Econ. Affairs and Finance 1974-77, for Relations with Parl. 1977; Conseiller général, Remiremont 1963-; Pres. Conseil Général des Vosges 1976-; Sénateur des Vosges 1977-; mem. European Parl. 1979-80; mem. R.P.R. (fmr. U.D.R.), Bureau Politique RPR 1979-; Mayor of Remiremont 1983-; Nat. Sec., R.P.R. in Charge of Problems in Society 1984-; Pres. Comm. for Finance, Budgetry Control and Econ. Accounts of the Nation to the Senate 1986-88. *Address:* Palais du Luxembourg, 75291 Paris cedex 06; 17 rue des Etats-Unis, 88200 Remiremont, France.

PONIATOWSKI, Prince Michel Casimir, L. EN D.; French civil servant and politician; b. 16 May 1922, Paris; s. of Prince Charles-Casimir Poniatowski and the late Princess (née Anne de Caraman-Chimay); m. Gilberte de Chavagnac 1946; three s. one d.; ed. Ecoles des Roches, Verneuil-sur-Avre, and Univ. de Paris; with Ministry of Finance 1948-56; Financial Attaché in Washington 1956-57; Asst. Dir. du cabinet to Minister of Finance 1957-58; Econ. and Financial Counsellor in Morocco 1958; Asst. Dir. du cabinet to Prés. du Conseil 1958; Dir. du cabinet to Sec. of State for Finance, later to Minister of Finance 1959-62; Dir. du Cabinet, Ministry of Finance 1962; Del. for Foreign Investment, Overseas Finance Admin. 1962; Head of Mission Ministry of Finance 1962-65, Dir. of Insurance 1963-67; Ind. Republican Deputy 1967-73; Sec.-Gen. Féd. des Républicains indépendants 1967-70, Pres. 1975-; Mayor of Isle-Adam 1971-; Minister of Health and Social Security 1973-74; Minister of State and of the Interior 1974-77; Roving Amb. (Personal Envoy of Pres.) 1977-81; mem. European Parl. 1979-; Pres. Comm. for Devt. and Cooperation, European Parl. 1979-, Inst. de Prospective Politique 1979-, Comm. for Energy, Research and Tech. to the European Parl. 1986; Chevalier, Légion d'honneur, Médaille militaire, Chevalier, Ordre national du Mérite, Croix de guerre 1939-45, Commdr. Isabela la Católica, Officier du Ouissam alaouite. *Publications:* L'avenir des pays sous-développés 1954, Histoire de la Russie d'Amérique et de l'Alaska 1959, Talleyrand aux Etats-Unis 1967, Les choix de l'espoir 1970, Cartes sur table 1972, Les Jagellons 1973, Conduire le changement 1975, Cadoudal, Moreau et Pichegru 1977, L'avenir n'est écrit nulle part 1978, Louis-Philippe et Louis XVIII 1980, L'histoire est libre 1982, Talley-rand et le Directoire 1982, Garnerin, premier parachutiste du monde 1983, Lettre ouverte au Président de la République 1983, L'Europe ou la Mort 1984, Le Socialisme à la Française 1985, Les Technologies Nouvelles, la chance de l'homme 1986, Talleyrand et le Consultat 1986. *Address:* 22 boulevard Jean Mermoz, 92200 Neuilly-sur-Seine, France. *Telephone:* 47.45.45.30.

PONIMAN, Gen. S.; Indonesian army officer and politician; b. 18 July 1926, Solo, Cen. Java; ed. Dutch Elementary School, Dutch Jr. High School and Army Staff and Command Coll.; held various army staff and command posts 1945-70; Commdr. Army Strategic Command (KOSTRAD) 1973; Commdr. of Territorial Defence, Command 1/Medan, N. Sumatra 1974; Deputy Commdr. of Army 1977; Commdr. of Army 1980; Minister of Defence and Security 1983-88. *Address:* c/o Ministry of Defence and Security, Jln. Merdeka Barat 13, Jakarta, Indonesia.

PONNAMPERUMA, Cyril Andrew, PH.D.: American professor of chemistry and laboratory director; b. 16 Oct. 1923, Galle, Ceylon (now Sri Lanka); s. of Grace Siriwardene and Andrew Ponnamperuma; m. Vallie Pal 1955; one d.; ed. Univs. of Madras, London and Calif. at Berkeley: Research Assoc., Lawrence Radiation Lab., Univ. of Calif. 1960-62; Research Scientist Chief, Chemical Evolution, Ames Research Center, NASA, Calif. 1962-70; Prof. of Chem., Univ. of Md. 1971-, Dir. Lab. of Chemical Evolution 1971-; Dir. Insts. of Fundamental Studies, Govt. of Sri Lanka, Colombo, Sri Lanka 1984-, Dir. Arthur Clarke Centre, Colombo 1984-, Science Adviser to Pres. of Sri Lanka 1984-; mem. American Chemical Soc., Astronomical Assen., A.A.A.S., Royal Inst. of Chem., Geochemical Soc., American Soc. of Biological Chemists, Radiation Research Soc.; Hon. D.Sc. (Sri Lanka) 1978, (Puget Sound) 1982, (Peradeniya) 1984, (Sri Jayawardhanapura) 1985; A. I. Oparin Gold Medal 1980. *Publications:* Origins of Life, Cosmic Evolution; 300 papers in the field of chem. and chemical evolution; Ed. of 16 books. *Address:* University of Maryland, Laboratory of Chemical Evolution, College Park, Md. 20742, U.S.A. *Telephone:* (301) 454-4059.

PONOMARYOV, Boris Nikolayevich; Soviet historian and politician; b. 17 Jan. 1905, Zaraisk, Ryazan region; ed. Moscow State Univ. and Red Professors' Inst.; Red Army 1919, Mil. Revolutionary Cttee. Zaraisk 1919-20; Young Communist League, Moscow Region 1920-22; Sec. Krasny Vostok Factory Party Org., Moscow Region 1922-23; mem. Propagandist Group, Cen. Cttee. of CPSU 1926-28; Asst. Dir. Red Profs.' Inst. 1933-36; Exec. Cttee. Communist Int. 1936-39; Asst. Dir. Marx-Engels-Lenin Inst. 1943-45; Cen. Cttee. CPSU 1944-46; First Deputy Chief Soviet Information Bureau, U.S.S.R. Council of Ministers 1946-49; Head of Dept., Cen. Cttee. CPSU 1949-61, mem. of Cen. Cttee. 1956-89, Secr. 1961, cand. mem. Political Bureau 1972-86, Deputy Pres. Cttee. for Party Control 1983-89; Deputy to U.S.S.R. Supreme Soviet 1958-; Chair. Foreign Affairs Comm., Soviet of Nationalities; corresp. mem. Acad. of Sciences of U.S.S.R. 1958, mem. 1962-; Order of Lenin (five times); Order of Red Banner of Labour (twice), Sixty Years of Armed Forces of U.S.S.R. Medal, Order of the October Revolution (U.S.S.R.), Order of Karl Marx (G.D.R.) 1980, Order of Victorious February (Czechoslovakia) 1981, and other decorations. *Publications:* Works on history of CPSU and int. workers' movements.

PONS, Bernard; French doctor and politician; b. 18 July 1926, Béziers; s. of Claude Pons and Véronique Vogel; m. Josette Cros 1952; five d.; ed. Faculté de Médecine, Montpellier; Gen. Practitioner Cahors 1952-67; elected Deputy for Lot, Nat. Assembly 1967, 1968, 1973, for Essonne 1978, for Paris 1981-86; Sec. of State, Ministry of Agric. 1969-73; Conseiller général, Canton of Carjac 1967-78; Municipal Councillor, Souillac 1971-; Regional Councillor, Ile-de-France 1978; mem. Rassemblement pour la République (fmrly. U.D.R.), Gen. Sec. 1979-84; mem. European Parl. 1979-85; Minister of Overseas Depts. and Territories 1986-88. *Leisure interests:* fishing, hunting, reading. *Address:* 14 rue François-Miron, 75004 Paris, France.

PONTECORVO, Bruno Maksimovich (brother of Guido and Gillo Pontecorvo, q.q.v.); Soviet (b. Italian) physicist; b. 22 Aug. 1913, Pisa, Italy; s. of Massimo Pontecorvo and Maria (née Maroni); ed. Pisa and Rome Univs.; Instructor Rome Univ. 1933-36; at scientific insts. in France 1936-40; in U.S.A. 1940-43; research at Chalk River, Canada, under E. Fermi, leading to devt. of neutron physics 1943-48; Assoc. Harwell Lab., U.K. 1948-50; went to U.S.S.R. 1950; mem. CPSU 1955-; Corresp. mem. U.S.S.R. Acad. of Sciences 1958-64, mem. 1964-; in charge of team at Joint Inst. for Nuclear Research, Dubna; U.S.S.R. State Prize 1954, Order of Lenin (twice), Order of the October Revolution 1983, Lenin Prize 1963, and other decorations. *Address:* Joint Institute for Nuclear Research, Dubna, c/o Head Post Office, P.O. Box 79, Moscow, U.S.S.R.

PONTECORVO, Gillo (brother of Bruno and Guido Pontecorvo, q.q.v.); Italian film director; b. 1919, Pisa; Golden Lion Award, Venice for La Battaglia di Algeri. *Films include:* Die Windrose ep Giovanna 1956, La Grande Strada Azzurra 1958, Kapò 1960, La Battaglia di Algeri (Battle of Algiers) 1966, Queimada! (Burn!) 1969, Ogro 1979. *Address:* via Massacciuc-coli 76, 00199 Rome, Italy.

PONTECORVO, Guido, DR.AGR., PH.D., F.R.S. (brother of Bruno and Gillo Pontecorvo, q.q.v.); British (b. Italian) geneticist and university professor; b. 29 Nov. 1907, Pisa; s. of Massimo Pontecorvo and Maria (née Maroni); m. Leonore Freyenmuth 1939 (died 1986); one d.; ed. Università degli Studi, Pisa, and Univ. of Edinburgh; Asst. and later Regent of Section, Ispettorato Compartimentale Agrario, Florence 1930-38; Research Student, Inst. of Animal Genetics, Edinburgh 1938-40, Dept. of Zoology, Univ. of Glasgow 1941-43; Lecturer, Inst. of Animal Genetics, Univ. of Edinburgh 1943-45; Lecturer, Sr. Lecturer, Reader, Dept. of Genetics, Univ. of Glasgow 1945-56, Prof. 1956-68; Hon. Dir. Medical Research Council Unit for Cell Genetics 1964-68; mem. staff, Imperial Cancer Research Fund 1968-75, Hon. Consultant Geneticist 1975-80; Jesup Lecturer, Columbia Univ. 1956, Messenger Lecturer, Cornell Univ. 1957, Leeuwenhoek Lecturer, Royal Soc. 1962; Gandhi Memorial Lecturer, Raman Inst. 1983; J. Weigle Memorial Lecturer, Calif. Inst. of Tech. 1984; Visiting Prof. Albert Einstein Coll. of Medicine, New York 1964, 1965, Washington State Univ. 1967; Royal Soc. Leverhulme Visiting Prof. Dept. of Biophysics, Rio de Janeiro 1969, Dept. of Biology, Pahlavi Univ., Iran 1974; Visiting Prof. Univ. Coll., London 1968-75, King's Coll., London 1969-70, Middlebury Coll., Vermont 1971, Univ. of Teheran 1975; Prof. Ospite Linceo, Scuola Normale Superiore, Pisa 1976-80; Raman Prof., Indian Acad. of Science 1982; Pres. Genetical Soc. 1964-65, Hon. mem. 1982; Vice-Pres. Inst. of Biology 1969-71; mem. Council, Soc. for Gen. Microbiology 1959-60; Fellow Royal Soc. of Edinburgh 1946 (mem. Council 1958-61), of London 1955 (mem. Council 1958-59); Fellow Linnean Soc. London 1971; Foreign mem., Indian Nat. Science Acad. 1984; mem. Indian Acad. of Sciences 1983; Foreign Assoc. N.A.S. (U.S.A.) 1984, Foreign mem. Danish Royal Acad. 1966; Hon. Foreign mem. American Acad. of Arts and Sciences 1958; Hon. mem. Peruvian Soc. Medical Genetics 1969; Hon. D.Sc. (Leicester) 1968, (East Anglia) 1974, (Camerino) 1974; Hon. LL.D. (Glasgow) 1978; Hansen Prize 1961; Darwin Medal (Royal Soc.) 1978, Campano d'Oro (Pisa) 1979. *Publication:* Trends in Genetic Analysis, numerous articles on genetics and high altitude botany. *Leisure interests:* alpine plant photography. *Address:* Imperial Cancer Research Fund, Lincoln's Inn Fields, London, W.C.2 (Office); 60 Thornhill Square, London, N1 1BE, England (Home). *Telephone:* 01-700 5320.

PONTI, Carlo, LL.D.; French (b. Italian) film producer; b. 11 Dec. 1913, Magenta, Milan; s. of the late Leone Ponti and Maria (née Zardone); m. 1st Giulania Fiastri 1946, one s. one d.; m. 2nd Sophia Loren (q.v.) 1966, two s.; ed. Università degli Studi, Milan; legal practice in office of Milan barrister 1935-38; film producer 1938-; French citizen 1965-; Major films produced: Roma Città Aperta 1945 (New York Critics Prize 1947), To Live in Peace 1945, Attila 1953, Ulysses 1953, La Strada 1954 (Oscar), War and Peace 1955, Two Women 1960, (Oscar Award for best foreign actress) Boccaccio '70 1961, Yesterday, Today, Tomorrow 1963 (Oscar), Marriage, Italian Style 1964, Casanova '70 1964, Lady L 1965, Dr. Zhivago 1965 (six Oscars), The 25th Hour 1966, Blow Up 1966 (Cannes Film Festival Award), The Girl and the General 1966, More than a Miracle 1966, Ghosts, Italian Style 1967, Smashing Time 1967, Diamonds for Breakfast 1967, Best House in London 1968, A Place for Lovers 1968, Zabriskie Point 1969, Sunflower 1969, Priest's Wife 1970, Love Stress 1971, Mortadella 1971, Red, White and ... 1972, Massacre in Rome 1973, Run Run Joe 1973, Verdict 1974, The Passenger 1974, Blood Money 1975, The Cassandra Crossing 1977, The Naked Sun 1979; Officier des Arts et des Lettres. *Address:* Chalet Daniel, Bürgenstock, Nidwalden, Switzerland; 32 Avenue George V, Paris 75008, France; Palazzo Colonna, 1 Piazza d'Ara Coeli 1, Rome, Italy.

PONTI, Michael; American concert pianist; b. 29 Oct. 1937, Freiburg, Germany; s. of Joseph Ponti and Zita Wüchner; m. 1st Carmen Wiechmann 1962 (divorced 1971); one s. two d.; m. 2nd Beatrice van Stappen 1984; studied under Prof. Gilmour McDonald and Prof. Erich Flinsch; début in Vienna 1964, in New York 1972; has toured extensively all over the world; over 80 recordings; Busoni Award, Italy 1964. *Address:* Heubergstrasse 32, D-8116 Eschenlohe, Federal Republic of Germany. *Telephone:* (08824) 594.

POOLE, 1st Baron, cr. 1958, of Aldgate; **Oliver Brian Sanderson Poole,** P.C., C.B.E., T.D.; British politician and banker; b. 11 Aug. 1911; s. of the late Donald Louis Poole; m. 1st Betty Margaret Gilkison 1933 (divorced 1951), one s. three d.; m. 2nd Daphne Heber Percy 1952 (divorced 1965); m. 3rd Barbara Ann Taylor 1966; ed. Eton Coll. and Christ Church, Oxford; served 1939-45 war (despatches thrice); M.P. for Oswestry Div. of Salop 1945-50; mem. Lloyds; Joint Treas. Conservative Party Org. 1952-55, Chair. 1955-57, Deputy Chair. 1957-59, Joint Chair. April-Oct. 1963, Vice-Chair. Oct. 1963- Oct. 1964; Chair. Thomas Stephens, Poole (Holdings); Chair. Whitehall Securities Corpn. Ltd.; Exec. Deputy Chair. Lazard Brothers Jan.-Oct. 1965, Chair. 1965-73; Chief Exec. S. Pearson 1973-75; Trustee, Nat. Gallery 1973-81; Hon. D.Sc. (City Univ.) 1970. *Address:* 24 Campden Hill Gate, Duchess of Bedford Walk, London, W.8, England.

POOS, Jacques F., D. ÈS SC. COMM. ET ECON.; Luxembourg politician; b. 3 June 1935, Luxembourg; m.; three c.; ed. Athénée Grand-Ducal, Luxembourg; ed. Univ. of Lausanne and Luxembourg Int. Univ.; Ministry of Nat. Economy 1959-62; Service d'Etudes et de Statistiques Economiques (STATEC) 1962-64; Dir. Imprimerie Coopérative 1964-76; Pres. SYTRA-GAZ 1970-76; Deputy 1974-76; Minister of Finance, Gov. IBRD, IMF, EIB 1976-79; Dir. Banque Continentale du Luxembourg S.A. 1980-82, Banque Paribas (Luxembourg) S.A. 1982-84; Vice-Pres. Parti Socialiste 1982-; Deputy Prime Minister, Minister of Foreign Affairs, of Foreign Trade and Co-operation, Minister of the Economy and Middle Classes and Minister of the Treasury 1984-. *Publications:* Le Luxembourg dans le Marché Commun 1961, Le modèle Luxembourgeois 1981, La Crise Economique et Financière; est-elle encore maitrisable? 1984. *Address:* Ministère des Affaires Etrangères, Luxembourg. *Telephone:* 556425.

POPA, Dumitru; Romanian politician; b. 27 Feb. 1925, Bucharest; m. Emilia Popa; two s.; ed. Acad. of Econ. Studies, Bucharest; joined Union of Communist Youth 1944; mem. Romanian CP 1945-; First Sec. Hunedoara Region Cttee. of Romanian CP 1963-65; First Sec. Bucharest Cttee RCP and Gen. Mayor of Bucharest 1966-72; mem. Cen. Cttee. 1965-84, Sec. 1979-80; Alt. mem. Exec. Cttee. of RCP 1966-69; mem. 1969-72; mem. Nat. Assembly 1961-; Sec. Grand Nat. Assembly 1961-65; mem. Nat. Council of the Socialist Unity Front 1968-72; Amb. to Democratic People's Repub. of Korea 1972-78; to Yugoslavia 1984-; Minister-State Sec. Ministry of Chemical Industry 1978-79, Minister of Industrial Constructions 1980-82. *Address:* Romanian Embassy, Kneza Miloša 70, Belgrade, Yugoslavia.

POPE-HENNESSY, Sir John Wyndham, Kt., C.B.E., F.B.A., F.S.A., F.R.S.L.; British museum director and art historian; b. 13 Dec. 1913, London; s. of the late Major-Gen. L. H. R. Pope-Hennessy and Dame Una Pope-Hennessy; ed. Balliol Coll., Oxford; joined staff Victoria and Albert Museum 1938, Keeper Dept. of Architecture and Sculpture 1954-66; Slade Prof. of Fine Art, Oxford Univ. 1956-57; Robert Sterling Clark Prof. of Art, Williams Coll., Williamstown, U.S.A. 1961-62; Slade Prof. of Fine Art, Cambridge Univ. 1964-65; Dir. Victoria and Albert Museum 1967-73, British Museum 1974-76; Consultative Chair. Dept. of European Paintings, Metropolitan Museum of Art, New York 1977-86; Prof. of Fine Arts, New York Univ. 1977-; Mitchell Prize 1981; Mangia d'Oro (Siena) 1982. *Publications:* Giovanni di Paolo 1937, Sassetta 1939, Sienese Quattrocento Painting 1947, A Sienese Codex of the Divine Comedy 1947, The Drawings of Domenichino at Windsor Castle 1948, A Lecture on Nicholas Hilliard 1949, Paolo Uccello 1950, Fra Angelico 1952, Italian Gothic Sculpture 1955, Italian Renaissance Sculpture 1958, Italian High Renaissance and Baroque Sculpture 1963, Catalogue of Italian Sculpture in the Victoria and Albert

Museum 1964, Italian Bronzes in the Kress Collection 1965, The Portrait in the Renaissance 1967, Essays on Italian Sculpture 1968, The Frick Collection Catalogue Vols. III and IV, Sculpture 1970, Raphael (The Wrightsman Lectures) 1970, Luca della Robbia 1980, The Study and Criticism of Italian Sculpture 1981, Benvenuto Cellini 1985, La Scultura Italiana del Rinscimento 1986, Catalogue of Italian Paintings in the Robert Lehman Collection 1986. *Leisure interest:* music. *Address:* Metropolitan Museum of Art, 5th Avenue at 82nd Street, New York, N.Y. 10028, U.S.A.; 28 via de'Bardi, Florence 50125, Italy.

POPESCU, Dumitru; Romanian politician and writer; b. 18 April 1928, Turnu Măgurele; m. Maria Popescu 1950; one s. two d.; ed. Acad. of Econ. Studies, Bucharest; mem. of the Romanian CP 1953-; Journalist on Contemporanul 1950-56; Ed.-in-Chief Scinteia Tineretului 1956-60; Dir. Agerpres (Romanian News Agency) 1960-62; Vice-Chair. State Cttee. for Culture and Art 1962-65; Ed.-in-Chief on Scinteia 1965-68; Pres. of the Council of Socialist Culture and Educ. 1971-76; Chair. Nat. Council of Romanian Radio-television 1976-; mem. of the Cen. Cttee. of RCP 1965-. Alt. mem. Exec. Political Cttee. 1968-69, mem. 1969-; Standing Bureau Exec., Political Cttee. RCP 1974-82; Sec. Cen. Cttee. of RCP 1968-81; Deputy to Grand Nat. Assembly 1965-; mem. Acad. of Social and Political Sciences 1970-, Nat. Council Front of Socialist Democracy and Unity, Standing Bureau, Supreme Council of Econ. and Social Devt. 1974-82, Chair. Man. Bd.; Rector Academia de partid pentru învăţămînt social-politic 1981-. *Publications:* Impresii de călător (Egypt, Iraq, Cuba) 1962, Drumuri europene 1965, Biletul la control (essays) 1968, Pentru cel ales (poems) 1968, Un om in Agora (poems) 1972, Iesirea din labirint (essays) 1973, Gustul sîmburelui (poems) 1974, Rază de Cobalt (poems) 1979, Pumnul şi palma (novel) vol. I 1980, vol. II 1981, vol. III 1982, Muzeul de ceară (novel) 1984, Vitralii incolore (novel) 1985. *Address:* Academia de Partid Pentru Învăţămînt social-politic, Bd. Armata Poporului 1-3, Bucharest (Office); Bd. Armata Poporului 1-3, Bucharest, Romania (Home).

POPESCU, Dumitru Radu; Romanian author; b. 19 Aug. 1935, Păpusa Village, Bihor County; ed. Colls. of Medicine and Philology, Cluj; reporter at the literary magazine Steaua 1956-69; ed.-in-chief of the literary magazine Tribuna 1969-82, Contemporanul 1982-; alt. mem. Cen. Cttee. Romanian CP 1968-79; mem. Cen. Cttee. Romanian CP 1979-; Chair. Romanian Writers' Union 1980-; Prize of the Writers' Union 1964, 1969, 1974, 1977, 1980; Prize of the Romanian Acad. 1970. *Major works include:* collections of short stories: Fuga (Flight) 1958, Fata de la miazăzi (A Girl from the South) 1964, Somnul pământului (The Earth's Sleep) 1965, Dor (Longing) 1966, Umbrela de soare (The Parasol) 1967, Prea mic pentru un război aşa de mare (Too Little for Such a Big War) 1969, Duios Anastasia trecea (Tenderly Anastasia Passed) 1967, Leul albastru (The Blue Lion) 1981; *novels:* Zilele săptămînii (Weekdays) 1959, Vara oltenilor (The Oltenians' Summer) 1964, F 1964, Vînătoarea regală (Royal Hunt) 1973, O bere pentru calul meu (A Beer for My Horse) 1974, Ploile de dincolo de vreme (Rains beyond Time) 1976, Impăratul norilor (Emperor of the Clouds) 1976; *plays:* Vara imposibilei iubiri (The Summer of Impossible Love) 1966, Vis (Dream) 1968, Aceşti îngeri trişti (Those Sad Angels) 1969, Pisica în noaptea Anului nou (Cat on the New Year's Eve) 1970, Pasărea Shakespeare (The Shakespeare Bird) 1973, Rezervaţia de pelicani (The Pelican Reservation) 1983, Iepurele şchiop (The Lame Rabbit) 1980, Orasul îngerilor (The Angel's City) 1985; *poems:* Clinele de fosfor (The Phosphorus Dog) 1981; *essays:* Virgule (Commas) 1978. *Address:* c/o Uniunea Scriitorilor, Calea Victoriei 115, Bucharest, Romania.

POPESCU, Ioan-Iovitz, PH.D.; Romanian professor of optics and plasma physics; b. 1 Oct. 1932, Burila-Mare; s. of Dumitru and Elvira Popescu; m. Georgeta-Denisa Chiru 1963; ed. Univ. of Bucharest; Asst. Prof. of Optics and Gaseous Electronics, Univ. of Bucharest 1955-60, Prof. Faculty of Physics 1972-, Dean 1972-77, Rector of Univ. 1981-; Head of Plasma Physics Laboratory, Inst. of Physics, Bucharest 1960-67, Scientific Deputy Dir. 1970-72, Dir. 1977-81; Alexander von Humboldt Dozentstipendium, Kiel Univ. 1967-69; Deputy to Grand Nat. Assembly 1980-; Alt. mem. Cen. Cttee. of Romanian Communist Party; Corresp. mem. Romanian Acad. 1974-; Labour Order of Romania 1964; Prize for Physics (Romanian Acad.) 1965; Scientific Merit Order 1981. *Publications:* Ionized Gases 1965, General Physics 1971-75, Plasma Physics and Applications 1981, numerous articles on optics and plasma physics. *Address:* University of Bucharest, Office of the Rector, Bd. Gheorghe-Gheorghiu Dej, Bucharest 5, Romania. *Telephone:* 14.57.44 (Office), 80.66.80 (Home).

POPJÁK, George Joseph, M.D., D.SC., F.R.S.C., F.R.S.; British biochemist; b. 5 May 1914, Kiskundorozsma, Hungary; s. of late George Popják and late Maria Mayer; m. Hasel Marjory Hammond 1941; ed. Royal Hungarian Francis Joseph Univ., Szeged, Hungary, and Postgraduate Medical School, Univ. of London; British Council Scholar 1939-41; Demonstrator, Dept. of Pathology, St. Thomas's Hospital, London 1941-47; Beit Memorial Fellow for Medical Research 1943-47; mem. Scientific Staff, Nat. Inst. for Medical Research, London 1947-53; Dir. Medical Research Council Experimental Radio-pathology Research Unit, Hammersmith Hospital, London 1953-62; Visiting Scientist, Nat. Heart Inst., Nat. Insts. of Health, Bethesda, Md., U.S.A. 1960-61; Joint Dir., Chemical Enzymology Lab., Shell Research Ltd. 1962-68; Assoc. Prof. in Molecular Sciences, Warwick Univ. 1965-68; Prof. of Biochem. Univ. of Calif. at Los Angeles Oct. 1968-84, Prof. Emer.

July 1984–; Foreign mem. Royal Flemish Acad. of Sciences and Fine Arts, Belgium; mem. American Acad. of Arts and Sciences 1971; Ciba Medal, Biochem. Soc. 1965; Stouffer Prize 1967; Davy Medal, The Royal Soc. 1968; Award in Lipid Chem., American Oil Chemists' Soc. 1977; Distinguished Scientific Achievement Award, American Heart Assoc., Greater Los Angeles Affiliate 1978–79. *Publications:* Lipids, Chemistry, Biochemistry and Nutrition (joint author) 1986; numerous articles in scientific journals, mainly on problems of lipid metabolism; monograph Chemistry, Biochemistry and Isotopic Trace Technique 1955. *Leisure interests:* music, sculpture and gardening. *Address:* Departments of Biological Chemistry and Medicine, Division of Cardiology, University of California, Los Angeles, Calif. 90024 (Office); 511 Cashmere Terrace, Los Angeles, Calif. 90049, U.S.A. (Home).

POPLE, John Anthony, M.A., PH.D., F.R.S.; British professor of theoretical chemistry; b. 31 Oct. 1925, Burnham, Somerset; s. of Keith Pople and Mary Jones; m. Joy Cynthia Bowers 1952; three s. one d.; ed. Univ. of Cambridge; Research Fellow Trinity Coll., Cambridge 1951–54, Lecturer in Math. 1954–58; Research Assoc., Nat. Research Council, Ottawa during summer 1956, 1957; Supt. Basic Physics Div., Nat. Physical Laboratory, Teddington (U.K.) 1958–64; Ford Visiting Prof. of Chem., Carnegie Inst. of Tech., Pittsburgh, Pa. 1961–62; Carnegie Prof. of Chemical Physics, Carnegie-Mellon Univ., Pittsburgh 1964–74, Acting Head, Dept. of Chem. 1967, John Christian Warner Univ. Prof. of Natural Sciences 1974–; mem. A.C.S. 1965–, Int. Acad. of Quantum Molecular Science 1967–; Foreign Assoc., Nat. Acad. of Sciences 1977; Fellow, American Physical Soc. 1970–, American Acad. of Arts and Sciences 1971–; Smith's Prizeman (Cambridge) 1950, Marlow Medal of Faraday Soc. 1958, A.C.S. Awards: Irving Langmuir 1970, Harrison Howe 1971, Gilbert Newton Lewis 1973, Pittsburgh 1975, Morley Medal, American Chemical Soc. 1976, Pauling Award 1977, Oesper Award, Univ. of Cincinnati Dept. of Chemistry 1984. *Publications:* co-author: High Resolution Magnetic Resonance 1959, Approximate Molecular Orbital Theory 1970, Ab initio Molecular Orbital Theory 1986; also over 200 publs. in scientific journals. *Leisure interest:* music. *Address:* Department of Chemistry, Carnegie-Mellon University, 4400 Fifth Avenue, Pittsburgh, Pa. 15213; 415 W, 100 Bryn Mawr Court, Pittsburgh, Pa. 15221, U.S.A. (Home).

POPOFF, Frank Peter, M.B.A.; American business executive; b. 27 Oct. 1935, Sofia, Bulgaria; s. of Eftim Popoff and Stoyanka Kossoroff; m. Jean Urse; three s.; ed. Indiana Univ.; with Dow Chemical Co. 1959–, Exec. Vice-Pres. 1985–87, Pres. and C.E.O. 1987–, also mem. Bd. of Dirs.; Exec. Vice-Pres., then Pres. Dow Chemical European subsidiary, Switzerland 1976–85; mem. Bd. of Dirs. Dow Corning Corpn., Chemical Bank & Trust Co., Midland, The Salk Inst. *Address:* Dow Chemical Co., 2030 Willard House, Dow Center, Midland, Mich. 48674, U.S.A.

POPOV, Nikolav Ivanovich; Soviet politician; b. 1936; ed. Leningrad Eng. Inst.; served in Soviet Army 1956–59; mem. CPSU 1959–; pres. of local cttee. Priozersky station 1959–60; party work in Leningrad Dist. 1960–71; Second, First Sec. of Vyborg City Cttee. (Leningrad) 1971–81; head of section, Sec. of Leningrad CPSU Dist. Cttee. 1981–83; Pres. of Dist. Exec. Cttee. 1983–; Deputy to U.S.S.R. Supreme Soviet; cand. mem. of CPSU Cen. Cttee. 1986–. *Address:* The Kremlin, Moscow, U.S.S.R.

POPOV, Oleg Konstantinovich; Soviet actor; b. 31 July 1930, Vyrubovo, Moscow Region; ed. Moscow State Circus School; clown on slack wire at Tbilisi Circus 1950; clown at Saratov Circus 1951; appeared in France, Britain, Poland, etc.; clown at Moscow Circus 1955–; People's Artist of R.S.F.S.R. and the U.S.S.R. 1969; Winner of Warsaw Int. Festival of Circus Art 1956, Oscar Prize, Brussels 1958; Order of Red Banner and other decorations. *Publication:* My Hero in the anthology Fires of the Manezh 1961. *Address:* All Union Organization of State Circuses, 15 Neglinnaya ulitsa, Moscow, U.S.S.R.

POPOV, Viktor Ivanovich, D.S.; Soviet diplomatist; b. 19 May 1918, Moscow; m. Natalia Aleksandrovna Popova; two s.; ed. Moscow Inst. of History and Philosophy, Higher Diplomatic School of U.S.S.R. Ministry of Foreign Affairs; joined Ministry of Foreign Affairs 1954, Counsellor, Democratic Repub. of Viet-Nam 1960–61, Embassy in Australia 1967–68, Minister-Counsellor, Embassy in U.K. 1968–80; Rector of Acad. of Diplomacy of U.S.S.R. and Amb. on special assignments, including Iran and Afghanistan, UN Gen. Assembly and UNESCO 1968–80, Amb. to U.K. 1980–86; mem. Cen. Auditing Comm. of CPSU 1981–; U.S.S.R. State Prize in History, Merited Scientific Worker of the R.S.F.S.R., many other Soviet and foreign awards. *Publications:* Anglo-Soviet Relations 1927–29, Anglo-Soviet Relations 1929–37, History of Diplomacy series (co-author) and other publications on international relations and U.S.S.R. foreign policy. *Leisure interests:* tennis, angling. *Address:* Ministry of Foreign Affairs, 32–34 Smolenskaya Sennaya Ploshchad, Moscow, U.S.S.R.

POPOV, Dr. Yevgeniy Pavlovich; Soviet automation specialist; b. 14 Feb. 1914, Moscow; ed. Bauman Higher Tech. Coll., Moscow; engineer-mechanic with an Air Force squadron 1939–43; mem. CPSU 1942–; teacher at A. F. Mozhaisky Acad. of Mil. Aviation and Eng., Leningrad 1943–64; Prof. 1948; Chair. Dept. of Automation and Remote Control, Mozhaisky Inst. 1949–; Chair. Section of Applied Problems, Presidium of U.S.S.R. Acad. of Sciences 1964–71; Head of Chair. at Bauman Higher Coll., Moscow 1971–; Head of Scientific Educational Centre "Robototechnika" 1981; corresp.

mem. U.S.S.R. Acad. of Sciences 1960–; U.S.S.R. State Prize 1949, 1972, Order of October Revolution; most important works concerned with the theory of automatic controls. *Address:* Bauman Higher College, 2-nd Baumanskaya St. 5, Moscow 107005, U.S.S.R.

POPP, Lucia; Austrian (b. Czech) soprano; b. 12 Nov. 1939, Uhorska Ves; ed. Bratislava Acad. of Music; joined Vienna State Opera 1963, subsequently became Prin. Soprano; début Salzburg Festival 1963, Covent Garden, London 1966, Metropolitan Opera, New York 1967; Australian tour 1969; also recital tours. *Address:* c/o Lydia Störle, Spitzingplatz 2, 8000 Munich 90, Federal Republic of Germany. *Telephone:* 691 25 08.

POPPER, Sir Karl (Raimund), Kt., C.H., M.A., PH.D., D.LIT., F.R.S., F.B.A.; British philosopher; b. 28 July 1902, Vienna, Austria; s. of Dr. Simon Siegmund Carl and Jenny (née Schiff) Popper; m. Josephine Anna Henninger 1930 (died 1985); ed. Vienna Univ.; Sr. Lecturer in Philosophy, Canterbury Univ. Coll., Christchurch, New Zealand 1937–45; Reader in Logic, London Univ. 1945–49, Prof. of Logic and Scientific Method 1949–69, Emer. 1969–; Head, Dept. Philosophy, Logic and Scientific Method, L.S.E. 1945–66; William James Lecturer, Harvard Univ. 1950; Fellow, Stanford Center for Advanced Study in the Behavioral Sciences 1956–57; Eleanor Rathbone Memorial Lecturer, Bristol Univ. 1956; Annual Philosophical Lecturer, British Acad. 1960; Shearman Lecturer, Univ. Coll. London 1961; Herbert Spencer Lecturer, Oxford Univ. 1961; Visiting Prof. Calif. and Minn. Univs. 1962, Indiana 1963, Univ. of Denver 1966; Farnum Lecturer, Princeton Univ. 1963, Inst. of Advanced Studies, Canberra 1963, Inst. of Advanced Study, Vienna 1964, Arthur Holly Compton Memorial Lecturer, Washington Univ. 1965; Henry D. Broadhead Memorial Lecturer, Univ. of Canterbury, Christchurch, N.Z. 1973; Visiting Fellow, Salk Inst. for Biological Studies 1966–67; Kenan Univ. Prof., Emory Univ. 1969; Ziskind Prof., Brandeis Univ. 1969; James Scott Lecturer, R.S.E. 1971; Romanes Lecturer, Oxford 1972; William Evans Prof., Univ. of Otago 1973; Visiting Erskine Fellow, Univ. of Canterbury 1973; Herbert Spencer Lecturer, Oxford 1973; Darwin Lecturer, Cambridge 1977; Tanner Lecturer, Univ. of Michigan 1978; First J.B. Morrell Memorial Lecturer, Univ. of York; Doubleday Lecturer, Smithsonian Inst. Washington D.C. 1979; First Peter Medawar Lecturer, Royal Soc., London 1986; Hon. Prof. Univ. of Vienna 1986; Dir. Ludwig Boltzmann Inst. for the Theory of Science, Vienna 1986; mem. Académie Int. de Philosophie de Science 1949–, Council Asscn. for Symbolic Logic 1951–55, Institut de France 1980–, Académie Européenne des Sciences, des Arts et des Lettres 1980–; Fellow, British Acad. 1958–, Royal Soc. 1976–; Assoc. Académie Royale de Belgique 1976–; Foreign mem. Accad. Nazionale dei Lincei 1981–, Hon. Foreign mem. American Acad. of Arts and Sciences 1966–; Hon. mem. Royal Soc. of New Zealand 1965–, Académie Int. d'Histoire des Sciences 1977–, Deutsche Akad. für Sprache und Dichtung 1979–; Hon. mem. Österreichische Akad. der Wissenschaften 1980–; Hon. mem. Soc. of Physicians in Vienna 1966; Foreign Assoc. N.A.S., Washington; Sr. Fellow Hoover Inst., Stanford; Pres. Aristotelian Soc. 1958–59, British Soc. for the Philosophy of Science 1959–61; Hon. LL.D. (Chicago, Denver); Hon. D.Lit. (Warwick); Hon. Litt.D. (Canterbury, N.Z., Salford, City Univ. of London, Guelph Ontario, Cambridge, Oxford); Dr. Rer. Nat. h.c. (Vienna), Dr. Phil. h.c. (Mannheim, Salzburg); Dr. rer. pol. h.c. (Frankfurt); Hon. Sc.D. (Gustavus Adolphus Coll., London Univ.); Hon. Fellow, L.S.E. 1972, Darwin Coll., Cambridge 1980; Grand Decoration of Honour in Gold (Austria) 1976; Ehrenzeichen für Wissenschaft und Kunst (Austria) 1980; Pour le Mérite (Fed. Repub. of Germany) 1980; Grand Cross of the Order of Merit (Fed. Repub. of Germany) 1983; Prize, City of Vienna 1965, Sonning Prize for services to European Civilization (Copenhagen) 1973; Lippincott Award, American Political Science Asscn. (for The Open Soc.) 1976, Dr. Karl Renner Prize (Vienna) 1978, Gold Medal for Distinguished Service to Science of the American Museum of Natural History, New York 1979, Leopold Lucas Prize, Univ. of Tübingen 1981, Prix Alexis de Tocqueville, Valognes, France 1984, Medal for Services to Science, City of Linz 1986, Int. Prize of Catalonia 1989. *Publications:* Logik der Forschung, The Open Society and Its Enemies, The Poverty of Historicism, The Logic of Scientific Discovery, Conjectures and Refutations: The Growth of Scientific Knowledge, Objective Knowledge: An Evolutionary Approach, Unended Quest: An Intellectual Autobiography, The Self and Its Brain: An Argument for Interactionism (with Sir John Eccles), Die beiden Grundprobleme der Erkenntnistheorie, The Open Universe: An Argument for Indeterminism, Quantum Theory and the Schism in Physics, Realism and the Aim of Science, Auf der Suche nach einer besseren Welt, Die Zukunst ist offen (with Konrad Lorenz); over 100 papers in journals of learned societies, trans. into 27 languages. *Leisure interests:* music, Jane Austen, Trollope. *Address:* c/o London School of Economics, Houghton Street, London, WC2A 2AE, England.

POREBSKI, Tadeusz, D.SC.TECH.; Polish mechanical engineer and politician; b. 16 April 1931, Bielsko; m.; one s.; ed. Wrocław Tech. Univ.; teacher Wrocław Tech. Univ. 1955–, Asst. 1955–61, lecturer 1961–65, Head, Research Centre of Science of Materials Inst. 1965–68, Asst. Prof. 1965–69, Prof. Extraordinary 1969–, Pro-Rector 1968–69, Rector 1969–80; mem. Team of scientific advisers on socio-economic affairs to First Sec. of Cen. Cttee. of Polish United Workers' Party (PZPR); mem. Youth Org. of Workers' Univ. Soc. 1947–48, Polish Youth Union 1948–55; mem. PZPR 1950–, mem. PZPR Voivodship Cttee., Wrocław 1971–, First Sec. PZPR

Voivodship Cttee., Wrocław 1980–83, deputy mem. PZPR Cen. Cttee. 1968–71, mem. 1971–, mem. Political Bureau of PZPR Cen. Cttee. 1981–, Chair. Science and Educ. Comm. of PZPR Cen. Cttee. 1981–; Sec. PZPR Cen. Cttee. 1983–88, Chair. Internal Comm. of PZPR Cen. Cttee. 1986–; Deputy to Seym 1980–; Chair. PZPR Deputies' Club; Vice-Marshal (Deputy Speaker) Seym 1988–; Chair. Socio-Econ. Council attached to Seym 1988–; Dr. h.c. (Kiev Tech. Univ.); Officer's and Commdr's Cross with Star, Order of Polonia Restituta, Order of Banner of Labour (1st Class) and other decorations. *Address:* Kancelaria Sejmu PRL, ul. Wiejska 34/6/8, 00-489 Warsaw, Poland.

PORRITT, Baron (Life Peer), cr. 1973, of Wanganui in New Zealand and of Hampstead in Greater London; **Arthur Porritt,** Bt., G.C.M.G., G.C.V.O., C.B.E.; British surgeon and administrator; b. 10 Aug. 1900, Wanganui, New Zealand; s. of Ernest Edward and Ivy Elizabeth (McKenzie); m. 1st Molly Bond 1926, 2nd Kathleen Mary Peck 1946; two s. one d.; ed. Wanganui Collegiate School and Otago Univ., New Zealand, Oxford Univ. and St. Mary's Medical School, London; St. Mary's Hosp. Surgical Staff 1936–65; War Service with R.A.M.C. Second World War; mem. Royal Medical Household 1936–67; Surgeon to Duke of York 1936, to Household 1937–46, to King George VI 1946–52, Sergeant-Surgeon to Queen Elizabeth 1953–67; Consulting Surgeon to the Army; Pres. Royal Coll. of Surgeons of England 1960–63; Pres. B.M.A. 1960–61 (Gold Medallist); Pres. Royal Soc. of Medicine 1966–67; mem. Int. Olympic Cttee. 1934–67 (now hon. mem. and Olympic Order 1986); Chair. British Commonwealth Games 1948–67, now Vice-Pres.; Gov.-Gen. of New Zealand 1967–72; Pres. Arthritis and Rheumatism Council 1974–; Vice-Pres. Royal Commonwealth Soc.; Dir. Sterling Winthrop Group and Sterling-Europa; Hon. Fellow, Royal Coll. of Surgeons of Edinburgh, Glasgow, Ireland, Australasia and Canada, American and South African Colls. of Surgeons, Royal Coll. of Physicians of U.K. and Australasia, Royal Coll. of Obstetricians and Gynaecologists, Royal Australian Coll. of Radiologists; Hon. LL.D. (St. Andrews, Birmingham, Otago and New Zealand), Hon. D.Sc. (Oxford), Hon. M.D. (Bristol); Bronze Medal 100 metres, Olympic Games 1924. *Publications:* Athletics (with D. G. A. Lowe) 1929, Essentials of Modern Surgery (with R. M. Handfield-Jones) 1939. *Address:* 57 Hamilton Terrace, London, NW8 9RG, England. *Telephone:* 01-286 9212.

PORTER, Andrew, M.A.; British music critic; b. 26 Aug. 1928, Cape Town, S.A.; s. of Andrew Ferdinand and Vera Sybil (Bloxham) Porter; ed. Diocesan Coll., Rondebosch, Cape Town, University Coll., Oxford; Music critic the Financial Times 1950–74; Ed. The Musical Times 1960–67; music critic The New Yorker 1972–; Visiting Fellow All Souls Coll., Oxford 1973–74; Bloch Prof., Univ. of Calif., Berkeley 1981; ASCAP–Deems Taylor Award 1975, 1978, 1982, Nat. Music Theater Award 1988; mem. American Acad. of Arts and Sciences 1984. *Publications:* A Musical Season 1974, Wagner's Ring 1976, Music of Three Seasons 1978, Music of Three More Seasons 1981, Verdi's "Macbeth": A Sourcebook (ed. with David Rosen) 1984, Musical Events: A Chronicle 1980–83 1987, 1983–86 1989. *Leisure interest:* architecture. *Address:* c/o The New Yorker, 25 West 43rd Street, New York, N.Y. 10036, U.S.A. *Telephone:* (212) 536 5400.

PORTER, Arthur T., M.A., PH.D., M.R.S.L.; Sierra Leonean professor and administrator; b. 26 Jan. 1924, Freetown; s. of Guy H. and Adina A. Porter; m. Rigmor Søndergaard Rasmussen 1953; one s. one d.; ed. Fourah Bay Coll., Sierra Leone, Cambridge Univ., Inst. of Educ., London and Boston Univ., U.S.A.; Asst. Dept. of Social Anthropology Edinburgh Univ. 1951–52; Lecturer in History Fourah Bay Coll. 1952–56; research in African Studies, Boston Univ. 1956–58; Prof. of Modern History Fourah Bay Coll., later Vice-Prin. 1960–64; Prin. Univ. Coll., Nairobi 1964–70; UNESCO Adviser on Ministry of Educ., Educ. Planning to Kenya Govt. 1970–74; Vice-Chancellor Univ. of Sierra Leone 1974–84; Fulbright Scholar-in-Residence, Bethany Coll., Kan. 1986–87; Hon. L.H.D. (Boston) 1969, Hon. LL.D. (Royal Univ. of Malta) 1969; Sierra Leone Independence Medal 1961; mem. Order of the Republic of Sierra Leone 1979; Yugoslav Flag with Gold Star, Synos Award Asscn. of Commonwealth Univs. 1985. *Publication:* Creoledom 1963. *Leisure interest:* photography. *Address:* New Cottage, 26B Spur Road, P.O. Box 1363, Freetown, Sierra Leone. *Telephone:* 31736.

PORTER, Eric Richard; British actor; b. 8 April 1928, London; s. of Richard John Porter and Phoebe Elizabeth Porter (née Spall); ed. L.C.C. and Wimbledon Tech. Coll.; first professional appearance in Shakespeare, Arts Theatre, Cambridge 1945; first appearance, London stage in Saint Joan 1946; Bristol Old Vic. Co. 1954, 1955–56; with Old Vic. Co. 1954–55; British tour with Lynne Fontanne and Alfred Lunt 1957, New York 1958; joined R.S.C. 1960: roles include Barabbas (The Jew of Malta), Shylock (The Merchant of Venice) 1965, Chorus (Henry V) 1965, Osip (The Government Inspector); title roles, King Lear, Dr. Faustus, Stratford 1968; toured Dr. Faustus with R.S.C. 1969; actor and Dir. My Little Boy—My Big Girl 1969, The Protagonist 1971, Capt. Hook, Mr. Darling in Peter Pan 1971, Twelfth Night, St. George's Elizabethan Theatre 1976; Big Daddy in Cat on a Hot Tin Roof 1988, King Lear 1989. *Films include:* The Fall of the Roman Empire 1964, The Pumpkin Eater 1964, The Heroes of Telemark 1965, Kaleidoscope 1966, The Lost Continent 1968, Hands of the Ripper 1971, Nicholas and Alexandra 1971, Anthony and Cleopatra 1972, The Last Ten Days of Hitler 1973, The Day of the Jackal 1973, The Belstone Fox 1973, Callan 1974, Hennessy 1975, The Thirty-Nine Steps 1978, Little Lord Fauntleroy

1980; many television appearances include title role, Cyrano de Bergerac, Jack Tanner (Man and Superman), Soames Forsyte (The Forsyte Saga), Separate Tables, Tolstoy, Macbeth 1970, When We Are Married, The Glittering Prizes, The Canal Children, The Winslow Boy, Anna Karenina, Alanbrooke (Churchill and the Generals), Polonius (Hamlet), The Crucible, The Sinbin, Neville Chamberlain, Churchill: The Wilderness Years, A Shilling Life, Jewel in the Crown, Moriarty (Sherlock Holmes), Fagin (Oliver Twist); Evening Standard Drama Award Best Actor of 1959, 1988, Guild of Television Producers and Directors Award to Television Actor of the Year 1967. *Leisure interests:* walking, cooking. *Address:* c/o London Management, 235/241 Regent Street, London, W1A 2JT, England.

PORTER, Sir George, Kt., M.A., PH.D., SC.D., P.R.S., F.R.S.; British professor of chemistry; b. 6 Dec. 1920, Stainforth; s. of late John Smith Porter and of Alice Ann Porter; m. Stella Brooke 1949; two s.; ed. Thorne Grammar School, Leeds Univ. and Emmanuel Coll., Cambridge; war service in R.N.V.R.; Demonstrator Physical Chemistry, Univ. of Cambridge 1949–52, Asst. Dir. of Research 1952–54; Prof. of Physical Chemistry, Univ. of Sheffield 1955–63, Firth Prof. and Head of Dept. of Chemistry 1963–66; Prof. of Chemistry, The Royal Institution, London 1963–66; Dir. The Royal Inst. 1966–85, Fullerian Prof. of Chemistry 1966–88, Emer. Prof. 1988–; Prof. of Photochemistry, Imperial Coll., London 1986–; Pres. The Royal Soc. 1985–; Chancellor Leicester Univ. 1985–; Pres. Comité Int. de Photobiologie 1968–72; Pres. Chemical Soc. 1970–72, Faraday Div. 1973–74, Nat. Asscn. for Gifted Children 1975–80; mem. Aeronautical Research Council 1964–66, of Council Open Univ. 1969–75, Science Museum Advisory Council 1970–73; Trustee, British Museum 1972–74; mem. Science Research Council 1976–80, Science Bd. 1976–80; Pres. Research and Devt. Soc. 1977–82; mem. R.S.A. Council 1978–80; Dir. of Applied Photophysics Ltd. 1971–; Pres. The Asscn. for Science Educ. 1985; Pres. British Asscn. for the Advancement of Science 1985–86; Foreign mem. Acad. of Sciences, Lisbon 1983, Inst. of Fundamental Studies, Sri Lanka 1985; Foreign Corresp. mem. La Real Acad. de Ciencias, Madrid 1978; Hon. mem. New York Acad. of Sciences 1968, Leopoldina Acad. 1970, Pontifical Acad. of Sciences 1974, Société de Chimie Physique (now Société Française de Chimie) 1979, Chemical Soc. of Japan 1982, American Philosophical Soc. 1986, Acad. dei Lincei 1988, Hungarian Acad. of Sciences 1988; Foreign Hon. mem. American Acad. of Arts and Sciences 1979; mem. Académie Int. de Lutèce 1979, U.S.S.R. Acad. of Sciences 1988, Acad. Europaea 1988; Foreign Assoc. U.S. Nat. Acad. of Sciences, Washington; Corresp. mem. Göttingen Acad. of Sciences; Hon. Fellow Inst. of Patentees & Investors 1970; Hon. Fellow, Emmanuel Coll., Cambridge; Hon. Prof. of Physical Chem., Univ. of Kent; Visiting Prof., Univ. Coll., London, Dept. of Chem. 1967–, Imperial Coll., London 1978–; Hitchcock Prof. Univ. of Calif. at Berkeley 1978; Robertson Memorial Lecturer 1978; Romanes Lecturer Oxford 1978; Hon. Prof. Chinese Acad. of Sciences, Dalian 1980; Counsellor, Inst. for Molecular Sciences, Okazaki, Japan 1980–83; Hon. D.Sc. (Univ. of Sheffield 1968, Univ. of Utah 1968, Univs. of East Anglia, Durham 1970, Univs. of Leicester, Leeds, Heriot-Watt, City Univ. 1971, Univs. of Manchester, St. Andrews, London 1972, Kent 1973, Oxford 1974, Hull 1980, Rio de Janeiro 1980, Instituto Quimico de Sarria, Barcelona 1981, Univs. of Pennsylvania, Coimbra, Portugal, Open Univ. 1983, Lille 1984, Univ. of Philippines 1985, Loughborough Univ. of Tech.) 1987, (Brunel) 1988; Dr. h.c. (Open Univ.) 1983; Hon. D.Univ. (Surrey) 1970, (Bologna) 1988; Hon. Freeman of the Salters' Co. 1981; Corday-Morgan Medal Chemical Soc. 1955; Liversidge Lecturer, Chem. Soc. 1969; shared with Prof. R. G. W. Norrish half of Nobel Prize for Chem. for work on photo-chem. 1967; Davy Medal, Royal Soc. 1971; Fairchild Distinguished Scholar, Calif. Inst. Tech. 1974; 1976 Kalinga Prize for the Popularisation of Science 1977; Robertson Prize of the Nat. Acad. of Sciences 1978; Rumford Medal (Royal Society) 1978; Communications Award of the European Physical Society 1978, Faraday Medal of Chemical Soc. 1980, Longstaff Medal of RSC 1981, Humphry Davy Lecturer at Royal Soc. 1985, Richard Dimbleby Lecture (BBC) 1988. *Publications:* Chemistry for the Modern World 1962, Progress in Reaction Kinetics (Ed.), and numerous scientific papers; B.B.C. Television series: Laws of Disorder 1965, Time Machines 1969–70, Natural History of a Sunbeam 1976. *Leisure interest:* sailing. *Address:* The Royal Society, 6 Carlton House Terrace, London, SW1Y 5AG, England.

PORTER, Sir Leslie, Kt.; British company executive; b. 10 July 1920, London; s. of Henry Alfred and Jane (Goldstein) Porter; m. Shirley Cohen 1949; one s. one d.; ed. Holloway Coll.; served British Army 1939–46; Man. Dir. J. Porter & Co. Ltd., importers and distributors 1946–60; joined Tesco Stores (Holdings) PLC, superstores, supermarkets, chain stores, furniture stores 1961, Man. Dir. and Deputy Chair. 1972–73, Chair. and Chief Exec. 1973–85, Pres. 1985–; Chair. Unicorn Heritage PLC; Chair. Sports Aid Foundation 1985–88, Hon. Vice-Pres. 1988–; Int. Vice-Pres. Museum of the Diaspora; mem. Lloyds 1966–; fmr. Pres. Inst. Grocery Distribution (IGD); mem. President's Council, Baptist Coll. of Hong Kong; Vice-Pres. Nat. Playing Fields Asscn.; Hon. Ph.D. *Leisure interests:* golf, yachting, tennis, bridge. *Address:* c/o Tesco PLC, Hammond House, 117 Piccadilly, London, W.1, England. *Telephone:* 01-629 2484.

PORTER, Robert; Australian professor of medical research; b. 10 Sept. 1932, S. Australia; s. of William J. and late Amy (née Tottman) Porter; m. Anne D. Steell 1961; two s. two d.; ed. Univs. of Adelaide and Oxford; House Physician and House Surgeon, Radcliffe Infirmary, Oxford 1959–60;

Univ. Lecturer in Physiology, Oxford 1961–67; Medical Tutor and Fellow, St. Catherine's Coll., Oxford 1963–67; Prof. of Physiology, Monash Univ. 1967–80; Dir. John Curtin School of Medical Research and Howard Florey Prof. of Medical Research, A.N.U. 1980–; Rhodes Scholar 1954; Radcliffe Travelling Fellow in Medical Science 1963–64; Sr. Fulbright Fellow, Washington Univ. School of Medicine, St. Louis 1973; Fogarty Scholar-in-Residence, Nat. Inst. of Health, Bethesda 1986–87. *Publications:* Corticospinal Neurones: Their Role in Movement (with C. G. Phillips) 1977; articles on neurophysiology. *Leisure interest:* sport. *Address:* John Curtin School of Medical Research, Australian National University, G.P.O. Box 334, Canberra City, A.C.T. 2601; 85 Brereton Street, Garran, A.C.T. 2605, Australia. *Telephone:* (062) 492597; (062) 810383.

PORTISCH, Lajos; Hungarian chess player; b. 4 April 1937; s. of Lajos Portisch Sr. and Anna Simon; mem. MTK-VM Sport Club; top ranking player of Hungary's selected team 1962–; nine times Hungarian champion; holder of Int. Grand Master title 1961–; European team Bronze Medallist 1961, 1965, 1973; team Silver Medallist 1970, 1977, 1980; Olympic Team Bronze Medallist 1956, 1966, Silver 1970, 1972, 1980, Gold 1978; qualified seven times as cand. for the individual chess world title; holder of Master Coach qualification; Labour Order of Merit (golden degree). *Publication:* Six Hundred Endings (co-author with B. Sárközi) 1973. *Leisure interest:* music. *Address:* Hungarian Chess Federation, 1055 Budapest, Néphadsereg utca 10, Hungary. *Telephone:* 116-616.

POSCH, Fritz (Friedrich), DR.PHIL.; Austrian historian; b. 30 March 1911, Weinreith bei Hartberg, Steiermark; s. of Franz Posch and Johanna Posch; m. Edeltraud Elsässer; ed. Univ. of Gras, Inst. für österreichische Geschichtsforschung, Vienna 1936–38; mil. service and prisoner-of-war 1940–48; with Land Govt. of Steiermark 1948–76, Dir. of Archives 1956–76; Hon. Prof. Univ. of Graz 1962; Pres. Styrian Historical Assen.; Chair. Comm. for the Historical Atlas of the Austrian Alpine Regions, Acad. of Sciences; mem. Austrian Acad.; Grosses Goldenes Ehrenzeichen der Republik Österreich, Österreichisches Ehrenkreuz für Wissenschaft und Kunst; many other awards and prizes. *Publications:* around 300 publs. including: Siedlungsgeschichte der Oststeiermark 1941, Die Besiedlung des Weizer Bodens 1956, Flammende Grenze 1968, Atlas zur Geschichte des steirischen Bauerntums 1976, Grosse geschichtliche Landeskunde der Steiermark 1978, Die Zinsregister des Chorherrenstiftes Vorau aus dem 15. Jahrhundert 1986. *Leisure interest:* mountain walking. *Address:* 8010 Graz, Theodor-Körner-Strasse 151; 8046 Rannach 44, Austria. *Telephone:* 0316/62-76-52 (Graz); 0316/69-14-053 (Rannach).

POSER, Hans August Louis, DR.PHIL.; German professor of geography; b. 13 March 1907, Hanover; s. of the late Friedrich Poser and Emilie Tönnies; m. Johanna von Stiepel 1933; three s.; ed. Univ. of Göttingen; Asst., Sr. Asst. Univ. of Göttingen 1930–36, Lecturer in Geography 1936–41; Navy and Army service 1939–45; Lecturer, Assoc. Prof. and Head, Geographical Inst. Tech. Univ. of Brunswick 1941–55, mem. Senate 1954–55; Prof. and Dir. Geographical Inst. Tech. Univ. of Hanover 1955–62, Dean, Faculty of Natural Sciences and Humanities 1957–58, mem. Senate 1957–61; Prof. and Dir. of Geographical Inst. Univ. of Göttingen 1962–71, Prof. Emer. 1971–; mem. numerous acads., learned socs. etc.; recipient of several awards and medals; Dr.rer.nat. h.c. (Technical Univ. Brunswick) 1986; Bundesverdienstkreuz 1982. *Publications:* several books and more than 85 articles on geomorphology, climatology of ice age, human and regional geography. *Leisure interests:* reading, collection of graphic art, gardening. *Address:* Ernst-Curtius-Weg 5, 3400 Göttingen, Federal Republic of Germany. *Telephone:* 0551-43845.

POSIBEYEV, Grigoriy Andreyevich; Soviet party official; b. 1935; ed. Leningrad Agric. Inst.; mem. CPSU 1959–; Komsomol posts 1959–65; Sec. of Leningrad Dist. Cttee. U.S.S.R. Komsomol 1965–67; First Sec. of Kingisepp Regional Cttee. of CPSU, Leningrad Dist. 1968–71; head of a dept., Leningrad Dist. Cttee. 1971–75, Sec. 1975–81; First Sec. of Dist. Cttee. in Mari A.S.S.R. 1981–; cand. mem. of Cen. Cttee. CPSU 1981–; Deputy to U.S.S.R. Supreme Soviet. *Address:* Central Committee of Communist Party of the Soviet Union, Kremlin, Moscow, U.S.S.R.

POSNETT, Sir Richard Neil, K.B.E., C.M.G., M.A.; British colonial administrator and diplomatist; b. 19 July 1919, Kotagiri, India; s. of Rev. Charles Walker Posnett and Phyllis (née Barker); m. Shirley Margaret Hudson 1959; two s. one d. (two s. one d. by previous marriage); ed. Kingswood School, St. John's Coll., Cambridge; R.A.F. 1940; Colonial Admin. Service, Uganda 1941–62; Chair. Uganda Olympic Cttee. 1954–58; Judicial Adviser 1960; Perm. Sec. for Social Devt., External Affairs, Trade and Industry 1961–63; Foreign Office 1964–66; U.K. Mission to UN 1966–70; briefly H.M. Commr., Anguilla 1969; Head of West Indian Dept., FCO 1970–72; Gov. and C.-in-C., Belize 1972–76; mission to Ocean Island (Banaba) 1977; FCO Adviser on Dependent Territories 1977–79; High Commr. in Uganda April–Nov. 1979; Gov. and C.-in-C. Bermuda 1981–83; U.K. Commr., Bd. of British Phosphate Commrs. 1978–81; Lord Chancellor's Panel of Ind. Inspectors 1983–; Gov. Kingswood School; Pres. Godalming-Joigny Friendship Assen.; mem. Royal Inst. of Int. Affairs, Royal African Soc., Royal Forestry Soc.; Fellow, Royal Commonwealth Soc.; K. St. J. 1972. *Publications:* articles in World Today and Uganda Journal. *Leisure interests:* skiing, growing trees. *Address:* Timbers, Northway, Godalming, Surrey, England. *Telephone:* (048 68) 6869.

POSNETTE, Adrian Frank, C.B.E., SC.D., F.R.S.; British research scientist; b. 11 Jan. 1914, Birmingham; s. of F. W. Posnette and E. Posnette (née Webber); m. Isabelle La Roche 1937; one s. two d.; ed. Cheltenham Grammar School, Christ's Coll. Cambridge and Imperial Coll. of Tropical Agriculture, Trinidad; Econ. Botanist, Gold Coast Govt. (Colonial Service) 1937–44; Head of Botany and Plant Pathology, W. African Cacao Research Inst. 1944–49; Virologist, E. Malling Research Station, England 1949–57, Head, Plant Pathology Dept. 1957–69, Deputy Dir. E. Malling Research Station 1969–72, Dir. 1972–79; Scientific Adviser, Chocolate Confectionery Alliance, London 1979–85; Hon. Prof. in Plant Sciences, Wye Coll., Univ. of London 1971–78; Jones-Bateman Cup, Royal Horticultural Soc. 1958, Victoria Medal of Honour 1982; Ridley Medal, Fruiterers' Co. 1978. *Publications:* Virus Diseases of Cacao in West Africa (in Annals of Applied Biology), Virus Diseases of Apples and Pears (Ed.) 1963, over 100 research papers on virus diseases of fruit crops in scientific journals. *Leisure interests:* gardening, ornithology. *Address:* Walnut Tree, East Sutton, Maidstone, Kent, ME17 3DR, England. *Telephone:* (0622) 843282.

POSOKHIN, Mikhail Vasiliyevich; Soviet architect and politician; b. 13 Dec. 1910, Tomsk; m. Galina Arkadeyevna Posokhina 1947; one s.; ed. Moscow Architecture Inst.; decorator of a theatre 1929; technician, work superintendent, architect, at construction of Kuznetsk iron and steel works 1928–35; Leading Architect, Moscow Design Dept. 1935–, Moscow Architecture Dept. 1938–60; Moscow Chief Architect 1960–; Chair. State Cttee. for Civil Eng. and Architecture and Vice-Chair. U.S.S.R. State Cttee. for Construction at U.S.S.R. Council of Ministers 1963–67; Head, Main Admin. of Architecture and Planning of Moscow, Chief Architect of Moscow 1967–80; Moscow Chief Architect and Academician-Sec., Section "Architecture and Monumental Art", U.S.S.R. Acad. of Arts 1980–88; Head of team working on gen. plan of Moscow to 1985 1971–; mem. CPSU 1961–; Deputy to U.S.S.R. Supreme Soviet (Soviet of Union) 1962–79, Deputy to Supreme Soviet, R.S.F.S.R. 1980–84; mem. Comm. for Construction and Bldg. Materials Industry, Soviet of Union, Presidium of U.S.S.R. Union of Architects, Soviet Peace Cttee., Cttee. U.S.S.R. Parl. Group; Fellow, U.S.S.R. Acad. of Arts 1979–; Hon. F.A.I.A. 1978–; State Prize 1949, 1980, Order of Red Banner of Labour, Order of Lenin (three times); prin. designs include multi-storeyed block of flats, Vosstaniy Square, Moscow 1948, Palace of Congresses in the Kremlin, Moscow 1961, U.S.S.R. Pavilion at Expo, Montreal 1967, Osaka 1970, U.S.S.R. Embassy in Brasília, Sports Complex "Olimpiyskiy" Moscow 1980, Complex of U.S.S.R. Acad. of Social Sciences 1985; People's Architect of U.S.S.R. *Publications:* A City for People 1973, sistemni analis i problemi razvitia gorodov 1983. *Leisure interest:* painting. *Address:* Executive Committee, Moscow City Soviet of Working People's Deputies, 13 Ulitsa Gorkogo, Moscow, U.S.S.R.

POSPELOV, Germogen Sergeyevich; Soviet automation specialist; b. 25 May 1914, Orekhovo-Zuevo, Moscow Dist.; s. of Sergei Alecseevich and Elizaveta Vasiljevna Pospelova; m. Muza Valentinovna Zenina 1946; one s.; ed. Moscow Energetics Inst.; mem. CPSU 1943; engineer with airborne regt. 1941–46; teacher at Zhukovsky Mil. Aviation Eng. 1946–64, Prof. 1957–; Deputy Chair. of Section of Applied Problems at Presidium of Acad. of Sciences 1964–70, Chair. 1970–73; head of Chair at Physical-Tech. Inst., Moscow 1969–; Head of Lab. at Computer Centre of Acad. of Sciences 1974–; corresp. mem. U.S.S.R. Acad. of Sciences 1984–; Chair. of Artificial Intelligence Council, Tech. Cybernetics Journal; State Prize 1972, Lenin Order 1984, various medals and orders. *Publications:* Goal-Programming Planning and Management 1976, Procedures and Algorithms of Complex Programmes Formation 1985, System Analysis and Artificial Intelligence 1980, Artificial Intelligence 1980, Artificial Intelligence—the Base of New Information Technology 1987. *Leisure interests:* touring, country skiing. *Address:* Computer Centre, U.S.S.R. Academy of Sciences, Moscow, U.S.S.R.

POSTEL-VINAY, André; French civil servant; b. 4 June 1911, Paris; s. of Marcel Postel-Vinay and Madeleine Delombre; m. Anise Girard 1946; four c.; ed. Univ. of Paris; Financial Inspector 1938; Gen. Man. Caisse Centrale de Coopération Economique 1944–72; Pres. de la Comm. des opérations de bourse 1973–74; Commdr. Légion d'honneur, Compagnon de la Libération, Membre du Conseil de l'Ordre de la Libération, Grand Croix de l'Ordre nat. du Mérite. *Address:* 7 place Pinel, 75013 Paris, France.

POSTGATE, John Raymond, D.PHIL., D.SC., F.R.S.; British professor of microbiology; b. 24 June 1922, London; s. of Raymond William and Daisy (née Lansbury) Postgate; m. Mary Stewart 1948; three d.; ed. Woodstock School, Kingsbury County School, Balliol Coll., Oxford; Sr. Research Investigator, Nat. Chemical Lab. 1949–50, Sr. Prin. 1950–59; Prin., Sr. Prin. Scientific Officer Microbiology Research Establishment 1959–63; Asst.-Dir. AFRC Unit of Nitrogen Fixation, Royal Veterinary Coll. 1963–65; Asst. Dir. AFRC Unit of Nitrogen Fixation, Univ. of Sussex 1965–80, Dir. 1980–87 and Prof. of Microbiology Univ. of Sussex 1965–87, Prof Emer. 1987–; Visiting Prof. Univ. of Ill. 1962–63, Ore. State Univ. 1977–78; Pres. Inst. of Biology 1982–84, Pres. Soc. for Gen. Microbiology 1984–87. *Publications:* Microbes and Man 1969, 1986, Biological Nitrogen Fixation 1972, Nitrogen Fixation 1978, 1987, The Sulphate-Reducing Bacteria 1979, 1984, The Fundamentals of Nitrogen Fixation 1982, A Plain Man's Guide to Jazz 1973. *Leisure interest:* listening to jazz and attempting to play it. *Address:* 1 Houndean Rise, Lewes, Sussex, BN7 1EG, England (Home). *Telephone:* (0273) 472675 (Home).

POSTNIKOV, Gen. Stanislav Ivanovich; Soviet military official; b. 1928; entered Soviet Army 1948; mem. CPSU 1957-; company commdr., battalion commdr., regimental commdr. 1951-67; graduated from Frunze Mil. Acad. 1961 and Mil. Acad. of Gen. Staff 1969; div. commdr. 1969-73; command posts 1975-79; Commdr. of Troops of Baltic Mil. Dist. 1979-; mem. of Cen. Cttee. and of Politburo of Latvian CP 1981-; mem. Cen. Auditing Comm. of CPSU 1981-; mem. Cen. Cttee. CPSU 1981-; Army Gen. 1986-. *Address:* Central Committee of Communist Party of Soviet Union, Kremlin, Moscow, U.S.S.R.

POSWICK, Charles, LL.D.; Belgian lawyer and politician; b. 6 Oct. 1924, Limbourg; s. of Jules Poswick and Marthe Roberti; Attaché, Cabinet of Prime Minister Eyskens 1949-50, later Asst. Chef de Cabinet, Ministry of Justice 1952-54; mem. of Parl. for Namur 1965-; Minister of Nat. Defence 1966-68; Vice-Pres. Parti de la Liberté et du Progrès (PLP) 1961-66, mem. Exec. Cttee. 1968-; Vice-Pres. Parl. 1977-, Pres. Nat. Defense Comm., Chamber of Reps. 1977-80; Pres. Conseil de la Communauté Française de Belgique 1984-85; Minister of Nat. Defence and of the Cabinet 1980; Pres. Conseil Régional Wallon 1985; partner Puissant Baeyens, Poswick and Co. (stockbrokers). *Address:* Puissant Baeyens, Poswick and Co., 36 rue Ravenstein, Brussels, Belgium. *Telephone:* 02-510 4511.

POTÁČ, Svatopluk, ING.; Czechoslovak banker and politician; b. 24 March 1925; ed. School of Economics, Prague; entered Státní Banka Československská 1952, Dept. Man. 1956-58, Chief Man. 1959-64, Deputy Gen. Man. 1964-69, Chair. of Bd. and Gen. Man. 1969-71, Pres. 1971-81; Deputy Prime Minister 1981-88; Chair. State Banking Comm. 1981; mem. Cen. Comm. of People's Control; mem. Scientific Council, Finance Research Inst.; mem. of Bd., Int. Bank for Econ. Co-operation, Moscow, Int. Investment Bank; Pres. of Directorate, Joint Stock Co. of the Czechoslovak Commercial Bank 1970-; Vice-Chair. Scientific Collegium of Econs. of Czechoslovak Acad. of Science; mem. Council for Int. Econ. Scientific and Technical Co-operation, State Comm. for Planning (fmr. Chair.), State Comm. for Wages, Cen. Cttee. CP of Czechoslovakia 1981-; Deputy of House of People, Fed. Assembly 1981-; Chair. Econ. Research Council of C.S.S.R. 1983-; Order of Labour 1975, Order of the Repub. of Czechoslovakia 1985. *Address:* Státní banka Československská, Prague 1, Na příkopě 28, Czechoslovakia.

POTAPENKO, Fyodor Ivanovich; Soviet diplomatist; b. 1927, Minsk; mem. of Cen. Comm. of Byelorussian CP 1960-69; Embassy Counsellor, Peking 1969-72; Counsellor, Ministry of Foreign Affairs 1972-75; Deputy Head, Far East Dept. at Ministry of Foreign Affairs 1975-80; Amb. to Singapore 1980-85, to Malaysia 1985-88. *Address:* Ministry of Foreign Affairs, Smolenskaya-Sennaya pl. 32/34, Moscow, U.S.S.R.

POTGIETER, Jacobus Ernst, B.A., B.D.; South African ecclesiastic (retd.); b. 12 May 1921, Benoni, Transvaal; m. Marthinet (Mercia) Van Der Merwe 1952; one s. one d.; ed. High School, Heidelberg, Univ. of Pretoria; began ministry in Dutch Reformed Church 1947, Student Pastor, Univ. of Pretoria 1955-68, Minister of Congregation, Pretoria 1968-80, Krokodilrivier (Brits) 1980-; Stated Clerk of Synod of N. Transvaal 1968-75, Moderator 1975-83; Stated Clerk Gen. Synod 1970-78, Assessor 1978-82, Moderator 1982-86. *Address:* P.O. Box 2021, Brits 0250, South Africa. *Telephone:* 01211-21989.

POTILA, Antti, M.SC.; Finnish business executive; b. 1 Nov. 1938, Kokemäki; s. of Erkki Potila and Helvi Potila (née Ekroos); m. Marjatta Rintala 1962; one d.; ed. Technical Univ. of Helsinki and Helsinki School of Econs. and Business Admin.; Sales Engineer, ASEA, Melbourne, Australia 1964; various positions with ÅOy Strömberg Ab 1964-78, Pres. and C.E.O. 1979-83; Chair. of Bd. of Orion Corpn. 1983-; Pres. and C.E.O. Rauma-Repola Corpn. 1984-86; Chair. and C.E.O. Finnair Oy 1987-, Chair subsidiaries of Finnair Oy 1987-; mem. Bd. of several Finnish cos. and industrial orgs.; Commr. of the Order of the Lion of Finland 1982. *Leisure interest:* aviation. *Address:* Finnair Oy, Mannerheimintie 102, 00250 Helsinki; Ullankatu 1 A 3, 00140 Helsinki, Finland (Home). *Telephone:* 0-81881 (Office); 0-637697 (Home).

POTTAKIS, Yannis A.; Greek politician; b. 1939, Corinth; m. Constantina (Alexopoulou) Pottaki; two s. one d.; ed. Univs. of Athens and Munich; founding mem. of Pasok; mem. Parl. 1977-; Alt. Minister of Nat. Economy July 1982-83, Minister of Finance 1983-84, of Agric. July 1985-; Chair. Council of Budget Ministers of EEC 1983. *Address:* Ministry of Agriculture, Odos Aharnon 2-6, Athens, Greece.

POTTER, Dennis (Christopher George), B.A.; British playwright, author and journalist; b. 17 May 1935; s. of Walter Potter and Margaret Potter; m. Margaret Morgan 1959; one s. two d.; ed. Bell's Grammar School, Coleford, Glos., St. Clement Danes Grammar School, New Coll., Oxford; Ed. Isis 1958; BBC TV (current affairs) 1959-61; Feature Writer, then TV Critic, Daily Herald 1961-64; Labour Parl. Cand. (East Herts) 1964; Leader Writer, The Sun Sept.-Oct. 1964 (then resgnd.); first TV play 1965; TV Critic, Sunday Times 1976-78. *TV plays:* Vote Vote Vote for Nigel Barton (also at Bristol Old Vic 1968; Soc. of Film and TV Arts Award 1966), Stand Up Nigel Barton, Where the Buffalo Roam, A Beast with Two Backs, Son of Man, Traitor, Paper Roses, Casanova, Follow the Yellow Brick Road, Only Make Believe, Joe's Ark, Schmoedipus, Late Call (adapted from novel by Angus Wilson) 1975, Brimstone and Treacle 1976 (not transmitted), Double Dare 1976, Where Adam Stood 1976, Pennies

from Heaven (sextet) 1978 (BAFTA Award 1978), Blue Remembered Hills 1979 (BAFTA Award 1980), Blade on the Feather, Rain on the Roof, Cream in my Coffee 1980 (Prix Italia 1982), Tender is the Night (sextet, from Scott Fitzgerald) 1985, The Singing Detective (six-part series) 1986, Visitors 1987, Christabel 1988, Lipstick on Your Collar (six-part series) 1989. *Screenplays:* Pennies from Heaven 1981, Brimstone and Treacle 1982, Gorky Park 1983, Dream Child 1985, Track 29 1987. *Stage play:* Sufficient Carbohydrate 1983. *Publications:* The Glittering Coffin 1960, The Changing Forest 1962; (plays) The Nigel Barton Plays 1968, Son of Man 1970, Brimstone and Treacle 1979, Sufficient Carbohydrate 1983, Waiting for the Boat (three plays) 1984; (novels) Hide and Seek 1973, Pennies from Heaven 1982, Blackeyes 1987. *Address:* Morecambe Lodge, Duxmere, Ross-on-Wye, Herefordshire, HR9 5BB, England. *Telephone:* (0989) 63199.

POTTER, Frank; Canadian international finance official; b. 20 July 1936; Exec. Dir. IBRD, IDA, Multilateral Guarantee Agency and Int. Finance Corpn. *Address:* 1818 H Street NW, Washington, D.C. 20433 (Office); Vinegar Hill Cottage, R.R.2 King, Ont., LOG 1KO, Canada (Home).

POTTER, Rev. Dr. Philip Alford, M.TH.; West Indian ecclesiastic; b. 19 Aug. 1921, Dominica; s. of the late Clement Potter and of Violet Peters; m. Doreen Cousins 1956 (died 1980); ed. Caenwood Theological Coll., Jamaica, Richmond Coll., England and London Univ.; Missionary and Overseas Sec. Student Christian Movement of Great Britain 1948-50; Minister, Methodist Church, Haiti 1950-54; World Council of Churches, Sec. Youth Dept. 1954-57, Exec. Sec. 1957-60, Dir. Comm. on World Mission and Evangelism 1967-72, Gen. Sec., Geneva 1972-84; Prof., United Theological Coll. of the West Indies, Kingston and Chaplain, Univ. of West Indies 1985-; Sec. for West Africa and West Indies, Methodist Missionary Soc., London 1961-66; Hon. Th.D. (Univ. of Hamburg 1971, Univ. of Geneva 1976, Theological Inst. of Romanian Orthodox Church 1977, Humboldt Univ., Berlin 1982, Univ. of Uppsala 1984, Univ. of Birmingham 1985); Hon. LL.D. (Univ. of West Indies) 1974; Niwano Peace Prize, Japan 1986. *Publications:* Key Words of the Gospel 1964, Explosives Lateinamerika (chapter in book edited by T. Tschuy); Review of Mission, Student World, 10 Fragen an die Weissen 1973, The Love of Power or The Power of Love 1974, Living the Christian Year 1975, Life in all its Fullness 1981; numerous articles in Ecumenical Review, International Review of Mission, Student World. *Leisure interests:* hiking, geology. *Address:* P.O. Box 136, Golding Avenue, Kingston 7, Jamaica.

POUILLOUX, Jean, D. ÈS L.; French university professor (retd.); b. 31 Oct. 1917, Le Vert; s. of F. Pouilloux and A. Kirner; m. Colette Fontaine 1940; two s. one d.; ed. Ecole Normale Supérieure; Prof. Univ. of Besançon 1954, Univ. Lumière, Lyons 1956, Prof. Emer. 1985-; Scientific Dir. C.N.R.S. 1975-82; mem. Acad. des Inscriptions et Belles Lettres, Pres. 1988; mem. Inst. de France, Acads. of Lyons, Bordeaux, Athens, Canada; Dr. h.c. (Salonica, Athens, Montreal). *Publications include:* Recherches sur l'histoire et les cultes de Tharos 1954-56, Recherches sur la forteresse de Rhamnonte 1954; publ. of works of Philon of Alexandria, reports of excavations in Delphi and Cyprus etc. *Leisure interests:* history, literature. *Address:* Maison de l'Orient, 7 rue Raulin, 69007 Lyons (Office); Pimotin, Tupin/Semans, 69420 Condrieu, France (Home). *Telephone:* 78.72.02.53 (Office); 74.59.51.19 (Home).

POUJADE, Pierre; French newspaper executive; b. 1 Dec. 1920, St. Céré; m. Yvette Seva 1944; three s. two d.; served in R.A.F., Second World War; after 1945 became publisher and bookseller, also active in politics; mem. St. Céré Municipal Council 1951; Founder Pres. Union de Défense de Commerçants et Artisans; Founder, Union et Fraternité Française; Founder Dir. Union et Défense (daily), Fraternité Française (weekly); Pres. Confédération Nat. des Travailleurs Indépendants 1970-; Pres. Nat. Assen. d'Assurance Maladie Obligatoire 1971-; Pres. Nat. Assen. l'Utilisation des Resources Energetiques Français (ANUREF) 1980-, Pres.-Founder l'Assen. Occitanie-Caraïbes; mem. Comm. Nat. de Carburants de Substitution 1983; mem. Conseil Economique et Social; creator of "La Vallée Heureuse" (gastronomic and tourist centre), La Bastide-l'Evêque; Founder and Pres. Centre de Formation Avicole, and Ferme Pieste, Château de Gouzou; Dir. Caisse Régionale, Midi-Pyrénées 1972-; f. Union pour la Défense des Libertés 1978; Croix du combattant volontaire, Medaille des Evadés. *Publications:* J'ai choisi le combat, A l'heure de la colère 1977, etc. *Leisure interest:* sport, particularly football and rugby. *Address:* "Vallée Heureuse", La Bastide-l'Evêque, 12200 Villefranche-de-Rouergue, France. *Telephone:* (65) 450205

POUJADE, Robert; French teacher and politician; b. 6 May 1928, Moulins (Allier); s. of Henri Poujade and Edmée (née Rival); m. Marie-Thérèse Monier 1953; one s.; ed. Ecole normale supérieure; Teacher of literature, Dijon 1954; Dept. Sec. of Fed. of Union of Democrats for Fifth Republic (U.N.R.) for Côte-d'Or 1958, mem. Cen. Cttee. and Exec. Bureau 1960, Sec.-Gen. 1968; Tech. Adviser to M. Maziol (Minister of Construction) Jan.-Feb. 1963; mem. Conseil Econ. et Social 1964-67; mem. Comm. for Econ. Devt. of Bourgogne Region 1965-73; Pres., Conseil régional Bourgogne of U.D.R., 1970-; Deputy for Côte-d'Or 1967-71, 1978-81, Pres. Conseil général 1981-; Sec.-Gen. UDR 1968-70; Minister for Protection of the Environment 1970-74; Insp. Gen. Public Instruction 1974-; M.P. for Côte-d'Or March 1986-; Mayor of Dijon 1971-; Vice-Pres. Association des

Maires de France 1983; Pres. Conservatoire du Littoral 1976–; Conseil nat. des villes d'art et d'histoire 1978, Comm. nationale des secteurs sauvegardés 1978–, Conseil d'administration de la Bibliothèque Nationale 1979; Chevalier, Légion d'honneur; Chevalier de l'Ordre national du Mérite; Chevalier des Palmes académiques; Commdr. des Arts et des Lettres; Rassemblement pour la République. *Publication:* Le Ministère de l'Impossible 1975. *Address:* Assemblée nationale, 75355 Paris; 10 boulevard Eugène Spuller, 21000 Dijon, France (Home).

POUKKA, (Kalle) Pentti, M.A.; Finnish newspaper editor; b. 13 Sept. 1919, Tampere; s. of Prof. Kalle Aukusti Poukka and Ina Irene Vihuri; m. Ejna Margarethe Jozua 1946; three s.; ed. Univ. of Helsinki; Publications Relations Officer Yhtyneet Paperitehtaat 1949–52; Research Worker, Taloudellinen Tutkimuskeskus; mem. Helsinki City Council 1965–, Chair. 1973–; Pres. Finnish Port Assen. 1968–74; Ed.-in-Chief Talouselämä 1954–55; Leader-writer and Economic Ed. Uusi Suomi 1955–57; Ed.-in-Chief Kauppalehti 1957–63, Uusi Suomi 1968. *Publications:* Teollisuuden rahoitus vv 1947–1952 (Financing Industry 1947–1952), Huomispäivän suomalainen (The Finn of Tomorrow), Porvarin Päiväkirja (Diary of a Bourgeois) 1969, Kapina Katsomossa (Revolt of the Audience) 1970, Purkkiin pantu ihminen (Canned Human) 1972, Tuntematon Sosialismi (Unknown Socialism) 1975. *Address:* Armas Lindgrenintie 11, 00570 Helsinki 1957, Finland. *Telephone:* 688949 (Home).

POULET, Georges M. Joseph; French government (overseas) official; b. 14 April 1914, Parnac, Indre; m. 1st Geneviève Duclos 1938, two s. one d.; m. 2nd Marjolaine Apestéguy 1967, one s. one d.; ed. Faculté de Droit, Paris, Coll. Chaptal de Paris and Ecole Nat. de la France d'Outre Mer; Head of Service of Political Affairs of Mauritania 1949–50; Sec.-Gen. of Mauritania 1955; Sec.-Gen., then Gov. of Polynesia 1957–59; Sec.-Gen. then High Commr. of New Caledonia 1960–64; Pres. Offices Postaux et Socs. Immobilières, Polynesia and New Caledonia; Gov. Territory of Islands of St. Pierre et Miquelon 1965–67; Head, French Mission of Co-operation, Chad 1967–71; Pres. Société d'Equipement, New Caledonia 1972; High Commr. Repub. of Comoros 1973; Econ. and Social Counsellor 1979–80; Counsellor of Foreign Trade of France 1981–87; Municipal Councillor of Saint Pierre 1984–; Officier, Légion d'honneur and other decorations. *Publications:* numerous publs. on Mauritania, Polynesia, New Caledonia etc. *Address:* BP 1100 Route de Galantry, 97500 Iles Saint Pierre et Miquelon. *Telephone:* (508) 41-31-53.

POUNCEY, Philip Michael Rivers, C.B.E., M.A., F.B.A.; British art historian; b. 15 Feb. 1910, Oxford; s. of the late Rev. G. E. Pouncey and Madeline Mary Roberts; m. 1937; two d.; ed. Marlborough Coll., Queens' Coll., Cambridge; Hon. Attaché at Fitzwilliam Museum, Cambridge 1931–33; Asst. at Nat. Gallery, London 1934–45; Asst. Keeper, Dept. of Prints and Drawings, British Museum 1945–54, Deputy Keeper 1954–66; Consultant on Italian paintings and drawings, Sotheby's 1966–. *Publications:* Catalogues of Italian drawings in the British Museum 1950, 1962, 1983 (co-author). *Leisure interest:* church music. *Address:* 5 Lower Addison Gardens, London, W14 8BG, England. *Telephone:* 01-603 3652.

POUND, Robert Vivian, B.A., M.A.(HON.); American physicist; b. 16 May 1919, Ridgeway, Ont., Canada; s. of V. E. Pound and Gertrude C. Prout; m. Betty Yde Andersen 1941; one s.; ed. Univ. of Buffalo and Harvard Univ.; Research Physicist, Submarine Signal Co., Boston, Mass. 1941–42; Staff mem. Radiation Laboratory, M.I.T. 1942–46; Jr. Fellow, Soc. of Fellows, Harvard Univ. 1945–48, Asst. Prof. 1948–50, Assoc. Prof. 1950–56, Prof. 1956–68, Mallinckrodt Prof. of Physics 1968–, Chair. Dept. of Physics 1968–72, Dir. Physics Labs. 1975–83; Zernike Prof. Groningen Univ. 1982; Visiting Prof. Coll. de France 1973, Univ. of Florida 1987; Visiting Fellow, Joint Inst. for Lab. Astrophysics, Univ. of Colorado 1979–80; Visiting Scientist Brookhaven Nat. Lab. 1986–87; Research Fellow, Merton Coll., Oxford 1980; mem. N.A.S.; Foreign Assoc. Académie des Sciences; Fellow, American Acad. of Arts and Sciences, American Physical Soc., A.A.A.S.; Fulbright Research Scholar, Oxford Univ. 1951; Fulbright Lecturer, Ecole Normale, Paris 1958; Guggenheim Fellow 1957–58, 1972–73; B. J. Thompson Memorial Award, Inst. of Radio Engineers 1948, Eddington Medal, Royal Astronomical Soc. 1965. *Publications:* Microwave Mixers 1948; papers on nuclear magnetism, electric quadrupole interactions, directional correlations of gamma rays, effect of gravity on gamma rays. *Address:* Lyman Laboratory of Physics, Harvard University, Cambridge, Mass. 02138 (Office); 87 Pinehurst Road, Belmont, Mass. 02178, U.S.A (Home). *Telephone:* (617) 495 2873 (Office); (617) 484 0254 (Home).

POUNDS, Kenneth Alwyne, C.B.E., PH.D., F.R.S.; British professor of space physics; b. 17 Nov. 1934, Leeds; s. of Harry Pounds and Dorothy Pounds (née Hunt); m. 1st Margaret Connell 1961; m. 2nd Joan Mary Millit 1982; three s. two d.; ed. Salt High School, Shipley, Yorks. and Univ. Coll. London; Dir. X-ray Astronomy Group, Univ. of Leicester 1973–, Prof. of Space Physics 1973–; mem. Int. Acad. of Astronautics. *Publications:* over 100 publs. in the scientific literature. *Leisure interests:* sport, music. *Address:* Department of Physics, University, Leicester, LE1 7RH (Office); 12 Swale Close, Oadby, Leics., LE2 4GF, England (Home). *Telephone:* (0533) 523509 (Office); (0533) 719370 (Home).

POUNGUI, Ange Edouard: Congolese economist and banker; began career in school, student unions; apptd. mem. Nat. Council for Revolution 1968,

then mem. Political Bureau, Minister for Finance 1971–73, Vice-Pres. Council of State and Minister for Planning 1973–76; Prime Minister of The Congo Aug. 1984–; worked for IMF and African Devt. Bank, then Dir.-Gen. Cen. African Bank 1976–79, then C.E.O. Congolese Commercial Bank. *Address:* Office du Premier Ministre, Brazzaville, Congo.

POUNTAIN, Sir Eric John, Kt., C.B.I.M., F.F.B., F.I.H.E.; British business executive; b. 5 Aug. 1933, Cannock Wood, Staffs.; s. of Horace and Elsie Pountain; m. Joan (née Sutton) 1960; one s. one d.; ed. Queen Mary's Grammar School, Walsall; joined F. Maitland Selwyn & Co., auctioneers and estate agents 1956, Jt. Principal 1959; f. Midland and General Devts. Ltd. (housebuilders) 1964; Chief Exec. John McLean & Sons Ltd. (following their takeover of Midland and General) 1969; Chief Exec. Tarmac Housing Div. (following takeover of John McLean by Tarmac Ltd.) 1974, Dir. Tarmac Ltd. 1977, Chief Exec. 1979, Deputy Chair. and Chief Exec. 1982, Chair. Tarmac PLC 1983–; non-exec. Dir. Glynwed Int. 1983–; non-exec. Dir. Beattie PLC 1984–, Deputy Chair. 1985–87, Chair. 1987–; non-exec. Dir. Midland Bank 1986–, IMI PLC 1988–. *Leisure interests:* farming, horse-breeding. *Address:* Edial House, Edial, Lichfield, Staffs., England.

POUPARD, H.E. Paul; French ecclesiastic; b. 30 Aug. 1930; ordained 1954; Titular Bishop of Usula 1979, Archbishop 1980; cr. Cardinal 1985; Deacon of S. Eugenio; Pres. Pontifical Council for Culture 1982; Pres. Pontifical Council for Dialogue with Non-Believers 1985. *Address:* Piazza San Calisto 16, 00153 Rome, Italy. *Telephone:* (06) 698 7393.

POVEDA BURBANO, Vice-Adm. Alfredo; Ecuadorean naval officer and politician; Minister of the Interior 1973–75; C.-in-C. of Navy 1975–79; Chief of Gen. Staff of Armed Forces Sept. 1975–Jan. 1976; Head of Mil. Junta which assumed power Jan. 1976; Pres. Supreme Council of Govt. 1976–79; Medalla de las Américas; Gran Cruz, Orden del Quetzal (Guatemala). *Address:* c/o Oficina del Presidente, Quito, Ecuador.

POWATHIL, Most Rev. Joseph, M.A., D.D.; Indian ecclesiastic; b. 14 Aug. 1930, Kurumpanadam; s. of Ulahannan Joseph Powathil; ordained R.C. Priest 1962; lecturer in Econs., St. Berchmans's Coll., Changanacherry 1963–72; Auxiliary Bishop of Changanacherry, Titular Bishop of Caesarea Philipi, 1972, consecrated Bishop 1972; 1st Bishop of Kanjirappally Diocese, Kerala 1977–86; Archbishop of Changanacherry 1985–; Chair. CBCI Comm. for Educ. and Clergy, KCBC Comm. for Educ., KCBC Comm. for Devt., Justice and Peace, SMBC Comm. for Ecumenism; mem. Pontifical Comm. for Dialogue with the Orthodox Syrian Church. *Address:* Archbishop of Changanacherry, Archbishop's House, Changanacherry 686 101, Kerala, India. *Telephone:* 20040.

POWELL, Anthony Dymoke, C.H., C.B.E.; British writer; b. 21 Dec. 1905, London; s. of Lieut.-Col. P. L. W. Powell, C.B.E., D.S.O., and Maud Mary Wells-Dymoke; m. Lady Violet Pakenham 1934; two s.; ed. Eton and Balliol Coll., Oxford; served Second World War in Welch Regiment and Intelligence Corps; mem. U.S. Acad. of Arts and Sciences; Hon. mem. Modern Languages Assen. of America; fmr. Trustee of Nat. Portrait Gallery; Orders of White Lion (Czechoslovakia), Léopold II (Belgium), Oaken Crown and Croix de Guerre (Luxembourg); James Tait Black Prize (for At Lady Molly's); Hon. D.Litt. (Sussex, Leicester, Kent, Oxford, Bristol); Hon. Fellow, Balliol Coll., Oxford 1974; W. H. Smith Award 1974; The Hudson Review Bennett Award 1984; Ingersoll Foundation T. S. Eliot Prize for Creative Writing 1984. *Publications:* Afternoon Men 1931 (performed as a play 1963), Venusberg 1932, From a View to a Death 1933, Agents and Patients 1936, What's Become of Waring 1939, John Aubrey and His Friends 1948, Selections from John Aubrey 1949, the Music of Time series: A Question of Upbringing 1951, A Buyer's Market 1952, The Acceptance World 1955, At Lady Molly's 1957, Casanova's Chinese Restaurant 1960, The Kindly Ones 1962, The Valley of Bones 1964, The Soldier's Art 1966, The Military Philosophers 1968, Books Do Furnish a Room 1971, Temporary Kings 1973, Hearing Secret Harmonies 1975, To Keep the Ball Rolling (memoir, incl. Infants of the Spring Vol. I 1976, Messengers of Day Vol. II 1978, Faces in my Time Vol. III 1980, The Strangers All are Gone Vol. IV 1982), A Dance to the Music of Time (novel-cycle, omnibus edn.) 1977, O, How the Wheel Becomes It! (novella) 1983, The Fisher King 1986, The Album of Music of Time (ed. Violet Powell) 1987. Plays: The Garden God, The Rest I'll Whistle 1971. *Address:* The Chantry, near Frome, Somerset, England. *Telephone:* (0373 84) 314.

POWELL, Sir (Arnold Joseph) Philip, Kt., C.H., O.B.E., R.A., R.I.B.A., A.A.DIPL.(HONS.); British architect; b. 15 March 1921, Bedford; s. of late Canon A. C. Powell and late Mary Winnifred (née Walker); m. Philippa Eccles 1953; one s. one d.; ed. Epsom Coll. and Architectural Assen. School of Architecture; in pvt. practice 1946–, as Powell, Moya and Partners, Architects; Treas. R.A.; won Westminster City Council's Pimlico Housing Competition (Churchill Gardens) 1946, Festival of Britain Vertical Feature (Skylon) Competition 1950; R.I.B.A. Bronze Medals, R.I.B.A. Awards, Housing Medals, Civic Trust Awards, Concrete Soc. Award, Carpenter's Award, R.I.B.A. Royal Gold Medal for Architecture 1974; mem. Royal Fine Art Comm. *Works include:* Churchill Gardens Flats, Westminster 1948–62; houses and flats at Gospel Oak, London 1954, houses at Chichester 1950, Toy's Hill 1954, Oxshott 1954, Leamington 1956, Baughurst (Hants.) 1954; "Skylon", Festival of Britain 1951; Mayfield School, Putney 1955, Plumstead Manor School, Woolwich 1970; extensions to Brasenose Coll.

Oxford 1961 and Corpus Christi Coll. Oxford 1969, picture gallery and undergraduates' rooms, Christ Church, Oxford 1967, new bldgs. at St. John's Coll. Cambridge 1967, Queens' Coll., Cambridge 1978; Chichester Festival Theatre 1961; Public Swimming Baths, Putney 1967; mental hosp. extensions, Fairmile 1957, Borocourt 1965, hospitals at Swindon, Slough, High Wycombe, Wythenshawe, Woolwich and Maidstone; British Pavilion at Expo 70, Osaka, Japan; Museum of London 1977; Dining rooms at Bath Acad. of Art 1970; Wolfson Coll., Oxford 1974; Headquarters, London & Manchester Assurance, nr. Exeter 1978, Nat. Westminster Bank, Shaftesbury Ave., London 1982, new bldgs. for Royal Holloway and Bedford New Coll., Egham 1986, Queen Elizabeth II Conf. Centre, Westminster 1986. *Address:* Powell, Moya and Partners, Architects, 21 Upper Cheyne Row, London, S.W.3; 16 The Little Boltons, London, S.W.10, England (Home).

POWELL, Colin Luther, M.B.A.; American army officer; b. 5 April 1937, New York; s. of Luther Powell and Maud A. McKoy; m. Alma V. Johnson 1962; one s. two d.; ed. City Univ. of New York and George Washington Univ.; commissioned U.S. Army 1958, Lieut. Gen. 1986; Commdr. 2nd Brigade, 101st Airborne Div. 1976–77; Exec. Asst. to Sec. Dept. of Energy 1979; Sr. Mil. Asst. to Sec. Dept. of Defense 1979–81; Asst. Div. Commdr. 4th Infantry Div. Fort Carson, Colo. 1981–83; Mil. Asst. to Sec. of Defense 1983–86; assigned to U.S. V Corps, Europe 1986–87; Nat. Security Adviser, White House, Washington 1987–88; C.-in-C. US Forces in Europe; Legion of Merit, Bronze Star, Air Medal, Purple Heart. *Address:* c/o White House, Washington, D.C. 20500, U.S.A.

POWELL, Enoch (see Powell, John Enoch).

POWELL, John, M.A., D.PHIL., C.ENG., F.I.E.E., F.R.S.(E), F.R.S.A.; British physicist and business executive; b. 4 Nov. 1923, Islip; s. of Algy and Constance Elsie Powell; m. Zena (née Steventon) Powell 1949; one s. one d.; ed. Bicester County School, No. 1 School of Tech. Training, R.A.F. and Queen's Coll., Oxford; Research Fellow, Nat. Research Laboratory, Ottawa 1952–54; Section Leader, Semi-Conductor Research and Devt., Marconi Research Laboratories; joined Texas Instruments (N. Europe) Ltd. 1957, Gen. Man. Tech. 1959, Product Group Man. 1960, Asst. Man. Dir. Operations 1962, Man. Dir. Northern Europe 1963, Asst. Vice-Pres. Texas Instruments Inc. 1968; Group Tech. Dir. EMI Ltd. 1971, Dir. for Commercial Electronics 1972, Deputy Man. Dir. 1973, Man. Dir. 1974–78, Group Vice-Chair. 1978–79, Consultant 1979–; mem. Honeywell Advisory Council 1978–81; mem. Finniston Cttee. of Inquiry into the Eng. Profession 1978–80, Physical Sciences Sub-Cttee. of Univ. Grants Cttee. 1979–85; Trustee, Radiological Research Trust; Faraday Lecturer 1978–79; Hon. mem. British Inst. of Radiology. *Leisure interests:* swimming, gardening, golf. *Address:* Kym House, 21 Buccleuch Road, Branksome Park, Poole, Dorset, BH13 6LD, England. *Telephone:* (0202) 763925.

POWELL, Rt. Hon. (John) Enoch, P.C., M.B.E., M.A., M.P.; British politician; b. 16 June 1912, Birmingham; s. of Albert Enoch and Ellen Mary (Breese) Powell; m. Margaret Pamela Wilson 1952; two d.; ed. King Edward's School, Birmingham, and Trinity Coll., Cambridge; Fellow Trinity Coll., Cambridge 1934–38; Prof. of Greek, Univ. of Sydney, N.S.W. 1937–39; army service rising to rank of Brig. 1939–46; Conservative mem. Parl. for Wolverhampton S.W. 1950–74, Ulster Unionist mem. Parl. for Down, South Oct. 1974–83, for South Down 1983–85, 1986–87; Parl. Sec. Ministry of Housing and Local Govt. 1955–57; Financial Sec. to Treasury 1957–58; Minister of Health 1960–63; Dir. Nat. Discount Co. 1964–68; mem. House of Commons Select Cttee. on Procedure 1976–. *Publications:* The Rendel Harris Papyri 1936, First Poems 1937, A Lexicon to Herodotus 1938, The History of Herodotus 1939, Casting-off, and other poems 1939, Herodotus, Book VIII 1939, Llyfr Blegywryd 1942, Thucydidis Historia 1942, Herodotus (transl.) 1949, One Nation (jointly) 1950, Dancer's End and The Wedding Gift (poems) 1951, The Social Services, Needs and Means 1952, Change is our Ally 1954, Biography of a Nation 1955, Saving in a Free Society 1960, Great Parliamentary Occasions 1960, A Nation Not Afraid 1965, A New Look at Medicine and Politics 1966, The House of Lords in the Middle Ages (with Keith Wallis) 1968, Freedom and Reality 1969, Still to Decide 1972, No Easy Answers 1973, Medicine and Politics: 1975 and After 1976, Wrestling with the Angel 1977, Joseph Chamberlain 1977, A Nation or No Nation 1978, Enoch Powell on 1992 1989. *Address:* 33 South Eaton Place, London, S.W.1, England. *Telephone:* 01-730 0988.

POWELL, Jonathan Leslie; British television producer; b. 25 April 1947, Faversham, Kent; s. of James Dawson Powell and Phyllis N. Sylvester (née Doubleday); ed. Sherborne School and Univ. of East Anglia; script ed. and producer of drama, Granada TV 1970–77; producer, drama serials, BBC TV 1977–83, Head of Drama Series and Serials 1983–; Controller BBC 1 Nov. 1987–; Royal TV Soc. Silver Award 1979–80. *Television serials include:* Testament of Youth 1979 (BAFTA award), Tinker, Tailor, Soldier, Spy 1979, Pride and Prejudice 1980, The Bell 1982, Smiley's People 1982 (Peabody Medal, U.S.A.), The Old Men at the Zoo 1983, Bleak House 1985, Tender is the Night 1985. *Address:* BBC Television, Wood Lane, London, W.12, England.

POWELL, Lewis Franklin, Jr., LL.M.; American judge; b. 19 Sept. 1907, Suffolk, Va.; s. of Lewis Franklin and Mary Lewis (Gwathmey) Powell, m. Josephine Rucker; one s. three d.; ed. Washington and Lee Univ. and Harvard Law School; mem. of law firm, Hunton, Williams, Gay, Powell

and Gibson, Richmond, Va. 1937–71; Pres. American Bar Asscn. 1964–65, American Coll. of Trial Lawyers 1969–70; Assoc. Justice of the Supreme Court of U.S.A. 1971–87; several hon. degrees; Legion of Merit (Bronze Star), Croix de Guerre avec palmes. *Address:* 1238 Rothesay Road, Richmond, Va. 23221, U.S.A. (Home).

POWELL, Michael James David, SC.D., F.R.S.; British professor of applied numerical analysis; b. 29 July 1936; s. of William James David Powell and Beatrice Margaret (née Page); m. Caroline Mary Henderson 1959; one s. (deceased) two d.; ed. Eastbourne Coll. and Peterhouse Cambridge; mathematician at A.E.R.E., Harwell 1959–76; John Humphrey Plummer Prof. of Applied Numerical Analysis, Cambridge Univ. 1976–, Professorial Fellow, Pembroke Coll. 1978–; George B. Dantzig Prize in Math. Programming 1982; Naylor Prize, London Math. Soc. 1983. *Publications:* Approximation Theory and Methods 1981; papers on numerical mathematics, especially approximation and optimization calculations. *Leisure interests:* canals, golf, walking. *Address:* 134 Milton Road, Cambridge, England.

POWELL, Michael L., F.R.G.S.; British film director; b. 30 Sept. 1905, Bekesbourne, Kent; s. of Thomas William and Mabel (née Corbett) Powell; m. 1st Frances Reidy 1943 (died 1983); two s.; m. 2nd Thelma Colbert Schoonmaker 1984; ed. King's School, Canterbury, Dulwich Coll.; joined Nat. Prov. Bank 1922; with Metro-Goldwyn-Mayer making Mare Nostrum in Mediterranean with Rex Ingram (dir.) 1925; worked on Ingram films The Magician 1926, The Garden of Allah 1927; brought to Elstree by painter and film dir. Harry Lachman 1928; worked on three Hitchcock silent films, including script of Blackmail (remade as first British sound film 1929); wrote scripts for Caste 1930, 77 Park Lane 1931; given chance to direct by Jerry Jackson 1931; dir. Two Crowded Hours and Rynox (40-minute melodramas); went on to make a dozen short features, including four for Michael Balcon at Shepherd's Bush Studios; directed Edge of the World 1937; given contract by Alexander Korda 1938; met Emeric Pressburger (q.v.) with whom wrote and directed The Spy in Black 1938, Contraband 1940; co-dir. The Thief of Baghdad 1939, The Lion has Wings 1939; producer and dir. 49th Parallel 1941 (Acad. Award 1942) from original story by Pressburger; formed The Archers Co. with Pressburger 1942 and together wrote, produced and directed 16 films, including The Life and Death of Colonel Blimp 1943, I Know Where I'm Going 1945, A Matter of Life and Death 1946, Black Narcissus 1946, The Red Shoes 1948 (for J. Arthur Rank); returned to Alexander Korda 1948 to make four films, including The Small Back Room 1948, The Tales of Hoffmann 1951, Oh Rosalinda (for EMI) 1955, returned to Rank to make The Battle of the River Plate 1956, Ill Met by Moonlight 1957; Archers Co. disbanded 1957; later directed Peeping Tom 1960, Honeymoon 1961, The Queen's Guards 1961, Bluebeard's Castle (Bartók opera) 1969, The Sorcerer's Apprentice (ballet film) 1955, They're a Weird Mob 1966, Age of Consent 1969 (both in Australia), The Boy Who Turned Yellow (from original story and script by Pressburger) 1972, Return to the Edge of the World 1978; fmr. assoc. of Francis Ford Coppola (q.v.), Zoetrope film co. *Theatre productions include:* produced and dir. The Fifth Column (Hemingway) 1945, The Skipper Next to God (Jan de Hartog) 1944, Heloise 1951, Hanging Judge 1952; TV series (several episodes) Espionage and The Defenders; Hon. Fellow British Asscn. of Film and Television Art, British Film Inst.; Hon. D.Litt. (East Anglia) 1978, (Kent) 1984; Hon. Dr. (Royal Coll. of Art) 1987; British Film Inst. Special Award (with Emeric Pressburger) 1978; Golden Lion Award of Venice Film Festival 1982. *Publications:* 200,000 Feet on Foula, Graf Spee, A Waiting Game 1975, The Red Shoes (with Emeric Pressburger) 1978, A Life in Movies (autobiog.) 1986. *Leisure interest:* leaning on gates. *Address:* Lee Cottages, Avening, Tetbury, Glos., GL8 8NJ, England.

POWELL, Sir Philip (see Powell, Sir (Arnold Joseph) Philip).

POWELL, Sir Richard Royle, G.C.B., K.B.E., C.M.G., B.A.; British banker, businessman and fmr. civil servant (retd. 1968); b. 30 July 1909, Walsall; s. of late Ernest Hartley Powell and late Florence Powell; ed. Queen Mary's Grammar School, Walsall, Sidney Sussex Coll., Cambridge; served Admiralty 1931–46; Under-Sec. Ministry of Defence 1946–48; Deputy Sec. Admiralty 1948–50; Deputy Sec. Ministry of Defence 1950–56, Perm. Sec. 1956–59; Perm. Sec. Bd. of Trade 1960–68; Chair. Alusuisse (U.K.) Ltd. 1969–84, Aeroprint Ltd. 1969–84, Sandoz Products 1977–87; fmr. Chair. Wilkinson Match Ltd., Hon. Pres. Jan. 1981–83; Dir. Ladbroke Group PLC 1980–86, Clerical Medical and General Life Assurance Soc. 1973–85, Whessoe PLC 1968–88, Bridgewater Paper Co. 1984–; Pres. Inst. for Fiscal Studies 1970–78; Hon. Fellow, Sidney Sussex Coll., Cambridge 1972. *Leisure interests:* music, opera, theatre. *Address:* 56 Montagu Square, London, W.1, England. *Telephone:* 01-262 0911.

POWELL, Robert; British actor; b. 1 June 1944, Salford, Lancs.; s. of John W. and Kathleen C. Powell; m. Barbara Lord 1975; one s. one d.; ed. Manchester Grammar School; first job, Victoria Theatre, Stoke-on-Trent 1964; *television roles include:* Doomwatch 1970, Jude the Obscure 1971, Jesus of Nazareth 1977, Pygmalion 1981, Frankenstein 1984, Hannay (series) 1988; *theatre roles include:* Hamlet 1971, Travesties (RSC) 1975, Terra Nova 1982, Private Dick 1982; *films include:* Mahler 1974, Beyond Good and Evil 1976, Thirty Nine Steps 1978, Imperative 1981, Jigsaw Man 1982, Shaka Zulu 1985, D'Annunzio 1987; Best Actor, Paris Film Festival

1980, Venice Film Festival 1982. *Leisure interests:* golf, tennis, cricket, computers. *Address:* 48 Flask Walk, Hampstead, London, N.W.3, England.

POWELL-JONES, John E., C.M.G.; British diplomatist (retd.); b. 14 April 1925, Cranleigh, Surrey; s. of Walter J. and Gladys M. (née Taylor) Powell-Jones; m. 1st Ann Murray 1949 (dissolved 1967), two s. one d.; m. 2nd Pamela Sale 1968; ed. Charterhouse and Univ. Coll., Oxford; joined Foreign Office 1949; served Bogotá 1950–52, Athens 1955–59, Léopoldville 1961–62; UN Dept., FO 1963–67; Canadian Nat. Defence Coll. 1967–68; Consul-Gen. Athens 1970–73; Amb. at Phnom Penh 1973–75; Royal Coll. of Defence Studies 1975; Amb. to Senegal, Guinea, Mali, Mauritania and Guinea-Bissau 1976–79, to Cape Verde 1977–79; Amb. and Perm. Rep. UN Conf. on Law of the Sea 1979–82; Amb. to Switzerland 1982–85; Chair. Inter Counsel Ltd. 1986–; elected Waverley Borough Councillor 1987–; Beit Prize (Oxford) 1948. *Leisure interests:* country pursuits. *Address:* Gascons, Gaston Gate, Cranleigh, Surrey, England (Home). *Telephone:* (0483) 274313.

POWERS, John A., B.A.; American business executive; b. 24 Oct. 1926, New York; m. Eileen Herlihy; one s. three d.; ed. St. Peter's Coll. and Harvard Univ.; various positions with McCann Erickson Inc. 1950–73; joined Heublein Inc. (a co. of RJR Nabisco, Inc.) 1973, Pres. and C.E.O. 1983–85, Chair. 1986–. *Address:* Heublein Inc., Farmington, Conn. 06034-0388, U.S.A.

POWIS, Alfred, O.C., B.COM.; Canadian business executive; b. 16 Sept. 1930, Montreal, P.Q.; s. of Alfred Powis Sr. and Sarah Champe McCulloch; m. Louise Margaret Finlayson 1977; two s. one d.; ed. Westmount High School and McGill Univ.; employee, Investment Dept., Sun Life Assurance Co. 1951–55; Internal Auditor, Noranda Inc. 1955, Asst. Treas. 1958, Asst. to Pres. 1962, Exec. Asst. 1963, Dir. 1964, Vice-Pres. 1966, Exec. Vice-Pres. 1967, Pres. and C.E.O. 1968–77, Chair. and Pres. 1977–82, Chair. and C.E.O. April 1982–, Hon. Pres. Copper Devt. Asscn. 1983–; also Dir., Noranda Aluminium Inc.; Vice-Pres. and Dir., Northwood Pulp Ltd., Brunswick Mining and Smelting Corpn. Ltd., Canadian Copper Refiners Ltd., Dir. Canada Wire & Cable Co. Ltd., Leaworth Holdings Ltd., Wire Rope Industries Ltd., Noranda Metal Industries, Noranda Manufacturing Ltd., Noranda Sales Corpn. Ltd., Noranda Exploration Co. Ltd., Noranda Australia Ltd., St. Lawrence Fertilizers Ltd., Placer Devt. Ltd., Quebec Smelters Ltd., Waite Amulet Mines Ltd., Empresa Fluorspar Mines Ltd., Kerr Addison Mines Ltd., Canadian Imperial Bank of Commerce, Ford Motor Co. of Canada Ltd., Gulf Canada Ltd., Sun Life Assurance Co., MacMillan Bloedel Ltd., Canadian Electrolytic Zinc Ltd., Gen. Smelting Co. of Canada Ltd., Brascan Ltd. 1982–, Northwood Mills Ltd.; Chair. Bd. of Trustees, Toronto Gen. Hosp. *Address:* Noranda Inc., P.O. Box 45, Commerce Court West, Toronto, Ont., M5L 1B6 (Office); 70 Woodlawn Avenue, West Toronto, Ont., M4V 1G7, Canada (Home). *Telephone:* 416-867-7111 (Office).

POWLES, Sir Guy Richardson, K.B.E., C.M.G., E.D., LL.B.; New Zealand public servant; b. 5 April 1905, Otaki; s. of Col. C. G. Powles, C.M.G., D.S.O.; m. Eileen Nicholls 1931; two s.; ed. Wellington Coll., Victoria Univ. Coll.; Barrister, Supreme Court of New Zealand 1927–40; war service, to rank of Col. 1940–46; Counsellor, Washington 1946–49; High Commr., Western Samoa 1949–60; High Commr. India 1960–62, Ceylon 1961–62, Amb. to Nepal 1961–62; Ombudsman, New Zealand 1962–75, Chief Ombudsman 1975–77; Resident Consultant, Int. Ombudsman Inst., Edmonton, Canada 1978; Race Relations Conciliator 1971–73; Pres. New Zealand Inst. of Int. Affairs 1965–71; Commr. Int. Comm. of Jurists, Geneva; Fellow, N.Z. Inst. of Public Admin. 1983; Patron New Zealand-India Soc., Environmental Defence Soc., New Zealand Foundation for Mental Health, New Zealand Foundation for Peace Studies, Coalition for Open Govt.; mem. Council Int. Freedom of Information Inst.; Hon. LL.D. *Leisure interests:* peace and arms control, reading and gardening. *Address:* 34A Wesley Road, Wellington C.1, New Zealand. *Telephone:* 738-068.

POYNTZ, Rt. Rev. Samuel Greenfield, M.A., B.D., PH.D.; Irish ecclesiastic; b. 4 March 1926, Manitoba, Canada; s. of Rev. James Poyntz and Catherine Greenfield; m. Noreen H. Armstrong 1952; one s. two d.; ed. Portora Royal School, Enniskillen and Trinity Coll., Dublin; curate, St. George's, Dublin 1950–52, Bray 1952–55, St. Michael and St. Paul, Dublin 1955–59; Incumbent, St. Stephen, Dublin 1959–67, St. Ann, Dublin 1967–70, St. Ann with St. Stephen, Dublin 1970–78; Archdeacon of Dublin 1974–78; Examining Chaplain, Archbishop of Dublin 1974–78; Bishop of Cork, Cloyne and Ross 1978–87; Bishop of Connor 1987–; Chair. Irish Council of Churches 1986–88; Vice-Pres. British Council of Churches 1987–; *Publications:* The Exaltation of the Blessed Virgin Mary 1953, Journey Towards Union 1975, Our Church—Praying with our Church Family 1983. *Leisure interests:* stamp collecting, rugby football. *Address:* Bishop's House, Deramore Park, Belfast, BT9 5JU, Northern Ireland.

POZSGAY, Imre, CAND.SC.; Hungarian politician; b. 26 Nov. 1933, Kóny; ed. Lenin Inst.; joined Hungarian Working People's Party 1950; evening lecturer in Marxism-Leninism for Bács County Cttee. of Hungarian Socialist Workers' Party (HSWP) 1957–65; Leader, later Ideological Sec., Agitation and Propaganda Dept. of Bács County Cttee., HSWP 1965–70; Section Leader, Agitation and Propaganda Dept. of HSWP Cen. Cttee. 1970; Deputy Chief Ed. Társadalmi Szemle (Social Review) journal of HSWP; Deputy Minister of Culture 1975–76, Minister 1976–80, Minister

of Culture and Educ. 1980–82; Gen. Sec. Nat. Council of the Patriotic People's Front 1982–88; mem. HSWP Cen. Cttee. 1980–, mem. Political Cttee. 1988–; Minister of State 1988–. *Publication:* Demokrácia és Kultura (Democracy and Culture) 1980. *Address:* Hungarian Socialist Workers' Party Central Committee, Széchenyi rakpart 19, 1387 Budapest, Hungary. *Telephone:* 111-400.

PRABHJOT KAUR; Indian poet and politician; b. 6 July 1924, Langaryal; d. of Nidhan Singh; m. Brig. Narenderpal Singh 1948; two d.; ed. Khalsa Coll. for Women, Lahore, and Punjab Univ.; first collected poems published 1943 (aged sixteen); represented India at numerous int. literary confs. 1956–; mem. Legis. Council, Punjab 1966–; Ed. Vikendrit; mem. Sahitya Akademi (Nat. Acad. of Letters), Exec. Bd. 1978; mem. Cen. Comm. of UNESCO, Nat. Writers Cttee. of India; received honours of Sahitya Shiromani 1964 and Padma Shri 1967; title of Rajya Kavi (Poet Laureate) by Punjab Govt. 1964, the Sahitya Akademi Award 1965, Golden Laurel Leaves, United Poets Int., Philippines 1967, Grand Prix de la Rose de la France 1968, Most Distinguished Order of Poetry, World Poetry Soc. Intercontinental, U.S.A. 1974; Woman of the Year, U.P.L.I., Philippines 1975, Sewa Sifti Award 1980, NIF Cultural Award 1982, Josh Kenya Award 1982, Delhi State Award 1983. *Publications:* 50 books, including: Poems: Supne Sadhran 1949, Do Rang 1951, Pankheru 1956, Lala (in Persian) 1958, Bankapasi 1958, Pabbi 1962, Khai 1967, Plateau (French) 1968, Wad-darshi Sheesha 1972, Madhiantar 1974, Chandra Yug 1978, Dreams Die Young 1979, Shadows and Light (Bulgarian) 1980, Him Hans 1982, Samrup 1982, Ishq Shara Ki Nasa 1983, Shadows (English and Danish) 1985; Short Stories: Kinke 1952, Aman de Na 1956, Zindgi de Kujh Pal 1982. *Leisure interests:* reading, travel. *Address:* D-203, Defence Colony, New Delhi 110024, India. *Telephone:* 626045.

PRADA, Michel André Jean Edmond; French civil servant; b. 2 April 1940, Bordeaux; s. of Robert and Suzanne (Bouffard) Prada; m. Annick Saudubray 1963; two s. three d.; ed. Lycée Montesquieu Bordeaux, Inst. d'Etudes Politiques de Bordeaux, Ecole Nat. d'Admin.; Inspecteur des Finances with Ministry of Econ. and Finance 1966–; Chargé de Mission, Inspection Générale des Finances 1969; Chargé de Mission, Direction de la Comptabilité Publique 1970, Asst. Director 1974, Head of Service 1977, Dir. de la Comptabilité Publique 1978–85; Dir. of Budget, Ministry of the Economy, Finance and the Budget 1986–88; Chevalier, Ordre nat. du Mérite. *Address:* 93 rue de Rivoli, 75001 Paris (Office); 2 rue Cart, 94160 Saint-Mandé, France (Home). *Telephone:* 374 95 33 (Home).

PRADIER, Henri Joseph Marie; French engineer; b. 5 Nov. 1931, Sainte-Colombe-lès-Vienne, Rhône; s. of Camille Pradier and Anne-Marie Côte; m. 1st Marie-France Michot (deceased), two s.; m. 2nd Brigitte Dapvril, one s. one d.; ed. Institution Robin, Vienne, Lycée du Parc, Lyons and Ecole Polytechnique; Consulting Engineer 1955–58; Shell Française 1958–67 and 1970–; Man. Dir. Shell du Maroc 1967–79, Vice-Pres. Distribution 1975–84; Man. Dir. Shell Française 1984–; Dir. Société pour l'Utilisation Rationnelle des Gaz (Butagaz) 1975–, Shell Chimie 1984–. *Leisure interests:* gardening, sailing, swimming. *Address:* Shell Française, 29 rue de Berri, 75008 Paris (Office); 52 rue du Ranelagh, 75016 Paris, France (Home).

PRADO ARANGUIZ, Jorge José; Chilean agriculturalist and politician; b. 25 March 1937, Santiago; m. Magdalena Lira Lecaros; two s.; ed. Colegio Padres Franceses, Universidad Católica de Chile; scholarships to study agricultural admin., org. of co-operatives and irrigation tech. in France, Norway and Israel; mem. Man. staff fruit-growing enterprise Casas de Pencahue, San Vicente de Tagua Tagua; partner of livestock enterprise Mapullay, Bucalemu, Santo Domingo; fmr. Man. and Dir. A.F.P. Planvital; active in farmers' unions; Vice-Chair. Confederacion de Productores Agrícolas 1973–75; mem. Bd. Sociedad Nacional de Agricultura 1967–, Vice-Chair. 1981–82; Minister of Agric. 1982–88. *Address:* Teatinos 40, Santiago, Chile. *Telephone:* 6965896.

PRADO VALLEJO, Julio; Ecuadorean lawyer, diplomatist and politician; b. 3 July 1924; ed. Univ. Cen. del Ecuador; Chargé d'Affaires, Brazil 1953–54, U.S.A. 1954–57; Pres. Inter-American Comm. for Econ. Co-operation 1956; Legal Adviser on Int. Agreements at Ministry of Finance 1958; Prof. at Univ. Cen. del Ecuador 1958–; Minister of Foreign Affairs 1967–68; Gran Oficial Cruzeiro do Sul (Brazil); Gran Cruz Al Mérito (Ecuador). *Publications:* Réplica a la peruanidad de Túmbez, Jáen y Mainas 1945, Demarcación de Fronteras - Ejecución del Protocolo de Rio de Janeiro de Enero 29 de 1942 1950. *Address:* Tamayo 1313 y Colón, Quito, Ecuador. *Telephone:* 238-375.

PRAEGER, Frederick Amos; American publisher; b. 16 Sept. 1916, Vienna, Austria; s. of Max M. Praeger and Manya Foerster; m. 1st Cornelia E. Blach 1946 (divorced 1959), three d.; m. 2nd Heloise B. Arons 1960 (divorced 1983), two d.; m. 3rd Kellie Masterson 1983; ed. Univ. of Vienna and Sorbonne, Paris; Assoc. Ed. R. Loewit Verlag, Vienna 1935–38; various positions 1938–41; civilian head of publs. br. information control div. U.S. Mil. Govt. Hesse, Germany 1946–48; Pres. Frederick A. Praeger Inc., 1950–68, Phaidon Publs., Inc., New York; Chair. Phaidon Publs., Ltd., London; Pres., C.E.O. and Editorial Dir. Westview Press, Boulder, Colo. 1975–; Dir. Pall Mall Press, London; Adjunct Prof. Grad. School of Librarianship, Denver Univ.; Assoc. Dir. Publishing Inst. 1976; Bronze Star; Hon. L.H.D. (Denver). *Address:* Westview Press, Inc., 5500 Central Avenue, Boulder, Colo., U.S.A.

PRAIN, Sir Ronald Lindsay, Kt., O.B.E.; British company director; b. 3 Sept. 1907, Iquiqui, Chile; s. of Arthur Lindsay Prain and Amy (née Watson) Prain; m. Esther Pansy Brownrigg 1938; two s.; ed. Cheltenham Coll.; Controller Diamond Die and Tool Control (Ministry of Supply) 1940–45, Quartz Crystal Control 1943–45; Chief Exec. Roan Selection Trust (R.S.T.) Int. Group of Copper Mining Cos. 1943–68, Chair. 1950–72; Chair. Botswana R.S.T. Group 1959–72; Chair. Merchant Bank of Cen. Africa Ltd. 1955–66, Merchant Bank (Zambia) Ltd. 1966–72; Dir. Pan Holding S.A., Metal Market and Exchange Ltd. 1943–65, Selection Trust Ltd. 1944–78, Int. Nickel Co. of Canada 1951–72, Wankie Colliery Ltd. 1953–63, Barclays Bank Int. Ltd. 1971–77, Monks Investment Trust Ltd., Foseco Minsep Ltd. 1969–80, and other cos.; Pres. British Overseas Mining Asscn. 1952, Inst. of Metals 1960–61, Cheltenham Coll. Council 1972–80; Hon. Pres. Copper Devt. Asscn.; Chair. Agricultural Research Council of Rhodesia and Nyasaland 1959–63; mem. Commonwealth Council of Mining and Metallurgical Insts. (Chair. 1961–74); mem. Council, Overseas Devt. Inst. 1960–80; Hon. mem. Inst. of Metals, BNF Metals Tech. Centre; Hon. Fellow, Inst. of Mining and Metallurgy, Metals Soc.; Trustee Inst. for Archeo-Metallurgical Studies; Gold Medal (Inst. of Mining and Metallurgy) 1968; Inst. of Metals Platininum Medal 1969. *Publications:* Selected Papers (4 vols.), Copper: The Anatomy of an Industry 1975, Reflections on an Era 1981, An Autobiography 1981. *Leisure interests:* cricket, real tennis, travel. *Address:* Waverley, Granville Road, St. George's Hill, Weybridge, Surrey, KT13 0QJ. *Telephone:* (0932) 842776.

PRAMOEDYA ANANTA TOER; Indonesian novelist; b. 20 Feb. 1925, Blora, East Java; worked with Domei Japanese news agency to 1945; studied as stenographer; wrote first book Sepulah Kepala Nika (Ten Chiefs of Nika), Jakarta 1945; manuscript lost before printing; 2nd Lieut., Indonesian revolution, Bekasi, east of Jakarta; with Voice of Free Indonesia producing Indonesian language magazine; arrested by Dutch July 1947; wrote first major works, Bukit Duri gaol; ed. Indonesian Library of Congress after release to 1951; arrested on order of Gen. A. H. Nasution (q.v.) in connection with book on overseas Chinese 1960; released 1961; aligned with communist-sponsored cultural groups; leading figure in Lekkra, Indonesian Communist Party cultural asscn.; arrested Nov. 1966; with first political prisoners on Buni island; released Jan. 1980; 7 novels (one published so far), one drama and 2 minor works composed in prison, Buni 1966–80; novels banned May 1981. *Novels include:* Keluarga Guerilya, Bumi Manusia (The World of Man) 1973, Anak Seluruh Bangsa (A Child of All Nations), Jajak Langkah (Strides Forward), Bumah Kaca (The Greenhouse).

PRAMOJ, Mom Rachawongse Kukrit; Thai politician; b. 20 April 1911; s. of Prince Khamrob and Mom Daeng Pramoj; brother of M. R. Seni Pramoj (q.v.); ed. Suan Kularb Coll., Trent Coll., U.K., Queen's Coll., Oxford; with Revenue Dept., Ministry of Finance; Siam Commercial Bank; Head of Gov.'s Office, Bank of Thailand, later Head of Issue Dept.; mem. Parl. 1946–76, Nat. Legis. Ass. 1977–; Deputy Minister of Finance 1947–48; Deputy Minister of Commerce; founded Siam Rath newspaper 1950; Leader Social Action Party; Speaker Nat. Ass. 1973–74; Prime Minister 1975–76, also Minister of the Interior Jan.-April 1976; mem. Cttee. to draft new constitution 1977–78; Dir. of Thai Studies, Thammasat Univ.; Pres. Exec. Cttee., Foundation for the Assistance of Needy Schoolchildren; appeared in film The Ugly American 1963. *Address:* National Legislative Assembly, Bangkok, Thailand.

PRAMOJ, Mom Rachawongse Seni, B.A.; Thai lawyer and politician; b. 26 May 1905, Ngor Swaga; s. of Prince Khamrob; brother of M. R. Kukrit Pramoj (q.v.); m. Usna Saligupta 1931; two s. one d.; ed. Trent Coll., U.K., Worcester Coll., Oxford; Judge, Appeal Court; Minister, Thai Embassy, Washington, D.C., Prime Minister 1945–46; law practice 1946–; Leader Democratic Party 1968–76; mem. Parl. 1969–76; Prime Minister Feb.-March 1975, April-Oct. 1976, also Minister of the Interior April-Oct. 1976; mem. Cttee. to draft new constitution 1977–78. *Publications:* several law books and English translations of Thai poetry. *Leisure interests:* golf, music, painting, poetry. *Address:* 219 Egamai Road, Bangkok, Thailand. *Telephone:* 3911632.

PRAPAS CHARUSATHIRA, General (see Charusathira, General Prapas).

PRATE, Alain; French civil servant and international official; b. 5 June 1928, Lille; m. Marie-José Alexis 1956; two s. one d.; ed. Ecole Nationale d'Administration; Asst. Insp. of Finances 1953–55, Insp. 1955–58; Del. to conf. on EEC 1957; Sec. of Monetary Cttee., EEC 1958–61; Dir. for Econ. Structure and Devt., Directorate-Gen. for Econ. and Financial Affairs, EEC 1961–65; Dir.-Gen. of Internal Market, EEC 1965; Technical counsellor for economic and financial questions in the Secretariat of the Presidency of the Repub. 1967–69; Head of Service, Inspectorate-General of Finance 1969–71, Dir.-Gen. Customs and Duties 1971–75; Dir. Crédit National 1975; Deputy Gov. Banque de France 1979–84; Vice-Pres. EIB 1984–; Officier de la Légion d'honneur, Officier de l'Ordre national du Mérite. *Publication:* Les batailles économiques du Général de Gaulle 1978, La France et sa monnaie 1987. *Address:* c/o European Investment Bank, 100 Boulevard Konrad Adenauer, 2950 Luxembourg.

PRATOLINI, Vasco; Italian writer; b. 19 Oct. 1913; Lugano Prize 1947; Viareggio Prize 1955, 1985; Feltrinelli Prize 1957; Marzotto Prize 1963. *Publications:* novels and stories: Via de' Magazzini 1942, Cronaca familiare 1947, Cronache di poveri amanti 1947, Le ragazze di San Frediano 1950, Metello 1955, Lo Scialo 1960, La costanza della ragione 1963, Allegoria e Derisione 1966, Il mannello di Natascia 1985. *Address:* Via F. S. Nitti, 46, Rome, Italy. *Telephone:* 3288521.

PRATT, Edmund T., Jr., B.S., M.B.A.; American chemical industry executive; b. 22 Feb. 1927, Savannah, Ga.; s. of Edmund T. Pratt, Sr. and Rose Miller; m. Jeanette Carneale 1951; two s.; ed. Duke Univ., Wharton School of Commerce and Finance, Univ. of Pennsylvania; served with U.S. Navy, World War II; intelligence officer 1952–54; Controller, IBM World Trade Corpn. 1958–62; Asst. Sec. U.S. Army 1962–64; joined Pfizer Inc. as controller (1964–67), Vice-Pres. Operations Pfizer Int. 1967–69, Chair. and Pres. 1969–71; Dir. and mem. Exec. Cttee. Pfizer Inc. 1969, Exec. Vice-Pres. 1970–71, Pres. 1971–72, Chair. and C.E.O. 1972–; Chair. Business Roundtable; mem. Emergency Cttee. for American Trade, New York State Business Council; Advisory Cttee. on Trade Negotiations; Dir. Chase Manhattan Corpn., Int. Paper Company, General Motors Corpn.; Trustee Cttee. for Econ. Devt.; mem. Bd. N.Y. Chamber of Commerce and Industry, Bd. of Trustees of Duke Univ., Bd. of Overseers of Wharton School of Commerce and Finance, Univ. of Pa., President's Export Council. *Address:* Pfizer Inc., 235 East 42nd Street, New York, 10017 N.Y., U.S.A. *Telephone:* 212-573-2323.

PRATT, (John) Christopher, C.C., R.C.A., B.F.A.; Canadian painter and printmaker; b. 9 Dec. 1935, St. John's, Newfoundland; s. of John Kerr Pratt and Christine Emily (Dawe) Pratt; m. Mary Frances West 1957; two s. two d.; ed. Prince of Wales Coll., St. John's Newfoundland, Memorial Univ. of Newfoundland, Glasgow School of Art, Scotland and Mount Allison Univ., Sackville, N.B.; taught as specialist in art, Memorial Univ. 1961–63; freelance artist 1963–; mem. Mount Carmel Town Council 1969–73, Postage Stamp Design Cttee., Ottawa 1970–73, The Canada Council 1975–81, Memorial Univ. Bd. of Regents 1972–75; Hon. D. Litt. (Memorial) 1972, Hon. LL.D. (Mount Allison) 1973. *Leisure interest:* offshore sailing. *Address:* Box 87, Mount Carmel, St. Mary's Bay, Newfoundland, AOB 2MO, Canada.

PRATT, Solomon Althanasius James, B.C.L., B.LIT., LL.B., M.A., M.SC., DIP.A-GR.ECONS.; Sierra Leonean politician; b. 25 Dec. 1921; s. of George Henry Pratt and Christiana Omotayo; m. Victoria Elizabeth Pratt 1944; one s. five d.; ed. Fourah Bay Coll., St. Catherine's, Oxford Univ., Univ. of London and Inner Temple; Economist, Sierra Leone Govt. 1949–52; Int. Civil Servant, Int. Labour Office, Geneva 1952–58; Chair. Riot Damages Comm. 1958–61; City Solicitor, Municipality of Freetown 1958–64; Gen. Man. Sierra Leone Railways and Econ. Advisor to the Govt. 1964–66; arrested and detained during Mil. Rule 1967; Parl. Rep. for Mountain Rural District 1968–; Minister of Econ. Devt. and Planning 1968–69; envoy of the Prime Minister to various countries and confs. 1969–71; Minister of State and Attorney-Gen. 1971, Minister of External Affairs 1971–73, of Devt. and Econ. Planning 1973–75; Attorney-General 1975–77; Minister of Econ. Planning 1977–78, of the Interior 1978–80, of Trade and Industry 1980–81, of Transport and Communications 1981; Pres. Sierra Leone UN Asscn.; Fellow, Victorian Coll. of Music; Insignia of Grand Commdr. of the Order of the Rokel. *Leisure interest:* church music. *Address:* c/o Ministry of Transport and Communications, Freetown, Sierra Leone.

PRAWER, Joshua, PH.D.; Israeli historian; b. 10 Nov. 1917, Bentzin, Poland; m. (wife deceased); one s.; ed. Hebrew Univ., Jerusalem; post-doctoral research, Paris and London 1949–50; Deputy Dean, Faculty of Humanities, Hebrew Univ. 1953–55, Prof. of History 1958–, Dean, Faculty of Humanities 1961–65; f. and Acad. Head, Haifa Univ. 1957–59, 1966–68; Co-founder, Faculty of Humanities and Social Sciences, Ben-Gurion Univ. 1970; Pro-Rector, Hebrew Univ. 1975–78; mem., Israel Acad. of Sciences and Humanities 1963, Chair. Humanities Section 1969–74; Vice-Pres. Int. Soc. of the Study of the Crusaders 1982; Fellow, Medieval Acad. of America 1966; Visiting Fellow, All Souls Coll., Oxford 1974; Corresp. mem. Acad. des Inscriptions et Belles Lettres 1976, Royal Historical Soc. 1984; Hon. Ph.D. (Montpellier) 1966; Prix Gustav Schlumberger (Acad. des Inscriptions et Belles Lettres, France) 1967; Prize for Humanities (Israel) 1969, Roths-child Prize for Humanites 1971, Chevalier ordre nat. du Mérite 1973. *Publications:* Histoire du Royaume Latin de Jerusalem, (2 vols.) 1969–71, The Latin Kingdom of Jerusalem: European Colonialism in the Middle Ages 1972, The World of the Crusaders 1972, Crusader Institutions 1980, Encyclopaedia Hebraica, 36 vols. (Ed.-in-Chief) 1969–83, The History of the Jews in the Latin Kingdom of Jerusalem 1988. *Address:* 6, Alkalai Street, Jerusalem; The Israeli Academy of Sciences and Humanities, Jerusalem, P.O. Box 4040, Israel. *Telephone:* 631180 (Home); 636211 (Office).

PRAWER, Siegbert Salomon, M.A., D.LITT., PH.D., LITT.D., F.B.A.; British university teacher and author; b. 15 Feb. 1925; s. of Marcus and Eleonora Prawer; brother of Mrs. Ruth Prawer Jhabvala (q.v.); m. Helga Alice Schaefer 1949; one s. two d. (and one s. deceased); ed. King Henry VIII School, Coventry, Jesus Coll., Christ's Coll., Cambridge; Adelaide Stoll Resident Student, Christ's Coll., Cambridge 1947–48; Asst. Lecturer, then Lecturer, then Sr. Lecturer, Univ. of Birmingham 1948–63; Prof. of German, Westfield Coll., London Univ. 1964–69; Taylor Prof. of German Language and Literature, Oxford 1969–86, Prof. Emer. 1986–; Co-editor,

Oxford Germanic Studies 1971–75, Anglica Germanica 1973–79; Visiting Prof. City Coll., New York 1956–57, Univ. of Chicago 1963–64, Harvard Univ. 1968, Hamburg Univ. 1969, Univ. of Calif., Irvine 1975, Otago Univ., N.Z. 1976, Univ. of Pittsburgh 1977, Australian Nat. Univ., Canberra 1980, Brandeis Univ. 1981–82; Resident Fellow, Knox Coll., Dunedin, N.Z. 1976; Fellow of Queen's Coll., Oxford 1969–, Dean of Degrees 1975–; Hon. Dir. London Univ. Inst. of Germanic Studies 1967–69, Hon. Fellow 1986; Pres. British Comparative Literature Assen. 1984–87; Hon. mem. Modern Languages Assen. of America 1986; Hon. D.Phil. (Cologne) 1985; Hon. D.Litt. (Birmingham) 1988; Goethe Medal 1973; Isaac Deutscher Memorial Prize 1977, Gundolf-Prize of the German Acad. 1986. *Publications:* German Lyric Poetry 1952, Mörike und seiner Leser 1960, Heine's Buch der Lieder: A Critical Study 1960, Heine: The Tragic Satirist 1962, The Penguin Book of Lieder 1964, The Uncanny in Literature (inaugural lecture) 1965, Heine's Shakespeare, a Study in Contexts (inaugural lecture) 1970, Comparative Literary Studies: An Introduction 1973, Karl Marx and World Literature 1976, Caligari's Children: The Film as Tale of Terror 1980, Heine's Jewish Comedy: A Study of His Portraits of Jews and Judaism 1983, Coalsmoke and Englishmen 1984, A. N. Stencl—Poet of Whitechapel 1984, Frankenstein's Island-England and the English in the Writings of Heinrich Heine 1986; edited: Essays in German Language, Culture and Society (with R. H. Thomas and L. W. Forster) 1969, The Romantic Period in Germany 1970, Seventeen Modern German Poets 1971; numerous articles on German, English and comparative literature. *Leisure interest:* portrait drawing. *Address:* The Queen's College, Oxford, England.

PRAWIRO, Radius, M.A.; Indonesian economist and banker; b. 29 June 1928, Yogjakarta; ed. Senior High School, Yogjakarta, Nederlandsche Economische Hoogeschool, Rotterdam, Econ. Univ. of Indonesia; Sec. Defence Cttee., Yogjakarta during revolution 1945; with Army High Command, Yogjakarta 1946–47; Angauta Tentara Pelajar (Army) 1948–51; Officer in Govt. Audit Office, Ministry of Finance 1953–65; Vice-Minister, Deputy Supreme Auditor, mem. Supreme Audit Office 1965–66; Gov. Bank Indonesia 1966–73; Chair. Indonesian Assen. of Accountants 1965–; Gov. IMF for Indonesia 1967–72, Alt. Gov. Asian Devt. Bank 1967–72; Minister of Trade 1973–78, of Trade and Co-operatives 1978–83, of Finance 1983–88, Co-ordinating Minister of Econs., Finance, Industry and Devt. Supervision March 1988–; Chair. Bd. of Govs. IBRD, IDA, IFC 1971–72; mem. Econ. Council of the Pres. 1968–, Nat. Econ. Stabilization Council 1968–, Gov. Bd. Christian Univ. of Indonesia, Supervisory Bd. Trisakti Univ. *Address:* Ministry of Finance, Jakarta; Jalan Imam Bonjol 4, Jakarta, Indonesia (Home).

PREBBLE, Richard William, B.A., LL.B.; New Zealand politician and lawyer; b. 7 Feb. 1948, U.K.; s. of Archdeacon K.R. Prebble; m. Nancy Prebble 1970; ed. Auckland Boys' Grammar School, Auckland Technical Inst. and Auckland Univ.; admitted as barrister and solicitor, N.Z. Supreme Court 1971; admitted to Bar, Fiji Supreme Court 1973; M.P. for Auckland Cen. 1975–; Jr. Opposition Whip 1978–79; Minister of Transport, of Railways, Minister of Civil Aviation and Meteorological Services, Minister of Railways, Minister of Pacific Island Affairs, Assoc. Minister of Finance 1984–87; Minister of State-Owned Enterprises, Postmaster-Gen., Minister of Works and Devt. and Minister of Pacific Island Affairs 1987–88; N.Z. Labour Party. *Leisure interests:* Polynesian and Melanesian culture, opera, drama. *Address:* Parliament Buildings, Wellington, New Zealand. *Telephone:* 749-116.

PREER, John Randolph, Jr, PH.D.; American professor of biology; b. 4 April 1918, Ocala, Fla.; m. Louise Brandau 1941; two s.; ed. Univ. of Florida, Gainesville; Assoc. Prof., subsequently Prof., Graduate School of Arts and Sciences, Univ. of Pa. 1947–67, Admissions Officer 1958–59; Prof., Ind. Univ. 1968–, Distinguished Prof. of Biology 1977–, Chair. Dept. of Biology 1977–79; mem. Genetics Study Section, Nat. Insts. of Health, Bethesda, Md. 1983–(87); Guggenheim Fellowship 1976; mem. N.A.S. *Publications:* numerous papers in scientific journals and contribs. to books and symposia. *Leisure interests:* astronomy, sailing. *Address:* Department of Biology, Indiana University, Bloomington, Ind. 47405, U.S.A. *Telephone:* (812) 335-3200.

PRELOG, Vladimir, DR. ING.; Swiss chemist; b. 23 July 1906, Sarajevo, Yugoslavia; s. of Milan and Maria (Cettolo) Prelog; m. Kamila Vitek 1933; one s.; ed. Inst. of Technology and School of Chemistry, Prague; Chemist, G. J. Driza Laboratories, Prague 1929–35; Lecturer (Dozent), Univ. of Zagreb 1935–40, Assoc. Prof. 1940–41; Privatdozent Eidgenössische Technische Hochschule 1942, Assoc. Prof. 1947–50, Prof. of Organic Chemistry 1950–76, Head of Laboratory of Organic Chemistry 1957–66; mem. Bd. CIBA-GEIGY Ltd., Basel 1960–78; mem. Papal Acad. of Science Leopoldina 1986–; Foreign mem. Royal Soc. (U.K.), Acad. of Sciences of U.S.S.R., N.A.S., American Acad. of Arts and Sciences, American Philosophical Soc., Accad. dei Lincei, Royal Irish Soc., Acad. Sciences, Paris, etc.; Werner Prize, Marcel Benoist Prize, Roger Adams Award, Stas Medal, Medal of Honour, Rice Univ., A. W. Hofmann Medal, Davy Medal Royal Soc., Nobel Prize 1975, and other prizes; Dr. h.c. (Zagreb, Liverpool, Cambridge, Brussels, Paris and Manchester Univs. and Inst. Químico Sarriá, Barcelona, Weizmann Inst., Rehovot). *Leisure interests:* swimming, skiing. *Address:* Universitätsstrasse 16, 8092, Zürich (Office); Bellariastrasse 33, 8002 Zürich, Switzerland (Home).

PREM CHAND, Lieut.-Gen. D.; Indian army officer (retd.) and United Nations official; b. 1916, Muzaffargarh, now West Pakistan; s. of the late Dewan and Mrs. Khem Chand; ed. Govt. Coll., Lahore and Staff Coll., Quetta; commissioned Indian Army 1937; served in Gen. Staff, Army HQ, New Delhi 1947, later apptd. Mil. Asst. to Chief of Army Staff; commanded Regimental Centre of First Gurkha Rifles; Instructor, Defence Services Staff Coll., Wellington; subsequently apptd. Deputy Dir. of Mil. Training, Dir. of Personnel Services, Dir. of Mil. Intelligence, New Delhi; Chief of Staff, HQ Western Command, Simla 1961, Commanded Brigade and Div. in Western Command; Gen.-Officer, Katanga Area, UN Operation in the Congo 1962–63; Commanded Div. in Eastern Command, Chief of Staff, HQ Eastern Command, Calcutta; Dir. Gen. Nat. Cadet Corps; retd. 1967 then held admin. post in industrial concern; Commdr. UN Force in Cyprus (UNFICYP) 1969–76; UN Sec. Gen.'s. Rep. for Rhodesia 1977; Commdr. desig. of UN Force for Namibia 1980–89; Head of UN Transition Assistance Group, Namibia 1989–; rank of Lieut.-Gen. 1974; Param Vishisht Seva Medal. *Leisure interests:* music and trekking. *Address:* c/o UN Information Centre, 55 Lodi Estate, New Delhi, India.

PREM TINSULANONDA, Gen.; Thai army officer and politician; b. 26 Aug. 1920; unmarried; ed. Suan Kularb School and Chulachomklao Royal Mil. Acad., Bangkok; started mil. career as Sub-Lieut. 1941; Commdr. Cavalry HQ 1968; Commdr.-Gen. 2nd Army Area 1974; Asst. C.-in-C. Royal Thai Army 1977; Deputy Minister of Interior, Govt. of Gen. Kriangsak Chomanan 1977; Minister of Defence 1979–87, later C.-in-C.; Prime Minister of Thailand 1980–88; Chair. Petroleum Authority of Thailand (PTT) 1981; Ramathipbodi Order, King of Thailand, Seri Maharajah Mangku Negara (Malaysia) 1984–. *Address:* c/o Office of the Prime Minister, Nakhon Pathom Road, Bangkok, Thailand.

PREMADASA, Ranasinghe; Ceylonese politician and local government official; b. 23 June 1924; m. Hema Wickrematunga 1964; one s. one d.; ed. Lorenz Coll., St. Joseph Coll., Colombo; began political career as member of Ceylon Labour Party and elected to Muncipal Council, Colombo 1950, Deputy Mayor 1955; joined United Nat. Party (U.N.P.) 1956; Third Mem. Colombo Cen. Constituency, House of Reps. 1960–65, Second Mem. 1965–70, First Mem. 1970–77; First Mem. Colombo Cen. Constituency, Nat. State Assembly 1977–; Parl. Sec. to Minister of Local Govt. 1965, Chief Whip of Govt. Parl. Group 1965, Parl. Sec. to Minister of Information and Broadcasting, and to Minister of Local Govt. 1966; Minister of Local Govt. 1968–70; Chief Whip of Opposition Parl. Group, House of Reps. (later Nat. State Assembly) 1970–77; Deputy Leader U.N.P. 1976–; Minister of Local Govt., Housing and Construction, and Leader of Nat. State Assembly July 1977–, Prime Minister of Sri Lanka 1978–88, Pres. of Sri Lanka Dec. 1988–; Minister of Highways 1981–88, of Buddha Sasana Feb. 1989–, of Defence Feb. 1989–, of Policy Planning and Implementation Feb. 1989–; mem. Emergency Civil Admin. 1984–; Del. to Buddha Sangayana, Burma 1955, to China and Soviet Union 1959, to Commonwealth Parl. Conf., Canberra, Australia 1970; successful negotiations with Friedrich Ebert Foundation (Fed. Repub. of Germany) to set up Sri Lanka Inst. in Sri Lanka 1965. *Publications:* numerous books in Sinhala. *Leisure interests:* photography, writing. *Address:* Office of the President, Republic Square, Colombo 1, Sri Lanka.

PREMAUER, Werner, DR.JUR.; German company executive; b. 27 July 1912, Berlin; s. of Otto Premauer and Katharina (née Frueh); m. Charlotte Schröder 1940; one s. two d.; ed. Univs. of Würzburg, Innsbruck, Erlangen, Munich; Asst. to Pres., Bayerische Vereinsbank 1947, Branch Man. Nuremburg 1948, Deputy mem. Bd. of Man. 1951, mem. 1953, Pres. 1968, Chair. Bd., Bayerische Vereinsbank 1976–, Nat. Cttee. of ICC, Council of ICC; Chair. and Dir. of numerous Cos.; Grosses Bundesverdienstkreuz, Bayerischer Verdienstorden, Commdr.'s Cross of Royal Swedish Order of Vasa. *Leisure interests:* mountaineering, skiing. *Address:* Bayerische Vereinsbank, Kardinal-Faulhaber-Strasse 14, D-8000 Munich 2, Federal Republic of Germany. *Telephone:* 089-2132-5575.

PRENDERGAST, Peter Thomas, D.F.A., M.F.A.; Welsh painter and draughtsman; b. 27 Oct. 1946, Abertridwr; s. of Martin and Mary Prendergast; m. Lesley A. Riding 1967; two s. two d.; ed. Cwmaber Sec. School, Cardiff Coll. of Art, Slade School of Fine Art and Reading Univ.; part-time lecturer, Liverpool Coll. of Art 1970–74; teacher, Ysgol Dyffryn Ogwen, Bethesda 1975–80; now part-time lecturer in Painting and Drawing at tech. coll.; rep. by Thos. Agnew of Bond St., London; one-man exhbns. Liverpool 1973, Bangor Univ. 1974, 1979, 1986, Welsh Arts Council Gallery 1975, Llandudno 1982, Durham 1982, Campden Arts Centre 1982, Swansea 1983, Bath 1987; group exhbns. at Tate Gallery 1984, Rocks and Flesh at Norwich Art School Gallery 1985, and elsewhere; represented in Group Wales exhbn., Czechoslovakia 1986–87, Artists in the Parks, Victoria and Albert Museum, London, Experience of Landscape, Arts Council of G.B. Touring exhbn.; painting of Bethesda reproduced in book Green Bridge: Short Stories from Wales. *Publications:* Road to Bethesda 1982, Hard Won Image 1984, Self Portrait 1988. *Leisure interests:* sport, music, reading. *Address:* 6 Upper Hill Street, Gerlan, Bethesda, Gwynedd, Wales, United Kingdom.

PRENTICE, Rt. Hon. Sir Reginald Ernest, Kt., J.P.; British politician, public affairs consultant and company director; b. 16 July 1923, Thornton Heath, Surrey; s. of Ernest George Edward Prentice and Elizabeth

Prentice; m. Joan Godwin 1948; one d.; ed. Whitgift School and London School of Econs.; temp. civil servant 1940-42; Royal Artillery 1942-46; student at London School of Econs. 1946-49; mem. staff Transport and Gen. Workers Union, Asst. to Legal Sec., in charge of Union's Advice and Service Bureau 1950-57; M.P. for East Ham (North) 1957-74, for Newham North-East 1974-79; Minister of State, Dept. of Educ. and Science Oct. 1964-66; Minister of Public Building and Works 1966-67, of Overseas Devt. 1967-69; Sec. of State for Educ. and Science 1974-75; Minister for Overseas Devt., with Cabinet rank June 1975-Dec. 1976 (resigned); resigned as Transport and Gen. Workers' Union-sponsored M.P. 1976; resigned from Labour Party and joined Conservative Party Oct. 1977; Conservative M.P. for Daventry 1979-87; Minister for the Disabled 1979-80; Pres. Assen. of Business Execs. *Publication:* (jt. author) Right Turn 1978. *Leisure interests:* walking, swimming and golf. *Address:* Wansdyke, Church Lane, Mildenhall, Marlborough, Wilts., England. *Telephone:* 0672-55397.

PRESCOTT, John Leslie, M.P., DIP. ECON POL. (OXON.); British trade unionist and politician; b. 31 May 1938; s. of John Herbert Prescott and Phyllis Prescott; m. Pauline Tilston 1961; two s.; ed. WEA correspondence courses, Ruskin Coll., Oxford, Hull Univ.; trainee chef 1953-55; steward in Merchant Navy 1955-63; Recruitment Officer, Gen. & Municipal Workers Union 1965; contested Southport for Labour 1966; Full-time official Nat. Union of Seamen 1968-70; M.P. Kingston upon Hull (East) 1970-83, Hull (East) 1983-; mem. Select Cttee. Nationalized Industries 1973-79, Council of Europe 1972-75, European Parl. 1975-79; P.P.S. to Sec. of State for trade 1974-76; Opposition Spokesman on Transport 1979-81, Regional Affairs and Devolution 1981-83, on Transport 1983-84, on Employment 1984-87, on Energy 1987-; mem. Shadow Cabinet 1983-; Labour. *Publication:* Not Wanted on Voyage 1966. *Address:* House of Commons, London, S.W.1. (Office); 365 Saltshouse Road, Sutton-on-Hull, North Humberside, England (Home).

PRESS, Frank, PH.D.; American geophysicist; b. 4 Dec. 1924, Brooklyn, New York; s. of Solomon and Dora (Steinholz) Press; m. Billie Kallick 1946; one s. one d.; ed. Coll. of City of New York and Columbia Univ.; Research Associate, Columbia Univ. 1946-49, Instructor, Geology 1949-51, Asst. Prof. of Geology 1951-52, Assoc. Prof. 1952-55; Prof. Geophysics, Calif. Inst. of Tech. 1955-65, Dir. Seismological Lab. 1957-65; Co-editor Physics and Chemistry of the Earth 1957-; Chair. Dept. of Earth and Planetary Sciences, M.I.T. 1965-77; Dir. Office of Science and Tech. Policy, Exec. Office of Pres., and Science and Tech. Adviser to Pres. 1977-80; Consultant to U.S. Navy 1956-57, U.S. Dept. of Defense 1958-62, NASA 1960-62, and 1965-; mem. U.S. del. Nuclear Test Ban Conf. Geneva 1959-61, Moscow 1963; Pres. Science Advisory Comm. 1961-64; Chair. Bd. of Advisors Nat. Center for Earthquake Research of the U.S. Geophysical Survey 1966-76; Planetology Subcomm. NASA 1966-70; Chair. Earthquake Prediction Panel Office of Science and Tech. 1965-66; Fellow American Acad. of Arts and Sciences 1966; Fellow Royal Astronomical Soc., mem. Nat. Acad. of Sciences 1958, Pres. 1981-; mem. Nat. Science Bd. 1970-77; fmr. Pres. American Geophysical Union; Chair. Cttee. on Scholarly Communication with People's Repub. of China 1975-77; mem. U.S.-U.S.S.R. Working Group in Earthquake Prediction 1973; fmr. mem. Exec. Council Nat. Acad. of Sciences; Hon. LL.D. (City Univ. of N.Y.) 1972, Hon. D.Sc. (Notre Dame Univ.) 1973, (Univ. of Rhode Island, of Arizona, Rutgers Univ., City Univ. of New York) 1979; Townsend Harris Medal Coll. of the City of New York; Royal Astronomical Soc. Gold Medal (U.K.) 1971; Day Medal Geological Soc. of America, Interior 1972; NASA Award 1973; Killian Faculty Achievement Award, M.I.T. 1975. *Publication:* Earth (with R. Siever) 1974. *Leisure interests:* skiing, sailing. *Address:* National Academy of Sciences, 2101 Constitution Avenue, N.W., Washington, D.C. 20418, U.S.A. *Telephone:* (202) 389-6231.

PRESS, Tamara Natanovna; Soviet athlete; b. 10 May 1937, Kharkov; mem. CPSU 1962-; ed. Leningrad Construction Engineering Inst. and Higher Party School of Cen. Cttee. of CPSU; women's champion in shot-put at Olympic Games 1960, 1964, at discus 1964, women's champion of Europe in discus throwing three times, between 1958-62, and sixteen times women's champion of U.S.S.R. between 1958-66; worked for All-Union Cen. Council of Trade Unions 1967-; Order of Lenin, Order of Badge of Honour, Honoured Master of Sports of U.S.S.R. 1960. *Address:* c/o All-Union Central Council of Trade Unions, Leninsky prospect 42, Moscow V-119, U.S.S.R.

PRESSLER, Larry, M.A., J.D.; American politician; b. 29 March 1942, Humboldt, S.D.; s. of Antone Pressler and Loretta Claussen; m. Harriet Dent 1982; ed. Univ. of South Dakota, Univ. of Oxford, England, Harvard Kennedy School of Govt. and Harvard Law School; Lieut. in U.S. Army, Viet-Nam 1966-68; mem. House of Reps. 1975-79; Senator from South Dakota Jan. 1979-, Chair. Senate Arms Control Cttee., mem. several other Senate Cttees.; Sec. U.S. Del. to Inter-Parl. Union 1981; Republican. *Publication:* U.S. Senators from the Prairie 1982. *Leisure interests:* running, tennis. *Address:* 407A Russell Senate Office Building, Washington, D.C. 20510; 700 New Hampshire Avenue, N.W., Washington, D.C. 20037, U.S.A. (Home).

PRESTON, Lewis T.; American banker; b. 5 Aug. 1926, New York, N.Y.; s. of Lewis Thompson and Priscilla (Baldwin) Preston; m. Gladys Pulitzer 1959; one s. five d.; ed. Harvard Univ.; joined J. P. Morgan & Co. Inc. 1951, Head of London offices 1966-68; Vice-Pres. Morgan Guaranty Trust Co. of New York 1961, Exec. Vice-Pres. and Head of Int. Banking Div. 1968-76; Chair. Morgan Guaranty Int. Finance Corpn. 1971-76; Vice-Chair. Bd., J. P. Morgan & Co., Morgan Guaranty 1976-78, Pres. 1978-79, Chair. Jan. 1980-, also Chair. Exec. Cttee.; mem. Fed. Advisory Council 1983-; Dir. Gen. Electric Co.; Trustee New York Univ., Guggenheim Museum; mem. Cttee. for Econ. Devt. *Leisure interests:* golf, tennis. *Address:* 23 Wall Street, New York, N.Y. 10015, U.S.A.

PRESTON, Peter John, M.A.; British journalist; b. 23 May 1938, Barrow-upon-Soar, Leicestershire; s. of John Whittle Preston and Kathlyn (née Chell); m. Jean Mary Burrell 1962; two s. two d.; ed. Loughborough Grammar School and St. John's Coll., Oxford; Editorial Trainee, Liverpool Daily Post 1960-63; Political Reporter, The Guardian 1963-64, Educ. Corresp. 1965-66, Diary Ed. 1966-68, Features Ed. 1968-72, Production Ed. 1972-75, Ed., The Guardian 1975-; mem. Scott Trust 1979-; Hon. D.Litt. (Loughborough) 1982. *Leisure interests:* football, films, four children. *Address:* The Guardian, 119 Farringdon Road, London, EC1R 3ER, England. *Telephone:* 01-278 2332.

PRESTON, Reginald Dawson, F.R.S., D.SC.; British professor of biophysics; b. 21 July 1908, Leeds; s. of Walter Cluderay and Eliza Preston (née Dawson); m. 1st Sarah Jane Pollard 1935 (deceased); m. 2nd Eva Frei 1963; one s. (deceased), two d.; ed. West Leeds High School, Univ. of Leeds and Cornell Univ., U.S.A.; Research Asst., Botany Dept., Univ. of Leeds 1931-32, 1851 Exhbn. Fellow 1932-35; Rockefeller Foundation Fellow, Cornell Univ. 1935-36; Asst. Lecturer, Lecturer, Sr. Lecturer, Botany Dept., Univ. of Leeds 1936-49, Reader in Plant Biophysics 1949-53, Prof. 1953-62, Prof. and Founder Head, Astbury Dept. of Biophysics 1962-73, Emer. Prof. 1973-, Dean of Science 1955-58, Chair. Bd. of Science and Tech. 1958-61, Library Cttee. 1964-73; School of Biological Sciences 1970-73; Visiting Prof., Botany Dept., Imperial Coll., Univ. of London 1976-79; Scientific Consultant to Hicksons Timber Impregnation Co. 1957-61; Fellow Inst. of Physics, Linnean Soc., Int. Acad. of Wood Science; Hon. Fellow Royal Microscopical Soc.; Hon. mem. Soc. for Experimental Biology, British Biophysical Soc., Int. Assoc. of Wood Anatomists; Anselme Payen Medal and Award, American Chemical Soc.; Distinguished Service Medal, Leeds Philosophy and Literature Soc. *Publications:* Molecular Architecture of Plant Cell Walls 1952, Physical Biology of Plant Cell Walls 1974; some 200 articles in scientific journals. *Leisure interests:* music, walking, gardening. *Address:* 117 St. Anne's Road, Leeds, LS6 3NZ, West Yorkshire, England. *Telephone:* (0532) 785248.

PRESTON, Simon John, MUS.B., M.A., A.R.C.M., F.R.A.M., F.R.C.C.O., F.R.C.M.; British organist and choirmaster; b. 4 Aug. 1938; ed. Canford School, King's Coll., Cambridge; Sub Organist Westminster Abbey 1962-67; Acting Organist St Albans Abbey 1967-68; Organist and Lecturer in Music, Christ Church, Oxford 1970-81; Organist and Master of the Choristers Westminster Abbey 1981-87; Conductor Oxford Bach Choir 1971-74; Hon. F.R.C.O.; Edison Award 1971; Grand Prix du Disque 1979. *Leisure interests:* croquet, squash. *Address:* Little Hardwick, Langton Green, Tunbridge Wells, Kent, England. *Telephone:* (0892) 862042.

PRETI, Luigi; Italian politician; b. 23 Oct. 1914; fmr. lawyer and Prof. of Philosophy and Pedagogy; mem. Constituent Assembly 1946-47, Chamber of Deputies 1947-, Vice-Pres. 1980-83; Pres. Internal Affairs Comm. Chamber of Deputies; Under-Sec. of State to Treas. (War Pensions Dept.) 1954; Minister for Finance 1958-59, 1966-68, of Foreign Trade 1962-63, without Portfolio Dec. 1963-66, for the Budget 1968-69, of Finance 1970-72, of Transport and Civil Aviation 1973-74, of the Merchant Navy March-Aug. 1979, of Transport 1979-80; Social Democrat. *Publications:* Il cocnetto di status 1942, Il Governo nella Costituzione della Repubblica 1954, Le lotte agrarie nella Valle Padana 1955, Diritto elettorale politico 1957, Giovinezza, giovinezza 1964, I miti della razza e dell'Impero 1968, Dialoghi della Nuova Frontiera 1970, Interpretazione di Dubcek 1971, Italia malata 1972, Un ebreo nel fascismo 1974, Il compromesso storico 1975, La sfida tra democrazia e autoritarismo 1980, Mussolini giovane 1982, Giolitti, i riformisti e gli altri 1985, Anno duemila, la pace nel mondo 1986. *Address:* Camera dei Deputati, Rome; Via P. Costa 34, 40125 Bologna, Italy.

PRÊTRE, Georges; French conductor; b. 14 Aug. 1924, Waziers; s. of Emile and Jeanne (Dérin) Prêtre; m. Gina Marny 1950; one s. one d.; ed. Lycée and Conservatoire de Douai, Conservatoire national supérieur de musique de Paris and Ecole des chefs d'orchestre; Dir. of Music, Opera Houses of Marseilles, Lille and Toulouse 1946-55, Dir. of music Opéra-comique, Paris, 1955-59, at l'Opéra 1959-; Dir.-Gen. of Music at l'Opéra 1970-71; conductor of the symphonic asscns. of Paris and of principal festivals throughout the world; also conducted at La Scala, Milan and major American orchestras; Conductor Metropolitan Opera House, New York 1964-65, La Scala, Milan 1965-66, Salzburg 1966; First Visiting Conductor, Vienna Symphony Orchestra 1985-; Officier, Légion d'honneur 1971, Haute Distinction République Italienne 1975, Commdr. République Italienne 1980; Officier, Légion d'honneur 1984. *Leisure interests:* riding, swimming, aviation. *Address:* Château de Vaudricourt, à Naves, par Castres, 81100 France. *Telephone:* (63) 59 06 91.

PREVIN, André George; American conductor, composer and pianist; b. (as Andreas Ludwig Priwin) 6 April 1929, Berlin, Germany; s. of Jack and

Charlotte (née Epstein) Previn; m. 1st Betty Bennett (divorced); two d.; m. 2nd Dory Langan 1959 (divorced 1970); m. 3rd Mia Farrow (q.v.) 1970 (divorced 1979); three s. three d.; m. 4th Heather Hales 1982; one s.; ed. Berlin and Paris Conservatories and Univ. of Calif.; Music Dir. Houston Symphony, U.S. 1967-69; Music Dir. and Principal Conductor, London Symphony Orchestra 1968-79, Conductor Emer. 1979-; composed and conducted approx. 50 film scores 1950-65; Guest conductor of most major world orchestras, also Royal Opera House, Covent Garden, Salzburg, Edinburgh, Osaka, Flanders Festivals; Music Dir. London South Bank Summer Music Festival 1972-74, Pittsburgh Symphony Orchestra 1976-84, Los Angeles Philharmonic Orchestra 1984-89; Music Dir. Royal Philharmonic Orchestra 1985-86, Prin. Conductor 1987-; series of television specials for BBC and for American Public Broadcasting Service; Television Critics Award 1972; Acad. Award for Best Film Score 1959, 1960, 1964, 1965. *Major works:* Symphony for Strings 1965, Overture to a Comedy 1966, Suite for Piano 1967, Cello Concerto 1968, Four Songs, Soprano and Orchestra 1968, Two Serenades for Violin 1969, Guitar Concerto 1970, Piano Preludes 1972, Woodwind Quintet 1973, Good Companions (musical) 1974, Song Cycle on Poems by Philip Larkin 1977, Every Good Boy Deserves Favour (music, drama, text by Tom Stoppard, q.v.) 1977, Pages from the Calendar (for Solo Piano) 1977, Peaches (for Flute and Strings) 1978, Principals 1980, Outings for Brass Quintet 1980, Reflections 1981, Piano Concerto 1984. *Publications:* Music Face to Face 1971, Orchestra (ed.) 1977, Guide to Music 1983. *Leisure interests:* collecting contemporary art, fencing, American folk art. *Address:* c/o Harrison/Parrott Ltd., 12 Penzance Place, London, W11 4PA, England.

PREY, Hermann; German opera and concert singer; b. 11 July 1929, Berlin; s. of Hermann Prey, Sr.; m. Barbara Pniok 1954; one s. two d.; ed. Humanistisches Gymnasium " Zum Grauen Kloster", Berlin, and Staatliche Musikhochschule, Berlin; at State Opera, Wiesbaden 1952, also Hamburg, Munich, Berlin, Vienna; guest appearances at La Scala, Milan, Metropolitan Opera, New York, Teatro Colón, Buenos Aires, San Francisco Opera; has sung at Festivals at Salzburg, Bayreuth, Edinburgh, Vienna, Tokyo, Aix-en-Provence, Perugia, Berlin, etc.; now with Munich State Opera; Prof., Musikhochschule, Hamburg 1982-; Meistersänger-Wettbewerb, Nuremberg 1952; Bayerischer Maximiliansorden 1986. *Publication:* Premierenfieber (memoirs) 1981. *Leisure interests:* riding, films. *Address:* Fichtenstrasse 14, 8033 Krailling vor München, Federal Republic of Germany.

PRICE, Charles Harry; American diplomatist; b. 1 April 1931, Kansas City, Mo.; s. of Charles Harry Price and Virginia (née Ogden) Price; m. Carol Ann Swanson 1969; two s. three d.; ed. Univ. of Mo.; Pres. and Dir. Linwood Securities Co., Kansas City 1960-81; Chair. and Dir. Price Candy Co., Kansas City 1969-81, American Bancorpn., Kansas City 1973-81; Chair. and C.E.O. American Bank and Trust Co., Kansas City 1973-81; Chair. and Dir. American Mortgage Co., Kansas City 1973-81; Dir. Earle M. Jorgensen & Co., Los Angeles, Swanson Broadcasting Co., Tulsa, Ameribanc, St. Joseph, Mo.; Amb. to Belgium 1981-83, to U.K. 1983-89; Dir. Hanson PLC, Texaco Inc., United Telecommunications Inc., New York Times 1989-; Dir. (non-exec.) B.A. 1989-; Vice-Chair. and mem. Exec. Cttee. Midwest Research Inst., Kansas City 1978-81; mem. Bd. of Dirs. Civic Council, Greater Kansas City 1979-80; Dir. St. Luke's Hosp., Kansas City 1970-81; mem. Heart Inst. Cttee., Kansas City, Int. Inst. Strategic Studies; Trustee, Sunset Hill School 1970-81; Hon. L.H.D. (Westminster Coll.) 1984; Hon. LL.D. (Univ. of Mo.) 1988. *Address:* One West Armour Boulevard, Suite 300, Kansas City, Mo. 64111, U.S.A. *Telephone:* (816) 931-4422.

PRICE, Don Krasher, A.B., B.A., B.LITT., LL.D., L.H.D., LITT.D., D.C.L.; American university professor; b. 23 Jan. 1910, Middlesboro, Ky.; s. of Don Krasher Price and Nell Rhorer Price; m. 1st Margaret (Helen) Gailbreath 1936 (died 1970), one s. one d.; m. 2nd Harriet Sloane Fels 1971; ed. Vanderbilt and Oxford Univs.; reporter Nashville Evening Tennessean 1930-32; mem. staff Home Owners' Loan Corpn. 1935-37, Social Science Research Council 1937-39, Public Admin. Clearing House 1939-53, U.S. Bureau of the Budget 1945-46, Hoover Comm. on Org. of Exec. Branch of Govt. 1947-48; Deputy Chair. Research and Devt. Board, U.S. Dept. of Defense 1952-53; Assoc. Dir. The Ford Foundation 1953-54, Vice-Pres. 1954-58; Dean, John Fitzgerald Kennedy School of Govt. (fmrly. Graduate School of Public Admin.) 1958-77, Harvard Univ. and Prof. of Govt., Harvard Univ. 1958-80, Prof. Emer. 1980-; Eastman Prof., Oxford Univ. 1985-86; mem. President's Advisory Cttee. on Govt. Org. 1959-61; Consultant to Exec. Office of the Pres. 1961-72; Herbert Spencer Lecturer, Oxford Univ. 1982; Trustee, Vanderbilt Univ., Twentieth Century Fund, Rhodes Scholarship Trust 1968-78, Petroleum Press Foundation (London) 1977-83; mem. American Asscn. for the Advancement of Science (Pres. 1967, Chair. of Bd. 1968); Senior mem. Inst. of Medicine; Hon. A.M., LL.D., L.H.D., Litt.D., D.C.L. (Oxford) 1983; Faculty Prize of Harvard Univ. Press for The Scientific Estate 1965. *Publications:* City Manager Government in the United States (with Harold and Kathryn Stone) 1940, Government and Science 1954, The Secretary of State (Editor) 1960, The Scientific Estate 1965, America's Unwritten Constitution 1983. *Leisure interests:* tennis, fishing. *Address:* 79 J. F. Kennedy Street, Cambridge, Mass. 02138; 984 Memorial Drive, Cambridge, Mass. 02138, U.S.A. (Home). *Telephone:* 617-876-2495 (Home).

PRICE, Frank; American television and cinema producer and executive; b. 17 May 1930, Decatur, Ill.; s. of William and Winifred (née Moran) Price; m. Katherine Huggins 1965; four s.; ed. Michigan State Univ., served with U.S.N. 1948-49; writer and story Ed., CBS-TV, New York 1951-53; with Columbia Pictures, Hollywood 1953-57, NBC-TV 1957-58; producer, writer, Universal Television, Calif. 1959-64, Vice-Pres. 1964-71, Sr. Vice-Pres. 1971-73, Exec. Vice-Pres. 1973-74, Pres. 1974-78, 1983-; Pres. Columbia Pictures 1978-79, Chair. and C.E.O. 1979-83; Chair. and C.E.O. MCA Motion Picture Group 1983-86, Price Entertainment 1987-; Exec. Producer The Virginian 1961-64, Ironside 1965, Kojak, Six Million Dollar Man, Bionic Woman, Rockford Files, Quincy, Rich Man, Poor Man. *Address:* Price Entertainment Inc., Columbia Plaza East, Suite 229, Burbank, Calif. 91505, U.S.A. *Telephone:* (818) 954-7717.

PRICE, Rt. Hon. George Cadle, P.C.; Belizean politician; b. 15 Jan. 1919; s. of William Cadle Price and Irene Price; ed. St. John's Coll., Belize City, and St. Augustin Seminary, Mississippi; City Councillor 1947-62; founder-mem. People's United Party (PUP) 1950, Sec. PUP 1950-56, Leader PUP 1956-; Pres. Gen. Workers' Union 1947-52; mem. Legislative Council, British Honduras (now Belize) 1954-65; mem. Exec. Council 1954-57, 1961-65; Mayor, Belize City 1956-62; mem. House of Reps. 1965-84, Cabinet 1965-84; fmr. mem. for Nat. Resources; First Minister 1961-63, leader of del. to London for self-Govt. constitutional talks; Premier 1964-81, Prime Minister of Belize 1981-84, Minister of Finance and Econ. Planning 1965-84, of Foreign Affairs 1981-84; mem. Privy Council 1982-; Chair. Reconstruction and Devt. Corpn.; Outstanding Alumnus Award (St. John's Coll.) 1971. *Address:* c/o House of Representatives, Belmopan, Belize.

PRICE, James Gordon, B.A., M.D.; British university professor; b. 20 June 1926, Brush, Colo., U.S.A.; s. of John Hoover Price and Laurette (Dodds) Price; m. Janet Alice McSween 1949; two s. two d.; ed. Univ. of Colorado; Intern, Denver Gen. Hosp.; pvt. practice, family medicine, Brush, Colo. 1952-78; Prof. and Chair. Dept. of Family Practice, Univ. of Kan. 1982-; nationally syndicated newspaper column, Your Family Physician 1973-86; Medical Ed., Curriculum Innovations 1973-; mem. Inst. of Medicine, N.A.S. *Leisure interest:* computer programming. *Address:* Department of Family Practice, University of Kansas Medical Center, 39th at Rainbow, Kansas City, Kan. 66103, U.S.A. *Telephone:* (913) 588-1900.

PRICE, Sir (James) Robert, K.B.E., D.PHIL., D.SC., F.A.A.; Australian organic chemist (retd.); b. 25 March 1912, Kadina, S. Australia; s. of E. J. Price; m. Joyce E. Brooke 1940; one s. two d.; ed. St. Peter's Coll., Adelaide and Univs. of Adelaide and Oxford; Head, Chem. Section, John Innes Horticultural Inst., U.K. 1937; Ministry of Supply (U.K.) 1939; Council for Scientific and Industrial Research (C.S.I.R.) Div. of Industrial Chem., Australia 1945; Officer in charge, Organic Chem. Section, Commonwealth Scientific and Industrial Research Org. (CSIRO) 1960, subsequently Chief Organic Chem. Div.; mem. Exec. CSIRO 1966; fmr. Chair. CSIRO 1970-77; Fellow, Australian Acad. of Science, Chair. Nat. Cttee. for Chem. 1966-69; Pres. Royal Australian Chem. Inst. (R.A.C.I.) 1962-64; mem. Council, Monash Univ. 1979-83; H. G. Smith Memorial Medal (R.A.C.I.) 1956, Leighton Memorial Medal (R.A.C.I.) 1969. *Publications:* numerous scientific papers and articles. *Leisure interest:* growing Australian native plants. *Address:* "Yangoora", 2 Ocean View Avenue, East R.S.D., Dromana, Victoria 3936, Australia.

PRICE, Leontyne; American soprano singer; b. 10 Feb. 1927, Laurel, Miss.; d. of James A. and Kate (Baker) Price; m. William Warfield 1952 (divorced 1973); ed. Central State Coll., Wilberforce, Ohio and Juilliard School of Music; appeared as Bess (Porgy and Bess), Vienna, Berlin, Paris, London, New York 1952-54; recitalist, soloist 1954-; soloist Hollywood Bowl 1955-59, 1966; opera singer NBC-TV 1955-58, San Francisco Opera Co. 1957-59, 1960-61, Vienna Staatsoper 1958, 1959-60, 1961; recording artist RCA-Victor 1958-; appeared Covent Garden 1958-59, 1970, Chicago 1959, 1960, 1965, Milan 1960-61, 1963, 1967, Metropolitan Opera, New York 1961-62, 1963-70, 1972, Paris Opéra as Aida 1968, Metropolitan Opera as Aida 1985 (retd.); numerous recordings; Fellow, American Acad. of Arts and Sciences; Hon. D.Mus. (Howard Univ., Cen. State Coll., Ohio); Hon. D.H.L. (Dartmouth); Hon. Dr. of Humanities (Rust Coll., Miss.); Hon. D.Hum.Litt. (Fordham); Presidential Medal of Freedom, Order of Merit (Italy), Nat. Medal of Arts 1985. *Address:* c/o Columbia Artists Management Inc., 165 West 57th Street, New York, N.Y. 10019, U.S.A.

PRICE, Margaret Berenice, C.B.E.; British opera singer; b. 13 April 1941, Tredegar, Wales; d. of late Thomas Glyn Price and of Lilian Myfanwy Richards; ed. Pontllanfraith Grammar School and Trinity Coll. of Music, London; operatic debut with Welsh Nat. Opera in Marriage of Figaro; renowned for Mozart operatic roles; has sung in world's leading opera houses and festivals; has made many recordings of opera, oratorio, concert works and recitals, and many radio broadcasts and television appearances; Hon. Fellow, Trinity Coll. of Music; Elisabeth Schumann Prize for Lieder, Ricordi Prize for Opera, Silver Medal of the Worshipful Co. of Musicians; Hon. D.Mus. (Wales) 1983. *Major roles include:* Countess in Marriage of Figaro, Pamina in The Magic Flute, Fiordiligi in Così fan Tutte, Donna Anna in Don Giovanni, Konstanze in Die Entführung, Amelia in Simone Boccanegra, Agathe in Freischütz, Desdemona in Otello, Elisabetta in Don Carlo, Aida and Norma. *Leisure interests:* cookery, reading, walking, swimming, driving. *Address:* c/o Bayerische Staatsoper München, Max Josef Platz 2, 8000 München 22, Federal Republic of Germany.

PRICE, Paul Buford, PH.D.; American physicist; b. 8 Nov. 1932, Memphis, Tenn.; s. of the late Paul Buford and Eva (Dupuy) Price; m. Jo Ann Baum 1958, one s. three d.; ed. Davidson Coll., Univ. of Virginia, Univ. of Bristol, Univ. of Cambridge; Physicist Gen. Electric Research Lab., New York 1960-69; Visiting Prof. Tata Inst. of Fundamental Research, Bombay, India 1965-66; Adjunct Prof. of Physics Rensselaer Polytechnic Inst. 1967-68; Prof. of Physics Univ. of Calif. at Berkeley 1969-, Chair. Dept. of Physics 1987-, Dir. Space Science Lab. 1979-85; NASA Consultant on Lunar Sample Analysis Planning Team; mem. Bd. Dirs. Terradex Corpn. 1978-86; Fellow and Chair. Cosmic Physics Div. American Physical Soc.; Fellow American Geophysical Union, American Astronomical Soc.; mem. Space Science Bd., N.A.S., Sec. Physical and Math. Sciences Class of N.A.S. 1985-88, Chair. Physics and Math. Scientific Class 1988-; Distinguished Service Award, (American Nuclear Soc.) 1964, Ernest O. Lawrence Memorial Award of Atomic Energy Comm. 1971, NASA Medal for Exceptional Scientific Achievement 1973; Hon. Sc.D. (Davidson Coll.) 1973. *Publications:* (jointly) Nuclear Tracks in Solids, numerous research papers in specialized journals. *Leisure interests:* skiing, travel. *Address:* 1056 Overlook Road, Berkeley, California, U.S.A. *Telephone:* (415) 642-4982 (Office); (415) 548-5206 (Home).

PRICE, Sir Robert (see Price, Sir James Robert).

PRICE, Vincent, B.A., B.S.A.; American actor; b. 27 May, 1911, St. Louis; s. of Vincent L. Price and Marguerite Wilcox; m. 1st Edith Barrett 1938 (divorced); one s.; m. 2nd Mary Grant 1939 (divorced); one d.; m. 3rd Coral Browne 1974; ed. Yale and London Univs. *Stage appearances include:* Victoria Regina 1935, Outward Bound 1939, Don Juan in Hell, Cocktail Party 1951, The Lady's Not for Burning 1952, Richard III 1954, Darling of the Day 1968, Oliver 1975, Diversions and Delights 1977-; Film debut in Service de Luxe 1938. *Films include:* Elizabeth and Essex 1939, Green Hell 1940, Tower of London 1940, Brigham Young 1940, Song of Bernadette 1943, Keys of the Kingdom 1944, Laura 1944, Czarina 1945, Dragonwyck 1946, Shock 1946, Long Night 1947, Three Musketeers 1948, Champagne for Caesar 1949, His Kind of Woman 1951, House of Wax 1953, The Mad Magician 1954, The Ten Commandments 1956, The Story of Mankind 1957, The Fly 1958, The Bat 1959, The House on Haunted Hill 1960, Fall of the House of Usher 1961, The Pit and the Pendulum 1961, Tales of Terror 1962, The Raven 1963, A Comedy of Terrors 1963, The Tomb of Ligeia 1964, City under the Sea 1965, Dr. Goldfoot and the Sex Machine 1965, House of a Thousand Dolls 1967, The Oblong Box 1969, Scream and Scream Again 1969, Cry of the Banshee 1970, The Abominable Dr. Phibes 1971, Dr. Phibes Rises Again 1971, Theatre of Blood 1973, Madhouse 1973, Basil, The Great Mouse Detective 1986, The Whales of August 1987, Backtrack 1989; narrator with various symphony orchestras; numerous TV appearances; mem. Bd. Archives of American Art, Whitney Museum Friends of American Art; art consultant Sears Roebuck & Co.; Commr. of U.S. Indian Arts and Crafts Board. *Publications:* I Like What I Know 1958, Book of Joe (with Mary Price) 1960, Treasury of American Art 1972, The Monsters (co-author) 1981; ed. (with V. Delacroix) Drawings of Delacroix. *Leisure interests:* collecting works of art, swimming. *Address:* 2121 Avenue of the Stars, Suite 1240, Los Angeles, Calif. 90067, U.S.A. (Office).

PRIDEAUX, Sir Humphrey Povah Treverbian, Kt., O.B.E., M.A.; British business executive; b. 13 Dec. 1915, London; s. of Walter Treverbian Prideaux and Marion Fenn (née Arbuthnot); m. Cynthia V. Birch Reynardson 1939; four s.; ed. St. Aubyns, Eton and Trinity Coll., Oxford; Regular army officer 1936-53; Dir. Navy, Army & Air Force Insts. 1956-63, Chair. 1963-73; Chair. Lord Wandsworth Foundation 1966, Trustee 1963-; Deputy Chair. Liebig's Extract of Meat Co. Ltd. 1968-69, Dir. 1966-69; Chair. Oxo Ltd. 1968-72; Dir. W. H. Smith & Son (Holdings) Ltd. 1969, Vice-Chair. 1977-81; Dir. Brooke Bond Oxo Ltd. 1969-70; Chair. Brooke Bond Liebig 1972-81; Pres. London Life Asscn Ltd. 1973-83, Dir. 1964-88; Vice-Chair. Morland & Co. 1981-82, Chair. 1983-; Dir. Grindlays (Holdings) PLC 1982-85; Dir. Grindlays Bank PLC 1984-85. *Leisure interests:* country pursuits. *Address:* Summers Farm, Long Sutton, Basingstoke, Hants.; also 124 Marsham Court, London, S.W.1, England. *Telephone:* (0256) 862295; 01-828 5378.

PRIDEAUX, Sir John Francis, Kt., O.B.E.; British banker; b. 30 Dec. 1911; s. of Walter Treverbian Prideaux and Marion Fenn (née Arbuthnot); m. Joan Brown 1934; two s. one d.; ed. St. Aubyns, Rottingdean and Eton Coll.; Middlesex Yeomanry, Second World War; Dir. Arbuthnot Latham and Co. Ltd. 1936, Chair. 1964-69; Chair. Arbuthnot Latham Holdings Ltd. 1969-74, Dir. Arbuthnot Latham Bank 1983-; Dir. Westminster Bank Ltd. (from 1968 Nat. Westminster Bank) 1955-81, Deputy Chair. 1962-69, Joint Deputy Chair. 1969-70, Chair. 1971-77, Chair. Int. Westminster Bank Ltd. 1969-77, Dir. 1977-81; Chair. and Treas., Bd. of Govs., St. Thomas' Hosp. 1964-74; Chair. Special Trustees for St. Thomas' Hosp. 1974-88; Chair. Cttee. of London Clearing Bankers 1974-76; Pres. Inst. of Bankers 1974-76; mem. Cttee. to Review the Functioning of Financial Insts. 1976-; Vice-Pres. British Bankers' Assen. 1972-77; D.L. for the County of Surrey 1976; Legion of Merit, U.S.A. *Address:* Arbuthnot Latham Bank Ltd., 131 Finsbury Pavement, London, EC2A 1AY;

Elderslie, Ockley, Surrey, England. *Telephone:* 01-628 9876 (Office); (0306) 711263 (Home).

PRIESS, Friedrich, D.IUR.; German banker (retd.); b. 19 Oct. 1903, Bremen; s. of Georg Priess and Paula Tönnesmann; m. Maria Büttner 1931; one s. three d.; ed. Univs. of Freiburg and Marburg; Lawyer, Bremen and legal adviser to N.V. Philips Gloeilampenfabrieken 1929-30; judge, Bremen 1930-37, Hamburg 1937-50; Vice-Pres. Landeszentralbank, Hamburg 1950-56; Partner, M. M. Warburg-Brinckmann, Wirtz & Co., Hamburg 1956-73; Chair. Advisory Bd., Deutsches Getreide-Kontor GmbH. *Address:* c/o M. M. Warburg-Brinckmann, Wirtz & Co., Ferdinandstrasse 75, 2000 Hamburg 1, Federal Republic of Germany. *Telephone:* 3 28 21.

PRIESTLEY, Charles Henry Brian, A.O., M.A., SC.D., F.A.A., F.R.S.; British meteorologist (retd.); b. 8 July 1915, Highgate, London; s. of Thomas Gordon Priestley and Muriel Brown; m. Constance Tweedy 1946; one s. two d.; ed. Mill Hill School and St. John's Coll. Cambridge; service in Meteorological Office, Air Ministry, at Porton (England), Suffield (Canada) and Dunstable (England), finishing as Officer-in-Charge Upper Air Analysis and Forecasting Branch 1939-46; Chief, Div. of Atmospheric Physics, Commonwealth Scientific and Industrial Research Org. (CSIRO) Australia 1946-73, Chair. Environmental Physics Research Labs. 1971-78; Prof. Meteorology, Monash Univ., Australia 1978-80; mem. Council, Australian Acad. of Science 1958-60, Vice-Pres. 1959-60; Vice-Pres. Royal Meteorological Soc. 1957-59; mem. Exec. Cttee. Int. Assen. for Meteorology and Atmospheric Physics 1954-60, Vice-Pres. 1967-75; mem. Advisory Cttee. World Meteorological Org. 1964-68, Chair. 1967-68; mem. numerous other int. scientific bodies; Visiting Research Scientist, Univ. of Chicago 1957; David Syme Medal, Univ. of Melbourne 1956; Buchan Prize, Royal Meteorological Soc. 1948, Symons Gold Medal, Royal Meteorological Soc. 1967, Int. Meteorological Org. Prize 1973, Rossby Research Medal 1974, Flinders Lecture 1976. *Publications:* Turbulent Transport in the Lower Atmosphere 1959; 60 scientific papers. *Leisure interests:* golf, bridge. *Address:* Flat 2, 862 Malvern Road, Armadale, Victoria 3143, Australia (Home).

PRIETO, Arnaldo da Costa; Brazilian civil engineer and politician; b. 13 Feb. 1930, Rio Grande do Sul; s. of Vicente B. Prieto and Henriqueta Maria Prieto; m. Irma Emilia Daudt Prieto; five s.; Pres. of Students Union of Rio Grande do Sul State; Titular Prof., Chair. of Topography, School of Eng., Pontífica Universidade Católica do Rio Grande do Sul; mem. Municipal Council, São Leopoldo 1960-63; Sec. of State for Labour and Housing, Rio Grande do Sul State 1963-67; Fed. Deputy 1967-71, 1971-75; Minister of Labour 1974-78; Dir. Housing Nat. Bank 1979-; Minister of Supreme Court of Audit 1980-. *Address:* SQS 207, Bloco K, Ap. 504, 70 253 Brasília, D.F., Brazil. *Telephone:* (00) (55) (61) 244-3297 and 223-7166.

PRIGENT, Michel; French editor; b. 29 Sept. 1950, Paris; s. of Jean Prigent and Germaine Morvan; m. Elisabeth Depierre 1974; two s.; ed. Lycées Henri IV and Louis-le-Grand, Ecole Normale Supérieure and Sorbonne, Paris; joined Presses Universitaires de France 1974, Sec. to Bd. of Dirs. 1978, Editorial Dir. 1985; Pres. Editeurs de Sciences Humaines et Sociales 1984. *Publications:* La liberté à refaire 1984, Le héros et l'Etat dans la tragédie de Pierre Corneille 1986. *Leisure interest:* walking. *Address:* Presses Universitaires de France, 108 boulevard Saint-Germain, 75006 Paris (Office); 17 rue de Tournour, 75006 Paris, France (Home). *Telephone:* 43.25.52.13 (Home).

PRIGOGINE, Ilya, PH.D.; Belgian university professor; b. 25 Jan. 1917, Moscow, U.S.S.R.; s. of Roman Prigogine and Julia Wichman; m. Marina Prokopowicz 1961; two s.; ed. Univ. Libre de Bruxelles; Prof. at Univ. Libre de Bruxelles 1947-; Dir. Instituts Internationaux de Physique et de Chimie 1959-; Prof., Enrico Fermi Inst. for Nuclear Studies and Inst. for the Study of Metals, Univ. of Chicago, U.S.A. 1961-66; Dir. Ilya Prigogine Center for Statistical Mechanics and Thermodynamics, Univ. of Texas 1967-; Special Adviser to Comm. of European Communities 1981; Chair. Rectory's Advisory Cttee., UN Univ.; Assoc. Dir. of Studies, Ecole des Hautes Etudes en Sciences Sociales, France 1987-; Hon. Prof. Banarashindu Univ. 1988; mem. Académie Royale de Belgique 1958, Pres. Classe des Sciences 1968-70; Foreign Hon. mem. American Acad. of Sciences and Arts 1960; Fellow Acad. of Sciences of New York 1962; mem. Romanian Acad. of Science 1965; mem. Royal Soc. of Sciences, Uppsala, Sweden 1967; Foreign Assoc. N.A.S (U.S.A.) 1967; mem. corresp. de la Soc. Royale des Sciences, Liège 1967; corresp. mem. Class of Physics and Mathematics, Acad. of Sciences, Göttingen 1970, Österreichische Akad. der Wissenschaften, Vienna 1971; mem. Deutsche Akad. der Naturforscher Leopoldina 1970, Acad. Int. de Philosophie des Sciences, Acad. Européenne des Sciences, des Arts et des Lettres, Paris 1980; foreign mem. Akad. der Wissenschaften der D.D.R., Berlin 1980; Hon. mem. Chemical Soc. of Poland 1971, Royal Chem. Soc. (Belgium) 1987, Biophysical Soc. (China); American Chem. Soc. Centennial Foreign Fellow 1976; mem. corresp. of Rheinische Westfälische Akad. der Wissenschaften, Düsseldorf, Foreign Fellow of the Indian National Science Acad. 1979; mem. Bd. Lawrence Hall of Sciences, Univ. of Calif. 1982; mem. Accademia Mediterranea delle Scienze, Catania, Italy 1982; Foreign mem. U.S.S.R. Acad. of Sciences 1982; Extraordinary Scientific mem. Max-Planck Foundation (Fed. Repub. of Germany) 1984; Dr. h.c. (Univs. of Newcastle-upon-Tyne 1966, Poitiers 1966, Chicago 1969, Bordeaux 1972, Uppsala 1977, Liège 1978, Aix-en-

Provence 1978, Georgetown 1980, Rio de Janeiro 1981, Cracow 1981, Stevens Inst. of Tech., Hoboken 1981, Heriot-Watt, Edinburgh 1985, François Rabelais, Tours, 1986, Nanjing 1986, Beijing 1986); Prix. Francqui 1955, Prix Solvay 1965; Svante Arrhenius Gold Medal, Acad. Royale des Sciences, Sweden 1969; Bourke Medal, Chemical Soc. 1972, Cothenius Gold Medal, Deutsche Akad. der Naturforscher Leopoldina (Halle) 1975, Rumford Medal 1976, Nobel Prize for Chem. 1977, Honda Prize 1983, and numerous other prizes and awards; Commandeur, Ordre des Arts et des Lettres (France). *Publications:* Traité de Thermodynamique, conformément aux méthodes de Gibbs et de De Donder (with R. Defay) 1944, 1950, Etude Thermodynamique des Phénomènes Irréversibles 1947, Introduction to Thermodynamics of Irreversible Processes 1962, The Molecular Theory of Solutions (with A. Bellemans and V. Mathot) 1957, Non-Equilibrium Statistical Mechanics 1962, Non-Equilibrium Thermodynamics, Variational Techniques and Stability (with R.´J. Donnelly and R. Herman) 1966, Kinetic Theory of Vehicular Traffic (with R. Herman) 1971, Thermodynamic Theory of Structure Stability and Fluctuations (with P. Glansdorff) 1971, Self-Organization in Non Equilibrium systems, from Dissipative Structures to order through fluctuations (with G. Nicolis) 1977, From Being to Becoming, Time and Complexity in the Physical Sciences 1980, La nouvelle alliance, les métamorphoses de la science (with I. Stengers) 1981, Order out of Chaos—Man's new Dialogue with Nature 1984, Exploring Complexity (with G. Nicolis) 1987. *Leisure interests:* music, arts. *Address:* avenue Fond'Roy 67, 1180 Brussels, Belgium. *Telephone:* 374-29-52.

PRIMAKOV, Yevgeniy Maksimovich; Soviet economist and historian; b. 29 Oct. 1929, Kiev; ed. Moscow Inst. of Oriental Studies; worked for State Comm. on Broadcasting and Television 1953–62; mem. CPSU 1959–; Columnist and Deputy Ed. (Asia and Africa Desk), Pravda 1962–70; Deputy Dir., then Dir. Inst. of World Econ. and Int. Relations, U.S.S.R. Acad. of Sciences 1970; elected to Congress of People's Deputies of the U.S.S.R. 1989; mem. CPSU Cen. Cttee. April 1989–; corresp. mem. U.S.S.R. Acad. of Sciences 1974, now mem.; specialist on Egypt and other Arab countries; Chief Ed. of and contributor to a number of collective works, including: International Conflicts 1972, The Energy Crisis in the Capitalist World 1975, Nasser Prize 1975. *Publications include:* The Arab Countries and Colonialism 1956; Egypt under Nasser (with I. P. Belyayev) 1975. *Address:* U.S.S.R. Academy of Sciences, Leninsky Prospekt 14, Moscow V-71, U.S.S.R.

PRIMATESTA, H.E. Cardinal Raúl Francisco; Argentine ecclesiastic; b. 14 April 1919, Capilla del Señor; ordained 1942; consecrated titular Bishop of Tanais 1957; Bishop of San Rafael 1961–65; Archbishop of Córdoba 1965–; created Cardinal by Pope Paul VI 1973. *Address:* Arzobispado, Avenida H. Irigoyen 98, Córdoba, Argentina.

PRINCE (Prince Rogers Nelson); American musician and actor; b. Minneapolis 1959; s. of John L. Nelson and Mattie (née Shaw) Nelson; singer, songwriter and actor; recipient three Grammy awards 1985; mem. Prince and the Revolution. *Albums include:* For You 1978, Dirty Minds 1979, Controversy 1981, 1999 1983, Purple Rain 1984, Around the World in a Day 1985 (Best Soul/Rhythm and Blues Album of the Year, Down Beat Readers' Poll 1985), Parade 1986, Sign of the Times 1987, Lovesexy 1988. *Films include:* Purple Rain 1984 (Acad. Award for Best Original Score), Under the Cherry Moon 1986. *Address:* c/o Tom Ross, Creative Artists Agency, 1888 Century Park East, Suite 1400, Los Angeles, Calif. 90067, U.S.A.

PRINCE, Harold S., LITT.D.; American theatrical director-producer; b. 30 Jan. 1928, New York; s. of Milton A. and Blanche (Stern) Prince; m. Judith Chaplin 1962; one s. one d.; ed. Emerson Coll.; co-produced Pajama Game 1954–56 (Antoinette Perry Award), Damn Yankees 1955–57 (Antoinette Perry Award), New Girl in Town 1957–58, West Side Story 1957–59, Fiorello! 1959–61 (Antoinette Perry Award, Pulitzer Prize), Tenderloin 1960–61, A Call on Kuprin 1961, They Might Be Giants 1961, Side by Side by Sondheim 1976; produced Take Her, She's Mine 1961–62, A Funny thing Happened on the Way to the Forum 1962–64 (Antoinette Perry Award), Fiddler on the Roof 1964–72 (Antoinette Perry Award), Poor Bitos 1964, Flora the Red Menace 1965; dir., producer She Loves Me! 1963–64, London 1964, Superman 1966, Cabaret 1966–69 (Antoinette Perry Award), London 1968, Zorba 1968–69, Company 1970–72 (Antoinette Perry Award), London 1972, A Little Night Music 1973–74 (Antoinette Perry Award) (London 1975), Pacific Overtures 1976; co-dir., producer Follies 1971–72; co-producer, dir. Candide 1974–75, Merrily We Roll Along 1981; dir. A Family Affair 1962, Baker Street 1965, Great God Brown 1972–73, The Visit 1973–74, Love for Love 1974–75, Ashmedai 1976, On the Twentieth Century 1978, Evita, London 1978, Broadway 1979, Los Angeles 1980, Chicago 1980, Australia 1980, Vienna 1981, Mexico City 1981, Sweeney Todd, the Demon Barber of Fleet Street 1979–80, London 1980, Silverlake 1980, Willie Stark 1981, A Doll's Life 1982, Play Memory, End of the World, Madame Rosa 1987. Operas: Madame Butterfly 1982, Candide 1982, Willie Stark 1982, Turandot 1983, Diamonds 1984, Grind 1985, The Phantom of the Opera (Tony Award for Best Dir. 1988) 1986; co-producer films The Pajama Game 1957, Damn Yankees 1958; dir. films Something for Everyone 1970, A Little Night Music 1978; mem. Council, Nat. Endowment Arts, League of New York Theatres; Critic Circle awards, Best Music Award, Evening Standard; Commonwealth Award 1982. *Address:* 1270 Avenue of Americas, New York 10020, N.Y., U.S.A. (Office).

PRINGLE, James Robert Henry, B.A.; British economist and journalist; b. 27 Aug. 1939, Surrey; s. of John and Jacqueline (née Berry) Pringle; m. Rita Schuchard 1966; ed. King's School, Canterbury, King's Coll., Cambridge, and London School of Econs.; asst. to Ed., then Asst. Ed. The Banker, London 1963–67; mem. editorial staff The Economist, London 1968; Asst. Dir., later Deputy Dir. Cttee. on Invisible Exports 1969–72; Ed. The Banker 1972–79; Exec. Dir. Group of Thirty, Consultative Group on Int. Econ. and Monetary Affairs, New York 1979–86; Sr. Fellow, World Inst. for Devt. Econs. Research of the UN Univ. 1986–. *Publications:* Banking in Britain 1973, The Growth Merchants 1977. *Leisure interests:* classical music, the theatre. *Address:* 27 Peel Street, London, W.8, England; World Institute for Development Economics Research, Annankatu 42c, Helsinki 00100, Finland. *Telephone:* 01-727 5801 (England); 3580-693-8506 (Finland).

PRINGLE, John Martin Douglas, M.A.; British journalist; b. 28 June 1912, Hawick, Scotland; s. of late J. Douglas Pringle; m. Celia Carroll 1936; one s. two d.; ed. Shrewsbury School, and Lincoln Coll., Oxford; mem. staff of Manchester Guardian 1934–39; served in Army 1940–44; Asst. Ed. Manchester Guardian 1944–48; joined staff The Times 1948; Ed. Sydney Morning Herald 1952–57, 1965–70; Deputy Ed. The Observer 1958–63; Managing Ed. Canberra Times 1964–65. *Publications:* China Struggles for Unity 1938, Australian Accent 1958, Australian Painting Today 1963, On Second Thoughts 1972, Have Pen: Will Travel 1973, The Last Shenachie 1976, The Shorebirds of Australia 1987. *Address:* 8/105A Darling Point Road, Darling Point, Sydney, N.S.W. 2027, Australia. *Telephone:* 328-7863.

PRIOR, Baron (Life Peer), cr. 1987, of Brampton in the County of Suffolk; **James Michael Leathes Prior,** P.C.; British politician and farmer; b. 11 Oct. 1927, Norwich; s. of the late C. B. L. and A. S. M. Prior; m. Jane P. G. Lywood 1954; three s. one d.; ed. Charterhouse and Pembroke Coll., Cambridge; M.P. for Lowestoft 1959–83, for Waveney 1983–87; Parl. Private Sec. to Pres. of Bd. of Trade 1963, to Minister of Power 1963–64, to Rt. Hon. Edward Heath 1965–70; Vice-Chair. Conservative Party 1965, 1972–74; Minister of Agric., Fisheries and Food 1970–72, Lord Pres. of Council 1972–74; Shadow Spokesman on Home Affairs March-June 1974, on Employment June 1974–79; Sec. of State for Employment 1979–81, for Northern Ireland 1981–84; Chair. GEC 1984–89; Dir. Barclays PLC 1984–, J. Sainsbury PLC 1984–, United Biscuits 1974–79, 1984–. *Publication:* A Balance of Power 1986. *Leisure interests:* cricket, tennis, golf, gardening. *Address:* 36 Morpeth Mansions, London, S.W.1; Old Hall, Brampton, Beccles, Suffolk, England. *Telephone:* 01-834 5543; Brampton 278.

PRISTAVKIN, Anatoliy Ignatevich; Soviet author; b. 17 Oct. 1931, Lyubertsy, Moscow; ed. Gorky Inst. of Literature; first works published 1954; mem. CPSU 1965–. *Publications:* Little Stories 1959, My Contemporaries 1959, Camp Fire in the Taiga 1964, A Lyrical Book 1969, A Cloud with a Silver Lining (Nochevala tuchka zolotaya) 1987. *Address:* U.S.S.R. Union of Writers, Ul. Vorovskogo 52, Moscow, U.S.S.R.

PRITCHARD, Baron (Life Peer), cr. 1975, of West Haddon in the County of Northamptonshire; **Derek Wilbraham Pritchard;** British business executive; b. 8 June 1910, Didsbury, Lancs.; s. of Frank Wheelton Pritchard and Ethel Annie Cheetham; m. Denise Arfor Huntbach 1941; two d.; ed. Clifton Coll., Bristol; took over family business of E. Halliday and Son Ltd., Manchester; Army Service, Second World War 1939–46; Dir. E. K. Cole Ltd. 1946–49; joined Ind Coope Ltd. as Man. Dir. Grants of St. James's Ltd. 1949, Chair. 1960–69; Dir. Samuel Montagu & Co. Ltd., Midland Bank Ltd., Paterson Zochonis and Co. 1977– and other cos.; Chair. British Nat. Export Council 1966–68; Deputy Chair. Allied Breweries 1967–68, Chair. 1968–70; Pres. Inst. of Dirs. 1968–74; non-exec. Chair. of Carreras 1970–72; Chair. Rothmans Int. Ltd. 1972–75; Pres. Abbeyfield Soc. 1970–80; Chair. The Dorchester Hotel 1976–79, Chair. Bd. of Trustees 1980–; Dir., fmr. Dir. numerous cos. *Leisure interests:* farming, fox-hunting. *Address:* 15 Hill Street, London, W1X 7FB (Office); West Haddon Hall, Northampton, NN6 7AU, England (Home). *Telephone:* 01-491 4366 (Office); (078 887) 210.

PRITCHARD, Sir John Michael, Kt., C.B.E.; British conductor; b. 5 Feb. 1921, London; s. of Albert Edward Pritchard and Amy Edith Pritchard (née Shaylor); ed. Sir George Monoux School, London; Conductor, Glyndebourne Festivals 1952–77, Principal Conductor, Glyndebourne Opera 1967–77, Musical Dir. 1969–77; Conductor and Musical Dir. Royal Liverpool Philharmonic Orchestra 1957–62; Principal Conductor and Artistic Dir. London Philharmonic Orchestra 1962–66; Co.-Dir. Opéra de Marseille 1966–68; Musical Dir. Glyndebourne Opera Festival 1969–77; Music Dir. Huddersfield Choral Soc. 1973–79; Chief Conductor, Cologne Opera Jan. 1978–; Joint Chief Guest Conductor, BBC Symphony Orchestra 1979–82, Prin. Conductor Oct. 1982–; Music Dir. Belgian Nat. Opera 1981–, San Francisco Opera 1986–; visiting conductor with principal orchestras and opera houses throughout the world; Shakespeare Prize, F.v.S. Foundation 1975. *Leisure interests:* good food and wine, theatre. *Address:* c/o Basil Horsfield, Estoril (B), Avenue Princesse Grace 31, Monte Carlo.

PRITCHARD, Sir Neil, K.C.M.G.; British diplomatist (retd.); b. 14 Jan. 1911, Widnes, Lancs.; s. of the late Joseph William and Lilian Pritchard; m. Mary Devereux Burroughes 1943 (died 1988); one s.; ed. Liverpool Coll.

and Worcester Coll., Oxford; Dominions Office 1933, Private Sec. to Perm. Under-Sec. 1936-38; Asst. Sec. Rhodesia and Nyasaland Royal Comm. 1938; Sec. Office of U.K. High Commr., Pretoria 1941-45; Principal Sec. Office of U.K. Rep., Dublin 1948-49; Asst. Under-Sec. of State, Commonwealth Relations Office (C.R.O.) 1951-54; Deputy U.K. High Commr., Canada 1954-57, Australia 1957-60; Acting Deputy Under-Sec. of State, C.R.O. 1961; High Commr. of U.K. in Tanganyika 1961-63; Deputy Under-Sec. of State, C.R.O. (later Commonwealth Office) 1963-67; Amb. to Thailand 1967-70. *Leisure interest:* golf. *Address:* Little Garth, Daglingworth, Cirencester, Glos., England.

PRITCHETT, Sir Victor Sawdon, Kt., C.B.E.; British author, critic; b. 16 Dec. 1900, Ipswich, Suffolk; s. of Sawdon Pritchett and Beatrice Martin; m. Dorothy Rudge Roberts 1936; one s. one d.; ed. Alleyn's School; Dir. of New Statesman 1960-78, has lectured in four univs. in U.S.A. including Princeton and Brandeis Univs.; Resident writer, Smith Coll. 1967, 1970-72; Clark Lectures, Cambridge 1969; Pres. PEN Int. 1974-76; Pres. Soc. of Authors 1977-; Hon. mem. American Acad. Arts and Letters, Nat. Inst. of Arts and Letters, N.Y.; Fellow, Vice-Pres. Royal Soc. of Literature; Hon. D.Lit. (Leeds) 1972 (Columbia Univ., New York and Sussex Univ.) 1978, (Harvard) 1985; named C.Lit. (R.S.L.) 1987; PEN Biography Award for Balzac 1974. *Publications:* Marching Spain, Clare Drummer, The Spanish Virgin, Shirley Sanz, Nothing Like Leather, Dead Man Leading, You Make Your Own Life, In My Good Books, It May Never Happen, Why Do I Write? (with Elizabeth Bowen and Graham Greene), The Living Novel, Mr. Beluncle, Books in General, The Spanish Temper, Collected Short Stories, When My Girl Comes Home, London Perceived, The Key to My Heart, Foreign Faces, New York Proclaimed, The Living Novel and Later Appreciations, Dublin, A Cab at the Door (autobiog.) 1968, Blind Love (short stories), George Meredith and English Comedy 1970, Midnight Oil (autobiog. Vol. II) 1971, Balzac 1973, The Camberwell Beauty (stories) 1974, Turgenev 1977, The Gentle Barbarian 1977, Selected Stories 1978, The Myth Makers (essays Vol. I) 1979, On the Edge of the Cliff (stories) 1979, The Tale Bearers 1980, Oxford Book of Short Stories (ed.) 1981, Collected Stories 1982, The Turn of the Years 1982, More Collected Stories 1983, A Man of Letters 1985, Chekhov 1988. *Address:* 12 Regent's Park Terrace, London, N.W.1, England.

PROBST, Raymond R., DR.IUR.; Swiss diplomatist (retd.) and business executive; b. 6 March 1919, Geneva; s. of Friedrich Probst and Suzanna Guigovsky; m. Annemarie Rey 1945; one s. one d.; ed. Univ. of Berne; Attaché, Dept. of Foreign Affairs 1942-47; Second Sec., Athens 1947-52; First Sec. Washington, D.C. 1952-56; Head, Political Div. West, Dept. of Foreign Affairs 1956-66; Amb. and del. of Swiss Govt. for Trade Rels. 1966-76; Amb. to U.S.A. 1976-80; Sec. of State for Foreign Affairs 1980-84; Pres. Swiss Foreign Rels. Asscn., Swiss Inst. for Study of Art, Swiss Chocolate Mfrs. Asscn., Carbura 1984-; Vice-Chair. Hoffman La Roche, Basle; mem. Int. Cttee. of Red Cross, Geneva; mem. Bd. Alusuisse, Sibra Holding, Financière Credit Suisse-First Boston. *Publications:* "Good Officer" in the Light of Swiss International Practice and Experience 1989, and several other publs. on defence matters, foreign affairs, int. law etc. *Leisure interests:* reading, art, skiing, swimming. *Address:* Brunnadernstrasse 76, 3006 Berne, Switzerland. *Telephone:* (031) 44.45.91 (Office); (031) 44.19.19 (Home)

PROCHNOW, Herbert Victor, B.A., M.A., PH.D.; American banker and writer; b. Wilton, Wisconsin; m. Laura Virginia Stinson 1928 (deceased); one s.; ed. Univ. of Wisconsin and Northwestern Univ.; with First Nat. Bank of Chicago 1929-73, rising from asst. cashier to Dir. 1960-68, Pres. 1962-68, Hon. Dir. 1968-73; Sec. Fed. Advisory Council of Fed. Reserve System 1945-; Consultant to Sec. of State 1955, 1957; Deputy Under-Sec. of State for Econ. Affairs 1955-56; Alt. Gov. for U.S. of World Bank and IMF 1955-56; Dir. Annual Summer Graduate School of Banking, Univ. of Wisconsin 1945-82; Chair. U.S. Del. Gen. Agreement on Tariffs and Trade, Geneva 1956; fmr. Asst. Prof. Business Admin., Indiana Univ., lectured Loyola and Northwestern Univs.; financial columnist, Chicago Tribune 1968-70; Pres. Chicago Asscn. of Commerce and Industry 1964, 1965; Commdr. of the Order of Vasa of Royal Govt. of Sweden 1965, Commdr., Cross of the Order of Merit of Germany 1968; several awards and hon. degrees. *Publications:* The Public Speaker's Treasure Chest (with Herbert V. Prochnow, Jr.) 1942, 1964, 1977, 1986, Great Stories from Great Lives 1944, Meditations on the Ten Commandments 1946, The Toastmaster's Handbook 1949, Term Loans and Theories of Bank Liquidity 1949, The Successful Speaker's Handbook 1951, 1001 Ways to Improve your Conversation and Speeches 1952, Meditations on the Beatitudes 1952, The Speaker's Treasury of Stories for all Occasions 1953, Speaker's Handbook of Epigrams and Witticisms 1955, Speaker's Treasury for Sunday School Teachers 1955, The Toastmasters and Speaker's Handbook 1955, A Treasury of Stories, Illustrations, Epigrams and Quotations for Ministers and Teachers 1957, Meditations on the Lord's Prayer 1957 (as Inspirational Thoughts on the Lord's Prayer 1970), The New Guide for Toastmasters and Speakers 1956, A Family Treasury of Inspiration and Faith 1958, The New Speaker's Treasury of Wit and Wisdom 1958, The Complete Toastmaster 1960, Effective Public Speaking 1960, Speaker's Book of Illustrations 1960, A Dictionary of Wit, Wisdom and Satire (with Herbert V. Prochnow, Jr.) 1962, 1000 Tips and Quips for Speakers and Toastmasters 1962, Practical Bank Credit (co-author) 1963, 1400 Ideas for Speakers

and Toastmasters 1964, The Successful Toastmaster (with Herbert V. Prochnow, Jr.) 1966, A Treasury of Humorous Quotations (with Herbert V. Prochnow, Jr.), Quotation Finders (with Everett M. Dirksen) 1971, A Speaker's Treasury for Educators, Convocation Speakers, etc., A Tree of Life, Speakers' Source Book, 1001 Quips, Stories and Illustrations for All Occasions 1973, The Speaker's and Toastmaster's Handbook 1973, The Changing World of Banking (with Herbert V. Prochnow, Jr.) 1974; co-author: The Next Century is America's 1938; editor American Financial Institutions 1951, Determining the Business Outlook 1954, The Federal Reserve System 1960, World Economic Problems and Policies 1965, The Five-Year Outlook for Interest Rates 1968, The One-Bank Holding Company 1969, The Eurodollar 1970, The Five-Year Outlook for Interest Rates in the U.S. and Abroad 1972, Dilemmas Facing the Nation 1979, The Toastmaster's Treasure Chest (with Herbert V. Prochnow Jr.) 1979, 1988, Bank Credit 1981, A Treasure Chest of Quotations for All Occasions 1983, Toastmaster's Quips and Stories 1983. *Address:* 1 First National Bank Plaza, Chicago, Ill. 60670; 2950 Harrison Street, Evanston, Ill. 60201, U.S.A.

PROCKNOW, Donald Eugene, B.S.; American company executive; b. 27 May 1923, Madison, S.D.; s. of Fred A. Procknow and Ruth (Trevor) Procknow; m. Esther Ehlert 1953; two s.; ed. Madison High School, S.D., South Dakota School of Mines and Tech., Univ. of Wisconsin; with Western Electric 1947-; Eng. Hawthorne Works, Chicago 1947-55; Asst. Supt. Devt. Eng., Hawthorne Works 1956-57; Supt. Precision Apparatus and Waveguide Shops, N.C. Works 1959-61; Asst. Works Man. N.C. Works 1961-62; Eng. of Mfg., New York HQ 1963-64; Gen. Man. Cen. Region, Service Div. West Chicago 1964-65; Vice-Pres. Western Electric 1965-69, Exec. Vice-Pres. and Dir. 1969-71, Pres., Dir. and Chief Admin. Officer 1971-72, Pres., and C.E.O. 1971-83, Dir. 1971-; Chair. Greater New York Councils, Boy Scouts of America; Hon. D.Eng. (S.D. School of Mines and Tech.) 1973, Hon. LL.D. (Oklahoma Christian Coll.) 1974, (Morris Harvey Coll., W. Va.) 1976. *Leisure interest:* scouting. *Address:* Western Electric, 222 Broadway, New York, N.Y. 10038, U.S.A. *Telephone:* (212) 571-2345.

PRODAN, David, D.HIST.; Romanian historian; b. 13 March 1902, Cioara (now Sāliste commune, Alba county); s. of Iliĕ Prodan and Ana Moţu; m. Florica Vlădescu 1940; ed. Univ. of Cluj-Napoca; archivist State Archives 1924-38; archivist 1938, Prin. Librarian 1938-41, Chief Librarian Central Univ. Library 1941-48; Prof. of History, Cluj-Napoca Coll. 1948-62; head of dept. Inst. of Nat. History Cluj—Sibiu 1948-62, head of dept. Inst. of History and Archaeology 1948-72; corresp. mem. Romanian Acad. 1948, mem. 1955; Hon. mem. American Historical Asscn. 1986-. *Publications:* Răscoala lui Horea în comitatele Cluj si Turda (Horea's Uprising in the Cluj and Turda Counties) 1938, Teoria imigraţiei românilor din Principatele Romăne în Transilvania în veacul al XVIII-lea (Theory of the Romanians' Immigration from the Romanian Principalities to Transylvania in the 18th Century) 1944, Iobăgia în domeniul Băii de Aries la 1770 (Serfdom on the Baia de Aries Estate in 1770) 1948, Supplex Libellus Valachorum 1948, Producţia fierului pe domeniul Hunedoarei în secolul al XVII-lea (The Production of Iron on the Hunedoara Estate in the 17th Century) 1960, Boieri şi Vecini în Tara Făgăraşului în sec. XVI-XVII (Boyars and Serfs in the Făgăraş County in the 16th-17th Centuries) 1963, Istoria României (Romania's History) vol. III (in collaboration) 1964, Iobăgia în Transilvania în secolul al XVI-lea (Serfdom in Transylvania in the 16th Century) 3 vols. 1967-68, Încă un Supplex Libellus Valachorum romănesc 1804 (Another Romanian Supplex Libellus Valachorum 1804) 1970, Die Aufhebung der Leibeigenschaft in Siebenbürgen 1970, Urbariile Tării Făgăraşului (Urbarii of the Făgăraş Country), vol. I, II, 1970, 1976, Răscoala lui Horea (Horea's Uprising) 2 vols. 1979. *Leisure interests:* music, arts, literature. *Address:* Strada Mică No. 1, Cluj-Napoca, Romania. *Telephone:* 30923.

PROFUMO, John Dennis, C.B.E.; British politician; b. 30 Jan. 1915; s. of the late Baron Albert Profumo, K.C.; m. Valerie Hobson 1954; one s.; ed. Harrow, Brasenose Coll., Oxford; with 1st Northamptonshire Yeomanry 1939; Brig. Chief of Staff, U.K. Mission in Japan 1945; M.P. (Kettering Div.) 1940-45, (Stratford-on-Avon) 1950-63; Parl. Sec., Ministry of Transport and Civil Aviation 1952-57, Parl. Under-Sec. of State for the Colonies 1957-58, for Foreign Affairs 1958-59; Minister of State for Foreign Affairs 1959-60; Sec. of State for War 1960-63; Dir. Provident Life Asscn. of London 1975-, Deputy Chair. 1978-82; mem. Bd. of Visitors, H.M. Prison, Grendon 1968-75; Chair. Toynbee Hall 1982-85, Pres. 1985-. *Leisure interests:* fishing, gardening, do-it-yourself.

PROKHOROV, Aleksandr Mikhailovich; Soviet physicist; b. 11 July 1916, Atherton, Australia; s. of Mikhail Ivanovich Prokhorov and Mariya Ivanovna Prokhorova; m. Galina Alekseyevna Shelepina; one s.; ed. Leningrad State Univ.; Physicist, P. N. Lebedev Inst. of Physics, U.S.S.R. Acad. of Sciences 1939-, Vice-Dir. 1972; Academician-Sec., Section Physics and Astronomy, U.S.S.R. Acad. of Sciences 1973-; Corresp. mem. U.S.S.R. Acad. of Sciences (Dept. of Pure and Applied Physics) 1960-66, mem. 1966-, mem. Presidium (Academician-Sec.) 1973-; mem. American Acad. of Arts and Sciences 1971; mem. CPSU 1950; Lenin Prize 1959; Nobel Prize for Physics for work in field of quantum electronics 1964; Chair. Soviet Nat. Cttee. U.R.S.I.; Ed.-in-Chief of Soviet Encyclopaedia 1969-; Lomosonov Gold Medal 1988; Hero of Socialist Labour 1969, 1986, Order of Lenin (twice), and other decorations. *Address:* P. N. Lebedev Institute of Physics, U.S.S.R. Academy of Sciences, 53 Leninsky Prospekt, Moscow, U.S.S.R.

PROKOFIYEV, Mikhail Alekseyevich; Soviet chemist and government official; b. 18 Nov. 1910, Voskresenskoe, Smolensk Region; ed. Moscow State Univ.; mem. CPSU 1941–; Deputy Dir. Chem. Research Unit, Moscow Univ. 1939–41, 1946–48; Deputy and First Deputy Minister of Higher and Specialized Secondary Educ. of U.S.S.R. 1951–66; R.F.S.F.R. Minister of Educ. 1966; Minister of Educ. of U.S.S.R. 1966–84; Deputy to U.S.S.R. Supreme Soviet 1966–; mem. Cttee. U.S.S.R. Parl. Group; mem. CPSU Cen. Cttee. 1971–; mem. Acad. of Pedagogical Sciences 1967–, Corresp. mem. U.S.S.R. Acad. of Sciences 1966–; Order of Lenin and other decorations. *Address:* c/o Ministry of Education of U.S.S.R., Moscow, U.S.S.R.

PROKOSCH, Frederic, PH.D.; American writer; b. 17 May 1908, Madison, Wis.; s. of Prof. Eduard Prokosch and Matilda Dapprich; ed. Yale Univ. and King's Coll., Cambridge. *Publications:* novels: The Asiatics 1935, The Seven Who Fled 1937, Night of the Poor 1939, The Skies of Europe 1941, The Conspirators 1943, Age of Thunder 1945, The Idols of the Cave 1946, Storm and Echo 1948, Nine Days to Mukalla 1953, A Tale for Midnight 1955, A Ballad of Love 1960, The Seven Sisters 1963, The Dark Dancer 1965, The Wreck of the Cassandra 1966, The Missolonghi Manuscript 1968, America, My Wilderness 1972, The Mermaid 1977, The Magic Carpet 1979; poems: The Assassins 1936, The Carnival 1938, Death at Sea 1940, Chosen Poems 1944, Some Poems of Hoelderlin (trans.) 1944, Voices (memoirs) 1983. *Leisure interests:* lepidoptery, book binding and printing, philately, bridge (tournament play). *Address:* Ma Trouvaille, 06 Plan de Grasse, France.

PROKOSHKIN, Yuriy Dmitriyevich; Soviet physicist; b. 19 Dec. 1929, Moscow; s. of Dmitriy and Bella Prokoshkin; m. Zinaida Prokoshkin 1958; two d.; ed. Moscow Univ.; mem. staff, Jt. Inst. for Nuclear Research, Dubna 1953–63; mem. CPSU 1963–; head of experimental physics dept. at Inst. for High-Energy Physics, Serpukhov 1963–; with others, conducted experiments on the discovery of antihelium-3 1968–72; most important works are on the physics of elementary particles; Professor; corresp. mem. U.S.S.R. Acad. of Sciences 1970–; Order of Red Banner of Labour, Kurchatov Gold Medal and Prize (U.S.S.R. Acad. of Sciences) 1965, Lenin Prize for Science 1986. *Publications:* Pion beta decay 1963, Observation of h-meson 1975, Observation of r(2510) meson with spin 6 1984, Observation of G(1590) Scalar Glueball Candidate 1987; and over 200 papers in scientific journals. *Address:* Institute for High-Energy Physics, Protvino, Serpukhov 142284, U.S.S.R. *Telephone:* 2280.

PROMYSLOV, Vladimir Fedorovich; Soviet construction engineer and politician; b. 28 July 1908, Oziory, Moscow Region; ed. Moscow Construction Engineering Institute; mem. CPSU 1928–; fmr. Deputy Chair. Council of Ministers, R.S.F.S.R. and Chair. State Cttee. of Council of Ministers of R.F.S.F.R. on Construction 1959–63; Deputy Chair. Council of Ministers of R.F.S.F.R. and Minister of Construction 1963; Chair. Exec. Cttee., Moscow City Soviet of Working People's Deputies 1963–; mem. Cen. Auditing Comm. of CPSU 1956–66; mem. Cen. Cttee. CPSU 1961–86; Deputy U.S.S.R. Supreme Soviet 1966–; mem. Foreign Affairs Comm. Soviet of Union; mem. Cttee. U.S.S.R. Parliamentary Group; Order of Lenin (three times), Order of the October Revolution and other decorations. *Address:* Moscow City Soviet, Ulitsa Gorkogo 13, Moscow, U.S.S.R.

PRONK, Johannes Pieter, D.ECON.; Netherlands politician; b. 16 March 1940, The Hague; s. of Johannes Pronk and Elisabeth H. v. Geel; m. Catharina Zuurmond; one s. one d.; ed. Gymnasium and Erasmus Univ.; Research Fellow, Netherlands Econ. Inst., Lecturer in Devt. Econs., Erasmus Univ. 1965–71; Prof. Univ. of Amsterdam 1989–; mem. Parl. 1971–73, 1978–80, 1986–; mem. European Parl. 1973; Minister of Devt. Co-operation 1973–77; Prof. Inst. of Social Studies, The Hague (Devt. Econs.) 1978–81, Deputy Sec.-Gen. UNCTAD 1980–85; Asst. Sec.-Gen. UN 1985–86; mem. Ind. Comm. on Int. Devt. Issues (ICIDI, Brandt Comm.) 1977–82; Deputy Chair. Labour Party of the Netherlands 1987–. *Address:* P.O. Box 87833, The Hague, Netherlands. *Telephone:* The Hague 182211 (Office).

PROSKURIN, Petr Lukich; Soviet author; b. 22 Jan. 1928, Kosytsy, Bryansk Dist.; first works publ. 1958. *Publications include:* Song of the Taiga 1960, Deep Wounds 1960, The Price of Bread 1961, Bitter Herbs 1964, Human Love 1965, Exit. Stories. A Novel 1971, Your Name: A Novel 1979, Afternoon Dreams 1985. *Address:* U.S.S.R. Union of Writers, ulitsa Vorovskogo 52, Moscow, U.S.S.R.

PROSSER, C. Ladd, PH.D.; American professor of physiology; b. 12 May 1907, Avon, New York; s. of Clifford James Prosser and Izora May Ladd; m. Hazel Blanchard 1934; one s. two d.; ed. Univ. of Rochester and Johns Hopkins Univ.; Postdoctoral Fellow, Harvard Medical School 1932–34; Asst. Prof., Clark Univ. 1934–39; Asst., subsequently Prof., Univ. of Ill. 1939–74, Prof. Emer. 1975–; Research Assoc., Manhattan Project 1942–45; Fellow American Acad. of Arts and Sciences; mem. N.A.S.; Guggenheim Fellow; Dr. h.c. (Clark Univ.) 1975. *Publications:* 200 papers in journals; Ed. 4 symposia; Author and Ed., Comparative Animal Physiology 1951, 1961, 1973; Author, Adaptational Biology: Molecules to Organisms 1986. *Address:* 205 East Michigan Street, Urbana, Ill. 61801 (Home); 524 Burrill

Hall, Physiology Department, University of Illinois, 407 S. Goodwin Street, Urbana, Ill. 61801, U.S.A. (Office).

PROSSER, Ian Maurice Gray, B. COMM., F.C.A., C.B.I.M.; British business executive; b. 5 July 1943, Bath; s. of Maurice and Freda Prosser; m. Elizabeth Herman 1964; two d.; ed. King Edward's School, Bath, Watford Grammar School and Univ. of Birmingham; Cooper Bros. (chartered accts.) 1964–69; Bass Charrington Ltd. 1969–82, Financial Dir. 1978; Vice-Chair. and Financial Dir. Bass PLC 1982–84, Vice-Chair. and Group Man. Dir. 1984–87, Chair. and C.E.O. 1987–; Dir. The Brewers' Soc., The Boots Co. PLC, Lloyds Bank PLC 1988–. *Leisure interests:* bridge, squash, gardening. *Address:* 30 Portland Place, London, W1N 3DF, England. *Telephone:* 01-637 5499.

PROTHEROE, Alan Hackford, M.B.E., T.D.; British journalist and broadcasting executive; b. 10 Jan. 1934, St. David's, Wales; s. of Rev. B. P. Protheroe and R. C. M. Protheroe; m. Anne Miller 1956; two s.; ed. Maesteg Grammar School, Glamorgan; Reporter, Glamorgan Gazette 1951–53; 2nd Lieut., The Welch Regt. 1954–56; Reporter, BBC Wales 1957–59, Industrial Corresp. 1959–64, Ed. News and Current Affairs 1964–70; Asst. Ed., BBC TV News 1970–72, Deputy Ed. 1972–77, Ed. 1977–80; Asst. Dir. BBC News and Current Affairs 1980–82; Asst. Dir.-Gen. BBC 1982–87; Man. Dir. The Services Sound and Vision Corpn. 1987–; Founder-mem. Assen. of British Eds., Chair. 1987; Dir., Visnews Ltd. 1982–87; Dir. Defence Public Affairs Consultants Ltd. 1987–; rank of Col. T.A.; F.B.I.M. *Publications:* contribs. to journals on media and defence affairs. *Leisure interest:* pistol and rifle shooting. *Address:* Amberleigh House, Chapman Lane, Flackwell Heath, Bucks., HP10 9BD, England. *Telephone:* (06285) 28492.

PROTOPAPAS, Nakos; Cypriot politician and fmr. civil engineer; b. 27 Aug. 1927, Phrenaros Village, Famagusta Dist.; ed. Paphos Gymnasium, Civil Eng. Inst. of Moscow, and Lomonosov Univ., U.S.S.R., Int. Inst. of Seismic Eng., Milan Polytechnic, Italy; studies also in Hungary and U.K.; pvt. practice 1962–64; joined Public Works Dept., Ministry of Communications and Works 1964, Nicosia Dist. Engineer 1984–87, rtd. as Sr. Exec. Engineer 1987; Minister of Communications and Works 1988–; Pres. Cyprus Civil Engineers' and Architects' Assen. 1974–88; Vice-Pres. Civil Servants' Trade Union 1985–. *Address:* Ministry of Communications and Works, Nicosia, Cyprus.

PROUT, Curtis, M.D.; American physician, teacher and administrator; b. 13 Oct. 1915, Swampscott, Mass.; s. of Henry B. Prout and Eloise D. Willett; m. 1st Daphne Brooks 1939 (divorced); m. 2nd Diane N. Emmons 1985; four d.; ed. Harvard Coll. and Harvard Medical School; internships and residency in pathology and medicine 1941–44; research fellowship 1944–45; private practice of internal medicine 1946–61, 1975–; Chief of Medicine, Harvard Univ. Health Services 1961–72; Assoc. Clinical Prof. of Medicine, Harvard 1975–82, Asst. Dean 1984–87; Dir. O.E.O. Prison Health Project, Boston 1972–74; Dir. Nat. Comm. on Correctional Health Care 1981–; Chair. Intern. Advisory Cttee. 1976–; Public mem. Board of Bar Overseers, Mass. 1979–85; various honours, awards and prizes. *Publications:* papers and chapters on research in malaria, infectious mononucleosis, longevity, educ. and health care of prisoners. *Leisure interests:* sailing, travelling, reading. *Address:* 319 Longwood Avenue, Boston, Mass. 02115 (Office); 115 School Street, Manchester, Mass. 01944, U.S.A.

PROWSE, Albert Richard Graham, B.COM., M.SC.; Australian economist and financial official; b. 1 May 1931; s. of A. B. Prowse; m. Barbara Elliott 1961; two s. one d.; ed. Melbourne High School, Melbourne Univ., Gonville and Caius Coll., Cambridge; Lecturer in Econs. Melbourne Univ. 1958–62; joined Commonwealth Service 1962; Sec. Prime Minister's Dept. 1967–69, Commonwealth Treas. 1969–81; Exec. Dir. IMF 1981–85; Under Treas. Treasury Dept. S. Australia 1985–. *Address:* 108 King William Street, Adelaide, 5000 South Australia (Office); 7 Kingston Terrace, North Adelaide, 5006 South Australia (Home).

PROXMIRE, William, M.A.; American politician; b. 11 Nov. 1915, Lake Forest, Ill.; s. of Theodore Stanley and Adele (Flanigan) Proxmire; m. Ellen Hodges; ed. Yale and Harvard Univs.; U.S. Army Intelligence Service 1941–46; State Assemblyman (Dem.) for Wisconsin 1951–52; Senator from Wisconsin 1957–89; Chair. Senate Banking Cttee. 1975–81; Pres. Artcraft Press, Waterloo, Wisconsin 1954–57; Democrat. *Publications:* Can Small Business Survive?, Uncle Sam, Last of the Big Time Spenders, You Can Do It!, The Fleecing of America.

PRUSSIA, Leland S., M.A.; American banker; b. 1929, San Jose, Calif.; s. of Leland Spencer Prussia and Doris E. Fowler; m. Vivian Blom; three s.; ed. Stanford Univ. and Harvard Business School; served U.S.A.F.; joined Bank of America as research economist 1956; Sr. Vice-Pres. in charge of Investment Securities Div. 1971; Exec. Vice-Pres. 1974, mem. Man. Cttee. 1976; Exec. Officer, World Banking Div. 1979–81; Chair. of Bd. BankAmerica Corpn. and Bank of America NT & SA 1981–86, Chair. Exec. Cttee. of BankAmerica Corpn. 1986–87; Dir. Hughes Aircraft Co.; numerous professional and civic appts.; Hon. D. Econ. (San Francisco) 1984. *Publication:* The Changing World of Banking. *Address:* Bank of America NT & SA, Executive Office 3001, P.O. Box 37000, San Francisco, Calif. 94137, U.S.A.

PRYCE, George Terry, C.B.I.M.; British business executive; b. 24 March 1934, Montgomery; s. of Edwin Pryce and Hilda Florence Pryce (née Price); m. Thurza Elizabeth Tatham 1957; two s. one d.; ed. Welshpool Boys' Grammar School, Nat. Coll. of Food Technology; various management positions in food industry; Tech. Dir. a large nat. frozen food co. early 1960s; Man. Dir. numerous cos. in food processing and manufacturing industry 1965-; Asst. Man. Dir. Dalgety (U.K.) Ltd. 1970-71, Man. Dir. 1971, mem. Bd. 1972, Chair. 1978-; Dir. Dalgety Ltd. 1972-, Man. Dir. 1978-, Chief Exec. 1981-; Chair. Dalgety Spillers Ltd. 1980-; Chief Exec. Dalgety PLC 1981-; Dir. H. P. Bulmer Holdings PLC; Fellow Inst. of Food, Science and Tech.; Gov. Nat. Coll. of Food Tech. 1981-. *Leisure interest:* golf. *Address:* 19 Hanover Square, London, W.1, England.

PRYCE, Maurice Henry Lecorney, M.A., PH.D., F.R.S.; British university professor; b. 24 Jan. 1913, Croydon, Surrey; s. of William John Pryce and Hortense E. Lecorney; m. 1st Susanne M. Born 1939 (dissolved 1959), one s. three d.; 2nd Freda M. Oldham 1961; ed. Royal Grammar School, Guildford, Trinity Coll., Cambridge, and Princeton Univ., U.S.A.; Fellow, Trinity Coll. and Faculty Asst. Lecturer Cambridge 1937; Reader in Theoretical Physics Liverpool Univ. 1939; Admiralty Signal Establishment 1941; Nat. Research Council of Canada (Atomic Energy) 1944; Univ. Lecturer and Fellow of Trinity Coll. Cambridge 1945; Visiting Prof. Princeton Univ. 1950-51; Wykeham Prof. of Physics, Oxford 1946-54; Henry Overton Wills Prof. of Physics, Bristol 1954-64; Prof. Univ. of Southern California 1964-68; Prof. of Physics (now Prof. Emer.), Univ. of British Columbia 1968-78, Prof. Emer. 1978-; Visiting Prof. Univ. of Sussex 1976-77; mem. Tech. Advisory Cttee. on Nuclear Fuel Waste Man. for Atomic Energy of Canada Ltd. 1978-. *Leisure interests:* walking, music. *Address:* c/o Physics Department, University of British Columbia, 2075 Westbrook Mall, Vancouver V6T 1W5 (Office); 4754 West 6th Avenue, Vancouver BC V6T 1C5, Canada (Home). *Telephone:* 604-224-1596 (Home).

PRYCE-JONES, Alan Payan, T.D.; British writer and editor; b. 18 Nov. 1908; s. of late Col. Henry Morris Pryce-Jones; m. 1st Thérèse Fould-Springer 1934 (died 1953); one s.; m. 2nd Mary Jean Kempner Thorne 1968 (died 1969); ed. Eton Coll. and Magdalen Coll., Oxford; Asst. Ed. The London Mercury 1928-32; Ed. The Times Literary Supplement 1948-59; served in France, Austria, Italy, Second World War 1939-45, Lieut.-Col. 1945; Trustee Nat. Portrait Gallery 1950-61; Dir. The Old Vic Trust 1950-61; mem. Council of Royal Coll. of Music 1956-61; Program Assoc. (Humanities and Arts) Ford Foundation 1961-63; Book Critic New York Herald-Tribune 1963-67; Theatre Critic, Theatre Arts 1963-. *Publications:* The Spring Journey 1931, People in the South 1932, Beethoven 1933, 27 Poems 1935, Private Opinion 1936, Prose Literature 1945-50, The Bonus of Laughter (autobiog.) 1987; libretto for Berkeley's opera Nelson 1954; The American Imagination (Ed.) 1960, Vanity Fair (libretto) 1962. *Leisure interests:* music, travelling. *Address:* 46 John Street, Newport, R.I. 02340, U.S.A.

PRYOR, David Hampton, LL.B.; American politician; b. 29 Aug. 1934, Camden, Ark.; s. of Edgar and Susan (née Newton) Pryor; m. Barbara Lunsford 1957; three s.; ed. Univ. of Arkansas; admitted to Arkansas Bar 1964; mem. Ark. House of Reps. 1961-66; served in Congress, House of Reps. 1966-72; Gov. of Arkansas 1974-79; Senator from Arkansas 1979-; mem. American Bar Asscn., Arkansas Bar Asscn.; Democrat. *Address:* 264 Russell Senate Office Building, Capitol Hill, Washington, D.C. 20510, U.S.A.

PTASHNE, Mark Stephen, PH.D.; American professor of biochemistry; b. 5 June 1940, Chicago, Ill.; s. of Fred Ptashne and Mildred Ptashne; ed. Reed Coll. and Harvard Univ.; Jr. Fellow, Harvard Soc. of Fellows 1965-68; Lecturer, Dept. of Biochemistry and Molecular Biology, Harvard Univ. 1968-71, Prof. 1971-, Chair. Dept. of Biochemistry and Molecular Biology 1980-83; Guggenheim Fellow 1973-74; Fellow American Acad. of Arts and Sciences; mem. N.A.S.; NATO Sr. Scientist Award 1977-78; Prix Charles-Léopold Mayer, Acad. des Sciences, Inst. de France (with W. Gilbert and E. Witkin) 1977; Eli Lilly Award 1975; shared Louisa Gross Horwitz Prize 1985; Gairdner Foundation Int. Award (with Charles Yanofsky) 1985; Feodor Lynen Lecturer 1988. *Publications:* A Genetic Switch 1986; 122 papers in scientific journals 1950-89. *Leisure interests:* classical music, opera. *Address:* Department of Biochemistry and Molecular Biology, Harvard University, 7 Divinity Avenue, Cambridge, Mass. 02138, U.S.A. *Telephone:* (617) 495-2336.

PU CHAOZHU; Chinese government official; Gov. of Yunnan 1983-85, Sec. Prov. CCP Cttee. 1985-; mem. 12th CCP Cen. Cttee. 1985, 13th Cen. Cttee. 1987. *Address:* Office of the Secretary, CCP, Kunming, Yunnan Province, People's Republic of China.

PU SHAN, PH.D.; Chinese academic; b. 27 Nov. 1923, Beijing; m. Chen Xiuying 1951; Dir. Inst. of World Econs. and Politics 1983-88; Pres. Chinese World Econ. Assen. 1985-; mem. Nat. Cttee., CCP Political Consultative Conf. 1988-. *Address:* Chinese Academy of Social Sciences, Beijing, People's Republic of China.

PU TA-HAI; Chinese government official; b. 3 April 1922, Meihsien, Kwangtung; m.; one s. two d.; ed. Chinese Mil. Acad., Chinese Army Command and Gen. Staff Coll. and Chinese Armed Forces Staff Coll.; Section Chief (Col.), Taiwan Peace Preservation H.Q. 1956-57; Dept.

Head (Col.), Gen. H.Q., Chinese Army 1957-60; Dept. Head (Maj.-Gen.), Personnel Div., Ministry of Nat. Defence 1963-68; Dept. Head (Maj.-Gen.), Taiwan Garrison Gen. H.Q. 1968-72; Dept. Head, Cen. Personnel Admin., Exec. Yuan 1972-78; Dir. Dept. of Personnel, Taipei City Govt. 1978-81, Taiwan Provincial Govt. 1981-84; Deputy Dir.-Gen. Central Personnel Admin., Exec. Yuan 1984, Dir.-Gen. 1984-. *Leisure interests:* tennis, badminton. *Address:* Office of the Director-General, Central Personnel Administration, Executive Yuan, 109 Huai Ning Street, Taipei, Taiwan. *Telephone:* (02) 361-7072.

PUAPUA, Rt. Hon. Dr. Tomasi, P.C.; Tuvalu politician; b. 10 Sept. 1938; m. 1971; two s. two d.; ed. Fiji School of Medicine and Univ. of Otago, N.Z.; medical practitioner; Prime Minister of Tuvalu Sept. 1981-, also Minister for Civil Service Admin., Local Govt. and Minister for Foreign Affairs. *Leisure interests:* athletics, rugby, tennis, volleyball, cricket, soccer, fishing, pig and poultry farming, gardening. *Address:* Office of the Prime Minister, Vaiaku, Funafuti, Tuvalu.

PUCCI, Emilio, Marchese di Barsento, M.A., DR.SOC.SC.; Italian couturier; b. 20 Nov. 1914, Naples; s. of Orazio Pucci and Augusta Pavoncelli; m. Cristina Nannini di Casabianca 1959; one s. one d.; ed. Reed Coll., Portland (Oregon) and Florence Univ.; Air Force torpedo-bomber pilot 1938-42; started his own fashion house 1950; Pres. Emilio Pucci, Florence, New York, Antico Setificio Fiorentino, Soc. Fiorentina Corse Cavalli, Soc. San. Giovanni Battista, Asscn. Proprietà Edilizia, Soc. San Giovanni di Dio, Cinquecento Fiorentino; Hon. Pres. Italian Shoe Stylists Asscn.; M.P. for Florence, Liberal Party 1963-72; City Counsellor, Florence 1964-; mem. Bd. of Dirs. S.I.N.A. Hotels, Finanziaria Banca Popolare di Novara; works under name "Emilio Pucci", New York; mem. Chamber of Deputies; Neiman Marcus Fashion Award 1954, Burdine Fashion Award 1955, Sports Illustrated "Sporting Look" Designer's Award 1961, Harper's Bazaar Medallion, Cavaliere del Lavoro al merito della Repubblica Italiana. *Leisure interests:* skiing, swimming, tennis, fencing and flying. *Address:* Palazzo Pucci, 6 Via dei Pucci, Florence, Italy. *Telephone:* 283-061-62.

PUCK, Theodore Thomas B.S., PH.D.; American professor of biophysics; b. 24 Sept. 1916, Chicago, Ill.; s. of Joseph and Bessie Puckowitz; m. Mary R. Hill 1946; three d.; ed. Univ. of Chicago; Univ. Fellow, Dept. of Chem., Univ. of Chicago 1938-40, Research Assoc., Dept. of Medicine 1941-45, Asst. Prof. Depts. of Medicine and Biochem. 1945-47; mem. Comm. on Airborne Infections, Army Epidemiological Bd., Office of Surgeon-Gen. 1944-46; Sr. Fellow, Calif. Inst. of Tech., Pasadena 1947-48; Prof. and Chair. Dept. of Biophysics, Univ. of Colorado Medical Center 1948-67; Research Prof. of Biochem., Biophysics and Genetics, Univ. of Colorado Medical Center 1967-; Research Prof. of American Cancer Soc. 1966-; Prof. Dept. of Medicine, Univ. of Colorado Health Sciences Center 1981-, Distinguished Prof., Dept. of Medicine, Univ. of Colorado 1986-; Dir. Eleanor Roosevelt Inst. for Cancer Research, Univ. of Colorado Medical Center 1962-; mem. N.A.S. 1960-, Editorial Bd., Encyclopaedia Britannica 1980-87, Paideia Group; Fellow, American Acad. for Arts and Sciences 1967-; Lasker Award 1958; Borden Award 1959; Stearns Award, Univ. of Colorado 1959; General Rose Memorial Hospital Award 1960; Distinguished Service Award of Univ. of Chicago Med. Alumni Assoc. 1969; Gross Horwitz Prize of Columbia Univ. in Cell Biology and Biochemistry 1973, Inst. of Med. 1974, Gordon Wilson Medal (American Clinical and Climatological Asscn.) 1977, Annual Award, Environmental Mutagen Soc. 1981, A.A.A.S. Award and Lectureship 1983, Heritage Foundation Scholar 1983, E. B. Wilson Medal of American Soc. for Cell Biology 1984, Bonfils-Stanton Award in Science 1984, A.R.C.S. Man of Science Award 1987, Hon. Award of Tissue Culture Asscn. 1987, Louisa Gross Horwitz Prize. *Publications:* The Mammalian Cell as a Micro organism: Genetic and Biochemical Studies in Vitro 1972; many papers (some jointly) in the field of somatic cell genetics, also airborne infection, virus interaction with host cells, mammalian cell biochemical genetics, human cytogenetics and mammalian radiation biology. *Leisure interests:* skiing, hiking, travel, music. *Address:* Eleanor Roosevelt Institute for Cancer Research, 1899 Gaylord Street, Denver, Colo. 80206 (Office); 10 South Albion Street, Denver, Colo. 80222, U.S.A. (Home). *Telephone:* 303-333-4515 (Office).

PUDKOV, Ivan Ivanovich; Soviet official; b. 1916; mem. CPSU 1945-; ed. Moscow Ordzhonikidze Aviation Inst.; various eng. and managerial posts until 1953; engineer and technologist with Ministry of Aviation 1953-68; First Deputy Minister for Construction of Light Industry 1968-77, Minister 1977; Deputy to U.S.S.R. Supreme Soviet 1979-; mem. Cen. Auditing Comm. of CPSU 1981-; Lenin Prize. *Address:* Ministry for Construction of Light Industry, Moscow, U.S.S.R.

PUGH, John Arthur, O.B.E.; British diplomatist; b. 17 July 1920, Hay-on-Wye; s. of late Thomas Arthur and of Dorothy Roberts Baker Pugh; ed. Brecon Grammar School and Bristol Univ.; served with R.N. 1941-45; Civil Service 1950-54; Gold Coast Admin. 1955-58; Adviser to Govt. of Ghana 1958-60; First Sec., High Comm., Lagos 1962-65, British Embassy, Bangkok 1965-68; British Perm. Rep. to UN Econ. Comm. for Asia and Far East 1965-68; Deputy High Commr. Ibadan, Nigeria 1971-73; Diplomatic Service Insp. 1973-76; High Commr., Seychelles 1976-80. *Leisure interests:* oriental ceramics and antiques, sea sports. *Address:* Pennybrin, Hay-on-Wye, Hereford (Home). *Telephone:* Hay 820 695 (Home).

PUGIN, Nikolay Andrevevich; Soviet politician; b. 1940; ed. Gorky Polytechnic; worker, foreman, at car factory 1958–75; mem. CPSU 1965–; sr. engineer at gear-box factory 1975–81; tech. dir. 1981–83; gen. dir. of Gorky Automobile Works 1981–86; Minister of Automobile Industry 1986–; mem. of CPSU Cen. Cttee. 1986–; Deputy to U.S.S.R. Supreme Soviet; State Prize 1985. *Address:* U.S.S.R. Ministry of Automobile Industry, Moscow, U.S.S.R.

PUGLIESE, Dr. Juan Carlos; Argentine politician and lawyer; b. 17 Feb. 1915; ed. Escuela Normal, Tandil; Magistrate 1933–40; Prov. Senator 1954; mem., later Pres. Tandil Town Council 1960–62; mem. Chamber of Deputies 1963–; Minister of Econs. 1964–66, March 1989–; Pres. Chamber of Deputies 1983–89. *Address:* Ministry of the Economy, Hipolito Yrigoyen 250, 1310 Buenos Aires, Argentina. *Telephone:* (1) 34-6411.

PUGO, Major-Gen. Boris Karlovich; Soviet politician; b. 1937, Moscow; s. of Karlis Pugo; ed. Riga Polytech. Inst.; engineer in Riga mechanical plant 1959–60; Sec. of Komsomol Cttee. of plant 1961; Sec. of Komsomol, Riga 1961–63; mem. CPSU 1963–; Head of a sector in Cen. Cttee. of All-Union Komsomol 1963–68; Head of Dept. for Org. Riga City Cttee., Latvian CP 1968–69; First Sec., Cen. Cttee. Latvian Komsomol, and mem. of Politburo, Cen. Cttee. of Latvian Komsomol 1969–70; Deputy to Supreme Soviet of Latvian S.S.R. 1969–71; mem. Cen. Cttee. of All-Union Komsomol 1970–74; Head of Dept. for Organizational Party Work, Cen. Cttee. Latvian CP 1974–75; Deputy to Latvian S.S.R. Supreme Soviet 1975–85; First Sec. of Riga City Cttee. Latvian CP 1975–76; mem. Cen. Cttee. Latvian CP 1976–; cand. mem. Politburo of Cen. Cttee. Latvian CP 1976–77, 1981–84; KGB work 1976–77; First Deputy Chair. of KGB, Latvian S.S.R. 1977–80, Chair. 1980–84; rank of Major-Gen. 1984–; First Sec. Cen. Cttee. Latvian CP, mem. of Politburo, Mil. Council, Baltic Mil. Dist. 1984–88; Chair. Party Control Cttee. 1988–; elected to Congress of People's Deputies of the U.S.S.R. 1989–; Deputy to Council of Nationalities, U.S.S.R. Supreme Soviet 1984–; mem. Presidium, Latvian S.S.R. Supreme Soviet 1985–; mem. Cen. Cttee. CPSU 1986–; Order of Red Banner, Order of Red Star, Badge of Honour, other medals. *Publications:* on Communist Party work etc. *Address:* Central Committee of the Communist Party of the Soviet Union, Staraya pl. 4, Moscow, U.S.S.R.

PUGSLEY, Sir Alfred Grenvile, Kt., O.B.E., D.SC.; British emeritus professor of civil engineering; b. 13 May 1903, Wimbledon; s. of H. W. Pugsley and Marian Clifford; m. Kathleen Mary Warner 1928; ed. Univ. of London; civil eng. apprentice, Royal Arsenal, Woolwich 1923–26; Technical Officer, Royal Airship Works, Cardington 1926–31; mem. Scientific and Tech. Staff, Royal Aircraft Establishment, Farnborough 1931–45; Prof. of Civil Eng., Univ. of Bristol 1945–68, now Emer. Prof. and Hon. Fellow; Chair. Aeronautical Research Council 1952–57; Pres. Inst. of Structural Engineers 1957–58; Hon. Fellow ICE, R.Ae.S.; Hon. D.Sc. (Belfast) 1965, (Cranfield) 1978, (Birmingham) 1982; Hon. D. Univ. (Surrey) 1968; Structural Engineers' Gold Medal 1968; Civil Engineers' Gold Medal 1979. *Publications:* The Theory of Suspension Bridges 1957, The Safety of Structures 1966, The Works of Isambard Kingdom Brunel (Ed. and contrib.) 1976. *Leisure interest:* local history. *Address:* 4 Harley Court, Clifton Down, Bristol, BS8 3JU, England. *Telephone:* (0272) 739400.

PUHAKKA, Matti Juhani; Finnish politician; b. 1945, Eno; industrial worker, Enso-Gutzeit Co., Inc. 1965–75, Rep. 1972–75; M.P. 1975–; mem. Social Democratic Party Cttee. 1978–; Chair. Social Cttee. of Parl. 1979–; Minister of Transport and Communications 1983; Second Minister, Ministry of Social Affairs and Health 1984–87, of Labour May 1987–. *Address:* Ministry of Labour, Eteläesplauadi 4, 00130 Helsinki, Finland.

PUJA, Frigyes; Hungarian politician; b. 1921, Battonya, County Békés; s. of János Puja and Danica Vrányés; m. Emma Répás; one d.; ed. Party Acad.; joined Communist Party 1944; Sec. of Party, District Battonya 1945–46; mem. Party Cttee., Deputy Head of Appointments Cttee., County Csanád 1946–49; Sub-Dept. Leader Cen. Bd. of Hungarian Working People's Party 1949–53; Amb. to Sweden 1953–55, to Austria 1955–59; Deputy Foreign Minister 1959–63; Head Foreign Dept., Cen. Cttee. of Hungarian Socialist Workers' Party 1963–68; mem. Cen. Cttee. HSWP 1966–88; First Deputy Foreign Minister 1968–73; Sec. of State for Foreign Affairs 1973; Minister of Foreign Affairs 1973–83; Amb. to Finland 1983–86; Labour Order of Merit, golden degree 1970. *Publications:* The Problems of Coexistence 1967, Unity and Debate in the International Communist Movement 1969, Why is the Warsaw Treaty Organization Necessary? 1970, The Road to Security 1971, Principles and Doctrines 1972, Socialist Foreign Policy 1973, The Liberated Battonya 1979, Characteristics and Perspectives of the Détente Process 1980, Hungarian Foreign Policy 1981, Flaming Years 1986 and various articles on int. affairs. *Address:* c/o Ministry of Foreign Affairs, Bem rkp. 47, 1027 Budapest, Hungary.

PUJOL I SOLEY, Jordi; Spanish pharmacologist, businessman and politician; b. 9 June 1930, Barcelona; s. of Florenci and Maria Pujol Soley; m. Marta Ferrusola 1956; seven s.; ed. privately; worked in pharmaceutical industry 1953–60; founded Banca Catalana group 1959, Man. Dir. 1959–76; mem. House of Reps. 1977; Adviser to Provisional Generalitat (Catalan govt.) 1977–80; mem. Catalan Parl. March 1980–; Pres. Generalitat de Catalunya May 1980–. *Publications:* Una política per Catalunya 1976, Construir Catalunya 1980. *Leisure interests:* reading, walking, cycling.

Address: Palau de la Generalitat, Plaça Sant Jaume, s/n Barcelona 2, Spain. *Telephone:* 317 19 32.

PULINCKX, Raymond; Belgian business administrator; b. 1924; ed. Inst. supérieur de Commerce de l'Etat, Anvers; Chef de Cabinet, Ministry of Econ. Affairs 1958–61; Dir.-Gen., Belgian Business Fed. 1961–62, Dir.-Gen. and Admin. 1962–70, Exec. Vice-Pres. 1970, now Man. Dir.; Chevalier de l'Ordre de Léopold, Commdr. de l'Ordre de la Couronne de Chêne, Officier de l'Ordre de la Couronne. *Address:* Fédération des Entreprises de Belgique, 4 rue Ravenstein, Brussels 1, Belgium.

PULITZER, Joseph, Jr., A.B.; American newspaper editor and publisher; b. 13 May 1913, St. Louis; s. of Joseph and Elizabeth (Wickham) Pulitzer; m. Louise Vauclain 1939 (died 1968); one s.; m. 2nd Emily S. Rauh 1973; ed. Harvard Univ.; Reporter San Francisco News 1935; mem. staff St. Louis Post-Dispatch 1936–48, Assoc. Ed. 1948–55, Ed. and Publr. 1955–; Vice-Pres. Pulitzer Publ. Co. 1940–55, Pres. 1955–; served U.S. Navy 1942–45. *Address:* St. Louis Post-Dispatch, Pulitzer Publishing Co., 1133 Franklin Avenue, St. Louis, Mo. 63101 (Office); 4903 Pershing Place, St. Louis, Mo. 63108, U.S.A. (Home).

PULLAI, Árpád; Hungarian politician; b. 3 Sept. 1925, Kecskemét; s. of Károly Pullai and Teréz Szentkirályi; m. Irén Györvári 1949; one s. one d.; fmr. County Sec., Hungarian Fed. of Democratic Youth; Hungarian Working People's Party 1948, fmr. First Sec. Debrecen Municipal Party Cttee., fmr. Ed. Party Life; Sec. Cen. Cttee. Hungarian Communist Youth Union 1958–61, First Sec. 1961–64; mem. Central Cttee. Hungarian Socialist Workers' Party 1962–88; Sec. of Cen. Cttee. 1966–76; Chief of Party and Mass Org. Dept. of Cen. Cttee. of HSWP 1964–66; mem. Parl. 1971, 1975; Minister of Posts and Communications 1976–83; Minister of Communications 1983–84. *Address:* c/o Ministry of Communications, 1400 Budapest, Dob utca 75/81, Hungary. *Telephone:* 220-220.

PUNGAN, Vasile, D.ECON.SC.; Romanian politician and diplomatist; b. 2 Nov. 1926, Bălăneşti, Gorj County; one d.; ed. Inst. of Economics, Bucharest; Dean of Faculty, Agronomical Inst. "Nicolae Bălcescu", Bucharest 1954; Gen. Dir., Ministry of Agriculture and Forestry 1955–58; Counsellor, Romanian Embassy, Washington 1959–62; Dir. and mem. Foreign Office Coll. 1963–66; Amb. to U.K. 1966–72; Counsellor of the Pres. of the Socialist Repub. of Romania 1973–78, 1979–82; mem. Grand Nat. Assembly (GNA) and Chair. GNA Comm. for Foreign Affairs and Int. Co-operation 1975–; Alt. mem. Cen. Cttee. of RCP 1972–79, mem. 1979–; Minister-Sec. of State at State Council 1979–82; Minister of Foreign Trade and Int. Econ. Co-operation 1982–86; Amb. to Bulgaria 1986–; Romanian decorations. *Address:* c/o Ministerul Afacerilor Externe, Bucharest, Romania. *Telephone:* 16.68.50.

PUNGOR, Ernö, PH.D.; Hungarian chemist; b. 30 Oct 1923, Vasszécsény; s.of József Pungor and Franciska Faller; m. Tünde Horváth; two s. one d.; ed. Pázmány Univ., Budapest; Corresp. mem. Hung. Acad. of Sciences 1967, mem. 1976–; Asst. Prof. Eötvös Univ., Budapest 1948–53, Assoc. Prof. 1953–62; Prof. Chemical Univ., Veszprém 1962–70; Dir. Inst. for Gen. and Analytical Chemistry, Tech. Univ., Budapest 1970–; Pres. Assen. of Eds. of European Chemical Journals 1977; mem. Int. Fed. of Scientific Eds. Assen. 1981; Chair. Working Party of Analytical Chemists of Fed. of European Chemical Socs. 1981; Chair. Analysis Div. of Hungarian Chemical. Soc.; Head Analysis Group, Hungarian Acad. of Sciences; Hon. mem. Czechoslovak Acad. Science Chemical Section 1966, Egyptian Pharmaceutical Soc. 1973, Austrian Analytical and Micro-analytical Soc. 1977, Chemical Soc. of Finland 1979, Analytical Chemical Soc. of Japan 1981; Hon. Prof., Agricultural Univ. of Lima 1973; Redwood Lecturer for English Soc. for Analytical Chemistry 1979; Robert Boyle Gold Medal (Royal Soc.) 1986, Talanta Gold Medal 1987, Excellent Inventor Gold Medal 1987, Gold Medal of Hungarian Acad. of Science 1988; pioneering work in the field of ion-selective electrodes and in flow-through analytical techniques; mem. IUPAC 1973; Vice-Pres. Electroanalytical Cttee. 1985; Dr. h.c. (Tech. Univ. of Vienna). *Leisure interest:* history. *Address:* Institute for General and Analytical Chemistry, Technical University, Budapest 1111, Gellért tér 4, Hungary. *Telephone:* 664-705.

PUNJALA, Shiv Shanker; Indian lawyer; b. 10 Aug. 1929, Mamidi Palli; s. of late Punjala Bashaiah and of Punjala Sathamma; m. Lakshmibai Punjala; two s. one d.; ed. Urdu Sharif Middle School, City Coll., Hyderabad, Hindu Coll., Amritsar; entered legal practice 1952, Sec. Hyderabad City Civil Court Bar Assen. 1958–61; mem., Vice-Pres. Bar Council, Andhra Pradesh 1965–, Chair. Disciplinary Cttee. 1970–; Third Govt. Pleader, High Court of Andhra Pradesh 1969, Second Govt. Pleader 1970, Principal Govt. Pleader 1972–74, Judge 1974–75; Sr. Advocate, Supreme Court, Sr. Counsel, Andhra Pradesh 1975–79; mem. Lok Sabha, Secunderabad Constituency 1979–, Minister of Law, Justice and Co. Affairs 1980–83. *Address:* c/o 402 'A' Wing, Shastri Bhavan, New Delhi 110011 (Office); Sree Sadan, 3-6-105 Himayat Nagar, Hyderabad 29, India (Home). *Telephone:* 384241/387908 (Office); 376599/372011 (Home).

PUOLANNE, Ulla Kaija, B.SC.(ECON.); Finnish politician; b. 28 June 1931, Lahti; financial officer, Puolanne eng. firm 1960–82; mem. Parl. 1975–; Chair. Conservative Party Parl. Group 1984–87; Second Minister of Finance 1987–. *Address:* Ministry of Finance, Snellmaninkatu 1A, 00170 Helsinki, Finland.

PURCELL, Edward Mills, PH.D.; American physicist (retd.); b. 30 Aug. 1912, Taylorville, Ill.; s. of Edward A. Purcell and Mary E. Mills Purcell; m. Beth Busser 1937; two s.; ed. Purdue Univ., Technische Hochschule, Karlsruhe, and Harvard Univ.; Instructor in Physics, Harvard 1938–40; Radiation Laboratory, M.I.T. 1940–46 (Faculty Instructor on leave of absence, Harvard 1941–45); Assoc. Prof. of Physics, Harvard 1945–49, Prof. of Physics 1949–58, Donner Prof. of Science 1958–60, Gerhard Gade Univ. Prof. 1960–80, Emer. Prof. 1980–; Sr. Fellow, Soc. of Fellows, Harvard Univ. 1950–71; Pres. American Physical Soc. 1970; mem. N.A.S., American Acad. of Arts and Sciences, American Philosophical Soc.; co-winner Nobel Prize in Physics 1952; Nat. Medal of Science 1980. *Address:* Lyman Laboratory of Physics, Harvard University, Cambridge, Mass. 02138; 5 Wright Street, Cambridge, Mass. 02138, U.S.A. *Telephone:* 617-495-2860.

PURDUM, Robert L., B.S.; American business executive; b. 1935, Wilmington, Ohio; m. Arlene Peterson; three s.; ed. Purdue Univ.; served U.S.N. and Indiana Toll Road Comm. 1956–62; joined Armco Inc. 1962, Dist. Eng., Metal Products Div. 1962–66, sales staff 1966–72, Dist. Man. 1972–76, Gen. Man. 1976–78; Pres. Midwestern Steel Div. 1978–80, Area Vice-Pres. 1980–82, Group Vice-Pres., C.E.O. Mfg. Services Group 1982–86, Exec. Vice-Pres. and C.O.O. 1986, Pres. and C.O.O. 1986–. *Leisure interests:* tennis, hunting, fishing, travel. *Address:* 300 Interpace Parkway, Parsippany, N.J. 07054 (Office); 26 Horizon Drive, Mendham, N.J. 07945, U.S.A. (Home). *Telephone:* 201-316-5200.

PURDY, James; American writer; b. 1923; ed. Chicago and Spain; Interpreter, editor and other posts in Cuba, Mexico, Washington, D.C. *Publications:* novels: Don't Call Me by My Right Name 1956, 63: Dream Palace 1956, Color of Darkness 1957, Malcolm 1959, The Nephew 1960, Cabot Wright Begins 1963, Eustace Chisholm and the Works 1967, Sleepers in Moon-Crowned Valleys (Part I Jeremy's Version 1970, Part II The House of the Solitary Maggot 1971), I Am Elijah Thrush 1972, In a Shallow Grave 1976, On Glory's Course 1983, Garments The Living Wear 1989; plays: Children is All 1962, Scrap of Paper 1981, The Berry-Picker 1981; An Oyster is a Wealthy Beast (story and poems) 1967, Mr. Evening 1968 (story and poems), On the Rebound 1970 (story and poems), The Running Sun (poems) 1971, Sunshine is an Only Child (poems) 1973, A Day after the Fair 1977 (stories and plays): Narrow Rooms (novel) 1978, Lessons and Complaints (poems) 1978, How I Became a Shadow (eight plays) 1979, Proud Flesh (plays) 1980, Mourners Below 1981, The Berry-Picker and Scrap of Paper (plays) 1981, Dawn 1985, Don't Let the Snow Fall (poem) 1985, In the Hollow of His Hand 1986, The Candles of your Eyes (collected stories) 1987, Are You in the Winter Tree? 1987; L.P. Recordings: 1963: Dream Palace 1968, Eventide and Other Stories 1969. *Address:* 236 Henry Street, Brooklyn, N.Y. 11201, U.S.A.

PURI, Ambrogio; Italian engineer and business executive; b. 26 Feb. 1920, Genoa; ed. Univ. of Genoa; began career with Cogne di Aosta; joined Istituto per la Riconstruzione Industriale (I.R.I.) Group 1947, Dir. Ilva 1956–58, Dir.-Gen. Rifornimenti Finsider 1958–62, Dir.-Gen. Italsider 1962–70, 1978–81, Pres. 1977–81; Pres. Italimpianti 1970–73, Pres. Ansaldo (responsible for electromechanical-nuclear section, Finmeccanica Group) 1973–76; Dir.-Gen. and Administrative Consultant, Finmeccanica, and Co-Dir.-Gen. for coordination of electromechanical-nuclear section 1976; Dir. Banco di Roma 1983–. *Address:* Banco di Roma, Via del Corso 307, 00186 Rome, Italy.

PURPURA, Dominick Paul, M.D.; American professor of neuroscience; b. 2 April, 1927, New York; s. of John R. Purpura and Rose Ruffino; m. Florence Williams 1948; three s. one d.; ed. Columbus Coll. and Harvard Medical School; Chair. and Prof., Dept. of Anatomy, Albert Einstein Coll. of Medicine 1967–74, Dept. of Neuroscience 1974–82, Prof. of Neuroscience 1982–, Dean, Albert Einstein Coll. of Medicine 1984–; Dir. Rose F. Kennedy Center for Research in Mental Retardation and Human Devt. 1972–82; Dean, Stanford Univ. School of Medicine 1982–84; Pres. Soc. for Neuroscience 1982–83, Int. Brain Research Org. 1986–, Vice-Pres. for Medical Affairs 1987–; mem. Inst. of Medicine (N.A.S.), N.A.S. *Publications:* numerous scientific papers. *Address:* Albert Einstein College of Medicine, Belfer Building, Room 312, 1300 Morris Park Avenue, Bronx, New York, N.Y. 10461, U.S.A. *Telephone:* (212) 430-2801.

PURVES, William, C.B.E., D.S.O.; British banker; b. 27 Dec. 1931, Kelso, Scotland; s. of Andrew Purves and Ida Purves; m. 1st Diana T. Richardson 1958 (divorced 1988); two s. two d.; m. 2nd Rebecca Jane Lewellen 1989; ed. Kelso High School; Nat. Bank of Scotland, Kelso 1948–54; joined the Hongkong and Shanghai Banking Corpn. 1954, Chief Accountant 1970–74, Man., Tokyo 1974–76, Sr. Man. Overseas Operations 1976–78, Asst. Gen. Man. Overseas Operations 1978–79, Gen. Man. Int. 1979–82, Exec. Dir. 1982–84, Deputy Chair. 1984–86, Chief Exec. 1986–, Chair. 1986–, mem. Exec. Council Hong Kong 1987–; Chair. British Bank of the Middle East 1986–; Hon. D. Univ. (Stirling) 1987. *Leisure interests:* golf, rugby. *Address:* The Hongkong and Shanghai Banking Corporation, GPO Box 64, Hong Kong (Office); 10 Pollock's Path, The Peak, Hong Kong (Home).

PUSEY, Nathan Marsh, A.M., PH.D.; American administrator; b. 4 April 1907, Council Bluffs, Iowa; s. of John Marsh and Rosa Drake Pusey; m. Anne Woodward 1936; two s. one d.; ed. Harvard Univ.; Asst. Harvard Univ. 1933–34; Sophomore Tutor, Lawrence Coll. 1935–38; Asst. Prof.

History and Literature, Scripps Coll., Claremont, Calif. 1938–40; Asst. Prof. Classics, Wesleyan Univ. 1940–43, Assoc. Prof. 1943–44; Pres. Lawrence Coll., Appleton, Wis. 1944–53; Pres. Harvard Univ. 1953–71, Andrew W. Mellon Foundation 1971–75, United Bd. for Christian Higher Educ. in Asia 1979–83; mem. American Acad. of Arts and Sciences; numerous honorary degrees. *Publications:* The Age of the Scholar 1963, American Higher Education 1945–1970 1978. *Leisure interests:* reading, gardening, sailing. *Address:* 200 East 66th Street, New York, N.Y. 10021, U.S.A. *Telephone:* (212) 371-8530.

PUTTNAM, David Terence, C.B.E.; British film producer; b. 25 Feb. 1941, London; s. of Leonard Arthur and Marie Beatrix Puttnam; m. Patricia Mary (née Jones) 1961; one s. one d.; ed. Minchenden Grammar School, London; advertising 1958–66, photography 1966–68, film production 1968–; Chair. Enigma Productions Ltd.; Dir. Nat. Film Finance Corpn. 1980–85, Anglia TV 1984–; Chair., C.E.O. Columbia Pictures, U.S.A. 1986–88; TV Presenter, Elstree: The British Hollywood 1989; Gov. Nat. Film and Television School; Pres. Council for Protection of Rural England 1986–; Hon. Special Lecturer in Drama, Bristol Univ. 1984–86, Hon. Prof. 1986–; Chair. Nat. Film and TV School 1988–; mem. Middx. Cricket Club; mem. Visiting Cttee., R.C.A. 1985–; Trustee, Tate Gallery 1986–; Special Jury Prize for The Duellists, Cannes 1977, two Acad. Awards and four BAFTA Awards for Midnight Express 1978, four Acad. Awards (including Best Film) three BAFTA Awards (including Best Film) for Chariots of Fire 1981, three Acad. Awards and nine BAFTA Awards for The Killing Fields 1985; Michael Balcon Award for outstanding contribution to the British Film Industry, BAFTA 1982; Hon. LL.D. (Bristol, Leicester); Chevalier, Ordre des Arts et des Lettres 1986. *Productions include:* That'll Be The Day, Mahler, Bugsy Malone, The Duellists, Midnight Express, Chariots of Fire, Local Hero, The Killing Fields, Cal, Defence of the Realm, Forever Young 1984, The Mission 1985, Mr Love 1986. *Publication:* Rural England: Our Countryside at the Crossroads 1988. *Leisure interests:* watching cricket, going to the cinema, following fortunes of Tottenham Hotspur Football Club. *Address:* Enigma Productions, 11/15 Queen's Gate Place Mews, London, SW7 5BG, England. *Telephone:* 01-581 8248/9.

PUYANA, Rafael; Colombian harpsichordist; b. 4 Oct. 1931, Bogotá; studied under Wanda Landowska; now lives in Paris but gives performances throughout the world; records for Philips and CBS. *Leisure interest:* collecting old keyboard instruments. *Address:* 88 rue de Grenelle, 75007 Paris, France.

PUŻYŃSKI, Stanislaw, M.D., D.SC.; Polish professor of psychiatry; b. 23 April 1936, Augustów; s. of Stefan Pużyński and Elzbieta Pużyński; m. Eliza Wójcik-Pużyńska 1960; one s. one d.; ed. Medical Acad. Białystok; Dept. of Psychiatry, Medical Acad. Białystok 1961–70; Head, Second Dept. of Psychiatry and Deputy Dir. Inst. of Psychiatry and Neurology, Warsaw 1970–, Prof. of Psychiatry 1979–; mem. numerous professional socs.; award of Scientific Council of Ministry of Health 1980. *Publications:* more than 100 publs. on psychiatry. *Leisure interests:* history, tourism. *Address:* Instytut Psychoneurologiczny, Al. Sobieskiego 1/9, 02-957 Warsaw (Office); ul. Czerniakowska 20 m.35, 00-714 Warsaw, Poland (Home). *Telephone:* 42 27 34.

PYAVKO, Vladislav Ivanovich; Soviet tenor; b. 1941; ed. State Institute of Theatrical Art; studied under R. Pastorino at La Scala, Milan; mem. CPSU 1978–; soloist with Bolshoi Opera 1965–; teacher of singing at State Institute of Theatrical Art 1980, Dean of School 1983–. People's Artist of U.S.S.R. 1983. *Major roles include:* Hermann in Queen of Spades, Grishka in The Legend of Kitezh . . . (Rimsky-Korsakov), Radames in Aida, Manrico in Trovatore, Cavaradossi in Tosca, Don José in Carmen, Nozdryov in Dead Souls (R. Shchedrin).

PYE, William Burns, A.R.C.A.; British sculptor; b. 16 July 1938, London; s. of Sir David Pye and Virginia Pye; m. Susan Marsh 1963; one s. two d.; ed. Charterhouse School, Wimbledon School of Art, Royal College of Art; Visiting Prof., California State Univ. 1975–76; Kinetic sculpture Revolving Tower 1970; made film Reflections 1971; sculpture 'Zemran' 1971; introduction of tensioned cables with less emphasis on volume 1972; combined working on commissions with smaller work and installations 1972–75; first visit to Far East for one-man show (retrospective) 1987; Slipstream and jetstream (water sculptures) commissioned by British Airports Authority, Gatwick Airport 1988; Balla Frois (100 ft. long water sculpture) commission for Glasgow Garden Festival 1988; Prix de Sculpture (Budapest) 1981, Vauxhall Mural Prize 1983, Peace Sculpture Prize 1984, A.B.S.A. award for best commission of new art in any medium 1988, Art at Work award for best site specific commission 1988. *Leisure interest:* playing the flute. *Address:* 43 Hambalt Road, Clapham, London, SW4 9EQ, England.

PYKA, Tadeusz, DR.ECON.SC.; Polish politician; b. 17 May 1930, Piekary Śląskie, Tarnowskie Góry District; ed. Acad. of Mining and Metallurgy, Cracow; Head of Casting Section, M. Buczek Foundry, Sosnowiec 1951–55; Deputy Dean, then Dean of Econ. Acad., Katowice 1955–64, Visiting Prof. 1967–; mem. Polish United Workers' Party 1953–81; First Sec. Town Cttee. PUWP, Bytom 1964–67; Second Sec. Voivodship Cttee. PUWP, Katowice 1967–74; Deputy mem. Cen. Cttee. 1964–71, mem. Cen. Cttee. 1971–80, Alt. mem. Political Bureau Feb.–Aug. 1980; Deputy to Seym 1972–80; Chair. Parl. Comm. for Foreign Trade 1972–74; First Vice-Chair. Planning

Comm. attached to Council of Ministers 1974–75; Deputy Chair. Council of Ministers 1975–80; Chair. Cttee. for Internal Market Affairs attached to Council of Ministers 1978–80; Head Govt. Comm. investigating workers grievances 1980–81; interned 1981–82, released Nov. 1982; Officer's Cross of Order Polonia Restituta 1969, Order of Banner of Labour (2nd Class) 1974 and other Polish and Foreign Awards. *Publications:* Programowanie optymalnych podziałów inwestycyjnych (Optimal Programming of Investment), Inwestycje hutnicze w Polsce i na świecie (Metallurgy Investment in Poland and the World) and other works on investment policy and economics.

PYM, Baron (Life Peer), cr. 1987, of Sandy in the County of Bedfordshire; **Francis Leslie Pym,** P.C., M.C., D.L.; British politician; b. 13 Feb. 1922, Abergavenny, Mon.; s. of Leslie Ruthven Pym and Iris Rosalind Orde; m. Valerie Fortune Daglish 1949; two s. two d.; ed. Eton and Magdalene Coll., Cambridge; served with 9th Queen's Royal Lancers (North African and Italian campaigns) 1942–46; mem. Liverpool Univ. Council 1949–53, Herefordshire County Council 1958–61; Hon. Fellow, Magdalene Coll.; M.P. for Cambridgeshire 1961–83; for Cambridgeshire S.E. 1983–87; Opposition Deputy Chief Whip 1967–70, Govt. Chief Whip and Parl. Sec. to Treasury 1970–73; Sec. of State for Northern Ireland 1973–74; Opposition Spokesman for Agriculture 1974–76, for House of Commons Affairs and Devolution 1976–78, for Foreign and Commonwealth Affairs 1978–79; Sec. of State for Defence 1979–81; Chancellor of Duchy of Lancaster, Paymaster-Gen. and Leader of the House of Commons Jan.–Sept. 1981; Lord Pres. of the Council and Leader of the House of Commons 1981–82; Sec. of State for Foreign and Commonwealth Affairs 1982–83; Pres. Cambridge Univ. Conservative Asscn. 1982–87, Atlantic Treaty Asscn. 1985–88; Chair. English-Speaking Union of the Commonwealth 1987–. *Publication:* The Politics of Consent 1984. *Leisure interest:* gardens. *Address:* Everton Park, Sandy, Beds., England.

PYNE, Natasha; British actress; b. 9 July 1946, Crawley, Sussex; d. of John Pyne and Iris Pyne; m. Paul Copley 1972; entered film industry 1961; mem. Young Vic Theatre Co. and Exchange Co., Manchester 1980–81; mem. BBC Radio Drama Co. 1985–87; stage plays include A Party for Bonzo (Soho Poly) 1985–87; films include The Idol, Taming of the Shrew, Breaking of Bumbo, One of Our Dinosaurs is Missing; TV plays include Father Dear Father (series), Hamlet, Silas Marner; BBC Play for Today: A Brush with Mr Porter on the Road to Eldorado 1981; Gems (Thames TV) 1987–88. *Leisure interests:* cycling, reading, cooking, travel. *Address:* c/o Kate Feast Management, 43A Princess Road, Regents Park, London, NW1 8JS, England. *Telephone:* 01-586 5502.

Q

QABOOS BIN SAID; Omani ruler; b. 18 Nov. 1940, Salalah; s. of late H.H. Said bin Taimur; 14th descendant of the ruling dynasty of Albusaid Family; m. 1976; ed. privately in U.K., R.M.A., Sandhurst; Sultan of Oman (following deposition of his father) July 1970-, also Prime Minister, Minister of Foreign Affairs, Defence and Finance; Hon. K.C.M.G. *Leisure interests:* reading, horse-riding, music. *Address:* The Palace, Muscat, Sultanate of Oman.

QADDAFI, Col. Mu'ammar al- (see Gaddafi, Col. Mu'ammar al-).

QADHAFI, Col. Mu'ammar al- (see Gaddafi, Col. Mu'ammar al-).

QASIMI, H. H. Sheikh Saqr bin Muhammad Al; Ruler of Ras Al-Khaimah; b. 1920; Ruler of Emirate of Ras Al-Khaimah 1948-; Chair. Rulers' Council of Trucial States -1971; mem. Supreme Council of United Arab Emirates 1972-. *Address:* The Ruler's Palace, Ras Al-Khaimah, United Arab Emirates.

QATAR, Emir of (see Thani, Sheikh Khalifa bin Hamad al-).

QAYSI, Riyadh Mehmoud Sami al-, LL.M., PH.D.; Iraqi diplomatist and lawyer; b. 20 Feb. 1939, Baghdad; m.; three c.; ed. Univs. of Baghdad and London; lecturer, Univs. of Baghdad and Mustansiriyah 1966-70; Vice-Dean, Coll. of Law and Politics, Univ. of Baghdad 1969; joined Ministry of Foreign Affairs 1970; First Sec. (later Counsellor), Perm. Mission of Iraq to UN 1970-75, rep. at Gen. Ass. 1970-74, 1979, Chair. Iraqi del. to Common Bureau of Co-ordination 1975, mem. Int. Law Comm. 1981-, Perm. Rep. to UN 1982-86; Amb. in Ministry of Foreign Affairs 1976-, Dir.-Gen. Legal Dept. 1979-82, Dir.-Gen. Foreign Services Inst. 1979-80. *Publications:* various legal works. *Address:* c/o Ministry of Foreign Affairs, Baghdad, Iraq.

QIAN HONG; Chinese swimmer; b. 1972; gold medallist, 100 metre butterfly, Pan-Pacific Swimming Championships, Brisbane 1987. *Address:* China Sports Federation, Beijing, People's Republic of China.

QIAN JIAZHU; Chinese economist and politician; b. 1909, Yiwu, Jiangsu Prov.; ed. Nat. Beijing Univ.; Lecturer in Econs. Beijing Univ. 1935; worked, and organised anti-Japanese socs. in South Western univs. 1937-42; Head of Hong Kong br. of Democratic Alliance 1946; apptd. perm. mem. Preparation Office of the Nat. Assen. of Industry and Commerce 1952; Vice-Dir. Admin. of Industrial and Commercial Man. of the State Council 1954-; mem. Cen. Cttee. of Democratic Alliance 1956-; mem. Science Planning Cttee. of State Council 1957-; Ed.-in-Chief of Cheng Ming magazine 1957-; mem. Nat. Cttee. of CPPCC 1959-66; inactive during the Cultural Revolution; mem. Cen. Cttee. Democratic Alliance 1983-; mem. 6th CPPCC 1983-; Asst. Chair. Econ. Construction Cttee. 1983-; Vice-Chair. Soc. for Research on the Chinese United Front Theory. *Publications include:* China's Internal Debt 1935, The Economic Situation in Kwangsi Province. *Address:* Chinese People's Political Consultative Conference, Beijing, People's Republic of China.

QIAN LINGXI; Chinese engineer; b. 16 July 1916, Wuxi, Jiangsu; one s. one d.; Pres. Dalian Inst. of Tech. 1981-, Chinese Soc. of Theoretical and Applied Mechanics 1982-. *Address:* Dalian University of Technology, Dalian, Liaoning 116024, People's Republic of China.

QIAN LINZHAO, PH.D.; Chinese scientist; b. 9 July 1906; ed. London Univ., and in France; went on a study tour to U.S.A. 1947-48; Deputy, 3rd NPC 1964; Vice-Pres., Univ. of Science and Tech. 1979-; mem. Dept. of Math. and Physics, Academia Sinica 1985-. *Address:* Room 205, Building 31, Zhong Guan Cun, Beijing 100080, People's Republic of China.

QIAN LIREN; Chinese party official; b. 1925; Deputy Sec.-Gen. All-China Fed. of Democratic Youth 1953; Deputy Dir. Int. Liaison Dept. China Fed. of Democratic Youth 1955; Sec.-Gen. All-China Students' Fed. 1956; Sec.-Gen. All-China Fed. of Youth 1959; Dir. Int. Liaison Dept. Communist Youth League 1959-Cultural Revolution; Dir. Int. Liaison Dept. All-China Fed. of Youth 1959-Cultural Revolution; Vice-Chair. All-China Fed. of Youth 1962; Perm. Rep. UNESCO 1978-81; Deputy Dir. Int. Liaison Dept., Cen. Cttee. CCP 1982-83; Dir. Int. Liaison Dept., Cen. Cttee. CCP 1983-; mem. CCP Cen. Cttee. 1985-; Dir. Renmin Ribao (People's Daily) 1985-. *Address:* Beijing, People's Republic of China.

QIAN MIN; Chinese politician; Minister of Fourth Ministry of Machine Building 1978-79, 1980-82; mem. NPC Standing Cttee. 1983-, Financial and Econ. Cttee. NPC 1983-; Head China-Zaire Friendship Group 1985-; Deputy Dir. Office of Industrial Streamlining Programme for Inland Provinces, State Council 1986. *Address:* State Council, Beijing, People's Republic of China.

QIAN QICHEN; Chinese diplomatist and state official; b. 1928, Tianjin; Second Sec. Embassy, U.S.S.R. 1960-62; Amb. to Guinea and Guinea Bissau 1974-76; Dir. Information Dept., Ministry of Foreign Affairs 1977-82; Vice-Minister, Foreign Affairs 1982-88, Minister April 1988-; alt. mem. 12th CCP Cen. Cttee. 1982, mem. 1985, mem. 13th Cen. Cttee. 1987-;

Chinese Special Envoy, 2-11th Round Sino-Soviet Consultations 1983-87; Deputy Dir. Comm. for Commemorating 40th Anniversary of UN 1985; Vice-Chair. Organizing Cttee. for Int. Year of Peace 1985. *Address:* Ministry of Foreign Affairs, 225, Chaonei Street, Dongsi, Beijing, People's Republic of China.

QIAN RENYUAN; Chinese chemist; b. 19 Sept. 1917, Changshu, Jiangsu; s. of Qian Nantie and Miao Lingfen; m. 1st Hu Miaozhen (divorced 1956), one s.; m. 2nd Ying Qicong 1961, one d.; Prof. of Chemistry 1951; Deputy Dir. Institute of Chemistry 1979-81, Dir. 1981-85; Pres. Chinese Chemical Soc. 1984-85; mem. Chemistry Div., Academia Sinica 1981. *Leisure interest:* classical music. *Address:* Institute of Chemistry, Academia Sinica, Zhong Guan Cun, Beijing, People's Republic of China. *Telephone:* 285505.

QIAN SANQIANG, PH.D.; Chinese physicist; b. 1910, Beijing; ed. Qinghua Univ.; m. He Cehui; with Curie Inst. Paris 1937-44; Prof. of Nuclear Physics 1948; Deputy Dir. Inst. of Modern Physics 1950-51, Dir. 1951-68; in political disgrace 1968-73; Dir. Div. of Math. and Physics, Chinese Acad. of Sciences 1981-85, Special Adviser 1985-; Pres. Soc. of Physics 1983; Vice-Chair. Nat. Academic Degrees Cttee. 1980-; Chair. Nat. Cttee. for Unifying Natural Science and Tech. Terms 1985-; mem. Presidium CPPCC 1983; Deputy Head Work Group for Science and Tech. 1983-; Vice-Chair. China Assen. for Science and Tech. 1980-. *Address:* Chinese Academy of Sciences, Beijing, People's Republic of China.

QIAN WEICHANG, PH.D.; Chinese nuclear physicist; b. 10 Sept. 1912, Wuxi Co., Jiangsu Prov.; m. Kong Xiangzhen; ed. California Inst. of Tech.; returned China 1946; mem. Standing Cttee. Democratic Youth League 1949-58; Dean of Studies, Qinghua Univ. 1950-55, Vice-Pres. 1956-58; Vice-Chair. Sino-Burmese Friendship Assen. 1952-59; Jiangsu Prov. Deputy to NPC 1954-59; mem. State Council Comm. for Scientific Planning 1957-58; purged 1958; rehabilitated 1972; Vice-Chair. CPPCC Nat. Cttee. 1987-; Pres. Shanghai Eng. Univ. Sept. 1983-. *Address:* Chinese People's Political Consultative Conference, Beijing, People's Republic of China.

QIAN XINZHONG, Maj.-Gen.; Chinese politician; b. 1911, Shanghai; Dir. Health Dept., South-West China Mil. Region 1950-53; mem. South-West China Mil. and Admin. Council (and Dir. of its Health Dept.) 1950-53, South-West China Admin. Council (and Dir. of its Health Dept.) 1953-54; mem. Medical Research Cttee., Ministry of Public Health 1955; mem. Scientific Planning Comm., State Council 1957-58; Vice-Minister of Public Health 1957-67, 1973-79, Minister 1979-82, Adviser 1982-; Minister of Family Planning May 1982-; Deputy for Jiangsu, 3rd NPC 1964; lost positions during Cultural Revolution; mem. Standing Cttee., 5th NPC March 1978-83; Chief Del. to 31st World Health Org. Conf., Geneva 1978; Deputy Head, Anti-schistosomiasis Leading Group, CCP Cen. Cttee. 1978-; Pres. Chinese Medical Assen. 1978-82; Deputy Leader, Cen. Cttee. group in charge of snail fever prevention in 13 S. China provinces 1979-; mem. Cen. Advisory Comm. 1985-, Presidium 6th NPC 1986; Hon. Pres. Bio-Medical Eng. Soc. 1980-, China Red Cross Soc. 1985-, China Assen. for the Blind and Deaf 1984-; Pres. Sports Fed. for the Disabled 1984-; UN Population Award 1983. *Address:* c/o State Council, Beijing, People's Republic of China.

QIAN XUESEN, PH.D.; Chinese physicist; b. 1910, Jiangsu; m. Jiang Ying; ed. Jiaotong Univ. Shanghai, California Inst. of Tech.; with M.I.T. 1935; Dir. Rocket Section, US Nat. Defence Science Advisory Bd. 1945; Prof., M.I.T. 1946; Dir. Inst. of Mechanics 1956; mem. 12th Cen. Cttee. CCP 1982-85; Vice-Minister Comm. for Science, Tech. and Industry for Nat. Defence 1984-88, Adviser 1988-; Chair. China Assen. for Science and Tech. 1986-; Hon. Pres. Astronautics Soc. 1980-, Soc. of Systems Eng. 1980-. *Address:* Chinese Academy of Sciences, Beijing, People's Republic of China.

QIAN YONGCHANG; Chinese politician; b. 1933; alt. mem. 12th Cen. Cttee. CCP 1982-87, mem. 13th Cen. Cttee. 1987-; Vice-Minister of Communications 1982-84, Minister 1984-. Chair. Bd. of Dirs., Hong Kong China Merchants Group 1985-. *Address:* Ministry of Communications, Beijing, People's Republic of China.

QIAN ZHENGYING, Miss; Chinese government official; b. 1922, Jiangsu; m. Huang Xinbai; ed. Dadong Univ., Shanghai; Vice-Minister of Water Conservancy 1952-58, of Water Conservancy and Electrical Power 1958; Minister of Water Conservancy and Electrical Power 1975-79, 1984-88, of Water Conservancy 1979-87, also of Power 1982-84; Adviser to State Council 1981-82, mem. 1982-; Adviser to State Flood Control HQ 1988-; mem. 11th Cen. Cttee. of CCP 1977, 12th Cen. Cttee. 1982, 13th Cen. Cttee. 1987; Gold Medal (Somalia). *Address:* State Council, Beijing, People's Republic of China.

QIAN ZHONGSHU, PH.D.; Chinese academic and writer; b. 1912, Wuxi Co., Jiangsu Prov.; s. of Qian Jibo; m. Yang Jiang; ed. Beijing Qinghua Univ., Oxford Univ.; returned to China 1937; ed. English quarterly Philobiblon 1946-48; researcher, Foreign Literature Inst. 1982-85; Vice-Pres., Chinese Social Sciences Acad. 1985-. *Publications:* Men, Beasts and Ghosts

1946, The Besieged Fortress (novel) 1947, Annotated Selection of Prose of the Song Dynasty 1958. *Address:* Chinese Social Sciences Academy, Jianguomenwai Street, Beijing, People's Republic of China.

QIANG XIAOCHU; Chinese party official; b. Shaanxi; Second Sec. CCP Cttee., Sungkiang 1951; mem. Prov. People's Govt., Sungkiang 1951; Chair. Sungkiang (when merged with Heilongjiang) 1952; Deputy Sec. CCP Cttee., Heilongjiang 1954, Sec. Secr., CCP Cttee. 1956; First Sec. Secr., CCP Sungari River Dist. Cttee. 1958; Alt. Sec. Secr., N.E. Bureau 1961; leading mem. 7th Ministry of Machine-Building 1976; First Sec. CCP Cttee., Jilin 1981; mem. 12th Cen. Cttee., CCP 1982–87; First Political Commissar, PLA Jilin Mil. Dist. 1982–; Sec. Cen. Cttee. for Discipline Inspection 1985–87; Deputy Head Leading Group for Rectification of Party Style within Cen. Depts. 1986–, mem. Cen. Advisory Comm. 1987–. *Address:* Communist Party Committee, Jilin Province, People's Republic of China.

QIAO SHI; Chinese party official; Sec. Afro-Asian Solidarity Cttee. 1965–Cultural Revolution; Deputy Dir. Int. Liaison Dept., CCP Cen. Cttee. 1978–82, Dir. 1982–83; mem. 12th Cen. Cttee., CCP 1982, 13th Cen. Cttee. 1985; mem. Politburo 1985, and Standing Cttee. of Politburo 1987–; Vice-Premier, State Council 1986; Alt. mem. Secr., Cen. Cttee. 1982–85, mem. 1985; Dir. Org. Dept., CCP Cen. Cttee. 1984–; Sec. Cen. Cttee. of Political Science and Law 1985–; Head Leading Group for Rectification of Party Style within Cen. Depts. 1986–; Sec. Cen. Comm. for Discipline Inspection 1987–. *Address:* International Liaison Department, Central Committee, Communist Party, Beijing, People's Republic of China.

QIAO SHIGUANG; Chinese artist; b. 1937, Guantao Co., Shandong Prov.; exponent of lacquer painting. *Address:* Central Academy of Arts and Crafts, Beijing, People's Republic of China.

QIAO XIAOGUANG; Chinese party official; b. 1918, Guangzong County, Hebei; Deputy Sec. CCP Guangxi 1953, Sec. 1961–66, 1974–76; First Sec. CCP of Guangxi and First Political Commissar, Guangxi Mil. District PLA 1977–; mem. 11th Cen. Cttee. CCP 1977, 12th Cen. Cttee. 1982; mem. CCP Cen. Advisory Comm. 1987–; Adviser, Chinese People's Asscn. for Friendship with Foreign Countries 1975–; Chair. Autonomous Regional CCPCC Cttee., Guangxi 1979–85; Rep. 4th Session 5th CCPC. *Address:* Regional Party Office of Guangxi, People's Republic of China. *Telephone:* 25674.

QIN CHUAN; Chinese newspaper editor; Deputy Ed.-in-Chief People's Daily, 1978–79, First Deputy Ed.-in-Chief 1979–82, Ed.-in-Chief 1982–83, Dir. 1983–85; Vice-Chair. Journalists' Asscn. 1983–; mem. 12th Cen. Cttee. CCP; Chair. Council of Int. Cultural Publ. Corpn. 1985. *Address:* People's Daily, Beijing, 2 Jin Tai Xi Lu, People's Republic of China.

QIN HEZHEN; Chinese party and government official; Sec. CCP Cttee., Shandong 1977–; Vice-Chair. Prov. Revolutionary Cttee., Shandong 1977–79; Deputy for Shandong, 5th NPC 1978; Vice-Gov. of Shandong 1979–83; Chair. Prov. People's Congress, Shandong 1983–85. *Address:* Chinese Communist Party Headquarters, Shandong Province, People's Republic of China.

QIN JIWEI, Gen.; Chinese army officer; b. 1912, Hongan, Hubei; Company Commdr. Red Army 1931; Deputy Commdr. Yunnan Mil. District, People's Liberation Army 1954; Deputy Commdr. Kunming Mil. Region, PLA 1955, Commdr. 1958; Lieut.-Gen. PLA 1955; Sec. CCP Yunnan 1966–68; Commdr. Chengdu Mil. Region, PLA 1973–76; mem. 10th Cen. Cttee. of CCP 1973; 2nd Political Commissar, Beijing Mil. Region, PLA 1975–78, First Political Commissar 1978–80, Commdr. Beijing Mil. Region 1980–; State Councillor 1988–; mem. 11th Cen. Cttee. of CCP 1977; Alt. mem. Politburo 12th Cen. Cttee. of CCP 1982–87; mem. 13th Cen. Cttee. CCP 1987–; First Sec. CCP Cttee. PLA Mil. Region 1981–. *Address:* PLA, Beijing Military Region, Beijing, People's Republic of China.

QIN WENCAI; Chinese industrialist; b. 25 Feb. 1925; Vice-Minister, Ministry of Petroleum Industry, Vice-Pres. Petroleum Corpn. of People's Repub. of China 1982; Chair. China Offshore Oil Service Co., Hong Kong 1985–; Pres. China Nat. Offshore Oil Corpn. 1982–87, Chair. Consultative Cttee. 1987–. *Address:* Jia 1, Sidao Kou Road, Haidian District, P.O. Box 9623, Beijing, People's Republic of China. *Telephone:* 2014906.

QIN YINGJI; Chinese party official; b. 1915, Tonglan Co., Guangxi (of Zhuang nationality); ed. Nationalities Coll. and Anti-Japan Mil. and Political Acad.; Regimental and Div. Commdr. New 4th Army, Sino-Japanese war; Dir. Public Security Dept., Prov. People's Govt., Hebei 1949–50; Council mem. Prov. People's Govt., Guangxi 1950; Dir. Public Security Dept., Guangxi, and Commdr. 6th Div., Public Security Forces 1950; Chair. Guixi Autonomous Zhou, Zhuang 1952–56; mem. Cen. S. China Admin. Council 1953–54; Deputy for Guangxi, 1st NPC 1954, 2nd 1959, 3rd 1964; Vice-Chair. Prov. People's Govt., Guangxi 1954–55; Vice-Gov. Guangxi Prov. 1955; Sec. CCP Cttee., Guangxi (Autonomous Region 1958–) 1957–Cultural Revolution; disappeared during Cultural Revolution; mem. Standing Cttee., Revolutionary Cttee., Guangxi Autonomous Region 1972–74, Vice-Chair. Revolutionary Cttee. 1974–79, also Sec. CCP Cttee. 1974–85; mem. 11th Cen. Cttee., CCP 1977, 12th Cen. Cttee. 1982–85; mem. Cen. Advisory Comm. 1987–; Chair. CPPCC, Guangxi 1979–; Chair. People's Govt.,

Guangxi Autonomous Region 1979–83. *Address:* Guangxi Autonomous Region, People's Republic of China.

QIN ZHAOYANG; Chinese writer; b. 1916, Hunei; Asst. Ed. People's Literature 1950; Deputy Dir. People's Literature Publishing House 1983–. *Publications:* On the Plain, Happiness, Advance across the Fields, Adventures of a little Swallow. *Address:* People's Literature Publishing House, Beijing, People's Republic of China.

QIN ZHONGDA; Chinese government official; b. 1923, Rongcheng Co., Shandong Prov.; Dir. a dept., Ministry of Petroleum and Chemical Industries 1978; Vice-Minister of Chemical Industry 1978, Minister 1982–; mem. 12th Cen. Cttee., CCP 1982–; Sec. Party Group, Ministry of Chemical Industry 1983–. *Address:* State Council, Beijing, People's Republic of China.

QU WU; Chinese politician; b. 1898, Weinan Co., Shaanxi Prov.; ed. Sun Yat-sen Univ., Army Acad. of U.S.S.R.; fmr. Head of Div. for Advisor's Affairs in Kuomintang Mil. Council; Instructor at Kuomintang Mil. Acad.; advisor to Kuomintang Del. 1949 peace negotiations with CCP, took part in pro-CCP Xinjiang revolt shortly after; served as Deputy Sec.-Gen. Govt. Admin. Council, Deputy Sec.-Gen. Standing Cttee. of NPC; Vice-Chair. of Nat. Cttee. CPPCC; Chair. Revolutionary Cttee. of Kuomintang 1987–. *Address:* Revolutionary Committee of the Kuomintang, Beijing, People's Republic of China.

QU XIAOGANG; Chinese musical composer; b. 16 Sept. 1952, Guizhou; s. of Qu Mengfei and Feng Gongheng; m. (divorced); farmer 1968–72; began viola study 1972; mem. Guiyang Beijing Opera Troupe 1972–78; student Dept. of Composition, Cen. Conservatory of Music 1978–83, Lecturer 1983–. *Works:* Mixed Chamber Music: Mong Dong 1984, Concerto for Percussion Instruments 1986, First Cello Concerto 1984–85, First Symphony 1986, The Mountain Song (for cello and orchestra) 1981, Girl of the Mountain (for violin and orchestra), The Mountain (symphonic suite), The Nether City (dance drama), Second String Quartet. *Leisure interests:* travelling, taking photographs, painting. *Address:* Department of Composition, Central Conservatory of Music, Baojia Jie Street, West District, Beijing, People's Republic of China.

QUADFLIEG, Will; German actor; b. 15 Sept. 1914, Oberhausen; ed. private drama studies; first stage appearances in Giessen, Gera, Düsseldorf; with Volksbühne, Berlin 1937–40, Schiller-Theater, Berlin 1940–45, Schauspielhaus, Hamburg 1946–50; guest appearances at Zürich, Salzburg Festival, Ruhr Festival and Burgtheater, Vienna; tours in Germany, Austria and Switzerland; noted for recitation of works of classical and contemporary poets; major stage roles in works of Goethe, Schiller, Shakespeare, Ibsen, Strindberg, etc. *Film appearances include:* Der Maulkorb, Der grosse Schatten, Lola Montez, Faust; mem. Freie Akad. der Künste, Hamburg, Deutsche Akad. der Darstellenden Künste, Frankfurt; Grosser Hersfeld Preis 1980; Medaille für Kunst und Wissenschaft 1984. *Publication:* Wir Spielen Immer. *Address:* 2860 Heilshorn, Federal Republic of Germany.

QUADRIO CURZIO, Alberto; Italian professor of economics; b. 25 Dec. 1937, Tirano-Valtellina; s. of Saverio F. Quadrio Curzio and Anna (Isella) Quadrio Curzio; m. Maria Luisa Bottasso 1964; one s. one d.; ed. Faculty of Political Sciences, Catholic Univ., Milan, St. John's Coll., Cambridge; Assoc. Prof. of Econs., Univ. of Cagliari 1965–68; Assoc. Prof. of Econs., Univ. of Bologna 1968–72, Prof. 1972–75, Chair., Faculty of Political Sciences 1974–75; Prof. of Econs., Catholic Univ., Milan 1976–, Dir. Centre of Econ. Analysis 1977–; Dir., Materie Prime (quarterly review) 1981–; Dir., Economia Politica (quarterly review); mem., Italian Nat. Research Council 1977–88; mem., Scientific Cttee., Nomisma 1981, Vice-Pres. 1982; mem. Council of the Italian Econ. Asscn. 1986–; St. Vincent Award 1984. *Publications:* Rendita e distribuzione in un modello economico plurisettoriale 1967, Investimenti in istruzione e sviluppo economico 1973, Accumulazione del Capitale e Rendita 1975, Protagonisti del Pensiero economico (with R. Scazzieri), 5 vols. 1977–83, Rent: Income Distribution, Order of Efficiency and Rentability 1980, The Gold Problem: Economic Perspectives 1982, Planning Manpower Education and Economic Growth 1983, Sui Momenti costitutivi della Economia Politica (with R. Scazzieri) 1983–84, Technological Scarcity: an Essay on Production and Structural Change 1986, The Exchange-Production Duality and the Dynamics of Economic Knowledge (with R. Scazzieri) 1986, Industrial Raw Materials: a Multi-Country, Multi-Commodity Analysis (with M. Fortis) 1986, The agro-technological system towards 2000: a European perspective (ed. with G. Antonelli) 1986, Produzione ed efficienza con tecnologie globali (with C. F. Manara and M. Faliva) 1987. *Leisure interest:* skiing. *Address:* Facoltà di Scienze Politiche, Università Cattolica, Largo Gemelli, 1-20123 Milan (Office); Via A. Saffi 31, 20123 Milan, Italy (Home). *Telephone:* 02/885 64 74 (Office); 02/469 41 08 (Home).

QUADROS, Jânio; Brazilian politician; b. 1917; ed. São Paulo School of Law; part-time high school teacher; practised law; mem. São Paulo City Council 1947–59; State Deputy 1950; Mayor, São Paulo City 1952–55, Nov. 1985–; Gov. São Paulo State 1955–59; Fed. Deputy 1959–60; Pres. of Brazil Jan.-Aug. 1961 (resgnd.); political rights suspended for 10 years, April 1964; arrested and banished to Corumba (near Bolivian border) July 1968. *Address:* Mayor's Residence, São Paulo, Brazil.

QUAISON-SACKEY, Alexander, M.A.; Ghanaian diplomatist; b. 9 Aug. 1924, Winneba; s. of late Alex Emanuel Sackey and of Alberta Quaison; m. Elsie Blankson 1951; four s. two d.; ed. Mfantsipim School, Exeter Coll., Oxford, London School of Economics and Lincoln's Inn, London; fmr. teacher at Mfantsipim School and with Gold Coast Secr.; Labour Officer Gold Coast 1952–55; Attaché British Embassy, Rio de Janeiro 1956; mem. Ghana del. to GATT, Geneva 1957; Head of Chancery and Official Sec. Ghana High Comm., London 1957–59; Perm. Rep. of Ghana to UN 1959–65; mem. UN Conciliation Comm. to the Congo (Léopoldville) 1961; Chair. UN Peacekeeping Cttee. 1965; Minister of Foreign Affairs 1965–66; mem. Convention People's Party; Vice-Pres. UN Gen. Ass. 1961–62, Pres. UN Gen. Ass. 1964–65; Amb. to Cuba 1961, to Mexico 1962; under house arrest 1966, released June 1966; practising Barrister-at-Law and Solicitor of the Supreme Court of Ghana 1966–77; Amb. to U.S.A. and Mexico 1978–80; Hon. LL.D. (Univ. of Calif.) 1965, (Tuskegee Inst.), Hon. Litt.D. (Montclair Coll.). *Publication:* Africa Unbound 1963. *Address:* Akumbia Lodge, P.O.B. 104, Winneba, Ghana (Home).

QUAN SHUREN; Chinese party and government official; b. 1931, Xinmin Co., Liaoning Prov.; Sec. CCP Cttee., Fushun City 1981–; Gov. of Liaoning 1983–86; Sec. CCP Prov. Cttee., Liaoning 1983–85, Deputy Sec. June 1985–86, Sec. 1986–; Alt. mem. 12th CCP Cen. Cttee. 1985–87, mem. 13th Cen. Cttee. 1987–. *Address:* Liaoning Provincial Committee, Shenyang, Liaoning Province, People's Republic of China.

QUAN ZHENGHUAN; Chinese mural artist, painter and university professor; b. 16 June 1932, Beijing; s. of Quan Liang-Su and Qin Xiao-Qing; m. Li Hua-Ji 1959; two d.; Prof. and mem. Academic Cttee., Cen. Acad. of Applied Arts; mem. Standing Cttee. of Artists' Assen. of China. *Murals include:* The Story of the White Snake (Beijing Int. Airport), Jin Wei filled the Ocean (Beijing Yian Jing Hotel). *Leisure interests:* Beijing Opera, old movies of 1930–1940s, football. *Address:* Central Academy of Applied Arts, Beijing, People's Republic of China. *Telephone:* 596391-244.

QUANDT, Bernhardt; German politician; b. 14 April 1903, Rostock; m.; joined Communist Party of Germany 1923; 10 years in concentration camp following active anti-fascist resistance from 1933; Minister of Agric. for Mecklenburg 1948–51; Prime Minister of Mecklenburg 1951–52; First Sec. Schwerin County Exec. of Socialist Unity Party and mem. Schwerin County Assembly 1952–74; mem. Cen. Cttee. Socialist Unity Party 1958–; mem. People's Chamber 1952–54, 1958–; mem. Council of State 1973–; decorations include Karl Marx Order, Grosser Stern der Volkerfreundschaft. *Address:* Staatsrat, Volkskammer, Berlin 1020, German Democratic Republic.

QUANT, Mary, O.B.E., F.S.I.A.; British (Welsh) fashion, cosmetic and textile designer; b. 11 Feb. 1934, London; d. of Jack and Mildred (née Jones) Quant; m. Alexander Plunket Greene 1957; one s.; ed. Goldsmiths Coll. of Art, London; started career in Chelsea, London 1954; Dir. of Mary Quant Group of cos. 1955–; mem. Design Council 1971–, U.K.–U.S.A. Bicentennial Liaison Cttee. 1973–, Advisory Council Victoria and Albert Museum 1976–78; restrospective exhbn. of 60's fashion, London Museum 1974; Sunday Times Int. Fashion Award; Rex Award (U.S.A.); Annual Design Medal, Soc. of Industrial Artists and Designers; Piavolo d'Oro (Italy); Royal Designer for Industry. *Publication:* Quant by Quant 1966. *Address:* Mary Quant Ltd., 3 Ives Street, London, S.W.3, England. *Telephone:* 01-584 8781.

QUARRIE, Donald; Jamaican athlete; b. 25 Feb. 1951, Kingston; competed Olympic Games, Munich 1972, reaching semi-final of 200 m.; Montreal 1976, won gold medal at 200 m. and silver medal at 100 m.; Moscow 1980, won bronze medal at 200 m.; competed Commonwealth Games, Edinburgh 1970, won gold medals at 100 m., 200 m. and 4×100 m. relay; Christchurch 1974 won gold medals at 100 m. and 200 m.; Edmonton 1978 won gold medal at 100 m.; one of only four men to break 20 secs. for 200 m.; World record holder for hand-timed 100 m., 200 m. and 220 yards. *Address:* c/o Jamaican Amateur Athletic Association, P.O. Box 272, Kingston 5, Jamaica, West Indies.

QUAYLE, James Danforth, B.S., J.D.; American politician; b. 4 Feb. 1947, Indianapolis; s. of James C. and Corinne (Pulliam) Quayle; m. Marilyn Tucker 1972; two s. one d.; ed. DePauw Univ., Greencastle, Ind., Indiana Univ.; served in Ind. Nat. Guard; court reporter Huntington Herald Press, Indiana 1965–69, Assoc. Publisher and Gen. Man. 1974–76; mem. Consumer Protection Div., Office of Attorney Gen., Ind. 1970–71; Administrative Asst. to Gov. of Ind. 1971–73; Dir. Indiana Inheritance Tax Div. 1973–74; admitted to Indiana bar 1974; teacher of business law Huntington Coll. 1975; mem. U.S. House of Reps. 1977–79; Senator from Indiana 1981–88; Vice-Pres. of U.S.A. Jan. 1989–; mem. Huntington bar assen.; mem. Hoosier State Press Assen.; Republican. *Address:* Office of the Vice-President, The White House, 1600 Pennsylvania Avenue, Washington, D.C. 20501; 7 North Jefferson Street, Huntington, Ind. 46750, U.S.A. (Home).

QUAYLE, Sir (John) Anthony, Kt., C.B.E.; British theatre director, producer and actor; b. 7 Sept. 1913, Ainsdale, Lancs.; s. of Arthur and Esther Overton; m. Dorothy Hyson 1947; one s. two d.; ed. Rugby and Royal Acad. of Dramatic Art; first stage appearance at Q Theatre 1931; joined the Old Vic Company 1932; first appearance in New York at Henry Miller Theatre 1936; with Old Vic at Elsinore 1937 and on tour of Continent and

Egypt 1939; served in Royal Artillery 1939–45; reappeared at the Criterion Theatre in The Rivals 1945; produced Crime and Punishment at the New Theatre 1946; produced and acted in Shakespeare's plays at Shakespeare Memorial Theatre, Stratford-on-Avon Feb. 1948–56; Dir. Shakespeare Memorial Theatre 1949–56; produced Harvey London 1948, directed 1975; produced Terence Rattigan's Who is Sylvia, Criterion Theatre, London Oct.1950; toured Australia with Shakespeare Memorial Theatre Company 1949–50 and Jan.-Oct. 1953; acted name part in Tamburlaine, New York Jan. 1956; acted in A View From The Bridge, London 1956; European tour of Titus Andronicus 1957; dir. and acted in The Firstborn, New York; acted in Long Day's Journey into Night, Edinburgh, London and Broadway 1958, Look After Lulu, Chin-Chin 1960, The Right Honourable Gentleman 1964, Incident at Vichy 1966, Sleuth, London 1970, New York 1970–71, Everyman 1974, The Old Country 1978, King Lear 1987, toured England with Devil's Disciple and Skin Game 1981, Hobson's Choice 1982; Dir. Lady Windermere's Fan, London 1966, Galileo, New York 1967, Harvey, London 1975, Old World (London) 1976–77, Do you Turn Somersaults? (U.S.A.) 1977–78, The Rivals (also acted) 1978, King Lear 1978, toured England with Heartbreak House 1980, A Coat of Varnish (also acted) 1982, Rules of the Game 1982; Actor/Dir. Clarence Brown Co., Tenn. 1975; f. Compass Theatre 1984, Dir. The Clandestine Marriage 1984, After the Ball is Over 1984, St. Joan, The Tempest 1985, Dandy Dick 1986, TV film Oedipus at Colonnus 1986, The Government Inspector 1988. *Films:* Woman in a Dressing Gown, The Man Who Wouldn't Talk, Ice Cold in Alex, Serious Charge, Tarzan's Greatest Adventure, The Challenge, The Guns of Navarone, H.M.S. Defiant 1961, Lawrence of Arabia 1962, The Fall of the Roman Empire 1964, Operation Crossbow, A Study in Terror, Anne of the Thousand Days, Bequest to the Nation, The Tamarind Seed, 21 Hours at Munich 1976, The Eagle Has Landed 1977, Murder by Decree 1978, Dial M for Murder 1981, After the Ball is Over 1985; also radio and TV plays including: Q.B.7, Moses 1974, Great Expectations 1974, Benjamin Franklin 1974, David and Saul 1975, Ice Age 1978, Henry IV, Parts I and II 1979, Masada 1979; directed colour production Caesar and Cleopatra for Nat. Broadcasting Co. Television; producer The Idiot (Nat. Theatre) 1970, TV films: Last Days of Pompeii 1983, Lace 1983, Beethoven 1983, Key to Rebecca 1984, Testament of John 1984, The Endless Game 1989, Confessional 1989; Hon. D.Litt. (Hull) 1987. *Publications:* Eight Hours from England 1945, On Such a Night 1947. *Address:* c/o International Creative Management Ltd., 388/396 Oxford Street, London, W1N 9HE, England. *Telephone:* 01-629 8080 (Office).

QUEFFÉLEC, Anne; French concert pianist; b. 17 Jan. 1948, Paris; d. of Henri Queffélec and Yvonne Pénau; m. Luc Dehaene 1983; one s.; ed. Conservatoire National, Paris (First Prize for Piano 1965, for Chamber Music 1966); since 1968 has played all over Europe, Japan (five tours), Israel, Africa, Canada and U.S.A.; has played with BBC Symphony, London Symphony, Royal Philharmonic, Bournemouth Symphony, Hallé, Scottish Chamber, City of Birmingham Symphony, Miami Symphony, Tokyo Symphony orchestras, Nouvel orchestre philharmonique de Radio-France, Orchestre de Strasbourg, etc., under conductors including Zinman, Groves, Leppard, Marriner, Boulez, Semkow, Skrowaczewski, Eschenbach, Gardiner, Pritchard, Atherton, etc.; has played at numerous festivals including Strasbourg, Dijon, Besançon, Bordeaux, Paris, King's Lynn, Bath, London Proms; First Prize, Munich Int. Piano Competition 1968; Prizewinner, Leeds Int. Piano Competition 1969; has made about 18 records for Erato-RCA, of music by Scarlatti, Chopin, Schubert, Fauré, Ravel, Debussy, Liszt, Hummel, Beethoven, Mendelssohn and Bach. *Leisure interests:* literature, walking, cinema, theatre, friends, humour, art exhibitions. *Address:* 15 avenue Corneille, 78600 Maisons-Lafitte, France.

QUELER, Eve; American conductor; b. New York; ed. Mannes Coll. of New York, City Coll. of New York, piano with Isabella Vengerov, conducting with Carl Bamberger, Joseph Rosstock, Walter Susskind and Igor Markevich; began as pianist, asst. conductor New York City Opera 1958 and 1965–70; later became a conductor; guest-conducted Philadelphia, Cleveland, Montreal Symphony, New Philharmonia, Australian Opera, Opéra de Nice, Opera de Barcelona, San Diego Opera, Edmonton Symphony, Nat. Opera of Czechoslovakia, Hungarian State, Hungarian Operahaz and various other orchestras; Music Dir. Opera Orchestra of New York 1967–; Musician of the Month, Musical American Magazine; Dr. h.c. (Russell Sage Coll., Colby Coll.); Martha Baird Rockefeller Fund for Music Award. *Recordings:* Puccini's Edgar, Verdi's Aroldo, Massenet's Le Cid, Boito's Nerone, Strauss' Guntram. *Publications:* articles in Musical America Magazine. *Leisure interest:* organic gardening. *Address:* c/o Shaw Concerts, 111 W. 57th Street, New York, N.Y. 10019, U.S.A.

QUENÉ, Theo; Netherlands civil servant; b. 29 July 1930, Oostzaan; s. of G. J. Quené and Th. A. M. Quené-Francois; m. 1st A. J. Boterenbrood 1956, 2nd Dr A. C. Ritter 1986; two s. two d.; ed. Agricultural Univ., Wageningen; Govt. Official Ministry of Housing and Physical Planning 1956–67, Dir.-Gen. for physical planning 1972–76, Sec.-Gen. 1976–78; Dir. Nat. Physical Planning Agency 1967–72; Chair. Scientific Council for Govt. Policy 1978–85; Chair. Socio-Economic Council 1985–; mem. Royal Acad. of Arts and Sciences 1971, numerous acads. in Netherlands and abroad; Kt. Order of the Dutch Lion. *Leisure interests:* nature protection, literature. *Address:* Bezuidenhoutseweg 60, P.O. Box 90405, 2509 LK The Hague

(Office); Keizersgracht 405, 1016 EK Amsterdam, The Netherlands (Home). *Telephone:* (070) 499501 (Office); (020) 253663 (Home).

QUENNELL, Peter, C.B.E.; British writer; b. 9 March 1905, Bickley, Kent; s. of late C. H. B. and M. Quennell; ed. Berkhamsted Grammar School and Balliol Coll., Oxford; fmr. Prof. of English Literature, Tokyo Bunrika Daigaku 1930; Ed. Cornhill Magazine 1944–51, History Today 1951–79. *Publications:* Baudelaire and the Symbolists, A Superficial Journey, Byron: The Years of Fame, Byron in Italy 1941, Caroline of England, Four Portraits 1945, Ruskin: The Portrait of a Prophet 1952, Spring in Sicily, The Singular Preference, Hogarth's Progress 1954, The Sign of the Fish 1960, Shakespeare: the Poet and His Background 1963, Alexander Pope: the Education of Genius 1968, Romantic England 1970, Casanova in London (essays) 1971, Samuel Johnson, his Friends and Enemies 1972, The Marble Foot (autobiog.) 1976, The Wanton Chase (autobiog.) 1980, Customs and Characters: Contemporary Portraits 1982; Editor: Aspects of 17th Century Verse, Memoirs of the Comte de Gramont (trans.), Letters of Madame de Lieven, Memoirs of William Hickey, Byron: A Self Portrait (1798-1824), Mayhew's London Labour and the London Poor (3 vols.), Marcel Proust: 1871-1922 1971, Vladimir Nabokov, his Life, his Work, his World 1979, A Lonely Business: A Self Portrait of James Pope-Hennessy 1981, The Pursuit of Happiness 1989. *Address:* 2 Chamberlain Street, Primrose Hill, London, N.W.1, England.

QUENTIN-BAXTER, R. Q., B.A., LL.B. ; New Zealand lawyer; b. 17 Jan. 1922, Christchurch; ed. Univ. of New Zealand; joined diplomatic staff, Dept. of External Affairs 1949; Deputy High Commr. in Canada 1957–58; Deputy Perm. Rep. New Zealand Mission to UN 1959–61; Counsellor, Tokyo 1961–64; Asst. Sec. for Legal, Consular and S. Pacific Affairs 1964–68, concurrently sr. Commr. for New Zealand, S. Pacific Comm.; Prof. of Jurisprudence and Constitutional Law, Victoria Univ. of Wellington 1968–85; Rep. to Comm. on Human Rights 1966–71 (Chair. 1969); mem. Int. Law Comm. 1972–; del. to various int. confs. and several sessions of UN Gen. Ass. *Address:* Faculty of Law, Victoria University of Wellington, Private Bag, Wellington, New Zealand.

QUESTIAUX, Nicole Françoise; French politician; b. 19 Dec. 1930, Nantes; d. of Pierre Valayer and Elisabeth Mills; m. Paul Questiaux 1951; one s. one d.; ed. Lycée de Casablanca, Morocco, Ecole nat. d'admin.; Auditer, Conseil d'Etat 1955, mem. 2nd sub-section, Disputes section, Maître des Requêtes 1962, Govt. Commr. assemblée du contentieux 1963–74; Pres. Joint Cttee. for Study of Problems relating to the Elderly 1969; Surrogate Govt. Commr. Tribunal des Conflits 1973–74; Conseiller d'Etat 1980–81; Minister of State May–June 1981, Minister of Nat. Solidarity 1981–82; Pres. 4th Sub-section Conseil d'Etat 1983–; Chevalier, Ordre nat. du Mérite. *Publications:* Le contrôle de l'administration et la protection des citoyens (with Guy Braibant and Céline Wiener) 1973, Traité du social; Situations, luttes politiques, institutions (with Jacques Fournier) 1976. *Address:* 13 avenue de Bretteville, 92200 Neuilly-sur-Seine, France (Home).

QUIE, Albert H.; American state governor; b. 18 Sept. 1923, Wheeling Township, Minn.; s. of Albert K. and Nettie (Jacobson) Quie; m. Gretchen M. Hansen 1948; four s. one d.; ed. Northfield High School and St. Olaf Coll., Northfield, Minn.; mem. Minnesota State Senate 1954–58; Rep. U.S. Congress 1958–78; Gov. of Minnesota 1979–83; 8 honorary doctorates and other awards; Ind. Republican. *Leisure interests:* training and showing saddle horses, reading. *Address:* c/o Room 130, State Capitol, St. Paul, Minn. 55155, U.S.A. (Office).

QUIJANO, Raúl Alberto; Argentine diplomatist; b. 13 Dec. 1923, Santa Fé; s. of Mateo Quijano and Sara Aldao de Quijano; m. Mercedes Santander 1963; one d.; ed. La Salle Coll., Buenos Aires and Univ. de Buenos Aires; Attaché, Argentine Foreign Service 1947, served in Perm. Mission to UN, in India and Pakistan; Third Sec., South Africa 1950; Second Sec., Perm. Mission to UN 1955, First Sec. 1958, Counsellor 1959, Minister 1963; Amb. and Dir.-Gen. of Political Affairs, Ministry of Foreign Affairs 1967; Amb. and Perm. Rep. to OAS 1969–75, 1979–84; Minister of Foreign Affairs 1976; Amb. to Paraguay 1984–; Chair. Int. Civil Service Comm. (UN) 1975–79; decorations from Govts. of Chile, Italy, Norway, Japan, Spain, Bolivia, Brazil. *Address:* Argentine Embassy, M. Lopez 2004, Asunción, Paraguay.

QUILES, Paul; French politician; b. 27 Jan. 1942, Saint Denis du Sig, Algeria; s. of René Quiles and Odette Tyrode; m. Josephe-Marie Bureau 1964; three d.; ed. Lycée Lyautey, Casablanca and Lycée Choptal et Louis le Grand, Paris; engineer, Shell Française 1973–78; Socialist Deputy to Nat. Ass. 1978–81, 1986–88; Minister of Town Planning and Housing 1983–85, and Transport 1984–85, of Defence 1985–86, of Posts, Telecommunications and Space May 1988–; mem. Econ. and Social Council 1974–75. *Address:* 22 boulevard Kellermann, 75013 Paris, France.

QUILLIOT, Roger, D. ÈS L.; French politician; b. 19 June 1925, Hermaville; s. of Adulphe Quilliot and Sidonie Lebel; m. Claire Trougnac 1948; two s.; ed. Collège de Béthune, Lycée Louis-le-Grand, Paris, Univs. of Lille and Paris; Teacher at Evreux 1949, Angers 1950, Savigny 1956; Municipal Councillor, Angers 1954; Sec. Fédération socialiste de Maine-et-Loire 1954–56; Prof. Univ. of Clermont-Ferrand 1963–; mem. Steering Cttee., French Section of Socialist Int. 1963–69; mem. Nat. Cttee., Fédération de la gauche démocratique et socialiste 1966–69; mem. Steering Cttee., Parti Socialiste

(and in charge of univ. affairs) 1969–79; Deputy Mayor, Clermont-Ferrand 1971, Mayor 1973–; Gen. Councillor, Clermont-Ferrand-Nord 1973–81, Vice-Pres. Gen. Council 1986; Senator (Puy-de-Dôme) 1974–81, Senator (Clermont-Ferrand) 1983–, Deputy March 1986, Senator Sept. 1986; Pres. Asscn. des maires des grandes villes de France 1977–83; Pres. Fédération nationale des Offices H.L.M. 1978–81; Minister of Housing May 1981–83, also of Urban Planning June 1981–83; Pres. Union nat. des H.L.M. 1985–. *Publications:* La mer et les prisons, Essai sur Albert Camus 1956, La société de 1960 et l'avenir politique de la France 1960, La liberté aux dimensions humaines 1967, Le parti socialiste S.F.I.O. et l'exercice du pouvoir 1972, L'homme sur le pavois (with Claire Quilliot) 1976, Une écharpe de maire 1982, Sur le Pavois 1986, Albert Camus (Ed.). *Address:* Mairie, 63000 Clermont-Ferrand (Office); 20 rue du Parc de Montjuzet, 63100 Clermont-Ferrand, France (Home).

QUINE, Willard Van Orman, M.A., PH.D., LL.D., L.H.D., D.LITT.; American philosophy professor; b. 25 June 1908, Akron, Ohio; s. of Cloyd R. Quine and Hattie van Orman Quine; m. Marjorie Boynton 1948; one s. three d.; ed. Oberlin Coll. and Harvard Univ.; Sheldon Travelling Fellow (Harvard) to Vienna, Prague and Warsaw 1932–33; Junior Fellow, Soc. of Fellows, Harvard 1933–36, Faculty Instructor in Philosophy 1936–41, Assoc. Prof. 1941–48, Prof. of Philosophy 1948–56, Edgar Pierce Prof. of Philosophy, Harvard Univ. 1956–78, Emer. Prof. 1978–; U.S.N.R. 1942–46; Visiting Prof. Univ. of São Paulo, Brazil 1942, George Eastman Visiting Prof., Oxford 1953–54; Shearman Lecturer, Univ. of London 1954; Pres. Asscn. for Symbolic Logic 1953–55; mem. Inst. for Advanced Study, Princeton 1956–57; Fellow, Center for Advanced Study in Behavioral Sciences, Stanford 1958–59; Gavin David Young Lecturer, Adelaide Univ., Australia 1959; Visiting Prof. Tokyo Univ. 1959; Fellow, Wesleyan Univ. Center for Advanced Study 1965; Fellow, American Acad. of Arts and Sciences, N.A.S., American Philosophical Soc.; Corresp. Fellow British Acad., Norwegian Acad.; Corresp. mem. Inst. de France; Visiting Prof. Rockefeller Univ. 1968, Coll. de France 1969; Paul Carus Lecturer, New York 1971, Saville Fellow, Oxford 1973–74; Pres. American Philosophical Asscn. 1958; mem. Inst. Int. de Philosophie, Acad. Int. de Philosophie des Sciences, Inst. Brasileiro de Filosofía, American Nat. Acad. of Sciences; Hon. D.Litt. (Oxford Univ.) 1970, (Cambridge Univ.) 1978 and 13 other hon. degrees; Butler Medal, Columbia Univ. *Publications:* A System of Logistic 1934, Mathematical Logic 1940, Elementary Logic 1941, O Sentido da Nova Lógica 1944, Methods of Logic 1950, From a Logical Point of View 1953, Word and Object 1960, Set Theory and its Logic 1963, The Ways of Paradox 1966, Selected Logic Papers 1966, Ontological Relativity 1969, Philosophy of Logic 1970, Web of Belief (with J. S. Ullian) 1970, The Roots of Reference 1973, Theories and Things 1981, the Time of My Life 1985, The Philosophy of W. V. Quine (co-author) 1986, Quiddities 1987, La Scienza e i Dati di Senso 1987, Pursuit of Truth 1989, Perspectives on Quine (co-author) 1989. *Leisure interests:* languages, geography. *Address:* 38 Chestnut Street, Boston, Mass. 02108, U.S.A. *Telephone:* 723-6754.

QUINN, Anthony Rudolph Oaxaca; American actor-director; b. 21 April 1916; s. of Frank and Nellie (Oaxaca) Quinn; m. 1st Katherine de Mille 1937 (divorced), one s. three d.; m. 2nd Iolanda Addoleri 1966; ed. Los Angeles; first appeared on stage 1936. *Films include:* Viva Zapata, Lust for Life, La Strada, Man from Del Rio, The Black Orchid, Warlock, Last Train from Gun Hill, Heller in Pink Tights, Savage Innocents, Guns of Navarone, Barabbas, Lawrence of Arabia, The Visit, Zorba the Greek, The Twenty-Fifth Hour, Guns for San Sebastian, The Secret of Santa Vittoria, The Shoes of the Fisherman, The Magus, A Dream of Kings, The Last Warrior, Flap, Across 110th Street, The Don is Dead 1973, The Marseille Contract 1974, Mohammed, Messenger of God (retitled The Message in the United Kingdom) 1976, The Children of Sanchez 1977, The Greek Tycoon 1977, The Passage 1978, Caravans 1979, Lion of the Desert 1981, High Risk 1982, Ghosts Can't Do It 1989; acted in musical version of Zorba the Greek, U.S.A. 1982–86; Dir. The Buccaneer 1958; Venice Film Festival Award for La Strada 1954, American Motion Picture Acad. Awards for Best Supporting Actor in Viva Zapata 1952, and Lust for Life 1956. *Publication:* The Original Sin (autobiog.). *Address:* c/o Mccartt, Orek, Barrett, 9200 Sunset Boulevard, 1009 Los Angeles, Calif. 90069, U.S.A.

QUINN, Ruairi, B.ARCH., M.R.I.A.I., R.I.B.A.; Irish architect and politician; b. 2 April 1946, Dublin; s. of Malachi and Julia Quinn; m. 1969 (separated 1983); one s. one d.; ed. Blackrock Coll. and Univ. Coll., Dublin; School of Ekistics, Athens 1970–71; Architects' Dept. Dublin Corpn. 1971–73; Partner, Burke-Kennedy Doyle and Partner 1973–82; mem. Dublin Corpn. 1974–77, 1981–82; mem. Seanad Eireann 1976–77, 1981–82; mem. Dail Eireann 1977–81, 1982–; Minister of State, Dept. of the Environment 1982–83; Minister for Labour and Minister for the Public Service 1983–87; mem. Irish Planning Inst. *Leisure interests:* athletics, reading. *Address:* Dail Eireann, Leinster House, Dublin 2, Ireland.

QUINN, William John, B.A., LL.B.; American lawyer and railway executive; b. 8 May 1911, St. Paul, Minn.; s. of William J. Quinn and Celina La Roque Quinn; m. Floy I. Heinen 1942; four s. four d.; ed. St. Thomas Coll., St. Paul (Minn.) and Univ. of Minnesota Law School; Law practice, St. Paul (Minn.) 1935–37, Asst. Dist. Attorney 1937–40; Attorney Soo Line Railroad 1940–42; Special Agent Fed. Bureau of Investigation 1942–45; Asst. Commercial Counsel Soo Line Railroad 1945, Commerce Counsel 1945–52, Asst.

Gen. Counsel 1952, Gen. Counsel 1952–53, Vice-Pres. and Gen. Counsel 1953–54; Gen. Solicitor Chicago, Milwaukee, St. Paul and Pacific Railroad Co. 1954–55, Vice-Pres. and Gen. Counsel 1955–58, Pres. 1958–66, Chair. and C.E.O. 1970–78; Pres. and C.E.O. Chicago Burlington & Quincy RR Co. 1966–70; Vice-Chair. Burlington Northern Inc. 1970–; Chair. Chicago Milwaukee Corpn. 1972–78, Pres. 1972–78; Chair. Bd. of Trustees, Loyola Univ. of Chicago; mem. Bd. of Dirs. St. Francis Hosp.; Hon. LL.D. (St. Thomas Coll., St. Paul, Minn.); Outstanding Achievement Award from Univ. of Minn. 1961. *Leisure interests:* golf, travel, viewing sports on television. *Address:* 111 West Washington Street, Suite 1250, Chicago, Illinois 60602 (Office); 1420 Sheridan Road, Apt. 4D, Wilmette, Illinois 60091, U.S.A. (Home). *Telephone:* 312-256-7622 (Home).

QUIÑONEZ AMEZQUITA, Mario Rafael; Guatemalan lawyer and diplomatist; b. 4 June 1933; s. of the late Hector Quiñones and of Elisa de Quiñones; m. Yolanda de Quiñones 1963; two s. two d.; ed. Univ. of San Carlos and Univ. of Rio Grande do Soul, Brazil; lawyer and notary with law firm of Viteri, Falla, Quiñones, Umaña, Orellana y Cáceres 1959–; Prof. of Law, Rafael Landívar Univ. 1962–, Dean Dept. of Legal and Social Sciences 1974–82; Vice-Pres. of Landívar Univ. 1978–82, Pres. March–Oct. 1982; Perm. Rep. to UN 1982–84; Minister of Foreign Affairs 1986–87; Vice-Pres. North and Cen. American Region, Union of Latin Notaries 1978; Pres. Asscn. of Lawyers and Notaries of Guatemala 1977; mem. Guatemala Del. UN Comm. on Int. Trade Law 1974. *Address:* 6A Calle 5-47, Zona 9, Guatemala City, Guatemala.

QUINTANA, Carlos, M.SC., M.B.A.; Mexican engineer; b. 1912, Puebla; s. of Miguel A. Quintana and María-Cruz Gómez-Daza; m. Lulu Pali Solomon 1944; three s. three d.; ed. Instituto Politécnico Nacional, Mexico, and Columbia and Harvard Univs., U.S.A.; fmr. Prof. of Engineering, Inst. Politécnico Nacional, Mexico City; in Dept. of Industrial Research, Bank of Mexico 1944–50; Man. Ayotla Textile S.A., Mexico 1948–49; Dir. Industrial Development Division, Econ. Comm. for Latin America (ECLA) 1950–60, Exec. Sec. ECLA 1967–72; Man. Industrial Programming, Nacional Financiera 1960–67; mem. Governing Council, Mexican Inst. for Tech. Research 1961–67; mem. Govt. Econ. Missions to Yugoslavia, Czechoslovakia, U.S.S.R. and Poland; mem. FAO Advisory Comm. on Pulp and Paper, Rome 1960–67; Asst. Sec.-Gen. UN 1967; Chair. of Bd. Centro Latinoamericano de Demografía; Man. Fondo Nacional de Fomento Industrial (Mexico) 1972; Gen. Credit Man. Nacional Financiera S.A. (official devt. bank of Mexico) 1974, Gen. Man. (Technical Advice) 1976. *Leisure interests:* music (piano), swimming. *Address:* Venustiano Carranza 25, México 1, D.F. (Office); Sierra Guadarrana 155, México 10, D.F., México (Home). *Telephone:* 520-86-99 (Home).

QUINTON, Baron (Life Peer) of Holywell in the City of Oxford and County of Oxfordshire, **Anthony Meredith Quinton,** F.B.A.; British academic; b. 25 March 1925, Gillingham, Kent; s. of the late Richard Frith Quinton and Gwenllyan Letitia Quinton; m. Marcelle Wegier 1952; one s. one d.; ed. Stowe School, Christ Church, Oxford; served in R.A.F., Flying Officer and Navigator 1943–46; Fellow, All Souls Coll., Oxford 1949–55, New Coll., Oxford 1955–78; Del., Oxford Univ. Press 1970–76; mem. Arts Council 1979–81; Visiting Prof., Swarthmore Coll., Pa. 1960, Stanford Univ., Calif. 1964, New School for Social Research, New York 1976–77; Dawes Hicks Lecturer, British Acad. 1971; Gregynog Lecturer, Univ. of Wales Aberystwyth 1973; T. S. Eliot Lecturer, Univ. of Kent, Canterbury 1976; Robbins Lecturer, Univ. of Stirling 1988; R.M. Jones Lecturer, Queen's Univ., Belfast 1988; Tanner Lecturer, Union of Warsaw 1988; Pres., Aristotelian Soc. 1975–76; Gov., Stowe School 1963–84, Chair. of Govs. 1969–75; Fellow, Winchester Coll. 1970–85; Pres. Trinity Coll., Oxford 1978–87; Emer. Fellow, New Coll., Oxford 1980; mem. Bd. of Eds. Encyclopaedia Britannica 1985–; mem. Peacock Cttee.; Chair. British Library 1985–. *Publications:* Political Philosophy (Ed.) 1967, The Nature of Things 1973, Utilitarian Ethics 1973, trans. of K. Ajdukiewicz's Problems and Theories of Philosophy (with H. Skolimowski) 1973, The Politics of Imperfection 1978, Francis Bacon 1980, Thoughts and Thinkers 1982. *Leisure interests:* sedentary pursuits. *Address:* 22 St. James's Square, London, SW1Y 4JH, England. *Telephone:* 01-930 4246.

QUINTON, John Grand, M.A., F.R.S.A.; British banker; b. 21 Dec. 1929; s. of William Grand and Norah May (née Nunn) Quinton; m. Jean Margaret Chastney 1954; one s. one d.; ed. Norwich School, St. John's Coll., Cambridge; Asst. Gen. Man. Barclays Bank Ltd. 1968, Local Dir. Nottingham Dist. Barclays Bank Ltd. 1969–71, Regional Gen. Man. 1971–75, Gen. Man. Barclays Bank Ltd. and Dir. Barclays Bank UK Ltd. 1975–, Dir. Barclays Bank PLC and Sr. Gen. Man. 1982–84, Deputy Chair. Barclays Bank PLC 1985–87, Chair. 1987–; Chair. Motability Finance Ltd. 1978–84, Gov. 1985; Chair. of the CEO of Cttee. of London Clearing Bankers 1982–83; Treas. Inst. of Bankers 1980–86; mem. City Capital Markets Cttee. 1981–86; mem. N.E. Thames Regional Health Authority 1974–87; mem. Accounting Standards Cttee. 1982–85; mem. Council, Royal Shakespeare Theatre 1988–. *Leisure interests:* tennis, gardening, music, occasional golf. *Address:* 54 Lombard Street, London, E.C.3., England.

QUIRK, Sir (Charles) Randolph, Kt., C.B.E., PH.D., D.LITT., FIL.DR., D.U., F.B.A.; British university professor and official; b. 12 July 1920, Isle of Man; s. of late Thomas and Amy Randolph Quirk; m. Gabriele Stein 1984; ed. Cronk y Voddy School, Douglas High School, Isle of Man, Univ. Coll., London;

served in R.A.F. 1940–45; Lecturer in English, Univ. Coll., London 1947–54; Commonwealth Fund Fellow, Yale Univ. and Univ. of Michigan, U.S.A. 1951–52; Reader in English Language and Literature, Univ. of Durham 1954–58, Prof. of English Language 1958–60; Quain Prof. of English, Univ. Coll., London 1960–81; Special Univ. Lectures, London 1960; Dir. Univ. of London Summer School of English 1962–67; Survey of English Usage 1959–; mem. Senate, Univ. of London 1970–78 (Chair. Academic Council 1972–75), Court 1972–75; Vice-Chancellor, Univ. of London 1981–85; Pres. Inst. of Linguistics 1983–86, British Acad. 1985–, Coll. of Speech Therapists 1987–; Gov. British Inst. of Recorded Sound, English-Speaking Union; Chair. Cttee. of Enquiry into Speech Therapy Services, British Council English Cttee. 1976–80, Hornby Educational Trust 1979–; mem. BBC Archives Cttee. 1975–, British Council 1983–; Lee Kwan Yew Fellow, Singapore 1985–86; Vice-Pres. Foundation of Science and Tech. 1986–; Hon. Degrees (Lund, Uppsala, Nijmegen, Paris, Liège, Reading, Leicester, Salford, Newcastle, Bath, Durham, Essex, Open Univ., Glasgow, Bar Ilan, Brunel, Sheffield); Fellow of Queen Mary Coll., Univ. Coll., London, Academia Europaea; Foreign Fellow, Royal Belgian Acad. Sciences 1975, Royal Swedish Acad. 1986; Hon. Fellow, Coll. of Speech Therapists, Inst. of Linguists; Hon. Master Grays Inn Bench 1983; Jubilee Medal (Inst. of Linguists) 1973. *Publications:* The Concessive Relation in Old English Poetry 1954, Studies in Communication (with A. J. Ayer, q.v. and others) 1955, An Old English Grammar (with C. L. Wrenn) 1955, Charles Dickens and Appropriate Language 1959, The Teaching of English (with A. H. Smith) 1959, The Study of the Mother-Tongue 1961, The Use of English (with supplements by A. C. Gimson and J. Warburg) 1962, Prosodic and Paralinguistic Features in English (with D. Crystal) 1964, A Common Language (with A. H. Marckwardt) 1964, Investigating Linguistic Acceptability (with J. Svartvik) 1966, Essays on the English Language—Medieval and Modern 1968, Elicitation Experiments in English (with S. Greenbaum) 1970, A Grammar of Contemporary English 1972 (with S. Greenbaum, G. Leech, J. Svartvik) 1972, The English Language and Images of Matter 1972, A University Grammar of English (with S. Greenbaum) 1973, The Linguist and the English Language 1974, Old English Literature: A Practical Introduction (with V. Adams, D. Davy) 1975, A Corpus of English Conversation 1980; contrib. to many others incl. Charles Dickens (ed. S. Wall) 1970, A New Companion to Shakespeare Studies 1971, The State of the Language 1980, Style and Communication in the English Language 1982, A Comprehensive Grammar of the English Language (with S. Greenbaum, G. Leech and J. Svartvik) 1985, Words at Work: Lectures on Textual Structure 1986; papers in linguistic and literary journals. *Address:* c/o The British Academy, Cornwall Terrace, London, NW1 4QP, England.

QUIRK, Desmond John; Australian business executive; b. 25 Oct. 1929; s. of the late John Robert Quirk and of Mavis Isabel Quirk; m. Audrey Ethel Quirk 1954 (deceased); three s.; ed. Armidale Teacher's Coll.; Man. Dir. Pioneer Int. Ltd.; Dir. Ampol Ltd., Ampol Exploration Ltd., Giant Resources Ltd., Pioneer Minerals Exploration Ltd. *Address:* 55 Macquarie Street, Sydney, N.S.W. 2000 (Office); 28 Lancaster Avenue, Stives, N.S.W. 2075, Australia (Home). *Telephone:* 27 9231 (Office); 449 4004 (Home).

QUIRK, James Patrick, A.O., PH.D.; Australian agricultural scientist; b. 17 Dec. 1924, Sydney; s. of J. P. Quirk; m. Helen M. Sykes 1950; one s. one d.; ed. Christian Brothers High School, Lewisham, St. John's Coll., Univ. of Sydney and Univ. of London; Research Scientist, CSIRO Div. of Soils, Soil Physics Section 1947; CSIRO Sr. Postgraduate Studentship, Physics Dept., Rothamsted Experimental Station, England 1950; Research Scientist, Sr. Research Scientist, CSIRO 1952–56; Reader in Soil Science, Dept. of Agricultural Chem., Waite Agricultural Research Inst., Univ. of Adelaide 1956–62; Carnegie Travelling Fellow, U.S.A. 1960; Foundation Prof. and Head, Dept. of Soil Science and Plant Nutrition, Univ. of W.A. 1963–74, Dir. Inst. of Agric. 1971–74, Dir., Waite Agricultural Research Inst. and Prof. 1974–; Commonwealth Visiting Prof., Oxford Univ. 1967; Fellow Australian Acad. of Science, Australian Inst. of Agricultural Science, Australian Acad. of Technological Science, American Soc. of Agronomy, Australian and N.Z. Asscn. for the Advancement of Science; Prescott Medal for Soil Science 1975, Medal of the Australian Inst. of Agricultural Science 1980, Farrer Memorial Medal 1982; Hon. D.Sc. Agr. (Louvain, Belgium) 1978. *Publications:* 200 scientific publs. *Leisure interests:* reading, tennis. *Address:* Waite Agricultural Research Institute, Glen Osmond, South Australia, 5064 (Office); 27 Fergusson Square, Toorak Gardens, South Australia, 5065 (Home). *Telephone:* (08) 972 2201 (Office); (08) 332 5631 (Home).

QUIROGA, Elena; Spanish writer; mem. Royal Spanish Acad. of Language; awarded Nadal Prize 1950. *Publications:* Viento del Norte 1951, La Sangre 1952, Algo Pasa en la Calle 1954, La Enferma 1954, La Careta 1955, Plácida, La Joven 1956, La Ultima Corrida 1958, Tristura 1960 (1960 Critics' Prize), Escribo tu Nombre 1965 (chosen to represent Spain in the Rómulo Gallegos literary competition), Grandes Soledades, La otra ciudad. *Address:* c/o Agencia Balcells, Diagonal 580, 08021 Barcelona, Spain.

QUONIAM, Pierre; French museum director; b. 6 Nov. 1920, Bois-Colombes; s. of René Quoniam and Marie-Louise (née Périé) Quoniam; m. Florence Roy 1946; one s. two d.; ed. Ecole des Hautes Etudes, Paris, Univ. of Paris and Ecole française d'archéologie et d'histoire de Rome;

Curator, Musée Bardo, Tunis 1948–53; Asst. in ancient history, Faculté des Lettres, Paris; lecturer, Faculté des Lettres, Lyon; Research Officer, Centre Nat. de la Recherche Scientifique (CNRS); Insp. Gen. of provincial museums 1962–72; Dir. Musée du Louvre 1972–78; Insp. Gen. of Museums of France 1978–87; Pres. Comité Culture de la Comm. nat. française de l'Unesco; Officier, Légion d'honneur, Commdr., Ordre nat. du Mérite, Commdr. des Arts et des Lettres. *Address:* 15 rue Gazan, 75014 Paris, France (Home).

QURAISHI, Abdul Aziz Bin Said Al, M.B.A., F.I.B.A. ; Saudi Arabian government official; b. 1930, Hail; s. of Zaid al-Quraishi and Sheikhah Abdul Aziz; m. Amal Abdul Aziz al-Turki 1965; one s. two d.; ed. Univ. of Southern California, U.S.A.; Gen. Man. State Railways 1961–68; Pres. Gen. Personnel Bureau 1968–74; Minister of State 1971–74; Gov. Saudi Arabian Monetary Agency 1974–83; fmr. Gov. for Saudi Arabia, IMF, Arab Monetary Fund; fmr. Alt. Gov. for Saudi Arabia, Islamic Devt. Bank; fmr. mem. Bd. of Dirs. Supreme Council for Petroleum and Mineral Affairs, Gen. Petroleum and Mineral Org., Public Investment Fund, Pension Fund, Man. Dir. Ali Zaid Al-Quraishi & Bros., Riyadh 1983–; Chair. Nat. Saudi Shipping Co., Riyadh 1983–; Vice-Chair. Saudi Int. Bank, London 1983–; mem. Int. Advisory Bd., Security Pacific Nat. Bank of Los Angeles 1983–; King Abdul Aziz Medal (Second Class), Order of Brilliant Star with Grand Cordon (Taiwan), Order of Diplomatic Merit, Gwan Ghwa Medal (Repub. of Korea), King Leopold Medal (Commdr. Class), Belgium, Emperor of Japan Award, Order of Sacred Treasure (First Class) 1980. *Address:* Malaz, Riyadh, Saudi Arabia (Office); P.O. Box 1848, Riyadh 11441, Saudi Arabia (Home).

QURESHI, Ishtiaq Husain, M.A., PH.D.; Pakistani scholar and politician; b. 20 Nov. 1903, Patiali; s. of Qazi Sadiq Husain Qureshi and Begum Altafunnisa Qureshi; m. Nayab Begum Qureshi 1920 (died 1965); one s.; ed. St. Stephen's Coll. (Univ. of Delhi), and Sidney Sussex Coll., Cambridge; Lecturer in History, St. Stephen's Coll. 1928; Reader in History Univ. of Delhi 1940, Prof. and Head of Dept. of History 1944, Dean of Faculty of Arts 1945; mem. for Bengal, Constituent Assembly of Pakistan 1947; Prof. of History and Head of Dept. of History, Punjab Univ. 1948; Deputy Minister of the Interior, Information and Broadcasting, Refugees and Rehabilitation, Govt. of Pakistan 1949, Minister of State 1950, Minister for Refugees and Rehabilitation, Information and Broadcasting 1951–53; Minister of Educ. 1953–55; mem. Advisory Council of Islamic Ideology 1962–63, Nat. Comm. on Educ. and Manpower 1968–69; mem. Tehrik-I-Istiqlal party (Vice-Pres. 1976–); Visiting Prof. Columbia Univ., New York 1955–60; Dir. Cen. Inst. of Islamic Research, Karachi 1960–62; Vice-Chancellor Univ. of Karachi 1961–71; Pres. Pakistan Inst. of Cen. and W. Asian Studies, Karachi 1970; Fellow Pakistan Acad. of Letters 1978 (Pres. 1979); Chair. Nat. Language Authority, Karachi 1979; Star of Pakistan 1964. *Publications:* The Administration of the Sultanate of Delhi 1941, The Pakistani Way of Life 1956, The Muslim Community in the Indo-Pakistan Subcontinent 1962, The Struggle for Pakistan 1965, The Administration of the Moghul Empire 1967, Ulema in Politics 1972, Education in Pakistan 1975, Akbar 1978, Perspectives of Islam and Pakistan 1979. *Leisure interests:* gardening, travel. *Address:* 3-B 4th Central Lane, Defence Housing Society, Karachi; Zeba Manzar, 1 Sharafabad, Shahid-i-Millat Road, Karachi 5, Pakistan. *Telephone:* 541211.

QURESHI, Moeen Ahmad, M.A., PH.D.; Pakistani economist and international official; b. 26 June 1930, Lahore; s. of Mohyeddin Ahmad Qureshi and Khursheed Jabin; m. Lilo Elizabeth Richter 1958; two s. two d.; ed. Islamia Coll. and Govt. Coll., Univ. of Punjab and Indiana Univ., U.S.A.; Social Science Consultant, Ford Foundation, Pakistan 1953; Hon. Lecturer, Univ. of Karachi 1953–54; Asst. Chief, Planning Comm., Govt. of Pakistan 1954–56, Deputy Chief 1956–58; Economist, IMF 1958–61, Div. Chief 1961–65, Adviser Africa Dept. 1965–66, Resident Rep. Ghana 1966–68, Sr. Adviser 1968–70; Econ. Adviser IFC 1970–74, Vice-Pres. 1974–77, Exec. Vice-Pres. 1977–81; Vice-Pres. Finance, World Bank 1979–80, Sr. Vice-Pres. Finance 1980–87, Sr. Vice-Pres. Operations 1987–. *Publications:* various articles in economic journals. *Leisure interests:* tennis, collecting antiques. *Address:* c/o The World Bank, 1818 H Street, N.W., Washington, D.C. 20433, U.S.A.

R

RAATIKAINEN, Kaisa; Finnish politician; b. 1928, Viitasaari; mem. Espoo City Council 1969–; M.P. 1970–87; mem. Presidential Electorate 1978, 1982; mem. Planning and Bldg. Council 1977–; Minister of the Interior 1984–87; Social Democratic Party. *Address:* c/o Ministry of the Interior, Hallituskatu 4, 00170 Helsinki 17, Finland.

RABAEUS, Bengt, M.A.; Swedish diplomatist; b. 4 May 1917, Vara; m. Birgitta M. Svensson 1946; three s.; ed. Kungliga Universitet i Uppsala; entered Foreign Service 1946, served Prague, Paris, Swedish Del. to UN (New York); Counsellor, Swedish Del. to OEEC, Paris 1957–59; Head of UN Political Div., Foreign Office, Stockholm 1959–61; First Counsellor, Paris 1961–62; Amb. to Algeria 1963–66; Deputy Sec.-Gen. European Free Trade Assen. (EFTA) 1966–72, Sec.-Gen. 1972–76; Deputy Perm. Under-Sec. of State, Ministry of Foreign Affairs 1976–78; Amb. and Perm. Rep. to European Communities 1978–83; Chair. Swedish Pulp and Paper Assen. 1983–. *Address:* Stureparken 3, S-114 26, Stockholm, Sweden.

RABASA, Emilio O.; Mexican lawyer and politician; b. 23 Jan. 1925; s. of Oscar Rabasa and Lilia M. de Rabasa; ed. Univ. Nacional Autónoma de México; Lecturer for 15 years, Univ. Nacional Autónoma de México; lawyer to Dept. of Banks and Money, Secr. of Finance; legal consultant to Heads of Agrarian Dept., Secr. of Agric. and Cattle, and to Secr. of Health and Nat. Assistance; Head of Legal Dept. of Banco Nacional de Credito Ejidal; Dir. Afianzadora Mexicana; Dir. Banco Cinematográfico 1965, concurrently Man. Dir. Compañiá Operadora de Teatros, Estudios Crurubusco, Películas Nacionales, CIMEX and PROCINEMEX; Amb. to U.S.A. 1970; Sec. of Foreign Affairs 1970–75. *Address:* c/o Secretaría de Relaciones Exteriores, Avenida Ricardo Flores Magón 1, Matelolco, D.F., Mexico.

RABASSA, Gregory, PH.D.; American professor of Romance languages; b. 9 March 1922, Yonkers, N.Y.; m. 1966; ed. Dartmouth Coll. and Columbia Univ.; Instructor in Spanish, Columbia Univ. 1947–52, Assoc. Instructor 1952–58, Asst. Prof. 1958–63, Assoc. Prof. of Spanish and Portuguese 1963–68; Prof. of Romance Languages, Queens Coll., Flushing, N.Y. 1968–86, Distinguished Prof. 1986–; Assoc. Ed. Odyssey Review 1961–64; mem. Renaissance Soc. of America, PEN Club and other professional assens.; Fulbright-Hays Fellow, Brazil 1965–66; Guggenheim Fellow 1988–; Nat. Book Award for translation 1967, New York Gov.'s Arts Award 1985, Wheatland Translation Prize 1988, etc.; Order of San Carlos (Colombia). *Address:* 136 East 76th Street, New York, N.Y. 10021, U.S.A.

RABB, Maxwell M., LL.B.; American diplomatist; b. 29 Sept. 1910, Boston; s. of Solomon and Rose (Kostick) Rabb; m. Ruth Creidenberg 1939; one s. three c.; ed. Harvard Univ.; practised law with Rabb and Rabb, Boston 1935–37, 1946–51; Admin. Asst. to Senator H. C. Lodge 1937–43, to Senator Sinclair Weeks 1944–45; legal, legis. and consultant to Sec. to Navy Forrestal 1945–46; consultant U.S. Senate Rules Cttee. 1952–53; Presidential Asst. and Sec. to Cabinet of Pres. Eisenhower 1953–58; partner Stroock, Stroock and Lavan law firm, New York 1958–; Amb. to Italy 1981–89; Hon. LL.D.; U.S. Commendation Ribbon, Order of Merit, Italy 1957, Cavaliere di Gran Croce (Italy) 1982. *Address:* American Embassy, APO New York 09794, U.S.A. *Telephone:* Rome (06) 4674.

RABEMANANJARA, Jacques; Madagascan writer and politician; b. c. 1913; mem. French Nat. Ass. as rep. for Madagascar 1946; initiated the Democratic Movt. for the restoration of Madagascan independence in harmony with France; arrested during the Madagascan insurrection of 1947 and exiled in France; helped to inaugurate the review and publishing house Présence africaine; winner of Le grand Prix de la Francophonie awarded by the Acad. Française 1988. *Publications: poems:* Dieux malgaches, Rites millénaires, Antsa, Lamba, Ode à Ranavalo, Antidote, Ordalies; *political works:* Témoignage malgache et colonialisme, Nationalisme et problèmes malgaches, Premiers jalons pour une politique de la culture.

RABETAFIKA, Joseph Albert Blaise, L. ÈS L., M.A.; Malagasy diplomatist; b. 3 Feb. 1932, Tananarive (now Antananarivo); m. Jeanne Razafintsalama 1955; one s. two d.; teacher in U.K., France and Madagascar 1953–59; joined Ministry of Defence, France 1960; mem. Madagascar del. to independence negotiations with France 1960; Counsellor in charge of cultural affairs and information, Madagascar diplomatic mission, France 1960–63; Perm. Del. to UNESCO, Paris 1961–63; Head, del. to IBE Confs., Geneva 1961–63; mem. del. to UN Gen. Ass. 1962–69; Dir. of Cabinet Foreign Ministry 1964–67; Consul-Gen., New York 1968–; Perm. Rep. to UN 1969–; Amb. to Canada 1970–, to Cuba 1974–; Vice-Pres. ECOSOC 1973; Chair. Group of 77 1973; Pres. Security Council 1985–86. *Leisure interests:* classical music, jazz, reading, violin playing. *Address:* Permanent Mission of Madagascar to the United Nations, 801 Second Avenue, Suite 404, New York, N.Y. 10017, U.S.A.

RABIN, Maj.-Gen. Itzhak; Israeli army officer and politician; b. 1 March 1922, Jerusalem; s. of Nehemia and Rosa (Cohen) Rabin; m. Leah Schlossberg 1948; one s. one d.; ed. Kadoorie Agricultural School, Kfar Tabor, and Staff Coll., England; Palmach commands 1943–48, including War of Independence; rep. Israel Defence Forces (I.D.F.) at Rhodes armistice negotiations; fmr. Head of Training Dept. I.D.F.; C.-in-C. Northern Command 1956–59; Head, Manpower Branch 1959–60; Deputy Chief of Staff and Head, Gen. Staff Branch 1960–64, Chief of Staff I.D.F. 1964–68; Amb. to U.S.A. 1968–73; mem. Knesset Jan. 1974–; Minister of Labour March-April 1974; Leader Labour Party 1974–77; Prime Minister 1974–77, also Minister of Communications 1974–75; Minister of Defence 1984–; Hon. Doctorates, Jerusalem Univ. 1967, Dropsie Coll. 1968, Brandeis Univ. 1968, Yeshiva Univ. 1968, Coll. of Jewish Studies, Chicago 1969, Univ. of Miami 1970, Hebrew Union Coll., Boston 1971. *Publication:* The Rabin Memoirs 1979. *Address:* c/o The Knesset, Jerusalem, Israel.

RABIN, Oskar; Soviet painter, now working 'underground'; b. 1928, Moscow; m. Valentina Kropovnitsky; one s.; Student of artist and teacher Yevgeny Kropovnitsky; worked in Riga 1946–48; thereafter student of Surikov Art Inst., Moscow; later expelled for unorthodox views; worked until 1958 as loader on railways and on construction sites, painting clandestinely; employed in arts & design centre 1958–67; since 1967 has devoted himself exclusively to painting; moving spirit of Leonozovo group outside Moscow, where he now lives; exhibited in "Festival of Youth" Exhbn., Moscow 1957; one-man show Grosvenor Gallery, London 1965; two open-air exhbns. in Cheremushki, outside Moscow and organized by s. (both officially bulldozed) 1974; "Twenty Russian Artists", Moscow (Bee-keeping Pavilion, VDNKh) 1975; "Unofficial Art in the Soviet Union", London 1977; other exhbns. in Fed. Repub. of Germany, Switzerland, Austria, France, Poland, USA (Chicago), Tbilisi, Denmark.

RABINOVITCH, B(enton) Seymour, PH.D., F.R.S.; Canadian professor emeritus of chemistry; b. 19 Feb. 1919, Montreal, P.Q.; s. of Samuel Rabinovitch and Rachel Shachter; m. 1st Marilyn Werby 1949 (deceased), 2nd Flora Reitman 1980; two s. two d.; ed. McGill Univ.; Royal Soc. of Canada Research Fellow 1946–47; Hilton Research Fellow 1947–48; Asst. Prof. Univ. of Washington, Seattle 1948–53, Asoc. Prof. 1953–57, Prof. Dept. of Chem. 1957–85, Prof. Emer. 1985–; Fellow, American Acad. of Arts and Sciences; mem. Silver Soc.; Guggenheim Fellowship 1961; Peter Debye Award; Michael Polyani Medal. *Publications:* 220 research papers. *Leisure interest:* silver smithing. *Address:* Department of Chemistry, University of Washington, Seattle, Wash. 98195, U.S.A. *Telephone:* 206-543-1636.

RABINOWITZ, Harry, M.B.E.; British composer and conductor; b. 26 March 1916, Johannesburg, S. Africa; s. of Israel Rabinowitz and Eva (née Kirkel) Rabinowitz; m. Lorna T. Anderson 1944; one s. two d.; ed. Athlone High School, Johannesburg and Guildhall School of Music, London; Conductor, BBC Radio 1953–60; Musical Dir. BBC Television Light Entertainment 1960–68; Head, of Music, London Weekend Television 1968–74; freelance composer and conductor 1977–; Music Dir. (TV) Julia and Friends 1986, Paul Nicholas and Friends 1987, series New Faces 1987; has appeared with London Symphony and Royal Philharmonic Orchestras in U.K. and with the Los Angeles Philharmonic and Boston Pops Orchestras in U.S.A.; Musical Dir. for world premières of Cats and Song & Dance; has composed and conducted several TV scores and conducted numerous film scores; awarded B.A.S.C.A. Gold Badge for Services to British Music 1985, Radio and TV Industries Award for Best TV Theme 1984. *Leisure interests:* listening to others making music, edible fungi hunting, wine-tasting. *Address:* Hope End, Holmbury St. Mary, Dorking, RH5 6PE, Surrey, England. *Telephone:* (0306) 730605.

RABINOWITZ, Jesse C., PH.D.; American professor of biochemistry; b. 28 April 1925, New York; s. of Julius Rabinowitz and Frances Pincus; ed. Polytechnic Inst. of Brooklyn, New York and Univ. of Wisconsin (Madison); U.S. Public Health Service Fellow, Univ. of Wis. Enzyme Inst. 1949–50, Univ. of Calif., Berkeley 1951–52; Chemist-Biochemist, Nat. Insts. of Health, Bethesda, Md. 1952–57; Assoc. Prof., Dept. of Biochemistry, Univ. of Calif., Berkeley 1957–63, Prof. 1963–, Chair. 1978–83; Guggenheim Fellow 1973; mem. N.A.S. *Publications:* more than 150 papers in scientific publs. *Address:* Department of Biochemistry, University of California, Berkeley, Calif. 94720, U.S.A. *Telephone:* (415) 642-0467.

RABKIN, Mitchell T., M.D.; American physician and hospital administrator; b. 27 Nov. 1930, Boston, Mass.; s. of Morris A. Rabkin and Esther Quint Rabkin; m. Adrienne M. Najarian 1956; one s. one d.; ed. Harvard Coll. and Harvard Medical School; trained in medicine, Mass. Gen. Hosp., Boston; U.S. Public Health Service, Nat. Inst. of Health, Bethesda, Md. 1957–59; Chief Resident in Medicine, Mass. Gen. Hosp. 1962, medical staff 1963–66; C.E.O. Beth Israel Hosp., Boston 1966–; Prof. of Medicine, Harvard Medical School 1985–; Hon. D.Sc. (Brandeis). *Address:* Beth Israel Hospital, Boston, Mass. 02215 (Office); 124 Canton Avenue, Milton, Mass. 02187, U.S.A. (Home). *Telephone:* 617-735-2222 (Office); 617-696-6614.

RABORN, Vice-Admiral William Francis, Jr.; American fmr. naval officer and business executive; b. 8 June 1905, Decatur, Texas; s. of William F. Raborn and Cornelia Moore; m. 1st Vance Barnes 1929 (deceased), 2nd Mildred T. Terrill 1955; one s. one d.; ed. U.S. Naval Acad.; Ensign U.S.

Navy 1928; Deputy Dir. Guided Missile Div., Office Chief Naval Operations 1952–54; Commanding Officer U.S.S. Bennington 1954–55; Asst. Chief Staff Commdr. Atlantic Fleet 1955; Dir. Special Projects, Fleet Ballistic Missile System (Polaris) 1955–62; Deputy Chief of Naval Operations (Devt.) 1962–63; Vice-Pres. Program Man. Aerojet Gen. Corpn. 1963–65; Vice-Pres. Gen. Rep. Aerojet Gen. Corpn. 1966–70; Dir. CIA 1965–66; Private Consultant 1970–; Pres. W. F. Raborn Co. Inc. *Leisure interest:* golf. *Address:* 1606 Crestwood Lane, McLean, Virginia 22101, U.S.A. (Office). *Telephone:* (703) 536-4492 (Office).

RABUKA, Brig.-Gen. Sitiveni Ligamamada, O.B.E., M.SC.; Fijian army officer and politician; b. 13 Sept. 1948, Nakobo; s. of Kolinio E.V. Rabuka and Salote Lomaloma; m. Suluweti Camamaivuna Tuiloma 1975; one s. two d.; ed. Provincial School Northern, Queen Victoria School, N.Z. Army schools, Indian Defence Services Staff Coll. and Australian Jt. Services Staff Coll.; Sr. Operational Plans Officer UNIFIL, Lebanon 1980–81; Chief of Staff, Fiji July-Dec. 1981; SO 1 Operations and Training, Fiji Army 1982–83, 1985–87; Commdr. Fiji Bn., Sinai 1983–85; staged coup 14 May 1987; Adviser on Home Affairs and Head of Security May–Sept. 1987; staged second coup 25 Sept. 1987; declared a Repub. 7 Oct. 1987; Commdr. and Head of Interim Mil. Govt. of Fiji Sept.-Dec. 1987; Commdr. Fiji Security Forces May 1987–; Minister for Home Affairs, Nat. Youth Service and Auxiliary Army Services Dec. 1987–. *Publication:* No Other Way 1988. *Leisure interests:* golf, rugby. *Address:* Fiji Military Forces, Box 102, Suva, Fiji. *Telephone:* 385222, 211401 (Office).

RABUKAWAQA, Sir Josua Rasilau, K.B.E., M.V.O.; Fijian diplomatist; b. 2 Dec. 1917, Nabouwala, Bua; s. of Dr. Aisea Rasilau and Adi Mereoni Dimaicakau; m. Mei T. Vuiwakaya 1944; three s. two d.; ed. Queen Victoria School, Fiji, Teachers' Training Coll., Auckland, N.Z.; teacher, Fiji 1938–52; Mortar Platoon Commdr. 1st Battalion Fiji Infantry Regt. Malayan Campaign 1954–55; Adjutant Fiji Mil. Forces 1955–56; Asst. Econ. Devt. Officer 1957–60; Dist. Officer, Commr., Fiji 1961–70; High Commr. to U.K. 1970–75, accred. to EEC Countries 1971–75; Amb. at Large to South Pacific Forum Countries 1977–80; Chief of Protocol, Fiji 1977–80; Man. Fiji Cricket Team in World Cup Competition, England 1979; R. B. Bennett Commonwealth Prize 1981. *Leisure interests:* rugby, cricket, music. *Address:* 6 Vunivivi Hill, Nausori, Fiji.

RACHKOV, Albert Ivanovich; Soviet politician and diplomatist; b. 1927; ed. Azov-Black Sea Inst. for the Mechanisation and Electrification of Agric. and CPSU Cen. Cttee. Higher Party School; mem. CPSU 1955–; combine-operator 1948–50; engineer, sr. engineer, man. of agric. div. in Kemerovo dist. 1956–65; work for CPSU Cen. Cttee. 1965–69, 1974–80; Sec. of Lipetsk Dist. Cttee. 1969–74; Second Sec. of Cen. Cttee. of Turkmenistan CP 1980–86; Amb. to People's Democratic Republic of Yemen 1986–; cand. mem. of CPSU Cen. Cttee. 1986–; Deputy to U.S.S.R. Supreme Soviet. *Address:* U.S.S.R. Embassy, Abyan Beach Road, Khormaksar, Aden, People's Democratic Republic of Yemen.

RACKER, Efraim, M.D.; American biochemist; b. 28 June 1913, Neu Sandez, Poland; m. Franziska Weiss 1945; one d.; ed. Univ. of Vienna; Research Asst. in biochemistry, Cardiff Mental Hosp., S. Wales 1938–40; Research Assoc., Dept. of Physiology, Univ. of Minn. 1941–42; Intern, Pneumonia Resident and Fellow, Harlem Hosp. New York 1942–44; Instructor, then Asst. Prof. of Microbiology, New York Univ. School of Medicine 1944–52; Assoc. Prof. of Biochem., Yale Univ. School of Medicine 1952–54; Chief, Div. of Nutrition and Physiology, Public Health Research Inst. of N.Y.C. 1954–66; Adjunct Prof. of Microbiology, N.Y. Univ. Bellevue Medical Center; Albert Einstein Prof. Section of Biochem., Molecular and Cell Biology, Cornell Univ. 1966–; mem. Nat. Acad. of Sciences, Hon. Ph.D. (Chicago); Nat. Medal of Science 1976. *Publications:* Mechanisms in Bioenergetics 1965, Membranes of Mitochondria and Chloroplasts 1970, A New Look at Mechanisms in Bioenergetics 1976, Science and the Cure of Diseases: Letters to Members of Congress 1979, Reconstitutions of Transporters, Receptors, and Pathological States 1985. *Leisure interests:* painting, tennis. *Address:* Section of Biochemistry, Molecular and Cell Biology, Cornell University, Wing Hall, Ithaca, N.Y. 14853, U.S.A. *Telephone:* (607) 255-4334.

RADCLIFFE, Percy; Manx politician (retd.); b. 14 Nov. 1916; s. of Arthur and Annie Radcliffe; m. Barbara Frances Crowe 1942; two s. one d.; mem. House of Keys (Lower House of Tynwald, Manx Parl.) for Ayre 1963–85; mem. Local Govt. Bd., Tynwald 1963, Chair. 1966–75; mem. Exec. Council 1976; Chair. Finance Bd. 1976–81; mem. Legis. Council (Upper House of Tynwald) 1980–; Chair. Gov.'s Exec. Council 1981–86; mem. Manx Agricultural Marketing Assćn. 1945–75; Pres. Royal Manx Agricultural Soc. 1962; mem. British Horse Driving Soc. 1979–. *Leisure interest:* driving hackney ponies. *Address:* "Kellaway", Sulby, Isle of Man. *Telephone:* (0624) 89 7257.

RADDA, George Karoly, M.A., D.PHIL., F.R.S.; British (b. Hungarian) professor of molecular cardiology; b. 9 June 1936, Gyor, Hungary; s. of Gyula Radda and Anna Bernolak; m. Mary O'Brien 1961; two s. one d.; ed. Pannonhalma and Eötvös Univ., Budapest and Merton Coll. Oxford; Research Assoc., Univ. of Calif., U.S.A. 1962–63; Lecturer in Organic Chem., St. John's Coll., Oxford Univ. 1963–64, Fellow and Tutor in Organic Chem., Merton Coll. 1964–84, Lecturer in Biochemistry, Oxford Univ.

1966–84, British Heart Foundation Prof. of Molecular Cardiology 1984–, Professorial Fellow, Merton Coll. 1984–; Chair. MRC Coll. Bd. 1988–; mem. MRC Council 1988–; Ed. Biochemicial and Biophysical Research Communications 1977–; Man. Ed. Biochimica et Biophysica Acta 1977–; Founder mem. Oxford Enzyme Group 1970–87; Hon. Dr. Med. (Berne) 1985; Colworth Medal, Biochemistry Soc. 1969, CIBA Medal and Prize 1983; Feldberg Prize 1982; British Heart Foundation Prize and Gold Medal for cardiovascular research 1982; Gold Medal, Soc. for Magnetic Resonance in Medicine 1984; Pres. Soc. for Magnetic Resonance in Medicine 1985–86; Hon. F.R.C.R. 1985; E.C. Slater Plenary Lecture 1985; Hon. Fellow American Heart Assćn. and Citation for int. achievement 1987, Buchanan Medal, Royal Soc. 1987; Hon. M.R.C.P. 1987. *Publications:* articles in books and scientific journals. *Leisure interests:* opera, jazz, swimming. *Address:* Merton College, Oxford and Department of Biochemistry, Oxford University, South Parks Road, Oxford, England. *Telephone:* (0865) 276310 (Coll.) and (0865) 275272 (Dept. of Biochemistry).

RADEMAKER GRÜNEWALD, Adm. Augusto Hamann; Brazilian naval officer and politician; b. 11 May 1905, Rio de Janeiro; s. of Jorge C. Rademaker and Anna Grünewald; m. Ruth Rademaker 1940; five c.; ed. naval college; served in Brazilian navy 1927–64, becoming Head of Cen. Command, Atlantic Defence Zone; mem. Revolutionary Command 1964; Minister for the Navy 1964–69, also for Transport and Public Works 1964–67; mem. ruling triumvirate Aug.-Oct. 1969; Vice-Pres. of Brazil 1969–74; numerous decorations. *Address:* Brasília, Brazil.

RADFORD, Courtenay Arthur Ralegh, M.A., D.LITT., F.S.A., F.B.A., F.R.HIST.S., F.R.S.A.; British archaeologist; b. 7 Nov. 1900, Hillingdon, Middx.; s. of late Arthur and Ada M. Radford (née Bruton); ed. St. George's School, Harpenden, and Exeter Coll., Oxford; Inspector of Ancient Monuments for Wales and Monmouthshire under Office of Works 1929–34; Dir. British School of Rome 1936–40; mem. German Archaeological Inst.; mem. Royal Comm. on Ancient Monuments in Wales and Monmouthshire 1935–46; mem. Royal Comm. on Historical Monuments in England 1954–76; Pres. Prehistoric Soc. 1954–58, Royal Archaeological Inst. 1960–63, Soc. for Medieval Archaeology 1969–71. *Address:* Culmcott, Uffculme, Devon, EX15 3AT, England. *Telephone:* Craddock (0884) 40251.

RADI, Essam Radi Abd al-Hamid; Egyptian engineer and politician; m.; two c.; ed. Faculty of Eng.; headed engineers of northern region of armed forces; held posts in Ministry of Irrigation in Egypt and Sudan; Gov. of Damietta 1980; Minister of Irrigation 1985–87, of Works and Water Resources Oct. 1987–. *Address:* Ministry of Works and Water Resources, Sharia Kasr El-Eini, Cairo, Egypt. *Telephone:* 24527.

RADNER, Roy, PH.D.; American economist; b. 29 June 1927, Chicago; s. of Ella and Samuel Radner; m. 1st Virginia Honoski (died 1976), m. 2nd Charlotte V. Kuh 1978; one s. three d.; ed. Hyde Park High School, Chicago and Univ. of Chicago; served U.S. army 1945–48; Research Assoc., Cowles Comm., Univ. of Chicago 1951–54, Asst. Prof. 1954–55; Asst. Prof. of Econs. Yale Univ. 1955–57; Assoc. Prof. of Econs. and Statistics, Univ. of Calif., Berkeley 1957–61, Prof. 1961–79, Chair. Dept. of Econs. 1965–69; Distinguished mem. tech. staff, AT & T Bell Labs. 1979–; Research Prof. of Econs. New York Univ. 1983–; Guggenheim Fellow 1961–62 and 1965–66; Overseas Fellow, Churchill Coll. Cambridge, England 1969–70; Assoc. Ed. Journal of Econ. Theory 1968–; Fellow American Acad. of Arts and Sciences, Econometric Soc. A.A.A.S.; mem. N.A.S., Inst. of Math. Statistics, American Econ. Assćn. *Publications:* Optimal Replacement Policy (with others) 1967, Decision and Organization (co-ed.) 1972, Economic Theory of Teams (with J. Marschak) 1972, Demand and Supply in U.S. Higher Education (with L. S. Miller) 1975, Education as an Industry (co-ed.) 1976, Mathematicians in Academia (with C. V. Kuh) 1980, Information, Incentives, and Economic Mechanisms (co-ed.) 1987, Perspectives on Deterrence 1989, and many articles. *Leisure interests:* music, backpacking, cross-country skiing. *Address:* AT & T Bell Laboratories, Room 2C-176, 600 Mountain Avenue, Murray Hill, N.J. 07974 (Office); 1 Park Place, Short Hills, N.J. 07078, U.S.A. (Home). *Telephone:* (201) 582-3517 (Office).

RĂDULESCU, Gheorghe, D.SC.(ECON.); Romanian economist and politician; b. 5 Sept. 1914, Bucharest; s. of Dumitru and Ana Rădulescu; m. Dorina Rădulescu 1938; one s.; ed. Acad. of Higher Commercial and Industrial Studies, Bucharest; Gen. Sec. and Deputy Minister for Foreign Econ. Relations 1948–52; Dir. Inst. for Econ. Research, Romanian Acad. of Sciences 1956–57; Deputy Minister of Trade and Minister of Home and Foreign Trade 1957–63; Deputy Chair. Council of Ministers 1963–79; Chair. Comm. for Econ. and Tech. Collaboration and Co-operation 1963–74; Vice-Pres. State Council 1979–; mem. Romanian CP 1933–, mem. Cen. Cttee. Romanian CP 1960–; mem. Exec. Political Cttee. Cen. Cttee. of Romanian CP 1965–; mem. Perm. Presidium Cen. Cttee. Romanian CP 1969–74; mem. Standing Bureau Exec. Political Cttee. 1977–; Perm. Rep. of Romania to Exec. Cttee. of Council for Mutual Econ. Assistance 1976–; Chair. Higher Court for Financial Control 1976–; mem. Grand Nat. Ass. 1961–, Defence Council 1969–74, Acad. of Social and Political Sciences 1970–, Nat. Council Front of Socialist Democracy and Unity 1980–; several Romanian orders including Hero of Socialist Labour 1971. *Publications:* numerous econ. studies, especially on home and foreign trade. *Leisure interest:* music. *Address:* Central Committee of the Romanian Communist Party, Str. Academiei 34, Bucharest, Romania. *Telephone:* 15 02 00.

RADYUKEVICH, Leonid Vladimirovich; Soviet politician and mining official; b. 1932; ed. Magnitogorsk Mining Inst.; foreman of works 1955–70; mem. CPSU 1959–; deputy chief engineer 1970–77; man. head of U.S.S.R. Minister of Ferrous Metallurgy 1977–79; Dir. of Magnitogorsk V.I. Lenin Metallurgical Combine 1979–85; U.S.S.R. First Deputy Minister of Ferrous Metallurgy 1985–; cand. mem. of CPSU Cen. Cttee. 1981–; Deputy to U.S.S.R. Supreme Soviet; State Prize 1969, 1982. *Address:* The Kremlin, Moscow, U.S.S.R.

RADZINOWICZ, Sir Leon, K.B., M.A., LL.D., F.B.A.; Polish-born British criminologist and law historian; b. 15 Aug. 1906, Łódź; m. 1st Irene Szereszewski 1933 (divorced 1955), 2nd Mary Ann Nevins 1958 (divorced 1979), 3rd Isolde Klarmann 1979; one s. one d.; ed. Cracow, Geneva, Paris, Rome and Cambridge Univs.; Lecturer, Geneva Univ. 1928–31; reported on Belgian penal system 1930; Lecturer, Warsaw Free Univ. 1932–36, Asst. Prof. 1936–39; visited England to report on English penal system for Polish Ministry of Justice 1938; Asst. Dir. of Research, Cambridge Univ. 1946–49, Fellow of Trinity Coll. 1948–, Dir. Dept. of Criminal Science 1949–59, Wolfson Prof. of Criminology 1959–73, Dir. Inst. of Criminology 1960–72; Vice-Pres. Int. Soc. for Social Defence; Vice-Pres. Assoc. Int. de Droit Pénal, Paris 1947–; Head UN Social Defence Section 1947–48; mem. Royal Comm. on Capital Punishment 1949–53, Home Office Advisory Council on Treatment of Offenders 1950–75, Royal Comm. on English Penal System 1964; Hon. Foreign mem. American Acad. of Arts and Sciences, Australian Acad. of Forensic Sciences; First Pres. British Acad. of Forensic Sciences; First Chair. Scientific Council, European Problems of Crime, Council of Europe 1963–69; Assoc. Fellow, Silliman Coll., Yale Univ. 1966–; Adjunct Prof. of Law and Criminology, Columbia Law School 1966–75; Walter E. Meyer Visiting Prof., Yale Law School 1962–63; Visiting Prof. Univs. of Va. 1968–69, of Philadelphia and Camden 1968–, Univ. of Penn. 1970–, Rutgers Univ. 1970–, Minnesota Law School 1977–, John Jay Coll. of Criminal Justice 1978–, Benjamin Cardozo Law School 1978–; Consultant to Ford Foundation on UN Criminology Inst. Rome 1962, to Ford Foundation and Bar Assocn., New York, on teaching and research in crime 1964–65, to Presidential Nat. Cttee. on Violence 1968, to Minister of Justice, N.S.W. and Nat. Justice and Crime, Canberra 1973, to Univ. of Cape Town Inst. of Crime 1972; Chief Rapporteur IX UN Crime Congress, Kayto 1970; Dir. Securicor 1974; Hon. mem. American Law Inst. 1981–; Visitor Princeton Inst. of Advanced Studies 1975; Hon. LL.D. (Edin.) 1988; J. B. Ames Prize and Medal, Harvard Law School 1950; Coronation Medal 1953; Bruce Smith Sr. Award for outstanding contribution to Criminal Justice Sciences of the U.S. 1976, Sellin-Glueck Award of the American Soc. of Criminology 1976, Joseph Andrews Award of American Law. Library Assocn. (with Roger Hood); Chevalier, Ordre de Léopold 1930. *Publications:* numerous books and articles in Polish, French, Italian and English on Criminology and Penology; History of English Criminal Law and Its Administration from 1750 Vol. I 1948, Vols. II and III 1956, Vol. IV 1968, Vol. V (with Roger Hood) 1986; In Search of Criminology 1961, The Need for Criminology 1965, Ideology and Crime 1966, Ed. Cambridge Studies in Criminology (52 vols.); ed. with Marvin E. Wolfgang Crime and Justice (3 vols.) 1971, with Roger Hood Criminology and the Administration of Criminal Justice: A Bibliography 1976, with Joan King The Growth of Crime 1977, The Cambridge Instutute of Criminology 1988. *Leisure interests:* travelling, dinner parties. *Address:* Rittenhouse Claridge, Apt. 2416, Rittenhouse Square, Philadelphia, Pa. 19103, U.S.A. *Telephone:* 215 546 9250.

RADZINSKY, Edvard Stanislavovich; Soviet dramatist; b. 23 Sept. 1936, Moscow; ed. Inst. of History and Archival Science, Moscow; *Plays include:* My Dream is India 1960, You're all of Twenty-Two, you Old Men! 1962, One Hundred and Four Pages on Love 1964, Kolobashkin the Seducer 1967, Socrates 1977. *Address:* c/o U.S.S.R. Union of Writers, ul. Vorovskogo 52, Moscow, U.S.S.R.

RAE, Alexander Lindsay, O.B.E., PH.D., M.AGR.SC., F.R.S.N.Z.; New Zealand professor of animal science; b. 3 Aug. 1923, Eltham; s. of Thomas Rae and Annie Rae; m. Fiona D. Thomas 1957; ed. Massey Agricultural Coll. and Iowa State Univ.; Jr. Lecturer in Sheep Husbandry, Massey Agricultural Coll. 1944-50; Prof. of Sheep Husbandry, Massey Univ. 1951-80, Prof. in Animal Science 1980–; Fellow, N.Z. Inst. of Agricultural Science; N.Z. Soc. of Animal Production McMeekan Memorial Award 1977; Sir Ernest Marsden Medal for Outstanding Service to Science 1982. *Publications:* research papers on animal genetics and breeding in scientific journals. *Leisure interest:* fishing. *Address:* Department of Animal Science, Massey University, Palmerston North (Office); 16 Wallace Place, Palmerston North, New Zealand (Home). *Telephone:* 063-69099 (Office); 063-78611 (Home).

RAFAEL, Gideon; Israeli diplomatist (retd.); b. Germany 5 March 1913; m. 1940; two c.; ed. Univ. of Berlin; immigrated 1934; mem. Kibbutz 1934-43; active in Haganah and war services 1939-42; Jewish Agency, Political Dept. 1943; in charge of preparation of Jewish case for Jewish Agency, Political Dept., Nuremberg War Crimes Trial 1945-46; mem. of Jewish Agency Comm. to Anglo-American Comm. of Enquiry 1946, and of Jewish Agency mission to UN Special Comm. for Palestine 1947; mem. Israel Perm. Del. to UN 1951-52; alt. rep. to UN 1953; rep. at UN Gen. Assemblies 1947-66; Counsellor in charge of Middle East and UN Affairs, Ministry for Foreign Affairs 1953-57; Amb. to Belgium and Luxembourg 1957-60, to the EEC 1959; Head of Israel Del. Int. Conf. Law of the Sea,

Geneva 1960; Deputy Dir.-Gen. Ministry for Foreign Affairs 1960-65; Perm. Rep. to UN 1967; Special Amb. and Adviser to Foreign Minister 1966-67; Dir-Gen. Ministry for Foreign Affairs 1967-71; Sr. Political Adviser to Minister of Foreign Affairs 1972-73, 1977-78; Amb. to U.K. (also accred. to Ireland) 1973-77; Head of Del. to UNCTAD III 1972. *Publications:* Destination Peace: Three Decades of Israeli Foreign Policy 1981 and numerous articles on int. affairs. *Address:* c/o Ministry of Foreign Affairs, Jerusalem, Israel.

RAFAELSON, Bob; American film director; b. 1933, New York. *Films directed include:* Head 1968, Five Easy Pieces 1970 (New York Film Critics Award), The King of Marvin Gardens 1972, Stay Hungry 1976, The Postman Always Rings Twice 1981, Black Widow 1987, Mountains of the Moon 1989. *Address:* 1400 N. Fuller Avenue, Hollywood, Calif. 90046, U.S.A.

RAFI, Brig. Gen. Mohammed; Afghan politician; b. 1944, Kabul; ed. Kabul Mil. Univ. and Mil. Acad. of the U.S.S.R.; mem. People's Democratic Party of Afghanistan 1973, mem. Cen. Cttee. 1978, Politburo 1981; fmr. Minister of Public Works, Defence and Deputy Pres. of Revolutionary Council of Afghanistan; Deputy Chair. Council of Ministers and Minister of Defence 1986-88; Vice-Pres. of Afghanistan June 1988–; Order of the Red Banner. *Address:* Office of the Vice-President, Kabul, Afghanistan.

RAFSANJANI, Hojatoleslam Hashemi; Iranian politician; b. 1934; Speaker, Islamic Consultative Ass. 1980–; Deputy Chair. Council of Experts (f. to appoint eventual successor to Ayatollah Khomeini); mem. Islamic Repub. Party; Acting C.-in-C. of the Armed Forces June 1988; Vice-Chair. Cttee. to revise the Constitution April 1989–. *Address:* c/o Islamic Republican Party, Dr. Ali Shariati Avenue, Teheran, Iran.

RAFTERY, Peter Albert, M.V.O., M.B.E.; British diplomatist; b. 8 June 1929; s. of John Raftery and Mary Glynn; m. 1st Margaret Frances Hulse 1949 (deceased); four d.; m. 2nd Fenella Jones 1975; ed. St. Ignatius Coll., London; joined India Office 1946, Commonwealth Relations Office 1949, New Delhi 1950, Peshawar 1956, Cape Town 1959, Kuala Lumpur 1963, Nairobi 1964; Asst. Political Agent, Bahrain 1968; First Sec. FCO 1973; Head of Chancery, Gaborone 1976; Head of E. Africa Dept., FCO 1980; Counsellor and Consul Gen., Amman 1982-85; High Commr. in Botswana 1986–. *Leisure interests:* tennis, squash. *Address:* c/o Foreign and Commonwealth Office, London, SW1A 2AH, England.

RAGON, Michel; French lecturer and writer; b. 24 June 1924, Marseille; s. of Aristide Ragon and Camille Sourisseau; m. Françoise Antoine 1968; worked in manual jobs since the age of 14; lived in Paris 1945–, bookseller on the Seine embankments 1954-64; art critic, architectural historian, novelist; lecturer at l'Ecole Nat. Supérieure des Arts Decoratifs à Paris 1972-85; Prix de l'Académie Française et de l'Académie d'Architecture. *Publications:* Histoire mondiale de l'architecture et de l'urbanisme modernes 1971-78, L'homme et les Villes 1975, L'espace de la mort 1981, L'art abstrait 1973-74, L'art pour quoi faire? 1971, 25 ans d'art vivant 1969, Histoire de la littérature prolétarienne en France 1974, L'accent de ma mère 1980, Ma soeur aux yeux d'Asie 1982, Les mouchoirs rouges de Cholet 1984, La Louve de Mervent 1985, Le Marin des Sables 1988. *Address:* 4 rue du Faubourg Poissonnière, 75010 Paris, France.

RAHMAN, Hamood-ur, B.A., LL.B.; Pakistani judge; b. 1 Nov. 1910, Patna, India; s. of late Dr. Daudur Rahman; m. Rabea Ashraf Ali 1941; five s. four d.; ed. St. Xavier's Coll., Calcutta, Univ. of London and Gray's Inn, London; called to the Bar, London 1937; joined Calcutta High Court 1938; Councillor of the Calcutta Corpn. 1940, Deputy Mayor of Calcutta 1943; Jr. Standing Counsel, Province of Bengal 1943-47; appeared for Province of E. Pakistan before Arbitration Tribunal, Delhi, India 1948; Legal Adviser, State Bank of Pakistan, Dacca 1950-53; Advocate-Gen. of E. Pakistan 1953-54; Judge, Dacca High Court 1954-60; Vice-Chancellor, Dacca Univ. 1958-60; mem. Int. Court of Arbitration, The Hague 1959-60; Judge, Supreme Court of Pakistan 1960-68, Chief Justice 1968-76; Chair. Comm. on Students' Problems and Welfare 1964, Law Reforms Comm. 1967, War Inquiry Comm. 1972; UN Cttee. on Crime Prevention and Control 1972, 1973; Chair. Council of Islamic Ideology, Pakistan 1974-77. *Address:* 194 Shadman, Phase 2, Lahore, Pakistan. *Telephone:* 415139.

RAHMAN, Janab M. Matiur, M.SC.; Bangladesh politician; ed. Dhaka Univ.; Lecturer, Political Science 1948; Pakistan Audit and Accounts Service 1949-71; detained in Pakistan 1972-73, then repatriated; Bangladesh rep. at numerous int. confs.; Sec. Ministry of Commerce 1976-82, Ministry of Industries 1984; Minister of Communications 1986-87; Amb. to Japan and Repub. of Korea 1982. *Address:* Ministry of Communications, Bhaban 7, 1st 9-Storey Bldg., 8th Floor, Dhaka, Bangladesh.

RAHMAN, Shah (Mohammad) Azizur; Bangladesh politician and lawyer; b. 23 Nov. 1925, Kushtia; Gen. Sec. All-India Muslim Students' Fed., All-Bengal Muslim Students' League 1945-47; Chair. East Pakistan Combined Opposition Party 1964; Leader Awami League Parl. Party and Deputy Leader of Opposition, Nat. Assembly of Pakistan 1965-69; Senior Advocate, Supreme Court of Bangladesh; mem. Bangladesh Parl. for Daulatpore, Kushtia Constituency; Leader of the House; Minister of Labour and Industrial Welfare 1978-79; Prime Minister 1979-82, also Minister of Educ. 1979-82, of Law and Parl. Affairs, Local Govt., Rural Devt. and Co-operatives, and Religious Affairs Feb.–March 1982; mem. Bangladesh Bar Council. *Address:* c/o Office of the Prime Minister, Dacca, Bangladesh.

RAHMAN, Tunku Abdul (see Abdul Rahman, Tunku).

RAHMAN KHAN, Ataur; Bangladeshi politician; b. 6 March 1905, Balia-Dhaka; s. of Emteazuddin Khan and Amatanessa Khanum; m. Syeda Akbamunessa Khanum 1941; three s. two d.; veteran activist in Bangladeshi politics; Opposition Leader in Parl. 1972–75; Leader of political party Bangladesh Jatiya League (fmr. Pakistan Nat. League) 1970–; mem. of seven party opposition alliance (led by Begum Khaleda Zia) –Jan. 1984; Prime Minister and concurrently Minister of Political and Parl. Affairs 1984–85. *Publications:* (In Bengali): Two Years of Ministry 1960, Ten Years of Despotism 1971, Nine Months of Prime Ministry. *Leisure interests:* reading, writing. *Address:* Bangladesh Jatiya League, 500A Dhanmondi R/A, Road No. 7, Dhaka, Bangladesh. *Telephone:* 505151, 507048, 506231.

RAHMANI, Chérif; Algerian politician; b. 16 Jan. 1945, Ain Oussera; m.; four c.; ed. Ecole Nat. d'Admin.; Inspecteur Gen.; Sec. Gen. to the Ministry of the Interior; Minister of Youth and Sport 1988–. *Address:* 3 place du 1er mai, Algiers, Algeria. *Telephone:* (2) 66-33-70.

RAHN, Hermann, PH.D.; American physiologist; b. 5 July 1912, E. Lansing, Mich.; s. of Otto Rahn and Bell S. Farrand Rahn; m. Katharine Wilson 1939; one s. one d.; ed. Cornell and Rochester, New York Univs.; Nat. Research Council Fellow, Harvard Univ. 1938–39; Instructor in Physiology, Univ. of Wyoming 1939–41; Asst. in Physiology, Univ. of Rochester School of Medicine 1941–42, Instructor 1942–46, Asst. Prof. 1946–50, Assoc. Prof. 1950–56; Lawrence D. Bell Prof. of Physiology and Chair. Dept. of Physiology, Univ. of Buffalo (since 1962 State Univ. of New York at Buffalo) 1956–72; Distinguished Prof. of Physiology 1973–; mem. N.A.S.; Fellow, American Acad. of Arts and Sciences; Pres. American Physiological Soc. 1963–64; mem. Council, Int. Union of Physiological Sciences 1965–74; Vice-Pres. 1971–74; hon. doctorates from Univs. of Paris, Yonsei (Seoul), Bern and Rochester. *Publication:* A Graphical Analysis of the Respiratory Gas Exchange (with W. O. Fenn) 1955, Blood Gases: Haemoglobin, Base Excess and Maldistribution (with others) 1973, and Ed. of other volumes. *Address:* Department of Physiology, State University of New York at Buffalo, Buffalo, N.Y. 14214 (Office); 75 Windsor Avenue, Buffalo, N.Y. 14209, U.S.A. (Home). *Telephone:* (716) 831-2619 (Office).

RAIDI; Chinese (Tibetan) party official; b. 1931, northern Tibet; ed. Cen. Nationalities Inst., Beijing; Sec. CCP Cttee., Nagu Region 1972; Sec. CCP Cttee., Tibet Autonomous Region 1975–77, Sec. 1977–; Chair. Peasants' Fed. of Tibet 1975; alt. mem. 11th CCP Cen. Cttee. 1977–82; Vice-Chair. Revolutionary Cttee., Tibet Autonomous Region 1977–79; Vice-Chair. People's Congress of Tibet 1979–83, Chair. 1986–; mem. 12th CCP Cen. Cttee. 1982. *Address:* Tibet Autonomous Region Chinese Communist Party, Lhasa, Tibet, People's Republic of China.

RAIMOND, Jean-Bernard; French diplomatist and politician; b. 6 Feb. 1926, Paris; s. of Henri Raimond and Alice Auberty; m. Monique Chabanel 1975; two d.; ed. Ecole Normale Supérieure and Ecole Nationale d'Admin-istration; C.N.R.S. 1951–53; Dept. of Political Affairs and Central Admin. of Ministry of Foreign Affairs 1956–66; Deputy Dir. Europe 1967; Asst. Dir. Office of Minister of Foreign Affairs 1967; Tech. Counsellor, Office of Prime Minister 1968–69; Sec.-Gen. Presidency of the Repub. 1969–73; Amb. to Morocco 1973–77; Dir. for N. Africa and the Levant 1977–78; Dir. Office of Minister of Foreign Affairs 1978; Dir.-Gen. for Cultural Relations, Ministry of Foreign Affairs 1979–81; Amb. to Poland 1982–84, to U.S.S.R. 1984–86; Minister of Foreign Affairs 1986–88; Amb. to Holy See, Rome 1988–; Officier, Légion d'honneur; Commdr. de l'Ordre Nat. du Mérite; Chevalier des Palmes Académiques; Order of Ouissan Alaouite (Morocco). *Address:* c/o 37 quai d'Orsay, 75007 Paris, France.

RAIMONDI, Ruggero; Italian opera singer; b. 3 Oct. 1941, Bologna; m. Isabel Maier 1987; operatic début in La Bohème at the Spoleto Festival 1964; début at Metropolitan Opera, New York in Ernani 1970; other engagements include Don Giovanni, Nozze di Figaro, Faust, Attila, Don Carlos, Boris Godunov and Don Quichotte: Films: Don Giovanni 1978, Six Characters in Search of an Author 1981, La Vie est un Roman 1982, Carmen 1983; produced Don Giovanni in Nancy in 1986; Officier des Arts et Lettres, Chevalier de l'Ordre de Malte, Commendatore della Repubblica Italiana. *Address:* c/o CAMI-Jack Mastroianni, 165 West 57th Street, New York, N.Y. 10019, U.S.A.

RAINE, Craig Anthony, B.A., B.PHIL.; British writer; b. 3 Dec. 1944, Shildon, Co. Durham; s. of Norman Edward and Olive Marie Raine; m. Ann Pasternak Slater 1972; three s. one d.; ed. Exeter Coll., Oxford; Poetry Ed. Faber and Faber Ltd. 1981–; Kelus Prize 1979, Southern Arts Literature Award 1979. *Publications:* The Onion, Memory 1978, A Martian Sends a Postcard Home 1979, A Free Translation 1981, Rich 1984, The Electrification of the Soviet Union (opera) 1986, A Choice of Kipling's Prose (ed.) 1987. *Address:* Faber and Faber Ltd., 3 Queen Square, London, WC1N 3AU, England. *Telephone:* 01-278 6881.

RAINE, Kathleen Jessie, M.A., F.R.S.L.; British poet; b. 1908; d. of late George Raine and Jessie Raine; m. Charles Madge (divorced); one s. one d.; ed. Girton Coll., Cambridge; Fellow, Girton Coll., Cambridge 1956–; co-Ed. Temenos (review); W. H. Smith Literary Award and other English and American poetry prizes and awards; Blake scholar; Hon. D.Litt. (Leicester) 1974, (Durham) 1979. *Publications:* Stone and Flower 1943, Living in Time 1946, The Pythoness 1949, The Year One 1952, Collected Poems 1956, The Hollow Hill (poems) 1965, Blake and Tradition (Andrew Mellon Lectures) 1969, Selected Writings of Thomas Taylor the Platonist (with George Mills Harper) 1969, William Blake, Selected Poems 1970, The Lost Country (poems) 1971, On a Deserted Shore (poems) 1972, Faces of Day and Night 1973, Farewell Happy Fields (autobiog.) 1973, The Land Unknown (autobiog.) 1975, The Oval Portrait (verse) 1977, The Lions Mouth (autobiog.) 1977, The Oracle in the Heart (poems) 1979, Collected Poems 1981, The Human Face of God 1982, The Presence (poems) 1988, Selected Poems 1988; criticism: Defending Ancient Springs 1967, Yeats, the Tarot and the Golden Dawn 1973, Death in Life and Life in Death 1973, David Jones and the Actually Loved and Known 1978, From Blake to a Vision 1978, Blake and the New Age 1979, The Inner Journey of the Poet and other papers 1982, L'imagination créatrice de William Blake 1986. *Address:* 47 Paultons Square, London, S.W.3, England.

RAINIER III, His Serene Highness Prince, Louis Henri Maxence Bertrand; Prince of Monaco; b. 31 May 1923; s. of the late Comte Pierre de Polignac and the late Princess Charlotte, Duchess of Valentinois; m. Grace Patricia Kelly 1956 (died 1982); one s. two d.; ed. Summerfields School, Hastings (England), Montpellier Univ., and Ecole Libre des Sciences Politiques, Paris; Hereditary Prince of Monaco 1944; succeeded his grandfather Prince Louis II 1949; founded Monaco Red Cross 1948, American Friends of Monaco 1952, Prix Rainier 1955, Grand Master, Ordre de St. Charles de Monaco, Grand Croix, Légion d'honneur, Belgian, Swedish, Greek, Lebanese, Italian, Netherlands and San Marino orders; served in French army as Lieut. and Col. 1944–45. *Address:* Palais de Monaco, Monte Carlo, Principality of Monaco.

RÄISÄNEN, Heikki Martti, M.A., D.THEOL.; Finnish professor of New Testament exegesis; b. 10 Dec. 1941, Helsinki; s. of Martti Olavi Räisänen and Saara Ilona Itkonen; m. Leena Marjatta Wright 1974; three s. one d.; ed. Univ. of Helsinki; lecturer in New Testament Exegesis, Univ. of Helsinki 1969–74, Acting Assoc. Prof. in Biblical Languages 1971–74, Prof. of New Testament Exegesis 1975–; Research Prof. Acad. of Finland 1984–89; Dir. Exegetical Inst., Univ. of Helsinki 1975–84, Vice-Dean of the Theological Faculty 1978–80; mem. Cttee. Finnish Exegetical Soc. 1969–85, Chair. 1980–85; mem. Finnish Acad. of Sciences 1978–, Cttee. Soc. for New Testament Studies 1986–89; Fulbright Visiting Scholar, Harvard 1970–71, Humboldt Visiting Scholar, Tubingen 1980–82. *Publications:* Die Mutter Jesu im Neuen Testament 1969, The Idea of Divine Hardening 1972, Das "Messiasgeheimnis" im Markus-evangelium 1976, Paul and the Law 1983, The Torah and Christ 1986, "The Messianic Secret" in Mark 1989. *Address:* Vantaanjäne 1 B 11, 01730 Vantaa, Finland.

RAISANI, Sardar Ghaus Bakhsh; Pakistani politician; b. 6 Sept. 1924, Kanak, Baluchistan; s. of late Nawab Sir Asadullah Khan Raisani; nine s. one d.; ed. Col. Brown Cambridge School, Dehra Dun; commissioned Indian Army 1945, served 1945–48; Chief of his tribe and of Sarawan tribes, Baluchistan 1949–; active in politics 1949–; Convenor, Baluchistan State Muslim League; mem. W. Pakistan Ass. 1956–58; mem. Baluchistan Ass. 1970–77; Leader of the Opposition 1972–74; f. and Convenor, Baluchistan United Front 1969; Gov. of Baluchistan 1971–72; Fed. Minister for Food and Agric. 1972–73; Sr. Minister Baluchistan Prov. Cabinet 1974–77; Pres. Pakistan People's Party Baluchistan 1974–77. *Leisure interests:* farming, hunting, angling, hiking. *Address:* Raisani House, Shahra-e-Nawab Raisani, Quetta, Pakistan. *Telephone:* 70661.

RAISMAN, John Michael, M.B.E., M.A.; British petroleum executive; b. 12 Feb. 1929, Lahore, India; s. of Sir Jeremy and Renee Mary (née Kelly) Raisman; m. Evelyn Anne Muirhead 1953; one s. three d.; ed. Rugby School, Queen's Coll., Oxford; joined Shell Int. Petroleum Co. Ltd. 1953, served in Brazil 1953–60; Gen. Man., Shell Panama 1960–62; Asst. to Exploration and Production Co-ordinator, Shell Int. Petroleum, Maatschappij 1963–65; Gen. Man., Shell Co. of Turkey Ltd. 1965–69; Pres. Shell Sekiyu KK 1970–73; Head of European Supply and Marketing, Shell Int. Petroleum 1974–77; Man. Dir., Shell U.K. Oil 1977–78; Deputy Chair. and Chief Exec., Shell U.K. Ltd. 1978–79, Chair. and Chief Exec. 1979–85; Chair. Shell Chemicals U.K. Ltd. 1979–85; Dir. Vickers 1981–, Glaxo Holdings PLC 1982–, Lloyds Bank 1985–, Lloyds Merchant Bank Holdings 1985–; Deputy Chair. British Telecom 1987–; mem. Pres.'s Cttee. of Confed. of British Industry (CBI), Chair. Europe Cttee. of CBI 1980–; Chair. Council of Industry for Man. Educ. (CIME) 1981–85; Chair. Oil Industry Emergency Cttee. (OIEC) 1981–85; Chair. Advisory Council, London Enterprise Agency 1979–85, Chair. Investment Bd. Electra Candover Partners 1985–, Electronics Industry DC 1986–; Gov. Nat. Inst. of Econ. and Social Research 1981–; mem. Governing Council of Business in the Community 1982–85; mem. Council, Inst. for Fiscal Studies 1982–, Governing Council of Business in the Community 1982–85; mem. Royal Comm. on Environmental Pollution 1986–87; Chair. Bd. Trustees R.A.; Pro-Chancellor Aston Univ. 1987–; Hon. D.Univ. (Stirling) 1983, Hon. LL.D. (Aberdeen) 1985, (Manchester) 1986. *Leisure interests:* golf, tennis, skiing. *Address:* Netheravon House, Netheravon Road South, Chiswick, London, W4 2PY, England.

RAJ, Dr. Kakkadan Nandanath, M.A., PH.D.; Indian economist; b. 13 May 1924, Trichur, Kerala; s. of K. N. Gopalan and Karthiayani Gopalan; m. Sarasamma Raj 1957; two s.; ed. Madras and London School of Econs.; Asst. Ed. Assoc. Newspapers of Ceylon 1947-48; Research Officer Balance of Payments Div., Dept. of Research, Reserve Bank of India 1948-50; Asst. Chief Econ. Div., Planning Comm. 1950-53; Prof. of Econs. Delhi School of Econs. 1953-73; Vice-Chancellor Delhi Univ. 1969-70; Fellow, Centre for Devt. Studies, Trivandrum 1973-83, Hon. Emer. Fellow 1983-; mem. Economic Advisory Council to Prime Minister 1983-87; Fellow Univ. Grants Comm. Nat. Fellow in Econs. 1971-73; Corresp. Fellow, British Acad.; Hon. Fellow, American Econs. Asscn., London School of Economics. *Publications:* The Monetary Policy of the Reserve Bank of India 1948, Employment—Aspects of Planning in Underdeveloped Economies 1956, Some Economic Aspects of the Bhakara-Nangal Project 1960, Indian Economic Growth: Performance and Prospects 1964, India, Pakistan and China: Economic Growth and Outlook 1966, Investment in Livestock in Agrarian Economics 1969. *Address:* Nandavan, Kumarapuram, Trivandrum 695011, Kerala State, India.

RAJA HAJI AHMAD, Raja Tan Sri Aznam, P.S.M., B.A.; Malaysian diplomatist; b. 21 Jan. 1928, Taiping; s. of Raja Haji Ahmad and Hajjah Zainab; m. Tengku Puan Sri Zailah Btd. T. Zakaria 1954; one s. two d.; ed. King Edward VII Coll. Taiping, Malay Coll. Kuala Kangsar, Univ. of Malaya in Singapore; joined Malayan Civil Service 1953, Foreign Service 1956; Second Sec. Bangkok 1957, First Sec. Cairo 1960-62; Principal Asst. Sec. Ministry of Foreign Affairs 1962-65; Deputy Perm. Rep. to UN 1965-68; High Commr. in India 1968-71; Amb. to Japan 1971-74, to U.S.S.R., Bulgaria, Hungary, Mongolia, Poland and Romania 1974-77, to France, Morocco, Portugal and Spain 1977-79; High Commr. in U.K. 1979-83. *Leisure interests:* reading, golf. *Address:* c/o Ministry of Foreign Affairs, Kuala Lumpur, Malaysia.

RAJAN, Mannaraswamighala Sreeranga, M.A., D.LITT; Indian university professor; b. 4 Aug. 1920, Badikayalapalli, Andhra Pradesh; s. of late M. V. Bhatrachar and Rangamma Rajan; m. Padma Rajan 1946; one s. two d.; ed. Univ. of Mysore and Columbia Univ. New York; govt. service 1944-47; Sec. Asian Relations Org. New Delhi 1947-48; Admin. Sec. and Research Sec. Indian Council of World Affairs 1949-59; joined Indian School of Int. Studies 1959; Research, Inst. of Commonwealth Studies, Univ. of London 1960-61; Prof. of Commonwealth Studies 1962-71, concurrently Dir. Indian School of Int. Studies 1965-71; Prof. of Int. Org. Jawaharlal Nehru Univ. 1971-84, Prof. Emer. 1986-; Presidential Adviser, Repub. of Nauru, Chief. Sec. and Sec. for External Affairs 1984-86; Asian Fellow, A.N.U., Canberra 1971-72; Fellow, UN Inst. for Training and Research, New York 1974-76. *Publications:* United Nations and Domestic Jurisdiction 1958, Post-War Transformation of the Commonwealth 1963, India in World Affairs 1954-56 1964, Non-alignment, India and the Future 1970, Sovereignty over Natural Resources 1978, The Expanding Jurisdiction of the United Nations 1982, India's Foreign Policy and Relations (with A. Appadorai) 1985, Studies on Non-alignment and the Non-aligned Movement 1986, India's Foreign Policy and Relations (with A. Appadorai) 1988, articles in books and learned journals. *Leisure interest:* cooking. *Address:* School of International Studies, Jawaharlal Nehru University, New Delhi, India. *Telephone:* 667676 (Office); 6411767 (Home).

RAJARATNAM, Sinnathamby; Singapore politician; b. 25 Feb. 1915, Ceylon (now Sri Lanka); ed. Raffles Inst., Singapore, King's Coll., London; brought to Malaya at age of six months; Assoc. Ed. Singapore Standard 1950-54; Editorial Staff Straits Times 1954-59; mem. Malayanization Cttee. 1955; mem. Minimum Standards of Livelihood Cttee. 1956; Convenor and Founder-mem. of People's Action Party; Assemblyman (now M.P.) for Kampong Glam constituency 1959-; Minister for Culture 1959-65, for Foreign Affairs 1965-80, also for Labour 1968-71, Second Deputy Prime Minister (with responsibility for Foreign Affairs) 1980-85; Sr. Minister, Prime Minister's Office 1985-88. *Address:* c/o Institute of Southeast Asian Studies, Heng Mui Keng Terrace, Pasir Panjang, Singapore 0511.

RAJBANSI, Amichand; South African politician; b. 14 Jan. 1942; m.; one s. four d.; fmr. school teacher, sports admin. and businessman; mem. S. African Indian Council (SAIC) 1974-, mem. Exec. 1974-76, 1979-81, Chair. Exec. Council 1981-; Chair. Ministers' Council, House of Dels. (Indian) 1984-88; Minister without Portfolio 1986-88; mem. Cen. Cabinet 1984-88; M.P. 1984-; mem. numerous educational, religious and cultural bodies. *Address:* c/o House of Delegates, Private Bag X 54323, Durban 4000, South Africa.

RAJNA, Thomas, D.MUS.; British composer and pianist; b. 21 Dec. 1928, Budapest; s. of late Dr. Nandor Rajna and Hella Eisen; m. Anne V. Campion 1966; two s. one d.; ed. Nat. Musical School, Budapest, Franz Liszt Acad. of Music, Budapest and Royal Coll. of Music, London; freelance composer, pianist and teacher, London 1951-63; Prof. of Piano, Guildhall School of Music 1963-70; Lecturer, Univ. of Surrey 1967-70; Sr. Lecturer in Piano, Univ. of Cape Town 1970-; compositions include film and ballet music, chamber music, two piano concertos, orchestral works etc.; commercial recordings of works by Stravinsky, Messiaen, Scriabin, Granados, Liszt and own compositions; Fellow, Univ. of Cape Town 1981; Liszt Prize, Budapest 1947, Artes Award (SABC) 1981; Hon. D.Mus. (Univ. of Cape

Town) 1981. *Leisure interests:* chess, swimming. *Address:* 10 Wyndover Road, Claremont, Cape 7700, South Africa.

RAKHIMBABAEVA, Zakhra; Soviet official; b. 1923, Uzbekistan; ed. Pedagogical Inst., Tashkent, Acad. of Social Sciences of CPSU Cen. Cttee.; Sec. of Komomsomol Dist. Cttee. 1942-46; mem. CPSU 1946-; Sec. of Cen. Cttee. of Uzbek CP 1946-51; First Deputy Minister of Culture of Uzbek S.S.R. 1955-56; mem. Cen. Cttee. of Uzbek CP 1956-71; Sec. and mem. of Politburo of Cen. Cttee. of Uzbek CP 1956-63; Minister of Culture of Uzbek S.S.R. 1963-67, 1981-. *Address:* Ministry of Culture, Tashkent, Uzbek S.S.R., U.S.S.R.

RAKHIMOVA, Ibodat; Soviet politician; b. 1922, Tadzhikistan; First Sec. Cen. Cttee. of Tadzhik Komsomol; Deputy Chair. Supreme Soviet of Tadzhik S.S.R., First Sec. Regional Cttee. of Tadzhik CP in Dushanbe, Deputy Head of Party Org., Tadzhik CP 1955-66; mem. Cen. Cttee. of Tadzhik CP 1956-, Sec. and mem. Politburo of Cen. Cttee. 1966-; Party Sec. for Ideology and Propaganda 1966-79; Sec. Presidium, Supreme Soviet of Tadzhik S.S.R. 1979-. *Address:* Supreme Soviet of Tadzhik S.S.R., Dushanbe, Tadzhik S.S.R., U.S.S.R.

RAKHMANIN, Oleg Borisovich; Soviet party official; b. 1924; mem. CPSU 1945-; served in Soviet Army 1939-45; with U.S.S.R. Foreign Ministry 1945-63; worked on Cen. Cttee. CPSU 1963-68; First Deputy Head of Dept. of Relations with Communist Workers' Parties and Socialist Countries, Cen. Cttee. CPSU 1968-89; mem. of Cen. Auditing Comm. CPSU 1971-76; Cand. mem. Cen. Cttee. CPSU 1976-81, mem. 1981-89. *Address:* The Kremlin, Moscow, U.S.S.R.

RAKOTOARIJAONA, Lieut.-Col. Désiré; Malagasy army officer and politician; b. 1934; Minister of Finance Feb.-June 1975; mem. Supreme Revolutionary Council 1975-88; Prime Minister 1977-88; mem. Front National pour la Défense de la Révolution Socialiste Malgache. *Address:* Office du Premier Ministre, Antananarivo, Madagascar.

RAKOTONIAINA, Justin; Malagasy teacher, diplomatist and politician; b. 1933, Betsileo; fmr. professor of Law, Univ. of Madagascar; Amb. to Algeria, also accred. to Tunisia and Guinea 1973-75; Minister of Nat. Educ. 1975-76; Prime Minister of Madagascar 1976-77; mem. Supreme Revolutionary Council. *Address:* c/o Office du Premier Ministre, Antananarivo, Madagascar.

RAKOWSKI, Mieczysław Franciszek, DR.HIST.; Polish journalist and politician; b. 1 Dec. 1926, Kowalewko, Szubin district; m. 1st Wanda Wiłkomirska (q.v.) 1952 (separated); two s.; m. 2nd Elżbieta Kępińska; ed. Higher School of Social Sciences, Cracow and Inst. of Social Sciences, Warsaw; worked at Cen. Cttee. of Polish United Workers' Party (PZPR) 1949-52, 1955-57; Sub-editor, Polityka 1957, Editor-in-Chief 1958-82; Chair. Gen. Board, Polish Journalists' Asscn. 1958-61; Deputy mem. Cen. Cttee., PZPR 1964-75, mem. Dec. 1975-; Deputy to Seym 1972-, Deputy Chair. PZPR Seym Deputies' Club 1980; Deputy Chair. Council of Ministers 1981-85; Chair. Cttee. for Trade Unions of Council of Ministers 1981-85; Vice-Marshal (Deputy Speaker) of Seym 1985-88; Chair. Socio-Econ. Council attached to Seym 1985-88; mem. Political Bureau PZPR Cen. Cttee. Dec. 1987-; Sec. PZPR Cen. Cttee. 1988; Chair. Council of Ministers (Prime Minister) 1988-; Presenter, TV programme Świat i Polityka (World and Politics); Chair. Polish Yachting Union; Order of Banner of Labour 1st and 2nd Class, Gold Cross of Merit, State Prize 2nd Class 1976, Commdr.'s Cross with Star of Order of Polonia Restituta, and other decorations. *Publications:* NRF z bliska (Fed. Rep. of Germany from a Short Distance) 1958, New World 1959, Socjal-demokratyczna Partia Niemiec w okresie powojennym 1949-54 (Social-Democratic Party of Germany in Post-war Period) 1960, Świat na zakręcie (The World in Turning) 1960, Zachód szuka ideologii (The West Looks for Ideology) 1961, Ameryka wielopiętrowa (Many-storied America), Klimaty w RFN (Climates of the Fed. Rep. of Germany), Polityka Zagraniczna PRL (The Foreign Policy of the Polish People's Republic) 1974, Dymisja Kanclerza (Chancellor's Dismissal) 1975, Spełnione i niespełnione 1978, Przesilenie grudniowe (December Crisis) 1981, Partnerstwo (Partnership) 1982, Czas nadziei i rozczarowań (Time of Hopes and Disappointments), Vol. 1 1985, Vol. 2 1987, Ein schwieriger Dialog 1986; co-author: The Polish Upswing 1971-75 1975. *Leisure interests:* joinery, angling, yachting. *Address:* Urząd Rady Ministrów, Al. Ujazdowskie 1/3, 00-583 Warsaw, Poland.

RALITE, Jack; French journalist and politician; b. 14 May 1928, Châlons-sur-Marne; m. Monique Pailler 1966; journalist on l'Humanité, Head of cultural dept., l'Humanité Dimanche; Deputy Mayor, Aubervilliers 1965-84, Mayor 1984-; mem. Nat. Ass. (for Seine-Saint-Denis) 1973-81, mem. Communist group; mem. Parl. Del. for French broadcasting 1974; Minister of Health 1981-83; Minister Del. attached to Minister of Social Affairs and Nat. Solidarity, in Charge of Employment 1983-84. *Address:* Hôtel de Ville, 93300 Aubervilliers, France.

RALL, David Platt, PH.D.; American government administrator; b. 3 Aug. 1926, Aurora, Ill.; s. of Edward Everett Rall and Nell Platt; m. Edith Levy 1954 (died 1987); one s. one d.; ed. North Cen. Coll., Naperville and Northwestern Univ.; Intern, Bellevue Hosp., New York 1952-53; Commissioned Officer, U.S. Public Health Service 1953-, Asst. Surgeon Gen. 1971-; Sr. Investigator, Lab. of Chemical Pharmacology, Nat. Cancer Inst., Bethesda, Md. 1953-55, Scientist, Clinical Pharmacology and Experimental Therapeutics Service, Gen. Medicine Br. 1956-58, Head of Service 1958-63, Chief, Lab. of Chemical Pharmacology 1963-69, Assoc. Scientific Dir. for Experimental Therapeutics 1966-71; Dir. Nat. Inst. of Environmental Health Sciences 1971-; Dir. Nat. Toxicology Program 1978-; Dept. of Health, Educ. and Welfare Distinguished Service Medal 1975; Arnold J. Lehman Award (Soc. of Toxicology) 1983. *Publications:* author and co-author of 160 scientific papers. *Address:* National Institute of Environmental Health Sciences, P.O. Box 12233, Research Triangle Park, N.C. 27709; 603 Brookview Drive, Chapel Hill, N.C. 27514, U.S.A. (Home). *Telephone:* (919) 541-3201.

RALL, J. Edward, M.D., PH.D.; American research scientist, physician and research administrator; b. 3 Feb. 1920, Naperville, Ill.; s. of Edward Everett Rall and Nell Platt; m. 1st Caroline Dumm 1944 (deceased), m. 2nd Nancy Lamontagne 1978; one s. one d.; ed. North Central Coll., Ill., Northwestern Univ., Chicago and Univ. of Minnesota; served U.S. army, Medical Corps 1946-48; Attending Physician, Memorial Hosp., New York City 1950-55; Assoc., Sloan-Kettering Inst., New York and Asst. Prof. of Medicine, Cornell Univ. 1951-55; Chief, Clinical Endocrinology Branch, Nat. Inst. of Arthritis, Metabolism and Digestive Diseases (later named Nat. Inst. of Arthritis, Diabetes and Digestive and Kidney Diseases—NIADDK), Nat. Insts. of Health 1955-62, assigned to Collège de France, Paris and Nat. Inst. for Medical Research, London, England 1961-62; Dir. Div. of Intramural Research, NIADDK 1962-83; Acting Deputy Dir. for Science, Nat. Insts. of Health 1981-82, Deputy Dir. for Intramural Research 1983-; mem. N.A.S., American Acad. of Arts and Sciences. *Publications:* over 150 biomedical research articles on thyroid gland and radiation. *Leisure interests:* pre-Columbian art, linguistics, music, theatre, gardening. *Address:* National Institutes of Health, Building 1, Room 122, Bethesda, Maryland 20892, U.S.A. (Office); 3947 Baltimore Street, Kensington, Md. 20895, U.S.A. (Home). *Telephone:* (301) 496-1921 (Office).

RALLIS, George J., LL.D.; Greek lawyer; b. 26 Dec. 1918; m. Helene Voultsos 1950; two d.; ed. Athens Univ.; served Reconnaissance Groups 1940-41 and Tank Corps 1945-48; elected Deputy for Athens 1950-58, 1961-67, 1974-; mem. Greek del. to European Council, Strasbourg 1953-58; Minister to Prime Minister's Office 1954-56, of Public Works and Communications 1956-58, of the Interior 1961-63, of Public Order April 1967; under house arrest April-May 1967, in prison and exile May-Sept. 1968; Minister to Prime Minister's Office and of Educ. 1974-77, for Co-ordination and Planning 1977-78, for Foreign Affairs 1978-80, Prime Minister of Greece 1980-81; mem. Popular Party 1950, Nat. Rally 1951, Nat. Radical Union 1956, New Democratic Party 1974-87; Medal of Valour, War Cross with two bars, D.S.M., and several foreign awards. *Publications:* John Rallis 1946, The Possibility of Increasing the Yield of Greek Agriculture 1952, Democracy and Communism 1959, The Truth about the Greek Politicians (in Greek) 1971, The Technique of Violence 1972, Ores Efthynis 1984. *Leisure interest:* golf. *Address:* 4 Kanari Street, Athens, Greece.

RAMA, Carlos M., PH.D.; Uruguayan writer, lawyer, professor and editor; b. 26 Oct. 1921, Montevideo; s. of Manuel Rama and Carolina Facal; m. Judith Dellepiane 1943; one s. one d.; ed. Univ. de la República and Univ. de Paris; Journalist 1940-48, 1972-; Exec. Sec. of Uruguayan Bar Asscn. 1940-49; Prof. of Universal History in secondary schools 1944-48; Ed. Nuestro Tiempo 1954-56, Gacetilla Austral 1971-73; Prof. of Sociology and Social Research, Prof. of Contemporary History, Prof. of Theory and Methodology of History, Univ. de la República 1950-72; Prof. of Latin American History, Univ. Autónoma de Barcelona 1973-; Pres. PEN Club Latinoamericano en España; Sec. Gen. Grupo de Estudios Latinoamericanos de Barcelona; Commdr., Order of Liberation (Spain); Officier des Palmes académiques (France). *Publications:* La Historia y la Novela 1947, 1963, 1970, 1974, Las ideas socialistas en el siglo XIX 1947, 1949, 1963, 1967, 1976, Ensayo de Sociología Uruguaya 1956, Teoría de la Historia 1959, 1968, 1974, 1980, Las clases sociales en el Uruguay 1960, La Crisis española del siglo XX 1960, 1962, 1976, Itinerario español 1961, 1977, Revolución social y fascismo en el siglo XX 1962, Sociología del Uruguay 1965, 1973, Historia del movimiento obrero y social latinoamericano contemporáneo 1967, 1969, 1976, Los afrouruguayos 1967, 1968, 1969, 1970, Garibaldi y el Uruguay 1968, Uruguay en Crisis 1969, Sociología de América Latina 1970, 1977, Chile, mil días entre la revolución y el fascismo 1974, España, crónica entrañable 1973-77, 1978, Historia de América Latina 1978, Fascismo y anarquismo en la España contemporánea 1979. *Leisure interest:* gardening. *Address:* c/o Monte de Orsá 7, Vallvidrera, Barcelona 17, Spain.

RAMA RAO, Nandamuri Taraka; Indian film actor and director and politician; b. 28 May 1923, Nimmakuru; s. of the late Lakshmayya Chowdhary and Mrs. Venkatramamma; ed. A.C. Coll., Guntur; appeared in first film Mana Desam 1949 since when he has played roles in more than 300 films with mythological, historical, folklore and social themes; has produced 20 films and dir. 11 of these; set up Ramakrishna Cine Studio at Hyderabad 1976; founder and first Pres. Telugu Desam Party 1982; mem. Andhra Pradesh Legis. Ass. 1983-; Chief Minister of Andhra Pradesh 1983-; Chair. Rashtriya Morcha (Nat. Front) Sept. 1988-. *Address:* Office of the Chief Minister, Raj Bhavan, Hyderabad, Andhra Pradesh, India.

RAMA RAU, Santha (see Rau, Santha Rama).

RAMACHANDRAN, Gopalasamudram Narayana, PH.D., D.SC., F.R.S., F.R.S.A.; Indian scientist and university professor; b. 8 Oct. 1922, Ernakulam, Kerala State; s. of G. R. Narayana Iyer and Lakshmi Ammal; m. Rajalakshmi Sankaran 1945; two s. one d.; ed. Maharaja's Coll., Ernakulam (Cochin), Indian Inst. of Science, Univs. of Madras and Cambridge; Lecturer in Physics, Indian Inst. of Science 1946-47, Asst. Prof. 1949-52; 1851 Exhbn. Scholar, Univ. of Cambridge 1947-49; Prof. Univ. of Madras 1952-70, and Head, Dept. of Physics 1952-70; Dean, Faculty of Science 1964-67; Prof. of Biophysics, Indian Inst. of Science 1970-77; Fogarty Int. Scholar, Nat. Insts. of Health, Washington 1977-78; Inst. Prof. of Mathematical Biology (later Mathematical Philosophy), Indian Inst. of Science 1978-81; part-time Prof. of Biophysics, Univ. of Chicago 1967-78; Distinguished Scientist, Center for Cellular and Molecular Biology, Hyderabad 1981-82; INSA Albert Einstein Prof., Indian Inst. of Science 1984-; Fellow, Indian Acad. of Sciences 1950-, mem. Council 1953-70, Sec. 1956-58, Vice-Pres. 1962-64; Dir. U.G.C. Centre of Advanced Study in Biophysics 1962-70; mem. Physical Research Cttee. 1959-; mem. Nat. Cttee. for Biophysics 1961-; Fellow, Nat. Inst. of Sciences (now Indian Nat. Science Acad.) 1963-; mem. Bd. of Scientific and Industrial Research, India 1962-65, Council Int. Union of Pure and Applied Biophysics 1969-72, Comm. on Macromolecular Biophysics 1969; Chair. Nat. Cttee. for Crystallography 1963-70; Sr. Visiting Prof., Univ. of Michigan 1965-66; Jawaharlal Nehru Fellow 1968-70; Hon. mem. American Soc. of Biological Chem. 1965-; Hon. foreign mem. American Acad. of Arts and Sciences 1970-; founder-mem. Third World Acad. (Rome); Hon. Fellow, Indian Inst. of Science 1984-; specialist in optics, crystal physics, X-ray crystallography biophysics and mathematical logic; Ed. Current Science 1950-58, Journal of the Indian Institute of Science 1973-78; mem. Editorial Bd. J. Molecular Biology 1959-66, Biochimica et Biophysica Acta 1965-72, Indian Journal of Pure and Applied Physics 1963-80, Int. Journal of Peptide and Protein Research 1969-82, Indian Journal of Biochemistry and Biophysics 1970-78, Biopolymers 1973-86, Connective Tissue Research 1973-84; Hon. D.Sc. (Rorkee Univ.) 1978, (Indian Inst. of Tech., Madras) 1985; Bhatnagar Memorial Prize 1961, Watumull Prize 1964, John Arthur Wilson Award 1967, Meghnad Saha Medal 1971, Ramanujan Medal 1972, J. C. Bose Award (U.G.C.) 1974, (Bose Inst.) 1975, Fogarty Medal 1978, C. V. Raman Medal 1983, Birla Award for Medicine 1985. *Publications:* Crystal Optics (in Handbuch der Physik, Vol 25, Berlin), Molecular Structure of Collagen (in International Review of Connective Tissue Research, Vol. I), Conformation of Polypeptides and Proteins, (Advances in Protein Chemistry, Vol. 23), Conformation of Polypeptide Chains (Annual reviews in Biochemistry, Vol. 39), Fourier Methods in Crystallography 1970, Biochemistry of Collagen (Ed.) 1976, Advanced Methods of Crystallography (Ed.), Aspects of Protein Structure, London (Ed.), Treatise on Collagen (Ed.), (two vols.) 1967, Conformation of Biopolymers, Vols. 1 and 2 (Ed.) 1967, Crystallography and Crystal Perfection (Ed.). *Leisure interests:* Indian and Western music, detective fiction, Eastern and Western philosophy. *Address:* Mathematical Philosophy Group, Indian Institute of Science, Bangalore 560012, India (Office); GITA, 10A Main Road, Mallaswaram West, Bangalore 560055, India (Home). *Telephone:* 344411, Ext. 461 (Office); 340362 (Home).

RAMACHANDRAN, Parthasarathi, M.A.; Indian politician; b. 15 July 1921, Korkai village in Cheyyar, Tamil Nadu; s. of A. Parthasarathi; m. Smt. Lakshmi 1949; three c.; ed. Voohese Coll., Vellore, Pachiayappa's Coll., Madras, Madras Univ.; Congress Volunteer, Indian Nat. Congress (later Org. Congress) 1936-37, mem. 1940-77; mem. Students Congress 1940-45; Convenor of Youth Congress in Madras 1953-55; lecturer, P.S.G. Arts Coll. in Coimbatore; mem. Tamil Nadu Legislative Assembly for Cheyyar 1957-62, for Peranamallur 1962-67, Chief Whip of Congress Party in Ass. 1957-67, Chair. Estimates Cttee. 1965-67, Vice-Chair. Co-ordinating Cttees. for planning forums set up in various colls. in Tamil Nadu; Sec. Tamil Nadu Org. Congress 1969-72, Pres. 1972-77; Pres. Janata Party in Tamil Nadu 1977-82; mem. Lok Sabha from Madras Cen. March 1977-; Minister for Energy 1977-79; Gov. of Kerala 1982-88; Chair. Food Corpn. of India 1981-82. *Address:* 55-B 7th Cross Street, Shastri Nagar, Madras 600020, India.

RAMADHANI, Most Rev. John Acland, B.A.; Tanzanian ecclesiastic; b. 1 Aug. 1932, Zanzibar; s. of Augustine Ramadhani and Mary Majaliwa; ed. Univ. of E. Africa, Queen's Coll. Birmingham and Univ. of Birmingham; Prin. St. Andrew's Teacher Training Coll., Korogwe 1967-69; Warden, St. Mark's Theological Coll., Dar es Salaam 1977-79; Bishop of Zanzibar and Tanga 1980-; Archbishop of the Prov. of Tanzania 1984-. *Leisure interest:* reading. *Address:* Diocese of Zanzibar and Tanga, P.O. Box 35, Korogwe, Tanzania. *Telephone:* Korogwe 22 (Office); Korogwe 68 (Home).

RAMAEMA, Col. Elias Phisoana; Lesotho police officer and politician; b. 10 Nov. 1933, Mapoteng, Berea Dist.; ed. Roma Coll.; joined police force 1959, transferred to Police Mobile Unit (PMU) 1968, later Lieut.-Col. in charge of Welfare; undertook specialized training overseas in 1978 and 1984; responsible for Ministries of Planning, Econ. Affairs and Manpower Devt., Information and Broadcasting, Public Service and Employment, Social Welfare and Pensions 1986-; awarded Medal for Meritorious Services and Medal for Gallantry. *Leisure interests:* soccer, farming, poultry. *Address:* The Military Council, Maseru, Lesotho.

RAMAHATRA, Lt.-Col. Victor; Malagasy army officer and politician; Prime Minister of Malagasy Repub. Feb. 1988–. *Address:* Office of the Prime Minister, Mahazoarivo, Antananarivo, Madagascar.

RAMALINGASWAMI, Vulimiri, M.D., D.SC. (OXON.), F.R.C.P.; Indian medical scientist; b. 8 Aug. 1921, Srikakulum, Andhra Pradesh; s. of Shri Gumpaswami and Sundaramma Ramalingaswami; m. Surya Prabha 1947; one s. one d.; ed. Univ. of Oxford, England; Pathologist for Indian Council of Medical Research at the Nutrition Research Labs., Coonor, South India 1947–54; Asst. Sec. and Deputy Dir. Indian Council of Medical Research 1954–57; Prof. of Pathology and Head of Dept., All-India Inst. of Medical Sciences, Ansari Nagar, New Delhi 1957–69, Dir. and Prof. of Pathology 1969–79; Dir.-Gen. Indian Council of Medical Research 1979–; Pres. Indian Nat. Science Acad. 1979–80; Jacobson Lecturer, Newcastle-upon-Tyne Univ. 1971, Jaques Parisot Lecturer, WHO 1975, Jawaharlal Nehru Memorial Lecturer 1975; Scholar-in-Residence, Fogarty Int. Centre, Nat. Insts. of Health, Bethesda, Md. 1976; Pres. Indian Asscn. for Advancement of Medical Educ. 1974–; Padma Bhushan 1971; Silver Jubilee Research Award, Medical Council of India 1974; Fellow, Indian Acad. of Medical Science 1961, Indian Nat. Science Acad. 1971 (Pres. 1979–), Royal Coll. Pathologists; Hon. Fellow, American Coll. of Physicians 1970–; Foreign Assoc., Nat. Acad. of Sciences, U.S.A. 1973–; D.Sc. h.c. (Andhra Univ.) 1967; Hon. Dr.Med. (Karolinska Inst.) 1974; Leon Bernard Foundation Award, WHO, Geneva 1976; J. C. Bose Medal, Indian Nat. Science Acad. 1977; Birla Award for Medical Research 1980. *Publications:* author and co-author of many papers, articles, lectures, monographs and books. *Leisure interests:* music, literature, sports. *Address:* Director-General's Office, Indian Council of Medical Research, Ansari Nagar, P.B. 4508, New Delhi 110029, India. *Telephone:* 373848 (Home).

RAMANANTSOA, Maj.-Gen. Gabriel; Malagasy army officer and politician; b. 13 April 1906, Tananarive; ed. Lycée de Tananarive, de Marseille, Ecole Spéciale Militaire, Saint-Cyr, Inst. des Hautes Etudes de Défense Nationale; Asst. to Chief Officer Ecole Mil. Préparatoire des Enfants de Troupe 1932; assigned to Colonial Infantry Regt. of Morocco, French Army 1931, 1935–36; rank of Capt. 1940; returned to Madagascar, organized Ecole Supérieure d'Educ. Physique, Fianarantsoa 1941, 1943–46; Dept. of Colonial Troops, Ministry of Defence, Paris 1946, 1953–59; in charge of War Veterans, Office of French High Comm., Madagascar 1948–53; served with French Army in Viet-Nam 1953; Lt.-Col., Col. 1959, Brig.-Gen. 1961, Maj.-Gen. 1967; participated in Franco-Malagasy negotiations for independence 1960; Chief of Gen. Staff of the Malagasy Armed Forces 1960–72; Head of Govt., Prime Minister, Minister of Defence, Minister of Planning 1972–75. *Address:* c/o Présidence de la République, Antananarivo, Madagascar.

RAMANUJAM, Gopala; Indian trade unionist; b. 28 May 1915; Founder-Sec. Tamilnadu Indian Nat. Trade Union Congress; Pres. Indian Nat. Textile Workers Fed. 1956, Indian Nat. Plantation Workers Fed. 1960; Pres. Indian Nat. Trade Union Congress 1958, 1959, 1986–, Gen. Sec. 1965–86; Man. Ed. Indian Worker 1965–78; Dir. Industrial Finance Corpn. 1968–72; Chair. Cotton Corpn. of India, Bombay 1974–76, Workers' Educ. Review Cttee. 1981–. *Publications:* From the Babul Tree, Industrial Relations—A Point of View, The Payment of Bonus Act, The Payment of Gratuity Act, The Third Party. *Address:* 1B Maulana Azad Road, New Delhi 110011 (Office); 45 Royapettah High Road, Madras 60014, India. *Telephone:* 844644.

RAMAPHOSA, Matamela Cyril; South African trade union leader; b. 1953, Johannesburg; ed. Sekano-Ntoane High School, Soweto, Univ. of Turfloop; Chair. Univ. br. S. African Students' Org. 1974; imprisoned under Section Six of Terrorism Act for 11 months, then for 6 months in 1976; returned to law studies and qualified 1981; apptd. legal adviser, Council of Unions of S. Africa; Gen.-Sec. Nat. Union of Mineworkers 1982–. *Address:* National Union of Mineworkers, P.O. Box 2424, Johannesburg 2000, South Africa.

RAMBERT, Charles Jean Julien, F.R.S.A.; French architect; b. 23 March 1924, Arrigny, Marne; s. of Jean Rambert; m. Françoise Coleda 1949; three s.; ed. Lycée Pierre-Corneille, Rouen, Inst. Saint-Aspais, Melun, and Ecole Nationale Supérieure des Beaux-Arts; Architect 1952–, Govt. registered architect 1953; Prof. of Construction and History of Art, Ecole de secrétariat technique du bâtiment 1957–82; Arbitrator-expert, Tribunal de Commerce 1960, and de Grande Instance, Versailles 1963, Cour d'Appel de Paris 1971–, Tribunal Administratif de Paris 1979–; Sec. Soc. of Registered Architects 1954–57, Gen. Sec. 1957, 1st Vice-Pres. 1968; Ed.-in-Chief L'Architecture française 1964–75; Counsellor, Ordre des Architectes de Paris 1964, Treas. 1969, Pres. 1976–78; Pres. Cie. des Experts-Architectes, Paris 1978; Asst. Dir. of Studies, Ecole Nat. Supérieure des Beaux Arts 1965, Prof. of History of Architecture 1969–; mem. Union Franco-Britannique des Architectes 1969; Fellow, Royal Soc. of Arts 1971; mem. Acad. d'Architecture 1978, Vice-Pres. 1981; Officier des Arts et Lettres 1967; Chevalier, Légion d'honneur, and other awards. *Publications:* Constructions scolaires et universitaires 1955, L'habitat collectif, Problème urbain 1957, Maisons familiales de plaisance 1959, Magasins 1961, Histoire de l'architecture civile en France 1963, French adapatation of World Architecture 1964, Architecture des origines à nos jours 1968, (English translation 1969), L'architecture française 1969, L'architecture occidentale 1974 (Audio-

visual series), Architecture hispano-mauresque 1980, L'architecture américaine des XIXe et XXe siècles: Chicago, New York. *Leisure interests:* history of art, literature, painting. *Address:* 179 rue de Courcelles, 75017 Paris; 48 rue Saint-Didier, 75016 Paris, France. *Telephone:* 783-35-51.

RAMEL, Baron Stig, M.A.; Swedish administrator; b. 24 Feb. 1927, Lund; s. of Malte Ramel and Elsa née Nyström; m. Ann Marie Wachtmeister 1953; two s. two d.; ed. studies in political science; attaché, Ministry of Foreign Affairs 1953; Swedish Embassy, Paris 1954–56; del. to OECD, Paris 1956–58; Swedish Embassy, Washington, D.C. 1958–60; Ministry of Foreign Affairs 1960–66; Vice-Pres. and Pres. Gen. Swedish Export Assscn. 1966–72; Exec. Dir. Nobel Foundation, Stockholm 1972–; mem. Royal Swedish Acad. of Sciences, King Charles XVI Gustaf Medal; Commdr. Order of Vasa Isabella Catholica and St. Olav, hon. doctorates from Gustavus Adolphus Coll. and Loretto Heights Coll. *Leisure interests:* literature, painting, skiing, orienteering. *Address:* Nobel Foundation, Sturegatan 14, Box 5232, S-102 45 Stockholm, Sweden. *Telephone:* 8-663 09 20.

RAMÍREZ MERCADO, Sergio; Nicaraguan politician and author; b. 1942, Masatepe, Masaya; s. of Pedro Ramírez Gutiérrez and Luisa Mercado Gutiérrez; m. Gertrudis Guerrero Mayorga; one s. two d.; ed. Univ. Autónoma de Nicaragua; was active in revolutionary student movt. and founding mem. of Frente Estudiantil Revolucionario 1962; mem. Cen. American Univ. Supreme Council (CSUCA), Costa Rica 1964, Pres. 1968; mem. Int. Comm. of FSLN (Sandinista Liberation Front) 1975; with Commdr. Luis Carrión prepared document detailing alleged crimes of Somoza dictatorship which was presented to US Congress 1976; undertook tasks on diplomatic front, propaganda and int. work on behalf of FSLN leading to overthrow of regime 1979; mem. Junta of Nat. Reconstruction Govt. 1979–; Vice-Pres. of Nicaragua 1984–. *Publications include:* Central American Story 1973, Charles Atlas also Dies 1977, the Nicaraguan Tale 1977, Time of Brilliance 1979, Castigo Divino 1988. *Address:* Office of the Vice-President, Managua, Nicaragua.

RAMÍREZ VÁZQUEZ, Pedro; Mexican architect; b. 16 April 1919, Mexico; s. of Dolores Vázquez and Max Ramírez; m. Olga Campuzano 1947; two s. two d.; ed. Univ. Nacional Autónoma de México; Prof. of Design and City Planning, Nat. School of Architecture, Univ. Nacional Autónoma de México; Sec. of Human Settlements and Public Works of Mexican Govt. 1976; Past Pres. Soc. of Mexican Architects and Nat. Coll. of Architects of Mexico; Chair. Organizing Cttee., Games of XIX Olympiad; Grand Prix of Twelfth Milan Triennial for prefabricated rural school project; Gold Medal, Eighth São Paulo Biennial for Nat. Museum of Anthropology, Mexico City. *Major works include:* co-author of design for Nat. School of Medicine, Univ. City; plans for several cities in Mexico; numerous prefabricated schools in Mexico (also used in S. America, Europe and Asia); buildings in Mexico City of Secr. of Labour, Nat. Labour Conciliation Bd., Nat. Inst. for Protection of Infancy, Secr. of Foreign Affairs, Aztec Stadium, Cia. Mexicana de Aviación, Owega Co., and Congress bldg.; Mexican pavilions at Brussels, Seattle and New York World Fairs; museums of Ciudad Juarez and Mexico City; Nat. Gallery of History and Nat. Gallery of Modern Art, Mexico City; Nat. Museum of Anthropology, Mexico City; Basilica of Guadalupe, Mexico City; Japanese Embassy, Mexico City; Gold Medal of the French Acad. of Architecture 1978. *Leisure interests:* industrial design and design of lead glass objects. *Address:* Avenida de las Fuentes 170, México 20, D.F., Mexico. *Telephone:* 595-4388.

RAMO, Simon, B.S., PH.D.; American engineering executive; b. 7 May 1913, Salt Lake City, Utah; s. of Benjamin and Clara (née Trestman) Ramo; m. Virginia May Smith 1937; two s.; ed. Univ. of Utah and Calif. Inst. of Tech.; with Gen. Electric Co., Schenectady 1936–46; Lecturer, Union Coll. 1941–46; Dir. Research Electronics Dept., Guided Missiles Research and Devt., Vice-Pres. and Dir. of Operations, Hughes Aircraft Co., Culver City 1946–53; Exec. Vice-Pres., Dir., Ramo-Wooldridge Corpn., L.A. 1953–58; Pres. Space Tech. Labs. Div. Ramo-Wooldridge Corpn. 1957–58; Scientific Dir. U.S.A.F. Ballistic Missiles Programme 1954–58; Dir. TRW Inc. 1954–, Exec. Vice-Pres. 1958–61, Vice-Chair. 1961–78, Chair. Exec. Cttee. 1969–78, Chair. Scientific and Tech. Cttee. 1978–, Chair. TRW-Fujitsu Co. 1980–; Research Assoc. Calif. Inst. of Tech. 1946, Visiting Prof. 1979–; Chair. Cen. for Study of American Experience, Univ. of Southern Calif. 1978–80; Faculty Fellow John F. Kennedy School of Govt., Harvard Univ. 1980–; mem. White House Energy Research and Devt. Advisory Council 1973–75; mem. U.S. State Dept. Cttee. on Science and Foreign Affairs 1973–75; Chair. President's Cttee. on Science and Tech. 1976–77; mem. Advisory Council to Sec. of Commerce 1976–77; Dir. Union Bancorp Inc., Union Bank, Atlantic Richfield Co., U.S. Chamber of Commerce; Trustee, Calif. Inst. of Tech., American Museum of Electricity; Consultant, President's Science Advisory Cttee.; Fellow, American Physical Soc., Inst. of Aeronautics and Astronautics, American Acad. of Arts and Sciences, American Asscn. for the Advancement of Science, American Astronautical Soc., Inst. for the Advancement of Eng., Inst. of Electrical and Electronic Engineers; Founder mem. Nat. Acad. of Eng.; mem. N.A.S. 1973–, Int. Acad. of Astronautics, American Philosophical Soc., Sr. Execs. Advisory Council, Nat. Industrial Conf. Board, Advisory Council on Japan/U.S. Econ. Relations, U.S. Chamber of Commerce Council on Trends and Perspective; Hon. D.Sc., D.Eng., LL.D.; Presidential Medal of Freedom 1983, and numerous other awards. *Publications:* Fields and Waves in Modern Radio (with J. R. Whinnery) 1944, 1953, Introduction to Microwaves 1945, Fields and Waves in Communication Electronics (with J. R. Whinnery and Theodore Van Duzer) 1965, Cure for Chaos 1969, Century of Mismatch 1970, Extraordinary Tennis for the Ordinary Player 1970, The Islands of E, Cono & My 1973, etc. *Leisure interests:* tennis, the violin. *Address:* TRW Inc., One Space Park, Redondo Beach, Calif. 90278, U.S.A. (Office).

RAMOS, Gen. Fidel; Phillippines army officer; b. 1928; s. of Narciso Ramos; m.; five d.; ed. Nat. Univ. Manila, U.S. Military Acad. West Point and Univ. of Illinois; active service in Korea and Vietnam; Deputy Chief of Staff 1981; Chief of Staff, Philippines Armed Forces Feb. 1986–; Minister of Defence Jan. 1988–; Legion of Honour 1987. *Address:* Ministry of Defence, Camp Aguinaldo, Quezon City, Manila, Philippines.

RAMPAL, Jean-Pierre Louis; French flautist; b. 7 Jan. 1922, Marseille; s. of Joseph and Andrée (née Roggero) Rampal; m. Françoise-Anne Bacque-yrisse 1947; one s. one d.; ed. Univ. de Marseille; world-wide tours 1945–; participant in major festivals in Rio de Janeiro, Aix, Menton, Salzburg, Edinburgh, Prague, Athens, Zagreb, Granada, Tokyo, etc.; Ed. for Ancient and Classical Music, Int. Music Co., New York City 1958–; Prof. Conservatoire Nat. de Musique de Paris; mem. French Musicological Soc.; Pres. Assen. Musique et Musiciens 1974–; Officier, Légion d'honneur; Officier de l'Ordre des Arts et Lettres de France; Grand Prix du Disque 1954, 1956, 1959, 1960, 1961, 1963, 1964, 1978; Oscar du Premier Virtuose Français 1956, Prix Edison 1969, Léonie Sonning Danish Music Prize 1978, Prix d'honneur du Prix Mondial du Disque de Montreux 1980. *Publication:* La Flute 1978. *Leisure interests:* tennis, deep-sea diving, movie-making. *Address:* 15 avenue Mozart, 75016 Paris, France. *Telephone:* 524-39-74.

RAMPHAL, Sir Shridath Surendranath, Kt., O.E., A.C., C.M.G., Q.C., S.C., LL.M., C.B.I.M., F.R.S.A.; Guyanese barrister, politician and international official; b. 3 Oct. 1928, New Amsterdam; s. of James I. Ramphal and Grace Ramphal (née Abdool); m. Lois Winifred King 1951; two s. two d.; ed. Queen's Coll., Georgetown, King's Coll., London, Harvard Law School; Crown Counsel, British Guiana 1953–54; Asst. to Attorney-Gen. 1954–56; Legal Draftsman 1956–58; Solicitor-Gen. 1959–61; Legal Draftsman, West Indies 1958–59; Asst. Attorney-Gen., West Indies 1961–62; Attorney-Gen., Guyana 1965–73; mem. Nat. Assembly 1965–75; Minister of State for External Affairs 1967–72, Minister of Foreign Affairs 1972–75, of Justice 1973–75; Commonwealth Sec.-Gen. 1975–(90); Chancellor Univ. of Guyana Dec. 1988–, Univ. of Warwick July 1989–; Queen's Counsel 1965 and Senior Counsel, Guyana 1966; mem. Council for Legal Educ., Univ., of the West Indies, Hon. Advisory Cttee. Centre for Int. Studies, New York Univ., Int. Comm. of Jurists, Bd. of Vienna Inst. of Devt., Int. Hon. Cttee. Dag Hammarskjold Foundation, Governing Body, Inst. of Devt. Studies, Sussex Univ., Ind. Comm. on Int. Devt. Issues, Ind. Comm. on Disarmament and Security Issues, Ind. Comm. on Int. Humanitarian Issues, World Comm. on Environment and Devt., South Comm., Bd. of Govs. World Maritime Univ., Int. Advisory Council of Television Trust for the Environment, Int. Bd. of United World Colls., Exec. Cttee. of Int. Inst. for Environment and Devt.; Patron One World Broadcasting Trust; Chair. Selection Cttee. of Third World Prize; Vice-Chair. Centre for Research on New Int. Econ. Order, Oxford; Vice-Pres. Royal Over-seas League; Hon. LL.D. (Panjab Univ.) 1975, (Southampton) 1976, (Univ. of the West Indies) 1978, (St. Francis Xavier Univ., Halifax, Canada) 1978, (Aberdeen) 1979, (Cape Coast, Ghana) 1980, (London) 1981, (Benin, Nigeria) 1982, (Hull) 1983, (Yale) 1985, (Cambridge) 1985, (Warwick) 1988, (York Univ., Ont., Canada) 1988; Hon. D.H.L. (Simmons Coll., Boston) 1982, Hon. D.C.L. (Oxon.) 1982, (East Anglia) 1983, (Durham) 1985, Hon. Dr. (Surrey) 1979, (Essex) 1980, Hon. D.Hum.Litt. (Duke Univ., U.S.A.) 1985, Hon. D.Litt. (Bradford) 1985, (Indira Gandhi Nat. Open Univ.) 1989, Hon. D. Sc. (Cranfield Inst. of Tech.) 1987; Arden and Atkin Prize, Gray's Inn 1952, Int. Educ. Award (Richmond Coll., London) 1988, R.S.A. Albert Medal 1988; John Simon Guggenheim Fellowship 1962; Hon. Bencher of Gray's Inn 1981; Fellow, King's Coll., London 1975, L.S.E. 1979, R.S.A. 1981, Magdalen Coll., Oxford 1982; Order of the Repub. (Egypt) 1973; Grand Cross, Order of the Sun (Peru) 1974; Grand Cross, Order of Merit (Ecuador) 1974. *Publications:* One World to Share: Selected Speeches of the Commonwealth Secretary-General 1975–79, Nkrumah and the Eighties (1980 Kwame Nkrumah Memorial Lectures), Sovereignty or Solidarity (1981 Callander Memorial Lectures), Some Light and Some in Darkness: The Long Shadow of Slavery (Wilberforce Lecture) 1983, The Message not the Messenger (STC Communication Lecture) 1985, The Trampling of the Grass (Econ. Comm. for Africa Silver Jubilee Lecture) 1985, For the South, a Time to Think 1986, Making Human Society a Civilised State (Corbishley Memorial Lecture) 1987, Inseparable Humanity: An Anthology of Reflections of Shridath Ramphal 1988, and contributions in journals of legal, political and international affairs, including International and Comparative Law Quarterly, Caribbean Quarterly, Public Law, Guyana Journal, The Round Table, Royal Society of Arts Journal, Foreign Policy, Third World Quarterly, International Affairs. *Leisure interests:* photography, cooking. *Address:* Commonwealth Secretariat, Marlborough House, Pall Mall, London, SW1Y 5HX, England. *Telephone:* 01-839 3411.

RAMPHUL, Indurduth; Mauritian banker; b. 10 Oct. 1931, Montagne Blanche; m. Taramatee Seedoyal 1962; one s. one d.; ed. Univ. of Exeter, England; Asst. Sec., Ministry of Finance 1966–67; Man., Bank of Mauritius 1967–70, Chief. Man. 1970–73, Man. Dir. 1973–82, Gov. 1982–. *Address:* Bank of Mauritius, P.O.B. 29, Sir William Newton Street, Port Louis; 9 Buswell Avenue, Quatre Bornes, Mauritius.

RAMPHUL, Radha Krishna; Mauritian diplomatist; b. 4 Jan. 1926, Curepipe; s. of Pundit Sookdev Ramphul and Rhikya Ramvarain; m. Leela Devi Lallah 1950; one s. one d.; ed. L.S.E., and Lincoln's Inn, London; Co. Sec. and Man. Sugar Estates 1946–50; helped organize Field Workers' Trade Union 1945–50; Dir. private firm in London 1955–69; Perm. Rep. to UN 1969–82; Rep. UN Comm. on Human Rights 1971–73, Preparatory Cttee. of Human Environment 1971, First and Second UN Decade, various confs. and all UN confs. on Laws of the Sea, Review Conf. Nuclear Weapons Non-Proliferation Treaty (Geneva, May 1975); Chair. African Group 1970–73, 1976–80; Vice-Pres. Gen. Ass., 25th session 1970, 35th session 1980–81; Vice-Chair. Law of the Sea Cttee.; Vice-Chair. Political and Security Cttee., 26th session 1971, Chair. 27th session 1972; Chair. of UN Comm. on Human Rights, 29th session 1973; Vice-Chair. Review Conf. Nuclear Weapons Non-Proliferation Treaty 1975; Rep. of Chair. Org. of African Unity at UN 1976–77; Chief Rep. of Mauritius to UN Security Council 1977–78 (Pres. Dec. 1977); mem. Indian Cultural Asscn., Int. Cultural Exchange, World Asscn. of World Federalists, Nat. Trust of U.K., Smithsonian Inst., U.S., World Wild Life Soc., Advisory Bd. of Eminent Persons on Disarmament Studies; Officier de l'Ordre du Mérite Centrafricain, Officier de l'Ordre national du Lion (Senegal). *Leisure interests:* chess, golf, riding, shooting, fishing, tennis, antique furniture, reading, swimming, paintings. *Address:* Port Louis, Mauritius.

RAMPLING, Charlotte; British actress; b. 1946, London; m. 2nd Jean-Michel Jarre (q.v.); two s.; film debut 1963. *Films include:* The Knack 1963, Rotten to the Core, Georgy Girl, The Long Duel, Kidnapping, Three, The Damned 1969, Skibum, Corky 1970, 'Tis Pity She's a Whore, Henry VIII and His Six Wives 1971, Asylum 1972, The Night Porter, Giordano Bruno, Zardoz, Caravan to Vaccares 1973, The Flesh of the Orchid, Yuppi Du 1974–75, My Lovely, Foxtrot 1975, Sherlock Holmes in New York, Orca—The Killer Whale, The Purple Taxi 1976, Stardust Memories 1980, The Verdict 1983, Viva la vie 1983, Beauty and Sadness 1984, He Died with his Eyes Open 1985, Max mon Amour, Max my Love 1985, Angel Heart 1987, Paris by Night 1988, Dead on Arrival 1989; numerous TV plays. *Address:* c/o Olga Horstig Primuz, 78 Champs Elysées, Paris 75008, France.

RAMSAY, Donald Allan, M.A., PH.D., F.R.S., F.R.S.C., F.A.P.S., F.C.I.C.; Canadian research scientist; b. 11 July 1922, London, U.K.; s. of Norman and (Thirza) Elizabeth (Beckley) Ramsay; m. Nancy Brayshaw 1946; four d.; ed. Latymer Upper School, London and St. Catharine's Coll., Cambridge; Jr. Research Officer, Nat. Research Council 1947–49, Asst. Research Officer 1949–54, Assoc. Research Officer 1954–61, Sr. Research Officer 1961–68, Prin. Research Officer 1968–87; mem. Canadian Asscn. of Physicists, Chem. Inst. of Canada; Queen Elizabeth II Silver Jubilee Medal 1977, Royal Soc. of Canada Centennial Medal 1982; Dr. h.c. (Reims) 1969, (Stockholm) 1982. *Publications:* numerous articles on molecular spectroscopy and structure. *Leisure interests:* organ-playing, sailing, fishing. *Address:* 100 Sussex Drive, Ottawa, Ont., K1A OR6, Canada (Office).

RAMSBOTHAM, Hon. Sir Peter (Edward), G.C.M.G., G.C.V.O.; British diplomatist and administrator; b. 8 Oct. 1919, London; s. of 1st Viscount Soulbury; m. 1st Frances Blomfield 1941 (died 1982); two s. one d.; m. 2nd Zaida Hall 1985; ed. Eton Coll. and Magdalen Coll., Oxford; entered diplomatic service 1948; served in Political Div., Allied Control Comm., Berlin 1948–50; First Sec., Foreign Office 1950–53; mem. U.K. del. to UN, New York 1953–57; Foreign Office 1957–63; Head of Chancery, British Embassy, Paris 1963–67; Foreign Office 1967–69; High Commr. to Cyprus 1969–71; Amb. to Iran 1971–74, to U.S.A. 1974–77; Gov. and C.-in-C. of Bermuda 1977–80; Dir. Commercial Union Assurance Co. 1980–, and Lloyds Bank Ltd. 1980–, Chair. Lloyds Bank Southern Region 1984–; Chair. Ryder-Cheshire Mission for the Relief of Suffering 1981–; Hon. LL.D. (Akron Univ.) 1975, (William and Mary Coll.) 1975, (Maryland Univ.) 1976, (Yale Univ.) 1977; Croix de guerre 1945, K.St.J. 1976. *Leisure interests:* gardening, fishing. *Address:* East Lane, Ovington, Alresford, Hants, England (Home). *Telephone:* (096 273) 2515.

RAMSEY, Norman Foster, M.A., PH.D., D.SC.; American scientist; b. 27 Aug. 1915, Washington, D.C.; s. of Brigadier-Gen. and Mrs. Norman F. Ramsey; m. 1st Elinor Stedman Jameson 1940 (died 1983); four d.; m. 2nd Ellie Welch 1985; ed. Columbia, Harvard and Cambridge Univs.; Assoc. Univ. of Illinois 1940–42; Asst. Prof. Columbia Univ. 1942–46; Research Assoc. M.I.T. Radiation Lab. 1940–43; Expert Consultant to Sec. of War 1942–45; Group Leader and Asscn. Division Head, Los Alamos Lab. of Atomic Energy Project 1943–45; Chief Scientist of Atomic Energy Lab., Tinian 1945; Assoc. Prof. Columbia Univ. 1945–47; Head Physics Dept., Brookhaven Nat. Lab. 1946–47; Assoc. Prof. Harvard Univ. 1947–50; Dir. Harvard Nuclear Lab. 1948–50 and 1952–53; Air Force Scientific Advisory Cttee. 1947–55; Dept. Defence Panel on Atomic Energy 1953–58; Prof. of Physics, Harvard Univ. 1950–, Sr. Fellow, Harvard Soc. Fellows 1970–; Higgins Prof. of Physics, Harvard Univ. 1966–; Scientific Adviser NATO 1958–59; Gen. Advisory Cttee., Atomic Energy Comm. 1960–72; Dir. Varian Associates 1963–66; Pres. Univs. Research Asscn. 1966–81; Eastman Prof.,

Oxford Univ. 1973–74; Luce Prof. of Cosmology, Mount Holyoke Coll. 1982–83, Prof. of Physics, Univ. of Va. 1983–84; Vice-Pres. American Physical Soc. 1977 (Pres. 1978); Chair. Physics Div. American Asscn. for Advancement of Science 1977; mem. N.A.S., American Acad. of Arts and Sciences, American Philosophical Soc.; Visiting Cttee. Nat. Bureau of Standards 1982–; Trustee, Carnegie Endowment for Int. Peace 1962– and the Rockefeller Univ. 1976–; Chair. Bd. of Govs., American Inst. of Physics 1980–86; Hon. D.Sc. (Case Western Reserve Univ.) 1968, (Middlebury Coll.) 1969, (Oxford Univ.) 1973, (Rockefeller Univ.) 1986; Presidential Order of Merit, Lawrence Award 1960, Davisson-Germer prize 1974, Award for Excellence in Science (Colombia Univ.) 1980, Medal of Honor of I.E.E. 1984, Monie Ferst Prize 1985, Rabi Prize 1985, Karl Compton Award 1986, Rumford Premium 1985, Oersted Medal 1988, Nat. Medal of Science 1988. *Publications:* Nuclear Moments 1953, Nuclear Two-Body Problems 1953, Molecular Beans 1955, 1985, Quick Calculus 1965, 1985; and numerous articles in the Physical Review. *Leisure interests:* skiing, walking, sailing, swimming, tennis, reading, conversation, music. *Address:* Lyman Physics Laboratory, Harvard University, Cambridge, Mass. 02178; 21 Monmouth Court, Brookline, Mass. 02146, U.S.A. *Telephone:* (617) 495-2864.

RANA, Damodar Shumshere Jung Bahadur, B.A.; Nepalese social worker and politician; b. July 1928, Palpa Tansen; s. of Lieut.-Gen. Madhab Shumshere J. B. Rana and Madhubi Kumari Rana; m. Bina Rana 1956; three s. one d.; ed. Missionary School, Darjeeling, Central Hindu School, Banaras and Banaras Hindu Univ.; Exec. mem. social orgs. in Nepal 1954–60; Chief Admin. Morang District 1961; Chair. Special Comm. Kosi Zone 1961, Commr. 1962–64; mem. Nat. Panchayat, mem. Exec. Cttee. and Foreign Affairs Cttee.; Amb. to the U.S.S.R. 1964–70, concurrently to Poland, Hungary and Czechoslovakia; Zonal Commr., Janakpur Zone 1970–71; Minister for Land Reform, Law and Justice 1978–79; Minister of State for Defence 1979; awarded Prabala Gorkha Dakchina Bahu and Subikhyat Trisakti Patt. *Address:* Phohara Durbar, Kathmandu, Nepal. *Telephone:* 11274.

RANA, Jai Pratap, M.SC.; Nepalese diplomatist; b. 6 June 1937, Tansen; m.; three c.; ed. London Univ. and the Fletcher School of Law and Diplomacy, U.S.A.; joined Ministry of Foreign Affairs 1961, Under-Sec. 1966, Jt. Sec. 1980–85; Second Sec., Embassy, London 1962–64, First Sec., Embassy, Washington 1966–68, First Sec., Nepal's Mission to the UN 1968–71; Counsellor and Deputy Chief of Mission in India 1975–80; Perm. Rep. to the UN 1985–. *Address:* Permanent Mission of the Kingdom of Nepal to the United Nations, 820 Second Avenue, Suite 1200, New York, N.Y. 10017, U.S.A. *Telephone:* 370-4188, 4189.

RANCE, Gerald Francis, O.B.E.; British diplomatist (retd.); b. 20 Feb. 1927, London; s. of Cecil Henry and Jane Carmel (née Beggs) Rance; m. Isabella Dorothy Keegan 1949; one d.; ed. Brompton Oratory; with Foreign Office 1943–45, worked in British Embassies in Belgrade, Rome, Bucharest 1951–57, British Consulates Gen., Istanbul, Munich 1957–63, with British Embassy in Kabul 1964–68, British Consulates Gen., New York, Dallas 1969–73, First Sec., FCO 1973–77, with British High Comms. Mbabane 1977–79, Nicosia 1980–83; High Commr. in Tonga 1984–87; with RCMP British Army 1945–48. *Leisure interests:* golf, tennis. *Address:* 1 Bruton Close, Chislehurst, Kent, England. *Telephone:* 01-467 3069.

RANCHOD, Bhadra, B.A., LL.B., LL.M., LL.D.; South African lawyer and diplomatist; b. 11 May 1944, Port Elizabeth; s. of Ghalloo Ranchod and Parvaty Ranchod; m. Viba M. Desai 1980; two d.; ed. Univs. of Cape Town, Oslo and Leiden; Sr. Lecturer, Dept. of Private Law, Univ. of Durban-Westville 1972, Prof. of Private Law 1974–, Dean, Faculty of Law 1976–79; Advocate of Supreme Court 1973–; mem. Bd. of Govs. S. African Broadcasting Corpn.; mem. S. African Law Comm.; mem. Human Sciences Research Council, numerous cttees. and public bodies etc.; Visiting Scholar, Columbia Univ., New York 1980–81; Amb. and Head of S. African Mission to European Communities 1986–. *Publications:* Foundations of the South African Law of Defamation (thesis) 1972, Law and Justice in South Africa 1986; about 50 papers on human rights issues. *Leisure interests:* jogging, reading, travel. *Address:* South African Mission to the European Communities, Mercator 6th Floor, rue de la Loi 26, 1040 Brussels (Office); 17 chemin du Putdael, St. Pierre-Woluwe, Brussels, Belgium (Home). *Telephone:* 231.17.25 (Office); 672.11.50 (Home).

RANDALL, Michael Bennett; British freelance journalist; b. 12 Aug. 1919; ed. St. Peter's School, Seaford, and Canford School; Asst. Ed., Sunday Chronicle 1952–53; Ed. Sunday Graphic 1953; Asst. Ed. Daily Mirror 1953–56; Asst. Ed. News Chronicle 1956–57; Asst. Ed. Daily Mail 1957–61, Deputy Ed. 1961–63, Ed. 1963–66; Man. Ed. (News) Sunday Times 1967–72, Senior Man. Ed. 1972–78; Hannen Swaffer Award as Journalist of 1965–66. *Publication:* The Funny Side of the Street 1988. *Address:* Flat One, 39 St. Anne's Crescent, Lewes, East Sussex, BN7 1SB, England.

RANDÉ, Dr Jenő, LL.D.; Hungarian journalist and diplomatist; b. 28 Aug. 1922, Rákospalota; s. of Jenő Szabó and Klára Nemes; m. Ilona Hajós; one s. two d.; ed. Budapest Univ.; Commentator Hungarian Radio 1945–60; Corresp. in New York 1957–60, London 1960–63; Political Ed.-in-Chief, Hungarian TV 1963–67; Dir. Press Dept., Hungarian Foreign Ministry 1968–70, 1974–78; Amb. to Egypt 1970–74, to Austria 1978–85; Sec.-Gen. World Fed. of Hungarians 1985–; Rózsa Ferenc Prize; Medal for Socialist

Work, Order White Rose (Finland), Commdr. Order Taj (Iran), Order of Repub. (Egypt); Grosses Silbernes Ehrenzeichen (Austria). *Publications:* New Yorkból jelentem (Reports from New York) 1958, Sputnik over New York 1960, A világ végétől a szent öbölig (From Land's End to Holy Loch) 1965, 1966, Fultontól Brüsszelig (From Fulton to Brussels) 1967, Tavasz Sziberiában (Spring in Siberia) with G. Baróti, A gépek forradalma (Revolution of the Machines) 1968. *Leisure interest:* angling. *Address:* World Federation of Hungarians, 1905 Budapest, Benczur utca 15, Hungary. *Telephone:* 225-405.

RANDLE, Sir Philip John, Kt., M.A., PH.D., M.D., F.R.C.P., F.R.S.; British biochemist and medical practitioner; b. 16 July 1926, Nuneaton; s. of Alfred J. and Nora A. Randle; m. Elizabeth A. Harrison 1952; one s. (deceased) three d.; ed. Sidney Sussex Coll., Cambridge and Univ. Coll. Hosp. Medical School, London; house physician and house surgeon, Univ. Coll. Hosp. 1951; MRC Research worker, Dept. of Biochem., Univ. of Cambridge 1952–55; Research Fellow, Sidney Sussex Coll. 1954–57; Lecturer in Biochem. Univ. of Cambridge 1955–64; Fellow and Dir. of Medical Studies, Trinity Hall, Cambridge 1957–64; Prof. and Head of Dept. of Biochem., Univ. of Bristol 1964–75; Prof. of Clinical Biochem. Univ. of Oxford and Fellow, Hertford Coll., Oxford 1975–; Minkowski Prize 1966, Ciba Medal 1984. *Publications:* numerous articles in scientific and medical journals. *Leisure interests:* travel, wherever and whenever possible. *Address:* Department of Clinical Biochemistry, John Radcliffe Hospital, Oxford, OX3 9DU, England. *Telephone:* (0865) 773115.

RANDOLPH, Denys, B.SC., C.ENG., C.B.I.M., F.R.S.A., M.R.AE.S., F.I.PROD.E., F.INST.D.; British company executive; b. 6 Feb. 1926, Ealing, London; s. of late Harry Beckham Randolph and Margaret Randolph; m. Marjorie Hales 1951; two d.; ed. Saint Paul's School, Hammersmith, Queen's Univ., Belfast; mil. service, Royal Engineers 1944–48; postgraduate apprenticeship 1952–54; Exec. Dir. Graviner Ltd. 1964–65, Wilkinson Sword (Int.) Ltd. 1965–66; Man. Dir. Hand Tools Div., Wilkinson Sword Ltd. 1966–69, Group Man. Dir. 1970–71, Chair. and Man. Dir. 1971–72, Chair. Wilkinson Sword Ltd. 1972–80, Pres. and Special Consultant 1980–; Chair. Graviner Ltd. 1969–79; Exec. Deputy Chair. British Match Corpn. (now Wilkinson Match Ltd.) 1973–75, Chair. Wilkinson Match Ltd. 1976–79; Dir. Duport Ltd. 1975–81; Chair. Inst. of Dirs. 1976–79, Vice-Pres. 1979–; Chair. Pains Fireworks Ltd. 1980–84, Woodrush Investments Ltd., Haddon Rockers Ltd. 1980–87; P.L.C. Peters Ltd. 1981–84, Peters Jackson Ltd. 1981–84; Gov. Admin. Staff Coll., Henley; Past Master, Worshipful Co. of Scientific Instrument Makers; Past Master, Worshipful Co. of Cutlers; mem. Royal Aeronautical Soc.; Fellow, Inst. of Production Eng., Royal Horticultural Soc. *Publication:* From Rapiers to Razor Blades: the Development of the Light Metals Industry. *Leisure interests:* yachting, golf, viticulture. *Address:* The Cottages, Rush Court, Wallingford, OX10 8LJ, England. *Telephone:* (0491) 36586.

RANDOLPH, Jennings, A.B.; American educator, executive and politician; b. 8 March 1902, Salem, W. Va.; s. of Ernest and Idell (née Bingman) Randolph; m. Mary Katherine Babb 1933; two s.; ed. Salem Coll.; Assoc. Ed. West Virginia Review 1925; Dir. Dept. of Public Speaking and Journalism, Dir. Athletics, Davis and Elkins Coll. 1926–32; Prof. of Public Speaking and Dean, Coll.of Business and Finance Admin., Southeastern Univ. 1936; mem. U.S. House of Reps. 1933–47; Asst. to Pres. and Dir. of Public Relations, Capital Airlines; Dean Coll. of Business and Financial Admin., Southeastern Univ.; U.S. Senator from W. Virginia 1958–84; mem. numerous Dels. including British-American Parl. Conf., Bermuda 1977, Agri-Energy Roundtable, Geneva 1981–84; several honorary degrees; numerous awards; Democrat. *Leisure interest:* sports. *Address:* 1730 Main Street, N.W., Suite 515, Washington, D.C. 20036, U.S.A.

RANGOONWALA, Mohamed Aly; Pakistani business executive; b. 20 May 1924, Rangoon, Burma; s. of V. M. Gany; m. Banu 1952; five s. one d.; joined father's business aged 12; began own business, Bombay 1940; moved to Pakistan 1948; became founder Chair. and Dir. several commercial, financial and business orgs.; served on Govt. bodies; extended business operations abroad (Asia, Europe, N. America) 1970; fmr. Chair. Nat. Bank of Pakistan, Fed. of Pakistan Chambers of Commerce and Industry; Pres. Pakistan Nat. Cttee., ICC 1976–; Pres. ICC 1981, mem. Presidency 1981–; Chair. World Memon Foundation, Z. V. M. Rangoonwala Trust; Star of Service (Pakistan); Grosse Verdienstkreuz (Fed. Repub. of Germany). *Address:* V. M. House, West Wharf, Karachi, Pakistan; c/o 123 George Street, London, W1H 5TB, England. *Telephone:* 201165 or 201660 (Karachi); 01-493 3266 or 493 3013 (London).

RANK, Sir Benjamin Keith, Kt., C.M.G., M.B., M.S., L.R.C.P., F.R.C.S., F.R.A.C.S., F.A.C.S.; Australian surgeon; b. 14 Jan. 1911, Heidelberg, Victoria; s. of Wreghitt Rank and Bessie Rank (née Smith); m. Barbara Lyle Facy 1938; one s. three d.; ed. Melbourne Univ.; war service 1939–46 (Lieut.-Col.); Hon. Plastic Surgeon, Royal Melbourne Hosp. 1946–66, Consulting Surgeon 1966–85, Chair. Bd. of Postgraduate Educ. 1968–75, mem. Bd. of Man. 1976–82, Medical Adviser to Bd. of Man. 1971–75; Consulting Plastic Surgeon to Dept. of Repatriation, also to Queen Victoria Hosp. and Royal Victorian Eye and Ear Hosp.; Chief Reparative Surgeon, Peter MacCallum Clinic 1964–79; Chair. Cttee. of Man., Victorian Plastic Surgery Unit, Preston and Northcote Community Hosp. 1966–86; Visiting Prof. Harvard

Univ. 1976; Pres. British Asscn. of Plastic Surgeons 1965; Pres. Royal Australasian Coll. of Surgeons 1966-68, Syme Orator 1976, Stawell Orator 1977; Pres. St. John's Ambulance Council, Victoria 1983-, Chair. 1978-83, mem. Motor Accident Bd., Victoria 1972-82; Foundation Chair. Australian Coll. of Speech Therapy, Hon. Fellow 1965; Hon. Fellow, Royal Coll. of Surgeons of Canada 1969, of Edinburgh 1973; Hon. D.Sc. (Punjabi Univ.) 1970; K.St.J. 1989. *Publications:* Surgery of Repair as Applied to Hand Injuries (co-author) 1963, Jerry Moore and Some of His Contemporaries 1975, Heads and Hands: an Era of Plastic Surgery 1987; more than 60 papers in British, American and Australian journals. *Leisure interests:* golf, gardening, painting. *Address:* 12 Jerula Avenue, Mount Eliza, Vic. 3930, Australia (Home).

RANK, Joseph McArthur; British business executive; b. 24 April 1918, Kingswood, Surrey; s. of the late Rowland Rank and of Margaret (née McArthur); m. The Hon. Moira, d. 3rd Baron Southborough; one s. one d.; ed. Loretto School; joined Mark Mayhew Ltd., Flour Millers 1936; Royal Air Force 1940-46; Joint Man. Dir. Joseph Rank Ltd. 1955-65; Deputy Chair. and Chief Exec. Ranks Hovis McDougall Ltd. 1965-69, Chair. 1969-81, Pres. 1981-88, Hon. Pres. April 1988-; Chair. British Nutrition Foundation Ltd. 1968-69; Chair. Millers Mutual Assen. 1969-; Dir. Royal Alexandra and Albert School 1952-, Chair. Governing Body 1975-84; Pres. Nat. Assen. of British and Irish Millers 1957-58, 1978; First High Sheriff of East Sussex 1974-75; Hon. F.R.C.P. 1978. *Address:* Landhurst, Hartfield, Sussex, England. *Telephone:* (089 277) 293.

RÁNKI, Dezsö; Hungarian pianist; b. 8 Sept. 1951, Budapest; s. of József Ránki and Edith Jecsmen; m. Edit Klukon 1979; ed. Ferenc Liszt Music Acad., Budapest (under Pál Kadosa); has given recitals and appeared with several leading orchestras throughout Europe; with Zoltán Kocsis (q.v.) toured U.S.A. with Budapest Symphony Orchestra under György Lehel 1971; Solo tour Philippines, Singapore, India 1975, Japan 1975, 1977, 1979, Spain, France, Britain (Queen Elizabeth Hall, London) 1978; has taught piano at Budapest Music Acad. since 1973; First Prize, Int. Schumann Competition, Zwickau, G.D.R. 1969, Grand Prix Int. du Disque (Paris) 1972, Liszt Prize 2nd Degree 1973, Kossuth Prize 1978. *Leisure interests:* gramophone records, sound tapes, Italian and Chinese food. *Address:* H-1073, Budapest VII, Kertész-utca 50; Interconcert Agency, Budapest V, Vörösmarty tér 1, Hungary. *Telephone:* 277-046 (Home); 184-664 (Agency).

RANKIN, Alick Michael, C.B.E.; British company director; b. 23 Jan. 1935, London; s. of Col. Niall Rankin and Lady Jean Rankin; m. 2nd Suzetta Nelson 1976; one s. three d.; ed. Eton Coll. and Oxford Univ.; Scots Guards 1953-55; worked in investment banking, Toronto, Canada 1956-59; with Scottish & Newcastle Breweries PLC 1960-, Chief Exec. 1983-, Deputy Chair. 1988-; Dir. (non-exec.) Christian Salvesen 1986-. *Leisure interests:* shooting, fishing, golf, tennis. *Address:* 3 Saxe-Coburg Place, Edinburgh, EH3 5BR, Scotland; 49 Pont Street, London, SW1X 0BD, England. *Telephone:* 031-332 3684; 01-581 1086.

RANNEY, Helen M., M.D.; American physician; b. 12 April 1920, Summer Hill, New York; d. of Alesia (Toolan) Ranney and Arthur C. Ranney; ed. Barnard Coll. and Coll. of Physicians and Surgeons, Columbia Univ.; Asst. Prof. of Clinical Medicine, Columbia Univ. 1958-60; Assoc. Prof. of Medicine, Albert Einstein Coll. of Medicine 1960-65, Prof. 1965-70; Prof. of Medicine, State Univ. of New York, Buffalo 1970-73; Prof. of Medicine, Dept. of Medicine, Univ. of Calif., San Diego 1973-, Chair. 1973-86; Distinguished Physician, Veterans Admin. Medical Center, San Diego 1986-; mem. N.A.S., Assen. of American Physicians, American Acad. of Arts and Sciences, American Soc. for Clinical Investigation. *Publications:* papers in medical journals concerned with haemoglobin. *Address:* Veterans Administration Medical Center (11F), 3350 La Jolla Village Drive, San Diego, Calif. 92161 (Office); 6229 La Jolla Mesa Drive, La Jolla, Calif. 92037, U.S.A. *Telephone:* (619) 453-7500 Ext. 3397.

RANTANEN, Jarmo Heikki Kullervo; Finnish politician; b. 20 June 1944, Orivesi; m. Marja-Liisa Palonen 1962; Asst. Sales Man. Kesoil Oy 1966-74; Real Estate Man. Tampere HAKA 1974-77; Man. Dir Pirkanmaa HAKA 1978-84; Regional Dir. STS Bank (Finnish Workers' Savings Bank) 1985; Mayor of Tampere 1985-; mem. Social Democratic Party (SPD) Cttee. 1984-; Minister of the Interior 1987-. *Address:* Ministry of the Interior, Kirkkokatu 12, 00170 Helsinki, Finland. *Telephone:* (90) 1601.

RANU, Harcharan Singh, C.ENG., PH.D., F.I.MECH.E.; Indian biomedical engineer; ed. Leicester Polytechnic, Univ. of Surrey, Middx. Hosp. Medical School and Polytechnic of Cen. London, M.I.T.; Asst. Engineer Coventry Gauge and Tool Co. 1964-65; Asst. to Chief Engineer Fabricom 1965-66; Research Scientist Nat. Inst. for Medical Research, London 1967-70; Research Fellow and lecturer Polytechnic of Cen. London 1967-76; Research Engineer Rubber and Plastics Research Assen. of Great Britain 1977; Asst. Prof. Wayne State Univ., Detroit 1977; Prof. of Biomedical Eng., La. Tech. Univ. 1982-; Consultant to Lincoln Gen. Hosp.; mem. A.S.M.E. 1978-, American Soc. of Biomechanics 1979-; Edwin Tate Award 1967, James Clayton Award (IME) 1974, 1975, 1976, Pres.'s Prize 1984. *Publications:* 95 papers, proceedings and chapters in professional journals, etc. *Address:* College of Engineering, Louisiana Technical University, P.O. Box 8502, Ruston, La. 71272, U.S.A.

RAO, Calyampudi Radhakrishna, M.A., SC.D., F.N.A., F.R.S.; Indian statistician; b. 10 Sept. 1920, Hadagali, Mysore State; s. of C. D. Naidu and A. Laxmikanthamma; m. Bhargavi Rao 1948; one s. one d.; ed. Andhra and Calcutta Univs.; Research at Indian Statistical Inst. 1943-46, Cambridge Univ. 1946-48; Prof. and Head of Div. of Theoretical Research and Training 1949-64; Dir. Research and Training School, Indian Statistical Inst. 1964-71, Sec. and Dir. 1972-76, Jawaharlal Nehru Prof. 1976-84; Univ. Prof., Univ. of Pittsburgh 1979-; Nat. Prof., India 1987-; Fellow, Inst. of Mathematical Statistics, U.S.A., Pres.-elect 1975-76, Pres. 1976-77; Treas. Int. Statistical Inst. 1961-65, Pres.-elect 1975-77, Pres. 1977-79; Pres. Int. Biometric Soc. 1973-75; Pres. Forum for Interdisciplinary Math.; Hon. Fellow, Royal Statistical Soc.; Fellow, American Statistical Assen., Econometric Soc., Third World Acad. of Sciences; Hon. Prof. Univ. of San Marcos, Lima; Hon. mem. Int. Statistical Inst.; Hon. Foreign mem. American Acad. Arts and Sciences 1975-; Hon. Fellow, King's Coll., Cambridge Univ.; Hon. Life mem. Biometric Soc.; Ed. Sankhya (Indian Journal of Statistics); Hon. D.Sc. (Andhra, Athens, Delhi, Leningrad, Philippines, Ohio State, Osmania and Tampere Univs.); Hon. D.Litt. (Delhi); Bhatnagar Memorial Award for Scientific Research; Padma Bhushan; Guy Silver Medal Royal Statistical Soc.; Meghnad Saha Gold Medal, Nat. Science Acad.; J. C. Bose Gold Medal. *Publications include:* Advanced Statistical Methods in Biometric Research, Linear Statistical Inference and its Application, Generalized Inverse of Matrices and its Applications, Characterization Problems of Mathematical Statistics; over 250 research papers in mathematical statistics. *Leisure interest:* writing humorous essays. *Address:* Department of Mathematics and Statistics, University of Pittsburgh, Pa. 15260, U.S.A.

RAO, Chandra Rajeswar; Indian politician; b. 6 June 1914; ed. Hindu High School, Masulipatam, and Banaras Hindu Univ.; at Vizagapatam Medical Coll. 1936-37; joined Communist Party, Andhra 1936; mem. Central Cttee. Communist Party of India 1948, Gen. Sec. 1950-51, 1964-; Order of Lenin 1974, Order of Friendship Among Peoples (U.S.S.R.), Georgi Dimitrov Order (Bulgaria), Star of People's Friendship (G.D.R.), Friendship Among Peoples Order (Czechoslovakia), Order of Sukhe Bator (Mongolia). *Address:* Communist Party of India, Ajoy Bhavan, Kotla Marg, New Delhi 110002, India. *Telephone:* New Delhi 3315546/3314058.

RAO, Chintamani Nagesa Ramachandra, M.SC., D.SC., PH.D., F.R.S.C., F.N.A., F.R.S.; Indian professor of chemistry; b. 30 June 1934, Bangalore; s. of H. Nagesa Rao; m. Indumati Rao 1960; one s. one d.; ed. Mysore, Banaras and Purdue Univs.; Lecturer, Indian Inst. of Science, Bangalore 1959-63; Prof. later Sr. Prof., Indian Inst. of Tech., Kanpur 1963-77, Dean of Research and Devt. 1969-72; Chair. Solid State and Structural Chem. Unit and Materials Research Lab., Indian Inst. of Science 1977-84, Dir. of Inst. 1984-; Visiting Prof. Purdue Univ., U.S.A. 1967-68, Oxford Univ. 1974-75; Fellow King's Coll. Cambridge Univ. 1983-84; Past Pres. IUPAC; Chair. Science Advisory Council to Prime Minister of India, Editorial Boards of eight int. journals; Foreign mem. Serbian and Slovenian Acads. of Science, Yugoslavia; Founding mem. Third World Acad. of Sciences; Vice-Pres., Indian Acad. of Sciences, Pres. Indian Nat. Science Acad., St. Catherine's Coll., Oxford 1974-75; American Chem. Soc. Centennial Foreign Fellow 1976; Jawaharlal Nehru Fellow, Indian Inst. of Tech.; Nehru Visiting Prof., Cambridge Univ.; Hon. D.Sc. (Purdue Univ., U.S.A.), (Bordeaux) 1982, 1983, (Sri Venkateswara) 1984, (Roorkee) 1985, (Banares) 1986, (Osmania, Mangalore) 1986, (Manipur) 1987; Royal Soc. of Chem. Medal (London) 1981; Marlow Medal, Faraday Soc. 1967; Bhatnagar Award 1968; Padma Shri 1974; Fed. of Indian Chamber of Commerce and Industry Award for Physical Sciences 1977, Sir C. V. Raman Award 1978, S. N. Bose Medal of Indian Nat. Science Acad. 1980, Padmavibhushan 1984. *Publications:* Ultraviolet Visible Spectroscopy 1960, Chemical Applications of Infra-red Spectroscopy 1963, Spectroscopy in Inorganic Chemistry 1970, Modern Aspects of Solid State Chemistry 1970, Solid State Chemistry 1974, Educational Technology in Teaching of Chemistry 1975, Phase Transitions in Solids 1978, Preparation and Characterization of Materials 1981, The Metallic and Non-Metallic States of Matter 1985, New Directions in Solid State Chemistry 1986; more than 500 original research papers. *Leisure interests:* gourmet cooking, general reading. *Address:* Director's Office, Indian Institute of Science, Bangalore 560012; AMBA 57, 8th Main Road, Malleswaram, Bangalore 560055, India (Home). *Telephone:* 341690 (Office); 341254 (Home).

RAO, Jalagam Vengala; Indian politician; b. 4 May 1922, Srikakulam Dist.; s. of the late Venkata Rao; m. Shrimati Mangayamma (deceased); two s.; Chair. Andhra Pradesh Chamber of Panchayal Raj 1959-64, mem. Legis. Ass. 1962-78, Minister of Home Affairs 1969-71, of Industries 1972-73, Chief Minister 1973-78; mem. Lok Sabha 1984; Union Minister of Industry Oct. 1986-. *Leisure interests:* reading, agriculture. *Address:* Ministry of Industry and Company Affairs, Udyog Bhavan, New Delhi 110011, India. *Telephone:* (11) 3011815.

RAO, Kona Prabhakara, B.A., LL.B.; Indian state governor; b. 10 July 1916, Bapatla, Andhra Pradesh; s. of Venkatrao I, Subhadramma; m. Padmavathi Rao; six s. four d.; mem. Andhra Pradesh (A.P.) State Ass. 1967, 1972, 1978; Chair. A.P. Tourism and Devt. Corpn.; Speaker, Legis. Ass. of A.P. 1981; Pres. PCC (I); Minister in Charge of Finance, Planning and Information; Gov. of Sikkim 1984-85, of Maharashtra 1985-86; actor and producer of several films. *Address:* Bapatla, Guntur District, Andhra Pradesh, India (Home). *Telephone:* 2577 (Home).

RAO, Raja; Indian writer; b. 21 July 1909; ed. Nizam Coll., Hyderabad, Univs. of Montpellier and Paris; Prof. of Philosophy, Univ. of Texas. *Publications:* Kanthapura, Cow of the Barricades, The Serpent and The Rope, The Policeman and the Rose (short stories in French and English), The Cat and Shakespeare, Comrade Kirillov (novels). *Address:* c/o Department of Philosophy, College of Humanities at Austin, University of Texas, Austin, Tex. 78712, U.S.A.

RAO, Vijayendra Kasturi Ranga Varadaraja, PH.D., D.LITT.; Indian economist and government official; b. 8 July 1908, Kancheepuram; s. of K. Kasturirangachar and Bharathi Bai; m. 1st Pramila 1931 (died 1955); 2nd Kamala 1962; one s. two d.; ed. Wilson Coll., Bombay, and Gonville and Caius Coll., Cambridge; Prin. and Prof. of Econs., L.D. Arts Coll., Ahmedabad 1937–42; Prof. and Head of Dept. of Econs., Delhi Univ. 1942–57; Dir. of Statistics, Govt. of India 1944–45; Planning Adviser, Govt. of India 1945–46; Food and Econ. Adviser, Embassy of India, Washington 1946–47; Founder and Dir. Delhi School of Econs., Delhi Univ. 1949–57, Vice-Chancellor, Delhi Univ. 1957–60, Emer. Prof. 1966–; Founder and Dir. Inst. of Econ. Growth 1960–63; mem. Indian Planning Comm. 1963–66; Chair. UN Sub-Comm. on Econ. Devt. 1947–50; mem. Parl. 1967–77; Union Minister for Transport and Shipping 1966–69; Minister of Educ. and Youth Services 1969–71; Founder, Dir. Inst. for Social and Econ. Change, Bangalore 1972–77 (retd.); Nat. Fellow, Indian Council of Social Science Research 1977–; Hon. Fellow Gonville and Caius Coll., Cambridge 1971; Hon. D.C.L. (Oxford) 1969; Padma Vibhushan Award 1974, Nat. Prof. 1984. *Publications:* Taxation of Income in India 1931, An Essay on India's National Income, 1925–29 1939, The National Income of British India, 1931–32 1940, War and Indian Economy 1943, India and International Currency Plans 1946, Post-war Rupee 1948, Foreign Aid and India's Economic Development 1962, Essays on Economic Development 1963, Greater Delhi—A Study in Urbanisation 1947–57 1965, Education and Human Resource Development 1966, Values and Economic Development, The Indian Challenge 1971, The Nehru Legacy 1971, Inflation and India's Economic Crisis (co-author) 1973, Growth with Justice in Asian Agriculture, Iran's Fifth Plan—An Attempted Economic Leap 1975, India's National Income 1950–51 to 1975–76, Swami Vivekanada—Prophet of Vedantic Socialism 1978, Many Languages and One Nation—The Problem of Integration 1979, Food, Nutrition and Poverty 1982; edited: Agricultural Labour in India 1961, Employment and Unemployment 1965, Bangladesh Economy—Problems and Prospects 1972, Planning for Change—Issues in Mysore's Development 1974, Indian Socialism: Retrospect and Prospect 1982, Food Nutrition and Poverty 1982, India's National Income 1950–80 1983, The Indian Crisis—Some Reflections 1985. *Leisure interests:* reading, writing. *Address:* "Dayanidhi", No. 1170A, 26A Main Road, 4th "T" Block, Jayanagar Bangalore 560041, India (Home). *Telephone:* 640146 (Home).

RAO SHOUKUN; Chinese army officer; served under Cheng Jun before 1944; Commdr. 18th Brigade, 6th Div., Cen. China Field Army 1946; Deputy Commdr. (rank of Vice-Adm.) PLA Shanghai Fleet; Head PLA unit, Shanghai 1961; Commdr. PLA E. Sea Fleet 1964; in PLA unit, Shanghai 1966; disappeared during Cultural Revolution; Commdr. N. China Sea Fleet 1979–80; Commdr. Jinan Mil. Region 1980–85; mem. Cen. Advisory Comm. 1983–; mem. Presidium 6th NPC 1986–. *Address:* c/o Office of the Commander, Jinan Military Region, People's Republic of China.

RAO XINGLI; Chinese agricultural worker; b. Oct. 1925, Hubei Prov.; s. of Rao Yunhe and Zhang Yueying; m. Guo Fenglan 1951; one s. four d.; Deputy for Hubei to 1st NPC 1954, to 2nd 1959, to 3rd 1964; singled out as model agricultural worker, special class 1956; Vice-Chair. Fed. of Poor and Lower-Middle Peasants of Hubei 1966–70; Vice-Chair. Revolutionary Cttee., Hubei 1968–77; mem. 9th CCP Cen. Cttee. 1969; Chair. Peasants' Fed., Hubei 1973–77; Vice-Chair. People's Congress, Hubei 1980; mem. 10th CCP Cen. Cttee. 1977, mem. 11th CCP Cen. Cttee. 1982. *Address:* Peasants' Federation, Wuhan, Hubei, People's Republic of China.

RAOUL, Major Alfred; Congolese army officer and politician; b. 1930; ed. Military Acad., Saint-Cyr, France; Adjutant to C.-in-C. of Congolese Armed Forces 1963–65; Dir. of Corps of Engineers 1965; Sec. in charge of Defence, Directorate of Nat. Revolutionary Council Aug. 1968; Prime Minister of Congo (Brazzaville) 1968–69, concurrently Minister of Defence 1968–69, concurrently Minister of State Planning and Admin. Sept.-Dec. 1969; Head of State 1968–69; Vice-Chair. Council of State 1969–71; sentenced to 10 years' imprisonment March 1972, released Aug. 1972; Amb. to Egypt 1978–80, to Belgium 1980–84, to EEC 1980–84; fmr. mem. Political Bureau of Congolese Workers' Party (P.C.T.); 2nd Sec. Cen. Cttee. of P.C.T. *Address:* c/o Ministry of Foreign Affairs, Brazzaville, People's Republic of the Congo.

RAPAI, Gyula: Hungarian politician and diplomatist (retd.); b. 1923, Kánya; s. of Mihály Rapai and Borbála Kisturi; m. Piroska Gáti 1949; two d.; ed. Soviet Communist Party High School, Moscow; joined Hungarian Communist Party 1945; Deputy Leader, later Head, Agitprop Dept., Hungarian Socialist Workers' Party Cen. Cttee. 1959–62; First Sec. Hungarian Socialist Workers' Party County Baranya Cttee. 1962–70; mem. Parl. 1966–70; mem. Nat. Council of Trade Unions 1966–70; Amb. to U.S.S.R.

1970–76; Dir. Kossuth Publishing House of Budapest 1976–82; Vice-Pres. Hungarian-Soviet Friendship Soc. 1977. *Address:* Vörösmarty tér 5, Budapest V. 1051, Hungary.

RÂPEANU, Valeriu; Romanian literary critic, historian and editor; b. 28 Sept. 1931, Ploiestiori, Prahova; s. of Gheorghe Râpeanu and Anastasia Râpeanu; m. Sanda Marinescu 1956; one s.; ed. Univ. of Bucharest; journalist 1954–69; Vice-Chair. of the Romanian Cttee. of Radio and TV 1970–72; Dir. Mihai Eminescu Publishing House, Bucharest 1972–; mem. Romanian Writers' Union; mem. Cen. Cttee. Romanian CP; mem. Int. Assoc. of Literary Critics; Corresp. mem. Acad. of Social and Political Sciences. *Publications:* the monographs George Mihail Zamfirescu 1958, Al. Vlahuţă 1964, Noi şi cei dinaintea noastră (Ourselves and Our Predecessors) 1966, Interferenţe spirituale (Spiritual Correspondences) 1970; Călător pe două continente (Traveller on Two Continents) 1970, Pe urmele tradiţiei (Following Traditions) 1973, Interpretări si inţelesuri (Interpretations and Significances) 1975, Cultură si istorie (Culture and History), two vols., 1979, 1981; Tărîmul unde nu ajungi niciodată (The Land You shall Never Reach) 1982, Scriitori dintre cele Două Razboaie (Writers between the two World Wars) 1986; ed. vols. by Nicolae Iorga, Gh. Brătianu, Al. Kiriţescu, Cella Delavrancea, Marcel Mihalovici; anthology of Romanian drama; essays on François Mauriac, Jean d'Ormesson, Marcel Proust, George Enescu, Monique Haas, Aaron Copland, André Malraux, Jean Cocteau. *Leisure interests:* music, art. *Address:* Editura Eminescu, Piaţa Scînteii 1, Bucureşti 71341, Romania.

RAPER, Kenneth Bryan; American professor of bacteriology and botany; b. 11 July 1908, Welcome, N.C.; s. of William Franklin Raper and Julia Crouse Raper; m. Louise Montgomery Williams; one s.; ed. Univ. of N.C. and George Washington and Harvard Univs.; Jr. Mycologist Bureau of Chem. and Soils, U.S. Dept. of Agric. (U.S.D.A.) 1929–36, Asst. Mycologist Bureau of Plant Industry 1936–40; Microbiologist, later Prin. Microbiologist N. Regional Research Lab., U.S.D.A., Peoria, Ill. 1940–53; Prof. of Bacteriology and Botany, Univ. of Wis. 1953–79, Prof. Emer. 1979–, mem. Cancer Research Cttee. 1956–60; Visiting Prof. of Botany, Univ. of Ill. 1946–53; Trustee, American Type Culture Collection, Washington, D.C. 1948–52, Chair. Exec. Cttee. 1956–60; mem. Merck Fellowship Board, Nat. Research Council 1953–57, Exec. Cttee. Div. of Biology and Agric. 1956–61; mem. Selection Cttee. for Senior Postdoctoral Fellowships, Nat. Science Foundation 1961–64, Chair. Biological Sciences 1962–64; Chair. U.S. Del. to Gen. Ass. of Int. Union of Biological Sciences (IUBS), London 1958, Prague 1964, Chair. U.S. Nat. Cttee. IUBS 1962–64; Chair. U.S. Nat. Cttee. for Int. Botanical Congress (Vice-Pres. XI Int. Botanical Congress), Seattle 1969; mem. N.A.S. (mem. of Council 1961–64), American Acad. of Arts and Sciences, American Philosophical Soc., A.A.A.S., Mycological Soc. of America (Pres. 1951), Soc. of Industrial Microbiologists (Pres. 1953), Soc. of American Microbiologists (Councillor 1954–58), etc.; Lasker Award (Co-Recipient) 1946, Distinguished Service Award, U.S.D.A. (Co-Recipient) 1947, Charles Thom Award, Soc. for Industrial Microbiology 1967, Distinguished Mycologist Award (Mycological Soc. of America) 1981, Hon. mem. American Soc. of Microbiologists, British Mycological Soc. 1984. *Publications:* Manual of the Aspergilli (with Charles Thom) 1945, Manual of the Penicillia (with Charles Thom) 1949, The Genus Aspergillus (with Dorothy I. Fennell) 1965, The Dictyostelids 1984; research papers on saprophytic fungi, industrial microbiology, and cellular slime molds. *Leisure interests:* photography, gardening. *Address:* c/o Department of Bacteriology, University of Wisconsin, Madison, Wis. 53706 (Office); 602 N. Segoe Road, Madison, Wis. 53705, U.S.A. (Home). *Telephone:* (608) 262-3055 (Office); (608) 233-7703 (Home).

RAPHAEL, Farid; Lebanese banker and government official; b. 28 Oct. 1933, Dlebta, Kesrouan; s. of Elie Raphael and Evelyne Khalife; m. Ilham Abdel Ahad 1970; one s. three d.; ed. Univ. of St. Joseph, Beirut, Univ. of Lyons, France; with Compagnie Algérienne de Crédit et de Banque, Beirut 1956–67; Founder and Gen. Man. Banque Libano-Française S.A.L. 1967–79, Chair. and Gen. Man. 1979–; Founder and Vice-Pres. Banque Libano-Française (France) S.A., Paris 1976–85, Chair. and Gen. Man. 1985–; Minister of Justice, Finance, Posts, Telephones and Telecommunications 1976–79. *Address:* Banque Libano-Française (France), 33 rue Monceau, 75008 Paris, France (Office); Baroudy Building, Hazmieh, Lebanon (Home).

RAPHAEL, Frederic Michael, M.A., F.R.S.L.; American writer; b. 14 Aug. 1931, Chicago, Ill.; s. of Cedric Michael Raphael and Irene Rose Mauser; m. Sylvia Betty Glatt 1955; two s. one d.; ed. Charterhouse, St. John's Coll., Cambridge; Lippincott Prize 1961, U.S. Acad. Award 1966, Royal TV Soc. Award 1976. *Publications:* novels: Earlsdon Way 1956, The Limits of Love 1960, Lindmann 1963, Orchestra and Beginners 1967, Like Men Betrayed 1970, April, June and November 1972, California Time 1975, The Glittering Prizes 1976, Heaven and Earth 1985, After the War 1988; short stories: Sleeps Six 1979, Oxbridge Blues 1980, Think of England 1986, After the War 1988; biography: Somerset Maugham and his World 1977, Byron 1982; essays: Cracks in the Ice 1979; translations: Catullus (with K. McLeish) 1978, The Oresteia of Aeschylus 1979; screenplays: Nothing But the Best 1965, Darling 1966, Far from the Madding Crowd 1968, Two for the Road 1968, Richard's Things 1980, Oxbridge Blues 1984. *Leisure interests:* tennis, travel. *Address:* Lagardelle, St. Laurent la Vallée, 24170 Belves, France; The Wick, Langham, Colchester, England. *Telephone:* (53) 28-42-63 (France); (0206) 322108.

RAPILLY, Yves Georges, L. EN D., DIPL.; French business executive; b. 24 April 1931, Saint-Brieuc; s. of Georges Rapilly and Marie-Françoise Helary; ed. Univ. of Paris; joined service juridique de la Soc. Anonyme des Automobiles Peugeot 1954, jt. Head 1958, Head 1964, mem. Exec. 1966, Finance Dir. 1972, Dir.-Gen. Peugeot S.A. 1986–; Pres. Soc. de Crédit à l'Industrie Automobile (SOCIA) 1977–, Société Financière de Banque 1983–, Société de Financement des Réseaux Automobile (SOFIRA) 1983–, Société PSA Finance Holding, Compagnie Générale de Crédit aux Particuliers (Crédipar) 1984–85; Chevalier Légion d'honneur. *Leisure interest:* skiing. *Address:* Peugeot S.A., 75 avenue de la Grande-Armée, 75116 Paris (Office); 185 avenue Victor-Hugo, 75116 Paris, France (Home).

RAPOPORT, Iosif Abramovich, DR.BIOL.SC.; Soviet geneticist; b. 1912, St. Petersburg (now Leningrad); ed. Leningrad Univ.; research asst. at U.S.S.R. Acad. of Sciences Inst. of Experimental Biology 1938–41; Red Army 1941–45; research asst. at U.S.S.R. Acad. of Sciences Inst. of Cytology 1945–48; palaeontologist with geological prospecting office of Ministry of Oil Industry 1948–57; researcher at Inst. of Chemical Physics 1957–65, Head of Dept. 1965–, Prof. 1971–; corresp. mem. of U.S.S.R. Acad. of Sciences 1979–; Lenin Prize for work on The Phenomenon of Chemical Mutagenesis and its Genetic Study 1984. *Address:* Institute of Chemical Physics of U.S.S.R. Academy of Sciences, Leningrad, U.S.S.R.

RAPOSO, Mario; Portuguese politician; b. Jan. 1929, Coimbra; ed. Univ. of Coimbra; Sub-Insp. for Social Assistance and Sec. to Minister of Finance, resigned to practise Law 1955; mem. Gen. Council, Ordem dos Advogados (Law Soc.) 1972–74, Chair. 1975–77; mem. Exec. Cttee. First Nat. Congress of Lawyers 1972; Cttee. for Judicial Reform, High Court of Justice 1974; Minister of Justice, Third Constitutional Govt.; mem. Ass. of the Repub. 1978–79, for Social Democratic Party (PSD) Dec. 1979–; Minister of Justice 1980–81, 1985–87. *Address:* c/o Ministério da Justiça, Praça do Comércio, Lisbon-2, Portugal.

RAPSON, Ralph, M.ARCH.; American architect; b. 13 Sept. 1914, Alma, Mich.; s. of Frank and Mable (née Nickols) Rapson; m. Mary Dolan; two s.; ed. Alma (Mich.) Coll., Univ. of Mich. Coll. of Architecture, and Cranbrook Acad. of Art; practising architect 1941–; f. Ralph Rapson and Assocs.; Head Dept. of Architecture Chicago Inst. of Design 1942–46; Assoc. Prof. of Architecture M.I.T. School of Architecture 1946–54 (leave of absence to execute designs in Europe for State Dept. 1951–53); Prof. and Head of School of Architecture, Univ. of Minnesota 1954–84; Visiting Prof. Univ. of Va.; mem. American Inst. of Architects, Int. Congress of Modern Architecture; Dir. Walker Art Gallery; fmr. Chair. Editorial Bd. Northwest Architect; numerous awards include Parker Medal 1951, American Inst. of Architects Honor Award for U.S. Embassy, Stockholm 1954, two Merit Awards 1955, Honour Award 1958. *Designs include:* projects for U.S. Government, several churches and schools, commercial, industrial and residential buildings, particularly U.S. Embassy, Stockholm, U.S. Embassy, Copenhagen, U.S. Consulate, Le Havre, St. Peter's Lutheran Church (Edina, Minn.), Fargo (N.D.) Civic Center, St. Paul (Minn.) Arts and Science Center, American Embassy, Beirut, Dr. William G. Shepherd House, St. Paul, Tyrone Guthrie Repertory Theatre, Minn. (Designs also executed for Embassies at Athens, The Hague and Oslo.) *Address:* 1503 Washington Avenue, S.E., Minneapolis, Minn. 55454 (Office); 1 Seymour Avenue, Minneapolis, Minn. 55404, U.S.A. (Home).

RASAPUTRAM, Warnasena, M.A., PH.D.; Sri Lankan central banker; b. 6 Sept. 1927, Matara; s. of Don Nicholas and Jane (née Ratnayake) Rasaputram; m. Jayanthi Sriya de Silva 1954; two s.; ed. Univs. of Ceylon and Wisconsin; Economist, Central Bank of Ceylon 1958–68; Consultant, Nat. Planning Dept. 1960–62; UN Expert, Econ. Planning (Nat. Accounts), Iraq 1965–67; Econ. Consultant, ECAFE, Bangkok 1967, 1969; Dir. of Econ. Research, Cen. Bank of Ceylon 1968–73, Asst. to Gov. 1974–75, Deputy Gov. 1975–76, Gov. and Chair. Monetary Bd. 1979–; Econ. Planning Expert, Asian Regional Team for Employment Promotion, ILO 1970–71; Dir. Air Ceylon 1973–75; Devt. Finance Corpn. 1974–76; UN Expert, Caribbean Regional Integration Advisory Team 1975; Alt. Ctee. Dir. IMF 1976–79. *Publications:* numerous papers on economics. *Leisure interests:* books, travel, photography. *Address:* Central Bank of Ceylon, 34–36 Janadhipathi Mawatha, Colombo (Office); Bank House, 206 Bauddhaloka Mawatha, Colombo 7, Sri Lanka (Home). *Telephone:* 27486 (Office); 81506 (Home).

RASHID BIN SAID AL-MAKTUM, Ruler of Dubai (see Maktoum, Rashid bin Said al-).

RASHID, Sheikh Mohammad, B.A., LL.B.; Pakistani lawyer and politician; b. 24 May 1915, Kalawala, Sheikhupura District; s. of late Sheikh Mehrdin; m. 1934; four s.; joined Muslim League 1940; imprisoned for political activities 1947; mem. Pakistan muslim League Council 1948–50; organized Azad Pakistan Party (later re-named Nat. Awami Party), Sec.-Gen. 1952; launched Kisan Morcha Movt. Lahore 1956; founder mem. Pakistan People's Party; Advocate, Supreme Court of Pakistan; mem. Nat. Ass.; Minister of Social Welfare, Health and Family Planning 1971–74, of Food and Agriculture, Co-operatives, Works, Underdeveloped Areas and Land Reforms 1974–77, of Agric., Co-operative and Land Reforms March–July 1977; imprisoned 1977–79. *Leisure interest:* reading. *Address:* 8 Zaldar Road, Ichhra, Lahore, Pakistan. *Telephone:* 21550.

RASMUSSEN, Anders Fogh; Danish politician; b. 26 Jan. 1953, Ginnerup, Jutland; ed. Univ. of Aarhus; mem. Folketing (Parl.) 1978–; Vice-Pres. Liberal Party 1986–; Minister of Fiscal Affairs 1987–; Pres. Liberal Youth Movement 1974–76. *Publication:* Opgør med skattesystemet 1979. *Address:* Ministry of Fiscal Affairs, Slotsholmsgade 12, 1216 Copenhagen K, Denmark. *Telephone:* (01) 92-33-66.

RASMUSSEN, Norman Carl, PH.D.; American nuclear engineer; b. 12 Nov. 1927, Harrisburg, Pa.; s. of Frederick Rasmussen and Faith Elliott; m. Thalia Tichenor 1952; one s. one d.; ed. Gettysburg Coll., Pennsylvania and Massachusetts Insts. of Technology; mem. Faculty, M.I.T. 1958–, Prof. of Nuclear Eng. 1965–, McAfee Prof. of Eng. 1983–, Head of Dept. 1975–81; mem. numerous advisory bodies etc. including Safety Advisory Bd. Three Mile Island Unit-2 Program 1980–; Fellow, A.A.A.S., American Nuclear Soc.; mem. N.A.S., Nat. Acad. of Eng. etc.; several awards and hon. degrees. *Publications:* Modern Physics for Engineers (co-author); articles in professional journals. *Address:* 77 Massachusetts Avenue, Cambridge, Mass. 02139 (Office); 80 Winsor Road, Sudbury, Mass. 01776, U.S.A. (Home).

RASMUSSEN, Poul Nørregaard, DR. PONT.; Danish professor of economics; b. 9 May 1922, Hylke; s. of Anders Rasmussen and Christine (née Nørregaard) Rasmussen; m. Karen Aase Bruun 1948 (died 1984); two d.; ed. Univs. of Aarhus and Copenhagen; Research Assoc. Univ. of Oslo 1947–48; Econ. Affairs Officer UN ECE, Geneva 1948–51; Reader in Econs., Univ. of Copenhagen 1951–56, Prof. 1956–88, Prof. Emer. 1988–. *Publications:* Forelaesninger om biblioteksbenyttelse og opgaveskrivning 1958, Matematik for økonomer (vols. 1 & 2) 1958–59, Om økonomiens metode 1963, Forelaesninger for økonomer om biblioteksbenyttelse og opgaveskrivning 1966, Noter og kommentarer til Don Patinkin: Money, Interest and Prices (with Niels Thygesen) 1967, The Economics of Technological Change 1976. *Address:* Strandboulevarden 32, 2100 Copenhagen Ø, Denmark. *Telephone:* (45-1) 42 82 68.

RASMUSSEN, Svend Erik, D. PHIL.; Danish professor of inorganic chemistry; b. 19 Nov. 1925, Esbjerg; s. of Svend Ove Rasmussen und Hilma Sophie (née Hellsten) Rasmussen; m. Clary Dorrit Hólmlund 1950; one s. one d.; ed. Univ. of Copenhagen and Queens Coll., Dundee; Asst. Lecturer Tech. Univ. of Denmark 1953–59; Prof. of Inorganic Chemistry, Univ. of Aarhus 1959; Gen. Sec. and Treasurer Int. Union of Crystallography 1972–81. *Publications:* numerous papers on crystallography in chemistry and crystallography journals. *Leisure interests:* travelling, skiing, literature. *Address:* Højkolvej 39, 8210 Aarhus V, Denmark. *Telephone:* 45 6155047.

RASMUSSEN, Viggo J.; Danish business executive; b. 20 Jan. 1915, Aalborg; s. of C. A. and Antonie Louise Rasmussen (née Andersen); m. Lydia Hansen 1939; one s. one d.; ed. Copenhagen School of Business Science; Danish Air Lines 1932–, Vice-Pres. 1947, Exec. Vice-Pres. Scandinavian Airlines System 1950–62; Pres. and Man. Dir. United Breweries (Tuborg Breweries and Carlsberg Breweries) 1962–71, mem. of the Bd. 1971–74, mem. Bd. of Tuborg Foundation; mem. Acad. of Tech. Sciences; Kt., First Degree, Order of Dannebrog, Kt., Order of Vasa, Commdr., Order of Merit of the Italian Republic. *Leisure interests:* antiques, paintings, ships. *Address:* Tuborg Breweries Ltd., Strandvejen 50, 2900 Hellerup (Home); 130 Store Kongensgade, DK-1264 Copenhagen K, Denmark.

RASPUTIN, Valentin Grigorovich; Soviet author; b. 15 March 1937, Ust-Uda (Irkutsk); ed. Irkutsk Univ.; first works published 1961; U.S.S.R. State Prize 1987. *Publications:* I Forgot to Ask Lyosha 1961, A Man of This World 1965, Bearskin for Sale 1966, Vasilii and Vasilisa 1967, Deadline 1970, Live and Remember, Stories, 1977, Fire 1987. *Address:* U.S.S.R. Union of Writers, Ul. Vorovskogo 52, Moscow, U.S.S.R.

RASSADIN, Stanislav Borisovich; Soviet literary critic; b. 4 March 1935, Moscow; ed. Moscow Univ. *Publications include:* Poetry of Recent Years 1961, Nikolai Nosov: A Bio-Critical Account 1961, Talk with the Reader: Essay on Literature 1962, The Role of the Reader 1965, Linden Alley 1966, Pushkin the Dramatist 1977, Fonvizin 1980.

RATAJCZAK, Henryk, M.SC., PH.D., D.SC.; Polish professor of chemistry; b. 30 Sept. 1932, Kadobno; m. Halina Opryszko 1972; one d.; ed. Technical Univ., Wrocław, Wrocław Univ., Univ. of Wales, Univ. of Salford, Sorbonne, Paris, Centre de Mécanique Ondulatoire Appliquée, Paris; Asst. in Physical Chem., Univ. of Wrocław 1956–59, Senior Asst. 1959–63, Adjunct 1963–70, Docent in Chemical Physics 1970–74, Extraordinary Prof. of Chem. 1975–, Head of Dept. of Theoretical Chem. and Chemical Physics 1969–79, Deputy Dir. of Research, Inst. of Chem. 1970–79, Dir. 1979–82, Rector Wrocław Univ. 1982–84; Visiting Prof. Univ. Salford, U.K. 1975–83, Univ. Paris 1977–78; Scientific Sec. of Spectroscopy Cttee., Polish Acad. of Sciences 1969–, Deputy Chair. 1979–; Corresp. mem. Polish Acad. of Sciences 1976–; Ed. for Eastern Europe, Journal of Molecular Structure, Advances in Molecular Relaxation and Interaction Processes; Editorial mem. Advisory Bd. of Chemical Physics Letters 1977–; Knight's Cross of Order of Polonia Restituta; Marie Sklodowska-Curie Prize 1976, Higher Educ. and Tech. Prize for Research, Ministry of Science 1970, 1973, 1978. *Publications:* Structural Studies of Some Hydrogen-bonded Ferroelectrics 1969, Dipole Moments of Hydrogen-bonded Complexes and Proton Transfer Effect 1969, On the Nature of Electron Donor Acceptor Interactions 1972,

Charge Transfer Properties of the Hydrogen Bond 1972, 1973, CNDO/2 Molecular Orbital Calculation of the Dewar Structure of Benzene 1972, of Pyridine 1974, of Pyrazine, Pyrimidyne and Pyridazine 1975, Charge Transfer Theory of Hydrogen Bonds: Relation Between Vibrational Spectra and Energy of Hydrogen Bonds 1976, Studies on the Lithium Bond 1976, SCF ab initio Calculations on the Lithium Fluoride-ethylene Complex 1977, Vibrational Polarized Spectra of Strongly Hydrogen-bonded Systems 1977, Influence of a.c. Electric Field on IR Spectra of Some Nematic Liquid Crystals with Positive and Negative Dielectric Anisotropy 1978, Molecular Orbital Calculations for the Glicine and HCl Crystals 1979, On Some Problems of Molecular Interactions 1980, Molecular Interactions Vols. 1 and 2 (Ed. with Prof. W. J. Orville-Thomas) 1980, Crystal structure of rubidium hydrogen bis-dibromoacetate 1980, Infra-red studies of complexes between carboxylic acids and tertiary amines in argon matrices 1980, On the non-additivity of the SCF interaction energy in the complex (LiH)$_3$ 1980, SCF ab initio study of the lithium bonded complexes 1980, Properties of strong hydrogen-bonded systems 1980, 13C chemical shifts of phenol derivatives: a correlation with electronic structures 1980, and over 80 articles on the theory, properties, structure and dynamics of molecular systems. *Leisure interests:* music, literature, sport. *Address:* Institute of Chemistry, Wrocław University, ul. Joliot-Curie 14, 50-383 Wrocław (Office); ul. Bystrzycka 71 m.9, Wrocław 54-215, Poland (Home). *Telephone:* 22-92-81 (Office); 55-98-99 (Home).

RATANOV, Anatoliy Petrovich; Soviet diplomatist; b. 8 March 1921, Buguruslan, Orenburg Region; mem. CPSU 1943–; worked for Young Communist League 1943–54; Ed. journal, Molodoi Kommunist (Young Communist) 1954–58; Perm. Rep. of U.S.S.R. Cttee. of Youth Orgs. to World Fed. of Democratic Youth 1958–60; First Sec., Phnom-Penh, Cambodia 1960–62, Counsellor 1962–63; Amb. to Cambodia 1965–68; on staff at Ministry of Foreign Affairs 1968–70; Amb. to Guinea 1970–73, to Ethiopia 1973–78; Order of Lenin, Red Banner of Labour, Badge of Honour, etc. *Address:* c/o Ministry of Foreign Affairs, Moscow, U.S.S.R.

RATEB, Aisha, PH.D.; Egyptian politician; b. 22 Feb. 1928; two s.; ed. Faculty of Law, Cairo Univ.; Jr. Lecturer, Faculty of Law, Cairo Univ., Lecturer 1957, then Prof. of Int. Law; Minister of Social Affairs 1971–76, of Social Affairs and Insurance 1976–77; Amb. Extraordinary, Ministry of Foreign Affairs 1978; Amb. to Denmark 1979–81, to Fed. Repub. of Germany 1981–84; Chair. Legis. Affairs Cttee. 1973–. *Address:* c/o Ministry of Foreign Affairs, Cairo, Egypt.

RATHBONE, Perry Townsend, A.B.; American museum director; b. 3 July 1911, Germantown, Pa.; s. of Howard Betts and Beatrice (Connely) Rathbone; m. Euretta de Cosson 1945; one s. two d.; ed. Harvard Univ.; Curator, Detroit Inst. of Arts 1936–40; Dir. City Art Museum, St. Louis 1940–55; Dir. Museum of Fine Arts, Boston 1955–72, Dir. Emer. and Consultant 1972–; Dir. Christie's Int. (fmrly. Christie's U.S.A.) 1973–; mem. American Asscn. of Museums and Asscn. of Art Museum Dirs., U.S. Nat. Comm. of Int. Council of Museums, American Acad. of Arts and Sciences, Visiting Cttee. Fogg Art Museum 1955–66, Rockefeller Panel on the Performing Arts 1962–63, Exec. Cttee. Art in the Embassies Prog.; Pres. Assn. of Art Museum Dirs. 1959–60, 1969–70; Vice-Chair. Mass. Art Comm. Bd. of Overseers, Fine Arts Prog. Brandeis Univ., Fine Arts Visiting Comm. Rhode Island School of Design; Special Adviser to the Ford Program in the Arts and Humanities; Trustee, New England Conservatory of Music, Museum of Science, Boston, Inst. of Contemporary Art, Boston, American Fed. of Arts 1959–80, Boston Arts Festival, Cape Cod Art Assn., Int. Exhibitions Foundation, Washington, D. C., Rhode Island School of Design, Charles Playhouse, Cosmopolitan Art Foundation 1974–, Royal Oak foundation 1975–, Opera Co. of Boston 1976–; Chevalier, Légion d'honneur and several hon. degrees. *Publications:* Charles Wimar: Painter of the Indian Frontier 1946, Max Beckmann 1948, Mississippi Panorama 1949, Westward the Way 1954, Lee Gatch 1960, Handbook of the Forsyth Wickes Collection 1968, Western Art 1970, Andrew Wyeth (in Japanese) 1974. *Leisure interests:* art, travel, historic preservation. *Address:* Christie's International, 502 Park Avenue, New York, N.Y. 10021; 130 Mount Auburn Street, Cambridge, Mass. 02138, U.S.A. (Office). *Telephone:* 212-546 1190 (Office).

RATHER, Dan, B.A.; American broadcaster and journalist; b. Oct. 1931, Wharton, Tex.; m. Jean Goebel; one s. one d.; ed. Sam Houston State Coll., Univ. of Houston, Tex., S. Tex. School of Law; writer and sports commentator with KSAM-TV; taught journalism for one year at Houston Chronicle; with CBS; with radio station KTRH, Houston for about four years; News and Current Affairs Dir. CBS Houston TV affiliate KHOU-TV late 1950s; joined CBS News 1962; Chief London Bureau 1965–66 ; worked in Viet-Nam; White House 1966; anchorman CBS Reports 1974–75; co-anchorman 60 Minutes CBS-TV 1975–81; anchorman Dan Rather Reporting CBS Radio Network 1977–; co-ed. show Who's Who CBS-TV 1977; anchorman Midwest desk CBS Nat. election night 1972–80; CBS Nat. Political Consultant 1964–; anchorman Man. Ed. CBS Evening News with Dan Rather 1981–; anchored numerous CBS News Special Programmes, including coverage of presidential campaigns in 1982 and 1984; as White House correspondent accompanied Pres. on numerous travels including visits to Middle East,. U.S.S.R., People's Repub. of China; five Emmy awards; Distinguished Achievement for Broadcasting Award, Univ. of S.

Calif. Journalism Alumni Assn, Bob Considine Award 1983. *Publications:* The Palace Guard 1974 (with Gary Gates), The Camera Never Blinks (with Mickey Herskowitz) 1977. *Address:* CBS News, 524 West 57th Street, New York, N.Y. 10019, U.S.A. (Office).

RATHKE, Heinrich Karl Martin Hans, DR.THEOL.; German ecclesiastic; b. 12 Dec. 1928, Mölln, Kreis Malchin; s. of Paul and Hedwig (née Steding) Rathke; m. Marianne Rusam 1955; six s. one d.; ed. Univs. of Kiel, Erlangen, Tübingen and Rostock; parish priest, Althof bei Bad Doberan 1954–55, Warnkenhagen, Mecklenburg 1955–62, Rostock Südstadt 1962–70; Priest in charge of community service and people's mission, Mecklenburg 1970–71; Bishop of the Evangelical-Lutheran Church of Mecklenburg 1971–84; Pastor in Crivitz/Mecklenburg July 1984–; Presiding Bishop of the United Evangelical Lutheran Church of the G.D.R. 1977–81. *Publication:* Ignatius von Antiochien and die Paulusbriefe 1967, Gemeinde heute und morgen 1979, Einstehen für Gemeinschaft in Christus 1980. *Address:* 2751 Schwerin, Münzstrasse 8; 2712 Crivitz, Kirchenstrasse 2, German Democratic Republic. *Telephone:* 2428.

RATLIFF, Floyd, PH.D.; American university professor; b. 1 May 1919, La Junta, Colo.; s. of Charles Frederick Ratliff and Alice Hubbard; m. Orma Vernon Priddy 1942; one d.; ed. Pueblo Junior Coll., Colorado Coll. and Brown Univ.; U.S. Army 1941–45; Nat. Research Council Postdoctoral Fellow, Johns Hopkins Univ. 1950–51; Instructor, Harvard Univ. 1951–52, Asst. Prof., 1952–54; Assoc., Rockefeller Inst. 1954–58, Assoc. Prof., Rockefeller Univ. 1958–66, Prof. 1966–; Pres. Harry Frank Guggenheim Foundation 1983–; mem. Nat. Acad. of Sciences, American Acad. of Arts and Sciences, American Philosophical Soc.; mem. Editorial Bd. Journal of General Physiology 1969–86; mem. Bd. of Scientific Counsellors of Nat. Eye Inst. 1970–73, Educ. Cttee. of the China Inst. in America 1977–; Hon. D.Sc. (Colo. Coll.) 1975; Howard Crosby Warren Medal (Soc. of Experimental Psychologists) 1966, Edgar D. Tillyer Award (Optical Soc. of America) 1976, Medal for Distinguished Service, Brown Univ. 1980, Pisart Vision Award, Distinguished Scientific Contribution Award of American Psychological Assn. 1984. *Publications:* Mach Bands: Quantitative Studies on Neural Networks in the Retina 1965, Studies on Excitation and Inhibition in the Retina (editor) 1974. *Leisure interests:* Oriental art (Chinese ceramics of the Sung dynasty). *Address:* Rockefeller University, 1230 York Avenue, New York, N.Y. 10021 (Office); 500 East 63rd Street, New York, N.Y. 10021, U.S.A. (Home). *Telephone:* (212) 570-8385 (Office); (212) 838-0060 (Home).

RATNER, Sarah, PH.D.; American biochemist; b. 9 June 1903, New York; unmarried; ed. Cornell and Columbia Univs.; Asst. Prof. of Biochemistry, Columbia Univ. Coll. of Physicians and Surgeons, New York 1946; Assoc. Prof., Dept. of Pharmacology, N.Y. Univ. Coll. of Medicine 1946–53, Research Prof., Biochemistry 1954–; mem. Dept. of Biochemistry, Public Health Research Inst. 1954–; Int. Fogarty Scholar in Residence, N.I.H., Bethesda, Md. 1978–79; enzyme discoveries of arginine and urea biosynthesis and mechanisms of action; mem. N.A.S., American Acad. of Arts and Sciences; hon. life mem. New York Acad. of Sciences, Harvey Soc.; several hon. degrees; Shoenheimer Award 1956, Neuberg Medal 1959, Garvan Medal 1961, Freedman Award 1975. *Publications:* 95 publs. in biochemistry journals. *Address:* Department of Biochemistry, The Public Health Research Institute, Inc., 455 First Avenue, New York, N.Y. 10016, U.S.A. *Telephone:* (212) 578-0817.

RATNOFF, Oscar Davis, A.B., M.D.; American professor of medicine; b. 23 Aug. 1916, New York; s. of Hyman L. Ratnoff and Ethel Davis Ratnoff; m. Marian Foreman 1945; one s. one d.; ed. Columbia Univ.; Intern Johns Hopkins Hosp., Baltimore, Md. 1939–40, Fellow in Medicine 1946–48, Instructor 1948–50, Instructor in Bacteriology 1945–50; Asst. Prof. in Medicine, Case Western Reserve Univ., Cleveland, Ohio 1950–56, Assoc. Prof. 1956–61, Prof. 1961–; Asst. Physician Univ. Hosps. of Cleveland 1952–56, Assoc. Physician 1956–57, Physician 1967–; Career Investigator American Heart Assn. 1960–; Hon. LL.D. (Aberdeen) 1980, Fellow A.A.A.S. 1982, Master American Coll. of Physicians 1983 and numerous other awards. *Publications:* Bleeding Syndromes 1960, Treatment of Hemorrhagic Disorders (Ed.) 1968, Disorders of Hemostasis (Ed.) 1984 and numerous scientific papers. *Address:* Department of Medicine, University Hospitals of Cleveland, Cleveland, Ohio 44106 (Office); 2916 Sedgewick Road, Shaker Heights, Ohio 44120, U.S.A. (Home). *Telephone:* (216) 844 3131 (Office); (216) 561 0986 (Home).

RATSIRAKA, Adm. Didier; Malagasy naval officer and politician; b. 4 Nov. 1936, Vatomandry; ed. Coll. Saint Michel, Tananarive (now Antananarivo), Lycée Henri IV, Paris, Ecole Navale, Lanveoc-Poulmic (France), Ecole des Officiers "Transmissions", Les Bormettes, and Ecole Supérieure de Guerre Navale, Paris; had several naval postings 1963–70; Mil. Attaché, Paris 1970–72; Minister of Foreign Affairs 1972–75; Pres. Supreme Council of Revolution June 1975–; Prime Minister and Minister of Defence June-Dec. 1975; Pres. Democratic Repub. of Madagascar Jan. 1976–; Sec.-Gen. Avant-garde de la révolution malgache 1976–, Front nat. pour la défense de la révolution socialiste malgache 1977–; Hon. Citizen, New Orleans, U.S.A. 1981. *Publications:* Stratégies pour l'an 2000. *Address:* Présidence de la République, Antananarivo, Madagascar.

RATTLE, Simon, C.B.E.; British conductor; b. 19 Jan. 1955, Liverpool; m. Elise Ross 1980; one s.; won Bournemouth John Player Int. Conducting

Competition 1973; has conducted Bournemouth Symphony Orchestra, Bournemouth Sinfonietta, New Philharmonia (now Philharmonia) Orchestra, Northern Sinfonia, London Philharmonic, London Sinfonietta, Berlin Philharmonic, Los Angeles Philharmonic, Stockholm Philharmonic, Toronto Symphony, etc.; début at Royal Festival Hall, London 1976, Royal Albert Hall, London 1976; Asst. Conductor, BBC Symphony Orchestra 1977; Queen Elizabeth Hall début 1977; Assoc. Conductor, Royal Liverpool Philharmonic Soc. 1977–80; Glyndebourne début 1977; Principal Conductor, London Choral Soc. 1979–84; Artistic Dir. South Bank summer music 1981–83; Jt. Artistic Dir. Aldeburgh Festival 1982–; Principal Guest Conductor, Los Angeles Philharmonic 1982–, Rotterdam Philharmonic 1981–84; Principal Conductor, City of Birmingham Symphony Orchestra Sept. 1980–. *Address:* c/o Harold Holt Ltd., 31 Sinclair Road, London, W14 0NS, England. *Telephone:* 01-603 4600.

RATTRAY, Alfred Adolphus, O.J., LL.B., F.C.A. A.C.I.S.; Jamaican lawyer and diplomatist; b. 19 Jan. 1925, St. Ann; s. of Septimus Augustus Rattray and Albertha (née Bailey); m. Cynthia Louise Weston 1951; two d.; ed. Excelsior High School, London Univ., Lincoln's Inn, London, L.S.E.; joined Civil Service 1945; Accountant and Man. Govt. Food Control Distribution Dept. 1947–51, rising to Asst. Under-Sec. 1953–64; with law firm Myers, Fletcher and Gordon 1964–80, Partner 1965–80 (on leave of absence 1975–80); founding Partner Rattray, Patterson, Rattray; engaged in business 1965–75; fmr. Chair. Bd., Jamaica Frozen Foods Ltd., Jamaica Fashion Export Guild Ltd., Guild Productions Ltd., New Kingston Hotel Ltd.: Dir. Bd. Sheraton Int. (Jamaica) Ltd., Island Holidays Ltd., Windsor Foods Ltd.; Deputy Chair. Jamaica Industrial Devt. Corpn. Ltd.; Dir. and Vice-Chair. West Indies Shipping Corpn.; fmr. Chair. Jamaica Port Authority; fmr. Pres. Jamaica Public Accountancy Bd.; Amb. to U.S.A., also to OAS 1975–80; Chair. Perm. Exec. Cttee of the Inter-American Econ. and Social Council 1978–80; part-time lecturer, Univ. of the West Indies 1961–75; mem. Excelsior School Bd. *Publications:* co-author: The Jamaican Companies Act 1965, The Public Accountancy Act 1968. *Leisure interests:* cricket, table tennis, fishing, bridge, reading. *Address:* 13 Caledonia Avenue, Cross Roads, Kingston 5, Jamaica.

RATUSHINSKAYA, Irina; Soviet poet; b. 4 March 1954; m. Igor Gerashchenko 1979; ed. Odessa Pedagogical Inst.; teacher Odessa Pedagogical Inst. 1976–83; arrested with husband, Moscow 1981; lost job, arrested again, 17 Sept. 1982, convicted of 'subverting the Soviet régime' and sentenced 5 March 1983 to seven years' hard labour; strict régime concentration camp Aug. 1983–Sept. 1986; released Sept. 1986; settled in U.K. 1986–; poetry appeared in samizdat publs., West European Russian language journals, translations in American and British press. *Publications include:* Poems (trilingual text) 1984, No, I'm Not Afraid 1986, Grey Is the Colour of Hope 1988.

RATZINGER, H.E. Cardinal Joseph Alois; German ecclesiastic; b. 16 April 1927, Marktl; s. of Joseph Ratzinger and Maria Peintner; ed. Univ. of Munich; Chaplain 1951; Prof. of Theology, Freising 1958, Bonn 1959, Münster 1963, Tübingen 1966, Regensburg 1969; Archbishop 1977; Cardinal 1977; Archbishop of München-Freising; Chair. Bavarian Bishops' Conf.; Prefect, Sacred Congregation for the Doctrine of the Faith Nov. 1981–; mem. Secr. Synod of Catholic Bishops 1983–; mem. Congregation for Public Worship 1985–. *Publications:* books and articles on theological matters. *Address:* Piazza del S. Uffizio 11, I-00120 Città del Vaticano. *Telephone:* (06) 6983296.

RAU, (Adolf) Wilhelm (Ludwig), DR. PHIL.; German professor of Indology; b. 15 Feb. 1922, Gera, Thuringia; s. of Rudolf Rau and Johanna Seifarth; m. Ruth Soreth 1930; one s. two d.; ed. Gymnasium Ruthenum, Gera and Leipzig and Marburg Univs.; Privatdozent (Indology), Marburg Univ. 1952–55; Research Fellow, Visvabharati Univ., Santiniketan, W. Bengal 1952–54; Prof. Extra-Ordinarius of Indo-European Linguistics, Univ. of Frankfurt/Main 1955–57; Prof. of Indian Philology, Marburg Univ. 1958–87; mem. Mainz Acad. and other learned socs. *Address:* Wilhelm-Röpke-Strasse 6, Block F, 1 Stockwerk, 3550 Marburg/Lahn (Office); Am Hofacker 16a, 3551 Gossfelden, Federal Republic of Germany (Home).

RAU, Johannes; German politician; b. 16 Jan. 1931, Wuppertal; s. of Ewald and Helene (Hartmann) Rau; m. Christina Delius 1982; one s. two d.; mem. North Rhine-Westphalian Diet 1958–, Minister-Pres. North Rhine-Westphalian Land 1978–; Chair. North Rhine-Westphalian Parl. Group Social Democratic Party (SPD) 1967–70, mem. Exec. Bd. 1968–, Chair. Dist. Bd. 1977–, mem. Presidency 1978–, Deputy Chair. 1982–; Pres. Bundesrat 1982–83; Lord Mayor, City of Wuppertal 1969–70; Minister of Science and Research, North Rhine-Westphalia 1970–78; Dr. h.c. (Düsseldorf) 1985, (Open Univ.) 1986, (Haifa) 1986; Grand Cross Order of Leopold II (Belgium) 1972, Grand Cross Order of Rio Branco (Brazil) 1978, Grand Officier, Ordre nat. du Mérite (France) 1980, Grand Cross Order of Merit of Federal Republic of Germany. *Publications:* Oberstufenreform und Gesamthochschule 1970 (co-author), Die neue Fernuniversität 1974. *Leisure interest:* stamp-collecting, especially Israeli stamps. *Address:* Haroldstrasse 2, D-4000 Düsseldorf 1 (Office); Katernberger Strasse 171, D-5600 Wuppertal 1, Federal Republic of Germany (Home).

RAU, Santha Rama; Indian writer; b. 24 Jan. 1923, Madras, Tamil Nadu; d. of late Sir Benegal Rama Rau and Lady Rama Rau (q.v.); m. 1st

Faubion Bowers 1951 (divorced 1966), one s.; m. 2nd Gurdon W. Wattles; two step-s. two step-d.; ed. St. Paul's Girls' School, London, and Wellesley Coll., U.S.A.; numerous journeys in Europe, India, America, Southeast Asia, Japan and Russia; fmr. teacher Hani Freedom School, Tokyo; English teacher at Sarah Lawrence Coll., Bronxville, N.Y. 1971–73; Hon. doctorates from Bates, Brandeis, Roosevelt and Russell Sage Colls.; Achievement Awards from Asia Soc., New York, The Secondary Educ. Bd., N.J., The Assen. of Indians in America. *Publications:* Home to India 1945, East of Home 1950, This is India 1953, Remember the House 1955, View to the South-East 1957, My Russian Journey 1959, A Passage to India (dramatization of E. M. Forster novel) 1962, Gifts of Passage (autobiog.) 1962, The Cooking of India 1969, The Adventuress 1971, A Princess Remembers 1976, An Inheritance 1979; numerous articles and short stories. *Leisure interests:* gardening, opera and swimming. *Address:* RR Box 200, Leedsville Road, Amenia, N.Y. 12501; 315 East 69th Street, New York, N.Y. 10021, U.S.A.

RAUCHFUSS, Wolfgang; German politician; b. 27 Nov. 1931, Grüna; fmr. mechanic; mem. SED 1951–, mem. SED Cen. Cttee. 1967; Deputy Minister of Foreign and Intra-German Trade 1961–65; Joint Deputy Chair. Council of Ministers Dec. 1965–, Minister for Supply of Materials 1974–; mem. Volkskammer 1967–; Vaterländischer Verdienstorden in Silver and other decorations. *Address:* Leipziger Strasse 5–7, 1086 Berlin, German Democratic Republic.

RAUSCHENBERG, Robert; American artist; b. 22 Oct. 1925, Port Arthur, Texas; s. of Ernest and Dora Rauschenberg; m. Susan Weil 1951 (divorced); one s.; ed. Kansas City Art Inst., Acad. Julien, Paris, Black Mountain Coll., North Carolina and Art Students League, New York; travel in Italy and North Africa 1952–53; Designer of stage-sets and costumes for Merce Cunningham Dance Company 1955–65, lighting for Cunningham Co. 1961–65; costumes and sets for Paul Taylor Dance Co. 1957–59; Choreography in America 1962–; affiliated with Leo Castelli Gallery, New York City 1957–, Sonnabend Gallery, New York and Paris; works in Tate Gallery, London, Albright-Knox Gallery, Buffalo, Whitney Museum of American Art, New York City, Andrew Dickson White Museum, Cornell Univ., Museum of Modern Art, N.Y., Goucher Coll. Collection, Towson, Maryland, Cleveland Museum of Art, Cleveland, Ohio, Kunstsammlung, Noedheim, Westfalen, Germany, etc.; numerous one-man shows in U.S.A. and Europe; exhbn. at Stedelijk Museum, Amsterdam 1968; travelling retrospective exhbn. organized by Smithsonian Inst. Nat. Collection of Fine Art 1976–78, retrospective exhbn. Staatliches Kunst-museum, Berlin 1980; mem. American Acad. and Inst. of Arts and Letters; First Prize Int. Exhbn. of Prints, Gallery of Modern Art, Ljubljana 1963, Venice Biennale 1964, Corcoran Biennial Contemporary American Painters 1965, Grammy Award 1984. *Address:* c/o Leo Castelli Gallery, 420 West Broadway, New York, N.Y. 10012, U.S.A.

RAVANEL, Jean, D. EN D.; French civil servant; b. 2 May 1920, Chamonix; s. of Louis and Ida (née Cachat) Ravanel; m. 1st Lydie Stapfer 1946 (divorced), two s. three d.; m. 2nd Marie Bonnerue 1981; ed. Faculty of Law, Grenoble Univ.; entered Civil Service 1945; Technical Adviser, Ministry of Public Works and Transport 1954–55; Dir. Cabinet of Minister of Agriculture 1958–62, and of Minister of Public Works and Transport 1962; Chair. Gen. Commissariat for Tourism 1963–70; Conseiller d'Etat 1968–; Pres. BVP (French Advertising Standards Authority) 1986–; Comm. de la concurrence 1986–; Chair. Ski France; Officier, Légion d'honneur, Ordre nat. du Mérite, Aeronautical Medal. *Publications:* Le Conseil d'Etat et le Parlement, Les délégués du personnel. *Address:* 48 rue Cortambert, 75116 Paris, France.

RAVEN, Peter Hamilton, PH.D.; American botanist, administrator and educator; b. 13 June 1936, Shanghai, China; m. Tamra Engelhorn 1968; one s. three d.; ed. Univ. of California, Berkeley and Univ. of California, Los Angeles; Nat. Science Foundation Postdoctoral Fellow, British Museum, London 1960–61; Taxonomist, Rancho Santa Ana Botanical Garden, Claremont, Calif. 1961–62; Asst. Prof., then Assoc. Prof. of Biological Sciences, Stanford Univ. 1962–71; Dir. Mo. Botanical Garden and Engelmann Prof. of Botany, Wash. Univ., St. Louis, Mo. 1971–; Chair. Nat. Museum Services Bd. 1984–; mem. Governing Bd. Nat. Research Council 1983–86, N.A.S. (Council 1983–86), Bd. World Wildlife Fund—U.S.A. 1983–, Nat. Geographic Soc. Comm. on Research and Exploration 1982–, N.A.S. Comm. on Human Rights 1984–87, Smithsonian Council 1985–(88), Int. Advisory Cttee., The Nature Conservancy 1985–; Pres. Org. for Tropical Studies 1985–86, American Inst. of Biological Sciences 1983–84; Fellow, American Acad. of Arts and Sciences, Calif. Acad. of Sciences, A.A.A.S., Linnean Soc. of London and John D. Raven and Catherine T. MacArthur Foundation Fellow, Washington Univ. 1985–(89); Foreign mem. Royal Danish Acad. of Sciences and Letters, Royal Swedish Acad. of Sciences; several hon. degrees; Distinguished Service Award, American Inst. of Biological Sciences 1981; Int. Environmental Leadership Medal of UNEP 1982, Int. Prize in Biology, Japanese Govt.; other awards and prizes. *Publications:* Papers on Evolution (with Ehrlich and Holm) 1969, Biology of Plants 1970, Principles of Tzeltal Plant Classification 1974, Biology 1985; more than 300 professional papers; Ed.: Coevolution of Animals and Plants 1975, Topics in Plant Population Biology 1979, Advances in Legume Systematics 1981; contribs. to many other publs. *Address:* Missouri Botanical Garden, P.O. Box 299, St. Louis, Mo. 63166-0299, U.S.A.

RAVEN, Simon Arthur Noel, M.A.; British author; b. 28 Dec. 1927, London; s. of A. G. Raven and E. K. Raven (née Christmas); m. Susan Mandeville Kilner 1951 (marriage dissolved 1957); one s.; ed. Charterhouse, King's Coll., Cambridge; Nat. Service 1946–48, served with Parachute Regt. and Officer Training School, Bangalore; research at Cambridge 1948–52; Lieut. in King's Shropshire Light Infantry 1953, served in Fed. Repub. of Germany and Kenya (rank of Capt. 1956), resgnd. 1957; since 1957 has worked as novelist, critic and playwright. *Publications include:* novels: The Feathers of Death 1959, Alms for Oblivion (10 vol. sequence) 1964–76, Shadows on the Grass (autobiography) 1982, September Castle (novel) 1985, Morning Star (Vol. 1 of The First-Born of Egypt sequence), The Face of the Waters, Before the Cock Crow 1986 (Vols. 2 and 3 of the First-Born of Egypt sequence), The Old School (memoirs) 1986, New Seed for Old (Vol. 4 of First-Born of Egypt sequence) 1988, The Old Gang 1988, Blood of My Bones (Vol. 5 of the First-Born of Egypt Sequence) 1989. TV dramatizations: The Pallisers 1974, Edward and Mrs Simpson 1978. *Leisure interests:* travel, reading, cricket, horse racing. *Address:* c/o Curtis Brown, 162–168 Regent Street, London, W1R 5TA, England.

RAVENS, Karl Friedrich; German politican; b. 29 June 1927, Achim; s. of Fritz and Anna Ravens (née Kipka); m. Inge-Lore Treichel 1953; one s.; ed. apprenticeship in aircraft building; car mechanic 1945–52, apprentice instructor 1952–61; Alderman 1956–, mem. Kreistag (local council) 1957–, Deputy Mayor 1961–72; mem. Parl. (Bundestag) 1961–78; mem. Nat. Exec. Social Democratic Party (SPD) 1968–69; Parl. Sec. of State to Minister for Housing and Town Planning 1969–72, to Fed. Chancellor Brandt 1972–74; Fed. Minister for Construction, Housing and Town Planning 1974–78; mem. Television Council, Second German Television (ZDF) 1974–; Grand Cross, Order of St. Olav (Norway) and other decorations. *Publications:* various essays on housing and urban politics in specialist periodicals. *Leisure interest:* gliding. *Address:* Glimmerweg 15, 3000 Hanover 91, Federal Republic of Germany.

RAVIROSA WADE, Leandro; Mexican civil engineer; b. 11 June 1920; ed. Univ. Nacional Autónoma de México; Head of Plano Regulador del Departamento del D.F. and afterwards head of planning in this region; Dir. of Harbour Construction in the Secretaría de Marina and Pres. of Cámara de la Construcción; formed the building consortium, Constructora Randales, S.A. for the Netzahualcóyotl dam (Malpaso Province); Sec. of Water Resources 1970–76. *Address:* c/o Secretaría de Agricultura y Recursos Hidráulicos, Insurgentes Sur 476, México, D.F., Mexico.

RAVITCH, Diane, PH.D.; American historian; b. 1 July 1938, Houston, Tex.; d. of Mr. and Mrs. Walter Silvers; m. Richard Ravitch 1960 (divorced 1986); two s.; ed. Wellesley Coll., and Columbia Univ.; Adjunct Prof. of History and Educ. Teachers' Coll., Columbia Univ. 1975–; participant on numerous public policy bodies; Hon. D.Hum.Litt. (Williams Coll.) 1984, (Reed Coll.) 1985, (Amherst Coll.) 1986, (State Univ. of New York) 1988. *Publications:* The Great School Wars: New York City 1805–1973 1974, The Revisionists Revised 1978, The Troubled Crusade: American Education 1945–1980 1983, The Schools We Deserve 1985, What Do Our 17-Year-Olds Know? (with Chester E. Finn, Jr.) 1987. 150 articles and reviews. *Address:* Box 177, Teachers' College, Columbia University, New York, N.Y. 10027, U.S.A.

RAWIRI, Georges; Gabonese government official and diplomatist; b. 10 March 1932, Lambarene, Gabon; m.; two c.; ed. Protestant school, Ngomo, and Lycée Jean-Baptiste Dumas, Ales.; Head Tech. Centre Garoua Radio Station 1957, Libreville Radio Station 1959; a founder of Radio Gabon 1959; Dir. Radiodiffusion Gabonaise 1960, Radio-Télévision Gabonaise 1963; Counsellor for Foreign Affairs 1963; Minister of Information, Tourism, Posts and Telecommunications 1963–64; Minister of State and Amb. to France 1964–71, also accred. to Israel, Italy, Spain, U.K., Malta 1965–71, and Switzerland 1967–71; Minister of State for Foreign Affairs and Co-operation 1971–74, of the Govt. Office 1974–75, of Transport 1975–79, Civil Aviation 1975–78 and the Merchant Navy 1975–79, Asst. to the Deputy Prime Minister 1978–79; Deputy Prime Minister, and Minister of Transport 1980–83, First Deputy Prime Minister, Minister for Transport and Public Relations 1983–86, First Deputy Prime Minister, Minister of Rail, Road and Inland Water Transport, Water and Forest Resources and Social Communications 1986–; Grand Officer de l'Ordre de l'Etoile Equatoriale and decorations from Mauritania, France, Malta and the Ivory Coast; Médaille d'Or des Arts, Sciences et Lettres; Grand Officier de l'Ordre Int. du Bien Public. *Address:* Ministère d'Etat de Transport, B.P. 3974, Libreville, Gabon.

RAWL, Lawrence G., B.E.; American business executive; b. Lyndhurst, N.J.; ed. Univ. of Oklahoma; joined Exxon Corpn. 1952, Producing Dept. New York 1960, Co-ordinator of Planning and Evaluation 1963, Asst. Man. East Texas Production Div. 1965, Operations Man. Production Dept. 1966, Exec. Asst. to Chair. of Bd. 1967–69, Dir. and Vice-Pres. 1972, Exec. Vice-Pres. Exxon U.S.A. 1976, Exec. Vice-Pres. Esso Europe 1978, Sr. Vice-Pres. Exxon 1980, Pres. 1985–87, Chair., C.E.O. Jan. 1987–; Dir. Chemical New York Corpn. and Chemical Bank, New York City Partnership, Inc., New York Chamber of Commerce and Industry, Business Council of N.Y. State, American Petroleum Inst.; mem. of Soc. of Petroleum Engineers, and others. *Address:* Office of the President, Exxon Corporation, 1251 Avenue of the Americas, New York, N.Y. 10020, U.S.A.

RAWLINGS, Flight-Lieut. Jerry; Ghanaian air force officer; b. 22 June 1947, Accra; s. of Madam Victoria Abbotoi; m. Nana Konado Agyeman; two d.; ed. Achimota School and Ghana Military Acad., Teshie; commissioned as Pilot Officer 1969, Flight-Lieut. 1978; arrested for leading mutiny of junior officers May 1979; leader mil. coup which overthrew Govt. of Supreme Mil. Council June 1979; Chair. Armed Forces Revolutionary Council (Head of State) June–Sept. 1979; retd. from armed forces Nov. 1979; leader mil. coup which overthrew Govt. of Dr. Hilla Limann (q.v.) Dec. 1981; Head of State Jan. 1982–; Chief of the Defence Staff Nov. 1982–; Chair. Provisional Nat. Defence Council Dec. 1981–. *Leisure interests:* boxing, diving (deep sea), swimming, horse riding, carpentry. *Address:* c/o Office of the Head of State, The Castle, Accra, Ghana.

RAWLINS, Surgeon-Vice-Adm. Sir John Stuart Pepys, K.B.E., F.R.C.P., F.F.C.M., F.R.A.E.S.; British consultant; b. 12 May 1922, Amesbury, Wilts.; s. of Col. Comdt. Stuart W. H. Rawlins and Dorothy P. Rawlins; m. Diana M. Freshney Colbeck 1944; one s. three d.; ed. Wellington Coll., Univ. Coll., Oxford and St. Bartholomew's Hosp., London; Surgeon-Lieut. R.N.V.R. 1947; Surgeon-Lieut. R.N., R.A.F. Inst. of Aviation Medicine 1951; R.N. Physiological Lab. 1957; Surgeon-Commdr. R.A.F. Inst. of Aviation Medicine 1961; H.M.S. Ark Royal 1964; US Naval Medical Research Inst. 1967; Surgeon-Capt. 1969; Surgeon-Commodore, Dir. of Health and Research (Naval) 1973; Surgeon-Rear-Adm. 1975; Dean of Naval Medicine and Medical Officer in charge of Inst. of Naval Medicine 1975–77; Acting Surgeon Vice-Adm. 1977; Medical Dir.-Gen. (Navy) 1977–80; Hon. Physician to H.M. The Queen 1975–80; Dir. Under Sea Industries Inc. 1981–83; Pres. Soc. for Underwater Tech. 1980–84; Chair. Deep Ocean Tech. Inc., Deep Ocean Eng. Inc. 1982–, Trident Underwater (Systems) Ltd. 1986–; consultant to Chemical Defence Establishment, Porton Down and British Airways PLC; Hon. Fellow, Univ. of Lancaster; numerous awards and medals. *Publications:* numerous papers in fields of aviation and diving medicine and underwater tech. *Leisure interests:* fishing, stalking, riding, judo. *Address:* Wey House, Standford Lane, Headley, Bordon, Hants, GU35 8RH, England. *Telephone:* Bordon 2830.

RAWLINSON OF EWELL, Baron (Life Peer), cr. 1978, of Ewell in the County of Surrey; **Peter Anthony Grayson Rawlinson,** Kt., P.C., Q.C.; British lawyer and politician; b. 26 June 1919, Birkenhead, Cheshire (now Merseyside); s. of Lieut.-Col. A. R. Rawlinson and Ailsa Grayson Rawlinson; m. 1st Haidee Kavanagh 1940; three d.; m. 2nd Elaine Angela Dominguez 1954; two s. one d.; ed. Downside and Christ's Coll., Cambridge; served in Irish Guards 1939–46; called to the Bar, Inner Temple 1946, Treas. 1984; mem. of Parl. 1955–78; Recorder of Salisbury 1961–62; Solicitor-Gen. 1962–64; mem. Bar Council 1966–68; Attorney-Gen. 1970–74; Attorney-Gen., Northern Ireland 1972–74; Leader Western Circuit 1975–82; mem. Senate, Inns of Court 1968; Chair. of the Bar 1975–76; Chair. of Senate, Inns of Court and Bar 1975–76, Pres. 1986–87; Recorder of Kingston-upon-Thames 1975–85; Chair. Owl Creek Investments 1985–; Dir. Pioneer Concrete Services 1985–, Daily Telegraph PLC 1985–; Hon. Fellow, Christ's Coll., Cambridge; Hon. mem. American Bar Assen.; Hon. Fellow, American Coll. of Trial Lawyers; Conservative. *Publications:* War Poems and Poetry today 1943, Public Duty and Personal Faith-the example of Thomas More 1978, A Price Too High (autobiog.) 1989. *Leisure interest:* painting. *Address:* 9 Priory Walk, London, SW10 9SP, England. *Telephone:* 01-370 1656.

RAWLS, John, PH.D.; American professor of philosophy; b. 21 Feb. 1921, Baltimore, Md.; s. of William Lee Rawls and Anna Abel Stump Rawls; m. Margaret Warfield Fox 1949; two s. two d.; ed. Kent School, Princeton and Cornell Univs.; served in U.S. Army 1943–46; Instructor, Princeton Univ. 1950–52; Fulbright Fellow, Oxford Univ., England 1952–53; Asst., then Assoc. Prof., Cornell Univ. 1953–59; Visiting Prof., Harvard Univ. 1959–60; Prof., M.I.T. 1960–62; Prof., Harvard Univ. 1962–, James Bryant Conant Univ. Prof. 1979–; mem. American Acad. of Arts and Sciences, American Philosophical Assen. (Vice-Pres. 1973, Pres. 1974), American Philosophical Soc., American Assen. of Political and Legal Philosophy (Pres. 1970–72). *Publications:* A Theory of Justice 1971; articles in professional journals. *Address:* 9 Winthrop Road, Lexington, Mass. 02173, U.S.A.

RAWSON, Merle R., B.S.; American business executive; b. 9 June 1924, Chicago, Ill.; m. Jane Rawson; two s. one d.; ed. York Community High School, Elmhurst, Ill., Bradley Univ., Ill., Univ. of Ill. and Northwestern Univ., Evanston, Ill.; Asst. to Plant Controller, John Wood Co. 1949; Asst. Controller Easy Laundry Appliances 1958; Controller O'Bryan Bros. 1961; joined Hoover Co. as Budget Dir. 1961; Controller Hoover Co. 1962, Controller and Asst. Treasurer 1963–64, Vice-Pres. and Treasurer 1964; Vice-Pres., Finance, Hoover Worldwide Corpn. 1965–69, Sr. Vice-Pres. 1969, Exec. Vice-Pres. 1971–75, Chair. and C.E.O. 1975–; Sr. Vice-Pres. and Treasurer, Hoover Co. 1969–75, Chair. and C.E.O. 1975–82, and Pres. 1982–88; Chair., Pres. and C.E.O. Worldwide Corpn. 1986–88; Chair. Hoover PLC, U.K. 1978–88; Dir. Hoover Co. and numerous subsidiaries; Dir. Soc. Bank of Eastern Ohio, N.A.; Soc. Corpn.; mem. Bd. of Dirs. Chicago Pacific Corpn. 1985–; mem. Council on Foreign Relations, New York, Advisory Council mem. Pace Univ., mem. Sr. Common Room, St. Edmund Hall (Oxford); Chevalier, Order of Leopold, Belgium 1980, Medal of the City of Paris 1983; Chevalier Légion d'honneur (France) 1986; Hon. Dr. of Public Services (Walsh Coll.) 1985. *Address:* Hoover Worldwide Corporation, North Canton, Ohio 44720, U.S.A.

RAY, Ajit Nath, M.A.; Indian judge; b. 29 Jan. 1912, Calcutta; s. of Sati Nath Ray and Kali Kumari Debi; m. Himani Mukherjee 1944; one s.; ed. Presidency Coll., Calcutta, Oriel Coll., Oxford and Gray's Inn, London; fmrly. practised as a barrister, Calcutta High Court; Judge, Calcutta High Court 1957-69; Judge, Supreme Court of India 1969-73, Chief Justice of India 1973-77; Hon. Fellow, Oriel Coll., Oxford; Pres. Int. Law Asscn. 1974-76, Vice-Pres. 1977-, Vice-Pres. Ramakrishna Inst. of Culture 1981-; mem. Int. Permanent Court of Arbitration 1976-; Pres. Governing Body Presidency Coll., Calcutta 1957-69; Founder-Pres. Soc. for the Welfare of the Blind 1958-80; Treas. Asiatic Soc. 1961-63, Vice-Pres. 1963-65; mem. Karma Samiti Visva Bharati Santiniketan 1963-65, 1967-69, Life mem. 1969-. *Address:* 15 Panditia Place, Calcutta 29, India. *Telephone:* 475213.

RAY, Dixy Lee, B.A., M.A., PH.D.; American marine biologist, administrator and politician; b. 3 Sept. 1914, Tacoma, Washington; d. of Alvis Marion Ray and Frances Adams Ray; ed. Mills coll., Oakland. Calif., Stanford Univ.; Teacher Oakland, Calif. public schools 1939-42; John Switzer Fellow, Stanford Univ. 1942-43; Van Sicklen Fellow, Stanford Univ. 1943-45; Assoc. Prof. of Zoology, Univ. of Washington 1945-76; Exec. Cttee. Friday Harbour Laboratories 1945-60; Special Consultant biological oceanography, Nat. Science Foundation 1960-63; Dir. of Pacific Science Centre, Seattle 1963-72; Visiting Prof., Stanford Univ. 1964-; Chief Scientist, Te Vega in Int. Indian Ocean Expedition 1964; Presidential Task Force on Oceanography 1969; mem. Atomic Energy Comm. 1972-75, Chair. 1973-75; Asst. Sec. of State Jan.-June 1975; Gov. (Democrat) Washington State 1977-81; Commentator KVI radio station, Seattle 1981-; Consultant TRW Eng. 1981-; mem. Marshall Fellowship Cttee.; Guggenheim Fellow 1952-53; Hon. degrees Mills Coll. 1967, St. Martins Coll. 1971, Hood Coll. 1973, Seattle Univ. 1972, Ripon Coll. 1974, St. Mary's Coll. 1974, Puget Sound Univ. 1974, Michigan State Univ. 1974, Union Coll. 1974, Northern Mich. Univ. 1974; Seattle Maritime Award 1967, William Clapp Award in Marine Biology 1958, Frances K. Hutchison Medal for service in conservation 1973, Francis Boyer Science Award 1974, YWCA 1974 Gold Medal Award, Outstanding Woman of Science Award, ARCS Foundation 1974; foreign mem. Danish Royal Soc. for Natural History 1965; UN Peace Medal 1973, Axel-Axelson Johnson Award, Swedish Royal Acad. of Science and Eng. 1974, American Exemplar Medal, Freedom Foundation at Valley Forge 1978, and numerous other degrees, awards and prizes. *Publications:* Marine Boring and Fouling Organisms 1959; numerous articles on public understanding of science and scientific papers on marine biology. *Leisure interests:* American Indian culture, boating, gardening, hiking. *Address:* 600 3rd Avenue, Fox Island, Wash. 98333, U.S.A. (Home). *Telephone:* (206) 549-2176.

RAY, Robert D., D.JUR.; American politician; b. 26 Sept.1928, Des Moines, Iowa; s. of the late Clark A. Ray and of Mrs. Mildred H. Ray; m. Billie Lee Hornberger 1951; three d.; ed. Drake Univ.; admitted to Ia. Bar 1954; partner Lawyer, Lawyer and Ray, Des Moines; Chair. Midwest Republican Chairmen's Asscn. 1965-68; Nat. Advisory Cttee. of Republican State Chairmen 1967; State Chair. of March of Dimes 1960-62; mem. of county, state and Nat. Bar Asscns. and Trial Lawyers' Asscns.; mem. Nat. Acad. of Practising Law Inst., Hon. Mem. Bd. of Trustees of American Acad. of Achievement; State Chair. of Republican Party 1963-67; Gov. of Iowa 1968-83; Pres. and C.E.O. Aegon NV. Ia. 1983-; Chair. Bd. of Dirs. Life Investors Inc. *Leisure interests:* sports, amateur photography.

RAY, Satyajit; Indian film director; b. 2 May 1921, Calcutta; s. of the late Sukumar Ray and Suprabha (née Das); m. Bijoya Das 1949; one s.; ed. Ballygunge Govt. School, Presidency Coll., Calcutta; Commercial artist in Calcutta before beginning his career in films; directed Pather Panchali 1954 (Cannes Int. Film Festival Award for "the most human document" 1956, Golden Laurel Award, Edinburgh Film Festival 1957), Aparajito 1956 (sequel to Pather Panchali, Grand Prix, Venice Film Festival 1957), The Philosopher's Stone, Jalsagar (The Music Room), Apur Sansar (The World of Apu), The Goddess 1961, Three Daughters 1961, Abhijan 1962, Kanchanjangha 1962, Mahanagar 1964, Charulata 1965, Kapurush-o-Mahapurush 1965, Nayak 1966, Chiriakhana 1968, The Adventures of Goopy and Bagha 1969, Days and Nights in the Forest 1969, Seemabaddha (Company Limited) 1970, Pratidwandi (The Adversary) 1971, Distant Thunder 1973, Golden Fortress 1974, The Middle Man 1975, Shratranj Ke Khilari (The Chessplayers) 1977, Elephant God, The Kingdom of Diamonds 1980, Pikoo 1982, The Home and The World 1984, Gana shatru (Public Enemy) 1989; composed the music for all his films since Three Daughters; editor Sandesh (children's magazine) 1961-; Magsaysay Award for Journalism and Literature 1967; Berlin Film Festival Prize for Distant Thunder 1973, Gold Medal, Légion d'honneur (France) 1989; Order of Yugoslav Flag 1971, Padma Bibushan 1976; Hon D.Litt. (Royal Coll. of Art, London) 1974, (Oxford) 1978, BFI Fellowship 1983. *Publications:* Our Films, Their Films 1977, Stories 1987. *Leisure interests:* listening to classical music (Indian and Western), reading science fiction. *Address:* Flat No. 8, 1/1 Bishop Lefroy Road, Calcutta 20, India. *Telephone:* 44-8747.

RAY, Siddhartha Sankar; Indian politican and lawyer; b. 20 Oct. 1920, Calcutta; s. of the late Sudhir Chandra Ray and Shrimati Aparna Devi (Das); m. Maya Bhattacharya 1947; ed. Presidency Coll., Calcutta; called to the Bar, Inner Temple, London; Senior Advocate, Supreme Court; fmr.

Minister of Law, Govt. of West Bengal; Leader of Opposition, West Bengal Govt. 1969; mem. Lok Sabha 1971-72, West Bengal Legis. Ass. 1972-77; Minister of Educ., Culture and Social Welfare and Minister in Charge, West Bengal Affairs, Govt. of India 1971-72; Chief Minister of West Bengal March 1972-77; Gov. of Punjab April 1986-; Admin of Chandigarh April 1986-; mem. Working Cttee. Congress Party, All India Congress Cttee., Congress Parl. Board; Pres. Bengal Cricket Asscn. 1982. *Leisure interests:* reading, sports. *Address:* 2 Beltala Road, Calcutta 700026, India. *Telephone:* 473465 (Home).

RAYES, Ghazi al; Kuwaiti diplomatist; b. 23 Aug. 1935; ed. Univ. of Cairo, Egypt; Third Sec. Ministry of Foreign Affairs 1962; Kuwaiti Embassy, Washington and Beirut 1965-67; Chair. Int. Affairs Section, Ministry of Foreign Affairs 1967-70; Counsellor, Kuwaiti Embassy, Beirut 1970-73; Amb. to Bahrain 1974-80, to United Kingdom Dec. 1980-. *Address:* Embassy of Kuwait, 46 Queen's Gate, London, S.W.7, England.

RAYNAUD, Jean Guillaume Marie, D. EN D.; French public servant; b. 27 May 1925, Vichy; s. of Guillaume Raynaud and Elisabeth Péligry; m. Marie-Thérèse Parent de Petkowski d'Ostoja 1951; one s. one d.; ed. Inst. d'Etudes Politiques de Paris, Ecole Nat. d'Admin.; Auditor, Cour des Comptes 1953; Tech. Adviser to Minister of the Interior July-Nov. 1957; Adviser to Cour des Comptes 1959; Tech. Adviser to Minister of Finance 1959-60; Chargé de mission, Office of Minister of Finance and Econ. Affairs 1960-62; Dir. of Educational, Univ. and Sports Facilities 1964-70; Dir.-Gen. Office français des techniques modernes d'éduc. 1970-76; mem. Haut conseil de l'audiovisuel 1973-76; Chief Adviser, Cour des Comptes 1979, Attorney-Gen. 1986-; Pres. Chambre régionale des comptes, Nord-Pas-de-Calais 1982-86; Chevalier, Légion d'honneur, Ordre Nat. du Mérite, Ordre Nat. du Mérite agricole; Commdr., des Palmes Académiques. *Publications:* Les Chambres régionales des comptes 1984, Les contrôles des Chambres régionales des comptes, La Cour des Comptes. *Address:* Cour des Comptes, 13 rue Cambon, 75100 Paris, France.

RAYNAUD, Pierre; French health inspector; b. 20 Oct. 1917, Paris; s. of Clément Raynaud and Lucienne Massinon; m. Denise Mouton 1940; one s. one d.; Dir. of hosps. 1945-63; Adviser to Ministry of Health 1956-58; expert in int. tech. co-operation 1962-68; Deputy Insp.-Gen. of Health 1963-71, Insp.-Gen. 1971-80; Pres. Fed. Hospitalière de France 1980-; founder, Hosp. Cttee. of European Community; Commdr., Légion d'Honneur, Commdr. Ordre Nat. du Mérite. *Publications:* Histoire des hôpitaux en France 1982. *Leisure interest:* collecting books. *Address:* 33 avenue d'Italie, 75013 Paris (Office); 10 rue Clément Hue, 78120 Rambouillet, France (Home). *Telephone:* 45-84-32-50 (Office); 34-83-11-23 (Home).

RAYNE, Baron (Life Peer), cr. 1976, of Prince's Meadow in Greater London; **Max Rayne,** Kt.; British company director; b. 8 Feb. 1918, London; s. of Phillip and Deborah Rayne; m. 1st Margaret Marco 1941 (dissolved 1960), one s. two d.; m. 2nd Lady Jane Antonia Frances Vane-Tempest-Stewart 1965, two s. two d.; ed. Cen. Foundation School and Univ. Coll., London; Royal Air Force 1940-45; Chair. London Merchant Securities PLC 1960-, Westpool Investment Trust PLC 1980-; Deputy Chair. First Leisure Corpn. PLC 1984-; dir. of other cos.; Gov. St. Thomas's Hospital 1962-74, Special Trustee 1974-; Gov. Royal Ballet School 1966-79, Malvern Coll. 1966-, Centre for Environmental Studies 1967-73; mem. Gen. Council King Edward VII's Hospital Fund for London 1966-; mem. Council St. Thomas's Hospital Medical School 1965-82, Council of Govs., United Medical Schools of Guy's and St. Thomas's Hospitals 1982-; Chair. London Festival Ballet Trust 1967-75, Nat. Theatre Bd. 1971-88; Founder Patron Rayne Foundation 1962-; Hon. Vice-Pres. Jewish Welfare Bd. 1966-; Vice-Pres. Yehudi Menuhin School 1987- (Gov. 1966-87); Hon. Fellow, Univ. Coll., London 1966, London School of Econs. 1974, Darwin Coll., Cambridge 1966, Royal Coll. of Psychiatrists 1977, King's Coll. Hosp. Medical School 1980, Univ. Coll. Oxford 1982, King's Coll., London 1983; Hon. LL.D., (London) 1968; Officier, Légion d'honneur. *Address:* 33 Robert Adam Street, London, W1M 5AH, England. *Telephone:* 01-935 3555.

RAYNER, Baron (Life Peer), cr. 1983, of Crowborough in the County of East Sussex; **Derek George Rayner,** Kt.; British businessman and civil servant; b. 30 March, 1926; s. of George Rayner and Hilda Rant; ed. City Coll., Norwich, Selwyn Coll., Cambridge; service in RAF 1946-48; joined Marks and Spencer 1953, Dir. 1967-, Jt. Man. Dir. 1973-82, Jt. Vice-Chair. 1982-83, Chief Exec. 1983-88, Chair. 1984-; Special Adviser to Govt. 1970, 1979-83; Chief Exec., Procurement Exec., Ministry of Defence 1971-72; Deputy Chair. Civil Service Pay Bd. 1978-80; Adviser Manpower Services Comm. 1981-82; mem. Design Council 1973-75, U.K. Permanent Security Comm. 1977-80, Royal Coll. of Art, British Maritime League; Chair. Coronary Artery Disease Research Asscn. 1985-; Vice-Pres. British-Israel Chamber of Commerce; Pres. Medical Coll. of St. Bartholomew's 1988; elected Hon. Fellow Selwyn Coll. 1983; Fellow, Inst. of Purchasing and Supply 1970. *Leisure interests:* food, music, gardening. *Address:* Michael House, Baker Street, London, W1A 1DN, England.

RAYNES, Edward Peter, M.A., PH.D., F.R.S.; British physicist; b. 4 July 1945, York; s. of Edward Gordon Raynes and Ethel Mary Raynes; m. Madeline Ord 1970; two s.; ed. St. Peter's School, York, Gonville and Caius Coll. and the Cavendish Lab., Cambridge; with Royal Signals and Radar

Establishment, Malvern 1971-, Deputy Chief Scientific Officer 1987-; Rank Opto-Electronic Prize 1980, Paterson Medal, Inst. of Physics 1986, Special Recognition Award, Soc. of Information Display 1987. *Publications:* numerous scientific publs. and patents; The Physics, Chemistry and Applications of Liquid Crystals (Jt. Ed.). *Leisure interests:* choral and solo singing. *Address:* Royal Signals and Radar Establishment, Malvern, Worcs., WR14 3PS (Office); 23 Leadon Road, Malvern, Worcs., WR14 2XF, England (Home).

RAZAFIMAHATRATRA, H.E. Cardinal Victor; Malagasy ecclesiastic; b. 8 Sept. 1921, Ambatofitorahana-Ambositra, Fianarantsoa; ordained priest 1956; Bishop of Farafangana 1971-76; Archbishop of Tananarive (Antananarivo) 1976-; cr. Cardinal 1976; mem. Sacred Congregation for the Evangelization of Peoples; entitled S. Croce in Gerusalemme. *Address:* Archevêché, Andohalo, 101 Antananarivo, Madagascar. *Telephone:* 20.726.

RAZAFIMBAHINY, Jules Alphonse; Malagasy jurist, economist and diplomatist; b. 19 April 1922, Mananjary; s. of Alphonse and Marguerite (née Ramasinoro) Razafimbahiny; m. Ravaoarisoa Razafy 1951; one s. one d.; ed. Institut de Droit des Affaires, Faculté de Droit, Paris, and Institut des Hautes Etudes Politiques, Paris, Collège des Sciences Sociales et Economiques, Paris; Pres. of Comm. of Overseas Countries associated with Econ. and Social Council of Common Market and EURATOM, Brussels 1958-60; Tech. Counsellor to Minister of State for Nat. Economy, Madagascar 1960-61; Minister Plenipotentiary 1962; First Sec.-Gen. OAMCE (Org. Africaine et Malgache de Co-opération Economique) later called OCAM (Org. Commune Africaine Malgache et Mauricienne) 1962-64; Dir.-Gen. Foreign Affairs (Tananarive) 1964-65; Amb. to U.K., Italy, Greece and Israel 1965-67; Sec. of State for Foreign Affairs (Econ. and African Affairs) 1967-69; Amb. to U.S.A. 1970-72, to Belgium and European Communities 1973-78 (also accred. to Netherlands, Luxembourg, German Democratic Rep., Switzerland and Holy See); Interregional Adviser, Dept. of Tech. Co-operation (DTCD) UN HQ, New York; UNDP Rep. in Burundi 1979-83; Dir. World Food Programme 1979, UN Information 1979; Resident Co-ordinator of UN System's activities for devt. of Burundi 1981-; fmr. Pres. Admin. Council, Soc. d'Energie, Madagascar, Pan-African Inst. of Devt.; mem. Editorial Board, Soc. for Int. Devt. (Washington, D.C.), Board, Coll. of Econ. and Social Studies and Institut d'Etudes de Développement Economique et Social; mem. Club de Dakar; Commdr., Ordre Nat. (Madagascar, Mauritania, Chad, Zaire, Comoro Islands), Officier, Ordre Nat. (Upper Volta, Gabon); Grand Croix de l'Ordre de Saint Sylvestre (Vatican), Grand Croix de l'Ordre nat. de la Répub. Italienne and other decorations. *Publications:* articles on economics. *Leisure interests:* music, painting, tennis. *Address:* c/o United Nations Development Programme, B.P. 1490, Bujumbura, Burundi.

RAZAFINDRABE, Armand; Malagasy diplomatist; b. 17 Sept. 1931, Tananarive (now Antananarivo); s. of Arthur Razafindrabe and Elisabeth Raheliarisoa; m. Françoise Gonin 1958; two d.; ed. Paris Univ.; Asst. Chief, Dept. of Econ. Affairs 1955, Chief of Dept. 1958-59; Admin. Officer, EEC 1959-60; Econ. and Commercial Counsellor, Embassy in Paris 1960-63; Perm. Rep. to EEC and Amb. to Belgium, Netherlands, Luxembourg and Switzerland 1963-73; Amb. to Japan 1974, 1983-88; Exec. Dir. IBRD, IFC, IDA 1974-82; head of del. negotiating Yaoundé Conventions with EEC 1963-68, to UNCTAD 1964,1968, 1972, to ECOSOC 1968, 1970, 1972; Chair. or Vice-Chair. of UN African Group, Group of 1977 and other bodies 1964, 1966, 1968, 1970, 1971, 1972; mem. Exec. Council GATT 1963-; Commdr., Ordre nat. Malgache; Grand Officer, Ordre de la Couronne de Belgique. *Leisure interests:* skiing, swimming, cooking, music, theatre. *Address:* 3101 New Mexico Avenue, N.W., Washington, D.C. 20016, U.S.A.; 13 rue Gilbert, Meyrin 1217, Geneva, Switzerland (Homes). *Telephone:* 82.77.12 (Geneva).

RAZAK, Dato Sri Mohamad Najib bin tun Haj Abdul, B.A.; Malaysian politician; b. 23 July 1954, Kuala Lipis, Pahang; m. Tengku Puteri Zainah bint Tengku Iskandar; three c.; ed. Univ. of Nottingham; Exec. Patronas 1974-78; Pengerusi Majuternak 1977-78; M.P. 1976-; Deputy Minister of Energy, Telecommunications and Posts 1978-80, of Educ. 1980-81, of Finance 1981-82; mem. State Ass. for Pakan constituency 1982; apptd. Menteri Besar Pahang 1982; Minister of Youth and Sports 1986-; mem. UMNO Supreme Council 1981-; Vice-Pres. UMNO Youth 1982-; Chair. Pahang Foundation 1982-86. *Address:* Ministry of Culture, Youth and Sports, 15th Floor, Wisma Keramat, Jalan Gurney, 50570 Kuala Lumpur, Malaysia.

RAZALEIGH HAMZAH, Tengku Tan Sri Datuk, P.S.M., S.P.M.K.; Malaysian politician and fmr. company executive; b. c. 1936; s. of late Tengku Mohamed Hamzah bin Zainal Abidin (fmr. Chief Minister of Kelantan); ed. Queen's Univ., Belfast, and Lincoln's Inn, London; Chair. of Kelantan Div. of United Malays' Nat. Org. (UMNO) in early 1960s; mem. Kelantan State Assembly for some years; Exec. Dir. Bank Bumiputra 1963, Chair., Man. Dir. 1970; Exec. Dir. PERNAS 1971-74; Chair. Malaysian Nat. Insurance; led trade mission to Beijing 1971; a Vice-Pres. UMNO 1975-; Pres. Assoc. Malay Chambers of Commerce until Oct. 1976; Chair. PETRONAS (Nat. Oil Co.) 1974-76; Minister of Finance 1976-84, of Trade and Industry 1984-87; Chair. IMF Meetings 1978-, Asram Devt. Bank 1977-, Islamic Devt. Bank 1977-. *Address:* c/o Ministry of Trade and Industry, Block 10, Government Offices Complex, Jalan Duta, Kuala Lumpur, Malaysia.

RÁZL, Stanislav; Czechoslovak politician; b. 13 April 1920, Sopotnice; one s. one d.; ed. School of Econs., Prague; worker 1939-44; Technician, Asscn. for Chem. and Metallurgical Production, Ústí-on-Elbe 1945-48; Technician, Gen. Man. of Chem. Industries, Prague 1948-51; Chief of Planning Dept., Deputy Minister, Ministry of Chem. Industry, Prague 1951-56; Enterprise Man., Asscn. for Chem. and Metallurgical Production, Ústí-on-Elbe 1956-63; Chief Technologist and Economist, Tech. Econs. Research Inst. 1963-65; Dir. of Devt. Dept., Ministry of Chem. Industry 1965-68, Minister of Chem. Industry 1968; Premier of Czech Socialist Repub. Jan.-Sept. 1969, Deputy Premier 1969-83; Minister of Planning 1969-71; Chair. Czech Planning Comm. 1971-83; Deputy to House of Nations, Fed. Assembly of C.S.S.R. 1969-71; Chair. Govt. Environmental Council 1971-77; Chair. Govt. Comm. for Complex Devt. of Krkonöse Region 1981-; Award of Merit in Construction 1960, Order of Labour 1975, Order of Repub. 1980. *Address:* Government Presidium of the Czech Socialist Republic, Prague 1, Lazarská 7, Czechoslovakia.

RAZUMOVSKY, Georgiy Petrovich; Soviet politician; b. 19 Jan. 1936; ed. Krasnodar Agricultural Inst.; agronomist on kolkhoz 1958-59; First Sec. Komsomol, Krasnodar Dist. 1959-61; mem. CPSU 1961-; section chief of Krasnodar Dist. Cttee. of CPSU 1961-64; Sec. CPSU cttee. on kolkhoz-sovkhoz production 1964-67; Head Dept. of Agric. Krasnodar Dist. Cttee. of CPSU 1967-71; Chief of section of a dept. Cen. Cttee. CPSU 1971-73; Chair. Exec. Cttee. of Krasnodar Dist. Workers' Soviet 1973-81; mem. Comm. on Consumer Goods 1974-79; Mandate Comm. 1979-84; Chair. Comm. on Agro-Industrial Complex 1984-85; Chair. Comm. on Legis. Proposals 1985-; Head of Dept. Agro-Industrial Complex of U.S.S.R. Council of Ministers 1981-83; First Sec. Krasnodar Dist. Cttee. CPSU and mem. of N. Caucasian Mil. Dist. 1983-85; Head of Dept. for Organizational Party Work of Cen. Cttee. CPSU 1985-; mem. Cen. Cttee. CPSU 1986-; Sec. Gen. Cttee. CPSU (responsible for cadre affairs) 1986-; mem. Politburo 1988-; elected to Congress of People's Deputies of the U.S.S.R. 1989; Order of Lenin 1986, Order of Red Banner 1981. *Address:* Central Committee of the Communist Party of the Soviet Union, Staraya pl. 4, Moscow, U.S.S.R.

READ, Air Marshal Sir Charles Frederick, K.B.E., C.B., D.F.C., A.F.C.; Australian air force officer (retd.); b. 9 Oct. 1918, Sydney; s. of Joseph F. Read and Ethel Mary Shelton; m. Betty Elsie Bradshaw 1946; three s.; ed. Sydney Grammar School and Imperial Defence Coll.; Dir. Operations, Royal Australian Air Force 1960-64; Commandant, R.A.A.F. Acad., Point Cook, Vic. 1966-68; Officer Commanding R.A.A.F. Richmond, N.S.W. 1968-69; Deputy Chief of Staff R.A.A.F. 1969-72, Chief of Staff 1972-75; retd. 1975. *Leisure interest:* yachting. *Address:* 2007 Pittwater Road, Bayview, N.S.W., Australia. *Telephone:* 997-1686.

READ, Sir John Emms, Kt., F.C.A., F.R.S.A., F.I.B.; British business executive; b. 29 March 1918, Brighton; s. of William E. and Daysie E. (née Cooper) Read; m. Dorothy M. Berry 1942; two s.; ed. Brighton, Hove and Sussex Grammar School and Admin. Staff Coll., Henley-on-Thames; Commdr. Royal Navy 1939-46; Adm.'s Sec. to Asst. Chief of Naval Staff, Admiralty 1942-45, Naval Sec., British Admiralty Tech. Mission, Ottawa 1945-46; Ford Motor Co. 1946-64, Dir. of Sales 1961-64; Exec. Dir. EMI Ltd. 1965, Man. Dir. 1966-69, Chief Exec. 1969-79, Deputy Chair. 1973-74, Chair. 1974-79; Deputy Chair. Thorn EMI Ltd. 1979-80, Dir. 1981-87; Chair. Trustee Savings Bank Cen. Bd. 1980-88, Trustee Savings Banks (Holdings) Ltd. 1980-86, TSB England and Wales 1983-86, TSB Group PLC 1986-88, (Dir. TSB England and Wales PLC 1986-88), United Dominions Trust Ltd. 1981-85; Dir. Dunlop Holdings Ltd. 1971-84, Thames Television Ltd. 1973-88 (Deputy Chair. 1981-88), Capitol Industries-EMI Inc., U.S.A. 1970-83, Group Five Holdings Ltd. 1984-, Wonderworld PLC 1986-, FI Group PLC 1989-, Nat. Youth Film Foundation 1987-; mem. P.O. Bd. 1975-77, Royal Naval Film Corpn. 1975-83, British Overseas Trade Bd. 1976-79; Chair. Electronics Econ. Devt. Comm. 1976-80, Armed Forces Pay Review Body 1976-83, Nat. Electronics Council 1977-80, Gov. Admin. Staff Coll., Henley 1974-; mem. Council of CBI 1977-, President's Cttee. 1977-84, Chair. Finance Cttee. 1978-84; Trustee, Westminster Abbey Trust 1978-87, Brain Research Trust 1982-; Pres. Sussex Assen. of Boys' Clubs 1982-, Cheshire Homes, Seven Rivers, Essex 1979-85; Chair. of Man. Inst. of Neurology 1980-; Vice-Pres. Inst. of Bankers 1982-; mem. Cttee. of London and Scottish Bankers 1986-88; mem. Governing Body, British Postgraduate Medical Fed. 1982-; Fellow, R.S.A. 1975-; Companion, Inst. of Radio Engineers, B.I.M.; Hon. D. Univ. (Surrey) 1987. *Leisure interests:* music, the arts, sport. *Address:* 41 Portman Square, London, W1H 9FH (Office); Muster House, 12 Muster Green, Haywards Heath, West Sussex, RH16 4AG, England (Home). *Telephone:* 01-935 7888 (Office); (0444) 413333 (Home).

READ, Piers Paul, M.A., F.R.S.L.; British writer; b. 7 March 1941, Beaconsfield; s. of Herbert Edward Read and Margaret Ludwig; m. Emily Albertine Boothby 1967; two s. two d.; ed. Ampleforth Coll., York and St. John's Coll., Cambridge; Artist-in-Residence, Ford Foundation, W. Berlin 1964; Sub-Ed. Times Literary Supplement, London 1965; Harkness Fellow Commonwealth Fund, New York 1967-68; Council mem. Inst. of Contemporary Arts (ICA), London 1971-75; Cttee. of Man. Soc. of Authors, London 1973-76; mem. Literature Panel Arts Council, London 1975-77; Adjunct Prof. of Writing, Columbia Univ., New York 1980; Sir Geoffrey Faber Memorial Prize, Somerset Maugham Award, Hawthornden Prize, Thomas

More Award (U.S.A.). *Publications:* Game in Heaven with Tussy Marx 1966, The Junkers 1968, Monk Dawson 1969, The Professor's Daughter 1971, The Upstart 1973, Alive: The Story of the Andes Survivors 1974, Polonaise 1976, The Train Robbers 1978, A Married Man 1979, The Villa Golitsyn 1981, The Free Frenchman 1986, A Season in the West 1988. *Leisure interest:* family life. *Address:* 50 Portland Road, London, W11 4LG, England. *Telephone:* 01-727 5719.

REAGAN, Nancy Davis (Anne Francis Robbins), B.A.; fmr. First Lady of the United States; b. 6 July 1923, New York; d. of Kenneth Robbins and Edith (née Luckett) Robbins, step-d. of Loyal Davis; m. Ronald Reagan (q.v.) 1952; one s. one d., one step-s. one step-d.; ed. Smith Coll., Mass.; contract actress Metro-Goldwyn-Mayer 1949-56; fmr. author syndicated column on prisoners-of-war and soldiers missing in action; civic worker active on behalf of Viet Nam war veterans, sr. citizens, disabled children and drug victims; Hon. Nat. Chair. Aid to Adoption of Special Kids 1977; one of Ten Most Admired American Women, Good Housekeeping Magazine 1977, Woman of Year, L.A. Times 1977, perm. mem. Hall of Fame of Ten Best Dressed Women in U.S., Lifetime Achievement Award, Council of Fashion Designers of U.S.A. 1988. *Films include:* The Next Voice You Hear 1950, Donovan's Brain 1953, Hellcats of the Navy 1957. *Publication:* Nancy 1980. *Address:* 34th Floor, Fox Plaza Tower, Century City, Los Angeles, Calif.; St. Cloud Road, Los Angeles, Calif., U.S.A. (Home).

REAGAN, Ronald Wilson; American politician and former actor; b. 6 Feb. 1911, Tampico, Ill.; s. of John Edward and Nelle (Wilson) Reagan; m. 1st Jane Wyman 1940 (divorced 1948), one s. one d.; m. 2nd Nancy (née Davis) Reagan (q.v.) 1952, one s. one d.; ed. Northside High School, Dixon, Ill., and Eureka Coll.; U.S. Air Force 1942-46; Gov. of Calif. 1967-74; Pres. of U.S.A. 1981-89; Dir. Nat. Review Bd. 1989-; Chair. Republican Govs. Asscn. 1969; fmr. film actor and producer, radio sports announcer (at Des Moines, Iowa) and Ed., Cen. Broadcasting Co.; operated horse-breeding and cattle ranch; Player and Production Supervisor, Gen. Electric Theater TV for eight years; fmr. Pres. Screen Actors Guild, Motion Picture Industry Council; mem. Bd. of Dirs. Cttee. on Fundamental Educ., St. John's Hosp.; Dr. h.c. (Notre Dame, Ind.) 1981, (Nat. Univ. of Ireland) 1984; numerous awards; Republican. *Films acted in include:* Love is on the Air 1937, Accidents Will Happen 1938, Dark Victory 1939, Hell's Kitchen 1939, Brother Rat and a Baby 1940, Santa Fé Trail 1940, International Squadron 1941, Nine Lives are Not Enough 1941, King's Row 1941, Juke Girl 1942, Desperate Journey 1942, This is the Army 1943, Stallion Road 1947, That Hagen Girl 1947, The Voice of the Turtle 1947, Night unto Night 1948, John Loves Mary 1949, The Hasty Heart (Great Britain) 1949, Louisa 1950, Storm Warning 1951, Bedtime for Bonzo 1951, Hong Kong 1952, Prisoner of War 1954, Law and Order 1954, Tennessee's Partner 1955, Hellcats of the Navy 1957, The Killers 1964. *Publications:* Where's the Rest of Me? (autobiography), reprinted as My Early Life 1981, Abortion and the Conscience of the Nation 1984. *Address:* 34th Floor, Fox Plaza Tower, Century City, Los Angeles, Calif.; St. Cloud, Los Angeles, Calif., U.S.A. (Home).

REBBECK, Denis, C.B.E., M.A., M.SC., PH.D., B.LITT., D.L., J.P., F.ENG.; British shipbuilder; b. 22 Jan. 1914, Belfast, N. Ireland; s. of late Sir Frederick and Lady Rebbeck; m. Rosamond Annette K. Jameson 1938; four s.; ed. Campbell Coll., Belfast and Pembroke Coll., Cambridge; Asst. Man. Harland and Wolff Ltd., Belfast 1939, Dir. 1946, Deputy Man. Dir. 1953-62, Man. Dir. 1962-70, Chair. 1965-66; Dir. D. and W. Henderson Ltd. and A. and J. Inglis Ltd. 1946-68, Chair. 1957-68; Dir. Iron Trades Employers' Insurance Asscn. Ltd. and Iron Trades Mutual Insurance Co. Ltd. 1950-84, Vice-Chair. 1969-72, Chair. 1972-84; Belfast Harbour Commr. 1962-85; Pres. Shipbuilding Employers' Fed. 1962-63; Vice-Pres. World Ship Soc. 1956-78, Pres. 1978-81; Dir. Colvilles Ltd., Glasgow 1963-67, Shipbuilding Corpn. Ltd., London 1963-73, Nat. Commercial Bank of Scotland Ltd. 1965-69, Royal Bank of Scotland Ltd. 1969-84, Nationwide Building Soc. 1980-89; Chair. Gen. Underwriting Agencies Ltd. 1984-; mem. Royal Yacht Squadron, Man. Bd., Eng. Employers Fed. 1963-75, Gen. Cttee., Lloyd's Register of Shipping 1962-85, Research Council and Chair. Design Cttee., British Ship Research Asscn. 1965-73, N. Ireland Econ. Council 1965-70; mem. Council of Royal Inst. of Naval Architects 1964-72; mem. Court of Assts. and Warden Worshipful Co. of Shipwrights, Prime Warden 1980-81; Dir. John Kelly Ltd. 1968-79, Deputy Chair. 1968-69, Chair 1969-79; Dir. Belships Co. Ltd. 1970-76, Chair. 1972-76; Special Consultant, Swan Hunter Group Ltd. 1970-79; Chair. Govt. Advisory Cttee. on Pilotage 1977-79; Chair. U.K. Pilotage Comm. 1979-83; Hon. Life mem. The Irish Port Authorities Asscn. 1985; Akroyd Stuart Award, Inst. of Marine Engineers 1943. *Leisure interests:* sailing and driving a vintage Rolls Royce. *Address:* The White House, Craigavad, Co. Down, BT18 0HE, N. Ireland, United Kingdom. *Telephone:* (023 17) 2294.

REBELO DE SOUSA, Dr. Baltasar; Portuguese politician; b. 16 April 1922, Lisbon; s. of Antonio J. and Joaquina L. Rebello de Souza; m. Maria Das Neves F. Duarte 1947; three s.; ed. Faculty of Medicine, Univ. of Lisbon; Under-Sec. of State for Educ. 1955-61; Vice-Pres. Overseas Council 1963-68; Gov.-Gen. of Mozambique 1968-70; Deputy to Nat. Assembly; Minister of Health and Corpns. 1970-73, in charge of Emigration Problems 1971-73, of Overseas Provs. 1973-74; Minister of Parl. Affairs 1982-83; Pres. Lusiada Acad. for Sciences, Literature and Arts S.P. Brazil 1984-(87);

mem. Portuguese dels. to int. orgs.; Dir. of enterprises-S.P. Brazil; Univ. Prof. Legal Medicine (Brazil); mem. Bd. of Dirs. Asscn. of Social Service and Portuguese League against Cancer; fmr. Prof. Inst. of Social Service; Grand Cross Ordem de Cristo, Ordem do Infante D. Henrique Portugal, Ordem do Cruzeiro do Sul, Ordem do Mérito Médico, Ordem do Mérito do Trabalho, Ordem Mérito Educativo (Brazil), Orden dos Cisneros (Spain), Grand Officer Ordem da Instrução Pública (Portugal), Ordem dos Santo Sepulchro's Cavaliers (Vatican), Grand Cross Ordem Colombo's Knights. *Publications:* Integral Preparation of Youth 1951, Unitary Concept of Medical Assistance and Social Assurance, Religion and Life 1952, Forms and Perspectives of Popular Culture 1956, A Big Land and a Great People, One Year of Gov. 1968, Social State—Reflections and Basic Concepts 1969, Pax Lusitana 1970, Social Political Perspectives (3 vols.) 1971, 1972, 1973; Legal Medicine Basics 1976. *Leisure interests:* African and sociology studies, travel, reading and writing. *Address:* Rua Matais Aires, 285 São Paulo, 001309 Brazil; Rua S. Bernardo 102, 1200 Lisbon, Portugal. *Telephone:* 608150 (Lisbon); 2576846/2116022/2116211/2116416/2116750 (São Paulo).

REBEYROLLE, Paul; French artist; b. 3 Nov. 1926; ed. Lycée Gay-Lussac, Limoges; exhbns. at Salon des Indépendants, Salon d'Automne, Salon de Mai, Salon de la Jeune Peinture (France); Dir. Salon de Mai; works in collections in England, Sweden, Belgium, U.S.A., Poland, Italy, Japan, etc.; rep. at Dunn Int. Exhibition, London 1963; First Prize, la Jeune Peinture 1950, Fénéon Prize 1951, First Prize at French Section, Paris Biennale 1959. *Address:* 9 rue Falguière, 75015 Paris, France.

REBLING, Eberhard, D.PHIL. German pianist and musicologist; b. 4 Dec. 1911, Berlin; m. Lin Jaldati; two d.; ed. Berlin Univ.; emigrated to Holland 1936; with resistance movement in Holland 1941-45; joined Netherlands CP 1946; Music Critic and Pianist, Amsterdam 1945-51; Sec.-Gen. Netherlands U.S.S.R. Soc. 1949-52; Chief Ed. periodical Musik und Gesellschaft, Berlin 1952-59; joined SED 1960; Rector Deutsche Hochschule für Musik Hanns Eisler, Berlin 1959-71, Prof. 1959-76; mem. Volkskammer 1963-, Steering Cttee. 1971-; Nat. prize 1954, Peace Medal 1964, Vaterländischer Verdienstorden in Gold and other decorations. *Publications:* Een eeuw Nederlandse Danskunst 1950, Den Lustelijcken Mey 1950, Johann Sebastian Bach 1951, Ballett gestern und heute 1956, Ballett, sein Wesen and Werden 1964, Ballet von A-Z 1966, Ballet heute 1970, Der Tanz der Völker 1972, Ballettfibel 1974, Marius Petipa 1975, Die Tanzkunst Indiens 1981. *Address:* 1251 Ziegenhals, Seestrasse 18, German Democratic Republic. *Telephone:* Zeuthen 836.

REBOCHO VAZ, Col. Camilo Augusto de Miranda; Portuguese army officer and administrator; b. 7 Oct. 1920, Avis; s. of Aurelio Rebocho Vaz and Marcelina da Conceição Miranda Vaz; m. Clotilde Gil da Assunção 1947; three s. two d.; ed. Univ. de Coimbra, Escola do Exército, Lisbon and Inst. de Altos Estudos Militares, Lisbon; mil. service in Portugal, Azores and Angola; 2nd Commdr., Infantry Regt., Luanda, Angola 1960; Commdr. of anti-terrorist activities 1961; Gov. District of Uige, Angola 1961-66; Gov. of Angola 1966-72; numerous military and civil decorations. *Publications:* Quatro Anos de Governo no Distrito de Uige, Angola 1967, Angola 1969, Dois Anos de Governo, Outros Dois Anos de Governo, Acção Governativa. *Leisure interest:* collecting shells and minerals. *Address:* c/o Ministério dos Negócios Estrangeiros, Lisbon, Portugal.

RECHENDORFF, Torben; Danish politician; b. 1 April 1937; teacher and prin. at various schools, Frederiksberg and Hørsholm 1960-81; Sec.-Gen. Conservative People's Party 1981; Minister of Ecclesiastical Affairs 1988-. *Address:* Ministry of Ecclesiastical Affairs, Frederiksholms Kanal 21, 1220 Copenhagen K, Denmark. *Telephone:* (01) 14-62-63.

RECKITT, Basil Norman, M.A., T.D.; British business executive (retd.); b. 12 Aug. 1905, St. Albans; s. of Norman and Beatrice Reckitt (née Hewett); m. 1st Virginia Carre-Smith 1928 (died 1961), 2nd Mary Holmes 1966; three d.; ed. Uppingham and King's Coll., Cambridge; joined Reckitt & Sons Ltd., Hull 1927, Dir. 1937-72, later Chair.; Dir. Reckitt & Colman Ltd. 1953-72, Vice-Chair. 1953-65, Deputy Chair. 1965-66, Chair. 1966-70; Royal Artillery 1938-44; Mil. Govt., Germany 1944-45; Sheriff, Kingston upon Hull 1970-71; Chair. of Council, Hull Univ. 1971-80, Pro-Chancellor 1980; Hon. LL.D. (Hull) 1967. *Publications:* History of Reckitt & Sons Limited, Charles I and Hull, The Lindley Affair, A History of the Sir James Reckitt Charity 1921-1979. *Address:* Haverbrack, Milnthorpe, Cumbria, England.

RECKTENWALD, Horst Claus, DR. RER. POL.; German professor of economics; b. 25 Jan. 1920, Spiesen; s. of Jacob Recktenwald and Maria Recktenwald; m. Hertha Joanni 1953; ed. Univ. of Mainz and foreign univs.; Prof. Technische Hochschule, Darmstadt 1958-59, Univ. of Freiburg im Breisgen 1959, Univ. of Erlangen-Nuremberg 1963-; mem. Leibniz-Akad. der Wissenschaft in Literatur; Grosses Bundesverdienstkreuz. *Publications include:* Klassiker der Nationalökonomie 1986, Die Nobel-Laureaten-Critical Thoughts 1989. *Leisure interest:* tennis. *Address:* 8500 Nuremberg-Laufamholz, Förrenbacher Strasse 15, Federal Republic of Germany. *Telephone:* 0911 501881.

REDAELLI SPREAFICO, Enrico; Italian iron and steel executive (retd.); b. 24 April 1911, Milan; ed. "Bocconi" Univ., Milan; joined Soc. Dalmine in IRI Group 1936; joined Finsider 1938, appointed Admin. Man. of Società Rejna, a firm in Finsider group 1943; Admin. Head, Società Cornigliano

1950, subsequently Admin. Man. and Asst. Gen. Man.; Gen. Man. Soc. Cornigliano 1958; Gen. Man. Italsider 1961, Man. Dir. 1962, 1972, Vice-Pres. 1972, Pres. 1973–77; Cavaliere del Lavoro; Grand Ufficiale dell'Ordine Equestre del Santo Sepolcro di Gerusalemme. *Address:* Via Alberto Mario 20, 20149 Milan, Italy (Home).

REDDAWAY, William Brian, C.B.E., M.A., F.B.A.; British economist; b. 8 Jan. 1913, Cambridge; s. of William Fiddian Reddaway and Kate Waterland (née Sills) Reddaway; m. Barbara A. Bennett 1938; three s. one d.; ed. Oundle School, and King's Coll., Cambridge; Asst. Bank of England 1934–35; Research Fellow in Econs. Univ. of Melbourne 1936–37; Fellow of Clare Coll., Cambridge 1938–; Bd. of Trade 1940–47; Lecturer, Cambridge Univ. 1947–55, Dir. Dept. of Applied Econs. 1955–70; Reader in Applied Econs. 1957–69, Prof. of Political Economy 1969–80; Econ. Adviser, Org. for European Econ. Co-operation (OEEC) 1951–52, Confederation of British Industries 1972–83; Econ. Consultant 1980–; Research Assoc. Centre for Int. Studies, New Delhi 1959–60; Visiting Lecturer, Econ. Devt. Inst., Washington 1966–67; Visiting Prof. Inst. of Devt. Studies, Dacca 1974–75; Head Inst. of Fiscal Studies Study on Sr. Man.'s Taxation 1977–79; mem. Royal Comm. on the Press 1961–62; mem. Nat. Bd. of Prices and Incomes 1967–71; Editor, London and Cambridge Economic Bulletin 1951–74, Economic Journal 1971–76; Regional Adviser, Econ. Comm., W. Asia 1979–80; Adam Smith Prize, Cambridge 1934. *Publications:* The Russian Financial System 1935, The Economics of a Declining Population 1939, The Measurement of Production Movements 1948, The Development of the Indian Economy 1962, The Effects of U.K. Direct Investment Overseas (interim report) 1967, (final report) 1968, The Effects of the Selective Employment Tax (first report) 1970, (final report) 1973, An Alternative Economic Strategy 1981, Some Key Issues for the Development of the Economy of Papua New Guinea 1986, and numerous articles in learned journals. *Leisure interests:* tennis, walking, skating, squash. *Address:* 12 Manor Court, Grange Road, Cambridge, CB3 9BE, England. *Telephone:* (0223) 350041.

REDDY, Kasu Brahmananda, B.A., B.L.; Indian politician; b. 28 July 1909, Chirumamilla; s. of Venkatakrishna and Sayamma Reddy; m. Raghavamma Reddy; ed. Madras Univ.; Pres. Guntur District Bd. 1936; mem. Madras Assembly 1946–52; Gen. Sec. Andhra Pradesh Congress Cttee. 1955; Minister of Finance and Planning, Andhra Pradesh 1960–62, of Finance and Co-operation 1962–64, Chief Minister 1964–71; Union Minister of Communications Jan.-Oct. 1974; Minister of Home Affairs 1974–77, of Industry 1979–80; Gov. Maharashtra Feb. 1988–; Pres. Indian Nat. Congress 1977–78 (resgnd.); mem. Lok Sabha for Narasaraopet 1977–79. *Address:* 6-3-1089, Rajabran Road, Somji Gowda, Hyderabad, India.

REDDY, Kolli Venkata Raghunatha, M.A., LL.B.; Indian lawyer and politician; b. 4 Sept. 1924; ed. V. R. Coll., Nellore, and Annamalai Univ. and Lucknow Univ.; mem. Senate Annamalai Univ. 1947–59; Advocate, Madras High Court 1950, Supreme Court 1958, also Andhra Pradesh High Court; mem. Rajya Sabha 1962–; Union Minister of State for Industrial Devt. and Company Affairs 1967–70, of Company Affairs 1970–72, of Labour and Rehabilitation 1973–77. *Publications:* Criminal Law—Procedural and Substantial. *Address:* 92 Shahjehan Road, New Delhi 110011, India.

REDDY, Marri Channa, M.B., B.S.; Indian agriculturist and politician; b. 13 Jan. 1919; ed. Chadarghat High School and Osmania Univ.; left medical practice to devote himself to politics in Hyderabad; held organizational posts in Indian Nat. Congress Party; leader in Hyderabad Congress; mem. Rajya Sabha 1950–51; Minister of Agriculture, Andhra Pradesh 1952, later Minister of Planning, Rehabilitation, Panchyat Raj, Industry and Commerce, Commercial Taxes, Education and Finance, Andhra Pradesh; Union Minister of Steel, Mines and Metals 1967–68; Gov. of Uttar Pradesh 1974–77; Chief Minister of Andhra Pradesh 1978–80; Gov. of Punjab 1982. *Address:* c/o Raj Bhavan, Chandigarh, Punjab, India.

REDDY, Neelam Sanjiva; Indian politician; b. 19 May 1913, Illuru village, Anantapur District, Andhra Pradesh; ed. Adyar Arts Coll., Anantapur; Sec. Andhra Pradesh Congress Cttee. 1936–46; active in Satyagraha movement; mem. and Sec. Madras Legislative Assembly 1946; mem. Indian Constituent Assembly 1947; Minister for Prohibition, Housing and Forests, Madras Govt. 1949–51; Pres. Andhra Pradesh Congress Cttee. 1951–52; mem. Rajya Sabha 1952–53, Andhra Pradesh Legislative Assembly 1953–64; Leader of Andhra Congress Legislature Party 1953–64; Deputy Chief Minister, Andhra Pradesh 1953–56, Chief Minister 1956–57; Pres. Indian Nat. Congress 1960–62; Chief Minister of Andhra Pradesh 1962–64; Union Minister of Steel and Mines 1964–65, of Transport, Aviation, Shipping and Tourism 1966–67; mem. Lok Sabha from Hindupur, Andhra Pradesh and Speaker of Lok Sabha 1967–69; cand. in presidential election 1969; engaged in agriculture 1969–77; mem. Cttee. of Janata Party Jan. 1977; Speaker of Lok Sabha March–July 1977; Pres. of India 1977–82; Hon. D.Litt. (Sri Venkateswara Univ.). *Address:* Illure, Anantapur, Andra Pradesh, India.

REDFORD, Robert; American actor; b. 18 Aug. 1937, Santa Monica, Calif.; ed. Van Nuys High School, Univ. of Colorado; *Films include:* War Hunt 1961, Situation Hopeless But Not Serious 1965, Inside Daisy Clover 1965, The Chase 1965, This Property is Condemned 1966, Barefoot in the Park 1967, Tell Them Willie Boy is Here 1969, Butch Cassidy and the Sundance Kid 1969, Downhill Racer 1969, Little Fauss and Big Halsy 1970,

Jeremiah Johnson 1972, The Candidate 1972, How to Steal a Diamond in Four Uneasy Lessons 1972, The Way We Were 1973, The Sting 1973, The Great Gatsby 1974, The Great Waldo Pepper 1974, Three Days of the Condor 1975, All the President's Men 1976, A Bridge Too Far 1977, The Electric Horseman 1980, Brubaker 1980, The Natural 1984, Out of Africa 1985, Legal Eagles 1986; Dir. Ordinary People 1980 (Acad. Award and Golden Globe Award for Best Dir. 1981), The Natural 1984, Milagro Beanfield War 1988 (also produced), Promised Land (exec. producer) 1988. *Address:* c/o Wildwood Enterprises, 100 Universal City Plaza, Universal City, Calif. 91608, U.S.A.

REDGRAVE, Vanessa, C.B.E.; British actress; b. 30 Jan. 1937; d. of the late Sir Michael Redgrave and Rachel Kempson; m. Tony Richardson (q.v.) 1962 (divorced 1967); two d.; ed. Queensgate School, London, and Central School of Speech and Drama; Evening Standard Award, Best Actress 1961 and Variety Club Award 1961; Award for Best Actress, Cannes Film Festival 1966 for Morgan—A Suitable Case for Treatment; Award for Leading Actress, U.S. Nat. Soc. of Film Critics and Best Actress Award, Film Critics' Guild (U.K.) for Isadora Duncan 1969; Acad. Award (Best Supporting Actress) for Julia 1978; Award (TV for Best Actress) for Playing for Time 1981; Laurence Olivier Award 1984; mem. Workers' Revolutionary Party (Cand. for Moss Side 1979); Fellow B.F.I. 1988. *Stage appearances in:* A Midsummer Night's Dream 1959, The Tiger and the Horse 1960, The Taming of the Shrew 1961, As You Like It 1961, Cymbeline 1962, The Seagull 1964, 1985, The Prime of Miss Jean Brodie 1966, Daniel Deronda 1969, Cato Street 1971, Threepenny Opera 1972, Twelfth Night 1972, Anthony and Cleopatra 1973, 1986, Design for Living 1973, Macbeth 1975, Lady from the Sea 1976 and 1979 (Manchester), The Aspern Papers 1984, Ghosts 1986, A Touch of the Poet 1988, Orpheus Descending 1988, A Madhouse in Goa 1989; *films include:* Morgan—A Suitable Case for Treatment 1965, Sailor from Gibraltar 1965, Camelot 1967, Blow Up 1967, Charge of the Light Brigade 1968, Isadora Duncan 1968, The Seagull 1968, A Quiet Place in the Country 1968, Dropout, The Trojan Women 1970, The Devils 1970, The Holiday 1971, Mary Queen of Scots 1971, Katherine Mansfield (BBC TV) 1973, Murder on the Orient Express 1974, Winter Rates 1974, 7% Solution 1975, Julia 1977, Agatha 1978, Yanks 1978, Bear Island 1979, Playing for Time (CBS TV) 1979, Playing for Time 1980, My Body My Child (ABC TV) 1981, Wagner 1982, The Bostonians 1983, Wetherby 1984, Prick Up Your Ears 1987, Comrades 1987, Consuming Passions 1988; produced and narrated documentary film The Palestinians 1977. *Publication:* Pussies and Tigers 1963. *Leisure interest:* changing the status quo. *Address:* 1 Ravenscourt Road, London, W.6, England. *Telephone:* 01-748 9105.

REDGROVE, Peter William, F.R.S.L.; British poet, author and analytical psychologist; b. 2 Jan. 1932; s. of Gordon G. Redgrove and late Nancy Lena Cestrilli-Bell; m. Penelope Shuttle; one d. (and two s. one d. by previous m.); ed. Taunton School and Queens' Coll., Cambridge; scientific journalist and editor 1954–61; Visiting Poet, Buffalo Univ., New York 1961–62; Gregory Fellow in Poetry, Leeds Univ. 1962–65; Resident Author and Sr. Lecturer in Complementary Studies, Falmouth School of Art 1966–83; O'Connor Prof. of Literature, Colgate Univ., New York; recipient of several awards. *Publications:* novels: In the Country of the Skin 1973, The Terrors of Dr Treviles 1974, The Glass Cottage 1976, The God of Glass 1979, The Sleep of the Great Hypnotist 1979, The Beekeepers 1980, The Facilitators, or, Madame Hole-in-the-Day 1982; psychology and sociology; The Wise Wound 1978, The Black Goddess and the Sixth Sense 1987; numerous vols. of poems, including The Collector and Other Poems 1960, The Force and Other Poems 1966, Dr. Faust's Sea-Spiral Spirit and Other Poems 1972, The Weddings at Nether Powers, and Other New Poems 1979, The Working of Water 1984, The Mudlark Poems and Grand Buveur 1986, In the Hall of the Saurians 1987, The Moon Disposes: Poems 1954–87 1987; anthologies and radio and television plays, etc; articles in magazines and journals. *Leisure interests:* work, photography, judo, yoga. *Address:* c/o David Higham Associates, 5–8 Lower John Street, Golden Square, London, W1R 4HA, England.

REDMAN, John B., C.B.E.; British business executive; b . 4 Oct. 1914, Leeds; s. of Bertram Redman and Margaret Redman; m. Doreen Culverwell (née Hunt) 1950; one s. one step-s.; ed. Felsted School, Essex; Sales Dir. Electrolux Ltd. 1962–67, Marketing Dir. 1967–69, Deputy Man. Dir. 1969–71; Man. Dir. 1972–79; Deputy Chair. and Chief Exec. Electrolux (U.K.) Group 1979–82, Chair. 1982–85. *Leisure interests:* supporting Yorkshire and England at most sports, walking. *Address:* 8 Bryanston Mews West, London, W1H 7FR, England. *Telephone:* 01-723 7407.

REDMOND, Walter T.; American business executive (retd.); b. 12 Aug. 1923, Battle Creek, Mich.; m. Jackie Redmond; ed. Michigan State Univ.; joined Kellogg Cos'. Industrial Eng. Dept. 1948, Comptroller's Dept. 1952, Comptroller 1961–67, Vice-Pres.-Controller 1967–72, Dir. 1972–, Exec. Vice-Pres. for Admin. 1975–80, Pres. and Chief Admin. Officer 1980–85, Vice-Chair. and Chief Admin. Officer 1985–87; mem. Leila Hospital Advisory Bd. 1971– (Chair. 1979–82); Trustee, Citizens Research Council of Mich. *Address:* Kellogg Co., 235 Porter Street, P.O. Box 3423, Battle Creek, Mich. 49016-3423, U.S.A. *Telephone:* (616) 966-2000.

REECE, Hon. Eric Elliott, A.C.; Australian trade unionist and politician; b. 6 July 1909, Mathinna; s. of G. O. Reece; m. Alice L. Hanigan 1936;

two s. (one deceased) two d.; ed. Launceston Jr. Tech. School; Organizer Australian Workers' Union, W. Tasmania 1935–46; mem. Fed. Exec. Australian Labor Party 40, 1949–59, Fed. Pres. 1952–53, 1954–55, Pres. Tasmanian Section 1948–59; Hon. Minister in charge of Housing and Building Supplies, Tasmania 1946–47; Minister for Lands and Works, Tasmania 1947–58, for Mines 1947–69; Premier of Tasmania 1958–69, Treas. 1959–69; Leader of the Opposition 1969–72; Premier, Treas., Minister for Mines, Tasmania 1972–75; mem. House of Ass. for Braddon, Tasmania 1946–75. *Leisure interest:* bowls. *Address:* 59 Howard Road, Glenorchy, Tasmania 7010, Australia.

REED, Ishmael Scott; American author; b. 22 Feb. 1938, Chattanooga; s. of Bennie S. Reed and Thelma Coleman; one s. one d.; Dir. Reed & Cannon Co.; Assoc. Fellow, Calhoun House, Yale Univ. 1983–; co-publr., Quilt magazine; Sr. Lecturer, Univ. of Calif. Berkeley; mem. usage panel, American Heritage Dictionary; Assoc. Ed. American Book Review; Exec. Producer Personal Problems (video soap opera); collaborator in multi media Bicentennial mystery, The Lost State of Franklin (winner Poetry in Public Places contest 1975); Chair. Berkeley Arts Comm.; Advisory Chair. Coordinating Council of Literary Magazines; Pres. Before Columbus Foundation; Nat. Endowment for Arts Writing Fellow 1974; Nat. Inst. of Arts and Letters Award 1975; Guggenheim Fellow 1975; Michaux Award 1978, ACLU Award 1978; mem. authors Guild of America, PEN. *Publications:* novels: The Free-Lance Pallbearers 1967, Yellow Back Radio Broke Down 1969, Mumbo Jumbo 1972, The Last Days of Louisiana Red 1974, Flight to Canada 1976, The Terrible Twos 1982, Cab Calloway Stands in For the Moon 1986; several vols. of poetry and essays. *Address:* c/o Avon Books Division, Hearst Corporation, 1790 Broadway, New York, N.Y. 02108, U.S.A.

REED, John Shedd, B.S.; American business executive; b. 9 June 1917, Chicago, Ill.; s. of Kersey C. Reed and Helen M. Shedd; m. Marjorie Lindsay 1946; three s. two d.; ed. Yale Univ., U.S. Naval Acad. and Harvard Business School; employee, Atchison, Topeka & Santa Fe Railway 1939; U.S.N.R. 1941–46; resumed career at Atchison, Topeka & Santa Fe Railway 1946, Vice-Pres. Finance 1959–64, Vice-Pres. Exec. Dept. 1964–67, Pres. 1967, Pres. and C.E.O. 1968; Chair. and C.E.O. AT & SF and Santa Fe Industries 1973–83; Chair. Citicorp 1984–; Chair. of Bd. Santa Fe Southern Pacific Corpn. 1987–88. *Leisure interests:* annual bicycle tour of Europe (mostly France), skiing, golf, tennis. *Address:* 224 South Michigan Avenue, Chicago, Ill. 60604, U.S.A. *Telephone:* 312-347-2700.

REED, Joseph Verner, B.A.; American United Nations official; b. 1937, New York; m.; two d.; ed. Deerfield Acad., Mass. and Yale Univ.; Asst. to Pres. of IBRD 1961–63, Asst. to Dir. 1965–68; employee Chase Manhattan Bank 1963–65, Admin. Asst. to Chair. of Bd. 1968–69, Vice-Pres. and Asst. to Chair. 1969–81; fmr. Amb. to Morocco; fmr. U.S. Rep. to UN ECOSOC with rank of Amb.; Under-Sec.-Gen. for Political and Gen. Ass. Affairs and Secr. Services UN, New York 1987–89; Chief of Protocol Jan. 1989–. *Address:* United Nations Plaza, New York, N.Y. 10017, U.S.A.

REED, Oliver; British actor; b. 13 Feb. 1938, Wimbledon; s. of Peter and Marcia Reed; m. 1st (divorced); one s. one d.; m. 2nd Josephine Burge 1985; ed. Ewell Castle. *Films include:* The Rebel 1960, No Love for Johnnie 1961, Pirates of Blood River 1962, The Damned 1962, The System 1964, The Brigand of Kandahar 1965, The Trap 1966, The Shuttered Room 1966, The Jokers 1966, Hannibal Brooks 1968, Oliver 1968, The Assassination Bureau 1969, Women In Love 1969, The Lady in the Car 1970, The Devils 1971, The Hunting Party 1971, Z.P.G. 1972, Sitting Target, Triple Echo 1972, The Three Musketeers 1973, The Four Musketeers 1974, 10 Little Indians 1974, Tommy 1975, The Sellout 1975, Great Scout and Cathouse Thursday 1976, Burnt Offerings 1976, The Prince and the Pauper 1977, Assault on Paradise 1977, The Big Sleep 1978, The Brood 1979, Omar Mukhtar 1979, Lion of the Desert 1980, The Great Question 1981, Venom 1981, Condorman 1981, The Sting II 1983, Castaway 1986, Captive 1986, The Adventures of Baron von Munchausen 1989; Vice-Pres. Rosslyn Park Rugby Club. *Publication:* Reed All About Me 1979. *Address:* 3 The Pines, Dorking, Surrey, RH4 2BE, England. *Telephone:* (0306) 888058.

REED, Richard John, SC.D.; American meteorologist; b. 18 June 1922, Braintree; s. of William Amber Reed and Gertrude Helen Volk; m. Joan Murray 1950; two s. one d.; ed. Calif. and Mass. Insts. of Tech.; Research Staff Mem., M.I.T. 1950–54; Asst. Prof., Univ.of Washington 1954–58, Assoc. Prof. 1958–63, Prof. Dept. of Atmospheric Sciences 1963–; Consultant, Nat. Meteorological Center, U.S. Weather Bureau 1961–62; Exec. Scientist, U.S. GARP Comm. 1968–69; Pres. American Meteorological Soc. 1972; Consultant, European Centre for Medium Range Weather Forecasts 1985–86; Trustee Univ. Corpn. for Atmospheric Research 1987–; mem. N.A.S. 1978–; Fellow, American Meteorological Soc.; Meisinger Award 1964, Second Half Century Award 1972, Charles Franklin Brooks Award 1983, Carl-Gustaf Rossby Research Medal 1988. *Publications:* Meteorology in Science in Contemporary China 1980; Ed. Journal of Applied Meteorology 1966–68; numerous scientific papers. *Leisure interests:* gardening, cultural events. *Address:* Department of Atmospheric Sciences, University of Washington, Seattle, Wash. 98195, U.S.A. *Telephone:* (206) 543-4575.

REED, Thomas Care, M.S.; American business executive and public official; b. 1 March 1934, New York, N.Y.; s. of Gordon and Naomi (Bradley) Reed;

ed. Cornell Univ. and Univ. of S. California; First Lieut., U.S.A.F. 1956–61; Experimental Physics staff, Lawrence Radiation Lab., Univ. of Calif. 1961–62, Consultant, 1962–67; Gen. Man. Supercon Ltd. 1963–65; Appointments Sec. Office of the Gov. of California 1967; Pres. Quaker Hill Devt. Corpn. 1965–; Asst. to Sec. and Deputy Sec. of Defence 1973, Dir. of Telecommunications and Command Control Systems, Dept. of Defence 1974–75, Sec. of the Air Force 1976–77, Special Asst. to the Pres. 1982–83; Vice-Chair. Pres. Comm. on Strategic Forces 1983–; Chair., C.E.O. River Oaks Agricorp 1982–. *Address:* Quaker Hill Development Corporation, 503 D Street, San Rafael, Calif. 94901, U.S.A.

REEDY, George Edward, Jr.; American government official and educationist; b. 5 Aug. 1917, East Chicago, Ind.; s. of George E. and Mary Mulvaney Reedy; m. Lillian Greenwald 1948 (died 1984); two s.; ed. Univ. of Chicago; Congressional Corresp. United Press, Washington, D.C. 1938–41, 1946–51; U.S. Army Air Corps 1942–45; Staff Dir. U.S. Senate Minority Policy Cttee. 1953–54, Majority Policy Cttee. 1955–60; Special Asst. to Vice-Pres. Lyndon B. Johnson 1961–63, Press Sec. to the Pres. 1964–65, Aide to the Pres. 1965–66, Special Consultant to the Pres. 1968–69; Pegram Lecturer, Brookhaven Nat. Radiation Lab. 1971; Adjunct Prof. of Political Science, State Univ. of New York 1971–72; Dean College of Journalism 1972–76; Lucius W. Nieman Prof. of Journalism, Marquette Univ. Sept. 1972–; American Specialist lecturing in South America 1976, Asia 1977, under U.S. State Dept. Cultural Exchange Program in India and Indonesia 1984, under U.S. Information Agency; mem. and chair. numerous govt. comms. and bds. of enquiry 1966–68; Vice-Pres. for Planning, Struthers Wells Corpn. 1966–; Fellow, Woodrow Wilson Int. Center for Scholars 1970–; Duke Univ. Fellow in Communications 1973–74; Poynter Fellow, Univ. of Indiana 1974, Hon. D.Cn.L., Episcopal Seminary Nashota 1981; Marquette Teaching Excellence Award 1985. *Publications:* Who Will Do Our Fighting for Us? 1969, The Twilight of the Presidency 1970, The Presidency in Flux 1973, Lyndon B. Johnson, A Memoir 1982, The U.S. Senate: Paralysis or Search for Consensus 1986, The Twilight of the Presidency: Johnson to Reagan (an update) 1987. *Leisure interests:* music, fishing. *Address:* College of Journalism, Marquette University, Milwaukee, Wisconsin (Office); 2535 North Stowell Avenue, Milwaukee, Wisconsin 53211, U.S.A. (Home). *Telephone:* (414) 224-7089 (Office).

REES, Albert Lloyd George, C.B.E., D.SC., PH.D., D.I.C., F.R.A.C.I., F.A.A.; Australian scientist; b. 15 Jan. 1916, Melbourne; s. of George P. Rees and Edith Targett; m. Marion Mofflin 1942; three d.; ed. Univs. of Melbourne and London; Lecturer in Chem., Univ. of W. Australia 1939; Beit Scientific Research Fellow, Imperial Coll., London 1939–41; Extra-Mural Research in Chem. Defence, Ministry of Supply, U.K., 1939–41; Research and Devt. Philips Electrical Industries, U.K. 1941–44; with Commonwealth Scientific and Industrial Research Org. (CSIRO) 1944–78, Chief Div. of Chemical Physics 1958–78; Chair. Chem. Research Labs. 1961–70; Chair. Independent Review of Defence Science and Tech. Org. (Australian Govt.) 1979–80; mem. Bureau and Exec. Cttee., Int. Union of Pure and Applied Chem. 1963–73, Vice-Pres. 1967–69, Pres. 1969–71; mem. Exec. Cttee. ICSU 1969–72, Gen. Cttee. ICSU 1972–76; Pres. Royal Australian Chem. Inst. (R.A.C.I.) 1967–68; mem. Council, Australian Acad. of Science 1963–68, 1969–73; mem. Bd. of Studies, Victoria Inst. of Colls. 1968–80, mem. Council 1978–80; mem. Cttee. of Inquiry into the Fluoridation of Victoria Water Supplies (Victorian Govt.) 1979–80; mem. Council, Gippsland Inst. of Advanced Educ. 1981–85; Fellow, Faculty of Science, Monash Univ. 1981–; Hon. D.App.Sc.; Liversidge Lecturer, Royal Soc. of N.S.W. 1952; Einstein Memorial Lecturer, Australian Inst. of Physics 1970; Rennie Medal 1946, H.G. Smith medal (R.A.C.I.) 1951, Leighton Memorial Medal (R.A.C.I.) 1970, Inaugural Ian Wark Medal and Lecturer, Australian Acad. of Science 1987. *Publications:* Chemistry of the Defect Solid State 1954, and many articles in learned journals. *Leisure interests:* golf, music, gardening. *Address:* 9 Ajana Street, North Balwyn, Victoria 3104, Australia. *Telephone:* 857-9358.

REES, Charles Wayne, D.SC., F.R.S.C., F.R.S.; British professor of organic chemistry; b. 15 Oct. 1927, Cairo, Egypt; s. of Percival C. Rees and Daisy A. Beck; m. Patricia M. Francis 1953; three s.; ed. Farnham Grammar School and Univ. Coll., Southampton; Lecturer in Organic Chem. Birkbeck Coll., London 1955–57, King's Coll., London 1957–63, Reader 1963–65; Prof. of Organic Chem. Univ. of Leicester 1965–69, Univ. of Liverpool 1969–78; Hofmann Prof. of Organic Chem., Imperial Coll., London 1978–; Tilden Lecturer, Royal Soc. of Chem. 1973–74, Pedler Lecturer 1984–85; August Wilhelm von Hofmann Lecturer, German Chem. Soc. 1985. *Publications:* some 300 research papers in scientific journals and 17 books. *Leisure interests:* music, wine, London. *Address:* Department of Chemistry, Imperial College, London, SW7 2AY, England. *Telephone:* 01-589 5111, Ext. 4502.

REES, David Allan, PH.D., D.SC., F.I.BIOL., F.R.S.C., F.R.S.; British scientist; b. 28 April 1936, Silloth; s. of James A. Rees and Elsie Bolam; m. Myfanwy Owen 1959; two s. one d.; ed. Hawarden Grammar School, Clwyd and Univ. Coll. of N. Wales, Bangor; Univ. of Edinburgh 1960, Asst. Lecturer in Chem. 1961, lecturer 1962–70, Section Man. 1970–72; Prin. Scientist Unilever Research, Colworth Lab. 1972–82; Assoc. Dir. (part-time) MRC Unit for Cell Biophysics Kings Coll., London 1980–82; Dir. Nat. Inst. for Medical Research 1982–87; Sec. MRC 1987–; Visiting Professorial Fellow,

Univ. Coll., Cardiff 1972–77; Hon. F.R.C.P. 1986; Colworth Medal, Biochem. Soc. 1970; Carbohydrate Award, Chem. Soc. 1970; Philips Lecture Royal Soc. 1984; mem. Royal Soc. Council 1986–; Hon. D.Sc. (Edinburgh) 1989. *Publications:* articles on carbohydrate biochem. and cell biology. *Leisure interests:* river cruising, reading, listening to music. *Address:* Medical Research Council, 20 Park Crescent, London, W1N 4AL, England. *Telephone:* 01-636 5422.

REES, Hubert, D.F.C., F.R.S., PH.D.; British professor of agricultural botany; b. 2 Oct. 1923, Llangennech, Wales; s. of Owen and Tugela Rees; m. Mavis Rosalind Hill 1946; one s. two d.; ed. Llandovery and Llanelli Grammar Schools and Univ. Coll. of Wales, Aberystwyth; served R.A.F. 1942–46; lecturer, Genetics Dept., Univ. of Birmingham 1950–59; Sr. lecturer, Univ. Coll. of Wales, Aberystwyth 1960–66, Reader 1966–67, Prof. of Agricultural Botany 1967–. *Publications:* Chromosome Genetics 1977, B Chromosomes 1982. *Leisure interest:* fishing. *Address:* Irfon, Llanbadarn Road, Aberystwyth, Wales. *Telephone:* (0970) 623668.

REES, Martin John, M.A., PH.D., F.R.S.; British professor of astronomy and experimental philosophy; b. 23 June 1942; s. of Reginald J. and Joan Rees; m. Caroline Humphrey 1986; ed. Shrewsbury School and Trinity Coll., Cambridge; Fellow, Jesus Coll., Cambridge 1967–69; Research Assoc. Calif. Inst. of Tech. 1967–68, 1971; mem. Inst. for Advanced Study, Princeton 1969–70; Visiting Prof. Harvard Univ. 1972, 1986–87; Prof. Univ. of Sussex 1972–73, Inst. for Advanced Study, Princeton 1982; Plumian Prof. of Astronomy and Experimental Philosophy, Univ. of Cambridge 1973–; Fellow, King's Coll., Cambridge 1969–72, 1973–; Dir. Inst. of Astronomy 1977–82, 1987–; Regents Fellow, Smithsonian Inst. 1984–; Foreign hon. mem. American Acad. of Arts and Sciences; Foreign Assoc. N.A.S.; mem. Academia Europaea 1989; Heinemann Prize, American Inst. of Physics 1984; Gold Medal (Royal Astronomical Soc.) 1987; Guthrie Medal, Inst. of Physics 1989. *Publications:* articles and reviews in scientific journals. *Address:* King's College, Cambridge, England. *Telephone:* (0223) 337548 (Office).

REES, Rt. Hon. Merlyn, P.C., M.P., M.SC.(ECON.); British lecturer and politician; b. 18 Dec. 1920, Cilfynydd; s. of late L. D. Rees and of E. M. Rees; m. Colleen Faith Cleveley 1949; three s.; ed. Harrow Weald Grammar School, Goldsmiths' Coll., London and London School of Econs.; served R.A.F. 1941–46, rank of Squadron Leader; Teacher, Harrow Weald Grammar School 1949–60; Labour Party Head Office 1960–62; Lecturer Luton Coll. of Tech. 1962–63; M.P. for Leeds South 1963–83, for Morley and Leeds South 1983–; Parl. Private Sec. to Chancellor of Exchequer 1964–65; Under-Sec. Ministry of Defence 1965–68, Home Office 1968–70; Opposition Spokesman for N. Ireland 1970–74; mem. Departmental Cttee. Investigating Official Secrets Act; Sec. of State for N. Ireland 1974–76; Home Sec. 1976–79, Opposition Spokesman for Home Affairs 1979–80, for Energy 1980–83, Co-ordinator of Econ. Planning; mem. Cttee. of Inquiry into events leading to Argentine invasion of the Falklands 1982; mem. Advisory Cttee. on Business Appointments. *Publications:* The Public Sector in the Mixed Economy 1973, Northern Ireland: A Personal Perspective 1985. *Leisure interest:* reading. *Address:* House of Commons, London, S.W.1, England.

REES, Mina, PH.D.; American mathematician and university administrator; b. 2 Aug. 1902, Cleveland; d. of Moses Rees and Alice L. Stackhouse; m. Dr. Leopold Brahdy 1955 (deceased); ed. Hunter Coll., Columbia Univ. and Univ. of Chicago; Instructor eventually Prof. of Math. and Dean of Faculty Hunter Coll. 1926–43, 1953–61; Tech. Aide and Exec. Asst. to Chief of Applied Maths. Panel, Office of Scientific Research and Devt. 1943–46; Head, Math. Branch, subsequently Dir., Math. Sciences Div., Office of Naval Research 1946–53; Prof. City Univ. of New York 1961–72, Dean of Graduate Studies 1961–68, Provost 1968–69, Pres. Graduate School 1969–72, Pres. Emer. 1972–; mem. Nat. Science Bd. 1964–70; Chair. Council of Graduate Schools in U.S. 1970; Pres. A.A.A.S. 1971; 19 hon. degrees; numerous awards including Achievement Award, American Assen. of Univ. Women 1965, President's Medal, Hunter Coll. 1970, and Elizabeth Blackwell Gold Medal 1971, Chicago Univ. Alumni Medal, Chancellor's Medal City Univ. of New York 1972, Nat. Acad. of Sciences Public Welfare Medal 1983, Columbia Univ. Public Service Medal 1983, New York Mayor's Award of Honor for Science and Tech. 1986. *Publications:* articles in journals. *Leisure interest:* painting. *Address:* 301 East 66th Street, New York, N.Y. 10021, U.S.A. (Home). *Telephone:* 212-879-9467 (Home).

REES-MOGG, Life Peer (cr. 1988), of Hinton Blewett in the County of Avon; **William,** Kt.; British journalist; b. 14 July 1928, Bristol; s. of late Edmund Fletcher and Beatrice (née Warren) Rees-Mogg; m. Gillian Shakespeare Morris 1962; two s. three d.; ed. Charterhouse and Balliol Coll., Oxford; Pres. Oxford Union 1951; Financial Times 1952–60, Chief Leader Writer 1955–60, Asst. Ed. 1957–60; City Ed. Sunday Times 1960–61, Political and Econ. Ed. 1961–63, Deputy Ed. 1964–67; Ed. of The Times 1967–81, Dir. The Times Ltd. 1968–81; Vice-Chair. BBC 1981–86; Chair. Arts Council 1982–88; Chair. Broadcasting Standards Council 1988–; mem. Exec. Bd. Times Newspapers Ltd. 1968–81, Dir. 1978–81; Dir. Gen. Electric March 1981–; Chair. and Propr. Pickering and Chatto Ltd. 1981–; Chair. Sidgwick and Jackson 1985–; Dir. M & G Group 1987–; mem. Int. Cttee. Pontifical Council for Culture 1983–; Hon. LL.D. (Bath) 1977. *Publications:* The Reigning Error: the Crisis of World Inflation 1974, An Humbler

Heaven 1977, How to Buy Rare Books 1985, Blood in the Streets (with James Dale Davidson) 1988. *Leisure interest:* art collecting. *Address:* 3 Smith Square, London, S.W.1; The Old Rectory, Hinton Blewett, Nr. Bristol, Avon, England.

REESE, Colin Bernard, M.A., PH.D., SC.D., F.R.S.; British professor of chemistry; b. 29 July 1930, Plymouth; s. of late Joseph and Emily Reese; m. Susanne L. Bird 1968; one s. one d.; ed. Dartington Hall School and Clare Coll., Cambridge; Research Fellow, Clare Coll. 1956–59, Harvard Univ. 1957–58; Official Fellow and Dir. of Studies in Chem., Clare Coll. 1959–73; Demonstrator in Chem., Univ. of Cambridge 1959–63, Asst. Dir. of Research 1963–64, Univ. Lecturer in Chem. 1964–73; Daniell Prof. of Chem., King's Coll., London 1973–. *Publications:* scientific papers mainly in chemistry journals. *Address:* Department of Chemistry, King's College, Strand, London, WC2R 2LS, England. *Telephone:* 01-836 5454.

REEVE, Anthony, C.M.G., M.A.; British diplomatist; b. 20 Oct. 1938, Wakefield; s. of Sidney Reeve and Dorothy (née Mitchell) Reeve; m. Pamela Margaret Angus 1964 (dissolved 1988); one s. two d.; ed. Queen Elizabeth Grammar School, Marling School and Merton Coll., Oxford; joined Lever Bros. and Assocs. 1962–65; entered Diplomatic Service 1965; Middle East Centre for Arab Studies 1966–68; Asst. Political Agent, Abu Dhabi 1968–70; First Sec. FCO 1970–73; First Sec., later Counsellor Washington 1973–78; Head of Arms Control and Disarmament Dept. FCO 1979–81, Southern Africa Dept. 1984–86; Counsellor, Cairo 1981–84; Asst. Under Sec. of State 1986–88; Amb. to Jordan Feb. 1988–. *Leisure interests:* writing, music. *Address:* c/o Foreign and Commonwealth Office, King Charles Street, London, SW1A 2AH, England.

REEVE, Christopher; American actor; b. 25 Sept. 1952, New York; TV appearances since 1973 include Anna Karenina 1985; appeared on stage in New York in Street Smart 1986. *Films include:* Somewhere in Time, Superman, Superman 2, Deathtrap, Monsignor, Superman 3, The Bostonians, The Aviator, Superman 4, Street Smart 1988. *Address:* c/o International Creative Management, 8899 Beverly Boulevard, Los Angeles, Calif. 90048, U.S.A.

REEVE, Michael David, M.A., F.B.A.; British academic; b. 11 Jan. 1943; s. of Arthur Reeve and Edith Mary Barrett; m. Elizabeth Klingaman 1970; two s. one d.; ed. King Edward's School, Birmingham, Balliol Coll., Oxford; Harmsworth Sr. Scholar, Merton Coll., Oxford 1964–65; Woodhouse Research Fellow, St. John's Coll., Oxford 1965–66; Tutorial Fellow, Exeter Coll., Oxford 1966–84, Emer. Fellow 1984–; Kennedy Prof. of Latin and Fellow Pembroke Coll., Univ. of Cambridge 1984–; Visiting Prof. Univ. of Hamburg 1976, McMaster Univ. 1979, Univ. of Toronto 1982–83; Ed., Classical Quarterly 1981–86. *Publications:* Longus, Daphnis and Chloe 1982, contributions to Texts and Transmission 1983, articles in European and American journals. *Leisure interests:* chess, music, gardening, mountain walking. *Address:* Pembroke College, Cambridge, CB2 1RF, England.

REEVES, Christopher Reginald, C.B.I.M.; British merchant banker; b. 14 Jan. 1936, Cardiff; s. of Reginald Reeves and Dora Tucker; m. Stella Jane Whinney 1965; three s.; ed. Malvern Coll.; served in Rifle Brigade, Kenya and Malaya 1955–58; Bank of England 1958–63; Hill Samuel & Co. Ltd. 1963–67; joined Morgan Grenfell & Co. Ltd. 1968, Dir. 1970, Head of Banking Div. 1972, Deputy Chair. 1975–84, Chief Exec. 1980–84, Chair. and Group Chief Exec. 1984–87; Vice-Chair. Merrill Lynch Europe Ltd. 1989–; Deputy Chair. London Bd. Westpac Banking Corpn.; Dir. Allianz Int. Insurance Co. Ltd., BICC PLC 1983–, The Inst. for Fiscal Studies 1983–87, Int. Freehold Properties SARL; Andrew Weir and Co. Ltd., Morgan Grenfell Group PLC 1983–87 (Deputy Chair. 1985–87), Oman Int. Bank 1984–; Gov. Dulwich Coll. Preparatory School; mem. City Univ. Business School Council; Vice-Pres. Centre for World Devt. *Leisure interests:* sailing, shooting, skiing. *Address:* 64 Flood Street, London, S.W.3, England.

REEVES, Marjorie Ethel, PH.D., D.LITT., F.R.HIST.S., F.B.A.; British university teacher (retd.); b. 17 July 1905, Bratton, Wilts.; d. of Robert John Reeves and Edith Sarah Whitaker; ed. Trowbridge Girls' High School, Wilts., St. Hugh's Coll. Oxford and Westfield Coll. London; History Mistress, Roan School for Girls, Greenwich, London 1927–29; History Lecturer, St. Gabriel's Coll., London 1931–38; Tutor, later Fellow, St. Anne's Coll. Oxford and Univ. Lecturer 1938–72, Vice-Prin. St. Anne's Coll. 1948–68. *Publications:* The Influence of Prophecy in the Later Middle Ages 1969, The Figurae of Joachim of Fiore 1972, Joachim of Fiore and the Prophetic Future 1976, Sheepbell and Ploughshare 1978, Joachim of Fiore and the Myth of the Eternal Evangel in the Nineteenth Century (with Warwick Gould) 1987, Competence, Delight and the Common Good: reflections on the crisis in higher education 1988; writes numerous books in the Then and There Series. *Leisure interests:* gardening, music. *Address:* 38 Norham Road, Oxford, OX2 6SQ and The Elms, Bratton, Wilts., BA13 4SX, England. *Telephone:* (0865) 57039 and (0380) 830235 (Bratton).

REEVES, Most Rev. Sir Paul Alfred, G.C.M.G., G.C.V.O., M.A., L.TH.; New Zealand ecclesiastic and administrator; b. 6 Dec. 1932; s. of D'Arcy Lionel and Hilda Mary Reeves; m. Beverley Watkins 1959; three d.; ed. Wellington Coll., Vic. Univ. of Wellington, St. John's Theological Coll., Auckland and St. Peter's Coll., Oxford; Deacon 1958; Priest 1960; Curate, Tokoroa, N.Z. 1958–59, St. Mary the Virgin, Oxford 1959–61, Kirkley St. Peter, Lowestoft

1961–63; Vicar, St. Paul, Okato, N.Z. 1964–66; Lecturer in Church History St. John's Coll., Auckland 1966–69; Dir. of Christian Educ. Diocese of Auckland 1969–71; Bishop of Waiapu 1971–79, of Auckland 1979; Primate and Archbishop of New Zealand 1980–85; Gov.-Gen. of New Zealand 1985–; Chair. Environmental Council 1974–76; Hon. Fellow St. Peter's Coll., Oxford 1980, Hon. D.C.L. (Oxon.) 1985; K.St.J. 1986. *Leisure interests:* swimming, sailing, jogging. *Address:* Government House, Private Bag, Wellington, New Zealand.

REFSHAUGE, Major-Gen. Sir William Dudley, A.C., Kt., C.B.E., E.D., M.B., B.S., F.R.C.O.G., F.R.A.C.S., F.R.A.C.P., F.R.A.C.M.A., F.R.A.C.O.G.; Australian health official; b. 3 April 1913, Melbourne; s. of Francis C. Refshauge and Margaret I. Brown; m. Helen E. Allwright 1942; four s. one d.; ed. Hampton High School and Scotch Coll., Melbourne and Melbourne Univ.; Resident Medical Officer, Alfred Hosp., Melbourne 1939, Women's Hosp. Melbourne 1946; Registrar, Women's Hosp. 1946–47, Medical Supt. 1948–51; Deputy Dir.-Gen. Army Medical Services 1951–55, Dir.-Gen. 1955–60; Commonwealth of Australia Dir.-Gen. of Health 1960–73; Chair. Nat. Health and Medical Research Council 1960–73, Commonwealth Council for Nat. Fitness 1960–73, Commonwealth Health Insurance Council 1960–73, etc.; mem. Exec. Bd., WHO 1967–70, Chair. 1969–70; Pres. World Health Assembly 1971; Sec.-Gen. World Medical Asscn. 1973–76; Patron Australian Sports Medicine Asscn., Totally and Permanently Incapacitated Asscn. (T.P.I.) 1983–, 2/2 Field Regt. Asscn. 1984–; Nat. Trustee Returned Services League of Australia 1963–73, 1976–; Chair. Bd. of Man. Canberra Girls Grammar School 1977; mem. Bd. of Dirs. Walter and Eliza Hall Inst. of Medical Research 1977–85, Nat. Cttee. Sir Robert Menzies Foundation 1979–; Hon. Consultant Australian Foundation on Alcoholism and Drugs of Dependence 1979–; Chair. Blood Transfusion Cttee., Red Cross Soc. (A.C.T.) 1980, Inst. of Ethics Cttee. 1983–; Pres. 1st Pan-Pacific Conf. on Drugs and Alcohol 1980; mem. Bd. of Dirs. Int. Council on Alcohol and Additions (I.C.A.A.) 1982–89, Deputy Pres. 1985–89; Chair. Interim Bd. of Man., Menzies School of Health Research, Darwin 1983–85, Chair. Bd. of Man. 1985–86; Deputy Chair. Research Grants Advisory Cttee. Menzies Foundation 1980–85; Chair. Planning Cttee., Centre for Population Health Research, Univ. of Tasmania 1986–87; Chair. Research into Drug Abuse Advisory Cttee. (Australian Drug Offensive) 1986–88. *Publications:* various pubs. in Medical Journal of Australia and New Zealand Medical Journal. *Leisure interests:* bowls, rug-making, gardening. *Address:* 26 Birdwood Street, Hughes, A.C.T. 2605, Australia. *Telephone:* 810943.

REGAN, Donald Thomas; American financial executive; b. 21 Dec. 1918, Cambridge, Mass.; s. of William F. and Kathleen (née Ahern) Regan; m. Ann Gordon Buchanan 1942; two s. two d.; ed. Harvard Coll.; U.S. Marine Corps 1940–46, attaining rank of Lt.-Col.; joined Merrill Lynch 1946, partner 1953; Vice-Pres. Merrill Lynch, Pierce, Fenner & Smith Inc. 1959, Exec. Vice-Pres. 1964, Chair. of Bd. and Chief Exec. Officer 1971–81; Chair. of Bd. and Chief Exec. Officer Merrill Lynch and Co. Inc. 1973–81; Pres. Regdon Assocs.; Sec. of the U.S. Treasury 1981–85, White House Chief of Staff 1985–87; Vice-Chair. Bd. of Dirs. of NYSE 1972–75; mem. Policy Cttee. of Business Roundtable 1978–80; Trustee, Cttee. for Econ. Devt. 1978–80, Charles E. Merrill Trust and Univ. of Pennsylvania; Hon. LL.D. (Hahnemann Medical Coll. and Hospital, Univ. of Penn., Tri-State Coll.). *Publications:* A View from the Street 1972, For the Record: From Wall Street to Washington 1988. *Address:* 11 Canal Center Plaza, Suite 301, Alexandria, Va. 22314, U.S.A.

REGAN, Hon. Gerald Augustine, Q.C.; Canadian politician; b. 13 Feb. 1929, Windsor, Nova Scotia; s. of Walter E. Regan and Rose M. Greene; m. A. Carole Harrison 1956; three s. three d.; ed. St. Mary's Univ. and Dalhousie Univ.; fmrly. practising lawyer; mem. Parl. for Halifax 1963–65, 1980–; Leader Liberal Party of Nova Scotia 1965–80; mem. Nova Scotia Legislature 1967–80; Premier of Nova Scotia 1970–78, Leader of the Opposition 1978–80; Minister of Labour and Sports 1980–81; Sec. of State and Minister responsible for Fitness and Amateur Sport 1981–82, for Int. Trade 1982–84, for Energy June–Sept. 1984; Pres. Hawthorne Devts. 1984–. *Leisure interests:* tennis, skiing. *Address:* P.O. Box 828, Station B, Ottawa, Ont., K1P 5P9; 2332 Georgina Drive, Ottawa, Ont., K2B 7M4, Canada.

REGGIANI, Serge; Italian-born French actor and singer; b. 2 May 1922, Reggio nell' Emilia; s. of Ferruccio Reggiani and Letizia Spagni; m. 1st Janine Darcey; one s. (deceased) one d.; m. 2nd Annie Noël; two s. one d.; ed. Conservatoire Nat. d'Art Dramatique; notable theatrical roles in Britannicus, Les parents terribles, Un homme comme les autres, Les trois mousquetaires, Les séquestrés d'Altona, etc.; Chevalier, Légion d'honneur. *Films include:* Le carrefour des enfants perdus, Les portes de la nuit, Manon, Les amants de Vérone, La ronde, Casque d'or, Napoléon, Les salauds vont en enfer, Les misérables, Marie Octobre, La grande pagaille, La guerre continue, Tutti a casa, Le Doulos, Le guépard, Marie-Chantal contre le Docteur Kah, Les aventuriers, La 25e heure, La mafia fait la loi, L'armée des ombres, Comptes à rebours, Touche pas à la femme blanche 1974, Vincent, François, Paul . . . et les autres 1974, Le chat et la souris 1975, Une fille cousue de fil blanc 1977, L'empreinte des géants, Fantastica, La terrasse 1980, Mauvais sang 1986. *Address:* c/o Charley Marouani, 4 avenue Hoche, 75008 Paris; c/o Artmédia, 10 avenue George V, 75008 Paris, France.

REGNIER, Charles; German actor and theatrical director; b. 22 July 1914, Freiburg; m. Pamela Wedekind 1941 (died 1986); one s. two d.; ed. school of dramatic art; acted in Vienna, Zürich, Hamburg, Cologne, Munich, Düsseldorf, Bochum and Wuppertal; appeared in many films; trans. works of Giraudoux, Cocteau, Maugham, Feydeau, Labiche, Mauriac, Colette, Barillet-Gredy, Dorin; German Critics' Prize 1955. *Address:* Seestrasse 6, 8193 Ambach/Starnbergersee, Federal Republic of Germany. *Telephone:* 08177-532.

REGO, Paula; British artist; b. 26 Jan. 1935, Lisbon, Portugal; d. of José Figueiroa Rego and Maria de San José Paiva Figueiroa Rego; m. Victor Willing; one s. two d.; ed. St. Julian's School, Carcavelos, Portugal, Slade School of Fine Art, University Coll. London; eight one-person exhbns. since 1979 in London, Lisbon, Amsterdam and Bristol; retrospective exhbns. at Gulbenkian Foundation, Lisbon 1989, Serpentine Gallery, London 1989; included in many mixed exhbns. in Paris, Rome, São Paulo, Tokyo, Madrid, Baden-Baden, New York, U.K. *Address:* 10 The Pryors, East Heath Road, London, NW3 1B5, England.

REHBERG, Poul Kristian Brandt, M.SC., D.PHIL.; Danish zoologist; b. 29 March 1895, Middelfart; s. of Adolf Boëtius and Marie Jakobe Rehberg (née Brandt); m. Ally Margrethe Madsen 1955; one d.; Asst. University Zoophysiological Lab., Univ. of Copenhagen 1921; Reader 1936; Prof. of Zoophysiology, Univ. of Copenhagen 1945–65; mem. Videnskabernes Selskab 1944; Defence Research Cttee. 1952–60; Chair. of Danish Cttee. Int. Union of Biological Sciences 1947–64; mem. Danish State Research Foundation 1952–61, Chair. Nat. Science section 1959–61; Chief Adviser, Civil Defence Research 1950–60; mem. Bd. and Exec. Politiken; Exec. mem. Danish Atomic Energy Comm. 1956, Chair. 1962–70; Vice-Pres. World Asscn. of World Federalists 1956, Acad. of Tech. Science, Copenhagen 1957; mem. NATO Science Cttee. 1957–60, Danish Science Advisory Council 1966–69; Bd. of Carlsberg Foundation 1960–71, Chair. 1969–72; mem. Bd. and Vice-Chair. United Breweries Carlsberg/Tüborg 1970–71; Chair. Research Fund for Congenital Diseases 1964–73; Hon. M.D. (Lund) 1950, Hon. M.V.D. (Copenhagen) 1958. *Publications:* Studies on Kidney Function 1926; various textbooks on physiology. *Address:* Høegsminde Parken 13, st. tv., DK 2900 Hellerup, Denmark. *Telephone:* 01-62-79-95.

REHFELD, Jens Frederik, D.M.SC.; Danish professor of clinical chemistry; b. 11 Oct. 1941, Aarhus; s. of Aage Rehfeld and Igrid Ipsen; m. Christine M. Aminoff 1963; two d.; ed. Univs. of Aarhus and Copenhagen; Resident in Medicine and Surgery, Bispebjerg Hospital, Copenhagen 1967–69; Univ. Research Fellow, Dept. of Clinical Chem. Bispebjerg Hospital 1969–73, Sr. Resident 1974–75; Prof. of Biochem. Univ. of Aarhus 1975–81; Prof. of Clinical Chem. and Chair. Dept. of Clinical Chem., Univ. of Copenhagen 1981–; Mack-Foster Award (Cambridge); Anders Jahre Prize (Oslo); Novo Prize (Copenhagen). *Publications:* 400 scientific publications about the biochemistry of hormonal peptides. *Leisure interests:* literature (fiction, biography), movies. *Address:* J.A. Schwartzgade 37, 2100 Copenhagen, Denmark. *Telephone:* 01-386823, 01-386633 (Ext. 2016).

REHNQUIST, William H., LL.B., M.A.; American judge; b. 1 Oct. 1924, Milwaukee, Wis.; s. of William Benjamin Rehnquist and Margery Peck Rehnquist; m. Natalie Cornell 1953; one s. two d.; ed. Stanford and Harvard Univs.; law clerk to U.S. Supreme Court Justice R. H. Jackson 1952–53; private practice, Evans, Kitchel and Jenckes, Phoenix, Ariz. 1953–57, Cunningham, Messenger, Carson & Elliott 1957–60, Powers & Rehnquist 1960–69; Asst. Attorney-Gen., Office of Legal Counsel, Dept. of Justice 1969–71; Assoc. Justice, Supreme Court of U.S.A. 1971–86, Chief Justice Sept. 1986–; Hon. Master of the Bench, Middle Temple, London 1986–; mem. American Bar Asscn., American Judicature Soc., etc. *Address:* Supreme Court of the United States, Washington, D.C. 20543, U.S.A.

REICH, John Theodore, PH.D.; Austrian-born American theatrical director; b. 30 Sept. 1906, Vienna; s. of Leopold Reich and Martha (Baxter) Reich; m. 1st Karoline Friederike van Kurzweil 1932 (deceased); m. 2nd Karen Ruth Lasker 1957 (died 1983); ed. Realgymnasium I, and Max Reinhardt School, Vienna, Vienna and Cornell Univs.; Dramaturg and Asst. Producer, Burgtheater, Vienna 1931–32; Dramaturg and Producer, Max Reinhardt Theatres, Vienna 1932–38; Asst. Producer, later Producer, Salzburg Festivals 1934–37; Asst., later Assoc. Prof. of Drama, Ithaca Coll., N.Y. 1938–45; Drama Dir. C.B.S. Television, New York 1945–46; Assoc. Prof. of Theatre, Smith Coll., Barnard Coll. 1947–51; Asst., later Assoc. Prof. of Theatre, Columbia Univ., Supervisor of Production Training, New York TV Workshop and also independent producer 1951–57; Head, Goodman Theatre and School of Drama, Chicago Art Inst. 1957–73; Dir. Ford Foundation's Theatre Communications Group 1965–72; Producing Dir. Goodman Theatre Resident Co. 1969–73; Prin. Guest Dir. Calif. Actor's Theatre, Missouri Rep. Theatre, Juilliard School; freelance Dir. Dallas Theatre Center, Miami Ring Theatre, Penn State Theatre, Asolo State Theatre, Great Lakes Shakespeare Festival, PAF Playhouse, etc.; Guest Dir. Utah Shakespearean Festival 1982, P.C.P.A. Theaterfest 1986, Delaware Theatre Co., Florida Studio Theatre; Guest Prof. State Univ. of New York 1983, Univ. of Wis.; Dr. h.c. (Lake Forest Coll., Ill.) 1972; Ford Foundation Award 1959; Chevalier, Ordre des Arts et Lettres 1964; Grand Badge of Honour, Austria 1971. *Publications:* Mary Stuart (adaptation of Schiller's play, with Jean Goldstone) 1958, Comedy of Words (adaptation of Schnitzler's play), The Salzburg Everyman 1983, Jonah (by Berreby, trans.), The Accident (by Durrenmatt, trans.); numerous other adaptations and articles. *Leisure interests:* music, hiking. *Address:* 79 Circle Drive, Syosset, N.Y. 11791, U.S.A.

REICH, Steve, M.A.; American composer; b. 3 Oct. 1936, New York; s. of Leonard Reich and June Carroll; m. Beryl Korot 1976; two s.; ed. Cornell Univ., Juilliard School of Music, Mills Coll.; studied composition with Berio and Milhaud; also studied at the American Soc. for Eastern Arts and in Accra and Jerusalem; set up his own ensemble 1966; Steve Reich and Musicians have completed sixteen European and American tours, with over 300 concerts 1971-; his music performed by major orchestras and ensembles in United States and Europe; recipient of three Rockefeller Foundation Grants 1975-81, a Guggenheim Fellowship and an award from the Koussevitzky Foundation 1981. *Major works include:* The Desert Music 1984, Tehillim 1982, Eight Lines for Chamber Orchestra 1985, Music for 18 Musicians, Vermont Counterpoint. *Recordings include:* Come Out, Violin Phase, It's Gonna Rain, Four Organs, Drumming, Six Pianos, Music for Mallet Instruments, Voices and Organ, Music for a Large Ensemble, Octet, and Variations for Winds, Strings and Keyboards. *Address:* c/o Helene Cann Reich Music Foundation, 175 Fifth Avenue, Suite 2396, New York, N.Y. 10010, U.S.A.

REICH-RANICKI, Marcel; German literary critic; b. 2 June 1920, Wloclawek; s. of David Reich and Helene Auerbach; m. Teofila Langnas 1942; one s.; in Berlin 1929-38; deported to Poland 1938; publrs., reader and literary critic, Warsaw until 1958; returned to Germany 1958; regular literary critic Die Zeit 1960-73; guest lecturer in U.S. univs. 1968-69; regular guest Prof. of Modern German literature in Univs. of Stockholm and Uppsala 1971-75; Man. Ed. Frankfurter Allgemeine Zeitung 1973-88; Hon. Prof. Univ. of Tübingen 1974-; Heine-Plakette 1976, Ricarda Huch Prize 1981, Goethe-Plakette 1984, Thomas-Mann-Preis 1987; Dr. Phil. h.c. *Publications:* Deutsche Literatur in West und Ost 1963, Literarisches Leben in Deutschland 1965, Literatur der kleinen Schritte 1967, Lauter Verrisse 1970, Uber Ruhestörer-Juden in der deutschen Literatur 1973, Zur Literatur der DDR 1974, Nachprüfung, Aufsätze über deutsche Schriftsteller von gestern 1977, Entgegnung, Zur deutschen Literatur der siebziger Jahre 1979, Betrifft Goethe 1982, Lauter Lobreden 1985, Nichts als Literatur, Aufsätze und Anmerkungen 1985, Mehr als ein Dichter, Über Heinrich Böll 1986, Thomas Mann und die Seinen 1987. *Leisure interests:* literature, music. *Address:* Gustav-Freytag-Strasse 36, 6000 Frankfurt am Main 1, Federal Republic of Germany. *Telephone:* 0611/561062.

REICHARDT, Robert Heinrich, D. PHIL; Austrian/Swiss professor of sociology, social philosophy and methodology of the social sciences; b. 2 May 1927, Basel; s. of Heinrich Reichardt and Magdalena (née Bachlehner) Reichardt; m. Dr. Isolde (née Dünhofen) Reichardt; ed. Univ. of Basel; Research Assoc. Princeton Univ. 1960-61; Asst. Inst. for Social Sciences, Univ. of Basel 1962-64; Dir. Dept. for Sociology, Inst. for Higher Studies, Vienna 1964-66; Prof. of Vienna 1966-; Exec. Dir. Inst. for Research on Socio-Econ. Devt., Austrian Acad. of Science 1977-84; mem. Austrian Acad. of Sciences 1978-; Co-operative Prize, Univ. of Basel 1960. *Publications:* Die Schallplatte als kulturelles und Ökon. Phänomen, Bedürfnisforschung im Dienste der Stadtplanung, Überleben wir den technischen Fortschritt (with others), Einführung in die Soziologie fur Juristen. *Leisure interests:* composition, playing the piano. *Address:* Institute for Sociology, Alserstrasse 33, 1080 Wien, Austria. *Telephone:* 43-51 08/31.

REICHSTEIN, Tadeus, DR. ING. CHEM.; Swiss chemist; b. 20 July 1897, Wloclaweck, Poland; s. of Isidor Reichstein and Gustava Brockman; m. Louise Henriette Quarls v. Ufford 1927; one d.; ed. Eidgenössische Technische Hochschule, Zürich; Asst. Eidgenössische Technische Hochschule, Zürich 1922-30, Prof. of Organic Chem. 1930-38; Prof. of Pharmacy Univ. of Basel 1938-46, Prof. of Organic Chem. 1946-67, Prof. Emer. 1967-; awarded Nobel Prize for Medicine and Physiology 1950, Copley Medal, Royal Soc. (U.K.) 1968; Dr. h.c. (Sorbonne, Geneva, Zürich, Abidjan, Basel, London and Leeds). *Leisure interests:* horticulture, botany. *Address:* Institut für Organische Chemie, St. Johanns-Ring 19, CH-4056, Basel; Weissensteinstrasse 22, CH-4059, Basel, Switzerland. *Telephone:* 061-576060.

REID, Alan Forrest, PH.D., F.A.A., F.T.S.; Australian scientist; b. 26 March 1931, New Zealand; s. of V. C. Reid; m.; five c.; ed. Univ. of N.Z., Christchurch, A.N.U., Canberra, Cornell Univ., New York; joined CSIRO 1959, research scientist 1972-82, Chief research scientist 1972-82, Chief Div. of Mineral Engineering 1982-84, Dir. Inst. of Energy and Earth Resources 1984-87, Inst. of Minerals, Energy and Construction 1988-; CSIRO Rivett Medal 1970. *Leisure interests:* music, art, gardening. *Address:* 105 Delhi Road, North Ryde, N.S.W. 2113; P.O. Box 93, North Ryde, N.S.W. 2113, Australia. *Telephone:* (02) 887-8822; (02) 887-8212.

REID, Escott Meredith, C.C.; Canadian diplomatist (retd.); b. 21 Jan. 1905, Campbellford, Ontario; s. of Rev. A. J. Reid and Morna Meredith Reid; m. Ruth Herriot; two s. one d.; ed. Toronto and Oxford Univs.; Rhodes Scholar 1927-30; Rockefeller Foundation Fellow 1930-32; Nat. Sec. of Canadian Inst. of Int. Affairs 1932-38; Acting Prof. of Govt. and Political Science, Dalhousie Univ., Halifax 1937-38; apptd. to Dept. of External Affairs 1939; served Ottawa, Washington, London; Asst. Under-Sec. of State for External Affairs 1947-48; Deputy Under-Sec. 1948-52; Acting Under-Sec. 1948-49; High Commr. in India 1952-57; Amb. to German Fed. Repub. 1958-62; Dir. S. Asia and Middle East Dept. of Int. Bank for Reconstruction and Devt. 1962-65; Prin., Glendon Coll. and Prof. of Political Science, York Univ., Toronto 1965-69; Consultant, Canadian Int. Devt. Agency, Ottawa 1970-72; Skelton-Clark Fellow, Queen's Univ., Kingston 1972-73; mem. Canadian Del. Int. Civil Aviation Conf. Chicago 1944, San Francisco 1945; Exec. Cttee. and Prep. Comm. of UN, London 1945; First, Second and Twelfth Sessions UN Gen. Ass.; Chair. Ass. Cttee. on Procedure and Org. 1947. *Publications:* The Future of the World Bank 1965, Strengthening the World Bank 1973, Time of Fear and Hope: The Making of the North Atlantic Treaty 1947-1949 1977, Envoy to Nehru 1981, On Duty, A Canadian at the Making of the United Nations 1945-46 1983, Hungary and Suez 1956: A View from New Delhi 1986, Radical Mandarin: Memoirs 1989. *Address:* R.R.2, Ste. Cécile de Masham, Quebec J0X 2W0, Canada. *Telephone:* 819-456-2805.

REID, Harry, J.D.; American politician; b. 2 Dec. 1939, Searchlight, Nevada; s. of Harry Reid and Inez Reid; m. Landra Joy Gould; five c.; ed. George Washington Univ.; City Attorney, Henderson, Nev. 1964-66; Trustee, Southern Nev. Memorial Hosp. Bd. 1967-69, Chair. Bd. of Trustees 1968-69; mem. Nev. Ass. 1969-70; Lieut.-Gov. of Nev. 1970-74; Chair. Nev. Gaming Comm. 1977-81; Congressman, U.S. House of Reps., Washington 1983-87; Senator from Nevada Jan. 1987-; mem. Bd. of Dirs. of American Cancer Soc., of Legal Aid Soc., of YMCA; Nat. Jewish Hosp., Humanitarian Award 1984; Hon. LL.D. (Southern Utah State Coll.) 1984; Democrat. *Address:* U.S. Senate, Washington, D.C. 20510, U.S.A.

REID, Sir Martin, K.B.E., C.M.G., M.A.; British diplomatist (retd.); b. 27 Aug. 1928, London; s. of the late Marcus Reid and Winifred Mary Stephens; m. Jane Elizabeth Harwood 1956; one s. three d.; ed. Merchant Taylors' School, and Brasenose Coll., Oxford; entered British Foreign Service 1953, and served in Paris, Rangoon, London, Georgetown and Bucharest 1954-70; Deputy High Commr., Malawi 1970-73; Prin. Pvt. Sec. to successive Secs. of State for Northern Ireland 1973-74; Head of Cen. and Southern African Dept., FCO 1974-78; Minister of British Embassy, S. Africa 1979-82; attached to Civil Service Selection Bd. 1983; British High Commr. to Jamaica and Amb. (non-resident) to Haiti 1984-87; Research Adviser, FCO 1987-88. *Leisure interests:* painting, chess. *Address:* 43 Carson Road, London, SE21 8HT, England.

REID, Sir Norman Robert, Kt., D.LITT., D.A., F.M.A., F.I.I.C.; British art gallery director; b. 27 Dec. 1915, London; s. of Edward Reid and Blanche Drouet; m. Jean Lindsay Bertram 1941; one s. one d.; ed. Wilson's Grammar School, London, Edinburgh Coll. of Art, and Edinburgh Univ.; Maj. Argyll and Sutherland Highlanders 1939-46; Tate Gallery 1946-79, Dir. 1964-79; Fellow, Int. Inst. for Conservation of Historic and Artistic Works, Sec.-Gen. 1963-65, Vice-Chair. 1966-79; Chair. British Council Fine Art Cttee. 1968-76; Officer, Order of Aztec Eagle (Mexico); mem. many cttees. *Leisure interests:* painting, gardening. *Address:* 50 Brabourne Rise, Park Langley, Beckenham, Kent, England (Home).

REID, Ogden Rogers, A.B.; American journalist and diplomatist; b. 24 June 1925, New York, N.Y.; s. of Ogden Reid and Helen Miles Rogers; m. 1949; six c.; ed. Yale Univ.; Reporter New York Herald Tribune 1950-51, various depts. 1952-53; Pres. and Ed. New York Herald Tribune S.A., Paris 1953-59, Dir. 1953-; Vice-Pres. New York Herald Tribune Inc. 1954-55; Pres. and Ed. New York Herald Tribune Inc. 1955-58, Dir. 1950; Amb. to Israel 1959-61; Chair. New York State Comm. Against Discrimination 1961-62; Dir. Panama Canal Co. 1956-59, Mass. Mutual Life Insurance Co. 1957-60; Congressman for Westchester County, N.Y. 1962-74; Nacional do Cruzeiro do Sul, Brazil 1956; Chair. Bard Coll. Center; Vice-Chair. Nat. Patent Devt. Corpn.; Trustee, Caribbean Cen. American Action; Chevalier, Légion d'honneur 1957; Hon. LL.D., Adelphi Coll. (N.Y.); Hon. Fellow, Bar-Ilan Univ., Israel 1959; Democrat. *Publication:* How Strong is America? The Score on National Defense (with Robert S. Bird) 1950. *Leisure interests:* sailing, skiing, hunting, fishing. *Address:* Ophir Hill, Purchase, N.Y. 10577, U.S.A. *Telephone:* 914-949-1291.

REID, Sir Robert Basil, Kt., C.B.E., M.A., F.INST.M., F.C.I.T.; British public transport executive; b. 7 Feb. 1921; s. of the late Sir Robert Niel Reid, K.C.S.I., K.C.I.E., and Lady A. H. Reid (née Disney); m. Isobel Jean McLachlan 1951 (died 1976); one s. one d.; ed. Malvern Coll., Brasenose Coll., Oxford; Commdr. Royal Tank Regt. 1941, rank of Capt. 1945; traffic apprentice, London and N. E. Railway 1947, Goods Agent, York 1958-60, Asst. Dist. Goods Man., Glasgow 1960-61, Dist. Passenger Man. 1961-63, Div. Commercial Man. 1963-67, Planning Man., Scottish Region 1967-68, Div. Man., Doncaster 1968-72, Deputy Gen. Man., E. Region, York 1972-74, Gen. Man., S. Region 1974-76, Exec. mem. for Marketing 1977-80, Chief Exec. (Railways), British Railways Bd. 1980-, Chair. 1983-; Dir., British Transport Hotels Ltd. 1977-83; Chair. Freightliner Co. Ltd. 1978-80; Pres. C.I.T. 1982-83; mem. UIC Bd. of Man., CBI Pres.'s Cttee., Governing Council and Bd. of Business in the Community; Companion B.I.M.; Freeman of City of London; Hon. Fellow, Brasenose Coll. 1984-. *Leisure interests:* golf, sailing, shooting. *Address:* British Railways Board, P.O. Box 100, 24 Eversholt Street, London, NW1 1DZ, England. *Telephone:* 01-928 5151.

REID, William Stanford, M.A., TH.M., PH.D.; Canadian ecclesiastic and professor of history; b. 13 Sept. 1913, Montreal; s. of Rev. William D. Reid and Daisy F. Stanford; m. Priscilla Lee 1940; no c.; ed. McGill Univ., Westminster Theological Seminary, Philadelphia, Pa., and Univ. of Pennsylvania; Minister, Fairmount Taylor Presbyterian Church, Montreal 1941–45; Founder and Minister, Presbyterian Church of Town of Mount Royal, Montreal 1945–51; Lecturer, subsequently Prof. of History, McGill Univ., Montreal 1941–65; Prof. and first Chair. Dept. of History, Univ. of Guelph 1965–70, Prof. of History 1970–78, Prof. Emer. 1979–; Visiting Lecturer, Presbyterian Theological Hall, Melbourne 1982–84; Hon. L.H.D. (Wheaton Coll.) 1975; Hon. D.D. (Presbyterian Coll., Montreal) 1978. *Publications:* The Church of Scotland in Lower Canada 1936, Skipper from Leith 1964, Economic History of Great Britain 1960, Trumpeter of God 1974, The Scottish Tradition in Canada 1976, John Calvin: His Influence on the Western World 1983. *Address:* Department of History, University of Guelph, Guelph, Ont. N1G 2W1 (Office); No. 906, 19 Woodlawn Road W., Guelph, Ont. N1H 7B1, Canada (Home). *Telephone:* (519) 824-4120 Ext. 3887 (Office); (519) 822-7032 (Home).

REID CABRAL, Dr. Donald J.; Dominican politician, lawyer and businessman; b. 9 June 1923, Santiago de los Caballeros; s. of William C. Reid and Auristela Cabral de Reid; m. Clara A. Tejera 1949; two d.; ed. Univ. de Santo Domingo; Pres. Reid & Pellerano C.A. 1949–; Pres. Automobile Dealers' Asscn. 1949–62; Vice-Pres. Council of State 1962–63; Minister of Foreign Affairs Sept.-Dec. 1963; Amb. to UN 1963; Amb. to Israel 1963; Pres. Triumvirate which ruled Dominican Repub. 1963–65; Minister of Foreign Affairs 1964; Minister of Armed Forces 1964–65; Sec. of State without Portfolio 1988–. *Leisure interests:* gardening, sailing, scuba-diving. *Address:* Cervantes 8, Santo Domingo, D.N., Dominican Republic. *Telephone:* 565-4481/4; 5-5677/8; 689-3389.

REILLY, Sir (D'Arcy) Patrick, G.C.M.G., O.B.E., M.A.; British diplomatist; b. 17 March 1909, Ootacamund, India; s. of Sir D'Arcy and Florence (née Wilkinson)Reilly; m. 1st Rachel Mary Sykes 1938 (died 1984), two d.; m. 2nd Ruth Norrington 1987; ed. Winchester Coll., and New Coll., Oxford; Fellow All Souls Coll., Oxford 1932–39, 1969–, Hon. Fellow, New Coll., Oxford 1972–; entered Diplomatic Service 1933; served Teheran 1935–38, Foreign Office 1938, Algiers 1943, Paris 1944, Athens 1945; Counsellor, Athens 1947; Imperial Defence Coll. 1949; Asst. Under-Sec. of State, Foreign Office 1950–53; Minister in Paris 1953–56; Deputy Under-Sec., Foreign Office 1956; Amb. to U.S.S.R. 1957–60; Deputy Under-Sec. Foreign Office 1960–64; Official Head U.K. Del. to UN Conf. on Trade and Devt.; Amb. to France 1965–68; Pres. London Chamber of Commerce and Industry 1972–75, Vice-Pres. 1975–; Chair. Banque Nat. de Paris Ltd. 1969–80, United Bank for Africa 1969–74, Univ. of London Management Cttee.; British Inst. in Paris 1970–79; Chair. Council, Bedford Coll., Univ. of London 1970–75; Hon. D.Litt. (Bath); Commdr., Légion d'honneur 1979. *Leisure interests:* travel, architecture, gardening. *Address:* Flat 2, 75 Warrington Crescent, London, W9 1EH, England. *Telephone:* 01-289 5384.

REINERT, Heinrich, DR.RER.OEC.; German business executive; b. 29 May 1920, Leipzig; m. 1952; one d.; fmrly. with Bayer AG and subsequently mem. Man. Bd. FINA Raffinerie AG and FINA Bitumenwerk 1960–; mem. Man. Bd. VEBA-Chemie AG 1967–; mem. Man. Bd. VEBA AG 1974–77, Chair. 1973; Chair. Supervisory Bd. Aral AG 1973–75, 1977. *Leisure interest:* hunting. *Address:* Ründerother Str. 46, 5250 Engelskirchen-Bickenbach, Federal Republic of Germany.

REINES, Frederick, M.E., M.S., PH.D.; American physicist; b. 16 March 1918, Paterson, N.J.; s. of Israel Reines and Gussie Cohen; m. Sylvia Samuels 1940; one s. one d.; ed. Stevens Inst. of Technology and New York Univ.; Staff mem. and Group Leader, Theoretical Div., Los Alamos Scientific Laboratory 1944–59; Prof. and Head, Dept. of Physics, Case Inst. of Tech. 1959–66; Dean of Physical Sciences Univ. of Calif., Irvine 1966–74, Prof. of Physics Univ. of Calif., Irvine 1966–87, Distinguished Prof. 1987–; Fellow, A.A.A.S., American Physical Soc., American Acad. of Arts and Sciences, N.A.S.; Hon. D.Sc. (Witwatersrand); Hon. D.Eng. (Stevens Univ.); Guggenheim Fellow 1958–59; Sloan Fellow 1959–63; Stevens Honor Award 1971, J. Robert Oppenheimer Memorial Prize 1981, Nat. Medal of Science 1983, Irvine Medal, Univ. of Calif. 1987. *Publications:* Papers on detection of free neutrino 1953–57, observation of high energy neutrinos in the cosmic radiation 1965, effects of nuclear explosions 1950, whole body counting of natural radioactivity in humans 1953, liquid scintillation counters 1952–66, stability of baryons 1954–87, observation of super nova neutrinos 1987. *Address:* University of California at Irvine, Irvine, Calif. 92717, U.S.A. *Telephone:* (714) 8567036.

REINHARDT, John Edward, M.S., PH.D.; American teacher and diplomatist; b. 8 March 1920, Glade Spring, Va.; s. of Edward Vinton Reinhardt and Alice Miller; m. Carolyn L. Daves 1947; three d.; ed. Knoxville Coll., Univs. of Chicago and Wisconsin; Instructor in English, Knoxville Coll. 1940–41, Fayetteville State Coll. 1941–42; U.S. Army 1942–46; graduate student 1946–50; Prof. of English, Virginia State Coll. 1950–56; Visiting Prof. of English, Atlanta Univ. 1953; Asst. Cultural Officer, American Embassy, Philippines 1956–58; Dir. American Cultural Center, Kyoto, Japan 1958–62; Dir. of Field Programs, American Embassy, Tokyo 1962–63; Cultural Attaché, Teheran 1963–66; Deputy Asst. Dir. of U.S. Information Agency for Far East 1966–68, for Africa 1968–70, for Far East 1970–71;

Amb. to Nigeria 1971–75; Asst. Sec. of State for Public Affairs 1975–77; Dir. U.S. Information Agency 1977–78, Int. Communication Agency 1978–80, Acting Dir. Nat. Museum of African Art, Smithsonian Inst. 1981–83, Acting Asst. Sec. for History and Art 1983, Asst. Sec. 1983–84; Dir. Div. of Int. Activities 1984–. *Leisure interests:* gardening, photography. *Address:* 6801 Laverock Court, Bethesda, Md. 20817, U.S.A.

REINHARDT, Max; British publisher; b. 30 Nov. 1915, Istanbul, Turkey; s. of Ernest and Frieda (née Darr) Reinhardt; m. 1st Margaret Leighton 1947 (divorced 1955); m. 2nd Joan MacDonald 1957; two d.; ed. Ecole des Hautes Etudes Commerciales, Paris, London School of Economics; Chair. Reinhardt Books Ltd. 1948–, Nonesuch Press Ltd. 1985–; Chair. The Bodley Head Group of Publishers 1957–87; Jt. Chair. Chatto, Virago, Bodley Head and Jonathan Cape Ltd. 1973–86; mem. Council, Publishers' Assocn. 1963–69, Royal Acad. of Dramatic Art 1965–. *Leisure interests:* swimming, bridge. *Address:* 16 Pelham Crescent, London, SW7 2NR, England. *Telephone:* 01-589 5527.

REIS, Mauricio Rangel; Brazilian agronomist and statistician; b. 2 March 1922, Rio de Janeiro; s. of Alfredo de Souza Reis and Maria Coeli Rangel Reis; m. Themis Lima Reis 1953; one s.; fmr. Sec.-Gen. Ministry of Agriculture; Deputy Head Inst. for Applied Econ. Research, Ministry of Planning and Gen. Co-ordination; well-known for his work in developing the Amazon region; Minister of the Interior 1974–78. *Address:* c/o Ministério de Interior, SAS, Quadra 1, Bloco A, Lotes 9/10, D.F., Brazil.

REISCHAUER, Edwin Oldfather, A.M., PH.D.; American historian and diplomatist; b. 15 Oct. 1910, Tokyo, Japan; s. of August Karl and Helen Oldfather Reischauer; m. 1st Adrienne Danton 1935 (died 1955), 2nd Haru Matsukata 1956; one s. two d.; ed. Oberlin Coll., Harvard Univ., and Univ. of Paris; studied in France, Japan, China 1933–38; Instructor Harvard 1938–42; Military Intelligence, Second World War; Special Asst. to Dir. Office of Far Eastern Affairs, Dept. of State 1945–46; Assoc. Prof. Far Eastern Languages 1946–50, Prof. 1950–61; Dir. Harvard-Yenching Inst. 1956–61; Amb. to Japan 1961–66; Prof. Harvard Univ. 1966–81, Prof. Emer. 1981–; Chair. Bd. Trustees, Harvard-Yenching Inst. 1969–83; Japan Foundation Prize 1975. *Publications:* Selected Japanese Texts for University Students (3 vols; compiler, with S. Elisseeff) 1942–47, Japan Past and Present 1946, Translations from Early Japanese Literature (with Joseph Yamagiwa) 1951, Wanted: An Asian Policy 1955, Ennin's Dairy: The Record of a Pilgrimage to China in Search of the Law 1955, Ennin's Travels in T'ang China 1955, The United States and Japan 1950, 1965, East Asia: The Great Tradition (with John K. Fairbank) 1960, East Asia: The Modern Transformation (with Fairbank and Craig) 1965, Beyond Vietnam: The United States and Asia 1967, Japan: The Story of a Nation 1970 and 1981, East Asia: Tradition and Transformation (with Fairbank and Craig) 1973, Toward the 21st Century: Education for a Changing World 1973, The Japanese 1977, Japan Society 1907–82, 1982, My Life Between Japan and America 1986, The Japanese Today: Change and Continuity 1988. *Address:* 863 Concord Avenue, Belmont, Mass. 02178, U.S.A. *Telephone:* (617) 484-7730.

REISS, Howard, PH.D.; American professor of chemistry; b. 5 April 1922, New York; s. of Isidor Reiss and Jean Goldstein; m. Phyllis F. Kohn 1945; one s. one d.; ed. New York and Columbia Univs.; Manhattan project, U.S. Army 1944–46; Instr., Asst. Prof. Boston Univ. 1949–51; mem. tech. staff, Cen. Research Lab. Celanese Corpn. of America 1951–52, Bell Telephone Labs. 1952–60; Asst. Dir. Edgar C. Bain Lab. for Fundamental Research, U.S. Steel Corpn. 1957; Assoc. Dir., Dir. Research Dept. Atomics Int. Div. North American Aviation Inc. 1960–62; Vice-Pres. Research, Pres., Dir. North American Aviation Science Center 1962–67; Vice-Pres. Research, Aerospace and Systems Group, North American Rockwell Corpn. 1967–68; Prof. of Chemistry, Univ. of Calif., L.A. 1968–; mem. N.A.S.; several awards and distinctions. *Publications:* The Methods of Thermodynamics 1965; articles in professional journals. *Leisure interests:* reading, carpentering, sports. *Address:* Department of Chemistry and Biochemistry, University of California, 405 Hilgard Avenue, Los Angeles, Calif. 90024 (Office); 16656 Oldham Street, Encino, Calif. 91436, U.S.A. (Home). *Telephone:* (213) 825-3029 (Office); (818) 784-4089 (Home).

REISS, Timothy James, M.A., PH.D., F.R.S.C.; British/Canadian professor of literature; b. 14 May 1942, Stanmore, Middx.; s. of James M. Reiss and Margaret J. Ping; divorced; three c.; ed. Hardye's School, Dorchester, Manchester Univ., Sorbonne, Paris and Univ. of Illinois; Instructor to Asst. Prof. Yale Univ. 1968–73; Assoc. Prof. Univ. de Montréal 1973–79, Prof. of Comparative Literature 1979–84; Prof. of Comparative Literature, Modern Languages and Philosophy, Emory Univ. 1983–86, Samuel C. Dobbs Prof. of Comparative Literature and French 1986–87; Prof. and Chair. of Comparative Literature New York Univ. 1987–; Canada Council Sr. Fellow 1987–78; Fellow Acad. of Literary Studies; other awards and visiting professorships. *Publications:* Toward Dramatic Illusion 1971, Tragedy and Truth 1980, The Discourse of Modernism 1982, The Uncertainty of Analysis 1988. *Address:* Department of Comparative Literature, New York University, 19 University Plaza, 4th Floor, New York, N.Y. 10003, U.S.A. *Telephone:* 212-998-8795.

REISZ, Karel; British film director; b. 21 July 1926, Ostrava, Czechoslovakia; s. of Dr. Josef and Frederika Reisz; m. 1st Julia Coppard (dissolved); m. 2nd Betsy Blair 1963; three s.; ed. Leighton Park School, Reading, and Emmanuel Coll., Cambridge; came to England 1939; served with Czechoslovak section of R.A.F. 1944–46; free-lanced as journalist, lecturer and teacher; Films Officer, Ford Motor Co.; now film dir. and producer. *Films:* Momma Don't Allow (Co-dir. with Tony Richardson) 1954, Every Day Except Christmas (producer) 1958, We Are the Lambeth Boys 1958 (Both for Fords), Saturday Night and Sunday Morning 1959, This Sporting Life (producer) 1962, Night Must Fall 1963, Morgan—A Suitable Case for Treatment 1965, Isadora 1969, The Gambler 1974, Dog Soldiers 1977, The French Lieutenant's Woman 1981, Sweet Dreams 1985, Everybody Wins 1989. *Publication:* The Technique of Film Editing 1953. *Leisure interest:* gardening. *Address:* Film Contracts, 2 Lower James Street, London, W.1, England.

REKOLA, Esko Johannes; Finnish lawyer and civil servant; b. 10 June 1919, Tampere; s. of Prof. Aarne Rekola and Laina Kouvo; m. 1st Raili Kilpeläinen 1945 (died 1973), three s.; m. 2nd Anna Liisa Sundquist 1974; ed. Helsinki Univ.; Chief of Taxation Dept., Ministry of Finance 1957–59, Chief of Budget Dept. 1959–63, 1964–65; Alt. Gov. Int. Bank for Reconstruction and Devt. 1962–66, Gov. 1976–78; Minister of Finance 1963–64; Chief of the Prime Minister's Office 1965–66; Gen. Man. Finnish State Railways 1966–73; Sec.-Gen. Ministry of Communications 1973–76; Minister of Finance 1976–77, of Economy 1977–79, for Foreign Trade 1979–82. *Address:* H Topeliuksenkatu 17A12, 00250 Helsinki 25, Finland. *Telephone:* 442454.

REKUNKOV, Aleksandr Mikhailovich; Soviet jurist and State official; b. 1920; ed. All-Union Law Inst.; mem. CPSU 1940–; served on war front 1941–45; public procurator in a series of regions of Rostov Dist. 1946–58; public procurator in Bryansk and Voronezh Dist. 1960–71; First Deputy Public Procurator of R.S.F.S.R. 1971–76; First Deputy Gen. Procurator of U.S.S.R. 1976–81; Procurator-Gen. 1981–88; Deputy to U.S.S.R. Supreme Soviet; mem. CPSU Cen. Cttee. –1989. *Address:* The Kremlin, Moscow, U.S.S.R.

RELLY, Gavin Walter Hamilton, M.A.; South African business executive; b. 6 Feb. 1926, Stellenbosch; m. Jane Margaret Glenton 1951; one s. two d.; ed. Diocesan Coll., Rondebosch and Trinity Coll., Oxford; joined Anglo American Corpn., Johannesburg 1949, Chair. Anglo American Corpn. (Cen. Africa) 1965–69; mem. Bd. Anglo American Corpn. of S.A. Ltd. 1965, Exec. Dir. 1966, Joint Deputy Chair. 1977–82, Chair. Jan. 1983–; mem. Bd. Hudson Bay Mining & Smelting Co. Ltd. 1970–83, Chair. 1970–73; Chair. Anglo American Industrial Corpn. 1973–83, AECI Ltd. Jan. 1983–; Dir. Minerals and Resources Corpn. Ltd. 1974–; Pres. South Africa Foundation 1981–82, Chair. Bd. of Trustees; Sr. Gov. Int. Exec. Service Corp. S.A. 1988–; Trustee Univ. of S.A. Foundation 1975–, Wits Foundation 1984–. *Address:* Anglo American Corpn. of South Africa Ltd., 44 Main Street, Johannesburg 2001, South Africa.

RELPH, Michael; British film producer, writer, designer and director; s. of late George Relph and Deborah (née Nansen) Relph; m. 1st Doris Gorden 1938, 2nd Maria Barry 1949; one s. one d.; fmr. Assoc. Producer and Producer, Ealing; Founder/Dir. Allied Film Makers; Chair. Film Production Asscn. of GB 1971–76, BFI Production Bd. 1971–76; Producer mem. Cinematograph Films Council 1971–76; Exec. in charge of Production, Kendon Films 1979–80; Art Dir., Ealing on films Champagne Charley, Nicholas Nickleby, Dead of Night, Saraband for Dead Lovers. *Films produced include:* The Captive Heart, Frieda, The Blue Lamp, Kind Hearts and Coronets, The Square Ring, I Believe in You (co-author, screenplay), The Ship That Died of Shame, The Rainbow Jacket, The Smallest Show on Earth, Sapphire, League of Gentlemen, Victim, Man in the Moon (co-author, screenplay), Life For Ruth, The Mind Benders, A Place to Go, (author, screenplay), Woman of Straw (co-author, screenplay), Masquerade (co-author, screenplay), The Assassination Bureau, The Man Who Haunted Himself (co-author), Scum, An Unsuitable Job for a Woman (co-producer), Heavenly Pursuits. *Films directed:* Davy, Rockets Galore. *Address:* The Lodge, Primrose Hill Studios, London, N.W.1, England. *Telephone:* 01-586 0249.

REMBISZ, Gabriela; Polish politician; b. 12 March 1937, Poznań; two d.; ed. secondary tech. school; production worker Stomil Poznań Tyres Works, Poznań 1961–, currently shift master; active in youth movt.; mem. Polish United Workers' Party (PZPR) 1976–; First Sec. PZPR Sectional Org. and mem. Exec. PZPR Plant Cttee. of Stomil Tyres Works, Poznań until 1986; mem. PZPR Cen. Cttee. 1986–, alt. mem. Political Bureau of PZPR Cen. Cttee. 1986–88, mem. 1988–; mem. Ind. Self-governing Trade Union of Stomil Employees; Badge for Services to City of Poznań. *Address:* Komitet Centralny PZPR, ul. Nowy Świat 6, 00-497 Warsaw, Poland.

REMEDIOS, Alberto Telisforo, C.B.E.; British opera singer; b. 27 Feb. 1935, Liverpool; s. of Albert and Ida Remedios; m. 1st Shirley Swindells 1958; m. 2nd Judith Hosken 1965; two s. one d.; studied with Edwin Francis, Liverpool; joined Sadler's Wells Opera Co. 1955; now sings regularly with English Nat. Opera and Royal Opera House, Covent Garden; has made numerous appearances in U.S.A., Canada, Argentina, Germany, France and Spain, and appeared in concert with major British orchestras; records include Wagner's Der Ring des Nibelungen and Tippett's A Midsummer Marriage; Queen's Prize, Royal Coll. of Music; First Prize, Int. Singing Competition, Sofia, Bulgaria. *Leisure interests:* football, motoring, record collecting. *Address:* c/o Ibbs & Tillett Ltd., 450 Edgware Road, London, W2 1EG, England. *Telephone:* 01-258 0525.

REMEZ, Brig.-Gen. Aharon; Israeli air force officer and diplomatist; b. 8 May 1919, Tel-Aviv; s. of David Remez; m. Rita Levy 1952; one s. three d.; ed. Harvard Business School, Woodrow Wilson School, Princeton; agricultural training in kibbutz, Givat Haim 1937–39; Emissary to Zionist Youth Movement, U.S.A. 1939–41; Royal Air Force 1942–47; mem. kibbutz Kfar Blum 1947–; Dir. of Planning and Operations, later Chief of Staff, Israel Air Force 1948; Commdr.-in-Chief Israel Air Force 1948–51; Head, Ministry of Defence Purchasing Mission, U.S.A. 1952–53; Aviation Adviser to Minister of Defence 1953–54; Man. Dir. Solel-Boneh Koor Industries and Crafts Co. Ltd. 1954–59; mem. Knesset 1955–57; Admin. Dir. Weizmann Inst. of Science, Rehovot 1959–60; Dir. Int. Co-operation Div., Ministry for Foreign Affairs 1960–64, Adviser on Int. Co-operation to Minister for Foreign Affairs 1964–65; Amb. to U.K. 1965–70; Dir.-Gen. Israel Ports Authority 1970–77; Chair. Israel Airports Authority 1977–81. *Publications:* articles on aviation, management and political topics. *Leisure interests:* sculpture, Do-It-Yourself hobbies. *Address:* Cottage 11, San Martin Street, Jerusalem 93341, Israel (Home).

REMICK, Lee; American actress; b. 14 Dec. 1935, Boston, Mass.; d. of Frank Remick and Pat Packard; m. 1st William Colleran 1957 (divorced 1969), one s. one d.; m. 2nd William R. Gowans 1970; ed. Hewitt School, New York; stage appearances in Anyone Can Whistle (musical), New York 1964, Wait Until Dark, New York 1966, Bus Stop, London 1976, I Do I Do 1983; *films include:* Face in the Crowd 1956, The Long Hot Summer 1957, These Thousand Hills 1958, Anatomy of a Murder 1959, Wild River 1959, Sanctuary 1960, Experiment in Terror (British title Grip of Fear) 1960, Days of Wine and Roses 1961, The Running Man 1962, The Wheeler Dealers 1963, The Travelling Lady 1963, The Hallelujah Trail 1964, No Way to Treat a Lady 1967, The Detective 1967, Hard Contract 1968, A Severed Head 1969, Loot 1969, Sometimes a Great Notion 1970, A Delicate Balance 1972, Hennessy 1975, The Omen 1976, Telefon 1977, The Medusa Touch 1977, The Europeans 1979, The Competition 1980, Tribute 1980; TV appearances in QB-VII, The Blue Knight, Jennie 1974, The Ambassadors 1977, Wheels (U.S.A. series) 1977–78, Haywire 1980, The Woman's Room 1980, The Letter 1981, Follies: Four Days 1986, Nutcracker 1987, The Vision (BBC) 1988; Golden Globe Award for The Blue Knight, Best TV Actress Award for Jennie, Soc. of Film and TV Arts 1974; Hon. D.H.L. (Emerson Coll.) 1977. *Address:* c/o International Creative Management Ltd., 8899 Beverly Boulevard, Los Angeles, Calif. 90048, U.S.A.

REMMELINK, Jan; Netherlands lawyer; b. 27 April 1922, Zelhem; m. J.A. Pol; one s.; ed. Utrecht Univ.; Deputy Clerk Co. Court of Justice 1946; Substitute Officer of Justice 1956; Attorney Gen. Supreme Court of the Netherlands 1968, Procurator Gen. 1988–; Professor of Criminal Law, Univ. of Groningen 1968; Professor Extraordinary Vrije Universiteit, Amsterdam; Ridder in de Orde van de Nederlandse Leeuw, Commandeur in de Orde van Oranje Massau. *Publications:* Uitleveringsrecht 1986, Hoofdwegen door het verkeersrecht 1988, numerous articles on criminal law. *Address:* Kazernestraat 52, Postbus 2030, 2500 EH The Hague, The Netherlands. *Telephone:* (070) 611311.

REMY, Pierre-Jean (pseudonym of Jean-Pierre Angremy); French diplomatist and author; b. 21 March 1937, Angoulême; s. of Pierre Angremy and Alice Collebrans; m. 2nd Sophie Schmit 1986; one s. one d.; ed. Lycée Condorcet, Inst. d'Etudes Politiques, Paris, Brandeis Univ. (U.S.A.) and Ecole Nationale d'Administration, Paris; served in Hong Kong 1963; Second Sec., Peking 1964, London 1966; First Sec. London 1968; Counsellor, Ministry of Foreign Affairs 1971; Dir. Programme Co-Ordination, O.R.T.F. 1972, Cultural Counsellor, French Embassy, London 1975–79; responsible for Theatre and Entertainment, French Ministry of Culture 1979–81; Dir.-Gen. Cultural and Scientific Affairs, Ministry of Foreign Affairs 1988–; Prix Renaudot for novel Le sac du palais d'été 1971, Grand Prix du Roman de l'Académie Française (for Une ville immortelle) 1986. *Publications:* Et Gulliver mourut de sommeil 1961, Midi ou l'attentat 1962, Gauguins à gogo 1971, Le sac du palais d'ete 1971, Urbanisme (poems) 1972, Une mort sale 1973, La vie d'Adrian Putney, poète 1973, Ava, La mort de Floria Tosca, Mémoires secrets pour servir à l'histoire de ce siècle 1974, Rêver la vie 1975, La figure dans la pierre 1976, Chine: Un itinéraire 1977, Les enfants du parc 1977, Si j'étais romancier 1977, Callas, une vie 1978, Les nouvelles aventures du Chevalier de la Barre 1978, Orient-Express 1979, Cordelia ou l'Angleterre 1979, Don Giovanni (Mozart/Losey) 1979, Pandora 1980, Salue pour moi le monde 1980, Un voyage d'hiver 1981, Don Juan 1982, Le dernier été 1983, Mata-Hari 1983, La vie d'un héro 1985, Une ville immortelle 1986; mem. Acad. Française; Chevalier, Ordre nat. du Mérite, Commdr. des Arts et des Lettres, Chevalier, Légion d'Honneur. *Leisure interest:* collecting 18th-century novels. *Address:* Ministry of Foreign Affairs, 64 Avenue Kleber, 75016 Paris; 100 rue de l'Université, 75007 Paris, France.

REN JIANXIN; Chinese lawyer; b. Aug. 1925, Shanxi Prov.; Secr. Cen. Comm. for Politics and Law 1949–53; Sec. Cen. Comm. for Legal System 1953–54; Sec. Legislation Bureau, State Council 1954–59; Dir. Dept. of Legal Affairs, China Council for the Promotion of Int. Trade (CCPIT), Standing mem. Research Cen. for Econ. Legislation under State Council, Sec. General China Foreign Trade and Maritime Arbitration Comm. 1960–81, Vice-Chair. 1981–88; Vice-Chair. CCPIT 1981–83; Vice-Pres. Supreme People's Court 1983–88, Pres. April 1988–; mem. Adjudication Cttee. SPC 1983–; Vice-Pres. China Law Soc. 1983–, China Econ. Law Inst., China

Int. Law Soc.; Pres. China Group AIPPI; Adviser China Consumers' Assen.; mem. Exec. Cttee. and Pres. for Asia, World Peace Through Law Centre (WPTLC) 1985-; mem. 13th CCP Cen. Cttee. 1987-. *Address:* Supreme People's Court, Beijing, People's Republic of China.

REN PING; Chinese papercut artist; b. 1962, Yanji, Jilin. *Address:* Cultural Exhibition Centre, Shandong, People's Republic of China.

REN RONG, Maj.-Gen.; Chinese military official; Head Propaganda Dept. Shaanxi-Gansu-Ningxia Border Region Govt. 1938; Political Commissar of a div. 9th Column of the Northeast Liberation Army 1947; Deputy Political Commissar 46th Corps, 4th Field Army 1951-52; Political Commissar 1952-; Deputy Dir. Political Dept. Chinese People's Volunteers in Korea 1957; mem. Ceasefire Comm. in Panmunjom 1960; Deputy Political Commissar Tibet Mil. Region 1965-70, Political Commissar 1970-75, First Political Commissar 1975-80; Vice-Chair. Tibet Revolutionary Cttee. 1968-79; alt. mem. 10th CCP Cen. Cttee. 1973; mem. 11th CCP Cen. Cttee. 1978; Deputy for Tibet to 5th NPC 1978-83; Chair. Tibet Prov. CPPCC 1979-80; Deputy Political Commissar Wuhan Mil. Region 1982-85. *Address:* Central Committee of the Chinese Communist Party, Beijing, China.

REN WUZHI; Chinese state official; b. 12 Sept. 1929, Xin Xian, Shanxi; s. of Ren Jin Huo and Ren Zhuo Huan; m. Zhang Miao Wen 1952; one s. two d.; Dir. State Bureau of Religious Affairs 1984-. *Leisure interests:* reading newspapers and books. *Address:* State Bureau of Religious Affairs, No. 22 XI An Men da Jie, Beijing, People's Republic of China.

REN ZHIBIN; Chinese soldier, party and government official; mem. Hubei-Henan-Anhui Border Region, New 4th Army, 1945; mem. Standing Cttee. CPPCC, Sec.-Gen. Shandong Prov. CCP Cttee., Council mem. Shandong Prov. People's Govt. 1951; Sec. Anhui Prov. CCP Cttee. 1964-67; purged after rebel seizure of power in Anhui Prov. Jan. 1967, rehabilitated Feb. 1974; Sec. Gen. Anhui Prov. CCP Cttee. 1977-78; alt. mem. 11th CCP Cen. Cttee. 1977-; mem. Cen Advisory Cttee. of CCP Cen Cttee. 1987-. *Address:* Central Advisory Committee of the Central Committee of the Chinese Communist Party, Zhongnanhai, Beijing, People's Republic of China.

REN ZHONGYI; Chinese government official; b. 20 Sept. 1914, Hebei Province; s. of Ren Yanfu and Han Qimei; m. Wang Xuan 1937; three s.; ed. China Univ., Beijing; Sec. Beijing N.W. Dist. Cttee. of CCP 1935-37; anti-Japanese guerrilla activity 1938-45; Sec. Dalian City Cttee. of CCP, Deputy Mayor of Dalian 1945-52; First Sec. Harbin City Cttee. of CCP, First Political Commisar of Harbin Garrison Command, Sec. Helongjiang Prov. Cttee. of CCP, Vice-Gov. Heilongjiang 1953-76; First Sec. Liaoning Prov. CCP Cttee., First Political Commissar of Liaoning Prov. Mil. Command 1977-80; First Sec. of Guangdong Prov. CCP Cttee., First Political Commissar of Guangdong Prov. Mil. Command 1980-85; mem. 11th, 12th CCP Cen. Cttees. 1973-85; mem. CCP Cen. Advisory Comm. 1985-. *Leisure interests:* wide interests, reading in particular. *Address:* c/o Guangdong Provincial Communist Party, People's Republic of China. *Telephone:* Guangzhou 750899.

RENAUD, Madeleine; French actress and author; b. 21 Feb. 1900; m. 1st Charles Gribouval, one s.; m. 2nd Jean-Louis Barrault (q.v.) 1940; ed. Lycée Racine and Paris Conservatoire; Pensionnaire, Comédie Française 1921-47; co-Dir. Compagnie Madeleine Renaud—Jean-Louis Barrault 1947-; plays in which she has acted important roles include Le soulier de satin, Occupe-toi d'Amélie, Les nuits de colère, Christophe Colombe, La dame aux camélias, Harold et Maude 1973, Oh les beaux jours 1976, Pas moi 1976, Wings 1979, Savannah Bay 1983, Lettre d'une mère à son fils 1983, Pense à l'Afrique 1984, Les salons 1986; *films include:* Jean de la lune, La maternelle, Remorques, Le ciel est à nous, Le plaisir, Dialogue des Carmélites, Le jour le plus long, Le diable par la queue 1968, L'humeur vagabonde 1971, La mandarine 1972; Commdr., Légion d'honneur, Commdr. des Arts et des Lettres. *Address:* 18 avenue du Président-Wilson, 75116 Paris, France.

RENCHARD, William S(hryock), A.B.; American banker; b. 1 Jan. 1908, Trenton, N.J.; s. of John A. and Lillian C. (Smith) Renchard; m. Alice Marie Fleming 1935; three d.; ed. Princeton Univ.; with the Nat. Bank of Commerce, New York 1928-29, the Guaranty Trust Co., New York 1929-30; joined the Chemical Bank 1930, Pres. and Dir. 1960-66, Chair. and C.E.O., 1966-73, Chair. Exec. Cttee. and Dir. 1973-78, Chair. Directors' Advisory Cttee. 1978-82, Hon. Dir. 1982-; official of many business and public bodies. *Leisure interest:* golf. *Address:* Chemical Bank, 30 Rockefeller Plaza, New York, N.Y. 10112, U.S.A.

RENDELL, Ruth, F.R.S.L.; British crime novelist; b. 17 Feb. 1930; d. of Arthur Grasemann and Ebba Kruse; m. Donald Rendell 1950, marriage dissolved 1975, remarried 1977; one s.; ed. Loughton County High School; Arts Council Nat. Book Award for Genre Fiction 1981. *Publications include:* From Doon with Death 1964, A Judgment in Stone 1976, The Lake of Darkness 1980, An Unkindness of Ravens 1985, Live Flesh 1986, Heartstones 1987, Talking to Strange Men 1987, Wolf to the Slaughter 1987, The Veiled One 1988, A Warning to the Curious—The Ghost Stories of M. R. James 1988, The Bridesmaid 1989, Suffolk 1989; (under-pseudonym Barbara Vine) A Dark-Adapted Eye 1986, A Fatal Inversion 1987, The House of Stairs 1988; three vols. of short stories. *Leisure interests:* reading, walking, opera. *Address:* Nussteads, Polstead, Suffolk, England.

RENDLE, Michael Russel, M.A.; British business executive; b. 20 Feb. 1931, Kuala Lumpur, Malaya; s. of late H. C. R. Rendle; m. Heather Rinkel 1957; two s. two d.; ed. Marlborough Coll. and New Coll., Oxford; joined Anglo-Iranian Oil Co. (now British Petroleum) 1954; served in U.K., Trinidad, Aden; Man. Dir. BP Trinidad 1967-70, BP Australia 1974-78; Dir. BP Trading (London) 1978-81; a Man. Dir. BP Co. 1981-86; Deputy Chair. Imperial Continental Gas Assn. 1986-87, British-Borneo Petroleum Syndicate 1986-; Dir. Willis Faber PLC 1985-, Petrofina SA 1986-87; mem. London Bd. Westpac Banking Corp. 1978-; mem. British Overseas Trade Bd. 1982-86, INSEAD Int. Council and U.K. Advisory Bd. 1984-86; Chair. UNICE Social Affairs Cttee. 1984-87; mem. Marlborough Coll. Council 1987-. *Leisure interests:* golf, music, various outdoor sports. *Address:* c/o Willis Faber PLC, 10 Trinity Square, London, EC3P 3AX, England. *Telephone:* 01-481 7152.

RENÉ, (France) Albert; Seychelles barrister and politician; b. 16 Nov. 1935, Seychelles; s. of Price René and Louisa Morgan; m. 1st Karen Handley 1956, one d.; m. 2nd Geva Adam 1975, one s.; ed. St. Louis Coll., Victoria, Seychelles Coll., St. Maurice, Switzerland, St. Mary's Coll., Southampton, U.K., King's Coll., London; called to Bar 1957; founder and Leader, Seychelles People's United Party 1964-; M.P. 1965-; Minister of Works and Land Devt. 1975-77; Prime Minister 1976-77; Pres. of Seychelles June 1977-, also C.-in-C., Minister of Econ. Devt. and Housing 1977-78, of Internal Affairs, Admin., Finance and Information 1977-79, of Finance 1977-78, of Youth and Community Devt. and Agric. 1978-80, of Health 1980-81, of Admin., Finance and Industries 1981-, of Planning and External Relations 1984-, of Defence 1986-, of Tourism 1988-; Order of the Golden Ark 1982. *Leisure interests:* gardening, fishing. *Address:* The State House, Victoria, Mahé, Seychelles. *Telephone:* 24391.

RENÉ, Louis; French surgeon; b. 21 Aug. 1918, Saint-Gilles, Gard; Head of Surgery, Hosp. of Croix-Saint-Simon, Paris 1955-84; Pres. Departmental Council of City of Paris 1973-85; Pres. Nat. Council, Ordre des Médecins 1987-, Int. Conf. of Medical Councils 1987, Nat. Cttee. of Medical Evaluation 1987; mem. Acad. de Chirurgie, Soc. française de médecine légale etc. *Address:* Conseil National de l'Ordre des Médecins, 60 boulevard de Latour-Maubourg, 75007 Paris, France.

RENFREW, Andrew Colin, PH.D., SC.D., F.B.A., F.S.A.; British professor of archaeology; b. 25 July 1937, Stockton-on-Tees; s. of the late Archibald Renfrew and of Helena D. Renfrew; m. Jane M. Ewbank 1965; two s. one d.; ed. St. Albans School, St. John's Coll., Cambridge, and British School of Archaeology, Athens; Lecturer in Prehistory and Archaeology, Univ. of Sheffield 1965-70, Sr. Lecturer 1970-72, Reader in Prehistory and Archaeology 1972; Prof. of Archaeology and Head of Dept., Univ. of Southampton 1972-81; Disney Prof. of Archaeology Univ. of Cambridge 1981-; Fellow of St. John's Coll., Cambridge 1981-86; Master of Jesus Coll., Cambridge 1986-; Visiting Lecturer, Univ. of Calif. at Los Angeles 1967; Rivers Memorial Medal, Royal Anthropological Inst. *Publications:* The Emergence of Civilization 1972, Before Civilization 1973, The Explanation of Culture Change 1973, British Prehistory 1974, Transformations: Mathematical Approaches to Culture Change 1979, Problems in European Prehistory 1979, An Island Polity 1982, Theory and Explanation in Archaeology 1982, Approaches to Social Archaeology 1984, The Archaeology of Cult 1985, Peer, Polity Interaction and Socio-Political Change 1986, Archaeology and Language: The Puzzle of Indo-European Origins 1987. *Leisure interests:* fine arts, coins. *Address:* Department of Archaeology, Downing Street, Cambridge, CB2 3DZ, England. *Telephone:* (0223) 333520.

RENGER, Annemarie; German politician; b. 7 Oct. 1919, Leipzig; d. of Fritz Wildung and Martha (née Scholz) Wildung; m. 1st Emil Renger 1938 (killed in 2nd World War), one s.; m. 2nd Aleksandar Renger-Lončarević 1965 (died 1973); private sec. to Dr. Kurt Schumacher 1945-52; managed SPD offices Berlin May-Dec. 1946; mem. Bundestag 1953-; SPD Parliamentary Group Man. 1969-72; Pres. Bundestag 1972-76, Jt. Vice-Pres. 1976-; mem. SPD 1945-; mem. Presidium 1961-73; mem. for ten years of advisory assembly of European Council and Assembly of West European Union; Vice-Pres. Int. Council of Social Democratic Women of the Socialist International 1972-76; Grosses Bundesverdienstkreuz. *Address:* Bundeshaus, 5300 Bonn, Federal Republic of Germany.

RENKE, Marian; Polish politician; b. 11 Feb. 1930, Piotrków Trybunalski; m.; two d.; ed. Łódź Univ. and Higher School of Social Sciences of PZPR Cen. Cttee., Warsaw; First Sec. Socialist Youth Union Cen. Cttee. 1957-64; Deputy Head, Foreign Dept. PZPR Cen. Cttee. 1965-71; Amb. to Cuba and Jamaica 1971-76, to Spain 1986-; Pres. Polish Sport Fed. 1976-78; Pres. Chief Cttee. for Physical Culture and Sport 1978-85, Pres. Polish Olympic Cttee. 1978-86; Deputy to Seym 1961-65; mem. Nat. Council of Culture 1983-86; Sec.-Gen. Assen. of Nat. Olympic Cttees. (ANOC) 1981-; Vice-Pres. European Assen. of Nat. Olympic Cttees. (ENOC) 1980-85; mem. Polish Workers' Party 1947-48, PZPR 1948-, alt. mem. PZPR Cen. Cttee. 1959-71; mem. Cen. Comm. for Party Control 1980-81; Polish and foreign decorations, including Commdr.'s and Officer's Cross of Order of Polonia Restituta, Order of Banner of Labour (2nd Class). *Publication:* Zagadnienia rozbrojeniowe w okresie międzywojennym 1918-1939 1966.

Leisure interests: swimming, skiing, tennis. *Address:* Embassy of the Polish People's Republic, Calle Guisando 23 bis, 28035 Madrid, Spain; ul. Mokotowska 3 m. 8, 00-640 Warsaw, Poland. *Telephone:* 209-16-05 (Madrid).

RENNERT, Wolfgang; German conductor, music and opera director; b. 1 April 1922, Cologne; s. of Dr. Alfred Rennert and Adelheid (née Nettesheim) Rennert; m. 1st Anny Schlemm 1957, 2nd Ulla Berkéwicz 1971 (divorced 1975); one s.; ed. Mozarteum Salzburg; Chief Conductor and Deputy Dir. of Music, Frankfurt 1953–67; Head of Opera, Staatstheater am Gärtnerplatz 1967–71; Perm. Guest Conductor, Berlin State Opera 1971–, Royal Opera, Copenhagen 1975–79; Dir. of Music and Dir. of Opera, Nat. Theatre, Mannheim 1980–85; guest appearances with Vienna State Opera, Munich and Hamburg Operas, Royal Opera House, Covent Garden, San Francisco Opera, Dallas Opera, Salzburg Festival, Munich Festival, Venice, Rome, Palermo and Lisbon Opera Houses. *Address:* D1000 Berlin (West) 45, Holbeinstrasse 58, Federal Republic of Germany. *Telephone:* 030-833 3094.

RENNIE, John Vernon Lockhart, F.R.S.S.A., PH.D.; South African professor (retd.); b. 26 Nov. 1903, Cape Town; s. of William Alexander Rennie and Esmerlada Elizabeth de Smidt; m. Beatrice Enid von Linsingen 1931; one s. two d.; ed. Univ. of Cape Town, Emmanuel Coll., Cambridge and Univ. Coll., London; Lecturer in Geology, Univ. of Cape Town 1929–30, Rhodes Univ. Coll. 1931–35 (became Rhodes Univ. 1951); Lecturer in Geography, Rhodes Univ. Coll. 1936–, Head of Geography Dept. 1937–62, Sr. Lecturer in Geography 1940–44, Prof. of Geography 1944–; Vice-Prin. and Pro-Vice-Chancellor, Rhodes Univ. 1951–53, 1957–70; Pres. S.A. Geographical Soc. 1944; mem. Nat. Council for Social Research 1954–58, 1964, Scientific Advisory Council 1964–69, Historical Monuments Comm. 1960–79; mem. Bd. of Trustees Albany Museum 1933–74, Chair. 1954–73; Hon. LL.D. (Rhodes Univ.) 1977; Gold Medal of Nat. Monuments Council 1980. *Publications:* 20 papers on South African invertebrate paleontology. *Leisure interest:* genealogy. *Address:* 7 Oatlands Road, Grahamstown, 6140, South Africa. *Telephone:* 22474.

RENOVICA, Milanko; Yugoslav politician; b. 1928, Sokolac; legal studies; mem. Bosnia-Hercegovina L.C. Cen. Cttee. and Bosnia-Hercegovina Presidency; Pres. Bosnia-Hercegovina Exec. Council 1974–82; Pres. Bosnia-Hercegovina Presidency 1983–85; mem. League of Communists of Yugoslavia (LCY) 1947–88, Pres. 1986–87. *Address:* c/o League of Communists of Yugoslavia, bul. Lenjina 6, Novi Beograd, Yugoslavia.

RENTCHNICK, Pierre, M.D.; Swiss physician and editor of medical publications; b. 17 July 1923, Geneva; s. of Jacques Rentchnick and Blanche (Spiegel) Rentchnick; m. Paule Adam 1948; one s.; ed. Univs. of Geneva and Paris; Ed.-in-Chief, Médecine et Hygiène, Geneva 1956–, Recent Results in Cancer Research, Heidelberg and New York 1962–83, Bulletin de l'Union internationale contre le cancer, Geneva 1962–80; f. Kiwanis-Club, Geneva 1966, Pres. 1976–77; f. Int. Soc. for Chemotherapy 1959; mem. New York Acad. of Sciences, Medical Soc. of Prague, French Soc. of Pathology. *Publications:* Esculape chez les Soviets 1954, Klinik und Therapie der Nebenwirkungen 1963, Esculape chez Mao 1973, Ces malades qui nous gouvernent 1976, Les orphelins mènent-ils le monde? 1978, Ces malades qui font l'Histoire 1983; numerous publs. on antibiotics in infectious diseases, on ethical problems, euthanasia etc. *Leisure interests:* skiing, golf, swimming, art (Netzuke). *Address:* 78 avenue de la Roseraie, 1211 Geneva 4 (Office); La Taupinière, chemin Bouchattet 8, 1291 Commugny, Vaud, Switzerland (Home). *Telephone:* 46 93 55 (Office); 76 22 64 (Home).

RENTZEPIS, Peter, PH.D.; American (b. Greek) scientist; b. 1 Dec. 1934, Kalamata, Greece; m. Alma Elizabeth Keenan; two s.; ed. Denison, Syracuse and Cambridge Univs.; mem. Tech. Staff Research Labs. Gen. Electric Co., New York, then mem. Tech. Staff, Bell Labs., N.J., Head, Physical and Inorganic Chem. Research Dept.; Presidential Chair. and Prof. of Chemistry, Univ. of Calif. 1985–; Adjunct Prof. of Chem., Univ. of Pa., of Chem. and Biophysics, Yale Univ. 1980–; Visiting Prof., Rockefeller Univ., 1971, M.I.T. –1975, of Chemistry Univ. of Tel-Aviv; mem. numerous academic cttees. and advisory bds. including U.S. Army Cttee. on Energetic Materials Research and Tech. 1982–83; Dir. NATO Advanced Study Inst. 1984; mem. Bd. of Dirs. KRIKOS—Science and Tech. for Greece, Bd. of Dirs. The Quanex Corpn. 1984; Fellow numerous acads. including N.A.S. 1978, membership cttee. 1984; Nat. Acad. of Greece 1980; American Chem. Soc. Peter Debye Prize in Physical Chemistry, American Physics Soc. Irving Langmuize Prize in Chemical Physics, Scientist of the Year 1978; Hon. Sc.D. (Denison) 1981, (Carnegie-Mellon) 1983; Hon. D.Phil. (Syracuse) 1980. *Publications:* over 200 on lasers, photochemistry, picosecond spectroscopy. *Address:* Department of Chemistry, University of California, Irvine, Calif. 92717, U.S.A. *Telephone:* 714-856 5934.

RENWICK, Sir Robin William, K.C.M.G., M.A.; British diplomatist; b. 13 Dec. 1937; s. of Richard Renwick and the late Clarice Henderson; m. Anne Colette Giudicelli 1965; one s. one d.; ed. St. Paul's School, Jesus Coll., Cambridge and Univ. of Paris (Sorbonne); army 1956–58; entered Foreign Service 1963; Dakar 1963–64; Foreign Office 1964–66; New Delhi 1966–69; Pvt. Sec. to Minister of State, Foreign and Commonwealth Office (FCO) 1970–72; First Sec., Paris 1972–76; Counsellor Cabinet Office 1976–78; Head Rhodesia Dept., FCO 1978–80; Political Adviser to Gov. of Rhodesia 1980; Visiting Fellow Center for Int. Affairs, Harvard 1980–81; Head of

Chancery, Washington 1981–84; Asst. Under-Sec. of State, FCO 1984–87; Amb. to S. Africa 1987–. *Publications:* Economic Sanctions 1981. *Leisure interest:* tennis, fishing, islands. *Address:* c/o Foreign and Commonwealth Office, London, S.W.1, England.

RESHETILOV, Vladimir Ivanovich; Soviet politician; b. 1937; ed. Dnepropetrovsk Eng. Inst.; sr. engineer at factory in Orenburg Dist. 1959–66; mem. CPSU 1963–; head of Dneprovskpromstroy trust 1966–73; First Deputy Pres. of Dnepropetrovsk City Exec. Cttee. 1973–77; chief engineer, head of Dneprometallurgstroy trust 1977–80; First Deputy, Deputy Minister of Heavy Industry Construction Enterprises for Ukrainian S.S.R. 1980–83; U.S.S.R. Deputy Minister of Heavy Industry Construction Enterprises 1983–86; U.S.S.R. Minister for Construction Jan.–Oct. 1986, for Construction in Northern and Western Regions of U.S.S.R. Oct. 1986–; cand. mem. of CPSU Cen. Cttee. 1986–; Deputy to U.S.S.R. Supreme Soviet. *Address:* The Kremlin, Moscow, U.S.S.R.

RESHETNEV, Mikhail Fedorovich, DR. TECH. SCI.; Soviet scientist in area of applied mechanics; b. 1924, Moscow; ed. Orzhonikidze Aviation Inst.; mem. CPSU 1951; Red Army 1942–45; engineer, chief engineer, head constructor 1950–77; Prof. 1975–; Gen Dir. of NPO 1977–; mem. of U.S.S.R. Acad. of Sciences 1984–; Hero of Socialist Labour 1974, Lenin Prize 1984. *Address:* Department of Applied Mechanics, U.S.S.R. Academy of Sciences, Leningrad, U.S.S.R.

RESHETNIKOV, Fedor Grigorevich; Soviet physical chemist; b. 25 Nov. 1919, Ukraine; s. of G. P. Reshetnikov and E. I. Reshetnikova; m. 1948; one d.; ed. Moscow Inst. of Non-Ferrous Metals, Dzerzhinsky Artillery Acad.; mem. CPSU 1947–; factory work 1944–45; scientific research work 1946–; Deputy Dir. All Union Scientific and Research Inst. 1966–, Corresp. mem. of U.S.S.R. Acad. of Sciences 1974–; U.S.S.R. State Prize 1951, 1975, 1985. *Leisure interest:* tourism. *Address:* All Union Scientific and Research Institute of Inorganic Materials, Rogov Street 5, Moscow 123060, U.S.S.R.

RESHTIA, Sayed Qassem; Afghan writer and diplomatist; b. 21 March 1913, Kabul; s. of Said Habib and Zainab Azimi; m. 1st Noorjahan Ziai 1930 (died 1946), one s. one d.; m. 2nd Golalai Kabir-Seraj 1971; ed. Istiqlal High School, Kabul, Financial and Banking Inst., Kabul, Kabul Univ. Coll. of Political Science; Clerk in Press Section, Ministry of Foreign Affairs 1931; Chief Clerk Foreign Relations Section, Ministry of Communications 1932; trans. at Afghan Acad. of Literature 1933, mem. 1934; Ed. Kabul Almanach and Kabul Magazine 1936–38; Vice-Pres. 1938, Dir.-Gen. of Publs.; Press Dept. 1940–44, Pres. 1948; Pres. Govt. Econ. Planning Bd. 1949–; Liaison Officer with UN Tech. Co-operation Mission in Afghanistan 1950; Govt. Co-operative Org. 1952, Bakhtar News Agency 1954; Minister of Information 1956–60, 1963–64, of Finance 1964–65; Afghan del. to UN 10th and 24th Gen. Assembly; Vice-Chair. of the Drafting Cttee. of Constitution 1964; Amb. to Czechoslovakia, Poland and Hungary 1960–62, to United Arab Repub. 1962–63 (also accred. to Lebanon, Sudan, Greece), to Japan 1970–73 (also accred. to Philippines) (retd.); Del. to 1st Afro-Asian Conf. (Bandung) 1955, 1st and 2nd Non-Aligned Conf. (Belgrade) 1961, (Cairo) 1965; accompanied the King of Afghanistan to United Arab Republic, Yugoslavia 1959, U.S.A. 1963, U.S.S.R. 1965; founding mem. Afghan Red Crescent Soc.; mem. Afghan Historical Soc. and Encyclopedia Soc.; Hon. Cultural Doctorate in int. diplomacy, World Univ. Round Table 1986. *Publications:* Afghanistan in the 19th Century, Jawani Afghan, Jamaluddin Afghani 1977, The Price of Liberty: The Tragedy of Afghanistan 1984, Between Two Giants (a Political History of Afghanistan in the 19th Century) 1989, and several novels. *Leisure interests:* reading and walking. *Address:* 13 rue des Boudines, Apt. 52, 1217 Meyrin, Switzerland. *Telephone:* 825614.

RESNAIS, Alain; French film director; b. 3 June 1922, Vannes; s. of Pierre and Jeanne (née Gachet) Resnais; m. Florence Malraux 1969; ed. Institut des Hautes Etudes Cinématographiques, Paris; Special Prize (Cannes) for Mon Oncle d'Amerique 1980; Grand Prix du Cinéma 1986; Légion d'honneur. *Short films directed (1948–59) include:* Van Gogh 1948, Guernica (with Robert Hessens) 1950, Les statues meurent aussi (with Chris Marker) 1952, Nuit et brouillard 1955. *Feature films include:* Hiroshima mon amour 1959, L'année dernière à Marienbad 1961, Muriel 1963, La guerre est finie 1966, Je t'aime, je t'aime 1968, Stavisky 1974, Providence 1977, Mon oncle d'Amérique 1980, La vie est un roman 1983, L'amour à mort 1984, Mélo 1986. *Address:* c/o Artmedia, 10 avenue George V, 75008 Paris; 70 rue des Plantes, 75014 Paris, France (Home).

RESNIK, Regina; American opera singer (mezzo-soprano); b. 30 Aug. 1924; d. of Samuel Resnik and Ruth Resnik; m. 1st Michael P. Davis 1947; one s.; m. 2nd Arbit Blatas 1975; ed. Hunter Col., New York; opera début as Lady Macbeth, New Opera Co. 1942; Mexico City 1943; New York City Opera 1943–44; Metropolitan Opera 1944–1983; sang 80 roles, soprano and mezzo-soprano, became regular mem. Royal Opera, London, Vienna State Opera, Bayreuth, Salzburg, San Francisco, Chicago, La Scala, Milan, Paris, Buenos Aires, Berlin, Brussels, etc.; Stage Dir. for maj. productions Hamburg, Venice, Sydney, Vancouver, Strasbourg, Warsaw, Lisbon, Madrid, Wiesbaden; appeared on Broadway in Cabaret 1987; President's Medal, Commdr. Ordre des Arts et des Lettres, France. *Address:* 50 West 56th Street, New York, N.Y. 10019, U.S.A.; 786 Giudecca, Venice, Italy.

RESTON, James; American (Scottish-born) journalist; b. 3 Nov. 1909, Clydebank, Scotland; m. Sarah Jane Fulton 1935; three s.; ed. Dayton, Ohio public schools and Illinois Univ.; first brought to U.S.A. 1910, permanently settled 1920–; began his career on Springfield (Ohio) Daily News and as sports publicity dir. for Ohio State Univ.; travelling Sec., Cincinnati Baseball Club; Sports Writer, Associated Press, New York 1934–37; Assoc. Press Corresp., London 1937–39; New York Times London Bureau 1939–41, Washington Bureau 1941–87; Dir. Office of War Intelligence Information Service, U.S. Embassy, London 1942; Asst. to Publisher, New York Times 1943, Acting Head, London Bureau 1943–45, Nat. Corresp. 1945, Diplomatic Corresp. 1946, Head of Washington Bureau 1953–64, Assoc. Ed. 1964–68, Exec. Ed. 1968–69, Vice-Pres. 1969–74, Dir. 1973–, Columnist 1973–; Co-publisher Vineyard Gazette 1968–; Hon. D.Litt. (Colgate, Oberlin, Brandeis, Harvard, Stanford, Miami, Glasgow, Michigan and Rutgers Univs.), Hon. LL.D. (New York), Hon. Dr. of Journalism (Northeastern Univ.) 1976, Hon. Dr. of Humane Letters (Yale) 1977; Hon. C.B.E. 1985; Pulitzer Awards 1945 and 1957, George Polk Memorial Award 1954, Raymond Clapper Award 1955, etc; Lovejoy Fellow 1974; Chevalier, Légion d'honneur, Medal of Liberty 1986, Helen B. Bernstein Award 1988. *Publications:* The Artillery of the Press 1967, Sketches in the Sand 1967. *Address:* c/o The New York Times, 1000 Connecticut Avenue, N.W., Washington, D.C. 20036, U.S.A. *Telephone:* (202) 862 0320.

RESWICK, James Bigelow, SC.D.; American engineer and administrator; b. 16 April 1922, Ellwood City, Pa.; s. Maurice Reswick and Katherine (Parker) Reswick; m. Irmtraud Orthlies Hoelzerkopf 1973; two s. (one deceased) one d.; ed. Massachusetts Inst. of Tech. and Rose Polytechnic Inst.; Assoc. Prof., Head Machine Design and Graphics Div., M.I.T. 1948–59; Leonard Case Prof. of Eng., Dir. of Eng. Design Center, Case Western Reserve Univ. 1959–70; Dir. Rehabilitation Eng. Center, Rancho Los Amigos Hosp., Prof. of Biomedical Eng. and Orthopaedics, Univ. of Southern Calif. and Dir. of Research Dept., Orthopaedics 1979–80; Assoc. Dir. of Tech., Nat. Inst. of Handicapped Research, U.S. Dept. of Educ. 1980–, Dir. of Research Sciences, Nat. Inst. on Disability and Rehabilitation Research 1988–; Dir. Rehabilitation Research and Devt. Evaluation Unit, Veterans Admin. Medical Center, Washington, D.C. 1984–; mem. Nat. Acad. of Eng.; Product Engineer Master Designer Award 1969. *Publications:* articles in scientific journals. *Leisure interest:* inventing (invented "Res-a-Tran" automatic wheelchair transmission). *Address:* National Institute on Disability and Rehabilitation Research, Division of Research Sciences, U.S. Department of Education, 400 Maryland Avenue, S.W. Washington, D.C. 20202-2645; 1003 Dead Run Drive, McLean, Va. 22101, U.S.A. (Home). *Telephone:* (301) 962-2367 (Office); (703) 442-8876 (Home).

RÉTORÉ, Guy; French theatre director; b. 7 April 1924; ed. Univ. of Paris; Public Relations Dept., S.N.C.F. until 1955; Actor and Producer, Théâtre de Boulevard until 1955; formed "La Guilde" (theatrical company), Menilmontant, East Paris 1954; opened Théâtre de Menilmontant 1958; Dir. Maison de la Culture, Menilmontant 1962–; Dir. Théâtre de l'Est Parisien (also gives concerts, ballets, films and conferences). *Plays produced include:* La fille du roi (Cosmos) 1955, Life and Death of King John 1956, Grenadiers de la reine (Farquhar, adapted by Cosmos) 1957, L'avare (Molière), Les caprices de Marianne (Musset), La fleur à la bouche (Pirandello), Le médecin malgré lui (Molière), Le manteau (Gogol, adapted by Cosmos) 1963, La Locandiera (Goldoni), Arden of Faversham 1964, Monsieur Alexandre (Cosmos) 1964, Macbeth (Shakespeare) 1964, Turcaret (Lesage) 1965, Measure for Measure (Shakespeare) 1965, Le voyage de Monsieur Perrichon (Labiche) 1965, Live Like Pigs (Arden), The Silver Tassie (O'Casey) 1966–67, Les 13 soleils de la rue St. Blaise (A. Gatti), La machine (Jean Cosmos) 1968–69, Lorenzaccio (Musset), L'opéra de quat'sous (Brecht), Major Barbara (Shaw) 1969–70, Les ennemis (Gorki), L'âne de l'hospice (Arden) 1970–71, Sainte Jeanne des abattoirs (Brecht) 1971–72, Macbeth (Shakespeare) 1972–73, Androclès et le lion 1974–75, Coquin de coq (O'Casey) 1975–76, L'ôtage (Claudel) 1976–77, Le camp du drap d'or 1980, Fin de partie, tueur sans gage 1981, Le Chantier 1982, Clair d'usine 1983, 325000 francs 1984, Entre passions et prairie (Denise Bonal) 1987; Officier des Arts et des Lettres. *Address:* 159 avenue Gambetta, 75020 Paris, France. *Telephone:* 43.63.20.96.

RETTEL, Jean, LL.D.; Luxembourg diplomatist; b. 12 Dec. 1925, Luxembourg; s. of Jean Rettel and Marie Hippert; m. Paule May 1966; one d.; ed. Univs. of Fribourg, Switzerland and Grenoble, France; practising lawyer, Luxembourg Bar 1950–54; joined Ministry of Foreign Affairs 1954; Sec. Bonn 1956–59; Counsellor and Deputy Chief, Div. of External Trade 1964–68; Chief Protocol and Legal Dept. 1968–69; Counsellor, Paris 1969–71, also Deputy Perm. Rep. to OECD; Perm. Rep. to UN 1972–76; Amb. to Switzerland 1976–86, also accred. to Austria 1976–78; Perm. Rep. to int. orgs. in Geneva 1977–86. *Leisure interests:* reading, sports, music. *Address:* c/o Ministry of Foreign Affairs, Foreign Trade and Co-operation, 5 rue Notre Dame, 2240 Luxembourg-Ville, Luxembourg.

RETTEDAL, Arne, Norwegian engineer and politician; b. 25 July 1926, Madla, Stavanger; ed. Norwegian Inst. of Tech.; started own eng. consulting firm 1961; Mayor of Stavanger 1965–67, 1972–81; Chair. Bd. Rogalandsbanken 1977–; mem. industrial council of Statoil (state-owned petroleum co.); Minister of Local Govt. and Labour 1981–86; Conservative. *Address:* c/o The Royal Ministry of Local Government and Labour, Møllergt. 43, Pb 8112 Dep, 0032 Oslo, Norway.

REUBER, Grant Louis, O.C., LL.D., PH.D., F.R.S.C.; Canadian banker; b. 23 Nov. 1927, Mildmay, Ont.; s. of Jacob Daniel Reuber and Gertrude Catherine Reuber; m. Margaret Louise Julia Summerhayes 1951; three d.; ed. Walkerton High School, Univ. of W. Ontario, Harvard Univ., Sidney Sussex Coll., Cambridge; with Econ. Research Dept. Bank of Canada 1950–52; Econ. and Int. Relations Div. Dept. of Finance 1955–57, Deputy Minister of Finance Govt. of Canada 1979–80; at Univ. of W. Ontario 1957–78, Asst. Prof. 1957–59, Assoc. Prof. 1959–62, Prof. Econ. Dept. 1962–78, Dean of Social Science 1969–74, Acad. Vice-Pres. and Provost, mem. Bd. of Govs. 1974–78; Chair. Ont. Econ. Council 1973–78; Sr. Vice-Pres. and Chief Economist Bank of Montreal 1978–79, Exec. Vice-Pres. 1980–81, Dir., Deputy Chair. and Deputy Chief Exec. 1981–83, Pres. 1983–87, Deputy Chair. 1987–. *Publications:* The Cost of Capital in Canada (with R. J. Wonnacott) 1961, (with R. E. Caves): Canadian Economic Policy and the Impact of International Capital Flows 1970, Private Foreign Investment in Development 1973, Canada's Political Economy 1980. *Leisure interests:* tennis, reading. *Address:* Bank of Montreal, First Bank Tower, First Canadian Place, Toronto, Ont. M5X 1A1 (Office); 98 Dunloe Road, Toronto, Ont. M5P 2T8, Canada (Home). *Telephone:* 416-867-4992 (Office).

REUT, Anatoliy Antonovich; Soviet politician; b. 1928; ed. Byelorussia Polytechnic, Minsk; factory work 1952–58; mem. CPSU 1955–; technologist, deputy dir. of Orzhonikidze Factory for Calculating Machines, Minsk 1958–62; head of section of Byelorussian Gosplan 1962–66; dir. of machine-tool factory, Minsk 1966–70, of computer factory, Minsk 1970–74; Second Sec. of Minsk City Cttee. 1974–75; U.S.S.R. First Deputy Minister of Radio Industry 1975–83; Deputy Pres. of Council of Ministers of Byelorussian CP and Pres. of Byelorussian State Planning Comm. 1983–85; First Deputy Pres. of U.S.S.R. State Planning Comm. (GOSPLAN), U.S.S.R. Minister 1985–; mem. of CPSU Cen. Cttee. 1986–. *Address:* The Kremlin, Moscow, U.S.S.R.

REUTER, Edzard; German business executive; b. 16 Feb. 1928, Berlin; s. of Ernst Reuter and Hanna Kleinert; ed. Univs. of Göttingen and Berlin; Asst. Prof., Free Univ. of Berlin 1954–56; various exec. posts in Bertelsmann Publishing Group 1957–64; with Daimler-Benz AG 1964–, various financial assignments, then Sec. 1964–71, Head of Corp. Planning and Org. 1971–73, deputy mem. Bd. of Man. 1973–76, full mem. 1976–, Chief Financial Officer 1980–87, Chair. 1987–; Chair. Supervisory Bd. AEG AG. *Address:* Daimler-Benz AG, Postfach 202, D-7000 Stuttgart 60; Taldorfer Str. 14A, D-7000 Stuttgart 70, Federal Republic of Germany.

REUTER, Paul; French international lawyer; b. 12 Feb. 1911, Metz; s. of Fery Reuter; m. Christiane Abram 1943; two s; Prof. law faculties of Nancy, Poitiers, Aix-en-Provence and Paris; at Ministry of Information 1944, of Justice 1945, of the Armed Forces 1948; legal adviser, Ministry of Foreign Affairs 1948; teacher Institut d'Etudes Politiques, Paris 1953, Acad. of Int. Law 1952, 1961, Faculty of Geneva 1981; mem. Perm. Cen. Opium Bd. 1948–68, Vice-Chair. 1953–69; mem. Int. Narcotics Control Bd. 1968–, Chair. 1974–83; Chair. Tribunal Suprême de Monaco; Chair. Perm. Court of Arbitration, Court for Nuclear Energy OECD 1985, UN Int. Law Comm. 1964–; mem. Inst. of Int. Law, Acad. Royale de Belgique; mem. various conciliation comms., arbitration tribunals, etc.; Croix de guerre, Commdr., Légion d'honneur, Commdr., Ordre nat. du Mérite, Commdr. des Palmes Académiques, Balzan, World Acad. of Arts and Sciences Award, Rufus Jones Award 1986. *Publications include:* Droit international public, Institutions internationales, Organisations européennes, La communauté européenne du charbon et de l'acier, Introduction au droit de traités, and numerous other books and articles. *Leisure interests:* the sea, music, gardening. *Address:* 72 rue du Cherche-Midi, 75006 Paris, France (Home). *Telephone:* 42-22-07-56 (Home).

REUTERSWÄRD, Carl Fredrik; Swedish artist, writer and sculptor; b. 4 June 1934, Stockholm; s. of Wilhelm Reuterswärd and Therese Ingestrom; m. 1st Anna Tesch 1958 (divorced 1968), two s. two d.; m. 2nd Mona Moller-Nielsen 1974, one s.; ed. Ecole de Fernand Leger, Paris and Royal Coll. of Art, Stockholm; first artist to use lasers 1965; Prof. Royal Coll. of Art, Stockholm 1965–70; since 1952 active in drawing, painting, sculpture, holography, scenography, graphics, design and architectural comms.; principal themes: Nonsens 1952–58; Cigars and Games 1958–63; Exercise 1958–64; Lazy Lasers and Holy Holos 1965–74; a trilogy: Kilroy (anybody) 1962–72, CAVIART (a somebody) 1972–82; works in public collections in Sweden, U.S.A., Fed. Repub. of Germany, France, England, Netherlands, Norway and Denmark, including National museum, Stockholm, Museum of Modern Art, New York, Städtische Kunsthalle, Düsseldorf, Musée National d'Art Moderne, Paris, Tate Gallery, London and Stedelijk Museum, Amsterdam; Non-Violence, bronze sculpture on perm. display in front of UN bldg., New York, since 1988. *Publications:* Kafka, Wahlstrom and Widstrand 1981, Caviart 1982, Making Faces 1984. *Address:* 6 rue Montolieu, 1030 Bussigny/Lausanne, Switzerland. *Telephone:* 021-7010514.

REUTOV, Olyeg Aleksandrovich; Soviet organic chemist; b. 5 Sept. 1920, Makeyevka, Donetsk Region; ed. Moscow Univ.; Soviet Army 1941–45; Instructor, Moscow Univ. 1945–54, Prof. 1954–;Head of own lab. at Moscow Univ.; research into physical organic chemistry and organometallic chemistry; Soviet expert on chemical and biological warfare, UN 1969–; Deputy Chair. Soviet Peace Cttee. 1974; Corresp. mem. U.S.S.R. Acad. of Sciences

1958-64, mem. 1964-; mem. CPSU 1942-. *Publications:* Theoretical Problems of Organic Chemistry 1956, Fundamentals of Theoretical Organic Chemistry 1967, Reaction Mechanisms of Organometallic Compounds (co-author) 1968, CH-Acids (co-author) 1978, Ambident Anions (co-author) 1983. *Address:* U.S.S.R. Academy of Sciences, 14 Leninsky Prospekt, Moscow, U.S.S.R.

REVEL, Jean-François; French writer; b. 19 Jan. 1924, Marseilles; m. 2nd Claude Sarraute 1966; one s. one d. by first marriage; one s. by second marriage; ed. Ecole Normale Supérieure and Sorbonne, Paris; teacher of French Literature, Institut Français, Mexico, later Florence 1952-56; teacher of Philosophy, Lille and Paris 1956-63; Literary Adviser Editions Julliard and Pauvert 1961-66, Editions Laffont 1966-77; Columnist of L'Express 1966-81; Dir. of L'Express 1978-81; Ed. and Columnist Le Point magazine 1982-; Chateaubriand Prize 1988. *Publications:* novel: Histoire de Flore 1957; essays: Pourquoi des philosophes? 1957, Pour l'Italie 1958, Le style du général 1959, Sur Proust 1960, La cabale des dévots 1962, En France 1965, Contrecensures 1966, Histoire de la philosophie occidentale Vol. I 1968, Vol. II 1970, Ni Marx ni Jésus 1970, Les idées de notre temps 1972, La tentation totalitaire 1976, Descartes inutile et incertain 1976, La nouvelle censure 1977, Un festin en paroles 1978, La grâce de l'état 1981, Comment les démocraties finissent 1983; Le rejet de l'etat 1984, Une anthologie de la poésie française 1984, Le terrorisme contre la démocratie 1987, La Connaissance inutile 1988. *Leisure interests:* riding, swimming. *Address:* 55 quai de Bourbon, 75004 Paris, France. *Telephone:* 43-54-65-87.

REVELLE, Roger, PH.D.; American university professor; b. 7 March 1909, Seattle, Wash.; s. of William R. and Ella R. (Dougan) Revelle; m. Ellen Virginia Clark 1931; one s. three d.; ed. Pomona Coll. and Univ. of California; teaching Asst., Pomona Coll. 1929-30, Univ. of Calif. 1930-31; Research Asst., Univ. of Calif., Scripps Inst. of Oceanography 1931-36, Instructor 1936-41, Asst. Prof. 1941-46, Assoc. Prof. 1946-48, Assoc. Dir. 1948-50, Acting Dir. 1950-51, Dir. 1951-64, Dir. Emer. 1964-, Prof. of Oceanography 1948-64; Dir. La Jolla Campus and Dean of School of Science and Eng. Univ. of Calif. 1958-61; Science Adviser to Sec. of Interior 1961-63; Univ. of Calif. Dean of Research 1963-64; Richard Saltonstall Prof. of Population Policy, Faculty of Public Health, Harvard Univ. 1964-79; Prof. of Science and Public Policy, Univ. of Calif., San Diego 1975-; Dir. Harvard Center for Population Studies 1964-75; mem. Int. Asscn. of Physical Oceanography (Pres 1963-67), A.A.A.S. (Pres. 1974), American Geophysical Union, N.A.S., American Acad. of Arts and Sciences, American Philosophical Soc.; mem. Naval Research Advisory Comm. 1959-, U.S. Nat. Comm. for UNESCO 1958-64 (Vice-Chair. 1961-64); mem. Cttee. on Climatic Changes and the Ocean of Intergovernmental Oceanographic Comm. and Scientific Cttee. on Oceanic Research (Chair. 1979-83); numerous hon. degrees; Albatross Medal, Swedish Royal Soc. of Science and Letters 1952; Agassiz Medal of Nat. Acad. of Sciences 1963; Order of Sitara-i-Imtiaz (Pakistan) 1964; Bowie Medal of American Geophysical Union; Vannevar Bush Award of Nat. Science Bd.; Tyler Environmental Prize (with E. O. Wilson); David Stone Medal, New England Aquarium Soc., Balzan Prize in Oceanography and Climatology 1986. *Publications:* over 200 scientific articles in professional publications. *Address:* University of California at San Diego, La Jolla, Calif. 92093; 7348 Vista Del Mar, La Jolla, Calif. 92037, U.S.A. (Home).

REVENKO, Grigoriy Ivanovich; Soviet politician; b. 1936; ed. Lvov Polytechnic; eng. and komsomol work 1958-62; mem. CPSU 1962-; Sec., Second Sec. of Odessa Dist. Komsomol 1962-64; instructor, Odessa CPSU Dist. Cttee. 1964-66; First Sec. Odessa Dist. Komsomol Cttee. 1966-68; Sec. of Komsomol Cen. Cttee. of Ukrainian CP 1968-72; work for Cen. Cttee. of Ukrainian CP 1972-75; Sec., Second Sec. of Kiev Dist. Cttee. 1975-84; work for CPSU Cen. Cttee. 1984-85; deputy head of dept. of CPSU Cen. Cttee. 1985-; First Sec. of Kiev Dist. Cttee. of Ukrainian CP 1985-; cand. mem. of CPSU Cen. Cttee. 1986-; Deputy to U.S.S.R. Supreme Soviet. *Address:* The Kremlin, Moscow, U.S.S.R.

REVERDIN, Olivier, D. ÈS L.; Swiss professor, politician and editor; b. 15 July 1913, Geneva; s. of Henri Reverdin and Gabrielle Bouthillier de Beaumont; m. Renée Chaponnière 1936; two s. one d.; ed. Univs. of Geneva and Paris, and Ecole Française d'Athènes; school teaching, Geneva and France 1938-41; Attaché Swiss Legation, Rome 1941-44; Lecturer and Asst. Prof. Ancient Greek Literature, Univ. of Geneva 1945-58, Ordinary Prof. 1958-83, Hon. Prof. 1983-; Parl. Ed. Journal de Genève, Berne 1945-54, and Man. Ed. 1955-59, Man. 1959-72, Chair. 1972-79; Deputy (Liberal) of Geneva at the Conseil des Etats 1955-71, at Conseil des Etats 1971-79; Chair. Fondation Hardt pour l'Etude de l'Antiquité Classique 1959-; Chair. Soc. Suisse des Sciences Humaines 1960-68; mem. Nat. Council for Scientific Research 1963-80, Chair. 1968-80; rep. Consultative Ass., Council of Europe 1964-74, Chair. of the Cultural and Scientific Cttee. 1966, of the Cttee. for Science and Tech. 1967-69, Pres. of the Ass. 1969-72; Chair. Fondation pour le Lexicon Iconographicum Mythologiae Classicae 1973-81; Vice-Pres. European Science Foundation 1974-77; Chair. Montres Rolex, S.A. 1976-, Sodeco Saia, S.A. 1975-, Fondation Baur Collections 1984-; Fondation Baur 1984; Hon. Fellow Acad. of Athens, Österreichische Akademie der Wissenschaften and Royal Belgian Acad. of Sciences, Arts and Humanities; Hon. Dr. h.c. (Heidelberg, Strasbourg);

Robert Schuman Medal. *Publications:* La religion de la cité platonicienne 1945, La guerre du Sonderbund vue par le Général Dufour 1948, 1987, Quatorze calvinistes chez les Topinambous 1957, La Crète, berceau de la civilisation occidentale 1960, Connaissance de la Suisse 1964, Entretiens sur l'Antiquité Classique, Vols. I-XXXIV (Ed.) 1954-88, La vision de Dorothéos 1984, Les premiers cours de grec au Collège de France 1984, Henri Estienne à Genève 1988. *Leisure interests:* horticulture, ornithology. *Address:* 8 rue des Granges, 1204 Geneva, Switzerland. *Telephone:* 022-215191.

REVOLLO BRAVO, H.E. Cardinal Mario; Italian ecclesiastic; b. 15 June 1919, Genoa; ordained 1943, elected to the titular Church of Tinisa di Numidia 1973, consecrated bishop 1973, prefect at Nueva Pamplona 1978, transferred Bogotá 1984; cr. Cardinal 1988. *Address:* Arzobispado, Carrera 7a N. 10-20, Bogotá, D.E., Colombia. *Telephone:* (91) 2437.700.

REXED, Bror A(nders), M.D.; Swedish physician and international civil servant; b. 19 June 1914, Gunnarskog; s. of Daniel Rexed and Agda née Andersson; m. 1st Dr. Ursula Schalling 1941, 2nd Anja-Riitta Ketokoski 1977; three s. two d.; ed. Karlstad Allmänna Läroverk, Karolinska Inst., Stockholm; Assoc. Prof. in Histology, Karolinska Inst. 1945-52; Prof. of Anatomy, Uppsala Univ. 1953-67; Dir.-Gen. Nat. Bd. of Health and Welfare, Stockholm 1967-78; Exec. Dir. and Asst. Sec.-Gen. UN Fund for Drug Abuse Control (UNFDAC), Vienna, Austria 1978-82; mem. UN Int. Narcotics Control Bd. 1982-; mem. or Chair. several Royal Cttees. on Medical Educ. 1946-65; Sec. to Swedish Medical Research Council 1951-62; mem. Nat. Research Advisory Council, and Science Adviser to Prime Minister 1962-67; Head of Swedish Dels. to WHO Gen. Ass. and to UN Comm. on Narcotic Drugs 1967-78; Chair. OECD Expert Group on Org. of Health Services 1972-74; Hon. M.D. (Oslo) 1969, (Helsinki) 1966, (Poznań) 1974; WHO Leon Bernard Prize for Social Medicine 1979. *Publications:* Post-natal Development of the Peripheral Nervous System 1945, Guidelines for the Control of Narcotic and Psychotropic Substances 1984; about 150 papers on neurohistology, neuropathology, public health and social medicine. *Leisure interests:* collecting ancient maps, golf. *Address:* Thomas Heftyes Gate 14C, 0264 Oslo 2, Norway (Home). *Telephone:* 02/391639.

REY, Fernando (Fernando Casado Arambillet Veiga); Spanish actor; b. 1912, La Coruna; s. of Fernando Casado Sr.; m. Mabel Karr; one s.; has appeared in many Spanish and European films including: La Gitanilla 1940, Eugenia de Montijo 1944, Reina Santa 1947, Don Quijote de la Mancha 1947, Bienvenido Mr. Marshall 1952, Tangier Assignment 1955, Parque de Madrid 1958, Sonatas 1959, Fabiola 1960, Viridania 1961, Los Palomas 1964, Don Quijote 1966, Cervantes 1967, Tristana 1970; other films include: Guns of the Magnificent Seven 1967, Satyricon 1969, Land Raiders 1969, The Adventurers 1970, The French Connection 1971, Antony and Cleopatra 1972, Discreet Charm of the Bourgeoisie 1972, French Connection II 1975, Quintet 1979, Padre Nuestro 1987; Best Actor Award, Cannes Film Festival 1972. *Address:* Orense 62, 28020 Madrid, Spain. *Telephone:* (91) 4560221.

REYES, Narciso G., A.B.; Philippine diplomatist and journalist; b. 6 Feb. 1914, Manila; m.; ed. Univ. of Santo Tomas; Assoc. Ed. Philippines Commonweal, Manila 1935-41; mem. Nat. Language Faculty, Ateneo de Manila 1939-41; Assoc. Ed. Manila Post 1945-47; Assoc. News Ed. Evening News, Manila 1947-48; Man. Ed. Philippine Newspaper Guild Organ 1947-48; Adviser to Philippine Mission to UN and Rep. of the Philippines to numerous ECOSOC sessions and UN Gen. Assemblies 1948-; Philippine Amb. to Burma 1958-62, to Indonesia 1962-67, to U.K. 1967-70; Perm. Rep. to UN 1970-77; Amb. to the People's Republic of China 1977-81; Sec-Gen. ASEAN 1980-82; Chair. 19th Session UN Social Devt. Comm. 1968-69; Pres. UN Devt. Programme Governing Council 1974; mem. UN Group on Disarmament and Devt. 1978-81; Pres. Philippine Council for Foreign Relations 1986-87, 1987-(89); Ed. Foreign Relations Journal 1985-; Chair. Bd. of Dirs., Eternal Educ. Plans 1988-. *Address:* 8 Lipa Road, Philamlife Homes, Quezon City, Manila, Philippines.

REYNOLDS, Albert; Irish politician; b. 3 Nov. 1935, Rooskey, Co. Roscommon; m. Kathleen Coén; two s. five d.; ed. Summerhill Coll., Sligo; fmr. Chair. C & D Petfoods; mem. Longford County Council 1974-79; mem. Dail 1977-; Minister for Posts and Telegraphs and Transport 1979-81; Minister for Industry and Energy March-Dec. 1982; Minister for Industry and Commerce 1987-88, for Finance and the Public Service Nov. 1988-; Fianna Fail. *Address:* Mount Carmel House, Dublin Road, Longford, Ireland.

REYNOLDS, Anna, F.R.A.M.; British opera and concert singer; b. 5 June 1936, Canterbury; d. of Paul Grey Reynolds and Vera Cicely Turner; ed. Benenden School, Royal Acad. of Music; studied with Professoressa Debora Fambri, Rome; has appeared at many int. festivals including Spoleto, Edinburgh, Aix-en-Provence, Salzburg Easter Festival, Vienna, Bayreuth, Tanglewood; has sung with leading orchestras all over the world including Chicago Symphony, New York Philharmonic, Berlin Philharmonic, London Symphony, etc.; has appeared in opera performances in New York Metropolitan, La Scala, Milan, Covent Garden, Bayreuth, Rome, Chicago Lyric Opera, Teatro Colón, Buenos Aires, Teatro Fenice, Venice and many others; has recorded for Decca, EMI, Polydor, Philips. *Leisure interests:*

REYNOLDS, Burt; American actor; b. 11 Feb. 1936, Waycross, Ga.; s. of Burt Reynolds Sr.; m. 1st Judy Carne (divorced 1965); m. 2nd Loni Anderson 1988; ed. Florida State Univ.; mem. Dirs. Guild of America. *Stage appearances include:* Mister Roberts, Look, We've Come Through, The Rainmaker; *films include:* Angel Baby 1961, Operation CIA 1965, Navajo Joe 1967, Impasse 1969, Skullduggery 1970, Deliverance 1972, Everything You've Always Wanted to Know about Sex But Were Afraid to Ask 1972, The Man Who Loved Cat Dancing 1973, Hustle 1975, Silent Movie 1976, Gator (also dir.) 1976, Nickelodeon 1976, Smokey and the Bandit 1977, Starting Over 1979, Cannonball Run 1981, Sharky's Machine (also dir.) 1981, City Heat 1984, Stick (also dir.) 1984, Rent A Cop 1987, Breaking In 1988, Switching Channels 1988; *television appearances include:* Riverboat, Pony Express, Gunsmoke, Hawk, Dan August. *Address:* c/o C.A.A., 1888 Century Park East, Suite 1400, Los Angeles, Calif. 90067, U.S.A.

REYNOLDS, David Parham; American industrial metals executive; b. 16 June 1915, Bristol, Tenn.; s. of late Richard Samuel Reynolds and Julia Louise Parham; m. Margaret Trezevant Harrison 1944; three d.; ed. Princeton Univ.; Reynolds Metals Co. (now Reynolds Aluminium), Louisville 1937–, Salesman 1937–41, Asst. Man. Aircraft Parts Div. 1941–44, Asst. Vice-Pres. 1944–46, Vice-Pres. 1946–58, Exec. Vice-Pres. 1958–75, Gen. Man. 1969–75, Vice-Chair. Bd., Chair. Exec. Cttee. 1975–76, C.E.O. 1976–86, Chair. Bd. 1986–88; Chair. Bd. Robertshaw Controls Co.; Dir. other cos. *Leisure interests:* golf, hunting, racing horses. *Address:* 8905 Tresco Road, Richmond, Va., U.S.A. (Home).

REYNOLDS, John Hamilton, PH.D.; American professor of physics; b. 3 April 1923, Cambridge, Mass.; s. of Horace Mason Reynolds and Catharine Whitford Coffeen; m. Anne Burchard Arnold 1975; two s. three d. (by previous marriage); ed. Harvard Coll. and Univ. of Chicago; Assoc. physicist, Argonne Nat. Laboratory 1950; Asst. Prof. to Prof. of Physics, Univ. of Calif. at Berkeley 1950–61, Prof. 1961–88, Emer. 1989–; Research Prof. Miller Inst. for Basic Research in Science 1959–61, 1967–68, Faculty Research Lecturer 1974; Guggenheim Fellow, Univ. of Bristol, England 1956–57, Nat. Science Foundation Sr. Postdoctoral Fellow and Visiting Prof. Univ. of São Paulo, Brazil 1963–64; Fulbright-Hays Research Award (Portugal) 1971–72; Chair. Dept. of Physics, Univ. of Calif. 1984–86; mem. N.A.S.; U.S.-Australia Co-operative Science Program award, (Perth) 1978–79; John Price Wetherill Medal of Franklin Inst., J. Lawrence Smith Medal of N.A.S., Leonard Medal, Meteoritical Soc., NASA Exceptional Scientific Achievement Medal; Guggenheim Fellow 1987. *Publications:* Research papers and reviews in fields of mass spectroscopy, isotope studies in meteorites, geochronology, solar system chronology, extinct radioactivity, and lunar samples. *Leisure interests:* swimming, hiking, brewing, microcomputers. *Address:* Department of Physics, University of California, Berkeley, Calif. 94720, U.S.A. *Telephone:* (415) 642-4863.

REYNOLDS, Joyce Maire, M.A., F.B.A.; British academic (retd.); b. 18 Dec. 1918, London; d. of William Howe Reynolds and Nellie Farmer Reynolds; ed. Walthamstow High School for Girls, St Paul's Girls' School, Hammersmith and Somerville Coll., Oxford; Temporary Admin. Officer, Board of Trade 1941–46; Rome Scholar, British School at Rome 1946–48; Lecturer in Ancient History, Kings Coll., Newcastle upon Tyne, Univ. of Durham 1948–51; Fellow, Lecturer and Dir. of Studies in Classics, Newnham Coll., Cambridge 1951–84; Univ. Asst. Lecturer, then Lecturer in Classics, Cambridge 1952–83, Reader in the Epigraphy of the Roman Empire 1983–84; Visiting mem. Inst. of Advanced Studies, Princeton, N.J., U.S.A. 1984–85; Visiting Prof., Univ. of Calif. at Berkeley, U.S.A. 1987; Visiting Lecturer, Univ. of Cape Town, S.A. 1987; Pres. Soc. for Libyan Studies 1982–85, Soc. for the Promotion of Roman Studies 1986–; Hon. Fellow Newnham Coll. 1984–; Hon. D. Litt. (Newcastle upon Tyne) 1984. *Publi-Newnham Coll. 1984–; Hon. D.Litt. (Newcastle upon Tyne) 1984. Publi-1951, Aphrodisias and Rome 1982, Jews and Godfearers at Aphrodisias (with R.F. Tannenbaum) 1987. Leisure interest:* walking. *Address:* Newn(with R. F. Tannenbaum) 1987. *Leisure interest:* walking. *Address:* Newn3PU, England (Home). *Telephone:* (0223) 335 700 (Office); (0223) 352 033 (Home).

REYNOLDS, Sir Peter William John, Kt., C.B.E.; British business executive; b. 10 Sept. 1929, Singapore; s. of Harry and Gladys Reynolds; m. Barbara Anne Johnson 1955; two s.; ed. Haileybury Coll.; with Unilever Ltd. 1950–70, Trainee, Man. Dir., then Chair., Walls Ltd.; Asst. Group Man. Dir. Ranks Hovis McDougall 1971, Group Man. Dir. 1972–81, Chair. 1981–; mem. Consultative Bd. for Resources Devt. in Agric. 1982–84; Dir. of Industrial Devt. Bd. for Northern Ireland 1982–, Guardian Royal Exchange 1986–; Chair. of Resources Cttee. of Food and Drink Fed. 1983–86; Dir. Boots Co. PLC 1986–, Guardian Royal Exchange PLC 1986–; mem. Peacock Cttee. *Leisure interests:* beagling, riding (occasionally), watching rugby football, reading, gardening. *Address:* Rignall Farm, Rignall Road, Great Missenden, Bucks, HP16 9PE, England. *Telephone:* (024 06) 4714.

RHALLYS, George J. (see Rallis, George J.).

RHEA, Alexander Dodson, III; American motor executive (retd.); b. 10 May 1919, Whitney, Tex.; s. of Alexander D. Rhea, Jr. and Annie Rhea;

m. Suzanne Menocal 1945; one s.; ed. Texas Christian Univ. and Princeton Univ.; U.S. Navy 1941–45, Lt.-Commdr. U.S.N.R.; Vice-Pres. Govt. Employees Insurance Co., Washington 1946–48; with Gen. Motors 1948–77, posts in S. America 1948–55, in Germany and N.Y. 1955–63; Regional Group Exec. 1963; Man. N.Y. Staff, Gen. Motors Overseas Operations 1966; Man. Dir., Gen. Motors Holden's Pty., Melbourne 1968–70; Chair. and Man. Dir. Vauxhall Motors Ltd. 1970–74; Chair. Gen. Motors European Advisory Council and Exec. Vice-Pres. and Dir., Gen. Motors Overseas Corpn. 1974–77. *Leisure interests:* reading, golf. *Address:* 580 Park Avenue, New York, N.Y. 10021, U.S.A.

RHEIMS, Maurice; French art critic; b. 4 Jan 1910, Versailles; s. of Gen. Léon and Jeanne (née Lévy) Rheims; m. Lili Krahmer 1951 (divorced); one s. two d.; ed. Ecole du Louvre, Sorbonne, Paris; Auctioneer, Paris 1935–72; mem. Acad. Française 1976–; Pres. Cultural Devt. Fund, Foundation of France; Vice-Pres. Admin. Council Nat. Library 1983–; Pres. prix Vasari 1986–; mem. Nat. Org. Cttee. European Architectural Heritage Year; Grand Officier, Légion d'honneur, Croix de guerre, Médaille de la Résistance, Officier des Arts et des Lettres, Commdr. Order of Merit (Italy). *Publications:* La vie étrange des objets 1960, La main, la vie de Gauguin, Vie de Toulouse-Lautrec (co-author), Le cheval d'argent, Un carpaccio en Dordogne, L'objet 1900, L'art 1900 ou le style Jules Verne, Dictionnaire des mots sauvages, La vie d'artiste, La sculpture au XIXème siècle 1971, Le luthier de Mantoue 1972, Les chefs d'oeuvre des musées de Province 1974, Haute curiosité 1975, Les collectionneurs 1981, Le Saint-Office 1983; film scripts Martin Soldat 1966, L'homme pressé 1977, L'enfer de la curiosité 1979, Amour de l'art 1984, Attila, laisse donc ta petite soeur tranquille 1985, Haarlem ... noir 1986. *Address:* 25 rue du Faubourg-Saint-Honoré, 75008 Paris, France. *Telephone:* 4265 5399.

RHINES, Peter Broomell, PH.D.; American university professor, oceanographer and atmospheric scientist; b. 23 July 1942, Hartford, Conn.; s. of Thomas B. Rhines and Olive S. Rhines; m. 1st Marie Lenos 1968 (divorced 1983); m. 2nd Linda Mattson Semtner 1984; one s.; ed. Loomis School, M.I.T., Trinity Coll., Cambridge, England; Sloan Scholar, M.I.T. 1960–63, N.S.F. Fellow 1963–64; Marshall Scholar, Cambridge 1964–67; Asst. Prof. of Oceanography M.I.T. 1967–71; Research Scientist, Cambridge Univ. 1971–72; mem. Scientific Staff, Woods Hole Oceanographic Inst. 1972–84, Dir. Center for Analysis of Marine Systems 1979–82, oceanographic research cruises 1972–84; Prof. of Oceanography and Atmospheric Sciences, Univ. of Washington, Seattle 1984–; Guggenheim Fellow, Christ's Coll. Cambridge, England 1979–80; Natural Environment Research Council Visiting Fellow, U.K. 1983; Fellow American Geophysical Union 1988, Queen's Fellow in Marine Sciences, Australia 1988; mem. N.A.S.; de Florez Award, M.I.T. 1963. *Publications:* research papers on general circulation of the oceans, waves and climate; contribs. to films on oceanography for BBC and Public Broadcasting System, U.S.A. *Leisure interests:* classical guitar, conversation and the out-of-doors. *Address:* School of Oceanography, University of Washington, WB-10, Seattle, Wash. 98195 (Office); 5753 61st Avenue N.E., Seattle, Wash. 98105, U.S.A. (Home).*Telephone:* (206) 522-5753 (Home).

RHOADS, James Berton, PH.D.; American archivist; b. 17 Sept. 1928, Sioux City, Iowa; s. of James H. and Mary K. Rhoads; m. S. Angela (Handy) Rhoads 1947; one s. two d.; ed. Univ. of California (Berkeley) and the American Univ., Washington, D.C.; held various positions in the Nat. Archives 1952–65; Asst. Archivist, Civil Archives 1965–66; Deputy Archivist of U.S.A. 1966–68; Archivist of U.S.A. 1968–79; Pres. Rhoads Assocs. Int. 1980–84; Dir. Graduate Program in Archives and Records Man., Western Washington Univ. 1984–; mem. Org. of American Historians; mem. Cttee. on Soviet-American Archival Co-operation 1986–, Bd. of Curators, Washington State Historical Soc. 1986–; Fellow, Soc. of American Archivists, Pres. 1974–75; Pres. Int. Council on Archives 1976–79; Vice-Pres. Intergovernmental Council on Gen. Information Program, UNESCO 1977–79, and mem. numerous other related orgs. *Publications:* numerous articles in professional journals. *Leisure interests:* reading, philately. *Address:* Rhoads, 3613 East Illinois Lane, Bellingham, Wash. 98226, U.S.A. *Telephone:* (206) 676-1235.

RHODES, Frank Harold Trevor, PH.D.; American geologist and university president; b. 29 Oct. 1926, Warwickshire, England; s. of Harold C. Rhodes and Gladys (Ford) Rhodes; m. Rosa Carlson 1952; four d.; ed. Univ. of Birmingham; Post-doctoral Fellow, Fulbright Scholar, Univ. of Ill. 1950–51, Visiting Lecturer in Geology summers of 1951–52; Lecturer in Geology, Univ. of Durham 1951–54; Asst. Prof., Univ. of Ill. 1954–55, Assoc. Prof. 1955–56, Dir. Univ. of Ill. Field Station, Wyoming 1956; Prof. of Geology and Head Dept. of Geology, Univ. of Wales, Swansea 1956–68, Dean Faculty of Science 1967–68; Prof. of Geology and Mineralogy, Coll. of Literature, Science and Arts, Univ. of Michigan 1968–77, Dean 1971–74, Vice-Pres. for Academic Affairs 1974–77; Pres. and Prof. of Geology, Cornell Univ. 1977–; numerous hon. degrees. *Publications:* The Evolution of Life 1962, Fossils 1963, Geology 1972, Evolution 1974, Language of the Earth 1981; over 70 major scientific articles and monographs, and some 40 articles on educ. *Address:* Office of the President, Cornell University, Ithaca, N.Y. 14853, U.S.A. *Telephone:* (607) 255-5201.

RHODES, John Jacob, B.S., LL.B.; American lawyer and politician; b. 18 Sept. 1916, Council Grove, Kan.; s. of John J. and Gladys Thomas Rhodes;

m. Mary Elizabeth (Betty) Harvey 1942; three s. one d.; ed. Kansas State Coll., Harvard Univ.; served Second World War, Col.; Partner, Rhodes, Killian & Legg, law firm, Mesa, Ariz. 1946–52; Vice-Pres., Dir. Farm Home, Life Insurance Co. 1951; Vice-Chair. Ariz. State Bd. of Public Welfare 1951–52; mem. Congress 1953–83; mem. Exec. Bd., Nat. Republican Congress Comm. 1953–62; Chair. Special Projects Sub-Cttee., Republican Policy Comm. 1961–65; Chair. Republican Policy Comm. 1965–73; Chair. Republican Platform Cttee. 1972; Perm. Chair. Republican Nat. Convention 1976, 1980; Nat. Co-Chair. Cttee. for a Responsible Fed. Budget 1983; Minority Leader, House of Reps. 1973–81; Counsel, law firm Hurton and Williams, Washington, D.C.; Dr. h.c. (Ariz., Ariz. State, Kansas State, Baker Univ.). *Publications:* The Futile System 1976, numerous articles. *Leisure interest:* golf. *Address:* Hurton and Williams, 2000 Pennsylvania Avenue, Washington, D.C. (Office); 860 W-Mountain View Drive, Mesa, Ariz. 85201, U.S.A. (Home). *Telephone:* (202) 955-1628 (Office); (602) 833-2267 (Home).

RIBEIRO, H.E. Cardinal António, TH.D.; Portuguese ecclesiastic; b. 21 May 1928, Celorico de Basto; s. of José Ribeiro and Ana Gonçalves; ed. Seminary of Braga and Pontifical Univ., Rome; ordained priest 1953; Prof. Univ. of Lisbon 1965–67; Auxiliary Bishop of Braga 1967; Auxiliary Bishop of Lisbon 1969; Patriarch of Lisbon 1971–; cr. Cardinal 1973. *Publications:* The Aevum According to Thomas Aquinas 1958, The Socialization 1964. *Leisure interests:* sport, philately, travel. *Address:* Campo dos Mártires da Pátria 45, 1198 Lisbon Codex, Portugal. *Telephone:* 56-39-01.

RIBERHOLDT, Gunnar; Danish diplomatist; b. 7 Nov. 1933, Naestved; s. of Poul G. Riberholdt and Erna M. Andersen; m. Kirsten H. Møller 1960; one s. one d.; ed. U.S. univs. and Univ. of Copenhagen; Ministry of Foreign Affairs 1958–62; Sec. of Embassy, Danish Perm. Mission to European Communities 1962–64, Deputy Head of Mission 1964–65; Head of Section, Ministry of Foreign Affairs 1965–69; Econ. Counsellor, Paris 1969–72; Dir. Ministry of Foreign Affairs 1973–75; Dir.-Gen. European Econ. Affairs 1975–77; Amb., Perm. Rep. of Denmark to European Communities 1977–84; Amb. to France 1984–. *Address:* 77 avenue Marceau, 75116 Paris, France. *Telephone:* 47 23 54 20.

RIBES, Pierre Raoul Martial, L. EN D.; French politician; b. 7 Aug. 1919, Ordizan; s. of Jean-Martial Ribes and Madeleine (née Dubuisson) Ribes; m. Jany Gordon 1956; three s.; ed. Lycée Janson-de-Sailly, Univ. of Paris; Dir. Cie. générale fiduciaire 1947–54, Asst. Dir.-Gen. 1954, Pres. and Dir.-Gen. 1955–; mem. Econ. and Social Cttee. 1964–67; Deputy for Les Yvelines, Nat. Assembly 1968–80; Vice-Pres. Nat. Ass. Cttee. for Finance, Gen. Econ. and the Econ. Plan; Head Temp. Mission for the Prime Minister May-Oct. 1976; Sec. of State for Posts and Telecommunications 1980–81; Dir. Political, Econ. and Social Publishing Co. (SEPES) 1974–; Chevalier, Légion d'honneur, Officier du Mérite agricole; affiliated to RPR. *Address:* 41 avenue Foch, 75116 Paris, France (Home).

RIBEYRE, Paul; French businessman and politician; b. 11 Dec. 1906, Aubagne; m. Andrée Offant 1939; three s. (and one s. and one d. deceased); Dir. La Reine Mineral Water Co. 1936–68; Mayor of Val-les-Bains 1945–80; Deputy from Ardèche to the two Constituent Nat. Assemblies 1945–46; Deputy for Ardèche, Nat. Assembly 1946–58; Senator for Ardèche 1958–80; Under-Sec. of State for Public Health and Population 1949, Minister of Public Health 1951–52, of Commerce 1953, of Justice 1953–54, of Industry 1957–58; Pres. Conseil Gen. de l'Ardèche 1958–79, fmr. Pres. Assocn. Parlementaire pour la Liberté de l'Enseignement; Pres. Club Européen de la Santé 1971–; Pres. Conseil Régional Rhônes-Alpes 1974–81; Officier, Légion d'honneur; mem. Directing Cttee. of Centre Democrat Party 1966–. *Leisure interests:* music, painting. *Address:* 9 rue Auguste Clément, 07600 Vals-les-Bains, France.

RIBIČIČ, Mitja; Yugoslav politician; b. 1919, Trieste; ed. Univ. of Ljubljana; mem. of Communist Party 1941–; mem. Cen. Cttee., League of Communists of Slovenia, League of Communists of Yugoslavia (LCY); mem. Presidium of Cen. Cttee. of LCY; mem. Slovene del. to Chamber of Nationalities of Fed. Ass.; has held various posts in the Slovene Govt. and the Yugoslav Fed. Govt.; Pres. Fed. Exec. Council 1969–71; mem. Presidency of Fed. Repub. 1971–74, Vice-Pres. 1973–74. *Address:* Savez komunista Jugoslavije, Bulevar Lenjina 6, Novi Beograd, Yugoslavia.

RIBICOFF, Abraham A. LL.B.; American lawyer and politician; b. 9 April 1910, New Britain, Conn.; m. Lois Mathes; one s. one d.; ed. New York Univ. and Univ. of Chicago; admitted to Conn. Bar 1933, New York Bar 1981, U.S. Supreme Court Bar 1981; U.S. Court of Appeals 1982; mem. Conn. Gen. Ass. 1939–42; Municipal Judge, Hartford, Conn. 1941–43, 1945–47; U.S. Rep., Conn. 1949–53; Gov. of the State of Conn. 1955–61; Sec. of Health, Educ. and Welfare under Pres. Kennedy 1961–62; U.S. Senator from Conn. 1963–81; Chair. Gov. Affairs Cttee. and Int. Trade Sub-cttee. of Finance Cttee.; del. to U.S. Mission to UN 1979; special counsel to law firm of Kaye, Scholer, Fierman, Hays & Handler, New York and Washington D.C. 1981–. *Publications:* Politics: The American Way (with Jon O. Newman) 1969, America Can Make It! 1972, The American Medical Machine 1972. *Address:* 425 Park Avenue, New York, N.Y. 10022, U.S.A.

RIBOUD, Antoine Amédée Paul; French business executive; b. 24 Dec. 1918, Lyons; s. of Camille Riboud and Hélène Frachon; m. Lucette

Hugonnard-Roche 1943; three s. one d.; ed. Ecole Supérieure de Commerce, Paris; joined Verreries Souchon-Neuvesel 1943, mem. Bd. of Dirs. and Sec.-Gen. 1952–62, Vice-Pres. 1962–65, Dir.-Gen. 1962–66, Pres. 1965–66; Pres. and Dir.-Gen. Soc. Boussois-Souchon-Neuvesel 1966–72; Pres. Boussois-Souchon-Neuvesel-Gervais-Danone 1973–; Vice-Pres. Cie. Gervais-Danone 1973–76, Pres. 1976–; Dir., later Dir.-Gen. Verreries de Gironcourt 1963–68; Dir., later Pres. and Dir.-Gen. Soc. des Eaux minérales d'Evian-les-Bains 1966–70; Vice-Pres. Glaverbel-Mecaniver, Brussels 1969–76, Pres. 1976–; Pres. and Dir.-Gen. Soc. européenne de brasseries 1970–76; Pres. Soc. moderne de boissons 1972–; Dir. Cie. financière de Paris et des Pays-Bas, Pricel, Cie. française Philips, Soc. des eaux minérales d'Evian, Dahlbusch, Vereenig de Glasfabrieken (Netherlands), Soc. pour l'exploitation et la vente des produits Fruité et Eva; Pres. Centre Nat. d'information pour la productivité des entreprises 1969–70, Asscn. Progrès et Environnement 1971–; mem. Loan Cttee. Crédit Nat., Cercle de l'Union; Officier des Arts et des Lettres. *Address:* 7 rue de Téhéran, 75008 Paris (Office); 13 rue Laurencin, 69002 Lyons, France (Home).

RICCI, Ruggiero; American violinist; b. 24 July 1918, San Francisco; s. of Pietro Ricci and Emma Bacigalupi; m. 1st Ruth Rink 1942; m. 2nd Valma Rodriguez 1957; m. 3rd Julia Whitehurst Clemenceau 1978; two s. three d.; ed. under Louis Persinger, Mischel Piastro, Paul Stassévitch and Georg Kulenkampff; debut with Manhattan Symphony Orchestra, New York 1929; first tour of Europe 1932; served U.S.A.F. 1942–45; Prof. of Violin, Univ. of Mich. 1982–; now makes annual tours of U.S.A. and Europe; has made 13 tours of S. America, five tours of Australia, two tours of Japan and three tours of U.S.S.R.; played the first performances of the violin concertos of Ginastera, Von Einem and Veerhoff; specializes in violin solo literature; Cavaliere Order of Merit (Italy). *Address:* School of Music, University of Michigan, 1100 Baits Drive, Ann Arbor, Mich. 48109, U.S.A.

RICE, Dorothy P., B.A.; American academic; b. 11 June 1922, Brooklyn, New York; d. of Gershon Pechman and Lena (Schiff); m. John D. Rice 1943; three s.; ed. Brooklyn Coll., New York, Univ. of Wisconsin, and George Washington Univ., Washington, D.C.; Dept. of Labor 1941–42; War Production Bd. 1942–44; Nat. War Labor Bd. 1944–45; Nat. Wage Stabilization Bd. 1945–47; Health Economist, Public Health Service 1947–49, Public Health Analyst 1960–62, 1964–65; Social Science Analyst, Social Security Admin. 1962–64; Chief, Health Insurance Research Branch 1965–72, Deputy Asst. Commr. Office of Research and Statistics 1972–76; Dir. Nat. Center for Health Stats. Hyattsville, Md. 1976–82; Prof.-in-Residence, Dept. of Social and Behavioural Sciences, Inst. for Health and Aging, Univ. of Calif., San Francisco 1982–, Inst. for Health Policy Studies, Univ. of Calif., San Francisco 1982–; numerous honours and awards. *Publications:* more than 100 articles in professional journals. *Address:* Institute for Health and Aging, Department of Social and Behavioral Sciences—N631, School of Nursing, University of California, San Francisco, Calif. 94143 (Office); 1055 Amito Avenue, Berkeley, Calif. 94705, U.S.A. (Home).

RICE, Stuart Alan, B.S., A.M., PH.D.; American professor of chemistry; b. 6 Jan. 1932, New York City; s. of Laurence Harlan Rice and Helen Rayfield; m. Marian Coopersmith 1952; two d.; ed. Brooklyn Coll. and Harvard Univ.; Asst. Prof. Dept. of Chem. and Inst. for the Study of Metals, Univ. of Chicago 1957–59, Assoc. Prof. Inst. for the Study of Metals (later James Franck Inst.) 1959–60, 1960–69, Louis Block Prof. of Chem. 1969, Louis Block Prof. of Physical Sciences 1969–, Chair. Dept. of Chemistry 1971–77, Frank P. Hixon Distinguished Service Prof. 1977–;Bourke Lecturer, Faraday Soc. 1964; Lecturer, numerous univs. in U.S.A. and abroad; Alfred P. Sloan Fellow 1958–62, Guggenheim Fellow 1960–61, Nat. Science Foundation Sr. Postdoctoral Fellow and Visiting Prof. Univ. Libre de Bruxelles 1965–66; Nat. Insts. of Health Special Research Fellow and Visiting Prof. H. C. Orsted Inst., Univ. of Copenhagen 1970–71; Fairchild Distinguished Scholar, Calif. Inst. of Tech. 1979; Dean, Div. of Physical Sciences, Univ. of Chicago 1981–; Baker Lecturer, Cornell Univ. 1985–86; Centenary Lecturer, Royal Soc. of Chemistry 1986–87; Fellow, American Acad. of Arts and Sciences; mem. N.A.S., Nat. Science Bd. 1980–; Foreign mem. Royal Danish Acad. of Science and Letters 1976; Hon. D.Sc. (Brooklyn Coll., Notre Dame Coll.) 1982; A. Cressy Morrison Prize in Natural Sciences, New York Acad. of Sciences 1955, American Chem. Soc. Award in Pure Chem. 1962, Marlow Medal, Faraday Soc. 1963, Llewellyn John and Harriet Manchester Quantrell Award 1970, Leo Hendrik Baekeland Award 1971, Peter Debye American Chem. Soc. Prize 1985, Joel Henry Hildebrand Award, American Chemical Soc., etc. *Publications:* Poly-electrolyte Solutions (with Mitsuru Nagasawa) 1961, Statistical Mechanics of Simple Liquids (with Peter Gray) 1965, Physical Chemistry (with R. S. Berry and John Ross) 1980; and 400 papers on chemical physics in scientific journals. *Leisure interests:* reading, carpentry. *Address:* The James Franck Institute, The University of Chicago, 5640 Ellis Avenue, Chicago, Ill. 60637 (Office); 5421 Greenwood Avenue, Chicago, Ill. 60615, U.S.A. (Home). *Telephone:* (312) 702-7199 (Office); 667-2679 (Home).

RICE, Tim(othy) Miles Bindon; British songwriter and broadcaster; b. 10 Nov. 1944, Amersham; s. of Hugh Gordon Rice and Joan Odette Rice; m. Jane Artereta McIntosh 1974; one s. one d.; ed. Lancing Coll.; with EMI Records 1966–68, Norrie Paramor Org. 1968–69; Founder and Dir. GRRR Books Ltd. 1976–, Pavilion Books Ltd. 1980–. *Lyrics for musicals* (music by Andrew Lloyd Webber, q.v.): Joseph and the Amazing Technicolor Dreamcoat 1968, Jesus Christ Superstar 1970, Evita 1976, Blondel (music by Stephen Oliver) 1983, Chess (music by Benny Andersson and Bjorn Ulvaeus) 1984, Cricket (with A. L. Webber) 1986. *Publications:* Evita (with Andrew Lloyd Webber) 1978; ed. Heartaches Cricketers' Almanack 1975-, Guinness Book of British Hit Singles and Albums 1977-, Lord's Taverners Sticky Wicket Book 1979, Guinness Book of Hits of the 70s 1980, Guinness Book of 500 Number One Hits 1982, Guinness Book of Hit Albums 1983-, Guinness Book of Hits of the 60s 1984, Guinness Hits Challenge 1984- (all Guinness books with Jo Rice, Paul Gambaccini and Mike Read), Treasures of Lords 1989. *Leisure interests:* cricket, history of popular music. *Address:* 196 Shaftesbury Avenue, London, W.C.2, England. *Telephone:* 01-836 1306.

RICE, Victor Albert; Canadian company executive; b. 7 March 1941, Hitchin, Herts., England; s. of Albert Edward and Rosina Emmeline (Pallant) Rice; financial posts in U.K. with Ford 1957-64, Cummins Engines 1964-67 and Chrysler 1968-70; Comptroller N. European Operations, Massey-Ferguson's Perkins Engines Group 1970, then Dir. Finance and Dir. Sales and Market Devt., Deputy Man. Dir. Operations 1974; Comptroller Massey-Ferguson Ltd., Toronto, Canada 1975, Vice-Pres. Staff Operations 1977; mem. Bd. of Dirs., Pres. and C.O.O. Massey-Ferguson (now Varity Corpn.) 1978-, Chair. and C.E.O. 1980-. *Leisure interests:* golf, music. *Address:* Varity Corporation, 595 Bay Street, Toronto, Ont. M5G 2C3, Canada. *Telephone:* (416) 593-3801.

RICH, Adrienne, A.B.; American writer; b. 16 May 1929, Baltimore; d. of Arnold Rich and Helen Elizabeth Jones; m. Alfred Conrad (died 1970); three s.; ed. Radcliffe Coll.; Teacher, New York poetry centre 1966-67; Visiting Lecturer, Swarthmore Coll. 1967-69; Adjutant Prof., Columbia Univ. 1967-69; Lecturer, City Coll. of New York 1968-70, Instructor 1970-71, Asst. Prof. of English 1971-72, 1974-75; Visiting Prof. of Creative Literature, Brandeis Univ. 1972-73; Prof. of English, Rutgers Univ. 1976-; Prof.-at-Large, Cornell Univ. 1981-; Lecturer and Visiting Prof, Scripps Coll. 1983-; Hon. Litt.D. (Wheaton Coll.) 1967, (Smith Coll.) 1979, (Brandeis Univ.) 1987, (Wooster Coll.) 1989; Yale Series of Younger Poets Award 1951; Guggenheim Fellow 1952, 1961; Ridgely Torrance Memorial Award, Poetry Soc. of America 1955; Shelley Memorial Award 1971; Nat. Book Award 1974, Ruth Lily Prize 1987, Brandeis Medal in Poetry 1987. *Publications:* A Change of World 1951, The Diamond Cutters and Other Poems 1955, Snapshots of a Daughter-in-Law 1963, Necessities of Life 1962-65, 1965-68 1969, Leaflets, Poems 1965-68, The Will to Change 1971, Diving into the Wreck 1973, Of Woman Born: Motherhood as Experience and Institution 1976, Selected Prose 1966-78 1979, A Wild Patience Has Taken Me This Far: Poems 1978-81 1981, The Fact of a Doorframe: Poems 1950-84 1984, On Lies, Secrets and Silence: Selected Prose 1979-85 1986, Your Native Land, Your Life 1986, Time's Power: Poems 1985-88 1989. *Address:* c/o W. W. Norton, 500 Fifth Avenue, New York, N.Y. 10036, U.S.A.

RICH, Alexander, M.D.; American molecular biologist; b. 15 Nov. 1924, Hartford, Conn.; s. of Max Rich and Bella Shub; m. Jane Erving King 1952; two s. two d.; ed. Harvard Coll. and Harvard Medical School; served U.S. Navy 1943-46; Research Fellow, Gates and Crellin Labs., Calif. Inst. of Tech. 1949-54; Chief of Section on Physical Chem., Nat. Inst. of Mental Health 1954-58; visiting Scientist, Cavendish Lab., Cambridge, U.K. 1955-56; Assoc. Prof. of Biophysics, M.I.T. 1958-61, Prof. 1961-, William Thompson Sedgwick Prof. of Biophysics 1974-; Fairchild Distinguished Scholar, Calif. Inst. of Tech., Pasadena 1976; Sr. Consultant, Office of Science and Tech. Policy, Exec. Office of the Pres. 1977-81; mem. Editorial Bd. Science 1963-69, Proceedings of the National Academy of Sciences 1973-78 and other journals; mem. Council of American Acad. of Arts and Sciences 1967-, Chair. Nominating Cttee. 1974-77; Chair. Cttee. on U.S.S.R. and E. Europe Exchange Program, N.A.S. 1973-76; mem. Biology Team of Viking Mars Mission, NASA 1969-80, Advisory Bd. of Acad. Forum, N.A.S. 1975-, Scientific Advisory Bd. of Stanford Synchrotron Radiation Project 1976-, U.S. Nat. Science Bd. 1976-, Bd. Govs. Weizmann Inst. of Science 1976-, Research Cttee., The Medical Foundation, Boston, Mass. 1976-80, U.S.-U.S.S.R. Jt. Comm. on Science and Tech., Dept. of State 1977-, Scientific Advisory Bd., Mass. Gen. Hospital 1978-, Scientific Review Cttee., Howard Hughes Medical Inst. 1978-, Visiting Cttee. to Div. of Medical Sciences, Harvard Univ. 1981-, Bd. of Dirs. Boston Medical Foundation 1981-, and other cttees.; mem. American Chem. Soc. and other socs., N.A.S. 1970- (mem. Exec. Cttee. 1985-); Fellow, Nat. Research Council 1949-51, American Acad. of Arts and Sciences 1959, Guggenheim Foundation 1963, A.A.A.S. 1965, mem. Pontifical Acad. of Sciences, The Vatican 1978, American Philosophical Soc. 1980; Foreign mem. French Acad. of Sciences 1984; Hon. Dr. (Rio de Janeiro) 1981; Skylab Achievement Award, NASA 1974; Theodore von Karmen Award 1976, Presidential Award, New York Acad. of Science 1977, James R. Killian Faculty Achievement Award, (M.I.T.) 1980, Jabotinsky Medal, New York 1980, and numerous other awards. *Publications:* Structural Chemistry and Molecular Biology 1968; 300 publications in the field of molecular structure of nucleic acid components, nucleic acids and polynucleotides, physical chem. of nucleotides and polynucleotides, molecular structure of proteins, mechanism of protein synthesis, molecular biology of the nucleic acids, X-ray crystallography, origin of life. *Leisure interests:* ocean sailing in small

boats, growing tomato plants, collecting fossils. *Address:* Department of Biology, Massachusetts Institute of Technology, Cambridge, Mass. 02139 (Office); 2 Walnut Avenue, Cambridge, Mass. 02140, U.S.A. (Home). *Telephone:* (617) 253-4715 (Office); (617) 547-1637 (Home).

RICH, Clayton, M.D.; American university administrator; b. 21 May 1924, New York; s. of Clayton Eugene Rich and Leonore (Elliot) Rich; m. 1st Mary Bell Hodgkinson 1953 (divorced 1974), one s.; m. 2nd Carolyn Sue Miller 1982 (divorced 1986); ed. Swarthmore Coll., Cornell Univ.; Intern, Albany Hosp., New York 1948-49, Asst. Resident 1950-51; Research Asst., Cornell Univ. Medical Coll. 1949-50; Asst. Rockefeller Univ. 1953-58, Asst. Prof. 1958-60; Asst. Prof. of Medicine, Univ. of Washington School of Medicine 1960-62, Assoc. Prof. 1962-67, Prof. 1967-71, Assoc. Dean 1968-71; Chief Radioisotope Service Veterans' Admin. Hosp., Seattle 1960-70, Assoc. Chief of Staff 1962-71, Chief of Staff 1968-70, Vice-Pres., Medical Affairs, Dean of School of Medicine; Prof. of Medicine, Stanford Univ. 1971-79, Carl and Elizabeth Naumann Prof. 1977-79; Chief of Staff Stanford Univ. Hosp. 1971-77, C.E.O. 1977-79; Sr. Scholar, Inst. of Medicine, N.A.S., Washington 1979-80; Provost Univ. of Okla. Health Sciences Center 1980-, Vice-Pres. for Health Sciences 1983-, Exec. Dean, Prof., Coll. of Medicine 1980-83; Fellow American Coll. of Physicians; mem. Asscn. of American Physicians, American Soc. of Mineral and Bone Research (Advisory Bd. 1977-80), Asscn. of American Medical Colls. (Exec. Council 1975-79), Inst. of Medicine, Endocrine Soc. *Publications:* numerous articles in medical journals. Address: Provost's Office, University of Oklahoma Health Services Center, P.O. Box 26901, Oklahoma City, Okla. 73190, U.S.A.

RICH, Frank Hart, Jr., A.B.; American journalist; b. 2 June 1949, Washington, D.C.; s. of Frank Hart Rich and Helene Aaronson; m. Gail Winston 1976; two s.; ed. Harvard Coll.; Film Critic and Sr. Ed. New Times Magazine 1973-75; Film Critic, New York Post 1975-77; Film and TV Critic, Time Magazine 1977-80; Chief Drama Critic, New York Times 1980-. *Address:* The New York Times, 229 West 43rd Street, New York, N.Y. 10036, U.S.A. *Telephone:* (212) 556 7414.

RICH, John Rowland, C.M.G., M.A.; British diplomatist (retd.); b. 29 June 1928, Durham; s. of Rowland William Rich and Phyllis Mary (née Chambers); m. Rosemary Ann Williams 1956; two s. one d.; ed. Sedbergh and Clare Coll. Cambridge; nat. service in Army 1949-51; joined H.M. Foreign, later Diplomatic Service 1951; served in Foreign Office, later FCO, Depts. and overseas at Addis Ababa 1953-56, Stockholm 1956-59, Bahrain 1963-66; Counsellor and Head of Chancery, Prague 1969-72; diplomatic service Inspector 1972-74; Counsellor (Commercial), Bonn 1974-78; Consul-Gen., Montreal 1978-80; Amb. to Czechoslovakia 1980-85, to Switzerland 1985-88. *Leisure interests:* walking, photographing wild orchids, gardening. *Address:* c/o National Westminster Bank, East Molesey, Surrey, KT8 9EZ, England.

RICH, Robert Graham, Jr., B.S.; American diplomatist; b. 15 Nov. 1930, Gainesville, Fla.; s. of Robert G. Rich and Lula A. Hawkins; m. Mary A. Cote; four d.; ed. Univ. of Florida and Cornell Univ.; naval officer, Korean War 1952-54; research engineer Sperry Rand Corpn. 1954-57; entered U.S. Foreign Service 1957; served in S. Korea, Indonesia and Dept. of State 1957-72; Nat. War Coll. 1972; Deputy Chief of Mission, U.S. Embassy, Trinidad & Tobago 1974-77; Dir. Office of Korean Affairs, Dept. of State 1977-81; Sr. Exec. Seminar in Nat. and Int. Affairs 1981-82; Deputy Chief of Missions, Manila 1982-87; Amb. to Belize 1987-; Dept. of State Superior Honor Awards (three). *Publication:* United States Troop Withdrawal from Korea: A Case Study in National Security Decision Making 1982. *Leisure interests:* sailing, reading, family. *Address:* United States Embassy, P.O. Box 286, Belize City, Belize. *Telephone:* 001-(501)-2-77161.

RICHARD, Christian Rémi; Malagasy politician and diplomatist; b. 3 May 1941, Morondava; s. of Georges and Blanche (née Grève) Richard; m. Eulalie Ralisiarivelo 1967; three s. three d.; Minister of Educ. Feb.-June 1975, of Youth 1976-77, also of Revolutionary Art and Culture June-July 1977, of Foreign Affairs 1977-83; Amb. to EEC 1984-, to Belgium, Luxembourg, the Netherlands and Switzerland 1984-86, 1987-; mem. Front National pour la Défense de la Révolution Socialiste Malgache. *Leisure interests:* football, hunting, photography, reading. *Address:* Embassy of Madagascar, 276 avenue de Turvuren, 1150 Brussels, Belgium.

RICHARD, Cliff, O.B.E.; British singer and actor; b. (as Harry Roger Webb) 14 Oct. 1940, India; s. of Roger and Dorothy Webb; ed. Riversmead School, Cheshunt; first successful record Move It 1958; plays guitar; own television series on BBC and ITV; various repertory and variety seasons; Top Box Office Star of Great Britain 1962-63, 1963-64; awarded Gold Discs (for sales over a million each) for Living Doll, The Young Ones, Bachelor Boy, Lucky Lips, Congratulations, Power to All Our Friends, Devil Woman, We Don't Talk Anymore, Daddy's Home, Mistletoe and Wine; also 30 Silver Discs (for sales over 250,000); Ivor Novello Award for Outstanding Achievement 1989. *Films:* Serious Charge 1959, Expresso Bongo 1960, The Young Ones 1961, Summer Holiday 1962, Wonderful Life 1964, Finders Keepers 1966, Two a Penny 1968, His Land, Take Me High 1973; appeared in musical Time, Dominion Theatre, London 1986-87. *Publications:* Questions 1970, The Way I See It 1972, The Way I See It

Now 1975, Which One's Cliff? 1977, Happy Christmas from Cliff 1980, You, Me and Jesus 1983, Mine to Share 1984, Jesus, Me and You 1985, Single-Minded 1988, Mine Forever 1989. *Leisure interests:* swimming, tennis. *Address:* c/o Gormley Management, P.O. Box 46c, Esher, Surrey, KT10 9AA, England. *Telephone:* (0372) 67752.

RICHARD, Ivor Seward, M.A., Q.C.; British lawyer, politician and diplomatist; b. 30 May 1932, Cardiff; s. of Seward Thomas and Isabella Irene Richard; m. Alison Mary Imrie 1962 (dissolved 1984); two s. one d.; ed. Cheltenham Coll., Pembroke Coll., Oxford; called to the Bar 1955; M.P. for Barons Court 1964-74; Parl. Pvt. Sec. to Sec. of State for Defence 1966-69; Under-Sec. of State for Defence for Army 1969-70; Queen's Counsel 1971; Perm. Rep. to UN 1974-79; Commr. of European Communities for Social Affairs, Employment, Education and Vocational Training Policy 1981-84; Chair. World Trade Centre Wales Ltd. (Cardiff) 1985-; Chair. Rhodesia Conf., Geneva 1976; Counsel to Chadbourne, Parke, Whiteside and Wolff, New York 1979-81; Hon. Fellow, Pembroke Coll. 1981-; Labour. *Publications:* Europe or the Open Sea 1971, We, the British 1983, and articles in various political journals. *Leisure interests:* playing piano, watching football, talking. *Address:* 11 South Square, Gray's Inn, London, WC1R 5EU, England. *Telephone:* 01-831 6974.

RICHARDS, Arthur L.; American diplomatist (retd.); b. 21 June 1907, Emmett, Ida.; s. of Arthur A. and Sedenia (Dunford) Richards; m. Ida Elizabeth Parker; two s. one d.; ed. Pasadena Jr. Coll., George Washington Univ. and Nat. War Coll.; joined Foreign Service 1930, Mexico, Washington, Teheran, Jerusalem, Cairo, Cape Town, Pretoria, Washington, Teheran 1930-52; Dir. Office of Greek, Turkish and Iranian Affairs, Dept. of State 1952-54; Consul-Gen. Istanbul 1954-56; Operations Co-ordinator, Dept. of State 1956-58; Special Asst. to Under-Sec. of State for Law of Sea 1958-60; Amb. to Ethiopia 1960-62; Deputy Rep. of U.S. to 18-Nation Disarmament Cttee., Geneva 1963-65; Dir. Washington Int. Center 1968-73; retd. 1973. *Address:* 4902 Rockmere Court, Sumner, Md. 20816, U.S.A.

RICHARDS, Sir Edward Trenton, Kt., C.B.E., J.P., M.P.; Bermudan politician; b. 4 Oct. 1908, Berbice, British Guiana; s. of late George A. Richards and Millicent (née Williams); m. Madree E. Williams 1940; one s. two d.; ed. Collegiate School and Queen's Coll., British Guiana; former teacher at Berkeley Inst., Bermuda; called to the Bar, Middle Temple, London 1946; mem. Bermudan House of Assembly 1948-76; fmr. Chair. Public Transportation Bd., Transport Control Bd., Jt. Parl. Cttee. investigating Racial Discrimination in Hotels and Restaurants, Berkeley Educ. Soc. 1956-72; mem. Bd. of Health, Bd. of Social Welfare and numerous other bds. and cttees.; Minister for Immigration and Labour and Deputy Govt. Leader 1968-71; Premier of Bermuda 1972-75; Bermudan rep. at Commonwealth Parl. Assen. Conf., Lagos 1962, Kuala Lumpur 1971; Head dels. to ILO confs., Geneva 1969, 70, 71; Hon. LL.D. (Wilberforce Univ., U.S.A.) 1960. *Leisure interests:* sport, reading, music. *Address:* "Wilton", Keith Hall Road, Warwick East, Bermuda. *Telephone:* 2-3645.

RICHARDS, Frederic Middlebrook, PH.D.; American biochemist; b. 19 Aug. 1925, New York; s. of George and Marianna Richards; m. Sarah Wheatland 1959; one s. two d.; ed. Mass Inst. of Tech. and Harvard Univ.; Research Fellow, Physical Chem., Harvard Univ. 1952-53; Nat. Research Council Fellow, Carlsberg Lab., Denmark 1954; Nat. Science Foundation Fellow, Cambridge Univ., U.K. 1955; Asst. Prof. of Biochemistry, Yale Univ. 1955-59, Assoc. Prof. 1959-62, Prof. 1963-, Chair. Dept. of Molecular Biology and Biophysics 1963-67, Dept. of Molecular Biophysics and Biochemistry 1969-73; mem. Council Int. Union of Pure and Applied Biophysics 1975-81; Dir. Jane Coffin Childs Memorial Fund for Medical Research 1976-; Corpn. mem. Woods Hole Oceanographic Inst. 1977-83; mem. Scientific Bd. Whitney Lab. for Experimental Marine Biology and Medicine, Nat. Advisory Research Resources Council N.I.H. 1983-; N.A.S., American Acad. of Arts and Sciences, American Chem. Soc., American Soc. of Biological Chemistry (Pres. 1978-80), Biophysical Soc. (Pres. 1972-73), American Crystallographic Assen.; Guggenheim Fellow 1967-68; Pfizer-Paul Lewis Award 1965; Kaj Linderstrøm-Lang Prize 1978. *Publications:* various articles in scientific journals in the general field of protein and enzyme chemistry. *Leisure interests:* sailing, skiing. *Address:* Department of Molecular Biophysics and Biochemistry, Yale University, P.O. Box 6666, 260 Whitney Avenue, New Haven, Conn. 06511 (Office); 69 Andrews Road, Guildford, Conn. 06437, U.S.A.

RICHARDS, (Isaac) Vivian Alexander ("Viv"); West Indian cricketer; b. 7 March 1952, St. John's, Antigua; s. of Malcolm Richards; m.; one s. one d.; ed. Antigua Grammar School; right-hand batsman, off-break bowler; début for Leeward Islands v. Windward Islands 1971-72; played for Somerset 1974-86, awarded county cap 1974; played for Queensland (Australia) in Sheffield Shield Competition 1976-77; toured (for West Indies) India, Sri Lanka and Pakistan 1974-75, Australia 1975-76, England 1976, Australia and New Zealand 1979-80, Australia 1981-82, England 1984, New Zealand 1986-87; Captain of West Indies 1985-; scored 1,710 runs in 11 Test matches in 1976 (record aggregate for a year); holds record for most sixes (26) hit in John Player League in one season 1977; Dr. h.c. (Exeter) 1986. *Publication:* (with David Foot) Viv Richards (autobiog.). *Leisure interests:* music, football. *Address:* c/o David Copp Management, P.O. Box 19, Sherborne, Dorset, DT9 3EF, England.

RICHARDS, Keith (Keith Richard); British musician and songwriter; b. 18 Dec. 1943, Dartford; s. of Bert Richards and Doris Richards; m. 1st Anita Pallenberg; one s. two d.; m. 2nd Patti Hansen 1983, two d.; ed. Sidcup Art School; lead guitarist, vocalist with the Rolling Stones 1962-; composer (with Mick Jagger q.v.), numerous songs and albums 1964-, including: The Rolling Stones Now! 1964, Aftermath 1966, Flowers 1967, Beggars' Banquet 1968, Let it Bleed 1969, Sticky Fingers 1971, Hot Rocks 1972, Exile on Main Street 1972, Goat's Head Soup 1973, It's Only Rock and Roll 1974, Metamorphosis 1975, Black and Blue 1976, Some Girls, Emotional Rescue 1980, Tattoo You 1981, Still Life 1982, Under Cover 1983, Dirty Work 1986, Talk is Cheap (solo) 1988; *Films:* Sympathy for the Devil 1970, Gimme Shelter 1970, Ladies and Gentlemen, the Rolling Stones 1974, Let's Spend the Night Together 1983.. *Address:* c/o Raindrop Services, 1776 Broadway, New York, N.Y. 10019, U.S.A.

RICHARDS, Sir Rex Edward, Kt., F.R.S., D.SC., M.A., D.PHIL.; British university administrator and professor of chemistry; b. 28 Oct. 1922, Colyton, Devon; s. of H. W. and E. N. Richards; m. Eva Edith Vago 1948; two d.; ed. Colyton Grammar School, St. John's Coll., Oxford; Fellow of Lincoln Coll., Oxford 1947-64; Dr. Lee's Prof. of Chem., Oxford 1964-70; Fellow of Exeter Coll., Oxford 1964-69; Warden Merton Coll., Oxford 1969-84; Vice-Chancellor Univ. of Oxford 1977-81; Chancellor Exeter Univ. 1981-; Tilden Lecturer 1962; Research Fellow, Harvard Univ. 1955; Hon. Fellow of St. John's Coll. and Lincoln Coll., Oxford 1968-, Merton Coll., Oxford 1984-; Assoc. Fellow, Morse Coll., Yale 1974-79; Chair. Oxford Enzyme Group 1969-83; Dir. Oxford Instruments Group 1982-; Dir. Leverhulme Trust 1985-; mem. Chem. Soc. Council 1957, 1988, Faraday Soc. Council 1963, Royal Soc. Council 1973-75, Advisory Bd. for Research Councils 1980-82, Advisory Council for Applied Research and Devt. 1984-87; Dir. IBM United Kingdom Holdings, IBM (U.K.) 1978-82; Chair. British Postgraduate Medical Fed.; Trustee of CIBA Foundation, Nat. Heritage Memorial Fund 1979-84, Tate Gallery 1982-88, Nat. Gallery 1982-; Hon. F.R.C.P. 1987; Hon.D.Sc. (East Anglia) 1971, (Exeter) 1975, (Leicester) 1978, (Salford) 1979, (Edinburgh) 1981; Hon. D.Litt. (Dundee) 1977, (Kent) 1987; Corday-Morgan Medal of Chemical Soc. 1954, Davy Medal, Royal Soc. 1976, Award in Theoretical Chem. and Spectroscopy, Chemical Soc. 1977, Epic Award 1982, Medal of Honour, Bonn Univ. 1983, Royal Medal, Royal Soc. 1986. *Publications:* numerous contributions to scientific journals. *Leisure interest:* contemporary art. *Address:* Leverhulme Trust, Lintas House, New Fetter Lane, London, EC4A 1NR (Office); 214 The Colonnades, Porchester Square, London, W2 6AS (Home); 13 Woodstock Close, Oxford, OX2 8DB, England (Home). *Telephone:* 01-882 6938 (Office); (0865) 513621 (Home).

RICHARDSON, Baron (Life Peer) cr. 1979, of Lee in the County of Devon, **John Samuel Richardson,** Bt., L.V.O., M.A., M.D., F.R.C.P.; British consultant physician; b. 16 June 1910, Sheffield; s. of Major John Watson Richardson and Elizabeth Blakeney; m. Sybil Trist 1933; two d.; ed. Charterhouse, Trinity Coll., Cambridge and St. Thomas's Hospital Medical School; various appointments at St. Thomas's Hospital and Royal Postgraduate Medical School; with R.A.M.C. during Second World War; Deputy Dir. to Medical Unit, St. Thomas's Hospital; Consulting Physician at St. Thomas's Hospital; Consultant Physician to Metropolitan Police 1957-80, London Transport Bd. 1964-80; Consultant Emer. to Army; Pres. Gen. Medical Council 1973-80; Chair. Council for Postgraduate Medical Educ. in England and Wales 1972-80, Armed Forces Medical Advisory Bd. 1975; mem. Council Royal Coll. of Physicians; fmr. Pres. Royal Soc. of Medicine, Int. Soc. for Internal Medicine, British Medical Assen.; Past-Master, Worshipful Soc. of Apothecaries of London; Hon. Fellow, Trinity Coll., Cambridge, Hon. F.R.C.P. (Edin., Ireland), Hon Fellow, Royal Coll. of Physicians and Surgeons (Glasgow), Royal Coll. of Psychiatrists, Royal Coll. of Surgeons of England, Royal Coll. of Gen. Practitioners, Faculty of Community Medicine; Hon. D.Sc. (Nat. Univ. of Ireland, Univ. of Hull), Hon. D.C.L. (Newcastle, Durham), Hon. LL.D. (Nottingham, Liverpool); Hadden Prize and Bristowe Medal, St. Thomas's Hospital 1936, Perkins Fellowship 1939-40; Hon. Bencher, Gray's Inn 1974, 1st De Lancy Law Prize (Royal Soc. of Medicine) 1978, Gold Medal B.M.A. 1980, Guthrie Medal, R.A.M.C. 1980; C. St. J. *Publications:* The Practice of Medicine 1960, Connective Tissue Disorders 1963, Anticoagulant Prophylaxis and Treatment (jointly) 1965. *Leisure interest:* gardening. *Address:* Windcutter, Lee, North Devon, England.

RICHARDSON, Elliot Lee, A.B., LL.B.; American lawyer and government official; b. 20 July 1920, Boston, Mass.; s. of Dr. Edward P. Richardson and Clara Shattuck Richardson; m. Anne Francis Hazard 1952; two s. one d.; ed. Harvard Coll. and Harvard Law School; Law Clerk, Supreme Court Justice Felix Frankfurter 1948-49; Asst. Sec. (Legislation), U.S. Dept. of Health, Educ. and Welfare 1957-59, Acting Sec. April-July 1958; U.S. Attorney for Mass. 1959-61; Special Asst. to U.S. Attorney-Gen. 1961; Lieut.-Gov. of Mass. 1965-67; Attorney-Gen. of Mass. 1967-69; U.S. Under-Sec. of State 1969-70; Sec. of Health, Educ. and Welfare 1970-72, of Defense 1972-73; Attorney-Gen. of U.S.A. May-Oct. 1973, resgnd.; Dir. Study of Operations of State and Local Govt., Woodrow Wilson Int. Center 1974; Amb. to U.K. 1975-76; Sec. of Commerce 1976-77; Amb.-at-large and Special Rep. of U.S. Pres. to Law of the Sea Conf. 1977-80; Sr. partner Milbank, Tweed, Hadley and McCloy, Washington 1980-; Chair. UN Assen. of U.S.A., Council on Ocean Law, Hitachi Foundation; hon.

degrees from Springfield Coll., Mass. Coll. of Optometry, Emerson Coll., Edin. and Univ. of New Hampshire; Hon. Bencher, Middle Temple 1975; Dr. h.c. (Edinburgh) 1986; Bronze Star, Purple Heart with Oak Leaf Cluster, Jefferson Award 1974, Thomas Hart Benton Award 1976. *Publications:* The Creative Balance 1976 and numerous articles. *Address:* Milbank, Tweed, Hadley and McCloy, 1825 Eye Street, N.W., Washington, D.C. 20006 (Office); 1100 Crest Lane, McLean, Va. 22101, U.S.A. (Home).

RICHARDSON, Frank H., PH.D.; American business executive; b. 15 March 1933, White River; s. of Clare C. Richardson and Mary Harrison Richardson; m. Marilyn Jean Duff 1958; one s. one d.; ed. S. Dakota School of Mines and Tech.; joined Shell as engineer 1955; various assignments in Exploration and Productions Operations and Shell Devt. Co.; Div. Engineer, Houston 1967, Eng. Man., Western E&P Region Production Dept., Houston 1971, Production Man., W. Coast Div., L.A. 1972, Div. Production Man., W. Div., Houston 1974, Gen. Man. Production 1975; Liaison, Shell Oil 1977, Vice-Pres. Corporate Planning 1978, Sr. Vice-Pres., Admin. 1980, Exec. Vice-Pres., Admin. 1982, Exec. Vice-Pres., Products 1983, Pres. and C.E.O. 1988-. *Address:* P.O. Box 2463, Houston, Tex. 77252, U.S.A.

RICHARDSON, George Taylor, B.COMM. LL.D.; Canadian business executive; b. 22 Sept. 1924, Winnipeg, Manitoba; s. of late James A. and late Muriel (née Sprague) Richardson; brother of Hon. James Armstrong Richardson (q.v.); m. Tannis Maree Thorlakson 1948; two s. one d.; ed. Grosvenor and Ravenscourt Schools, Winnipeg, and Univ. of Manitoba; joined family firm of James Richardson and Sons, Ltd., Winnipeg 1946, Vice-Pres. 1954, Pres. 1966-; Chair. Richardson Greenshields of Canada; Dir. Pioneer Grain Co. Ltd., and other subsidiaries of James Richardson and Sons, Ltd.; Dir. INCO Ltd., United Canadian Shares Ltd., Canada Packers Inc.; mem. Winnipeg Commodity Exchange, Chicago Bd. of Trade and other major N. American commodity exchanges; Hon. LL.D. (Manitoba). *Leisure interests:* hunting, helicopter flying. *Address:* James Richardson and Sons Ltd., Richardson Building, 1 Lombard Place, Winnipeg, Manitoba, R3B 0Y1 (Office); Briarmeade, Lot 197, St. Mary's Road, St. Germain, Manitoba, R0G 2A0, Canada (Home). *Telephone:* 934-5811 (Office); 253-4221 (Home).

RICHARDSON, Gordon Dalyell, O.B.E., M.A., F.L.A.A.; Australian librarian (retd.); b. 23 Nov. 1917, N.S.W.; s. of L. E. D. and Wilga (née Dale) Richardson; m. 1st Yvonne L. Spence 1940 (died 1965); m. 2nd Ruth Robertson 1966; one s. two d.; ed. Sydney Univ.; Asst., Public Library, N.S.W. 1934-40; Infantry Officer, Australian Imperial Force 1940-45; Deputy Prin. Librarian, N.S.W. 1954-56; Mitchell Librarian 1958-73; Prin. Librarian and Sec. Library of N.S.W. 1959-73; Exec. mem. Library Bd. of N.S.W. 1959-73; Prin. Archivist, N.S.W. 1961-73; Vice-Pres. Library Assocn. of Australia 1964-66, Pres. 1967-68; Chair. Standing Cttee. Australian Advisory Council on Bibliographical Services 1970-72; Pres. Inverness Field Club 1987-; J. A. Ferguson Memorial Lecture 1975; Hon. Fellow Royal Australian Historical Soc. 1978. *Publications:* numerous papers on librarianship and archives. *Leisure interests:* gardening, family history. *Address:* 16 Eriskay Road, Inverness IV2 3LX, Scotland. *Telephone:* (0463) 221607.

RICHARDSON, Graham; Australian politician; b. 27 Sept. 1949, Kogarah, Sydney; m.; two c.; ed. Marist Brothers Coll., Kogarah; state organiser Australian Labor Party, N.S.W. 1971-76, Gen. Sec. 1976-83, State Campaign Dir. 1976-; Vice-Pres. Nat. Labor Party 1976, Del. to Nat. Conf. 1977-, convenor Nat. Industrial Platform Cttee.; Senator for N.S.W. March 1983; Minister for the Environment and the Arts July 1987-, for Sports, Tourism and Territories Jan. 1988-; Chair. Senate Estimates Cttee. 1986, Senate Select Cttee. on TV Equalisation; mem. several senate cttees. and three ministerial cttees. *Leisure interests:* golf, reading, skiing. *Address:* Department of the Arts, Sport, the Environment, Tourism and Territories, Silverton Centre, Moore Street, Canberra City, A.C.T. 2601, Australia.

RICHARDSON, Ian William, C.B.E., F.R.S.A.M.D.; British actor; b. 7 April 1934, Edinburgh; s. of John and Margaret (Drummond) Richardson; m. Maroussia Frank 1961; two s.; ed. Tynecastle, Edinburgh, Royal Scottish Acad. of Music and Drama, Glasgow Univ.; joined Birmingham Repertory Theatre Co. 1958, playing leading parts including Hamlet; joined R.S.C., Stratford and Aldwych 1960-75, parts including: Aragon (Merchant of Venice), Sir Andrew Aguecheek (Twelfth Night) 1960, Malatesti (Duchess of Malfi) 1960, Oberon (A Midsummer Night's Dream) 1961, Tranio (Taming of the Shrew) 1961, The Doctor (The Representative) 1963, Edmund (King Lear) 1964, Antipholus of Ephesus (Comedy of Errors) 1964, Herald and Marat (Marat/Sade) 1964, 1965, Ithamore (The Jew of Malta) 1964, Ford (Merry Wives of Windsor) 1964, 1966, 1969, Antipholus of Syracuse (Comedy of Errors) 1965, Chorus (Henry V) 1965, Vindice (The Revengers Tragedy) 1965, 1969, Coriolanus 1966, Bertram (All's Well That Ends Well) 1966, Malcolm (Macbeth) 1966, Cassius (Julius Caesar) 1968, Pericles 1969, Angelo (Measure for Measure) 1970, Buckingham (Richard III) 1970, Proteus (Two Gentlemen of Verona) 1970, Prospero (The Tempest) 1970, Richard II/Bolingbroke (Richard II) 1973, Berowne (Love's Labour's Lost) 1973, Iachimo (Cymbeline) 1974, Shalimov (Summer Folk) 1974, Ford (Merry Wives of Windsor) 1975, Richard III 1975, Tom Wrench (Trelawny), Sadler's Wells 1971-72, Henry Higgins (My Fair Lady), Broadway 1974; Jack Tanner (Man and Superman), Shaw Festival Theatre, Niagara-on-the Lake, Canada, The Government Inspector, Romeo and Juliet, Old Vic

1979, Lolita (New York) 1981; tours with R.S.C. to Europe, U.S.A., U.S.S.R., Japan; film roles include Capt. Fitzroy (The Darwin Adventure) 1971, Priest (Man of la Mancha) 1972, Marat/Sade, Hound of the Baskervilles 1982, The Sign of Four 1982, Whoops Apocalypse 1986, The Fourth Protocol 1986, Asking for Trouble 1986, Burning Secret 1988; TV appearances include Anthony Beavis (Eyeless in Gaza) 1971, Voyage Round My Father, Canterbury Tales, Danton's Death (BBC) 1977, Sorry (BBC) 1978, Ike—The War Years (ABC TV, U.S.A.) 1978, Tinker, Tailor, Soldier, Spy (BBC) 1979, Churchill and His Generals (BBC) 1979, Private Schulz (BBC) 1980, A Cotswold Death (BBC) 1981, The Woman in White (BBC serial) 1982, Underdog 1982, Salad Days 1982, Brass 1983, Mistral's Daughter, The Master of Ballantrae 1984, Six Centuries of Verse 1984, Nehru (Mountbatten—the Last Viceroy) 1985, Monsieur Quixote 1985, Star Quality 1985, Blunt 1986, Porterhouse Blue 1986, Devil's Disciple 1986, Troubles 1988, Pursuit (TV mini-series) 1988, The Winslow Boy 1989; James Bridie Gold Medal (R.S.A.M.D.); Tony Nomination, New York; Drama Desk Award, New York, Royal Television Soc. Award 1981/82. *Publication:* Preface to Cymbeline 1976, Preface to The Merry Wives of Windsor 1988. *Leisure interests:* archaeology, music, books, cinematography, travel. *Address:* c/o London Management, 235-241 Regent Street, London, W.1, England.

RICHARDSON, Peter Damian, PH.D., F.R.S., A.C.G.I., D.I.C.; British mechanical engineer; b. 22 Aug. 1935, West Wickham; s. of Reginald W. Richardson and Marie S. Richardson; ed. Imperial Coll. London; demonstrator Dept. of Mechanical Eng., Imperial Coll. 1955-58; went to U.S.A. 1958; Visiting Lecturer Brown Univ. 1958-59, Research Assoc. 1959-60, Asst. Prof. of Eng. 1960-65, Assoc. Prof. 1965-68, Prof. 1968-84, Prof. of Eng. and Physiology 1984-; Chair. Exec. Cttee. Center Biomedical Eng. 1972-; Consultant to Industry U.S. Govt. Agencies; recipient of Sr. Scientist Award Alexander Von Humboldt Foundation 1976; mem. American Soc. of Eng., American Soc. of Artificial Internal Organs, European Soc. of Artificial Organs, Biomedical Eng. Soc. *Publications:* contribs. to many professional journals. *Address:* Box D, Brown Univ., Providence, R.I. 02912, U.S.A.

RICHARDSON, Tony; British stage and film producer; b. 5 June 1928, Shipley, Yorks.; s. of Clarence Albert Richardson and Elsie Evans Campion; m. Vanessa Redgrave (q.v.) 1962 (divorced 1967); three d.; ed. Wadham Coll., Oxford; Artistic Dir. Royal Court Theatre 1956; Dir. Woodfall Film Productions Ltd. 1958-. *Plays:* produced or directed include: Look Back In Anger, The Chairs, Pericles and Othello (Stratford), The Entertainer, Luther, The Seagull, St. Joan of the Stockyards, Hamlet, Threepenny Opera, I Claudius, Arturo Ui, A Taste of Honey, Lady From the Sea, As You Like It (Los Angeles), Toyer. *Films:* (produced or directed): Look Back In Anger 1958, The Entertainer 1959, Saturday Night and Sunday Morning 1960, A Taste of Honey 1961, The Loneliness of the Long Distance Runner 1962, Tom Jones 1963, The Loved One 1964, Mademoiselle 1965, The Sailor from Gibraltar 1965, Red and Blue 1966, The Charge of the Light Brigade 1967, Laughter in the Dark 1968, Hamlet 1969, Ned Kelly 1969, A Delicate Balance 1973, Dead Cert 1973, Joseph Andrews 1977, Death in Canaan 1978, The Border 1981, The Hotel New Hampshire 1984, Penalty Phase (TV) 1986, Antony and Cleopatra 1987, Shadow on the Sun (TV) 1988. *Leisure interests:* tennis, travelling. *Address:* 1478 North Kings Road, Los Angeles, Calif. 90069, U.S.A.

RICHARDSON, William Chase, M.B.A., PH.D.; American university administrator; b. 11 May 1940, Passaic, N.J.; s. of Henry B. and Frances (Chase) Richardson; m. Nancy Freeland 1966; two d.; ed. Trinity Coll., Hartford, Conn. and Univ. of Chicago; Research Assoc., Instr. Univ. of Chicago 1967-70; Asst. Prof. Univ. of Washington, School of Public Health and Community Medicine 1971-73, Assoc. Prof. 1973-76, Prof. of Health Services 1976-84, Chair. Dept. of Health Services 1973-76, Graduate Dean, Vice-Provost for Research, 1981-84; Exec. Vice-Pres., Provost, and Prof. Dept. of Family and Community Medicine, Pennsylvania State Univ. 1984-; mem. Inst. of Medicine, N.A.S.; Fellow American Public Health Asscn.; Trinity Whitlock Award; Mary H. Bachmeyer Award (Univ. of Chicago); Kellogg Fellow. *Publications:* articles in professional journals. *Address:* 201 Old Main, Pennsylvania State University, University Park, Pa. 16802; 900 Outer Drive, State College, Pa. 16801, U.S.A. *Telephone:* (814) 865-2505; (814) 466-3153.

RICHARDSON OF DUNTISBOURNE, Baron (Life Peer), cr. 1983; **Gordon William Humphreys Richardson**, K.G., P.C., M.B.E.; British banker; b. 25 Nov. 1915, London; s. of John Robert and Nellie Richardson (née Humphreys); m. Margaret Alison Sheppard 1941; one s. one d.; ed. Nottingham High School, and Gonville and Caius Coll., Cambridge; S. Notts. Hussars Yeomanry 1939, Staff Coll., Camberley 1941; called to the Bar, Gray's Inn 1947; mem. Bar Council 1951-55; Industrial and Commercial Finance Corpn. Ltd. 1955-57; Dir. J. Henry Schroder and Co. 1957-62; Chair. J. Henry Schroder Wagg and Co. Ltd. 1962-72; Chair. Schroders Ltd. 1965-73, J. Henry Schroder Banking Corpn. (U.S.A.) 1967-69, Schroders AG (Switzerland) 1967, Schroders Inc. (U.S.A.) 1969-73; Dir. Bank of England 1967-73, Gov. 1973-83; Dir. BIS 1983-; Chair. Cttee. on Turnover Taxation 1963-64; Vice-Chair. Legal and Gen. Assurance Soc. Ltd. 1959-70, Lloyds Bank Ltd. 1962-66; Dir. Rolls-Royce (1971) Ltd. 1971-73, ICI 1972-73; mem. Int. Advisory Bd. Chemical Bank July 1986-, Chair. July

1986–; Chair. Morgan Stanley Int. Inc. 1986–; mem. Co. Law Amendment Cttee. 1959–62; mem. Court, London Univ. 1962–65; mem. Nat. Econ. Devt. Council 1971–73, 1980–83; Chair. Industrial Devt. Advisory Bd. 1972–73, "Group of Ten" 1982–83; Chair. "Group of 30" 1985–, Dir. Glyndebourne Arts Trust 1982–88, Royal Opera House 1983–88; Chair. Pilgrim Trust 1984–; Hon. Master of Bench of Gray's Inn 1973; one of H.M. Lieuts. for City of London 1974–; High Steward of Westminster 1985–; Deputy Lieut. for Glos. 1983–; Hon. Fellow, Wolfson Coll., and Gonville and Caius Coll., Cambridge Univ.; Hon. D.Sc. (The City Univ.) 1975, (Univ. of Aston in Birmingham) 1979, Hon. LL.D. (Cambridge) 1979, Hon. D.C.L. (East Anglia) 1984; Benjamin Franklin Medal (Royal Soc. of Arts) 1984. *Leisure interests:* reading, walking. *Address:* c/o Kingsley House, 1a Wimpole Street, London, W1M 7AA, England. *Telephone:* 01-709 3004.

RICHER, Yvon (François); Canadian librarian; b. 2 July 1943, Hull, Quebec; s. of François Richer and Yvette Villeneuve; m. Suzanne Naubert 1967; one s.; ed. Univs. of Ottawa and Toronto; Sr. Cataloguer Laval Univ. Library 1965–68, Head Catalogue Dept. 1968–71, Head Processing Div. 1971–75; Asst. Dir. (Systems) Catalogue Branch, Nat. Library of Canada 1975–76; Assoc. Univ. Librarian Univ. of Ottawa 1976–78, Univ. Chief Librarian 1978–. *Address:* Morriset Library, 65 Hastey Street, Ottawa, Ont., K1N 9AB (Office); 40 Eastpark Drive, Ottawa, Ont., K1B 3Z9, Canada (Home).

RICHLER, Mordecai; Canadian writer; b. 1931, Montreal; s. of Moses Isaac Richler and Lily Rosenberg; m. Florence Wood 1960; three s. two d.; ed. Montreal Hebrew Acad., Baron Byng High School and Sir George Williams Univ.; Canada Council Junior Arts Fellowship 1959, 1960; Fellowship in Creative Writing, Guggenheim Foundation, New York 1961, Canada Council, Sr. Arts Fellowship 1967, Paris Review Humour Prize 1968, Writer-in-residence, Sir George Williams Univ. 1968–69; Visiting Prof. Carleton Univ., Ottawa 1972–74; Editorial Bd., Book-of-the-Month Club, New York 1976; Canadian Gov.-Gen.'s Award for Fiction 1969, 1972, Golden Bear, Berlin Film Festival 1974. *Publications:* (novels) The Acrobats 1954, Son of a Smaller Hero 1955, A Choice of Enemies 1957, The Apprenticeship of Duddy Kravitz 1959, The Incomparable Atuk 1963, Cocksure 1968, St. Urbain's Horseman 1971, Images of Spain 1978, Joshua Then and Now 1980; (stories) The Street 1972; (film scripts) No Love for Johnnie, Life at the Top, The Apprenticeship of Duddy Kravitz, etc.; (TV plays) The Trouble with Benny, etc.; (essays) Hunting Tigers under Glass 1969, Shovelling Trouble 1973, Home Sweet Home 1984; Canadian Writing Today (editor) 1970; (for children) Jacob Two-Two Meets the Hooded Fang 1975, The Best of Modern Humour (Ed.) 1983, Jacob Two-Two and the Dinosaur 1987. *Leisure interest:* poker. *Address:* Appartment 80c, 1321 Sherbrooke Street West, Montreal, Quebec, Canada. *Telephone:* 514-288-2008.

RICHMOND, Sir John Christopher Blake, K.C.M.G.; British diplomatist; b. 7 Sept. 1909, Hitcham; s. of Ernest Tatham and Margaret Muriel Richmond (née Lubbock); m. Diana Margaret Lyle Galbraith 1939; two s. three d.; ed. Lancing Coll., Hertford Coll., Oxford, and Univ. Coll., London; on archaeological expeditions, Beisan, Jericho, Tel El Duweir, Ithaca 1931–36; H.M. Office of Works 1937–39; served in Middle East in Second World War 1939–46; Dept. of Antiquities, Palestine Govt. 1946–47; British Foreign Service, Oriental Sec., Baghdad 1947–51; Foreign Office 1951–53; Counsellor, Amman 1953–55; Consul-Gen. Houston, Texas 1955–58; British Property Comm., Cairo 1959; Political Agent, Kuwait 1959–61; Amb. to Kuwait 1961–63; Amb. to Sudan 1965–66; Lecturer in Modern Near East History, Durham Univ. 1966–74, retd; Supernumerary Fellow, St. Antony's Coll., Oxford 1963–64. *Publication:* Egypt 1798-1952 1977. *Leisure interest:* carpentry and joinery. *Address:* 21 The Avenue, Durham City, England. *Telephone:* 091 384 7257.

RICHMOND, Julius B., M.D.; American physician; b. 26 Sept. 1916, Chicago, Ill.; s. of Jacob Richmond and Anna (Dayno) Richmond; m. Rhee Chidekel 1937 (died 1985); two s. (one deceased); ed. Univ. of Illinois; Intern, Cook County Hosp. Chicago 1939–41; Resident, Municipal Contagious Diseases Hosp. Chicago 1941–42, 1946; mem. Faculty, Univ. of Ill. Medical School 1946–52, Prof. of Paediatrics 1950–53, Dir. Inst. of Juvenile Research 1952–53; Prof., Chair. Dept. of Paediatrics, Coll. of Medicine, State Univ. of New York at Syracuse 1953–65, Dean, Medical Faculty and Chair. Dept. of Paediatrics 1965–70; Prof. of Child Psychiatry and Human Devt., Prof., Chair. Dept. of Preventive and Social Medicine, Harvard Medical School 1971–77; Psychiatrist-in-Chief, Children's Hosp. Medical Center, Boston 1971–77; Dir. Judge Baker Guidance Center, Boston 1971–77; Asst. Sec. Health and Surgeon-Gen. Dept. of Health and Social Services 1977–81; Prof. of Health Policy Harvard Medical School and Harvard School of Public Health 1981–; Adviser on Child Health Policy, Children's Hosp. Medical Center 1981–; Dir. Div. of Health Policy, Research and Educ. 1983–; several awards and hon. degrees. *Publications:* seven books on paediatrics. *Address:* Harvard Medical School, Division of Health Policy, Research and Education, 641 Huntington Avenue, Room 316, Boston, Mass. 02115 (Office); 79 Beverly Road, Chestnut Hill, Mass. 02167, U.S.A. (Home). *Telephone:* (617) 732-1410 (Office); (617) 277-4830 (Home).

RICHMOND, Sir Mark Henry, Kt, SC.D., F.R.S.; British academic; b. 1 Feb. 1931, Sydney, Australia; s. of Harold Sylvester Richmond and Dorothy Plaistowe Tegg; m. Shirley Jean Townrow 1958; one s. two d.; ed. Epsom Coll., Clare Coll., Univ. of Cambridge; mem. scientific staff, Medical Research Council 1958–65; Reader in Molecular Biology, Univ. of Edinburgh 1965–68, Prof. of Bacteriology, Univ. of Bristol 1968–81, Vice-Chancellor and Prof. of Molecular Bacteriology, Victoria Univ. of Manchester 1981–; mem. Public Health Laboratory Service Bd. 1976–85; Chair. Cttee. of Vice-Chancellors and Prins. of the U.K. 1987–, Microbiological Food Safety Cttee. 1989–; mem. and fmr. mem. numerous bds.; Robert Koch Award 1977. *Publications:* numerous scientific articles. *Leisure interests:* gardening, hill walking, opera. *Address:* Vice-Chancellor's Office, University of Manchester, Oxford Road, Manchester, M13 9PL, England. *Telephone:* (061) 273 3333.

RICHTER, Burton, PH.D.; American physicist; b. 22 March 1931, Brooklyn, New York; s. of Abraham and Fannie (Pollack) Richter; m. Laurose Becker 1960; one s. one d.; ed. Mass. Inst. of Technology; Stanford Univ. 1956–, Research Assoc. in Physics, High Energy Physics Lab., Stanford Univ. 1956–59; mem. group building first electron storage ring and conducting a colliding beam experiment extending validity of quantum electrodynamics; Asst. Prof., Stanford Univ. 1959–63, Assoc. Prof. 1963–67; worked at Stanford Linear Accelerator Centre 1963–; set up a group which built a high energy electron positron machine (SPEAR) and has continued to develop new accelerator and detector techniques including most recently the SLAC linear collider; Full Prof., Stanford Univ. 1967–, Paul Pigott Prof. of Physical Science 1980; Tech. Dir. Stanford Linear Acceleration Center 1982–84, Dir. 1984–; sabbatical year at European Org. for Nuclear Research (CERN), Geneva 1975–76; Loeb Lecturer, Harvard Univ. 1974, De Shalit Lecturer, Weizmann Inst. 1975; N.A.S. 1976; E. O. Lawrence Award 1975, Nobel Prize for Physics (jointly with Samuel Ting, q.v.) for discovery of the heavy, long-lived "psi" particle 1976. *Publications:* over 300 articles in various scientific journals 1963–89. *Address:* Stanford Linear Accelerator Center, P.O. Box 4349, Stanford University, Stanford, Calif. 94305, U.S.A.

RICHTER, Gerhard; German artist; b. 9 Feb. 1932, Dresden; s. of Horst and Hildegard Richter; m. 1st Marianne (née Eufinger); m. 2nd Isa (née Genzken) 1982; one d.; ed. Staatliche Kunstakademien Dresden and Düsseldorf; Visiting Prof. Kunstakademie Hamburg 1967, Coll. of Art, Halifax, Canada 1978; Prof. Staatliche Kunstakademie Düsseldorf 1971–; mem. Akad. der Künste, Berlin; one-man shows in galleries and museums all over world 1964–; paintings in public collections in Berlin, Cologne, Basle, Paris, New York, Chicago, Toronto, London, etc.; Kunstpreis Junger Westen 1966, Arnold Bode Preis 1982, Kokoschka Prize (Austria) 1985. *Address:* Kaiserswerther Strasse 115, 4000 Düsseldorf 30, Federal Republic of Germany. *Telephone:* 0211-45 15 62.

RICHTER, Hans Werner; German writer; b. 12 Nov. 1908, Ostseebad Bansin; s. of Richard Richter and Anna Knuth; m. Anthonie Lesemann 1942; P.O.W. in U.S.A., Second World War; freelance writer 1945–; Founder, founder mem. Group 1947; Hon. Prof. (Berlin) 1979; Dr. h.c. (Karlsruhe) 1978; Fontane Prize 1950, Rene Schickele Prize 1952, Kulturpreis des DGB (German Fed. of Trade Unions) 1972, Kulturpreis des BDI (Fed. of German Industry) 1982, Grosser Literarischer Preis, Bayerische Akad. der Schönen Künste 1986, Literaturpreis, Bayerische Akademie der Künste 1986, Andreas Gryphius Preis 1986. *Publications include:* Die Geschlagenen 1949, Sie fielen 270aus Gottes Hand 1951, Spuren im Sand 1953, Du sollst nicht töten 1955, Linus Fleck oder der Verlust der Würde 1958, Almanach der Gruppe 1947 1947–1962 1962, Bestandsaufnahme—Eine deutsche Bilanz 1962, Walther Rathenau— Reden und Schriften 1964, Plaedoyer für eine neue Regierung oder Keine Alternative 1965, Menschen in freundlicher Umgebung 1965, Doda 1964, Karl Marx in Samarkand 1966, Blinder Alarm 1970, Rose weiss, Rose rot 1971, Briefe an einen jungen Sozialisten 1974, Die Flucht nach Abanon 1980, Die Stunde der falschen Triumphe 1981, Ein Julitag 1982, Im Etablissement der Schmetterlinge 1986, Reisen durch meine Zeit 1989. *Address:* Flossmannstrasse 13, 8000 Munich 60, Federal Republic of Germany. *Telephone:* 089/880486.

RICHTER, Horst-Eberhard, M.D., D.PHIL.; German professor of psychological medicine; b. 28 April 1923, Berlin; s. of Otto and Charlotte Richter; m. Bergrun Luckow 1947; one s. two d.; ed. Berlin Univ.; Dir. Advisory and Research Centre for Childhood Emotional Disturbances, Wedding Children's Hosp., Berlin 1952–62; Physician, Psychiatric Clinic, W. Berlin Free Univ. 1955–62; Dir. Berlin Psychoanalytic Inst. 1959–62; Chief of Dept. of Psychosomatic Medicine, Univ. of Giessen, Fed. Repub. of Germany 1962–, Dir. Centre for Psychosomatics 1973–; Research Prize, Swiss Soc. of Psychosomatic Medicine 1970; Theodor-Heuss Prize 1980. *Publications:* Eltern, Kind und Neurose 1963, Herzneurose (with D. Beckmann) 1969, Patient Familie 1970, Giessen-Test (with D. Beckmann) 1972, Die Gruppe 1972, Lernziel Solidarität 1974, The Family as Patient 1974, Flüchten oder Standhalten 1976, Der Gotteskomplex 1979, Alle redeten vom Frieden 1981, Sich der Krise Stellen 1981, Zur Psychologie des Friedens 1982, Die Chance des Gewissens 1986. *Address:* Friedrichstrasse 33, 6300 Giessen, Federal Republic of Germany. *Telephone:* 0641/702 2461.

RICHTER, Svyatoslav Theofilovich; Soviet pianist; b. 20 March 1915, Zhitomir, Ukraine; m. Nina Dorliak; ed. Moscow State Conservatoire; won First Prize at the Third U.S.S.R. Competition of Executant Musicians 1945; extensive tours all over the world; Order of Lenin, Hero of Socialist Labour 1975, Order of the October Revolution 1981 and other decorations.

Repertoire includes works by: Bach (cycle of 48 Preludes and Fugues), Beethoven, Schubert, Rachmaninov, Skryabin, Prokofiev, Ravel, Debussy, Mozart, Schumann, Rubinstein, Myaskovsky, Shostakovich, etc. *Address:* c/o Victor Hochhauser Ltd., 3 Oak Hill Way, London, N.W.3, England; Moscow State Philharmonic Society, 31 Ulitsa Gorkogo, Moscow, U.S.S.R.

RICHTER PRADA, Gen. Pedro; Peruvian politician and army officer; fmr. Chief of Staff of the Army, fmr. Minister of the Interior; Chair. Joint Chiefs of Staff Jan. 1978-81; Prime Minister, Minister of War and C.-in-C. of Armed Forces of Peru 1978-80; Pres. Mokichi Okada Foundation, Peru 1981-. *Address:* c/o Oficina del Primer Ministro, Lima, Peru.

RICK, Charles Madeira, Jr., PH.D.; American professor and geneticist; b. 30 April 1915, Reading, Pa.; s. of late Charles M. Rick and Miriam C. (Yeager) Rick; m. Martha Elizabeth Overholts 1938 (died 1983); one s. one d.; ed. Pennsylvania State and Harvard Univs.; Asst. Plant Breeder, W. Atlee Burpee Co., Lompoc, Calif. 1937-40; Instructor and Asst. Geneticist, Univ. of Calif. at Davis 1940, other academic ranks, then Prof. and Geneticist 1955-; mem. Genetics Study Section of Nat. Insts. of Health 1958-62; Co-ordinator Tomato Genetics Co-operative 1950-82; Visiting Lecturer, N. C. State Univ. 1956, Univ. de São Paulo, Brazil 1965, Faculty Research Lecturer, Univ. of Calif. 1961, Carnegie Visiting Prof., Univ. of Hawaii 1963; Visiting Scientist, Univ. of Puerto Rico 1968; Visiting Prof. Univ. de Rosario, Argentina 1980; mem. Panel in Genetic Biology, Nat. Science Foundation 1971-72; Nat. Plant Genetics Resources Board, U.S. Dept. of Agric. 1975-82; mem. N.A.S.; Guggenheim Fellow 1948, 1950; Centennial Lecturer Ontario Agricultural Coll., Univ. of Guelph 1974; Vaughan Research Award of American Soc. for Horticultural Science 1946, Campbell Award of A.A.A.S. 1959, M. A. Blake Award, American Soc. Horticultural Science 1974; Merit Award, Botanical Soc. of America 1976, Frank N. Meyer Memorial Medal, American Genetics Assen. 1982, Thomas Roland Medal, Mass. Horticultural Soc. 1983, Distinguished Econ. Botanist, Soc. for Econ. Botany 1987, Genetic and Plant Breeding Award, Nat. Council of Commercial Plant Breeders 1987. *Publications:* 150 papers in research journals; and 142 research notes in Reports of Tomato Genetics Co-operative. *Leisure interests:* gardening, photography. *Address:* Department of Vegetable Crops, University of California, Davis, Calif. 95616 (Office); 8 Parkside Drive, Davis, Calif. 95616, U.S.A. (Home). *Telephone:* (916) 752-1737 (Office); (916) 756-1387 (Home).

RICKETT, Sir Denis Hubert Fletcher, K.C.M.G., C.B.; British fmr. civil servant and banker; b. 27 July 1907, Sutton, Surrey; s. of late Hubert Cecil Rickett and of Mabel Fletcher; m. Ruth Pauline Armstrong 1946; two s. one d.; ed. Rugby School and Balliol Coll., Oxford; joined staff of Econ. Advisory Council 1931; Offices of the War Cabinet 1939; Pvt. Sec. to Minister of Production 1943-45; Asst. (for work on atomic energy) to Chancellor of the Exchequer 1945-47; transferred to Treasury 1947; Prin. Pvt. Sec. to the Prime Minister 1950-51; Minister (economic) to U.S.A. and Head of U.K. Treasury and Supply Del. 1951-54; Third Sec., Treasury 1954-60, Second Sec. 1960-68; Vice-Pres. IBRD 1968-74; Dir. Schroder Int. 1974-79, De La Rue Co. 1974-77; Adviser J. Henry Schroder Wagg & Co. 1974-79; Fellow of All Souls Coll., Oxford 1929-49. *Leisure interest:* music. *Address:* 9 The Close, Salisbury, Wilts., England.

RICKS, Christopher Bruce, F.B.A.; British professor of English literature; b. 18 Sept. 1933; s. of James Bruce Ricks and Gabrielle Roszak; m. 1st Kirsten Jensen 1956 (dissolved), two s. two d.; m. 2nd Judith Aronson 1977, one s. two d.; ed. King Alfred's School, Wantage, Oxon., Balliol Coll., Univ. of Oxford; 2nd Lieut. Green Howards 1952; Andrew Bradley Jr. Research Fellow Balliol Coll. Univ. of Oxford 1957, Fellow Worcester Coll. 1958-68; Prof. of English Bristol Univ. 1968-75; Fellow Christ's Coll., Prof. of English Univ. of Cambridge 1975-86, King Edward VII Prof. of English Literature 1982-86, Prof. of English, Boston Univ. 1986-; Visiting Prof. at Univs. of Berkeley and Stanford 1965, Smith Coll. 1967, Harvard Univ. 1971, Wesleyan 1974, Brandeis 1977, 1981, 1984, U.S.A.; Vice-Pres. Tennyson Soc.; George Orwell Memorial Prize 1979; Beefeater Club Prize for Literature 1980. *Publications:* Milton's Grand Style 1963, The Poems of Tennyson (Ed.) 1969, Tennyson 1972, Keats and Embarrassment 1974, The State of the Language (Ed. with Leonard Michaels) 1980, The Force of Poetry 1984, The New Oxford Book of Victorian Verse 1987 (Ed.), Collected Poems and Selected Prose of A. E. Housman (Ed.) 1988, T.S. Eliot and Prejudice 1988. *Address:* 39 Martin Street, Cambridge, Mass. 02138, U.S.A.; Lasborough Cottage, Lasborough Park, nr. Tetbury, Glos., England. *Telephone:* (617) 354-7887 (U.S.A.); (066 689) 252 (England).

RICO, Francisco, PH.D.; Spanish professor of medieval literature; b. 28 April 1942, Barcelona; s. of the late Cipriano Rico and of María Manrique; m. Victoria Camps 1966; three s.; ed. Univ. of Barcelona; Prof. of Medieval Literature, Autonomous Univ. of Barcelona 1971-; Visiting Prof. The Johns Hopkins Univ. 1966-67, Princeton Univ. 1981, Scuola Normale Superiore 1987; Gen. Dir. Centre of Spanish Letters, Ministry of Culture 1985-86; Ed. Book Series: Letras e idéas, Filologia, Letras hispanicas; mem. Royal Spanish Acad. 1986-. *Publications:* El pequeño mundo del hombre 1970, The Spanish Picaresque Novel and the Point of View 1970, Vida u obra de Petrarca (Vol. 1) 1974, Historia y crítica de la literatura espanola (8 vols.) 1980-84. *Leisure interest:* contemporary literature. *Address:* Santa Teresa 38, 08190 St. Cugat del Vallès, Barcelona; Apartado 1, Universidad

Autónoma de Barcelona, 08193 Bellaterra-Barcelona, Spain. *Telephone:* 674 07 08; 581 15 26.

RIDDICK, Frank Adams, Jr., M.D.; American physician; b. 14 June 1929, Memphis; s. of Frank Adams Riddick Sr. and Falba Crawford Riddick; m. Mary Belle Alston 1952; two s. one d.; ed. Vanderbilt and Washington Univs.; Staff Physician, Ochsner Clinic, New Orleans 1961-, Asst. Medical Dir. 1969-73, Assoc. Medical Dir. 1973-75, Medical Dir. 1975-, Trustee, Alton Ochsner Medical Foundation 1974-; Clinical Prof. of Medicine, Tulane Univ., New Orleans 1977-; Chair. Council on Medical Educ., American Medical Assen. 1982-84; Distinguished Physician Award, American Soc. of Internal Medicine 1980; Physician Exec. Award, American Coll. of Medical Group Admins. 1984. *Publications:* 56 scientific papers. *Leisure interest:* travel. *Address:* Ochsner Clinic, 1514 Jefferson Highway, New Orleans, La. 70121; 1923 Octavia Street, New Orleans, La. 70115, U.S.A. (Home) *Telephone:* (504) 838-4001 (Office); (504) 897-1737 (Home).

RIDGE, Anthony Hubert, B.A. (CANTAB.); British international civil servant; b. 5 Oct. 1913, London; s. of Timothy L. and Magdalen Ridge (née Hernig); m. Marjory J. Sage 1938; three s. one d.; ed. Christ's Hospital, Jesus Coll., Cambridge; held posts in GPO 1937-63; Deputy Dir.-Gen. Int. Bureau, Universal Postal Union 1964-73, Dir.-Gen. 1973-74. *Leisure interests:* music, gardening, walking, "popular" science, transport systems. *Address:* Staple, Postling, Hythe, Kent, CT21 4HA, England.

RIDGWAY, General Matthew B., D.S.C. (with O.L.C.), D.S.M. (with 3rd O.L.C.); American army officer (retd.); b. 3 March 1895, Fort Monroe, Va.; s. of Thomas Ridgway and Ruth Starbuck Bunker; m. Mary Princess Anthony 1947; one s. (deceased); ed. U.S. Military Acad.; commissioned Lieut. U.S. Army 1917 and advanced through grades to Lieut.-Gen. 1945, Gen. 1951; technical adviser to Gov.-Gen. of Philippines 1932-33; Asst. Chief of Staff 6th Corps Area 1935-36, Deputy Chief of Staff Second Army 1936; Asst. Chief of Staff Fourth Army 1937-39; accompanied Gen. Marshall to Brazil 1939; War Plans Div., War Dept. Gen. Staff 1939-42; Asst. Div. Commdr. 82nd Infantry Div. 1942, Div. Commdr. 1942; Commdg. Gen. 82nd Airborne Div., Sicily, Italy, Normandy 1942-44; Commdr. 18th Airborne Corps, Belgium, France, Germany 1944-45; Commdr. Luzon Area 1945; Commdr. Mediterranean Theatre of Operations and Deputy Supreme Allied Commdr. Mediterranean Sept. 1945-Jan. 1946; Sr. U.S. Army mem. Mil. Staff Cttee., UN 1946-48; Chair. Inter-American Defence Bd. 1946-48; C.-in-C. Caribbean Commd. 1948-49; Deputy Army Chief of Staff for Admin. 1949-50; Commdr. Eighth Army in Korea 1950-51; Commdr. UN Command in Far East, C.-in-C. Far East and Supreme Commdr. Allied Powers in Japan 1951-52; Supreme Allied Commdr., Europe 1952-53; Chief of Staff U.S. Army 1953-55; Chair. Bd. of Trustees, Mellon Inst. of Industrial Research 1955-60; Presidential Medal of Freedom 1986. *Publications:* Soldier 1956, The Korean War 1967. *Leisure interests:* hunting, fishing, gardening, travel. *Address:* 918 West Waldheim Road, Fox Chapel, Pittsburgh, Pa. 15215, U.S.A. (Home). *Telephone:* (412) 781-4833.

RIDING, Laura (Jackson); American writer; b. 16 Jan. 1901, New York City; d. of Nathaniel S. and Sarah Reichenthal; legally adopted surname Riding 1927; m. Schuyler B. Jackson 1941 (died 1968); ed. Cornell Univ.; mem. Fugitives (Southern U.S. poets) in early career; writing activities long centred in poetry; expanded linguistic norm of poems, affecting style of many other poets; lived abroad 1926-39, seeking in varied writing and work with others, including printing, publishing (partner in Seizin Press), to outline ground of moral unity for modern sensibility; renounced poetry and literary affiliations on return to U.S.A., seeing language itself as essential moral meeting-ground; long work with husband on language-study issued in book part-finished when he died, completed alone under a Guggenheim fellowship; Mark Rothko Appreciation Award 1971, Nat. Endowment for Arts Fellowship 1979. *Publications include:* The Close Chaplet (first of 9 vols. of poems) 1926, Survey of Modernist Poetry 1927, Contemporaries and Snobs 1928, Anarchism is Not Enough 1928, Experts are Puzzled 1930, Progress of Stories 1935, Essays, Critical Notes, Poems, Epilogue 1935-37, A Trojan Ending 1937, 1984 (Spanish ed. 1986), Collected Poems 1938, Lives of Wives 1939, 1988; edited Epilogue 1935-37, The World and Ourselves 1938; later publs., contrib. to Chelsea 1962-, Civiltà delle Macchine 1963, Art and Literature 1965, The Private Library 1972, 1973, Denver Quarterly 1974-, Antaeus 1974-, Univ. of Toronto Quarterly 1977, Poetry Nation Review 1979-, Massachusetts Review 1980, 1983, Grand Street 1982, 1983, Glasgow Magazine 1983, Sulfur 1984-; Selected Poems: In Five Sets U.K. 1970, U.S.A. 1973; The Telling (expanded book form) U.K. 1972, U.S.A. 1973; contribs. in anthology Revolution of the Word 1975; Rational Meaning: a New Foundation for the Definition of Words (delayed publ.); It Has Taken Long, Selected Writings (volume-length, Chelsea) 1977; Collected Poems U.K., U.S.A. 1980, Description of Life (story) 1980, Progress of Stories (enlarged) U.K., U.S.A. 1982, Communications of Broad Reference 1983. *Address:* Box 35, Wabasso, Fla. 32970, U.S.A.

RIDLEY, Rt. Hon. Nicholas; P.C., M.P.; British politician; b. 17 Feb. 1929, Newcastle upon Tyne; s. of 3rd Viscount Ridley and Viscountess Ridley; m. 1st Hon. Clayre Campbell (dissolved 1972), 2nd Judy Kendall 1979; three d.; ed. Eton Coll. and Balliol Coll., Oxford; Brims & Co., Ltd. (civil engineering contractors), Newcastle upon Tyne 1950-59, Dir. 1954-70; Dir. Heenan Group Ltd. 1961-68, Ansonia Finance 1973-79, Marshall Andrew

1975–79; M.P. for Cirencester and Tewkesbury 1959–; Parl. Pvt. Sec. to Minister of Educ. 1962–64; Parl. Sec. to Ministry of Tech. June–Oct. 1970; Parl. Under-Sec. of State, Dept. of Trade and Industry 1970–72; Minister of State, FCO 1979–81; Financial Sec. to the Treasury 1981–83; Sec. of State for Transport 1983–86, for the Environment 1986–; del. to Council of Europe and WEU 1962–66; mem. Royal Comm. on Historical Manuscripts 1967–69; Conservative. *Leisure interests:* painting, fishing, gardening. *Address:* Old Rectory, Naunton, Cheltenham, Glos., England.

RIEBER-MOHN, Georg Frederik; Norwegian lawyer; b. 13 Aug. 1945, Lillehammer; m. Kari Nergaard 1967; two s. one d.; ed. Univ. of Oslo; Deputy Gov. Western Prison Dist. 1971–74; Asst. Judge, Magistrates' Court of Stavanger 1975–76; Dist. Attorney (Regional Head of Prosecutions) 1976–80; Gen. Dir. Prison and Probation Service 1980–85; Judge, Appeal Court 1985–86; Gen. Dir. of Public Prosecutions 1986–. *Leisure interest:* salmon fishing. *Address:* Karl Johans Gate 12, Postbox 8002 DEP, 0030 Oslo 1 (Office); Konglefaret 51, 1343 Eiksmarka, Norway (Home). *Telephone:* 02 330270 (Office); 02 2409 66 (Home).

RIEDLBAUCH, Vaclav; Czechoslovak composer; m.; two c.; ed. Junior Music Acad. and the Acad. of Arts, Prague; Sr. Lecturer in Composition, Acad. of Arts; composed Macbeth as the basis of an eighty minute ballet, a quartet for four saxophones (chamber music), and The Vision (a symphonic poem) *Address:* Academy of Arts, 116 65 Prague, Smetanovo nábř. 2, Czechoslovakia.

RIEFENSTAHL, Leni; German film director, photographer and writer; b. 22 Aug. 1902; d. of Alfred and Bertha Riefenstahl; ed. Kunstakademie, Berlin; solo dancer 1920s; acted in films 1920s and 1930s; directed first film 1932; Silver Medal Venice Biennale (for The Blue Light) 1932, Gold Medal 1937, 1938. *Films include:* The White Hell of Pitz Palu (actor) 1929, The Blue Light (actor/dir.) 1932, S.O.S. Iceberg (actor) 1933, Triumph of the Will (dir., documentary of Nuremberg Rally) 1934, Olympische Spiele (dir., documentary of Berlin Olympic Games) 1936, Tiefland 1945. *Publications:* The Last of the Nuba 1974, People of the Kau 1976, Coral Gardens 1978, Mein Afrika (photographs) 1982. *Address:* Tengstrasse 20, 8000 München 40, Federal Republic of Germany. *Telephone:* (089) 278 0165.

RIEGLE, Donald W., Jr., M.B.A.; American politician; b. 4 Feb. 1938, Flint, Mich.; s. of Donald Wayne and Dorothy (née Fitchett) Riegle; m. 3rd Lori L. Hansen 1978; four c.; ed. Flint Cen. High School, Flint Jr. Coll., Western Michigan Univ., Univ. of Michigan, Michigan State Univ., Harvard; Sr. Pricing Analyst, IBM Corpn. 1961–64; mem. faculty, Mich. State Univ., Boston Univ., Harvard Univ., Univ. of Southern Calif.; mem. U.S. House of Reps. 1967–76, mem. House Cttee. on Appropriations 1967–73; changed party affiliation from Republican to Democrat Feb. 1973; mem. Special Task Force of House of Reps. on Energy and Econ. 1975–; later mem. House Cttee. on Int. Relations, Sub-Cttee. on Int. Political and Mil. Affairs, Sub-Cttee. on Int. Security and Scientific Affairs; U.S. Senator from Mich. 1977–; Hon. LL.D. (Defiance Coll., Ohio, St. Benedict's Coll., Kan., Schoolcraft Coll. Mich.). *Publication:* O Congress (with T. Armbrister) 1972. *Address:* 105 Dirksen Senate Office Building, Capitol Hill, Washington, D.C. 20510, U.S.A.

RIEGLER, Josef: Austrian politician; Minister of Agric. and Forestry Jan. 1987–; Vice-Chancellor April 1989–; Leader Österreichische Volkspartei (Austrian People's Party) April 1989–. *Address:* Österreichische Volkspartei, Karntnerstrasse 51, 1010 Vienna, Austria.

RIEGNER, Gerhart M.; Swiss administrator; b. 12 Sept. 1911, Berlin; ed. Univs. of Berlin, Freiburg, Heidelberg, Paris, Graduate Inst. of Int. Studies, Geneva, and Acad. for int. Law, The Hague; Legal Sec. World Jewish Congress 1936–39, Dir. Geneva Office 1939–48, mem. World Exec. 1948–60, Dir. of Coordination 1960–65, Sec.-Gen. 1965–83, Co-Chair. Governing Bd. 1983–; Int. Chair. World Univ. Service 1949–55; Pres. Conf. of non-Govt. Orgs. at UN 1953–55, Conf. of non-Govt Orgs. in Consultative Status with UNESCO 1956–58. *Publications:* articles on legal matters, Jewish affairs and Christian-Jewish relations. *Address:* World Jewish Congress, 1 rue Varembé, Geneva (Office); 25 Avenue Wendt, Geneva, Switzerland (Home).

RIENÄCKER, Günther, DR.PHIL.; German chemist; b. 13 May 1904, Bremen; s. of Franz and Frieda (née Kröger) Rienäcker; m. Lotte Christiansen 1931; two s. one d.; ed. Univ. of Munich; Prof. Univ. of Göttingen 1936–42; Prof. and Dir. Inst. of Inorganic Chem., Univ. of Rostock 1942–54; Prof. of Inorganic Chem., Univ. of Berlin 1954–, Dir. 1st Chemical Inst. 1954–62; mem. Akad. der Wissenschaften der D.D.R., Dir. of its Inst. for Research into Catalysts 1951–69, Gen. Sec. 1957–68; mem. Exec. Council, Kulturbund der D.D.R., Deutsche Akad. der Naturforscher Leopoldina; Hon. mem. Hungarian Acad. of Sciences; Foreign mem. Acad. of Sciences, U.S.S.R.; mem. Inst. d'Egypte, Cairo; Dr. Rer. Nat. h.c. (Rostock) 1969, (Leuna-Merseburg) 1974, (Humboldt Univ., Berlin) 1984; Nat. Prize 1955, many other prizes and awards; Vaterländischer Verdienstorden in Gold; Ed. Zeitschrift anorganische allgemeine Chemie. *Leisure interests:* chemistry, music. *Address:* 1162 Berlin-Friedrichshagen, Werlsee Strasse 39A, German Democratic Republic. *Telephone:* 4829741.

RIESENHUBER, Heinz Friedrich, DR.RER.NAT.; German politician; b. 1 Dec. 1935, Frankfurt; s. of Karl and Elisabeth (née Birkner) Riesenhuber;

m. Beatrix Walter 1968; two s. two d.; ed. Gymnasium in Frankfurt and Univs. of Frankfurt and Munich; with Erzgesellschaft mbH, c/o Metallgesellschaft, Frankfurt 1966–71; Tech. Man. Synthomer-Chemie GmbH, Frankfurt 1971–82; Chair. Frankfurt Branch 1973–78; mem. Bundestag 1976–; Fed. Minister for Research and Technology 1982–. *Publications:* articles in specialist journals. *Leisure interest:* reading. *Address:* Bundesministerium für Forschung und Technologie Heinemannstrasse 2, 5300 Bonn 2, Federal Republic of Germany. *Telephone:* 0228 59-3010.

RIESMAN, David, A.B., LL.B., LL.D., D.LIT., ED.D.; American social scientist; b. 1909, Philadelphia, Pa.; s. of Dr. David and Eleanor L. (Fleisher) Riesman; m. Evelyn Hastings Thompson 1936; two s. two d.; ed. Harvard Univ. and Harvard Law School; Law clerk to Mr. Justice Brandeis, Supreme Court 1935–36; Practised law 1936–37; Prof. of Law, Buffalo Univ. 1937–41; Deputy Asst. Dist. Attorney, N.Y. County 1942–43; Asst. Treas. Sperry Gyroscope Co. 1943–46; Prof. Social Sciences, Chicago Univ. 1946–58; Prof. Social Sciences, Harvard 1958–81; mem. Pres.'s Task Force on Educ. 1965–68, Carnegie Comm. on Future of Higher Educ. 1967–75; Fellow, Center for Advanced Study in the Behavioral Sciences, Stanford 1968–69; mem. Inst. for Advanced Study, Princeton 1971–72; on bd. of eds., Sociology of Educ., Tech. and Culture, Universities Quarterly; Sponsor, Fed. of American Scientists; numerous hon. degrees. *Publications:* The Lonely Crowd 1950, Faces in the Crowd 1952, Thorstein Veblen: A Critical Interpretation 1953, Individualism Reconsidered 1954, Constraint and Variety in American Education 1956, Abundance for what? 1964, The Academic Revolution (with Christopher Jencks) 1968, Academic Values and Mass Education (with Joseph Gusfield and Zelda Gamson) 1970, Education and Politics at Harvard (with Seymour M. Lipset) 1975, The Perpetual Dream—Experiment and Reform in the American College (with G. Grant) 1978, On Competence: A Critical Analysis of Competence-Based Reforms in Higher Education (with G. Grant and others) 1979, On Higher Education: The Academic Enterprise in an Era of Rising Student Consumerism 1980. *Address:* 49 Linnaean Street, Cambridge, Mass. 02138, U.S.A. (Home).

RIFA'I, Zaid al-, M.A.; Jordanian diplomatist; b. 27 Nov. 1936, Amman; s. of Samir Pasha al-Rifa'i and Alia Shukry; m. Muna Talhouni 1965; one s. one d.; ed. Victoria Coll., Cairo, and Harvard and Columbia Univs.; joined diplomatic service 1957; Attaché, Ministry of Foreign Affairs 1957; Sec., Embassy, Cairo 1957; Sec. Jordanian Del. to UN 1957–59; Chief of Royal Protocol 1965; Sec.-Gen. of Royal Court and Private Sec. to H.M. King Hussein 1967; Chief of Royal Court 1969; Amb. to U.K. 1970–72; Political Adviser to King Hussein 1972–73; Prime Minister of Jordan 1973–76, 1985–89; Minister for Foreign Affairs and Defence 1973–76, of Defence 1985–89; Medal of Independence, Order of the Jordanian Star, Order of the Renaissance (Egypt). *Leisure interests:* music, reading, bridge, water-skiing, sailing, tennis. *Address:* Jabal Amman, Amman, Jordan. *Telephone:* 44565.

RIFBJERG, Klaus; Danish author; b. 15 Dec. 1931, Copenhagen; s. of Thorvald Rifbjerg and Lilly Nielsen; m. Inge Merete Gerner 1955; one s. two d.; ed. Princeton Univ., U.S.A., and Univ. of Copenhagen; Literary critic, Information 1955–57, Politiken 1959–65 (Copenhagen daily newspapers); Literary Dir. Gyldendal Publrs. 1984–; Prof. of Aesthetics, Lærerhøjskole, Copenhagen 1986; Aarstrup Medal 1964, Danish Critics' Award 1965, Grant of Honour from the Danish Dramatists 1966, Danish Acad. Award 1966, Golden Laurels 1967, Soren Gyldenal Award 1969, Nordic Council Award 1970, Grant of Honour from the Danish Writers' Guild 1973, PH Prize 1979, Holberg Medal 1979, H.C. Andersen Prize 1988. *Publications:* novels: Den Kroniske Uskyld 1958, Operaelsken 1966, Arkivet 1967, Lonni Og Karl 1968, Anna (Jeg) Anna 1970, Marts 1970 1970, Leif den Lykkelige JR. 1971, Til Spanien 1971, Lena Jorgensen, Klintevej 4, 2650 Hvidovre 1971, Brevet til Gerda 1972, R.R. 1972, Spinatfuglene 1973, Dilettanterne 1973, Du skal ikke vaere ked af det Amalia 1974, En hugorm i solen 1974, Vejen ad hvilken 1975, Tak for turen 1975, Kiks 1976, Tango 1978, Dobbeltgœnger 1978, Drengene 1978, Joker 1979, Voksdugshjertet 1979, Det sorte hul 1980, Detsorte kul 1980, Falsk Forår 1984, Engel 1987; short stories: Og Andre Historier 1964, Rejsende 1969, Den Syende Jomfru 1972, Sommer 1974; non-fiction: I Medgang Og Modgang 1970; plays: Gris Pa Gaflen 1962, Hva's Skal Vi Lave 1963, Udviklinger 1965, Hvad en Mand Har Brug For 1966, Voks 1968, Ar 1970, Narrene 1971, Svaret Blaeser i Vinden 1971, Det Korte af det lange 1976, Twist 1976, Et bortvendt ansigt 1977, Deres majestæt! 1977; poems: Livsfrisen 1979 and several other vols. of poetry; twenty radio plays. *Address:* c/o Gyldendal Publishers, 3 Klareboderne, 1001 Copenhagen (Office); Kristianiagade 22, 3 Sal Th. DK-2100, Copenhagen, Denmark (Home).

RIFKIN, Joshua, B.S., M.F.A.; American musician; b. 22 April 1944, New York; s. of Harry H. Rifkin and Dorothy Helsh; one d.; ed. Juilliard School of Music and New York, Göttingen and Princeton Univs.; Musical Adviser, Assoc. Dir. Nonesuch Records 1966–75; Asst., Assoc. Prof. of Music, Brandeis Univ. 1970–82; Dir. The Bach Ensemble 1978–; Visiting Prof. Yale Univ. 1982–83, Princeton Univ. 1988, Stanford Univ. 1989; Fellow, Inst. for Advanced Study, Berlin 1984–86; made several recordings of

Rags by Scott Joplin, Bach's Mass in B minor 1982, Bach's Magnificat 1983, numerous Bach cantatas 1986-; Gramophone Award 1983. *Publications:* articles in musical journals and the New Grove Dictionary of Music and Musicians. *Leisure interests:* food and wine, cinema, daughter. *Address:* 61 Dana Street, Cambridge, Mass. 02138, U.S.A. *Telephone:* (617) 876-5987.

RIFKIND, Rt. Hon. Malcolm Leslie, P.C., Q.C., M.P., LL.B., M.SC.; British politician; b. 21 June 1946; s. of E. Rifkind; m. Edith Steinberg 1970; one s. one d.; ed. George Watson's Coll. and Univ. of Edinburgh; lecturer, Univ. of Rhodesia 1967-68; called to Scottish Bar 1970; mem. Parl. for Edinburgh, Pentlands 1974-; Parl. Under-Sec. of State, Scottish Office 1979-82, FCO 1982-83; Minister of State, FCO 1983-86; Sec. of State for Scotland Jan. 1986-; Conservative. *Address:* House of Commons, London, S.W.1, England.

RIGBY, Jean Prescott, A.R.A.M., A.R.C.M.; British opera singer; b. 22 Dec. 1954, Fleetwood, Lancs.; d. of Thomas Boulton Rigby and Margaret Annie Rigby; ed. Elmslie Girls' School, Blackpool, Birmingham School of Music, R.A.M. and Opera Studio; studies piano and viola at Birmingham then singing at R.A.M. with Patricia Clark, with whom she continues to study; Prin. Mezzo-Soprano, English Nat. Opera 1982-, roles have included Mercedes, Marina, Lucretia and Dorabella, future roles include Carmen 1987; début Covent Garden 1983, roles have included Tebaldo, Mercedes and Hippolyta, future plans include second Lady, Magic Flute and Olga, Eugene Onegin 1988; Glyndebourne début 1984, sang Nancy in Albert Herring and Mercedes in Carmen 1985; TV appearances in Così fan Tutte and film on Handel; also sings concert repertoire and has made recordings with Giuseppe Sinopoli; numerous prizes and scholarships at R.A.M. including Countess of Munster, Leverhulme, Peter Stuyvesant, R.S.A. scholarships and the Prin.'s Prize; Royal Overseas League and Young Artists' Competition 1981. *Leisure interests:* theatre, sport, British heritage. *Address:* c/o English National Opera, London Coliseum, St. Martin's Lane, London, WC2N 4ES, England.

RIGG, (Enid) Diana (Elizabeth), C.B.E.; British actress; b. 20 July 1938, Doncaster, Yorks.; d. of Louis and Beryl (Helliwell) Rigg; m. 1st Menahem Gueffen 1973 (divorced 1976); m. 2nd Archibald Hugh Stirling 1982, one d.; ed. Fulneck Girls' School, Pudsey, Yorks, R.A.D.A.; Professional debut as Natella Abashwilli (The Caucasian Chalk Circle), York Festival 1957; repertory Chesterfield and Scarborough 1958; Dir. United British Artists 1982-; mem. Arts Council Cttee. 1986; Assoc. Artist of R.S.C., Stratford and Aldwych 1959-64. *Roles there included:* Andromache (Troilus and Cressida), 2nd Ondine, Violanta and Princess Bertha (Ondine), Philippe Trincant (The Devils), Gwendolen (Becket), Bianca (The Taming of the Shrew), Madame de Tourvel (The Art of Seduction), Helena (A Midsummer Night's Dream), Adriana (Comedy of Errors), Cordelia (King Lear), Nurse Monika Stettler (The Physicists), Lady Macduff (Macbeth); toured Eastern Europe, U.S.S.R., U.S.A. in King Lear, Comedy of Errors 1964; Viola (Twelfth Night), Stratford 1966; mem. Nat. Theatre 1972. *Roles there included:* Dottie Moore (Jumpers) 1972, Hippolita ('Tis Pity She's A Whore) 1972, Lady Macbeth (Macbeth) 1972, Célimène (The Misanthrope), Washington and New York 1973, 1975, The Governor's Wife (Phaedra Britannica) 1975, rejoined Nat. Theatre at the Lyttelton to play Ilona in The Guardsman 1978. *Other stage appearances include:* Heloise (Abelard and Heloise) London 1970, Los Angeles, New York 1971, Eliza Doolittle (Pygmalion) London 1974, Ruth Carson (Night and Day) London 1978, Colette, Seattle and Denver 1982, Hesione Hushabye (Heartbreak House) London 1983, Rita in Little Eyolf, London 1985, Cleopatra in Antony and Cleopatra, Chichester 1985, Wildfire, London 1986, Follies 1987. *TV appearances include:* Sentimental Agent 1963, A Comedy of Errors 1964, The Hothouse 1964, Emma Peel (The Avengers) 1965-67, Women Beware Women 1965, Married Alive 1970, Diana (U.S. series) 1973, In This House of Brede 1975, Three Piece Suite 1977, Clytemnestra in The Serpent Son 1979, The Marquise 1980, Hedda Gabler 1981, Rita Allmers in Little Eyolf 1982, Reagan in King Lear 1983, Witness for the Prosecution 1983, Bleak House 1984, A Hazard of Hearts 1987, Worst Witch 1987, Unexplained Laughter 1989. *Films include:* A Midsummer Night's Dream 1969, The Assassination Bureau 1969, On Her Majesty's Secret Service 1969, Julius Caesar 1970, The Hospital 1971, Theatre of Blood 1973, A Little Night Music 1977, The Great Muppet Caper 1981, Evil under the Sun 1982; Plays and Players Award for Best Actress (Phaedra Britannica 1975, Night and Day 1978). *Publication:* No Turn Unstoned 1982. *Leisure interests:* reading, writing, cooking, travel. *Address:* c/o London Management, 235 Regent Street, London, W1A 2JT, England.

RIGGS, Lorrin Andrews, A.B., M.A., PH.D.; American psychologist; b. 11 June 1912, Harput, Turkey; s. of Ernest Wilson and Alice (Shepard) Riggs; m. Doris Robinson 1937; two s.; ed. Dartmouth Coll. and Clark Univ.; N.R.C. Fellow, Biological Sciences, Univ. of Pa. 1936-37; Instructor Univ. of Vermont 1937-38, 1939-41; with Brown Univ. 1938-39, 1941-, Research Assoc., Research Psychologist Nat. Defence Research Cttee., Asst. Prof., Assoc. Prof. 1938-51, Prof. of Psychology 1951-; L. Herbert Ballou Foundation Prof. of Psychology 1960-68, Edgar J. Marston Univ. Prof. of Psychology 1968-77, Prof. Emer. 1977-; Guggenheim Fellow, Univ. of Cambridge 1971-72; mem. American Psychological Assen. (Div. Pres. 1962-63), Eastern Psychological Assen. (Pres. 1975-76), A.A.A.S. (Chair.

and Vice-Pres. Section 1 1964), Optical Soc. of America, N.A.S., American Physiological Soc., Int. Brain Research Org., Soc. for Neuroscience, Soc. of Experimental Psychologists, American Acad. of Arts and Sciences, Assen. for Research in Vision and Ophthalmology (Pres. 1977); Howard Crosby Warren Medal, Soc. of Experimental Psychologists 1957, Jonas S. Friedenwald Award, Assen. for Research in Ophthalmology 1966, Edgar D. Tillyer Award, Optical Soc. of America 1969, Charles F. Prentice Award, American Acad. of Optometry 1973, Distinguished Scientific Contribution Award, American Psychological Assen. 1974, Kenneth Craik Award, Cambridge Univ. 1979, Frederick Ives Medal, Optical Soc. of America 1982. *Publications:* Numerous scientific articles on vision and physiological psychology. *Address:* Hunter Laboratory of Psychology, Brown University, Providence, R.I. 02912, U.S.A.

RIGHI-LAMBERTINI, H.E. Cardinal Egano; Italian ecclesiastic; b. 22 Feb. 1906, Casalecchio di Reno, Bologna; ordained priest 1929; Titular Archbishop of Doclea 1960-79; cr. Cardinal 1979; mem. Council for the Public Affairs of the Church, Sacred Congregation for the Bishops, Secretariat for Non-Christians; Hon. Pres. Cen. Comm. for Sacred Art in Italy; Deacon of S. Giovanni Bosco in Via Tuscolana. *Address:* 00193 Roma, Piazza della Città Leonina 9, Italy. *Telephone:* 65.94.63.

RIGOUT, Marcel; French politician; b. 10 May 1928, Verneuil-sur-Vienne; s. of Joseph Rigout and Marie Lagarde; lathe turner; Political Ed. L'Echo du Centre; mem. Cen. Cttee., French Communist Party 1961-; Deputy (Haute-Vienne) to Nat. Ass. 1967-68, 1973-81, 1986-; Vice-Chair. Communist group in Nat. Ass.; elected Gen. Councillor, Pierre-Buffière 1971, re-elected 1976, 1982; Vice-Pres. Gen. Council of Haute-Vienne; Minister of Vocational Training 1981-84. *Publication:* L'Autre chance 1983. *Address:* Assemblée nationale, 75355 Paris; 87260 Saint-Genest-sur-Roselle, France. (Home).

RIIS, Povl, M.D.; Danish physician and professor of medicine; b. 28 Dec. 1925, Copenhagen; s. of Lars Otto and Eva Elisabeth (née Erdmann) Riis; m. Else Harne 1954; one s. three d.; ed. Univ. of Copenhagen; Specialist in internal medicine 1960, gastroenterology 1963; Head of Medical Dept. B, Gentofte Univ. Hosp. 1963-76; Prof. of Internal Medicine, Univ. of Copenhagen 1974-; Head of Gastroenterological Dept. C, Herlev Univ. Hosp. 1976-; Asst. Ed. Journal of the Danish Medical Assen. 1957-67, Chief Ed. 1967-; Ed. Bibliothek for Laeger 1965-, Danish Medical Bulletin 1968-; mem. Bd., Danish Soc. for Internal Medicine 1962-67, Danish Anti-Cancer League 1970-75, Danish Soc. for Theoretical and Applied Therapy 1972-77, Int. Union against Cancer 1978-86; mem. Danish Medical Research Council 1968-74, Chair. 1972-74; mem. Danish Science Advisory Bd. 1972-74, Co-Chair. 1974; mem. Nordic Scientific Co-ordination Cttee. for Medicine 1968-72, Chair. 1970-72; Chair. Nordic Medical Publs. Cttee. 1970-72; Vice-Pres. European Science Foundation (ESF) 1974-77, mem. Exec. Council 1977-; Chair. ESF Cttee. on Genetic Manipulation 1975-77, Chair. ESF Liaison Cttee. on General Manipulation 1977-; mem. Council for Int. Org. of Medical Sciences Advisory Cttee. 1977; mem. Trustees Foundation of 1870 1976, Trier-Hansen Foundation 1977; hon. mem. Icelandic Medical Assen. 1978; Chair. Danish Central Scientific-Ethical Cttee. 1979, Nat. Medical Bd. Danish Red Cross 1985-; Danish Foreign Office del. Helsinki negotiations, Hamburg 1980; mem. Int. Cttee. of Medical Journal Eds. 1980, Editorial Bd., Acta med. Scand. 1980, Ethic Bd., Danish Medical Assen. 1980-82, WHO European Advisory Cttee. for Medical Research 1980-85; Vice-Dean Faculty of Medicine, Univ. of Copenhagen 1979-82; Chair. Nat. Medical Bd. of Danish Red Cross; Chair. Int. Org. of Inflammatory Bowel Diseases 1986; Alfred Benzon Prize, August Krogh Prize 1974, Christensen-Ceson Prize 1976, Klein-Prize 1980, Barfred-Pedersen Prize 1980, Hagedorn Prize 1983, Nordic Gastro Prize 1983. *Publications:* Contributor: Handbook of Scientific Methodology (in Danish) 1971-, World Medical Assen. Helsinki Declaration 1975, We Shall All Die—but how? (in Danish) 1977; Author: Handbook of Internal Medicine (in Danish) 1968, Grenzen der Forschung 1980; Community and Ethics (in Danish) 1984, Medical Ethics (in Danish) 1985, Ethical Issues in Preventive Medicine 1985, Medical Science and the Advancement of World Health 1985, Bearing and Perspective 1988, Face Death 1989; Ed. Nordic Medicine 1984; many articles in medical journals; lyrics to contemporary Danish compositions. *Leisure interests:* tennis, music, mountain walking. *Address:* Herlev University Hospital, 2730 Herlev (Office); Nerievej 7, 2900 Hellerup, Denmark (Home). *Telephone:* 02-942733 (Office); 01-62 9688 (Home).

RIKER, William H., PH.D.; American professor of political science; b. 22 Sept. 1920, Des Moines, Ia.; s. of Ben H. Riker and Alice Lenox Riker; m. Mary Elizabeth Lewis 1943; one s. two d.; ed. DePauw Univ. and Harvard Univ.; Asst. Prof. Lawrence Univ. 1948-62; Prof. and Chair. Political Science, Univ. of Rochester 1962-78, Dean of Graduate Studies 1978-83, Wilson Prof. of Political Science 1970-; Visiting Research Prof. Political Economy, Washington Univ. 1983-84; Ford Fellow 1952-53; Rockefeller Fellow 1955-56; Fellow, Center for Advanced Study in Behavioral Sciences 1960-61; Guggenheim Fellow 1983-84; Hon. D.Litt. (Lawrence Univ.) 1975, (DePauw Univ.) 1979, (Stony Brook) 1985, Hon. Ph.D. (Univ. of Uppsala) 1978, Uihlein Award for Undergraduate Teaching 1962. *Publications:* Soldiers of the States 1958, The Theory of Political Coalitions 1963, Federalism 1964, An Introduction to Positive Political Theory 1973, Liberalism against Populism: A Confrontation between the Theory of Democracy and the Theory of Social Choice 1982, The Art of Political Manipulation 1986, The Development of American Federalism 1987. *Address:* Department of Political Science, University of Rochester, Rochester, N.Y. 14627 (Office); 75 Windermere Road, Rochester, N.Y. 14610, U.S.A. (Home). *Telephone:* (716) 275-5519 (Office); (716) 288-2988 (Home).

RIKLIS, Meshulam; American (b. Turkish) business executive; b. 2 Dec. 1923, Istanbul, Turkey; s. of Pinhas and Betty (Guberer) Riklis; m. 1st Judith Stern 1944; one s. two d.; m. 2nd Pia Zadora 1977; one d.; ed. High School, Israel, Univ. of Mexico and Ohio State Univ.; Co-Dir. Youth Activities and Mil. Training, Hertzlia High School, Tel-Aviv 1942; went to U.S. 1947, naturalized 1955; Teacher of Hebrew, Talmud Torah School, Minneapolis 1951; Research Dept., Piper, Jaffray and Hopwood 1951–53, Sales Rep. 1953–56; Chair., C.E.O. Rapid Electrotype Co., American Colortype Co. 1956–57; Pres. Rapid-American Corpn. 1957–, Chair. 1958–; Vice-Chair. McCrory Corpn. 1960–69, Vice-Chair. Exec. Cttee. and Dir. 1970–, Chair. 1975–; owner Riviera Hotel, Las Vegas. *Address:* 725 Fifth Avenue, New York, N.Y. 10022 (Office); 781 Fifth Avenue, New York, N.Y. 10022, U.S.A. (Home).

RILEY, Bridget, C.B.E., A.R.C.A.; British artist; b. 24 April 1931, London; d. of John Fisher and the late Bessie Louise (née Gladstone) Riley; ed. Cheltenham Ladies' Coll., Goldsmiths Coll. of Art and Royal Coll. of Art, London; first one-woman exhbn. in London at Gallery One 1962, followed by others in England, America, Switzerland, Australia and Japan; has exhibited in group shows in Australia, Italy, France, Holland, Germany, Israel, America, Japan and Argentina; represented Great Britain at Biennale des Jeunes, Paris 1965, at Venice Biennale 1968; retrospective exhbn. Europe and U.K. 1970–72; second retrospective exhbn. touring America, Australia and Japan 1978–80; Arts Council Touring Exhbn. 1984–85; paintings, drawings, and prints in public collections in England, Ireland, Switzerland, Netherlands, Austria, Germany, Japan, Israel, America, Australia and New Zealand; Trustee, Nat. Gallery 1981–; AICA Critics Prize 1963; Prize in Open Section, John Moores Liverpool Exhbn. 1963; Peter Stuyvesant Foundation Travel Bursary to U.S.A. 1964; Major Painting Prize, Venice Biennale 1968; Prize at Tokyo Print Biennale 1971; Gold Medal at Grafikk-bienniale, Fredrikstad, Norway 1980; founder mem. and fmr. Dir. S.P.A.C.E. Ltd.; Hon. Dr. of Letters (Manchester Univ.) 1976, Dr. h.c. (Ulster) 1986. *Address:* c/o Mayor Rowan Gallery, 31a Bruton Place, London, W1X 7AB, England. *Telephone:* 01-499 3011.

RILEY, Sir Ralph, Kt., M.A., D.SC., PH.D., F.R.S.; British scientist; b. 23 Oct. 1924, Scarborough; s. of Ralph and Clara Riley; m. Joan Elizabeth Norrington 1949; two d.; ed. Univ. of Sheffield; Demonstrator, Dept. of Botany, Univ. of Sheffield 1951–52, with Plant Breeding Inst., Cambridge 1952–78, Head, Cytogenetics Dept. 1955–71, Dir. of Inst. 1971–78; Sec. and Deputy Chair., Agricultural and Food Research Council, London 1978–85; mem. Indian Science Acad., N.A.S., Agric. Acad. of France. *Publications:* scientific papers and reviews on plant breeding and the cytology and genetics of crop plants. *Address:* 16 Gog Magog Way, Stapleford, Cambridge, CB2 5BQ, England.

RILEY, Richard Wilson, LL.B.; American state governor; b. 2 Jan. 1935, Greenville, South Carolina; s. of E. P. and Martha Dixon Riley; m. Ann Yarborough 1957; three s. one d.; ed. Greenville Sr. High School, Furman Univ. and South Carolina School of Law; Lieut. in U.S. Navy; Legal Counsel to U.S. Senate Cttee. of Olin D. Johnston 1960; with family law firm 1961–62; mem. S.C. House of Reps. 1962–66, S.C. Senate 1966–76; S.C. State Chair. for Jimmy Carter's Presidential Election Campaign 1976; Gov. of South Carolina 1979–87. *Address:* c/o Office of the Governor, State House, Columbia, S.C. 29201, U.S.A.

RILEY, Terry Mitchell, M.A.; American composer, pianist and raga singer; b. 24 June 1935, Colfax, Calif.; s. of Wilma Ridlofi and Charles Riley; m. Ann Yvonne Smith 1958; three c.; ed. San Francisco State Univ. and Univ. of California, and pvt. studies with Duane Hampton, Adolf Baller and Pandit Pran Nath; taught music composition and N. Indian Raga at Mills Coll. 1971–83; freelance composer and performer 1961–; launched Minimal Music movt. with composition and first performance of In C 1964; John Simon Guggenheim Prize 1980. *Publications:* The Harp of New Albion for Solo Piano in Just Intonation, Salome Dances for Peace (string quartet), Cadenza on the Night Plain, Sunrise of the Planetary Dream Collector, Sri Camel, a Rainbow in Curved Air, In C, The Ten Voices of the Two Prophets, Persian Surgery Dervishes. *Leisure intersts:* music, gardens and orchards. *Address:* 13699 Moonshine Road, Camptonville, Calif. 95922, U.S.A. *Telephone:* (916) 288-3522.

RILLING, Helmuth, D.PHIL., D.THEOL.; German conductor, professor of music and church music director; b. 28 May 1933, Stuttgart; s. of Eugen Rilling and Hildegard Plieninger; m. Martina Greiner 1967; two d.; ed. protestant theological seminars of Schöntal and Urach; Staatliche Hochschule für Musik, Stuttgart, studied organ with Fernando Germani, Conservatorio di Santa Cecilia, Rome and conducting with Leonard Bernstein, New York; organist and choirmaster, Gedächtniskirche, Stuttgart 1957–; taught organ and conducting, Berliner Kirchenmusikschule, Berlin-Spandau and Dir., Spandauer Kantorei 1963–66; Prof. of Conducting, Staatliche Hochschule für Musik, Frankfurt 1966–85; taught at Ind. Univ., Bloomington, U.S.A. 1976–77; Dir. Frankfurter Kantorei 1969–81; f. Summer Festi-

val (now Oregon Bach Festival), Eugene, U.S.A. 1970; Founder and Dir. Gächinger Kantorei, Stuttgart 1954–, Figuralchor of the Gedächtniskirche, Stuttgart 1957–, Bach-Collegium Stuttgart 1965–, Sommer Acad. Johann Sebastian Bach Stuttgart 1979–, Int. Bach Acad. Stuttgart 1981–, Bach Acad. Tokyo and Buenos Aires 1983–; world-wide int. appearances with own ensembles and as guest conductor and guest prof.; regular co-operation with Israel Philharmonic Orchestra, The Cleveland Orchestra, Boston Symphony Orchestra, Toronto Symphony Orchestra; Distinguished Service Award (Univ. of Oregon) 1985. *Publications:* Johann Sebastian Bach, Matthäus-Passion; Einführung und Studienanleitung 1975, Johann Sebastian Bach's H-moll-Messe 1979. *Recordings:* all the sacred cantatas and oratorios of J.S. Bach and many others. *Address:* Im Greutle 19, D-7250 Leonberg 7, Federal Republic of Germany.

RIMAN, Josef; Czechoslovak scientist; b. 30 Jan. 1925; ed. Faculty of Medicine, Charles Univ., Prague; Dir. Inst. of Molecular Genetics, Czechoslovak Acad. of Scientists 1974; mem. Czechoslovak Acad. of Sciences 1977–, Pres. 1985–; cand. mem. ideological comm. CP of Czechoslovakia; Klement Gottwald State Prize (twice) and other state orders. *Address:* Czechoslovak Academy of Sciences, 111 42 Prague 1, Národní Tř. 3, Czechoslovakia.

RIMINGTON, Claude, M.A., PH.D., D.SC., F.R.S.; British university professor (retd.); b. 17 Nov. 1902, London; s. of George Garthwaite Rimington and Hilda Klyne; m. Soffi Andersen 1929; one d.; ed. Cambridge and London Univs.; Biochemist, Woollen Industries' Research Assen., Leeds 1928–31; Empire Marketing Bd. Research Fellow at Onderstepoort Veterinary Research Lab., Pretoria, S.A. 1931–36; Scientific Research Officer, Div. of Veterinary Services, Govt. of Union of S.A. 1936–37; Biochemist on staff of Nat. Inst. for Medical Research of Medical Research Council of Great Britain 1937–45; Prof. of Chemical Pathology, Univ. of London, and Head of Dept. of Chemical Pathology, Univ. Coll. Hospital Medical School 1945–67, Emer. Prof. Univ. of London 1967–; Hon. F.R.C.P.(E); mem. Norwegian Acad. of Science and Letters 1988–; Graham Gold Medal for Medical Research, Univ. of London. *Publications:* (Co-author) Diseases of Porphyrin Metabolism 1962, Disorders of Porphyrin Metabolism 1987; numerous articles on biochemistry, chem. and chemical pathology. *Leisure interests:* literature, languages. *Address:* Askerøy, Vestre Sandøy 4915, Norway.

RINCHIN, Lodongiin; Mongolian agronomist, politician and diplomatist; b. 25 July 1929, Gobi Altai Aimag; ed. Agricultural Inst., U.S.S.R.; Agronomist, Chief Agronomist, Ministry of Livestock Husbandry 1955–60; Deputy Minister, First Deputy Minister of Agric. 1960–67; Chair. Supreme Council, Agric. Co-operative Bd. 1967–70; Minister for Foreign Affairs 1970–76, of Agric. 1976–80; Amb. to Yugoslavia 1981–84; mem. Cen. Cttee. Mongolian People's Revolutionary Party (MPRP) 1961–; Head of MPRP Cen. Cttee. Dept. for Int. Relations Jan. 1985–; Deputy to Great People's Hural (Ass.); mem. Presidium, Great People's Hural July–Dec. 1987; Chair. Great People's Hural 1987–; various state orders and medals. *Address:* Central Committee of the Mongolian People's Revolutionary Party, Ulaanbaatar, Mongolia.

RING, Sir Lindsay Roberts, G.B.E., J.P.; British executive; b. 1 May 1914, London; s. of George Arthur Ring and Helen Rhoda Mason Ring (née Stedman); m. Hazel Doris Nichols 1940; two s. one d.; ed. Dulwich Coll. and Mecklenburg, Germany; served Europe and Middle East, Major, Royal Army Service Corps 1939–45; Underwriting mem. Lloyd's 1964; Chair. Ring and Brymer (Birchs) Ltd.; Chair. Hotel and Catering Trades Benevolent Assen. 1962–71; mem. Bd. of Verge of Royal Palaces; Gov. Farrington's School; Hon. Treas. Church Army Housing; mem. Court of Assts., Armourers' and Braziers' Co., Master 1972; Common Councilman for Ward of Bishopsgate, City of London 1964–68; Alderman for Ward of Vintry 1968–74; Sheriff, City of London 1967–68; Lord Mayor of London 1975–76; mem. Gaming Bd. for Great Britain 1977–83, Northern Ireland Devt. Agency 1977; Gov. The Hon. The Irish Soc. 1980–84; Hon. D.Sc. (City Univ., London) 1976, Hon. D.Litt. (Ulster Univ.) 1976; Freeman, City of London 1935; Hon. Freeman of Coleraine (Londonderry); Hon. Col. 151st Transport Regt. Greater London Royal Corps of Transport (V); Fellow, Hotel and Catering Inst.; Commdr. Légion d'honneur, Order Rio Branca (Brazil), Diego de Losada (Venezuela); K.St.J. *Leisure interest:* gardening. *Address:* Chalvedune, Wilderness Road, Chislehurst, Kent, BR7 5EY, England. *Telephone:* 01-467 3199.

RINGADOO, Sir Veerasamy, Kt., G.C.M.G., BAR.-AT-LAW ; Mauritius politician; b. 1920, Port Louis; s. of Nagaya Ringadoo; m. Lydie Vadamootoo 1954; one s. one d.; ed. Port Louis Grammar School and London School of Econs., England; called to the Bar 1949; elected Municipal Councillor 1956; elected mem. Legis. Council for Moka-Flacq 1951–67; Minister for Labour and Social Security 1959–64, for Educ. 1964–67, of Agric. and Natural Resources 1967–68, of Finance 1968–82; Gov.-Gen. of Mauritius Jan. 1986–; attended London Constitutional Conf. 1965; First mem., Legis. Assembly (M.L.A.) for Quartier Militaire and Moka 1967–86 (Lab); Gov. IMF; Chair. African Devt. Bank and African Devt. Fund 1977–78; Officer, Ordre National Malgache 1969, Médaille de l'Assemblée Nat. Française 1971; Hon. Fellow L.S.E. 1976; Hon. LL.D. (Mauritius) 1975, Hon. D.Litt. (Andhra Univ., India) 1978. *Address:* Government House, Port Louis,

Corner of Farquhar and Sir Celicourt Antelme Streets, Quatre-Bornes, Mauritius (Home).

RINGBOM, Sixten, FIL.DR.; Finnish professor of history and theory of art; b. 27 July 1935, Turku; s. of Lars-Ivar Ringbom and Olga Ringbom; m. Marianne Fortelius 1959; one s. one d.; ed. Svenska Klassiska Lyseum, Åbo, Åbo Akad., Warburg and Courtauld Insts. London; Asst. Librarian, Donner Inst. Åbo Akad. 1959–63, Sr. Asst. Librarian 1963–70; Prof. of History and Theory of Art, Åbo Akad. 1970–; Research Prof. Acad. of Finland 1986–(91); Visiting Prof. Washington Square Coll., New York Univ. 1966–67; Fellow-in-residence, NIAS Netherlands Inst. for Advanced Study in the Humanities and Social Sciences 1986–87. *Publications:* Icon to Narrative: the Rise of the Dramatic Close-Up in 15th Century Devotional Painting 1965, The Sounding Kosmos 1970, Konsten i Finland (ed. and contrib.) 1978, Stone, Style and Truth 1988. *Address:* Konsthistoriska institutionen, Åbo Akademi, 20500 Åbo (Office); Blåbärsvägen 13, 20720 Åbo, Finland (Home). *Telephone:* (358-21) 654582 (Office); (358-21) 360905 (Home).

RINGWOOD, Alfred Edward, PH.D., F.R.S.; Australian scientist; b. 19 April 1930, Melbourne; m. Gun Ivor Carlson 1960; one s. one d.; ed. Geelong Grammar School, Melbourne Univ., Trinity Coll., Harvard Univ.; Sr. Research Fellow, Dept. of Geophysics, A.N.U. 1959, Sr. Fellow 1960, Personal Prof. in Geophysics 1963–67, Prof. of Geochemistry 1967–; Prin. Investigator for Lunar Samples, NASA 1968–; Dir. Research School of Earth Sciences, A.N.U. 1978–84; Andrew White Prof.-at-Large, Cornell Univ. 1974–80; Fellow, Australian Acad. of Science 1966–, mem. of council 1969–72, Vice-Pres. 1971–72; Foreign Assoc. N.A.S. 1975; Fellow, American Geophysical Union 1969; Foreign mem. Geological Soc. of London 1967; Hon. mem. All-Union Mineralogical Soc., U.S.S.R. 1975; Fellow, Meteoritical Soc. 1972; various honours. *Publications:* Composition and Petrology of the Earth's Mantle 1975, Safe Disposal of High Level Nuclear Reactor Wastes: A New Strategy 1978, Origin of the Earth and Moon 1979, and 232 scientific papers. *Address:* Research School of Earth Sciences, Australian National University, P.O. Box 4, Canberra, A.C.T. 2601 (Office); 3 Vancouver St., Red Hill, A.C.T., Australia (Home). *Telephone:* 49 3420 (Office).

RINSER, Luise; German author; b. 30 April 1911, Pitzling/Oberbayern; d. of Joseph and Luise Rinser; m. 1st Horst-Guenther Schnell 1939 (deceased), two s.; m.; 2nd Carl Orff (died 1982); School teacher 1935–39; works banned 1941; imprisoned 1944–45; after World War II became literary critic of Neue Zeitung, Munich; now free-lance writer; mem. Akad. der Künste, PEN Centre of Fed. Repub. of Germany. *Publications:* novels: Die gläsernen Ringe 1940, Mitte des Lebens 1950, Daniela 1953, Abenteuer der Tugend 1957, Ich Bin Tobias 1968; Der schwarze Esel 1974; Mirjam 1983; short stories: Ein Bündel weisser Narzissen 1956; essays: Schwerpunkt, Über die Hoffnung, Vom Sinn der Traurigkeit, Unterentwickeltes Land Frau, Wie, wenn wir ärmer würden 1974, Dem Tode geweiht 1974; letters: Hochzeit der Widersprüche 1973; diaries: Gefängnis/Tagebuch 1946, Baustelle 1970, Grenz-Übergänge 1972, Kriegsspielzeug 1978, Winterfrühling 1982; play: Philemon; travel: Wenn die Wale kämpfen 1976, Khomeini und der islamische Gottesstaat 1979, Nordkoreanisches Reise-Tagebuch 1981; Bruder Feuer (for young people) 1975; autobiography: Den Wolf umarmen 1981, Im Dunkeln Singen (diary) 1984, Geschichten aus der Löwengrube (short stories) 1986, Silberschuld (novel) 1987, Das Geheimnis des Brunnens, Das Squirrel (for children). *Leisure interests:* politics, theology. *Address:* I-00040 Rocca di Papa, Rome, Italy. *Telephone:* 949087.

RINTZLER, Marius Adrian; German opera and concert singer; b. 14 March 1932, Bucharest, Romania; m. Sanda Dragomir 1964; ed. Acad. of Music, Bucharest; soloist with Bucharest Philharmonic 1959; début in opera in Bucharest as Don Basilio in Il Barbiere di Siviglia 1964; went to Germany 1966; leading bass at Düsseldorf's Deutsche Oper am Rhein 1968–; guest singer with major opera cos., including Metropolitan, San Francisco, Glyndebourne, Paris, Brussels, Munich; Repertoire includes various roles in Richard Strauss' Rosenkavalier (Ochs), Capriccio (La Roche), Schweigsame Frau (Morosus), in Rossini's La Cenerentola (Don Magnifico), Il Barbiere (Bartolo), in Richard Wagner's Ring (Alberich), in Mozart's Don Giovanni (Leporello), Die Entführung (Osmin); appears with major symphony orchestras in Europe and U.S.A., including London Philharmonia, Berlin Philharmoniker, Cleveland Symphony; also gives recitals, TV appearances in England, Germany and France. *Address:* Friedingstrasse 18, 4-Düsseldorf 12, Federal Republic of Germany. *Telephone:* 29 70 83.

RIOPELLE, Jean-Paul, C.C.; Canadian painter; b. 1923, Montreal, Que.; settled in Paris 1947; participated in L'Imaginaire exhbn., Galerie du Luxembourg 1947, Surrealist exhbn., Galerie Maeght 1947; one-man shows, Paris 1949, New York 1954, London 1956, Ottawa 1963, Musée d'Art Moderne, Paris 1971; chosen by J. J. Sweeney for Younger European Painters Exhbn., Guggenheim Museum, New York 1953–54; works in the Tate Gallery and Nat. Gallery of Canada and in private collections; UNESCO Award 1962; Canada Council Medal 1966. *Address:* 10 rue Frémincourt, Paris 75015, France.

RÍOS, Juan; Peruvian poet, dramatist, journalist and critic; b. 28 Sept. 1914, Barranco, Lima; s. of Rogelio Ríos and Victoria Rey (de Ríos); m.

Rosa Saco 1946; one d.; National Prize for Playwriting 1946, 1950, 1952, 1954, 1960; Nat. Poetry Prize 1948, 1953; Writers' Fellowship, UNESCO, Europe and Egypt 1960–61; mem. Academia Peruana de la Lengua Correspondiente a la Española. *Publications:* Canción de Siempre 1941, Malstrom 1941, La Pintura Contemporánea en el Perú 1946, Teatro (I) 1961, Ayar Manko 1963, Primera Antología Poetica 1982. *Address:* Bajada de Baños 109, Barranco, Lima 04, Peru. *Telephone:* 671799 (Lima).

RÍOS MONTT, Gen. Efraín; Guatemalan army officer and politician; b. 1927; joined army 1943; defence posting, Washington, D.C. 1973; contested presidential election for Christian Democratic coalition 1974; Mil. Attaché, Madrid; fmr. Commdr. Honour Guard Brigade; Dir. Mil. Acad.; installed as leader of mil. junta after coup March 1982; Minister of Nat. Defence March–Sept. 1982; Pres. of Guatemala, also C.-in-C. of the Army 1982–83; overthrown Aug. 1983.

RIPA DI MEANA, Carlo; Italian politician and journalist; b. 15 Aug. 1929, Marina di Pietrasanta, Lucca; journalist on Il Lavoro (weekly journal of the Confederazione Generale Italiana del Lavoro) and on L'Unità (Italian daily) 1950–53; co-f. and ran weekly Nuova Generazione 1953–56; co-f. and Ed. magazine Passato e Presente 1957; publisher's ed. for Feltrinelli and Rizzoli 1958–66; resgnd. from Italian CP 1957, joined Italian Socialist Party 1958; Sec.-Gen. Club Turati, Milan 1967–76; Regional Councillor, Lombardy, Leader, Socialist Party group in the Council 1970–82; mem. bd. La Scala Theatre, Milan 1970–74; Chair. Venice Biennale 1974–79; head of int. relations, Italian Socialist Party 1979–80; mem. European Parl. 1979–; mem. Comm. of the European Communities (responsible for Citizen's Europe, information, culture and tourism) 1985–89, (responsible for communication) 1986–89, (responsible for Environment and Nuclear Safety) Jan. 1989–; Chair. Istituto per la Cooperazione economica internazionale e i problemi dello sviluppo 1983–. *Publications:* Un viaggio in Viet-Nam 1956, Dedicato a Raymond Roussel e alle sue impressioni d'Africa 1965, Il governo audiovisivo 1973. *Address:* Commission of the European Communities, 200 rue de la Loi, 1049 Brussels, Belgium.

RIPLEY, S. Dillon, B.A., PH.D.; American museum director and zoologist; b. 20 Sept. 1913, New York; s. of Louis Arthur Ripley and Constance Baillie (Rose); m. Mary Moncrieffe Livingston 1949; three d.; ed. St. Paul's School, Concord, N.H., and Yale and Harvard Univs.; Zoological Collector, Acad. of Natural Science, Philadelphia 1936–39; Voluntary Asst. American Museum of Natural History, New York 1939–40; Asst. Harvard Univ. 1941–42; Asst. Curator Birds, Smithsonian Inst. 1942, Sec. 1964–84, Sec. Emer. 1984–; Lecturer and Assoc. Curator Yale Univ. 1946–52, Asst. Prof. 1949–55, Assoc. Prof. Zoology 1955–61, Prof. of Biology 1961–64; Dir. Peabody Museum of Natural History 1959–64; Guggenheim Foundation Fellow 1954; Fellow or mem. of numerous scientific socs. in U.S. and abroad, including Nat. Acad. of Sciences, American Philosophical Soc., American Acad. of Arts and Sciences and British Ornithologists' Union; Hon. M.A. (Yale Univ.), Hon. D.H.L. (Marlboro Coll.,Williams Coll.), Hon. D.Sc. (George Washington Univ. Catholic Univ., Ma. Univ., Cambridge Univ., Trinity Coll. and Brown Univ.), Hon. LL.D. (Dickinson Coll., Hofstra Univ., Yale Univ., Gallaudet Coll., Johns Hopkins Univ., Harvard Univ.), Hon. D.Eng. (Stevens Inst. Tech.); New York Zoological Soc. Medal 1966, Royal Zoological Soc. of Antwerp Medal 1970, F. K. Hutchinson Medal, Garden Club of America 1979; Order of White Elephant and Freedom Medal (Thailand), Officier, Ordre des Arts et Lettres, Légion d'honneur (France), Officier, Ordre Léopold (Belgium), Commdr., Order of Merit (Poland), Commdr. Dannebrog (Denmark), Golden Ark (Netherlands), Grand Cross del Mérito Civil (Spain), Holland Soc. Medal 1977, Henry Shaw Medal, St. Louis Botanical Garden 1982, Gold Medal, New York Inst. of Social Sciences 1982, Order of the Sacred Treasure (Japan) 1982, Order of Oranje-Nassau (Netherlands), Hon. K.B.E. 1979, Olympia Prize 1984, Presidential Medal of Freedom 1985. *Publications:* The Trail of the Money Bird 1947, Search for the Spiny Babbler 1953, A Paddling of Ducks 1959, A Synopsis of the Birds of India and Pakistan 1961, Ornithological Books in the Yale Library (Co-Author) 1961, Land and Wildlife, Tropical Asia 1964, Handbook of the Birds of India and Pakistan (Co-author), Vol. I 1968, Vols. II and III 1969, Vol. IV 1970, Vol. V 1972, Vol VI 1971, Vol. VII 1972, Vol. VIII, Vol. IX 1973, Vol. X 1974 (Compact ed. 1983), The Sacred Grove/Essays on Museums 1969. The Paradox of the Human Condition 1975, Rails of the World 1977, A Pictorial Guide to Birds of the Indian Subcontinent 1983; contributions to numerous journals. *Leisure interests:* travel, observing and collecting waterfowl, especially watching ducks. *Address:* 2324 Massachusetts Avenue, N.W., Washington, D.C. 20008; Summer: Paddling Ponds, Litchfield, Conn. 06759, U.S.A. (Homes). *Telephone:* (202) 232-3131 (Home); (203) 567-8208 (Summer).

RIPPON, Angela; British journalist, producer and newsreader; b. 12 Oct. 1944, Plymouth, Devon; d. of John and Edna Rippon; m. Christopher Dare 1967; ed. Plymouth Grammar School; Ed., Producer and Presenter, Westward Television (ITV) 1967–73; Presenter and Reporter, BBC TV Plymouth 1966–69; Reporter, BBC TV Nat. News 1973–75, Newsreader 1975–81; Presenter TV-am Feb.–April 1983; Arts and Entertainment Corresp. for WNEV-TV, Boston, 1984–85; Vice-Pres. Int. Club for Women in TV 1979–; Dir. Nirex. 1986–; Newsreader of the Year 1975, 1976, 1977; TV Personality of the Year 1977. *TV appearances include:* Angela Rippon Reporting (documentary), Antiques Roadshow, In the Country, Compere,

Eurovision Song Contest 1976, Royal Wedding 1981, Masterteam (BBC) 1985, 1986, 1987, Come Dancing 1988-, What's My Line? 1988-. *Publications:* Riding, In the Country, Victoria Plum (children's stories), Mark Phillips—The Man and his Horses 1982, Angela Rippon's West Country 1982, Badminton: A Celebration 1987. *Leisure interests:* cooking, gardening, riding. *Address:* c/o I.M.G., The Pier House, Strand on the Green, London, W4 3NN, England. *Telephone:* 01-994 1444.

RIPPON OF HEXHAM, Baron (Life Peer) cr. 1987, of Hesleyside in the County of Northumberland; **Geoffrey Rippon**, P.C., Q.C., M.A., M.P.; British barrister and politician; b. 28 May 1924; m. Ann Leyland Yorke 1946; one s. three d.; ed. King's Coll., Taunton and Brasenose Coll., Oxford; called to Bar, Middle Temple 1948; mem. Surbiton Borough Council 1945-54, Mayor 1951- 52; mem. London County Council 1952-61; M.P. for Norwich 1955-64, for Hexham 1966-87; Parl. Sec. Ministry of Aviation 1959-61; Jt. Parl. Sec. Ministry of Housing and Local Govt. 1961-62; Minister of Public Building and Works 1962-64; Leader of U.K. Del. to the Council of Europe and W.E.U. 1967-70; Dir. Fairey Co. Ltd. 1964-70; Dir. Bristol Aeroplane Co. 1964-68; Dir. and Chair. Holland and Hannen & Cubitts 1964-68; Deputy Chair. Drake & Scull Ltd. 1968-70; Chair. Dun and Bradstreet (U.K.) 1975-, Chair. Britannia Arrow 1977-, Chair. Brasseys Publishers Ltd. 1977-, Robert Fraser Group 1986-; Minister of Tech. June-July 1970; Chancellor of Duchy of Lancaster in charge of negotiations for British entry to Common Market 1970-72; Sec. of State for the Environment 1972-74; Leader, Conservative Group, European Parl. 1977-79; Chair. Parl. Foreign and Commonwealth Affairs Cttee., Conservative Party 1979-81; Pres. British section, European League for Econ. Co-operation 1969-83, Chair. 1983-; Chair. British Council of the European Movt. 1982-86, Jt. Pres. 1986-; Dir. Groupe Bruxelles, Lambert 1984-; mem. Court Univ. of London 1958-; Pres. Assen. of Dist. Councils 1986-; Hon. Fellow, Brasenose Coll., Oxford; Master of the Bench, Middle Temple. *Publications:* Forward from Victory (co-author) 1943, The Rent Act 1957. *Address:* 2 Paper Buildings, Temple, London, E.C.4 (Office); Mantle Hill, Hesleyside, Hexham, Northumberland, England (Home). *Telephone:* 01-353 5835 (Office).

RIS, Hans, PH.D.; American professor of zoology; b. 15 June 1914, Bern, Switzerland; s. of August Ris and Martha Ris; m. 1st Hania W. Wislicka 1947 (divorced 1971), one s. one d.; m. 2nd Theron Caldwell 1980; ed. Univs. of Bern, Switzerland, Rochester and New York and Columbia and Yale Univs.; Lecturer in Zoology, Col. Univ. 1941-42; Asst. Prof. of Biology, Johns Hopkins Univ. 1942-44; Asst. then Assoc. Prof. of Physiology, Rockefeller Inst., New York 1944-49; Assoc. Prof. of Zoology, Univ. of Wis., Madison 1949-53, Prof. 1953-84, Prof. Emer. 1984-, Dir. Madison High Voltage Electron Microscope Facility 1969-86; Fellow American Acad. of Arts and Sciences; mem. N.A.S. *Publications:* 100 publs. of original research results in scientific journals 1938-. *Leisure interests:* reading, photography, hiking, camping, skiing. *Address:* Zoology Research, University of Wisconsin, 1117 W. Johnson, Madison, Wis. 53706; 5542 Riverview Drive, Waunakee, Wis. 53597, U.S.A. (Home). *Telephone:* (608) 262-2694 (Office); (608) 849-7341 (Home).

RISCHBIETER, Karlos; Brazilian central banker; b. 24 Oct. 1927, Blumenau; s. of Luiz and Helga (Ebert) Rischbieter; m. Francisca Maria Rischbieter 1958; one s. one d.; ed. Eng. School, Paraná Fed. Univ., courses in Paris and Curitiba, Paraná; engineer and adviser to private cos. 1953-61; Head of Planning Area in Paraná State Devt. Co. (CODEPAR) 1962, then Admin. Dir., Financial Dir. then Pres. CODEPAR until 1965; Adviser to Pres. of Brazilian Coffee Inst., also Rep. of Inst. in Hamburg 1965-67; mem. Planning Advisory Council (CONSPLAN) in Ministry of Planning 1965-67; Pres. Bank of Devt. of State of Paraná (BADEP) 1972-74, Fed. Savings Bank (CEF) 1974-77, Banco do Brasil 1977-79; Minister of Finance 1979-80; Chair. Volvo do Brasil, MPM Propaganda; mem. of bd. Artex S.A., Refripar S.A., Climax S.A., Lacta S.A., Sicom S.A.; Commdr. Order of Rio Branco; Commdr. Aeronautical Order of Merit. *Leisure interests:* painting, classical music, opera. *Address:* Rua Comendador Araujo 145-51, 80 000 Curitiba Pr., Brazil.

RISCHEL, Jørgen; Danish professor of phonetics; b. 10 Aug. 1934, Kullerup; s. of Ejner Rischel and Gunnild Rischel; m. Anna-Grethe Rischel 1961; three d.; ed. Univs. of Copenhagen, Iceland and Oslo; lecturer in Danish, Univ. of Bergen, Norway 1960-61; Assoc. Ed. Norwegian-English Dictionary Project, Univ. of Wis. 1961-62; Asst. Prof., later Assoc. Prof. Univ. of Copenhagen 1963-78, Prof. of Linguistics 1978-81, Prof. of Phonetics 1981-; Visiting Prof. Univ. of Calif. 1978; mem. Royal Danish Acad. of Sciences and Letters 1978-, Danish Research Council for the Humanities 1988-. *Publications:* The Lepchas (with Halpdan Siiger) Vol. II 1967, Topics in West Greenlandic Phonology (Essay) 1974, Pioneers of Eskimo Grammar (with Knut Bergsland) 1987, co-author of various dictionaries and ed. of works on the Faroe Islands in the 17th century. *Leisure interests:* music, travelling (under primitive conditions to remote areas). *Address:* Institute of General and Applied Linguistics, University of Copenhagen, 80 Njalsgade, 2300 Copenhagen S (Univ.); 57 Stenhojgaardsvej, 3460 Birkerød, Denmark (Home). *Telephone:* (01) 542211 (Univ.); (02) 816803 (Home).

RISHBETH, John, O.B.E., SC.D., F.R.S.; British plant pathologist; b. 10 July 1918, Cambridge; s. of Prof. and Mrs. O. H. T. Rishbeth; m. Barbara

Sadler 1946; one s. one d.; ed. St. Lawrence Coll. Ramsgate and Christ's Coll. Cambridge; Chemist, Royal Ordnance Factories 1940-43; Bacteriologist, Scientific Advisers Div. Ministry of Food 1943-45; Demonstrator in Botany, Univ. of Cambridge 1947-49; Plant Pathologist, West Indian Banana Research Scheme 1950-52; Lecturer in Botany, Univ. of Cambridge 1953-73, Reader in Plant Pathology 1973-84 (retd.); Fellow, Corpus Christi Coll. Cambridge 1964-; Visiting Prof. N. Carolina State Univ. 1967; Dr. h.c. (Royal Veterinary and Agric. Univ. Copenhagen) 1976. *Publications:* papers in professional journals. *Leisure interests:* natural history, gardens, mountain walking, tennis. *Address:* 36 Wingate Way, Cambridge, CB2 2HD, England. *Telephone:* (0223) 841298.

RISHTYA, Kassim (see Reshtia, Sayed Qassem).

RISK, Sir Thomas Neilson, Kt., B.L.; British banker; b. 13 Sept. 1922, Glasgow; s. of late Ralph Risk and Margaret N. Risk; m. Suzanne Eiloart 1949; four s.; ed. Kelvinside Acad. and Glasgow Univ.; Partner, Maclay, Murray & Spens (Solicitors), Glasgow and Edin. 1950-81; Gov. Bank of Scotland 1981-; Dir. Standard Life Assurance Co. 1965-88, Chair. 1969-77; Dir. The British Linen Bank Ltd. 1968-, Gov. 1977-86; Chair. Scottish Financial Enterprise 1986-; Dir. Barclays Bank PLC 1983-85, Howden Group PLC 1971-87, Merchants Trust PLC, MSA (Britain) Ltd., Shell U.K. Ltd. 1982-, Bank of Wales PLC 1986-; Hon. LL.D. (Glasgow) 1985. *Leisure interests:* golf, reading. *Address:* 10 Belford Place, Edin., EH4 3DH, Scotland. *Telephone:* 031-243 5511 (Office); 031-332 9425 (Home).

RIŠKO, Ján, PHDR.; Czechoslovak journalist; b. 6 Feb. 1930, Lúky, Povážska Bystrica Dist.; ed. Coll. of Political and Econ. Sciences, Prague 1949-53; Ed., daily newspaper Mladá fronta, Prague 1953-56; mem. Cen. Cttee. Union of Slovak Journalists 1953-67, Chair. 1983-; head, foreign desk, daily newspaper Smena, Bratislava 1956-59; head, foreign desk, Pravda, Bratislava 1960-67; Ed. Czechoslovak News Agency, Corresp. and head of office in Moscow 1967-70; official, Secr. of Cen. Cttee. CP of Czechoslovakia, Prague 1970; Alt. mem. Cen. Cttee. CP of Czechoslovakia 1981-; Dir.-Gen. Czechoslovak Radio, Prague 1970-; mem. House of the Nations, Fed. Assembly 1986-; Chair. Programme Comm., Int. Radio and TV Org. (OIRT) 1973-; Chair. Czechoslovak Union of Journalists 1983-; Award For Merits in Construction 1970, Ordre du Travail 1980. *Address:* Vinohradská 12, Prague 2, Czechoslovakia.

RITBLAT, John Henry, F.S.V.A.; British business executive; b. 3 Oct. 1935; m. Isabel Ritblat 1960 (died 1979); two s. one d.; ed. Dulwich Coll., Coll. of Estate Management, London Univ.; Chair. The British Land Co. Ltd.; Co-founder and Sr. Partner Conrad Ritblat & Co., Consultant Surveyors and Valuers 1958, Chair. and Man. Dir. 1970-; Man. Dir. Union Property Holdings (London) Ltd. 1969, Crown Estates Paving Commn. 1969-. *Leisure interests:* golf, skiing, squash, books, architecture. *Address:* 10 Cornwall Terrace, Regent's Park, London, NW1 4QP, England. *Telephone:* 01-486 4466.

RITCHIE, Cedric E., O.C.; Canadian banker; b. 22 Aug. 1927, Upper Kent, N.B.; s. of E. Thomas Ritchie and Marion (née Henderson) Ritchie; m. Barbara Binnington 1956; ed. Bath High School, N.B.; joined The Bank of Nova Scotia, Bath N.B. 1945, served various branches in the Maritime Provs. and Montreal, Asst. Insp. 1954-56, Chief Accountant 1960-63, Asst. Gen. Man. Admin. 1963-66, Jt. Gen. Man. 1966-68, Chief Gen. Man. Int. 1968-70, Chief Gen. Man. 1970-72, elected a Dir. 1972, Pres. 1972-79, C.E.O. 1972-, Chair. of Bd. Dec. 1974-; Chair. and Dir. numerous other banks and trust cos. *Leisure interests:* golf, skiing, curling. *Address:* The Bank of Nova Scotia, General Office, 44 King Street, West, Toronto M5H 1H1, Canada.

RITCHIE, J. Murdoch, PH.D., D.SC., F.R.S.; British professor of pharmacology; b. 10 June 1925, Aberdeen, Scotland; s. of Alexander Farquharson and Agnes Jane Bremner; m. Brenda Rachel Bigland 1951; one s. one d.; ed. Univs. of Aberdeen and London; Research Physicist in Radar at Telecommunications Research Establishment, Malvern 1944-46; Jr. Lecturer in Physiology, Univ. Coll. London 1949-51; mem. of staff, Inst. for Medical Research, Mill Hill 1951-56; Asst. Prof. of Pharmacology, Albert Einstein Coll. of Medicine, New York, U.S.A. 1956-57, Assoc. Prof. 1958-63, Prof. 1963-68; Prof. and Chair. Dept. of Pharmacology, Yale Univ. School of Medicine, U.S.A. 1968-74, Dir. Div. of Biological Sciences 1975-78, Eugene Higgins Prof. of Pharmacology 1968-; Hon. M.A. (Yale) 1968; Hon. D. Sc. (Aberdeen) 1987; Fellow Univ. Coll. London; Van Dyke Memorial Award 1983. *Publications:* numerous scientific articles in Journal of Physiology, Proceedings of Royal Soc., Nature, Proceedings of N.A.S., U.S.A. *Leisure interests:* chess, skiing and squash. *Address:* Department of Pharmacology, Yale University School of Medicine, 333 Cedar Street, New Haven, Conn. 06510; 47 Deepwood Drive, Hamden, Conn. 06517, U.S.A. *Telephone:* (203) 785-4567 (Univ.); (203) 777-0420 (Home).

RITCHIE, James Martin, F.R.S.A., F.B.I.M.; Scottish business executive; b. 29 May 1917, Glasgow; s. of late Sir James and of Lady Ritchie; m. Noreen M. L. Johnston 1939; three s.; ed. Strathallan School; joined Andrew Ritchie & Son Ltd., Glasgow (family business) 1934, Dir. 1938; war service 1939-45; rejoined Andrew Ritchie & Son Ltd. 1945, Man. Dir. 1950; Gen. Man. Bowater-Eburite Ltd. (after merger) 1956; Dir. Bowater Paper Corpn. Ltd. 1959, Man. Dir. 1964, Deputy Chair. 1967, Chair. 1969-72; Vice-Chair. British Enkalon Ltd. 1974-75, Chair. 1975-83; fmr. Dir. Vickers Ltd.,

British Enkalon Ltd., Haymills Holdings Ltd. (Chair. 1977–83), Sun Alliance and London Insurance Group; Councillor (Conservative), South Bucks. Dist. Council 1980–. *Leisure interest:* golf. *Address:* The Court House, Fulmer, Bucks., England. *Telephone:* (028 16) 2585.

RITHAUDDEEN AL-HAJ BIN TENGKU ISMAIL, Y.M. Tengku Ahmad; Malaysian barrister and politician; b. 24 Jan. 1932; mem. of Royal family of Kelantan; ed. Nottingham Univ. and Lincoln's Inn, U.K.; Circuit Magistrate in Ipoh 1956–58, Pres. of Sessions Court 1958–60; Deputy Public Prosecutor and Fed. Counsel 1960–62; mem. Council of Advisers to Ruler of State of Kelantan (MPR), resgnd. to enter pvt. practice; Chair. East Coast Bar Cttee. of Malaya; Chair. Sri Nilam Co-operative Soc., Malaysia; mem. Malayan Council 1967, 1968, 1969, 1970; Sponsor, Adabi Foundation; Sponsor, Kelantan Youth; Adviser, Kesatria; Chair. Farmers' Org. Authority; Minister with Special Functions Assisting Prime Minister on Foreign Affairs 1973–75; mem. Supreme Council, United Malays' Nat. Org. June 1975–; Minister for Foreign Affairs 1975–81, 1984–86, for Trade and Industry 1981–83, for Information 1986–87, of Defence 1987–. *Address:* Ministry of Defence, Jalan Padang Tembak, 50634 Kuala Lumpur, Malaysia. *Telephone:* (03) 2921333.

RITT, Martin; American film director; b. 2 March 1920, New York; s. of Morris and Rose Ritt; ed. Elon Coll.; numerous Broadway acting appearances 1937–55; appeared in films: Winged Victory 1944, End of the Game 1976, Hollywood on Trial 1977; directed numerous productions on Broadway incl. Mr. Peebles and Mr. Hooker 1946, Yellow Jack 1947, The Big People 1947, Set My People Free 1948, The Man 1950, Cry of the Peacock 1950, Golden Boy 1954, Boy Meets Girl 1954, The Front Page 1954, A View from the Bridge 1955, A Memory of Two Mondays 1955; films directed: A Man is Ten Feet Tall 1956, Edge of the City 1956, The Down Payment 1957, The Long Hot Summer 1957, The Sound and the Fury 1958, The Black Orchid 1959, Five Branded Women 1960, Paris Blues 1961, Adventures of a Young Man 1962, Hud 1963, The Outrage 1964, The Spy Who Came in from the Cold 1965, Hombre 1967, The Brotherhood 1968, The Molly Maguires 1969, The Great White Hope 1970, Sounder 1972, Pete'n'Tillie 1972, Conrack 1974, The Front 1976, Casey's Shadow 1977, Back Roads 1981, City Heat 1984, Nuts 1987; mem. Screen Dirs. Guild, American Fed. of TV and Radio Artists, Screen Actors Guild; Peabody Award. *Address:* Martindale, 9200 Sunset Boulevard, Los Angeles, Calif. 90069, U.S.A.

RITTER, Gerhard A., DR.PHIL.; German professor of modern history; b. 29 March 1929, Berlin; s. of Wilhelm and Martha (née Wietasch) Ritter; m. Gisela Kleinschmidt 1955; two s.; ed. Arndt-Oberschule, Berlin, Univ. of Tübingen, Free Univ., Berlin; research, Univ. of Oxford, England 1952–54; Asst. Free Univ., Berlin 1954–61, Prof. of Political Science 1962–65; Prof. of Modern History, Univ. of Münster 1965–74; Prof. of Modern History, Univ. of Munich 1974–; fmr. Guest Prof., Washington Univ., St. Louis, Mo., Univ. of Oxford, Univ. of Calif. (Berkeley), Tel-Aviv Univ.; mem. Senate and Main Cttee., Deutsche Forschungsgemeinschaft (German Research Soc.), Bonn 1973–76; Chair. Asscn. of Historians of Germany 1976–80; mem. Bavarian Acad. of Sciences, Munich, Comm. for History of Parliamentarism and Political Parties, Historische Kommission, Berlin. *Publications:* Die Arbeiterbewegung im Wilhelminischen Reich 1959, Parlament und Demokratie in Grossbritannien 1972, Das Deutsche Kaiserreich 1871–1914 1981, Deutsche Sozialgeschichte 1870–1914 (with Jürgen Kocka) 1982, Arbeiterbewegung, Parteien und Parlamentarismus 1976, Die II Internationale 1918/19. Protokolle, Memoranden, Berichte und Korrespondenzen 1980, Staat, Arbeiterschaft und Arbeiterbewegung in Deutschland 1980, Sozialversicherung in Deutschland und England 1983, Die deutschen Parteien 1830–1914 1985. *Address:* Institut für Neuere Geschichte, Franz-Joseph-Strasse 10, D-8000 Munich 40 (Office); Bismarckweg 3, D-8137 Berg/Starnberger See 3, Federal Republic of Germany (Home). *Telephone:* Munich 2180-2960 (Office).

RITTER, Jorge Eduardo, PH.D.; Panamanian diplomatist and politician; b. 1950; m.; two c.; ed. Pontificia Univ., Colombia; Clerk to Legis. Comm. 1973–77; Lecturer in Constitutional and Civil Law Univ. of Panama; fmr. mem. Governing Council Inst. for Human Resources Training and Devt.; Vice-Minister of Labour and Social Welfare 1977–78; Pvt. Sec. and Adviser to Pres. of Panama 1978–81; Minister of Foreign Affairs (desig.) 1981; teacher Nat. Political Training Coll. of the Guardia Nacional 1981; Minister of Interior and Justice 1981–82; Amb. to Colombia 1982–86; Perm. Rep. to UN 1986–88; Minister of Foreign Affairs April 1988–; Chair. Exec. Council Nat. Telecommunications Inst. 1981; Chair. Bd. Civil Aviation Authority 1981–82; mem. Bd. Banco Ganadero 1980–; Ritter, Diás y Asociados 1982–; Banco Interoceánico de Panama 1985–. *Address:* Ministry of Foreign Affairs, Panama 4, Panama. *Telephone:* 27 0013.

RITTNER, Luke Philip Hardwick; British arts administrator; b. 24 May 1947, Bath; s. of Stephen Rittner and Joane Rittner; m. Corinna Frances Edholm 1974; one d.; ed. Blackfriars School, Laxton, City of Bath Tech. Coll., Dartington Coll. of Arts and London Acad. of Music and Dramatic Art; Asst. Admin. Bath Festival 1968–71, Jt. Admin. 1971–74, Admin. Dir. 1974–76; Assoc. Dir. Business Sponsorship of the Arts 1976–83, Sec.-Gen. Arts Council of Great Britain 1983–; Gov. Urchfont Manor, Wiltshire Adult Educ. Centre 1982–83; mem. Music Panel, British Council 1979–83, Council

Victoria and Albert Museum 1980–83; Trustee Bath Preservation Trust 1968–73, Theatre Royal, Bath 1979–82; Foundation Trustee Holburne Museum, Bath 1981–. *Leisure interests:* the arts. *Address:* c/o Arts Council of Great Britain, 105 Piccadilly, London W1V 0AU, England. *Telephone:* 01-629 9495.

RIVAS-MIJARES, Gustavo, M.SC., DR.ING.; Venezuelan environmental engineer; b. 7 Nov. 1922, Valencia; s. of J. A. Rivas-Montenegro and Amparo Mijares de Rivas; m. Ligia Cardenas 1946; four c.; ed. Liceo Pedro Gual, Valencia, Univ. Central de Venezuela, Caracas and Univ. of Michigan; Prof. of Sanitary Eng., Faculty of Eng., Univ. Central de Venezuela 1945–85, Dean, Grad. School 1973–76; Pres. Nat. Acad. of Physics, Mathematics and Natural Science 1981–85; Dir. Nat. Council of Scientific and Tech. Research 1968–72; fmr. Dir. Venezuela Inst. of Scientific Research; Foreign Assoc. Nat. Acad. of Eng., U.S.A., Mexico, Spain; several awards. *Publications:* author and co-author of several books and 116 research papers. *Address:* Urb. Santa Rosa de Lima, Calle C, Res. Jarama, Apt. 7-A, Caracas, Venezuela. *Telephone:* 917156.

RIVERS, Larry; American artist; b. 1923, New York; m. 1st Augusta Berger 1945 (divorced), two s.; m. 2nd Clarice Price 1961, two c.; ed. New York Univ.; studied with Hans Hofmann; one-man exhbns. New York galleries 1949–; exhibited in group shows, Vanguard Gallery, Paris 1953, American Fed. of Arts travelling exhbn. 1954–55, Museum of Modern Art, New York 1956, Museum de Arte Moderne, São Paulo, Brazil 1957, Art Inst., Chicago, Minneapolis Inst. of Arts, special exhbn. sponsored by Museum of Modern Art, Japan, Museum Mexico City, Hirshhorn Gallery, Washington, Los Angeles Co. Museum, Museum Caracas, Venezuela 1979–80, Hanover Museum, Fed. Repub. of Germany 1980; works in perm. collections, William Rockhill Nelson Gallery of Art, Kansas City, Minneapolis Inst. of Arts, State Univ. Coll. of Educ., New Paltz, New York, Brooklyn Museum of Art, Metropolitan Museum of Art, Museum of Modern Art, Whitney Museum of American Art, New York, R.I. School of Design, Providence, N.C. Museum of Art, Raleigh, Corcoran Gallery of Art, Washington; works in pvt. collections; Stage Designer The Toilet (play); appeared in film Pull My Daisy; mural History of the Russian Revolution; special awards Corcoran Gallery of Art 1954, Arts Festival, Spoleto, Italy, Newport, R.I. 1958. *Publication:* Drawings and Digressions 1979. *Address:* c/o Marlborough Gallery, 40 West 57th Street, New York, N.Y. 10022, U.S.A.

RIVET, Albert Lionel Frederick, M.A., F.B.A., F.S.A.; British emeritus professor; b. 30 Nov. 1915, London; s. of Albert Robert Rivet and Rose Mary Rivet (née Bulow); m. Audrey Catherine Webb 1947; one s. one d.; ed. Felsted School and Oriel Coll. Oxford; schoolmaster 1938–39; served Air Raid Precautions then Army 1939–46; bookseller 1946–51; Asst. Archaeology Officer, Ordnance Survey 1951–64; Lecturer in Classics, Univ. of Keele 1964–67, Reader in Romano-British Studies 1967–74, Prof. of Roman Provincial Studies 1974–81, Emer. Prof. 1981–; Pres. Soc. for the Promotion of Roman Studies 1977–80; mem. Royal Comm. on Historical Monuments of England 1979–85; Corresp. mem. Deutsches Archäologisches Institut. *Publications:* 3rd Edn. O.S. Map of Roman Britain 1956, Town and Country in Roman Britain 1958, O.S. Map of Southern Britain in the Iron Age 1962, The Iron Age in Northern Britain (Ed.) 1966, The Roman Villa in Britain (Ed.) 1969, The Place-Names of Roman Britain (with C. Smith) 1979, Gallia Narbonensis 1988; many contribs. to atlases, encyclopaedias and journals in Britain, France, Germany, Italy and U.S.A. *Leisure interest:* writing. *Address:* 7 Springpool, The University, Keele, Staffs., ST5 5BN, England.

RIVETTE, Jacques; French film director; b. 1 March 1928, Rouen; s. of André and Andrée (née Amiard) Rivette; ed. Lycée Corneille, Rouen; journalist and critic on Cahiers du Cinéma 1953–82; Asst. to Jacques Becker and Jean Renoir 1954; Dir. of Films 1956–; Grand Prix nat. 1981. *Films:* Le coup du berger (director) 1956, Paris nous appartient (author and director) 1958–60, Suzanne Simenon, La Religieuse de Diderot 1966, L'Amour fou 1968, Out One: Spectre 1973, Céline et Julie vont en bateau 1974, Le vengeur, Duelle 1976, Le pont du Nord 1982, Merry-go-round 1983, Wuthering Heights 1984, L'amour par terre 1984, The Gang of Four (Berlin Film Award 1989) 1988; Dir. La religieuse (theatre) 1963; Chevalier, Ordre nat. du Mérite; Grand Prix nat. du Cinéma 1981. *Address:* 20 boulevard de la Bastille, 75012 Paris, France.

RIVLIN, Moshe; Israeli executive; b. 16 Jan. 1925, Jerusalem; s. of Yitzhak and Esther Rivlin; m. Ruth Moav (Horbaty) 1960; two d.; ed. Teachers' Seminary, Graduate Aluma Inst. for Jewish Studies, Mizrachi Teacher's Coll. and School for Political Science, Hebrew Univ., Jerusalem; Major in ZAHAL 1948–49; Consul in U.S.A. 1952–58; Dir. Information Dept., The Jewish Agency 1958–60, Sec.-Gen. 1960–66, Dir.-Gen. and Head of Admin. and Public Relations Dept. 1966–71; elected Dir.-Gen. of reconstituted Jewish Agency 1971–77; Assoc. mem. Exec., World Zionist Org. 1971; Chair. Keren Kayemeth Le Israel 1977–; Nat. Chair. Haganah Veterans Assen. in Israel 1972–82; mem. Bd. of Govs. Ben-Gurion Univ., Coll. for Public Admin., Jewish Telegraphic Agency; mem. Exec. Cttee. Yad Ben-Zvi, mem. Council Yad Ben-Gurion; mem. Bd. of Dirs. Jerusalem Post, Beit Hatfutzot, Hebrew Univ. *Address:* Keren Kayemeth Le Israel, P.O. Box 283, Jerusalem; 34 Hapalmach Street, Jerusalem, Israel (Home). *Telephone:* 02/244023 (Office); 02/635173 (Home).

RIVOYRE, Christine Berthe Claude Denis de, L. ÈS L.; French journalist and author; b. 29 Nov. 1921, Tarbes; d. of François Denis de Rivoyre and Madeleine née Ballande; ed. Inst. du Sacré Coeur, Bordeaux and Poitiers, Faculté des lettres, Paris and Univ. of Syracuse, U.S.A.; journalist Le Monde (daily) 1950-55; Literary Dir. Marie-Claire (monthly magazine) 1955-65; mem. Haut Comité de la Langue française, Conseil Supérieur des Lettres, Prix Medicis Jury; Chevalier, Légion d'honneur, Chevalier des Arts et des Lettres; Prix Paul Morand (Académie française) 1984. and other awards. *Publications:* L'alouette au miroir 1956, La mandarine 1957, La tête en fleurs 1960, La glace à l'ananas 1962, Les sultans 1964, Le petit matin 1968, Le seigneur des chevaux (with A. Kalda) 1969, Fleur d'agonie 1970, Boy 1973, Le voyage à l'envers 1977, Belle alliance 1982, Reine-Mère 1985. *Address:* Dichats Ha, Onesse-Laharie, 40110 Morceux, France.

RIX, Timothy John, B.A., C.B.I.M., F.R.S.A.; British publisher; b. 4 Jan. 1934, Maidenhead, Berks.; s. of late Howard T. and of Marguerite Selman Rix; m. 1st Wendy E. Wright 1960 (dissolved 1967), 2nd Gillian née Greenwood 1968; one s. two d.; ed. Radley Coll., Clare Coll., Cambridge and Yale Univ.; joined Longman Green & Co. Ltd. 1958, Overseas Educ. Publr. 1958-61, Publishing Man. Far East and S.E. Asia 1961-63, Head, English Language Teaching Publishing 1964-68, Div. Man. Dir. 1968-72, Jt. Man. Dir. 1972-76, Chief Exec. Longman Group Ltd. 1976-88, Chair. 1984-88; Chair. Addison-Wesley-Longman Group Ltd. 1988-; Dir. Pearson Longman Ltd. (now Pearson PLC) 1979-83, Goldcrest Television 1981-83, Yale Univ. Press Ltd., London 1984; mem. British Library Bd. 1986, British Council Bd. 1988; Chair. Book Trust 1986-88; other professional appointments. *Publications:* articles on publishing in trade journals. *Leisure interests:* reading, landscape, wine. *Address:* 24 Birchington Road, London, N8 8HP, England. *Telephone:* 01-348 4143.

RIZZOLI, Angelo; Italian publisher; b. 12 Nov. 1943, Como; s. of Andrea and Lucia (née Solmi) Rizzoli; m. Eleonora Giorgi 1979; one c.; ed. univ.; Pres. and Man. Ed. Rizzoli Editore 1978-; Pres. Cineriz Distributori Associati 1978-, Rizzoli Film 1978-. *Address:* Via Angelo Rizzoli 2, 20132 Milan, Italy (Office). *Telephone:* 02-25-841.

ROA BASTOS, Augusto; Paraguayan writer and journalist; b. 1917; ed. Asunción; returned to Paraguay after 40 years in exile March 1989; awarded John Simon Guggenheim Memorial Foundation 1971. *Publications:* Poetry: El Ruiseñor y la Aurora 1936, El Naranjal Ardiente 1947-49; Novels: El Trueno entre las Hojas 1953, Hijo de Hombre 1960, El Baldío 1966, Los Pies sobre el Agua 1967, Madera Quemada 1967, Moriencia 1969, Cuerpo Presente y otros cuentos 1971, Yo el Supremo 1974, Los Congresos 1974, El Somnámbulo 1976; Screenplays: El Trueno entre las Hojas 1955, Hijo de Hombre 1960, Shunko 1960, Alias Gardelito 1963, Castigo al Traidor 1966, El Señor Presidente 1966, Don Segundo Sombra 1968. *Address:* Berutti 2828, Martínez, Buenos Aires, Argentina.

ROA-KOURI, Raúl; Cuban diplomatist; b. 9 July 1936, Havana; s. of Raúl Roa and Ada Kouri; m. María Rodríguez de Roa-Kouri 1976; two d. (previous marriage); ed. Univ. of Havana, Columbia Univ. in New York, U.S.A.; Deputy Perm. Rep. to UN 1959-60; Amb. to Czechoslovakia 1961-63, to Brazil 1963-64; Dir. of Trade Policy, Ministry of Foreign Trade 1964-66; Dir.-Gen. of Int. Dept. Ministry for Food Industries 1967-70; Dir.-Gen. of Nat. Cttee. for Econ., Scientific and Tech. Co-operation 1971-72; Perm. Sec. CMEA Nat. Cttee. for Econ. Scientific and Tech. Co-operation 1972-76; Sr. Political Adviser to Vice-Pres. of Council of State in charge of Foreign Affairs 1976-78; Perm. Rep. to UN 1978-84; Vice-Minister of Foreign Affairs 1984-; mem. Scientific Council, Center for Int. Econ. Research, Havana Univ. 1986-. *Leisure interests:* music, literature, tennis, writing. *Address:* c/o Ministry of Foreign Affairs, Havana, Cuba.

ROACH, Maxwell Lemuel; American jazz musician; b. 10 Jan. 1924, Elizabeth City, N.C.; s. of Alphonzo Roach and Cressie (née Saunders) Roach; m. 1st Mildred Wilkinson 1949 (divorced); one s. one d.; m. 2nd Abbey Lincoln 1962 (divorced); ed. Manhattan School of Music, New England Conservatory of Music; Prof. of Music, Univ. of Massachusetts 1973-; specialized in percussion instruments, with Charlie Parker 1946-48, later with Thelonius Monk, Bud Powell, Dizzy Gillespie, etc.; Co-leader Maw Roach-Clifford Brown Quintet 1954-56; appearances at Paris Jazz Festival 1949, Newport Jazz Festival 1972; composer and choreographer Freedom Now suite; received Best Record of Year Award, Down Beat magazine 1956, and other awards; mem. Jazz Artists Guild Inc. *Address:* c/o Willard Alexander Inc., 660 Madison Avenue, New York, N.Y. 10021, U.S.A.

ROBARDS, Jason Nelson, Jr.; American actor; b. 26 July 1922, Chicago; s. of Jason Nelson Robards and Hope Robards (née Glanville); m. 1st Eleanor Pitman 1948; two s. one d.; m. 3rd Lauren Bacall 1961 (divorced); one s.; m. 4th Lois O'Connor 1970; two s.; ed. American Academy of Dramatic Arts; served with U.S. Navy 1939-46; *Broadway plays include:* Stalag 17 1951-53, The Chase 1952, The Iceman Cometh 1956, Long Day's Journey into Night 1956-58, 1976, Henry IVth Part 1 1958, Macbeth, The Disenchanted 1958-59, Toys in the Attic 1960, Big Fish, Little Fish 1961, A Thousand Clowns 1962, After the Fall 1964, But for Whom, Charlie 1964, Hughie 1964, The Devils 1965, We Bombed in New Haven 1968, The Country Girl 1972, A Moon for the Misbegotten 1973, A Touch of the Poet

1977-78, You Can't Take it with You 1983; *films include:* The Journey 1959, By Love Possessed 1961, A Thousand Clowns, Big Hand for the Little Lady 1966, Any Wednesday 1966, St. Valentine's Day Massacre 1967, The Night They Raided Minsky's 1968, The Loves of Isadora 1969, Once Upon a Time in the West 1969, Ballad of Cable Hogue 1970, Johnny Got His Gun 1971, Murder in the Rue Morgue 1971, The War Between Men and Women 1972, Pat Garrett and Billy the Kid 1973, All the President's Men 1976, Julia 1977, Comes a Horseman 1978, Hurricane 1979, Melvin and Howard 1979, Max Dugan Returns 1982, Something Wicked This Way Comes 1983, The Iceman Cometh 1985, Square Dance 1987, The Good Mother 1988, Black Rainbow 1989, Parenthood 1989; *television films include:* For Whom the Bell Tolls 1959, The Iceman Cometh 1961, One Day in the Life of Ivan Denisovitch 1968, Washington Behind Closed Doors 1977, The Last Year 1980, The Day After 1983, Sakharov 1984; Johnny Bull 1986; Bd. Dirs. American Academy of Dramatic Arts 1957-; ANTA Award for Outstanding Contribution to Living Theater 1959; Perry Award as Best Actor 1959, Academy Awards for Best Supporting Actor 1976, 1977; New York Film Critics Circle Award for Best Supporting Actor 1976. *Address:* c/o STE Representation Ltd., 888 Seventh Avenue, New York, N.Y. 10019, U.S.A.

ROBB, Charles Spittal, B.B.A., J.D.; American lawyer and politician; b. 26 June 1939, Phoenix, Ariz.; s. of James Spittal Robb and Frances Howard (née Woolley) Robb; m. Lynda Bird Johnson (d. of late Pres. Lyndon B. Johnson) 1967; three d.; ed. Cornell Univ., Univ. of Wisconsin and Univ. of Virginia; admitted to Va. Bar 1973; law clerk to John D. Butzner, Jr., U.S. Court of Appeals 1973-74; admitted to U.S. Supreme Court Bar 1976; Attorney, Williams, Connolly and Califano 1974-77; Lieut.-Gov. of Virginia 1978-82, Gov. 1982-86; Chair. Democratic Govs. Asscn. 1984-85, Democratic Leadership Council 1986-; Chair Educ. Comm. of the States, Educ. Sub-Cttee. of the Nat. Govs. Assn's. Standing Cttee. on Human Resources; Chair. Southern Govs. Assn. 1984-85; Pres. Council of State Govts. 1985-86; Partner, Hunton and Williams 1986-; mem. Bd. various educational insts.; mem. American, Va. Bar Assns., Va. Trial Lawyers' Assn.; Bronze Star, Viet-Nam Service Medal with four stars, Vietnamese Cross of Gallantry with Silver Star; Raven Award 1973; Seven Socs. Org. Award, Univ. of Va. *Address:* Hunton and Williams, 3050 Chain Bridge Road, Fairfax, Va. 22030, U.S.A.

ROBB, John, M.B., F.R.C.S.; Irish surgeon and politician; b. 24 Feb. 1932, Downpatrick; s. of John Charles Robb and Jessie Robb (née Wilson); m. Sylvia Sloan 1968; two s. two d.; ed. Merchiston Castle School, Edin., Scotland, Queen's Univ. Belfast, Northern Ireland; Chair. Jr. Hosp. Staff Group, Northern Ireland 1962-63; lecturer in Surgery, Dept. of Surgery, Queen's Univ. and Royal Victoria Hosp. 1964-66; Medical Officer, Long Bone Trauma Unit, King Edward VIII Hosp., Durban, S.A. 1966-67; Medical Officer, Accident Emergency and Orthopaedics, Baragwanath Hosp., Soweto, S.A. 1967; Consultant Surgeon, Royal Vic. Hosp., Belfast, Northern Ireland 1968-72; Harare Hosp., Harare (then Salisbury, Rhodesia) 1979; now Consultant Surgeon, Route Hosp., Ballymoney, Co. Antrim; Sec. Postgraduate Surgical Training Cttee. Northern Ireland 1964-66; Undergraduate and Postgraduate Examiner, Royal Coll. of Surgeons Ireland 1968-74; Founder-mem. New Ireland Movement 1972; mem. Council New Univ. of Ulster 1973-76; mem. Radio Telefis Eireann Governing Authority 1973-76; Gov. Irish Foundation for Human Devt. 1975-; mem. Cttee. Ulster People's Coll. Assn. 1979-84; Chair. New Ireland Group 1982-, Viking Surgeons' Club 1987; Senator (Dublin) 1982-. *Publications:* articles on surgery, several pamphlets on Irish political problems. *Address:* 85 Charlotte Street, Ballymoney, Co. Antrim, Northern Ireland. *Telephone:* 02656-62235.

ROBBE-GRILLET, Alain; French writer, film-maker and agronomist; b. 18 Aug. 1922, Brest; s. of Gaston Robbe-Grillet and Yvonne Canu; m. Catherine Rstakian 1957; ed. Lycée Buffon, Lycée St. Louis and Inst. Nat. Agronomique, Paris; Chargé de Mission, Inst. Nat. de la Statistique 1945-48; Engineer Inst. des Fruits Tropicaux (Guinea, Morocco, Martinique and Guadeloupe) 1949-51; Literary Adviser Editions de Minuit 1955-85; Chevalier, Légion d'honneur; Officier Ordre nat. du mérite; Prix Louis Delluc 1963. *Publications:* Novels: Les gommes 1953, Le voyeur 1955, La jalousie 1957, Dans le labyrinthe 1959, La maison de rendez-vous 1965, Projet pour une révolution à New York 1970, Topologie d'une cité fantôme 1976, La belle captive 1977, D'un régicide 1978, Souvenirs du triangle d'or 1978, Djinn 1981, Le miroir qui revient 1984, Angélique ou l'enchantement 1988; short stories: Instantanés 1962; essay: Pour un nouveau roman 1964; films: L'année dernière à Marienbad 1961; films directed: L'immortelle 1963, Trans-Europ-Express 1967, L'homme qui ment 1968, L'Eden et après 1970, Glissements progressifs du plaisir 1974, Le jeu avec le feu 1975, La belle captive 1983. *Address:* 7 rue Bernard-Palissy, 75006 Paris (Office); 18 boulevard Maillot, 92200 Neuilly-sur-Seine, France (Home). *Telephone:* 722-31-22 (Home).

RÖBBELEN, Gerhard Paul Karl, DR.RER.NAT.; German professor of plant genetics; b. 10 May 1929, Bremen; s. of Ernst Röbbelen and Henny Röbbelen; m. Christa Scherz 1957; two s. one d.; ed. Univs. of Göttingen and Freiburg; Asst. Prof. Inst. of Agronomy and Plant Breeding, Univ. of Göttingen 1957-62, Prof. and Head Div. of Cytogenetics 1967-70, Dir. of Inst. 1970-, Dean Faculty of Agric. 1971-72; Visiting Prof. Univ. of Miss.,

Columbia 1966–67; Ed. Journal of Plant Breeding 1976–; mem. German Soc. for Genetics (Pres. 1964–70, 1977–79), European Asscn. for Research in Plant Breeding—EUCARPIA (Chair. Section for Oil and Protein Crops 1977–86, Pres. 1986–), German Botanical Soc., Asscn. for Applied Botany, Genetics Soc. of Canada, Soc. for Genetics, Munich, German Agricultural Soc., German Soc. for Quality Research, Acad. of Sciences, Göttingen 1981–; Hon. Dr. Agric. (Kiel) 1976. *Publications:* over 200 articles on research into plant breeding. *Leisure interests:* music, mountain climbing, gardening. *Address:* 8 Von Sieboldsrasse, 3400 Göttingen (Office); 9 Tuckermannweg, 3400 Göttingen, Federal Republic of Germany.

ROBBINS, Frederick Chapman, A.B., B.S., M.D.; American scientist and university professor; b. 25 Aug. 1916, Auburn, Ala.; s. of William J. and Christine (Chapman) Robbins; m. Alice Havemeyer Northrop 1948; two d.; ed. Univ. of Missouri and Harvard Medical School; served U.S. Army 1942–46; Senior Fellow, Nat. Research Council 1948–50; Research Fellow, Harvard Medical School 1948–50; Instructor, Harvard Medical School 1950–51, Assoc. (Pediatrics) 1951–52; Assoc., Research Div. of Infectious Disease, Children's Medical Center, Boston 1950–52; Assoc. Physician and Assoc. Dir. of Isolation Services, Children's Hospital, Boston 1950–52; Research Fellow, Boston Lying-in Hospital 1950–52; Asst. Children's Medical Service, Mass. Gen. Hospital, Boston 1950–52; Dir. Dept. of Pediatrics and Contagious Diseases, Cleveland Metropolitan Gen. Hospital 1952–66; Prof. of Pediatrics, Case Western Reserve Univ. School of Medicine, Cleveland 1952–80, Dean 1966–80, Dean Emer. 1980–, Prof. Emer. 1987–; Assoc. Pediatrician Univ. Hospitals, Cleveland 1952–66; Pres. Inst. of Medicine, N.A.S. 1980–85; mem. Nat. Acad. of Sciences 1972, American Philosophical Soc. 1972; Hon. D.Sc. (John Carroll and Mo. Univs.); Hon. LL.D. (New Mexico) 1968; Bronze Star 1945; First Mead Johnson Award (jointly) 1953; Nobel Prize for Physiology and Medicine (jointly) 1954; Medical Mutual Honor Award for 1969. *Publications:* various scientific papers related to virus and rickettsial diseases, especially 'Q' fever in the Mediterranean area and cultivation of poliomyelitis viruses in tissue culture. *Address:* 2626 West Park Boulevard, Shaker Heights, Ohio 44120, U.S.A. (Home).

ROBBINS, Harold (pseudonym of Francis Kane); American author; b. 21 May 1916, New York; m. 1st Lillian Machnivitz (dissolved); m. 2nd Grace Palermo; two d.; ed. George Washington High School, New York; food and commodity dealer, New York until 1940; Shipping Clerk, later Dir. of Budget and Planning, Universal Pictures, New York 1940–46. *Publications:* Never Love a Stranger 1948, The Dream Merchants 1949, A Stone for Danny Fisher 1951, Never Leave Me 1953, 79 Park Avenue 1955, Stiletto 1953, The Carpetbaggers 1961, Where Love Has Gone 1962, The Adventurers 1966, The Inheritors 1969, The Betsy 1971, The Pirate 1974, The Lonely Lady 1976, Dreams Die First 1977, Memories of Another Day 1979, Goodbye, Janette 1981, Spellbinder 1982, Descent from Xanadu 1984, The Storyteller 1985, Piranha 1986. *Address:* c/o New English Library, 47 Bedford Square, London, WC1B 3DP, England.

ROBBINS, Herbert Ellis, PH.D.; American university professor; b. 12 Jan. 1915, Newcastle, Pa.; m. 1st Mary Dimock 1943 (divorced 1955); two d.; m. 2nd Carol Hallett 1966; two s. one d.; ed. Harvard Univ.; U.S. Navy 1942–46; Prof. N.C. Univ. 1946–53, Columbia Univ. 1953–86, Rutgers Univ. 1986–; Hon. D.Sc. (Purdue) 1974; Guggenheim Fellow 1952, 1975. *Publications:* Selected Papers 1985; Co-author: What is Mathematics? 1941, Great Expectations 1971. *Address:* Rutgers University, Hill Center, Busch Campus, New Brunswick, N.J. 08903, U.S.A.

ROBBINS, Jerome; American choreographer and director; b. 11 Oct. 1918, New York; s. of Harry and Lena Robbins; ed. New York Univ.; Dancer in Broadway choruses 1938–40; American Ballet Theatre soloist 1941–46; Choreographer, New York City Ballet 1949–, Assoc. Artistic Dir. 1949–59, Ballet Master 1969–83, Co-Ballet Master 1983–; formed Ballets: U.S.A.; touring U.S. and Europe 1958–; mem. Nat. Council on the Arts 1974–80, Dance Panel, N.Y. State Council on the Arts 1973–77; Antoinette Perry (Tony) Award for Fiddler on the Roof 1965, Kennedy Center Award 1981, two Acad. Awards, Nat. Medal of Arts 1988, and others. *Choreographed:* Ballets: Fancy Free 1944, Interplay 1945, Facsimile 1947, Pas de Trois 1947, The Cage 1951, Fanfare 1953, Afternoon of a Faun 1953, The Concert 1956, N.Y. Export op. Jazz 1958, Moves 1961, Events 1961, Les Noces 1965, Dances at a Gathering 1970, Requiem Canticles 1972, In the Night, The Dybbuk Variations 1974, Mother Goose 1975, Other Dances 1976, Opus 19 "The Dreamer" 1979, Suite of Dances 1980, Rondo 1981, Pas de Deux from Tchaikovsky First Piano Concerto 1981, Piano Pieces 1981, The Gershwin Concerto 1982, Four Chamber Works 1982, Glass Pieces 1983, I'm Old Fashioned 1983, Antique Epigraphs 1984, Eight Lines 1985, In Memory Of . . . 1985, Quiet City 1986, Piccolo Balleto 1986, and many others; Musicals include: On the Town 1945, High Button Shoes 1947, Call Me Madam 1950, The King and I 1951 (film 1956), The Pajama Game (co-dir.) 1954, Bells are Ringing (dir.) 1956, West Side Story (dir. and choreographer) 1957, (film 1960), Gypsy (dir. and choreographer) 1959, Oh Dad, Poor Dad (dir.) 1962, Fiddler on the Roof (dir. and choreographer) 1964, Jerome Robbins Broadway (Dir. and choreographer) 1989; Opera: The Tender Land 1954. *Address:* c/o New York City Ballet, New York State Theatre, Lincoln Center, New York, N.Y. 10023, U.S.A.

ROBENS OF WOLDINGHAM, Baron, cr. 1961 (Life Peer), of Woldingham in the County of Surrey; **Alfred Robens,** P.C., D.C.L., LL.D.; British politician; b. 18 Dec. 1910, Manchester; s. of George and Edith Robens; m. Eva Powell 1937; ed. Council School; Official of Union of Distributive and Allied Workers 1935–45; Manchester City Councillor 1942–45; Labour M.P. for Wansbeck Div. of Northumberland 1945–50, Blyth 1950–60; Parl. Pvt. Sec. to Minister of Transport 1945–47; Parl. Sec. Minister of Fuel and Power 1947–51; Minister of Labour April–Oct. 1951; Labour Relations Consultant, Atomic Power Construction Ltd. 1960; Deputy Chair. Nat. Coal Bd. 1960–61, Chair. 1961–71; Chair. Johnson Matthey and Co. Ltd. 1971–83, Hon. Pres. 1983–86; Chair. Vickers Ltd. 1971–79, St. Regis Newspapers 1975–80, Snamprogetti 1980–, Alfred Robens Associates 1984–; Dir. American Medical (Europe) Ltd. 1981–; mem. NEDC 1962–71; Pres. Advertising Asscn. 1963–67; Chair. Foundation on Automation and Employment 1970; Chair. Council of the Manchester Business School 1970–79; mem. Royal Comm. on Trade Unions and Employers' Asscns. 1965–68; Chair. Govt. Enquiry into Safety and Health of People at Work; Chair. Eng. Industries Council 1976–80; Gov. Queen Elizabeth's Training Coll. for the Disabled 1951–80; Chair. of Govs. Guy's Hosp. 1965–74; Dir. J. H. Sankey and Son Ltd., Bank of England 1966–81, St. Regis Paper Co. (U.K.) 1971–81, St. Regis Int. (U.K.) 1971–81, Trust-House-Forte 1971–85, Times Newspapers Holdings Ltd. 1980–83; Chair. It. Econ. Mission to Malta 1967; Chancellor, Univ. of Surrey 1966–77; Fellow, Manchester Coll. of Science and Tech. 1965–; Hon. D.C.L. (Newcastle, Manchester), Hon. LL.D. (Leicester, London and Manchester Univs.); Mackintosh Medal, Advertising Asscn. 1970, Albert Medal of R.S.A. 1977. *Publications:* Human Engineering 1970, Ten Year Stint 1971. *Leisure interest:* gardening. *Address:* House of Lords, London, S.W.1, England.

ROBERT, Jacques Frédéric, D. EN D.; French professor of law; b. 29 Sept. 1928, Algiers, Algeria; s. of Frédéric and Fanny Robert; m. Marie-Caroline de Bary 1958; two s. two d.; ed. Lycée E. F. Gautier, Algiers, Univs. of Algiers and Paris, C.N.R.S.; Prof. of Law, Univs. of Algiers 1956–60, Rabat, Morocco 1960–62, Grenoble 1962–65; Dir. Maison franco-japonaise, Tokyo 1965–68; Prof. of Law, Univ. of Nanterre 1968–69, Univ. of Paris II 1969–; Contributor, Le Monde and La Croix 1971–; Pres. Univ. of Paris II (Panthéon) 1979–85; Pres. of Centre français de droit comparé 1985–; mem. Conseil Constitutionnel 1989–; Prix Paul Deschanel 1954; Chevalier, Légion d'honneur; Order of the Sacred Treasure (Japan); Officier des Palmes académiques; Chevalier, Ordre nat. du Mérite; Commdr., Order of Honour (Austria). *Publications:* Les violations de la liberté individuelle 1954, La monarchie marocaine 1963, Le Japon 1970, Introduction à l'Esprit des Lois 1973, Libertés publiques 1976; L'Esprit de défence 1988. *Leisure interests:* music, photography, tennis. *Address:* Université de Paris II, 12 place du Panthéon, 75005 Paris (Office); 14 Villa Saint-Georges, 92160 Antony, France (Home). *Telephone:* 325 26 73 (Office); 666 12 32 (Home).

ROBERTO, Holden (see Holden, Roberto).

ROBERTS, Burnell R., M.B.A.; American business executive; b. 6 May 1927, Wis.; s. of Roy and Anna Mae (née Jones) Roberts; m. Karen Ragatz 1953; two s. two d.; ed. Univ. of Wis. and Harvard Graduate School of Business; with Bendix Aviation Corpn. 1953–58, Gen. Tire and Rubber Co. 1957–62 (Treas. and Controller subsidiary, A. M. Byers Co., Pittsburgh 1962–66); Asst. to Exec. Vice-Pres. Mead Corpn. 1966–68, Controller and Vice-Pres. (Finance) 1968–71; Group Vice-Pres. Merchants Group 1971–74; Group Vice-Pres. Mead Paper 1974–; Sr. Vice-Pres. Mead Corpn. 1979–81, Pres. 1981–, Chair. and C.E.O. April 1982–; Dir. several cos. *Leisure interests:* tennis, reading. *Address:* The Mead Corporation, Courthouse Plaza, N.E., Dayton, Ohio 45463, U.S.A. (Home). *Telephone:* (513) 222-6323.

ROBERTS, Chalmers McGeagh, A.B.; American journalist; b. 18 Nov. 1910; m. Lois Hall 1941; two s. one d.; ed. Amherst Coll.; Reporter Washington Post, D.C. 1933–34, Associated Press, Pittsburgh Bureau 1934–35, Toledo News-Bee 1936–38, Japan Times, Tokyo 1938–39; Asst. Man. Ed. Washington Daily News 1939–41; Sunday Ed. Washington Times-Herald 1941; Office of War Information, London and Washington 1941–43; U.S. Army Air Force 1943–46; Life magazine 1946–47; Washington Star 1947–49; Washington Post 1949–71, Chief Diplomatic corresp. 1954–71, Contrib. columnist 1971–, San Diego Union contrib. columnist 1977–87; Hon. Dr. of Humane Letters 1963. *Publications:* Washington Past and Present 1950, Can We Meet the Russians Half Way? 1958, The Nuclear Years: the Arms Race and Arms Control, 1945–70 1970, First Rough Draft: a Journalist's Journal of Our Times 1973, The Washington Post: The First 100 Years 1977. *Address:* 6699 MacArthur Boulevard, Bethesda, Md. 20816, U.S.A. (Office and Home).

ROBERTS, Sir Denys Tudor Emil, K.B.E., Q.C., M.A., B.C.L.; British administrator and judge; b. 19 Jan. 1923, London; s. of William David Roberts and Dorothy Eliza Morrison; m. 1st B. Marsh 1949, one s. one d.; m. 2nd Fiona Alexander 1985; ed. Aldenham School, Wadham Coll., Oxford and Lincoln's Inn; Captain, Royal Artillery 1943–46; English Bar 1950–53; Crown Counsel, Nyasaland (now Malawi) 1953–59; Attorney-Gen., Gibraltar 1960–62; Solicitor-Gen., Hong Kong 1962–66, Attorney-Gen. 1966–73, Colonial Sec. 1973–76, Chief Sec. 1976–78, Chief Justice Hong Kong and Brunei 1979–87, of Brunei 1979–; mem. Court of Appeal for Bermuda 1988–; Seri Paduka Makhota Brunei. *Publications:* five novels 1955–65.

Leisure interests: writing, cricket, tennis, walking. *Address:* Supreme Court, Bandar Seri Begawan, Brunei.

ROBERTS, Derek Harry, C.B.E., B.SC., F.R.S., F.ENG.; British physicist and business executive; b. 28 March 1932, Manchester; s. of Harry Roberts and Alice Roberts (née Storey); m. Winifred Short 1958; one s. one d.; ed. Manchester Cen. High School and Manchester Univ.; Research Scientist, Plessey Co. 1953–67; Gen. Man. Plessey Semiconductors 1967–69; Dir. Plessey Allen Clark Research Centre 1969–73; Man. Dir. Plessey Microsystems Div. 1973–79; Dir. of Research, The General Electric Co. PLC 1979–83, Tech. Dir. 1983–85, Deputy Man. Dir. (Tech.) 1985–88, Dir. 1988–; Provost Univ. Coll., London April 1989–; Visiting Prof., Univ. Coll. London 1979; Hon. D.Sc. (Bath) 1982, (Loughborough) 1984, (City) 1985, (Lancaster) 1986, (Manchester) 1987, D.Univ. (Open) 1984. *Publications:* about 25–30 tech. papers in learned soc. journals. *Leisure interest:* gardening. *Address:* The General Electric Company PLC, 1 Stanhope Gate, London, W1A 1EH; The Old Rectory, Maids Moreton, Buckingham, England. *Telephone:* 01-493 8484; (0280) 813470.

ROBERTS, Sir Frank Kenyon, G.C.M.G., G.C.V.O., M.A.; British diplomatist (retd.), international official and businessman; b. 27 Oct. 1907, Buenos Aires, Argentina; s. of Henry George Roberts and Gertrude Kenyon; m. Celeste Leila B. Shoucair 1937; ed. Bedales and Rugby Schools and Trinity Coll., Cambridge; Third Sec. Foreign Office 1930–32, British Embassy, Paris 1932–35; Second Sec. Cairo 1935–37, Foreign Office 1937–45 (First Sec. 1941, Head of Central Dept. 1941–45, Acting Counsellor 1943); Chargé d'Affaires to Czechoslovak Govt. in London 1943; Minister to U.S.S.R. 1945–47; Pvt. Sec. to Foreign Sec. 1947–49; mission to Moscow 1948; Deputy High Commr. in India 1949–51; Deputy Under-Sec. of State, Foreign Office 1951–54; Amb. to Yugoslavia 1954–57; U.K. Perm. Rep. on N. Atlantic Council 1957–60; Amb. to U.S.S.R. 1960–62, to Fed. Repub. of Germany 1963–68; Advisory Dir. Unilever Ltd. 1968–80; Dir. Dunlop Holdings Ltd. 1970–79, Hoechst (U.K.), Amalgamated Metal Corpn., Mercedes-Benz (U.K); fmr. adviser on Int. Affairs to Lloyds; Pres. British Atlantic Cttee. 1969–81, Vice-Pres. 1982–; Pres. Atlantic Treaty Assen. 1969–73, Vice-Pres. 1973–; Chair. European-Atlantic Group 1970–73, Pres. 1973–82; Hon. Gov. Atlantic Inst. for Int. Affairs; mem. Review Cttee. on Overseas Representation 1968–69; mem. Council of the Royal Inst. for Int. Affairs 1968–83; Pres. German Chamber of Industry and Commerce 1971–74, Vice-Pres. 1974–; Grand Cross of German Order of Merit. *Leisure interests:* golf, reading, travelling, international relations. *Address:* 25 Kensington Court Gardens, London, W8 5QF, England. *Telephone:* 01-937 1140.

ROBERTS, George A., D.SC.; American business executive; b. 18 Feb. 1919, Uniontown, Pa.; s. of Jacob Earle Roberts and Mary Mildred Bower; m. 1st Betty E. Matthewson 1941; m. 2nd Jeanne Polk Roberts 1971; two s. one d.; ed. Carnegie Inst. of Tech.; Pres. and Chair. Bd., Vasco Metals Corpn. until 1966; Pres. and mem. Bd. of Dirs., Teledyne Inc. (following merger with Vasco Metals) 1966–, C.E.O. 1987–; fmr. Int. Pres. American Soc. for Metals, Pres. American Soc. for Metals Foundation for Educ. and Research, Trustee Council for Profit Sharing Industries, Trustee Trade Relations Council and Chair. Bd. Metallurgy-Ceramics Foundation Inc.; mem. Bd. of Trustees, Carnegie-Mellon Univ.; Fellow, Metallurgical Soc. of the American Inst. of Mining, Metallurgical and Petroleum Engineers and the American Soc. for Metals (Gold Medal 1977); mem. Nat. Acad. of Eng. *Publications:* Tool Steels; many technical papers. *Address:* 1901 Avenue of the Stars, Suite 1800, Los Angeles, Calif. 90067, U.S.A.

ROBERTS, John D., PH.D.; American chemist and educator; b. 8 June 1918, Los Angeles, Calif.; s. of Allen Andrew Roberts and Flora Dombrowski; m. Edith M. Johnson 1942; three s. one d.; ed. Univ. of California at Los Angeles; Instructor Univ. of Calif. at Los Angeles; Nat. Research Fellow in Chem., Harvard Univ. 1945–46, Instructor 1946; Instructor M.I.T. 1946–47, Asst. Prof. 1947–50, Assoc. Prof. 1950–53; Guggenheim Fellow, Calif. Inst. of Technology 1952–53, Prof. of Organic Chem. 1953–72, Inst. Prof. of Chem. 1972–, Chair. Div. of Chem. and Chemical Eng. 1963–68, Acting Chair. 1972–73, Dean of the Faculty 1980–83, Vice-Pres. and Provost 1980–83; Visiting Prof. Ohio State Univ. 1952, Harvard Univ. 1959–60, Univ. of Munich 1962; Distinguished Visiting Prof. Univ. of Iowa 1967; Visiting Prof. Stanford Univ. 1973; mem. N.A.S., Chair. Section of Chem. 1968–71, of Math. and Physical Sciences 1976–78, Class I 1977–79, Counsellor 1980–83; mem. American Philosophical Society 1974, Counsellor, Class I 1983–86; Dr. h.c. (Munich and Temple Univ.); American Chemical Soc. Award in Pure Chem. 1954, Harrison Howe Award 1957, Roger Adams Award 1967, Univ. of Calif. at Los Angeles Alumni Achievement Award 1967, Nichols Medal 1972, Richard C. Tolman Medal 1975, Michelson-Morley Award 1976, James F. Norris Award 1979, Pauling Award 1980, Richards Medal 1982, Willing Gibbs Gold Medalist 1983, Golden Plate Award, American Acad. of Achievement 1983, Priestley Medal 1987. *Publications:* Nuclear Magnetic Resonance 1958, Spin-Spin Splitting in High Resolution Nuclear Magnetic Resonance Spectra 1961, Molecular Orbital Calculations 1961, Basic Principles of Organic Chemistry 1965, Modern Organic Chemistry 1967, Organic Chemistry, Methane to Macromolecules 1971; and numerous articles 1940–. *Leisure interests:* tennis, skiing, sailing, classical music, colour photography. *Address:* Gates and Crellin Laboratories, California Institute of Technology, Pasadena, Calif. 91125, U.S.A. *Telephone:* (213) 795-6841.

ROBERTS, John M., PH.D.; American professor of anthropology; b. 8 Dec. 1916, Omaha, Neb.; s. of John M. Roberts and Ruth E. Kohler; m. 1st Marie L. Kotouc 1941 (deceased); m. 2nd Joan Marilyn Skutt 1961; two s. two d.; ed. Univs. of Neb., Chicago and Yale; U.S. Army 1942–45; Asst. Prof. of Anthropology Univ. of Minn. 1947–48; Asst. Prof., Dept. of Social Relations Harvard 1948–53; Assoc. Prof. of Anthropology Univ. of Neb. 1953–55, Prof. 1955–58; Prof. of Anthropology Cornell Univ. 1958–71; Andrew W. Mellon Prof. Emer. of Anthropology, Univ. of Pittsburgh 1971–87, also Adjunct Prof. of Sociology; mem. N.A.S.; Fellow Center for Advanced Study in the Behavioral Sciences 1956–57, American Acad. of Arts and Sciences. *Publications:* Three Navaho Households 1951, Zuni Law (co-author) 1954, The Language of Experience (co-author) 1956; monographs, chapters and articles. *Leisure interest:* limited travel. *Address:* 122 Kent Drive, Pittsburgh, Pa. 15241, U.S.A. (Home). *Telephone:* (412) 833-7467 (Home).

ROBERTS, John Morris, D.PHIL.; British historian; b. 14 April 1928, Bath, Somerset; s. of late Edward Henry Roberts and Dorothy Julia Hallett; m. Judith Armitage 1964; one s. two d.; ed. Taunton School, Keble Coll., Univ. of Oxford; nat. service 1949–50; Prize Fellow Magdalen Coll., Univ. of Oxford 1951–53, Tutorial Fellow Merton Coll. 1954–79, Warden 1984–; Vice-Chancellor Univ. of Southampton 1979–85; mem. Bd. of Govs. BBC 1988–; Hon. Fellow, Keble Coll., Univ. of Oxford; Hon. D.Litt. (Southampton) 1987. *Publications:* various historical books and articles. *Leisure interest:* music. *Address:* Merton College, Oxford, OX1 4JD, England.

ROBERTS, Lewis Edward John, C.B.E., M.A., D.PHIL., F.R.S.; British research scientist; b. 31 Jan. 1922, Cardiff; s. of Rev. W.E. and L.L. Roberts; m. Eleanor M. Luscombe 1947; one s.; ed. Swansea Grammar School, Jesus Coll., Oxford and Clarendon Lab., Oxford; Scientific Officer, Chalk River Labs., Ont. 1946–47; Scientist, Atomic Energy Research Establishment (AERE) Harwell 1947–54; Commonwealth Fund Fellow, Univ. of Calif. (Berkeley) 1967–75; Asst. Dir. AERE, Harwell 1967–75, Dir. 1975–86; mem. UKAEA 1979–86; Wolfson Prof. of Environmental Risk Assessment, Univ. of E. Anglia 1986–. *Publications:* Nuclear Power and Public Responsibility 1984; papers in scientific journals on solid state chemistry and thermodynamics, surface chem., radioactive waste man. *Leisure interests:* reading, gardening. *Address:* Environmental Sciences Department, University of East Anglia, Norwich, NR4 7TJ, England.

ROBERTS, Michael, D.PHIL., F.B.A., F.R.HIST.S., M.R.I.A.; British professor of modern history; b. 21 May 1908; s. of Arthur Roberts and Hannah Elizabeth Landless; m. Ann McKinnon Morton 1941; one d.; ed. Brighton Coll., Worcester Coll., Oxford; Lecturer, Merton Coll. Oxford 1932–34; Prof. of Modern History, Rhodes Univ., S.A. 1935–53, Public Orator 1951–53; Lieut. S.A. Int. Corps 1942–44; British Council Rep., Stockholm 1944–46; Prof. of Modern History, Queen's Univ., Belfast 1954–73; A. L. Smith Lecturer, Oxford 1962, Enid Muir Memorial Lecturer, Univ. of Newcastle upon Tyne 1965, Creighton Lecturer in History, Univ. of London 1965, Stenton Lecturer, Univ. of Reading 1969; James Ford Special Lecturer, Oxford 1973, Wiles Lecturer, Queen's Univ., Belfast 1977; Procter Visiting Fellow, Princeton Univ. 1931–32; Hugh Le May Visiting Fellow, Rhodes Univ. 1960–61; Visiting Fellow, All Souls Coll., Oxford 1968–69; Honnold Visiting Fellow, Pomona Coll., Calif. 1978; Visiting Fellow, Trevelyan Coll., Durham 1981; Leverhulme Faculty Fellow in European Studies 1973; Hon. Fellow, Worcester Coll., Oxford; Foreign mem. Royal Swedish Acad. of Letters, History and Antiquities, Royal Swedish Acad. of Science; Hon. mem. Samfundet för utgivande av handskrifter rörande Skandinaviens historia; Hon. Fil. dr. (Stockholm) 1960, Hon. D.Lit. (Queen's Univ., Belfast) 1977, (Rhodes Univ.) 1988; Chevalier, Order of North Star (Sweden), The King's Medal (Sweden) 1981. *Publications:* The Whig Party 1807–1812 1939, The South African Opposition 1939–45 1947 (with A. E. G. Trollip), Gustavus Adolphus: A History of Sweden 1611–1632 Vol. I 1953, Vol. II 1958, Essays in Swedish History 1967, The Early Vasas: A History of Sweden 1523–1611 1968, Sweden as a Great Power 1611–1697 1968, Sverige och Europa 1969, Gustav Vasa 1970, Gustavus Adolphus and the Rise of Sweden 1973, Sweden's Age of Greatness (edited) 1973, Macartney in Russia 1974, The Swedish Imperial Experience 1560–1718 1979, British Diplomacy and Swedish Politics 1758–1773 1980, Sverige som stormakt 1980, The Age of Liberty: Sweden 1719–1772 1986, Swedish Diplomats at Cromwell's Court 1988, also translations from the Swedish of works by Nils Ahnlund, F. G. Bengtsson, Gunnar Wennerberg, Birger Sjöberg, Carl Michael Bellman and Anna Maria Lenngren, and articles in periodicals. *Leisure interest:* music. *Address:* 1 Allen Street, Grahamstown 6140, Cape Province, South Africa. *Telephone:* Grahamstown 24855.

ROBERTS, Paul Harry, M.A., PH.D., SC.D. (Cantab.), F.R.S.; British professor of mathematics; b. 13 Sept. 1929, Aberystwyth, Wales; s. of Percy Harry Roberts and Ethel Frances Roberts (née Mann); ed. Ardwyn Grammar School, Univ. Coll. of Wales, Gonville and Caius Coll., Cambridge (George Green Student 1951–54); Scientific Officer, Atomic Weapons Research Establishment (AWRE), Aldermaston 1955–56; ICI Fellow in Physics, Univ. of Durham 1956–59, Lecturer in Physics 1959–61; Assoc. Prof. of Astronomy, Univ. of Chicago 1961–63; Prof. of Applied Mathematics, Univ. of Newcastle upon Tyne 1963–86; Prof. of Math., Univ. of Calif. (L.A.) 1986–; Ed. Geophysical and Astrophysical Fluid Dynamics 1976–. *Publi-*

cations: An Introduction to Magnetohydrodynamics 1967, The Fluid Mechanics of Astrophysics and Geophysics (Ed.). *Leisure interests:* chess, playing bassoon. *Address:* Department of Mathematics, University of California (Los Angeles), Calif. 90024, U.S.A. *Telephone:* (213) 206-2707, (213) 825-7764.

ROBERTS, Rev. Richard Frederick Anthony, C.B.E.; Bahamian diplomatist and ecclesiastic; b. 12 May 1932; s. of Enoch Pedro and Gladys Raine (Archer) Roberts; m. Melvern Hollis (Bain) Roberts 1960; one s. two d.; ed. St. John's Coll.; Personnel Officer Bahamas Airways 1963-67; Exec. Dir. and Partner Venn Livingstone Roberts (public relations) 1967-68; Personnel Dir. New Providence Devt. Co. Ltd. 1968; mem. Parl. for Centreville constituency 1968-77; Parl. Sec. to Ministry of Finance 1969-72, to Ministry of Agric. 1971-72; Minister of Agric. and Fisheries 1972-73, of Home Affairs 1973, of Agric., Fisheries and Local Govt. 1974-77; High Commr. in U.K. 1979-84; ordained deacon 1987, priest 1988; Asst. Priest, St. Barnabas Anglican Church, Nassau, Bahamas 1988-; previous activities include Pres. Airline Workers Union, Sec.-Gen. Amalgamated Building Constructional Eng. Trade Union, Asst. Gen. Sec. Bahamas Fed. of Labour, Pres. Bahamas TUC, Gen. Sec. Bahamas TUC, Asst. Gen. Sec. Progressive Liberal Party (PLP), First Vice-Chair. PLP; Chair. Maritime Bd., Vice-Chair. Bahamas Agricultural Corpn., Sec. Methodist Preachers Cttee. *Leisure interests:* fishing, reading, sports, religion. *Address:* Carmichael Road, P.O. Box 565, Nassau, Bahamas (Home).

ROBERTS, Roy Ernest James, C.B.E., C.B.I.M., F.ENG., F.I.D., F.R.S.A., F.I.MECH.E., F.I.PROD.E.; British engineer and business executive; b. 14 Dec. 1928, Surrey; s. of Douglas Henry and Elsie Florence (née Rice) Roberts; m. Winson Madge Smith 1950; two s.; ed. Farnham Grammar School, Royal Aircraft Establishment, Farnborough; with Guest, Keen and Nettlefolds (GKN) 1951-55; Asst. to Dirs., C & B Smith Ltd. 1956-57, Works Dir. 1958-66, Dir. and Gen. Man. 1966-70 (acquired by GKN 1966); Man. Dir. GKN Cwmbran Ltd. 1970-72, Man. Dir. GKN Eng. Ltd. 1972-73, Chair. GKN Building Supplies and Services Ltd. 1974-77; mem. main Bd. of GKN 1975-88, Group Man. Dir. GKN PLC 1980-87, Deputy Chair. (non-exec.) 1987-88; part-time mem. U.K.A.E.A. 1981-88; Vice-Pres. Inst. of Production Eng. 1983-88; mem. of Court and Council Cranfield Inst. of Tech. 1983-; Vice-Pres. Eng. Employers' Fed. 1988-; Deputy Chair. Dowty Group PLC 1986-; Deputy Chair. Simon Eng. PLC 1986-87, Chair. June 1987-; mem. Eng. Council 1986-88; Pres. Inst. of Mech. Eng. 1989-; mem. Council Fellowship of Eng. 1987-. *Leisure interests:* music, walking, shooting, fishing. *Address:* Simon Engineering PLC, Buchanan House, 3 St. James's Square, London, SW1Y 4JU, England. *Telephone:* 01-925 0666.

ROBERTS, Walter Orr, PH.D.; American solar astronomer; b. 20 Aug. 1915, West Bridgewater, Mass.; s. of Ernest Marion and Alice Elliot (Orr) Roberts; m. Janet Naomi Smock 1940; three s. one d.; ed. public schools, Brockton, Mass., Amherst Coll. and Harvard Univ.; est. and directed solar coronagraph station of Harvard Coll. Observatory, Climax, Colorado 1940-46; Dir. High Altitude Observatory, Boulder, Colorado 1946-60; Prof. of Astro-geophysics, Univ. of Colo., Boulder 1957-; Dir. Nat. Center for Atmospheric Research, Boulder 1960-68, Research Assoc. 1975-; Pres. Univ. Corpn. for Atmospheric Research, Boulder 1960-73, Trustee 1960-75, Pres. Emer. 1980-; Pres. A.A.A.S. 1968; Trustee, The MITRE Corpn. 1960-87, Amherst Coll. 1964-70, Kettering Foundation 1964-70, Max C. Fleischmann Foundation 1967-79, Aspen Inst. for Humanistic Studies 1970-, Int. Fed. of Insts. for Advanced Study 1971-; Dir. Program on Science, Tech. and Humanism, Aspen Inst. for Humanistic Studies 1974-77; Dir. Program on Food, Climate and the World's Future, Aspen Inst. for Humanistic Studies 1977-81; Head of Sub-cttee. of U.S.-U.S.S.R. Co-operative Programme on Man's Impact on the Environment 1973-75; mem. Editorial Bd. Journal of Planetary and Space Science, U.S.-Japan Cttee. on Scientific Co-operation 1968-74, Environmental Group, UN Asscn. of U.S.A. 1970-75; fmr. mem. Advisory Cttee. World Meteorological Org., Geophysics Bd. of N.A.S.; Gen. mem. Bd. of Dirs., Int. Inst. for Environment and Devt. Affairs 1971-76, mem. Cttee. on Int. Environmental Programs of the N.A.S. 1971-75, Defense Science Bd., Dept. of Defense 1972-75; Sec. Marconi Int. Fellowship Council 1974-82; mem. Bd. of Dirs. Air Force Acad. Foundation 1973-81, mem. Founding Bd. Civilian/Mil. Inst. 1975-81, Chair. Task Force on Science and Tech. 1975-82; Dir. Worldwatch Inst. 1975-86; Trustee, Upper Atmosphere Research Corpn. 1971-74; Vice-Pres. American Philosophical Soc. 1981-86; Hon. D.Sc. (Ripon Coll., Amherst Coll., The Colorado Coll., C. W. Post Coll. of L.I. Univ., Carleton Coll., Southwestern at Memphis, Colo., Denver and Alaska Univs.); Hodgkins Medal, Smithsonian Inst. 1973, The Mitchell Prize 1979, Int. Environment Leadership Medal 1982, Boulder County Award in Science 1986, Bonfils-Stanton Foundation Award in Science 1986, ARCS Foundation's Man of Science 1986. *Leisure interests:* music, gardening, flying. *Address:* University Corporation for Atmospheric Research, P.O. Box 3000, Boulder, Colo. 80307 (Office); 1829 Bluebell Avenue, Boulder, Colo. 80302, U.S.A. (Home). *Telephone:* (303) 494-5151 (Office).

ROBERTS-JONES, Ivor, C.B.E., R.A.; British sculptor; b. 2 Nov. 1913, Oswestry; s. of William Roberts-Jones and Florence Owles; m. Monica Booth 1940; one d.; ed. Oswestry Grammar School, Worksop Coll., Goldsmith's Coll. Art School and Royal Acad. Schools; served in armed forces 1939-46; taught sculpture at Goldsmith's Coll. Art School 1946-64,

Head of Sculpture Dept. 1964-77; elected Royal Academician 1972; exhbns. include R.A., Arts Council travelling exhbns., Battersea Park, London, Nat. Museum of Wales; major works of sculpture include Sir Winston Churchill, Parliament Square, London 1973, Oslo 1975, New Orleans 1976, Janus Rider Group at Harlech Castle 1982; works purchased by Tate Gallery, Nat. Portrait Gallery, Nat. Museum of Wales, Beaverbrook Foundation, Arts Council, etc.; public portrait comms. include memorial statue to Augustus John, Fordingbridge 1965 and Earl Attlee, Members' Lobby, House of Commons 1979; other portrait comms. include H.R.H. The Prince of Wales, H.R.H. The Duke of Edinburgh, Yehudi Menuhin, Somerset Maugham, and many others; Hon. LL.D. (Wales) 1983. *Address:* The Bridles, Hall Lane, Shimpling, nr. Diss, Norfolk, England. *Telephone:* (0379) 740204.

ROBERTSON, Alan, O.B.E., F.R.S., D.SC.; British geneticist; b. 21 Feb. 1920; s. of late John Mouat Robertson and Annie Grace; m. Margaret Sidney 1947; two s. one d.; ed. Liverpool Inst., Gonville and Caius Coll., Cambridge; Operational Research Section, Coastal Command, R.A.F. 1943-46; Agricultural Research Unit of Animal Genetics, Edinburgh 1947-85, Deputy Chief Scientific Officer 1966-85; Hon. Prof., Edinburgh Univ. 1967; Foreign Assoc., N.A.S., U.S.A. 1979; Hon. Dr.rer.nat. (Univ. of Hohenheim) 1968, Dr. h.c. (Norway) 1984, (Agric. Univ., Denmark) 1986, (State Univ., Liège, Belgium) 1986; Gold Medal, Royal Agricultural Soc. 1958. *Publications:* papers in scientific journals. *Leisure interests:* gardening, tennis. [*Died 25 April 1989.*]

ROBERTSON, Harold Rocke, C.C., M.D., C.M., F.R.C.S., F.A.C.S., F.R.S.C., D.C.L., LL.D., D.SC.; Canadian surgeon; b. 4 Aug. 1912, Victoria, B.C.; s. of Harold Bruce Robertson and Helen McGregor Rogers; m. Beatrice Roslyn Arnold 1937; three s. one d.; ed. St. Michael's School, Victoria, B.C., Ecole Nouvelle, Coppet, Switzerland, Brentwood Coll., Victoria, B.C., and McGill Univ.; Chief of Surgery, Shaughnessy Hospital, D.V.A., Vancouver 1945-59; Chief of Surgery, Vancouver Gen. Hospital 1950-59; Prof. of Surgery, Univ. of B.C. 1950-59; Surgeon-in-Chief, Montreal Gen. Hospital 1959-62; Prof. of Surgery, Chair. of Dept., McGill Univ. 1959-62; Prin. and Vice-Chancellor, McGill Univ. 1962-70; Pres. Conf. of Rectors and Prins. of Quebec Univs. 1968; mem. Science Council of Canada 1976-82; 13 hon. degrees. *Publications:* Numerous articles in medical journals and medical textbooks. *Leisure interest:* gardening. *Address:* R.R.2 Mountain, Ont. K0E 1S0, Canada.

ROBERTSON, Iain Samuel, C.A., LL.B.; British civil servant; b. 27 Dec. 1945, Glasgow; s. of Alfred Robertson and Kathleen Robertson; m. Morag Robertson 1972; two s. two d.; ed. Jordanhill Coll., Glasgow Univ. and Inst. of Chartered Accountants of Scotland; industry and professional practice 1966-72; Civil Servant 1972-83; Dir. Locate in Scotland 1983-86; Chief Exec. Scottish Devt. Agency 1987-; Chair. Scottish Devt. Finance Ltd. 1987- (Dir. 1983-87), The Glasgow Garden Festival 1988 Ltd. 1987-89; Dir. Selective Assets Trust PLC 1988-. *Address:* Scottish Development Agency, 120 Bothwell Street, Glasgow, G2 7JP (Office); 7 Douglas Gardens, Bearsden, Glasgow, G61 2SJ, Scotland (Home). *Telephone:* 041-248 2700 (Office); 041-942 0819 (Home).

ROBERTSON, John Monteath, C.B.E, PH.D., D.SC., LL.D., F.R.I.C., F.INST.P., F.R.S., F.R.S.E.; British professor of chemistry; b. 24 July 1900, Perthshire, Scotland; s. of William Robertson and Jane Monteath; m. Stella Kennard Nairn 1930; two s. one d.; ed. Perth Acad. and Glasgow Univ.; Commonwealth Fellow, U.S.A. 1928-30; mem. of staff, Davy Faraday Research Laboratory, The Royal Institution, London 1930-39; Sr. Lecturer in Physical Chemistry, Univ. of Sheffield 1939-41; Scientific Adviser (Chemical) H.Q. Bomber Command, R.A.F. 1941-42; Gardiner Prof. of Chem. and Dir. of the Chemical Laboratories, Univ. of Glasgow 1942-70, Emer. Prof. 1970-; mem. Univ. Grants Cttee. 1960-64; Corresp. mem. Turin Acad. of Sciences; Pres. Chemical Soc. 1962-64; Hon. LL.D. (Aberdeen), Hon. D.Sc. (Strathclyde); Davy Medal, Royal Soc. 1960, Longstaff Medal, Chem. Soc. 1966, Paracelsus Medal, Swiss Chemical Soc. 1971, Gregory Aminoff Medal, Swedish Royal Soc. 1983. *Publications:* Organic Crystals and Molecules 1953, Organic Structure Reports (Editor) 1940-53, 1957, 1960, 1961, Computing Methods and the Phase Problem (Editor) 1961, International Review of Science, Physical Chemistry Vol. II (Editor) 1972, 1975; about 300 research papers in Journal of the Chemical Society and Proceedings of the Royal Society, etc. *Leisure interest:* travel. *Address:* 11A Eriskay Road, Inverness, IV2 3LX, Scotland. *Telephone:* (0463) 225561.

ROBERTSON, Lewis, C.B.E., F.R.S.E.; British industrialist and administrator; b. 28 Nov. 1922, Dundee, Scotland; s. of John Robertson and Margaret Robertson (née Arthur); m. Elspeth Badenoch 1950; three s. one d.; ed. Trinity Coll., Glenalmond, and trained as accountant; R.A.F. Intelligence 1942-46; worked in textile industry, Chair. and Man. Dir. Scott & Robertson PLC 1946-70; Chief Exec. and Deputy Chair. Grampian Holdings PLC 1971-76; Deputy Chair. and Chief Exec. Scottish Devt. Agency 1976-81; Dir. Scottish & Newcastle Breweries PLC 1975-87, Whiteman Int., S.A., Geneva 1987-; Chair. F.H. Lloyd Holdings PLC 1982-87, Triplex PLC 1983-87, Triplex Lloyd PLC 1987-, Girobank Scotland 1984-, Borthwicks PLC 1985-89, F.J.C. Lilley PLC 1986-; Trustee (Exec. Cttee.), Carnegie Trust for the Univs. of Scotland 1963-; mem. British Council (Chair. Scottish Advisory Cttee.) 1978-87, Restrictive Practices Court 1983-; Hon. LL.D. (Dundee) 1971. *Leisure interests:* work, computer use, things Italian, music, literature. *Address:* 32 Saxe Coburg Place, Edin., EH3 5BP, Scotland (Office).

ROBERTSON, Robert Gordon, P.C., C.C., M.A., D.C.L., LL.D., F.R.S.C.; Canadian government official; b. 19 May 1917, Sask.; s. of John G. Robertson and Lydia A. Paulson; m. Beatrice M. Lawson 1943; one s. one d.; ed. Univs. of Saskatchewan, Toronto and Oxford (U.K.); Third Sec. Dept. of External Affairs 1941-43; Asst. to Under-Sec. of State for External Affairs 1943-45; Sec. to Office of Prime Minister 1945-49; mem. Cabinet Secr., Privy Council Office 1949-51; Asst. Sec. to Cabinet, Privy Council Office 1951-53; Deputy Minister of Northern Affairs and Nat. Resources and Commr. of the Northwest Territories 1953-63; Clerk of Privy Council and Sec. to Cabinet 1963-75; Sec. to Cabinet for Federal-Provincial Rels. 1975-79; Pres. Inst. for Research on Public Policy 1980-84; Fellow in Residence 1984-; Hon. Fellow, Exeter Coll., Oxford; Chancellor, Carleton Univ. 1980-; mem. Queen's Privy Council for Canada. *Publications:* numerous articles on government, constitutional reform and public policy. *Leisure interests:* skiing, gardening. *Address:* The Institute for Research on Public Policy, 275 Slater Street, 5th Floor, Ottawa, Ont. K1P 5H9 (Office); 20 Westward Way, Ottawa, Ont. K1L 5A7, Canada (Home).

ROBERTSON, Sir Rutherford Ness, Kt., A.C., C.M.G., D.SC., PH.D., F.R.S.; Australian botanist; b. 29 Sept. 1913, Melbourne; s. of Rev. J. Robertson; m. Mary Rogerson 1937; one s.; ed. St. Andrew's Coll., Christchurch, New Zealand, Sydney Univ., and St. John's Coll., Cambridge; Asst. Lecturer, later Lecturer in Botany, Sydney Univ. 1939-46; Sr. Research Officer, later Chief Research Officer, Commonwealth Scientific and Industrial Research Org. (C.S.I.R.O.), Div. of Food Preservation 1946-59, mem. Exec. of C.S.I.R.O. 1959-62; Visiting Prof. Univ. of Calif. 1958-59; Prof. of Botany, Univ. of Adelaide 1962-69; Chair. Australian Research Grants Cttee. 1965-69; Master, Univ. House, Australian Nat. Univ., Canberra 1969-72, Pro-Chancellor 1984-86; Dir. Research School of Biological Sciences 1972-78; Hon. Visitor Sydney Univ. 1979-86; Deputy Chair. Australian Science and Tech. Council 1977-81; Fellow, Australian Acad. of Science 1954, Pres. 1970-74; Foreign Assoc. U.S. Acad. of Sciences 1962; Pres. Australian and New Zealand Assen. for the Advancement of Science 1965; Pres. 13th Int. Botanical Congress 1981; Foreign mem. American Philosophical Soc. 1971; Hon. mem. Royal Soc. of New Zealand 1971; Hon. Foreign mem. A.A.A.S. 1973; Hon. Fellow, St. John's Coll. Cambridge 1973, Royal Soc., Edinburgh 1983; Hon. D.Sc. (Tasmania) 1965, (Monash) 1970, (Australian Nat. Univ.) 1979; Hon. Sc.D. (Cambridge) 1969; Clarke Memorial Medal, Royal Soc. of N.S.W. 1954; Farrer Memorial Medal 1963; A.N.Z.A.A.S. Medal 1968; Mueller Medal 1970; Burnet Medal 1975. *Publications:* Electrolytes in Plant Cells (co-author) 1961, Protons, Electrons Phosphorylation and Active Transport 1968, The Lively Membranes 1983. *Leisure interests:* reading, watercolours. *Address:* P.O. Box 9, Binalong, N.S.W. 2584, Australia. *Telephone:* (06) 2274373.

ROBICHAUD, Hon. Louis Joseph, C.C., P.C., Q.C., B.A.; Canadian politician; b. 21 Oct. 1925, St. Anthony, Kent County, N.B.; s. of Amédée and Annie (née Richard) Robichaud; m. Lorraine Savoie 1951; three s. one d.; ed. Sacred Heart and Laval Univs.; private law practice 1951-60; mem. N.B. Legislature 1952-71, Leader of Opposition 1958-60, 1970-71; Premier of N.B. 1960-70, Attorney-Gen. 1960-65, Minister of Youth 1968-70; mem. Senate Dec. 1973-; numerous hon. degrees; Liberal. *Address:* 7 Pineland Avenue, Nepeau, Ont., K2G 0A5, Canada. *Telephone:* (613) 727-0058.

ROBIN, Gabriel Marie Louis; French diplomatist; b. 25 Aug. 1929, Molières-sur-Cèze; s. of Charles Robin and Camille (née Rolland) Robin; m. Aleth Pelissonnier 1961; one s. one d.; ed. Coll. Saint-Stanislaus, Nimes, Lycée d'Alès, Ecole normale supérieure and Ecole nat. d'admin; Schoolteacher 1953-56; Second Sec., Embassy 1961-65, First Sec. 1965-67; Second Counsellor, Perm. Rep. to the EEC 1967-69; Tech. Adviser to the Prime Minister 1969; Deputy Dir. Central Admin. 1969-72; First Counsellor, London 1972-73; Tech. Adviser, Secr. Gen. of the Pres. 1973-79; Dir. of Political Affairs, Ministry of Foreign Affairs 1979-81; Amb. and Perm. Rep. to NATO Feb. 1987-; Chevalier Légion d'honneur, Officier ordre nat. du Mérite. *Publications:* La Crise de Cuba, du mythe à l'histoire 1984, La Diplomatie de Mitterrand ou le triomphe des apparences 1985. *Leisure interest:* tennis. *Address:* Délégation Permanente de la France a l'OTAN, Boulevard Leopold III, 1110 Brussels, Belgium (Office); 45 bis Hameau Boileau, 75016 Paris, France (Home).

ROBINET, Hervé Jean, LL.D.; Belgian diplomatist; b. 1 May 1923, Ougrée, Liège; m. Simone Vanhorenbeeck 1979; ed. Univ. of Liège; entered diplomatic service 1950; served Pvt. Sec.'s Office, Ministry of Foreign Affairs (twice); held posts in Perm. Mission of Belgium at UN, Geneva and EEC, Brussels; Minister Plenipotentiary 1978-; Deputy Perm. Rep. to European Communities, Brussels until 1979; Perm. Rep. to OECD 1979-83, Amb. 1979-. *Address:* c/o Ministère des Affaires Etrangères, Brussels, Belgium.

ROBINS, Lee Nelken, M.A., PH.D.; American professor of sociology in psychiatry; b. 29 Aug. 1922, New Orleans, La.; m. Eli Robins M.D.; four s.; ed. Radcliffe Coll. and Harvard Univ.; Research Assoc. Inst. for Urban and Regional Studies, Washington Univ. Medical School, St. Louis, Mo. 1962-63, Research Assoc. Prof. Dept. of Psychiatry 1962-66, Research Prof. of Sociology in Psychiatry 1966-68, Prof. of Sociology in Psychiatry 1968-, Prof. Dept. of Sociology 1969-; NIMH Special Research Fellowship,

Washington Univ. 1968-70; mem. Inst. of Medicine (N.A.S.); Research Scientist Award 1970. *Publications include:* Deviant Children Grown Up: A Sociological and Psychiatric Study of Sociopathic Personality 1966, Studying Drug Abuse 1985. *Address:* Washington University School of Medicine, Department of Psychiatry, 4940 Audubon Avenue, St. Louis, Mo. 63110, U.S.A. *Telephone:* 314-362-2469.

ROBINS, Robert Henry, M.A., D.LIT., F.B.A.; British professor of general linguistics; b. 1 July 1921, Broadstairs; s. of Dr. J. N. Robins and Muriel W. Robins; m. Sheila M. Fynn 1953 (died 1983); ed. Tonbridge School and New Coll. Oxford; Lecturer in Linguistics, SOAS Univ. of London 1948-55; Reader in Gen. Linguistics, Univ. of London 1955-65, Prof. 1966-86, Prof. Emer. 1986-; Visiting Prof. Univs. of Washington, Hawaii, Minn., S. Fla. and Salzburg 1963-79; Hon. Sec. Philological Soc. 1961-88, Pres. 1988-; Pres. Perm. Int. Cttee. of Linguistics 1977-; Hon. mem. Linguistic Soc. of America. *Publications:* eight books on linguistics. *Leisure interests:* travel, gardening. *Address:* School of Oriental and African Studies, University of London, London, WC1H 0XG (Office); 65 Dome Hill, Caterham, Surrey, CR3 6EF, England (Home). *Telephone:* 01-637 2388 (Office); (0883) 43778 (Home).

ROBINSON, Sir Albert Edward Phineas, Kt., M.A.; British business executive; b. 30 Dec. 1915, Durban; s. of Charles Phineas and Mabel Victoria Robinson; m. 1st Mary J. Bertish 1944 (died 1973), four d.; m. 2nd Mrs. M. L. Royston-Pigott (née Barrett) 1975; ed. Durban High School and Stellenbosch, L.S.E., Trinity Coll., Cambridge and Leiden Univs.; Barrister-at-Law, Lincoln's Inn; Imperial Light Horse, N. Africa 1940-43; mem. Johannesburg City Council and Leader United Party in Council 1945-48; United Party M.P., South African Parl. 1947-53; perm. resident in S. Rhodesia (now Zimbabwe) 1953; Dir. banks, building socs., several financial and industrial cos. 1953-61; Chair. Cen. African Airways Corpn. 1957-61; mem. Monckton Comm. 1960; High Commr., Fed. of Rhodesia and Nyasaland in the U.K. 1961-63; Deputy Chair. Gen. Mining and Finance Co. Ltd. 1963-71; Chair. Johannesburg Consolidated Investment Co. Ltd. 1971-80, Rustenburg Platinum Mines Ltd. 1971-80; Dir. Anglo-American Corpn. of South Africa Ltd. 1965-88; Chancellor, Univ. of Bophuthatswana. *Address:* 36 Smits Road, Dunkeld, Johannesburg, South Africa.

ROBINSON, (Arthur Napoleon) Raymond, M.A., LL.B., M.P.; Trinidad and Tobago barrister, economist and politician; b. 16 Dec. 1926, Calder Hall; s. of James Andrew Robinson and Emily Isabella Robinson; m. Patricia Jean Rawlins 1961; one s. one d.; ed. Bishop's High School, Tobago, St. John's Coll., Oxford and Inner Temple, London; M.P. West Indies 1958-61; Rep. of Trinidad and Tobago Council of Univ. of West Indies 1959-61; Minister of Finance and Gov. for Trinidad Bd. of Govs. of IMF and IBRD 1961-67; Deputy Leader, People's Nat. Movement 1967-70; Minister of External Affairs 1967-68; Consultant to the Foundation for the Establishment of an Int. Criminal Court 1971; Chair. Democratic Action Congress 1971-; Rep. for Tobago East, House of Reps. 1976-80; Chair. Tobago House of Ass. 1980-; Leader Nat. Alliance for Reconstruction Feb. 1986-; Prime Minister of Trinidad and Tobago Dec. 1986-, also Minister of Finance and the Economy; Expert Consultant to UN Secr. on Crime Prevention May 1981-; Visiting Scholar, Harvard Univ. 1971; Studentship Prize, Inner Temple; Distinguished Int. Criminal Law Award 1977. *Publications:* The New Frontier and the New Africa 1961, Fiscal Reform in Trinidad and Tobago 1966, The Path of Progress 1967, The Teacher and Nationalism 1967, The Mechanics of Independence 1971, Caribbean Man 1986 and contributions to Encyclopaedia Britannica. *Leisure interests:* walking, swimming, travel, reading, modern music. *Address:* Office of the Prime Minister, Whitehall, 29 Maraval Road, Port Clair, Port of Spain; 21 Ellerslie Park, Maraval, Trinidad; Robinson Street, Scarborough, Tobago, Trinidad and Tobago. *Telephone:* 622-3141 (Port of Spain); 62-25544 (Trinidad); 639-2281 (Tobago).

ROBINSON, Basil William, M.A., F.B.A., F.S.A.; British museum curator (retd.); b. 20 June 1912, London; s. of William Robinson and Rebecca Frances Mabel (née Gilbanks) Robinson; m. 1st Ailsa Mary Stewart 1945 (died 1954); m. 2nd Oriel Hermione Steel 1958, one s. one d.; ed. Winton House, Winchester, Winchester Coll., Corpus Christi Coll., Oxford; taught at Holyrood School, Bognor Regis 1936-39; Asst. Keeper Victoria & Albert Museum 1939; war service 1940-46; Deputy Keeper, Dept. of Metalwork, Victoria & Albert Museum 1946-54, Keeper 1966-72, Keeper Emer. 1972-76; Consultant Sotheby's 1976-; Uchiyama Memorial Prize (Japan) 1983; Pres. Royal Asiatic Soc. 1970-73. *Publications:* Descriptive Catalogue of the Persian Paintings in the Bodleian Library 1958, Kuniyoshi 1961, Arts of the Japanese Sword 1961, Persian Miniature Paintings 1967, Persian Paintings in the India Office Library 1976, Persian Paintings in the John Rylands Library 1980, Kuniyoshi: The Warrior Prints 1982, The Aldrich Book of Catches 1989. *Leisure interests:* singing catches. *Address:* 41 Redcliffe Gardens, London, SW10 9JH, England. *Telephone:* 01-352 1290.

ROBINSON, Sir (Edward) Austin (Gossage), Kt., C.M.G., O.B.E., F.B.A., M.A.; British economist; b. 20 Nov. 1897, Farnham; s. of late Rev. A. G. Robinson (Canon of Winchester Cathedral) and Edith (née Sidebotham) Robinson; m. Joan (née Maurice) Robinson 1926 (died 1983); two d.; ed. Marlborough Coll. and Christ's Coll., Cambridge; Fellow of Corpus Christi Coll. Cambridge 1923-26; Tutor to H.H. the Maharajah of Gwalior 1926-28; Univ.

Lecturer Cambridge 1929; Fellow of Sidney Sussex Coll. Cambridge 1931–; mem. Econ. Section War Cabinet 1939–42; Chief Econ. Adviser and Head of Programmes Div., Ministry of Production 1942–45; mem. Reparations Mission, Moscow and Berlin 1945; Econ. Adviser, Bd. of Trade 1945–46; Cen. Econ. Planning Staff 1947–48; mem. U.K. Del. to OEEC 1948; Reader in Econs. Univ. of Cambridge 1949, Prof. of Econs. 1950–65, Emer. 1966–; Sec. Royal Econ. Soc. 1946–72; Treas. Int. Econ. Assen. 1950–59, Pres. 1959–62; mem. Exec. Council Dept. Scientific and Industrial Research 1954–59; OEEC Adviser on Italian Devt. 1954–58; Chair. OEEC Energy Advisory Comm. 1957–60; Dir. of Econs., Ministry of Power 1967–68; Joint Ed. The Economic Journal 1944–72. *Publications:* The Structure of Competitive Industry 1932, Monopoly 1940; Ed. or Jt. Editor: Economic Consequences of the Size of Nations 1960, Economic Development of Africa South of the Sahara 1963, Problems in Economic Development 1965, The Economics of Education (with J. E. Vaizey) 1966, Backward Areas in Advanced Countries 1969, Economic Development in South Asia 1970, Economic Prospects of Bangladesh 1973, Appropriate Technologies for Third World Development 1979, Employment Policy in a Developing Country 1983. *Leisure interest:* visiting developing countries. *Address:* Sidney Sussex College, Cambridge, England. *Telephone:* 0223 357548.

ROBINSON, James D., III, M.B.A.; American company executive; b. 19 Nov. 1935, Atlanta, Ga.; m. 1st Bettye Bradley (divorced); one s. one d.; m. 2nd Linda Gosden 1984; ed. Georgia Inst. of Tech., Harvard Graduate School of Business Admin.; Officer, U.S. Naval Supply Corps 1957–59; various depts. of Morgan Guaranty Trust Co. 1961–66, Asst. Vice-Pres. and Staff Asst. to Chair. and Pres. 1967–68; Gen. Partner, Corp. Finance Dept., White, Weld & Co. 1968–70; Exec. Vice-Pres. American Express Co. 1970–75, Dir. April 1975–, Pres. 1975–77, March 1989–, Chair. of Bd. and C.E.O. April 1977–, C.O.O. April 1989–; Pres. and C.E.O. (Banking), American Express Int. Banking Corpn. 1971–73, Vice-Chair. 1973–75, Dir. 1973–, Chair., C.E.O. American Express Int. Banking Corpn. 1983–84; Chair. American Express Credit Corpn. 1973–75; also Dir. various subsidiaries; Chair. N.Y. State Savings Bond Cttee. 1980–81; Dir. Gen. Motors 1986–, Fireman's Fund American Insurance Co., Coca-Cola Co., Union Pacific Corpn., Trust Co. of Ga., Bristol Myers Co., United Way of Tri-State; Vice-Pres. Memorial Hosp. for Cancer and Allied Diseases; mem. Bd. of Trustees, The Brookings Inst.; mem. Bd. of Overseers, Bd. of Managers, Memorial Sloan-Kettering Cancer Center; mem. Bd. of Dirs. New York Chamber of Commerce and Industry; mem. Council on Foreign Relations, Rockefeller Univ. Council, The Business Council. *Address:* American Express Co., 65 Broadway, New York, N.Y. 10004, U.S.A.

ROBINSON, John Foster, C.B.E., D.L., T.D.; British business executive; b. 2 Feb. 1909, Bristol; s. of the late Sir Foster Gotch Robinson and Marguerite Victoria M. Clarke; m. 1st Margaret Paterson 1935 (died 1977), two s. two d.; m. 2nd Mrs. Joan de Moraville 1979; ed. Harrow and Christ Church Coll., Oxford; Dir. E. S. and A. Robinson Ltd. 1943–48, Man. Dir. 1948–58, Deputy Chair. 1958–61, Chair. E. S. and A. Robinson (Holdings) Ltd. 1961–; Deputy Chair. Dickinson Robinson Group Ltd. (now DRC PLC) 1966–68, Chair. 1968–74, Hon. Pres. 1974–; Chair. John Dickinson and Co. Ltd. 1968–74; Dir. Eagle Star Insurance Co. Ltd. 1968–; mem. S.W. Regional Bd. Nat. Westminster Bank Ltd. 1969–76; Dir. Bristol and West Building Soc., Nat. Westminster Bank Ltd.; D.L. Glos. 1972; High Sheriff, Avon 1975. *Leisure interests:* shooting, fishing, cricket, golf. *Address:* Honor Farm, Failand Lane, Portbury, Bristol, BS20 9SR, England.

ROBINSON, Rt. Hon. Sir Kenneth, Kt., P.C.; British politician and administrator; b. 19 March 1911, Warrington; s. of late Clarence Robinson and Marion Robinson (née Linnell); m. Helen Elizabeth Edwards 1941; one d.; ed. Oundle School; Insurance Broker, Lloyds' 1927–40; Naval Service 1941–46; Co. Sec. 1946–49; M.P. 1949–70; Asst. Whip 1950–51, Opposition Whip 1951–54; Minister of Health 1964–68; Minister for Planning and Land, Ministry of Housing and Local Govt. 1968–69; mem. Finance Cttee. The Nat. Trust 1977–86, Council of R.S.A. 1977–; Chair. English Nat. Opera 1972–77, Arts Council of Great Britain 1977–82; Man. Dir. Personnel, British Steel Corpn. 1971–74; Chair. London Transport Exec. 1975–78; Chair. Young Concert Artists Trust 1983–; Chair. Carnegie Council for Arts and Disabled People 1985–88; Fellow Chartered Inst. of Transport, Hon. Fellow Royal Coll. Gen. Practitioners; Hon. D.Litt. (Liverpool) 1980; Labour. *Publications:* Wilkie Collins, a Biography 1951, Policy for Mental Health 1958, Patterns of Care 1961, Look at Parliament 1962. *Leisure interests:* listening to music, reading, looking at pictures. *Address:* 12 Grove Terrace, London, N.W.5, England.

ROBINSON, Kenneth Ernest, C.B.E., D.LITT., LL.D., F.R.HIST.S.; British historian and university administrator; b. 9 March 1914, London; s. of late Ernest and Isabel Robinson; m. Stephanie Christine S. Wilson 1938; one s. one d.; ed. Monoux Grammar School, Walthamstow, Hertford Coll., Oxford, and London School of Econs.; entered Colonial Office 1936; Asst. Sec. 1946–48, resigned; Fellow of Nuffield Coll. 1948–57, Hon. Fellow 1984–; Reader in Commonwealth Govt., Oxford 1948–57; Leverhulme Research Fellow 1952–53; Reid Lecturer, Acadia Univ. 1963; part-time mem., Directing Staff, Civil Service Selection Bd. 1951–56, Chair. Panel 1972–77; Prof. of Commonwealth Affairs and Dir. of Inst. of Commonwealth Studies, Univ. of London 1957–65, Hon. Life mem. 1980–; mem. Colonial Econ. Research Cttee. 1949–62, Colonial Social Science Research Council

1958–62, Councils of Overseas Devt. Inst. 1960–65, Royal Inst. of Int. Affairs 1962–65, Int. African Inst. 1960–65, African Studies Assen. of U.K. 1963–65, 1978–81, Assen. of Commonwealth Univs. 1967–69, Royal Asiatic Soc. Hong Kong Branch 1965–69, Hong Kong Man. Assen. 1966–72, Univ. of Cape Coast 1972–74, Inter-Univ. Council for Higher Educ. Overseas 1973–79, Royal Commonwealth Soc. 1974–87 (Vice-Pres. 1983), Royal African Soc. 1983– (Vice-Pres. 1987); Gov. L.S.E. 1959–65; Vice-Chancellor, Univ. of Hong Kong 1965–72; Hallsworth Research Fellow, Manchester Univ. 1972–74; Callander Lecturer, Aberdeen Univ. 1979; Dir. Survey of Resources for Commonwealth Studies, Univ. of London 1974–75; J.P. Hong Kong 1967–72; Corresp. mem. Acad. des Sciences d'Outre-Mer, Paris; Hon. LL.D. (Chinese Univ. of Hong Kong) 1969; Hon. Dr. (Open Univ.) 1978; Ed. Journal of Commonwealth Political Studies 1961–65; Special Commonwealth Award, Ministry of Overseas Devt. 1965. *Publications:* Africa Today (co-author) 1955, Africa in the Modern World (co-author) 1955, Five Elections in Africa (with W. J. M. Mackenzie) 1960, Essays in Imperial Government (with A. F. Madden) 1963, The Dilemmas of Trusteeship 1965, A Decade of the Commonwealth (with W. B. Hamilton and C. Goodwin) 1966, University Co-operation and Asian Development (co-author) 1967, L'Europe au XIXe et XXe siècles, Vol. VII (co-author) 1967, Experts in Africa (co-author) 1980, Perspectives in Imperialism and Decolonisation (co-author) 1984. *Address:* The Old Rectory, Church Westcote, Oxford, OX7 6SF, England. *Telephone:* (0993) 830586.

ROBINSON, Paul Heron, Jr.; American businessman and diplomatist; b. 22 June 1930, Chicago, Ill.; s. of Paul Heron Robinson and Virginia Jane Croft; m. Martha Bidwell 1953; one d.; ed. Univ. of Illinois, Coll. of Commerce; Officer U.S.N. 1953–55; f. Robinson Inc. 1960, Robinson Coulter Ltd. (London) 1974, Robinson Thomson (Australia) Ltd. 1980, Robinson Thomson (N.Z.) Ltd. 1980; Amb. to Canada 1981–85; Korean, UN and Nat. Service medals. *Leisure interests:* horseback riding, history. *Address:* c/o Department of State, 2210 C. Street, N.W., Washington, D.C. 20520, U.S.A.

ROBINSON, Peter David, M.P.; British politician; b. 29 Dec. 1948; s. of David McCrea Robinson and Sheliah Robinson; m. Iris Collins 1970; two s. one d.; ed. Annadale Grammar School, Castlereagh Further Educ. Coll.; Gen. Sec. Ulster Democratic Unionist Party 1975–79, Deputy Leader 1980–; M.P. for Belfast E., Northern Ireland Ass. 1982–86 (resigned seat Dec. 1985 in protest against Anglo-Irish Agreement; re-elected Jan. 1986); M.P. for Belfast E., House of Commons, 1979–; mem. Castlereagh Borough Council 1977, Deputy Mayor 1978, Mayor 1986; Democratic Unionist. *Publications:* Ulster—the facts 1982 (jtly.); booklets: The North Answers Back 1970, Capital Punishment for Capital Crime 1978, Self Inflicted 1981, Ulster in Peril 1981, Savagery and Suffering 1981. *Address:* 51 Gransha Road, Dundonald, Northern Ireland.

ROBINSON, Raymond (see Robinson, Arthur Napoleon Raymond).

ROBINSON, Thomas Lloyd, T.D., LL.D.; British company director; b. 21 Dec. 1912, Swansea; s. of Thomas Rosser Robinson and Rebe Francis-Watkins; m. Pamela Rosemary Foster 1939; one s. two d.; ed. Wycliffe Coll., Stonehouse, Glos.; served war 1939–45, Royal Warwickshire Regt., 61st Div. and SHAEF; Staff Coll. Camberley; Dir. E. S. and A. Robinson Ltd. 1952, Jt. Man. Dir. 1958; Deputy Chair. E. S. and A. Robinson (Holdings) Ltd. 1963; Dir. Legal & General Group PLC 1970–83, Vice-Chair. 1978–83; Chair. Legal & General South and West Advisory Bd. 1972–84; Dir. West of England Trust Ltd. 1973–80, Van Leer Groep Stichting, Netherlands 1977–81; Chair. Dickinson Robinson Group Ltd. 1974–77, Hon. Pres. 1988–; Dir. Bristol Waterworks Co. 1978–84; Chair. Council of Govs., Wycliffe Coll. 1970–82, Pres. 1988–; Master, Soc. of Merchant Venturers 1977–78; High Sheriff of Avon 1979–80; Pres. Gloucestershire County Cricket Club 1980–83; Pro-Chancellor Bristol Univ. 1983–; Pres. Warwicks. Old County Cricketers' Assen. 1989. *Leisure interests:* reading, golf, music. *Address:* Lechlade, 23 Druid Stoke Avenue, Stoke Bishop, Bristol, BS9 1DB, England. *Telephone:* Bristol 681957.

ROBLES, Marco Aurelio; Panamanian politician; b. 8 Nov. 1905; fmr. govt. official; Minister of Govt. and Justice 1960–64; Pres. of Panama 1964–68. *Address:* Panama City, Panama.

ROBLES, Marisa, H.R.C.M., F.R.C.M.; British concert harpist; b. 4 May 1937, Madrid, Spain; m. 3rd David W. Bean 1985; two s. one d. from previous marriages; ed. Madrid Royal Conservatoire of Music; Prof. of the Harp, Madrid Conservatoire 1958–; Harp Tutor to Nat. Youth Orchestra of G.B. 1964–69; Prof. of Harp Royal Coll. of Music, London 1969–; soloist with James Galway (q.v.) Albert Hall, London 1978; played with major orchestras including New York Philharmonic 1984; tours in Europe, U.S.A., Australia, Japan, S. America, Canada; made various records and appeared in many musical programmes on television. *Publications:* several harp pieces and arrangements. *Leisure interests:* theatre, indoor plants, nature in general, cooking, spending private time with family. *Address:* 38 Luttrell Avenue, London, SW15 6PE, England.

ROBLIN, Duff, P.C., C.C.; Canadian politician; b. 17 June 1917, Winnipeg, Man,; m. Mary L. Mackay; two c.; ed. Univs. of Manitoba and Chicago; Wing Commdr. R.C.A.F. 1940–46; mem. Man. Legis. 1949–68; Premier of Man. 1958–67; mem. of Senate 1978–; Leader of Govt. in the Senate

1984–86; Progressive Conservative Party. *Address:* The Senate, Ottawa, Ont., K1A 0A4, Canada.

ROBSON, Sir James Gordon, Kt., C.B.E., M.B., CH.B., F.F.A.R.C.S., F.R.C.S., D.SC.; British professor of anaesthetics; b. 18 March 1921, Stirling, Scotland; s. of James C. Robson and Freda E. Howard; m. 1st Martha G. Kennedy 1945 (died 1975); one s.; m. 2nd Jennifer Kilpatrick 1984; ed. High School of Stirling and Univ. of Glasgow; Wellcome Research Prof. of Anaesthetics, McGill Univ., Montreal 1956–64; Dir. and Prof. of Anaesthetics, Royal Postgraduate Medical School, Univ. of London 1964–86; Dean, Faculty of Anaesthetists, Royal Coll. of Surgeons 1973–76; Vice-Pres. Royal Coll. of Surgeons 1977–79, Master, Hunterian Inst. 1982–88; Consultant Adviser in Anaesthetics to Dept. of Health and Social Security 1975–84; Chair. Medical and Survival Cttee. R.N.L.I. 1988– (mem. 1981–), mem. Cttee. Man. 1988–; Civilian Consultant to the Army in Anaesthetics 1982–88; Chair. Advisory Cttee. on Distinction Awards 1984–; Pres. Scottish Soc. of Anaesthetists 1985–86; Pres. Royal Soc. of Medicine 1986–88. *Publications:* numerous articles in learned journals on neurophysiology, anaesthesia, pain and central nervous system mechanisms of respiration. *Leisure interests:* golf, wet fly fishing. *Address:* Brendon, Lyndale, London, NN2 2NY, England.

ROBSON John Adam, C.M.G., PH.D.; British diplomatist; b. 16 April 1930, Watford; s. of Air Vice-Marshal Adam H. Robson, C.B., M.C., and Vera M. Purvis; m. Maureen Bullen 1958; three d.; ed. Charterhouse and Gonville & Caius Coll. Cambridge; Research Fellow, Gonville & Caius Coll. 1954–58; Asst. Lecturer, Univ. Coll. London 1958–60; entered H.M. Foreign (later Diplomatic) Service 1961; served Bonn, Lima, Madras, Lusaka, Oslo; Royal Coll. of Defence Studies 1975; Amb. to Colombia 1982–87, to Norway 1987–. *Publication:* Wyclif and the Oxford Schools 1961. *Leisure interests:* gardening, travel. *Address:* Foreign and Commonwealth Office, King Charles Street, London, S.W.1, England.

ROBUCHON, Joël; French chef and restaurateur; b. 7 April 1945, Poitiers; m.; one s. one d.; Apprenti 1960–63, Commis 1963–64, Chef de Partie 1965–69, Chef 1970–78, Dir. Hotel Nikko de Paris 1978–81, Proprietor and Chef Restaurant Jamin, Paris 1981–; numerous demonstrations overseas; Officier du Mérite Agricole; Chevalier des arts et des Lettres; Chevalier, Ordre National du Mérite; professional awards include: Trophée National de l'Académie Culinaire de France 1972, Meilleur Ouvrier de France 1976, Lauréat du Prix Hachette 1985, chef de l'Année 1987; also some 15 gold, silver and bronze medals. *Publication:* Ma cuisine pour vous. *Address:* Restaurant Jamin, 32 rue de Longchamp, 75116 Paris, France. *Telephone:* (1).47.27.12.27.

ROCARD, Michel Louis Léon, L. ÈS L.; French politician; b. 23 Aug. 1930, Courbevoie; s. of Yves Rocard and Renée Favre; m. 2nd Michèle Legendre 1972; three s. one d.; ed. Lycée Louis-le-Grand, Paris, Univ. of Paris, Ecole Nat. d'Admin.; Nat. Sec. Asscn. des Etudiants socialistes, French Section of Workers' Int. (Socialist Party) 1955–56; Insp. des Finances 1958, Econ. and Financial Studies Service 1962–, Head of Budget Div., Forecasting Office 1965, Insp. Gen. des Finances 1985; Sec.-Gen. Nat. Accounts and Budget Comm. 1965; Nat. Sec. Parti Socialiste Unifié (PSU) 1967–73; Cand. in first round of elections for presidency of French Repub. 1969; Deputy (Yvelines) to Nat. Assembly 1969–73, 1978–81; left PSU to join Parti Socialiste (PS) 1974, mem. Exec. Bureau 1975–81, 1986–, Nat. Sec. in charge of public sector 1975–79; Mayor of Conflans-Sainte-Honorine 1977–88; Minister of State, Minister of Planning and Regional Devt. 1981–83, of Agric. 1983–85; Prime Minister of France May 1988–; M.P. for Yvelines 1986–88. *Publications:* Le PSU et l'avenir socialiste de la France 1969, Des militants du PSU présentés par Michel Rocard 1971, Questions à l'Etat socialiste 1972, Un député, pourquoi faire? 1973, Le marché commun contre Europe (with B. Jaumont and D. Lenègre) 1973, L'inflation au coeur (with Jacques Gallus) 1975, Parler vrai 1979, A l'épreuve des faits: textes politiques (1979–85) 1986. *Leisure interests:* skiing, sailing. *Address:* 57 rue de Varenne, 75700 Paris, France.

ROCHAS DA COSTA, Celestino; Sao Tomé and Príncipe politician; fmrly. Minister of Labour, Educ. and Social Security; Prime Minister of São Tomé and Príncipe Jan. 1988–; mem. Movimento de Libertacão de São Tomé e Príncipe (MLSTP). *Address:* Oficina del Primer Ministre, São Tomé, São Tomé and Príncipe.

ROCHDALE, Viscount, cr. 1960 (2nd Baron, cr. 1913); **John Durival Kemp,** O.B.E., T.D., D.L., B.A.; British industrialist; b. 5 June 1906, Rochdale, Lancs.; m. Elinor Dorothea Pease 1931; one s.; ed. Eton Coll., and Trinity Coll., Cambridge; Man. and later Dir., Kelsall & Kemp Ltd., Rochdale 1928–39; served with British Expeditionary Force in France 1939–40; attached to U.S. Forces in Pacific with rank of Col. 1944; later with Combined Operations Command, India; Brig. 1945; mem. Cen. Transport Consultative Cttee. 1952–57; Pres. Nat. Union of Mfrs. 1953–56; Vice-Pres. British Productivity Council 1955–56; Gov. BBC 1954–59; Dir. Consett Iron Co. 1956–67; Chair. The Cotton Bd. 1957–62; Chair. Kelsall & Kemp Ltd., Rochdale 1950–71, Harland and Wolff Ltd., Belfast 1971–75; Dir. Nat. and Commercial Banking Group Ltd. 1971–77; Chair. Cttee. of Enquiry into the Major Ports of Great Britain 1961–62; Deputy Chair. William & Glyn's Bank Ltd. 1973–77; Pres. British Legion (N.W. Area) 1954–61, Econ. League 1963–69, N.-W. Industrial Devt. Asscn. 1974–84; mem. Western

Hemisphere Exports Council 1953–64; mem. and Past Upper Bailiff, Worshipful Co. of Weavers; Chair. Nat. Ports Council 1963–67, Cttee. of Inquiry into Shipping Industry 1967–70; Chair. Rosehill Arts Trust Ltd. 1971–78; Dir. Cumbria Rural Enterprise Agency 1986–; Textile Inst. Medal 1986. *Leisure interests:* forestry, music, gardening. *Address:* Lingholm, Keswick, Cumbria, England. *Telephone:* Keswick 72003.

ROCHE, (Eamonn) Kevin; American architect; b. 14 June 1922, Dublin, Ireland; s. of Eamon and Alice (Harding) Roche; m. Jane Tuohy 1963; two s. three d.; ed. Nat. Univ. of Ireland and Illinois Inst. of Tech.; with Eero Saarinen & Assocs. 1950–66, Chief Designer 1954–66; Partner, Kevin Roche, John Dinkeloo and Assocs. 1966–; Academician Nat. Inst. of Arts and Letters, American Acad. in Rome 1968–71; mem. Fine Arts Comm., Washington, D.C., Acad. d'Architecture; Academician Nat. Acad. of Design; mem. Bd. of Trustees, Woodrow Wilson Int. Center for Scholars, Smithsonian Inst. Accad. Nazionale Di San Luca 1984; LL.D. h.c. (Ireland Nat. Council for Educational Awards); Brunner Award, Nat. Acad. of Arts and Letters 1965, Brandeis Univ. Creative Arts Award 1967, ASID 1976 Total Design Award, Académie d'Architecture 1977 Grand Gold Medal, Pritzker Architecture Prize 1982 and other awards. *Major works include:* IBM World Fair Pavilion, New York; Oakland Museum; Rochester Inst. of Tech.; Ford Foundation Headquarters, New York; Fine Arts Center, Univ. of Mass.; Power Center for the Performing Arts, Univ. of Mich.; Creative Arts Center, Wesleyan Univ., Middletown, Conn.; Coll. Life Insurance Co. of America Headquarters, Indianapolis; Six new wings, Master Plan, Metropolitan Museum of Art, New York; Office Complex, UN Devt. Corpn., New York; Denver Center for the Performing Arts, Denver, Colo.; John Deere & Co., West Office Bldg., Moline, Ill.; Union Carbide Corpn. World HQ, Conn.; General Foods Corpn. HQ, Rye, N.Y.; John Deere Insurance Co. Headquarters, Moline, Ill.; Bell Telephone Labs., Holmdel, N.J., Morgan Bank Headquarters, New York; Northern Telecom HQ, Atlanta, Ga.; E. F. Hutton Headquarters, New York; Bouygues HQ, Paris, IBM Hudson Hills Computer Research Lab., New York 1984, UNICEF HQ, New York 1984, Leo Burnett Company HQ, Chicago 1985, Corning Glass Works HQ, Corning, N.Y. 1986, Merck and Co. HQ, Readington, N.J. 1987, The Jewish Museum 1988. *Address:* 20 Davis Street, P.O. Box 6127, Hamden, Conn. 06517, U.S.A.

ROCHE, James M.; American motor executive; b. 16 Dec. 1906, Elgin, Ill.; s. of Thomas E. and Gertrude (Bull) Roche; m. Louise McMillan 1929; two s. one d.; ed. La Salle Univ., Chicago; Gen. Motors 1927–; Statistician, Cadillac Sales and Service Branch, Chicago 1927; Head of Business Man. Dept., Cadillac Motor Car Div., Detroit 1935; Gen. Sales Manager, Cadillac Motor Car Div. 1950–57, Gen. Man. 1957–60; Vice-Pres. Gen. Motors 1957–60, Vice-Pres. (Gen. Motors Marketing Staff) 1960–62, Exec. Vice-Pres. and Dir. 1962–65; Pres., C.O.O., Chair. Exec. Cttee., Dir. and mem. Finance Cttee. Gen. Motors 1965–67, Chair. 1967–72, now Dir.; Dir. Pepsico Inc., Jack Eckerd Corpn., New York Stock Exchange. *Leisure interests:* reading, music, fishing. *Address:* 425 Dunston Road, Bloomfield Hills, Mich. 48013, U.S.A.

ROCHE, Jean Casimir Henri Hilaire, D. EN MED., D. ES SC.; French university professor; b. 14 Jan. 1901, Sorgues; s. of Gaston Roche and Marie Lointier; m. Elisabeth Mathilde Barman 1937; three s. (one deceased) two d. (one deceased); Asst. in Physiology, Montpellier Univ. 1920–23; Lecturer in Biochem., Univ. of Strasbourg 1925–30; Prof. of Biochem., Univ. of Lyon 1930–31, Marseilles Univ. 1931–47; Hon. Prof. 1948; Dir. of Laboratory Comparative Biochem., Ecole des Hautes Etudes, Paris 1941–; Prof of Biochem., Coll. de France, Paris 1947–72; Rector, Univ. of Paris 1961–69; Dir. Laboratoire Maritime, Coll. de France, Concarneau, Brittany and Pres. Inst. des Hautes Etudes, Tunis (Univ. of Paris); Rector, Gen. Del. of Minister of Educ. to Univ. Int. Affairs 1970–72; Vice-Pres. Int. Assocn. of Univs.; Pres. Soc. of Friends of Univs. of Paris; mem. Acad. des Sciences, Acad. de Médecine; Hon. mem. Accademia dei Lincei (Rome), Royal Soc., Edinburgh, Royal Acad. of Sciences, Sweden, Denmark, Nat. Acad. of Sciences (Argentina), Belgian Acad. of Medicine, Bulgarian Acad., Hungarian Acad., Romanian Acad., Serbian Acad. of Arts and Sciences; Hon. D.C.L. (Oxford), Hon. D.SC. (London, Frankfurt, New York, Bucharest, Montreal, Southampton, Pamplona, Bradford, Boston), D. Med. (Naples, Liège, Buenos Aires, São Paulo-Campinas, Madrid), D. Phil. (Tel Aviv). *Publications.* Essai sur la biochimie générale et comparée des pigments respiratoires 1936, Précis de chimie 1934. *Leisure interest:* archaeology. *Address:* 6 boulevard Jourdan, 75014 Paris, France. *Telephone:* 45-89-92-60.

ROCHE, John P., PH.D., LITT.D., LL.D., D.H.L.; American professor of politics and history; b. 7 May 1923, Brooklyn, N.Y.; s. of Walter John and Ruth Pearson Roche; m. Constance Ludwig 1947; one d; ed. Hofstra Coll. and Cornell Univ.; Instructor, then Assoc. Prof. of Political Science, Haverford Coll. 1949–56; Prof. of Politics and History, Brandeis Univ. 1956–73, Chair. Dept. of Politics 1956–59, 1961–65, Dean, Faculty of Arts and Sciences 1958–60, Henry R. Luce Prof. of Civilization and Foreign Affairs and Academic Dean, Fletcher School of Law and Diplomacy 1973–85, Acting Dean 1978–79, Dean ad interim 1985–86; John M. Olin Distinguished Prof. of American Civilization 1986–; Visiting appts.: Swarthmore Coll., Cornell and Columbia Univs. and M.I.T. and Lecturer, Univ. of Aix-en-Provence; Fellow, Fund for the Advancement of Educ. 1954–55, Rockefeller Foundation 1961-62, 1965-66; Nat. Chair. Americans for Democratic Action 1962-65; Consultant to Vice-Pres. Hubert H. Humphrey and U.S. Dept. of State 1964-66; Special Consultant to the Pres. of the U.S. 1966-68; mem. Presidential Comm. on Int. Radio Broadcasting 1972-73, U.S. Gen. Advisory Cttee. on Disarmament 1982-; Mass. Advisory Comm., U.S. Civil Rights Comm. 1984-86; Trustee, Woodrow Wilson Center for Scholars, Smithsonian Inst., Dubinsky Foundation; mem. U.S. Bd. for Int. Broadcasting 1974-78; mem. Sub-Cttee. on Prevention of Discrimination and Protection of Minorities, UN Human Rights Comm. 1983-, Council of Foreign Relations, Mass. Historical Soc. *Publications:* The Dynamics of Democratic Government (with Murray S. Stedman, Jr.) 1954, Aspects of Liberty 1958, Courts and Rights 1961, The American Image: The Political Process (with Leonard W. Levy) 1963, The Quest for the Dream: The Development of Civil Liberties and Human Relations in Modern America 1963, Shadow and Substance: Essays on the Theory and Structure of Politics 1964, The Crossroad Papers 1965, The Dynamics of Modern Government (with Meehan and Stedman) 1966, John Marshall: Major Opinions and Other Writings (Editor) 1967, Sentenced to Life: Reflections on Politics, Education and Law 1974, The American Revolution—A Heritage of Change (co-author) 1975, The Vietnam Legacy (contributor) 1976, American Nationality 1607-1978: An Overview 1979, Political Power and Legitimacy 1979, Intelligence Policy and National Security (contributor) 1982, The History and Impact of Marxist-Leninist Organization Techniques 1984, National Security Policy: The Decision Making Process (contrib.), Was Everyone Terrified? The Mythology of "McCarthyism" 1989 and numerous articles on law and politics. *Address:* Fletcher School of Law and Diplomacy, Medford, Mass. 02155 (Office); 15 Bay State Road, Weston, Mass. 02193, U.S.A. (Home). *Telephone:* (617) 381-3633 (Office); (617) 899-5085 (Home).

ROCHE, Kevin (see Roche, Eamonn Kevin).

ROCHE, Marcel M.D., M.A.; Venezuelan parasitologist; b. 15 Aug. 1920, Caracas; s. of Luis and Beatrice Roche; m. 1st María Teresa Rolando 1948 (deceased), one s. three d.; m. 2nd Flor Blanco-Fombona 1972; ed. Coll. Sainte Croix de Neuilly, St. Joseph's Coll., Philadelphia, Johns Hopkins Univ., Baltimore, and Harvard School of Medicine, Boston; Intern, Johns Hopkins Hospital, Baltimore 1946-47; Asst. Resident, Peter Bent Brigham Hospital, Boston 1947-48; Research Fellow, Harvard School of Medicine, Boston 1948-50; Research work, New York Public Health Research Inst. 1950-51; Dir. Luis Roche Inst. for Medical Research 1952-58; Dir. Venezuelan Inst. for Scientific Research 1958-69, Chief of Dept. of Physiopathology 1958-69; Pres. Consejo Nacional de Investigaciones Científicas y Tecnológicas 1969-72; Simón Bolívar Prof. of Latin American Studies, Univ. of Cambridge 1970-71; D.Sc. (h.c.); Ed. Interciencia 1976-; Head, Dept. of Science Studies IVIC 1975-; Perm. Delegate of Venezuela at UNESCO 1984; UNESCO's Kalinga Prize for Popularization of Science 1987. *Publications:* Bitácora 1963, La Ciencia entre Nosotros 1969, Rafael Rangel 1974, Descubriendo a Prometeo 1975, numerous papers on environmental and tropical medicine. *Leisure interests:* playing the 'cello, writing poetry. *Address:* Calle Nuñez Ponte, 88, Lomas del Mirador, Caracas 1060, Venezuela. *Telephone:* 923224 (Office); 929972 (Home).

ROCHER, Guy, C.C., PH.D., F.R.S.C.; Canadian professor of sociology; b. 20 April 1924, Berthierville, P.Q.; s. of late Barthélemy Rocher and of Jeanne Magnan; m. 1st Suzanne Cloutier 1949, 2nd Claire-Emmanuèle Depocas 1985; four d.; ed. Univ. of Montreal, Univ. Laval and Harvard Univ.; Asst. Prof. Univ. Laval 1952-57, Assoc. Prof. 1957-60; Prof. of Sociology, Univ. of Montreal 1960-; Deputy Minister of Cultural Devt. Govt. of Quebec 1977-79, of Social Devt. 1981-82; mem. Royal Comm. on Educ. in Quebec 1961-66; Vice-Pres. Canada Council of Arts 1969-74; Pres. Radio-Quebec 1979-81; mem. American Acad. of Arts and Sciences. *Publications:* Introduction à la Sociologie Générale 1969, Talcott Parsons et La Sociologie Américaine, Le Québec en Mutation 1973, Ecole et Société au Québec 1975, Entre les Rêves et l'Histoire 1989. *Leisure interests:* tai-shi, skiing, swimming, concerts, reading. *Address:* 1° Faculté de Droit, Université de Montréal, C.P. 6128, Succursale 'A', Montreal, P.Q., H3C 3J7 (Office); 2° 4670 de Grand-Pré, Montreal, P.Q., H2T 2H7, Canada.

ROCHESTER, George Dixon, PH.D., F.R.S., F.INST.P.; British professor of physics; b. 4 Feb. 1908, Wallsend; s. of Thomas and Ellen Rochester; m. Idaline Bayliffe 1938; one s. one d.; ed. Wallsend Secondary School, Univs. of Durham, Stockholm and California; Earl Grey Scholar, Durham Univ. 1926-29; Earl Grey Fellow, Stockholm Univ. 1934-35; Commonwealth Fund Fellow Univ. of Calif. 1935-37; Asst. Lecturer, Manchester Univ. 1937-46, Lecturer 1946-49, Sr. Lecturer 1949-53, Reader 1953-55; Prof. of Physics, Durham Univ. 1955-73, Emer. 1973-; Scientific Adviser in Civil Defence, N.W. Region 1952-55; mem. Council of Council for Nat. Academic Awards (CNAA) 1964-74; Second Pro-Vice-Chancellor, Durham Univ. 1967-69, Pro-Vice-Chancellor 1969-70; Hon D.Sc. (Newcastle) 1973, (CNAA) 1975, Hon. Fellowship (Newcastle upon Tyne Polytechnic) 1977; C.V. Boys Prizeman 1956; Symons Memorial Lecturer, Meteorological Soc. 1962. *Publications:* (with J. G. Wilson) Cloud Chamber Photographs of the Cosmic Radiation 1952; also scientific papers on elementary particles, cosmic rays, spectroscopy and the history of science. *Leisure interests:* church, reading, walking, television. *Address:* 18 Dryburn Road, Durham, DH1 5AJ, England. *Telephone:* Durham 386 4796.

ROCKEFELLER, David, B.S., PH.D.; American banker b. 12 June 1915, New York; s. of John Davison Jr. and Abby Greene (née Aldrich) Rockefeller; brother of Laurance (q.v.); m. Margaret McGrath 1940; two s. four d.; ed. Harvard Univ. and Univ. of Chicago; Sec. to Mayor Fiorello H. La Guardia, New York 1940-41; Asst. Regional Dir. U.S. Office of Defense 1941-42; Officer of Defense, Health and Welfare, U.S. Army 1942-45; Foreign Dept. Chase Nat. Bank 1946-48, Second Vice-Pres. 1948-49, Vice-Pres. 1949-51, Sr. Vice-Pres. 1951-55; Exec. Vice-Pres. Chase Manhattan Bank 1955-57, Dir. 1957-81, Vice-Chair. Bd. of Dirs. 1957-61, Pres and Chair. Exec. Cttee. 1961-69, C.E.O. 1969-80, Chair. of Bd. 1969-81, Chair. Int. Advisory Cttee. 1981-; Chair. Rockefeller Univ. 1950-75, Chair Exec. Cttee. 1975-, Council on Foreign Relations and other chairmanships; Vice-Chair. Museum of Modern Art; Trustee Rockefeller Brothers Fund, Vice-Chair. 1969-80; Rockefeller Family Fund, John F. Kennedy Library, Chicago Univ., Life Trustee 1966-; Dir. Rockefeller Center Inc., New York Clearing House 1971-79, Int. Exec. Service Corps, Chair. 1964-68, Council of the Americas, Chair. 1965-70, Center for Inter-American Relations, Chair. 1966-70; Hon. LL.D. from 11 univs.; Hon. D.Eng. (Colorado School of Mines) 1974; numerous American and foreign awards. *Publications:* Unused Resources and Economic Waste 1940, Creative Management in Banking 1964. *Address:* 30 Rockefeller Plaza, New York, N.Y. 10112, U.S.A.

ROCKEFELLER, James S.; American businessman; b. 8 June 1902, New York; s. of William G. and Elsie (Stillman) Rockefeller; m. Nancy Carnegie 1925; two s. two d.; ed. Yale Univ.; worked with Brown Brothers & Co. 1924-30; joined Nat. City Bank of New York (now Citibank) 1930, Asst. Cashier 1931, Asst. Vice-Pres. 1933, Vice-Pres. 1940, Sr. Vice-Pres. 1948, Exec. Vice-Pres. 1952, Pres. and Dir. 1952-59, Chair. and Dir. 1959-67; served with U.S. Army 1942-46; Dir. Cranston Print Works Co.; Pres. and Dir. Indian Spring Land Co.; Vice-Pres. and Dir. Indian Rock Corpn.; mem. Bd. of Overseers, Memorial Hosp. for Cancer and Allied Diseases, New York; Trustee of Estate of William Rockefeller, American Museum of Natural History; Hon. Dir. NCR Corpn. *Leisure interests:* farming, shooting, fishing. *Address:* Room 2900, 399 Park Avenue, New York, N.Y. 10043, U.S.A. *Telephone:* (212) 559-4444.

ROCKEFELLER, John Davison, IV, B.A.; American state governor; b. 18 June 1937, New York; s. of John Davison III and Blanchette F. (Hooker) Rockefeller; m. Sharon Percy 1967; three s. one d.; ed. Harvard and Yale Univs. and Int. Christian Univ., Tokyo; mem. Nat. Advisory Council, Peace Corps 1961, Special Adviser to Dir. 1962, Operations Officer in Charge of work in Philippines until 1963; Bureau of Far Eastern Affairs, U.S. State Dept. 1963, later Asst. to Asst. Sec. of State for Far Eastern Affairs; consultant, President's Comm. on Juvenile Delinquency and Youth Crime 1964, White House Conf. on Balanced Growth and Econ. Devt. 1978-, Pres.'s Comm. on Coal 1980-; field worker, Action for Appalachian Youth Program 1964; mem. W. Va. House of Dels. 1966-68; Sec. of State, W. Va. 1968-72; Pres. W. Va. Wesleyan Coll., Buckhannon 1973-75; Gov. of W. Va. 1977-85, Senator from W. Va. Jan. 1985-; Republican. *Publications:* articles in magazines. *Address:* 241 Dirksen Senate Office Building, Washington, D.C. 20510, U.S.A.

ROCKEFELLER, Laurance Spelman, A.B.; American conservationist and business executive; b. 26 May 1910, New York; s. of John Davison Jr. and Abby Greene (née Aldrich) Rockefeller; brother of David (q.v.); m. Mary French 1934; one s. three d.; ed. Princeton Univ.; served in U.S.N.R. 1942-45; Dir. Eastern Airlines 1938-60, 1977-81, Advisory Dir. 1981-; Chair. Rockefeller Center 1953-56, 1958-66 (now Dir.), Hudson River Valley Comm. 1965-66, New York Zoological Soc. 1970-75 (Hon. Chair. 1975-), Rockefeller Brothers Fund 1958-80 (Vice-Chair. 1980-82, now Pres. and Advisory Trustee), Citizens' Advisory Cttee. on Environmental Quality 1969-73 (mem. 1973-79); Pres. American Conservation Asscn., Jackson Hole Preserve Inc., Palisades Interstate Park Comm. 1970-77 (Commr. Emer. 1978-); Dir. Reader's Digest Assen. 1973-; Trustee Emer., Princeton Univ.; Trustee Alfred P. Sloan Foundation 1960-82, Nat. Geographical Soc.; mem. Nat. Cancer Advisory Bd. 1972-79, Memorial Sloan-Kettering Cancer Center (Chair. 1975-82, Hon. Chair. 1982-); Commdr., Ordre Royal du Lion (Belgium) 1950, Hon. O.B.E. and several American awards. *Address:* c/o Rockefeller Brothers Fund, 1290 Avenue of Americas, New York, N.Y. 10104, U.S.A.

RODDIE, Ian Campbell, C.B.E., T.D., D.SC., M.D., F.R.C.P.I.; British professor of physiology; b. 1 Dec. 1928, N. Ireland; s. of late Rev. J. R. W. Roddie and of Mary H. (Wilson) Roddie; m. 1st Elizabeth A. G. Honeyman 1958 (deceased); 2nd Katherine O'Hara 1974 (divorced); 3rd Janet Doreen Saville 1987; two s. four d.; ed. Methodist Coll. Belfast and Queen's Univ. Belfast; Resident Medical Officer, Royal Victoria Hosp., Belfast 1953-54; Lecturer in Physiology, Queen's Univ. of Belfast 1957-60, Reader 1962-64, Dunville Prof. of Physiology 1964-87, Pro-Vice-Chancellor 1984-87; Visiting Prof., Chinese Univ. of Hong Kong 1986-87; Health Consultant, Asian Devt. Bank, Manila 1987-; mem. Royal Irish Acad.; Harkness Fellowship 1960; Conway Bronze Medal 1977. *Publications:* Physiology for Practitioners 1971, Multiple Choice Questions in Human Physiology 1971, The Physiology of Disease 1975. *Leisure interest:* gardening. *Address:* 1A Residence 13, The Chinese University of Hong Kong, Shatin, N.T., Hong Kong. *Telephone:* (0) 699 4512.

RODDIS, Louis Harry, Jr.; American business executive; b. 9 Sept. 1918, Charleston, S.C.; s. of the late Louis H. Roddis and of Winifred Stiles Roddis; m. Alice Stets Garner 1964; one s. eight d.; ed. U.S. Naval Acad. and Massachusetts Inst. of Tech.; former U.S. Naval Officer; helped to develop a prototype ship propulsion reactor and participated in design of U.S.S. Nautilus and other early naval nuclear projects; with Div. of Reactor Devt. U.S. Atomic Energy Comm. 1955–58; Pres. Pa. Electric Co. (subsidiary of Gen. Public Utilities Corpn.) 1958–67, Chair. of Bd. 1967–69; Dir. Nuclear Activities of Gen. Public Utilities Corpn.1967–69; Pres. and mem. Bd. of Trustees, Consolidated Edison Co. of New York Inc. 1969–73, Vice-Chair. 1973–74; Pres., C.E.O. John J. McMullen Assocs., Inc. 1975–76, Consulting Engineer 1976–; fmr. Dir. Gould Inc., Hammermill Paper Co., Research-Cottrell Inc., The Detroit Edison Co.; mem. Advisory Comm. Rockefeller Univ. 1972–86; active in a wide variety of public services, charitable, industrial and trade orgs.; consultant to several govt. agencies; Dir. and Past Pres. Atomic Industrial Forum, American Nuclear Soc.; mem. Nat. Acad. of Eng. and other professional socs; Fellow, Royal Inst. of Naval Architects, American Soc. of Mechanical Engineers, A.A.A.S., American Nuclear Soc.; Outstanding Service Award, U.S. Atomic Energy Comm. 1957, Exceptional Service Award, U.S. Dept. of Energy 1984. *Leisure interest:* sailing. *Address:* P.O. Box 1513, Charleston, S.C. 29402, U.S.A. *Telephone:* (803) 723-0319.

RODE, Ebbe; Danish actor; b. 10 May 1910; s. of Helge and Edith Rode; m. Nina Pens 1959; mem. staff Dagmarteatret 1931, Royal Theatre, Copenhagen 1932–57, 1965–; guest actor at theatres in Denmark, Iceland, Norway and Sweden; Kt. of the Order of Dannebrog. *Leading roles in plays including:* Etienne, Topaze, Winterset, Ah! Wilderness, Waterloo-Bridge, Caesar and Cleopatra, Dolls House, Pygmalion, Otto Frank, The School for Scandal, The Price, The Father; has acted in numerous films and on television and radio. *Publications:* My Meeting with Albert Schweitzer in His Hospital, numerous speeches, poems, memoirs, articles and books about actors and acting. *Address:* Solbakken 28, 2830 Virum; The Royal Theatre, Copenhagen, Denmark.

RODENSTOCK, Rudolf (Rolf), DR.RER.POL.; German manufacturer; b. 1 July 1917; ed. Tech. Univ., Munich; Prof. with special duties, Univ. of Munich 1956; proprietor of Optische Werke G. Rodenstock, Munich; Pres. Industrie- und Handelskammer, Munich 1971–; Vice-Pres. Bundesverband der Deutschen Industrie (Fed. of German Industries), Köln 1984– (Pres. 1978–84), Vereinigung der Arbeitgeberverbände in Bayern, Munich 1977– (Chair. 1955–77); Chair. shareholders' meeting FAZ GmbH, Frankfurt, Advisory Bd., Bayerische Hypotheken -und Wechselbank, Munich; mem. Supervisory Bd. Bayernwerk AG, Munich, Deutsche Spezialglas AG, Grünenplan, Gerling-Weltsicherungs-Pool AG, Cologne, Münchener Rückversicherungs-Gesellschaft, Munich. *Address:* Isartalstrasse 43, 8000 Munich 5, Federal Republic of Germany.

RODERICK, David Milton, B.S.; American business executive; b. 3 May 1924, Pittsburgh, Pa.; s. of Milton S. and Anna (née Baskin) Roderick; m. Elizabeth J. Costello 1948; two s. one d.; ed. Univ. of Pittsburgh; Asst. to Dir. Statistics U.S. Steel Corpn. Pitts. 1959–62, accounting consultant Int. projects 1962–64, Vice-Pres. Accounting 1964–67, Vice-Pres. Int. Div. 1967–73, Chair. Finance Cttee. 1973–75, Pres. 1975–79, Chair. and C.E.O. 1979–, Dir. 1975– (co. now named USX Corpn. 1986); Dir. Procter and Gamble Co., Aetna Life and Casualty Co., Marathon Oil Co., Texas Oil and Gas Corpn., Texas Instruments Inc.; mem. Bd. Dirs. Nat. Action Council for Minorities in Eng.; mem. advisory council Japan-U.S. Econ. Relations; mem. American Iron and Steel Inst.; Chair. Int. Iron and Steel Inst. *Publication:* Industrial Internal Auditing (co-author). *Address:* 600 Grant Street, Pittsburgh, Pa. 15230, U.S.A. (Office).

RODGER, Stanley Joseph, M.P.; New Zealand politician; b. 13 Feb. 1940, Dunedin; m. Anne Patricia O'Connor 1968; two c.; ed. King Edward Tech. Coll.; with Ministry of Works and Devt. and Housing Corpn. 1957–75; Pres. Public Service Asscn. 1970–74, Asst. Sec. 1976–78; Chair. Combined State Unions 1970–74; M.P. for Dunedin N. 1978–; Minister of Labour and State Services July 1984–, of Immigration Aug. 1987–, of State-owned Enterprises and Railways Nov. 1988–; fmr. Vice-Pres. UN Asscn.; fmr. mem. Industrial Relations Advisory Council; fmr. Pres. Wellington Regional Council of Labour Party; fmr. mem. Parl. Select Cttee. on Labour and Educ. Labour. *Address:* House of Representatives, Wellington, New Zealand.

RODGERS, Joe; American diplomatist and business executive; b. 12 Nov. 1933, Bay-Minette, Ala.; m. Helen Martin; two c.; ed. Alabama Univ.; man. of several construction firms, Tennessee, then Pres. American Constructor Inc., Nashville 1979–85; Proprietor, JMR Investments, Nashville 1976–; mem. Presidential Advisory Cttee. on overseas intelligence activities 1981–85; Amb. to France 1985–89. *Address:* State Department, 2201 C Street, N.W., Washington, D.C. 20520, U.S.A.

RODGERS, John, M.S., PH.D.; American professor of geology; b. 11 July 1914, Albany, N.Y.; s. of Henry D. and Louise W. (Allen) Rodgers; unmarried; ed. Albany Acad., Cornell and Yale Univs.; Dept. of Geology, Cornell Univ. 1935–36, Instructor 1936–37; Field Geologist, U.S. Geological Survey 1938–, in full time employment 1940–46; Scientific Consultant, U.S. Army Corps. of Engineers 1944–46; Instructor, Yale Univ. 1946–47, Asst.

Prof. 1947–52, Assoc. Prof. 1952–59, Prof. 1959–, Silliman Prof. of Geol. 1962–85, Emer. 1985–; Gen. Sec. Int. Comm. on Stratigraphy 1952–60; Sr. Fellow, Nat. Science Foundation 1959–60; Commr. Conn. Geol. and Nat. History Survey 1960–71; Visiting Lecturer, Coll. de France 1960; Exchange scholar Soviet Union 1967; Asst. Ed. American Journal of Science 1948–54, Ed. 1954–; mem. N.A.S., American Philosophical Soc.; Hon. mem. Soc. of London 1970; Pres. Conn. Acad. of Arts and Sciences 1969, Geol. Soc. of America 1970; Hon. mem. Soc. Géologique de France 1973; Hon. Foreign mem., U.S.S.R. Acad. of Sciences 1976; Foreign Corresp. mem. Acad. real de Ciencias, Barcelona 1976; John Simon Guggenheim Fellow (Australia) 1973–74; Medal of Freedom, U.S. Army 1946, Penrose Medal (Geological Soc. of America) 1981, James Hall Medal (N.Y. State Geological Survey) 1986, Prix Gaudry, Société géologique de France 1987, Médaille Paul Fourmarier, Acad. Royale des Sciences, Lettres et Beaux Arts de Belgique 1987. *Publications:* Principles of Stratigraphy (with C. Dunbar) 1957, The Tectonics of the Appalachians 1970, The Harmony of the World (record, with W. Ruff) 1979; many articles on geology. *Leisure interests:* music (piano), travel, reading (history, philosophy). *Address:* Department of Geology, Yale University, P.O. Box 6666, New Haven, Conn. 06511, U.S.A. *Telephone:* (203) 432-3128.

RODGERS, H. E. Patricia Elaine Joan, M.A., D.POL.SC.; Bahamian diplomatist; b. Nassau; ed. School of St. Helen & St. Catherine, Abingdon, Univ. of Aberdeen, Graduate Inst. of Int. Relations, St. Augustine, Trinidad, Inst. Universitaire des Hautes Etudes Int., Univ. of Geneva; Counsellor and Consul, Washington, D.C. 1978–83; Alt. Rep. to OAS 1982–83; Deputy High Commr. (Acting High Commr.) in Canada 1983–86, High Commr. 1986–88; High Commr. in U.K. 1988–; mem. Bahamas Del. to UN Conf. on Law of the Sea 1974, 1975, OAS Gen. Ass. 1982, Caribbean Co-ordinating Meeting (Head of Del.), OAS 1983, Canada/Commonwealth Caribbean Heads of Govt. Meeting 1985, Commonwealth Heads of Govt. Meeting Nassau 1985, Vancouver 1987; Adviser to Bahamas Del., Annual Gen. Meetings of World Bank and IMF 1978–82. *Publications:* Mid-Ocean Archipelagos and International Law; A Study of the Progressive Development of International Law 1981. *Leisure interests:* folk art, interior decorating, theatre, gourmet cooking. *Address:* The High Commission of the Commonwealth of the Bahamas, Bahamas House, 10 Chesterfield Street, London, W1X 8AH, England. *Telephone:* 01-408 4488.

RODGERS, Rt. Hon. William Thomas, P.C., M.A.; British politician and administrator; b. 28 Oct. 1928, Liverpool; s. of William Arthur and Gertrude Helen Rodgers; m. Silvia Schulman 1955; three d.; ed. Sudley Road Council School, Quarry Bank High School, Liverpool and Magdalen Coll., Oxford; Gen. Sec. Fabian Soc. 1953–60; Labour Cand. for Bristol West 1957; Borough Councillor, St. Marylebone 1958–62; M.P. for Stockton-on-Tees 1962–74, for Stockton Div. of Teeside 1974–83; Parl. Under-Sec. of State, Dept. of Econ. Affairs 1964–67, Foreign Office 1967–68; Leader, U.K. del. to Council of Europe and Ass. of WEU 1967–68; Minister of State, Bd. of Trade 1968–69, Treasury 1969–70; Chair. Expenditure Cttee., on Trade and Industry 1971–74; Minister of State, Ministry of Defence 1974–76; Sec. of State for Transport 1976–79; Opposition Spokesman for Defence 1979–80; left Labour Party March 1981; Co-founder Social Democratic Party March 1981, mem. Nat. Cttee. 1982–87, Vice-Pres. 1982–87; Dir.-Gen. R.I.B.A. Dec. 1987–. *Publications:* Hugh Gaitskell 1906–1963 (Ed.) 1964, The People Into Parliament (co-author) 1966, The Politics of Change 1982, Ed. and co-author Government and Industry 1986. *Leisure interests:* reading, walking, cinema. *Address:* 48 Patshull Road, London, NW5 2LD, England (Home).

RODIN, Judith, PH.D.; American professor of psychology, psychiatry and medicine; b. 9 Sept. 1944, Philadelphia, Pa.; d. of Morris Rodin and Sally (Winson) Seitz; m. Nicholas Neijelow 1978; one s.; ed. Univ. of Pennsylvania and Columbia Univ.; Nat. Science Foundation Postdoctoral Fellow, Univ. of Calif. 1971; Asst. Prof. of Psychology, New York Univ. 1970–72; Asst. Prof. Yale Univ. 1972–75, Assoc. Prof. 1975–79, Dir. Grad. Studies 1978–83, Prof. of Psychology 1979–83, Prof. of Psychiatry 1980, Philip R. Allen Prof. of Psychology 1984; Chair. John D. & Catherine T. MacArthur Foundation Research Network on Health-Promoting and Health-Damaging Behaviour 1984–. *Publications:* Women and Weight: A normative discontent (with others) 1985; articles in professional journals. *Address:* Department of Psychology, Yale University, 2 Hillhouse Avenue, New Haven, Conn. 06520 (Office); 10 Maple Street, Stratford, Conn. 06497, U.S.A. (Home).

RODINO, Peter Wallace, Jr.; American politician; b. 7 June 1909, Newark, N.J.; s. of Peter and Margaret (Gerard) Rodino; m. Marianna Stango 1941; one s. one d.; ed. New Jersey Law School; admitted to N.J. Bar 1938; mem. House of Reps. for N.J. 1948–74; Chair. House Judiciary Cttee. 1973; Del. N. Atlantic Assembly 1962–, Intergovernmental Cttee. for European Migration 1962–72 (Chair. 1971–72); mem. Pres. Select Comm. on Western Hemisphere Immigration; Chair. Impeachment investigation of Pres. Richard Nixon 1973–74; 13 hon. degrees; Bronze Star, Kt., Order of the Crown (Italy), Grand Kt., Order of Merit (Italy), and numerous other awards and decorations. *Address:* Rayburn House Office Building, Washington, D.C. 20515; 205 Grafton Avenue, Newark, N.J. 07104 (Home).

RODIONOV, Aleksey Alekseyevich; Soviet diplomatist; b. 27 March 1922, Pesochnoye, Gorky Region; ed. U.S.S.R. Finance and Econs. (Correspondence) Inst.; Young Communist League and CP work 1940–64; First Sec. Omsk City Cttee., CPSU 1953–60; Sec. Omsk Regional Cttee., CPSU

1960–62; Diplomatic Service 1964–; Minister-Counsellor, New Delhi 1964–66; Amb. to Burma 1966–68; Minister of Foreign Affairs of R.S.F.S.R. 1968–71; Amb. to Pakistan 1971–74, to Turkey 1974–83, to Canada 1983–; Order of the October Revolution, Order of Red Banner (four times), Order of Friendship of Peoples. *Address:* Embassy of the U.S.S.R., 285 Charlotte Street, Ottawa, K1N 8L5, Canada.

RODIONOV, Nikolay Nikolayevich; Soviet politician; b. 30 April 1915; ed. Moscow Steel Inst.; Engineer, Magnitogorsk and Leningrad 1941–48; mem. CPSU 1944–; party work, Leningrad 1948–54; Second Sec. Leningrad City Cttee. CPSU 1954–56, First Sec. 1957–60; Second Sec. Leningrad Dist. Cttee. 1956–57; Second Sec. Cen. Cttee. CP Kazakhstan 1960–62; Deputy Chair. Council of Nat. Economy, Leningrad Econ. Region 1962–65; First Sec. Chelyabinsk Regional Cttee. of the CPSU 1965–70; Deputy Minister of U.S.S.R. for Foreign Affairs 1970–; Amb. to Yugoslavia 1978–86; Cand. mem. Cen. Cttee. CPSU 1961–66, mem. 1966–; Deputy to U.S.S.R. Supreme Soviet 1958–70; Order of Lenin, Order of October Revolution and other decorations. *Address:* The Kremlin, Moscow, U.S.S.R.

RODRÍGUEZ, Gen. Andrés; Paraguayan officer and politician; b. 1924; m. Nelida Reig; Col. 1961; Commdr. Cavalry Div., Asuncion 1961–; Head First Army Corps; led successful coup d'etat Feb. 1989; Pres. of Paraguay Feb. 1989–. *Address:* Casa Presidencial, Avenida Mariscal López, Asunción, Paraguay.

RODRIGUEZ CAMPOS, Orestes, D. EN FIL.; Peruvian politician and professor of economics; b. 6 Dec. 1927; m. Elvira Kadota Falcon de Rodriguez; two s. one d.; ed. Univ. Nacional Mayor de San Marcos; Full Prof. of Econs., Univ. Nacional Federico Villarreal, Dir. Gen. Studies, Head Dept. of Econs., Dir. Acad. Programme for Econs., Vice-Rector, then Rector; Pres. Regional Council of Rectors, Zona Costa; Pres. Univ. Fed., Univ. Rector Univ. Popular Gonzáles Prada del PAP; Nat. Deputy for Dept. of Ancash; Pres. Directorate Corporación Nacional de Desarrollo (CONADE); Minister of State for Labour and Social Welfare 1987–. *Publications:* Economia de Mercado, Plan de Gobierno y Presupuesto Nacional, Inflacion y Crisis Economica. *Address:* Ministerio de Trabajo y Promocion Social, S/N Avda. Salaverry, Jesus Maria, Lima, Peru. *Telephone:* 322510.

RODRÍGUEZ LARA, Maj.-Gen. Guillermo; Ecuadorean army officer; b. 4 Nov. 1923; ed. Quito Mil. Acad. and studies abroad; C.-in-C. of Army 1971; President of Ecuador (following coup d'état) 1972–76.

RODRÍGUEZ RODRÍGUEZ, Carlos Rafael; Cuban journalist, writer and politician; b. 23 May 1913, Cienfuegos, Cuba; s. of Pedro and Antonia Rodríguez; m. 3rd Mirta Rodríguez 1975; two c.; mem. Partido Comunista 1932–, Exec. Cttee. 1940–; Dir. Escuela Económica, Univ. de la Habana 1960–62, Prof. Emer. 1983–; Ed. Hoy 1959–62; Pres. Nat. Land Reform Inst. (Minister of Agric.) 1962–65; mem. Cen. Cttee. and Nat. Secr. Cuban CP 1966; Vice-Pres. Council of Ministers 1971–, Council of State 1976–; mem. Exec. Cttee. of the Govt. 1976; mem. Exec. Cttee. COMECON 1972–, Pres. 1983–84; mem. Political Bureau Cuban CP 1976–; mem. South Comm. 1987. *Publications:* Marxism in Cuban History 1943, José de la Luz y Caballero 1947, José Martí, Guide of His Time and Anticipator of Ours 1953, Employment in Cuba 1954, Welles' Mission 1957, The Working Class and the Cuban Revolution 1960, Four Years of Agrarian Reform 1962, José Antonio Mestre (Philosophy in Havana) 1963, The Economic Situation of Cuba 1965–66, Financing and Other Problems of Agriculture and Cattle Development 1966, Agriculture and Animal Production in Cuba 1967, Lenin and the Colonial Matter 1970, Martí, Contemporary and Companion 1973, Cuba during the Transition to Socialism 1959–63 1978, Letra con Filo Vols. I and II 1983, Vol. III 1988, Words in the Seventies 1984, Letra con Filo Vol. III 1987. *Address:* Palacio de la Revolución, Ciudad de la Habana, Cuba.

RODRÍGUEZ Y RODRÍGUEZ, Jesús; Mexican financial official; b. 2 March 1920, México, D.F.; ed. Univ. Nacional Autónoma de México; joined Secr. of Finance and Public Credit 1942, Under-Sec. for Finance and Credit 1959–70; Exec. Dir. for Mexico, Panama and Dominican Repub., IDB 1971–79; Prof. of Admin. Law, Univ. Nacional Autónoma de México; First Vice-Pres. Inter-American Econ. and Social Council; Acting Chair. Inter-American Cttee. on Alliance for Progress; del. to numerous int. confs. *Address:* c/o Universidad Nacional Autónoma de México, Ciudad Universitaria, Villa Obregón, México 20 D.F., Mexico.

ROEG, Nicolas Jack; British film director; b. 15 Aug. 1928, London; s. of Jack Nicolas Roeg and Mabel Roeg; m. 1st Susan Rennie Stephen 1957, 2nd Theresa Russell; six s.; ed. Mercers School; started in film industry as clapper-boy. *Principal films:* as cinematographer: The Caretaker 1963, The Masque of the Red Death, Nothing but the Best 1964, Fahrenheit 451 1966, Far from the Madding Crowd 1967, Petulia 1968; Dir: Performance 1968, Walkabout 1970, Don't Look Now 1972, The Man who Fell to Earth 1975, Bad Timing 1979, Eureka 1983, Insignificance 1984, Castaway 1985, Track 29 1987, Aria (Sequence) 1988. *Address:* c/o Terence Baker, 19 Jermyn Street, London, W.1, England. *Telephone:* 01-439 2971.

ROEM, Mohammad; Indonesian politician; b. 16 May 1908, Parakan, Kedu Central Java; s. of Dzoelkarnain Djojosasmito and Siti Tarbiyah; m. Markisah Dahlia 1932; one s. one d.; ed. Law School, Batavia (now Jakarta); Solicitor in private practice, Jakarta 1940–67; fmr. leader of Islamic Youth

Movement; Indonesian Minister of the Interior 1946–48; mem. del. in Dutch-Indonesian talks leading to Agreement Linggajati 1947, Renville Agreement 1948; Chair. Indonesian del. leading to Van Roijem-Roem Statements 1949; Deputy Chair. Round Table Conf. with Netherlands Govt. 1949; first High Commr. of Indonesia to the Netherlands 1950; Minister of Foreign Affairs 1950–51, of Home Affairs 1952–53; First Vice-Premier 1956–57; mem. Exec. Cttee. Masjumi Party 1945–62, Third Deputy Chair. 1959; Pres. Islamic Univ., Medan 1953–62; detained 1962–66; founder-mem. Partai Muslimin Indonesia 1967, Chair. 1968–72; mem. World Muslim Congress 1975–; mem. Bd. Dirs. Asian Conf. for Religion and Peace; Vice-Chair. Bd. of Curators, Islamic Medical Faculty, Jakarta. *Publications:* Bunga Rampai Sejarah I (1972), II (1977). *Leisure interests:* swimming, horse-riding. *Address:* c/o Jalan Teuku Cik Ditiro 58, Jakarta-Pusat, Indonesia. *Telephone:* 343393.

ROEMER, Charles Elson, III, B.A., M.B.A.; American politician; b. 4 Oct. 1943, Shreveport, La.; s. of Charles E. Roemer and Adeline (née McDade) Roemer; m. Patti Crocker; two s. one d.; ed. Harvard Univ.; Vice-Pres. Sales, Innovative Data Systems Inc.; partner Scopena Plantation; mem. 97th–100th Congresses from 4th Dist. La. 1981–87; Gov. of Louisiana 1988–; Chair. Bossier Heart Fund Drive 1973; fmr. Vice-Pres. La. Alliance for Good Govt.; Trustee Physicians and Surgeons Hosp., Alliance for a Better Community; Chair. Minuteman Org.; mem. Bd. of Dirs. Diabetic Bd., N. La.; Del. La. Constitutional Convention 1972; Democrat. *Address:* Office of Governor, P.O. Box 94004, Baton Rouge, La. 70804-9004, U.S.A.

ROESKY, Herbert W., DR. SC.; German professor of inorganic chemistry; b. 6 Nov. 1935, Laukischken; s. of Otto Roesky and Lina Roesky; m. Christel Roesky 1964; two s.; ed. Univ. of Göttingen; lecturer 1970, Prof. of Inorganic Chem., Univ. of Frankfurt 1971–80, Exec. Dir. Frankfurt 1973–76; Dir. Inst. of Inorganic Chem., Univ. of Göttingen 1980–, Dean Dept. of Chem. 1985–87; Visiting Prof. Univ. of Auburn, U.S.A. 1984, Tokyo Inst. of Tech. 1987; mem. Gesellschaft Deutscher Chemiker, American Chemical Soc., Chemical Soc., London, Gesellschaft Deutscher Naturforscher und Ärzte, Deutsche Bunsen-Gesellschaft für Physikalische Chemie, Selection Bd.; Alexander von Humboldt-Stiftung 1973–84, editorial bd. of Inorganic Syntheses, Journal of Fluorine Chemistry; Wöhler Prize 1960, French Alexander von Humboldt Prize 1986, Leibniz Prize 1987. *Publications:* more than 400 learned papers and articles. *Leisure interest:* antique collecting. *Address:* Institute of Inorganic Chemistry, University of Göttingen, Tammannstrasse 4, D-3400 Göttingen, Federal Republic of Germany. *Telephone:* (0551) 393001.

ROESTAM, Soepardjo; Indonesian politician; b. 12 Aug. 1926, Sokoraja, Cen. Java; ed. Jr. High School, Purwokerto, Army Staff and Command Coll., Bandung and Infantry School, Fort Benning, U.S.A.; Mil. attaché, Netherlands 1952, Malaysia 1952–62; Head, Asia-Pacific Directorate, Dept. of Foreign Affairs 1967–71; Amb. to Yugoslavia 1971–72, to Malaysia 1972–74; Gov. of Cen. Java 1974–83; Minister of Home Affairs 1983–88, Minister Co-ordinator for Public Welfare March 1988–. *Address:* Ministry of Public Welfare, Jln. Merdeka Barat 3, Jakarta, Indonesia.

ROGÉ, Pascal; French pianist; b. 6 April 1951, Paris; ed. Paris Conservatoire; début Paris 1969, London 1969; First Prize, Marguérite Long-Jacques Thibaud Int. Competition 1971; specialist in Ravel, Poulenc, Debussy, Satie; soloist with leading orchestras; exclusive recording contract with Decca, London. *Leisure interests:* reading, tennis, riding. *Address:* c/o Balmer/Dixon Management, Granitweg 2, Zürich 8006; 17 avenue des Cavaliers, 1224 Geneva, Switzerland.

ROGER OF TAIZÉ, Brother (Roger Louis Schutz-Marsauche); French/Swiss monk; b. 22 May 1915, Provence, Switzerland; s. of Charles Schutz and Amélie Marsauche; ed. theological studies in Lausanne and Strasbourg; founder and Prior of Taizé (int. ecumenical, monastic community) 1940–; arrived in Taizé 1940; lived alone there for two years sheltering Jews and political refugees; first fraternity of brothers outside Taizé formed 1951; there are now fraternities living among the poor on every continent; attended Second Vatican Council 1962–65; lived in poor neighbourhood in Calcutta 1976; visited Lebanon and launched Pilgrimage of Trust on Earth 1982; Templeton Prize for Religion 1974; German Publrs. and Booksellers Peace Prize 1974; UNESCO Prize for Peace Educ. 1988; Dr. h.c. (Catholic Theol. Acad. of Warsaw) 1986. *Publications:* Parable of Community, basic texts of Taizé (contains The Rule of Taizé); journal in six vols.; with Mother Theresa of Calcutta: Meditations on the Way of the Cross, Mary, Mother of Reconciliations. *Address:* Taizé Community, 71250 Cluny, France. *Telephone:* 85.50.14.14.

ROGERS, Benjamin, B.A., M.SC. (ECON.); Canadian fmr. diplomatist; b. 3 Aug. 1911, Vernon, B.C.; s. of Reginald Heber and Anna (Fraser) Rogers; m. Frances Morrison 1939; one s.; ed. Dalhousie Univ., and Univ. of London; with Royal Inst. of Int. Affairs, London 1935–36; Acting Nat. Sec. Canadian Inst. of Int. Affairs 1937–38; entered Dept. of External Affairs 1938; served Australia 1939–43, U.S.A. 1943–44, Brazil 1944–48, Dept. of External Affairs 1948–50; Chargé d'affaires, Prague 1950–52; Dept of External Affairs 1952–55; Amb. to Peru 1955–58, Amb. to Turkey 1958–60; Deputy High Commr. to U.K. 1960–64; Amb. to Spain and Morocco 1964–69; Amb. to Italy and High Commr. to Malta 1970–72; Chief of Protocol, Dept. of External Affairs 1972–75; retd. *Publication:* Canada

Looks Abroad (with R. A. McKay) 1938. *Leisure interests:* skiing, writing. *Address:* 10-140 Ridean Terrace, Ottawa K1M 0Z2, Canada. *Telephone:* (613) 748-5471.

ROGERS, Gen. Bernard William, M.A.; American army officer; b. 16 July 1921, Fairview, Kan.; s. of late W. H. Rogers and Mrs. Rogers; m. Ann Ellen Jones 1944; one s. two d.; ed. Kansas State Coll., U.S. Mil. Acad., Univ. of Oxford, U.S. Army Command and Gen. Staff Coll., U.S. Army War Coll.; Commdg. Officer, Third Bn., Ninth Infantry Regt., Second Infantry Div., Korea 1952-53; Commdr., First Battle Group, 19th Infantry, 24th Infantry Div., Augsburg, Fed. Repub. of Germany 1960-61; Exec. Officer to the Chair., Joint Chiefs of Staff, the Pentagon 1962-66; Asst. Div. Commdr., First Infantry Div., Repub. of Viet-Nam 1966-67; Commdt. of Cadets, U.S. Mil. Acad. 1967-69; Commdg. Gen., Fifth Infantry Div., Fort Carson, Colo. 1969-70; Chief of Legis. Liason, Office of the U.S. Sec. of the Army 1971-72; Deputy Chief of Staff for Personnel 1972-74; Commdg. Gen., U.S. Army Forces Command, Fort McPherson, Ga. 1974-76; Chief of Staff, U.S. Army 1976-79, Supreme Allied Commdr. Europe, NATO 1979-87; Rhodes Scholar 1947-50; Hon. Fellow Univ. Coll., Oxford; Hon. LL.D. (Akron, Boston), Hon. D.C.L. (Oxford) 1983; D.S.C., D.D.S.M., Silver Star, Legion of Merit, Bronze Star, Air Medal. *Publications:* Cedar Falls-Junction City: a Turning Point 1974, NATO's Strategy: An Undervalued Currency 1985, The Realities of NATO Strategy 1985, NATO's Conventional Defense Improvements Initiative: A New Approach to an Old Challenge, NATO's 16 Nations 1986, Western Security and European Defence RUSI 1986, NATO and U.S. National Security: Misperception Versus Reality 1987, Soldat und Technik 1987, Arms Control and NATO, The Council for Arms Control 1987, Arms Control: for NATO, the Name of the Game is Deterrence, Global Affairs 1987; contribs. to Atlantic Community Quarterly 1979, Foreign Affairs 1982, NATO Review 1982, 1984, RUSI 1982, Strategic Review, Nato's 16 Nations 1983, Géopolitique 1983, Europa Archiv 1984, Leaders Magazine 1984. *Leisure interests:* golf, reading. *Address:* c/o SHAPE Liaison Office, Room 1A 711, Pentagon, Washington, D.C. 20310, U.S.A.

ROGERS, Ginger (Virginia Katherine McMath); American actress; b. 16 July 1911, Independence, Mo.; d. of William Eddins McMath and Lela Emogen Owens; m. 1st Edward Jackson Culpepper (divorced), m. 2nd Lew Ayers (divorced), m. 3rd Jack Briggs (divorced), m. 4th Jacques Bergerac (divorced), m. 5th G. William Marshall (divorced); no c.; commenced dancing career as performer in stage shows on cinema circuit, later graduating to musical shows on Broadway and films; Acad. Award Best Actress for Kitty Foyle 1940. *Stage appearances include:* Top Speed 1929, Girl Crazy 1930, Hello Dolly 1965, Mame (London) 1969. *Films include:* Young Man of Manhattan 1930, Flying Down to Rio (the first of ten musicals co-starring Fred Astaire, q.v.) 1933, Gold Diggers of 1933 1933, Forty Second Street 1933, Gay Divorcee 1934, Roberta 1935, Top Hat 1935, Follow the Fleet 1936, Swing Time 1936, Shall We Dance 1937, Stage Door 1937, Carefree 1938, Vivacious Lady 1938, The Story of Vernon and Irene Castle 1939, Kitty Foyle 1940, Tom, Dick and Harry 1941, The Major and the Minor 1942, Lady in the Dark 1944, Weekend at the Waldorf 1945, It Had to Be You 1947, The Barkleys of Broadway 1949, We're Not Married 1952, Monkey Business 1952, Forever Female 1954, Black Widow 1954, Tight Spot 1955, Oh Men, Oh Women 1957, The Confession 1965; Dir. Babes in Arms (play) 1987. *Leisure interests:* oil painting, tennis, golf. *Address:* Rogers Rogue River Ranch, 18745 Highway No. 62, Eagle Point, Ore. 97524, U.S.A.

ROGERS, John; Irish lawyer; b. 24 Dec. 1949; s. of Tom and Phil (née Conneally) Rogers; m. Beth Royds 1979; two s. one d.; ed. Catholic Univ. School, Rockwell Coll., Trinity Coll., Dublin and King's Inns, Dublin; called to the Irish Bar 1973 and practised thereafter on Dublin Circuit; Dir. of Free Legal Advice Centres 1971-73; Lecturer in Labour Law, Coll. of Industrial Relations, Dublin 1981-83; called to Inner Bar 1984; Attorney-Gen. of Ireland 1984-87. *Leisure interests:* bird-watching, hill-walking, winter bathing, pedigree cattle, vernacular architecture. *Address:* c/o Office of the Attorney-General, Government Buildings, Dublin 2, Ireland.

ROGERS, Martin Hartley Guy, B.A.; British diplomatist; b. 11 June 1925, Birmingham; s. of Canon Guy Rogers, M.C., B.D., and Marguerite Inez (Hartley) Rogers; m. Jean Beresford Chinn 1959; one s. three d.; ed. Marlborough Coll. and Jesus Coll., Cambridge; Commonwealth Relations Office 1949-51, 1954-56, 1958-60, 1963-68; High Comm. Karachi 1951-53; seconded to Nigerian Govt. 1956-57; Nat. Defence Coll. Canada 1960-61; High Comm. Ottawa 1961-63; Deputy High Commr. Bombay 1968-71, Kaduna 1972-75; High Commr. in the Gambia 1975-79; Asst. Dir. Civil Service Selection Bd. 1979-85. *Leisure interests:* golf, bridge. *Address:* Croftside, Harrow Road East, Dorking, Surrey, England. *Telephone:* Dorking 883789.

ROGERS, Paul; British actor; b. 22 March 1917, Plympton, Devon; s. of Edwin and Dulcie Myrtle Rogers; m. 1st Jocelyn Wynne 1939 (divorced 1955), two s.; m. 2nd Rosalind Boxall 1955, two d.; ed. Newton Abbot Grammar School, Devon and Michael Chekhov Theatre Studio; first stage appearance at Scala Theatre 1938; Stratford-on-Avon Shakespeare Memorial Theatre 1939; Royal Navy 1940-46; with Bristol Old Vic Co. 1947-49, London Old Vic 1949-53, 1955-56. *Plays include:* The Merchant of Venice 1952, The Confidential Clerk 1953, Macbeth 1954, The Taming of the

Shrew; toured Australia as Hamlet 1957; The Elder Statesman 1958, King Lear 1958, Mr. Fox of Venice 1959, The Merry Wives of Windsor 1959, A Winter's Tale 1959, One More River 1959, JB 61, Photo Finish 1962, The Seagull 1964, Season of Goodwill 1964, The Homecoming 1965, 1968, Timon of Athens (Stratford) 1965, The Government Inspector 1966, Henry IV (Stratford) 1966, Plaza Suite 1969, The Happy Apple 1970, Sleuth (London 1970, New York 1971), Othello (Old Vic) 1974, Heartbreak House (Nat. Theatre) 1975, The Marrying of Ann Leete (Aldwych) 1975, The Return of A. J. Raffles (Aldwych) 1975, The Zykovs (Aldwych) 1976, Volpone, The Madras House (Nat. Theatre) 1977, Half Life (Nat. Theatre), Eclipse (Royal Court Theatre) 1978, Merchant of Venice (Birmingham Repertory Co.) 1979, You Never Can Tell (Lyric, Hammersmith) 1979, The Dresser (New York) 1981-82, The Importance of Being Earnest (Nat. Theatre) 1982, A Kind of Alaska (Nat. Theatre) 1982, The Applecart (Haymarket) 1986, Danger: Memory! 1986, King Lear 1989. *Films include:* A Midsummer Night's Dream 1968, The Looking-Glass War 1969, The Reckoning 1969, The Homecoming 1973, The Abdication 1975, Mr. Quilp 1975. *TV film:* Porterhouse Blue 1986. *Address:* 9 Hillside Gardens, Highgate, London, N.6, England. *Telephone:* 01-340 2656.

ROGERS, Richard George, A.A.DIPL., M.ARCH., R.A.; British architect; b. 23 July 1933; m. 1st Su Brumwell 1960; three s.; m. 2nd Ruth Elias 1973; two s.; ed. Architectural Asscn., London, Yale Univ.; Fulbright, Edward D. Stone and Yale Scholar; winner of Int. Competition from 680 entries for Pompidou Centre, Paris 1977; winner Lloyd's Int. Competition for Lloyd's HQ, London 1978; Chair. Richard Rogers and Partners, Rogers PA Tech. Science Centre, Piano and Rogers, France; Dir. River Café, Thames Wharf Studios. *Projects include:* PA Tech. Centre, Phases 1, 2 and 3, Cambridge 1970-84, Music Research Centre, Paris 1977, Cummins/Fleetguard Factory, Quimper, France 1980, Inmos Microprocessor Factory, Newport 1982, World HQ for the Wellcome Foundation, U.K. 1986, PA Tech. Science Lab., Princeton 1984, Urban Conservation, Florence 1984, London Docklands Devt. Corpn., Strategic Plan for Royal Docks 1984, Citicorp Investment Bank Ltd., Billingsgate Market Conversion 1985, Groupe de Recherche et de Construction, Paris, Nantes; Visiting Lecturer UCLA, Princeton, Columbia, Harvard and Cornell Univs.; Saarinen Prof. Yale Univ. 1985; Trustee Tate Gallery 1981-89 (Chair. 1984-88); mem. R.I.B.A. Council, UN Architect's Cttee.; Hon. F.A.I.A., Hon. Dr. (RCA); mem. Royal Acad. of Art, The Hague; Royal Gold Medal R.I.B.A. 1985; Chevalier Nat. Légion d'honneur 1986; Hon. Fellow American Inst. of Arch. 1986. *Publications:* Techniques and Architecture 1983, Richard Rogers and Architects 1985. *Address:* Thames Wharf, Rainville Road, London, W6 9HA, England. *Telephone:* 01-385 1235.

ROGERS, William P., LL.B.; American lawyer and government official; b. 23 June 1913, Norfolk, N.Y.; s. of Harrison Alexander and Myra (Beswick) Rogers; m. 1936; three s. one d.; ed. Canton High School, New York, Colgate Univ. and Cornell Univ. Law School; joined law firm of Cadwalader, Wickersham and Taft, New York 1937; Asst. Dist. Attorney, County 1938-42, 1946-47; officer in U.S. Navy 1942-46; Chief Counsel, Senate War Investigating Cttee. 1947-48, Senate Perm. Investigating Cttee. 1948-50; mem. law firm of Dwight, Royall, Harris, Koegel and Caskey 1950-53; Deputy Attorney Gen. of the U.S. 1953-57, Attorney Gen. 1957-61; U.S. Rep., Gen. Ass. UN 1965; U.S. Rep., UN Ad Hoc Cttee. on S.W. Africa 1967; mem. Pres. Comm. on Law Enforcement and Admin. of Justice 1965-67; with Royall, Koegel, Rogers and Wells 1961-69; U.S. Sec. of State 1969-73; with law firm of Rogers and Wells 1973-; Head Comm. to Investigate Challenger Disaster 1986; Chair. Advisory Bd. Merrill Lynch. *Address:* 200 Park Avenue, New York, N.Y. 10017; c/o Rogers and Wells, 1737 H Street, N.W., Washington, D.C.20006, U.S.A. (Offices).

RÓG-ŚWIOSTEK, Mieczysław Jan, M.A.; Polish journalist and politician; b. 24 Feb. 1919, Borsuki; s. of Jan and Marianna Dziura; m. Barbara Jampolska 1945; two d.; ed. Higher School of Social Sciences of Polish United Workers' Party (PZPR) Cen. Cttee., Warsaw; during Nazi occupation mem. Armed Struggle Union 1940-42, organizer, captain of People's Army in Kielce Region, Chief of Staff "Swit" People's Army Second Brigade, mem. Staff of Third Dist. of People's Army 1944; First Sec. Town Cttee. of Polish Workers' Party, Radom 1945; Second Sec. Voivodship Cttee. Polish Workers' Party, Kielce 1945-46; Chief, Polish repatriation Mission in U.S. Occupation Zone of Germany 1945-46; Sr. instructor Admin. Dept. of Cen. Cttee., Polish Workers' Party 1946-48 and of PZPR Cen. Cttee. 1948-49; Ed.-in-Chief, daily Chłopska Droga 1949-53; Dir. Dept. of Agricultural Science and Propaganda at Ministry of Agric. 1953-57; Ed.-in-Chief, daily Słowo Ludu, Kielce 1957-58 and daily Chłopska Droga, Warsaw 1958-86; mem. Main Bd. of Polish Journalists' Assen. 1956-81, Vice-Pres. Main Bd. 1964-74; mem. Presidium Main Bd. of Union of Fighters for Freedom and Democracy 1964-; Deputy to Seym 1965-85; Pres. Polish-Japanese Soc. 1978-; mem. Council of State 1981-85; mem. Polish Workers' Party 1943-48, PZPR 1948-, deputy mem. PZPR Cen. Cttee. 1964-80, mem. PZPR Cen. Cttee. 1980-81; Commdr.'s Cross with Star, Officer's and Kt.'s Cross, Order of Polonia Restituta, Order of Cross of Grunwald (3rd Class), Order of Banner of Labour (1st and 2nd Class), Soviet Order of Great Patriotic War (1st class), U.S.A. Medal of Freedom, Grand Cordon, Order of the Sacred Treasure 1st Class (Japan) 1987, and other decorations. *Publications:* Moje spotkanie z Japonią 1976, Czas przeszły i teraźniejszy 1982, numerous articles in Warsaw dailies. *Leisure interests:* reading, swimming, hunting, photography. *Address:* ul. Ikara 17m. 13, 02-705 Warsaw, Poland (Home). *Telephone:* 43-26-46.

ROH TAE WOO; Korean politician; b. 4 Dec. 1932, Taegu; m. Roh (née Kim) Ok Sook; one s. one d.; ed. Taegu Tech. School, Kyongbuk High School, Korean Mil. Acad., U.S. Special Warfare School, Repub. of Korea War Coll.; served in Korean War 1950; Commanding Gen. 9th Special Forces Brigade 1974-79, 9th Infantry Div. Jan.-Dec. 1979, Commdr. Capital Security Command 1979-80, Defence Security Command 1980-81, Four-Star Gen. 1981, retd. from army July 1981; Minister of State for Nat. Security and Foreign Affairs 1981-82, Minister of Sports 1982, of Home Affairs 1982; Pres. Repub. of Korea Feb. 1988-; mem. Nat. Ass. 1985; Chair. Democratic Justice Party 1985-87, Pres. Aug. 1987-; Pres. Seoul Olympic Organising Cttee. 1983, Korean Amateur Sports Asscn. 1984, Korean Olympic Cttee. 1984; numerous decorations. *Leisure interests:* tennis, swimming, golf, music, reading. *Address:* 108-17 Yonhui-Dong, Sodaemun-Gu, Seoul, Republic of Korea.

ROHDE, Helmut; German journalist and politician; b. 9 Nov. 1925, Hanover; m. 1st Hanna Müller 1950; one s.; m. 2nd Ruth Basenaü 1983; ed. Acad. for Labour, Political Studies and Econs.; journalist, German Press Agency; Press Officer, Ministry for Social Affairs, Lower Saxony; mem. Parl. (Bundestag) 1957-; mem. European Parl. 1964-; Parl. State Sec. Fed. Ministry of Labour and Social Affairs 1969-74; Chair. SPD Working Group for Issues Concerning Employees 1973-84; Fed. Minister for Educ. and Science 1974-78; Deputy Chair. SPD, Bundestag 1979; Paul Klinger Prize 1974, Gold Medal, Asscn. of War-Blinded. *Publications:* Sozialplanung—Theorie und Praxis der deutschen Sozialdemokratie, Gesellschaftspolitische Planung und Praxis, Für eine soziale Zukunft, and numerous articles on social and education policy. *Leisure interests:* modern art, music, modern jazz. *Address:* Munzelerstrasse 14c, 3 Hannover, Federal Republic of Germany. *Telephone:* 42-39-55.

ROHLÍČEK, Rudolf, DR.SC.; Czechoslovak politician; b. 14 July 1929, Malacky; ed. School of Economics, Bratislava; Head of Dept., Investment Bank, Bratislava 1948-58; Chief Sec. District Cttee., CP of Slovakia 1958-60; post-graduate studies 1960-63; official, Cen. Cttee., CP of Czechoslovakia 1963-64; various offices, Cen. Cttee., CP of Slovakia 1964-67; Head of Dept., Cen. Cttee., CP of Czechoslovakia 1967-69; Minister of Finance, Fed. Govt. 1969-73, Deputy Prime Minister 1973-86; First Deputy Prime Minister 1986-; Head of Czechoslovak del. to CMEA Perm. Comm. for Financial Questions 1970-73, Perm. Rep. to CMEA 1973-; Deputy, House of People, Fed. Assembly Č.S.S.R. 1971-; Chair. Č.S.S.R. Govt. Comm. for Questions of Rationalization of State Admin. 1970-74; Chair. Council for Int. Econ. and Scientific Tech. Co-operation 1974-; mem. Cen. Cttee. of CP of Czechoslovakia 1971-; mem. Secr. Oct. 1988-; Chair., Govt. Cttee. for Foreign Tourism 1976-82; Chair. Czechoslovak Section of the Czechoslovak-Soviet Inter-Govt. Comm. 1983-; Chair. Govt. Cttee. for Questions of Planned Man. of Nat. Economy 1985-; Order of Labour 1973, Order of Victorious February 1979. *Publications:* Finance and Technical Progress 1966, Finance and Efficiency 1974. *Address:* Government Presidium of Czechoslovakia, nábř. kpt. Jaroše 4, Prague, Czechoslovakia.

ROHMER, Eric (pseudonym of Maurice Henri Joseph Schérer); French film director; b. 21 March 1920, Tulle, Corrèze; s. of Désiré Schérer and Jeanne Monzat; m. Thérèse Barbet 1957; ed. in Paris; School teacher and journalist until 1955; film critic of Revue du cinéma, Arts, Temps modernes, La Parisienne 1949-63; founder (with others) and fmr. co-editor of La Gazette du cinéma (review); fmr. co-editor of Cahiers du cinéma; co-dir. Soc. des Films du Losange 1964-; made educational films for French TV 1964-70; Officier des Arts et des Lettres; Prix Max-Ophuls 1970 (for Ma nuit chez Maud); Prix Louis-Delluc 1971, Prix du Meilleur Film du Festival de Saint-Sébastien 1971, Prix Méliès 1971 (all for Le genou de Claire), Prix Speciale Soc. des Auteurs et Compositeurs 1982, Best Dir. Award, Berlin Film Festival 1983, Officier, Légion d'honneur. *Wrote and directed:* Présentation ou Charlotte et son steak 1951, Véronique et son cancre 1958, Le signe du lion (first feature) 1959, La boulangère de Monceau 1962, La carrière de Suzanne 1963, La collectionneuse 1966, Ma nuit chez Maud 1969, Le genou de Claire 1970, L'amour l'après-midi 1972, La Marquise d'O 1976, Percival le Gallois 1978, La Femme de l'Aviateur, Le Beau Mariage 1982, Pauline à la Plage 1982, Les Nuits de la pleine Lune 1984, Le Rayon Vert 1985, Four Adventures of Reinette and Mirabelle 1987, My Girlfriend's Boyfriend 1988. *Publications:* Alfred Hitchcock, Charlie Chaplin 1973, Six contes moraux 1974, L'organisation de l'espace dans le "Faust" de Murnau 1977. *Address:* 26 avenue Pierre-1er-de-Serbie, 75116 Paris, France.

ROHNER, Georges; French artist; b. 20 July 1907, Paris; m. Suzanne Guy 1943; two s.; ed. Atelier Lucien Simon; mil. service and painting, Guadeloupe 1934; prisoner-of-war 1940; exhbns. in Philadelphia 1949, Galérie Framond, Paris 1951, 1953, 1956; Prof. Ecole Nat. Supérieure des Arts Décoratifs 1962-; mem. Inst. de France (Acad. des Beaux Arts, Chair. of Ingres) 1962-; exhbns. in London 1973, New York 1974, Galérie Framond, Paris 1983-84; Retrospective, Musée de Quimper 1987; Légion d'Honneur. *Address:* c/o Galérie Framond, 3 rue des Saints Pères, 75006 Paris, France. *Telephone:* 42.60.74.77.

ROHRER, Heinrich, PH.D.; Swiss physicist; b. 6 June 1933, Buchs, St. Gallen; m. Rose-Marie Egger 1961; two d.; ed. Swiss Federal Inst. of Technology; post-doctoral research, Rutgers Univ., N.J.; IBM Research Lab., Rüschlikon 1963-, Man. Physics Dept.; sabbatical, Univ. of Calif. Santa Barbara 1974-75; Nobel Prize for Physics (with Ernst Ruska and Gerd Binnig) for work in pioneering devt. of electronic microscope 1986; IBM Fellow 1986; Hon. D.Sc. (Rutgers Univ.) 1987. *Address:* IBM Research Laboratory, Säumerstrasse 4, 8803 Rüschlikon, Zürich, Switzerland. *Telephone:* 41-1-72 48 111.

RÖHRS, Karl, DR.RER.POL.; German business executive; b. 14 Dec. 1910, Freilingen, Niedersachsen; s. of August and Emma (née Sasse) Röhrs; m. Marga Dücker 1936; ed. Univs. of Berlin and Hamburg; joined Vereinigte Aluminium-Werke AG (VAW) 1937, Deputy mem. Man. Bd. 1946, mem. 1951, Chair. Man. Bd. 1962-68, Chair. Supervisory Bd. 1969-85; mem. Man. Board, Vereinigte Industrie-Unternehmungen AG 1951-76. *Address:* Im Hohn 29, 5300 Bonn-Bad Godesberg, Federal Republic of Germany.

ROIZMAN, Bernard, SC.D.; American professor of virology; b. 17 April 1929, Romania; m. Betty Cohen 1950; two s.; ed. Temple Univ., Phila., The Johns Hopkins Univ., Baltimore; Instructor of Microbiology, Johns Hopkins Univ. 1956-57, Research Assoc. 1957-58, Asst. Prof. 1958-65; Assoc. Prof. of Microbiology, Univ. of Chicago 1965-69, Prof. 1969-70, Prof. of Microbiology and Biophysics 1970-, Chair. Interdepartmental Cttee. on Virology 1969-85, Joseph Regenstein Prof. of Virology 1981-83, Joseph Regenstein Distinguished Service Prof. of Virology 1984-; Chair. Dept. of Molecular Genetics and Cell Biology 1985-; fmr. ed. of numerous specialist scientific publs. and mem. Editorial Bd. Journal of Virology 1970-, Intervirology 1972-85, Virology 1976-78, 1983-, Microbiologica 1978-; mem. or fmr. mem. numerous grant review panels, int. panels, including Chair. Herpesvirus Study Group, Int. Cttee. for Taxonomy of Viruses 1971-, Scientific Advisory Bd., Showa Univ. Inst. of Biomedical Research 1983-; mem. Int. Microbial Genetics Comm., Int. Asscn. of Microbiological Sciences 1979-86; mem. Scientific Advisory Cttee. Int. Asscn. for the Study and Prevention of Virus Associated Cancers 1983-; numerous nat. panels on vaccines, cancers; Scholar in Cancer Research at American Cancer Soc., Inst. Pasteur (with Andre Lwoff), Paris 1961-62; Travelling Fellow Int. Agency for Research Against Cancer (with Dr. Klein), Stockholm, Sweden 1970; mem. American Asscn. of Immunologists, Soc. for Experimental Biology and Medicine, American Soc. for Microbiology, for Biological Chemists, Soc. for Gen. Microbiology (U.K.), American Soc. for Virology; mem. N.A.S. 1979-; numerous awards. *Publications:* author or co-author of approx. 300 papers in scientific journals and books, Ed. or Co-Ed. of 6 books. *Address:* Viral Oncology Laboratories, University of Chicago, 910 East 58th Street, Chicago, Ill. 60637 (Office); 5555 South Everett Avenue, Chicago, Ill. 60637, U.S.A. (Home). *Telephone:* (312) 702-1898 (Office).

ROJAS, Francisco Jose; Mexican government official; b. 1944, Mexico City; ed. Nat. Univ. of Mexico and postgraduate studies in Tel Aviv and Mexico; Head of Budgetary Control and Asst. Man. of Finance, Office of Controller-Gen. 1971-72; various posts at Ministry of Finance 1973-76; Head of Advisers to Minister of Finance 1977-79; Ministry of Programming and Budget 1979-83; Controller-Gen. 1983-86; mem. Mexican Inst. of Public Accountants., Soc. of Accountants. *Publications:* many specialized articles. *Address:* c/o Secretaria de Hacienda y Credito Publico, Palacio Nacional, Mexico, D.F., Mexico.

ROJAS DE MORENO DÍAZ, María Eugenia; Colombian politician; b. 1934; d. of the late Gen. Gustavo Rojas Pinilla (Pres. of Colombia 1953-57); m. Samuel Moreno Díaz; two s.; fmr. mem. of the Senate; Majority Leader, Bogotá City Council; Leader, Alianza Nacional Popular (ANAPO) 1975-. *Address:* c/o El Senado, Bogotá, D.E., Colombia.

ROJO, Luis Angel, PH.D.; Spanish economist; b. 6 May 1934, Madrid; s. of Luis Rojo and Luisa Duque de Rojo; m. Concepción de Castro 1958; two s. one d.; ed. Univ. of Madrid and London School of Econs.; economist, Research Dept. Ministry of Commerce 1959-68; Asst. Prof. Dept. of Econ. Analysis, Faculty of Econs., Univ. of Madrid, 1959-65, Prof. of Econ. Analysis 1966-84; Gen. Dir. of Research and Studies, Bank of Spain 1971-88, Deputy Gov. 1988-; mem. Royal Acad. of Moral and Political Sciences; First Int. Prize "Rey Juan Carlos I" for Econs. 1986. *Publications:* Keynes y el pensamiento macroeconómico actual 1965, El Nuevo Monetarismo 1971, Renta, precios y balanza de pagos 1975, Marx: Economía y sociedad (with V. Pérez Díaz) 1984, Keynes: su tiempo y el nuestro 1984. *Leisure interests:* San Agustín, 9 28014 Madrid, Spain. *Telephone:* 532 49 47.

RØKKE, Mona; Norwegian lawyer, police officer and politician; b. 3 March 1940, Drammen; ed. Univ. of Oslo; fmrly. in business in Drammen and Oslo; Deputy Asst. Chief, Drammen Police 1971-73, 1976-77; Deputy judge, Kongsberg, Buskerud 1973-74; lawyer, Drammen 1975-76; mem. Municipal Council, Drammen 1972, Municipal Exec. Bd. 1976; mem. Storting 1977-; Minister of Justice 1981-86; Conservative. *Address:* c/o Ministry of Justice, Akersgaten 42, Pb. 8005, Oslo, Norway.

ROLANDIS, Nicos A.; Cypriot barrister, company executive and politician; b. 10 Dec. 1934, Limassol; m. Lelia Aivaliotis; one s. two d.; ed. Pancyprian Gymnasium Nicosia, Middle Temple, London; called to the bar, Middle Temple 1956; practised law in Cyprus for a short time then entered business; exec. positions with many industrial and commercial cos.; active in politics 1976-, founder mem. Democratic Camp (now Democratic Party), founder and Chair. Liberal Party 1986; Minister of Foreign Affairs March 1978-83. *Address:* 13 Agapis Street, Nicosia, Cyprus. *Telephone:* 389596.

ROLL OF IPSDEN, Baron (Life Peer), cr. 1977, of Ipsden in the County of Oxford; **Eric Roll,** K.C.M.G., C.B., PH.D., B.COM.; British banker and former civil servant; b. 1 Dec. 1907, Austria; s. of Mathias and Fany (Frendel) Roll; m. Winifred Taylor 1934; two d.; ed. Univ. of Birmingham; Asst. Lecturer, Univ. Coll., Hull 1930, Prof. of Econs. and Commerce 1935-39; Special Fellow, Rockefeller Foundation 1939-41; Deputy mem., Combined Food Bd. 1941-46; Asst. Sec. Ministry of Food 1946-47, The Treasury 1947, Under-Sec. 1948-53; Chair. Econ. Cttee., OEEC 1948-53; Minister, U.K. del. to NATO 1952-53; Under-Sec. Ministry of Agric., Fisheries and Food 1953-57; Exec. Dir. Int. Sugar Council 1957-59; Deputy Sec. Ministry of Agric., Fisheries and Food 1960-61; Deputy Leader, U.K. del. to EEC Brussels Conf. 1961-63; Econ. Minister and Head of U.K. Treasury del., Washington 1963-65; Exec. Dir. for U.K., IMF, IBRD, Perm. Under-Sec. of State, Dept. of Econ. Affairs 1964-66; Chair. S. G. Warburg & Co. Ltd. 1974-84, Jt. Chair. 1984-87, Pres. S. G. Warburg Group PLC 1987-; Chair. Mercury Securities 1974-84, Pres. 1984-87; Dir. Bank of England 1968-77, Peugeot Talbot Motor Co. Ltd. 1967-87; Chair. NEDC Cttee. on Finance for Industry 1975-80; Hon. Chair. Book Devt. Council; Chancellor, Southampton Univ. 1974-84; Hon. D.Sc. (Hull, Birmingham), Hon. LL.D. (Southampton). *Publications:* An Early Experiment in Industrial Organization 1930, Spotlight on Germany 1933, About Money 1934, Elements of Economic Theory 1935, Organized Labour (co-author) 1938, The British Commonwealth at War (co-author) 1943, The Combined Food Board 1957, The World after Keynes 1968, A History of Economic Thought 1973, Uses and Abuses of Economics 1977, Crowded Hours 1985. *Leisure interests:* reading, music. *Address:* c/o S. G. Warburg Group PLC, 2 Finsbury Avenue, London, EC2M 2PA, England.

ROLLEFSON, Ragnar, M.A., PH.D.; American physicist; b. 23 Aug. 1906, Chicago, Ill.; s. of Carl J. and Marie (Krohn) Rollefson; m. Erna Brambora 1936; two s. two d.; ed. Univ. of Wisconsin; Instructor in Physics, Univ. of Wis. 1930-36, Asst. Prof. 1936-42, Assoc. Prof. 1942-46, Prof. 1946-76, Emer. 1976-, Chair. Physics Dept. 1947-51, 1952-56, 1957-61; with Radar Laboratory, M.I.T. 1942-45; Chief Scientist, Naval Research Laboratory Field Station 1946, Lincoln Lab. M.I.T. 1951-52, Chief Scientist, U.S. Army 1956-57; Acting Dir. Univ. Research Asscn. Devt. Laboratory 1957-60; Dir. Int. Scientific Affairs, State Dept. 1962-64. *Leisure interests:* sports, travel. *Address:* Department of Physics, University of Wisconsin, Madison, Wis. (Office); 4206 Wanetah Trail, Madison, Wis., U.S.A. (Home). *Telephone:* 274-0635.

RÖLLER, Wolfgang, DR. RER. POL.; German bank executive; b. 20 Oct. 1929, Uelsen, Lower Saxony; ed. Univs. of Berlin and Frankfurt; joined Dresdner Bank AG, Frankfurt/Main, Deputy mem. Bd. of Man. Dirs. 1971-73, Full mem. 1973-85, Chair. 1985-; Chair. Supervisory Bd. ABD Securities Corpn., New York, Bank für Handel und Industrie AG, Berlin, Deutscher Investment-Trust Gesellschaft für Wertpapieranlagen m.b.H., Frankfurt, Dresdnerbank Investment Man. Kapitalanlageges. m.b.H., Frankfurt, Dresdner-ADB Securities Ltd., Hong Kong/Tokyo; mem. Supervisory Bd. Allianz AG Holding, Munich, Daimler-Benz AG, Stuttgart, Degussa AG, Frankfurt, Deutsche BP AG, Hamburg, Henkel KGaA, Düsseldorf; Fried. Krupp G.m.b.H., Essen; Metallgesellschaft AG, Frankfurt, Rheinisch-Westfälisches Elektrizitätswerk AG, Essen; mem. other supervisory, advisory and man. bds.; Vice-Chair. Bd. Frankfurt Stock Exchange, Chair. Admissions Cttee. 1986-; Pres. Asscn. of German Banks 1987-. *Address:* Dresdner Bank AG, Jürgen-Ponto-Platz 1, D-6000 Frankfurt/Main 11, Federal Republic of Germany.

ROLLIER, François; French motor executive; b. 2 Feb. 1915, Paris; m. Louise Germain de Montauzan 1941; five c.; ed. Faculté de Droit, Paris; admitted to Annecy Bar 1945; joined Soc. Michelin 1956; Man. Cie. Générale des Etablissements Michelin, Manufacture Française des Pneumatiques Michelin; Deputy Chair. Citroën S.A. June-Dec. 1970, Chair. 1971-76, Pres. Advisory Council 1982-; Pres. Soc. de Participation et de Développement Industriel (PAREDI) 1971-; Pres., Dir.-Gen. Citroën Hispania 1973-76; Dir. Banque Nat. de Paris 1973-75, Cie. Financière Michelin, Geneva, Soc. Aussedat-Rey 1976-; Médaille militaire, Croix de guerre. *Address:* 14-16 rue Singer, 75016 Paris and 12 rue Jean-Mermoz, Annecy-le-Vieux, 74000 Annecy, France (Homes).

ROLLINS, Reed Clark, B.A., M.S., PH.D.; American botanist; b. 7 Dec. 1911, Lyman, Wyoming; s. of William Clarence Rollins and Clara Rachel Slade Rollins; m. 1st Alberta Fitz-Gerald 1939 (divorced 1975); 2nd Kathryn W. Roby 1978; one s. one d.; ed. Univ. of Wyoming, State Coll. of Washington, Harvard Univ.; Teaching Fellow, State Coll. of Washington 1934-36; teaching asst., summer school Univ. of Wyoming 1935, in biology, Harvard 1936-37; instructor biology, asst. curator, Dudley Herbarium, Stanford 1940-41; Asst. Prof., Curator 1941-47, Assoc. Prof., Curator 1947-48; Assoc. geneticist, Guayule Research Project, Dept. of Agric. 1943-45; Principal Geneticist, Stanford Research Inst. 1946-47; geneticist div. rubber plant investigations, Dept. of Agric. 1947-48; Assoc. Prof., Botany 1948-54 and Dir., Gray Herbarium, Harvard Univ. 1948-78; Asa Gray Prof. of Systematic Botany, Harvard Univ. 1954-82, Emer. 1982-; Super-

visor, Bussey Inst., Harvard Univ. 1967-78; Fellow, Soc. of Fellows, Harvard Univ. 1937-40; mem. N.A.S., American Soc. of Naturalists (Vice-Pres. 1960, Pres. 1966), A.A.A.S., American Inst. of Biological Sciences, Genetics Soc. of America; Chair. Inst. of Plant Sciences, Harvard Univ. 1965-69; Chair. Admin. Cttee. Farlow Library and Herbarium, Harvard Univ. 1974-78; Chair. Botany Section, N.A.S. 1977-80; Pres. Section of Nomenclature, XIII Int. Botanical Congress, Sydney 1981; Centenary Medal, French Botanical Soc., Certificate of Merit, Botanical Soc. of America, Congress Medals XI and XII Int. Botanical Congress, Gold Seal, Nat. Council of State Garden Clubs 1981. *Publications:* Revised edition of Fernald and Kinsey's Edible Wild Plants of Eastern North America, The Genus Lesquerella (Cruciferae) in North America (with E. Shaw), articles and technical papers in professional journals. *Address:* Gray Herbarium, 22 Divinity Avenue, Cambridge, Mass. 02138 (Office); 19 Chauncy Street, Cambridge, Mass. 02138, U.S.A. (Home). *Telephone:* (617) 495-2364 (Office); (617) 876-5442 (Home).

ROLSHOVEN, Hubertus, DR. ING; German mining executive and administrator; b. 15 Feb. 1913, Schellerten; s. of Franz and Therese (Meulenbergh) Rolshoven; m. Sofie Dorothea von Wunsch 1940; four s.; ed. Univs. of Tübingen and Bonn, Tech. Hochschulen Aachen and Berlin; Engineer, Bochum 1945-47; Works Man. Consolidation Colliery, Gelsenkirchen 1947-53; Man. Mining Works, Essen 1953-56; Man. Dir. Man. Bd., Hansa Bergbau A.G., Dortmund 1956-57; Chair. Man. Bd. Saarbergwerke A.G., Saarbrücken 1957-69; Prof. Saarland Univ.; Dir. European Acad. Otzenhausen; Pres. Inst. für regional-politische Zusammenarbeit in innergemeinschaftlichen Grenzräumen, VDI-Gesellschaft Energietechnik. *Publications:* Beobachtungen über die Geologie des Kunnitales und des oberen Ramistales im Cercergebirge 1939, Der Steinkohlenbergbau an der Saar 1960, Wirtschaftsgrundlagen im Montandreieck-Saar-Lothringen-Luxemburg 1965, Das Industriedreieck Saar-Lothringen-Luxemburg, Rohstoffwirtschaft und Rohstoffpolitik 1968, Rohstoffe für die Welt von morgen, Mineralrohstoffe: Grundlage der Industriewirtschaft 1972, Energierohstoffe: Mangel oder Überfluss? 1978, Rohstoffwirtschaft und Bergbaustudium 1981. *Leisure interests:* hunting, riding, history. *Address:* Haus Blauberg, 6600 Saarbrücken 6, Federal Republic of Germany. *Telephone:* (0681) 85 41 05.

ROMAHI, Seif al-Wady al-, M.A., PH.D.; Abu Dhabi diplomatist; b. 28 Dec. 1938, Museira'a, Palestine; s. of Ahmed al-Hajj Abdul-Nabi; m.; three c.; ed. Lebanese State Univ. and Univ. of Southern Illinois; Area Educ. Supt., Ministry of Educ., Qatar 1960-64; Deputy Dir. Office of the Ruler of Abu Dhabi 1968-70; Dir. League of Arab States Office, Dallas, Tex. 1970-72; Minister Plenipotentiary, Foreign Ministry, Abu Dhabi, U.A.E., with U.A.E. Embassies in Libya and Japan 1973-86; Visiting Prof. Jochi (Sophia) Univ. Tokyo 1977-80; Supervisor of Diplomatic Training, Ministry of Foreign Affairs 1980-83, 1986-; seconded to Nat. Bank of Abu Dhabi as Chief Rep. in N. Asia while concurrently Visiting Prof. Jochi (Sophia) Univ. and Int. Univ. of Japan 1984-86; mem. numerous U.A.E. dels. to int. confs.; mem. or fellow, Acad. of Islamic Research, India, Japanese Acad. of Oriental Studies, British Soc. for Middle Eastern Studies, Middle East Inst., Washington, D.C., Middle East Studies Asscn. of N. America, Japan Middle East Studies Asscn., etc.; Order of Independence (Jordan) and other honours and awards. *Publications:* several books and articles in professional journals. *Leisure interests:* calligraphy, travel, poetry, listening to music, drawing, reading and research. *Address:* P.O. Box 8222, Abu Dhabi, United Arab Emirates (Permanent Address).

ROMAN, Herschel Lewis, PH.D.; American professor of genetics; b. 29 Sept. 1914, Szumsk, Poland; s. of Isadore Roman and Anna Bluwstejn; m. Caryl Kahn Roman 1938; two d.; ed. Univ. of Missouri; Instructor to Prof. of Botany, Univ. of Washington, Seattle, Wash. 1942-52; Prof. of Botany, Univ. of Washington, 1952-59, Chair. and Prof. of Genetics 1959-80, Prof. 1980-83, Emer. 1983-; mem. N.A.S., American Acad. of Arts and Sciences; Pres. Genetics Soc. of America 1968; Guggenheim Fellow, Univ. of Paris 1952-53, Fulbright Scholar 1956-57; Ed. Annual Review of Genetics 1965-84; Visiting Prof. Australian Nat. Univ., Canberra 1966; Gold Medal (Emil Christian Hansen Foundation, Copenhagen) 1980, Thomas Hunt Morgan Medal of Genetics Soc. of America 1985; Dr. h.c. (Univ. of Paris) 1985. *Publications:* papers on cytogenetic studies in maize 1947-51, on the genetics of yeast 1951-. *Leisure interests:* gardening, tourism. *Address:* Department of Genetics, University of Washington, Seattle, Wash. 98195; 5619 77th Street, N.E., Seattle, Wash. 98115, U.S.A. (Home). *Telephone:* (206) 543-1657 (Office); (206) 525-8224 (Home).

ROMANIK, Jerzy; Polish politician; b. 21 Sept. 1931, Zakopane; m. Janina Surma 1958; two d.; mechanic in State Agricultural Machinery Centre, Grodków 1948-55; tractor mechanic in State Agricultural Machinery Centre, Kopice 1955-58; successively miner, foreman, blaster, cutter and loading machine operator in Siemianowice Coal Mine 1958-; many years' activist of Miners' Trade Union; mem. Polish Youth Union 1948-56; mem. Polish United Workers' Party (PZPR) 1971-, mem. Plenum PZPR Town Cttee., Siemianowice 1978-, deputy mem. PZPR Cen. Cttee. 1980-81, mem. PZPR Cen. Cttee. 1981-, mem. Political Bureau of PZPR Cen. Cttee. 1981-86, Chair. Mining Comm. of PZPR Cen. Cttee. 1981-86; Order of Banner of Labour (2nd Class). *Leisure interest:* sport. *Address:* Komitet Centralny PZPR, ul. Nowy Świat 6, 00-497 Warsaw, Poland.

ROMANO, John, M.D., D.SC.; American professor of psychiatry; b. 20 Nov. 1908, Milwaukee, Wis.; s. of Nicholas Vincent Romano and Frances Louise Notari Romano; m. Miriam Modesitt Romano 1933; one s.; ed. Marquette Univ., Milwaukee; Instructor in Medicine, Harvard Medical School 1939–42; Prof. and Chair., Dept. of Psychiatry, Coll. of Medicine, Univ. of Cincinnati 1942–46; Prof. and Chair., Dept. of Psychiatry, School of Medicine and Dentistry, Univ. of Rochester 1946–71, Distinguished Univ. Prof. of Psychiatry 1968–79, Prof. Emer. 1979–; mem. New York Acad. of Medicine, New York Acad. of Sciences, Health Sciences Bd., Inst. of Medicine 1984–. *Leisure interest:* medical history. *Address:* Department of Psychiatry, University of Rochester Medical Center, 300 Crittenden Boulevard, Rochester, N.Y. 14642; 240 Chelmsford Road, Rochester, N.Y. 14618, U.S.A. (Home). *Telephone:* (716) 275-3047; (716) 244-7714 (Home).

ROMANO Sergio, LL.D.; Italian diplomatist and historian; b. 7 July 1929, Vicenza; s. of Romano Romano and Egle Bazzolo; m. Mary Anne Heinze 1954; two s. one d.; ed. Liceo C. Beccaria, Milan, Univ. of Milan, Univ. of Chicago; Foreign Corresp. and film critic for Italian radio and newspapers, Paris, London and Vienna 1948–52; entered Italian Foreign Service 1954; Vice-Consul, Innsbruck, Austria 1955; Sec., Italian Embassy, London 1958–64; Private Sec. to Minister of Foreign Affairs 1964; mem. Diplomatic Staff of the Pres. of the Repub. 1965–68; Counsellor (later Minister), Italian Embassy, Paris 1968–77; Dir.-Gen. of Cultural Relations, Ministry of Foreign Affairs 1977–83; Guest Prof. Faculty of Political Sciences, Univ. of Florence 1981–83; Italian Perm. Rep. Atlantic Council, Brussels 1983–85, Amb. to U.S.S.R. 1985–89; mem. Advisory Cttee., Italian Encyclopaedia; Grand' Ufficiale of the Italian Order of Merit, Commdr. Légion d'honneur, other European and Latin-American honours. *Publications:* Crispi, Progetto per una Dittatura 1973, 1986, La Quarta Sponda 1977, Histoire de l'Italie du Risorgimento à nos jours 1977, Italie 1979, Giuseppe Volpi, Industria e Finanza tra Giolitti e Mussolini 1979, La Francia dal 1870 ai nostri giorni 1981, Benedetto Croce, La Philosophie comme histoire de la Liberté (Ed.) 1983, La Lingua e il Tempo 1983, Giovanni Gentile, La Filosofia al Potere 1984, Florence, Toscane 1988.

ROMANOV, Grigoriy Vasilyevich; Soviet politician; b. 7 Feb. 1923; ed. Leningrad Shipbuilding Inst.; mem. CPSU 1944–; Army service 1941–45; Designer, head of section, Construction Bureau, Ministry of Shipbuilding Industry 1946–54; Party official 1954–61; Sec. Leningrad City Cttee. CPSU 1961–62; Sec. Leningrad Region Cttee. CPSU 1962–70; First Sec. 1970–85; mem. CPSU Cen. Cttee. 1966–86, Cand. mem. Politburo 1973–76, mem. 1976–86; Deputy to U.S.S.R. Supreme Soviet 1966–85, mem. Presidium 1970–85; Sec. CPSU Cen. Cttee. 1983–85; Order of Lenin and various decorations. *Address:* The Kremlin, Moscow, U.S.S.R.

ROMANSKY, Monroe James, M.D., F.A.C.P.; American physician and professor of medicine; b. 16 March 1911, Hartford, Conn.; s. of Benjamin Romansky and Henrietta Levine Romansky; m. Evelyn Muriel Lackman 1943; four s.; ed. Univ. of Maine, Univ. of Rochester School of Medicine; Intern, Strong Memorial Hosp., Univ. of Rochester, N.Y. 1937–38, Asst. Resident 1938–39, Chief Resident 1940–41; James Gleason Research Fellow, Univ. of Rochester 1939–40; Instructor, Investigator for Surgeon Gen. U.S. Army, at Univ. of Rochester 1941–42; Medical Corps, U.S. Army 1942–46; Chief of Biochem. and Antibiotic Research, Walter Read Army Hosp., Washington, D.C. 1942–46; Assoc. Prof. George Washington Univ. School of Medicine 1946–57; Prof., George Washington Univ. Medical Center 1957–, Dir. of Infectious Diseases Div. and Research Lab. 1950–69; Dir. George Washington Univ. Medical Div. at D.C. Gen. Hosp. 1950–69; Consultant, Walter Reed Army Hosp. 1946–, Veterans Admin. Hosp. 1952–, Nat. Inst. of Health 1953–, to Surgeon Gen. U.S.A.F. 1966–; mem. Editorial Board, Antimicrobial Agents and Chemotherapy 1961–72; mem. Trustees Council, Univ. of Rochester 1965–; Diplomate, American Bd. of Internal Medicine, Examiner 1965, 1967, 1969; mem. Infectious Diseases Soc. (Founding Council 1963–66), American Soc. of Internal Medicine, American Fed. for Clinical Research, Soc. for Experimental Biology and Medicine, American Soc. of Microbiology, Soc. of Medical Consultants to Armed Forces; Army Legion of Merit. *Publications:* numerous publs. on subjects in antibiotics and infectious diseases and nutrition in obesity. *Address:* 5480 Wisconsin Avenue, Chevy Chase, Md. 20815 (Office); 6609 32nd Place, N.W., Washington, D.C. 20015, U.S.A. (Home).

ROMANUS, Sven Einar; Swedish judge; b. 19 Jan. 1906, Karlstad; s. of Anton and Reidunn (Lindboe) Romanus; m. Alfhild Sandfaerhus 1932; one s. two d.; ed. Univ. of Stockholm; Justice, Supreme Court 1951–69, Chief Justice 1969–73; Minister of Justice 1976–79; Chair. Swedish Nat. Council for Radioactive Waste 1980–81, Swedish Nat. Bd. for Spent Nuclear Fuel 1981–84; Commdr. Grand Cross, Order of North Star, King's Medal of the Seraphim. *Address:* Kummelvaegen 14, 16139 Bromma, Sweden. *Telephone:* 08-25 98 62.

ROMÁNY, Pál, D.SC.; Hungarian agronomist and politician; b. 1929, Szajol; s. of Pál Romány and Jolán Tasi; m. Erzsébet Markó 1957; one d.; ed. Gödöllö Univ. of Agronomy; joined Hungarian CP 1949; various posts in Ministry of Agric. and in State Farm Admin., Pest-Nógrád County 1952–58, later Chair. Bd. for State Farms, Borsod-Heves County; Deputy Leader, Dept. of Political Econ., Hungarian Socialist Workers' Party, Sec. Cen. Cttee. Bd. on Co-operative Policy 1967–70, Pres. 1974–75; First Sec. Bács-Kiskun County Cttee. 1970, mem. Cen. Cttee. 1970–, Head of Cen. Cttee.

Dept. for Regional Econ. Devt. 1973–75; Minister of Agric. and Food 1975–80; First Sec. County Bács-Kiskun Party Cttee. 1980–88; Chair. Univ. Political Sciences 1980–, Comm. for Agric. History, Hungarian Acad. of Sciences 1971–87; Rector Political Acad. of the HSWP 1987–; Tessedik Sámuel Memorial Medal 1973. *Address:* Ajtósi Dürer 19-21, 1146 Budapest, Hungary.

ROMER, Roy R., B.S., LL.B.; American politician; b. 31 Oct. 1928, Garden City, Kan.; s. of Irving Rudolph and Margaret Elizabeth (née Snyder) Romer; m. Beatrice Miller 1952; five s. two d.; ed. Colorado State Univ., Univ. of Colorado, Yale Univ.; farmed in Colo. 1942–52; admitted to Colo. Bar 1952; independent practice, Denver 1955–66; mem. Colo. House of Reps. 1958–62, Colo. Senate 1962–66; Commr. for Agric. for Colo. 1975; State Treas. 1977–86; Gov. of Colorado 1987–; owner Arapahoe Aviation Co., Colo. Flying Acad., Geneva Basin Ski Area, Chain Farm Implement and Industrial Equipment Stores in Colo.; Gov. Small Business Council; mem. Agric. Advisory Cttee., Colo. Bd. of Agric., Colo. Bar Asscn.; Democrat. *Address:* Office of the Governor, State Capital Building, Room 136, Denver, Colo. 80203, U.S.A.

ROMERO, Pepe; American (naturalized) classical guitarist; b. 3 Aug. 1944, Malaga, Spain; s. of Celedonio Romero and Angelita (née Gallego) Romero; m. 1st Kristine Eddy 1965; m. 2nd Carissa Sugg 1987; one s. three d.; ed. various music acads. in U.S.A., including Music Acad. of the West; began career in Seville, Spain, as part of Romero Quartet 1951, re-formed in U.S.A. 1960; averages 200–250 concerts a year world-wide; recordings number more than 50 solos, plus others with the Romero Quartet and various orchestras; artist-in-residence Univ. of Southern Calif. 1972, Univ. of Calif., San Diego 1984. *Publications:* Guitar Method, Guitar Transcriptions for 1, 2 and 4 guitars. *Leisure interests:* photography, chess.

ROMERO-BARCELÓ, Carlos Antonio, B.A., LL.B., J.D.; Puerto Rican lawyer and politician; b. 4 Sept. 1932, San Juan, Puerto Rico, s. of Antonio Romero-Moreno and Josefina Barceló-Bird; m. 1st, two s.; m. 2nd Kathleen Donnelly 1966, one s., one d.; ed. Phillips Exeter Acad., N.H., Yale Univ., Univ. of Puerto Rico; admitted to bar, San Juan, Puerto Rico 1956; Pres. Citizens for State 51 1965–67; Mayor of San Juan 1969–77; Pres. New Progressive Party 1974–86, Nat. League of Cities 1974–75; Gov. of Puerto Rico 1977–85; Chair. Southern Govs. Conf. 1980–81; mem. Council on Foreign Affairs 1985–, Int. Platform Asscn. 1985–; Hon. LL.D. (Univ. of Bridgeport, Conn.) 1977; James J. and Jane Hoey Award for Interracial Justice, Catholic Interracial Council of N.Y. 1977; Special Gold Medal Award, Spanish Inst., New York 1979; U.S. Attorney-General's Medal 1981. *Publications:* Statehood is for the Poor 1973, Statehood for Puerto Rico, Vital Speeches of the Day 1979, Puerto Rico, U.S.A.: The Case for Statehood, Foreign Affairs 1980, The Soviet Threat to the Americas, Vital Speeches of the Day 1981. *Leisure interests:* reading, horse riding, tennis, swimming, water sports. *Address:* Royal Bank Center Suite 807, Hato Rey, 00918 Puerto Rico; P.O. Box 4109, San Juan, 00936 Puerto Rico, U.S.A. *Telephone:* 766-2500.

ROMERO HERRERA, Carlos; Spanish politician; b. 1941, Fuentesaúco; ed. Madrid Univ., Ecole des Hautes Etudes Européennes and the Sorbonne, Paris; worked on rural devt., Ministry of Agric. 1970–77; Asst. Dir.-Gen. of Production and Employment, Ministry of Econ. in Dept. of Employment Policy, Ministry of Econ. and Commerce; Minister of Agric., Fishing and Food Dec. 1982–. *Address:* Ministerio de Agricultura, Pesca y Alimentación, Paseo de la infanta Isabel 1, Madrid 7, Spain (Office).

ROMERO KOLBECK, Gustavo, M.A.; Mexican economist and public official; b. 3 July 1923, Mexico City; s. of Gustavo and Ana María (de Romero) Kolbeck; m. Leonor Martínez 1950; one s. two d.; ed. Nat. Univ. of Mexico, George Washington Univ. and Chicago Univ.; Prof. at Nat. School of Econs. 1949, Nat. Univ. of Mexico 1966; Dir. School of Econs. Anahuac Univ. 1967–70; Economist Bank of Mexico 1944–45; Research Dept. of Banco de Comercio 1946; Head of Dept. of Econ. Studies, Banco Nacional de México 1949–54; Deputy Dir. and Dir. of Public Investments, Ministry of Programming and Budget 1954–62; Founder and Dir., Centre for Econ. Study of Private Sector 1963–65; mem. Bd. of Govs. CONCANACO 1967; Dir. and Founder of journals Business Trends and Expansión 1967–69; Amb. to Japan 1971–73, to U.S.S.R. 1982–83; Dir.-Gen. Financiera Nacional Azucarera S.A. 1973, Nacional Financiera, S.A. 1974–76, Bank of Mexico 1976–82; Alt. Gov. World Bank 1974–76, IMF and IADB 1976–82; Dir.-Gen. Banco Obrero, S.A. 1983–; decorations from Japan, France, Fed. Repub. of Germany, Brazil and other countries. *Leisure interests:* swimming, reading. *Address:* Rubén Darío 45-2, Cd. Rincón del Bosque 11580, México D.F., Mexico (Home). *Telephone:* 531-37-11 (Home).

ROMERO MENA, Gen. Carlos Humberto; Salvadorian army officer and politician; b. Chalatenango; s. of late José María Romero and of Victoria Mena de Romero; m. Gloria Guerrero de Romero; two s. two d.; ed. Capitán General Gerardo Barrios Mil. School, Escuela de Armas y Servicios, Escuela de Comando y Estado Mayor Manuel Enrique Araujo; Section Commd., Adjutant, and Paymaster, Capt.-Gen. Gerardo Barrios Mil. School and other mil. bodies; Regt. Commdr. Cavalry; Second Officer 1st Infantry Regt.; Sub-Dir. Escuela de Armas y Servicios and Head Dept. Personnel, Gen. Staff Armed Forces; Mil. Attaché to Embassy, Mexico; Head of Staff of Presidency of Repub.; Minister Defence and Public

Security; Pres. Cen. American Defense Council 1973-77; Pres. of Repub. of El Salvador 1977-79 (overthrown in coup); del. 7th Conf. of American Armies 1966, 2nd Conf. of Cen. American Defense Council 1960, 6th Conf. of American Intelligence Officials 1967; Partido de Conciliación Nacional.

ROMITA, Pier Luigi, DR.ENG.; Italian politician; b. 27 July 1924, Turin; s. of Giuseppe Romita and Maria Stella; m. Antonia Magri 1961; one d.; ed. Univ. of Rome; mem. Italian Parl. 1958-; Prof. of Agricultural Hydraulics, Milan Univ. 1963-; Under-Sec. for Public Works 1963, for Public Educ. 1966, for Internal Affairs 1968, for Public Educ. 1970; Minister of Scientific and Technological Research 1972-73, 1980-81, 1981-82, of Regional Affairs 1983-84, of the Budget 1984-88; Sec.-Gen. Partido Socialista Democratico 1976-78. *Address:* c/o Ministry of the Budget, Via XX Settembre 97, 00100 Rome, Italy.

ROMITI, Cesare, B.ECON.; Italian businessman; b. 24 June 1923, Rome; joined B.P.D. (Bombrini, Parodi e Delfino) 1947; Man. Dir. and Gen. Man. Alitalia 1970; Man. Dir. and Gen. Man. financial offices of IRI Italstat 1973; Head of Cen. Office for Finance, Planning and Control, Fiat 1974, Man. Dir. April 1976-; Head of Components Group, Fiat S.p.A. Jan. 1979-; Chair. Gilardini 1976-, SNIA-BDP 1984-, Gemina 1985-. *Address:* 10 Corso Marconi, 10125, Turin, Italy.

ROMPE, Robert, DR.PHIL.; German physicist; b. 10 Sept. 1905, St. Petersburg (now Leningrad), Russia; m. Elisabeth Baumgarten 1947; three s. two d.; ed. Technical Univ., Berlin-Charlottenburg and Bonn Univ.; mem. CP 1932, Socialist Unity Party (SED), mem. Cen. Cttee. 1946-; Head of High Schools and Science Section, Cen. Admin. for Educ. 1945-49; Prof. of Physics and Dir. II Physical Inst. of Humboldt Univ., Berlin 1946-68; mem. G.D.R. Acad. of Sciences and Dir. of its Inst. für Strahlungsquellen 1949-58; mem. Exec. Cttee. Forschungsgemeinschaft der naturwissenschaftlichen, technischen und medizinischen Institut, G.D.R. Acad. of Sciences 1957-68; mem. Research Council of G.D.R. 1957-; Deputy Pres. Council for Peaceful Use of Atomic Energy 1955-63; mem. Cen. Cttee. SED 1958; Chair. Physics Soc. G.D.R. 1970-; Foreign mem. Czechoslovak Acad. of Sciences; Hon. mem. Ungarische Akad. der Wissenschaften; Hon. Dr. Ing.; Dr. rer. nat. h.c.; Nat. Prize 1951; Vaterländischer Verdienstorden in Silver and Gold 1955, 1970; Euler Medal of U.S.S.R. Acad. of Sciences 1957, Verdienter Wissenschaftler des Volkes 1975, Karl-Marx-Orden 1980, Stern der Völkerfreundschaft 1985 and other decorations. *Address:* Gersweiler Strasse 7, Berlin-Müggelheim, 1168, German Democratic Republic. *Telephone:* 6568264.

ROMUALDEZ, Eduardo Z.; Philippine financial administrator and diplomatist; b. 22 Nov. 1909, Tolosa, Leyte; m. Concepción A. Veloso; ed. Univs. of the Philippines and Santo Tomás, and Georgetown Univ., Washington, D.C.; Pres. Bankers Assen. of the Philippines 1950-53; Dir. Chamber of Commerce of the Philippines 1950-52; Regional Vice-Pres. American Bankers' Assen. 1951-56; Chair. Bd. of Dirs., Philippine Air Lines (PAL) 1954-62, Pres. 1961-62; mem. Monetary Bd. Cen. Bank of the Philippines 1954-61, Pres. 1966-70; Alt. Gov. IMF 1956-61, IBRD 1956-61, 1966-70, IFC 1957-61; Chair. Rehabilitation Finance Corpn. 1954-57, Nat. Econ. Devt. Council 1956-58, 1968-69, Devt. Bank of the Philippines 1958, Tax Comm. 1959-61, 1966-70, Bd. of Industries 1966-70; Pres. Philippine Trust Co. 1947-54, 1962-, Fidelity and Surety Co. of the Philippines Inc. 1947-54, 1962-65, Philippines Nat. Bank 1959-61; Sec. of Finance, Repub. of the Philippines 1966-70; Chair. Asian Devt. Bank 1966-68; Amb. to U.S.A. 1971-82 (also accred. to Dominican Repub. and the Bahamas 1979); mem. numerous cttees., etc., and del. to many int. confs. *Address:* c/o Ministry of Foreign Affairs, Manila, Philippines.

RONAN, Sean G., M.A., LL.B.; Irish civil servant and diplomatist; b. 11 Jan. 1924, Cork; s. of John Ronan and Mary Hogan; m. Brigid Teresa McGuinness 1949; three d.; ed. Nat. Univ. of Ireland, Univ. Coll., Dublin; Exec. Officer Revenue Commrs. 1942-46; Admin. Officer Ministry of Finance 1946-49; Third Sec. Ministry of Foreign Affairs 1949-51, First Sec. 1951-55; Consul-Gen., Chicago 1955-60; Counsellor Ministry of Foreign Affairs 1960-64; Asst. Sec.-Gen. for Political, UN and Cultural Affairs and Information, Ministry of Foreign Affairs 1964-72; Amb. to Fed. Repub. of Germany 1972-73, to Greece 1977-84, to Israel (non-resident) 1979-84, to Japan and Repub. of Korea 1984-; Dir.-Gen. for Information, Comm. of European Communities 1973-77; Great Order of Merit with Star of Fed. Rep. of Germany 1973. *Leisure interests:* literary and cultural. *Address:* Embassy of Ireland, Kowa 25 Building, 8-7 Sanbancho, Chiyoda-ku, Tokyo 102, Japan. *Telephone:* 263-0695.

RONAY, Egon, LL.D.; British publisher and journalist; b. Pozsony, Hungary; m. 2nd Barbara Greenslade 1967; one s. (and two d. by previous marriage); ed. School of Piarist Order, Budapest, Univ. of Budapest and Acad. of Commerce, Budapest; trained in kitchens of family catering firm and abroad; managed 5 restaurants within family firm; emigrated from Hungary 1946; Gen. Man. 3 restaurants in London before opening own restaurant The Marquee 1952-55; gastronomic and good living columnist, Sunday Times, weekly columnist on eating out, food, wine and tourism, Daily Telegraph and later Sunday Telegraph 1954-60; weekly column, The Evening News 1968-74; mem. Acad. des Gastronomes (France) 1979; Pres. British Acad. of Gastronomy; founder and, until 1985, publr. of the Egon

Ronay Guides. *Address:* 37 Walton Street, London, SW3 2HT, England. *Telephone:* 01-584 1384.

RØNBECK, Sissel; Norwegian politician; b. 24 May 1950, Hammerfest; m.; Travel Sec. for AUF (Norwegian Labour Youth League) 1970-72, Chair. 1975-77; mem. of Storting 1977; Minister of Consumer Affairs and Govt. Admin. 1979-81, of the Environment May 1986-; Head, Labour Party's Women's Secr. 1985-; Chair. Storting's Standing Cttee. on Church and Educ. 1985-. *Address:* Ministry of Environment, P.O. Box 8013, Dep., Oslo 1, Norway. *Telephone:* (2) 11-90-90.

RONDELLI, Lucio; Italian banker; b. 12 May 1924, Bologna; one s.; ed. Univ. of Bologna; joined Credito Italiano 1947, apptd. Officer 1951, Asst. Man. 1954, Deputy Man. 1959, Man. Venice Br. then Genoa Br. 1961, Deputy Gen. Man. 1966, Gen. Man. 1967, Man. Dir. 1969-; Chair. Credito Italiano Finance Corpn. Ltd., Nassau and Credito Italiano Int. Ltd., London; Dir. Banque Transatlantique S.A., Paris and Mediobanca S.p.A., Milan; mem. Banking Cttee. ICC, Italian Section, Rome; Hon. mem. Forex Club Italiano; Cavaliere di Gran Croce dell'Ordine al Merito. *Publications:* articles on econ. policy in newspapers and journals. *Address:* Credito Italiano Direzione Centrale, Piazza Cordusio, 20121 Milan, Italy. *Telephone:* 02-88621.

RONG YIREN; Chinese financial company executive and government official; b. 1 May 1916, Wuxi, Jiangsu; s. of Rong Deshen; m. Yang Jinaqing 1936; five c.; ed. St. John's Univ., Shanghai; Man. Mow Sing Flour Mills, Wuxi 1937-49; Vice-Pres. Foh Sing Flour Mills, Shanghai 1947-55; Pres. Sung Sing Textile Printing and Dyeing Co., Shanghai 1950-55; Vice-Mayor Shanghai 1957-66; Vice-Minister, Ministry of Textile Industry 1959-66; mem. 2nd, 3rd, 4th, 5th Nat. Cttees. of CPPCC; mem. 1st, 2nd, 3rd, 4th, 5th NPC 1954-62; Chair. China Int. Trust and Investment Corpn., Beijing 1979-; Vice-Chair. Song Chingling Foundation, Beijing 1983-; Chair. All-China Fed. of Industry and Commerce April 1988-; Hon. Adviser China Soccer Assen. 1984-; Vice-Chair. Nat. Cttee. CPPCC 1978-82, Standing Cttee. 6th NPC 1982-86, Exec. Chair. 1986-; Chair. Bd. of Trustees Jinan Univ. Guangzhou 1985-; Hon. Chair. Bd. of Trustees Jiang Nan Univ., Wuxi 1985-; mem. All China Assen. of Industry and Commerce (Vice-Chair. 1953). *Publications:* articles and speeches on China's devt. and related matters. *Leisure interests:* walking, rose-gardening, spectator sports, including soccer. *Address:* China International Trust and Investment Corporation, 19 Jiangoumen Wai Dajie, Beijing, People's Republic of China. *Telephone:* 5001810.

RONNEBURGER, Uwe; German farmer and politician; b. 23 Nov. 1920, Kiel; m.; five c.; private farmer 1948-; active in local govt. and church affairs in Schleswig-Holstein; mem. FDP 1957-; Deputy Chair. 1976-82, now Fed. Cen. Cttee.; Deputy Chair. of FDP Parl. Group 1973-75, April 1983-; fmr. Chair. Cttee. for Interior German Relations, FDP Rep. on Defence Cttee. of Bundestag; mem. Landtag of Schleswig-Holstein 1975-80; mem. Bundestag 1972-75, 1980-; mem. Synod, Evangelical Church of Germany 1972-. *Address:* Bundestag, D-5300 Bonn; Staatshof, 2251 Tetenbüll-über-Husum, Federal Republic of Germany.

RONSON, Gerald Maurice; British business executive; b. 26 May 1939; s. of Henry Ronson and Sarah Ronson; m. Gail Ronson 1967; four d.; Chief Exec. Heron Corpn. PLC 1976-, Chair. 1979-; Chair. and Chief Exec. Heron Int. PLC 1983-. *Leisure interests:* yachting, shooting. *Address:* Heron House, 19 Marylebone Road, London, NW1 5JP, England (Office). *Telephone:* 01-486 4477.

ROOD, Johannes (Jon) Joseph Van, PH.D., M.D.; Netherlands immunologist; b. 7 April 1926, The Hague; s. of Albert van Rood and Rientje Röell; m. Sacha Bsse. van Tuyll van Serooskerken 1957; one s. two d.; ed. Univ. of Leiden; worked in bloodbanking 1952-; in charge of Bloodbank and foundation of Dept. of Immunohaematology, Univ. Hospital, Leiden 1957; work in tissue typing 1958-; worked on antibody synthesis in Public Health Research Inst., New York 1962; lecturer in Immunohaematology, Univ. of Leiden 1965-, Prof. in Internal Medicine 1969-; Founder Eurotransplant 1967. *Publications:* Leukocyte Antibodies in Sera of Pregnant Women 1958, Platelet Survival 1959, Erythrocyte Survival with DFP 32 1961, Leukocyte Groups, the Normal Lymphocyte Transfer Test and Homograft Sensitivity 1965, Platelet Transfusion 1965, The Relevance of Leukocyte Antigens 1967, A Proposal for International Co-operation: EURO-TRANSPLANT 1967, Transplantation of Bone-marrow cells and Fetal Thymus in an Infant with Lymphonenic Immunological Deficiency 1969, The 4a and 4b Antigens: Do They or Don't They? 1970, Anti HL-A 2 Inhibitor in Normal Human Serum 1970, HL-A Identical Phenotypes and Genotypes in Unrelated Individuals 1970, HL-A and the Group Five System in Hodgkin's Disease 1971, The (Relative) Importance of HL-A Matching in Kidney Transplantation 1971, Simultaneous Detection of Two Cell Populations by Two Colour Fluorescence and Application to the Recognition of B Cell Determinants 1976, HLA-linked Control of Suscepti-bility to Tuberculoid Leprosy and Association with HLA-DR types 1978. *Address:* Department of Immunohaematology, University Hospital, Leiden, Netherlands. *Telephone:* 071-147222/4800.

ROOKE, Sir Denis Eric, Kt., C.B.E., B.SC.(ENG.), F.R.S., F.ENG.; British engineer and executive; b. 2 April 1924, London; s. of F. G. Rooke; m. Elizabeth Brenda Evans 1949; one d.; ed. Westminster City School, Addey and

Stanhope School, Univ. Coll., London; served with Royal Electrical and Mechanical Engineers in U.K. and India 1944-49; joined S.E. Gas Bd. 1949, Asst. Mechanical Engineer 1949, Deputy Man. of Works 1954, Devt. Engineer 1959; seconded to N. Thames Gas Bd. 1957; mem. tech. team aboard Methane Pioneer 1959; Devt. Engineer, Gas Council 1960 (name changed to British Gas Corpn. 1973, and to British Gas PLC 1986), mem. for Production and Supply 1966-71, Deputy Chair. 1972-76, Chair. 1976-89; mem. Offshore Energy Tech. Bd. 1975-78; mem. Nat. Econ. Devt. Council (NEDC) 1976-80, U.K. Energy Comm. 1977-79; part-time mem. British Nat. Oil Corpn. (BNOC) 1976-82; Pres. Welding Inst. 1981-83; Chair. Council for Nat. Academic Awards 1978-83; Trustee Science Museum 1984-; Commr. Royal Comm. for the Exhbn. of 1851 1984-; Pres. Fellowship of Eng. 1986-; Chancellor Loughborough Univ. of Tech. 1989-; Fellow, Univ. Coll. London 1972, Inst. of Chemical Engineers; Hon. Fellow, Inst. of Chemical Engineers; Hon. Fellow, Inst. of Gas Engineers (Pres. 1975-76), Inst. of Mechanical Engineers, Inst. of Energy; Master Worshipful Co. of Eng. 1985-86; Hon. D.Sc. (Salford) 1978, (Leeds) 1980, (City Univ.) 1985, (Durham) 1986, (Cranfield Inst. of Tech.) 1987; Hon. D.Tech. (Council for Nat. Acad. Awards) 1986; Hon. LL.D. (Bath) 1987. *Publications:* numerous papers to learned socs. and professional asscns. *Leisure interests:* photography, listening to music. *Address:* British Gas PLC, Rivermill House, 152 Grosvenor Road, London, SW1V 3JL (Office); 23 Hardy Road, Blackheath, London, SE3 7NS, England (Home). *Telephone:* 01-821 1444 (Office).

ROONEY, Denis Michael Hall, C.B.E., M.A., F.ENG., F.I.E.E., F.I.MECH.E.; British business executive (retd.); b. 9 Aug. 1919, Liverpool; s. of Frederick and Ivy Rooney; m. 1st Ruby Teresa Lamb 1942 (died 1984), three s. three d.; m. 2nd Muriel Franklin 1986, one step-d.; ed. Stonyhurst Coll., Downing Coll., Cambridge; Deputy Man. Dir. Balfour Beatty Ltd. 1969-72, Man. Dir. 1973-77, Chair. 1975-80; Exec. Dir. BICC Ltd. 1973-80, Exec. Vice-Chair. 1978-80, Chair. BICC Int. Ltd. 1978-80; Chair. S.E. Asia Trade Advisory Group, British Overseas Trade Bd. (BOTB) 1975-79, mem. Overseas Projects Bd., BOTB 1976-79; mem. BOTB 1979-80; mem. British Overseas Trade Advisory Council 1976-80; mem. Export Group for Construction Industries 1964-80, Deputy Chair. 1979-80; Deputy Chair. Metal Manufacturers Ltd. (Australia) 1978-80; mem. Council, Christian Asscn. of Business Execs. 1979-80, mem. Advisory Council 1980-; Chair. Nat. Nuclear Corpn. Ltd. 1980-81; industrial consultant 1982-87; consultant, Goddard, Kay, Rogers 1983-85; Chair. Laserfix Ltd. 1984-86; mem. Council Inst. of Business Ethics 1986-; Hon. Treas. W. London Cttee. for the Protection of Children 1988-; Liveryman, Worshipful Co. of Turners. *Leisure interest:* golf. *Address:* 36 Edwardes Square, London, W.8, England.

ROOSA, Robert V., A.B., M.A., PH.D.; American banker and fmr. government official; b. 21 June 1918, Marquette, Mich.; s. of Harvey Mapes Rosa and Ruth Lagerquist; m. Ruth Grace Amende 1946; two d.; ed. Univ. of Michigan; teacher of Econs., Michigan, Harvard, M.I.T. 1939-43; Fed. Reserve Bank of New York 1946-60, Vice-Pres. Research Dept. 1956-60; Under-Sec. for Monetary Affairs, U.S. Treas. 1961-64; Chair. The Brookings Inst. 1975-, Partner Brown Bros. Harriman and Co. 1965-; Dir. American Express Co. 1966, Texaco Inc. 1969, Owens-Corning Fiberglas Corpn. 1969; Trustee The Rockefeller Foundation 1967; mem. American Acad. of Arts and Sciences, American Philosophical Soc.; Ind. Democrat. *Publications:* Money, Trade and Economic Growth (Editor) 1951, Federal Reserve Operations in the Money and Government Securities Markets 1956, Monetary Reform for the World Economy 1965, The Dollar and World Liquidity 1967, The Balance of Payments: Free Versus Fixed Exchange Rates (with Milton Friedman) 1967. *Address:* Brown Bros. Haniman and Co., 59 Wall Street, New York, N.Y. 10005 (Office); 30 Woodlands Road, Harrison, N.Y. 10528, U.S.A. (Home). *Telephone:* (212) 483 5318 (Office); (914) 967-7646 (Home).

ROOTES, 2nd Baron, cr. 1959, of Ramsbury; William Geoffrey Rootes, F.B.I.M., F.R.S.A., C.ST.J.; British company director; b. 14 June 1917; s. of 1st Baron Rootes, G.B.E.; m. Marian Slater (née Hayter) 1946; one s. one d.; ed. Harrow and Christ Church, Oxford; War Service 1939-45, R.A.S.C.; rejoined Rootes Motors 1946, Man. Dir. 1962-67, Deputy Chair. 1965-67, Chair. 1967-70; Chair. Chrysler U.K. 1967-73; Dir. First Nat. City Trust Co. (Bahamas) Ltd.; Pres. Motor and Cycle Trades Benevolent Fund 1968-70, Motor Industry Research Asscn. 1970-71, Inst. of Motor Industry 1973-75; mem. Nat. Advisory Council, Motor Mfg. Industry 1964-71,Nat. Econ. Devt. Cttee., Motor Mfg. Industry 1968-73, British Nat. Export Council (Chair. American Cttee. 1969-71), Council, CBI 1967-74, Europe Cttee., CBI 1972-76, Council Inst. of Dirs. 1953-, Council Warwick Univ. 1956-74, Council Soc. of Motor Mfrs. (Pres. 1960-61, Chair. Exec. Cttee. 1972-73); Dir. Lucas Industries Ltd. 1973-85, Rank Hovis McDougall Ltd. 1973-84; Chair. Game Conservancy 1975-79; Vice-Pres. British Field Sports Soc. 1977-; mem. U.K. Council, Trustee World Wildlife Fund 1979-88; mem. Council for Game Conservancy. *Leisure interests:* shooting, fishing, ornithology. *Address:* North Standen House, Hungerford, Berks., England.

ROPER, Warren Richard, M.SC., PH.D., F.R.S., F.R.S.N.Z., F.N.Z.I.C.; New Zealand professor of chemistry; b. 27 Nov. 1938, Nelson; s. of Richard J. Roper and Nancy L. Robinson; m. Judith D. C. Miller 1961; two s. one d.; ed. Nelson Coll., Univ. of Canterbury and Univ. of N. Carolina; lecturer, Univ. of Auckland 1966, Prof. of Chem. 1984-; Visiting Lecturer, Univ. of

Bristol 1972; Visiting Prof. Univ. of Leeds 1983, Univ. of Rennes 1984, 1985, Stanford Univ. 1988; Centenary Lecturer, Royal Soc. of Chem. 1988; Royal Soc. of Chem. Award in Organometallic Chem. 1983; I.C.I. Medal (N.Z. Inst. of Chem.) 1984. *Publications:* over 100 original papers and reviews in scientific journals. *Leisure interests:* listening to music (especialy opera), walking. *Address:* Department of Chemistry, The University of Auckland, Private Bag, Auckland (Office); 26 Beulah Road, Auckland 10, New Zealand (Home). *Telephone:* (09) 737 999 Ext. 8320 (Office); (09) 478 6940 (Home).

ROQUEMAUREL, Marquis Ithier de; French business executive; b. 15 Sept. 1914, Villetoureix, Dordogne; s. of late Marquis de Roquemaurel and Madeleine Meunier du Houssoy; m. Claude du Pouget de Nadaillac 1938; two s. one d.; ed. Coll. Stanislas, Paris and Ecole Cen. des Arts et Manufactures, Paris; Pres./Dir.-Gen. Brodard and Taupin (printers) 1950- (Hon. Pres. 1980); Dir. Ancienne Société Anonyme de Rotogravure d'Art, Brussels 1954-74, Agence et Messageries de Presse, Belgium (also Pres.) 1959-, Société d'Etudes et de Publications Economiques 1962-, Réalités in America (also Pres./Dir.-Gen.) 1962-73, Office d'Editions Générales-Presse 1963-; Man. F.E.P. (France Editions & Publications) 1964-76; Dir. Librairie Hachette 1955-, Deputy Dir.-Gen. 1964-67, Pres./Dir.-Gen. 1967-76 (Hon. Pres. 1980); Man. Société de Gérance d'intérêts de presse 1967-76, Télé-7 Jours 1968-; Dir. Crédit Foncier Franco-Canadien 1968-79, Cie. Française d'Exploitations Commerciales 1968-80, Femmes d'Aujourd'hui, Belgium 1968-74, Sociedad General Española de Librería, Spain 1968-80; mem. admin. council, France-Canada Chamber of Commerce 1969-; Officier, Légion d'honneur, Ordre du Cèdre, Chevalier, Ordre de Leopold, Croix de guerre and many other decorations. *Leisure interests:* yachting, horse riding. *Address:* 23 rue de Berri, 75008 Paris (Office); 12 place Joffre, 75007 Paris, France (Home). *Telephone:* 562-44-55 (Office); 45 67 70 81 (Home).

ROS, Enrique Jorge, LL.D.; Argentine diplomatist; b. 16 July 1927; ed. Univs. Buenos Aires and Paris; practised as lawyer 1949-54; joined Diplomatic Service 1954; Perm. Mission to OAS 1956-58, to UN 1959-63; Chargé d'Affaires, The Hague 1965-67; Embassy, London 1967-71; Head of Mission, Beijing 1973-75; Amb. to Israel 1976-77, to UN 1977-80; Dir.-Gen. Foreign Policy Bureau, Ministry of Foreign Affairs 1980, Under-Sec. for Foreign Affairs 1980-82; Amb. to Spain 1982-84, to Japan 1984-; decorations from Bolivia, Brazil, Chile, Colombia, Ecuador, Paraguay, Peru, Venezuela, Japan. *Leisure interest:* reading. *Address:* Ministry of Foreign Affairs, Arenales 761, Buenos Aires, Argentina. *Telephone:* 31-0071/9.

RÖSCH, Jean; French astronomer; b. 5 Jan. 1915; s. of Dr. Gabriel Rösch and Lucile Forgues; m. Raymonde Postel 1937; ed. Lycée in Algiers and Ecole Normale Supérieure, Paris; Astronomical Asst. Observatory of Bordeaux 1940-43, Assoc. Astronomer 1943-47, Dir. Pic du Midi Observatory 1947-81; lecturer, Univ. of Bordeaux 1943-63; Prof. of Astronomy, Univ. de Paris à la Sorbonne (now Univ. Pierre et Marie Curie) 1963-83, now Prof. Emer.; research on astronomical subjects including binocular vision, the solar system and telescopic images, and choice of sites for observatories; Pres. and mem. numerous astronomical comms.; Pres. Soc. Astronomique de France 1966-69; Corresp. Bureau des Longitudes 1968-; Founder mem. Acad. Nat. Air et Espace; Prix Benjamin Valz, Acad. des Sciences 1942, Médaille Janssen, Acad. des Sciences 1944, Prix Ancel, Acad. des Sciences 1971, Prix des Trois Physiciens 1974, Prix Deslandres, Acad. des Sciences 1986; Officier, Légion d'honneur, Commdr. Palmes académiques, Commdr. Mérite Nat. Mauritanie. *Publications:* Numerous works on astronomy. *Leisure interest:* mountaineering. *Address:* Observatoire du Pic du Midi, 65200 Bagnères-de-Bigorre; and Institut d'Astrophysique, 98 bis boulevard Arago, 75014 Paris, France. *Telephone:* 62-95-19-69 (Bagnères); 46-33-60-40 (Paris).

RÖSCH, Otto; Austrian politician; b. 24 March 1917, Vienna; s. of Otto and Marie (née Gusenbauer) Rösch; m. Elfriede Rösch 1938 (dissolved); one s. three d.; ed. Volksschule, Vienna, Bundeserziehungsanstalt Traiskirchen, and Univs. of Vienna and Graz; Mil. service 1940-45; Sec. (for region of Styria) to Asscn. of Socialist Municipal Reps. 1949; mem. Bundesrat 1951; mem. Styrian Assembly 1953; mem. Lower Austrian Assembly and Sec. of State, Fed. Ministry of Defence 1959-66; mem. Lower Austrian Provincial Govt. 1966; Fed. Minister of Interior 1970-77, of Defence 1977-83; Grosses Silbernes Ehrenzeichen, Silbernes Komturkreuz; Socialist Party. *Publications:* articles in the press and political documents. *Leisure interests:* films, skiing. *Address:* Bundesministerium für Landesverteidigung, Vienna, Austria.

ROSE, Bram, M.D., PH.D., F.R.S.(C.), F.A.C.P., F.R.C.P.; Canadian physician; b. 21 April 1907; m. Rosa Mary Johnson 1940; two s. one d.; ed. Westmount High School and McGill Univ.; Research Asst. McGill Univ. Clinic 1936-39, Research Assoc. 1939-40; R.C.A.F. 1940-46; Asst. Physician, Royal Victoria Hospital, Montreal 1942; Asst. Prof. of Medicine, McGill Univ. Clinic 1950; Assoc. Physician Royal Victoria Hospital 1951; Assoc. Prof. of Medicine, McGill Univ. Clinic 1955; Physician, Royal Victoria Hospital 1961; Prof. of Experimental Medicine, McGill Univ. Clinic 1963-75, Prof. Emer. 1978-; Consultant in Allergy and Dir. of Allergy Lab., Queen Mary Veterans Hospital 1949-; Hon. Consultant in Medicine, Jewish Gen. Hospital, Montreal 1957-; Regional Cons., Jewish Nat. Home for Asthmatic Children, Denver 1959-; Dir. Div. of Immunochemistry and Allergy, Univ.

Clinic, Royal Victoria Hospital 1955-78; fmr. Pres. Canadian Soc. of Immunology; Past Pres. of Canadian and American Acads. of Allergy, Int. Asscn. of Allergology; mem. Training Grant Cttee., Nat. Inst. of Allergy and Immunology, Nat. Inst. of Health, Bethesda, Maryland, Bd. Trustees Trudeau Inst., Saranac Lake, N.Y. 1950- (Chair. Scientific Advisory Bd. 1960-63), Grants Cttee. on Immunology and Transplantation, Nat. Research Council, Ottawa 1968-72, Centenial Fellowships Selection Cttee., Medical Research Council, Ottawa, 1972-77; First Harry Webster Thorp Prof. of Medicine 1974-78; First Harry Alexander Visiting Prof. of Medicine, Washington Univ. 1973; Hon. mem. British, French, Australian, Mexican, Brazilian, Argentinian Acads. of Allergy and Immunology; Centennial Medal 1967, Jubilee Medal 1977; Satellite Symposium held in his honour, 6th Int. Congress of Immunology, on Regulation IgE Synthesis, Toronto 1986; Guest of Honour, XX Congresso Brasileiro de Alergia e Imunopatologia, Rio de Janeiro 1986. *Publications:* over 150 works, on histamine, cardiac catheterization, metabolism, shock, (blackout) acceleration in aircraft, ACTH, cortisone, immunoglobulins, and immune mechanisms in disease; Section Ed. of Immunological Diseases 1966, 1971, 1978. *Leisure interests:* music, skiing, electronics. *Address:* R.R. 3 Magog, Quebec J1X 3W4, Canada (Home). *Telephone:* (819) 843-5817.

ROSE, Sir Clive (Martin), G.C.M.G., M.A., F.R.S.A.; British diplomatist (retd.); b. 15 Sept. 1921; s. of the late Bishop Alfred Rose; m. Elisabeth MacKenzie Lewis 1946; two s. three d.; ed. Marlborough Coll. and Christ Church, Oxford; Rifle Brigade (rank of Maj., mentioned in despatches), Europe, India, Iraq 1941-46; Commonwealth Relations Office 1948; High Comm. Madras 1948-49; Foreign Office 1950; served in Bonn, Montevideo, Paris, Washington and London 1950-73; Imperial Defence Coll. 1968; Amb. and Head of UK Del. to Mutual and Balanced Force Reduction talks, Vienna 1973-76; Deputy Sec. to Cabinet Office 1976-79; U.K. Perm. Rep. on N. Atlantic Council 1979-82; mem. Advisory Council, Control Risks Ltd. 1983-; Dir. Control Risks Information Services Ltd. 1986-; Pres. Asscn. of Civil Defence and Emergency Planning Officers 1987-; mem. Advisory Bd. Royal Coll. for Defence Studies 1985-; Chair. Council Royal United Services Inst. 1983-86, Vice-Pres. 1986-. *Publications:* Campaigns Against Western Defence: NATO's Adversaries and Critics 1985, The Soviet Propaganda Network: a Directory of Organisations Serving Soviet Foreign Policy 1988. *Address:* Chimney House, Lavenham, Suffolk, CO10 9QT, England.

ROSE, Eliot Joseph Benn, C.B.E.; British publisher; b. 7 June 1909, London; s. of Col. E.A. and Mrs. Julia E. Rose; m. Susan P. Gibson 1946; one s. one d.; ed. Rugby, and New Coll., Oxford; served R.A.F. 1939-45; Literary Ed. The Observer 1948-51; Dir. Int. Press Inst., Zürich 1952-62; Dir. Survey of Race Relations in Britain 1963-69; Editorial Dir., Westminster Press 1970-74; Chair. Penguin Books Ltd. 1973-80; Dir. Pearson Longman 1974-81; Chair. InterAction Trust 1968-84, Runnymede Trust; Consultant to UNICEF 1981-. *Publication:* Colour and Citizenship 1969. *Leisure interest:* music. *Address:* 37 Pembroke Square, London, W.8, England. *Telephone:* 01-937 3772.

ROSE, Comte François Jean-Baptiste Hubert Edouard Marie de Tricornot de; French diplomatist (retd.); b. 3 Nov. 1910; m. Yvonne Daday 1933; two d.; ed. Ecole Libre des Sciences Politiques, Paris; Sec. Embassy to U.K. 1937, Italy 1945-46; mem. French del. to UN 1946-50; Minister-Counsellor, Spain 1952-56; Ministry of Foreign Affairs, Paris 1956-60; mem. Atomic Energy Comm. (Paris) 1950-64; Pres. European Nuclear Research Org. (CERN) 1958-60; Asst. to Chief of Staff, Nat. Defence 1961-62; Amb. to Portugal 1964-69; Amb. and Perm. Rep. to N. Atlantic Council 1970-75; Amb. de France 1974; Vice-Pres. Council of Int. Inst. Strategic Studies (London); mem. Trilateral Comm. (European Group); mem. Exec. Bd. French Red Cross; Officier, Légion d'honneur, Commdr. Ordre nat. du Mérite, Croix de guerre. *Publications:* La France et la défense de l'Europe 1976, European Security and France 1984, La paix. Pourquoi pas? (with J. D. Remond and Chantal Ruiz-Barthélémy) 1986. *Leisure interests:* golf, skiing, shooting. *Address:* 5 rue du Faubourg Saint-Honoré, 75008 Paris, France (Home).

ROSE, Richard, B.A., D.PHIL.; American author and professor of public policy; b. 9 April 1933, St. Louis, Mo.; s. of Charles Imse and Mary Conely Rose; m. Rosemary J. Kenny 1956; two s. one d.; ed. Clayton High School, Mo., Johns Hopkins Univ., L.S.E., Oxford; worked in political public relations, Miss. Valley 1954-55; Reporter St. Louis Post-Dispatch 1955-57; lecturer in Govt., Univ. of Manchester 1961-66; Prof. of Politics Strathclyde Univ. 1966-82, Prof. of Public Policy and Dir., Centre of Public Policy 1976-; Consultant Psephologist, The Times, Ind. Television, Daily Telegraph, etc. 1964-; Sec. Cttee. on Political Sociology, Int. Sociology Asscn. 1970-85; Founding Mem. European Consortium for Political Research 1970; Mem. U.S./U.K. Fulbright Comm. 1971-75; Guggenheim Fellow 1974; Visiting scholar at various insts., Europe, U.S.A.; mem. Home Office Working Party on Electoral Register 1975-77; Co-Founder British Politics Group 1974-; Convenor Work Group on U.K. Politics, Political Studies Asscn. 1976-88; mem. Council Int. Political Science Asscn. 1976-82; Tech. Consultant OECD; Dir. S.S.R.C. Research Programme, Growth of Govt. 1982-86; Chair. and Ed. Journal of Public Policy 1981-; Hon. Vice-Pres. U.K. Political Studies Asscn. *Publications:* numerous books on politics and public policy including Politics in England, Public Employment in Western

Nations, Taxation by Political Inertia, Understanding Big Government, Do Parties Make a Difference?, Presidents and Prime Ministers, The Postmodern Presidents, Voters Begin to Choose: International Almanac of Electoral History, Northern Ireland: Time of Choice; many papers in academic journals. *Leisure interests:* architecture, music, writing. *Address:* Centre for the Study of Public Policy, Livingstone Tower, Richmond Street, Glasgow, G1 1XH (Office); Bennochy, 1 East Abercromby Street, Helensburgh, Dunbartonshire, G84 7SP, Scotland (Home). *Telephone:* 041 552 4400 (Office); Helensburgh (0436) 72164 (Home).

ROSEAU, Maurice Edmond Adolphe, PH.D.; French professor of science; b. 3 Nov. 1925, Asnières; s. of Marcel Roseau and Cécile Roseau; m. Marie-Françoise Louet 1960; one s. two d.; ed. Lycée Condorcet, Paris, Ecole Normale Supérieure and Univ. of Paris; French army N. Africa 1944-45; teacher in maths. in Lycée, Le Mans 1948-49; Research Fellow Nat. Centre for Scientific Research 1949-52; Assoc. Prof. at Univ. of Caen 1952-54, Univ. of Poitiers 1954-57; temp. mem. at Inst. of Math. Sciences, Univ. of New York 1957-58; Prof. at Univ. of Lille 1958-62, Univ. of Paris 1962-; Visiting Prof. Univ. Of Calif., Berkeley 1967, 1978, Catholic Univ. of Rio de Janeiro 1971, Univ. of Louvain 1974; mem. of Acad. des Sciences 1982; Scientific Adviser at Nat. Inst. for Research in Transportation and Safety 1983-; mem. Higher Council for Research and Tech. 1987-. *Publications:* Vibrations non linéaires et théorie de la stabilité 1966, Solutions périodiques ou presque périodiques de la mécanique non linéaire 1970, Equations différentielles 1976, Asymptotic Wave Theory 1976, Vibrations des systèmes mécaniques 1984, and numerous papers on waves and vibrations. *Address:* 144 Avenue du Général Leclerc, Sceaux, 92330, France (Home); *Telephone:* (1) 43 50 77 64 (Home).

ROSEMAN, Saul, M.S. PH.D.; American biochemist; b. 9 March 1921, Brooklyn, N.Y.; s. of Emil and Rose (née Markowitz) Roseman; m. Martha Ozrowitz 1941; one s. two d.; ed. City Coll. of New York and Univ. of Wisconsin; Instructor to Asst. Prof., Univ. of Chicago 1948-53; Asst. Prof. to Prof. of Biological Chem. and Chemist, Rackham Arthritis Research Unit, Univ. of Mich. 1953-65; Prof. of Biology, Johns Hopkins Univ. 1965-, Chair. Dept. of Biology 1969-73, 1988-, Dir., McCollum-Pratt Inst. 1969-73, 1988-; Ralph S. O'Connor Prof. of Biology; Consultant, Nat. Cystic Fibrosis Research Foundation. Nat. Science Foundation, American Cancer Soc., Hosp. for Sick Children, Toronto; mem. American Soc. of Biological Chemists, American Acad. of Arts and Sciences, American Chemical Soc., Nat. Acad. of Sciences, A.A.A.S., Biophysical Soc., American Asscn. of Univ. Profs.; Scientific Counsellor to Nat. Cancer Inst.; Counsellor to American Soc. of Biological Chemists; mem. Editorial Bd.: Journal of Biological Chemistry 1962-75, Journal of Lipid Research 1967-, Journal of Membrane Biology 1969-, Biochimica et Biophysica Acta 1971-, Biochemistry 1977-; Hon. mem. Biochemical Soc. of Japan; Hon. M.D. (Univ. of Lund, Sweden) 1984; Sesquicentennial Award (Univ. of Mich.) 1967, 15th Annual T. Duckett Jones Memorial Award, Helen Hay Whitney Foundation 1973, Rosensteihl Award (Brandeis Univ.) 1974, Gairdner Foundation Int. Award 1981, Townsend Harris Medal, City Coll. of New York 1987. *Publications:* over 180 original articles in scientific journals. *Leisure interests:* sailing, music, reading, athletics. *Address:* Department of Biology and McCollum-Pratt Institute, The Johns Hopkins University, Md. 21218 (Office); 8206 Cranwood Court, Baltimore, Md. 21208. U.S.A. (Home). *Telephone:* 338-7333 (Office); 486-7439 (Home).

ROSEN, Charles, PH.D.; American pianist; b. 5 May 1927, New York City; s. of Irwin Rosen and Anita Gerber; ed. Juilliard School of Music, Princeton Univ.; studied piano with Moriz Rosenthal and Hedwig Kanner-Rosenthal 1938-45; recital début, New York 1951; first complete recording of Debussy Etudes 1951; première of Double Concerto by Elliott Carter, New York 1961; has played recitals and as soloist with orchestras throughout America and Europe; has made over 35 recordings including Stravinsky: Movements with composer conducting 1962, Bach: Art of Fugue, Two Ricercars, Goldberg Variations 1971, Beethoven: Last Six Sonatas 1972, Boulez: Piano Music, Vol. I, Diabelli Variations, Beethoven Concerto No. 4, 1979, Schumann: The Revolutionary Masterpieces; Prof. of Music, State Univ. of N.Y. 1972-; Nat. Book Award 1972; Edison Prize, Netherlands 1977; Guggenheim Fellowship 1974; Messenger Lectures, Cornell Univ. 1975, Bloch Lectures, Univ. of Calif., Berkeley 1977, Gauss Seminars, Princeton Univ. 1978; Norton Prof. of Poetry, Harvard Univ. 1980-81; Dr. Mus. h.c. (Trinity Coll., Dublin 1976, Leeds Univ. 1976, Durham Univ.). *Publications:* The Classical Style: Haydn, Mozart, Beethoven 1971, Schoenberg 1975, Sonata Forms 1980, Romanticism and Realism (with Henri Zerner) 1984, The Musical Language of Elliott Carter 1985 and several articles. *Address:* 101 West 78th Street, New York, N.Y. 10024, U.S.A.

ROSÉN, Haiim B., PH.D.; Israeli professor of linguistics; b. 4 March 1922, Vienna, Austria; s. of late Georg Rosenrauch and Olga Gerstl; m. Hannah Steinitz 1953; one s.; ed. schools in Vienna, Hebrew Univ., Jerusalem, Ecole Pratique des Hautes Etudes and Coll. de France, Paris; went to Palestine 1938; school-teacher, Tel Aviv 1944-49; mem. Faculty, Hebrew Univ. Jerusalem 1951-, Prof. of Gen. and Indo-European Linguistics 1968-, Head, Dept. of Linguistics 1973-86; Prof. of Classics and Hebrew Linguistics, Tel Aviv Univ. 1962-; mem. Israeli Nat. Acad. of Sciences and Humanities; visiting professorships at Univ. of Chicago, Univ. of Paris, Coll. de France etc.; Israel State Prize in the Humanities 1978. *Publi-*

cations: about 150 books and articles on classical phlilology, Indo-European and Hebrew linguistics. *Address:* 13, r. Bruria, Jerusalem 93184, Israel. *Telephone:* (972) (2) 634-236.

ROSEN, Milton William, B.S.; American engineer and physicist; b. 25 July 1915, Philadelphia, Pa.; s. of Abraham and Regina (Weiss) Rosen; m. Josephine Haar 1948; three d.; ed. Univ. of Pennsylvania, Univ. of Pittsburgh, and California Inst. of Tech.; Engineer Westinghouse Electric and Mfg. Co. 1937–38; Engineer-physicist Naval Research Lab., Washington 1940–58, Scientific Officer Viking Rocket 1947–55, Head Rocket Devt. Branch 1953–55, Tech. Dir. Project Vanguard (earth satellite) 1955–58; Engineer NASA 1958–74; Chief Rocket Vehicle Devt. Programs 1958–59, Asst. Dir. Launch Vehicle Programs 1960–61, Dir. Launch Vehicles and Propulsion 1961–63; Sr. Scientist, Office of DOD and Interagency Affairs, NASA 1963–72; Deputy Assoc. Admin. for Space Science (Eng.) 1972–74; Exec. Sec. Space Science Bd. 1974–78; Exec. Sec. Cttee. on Impacts of Stratospheric Change, Nat. Acad. of Sciences 1978–80, Cttee. on Underground Coal Mine Safety 1980–83; Exec. Dir. Space Applications Board 1983–85; Chair. Greater Washington Assen. of Unitarian Churches 1966–68; Study Leader, Inst. for Learning in Retirement, American Univ., Washington, D.C. *Publication:* The Viking Rocket Story 1955. *Leisure interests:* music, art collecting, rug making. *Address:* 5610 Alta Vista Road, Bethesda, Md. 20817, U.S.A. *Telephone:* (301) 530-1497.

ROSENBERG, Pierre Max; French curator; b. 13 April 1936, Paris; s. of Charles Rosenberg and Gertrude Rosenberg; m. Béatrice de Rothschild 1981; ed. Lycée Charlemagne, Faculté de droit de Paris and Ecole du Louvre; Chief Curator Dept. des Peintures, Musée du Louvre 1983–; Curator Musée Nat. de l'Amitié et des Relations franco-américaines de Blérancourt; Chevalier des Arts et des Lettres, ordre nat. du Mérite. *Publications:* numerous works on 17th and 18th centuries. *Address:* Musée du Louvre, 34 quai du Louvre, 75058 Paris (Office); 35 rue de Vaugirard, 75006 Paris, France (Home).

ROSENBLITH, Walter Alter; American scientist and university professor; b. 21 Sept. 1913, Vienna, Austria; s. of David A. and Gabriele (Roth) Rosenblith; m. Judy O. Francis 1941; one s. one d.; ed. Berlin, Lausanne, Paris, Bordeaux Univs.; Research Engineer, France 1937–39, N.Y. Univ. 1939–40; Teaching Fellow in Physics, Univ. Calif. (Los Angeles) 1940–43; Asst. Prof., Assoc. Prof., Acting Head, Dept. of Physics, S. Dak. School of Mines and Tech. 1943–47; Research Fellow, Harvard Univ., Psycho-Acoustic Laboratory 1947–51; Assoc. Prof., Communications Biophysics, M.I.T. 1951–57, Prof. 1957–, Inst. Prof. 1975–; Research Assoc. in Otology, Harvard Medical School and Massachusetts Eye and Ear Infirmary 1957–; Chair. M.I.T. Faculty 1967–69; Assoc. Provost M.I.T. 1969–71, Provost 1971–80; Dir. Kaiser Industries 1968–76, SofTech. Inc. 1981–87; Fellow, Acoustical Soc. of America, World Acad. of Art and Science, American Assen. for the Advancement of Science, Soc. of Experimental Psychologists, Inst. of Electrical and Electronic Engineers; mem. Nat. Acad. of Eng., Nat. Acad. of Sciences (Foreign Sec. 1982–86), Inst. of Medicine (also Council mem. 1970–76), American Acad. of Arts and Sciences, Biophysical Soc., Soc. for Neuroscience, American Otological Soc., Life Science Panel, Pres.'s Science Advisory Cttee. 1961–66; Cen. Council, Exec. cttee. and Hon. Treas. Int. Brain Research Org. (UNESCO) 1960–68, Council Int. Union for Pure and Applied Biophysics 1961–69; Inaugural Lecturer, Tata Inst. for Fundamental Research 1962; Weizmann Memorial Lectures 1962; Consultant, WHO 1964–65, Carnegie Corpn. of New York 1986–; mem. Nat. Acad. of Sciences—Nat. Research Council Brain Science Cttee. 1965–68, Pres.'s Cttee. on Urban Housing 1967–68, Bd. Foreign Scholarships 1978–81 (Chair. 1980–81), Bd. of Trustees, Brandeis Univ. 1979–; Chair. Science Advisory Council, Callier Center for Communication Disorders 1968–86, mem. Bd. of Govs. Weizmann Inst. of Science 1973–86, Advisory Cttee. to Dir. Nat. Inst. of Health 1970–74, Nat. Research Council Gov. Bd. 1974–76; USIA Advisory Panel on Int. Educational Exchange 1982–86; Chair. Research Cttee., Health Effects Inst. 1981–; U.S. Co-ordinator, U.S.-France Science and Tech. Program 1979–82; mem. Council on Foreign Relations 1983–; Vice-Pres. Int. Council of Scientific Unions 1984–88; Chair. Int. Advisory Panel of Chinese Univ. Devt. Project II 1986–; Hon. Sc.D. (Univ. of Pa.) 1976, (S. Dak. School of Mines and Tech.) 1980, (Brandeis Univ.) 1988, Dr. h.c. (Fed. Univ. of Rio de Janeiro) 1976, Chevalier Legion d'honneur 1982. *Publications:* Noise and Man (with K. N. Stevens) 1953, Processing Neuroelectric Data (Editor) 1959, Sensory Communication (Editor) 1961, and contributor of numerous articles and chapters to professional publications. *Address:* Massachusetts Institute of Technology, Cambridge, Mass. 02139; 164 Mason Terrace, Brookline, Mass. 02146, U.S.A. (Home).

ROSENBROCK, Howard Harry, D.SC., F.ENG., F.R.S.; British professor of control engineering; b. 16 Dec. 1920, Ilford, Essex; s. of Henry F. Rosenbrock and Harriett E. (née Gleed) Rosenbrock; m. Cathryn J. Press 1950; one s. two d.; ed. Slough Grammar School and Univ. Coll., London; R.A.F.V.R. 1941–46; Electrical Research Assen. 1949–51; John Brown & Co. 1951–54; Constructors John Brown Ltd., latterly Research Man. 1954–62; A.D.R. Cambridge Univ. 1962–66; Prof. of Control Eng., UMIST, Manchester 1966–87, Emer. Prof. 1987–; Moulton Medal, Inst. of Chemical Engineers 1957; Inst. of Electrical Eng. Heaviside Premium 1967; Sir Harold Hartley Medal, Inst. of Measurement and Control 1970; Inst. of

Electrical and Electronic Engs. Control Systems Science and Eng. Award 1982, Inst. of Electrical Eng. Control Achievement Award 1988. *Publications:* Computational Techniques for Chemical Engineers (with C. Storey) 1966, Mathematics of Dynamical Systems 1970 (with C. Storey), State-Space and Multivariable Theory 1970, Computer-Aided Control System Design 1974. *Leisure interests:* microscopy, photography, 17th and 18th Century Literature. *Address:* UMIST, P.O. Box 88, Manchester, M60 1QD (Office); Linden, Walford Road, Ross-on-Wye, Herefordshire, HR9 5PQ, England. *Telephone:* 061-236 3311 Ext. 2129 (Office); (0989) 65372 (Home).

ROSENDE SUBIABRE, Hugo; Chilean lawyer, university teacher and politician; b. 9 May 1916, Chillan; m. Marta Alvarez; five c.; ed. Instituto de Humanidades, Universidad Católica de Chile; Prof. of Civil Law, Univ. Católica 1941, Universidad de Chile 1942; fmr. Conservative M.P. for Santiago; Dean Faculty of Law, Univ. de Chile 1976–83; practised as lawyer in Supreme Court of Justice until 1983; Minister of Justice 1983–. *Address:* Compañía 111, Santiago, Chile. *Telephone:* 6968151.

ROSENFELT, Frank Edward, B.S., LL.B.; American company executive; b. 15 Nov. 1921, Peabody, Mass.; s. of Samuel and Ethel (Litvack) Rosenfelt; m. Judith Roman 1943; two s. one d.; ed. Cornell Univ.; served with U.S. Army (decorated Purple Heart); admitted to N.Y. and Mass. Bars 1950, Calif. Bar 1971; Attorney RKO Radio Pictures 1950–55; joined Metro-Goldwyn-Mayer Inc. 1955, Pres. and C.E.O. and Dir. 1973–; Chair. of Bd. and C.E.O. Metro-Goldwyn-Mayer Film Co. 1980–83, Vice-Chair. Emer. 1983–85; Vice-Chair. MGM/UA Entertainment Co. 1985–; mem. Acad. Motion Picture Arts and Sciences (Bd. of Govs. 1977–85); mem. Bd. Eds. Cornell Law Quarterly 1948–50. *Address:* UIP House, 45 Beadon Road, Hammersmith, London, W.6, England.

ROSENNE, Meir, PH.D.; Israeli diplomatist; b. 19 Feb. 1931, Jassy, Romania; s. of Jacob Rosenhaupt and Fanny Baratz; m. Vera Ayal 1959; two d.; ed. Inst. d'Etudes Politiques, Paris, Faculté de Droit, Paris, and Inst. des Hautes Etudes Int.; served Consulate-Gen. of Israel, Paris 1953–57; E. European Desk, Ministry of Foreign Affairs 1957–61; Consul, New York, Del. to UN Gen. Assembly, Human Rights Comm. 1961–67; Ministry of Foreign Affairs 1967–69; Co-ordinator and Dir. of Foreign Relations, Atomic Energy Comm. 1969–71; Legal Adviser, Ministry of Foreign Affairs 1971–79; mem. del. of Israel to Geneva Peace Conf. 1973, negotiations with Egypt 1974, with Syria 1974, with U.S.A. and Egypt 1975, Camp David 1978 and Washington talks 1979; Amb. to France 1979–83; Amb. to U.S.A. 1983–87. *Leisure interest:* volley-ball. *Address:* c/o Ministry of Foreign Affairs, Hakirya, Romema, Jerusalem, Israel.

ROSENNE, Shabtai, LL.B., PH.D.; Israeli lawyer and diplomatist (retd.); b. 24 Nov. 1917, London, England; s. of Harry and Vera Rowson; m. Esther Schultz 1940; two s.; ed. London Univ. and Hebrew Univ. of Jerusalem; Advocate (Israel), Political Dept., Jewish Agency for Palestine 1946–48; Legal Adviser, Ministry of Foreign Affairs 1948–66; Deputy Perm. Rep. to UN 1967–71; Perm. Rep. to UN, Geneva 1971–74; Ministry of Foreign Affairs 1974–82; mem. Israeli del. to UN Gen. Assemblies 1948–83, Vice-Chair. Legal Cttee. Gen. Assembly 1960; mem. Israeli del. to Armistice Negotiations with Egypt, Jordan, Lebanon and Syria 1949; mem. Israel del. to UN Conf. on Law of the Sea 1958, 1960, Chair. 1973, 1978–82; Chair. Israel del. to UN Conf. on Law of Treaties 1968, 1969, mem. other UN confs.; Govt. Rep. before Int. Court of Justice in several cases; mem. Int. Law Comm. 1962–71, UN Comm. on Human Rights 1968–70; Visiting Prof., Bar Ilan Univ. 1974–; Arthur Goodhart Visiting Prof. of Legal Science, Cambridge 1985–86; Bella van Zuylen Visiting Prof., State Univ. of Utrecht 1986–87, Univ. of Amsterdam 1987; mem. Inst. of Int. Law 1963–, Rapporteur, Termination and Modification of Treaties 1965; Fellow Jewish Acad. of Arts and Sciences 1981; Hon. mem. American Soc. of Int. Law 1976; Israel Prize 1960; Certificate of Merit, American Soc. of Int. Law 1968. *Publications:* International Court of Justice 1957, The Time Factor in Jurisdiction of the International Court of Justice 1960, The Law and Practice of the International Court (2 vols.) 1965, The Law of Treaties: Guide to the Vienna Convention 1970, The World Court: What It Is And How It Works 1973, Documents on the International Court of Justice 1974, 1979, Procedure in the International Court 1983, Practice and Methods of International Law 1984; numerous articles, mainly on law. *Address:* P.O. Box 3313, Jerusalem 91 033, Israel. *Telephone:* (972)-2-526401.

ROSENTHAL, Abraham Michael; American newspaperman; b. 2 May 1922, Sault St. Marie, Ont., Canada; s. of Harry and Sarah (née Dickstein) Rosenthal; m. 1st Ann Marie Burke 1949; three s.; m. 2nd Shirley Anderson 1988; New York Times 1944–, UN Bureau 1946–54, New Delhi 1954–58, Warsaw 1958–59, Geneva 1959–61, Tokyo 1961–63, Metropolitan Ed. 1963–66, Asst. Man. Ed. 1966–68, Assoc. Man. Ed. 1968–69, Man. Ed. 1969–77, Exec. Ed. 1977–86, Assoc. Ed. and columnist 1986–87, columnist 1987–; Ed. at large, Ed. Consultant G.P. Putnam 1988–; Pulitzer Prize 1960, Nat. Press Foundation Award 1986. *Publications:* 38 Witnesses, One More Victim (co-author). *Address:* New York Times, 229 West 43rd Street, New York, N.Y. 10036, U.S.A.

ROSENTHAL, Jean, L. ÈS L.; French publisher; b. 2 Aug. 1923, Paris; s. of Marcel Rosenthal and Yvonne La Touche; m. Françoise Moreau 1975; ed. Lycée Condorcet, Sorbonne Univ.; entered journalism 1946, translations field 1949; Dir. Overseas Rights, Edns. Robert Laffont, Paris 1962; Pres.

Edns. Stock, Paris 1981-; Chevalier des Arts et des Lettres, Chevalier Ordre de la Croix du Sud (Brazil). *Publications:* trans. of Saul Bellow, John Le Carré, Herman Wouk, Henry Miller, Philip Roth, Ken Follett, etc. *Address:* 23 square Vergennes, 75015 Paris, France. *Telephone:* 48.28.34.63.

ROSENTHAL, Philip, M.A.; German ceramics and glass executive and politician; b. 23 Oct. 1916, Berlin; s. of Dr. Philipp and Maria (née Frank) Rosenthal; m. 4th Lavinia McLeod Day; two s. three d.; ed. Wittelsbacher Gymnasium, Munich, St. Laurence Coll., Ramsgate, and Exeter Coll., Oxford; Advertising Man. Rosenthal AG 1950-58, Chair. Man. Bd. Rosenthal AG, Selb 1958-70, 1972-81; Chair. Advisory Bd. Rosenthal Isolatoren GmbH, Selb until 1970; SPD mem. of Parl. 1969-83; Parl. Sec of State at Ministry of Econs. and Finance 1970-71; Chair. SPD-comm. on workers' capital sharing; SPD Spokesman on Communications 1983-; Pres. German Design Council, Darmstadt; Hermann Lindrath Prize 1980: Gläserne Letter, Economic Press Club of Munich Prize 1981, Grosses Bundesverdienstkreuz 1982. *Publications:* Einmal Legionär, publications on design, co-determination and capital sharing. *Leisure interests:* mountaineering, walking, rowing. *Address:* 8672 Erkersreuth, Schloss Erkersreuth, Selb/Oberfranken, Federal Republic of Germany. *Telephone:* Selb 721.

ROSENTHAL, Thomas Gabriel, M.A.; British publisher, critic and broadcaster; b. 16 July 1935; s. of Erwin I. J. Rosenthal; m. Ann Judith Warnford-Davis; two s.; ed. Perse School, Cambridge and Pembroke Coll., Cambridge; served R.A. 1954-56; joined Thames and Hudson Ltd 1959, Man. Dir. Thames and Hudson Int. 1966; joined Martin Secker and Warburg Ltd. as Man. Dir. 1971, Dir. Heinemann Group of Publrs. 1972-84, Man. Dir. William Heinemann Int. Ltd. 1979-84, Chair. World's Work Ltd. 1979-84, Heinemann Zsolnay Ltd. 1979-84, Kaye and Ward Ltd. 1980-84, William Heinemann, Australia and S.A. 1981-82, Pres. Heinemann Inc. 1981-84; Jt. Man. Dir. and Jt. Chair. André Deutsch Ltd. 1984-, Sole Man. Dir. 1987-; Chair. Frew McKenzie (Antiquarian Booksellers) 1985-; Art Critic The Listener 1963-66; Chair. Soc. of Young Publrs. 1961-62; mem. Cambridge Univ. Appointments Bd. 1967-71, Exec. Cttee. Nat. Book League 1971-74, Cttee. of Man. Amateur Dramatic Club, Cambridge (also Trustee), Council R.C.A. 1982-87, Exec. Council Inst. of Contemporary Arts 1987-; Trustee Phoenix Trust. *Publications:* Monograph on Jack B. Yeats 1964, Monograph on Ivon Hitchens (with Alan Bowness) 1973; A Reader's Guide to European Art History 1962, A Reader's Guide to Modern American Fiction 1963, Monograph on Arthur Boyd (with Ursula Hoff) 1986; articles in journals and newspapers. *Leisure interests:* opera, pictures, bibliomania. *Address:* André Deutsch Ltd., 105 Great Russell Street, London, WC1, England. *Telephone:* 01-580 2746.

ROSENZWEIG, Mark Richard, PH.D.; American physiological psychologist and neuroscientist; b. 12 Sept. 1922, Rochester, New York; s. of Jacob Z. Rosenzweig and Pearl Grossman Rosenzweig; m. Janine S. A. Chappat 1947; one s. two d.; ed. Univ. of Rochester and Harvard Univ.; served U.S. Navy 1944-46; Asst. Prof., Univ. of Calif., Berkeley 1951-56, Assoc. Prof. 1956-60, Prof. 1960-; main area of interest: neural mechanisms of learning and memory formation; main findings: plastic anatomical and neurochemical responses of the nervous system of vertebrates to training and differential experience, requirement of protein synthesis in brain for formation of long-term memory; Fellow A.A.A.S., American Psychological Asscn.; Charter mem. Int. Brain Research Org., Soc. for Neuroscience; mem. N.A.S., American Physiological Soc., Société Française de Psychologie; mem. Exec. Cttee., Int. Union of Psychological Science, Vice-Pres. 1980-84, Pres. 1988-(92), Chair. U.S. Nat. Cttee. (N.A.S.-N.R.C.) 1985-; mem. Int. Cttee. on Social Science Information and Documentation 1972-80 (Pres. 1976-78); Chair. Advisory Cttee. for Int. Council of Scientific Unions (N.A.S.-N.R.C.) 1985-88; Ed. Annual Review of Psychology 1968-; Dr. h.c. (Université René Descartes, Sorbonne, Paris) 1980; Distinguished Scientific Contrib. Award (American Psychological Asscn.) 1982. *Publications:* Psychology: An introduction (with P. H. Mussen) 1973, 1977, 1979, Biologie de la Mémoire 1976, Neural mechanisms of learning and memory (Co-Ed. with E. L. Bennett) 1976, Physiological Psychology (with A. L. Leiman) 1982, 1989, Psychophysiology: Memory, motivation and event-related potentials in mental operations (Co-Ed. with R. Sinz) 1983; book chapters and articles in scientific journals. *Leisure interests:* travel, photography. *Address:* Department of Psychology, 3210 Tolman Hall, University of California, Berkeley, Calif. 94720, U.S.A. *Telephone:* (415) 642-7132.

ROSENZWEIG-DÍAZ, Roberto de; Mexican diplomatist; b. 30 June 1924, The Hague, Netherlands; s. of Alfonso de Rosenzweig-Díaz and Elisa Azmitia de Rosenzweig-Díaz; m. Margarita Olloqui de Rosenzweig-Díaz 1951; one d.; ed. Ecole des Roches, France, High School in Panama Canal Zone, Colegio Franco-Mexicano, Mexico, Exeter Coll., Oxford, England; Foreign Service, serving 1946-47 as Third Sec., London, Second Sec., Paris, First Sec., Rio de Janeiro, Minister Counsellor, Paris; Amb. to El Salvador, later to Egypt 1968-74; Adviser and Alt. del. to UN Gen. Assembly 1954-60, Head of Del. 1976; served Drugs Comm. of ECOSOC, Fourth Cttee. of Gen. Assembly 1970, 1973, 1975; Perm. Rep. to UN and Amb. to Bahamas 1976-78, to the Netherlands 1978-81, to Austria 1981-86, to Venezuela 1986-; Chair. Int. Atomic Energy Agency 1983-84; Kt. Commdr., Orden del Cruzeiro do Sul (Brazil), Ordre nat. du Mérite (France), José Matías Delgado Nat. Order, Gran Cruz de Plata and other decorations. *Address:* Mexican Embassy, Quinta Mexico, Av. Principal de Valle Arriba,

Caracas, Venezuela; Miguel Laurent 607, Col. del Valle, Mexico (Home). *Telephone:* 688-07-03 (Home).

ROSHOLT, (Aanon) Michael; South African chartered accountant and business executive; b. 1920, Johannesburg; m. Beatrice Ash 1948; three s.; ed. Michaelhouse School; commissioned as Lieut., Natal Field Artillery, World War II, prisoner-of-war 1942-45; joined firm of C.A.s Goldby, Panchaud and Webber, and later became Sr. Partner; non-exec. mem. Bd., Thos. Barlow and Sons Ltd. 1961-63, Joint Deputy Chair. 1963-68, Jt. Deputy Chair. and Man. Dir. 1968-72; Vice-Chair. and Chief Exec., Barlow Rand Ltd. 1972-79, Chair. 1979-; Deputy Chair. Standard Bank of S.A. Ltd.; Vice-Chair. Standard Bank Investment Corpn. Ltd; Dir. S.A. Breweries, S.A. Mutual Life Assurance Soc., ASA Ltd.; Chair. Ash Bros; Chancellor Univ. of Witwatersrand 1982-; Gov. and Dir. S.A. Urban Foundation; Chair. Residential Devt. and Construction Div. of Urban Foundation, Michaelhouse School Trust; African Children's Feeding Scheme; Patron Natal Univ. Devt. Foundation; Trustee S.A. Foundation; Dir. Family Housing Assen.; Patron S.A. Soc. for Co-operative Educ.; Nat. Fund-Raising Chair. New Era Schools Trust; Vice-Chair. Job Creation S.A.; Fellow Free Market Foundation; Hon. Fellow and Trustee Coll. of Medicine of S.A.; Hon. D.Econ. (Natal); Paul Harris Fellowship (Rotary). *Leisure interests:* squash, golf, fishing, photography, ornithology, reading. *Address:* Barlow Rand Ltd., P.O. Box 782248, Sandton, 2146 South Africa.

ROSICKÝ, Bohumír, DR.RER.NAT., DR.SC.; Czechoslovak professor of parasitology; b. 18 April 1922, Brno; ed. Charles Univ., Prague; mem. of staff, Rovnost (Brno daily paper) 1945-46; Chemical Research Worker, Lab. Head in chemical industry 1947-50; specialist, Cen. Biological Inst., Prague 1950-53; Head, Dept. of Parasitology, Biological Inst., Czechoslovak Acad. of Sciences, Prague 1954-61; Dir. Inst. of Parasitology, Prague 1962-80, Inst. of Hygiene and Epidemiology 1980-; Prof. Natural Sciences, Comenius Univ., Bratislava 1965-; corresp. mem. Czechoslovak Acad. of Sciences 1960-70, Academician 1970-, Vice-Pres. 1970-77; Deputy to Czech Nat. Council 1969-, mem. Presidium 1976-; WHO Consultant, India 1964-65; mem. Joint WHO/FAO UN Panel of Zoonoses; Corresp. mem. Bulgarian Acad. of Sciences 1974; State Prize 1954; Klement Gottwald State Prize (with team) 1956, 1972, G. Mendel Gold Medal 1970, Silver Plaque of Czechoslovak Acad. of Sciences 1972, Order of Cyril and Method (Bulgaria) 1972, Krzyz Oficerski (Poland) 1973, Order of Labour 1982. *Publications:* Modern Insecticides (co-author) 1951, Czechoslovak Fauna-Aphaniptera 1957, Parasitologische Arbeitsmethoden (co-author) 1965; 130 papers on ecology, taxonomy, entomology, medical zoology and parasitology. *Address:* Ceskoslovenská Akademie Věd, 111 42 Prague 1, Národní Tř. 3, Czechoslovakia.

ROSKILL, Baron; (Life Peer), cr. 1980, of Newtown in the County of Hampshire; **Rt. Hon. Eustace Wentworth Roskill,** Kt., P.C., M.A., D.L.; British judge; b. 6 Feb. 1911, London; s. of late John Henry Roskill, K.C., and Sybil Mary Wentworth (Dilke) Roskill; m. Elisabeth Wallace Jackson 1947; one s. two d.; ed. Winchester Coll., Exeter Coll., Oxford; Harmsworth Law Scholar, Middle Temple 1932; called to the Bar, Middle Temple 1933, Ministry of War Transport 1939-45, Q.C. 1953, Chair. Hampshire Quarter Sessions 1960-71, Judge of High Court (Queen's Bench Div.) 1962-71, Vice-Chair. Parole Bd. 1967-69, Lord Justice of Appeal 1971-80, Lord of Appeal in Ordinary 1980-86; Pres. Senate of Four Inns of Court 1972-74; Treas. Middle Temple 1980; Hon. Bencher, Inner Temple 1980; Chair. Third London Airport Comm. 1968-70, London Int. Arbitration Trust Ltd. 1981-, Fraud Trials Cttee. 1983-85, Appeal Cttee. Panel on Takeover and Mergers 1987-; Hon. Fellow, Exeter Coll., Oxford 1963; Fellow Winchester Coll. 1981-86. *Leisure interests:* gardening, music, swimming. *Address:* New Court, Temple, London, E.C.4; Heatherfield, Newtown, Newbury, Berks., RG15 9DB, England. *Telephone:* 01-353 8870; (0635) 40606 (Home).

ROSOMAN, Leonard Henry, O.B.E., R.A., F.S.A.; British artist and teacher; b. 27 Oct. 1913, London; s. of Henry Edward Rosoman and Lillian Blanche (née Spencer); m. Jocelyn Rickards 1963 (divorced 1968); ed. Deacons School, Peterborough, Durham Univ., R.A. Schools and Cen. School of Art and Design, London; taught Reimann School, London 1937-39; Official War Artist to Admiralty 1943-45; taught Camberwell School of Art, London 1946-47; taught Edin. Coll. of Art 1947-56, Chelsea School of Art, London 1956-57, R.C.A., London 1957-78; freelance artist 1978-; designed and painted vaulted ceiling in Lambeth Palace Chapel, London; exhbns. at Rowland Browse & Delbanco and Fine Art Soc., London, Lincoln Center and Touchstone Gallery, New York, State Univ. of New York at Albany, Oldham Art Gallery and David Paul Gallery, Chichester; Winston Churchill Fellow 1966-67; Hon. A.R.C.A.; Hon. mem. Royal Scottish Soc. of Painters in Water Colours, Royal W. of England Acad. *Leisure interest:* travelling as much as possible. *Address:* 7 Pembroke Studios, Pembroke Gardens, London, W8 6HX, England. *Telephone:* 01-603 3638.

ROSS, André Louis Henry, L. EN D.; French diplomatist; b. 13 March 1922, Calais; s. of René Ross and Yvonne Alexander; m. Thérèse Anne Guéroult 1951; ed. Univ. of Paris and Ecole nat. d'admin.; 1st Counsellor, Bangkok 1964-66; Amb. to Laos 1968-72, Zaire 1972-78, India 1979-83, Japan 1983-85; Sec.-Gen. Ministry of Foreign Affairs 1985-87; Amb. of France 1985; Adviser and mem. Bd., Indosuez Bank 1987-; mem. Council of French Museums 1988-; Commdr., Légion d'honneur, ordre nat. du

Mérite. *Leisure interests:* the arts and math. *Address:* 1 rue de Fleurus, 75006 Paris, France. *Telephone:* (1) 45 48 55 60.

ROSS, Sir Archibald David Manisty, K.C.M.G., M.A.; British businessman and diplomatist (retd.); b. 12 Oct. 1911, Budleigh Salterton, Devon; s. of late John Archibald Ross, I.C.S., and of Dorothea Manisty; m. Mary Melville Macfadyen 1939; one s. one d.; ed. Winchester, and New Coll., Oxford; Diplomatic Service 1936-71; Minister, Rome 1953-56; Asst. Under-Sec. of State 1956-60; Amb. to Portugal 1961-66, to Sweden 1966-71; Chair., Alfa-Laval Co. Ltd., Saab (U.K.), Scania (U.K.) 1972-82, Ericsson Information Systems 1981-86, Anglo-Swedish Arts Foundation 1983-; mem. Council Royal Agric. Soc. of England 1980-85; Grand Cross, Order of the North Star, Sweden 1981. *Leisure interests:* tennis, music. *Address:* 17 Ennismore Gardens, London, S.W.7, England.

ROSS, (Claud) Richard, C.B., M.A.; British financial executive and economist; b. 24 March 1924, Steyning, Sussex; s. of Claud Frederick and Frances Muriel Ross; m. Leslie Beatrice Arnell 1954; two d.; ed. Ardingly Coll. and Hertford Coll., Oxford; served in Royal Engineers 1942-47; Fellow Hertford Coll. Oxford and Lecturer in Econs. 1951, 1955-63; Econ. Adviser to H.M. Treasury 1952-55; Dean, School of Social Studies and Prof. of Econs., Univ. of East Anglia 1963-68; Special Consultant to OECD 1968-71; Deputy Sec., Cen. Policy Review Staff, Cabinet Office 1971-78; Vice-Pres. EIB and Vice-Chair. Bd. of Dirs. 1978-; mem. East Anglia Regional Econ. Planning Council 1966-69, Deputy Chair. 1967-69. *Publications:* Financial and Physical Problems of Development in the Gold Coast (with D. Seers) 1952, articles on economics. *Address:* European Investment Bank, 100 boulevard Konrad Adenauer, 2950 Luxembourg; 2A Oliver's Wharf, 64 Wapping High Street, London, E.1, England. *Telephone:* 43 79-1 (Office).

ROSS, Diana; American singer and actress; b. 26 March 1944, Detroit; d. of Fred and Ernestine Ross; m. 1st Robert Ellis Silberstein 1971 (divorced 1976); three d.; m. 2nd Arne Naess 1985; fmr. lead singer Diana Ross and the Supremes; solo singer 1970-; numerous records with Supremes and solo; TV specials. *Films include:* Lady Sings the Blues 1972, Mahogany 1975, The Wiz 1978; citation from Vice-Pres. Humphrey for efforts on behalf of Pres. Johnson's Youth Opportunity Programme; from Mrs. Martin Luther King and Rev. Abernathy for contribution to Southern Christian Leadership Conf. cause; Billboard, Cash Box and Record World magazine awards as world's outstanding female singer; Grammy Award 1970; Female Entertainer of the Year, Nat. Assen. for the Advancement of Colored People 1970; Cue Award as Entertainer of the Year 1972; Golden Apple Award 1972; Gold Medal Award, Photoplay 1972; Antoinette Perry Award 1977; Golden Globe Award 1972. *Albums include:* I'm Still Waiting 1971, Touch Me In The Morning 1973, Why Do Fools Fall in Love? 1981, Eaten Alive 1984, Chain Reaction 1986, Workin' Overtime 1989. *Address:* RTC Management, P.O. Box 1683, New York, N.Y. 10185, U.S.A.

ROSS, Rt. Hon. Lord; Donald MacArthur Ross, M.A., LL.B., F.R.S.E.; British lawyer; b. 29 March 1927, Dundee; s. of John Ross and Jessie MacArthur Thomson; m. Dorothy M. Annand 1958; two d.; ed. High School of Dundee and Univ. of Edinburgh; nat. service with Black Watch 1947-49; T.A. rank of Capt. 1949-58; Advocate 1952; Q.C. (Scotland) 1964; Vice-Dean, Faculty of Advocates 1967-73, Dean 1973-76; Sheriff Prin. of Ayr and Bute 1972-73; Senator, Coll. of Justice, Scotland and Lord of Session 1977-; Lord Justice Clerk of Scotland 1985-; Deputy Chair. Boundary Comm. for Scotland 1977-85; mem. Scottish Cttee. of Council on Tribunals 1970-76, Cttee. on Privacy 1970; Chair. Court of Heriot Watt Univ. 1984- (mem. 1978-); Hon. LL.D. (Edinburgh) 1987, Hon. D.Univ. (Heriot Watt) 1988. *Publication:* contrib. to Stair Memorial Encyclopaedia of Scots Law. *Leisure interests:* gardening, walking. *Address:* Parliament House, Edinburgh, EH1 1RQ, Scotland. *Telephone:* 031 225 2595.

ROSS, Ian Gordon, M.SC., PH.D., F.A.A.; Australian professor of chemistry; b. 5 July 1926, Sydney; s. of Gordon R. Ross and Isabella M. Jenkins; m. Viola Bartlett 1975; ed. Univs. of Sydney and London; Research Assoc., Fla. State Univ. 1953; lecturer, then Reader in Physical Chem., Univ. of Sydney 1954-67, Prof. of Chem. 1968-; Pro Vice-Chancellor Australian Nat. Univ. 1975, Deputy Vice-Chancellor 1977-; Chair. Australian Research Grants Cttee. 1972-79, Inquiry into Govt. Labs. 1982-83, Australian & New Zealand Assen. for the Advancement of Science 1984-86; H.G. Smith Medal, Royal Australian Chem. Inst. 1972. *Publications:* scientific papers on theoretical chemistry and molecular spectroscopy. *Address:* RMB 2039, Queanbeyan, N.S.W. 2620, Australia. *Telephone:* (06) 297-3510.

ROSS, Ian Munro, PH.D., F.I.E.E.E.; American (b. British) electrical engineer; b. 15 Aug. 1927, Southport, England; m. Christina Leinberg 1955; one s. two d.; ed. Gonville and Caius Coll. Cambridge, England; went to U.S.A. 1952, naturalized 1960; with AT&T Bell Labs. (and affiliates) 1952-, Exec. Dir., Network Planning Div. 1971-73, Vice-Pres., Network Planning and Customer Services 1973-76, Exec. Vice-Pres., Systems Eng. and Devt. 1976-79, Pres. 1979-; Dir., Thomas & Betts Corpn., B. F. Goodrich Co.; Liebmann Memorial Prize, I.E.E.E. 1963; Public Service Award, NASA 1969, 1975, I.E.E.E. Medal of Honour 1988; Fellow, American Acad. of Arts and Sciences; mem. Nat. Acad. of Eng. *Address:* AT&T Bell Laboratories, Crawfords Corner Road, Holmdel, N.J. 07733-1988, U.S.A. *Telephone:* (201) 949-3242.

ROSS, Sir Lewis Nathan, Kt., C.M.G., F.C.A.; New Zealand company director and banker; b. 7 March 1911, Auckland; s. of Robert and Raie Ross; m. Ella M. Burns; one d. two s.; ed. Auckland Grammar School, Univ. of Auckland; commenced practice as a chartered accountant in Auckland 1932; Pres. Assoc. Chambers of Commerce of N.Z. 1956-57, N.Z. Soc. of Accountants 1972-73; Chair. Govt. Cttee. to Review Taxation in N.Z. 1966-67; mem. Nat. Devt. Council 1969-74; Chair. Bank of N.Z. 1966-87; Dir. Revertex Industries Ltd., James Hardie Impey Ltd. and several other cos.; Chair. Aotea Centre Trust Bd. 1984-; Hon. LL.D. (Auckland) 1983. *Publications:* Taxation: principles, purpose and incidence 1972; one research lecture, several booklets and articles on finance and taxation. *Address:* Achilles House, Customs Street, P.O. Box 881, Auckland (Office); 4/198 Remuera Road, Remuera, Auckland, New Zealand (Home). *Telephone:* 798-665 (Office); 547-449 (Home).

ROSS, Richard (see Ross, Claud Richard).

ROSS, Steven J.; American business executive; b. 1927, New York; ed. Paul Smith's Coll.; Pres., Dir. Kinney Services Inc. 1966-72; Chair., Pres., C.E.O. Warner Communications Inc. (merger with Time Inc. 1989) 1972-; Bd. of Dirs. New York Convention, N.Y. State Alliance to Save Energy. *Address:* 75 Rockefeller Plaza, New York, N.Y. 10019, U.S.A.

ROSSI, H.E. Cardinal Agnelo; Brazilian ecclesiastic; b. 4 May 1913; ordained priest 1937; Bishop of Barra do Pirai 1956; Archbishop of São Paulo 1964; cr. Cardinal 1965; Prefect, Sacred Congregation for the Evangelization of the People 1970-84; Titular Bishop of Ostia and Sabina-Poggio Mirteto; Pres. Admin. of Patrimony of Holy See 1984-; Grand Chancellor Pontificia Universitas Urbaniana; mem. Congregations for Catholic Educ., for the Cause of the Saints, for the Religious and for Secular Insts., for the Clergy, for Oriental Churches, for the Bishops, and others. *Address:* 00120, Vatican City, Italy.

ROSSI, Bruno B.; American professor; b. 13 April 1905, Venice, Italy; s. of Rino Rossi and Lina Minerbi Rossi; m. Nora Lombroso 1938; one s. two d.; ed. Univs. of Padua and Bologna; Asst. Univ. of Florence 1928-32; Prof. Univ. of Padua 1932-38; Assoc. Prof. Cornell Univ., Ithaca, N.Y. 1940-43; Staff mem. Los Alamos Lab., N.M. 1943-46; Prof. of Physics, M.I.T. 1946-70, Inst. Prof. 1966, Inst. Prof. Emer. 1970-; Hon. Prof. Univ. Mayor de San Andrés, La Paz, Bolivia; Hon. Fellow Tata Inst. Fundamental Research, Bombay 1971; mem. Physics Cttee. of NASA; mem. N.A.S.; Dr. h.c. (Palermo, Durham 1974, Univ. of Chicago 1977; Research Corpn. Scientific Award; Order of Merit of the Repub. of Italy; Italian Physical Soc. Gold Medal 1970; Int. Feltrinelli Award, Accademia dei Lincei, Cresson Medal, Franklin Inst., Philadephia 1974, Rumford Prize, American Acad. of Arts and Sciences 1976, Nat. Medal of Science 1985, Wolf Prize 1987. *Publications:* Ionization Chambers and Counters (Co-Author) 1949, High Energy Particles 1952, Optics 1957, Cosmic Rays 1964, Introduction to the Physics of Space (Co-Author) 1970; about 150 papers. *Address:* Massachusetts Institute of Technology, 77 Massachusetts Avenue, Cambridge, Mass. (Office); 221 Mount Auburn Street, Cambridge, Mass. 02138, U.S.A. (Home). *Telephone:* (617) 253-4283 (Office); (617) 864-9617 (Home).

ROSSINI, Frederick Dominic, M.S., PH.D., D.SC., D.ENG.SC., LITT.D.; American chemist; b. 18 July 1899, Monongahela, Pa.; s. of Martino and Costanza Rossini; m. 1st Anne K. Landgraff 1932 (died 1981); one s.; 2nd Dorothy T. Purcell 1983; ed. Carnegie Inst. of Tech., and Univ. of Calif.; Asst. in Physics, Carnegie Inst. of Tech. 1923-24, Asst. in Mathematics 1924-26; Teaching Fellow in Chem., Univ. of Calif. 1926-28; Physical Chemist, Nat. Bureau of Standards 1928-50, Chief of Section on Thermochem. and Hydrocarbons 1936-50, Lecturer in Chemical Thermodynamics, Graduate School Nat. Bureau of Standards 1934-50; Dir. American Petroleum Inst. Research Projects 1935-60; Silliman Prof., Head Dept. of Chem., Dir. Chemical and Petroleum Research Lab., Carnegie Inst. of Tech. 1950-60; Dean, Coll. of Science and Assoc. Dean Graduate School. Univ. of Notre Dame 1960-67, Vice-Pres. for Research 1967-71; Prof. of Chem., Rice Univ. 1971-78; Bd. of Editors Journal of American Chemical Society 1946-56; Comm. on Thermochem., Int. Union of Pure and Applied Chem. 1934-61; Pres. Comm. on Chemical Thermodynamics 1952-61; Consultant Nat. Science Foundation 1952-62; Chair. Div. of Petroleum Chem., American Chemical Soc. 1954; Marburg Lecturer American Soc. for Testing Materials 1953; Chair. Div. Chem. and Chemical Tech., Nat. Research Council 1955-58; Pres. Albertus Magnus Guild 1961-65, Assen. Midwest Univ. 1967-68, Cttee. on Data for Science and Tech. of the Int. Council of Scientific Unions 1966-75, World Petroleum Congresses 1967-75; Vice-Pres. Argonne Univ. Assen. 1968-70; mem. Nat. Acad. of Sciences; Dr. h.c. (Univ. of Lund, Sweden) 1974; awards include Priestley Medal (American Chem. Soc. 1971), Redwood Medal (Inst. of Petroleum, U.K.) 1972, Carl Engler Medal (Deutsche Gesellschaft für Mineralölwissenschaft und Kohlechemie, Fed. Repub. of Germany) 1976, Nat. Medal of Science (U.S.A.) 1977. *Publications:* 11 books and 253 papers. *Address:* 605 South U.S. Highway 1, T900, Juno Beach, Fla. 33408, U.S.A. *Telephone:* (407) 622-5710.

ROSSINOT, André, D. EN MED.; French doctor and politician; b. 29 May 1939, Briey, Meurthe-et-Moselle; s. of Lucien Rossinot and Jeanne Fondeur; m. 3rd Françoise Cordelier 1985; three c. from previous marriages; ed. Lycée Poincaré and Faculty of Medicine, Nancy; ear, nose and throat specialist in private practice; Town Councillor, Nancy 1969-71; Mayor of Nancy 1983-; Deputy to Nat. Ass. (UDF) 1978-86; Pres. Parti Radical 1983-; Minister for Relations with Parliament 1986-88. *Address:* Hôtel de Ville, place Stanislas, 54000 Nancy, France.

ROSTA, Endre, D.IUR.; Hungarian jurist; b. 18 July 1909, Berettyószéplak; m. Simone Pasche 1946; three d.; ed. Budapest and Graz; Official, Cen. Cttee. Hungarian CP 1945-48, later Hungarian Working People's Party; Head of Press Dept. of Prime Minister's Office; Judge, later Vice-Pres. High Court for Econ. Affairs; science-policy and legal adviser Hungarian Acad. of Sciences Research Inst. for Computer Technology and Automation and Centre of Computer Technology and Org., Hungarian Telecommunications Assen.; Exec. Chair. Inst. for Cultural Relations 1961-69, Chair. 1970-77; Labour Order of Merit golden degree. *Leisure interests:* logic, mathematics. *Address:* H-1124 Budapest, Stromfeld Aurél ut 34, Hungary. *Telephone:* 563-121.

ROSTOW, Eugene Victor, LL.D. (brother of Walt Whitman Rostow, q.v.); American lawyer, economist and government official; b. 25 Aug. 1913, Brooklyn, N.Y.; s. of Victor A. and Lillian Rostow; m. Edna B. Greenberg 1933; two s. one d.; ed. Yale Coll., King's Coll., Cambridge, and Yale Law School; admitted to N.Y. Bar 1938, practised in New York City 1937-38; mem. Faculty, Law School, Yale 1938-, Prof. of Law 1944-84, Sterling Prof. of Law and Public Affairs 1964-84, Dean 1955-65 (on leave 1966-69), Prof. Emer., Sr. Research Scholar 1984-; Visiting Prof., Univ. of Chicago 1941; Pitt Prof. of American History and Insts., Professorial Fellow, King's Coll., Cambridge 1959-60; Guggenheim Fellow 1959-60; Adviser to Dept. of State 1942-44, 1961-66; Asst. Exec. Sec. Econ. Comm. for Europe, UN 1949-50; Under-Sec. of State for Political Affairs, Dept. of State 1966-69; Eastman Visiting Prof. and Fellow of Balliol Coll., Oxford 1970-71; Visiting Research Prof. of Law and Diplomacy Nat. Defense Univ., Washington 1984-; Pres. Atlantic Treaty Assen. 1973-76; Dir. Arms Control and Disarmament Agency 1981-83; Fellow, A.A.A.S.; Hon. LL.D. (Cambridge); Kt. Commdr., Order of the Crown, Belgium, Chevalier, Légion d'honneur. *Publications:* Planning for Freedom 1959, The Sovereign Prerogative 1962, Law, Power and the Pursuit of Peace 1968, Peace in the Balance 1972, Is Law Dead? (Ed.)1971, The Ideal in Law 1978. *Address:* 208 St. Ronan Street, New Haven, Conn. 06511; National Defense University, Ft. L. J. McNair, Washington, D.C. 20319, U.S.A.

ROSTOW, Walt Whitman, PH.D.; American economist; b. 7 Oct. 1916, New York, N.Y.; s. of Victor A. and Lillian H. Rostow; brother of Eugene Victor Rostow (q.v.); m. Elspeth Vaughan Davies 1947; one s. one d.; ed. Yale and Oxford Univs.; Instructor in Econs. Columbia Univ. 1940-41; Maj., U.S. Army 1942-45; Asst. Chief German-Austrian Econ. Div. State Dept. 1945-46; Harmsworth Prof. of American History, Oxford Univ. 1946-47; Asst. to Exec. Sec. UN Econ. Comm. for Europe 1947-49; Pitt Prof. of American History Cambridge Univ. 1949-50; Prof. of Econ. History M.I.T. and Staff mem. M.I.T. Center for Int. Studies 1951-60; Deputy Special Asst. to the Pres. for Nat. Security Affairs Jan.-Nov. 1961; Counsellor and Chair. Policy Planning Council, Dept. of State 1961-66; Special Asst. to the Pres., The White House 1966-69; currently Prof. of Econs. and History, Univ. of Texas; Legion of Merit, Hon. O.B.E. (U.K.), Presidential Medal of Freedom (with distinction) 1969. *Publications:* The American Diplomatic Revolution 1947, Essays on the British Economy of the XIX century 1948, The Process of Economic Growth 1952, The Growth and Fluctuation of the British Economy 1790-1850 (with A. D. Gayer and A. J. Schwartz) 1953, The Dynamics of Soviet Society (with A. Levin and others) 1953, The Prospects for Communist China (with others) 1954, An American Policy in Asia (with R. W. Hatch) 1955, A Proposal: Key to an Effective Foreign Policy (with Max F. Millikan) 1957, The United States in the World Arena 1960, The Stages of Economic Growth 1960, View from the Seventh Floor 1964, A Design for Asian Development 1965, East-West Relations: Is Detente Possible? (with William E. Griffith) 1969, Politics and the Stages of Growth 1971, The Diffusion of Power 1972, How it All Began 1975, The World Economy: History and Prospect 1978, Getting from Here to There 1978, Why the Poor Get Richer and the Rich Slow Down 1980, British Trade Fluctuations 1868-1896 1981, Pre-Invasion Bombing Strategy: General Eisenhower's Decision of March 25th, 1944 1981, The Division of Europe after World War II: 1946 1981, Europe after Stalin: Eisenhower's Three Decisions of March 11th, 1953 1982, Open Skies: Eisenhower's Proposal of July 21st, 1955 1982, The Barbaric Counter-Revolution: Cause and Cure 1983, Eisenhower, Kennedy and Foreign Aid 1985, The United States and the Regional Organization of Asia and the Pacific: 1965-85 1986, Rich Countries and Poor Countries: Reflections from the Past, Lessons for the Future 1987, Essays on a Half Century: Ideas, Politics, and Action 1988. *Leisure interest:* tennis. *Address:* 1 Wildwind Point, Austin, Tex., 78746, U.S.A.

ROSTROPOVICH, Mstislav Leopoldovich; Soviet-born 'cellist, conductor and accompanist; b. 27 March 1927, Baku, Azerbaizhan S.S.R.; s. of Leopold Rostropovich and Sofia Fedotova; m. Galina Vishnevskaya (q.v.) 1955; two d.; ed. Moscow Conservatoire; 'cello début (U.S.S.R.) 1940; numerous concert tours in U.S.S.R. and abroad as soloist and 'cellist in trio with Emil Gilels (q.v.) and Leonid Kogan (q.v.) since 1947; début in U.S.A. as 'cellist 1955, as conductor 1975; Music Dir. Nat. Symphony Orchestra (Washington, D.C.) 1977-; Joint Artistic Dir. Aldeburgh Festival (U.K.)

1977-; mem. Union of Soviet Composers 1950-78, 1989-; Prof. Moscow and Leningrad Conservatoires 1960-78; among composers who have written works for him are Prokofiev, Shostakovich, Miaskovsky, Khachaturian, Kabalevsky, Britten, Piston and Bernstein; Hon. mem. Acad. of St. Cecilia (Rome), A.A.A.S.; Hon. F.R.A.M.; Hon. K.B.E. 1987; Hon. D.Mus. (Oxford) 1980; hon. degrees (including Humanities, Law, Letters, Music) from 21 univs.; First Prize at All-Union Competition of Musicians 1945, Int. 'Cellist Competition 1947, 1950, 'Cellist Competition 1949, U.S.S.R. State Prize 1951, People's Artist of the U.S.S.R., Lenin Prize 1964, Gold Medal, Royal Philharmonic Soc. (U.K.), Siemens Prize (Fed. Repub. of Germany), Sonning Prize (Denmark), Albert Schweitzer Music Award 1985; Commdr., Ordre des Arts et des Lettres (France), Légion d'honneur, Presidential Medal of Freedom 1987. *Address:* c/o National Symphony Orchestra, John F. Kennedy Centre for the Performing Arts, Washington, D.C. 20566, U.S.A. *Telephone:* (202) 785-8100.

ROSZKOWSKI, Janusz; Polish journalist; b. 11 March 1928, Łapy; s. of Stefan Roszkowski and Aleksandra Pieńkowska; m. Natalia Roszkowska 1960; one s.; ed. Acad. of Political Sciences, Warsaw; journalist Polish Press Agency (PAP) Warsaw 1953-; reporter 1953-61, corresp. in Berlin 1961-63, in Bonn 1963-67, Deputy Ed.-in-Chief Home Section 1967-68, Ed.-in-Chief Home Section 1968-71, Deputy Ed.-in-Chief PAP 1969-71, Ed.-in-Chief (acting) 1971-72, Ed.-in-Chief PAP 1972-86; Pres. Polish Cttee. for Radio and TV 1986-; Vice-Pres. Gen. Bd. Polish Journalists Assen. 1971-74, 1978-80, European Press Agencies Assen. 1979-82, Pres. 1982-83; mem. Polish Journalists' Assen. 1954-82, Assen. of Journalists of Polish People's Repub. 1982-; mem. Polish Workers' Party 1947-48, PZPR 1948-, alt. mem. Cen. Cttee. PZPR 1971-81, Bolesław Prus Award 1st Class 1973, Juliusz Fuczik Hon. Medal of Int. Journalist Assen., Order of Banner of Labour (Second Class), Commdr.'s Cross, Order of Polonia Restituta. *Publications:* literary critic, regular contributions to weekly Kultura 1967-76. *Leisure interests:* reading historical books, films, wanderings, angling, bibliophilism. *Address:* ul. Lądowa 1/3 m. 14, 00-759 Warsaw, Poland. *Telephone:* 41-07-94 (Home); 44-62-60 (Office).

ROTA, Gian-Carlo, PH.D.; American (b. Italian) professor of applied mathematics and philosophy; b. 27 April 1932, Milan; s. of Dr. Giovanni Rota and Gina Facoetti Rota; m. Teresa Rondon 1956 (divorced 1979); no c.; ed. Princeton Univ., Yale Univ.; early years in Italy and Quito, Ecuador, arrived in U.S.A. 1950, naturalized U.S. Citizen 1961; Benjamin Pierce Instructor, Harvard Univ. 1957-59, Asst. Prof., then Assoc. Prof., then Prof. of Math. M.I.T. 1959-73, Prof. of Applied Math. and Philosophy 1973-; Prof. Rockefeller Univ. 1965-67; Fellow Los Alamos Lab. 1966, 1971-; mem. N.A.S., American Acad. of Arts and Sciences, Academia Argentina de Ciencias, Dr. h.c. (Strasbourg) 1984. *Publications:* Chief Ed. Encyclopaedia of Mathematics (30 vols. to date), Ed. Advances in Mathematics, about 100 papers in specialized journals. *Leisure interest:* languages. *Address:* 2-351 Massachussets Institute of Technology, Cambridge, Mass. 02139 (Office); 10 Emerson Place APT 16c, Boston, Mass. 02114, U.S.A. (Home). *Telephone:* (617) 253-4333 (Office).

ROTBERG, Eugene Harvey, LL.B.; American World Bank official; b. 19 Jan. 1930, Philadelphia, Pa.; s. of Irving Bernard Rotberg and Blanche Grace Rotberg; m. Dr. Iris Sybil Comens 1954; two d.; ed. Temple Univ. and Univ. of Pennsylvania.; mem. Pennsylvania and D.C. Bar; with U.S. Securities and Exchange Comm. 1957-68, Chief Counsel, Office of Policy Research, Sec. 1963-66; Assoc. Dir. Markets and Regulation, Sec. 1966-68; Vice-Pres. and Treas. IBRD and affiliates (IDA and IFC) 1969-87; Exec. Vice-Pres. Merrill Lynch and Co. 1987-; Professorial Lecturer in Law, George Washington Univ. Law School 1965-; Trustee, Hofstra Univ.; Distinguished Service Award, U.S. Govt. (Securities and Exchange Comm.) 1968; Alumni Award, Temple Univ. 1969; *Leisure interests:* theatre, travel. *Address:* Merrill Lynch and Co. Inc., World Financial Center, New York, N.Y. 10281-1206; 7211 Brickyard Road, Potomac, Md. 20854, U.S.A. (Home).

ROTBLAT, Joseph, C.B.E., M.A., D.SC., PH.D., F.INST.P.; British (b. Polish) physicist; b. 4 Nov. 1908, Warsaw; s. of the late Z. Rotblat; ed. Univ. of Warsaw; Research Fellow, Radiological Lab. of Scientific Soc. of Warsaw 1933-39; Asst. Dir. of Atomic Physics, Inst. of Free Univ. of Poland 1937-39; Oliver Lodge Fellow, Univ. of Liverpool 1939-40; Lecturer, later Sr. Lecturer, Dept. of Physics, Univ. of Liverpool 1940-49, Dir. of Research in Nuclear Physics, Univ. of Liverpool 1945-49; Prof. of Physics in Univ. of London, at St. Bartholomew's Hosp. Medical Coll. 1950-76, Emer. 1976-; Sec.-Gen. of the Pugwash Confs. 1957-63; mem. WHO Man. Group; Ed. Physics in Medicine and Biology; Pres. Hosp. Physicists' Assen.; British Inst. of Radiology; Pres. Int. Youth Science Fortnight; mem. Polish Acad. of Sciences, A.A.A.S.; Foreign Hon. mem. American Acad. of Arts and Sciences; Hon. Fellow UMIST; Hon. D.Sc. (Bradford) 1973, Dr. h.c. (Univ. of Moscow); Bertrand Russell Soc. Award 1983; Order of Merit (Poland). *Publications:* Atomic Energy, a Survey 1954, Atoms and the Universe 1956, 1973, Science and World Affairs 1962, Aspects of Medical Physics 1966, Pugwash 1967, Scientists in the Quest for Peace 1972, Nuclear Reactors: To Breed or Not to Breed? 1977, Nuclear Energy and Nuclear Weapon Proliferation 1979, Nuclear Radiation in Warfare 1981, Scientists, the Arms Race and Disarmament 1982, The Arms Race at a Time of Decision 1984, Nuclear Strategy and World Security 1985, World Peace and the Developing Countries 1986, Strategic Defence and the Future of the Arms Race 1986, Coexistence, Co-operation and Common Security 1987. *Leisure interests:* travel, music. *Address:* 8 Asmara Road, London, NW2 3ST, England. *Telephone:* 01-435 1471.

ROTENSTREICH, Nathan, M.A., PH.D.; Israeli professor of philosophy; b. 31 March 1914, Sambor, Poland; s. of Fischel Rotenstreich; two d.; ed. Hebrew Univ. of Jerusalem and Univ. of Chicago; Research Assoc. in Philosophy, Hebrew Univ. of Jerusalem 1949, Sr. Lecturer 1951, Prof. 1955-, Dean, Faculty of Humanities 1957-61, Rector 1963-69; mem. Israel Acad. of Sciences and Humanities, Chair. Humanities Section 1974-80, 1983-86, Vice-Pres. 1986-; mem. Int. Inst. of Philosophy; Foreign Assoc. U.S. Nat. Acad. of Educ.; Assoc. mem. Center for Study of Democratic Insts., U.S.A.; Visiting Prof. City Coll., New York 1970-71, Harvard Univ. 1980-81; Israel Prize in the Humanities 1963; Ph.D. h.c. (Jewish Theological Seminary, U.S.A.) 1975, (Hebrew Union Coll.) 1982, (Haifa Univ.) 1986. *Publications:* numerous books and over 100 articles in magazines and professional journals in Israel, Europe and U.S.A. *Leisure interest:* reading. *Address:* Israel Academy of Sciences and Humanities, P.O. Box 4040, Jerusalem, Israel 91-040. *Telephone:* (02) 636-211.

ROTERS, (Rudolf) Eberhard; German museum director; b. 15 Feb. 1929, Dresden; s. of late Rudolf Roters and Johanna Löwe; m. Hanna M. Lutze 1963; two d.; ed. Halle/Saale and Freie Univ. Berlin; mem. staff, Ehem. Staatliche Museen, Berlin 1958-65; Asst. Nat. Gallery 1962-; Gen. Sec. Deutsche Gesellschaft für Bildende Kunst (Kunstverein Berlin) 1965-69; Exhbn. Dir. Kunsthalle Nürnberg 1969-71; Gen. Sec. Akad. der Künste, Berlin 1972-76; Dir. Berlinische Galerie 1976-87; mem. Akad. der Künste, Dir. Abteilung Bildende Kunst 1983-86, Deputy Dir. 1986-; Bundesverdienstkreuz; Ernst Reuter Plakette in Silber 1987. *Publications:* Maler am Bauhaus 1965, Europäischer Expressionisten 1970, Berlin 1910-1933. Die visuellen Künste 1983, Galerie Ferdinand Möller 1984, E.T.A. Hoffman 1984; numerous other publs. on 19th and 20th Century Art. *Address:* 1000 Berlin 30, Regensburger Strasse 10, Federal Republic of Germany.

ROTH, Klaus Friedrich, B.A., M.SC., PH.D., F.R.S.; British mathematician; b. 29 Oct. 1925, Breslau, Germany; s. of the late Dr. Franz Roth and Mathilde Roth (née Liebrecht); m. Dr. Melek Khairy 1955; ed. St. Paul's School, London, Peterhouse, Cambridge, and Univ. Coll., London; Asst. Master Gordonstoun School 1945-46; postgraduate student Univ. Coll., London 1946-48; mem. Mathematics Dept. Univ. Coll., London 1948-66 (title of Prof. in Univ. of London conferred 1961); Prof. of Pure Mathematics (Theory of Numbers), Imperial Coll., London 1966-88, Visiting Prof. 1988-; Visiting Lecturer, M.I.T. 1956-57, Visiting Prof. 1965-66; Fellow of Univ. Coll. London 1979; Foreign Hon. mem. A.A.A.S. 1966-; Fields Medal Int. Congress of Mathematicians 1958, De Morgan Medal (London Mathematics Soc.) 1983. *Publications:* papers in journals of learned societies. *Leisure interests:* chess, cinema, ballroom dancing. *Address:* Department of Mathematics, Imperial College of Science and Technology, 180 Queen's Gate, London, SW7 2BZ (Office); 24 Burnsall Street, London, SW3 3ST, England (Home). *Telephone:* 01-589 5111 (Office); 01-352 1363 (Home).

ROTH, Sir Martin, Kt., M.D., F.R.C.P., F.R.C PSYCH.; British professor of psychiatry; b. 6 Nov. 1917, Budapest, Hungary; s. of the late Samuel Simon Roth and the late Regina Roth; m. Constance Heller 1945; three d.; ed. St. Mary's Hospital Medical School, London and McGill Univs.; Dir. of Clinical Research, Graylingwell Hosp. 1950-55; Visiting Asst. Prof. McGill Univ. 1954; Prof. of Psychological Medicine, Univ. of Newcastle upon Tyne (fmrly. Durham Univ.) 1956-77; Prof. of Psychiatry, Univ. of Cambridge 1977-85, Prof. Emer. 1985-; Fellow Trinity Coll., Cambridge 1977-; Hon. Physician Royal Victoria Infirmary, Newcastle upon Tyne 1956-; mem. Medical Research Council 1964-68; mem. Clinical Research Bd. 1964-70, Chair. Grants Cttee. 1968-70; Co-Ed. British Journal of Psychiatry 1968, Psychiatric Developments 1983-; mem. Cen. Health Services Council, Standing Medical Advisory Cttee., Dept. of Health and Social Security 1968-75; Visiting Prof. Swedish univs. 1967; Mayne Guest Prof. Univ. of Queensland 1968; Pres. Section of Psychiatry, Royal Soc. of Medicine 1968-69; First Pres. Royal Coll. of Psychiatrists 1971-75; Hon. mem. Soc. Royale de Médecine Mentale de Belgique 1970, Canadian Psychiatric Asscn. 1972; Corresp. mem. Deutsche Gesellschaft für Psychiatrie und Nervenheilkunde 1970; Adolf Meyer Lecturer, American Psychiatric Assen. 1971; Visiting Prof. Univ. of Iowa 1976, Univ. of Indianapolis 1976; Distinguished Fellow American Psychiatric Assen. 1972, Linacre Lecturer, St. John's Coll. Cambridge 1984; Hon. Fellow Australian and New Zealand Coll. of Psychiatrists 1974, Royal Coll. of Psychiatrists 1975, Hon. Sc.D. (Dublin) 1977, Anna Monika Award 1977, Paul Hoch Award 1979, Gold Medal, Soc. of Biological Psychiatry 1980, Golden Florin, City of Venice 1979, Leonard Cammer Memorial Award 1981, Kesten Award (Univ. of S. Calif.) 1983, Sandoz Prize, Int. Gerontological Assen. 1985, Kraepelin Medal, Max-Planck Inst., Munich, Salmon Medal, N.Y. Acad. of Medicine. *Publications:* Clinical Psychiatry (with W. Mayer-Gross and Eliot Slater) 1954, Italian, Spanish, Portuguese and Chinese trans.; Editor: Psychiatry, Genetics and Pathography: A Tribute to Eliot Slater 1979, Psychiatry, Human Rights and the Law 1985, Alzheimer's Disease and Related Disorders (with Iversen), Reality of Mental Illness (with J. Kroll), CAMDEX-Cambridge Examination for Mental Disorders of the Elderly (with Mountjoy, Huppert and Tym). *Leisure interests:* literature, music,

swimming. *Address:* Trinity College, Cambridge, CB2 1TQ, England. *Telephone:* Cambridge 63128.

ROTH, Philip, M.A.; American writer; b. 19 March 1933, Newark, N.J.; s. of Bess Finkel Roth and Herman Roth; m. Margaret Martinson 1959 (died 1968); ed. Bucknell Univ. and Univ. of Chicago; in U.S. Army 1955-56; Lecturer in English, Univ. of Chicago 1956-58; Visiting Lecturer, Univ. of Iowa Writers' Workshop 1960-62; Writer-in-Residence, Princeton Univ. 1962-64, Univ. of Pa. 1967-80; Distinguished Prof. of Literature, Hunter Coll. 1989-; Visiting Lecturer, State Univ. of N.Y., Stony Brook 1967, 1968; Houghton Mifflin Literary Fellow 1959; Guggenheim Fellowship Grant 1959-60, Rockefeller Grant 1965, Ford Foundation Grant 1966; mem. Nat. Inst. of Arts and Letters 1970-; Daroff Award of Jewish Book Council of America 1959, Award of Nat. Inst. of Arts and Letters 1959, Nat. Book Award for Fiction 1960. *Publications:* Goodbye Columbus (novella and stories) 1959; novels: Letting Go 1962, When She Was Good 1967, Portnoy's Complaint 1969, Our Gang 1971, The Breast 1972, The Great American Novel 1973, My Life as a Man 1974, Reading Myself and Others (essays) 1975, The Professor of Desire 1977, The Ghost Writer 1979, A Philip Roth Reader 1980, Zuckerman Unbound 1981, The Anatomy Lesson 1983, The Prague Orgy 1985, Zuckerman Bound 1985, The Counterlife 1986, The Facts: A Novelists Autobiography 1988. *Address:* c/o Farrar, Straus and Giroux, 19 Union Square West, New York, N.Y. 10003, U.S.A.

ROTH, William George; American business executive; b. 3 Oct. 1938, Lamberton, Minn.; s. of Euclair Ford and Kathryn (née Kluegel) Roth; m. Patricia E. Gibson 1960; two s.; ed. Univ. of Notre Dame and Purdue Univ.; with the Trane Co., La Crosse, Wis. 1961-85, Vice-Pres., Gen. Man. 1973-77, Deputy Chair. 1977-78, Chair. and C.E.O. 1978-85; Pres. American Standard Inc., New York 1985-87; C.E.O. Dravo Corpn., Pitts. 1987-; Dir. Norwest Corpn., G. Heileman Brewing; mem. NAM (Bd. of Dirs. 1978-). *Address:* Dravo Corporation, 1 Oliver Plaza, Pittsburgh, Pa. 15222, U.S.A.

ROTH, William V., Jr.; American politician; b. 22 July 1921, Great Falls, Mont.; s. of William V. and Clara Nelson Roth; m. Jane Richards 1965; one s. one d.; ed. Univ. of Oregon and Harvard Univ.; admitted to Del. Bar and U.S. Supreme Court; fmr. Congressman from Delaware; mem. Republican Nat. Cttee. 1961-64; Senator from Delaware 1971-; Chair. Senate Govt. Affairs Cttee. 1981. *Address:* Hart Senate Office Building, Washington, D.C., 20510, U.S.A.

ROTHÉ, Jean-Pierre-Edmond, D. ES SC.; French university professor; b. 16 Nov. 1906, Nancy; s. of Edmond Rothé and Marguerite Tilly; m. Marguerite Méjan 1942; two s. two d.; Asst. Faculty of Sciences, Strasbourg Univ. 1928, Asst. Prof. 1937, Prof. 1945-76, Hon. Prof. 1976-; Dir. Inst. de Physique du Globe de Strasbourg 1946-76; Hon. Sec.-Gen. Int. Assen. of Seismology of Int. Union of Geodesy and Geophysics; fmr. Dir. Int. Bureau of Seismology; prize-winner, Acad. of Sciences (Paris) 1934, 1979; Gold Medal, Science Council of Japan 1986; Chevalier, Légion d'honneur. *Publications:* Contribution à l'étude des anomalies de champ magnétique terrestre 1937, Séismes et volcans 1946, 1958, 1962, 1968, 1972, 1977, 1984, Prospection géophysique, Vol. I 1949, Vol. II 1951, La radioactivité de Vosges hercyniennes 1957, The Seismicity of the Earth (1953-1965) 1969, Earthquakes and Reservoir Loadings 1969, Séismes artificiels 1970, Séismicité de la France 1972, 1984. *Leisure interests:* tennis, skiing. *Address:* 160 rue d'Alco, 34080 Montpellier, France. *Telephone:* 67-75-81-42.

ROTHELL, George Edwin, B.S.; American banker; b. 17 Dec. 1930, Norfolk, Neb.; s. of Frank Stephen and Margaret Anna (Howorth) Rothell; m. Elaine Marie Jones; one d.; ed. Univ. of Neb.; Vice-Pres. Bank of America, Los Angeles 1960-72; Man. Dir. Western American Bank (Europe) Ltd., London 1972-77; Exec. Vice-Pres. United Calif. Bank 1977-78, Pres. 1978-80; Pres. First Interstate Bancorp. 1980-85, Vice-Chair., Dir. 1985-; Dir. First Interstate Banks of Nev., Wash. and Idaho. *Address:* First Interstate Bancorp., P.O. Box 54068, Los Angeles, Calif. 90054, U.S.A.

ROTHENBERG, Susan, B.F.A.; American artist; b. 20 Jan. 1945, Buffalo, New York; d. of Leonard Rothenberg and Adele Cohen; m. George Trakas 1971; one d.; ed. Cornell and George Washington Univs. and Corcoran Museum School; one-woman exhbns. include Akron Art Museum 1981-82, Stedelijk Museum, Amsterdam 1982, San Francisco Museum of Art 1983, Carnegie Inst. Museum of Art, Pittsburg 1984, Los Angeles County Museum of Art 1983, Inst. of Contemporary Art, Boston 1984, Aspen Center for the Visual Arts 1984, Willard Gallery 1976, 1977, 1979, 1981, 1983; has participated in numerous group exhbns. at Museum of Modern Art, Whitney Museum of American Art, Venice Biennale and galleries in Germany, Denmark, Spain, Finland etc.; work exhibited in several public collections in U.S.A. and Netherlands; Guggenheim Fellow 1980. *Address:* c/o Willard Gallery Inc., 14 East 75 Street, New York, N.Y. 10021-2657, U.S.A.

ROTHENBERGER, Anneliese; German opera singer (soprano); b. 19 June 1926, Salenstein; d. of Josef Rothenberger and Sophie Häffner; m. Gerd W. Dieberitz 1954; ed. Real- und Musikhochschule, Mannheim; début, Coblenz Theatre 1947; with State Opera Hamburg, Munich, Vienna 1948-70; Guest singer at La Scala, Milan, Metropolitan Opera, New York, Salzburg Festival, etc.; TV Special 1969-; Distinguished Service Cross 1st Class, Great Cross. *Films:* Die Fledermaus 1955, Der Rosenkavalier,

Publication: Melody of My Life 1973. *Leisure interests:* driving, books, painting. *Address:* 8268 Salenstein am Untersee, Switzerland.

ROTHENSTEIN, Sir John Knewstub Maurice, Kt., C.B.E., M.A., PH.D., F.M.A.; British writer and art director; b. 11 July 1901, London; s. of Sir William Rothenstein and Alice M. Knewstub; m. Elizabeth Kennard Whittington Smith 1929; one d.; ed. Bedales School, Worcester Coll., Oxford, and Univ. Coll. London; Asst. Prof. of Art History Univ. of Kentucky 1927-28, Univ. of Pittsburgh 1928-29; Dir. of City Art Galleries Leeds 1932-34, Sheffield 1933-38; Dir. and Keeper Tate Gallery 1938-64; mem. British Council 1938-64; mem. Art Panel, Arts Council Great Britain 1942-52, 1954-56; mem. Advisory Cttee. on decoration of Westminster Cathedral 1953-; mem. Council Friends of the Tate Gallery 1958-; Hon. Fellow, Worcester Coll., Oxford 1963-; Fellow, Univ. Coll. London 1971; Rector Univ. of St. Andrews 1964-67; Pres. Friends of Bradford Art Galleries and Museums 1972-; Ed. The Masters 1965-67; Visiting Prof. of Art History, Fordham Univ., N.Y. 1967-68, Agnes Scott Coll., Georgia 1969-70; Distinguished Prof., Brooklyn Coll. of the City Univ., New York 1971 and 1972; Regents' Lecturer, Univ. of Calif. at Irvine 1973; Pres. Friends of the Stanley Spencer Gallery 1981-; Hon. LL.D. (New Brunswick 1961, St. Andrews 1964); Kt. Commdr., Order of Aztec Eagle (Mexico) 1953, Order of St. Gregory the Great 1976. *Publications:* The Portrait Drawings of William Rothenstein, 1889-1925 1926, Eric Gill 1927, The Artists of the 1890's 1928, Morning Sorrow (novel) 1930, Sixteen Letters from Oscar Wilde (editor) 1930, British Artists and the War 1931, Nineteenth Century Painting 1932, An Introduction to English Painting 1933, The Life and Death of Conder 1938, Augustus John 1944, Edward Burra 1945, Manet 1945, Foreign Pictures in the Tate Gallery 1949, Turner 1949, 1960, London's River, an Anthology (with Father Vincent Turner, S.J.) 1951, Modern English Painters, Vol. I Sickert to Smith 1952, Vol. II, Lewis to Moore 1956, Vol. III, Wood to Hockney 1974, The Moderns and their World (introduction) 1957, The Tate Gallery 1958, 1962, British Art since 1900: an Anthology 1962, Matthew Smith 1962, Paul Nash 1962, Augustus John 1963, Sickert 1963, Turner (with Martin Butlin) 1964, Francis Bacon (with Ronald Alley) 1964, Summer's Lease (autobiography I) 1965, Brave Day, Hideous Night (II) 1966, BBC TV: Collection and Recollection 1968, Churchill the Painter (COI) 1968, Time's Thievish Progress (III) 1970, Victor Hammer: Artist and Craftsman 1978, Stanley Spencer the Man: Correspondence and Reminiscences (editor) 1979, John Nash 1984, Stanley Spencer 1989. *Address:* Beauforest House, Newington, Dorchester-on-Thames, Oxfordshire, OX9 8AG, England.

ROTHENSTEIN, Michael, R.A.; British artist; b. 1908, London; s. of Sir William Rothenstein and Alice Rothenstein; m. 1st Bett Fitzgerald 1935; one s. one d.; m. 2nd Diana Arnold Forster 1958; self-taught, with brief interlude at Cen. School of Art, London; First Prize Giles Bequest Colour Prints 1954 and 1956; Graven Image Exhbn. Award 1963; Purchase Award, Lugano Biennale VIII 1964; Grand Prix, Norwegian Int. Print Biennale 1976; frequent one-person shows in U.K. and abroad; int. exhbns. in Cracow, Ljubljana, W. Berlin, Fredrikstade; works in Tate Gallery, London and Museum of Modern Art, New York. *Publications:* Frontiers of Printmaking 1966, Relief Printing 1970, Suns and Moons 1972, Seven Colours (with Edward Lucie Smith) 1975, Song of Songs 1979. *Leisure interests:* travel, reading. *Address:* Columbia House, Stisted, Braintree, Essex, England. *Telephone:* (0376) 25444.

ROTHERHAM, Leonard, C.B.E., D.SC., F.R.S.; British scientist; b. 31 Aug. 1913, Sutton-in-Ashfield; m. Nora M. Thompson 1937; one s. two d.; ed. Strutt School, Belper and Univ. Coll., London; Prin. Physicist, Brown-Firth Research Labs. 1935-46; Head of Metallurgy Dept., Royal Aircraft Establishment 1946-50; Asst. Controller, Dept. of Atomic Energy (Production), later Dir. Research and Devt., U.K.A.E.A. (Industrial Group) 1950-58; mem. Bd. Cen. Electricity Generating Bd. and Head of Research, Electrical Council and Electrical Supply Industry 1958-69; Vice-Chancellor, Univ. of Bath 1969-77; Dir. Chemring PLC 1976-; Tech. Adviser, Wolfson Foundation 1976-87; mem. Gov. Body, Imperial Coll., London 1977-; has served on various govt. advisory councils etc.; Pres. Inst. of Metallurgists 1964, Inst. of Metals 1965; Hon. Fellow, Welding Inst.; Hon. Life mem. American Soc. of Mech. Engs.; Fellow, Univ. Coll., London, Imperial Coll., London; Hon. Prof., Univ. of Bath; Hon. LL.D. (Bristol) 1972, Hon. D.Sc. (Bath) 1976. *Publications:* Research and Innovation 1984, monographs, lectures, etc. *Leisure interests:* gardening, golf. *Address:* Westhanger, Horningsham, Warminster, Wilts., BA12 7LH, England. *Telephone:* (09853) 315.

ROTHERMERE, 3rd Viscount, cr. 1919, of Hemsted; **Vere Harold Esmond Harmsworth,** Bt.; British newspaper owner; b. 27 Aug. 1925, London; s. of 2nd Viscount Rothermere and Margaret Hunam Redhead; m. Mrs. Patricia Evelyn Beverley Brooks (née Matthews) 1957; one s. two d. (one step-d.); ed. Eton, Kent School, Conn., U.S.A.; Gen. Man. Daily Sketch 1955-63; Vice-Chair. Assoc. Newspapers Group Ltd. 1963-71, Chair. 1971-; Chair. Daily Mail and Gen. Trust Ltd. 1978-, Evening Standard Co. Ltd. 1985-; Dir. Consolidated Bathurst (Canada); Chair. U.K. Section Commonwealth Press Union 1977-83, Pres. 1983; Patron, London School of Journalism 1980-; Trustee, Reuters Ltd., Visnews; Fellow, Royal Soc. of Arts, British Inst. of Man.; Commdr., Order of Lion (Finland), Commdr., Order of Merit (Italy). *Leisure interests:* painting, sailing, reading. *Address:*

New Carmelite House, Carmelite Street, London, E.C.4, England.; London Daily Mail, 220 East 42nd Street, New York, N.Y. 10017, U.S.A.; 36 rue de Sentier, 75002 Paris, France. *Telephone:* 01-353 6000 (London), (212) 986-1950 (New York), 508-4841 (Paris).

ROTHSCHILD, 3rd Baron, cr. 1885; **Nathaniel Mayer Victor Rothschild,** G.B.E., G.M., PH.D., SC.D., F.R.S.; British scientist and public servant; b. 31 Oct. 1910, London; s. of Nathaniel Charles Rothschild and Rozsika v. Wertheimstein; m. 1st Barbara J. Hutchinson 1933 (divorced 1946); one s. two d.; m. 2nd Teresa G. Mayor 1946; one s. (and one s. deceased) two d.; ed. Harrow and Trinity Coll., Cambridge; Fellow of Trinity Coll., Cambridge 1935-39; Mil. Intelligence 1939-45; B.O.A.C. 1946-48; Chair. Agric. Research Council 1948-58; Chair. Risby Fruit Farms Ltd. 1949-; mem. BBC Gen. Advisory Council 1952-56; Asst. Dir. of Research, Dept. of Zoology, Cambridge Univ. 1950-70; Vice-Chair. Shell Research Ltd. 1961-63, Chair. 1963-70; Research Co-ordinator of Royal Dutch Shell Group of Cos. 1965-70; mem. Council for Scientific Policy 1965-67, Cen. Advisory Council for Science and Technology 1969; Dir.-Gen. Cen. Policy Review Staff, Cabinet Office 1971-74; Chair. Rothschilds Continuation 1976-88, Rothschilds Continuation Holdings A.G. 1982-88, Biotechnology Investments Ltd. 1981-; Dir. N. M. Rothschild & Sons Ltd. 1976- (Chair. 1975-76), Rothschild Inc. 1976-85; Chair. Royal Comm. on Gambling 1976-78; delivered 4th Royal Soc. Tech. Lecture 1970, Dimbleby Lecture 1978; Fellow, Royal Statistical Soc.; Hon. Fellow, Trinity Coll., Cambridge, Weizmann Inst. of Science, Israel, Bellairs Research Inst. of McGill Univ., Barbados, Wolfson Coll., Cambridge, Inst. of Biology, Imperial Coll. of Science and Tech.; Fellow Royal Statistical Soc. 1984; Hon. D.Sc. (Newcastle, Manchester, Technion, Haifa, City Univ., London, Bath), Hon. Ph.D. (Tel-Aviv Univ., Hebrew Univ., Bar-Ilan Univ.), Hon. LL.D. (Univ. of London), Hon. D. (York Univ.); American Legion of Merit, American Bronze Star, Melchett Medal 1971, R.S.A. Medal 1972. *Publications:* The History of Tom Jones, A Framework for Government Research and Development 1971, The Rothschild Library 1954, Fertilization 1956, A Classification of Living Animals 1961, The Rothschild Family Tree 1973, 1981, Meditations of a Broomstick 1977, You Have it Madam 1980, An Enquiry into the Social Science Research Council 1982, The Shadow of a Great Man 1982, Random Variables 1984, Probability Distributions 1986. *Leisure interests:* golf, jazz.

ROTHSCHILD, Edmund Leopold de; British merchant banker; b. 2 Jan. 1916, London; s. of Lionel N. de Rothschild and Marie Louise Beer; m. 1st Elizabeth E. Lentner 1948 (deceased 1980); two s. two d.; m. 2nd Anne Evelyn, widow of late J. Malcom Harrison 1982; Deputy Chair. British Newfoundland Corpn. Ltd. 1963-69, Churchill Falls (Labrador) Corpn. Ltd. 1966-69; Chair. Tokyo Pacific Holdings (Seaboard) N.V., Tokyo Pacific Holdings N.V., Straflo Ltd. 1975-, AUR Hydropower Ltd. 1980-; Dir. N. M. Rothschild & Sons Ltd. 1975-, Exbury Gardens Ltd.; Pres. Asscn. of Jewish Ex-Servicemen and Women; Vice-Chair. Cen. British Fund for Jewish Relief and Rehabilitation; mem. Council Royal Nat. Pension Fund for Nurses; Trustee, Queen's Nursing Inst., British Freedom from Hunger Campaign; Vice-Pres. Council of Christians and Jews; Pres. Research Into Ageing; Hon. Life Vice-Pres. BRINCO Ltd. 1979-; Hon. LL.D. (Memorial Univ. of Newfoundland) 1961; Hon. D.Sc. (Salford) 1983; Order of the Sacred Treasure, 1st Class (Japan) 1973. *Publications:* Window on the World 1949. *Leisure interests:* gardening, shooting, fishing, photography. *Address:* N. M. Rothschild & Sons Ltd., New Court, St. Swithins Lane, London, EC4P 4DU; Exbury House, Exbury, Nr. Southampton, 5O4 1AF, England. *Telephone:* 01-280 5000; (0703) 893-145.

ROTHSCHILD, Baron Elie Robert de, F.R.S.M.; French banker; b. 29 May 1917, Paris; s. of Baron Robert and Nelly (née Beer) de Rothschild; m. Liliane Fould-Springer 1942; one s. two d.; ed. Lycée Louis le Grand, Faculty of Law, Univ. de Paris; Pres. Rothschild Bank, Zürich, Assicurazioni Generali Trieste et Venise; Officier, Légion d'honneur, Croix de guerre, Ufficiale Ordine al Merito della Repubblica Italiana. *Leisure interests:* breeding, gardening. *Address:* 32 Ormonde Gate, London, S.W.3, England.

ROTHSCHILD, Baron Guy Edouard Alphonse Paul de; French banker; b. 21 May 1909, Paris; s. of the late Baron Edouard and Germaine (née Halphen) de Rothschild; m. 1st Alix Schey de Koromla 1937 (dissolved 1956), one s.; m. 2nd Baronne Marie-Hélène van Zuylen van Nyevelt, one s.; ed. Lycées Condorcet and Louis-le-Grand, Univ. de Paris; Pres. Compagnie du Nord (fmr. Cie. du chemin de fer du Nord) 1949, Dir., Exec. Pres. 1968-; Pres., Dir.-Gen. Soc. minière et métallurgique de Penarroya 1964-71; Pres., Dir.-Gen. Banque Rothschild-Paris 1968-78; Pres., Dir.-Gen. Imetal (fmr. Soc. Le Nickel) 1971-79; Dir. Rothschild Inc., Centro Asegurador S.A.; Pres. Fonds juif unifié 1950-82; Officier, Légion d'honneur, Croix de guerre. *Publication:* The Whims of Fortune (autobiog.) 1985. *Leisure interests:* breeding and racing horses. *Address:* 2 rue St. Louis en l'Ile 75004, Paris, France.

ROTHSCHILD, Baron Robert, DR.RER.POL.; Belgian diplomatist (retd.); b. 16 Dec. 1911, Brussels; s. of Bernard Rothschild and Marianne von Rynveld; one d.; ed. Univ. of Brussels and Acad. of Int. Law, The Hague; entered Foreign Office 1937; served Lisbon 1941, Chongqing 1944, Shanghai 1946, Washington, D.C. 1950; Deputy Permanent Rep. to NATO 1952; Chef de Cabinet, Foreign Office 1954-58; Amb. to Yugoslavia 1958-

60; Deputy Chief of Diplomatic Mission to the Republic of Congo 1960; Chef de Cabinet, Foreign Office 1961-64; Amb. to Switzerland 1964-66, to France 1966-73, to U.K. and Perm. Rep. to W.E.U. Council 1973-76; awards include Commdr., Order of Leopold (Belgium), Commdr., Légion d'honneur, Hon. K.C.M.G. (U.K.). *Publication:* La Chute de Chiang-Kai-shek 1972, Peace for Our Time 1988. *Leisure interests:* gardening, travel. *Address:* 43 Ranelagh Grove, London, S.W.1; 1 rue Ernest Dereume, Rixensart, Belgium. *Telephone:* 01-730 6352 (London).

RÖTZSCH, Helmut, M.A., PH.D.; German librarian; b. 17 Dec. 1923, Leipzig; s. of late Karl and Helene Rötzsch; m. Ursula Heinz 1951; one s.; ed. Buchhändler-Lehranstalt, Leipzig, and Karl Marx Univ., Leipzig; Dir. of Admin. and Personnel Dept., Deutsche Bücherei 1950-53, Dir. of Acquisition Dept. 1953-59, Deputy Dir.-Gen. 1959-61, Dir.-Gen. 1961-; Town Councillor, Leipzig 1961-; Pres. Bibliotheksverband der DDR 1968-74, mem. of presidency 1964-; titular Prof. of Library and Information Science, Oberbibliotheksrat; Distinguished Service Medal of G.D.R. 1959, Nat. Distinguished Service Bronze Medal of G.D.R. 1964, Wilhelm Bracke Gold Medal 1973, Order Banner of Labour 1976, Nat. Distinguished Service Silver Medal of G.D.R. 1980, Nat. Distinguished Service Gold Medal of G.D.R. 1988. *Publications:* Der Börsenverein der Deutschen Buchhändler zu Leipzig und die Deutsche Bücherei 1962, Die Deutsche Bücherei—die deutsche Nationalbibliothek 1962, Anton Graff und seine Buchhändlerporträts 1965, Die Deutsche Bücherei in Leipzig (Co-author) 1987; Editor: Deutsche Bücherei 1912-62, Jahrbuch der Deutschen Bücherei 1965-, Beiträge zur Geschichte des Buchwesens 1965-. *Address:* Karl-Rothe-Strasse 15, DDR-7022 Leipzig, German Democratic Republic. *Telephone:* 52206.

ROUARD, Pierre, D. ÈS SC.; French professor of physics (retd.); b. 25 Oct. 1908, Marseille; s. of Adolphe Rouard and Rose Petit; m. Lucrèce Kohler 1946; ed. Faculty of Sciences, Marseille; held Chair. in Physics, Faculty of Sciences, Clermont-Ferrand 1942-44; Prof., Faculty of Sciences, Marseille 1944-78, Assessor to Dean of Faculty 1949-58, Dean 1958-69; Pres. Ass. of Deans of Science Faculties 1961-67; Dir. Cen. d'Etudes des Couches Minces; Dir. Lab., Ecole Pratique des Hautes-Etudes, Paris 1968-78; mem. Nat. Cttee. for Scientific Research 1950-66, French Cttee. for Physics 1959-66, Scientific Council of Commissariat à l'Energie Atomique 1960-70, Conseil Supérieur de l'Education Nat. and its Perm. Section 1967-71; mem. Acad. of Sciences (Institut de France) 1970-; Prix de Parville (Acad. of Sciences) 1951. *Publications:* Propriétés optiques des lames minces solides 1952, Applications optiques des lames minces solides 1952, Electro-acoustique 1960, Optical Constants of Thin Films 1964, Optical Properties of Thin Metal Films 1977. *Address:* 58 boulevard Tellène, 13007 Marseille, France. *Telephone:* 91 31 03 72.

ROUCH, Jean, PH.D.; French anthropologist and film-maker; b. 31 May 1917, Paris; s. of Jules Rouch and Lucienne (née Gain); m. Jane Margaret George 1952; started career as civil engineer, Head of Public Works Dept., Niger 1942; C.O., Reconnaissance Section, Engineer Corps, First French Army 1944-45; made first ever canoe journey down Niger River from source to sea (with Jean Sauvy and Pierre Ponty) 1946-47; studied Songhay people of Niger and the Dogon of Mali; has made over 100 films, including Circoncision (Grand Prix, Festival du film maudit, Biarritz 1949), Les Maîtres Fous (Grand Prix, Venice Int. Film Festival 1957), Moi, un Noir (Prix Louis Delluc 1958), Chronique d'un Eté (with Edgar Morin; Prix internationale de la Critique, Cannes 1961) La Chasse au Lion à l'Arc (prizewinner, Venice Documentary Film Festival 1965), Le Vieil Anaï (Int. Critics' Prize, Venice 1980) and Dionysos (Official choice, Venice Festival 1984); Dir. of Research, Cen. Nat. de la Recherche Scientifique, Paris 1966-86; Head of Int. Anthropological Film Cttee. 1953-86; Gen. Sec. Cinémathèque Française 1985-86; Visiting Prof., Harvard Univ., U.S.A. (summer school) 1980-86; Chevalier, Légion d'Honneur; Croix de guerre; Hon. PH.D. (Leyden) 1980. *Publications:* four major vols. about the Songhay people of the Niger river 1954-57. *Leisure interests:* swimming, bicycling, canoeing on African rivers, drawing and painting. *Address:* Musée de l'Homme, Place de Trocadero, 75016 Paris (Office); 168 boulevard du Montparnasse, 75014 Paris, France (Home). *Telephone:* 47043820 (Office); 43354862 (Home).

ROUDY, Yvette; French politician; b. 10 April 1929, Pessac; d. of Joseph Saldou and Jeanne Dicharry; m. Pierre Roudy 1951; ed. Collège technique de jeunes filles, Bordeaux, Centre nat. de télé-enseignement, Vanves; sec. 1948-52; translator with an American co. 1952-63; began literary translations 1964; Sec.-Gen. Mouvement démocratique féminin; f. and Ed.-in-Chief, La Femme du 20 ème siecle, joined Convention des institutions républicaines 1965, mem. Exec. Bureau; worked in Parti Socialiste 1971-76, in charge of women's section, f. Training Section, mem. Steering Cttee. and Nat. Sec. (elected 1979); Cand. in legis. elections 1978; mem. European Parl. 1979-81; Minister-Del. in charge of Women's Rights, attached to Prime Minister 1981-85, Minister 1985-86; Deputy to Nat. Ass. for Calvados 1986-; Socialist. *Publications include:* La Réussite de la femme 1969, la Femme en marge 1975, A Cause d'elles 1985. *Leisure interests:* tennis, swimming. *Address:* Assemblée nationale, 75355 Paris; Parti socialiste, 1 rue de Solférino, 75333 Paris, France.

ROUILLON, Fernand; French diplomatist; b. 11 Dec. 1920, Condrieu (Rhône); s. of Albert and Marguerite (née Bassieux) Rouillon; m. Annick

Chavoix 1946; one s. eight d.; ed. Tivoli Coll., School of Political Sciences, Bordeaux Univ.; with Ministry of Foreign Affairs 1944-; Dept. of Econ. Affairs 1944-47; Attaché, Tunis 1947-51, London (NATO) 1951-52, Attaché, Second Sec., Ottawa 1952-56; Dept. of Eastern Europe 1956-58, of Cultural Affairs 1958-60; First Sec., Rabat 1960-63, Second, then First Counsellor, UN 1963, First Counsellor, Athens 1968; Asst. Dir. Dept. of Middle East 1970-75; Amb. to Syria 1975-81, to Turkey 1982-86; Officier, Légion d'honneur, Commdr., Ordre nat. du Mérite. *Leisure interest:* bridge. *Address:* 7 place de Séoul, 75014 Paris; A.C.T.E., 128 Faubourg St. Honoré, 75008 Paris, France. *Telephone:* 43.22.85.80 (place de Séoul); 42.56.27.55 (Faubourg St. Honoré).

ROUILLY, Jean, L. EN D.; French television executive; b. 21 Dec. 1943, Villennes-sur-Seine; s. of Roger Rouilly and Nicole Antigna; m. Annyck Graton 1987; ed. Lycées Jules Verne and Georges Clémenceau, Faculté de Droit, Bordeaux and Inst. d'Etudes Politiques, Bordeaux; Asst. to the Dir., Office de Radiodiffusion-Télévision Francaise, 1966-70, Admin. Documentary Programmes 1970-72, Gen. Man. to Del. Gen. of TV Production 1972-74; Sec.-Gen. Production, Antenne 2 1975-81, Asst. Dir. Finance 1981-85, Production Man. 1985-87, Dir.-Gen. Programme Production 1987-; Asst. Dir.-Gen. Antenne 2 1987-; Dir. Films A2 1981-87, Dir.-Gen. 1987-; Sec.-Gen. TV5 1983-85. *Address:* Antenne 2, 22 avenue Montaigne, 75387 Paris Cedex 08 (Office); 48 Quai Le Gallo, 92100 Boulogne, France (Home). *Telephone:* 42 99 41 23 (Office).

ROULEAU, Joseph-Alfred, O.C.; Canadian bass singer; b. 28 Feb. 1929, Matane, Quebec; s. of Joseph-Alfred Rouleau and Florence Bouchard; m. Renée Moreau; one s. two d. (one from previous marriage); ed. Coll. Jean De Brebeuf, Montreal, Univ. of Montreal, Conservatoire of Music, Province of Quebec; three years in Milan for singing studies; debut in Montreal 1955, at Royal Opera House, Covent Garden 1957-, has sung over 30 roles at Covent Garden; guest artist at principal Opera Houses all over the world; tours of Canada 1960, Australia (with Joan Sutherland) 1965, Russia 1966, 1969, Romania, S. Africa 1974, 1975, 1976; Paris Opera 1975, Metropolitan Opera, New York 1984, 1985, 1986, San Francisco 1986, 1987; Prof. of Voice, Univ. of Quebec (U.Q.A.M.) 1980-, mem. Admin. Bd.; mem. Bd. Corpn. of Montréal Opéra Co. 1980-; recordings for E.M.I. include: Scenes from Anna Bolena, Ruddigore, Romeo et Juliette (Gounod); for L'oiseau lyre: L'enfance du Christ (Berlioz); for Decca: Semiramide, Boris Godunov, Renard (Stravinsky), and recording of French operatic arias with Royal Opera House Orchestra; several awards including Prix Calixa-Lavallée 1967 (La Société St. Jean Baptiste, Montreal), Order of Canada 1977. *Major roles include:* Boris Godunov (Boris Godunov), Philip II (Don Carlo), Basilio (Barber of Seville), Mephisto (Faust), Dosifei (Khovanschina), Don Quixote (Don Quixote), Inquisitore (Don Carlo), Ramfis (Aida), Prince Gremin (Onegin), Father Capulet (Roméo et Juliette). *Leisure interests:* tennis, golf, reading. *Address:* University of Quebec in Montreal, 1700 Rue Berri, Montreal, Que. H2L 4E7; 32 Lakeshore Road, Beaconsfield, Que. H9W 4H3, Canada (Home). *Telephone:* (514) 697-7266, (514) 282-4898.

ROUMAJON, Yves Pierre Jean; French psychiatrist; b. 13 Dec. 1914, Aix-en-Provence; s. of late Joseph Roumajon and Camille Guilbaud; m. 1954; one s.; ed. Lycée Champollion, Coll. Municipal de Chalons-sur-Marne, Lycée Faidherbe, Lille, and Lycée Louis-le-Grand, Paris; fmr. Intern, Hôpitaux Psychiatriques de la Seine; Medical Head of Psychiatric Service, Choquan Hospital, S. Viet-Nam 1950-52; Head of Clinic, Faculty of Medicine 1953; Doctor, Seine Centre for Educational Guidance for Children and Adolescents 1953-60; Psychiatrist, Educ. Service for Young Prisoners, Fresnes Prison 1958-70; medical Dir. C.M.P. Vauhallan 1970-79, Hon. Expert 1984; Expert at Paris Court of Appeal 1958-, and Court of Cassation 1963-; mem. Bd. of Dirs. Int. Soc. of Criminology 1963, Treas. 1972; mem. Comm. for the revision of French Penal Code 1981-; Pres. Asscn. française de Criminologie 1969, Hon. Pres. 1981-; Officier, Légion d'honneur, Croix de guerre 1939-45, etc. *Publications:* Ils ne sont pas nés délinquants 1977, Enfants perdus, Enfants punis en France depuis St. Louis 1989. *Address:* Les Erables, 37 Avenue Gallieni, 92190 Meudon Bellevue, France. *Telephone:* 45.07.84.65.

ROURKE, Mickey (Philip Andre); American actor; b. 1955, New York; m.; ed. Actors' Studio, New York. *Film appearances include:* Fade to Black, 1941 1979, Heaven's Gate 1980, Body Heat 1981, Diner 1982, Eureka 1983, Rumblefish 1983, Rusty James 1983, The Pope of Greenwich Village 1984, 9½ Weeks 1984, Year of the Dragon 1985, Angel Heart 1986, A Prayer for the Dying 1986, Barfly 1987. *Address:* c/o Progressive Artists Agency, 400 S. Beverly Drive, Suite 216, Beverly Hills, Calif. 90212, U.S.A.

ROUSE, Irving, B.S., PH.D.; American professor of anthropology; b. 29 Aug. 1913, Rochester, N.Y.; s. of B. Irving Rouse and Louise Bohachek; m. Mary Mikami 1939; two s.; Asst., then Assoc. Curator, Peabody Museum of Natural History, Yale Univ. 1938-62, Curator 1977-85, Curator Emer. 1985-, Instructor to Assoc. Prof. 1939-54, Prof. of Anthropology 1954-69; Charles J. MacCurdy Prof. of Anthropology (Yale Univ.) 1969-84, Prof. Emer. 1984-, fmr. Chair. Dept. of Anthropology; Pres. Soc. for American Archaeology 1952-53, American Anthopology Asscn. 1967-68; mem. American Acad. of Arts and Sciences, Nat. Acad. of Sciences, Royal Anthropological Inst., Soc. of Antiquaries of London; Pres. Asscn. for Field Archaeology 1977-79; A. Cressy Morrison Prize in Natural Sciences, Viking

Fund Medal in Anthropology, Distinguished Service Award, American Anthropological Assen. *Publications:* Prehistory in Haiti 1939, Culture of the Ft. Liberté Region, Haiti 1941, Archeology of the Maniabón Hills, Cuba 1942, A Survey of Indian River Archaeology, Florida 1951, Porto Rican Prehistory 1952, An Archaeological Chronology of Venezuela (with J. M. Cruxten) 1958, Venezuelan Archaeology (with J. M. Cruxent) 1963, Introduction to Prehistory 1972, Migrations in Prehistory 1986. *Leisure interests:* singing, swimming. *Address:* Department of Anthropology, Yale University, New Haven, Conn. 06520 (Office); 12 Ridgewood Terrace, North Haven, Conn. 06473, U.S.A. (Home). *Telephone:* (203) 432-3690.

ROUSSEL, Claude; French journalist (retd.); b. 7 Feb. 1919, Paris; s. of Pierre Roussel; m. Aasa Billquist 1955; one s. one d.; ed. Lycée Louis-le-Grand, Ecole Normale Supérieure; French Resistance 1941–44; co-founder Agence Information et Documentation and of Agence France-Presse 1944; Asst. Sec.-Gen., later Sec.-Gen. Agence France-Presse 1944–51, Dir. in Scandinavia 1951–54, Sec.-Gen. 1954–75, Pres.-Dir.-Gen. 1975–78; Pres. Union Européenne des Agences Photographiques 1960–65; fmr. Insp.-Gen. Communications, Ministry of Culture and Communications; Chevalier, Légion d'honneur. *Leisure interests:* tennis, swimming, skiing. *Address:* 13 rue Nicolo, 75016 Paris, France.

ROUSSELET, André Claude Lucien, L.EN D.; French business executive; b. 1 Oct. 1922, Nancy; s. of Marcel and Yvonne (née Brongniart) Rousselet; m. Catherine Roge (divorced); two s. one d.; ed. Lycée Claude Bernard, Paris, Faculte de Droit, Paris and Ecole Libre des Sciences Politiques; Chef de Cabinet, Prefects of Ariege and L'Aube 1944; Sub-prefect of Condom 1946, Pointe-à-Pitre 1948, Issoudun 1935; Chef de Cabinet, Minister of the Interior 1954; Special Asst. Office of Minister of Posts and Telecommunications 1955; Chef de Cabinet, Minister of Justice 1956; Dept. of External Relations, Simca 1958; Pres.-Dir.-Gen. Société nouvelles des autoplaces G7 1962–67, 1972–; Deputé for Haute-Garonne 1967–68; Man. Galérie de France and Dir. du Cabinet, Pres. of Repub. 1981–82; Pres.-Dir.-Gen. Agence Havas 1982–86 (now Dir.); Pres.-Dir.-Gen. Canal Plus. *Leisure interests:* golf, tennis, painting. *Address:* Havas, 136 avenue Charles-de-Gaulle, 92522 Neuilly-sur-Seine; 28 rue Henri Barbusse, 92110 Clichy, France.

ROUSSELLE, Regis; French stockbroker; b. 25 Jan. 1948, Rheims; ed. Ecole des Arts et Manufactures and Faculté des Sciences Econs.; Chair. Finance Eng. 1974–81; Stockbroker Meeschaert-Rousselle 1981–87, Chair. 1988–; Chair. Soc. des Bourses Françaises 1988–, Conseil des Bourses de Valeurs 1988–; Coll. mem. Comm. des Opérations de Bourse 1988–. *Address:* 16 Boulevard Montmartre, 75009 Paris, France.

ROUSSIN, André Jean Paul, B. ÉS L.; French playwright; b. 22 Jan. 1911; m. Lucienne Deluy 1947; one s.; ed. Inst. Mélizan, Marseille; left journalism to found "Le Rideau Gris" with Louis Ducreux; mem. Acad. Française 1973–; Officier, Légion d'honneur, Commdr., Ordre des Arts et des Lettres, Commdr., Ordre nat. du Mérite. *Plays include:* Am-stram-gram, Une grande fille toute simple 1944, Jean-Baptiste le mal-aimé, Le tombeau d'Achille 1945, La sainte famille, La petite hutte, Les oeufs d'Autriche 1950, Nina, Bobosse, La main de César, Le mari, la femme et la mort, L'amour fou, Lorsque l'enfant paraît, La mamma 1957, Une femme qui dit la vérité, Les Glorieuses, L'Ecole des autres, Un amour qui ne finit pas, La voyante, La locomotive, On ne sait jamais, La claque 1972, La vie est trop courte 1981; screenplays: Une grande fille toute simple, Lorsque l'enfant paraît, Nina, Bobosse; other works: Le rideau rouge 1982, Le rideau gris et habit vert; (essays) Patience et impatiences 1953, Un contentement raisonnable 1965, La boîte à couleurs 1974. *Address:* 12 place des Victoires, 75002 Paris, France (Home).

ROUX, Abraham Johannes Andries, D.SC.(ENG.), M.SC., M.I.MECH.E.; South African nuclear scientist; b. 18 Oct. 1914, Bethlehem, Orange Free State; s. of Abraham J. A. Roux and Anna S. Naude; m. Ulrica Prinsloo 1939; one s. one d.; ed. Univ. of the Witwatersrand; Lecturer, Dept. of Mechanical Eng., Witwatersrand Univ. 1939–43; Sr. Lecturer, Stellenbosch Univ. 1944–46; Prin. Research Officer, Nat. Building Research Inst., Council for Scientific and Industrial Research (CSIR) 1946–51, Officer in Charge CSIR Mech. Engineering Research Unit 1952; Dir. Nat. Physical Research Lab. 1952–55, Nat. Mech. Eng. Research Inst., CSIR 1955–57, Vice-Pres. CSIR 1957–69; Part-time Dir. Atomic Energy Research Programme 1957–59, Dir. of Research, Atomic Energy Bd. 1959–60, Dir. Atomic Energy Bd. 1960–64, Dir.-Gen. 1964–67, Chair. 1967–70, Pres. 1971–79; Chair. Nat. Inst. for Metallurgy 1967–76, UCOR 1970–; Vice-Chair. S.A. Akad. vir Wetenskap en Kuns 1961, Chair. 1963; mem. Bd. of Dirs. Nuclear Fuels Corpn. 1968–77; Dir. Vaal Reefs Mining and Exploration Co. 1979–; mem. Prime Minister's Scientific Advisory Council 1962–79, Univs. Advisory Cttee. 1966–74, 1976–, CSIR 1966–79, S.A. Council of Professional Engs. 1968, Prime Minister's Planning Advisory Cttee. 1974–79, Cttee. on Energy Policy, Dept. of Planning and the Environment 1974–; Hon. mem. S.A. Inst. of Mining and Metallurgy; Hon. D.Sc. (Stellenbosch, Orange Free State Univs.); Hon. D.Sc.Eng. (Univ. of Pretoria, Univ. of Witwatersrand); Hendrik Verwoerd Award (with Dr. W. L. Grant, q.v.); M. T. Steyn Prize for Scientific and Tech. Achievement, State President's Decoration for Meritorious Service 1980. *Publications:* Mechanical Engineering Research in South Africa 1952, Mechanical Engineering in Relation to Industry 1955–57, Developments in the Field of Nuclear Power and their Impact

on South Africa 1958, The Atomic Energy Research and Development Programme of South Africa 1959, Science, Industry and the Professional Society 1960, The First Reactor Installation of the Republic of South Africa 1962, South Africa's Programme of Nuclear Research 1962, The Scope of Research and Development in the Field of Radioisotopes and Nuclear Radiation in South Africa 1964, Nuclear Engineering in South Africa 1964, Power Generation in South Africa with Special Reference to the Introduction of Nuclear Power (Co-author) 1966, Nuclear Energy in South Africa 1967, Energy for the Coming Century—Nuclear Energy 1969, Policy Aspects of the Introduction of Nuclear Power in South Africa (Co-author) 1969, South Africa's Position in the World Energy Picture 1973, Exploitation of South Africa's Mineral Potential 1974, The South African Uranium Enrichment Project 1975, Nuclear Fuel Cycle Developments in South Africa 1976. *Leisure interest:* golf. *Address:* 79 Stella Street, Brooklyn, Pretoria 0002, South Africa (Home).

ROUX, Ambroise Marie Casimir; French business executive; b. 26 June 1921, Piscop, Val d'Oise; s. of André Roux and Cécile Marcilhacy; m. Françoise Marion 1946; one s. one d.; ed. Collège Stanislas, Paris, Ecole Polytechnique, Ecole des Ponts et Chaussées, Ecole Supérieure de l'Electricité; Engineer, Civil Eng. Dept. 1944–51; Exec. Dir. Office of Sec. of State for Industry and Commerce, Industry Dept. 1952–55; Asst. Gen. Man. Compagnie Générale d'Electricité, Paris 1955–63, Gen. Man. 1963, Dir. 1966, Chair. of Bd. 1970–82, Hon. Chair. 1982–; Vice-Chair. Crédit Commercial de France 1974–82; Hon. Chair. Pétrofigaz, AFNOR 1972–79; Chair. of Board, Cie. Industrielle des Télécommunications CIT-ALCATEL 1966–82, Hon. Chair. 1982–, Cie. Electro Financière 1969–82, Hon. Chair. 1982–; Dir. Société La Radiotechnique, Cie Forestière Occidentale, Mines de Kali St. Thérèse, Co. Générale des Eaux, CEP Communication, Société du Louvre, Cie Financière, PARIBAS, Groupe de la Cité, Schneider SA; Vice-Chair. Fed. French Industries 1966–74, First Vice-Chair. 1975–82, Hon. First Vice-Chair. 1982–; Chair. AGREF 1976–82, Assen. Française des Entreprises Privées (AFEP) 1983–; Dir. Barclays Bank 1982–, Vice-Chair. 1986–; Vice-Chair. Sté Plantations des Terres-Rouges 1985–; Dir.-Gen. Occidentale 1979–87, Chair. 1987–; Chair. Hoche-Friedland 1988–; Grand Officier, Légion d'honneur, Commdr., Mérite commercial, Commdr. de l'Instruction publique. *Address:* 17 place des Etats-Unis, 75116 Paris, France (Home). *Telephone:* 47-63-53-11 (Office).

ROUX, David Gerhardus, PH.D., F.R.S.S.A.; South African scientist; b. 14 June 1920, Paarl, Cape Prov.; s. of David G. Roux and Louisa (née Alant) Roux; m. Valerie van Deventer 1949; one s. three d.; ed. Boys High School, Wellington, Rhodes Univ., Heidelberg Univ., Cambridge Univ. and Harvard Univ.; Prin. Research Scientist, Leather Industries Research Inst., Grahamstown 1947–67; Prof. and Head Dept. of Chemistry, Univ. of the O.F.S., Bloemfontein 1968–85; Exec. Dir., Foundation for Research Devt., CSIR, Pretoria 1986–; Charles Bullard Fellow, (Harvard) 1963; Havenga Prize (S.A. Acad.) 1968; Gold Medal (S.A. Chem. Inst.) 1978; Leon Fox Foundation award 1984. *Publications:* numerous articles in scientific journals. *Address:* Foundation for Research Development, CSIR, Box 395, Pretoria 0001 (Office); 13 Theron Street, Fernkloof, Hermanus 7200, South Africa (Home). *Telephone:* (012) 841-2426 (Office); (02831) 21931 (Home).

ROUX, Jacques; French diplomatist; b. 1 March 1907, Avignon; s. of Pierre Roux and Jeanne Sivan; m. Consuelo Eyre 1964 (deceased); ed. Coll. Saint-Joseph, Avignon, Facultés de droit d'Aix-en-Provence et de Paris, Ecole libre des sciences politiques; Diplomatic Service, London 1934–37; Ministry of Foreign Affairs 1937; Sec. Chongqing 1945, Counsellor Nanjing 1946; Dir. of Asian Dept., Ministry of Foreign Affairs 1952–56, Asst. Dir.-Gen. of Political Affairs 1956, 1957–63, Asst. Dir. Office of Minister 1956–57; Amb. to United Arab Repub. (now Egypt) 1963–68, to Switzerland 1969–72; Minister of Monaco, Berne 1974–, Amb. 1982–; Commdr., Légion d'honneur. *Address:* 65 Elfenaustrasse, 3074 Muri/Berne; 39 chemin de Chamblandes, 1009 Pully, Switzerland. *Telephone:* 222858.

ROUX, Jean-Louis, O.C.; Canadian actor, author and theatre director; b. 18 May 1923, Montreal; s. of Louis Roux and Berthe Leclerc; m. 1950; one s.; ed. Coll. Sainte-Marie and Univ. de Montréal; mem. Les Compagnons de Saint Laurent theatrical co. 1939–42, Ludmilla Pitoëff theatrical co. 1942–46; founder, Théâtre d'Essai, Montreal 1950; co-founder, Théâtre du Nouveau Monde 1951, Sec.-Gen. 1953-63, Artistic Dir. 1966–82; Dir.-Gen. Nat. Theatre School of Canada 1981–87; has appeared in more than 200 roles (in both French and English) on stage (Montreal, Stratford, Paris), TV, cinema, and radio and directed more than 50 theatrical productions; Hon. Dr. (Univ. of Laval); Molson Award, World Theatre Award; Grand Prix du Québec; Chevalier, Ordre Nat. du Québec. *Leisure interests:* theatre, chess, swimming, walking. *Address:* 4145 Blueridge Crescent, Apt. 2, Montreal, Quebec, H3H 1S7, Canada. *Telephone:* (514) 937-2505.

ROWE-HAM, Sir David (Kenneth), G.B.E., J.P., F.C.A., F.C.I.S.; British accountant; b. 19 Dec. 1935; s. of Kenneth Henry Rowe-Ham and Muriel Phyllis Rowe-Ham; m. Sandra Celia Glover (née Nicholls); three s. ed. Dragon School, Charterhouse; mem. Stock Exchange 1964–84; Sr. Partner, Smith Keen Cutler 1972–82; Dir. The Nineteen Twenty Eight Investment Trust 1984–86; Regional Dir. (London W.) Lloyds Bank PLC 1985–; Dir. W. Canning PLC 1981–86, Consultant 1986–; Dir. Savoy Theatre Ltd. 1986–; Chair. Advisory Panel, Guinness Mahon Fund Managers Ltd. 1987–; Consultant, Touche Ross & Co. 1984–; Chair. Asset Trust PLC 1982–; Lord Mayor of London 1986–87; Chair. Political Council, Jr. Carlton Club 1977, Deputy Chair. Carlton Political Cttee. 1977–79; Chair. Birmingham Municipal Bank 1970–72; mem. Prince's Youth Business Trust Council 1987–; Gov. Royal Shakespeare Trust; Trustee, Friends of D'Oyly Carte; Gov., Christ's Hosp.; Royal Soc. of St. George; Hon. D.Litt. (City Univ.) 1986; Pedro Ernesto Medal, Rio de Janeiro 1987; K.St.J. 1986; Commdr. de l'Ordre du mérite 1984; Commdr. Order of the Lion, Malawi 1985; Order of the Aztec Eagle (Class II), Mexico 1985; Order of King Abdul Aziz (Class I) 1987; Grand Officier du Wissam Alouite 1987, Order of Diego Losada of Caracas 1987. *Leisure interests:* theatre, shooting. *Address:* Hill House, 1 Little New Street, London, EC4A 3TR, England. *Telephone:* 01-936-3000.

ROWICKI, Witold; Polish conductor and composer; b. 26 Feb. 1914, Taganrog, U.S.S.R.; s. of Jan and Nadieżda Rowicki; m. Joanna Nowak 1939; one s. one d.; ed. Cracow Conservatoire; debut as conductor 1932; appearances as soloist and in chamber ensembles 1932–45; Founder, Musical Dir. and Chief Conductor Radio Symphony Orchestra, Katowice 1945–50; Prof. Higher State School of Music, Warsaw 1952–54; Organizer, Musical Dir. and Chief Conductor Warsaw Philharmonic Orchestra, now Nat. Philharmonic Orchestra 1950–55, 1958–77; Dir. Teatre Wielki Opera Centre 1965–70; Dir. summer courses of interpretation for conductors, Vienna 1976–78; conducted in many European, African, Asian, North and South American countries, and Australia; Grand Prix du Disque, Acad. Charles Cros, Paris 1959, Minister of Culture and Art Prize 1963, 1977 (1st Class), Grand Prix Belge 1965, Edison Prize, Amsterdam 1965, Grand Prix Nat. du Disque, Paris 1966, State Prize (1st Class) 1966, Award of Union of Composers 1962, Officer, Commdr. and Commdr. with Star, Cross of Polonia Restituta, Order of the Banner of Labour (1st class), 1959, 1978 (twice), etc. *Leisure interests:* archaeology, politics. *Address:* Ul. Chocimska 35 m. 12, 00-791 Warsaw, Poland. *Telephone:* 49-80-64.

ROWLAND, Frank Sherwood, PH.D.; American professor of chemistry; b. 28 June 1927, Delaware; s. of Sidney A. Rowland and Margaret Lois Drake Rowland; m. Joan Lundberg 1952; one s. one d.; ed. Chicago and Ohio Wesleyan Univs.; Instructor in Chemistry, Princeton Univ. 1952–56; Asst. to Prof., Kansas Univ. 1956–64; Prof., Univ. of Calif. Irvine 1964–, Daniel G. Aldrich Endowed Prof. of Chemistry 1985–; Guggenheim Fellow 1962, 1974; mem. American Acad. of Arts and Sciences 1977–, N.A.S. 1978–; Tyler Prize in Ecology and Energy (now called World Prize for Environmental Achievement), Japan Prize in Environmental Science and Tech. (jtly. with Elias J. Corey, q.v.) 1989; numerous other awards, lectureships and cttee. memberships. *Publications:* articles in scientific journals. *Leisure interests:* athletics, opera. *Address:* 4807 Dorchester Road, Corona del Mar, Calif. 92625, U.S.A. (Home). *Telephone:* (714) 760-1333.

ROWLAND, Air Marshal Sir James Anthony, A.C., K.B.E., D.F.C., A.F.C., B.E., C.ENG., F.R.AE.S., F.I.E. (Aust.); Australian air force officer (retd.); b. 1 Nov. 1922, Armidale, N.S.W.; s. of Commdr. Louis Claude Rowland and Elsie Jean Wright; m. Faye Alison Doughton 1955; one d.; ed. Univ. of Sydney; Master Bomber, Pathfinder Force, Bomber Command R.A.F. 1944; with R.A.A.F.; Chief Test Pilot, Aircraft Research and Devt. Unit 1951–54; Officer Commanding Research and Devt. 1958–60; Chief Tech. Officer, No. 82 Wing 1957, Mirage Mission, Paris 1961–64; Commanding No. 3 Aircraft Depot, Amberley 1967–68; Sr. Eng. Staff Officer, HQ Operational Command 1969–70; with Dept. of Air: Dir.-Gen. of Aircraft Eng. 1972, Air Mem. for Tech. Services 1973–74; Chief of Air Staff, R.A.A.F. 1975–79; mem. Admin. Appeals Tribunal 1979–80; Gov. N.S.W. 1981–89; Consultant Office Française d'Exportation de Matériel Aéronautique (OFEMA), Australia 1980; Councillor, Royal Aeronautical Soc., Australian Branch 1973–75; Hon. D. Eng. (Sydney Univ.) 1983; K.St.J. *Publications:* official reports, contributions to journals. *Leisure interests:* carpentry, history, surfing. *Address:* 35 Trapper's Way, Clareville, Sydney, N.S.W. 2107, Australia.

ROWLAND, John Russell; Australian diplomatist; b. 10 Feb. 1925, Armidale, N.S.W.; s. of L. C. and E. J. Rowland; m. Moira Enid Armstrong 1956; one s. two d.; ed. Cranbrook School, Sydney, and Univ. of Sydney; Dept. of External Affairs 1944–, served Moscow 1946–48, Saigon 1952, 1954–55, Washington 1955–56, London 1957–59; Asst. Sec., Dept. of External Affairs 1961–65; Amb. to U.S.S.R. 1965–68, First Asst. Sec. Dept. of External Affairs 1969; High Commr. in Malaysia 1969–72, Amb. to Austria, Czechoslovakia, Hungary and Switzerland 1973–74, to France 1978–82; Deputy Sec., Dept. of Foreign Affairs 1975–78; Visiting Fellow, A.N.U. 1983–84. *Publications:* The Feast of Ancestors 1965, Snow 1971 (poetry), Times and Places 1976 (poetry), The Clock Inside 1979 (poetry), The Sculptor of Candles (Verse trans.) 1985. *Address:* 15 Grey Street, Deakin, A.C.T. 2600, Australia.

ROWLAND, Roland W. ("Tiny"); British businessman; b. (as R. W. Fuhrhop) 1917, India; joined Lonrho (fmrly. London and Rhodesian Mining and Land Co.) 1961, now Chief. Exec. and Man. Dir. Lonrho (subsidiaries in Nigeria, Malawi, Kenya, Zimbabwe, Zambia); Deputy Chair. The Observer Ltd. 1981–83, Chair. 1983–. *Publication:* A Hero from Zero: The Story of Kleinwart Benson and Mohammed Fayed 1988. *Address:* Lonrho PLC, Cheapside House, 138 Cheapside, London, EC2V 6BL, England.

ROWLING, Rt. Hon. Sir Wallace Edward, K.C.M.G., P.C., M.A.; New Zealand politician; b. 15 Nov. 1927, Motueka, South Island; s. of A. Rowling; m.

Glen Elna Reeves 1951; two s. one d.; ed. Nelson Coll. and Canterbury Univ.; fmr. Educ. Officer, N.Z. Army and Col. Commdt. Royal N.Z. Army Educ. Corps; mem. Parl. for Buller 1962–72, Tasman 1972–84; Pres. Labour Party 1970–73; Minister of Finance 1972–74; Prime Minister 1974–75, also Minister of Foreign Affairs, of Legis. Dept., in charge of N.Z. Security Intelligence Dept., the Audit Dept; Leader of Opposition 1975–83; Amb. to U.S.A. 1985–; Pres. Asia Pacific Socialist Org. 1977–; Hon. LL.D. (Canterbury) 1987. *Leisure interests:* golf, badminton. *Address:* New Zealand Embassy, Observatory Circle N.W., Washington, D.C. 20008, U.S.A.; 15 Waverley Street, Richmond, New Zealand.

ROWLINSON, John Shipley, F.ENG., F.R.S.; British scientist and university professor; b. 12 May 1926, Handforth, Cheshire; s. of Frank Rowlinson and Winifred Jones; m. Nancy Gaskell 1952; one s. one d.; ed. Trinity Coll., Univ. of Oxford; Research Assoc., Univ. of Wis. 1950–51; Research Fellow, then Lecturer, then Sr. Lecturer in Chem., Univ. of Manchester 1951–60; Prof. of Chemical Tech., Univ. of London 1961–73; Dr. Lee's Prof. of Chem., Univ. of Oxford 1974–; Fellow Exeter Coll., Oxford 1974–; Meldola Medal, Royal Inst. of Chem. 1954; Marlow Medal, Faraday Soc. 1956; Hoffman Lecturer, Gesellschaft Deutscher Chemiker 1980, Faraday Lecturer 1983, Lennard-Jones Lecturer, Royal Soc. of Chem. 1985, Mary Upson Prof. of Eng., Cornell Univ. 1988. *Publications:* Liquids and Liquid Mixtures (jtly.) 1982 (3rd edition), The Perfect Gas 1963, Thermodynamics for Chemical Engineers (jtly.) 1975, Molecular Theory of Capillarity (jtly.) 1982. *Leisure interest:* mountaineering. *Address:* Physical Chemistry Laboratory, South Parks Road, Oxford, OX1 3QZ (Office); 12 Pullens Field, Headington, Oxford, OX3 0BU, England (Home). *Telephone:* (0865) 275401 (Office); (0865) 67507 (Home).

ROWNTREE, Sir Norman Andrew Forster, Kt., B.SC., C.ENG., F.I.C.E.; British engineer; b. 11 March 1912; s. of Arthur Thomas and Ethel (née Forster) Rowntree; m. Betty Thomas 1939; two s. one d.; ed. Tottenham Co. School, Univ. of London; Consulting Engineer 1953–64; mem. and Dir. Water Resources Bd. 1964–73; Prof. of Civil Eng. UMIST 1975–79; mem. Advisory Council for Applied Research and Devt. 1976–80, Meteorological Office Cttee. 1979–80; Consultant to Allot and Lomax, Consulting Engineers 1979–86; mem. Comm. for Commonwealth Scholarship 1979–80, Scientific Council, Centre de Formation Int. à la Gestion des Resources en Eau, France 1977–80 (Hon. Vice-Pres. 1980–86), Expert Advisory Cttee., N.J. Water Supply Master Plan, U.S.A. 1976–80; Pres. Inst. of Water Engineers 1962–63; Vice-Pres. Inst. of Civil Engineers 1972–75, Pres. 1975–76; Visiting Prof. King's Coll., London 1972–75; Council of Eng. Insts. Graham Clark Lecturer 1972; Inst. of Mechanical Engineers Hawksley Lecturer 1976; Gold Medal, Soc. of Chemical Industry 1977. *Address:* 97 Quarry Lane, Kelsall, Tarporley, Cheshire, CW6 0NJ, England. *Telephone:* (0829) 51195.

ROWNY, Lieut.-Gen., The Hon. Edward Leon, B.C.E., M.A., M.S., PH.D.; American army officer; b. 3 April 1917, Baltimore, Md.; s. of Gracyan J. and Mary Ann (née Rodgers) Rowny; m. Mary Rita Leyko 1941; four s. one d.; 2nd Lieut. U.S. Army 1941; eventually Lieut.-Gen. 1970; in African campaign 1942, European and Middle Eastern Campaigns 1944–45; Korea 1950–52; Viet-Nam 1962–63; Special Asst. Tactical Mobility Dept. of army 1963–75; Commdg. Gen. 24th Infantry Div., Europe 1965–66; Deputy Chief of Staff Logistics, Europe 1968–69; Deputy Chief of Research and Devt. 1969–70; Commdg. Gen. Intelligence Corps, Korea, 1970–71; Deputy Chair. Mil. Comm. NATO 1971–73; Joint Chiefs of Staff rep. to SALT del., Geneva 1973–79; Chief Arms Control Negotiator 1981–85; Special Adviser to Pres. 1985–89; Special Counsellor to State Dept. April 1989–; Pres. Nat. War Coll. Alumni Asscn. 1987–88; D.S.M., Silver Star with two oak leaf clusters, Legion of Merit with four oak clusters, Combat Infantry Badge with star. *Address:* Department of State, Washington, D.C. 20520, U.S.A.

ROWSE, Alfred Leslie, D.LITT., F.R.S.L., F.B.A.; British historian, poet and writer; b. 4 Dec. 1903, St. Austell, Cornwall; ed. in Cornwall, and Christ Church, Oxford; Fellow British Acad.; Emer. Fellow All Souls Coll., Oxford; Benson Medal, Royal Soc. of Literature 1982. *Publications:* Sir Richard Grenville of the Revenge 1937, Tudor Cornwall 1941, Poems of a Decade 1931–41, A Cornish Childhood 1942, The Spirit of English History 1943, Poems Chiefly Cornish 1944, The English Spirit 1944, West Country Stories 1945, The Use of History 1946, Poems of Deliverance 1946, The End of an Epoch 1947, The England of Elizabeth 1950, The English Past 1951 (revised edn. entitled Times, Persons, Places 1965), Lucien Romier's History of France trans. and completed 1953, The Expansion of Elizabethan England 1955, The Early Churchills 1956, The Later Churchills 1958, Poems Partly American 1959, The Elizabethans and America 1959, St. Austell: Church, Town, Parish 1960, Appeasement: A Study in Political Decline 1961, Ralegh and the Throckmortons 1962, William Shakespeare: A Biography 1963, Christopher Marlowe: A Biography 1964, A Cornishman at Oxford 1965, Shakespeare's Southampton 1965, Bosworth Field and the Wars of the Roses 1966, Poems of Cornwall and America 1967, Cornish Stories 1967, A Cornish Anthology 1968, The Cornish in America 1969, The Elizabethan Renaissance: Vol. I The Life of the Society 1971, Vol. II The Cultural Achievement 1972, The Tower of London in the History of the Nation 1972, Strange Encounter: Poems 1972, Shakespeare the Man 1973, Simon Forman: Sex and Society in Shakespeare's Age 1974, Windsor Castle in the History of the Nation 1974, Victorian and Edwardian Cornwall (with Sir John Betjeman) 1974, Oxford in the History of the Nation 1975, Discoveries and Reviews from Renaissance to Restoration 1975, Jonathan Swift—Major Prophet 1975, A Cornishman Abroad 1976, Brown Buck: A Californian Fantasy 1976, Matthew Arnold: Poet and Prophet 1976, Shakespeare the Elizabethan 1976, Homosexuals in History: Ambivalence in Society, Literature and the Arts 1977, Milton the Puritan 1977, Heritage of Britain 1977, The Road to Oxford: Poems 1978, The Poems of Shakespeare's Dark Lady (ed. with introduction) 1978, The Byrons and Trevanions 1978, The Annotated Shakespeare (ed. 3 vols.) 1978, Roper's Life of Sir Thomas More (ed. with letters and introduction) 1979, A Man of the Thirties 1979, Portraits and Views 1979, Story of Britain 1979, Memories of Men and Women 1980, A Life: Collected Poems 1981, Eminent Elizabethans 1983, Shakespeare's Sonnets, with prose versions (revised edition) 1984; Shakespeare's Characters: A complete Guide 1984, Night at the Carn and Other Stories 1984, Glimpses of the Great 1985, Shakespeare's Self-Portrait 1985, A Quartet of Cornish Cats 1986, Stories from Trenarren 1986, Reflections on the Puritan Revolution 1986, The Little Land of Cornwall 1986, In Shakespeare's Land 1986, Court and Country: Studies in Tudor Social History 1987, The Poet Auden: A Personal Memoir 1987, Quiller Couch: A Portrait of Q 1988, Friends and Contemporaries 1989, Shakespeare the Man (revised) 1988, The Contemporary Shakespeare (ed.), A. L. Pawse's Cornwall 1988, Transatlantic: Later Poems 1989, The Controversial Collensos 1989, Discovering Shakespeare 1989. *Leisure interests:* seeing historic places, gardening. *Address:* Trenarren, St. Austell, Cornwall, England.

ROWSON, Lionel Edward Aston, O.B.E., M.A., F.R.S., F.R.C.V.S.; British veterinary scientist (retd.); b. 28 May 1914, Stafford; s. of Lionel F. Rowson and Maud Ann Aston; m. Audrey Kathleen Foster 1942; two s. two d.; ed. Edward VIth School, Stafford, Royal Veterinary Coll., London; Gen. Practice, Cannock, Staffs. 1938-40; Pathology Lab., Univ. of Cambridge 1940-42, Dir. Artificial Insemination Centre, 1942-84, also Deputy Dir. Unit of Reproductive Physiology, then Officer-in-Charge (retd. 1979); Hon. Sc.D. (Cambridge) 1986; Thomas Baxter Prize for Contrib. to the Dairy Industry 1956; Dalrymple-Champneys Cup and Medal, British Veterinary Assoc. 1975; Bledisloe Medal 1978; Gold Medal, Accad. Nazionale di Agricoltura, Milano 1978; Foreign Corresp. Acad. Royale de Médecine de Belgique 1978, hon. foreign mem. 1984, Pioneer Award, Int. Embryo Transfer Soc. 1985. *Publications:* numerous scientific papers. *Leisure interest:* horse breeding. *Address:* The Grove, Water Lane, Histon, Cambridge, CB4 4LR, England (Home). *Telephone:* (022023) 2534.

ROY, Claude; French writer; b. 28 Aug. 1915, Paris; s. of Félicien and Germaine (née Delaville) Roy; m. 2nd Loleh Bellon 1962; one s. from previous marriage; ed. Univ. of Paris; war service 1939-40; imprisoned and escaped 1940; in the Unoccupied Zone of France 1940-43; contributed to the review Poésie 1940, 1941, etc., and to the review Fontaine; mem. Resistance in Southern Zone, Les Etoiles movement; contributed to the clandestine Press Les Lettres Françaises; War Corresp. after the Liberation; Croix de guerre; Prix Fémina-Vacaresco 1970. *Publications:* L'enfance de l'art 1941, Clefs pour l'Amérique, Clefs pour la Chine, Descriptions critiques, La nuit est le manteau des pauvres, Le soleil sur la terre, Le malheur d'aimer, Le journal des voyages, L'homme en question, Gérard Philipe (with Anne Philipe), Léone et les siens, L'amour du théâtre, La dérobée, Jean Vilar, Défense de la littérature 1968, Le verbe aimer 1969, Moi je (memoirs) 1969, Nous (memoirs 1944-56) 1972, Le soleil des romantiques 1974, Enfantasques 1974, Somme toute 1976 (memoirs 1955-75), Nouvelles enfantasques 1978, La traversée du Pont des Arts 1979, Sais-tu si nous sommes encore loin de la mer? 1979, Sur la Chine 1979, Les Chercheurs de dieux 1980, Permis de Séjour 1983, À la lisière du temps 1985, Temps variable avec éclaircies 1985, L'Ami lointain 1987, Le Voyage d'automne 1987. *Address:* Editions Gallimard, 5 rue Sébastien-Bottin, 75007 Paris, France.

ROYAL, H.R.H. The Princess; Anne Elizabeth Alice Louise, G.C.V.O.; b. 15 Aug. 1950; d. of Queen Elizabeth II and Prince Philip, Duke of Edinburgh; m. Capt. Mark Anthony Peter Phillips 1973; one s., Peter Mark Andrew, b. 15 Nov. 1977, one d., Zara Anne Elizabeth, b. 15 May 1981; ed. Benenden School, Kent; Col.-in-Chief, 14th/20th King's Hussars, Worcs. and Sherwood Foresters Regt. (29th/45th Foot), Royal Regina Rifles, 8th Canadian Hussars (Princess Louise's), Royal Corps of Signals, The Canadian Armed Forces Communications and Electronics Branch, The Royal Australian Corps of Signals, The Royal Scots, Royal New Zealand Corps of Signals; Royal New Zealand Nursing Corps, The Grey and Simcoe Foresters Militia; Chief Commdt., W.R.N.S.; Hon. Air Commodore, R.A.F. Lyneham; Pres. W.R.N.S. Benevolent Trust, British Acad. of Film and Television Arts, Hunters' Improvement and Light Horse Breeding Soc., Save the Children Fund, Windsor Horse Trials, The Royal School for Daughters of Officers of the Royal Navy and Royal Marines (Haslemere), British Olympic Assen., Council for Nat. Acad. Awards; Patron, Assen. of Wrens, Riding for the Disabled Assen., Jersey Wildlife Preservation Fund, The Royal Corps of Signals Assen., The Royal Corps of Signals Inst., Missions to Seamen, British Knitting and Clothing Export Council, The Army and Royal Artillery Hunter Trials, Gloucs. and North Avon Fed. of Young Farmers' Clubs, Royal Lymington Yacht Club, Royal Port Moresby Soc. for the Prevention of Cruelty to Animals, Horse of the Year Ball, Benenden Ball, British School of Osteopathy, the Royal Tournament,

Communications and Electronics Branch Inst., All England Women's Lacrosse Assen., Home Farm Trust; Vice-Patron, British Show Jumping Assen.; Commdt.-in-Chief, St. John Ambulance and Nursing Cadets, Women's Transport Service; Freeman of the City of London, of the Fishmongers' Co., Master Warden Farriers' Co., Master and Hon. Liveryman, Carmen's Co., Hon. Liveryman Farriers' Co.; Hon. Freeman, Farmers' Co., Loriners' Co.; Yeoman, Saddlers' Co.; Hon. mem., British Equine Veterinary Assen., Royal Yacht Squadron, Royal Thames Yacht Club, Minchinhampton Golf Club; Hon. Life mem. RNVR Officers' Assen.; Life mem. Royal British Legion Women's Section, Royal Naval Saddle Club; mem. Island Sailing Club; Visitor, Felixstowe Coll.; official visits abroad to the 14th/20th King's Hussars in Fed. Repub of Germany 1969, 1975, to see the work of the Save the Children Fund in Kenya 1971, to the 2,500th anniversary celebrations of the Iranian monarchy 1971, to 14th/20th King's Hussars and to see the work of the Save the Children Fund, Hong Kong 1971, to S.E. Asia 1972, Munich 1972, Yugoslavia 1972, Ethiopia and the Sudan 1973, to visit Worcs. and Sherwood Foresters Regt. in Berlin 1973, in Hereford, Fed. Repub. of Germany 1974, to Canada 1974, to Australia 1975, to U.S.A. 1977, to Fed. Repub. of Germany, and Norway 1978, to Portugal, Fed. Repub. of Germany, Thailand, Gilbert Islands, New Zealand, Australia and the Bahamas, Canada 1979, to Royal Corps of Signals in Cyprus, France, Belgium and Fiji 1980, Royal Corps of Signals in Berlin, Nepal, Worcestershire and Sherwood Foresters Regiment and 14th/20th King's Hussars in Fed. Repub. of Germany; U.S.A., Canada and tour of Africa, North Yemen and Lebanon 1982, to France, Japan, Hong Kong, Singapore, Pakistan, Australia, Netherlands and B.A.O.R. 1983, U.S.A., Africa, India, Bangladesh, Fed. Repub. of Germany, U.A.E. 1984; Chancellor, Univ. of London 1981-; has accompanied the Queen and the Duke of Edinburgh on several State Visits; has taken part in numerous equestrian competitions including Montreal Olympics 1976, Horse of the Year Show, Wembley and Badminton Horse Trials; winner of Raleigh Trophy 1971 and Silver Medal in 1975 in Individual European Three Day Event; Sportswoman of the Year, Sports Writers' Assen., Daily Express, World of Sport, BBC Sports Personality 1971. *Address:* Buckingham Palace, London, S.W.1, England.

ROYER, Jean; French politician; b. 31 Oct. 1920, Nevers; s. of Léon-Antoine Royer and Odette Bourgoin; m. Lucienne Leux 1944; two s. two d.; ed. Ecole primaire supérieure Paul-Louis-Courier, Tours and Univ. de Poitiers; teacher at Langeais 1945-48, at Sainte-Maure 1950-54, at Tours 1954-58; del. of RPF (Rassemblement du Peuple Français) 1947-51; Ind. Deputy to Nat. Ass. 1958-73, May 1976-; Mayor of Tours 1959•; Councillor for Tours-ouest Dist. 1961-; Minister of Commerce, Trades and Crafts 1973-74, of Posts and Telecommunications March-May 1974; Presidential cand. 1974. *Address:* Assemblée Nationale, 75355 Paris; 62 rue des Pierres-Plates, Saint-Avertin, 37110 Chambray-les-Tours, France.

ROYO SÁNCHEZ, Arístides, PH.D.; Panamanian lawyer and politician; b. 14 Aug. 1940, La Chorrera; s. of Roberto Royas and Gilma Sánchez; m. Adele Ruíz 1963; one s. two d.; ed. Nat. Institute, Panama City, Univs. of Salamanca and Bologna; Gen. Sec. of the Gen. Solicitorship of the Repub. of Panama 1965-68; Prof. of Consular, Notariate and Mercantile Law, Univ. of Panama 1966-69, then Prof. of Criminal Law, research 1967-71; mem. Law Codification Comm. 1969; mem. drafting comms. for Penal Code 1970, Constitution 1972; mem. Legis. Comm. of Nat. Council of Legislation 1972-73; Gen. Sec. School of Lawyers of Panama 1973; mem. Morgan & Morgan (lawyers) 1968-; a negotiator of Torrijos-Carter Canal Treaties between Panama and U.S.A. 1977; mem. Org. Comm. of Democratic Revolutionary Party; Minister of Educ. 1973-78; Pres. of Panama 1978-82; Amb. to Spain 1982-85; Grand Cross, Alfonso X the Wise (Spain) 1977, Extraordinary Grand Cross, Vasco Núñez de Balboa (Panama) 1978; Grand Collar, Order of Manuel Amador Guerrero (Panama) 1978; Grand Collar, Order of Isabel la Católica (Spain) 1979; Grand Cross, Légion d'honneur 1979; Extraordinary Grand Cross, Order of Boyaca (Colombia) 1979; Dr. h.c. Univ. San Martín de Porres, Lima, Peru 1979; hon. mem. Spanish Law Soc. 1979. *Publications:* Philosophy of Law in Cathrein and Del Vecchio 1963, History of Spanish Commercial Code 1964, The Responsibility of the Vettore in Sea Shipping 1965, Extraterritoriality of the Panamanian Criminal Law 1967, Project of Criminal Code of Panama, The Participation of Labourers in the Utilities of Enterprises, Revolution or De Facto Government, Manager in the Enterprise 1970, Commentaries to the Law on Retiring Funds for Journalists 1971, The Technician and the Politician in Public Administration 1973, Popular Consultation of the Law 1972. *Leisure interests:* reading, writing, skiing, jogging. *Address:* Morgan and Morgan, P.O. Box 1824, Panama City 1 (Office); P.O. Box 3333, Panama City 4, Republic of Panama (Home). *Telephone:* (507) 63-8822 (Office); (507) 69-1025 (Home).

ROYSTER, Vermont Connecticut, A.B., LL.D.; American journalist; b. 30 April 1914, Raleigh, N.C.; s. of Wilbur H. and Olivette B. Royster; m. Francis Claypole 1937; two d.; ed. Univ. of North Carolina; Reporter New York City News Bureau 1936, Wall Street Journal 1936; Washington Corresp. Wall Street Journal 1936-41, 1945-46, Chief Washington Corresp. 1946-48, Editorial Writer and Columnist 1946-48, Assoc. Ed. 1948-51, Sr. Assoc. Ed. 1951-58, Ed. 1958-71, Contrib. Ed. and Columnist 1971-; Sr. Vice-Pres. Dow Jones & Co. Inc. 1960-71, Dir. 1970-; Pres. American Soc. of Newspaper Editors 1965-66; Kenan Prof. Journalism and Public Affairs,

Univ. of N. Carolina 1971–86; Sr. Fellow, Inst. of Policy Sciences, Duke 1973–85; frequent radio and TV appearances; served U.S. Navy 1941–45; mem. Pulitzer Bd. for Prizes in Journalism and Letters 1968–76; UNC Prof. Emer. 1983–; Hon. Litt.D. (Temple Univ.), Hon. L.H.D. (Elon Coll., N.C.); Pulitzer Prize for editorial writing 1953, 4th Estate Award for Lifetime Contribution to Journalism, Nat. Press Club (Washington, D.C.) 1978, Pulitzer Prize for Commentary 1984, Presidential Medal of Freedom 1986 and other awards. *Publications:* Journey through the Soviet Union 1964, A Pride of Prejudices 1967, My Own, My Country's Time (memoirs) 1983, The Essential Royster: A Half Century of a Journalist's Eye 1985. *Leisure interest:* boating. *Address:* 903 Arrowhead Road, Chapel Hill, N.C. 27514, U.S.A.

ROZANOV, Evgeny Grigorevich; Soviet architect; b. 8 Nov. 1925, Moscow; s. of Grigory Alexandrovich Rozanov and Anastasiya Nikolaevna Rozanova; m. Aida Iljenkova 1952; one s.; ed. Moscow Inst. of Architecture; mem. CPSU 1964–; Dir. of Mezentsev Inst. of Experimental Architecture 1970–85; major bldgs. designed in Essentuki, Vladivostok, Tashkent, Moscow (notably Dinamo Sports Centre); teacher of architecture at Moscow Architectural Inst. 1960–85; Chair. State Cttee. on Architecture and Town Planning 1987–; Sec. of U.S.S.R. Union of Architects 1981–; elected to Congress of People's Deputies of the U.S.S.R. 1989; Khamza Uzbek State Prize 1970, U.S.S.R. State Prize 1975, 1980; mem. U.S.S.R. Acad. of Arts 1983, People's Architect of U.S.S.R. 1983. *Leisure interests:* painting, sculpture, music. *Address:* 24 Pushkinskaya ul., 103824 Moscow, U.S.S.R.

ROZES, Simone, L. EN D.; French lawyer; b. 29 March 1920, Paris; d. of Léon Ludwig and Marcelle Cetre; m. Gabriel Rozes 1942; one s. one d.; ed. Lycée de Sèvres, Lycée de St.-Germain-en-Laye, Univ. of Paris, Ecole Libre des Sciences Politiques; trainee lawyer, Paris 1947–49; Surrogate Judge, Bourges 1949–50; attaché, Justice Dept. 1951–58; Admin. Chief, Cabinet of the Minister of Justice 1958–62, Judge 1962, Vice-Pres. Tribunal de Grande Instance de Paris 1969–73, Pres. 1976–81; Dir. Reformatory Educ. 1973–76; mem. Crime Prevention and Control Cttee. UN 1977–; Advocate-Gen. European Court of Justice 1981–82; First Advocate Gen. 1982–84; Pres. Cour de Cassation 1984–88; Pres. Int. Soc. of Social Defence, Soc. of Comparative Law; Officier, Légion d'honneur; Officier, Ordre nat. du Mérite; Médaille de l'Educ. Surveillée; Médaille de l'Admin. Pénitentiaire; Commdr. Cross, Order of Merit (Fed. Repub. of Germany). *Leisure interests:* skiing, mountaineering. *Address:* c/o Cour de Cassation, 5 quai de l'Horloge, 75001 Paris, France.

RÓŻEWICZ, Tadeusz; Polish poet and playwright; b. 9 Oct. 1921, Radomsko; ed. Univ. of Cracow; fmr. factory worker and teacher; Corresp. mem. Bavarian Acad. of Fine Arts 1982–, Acad. of Arts (G.D.R.); State Prize for Poetry 1955, 1956; Literary Prize, City of Cracow 1959; Prize of Minister of Culture and Art 1962, State Prize 1st Class 1966; Alfred Jurzykowski Foundation Award, New York 1966; Austrian Nat. Prize for European Literature 1982; Prize of Minister of Foreign Affairs 1974, 1987; Golden Wreath Prize for poetry (Yugoslavia) 1987; Commdr. Cross of Order Polonia Restituta 1970, Medal of 30th Anniversary of People's Poland 1974, Order of Banner of Labour (2nd class) 1977. *Publications:* 15 vols. of poetry including Niepokój (Faces of Anxiety), Czerwona rękawiczka (The Red Glove), Czas który idzie (The Time Which Goes On), Równina (The Plain), Srebrny kłos (The Silver Ear), Rozmowa z księciem (Conversation with the Prince), Zielona róza (The Green Rose), Nic w płaszczu Prospera (Nothing in Prosper's Overcoat), Twarz (The Face), Duszyczka (A Little Soul), Poezje (Poetry) 1987. *Plays include:* Kartoteka (The Card Index), Grupa Laokoona (Laocoon's Group), Świadkowie albo nasza mała stabilizacja (The Witnesses), Akt przerywany (The Interrupted Act), Śmieszny staruszek (The Funny Man), Wyszedł z domu (Gone Out), Spaghetti i miecz (Spaghetti and the Sword), Stara kobieta wysiaduje (The Old Woman Broods), Na czworakach (On All Fours), Do piachu (Down to Sand), Białe małżeństwo (White Marriage), Odejście Głodomora (Starveling's Departure), Na powierzchni poematu i w środku: nowy wybór wierszy, Pułapka (The Trap), Próba rekonstrukcji, Tarcza z pajeczyny. *Prose includes:* Opowiadania wybrane (Selected Stories). *Address:* Ul. Januszewicka 13 m. 14, 53-136 Wrocław, Poland. *Telephone:* 67-71-38.

ROZHDESTVENSKY, Gennadiy Nikolayevich; Soviet conductor; b. 4 May 1931, Moscow; m. Viktoria Postnikova; ed. Moscow State Conservatoire; Asst. Conductor, Bolshoi Theatre 1951, Conductor 1956–60, Prin. Conductor 1965–70; Chief Conductor of U.S.S.R. Radio and TV Symphony Orchestra 1961–74; Chief Conductor Stockholm Philharmonia 1974–77, Moscow Chamber Orchestra 1974–83; Founder, Artistic Dir., Chief Conductor, State Symphony Orchestra of Ministry of Culture, U.S.S.R. 1983–; Prin. Conductor BBC Symphony Orchestra 1978–82, Vienna Symphony Orchestra 1982–83; has been guest conductor of numerous orchestras throughout Europe, America and Asia; Prof. of Conducting, Moscow State Conservatoire 1965–; Hon. mem. Swedica Royal Acad. 1975; Merited and People's Artist of the R.S.F.S.R. 1966, Lenin Prizewinner 1970, Order of Red Banner of Labour (twice) and other decorations. *Leisure interest:* music. *Address:* c/o Victor Hochhauser Ltd., 4 Holland Park Avenue, London, W.11, England.

ROZHDESTVENSKY, Robert Ivanovich; Soviet author and poet; b. 20 June 1932, Kosikha Village, Altai Dist.; s. of Ivan Ivanovich Rozhdestvensky and Vera Pavlovna Rozhdestvenskaya; m. Alla Borisovna Kireewa

1953; two d.; ed. Gorky Inst. of Literature, Moscow; writer and poet 1950–; Order of Red Banner, Order of Lenin, State Prize 1979 and several medals. *Publications include:* poetry: Flags of Spring 1955, To My Contemporary 1962, Radius of Action 1965, Vera's Son 1966, The Dedication 1970, Requiem 1970, In All Earnestness 1970, The Artist Aleksandra Bill 1970, The Heart's Radar 1971, The Return: Verse of Several Years 1972, The Line 1973, In the Twenty Years 1973, Before the Holiday: Verse and Poems 1974, Selected Works 1974, Two Hundred and Ten Steps 1978, The Voice of the Town 1979, The Seventies 1979, This is the Time 1980, Everyday Miracle 1983, To My Friends 1986, Age 1988; verse translated into many languages. *Leisure interest:* history of Moscow. *Address:* U.S.S.R. Union of Writers, Ulitsa Vorovskogo 52, Moscow; Ap. 69, Ul. Gorkogo 9, 103009 Moscow, U.S.S.R. *Telephone:* 229 64 97.

ROZOV, Viktor Sergeevich; Soviet dramatist; b. Aug. 1913, Yaroslavl; worked initially as actor in Kostroma and Moscow; served in Red Army 1941–45; U.S.S.R. State Prize 1967. *Works include:* plays: Her Friends 1949, Pages from Life 1953, In Search of Joy 1957, Uneven Fight 1960, Before Supper 1962, The Immortals (made into film The Cranes are Flying) 1957, A Traditional Meeting 1967, From Evening till Noon 1970, How Things Stand 1973, The Little Cabin 1982 (banned, then performed Moscow 1987).

ROZOVSKY, Mark; Soviet theatre-director and script-writer; b. 1937, Petropavlovsk; ed. Moscow Univ., f. and managed 'Our Home', (650 seat amateur studio theatre) with fellow students of Moscow Univ. 1958–70; theatre officially disbanded 1970; freelance 1970–; wrote 3 books on theatre, dir. versions of Karamzin, Kafka, Dostoevsky and others in Leningrad, Moscow and Riga 1970–74, dir. Orpheus and Eurydice (rock-opera) 1975, and a musical adaptation of 'Strider' jointly with Georgii Tovstonogov (q.v.), by L. N. Tolstoy for Gorky Theatre, Leningrad; Theatre of Nations Prize Hamburg and Avignon 1979. *Other productions include:* Amadeus (P. Shaffer) for Moscow Arts Theatre; libretto for opera about Mayakovsky; work for TV including documentary on Meyerhold, Triumphal Square 1984; works for Gorky Theatre Leningrad and Theatre of Russian Drama, Riga, Latvia, and his own Second Studio Theatre, Moscow. *Address:* c/o Gorky Theatre, Leningrad, U.S.S.R.

RU ZHIJUAN; Chinese writer; b. Oct. 1925, Shanghai; s. of Ru Pang-shi; m. Wang Xiao-ping 1950; one s. two d.; orphaned at early age; joined a theatrical troupe in CCP forces 1943; mem. editorial bd. Literary Monthly 1955, Shanghai Literature 1979. *Publications include:* The Path Through The Grassland, Tall White Poplar (short stories), Quiet Maternity Hospital (short stories), The Man Who Cherishes Flowers Has Gone Away (essays), She Comes From That Way (novel). *Leisure interest:* going to the movies. *Address:* 675 Ju Lu Road, Shanghai, People's Republic of China. *Telephone:* 315126.

RUAN BOSHENG; Chinese party official; b. 1912, Tangshan Co., Hebei Prov.; joined CCP 1937; Deputy Sec. CCP Tangshan City Cttee. 1952; Chair. Tangshan City Trade Union Council 1952; Vice-Gov. Hebei Prov. 1955, 1958; Sec. CCP Cttee., Jilin Prov. 1965, 1971; Vice-Chair. Prov. Revolutionary Cttee., Jilin 1968; Alt. mem. 9th Cen. Cttee., CCP 1969, mem. and Alt. mem. 10th Cen. Cttee., 1973, mem. 11th Cen. Cttee. 1977; Chair. Prov. People's Congress, Shanxi 1979–, Sec. CCP Cttee., Shanxi 1979–85. *Address:* People's Republic of China.

RUAN CHONGWU; Chinese party and state official; b. 1933; ed. Moscow Auto-Eng. Inst.; Deputy Dir. Shanghai Materials Research Inst.; Deputy Sec. Shanghai Municipal Scientific Workers' Asscn.; Science and Tech. Counsellor, Chinese Embassy in Bonn 1978; Vice-Mayor Shanghai 1983–85; Sec. CCP, Shanghai Municipality 1983–85; mem. 12th CCP Cen. Cttee. 1985, 13th Cen. Cttee. 1987–; Minister of Public Security 1985–87; Vice-Minister Science and Tech. Comm., State Council April 1987–. *Address:* 14 Dong Chang An Street, Beijing, People's Republic of China.

RUBBIA, Carlo; Italian professor of physics; b. 31 March 1934, Gorizia; ed. high school, Pisa and Columbia and Rome Univs.; research physicist. CERN 1960–, mem. CERN 1985–, Dir.-Gen. Jan. 1989–; Prof. of Physics, Harvard Univ. 1972–; mem. Papal Acad. of Science 1986–; Nobel Prize for Physics 1984, Leslie Prize for exceptional achievements 1985, Jesolo d'Oro 1986. *Address:* Organisation Européenne pour la Recherche Nucléaire (CERN), EP Division, 1211 Geneva 23, Switzerland.

RUBEN, Vitaliy Petrovich; Soviet politician; b. 26 Feb. 1914, Moscow; ed. Yaroslav Agricultural Coll., Higher Party School; worked as agronomist and teacher until 1941; party work 1941–44; worked with Cen. Cttee. CP of Latvia 1944–47; Second Sec. Daugavpils Regional Cttee. CP of Latvia 1947–48; attended CPSU School 1948–51; Cen. Cttee. CP of Latvia, Councils of Agric. and State Planning Cttee. of Latvia 1951–61; Deputy Chair. Council of Ministers, Latvian S.S.R. 1961–62, Chair. 1962–70; Presidium of Supreme Soviet of Latvian S.S.R. 1970–74; Vice-Chair. Presidium of U.S.S.R. Supreme Soviet 1970–74; Cand. mem. Cen. Cttee. CPSU 1966–76, mem. 1976–; Deputy to U.S.S.R. Supreme Soviet 1962–; Chair. Soviet of Nationalities, U.S.S.R. Supreme Soviet 1974–84; Order of Lenin (three times), Order of the October Revolution, Badge of Honour and other decorations. *Address:* Soviet of Nationalities, U.S.S.R. Supreme Soviet, The Kremlin, Moscow, U.S.S.R.

RUBENIS, Juris Y.; Soviet politician; b. 15 April 1925, Latvia; ed. Latvian State Univ. and Party High School of Cen. Cttee. of CPSU; mem. CPSU 1953–; served in Soviet Army 1943; engineer at Riga Compressor Works 1951–52; leading Komsomol posts in Latvia 1952–55; CPSU work 1955–58; First Sec. Liepaya City Cttee. of Latvian CP 1960–63, Riga City Cttee. 1963–66; mem. Cen. Cttee. of Latvian CP 1961–; mem. for Industry, Politburo of Cen. Cttee. of Latvian CP 1962–63, cand. mem. Politburo of Cen. Cttee. 1963–66, mem. 1966–; Sec. Cen. Cttee. of Latvian CP 1966–70; Chair. Council of Ministers of Latvian S.S.R. 1970–88; Deputy to U.S.S.R. Supreme Soviet 1970–; cand. mem. Cen. Cttee. of CPSU 1971–; Order of Lenin (three times), Order of October Revolution, Order of Red Banner of Labour. *Address:* Council of Ministers of Latvian S.S.R., Riga, Latvian S.S.R., U.S.S.R.

RUBENS, Bernice Ruth, B.A.; British author; b. 26 July 1928, Cardiff; d. of Eli and Dorothy Reuben; m. Rudi Nassauer 1947; two d.; ed. Cardiff High School for Girls and Univ. of Wales, Cardiff; author and dir. of documentary films on Third World subjects; Fellow Univ. Coll., Cardiff; Booker Prize 1970; American Blue Ribbon (documentary film) 1972. *Publications:* novels: Set on Edge 1960, Madame Sontsatzka 1962, Mate in Three 1964, The Elected Member 1968, Sunday Best 1970, Go Tell the Lemming 1972, I Sent a Letter to my Love 1974, Ponsonby Post 1976, A Five-year Sentence 1978, Spring Sonata 1979, Birds of Passage 1980, Brothers 1982, Mr. Wakefield's Crusade 1985, Our Father 1987. *Leisure interest:* playing 'cello. *Address:* 16A Belsize Park Gardens, London, NW3 4LD, England.

RUBENSTEIN, Edward, M.D.; American professor of medicine; b. 5 Dec. 1924, Cincinnati; s. of Louis Rubenstein and Nettie Nathan; m. Nancy Ellen Millman 1954; three s.; ed. Cincinnati Univ. Coll. of Medicine; Laboratory Asst., Dept. of Physiology, Cincinnati Univ. 1947; Intern, then Jr. Asst., then Sr. Asst. Resident in Medicine, Cincinnati Gen. Hosp. 1947–50, Medical Chief, Psychosomatic Service 1953–54; Research Fellow, May Inst., Cincinnati 1950; Chief of Medicine, U.S.A.F. Hosp., March Airforce Base 1950–52; Sr. Asst. Resident in Medicine, Barnes Hosp., St. Louis 1952–53; Chief, Clinical Physiology Unit, San Mateo Co. Gen. Hosp. 1955–63, Chief of Medicine 1960–70; Prof. of Medicine and Assoc. Dean of Postgraduate Medical Educ., Stanford Univ. School of Medicine 1971–; Ed.-in-Chief Scientific American 1978–; mem. Inst. of Medicine of N.A.S.; Master, American Coll. of Physicians; T.V. documentary Being Human 1979; research in synchrotron radiation. *Publications:* Intensive Medical Care 1971; numerous scientific papers. *Address:* Medical School Office Bldg., Suite X365, Stanford Univ. School of Medicine, Stanford, Calif. 94305, U.S.A. *Telephone:* (415) 723 7188.

RUBIK, Ernő; Hungarian architect, designer and inventor; b. 13 July 1944, Budapest; s. of Ernő Rubik Sr. and Magdolna Szántó; m. 1st Rózsa Kovács 1977 (divorced 1985), one s. one d.; m. 2nd Ágnes Hégley 1985; one d.; ed. Technical Univ. and Acad. of Applied Arts, Budapest; consecutively Asst. Assoc., then Prof., Acad. of Applied Arts, Dir. of Postgraduate Studies 1983–; Hon. Prof. Acad. of Crafts and Design, Budapest 1987; Inventor Rubik's Cube and other games and puzzles; Pres. Rubik Studio; Labour Order of Merit Gold Medal of the Hungarian People's Repub., Toy of the Year award 1981–82 of United Kingdom, Fed. Repub. of Germany, Italy, Sweden, Finland, France, U.S.A.; State Prize 1983; mem. Hungarian Peace Council. *Publications:* co-author and editor of A büvös kocka (The Magic Cube) 1981, Rubik's Magic 1986, Rubik's Cubic Compendium 1987. *Leisure interests:* swimming, skiing, sailing. *Address:* Rubik Studio, 1122 Budapest, Városmajor u. 74, Hungary. *Telephone:* 558-337.

RUBIN, Louis Decimus, Jr., PH.D.; American professor of English, publisher and writer; b. 19 Nov. 1923, Charleston, S.C.; s. of Louis Decimus Rubin, Sr. and Janet Weinstein Rubin; m. Eva Maryette Redfield 1951; two s.; ed. High School of Charleston, Coll. of Charleston, Univ. of Richmond and Johns Hopkins Univ.; U.S. Army 1943–46; instructor in English Johns Hopkins Univ. 1948–54; Exec. Sec. American Studies Asscn. 1954–56 (also fmr. Vice-Pres.); Assoc. Ed. News Leader, Richmond, Va. 1956–57; Assoc. Prof. of English, then Prof. and Chair. English Dept. 1957–67; Prof. of English Univ. of N.C. at Chapel Hill 1967–, Univ. Distinguished Prof. 1972–; Visiting Prof. La. State Univ., Univ. of Calif. at Santa Barbara, Harvard Univ.; lecturer, Aix-Marseille at Nice, Kyoto Summer American Studies Seminars; USICA, Austria, Germany; Ed. Southern Literary Studies Series, Louisiana State Univ. Press 1965–; Co-Ed. Southern Literary Journal 1968–; Pres. and Ed.-in-Chief Algonquin Books, Chapel Hill 1982–; fmr. Pres. Soc. for Study of Southern Literature; fmr. Chair. American Literature Section, Modern Language Assn.; mem. S.C. Acad. of Authors, Fellowship of Southern Writers; Hon. D.Litt. (Richmond, Clemson). *Publications:* author: Thomas Wolfe: The Weather of His Youth 1955, No Place on Earth 1959, The Faraway Country 1964, The Golden Weather (novel) 1961, The Curious Death of the Novel 1967, The Teller in the Tale 1967, George W. Cable 1969, The Writer in the South 1972, William Elliott Shoots a Bear 1975, The Wary Fugitives 1978, Surfaces of a Diamond (novel) 1981, A Gallery of Southerners 1982, The Even-Tempered Angler 1984; editor: Southern Renascence 1953, Idea of an American Novel 1961, South 1961, Comic Imagination in American Literature 1973, The Literary South 1979, American South 1980, The History of Southern Literature 1985, An Apple for My Teacher 1986. *Leisure interests:* sailing, baseball, classical music, reading. *Address:* Algon-

quin Books, P.O. Box 2225, Chapel Hill, N.C. 27515; University of North Carolina, Chapel Hill, English Department, N.C. 27514 (Offices); 702 Gimghoul Road, Chapel Hill, N.C. 27514, U.S.A. (Home). *Telephone:* (919) 967-0108 (Office); (919) 962-4005 (University); (919) 929-3410 (Home).

RUBIN, Vera Cooper, PH.D.; American astronomer; b. 23 July 1928, Philadelphia; d. of Philip Cooper and Rose Applebaum Cooper; m. Robert J. Rubin 1948; three s. one d.; ed. Vassar Coll., Cornell Univ., Georgetown Univ.; Research Assoc. to Asst. Prof. Georgetown Univ. 1955–65; mem. Staff Dept. of Terrestrial Magnetism, Carnegie Inst., Wash. 1965–; Distinguished Visiting Astronomer, Cerro Tololo Inter-American Observatory 1978, Chancellor's Distinguished Prof. Astronomy Univ. of Calif., Berkeley 1981; Pres.'s Distinguished Visitor, Vassar Coll. 1987; B. Tinsley Visiting Prof., Univ. of Texas 1988; has observed at Kitt Peak Nat. Observatory, Lowell, Palomar, McDonald, Las Campanas, Chile observatories; Assoc. Ed. Astronomical Journal 1972–77, Astrophysical Journal of Letters 1977–82; mem. Council American Astronomical Soc. 1977–80; mem. Editorial Bd. Science Magazine 1979–; mem. Council Smithsonian Inst. 1979–; Pres. Galaxy Comm. Int. Astronomical Union 1982–85; mem. N.A.S., American Acad. of Arts and Sciences; Hon. D.Sc. (Creighton Univ.) 1978, (Harvard Univ.) 1988. *Publications:* over 100 scientific papers on the dynamics of galaxies in specialist journals. *Leisure interests:* family, garden, hiking, travel. *Address:* Department of Terrestrial Magnetism, Carnegie Institution of Washington, 5241 Broad Branch Road, N.W., Washington, D.C. 20015, U.S.A.

RUBIN, H.E. Cardinal Władysław; Polish ecclesiastic; b. 20 Sept. 1917, Toki, Lwów (now Lvov, U.S.S.R.); ordained priest 1946; Titular Bishop of Serta 1964–79; cr. Cardinal 1979; Prefect, Sacred Congregation for the Eastern Churches 1980–85; mem. Sacred Congregations for the Doctrine of the Faith and for the Causes of Saints; mem. Supreme Tribunal for the Apostolic Signatura, Secr. for Promoting Christian Unity, Pontifical Comm. for the Revision of Oriental Canon Law, Sacred Congregation for the Doctrine of the Faith, for Religious and Secular Insts., for the Evangelization of the People, for the Causes of the Saints, for Catholic Educ., Supreme of the Apostolic Signature, Secr. for Christian Unity, Pontifical Comm. for the Revision of the Codex of the Eastern Canonical Law; Deacon of S. Maria in Via Lata. *Address:* Palazzo dei Convertendi, Via della Conciliazione 34, 00193 Rome, Italy. *Telephone:* 698.4732, 698.4662.

RUBIN, William, PH.D.; American curator and art historian; b. 11 Aug. 1927, New York; ed. Univ. of Paris, Columbia Univ.; Prof. of Art History Sarah Lawrence Coll. 1952–67, City Univ. of New York 1960–68; Adjunct Prof. Art History, Inst. of Fine Arts, New York Univ. 1968–; Chief Curator Painting and Sculpture, Museum of Modern Art, New York 1968–, Dir. Painting and Sculpture 1973–88; exhbns. arranged include: Dada, Surrealism and their Heritage 1968, New American Painting and Sculpture 1969, Stella 1970, Miro 1973, Picasso: A Retrospective 1980, Giorgio DeChirico 1982, Primitivism in 20th Century Art 1984; American Ed. Art Int. Magazine 1959–64; Trustee Sarah Lawrence Coll. 1980–; Chevalier Légion d'honneur, Officier des Arts et Lettres (Paris) 1979. *Publications:* Matta 1957, Modern Sacred Art and the Church of Assy 1961, Dada, Surrealism and their Heritage 1966, Dada and Surrealist Art 1969, Frank Stella 1970, Picasso in the Collection of the Museum of Modern Art 1973, The Paintings of Gerald Murphy 1974, Anthony Caro 1975, (with Carolyn Lanchner) André Masson 1976, Paris-New York: Situation de l'Art 1978; ed. (with Carolyn Lanchner) Cézanne: The Late Work 1977, Picasso: A Retrospective 1980. *Address:* Museum of Modern Art, 11 W 53rd Street, New York, N.Y. 10019, U.S.A.

RUBINSTEIN, Amnon, PH.D.; Israeli politician and lawyer; b. 1931, Tel Aviv; m.; two c.; ed. law faculty, Hebrew Univ., London School of Econs., U.K.; mil. service Israeli Defence Forces; fmr. Dean Faculty of Law and Prof. of Law, Tel Aviv Univ.; elected to Ninth Knesset (Parl.), mem. Foreign Affairs and Security Cttee. –1981, to Tenth Knesset, mem. Econs. Cttee., Chair. Shinui Faction 1983; Minister of Communications 1984–87; Shinui Party. *Address:* c/o Ministry of Communications, Hakirya, Jerusalem.

RUBOTTOM, Roy Richard, Jr.; American diplomatist, educator and university administrator; b. 13 Feb. 1912, Brownwood, Tex.; s. of Roy Richard Rubottom and Jennie Eleanor Watkins; m. Billy Ruth Young 1938; two s. one d.; ed. Southern Methodist and Texas Univs.; in commerce 1935–37, Asst. Dean, Student Life Tex. Univ. 1937–41; served in U.S. Navy (Commdr.) 1941–46; Naval liaison officer, Mexico 1943–45; Naval Attaché, Paraguay 1945–46; Appointed Foreign Service Officer 1947; Embassy Sec. and Consul, Bogotá 1947–49; in charge Mexican Affairs, State Dept. 1950–52; Dir. Mid-American Affairs 1952–53; 1st Sec., Madrid Embassy 1953–54; Dir. Operations Mission, Madrid 1954–56; Deputy Asst. Sec. and Acting Asst. Sec., of State for Inter-American Affairs 1956; Asst. Sec. 1957–60; Amb. to Argentina 1960–61; faculty adviser for State Dept., Naval War Coll. 1961–64; Vice-Pres. Southern Methodist Univ., Tex. 1964–71; Prof. Emer. of Political Science 1975–, Dir. Center of Ibero-American Civilizations 1975–77; Pres. Univ. of the Americas 1971–73; Dir. Office of Int. Affairs, Dallas 1985–87; Hon. LL.D. (South-western Coll., Winfield, Kansas) 1968. *Publication:* Spain and the U.S. since World War Two (co-author) 1984. *Leisure interests:* swimming, travel, reading.

Address: Southern Methodist University, Dallas, Tex. 75275; 3429 University Blvd., Dallas, Tex 75205, U.S.A. (Home).

RUBTSOV, Nikolay Fyodorovich; Soviet politician; b. 1931; ed. Rostov Univ. and CPSU Cen. Cttee. Higher Party School; Pres. of trades-union cttee. of Rostov Univ. 1953–54; mem. CPSU 1954–; First Sec. of Komsomol Regional Cttee., deputy head of dept. of Rostov Dist. Komsomol Cttee., Sec. of Kirov Regional Cttee. 1954–58; Sec., Second, First Sec. of Rostov Komsomol Dist. Cttee. 1958–61; head of section of Komsomol Cen. Cttee. 1966–83; head of Secr. of Presidium of U.S.S.R. Supreme Soviet 1983–; mem. of CPSU Cen. Auditing Comm. 1986–. *Address:* The Kremlin, Moscow, U.S.S.R.

RUCKELSHAUS, William Doyle; American government official; b. 24 July 1932, Indianapolis, Ind.; s. of John K. and Marion (Doyle) Covington Ruckelshaus; m. Jill E. Strickland 1962; one s. four d.; ed. Portsmouth Priory School, R.I. and Princeton and Harvard Univs.; served with U.S. Army 1953–55; admitted to Indiana Bar 1960; attorney with Ruckelshaus, Bobbit & O'Connor 1960–68; Partner Ruckelshaus, Beveridge, Fairbanks & Diamond (fmrly. Ruckelshaus, Beveridge & Fairbanks), Sr. Partner 1974–76; Deputy Attorney-Gen. Ind. 1960–65; Minority Attorney, Ind. State Senate 1965–67; mem. Ind. House of Reps. 1967–69; Asst. Attorney-Gen., U.S. Civil Div., Dept. of Justice 1969–70; Dir. Environmental Protection Agency 1970–73; Acting Dir. FBI 1973; Deputy Attorney-Gen. 1973; Sr. Vice-Pres. Weyerhaeuser Co. 1976–83; Dir. Environmental Protection Agency 1983–84; mem. firm Perkins Coie, Seattle 1985–; fmr. mem. Bd. Dirs. Cummins Engine Co., Inc., Peabody Int. Corpn., Church and Dwight Co. Inc., Nordstrom, Inc.; fmr. Chair. Bd. Geothermal Kinetics Inc., Trustees of Urban Inst.; mem. Bd. American Paper Inst., Council on Foreign Relations, Twentieth Century Fund; Trustee, Pacific Science Center Foundation, Seattle Chamber of Commerce, The Conservation Foundation, Seattle Art Museum; mem. Public Interest Advisory Cttee. Harvard Univ. Medical Project, Bd. of Overseers, Harvard J.F.K. School of Govt., Bd. of Regents, Seattle, Univ.; mem. several U.S. bar assocs. *Publication:* Reapportionment—A Continuing Problem 1963. *Leisure interests:* tennis, fishing, reading. *Address:* Perkins and Coie, 1900 Washington Building, Seattle, Wash. 98101 (Office); 1015 Evergreen Point Road, Medina, Wash. 98039, U.S.A. (Home). *Telephone:* (206) 453-0863 (Home).

RUDA, José María, LL.D.; Argentine lawyer and diplomatist; b. 9 Aug. 1924, Buenos Aires; s. of José Maria Ruda and Margarita Comas de Ruda; m. 1st Maria Haydée Arnold 1949 (died 1980), m. 2nd Ruth Guevara Achaval 1983; five c.; ed. Univ. de Buenos Aires and New York Univ.; Office of Legal Affairs, UN Secr. 1951–55; Sec. of State, Salta Prov., Argentina 1956–57; Counsellor, La Paz 1957–60; mem. Argentine Del. to UN 1959, Chair. Argentine Del. 1965, Perm. Rep. to UN 1966–70; Assoc. Prof. of Int. Law, Univ. de Buenos Aires 1959–71, Prof. of Int. Law 1971–; Under-Sec. of State for Foreign Affairs and Worship 1970–73; Visiting Prof. Colegio de México 1963; mem. Int. Law Comm. of UN 1964–73; Judge, Int. Court of Justice 1973–, Pres. 1988–; mem. ILO Panel of Experts 1978–, Pres. 1988; Del. to numerous int. confs. *Publications include:* The Powers of the General Assembly of the UN in Political and Security Matters 1956, Jurisdiction of the International Court 1959, Relations Between the United Nations and the Organization of American States in Connexion with International Peace and Security 1959 A Study in Politics and Law: The United Nations 1962, The Evolution of International Law, International Instruments 1976. *Address:* International Court of Justice, Peace Palace, The Hague, Netherlands; Callao 1707, Buenos Aires, Argentina.

RUDDLE, Francis Hugh, PH.D.; American professor of biology and human genetics; b. 19 Aug. 1929, West New York, N.J.; s. of Thomas Hugh Ruddle and Mary Henley (Rodda); m. Nancy Marion Hartman 1964; two d.; ed. Wayne State Univ., Detroit and Univ. of California, Berkeley; Research Assoc., Child Research Center of Mich., District 1953–56; Nat. Insts. of Health Postdoctoral Fellow, Dept. of Biochemistry, Univ. of Glasgow, Scotland 1960–61; Asst. Prof., Yale Univ. 1961–67, Assoc. Prof. 1967–72, Prof. of Biology and Human Genetics 1972–, Chair. Dept. of Biology 1977–83, Ross Granville Harrison Prof. of Biology 1983–; Pres. American Soc. of Human Genetics 1985; Pres. American Soc. of Cell Biology 1986; Fellow A.A.A.S.; mem. N.A.S., American Genetic Assocn., American Soc. of Biological Chemists, American Soc. of Zoologists, Genetics Soc. of America. *Leisure interest:* boating. *Address:* Department of Biology, Yale University, Kline Biology Tower, P.O. Box 6666, New Haven, Conn. 96511-8112, U.S.A. *Telephone:* (203) 436-0418.

RUDDOCK, Joan Mary, B.SC., A.R.C.S.; British politician and anti-nuclear campaigner; b. 28 Dec. 1943; d. of Ken and Eileen Anthony; m. Dr. Keith Ruddock 1963; ed. Pontypool Grammar School for Girls and Imperial Coll. London; worked for Shelter (nat. campaign for the homeless) 1968–73; Dir. Oxford Housing Aid Centre 1973–77; Special Programmes Officer with unemployed young people, Manpower Services Comm. 1977–79; Organiser, Reading Citizens Advice Bureau 1979–87; Chair. Campaign for Nuclear Disarmament (CND) 1981–85, Vice-Chair. 1985–; M.P. for Deptford 1987–; Frank Cousins Peace Award 1984; Labour. *Address:* House of Commons, Westminster, London, S.W.1, England.

RUDÉ, George Frederic Elliot, PH.D., F.R.HIST.S.; British professor of history (retd.); b. 8 Feb. 1910, Oslo, Norway; m. Doreen F. C. De La

Hoyde 1940; no c.; ed. Shrewsbury School, Trinity Coll. Cambridge and Univ. of London; school-teacher (modern languages and history) 1931–54; Sr. Lecturer in History, Univ. of Adelaide 1959–62, Prof. 1963–67; Prof. of History, Flinders Univ. Adelaide 1968–70, Concordia Univ. Montreal 1970–88; Visiting Prof. Univs. of Tokyo and Stirling 1968–70; Alexander Prize (Royal Historical Soc.) 1955. *Publications:* The Crowd in the French Revolution 1959, Wilkes and Liberty 1962, The Crowd in History 1964, Revolutionary Europe 1964, Robespierre 1975, Protest and Punishment 1978, Ideology and Popular Protest 1980, Crime and Society in 19th Century Britain 1985, The French Revolution after 200 years 1988. *Leisure interests:* walking, travel, debating. *Address:* 24 Cadborough Cliff, Rye, Sussex, TN31 7EB, England. *Telephone:* (0797) 223442.

RUDING, H. O. (Onno), DR. ECON.; Netherlands politician, economist, banker and international official; b. 15 Aug. 1939, Breda; s. of Dr. R. Ruding and A. M. Ruding (née Fehmers); m. Renée V. Hekking 1971; one s. one d.; ed. grammar school (Gymnasium) in Breda, Netherlands School of Econs. at Rotterdam; Head of Int. Monetary Affairs Div., Treasury-Gen. of Ministry of Finance 1965–70; Joint Gen. Man. Amsterdam-Rotterdam Bank, N.V., Head of Securities Underwriting, New Issue and Corp. Finance Dept. 1971–76; Exec. Dir. for Cyprus, Israel, Netherlands, Romania and Yugoslavia, IMF, Washington, D.C., U.S.A. 1977–80; mem. Bd. of Man. Dirs. Amsterdam-Rotterdam Bank N.V., Amsterdam Jan. 1981–82; Chair. AMRO Int. 1981–82; Minister of Finance Nov. 1982–; Chair. IMF Policy Making Interim Cttee. Jan. 1985–. *Publication:* Towards an Integrated European Capital Market? 1969. *Leisure interests:* history, golf, chess. *Address:* Ministry of Finance, Korte Voorhout 7, 2511 The Hague (Office); Wilhelminaplein 5, 2243 HE Wassenaar, Netherlands (Home). *Telephone:* (070) 462966 (Office); (01751) 78644 (Home).

RUDINI, Gen.; Indonesian army officer; b. 15 Dec. 1929, Malang, E. Java; s. of R. I. Poespohandojo and R. A. Koesbandijah; m. Oddyana Rudini 1959; one s. two d.; ed. Breda Mil. Acad., Netherlands, reaching rank of Second Lieut.; Commdr. Kostrad Infantry/Airborne Brigade 1972–73; Commdr. Indonesian contingent of UN Peace-keeping Force in Middle East 1973–76; Commdr. Kostrad Airborne Combat 1976–81; Commdr. N. and Cen. Sulawesi Mil. Region, Manado 1981, later Commdr. of Kostrad; Chief of Staff, Indonesian Army 1983–88; Minister of Home Affairs March 1988–. *Leisure interests:* sport, music. *Address:* Ministry of Home Affairs, Jalan Merdeka Utara 7, Jakarta Pusat, Indonesia.

RUDMAN, Warren Bruce, LL.B.; American lawyer and politician; b. 18 May 1930, Boston, Mass.; s. of Edward G. and Theresa (née Levenson) Rudman; m. Shirley Wahl 1952; one s. two d.; ed. Valley Forge Mil. Acad., Syracuse Univ., Boston Coll. Law School; rank of Capt. U.S. Army 1952–54; admitted to N.H. Bar, mem. law firm Stein, Rudman and Gormley 1960–69; Attorney-Gen. N.H., Concord 1970–76; Partner Sheehan, Phinney, Bass and Green 1976–80; Fiscal Agent Gov. Walter Peterson's campaign 1968, Special Counsel to Gov. Peterson 1969–70; Republican Senator from N.H. 1980–; Founder, Chair. Bd. Trustees Daniel Webster Jr. Coll., New England Aeronautical Inst. 1965–81; Sr. Advisory Cttee., John F. Kennedy School of Govt., Harvard Univ.; mem. American Legion, Sub-Cttee. on Defence Co-operation of the North Atlantic Ass., Sec. of State's Advisory Panel on Overseas Security; Bronze Star. *Address:* 530 Hart Senate Office Building, Washington, D.C. 20510, U.S.A. *Telephone:* (202) 224-3324.

RUDNICKI, Adolf; Polish writer; b. 19 Feb. 1912, Warsaw; ed. Commercial School, Warsaw; soldier, Polish campaign 1939; mem. Resistance 1942–44, Warsaw insurrection 1944; Co-editor Kuźnica 1945–49; State Prize 1955, 1966, Officer's Cross, Order of Polonia Restituta 1956. *Publications:* Szczury (Rats), Żołnierze (Soldiers), Niekochana (The Unloved One), Lato (Summer), Ucieczka z Jasnej Polany (Flight from Yasna Polyana), Żywe i martwe morze (Living and Dead Seas), Pałeczka czyli każdemu to na czym mu mniej zależy (The Baton, or To Each What He Least Cares For), Niebieskie kartki (Blue Pages, 8 vols. of short stories and essays), Krowa (The Cow), Złote okna (Golden Windows), Młode cierpienia (The Young Sufferings), Manfred (drama), 50 opowiadań (50 stories), Wybór opowiadań (selected stories) 1976, Niekochana i inne opowiadania (The Unloved One and other stories) 1976, Noc będzie chłodna, niebo w purpurze (Night Will Be Chilly, Sky Will Be Purple) 1977, Daniela naga 1978, Rogaty warszawiak 1981, St. jeden 1984. *Address:* Ul. Kanonia 16/18m. 4, 00-278 Warsaw, Poland. *Telephone:* 31-3609.

RUDNICKI, Zbigniew, D.JUR.; Polish politician; b. 1 Dec. 1928, Stanisławów; s. of Karol and Maria Rudnicka; m. Urszula Rudnicka 1952; one d.; ed. Acad. of Commerce, Poznań, and Law Faculty of Poznań Univ.; worked in Poznań Land Engineering Building Establishment, Poznań 1948–49, in Chamber of Handicrafts, Poznań 1949–56; mem. Democratic Party (SD) 1952–; Sec. SD Town Cttee., Poznań 1956–61, Chair. 1961–66; Deputy Chair. SD Voivodship Cttee., Poznań 1967–71, Chair. 1971–73; mem. Presidium SD Cen. Cttee. 1973–81, 1985–, Sec. 1973–80, Deputy Chair. 1980–81; Deputy Chair. Presidium of Town Nat. Council, Poznań 1961–73; Deputy to Seym 1976–85; Minister of Telecommunications 1980–81; Pres. Cen. Union of Handicrafts 1982–; mem. Supreme Co-operative Council 1983–; Order of Banner of Labour (1st and 2nd Class), Kt.'s and Officer's Cross, Order of Polonia Restituta, and other decorations. *Leisure interest:* gardening. *Address:* Centralny Związek Rzemiosła, ul. Miodowa 14, 00-246 Warsaw, Poland. *Telephone:* 31-14-61 (Office); 43-50-84 (Home).

RUDOLF, Tadeusz, M.ECON.; Polish politician; b. 22 Jan. 1926, Bochnia; ed. Higher School of Social Sciences, Warsaw and Party School, Cen. Cttee. PZPR, Warsaw; worked in Cable Factory, Cracow 1944; active mem. Fighting Youth Union and Polish Youth Union; mem. PPR 1945-48, PZPR 1948-; First Sec. PZPR Town Cttee., Zakopane 1948-50; Chair. Comm. for Youth Questions, PZPR Voivodship Cttee., Warsaw 1957; Sec. Cen. Cttee., Socialist Youth Union, 1957-64; Deputy Chief Organizational Dept., Cen. Cttee. of PZPR 1964-68; 1st Sec. Voivodship Cttee., Kielce 1968-72; Deputy to Seym 1969-76; Chair. Seym Comm. of Econ. Plan, Budget and Finance 1973-74; Deputy mem. Cen. Cttee., PZPR 1968-71, mem. 1971-81; Vice-Chair. Cen. Council of Trade Unions 1972-74; Minister of Labour, Wages and Social Affairs 1974-79; mem. Council of Ministers, First Deputy Chair. Planning Comm. attached to Council of Ministers 1979-81; Order of Banner of Labour 1st Class and others.

RUDOLPH, Frederick, M.A., PH.D., LITT.D.; American historian; b. 19 June 1920, Baltimore, Md.; s. of Charles F. Rudolph and Jennie H. Swope; m. Dorothy Dannenbaum 1949; two d.; ed. Wyoming Seminary, Williams Coll. and Yale Univ.; U.S. Army 1942-46; Instr. Williams Coll. 1946-47; Asst. Instr. Yale Univ. 1949-50; mem. Williams Faculty 1951-, Prof. 1961-82, Mark Hopkins Prof. of History 1964-82, Prof. Emer. 1982-; Visiting Lecturer, Harvard 1960, 1961; Visiting Prof. Univ. of Calif. Berkeley 1983; Exec. Ed. Change 1980-84, Consultant Ed. 1985-; Guggenheim Fellow 1958-59, 1968-69; other honours and awards. *Publications:* Mark Hopkins and the Log 1956, The American College and University: A History 1962, Curriculum: A History of the American Undergraduate Course of Study Since 1636 1977. *Address:* 320 Stetson Hall, Williams College, Williamstown, Mass. 01267 (Office); 234 Ide Road, Williamstown, Mass. 01267, U.S.A. (Home). *Telephone:* 413-597-2416 (Office); 413-458-4416 (Home).

RUDOLPH, Paul Marvin, M.ARCH.; American architect; b. 23 Oct. 1918; ed. Alabama Polytechnic Inst., and Harvard Univ.; Fellow in Architecture, Harvard Univ. 1941-42; Officer in Charge, Ship Construction, U.S. Naval Reserve, Brooklyn Navy Yard 1943-46; Partner, architectural firm of Twitchell & Rudolph, Sarasota (Florida) 1947-51; architectural practice Sarasota, Cambridge, Newhaven 1952-65; Boston, N.Y. 1965-; Chair. Dept. of Architecture, Yale Univ. 1958-65; numerous honours and awards including Best House of the Year Award, A.I.A. 1949, Outstanding Young Architects Award, São Paulo Int. Competition 1954, house chosen by Architectural Record as one of fifty most significant buildings completed since 1900 1956, Arnold Brunner Prize in Architecture, American Acad. of Arts and Letters 1958, Boston Arts Festival Award for Commercial Building; Award of Merit A.I.A. Honors Award 1962, 1964, First Honor Award A.I.A. Honors Award 1964, Architectural Record Award of Excellence for House Design 1963. *Important projects include:* Good Design Exhibition (Chicago Merchandise Mart and New York Museum of Modern Art) 1951, U.S. Embassy, Amman, Jordan 1954, Art, Music and Drama Building, Wellesly Coll., Mass., Junior-Senior High School, Sarasota, Blue Cross-Blue Shield Inc. Headquarters Building, Boston, Greeley Memorial Laboratory, Yale Forestry School 1957, Arts and Architecture Building, Yale Univ., Church Street Redevelopment Project, New Haven, Conn., Tuskegee Inst., Montgomery, Ala. 1958, work at Yale 1960, Auburn 1961, and Endo Laboratories, Garden City, N.Y., Parking Garage, New Haven, Conn., I.B.M. Components Div. Facilities, East Fishkill, N.Y., Elderly Housing, New Haven, Creative Arts Center for Colgate Univ., N.Y., New Town of Stafford Harbor, Virginia 1967, Orange County Govt. Center, Goshen, N.Y. 1967, New Haven Govt. Center 1968, Corporate Headquarters and Research for Burroughs Wellcome & Co. (U.S.A.) Inc. 1969, Office Bldg. for Daiei House & Co., Nagoya, Japan 1971, Harrington Cancer Care Center, Amarillo, Texas 1978, office bldgs. in Fort Worth, Texas 1979, three apartment bldgs. in Singapore 1979-80. *Address:* 54 West 57th Street, New York, N.Y. 10019, U.S.A.

RUDOWSKI, Witold Janusz; Polish professor of surgery; b. 17 July 1918, Piotrków Trybunalski; s. of Maksymilian and Stefania Rudowski, judge of Supreme Court of Poland and Stefania Rudowska; m. 1940; two s. one d.; ed. Clandestine Univ., Warsaw 1943; Assoc. Prof. of Surgery, Warsaw Univ. 1954-61, Prof. Extraordinary 1961-70, Prof. 1971-; Consultant Surgeon and Sr. Research Worker, Madame M. Curie Cancer Insts. in Warsaw 1948-64; Dir. and Head, Dept. of Surgery, Inst. of Haematology and Blood Transfusion, Warsaw 1964-; Deputy Head Dept. of Medical Sciences of Polish Acad. of Sciences 1973-; Chair. Scientific Council to Minister of Health and Social Welfare 1970-75, mem. Presidium 1979-; Expert WHO 1965-; mem. and First Vice-Chair. Exec. Bd. 1985-; Vice-Pres. Int. Fed. of Surgical Colls., Pres. 1975-78; Deputy Chair. Polish Haematological Soc. 1966-; Pres. Polish Surgeons' Soc. 1980-83; Hon. Corresp. mem. N. Pacific Surgical Assocn. 1974, Italian Soc. of Surgical Research 1975, Polish Acad. of Sciences 1973-83, mem. 1983-, Hon. mem. W. African Coll. of Surgeons 1975, Czechoslovakian Soc. of Physicians, Surgical Section; Hon. Fellow, American Coll. of Surgeons 1971, Royal Coll. of Surgeons of Edinburgh 1972, Royal Coll. of Surgeons of England 1973, Royal Coll. of Physicians and Surgeons of Canada 1974, Coll. of Dutch Surgeons, Swedish Surgical Soc., Royal Coll. of Surgeons in Ireland 1978, Royal Australasian Coll. of Surgeons 1979, Swiss Surgical Soc. 1983, German Surgical Assocn. 1984, Italian Surgical Assocn. 1984; Dr. h.c. (Poznań Medical Acad.) 1975, (Warsaw Medical Acad.) 1979, (Łódź Medical Acad.) 1980, Wrocław Medical Acad. 1982, Edinburgh Univ. 1983; Silver Cross of Virtuti Militari 1944, Gold

Cross of Merit 1956, Commdr., Cross Order of Polonia Restituta 1979, Medal for Warsaw 1970, State Prize (2nd class) 1972, State Prize (2nd class, collective) 1978, Hon. Meritorious Physician of People's Poland 1980. *Publications:* Burn-Therapy and Research 1976, Disorders of Hemostasis in Surgery 1978, Surgery of the Spleen 1987; and 500 papers in Polish and other languages on cancer, clinical pathophysiology, burns and blood transfusion. *Leisure interests:* literature, classical music, photography. *Address:* Aleja Armii Ludowej 17 m.1, 00-632 Warsaw, Poland. *Telephone:* 49-85-06 (Office); 25-44-39 (Home).

RUDZIŃSKI, Witold; Polish musicologist and composer; b. 14 March 1913, Siebież; s. of Henryk and Maria Rudziński; m. Nina Rewieńska 1958; one s. two d.; ed. Wilno Univ. and Wilno Conservatoire and Paris; Prof. Wilno Conservatoire 1939-42, Łódż Conservatoire 1945-47, Extraordinary Prof. 1964, Ordinary Prof. 1983; Dir. Dept. of Music, Ministry of Culture 1947-48; Ed. Muzyka 1951-54; Prof. State Higher School of Music, Warsaw 1957-83; Chief Dept. of Theory of Music; Pres. Warsaw Branch of Polish Composers Union 1963-69, 1977-83; Officer and Commdr., Cross of Polonia Restituta; Special Award, Monaco 1963, First Prize, Edward Grieg Competition, 1965, Minister of Culture and Art Prize, 1st Class 1976, 1978, 1981, Prize of Chair. Council of Ministers 1984, etc.; works include Piano Concerto, two Symphonies, Symphonic Suite, two String Quartets, two Sonatas for piano and violin, cantata, flute quartet, song cycle, chamber works for piano, flute, 'cello, woodwind and percussion instruments; Operas: Janko Muzykant, Komendant Paryża (Commander of Paris), Odprawa posłów greckich (Dismissal of the Greek Envoys), Sulamita (Sulamith), Chłopi (The Peasants), The Ring and the Rose; music poem Dach świata (Roof of the World) for recitative and orchestra; Gaude Mater Polonia for solo voice, choir, recitative and orchestra; Lipce (oratorio). *Publications:* Muzyka dla wszystkich (Music for Everybody), monographs on Moniuszko and Bartok, studies in musical rhythm. *Leisure interests:* history, biography, linguistics. *Address:* ul. Narbutta 50 m. 6, 02-541 Warsaw, Poland. *Telephone:* 49 34 77.

RUELLE, David Pierre, PH.D.; French (b. Belgian) research mathematician and physicist; b. 20 Aug. 1935, Ghent, Belgium; s. of Pierre Ruelle and Marguerite de Jonge; m. Janine Lardinois 1960; one s. two d.; ed. high school at Mons and Free Univ. of Brussels; Research Asst. and Privatdozent, Eidgenössische Technische Hochschule, Zürich 1960-62; mem. Inst. for Advanced Study, Princeton 1962-64; Prof. Inst. des Hautes Etudes Scientifiques, Bures-sur-Yvette 1964-; mem. Acad. des Sciences; Dannie Heineman Prize 1985; Boltzmann Medal 1986; Chevalier, Légion d'Honneur 1989. *Publications:* Statistical Mechanics: Rigorous Results 1969, Thermodynamic Formalism 1978, Elements of Differentiable Dynamics and Bifurcation Theory 1989. *Address:* I.H.E.S., 91440 Bures-sur-Yvette (Office); 1 avenue Charles-Comar, 91440 Bures-sur-Yvette, France (Home). *Telephone:* (1) 6907 4853 (Office); (1) 6907 6152 (Home).

RUETHER, Rosemary Radford, PH.D.; American professor of theology; b. 2 Nov. 1936; d. of Robert A. Radford and Rebecca C. Ord; m. Herman J. Ruether 1957; one s. two d.; ed. Scripps Coll. Claremont, Calif. and Claremont Grad. School; Howard Univ. School of Religion 1965-76; Ga. Harkness Prof. of Theology, Garrett-Evangelical Seminary and mem. Grad. Faculty, Northwestern Univ. Evanston, Ill. 1976-; Visiting Prof. Harvard Divinity School 1972-73; Fulbright Scholar, Sweden 1984; 8 hon. degrees. *Publications:* author or ed. of 22 books. *Leisure interests:* painting, swimming. *Address:* Garrett Seminary, 2121 Sheridan Road, Evanston, Ill., U.S.A. *Telephone:* 312-866-3953.

RUFFINI, Attilio; Italian politician; b. 31 Dec. 1924, Mantua; ed. Catholic Univ. of Milan; joined Democrazia Cristiana (DC) 1945, later Head of Political Secretariat, then Deputy Sec. of Party; mem. Chamber of Deputies for Palermo 1963-; Under-Sec. in Ministry of Educ., later at Treasury; Minister of Transport 1976-77, of Defence 1977-79, of Foreign Affairs Jan.-March 1980. *Publications:* I valori cristiani della Resistenza, Fondamento e significato dell'unita politica dei cattolici. *Address:* Camera dei Deputati, Piazza Montecitorio, 1-00100 Rome, Italy.

RUGAMBWA, H.E. Cardinal Laurean; Tanzanian ecclesiastic; b. 12 July 1912, Bukongo; s. of D. Rushubirwa and A. Mukaboshezi; ed. Rubya Seminary, Katigondo Seminary, De Propaganda Fide Univ., Rome; ordained Priest 1943; missionary work in E. Africa; studied canon law in Rome; Bishop of Rutabo 1952; created Cardinal by Pope John XXIII 1960; transferred to Bukoba Diocese 1960; Archbishop of Dar es Salaam Archdiocese 1969-; Hon. LL.D. (Notre Dame, St. Joseph's Coll.), Philadelphia, Rosary Hill Coll.), Hon. L.H.D. (Coll. of New Rochelle), Hon. Dr. (Catholic Univ. of America, Georgetown Univ., Washington); mem. Comm. for Revision of Canon Law; mem. Knights of Columbus, Sacred Congregation for the Causes of Saints. *Address:* Archbishop's House, St. Joseph, P.O. Box 167, Dar es Salaam, Tanzania. *Telephone:* Dar es Salaam 22031 (Office); 68734 (Home).

RUGGIERO, Renato; Italian diplomatist; b. 9 April 1930, Naples; ed. Univ. of Naples; entered Diplomatic Service 1955; served São Paulo, Moscow, Washington; Counsellor, Belgrade 1966; Counsellor for Social Affairs, Perm. Mission to European Communities 1969; Chef de Cabinet Pres. of Comm. of European Communities 1970-73, Dir.-Gen. of Regional Policy 1973-77, Comm. Spokesperson 1977; Co-ordinator EEC Dept., Ministry of Foreign Affairs 1978; Diplomatic Counsellor of Pres. of Council 1979; Chef de Cabinet of Minister of Foreign Affairs 1979; Perm. Rep. to European Communities 1980–84; Dir.-Gen. for Econ. Affairs, Ministry of Foreign Affairs 1984–85; Sec.-Gen. Ministry of Foreign Affairs 1985–87, Minister of Foreign Trade July 1987–; Personal Rep. of Pres. of Council, Econ. Summits Bonn 1978, Tokyo 1979, Venice 1980, London 1984, Bonn 1985, Tokyo 1986, Venice 1987; Pres. Exec. Cttee. OECD; Kt., Grand Cross, Order of Merit. *Address:* Ministry of Foreign Trade, Viale America 341, EUR, 00100 Rome, Italy. *Telephone:* (06) 36911.

RUHFUS, Jürgen, DR. IUR.; German civil servant and diplomatist; b. 4 Aug. 1930, Bochum; m. Karin Engel 1958; three d.; with Fed. Foreign Office, Bonn 1955; Consulate Gen., Geneva 1956–57, Dakar 1958–59; Embassy, Athens 1960–63; Deputy Spokesman of the Fed. Foreign Office 1964, Official Spokesman 1966; Amb. to Kenya 1970-73; Asst. Under-Sec. in Fed. Foreign Office 1973–76, Adviser on Foreign Affairs and Defence to Fed. Chancellor 1976–80; Amb. to U.K. 1980–83; Head of Political Directorate—Gen. Fed. Foreign Office, Jan.-June 1984; State Sec. Fed. Foreign Office 1984–87; Amb. to U.S.A. 1987–; Hon. K.B.E., Commdr. Cross and Kt. Commdr's Cross of the Order of Merit (Fed. Repub. of Germany). *Leisure interests:* golf, tennis, skiing, shooting. *Address:* Embassy of the Federal Republic of Germany, 4645 Reservoir Road, N.W., Washington, D.C. 20007, U.S.A. *Telephone:* (202) 298-4201.

RUI XINGWEN; Chinese government official; Minister of Urban and Rural Construction Environmental Protection 1984–85; Vice-Minister State Planning Comm. -1985; Head Leading Group for Restructuring Managerial Systems of Construction Industry 1984; First Sec. Party Cttee., PLA Shanghai Garrison 1985; Sec. CCP Shanghai 1985–87; mem. CCP Cen. Cttee. 1982-, mem. Secr. of Cen. Cttee. 1987-. *Address:* State Council, Beijing, People's Republic of China.

RUIJGH, Cornelis Jord, D.PHIL.; Netherlands professor of Greek; b. 28 Nov. 1930, Amsterdam; s. of Jord Ruijgh and Trijntje Swart; ed. Univ. of Amsterdam and Ecole Pratique des Hautes Etudes, Paris; Asst. in Greek Philology, Univ. of Amsterdam 1954–66, lecturer, Ancient Greek Language 1966–69, Prof. of Ancient Greek Language, Dialectology and Mycenology 1969–; mem. Royal Netherlands Acad.; mem. Int. Perm. Cttee. of Mycenean Studies 1970–; Prix Zographos; Michael Ventris Memorial Award. *Publications:* L'élément achéen dans la langue épique, 1957, Etudes sur le grammaire et le vocabulaire du grec mycénien 1967 etc. *Leisure interest:* music. *Address:* Keizersgracht 800, 1017 ED Amsterdam, Netherlands. *Telephone:* 020-247995.

RUKEYSER, Louis Richard, A.B.; American economic broadcaster, lecturer, columnist and author; b. 30 Jan. 1933, New York; s. of Merryle Stanley Rukeyser and Berenice Helene Simon; m. Alexandra Gill 1962; three d.; ed. Princeton Univ.; reporter, Baltimore Sun Newspapers 1954-65, Chief Political Corresp. Evening Sun 1957–59, Chief London Bureau of The Sun 1959–63, Chief Asian Corresp. 1963–65; Sr. Corresp. and Commentator ABC News 1965–73, Paris Corresp. 1965–66, Chief London Bureau 1966–68, Econ. Ed. and Commentator 1968–73; Presenter Wall St. Week (PBS-TV programme) 1970–; nationally syndicated econ. columnist McNaught Syndicate 1976-86, Tribune Media Services 1986-; also lecturer; Hon. Litt. D. (N.H. Coll.) 1975; Hon. LL.D. (Moravian Coll.) 1978, (Mercy Coll.) 1984; Hon. D.B.A. (Southeastern Mass. Univ.) 1979; Hon. L.H.D. (Loyola Coll.) 1982; Overseas Press Club Award 1963, G. M. Loeb Award (Univ. of Conn.) 1972, George Washington Honor Medal Freedoms Foundation 1972, 1978, Janus Award for Excellence in Financial News Programming 1975, New York Financial Writers Asscn. Award 1980. *Publications:* How to Make Money in Wall Street 1974, What's Ahead for the Economy: The Challenge and the Chance 1983, Louis Rukeyser's Business Almanac 1988. *Address:* 586 Round Hill Road, Greenwich, Conn. 06831, U.S.A.

RUMOR, Mariano; Italian politician; b. 16 June 1915, Vicenza (Venezia); mem. of Parl. 1948–; Deputy Sec. Christian Democrat Party 1954-64, Sec.-Gen. 1964–65, now Political Sec.; fmr. Under-Sec. for Agric., fmr. Under-Sec. to the Presidency; Minister of Agric. 1959–63, of Interior 1963; Pres. European Union of Christian Democrats 1965–; Prime Minister of Italy 1968–69, 1969–70, March-July 1970, 1973–74; Minister of Interior 1972-73, of Foreign Affairs 1974–76; mem. European Parl. 1979-84. *Address:* viale Milano 74, 1-36100 Vicenza, Italy.

RUMSFELD, Donald H., A.B.; American fmr. government official; b. 9 July 1932, Chicago; s. of George and Jeannette (née Husted) Rumsfeld; m. Joyce Pierson 1954; one s. two d.; ed. Princeton Univ.; mem. 88th-91st Congresses; Republican; Dir. Office of Econ. Opportunity 1969–70; Dir. Cost of Living Council, Counsellor to Pres. 1971–73; Amb. to NATO 1973–74; White House Chief of Staff 1974–75; Sec. of Defense 1975–77; mem. Cabinet 1969-72, 1974–77; Pres. and C.E.O. G. D. Searle and Co., Skokie, Ill. 1977–85; Sr. Adviser, William Blair and Co. 1985–; Pres. Special M.E. Envoy 1983–84; Chair. Inst. for Contemporary Studies 1986–; Chair. Eisenhower Exchange Fellowships 1986–; mem. Presidential Advisory Cttee. on Arms Control 1982–86, Nat. Econ. Comm. 1988–89; mem. Bd. of Dirs. Sears Roebuck and Co., Kellogg Co., Rand-Corpn.; Hon. Dr. (Ill. Coll., Lake Forest Coll., Park Coll., Tuskegee Inst.); Presidential Medal of Freedom, Woodrow Wilson Award. *Leisure interests:* sports, history

and reading. *Address:* c/o William Blair and Co., 135 South LaSalle Street, Suite 1740, Chicago, Ill. 60603, U.S.A.

RUMYANTSEV, Aleksey Matveyevich; Soviet journalist and politician; b. 18 Feb. 1905, Mintsovo, Galich Dist., Kostroma Region; s. of M. S. Rumyantsev and E. K. Rumyantseva; m. Alexandra Mazlach 1928; one s. one d.; ed. Kharkov Economics Inst.; Commissariat of Agric., later Justice, Ukraine 1926–30; Dir. Inst. of Econs., U.S.S.R. Acad of Sciences, Head Social Science Dept., Ukrainian Acad. of Sciences 1930–43; mem. CPSU 1940–; party work, Kharkov Regional Cttee., Communist Party of Ukraine 1943–52; on staff of Cen. Cttee. CPSU 1952–55; Ed.-in-Chief Kommunist 1955–58, Problemy Mira i Sotsialisma (Problems of Peace and Socialism) 1958–64, Pravda Nov. 1964–65; Sec. Econ. Branch of the U.S.S.R. Acad. of Sciences 1965–67; Dir. Inst. of Concrete Investigations, Acad. of Sciences 1968–71; Corresp. mem. U.S.S.R. Acad. of Sciences 1960–66, mem. 1966–, Vice-Pres. 1967–71, mem. Presidium 1971–79; mem. Cen. Cttee. of CPSU 1952–59, 1961–76; Corresp. mem. Acad. Sciences of G.D.R.; Order of Lenin (twice), Order of October Revolution and others. *Publications:* (in Russian) Origin of Private Property 1947, On the Subject of Political Economy 1960, On the Categories and Laws of the Political Economy of the Formation of Communism 1966, The Leninist Pattern and the Development of Political Economy 1967, Problems of the Contemporary Science of Society 1969, Sources in the Evolution of the Ideas of Mao Tse-Tung 1972, The Main Goal of Socialist Economy 1986, The Primitive Stage of Economy 1987. *Leisure interest:* History of Ancient Russia. *Address:* Institute of World Economics and International Relations, Profsoyuznaya 23, Moscow, U.S.S.R.

RUNCIE, Most Rev. and Rt. Hon. Robert Alexander Kennedy, P.C., M.C., M.A.; British ecclesiastic; b. 2 Oct. 1921; s. of Robert Dalziel and Anne Runcie; m. Angela Rosalind Turner 1957; one s. one d.; ed. Merchant Taylors', Crosby, Brasenose Coll., Oxford, and Westcott House, Cambridge; served in Scots Guards, World War II; Deacon 1950; Priest 1951; Curate, All Saints, Gosforth 1950–52; Chaplain, Westcott House, Cambridge 1953–54, Vice-Prin. 1954–56; Fellow, Dean and Asst. Tutor, Trinity Hall, Cambridge 1956–60; Vicar of Cuddesdon and Prin. of Cuddesdon Theological Coll. 1960-70; Canon and Prebendary of Lincoln 1969; Bishop of St. Albans 1973-80; Archbishop of Canterbury Feb. 1980–; Chair. BBC and IBA Cen. Religious Advisory Cttee. 1973–80; Anglican Chair., Anglican-Orthodox Joint Doctrinal Comm. 1973–80; Select Preacher, Cambridge 1957, 1975 and Oxford 1959, 1973; Hon. Fellow, Trinity Hall, Cambridge 1975, Brasenose Coll., Oxford 1978; Teape Lecturer, St. Stephen's Coll., Delhi 1962; Visitor of King's Coll., Pres. Royal School of Church Music 1980; Hon. D.D. (Oxford) 1980, (Cambridge) 1981, (Univ. of South Sewanee) 1981, (Durham) 1982, (St. Andrews) 1989, Hon. D.C.L. (Univ. of Kent) 1982, (Univ. of West Indies) 1984, (Berkeley Divinity School) 1986, (Yale) 1986; Hon. D.Litt. (Univ. of Keele) 1981, (Univ. of Liverpool) 1983; Freedom of St. Albans, of the City of London, of Canterbury; Hon. Master of the Bench of Grays Inn 1980; Patron of Christian Unity Award, Council of Christian Unity, Yale Univ. 1986; Cross of the Order of the Holy Sepulchre, Greek Orthodox Church 1986. *Publications:* Cathedral and City: St. Albans Ancient and Modern (Ed.) 1977, Windows unto God 1983, Seasons of the Spirit 1983, One Light for One World 1988. *Leisure interests:* travel, reading novels. *Address:* Lambeth Palace, London, SE1 7JU; The Old Palace, Canterbury, Kent, England. *Telephone:* 01-928 8282 (London).

RUNCIMAN, The Hon. Sir Steven (James Cochran Stevenson), Kt., C.H., M.A., F.B.A.; British historian; b. 7 July 1903, Northumberland; s. of 1st Viscount Runciman and Hilda Stevenson; ed. Eton Coll., and Trinity Coll., Cambridge; Fellow Trinity Coll., Cambridge 1927–38; Lecturer Cambridge Univ. 1931–38; Press Attaché, British Legation, Sofia 1940–41; Prof. of Byzantine Studies, Istanbul Univ. 1942–45; Rep. of British Council, Greece 1945–47; Chair. Anglo-Hellenic League 1951–67; Trustee, British Museum 1960–67; Fellow British Acad. 1957; Hon. Fellow Trinity Coll., Cambridge; Foreign mem. American Philosophical Soc. 1965; Kt., Commdr. Order of the Phoenix (Greece); Hon. Litt.D. (Cambridge, Chicago, Durham, London, Oxford, St. Andrews and Birmingham, New York); Hon. LL.D. (Glasgow); Hon. D. Phil. (Salonika); Hon. D.D. (Wabash, U.S.A.); Hon. D. Litt. Hum. (Ball State, U.S.A.); Silver PEN award 1969, Wolfson Literary Award for History 1982; C.L. (R.S.L.) 1987; Apptd. by Oecumenical Patriarch, Grand Orator of the Great Church 1970. *Publications:* The Emperor Romanus Lecapenus 1929, The First Bulgarian Empire 1930, Byzantine Civilisation 1933, The Medieval Manichee 1947, History of the Crusades (3 vols.) 1951–54, The Eastern Schism 1955, The Sicilian Vespers 1958, The White Rajahs 1960, The Fall of Constantinople 1453 1965, The Great Church in Captivity 1968, The Last Byzantine Renaissance 1970, The Orthodox Churches and the Secular State 1972, Byzantine Style and Civilization 1975, The Byzantine Theocracy 1977, Mistra 1979. *Address:* Elshieshields, Lockerbie, Dumfriesshire, Scotland. *Telephone:* (0387) 810-280.

RUNCIMAN OF DOXFORD, 2nd Viscount, cr. 1937; **Walter Leslie Runciman,** Bt., A.F.C., O.B.E., M.A.; British shipowner and industrialist; b. 26 Aug. 1900, Newcastle upon Tyne; s. of 1st Viscount Runciman of Doxford, P.C.; m. 2nd Katherine Schuyler Garrison 1932; one s.; ed. Eton and Trinity Coll., Cambridge; Pres. Royal Inst. of Naval Architects 1951–61; Chair. North of England Shipowners' Asscn. 1931–32; Chair. Council, Armstrong Coll., Durham Univ. 1935–37; Dir.-Gen. British Overseas Airways Corpn.

1940–43; Air Attaché, Teheran 1943–46; Pres. Chamber of Shipping of the U.K. 1952, Chair. Gen. Council of British Shipping 1952; Chair. Trustees, Nat. Maritime Museum 1963–73; Pres. Iran Soc. 1979–; Hon. D.C.L. (Durham). *Leisure interests:* sailing, shooting. *Address:* 46 Abbey Lodge, Park Road, London, N.W.8, England.

RUNCORN, Stanley Keith, M.A., SC.D., PH.D., F.R.S.; British physicist; b. 19 Nov. 1922, Southport, Lancs.; s. of W. H. Runcorn and Lily Idena Roberts; unmarried; ed. George V Grammar School, Southport and Gonville and Caius Coll., Cambridge; Experimental Officer, Radar Research and Devt. Establishment, Malvern 1943–46; Asst. Lecturer, Univ. of Manchester 1946–48, Lecturer 1948–49; Asst. Dir. of Research in Geophysics, Cambridge Univ. 1950–55; Fellow, Gonville and Caius Coll., Cambridge 1948–55; Prof. of Physics and Head of School of Physics, King's Coll. Univ. of Durham 1956–63; Univ. of Newcastle upon Tyne 1963–; recipient lunar samples from Apollo missions; Rutherford Memorial Lecturer, Kenya, Tanzania and Uganda 1970; Du Toit Memorial Lecture (South Africa) 1972; Hitchcock Foundation Prof. Univ. of Calif. at Berkeley 1981; Pres. Section A (Physics and Mathematics) British Assen. 1980–81; mem. Pontifical Acad. of Sciences 1981, Royal Norwegian Acad. of Science and Letters 1985; Hon. mem. Royal Netherlands Acad. of Science 1975, European Geophysical Soc. 1977; Hon. D.Sc. (Utrecht) 1969, (Ghent) 1971, (Paris Univ.) 1979, (Bergen) 1980; Foreign Fellow, Indian Nat. Science Acad. 1980; Vetlesen Prize, Columbia Univ. 1971; Napier Shaw Prize, Royal Meteorological Soc. 1959, Charles Chree Medal and Prize, Inst. of Physics 1969, John Adams Fleming Medal, American Geophysical Union 1983, Gold Medal (Royal Astronomical Soc.) 1984, Wegener Medal, European Union of Geosciences 1987. *Publications:* Ed. of Continental Drift 1962, Methods & Techniques in Geophysics (2 vols.) 1966, Mantles of the Earth and Terrestrial Planets 1968, The Application of Modern Physics to the Earth & Planetary Interiors 1969, Palaeogeophysics 1970; Co-Ed. of Physics and Chemistry of the Earth (Vols. 1-7) 1956–66, Methods in Palaeomagnetism 1967, Magnetism and the Cosmos 1967, Palaeogeophysics 1970, The Moon 1971; Author of approximately 150 scientific papers. *Address:* School of Physics, University of Newcastle upon Tyne, Newcastle upon Tyne, NE1 7RU; 16 Moorside Court, Fenham, Newcastle upon Tyne, England (Home). *Telephone:* (091) 232 8511 (Office).

RUPERT, Anthony Edward, M.SC., F.I.A.M.; South African business executive; b. 4 Oct. 1916, Graaff Reinet; s. of late John P. Rupert and Hester A. van Eeden; m. H. Goote 1941; two s. one d.; ed. Volks High School, Graaff Reinet, Pretoria Univ. and Univ. of S.A.; Lecturer in Chem., Pretoria Univ. 1939–41; Founder and Chair. Rembrandt Group of Cos. (tobacco) 1948–; Chair. Tech. and Industrial Investments Ltd. 1950–; Pres. S.A. Nature Foundation; Chair. Historical Homes of S.A. Ltd., Small Business Devt. Corpn.; Dir. S.A. Reserve Bank, Cape Wine and Distillers Ltd.; Vice-Pres. Bd. of Govs. Urban Foundation; Fellow of the Int. Acad. of Man.; Chancellor Univ. of Pretoria; mem. South African Chemical Inst., South African Inst. of Man., South African Acad. for Arts and Science; Vice-Pres. World Wildlife Fund for Nature; Hon. Prof. in Business Admin. at Univ. of Pretoria; Hon. mem. Lesotho Medical Assen., Hon. D.Sc. (Pretoria), Hon. D.Comm. (Stellenbosch), Hon. LL.D. (Univ. of Cape Town), Hon. D.Lit. (Univ. of Natal); Decoration for Meritorious Service 1980. *Publications:* Progress through Partnership, Leaders on Leadership, Inflation—How to Curb Public Enemy Number One, Priorities for Coexistence. *Leisure interests:* research, conservation, art. *Address:* 34 Alexander Street, P.O. Box 456, Stellenbosch (Office); 13 Thibault Street, Mostertsdrift, Stellenbosch, South Africa (Home). *Telephone:* Stellenbosch 2331 (Office).

RUPIA, Paul Milyango, B.A., M.P.A.; Tanzanian diplomatist and civil servant; b. 21 July 1936, Shinyanga; s. of the late John Rupia and Lois Rupia; m.; two s. three d.; ed. Cuttington Coll., Liberia, New York Univ., U.S.A.; Asst. Sec. Ministry of Foreign Affairs 1963; Foreign Service Officer, Embassy, Ethiopia 1964–68; Deputy High Commr. in U.K. 1968–70; mem. Tanzanian dels. to UN Gen. Assembly 1970, 1972–77, 1979–80; Counsellor, Ministry of Foreign Affairs 1971–72, Dir. African and Middle East Div. 1972–74; Alt. Rep. of Tanzania to UN 1975; Amb. to Ethiopia 1976–81; Perm. Rep. of Tanzania to UN 1981–84; Prin. Sec., Ministry of Foreign Affairs 1984–86, Prin. Sec. to the Pres. July 1986–; mem. Tanzanian dels. in Council of Ministers and summit meetings of OAU, OAU missions to Djibouti and Somalia 1976; Visiting Lecturer, Centre for Foreign Relations, Dar es Salaam Aug. 1979, Zimbabwe Diplomatic Course, Commonwealth Secr., Salisbury (now Harare) Aug. 1980. *Address:* State House, P.O. Box 9120, Dar-es-Salaam, Tanzania. *Telephone:* 21085.

RUSCHA, Edward Joseph; American artist; b. 16 Dec. 1937, Omaha, Neb.; s. of Edward Joseph Ruscha and Dorothy Driscoll; m. Danna Knego 1967; one s.; ed. Chouinard Art Inst., Los Angeles; first one-man exhbn. Los Angeles 1963; produced first film, Miracle, Los Angeles 1975; major restrospective exhbn., San Francisco Museum of Modern Art 1982, Musée St. Pierre, Lyons, France 1985; first public comm., for Miami Dade Cultural Center's Main Library, Miami, Fla. 1985; Guggenheim Foundation Fellowship 1971. *Publications:* (books) Twenty-six Gasoline Stations 1963, Various Small Fires and Milk 1964, Some Los Angeles Apartments 1965, The Sunset Strip 1966, Royal Road Test 1967, Business Cards 1968, Nine Swimming Pools 1968, Crackers 1969, Real Estate Opportunities 1970, A Few Palm Trees 1971, Colored People 1972, Hard Light 1978, *Address:* 1024 3/4 N. Western Avenue, Hollywood, Calif. 90029, U.S.A.

RUSH, Kenneth, A.B., J.D.; American lawyer, diplomatist and businessman; b. 17 Jan. 1910, Walla Walla, Wash.; s. of David C. and Emma K. (Kidwell) Rush; m. Jane Gilbert Smith 1937; three s. one d.; ed. Univ. of Tennessee, and Yale Univ. Law School; Assoc. Chadbourne, Stanchfield & Levy 1932–36; Union Carbide Corpn. 1937–69, Vice-Pres. 1949–61, Dir. 1958–69, Exec. Vice-Pres. 1961–66, Pres. 1966–69, mem. Exec. Cttee. 1966–69; Asst. Prof. of Law, Duke Univ. Law School 1936–37; Dir. American Sugar Co. (now Amstar Corpn.) 1962–69; Chair. Manufacturing Chemists Assen. 1966–67; Dir. Bankers Trust Co. 1966–69, Bankers Trust New York Corpn. 1966–69; mem. Council on Foreign Relations, Public Advisory Cttee. on U.S. Trade Policy of L. B. Johnson 1968–69; Supreme Court Comm. on Judicial Fellows; Chair. Personnel Cttee., mem. Audit and Planning Comm. Smithsonian Inst.; Amb. to Fed. Repub. of Germany 1969–72; Negotiator of Quadripartite Agreement on Berlin 1971; Deputy Sec. of Defense 1972–73; Deputy Sec. of State 1973–74; Acting Sec. State Sept. 1973; Counsellor to the Pres. for Econ. Policy 1974; mem. Nat. Security Council; Chair. Council on Int. Econ. Policy, the President's Cttee. on East-West Trade Policy, President's Food Cttee., President's Cttee. on Energy, Council for Wages and Price Stability 1974; Chair. Joint Presidential-Congressional Steering Cttee. for Conf. on Inflation Sept. 1974; Amb. to France 1974–77; Gov. American Red Cross 1972–74; Chair. Bd. of Foreign Service 1973–74; Trustee, The Taft School 1957–62, Foundation for Commemoration of Constitution 1986, Richard Nixon Presidential Archives Foundation 1984; Dir. El Paso Co. 1977–83, Alliance to Save Energy 1977–; Chair. The Atlantic Council 1977–85, Supreme Court Historical Soc. 1983–, Youth for Understanding 1983, Presidential Comm. for German-American Tricentennial 1983–84, Council of American Ambs. 1983; Hon. LL.D. (Tusculum Coll.) 1961, Hon. D.H. (The Citadel) 1982; Grand Cross, Order of Merit, Germany 1972; Dept. of Defense Medal for Distinguished Public Service 1973, Gold Medal, French Senate 1977. *Address:* 200 North Ocean Boulevard, Delray Beach, Fla. 33483, U.S.A. *Telephone:* (407) 276-5939.

RUSHDIE, (Ahmed) Salman, M.A., F.R.S.L.; British writer; b. 19 June 1947, Bombay, India; s. of Anis Ahmed and Negin (née Butt) Rushdie; m. 1st Clarissa Luard 1976 (divorced 1987); one s.; m. 2nd Marianne Wiggins 1988; one step-d.; ed. Cathedral and John Connon Boys' High School, Bombay, Rugby School, England, King's Coll., Cambridge; British citizen 1964; mem. Footlights revue, Univ. of Cambridge 1965–68; actor, fringe theatre, London 1968–69; advertising copy-writer 1969–73; wrote first published novel Grimus 1973–74; part-time advertising copy-writer while writing second novel 1976–80; mem. Int. PEN 1981–, Soc. of Authors 1983–, Exec. Cttee. Nat. Book League 1983–, Council Inst. of Contemporary Arts 1985–, British Film Inst. Production Bd. 1986–; Hon. Spokesman Charter 88 1989; Exec. mem. Camden Cttee. for Community Relations 1977–83; Booker McConnell Prize for Fiction 1981; Arts Council Literature Bursary 1981, English Speaking Union Literary Award 1981, James Tait Black Memorial Book Prize 1981, Prix du Meilleur Livre Etranger for Shame 1984. *Publications:* Grimus 1975, Midnight's Children 1981, Shame 1983, The Jaguar Smile: A Nicaraguan Journey 1987, The Satanic Verses 1988, and has written articles for New York Times, Washington Post, The Times and Sunday Times, etc. *Leisure interests:* films, chess, table tennis, involvement in politics, especially race relations. *Address:* c/o Deborah Rogers Ltd., 49 Blenheim Crescent, London, W.11, England.

RUSHDY, Maj.-Gen. Ahmed; Egyptian police officer and politician; b. 1924, Menufia; m.; four c.; ed. Police Acad.; fmr. career police officer; Chief State Security Bureau of Investigations for Cairo 1976–78; Asst. to Minister of Interior for Central Region 1978; Minister of Interior 1985–86; several orders and decorations. *Address:* c/o Ministry of the Interior, Cairo, Egypt.

RUSINEK, Michał; Polish writer; b. 29 Sept. 1904, Cracow; s. of Piotr and Maria Rusinek; m. Josephine Rusinek 1932; two d.; ed. Cracow Univ.; Dir. Bureau of Polish Acad. of Letters, Warsaw 1934–39; prisoner at Mauthausen concentration camp during the war; Head of Dept. Ministry of Culture and Art 1946–48; Sec.-Gen. of Polish PEN Club 1946–73; Vice-Pres. Polish Writers Union, Warsaw 1956–60; Vice-Pres. Union of Polish Authors and Composers; Hon. Chair. Int. Writers' Fund, London PEN Club; Hon. Citizen Rio de Janeiro; Hon. mem. Brasilian Acad. of Literature; mem. Nat. Council of Culture; Vice-Chair. Chief Council, Union of Fighters for Freedom and Democracy, ZBoWiD, 1980–; Pres. Polish Centre Société Européenne de Culture (SEC) 1981–, Vice-Pres. Exec. Council 1982–; Man. Dir. Authors Agency 1964–72; fmr. Ed.-in-Chief Polish Literature—Littérature Polonaise; Literary Prize of Cracow 1934; Literary Pietrzak Prize 1976; Literary Prize of Warsaw 1986; Literary Prize (1st Class), Ministry of Culture and Art 1987; Gold Cross of Merit 1947; Kt.'s Cross of Polonia Restituta 1956, Nat. Educ. Comm. Medal, Commdr.'s Cross of Polonia Restituta 1959; Order of Banner of Labour, 1st Class 1970, Commdr.'s Cross with Star, Order of Polonia Restituta 1982, Cross-Oświęcim (Auschwitz) etc. *Publications:* novels: Burza nad brukiem, Człowiek z bramy, Ziemia miodem płynąca, Pluton z Dzikiej Łąki, Z barykady w dolinę głodu, Wiosna admirała, Muszkieter z Itamariki, Królestwo pychy, Niebieskie ptaki, Zielone złoto, Kolorowe podróże, Prawo jesieni, Igraszki Nieba, Malowane życie, Opowieści niezmyślone, Ziemia Kopernika, Dzika plaża, Opowieści niezmyślone dawne i nowe 1976, Raj Nieutracony 1979, Moja Wieża Babel 1982, Opowiadania Zebrane 1987; plays: Kobieta we mgle, Pawilon pod sosnami, Jedna ojczyzna, Dwie Ewy; screenplay for Pierwszy start; books translated into 21 languages. *Leisure interests:* chess, gardening (roses). *Address:* Ul. Odolańska 30, 02-562 Warsaw, Poland. *Telephone:* 45-03-21.

RUSK, Dean, M.A.; American fmr. Secretary of State; b. 9 Feb. 1909, Cherokee Co., Ga.; s. of Robert Hugh Rusk and Frances Elizabeth (née Clotfelter) Rusk; m. Virginia Foisie 1937; two s. one d.; ed. Davidson Coll., N.C., St. John's Coll., Oxford, and Univ. of California Law School; Assoc. Prof. of Govt., Mills Coll. Calif. 1934-38, Dean of Faculty 1938-40, mil. service 1940-46; Asst. Chief Div. of Int. Security Affairs, U.S. Dept. of State 1946; Special Asst. to Sec. of War 1946-47; Dir. of Office of UN Affairs 1947-49, Asst. Sec. of State 1949, Deputy Under-Sec. of State 1949-50, Asst. Sec. of State for Far Eastern Affairs 1950-52; Pres. The Rockefeller Foundation 1952-61; Sec. of State 1961-69; Sibley Prof. of Int. Law, Univ. of Georgia 1970-; Pres. Gen. Educ. Bd. 1952-61; mem. Asscn. of American Rhodes Scholars, American Soc. of Int. Law, Council on Foreign Relations; awards include Legion of Merit with Oak Leaf Cluster and Cecil Peace Prize 1933; Hon. K.B.E. 1976; Hon. LL.D. (18 univs. and colls.); Hon. L.H.D. (3 univs. and colls.); Hon. D.C.L. Oxon, 1962, Hon. Fellow (St. John's Coll., Oxford); Democrat. *Address:* University of Georgia, Athens, Ga. (Office); 1 Lafayette Square, 620 Hill Street, Athens, Ga. 30606, U.S.A. (Home).

RUSSELL, Sir Archibald Edward, Kt., C.B.E., F.R.AE.S., F.A.I.A.A., F.R.S.; British aircraft engineer and executive (retd.); b. 30 May 1904, Wotton-under-Edge, Glos.; m.; one s. one d.; ed. Bristol Univ.; joined The Bristol Aeroplane Co. Ltd. 1926, Chief Engineer of Aircraft Div. 1943, elected to the Bd. 1951, assumed title of Chief Engineer (Aircraft) 1955, Dir. and Chief Engineer of Bristol Aircraft Ltd. 1956, Tech. Dir. Filton Div. of British Aircraft Corpn. 1960-69, Man. Dir. Filton Div. 1966-69, then Chair. 1967-69; fmr. Dir. of British Aircraft Corpn. Ltd. and British Chair. of Anglo-French Concorde Cttee. of Dirs. (Aircraft) 1965-69; Vice-Chair. BAC-Sud Aviation Concorde Cttee. 1969-70; Hon. D.Sc. (Bristol Univ.) 1951. *Address:* 2 Glendower House, Clifton Park, Bristol, BS9 1BP, England. *Telephone:* (0272) 39208.

RUSSELL, Donald Stuart, A.B., LL.B.; American lawyer and politician; b. 22 Feb. 1906, Lafayette Springs, Miss.; s. of Jesse and Lula (née Russell) Russell; m. Virginia Utsey 1929; three s. one d.; ed. Univ. of Mich.; admitted to S.C. Bar 1928; legal practice 1930-42; mem. Price Adjustment Board, War Dept., Wash. 1942; Asst. to Dir. Econ. Stabilisation 1942, Asst. to Dir. War Mobilisation 1943; U.S. Army 1944; Deputy Dir. Office of War Mobilisation Reconversion 1945; Asst. Sec. of State 1945-47; Pres. Univ. of S.C. 1952-57; legal practice 1957-62; Gov. of S.C. 1962-65; Senator from S.C. 1965-66; Fed. Judge (Fourth Circuit) 1966-71; U.S. Circuit Appeals Judge 1971-; Trustee, Converse Coll., Spartanburg, S.C., Benedict Coll., Columbia, S.C.; Trustee Emer. Emory Univ., Atlanta; Democrat. *Address:* U.S. Court of Appeals, P.O. Box 1985, Spartanburg, S.C. 29301, U.S.A.

RUSSELL, George, C.B.E., B.A.; British business executive; b. 25 Oct. 1935; s. of William H. and Frances A. Russell; m. Dorothy Brown 1959; three d.; ed. Gateshead Grammar School, Durham Univ.; Vice-Pres. and Gen. Man. Welland Chemical Co. of Canada Ltd. 1968, St. Clair Chemical Co. Ltd. 1968; Man. Dir. Alcan UK Ltd. 1976; Asst. Man. Dir. Alcan Aluminium (UK) Ltd. 1977-81, Man. Dir. 1981-82; Man. Dir. and C.E.O. British Alcan Aluminium 1982-86; Group Chief Exec. Marley Plc 86-; Deputy Chair. Channel Four TV 1987-; Chair. Ind. TV News (I.T.N.) 1988-; Chair. Luxfer Holdings Ltd. 1976, Alcan UK Ltd. 1978; Dir. Alcan Aluminiumwerke GmbH, Frankfurt 1982-, Northern Rock Building Soc. 1985-, Alcan Aluminium Ltd. 1987-; Visiting Prof. Univ. of Newcastle upon Tyne 1978; mem. Northern Industrial Devt. Bd. 1977-80, Washington Devt. Corpn. 1978-80, IBA 1979-86, Civil Service Pay Research Unit 1980-81, Widdicombe Cttee. of Inquiry into Conduct of Local Authority Business 1985; Trustee Beamish Devt. Trust 1985-; Hon. D. Eng. (Newcastle upon Tyne) 1985. *Leisure interests:* tennis, badminton, bird watching. *Address:* 46 Downshire Hill, London NW3 1NX, England. *Telephone:* 01-435 7742.

RUSSELL, Admiral James Sargent; American naval officer; b. 22 March 1903, Tacoma, Wash.; s. of Ambrose J. Russell and Loella J. Sargent; m. 1st Dorothy Johnson 1929 (deceased 1965), 2nd Geraldine Haus Rahn 1966; two s.; ed. Naval Acad., Annapolis and Calif. Inst. of Tech.; Merchant Marine 1918-22; U.S. Navy 1926-65, Naval Aviator 1929-65, Admiral 1958-65; Aircraft Carrier Desk, Bureau of Aeronautics 1939-41, Dir. of Military Requirements 1943-44; C.O. of Aircraft Squadron 1942; Chief of Staff to Commdr. Carrier Div. 2, Pacific Campaigns 1944-45; C.O. of U.S.S. Bairoko 1946-47, U.S.S. Coral Sea 1951-52; Deputy Dir., Mil. Application, Atomic Energy Comm. 1947-51; Office of Chief of Naval Operations 1952-54; Commdr. Carrier Div. 17 and 5, Pacific Fleet 1954-55; Chief, Bureau of Aeronautics 1955-57; Deputy Commdr. Atlantic Fleet 1957-58; Vice-Chief of Naval Operations 1958-61; C.-in-C. NATO Forces in Southern Europe 1962-65; recalled to active duty to direct review of safety in aircraft-carrier operations 1967, and to chair an evaluation group in Viet-Nam 1968; Consultant to Boeing Co. 1965-79; Dir. Alaska Airlines 1965-70, Airtronics Inc. 1965-72, Tacoma Boatbuilding Co. 1980-85; Collier Trophy 1956; D.F.C., D.S.M., etc. *Publications:* articles on naval aviation. *Leisure interests:* aviation, swimming, sailing, gardening. *Address:* 7734 Walnut Avenue, S.W., Tacoma, Wash. 98498, U.S.A. *Telephone:* (206) 588-9356.

RUSSELL, John, O.B.E., B.A.; British art critic; b. 22 Jan. 1919, Fleet, Hants.; s. of Isaac J. Russell and Harriet E. (née Atkins) Russell; m. 3rd Rosamund Bernier 1975; ed. Magdalen Coll., Oxford; Hon. attaché Tate Gallery, London 1940; with Ministry of Information 1941, Intelligence Div. Admiralty 1942-46; mem. editorial staff Sunday Times 1946-74; moved to U.S. 1974; Art Critic New York Times 1974-82, Chief Art Critic 1982-; awarded Empire Grand Medal of Honour, Austria, Officier des Arts et Lettres, France, Order of Merit, Fed. Repub. of Germany. *Publications include:* Shakespeare's Country 1942, Switzerland 1950, Braque 1959, Erich Kleiber: A Memoir 1956, Paris 1960, Max Ernst 1967, Vuillard 1971, Francis Bacon 1971, Seurat 1965, Henry Moore 1968, The Meanings of Modern Art 1981, (revised 1984); contrib. to numerous books. *Address:* c/o New York Times, 229 W 43rd Street, New York, N.Y. 10036, U.S.A.

RUSSELL, Ken; British film director; b. 3 July 1927, Southampton; s. of Henry Russell and Ethel Smith; m. 1st Shirley Russell; four s. one d.; m. 2nd Vivian Jolly 1984; one d.; ed. Nautical Coll., Pangbourne; fmr. actor and freelance magazine photographer; has directed many television documentaries for BBC which have been shown all over the world; has directed the following television documentaries: Elgar, Bartok, Debussy, Henri Rousseau, Isadora Duncan, Delius, Richard Strauss, Clouds of Glory; films: French Dressing 1964, Billion Dollar Brain 1967, Women in Love 1969, The Music Lovers 1970, The Devils 1971, The Boyfriend 1971, Savage Messiah 1972, Mahler 1973, Tommy 1974, Lisztomania 1975, Valentino 1977, Altered States 1981, Gothic 1986, Aria (segment) 1987, Salome's Last Dance 1988, The Lair of the White Worm 1988, The Rainbow 1989; theatre: Rake's Progress (Stravinsky) 1982, Die Soldaten (Zimmerman) 1983. *Leisure interest:* music. *Address:* c/o ICM, 8899 Beverly Boulevard, Los Angeles, Calif. 90048, U.S.A.

RUSSELL, Philip Welsford Richmond, M.B.E., B.A., L.TH.; South African ecclesiastic; b. 21 Oct. 1919, Durban; s. of Lesley Richmond Russell and Clarice Louisa (née Welsford) Russell; m. Violet Eirene Hogarth 1945; one s. three d.; ed. Durban High School, Rhodes Univ. Coll., St. Paul's Theological Coll.; Deacon 1950; ordained Anglican priest 1951; St. Peter's Parish, Pietermaritzburg 1950-54; incumbent, Parishes of Greytown 1954-57, Ladysmith 1957-61, Kloof 1961-66; Archdeacon of Pinetown 1962-66; Bishop Suffragan, Diocese of Cape Town 1966-70; Bishop of Port Elizabeth 1970-74, of Natal 1974-81; Archbishop of Cape Town 1981-86. *Publication:* Tools for the Job (with Bishop Lawrence Zulu). *Leisure interests:* climbing, jogging. *Address:* 400 Currie Road, Durban, Natal, South Africa.

RUSSELL, Sir Spencer Thomas, Kt., F.C.A., F.C.I.S., F.N.Z.I.M.; New Zealand banker; b. 5 Oct. 1923, Waimate; s. of Thomas Spencer Russell; m. Ainsley Coull 1953; three s.; ed. Wang Coll. School; served in 2nd N.Z. Expeditionary Force, World War II; Man., Overseas Dept., Nat. Bank of N.Z. 1956-60, Asst. to Gen. Man. 1960-66, Asst. Gen. Man. and Chief Man., London 1966-76, Chief Exec. and Dir. 1976-83; Gov. Reserve Bank of N.Z. 1984-; fmr. Pres., Wellington Chamber of Commerce; fmr. mem. Dominion Exec., N.Z. Returned Services Asscn. *Leisure interests:* golf, gardening. *Address:* Governor's Office, Reserve Bank of New Zealand, 2 The Terrace, Wellington, New Zealand. *Telephone:* 722 029.

RUSSELL, William L(awson), PH.D.; American geneticist; b. 19 Aug. 1910, Newhaven, England; s. of Robert Lawson Russell and Ellen Frances Frost; m. 1st Elizabeth B. Shull 1936, m. 2nd Liane R. Brauch 1947; four s. two d.; ed. Oriel Coll. Oxford, England and Univ. of Chicago, U.S.A.; Research Assoc., Jackson Lab., Bar Harbour, Maine 1937-47; Prin. Geneticist, Oak Ridge Nat. Lab. 1947-77, Consultant 1977-; Del. to UN Confs. on Peaceful Uses of Atomic Energy 1955, 1958, 1971; Scientific Adviser, UN Scientific Cttee. on Effects of Atomic Radiation 1962-; Pres. Genetic Soc. of America 1965; mem. N.A.S.; Roentgen Medal; Enrico Fermi Award. *Publications:* numerous scientific journal articles and book chapters on genetic effects and hazards of radiation and chemicals. *Leisure interests:* statutory preservation of wilderness areas, hiking, canoeing. *Address:* Biology Division, Oak Ridge National Laboratory, P.O. Box Y, Oak Ridge, Tenn. 37831; 130 Tabor Road, Oak Ridge, Tenn. 37830, U.S.A. (Home). *Telephone:* (615) 574-0858 (Office); (615) 482-2153 (Home).

RUST, Josef, DR.JUR.; German business executive; b. 12 Nov. 1907, Bremen-Blumenthal; s. of Wilhelm R. and Maria (née Immenkamp) Rust; m. Elisabeth Dartsch 1938; two c.; ed. Univs. of Göttingen, Munich and Berlin; Assessor, Oldenburg Bar; with State Ministry of the Economy 1934; again at Oldenburg Bar 1945-48; Finance Ministry of Lower Saxony 1948; Dir. Dept. of Econ. and Finance, Fed. Chancellory 1949-52; Dir. Dept. of Raw Materials Industry, Fed. Ministry of the Economy 1952-55; Sec. of State, Fed. Ministry of Defence 1955-59; Chair. Man. Bd., Wintershall AG 1959, Chair. Supervisory Bd. 1969-78, then mem. Supervisory Bd.; mem. Supervisory Bd., Volkswagenwerk AG, Chair. 1966-74; fmr. mem. supervisory boards of various other German companies. *Leisure interest:* hunting. *Address:* 35 Kassel-Wilhelmshöhe, Kurhausstrasse 8, Federal Republic of Germany.

RUTHERFORD, Jack Dow, M.B.A.; American business executive; b. 5 Oct. 1933, Greenland; s. of James A. and Leslie (Williams) Rutherford; m. Marilyn Pagett 1952; two d.; ed. Wayne State, Michigan State and Harvard Univs.; Plant Man., Romeo, Mich. Ford Motor Co. 1952-78; Sr. Vice-Pres., Agricultural Equipment Group, Int. Harvester Co. 1978, Sr. Vice-Pres.

and Gen. Man. Components Group 1980, Pres. Admin. Services Group 1982, Pres. Int. and Components Group 1982, Pres. Int. Harvester Co. 1983–85, C.O.O. 1983, 1984, Vice-Chair. 1984–. *Address:* 207 Glendale, Bay View, Mich. 49770, U.S.A. (Homes). *Telephone:* (312) 323-8241; (616) 347-4026 (Homes).

RUTHVEN, Kenneth Knowles, PH.D., F.A.H.A.; British professor of English; b. 26 May 1936; ed. Univ. of Manchester; Asst. Lecturer, Lecturer, Sr. Lecturer Univ. of Canterbury, Christchurch, N.Z. 1961–72, Prof. of English 1972–79; Prof. of English, Univ. of Adelaide 1980–85, Univ. of Melbourne, Vic., Australia 1985–. *Publications:* A Guide to Ezra Pound's Personae 1969, The Conceit 1969, Myth 1976, Critical Assumptions 1979, Feminist Literary Studies: An Introduction 1984. *Address:* English Department, University of Melbourne, Parkville, Vic. 3052, Australia. *Telephone:* 344-5506.

RUTKOWSKI, Antoni, D.TECH.SC.; Polish expert in food science; b. 13 Nov. 1920, Poznań; s. of Witold Rutkowski and Wanda (née Pokrzywnicka); m. Zofia Kaźmierczak 1948; two d.; ed. Poznań Univ. 1948; Staff Poznań Univ. 1946–54, Asst., Lecturer in Food Tech. Dept. 1954; Asst. Prof., Dir. Fat Industry Inst., Warsaw 1954–59; Deputy Dir., Gen. Chemistry Inst., Warsaw 1960–69, Extraordinary Prof. 1961, Ordinary Prof. 1969; Head, Dept. of Food Tech., Agric. Univ., Olsztyn 1960–69; Deputy Dir. Food and Nutrition Inst., Warsaw 1969–73; with Main School of Farming, Agric. Univ., Warsaw: Head, Dept. on Meat and Fat Tech. 1973–82, Dir. Food Tech. Inst. 1977–82, Head, Dept. of Processing Tech. of Oleiferous Seeds 1982–; Chair. Food Tech. and Chemistry Cttee. of Polish Acad. of Sciences 1969–71, 1978–85; corresp. mem. Polish Acad. of Sciences 1971–83, mem. 1983–; Deputy Sec., Agric. and Forestry Sciences Dept. of Polish Acad. of Sciences 1972–77, Sec. of Dept. and mem. Presidium 1984–; Chair. Science and Tech. Council of Minister of Food Ind. 1969–81, Vice-Chair. Science and Tech. Council of Minister of Agric. and Food Economy 1981–; Expert FAO; mem. Polish United Workers Party (PZPR) 1963–; Hon. mem. Hungarian Asscn. of Food Industries 1977; mem. Exec., Int. Union of Food Science Tech. 1982–87, Vice-Pres. 1987–; Foreign mem. All-Union Acad. of Agric. Sciences (U.S.S.R.) 1984; Dr. h.c. (Agric. Univ., Poznań) 1983, (Agric. Univ. Olsztyn) 1986; Commdr.'s and Officer's Crosses of Order of Polonia Restituta, Order of Banner of Labour (Second Class) and other decorations. *Publications:* numerous works on chemistry of food products, including on vegetable oils and post-extractive oil-meals, mostly rapeseed oils and their nutritive value; 11 books and acad. handbooks, numerous scientific works. *Leisure interests:* travel, photography. *Address:* ul. Marszałkowska 9/15 m. 32, 00–626 Warsaw, Poland. *Telephone:* 25-11-61 (Home), 20-33-71 (Office).

RUTT, Rt. Rev. Cecil Richard, C.B.E., M.A., D.LITT.; British ecclesiastic; b. 27 Aug. 1925, Langford, Beds.; s. of Cecil Rutt and Mary Hare Turner; m. Joan M. Ford 1969; no c.; ed. Huntingdon Grammar School, Kelham Theological Coll. and Pembroke Coll., Cambridge; RNVR 1943–46; ordained 1951; curate St. George's, Cambridge 1951–54; Church of England Mission to Korea 1954–74, consecrated Bishop 1966, Bishop of Taejon, Repub. of Korea 1968–74; Bishop of St. Germans, Cornwall 1974–79; Bishop of Leicester 1979–; Chaplain, Order of St. John of Jerusalem 1978; Hon. D.Litt. (Confucian Univ., Seoul) 1974; Tasan Cultural Award (for writings on Korea) 1964, Order of Civil Merit, Peony Class (Korea) 1974. *Publications:* Korean Anglican Hymnal (ed.) 1961, Korean Works and Days 1964, P'ungnyu Han'guk (in Korean) 1965, An Anthology of Korean Sijo 1970, The Bamboo Grove 1971, James Scarth Gale and His History of the Korean People 1972, Virtuous Women 1974, A History of Hand Knitting 1987; contributions to various Korean and liturgical publications. *Address:* Bishop's Lodge, 10 Springfield Road, Leicester LE2 3BD, England. *Telephone:* (0533) 708985.

RUTTER, John Milford, M.A., MUS.B.; British composer and conductor; b. 24 Sept. 1945, London; m. JoAnne Redden 1980; one s. one step-d. ; ed. Highgate School and Clare Coll., Cambridge; Dir. of Music Clare Coll., Cambridge 1975–79, part-time lecturer in Music, Open Univ. 1975–87; Founder and Dir. The Cambridge Singers 1981–; Hon. Fellow Westminster Choir Coll., Princeton. *Compositions include:* choral: The Falcon 1969, Gloria 1974, Bang! (opera for young people) 1975, The Piper of Hamelin (opera for young people) 1980, Requiem 1985, numerous carols, anthems and songs; orchestral works and music for TV; ed. and recorded original version of Fauré Requiem 1984. *Address:* Old Lacey's, St. John's Street, Duxford, Cambridge, England. *Telephone:* (0223) 832474.

RUTTER, Michael Llewellyn, C.B.E., M.D., F.R.C.P., F.R.C.PSYCH., F.R.S.; British professor of child psychiatry; b. 15 Aug. 1933; s. of Llewellyn Charles Rutter and Winifred Olive Rutter; m. Marjorie Heys 1958; one s. two d.; ed. Birmingham Univ. Medical School, training in pediatrics, neurology and internal medicine 1955–58; practised at Maudsley Hosp. 1958–61; Nuffield Medical Travelling Fellow, Albert Einstein Coll. of Medicine, New York 1961–62; scientist with MRC Social Psychology Research Unit 1962–65; Sr. Lecturer, then Reader, Univ. of London Inst. of Psychiatry 1966–73, Prof. of Child Psychiatry 1973–; Hon. Dir. MRC Child Psychiatry Unit 1984–; Fellow Center for Advanced Study in Behavioral Sciences, Stanford Univ. 1979–80; guest lecturer at many insts. in Britain and America; Hon. Fellow British Psychological Soc. 1978, Hon. Fellow American Acad. of Pediatrics 1981, Hon. D.SC. (Leiden) 1985; numerous awards

U.K. and U.S.A. *Publications:* Children of Sick Parents 1966, jtly. A Neuropsychiatric Study in Childhood 1970, ed. jtly. Education, Health and Behaviour 1970, ed. Infantile Autism 1971, Maternal Deprivation Reassessed 1981, ed. jtly. The Child with Delayed Speech 1972, Helping Troubled Children 1975, jtly. Cycles of Disadvantage 1976, ed. jtly. Child Psychiatry 1977, (2nd ed. as Child and Adolescent Psychiatry 1985), ed. jtly. Autism 1978, Changing Youth in a Changing Society 1979, jtly. Fifteen Thousand Hours: Secondary Schools and Their Effect on Children 1979, ed. Scientific Foundations of Development Psychiatry 1981, A Measure of Our Values: Goals and Dilemmas in the Upbringing of Children 1983, jtly. Lead versus Health 1983, jtly. Juvenile Delinquency 1983, ed. Developmental Neuropsychiatry 1983, ed. jtly. Stress, Coping and Development 1983, ed. jtly. Depression and Young People 1986. *Leisure interests:* fell walking, tennis, wine tasting, theatre. *Address:* 190 Court Lane, Dulwich, London, SE21 7ED, England.

RUUSUVUORI, Aarno Emil; Finnish architect; b. 14 Jan. 1925, Kuopio; s. of Armas Ruusuvuori and Aune Hämäläinen; m. Anna Maria E. Jäämeri 1970; two d.; ed. Helsinki Tech. Univ.; Asst. in Architecture, Helsinki Tech. Univ. 1952–59, Acting Prof. of Architecture 1959–63, Prof. 1963–66; own drawing office 1952–; Ed. Architect-Arkitekten (magazine) 1952–55, Chief Ed. 1956–57; Dir. Museum of Finnish Architecture 1975–78, 1983–88; State Prof. of Art 1978–83; Pres. Finnish Asscn. of Architects (SAFA) 1982; Hon. Fellow American Inst. of Architects 1982; Väinö Vähäkallio Award 1955, Commdr. Order of the Lion of Finland 1983. *Principal works include:* Parish Cens.: Hyvinkää Church 1961, Huutoniemi Church 1963, Tapiola Church 1964; Printing Works of Weilin and Göös 1964–66, Police HQ, Mikkeli 1968, Helsinki City Hall (renovation) 1970, Rauhanummi Chapel, Hyvinkää 1972, Paragon Office Building 1973, REDC Building, Addis Ababa, Ethiopia 1976, Parate Printing Works 1979, Hotel Al Rashid, Riyadh, Saudi Arabia 1980. *Leisure interest:* fishing. *Address:* Annankatu 15 B 10, 00120 Helsinki 12 (Office); Vatakuja 2 C 30, 00200 Helsinki 20, Finland (Home). *Telephone:* 646 106 (Office); 692 3553 (Home).

RŮŽEK, Miloslav, PH.DR.; Czechoslovak diplomatist; b. 25 Jan. 1923, Kamenná Lhota; m. Věra Černohlávková 1949, two s. two d.; ed. Charles Univ., Prague; Local Govt. 1945–49, Ministry of Education and Culture 1949–50, Foreign Trade 1950–54, of Foreign Affairs 1954–; Counsellor, London 1954–57; Section Head, Ministry of Foreign Affairs 1957–59, 1963–66; Amb. to U.S.A. 1959–63, to U.K. 1966–71; Deputy Minister of Foreign Affairs 1971–75; Perm. Rep. to UN, Geneva 1975–82; mem. Inst. of Int. Relations 1982–; Distinction "For Merits in Construction" 1973. *Address:* Nerudova 3, 1-Malá Strána, 118.50, Prague, Czechoslovakia.

RYABINKINA, Yelena Lvovna; Soviet ballet dancer; b. 1941, Moscow; m. 1st Eduard Martzevich 1964 (divorced 1972), 2nd Jurij Fidler 1974; ed. Bolshoi Theatre Ballet School, State Inst. of Theatrical Art 1984; joined Bolshoi Theatre Ballet Company 1959; Hon. Actress of R.S.F.S.R.; principal roles: Odette-Odille (Swan Lake), Raimonde (Raimonde), Mirta (Giselle), Kitri (Don Quixote), Vanina Vanini (Vanina Vanini), Persian Dance (Khovanshchina), Zarema (Fountain of Bakhchisarai), etc. *Address:* State Academic Bolshoi Theatre of the U.S.S.R., Ploshchad Sverdlova, Moscow, U.S.S.R.

RYABOV, Yakov Petrovich; Soviet politician; b. 24 March 1928, Ruzaevka Region, Mordovian A.S.S.R.; construction engineer, Sverdlovsk 1946–58; ed. Ural Polytechnical Inst., Sverdlovsk 1952; mem. CPSU 1954; political post in turbine engine plant, Sverdlovsk 1958–60; First Sec. Ordzhonikidze Regional Cttee. CPSU 1960–63; First Sec. Sverdlovsk City Cttee, CPSU 1963–66; Deputy to R.S.F.S.R. Supreme Soviet 1963–75; Second Sec., Sverdlovsk Dist. Cttee. CPSU 1966–71, First Sec. 1971–76; mem. Presidium of R.S.F.S.R. Supreme Soviet 1967–75; mem. Cen. Cttee. CPSU 1971–; Deputy to the Council of the Union, U.S.S.R. Supreme Soviet 1972–; Sec. (for defence industry) of Cen. Cttee. CPSU 1976–79; First Deputy Chair. of U.S.S.R. Gosplan 1979–83; Chair. U.S.S.R. State Comm. for Foreign Econ. Relations (GKES) 1983–84; Deputy Chair. U.S.S.R. Council of Ministers 1984–86, Chair. of Soviet Section of Soviet-Iraqi Comm. for Econ. Co-operation 1984–; Order of Lenin (three times) and numerous other medals. *Publications include:* many articles on economic planning, natural resources supply and a book on COMECON. *Address:* The Kremlin, Moscow, U.S.S.R.

RYAN, Alan James, M.A., F.B.A.; British professor of politics and author; b. 9 May 1940, London; s. of James W. Ryan and Ivy Ryan; m. Kathleen Alyson Lane 1971; one d.; ed. Christ's Hospital and Balliol Coll. Oxford; Fellow, New Coll. Oxford 1969–88; Reader in Politics, Univ. of Oxford 1978–88; Prof. of Politics, Princeton Univ. 1988–; Visiting Prof., City Univ. of New York, Univs. of Texas, Calif., Witwatersrand Univ., Univ. of Cape Town 1967–; Visiting Fellow, Australian Nat. Univ.; de Carle Lecturer, Univ. of Otago; del. Oxford Univ. Press 1982–87. *Publications:* The Philosophy of John Stuart Mill 1970, The Philosophy of the Social Sciences 1970, J. S. Mill 1974, Property and Political Theory 1984, Property 1987, Russell: A Political Life 1988. *Leisure interest:* dinghy sailing. *Address:* 77 Overbrook Drive, Princeton, NJ 08540, U.S.A.; 21 Cunliffe Close, Oxford, England.

RYAN, Frank, M.B.A.; American business executive; b. 15 Sept. 1931, Philadelphia; s. of Frank J. Ryan and Mildred (née Showers) Ryan; m.

Jane E. Loughran 1955; two s. two d.; ed. Villanova Univ. and Lehigh Univ.; joined Air Products and Chemicals Inc. 1957, Asst. Gen. Man. Industrial Gas Div. 1966, Gen. Man. Agricultural Chemicals Div. 1968, Vice-Pres. 1971, Group Vice-Pres. 1978, Pres. and C.O.O. July 1988–; J. Stanley Morehouse Memorial Award (Villanova Univ.); Dr. h.c. (Villanova Univ.). *Leisure interests:* golf, tennis, boating. *Address:* Air Products and Chemicals Inc., Allentown, Pa. 18195 (Office); 2898 Fairfield Drive, Allentown, Pa. 18103, U.S.A. (Home). *Telephone:* (215) 481-6889 (Office); (215) 435-2817 (Home).

RYAN, Peter Allen, B.A., M.M.; Australian publisher; b. 4 Sept. 1923, Melbourne; s. of Emmett F. and Alice D. Ryan; m. Gladys A. Davidson 1947; one s. one d.; ed. Malvern Grammar School, Melbourne and Univ. of Melbourne; mil. service 1942–45; Dir. United Service Publicity Pty. Ltd. 1953–57; Public Relations Man., Imperial Chemical Industries of Australia and New Zealand Ltd. 1957–61; Asst. to Vice-Chancellor, Univ. of Melbourne 1962; Dir. Melbourne Univ. Press 1962–; mem. Solicitors Disciplinary Tribunal 1984–. *Publications:* Fear Drive My Feet 1959, The Preparation of Manuscripts 1966, Encyclopaedia of Papua and New Guinea (Gen. Ed.) 1972, Redmond Barry 1973. *Leisure interests:* reading, writing, riding. *Address:* 268 Drummond Street, Carlton, Vic. 3053, Australia. *Telephone:* 347-3455.

RYAN, Richie, B.A.; Irish lawyer and fmr. politician; b. 1929, Dublin; s. of James R. Ryan and Irene Boyle; m. Mairéad King 1956; three s. two d.; ed. Synge St. Christian Brothers' School, Dublin, Univ. Coll., Dublin, Inc. Law Soc. of Ireland Law School; Personal Asst. to Minister for Justice 1954–57; mem. Dáil (House of Reps.) 1959–82; mem. Dublin Health Authority (Chair. 1967–68), mem. Eastern Health Bd. 1967–73; mem. Dublin City Council 1960–73; Commr. of Irish Lighthouses Authority 1960–; Del. to Consultative Assembly, Council of Europe 1968–73; Amnesty Int. Rep. in Middle East 1969–70; mem. of European Parl. 1973, 1977–86, Vice-Pres. Budget Cttee.; fmr. Trustee of Fine Gael Party and Spokesman on Foreign Affairs; Minister for Finance, Minister for the Public Service 1973–77; Chair. Bd. Govs. IMF, World Bank and IDA 1976–77; Gov. IMF, World Bank and European Investment Bank 1973–77; Pres. EEC Council of Ministers of Finance and Economy 1975; Rep. EEC in U.S.A., Saudi Arabia, Kuwait, U.A.E., Iran and Bahrain 1975, 1976; Del. to Inter-Parl. Union, Iran 1966; mem. Jt. Ass. European Parl. and ACP States 1979–86; Irish mem. of Court of Auditors of European Communities; fmr. Vice-Pres. European Union of Christian Democrats; mem. Inc. Law Soc. of Ireland, Inst. of Taxation in Ireland, Amnesty Int. (Irish Section). *Leisure interests:* reading, theatre, music. *Address:* European Court of Auditors, 12 Rue Alcide de Gasperi, 1615 Luxembourg. *Telephone:* Luxembourg (352) 4398-370.

RYAN, Susan Maree, M.A.; Australian politician; b. 10 Oct. 1942, Camperdown, N.S.W.; m.; one s. one d.; ed. Brigidine Convent, Marouba, Univ. of Sydney and Australian Nat. Univ., Canberra; fmrly. worked as school teacher, later as research officer and tutor with Canberra Coll. of Advanced Educ. and lecturer in adult educ. at Australian Nat. Univ.; Nat. Exec. Officer, Australian Council of State School Orgs. and Consultant, Australian Schools Comm. 1973–75; foundation mem. Women's Electoral Lobby; Senator 1974–; Minister for Educ. and Minister assisting Prime Minister in Women's Affairs 1983–87, Special Minister of State, Minister Assisting the Prime Minister on the Status of Women and the Bicentenary, and Minister Assisting the Minister of Community Services and Health July–Dec. 1987; fmrly. Minister of Youth Affairs; Publr. Penguin Books, Melbourne Dec. 1987–; Australian Labor Party. *Leisure interests:* reading, theatre, music, travel, swimming, tennis. *Address:* c/o House of Representatives, Canberra, A.C.T. 2600, Australia.

RYAZANOV, Eldar; Soviet film director; b. 1927; studied at VGIK under Pyriev; writes most of his own scripts (often together with playwright Emil Braginsky). *Films include:* Voices of Spring 1955, Carnival Night 1956, The Girl without an Address 1957, How Robinson was Created 1961, The Hussar Ballad 1962, Let Me Make a Complaint 1964, Look out for the Cars 1966, The Zigzag of Success 1968, The Old Rascals 1971, The Amazing Adventures of Italians in Russia 1973, The Irony of Fate 1975, An Unofficial Romance 1978, Garage 1979 and many films for TV.

RYBAKOV, Aleksei Mironovich; Soviet politician; b. 1 April 1925; worked as an accountant and on a collective farm 1941–42; served in Red Army 1942–44; teacher of maths. and sec. of a komsomol in Orenburg 1944–46; mem. CPSU 1945–; engineer 1946–48; political work at Velikie Luki, Kalinin 1950–57; Second Sec. Velikie Luki City Cttee. CPSU, Pskov Dist. 1962–66, First Sec. 1966–71; Deputy to R.S.F.S.R. Supreme Soviet 1972–75; First Sec. of Pskov Dist. Cttee. CPSU and mem. Mil. Council, Leningrad Mil. Dist. 1971–; Deputy to Council of the Union, U.S.S.R. Supreme Soviet 1974–; cand. mem. Cen. Cttee. CPSU 1976–89; Order of Lenin 1985. *Address:* The Kremlin, Moscow, U.S.S.R.

RYBAKOV Anatoliy Naumovich; Soviet writer; b. 1 Jan. 1911, Chernigov; ed. Moscow Inst. of Railway Engineers; Red Army 1941–45; various orders and decorations. *Publications:* The Dagger 1948; The Bronze Bird 1956, The Drivers 1950 (U.S.S.R. State Prize), Ekaterina Voronina 1955, Summer in Sosnyaki 1964; The Adventures of Krosh 1960, Krosh's Vacation 1966, The Unknown Soldier 1970, Selected Works 1971, 1973, Children of

Arbat 1987. *Address:* U.S.S.R. Union of Writers, Ul. Vorovskogo 52, Moscow, U.S.S.R.

RYBAKOV, Boris Aleksandrovich; Soviet historian and archaeologist; b. 3 June 1908, Moscow; ed. Moscow Univ.; Dir. archaeological expeditions at Vyshgorod, Moscow, Zvenigorod, Chernigov, etc. 1932–; Assoc. Inst. of History of Material Culture, U.S.S.R. Acad. of Sciences 1936–39; lecturer, Moscow Univ. 1938–43, Prof. 1943–; Dir. Inst. of History of Material Culture, now Inst. of Archaeology, U.S.S.R. Acad. of Sciences 1943–; Pres. U.S.S.R.-Greece Soc.; Corresp. mem. U.S.S.R. Acad. of Sciences 1953–58, mem. 1958–; Bureau mem. Dept. of Historical Science, U.S.S.R. Acad. of Sciences 1957–, Sec. 1973–75; Bureau mem. Nat. Cttee. of Soviet Historians 1957–; Foreign mem. Czechoslovak Acad. of Sciences, Polish Acad. of Sciences 1970; State Prize 1949, 1952; Hero of Socialist Labour 1978. *Publications include:* The Radimichians 1932, Chernigov Antiquities 1949, Russian Systems of Linear Measurements from 11th–15th Century 1949, Handicraft of Ancient Russia 1948, Three Bogatyrs 1969, The "Slovo" and its Contemporaries 1970, Russian Applied Art of the X-XIII Centuries 1971, Russian Chroniclers and the Author of the "Slovo" 1972, Poland and Russia XVII–XIX Centuries 1974, Russian Maps of Muscovy from 15th to Beginning of 16th Centuries 1974, The 1073 Chronicle of Syatoslav 1977, Cultural Exchange in Eastern Europe in the 16th Century 1976. *Address:* Institute of Archaeology, U.S.S.R. Academy of Sciences, 19 Dm. Ulyanov, Moscow, U.S.S.R.

RYBAR, Stefan; Czechoslovak politician; b. 24 Aug. 1939, Zahorska Bystrica, Bratislava Dist.; ed. Vocational Training School, Bratislava and (later) Advanced School of Politics of CP of Czechoslovakia Cen. Cttee., Prague; worker and shift-leader, Slovnaft Nat. Enterprise, Chair. Enterprise Party Cttee. 1976; Sec. Party Ward Cttee., Bratislava 2 1978–80, Leading Sec. 1980–85; elected Sec. Bratislava CPSL City Cttee. 1985, Leading Sec. 1988–; mem. CPSL Presidium 1988–. *Address:* c/o RYC Presidium, CPSL, Prague, Czechoslovakia.

RYBICKI, Zygmunt, M.A., LL.D.; Polish university professor; b. 15 May 1925, Panki; s. of Stanisław and Maria Górska; m. Maria Warowna 1952; two d.; ed. Univ. of Warsaw; in Polish Partisan Army 1942–45; Civil Office of Pres. of Poland 1947; Scientific worker Acad. of Political Sciences 1948–50, Faculty of Law, Warsaw Univ. 1950–; Asst. Prof. of Admin. Law, Univ. of Warsaw 1959–64, Extraordinary Prof. 1964–69, Prof. 1969–; Dir. of Dept., Ministry of Higher Educ. 1963–65; Pro-Rector Warsaw Univ. 1965–69, Rector 1969–80; Under-Sec. of State in Office of Council of Ministers 1980–85, Sec. of State 1985–; Pres. Popular Knowledge Soc. 1969–77; mem. Cen. Cttee., Polish United Workers' Party 1971–81; mem. Cen. Bd. Assn. of Fighters for Freedom and Democracy; Pres. Cttee. of Legal Science, Polish Acad. of Sciences 1972–77; mem. Int. Political Sciences Assn., American Assn. for Public Admin. Sciences, Assn. du Droit Comparé; Kt.'s, Officer's and Commdr.'s Cross with Star Order of Polonia Restituta, Cross for Valour, Partisan Cross, Golden Cross of Merit, S. Vavilov Medal (U.S.S.R.) 1973, Commdr. Nat. Order of Merit (France) 1975, Commdr. Order of Henry the Navigator (Portugal) 1976, Grand Officer Cross of Crown Order (Belgium) 1977, Order of the Banner of Labour (1st class) 1977; Prize of Polish Inst. of Int. Affairs (for Econ. Admin. in Poland) 1976. *Publications:* Council of Workers' Delegates in Poland 1918–19 1962, The Structure and Functioning of Nat. Councils in the Polish People's Republic 1965, Administrative Law: Aspects of Planned Economy 1968, System of Local Government in Poland 1971, Economic Administration in COMECON Countries (Council of Mutual Economic Assistance) 1974, Economic Administration in Poland 1975, Administrative Law and Public Administration (co-author) 1984, Essays on Administration, Legal and Organizational Problems 1988. *Leisure interest:* touring. *Address:* Office of Council of Ministers, Warsaw (Office); Wiktorii Wiedeńskiej 6 m. 3, 02-954 Warsaw, Poland (Home). *Telephone:* 42-25-75 (Home).

RYCHLEWSKI, Jan, D.ENG.; Polish scientist; b. 23 May 1934, Moscow, U.S.S.R.; m.; one c.; ed. Tech. Univ., Warsaw; Dr. of Tech. Sciences 1964–65, Asst. Prof. 1965–70, Extraordinary Prof. 1970–86, Ordinary Prof. 1986–; Scientist, Inst. of Fundamental Technological Problems, Polish Acad. of Sciences (IPPT PAN) 1958–79, fmr. Head of Lab. of Math. Theory of Plasticity, Dept. of Continuous Mediums Mechanics; Co-organizer of S. Banach Math. Centre, Warsaw; Corresp. mem. Polish Acad. of Sciences 1973–, mem. Presidium and Sec. of III (Dept. of Mathematical, Physical and Chemical Sciences) 1978–80; Chair. Cttee. for Research on Outer Space; Vice-Pres. Int. Aeronautics Fed. 1982–; mem. Polish United Workers' Party (PZPR) 1952–; First Deputy Chief of Dept. of Science and Educ., Cen. Cttee. PZPR 1972–78; Gold Cross of Merit, Knight's Cross of Order of Polonia Restituta and other decorations. *Publications:* over 50 works on problems of mechanics of continuous mediums, including Plastyczność ciał o skokowej niejednorodności 1966, Niewrażliwość materiałów na zmiany dróg odkształcenia 1972, Teoria materiałów 1975; Co-author Teoria plastyczności 1962. *Leisure interests:* sport, tennis. *Address:* Al. Niepodległości 132 m. 70, 02-554 Warsaw, Poland.

RYCKMANS, Pierre, PH.D.; Belgian professor of Chinese studies; b. 28 Sept. 1935, Brussels; m. Chang Han-fang; three s. one d.; ed. Univ. of Louvain; Prof. of Chinese Studies, Univ. of Sydney 1987–. *Publications:* (under pen-name Simon Leys) The Chairman's New Clothes: Mao and the Cultural Revolution 1977, Chinese Shadows 1977, The Burning Forest

1985, La Mort de Napoléon 1986, Early Confucian Philosophers 1989. *Address:* Chinese Studies, University of Sydney, Sydney, N.S.W. 2006, Australia.

RYCROFT, Hedley Brian, F.R.S.S.A., PH.D.; South African professor of botany; b. 26 July 1918, Natal; s. of Frederick and Winifred Rycroft; m. 1st Maureen Starke 1947 (divorced 1973), 2nd Joan Stucke 1976; two s. one d.; ed. Nat. Univ. Coll., Univ. of Stellenbosch and Univ. of Cape Town; Forest Research Officer 1945–83; Lecturer in Forestry, Univ. of Stellenbosch 1945–83; Prof. of Botany, Univ. of Cape Town 1954–83; Dir. Nat. Botanic Gardens of S.A. 1954–83; Dir. Skyline Botanic Garden and Arboretum, Natal 1983–86; Dir. Herborium, Univ. of Fort Hare, Ciskei 1988–. *Publications:* Trees of the Tsitgikuma 1970, Kirstenbosch 1980. *Leisure interests:* breeding dogs, forest vegetation of Ciskei. *Address:* Little Timbers, P.O. Box 5, Hogsback 5312, E. Cape, South Africa. *Telephone:* (0020) 813.

RYDBECK, Olof, B.A., B.L.; Swedish diplomatist and radio administrator; b. 15 April 1913, Djursholm; s. of Oscar Rydbeck and Signe Olson; m. Monica Schell 1940; one s. one d.; ed. Djursholm Secondary School, Uppsala Univ.; Attaché Ministry for Foreign Affairs 1939, Berlin 1940, Ankara 1941; Second Sec. Ministry for Foreign Affairs 1943–45, Washington 1945–46; First Sec. Washington 1946–50, Bonn 1950–53; Head of Press Section Ministry for Foreign Affairs 1953–55; Dir.-Gen. Swedish Broadcasting Corpn. 1955–70; mem. Bd. for Psychological Defence Preparedness 1954–70, Bd. of Dirs. Stockholm Concert Soc. 1955–62, Cen. Cttee. Swedish Red Cross 1955–70, Council Swedish Inst. 1956–70, R.A.M. 1962–; Bd. of Dirs. T.T. (Swedish Central News Agency) 1967–70, Inst. of Int. Affairs 1967–; Chair. Int. Broadcasting Inst. 1967–70, mem. 1970–, UNESCO Advisory Cttee. on Outer Space Communications 1967–70; Pres. European Broadcasting Union 1961–64, Hon. Chair. 1964–; Perm. Rep. to UN 1970–76; Amb. to U.K. 1976–79; Commr.-Gen. UNRWA 1979–85; Chair. Govt. Comm. investigating certain arms exports 1987–88. *Leisure interests:* music, literature. *Address:* 3 Avenue Général de Gaulle, 69260 Charbonnières-les-Bains, France. *Telephone:* 78 87 05 17.

RYDER OF EATON HASTINGS, Baron (Life Peer), cr. 1975, of Eaton Hastings, Oxfordshire; **Sydney Thomas Franklin (Don) Ryder,** Kt.; British business executive; b. 16 Sept. 1916, Ealing, London; s. of John Ryder; m. Eileen Winifred Dodds 1950; one s. one d.; Ed. Stock Exchange Gazette 1950–60; Joint Man. Dir. Kelly Iliffe Holdings and Assoc. Iliffe Press 1960–61, Sole Man. Dir. 1961–63; Dir. Int. Publishing Corpn. 1963–70; Man. Dir. Reed Paper Group 1963–68, Chair., Chief Exec. Reed Int. 1968–74; Industrial Adviser, Cabinet Office 1974–; Chair. Nat. Enterprise Bd. 1975–77; Dir. Metropolitan Estate Property Corpn. Ltd. 1972–75; part-time mem. British Gas Corpn. 1973–78; mem. of Council and Bd. of Fellows, B.I.M. 1970–, Cranfield Inst. of Tech. 1970–74, Industrial Soc. 1971–, N.E.D.C. 1975–77; Pres. Nat. Materials Handling Centre 1970–77; Vice-Pres. Royal Soc. for Prevention of Accidents 1973–. *Leisure interests:* sailing, squash, chess. *Address:* House of Lords, London, S.W.1, England.

RYDER OF WARSAW, Baroness (Life Peer), cr. 1978, of Warsaw in Poland and of Cavendish in the County of Suffolk; **Susan Ryder,** C.M.G., O.B.E.; British social worker; b. 3 July 1923, Leeds; d. of Charles and Elizabeth Ryder; m. Group Capt. Leonard Cheshire (q.v.) 1959; one s. one d.; ed. Benenden School, Cranbrook, Kent; served World War II with First Aid Nursing Yeomanry and Special Operations Exec. 1939–45; Founder, Sue Ryder Foundation for the Sick & Disabled of all age groups; co-founder, Mission for the Relief of Suffering; Trustee, Leonard Cheshire Foundation; Hon. LL.D. (Liverpool) 1973, (Exeter) 1980, (London) 1981, (Leeds) 1984, Hon. D.Litt. (Reading) 1982, Hon. D.C.L. (Kent) 1986, Hon. D.Jur. (Cambridge) 1989; Officer's Cross, Order of Polonia Restituta 1965, Medal of Yugoslav Flag with Gold Wreath and Diploma 1971, Golden Order of Merit (Poland) 1976, Order of Smile (Poland) 1981. *Publications:* And the Morrow is Theirs (autobiog.) 1975, Child of My Love (autobiog.) 1986; Remembrance (annual magazine of Sue Ryder Foundation). *Leisure interests:* music, architecture, building. *Address:* Sue Ryder Home, Cavendish, Suffolk, CO10 8AY, England.

RYDIN, Bo, B.SC.; Swedish business executive; b. 7 May 1932; s. of Gunnar and Signe (née Höög) Rydin; m. Monika Avréus 1955; with Stockholms Enskilda Bank 1956–57; Marma-Långrör AB 1957–60; A.B. Gullhögens Bruk 1960, Pres. and C.E.O. 1965–71; Pres. and C.E.O. Svenska Cellulosa Aktiebolaget 1972–88, Chair. and C.E.O. 1988–; mem. Bd. Insurance Co. Skandia, Svensk Interkontinental Lufttrafik AB (SILA), ABA, Employers' Fed. of Swedish Forest Industries, Svenska Handelsbanken, Papierwerke Waldhof-Aschaffenburg AG, Papeteries Léon Clergeau SA, Bd. Swedish Telecommunications, Nobel Industries; mem. Bd. Swedish Employers' Fed., Mölnlycke, Transatlantic Corpn., Korsselbränna; Vice-Chair. Industrivärden. *Leisure interests:* golf, hunting. *Address:* Svenska Cellulosa Aktiebolaget, 851 88 Sundsvall, Sweden.

RYE, C. Richard, B.COM.; Australian civil servant; b. 1935; ed. Univ. of Melbourne; joined Australian Bureau of Statistics 1953; transferred to Treasury 1968, Asst. Sec., Econ. Branch 1970; Minister for Financial Affairs, Embassy, Washington D.C. 1975–76; First Asst. Sec. Gen. Financial and Econ. Policy Div., Treasury 1976–79; Deputy Sec. for Econ. Affairs 1979–1983; Deputy Sec. of the Treasury 1983–85; Exec. Dir. IMF 1985–. *Address:* c/o IMF, 700 19th Street, N.W., Washington, D.C. 20431, U.S.A.

RYKOV, Vasily Nazarovich; Soviet official and diplomatist; b. 1918; ed. Novocherkassk Industrial Inst.; Sec. of CPSU section in plant, Irkutsk 1941–46; Sec. of CPSU section at research Inst. 1946–56; First Sec. of Regional Cttee. of Leningrad CPSU, Moscow 1956–61; mem. of Politburo, Second Sec. of Cen. Cttee. of Turkmen CP 1963–75; Cand. mem. of Cen. Cttee. of CPSU 1966–71, mem. 1971–89; Amb. to Algeria 1975–84. Order of Red Banner. *Address:* Ministry of Foreign Affairs, Moscow, U.S.S.R.

RYRIE, Sir William Sinclair, K.C.B., M.A.; British civil servant and treasury official; b. 10 Nov. 1928, Calcutta, India; s. of Rev. Dr. Frank and Mabel M. Ryrie; m. 1st Dorrit Klein 1953 (dissolved 1969), two s. one d.; m. 2nd Christine G. Thomson 1969, one s.; ed. Heriot's School, Edinburgh, Edinburgh Univ.; army service, Lieut. Intelligence Corps in Malaya 1951–53 (dispatches 1953); joined Colonial Office as Asst. Prin. 1953; seconded to Govt. of Uganda 1956–58; Prin., UN Affairs, Colonial Office 1959–63; Prin., Balance of Payments Div. of H.M. Treasury 1963–66, Asst. Sec. for Int. Monetary Affairs 1966–69; Prin. Private Sec. to Chancellor of the Exchequer 1969–71; Under-Sec., Public Sector Group in Treasury 1971–75; Econ. Minister, Embassy in U.S.A. and Exec. Dir. of IMF, IBRD, IDA, IFC 1975–79; Second Perm. Sec., Domestic Economy Sector, H.M. Treasury 1980–82; Perm. Sec. Overseas Devt. Admin. 1982–84; Exec. Vice-Pres. Int. Finance Corpn. Oct. 1984–. *Leisure interests:* music, photography. *Address:* 1818 H. Street, Washington, D.C. 20433, U.S.A.; Hesper House, Wells Park Road, London, SE26 6RQ, England (Home). *Telephone:* 01-699 5242 (Home).

RYSANEK, Leonie; Austrian soprano; b. 14 Nov. 1926, Vienna; d. of Peter and Josefine (née Hoeberth) Rysanek; m. Ernst Ludwig Gausman 1968; ed. Vienna Conservatory; roles include Sieglinde (Die Walküre) Bayreuth 1951, Senta (Der fliegende Holländer) San Francisco 1956, Lady Macbeth, Metropolitan Opera 1959, Crysothemis (Elektra) Paris 1973, Medea, Athens 1973, Gioconda, Berlin 1974, die Kaiserin (Die Frau ohne Schatten) Salzburg Festival 1974, (Salome) 1974, (Die Walküre) 1975, Kundry (Parsifal) Hamburg 1977, Santuzza (Cavalleria Rusticana) Munich 1978, Kostelnicka (Jenůfa) Sydney 1985; also frequent appearances in New York, Munich, Milan, London, Edinburgh, Aix-en-Provence, Hamburg, Budapest, Vienna, Paris, Moscow, San Francisco, Bayreuth, Japan, Australia; Kammersängerin of Austria and Bavaria; Chappel Gold Medal of Singing (London), Silver Rose (Vienna Philharmonic), Austrian Gold Cross (1st Class) for Arts and Science, Cigale d'or (France) 1976; Lotte Lehman Ring 1979, Croix de l'Ordre de Malte, Paris 1983, Ehren-Ring der Stadt Wien 1987; hon. mem. Vienna Staatsoper. *Address:* c/o Herbert H. Breslin Inc., 119 West 57th Street, New York, N.Y. 10019, U.S.A.

RYSSDAL, Rolv Einar Rasmussen, CAND.JUR.; Norwegian judge; b. 27 Oct. 1914, Bergen; s. of Anders Rasmussen Ryssdal and Martha Seim; m. Signe Marie Stray 1954; two s. one d.; ed. Oslo Univ.; Deputy Crown Prosecutor, Attorney-Gen.'s Office 1945; called to the Bar of the Supreme Court 1948; Under-Sec. of Justice 1956; Justice, Supreme Court 1964, Chief Justice 1969–84; Judge European Court of Human Rights 1973–, Vice-Pres. 1981–86, Pres. 1986–; Commdr. with Star, Order of St. Olav (Norway); Commdr. 1st Class, Order of Dannebrog (Denmark); Commdr. Order of Nordstjerne (Sweden). *Address:* European Court of Human Rights, B.P. 431, R6-67006 Strasbourg Cedex, France; Øvre Ullern terrasse 34, Oslo 3, Norway (Home).

RYSTE, Ruth Anlaug; Norwegian politician; b. 24 July 1932, Bamble; d. of Hans and Christine Skaugen; m. Øyvind Ryste 1954; Official, then Head of Section, Bamble Insurance Office 1950–70; Sec. Norwegian Inst. of Tech. 1970–73; Personal Sec. of Minister of Consumer Affairs and Admin. 1973–75; Sec., Civil Servants Asscn. 1975–76; Minister of Social Affairs 1976–79; mem. of Bamble Local Bd.; mem. Norwegian Confed. of Trade Unions 1969–71; mem. Bd. of Nat. Theatre 1975–; mem. Cen. Bd. Norwegian Labour Party 1976–; Dir. Norwegian Refugee Council 1980–82, Norwegian Govt. Refugee Agency 1982–. *Address:* Vassfaret 12, Oslo 3, Norway (Home). *Telephone:* (02) 42 97 90 (Office); 14 18 96 (Home).

RYTKHEU, Yuriy Sergeyevich; Soviet writer; b. 8 March 1930, Uellen, Chukotka N.O., Magadan Region; ed. Leningrad Univ.; foremost Chukchi writer; works have been translated into Russian; started writing for the newspaper Soviet Chukotka 1947; mem. CPSU 1967–; Badge of Honour; Order of Friendship of Peoples 1980. *Publications:* Short stories: Friends and Comrades, People of our Coast 1953, When the Snow Melts (novel) 1960, The Sorceress of Konerga 1960, The Saga of Chukotka 1960, Farewell to the Gods (short stories) 1961, Nunivak (tales) 1963, The Magic Gauntlet (novel) 1963, In the Vale of the Little Sunbeams (novel) 1963, The Walrus of Dissent (stories) 1964, Blue Peppers (stories) 1964, Wings Are Becoming Stronger in Flight (novel) 1964, Bear Stew (verses) 1965, The Finest Ships 1967, Dream at the Onset of Rust 1969, Frost on the Threshold 1970, The Harpoon Thrower 1971, Dream in the Mist (novel) 1972, White Snows (novel) 1976, When the Whales Depart 1976. *Address:* Union of Writers of the U.S.S.R., Ul. Vorovskogo 52, Moscow, U.S.S.R.

RYUYTEL, Arnold Fyodorovich, CAND. AGRIC. SC.; Soviet politician; b. 1928; ed. Estonian Agric. Acad.; sr. agronomist, Saaremaa Dist., Estonian S.S.R. 1949–50; Deputy Dir. of Estonian Inst. of Livestock-breeding and Veterinary Science 1955–63; mem. CPSU 1964–; Dir. of Tartu State Collective Farm 1963–69; Rector of Estonian Agric. Inst. 1969–72; Sec. of

Cen. Cttee. of Estonian CP 1977–79; First Deputy Pres. of Council of Ministers 1979–83; Pres. of Presidium of Supreme Soviet of Estonian S.S.R. 1983–84; Deputy Pres. of U.S.S.R. Presidium of Supreme Soviet 1984–; mem. of CPSU Cen. Inspectorate Cttee. 1986–; Deputy to U.S.S.R. Supreme Soviet. *Address:* The Kremlin, Moscow, U.S.S.R.

RYZHKOV, Nikolai Ivanovich; Soviet party economist; b. 28 Sept. 1929; mem. CPSU 1956–; mem. Cen. Cttee. CPSU in charge of Heavy Industry 1981–; Sec. of Cen. Cttee. CPSU 1977, mem. Secr. CPSU 1982–85, mem. Politburo April 1985–; Chair. Council of Ministers Sept. 1985–; First Deputy Chair. of Gosplan 1978–82; mem. CPSU Cen. Cttee. 1986–; elected to Congress of People's Deputies of the U.S.S.R. 1989; Order of Lenin (twice), Order of Red Banner of Labour (twice) and other decorations. *Address:* The Kremlin, Moscow, U.S.S.R.

RZHEVSKY, Vladimir Vasilevich; Soviet mining specialist; b. 1919, Moscow; ed. Moscow Mining Inst.; mem. CPSU 1943; served in Soviet Army 1941–47; Prof. 1958; Corresp. mem. of U.S.S.R. Acad. of Sciences 1966, mem. 1981; Sr. Inspector of Higher and Intermediate Specialised Educ. with Ministry of Educ. 1950–53; mem. of staff of Moscow Mining Inst. (Dean, Prof., Head of Faculty) 1953–62, Rector 1962–; Pro-rector of Patrice Lumumba Univ., Moscow 1960–62; also Head of Section at U.S.S.R. Acad. of Sciences Inst. for Research into Complex Mining 1977–. *Address:* U.S.S.R. Academy of Sciences Institute for Research into Complex Mining, Ul. Volodarskogo. 38, Moscow, U.S.S.R.

S

SÁ, Angelo Calmon de; Brazilian banker and politician; b. 1 Nov. 1935, Salvador-Bahia; s. of Francisco de Sá and Maria dos Prazeres Calmon de Sá; m. Ana Maria Carvalho 1962; two s. two d.; ed. Univ. Federal da Bahia; Sec. of Industry and Commerce, Bahia State 1967-70, Sec. of Finance 1970-71; Minister of Industry and Commerce 1977-79; Pres. Banco do Brasil S.A. 1974-77, mem. Bd. of Dirs. 1987-; mem. Bd. of Dirs. Banco Econômico S.A. 1977-, Pres. and C.E.O. 1979-; Chair. Brazilian Cocoa Trade Comm. (Comcauba) 1980-; Dir. Nordeste Quimica S.A. 1980-, American Express Int. Bank Ltd., New York 1982-, Associação de Exportadores Brasileiros 1982-; mem. Int. Advisory Council Wells Fargo Bank, San Francisco 1979-; mem. Nat. Monetary Council, representing pvt. sector 1979-86; Vice-Pres. Bahia Chamber of Commerce 1981-; Dir. Brazilian Exporters' Asscn. 1982-; Pres. Brazil section, Brazil-U.S. Business Council 1984-87, mem. Exec. Cttee. 1987-; mem. Bd. of Trustees, Eisenhower Exchange Fellowships Inc.; several Brazilian honours. *Publication:* study on the Bank of Brazil as an agent of development and a factor of national integration. *Leisure interests:* riding, tennis, golf. *Address:* Banco Econômico S.A., Rua Miguel Calmon, 285, Edf. Goes Calmon, 11°, 40.015 Salvador-Bahia, Brazil.

SAARINEN, Aarne; Finnish politician; b. 5 Dec. 1913, Degerby; s. of Armas R. Saarinen and Maria Tomminen; m. Helmi Aho 1933; three c.; fmr. mason; fmr. mem. Social-Democratic Party; Joined Finland-U.S.S.R. Soc. 1940; mem. Finnish Communist Party 1944, mem. Cen. Cttee. 1957-, mem. Political Bureau 1964-, Chair. Finnish Communist Party 1966-82; Officer Building Workers' Union 1945, Sec. for Educ. 1947-50, Pres. 1954-66; mem. Diet 1962-; mem. Gen. Council of World Fed. of Trade Unions 1961-69; Vice-Pres. Finnish People's Democratic League 1973-, Finnish Peace Cttee. *Address:* Suomen Kommunistinen Puolue, Sturenkatu 4, 00510 Helsinki 51, Finland. *Telephone:* 750844.

SABA, Elias, B.LITT.; Lebanese economist and politician; b. 1932, Lebanon; s. of Shukri Saba and Guilnar Abou Haidar; m. Hind Sabri Shurbagi 1960; five d.; ed. American Univ. of Beirut and Univ. of Oxford; Econ. Adviser to Ministry of Finance and Petroleum, Kuwait and Kuwait Fund for Arab Econ. Devt. 1961-62; Chair. Dept. of Econs., American Univ. of Beirut 1963-67; Assoc. Prof. of Econs., American Univ. of Beirut 1967-69; Deputy Prime Minister of the Lebanon, Minister of Finance and of Defence 1970-72; Econ. and Financial Adviser to the Pres. 1972-73; Chair., Gen. Man. St. Charles City Centre S.A.R.L. 1974-; Vice-Chair. Banque du Crédit Populaire, Chair. Allied Bank, Beirut 1983; Chair., C.E.O. The Associates, S.A.R.L. 1981-; mem. Nat. Dialogue Cttee. 1975. *Publication:* Postwar Developments in the Foreign Exchange Systems of Lebanon and Syria 1962. *Leisure interests:* hunting, vintage and classic cars. *Address:* P.O. Box 5292, Ayoub Centre, Ashrafieh, Beirut, Lebanon.

SABA, Hanna, D. EN D.; Egyptian jurist and diplomatist; b. 23 July 1909, Damietta; s. of S. Saba Bey and Catherine Fackr; m. Carmen Sednaoui 1937; one s. two d.; ed. Coll. of Jesuit Fathers, Cairo, Faculté de Droit, Paris, and Ecole libre des Sciences politiques, Paris; Ministry of Foreign Affairs, Cairo 1942, Counsellor 1946, Minister 1952; Dir. of Treaties Div., UN Secr. 1946-50; Juridical Adviser, UNESCO 1950-67; Asst. Dir.-Gen. of UNESCO 1967-71, Alt. Chair. Appeals Bd. 1973; Vice-Chair. Council of Arbitration, Franco Arab Chamber of Commerce; mem. Gov. Bd. Int. Inst. of Human Rights; Grand Officer of Merit (Egypt); Officer of the Nile; Grand Cross of Merit; Ordre de Malte. *Publications:* L'Islam et la nationalité 1932, L'évolution dans la technique des traités, Les droits économiques et sociaux dans le projet de pacte des droits de l'homme, Les ententes et accords régionaux dans la Charte des Nations Unies (Course at Acad. of Int. Law, The Hague 1952), L'activité quasi-législative des institutions spécialisées des Nations Unies (Course at Acad. of Int. Law, The Hague 1964). *Leisure interest:* golf. *Address:* 3 boulevard de la Saussaye, Neuilly-sur-Seine 92200; Le Moulin des Roberts Gordes 84220, France. *Telephone:* 47.22.62.63 (Neuilly); (90) 72.22.78 (Le Moulin des Roberts Gordes).

SABA, Shoichi, B.ENG., F.I.E.E.E.; Japanese business executive; b. 28 Feb. 1919; s. of Wataru and Sumie Saba; m. Fujiko Saito 1945; two s. one d.; ed. Tokyo Imperial Univ.; Pres. Toshiba Corpn. 1980-86, Chair. 1986-87, Adviser 1987-; Dir. ICI (U.K.) 1985- and numerous other bodies; Vice-Chair. KEIDANREN 1986-; Chair. Electronic Industries Asscn. of Japan 1986-87, The Japan Inst. of Industrial Eng. 1982-88; Progress Prize (Inst. of Electrical Engineers of Japan) 1958; Blue Ribbon Medal (Govt. of Japan) 1980. *Leisure interests:* golf, yachting. *Address:* 8-26-38, Kinuta, Setagaya-ku, Tokyo 157, Japan. *Telephone:* 03-416-4315.

SABAH, Sheikh Ali Khalifa al-, M.SC.; Kuwaiti politician; b. 22 Oct. 1945; ed. Victoria Coll., Cairo, Univs. of San Francisco and London; Head, Econs. Dept., Ministry of Finance and Oil 1968-73; Asst. Under-Sec. Ministry of Finance and Oil 1973-75; Under-Sec. Ministry of Finance 1975-78; Chair. Int. Gulf Bank 1976-78; Pres. OPEC, Chair. Dollar Cttee. 1978; Minister of Oil 1978-83, of Finance 1984-85, of Oil 1985-; Chair. Bd. Dirs. Kuwait Petroleum Corpn. 1980-. *Address:* c/o Ministry of Oil, P.O. Box 5077, Kuwait City, Kuwait.

SABAH, Sheikh Jaber al-Ahmad al-Jaber al-; Amir of Kuwait; b. 1928, Kuwait; ed. Almubarakiyyah School, Kuwait, and private tutors; Gov. of Ahmadi and Oil areas 1949-59; Pres. Dept. of Finance and Economy 1959; Minister of Finance, Industry and Commerce 1963, 1965; Prime Minister 1965-67; Crown Prince 1966-77; Amir Jan. 1978-, succeeding his uncle. *Address:* Sief Palace, Amiry Diwan, Kuwait (official residence).

SABAH, Sheikh Jaber al-Ali al-Salem al-; Kuwaiti politician; b. 29 June 1926; Pres. Dept. of Electricity, Water and Gas 1952-63; mem. High Exec. Cttee. to organize establishments and depts. 1954; mem. Defence High Council; Minister of Information 1964-71, 1975-81; Deputy Prime Minister 1975-81; Chair. Kuwait Int. Petroleum Investment Co. Jan. 1981-. *Address:* c/o Council of Ministers, Kuwait City, Kuwait.

SABAH, Sheikh Saad al-Abdullah al-Salem al-; Kuwaiti Crown Prince and politician; b. 1930, Kuwait; m. Sheikha Latifah Fahad al-Sabah; one s. four d.; ed. Kuwait govt. schools and Hendon Coll., U.K.; Deputy Chief, Police and Public Security Dept. 1959, Chief 1961; Minister of Interior 1961, and of Defence 1965; Crown Prince Jan. 1978-; Prime Minister Feb. 1978-; Ex-officio Chair. Supreme Defence Council, Supreme Petroleum Council, Civil Service Council, Supreme Housing Council. *Leisure interests:* fishing, gardening, photography. *Address:* Office of The Crown Prince and Prime Minister, P.O. Box 4, Safat, 13001 Kuwait City, Kuwait.

SABAH, Sheikh Sabah al-Ahmad al-Jaber al-; Kuwaiti politician; b. 1929; ed. Mubarakiyyah Nat. School, Kuwait and privately; mem. Supreme Cttee. 1955-62; Minister of Public Information and Guidance and of Social Affairs 1962-63, of Foreign Affairs 1963-, acting Minister of Finance and Oil 1965, Minister of the Interior 1978; Deputy Prime Minister Feb. 1978-; acting Minister of Information 1981-84. *Address:* Ministry of Foreign Affairs, P.O. Box 3, Safat, al-Sour Street, Kuwait.

SABAH, Sheikh Salim al-Sabah al-Salim al-; Kuwaiti diplomatist; b. 18 June 1937; s. of the late Sheikh Sabah al-Salim al-Sabah, Amir of Kuwait; ed. Secondary School Kuwait, Gray's Inn, London, and Christ Church, Oxford; joined Foreign Service 1963; fmr. Head Political Dept. Ministry of Foreign Affairs; Amb. to the U.K. 1965-70; also to Norway, Denmark and Sweden 1968-70; Amb. to U.S.A. 1970-75, also accred. to Canada; Minister of Social Affairs and Labour 1975-78, of Defence 1978-87, of the Interior 1987-. *Address:* Ministry of the Interior, P.O.B. 4/11, Safat, Kuwait.

SABAH, Sheikh Saud Nasir al-; Kuwaiti diplomatist; b. 3 Oct. 1944, Kuwait; s. of Sheikh Nasir Saud Al-Sabah; m. Awatif S. Al-Sabah 1962; three s. two d.; Barrister-at-Law, Gray's Inn, Legal Dept., Ministry of Foreign Affairs; Rep. to Sixth Cttee., UN Gen. Ass. 1969-74, to Seabed Cttee. 1969-73; Pres. IMCO 1977-78; Vice-Chair. del. to Conf. on Law of the Sea 1974-75; rep. of del. to Conf. on Law of Treaties 1969; Amb. to U.K., also accred. to Denmark, Norway and Sweden 1975-80, to U.S.A., also accred. to Canada and Venezuela 1981-. *Address:* Embassy of Kuwait, 2940 Tilden Street, N.W., Washington, D.C. 20008, U.S.A. *Telephone:* (202) 966-0702.

SABATIER, Robert; French writer; b. 17 Aug. 1923, Paris; s. of Pierre Sabatier and Marie Exbrayat; m. Christiane Lesparre 1957; fmr. manual worker and factory exec.; produced journal La Cassette; Lauréat de la Soc. des gens de lettres 1961; Grand Prix de Poésie de l'Académie française 1969 for Les châteaux de millions d'années; Antonin-Artaud Prize and Prix Apollinaire for poems Les fêtes solaires; mem. l'Académie Goncourt. *Publications:* Alain et le nègre 1953, Le marchand de sable 1954, Le goût de la cendre 1955, Les fêtes solaires 1955, Boulevard 1956, Canard au sang 1958, Saint Vincent de Paul, Dédicace d'une navire 1959, La Sainte-Farce 1960, La mort du figuier 1962, Dessin sur un trottoir 1964, Les poisons délectables (poems) 1965, Le Chinois d'Afrique 1966, Dictionnaire de la mort 1967, Les châteaux de millions d'années (poems) 1969, Les allumettes suédoises 1969, Trois sucettes à la menthe 1972, Noisettes sauvages 1974, Histoire de la poésie française des origines à nos jours (8 vols.) Icare et autres poèmes 1976, Les enfants de l'été 1978, Les fillettes chantantes 1980, L'oiseau de demain 1981, Les années secrètes de la vie d'un homme 1984, David et Olivier 1986. *Address:* 64 boulevard Exelmans, 75016 Paris, France.

SABATINI, Gabriela; Argentinian tennis player; b. 16 May 1970, Buenos Aires; coached by Angel Gimenez; won French and Italian Jr. and Orange Bowl 18s 1984; reached semi-finals French Open, won Japan Open 1985; reached semi-finals Wimbledon, runner-up French Open 1986; reached semi-finals French Open, runner-up Italian Open, winner Tokyo and Brighton, runner-up French Open doubles (with Steffi Graf) 1987.

SÁBATO, Ernesto; Argentinian writer; b. 24 June 1911, Rojas; m. Matilde Kusminsky-Richter; two s.; ed. Univ. Nacional de la Plata; fmr. Dir. of Cultural Relations, Argentina; has lectured in following Univs.: Paris, Columbia, Berkeley, Madrid, Warsaw, Bucharest, Bonn, Milan, Pavia, Florence, etc.; Pres. Comisión Nacional sobre Desaparición de Personas

(CONADEP) 1984; mem. the Club of Rome, Ribbon of Honour, Argentine Soc. of Letters; Prize of the Inst. of Foreign Relations (Stuttgart) 1973, Grand Prize of Argentine Writers' Soc. 1974, Prix Meilleur Livre Etranger for Abaddon el Exterminador (Paris) 1977; Chevalier, Ordre des Arts et des Lettres (France), Chevalier, Légion d'honneur 1978, Gran Cruz de la República Española, Gabriela Mistral Prize 1984, Cervantes Prize, Madrid 1984, Jerusalem Literary Prize 1989. *Publications:* Uno y el Universo 1945, Hombres y Engranajes 1951, Heterodoxia 1953, El escritor y sus fantasmas 1963, Tres Aproximaciones a la Literatura de Nuestro Tiempo 1969 (essays); El Túnel 1947, Sobre Héroes y Tumbas 1961, Abaddon el Exterminador 1976 (novel). *Address:* Langeri 3135, Santos Lugares, Argentina. *Telephone:* 757-1373.

SÁBATO, Jorge Federico, D.JUR.; Argentinian politician; b. 25 May 1938, La Plata; ed. Univ. de Buenos Aires, Univ. of Paris; researcher, C.N.R.S., Paris; researcher in Political Science; Prof. Faculties of Econs. and Eng., Univ. de Buenos Aires; Expert UN and OAS projects in Brazil, Peru, Ecuador, Colombia and Venezuela; Sec. of State and Adviser to Pres. 1983-84; Sec. of State for Foreign Affairs 1984-85, Int. Relations and Culture 1985-87; Minister of Educ. and Justice 1987-; holds numerous decorations, including Gran Cruz de la Orden del Mérito Civil (Spain) 1985, Gran Cruz, Orden de la República Italiana 1985, Gran Cruz, Orden del Mérito (Fed. Repub. of Germany) 1987. *Publications:* various books and articles on science of politics. *Address:* Ministerio de Educación y Justicia de la Nación, Buenos Aires, Argentina.

SABATTANI, H.E. Cardinal Aurelio; Italian ecclesiastic; b. 18 Oct. 1912, Imola; ordained priest 1935; former Prelate of Loreto –1971; Prefect of Holy See's Supreme Tribunal 1983-; cr. Cardinal 1983. *Address:* Piazza S. Marta, 00120 Vatican City, Italy. *Telephone:* (06) 6984615.

SABBAGH, Hussein Rashid al-, B.A.; Bahraini diplomatist; b. 1938; m.; three c.; ed. Univ. of Cairo, Egypt; lecturer, Univ. of Cairo 1963-68; joined Ministry of Information, Bahrain 1968, Supt. of News and Culture Affairs 1970-75; joined Ministry of Foreign Affairs 1975; First Sec., Embassy in U.K. 1975-76; Chargé d'affaires, Lebanon 1976-79, Counsellor 1979; Amb. to Iran 1979-82; Perm. Rep. to UN 1982-87.

SABBAH, Michel; Palestinian ecclesiastic; b. 1933, Nazareth; ed. Patriarchate Seminary of Beit-Jala and in Beirut and Paris; ordained priest 1955; fmr. Dir. Gen. of Schools, Patriarchate of Jerusalem; priest, Misdar, nr. Amman; Pres. Frères Univ. Bethlehem; Latin (Roman Catholic) Patriarch of Jerusalem 1988-. *Address:* Office of the Latin Patriarch, Jerusalem, Israel.

SABIN, Albert B(ruce), B.S., M.D.; American virologist (retd.); b. 26 Aug. 1906, Bialystok, Russia; s. of Jacob and Tilly Krugman Sabin; m. 1st Sylvia Tregillus (deceased) 1935, 2nd Jane Blach Warner (divorced) 1967, 3rd Heloisa Dunshee de Abranches 1972; two d.; ed. New York Univ.; Research Assoc. in bacteriology, New York Univ. Coll. of Medicine 1926-31; House Physician, Bellevue Hospital, N.Y. City 1932-33; Fellow in Medicine, Nat. Research Council, Lister Inst. (England) 1934; Asst., Rockefeller Inst., N.Y.C. 1935-37, Assoc. 1937-39; Assoc. Prof. of Research Pediatrics, Univ. of Cincinnati Coll. of Medicine 1939-46, Prof. 1946-60, Distinguished Service Prof. 1960-70, Emer. 1971-; Pres. Weizmann Inst. of Science 1970-72; Fogarty Scholar, Nat. Insts. of Health 1973; Expert Consultant Nat. Cancer Inst. 1973-74; Distinguished Research Prof. of Biomedicine, Medical Univ. S.C. 1974-82, Distinguished Prof. Emer. 1982-, Univ. of Cincinnati 1971-; Visiting Prof. School of Medicine Georgetown Univ. 1983; Sr. Expert Consultant, Fogarty Int. Center, Nat. Insts. of Health 1984-86; Consultant, Surgeon Gen., U.S. Army 1974-; Consultant to Asst. Sec. for Health, Dept. of Health, Educ. and Welfare (U.S.A.) 1975-77, WHO Advisory Panel 1975-; developer of oral polio vaccine; Medical Corps U.S. Army, Second World War; mem. U.S. Army Medical Research and Devt. Advisory Panel 1974-79, Advisory Panel on Medical Research, Pan American Health Org. (Washington D.C.) 1973-76; mem. Nat. Acad. of Sciences (U.S.A.); Fellow A.A.A.S.; hon. mem. numerous acads. and socs.; numerous hon. degrees; Hon. Fellow, Royal Soc. of Health, London; Int. Antonio Feltrinelli Prize 1964, Lasker Award 1965, Royal Soc. of Health Gold Medal 1969, Nat. Medal of Science (U.S.A.) 1971, Distinguished Civilian Service Medal, U.S. Army 1973, Statesman in Medicine Award 1973, Medal of Liberty 1986, Presidential Medal of Freedom 1986, Order of Friendship Among Peoples, U.S.S.R. 1986, and numerous awards and honours for work in medical research. *Leisure interests:* foreign affairs, music, art, philosophy. *Address:* Sutton Towers, Apartment 1001, 3101 New Mexico Avenue, N.W., Washington, D.C. 20016, U.S.A. (Home). *Telephone:* (202) 363-8066 (Home).

SABIROVA, Malika Abdurakhmanovna; Soviet ballerina; b. 1942, Tadzhikistan; ed. Leningrad Vaganova Choreographic School; soloist with Tadzhik S. Aini Opera and Ballet Theatre 1961-; numerous guest performances abroad; Silver Medal, Varna 1964; First Prize and Gold Medal in first int. Ballet Competition in Moscow 1957; Rudaki State Prize of the Tadzhik S.S.R. 1967; Lenin Komsomol Prize 1970; People's Artist of the U.S.S.R. 1974.

SABISTON, David Coston, Jr., M.D.; American professor of surgery; b. 4 Oct. 1924, Onslow County, N.C.; s. of David Coston and Marie (Jackson) Sabiston; m. Agnes Barden 1955; three d.; ed. Univ. of N.C. and Johns Hopkins Univ. School of Medicine; Intern, Asst. Resident, Chief Resident in Surgery, Johns Hopkins Hospital 1947-53; Asst. Prof., Assoc. Prof., Prof. of Surgery, Johns Hopkins Univ. School of Medicine 1953-64; Howard Hughes Investigator 1955-61; James Buchanan Duke Prof. of Surgery and Chair. of Dept., Duke Univ. Medical Center 1964-; Fulbright Research Scholar, Univ. of Oxford 1961; Research Assoc. Hosp. for Sick Children, London 1961; mem. or fellow of numerous professional orgs.; Hon. mem. Colombian Surgical Soc., German Soc. for Surgery, Japanese Coll. of Surgeons; Hon. F.R.C.S.; Hon. F.R.C.S.E., F.R.A.C.S.; Hon. Fellow, Asociación de Cirugía del Litoral Argentino, Brazilian Coll. of Surgeons, Royal Coll. of Physicians and Surgeons of Canada; several achievement awards. *Publications:* Gibbon's Surgery of the Chest (Co-Ed.) 1969, Textbook of Surgery (Ed.) 1972, Essentials of Surgery (Ed.). *Address:* Duke University Medical Center, Durham, N.C. 27710 (Office); 1528 Pinecrest Road, Durham, N.C. 27705, U.S.A. (Home). *Telephone:* 919-684-2831 (Office).

SABOURET, Yves Marie Georges; French civil servant; b. 15 April 1936, Paris; s. of Henri and Colette (née Anthoine) Sabouret; m. Anne de Caumont la Force 1965; one s. two d.; ed. Ecole Nat. d'Admin.; Inspecteur des finances 1964-81; technical counsellor, Office of Minister of Supply and Housing 1968-69; Dir. Office of Minister of Labour, Employment and Population 1969-72; Counsellor for Social and Cultural Affairs to Prime Minister Pierre Messmer 1972-74; Conseiller gén., Côtes du Nord (Canton de Matignon) 1973-; Pres. Société de développement régional de la Bretagne 1977-; Vice-Pres., Société Matra 1979-; Dir.-Gen. Hachette 1981-87, Vice-Pres. 1987-; Pres. Atlas Copco France 1984-. *Address:* Atlas Copco France, 326 rue du Général Leclerc, BP 11, 95130 Franconville, France.

SABOURIN, Louis, LL.L., PH.D., F.R.S.C.; Canadian academic; b. 1 Dec. 1935, Quebec City; s. of Rolland Sabourin and Valeda Caza; m. Agathe Lacerte 1959; one s. two d.; ed. Univ. of Ottawa, Univ. of Paris, France, Institut d'Etudes Politiques de Paris, France, Columbia Univ., U.S.A.; Prof. Dir. Dept. of Political Science, Univ. of Ottawa, Dean of Faculty of Social Science; Founder and Dir. Inst. of Int. Co-operation and Devt., Visiting Sr. Research Fellow Jesus Coll., Oxford, and Queen Elizabeth House, England 1974-75; Pres. OECD Devt. Centre, Paris 1977-82; Prof. Int. Economic Orgs., Ecole Nationale d'Administration Publique, Univ. of Quebec 1983-, Dir. Groupe d'Etude, de Recherche et de Formation Internationales 1983-; Visiting Prof. University of Paris (Sorbonne) 1982; founding mem. Asia-Pacific Foundation, Montreal Council of Foreign Relations, Pontifical Comm. on Justice and Peace; Ford Int. Fellow 1962, Canada Council Scholar 1963. *Publications:* Le système politique du Canada 1969, Dualité culturelle dans les activités internationales du Canada 1970, Canadian Federalism and International Organizations 1971, Le Canada et le développement international 1972, Allier la théorie à la pratique: le développement de la Chine nouvelle 1973, International Economic Development: Theories, Methods and Prospects 1973, The Challenge of the Less Developed Countries 1981, La crise économique: contraintes et effets de l'interdépendance pour le Canada 1984, numerous articles. *Leisure interests:* music, travel, wine-tasting (Grand officier du Tastevin), skiing, tennis, cycling. *Address:* Groupe d'Etude, de Recherche et de Formation Internationales (GERFI), 4835 Christophe Colomb, Montreal, Quebec (Office); 35 Terrasse Les Hautvilliers, Outremont, Quebec, Canada (Home). *Telephone:* (514) 522-3641 (Office); (514) 271-3496 (Home).

SABRI, Wing-Commdr. Ali; Egyptian air force officer and politician; b. 30 Aug. 1920; ed. Mil. Acad. and Air Force Acad.; fought in Palestine War 1948; Minister for Presidential Affairs, Egypt 1957-58, U.A.R. 1958-62; Pres. Exec. Council 1962-64, Prime Minister 1964-65, Vice-Pres. of Repub. 1965-67; Sec.-Gen. Arab Socialist Union 1965-67, 1968-70; Deputy Prime Minister and Minister of Local Govt. June-Oct. 1967; Resident Minister for Suez Canal Zone 1967-68; Vice-Pres. of Egypt 1970-71; charged with treason and sentenced to death Dec. 1971; sentence later commuted to life imprisonment; released May 1981.

SACHER, Paul; Swiss musician; b. 28 April 1906, Basel; m. Maja Stehlin 1934; ed. Univ. and Conservatoire of Basel; founder of Basel Chamber Orchestra 1926, with Chamber Choir 1928; founder of Schola Cantorum Basiliensis 1933; conductor of Collegium Musicum Zürich 1941-; Dir. Basel Acad. of Music 1954-69; constituted Paul Sacher Foundation 1973, containing musical autographs and archives; has conducted in almost all European countries; has been responsible for many first performances of musical works and commissioned works by Bartók, Britten, Henze, Hindemith, Honegger, Martín, Martinu, Strauss and Stravinsky; Hon. Pres. Asscn. of Swiss Musicians; Hon. mem. I.S.C.M.; Corresp. mem. Bayerische Akad. der Schönen Künste; Dr. Phil. h.c. of Basel Univ., Hon. D.Mus. (Oxford, Birkbeck Coll.) 1988; Schönberg Medal 1953; Mozart Medal 1956, Litteris et artibus Medal 1st Class (Vienna) 1972; Kunstpreis der Stadt Basel 1972; Béla Bartók Memorial Medal 1981; Gold Medal for Cultural Merit, Canton of Zürich 1981; Officier de l'Ordre des Arts et des Lettres 1984, Commendatore, Ordine al Merito (Italy) 1985, Officier, Légion d'honneur. *Publications:* Articles in reports of Basel Chamber Orchestra, and book on Adolf Hamm (organist). *Leisure interests:* trees, gardening, books. *Address:* Schönenberg, 4133 Pratteln BL, Basel, Switzerland. *Telephone:* 061-815100.

SACHS, Robert Green, PH.D.; American professor of physics; b. 4 May 1916, Hagerstown, Md.; s. of Harry M. and Anna (Green) Sachs; m. 1st Selma Solomon 1941, 2nd Jean K. Woolf, 3rd Carolyn L. Wolf 1968; two s. three d., one step s. two step d.; ed. Baltimore City Coll., and Johns Hopkins Univ.; Research Fellow, George Washington Univ. 1939-41, and Lecturer, Univ. of Calif. (Berkeley) 1941; Instructor, Purdue Univ. 1941-43; Section Chief, Ballistic Research Lab. Aberdeen (Md.) Proving Ground 1943-46; Dir. Theoretical Physics Div., Argonne Nat. Lab. 1946-47; Assoc. Prof. of Physics, Univ. of Wisconsin 1947-48, Prof. 1948-64; Assoc. Dir. Argonne Nat. Lab. 1964-68; Prof. of Physics, Univ. of Chicago 1964-86, Prof. Emer. 1986-, Dir. Enrico Fermi Inst. 1968-73, 1983-86; Vice-Pres. Chair. A.A.A.S., Physics Section 1970-71; Dir. Argonne Nat. Lab. 1973-79; Visiting Prof., Princeton Univ. 1955-56, Univ. of Paris 1959-60, Tohoku Univ., Japan Sept.-Nov. 1974; mem. N.A.S., Chair. Physics Section 1977-80, Chair. Class 1 (Mathematical and Physical Sciences) 1980-83; Fellow, American Acad. of Arts and Sciences, Chair. Midwest Center Council and Vice-Pres. 1980-83; Guggenheim Fellowship 1959-60; Hon. D.Sc. (Purdue Univ.) 1967, (Univ. of Ill.) 1977, (Elmhurst Coll.) 1987. *Publications:* Nuclear Theory 1953, National Energy Issues—How Do We Decide? 1980, The Nuclear Chain Reaction—Forty Years Later 1984, The Physics of Time Reversal 1987, numerous articles in scientific journals. *Leisure interest:* sailing. *Address:* The Enrico Fermi Institute, Univ. of Chicago, 5630 South Ellis Avenue, Chicago, Ill. 60637; 5490 South Shore Drive, Chicago, Ill. 60615, U.S.A. (Home). *Telephone:* (312) 702-7478 (Office); (312) 752-2077 (Home).

SACKS, Oliver Wolf, B.M., B.CH.; British neurologist and writer; b. 9 July 1933, London; s. of Dr. Samuel Sacks and Dr. Muriel Elsie (Landau) Sacks; ed. St. Paul's School, London and Queen's Coll., Oxford; Resident, Univ. of Calif., L.A. 1962-65; Consultant Neurologist, Bronx State Hosp., New York 1965-, Beth Abraham Hosp., Bronx 1965-, Headache Unit, Montefiore Hosp., Bronx 1966-68, several clinics and homes for the aged and chronically ill, New York 1966-; Consultant Neurologist and mem. Medical Advisory Bd., Gilles de la Tourette Syndrome Asscn., New York 1974-; Instructor in Neurology, Albert Einstein Coll. of Medicine, Bronx, New York 1966-75, Asst. Clinical Prof. of Neurology 1975-78, Assoc. Clinical Prof. 1978-85, Clinical Prof. 1985-; Hawthornden Prize (for Awakenings) 1974. *Publications:* Migraine 1970, Awakenings 1973, A Leg to Stand On 1984, The Man Who Mistook His Wife For A Hat 1985, Seeing Voices: A Journey Into The World of the Deaf 1989. *Address:* 119 Horton Street, City Island, Bronx, New York, N.Y. 10464, U.S.A. *Telephone:* (212) 885-2068.

SADANAGA, Ryoichi, D.SC.; Japanese mineralogist and crystallographer; b. 25 June 1920, Osaka; m. Sakiko Iwata 1945; two d.; ed. Univ. of Tokyo; Prof. of Mineralogy, Univ. of Tokyo 1959-81, Prof. Emer. 1981-; mem. Japan Acad. 1981-. *Publication:* Introduction to Crystallography 1986. *Address:* 4-1-4 Suimeidai, Kawanishi-shi, Hyogo-ken, 666-01 Japan. *Telephone:* (0727) 92 5100.

SADDHATISSA, Ven. Hammalava, M.A., PH.D., D.LITT.; British professor of Pali and Buddhist philosophy (retd.); b. 28 May 1914, Ceylon (Sri Lanka); s. of Bandara and Ukkumenike Mapa Banneheka; unmarried; ed. Vidyodaya Coll., Benares Hindu Univ., School of Oriental & African Studies, London and Univ. of Edinburgh; Prin., Vikramasila Coll. Sri Lanka 1940-44; Sr. Lecturer in Pali, Mahabodhi Coll., Sarnath, India 1950-53; Prof. of Pali, Benares Hindu Univ. 1956-57; Head, London Buddhist Vihara, London 1957-; lecturer, Univ. of London 1958-60; Prof. of Pali and Buddhist Philosophy, Univ. of Toronto 1966-69; Visiting Lecturer, Univ. of Oxford 1973; lecture tours in Europe, U.S.A., Japan, Korea, India; est. Theravada Centres in Europe and England; Pres. British Mahabodi Soc.; Vice-Pres., Pali Text Soc., London; Patron, Council of World Religions, N.Y.; Hon. D.Litt. (Kelaniya Univ.) 1979, (Jayavardhanapura Univ.) 1981, (Peradeniya Univ.) 1981. *Publications include:* Buddhist Ethics 1970, The Buddha's Way 1971, The Life of the Buddha 1976; translations, critical editions of texts etc. *Leisure interests:* reading religious books and philosophy. *Address:* 5 Heathfield Gardens, London, W4 4JU, England. *Telephone:* 01-995 1711.

SADIE, Stanley John, C.B.E., M.A., PH.D., MUS.B.; British writer on music; b. 30 Oct. 1930, Wembley; s. of David Sadie and Deborah Sadie (née Simons); m. 1st Adèle Bloom 1953 (died 1978), two s. one d.; m. 2nd Julie Anne McCornack Vertrees, one s. one d.; ed. St. Paul's School, London, Gonville and Caius Coll., Cambridge; Prof. Trinity Coll. of Music 1957-65; Music Critic, The Times 1964-81; Ed., The Musical Times 1967-87, New Grove Dictionary of Music and Musicians, Master Musicians series 1976-; Music Consultant to Man and Music (Granada TV series) 1984-; broadcaster on musical subjects; Ed. of 18th-century music; mem. Critics' Circle, Int. Musicological Soc. (mem. Directorium), American Musicological Soc., Royal Musical Asscn., (Vice-Pres.), Hon. D.Litt. (Leicester) 1981; Hon. R.A.M. *Publications:* Handel 1962, Mozart 1966, The Pan Book of Opera/The Opera Guide (with A. Jacobs) 1964, Beethoven 1967, Handel 1968, Handel Concertos 1972, The New Grove Dictionary of Music and Musicians, 20 vols. (Ed.) 1980, Mozart (The New Grove) 1982, The New Grove Dictionary of Musical Instruments, 3 Vols. (Ed.) 1984, The Cambridge Music Guide (with A. Latham) 1985, Mozart Symphonies 1986, The New Grove Dictionary of American Music, 4 Vols. (Co-Ed.) 1986, The Grove Concise Dictionary

of Music 1988, and contribs. to various music periodicals and journals. *Leisure interests:* watching cricket, drinking (coffee, wine), canal boating. *Address:* 12 Lyndhurst Road, London, NW3 5NL, England. *Telephone:* 01-435 2482.

SADIK, Nafis, M.D.; Pakistani official; b. 18 Aug. 1929, Jaunpur, India; d. of Iffat Ara and Mohammad Shoaib; m. Azhar Sadik 1954; three c. and two adopted c.; ed. Loretto Coll. Calcutta, Calcutta Medical Coll., Dow Medical Coll. Karachi and Johns Hopkins Univ.; Intern, Gynaecology and Obstetrics, City Hosp., Baltimore, Md. 1952-54; civilian medical officer in charge of women's and children's wards in various Pakistani armed forces hosps. 1954-63; Resident, Physiology, Queens Univ., Kingston, Ont. 1958; Head, Health Section, Planning Comm., on Health and Family Planning, Pakistan 1964; Dir. of Planning and Training, Pakistan Cen. Family Planning Council 1966-68, Deputy Dir.-Gen. 1968-70, Dir.-Gen. 1970-71; Tech. Adviser, UN Population Fund (UNFPA) 1971-72, Chief, Programme Div. 1973-77, Asst. Exec. Dir. 1977-87, Exec. Dir. UNFPA 1987-; Fellow ad eundem, Royal Coll. of Obstetricians and Gynaecologists; Hugh Moore Award 1976. *Publications:* Population: National Family Planning Programme in Pakistan 1968, Population: the UNFPA Experience (ed.) 1984; articles in professional journals. *Leisure interests:* bridge, reading, theatre. *Address:* United Nations Population Fund, 220 East 42nd Street, New York, N.Y. 10017, U.S.A.

SADLI, Mohammad, M.SC., PH.D.; Indonesian politician; b. 10 June 1922; m. Saparinah Subali 1954; ed. Univs. of Gadjah Mada and Indonesia, Massachusetts Inst. of Tech., Univ. of California (Berkeley) and Harvard Univ.; lecturer, later Prof. of Econs., Univ. of Indonesia 1957, 1978-, Army Staff Coll. 1958-65, Navy Staff Coll. 1958-65; Dir. Inst. of Econ. and Social Research, Faculty of Econs., Univ. of Indonesia 1957-63; Asst. to Pres., Univ. of Indonesia 1963-64; mem. Gov. Council, UN Asian Inst. of Devt. and Planning 1963-64; Chair. Indonesian Economists Assocn. 1966-72; Chair. Tech. Cttee. for Foreign Investment 1967-73; Minister of Manpower 1971-73, of Mines 1973-78; Chair. Bd. of Govt. Commrs. PERTAMINA State Oil Co. 1973-78; Adviser, Bapindo (State Devt. Bank) 1978-; Assoc., Faculty, Lemhamas (Nat. Defence Inst.) 1978-; Chair. Bd., P.T. Aneka Tambang (state mining co.) 1979-; Assoc., P.T. Indoconsult 1979-; mem. UN Group on Multinat. Cos. 1973-74. *Leisure interests:* reading, golf, bowling. *Address:* Universitas Indonesia, Salemba Raya 4, Jakarta (Office); Brawijaya IV, 24 Kebayoran Baru, Jakarta-Selatan, Indonesia (Home). *Telephone:* 772599 (Home).

SADOVE, A. Robert, PH.D.; American international finance official; b. 8 Sept. 1921, Lake Placid, N.Y.; m.; one s. three d.; ed. Harvard Univ.; Staff economist, Gass, Bell and Associates (Consulting Economists) 1950-56; Adviser, German-Israel Reparations Mission, Cologne 1952-53; Industrial Devt. Adviser, Govt. of Israel 1953-54; Asst. Prof. of Econs., George Washington Univ. 1954-56; Economist, Transportation Div., Public Utilities Div. and Econs. Dept. IBRD 1956-62, Econ. Adviser Projects Dept. 1962-68; Dir. Transportation Projects Dept. and Acting Dir. Tourism Projects Dept. 1968-69, Special Projects Dept. IBRD 1969-72, Urban Projects Dept. 1972-74, Special Studies, E. Asia and Pacific 1974-, Special Operations, Office of the Vice-Pres. Projects Staff 1975-; Admin. World Bank Graduate Scholarship Program 1986-. *Address:* International Bank for Reconstruction and Development, 1818 H Street, N.W. Washington, D.C. 20433, U.S.A.

SADOWSKI, Wiesław; Polish economist and politician; b. 2 Jan. 1922, Warsaw; m. Stefania Sadowski 1947; one d.; ed. Main School of Commerce, Warsaw; scientific worker at Main School of Planning and Statistics, Warsaw 1945-, Prof. 1960-, Rector 1965-78; Corresp. mem. Polish Acad. of Sciences (PAN) 1969-; mem. numerous Polish and foreign scientific asscns., incl. Int. Statistical Inst.; Deputy to Seym 1969-80; Pres. Cen. Statistical Office (GUS) 1980-89; Order of Banner of Labour (1st Class), Commdr.'s and Officer's Cross, Order of Polonia Restituta, Meritorious Teacher of People's Poland and other decorations. *Publications:* numerous works on statistics and econometrics. *Leisure interest:* music. *Address:* Al. Na Skarpie 19 M 3, 00-488 Warsaw, Poland.

SAEMALA, Francis Joseph, B.A.; Solomon Islands civil servant and diplomatist; b. 23 June 1944; ed. Victoria Univ., Wellington, N.Z.; Head of Planning, Cen. Planning Office 1976; Sec. to Independence Timetable Talks del. and Jt. Sec. to Constitutional Conf. in London 1977; Special Sec. to Chief Minister 1976, to Prime Minister 1978-81; Sec. to Leader of the Opposition 1981-82; Perm. Sec. Ministry of Foreign Affairs and Int. Trade 1982-83; Perm. Rep. to UN 1983-. *Address:* Permanent Mission of Solomon Islands to the United Nations, 820 Second Avenue, Suite 800A, New York, N.Y. 10017, U.S.A.

SÁENZ DE COSCULLUELA, Javier; Spanish politician; b. 11 Oct. 1944, Logroño; m.; two s.; ed. Barcelona Univ.; practised Barcelona, specializing in labour law and labour relations, advising trade unions; active opponent of Franco regime; mem. Socialist Party (PSOE) 1972-; detained several times for political activities; M.P. 1977-; joined Fed. Exec., PSOE, with responsibility for Parl. Relations 1981, Fed. Exec. Sec. 1981-; fmr. Pres. Parl. Socialist Group, Chair. Spanish Del. to IPU; Minister for Public Works and Urban Environment 1986-. *Address:* Ministerio de Obras

Públicas y Urbanismo, Nuevos Ministerios, Paseo de la Castellana s/n, Madrid 3, Spain. *Telephone:* Madrid 253 1600.

SAFDIE, Moshe, B.ARCH., F.R.A.I.C.; Canadian (b. in Israel) architect; b. 14 July 1938, Haifa; s. of Leon Safdie and Rachael Esses; m. Nina Nusynowicz 1959 (divorced 1981), one s. one d.; m. 2nd Michal Ronnen 1981; two d.; ed. McGill Univ. Montreal, Canada; with Van Ginkel & Assocs., Montreal 1961–62; Louis I. Kahn, Philadelphia 1962–63; architect, planner Canadian Corpn. for 1967 World Exhbn. 1963; Moshe Safdie & Assocs., Montreal 1964–, Moshe Safdie and Assocs. Inc., Boston 1978–; commissioned to execute Habitat '67 1964; Coldspring New Town, Baltimore; Mamilla Business District, Jerusalem; Musée Nat. de la Civilisation, Quebec City; Robina New Town, Gold Coast, Australia; Colegio Hebreo Maguen David, Mexico City; National Gallery of Canada, Ottawa; Toronto Ballet Opera House; Ottawa City Hall; Visiting Prof. McGill Univ. 1970–71; Davenport Prof. of Architecture, Yale Univ. 1971–72; Dir. Urban design program of Harvard Univ. 1978–; Hon. LL.D. (McGill Univ.) 1982, Dr. h.c. (Laval Univ.) 1988; Lieut.-Gov. Gold Medal (Canada) 1961, Massey Medal for Architecture (Canada) 1969, A.R.I.A. Sinergy Award (U.S.A.) 1970, Urban Design Concept Award (U.S.A.) 1980, Int. Design Award in Urban Design (U.S.A.) 1980, Rechter Prize for Architecture 1982; Fellow mem. Royal Architectural Inst. Canada, Order of Architects of Que., Ont. Assen. Architects. *Publications:* Beyond Habitat 1970, The Japan Architect 1970, The Coldspring Presentation 1972, Horizon 1973, For Everyone a Garden 1974, Form and Purpose 1982, Jerusalem: The Future of the Past 1989. *Address:* 100 Properzi Way, Somerville, Mass. 02143-3798, U.S.A.; 3601 University Street, Montreal, Quebec, Canada.

SAFFAR, Salman Mohamed al-, PH.D.; Bahraini diplomatist; b. 1931, Bahrain; m.; ed. Baghdad Univ., Iraq and Sorbonne, Paris; Primary School teacher, Bahrain 1949–54, Secondary school teacher 1959–60; with Ministry of Foreign Affairs 1960–; Permanent Rep. to UN 1971–81; Amb. to France Nov. 1982–. *Address:* Embassy of Bahrain, 15 avenue Raymond Poincaré, 75116 Paris, France.

SAFIRE, William; American journalist and author; b. 17 Dec. 1929, New York; s. of Oliver C. Safir and Ida Panish; m. Helene Belmar Julius 1962; one s. one d.; ed. Syracuse Univ.; journalist, New York Herald Tribune Syndicate 1949–51; Corresp. WNBC-WNBT, Europe and Middle East 1951, Radio and TV Producer, WNBC, New York 1954–55; Vice-Pres. Tex McCrary Inc. 1955–60; Pres. Safire Public Relations Inc. 1960–68; Special Asst. to Pres. Nixon, Washington 1968–73; Columnist, New York Times, Washington 1973–; Pulitzer Prize for Distinguished Commentary 1978. *Publications:* The Relations Explosion 1963, Plunging into Politics 1964, Safire's Political Dictionary 1968, Before the Fall 1975, Full Disclosure 1977, Safire's Washington 1980, On Language 1980, What's the Good Word? 1982, Good Advice (with Leonard Safir) 1982, I Stand Corrected 1984, Take My Word for It 1986, Freedom (novel) 1987, You Could Look It Up 1988. *Address:* c/o New York Times, 1627 Eye Street, N.W. Washington, D.C. 20006, U.S.A.

SAFRONCHUK, Vasiliy Stepanovich; Soviet diplomatist; b. 16 Feb. 1925, Krivoi Rog, Ukraine; ed. Moscow Inst. of International Relations; lecturer, researcher at Moscow Inst. of Int. Relations 1955–59; First Sec. Counsellor at Soviet Embassy in U.K. 1959–64; Counsellor, Deputy Chief of Second European Dept., Foreign Ministry Moscow 1964–67; Amb. to Ghana 1967–71; Deputy Perm. Rep. of U.S.S.R. to UN 1971–76; Deputy Chief Second European Dept., Foreign Ministry, Moscow 1976–79; Minister-Counsellor, Soviet Embassy, Afghanistan 1979–82; Head, Middle East Dept. in Foreign Ministry, Moscow 1982–85; First Deputy Perm. Rep. of U.S.S.R. to UN 1985–86; Under-Sec.-Gen. for Policy and Sec. Council Affairs, UN 1987–. *Address:* United Nations, P.O. Box 20, New York, N.Y. 10163-0020, U.S.A.

SAGAN, Carl Edward, PH.D., SC.D.; American educator, author and astronomer; b. 9 Nov. 1934, New York; s. of Samuel and Rachel Sagan; m. 1st Linda Sagan (divorced 1980), three s.; m. 2nd Ann Druyan 1981; ed. Univ. of Chicago; Miller Research Fellow, Univ. of Calif. at Berkeley 1960–62; Asst. Prof. of Genetics, Stanford Univ. Medical School 1962–63; Asst. Prof. of Astronomy, Harvard Univ., and Astrophysicist, Smithsonian Astrophysical Observatory 1962–68; numerous visiting lectureships at univs. and scientific assens. 1967–; Dir. Lab. for Planetary Studies, Cornell Univ. 1968–, Prof. of Astronomy and Space Sciences 1970–, David Duncan Prof. 1976–, Assoc. Dir. Center for Radiophysics and Space Research 1975–; Visiting Assoc., California Inst. of Tech. 1971–72, 1976–77; Chair. Div. for Planetary Sciences, American Astronomical Soc. 1975–76, Astronomy Section of A.A.A.S. 1975–76, Planetology Section, American Geophysical Union 1980–82; Ed.-in-Chief ICARUS: Int. Journal of Solar System Studies 1968–79; Vice-Chair. Working Group on Moon and Planets of Cttee. on Space Research (COSPAR) of ICSU 1968–74; mem. various advisory bds., NASA 1959–, Investigator of Mariner, Viking, Voyager interplanetary missions 1962, 1971–72, 1976, 1979–81, lecturer Apollo flight crews 1969–72, Chair. NASA Study Group on Machine Intelligence and Robotics 1977–79; Chair. U.S. del. to joint conf. of U.S. and Soviet Acads. of Science on Communication with Extraterrestrial Intelligence 1971; Pres. Carl Sagan Productions: Science for the Media 1977–; Pres. CETI Foundation 1978–; Pres. The Planetary Soc. 1979–; Creator and Presenter Cosmos TV series 1980; mem. or Fellow Int. Astronomical Union, American Astronomical Soc., American Geophysical Union, American Physical Soc., Int. Acad. of

Astronautics, Int. Soc. for Study of Origins of Life, American Astronautical Soc. (Dir. 1976–79), American Acad. of Arts and Sciences, British Interplanetary Soc.; mem. Council Smithsonian Inst. 1975–; numerous hon. degrees; NASA Medals 1972, 1977, 1981, Prix Galabert 1973, Campbell Award 1974, Klumpke-Roberts Prize 1974, Joseph Priestley Award 1975, Newcomb Cleveland Prize 1977, Pulitzer Prize 1978, Washburn Medal Boston Museum of Science 1978, Explorers Club 75th Anniversary Award 1980, George Foster Peabody Award 1981, Glenn Seaborg Prize 1981, A.S.M.E. Roe Medal 1981, Honda Foundation Prize 1985. *Publications:* Atmospheres of Mars and Venus 1961, Intelligent Life in the Universe 1966, Planets 1966, Planetary Exploration 1970, The Air War in Indochina 1971, UFOs: A Scientific Debate 1972, The Cosmic Connection 1973, Communication with Extraterrestrial Intelligence 1973, Mars and the Mind of Man 1973, Other Worlds 1975, The Dragons of Eden 1977, Murmurs of Earth: The Voyager Interstellar Record 1978, Broca's Brain 1979, Cosmos 1980, Contact 1985, Comet (novel) 1986; 350 scientific papers and articles. *Address:* Space Sciences Building, Cornell University, Ithaca, N.Y. 14853, U.S.A. *Telephone:* (607) 256-4971, 4972.

SAGAN, Françoise (pseudonym of Françoise Quoirez); French writer; b. 21 June 1935, Cajarc; d. of Pierre and Marie (née Laubard) Quoirez; m. 1st Guy Schoeller 1958; m. 2nd Robert Westhoff 1962, one s.; ed. Couvent des Oiseaux et Couvent du Sacré Coeur, Paris; Prix des Critiques pour Bonjour tristesse 1954. *Publications:* Bonjour tristesse 1954, Un certain sourire 1956, Dans un mois, dans un an 1957, Aimez-vous Brahms . . . 1959, La chamade 1965, Le garde du coeur 1968, Un peu de soleil dans l'eau froide 1969, Des bleus à l'âme 1972, Il est des parfums (with Guillaume Hanoteau) 1973, Les merveilleux nuages 1973, Un profil perdu 1974, Réponses 1975, Des yeux de soie 1976, La femme fardée, Musique de scène 1981, De guerre lasse 1985, Un sang d'aquarelle 1987, Dear Sarah Bernhardt 1988; scenario for the ballet Le rendez-vous manqué (with Michel Magne); own film adaption of Dans un mois, dans un an; Dir. Les fougères bleues (film) 1976; *Plays:* Château en Suède 1959, Les violons parfois ... 1961, La robe mauve de valentine 1963, Bonheur, impair et passe 1964, Le cheval évanoui 1966, L'écharde 1966, Un piano dans l'herbe 1970, Zaphorie 1973, Le lit défait 1977, Pol Vandromme 1978, Il fait beau jour et nuit 1978, Le chien couchant 1980, Un orage immobile 1983. *Address:* Equemauville, 14600 Honfleur, France.

SAGATELYAN, Mikhail; Soviet journalist and writer; b. 1927; ed. Moscow Inst. of Int. Relations; worked in Washington as journalist 1959–65; Vice-Chair. Foreign Comm. of the Union of U.S.S.R. Writers. *Publications include:* Journey into Imperialism 1985, Anti-Morality 1986. *Address:* U.S.S.R. Union of Writers, ulitsa Vorovskogo 52, Moscow, U.S.S.R.

SAGDEEV, Roald Zinnurovich, D.SC.; Soviet physicist; b. 26 Dec. 1932, Moscow; ed. Moscow State Univ.; Research Worker, Inst. of Atomic Energy, U.S.S.R. Acad. of Sciences 1956–61; Head of Lab., Inst. of Nuclear Physics, Siberian Dept., Acad. of Sciences 1961–70, Inst. of High Temperature Physics of U.S.S.R. Acad. of Sciences 1970–73; Prof. Novosibirsk State Univ. 1964–; Dir. Inst. of Space Research 1973–; Corresp. mem. U.S.S.R. Acad. of Sciences 1964, mem. 1968–; Order of October Revolution, Order of Red Banner, and other decorations. *Address:* Institute of Space Research, Profsoyuznaya 88, Moscow, U.S.S.R.

SAGET, Louis Joseph Edouard; French government official; b. 27 April 1915, Paris; s. of Pierre and Jeanne (née Barbare) Saget; m. Anne Vincens 1940; five c.; ed. Lycée Janson-de-Sailly, Paris; Mayor of Tananarive 1954–56; First Counsellor, French Embassy, Madagascar 1959–60; High Commr. in Comoro Islands 1960–62; Commissaire aux Comptes, European Launcher Devt. Org. 1963–66; Gov. of French Somaliland 1966–67; High Commr. in Djibouti 1967–69; Conseiller maître à la Cour des Comptes 1970–84; Pres. Agence nat. pour l'amélioration de l'habitat 1971–78, Comm. de terminologie du ministère de la Défense 1973–87; Investigator, Comité central d'enquête sur le coût et le rendement des services publics 1974–84; mem. Electoral Comm. for French living abroad 1977–88, Cttee. for Fiscal Matters, Customs and Exchange 1987–; Officier Légion d'honneur, Commdr. Nat. du Mérite, Croix de guerre, Commdr. de l'Etoile noire, Commdr. de l'Ordre nat. Malgache, Grand Commdr. of the Order of the Star of Ethiopia, Commdr. de l'Etoile equatoriale de Gabon, Nat. Order of Upper Volta, Order of the Leopard of Zaire, Grand Officier Ordre du Croissant Vert des Comores. *Leisure interest:* nature. *Address:* 13 rue Cambon 75001 Paris (Office); 1 rue de Laborde, 91660 Méréville, France (Home).

SÁGHY, Vilmos, ECD.; Hungarian economist and politician; b. 9 Jan. 1922, Győrzámoly, Győr County; s. of Zsigmond Sághy and Rozália Pécsi; m. Ágnes Kertész 1949; two s.; ed. Econ. and Tech. Acad. and Univ. of Agronomy; began career as Head of Div. in a company; First Asst. in Econ. and Tech. Acad.; various posts in party admin. 1952–54; Deputy Minister of Food 1954–63; Vice-Pres. Nat. Planning Office 1963–67; First Deputy Minister of Agric. and Food 1967–70; First Deputy Minister, then Sec. of State for Internal Trade 1970–76, Minister 1976–82; recipient of several Hungarian and foreign awards. *Leisure interests:* handicrafts, gardening. *Address:* c/o Ministry of Internal Trade, Vigadó-utca 6, Budapest V, Hungary. *Telephone:* 185-044.

SAGLIO, Jean-François; French mining engineer; b. 29 July 1936, Toulon; s. of Georges Saglio; m. Odile Bertrand 1968; two s. one d.; ed. Ecole

Polytechnique and Ecole Supérieure des Mines, Paris; Engineer, Govt. Del. Algiers 1960–61; Mining Engineer, Mines de Metz 1961–66; founder/Dir. Agence de Bassin Rhin-Meuse, Metz 1966–69; Adviser, Cabinet of Pres. of France 1969–73; Head, Perm. Secr. for Study of Water Problems of Paris 1971–73; Dir. in charge of Pollution and Nuisance, Ministry of Environment 1973–78; Pres. Dir.-Gen. Agence Foncière et Technique de la Région Parisienne 1979–81; Dir. of Innovation and Valorization of Research, Elf Aquitaine, also Dir. of New Projects 1981–84; Pres. Dir.-Gen. INOVELF 1981–84; Asst. Dir.-Gen. Société Elf-France 1984; Asst. Dir.-Gen. Refineries and Distribution, Société Nat. Elf Aquitaine 1984; now Dir.-Gen. of Industry, Ministry of Industry, Posts & Telecommunications and Tourism. *Address:* Ministère de l'Industrie, des P & T et du Tourisme, Direction Générale de l'Industrie, 32 rue Gersant, 75017 Paris (Office); 143 rue de la Pompe, 75116 Paris, France (Home). *Telephone:* 45.72.80.80 (Office); 45.53.05.44 (Home).

SAHADE, Jorge, PH.D.; Argentinian astrophysicist; b. 23 Feb. 1915, Alta Gracia; s. of Nallib Jorge Sahade and María Cassab; m. 1st Myriam Stella Elkin Font 1948 (died 1974), one s. one d.; m. 2nd Adela Emilia Ringuelet 1975; ed. Colegio de Monserrat, Córdoba, Univ. of Córdoba, Univ. of La Plata; Fellow Univ. of La Plata at Univ. of Chicago (Yerkes Observatory) 1943–46; Prof. Univ. of Córdoba 1948–55, Dir. Córdoba Observatory 1953–55; Guggenheim Fellow Univ. of Calif., Berkeley 1955–57, Research Astronomer 1957–58, 1960; Prof. and Head Div., Univ. of La Plata Observatory 1958–71, in charge of two-m. telescope project 1958–69, Dir. Observatory 1968–69, Dean Faculty of Exact Sciences 1969; Pres. Argentine Astronomical Asscn. 1963–69, Comm. 29 Astronomical Union 1964–67, Rotary Club La Plata Centro 1967–68; Chair. COSPAR Advisory Panel on Space Research in Developing Countries 1973–79, Pres. 1979–82; Vice-Pres. Exec. Cttee. Int Astronomical Union 1967–73, Pres. 1985–88, Adviser 1988–(91), Vice-Pres. Comm. 38 1988–(91); Dir. Inst. of Astronomy and Space Physics, Buenos Aires 1971–74; mem. Bd. Dirs. Nat. Research Council 1969–73, Exec. Bd. ICSU 1972–76, Gen. Cttee. 1972–80, COSTED 1973–79; Visiting Prof. at numerous univs.: Indiana, Sussex, Mons, Collège de France, Int. School for Advanced Study, Trieste, San Marcos (Peru), Porto Allegre (Brazil); Visiting Astronomer Dominion Astrophysical Observatory, Victoria, B.C., later Visiting Research Officer; Visiting Scientist Max-Planck Institut-für-Astrophysik, Fed. Repub. of Germany, Cerro Tololo Interamerican Observatory, Chile, Trieste Observatory; Guest Investigator at numerous observatories; Hon. Prof. Univ. of San Marcos, Peru 1987; Hon. mem. Argentine Asscn. of Friends of Astronomy 1970, Argentine Astronomical Asscn. 1985; Assoc. Royal Astronomical Soc., U.K. 1970; Corresp. mem. Nat. Acad. of Sciences, Buenos Aires 1970, Nat. Acad. of Sciences, Córdoba 1972, Foreign Corresp. mem. Royal Acad. of Exact, Physical and Natural Sciences, Madrid 1972; Dr. h.c. (Córdoba) 1987; Golden Planetarium Award 1973, Konex Award 1983, Diploma of Recognition, World Cultural Council 1987; Asteroid (2605)=1974 QA named Sahade at the proposal of the discoverer 1986. *Publications:* 170 research papers in int. journals. *Address:* C.C. 677, Observatorio Astronómico, FCAG, Universidad Nacional de La Plata, 1900 La Plata (Office); 49-342, 1900 La Plata, Argentina (Home). *Telephone:* (54-21) 249790 (Office); (54-21) 31063 (Home).

SAHGAL, Nayantara; Indian writer; b. 10 May 1927, Allahabad; d. of Ranjit Sitaram and Vijaya Lakshmi Pandit; m. 1st Gautam Sahgal 1949 (divorced 1967), one s. two d.; m. 2nd E. N. Mangat-Rai 1979; ed. Wellesley Coll., U.S.A.; Scholar-in-Residence, holding creative writing seminar, Southern Methodist Univ., Dallas, Texas 1973, 1977; Adviser English Language Bd., Sahitya Akademi (Nat. Acad. of Letters), New Delhi; mem. Indian Del. to UN Gen. Ass. 1978; mem. Nat. Exec., People's Union for Civil Liberties; Fellow, Radcliffe Inst. (Harvard Univ.) 1976, Wilson Int. Centre for Scholars, Washington, D.C. 1981–82, Nat. Humanities Center, N.C. 1983–84. *Publications:* Prison and Chocolate Cake 1954, A Time to be Happy 1958, From Fear Set Free 1962, This Time of Morning 1965, Storm in Chandigarh 1969, History of the Freedom Movement 1970, The Day in Shadow 1972, A Situation in New Delhi 1977, A Voice for Freedom 1977, Indira Gandhi's Emergence and Style 1978, Indira Gandhi: Her Road to Power 1982, Rich Like Us (awarded Sinclair Prize 1985; Sahitya Akad. Award 1987) 1985, Plans for Departure 1985 (awarded Commonwealth Writers' Prize 1987), Mistaken Identity 1988. *Leisure interests:* reading (novels, politics, philosophy), music (Indian, Western, Classical), walking. *Address:* 181B Rajpur Road, Dehra Dun, 248009 Uttar Pradesh, India.

SAHL, Mort(on) Lyon, B.S.; American comedian; b. 11 May 1927, Montreal, Canada; s. of Harry Sahl; m. 1st Sue Babior 1955 (divorced 1957); m. 2nd China Lee; one c.; ed. Compton Jr. Coll., Univ. of Southern California; Ed. Poop from the Group; magazine writing; many night club engagements; radio and TV performances, including Comedy News TV show, Steve Allen Show, Jack Paar Show, Eddie Fisher Show, Nightline, Wide Wide World; monologues on long-playing records; in Broadway revue, The Next President 1958; one-man show Broadway 1987; films include: In Love and War 1958, All the Young Men 1960, Doctor, You've Got to be Kidding 1967, Nothing Lasts Forever 1984; TV film: Inside the Third Reich 1982. *Publication:* Heartland 1976. *Address:* c/o Stanley Weinstein Arts Management, 210 Rutgers Lane, Parsippany, N.J. 07054, U.S.A.

SAHLIN, Mauritz; Swedish business executive; b. 14 June 1935, Karlskoga; m. Ulla Hilding; four c.; ed. Royal Inst. of Tech., Stockholm;

Bulten-Kanthal, Hallstahammar 1960–72; joined AB SKF, Göteborg 1972, Man. Dir. SKF GmbH, Germany 1973–78, Man. Dir. SKF Europe 1978–85, Man. Dir. SKF Group 1985–; Chair. Ovako Steel AB 1986–. *Address:* AB SKF, 41550 Göteborg (Office); Götabergsgatan 34, 411 34 Göteborg, Sweden (Home). *Telephone:* 031-371000 (Office); 031-204572 (Home).

SAID, Ali; Indonesian lawyer and politician; b. 12 June 1927, Malang, E. Java; ed. Mil. Law Acad. and Jakarta Mil. Law Inst.; Mil. Prosecutor 1960; Chief Judge for trial of communist leaders and activists, Jakarta; Sec. to Team for Combat of Corruption; Attorney-Gen. 1979; Minister of Justice 1981–85. *Address:* c/o Ministry of Justice, Jln. Hayam Wuruk, 7, Jakarta, Indonesia.

SAID, Edward W., M.A., PH.D.; American university professor; b. Nov. 1935, Jerusalem; m. Mariam Cortas 1970; one s. one d.; ed. Victoria Coll., Cairo, Mt. Hermon School, Mass., Princeton and Harvard Univs.; instructor in English, Columbia Univ. 1963–65, Asst. Prof. of English and Comparative Literature 1967–69, Prof. 1969–74, Parr Prof. 1977–; Visiting Prof. of Comparative Literature, Harvard Univ. 1974, of Humanities, Johns Hopkins Univ. 1979; Editor, Arab Studies Quarterly; Chair. Bd. of Trustees, Inst. of Arab Studies; mem. Palestine Nat. Council, Council on Foreign Relations, New York, Acad. of Literary Studies, PEN Club, New York; Fellow, Center for Advanced Study in Behavioral Science, Stanford 1975–76; Bowdoin Prize (Harvard Univ.); Lionel Trilling Award 1976. *Publications:* Joseph Conrad and the Fiction of Autobiography, Beginnings: Intention and Method, Orientalism, The Question of Palestine, Literature and Society, Covering Islam 1981, The World, the Text and the Critic 1983, After the Last Sky 1986. *Address:* 419 Hamilton Hall, Columbia University, New York, N.Y. 10027, U.S.A.

SAID, Faisal bin Ali al-; Omani diplomatist and politician; b. 1927, Muscat; attached to Ministry of Foreign Affairs, Muscat 1953–57; lived abroad 1957–70; Perm. Under-Sec. Ministry of Educ. 1970–72; Minister of Econ. Affairs 1972; Perm. Rep. to UN, Amb. to U.S.A. 1972–73; Minister of Educ. 1973–76, of Omani Heritage 1976–, of Culture 1979–. *Address:* Ministry of Culture, P.O. Box 668, Muscat, Oman.

SAID, Hakim Mohammed; Pakistani physician; b. 9 Jan. 1920; s. of late Hakim Abdul Majeed and Rabia Begum; m. Nemat Begum 1943 (deceased); one d.; ed. Ayurvedic and Unani Tibbi (Medical) Coll., Delhi; Founder, Sec.-Gen. Soc. for Promotion of Eastern Medicine 1956; Founder, Pres. Coll. of Eastern Medicine, Karachi 1958; Pres. Inst. of Health and Medical Research, Hamdard Foundation, Soc. for the Promotion and Improvement of Libraries, Hamdard Acad., Pakistan Historical Soc., Ibn-i-Khaldun Educ. Soc., Inst. of Cen. and West Asian Studies Karachi Univ.; Chair. Hamdard Waqf Labs.; organized Health of the Nation Conf., Karachi 1971, formed Nat. Health Cttee.; mem. Exec. Cttee. Union Int. d'Education pour la Santé, Paris until 1976; Adviser to Pres. of Pakistan on Tibb (Traditional Medicine) 1979–82; mem. numerous socs.; participant, organizer many int. confs. and congresses; mem. New York Acad. of Sciences, British Soc. for the History of Science; Assoc. mem. Royal Soc. of Health, U.K.; Fellow Royal Acad. of Islamic Civilization Research, Jordan; Hon. D.Sc. (Medicine Alternativa International) 1984; Sitara-i-Imtiaz (Award for Social and Educ. Service, Govt. of Pakistan) 1966, Sadiq Dost (Award from people of Bahawalpur), Islamic Medicine Prize from Kuwait Foundation for the Advancement of Sciences 1982. *Publications include:* Medicine in China, Europe Nama, Germany Nama, Wonders of the Human Body, Health of the Nation, The Employer and Employee, Tazkàr-i-Muhammad, Pharmacopoeia of Eastern Medicine, Main Currents of Contemporary Thought in Pakistan (2 vols.), Maqalat-i-Sham-i-Hamdard, Maqalat-i Ibn al-Haitham, Pharmacographia Indica, Al-Biruni Commemorative Volume, Greco-Arab Medicine and Modern Western Medicine—Conflict or Symbiosis, Ek Musafir Char Mulk, Al-Biruni, His Times, Life and Works, Safar Nama Roos, Switzerland Men Merey Chand Shab-O-Roz, Diseases of the Liver—Greco-Arab Concepts, Proceedings of the International Symposium on New Researches in Biology and Genetics: Problems of Science and Ethics, Proceedings of the Int. Conf. on History and Philosophy of Science, Greco-Arab Concepts on Cardiovascular Diseases, Korea Kahani. *Leisure interest:* tennis. *Address:* Hamdard Foundation Pakistan, Hamdard Centre, Nazimabad, Karachi 18 (Office); 58/1 Upper Sind Colony, Karachi 5, Pakistan (Home). *Telephone:* 616001-5 (Office); 410612 (Home).

SAIER, Oskar, DR.JUR.CAN.; German ecclesiastic; b. 12 Aug. 1932, Wagensteig; s. of Adolf and Berta Saier; ed. Univs. of Freiburg and Tübingen; curate 1957; Asst. Kanonist. Inst. Univ. of Munich 1963; Bishop of Freiburg 1972, Archbishop 1978–; Chair. Pastoral Comm. of German Conf. of Bishops 1979; mem. Vatican Congregation for the Clergy 1984; Second Chair. of German Conf. of Bishops 1987; Freeman of Buchenbach 1972, of St. Peter, Black Forest 1977, and of Bethlehem, Israel 1984. *Publication:* Communio in der Lehre des Zweiten Vatikanischen Konzils 1973. *Address:* Herrenstrasse 35, D-7800 Freiburg, Federal Republic of Germany. *Telephone:* 0761/2188-1.

SAIF AL-ISLAM, Mohamed al-Badr, H.R.H.; fmr. Imam of the Yemen; b. 1927; ed. Coll. for Higher Education, Sana'a (Yemen); Minister for Foreign Affairs 1955–61, and Minister of Defence and C.-in-C. 1955–62; succeeded to Imamate on the death of his father, Imam Ahmed Sept. 1962; in hills, Yemen, leading Royalist Forces in civil war 1962–68; replaced by

Imamate Council May 1968; in exile in Saudi Arabia 1968-. *Address:* Jeddah, Saudi Arabia.

SAIFUDIN (see Seypidin).

SAIGH, Nassir M. Al-, D.B.A.; Saudi Arabian expert on business administration; b. 10 Oct. 1942, Riyadh; s. of Mohammed Al-Saigh and Noura Al-Saigh; ed. Univ. of Kentucky, Lexington, Univ. of Indiana, Bloomington, King Saud Univ., Riyadh; Chair. Business Admin. Dept., King Saud Univ. 1980-83, Asst. Prof., Faculty of Admin. Sciences 1979-80; Chief Ed., Arab Journal of Admin. 1983-; Dir.-Gen. Arab Org. of Admin. Sciences 1983-. *Publications:* Administrative Reform in the Arab World: Readings 1986, Public Administration and Administrative Reform in the Arab World 1986. *Leisure interest:* reading. *Address:* Arab Organization of Administrative Sciences, P.O. Box 17159, Amman, Jordan. *Telephone:* 813635 (Office); 687327 (Home).

SAILI FAASOOTAULOA, Tuaopepe Falesa Pualagi Sam, C.P.A.; Western Samoan politician; b. 3 May 1936, Alamagota; m. 1st Amy Papalii 1959 (divorced 1968), three s. two d.; m. 2nd Metotagivale Leaupepe 1968, three s. five d.; ed. Victoria Univ. Wellington, N.Z.; Auditor, Govt. of Samoa 1963-65; established pvt. practice Saili, Lam Sam and Kelemete (accounting and auditing firm) 1965; mem. Parl. 1972-; Minister of Finance 1973-75, 1985-; Gen. Man. Western Samoa Trust Estates Corpn. 1983-85; Lay Preacher, Congregational Christian Church of Samoa 1975-. *Leisure interests:* represented Western Samoa in rugby, cricket and tennis. *Address:* Ministry of Finance, P.O. Box 44, Apia, Western Samoa.

SAINER, Leonard, LL.B.; British solicitor and business executive; b. 12 Oct. 1909, London; s. of Archer and Sarah Sainer; ed. Central Foundation School, Univ. Coll. London, L.S.E.; Consultant, Titmuss, Sainer and Webb (solicitors); Dir. (fmly. Chair.) Sears PLC; Dir. First Nat. Finance Corpn. Ltd. *Address:* Sears PLC, 40 Duke Street, London, W1A 2HP; Titmuss, Sainer and Webb, 2 Serjeants' Inn, London, EC4Y 1LT; 26 Chester Terrace, Regent's Park, London, N.W.1, England (Home).

SAINJU, Mohan Man, B.A., B.L., PH.D.; Nepalese government official; b. 28 March 1941, Palpa; s. of late Lalit Man Sainju and Ganesh Kumari Sainju; m. Madhuri Sainju 1964; one s. one d.; ed. Tribhuwan Univ. Kathmandu and Univ. of North Carolina; officer on special duty, Ministry of Econ. Planning 1963; Dir. and Chief Dir. Dept. of Land Reform 1964; Jt.-Sec. Ministry of Food, Agric. and Land Reform 1967; Chief Specialist, Centre for Econ. Devt. and Admin. Tribhuwan Univ. 1972, Rector 1973; Perm. mem. Nat. Planning Comm. 1976, Vice-Chair. 1982-; Maherdra Vidya Bhushan; Gorakha Dakshin Bahu, Trishkti Patta. *Publication:* book on land reform in Nepal. *Leisure interests:* reading, badminton. *Address:* Singh Durbar, Kathmandu (Office); Cantoo Sanepa, Lalitpur, Kathmandu, Nepal (Home).

SAINSBURY, Baron (Life Peer), cr. 1962, of Drury Lane; **Alan John Sainsbury;** British retail executive; b. 13 Aug. 1902; s. of John Benjamin and Mabel Miriam Sainsbury; m. 1st Doreen Davan Adams 1925 (dissolved), three s.; m. 2nd Anne Elizabeth Lewy 1944, one d.; ed. Haileybury School; J. Sainsbury Ltd. (grocery and provision firm) 1921-, Chair. 1956-67, Jt. Pres. 1967-; mem. Williams' Cttee. on Milk Distribution 1947-48, Food Research Advisory Cttee. 1960-70, (Chair. 1965-70), Econ. Devt. Cttee. for the Distributive Trades (N.E.D.C.) 1964-68, Exec. Cttee. PEP 1970-76; Vice-Pres. Royal Soc. for Encouragement of Arts, Manufacturers and Commerce 1962-66, The Asscn. of Agriculture 1965-73; Pres. Grocer's Inst. 1963-66, Dir. 1966-; Pres. Pestalozzi Children's Village Trust 1963-, Multiple Shops Fed. 1963-65, Royal Inst. Public Health and Hygiene 1965-70; Chair. Cttee. of Inquiry into relationship of pharmaceutical industry with Nat. Health Service 1965-67; mem. Labour Party 1945-81; joined SDP 1981; mem. Court of Univ. of Essex 1966-76; Gov. City Literary Inst. 1967-69; Pres. Distributive Trades Educ. and Training Council 1975-83; Vice-Pres. Parl. Group for World Govt. 1982-; Chair. of Trustees, Overseas Students Advisory Bureau, Uganda Asian Relief Trust 1972-74; mem. Council English Stage Co. 1975-, Writers and Scholars Educ. Trust 1975-; fmr. mem. House of Lords Select Cttee. on European Communities; Hon. Fellow, Inst. of Food Science and Technology. *Address:* J. Sainsbury PLC, Stamford House, Stamford Street, London, SE1 9LL, England. *Telephone:* 01-928-6775.

SAINSBURY, Baron (Life Peer), cr. 1989, of Preston Candover; **John Davan**, M.A.; British business executive; b. 2 Nov. 1927, London; s. of A. J. (later Baron) Sainsbury (q.v.); m. Anya Linden 1963; two s. one d.; ed. Stowe School and Worcester Coll., Oxford; Dir. J. Sainsbury Ltd. 1958-, Vice-Chair. 1967-69, Chair. 1969-; Dir. Royal Opera House, Covent Garden 1969-85, 1987-, The Economist 1972-80, Royal Opera House Trust 1974-84; Chair. Friends of Covent Garden 1969-81, Benesh Inst. of Choreology 1986-87; Vice-Pres. Contemporary Arts Soc. 1984-; mem. Council, Retail Consortium 1975-79; mem. Nat. Cttee. for Electoral Reform 1976-85; Jt. Hon. Treas. European Movement 1972-75, a Pres. 1975-; Gov. Royal Ballet School 1965-76, 1987-; Trustee Nat. Gallery 1976-83, Westminster Abbey Trust 1977-83; Fellow, Inst. of Grocery Distribution 1973-; Hon. Bencher, Inner Temple 1985; Hon. D.Sc. (London) 1985. *Address:* c/o J. Sainsbury PLC, Stamford House, Stamford Street, London, SE1 9LL, England. *Telephone:* 01-921 6000.

SAINT BRIDES, Baron (Life Peer), cr. 1977, of Hasguard in the County of Dyfed; **(John) Morrice (Cairns) James**, P.C., G.C.M.G., C.V.O., M.B.E.; British diplomatist; b. 30 April 1916; s. of Lewis Cairns James and Catherine Mary James; m. 1st Elizabeth Piesse (died 1966), 2nd Geneviève Sarasin 1968; one s. two d.; ed. Bradfield, Oxford Univ.; joined Dominions Office 1939; Royal Navy, Royal Marines Second World War; staff of U.K. High Comm. in S. Africa 1946-47; Commonwealth Relations Office, London 1947-52; Deputy U.K. High Commr., Lahore 1952-53; Imperial Defence Coll. 1954; Deputy U.K. High Commr., Pakistan 1955-56, India 1958-61, U.K. High Commr., Pakistan 1961-66, Privy Councillor 1968; Deputy Under-Sec. of State, Commonwealth Office, London 1966-68, Perm. Under-Sec. of State 1968; High Commr. to India 1968-71; High Commr. to Australia 1971-76; Visiting Fellow, Dept. of Political Science, Univ. of Chicago 1978-79; Fellow, Center for Int. Affairs, Harvard Univ. 1979-80; Distinguished Diplomat in Residence, Foreign Policy Research Inst., Philadelphia 1981; Visiting Scholar, Univ. of Texas 1982-83; Distinguished Visiting Prof. of Int. Studies, Rhodes Coll., Memphis 1983-84; Visiting Fellow Center for Int. Security and Arms Control, Stanford Univ. 1984-89; attended (as hon. mem. of U.S. del.) Second, Third and Fourth Annual Confs. FPRI/Soviet Inst. for the U.S.A., Zvinigorod, U.S.S.R. 1981, Valley Forge, U.S.A. 1982, Moscow, U.S.S.R. 1984; visited Beijing with team from CISAC, Stanford Univ. for talks with Chinese Inst. for Int. Affairs Sept. 1985; Hon. mem., U.S. del., talks between CISAC and Soviet Inst. for Far Eastern Affairs Oct. 1986, Sept. 1987 and June 1988; King of Arms of the Most Distinguished Order of Saint Michael and Saint George 1975-86. *Leisure interest:* meeting new and intelligent people. *Address:* Cap Saint-Pierre 83990, Saint-Tropez, France. *Telephone:* (94) 97-14-75.

ST. JOHN, (Harold) Bernard, Q.C.; Barbados lawyer and politician (retd.); b. 16 Aug. 1931, Christ Church; m. Stella Hope; one s. two d.; ed. Boys' Foundation, Harrison Coll., Univ. of London, Inner Temple; called to Bar 1954; private legal practice, Barbados and Eastern Caribbean 1954-; Q.C. 1969; Legal Adviser to Southern Dist. Council; Pres. Barbados Bar Asscn.; mem. Senate 1964-66, 1971-76; mem. House of Ass. 1966-71, 1976-; Chair. Barbados Labour Party 1966-71; Leader of the Opposition 1970-71; Minister of Trade, Tourism and Industry 1976-86, also Deputy Prime Minister, Prime Minister and Minister of Finance 1985-86; Trustee, Barbados Labour Party 1986-; Chair. Caribbean Tourism Research Cen. 1977-79; Pres. ACP (African, Caribbean and Pacific) Council of Ministers 1979; Pres. Latin American Council of Ministers 1980. *Leisure interest:* fishing. *Address:* 3 Enterprise, Christchurch, Barbados (Home).

ST. JOHN OF FAWSLEY, Baron (Life Peer), cr. 1987, of Preston in the County of Northampton; **Norman Antony Francis St. John-Stevas**, P.C., M.A., B.C.L., PH.D., M.P., F.R.S.L.; British politician, barrister, author and journalist; b. 18 May 1929; ed. Ratcliffe, Fitzwilliam Coll., Cambridge, Christ Church, Oxford, and Yale; Barrister, Middle Temple 1952; Lecturer, King's Coll., London 1953-56; Tutor in Jurisprudence, Christ Church, Oxford 1953-55, Merton Coll., Oxford 1955-57; Founder mem. Inst. of Higher European Studies, Bolzano 1955; Legal Adviser to Sir Alan Herbert's Cttee. on Book Censorship 1954-59; Legal and Political Corresp., The Economist 1959-64; Conservative M.P. for Chelmsford 1964-87; Sec. Conservative Party Home Affairs Cttee. 1969-72; mem. Fulbright Comm. 1961; Parl. Select Cttee. Race Relations and Immigration 1970-72; Parl. Under-Sec. for Educ. and Science 1972-73; Minister of State for the Arts 1973-74; mem. Parl. Select Cttee. on Race Relations and Immigration 1970-72, on Civil List 1971-83, on Foreign Affairs 1983-87; mem. Shadow Cabinet 1974-79, Shadow Leader of the House of Commons 1978-79, Opposition Spokesman on Educ. 1974-78, Science 1974-78 and the Arts 1974-79; Chancellor of the Duchy of Lancaster 1979-81; Leader of the House of Commons 1979-81; Minister for the Arts 1979-81; Vice-Chair. Cons. Parl. N. Ireland Cttee. 1972-87; Vice-Chair. Cons. Group for Europe 1972-75; Chair. Royal Fine Art Comm. 1985-; Vice-Pres. Theatres Advisory Council 1983-; founder mem. Christian-Social Inst. of Culture, Rome 1969; mem. Council RADA 1983-, Nat. Soc. for Dance 1983-, Nat. Youth Theatre 1983- (Patron 1984-), Royal Coll. of Art 1985-; Trustee Royal Philharmonic Orch. 1985-, Decorative Arts Soc. 1984-; Hon. Sec. Fed. of Conservative Students 1971-73; Ed. The Dublin (Wiseman Review) 1961; Romanes Lecturer, Oxford 1987; Hon. D.D. (Susquehanna, Pa) 1983, Hon. D.Litt. (Schiller) 1985, (Bristol) 1988; Silver Jubilee Medal 1977; Kt. Grand Cross, St. Lazarus of Jerusalem 1963; Cavaliere Ordine al Merito della Repubblica (Italy) 1965, Commendatore 1978. *Publications:* Obscenity and the Law 1956, Walter Bagehot 1959, Life, Death and the Law 1961, The Right to Life 1963, Law and Morals 1964, The Literary Essays of Walter Bagehot 1965, The Historical Essays of Walter Bagehot 1968, The Agonising Choice 1971, The Political Essays of Walter Bagehot 1974, The Economic Works of Walter Bagehot 1978, Pope John Paul, His Travels and Mission 1982, The Two Cities 1984. *Leisure interests:* reading, talking, listening to music, travelling, walking, appearing on television. *Address:* 34 Montpelier Square, London, S.W.1, England. *Telephone:* 01-589 3001.

ST. JOSEPH, John Kenneth Sinclair, C.B.E., M.A., PH.D., LITT.D., F.B.A., F.S.A., F.G.S.; British academic; b. 1912, Cookley, Worcs.; s. of the late John D. St. Joseph and Irma R. (née Marris) St. Joseph; m. Daphne M. March 1945; two s. two d.; ed. Bromsgrove School, Worcs., and Selwyn Coll., Cambridge; research student, Selwyn Coll., Cambridge 1934-37; Harkness Scholar 1934; Goldsmith's Co. Sr. Student 1935-37; Dept. of Scientific and

Industrial Research Sr. Research Award 1936-37; Fellow, Selwyn Coll. 1939-, Lecturer in Natural Sciences and Dean 1939-62, Tutor 1945-62, Librarian 1946-62, Vice-Master 1974-80; Univ. Demonstrator in Geology, Cambridge 1937-45, Univ. Lecturer 1945-48; Operational Research, Ministry of Aircraft Production 1942-45; Leverhulme Research Fellow 1948-49; Curator in Aerial Photography, Cambridge 1948-62, Dir. in Aerial Photography 1962-80; Prof. of Aerial Photographic Studies, Univ. of Cambridge and Professorial Fellow, Selwyn Coll. 1973-80, Prof. Emer. 1980-; mem. Ancient Monuments Bd. (England) 1969-85, Royal Comm. on Historical Monuments (England) 1972-81; hon. corresp. mem. German Archaeological Inst.; Hon.Sc.D. (Trinity Coll., Dublin); Hon. LL.D. (Dundee); Dr. h.c. (Amsterdam). *Publications:* several books and book chapters. *Leisure interests:* gardening, lumbering. *Address:* Histon Manor, Cambridge, CB4 4JJ, England. *Telephone:* Histon 2383.

SAINT LAURENT, Yves (Henri Donat Mathieu); French couturier; b. 1 Aug. 1936, Oran, Algeria; s. of Charles Mathieu Saint Laurent and Lucienne Andrée Wilbaux; ed. Lycée d'Oran; career dedicated to haute couture; designer; partner and successor of Christian Dior 1954; shareholder Yves Saint Laurent S.A. 1962-; works include: costume sketches for Roland Petit's ballets Chants de Maldoror 1962, Adagio and Variations, Notre Dame de Paris 1965; sketches for costumes for le Mariage de Figaro (Compagnie Madeleine Renaud—Jean Louis Barrault) 1964, scenery and costumes for Zizi Jeanmaire's shows at the Alhambra 1962 and Théâtre National de Paris 1963, costumes for Edward Albee's A Delicate Balance (Théâtre de France) 1967; films: costumes for Luis Buñuel's Belle de Jour 1967, La Chamade (from the novel by Françoise Sagan) 1968, Alain Resnais' Stavisky 1974; exhbns.: Beijing Museum of Fine Arts 1985, Museum of Arts and Fashion, Paris 1986; Oscars from Neiman-Marcus (Dallas) 1958, Harper's Bazaar 1966, Oscar of fashion for his entire work 1985. *Publication:* illustrated book La Vilaine Lulu 1967. *Address:* 5 avenue Marceau, 75116 Paris (Office); 55 rue de Babylone, 75007 Paris, France (Home).

SAITO, Eishiro; Japanese steel industry executive; b. 22 Nov. 1911, Niigata City; s. of Tooru and Tome Saito; m. Toshiko Kato 1939; one s. one d.; ed. Tokyo Imperial Univ.; joined Japan Iron and Steel Co. Ltd. 1941; Dir. Yawata Iron and Steel Co. Ltd. 1961, Man. Dir. 1962, Sr. Man. Dir. 1968; Sr. Man. Dir. Nippon Steel Corpn. 1970, Exec. Vice-Pres. 1973, Rep. Dir. and Pres. 1977-81, Chair. and Rep. Dir. 1981-87; Hon. Chair. and Advisor June 1987-; Chair. Japan Fed. of Econ. Orgs. 1986-; Hon. Chair. Kozai Club (Steel Materials Club), Japan Iron and Steel Exporters' Asscn., Int. Iron and Steel Inst. 1977; Hon. Chair. Japan Iron and Steel Fed.; Blue Ribbon Medal, First Class Order of the Sacred Treasure, Ordem de Rio Branco, Order of Bernard O'Higgins, Grossen Stern der Völkerfreundschaft, Orden de Mayo Gran Cruz. *Leisure interests:* golf, "Go", reading. *Address:* 1-18-808, Hiroo 4-chome, Shibuya-ku, Tokyo 150, Japan (Home).

SAITO, Juro; Japanese politician; b. 1940; Pvt Sec. to Minister of Health and Welfare; Parl. Vice-Minister of Finance; Chair. of Cttee. on Commerce and Industry and of Cttee. on Rules and Admin., House of Councillors; Chair. Liberal Democratic Party House of Councillors Diet Affairs Cttee.; Minister of Health and Welfare 1986-87; Liberal Democratic Party. *Address:* c/o Ministry of Health and Welfare, 2-2 Kasumigaseki 1-chome, Chiyoda-ku, Tokyo, Japan.

SAITO, Kunikichi; Japanese politician; b. 1909; specialized in welfare and medical affairs, Labour Ministry; mem. for Fukushima Prefecture, House of Representatives; Deputy Sec.-Gen. Liberal Democratic Party (LDP), Chair. House of Representatives Finance Cttee., Deputy Chief Cabinet Sec., Parl. Vice-Minister of Finance, Minister of Health and Welfare 1972-74, July-Sept. 1980; Sec.-Gen. of LDP 1978-80; Dir.-Gen. Admin. Man. Agency 1982-83. *Address:* House of Representatives, Tokyo, Japan.

SAITO, Nobufusa, D.SC.; Japanese nuclear chemist; b. 28 Sept. 1916, Tokyo; m. Haruko Umeda 1944; one s. two d.; ed. Tokyo Imperial Univ.; fmr. Asst. Prof., Kyushu and Seoul Univs., Prof. of Inorganic Chem., Tokyo Univ. 1956-65; Chief Researcher, Inst. of Physical and Chemical Research 1959-76; fmr. Consultant to Int. Atomic Energy Agency (I.A.E.A.), Dir. of Isotopes Div. 1963-65; Prof. Inorganic and Nuclear Chem., Tokyo Univ. 1965-77, Dir. Radioisotope Centre 1970-77; Prof. Inorganic and Analytical Chem. Toho Univ. 1978-87, Dean, Faculty of Science 1979-82; Dir. Radioisotopes Assocn. 1967-; Tech. Adviser, Japan Atomic Energy Research Inst. 1966-; mem. Chemical Soc. of Japan (Vice-Pres. 1976-78, Pres. 1981-82), American Chemical Soc., Atomic Energy Soc. of Japan, Japan Soc. for Analytical Chem., Pres. 1979-80, Hon. mem. 1980-; Chem. Soc. of Japan Award 1974; Nat. Purple Ribbon Medal for Chemistry 1979; Royal Decoration of Second Order of Sacred Treasure 1987. *Leisure interests:* music, travel. *Address:* 5-12-9, Koshigoe, Kamakura 248, Japan. *Telephone:* 0467-31-3178.

SAITO, Shigeyoshi; Japanese politician; b. 9 Aug. 1918, Shizuoka Pref.; ed. Waseda Univ.; Vice-Pres. Daishowa Paper Mfg. Co. 1961-64; Mayor, Yoshihara City, Shizuoka Pref. 1964-66, Fuji City, Shizuoka Pref. 1966-69; mem. House of Reps. 1969-; Parl. Vice-Minister of Labour 1976; Minister of Construction 1980-81. *Address:* c/o Liberal-Democratic Party, 7, 2-chome, Hirakawacho, Chiyoda-ku, Tokyo, Japan.

SAKALAUSKAS, Vitautas Vladovich; Soviet party official and politician; ed. Engineering Inst.; mem. CPSU 1960-; Deputy Dir. of Lithuanian S.S.R. Sovnarkhoz (Econ. Planning Org.) 1963-65; Deputy Head, Head of Section of Cen. Cttee. of Lithuanian CP 1965-69; Pres. of Exec. Cttee. of Vilnius City Cttee. of Lithuanian CP 1969-74; First Sec. of Vilnius City Cttee. of Lithuanian CP 1974-83; First Deputy Pres. of Council of Ministers of Lithuanian S.S.R. 1983-84, Chair. Nov. 1985-; party work for Cen. Cttee. of CPSU 1984-85; Cand. mem. of Cen. Cttee. of CPSU 1986-. *Address:* Council of Ministers, Vilnius, Lithuanian S.S.R., U.S.S.R.

SAKAMOTO, Tomokazu, B.A.; Japanese broadcasting executive; b. 28 March 1917, Kanda, Tokyo; ed. Waseda Univ.; joined Nippon Hoso Kyokai (Japan Broadcasting Corpn.) 1939, Head of Scripts Section 1949, Man. Literary Arts Div., Radio Dept. 1956, Radio and TV Programming 1957, Deputy Dir. Entertainment 1960, Dir. 1965, Deputy Dir.-Gen. Broadcasting 1968-71, Man. Dir. and Dir.-Gen. 1971-73, Exec. Vice-Pres. 1976, Pres. 1976-82; Grosses Silbernes Ehrenzeichen (Austria) 1976, Order of Aguila Azteca (Mexico) 1981. *Address:* 2-34-24, Kamiasoo, Asao-ku, Kawasaki-shi, Japan (Home).

SAKATA, Michita; Japanese politician; b. 1916, Kyu-Shu; s. of Michio and Yo Sakata; m. Michiyo Sakata 1948; two s. two d.; ed. Tokyo Imperial Univ.; fmr. Private Sec. to Minister of Commerce and Industry; fmr. Parl. Vice-Minister for Transport; fmr. Minister of Health and Welfare; fmr. Minister of Educ.; mem. House of Reps., Speaker 1985-86; Dir. Defence Agency 1974-76; Minister of Justice 1981-82; Liberal Democrat. *Leisure interests:* music, painting. *Address:* Dai-ichi Gi-in-kaikan, 2-2-1, Nagato-cho, Chiyoda-ku Tokyo, Japan. *Telephone:* Tokyo 581-4877.

SAKHAROV, Andrey Dmitriyevich, D.PHIL.; Soviet nuclear physicist; b. 21 May 1921, Moscow; m. 2nd Yelena Bonner 1971; one s. one d.; ed. Moscow State Univ.; Physicist, P.N. Lebedev Physics Inst., Acad. of Sciences 1945-; mem. Acad. of Sciences of U.S.S.R. (Dept. of Nuclear Physics) 1953-, elected to Presidium 1988; mem. American Acad. of Arts and Sciences 1969-, Foreign Assoc. N.A.S. 1972-; with Igor Tamm achieved important breakthrough in field of controlled nuclear fusion leading to devt. of Soviet hydrogen bomb; formed Human Rights Cttee. 1970; freed from internal exile Dec. 1986; Hon. Pres. Int. League for Human Rights 1986-; elected to Congress of People's Deputies of the U.S.S.R. 1989; Eleanor Roosevelt Peace Award 1973, Cino del Duca Prize 1974, Reinhold Niebohr Prize, Univ. of Chicago 1974, Nobel Peace Prize 1975; Hero of Socialist Labour, Order of Lenin, Laureate of U.S.S.R. (stripped of U.S.S.R. awards Jan. 1980); Fritt Ord Prize 1980; Foreign Assoc. French Acad. of Science 1981; Hon. Citizen of Florence 1989; Hon. D.Sc. (Oxford) 1989. *Publications include:* Progress, Peaceful Co-existence and Intellectual Freedom 1968, Sakharov Speaks 1974, My Country and the World 1975, Alarm and Hope 1979, and basic works on problems of theoretical physics. *Address:* U.S.S.R. Academy of Sciences, Leninsky prospekt 14, Moscow; 486 Chkalov Street, Moscow, U.S.S.R. (Home).

SAKHNYUK, Ivan Ivanovich; Soviet party official; First Sec. of Kharkov City Cttee. of Ukrainian CP 1973-76; mem. Cen. Cttee. of Ukrainian CP 1976-; First Sec. of Kharkov Dist. Cttee. of Ukrainian CP 1976-; mem. Cen. Cttee. CPSU 1976-; Head of Section of Cen. Cttee. CPSU 1980-; Head of Cen. Cttee. Dept. of Agricultural Machine Building 1983—. *Address:* c/o Ministry of Agricultural Machine Building, Moscow, U.S.S.R.

SAKURAUCHI, Yoshio; Japanese politician; b. 1912; ed. Keio Univ.; returned to House of Reps. twelve times, House of Councillors once; fmr. Pres. Japanese Electro-Chemical Assocn.; Parl. Vice-Minister of Justice; Minister of Int. Trade and Industry 1964-65; Chair. House of Reps. Foreign Affairs Cttee. 1971; Minister of Agric. and Forestry 1972-73; Chair. Policy Research Council, Liberal-Democratic Party (LDP) Sept.-Dec. 1976; Minister of Construction and Dir.-Gen. Nat. Land Agency 1977-78; Sec.-Gen. LDP 1979-81; Minister of Foreign Affairs 1981-82. *Address:* c/o Liberal-Democratic Party, 7, 2-chome, Hirakawacho, Chiyoda-ku, Tokyo, Japan.

SALA, Marius, PH.D.; Romanian linguist; b. 8 Sept. 1932, Vaşcău, Bihor Co.; s. of Sabin Sala and Eleonora Tocoianu; m. Florica Sala 1958; one d.; ed. Coll. of Philology, Bucharest Univ.; researcher, Inst. of Linguistics, Bucharest 1955-; Visiting Prof. Heidelberg 1971, Málaga 1968, 1970, 1973, 1979, Madrid 1978, 1981, 1987, Mexico City 1984; Corresp. mem. Royal Acad. Spain 1978; Corresp. mem. Mexican Inst. of Culture 1981; mem. Int. Cttee. of Onomastic Studies 1969; mem. Int. Cttee. of the Mediterranean Linguistic Atlas 1960; mem. Man. Junta of the Int. Assocn. of Hispanists 1974-80; mem. Cttee. Soc. of Romance Linguistics 1974-80; mem. Perm. Int. Cttee. of Linguists 1987-; Prize of Romanian Acad. 1970; Prize of Mexican Acad. Centennial 1976. *Publications:* Contribuţii la fonetica istorică a limbii române (Contributions to the Historical Phonetics of the Romanian Language) 1970, Estudios sobre el judeo-español de Bucarest, Mexico City 1970, Phonétique et Phonologie du Judéo-Espagnol de Bucharest, The Hague 1971, Le judéo-espagnol, The Hague 1976, Contributions à la phonétique historique du roumain, Paris 1976, El léxico indígena del español americano, Apreciaciones sobre su vitalidad (co-author), Mexico-Bucharest 1977, El español de América, (Vol. 1), Léxico (co-author), Bogotá 1981, Limbile lumii. Mică enciclopedie (The Languages of the World: A concise encyclopaedia) (co-author), 1981, Les langues du monde (Petite Encyclopédie) (co-author), Paris 1984, Etimologia si Limba

Română (Etymology and the Romanian Language) (co-author) 1987, Vocabularul Reprezentativ Al Limbilov Romanice (The Representative Vocabulary of the Romance Languages) (co-author) 1988, El problema de las lenguas en contacto, Mexico City 1988. *Leisure interests:* philately, cooking. *Address:* Institutul de lingvistică, Str. Spiru Haret 12, 79515 Bucharest, Romania.

SALACROU, Armand Camille; French playwright; b. 9 Aug. 1899; ed. Faculty of Medicine, Faculty of Letters, Faculty of Law, Paris; thirty plays produced in Paris, first performance in Théâtre de l'Oeuvre 1925, first included in repertoire of Comédie-Française 1944; fmr. Pres. Soc. des Auteurs et Compositeurs Dramatiques; fmr. Pres. of Int. Theatre Inst. (UNESCO); Pres. Int. Confed. of Writers' and Composers' Asscns. 1975-; mem. Acad. Goncourt; Grand Officier, Légion d'honneur; Commdr. des Palmes Académiques, des Arts et des Lettres. *Plays:* Le pont de l'Europe 1927, Atlas-Hotel 1931, Une femme libre 1934, L'inconnue d'Arras 1935, La terre est ronde 1938, Histoire de rire 1939, Les fiancés du Havre 1944, Les nuits de la colère 1946, L'Archipel Lenoir 1947, Les invités du Bon Dieu, Sens interdit 1953, Le miroir, Une femme trop honnête 1956, Boulevard Durand 1960, Comme les chardons 1964, Dans la salle des pas perdus (memoirs), etc. *Address:* Villa Maritime, 8 rue Guy de Maupassant, 76600 Le Havre, France.

SALAH, Abdullah A.; Jordanian diplomatist; b. 31 Dec. 1922, Jordan; m. Fadwa Dajani 1960; one d.; ed. Bishop Gobat's School, Jerusalem, and American Univ. of Beirut; Field Educ. Officer, UN Relief and Works Agency (UNRWA), Jordan 1952-62; Amb. to Kuwait 1962-63, to India 1963-64, to France 1964-66, 1967-70; Minister of Foreign Affairs Dec. 1966-67, 1970-72; Amb. to U.S.A. (also accred. to Mexico) 1973-80, to Switzerland (also accred. to Austria) 1980-83; Perm. Rep. to UN 1983-; several decorations. *Address:* Jordan Mission to the UN, 866 United Nations Plaza, New York, N.Y. 10017 (Office); 126 East 72nd Street, New York, N.Y. 10021, U.S.A. (Home). *Telephone:* (212) 752-0135 (Office); (212) 517-5665 (Home).

SALAM, Abdus, M.A., PH.D., D.SC., F.R.S.; Pakistani university professor; b. 29 Jan. 1926, Jhang; ed. Govt. Coll., Lahore, St. John's Coll., Cambridge and Cavendish Lab., Cambridge; Prof. of Mathematics, Govt. Coll., Lahore 1951-54; Head, Mathematics Dept., Panjab Univ., Lahore 1952-54; lecturer, Univ. of Cambridge 1954-56; Prof. of Theoretical Physics, Imperial Coll. of Science and Technology, Univ. of London 1957-; Scientific Sec. Geneva Confs. on Peaceful Uses of Atomic Energy 1955, 1958; mem. Pakistan Atomic Energy Comm. 1958-74, Pakistan Science Council 1963-75, Chief Scientific Adviser to Pres. 1961-74; Pres. Pakistan Asscn. for Advancement of Science 1961-62; Chair. Pakistan Space and Upper Atmosphere Cttee. 1962-63; Gov., Int. Atomic Energy Agency 1962-63; Founder and Dir. Int. Centre for Theoretical Physics, Trieste 1964-; mem. UN Advisory Cttee. on Science and Tech. 1964-75, Chair. 1971-72; mem. UN Panel and Foundation Cttee. for UN Univ. 1970-73; Vice-Pres. IUPAP 1972-78; mem. Scientific Council Stockholm Int. Peace Research Inst. (SIPRI) 1970-; mem. Bd. Pakistan Sciences Foundation 1973-77; mem. London and American Physical Socs., European Acad. of Science, Arts and Humanities, Paris 1980, Pontifical Acad. of Sciences 1981; founder mem. Third World Acad. of Sciences 1983; Foreign mem. American Acad. of Art and Sciences 1971, U.S.S.R. Acad. of Sciences 1971, Accademia Nazionale dei Lincei (Rome) 1979, Accademia Tiberina (Rome) 1979, Iraqi Acad. (Baghdad) 1979, Acad. of Kingdom of Morocco 1980, Accademia Nazionale delle Scienze (dei XL) (Rome) 1980; Assoc. mem. Josef Stefan Inst., Ljubljana 1980; Corresp. mem. Acad. of Sciences, Lisbon 1981, Yugoslav Acad. of Sciences and Arts, Zagreb 1983; Hon. mem. Korean Physics Soc., Seoul 1979; Fellow Pakistan Acad. of Sciences 1954, Royal Swedish Acad. of Sciences 1970, Bangladesh Acad. of Sciences 1980; Hon. Fellow St. John's Coll., Cambridge 1971, Tata Inst. of Fundamental Research, Bombay 1979, Ghana Acad. of Arts and Sciences 1984; Foreign Fellow Indian Nat. Science Acad. 1980; Hon. Life Fellow Physical Soc., London 1986-; Hon. D.Sc. from 30 univs.; many awards including Hopkins Prize (Cambridge Univ.) 1958, Adams Prize (Cambridge Unv.) 1958, Maxwell Medal and Award (Physical Soc., London) 1961, Hughes Medal (Royal Soc., London) 1964, Atoms for Peace Award 1968, Guthrie Medal and Prize 1976, Royal Medal (Royal Soc., London) 1978, Matteuci Medal (Accademia Nazionale dei Lincei, Rome) 1978, John Torrence Tate Medal (American Inst. of Physics) 1978, Einstein Medal (UNESCO) 1979, Joint Winner Nobel Prize for Physics 1979, Peace Medal (Charles Univ., Prague) 1981, Lomonosov Gold Medal (U.S.S.R. Acad. of Sciences) 1983, Premio Umberto Biancamano (Italy) 1986, Dayemi Int. Peace Award (Bangladesh) 1986; Order of Nishan-e Imtaz 1979, Order of Andres Bello (Venezuela) 1980, Order of Istiqlal (Jordan) 1980, Cavaliere di Gran Groce dell'Ordine del Merito (Italy) 1980. *Publications:* Symmetry Concepts in Modern Physics 1966, Aspects of Quantum Mechanics (Ed. with E. P. Wigner) 1972, Ideals and Realities: selected essays of Abdus Salam 1984, Supergravity in Diverse Dimensions, Vols. I and II 1987; and about 250 papers on physics of elementary particles. *Address:* Department of Physics, Imperial College of Science and Technology, London, S.W.7, England; International Centre for Theoretical Physics, P.O. Box 586, 34100, Trieste, Italy. *Telephone:* 01-589 5111, ext. 6971, and Trieste 2240-250.

SALAM, Saeb; Lebanese politician; b. 1905, Beirut; s. of Selim and Koulthoum Salam; m. Tamima Mardam Bey 1941; three s. two d.; ed.

American Univ. of Beirut, L.S.E.; elected Provisional Head, Lebanese Govt. 1943; Deputy 1943-47, 1951, 1960; Minister of Interior 1946, 1960-61, 1970-73, of Foreign Affairs 1946; Prime Minister 1952, 1953, 1960-61, 1970-73, concurrently Minister of Defence 1961; mem. Nat. Dialogue Cttee. 1975; pioneer Lebanese civil aviation 1945, f. and Hon. Pres. Middle East Airlines Co., Beirut 1945-56; Pres. Nat. Fats and Oil Co. Ltd., Beirut; Pres. Makassed Philanthropic Islamic Asscn. 1958-82, Hon. Pres. 1982-; mem. Lebanese Reconciliation Conf. Geneva 1983, Lausanne 1984; Medal of the Nat. Struggle of Lebanon, Order of the Cedar of Lebanon, numerous foreign decorations. *Leisure interests:* hunting, swimming, reading, riding. *Address:* Rue Moussaitbé, B.P. 3147, Beirut, Lebanon.

SALAMONE, Ottavio, LL.B., DR.RER.POL.; Italian banker; b. 4 Feb. 1930, Palermo; s. of Nicola Salamone and Maria Etele Calapso; m. Giuseppina Salamone 1958; three d.; Man. Banco di Sicilia, Brussels 1960-64; Paris 1965-67, Chief Economist of the Bank and Head of Strategic Planning 1968-78, Head of Int. Div. 1978-83, Deputy Chief Executive 1983-85; Dir. Gen. and Chief Exec. 1985-; mem. Bd. of Dirs. Italian Bankers Asscn. *Publications:* numerous articles on int. econs. and finance. *Leisure interest:* classical music. *Address:* Banco di Sicilia, Via Generale Magliocco 1, 90141 Palermo, Italy (Office). *Telephone:* (091) 274331 (Office).

SALAZAR LÓPEZ, H.E. Cardinal José; Mexican ecclesiastic; b. 12 Jan. 1910, Ameca, Guadalajara; ordained 1934; consecrated titular Bishop of Prusiade 1961; transferred to Zamora 1967; Archbishop of Guadalajara 1970-; created Cardinal by Pope Paul VI 1973; Pres. Mexican Episcopal Conf. 1973-. *Address:* Palacio Arzobispal, Apartado Postal I-331, Guadalajara, Jal., Mexico.

SALCEDO-BASTARDO, José Luis; Venezuelan writer and diplomatist; b. 15 March 1926, Carúpano, Sucre; s. of Joaquín and Catalina (née Bastardo) Salcedo-Arocha; m. María Cecilia Avila 1968; four s.; ed. Universidad Central de Venezuela, Univ. de Paris and L.S.E.; Teacher of Social Sciences 1945; Chief Ed. Revista Nacional de Cultura 1948-50; Asst. lecturer, Universidad Central de Venezuela 1949; Founder Rector, Univ. of Santa María, Caracas 1953; Senator for State of Sucre mem. Senate Foreign Relations Cttee. 1958; Amb. to Ecuador 1959-61, to Brazil 1961-63; Prof. of Sociology, Univ. Central de Venezuela 1964; Pres. Nat. Inst. of Culture and Fine Arts 1965-67; Vice-Pres., Supreme Electoral Council 1970-74; Amb. to France 1974-76, to U.K. 1984-87, to G.D.R. 1987-; Sec.-Gen. to Presidency 1976-77; Minister of State for Science, Tech. and Culture 1977-78. *Publications:* Por el Mundo Sociológico de Cecilio Acosta 1945, En Fuga hacia la Gloria 1947, Visión y Revisión de Bolívar 1957, Biografía de Don Egidio Montesinos 1957, Tesis para la Unión 1963, Bases de una Acción Cultural 1965, Historia Fundamental de Venezuela 1970, La Conciencia del Presente 1971, Carabobo: Nacionalidad e Historia 1972, Bolívar: Un Continente y un Destino 1972, El Primer Deber 1973, Despolitizar la Historia: una tarea para el desarrollo 1973, De la Historia y los Deberes 1975, Bolívar y San Martín 1975, Un Hombre Diáfano 1976, Crucible of Americanism (Miranda's London House) 1979, Concordancias Ideológicos y Literarias en Bolívar 1981, Andrés Bello Americano 1982, Reiteración Bolivariana 1983, Andrés Eloy Blanco para jóvenes 1983, Simón Bolívar, L'unico scopo e la libertá 1983, Simón Bolívar: La Esperanza del Universo 1983, Bolívar, el Nacer Constante 1986. *Leisure interest:* travelling abroad. *Address:* 1080 Berlin, Unter den Linden 63-65, German Democratic Republic; Apartado Postal 2777, Caracas, Venezuela.

SALCHER, Herbert, DR.JUR., DR.RER.POL.; Austrian politician and lawyer; b. 3 Nov. 1929, Innsbruck; s. of Oswald and Frieda (née Hocheder) Salcher; m. Edith Durnes 1956; one s. one d.; ed. Innsbruck; joined Tirol area health insurance org. for workers and employees, Innsbruck 1950-70, Head of law dept. 1955-, Deputy Dir. 1962-; mem. (later Prov. Chair. for Tirol) Socialist Youth 1946-; mem. Socialist Party of Austria 1950-, Prov. Chair. for Tirol and mem. Fed. Party Presidium 1969-85; mem. Innsbruck area council 1960-69; Prov. Deputy Leader in Tirol (responsible for health and social affairs) 1970-85; Fed. Minister for Health and Environment 1979-81, for Finance 1981-84; mem. OGB (Union of Private Employees) Prov. Exec. in Tirol; Ehrenzeichen des Landes Tirol 1977; Hon. Senator, Univ. of Innsbruck 1979. *Leisure interest:* football. *Address:* 6020 Innsbruck, Kärtner Strasse 64, Austria.

SALEH, Lt.-Col. Ali Abdullah; Yemeni army officer and politician; b. c. 1942; participated in 1974 coup; Security Chief, Taiz Province until June 1978; mem. Provisional Presidential Council, Deputy C.-in-C. of Armed Forces June-July 1978; Pres. of Yemen Arab Repub. and C.-in-C. of Armed Forces July 1978-. *Address:* Office of the President, Sana'a, Yemen Arab Republic.

SALEH, Rachmat; Indonesian politician; b. 1 May 1930, Surabya, E. Java; ed. Univ. of Indonesia, Jakarta; joined Bank of Indonesia 1956; Reserve Bank of India, Bombay 1957; temporary rep. of Bank of Indonesia in U.S.A. 1958; Asst. Sec. to Bank of Indonesia Rep. in Netherlands; various posts with Bank of Indonesia, Jakarta 1960-66, Dir. 1966, Gov. 1978; Minister of Trade 1983-88. *Address:* c/o Ministry of Trade, Jln. Moh. Ihkwan Rais, 5, Jakarta, Indonesia.

SALEHKHOU, Ghassem, PH.D.; Iranian diplomatist and international financial official; b. 27 March 1941, Teheran; s. of Mohammad Hassan and Essmat; m. Simin Khatib Damavandi 1964; one s.; ed. Nat. Univ. of Iran,

Fairleigh Dickinson Univ., N.J., U.S.A., New School for Social Research, New York; Econ. Expert, Plan Org., Teheran 1964-65; Research Asst., Dept. of Social Science, Fairleigh Dickinson Univ., N.J. 1967-68, Instructor 1968-72; Pres. Saleh Int. Inc., U.S.A. 1972-75; Econ. Expert, Bureau of Int. Econ., Plan and Budget Org., Teheran 1975-76; Man. Dir. Protrade Iran S.S.K., Teheran 1976-79; Lecturer Faculty of Econs., Univ. of Teheran 1976-79, Centre for Gen. Educ., Industrial Univ., Teheran 1977-79; Exec. Dir. Shirin Khorasan, Teheran 1976-79; Amb. to Japan 1979-82; Adviser to Gov. Bank Markazi Iran (Cen. Bank) 1982; Exec. Dir. IMF, Washington, D.C. 1982-88. *Publications:* Commercialization of Technology in Developing Countries, Fundamentals of Productivity in Contrasting Economic Systems. *Leisure interests:* photography, antiques, handicrafts, tennis, religious studies. *Address:* c/o International Monetary Fund, 700 19th street, N.W., Washington, D.C. 20431, U.S.A.

SALEK, Lieut.-Col. Mustapha Ould; Mauritanian army officer and politician; ed. Saumur Mil. Acad., France; Chief of Staff of Armed Forces 1968-69, March 1978; fmr. Dir. Société Nat. d'Import/Export (SONIMEX); Commdr. Third Mil. Region 1977; Head of State and Chair. Mil. Cttee. for Nat. Recovery (later for Nat. Salvation) 1978-79; sentenced to 10 years' imprisonment for plotting against Pres. Haidalla March 1982.

SALEM, Elie; Lebanese academician and politician; b. 1930, Bterram Koura; Dean of Science and Arts, Prof. of Political Science, American Univ., Beirut 1974-82; lecturer on Middle East, Johns Hopkins Univ., U.S.A.; Deputy Prime Minister and Minister of Foreign Affairs 1982-84. *Address:* c/o Ministry of Foreign Affairs, Beirut, Lebanon.

SALET, Francis; French museum director; b. 12 Feb. 1909, Paris; s. of Pierre Salet and Marie Thérèse Bazin; m. Denise Brosselin 1938; six c.; Asst. Musée du Louvre 1942; Conservateur, Musées Nationaux 1945, Conservateur en Chef 1964; Insp.-Gen. of Museums 1974; Conservateur, Domaine de Chantilly; mem. Inst. de France; Officier, Légion d'Honneur, Commdr. des Arts et des Lettres; Grand Prix nat. du Patrimoine 1988. *Publications:* books and articles on the art of the Middle Ages. *Leisure interest:* history of art. *Address:* 49 rue de Bellechasse, 75007 Paris, France.

SALIFOU, Illa; Niger diplomatist; b. 17 Feb. 1932, Madaoua; s. of Salifou and Larba Mayaki; m. Bernadette Soares 1955; five s. two d.; ed. Univ. Inst. for Higher Int. Studies; Dir. Admin. and Legislative Div., Ministry of Justice 1960-61; First Sec., later Counsellor, Washington, D.C. until 1966; Dir. de Cabinet, Ministry of Foreign Affairs and Co-operation 1968-70, 1971-74, Tech. Counsellor, Dir. Consular and Admin. Affairs 1970-71; Perm. Rep. to UN 1974-76; Amb. to U.S.A. 1974-76, to U.S.S.R., Poland, Romania, Yugoslavia, Czechoslovakia, India, German Democratic Repub. 1976-79; Sec.-Gen. Ministry of Foreign Affairs and Co-operation 1979-80; Personnel Man., Agence de Coopération Culturelle et Technique (ACCT) Paris 1981-. *Leisure interests:* photography, music, reading. *Address:* ACCT, 13 Quai André Citroën, 75015 Paris, France. *Telephone:* 575-62-41.

SALIM, Salim Ahmed; Tanzanian diplomatist; b. 1942, Zanzibar; ed. Lumumba Coll., Zanzibar and Univ. of Delhi; Publicity Sec. of UMMA Party and Chief Ed. of its official organ Sauti ya UMMA 1963; Exec. Sec. United Front of Opposition Parties and Chief Ed. of its newspaper; Sec. Gen. All-Zanzibar Journalists Union 1963; Amb. to United Arab Repub. 1964-65; High Commr. to India 1965-68; Dir. African and Middle East Affairs Div., Ministry of Foreign Affairs 1968-69; Amb. to People's Repub. of China and Democratic People's Repub. of Korea June-Dec. 1969; Perm. Rep. to UN 1970-80 (Pres. of Gen. Ass. 1979), also High Commr. to Jamaica, accred. to Guyana, Trinidad and Tobago, and Amb. to Cuba 1971-80; Chair. UN Special Cttee. on Decolonization 1972-79; Minister of Foreign Affairs 1980-84, Prime Minister of Tanzania 1984-85, Deputy Prime Minister, Minister of Defence and Nat. Service 1986-; a fmr. Vice-Pres. of Tanzania; fmr. del. of Tanzania at UN Gen. Ass. and other int. confs. *Address:* Office of the Prime Minister, Dar-es-Salaam, Tanzania.

SALIMOV, Akil Umurzakovich; Soviet official; b. 1928, Uzbekistan; ed. Tashkent Polytech. Inst., Cand. Tech. Science 1954; lecturer, Dean, Pro-rector of Tashkent Polytech. Inst. 1954-65; Deputy Head of Dept. of Science and Educational Insts. with Cen. Cttee. of Uzbek CP 1965-66, Head 1966-70; Sec. of Uzbek CP 1970-83; Deputy to U.S.S.R. Supreme Soviet 1983-; Pres. Praesidium of Supreme Soviet of Uzbek CP and Deputy-Pres. U.S.S.R. Supreme Soviet 1983-87; Rector Tashkent Inst. for Irrigation Engineers and Agricultural Mechanisation Dec. 1986-. *Address:* The Kremlin, Moscow, U.S.S.R.

SALINAS DE GORTARI, Carlos, PH.D.; Mexican politician; b. 1948, Mexico City; ed. Nat. Univ. of Mexico and Harvard Univ.; Asst. Prof. of Statistics, Nat. Univ. of Mexico 1970; Research Asst. Harvard Univ. 1974; taught Public Finance and Fiscal Policy in Mexico 1976, 1978; Asst. Dir. of Public Finance, Ministry of Finance 1971-74, Head of Econ. Studies 1974-76, Asst. Dir. of Financial Planning 1978, Dir.-Gen. 1978-79; Dir.-Gen. of Econ. and Social Policy, Ministry of Programming and Budget 1979-81; Dir.-Gen. Inst. of Political, Social and Econ. Studies 1981-82; Minister of Planning and Fed. Budget 1982-87; named as Pres. Cand. by Partido Revolucionario Institucional (PRI) 1987-; Pres. of Mexico Dec. 1988-. *Publications:* numerous articles and essays. *Address:* Palacio de Gobierno, México, D.F., Mexico.

SALINAS IZAGUIRRE, Abel; Peruvian politician, engineer and economist; b. 12 May 1930, Puerto Supe; Dir. Nat. Housing Corpn. 1961; Prof. of Econ. Planning, Latin American Inst. of Econ. and Social Planning, Chile 1965; Prof. of Project Preparation and Evaluation, Faculty of Econs., Universidad Nacional Federico Villareal 1966; Chair. Lima Public Works Bd. 1970; mem. Higher Council of Nat. Econ. Devt. Fund 1971; Lima Prov. Councillor 1983; Minister of the Interior 1985-87, of Energy and Mines 1987-88, of Economy and Finance Sept. 1988-; mem. Colegio de Ingenieros del Perú, Colegio de Economistas del Perú, Asociación Electrotécnica Peruana, Instituto de Desarrollo Económico y Social de Argentina, Centro de Estudios de Desarrollo Económico del Paraguay. *Address:* Plaza 30 de Agosto 150, San Isidro, Lima, Peru. *Telephone:* 416990.

SALINGER, J(erome) D(avid); American author; b. 1 Jan. 1919, New York; s. of Sol and Miriam (née Jillich) Salinger; m. Claire Douglas 1953 (divorced 1976); one s. one d.; ed. Manhattan public schools and a military coll.; travelled in Europe 1937-38; army service with 4th Infantry Div. (Staff Sergeant) 1942-46; mem. Légion d'honneur. *Publications:* The Catcher in the Rye 1951, Franny and Zooey, Raise High the Roof Beam, Carpenters and Seymour—An Introduction 1963 (novels), For Esme with Love and Squalor 1953 (stories); numerous stories, mostly in the New Yorker 1948-. *Address:* c/o Harold Ober Associates Inc., 40 E. 49th Street, New York, N.Y. 10017, U.S.A.

SALINGER, Pierre Emil George, B.S.; American journalist and politician; b. 14 June 1925, San Francisco; s. of the late Herbert Edgar Salinger and of Jehanne Bietry Carlson; m. 3rd Nicole Helene Gillmann 1965 (divorced 1988); three s. one d.; ed. Univ. of San Francisco; San Francisco Chronicle 1942-55; U.S. Navy Second World War; Press Officer, Calif., Stevenson for Pres. Campaign 1952, Richard Graves for Gov. (Calif.) 1954; West Coast Ed., Contributing Ed. Collier's Magazine 1955-56; Investigator, Senate Labor Rackets Cttee. 1957-59; Press Sec. to Senator John F. Kennedy 1959-61, to Pres. John F. Kennedy 1961-63, to Pres. Lyndon Johnson 1963-64; U.S. Senator from Calif. 1964-65; Dir. Nat. Gen. Productions 1965-; Vice-Pres. Nat. Gen. Corpn. 1965-, Continental Airlines 1965-68; Chair. Great America Man. and Research Co. Int. (Gramco) 1968-, Deputy Chair. Gramco (U.K.) Ltd. 1970-71; Sr. Vice-Pres. Amprop Inc. 1969; Roving Ed. L'Express, Paris 1973-78; Roving reporter in Europe for ABC (TV) 1977-87 (Adviser on Foreign Affairs 1987-); Bureau Chief, ABC News, Paris 1977; Chief Foreign Corresp. ABC News 1983-87; lecturer at over 60 U.S. univs. and colls. 1965-69; Trustee, Robert F. Kennedy Memorial Foundation, American Coll. in Paris (now American Univ. in Paris) 1973-88; Officier, Légion d'honneur 1978; Democrat. *Publications:* A Tribute to John F. Kennedy 1964, With Kennedy 1966, A Tribute to Robert F. Kennedy 1968, On Instructions of my Government (novel) 1971, Je suis un américain 1975, La France et le nouveau monde 1976, Venezuelan Notebooks 1978, America Held Hostage: The Secret Negotiations 1981, The Dossier (novel, with Leonard Gross) 1984, Above Paris (with Robert Cameron) 1984, Mortal Games (novel, with Leonard Gross) 1988. *Address:* c/o ABC News, 44 West 66th Street, New York, N.Y. 10023, U.S.A.

SALIS, Jean Rodolphe de, D. ÈS L.; Swiss professor; b. 12 Dec. 1901, Berne; m. Elsie Huber 1940; one s.; ed. Gymnase de Berne and Univs. of Montpellier, Berne, Berlin and Paris; corresp. of Der Bund in Paris 1930-35; syndicated corresp. of the foreign press in Paris 1931-35; Prof. of History, Swiss Inst. of Tech., Zürich 1935-68; commentator of Radio Beromuenster ("Weltchronik") 1940-47; observer at First Gen. Ass. of UNESCO 1946; Prof. Univ. of Vienna, Summer 1947; mem. of University Comm. (Germany, British Zone) 1948; Del. to UNESCO Gen. Conf. 1954, 1960; Pres. Pro Helvetia Foundation 1952-64; Dr. h.c. (Geneva) 1959, (Vienna) 1981, (Hamburg) 1983, (Lausanne) 1985; Officier, Légion d'honneur; Grosses Silbernes Ehrenzeichen Oesterreich, Grosses Bundesverdienstkreuz. *Publications:* Sismondi, la vie et l'oeuvre d'un cosmopolite philosophe (2 vols.) 1932, Rainer Maria Rilkes Schweizer Jahre 1936, Giuseppe Motta, Dreissig Jahre eidgenössiche Politik 1941, Fritz Wotruba 1947, Weltgeschichte der neuesten Zeit, 6 Vols. 1980, Im Lauf der Jahre 1962, Weltchronik 1939-45, Schwierige Schweiz 1968, Grenzüberschreitungen, Ein Lebensbericht (Vol. I) 1975, (Vol. II) 1978, Notizeneines Müssigängers 1983, Innen und Aussen 1987. *Leisure interests:* music, theatre, hunting. *Address:* Schloss Brunegg, Aargau; Claussiusstrasse 34, Zurich, Switzerland. *Telephone:* 56-11-44, 251-20-21.

SALISBURY, Harrison Evans, B.A.; American journalist; b. 14 Nov. 1908; s. of Percy P. and Georgiana E. Salisbury; m. 1st Mary Hollis 1933 (divorced), two s.; m. 2nd Charlotte Rand 1964; ed. Univ. of Minnesota; United Press Int. 1930-48; Moscow Corresp., New York Times 1949-54, Nat. Affairs Ed. 1961-63, Asst. Man. Ed. 1964-72, Assoc. Ed. 1972-74; mem. American Acad. of Arts and Sciences 1969-, Nat. Inst. of Arts and Letters 1972- (Pres. 1975-76); Pres. Authors' League 1980-; mem. American Acad. of Arts and Letters 1985-; Pulitzer Prize for Int. Correspondence 1955; George Polk Memorial Journalism Award 1958, 1967. *Publications:* Russia on the Way 1946, American in Russia 1955, The Shook-Up Generation 1959, To Moscow—and Beyond 1960, Moscow Journal 1961, A New Russia? 1962, The Northern Palmyra Affair 1962, Orbit of China 1967, Behind the Lines—Hanoi 1967, The Soviet Union: The 50 Years 1967, The 900 Days, The Siege of Leningrad 1969, The Coming War

Between Russia and China 1970, The Many Americas Shall be One 1971, The Eloquence of Protest 1972, To Peking—and Beyond 1973, The Gates of Hell 1975, Travels around America 1976, Black Night, White Snow—Russia's Revolutions 1905-1917 1978, Without Fear or Favor: The New York Times and Its Times 1980, One Hundred Years of Revolution, Journey of Our Times: A Memoir 1983, The Long March: The Untold Story 1985, A Time of Change: A Reporter's Tale of Our Times 1988. *Address:* c/o Harper and Row Inc., 10 East 53rd Street, New York, N.Y. 10022; Box 70, Taconic, Conn. 06079, U.S.A. (Home). *Telephone:* (203) 824-7074 (Home).

SALK, Jonas Edward, B.SC., M.D.; American scientist; b. 28 Oct. 1914, New York; s. of Daniel Salk and Dora Press; m. 1st Donna Lindsay 1939 (dissolved 1968), 2nd Francoise Gilot 1970; three s.; ed. New York Univ. Coll. of Medicine and Coll. of New York City; Fellow in Chem., New York Univ. Coll. of Medicine 1935-36, Christian A. Herter Fellow 1936-38, Fellow in Bacteriology 1939-40; Intern, Mt. Sinai Hosp., New York 1940-42; Nat. Research Council Fellow, School of Public Health, Univ. of Michigan 1942-43, Research Fellow in Epidemiology 1943-44, Research Assoc. in Epidemiology 1944-46, Asst. Prof. 1946-47; Assoc. Prof. of Bacteriology, of Virus Research, School of Medicine, Univ. of Pittsburgh 1947-49, Dir. of Virus Research Lab. 1947-63, Research Prof. 1949-55; Commonwealth Prof. Preventive Medicine 1955-57; Commonwealth Prof. Experimental Medicine 1957-63; Dir. Salk Inst. for Biological Studies 1963-75, Resident Fellow 1963-84, Founding Dir. 1975-, Distinguished Prof. in Int. Health Sciences 1984-; Consultant to Sec. of War in Epidemic Diseases 1944-47; Consultant to Sec. of Army in Epidemic Diseases 1947-54; Adjunct Prof. of Health Sciences in Depts. of Psychiatry, Community Medicine and Medicine, Univ. of Calif., San Diego 1970-; specialist polio research; mem. American Epidemiological Soc., American Soc. for Clinical Investigation, Soc. for Experimental Biology and Medicine; Fellow of American Public Health Asscn., A.A.A.S., Asscn. American Physicians, American Acad. of Arts and Sciences; Hon. Fellow, American Acad. of Pediatrics, Royal Soc. of Health, Weizmann Inst., Univ. of Calif., San Diego, All India Inst. of Med. Sciences; several hon. degrees; Jawaharlal Nehru Award for Int. Understanding 1976, Harry S. Truman Good Neighbor Award 1983, and many other awards and prizes. *Publications:* Man Unfolding 1972, The Survival of the Wisest 1973, World Population and Human Values: A New Reality (joint author) 1981, Anatomy of Reality: Merging of Intuition and Reason 1983, and over 90 scientific papers. *Address:* The Salk Institute for Biological Studies, P.O. Box 85800, San Diego, Calif. 92138, U.S.A. *Telephone:* 619-453-4100.

SALKIND, Alexander; Russian film producer; b. Danzig; father of Ilya Salkind (q.v.); worked in Germany with his father, producer Miguel Salkind; moved to Mexico 1945, to Spain 1950. *Films include:* Black Jack, Austerlitz, The Trial, The Life of Cervantes, Light at the Edge of the World, Bluebeard, The Three Musketeers, The Four Musketeers, The Twist, The Prince and the Pauper, Superman, Superman 2, Superman 3, Supergirl, Santa Claus: The Movie. *Address:* Pinewood Studios, Pinewood Road, Iver Heath, Bucks., England.

SALKIND, Ilya; film producer; b. 1947, Mexico; s. of Alexander Salkind (q.v.); Assoc. Producer, Cervantes, The Light at the Edge of the World, Spain, 1974. *Films include:* Bluebeard, The Three Musketeers, The Four Musketeers, The Twist, The Prince and the Pauper, Superman, Superman 2, Superman 3, Supergirl, Santa Claus: The Movie. *Address:* Pinewood Studios, Pinewood Road, Iver Heath, Iver, Bucks., England.

SALLAH, Ousman Ahmadou, B.A.; Gambian diplomatist; b. 26 July 1938, Kudang; s. of Ahmadou Jabel Sallah and Haddy Sallah; m. Ramou Sallah 1966; two s. two d.; ed. Trinity Coll., Hartford, Conn., School of Int. Affairs, Columbia Univ., New York; Asst. Sec., Prime Minister's Office 1967; Asst. Sec. Ministry of External Affairs 1967-68, Deputy Perm. Sec. 1973-74; First Sec., Head of Chancery and Acting High Commr., London 1971; Amb. to Saudi Arabia (also accred. to Egypt, Iran, Kuwait, Qatar and U.A.E.) 1974-79, to U.S.A. 1979-83; Perm. Rep. to UN 1979-83, 1987-; Perm. Sec. Ministry of External Affairs and Head of Gambian Diplomatic Service 1982-; Hon. LL.D. (Trinity Coll., Hartford); Diploma in Int. Relations and Diplomacy from UNITAR. *Leisure interest:* tennis. *Address:* Permanent Mission of the Gambia to the United Nations, 19 East 47th Street, New York, N.Y. 10017, U.S.A.; P.O. Box 667, Banjul, The Gambia. *Telephone:* 93-2184 (Home).

SALLAL, Marshal Abdullah as-; Yemeni army officer and politician; b. 1917; ed. in Iraq; returned to Yemen from Iraq 1939; imprisoned 1939; Army Service 1940-48, 1955-67; imprisoned 1948-55; Gov. of Hodeida 1959-62; Chief of Staff to Imam Mohammed Sept. 1962; led coup against the Imam and proclaimed a repub. Sept. 1962; Pres. of the Revolutionary Council, Commdr.-in-Chief of the Republican forces, Yemeni Civil War 1962-67, concurrently Prime Minister 1962-67, Minister of Foreign Affairs 1963-64; deposed Nov. 1967; now living in Egypt.

SALLAM, Mohamed Abdulaziz, B.A.; Yemeni diplomatist; b. 15 Dec. 1933, Taiz; s. of Abdulaziz Mohamed Sallam and Hend Abdullah Ali; m. Maryam Ahmed al-Awami 1960; three s.; ed. secondary school in Helwan, Egypt, Stockbridge School, Mass. and Temple Univ., Philadelphia, Pa., U.S.A.; engaged in private sector 1960-61; Instructor, Belguis Coll. 1961-62; Dir.-

Gen. Ministry of Public Health 1962-63; Minister and Chargé d'affaires, Embassy in Baghdad 1963-64; Deputy Minister of Foreign Affairs 1964-65; Chair. Board, Yemen Drug Co. 1965-66; Minister of Foreign Affairs 1966-67; Dir.-Gen. Office of the Prime Minister 1970-71; Amb. in Ministry of Foreign Affairs 1971-73; Minister with rank of Amb., Embassy in London 1973-75; Amb., Deputy Perm. Rep. to UN 1975-76, Perm. Rep. 1976-78, 1982-85; Chief of Cabinet for Tech. Affairs in Office of the Prime Minister 1978-82; leader of dels. to various int. confs. incl. UN Gen. Ass. 1965, Fifth Emergency Special Session, Fourth Summit Conf. of Arab League 1967. *Leisure interests:* chess, music. *Address:* 78 Hedda Road, Sana'a, Yemen Arab Republic (Home). *Telephone:* 77420 (Home).

SALLE, David, M.F.A.; American artist; b. 1952, Okla.; s. of Alvin S. Salle and Tillie D. (née Brown) Salle; ed. California Inst. of Arts; one-man shows include: Project Inc., Cambridge, Mass. 1975, Foundation Corps de Garde, Groningen, Holland 1976, 1978, Artists Space, New York 1976, Foundation de Appel, Amsterdam 1977, The Kitchen, New York 1977, 1979, Mary Boone Gallery, New York 1981-83, Lucio Amelio Gallery, Naples 1981, Mario Diacono, Rome 1982, Anthony D'Offay Gallery, London 1982, Akira Ikeda Gallery, Tokyo 1983, Castelli Graphics, New York 1984, Gagosian Gallery, Los Angeles 1984; retrospective exhbn. Museum of Contemporary Art, Chicago 1987; group shows include: Serial Gallerie, Amsterdam 1977, Studio Cannaviello, Milan 1979, Grand Palais, Paris 1980, Nigel Greenwood Gallery, London 1981, Kunsthallen, Göteborg, Sweden 1981, New York Public Library 1982, Whitney Museum of American Art, New York 1982-83, Kassel 1982, Venice 1982, Stockholm 1983, Madrid 1983, São Paulo 1983, London (Tate Gallery) 1983, Pace Gallery 1983. *Address:* c/o Leo Castelli Gallery, 420 W. Broadway, New York, N.Y. 10012, U.S.A.

SALLINGER, Rudolf; Austrian business executive; b. 3 Sept. 1916; ed. Technische Hochschule, Vienna; Proprietor of stonemason's firm, Vienna 1943-; Head of Guild of Stone-Masons, Vienna 1950, later Deputy Head of Fed. of Guilds; Chair. Trade Section, Chamber of Commerce, Vienna; Pres. Chamber of Commerce, Vienna 1960-64; Pres. Fed. Econ. Chamber 1964-; Pres. Austrian Nat. Cttee. for Int. Trade; mem. Nationalrat 1966-; numerous decorations. *Address:* Bundeskammer der gewerblichen Wirtschaft, 1045 Vienna, Wiedner Hauptstrasse 63, Austria.

SALMAN IBN ABDUL AZIZ, H.R.H. Prince; Saudi Arabian politician; b. 13 Dec. 1936; s. of the late King Abdul Aziz ibn Saud; m.; brother of H.R.H. King Fahd (q.v.); Gov. of Riyadh 1962-; Chair. Bd. Riyadh Water and Sanitary Drainage Authority, and numerous other orgs.; active in Abdul Aziz Foundation. *Leisure interest:* reading. *Address:* Office of the Governor, Riyadh, Saudi Arabia.

SALMAN, Salah, M.D., F.A.C.S.; Lebanese physician and government official; b. 24 Jan. 1936, Beirut; ed. American Univ. of Beirut School of Medicine, Johns Hopkins Univ. School of Medicine, U.S.A.; Minister of Public Health March–June 1972; Assoc. Prof. and Chair. of Dept of Otolaryngology, American Univ. of Beirut 1974-; Minister of the Interior, Housing and Co-operatives 1976-79; Penrose Award, Faculties of Medical Sciences 1961. *Publications:* 19 papers in int. and local medical journals in otolaryngology and allied subjects. *Address:* American University of Beirut, Lyon Street, Najjar Building, Beirut, Lebanon (Home).

SALMANOV, Grigory Ivanovich; Soviet military official; b. 1922; ed. Higher Mil. Acad. and Gen. Staff Mil. Acad.; mem. CPSU 1944-; served in Soviet Army 1940-; rank of Gen.; various sr. posts 1949-69; Commdr. of Kiev Mil. Dist 1969-75, Transbaikal 1978-; Deputy Commdr.-in-Chief of U.S.S.R. Ground Forces 1975-78; Deputy to Supreme Soviet 1970-; mem. Cen. Cttee. Ukrainian CP 1971-76; cand. mem. Cen. CPSU 1971-76; mem. 1981-; Order of Red Star. *Address:* The Kremlin, Moscow, U.S.S.R.

SALMERÓN, Fernando; Mexican philosopher; b. 30 Oct. 1925, Córdoba, Veracruz; s. of Prof. Fernando A. Salmerón and Ana María Roíz de Salmerón; m. Alicia V. Castro 1952; four s. two d.; ed. University of Veracruz, Autonomous Univ. of Mexico (UNAM), Albert Ludwig Univ., Fed. Repub. of Germany; Dir. Faculty of Philosophy, Univ. of Veracruz 1956-58, Rector 1961-63; Dir. Inst. of Philosophical Investigations (UNAM) 1966-78, Investigator of Complete Time 1981-; Rector Iztapalapa Section, Metropolitan Autonomous Univ. 1978-79, Gen. Rector 1979-81; mem. Colegio Nacional 1972-; hon. Dr. Univ. of Veracruz, Investigador Nacional 1984. *Publications include:* Las Mocedades de Ortega y Gasset 1959, Cuestiones educativas y páginas sobre México 1962, La Filosofía y las actitudes morales 1971, Etica y análisis (ed.) 1985, Ortega y Gasset (ed.) 1984, Ensayos filosóficos 1988. *Address:* El Colegio Nacional, Luis González Obregón 23, México 1, D.F. (Office); Congreso 70, Tlalpan, 1400 México D.F., Mexico (Home). *Telephone:* 573 21 65 (Home).

SALMON, Baron (Life Peer), cr. 1972, of Sandwich, Kent; **Cyril Barnet Salmon,** P.C.; British judge; b. 28 Dec. 1903, London; s. of Montague Salmon and Marian Trevor; m. 1st Rencie Anderfelt 1929 (died 1942), 2nd Jean, Lady Morris 1946; one s. one d.; ed. Mill Hill and Pembroke Coll., Cambridge; called to the Bar, Middle Temple 1925, Master, Treasurer 1972, Hon. Fellow; Q.C. 1945; Judge, High Court of Justice, Queen's Bench Div. 1957-64; Lord Justice of Appeal 1964-72; Lord of Appeal in Ordinary 1972-80; Commissary of Cambridge Univ. 1979-; Chair. Royal Comm. on Standards of Conduct in Public Life 1974-76; Gov. Mill Hill School; Hon. Fellow, Pembroke Coll., Cambridge; Hon. D.C.L. (Kent) 1978. *Leisure* *interests:* fishing, golf. *Address:* Manwood Place, Sandwich, Kent, England. *Telephone:* Sandwich 2244.

SALMON, Brian Lawson, C.B.E.; British business executive (retd.); b. 30 June 1917, London; s. of Julius Salmon and Emma Constance Gluckstein; m. Annette Wilson Mackay 1946; two s. one d.; ed. Malvern Coll.; joined J. Lyons & Co. 1935, Dir. 1961–, Jt. Man. Dir. 1967–69, Deputy Chair. 1969–72, Chair. 1972–77; Vice-Chair. Bd. of Govs., Westminster Hospital Group 1963–74; a Vice-Chair. Royal Coll. of Nursing 1972; Chair. Cttee. on Sr. Nursing Staff Structure 1963–66, Camden and Islington Area Health Authority (Teaching) 1974–77; Chair. Supply Bd. Working Group, Dept of Health and Social Security 1977. *Leisure interests:* theatre, ballet. *Address:* 34 Kingston House North, Princes Gate, London, SW7 1LN, England. *Telephone:* 01-589 1382.

SALMON, Geoffrey Isidore Hamilton, C.B.E.; British businessman; b. 14 Jan. 1908, London; s. of Harry and Lena (née Gluckstein) Salmon; m. Peggy Rica (née Jacobs) 1936; two s. one d.; ed. Malvern Coll. and Jesus Coll., Cambridge; Hon. Catering Adviser to the Army 1959–71; Chair. J. Lyons & Co. Ltd. 1968–72, Pres. 1972–77. *Address:* 10 Stavordale Lodge, 12 Melbury Road, London, W14 8LW, England. *Telephone:* 01-602 3425.

SALMON, John Tenison, D.SC., F.R.E.S., F.R.P.S., F.R.S.N.Z.; New Zealand professor of zoology and author (retd.); b. 28 June 1910, Wellington; s. of Charles T. Salmon and Marie Salmon; m. Pamela N. Wilton 1948; four s.; ed. Wellington Coll. and Victoria Univ. of Wellington; entomologist, Dominion Museum 1934–48; Sr. Lecturer in Biology, Vic. Univ. of Wellington 1948–58, Assoc. Prof. of Zoology 1958–64, Prof. and Head, Dept. of Zoology 1965–76, Dean of Science 1971–72; mem. Nature Conservation Council of N.Z. 1962–84; Nuffield Travelling Research Fellow 1950–51; Carnegie Travelling Fellow 1958; hon. mem. American Entomological Soc.; has held numerous hon. positions in learned socs. etc. *Publications include:* Heritage Destroyed 1960, New Zealand Flowers and Plants in Colour 1963, The Native Trees of New Zealand 1980, Field Guide to the Alpine Plants of New Zealand 1985, A Field Guide to the Native Trees of New Zealand 1986; numerous scientific papers, magazine articles etc. *Leisure interests:* photography, gardening, tramping. *Address:* Rongonui, 60 Harvey Street, Taupo, New Zealand. *Telephone:* 85-187.

SALMON, Neil Lawson, C.B.I.M.; British business executive; b. 17 Feb. 1921, London; s. of Julius and Mimi Salmon; m. Yvonne Helene Isaacs 1944; one s. one d.; ed. Malvern Coll., Institut Minerva, Zürich, Switzerland; joined J. Lyons and Co. Ltd. 1938, Dir. 1965–81, Joint Man. Dir. 1967–69, Group Man. Dir. 1969–72, Deputy Chair. 1972–77, 1978–81, Chair. 1977–78; Dir. Allied Breweries 1978–81; Lay mem. of Restrictive Practices Court 1971–; part-time mem. of Monopolies and Mergers Comm. 1980–; mem. Council British Inst. of Man. 1974–88; Chair. Professional Standards Cttee. 1982–88. *Leisure interests:* opera, ballet, theatre, wine. *Address:* Eldon House, 1 Dorset Street, London, W1H 3FB, England. *Telephone:* 01-581 4501.

SALMON, Robert; French journalist; b. 6 April 1918, Marseille; s. of Pierre Salmon; ed. Lycée Louis le Grand, Ecole Normale Supérieure and at the Sorbonne; Founder Mouvement de Résistance et Défense de la France; mem. Comité Parisien de Libération; Leader Paris Div., Mouvement de Libération Nationale; mem. Provisional Consultative Ass. 1944, First Constituent Ass. 1945; Founder Pres. and Dir. Gen. France-Soir 1944; fmr. Pres. Soc. France-Editions (Elle, Le Journal de Dimanche, Paris-Presse, etc.), Hon. Pres. 1976–; fmr. Pres. Soc. de Publications Economiques (Réalités, Connaissance des Arts, Entreprise, etc.); Sec.-Gen. Féd. Nat. de la Presse 1951–77; Hon. Pres. French Cttee. Int. Press Inst.; Dir. Fondation Nat. des Sciences Politiques 1973–; Prof. Inst. d'Etudes Politiques, Univ. of Paris, and Ecole Nat. d'Admin.; Dir. Fondation nat. des sciences politiques 1973–, mem. Haut Conseil de l'audiovisuel 1973–82; mem. Comm. de la République Française pour l'UNESCO 1979–; Commdr., Légion d'honneur, Croix de guerre, Rosette de la Résistance, Médaille des évadés. *Publications:* Le sentiment de l'existence chez Maine de Biran 1943, Notions élémentaires de psychologie 1947, L'organisation actuelle de la presse française 1955, Information et publicité 1956, L'information économique, clé de la prosperité 1963. *Address:* 53 avenue Foch, 75116 Paris, France.

SALOLAINEN, Pertti Edvard, M.SC. (ECON.); Finnish politician; b. 19 Oct. 1940, Helsinki; m. Anja Sonninen 1964; TV journalist, Finnish Broadcasting Co. 1962–66, corresp. in London 1966–69; journalist, BBC, London 1966; Head of Dept. Finnish Employers' Confed. 1969– (on leave of absence 1975–); mem. Parl. 1970–; Minister for Foreign Trade 1987–; Nat. Coalition Party. *Address:* Ministry of Foreign Trade, Helsinki, Finland.

SALOMONS, Jean-Pierre (Pseudonym Jean-Pierre Aumont); French actor and playwright; b. 5 Jan. 1911, Paris; m. 1st Maria Montez 1942, 2nd Marisa Pavan 1956; two s. one d.; ed. Lycées Rollin and Buffon, Paris and Conservatoire nat. d'art dramatique; Officier Légion d'honneur, ordre nat. du Mérite, Croix de guerre. *Stage appearances include:* Britannicus, la Machine infernale, Jules César, Flora, Tovaritch, Coup de soleil 1982, Pense à l'Afrique 1984; *films include:* Maman Colibri, Les Anges meurtriers, la Vie commence demain, le Diable à quatre heures, les Sept Péchés capitaux, la Nuit américaine 1972, le Chat et la Souris, Mahogany 1976, Nana, le désir: la Java des ombres 1983, l'Age Vermeil (TV) 1984. *Publications:*

l'Empéreur de Chine, l'Ile heureuse, un Beau Dimanche, Julius Caesar, The Infernal Machine, Gigi, On Golden Pond. *Leisure interest:* writing. *Address:* 4 Allée des Brouillards, 75018 Paris, France.

SALONEN, Esa-Pekka; Finnish conductor and composer; b. 30 June 1958, Helsinki; ed. Sibelius Acad., Helsinki; studied composition with Rautavaara and conducting with Panula; studied in Italy 1979–81; Prin. Guest Conductor, Philharmonia Orchestra 1984, Oslo Philharmonic Orchestra 1985–; Prin. Conductor Swedish Radio Symphony Orchestra 1985; Artistic Adviser New Stockholm Chamber Orchestra 1986. *Compositions:* orchestral: Concerto (for Alto Saxophone and Orchestra) 1980–81, Giro 1981; Chamber Music: YTA 1 (for Alto flute), YTA II (for Piano) 1985, YTA III (for Cello) 1987, Floof (for Soprano and Chamber Ensemble) 1988; radiophonic music: Baalal 1982. *Address:* c/o Van Walsum Management, 40 St. Peter's Road, London, W6 9BH, England.

SALPETER, Edwin E., M.SC., PH.D.; American physicist and professor; b. 3 Dec. 1924, Vienna, Austria; s. of Jakob L. and Friedericke Salpeter; m. Miriam M. Mark 1950; two d.; ed. Sydney Boys' High School, Australia and Univ. of Birmingham, England; Dept. of Scientific and Industrial Research Fellow, Univ. of Birmingham, England 1948–49; Research Assoc., then Assoc. Prof., Cornell Univ., U.S. 1949–56, Prof. of Physics and Astrophysics 1956–71, J. G. White Distinguished Prof. of Physical Sciences 1971–; mem. Nat. Science Bd. 1978–84; Visiting Prof. A.N.U. 1954, Sydney Univ. 1960, Cambridge Univ. 1968; mem. N.A.S., American Acad. of Arts and Sciences, American Philosophical Soc., Deutsche Akad. Leopoldina; Hon. D.Sc. (Chicago and Case Western Reserve Univs.). *Publications:* One book and over 100 scientific papers on quantum mechanics, plasma physics and theoretical astrophysics. *Leisure interests:* tennis, skiing, photography. *Address:* Laboratory of Nuclear Studies, Cornell Univ., Ithaca, N.Y. 14853 (Office); 116 Westbourne Lane, Ithaca, N.Y. 14850, U.S.A. (Home). *Telephone:* 607-255-3302.

SALT, George, SC.D., F.R.S.; British zoologist; b. 12 Dec. 1903, Loughborough; s. of Walter Salt and Mary Cecilia Hulme; m. Joyce Laing 1939; two s.; ed. Univs. of Alberta, Harvard and Cambridge; Entomology with United Fruit Co., Repub. of Colombia 1926–27, with Imperial Inst. of Entomology 1928–31; Royal Soc. Moseley Research Student 1932–33; Fellow, King's Coll., Cambridge 1933–; Lecturer in Zoology, Cambridge Univ. 1937–65; Dean, King's Coll. 1939–45, Tutor for Advanced Students 1945–51; Reader in Animal Ecology, Univ. of Cambridge 1965–71; Visiting Prof. Univ. of Calif. 1966; Murchison Grant, Royal Geographical Soc. 1951; Fellow of Royal Soc. 1956; Pres. Cambridge Philosophical Soc. 1970–72. *Publications:* Experimental Studies in Insect Parasitism 1–16 1934–72, Ecology of Upper Kilimanjaro 1954, Defence Reactions of Insects to Metazoan Parasites 1963, Resistance of Insect Parasitoids to the Defence Reactions of their Hosts 1968, The Cellular Defence Reactions of Insects 1970, and numerous scientific papers. *Leisure interests:* mountaineering, gardening, calligraphy and palaeography. *Address:* King's College, Cambridge; 21 Barton Road, Cambridge, CB3 9LB, England (Home). *Telephone:* 350411 (King's Coll.).

SALTER, John Rotherham, M.A., F.B.I.M., F.R.S.A., F.R.G.S., A.C.I.ARB.; British solicitor and international business lawyer; b. 2 May 1932, London; s. of Herbert Salter and Nora Salter; m. Cynthia Brewer 1961; one s. two d.; ed. Queen Elizabeth's School, Ashridge Coll., Lincoln Coll., Oxford and King's Coll. London; Lieut. R.A. 1951–53; partner, Denton Hall Burgin & Warrens 1961–; Vice-Chair. IBA Cttee. of Energy and Natural Resources Law 1976–79, IBA Cttee. on Int. Environmental Law 1979–82; Chair. Section on Business Law, Int. Bar Asscn. 1986–88; Treas. Anglo-American Real Property Inst. 1985–86; Trustee, Petroleum Law Educ. Trust 1980–, IBA Educ. Trust 1983–; consultant, UNIDO 1983–84; Chair. The Silver Soc. 1986–87; Freeman of London and of Glasgow. *Publications:* Planning Law for Industry (jt. ed.) 1981, U.K. Onshore Oil and Gas Law 1986; contrib. to U.K. Oil and Gas Law 1984, Halsbury's Laws of England (Vol. 58) 1986, Law of the European Communities 1986; numerous articles and publs. for Int. Bar Asscn. *Leisure interests:* the arts, archaeology, sailing. *Address:* Five Chancery Lane, London, WC2A 1LF, England. *Telephone:* 01-242 1212.

SALTER, Lionel Paul, M.A., MUS.B., L.R.A.M.; British musicologist; b. 8 Sept. 1914, London; s. of Morris Salter; m. Christine Fraser 1939; three s.; ed. Owen's School, London Acad. of Music, Royal Coll. of Music, St. John's Coll., Cambridge; Music Asst. in films 1936–38, and in TV 1937–39; during army service, Guest Conductor for Radio France Symphony Orchestra 1943–44; then various BBC posts as Asst. Conductor with Theatre Orchestra 1945–46, Producer, Gramophone Dept. 1946–48, European Music Supervisor 1948–53, Artists' Man. 1953–55, Head of Overseas Music 1956, of TV Music 1956–63, of Opera 1963–67, Asst. Controller, Music 1967–74; Chair. radio Music Group, European Broadcasting Union 1965–74; Programme Ed., Edinburgh Int. Festival 1951–55, and for BBC Promenade Concerts 1968–74; Ed. BBC Music Guides 1967–75; Ed. Associated Bd. of Royal Schools of Music 1977–; Vice-Chair. British Fed. of Music Festivals 1984–87; performs as harpsichordist, pianist and conductor. *Publications:* numerous musical works; books and articles on music; opera translations. *Address:* 26, Woodstock Road, London, NW11 8ER, England. *Telephone:* 01-458 3568.

SALTYKOV, Aleksey; Soviet film director; b. 1934; ed. All-Union State Cinematography Inst., Moscow; *Films include:* My Friend Kolka 1961 (with A. Mitta), Beat the Drum 1962 (Mosfilm), The Chairman 1964, The Kingdom of Women 1967, The Director 1969 (all three with scripts by Yuriyn Nagibin, q.v.), The Siberian Woman 1972, A Point of No Return 1974, And There Was an Evening and a Morning 1971.

SALTZMAN, Charles Eskridge, B.S., B.A., M.A.; American investment banker; b. 19 Sept. 1903, Zamboanga, Philippines; s. of Major Gen. Charles McKinley Saltzman and Mary Eskridge Saltzman; m. 1st Gertrude Lamont 1931 (divorced), 2nd Cynthia Southall Myrick 1947 (divorced), 3rd Clotilde Knapp McCormick 1978; two s. (one deceased) two d.; ed. Cornell Univ., U.S. Military Acad., and Oxford Univ. (Rhodes Scholar); with New York Telephone Co., successively Commercial Engineer, Commercial Asst. Man., Commercial Man., Directory Production Man. 1930–35; with New York Stock Exchange 1935–49, beginning as Asst. to Exec. Vice-Pres., later Sec. and Vice-Pres.; on mil. leave of absence 1940–46; served as 2nd Lieut. Corps of Engineers, U.S. Army 1925–30; Commissioned 1st Lieut. New York Nat. Guard 1930, advanced to Lieut.-Col. 1940, on active duty in U.S. Army 1940–46; serving overseas 1942–46, Brig.-Gen. 1945; Major-Gen., retd.; on leave of absence from New York Stock Exchange for government service 1947–49; Special Asst. to Sec. of State 1947; Asst. Sec. of State for occupied areas 1947–49; Gen. Partner, Henry Sears & Co. 1949–56 (on leave of absence for govt. service June 1954–Jan. 1955); Under-Sec. of State for Admin. June 1954–Jan. 1955; partner Goldman Sachs & Co. 1956–, Ltd. Partner 1973–; Nat. Pres. English-Speaking Union of United States 1961–66; Hon. D.Mil.Sc. (Citadel, Charleston, S.C) 1984; awarded D.S.M. (U.S.), L.M. (U.S.), O.B.E. (U.K.), Croix de guerre with Gold Star (France), Bronze Medal (Italy), Ouissam Alouitte (Morocco), Cross of Merit with Swords (Poland), The War Medal (Brazil); Grand Officer, Order of the Crown of Italy. *Leisure interests:* travel, biography, history. *Address:* 85 Broad Street, New York, N.Y. 10004 (Office); 30 East 62nd Street, New York, N.Y. 10021, U.S.A. (Home). *Telephone:* (212) 902 6919 (Office); (212) 759-5655 (Home).

SALVATICI, Nilo; Italian banker; b. 10 March 1922, Monticiano; s. of Arturo Salvatici and Serafina Mugelli; m. Dina Branconi 1946; two c.; served for 43 years with Bank Monte dei Paschi de Siena, retiring with title of Cen. Man.; Deputy Chair. Monte dei Paschi di Siena 1983–; mem. Bd. of Dirs. Italian Int. Bank, Banque du Sud, Tunis, Istituto Federale di Credito Agrario per la Toscana, Finbancaria, S.p.A., Milan, Mediocredito regionale del Lazio, Rome, Italsiel S.p.A., Rome, Cassa di Previdenza del Monte dei Paschi di Siena, A.L.M.A. S.p.A. and I.B.A., Vienna; Commendatore della Repubblica Italiana. *Leisure interests:* numismatics, philately. *Address:* 57 Strada Terrensano de Belcaro, 53100 Siena, Italy. *Telephone:* 0577/ 47 074.

SALVETTI, Carlo; Italian physicist; b. 30 Dec. 1918, Milan; s. of Adriano Salvetti; m. Piera Pinto 1951; two d.; ed. Univ. of Milan; fmr. Prof. of Theoretical Physics, Univ. of Bari; Dir.-Gen. Nuclear Study Centre, Ispra 1957–59; Dir. Int. Atomic Energy Agency (IAEA) Research Div. 1959–62; Gov. for Italy to IAEA 1962–64, 1968–70, Chair. Bd. of Govs. IAEA 1963–64; Chair. European Atomic Energy Soc. 1967–68, mem. EAES Council 1963–72; Chair. Euratom Scientific and Technical Cttee. 1969–70, mem. 1967–73; Chair. ENEA-OECD Steering Cttee. 1969–73; Chair. ANS, Italian Section 1971–75; Prof. of Gen. Physics, Univ. of Milan; Vice Pres. Italian Nat. Cttee. for Nuclear Energy (C.N.E.N.) 1964–81; Vice-Chair. Italian Forum for Nuclear Energy (FIEN) 1965–; Consultant to ENEA 1981–; Chair. Italian Cttee. for Ind. Application of Radioisotopes (COMISO-TOP) 1966–; Chair. Italian Nuclear Soc. (SNI) 1975–79; mem. Bd. European Nuclear Soc. (ENS) 1975–, Chair. 1979–81, Hon. Fellow 1986–; mem. Consultative Cttee. on Fusion (CCF) within Comm. of European Communities 1976–81; Fellow, American Nuclear Soc. 1970–. *Publications:* over 100 scientific and technical articles on nuclear physics, reactor theories and energy problems. *Leisure interests:* golf, painting. *Address:* Via Gramsci 38, I-00197 Rome, Italy. *Telephone:* (06) 3600960.

SALZMAN, Herbert, B.A.; American diplomatist, company executive and private investor; b. 2 May 1916, New York, N.Y.; s. of William and Minnie (Reich) Salzman; m. Rita Fredricks 1947; two s.; ed. Yale Univ., Harvard Business School, Columbia Graduate School of Business; served in U.S. Navy (Ensign to Lieut.-Commdr.) 1941–46; Vice-Pres. Production, Standard Bag Corpn. 1946–55, Vice-Pres. Sales 1955–59, Pres. 1959–66; Asst. Admin. Agency for Int. Devt. (AID) 1966–71; Acting Pres. Overseas Private Investment Corpn. 1969–71, Exec. Vice-Pres. 1971–73, Dir. 1973–77; Dir. Kennedy Center Productions Inc. 1972–; mem. Visiting Comm. Middle East Center, Univ. of Chicago 1964–70, Center for Int. Affairs, Harvard 1975–81; U.S. Amb. to OECD 1977–81; Vice-Chair. and Trustee, Forum Theater, Kennedy Center for the Performing Arts 1976–79; Dir. Starwood Corpn. 1976–77, 1981-84, New York Commr. for Int. Business 1983–84; Partner Bradford Assocs. 1984–. *Publications:* How to Reduce and Manage the Political Risks of Investment in Less Developed Countries 1975. *Leisure interests:* skiing, tennis. *Address:* Bradford Associates, 22 Chambers Street, Princeton, N.J. 08540, U.S.A. (Office); Haus Linard, 7250 Klosters, Switzerland (Home). *Telephone:* (609) 921-3880 (Office).

SALZMAN, Pnina; Israeli pianist; b. 1923, Tel-Aviv; m. Igal Weissmann 1947; one d.; ed. Ecole normale de musique and Conservatoire national de musique, Paris; gave first concert in Paris at age of twelve; since then has given concerts in Israel, Japan, U.S.S.R., S. Africa, Australia, New Zealand, France, Britain, Belgium, Denmark, Sweden, Norway, Finland, U.S.A., etc., under baton of Sir Malcolm Sargent, Charles Munch, Koussevitsky, etc.; over 300 concerts with Israeli orchestras and regular performances with orchestras all over the world; fmr. Prof. of Piano, Tel-Aviv Univ. *Leisure interests:* gardening, painting, graphology. *Address:* 20 Dubnov Street, Tel-Aviv, Israel. *Telephone:* 261993.

SAMAD, Datuk Shahrir Abdul, B.ECONS., M.B.A.; Malaysian politician; b. 22 Nov. 1949, Kuantan, Pahang; m. Datin Sharizan Abdullah; ed. Univ. of Malaya; bank officer, Chartered Bank 1972–73; Political Sec. to Minister of Trade and Industry 1973–75; Political Sec. Prime Minister's Dept. 1975–78; mem. Parl. 1978–; Parl. Sec. to Prime Minister's Dept. 1978–80; Deputy Minister of Finance 1980; Minister of Fed. Territory 1983–86, of Welfare 1986–87; mem. Nat. Exec. Cttee. UMNO Youth Malaysia 1980; Darjah Paduka Johor, Pingat Ibrahim Sultan Johor. *Address:* c/o Ministry of Welfare, Wisma Shen, Jalan Masjid India, 50562 Kuala Lumpur, Malaysia.

SAMARAKIS, Antonis; Greek author; b. 16 Aug. 1919, Athens; s. of Evripidis Samarakis and Adriani Pantelopoulos; m. Eleni Kourebanas 1963; ed. Univ. of Athens; Chief of Emigration, Refugees and Technical Assistance Depts., Ministry of Labour 1935–40, 1944–63; active in resistance movt. during second World War; has served on many humanitarian missions in many parts of the world for ILO, UNHCR, ICEM and Council of Europe; Expert on social and labour problems (many African countries, chiefly Guinea) ILO 1968–69; denied a passport Oct. 1970; mem. PEN, Nat. Soc. of Authors; Officier, Ordre de Léopold II (Belgium); hon. citizen of San Francisco and New Orleans; Greek Nat. Book Award 1962, Greek Prize of the Twelve 1966, Grand Prix de la Littérature policière (France) 1970, Europalia Prize for Literature 1982. *Publications:* short stories: Wanted: Hope 1954, I Refuse 1961, The Jungle 1966, The Passport (in Nea Kimina 2) 1971; novels: Danger Signal 1959, The Flaw 1965; contributor to The Child's Song (anthology of poems for children); works have been translated into 16 languages and frequently adapted for cinema and television. *Leisure interest:* travel. *Address:* 53 Taygetou and Ippolytu Streets, Athens 806, Greece. *Telephone:* 202-9044 (Home).

SAMARANCH TORELLO, Juan Antonio; Spanish international sports official and diplomatist; b. 17 July 1920, Barcelona; s. of Francisco Samaranch and Juana Torello; m. María Teresa Salisachs Rowe 1955; one s. one d.; ed. German Coll., Higher Inst. of Business Studies, Barcelona; mem. Spanish Olympic Cttee. 1954–, Pres. 1967–70; mem. Int. Olympic Cttee. 1966–, Vice-Pres. 1974–78, Pres. July 1980–; Amb. to U.S.S.R. (also accred. to Mongolia) 1977–80; Pres. Int. Boat Show; numerous decorations from many countries. *Leisure interest:* philately. *Address:* International Olympic Committee, Château de Vidy, 1007 Lausanne, Switzerland; Avda. Pau Casals, 24, Barcelona 21, Spain (Home). *Telephone:* (41) (21) 25-32-71 (Switzerland); 209-07-22 (Home).

SAMARAPUNGAVAN, Subrahmanyan, B.SC.ENG.; Indian steel industry executive; b. 2 Oct. 1928, Tuticorin; s. of K. and Visalakshi Subrahmanyan; m. Lioubov Levitina 1960; one s. one d.; ed. Calcutta and Banaras Hindu Univs.; Steel Melting Shop, Tata Iron and Steel Co. 1951–56; Jr. Engineer Steel Melting Shop, Bhilai Steel Plant 1956–60, in charge of design work, Cen. Eng. and Design Bureau (now MECON) 1960–71, Asst. Gen. Supt. (Iron and Steel) Bhilai Steel Plant 1971–74; Gen. Supt. Bokaro Steel Plant 1974–76; Man. Dir. Bokaro Steel Ltd. 1976–81, Indian Iron and Steel Co. March-Nov. 1981; Chair. Steel Authority of India Ltd. 1981–85; Pres. Indian Inst. of Metals 1982; mem. Public Enterprise Selection Bd. 1982; Fellow Inst. of Eng. of India; Merit Certificate, Bhilai Steel Plant 1963. *Publications:* articles on iron and steel. *Leisure interests:* reading, dramatics. *Address:* c/o Ispat Bhavan, Lodi Road, New Delhi 110003, India (Office). *Telephone:* 622906 (Home).

SAMBURSKY, Shmuel, PH.D.; Israeli professor of history; b. 30 Oct. 1900, Königsberg, Germany; s. of Menahem Sambursky and Selma Sambursky; m. 1st Esther Rabinowitz 1923; one d.; m. 2nd Miriam Grünstein 1938; ed. Univs. of Königsberg and Berlin; emigrated to Palestine 1924; teacher of Physics and Math., Yellin Teacher's Seminary 1924–28; Instructor in Physics, Hebrew Univ. of Jerusalem 1928–49, Assoc. Prof. 1949–57, Chair. Dept. of the History and Philosophy of Science 1957–, Dean of the Faculty of Science 1957–59, Eleanor Roosevelt Prof. of the History and Philosophy of Science 1960–; Exec. Sec. Palestine Bd. for Scientific and Industrial Research 1945–48; Dir. Research Council of Israel 1949–56; Visiting Fellow, St. Catherine's Coll., Oxford 1965, All Souls Coll., Oxford 1967; Visiting Prof., Univ. of Heidelberg 1968; mem. Israel Acad. of Sciences and Humanities 1962; corresp. mem. Heidelberg Acad. of Science 1977; Israel Prize for the Humanities 1968. *Publications:* The Physical World of the Greeks 1956, Physics of the Stoics 1959, The Physical World of Late Antiquity 1961, Physical Thought from the Presocratics to the Quantum Physicists 1974, The Concept of Time in Late Neoplatonism (with S. Pines) 1971, The Concept of Place in Late Neoplatonism 1982. *Leisure interest:* reading. *Address:* c/o Israel Academy of Sciences and Humanities, P.O. Box 4040, Jerusalem 91040; Magnes Square 3, Jerusalem 92-304, Israel (Home). *Telephone:* 02-636211 (Office); 02-631135 (Home).

SAMIOS, Nicholas Peter, PH.D.; American physicist; b. 15 March 1932, New York; s. of Peter and Niki Samios; m. Mary Linakis 1958; two s. one d.; ed. Columbia Coll., Columbia Univ., New York; Instructor, Dept. of Physics, Columbia Univ. 1956–59, Adjunct Prof. 1970–; Asst. Physicist Brookhaven Nat. Lab. Dept. of Physics 1959–62, Assoc. Physicist 1962–64, Physicist 1964–68, Group Leader of the Nuclear Interactions Group (now New Group) 1965–75, Sr. Physicist 1968–, Chair. Dept. of Physics 1975–81, Deputy Dir. 1981, Acting Dir. 1982, Dir. May 1982–; Adjunct Prof. Stevens Inst. of Tech. 1969–75; mem., fmr. mem. or fmr. chair. numerous specialist cttees. and bds.; Fellow American Physical Soc. 1964–, mem. Exec. Cttee. 1976–1977; mem. New York Acad. of Sciences 1980–; Fellow American Acad. of Arts and Sciences 1981–; mem. N.A.S.; mem. Int. Cttee. for Future Accelarators (ICFA) 1984–; E. O. Lawrence Memorial Award, New York Acad. of Sciences 1980. *Address:* Brookhaven National Laboratory, Upton, New York, N.Y. 11973-5000, U.S.A. *Telephone:* (516) 282-2772.

SAMMET, Rolf, DR.RER.NAT.; German chemicals executive; b. 21 Feb. 1920, Stuttgart; s. of Dr. Paul and Else (née Hillman) Sammet; m. Hilde Beckerwerth; one s. two d.; ed. Gymnasium and Technische Hochschule, Stuttgart and Technische Hochschule, Munich; Asst. Inst. for Organic Chemistry 1945–47; joined Hoechst AG 1949, Divisional Adviser, Dept. of Tech. Man. 1952–54, Man. 1957, Departmental Dir. 1960; Deputy mem. of Bd., Hoechst AG 1962, C.E.O. 1966–85, Chair. Man. Bd. 1969–85, Chair. Supervisory Bd. 1985–; Hon. Prof. Univ. Frankfurt/Main 1975–; Dr. Ing. E.h. (Univ. of Stuttgart); Dr. rer. nat. h.c. (Göttingen). *Address:* Hoechst AG, 6230 Frankfurt/Main–80, Federal Republic of Germany. *Telephone:* Frankfurt 305-7892.

SAMOILOV, Vladimir Yakovlevich; Soviet actor; b. 1924; ed. Odessa Theatre School; active service in World War II; acted with Ivanov Theatre, Odessa, Lunacharsky Theatre, Kemerovo, and Gorky Theatre, Gorky 1948–69, Mayakovsky Theatre 1969–; State Prize 1976, People's Artist of U.S.S.R. 1984. *Roles include:* Richard III (Shakespeare), Satin, Suslov in Gorky's plays Lower Depths and Summer Folk, Velikatov in Ostrovsky's Actors and Admirers, Korzukhin in Bulgakov's Flight etc. *Films include:* The 26 Commissars of Baku, The Stars Won't Stop Shining, The Prize (State Prize 1976), An Especially Important Mission, etc. *Address:* Mayakovsky Theatre, Moscow, U.S.S.R.

SAMOILOVA, Tatyana Yevgeniyevna; Soviet film actress; b. 4 May 1934, Leningrad; ed. Shchukin Theatre School; Honoured Art Worker of the R.S.F.S.R.; Order of the Badge of Honour; *Roles include:* Maria (The Mexican) 1955, Veronika (The Cranes Are Flying) 1957, Tanya (The Unsent Letter) 1960, Natasha (Leon Garros Looks for a Friend) 1960, Alba (Alba Regia) 1961, Sonia (They Went East) 1964, Anna (Anna Karenina) 1978.

SAMOJLIK, Bazyli, D.ECON; Polish economist and politician; b. 5 Nov. 1943, Józefowo, Białystok Voivodship; ed. Main School of Planning and Statistics, Warsaw; Teacher, Main School of Planning and Statistics, Warsaw 1965–78; worked at Dept. of Planning and Econ. Analyses of Polish United Workers' Party (PZPR) Cent. Cttee. 1978–80, Econ. Advisor to Chair. of Council of Ministers 1980–83; Chief of Prime Minister's Advisors' Team 1983–86; Minister of Finance 1986–88; mem. PZPR 1967–; fmr. mem. Comm. for Econ.-Financial Solutions Planning of Acads. of Sciences of Socialist States; fmr. mem. team for system prices, duties and wages solutions of Econ. Reform Comm.; mem. Secr. of Econ. Reform Comm.; Awards from Minister of Science, Higher Educ. and Tech.; Oskar Lange Award; Gold Cross of Merit and other decorations. *Leisure interest:* sport. *Address:* c/o Ministerstwo Finansów, ul. Świętokrzyska 12, 00-044 Warsaw, Poland.

SAMPEDRO, José Luis; Spanish economist and novelist; b. 1 Feb. 1917, Barcelona; s. of Luis and Matilde Sampedro; m. Isabel Pellicer Iturrioz 1944; one d.; ed. Madrid Univ.; Civil Service, Ministry of Finance 1935–50, 1957–62; Asst. Prof. of Econ. Structure, Madrid Univ. 1947–55, Prof. 1955–69; Economist, Ministry of Commerce 1951–57; Adviser to Spanish Del. to UN 1956–58; Special Prof. of Econ. Sociology, Madrid Univ. 1962–65; Asst. Gen. Dir. Banco Exterior de España 1962–69; Visiting Prof. Univ. of Salford 1969–70, Univ. of Liverpool 1970–71; Econ. Adviser Customs Bureau, Ministry of Finance 1971–79; nominated mem. Senate 1977–79; Econ. Adviser Banco Exterior de España 1979–81; Vice-Pres. Fundacion Banco Exterior de España 1981–84; Spanish Nat. Award for new playwrights 1950. *Publications:* Economics: Principles of Industrial Location 1954, Effects of European Economic Integration 1957, Economic Reality and Structural Analysis 1958, The European Future of Spain 1960, Regional Profiles of Spain 1964, Decisive Forces in World Economics 1967, Economic Structure 1969, Conscience of Underdevelopment 1973, Inflation Unabridged 1976; Fiction: Congreso en Estocolmo (Congress in Stockholm) 1952, El Río que nos lleva (The River which Carries Us) 1962, El Caballo Desnudo (The Naked Horse) 1970, Octubre, Octubre (October, October) 1981, La Sonrisa Etrusca (Etruscan Smile) 1985; plays: La Paloma de Cartón (The Paper Dove) 1950, Un sitio para vivir (A Place to Live in) 1956. *Leisure interests:* human communication. *Address:* Cea Bermúdez 51, 28003 Madrid, Spain. *Telephone:* 244-2860.

SAMPER, Armando; Colombian agricultural economist; b. 9 April 1920, Bogotá; s. of late Daniel Samper Ortega and of Mayita Gnecco de Samper; m. Jean K. de Samper 1945; two s. two d.; ed. Cornell Univ., U.S.A.; research and teaching posts in agricultural econs., Colombia 1943–49; Inter-American Inst. of Agricultural Sciences of OAS, Turrialba, Costa Rica 1949–69, Head of Scientific Communications Service 1949–54, Dir. of Regional Services 1955–60, Dir. of Inst. 1960–69; Visiting Prof. Univ. of Chicago 1954–55; Minister of Agric. 1966–67, 1969–70; Agricultural Adviser, Banco de la República, Bogotá 1970–72; Chancellor Univ. de Bogotá 1971; FAO Asst. Dir.-Gen. for Latin American Affairs, Santiago, Chile 1972–74; Pres. Nat. Corpn. for Forestry Research and Devt. (CONIF), Bogotá 1975–77, Consultant 1978–; Dir.-Gen. Colombian Sugar Cane Research Centre 1978–; mem. Latin American Plant Science Asscn., Colombian Asscn. of Professional Agriculturists, Soc. for Int. Devt., Int. Asscn. of Agricultural Econs., Econ. Soc. of Friends of the Country, Int. Inst. of Tropical Agric., Colombian Acad. of Sciences. *Publications:* Importancia del Café en el Comercio Exterior de Colombia 1948, A Case Study of Cooperation in Secondary Education in Chile 1957, Política de Transformación Rural 1967, Memoria del Ministro de Agricultura al Congreso Nacional 1966–67, Desarrollo Institucional y Desarrollo Agrícola (3 vols.) 1969, El Cuatrenio de la Transformación Rural 1966–70. *Address:* Apartado Aéreo 100-286, Bogotá, Colombia. *Telephone:* 256-73-01 (Office).

SAMPHAN, Khieu (see Khieu Samphan).

SAMPSON, Anthony (Terrell Seward) M.A.; British writer and journalist; b. 3 Aug. 1926, Billingham, Durham; s. of Michael Sampson and Phyllis (née Seward) Sampson; m. Sally Bentlif 1965; one s. one d.; ed. Westminster School and Christ Church, Oxford; served with Royal Navy 1944–47; Sub Lieut. R.N.V.R. 1946; Ed. Drum magazine, Johannesburg 1951–55; Editorial Staff, The Observer 1955–66, Chief American Corresp. 1973–74, Ed. The Observer Colour Magazine 1965–66; Assoc. Prof. Univ. of Vincennes, Paris 1968–70; Contributing Ed. Newsweek 1977–; Editorial Adviser, Brandt Comm. 1979; Dir. The New Statesman 1979–83; Ed. The Sampson Letter 1984–86; awarded Prix Int. de la Presse for The Seven Sisters 1976. *Publications:* Drum, a Venture into the New Africa 1956, The Treason Cage 1958, Commonsense about Africa 1960, (with S. Pienaar), Anatomy of Britain 1962, Anatomy of Britain Today 1965, South Africa: Two Views of Separate Development 1966, Macmillan: a Study in Ambiguity 1968, The New Anatomy of Britain 1971, The Sovereign State: the Secret History of ITT 1973, The Seven Sisters 1975, The Arms Bazaar 1977, The Money Lenders 1981, The Changing Anatomy of Britain 1982, Empires of the Sky 1984, The Oxford Book of Ages (with Sally Sampson) 1985, Black and Gold: Tycoons, Revolutionaries and Apartheid 1987. *Leisure interest:* gardening. *Address:* 27 Ladbroke Grove, London W.11; Quarry Garden, Wardour, nr. Tisbury, Wiltshire, England. *Telephone:* 01-727 4188 (London); Tisbury 870407 (Wiltshire).

SAMUELSON, Paul Anthony, PH.D., LL.D., D.LITT., D.SC.; American economist; b. 15 May 1915, Gary, Ind.; s. of Frank Samuelson and Ella Lipton; 1st Marion E. Crawford 1938; four s. (including triplets) two d.; m. 2nd Risha Eckaus 1981; ed. Hyde Park High School Chicago, Univ. of Chicago and Harvard Univ.; Prof. of Econs. at M.I.T. 1940–, Inst. Prof. 1966–85, Prof. Emer. June 1986–, Gordon Y. Billard Fellow 1986–, mem. Radiation Lab. Staff 1944–45; Visiting Prof. of Political Economy, New York Univ. 1986–; Consultant to Nat. Resources Planning Bd. 1941–43, to War Production Bd. 1945, to U.S. Treasury 1945–52, 1961–, to Rand Corpn. 1949–75, to Council of Econ. Advisers 1960–68, to Fed. Reserve Bd. 1965–, to Loomis, Sayles & Co. Boston and to Burden Investors Services Inc.; Research Advisory Bd. Cttee. for Econ. Devt. 1960; Advisory Bd. to Pres. Eisenhower's Comm. on Nat. Goals 1960; Nat. Task Force on Econ. Educ. 1960–61; Special Comm. on Social Sciences of Nat. Science Foundation 1968–; Comm. on Money and Credit; Econ. Adviser to Pres. Kennedy during election campaign; author of report to Pres. Kennedy on State of American Economy 1961; on Editorial Bd. of Econometrica; Guggenheim Fellow 1948–49; numerous hon. degrees including D.Sc. (City of London Univ.) 1980; mem. American Acad. of Arts and Sciences, American Economic Asscn. (Pres. 1961), Int. Econ. Asscn. (Pres. 1965–68, lifetime hon. Pres.); Fellow American Philosophical Soc., Econometric Soc. (Council mem., Vice-Pres. 1950, Pres. 1951); Corresp. Fellow British Acad.; several awards including Nobel Prize for Economic Science 1970, Albert Einstein Commemorative Award 1971. *Publications:* Foundations of Economic Analysis 1947 (2nd edn. 1961, enlarged edn. 1983), Economics 1948, 1952, 1955, 1958, 1961, 1964, 1967, 1970, 1973, 1976, 1980, 1985 (21 translations), Readings in Economics (with R.L. Bishop and J.R. Coleman) 1952, 1955, 1958, 1967, 1973, Linear Programming and Economic Analysis 1958, Collected Scientific Papers, I and II 1966, III 1972, Collected Scientific Papers of Paul A. Samuelson (vols. I–V) 1965, 1972, 1978, 1987; author and joint author of numerous articles on economics. *Leisure interest:* tennis. *Address:* Massachusetts Institute of Technology, Cambridge, Mass. 02139; 75 Clairemont Road, Belmont, Mass. 02178, U.S.A. (Home). *Telephone:* 617-253-3368 (M.I.T.).

SAN YU, Brig.-Gen. U; Burmese army officer and politician; b. 1919, Prome; ed. Univ. of Rangoon and an American mil. coll.; commissioned 1942, served in Second World War; Mil. Sec. to Chief of Gen. Staff 1956–59; Officer commanding the North and Northwest mil. areas; mem. Revolutionary Council, Deputy Chief of Gen. Staff, Commdr. of Land Forces and Minister of Finance and Revenue 1963; Gen. Sec. Cen. Organizing Cttee., Burmese Socialist Programme Party 1965–78, re-elected 1978;

Minister of Nat. Planning, Finance and Revenue 1969-72; Deputy Prime Minister 1971-74; Minister of Defence 1972-74; Chief of Gen. Staff 1972-74; Sec. Council of State 1974-81; Pres. of Burma and Chair. Council of State 1981-88; Vice-Chair. Burma Socialist Programme Party 1985-88, Socialist Econ. Planning Cttee. -1988. *Address:* Council of State, Rangoon, Burma.

SANBAR, Moshe, M.A.(ECON.); Israeli banker and economist; b. 29 March 1929, Kecskemét, Hungary; s. of Shlomo and Miriam (Klausner) Sandberg; m. Bracha Rabinovich 1951; two d.; ed. Univ. of Budapest and Hebrew Univ., Jerusalem; immigrated to Israel 1948; Project Dir. Israel Inst. of Applied Social Research and later Deputy Dir. 1951-58; Lecturer in Statistics, Hebrew Univ., Jerusalem 1957-61; Deputy Dir. Internal State Revenue Div., Ministry of Finance 1958-63; Econ. Adviser to Ministry of Finance 1963-68; Dir. of the Budgets, Ministry of Finance 1964-68; Deputy Chair. and later Chair., Industrial Devt. Bank of Israel 1968-71; Chief Econ. Adviser to Minister of Finance 1969-71; Deputy Minister of Trade and Industry 1970-71; Gov. Bank of Israel 1971-76; Chair. Electrochemical Inds. (Frutarom) Ltd., Haifa 1976-81, Independent Mortgage Bank 1981-83, Tzelon Industries (Aluminium) 1981-, M.G. Industries (Rubber) 1984-, La Nationale Insurance Co. 1985, Solel Boneh Ltd. (Construction) 1986, Bank Leumi Le Israel Ltd. 1988-; mem. various bds. of dirs.; Chair. HABIMA Nat. Theatre 1969-81, Coll. of Admin. 1972-, Museum Janco-Dada 1980-; Hon. Chair. World Org. of Hungarian Jews 1975-. *Publications:* My Longest Year (Yad Vashem Prize) 1966, The Political Economy of Israel 1948-1982; numerous articles in professional journals. *Address:* 44 Pincas Street, Tel-Aviv, Israel (Home). *Telephone:* (03) 642-698 (Office); (03) 446-060 (Home).

SÁNCHEZ, Luis Alberto; Peruvian politician and writer; b. 12 Oct. 1900, Lima; m. Rosa Dergan; six c.; on staff of Mercurio Peruano, Revista Hogar and Revista Mundial 1919-31; f. la Tribuna 1931; Deputy Ed. Ercilla (Chile) 1934; Man. Editorial Ercilla 1939; Rector Universidad Nacional Mayor de San Marcos 1946-61, 1961; Chair. Political Cttee. of Partido Aprista Peruano 1984; Deputy for Lima 1945; elected Senator 1963, 1980 and 1985; mem. Constituent Ass. 1931 and 1978; Pres. a.i. Constituent Ass. 1979; First Vice-Pres. 1985-; Prime Minister of Peru May 1989-; taught in various univs. in Latin America, U.S.A., France, Israel and Lebanon 1930-59; mem. Lima Coll. of Lawyers, Peruvian Journalists' Assen., Academia Peruana de la Lengua, Real Academia de la Lengua Española, Instituto Iberoamericano de Literatura (Madrid); many decorations. *Publications:* approx. 70 works of literature, history, philosophy and politics since 1919, including Haya de la Torre, or El Politíco, Historia Contemporánea, Historia de la Literatura Americana, La Literatura en el Perú, Historia General de América, Perú: Retrate de un país adolescente, Testimonio Personal: Memoria de un peruano del Siglo XX, Bolívar. *Address:* Prime Minister's Office, Ucayali 363, Lima, Peru.

SÁNCHEZ HERNÁNDEZ, Col. Fidel; Salvadorian army officer and politician; b. 7 July 1917; Mil. Attaché, Washington 1960-62; Minister of Interior 1962-66; Pres. of El Salvador 1967-72; fmr. Leader of Partido de Conciliación Nacional (PCN).

SÁNCHEZ-VILELLA, Roberto; Puerto Rican politician; b. 19 Feb. 1913, Mayaguez; s. of Luis Sánchez-Frasqueri and Angela Vilella-Vélez; m. Jeanette Ramos-Buonomo 1967; one s. three d.; ed. Ohio State Univ.; Sub-Commr. of the Interior 1941-42; Dir. Transportation Authority of Puerto Rico 1942-45; Special Asst. to Pres. of Senate 1946-47; Resident Engineer Caribe Hilton Hotel 1947-48; Exec. Sec. to Govt. 1949-51; Sec. of State 1952-64; Gov. Puerto Rico 1965-69; Prof. School of Public Admin. 1974-; fmr. Pres. People's Party; mem. Puerto Rico Coll. of Engineers, American Soc. of Public Administrators; Hon. LL.D. (Ohio State Univ.) 1966. *Leisure interests:* reading, dominoes. *Address:* 414 Muñoz Rivera Avenue, Suite 7-A, Stop 31-1/2, Hato Rey, Puerto Rico 00918 *Telephone:* 753-9156.

SANCHO-ROF, Juan, D.CHEM.ENG.; Spanish businessman; b. 9 Feb. 1940, Madrid; m. Paloma Suils; two s. three d.; ed. Universidad Complutense de Madrid and Instituto de Estudios Superiores de la Empresa, Barcelona; Technical-Commercial post Petronor S.A. (Petroleos del Norte) 1970-76, Deputy Gen. Man. 1976-85; Chair. and C.E.O. Repsol Petroleo S.A. 1985-. *Publications:* several technical works. *Address:* José Abascal 4, 28003 Madrid, Spain. *Telephone:* 446-52 00 (Office); 446-60 70 (Home).

SAND, Ulf; Norwegian politician; b. 22 May 1938, Oslo; s. of Thormod Sand and Erna Løvdal; m. Sidsel Bye 1967; two s.; Planning Div., Ministry of Finance 1963-66; Under-Sec. of State, Ministry of Wages and Prices 1972, 1973-77; Econ. Dept., Norwegian Fed. of Trade Unions (LO) 1966-71, Research Dir. 1972-73, Dir. Econ. Dept. 1977-79, 1981-83; Minister of Finance 1979-81; Dir. State Educational Loan Fund 1983-; mem. Nat. Exec. Cttee. Labour League of Youth 1964-69; Chair. Labour Party Cttee. on Political and Econ. Affairs, Cttee. on Tax Policy. *Address:* c/o State Educational Loan Fund, Økernveien 195, Økern, 0510 Oslo 5, Norway.

SANDAGE, Allan Rex, PH.D., D.SC.; American astronomer; b. 18 June 1926, Iowa City; s. of Charles H. Sandage and Dorothy M. Briggs; m. Mary L. Connelly 1959; two s.; ed. Univ. of Illinois and California Inst. of Tech.; staff mem. Mount Wilson and Palomar Observatories 1952-; Asst. Astronomer Hale Observatories, Calif. 1952-56, Astronomer 1956-; Sr. Research Astronomer Space Telescope Scientific Inst. 1986-; Homewood Prof. of Physics, Johns Hopkins Univ., Baltimore 1987-88; Hitchcock Prof. Univ.

of Calif. at Berkeley 1988-; Visiting Astronomer, Univ. of Hawaii 1986; Visiting Lecturer, Harvard Univ. 1957; Consultant, Nat. Science Foundation 1961-63; mem. Cttee. on Science and Public Policy 1965; Philips Lecturer, Haverford Coll. 1968; Research Assoc. Australian Nat. Univ. 1968-69; Fulbright-Hayes Scholar 1972; fmr. mem. N.A.S., mem. American Acad. of Arts and Sciences, A.A.A.S., Royal and American Astronomical Socs.; numerous hon. degrees; Helen Warner Prize of American Astronomical Soc. 1960, Russell Prize 1973; Eddington Medal, Royal Astronomical Soc. (U.K.) 1963; Pope Pius XI Gold Medal, Pontifical Acad. of Sciences 1966; Gold Medal, Royal Astronomical Soc. (U.K.) 1967, Rittenhouse Medal 1968, Nat. Medal of Scientific Merit 1971, Elliott Gresson Medal, Franklin Inst. 1973, Gold Medal of Pacific Astronomical Soc. 1975. *Publications:* numerous scientific papers and Hubble Atlas of Galaxies. *Leisure interest:* gardening. *Address:* Hale Observatories, 813 Santa Barbara Street, Pasadena, Calif. 91106 (Office); 8319 Josard Road, San Gabriel, Calif. 91775, U.S.A. (Home). *Telephone:* (213) 285-5086 (Home).

SANDBERG, Sir Michael Graham Ruddock, C.B.E.; British banker; b. 31 May 1927, Thames Ditton, Surrey; s. of late Gerald Arthur Clifford and Ethel Marion (née Ruddock) Sandberg; m. Carmel Mary Roseleen Donnelly; two s. two d.; ed. Saint Edward's School, Oxford; mil. service 1945-48, commissioned into 6th DCO Lancers, Indian Army, later 1st King's Dragoon Guards; joined Hongkong and Shanghai Banking Corpn. 1948, Deputy Chair. 1973-77, Chair. 1977-86; Chair. British Bank of the Middle East 1980-86; Dir. Marine Midland Banks, Inc. 1980-87; Pres. Surrey County Cricket Club 1988-89; mem. of Exec. Council of Hong Kong 1978-86; Treasurer Univ. of Hong Kong 1977-86; Chair. of Stewards, Royal Hong Kong Jockey Club 1972-86; Hon. LL.D. (Hong Kong) 1984, (Pepperdine) 1986. *Leisure interests:* horse racing, cricket, horology. *Address:* c/o The Hongkong and Shanghai Banking Corporation, 1 Queen's Road Central, Hong Kong.

SANDBLOM, (John) Philip, M.D., M.S.; Swedish professor of surgery and university administrator; b. 29 Oct. 1903, Chicago, Ill., U.S.A.; s. of Dr. John N. Sandblom and Ellen Chinlund; m. Grace Schaefer 1932; three s. two d.; ed. Northwestern Univ. and Karolinska Institutet, Stockholm; Assoc. Prof. of Surgery, Karolinska Institutet, Stockholm 1944; Surgeon-in-Chief, Crown Princess Louise's Children's Hospital 1945-50; Prof. of Surgery and Head of Dept. of Surgery, Lund Univ. 1950-70, Vice-Chancellor of Lund Univ. 1957-68; Visiting Prof. Univ. of Calif., San Diego 1972-73, Univ. of Lausanne 1973-80, Univ. of Taipei 1982; mem. of Board, Soc. for Modern Art 1936-46, Gen. Art Soc. 1943-70; Treas. Swedish Surgical Soc. 1946-52, Pres. 1957-58, 1970; mem. Insurance Advisory Bd. 1947-50; Pres. Soc. Int. de Chirurgie 1967; Hon. Fellow, American Coll. of Surgeons, Royal Coll. of Surgeons of England, Edinburgh, and in Ireland; Hon. mem. American Surgical Assen., Southern Surgical Assen., Soc. Int. de Chirurgie, Assen. of Surgeons of Great Britain and Ireland, Swedish, Danish, French, Italian, Northern, Swiss and Finnish Surgical Socs.; Corresp. mem. Deutsche Gesellschaft für Chirurgie and Norwegian Surgical Soc.; Ph.D. h.c. and many hon. degrees. *Publications:* Function of the Human Gall Bladder 1932, Function of the Sphincter Oddi., Tensile Strength of Healing Wounds 1944, Hemobilia 1972, The Responsibility of Society to Surgery, The Role of the University in the World of Violence, The Difference in Men, Portal Hypertension, 100 Years of Surgical Research, Creativity and Disease; teaching film: Atraumatic Surgical Technique 1976, and various papers. *Leisure interests:* collecting works of modern art, sailing, skiing. *Address:* 2 chemin des Bluets, 1009 Pully Lausanne, Switzerland. *Telephone:* 021-296877.

SANDER, Michael Arthur, B.SC.; South African business executive; b. 2 Oct. 1941, Germiston; s. of Norman William Henry Sander and Nora McLaverty; m. Pamela Wendy Mills; ed. Durban High School, Univ. of Natal; joined AECI Ltd. as Overseas Industrial Bursar, and seconded to ICI Heavy Organic Chemicals Div., Teeside, U.K. 1963-65; then returned to AECI Devt. Dept. and became involved in new project devt.; appointed Gen. Man., Anikem (Pty.) Ltd. 1970; moved to subsidiary Co. Rand Carbide as Devt. Man. 1977; Man. Dir. AECI Chlor-Alkali and Plastics Ltd. 1982, Chair. 1984; Exec. Dir. AECI Ltd. 1984, Man. Dir. 1985-; currently Dir. of a number of AECI group subsidiary and Assoc. Cos. *Leisure interests:* shooting, fishing, photography, music. *Address:* Carlton Centre, P.O. Box 1122, Johannesburg 2000, South Africa. *Telephone:* (011) 223-9111.

SANDERLING, Kurt; German musical conductor; b. 19 Sept. 1912, Arys; m. 1st Nina Bobath 1941, m. 2nd Barbara Wagner 1963; three s.; Conductor Leningrad Philharmonic 1941-60, Chief Conductor Berlin Symphony Orchestra 1960-77; Guest Conductor (mainly in Europe and N. America); many awards and prizes (U.S.S.R. and G.D.R.). *Address:* Am Iderfenngraben 47, 1110 Berlin, German Democratic Republic. *Telephone:* 4893458.

SANDERS, Donald Neil, C.B., B.ECON.; Australian banker; b. 21 June 1927, Sydney; s. of L. G. Sanders; m. Betty Elaine Constance 1952; four s. one d.; ed. Wollongong High School, Univ. of Sydney; Commonwealth Bank of Australia 1943-60; Australian Treasury 1956-57; Bank of England 1960; with Reserve Bank of Australia 1960-87, Supt., Credit Policy Div. of Banking Dept. 1964-66, Deputy Man. of Banking Dept. 1966-67, of Research Dept. 1967-70; Australian Embassy, Washington D.C. 1968; Chief Man. of Securities Markets Dept. 1970-72, of Banking and Finance Dept. 1972-74, Adviser and Chief Man. 1974-75, Deputy Gov. and Deputy

Chair. of Bd. 1975-87; Man. Dir. Commonwealth Banking Corpn. 1987-; C.E.O. Commonwealth Bank of Australia 1987-; Chair. Australian European Finance Corpn. Ltd. *Address:* Commonwealth Banking Corporation, Cnr. Pitt Street and Martin Place, Sydney, N.S.W. 2000, Australia.

SANDERS, Ronald; Antigua and Barbuda diplomatist, broadcaster and consultant; b. 26 Jan. 1948, Guyana; s. of Joseph Sanders; m. Susan Ramphal 1975; ed. Sacred Heart R.C. School, Guyana, Westminster School, England and Boston Univ., U.S.A., Univ. of Sussex; Man. Dir. Guyana Broadcasting Service, Public Affairs Adviser to Prime Minister of Guyana 1973-76; Lecturer in Communications, Univ. of Guyana 1975-76; Consultant to Pres. of Caribbean Devt. Bank, Barbados 1977-78; Special Adviser to the Minister of Foreign Affairs 1978-82; Deputy Perm. Rep. to the UN, New York 1982-83; Amb. Extraordinary and Plentipotentiary accred. to UNESCO 1983-87; High Commr. in U.K. 1984-87 (also accred to Fed. Repub. of Germany 1986-87); ed. Caribbean Broadcasting Union 1975-76; Chair. Caribbean Sub-Group at UNESCO 1983-85; mem. Bd. of Dirs. of Caribbean News Agency 1976-77; mem. Inter-Governmental Council of the Int. Programme for the Devt. of Communications at UNESCO 1983-87; mem. Exec. Bd. UNESCO 1985-(89); Visiting Fellow, Oxford Univ. 1987-89. *Publications:* Broadcasting in Guyana 1978, Antigua and Barbuda: Transition, Trial, Triumph 1984, Inseparable Humanity: Anthology of Reflections of the Commonwealth Secretary-General (Ed.) 1988, several articles on media ownership and control, communication and development and Antarctica. *Leisure interests:* reading, West Indian history, cinema. *Address:* 24 Chelmsford Square, London, NW10 3AR, England. *Telephone:* 01-459 3154.

SANDIFORD, Lloyd Erskine, P.C., B.A.(HONS.), M.A.; Barbados politician; b. 24 March 1937; s. of Cyril G. Sandiford and Eunice Sandiford; m. Angelita P. Ricketts 1963; one s. two d.; ed. Harrison Coll., Barbados, Univ. Coll. of the W. Indies, Jamaica and Univ. of Manchester; Asst. Master, Modern High School, Barbados 1956-57, Kingston Coll., Jamaica 1960-61; part-time Tutor and Lecturer, Univ. of W. Indies, Barbados 1963-65; Sr. Grad. Master, Harrison Coll. 1964-66; Asst. Tutor, Barbados Community Coll. 1976-86; mem. Barbados Senate 1967-71, House of Ass. 1971-; Personal Asst. to Prime Minister 1966-67; Minister of Educ. 1967-71, of Educ., Youth Affairs, Community Devt. and Sport 1971-75, of Health and Welfare 1975-76; Deputy Prime Minister and Minister of Educ. and Culture 1986-87; Prime Minister and Minister of Econ. Affairs June-July 1987, Aug. 1987-; mem. Democratic Labour Party, Pres. 1974-75; founder, Acad of Politics. *Leisure interests:* choral singing, reading. *Address:* Office of the Prime Minister, Bay Street, St. Michael, Barbados.

SANDILANDS, Sir Francis Edwin Prescott, Kt., C.B.E., M.A.; British insurance executive; b. 11 Dec. 1913, Chatham; s. of the late Lt.-Col. Prescott Sandilands and of Gladys Baird Murton; m. Susan Gillian Jackson 1939; two s.; ed. Eton and Corpus Christi Coll., Cambridge; joined Commercial Union Group of insurance cos. 1935, Chief Gen. Man. 1958-72, Vice-Chair. 1968-72, Chair. 1972-83; Chair. Royal Trust Co. of Canada (U.K.) 1974-84, British Insurance Assen. 1965-67, Cttee. on Inflation Accounting (Sandilands Cttee.) 1974-75, Cttee. on Invisible Exports 1976-83; Dir. Plessey Co. Ltd. 1976, Royal Opera House Trust 1975-85; Pres. Insurance Inst. of London 1969-70; Dir. Lewis and Peat 1983-; Treas. Univ. Coll. London 1973-81; Hon. Fellow, Corpus Christi Coll., Cambridge 1975, Univ. Coll., London 1981; Commdr., Order of Crown of Belgium. *Leisure interests:* music, medieval history, gardening. *Address:* 53 Cadogan Square, London, S.W.1, England (Home). *Telephone:* 01-235 6384 (Home).

SANDLE, Michael Leonard, A.R.A., D.F.A.; British artist; b. 18 May 1936, Weymouth, Dorset; s. of Charles E. and Dorothy G. (née Vernon) Sandle; m. 1st Cynthia D. Koppel 1971 (divorced 1974), 2nd Demelza Spargo 1988; ed. Douglas High School, Isle of Man, Douglas School of Art and Tech. and Slade School of Fine Art; studied lithography, Atelier Patris, Paris 1960; began sculpture 1962; held various teaching posts in U.K. 1961-70 including Leicester and Coventry Colls. of Art; resident in Canada 1970-73; Visiting Prof. Univ. of Calgary 1970-71; Visiting Assoc. Prof. Univ. of Victoria, B.C. 1972-73; Lecturer in Sculpture, Fachhochschule für Gestaltung, Pforzheim, Fed. Germany 1973-77, Prof. 1977-80; Prof. Akad. der Bildenden Kunste, Karlsruhe 1980-; various exhbns. in U.K. and internationally since 1957 including V. Biennale, Paris 1966, Documenta IV, Kassel 1968, Documenta VI 1977; works in many public collections in U.K., Germany, Australia, U.S.A. etc. *Address:* Schloss Scheibenhardt, 7500 Karlsruhe, Federal Republic of Germany. *Telephone:* Karlsruhe 86 86 33.

SANDOUNGOUT, Marcel; Gabonese trade unionist and diplomatist; b. 25 Oct. 1927; fmr. trade unionist, Gabon; fmr. Chef de Cabinet to Minister of Planning for Agric.; Chief, Div. for Int. Orgs., Ministry of Foreign Affairs 1960; mem. Nat. Ass. 1961, Chair. Cttee. for Foreign Affairs and Defence, 1961, 1962; Del. to Defence Council of African and Malagasy Union 1961, 1962; Minister of Health and Social Affairs May-Dec. 1962, for Public Works, Tourism and Posts and Telecommunications 1963-64; Amb. to Fed. Repub. of Germany, Belgium, Netherlands, Norway, Denmark, Sweden and Luxembourg 1964-66; Perm. Rep. to GATT and EEC 1964-66; Perm. Rep. to UN 1967-68; Amb. to Dahomey and Senegal 1969-71, to Ivory Coast 1971-72, to France (also accred. to Austria, Switzerland and Tunisia) 1972-79. *Address:* c/o Ministère des Affaires Etrangères, Libreville, Gabon.

SANDOVAL, Arturo; Cuban jazz trumpeter; b. 1949, Artemisa; m. Marianela Sandoval; one s.; ed. Nat. School of Art; began trumpet playing aged 12 and made first public appearances in Cuba aged 13; played in group with Chucho Valdez until 1981; formed own group in 1981 and now undertakes annual maj. world tour; festival appearances at Tokyo, Newport, Montreux, Antibes, Chicago, the Hague and the Hollywood Bowl; several record albums.

SANEYEV, Viktor; Soviet athlete; b. 24 Oct. 1945, Sukhumi, Georgian SSR; m. Tatiana Saneyeva 1972; one s.; ed. Malygina Boarding School, Gantiardi Boarding School, Sukhumi Inst. of Subtropical Cultures, Tbilisi Inst. of Physical Educ.; int. athlete 1964-; won Olympic gold medals in triple jump, Mexico 1968, Munich 1972, Montreal 1976, silver medallist, Moscow 1980; European triple jump champion 1969, 1974, silver medallist 1971, 1978; European Indoor champion 1970, 1972, 1975, 1976, 1977; European and Olympic record holder; World record holder 1968-1972, 1972-1975; Order of Lenin, Red Banner of Labour, Friendship of Peoples, Master of Sport. *Address:* c/o Light Athletic Federation, Skatertnyi per 4, Moscow G.69, U.S.S.R.

SANFORD, Charles Steadman, Jr., M.B.A.; American banker; b. 8 Oct. 1936, Savannah, Ga.; s. of Charles S. Sanford and Ann Lawrence; m. Mary McRitchie 1959; one s. one d.; ed. Univs. of Georgia and Pennsylvania; Exec. Vice-Pres. Bankers Trust Co. 1974, mem. Man. Cttee. 1979, Pres. 1983, Deputy Chair. 1986, Chair. of Bd. 1987-. *Address:* Bankers Trust Company, 280 Park Avenue, New York, N.Y. 10017 (Office); 11 Langdon Terrace, Bronxville, N.Y. 10708, U.S.A. (Home). *Telephone:* (212) 850-1045 (Office); (914) 961-5336 (Home).

SANFORD, Terry, A.B., J.D.; American university president, lawyer and politician; b. 20 Aug. 1917, Laurinburg, N.C.; s. of the late Cecil L. Sanford and of Elizabeth Martin Sanford; m. Margaret Rose Knight 1942; one s. one d.; ed. Presbyterian Junior Coll., Univ. of North Carolina and Univ. of N.C. School of Law; attorney at law and partner in private law firm N.C. 1948-60; Partner Sanford, Adams, McCullough & Beard 1965-86; mem. N.C. State Ports Authority 1950-53; Senator from North Carolina 1953-55, Jan. 1987-; Gov. N.C. 1961-65; mem. Bd. of Trustees Methodist Coll. Fayetteville 1958- (Chair. 1958-68), Shaw Univ. 1965-76, Univ. of N.C. 1961-72 (Chair. 1961-65); Pres. Duke Univ. 1969-85, Pres. Emer. 1985-; Trustee Howard Univ. 1971-86, Berea Coll. 1968-73; mem. of Bd., Cities Service Co. 1971-79, ITT Corpn. 1976-86, American Stock Exchange 1977-83, Cadmus Communications Corpn. 1979-86, Prudential-Bache Mutual Funds 1983-86, Golden Corral Corpn. 1984-86; mem. American Bar Assen., North Carolina Bar Assen., District of Columbia Bar; fmr. mem. of numerous orgs. concerned with regional and urban problems, educ., children and youth, health, arts. *Publications:* But What About People? 1966, Storm Over the States 1967, A Danger of Democracy 1981. *Address:* U.S. Senate, Capitol Hill, Washington, D.C. 20510; 2500 Auburn Street, Durham, N.C. 27707, U.S.A.

SANGARE, N'Faly, M.A. ECON.; Guinean economist and diplomatist; b. 14 Oct. 1933, Kankan; m. Aïssatou Bah 1963; five c.; ed. Univ. of Paris; Deputy Dir. Crédit Nat., Conakry, Guinea 1963-67; Dir. of Issue, Cen. Bank of Guinea 1963-67, Dir.-Gen. 1967-69, Gov. 1969-75; Minister of Banking and Insurance 1974-75, of Planning and Co-operation 1975-78; Amb. to Benelux and the EEC, Brussels 1978-80; Alt. Exec. Dir., IMF 1981-82, Exec. Dir. 1982-84; several foreign decorations. *Leisure interests:* reading, music. *Address:* 5823 Magic Mountain Drive, Rockville, Md. 20852, U.S.A. (Home). *Telephone:* (202) 477 3776 (Office).

SANGER, David John, F.R.A.M., F.R.C.O., A.R.C.M.; British organist; b. 17 April 1947, London; s. of Stanley C. Sanger and Ethel L. F. Sanger; ed. Eltham Coll., London and Royal Acad. of Music; studied organ in Paris with Marie-Claire Alain and later with Susi Jeans 1966-68; First Prize, Int. Organ Competition, St. Albans 1969, since when has been freelance soloist and teacher of organ; has performed throughout Europe and in U.S.A. and Canada; Prof. of Organ, Royal Acad. of Music 1983-; First Prize, Int. Organ Competition, Kiel 1972; has recorded six organ symphonies of Louis Vierne and complete organ works of César Franck. *Leisure interests:* fell-walking, tennis, swimming, photography, choir-training, singing. *Address:* Old Wesleyan Chapel, Embleton, Nr. Cockermouth, Cumbria, CA13 9YA, England. *Telephone:* (059 681) 628.

SANGER, Frederick, O.M., C.H., C.B.E., PH.D., F.R.S.; British research biochemist; b. 13 Aug. 1918, Rendcomb, Glos.; s. of Frederick Sanger and Cicely Crewdson; m. Joan Howe 1940; two s. one d.; ed. Bryanston School and St. John's Coll., Cambridge; biochemical research at Cambridge 1940-; Beit Memorial Fellowship 1944-51; mem. Scientific Staff, Medical Research Council 1951-83, retd., Fellow, King's Coll., Cambridge 1954-; Hon. Foreign mem. American Acad. of Arts and Sciences 1958-; hon. mem. American Soc. of Biological Chemists, Japanese Biochemical Soc.; corresp. mem. Asociación Química de Argentina; mem. Acad. of Science of Argentina and Brazil, World Acad. of Arts and Science, Russell Cttee. against Chemical Weapons 1981-; foreign assoc. N.A.S. (U.S.A.), French Acad. of Sciences; Corday-Morgan Medal and Prize, Chemical Soc. 1951, Nobel Prize for Chemistry 1958 and (jointly) 1980, Alfred Benzon Prize 1966; Royal Medal (Royal Soc.) 1969; Hopkins Memorial Medal 1971; Gairdner Foundation Annual Award 1971, 1979, Hanbury Memorial Medal 1976, William Bate

Hardy Prize 1976, Copley Medal 1977, G. W. Wheland Award 1978, Louisa Gross Horwitz Prize 1979, Albert Lasker Basic Medical Research Award, Columbia Univ. (with W. Gilbert, q.v.) 1979, Gold Medal, Royal Soc. of Medicine 1983; Hon. D.Sc. (Leicester, Oxford, Strasbourg, Cambridge 1983). *Publications:* various papers on protein and nucleic acid structure and metabolism in scientific journals. *Leisure interests:* boating, gardening. *Address:* Far Leys, Fen Lane, Swaffham Bulbeck, Cambridge, CB5 0NJ, England (Home). *Telephone:* (0223) 811610.

SANGER, Ruth Ann, PH.D., F.R.S.; British medical research scientist; b. 6 June 1918, Southport, Queensland; d. of Hubert Sanger and Katharine M. Ross (Cameron); m. Robert Russell Race, C.B.E., F.R.C.P., F.R.S. (q.v.) 1956; no c.; ed. Abbotsleigh, Sydney and Sydney and London Univs.; mem. of scientific staff, Red Cross Blood Transfusion Service, Sydney 1941–46, Medical Research Council Blood Group Unit, Lister Inst., London 1946–83, Dir. 1973–83; Karl Landsteiner Award, American Asscn. of Blood Banks (with Dr. R. R. Race) 1957, Philip Levine Award, American Soc. of Clinical Pathologists (with Dr. R. R. Race) 1970, Gairdner Award, Toronto 1972, Oliver Memorial Award 1973. *Publications:* Blood Groups in Man (with Dr. R. R. Race) 1950; many papers on blood groups in medical and scientific journals. *Address:* 22 Vicarage Road, East Sheen, London, SW14 8RU, England. *Telephone:* 01-876 1508.

SANGUINETI, Edoardo; Italian writer; b. 9 Dec. 1930, Genoa; s. of Giovanni Sanguineti and Giuseppina Cocchi; m. Luciana Garabello 1954; three s. one d.; ed. Univ. degli Studi, Turin; Prof. of Italian Literature, Univ. of Salerno 1968–74, Genoa 1974–; Town Councillor of Genoa 1976–81; mem. Chamber of Deputies 1979–83. *Publications:* Laborintus 1956, Opus metricum 1960, Interpretazione di Malebolge 1961, Tre studi danteschi 1961, Tra liberty e crepuscolarismo 1961, Alberto Moravia 1962, K. e altre cose 1962, Passaggio 1963, Capriccio italiano 1963, Triperuno 1964, Ideologia e linguaggio 1965, Il realismo di Dante 1966, Guido Gozzano 1966, Il Giuoco dell' Oca 1967, Le Baccanti di Euripide (trans.) 1968, Fedra di Seneca (trans.) 1969, T.A.T. 1969, Teatro 1969, Poesia Italiana del Novecento 1969, Il Giuoco del Satyricon 1970, Orlando Furioso (with L. Ronconi) 1970, Renga (with O. Paz, J. Roubaud, C. Tomlinson) 1971, Storie Naturali 1971, Wirrwarr 1972, Catamerone 1974, Le Troiane di Euripide (trans.) 1974, Giornalino 1976, Postkarten 1978, Le Coefore di Eschilo (trans.) 1978, Giornalino secondo 1979, Stracciafoglio 1980, Edipo tiranno di Sofocle (trans.) 1980, Scartabello 1981, Segnalibro 1982, Alfabeto apocalittico 1984, Scribilli 1985, Faust, un travestimento 1985, Novissimum Testamentum 1986, La missione del critico 1987, Bisbidis 1987, Ghirigori 1988. *Address:* Via Pergolesi 20, 16159 Genoa, Italy. *Telephone:* 010-444050.

SANGUINETTI, Julio María; Uruguayan politician and lawyer; b. 1936; m. Marta Canessa; one s. one d.; mem. Gen. Ass. 1962–73; Minister of Labour and Industry 1969–72, of Educ. and Culture 1972–73; then Pres. Comisión Nacional de Artes Plasticas; then Pres. of UNESCO Comm. for promotion of books in Latin America; Pres. of Uruguay March 1985–; Leader Colorado Party 1981–; Pres. Nat. Fine Arts Council. *Address:* Oficina del Presidente, Montevideo, Uruguay.

SANKEY, John Anthony, C.M.G., M.A.; British diplomatist; b. 8 June 1930, London; m. Gwendoline Putman 1958; two s. two d.; ed. Cardinal Vaughan School, Kensington, Peterhouse, Cambridge, NATO Defence Coll., Rome; Colonial Office 1953–61; First Sec., U.K. Mission to UN, New York 1961–64; First Sec. FCO 1964–68; Deputy High Commr. in Guyana 1968–71; Counsellor, Singapore 1971–73; Deputy High Commr. in Malta 1973–75; Counsellor, The Hague 1975–79; Special Counsellor for African Affairs, FCO 1980–82; High Commr. in Tanzania 1982–85; Perm. Rep. to the UN in Geneva and to GATT 1985–. *Leisure interest:* walking in the Jura. *Address:* United Kingdom Mission, 37–39 rue de Vermont, 1211 Geneva 20, Switzerland.

SANO, Kenjiro; Japanese business executive; b. 5 Oct. 1920, Tokyo; s. of Seisaku Sano and Kou Sano; m. Sadako Komazaki 1944; one s. one d.; ed. Univ. of Tokyo; entered Diesel Motors Kogyo Co., Ltd. (now Isuzu Motors Ltd.) 1948, Dir. Isuzu Motors Ltd. 1970, Exec. Dir. 1973, Man. Dir. 1977, Exec. Vice-Pres. 1982, Chair. 1984–; Blue Ribbon Medal. *Leisure interests:* golf, reading. *Address:* Isuzu Motors Ltd., 22-10, Minami-oi 6-chome, Shinagawa-ku, Tokyo (Office); 22-18 Iwabuchi-cho, Kita-ku, Tokyo, Japan (Home). *Telephone:* 03-762-1111 (Office); 03-901-2111 (Home).

SANSBURY, Rt. Rev. Cyril Kenneth, D.D.; British ecclesiastic; b. 21 Jan. 1905; m. Ada Ethelreda Mary Wamsley 1931; one s. two d.; ed. St. Paul's School, London, Peterhouse, Cambridge, and Westcott House, Cambridge; ordained Deacon 1928, Priest 1929; Curate, Diocese of Southwark 1928–32; Missionary in Japan 1932–41; Prof. Central Theological Coll., Tokyo, and Chaplain, St. Andrew's Church, Tokyo 1934–41; Chaplain, Royal Canadian Air Force 1941–45; Warden, Lincoln Theological Coll. 1945–52; Canon and Prebendary, Lincoln Cathedral 1948–53; Warden, St. Augustine's Coll., Canterbury 1952–61; Hon. Canon of Canterbury 1953–61; Bishop of Singapore and Malaya 1961–66; Gen. Sec. British Council of Churches 1966–73; Asst. Bishop, Diocese of London 1966–73; Priest-in-charge St. Mary in the Marsh, Norwich 1973–84. *Address:* 67C The Close, Norwich, NR1 4DD, England. *Telephone:* 0603-618808.

SANT, Lorry, M.P.; Maltese politician; b. 26 Dec. 1937, Paola; s. of John Sant and Mary Levanzin; m. Carmen Pace 1968; ed. St. Michaels School,

H.M. Naval Dockyard Tech. Coll.; Sec. Labour League of Youth; Sec. Metal Workers Union 1960–71; mem. House of Reps. 1962, 1966; Minister of Public Bldgs. and Works 1971–87, of Water Works 1975–87, of Works and Sport 1976–87, of the Interior 1981–83, of Works and Housing 1983–87. *Address:* c/o House of Representatives, Valletta, Malta.

SANTANDER, Teresa, PH.D.; Spanish librarian; b. 11 June 1925, Salamanca; ed. Univ. of Salamanca, PH.D; Instructor in Greek Language, Instituto Nacional de Enseñanza Media "Lucia de Medrano", Salamanca 1949–50; Asst., Archives, Libraries and Museums, Univ. of Salamanca 1955; then mem. of Corps of Professional Archivists, Librarians and Archaeologists 1958; Dir. León Public Library and León Libraries Prov. Co-ordinating Centre 1958–60; Librarian, Univ. of Salamanca 1960–74, Dir. of Library and Archives 1974–88; mem. Centro de Estudios Salmantinos. *Publications:* Indice de médicos españoles (with Luis S. Granjel) 1957, La creación de la cátedra de Cirugía en la Universidad de Salamanca 1965, Un manuscrito desconocido de Plotino en Salamanca 1969, Hipócrates en España (16th century) 1971, La iglesia de San Nicolás y el antiguo teatro anatómico de la Universidad de Salamanca 1983, Escolares médicos en Salamanca 1984. *Address:* Calle de Zamora 44, 1°, 37002 Salamanca, Spain.

SANTELLI, Claude Jean Xavier, L. ÈS L.; French playwright, television director and producer; b. 17 June 1923, Metz, Moselle; s. of late César Santelli and of Elisa Franceschi; m. Olympe Collet 1949; ed. Lycées Montaigne, Louis-le-Grand, Paris, Univ. de Paris; actor in occupied Germany 1944–49; French teacher École pratique de l'Alliance française, Conf. Organizer Union des sciences politiques 1949–55; playwright 1954–, for TV 1956–; producer and presenter, Livre, mon Ami 1958–68, producer Théâtre de la Jeunesse 1960–66; mem. controlling Cttee. Organization de la Radiodiffusion-Télévision Française (O.R.T.F.) 1965–74, Controller of New Year programmes 1964, 1968; mem. Council of Cultural Devt. 1971–73; Pres. Soc. des auteurs et compositeurs dramatiques 1982–84, 1986–; plays include le Fantôme (after Plautus) 1954, la Famille Arlequin (prix Molière) 1955, Lope de Vega 1958; producer of first French TV serial le Tour de France par deux enfants 1957–58; Writer and Dir. Lancelot du lac, Producer TV programmes les Cent livres des hommes 1970, la Porte ouverte 1971, la Légende du siècle 1972, Screenplay and Dir. Histoire vraie, Histoire d'une fille de ferme 1973, Madame Baptiste, la Confession d'un enfant du siècle 1974, le Père Amable, Première Neige 1975, Author and Dir. la Vérité de Madame Langlois 1977, la Chaine 1979, le Neveu de Rameau 1980, Jacques le fataliste et son maître 1984; Dir. theatrical production of La tour de Nesle 1986; numerous adaptations for children's drama programmes; Chevalier, Légion d'honneur, ordre nat. du Mérite, Médaille de la Résistance, Officier, Arts et Lettres. *Address:* 36 rue des Alouettes, 75019 Paris (Office); 110 boulevard Saint-Germain, 75006 Paris, France (Home).

SANTER, Jacques, D. EN D; Luxembourg politician; b. 18 May 1937, Wasserbillig; m. Danièle Binot; two s.; ed. Athénée de Luxembourg, Univs. of Paris and Strasbourg and Inst. d'Etudes Politiques, Paris; advocate, Luxembourg Court of Appeal 1961–65; attaché, Office of Minister of Labour and Social Security 1963–65; Govt. attaché 1965–66; Parl. Sec. Parti Chrétien-Social 1966–72, Sec.-Gen. 1972–74, Pres. 1974–82; Sec. of State for Cultural and Social Affairs 1972–74; mem. Chamber of Deputies 1974–79; mem. European Parl. 1975–79, Vice-Pres. 1975–77; Municipal Magistrate, City of Luxembourg 1976–79; Minister of Finance, of Labour and of Social Security 1979–84; Prime Minister, Minister of State and Minister of Finance July 1984–. *Leisure interests:* walking, swimming. *Address:* Hotel de Bourgogne, 4 rue de la Congrégation, L-2910 Luxembourg (Office); 69 rue J.-P. Huberty, 1742 Luxembourg (Home). *Telephone:* 478-1 (Office).

SANTER, Rt. Rev. Mark, M.A.; British ecclesiastic; b. 29 Dec. 1936, Bristol; s. of Rev. Canon E. A. R. Santer and Phyllis C. Barlow; m. Henriette Cornelia Weststrate 1964; one s. two d.; ed. Marlborough Coll., Queens' Coll. and Westcott House, Cambridge; Curate All Saints Cuddeson 1963–67; Tutor Cuddeson Coll., Oxford 1963–67; Dean and Fellow Clare Coll., Cambridge 1967–72; Asst. Lecturer in Divinity, Univ. of Cambridge 1968–72; Principal Westcott House 1973–81; Area Bishop of Kensington 1981–87; Bishop of Birmingham 1987–; Co-Chair. Anglican/R.C. Int. Comm. 1983–; Hon. Fellow Clare Coll. 1987. *Publications:* Documents in Early Christian Thought (with M. F. Wiles) 1975, Their Lord and Ours (Ed.) 1982. *Address:* Bishop's Croft, Old Church Road, Harborne, Birmingham, B17 0BG, England. *Telephone:* (021) 427-1163.

SANTOS, Corentino Virgilio; Cape Verde banker and diplomatist; b. 12 Dec. 1946, São Vicente; s. of Virgilio Santos and Joseph Ana Ramos; one s. one d.; ed. Technical Univ. of Lisbon, Portugal; served as Sr. Technician on Industrial Economy, Office of Sec. of State for Industry; apptd. Under-Sec. for Finance during transition to independence of Cape Verde 1974; Gov. Bank of Cape Verde 1975–84; Perm. Rep. to UN 1984–87. *Publication;* study on financial structures of Portuguese industry (co-author) 1973. *Leisure interests:* reading, sport. *Address:* c/o Ministry of Foreign Affairs, Praça 10 de Mayo, CP60, Praia, São Tiago, Cape Verde.

SANTOS, João Oliveira, LL.D.; Brazilian international trade and banking expert; b. 26 Oct. 1914, Rio de Janeiro; s. of João Barbosa dos Santos and Albertina de Oliveira Santos; m. Margarita Beatriz Williams 1959; two s. one d.; ed. Universidade do Brasil and American Univ., Washington, D.C.;

at Ministry of Labour, Industry and Commerce, Brazil 1935, 1942, 1950–54; on active service in Brazilian Air Force 1943–45; Lecturer American Univ., Washington 1945–46; Deputy Dir. and Acting Dir. Dept. of Econ. and Social Affairs, Gen. Secr. OAS, Washington, D.C. 1955–58; Sec.-Gen. Latin American Coffee Agreement 1958–59, Coffee Study Group, Wash. 1958–75, Int. Coffee Agreement, Washington, D.C. 1959–63; Exec. Dir. Int. Coffee Org., London 1963–68; Operations Man. and Vice-Pres. in charge of the fund for Special Operations, Inter-American Devt. Bank, Washington, D.C. 1968–74; Consultant on Commodities for UN 1962, mem. Bd. of Industries 1975–; Order of the Sun of Peru, Order of Honour, Merit of Haiti and Order of Rubén Darío of Nicaragua, Order of San Carlos (Colombia), Order of Merit (Ecuador), Order of José Matias Delgado (El Salvador), Order of Duarte Sánchez y Mella (Dominican Republic), Order Infante Don Henrique (Portugal), Medal Santos Dumont (Brazil) and others. *Address:* 7214 Park Terrace Drive, Alexandria, Virginia, 22307, U.S.A. *Telephone:* (703) 765-3092.

SANTRY, Arthur J., Jr.; American business executive; b. 1 Aug. 1918, Brookline, Mass.; s. of Arthur Joseph and Suzanne (née Cawley) Santry; m. Julia Timmins 1955; four s. one d.; ed. Williams Coll. and Harvard Law School; fmr. Partner, Putnam, Bell, Santry and Ray (law firm), Boston, Mass.; joined Combustion Eng. Inc. 1956, Dir. 1957, Pres and C.E.O. 1963–82, Chair. 1982–88; Dir. Bristol-Myers Co., Jenney Oil Co., Inc., Putnam Trust Co., Amax Inc., The Singer Co. *Address:* Combustion Engineering Inc., 900 Long Ridge Road, P.O. Box 9308, Stamford, Conn. 06904, U.S.A.

SAOUMA, Edouard; Lebanese agricultural engineer and international official; b. 6 Nov. 1926, Beirut; m. Inès Forero; one s. two d.; ed. St. Joseph's Univ. School of Eng., Beirut, Ecole nat. Supérieure d'Agronomie, Montpellier, France; Dir. Tel Amara Agricultural School 1952–53, Nat. Centre for Farm Mechanization 1954–55; Sec.-Gen. Nat. Fed. of Lebanese Agronomists 1955; Dir.-Gen. Nat. Inst. for Agricultural Research 1957–62; mem. Governing Board, Nat. Grains Office 1960–62; Lebanese del. to FAO 1955–62, Deputy Regional Rep. for Asia and Far East 1962–65, mem. of Secr. 1963–, Dir. Land and Water Devt. Div. 1965–75, Dir.-Gen. of FAO 1976–82, 1982–; Minister of Agric., Fisheries and Forestry Oct.–Nov. 1970; Hon. Prof. of Agronomy, Agric. Univ. of Beijing; Accademico Corrispondente dell' Accademia Nazionale di Agricoltura (Italy); Dr. h.c. (Univs. of Gembloux, Belgium, Jakarta, Seoul, Uruguay, La Molina, Peru, Warsaw, Los Baños, Philippines, Punjab, Faisalabad, Nicaragua, Gödöllo Univ. of Agricultural Science, Hungary, Beijing Univ. of Agric., Prague); Order of the Cedar (Lebanon), Said Akl Prize (Lebanon); Chevalier du Mérite agricole (France), Grand Croix, Ordre nat. du Tchad, du Ghana, de la Haute Volta (Burkina Faso), Gran Cruz al Mérito Agrícola (Spain), Kt. Commdr. Order of Merit (Greece), Orden del Mérito Agrícola (Colombia), Gran Oficial del Orden de Vasco Nuñez de Balboa (Panama), Orden al Mérito Agricola (Peru), Order of Merit (Egypt, Mauritania), Grand Officier, Ordre de la République (Tunisia), Grand Officier, Ordre Nat. (Madagascar). *Publications:* technical publs. in agriculture. *Address:* Food and Agriculture Organization of the United Nations, Via delle Terme di Caracalla, 00100 Rome, Italy. *Telephone:* 57971.

SAPORTA, Marc, LL.D.; French writer; b. 20 March 1923; ed. Univs. of Paris and Madrid; worked in the Dept. of Cultural Activities UNESCO 1948–53, Asst. Ed. Informations et Documents 1954–71, Ed. 1971–78; Ed.-in-Chief Dept. of Publs. U.S. Information Agency (Paris) 1978–84; Literary Critic L'Express 1954–71, La Quinzaine Littéraire 1966–71. *Publications:* Les lois de l'air 1953, La convention universelle du droit d'auteur de l'UNESCO 1952, Le grand défi: U.S.A.-U.R.S.S., I 1967, II 1968 (Ed. and Co-Author), Histoire du roman américain 1970, La vie quotidienne contemporaine aux U.S.A. 1972, Go West 1976, William Faulkner (Ed. and jt. author) 1983, Henry James (Ed. and jt. author) 1983, I. B. Singer (Ed. and jt. author) 1984, Nathalie Sarraute (Ed. and jt. author) 1984, Marguerite Duras (Ed. and jt. author) 1985, Vivre aux Etats-Unis 1986, André Breton ou le Surréalisme Même (Ed. and Co-Author) 1988, Israel 1988; novels: Le furet 1959, La distribution 1961, La quête 1961, Composition numéro un 1962, Les invités 1964. *Address:* 9 rue Saint-Didier, 75116 Paris, France.

SARABHAI, Mrinalini; Indian dancer and choreographer; b. 1935; m. Dr. Vikram A. Sarabhai; one s. one d.; studied under Meenakshi Sundaram Pillai; founder/Dir. Darpana Acad. of Performing Arts, Ahmedabad 1949; Chair. Handicrafts & Handloom Devt. Corpn. of Gujarat State; mem. Sangeet Natak Acad., New Delhi; Hon. Consultant, Nat. Centre for Performing Arts, Bombay; Pres. Alliance Française; adviser to many arts and cultural insts. in India; Vishwa Gurjari award 1984; Deshikothama award (Vishwa Bharati Univ. Shantiniketan) 1987. *Publications:* one novel, textbook on Bharata Natyam, a book on various classical dance-dramas, children's books and articles in newspapers and journals. *Address:* Darpana Academy of Performing Arts, Ahmedabad 380013, Gujarat, India. *Telephone:* 445189.

SARAIVA GUERREIRO, Ramiro Elysio; Brazilian diplomatist; b. Salvador; s. of José Affonso Guerreiro and Esther Saraiva Guerreiro; m. Gloria Vallim Guerreiro 1947; one s. one d.; ed. Univ. of Brazil and Rio Branco Inst. (Diplomatic Acad.); Foreign Service 1945; Brazilian Mission to UN 1946–69; Embassies, La Paz 1950–51, Washington 1956–58; Minister-

Counsellor, Montevideo 1966–67, deputy del. to Meeting of Chiefs of American States 1967; del. Emergency Special Session of UN Gen. Ass. 1967; Asst. Sec.-Gen. of Int. Orgs., Ministry of Foreign Affairs 1967–79; mem. del. to numerous UN Gen. Assemblies; Under Sec.-Gen. of External Policy 1969; Rep. at meetings of Comm. of Sea Bed and Ocean Floor 1969–72; Chief of del. UN Conf. on Law of the Sea 1968–77, 26th Session of GATT 1970, Geneva 1970–74, Disarmament Cttee. 1970–74, Chief of Section of Brazilian-German Cttee. on Econ. Co-operation and Science and Tech. 1974, 1975, 1977; Amb. to France 1978–79; Minister of Foreign Affairs 1979–85; Chief of Dels. to 24th–28th UN Gen. Assemblies 1979–83; mem. Geographical Soc. (Rio de Janeiro), American Soc. of Int. Law, Brazilian Soc. of Air Law, Argentine Council for Int. Relations. *Leisure interests:* reading, golf. *Address:* c/o Ministério das Relações Exteriores, Esplanada dos Ministérios 70170, Brasília, DF, Brazil.

SARASIN, Alfred Emanuel; Swiss banker; b. 13 April 1922, Basel; s. of Bernhard and Rosemarie Sarasin-La Roche; m. Colette de Loriol 1950; two d.; ed. secondary educ. in Geneva and New York; Partner, A. Sarasin & Cie., bankers 1950–; mem. Bd., Swiss Bankers' Assen. 1958–86, Chair. 1965, then Pres.; fmr. Pres. Basel Stock Exchange for seven years; Liberal mem. Great Council of Canton of Basel City for five years, resgnd; Pres. Soc. Int. Pirelli S.A., Union Trading Co. Ltd., Grands Magasins Jelmoli S.A., Kraftwerke Brusio S.A., Hero Conserven Lenzburg; mem Bd. of about 20 industrial and commercial cos.; mem. Bd., Basel, Swiss and Int. Chambers of Commerce. *Leisure interests:* shooting, fishing. *Address:* Freiestrasse 107, CH-4002 Basel, Switzerland. *Telephone:* 23-00-55 (Office).

SARASIN, Arsa; Thai diplomatist; b. 1936; s. of Pote Sarasin (former Prime Minister of Thailand, q.v.); ed. Boston Univ.; Perm. Sec. Ministry of Foreign Affairs until 1986; Amb. to U.S.A. 1986–88. *Address:* c/o Ministry of Foreign Affairs, Saranrom Palace, Bangkok 10200, Thailand.

SARASIN, Pote; Thai lawyer, politician and international administrator; b. 25 March 1907, Bangkok; m.; five s. one d.; ed. Wilbraham Acad., Mass., and Middle Temple, London; practised law in Thailand 1933–45; mem. Senate 1948–50; Deputy Minister of Foreign Affairs 1948, Minister of Foreign Affairs 1948–50; rep. Thailand on UN Korea Comm. 1950; Amb. to U.S.A. 1952–57; Del. to UN 1952–55; Prime Minister 1957–58; Sec.-Gen. SEATO 1957–63; Minister of Econ. Affairs and Nat. Devt., Thailand 1963–68; Minister of Econ. Affairs 1968–69; Vice-Chair. United Thai People's Party 1968; Deputy Prime Minister and Minister of Nat. Devt. 1969–71; mem. Nat. Exec. Council and Dir. Econ., Finance and Industry Affairs 1971–72; mem. Thai Bar Assen. *Address:* Saha-Pracha-Thai, 1/226, Sri Ayudhya, Dusit, Bangkok, Thailand.

SARBANES, Paul Spyros, B.A., LL.B.; American lawyer and politician; b. 3 Feb. 1933, Salisbury, Md.; s. of Spyros P. and Matina (née Tsigounis) Sarbanes; m. Christine Dunbar 1960; two s. one d.; ed. Princeton Univ., Balliol Coll., Oxford, Harvard Law School; Rhodes Scholar, Balliol Coll., Oxford 1954–57; admitted to Maryland Bar 1960; Law Clerk to Circuit Judge 1960–61; Assoc., Piper and Marbury, Baltimore 1961–62; Admin. Asst. to Chair. Council of Econ. Advisers 1962–63; Exec. Dir. Charter Revision Comm., Baltimore 1963–64; Assoc., Venable, Baetjer & Howard, Baltimore 1965–70; mem. Md. House of Dels. 1967–71, U.S. House of Reps. 1971–76, Senator from Maryland Jan. 1977–; Democrat. *Address:* United States Senate, Capitol Hill, Washington, D.C. 20510, U.S.A.

SARDANIS, Andreas Sotiris; Zambian company director; b. 13 March 1931, Cyprus; m. Danae Gavas 1962; two s.; ed. in Cyprus; emigrated to Zambia 1950; managerial posts in trading and transport undertakings 1950–62; Chair. and Man. Dir. Industrial Devt. Corpn. 1965–70; Perm. Sec. Ministry of Commerce, Industry and Foreign Trade 1968; later Perm. Sec. Ministry of Trade, Industry and Mines, and Perm. Sec. Ministry of Devt. and Finance; Man. Dir. Zambia Industrial and Mining Corpn. Ltd. (ZIMCO) and Chair. of its subsidiaries, Indeco Ltd, and Mindeco Ltd. 1970–71; Perm. Sec., Ministry of State Participation April–Dec. 1970; Man. Dir. Sardanis Assocs. 1971–76; Chair. ITM Int. S.A. 1976–. *Address:* 126 East 56th Street, New York, N.Y. 10022, U.S.A.; 16 Grosvenor Place, London, W1X 9FB, England; Chaminuka, P.O. Box 32946, Lusaka, Zambia. *Telephone:* 212 980 9110 (New York); 01-629 8899 (London); 219327 (Lusaka).

SAREI, Sir Alexis Holyweek, Kt., C.B.E., J.C.D.; Papua New Guinea ecclesiastic and diplomatist; b. 25 March 1934, Buka; m. Claire Dionne 1972; three s. three d. (all adopted); ed. Univ.; Roman Catholic Priest 1966–71; Pvt. Sec. to Chief Minister 1972–73; Dist. Commr. 1973–75; Warden, Univ. of Papua New Guinea 1972; Premier, N. Solomons Prov. Govt. 1976–80; High Commr. in U.K. (also Amb. to other European and Middle Eastern countries) 1980–83; Perm. Rep. to U.N. and Amb. to U.S.A. 1983–86; Papua New Guinea Independence Medal. *Publication:* The Practice of Marriage Among the Solos 1974. *Leisure interests:* music, all sports, writing letters, swimming, hunting. *Address:* c/o Ministry of Foreign Affairs, Port Moresby, Papua New Guinea.

SARGAN, John Denis, M.A., F.B.A.; British academic (retd.); b. 23 Aug. 1924, Doncaster; s. of H. and G. A. Sargan; m. Phyllis Mary Millard 1953; two s. one d.; ed. St. John's Coll., Cambridge; Lecturer, then Reader in Econ. Statistics, Leeds Univ. 1948–63; Reader, then Prof. of Econometrics, L.S.E. 1963–84; Prof. Emer. 1984–; Pres. Econometric Soc. 1980; Fellow, American Acad. of Arts and Sciences 1987–. *Publications:* numerous articles on econometrics. *Leisure interests:* theatre, music. *Address:* 49

Dukes Avenue, Theydon Bois, Epping, CM16 7HQ, England. *Telephone:* (037881) 2222.

SARGENT, John Turner; American publisher; b. 26 June 1924; m. 1st Neltje Doubleday 1953 (divorced), one s. one d.; m. 2nd Elizabeth Nichols Kelly 1985; Doubleday and Co. Inc., Ed. 1949–50, Advertising and Publicity, Trade Sales man. 1950–60, Vice-Pres. and Dir. 1960–61, Pres. 1961–78, Chair. Bd. 1978–; Dir. Grumman Corpn., Atlantic Mutual Cos.; Trustee East River Savings Bank, New York Public Library, New York Zoological Soc., American Acad. in Rome, Kips Bay Boys Club, Alger Fund, Castle Convertible Fund. *Address:* Doubleday and Co. Inc., 245 Park Avenue, New York, N.Y. 10017 (Office); Halsey Lane, Watermill, N.Y. 11976, U.S.A. (Home).

SARGENT, Wallace Leslie William, PH.D., F.R.S.; British astronomer; b. 15 Feb. 1935, Elsham, Lincs.; s. of Leslie and Eleanor Sargent; m. Anneila I. Cassells 1964; two d.; ed. Scunthorpe Tech. High School and Manchester Univ.; Research Fellow in Astronomy, Calif. Inst. of Tech. 1959–62; Senior Research Fellow, Royal Greenwich Observatory 1962–64; Asst. Prof. of Physics, Univ. of Calif., San Diego 1964–66; Asst. Prof. of Astronomy, Calif. Inst. of Tech. 1966–68, Assoc. Prof. 1968–71, Prof. 1971–81, Exec. Officer for Astronomy 1975–81, Ira S. Bowen Prof. of Astronomy 1981–; Fellow, American Acad. of Arts and Sciences; Alfred P. Sloan Foundation Fellow 1968–70; George Darwin Lecturer, Royal Astronomical Soc. 1987; Helen B. Warner Prize, American Astronomical Soc. 1969. *Publications:* numerous papers in scientific journals. *Leisure interests:* reading, gardening, watching sports, oriental rugs. *Address:* Department of Astronomy 105–24, California Institute of Technology, Pasadena, Calif. 91125 (Office); 400 South Berkeley Avenue, Pasadena, Calif. 91107. U.S.A. (Home). *Telephone:* (818) 356-4055 (Office); (818) 795-6345 (Home).

SARGESON, Alan McLeod, PH.D., F.A.A., F.R.S.; Australian professor of inorganic chemistry; b. 13 Oct. 1930, Armidale, N.S.W.; s. of Herbert L. Sargeson and Alice McLeod; m. Marietta Anders 1959; two s. two d.; ed. Maitland Boys' High School and Univ. of Sydney; Lecturer, Dept. of Chem., Univ. of Adelaide 1956–57; Research Fellow, John Curtin School of Medical Research, A.N.U. 1958; Fellow, A.N.U. 1960, Sr. Fellow, Research School of Chem. 1967, Professorial Fellow 1968–78, Prof. 1978–, Dean 1986–88; Foreign mem. Royal Danish Acad. of Arts and Sciences. *Leisure interest:* swimming. *Address:* Research School of Chemistry, Australian National University, G.P.O. Box 4, Canberra, A.C.T. 2601, Australia. *Telephone:* (062) 493718.

SARKISIAN, Sos Artashesovich; Soviet actor; b. 1929, Armenia; ed. Yerevan Theatre Inst.; acted with Sundukian Theatre 1954–; acted in films 1960–; People's Artist of Armenian S.S.R. 1972, Armenian State Prize for work in the theatre 1979, People's Artist of U.S.S.R. 1985. *Roles include:* The Triangle (Armenian State Prize 1975), Solaris, Gikor and others. *Address:* Sundukian Theatre, Yerevan, U.S.S.R.

SARKISOV, Babken Yesayevich; Soviet politician; b. 1913; mem. CPSU 1939–, mem. Cen. Cttee. 1981–; mem. Cen. Cttee. of Armenian CP 1956–, Sec. and mem. Politburo 1956–61; Deputy to Supreme Soviet of Armenian S.S.R. 1959; Chair. State Cttee. on Science and Tech., Council of Ministers of Armenian S.S.R. 1961; Chair. State Cttee. for the Co-ordination of Scientific Research, Council of Ministers of the Armenian S.S.R. 1961–65; Minister of Motor Transport of Armenian S.S.R. 1966–70; Chair. State Cttee. on Pricing, Council of Ministers of Armenian S.S.R. 1970–75; Pres. Presidium Supreme Soviet of Armenian S.S.R. 1975–86, Vice-Chair. Presidium of U.S.S.R. Supreme Soviet 1977–86; mem. Cen. Auditing Comm. of CPSU 1976–. *Address:* Supreme Soviet of Armenian S.S.R., Yerevan, Armenian S.S.R., U.S.S.R.

SARLÓS, István; Hungarian politician; b. 30 Oct. 1921, Budapest; ed. Budapest Univ.; joined Working-Class Movement and the Social Democrat Party 1939; held various mass organizational and Party positions 1945–59; First Sec. of 6th Dist. Cttee. Hungarian Socialist Workers' Party 1959–63, mem. Cen. Cttee. 1966–; Chair. Budapest Metropolitan Council Exec. Cttee. 1963–70; head of Editorial Bd. daily Népszabadság 1970–74; Gen. Sec. Patriotic People's Front 1974–82; Vice-Pres. Council of Ministers 1982–84; Pres. of Parl. 1984–88; mem. Political Cttee. 1975–85, M.P. 1963–88; Vice-Pres. Pres. Council of the Hungarian People's Repub. 1988–; Labour Order of Merit, Order of Merit of the Hungarian People's Repub. 1981. *Publication:* Haza, haladás, humanizmus (Fatherland, Progress, Humanism) 1981. *Address:* Parliament Building, Kossuth Lajos tér 1, Budapest V, Hungary. *Telephone:* 123-500.

SARNEY, José; Brazilian politician; b. 1930; Asst. to Maranhão State Gov. 1950; Maranhão State Rep. 1956, re-elected 1958, 1962; elected Gov. of Maranhão 1965; state senator (Arena Party, now Partido Democrático Social (PDS)) 1970; Nat. Pres. Arena 1970; fmr. Chair. PDS; mem. Partido Frente Liberal 1984–; acting Pres. of Brazil March–April 1985, Pres. April 1985–; mem. Brazilian Acad. of Letters. *Publication:* Tales of Rain and Sunlight 1986. *Leisure interests:* literature, painting. *Address:* Oficio do Presidente, Palácio do Planalto, Praça dos Tres Podêres, 70.150 Brasília, D.F., Brazil.

SARPANEVA, Timo Tapani; Finnish designer; b. 31 Oct. 1926; s. of Akseli Johannes Sarpaneva and Martta Sofia Karimo; m. 1st Ann-Mari

Holmberg (divorced); m. 2nd Marfatta Svennerig; three s. one d.; ed. Industrial Art Inst., Helsinki; Designer for A. Ahlström Oy, Iittala Glassworks 1950–; Teacher in Textile Printing and Design, Industrial Art Inst. Helsinki 1953–57; Artistic Dir. Porin Puuvilla Cotton Mill 1955–66; AB Kinnasand Textile Mill, Sweden 1964–; Designer for Juhava Oy, Jughans AG, Fed. Repub. of Germany, Opa Oy, Primo Oy, Rosenlew Oy, Roserthal AG, Fed. Repub. of Germany, Villayhnymä; invited by Brazilian Govt. to lecture on and exhibit Finnish art glass 1958; exhbn. architect for Finnish industrial art exhbns. in most European countries, Japan and U.S.A.; architect for Finnish Section, Expo 1967, Montreal; private exhbns. in Finland, Sweden, Norway, Denmark, Iceland, Netherlands, England, Germany, France, Italy, U.S.A., Brazil, U.S.S.R.; mem. Bd. of Dirs. Asscn. of Arts and Crafts, State Cttee. of Design, Bd. of Inst. of Industrial Design; numerous awards, including three Grand Prix at Milan Triennali; Hon. Dr. of Design, Royal Coll. of Art, London 1967; Commdr., Order of Lion of Finland. *Address:* Via Navegna 7, Minusio, Locarno, Switzerland.

SARR, Samuel Jonathan Okikiola, M.B.E.; Gambian diplomatist; b. 13 April 1921, Banjul; s. of John Williamson Sarr and Constance Olivine Sarr; m. Wilhelmina Filicia Sarah Conteh 1970; one s. two d.; ed. Methodist Boys' High School; various posts, BOAC and W. African Airways Corpn. 1942–57; mem., Gambia Oilseeds Marketing Bd. 1958–69, Dist. Sales Man. for The Gambia, Senegal, Sierra Leone, Liberia and Ghana 1965–70; mem., The Gambia Tourist Bd. 1967–71; Pres. The Gambia Tourist Asscn. 1967–71; Amb. to Senegal (also accred. to Guinea, Liberia, Sierra Leone, Mali, Mauritania and Guinea Bissau) 1971–74; High Commr. in Nigeria (also accred. to Ghana, Cameroon, Gabon and Togo) 1974–83, Dean of Diplomatic Corps; High Commr. in the U.K. 1983–87, also accred. to Austria, Denmark, Norway, Sweden, Switzerland and the Holy See; Chair., Econ. Community of W. African States High Commrs. and Ambs. in Nigeria 1981–83. *Leisure interests:* cricket, tennis, football, reading. *Address:* Ministry of Foreign Affairs, Banjul, The Gambia.

SARRAUTE, Nathalie, L. ÈS L., L. EN D.; French writer; b. 18 July 1900, Ivanovo, Russia; d. of Ilya Tcherniak and Pauline Chatounovski; m. Raymond Sarraute 1925; three d.; ed. Univs. of Paris and Oxford; Prix International de Littérature 1964, Grand Prix national 1982; Dr. h.c. (Dublin) 1976, (Canterbury) 1980. *Publications:* Tropismes 1939, Portrait d'un inconnu 1948, Martereau 1953, L'ère du soupçon 1956, Le Planétarium 1959, Les fruits d'or 1963, Le silence 1965, Le mensonge 1966, Entre la vie et la mort 1968, Isma 1970, Vous les entendez? 1972, C'est beau 1975, Disent les imbéciles 1976, Elle est là 1978, L'usage de la parole 1980, Pour un oui ou pour un non 1982, Enfance 1983, Paul Valéry et l'enfant d'éléphant 1985 (trans. into 25 languages). *Address:* 12 avenue Pierre 1er de Serbie, 75116 Paris, France.

SARRE, Claude-Alain; French industrialist; b. 10 April 1928, Douai; s. of Henri Sarre and Claudine Vau; m. Simone Allien 1952; two s. one d.; ed. Inst. d'Etudes Politiques, Paris; with Cie. Air France; joined Soc. André Citroën 1955, Commercial Dir. 1968, Chair., Man. Dir. Soc. Automobiles Citroën and Soc. Commerciale Citroën 1968–70; joined Lainière de Roubaix-Prouvost Masurel S.A. 1970, Pres., Dir.-Gen. 1972–77; Chair. Inst. de Devt. industriel 1975–77; Dir. Soc. Sommer-Allibert 1976; Pres. and Dir. Gen. Nobel-Bozel 1978–82; Dir. gen. Conseil national du patronat français 1983–; Chevalier, Légion d'honneur. *Address:* 18 rue Murillo, 75008 Paris, France. *Telephone:* 42.27.80.75.

SARRE, Massamba, L. EN D.; Senegalese diplomatist; b. 6 Oct. 1935, St. Louis; m.; four c.; ed. Law Colls. Dakar, Senegal and Grenoble, France; Asst. Coll. of Law and Econ. Sciences, Dakar 1959; Asst. Sec.-Gen. to Minister of Foreign Affairs 1960–62, Sec.-Gen. 1962–64, Cabinet Dir. 1964–68; Amb. to Morocco 1968–72, accred. to Turkey, Pakistan, Afghanistan, Bahrain and Qatar 1972–79, to Tunisia 1979–80; Perm. Rep. to UN 1980–88; del. at numerous confs. of UN, OAU, Non-Aligned Countries and Islamic Conf. *Address:* c/o Ministry of Foreign Affairs, place de l'Indépendance, Dakar, Senegal.

SARTORIUS, Norman, M.D., PH.D., D.P.M.; Yugoslav psychiatrist and psychologist; b. 28 Jan. 1935, Minster; s. of Dr Feodora Sartorius-Fischer and Mirko Sartorius; m. Vera Sartorius 1963; one d.; ed. Univ. of Zagreb, Univ. of London; Consultant, Dept. of Psychiatry, Univ. of Zagreb 1959–64; Research Fellow, Inst. of Psychiatry, Univ. of London 1964–65; WHO Consultant in psychiatric epidemiology 1967–68; Medical Officer in charge of Epidemiological and Social Psychiatry and Standardization of Psychiatric Diagnosis, Classification and Statistics, WHO 1969–73, Chief, Office of Mental Health 1974–76, Dir. Div. of Mental Health 1976–; Visiting Prof. Belgrade, Geneva, London; Prof. Univ. of Zagreb; Hon. Fellow Royal Coll. of Psychiatrists, U.K.; Corresp. mem. Royal Spanish Acad. of Medicine; Hon. mem. of numerous professional and scientific orgs.; Dr. h.c. (Umea); Rema Lapouse medal. *Publications:* more than 160 articles, several books (author or Ed.) on schizophrenia, transcultural psychiatry, mental health policy,. scientific methodology. *Leisure interests:* chess, reading. *Address:* Division of Mental Health, World Health Organization, CH-1211 Geneva 27, Switzerland. *Telephone:* (22) 913617.

SARTZETAKIS, Christos A., LL.D.; Greek lawyer and politician; b. 6 April 1929, Salonika; m.; one d.; ed. Salonika Univ. and Law Faculty, Paris (Sorbonne); called to Bar 1954; apptd. J.P. 1955, Judge of 1st Instance

1956; Investigating Magistrate in Lambrakis affair (which inspired Vasilis Vasilikos' novel Z, later made into film) 1963–64; postgraduate studies Paris 1965–67; mem. Société de Législation Comparée, Paris 1966–; fmr. mem. Admin. Council Hellenic Humanistic Soc. recalled by junta and posted to Volos Court of Misdemeanours 1967–69; arrested and detained for 50 days on unspecified charges 1969; reinstated as an Appeal Judge 1974; Sr. Appeal Judge, Nauplion 1981, Justice of Supreme Court 1982–85; Pres. of Greece 1985–; mem. Société de Législation Comparée, Paris 1966–; fmr. mem. Admin. Council Hellenic Humanistic Soc. *Address:* Office of the President, Athens, Greece.

SARY IENG (see Ieng Sary).

SASS, Sylvia; Hungarian soprano; b. 12 July 1951, Budapest; ed. Franz Liszt Acad. of Music, Budapest; joined Hungarian State Opera; subsequently sang in Vienna, Salzburg and Hamburg; U.K. début with Scottish Opera, Glasgow (Desdemona in Verdi's Otello) 1975, Covent Garden, London (in I Lombardi) 1976, Metropolitan Opera, New York (Tosca) 1977; also gives recitals. *Address:* c/o Dido Senger, 103 Randolph Avenue, London, W9 1DL, England. *Telephone:* 01-289 3736.

SASSER, James Ralph, J.D.; American politician; b. 30 Sept. 1936, Memphis, Tenn.; s. of Joseph Ralph and Mary Nell (née Gray) Sasser; m. Mary Ballantine Gorman 1962; one s. one d.; ed. Vanderbilt Univ.; served U.S. Marine Corps Reserve 1958–65; partner Goodpasture, Carpenter, Woods and Sasser, Nashville 1961–76; Chair. Tennessee Democratic State Cttee. 1973–76; Senator from Tennessee Jan. 1977–. *Address:* 298 Russell Senate Office Bldg., Washington, D.C. 20510, U.S.A.

SASSMANNSHAUSEN, Günther, DIP.GEOLOGY; German businessman; b. 3 June 1930, Weidenau; joined Preussag AG, Hanover 1955, Tech. Dir. 1960, Asst. Dir. 1965, mem. Bd. of Dirs. 1968, fmr. Pres. and Chief Exec. Dir.; Chair. Amalgamated Metal Corpn. Ltd., London; Pres. Nirtschaftsvereinigung Metalle, Düsseldorf; mem. Supervisory Bd., Salzgitter AG 1983–; Hon. Dr.Ing. *Address:* P.O. Box 4827, 3000 Hanover, Federal Republic of Germany.

SASSOON, David; British fashion designer; b. 5 Oct. 1932, London; s. of George Sassoon and Victoria Gurgi; unmarried; ed. Chelsea Coll. of Art and Royal Coll. of Art; designer, Belinda Bellville 1958; first ready-to-wear collection 1963; Dir. Belinda Bellville 1964; Licencee Vogue Butterick U.S.A. 1966 (became Bellville Sassoon 1970); Dir. and sole shareholder Bellville Sassoon 1983–; Licencee, Japan 1988. *Leisure interests:* theatre, ballet. *Address:* Bellville Sassoon, 73 Pavilion Road, London, S.W.1, England.

SASSOON, Vidal; hair stylist; b. 17 Jan. 1928, London; s. of Nathan and Betty (Bellin) Sassoon; two s. two d.; ed. New York Univ.; served with Palmach Israeli Army; cr. a form of hairstyling based on Bahaus and geometric forms; Founder and Chair. Vidal Sassoon Inc.; Pres. Vidal Sassoon Foundation; f. Vidal Sassoon Centre for the Study of Anti-Semitism and Related Bigotries at Hebrew Univ., Jerusalem; awards include French Ministry of Culture award, award for services rendered, Harvard Business School, Intercoiffure Award, Cartier, London 1978; Fellow Hair Artists Int. *Address:* 2049 Century Park East, Los Angeles, Calif. 90067, U.S.A. (Office).

SASSOU-NGUESSO, Col. Denis; Congolese army officer and politician; b. 1943; mem. Council of State 1976–77; First Vice-Pres., Mil. Cttee. of the Parti Congolais du Travail (PCT), charged with the co-ordination of PCT activities 1977–79, concurrently Minister of Nat. Defence; President of the Congo People's Republic March 1979–, also Minister of Defence and Security; Pres. Cen. Cttee. PCT. *Address:* Office du Président, Comité Militaire du Parti Congolais du Travail, Brazzaville, Congo People's Republic.

SATANOWSKI, Robert; Polish conductor; b. 20 June 1918, Łódź; m.; two c.; ed. Faculty of Conducting, Theory and Composition, Higher State School of Music, Łódź 1951; studied with W. Felsenstein, Herbert von Karajan 1958–60; conductor, State Philharmonic in Lublin 1951–54, Artistic Dir. State Philharmonic in Bydgoszcz 1954–58; Generalmusikdirektor, Städtische Bühner, Karl-Marx-Stadt, G.D.R. 1960–62; Dir., Artistic Dir. State Philharmonic 1961–63 and State Opera, Poznań 1963–69; Artistic Dir. Poznań Chamber Orchestra 1962–69; perm. visiting conductor Zurich Opera 1967–70; Generalmusikdirektor Rhine Symphony Players, Krefeld Opera (Fed. Repub. of Germany) 1969–76; Dir., Artistic Dir., Cracow Music Theatre 1975–77, State Opera in Wrocław 1976–81; Dir., Artistic Dir. Great Theatre in Warsaw 1981–; Deputy to Sejm 1985–; mem. Polish Musicians' Asscn., Pres. 1965–70, 1981–88; Maj.-Gen. 1988; numerous Polish and foreign decorations including Commdr.'s Cross with Star and Knight's Cross of Polonia Restituta Order, Order of Grunwald Cross (3rd Class), Order of Banner of Labour, (1st Class), Cross of Valour, Partisan Cross. *Address:* Teatr Wielki, Pl. Teatralny 3, 00-077 Warsaw, Poland. *Telephone:* 26-32-89.

SATARAWALA, Kershasp Tehmurasp, M.A.; Indian administrator and diplomatist; b. 15 Feb. 1916, Satara, Maharashtra; s. of Tehmurasp P. Satarawala and Meherbai H. Chhibber; m. Frainy Bilimoria 1947; three d.; ed. Bilimoria High School, Panchagani, Wadia Coll., Poona and Govt. Coll., Lahore; Fellow, Nuffield Foundation, London; in Indian Army during

Second World War; Indian Admin. Service 1947–75; with Indian Airlines 1967–71, Man. Dir., later Chair.; Adviser to Govs. of Gujarat, Orissa, Jammu and Kashmir 1971–80; Special Sec. Foreign Trade Ministry, later Sec. Steel and Mines Ministry 1972–73; Sec.-Gen. Family Planning Asscn. of India 1976–81; Chair. Gujarat Aromatics Ltd. 1977–83; mem. Indian Wild Life Bd. 1976–81, Nat. Cttee. on Environmental Planning 1980–83, Minorities Comm. 1981–83; Co-ordinator IX Asian Games, New Delhi 1982, Non-aligned Summit Meeting, New Delhi 1983; Lieut.-Gov. of Goa, Daman and Diu and Admin., Dadra and Nagar Haveli 1983–84; Gov. of Punjab 1984–85; Amb. to Mexico, Guatemala and El Salvador 1985–; Padma Bhushan. *Publications:* Plan on Tourism and Civil Aviation for Gujarat 1972, Gir Lion Sanctuary 1972, Perspective Plan of Gujarat 1974–84; articles on industrial devt., environment, etc. *Leisure interests:* classical music, trekking, golf. *Address:* Embassy of India, Avenida Musset 325, Colonia Polanco, 11550 Mexico D.F.; 423 Kirti Apartments, Narangi Bang Road, Pune 411001, India. *Telephone:* 254-23-49; 663-213.

SATHE, Vasant P., B.A., LL.B.; Indian politician; b. 5 March 1925, Nasik, Maharashtra; s. of Purushottam Sathe and Shrimati Indira; m. Jayashri Sathe 1949; one s. two d.; ed. Bhonsale Mil. School, Nagpur Univ.; took part in Quit India Movement and was imprisoned 1942; associated with Socialist Party and PSP until 1964; joined Congress Party 1964; Pres. Madhya Pradesh Textile Workers' Fed. 1956–60, Vidarbha Textile Workers' Fed. 1960–65; mem. Lok Sabha 1972–; Minister of Information and Broadcasting, Govt. of India 1980–82, of Chemicals and Fertilizers 1982–85, of Steel, Mines and Coal 1985–86, of Energy 1986–, of Mines and Steel (Acting) 1987–88, of Communications Feb.–June 1988; Sr. adviser, Indian del. to 25th UN Gen. Ass.; mem. inter-parl. del. to Tokyo 1964; Vice-Pres. Maharashtra Congress (I) Cttee.; mem. All India Congress Cttee.; mem. Maharashtra State Congress (I) Parl. Bd. *Publication:* Towards Social Revolution: A Case for Economic Democracy 1985. *Leisure interests:* music, folk dances, economics. *Address:* Ministry of Energy, 2 Krishna Menon Marg, New Delhi 110 011, India.

SATO, Megumu; Japanese politician; b. 28 Feb. 1924; ed. Kyoto Univ.; joined Ministry of Posts and Telecommunications; mem. House of Reps. 1969–; Parl. Vice-Minister for Home Affairs 1974–75, for Post and Telecommunications 1976, Minister 1984–85; Liberal Democratic Party. *Publication:* Ohshu Zakki Sekai no Tabi kara. *Leisure interests:* Go, sport. *Address:* c/o Ministry of Posts and Telecommunications, 1-3, Kasumigaseli, Chiyoda-ku, Tokyo 100, Japan. *Telephone:* 3-504-4798.

SATO, Moriyoshi; Japanese politician; b. 28 March 1922; ed. Chuo Univ.; Private Sec. to two Govt. Ministers; mem. of House of Reps. 1969–; Parl. Vice-Minister for Transport 1975–76, for Nat. Lamd Agency 1976–77; Deputy Sec.-Gen. Liberal Democratic Party 1977–78, Vice-Chair. Policy Affairs Research Council; Minister of Agric. Forestry and Fisheries 1984–85. *Leisure interest:* reading. *Address:* c/o Ministry of Agriculture, Forestry and Fisheries, 1-2, Kasumigaseki, Chiyoda-ku, Tokyo 100, Japan.

SATO, Takashi; Japanese politician; b. Dec. 1927, Niigata Pref.; m.; two s.; ed. Tokyo Univ. of Agric.; mem. House of Councillors 1967; Parl. Vice-Minister for Agric. and Forestry 1972; Chair. House of Councillors Standing Cttee. on Agric., Forestry and Fisheries 1974, 1978; mem. House of Reps. 1976 (five terms); Minister of Agric., Forestry and Fisheries 1987–88; Liberal-Democratic Party (LDP). *Leisure interests:* judo, noh chant. *Address:* Kudan Shukusha, 2-14-3 Fujimi, Chiyoda-ku, Tokyo, Japan.

SATOWAKI, H.E. Cardinal Joseph Asajiro; Japanese ecclesiastic; b. 1 Feb. 1904, Shittsu, Nagasaki; ordained priest 1932; Bishop of Kagoshima 1955–68; Archbishop of Nagasaki 1968–; cr. Cardinal 1979; mem. Sacred Congregations for the Evangelization of Peoples, the Oriental Churches, the Clergy, Catholic Educ., the Bishops; entitled S. Maria della Pace. *Address:* Catholic Center, 10-34 Uenomachi, Nagasaki-shi, Japan. *Telephone:* (0958) 46-4246.

SATPATHY, Nandini; Indian politician, social worker and short-story writer; b. 9 June 1931, Cuttack; d. of Kalindi Charan and Ratnamani Panigrahi; m. Shri Debendra Satpathy; two s.; ed. Ravenshaw Coll., Cuttack; Leader of the students' movements in Orissa and Sec. Girls Students' Asscn. 1948–49; took part in many welfare activies, organized and became Sec. of the Orissa Women's Relief Cttee.; organized Orissa branch, Asscn. of Social and Moral Hygiene in India 1958; associated with numerous nat. welfare, literary and other orgs.; mem. Rajya Sabha (Upper House) 1962–72; Deputy Minister for Information and Broadcasting 1966–69; Deputy Minister attached to Prime Minister 1969–70, Minister of State for Information and Broadcasting 1971–72; Leader Indian film del. to Moscow 1966, 1968 and Tashkent 1972; del. Gen. Conf. UNESCO, Paris 1972; mem. Indian del. to Commemorative Session UN, New York 1970; Chief Minister of Orissa 1972–73, 1974–76; resgnd from Congress Party Feb. 1977; mem. All India Janata Party Exec. Cttee., Orissa Legis. Ass.; fmr. mem. Working Cttee. of the All India Congress Cttee. and Advisory Council Youth Congress; Chair. Orissa Flood and Cyclone Relief Cttee.; Chair. Children's Film Soc., Bombay; mem. Bd. of Dirs. Int. Centre of Films for Children and Young People, Paris 1968–; Ed. Dharitri (Mother Earth) and Kalana (Assessment), monthly magazines; received many literary prizes. *Publications:* Ketoti Katha, collection of short stories. *Leisure* *interests:* reading and story writing. *Address:* 107 Surya Nagar, Bhubaneswar, Orissa, India. *Telephone:* 53200, 50784.

SAUD AL-FAISAL, H.R.H. Prince, B.A.(ECONS.); Saudi Arabian diplomatist and politician; b. 1941, Riyadh; s. of late King Faisal; ed. Princeton Univ., U.S.A.; fmr. Deputy Minister of Petroleum and Mineral Resources 1971–74; Minister of State for Foreign Affairs March-Oct. 1975, Minister of Foreign Affairs Oct. 1975–; leader del. to UN Gen. Ass. 1976; Special Envoy of H.M. King Khaled in diplomatic efforts to resolve Algerian-Moroccan conflict over Western Sahara, and the civil war in Lebanon; mem. Saudi Arabian del. to Arab restricted Summit, Riyadh, Oct. 1976 and to full Summit Conf. of Arab League, Oct. 1976; Founding mem. King Faisal's Int. Charity Soc. *Leisure interest:* reading. *Address:* Ministry of Foreign Affairs, Riyadh-Nasseriya Street, Riyadh 11124, Saudi Arabia. *Telephone:* (1) 406-7777.

SAUDI ARABIA, King of (see Fahd ibn Abdul Aziz).

SAUERLÄNDER, Willibald, DR.PHIL.; German art historian; b. 29 Feb. 1924, Waldsee; m. Brigitte Rückoldt 1957; one s.; ed. Univ. of Munich; Visiting mem. Inst. for Advanced Study, Princeton 1961–62; Prof. of History of Art, Univ. of Freiburg/Br. 1962–70; Dir. Zentralinst. für Kunstgeschichte, Munich 1970–89; Visiting Prof. Inst. of Fine Arts, New York Univ. 1964–65, Collège de France, Paris 1981, Madison/Wis. Univ. 1982, Harvard 1984–85; Visiting mem. Princeton 1973; mem. Bayerische Akad. der Wissenschaften, Medieval Acad. of America, Soc. Nat. des Antiquaires de France, Royal Soc. of Antiquaries, London; Dr. h.c. *Publications:* Die Kathedrale von Chartres 1954, Jean-Antoine Houdon: Voltaire 1963, Gotische Skulptur in Frankreich 1140-1270 1970, Das Königsportal in Chartres 1984. *Address:* c/o Zentralinstitut für Kunstgeschichte, Meiserstrasse 10, D-8000 Munich 2, Federal Republic of Germany. *Telephone:* 089/5591-546.

SAUGUET, Henri, (pseudonym of Henri Poupard); French composer; b. 18 May 1901, Bordeaux; s. of Auguste Poupard and Isabelle Sauguet; one adopted s.; ed. schools in Bordeaux; studied under J. Canteloube, C. Koechlin and Eric Satie; music critic for various journals 1928–48; Founder and Pres. Union Nat. des Compositeurs 1976–; Hon. Pres. Comité Nat. de la Musique 1969–70, Soc. des Auteurs et Compositeurs Dramatiques; Assoc. mem. Acad. of Bordeaux; mem. Inst. de France (Acad. des Beaux-Arts); Assoc. mem. Inst. of Arts of U.S.A.; mem. many other musical orgs. etc.; Commdr. Légion d'Honneur, Ordre Nat. Du Mérite, Commdr. des Arts et des Lettres, Order of Leopold (Belgium). *Compositions include:* symphonies, concertos, cantatas, quartets, trios, sonatas, theatre music, ballet music and numerous scores for film, radio, TV etc. *Address:* 36 rue la Bruyère, 75009 Paris; "La maison des chants", Fargues, 33230 Coutras, France. *Telephone:* 45.26.68.13.

SAUKKONEN, (Veikko Antti) Juhani; Finnish clergyman and politician; b. 22 June 1937, Viipuri; s. of Eino Vilho Saukkonen and Sirkka Elina Repo; m. Taimi Tuulikki Tervonen 1963; Curate, Parikkala Parish 1966–77, Sr. Clergyman 1977–; M.P. 1972–; Minister of Defence 1982–83; mem. Centre Party. *Address:* c/o Ministry of Defence, Et. Makasiinikatu 8, 00130 Helsinki 13, Finland. *Telephone:* 625 801.

SAUL, Bruno Eduardovich, CAND.ECON.SC.; Soviet politician; b. 1932; ed. Leningrad Electro-Tech. Inst. Higher Party School of Cen. Cttee. CPSU; mem. CPSU 1960–; worked for Estonian S.S.R. Ministry of Transport 1956–66; Deputy Minister of Transport of Estonian S.S.R. 1966–69, Minister 1969–75, Deputy Chair. of Council of Ministers of Estonian S.S.R. 1975–83, Chair. 1984–88; Sec. of Cen. Cttee. of Estonian CP 1983–84; Deputy to U.S.S.R. Supreme Soviet; Cand. mem. CPSU Cen. Cttee.; U.S.S.R. State Prize 1981. *Address:* Council of Ministers, Tallinn, Estonian S.S.R., U.S.S.R.

SAUL, Eduard; Czechoslovak economist and politician; b. 8 March 1929, Kuřim, Brno-venkov; ed. Prague School of Econs. and Univ. of Tech., Brno; Design Engineer, Head of Dept. for Tech. Devt. and Research, Deputy Dir. for Tech., TOS Kuřim enterprise 1955–71; Dir. Žďárské Machine Works and Iron Foundry, Žďár nad Sázavou 1972–80; First Deputy to Minister of Gen. Eng. 1980–81, Minister of Metallurgy and Heavy Eng. 1981–88; Order of Labour 1975, Soviet Order of Friendship of the Nations, Hungarian Order of Labour. *Address:* Ministerstvo hutnictví a těžkého strojírenství, Na Františku 32, Prague 1, Czechoslovakia.

SAUL, Ralph Southey, B.A., LL.B.; American lawyer, stock exchange official and insurance executive; b. 21 May 1922, Brooklyn, N.Y.; s. of Walter Emerson and Helen Douglas; m. Bette Jane Bertschinger 1956; one s. one d.; ed. Univ. of Chicago and Yale Law School; war service, U.S.N.R. 1943–46; attached to American Embassy, Prague 1947–48; admitted to D.C. Bar 1951, to New York Bar 1952; Assoc., firm of Lyeth and Voorhees, New York City 1951–52; Asst. Counsel to Gov. of New York State 1952–54; Staff Attorney, Radio Corpn. of America 1954–58; with Securities and Exchange Comm. 1958–65, Dir. Div. of Trading and Markets 1963–65; Vice-Pres. for Corporate Devt., Investors Diversified Services, Inc. 1965–66; Pres. American Stock Exchange 1966–71; Vice-Chair. First Boston Corpn. 1971–74; Chair., C.E.O. INA Corpn., Phila., 1975–81; Chair. CIGNA Corpn. (formerly Connecticut Gen. and INA Corpn.) 1981–84, Peers and Co. 1985–, mem., Bd. of Dirs. Drexel Burnham 1989–. *Address:* 549 Avonwood Road, Haverford, Pa. 19041, U.S.A.

SAULNIER, Air Chief Marshal Jean-Michel; French air force officer; b. 15 Nov. 1930, Parcé-sur-Sarthe; ed. Ecole de l'air; served in Far East 1952–54; subsequently at various French bases as fighter pilot; Ecole d'application militaire de l'énergie atomique, Cherbourg 1961–65; C.O. Dijon base 1965; Gen. Staff post, then C.O. Luxeuil nuclear air base 1971; Chef de cabinet to Air Force Chief of Staff 1973–76; C.O. Air Force Officers' School, Salon-de-Provence 1976–79; Commdr. Strategic Air Force squadrons 1979–81; Special Chief of Staff, Defence Cabinet 1981–85; Chief of Defence Staff 1985–; Grand Officier, Légion d'honneur. *Address:* Ministère de la Défense, 231 boulevard Saint-Germain, 75007 Paris, France.

SAUNDERS, Ernest Walter, M.A., F.INST.M.; British business executive; b. 21 Oct. 1935, Vienna, Austria; m. Carole A. Stephings 1963; two s. one d.; ed. St. Paul's School, London, and Emmanuel Coll., Cambridge; Man. Dir. Beecham Products Int., Dir. Beecham Products 1966–73; Chair. European Div. Great Universal Stores 1973–77; Pres. Nestlé Nutrition SA and mem. Man. Cttee., Nestlé SA, Vevey, Switzerland 1977–81; Chief Exec. and Deputy Chair. Guinness PLC 1981–86, Chief Exec. and Chair. 1986–87; Chair. Arthur Guinness Son & Co. (G.B.) Ltd., 1982–87, Guinness Brewing Worldwide 1982–87, Guinness-Harp Corpn. 1983–86, Martin Retail Group 1984–86, Distillers Co. Ltd. 1986–87; charged with fraud in connection with illegal share dealings Oct. 1987; Dir. Queens Park Rangers Football & Athletic Club 1983–, Brewers' Soc. 1983–; fmr. Chair. C.E.O. Arthur Bell & Sons PLC. *Leisure interests:* skiing, tennis, football. *Address:* c/o Guinness PLC, 39 Portman Square, London, W1H 9HB, England. *Telephone:* 01-486 0288.

SAUNDERS, Sir John Anthony Holt, Kt., C.B.E., D.S.O., M.C.; British banker (retd.); b. 1917, London; m. Enid Mary Durant Cassidy; two d.; ed. Bromsgrove School; British Army 1940–45; rejoined Hongkong and Shanghai Banking Corpn. 1945, Chair. 1964–72, Chair. London Advisory Cttee. 1972–77; mem. Exec. Council Hong Kong Govt. 1966–72; Chair. of Stewards, Royal Hong Kong Jockey Club 1967–72. *Leisure interest:* travel. *Address:* The Dairy House, Maresfield Park, Uckfield, Sussex, England.

SAUNDERS, Sir Owen, Kt., F.R.S.; British professor of mechanical engineering (retd.); b. 24 Sept. 1904, London; s. of Alfred George Saunders and Margaret Elle Jones; m. 1st Marion McKechney 1935 (died 1980); m. 2nd Daphne Holmes 1981; one s. two d.; ed. Birkbeck Coll., Trinity Coll., Cambridge; Prof. of Mechanical Eng., Imperial Coll. 1946–64, Pro-Rector 1964–66, Acting Rector 1966–67; Vice-Chancellor, Univ. of London 1967–69; Max Jakob Award; Melchett Medallist. *Publications:* The Calculation of Heat Transfer 1932; papers in proceedings of the Royal Soc. *Leisure interests:* music, bridge. *Address:* Oakbank, Sea Lane, Middleton-on-Sea, Sussex, England. *Telephone:* (0243) 692966.

SAUNDERS, Stuart John, M.D., F.R.C.P., F.C.P.S.A.; South African physician; b. 28 Aug. 1931, Cape Town; s. of Lilian Emily and the late Albert Frederick Saunders; m. 1st Noreen Merle Harrison 1956 (died 1983), one s. one d.; m. 2nd Anita Louw 1984; ed. Christian Brothers Coll. and Univ. of Cape Town; Registrar in Pathology and Medicine, Groote Schuur Hosp. and Univ. of Cape Town 1955–58; Research Asst. Royal Postgraduate Medical School, London 1959–60; Lecturer and Sr. Lecturer, Groote Schuur Hosp. and Univ. of Cape Town 1961–70; Fellow in Medicine Harvard Medical School and Mass. Gen. Hosp. 1963–64; Prof. and Head of Medicine Dept. Groote Schuur Hosp. and Univ. of Cape Town 1971–80; Deputy Principal for Planning, Univ. of Cape Town 1978–80, Vice-Chancellor and Prin. Univ. of Cape Town 1981–; Past Pres. S.A. Inst. of Race Relations; Adams Fellowship; Oppenheimer Memorial Trust Advanced Study Grant; Life Fellow (Univ. of Cape Town). *Publications:* numerous scientific publications particularly in the field of liver diseases. *Leisure interests:* reading, fishing. *Address:* University of Cape Town, Rondebosch, Cape Town 7700; and "Glenara", Burg Road, Rondebosch 7700, Private Bag, Cape Province, South Africa. *Telephone:* 650 2105/6 (Office); 686 3895 (Home).

SAUNIER-SEÏTÉ, Alice Louise, D. ÈS L.; French educator and politician; b. 26 April 1925, Saint-Jean-le-Centenier; d. of Daniel-René and Marie-Louise (Lascombe) Saunier; m. 1st Elie-Jacques Picard 1947, two s.; m. 2nd Jérôme Seïté (deceased); ed. Lycée de Tournon, Facultés des Lettres et des Sciences de Paris, Ecole nat. des langues orientales vivantes; Attachée, then Chargée de recherche, Nat. Centre for Scientific Research (C.N.R.S.) 1958–63; lecturer in geography, faculté des lettres, Rennes 1963–65, Prof. 1965–69; mem. Nat. Cttee. for Scientific Research 1963–70; mem. Perm. Section C.N.R.S. 1967–70; Dir. Collège littéraire universitaire, Brest 1966–68, Dean of faculté des lettres, 1968–69; Dir. Inst. universitaire de technologie, Sceaux 1970–73; Prof. Univ. of Paris XI 1969–73, Vice-Pres. 1970–71; Rector, Acad. of Reims 1973–76; Sec. of State for Univs. 1976–77, Minister of Univs. 1978–81, of the Family and Women's Affairs 1981; Prof. of Geographic Organization of Space, Conservatoire des Arts et Metiers 1981–; Municipal Councillor, Manso 1971–83, Deputy Mayor 1977–83; Vice-Pres. Nat. Movt. of Local Reps. 1985–; mem. Council, Inst. Océanographique; mem. Jury, Prix Mémorial Mérimée; Conseiller de Paris; mem. Soc. des Explorateurs français; Assoc. mem. Institut d'Egypte, Acad. of Sciences, Iceland; Officier de la Légion d'honneur; Medaille d'or de la jeunesse et des sports; Medal of C.N.R.S.; Medal of Société de géographie de Paris; decorations from Cameroon, Ivory Coast, Egypt, Gabon, Greece, Indonesia, Iceland, Luxembourg, Portugal and Sweden. *Publications:* Les vallées septentrionales du Massif de l'Oetztal 1963,

Südföhn d'Innsbruck (contrib.) 1965, En première ligne 1982, Remettre l'état à sa place 1984, Une Europe à la carte 1985. *Leisure interest:* fencing. *Address:* CNAM, 292 rue Saint-Martin, 75141 Paris Cedex 03, France. *Telephone:* (1) 42.71.24.14.

SAUR, Klaus Gerhard; German publisher; b. 27 July 1941, Pullach; s. of Karl-Otto Saur and Veronika Saur; m. Lilo Stangel 1977; one s. one d.; ed. High School, Icking and Commercial High School, Munich; Marketing Man. Vulkan-Verlag, Essen 1962; Publishing Man. K.G. Saur, Munich 1963, Publishing Dir. 1966; Pres. K.G. Saur New York and K.G. Saur, London 1977; Chief Exec. Butterworths European Div. and Man. Dir. K.G. Saur Munich 1988–; founder World Guide to Libraries, Publrs. Int. Directory; Hon. Fellow, Tech. Univ. of Graz; Hon. Medal, City of Munich 1988; Dr. Phil. h.c. (Marburg) 1985. *Leisure interests:* special German exile literature 1933–45, int. politics, history of publishing and book trade. *Address:* Josefinenstrasse 22, 8000 Munich 71, Federal Republic of Germany. *Telephone:* 089 7910460.

SAURA, Carlos; Spanish film director; b. 1932, Aragon; m.; two c.; ed. film school in Madrid. *Films include:* La Prima Angelica, La Caza (Silver Bear, Berlin Film Festival), Blood Wedding, Carmen (flamenco version), El Amor Brujo. *Address:* Atocha 43, 28012 Madrid, Spain. *Telephone:* (91) 2275227.

SAUVAGNARGUES, Jean Victor; French diplomatist and politician; b. 2 April 1915, Paris; m. Lise Marie L'Evesque 1948; two s. two d.; ed. Ecole Normale Supérieure; entered Ministry of Foreign Affairs 1941, attached to French Embassy, Bucharest, later on staff of Gen. de Gaulle 1945–46; Head of Political Service for German Affairs 1946–49, Deputy Dir. for Central Europe 1949–54; in office of Antoine Pinay, Minister of Foreign Affairs 1955–56; Dir. Gen. for Moroccan and Tunisian Affairs Jan.-March 1956; Amb. to Ethiopia 1956–60; Dir. for Middle Eastern Affairs and African Affairs; Amb. to Tunisia 1962–70, to Fed. Repub. of Germany 1970–74, to U.K. 1978–81; Minister of Foreign Affairs 1974–76; Commdr., Légion d'honneur, Commdr., Ordre nat. du Mérite; G.C.M.G. *Address:* 14 avenue Pierre 1er de Serbie, 75116 Paris, France.

SAUVAN, Henri Léon; French airline executive; b. 29 April 1923, Paris; s. of Léon and Anna (née Merlino) Sauvan; m. Christiane Dusanter 1945; two s. two d.; ed. Lycée Condorcet, Faculté de Droit, Ecoles des Hautes Etudes Commerciales; joined Air France 1947, Asst. Man. 1947–52, Head of Budget Service 1952–64, Asst. to Vice-Pres. (Man. Control and Budgets) 1964–66, Vice-Pres. (Route Programming and Agreements) 1968–72, Vice-Pres. (Corporate Planning, Route Programming and Agreements) 1972–74, Sec.-Gen. 1974–82, Pres. Air France 1983–88; Chevalier, Légion d'Honneur; Officier, Ordre nat. du Mérite. *Address:* 21 ter boulevard d'Argenson, 92200 Neuilly-sur-Seine, France (Home).

SAUVÉ, H.E. Jeanne (Benoit), P.C., C.C., C.M.M., C.D.; Canadian politician and journalist; b. 26 April 1922, Prud'Homme, Sask.; d. of Charles Albert Benoit and Anna Vaillant; m. Maurice Sauvé 1948; one s.; ed. Univs. of Ottawa and Paris; Nat. Pres., Jeunesse Etudiante Catholique, Montreal 1942–47; Founder Del. to int. confs., Fédération des Mouvements de Jeunesse du Québec 1947; Student, London and French Teacher, London Co. Council 1948–50; Asst. to Dir., Youth Section, UNESCO, Paris 1951; Journalist and Broadcaster, CBC, Contrib. to CTV, NBC and CBS 1952–72; Union des Artistes, Montreal, mem. Bd. 1961–, Vice-Pres. 1968–70; Canadian Inst. on Public Affairs, Vice-Pres. 1962–64, Pres. 1964; mem. Canadian Centennial Comm. 1966; Gen. Sec., Fédération des Auteurs et des Artistes du Canada 1966–72; mem. Bd., Montreal YMCA 1968; Dir., Bushnell Communications Ltd., Ottawa 1969–72; Dir., CKAC Radio Station, Montreal 1969–72; free-lance editorial contribs. to Montreal Star and Toronto Star 1970–72; M.P. for Montreal-Ahuntsic (now Montreal Laval-les-Rapides) 1972–84; Minister of State in charge of Science and Tech. 1972–74, for Environment 1974–75, of Communications (with responsibility for French-speaking countries in Dept. of External Affairs) 1975–79; Speaker of House of Commons 1980–84; Gov.-Gen. of Canada Dec. 1983–, C.-in-C. 1983–; Chancellor and Prin. Companion Order of Canada; Chancellor and Commdr. Order of Mil. Merit; lecture tours in Canada and U.S.A.; named one of seven founding mems. of the Inst. of Political Research by the Rt. Hon. Pierre Trudeau 1972; D.Sc. h.c. (New Brunswick Univ.) 1974; Hon. LL.D. (Calgary Univ.) 1982; Hon. D.H.L. (Mount St. Vincent, Halifax) 1983; Hon. D.Iur. (McGill), Hon. LL.D. (Toronto, Queen's), D.Univ. (Ottawa, Laval, Montreal). *Address:* Government House, 1 Sussex Drive, Ottawa, Ont., K1A 0A1, Canada. *Telephone:* 993-8200.

SAUVY, Alfred; French economist, sociologist and demographer; b. 31 Oct. 1898, Villeneuve de la Raho; s. of Louis Sauvy and Jeanne Tisseyre; m. Marthe Lamberet 1932; one d.; ed. Ecole Polytechnique; Dir. Institut de Conjoncture 1937–45; Sec.-Gen. for Family and Population 1945; Dir. Inst. Nat. d'Etudes Démographiques 1945–62; mem. UN Population Comm. 1947–; Pres. UN Population Comm. 1950–53; Pres. Soc. de Statistique de Paris 1947; Prof. of Econs. and Opinion, Inst. of Political Studies 1942–58; Dir. Institut de Démographie de l'Université de Paris 1957–69; Prof. Social Demography (Life of Populations), Coll. de France 1959–69, Hon. Prof. 1970; Prof. of Economy and Population, Univ. of Paris 1962–75, Univ. of Louvain 1974–76, Ecole Polytechnique 1975; mem. Int. Statistical Inst., Haute Comité de la Population 1977–; Pres. Int. Population Union 1961–63;

Dr. h.c. Geneva, Brussels, Liège, Utrecht, Palermo, Montreal and Barcelona Univs.; Grand Officier, Légion d'honneur, Grand Croix de l'Ordre nat. du Mérite. *Publications:* principal works: Essai sur la conjoncture et la prévision économique 1938, Richesse et population 1944, Le pouvoir et l'opinion 1949, Théorie générale de la population 1952–66, L'opinion publique 1956, La nature sociale 1957, La montée des jeunes 1959, Le plan Sauvy 1960, Fertility and Survival 1961, Mythologie de notre temps 1965, 1971, Histoire économique de la France entre les deux guerres Vol. 1 (1918-1931) 1965, Vol. II De Pierre Laval à Paul Reynaud 1967, Vol. III 1971, Vol. IV 1975, Les quatres roues de la fortune 1968, Socialisme en liberté 1970, General Theory of Population 1970, La révolte des jeunes 1970, De Paul Reynaud à Charles de Gaulle 1972, Croissance zéro? 1973, 1975, Vers l'enseignement pour tous 1974, La fin des riches 1975, L'économie du diable 1976, Eléments de démographie 1977, Coût et valeur de la vie humaine 1977, La tragédie du pouvoir, La vie économique des Français de 1939 à 1945 1978, Humour et politique 1979, La machine et le chômage 1980, La vie en plus 1981, Mondes en marche 1982, le travail noir et l'économie de demain 1984, De la rumeur à l'histoire 1985, Sur l'humour. *Leisure interests:* theatre, humour, ancient books on economy and population, sport. *Address:* 76 rue Lepic, 75018 Paris, France. *Telephone:* 460-6-33-21.

SAVALAS, Telly (Aristotle), B.A.; American actor; b. 21 Jan. 1926, Long Island, N.Y.; s. of the late Nicholas Constantine and of Christina (née Kapsallis) Savalas; m. 1st Katherine Nicolaides, one d.; m. 2nd Marilynn Gardner 1960 (divorced 1974), two d.; m. 3rd Sarah Adams 1974, one s.; m. 4th Julie Hovland 1984; one s.; ed. Columbia Univ.; worked with Voice of America radio broadcasts; joined U.S. State Dept., became Exec. Dir. of Information Services; worked on television network documentaries; began film acting career 1960; began appearances in television series Kojak in U.S.A. 1973, in U.K. 1974. *Films include:* Birdman of Alcatraz 1962, Genghis Khan 1965, The Battle of the Bulge 1965, The Greatest Story Ever Told 1965, Beau Geste 1966, The Dirty Dozen 1967, The Scalphunters 1968, Buona Sera Mrs. Campbell 1968, The Assassination Bureau 1968, On Her Majesty's Secret Service 1969, Crooks and Coronets 1969, Mackenna's Gold 1969, Kelly's Heroes 1970, A Town Called Bastard 1970, Pancho Villa 1971, Horror Express 1972, Inside Out 1975, Diamond Mercenaries 1975, Capricorn One 1977, Beyond the Poseidon Adventure 1979, The Border 1979, My Palikari 1980, Cannonball Run II 1983, The Dirty Dozen III 1987. *Address:* c/o International Creative Managements, 22 Grafton Street, London W.1, England; 333 Universal City Plaza, Universal City, Calif. 91608, U.S.A. *Telephone:* 01-629 8080 (London Agent).

SAVARIMUTHU, Rt. Rev. Tan Sri John Gurubatham, P.S.M., B.D.; Malaysian ecclesiastic; b. 29 Nov. 1925, Kulasekharapatnam, India; s. of the late John Gurubatham and Koilpillai Gurubatham; m. Puan Sri Catherine Edith Yesadian; two s. one d.; ed. Madras Univ., Serampore Univ. and St. Augustine's Coll., Canterbury, England; Asst. Curate St. Mark's Church, Seremban 1952–55; curate St. Mary's Church, Portsea, Portsmouth, England 1963, St. George's Cathedral, Kingston, Ont., Canada 1963; Vicar of Negri Sembilan 1956–62, S. Johore 1964–70, St. James' Church, Kuala Lumpur 1971–72; Bishop's Examining Chaplain 1964–70; Visiting Lecturer St. Peter's Hall, Singapore 1964–70; Archdeacon of South 1970–71, and of whole Diocese 1972, Dir. of Theological Training, Diocese of W. Malaysia 1971–72, Vicar-Gen. 1972–73, Bishop of W. Malaysia (Anglican/Episcopal Church) March 1973–; Nat. Chair. Church Union Negotiating Cttee. 1973–75; Nat. Pres. Council of Churches of Malaysia 1979–83; Chair. Council of the Church of E. Asia Theological Comm. 1979–87, Provincial Sec. CCEA 1979–83, Episcopal Chair. (Presiding Bishop) CCEA Nov. 1987–; Nat. Vice-Pres. Council of Churches of Malaysia and Singapore 1973–75; Panglima Setia Mahota 1980. *Leisure interests:* reading, swimming, walking. *Address:* Diocesan Office, 9 Jalan Tengah, 50450 Kuala Lumpur; Rumah Bishop, 14 Persiaran Stonor, 50450 Kuala Lumpur, West Malaysia. *Telephone:* 03-2427303 (Office); 03-2421850 (Home).

SAVCHENKO, Arkadiy Markovich; Soviet opera singer; b. 1936; ed. Moscow Conservatoire; soloist with Byelorussion Bolshoi Theatre 1960–; baritone; People's Artist of U.S.S.R. 1985. *Roles include:* Yevgeny in Tchaikovsky's Yevgeny Onegin, Kizgaylo in Smolsky's Ancient Legend, Telramud in Wagner's Lohengrin, Malatesta in Donizetti's Don Pasquale, etc. *Address:* Bolshoi Teatr, Minsk, U.S.S.R.

SAVIĆ, Pavel; Yugoslav physical chemist; b. 10 Jan. 1909, Salonika, Greece; s. of Petar and Ana (née Trpković) Savić; m. Branka Božinović 1934; one d.; ed. Univ. of Belgrade; Asst. Prof., Univ. of Belgrade 1932–34; worked with Mme. Joliot-Curie at Inst. for Radium, Paris, 1935–39; discovered together fission of uranium nucleus and thence basis for practical use of nuclear energy; lecturer, Univ. of Belgrade 1940–41; active in People's Liberation War 1941–45; Prof. of Physical Chemistry, Univ. of Belgrade 1945–66; Inst. for Physical Problems, Acad. of Sciences of U.S.S.R. 1945–46; Head, Physical Chem. Inst., Univ. of Belgrade, 1947–66; founder of Boris Kidrič Inst. for Nuclear Sciences, Vinča, Pres. the Scientific Council 1948–58; Vice-Pres. Fed. Comm. for Nuclear Energy 1955–60; Pres. Serbian Acad. of Sciences and Arts 1971–81; mem. Yugoslav Acad. of Sciences, Nat. Acad. of Sciences, New York; Foreign mem. Acad. of Sciences of U.S.S.R.; hon. mem. Hungarian Acad. of Sciences; corresp. mem. Slovenian Acad. of Sciences and Arts; mem. Macedonian Acad. of

Sciences and Arts, Acad. of Sciences and Arts of Bosnia and Herzegovina, Athens Acad. of Sciences; numerous Yugoslav and foreign awards and decorations, including Order of Labour, First Class 1954 and Officier de la Légion d'honneur 1965 and 1976; Rutherford Medal 1979, Lomonosov Medal (Gold) 1982, Kurnakov Medal 1982, D.I. Mendeljejev Medal (Silver) 1984; Order of Hero of Socialist Labour 1979. *Publications:* The Behaviour of Materials under High Pressures, Vols. I-IV (with R. Kašanin) 1962-64, Od atoma do nebeskih tela 1970, Nauka i društvo 1978; also many papers on nuclear physics. *Address:* Bulevar Revolucije 257/III, Entrance 5, Flat 32, Belgrade, Yugoslavia.

SAVIMBI, Dr. Jonas; Angolan nationalist leader; b. 1934; ed. Univ. of Lausanne; fmr. Sec.-Gen. União das Populações de Angola (UPA); Foreign Minister of Governo Revolucionário de Angola no Exilio (GRAE) 1962-64; resgnd. from GRAE at OAU meeting, Cairo July 1964; studied at Univ. of Lausanne 1964-65; moved to Lusaka; founded União Nacional para a Independência Total de Angola (UNITA) near Luso, March 1966; Pres. UNITA March 1966-; Leader UNITA forces in guerrilla war against the Portuguese and in Angolan civil war against MPLA forces after Portuguese withdrawal in Nov. 1975; proclaimed Pres. of People's Democratic Repub. of Angola Nov. 1975 (rival MPLA regime is recognized internationally); engaged in guerrilla activities against MPLA 1976-.

SAVIN, Anatoliy Ivanovich, D.TECH.SC.; Soviet specialist in radio analysis and systems analysis; b. 1920; ed. Bauman Tech. Inst., Moscow; mem. CPSU 1944-; formerly employed as engineer and constructor; constructor with machine-bldg. plant 1944-51; positions of responsibility on eng. side of radio-tech. industry 1951-; corresp. mem. Acad. of Sciences 1979, mem. 1984-; Prof. 1984; main research has been on complex radio-tech. automatized informational systems; inventor of cosmic radio-telescope KRT-10; Lenin Prize 1972, Hero of Socialist Labour 1976, State Prizes 1946, 1949, 1951, 1981. *Address:* Academy of Sciences, Leningrad, U.S.S.R.

SAVINKIN, Nikolai Ivanovich; Soviet politician b. 11 Dec. 1913; ed. Kashira Tech. Inst. for Mechanization of Agric., Lenin Mil. Political Acad., Moscow; political posts in Red Army in Transbaikal Region 1935-50; mem. CPSU 1937-; sr. posts in Cen. Cttee. CPSU, including that of deputy head of Dept. of Admin. Organs of Cen. Cttee. CPSU 1950-60, First Deputy Head 1960-68, Head 1968-; mem. Cen. Auditing Comm. CPSU 1966-71; mem. Council of Nationalities 1970-; cand. mem. Cen. Cttee. CPSU 1971-81, mem. 1981-89; Hero of Socialist Labour 1964, Orders of Lenin 1964, 1973, 1983. *Publications include:* numerous articles on Party work, on national security, and Party Work in the Army. *Address:* The Kremlin, Moscow, U.S.S.R.

SAVOY, Guy; French chef and restaurateur; b. 24 July 1953, Nevers; m. Marie Danielle Amann 1975; one s. one d.; for three years Chef at La Barrière de Clichy, Paris; Proprietor Restaurant Guy Savoy, Paris 1980-, Restaurant Le Bistrot de l'Etoile 1988-. *Publications:* Les Légumes gourmands 1985, La Gourmandise apprivoisée 1987. *Leisure interest:* modern painting. *Address:* Restaurant Guy Savoy, 18 rue Troyon, 75017 Paris; Le Bistrot de l'Etoile, 13 rue Troyon, 75017 Paris, France. *Telephone:* (Guy Savoy) 43.80.40.61, 43.80.35.22; (Bistrot de l'Étoile) 42.67.25.95.

SAW MAUNG, Gen.; Burmese army officer and politician; Chief of Staff Defence Forces; led coup d'état Sept. 1988; Prime Minister, Minister of Defence and Foreign Affairs Sept. 1988-; Chair. State Law and Order Restoration Council Sept. 1988-. *Address:* Office of the Prime Minister, Rangoon, Burma.

SAWALLISCH, Wolfgang; German conductor; b. 26 Aug 1923, Munich; ed. Wittelsbacher Gymnasium, Munich; studied under Profs. Ruoff, Haas and Sachsse; mil. service 1942-46, P.O.W. in Italy; conductor Augsburg 1947-53; Musical Dir. Aachen 1953-58, Wiesbaden 1958-60, Cologne Opera 1960-63; Conductor Hamburg Philharmonic Orchestra 1960-73, Hon. mem. 1973-; Prin. Conductor Vienna Symphony Orchestra 1960-70, Hon. mem. and hon. conductor 1980; Prof. Staatliche Hochschule für Musik, Cologne 1960-63; Musical Dir. Bayerische Staatsoper Munich 1971-; Prin. Conductor Bayerisches Staatsorchester; Perm. Conductor Teatro alla Scala, Milan; conducted at many Festivals; recordings in Germany, U.S.A. and Britain; Hon. Conductor NHK Symphony Orchestra, Tokyo 1967; Artistic Dir. Suisse Romande Orchestra, Geneva 1973-80; Dir. Bayerische Staatsoper, Munich 1982-; Accademico Onorario Santa Cecilia; Österreichisches Ehrenkreuz für Kunst und Wissenschaft, Bayerischer Verdienstorden, Bruckner-Ring of Vienna Symphony Orchestra 1980, Verdienstkreuz (Fed. Repub. of Germany), Bayerische Maximiliansorden für Wissenschaft und Kunst 1984, Orden der aúfgehenden sonne am Halsband, Japan. *Address:* c/o Bayerische Staatsoper, Postfach 745, D-8000 Munich 1, Federal Republic of Germany. *Telephone:* 2185-367.

SAWDY, Peter Bryan; British company executive; b. 17 Sept. 1931, London; s. of Alfred Eustace Leon and Beatrice (Lang) Sawdy; m. Anne Stonor 1955; two d.; ed. Ampleforth Coll., London School of Econs. (external); nat. service, commissioned Queen's Regt., also served Parachute Regt. Egypt and Iraq 1951-53; Exec. Trainee, Brooke Bond Group 1953; Buying Exec., Brooke Bond Ceylon Ltd. 1956, Chair. 1964; Dir. Brooke Bond Group 1965; Dir. Brooke Bond Liebig Ltd. 1968, Man. Dir. 1975-77; Chief Exec. Brooke Bond Liebig Group 1977-; Dir. Costain Group 1979-; Deputy Chair. and Chief Exec. Brooke Bond Group 1981-. *Leisure inter-*

ests: squash, golf, 20th-century literature. *Address:* 18 Elm Park Road, London, S.W.3, England.

SAWICKI, Roman Mieczyslaw, PH.D., F.R.S.; British entomologist; b. 20 Aug. 1930, Wilno, Poland; ed. Univ. of London; Research Asst. Chelsea Coll. of Science, Univ. of London 1954-56; Scientific Officer, Insecticides and Fungicides Dept. Rothamsted Experimental Station 1956, Sr. Prin. Scientific Officer 1976-, leader Resistance Research Group 1976-. *Publications:* numerous papers in scientific journals. *Address:* Department of Insecticides and Fungicides, AFRC Institute of Arable Crops Research, Rothamsted Experimental Station, Harpenden, Herts., AL5 2JQ, England. *Telephone:* 05827 63133.

SAWYER, Charles Henry, PH.D.; American anatomist and educator; b. 24 Jan. 1915, Ludlow, Vt.; s. of John Guy Sawyer and Edith Mabel (Morgan) Sawyer; m. Ruth Eleanor Shaeffer 1941; one d.; ed. Middlebury Coll., Cambridge Univ., England and Yale Univ.; Instructor in Anatomy, Stanford Univ. 1941-44; Assoc., Asst. Prof., Assoc. Prof., Prof. of Anatomy, Duke Univ. 1944-51; Prof. of Anatomy, U.C.L.A. 1951-85, Chair. Dept. 1955-63, Acting Chair. Univ. 1968-69, Emer. Prof. of Anatomy 1985-; Fellow American Acad. of Arts and Sciences; mem. N.A.S.; Hon. mem. Hungarian Soc. of Endocrinology and Metabolism, Japan Endocrine Soc.; Koch Award (Endocrine Soc.) 1973, Hartman Award (Soc. for Study of Reproduction) 1977, Henry Gray Award (American Assen. of Anatomists) 1983. *Publications:* over 300 major scientific publs., principally on neuroendocrinology of reproduction; (Sr. Ed.) Steroid Hormones and Brain Function 1971. *Leisure interests:* music (symphonic, chamber and piano). *Address:* Department of Anatomy, University of California at Los Angeles School of Medicine, Los Angeles, Calif. 90024; 466 Tuallitan Road, Los Angeles, Calif. 90049, U.S.A. (Home). *Telephone:* (213) 825-9569 (University).

SAWYER, John Stanley, M.A., F.R.S.; British meteorologist (retd.); b. 19 June 1916, Wembley, Middx.; s. of late Arthur Stanley Sawyer and Emily Florence Frost; m. Betty Vera Beeching (née Tooke) 1951; one d.; ed. Jesus Coll., Univ. of Cambridge; with Meteorological Office 1937-76, Dir. of Research 1965-76; Pres. Royal Meteorological Soc. 1963-65; Pres. Comm. for Atmospheric Sciences, World Meteorological Org. 1968-73; mem. Council, Natural Environment Research Council 1975-81; Symons Medal, Royal Meteorological Soc. 1971; Int. Meteorological Org. Prize 1973. *Publications:* numerous scientific papers in meteorological journals. *Leisure interest:* gardening. *Address:* Ivy Corner, Corfe, Taunton, Somerset, TA3 7AN, England. *Telephone:* (082342) 612.

SAXBE, William B., LL.D.; American lawyer and politician; b. 25 June 1916, Mechanicsburg, Ohio; s. of Bart Rockwell Saxbe and Faye Henry Carey; m. Ardath (Dolly) Kleinhans 1940; two s. one d.; ed. Mechanicsburg High Schools and Ohio State Univ.; mem. Ohio House of Reps. 1947-54 (Majority Leader 1951-52, Speaker of the House 1953-54); Chair. Ohio Program Comm. 1953; Ohio Attorney-Gen. 1957-58, 1963-68; Chair. Ohio Crime Comm. 1969-70, Ohio Alliance for Energy, Growth and Jobs; Senator from Ohio 1969-74; Attorney-Gen. 1973-74; Amb. to India 1975-76; partner law firm Chester, Saxbe, Hoffman & Wilcox, Columbus, Ohio 1977-81; with Jones, Day, Reavis & Pogue, Cleveland 1981-84, with Pearson, Ball and Dowd, Washington 1984-; Dir. First Ohio Bank Group, Columbus, Mohawk Rubber Co., Hudson, Big Drum Inc., Columbus, Ohio Acceleration Corpn.; mem. Cttee. on Armed Services, Govt. Operations, Post Office, Civil Service and Special Cttee. on Ageing; Republican. *Address:* 16 South Main Street, Mechanicsburg, Ohio 43044 (Office); Route 2, Mechanicsburg, Ohio 43044, U.S.A. (Home).

SAXENA, Surrendra Kumar, PH.D.; Indian international co-operative official; b. 3 April 1926; m. Ingalill Gunnel Amanda Friberg; one s. two d.; ed. Univ. of Agra, Inst. of Social Studies, The Hague, Municipal Univ., Amsterdam; Asst. Prof, Dept. of Econs., Birla Coll. 1949-52; Research Fellow, Inst. of Social Studies, The Hague 1955-56; with ICA Regional Office and Educ. Centre for S.E. Asia 1959-61, Regional Officer 1961-68; Dir. Int. Co-operative Alliance (ICA) 1968-81; Sr. Consultant to Swedish Co-operative Centre, Stockholm 1981-; Consultant Faculty of Environmental Sciences, York Univ., Toronto; Vice-Pres. Union of Int. Assocns., Brussels; Dr. h.c. Univ. of Sherbrooke, Canada; Severin Jorgensen Prize (Copenhagen) 1978, Indian Co-operative Movement Medal 1979, Highest Medal of Yugoslavia Co-operative Union 1980. *Publications:* Nationalisation and Industrial Conflict: Example of British Coal Mining 1955, Agricultural Co-operation in S.E. Asia 1961, Role of Foreign Aid in Development of Co-operative Processing 1965, Activities and Role of the International Co-operative Alliance in S.E. Asia 1966, The International Co-operative Alliance and Co-operative Trade 1967. *Leisure interests:* golf, Indian music. *Address:* 56 Raymerville Drive, Markham, Ont. L3P 4J5, Canada. *Telephone:* 416-294-9747 (Home).

SAY, Rt. Rev. Richard David, K.C.V.O., D.D.; British ecclesiastic; b. 4 Oct. 1914, London; s. of Commdr. Richard Say, O.B.E., R.N.V.R., and Kathleen Mary Wildy; m. Irene Frances Rayner, O.B.E., J.P., 1943; two s. (one deceased) two d.; ed. Univ. Coll. School, Christ's Coll., Cambridge and Ridley Hall, Cambridge; Curate of St. Martin-in-the-Fields 1943-50, Gen. Sec., Church of England Youth Council 1944-47; Gen. Sec., British Council of Churches 1947-55; Rector of Hatfield and Domestic Chaplain to

Marquess of Salisbury, K.G. 1955–61; Hon. Canon of St. Albans 1957–61; Bishop of Rochester 1961–88; Asst. Bishop of Canterbury 1988–; Church of England del. to World Council of Churches 1948, 1954, and 1961; Sub-Prelate of the Order of St. John of Jerusalem; Chaplain to the Pilgrims of G.B. 1968–; mem. House of Lords 1969–88; High Almoner to H.M. the Queen 1970–88; Deputy Pro-Chancellor, Univ. of Kent 1977–83, Pro-Chancellor 1983–; Court of Ecclesiastical Causes Reserved 1984–; Chair. Age Concern England 1986–; Vice-Pres. UNA, G.B. and Northern Ireland 1986–; Hon. D.C.L. (Kent) 1987; Hon. mem. Inst. of Royal Engineers 1986; Hon. Freeman Borough of Tonbridge and Malling 1987, Borough of Rochester Upon Medway 1988–. *Leisure interests:* history, travel. *Address:* 23 Chequers Park, Wye, Ashford, Kent, TN25 5BR, England. *Telephone:* (0233) 812230.

SAYED, Dr. As-Sayed Ali As-, PH.D.; Egyptian politician; b. Oct. 1927, Alexandria; ed. Univ. of Alexandria; mem. People's Ass. 1971–, Deputy Speaker 1972–79; mem. Shoura Council; Minister of State for People's Ass. and Shoura Council Affairs 1985–87. *Address:* Majlis al-Sha'ab, Cairo, Egypt.

SAYED, Gamal As, PH.D.; Egyptian electronics engineer and politician; b. 1918; ed. Military Acad., Faculty of Eng. in U.K. and Czechoslovakia, and Staff Coll. of Supreme Mil. Acad.; played prominent role in Oct. 1973 War; fmr. mem. Bd. Arab Industrialization Org.; Asst. to Minister of Defence for Tech. Affairs 1979; Minister of State for Mil. Production 1982–. *Address:* Ministry of Military Production, 5 Sharia Ismail Abaza, Kasr El-Eini, Cairo, Egypt. *Telephone:* 27487.

SAYED, Mostafa Amr El-, PH.D.; American professor of chemistry; b. 8 May 1933, Zifta, Egypt; s. of Amr El-Sayed and Zakia Ahmed; m. Janice Jones 1957; three s. two d.; ed. Ein Shams Univ., Cairo, Egypt, Florida State, Yale and Harvard Univs., Calif. Inst. of Tech.; Asst. Prof., Univ. of Calif., Los Angeles 1961–64, Assoc. Prof. 1964–67, Prof. 1967–; Consultant to Space Tech. Lab. on Laser Tech. 1962–63, Electro-Optical Systems on Laser Tech. 1963–66, N. American Aviation on the Minuteman Program 1964–65, Navy Electronics Labs. on Dye and Liquid Lasers 1969–73, Ford Research Labs. 1970, Northrop Corpn. on Molecular Energy Transfer 1979–81; Vice-Pres. Egyptian American Scholars 1977–; Pres. Arab Physical Soc. 1979–; Ed. Journal of Physical Chem., American Chemical Soc. 1980–; Jt. Ed. Int. Reviews in Physical Chem. 1984–; mem. Physical Chem. Div., IUPAC 1985–; mem. N.A.S., American Acad. of Arts and Sciences; Trustee Bd. of Trustees of Associated Univs. Inc. 1988–; Alfred P. Sloan Fellow 1965–71; John Simon Guggenheim Memorial Foundation Fellow 1967-68; Fresenius Nat. Award in Pure and Applied Chem. 1967, Alexander von Humboldt Sr. U.S. Scientist Award, West German Govt. 1982. *Publications:* many articles in scientific journals. *Address:* Department of Chemistry and Biochemistry, University of California, Los Angeles, Calif. 90024 (Office); 3325 Colbert Avenue, Los Angeles, Calif. 90066, U.S.A. (Home). *Telephone:* (213) 825-1352 (Office); (213) 391-2272 (Home).

SAYER, Guy Mowbray, C.B.E., J.P.; British banker (retd.); b. 18 June 1924, London; s. of the late Geoffrey Robley Sayer and Winifred Lily Sayer; m. Marie Anne Sophie Mertens 1951; one s. two d.; ed. Hong Kong, Shrewsbury School, England; with The Hongkong and Shanghai Banking Corpn. 1946–77, Staff Controller, Head Office 1968, Gen. Man. 1969, Dir. 1970, Deputy Chair. 1971, Chair. 1972–77, mem. London Advisory Cttee.; Dir. World Maritime Ltd., Bermuda, World Shipping and Investment Ltd., Bermuda, World Finance Int. Ltd., Hong Kong 1977–; Gov. Sutton's Hosp. in Charterhouse; Hon. LL.D. (Univ. of Hong Kong) 1978; Fellow, Inst. of Bankers, London; Liveryman, Worshipful Co. of Innholders, Freeman of the City of London. *Leisure interests:* golf, walking. *Address:* 5 Pembroke Gardens, London, W.8, England.

SAYLES, George Osborne, D.LITT., LL.D., F.B.A.; British academic; b. 20 April 1901, Chesterfield; s. of Rev. L. P. Sayles and Margaret Brown; m. Agnes Sutherland 1936; one s. one d.; ed. Glasgow Univ. and Univ. Coll. London; Prof. of Modern History, Queen's Univ. of Belfast 1945–53; Burnett-Fletcher Prof. of History, Aberdeen Univ. 1953–62; Sr. Research Fellow, Inst. of Advanced Legal Studies, Univ. of London 1962–67; first Kenan Prof. of History, New York Univ., U.S.A. 1967; Hon. D.Litt. (Trinity Coll. Dublin), Hon. LL.D. (Glasgow); Ames Medal, Harvard Law Faculty. *Publications:* Select Cases in Court of King's Bench 1272–1422 (7 vols.) 1936–72, Medieval Foundations of England 1948, The King's Parliament of England 1974, Fleta (3 vols.) 1955–1984, The English Parliament in the Middle Ages, The Functions of the Medieval Parliament of England 1988, and many other works. *Leisure interest:* travel. *Address:* Warren Hill, Crowborough, Sussex, TN6 1RA, England. *Telephone:* (089 26) 661439.

SCALES, John Tracey, O.B.E., L.R.C.P., F.R.C.S., C.I.MECH.E.; British professor and medical practitioner; b. 2 July 1920, Colchester; s. of W.L. Scales; m. Cecilia May Sparrow 1945; two d.; ed. Haberdasher's Askes School, London, King's Coll., London, Univs. of Glasgow and Birmingham, Charing Cross Hosp. Medical School; Capt. R.A.M.C. 1945–47; House Surgeon Royal Nat. Orthopaedic Hosp., Stanmore 1947, M.O. Plastics Unit 1949, Hon. Sr. Registrar 1952, Consultant in Orthopaedic Prosthetics 1978; lecturer Inst. of Orthopaedics, Univ. of London 1951, Sr. Lecturer 1952, Reader Biomedical Eng. 1968, Prof. 1974, Emer. Prof. 1985–; Hon. Consultant Royal Nat. Orthopaedic Hosp., Stanmore, Royal Orthopaedic Hosp.,

Birmingham, Mount Vernon Hosp., Middx.; Hon. Dir. Dept. of Research in Plastic Surgery, Mount Vernon Hosp.; Thomas Henry Green Prize in Surgery, Robert Danis Prize, S.G. Brown Award (Royal Soc.), James Berrie Prize, Jackson Burrows Medal, Donald Julius Green Prize (Inst. of Mech. Eng.). *Publications:* numerous articles and scientific papers. *Leisure interests:* dogs, Goss china. *Address:* Royal National Orthopaedic Hospital, Brockley Hill, Stanmore, Middx., HA7 4LP (Office); 17 Brockley Avenue, Stanmore, Middx. HA7 2AX, England (Home). *Telephone:* 01-954 2300 (Office); 01-958 8773 (Home).

SCALFARI, Eugenio, D.IUR.; Italian editor; b. 6 April 1924, Civitavecchia; m. Simonetta de Benedetti 1959; two d.; contrib. Il Mondo, L'Europeo 1950–; Promoter Partito Radicale 1955–, L'Espresso 1955–, Ed.-in-Chief 1963–68, Man. Dir. 1970–75; Promoter La Repubblica 1976–, Ed.-in-Chief and Dir. 1988–; Deputy Parl. 1968–72; Siena Award 1985, Journalist of the Year Award 1986. *Publications:* Rapporto sul Neocapitalismo Italiano, Il Potere Economico in URSS, L'Autunno della Repubblica, Razza Padrona, Interviste ai Potenti, L'Anno di Craxi, La Sera Andavamo in Via Veneto. *Address:* Piazza dell'Indipendenza 11/B, 00185 Roma, Italy. *Telephone:* (06) 49821.

SCALFARO, Oscar Luigi; Italian politician and lawyer; b. 9 Sept. 1918, Novara; ed. Università Cattolica del Sacro Cuore, Milan; elected Christian Democrat (D.C.) M.P. for Turin-Novara-Vercelli 1948; Sec. then Vice-Chair. Parl. Group and mem. Nat. Council of D.C., mem. of D.C. Cen. Office during De Gasperi's leadership, Under-Sec. of State at Ministry of Labour and Social Security in Fanfani Govt., Under-Sec. in Ministry of Justice, Under-Sec. in Ministry of Interior 1959–62; Minister of Transport and Civil Aviation in Moro, Leone and Andreotti Govts. Minister of Educ. in second Andreotti Govt.; Vice-Chair. House of Deputies; Minister of the Interior 1983–87. *Address:* c/o Ministry of the Interior, Palazzo Viminale, Via Depretis, 00100 Rome, Italy.

SCALI, John Alfred, B.S.; American journalist; b. 27 April 1918, Canton, Ohio; s. of Paul M. and Lucy (Leone) Scali; m. 1st Helen Lauinger Glock 1945 (divorced 1973); three d.; m. 2nd Denise Y. St. Germain 1973; ed. Boston Univ.; Reporter Boston Herald 1942 and Boston Bureau, United Press (UP) 1942–43; Associated Press, War Corresp. European Theatre of Operations 1944 and later Diplomatic Corresp., Wash. Bureau 1945–61; Diplomatic Corresp. ABC Television and Radio, Wash. 1961–71; Sr. Corresp. ABC News, Washington 1975–; Special Consultant for Foreign Affairs to the Pres. 1971–73; Amb., Perm. Rep. to UN 1973–75; mem. A.F.T.R.A.; hon. degrees (Malone, York Colls.) 1974; Journalism Award, Univ. of S. Calif. 1964; special award, Wash. Chapter Nat. Acad. of Arts and Sciences 1964; John Scali Award created by Washington Chapter of A.F.T.R.A. 1964; Man of the Year award in Journalism, Boston Univ. 1965; special award Overseas Press Clubs 1965; Rizzuto Gold Medal Award 1974. *Address:* 1717 De Sales Street, N.W., Washington, D.C. 20036, U.S.A.

SCALIA, Antonin, A.B., LL.B.; American judge; b. 11 March 1936, Trenton, N.J.; s. of S. Eugene and Catherine L. (Panaro) Scalia; m. Maureen McCarthy 1960; five s. four d.; ed. Univ. of Fribourg, Switzerland and Harvard Univ.; called to Bar, Ohio 1962, Virginia 1970; Assoc. Jones, Day, Cockley & Reavis, Cleveland 1961–67; Assoc. Prof. Univ. of Va. Law School 1967–70, Prof. 1970–74; Gen. Counsel Office of Telecommunications Policy, Exec. Office of President 1971–72; Chair. Admin. Conf. U.S., Washington 1972–74; Asst. Attorney Gen., U.S. Office of Legal Counsel, Justice Dept. 1974–77; Prof. Law School, Univ. of Chicago 1977–82; Visiting Prof. Georgetown Law Center 1977, Stanford Law School 1980–81; Judge, U.S. Court of Appeals (D.C. Circuit) 1982–86; Judge, U.S. Supreme Court 1986–; Hon Master of the Bench, Inner Temple, London 1986; mem. numerous advisory councils etc. *Address:* U.S. Supreme Court, Washington, D.C. 20001; 6713 Wemberly Way, McLean, Va. 22101, U.S.A.

SCAMMON, Richard M.; American psephologist; b. 17 July 1915, Minneapolis, Minn.; s. of Dr. Richard E. and Mrs. Julia (Simms) Scammon; m. Mary Stark Allen 1952; one d.; ed. Univ. of Minnesota, London School of Econs., Univ. of London and Univ. of Michigan; Research Sec., Radio Office, Univ. of Chicago 1939–41; Army Service 1941–46; Chief, Political Activities Branch, Civil Admin. Div., Office of Military Govt. U.S. (Germany) 1946–48; Chief, Div. of Research for Western Europe, Dept. of State 1948–55; Dir. Elections Research Center, Washington 1955–61, 1965–; Dir. of the Census 1961–65; Chair. U.S. Del. to Observe Elections in U.S.S.R. 1958, Chair. Pres.'s Comm. on Registration and Voting Participation 1963, OAS Electoral Mission to the Dominican Repub. 1966; Pres. Nat. Council on Public Polls 1969–70; Chair. Select Comm. on Western Hemisphere Immigration 1966–68; mem. U.S. Del. to UN Gen. Ass. 1973; Consultant, State Dept. (West Bank autonomy) 1979–80, (El Salvador) 1981–82; mem. Nat. Bipartisan Comm. on Cen. America 1983–84; mem. Editorial Bd. Public Opinion, World Affairs, Electoral Studies; Chief elections consultant, NBC News; mem. Bd. of Dirs. Int. Foundation for Electoral Systems 1987–. *Publications:* Editor, America Votes Vol. 1 1956, Vol. 2 1958, Vol. 3 1960, Vol. 4 1962, Vol. 5 1964, Vol. 6 1966, Vol. 7 1968, Vol. 8 1970, Vol. 9 1972, Vol. 10 1973, Vol. 11 1975, Vol. 12 1977, Vol. 13 1979, Vol. 14 1981, Vol. 15 1983, Vol. 16 1985, Vol. 17 1987, Vol. 18 1989; Ed. America at the Polls 1965, (1988), Co-Author This U.S.A. 1965, The Real Majority 1970. *Address:* 5508 Greystone Street, Chevy Chase, Maryland 20815, U.S.A. *Telephone:* (202) 659-9490.

SCANLON, Baron (Life Peer), cr. 1979, of Davyhulme in the County of Greater Manchester; **Hugh Parr Scanlon;** British trade unionist; b. 26 Oct. 1913, Australia; m. Nora Markey 1943; two d.; ed. Stretford Elementary School, Nat. Council of Labour Colls.; apprentice; instrument maker; Shop Steward, Convener Associated Electrical Industries, Trafford Park; Div. Organizer Amalgamated Eng. Union, Manchester 1947-63, mem. Exec. Council AEU London 1963-67; Pres. Amalgamated Union of Engineering Workers (AUEW) 1967-78; fmr. Vice-Pres., mem. Exec. Cttee. Int. Metalworkers' Fed.; fmr. mem. Nat. Econ. Devt. Council (NEDC); fmr. mem. Metrication Bd.; fmr. Pres. European Metalworkers' Fed.; Chair., Chief Exec. Eng. Industry Training Bd. 1975-82; mem. Advisory Council for Applied Research and Devt. 1982-; mem. British Gas Corpn. 1976-82, Govt. Cttee. of Inquiry into Teaching of Maths in Primary and Secondary Schools in England and Wales 1978-; Hon. D.C.L. *Leisure interests:* golf, swimming, gardening. *Address:* 23 Seven Stones Drive, Broadstairs, Kent, England.

SCANNELL, Vernon, F.R.S.L.; British freelance author, poet and broadcaster; b. 23 Jan. 1922; ed. Leeds Univ.; served with Gordon Highlanders 1940-45; various jobs including teacher, Hazelwood Prep. School 1955-62; Southern Arts Assen. Writing Fellowship 1975-76; Visiting Poet, Shrewsbury School 1978-79; Resident Poet, King's School, Canterbury 1979. *Publications:* several novels including The Fight 1953, A Lonely Game (for younger readers) 1979 and Ring of Truth 1983; volumes of poetry including The Masks of Love 1960 (Heinemann Award), A Sense of Danger (Ed., with Ted Hughes and Patricia Beer) 1962; New Poems, a PEN anthology 1962; Walking Wounded: poems 1962-65, 1968, Epithets of War: poems 1965-69, 1969; Mastering the Craft (Poets Today Series) 1970, Pergamon Poets, No. 8 (with J. Silkin) 1970, Selected Poems 1971, The Winter Man: new poems 1973, The Apple Raid and other poems 1974 (Cholmondeley Poetry Prize), The Loving Game 1975, New and Collected Poems 1950-80, 1980, Winterlude and other poems 1982, Funeral Games (poems) 1987; *(criticism)* Not Without Glory: poets of World War II 1976, How to Enjoy Poetry 1982, How to Enjoy Novels 1984; *(autobiography)* The Tiger and the Rose 1971, A Proper Gentleman 1977, Argument of Kings (autobiog.) 1987; Sporting Literature: an Anthology 1987, The Clever Potato, Poems for Children 1988, Soldiering On, Poems of Military Life 1989. *Leisure interests:* listening to radio (mainly music), drink, boxing (as a spectator), films, reading. *Address:* 51 North Street, Otley, W. Yorks., LS21 1AH, England. *Telephone:* (0943) 467176.

SCARAMUZZI, Franco; Italian agricultural scientist; b. 26 Dec. 1926, Ferrara; s. of Donato Scaramuzzi and Alberta Rovida; m. Maria Bianca Cancellieri 1955; one s. one d.; Prof. of Pomology, Univ. of Pisa 1959, Univ. of Florence 1969-; Rector Magnificus, Univ. of Florence 1979-; Pres. Int. Soc. of Horticultural Science, Italian Acad. of Vine and Wine, Accademia Economica Agraria dei Georgofili; mem. Soviet Acad. of Agricultural Sciences. *Address:* Piazza San Marco 4, 50121 Florence (Office); Viale Amendola 38, 50121 Florence, Italy (Home). *Telephone:* 055/ 29-64-14 (Office); 055/ 24-19-34 (Home).

SCARASCIA-MUGNOZZA, Carlo, DR.JUR.; Italian lawyer; b. 19 Jan. 1920, Rome; m. Edda Alfano 1951; three d.; mem. Chamber of Deputies 1953; Vice-Pres. Christian Democrat Parl. Group 1958-62; Leader, Italian del. to UNESCO 1962; Sec. of State for Educ. 1962-63, for Justice June-Dec. 1963; mem. European Parl. 1961, Chair. Political Cttee. 1971-72; Vice-Pres. of Comm. of the European Communities, Commr. for Agriculture 1972-73; Commr. for Press and Information, Transport Policy, Environment and Consumer Protection, Relations with the European Parl. 1973-77; Pres. Int. Centre for Advanced Mediterranean Agronomic Studies, Paris; Councillor of State; Pres. National Dance Acad. *Address:* Via Proba Petronia 43, 00136 Rome, Italy. *Telephone:* (06) 345 3114.

SCARF, Herbert Eli, PH.D.; American economist; b. 25 July 1930, Philadelphia, Pa.; s. of Louis H. Scarf and Lena Elkman; m. Margaret Klein 1953; three d.; ed. Temple Univ. and Princeton Univ.; employee of Rand Corpn., Santa Monica, Calif. 1954-57; Asst. and Assoc. Prof., Dept. of Statistics, Stanford Univ., Calif. 1957-63; Fellow, Center for Advanced Study in the Behavioral Sciences, Stanford, Calif. 1962-63; Prof. of Econs., Yale Univ. 1963-70, Stanley Resor Prof. of Econs. 1970-78, Sterling Prof. of Econs. 1979-; Dir. Cowles Foundation for Research in Econs. 1967-71, 1981-84, Dir. Div. of Social Sciences 1971-72, 1973-74; Visiting Prof., Stanford Univ., Calif. 1977-78, Mathematical Sciences Research Inst. Spring 1986; Ford Foundation Sr. Faculty Fellowship 1969-70; Fellow Econometric Soc., Pres. 1983; Fellow American Acad. of Arts and Sciences; mem. N.A.S.; Hon. L.H.D. (Chicago) 1978; Lanchester Prize, (Operations Research Soc. of America) 1974, Von Neumann Medal 1983. *Publications:* Studies in the Mathematical Theory of Inventory and Production (with K. Arrow and S. Karlin) 1958, The Optimality of (S, s) Policies in the Dynamic Inventory Problem 1960, The Computation of Economic Equilibria (with Terje Hansen) 1973, Applied General Equilibrium Analysis (with John Shoven, eds.) 1984; articles in learned journals. *Leisure interests:* music, reading, hiking. *Address:* Cowles Foundation for Research in Economics, Yale University, Box 2125 Yale Station, New Haven, Conn. 06520 (Office); 88 Blake Road, Hamden, Conn. 806517, U.S.A. (Home). *Telephone:* (203) 432-3693 (Office); (203) 776-9197 (Home).

SCARFE, Gerald A.; British cartoonist; b. 1 June 1936, London; m. Jane Asher; has contributed cartoons to Punch 1960-, Private Eye 1961-, Daily Mail 1966-, The Sunday Times 1967-, Time 1967-; exhibited at Grosvenor Gallery (group exhbns.) 1969, 1970, Pavilion d'Humour, Montreal 1969, Expo 1970, Osaka 1970; one-man exhbns. Waddell Gallery, New York 1968, 1970, Vincent Price Gallery, Chicago 1969, Grosvenor Gallery 1969, Nat. Portrait Gallery 1971, Royal Festival Hall 1983, Langton Gallery 1986; animation and film directing BBC 1969-; Zagreb Prize for BBC film Long Drawn Out Trip 1973; *Theatre design:* Ubu Roi (Traverse Theatre) 1957, What the Butler Saw (Oxford Playhouse) 1980, No End of Blame (Royal Court, London) 1981, Orpheus in the Underworld (English Nat. Opera, Coliseum) 1985, Who's a Lucky Boy (Royal Exchange, Manchester) 1985. *Publications:* Gerald Scarfe's People 1966, Indecent Exposure 1973, Expletive Deleted: The Life and Times of Richard Nixon 1974, Gerald Scarfe 1982, Father Kissmass and Mother Claus 1985, Scarfe by Scarfe (autobiog.) 1986, Gerald Scarfe's Seven Deadly Sins 1987, Line of Attack 1988. *Leisure interests:* drawing, painting, sculpting. *Address:* 10 Cheyne Walk, London, S.W.3, England.

SCARGILL, Arthur; British trades union official; b. 11 Jan. 1938, Worsborough, Yorks.; s. of the late Harold Scargill and of Alice Scargill; m. Anne Harper 1961; one d.; ed. White Cross Secondary School; worked first in a factory, then Woolley Colliery 1955; mem. Barnsley Young Communist League 1955-62; mem. Nat. Union of Mineworkers (N.U.M.) 1955-, N.U.M. Branch Cttee. 1960, Branch del. to N.U.M. Yorks. Area Council 1964, mem. N.U.M. Nat. Exec. 1972-, Pres. Yorks. N.U.M. 1973-82, Pres. N.U.M. April 1982-; Chair. N.U.M. Int. Cttee.; Pres. Int. Miners Org. Sept. 1985-; mem. Labour Party 1966-; mem. T.U.C. Gen. Council 1986-88. *Address:* National Union of Mineworkers, St. James' House, Vicar Lane, Sheffield, S1 2EX, England. *Telephone:* (0742) 700388.

SCARMAN, Baron (Life Peer), cr. 1977, of Quatt in the County of Salop (Shropshire); **Leslie George Scarman,** Kt., P.C., O.B.E., Q.C.; British judge; b. 29 July 1911, London; s. of George Charles and Ida Irene Scarman; m. Ruth Clement Wright 1947; one s.; ed. Radley Coll. and Oxford Univ.; Harmsworth Law Scholar, Middle Temple 1936; R.A.F. (Volunteer Reserve) 1940-45; Q.C. 1957; Judge, High Court of Justice, England 1961; Chair. Law Comm. for England and Wales 1965-72; Lord Justice of Appeal 1973-77, Lord of Appeal in Ordinary 1977-86 (retd.); Chancellor of Univ. of Warwick 1981-89; Pres. Royal Inst. of Public Admin. 1981-, Constitutional Reform Centre 1984-; Hon. LL.D. (London, Warwick, Kent, Exeter, City of London, Cambridge, Wales); Hon. D.C.L. (Oxford, Freiburg); Hon. D. Univ. (Brunel) 1987. *Publications:* Pattern of Law Reform 1967, English Law—the New Dimension 1974, Scarman Report on the Brixton Riots 1981. *Leisure interests:* music, walking, gardening, history. *Address:* House of Lords, London, S.W.1, England. *Telephone:* 219-3000.

SCARPALEZOS, Spyros-Constantin, PH.D., M.D.; Greek neurologist and psychiatrist; b. 3 Oct. 1912, Athens; m. Corinna Montesantou 1941; one s.; ed. Athens Univ. Medical School; Lecturer, Dept. of Neurology and Psychiatry, Athens Univ. Medical School 1939-46, Sr. Lecturer 1949-51, Assoc. Prof. 1951-55, Dir.-in-Charge 1955-57, Prof. and Chair. of Dept. 1964-80; Dir., Dept. of Neurology, Evangelismos Hosp., Athens 1957-64; in pvt. practice 1981-; Pres. Hellenic Soc. of Electroencephalography and Clinical Neurophysiology 1976-, of Neurology and Psychiatry 1967-69, 1982-, Franco-Hellenic Medical Assen. 1980-; Officier de l'ordre de la santé publique de France, Officier Légion d'honneur; Silver Medal, Paris Univ. *Publications:* Friedreich's Disease 1939, L'Hérédité Similaire dans la Maladie de Parkinson 1984, La Prédisposition Constitutionnelle dans les Maladies du Système Nerveux 1949, Electroencephalography of Brain Tumours 1951, Polymyositis 1961, Textbook of Neurology (in Greek) 1969, Investigation Neurophysiologique dans la Sclérose en Plaques 1986. *Leisure interests:* collecting ancient Greek objects and modern art. *Address:* 2a Lykiou Street, 106 74 Athens, Greece. *Telephone:* 7214.922.

SCELBA, Mario, D.JUR.; Italian politician; b. 5 Sept. 1901, Caltagirone; m. Nerina Palestini 1929; one d.; ed. Rome Univ.; Founder mem. Italian People's Party 1919; practised as lawyer after suppression of People's Party 1926-; re-entered politics 1941 and became one of founders of Christian Democrat Party and newspaper Il Popolo; Minister for Posts and Telecommunications 1945-47; Minister of the Interior 1947-53, 1960-62; Prime Minister and Minister of the Interior 1954-55; mem. Chamber of Deputies; Deputy to the European Parl. Ass. 1958-79, Pres. 1969-71; Pres. Nat. Council of the Christian Democrat Party 1966; mem. Senate; Pres. Senate's Comm. on Foreign Affairs; hon. degrees Univ. of Ottawa, Columbia Univ. (Washington), Fordham Univ. and St. John's Univ. (New York). *Address:* Via Barberini 47, Rome, Italy (Home). *Telephone:* 48-54-56 (Home).

SCHABRAM, Hans, DR.PHIL.; German professor of medieval English; b. 27 Sept. 1928, Berlin; s. of Paul Schabram and Lucia Schabram; m. Candida Larisch 1956; two s. one d.; ed. Univs. of Berlin and Cologne; Asst. English Dept. Univ. of Heidelberg 1957-63; Prof. of Medieval English Language and Literature Univ. of Giessen 1964-69, Univ. of Göttingen 1968-; mem. Akad. der Wissenschaften, Göttingen. *Publications:* 55 publs. on English Philology since 1956. *Address:* Seminar für Englische Philologie der Universität, Humboldtallee 13, 3400 Göttingen (Office); Michaelisweg 10, 3400

Göttingen, Federal Republic of Germany. *Telephone:* 0551-397571 (Office); 0551-55444 (Home).

SCHACHMAN, Howard Kapnek, PH.D.; American educator and biochemist; b. 5 Dec. 1918, Philadelphia, Pa.; s. of Morris H. and Rose Kapnek Schachman; m. Ethel H. Lazarus 1945; two s.; ed. Mass. Inst. of Technology and Princeton Univ.; Fellow, Nat. Inst. of Health 1946-48; Instructor (Biochem.), Univ. of Calif., Berkeley 1948-50, Asst. Prof. 1950-54, Assoc. Prof. 1955-59, Prof. of Biochem. and Molecular Biology 1959-, Research Biochemist to Virus Lab. 1959-; Chair. Dept. of Molecular Biology and Dir. Virus Lab. 1969-76; Pres. (elect) American Soc. of Biological Chemists 1986, Pres. 1987-88; mem. N.A.S., A.A.A.S., American Acad. of Arts and Sciences; Scholar-in-Residence Fogarty Int. Center, NIH 1977-78; Pres. Fed. of American Socs. for Experimental Biology 1988-89; mem. Scientific Council and Scientific Advisory Bd. of Stazione Zoologica Naples, Italy 1988-, Bd. of Scientific Consultants of Memorial Sloan-Kettering Cancer Center 1988-; Hon. D.Sc. (Northwestern Univ.) 1974; Calif. Section Award, American Chemical Soc. 1958; E. H. Sargent & Co. Award for Chemical Instrumentation, American Chemical Soc. 1962; John Scott Award, City of Philadelphia 1964; Warren Triennial Prize, Mass. Gen. Hosp. 1965, Merck Award, American Soc. of Biological Chemists 1986. *Publications:* Ultracentrifugation in Biochemistry 1959; articles. *Leisure interest:* sports. *Address:* Molecular Biology and Virus Laboratory, University of California, Berkeley, Calif. 94720, U.S.A. *Telephone:* (415) 642-7046.

SCHADEWALDT, Hans, DR. MED.; German professor of medical history; b. 7 May 1923, Kottbus; ed. Univs. of Tübingen, Würzburg and Königsberg; lecturer Univ. of Freiburg 1961-63; Prof. History of Medicine, Univ. of Düsseldorf 1963-, Dean, Faculty of Medicine 1976-77; Officier Ordre du Mérite Culturel, Monaco; Officier Ordre des Palmes Académiques, Paris; Bundesverdienstkreuz (1st Class). *Publications:* Michelangelo und die Medizin seiner Zeit 1965, Die berühmten Ärzte 1966, Kunst und Medizin 1967, Der Medizinmann bei den Naturvölkern 1968, Geschichte der Allergie 1979-83, Die Chirurgie in der Kunst 1983. *Address:* Brehmstrasse 82, D-4000 Düsseldorf, Federal Republic of Germany. *Telephone:* 0211 623163; 0211 3113940.

SCHAEBERLE, Robert M.; American business executive; b. 1923, New Jersey; s. of Frederick Schaeberle and Bertha Thieleman; m. Barbara J. Slockbower 1945; three c.; ed. Dartmouth Coll.; served U.S. Navy, World War II (rank of Lieut.-Commdr.); joined Nabisco Inc. 1946, Controller 1960, Vice-Pres. and Asst. to Pres. 1962, Vice-Pres. for Finance 1964, Exec. Vice-Pres. 1964-66, Pres. 1966-73, C.O.O. 1972-73, Chair. of Bd. and C.E.O. 1973-81 (co. merged with Standard Brands to form Nabisco Brands), Chair. and C.E.O. 1981-83, Chair. 1983-87, Dir. and mem. Exec. Cttee.; Dir. Libbey-Owens Ford Co.; mem. Advisory Bd., Chemical Bank New York Trust Co., Emergency Cttee. for American Trade; Dir. of several cos. *Address:* c/o Nabisco Inc., River Road, East Hanover, New Jersey 07936, U.S.A.

SCHAEFER, George Anthony, B.S.; American tractor executive; b. 13 June 1928, Covington, Ky.; s. of George Joseph Schaefer and the late Marie Cecilia Sandheger; m. Barbara Ann Quick 1951; one s. one d.; ed. St. Louis Univ. High School, St. Louis Univ.; joined Caterpillar Tractor Co. (now Caterpillar Inc.), Ill. 1951, Graduate Accounting Trainee 1951-52, Staff Auditor, Gen. Offices 1952-56, Auditing Procedures and Machine Accounting Man., San Leandro Plant 1956-59, Asst. Chief Accountant 1960-62, Finance and Accounting Man., Caterpillar France, S.A. 1962-68, Div. Man. Corporate Accounting, Accounting, Gen. Offices 1968-69, Div. Man. Mfg. Systems Devt. 1969-70, Man. Mfg. Systems Devt., Gen. Offices 1970-73, Man. Decatur Plant 1973-76, Vice-Pres. Financial and Data Processing 1976-81, Exec. Vice-Pres. 1981-84, Div. 1983-, Vice-Chair. 1984-85, Chair., C.E.O. Feb. 1985-. *Address:* Caterpillar Inc., 100 N.E. Adams Street, Peoria, Ill. 61629, U.S.A. *Telephone:* (309) 675-1000.

SCHAEFER, William Donald, LL.M., J.D.; American politician; b. 2 Nov. 1921, Baltimore; s. of William Henry Schaefer and Tululu Skipper; ed. Baltimore Univ.; law practice, Baltimore 1943-; mem. Baltimore City Council 1955-67, Pres. 1967-71; Mayor 1971-87; Gov. of Maryland Jan. 1987-; Hon. LL.D. (Baltimore) 1976, (Md.) 1981, (Morgan State) 1983; Hon. J.D. (Loyola Coll.) 1976; Hon. D.H.L. (Towson) 1983; numerous awards including: Jefferson Award 1979, Michael A. DiNunzio Award 1981; Distinguished Mayor Award, Nat. Urban Coalition 1982; mem. Nat. History Soc., American Public Works Assocn. and American Inst. of Banking; Democrat. *Address:* State Capitol, Annapolis, Md. 21401, U.S.A.

SCHAEFERS, Wolfgang Friedrich Wilhelm, DR.ING.; German engineer and executive; b. 11 Dec. 1930, Oberhausen; s. of Friedrich and Adele (née Verhufen) Schaefers; m. Christel Weingarten 1954; two s.; ed. Rheinisch-Westfälische Technische Hochschule, Aachen; Works Man. with Mannesmann AG 1961-62; mem. Man. Bd. Verein Deutscher Eisenhüttenleute 1962-64 (also currently); Technical Works Man. Rheinstahl Hüttenwerke AG 1964-69; mem. Man. Bd. Rheinstahl AG (Thyssen Industrie AG from April 1976) 1969-75, Spokesman 1975-76, Chair. 1976-80; Chair. Supervisory Bd. Thyssen Nordseewerke GmbH, Thyssen Schalker Verein GmbH, Thyssen Giesserei AG, Österreichische Salen-Kunststoffwerk Gesellschaft mbH; Chair. Advisory Bd. Thyssen Industrie AG Henschel; Vice-Chair. Supervisory Bd. Henschel Flugzeug-werke AG; mem. Supervisory Bd.,

Messerschmitt-Bölkow-Blohm GmbH, München; mem. Max-Planck-Gesellschaft zur Förderung der Wissenschaften e.V. Deutsch-Türkische Gesellschaft für Kultur, Wirtschaft und Handel e.V. and other socs.; Special mem. South African Inst. of Foundrymen; Cttee. or Bd. positions with nine firms and asscns. in steel and other sectors. *Publications:* numerous publs. on technical subjects, including steel production. *Leisure interests:* sailing, hunting. *Address:* Poeppinghausstr. 8, 466 Gelsenkirchen-Buer, Federal Republic of Germany (Home). *Telephone:* 39 65 81.

SCHAEFFER, Bogusław; Polish composer and playwright; b. 6 June 1929, Lwów (now Lvov, U.S.S.R.); s. of Władysław and Julia Schaeffer; m. Mieczysława Hanuszewska 1953; one s.; ed. State Higher School of Music, Jagiellonian Univ., Cracow; wrote first dodecaphonic music for orchestra, Music for Strings: Nocturne 1953; Assoc. Prof. State Higher School of Music, Cracow 1963-86, Extraordinary Prof. 1986-; Chief Ed. Forum Musicum 1967-; leads Int. Summer Courses for New Composition in Salzburg (Austria) 1976-; G. Fitelberg Prize 1959, 1960, 1964; A. Malawski Prize 1962; Minister of Culture and Arts Prize 1971, 1980, Union of Polish Composers Prize 1977; Knight's Cross of Polonia Restituta Order, Gold Cross of Merit. *Publications:* Nowa Muzyka. Problemy współczesnej techniki kompozytorskiej (New music. Problems of contemporary technique in composing) 1958, Klasycy dodekafonii (Classics of dodecaphonic music) 1964, Leksykon kompozytorów XX wieku (Lexicon of 20th century composers) 1965, W kręgu nowej muzyki (In the sphere of new music) 1967, Mały informator muzyki XX wieku 1975, Introduction to Composition (in English) 1975, Historia muzyki (Story of Music) 1980. *Chief works:* Extrema, Tertium datur, Scultura, S'alto for alto saxophone, Collage and form, Electronic music, Visual music, Heraclitiana, Missa elettronica, Jangwa, also film and theatre music, Miserere, Organ Concerto. *Leisure interests:* literature, theatre. *Address:* Osiedle Kolorowe 4, 31-938 Cracow, Poland. *Telephone:* 44-19-60.

SCHAEFFER, Pierre; French engineer, writer and composer; b. 14 Aug. 1910; s. of Henri Schaeffer and Lucie Labriet; m. 1st Elisabeth Schmitt (deceased); one d.; m. 2nd Jacqueline de Lisle 1962; one s.; ed. Ecole Polytechnique and Ecole supérieure d'électricité et des télécommunications; fmr. Dir. of Research, Office de Radiodiffusion-Télévision Française 1959; a leader of movement for development of "musique concrète" (works include Symphonie pour un homme seul and music for films); fmr. Assoc. Prof., Conservatoire nat. de Musique; mem. Admin. Council, Acad. de France in Rome 1979-; Officier, Légion d'honneur, Chevalier des Palmes académiques, Commdr. des Arts et des Lettres. *Publications:* Amérique, nous t'ignorons (essay) 1946, Les enfants de coeur (novel) 1949, A la recherche d'une musique concrète 1952, Traité des objets musicaux 1966, La musique concrète 1967, Solfège de l'objet sonore 1967, L'observateur observe 1967, 1975, Le gardien de volcan 1969, L'avenir à reculons 1970, Machines à communiquer, Vol. I Genèse des simulacres 1970, Vol. II Pouvoir et communication 1972, Le trièdre fertile 1975, Les antennes de Jéricho 1978, Oeuvres de musique concrète et électronique 1977-78, Excusez-moi je meurs (short stories) 1981, Prélude choral et fugue (novel) 1983, Faber et sapiens (essay) 1985. *Leisure interest:* philosophy. *Address:* 13 rue des Petits-Champs, 75001 Paris, France. *Telephone:* 296-55-77.

SCHAETZEL, John Robert; American writer and business consultant; b. 28 Jan. 1917, Holtville, Calif.; m. Imogen Schwope 1945; two d.; ed. Pomona Coll., Calif., Univ. of Mexico and Harvard Univ.; Admin. Asst., Bureau of the Budget 1942; Special Asst. to Dir. of Office of Int. Trade Policy, Dept. of State 1945-50; Special Asst. to Asst. Sec. of State for Econ. Affairs 1950-54; Nat. War Coll. 1954-55; Officer in charge of peaceful uses of atomic energy, Office of Special Asst. to Sec. for Disarmament and Atomic Energy 1955-59; mem. Presidential Task Force 1960-61; Special Asst. to Under-Sec. of State for Econ. Affairs 1961, to Under-Sec. of State 1961-62; Deputy Asst. Sec. of State for Atlantic Affairs 1962-66; Amb. to European Communities 1966-72, resgnd.; Pres. Council on U.S. Int. Trade Policy; Chair. Task Force on Consultation for Trilateral Comm.; mem. Advisory Council, Johns Hopkins Bologna Center; Pres. American Council for Jean Monnet Studies Inc.; Consultant Gen. Accounting Office, C.I.A., Brookings Inst.; mem. Council on Foreign Relations, New York; mem. Bd. Woodrow Wilson Fellowship Foundation; Rockefeller Public Service Award 1959. *Publications:* The Unhinged Alliance—America and the European Community 1975; numerous articles for many journals. *Address:* 2 Bay Tree Lane, Bethesda, Md. 20816, U.S.A. *Telephone:* (301) 229-0957.

SCHAFF, Adam, PH.D.; Polish sociologist and philosopher; b. 10 March 1913, Lwów (now Lvov, U.S.S.R.); s. of Maks Schaff and Ernestina Schaff de domo Felix; m. Anna Schaff 1935 (died 1975), one d.; m. 2nd Teresa Schaff 1976; ed. Lwów Univ. and Ecole des Sciences Politiques et Economiques, Paris; scientific work in U.S.S.R. 1940-45; Prof. Łódź Univ. 1945-48; Prof. of Philosophy, Warsaw Univ. 1948-70; Dir. Polish United Workers' Party Inst. of Social Sciences 1950-57; mem. Polish Acad. of Sciences (Chair. Philosophy Cttee. 1951-68, Dir. Inst. of Philosophy and Sociology 1957-68); Visiting Prof., Univ. of Vienna 1969-72, Hon. Prof. of Philosophy 1972-; mem. Bulgarian Acad. of Sciences; mem. Polish Workers' Party 1944-48, Polish United Workers' Party 1948-84 (mem. Cen. Cttee. 1959-68); mem. Exec. Cttee. Int. Fed. of Philosophical Asscns.; mem. of Int. Inst. of Philosophy, Paris; mem. Royal Acad. of Political and Moral Sciences, Madrid; Hon. Pres. Bd. of Dirs. of the European Centre for

Social Sciences in Vienna; Ed. Myśl Współczesna (Contemporary Thought) 1946-51, Myśl Filozoficzna (Philosophical Thought) 1951-56; Dr. h.c. (Mich. Univ., Ann Arbor) 1967; Dr. h.c. (Sorbonne) 1975, (Univ. de Nancy) 1982; State Prizes, 1st and 2nd Class. *Publications:* Pojęcie i słowo (Concept and Word) 1946, Wstęp do teorii marksizmu (Introduction to the Theory of Marxism) 1947, Narodziny i rozwój filozofii marksistowskiej (Birth and Development of Marxist Philosophy) 1949, Z zagadnień marksistowskiej teorii prawdy (Some Problems of the Marxist Theory of Truth) 1951, Obiektywny Charakter Praw Historii (The Objective Character of Historical Laws) 1955, Wstęp do Semantyki (Introduction to Semantics) 1960, Filozofia Człowieka (A Philosophy of Man) 1962, Język i poznanie (Language and Cognition) 1963, Marksizm a jednostka ludzka (Marxism and the Human Individual) 1965, Szkice z filozofii języka (Essays in the philosophy of Language) 1967, Historia i Prawda (History and Truth) 1970, Gramatyka generatywna a koncepcja wrodzonych idei (Generative Grammar and Conception of Innate Ideas) 1972, Strukturalizm i Marksizm (Structuralism and Marxism) 1975, Entfremdung als soziales Phänomen (Alienation as a Social Phenomenon) 1977, Stereotypen und das menschliche Handeln 1980, Die Kommunistische Bewegung am Scheideweg 1982, Polen Heute 1983, Wohin führt der Weg? 1985, Perspektiven des Modernen Sozialismus 1988. *Leisure interest:* tennis. *Address:* Aleja I Armii W.P. 2/4 m. 24, 00-582 Warsaw, Poland; Flossgasse 2/28, A-1020 Vienna, Austria. *Telephone:* 28-18-32 (Warsaw); 33-50-253 (Vienna).

SCHAFFNER, Franklin James: American film director and producer; b. 30 May 1920, Tokyo, Japan; s. of Paul Franklin and Sarah (née Swords) Schaffner; m. Helen Jean Gilchrist 1948; two d.; ed. Franklin and Marshall Coll.; served in U.S.N.R. 1942-46, final rank Lieut.; dir. numerous television programmes including Studio One 1948-51, Person to Person 1956-58, Playhouse 90 1958-60. *films include:* The Stripper 1963, The Best Man 1964, The War Lord 1965, The Double Man 1967, Planet of the Apes 1968, Patton 1969, Nicholas and Alexandra 1971, Papillon 1973, Islands in the Stream 1977, The Boys from Brazil 1978, Yes, Giorgio 1981, Sphinx 1981, Lionheart 1987; also dir. Advise and Consent, Broadway 1961; numerous awards, including Variety Critics Poll Award for Advise and Consent, Dirs. Guild of America Award, and Oscar for Patton, 1971; mem. Dirs. Guild of America, Nat. Acad. TV Arts and Sciences. *Address:* c/o Chasin-Park-Citron Agency, 9255 Sunset Boulevard, Los Angeles, Calif. 90069, U.S.A.

SCHAFFSTEIN, Friedrich, DR. JUR.; German professor of law; b. 28 July 1905, Göttingen; s. of Dr. Karl Schaffstein; ed. Univs. of Innsbruck and Göttingen; teacher in criminal law Univ. of Göttingen 1927-33, Prof. of Criminal Law, Leipzig 1933-35, Univ. of Kiel 1935-41, Univ. of Strasbourg 1941-45, Verwaltungs-akademie Lüneburg 1946-50; Prof. of Law (Criminal and Criminology) Univ. of Göttingen 1953-70, Prof. Emer. 1970-; mem. Akademie der Wissenschaften, Göttingen. *Publications:* Die Entwicklung der allgemeiner Lehren vom Verbrechen im gemeinen Strafrecht 1930, Wilhelm von Humboldt 1952, Die Strafrechtswissenschaft im Zeitalter des Humanismus 1954, Jugendstrafrecht (9th edn.) 1987, Abhandlungen zur Strafrechtsgeschichte und Wissenschaftsgeschichte 1987. *Address:* Ewaldstrasse 103, 3400 Göttingen, Federal Republic of Germany. *Telephone:* 0551-57053.

SCHAIRER, George Swift, M.S.; American aircraft and missile design engineer; b. 19 May 1913, Wilkinsburg, Pa.; s. of Otto Sorg and Elizabeth Blanch Swift Schairer; m. Mary Pauline Tarbox 1935; two s. two d.; ed. Oakmont Public School, Oakmont, Pa., Summit New Jersey High School, Swarthmore Coll., Mass. Inst. of Tech., and Advanced Management Program, Hawaii Univ.; Automotive Engineer, Bendix Aviation Corpn., South Bend, Ind. 1935-37; Engineer, Consolidated Vultee Aircraft Corpn., San Diego 1937-39; Chief Aerodynamist, Boeing Co. 1939-46, Staff Engineer (Aerodynamics and Power Plant) 1946-51, Chief of Technical Staff 1951-56, Asst. Chief Engineer 1956-57, Dir. of Research 1957-59, Vice-Pres. (Research and Devt.) 1959-71, Vice-Pres. Research 1971-78 (retd.); consultant The Boeing Co. 1978-; mem. N.A.S. 1968-, Nat. Acad. of Eng., Int. Acad. of Astronautics; Hon. Fellow, A.I.A.A.; official of numerous other orgs.; Sylvanus Albert Reed Award, Inst. of Aeronautical Sciences 1949; Daniel Guggenheim Medal 1967; Hon. D.Eng. (Swarthmore Coll.) 1958. *Publications:* numerous papers on aeronautics and related subjects. *Leisure interests:* sailing, model airplane building, photography, fine arts. *Address:* 4242 Hunts Point Road, Bellevue, Wash., U.S.A. (Home). *Telephone:* (206) 454-3602 (Home).

SCHALL HOLBERG, Britta; Danish politician; b. 25 July 1941, Næstved; d. of Preben Schall Holberg; ed. N. Zahle's Teacher Training Coll., Copenhagen; owner of the Hagenskov estate on Funen; fmr. Deputy Mayor of Assens and Deputy Chair. of Fed. of Danish Social Cttees.; Minister for the Interior 1982; M.P. 1984-; Liberal. *Address:* c/o Ministry of the Interior, Christiansborg Slotsplads 1, 1218 Copenhagen K, Denmark. *Telephone:* (01) 11-69-00.

SCHALLER, François; Swiss professor of economics and business executive; b. 3 Dec. 1920, Porrentruy; s. of Georges Schaller and Laetitia Crevoisier; m. Claudine Jobin 1952; two s. three d.; ed. Univs. of Lausanne and Berne; lecturer in political economy, Univ. of Berne 1954-86, Univ. of Lausanne 1963-86, Univ. of Neuchâtel 1967-70, Fed. Polytechnic of Lausanne 1971-73; mem. Council, Banque Nat. Suisse 1973-, Vice-Pres. Bd.

1978-86, Pres. 1986-89; mem. several non-govt. comms.; business interests in industry, transport and banking; hon. Council mem. Institut des Hautes Etudes économiques et sociales, Brussels. *Publications:* Le droit au travail et les problèmes économiques d'après guerre 1946, De la charité privée aux droits économiques et sociaux du citoyen 1950, La notion de productivité 1975 (in Italian 1976), various articles in economic journals. *Address:* 1 chemin de Clair-Matin, CH 1066 Epalinges, Switzerland. *Telephone:* 784-1982.

SCHALLY, Andrew Victor, PH.D.; American medical researcher; b. 30 Nov. 1926, Wilno, Poland (now Vilnius, U.S.S.R.); s. of Casimir Peter and Maria (Lacka) Schally; m. 1st Margaret Rachel White, one s. one d.; m. 2nd Ana Maria de Medeiros-Comaru 1976; ed. Bridge of Allen, Scotland, London Univ., McGill Univ., Montreal, Canada; Asst. Prof. of Physiology and Asst. Prof. of Biochem., Baylor Univ. Coll. of Medicine, Houston, Tex. 1960-62; Chief, Endocrine and Polypeptide Labs., Veterans Admin. Hosp., New Orleans, La. 1962-; Sr. Medical Investigator, Veterans Admin. 1973-; Assoc. Prof. of Medicine, Tulane Univ. School of Medicine, New Orleans, La. 1962-67, Prof. of Medicine 1967-; Charles Mickle Award 1974, Gairdner Foundation Award 1974, Edward T. Tyler Award 1975, Borden Award in the Medical Sciences (Asscn. of American Medical Colls.) 1975, Lasker Award 1975, shared Nobel Prize for Physiology or Medicine with Roger Guillemin (q.v.) for discoveries concerning peptide hormones 1977. *Publications:* numerous scientific papers, particularly concerning hormones and cancer. *Leisure interest:* swimming. *Address:* Veterans Administration Hospital, 1601 Perdido Street, New Orleans, La. 70146 (Office); 5025 Kawanee Avenue, Metairie, La. 70002, U.S.A. (Home). *Telephone:* (504) 589-5230 (Office).

SCHANBERG, Sydney Hillel, B.A.; American journalist; b. 17 Jan. 1934, Clinton, Mass.; s. of Louis and Freda (née Feinberg) Schanberg; two d.; ed. Harvard Univ.; joined New York Times 1959, reporter 1960, Bureau Chief, Albany, New York 1967-69, New Delhi, India 1969-73, S.E. Asia Corresp., Singapore 1973-75, City Ed. 1977-80, Columnist 1981-85; Columnist Newsday newspaper, New York 1986-; numerous awards, including Page One Award for Reporting 1972, George Polk Memorial Award 1972, Overseas Press Club Award 1972, Bob Considine Memorial Award 1975, Pulitzer Prize 1975. *Address:* 164 West 79th Street, Apt. 12-D, New York, N.Y. 10024, U.S.A.

SCHARANSKY, Natan (b. Anatoly); Israeli (b. Soviet) computer scientist and human rights activist; b. 20 Jan. 1948, Donetsk, U.S.S.R.; m. Natalya (now Avital) Stiglitz 1974; a leading spokesman for Jewish emigration movt. in U.S.S.R.; arrested by Soviet authorities for dissident activities 1977; received 13-year prison sentence on charges of treason 1978; following worldwide campaign, Soviet authorities released him in exchange for eastern spies held in West and he took up residence in Israel Feb. 1986; Perm. Rep. (desig.) of Israel to UN 1989-. *Publication:* Fear No Evil 1988. *Address:* 800 Second Avenue, New York, N.Y. 10021, U.S.A.

SCHARF, Kurt Franz Wilhelm, TH.D., D.D.; German ecclesiastic; b. 21 Oct. 1902, Landsberg/Warthe; s. of Johannes Scharf and Margarethe Rüdel; m. 1st Ingeborg Sommerwerck 1928 (died 1929), one d.; m. 2nd Renate Scharf 1933, one s. three d.; ed. Tübingen, Jena and Halle/Saale Univs.; Pastor Friesack 1928, Sachsenhausen 1933; Präses Brotherhood of Brandenburg Confessional Churches 1933; Chair. Conf. of Brotherhoods of Confessional Churches in Germany 1938; several times arrested and forbidden to preach and publish by Nazi regime; Präses Brandenburg Confessional Synod 1935; Provost Berlin-Brandenburg Prov. 1945; Chair. United Evangelical Church 1955; Chair. Protestant Church in Germany 1961-67, Deputy Chair. 1967-79; Bishop of Berlin-Brandenburg (Protestant Church) 1966-76; Vice-Pres. United World Bible Soc. 1966-69; mem. Cen. Cttee. World Council of Churches 1968-75; Ed. Rundbriefe der Bekennenden Kirche 1933-45 (illegal 1935-45); Hon. Th.D. Humboldt Univ., Berlin; Hon. D.D. Eden Seminary, Webster Groves (Mass.), Christliche Akademie (Warsaw); Buber-Rosenzweig Medal, Jüdisch-Christlicher Koordinierungsrat, Kopernikusmedaille, Ernst-Reuter-Medaille der Stadt Berlin West, Gustav-Heinemann-Preis, Dr. Leopold-Lucas-Preis der Universität Tübingen, Goldenes Athos-Kreuz des Ökumenischen Patriarchates (Istanbul), Augustin Cross of Archbishop of Canterbury. *Publications:* Für ein politisches Gewissen der Kirche 1972, Brücken und Breschen 1977, Streit mit der Macht 1983, Widerstehen und Versöhnen 1987. *Leisure interests:* chess, poetry. *Address:* Am Hirschsprung 35, 1000 Berlin 33, Federal Republic of Germany. *Telephone:* 030-831 26 00.

SCHARRER, Berta Vogel, PH.D.; American professor of anatomy; b. 1 Dec. 1906, Munich, Germany; d. of Karl Vogel and Johanna Greis; m. Dr. Ernst Albert Scharrer 1934 (deceased); ed. Univ. of Munich; Research Assoc., Research Inst. of Psychiatry, Munich 1931-34, Univ. of Frankfurt Neurological Inst. 1934-37, Univ. of Chicago, U.S. 1937-38, Rockefeller Inst. 1938-40; Instructor and Fellow, Western Reserve Univ., Cleveland, Ohio 1940-46; Asst. Prof. (Research) and John Simon Guggenheim Fellow, Univ. of Colo. 1946-54; Prof. Albert Einstein Coll. of Medicine, New York 1955-77, Prof. Emer. of Anatomy and Neuroscience 1978-; mem. N.A.S., American Acad. of Arts and Sciences, Deutsche Akad. der Naturforscher Leopoldina, Royal Netherlands Acad. of Arts and Sciences; hon. mem. European Soc. for Comparative Endocrinology, Int. Soc. for Neuroendocrinology, Israel Soc. for Anatomical Sciences, Anatomische Gesellschaft;

Pres. American Asscn. of Anatomists 1978-79; Fellow, A.A.A.S. 1980; Dr. med. h.c. (Univ. of Giessen, Fed. Repub. of Germany) 1976; Hon. Dr. Sc. (Northwestern Univ.) 1977, (Univ. of N.C.) 1978, (Smith Coll.) 1980, (Harvard Univ.) 1982, (Yeshiva Univ., New York) 1983, (Mount Holyoke Coll.) 1984, (State Univ. of New York) 1985; Dr. of Laws h.c. (Univ. of Calgary) 1982; Kraepelin Gold Medal 1978, F. C. Koch Award 1980, Schleiden Medal, Leopoldina 1983. *Publications:* Neuroendocrinology (with E. Scharrer) 1963; and other publications in the fields of comparative neuroendocrinology and neurosecretion. *Leisure interests:* music, reading. *Address:* Department of Anatomy, Albert Einstein College of Medicine, 1300 Morris Park Avenue, Bronx, N.Y. 10461, U.S.A. *Telephone:* (212) 430-2835.

SCHATZMAN, Evry; French research scientist; b. 16 Sept. 1920, Neuilly; s. of Benjamin Schatzman and Cécile Kahn; four c.; ed. Ecole Normale Supérieure; Research Assoc. Centre Nat. de la Recherche Scientifique (C.N.R.S.) 1945, Head of Research 1948; Prof. Univ. of Paris 1954; Dir. of Research, C.N.R.S. 1976-; Prix Holweck 1976; mem. Acad. of Sciences 1985-; Médaille d'Or, C.N.R.S. 1983. *Publications:* Astrophysique Générale 1957, Structure de l'Univers 1968, Science et Société 1971, Les enfants d'Uranie 1986, Le message du photon voyageur 1987, La science menacée 1989, Les Etoiles 1989. *Address:* 11 rue de l'Eglise, Dompierre, 60420 Maignelay-Montigny, France. *Telephone:* 44.51.24.14.

SCHÄUBLE, Wolfgang, D.JUR.; German politician and lawyer; b. 18 Sept. 1942, Freiburg; s. of Karl Schäuble and Gertrud (née Göhring) Schäuble; m. Ingeborg Hensle 1969; one s. three d.; ed. Univs. of Freiburg and Hamburg; Regional Pres., Junge Union, S. Baden 1969-72; worked in admin. of taxes, Baden-Württemberg 1971-72; mem. Bundestag 1972-, Exec. Sec. CDU/CSU Parl. group 1981-84; mem. parl., European Council 1975-84; Chair. CDU Cttee. on Sport 1976-84; Regional Vice-Pres., CDU, S. Baden 1982-; Minister with special responsibility and Head of Chancellery 1984-89, of Interior April 1989-; legal practice in Offenburg 1978-84; Chair. Arbeitsgemeinschaft Europäischer Grenzregionen (AGEG) 1979-82; Grosses Bundesverdienstkreuz; Commdr., Ordre nat. du Mérite. *Leisure interests:* tennis, chess, music. *Address:* Ministry of the Interior, Grautheindorfer Strasse 198, 5300 Bonn 1, Federal Republic of Germany. *Telephone:* (0228) 6811.

SCHAUFUSS, Peter; Danish ballet dancer, producer, choreographer and artistic director; b. 26 April 1950, Copenhagen; s. of Frank Schaufuss and Mona Vangsaae; ed. Royal Danish Ballet School; apprentice 1965; soloist Nat. Ballet of Canada 1967-68, 1977-83; Royal Danish Ballet 1969-70; prin. London Festival Ballet 1970-74; New York City Ballet 1974-77; guest appearances in Canada, Denmark, France, Germany, Italy, Japan, U.K., U.S.A., Austria, South America; Presented BBC TV series 'Dancer'; numerous TV appearances; *created following roles:* 1975: Rhapsodie Espagnole, The Steadfast Tin Soldier (Balanchine); 1980: Phantom of the Opera (Petit); 1982: Verdi Variations, Orpheus (MacMillan); *produced Bournonville Ballets:* La Sylphide (London Festival Ballet, Stuttgart Ballet, Roland Petit's Ballet de Marseille, Deutsche Oper Berlin, Teatro Comunale Firenze), Napoli (Nat. Ballet of Canada), Folktale (Deutsche Oper Berlin), Dances from Napoli (London Festival Ballet), Bournonville (Aterballetto), The Nutcracker (London Festival Ballet); Solo Award, 2nd Int. Ballet Competition, Moscow 1973, Star of the Year Award 1978 by Abendzeitung, Munich, Evening Standard Award 1979, Soc. of West End Theatres Ballet Award (now Olivier) 1979. *Address:* c/o London Festival Ballet, 39 Jay Mews, London, SW7 2ES, England.

SCHAWLOW, Arthur Leonard, PH.D., LL.D., D.SC.; American professor of physics; b. 5 May 1921, Mount Vernon, N.Y.; s. of Arthur and Helen (Mason) Schawlow; m. Aurelia Keith Townes 1951; one s. two d.; ed. Univ. of Toronto; Postdoctoral Fellow and Research Assoc., Columbia Univ. 1949-51; Research Physicist, Bell Telephone Labs. 1951-61; Visiting Assoc. Prof., Columbia Univ. 1960; J. G. Jackson—C. J. Wood Prof. of Physics, Stanford Univ. 1961-, Chair. Dept. of Physics 1966-70; Dir. Optical Soc. of America 1966-69, Pres. 1975; mem. Council, American Physical Soc. 1966-70, hon. mem. 1982, Chair. Div. of Electron and Atomic Physics 1974, Vice-Pres. Elect 1979, Vice-Pres. 1980, Pres. 1981; mem. N.A.S.; Fellow, American Acad. of Arts and Sciences; hon. doctorates from Univs. of Ghent, Toronto, Bradford, Alabama, Trinity Coll. Dublin, Lund; Thomas Young Medal and Prize (Inst. of Physics and Physical Soc. U.K.), Ballantine Medal (Franklin Inst.), Liebmann Prize (Inst. of Electrical and Electronic Engineers); Calif. Scientist of the Year 1973; Geoffrey Frew Fellowship (Australian Acad. of Sciences) 1973; Frederic Ives Medal (Optical Soc. of America) 1976; Marconi Int. Fellowship 1977; shared Nobel Prize in Physics for devt. of laser spectroscopy 1981; Schawlow Medal (Laser Inst. of America) 1982. *Publications:* Microwave Spectroscopy (with C. H. Townes) 1955, and over 190 scientific papers. *Leisure interest:* jazz music. *Address:* Department of Physics, Stanford University, Stanford, Calif. 94305; 849 Esplanada Way, Stanford, Calif. 94305, U.S.A. (Home).

SCHECKTER, Jody David; South African racing driver; b. 21 Jan. 1950, East London, nr. Durban; m. Pam Bailey; one s.; raced karts from age of 11, graduated to motorcycles and racing cars; won S.A. Formula Ford Sunshine Series in 1970, competed in Britain from 1971; World Champion 1979, runner-up 1977, third 1974 and 1976; *Grand Prix wins:* 1974 Swedish (Tyrrell-Ford), 1974 British (Tyrrell-Ford), 1975 South African (Tyrrell-Ford), 1976 Swedish (Tyrrell-Ford), 1977 Argentine (Wolf-Ford), 1977 Monaco (Wolf-Ford), 1977 Canadian (Wolf-Ford), 1979 Belgian (Ferrari),

1979 Monaco (Ferrari), 1979 Italian (Ferrari); retd. 1980. *Leisure interest:* keeping fit. *Address:* Monte Carlo, Monaco.

SCHEEL, Walter; German politician; b. 8 July 1919, Solingen; m. 2nd Dr. Mildred Wirtz 1969 (died 1985); two s. two d.; m. 3rd Barbara Wiese 1988; ed. Reform-Gymnasium, Solingen; served German Air Force, World War II; fmr. head of market research org.; mem. Landtag North Rhine-Westphalia 1950-53; mem. Bundestag 1953-74, Vice-Pres. 1967-69; Fed. Minister for Econ. Co-operation 1961-66; Chair. of Free Democrats 1968-74 (Hon. Chair. 1979); Vice-Chancellor, Minister of Foreign Affairs 1969-74; Pres. Fed. Repub. of Germany 1974-79; mem. European Parl. 1958-69; Pres. Bilderberg Conf. -1985; Chair. German Council of European Movt. -1985; Chair. Bd. of Trustees, Friedrich Naumann Foundation; Chair. Admin. Council, Germanic Nat. Museum, Nuremberg, Cttee. European Music Year 1983-86, Supervisory Bd., German Finance Co. for Investments in Developing Countries 1980, Directory for Thoroughbreds and Races 1982; Pres. Europa-Union Deutschland 1980-; mem. Supervisory Bd. ROBECO Group 1982-, Supervisory Bd. Thyssen AG 1980, Supervisory Bd. Thyssen Stahl AG 1983; Hon. Pres. German Fed. of Artists; Theodor Heuss Prize 1971, Peace Prize (Kajima Inst., Tokyo) 1973; numerous hon. degrees and awards from Germany and abroad; Fondation du Mérite Européen 1984. Grosses Bundesverdienstkreuz (special class). *Publications:* Konturen einer neuen Welt 1965, Schwierigkeiten, Ernüchterung und Chancen der Industrieländer 1965, Formeln deutscher Politik 1968, Warum Mitbestimmung und wie 1970, Die Freiburger Thesen der Liberalen (with K.-H. Flach and W. Maihofer) 1972, Bundestagreden 1972, Reden und Interviews 1972-79, Vom Recht des anderen—Gedanken zur Freiheit 1977, Die Zukunft der Freiheit 1979, Nach 30 Jahren; Die Bundesrepublik Deutschland, Vergangenheit, Gegenwart, Zukunft 1979, Die andere deutsche Frage 1981, Wen Schmerzt noch Deutschlands Teilung? 1986. *Leisure interest:* modern art. *Address:* Lindenalle 23, 5000 Cologne-Marienburg, Federal Republic of Germany.

SCHEER, François, D.E.S.; French diplomatist; b. 13 March 1934, Strasbourg; s. of Alfred Scheer and Edmée Lechten; m. 2nd Nicole Roubaud 1985; two s. four d.; ed. Faculty of Law, Univ. of Paris, Inst. d'Etudes Politiques de Paris, Ecole Nat. d'Admin. Second Sec. Embassy, Algiers 1962-64; Direction des Affaires Economiques et Financières, Admin. Cen. 1964-67; Cultural Attaché Embassy, Tokyo 1967-71; Counsellor for Foreign Affairs 1968; Deputy Dir. for Budget 1971, also for Financial Affairs 1972-76; Amb. to Mozambique and Swaziland 1976-77; Perm. Rep. to European Community 1977-79, Dir. of Cabinet to the Pres. of the Ass. of the European Community 1979-81; Dir. of Cabinet of Minister of Foreign Affairs 1981-84; Amb. to Algeria 1984-86; Amb. and Perm. Rep. for France to the European Community 1986-88; Dir. Ecole Nat. d'Admin. 1965-66, Inst. d'Etudes Politiques, Paris 1965-67; Chevalier Légion d'Honneur; Officier Ordre Nat. du Mérite. *Address:* 8 rue Maison Dieu, 75014 Paris, France.

SCHEFFLER, Israel, PH.D.; American philosopher and educator; b. 25 Nov. 1923, New York; s. of Leon Scheffler and Ethel Grünberg Scheffler; m. Rosalind Zuckerbrod 1949; one s. one d.; ed. Brooklyn Coll., Jewish Theological Seminary and Univ. of Pennsylvania; mem. Faculty, Harvard Univ. 1952-, Prof. of Educ. 1961-62, Prof. of Educ. and Philosophy 1962-64, Victor S. Thomas Prof. of Educ. and Philosophy 1964-, Hon. Research Fellow in Cognitive Studies 1965-66, Co-Dir. Research Center for Philosophy of Educ. 1983-; Fellow Center for Advanced Study in Behavioral Sciences, Palo Alto, Calif. 1972-73; Guggenheim Fellow 1958-59, 1972-73. *Publications:* The Language of Education 1960, The Anatomy of Inquiry 1963, Conditions of Knowledge 1965, Science and Subjectivity 1967, Reason and Teaching 1973, Four Pragmatists 1974, Beyond the Letter 1979, Of Human Potential 1985, Inquiries 1986. *Leisure interest:* reading. *Address:* Larsen Hall, Harvard University, Cambridge, Mass. 02138; Emerson Hall, Harvard University, Cambridge, Mass. 02138, U.S.A. *Telephone:* (617) 495-3569 (Larsen Hall); (617) 495-4669 (Emerson Hall).

SCHEIBE, Erhard A.K., DR. RER. NAT.; German professor of philosophy; b. 24 Sept. 1927, Berlin; s. of Albert Scheibe and Maria (née Heidenreich) Scheibe; m. Maria Elgert-Eggers 1958; two s. one d.; ed. Berlin and Singen High Schools, Univ. of Göttingen; Asst. Max Planck Inst. of Physics, Göttingen 1956-57; Asst. and lecturer Univ. of Hamburg 1957-64; Prof. of Philosophy, Univ. of Göttingen 1964-83, Univ. of Heidelberg 1983-; mem. Acad. of Sciences, Göttingen, Acad. of Sciences and Literature, Mainz, Int. Acad. of Philosophy and Sciences, Brussels. *Publications:* Die kontingenten Aussagen in der Physik 1964, The Logical Analysis of Quantum Mechanics 1973. *Leisure interests:* music, art, literature. *Address:* Philos. Seminar, Marsiliusplatz 1, 6900 Heidelberg (Univ.); Am. Büchsenackerhang 39, 6900 Heidelberg, Federal Republic of Germany (Home). *Telephone:* 06221-542483 (Univ.).

SCHEIDER, Wilhelm, DR.RER.POL.; German business executive; b. 11 March 1928, Butow; ed. high school and Univs. of Kiel and Münster; Man. Iron and Steel Trade Asscn., Saar 1959-67; Gen. Man. Walzstahlkontor Süd GmbH, Saarbrücken 1967-71; mem. Man. Bd. Neunkircher Eisenwerk AG 1971-73; Deputy Chair. Fried. Krupp Hüttenwerke AG (now Krupp Stahl AG), Bochum 1973-78, Chair. Man. Bd. 1978-80; Chair. Man. Bd. Fried. Krupp GmbH 1980-; Chair. and mem. several cos. *Address:* Fried.

Krupp GmbH, Altendorfer Strasse 103, 4300 Essen, Federal Republic of Germany. *Telephone:* 188 21 00.

SCHELER, Werner, DR.SC.MED.; German molecular pharmacologist; b. 12 Sept. 1923, Coburg; s. of Karl and Elise (née Vogel) Scheler; m. Ingeborg Fischbach 1960; three d.; ed. Friedrich Schiller Univ., Jena and Humboldt Univ., Berlin; scientific asst., Humboldt Univ. 1951–54, Berlin Acad. of Sciences 1954–59; Asst. Prof. and Prof., Univ. of Greifswald 1959–71, Rector 1966–70; Dir. Research Centre of Molecular Biology and Medicine, Berlin Acad. of Sciences 1971–79; Pres. Acad. of Sciences of G.D.R. 1979–; mem. Research Council of G.D.R., Medical Research Council, Council of Higher Educ.; mem. Deutsche Akad. der Naturforscher Leopoldina; Foreign mem., Acads. of Sciences of Czechoslovakia, Bulgaria, U.S.S.R., U.S.S.R. Acad. of Med. Sciences; Nat. Prize for Science and Tech.; Dr. h.c. (Vilnius, Greifswald). *Publication:* Grundlagen der allgemeinen Pharmakologie 1969, 1980. *Address:* 22/23 Otto-Nuschke-Strasse, DDR-1086 Berlin (Office); 47 Lienhardweg, DDR-1170 Berlin, German Democratic Republic.

SCHELL, Maximilian; Swiss actor; b. 8 Dec. 1930, Vienna; s. of Hermann Ferdinand Schell and Margarete Noe von Nordberg; m. Natalya Andreichenko 1985; one d.; ed. Humanistisches Gymnasium, Basel, Freies Gymnasium, Zürich, and Univs. of Zürich, Basel and Munich; Corporal, Swiss Army 1948–49; various appearances on stage in Switzerland and Germany 1952–55; German début in Children, Mothers and a General 1955; American film début in Young Lions 1958; on Broadway stage in Interlock 1958; Critics Award (Broadway) 1958; New York Critics Award 1961, 1978; Golden Globe Award 1961, 1974; Acad. Award 1961, 1970, 1971, 1978, 1985; Silver Award San Sebastian 1970, 1975; German Fed. Award 1971, 1979, 1980; Film Critics' Award, Chicago 1973; Golden Cup 1974; Bavarian Film Prize 1984. *Principal films acted in:* Judgment at Nuremberg 1961, Five Finger Exercise 1961, Reluctant Saint 1962, Condemned of Altona 1962, Topkapi 1964, Return from the Ashes 1965, Beyond the Mountains 1966, The Deadly Affair 1966, Counterpoint 1966, Krakatoa, East of Java 1967, The Castle 1968, First Love 1969, Pope Joan 1971, Paulina 1880 1971, The Pedestrian 1973, The Odessa File 1974, The Man in the Glass Booth 1975, Assassination 1975, Cross of Iron 1977, Julia 1977, Avalanche Express 1978, The Black Hole 1979, The Diary of Anne Frank 1980, The Chosen 1980, Les îles 1983, Phantom of the Opera 1983, Man Under Suspicion 1983, The Assisi Underground 1984, Peter the Great 1985, The Rosegarden 1989; Producer, Dir. First Love 1969, Tales from the Vienna Woods 1979, Dir. and wrote screenplay End of the Game 1975; Dir. Volkstheater, Munich 1981–. *Principal plays acted in:* Hamlet, Prince of Homburg, Mannerhouse, Don Carlos, Sappho (Durrell), A Patriot for Me, The Twins of Venice, Old Times, Everyman 1978/79/80; Dir. All for the Best, A Patriot for Me, Hamlet, Pygmalion, La Traviata 1975, Tales from the Vienna Woods, Nat. Theatre 1977, The Undiscovered Country, Salzburg Festival 1979/80, Der Seidene Schuh, Salzburg Festival 1985. *Address:* Keplerstrasse 2, 8 Munich 80, Federal Republic of Germany. *Telephone:* 089-478577.

SCHELLING, Friedrich Wilhelm Eugen Eberhard von; German banker; b. 3 May 1906, Berlin; s. of Ulrich and Lina (von Jagemann) von Schelling, great-grandson of F. W. J. von Schelling, philosopher (1775–1854); m. Hildegard Oelkers 1932; one s. one d.; ed. Kaiserin Augusta Gymnasium, Berlin and Univs. of Heidelberg and Berlin; Judge, Berlin 1931–32; Reichsbank, Berlin 1932–45; Reichsbankdirektor, Hamburg 1946–48; Bank deutscher Länder, Frankfurt (Main) 1948–57; Pres. of Landeszentralbank of Free and Hanseatic City of Hamburg 1957–74; Grosses Bundesverdienstkreuz mit Stern. *Publication:* Die Bundesbank in der Inflation 1975, Wir brauchen Grundlagenforschung zum neuen Weltwährungsystem (article) 1979. *Address:* Kaspar-Ohm-Weg 16, 2000 Hamburg 65, Federal Republic of Germany. *Telephone:* 5-36-11-90 (Home).

SCHELLING, Thomas Crombie, PH.D.; American university professor; b. 14 April 1921, Oakland, Calif.; s. of John M. Schelling and Zelda M. Ayres Schelling; m. Corinne Tigay Saposs 1947; four s.; ed. Univ. of California at Berkeley and Harvard Univ.; Fiscal Analyst, U.S. Bureau of the Budget 1945–46; Econ. Econs. Co-operation Admin., Copenhagen and Paris 1948–50, Exec. Office of the Pres. 1951–53; Assoc. Prof. and Prof. of Econs., Yale Univ. 1953–58; Lucius N. Littauer Prof. of Political Economy, Harvard Univ. 1958–; Sr. Staff mem. The Rand Corpn. 1958–59; Fellow American Acad. of Arts and Sciences; mem. N.A.S., Inst. of Medicine. *Publications:* National Income Behavior 1951, International Economics 1958, Strategy of Conflict 1960, Strategy and Arms Control (with Morton H. Halperin) 1961, Arms and Influence 1967, Micromotives and Macrobehavior 1978, Choice and Consequence 1984. *Leisure interests:* running, hiking. *Address:* Kennedy School of Government, 79 Kennedy Street, Cambridge, Mass. 02138 (Office); 20 Oakland Street, Lexington, Mass. 02173, U.S.A. (Home). *Telephone:* (617) 495-1185 (Office); (617) 862-9575 (Home).

SCHELLOW, Erich; German actor; b. 27 Feb. 1915, Berlin; s. of Erich Schellow and Martha Schellow; m. Elke von Klopmann 1983; one s.; ed. Drama School of Prussian State Theatre, Berlin; actor Volkstheater, Hamburg-Altona 1937–40, Prussian State Theatre, Berlin 1941–44, Schauspielhaus, Hamburg 1945–48, Staate-Bühnen, Berlin 1948–; guest appearances, Burgtheater, Vienna 1963–64, Salzburg Festival 1965; mem. Akad. der Künste, Berlin; Staatsschauspieler; Berlinerkunstpreis, Kritiker-

preis; Bundesverdienstkreuz. *Leisure interest:* diving. *Address:* 1000 Berlin 33, Schweinfurthstrasse 76A, Federal Republic of Germany. *Telephone:* 824 1407.

SCHENCK, Michael U. R. von, DR. IUR.; Swiss diplomatist; b. 21 April 1931, Basel; s. of Dr. Ernst von Schenck and Selma Oettinger; ed. Humanistisches Gymnasium and Univ., Basel, and in Lausanne; Swiss Trade Fair 1950–55; Die Woche 1950–55; Swiss Foreign Ministry 1957–67, Del. to OECD 1958, Del. to UN 1959–61, UN Narcotics Conf. 1961, Swiss Tech. Assistance Authority 1961–67; Founder and Dir. Swiss Volunteers for Devt. 1962–67; Sec.-Gen. Int. Sec. for Volunteer Service (ISVS) 1967–71; Harvard Univ. 1972–73; Rep. to IAEA and UNIDO, Swiss Embassy, Vienna 1973–77; Head Econ. Dept., Swiss Embassy, Bonn 1977–79; Amb. to Ghana (also accred. to Liberia, Sierra Leone and Togo) 1979–83, to Finland 1983–86, to Bulgaria 1987–. *Publications:* Der Statutenwechsel im internationalen Obligationenrecht 1955, Volunteer Manpower for Development 1967, Conferencia Regional sobre Servicio Voluntario 1968, An International Peace Corps 1968, Youth Today 1968, Youth's Role in Development 1968, International Volunteer Service 1969. *Leisure interests:* skiing, hiking. *Address:* c/o Ministry of Foreign Affairs, Berne, Switzerland.

SCHENKER, Joseph G., M.D.; Israeli physician; b. 20 Nov. 1933, Cracow, Poland; s. of the late Itzhak Schenker; m. Ekaterina Idels 1959; two s.; ed. Herzlia High School, Tel Aviv and the Hebrew Univ. of Jerusalem; Exec. Chief of Teaching Obstetrics and Gynaecology, Hebrew Univ. Medical School 1977–84; Chair. Dept. of Obstetrics and Gynaecology, Hadassah Univ. Hosp. 1978; Pres. Israel Soc. of Obstetrics and Gynaecology 1979; Pres. of the Council of Israel Medical Assen. 1980; Chair. of Directory, Bd. Examination in Obstetrics and Gynaecology, State of Israel 1979–83, of Advisory Cttee. 1979–86; Acting Chair. of Hadassah Org. of Heads of Depts. 1983–; Chair. Residency Programme, Medical Council 1987, of Cttee. Licensing Physicians, Ministry of Health 1987; Pres. of Int. Soc. for Study of Pathophysiology 1983. *Publications:* Ed. Recent Advances in Pathophysiological Conditions in Pregnancy 1984, The Intrauterine Life-Management and Therapy 1986; about 250 articles in scientific journals. *Leisure interests:* history, chess. *Address:* Department of Obstetrics and Gynaecology, Hadassah University Hospital, P.O. Box 12000, Jerusalem 91120; 5 Mendale Street, Jerusalem 92147, Israel (Home). *Telephone:* 02-446424; 02-637775 (Home).

SCHEPISI, Frederic Alan; Australian film writer and director; b. 26 Dec. 1939, Melbourne; s. of Frederic Thomas and Loretto Ellen (née Hare) Schepisi; m. 1st Joan Mary Ford 1960; m. 2nd Rhonda Elizabeth Finlayson 1973; two s. four d.; ed. Assumption Coll., Kilmore, Vic., Marist Brothers' Juniorate, Macedoni, Vic., Marcellini Coll., Melbourne; TV Production Man., Daton Advisory Service, Melbourne 1961–64; Victorian Man. Cinesound Productions, Melbourne 1964–66; Man. Dir., The Film House, Melbourne 1964–66, Chair. 1979–; Australian Film Awards Best Film (for The Devil's Playground). *Films:* The Devil's Playground 1975, The Chant of Jimmie Blacksmith 1978, Barbarosa 1981, Iceman 1983, A Cry in the Dark 1988. *Leisure interests:* tennis, swimming. *Address:* 159 Eastern Road, South Melbourne, Vic., Australia. *Telephone:* 699-9722.

SCHERAGA, Harold A., PH.D.; American professor of chemistry; b. 18 Oct. 1921, Brooklyn, New York; s. of Samuel and Etta Scheraga; m. Miriam Kurnow 1943; one s. two d.; ed. City Coll. of New York and Duke Univ.; American Chemical Soc. Postdoctoral Fellow Harvard Medical School 1946–47; Instructor of Chem. Cornell Univ. 1947–50, Asst. Prof. 1950–53, Assoc. Prof. 1953–58, Prof. 1958–, Todd Prof. 1965–, Chair. Chem. Dept. 1960–67; Guggenheim Fellow and Fulbright Research Scholar Carlsberg Lab., Copenhagen 1956–57, Weizmann Inst., Rehovoth, Israel 1963; Nat. Inst. of Health Special Fellow Weizman Inst., Rehovoth, Israel 1970; Visiting Lecturer Wool Research Labs. C.S.I.R.O., Australia Dec. 1959; Visiting Prof. Weizmann Inst., Rehovoth, Israel 1992–73, Japan Soc. for the Promotion of Science 1977; Regional Dir. Nat. Foundation for Cancer Research 1982–; mem. N.A.S., American Acad. of Arts and Sciences; Vice-Chair. Cornell Section American Chemical Soc. 1954–55, Chair. 1955–56, Councillor 1959–62; mem. Advisory Panel in Molecular Biology Nat. Science Foundation 1960–62; mem. Ed. Bd. numerous scientific journals; mem. Biochem. Training Cttee., Nat. Insts. of Health 1963–65, Fogarty Scholar 1984, 1986, 1988, 1989; mem. Comm. on Molecular Biophysics Int. Union for Pure and Applied Biophysics 1967–69; mem. Comm. on Macromolecular Biophysics, Int. Union for Pure and Applied Biophysics 1969–75, Pres. 1972–75; mem. Comm. on Subcellular and Macromolecular Biophysics, Int. Union for Pure and Applied Biophysics 1975–81; mem. Exec. Comm. Div. of Physical Chem. American Chemical Soc. 1966–69; Vice-Chair. Div. of Biological Chem. American Chemical Soc. 1970, Chair. 1971; mem. Council Biophysical Soc. 1967–70; mem. Research Career Award Cttee. Nat. Inst. of Health 1967–71; mem. Bd. of Governors Weizmann Inst., Rehovoth, Israel 1970–; hon. life mem. New York Acad. of Sciences 1985; American Chemical Soc. Eli Lilly Award in Biochem. 1957; Welch Foundation Lecturer 1962; Harvey Lecturer 1968; Gallagher Lecturer 1968–69, Lemieux Lecturer 1973, Hill Lecturer 1976, Venable Lecturer 1981; Hon. Sc.D. (Duke Univ.) 1961, (Univ. of Rochester) 1988; Townsend Harris Medal C.C.N.Y. 1970; Nichols Medal, N.Y. Section, American Chem. Soc. 1974; City Coll. Chem. Alumni Scientific Achievement Award Medal 1977; American Chem. Soc. Kendall Award in colloid chem. 1978; Linderstrøm-Lang Medal 1983, Kowalski Medal 1983, Pauling Medal, American Chemical Soc. 1985. *Publications:* Protein Structure 1961, Theory of Helix-Coil Transitions in Biopolymers 1970; 750 articles; research on physical chem. of proteins and other macromolecules; structure of water; chemistry of blood clotting. *Leisure interests:* golf, skiing. *Address:* Baker Laboratory of Chemistry, Cornell University, Ithaca, N.Y. 14853-1301; 212 Homestead Terrace, Ithaca, N.Y. 14850, U.S.A. (Home). *Telephone:* (607) 255-4034 (Office); (607) 272-5155 (Home).

SCHERER, H.E. Cardinal Alfredo Vicente; Brazilian ecclesiastic; b. 5 Feb. 1903, Bom Princípio, Rio Grande do Sul; s. of Pedro and Ana Oppermann Scherer; ed. primary school, Seminário Cen. de São Leopoldo and Pontifical Gregorian Univ., Rome; ordained priest in Rome 1926; Pvt. Sec. to Archbishop of Porto Alegre 1927-33; organizer of Parishes of Tapes and Barra do Ribeiro 1933-35; Parish Priest São Geraldo, Porto Alegre 1935-46; Auxiliary Bishop of Porto Alegre 1946; Archbishop of Porto Alegre 1946-82, Archbishop Emer. 1982-; cr. Cardinal 1969. *Address:* c/o Residência Arquiepiscopal, Rue Espírito Santo 95, Porto Alegre, RS, Brazil.

SCHERMERS, Henry G., LL.D; Netherlands professor of law; b. 27 Sept. 1928, Epe; s. of Petrus Schermers and Amelia M. Schermers Gooszen; m. Hotsche A.C. Tans 1957; one s. two d.; mil. service 1948-50; Int. Org. Dept., Ministry of Foreign Affairs 1953-56, Office of Legal Adviser 1956-63; Prof. of Law, Univ. of Amsterdam 1963-78, Univ. of Leiden 1978-; Dir. Int. Course in European Integration 1965-81; Pres. Acad. Council Asser Inst., The Hague 1977-; Ed. Common Market Law Review 1978-; Visiting Prof. Univ. of Mich. 1968-69, Queen Mary Coll., London 1988; Dean Leiden Law School 1985-87; mem. European Comm. of Human Rights; Officer, Crown of Belgium. *Publications:* International Institutional Law 1972, Judicial Protection in the European Communities 1976. *Leisure interests:* sports, youth, carpentry. *Address:* Hugo de Grootstraat 27, Leiden (Office); Herengracht 15, 2312 LA, Leiden, Netherlands (Home). *Telephone:* 071-149641 (Office); 071-124294 (Home).

SCHERRER-BYLUND, Paul, PH.D.; Swiss librarian and writer; b. 18 Aug. 1900, St. Gallen; s. of Gustav Hermann Scherrer and Sophie Gehrig; m. 1st Tamara Wintsch 1929, 2nd Barbro Bylund 1963; two s. one d.; ed. Univs. of Munich, Berlin and Glasgow; Asst. Librarian Univ. Library of Basel 1928-31, Librarian 1931-47; Chief Librarian, Library of Swiss Fed. Inst. of Technology, Zürich 1947-52, Dir. 1953-62; Dir. Cen. Library Zürich Univ. 1963-71; fmr. Vice-Pres. Swiss Asscn. of Librarians and fmr. Pres. Swiss Soc. of Bibliophiles; fmr. Pres. Gottfried-Keller-Gesellschaft; Hon. mem. Int. Asscn. Bibliophily, Swiss Soc. of Bibliophiles, Naturforschende Gesellschaft, Zürich; Award of Kulturförderungskommission, Zurich 1973. *Publications include:* Thomas Murners Verhältnis zum Humanismus, untersucht auf Grund seiner "Reformatio poetarum" 1929, Zwei neue Schriften Thomas Murners 1929, Zum Kampfmotiv bei Thomas Murner 1935, Erasmus im Spiegel von Thomas Murners Reformationspublizistik 1936, Die Toten in der deutschen Lyrik zweier Weltkriege 1944, Sub aeternitatis specie 1953, Vom Werden und von den Aufgaben der Bibliotheken technischer Hochschulen 1955, Die Gründung der Eidg. Polytechnicums und das schweizerische Nationalbewusstsein 1955, Bibliotheken und Bibliothekare als Träger kultureller Aufgaben 1956, Epigonen-Angst 1957, Vornehmheit, Illusion und Wirklichkeit als Grundmotive des "Felix Krull" 1958, Bruchstücke der Buddenbrooks-Urhandschrift 1958, Die Bibliothek des deutschen Patentamtes und die kulturellen Aufgaben technischer Bibliotheken 1959, Aus Thomas Manns Vorarbeiten zu den Buddenbrooks 1959, Thomas Manns Mutter liefert Rezepte für die Buddenbrooks 1959, Thomas Mann und die Wirklichkeit 1960, Ueber den Sinn des Thomas Mann Archivs 1961, Von der Macht und der Sendung des Buchdrucks 1961, Die Zeit im bibliothekarischen Beruf 1965, Die Stellung des Bibliothekars in der modernen Gesellschaft 1967, Schweizerische Gesichtspunkte zum Problem der Universalbibliothek 1967, Tradition und Technik in den Bibliotheken 1968, Gottfried Keller "Wildling des Glaubens" 1969, Gottfried Keller und die Buchillustration 1972. *Leisure interest:* collecting books. *Address:* Beckhammer 32, CH Zürich 8057, Switzerland (Home). *Telephone:* 01-3622710.

SCHEUCH, Erwin K., DR.RER.POL.; German sociologist; b. 9 June 1928, Cologne; s. of Otto Wilhelm Scheuch and Cecilie Bauschert; m. Ute Pulm 1985; two s.; ed. Univ. of Conn., U.S.A., Univs. of Frankfurt and Cologne; Research Asst. UNESCO Inst. for Social Research, Cologne 1951-53, Inst. for Social Research, Univ. of Cologne 1953-58; Instructor Univ. of Cologne 1961; Lecturer in Social Relations, Harvard Univ. 1962-64; Prof. of Sociology, Univ. of Cologne 1965-; Visiting Prof. of Sociology, Berlin 1965, Inst. for Advanced Studies, Princeton 1973-74, Auckland Univ. 1977, Univ. of Penn. 1975, Stockholm Univ. 1979, Paris 1981; Dir. Cen. Archive for Empirical Social Research 1964-, Inst. of Applied Social Research 1965-; Rockefeller Foundation Fellow, Columbia Univ., Univ. of Mich., Univ of Calif., Berkeley, Univ. of Chicago 1959-60; Bundesverdienstkreuz. *Publications:* Soziologie der Wahl 1965, Wiedertäufer der Wohlstandsgesellschaft 1969, Die alte Rechte und die Neue Linke 1970, Hasch und LSD als Modedronge 1973, Grundbegriffe der Soziologie (2nd edn.) 1975, Kulturintelligenz als Machtfaktor 1976, Wird die Bundesrepublik unregierbar? 1976, Das Forschungsinstitut 1978, Historical Social Research 1979, Datenzugang und Datenschutz 1981, Gesundheitspolitik zwischen Staat und Selbstver-

waltung 1982, Empirische Sozialforschung in der modernen Gesellschaft 1983, Zwischen Wohlstand und Bankrott 1984, (with Ute Scheuch) China und Indien 1987, Die nervöse Gesellschaft 1989. *Leisure interest:* tennis. *Address:* Apt. 4111, Uni Center, 5000 Cologne 41, Federal Republic of Germany (Home). *Telephone:* (0221) 427934 (Home).

SCHEVILL, James, B.S.; American professor of English, poet and playwright; b. 10 June 1920, Berkeley, Calif.; s. of Rudolph Schevill and Margaret Erwin Schevill; m. 1st Helen Shaner 1942; two d.; m. 2nd Margot Blum 1966; ed. Harvard and Brown Univs.; with U.S. Army 1942-46, rank of Capt.; teacher, Calif. Coll. of Arts and Crafts 1951-58, Pres. of Faculty Ass. 1956; San Francisco State Univ. 1959-68, Prof. of English 1968; Prof. of English, Brown Univ. 1968-; Pres. Rhode Island Playwrights' Theatre 1984; Co-Dir., Dir. Creative Writing Program, Brown Univ. 1972-75; Dir. The Poetry Centre, San Francisco State Univ. 1961-68, Prof. of English 1968-; mem. Bd. Trinity Square Repertory Co., Providence, Rhode Island 1975-; Hon. M.A. (Browns) 1970; Hon. L.H.D. (Rhode Island Coll.) 1986; numerous awards including Ford Foundation grant in theatre to work with Joan Littlewood's Theatre Workshop in London 1960-61, William Carlos Williams Award for The Stalingrad Elegies 1965, Guggenheim Fellowship in Poetry 1981, McKnight Fellowship in Playwriting 1984. *Publications: poetry:* Tensions 1947, The American Fantasies 1951, The Right To Greet 1955, Selected Poems 1945-59 1959, Private Dooms and Public Destinations: Poems 1945-62 1962, The Stalingrad Elegies 1964, Release 1968, Violence and Glory: Poems 1962-68 1969, The Buddhist Car and Other Characters 1973, Pursuing Elegy 1974, The Mayan Poems 1978, Fire of Eyes: A Guatemalan Sequence 1979, The American Fantasies: Collected Poems 1945-81 1983, Performance Poems 1984, The Invisible Volcano 1985, Collected Poems, Vol. II, 1945-1986, Ambiguous Dancers of Fame 1987; *plays:* High Sinners, Low Angels 1953, The Bloody Tenet 1957, Voices of Mass and Capital A 1962, The Black President and Other Plays 1965, Lovecraft's Follies 1969, Cathedral of Ice 1975, Wastepaper Theatre Anthology (Co.-Ed.) 1978, Collected Short Plays 1986, Oppenheimer's Chair 1985, Time of the Hand and the Eye 1986; *other publications:* Sherwood Anderson: His Life and Work (biog.) 1951, The Roaring Market and the Silent Tomb (biog.) 1956, The Cid (trans.) 1961, Breakout: In Search of New Theatrical Environments 1973, The Arena of Ants (novel) 1976, Six Historians by Ferdinand Schevill (Ed.) 1956; numerous readings 1960-84. *Address:* 17 Keene Street, Providence, R.I. 02906, U.S.A. *Telephone:* (401) 421-7038.

SCHIAVINATO, Giuseppe, Dr.; Italian professor of mineralogy; b. 10 Dec. 1915, Padua; s. of Leopoldo and Melania Marcolin; m. Zora Rebula 1943; Asst. in Mineralogy, Univ. of Padua 1943-51; Prof. of Mineralogy, Univ. of Bari 1951-55, Pres. Faculty of Mathematical, Physical and Natural Sciences 1953-55; fmr. Prof. of Mineralogy, Inst. of Mineralogy, Petrography and Geochemistry, Università degli Studi di Milano, Pres. Faculty of Science 1960-66, Rector 1972-85; Pres. Consiglio Naz. delle Ricerche 1971-72; mem. Acad. Nazionale dei Lincei, Accad. Naz. delle Scienze and other nat. acads.; Cavaliere di Gran Croce dell'ordine della Repubblica and other decorations. *Publications:* more than 60 papers on crystallography, mineralogy and petrography. *Leisure interest:* alpinism. *Address:* c/o Academia Nazionale dei Lincei, Palazzo Corsini, Via della Lungara 10, 00165 Rome, Italy.

SCHICKEL, Richard, B.S.; American writer; b. 10 Feb. 1933, Milwaukee; s. of Edward J. Schickel and Helen (née Hendricks) Schickel; three d.; ed. Univ. of Wisconsin; St. Ed. Look Magazine 1957-60, Show Magazine 1960-63; self-employed 1963-; Film Critic Life Magazine 1965-72, Time Magazine 1973-; Consultant Rockefeller Foundation 1965; Lecturer in History of Art, Yale Univ. 1972, 1976; Guggenheim Fellow 1964; mem. Nat. Soc. of Film Critics, N.Y. Film Critics. *Publications:* The World of Carnegie Hall 1960, The Stars 1962, Movies: The History of an Art and an Institution 1964, The Gentle Knight 1964, The Disney Version 1968, The World of Goya 1968, Second Sight: Notes on Some Movies 1972, His Pictures in the Papers 1974, Harold Lloyd: The Shape of Laughter 1974, The Men Who Made the Movies 1975, The World of Tennis 1975, The Fairbanks Album 1975, Another I, Another You 1978, Singled Out 1981, Cary Grant: A Celebration 1984, D. W. Griffith: An American Life 1984, Intimate Strangers: The Culture of Celebrity 1985; Co-Ed. Film 1967-68; Producer, Dir., Writer: TV The Man Who Made the Movies 1973, Funny Business 1978, Into the Morning: Willa Cather's America 1978, The Horror Show 1979, James Cagney: That Yankee Doodle Dandy 1981; Producer, Writer: TV Life Goes to the Movies 1976, SPFX 1980. *Address:* 311 E. 83rd Street, New York, N.Y. 10028, U.S.A.

SCHIFF, Andras; Hungarian concert pianist; b. 21 Dec. 1953, Budapest; s. of Odon Schiff and Klara Schiff (Csengeri); ed. Franz Liszt Acad. of Music, Budapest, with Prof. Paul Kadosa and Ferenc Rados, and privately with George Malcolm; recitals in London, New York, Paris, Vienna, Munich, Florence; concerts with New York Philharmonic, Chicago Symphony, Vienna Philharmonic, Concertgebouw, Orchestre de Paris, London Philharmonic, London Symphony, Royal Philharmonic, Israel Philharmonic, Philadelphia, Washington Nat. Symphony; played at Salzburg, Edin., Aldeburgh and Tanglewood Festivals; exclusive recording contract with Decca; recordings include Bach Goldberg Variations, Bach Partitas, Mendelssohn Concertos 1 and 2, Schubert Trout Quintet, Schumann and Chopin 2,

Mozart concertos K456 and K453, Bach Two- and Three-part Inventions, Bach Well-Tempered Clavier, Beethoven Violin and Piano Sonatas with Sandor Vegh, Tchaikovsky Piano Concerto; Prizewinner at 1974 Tchaikovsky Competition in Moscow and Leeds Piano Competition 1974; Liszt Prize 1977. *Leisure interests:* literature, languages and soccer. *Address:* c/o Terry Harrison Artists Management, 9a Penzance Place, London, W11 4PE, England.

SCHIFF, Emile Louis Constant; Netherlands diplomatist; b. 2 March 1918; ed. Rijksuniversiteit, Leiden; Second Sec., Washington 1945-49; Second, later First Sec., Madrid 1949-52; Pvt. Sec. to Ministers of Foreign Affairs, The Hague 1952-54; Counsellor Perm. Mission to UN 1955-59; Minister, Washington 1959-64; Amb. to Indonesia 1965-68; Sec.-Gen. Ministry of Foreign Affairs 1968-77; Amb. to Australia 1977-83; Kt., Order of Netherlands Lion, Commdr., Order of Orange-Nassau and many foreign awards. *Leisure interest:* golf. *Address:* Neuhuyskade 28, 2596 XL, The Hague, Netherlands. *Telephone:* 24-74-84.

SCHIFFER, Menahem Max, PH.D.; American professor of mathematics; b. 24 Sept. 1911, Berlin, Germany; s. of Chaim and Miriam (née Alpern) Schiffer; m. Fanya Rabinovics 1937; one d.; ed. Oberrealschule, Berlin, Berlin Univ. and Hebrew Univ., Jerusalem; Jr. Asst. Hebrew Univ., Jerusalem 1934-38, Sr. Asst. 1938-43, Lecturer 1943-46; Visiting Lecturer Harvard Univ. 1946-49, Princeton Univ. 1949-50; Prof. Hebrew Univ., Jerusalem 1950-51; Prof. of Math. Stanford Univ. 1951-77; mem. N.A.S., American Acad. of Arts and Sciences; Foreign mem. Finnish Acad. of Sciences 1975; Hon. D.Sc. (Israel Inst. of Tech.) 1973. *Publications:* Coauthor: Kernel Functions in Mathematical Physics 1953, Functionals of Finite Riemann Surfaces 1954, Introduction to General Relativity 1965; numerous articles in mathematical journals. *Leisure interests:* history, philosophy, rare books, walking, travel, music. *Address:* 3748 Laguna Avenue, Palo Alto, Calif. 94306, U.S.A. *Telephone:* (415) 493-9154.

SCHILLER, Karl, DR. RER. POL.; German economist and politician; b. 24 April 1911, Breslau; m. 4th Vera Schiller; four c.; ed. Univs. of Kiel, Frankfurt am Main, Berlin and Heidelberg; Univ. Asst., Heidelberg 1934-35; Head of Research Group Inst. for World Econs., Kiel 1935-41; Army Service 1941-45; Visiting Prof. Univ. of Kiel 1945-46; Prof. of Econs., Dir. of Social Econ. Seminars and Inst. for Foreign Trade and Overseas Commerce, Univ. of Hamburg 1947-72, Rector Univ. of Hamburg 1956-58; mem. Council of Scientific Advisers Fed. Ministry of Econs. 1947-; mem. Council of Scientific Advisers Fed. Ministry of Econ. Co-operation 1963-66; Senator for Econs., Hamburg 1948-53, Berlin 1961-65; mem. Bundesrat 1949-53, 1961-65; Deputy Chair. Econ. Cttee., Exec. Cttee. of SPD 1962-64, Chair. 1964-72, mem. Exec. Cttee. SPD 1964-72, mem. Presidium 1966-72, mem. Bundestag 1965-72, Deputy Chair. and Econ. Spokesman of SPD Parl. Group 1965-66; Fed. Minister of Econs. 1966-71, of Econs. and Finance 1971-72 (resgnd.); Pres. Econ. Devt. of Equatorial and Southern Africa (EDESA) 1973-79; mem. Ford European Advisory Council 1976-; Hon. Senator Univ. of Hamburg 1983; Alexander Ruestow Plaque 1976; Ludwig Erhard Prize 1978; Buergermeister Stolten Plaque 1986; Bernhard Harms Plaque 1989. *Publications:* Aufgaben und Versuche: Zur neuen Ordnung von Wirtschaft und Gesellschaft 1953, Der Ökonom und die Gesellschaft: Das freiheitliche und soziale Element in der Wirtschaftspolitik 1964, Berliner Wirtschaft und deutsche Politik, Reden und Aufsätze 1961-1964 1964, Reden zur Wirtschafts- und Finanzpolitik 1966-1972, Aufgeklärte Marktwirtschaft-Kollektive Vernunft in Politik und Wirtschaft 1969, Betrachtungen zur Geld- und Konjunkturpolitik 1984; numerous economic and political articles. *Address:* 2112 Jesteburg, Reindorfer Strasse 84, Federal Republic of Germany.

SCHILPP, Paul Arthur, B.D., PH.D.; American (b. German) university professor, philosopher and writer; b. 6 Feb. 1897, Dillenburg, Hessen, Germany; s. of the Rev. Hermann and Emilie (Dittmar) Schilpp; m. 2nd E. Madelon Golden 1950; one s. one d.; ed. Bayreuth Gymnasium, Baldwin-Wallace Coll. (Ohio), Northwestern Univ., Garrett Theol. Seminary, Evanston, and Stanford Univ.; Prof. of Psychology and Religious Educ., Coll of Puget Sound 1922-23, Prof. of Philosophy, Coll. of the Pacific 1923-34; lecturer of Philosophy, Northwestern Univ. 1936-37, Assoc. Prof. 1937-50, Prof. 1950-65, Prof. Emer. 1965-; Distinguished Visiting Research Prof. of Philosophy Southern Ill. Univ., Carbondale 1965-80, Emer. Prof. 1980-; Visiting Prof., Ohio State Univ. 1931, Univ. of Munich 1948, Pacific Philosophy Inst. 1954; Founder, Pres. and Ed. Library of Living Philosophers; Watumull Foundation Research Fellowship for India 1950-51; Pres. American Philosophical Asscn. (Western Div.) 1958-59; Memorial Lecturer, Arizona State Univ. 1963; Hon. Litt.D. (Baldwin-Wallace Coll.); Hon. L.H.D. (Springfield Coll., Mass.) 1963, (Kent State Univ., Ohio) 1975, (Southern Ill.) 1982; Bertrand Russell Award, Bertrand Russell Soc. 1980. *Publications:* Do We Need a New Religion? 1929, Kant's Pre-Critical Ethics 1938, The Quest for Religious Realism 1938, Lamentations on Christmas 1945, Human Nature and Progress 1954, The Crisis in Science and Education 1963; Ed. and Contributor Higher Education Faces the Future 1930, Theology and Modern Life 1940, Library of Living Philosophers (17 vols. so far published) 1939-82, The Student Seeks an Answer 1960, New Frontiers of Christianity 1962, In Albert Schweitzer's Realms 1962, Religion Ponders Science 1964, The World of Philosophy (Pakistan) 1966, The Critique of War 1969, Value and Valuation 1972; Ed. Albert

Einstein: Autobiographical Notes 1979. *Leisure interests:* chess, travel, music. *Address:* Department of Philosophy, Southern Illinois University, Carbondale, Ill. 62901, U.S.A.; and 9 Hillcrest Drive, Carbondale Ill. *Telephone:* (618) 536-6641 (Office); (618) 549-6335 (Home).

SCHILTZ, Hugo, D. EN D.; Belgian politician; b. 28 Oct. 1927, Borsbeek; lawyer at Antwerp Bar 1953-; Deputy in House of Reps., 1965-; Vice-Pres. Volksunie (VU) 1981-; Minister of Finance and of the Budget 1981-85; Deputy Prime Minister and Minister of the Budget and of Scientific Policy 1988-. *Address:* Ministry of the Budget, 26 rue de la Loi, 1040 Brussels, Belgium. *Telephone:* (02) 230-15-80.

SCHILY, Otto; German lawyer and politician; b. 20 July 1932, Bochum; s. of Frans Schily; two c.; ed. Munich, Hamburg and Berlin Univs.; mem. Bundestag 1983-86, 1987-; mem. Presidium Neue Gesellschaft für bildende Kunst; Adviser, Humanist Union. *Address:* Bundeshaus, 5300 Bonn 1, Federal Republic of Germany. *Telephone:* 0228-161.

SCHIMBERNI, Mario, B.ECON.; Italian industrial executive; b. 10 March 1923, Rome; s. of Tommaso Schimberni and Lina Ludovici; m. Angela Peppicelli; ed. Rome Univ.; lecturer in Industrial and Commercial Techniques, Rome Univ. 1946-54; various admin., financial and managerial posts with Bomprini Parodi Delfino 1954-64, Gen. Man. 1964-70, SNIA Viscosa 1970-72, Man. Dir. 1972-75; Pres. Montefibre 1975-77; Deputy Chair. Montedison (now Montecatini Edison) 1977-80, Chair. 1980-87; Chair. CEFIC 1982-, Montedison Int. Holding Co. 1978-88, Erbamont N.V. 1983-; Deputy Chair. Hirmont Inc. 1983; Special Commr. Nat. Railway Authority 1988-. *Address:* Foro Buonaparte 31, Milan, Italy. *Telephone:* (02) 63331-5210.

SCHINDEL, Ulrich, DR. PHIL.; German professor of classical philology; b. 10 Sept. 1935, Frankfurt/M.; s. of Ernst Schindel and Erika Vogt; m. Mette Lietzmann 1963; two s. one d.; ed. Univs. of Göttingen, Munich and Hamburg; univ. teacher in Greek, Göttingen 1962-71, lecturer in Classical Philology 1971, Dozent 1971-74, Asst. Prof. 1974-77, Prof. 1977-; mem. Akad. der Wissenschaften Göttingen 1977. *Publications:* Demosthenes im 18 Jh. 1963, Die latein. Figurenlehren des 5.-7. Jahres 1975, Aeschinis Orationes 1978, Der Mordfall Herodes 1980, Demosthenes, Wege der Forschung, (ed.) 1987, Anonymus Ecksteinii, (ed.) 1987. *Address:* Seminar für Klassische Philologie der Universität Göttingen, Platz der Göttinger Sieben 5, Göttingen (Office); Albert-Schweitzerstrasse 3, 34 Göttingen, Federal Republic of Germany (Home). *Telephone:* 0511 394692 (Office); 0511 24530 (Home).

SCHINDLER, Alexander Moshe; American Rabbi; b. 4 Oct. 1925, Munich, Germany; s. of Eliezer Schindler and Sali Hoyda; m. Rhea Rosenblum 1956; two s. three d.; ed. Coll. of City of New York, Hebrew Union Coll.; Asst. Rabbi, Temple Emmanuel, Worcester, Mass. 1953-56, Assoc. Rabbi 1956-59; Dir. New England Council, Union of American Hebrew Congregations 1959-63, Nat. Dir. of Educ. 1963-67, Vice-Pres. 1967-72, Pres. 1973-; mem. Exec. Bd. Conf. of Pres. of Maj. Jewish American Orgs. 1967-, Chair. 1976-78; mem. Exec. Bd. Hebrew Union Coll., Jewish Inst. of Religion 1967-; mem. Exec. Bd. Memorial Foundation of Jewish Culture 1967-; Vice-Pres. World Jewish Congress; mem. Exec. Cttee. American Section, World Zionist Org. 1973-; Vice-Pres. World Union for Progressive Judaism; founding bd. Dimensions; Townsend Harris Medal, Coll. of City of New York 1979; Hon. D.D.; Bronze Star, Purple Heart. *Publication:* From Discrimination to Extermination 1950. *Address:* 838 Fifth Avenue, New York, N.Y. 10021, U.S.A.

SCHIRMBECK, Heinrich; German author, cultural and natural philosopher; b. 23 Feb. 1915, Recklinghausen; s. of Heinrich Schirmbeck and Elise Graebe; m. 1st Ursula Possekel 1940 (divorced), 2nd Evelyne Rossberg 1966 (divorced); three s. two d.; ed. Recklinghausen Gymnasium; former bookseller and later newspaper ed., free-lance radio contrib. 1950-; mem. Deutsche Akad. für Sprache und Dichtung, Darmstadt, Akad. der Wissenschaften und der Literatur, Mainz (Literaturpreis 1950); mem. German PEN centre; Förderpreis zum Immermann-Preis der Stadt Düsseldorf 1962. *Publications include:* Ärgert Dich Dein Rechtes Auge 1957, Der Junge Leutnant Nikolai 1958, Bausteine zu einer Poetik im Atomzeitalter 1964, Ihr werdet sein wie Götter 1966, Die Pirouette des Elektrons 1980, Für eine Welt der Hoffnung 1988 and many other novels, novellas, short stories, essays etc. *Leisure interests:* classical music, literature, philosophy, ecology, wandering. *Address:* Park Rosenhöhe 13, 6100 Darmstadt, Federal Republic of Germany. *Telephone:* 06151/712583.

SCHIRMER, Hans Heinrich Theodor, DR.PHIL.; German diplomatist; b. 9 Jan. 1911, Berlin; s. of Lt.-Gen. Hermann and Henrietta (née Hansen) Schirmer; m. Gabrielle Archard 1951; one s. one d.; ed. Univ. of Heidelberg; Foreign Service, Berlin 1939-43; mil. service and prisoner-of-war 1943-46; Head, Foreign Affairs Div., Press and Information Office of German Fed. Govt. 1950-55; Counsellor Cairo 1955-60; Consul-Gen. Hong Kong 1961-62; Asst. Sec. Press and Information Office 1966-68; Amb. to Australia 1968-70, to Austria 1970-74; Rep. of Fed. Repub. of Germany in European-Arab Dialogue; Grosses Bundesverdienstkreuz. *Leisure interests:* history, ornithology, swimming. *Address:* Auswärtiges Amt, 5300 Bonn 1, Adenaueralle 120, Federal Republic of Germany.

SCHIRNER, Jochen; German business executive; b. 27 Feb. 1939; s. of Karl Schirner and Inge Schirner; m. Marietheres Schirner 1962; two s. one d.; joined Rheinische Blattmetall AG (now VAW-Leichtmetall GmbH) 1963–, Head Business Man. Dept. 1969, Dir. 1974, Chair. Bd. of Dirs. Jan. 1986–. *Address:* Vereinigte Aluminium-Werke AG, Georg-von-Boeselager Strasse 25, 5300 Bonn 1, Federal Republic of Germany. *Telephone:* 0228 552-02.

SCHLAG, Edward William, PH.D.; American professor of physical chemistry; b. 12 Jan. 1932, Los Angeles; s. of Hermann Schlag and Hilda Nolte; m. Angela Gräfin zu Castell-Castell 1955; one s. two d.; ed. Occidental Coll. and Univ. of Washington; post-doctoral research, Univ. of Bonn 1958; research scientist, film dept. E.I. du Pont de Nemours, Buffalo 1959; tech. adviser, Buffalo 1960–62; Asst. Prof. of Chemistry, Northwestern Univ. 1960–64, Assoc. Prof. 1964–69, Prof. 1969–71; Prof. of Physical Chem. Tech. Univ. Munich 1971–, Dean, Faculty of Chem. 1982–84; mem. numerous cttees.; Fellow, American Physical Soc., Deutsche Bunsengesellschaft; mem. Bayrische Akad. der Wissenschaften; Alfred P. Sloan Fellow 1965; Hon. D.Phil. (Hebrew Univ. of Jerusalem) 1988. *Address:* Institut für Physikalische und Theoretische Chemie, Technische Universität München, Lichtenbergstrasse 4, 8046 Garching bei München (Office); Osterwaldstrasse 91, 8000 Munich 40, Federal Republic of Germany (Home).

SCHLEBUSCH, Alwyn Louis, B.A., LL.B.; South African politician; b. 16 Sept. 1917, Lady Grey, Cape Prov.; m. Isabella E. Krause 1942; two s. two d.; ed. Kroonstad, Univ. of Stellenbosch, Univ. of Pretoria; fmr. Attorney and later Mayor, Henneman 1948–49, 1951–52; Farmer 1953–; mem. Prov. Council, Orange Free State 1958–62; M.P. for Kroonstad 1962–80; Deputy Speaker House of Assembly 1974, Speaker 1974–76; Leader Nat. Party, Orange Free State 1977–80; Minister of Public Works and Immigration 1976–78, and of the Interior 1978–79, of Justice and the Interior 1979–80, in charge of Comm. for Admin. 1979–80; Vice-Pres. of South Africa 1980–84; Chair. (ex officio) Pres.'s Council 1980–86; Minister in Office of the Pres. in charge of the Comm. for Admin. and the S.A. Broadcasting Corpn. 1986–88; fmr. Chair. Prime Minister's Comm. of Enquiry into Certain Orgs. *Address:* c/o Office of the State President, Pretoria, South Africa.

SCHLEIMINGER, Günther, D.ECON.; German international finance official; b. 26 April 1921, Magdeburg; s. of Max Schleiminger and Ilse Kessler; m. Ingrid Bettlewski; two c.; ed. Univs. of Königsberg (now Kaliningrad, U.S.S.R.), Berlin and Kiel; war service 1940–45; German Fed. Ministry for the Marshall Plan 1950–52; Fed. German Del. to Org. for European Econ. Co-operation (OEEC), Paris, and Chair. Alt. mems. of European Payments Union (EPU) Man. Bd. 1952–58; Deputy Head Dept. of Int. Orgs., Deutsche Bundesbank, Fed. Repub. of Germany 1958–68; Alt. mem. Monetary Cttee. EEC 1958–65; German mem. EMA Bd. of Man. 1960–68; Sec. to Group of Ten 1963–64; Exec. Dir. IMF for Fed. Repub. of Germany 1968–74; Sec.-Gen. B.I.S., Basle 1975–77, Asst. Gen. Man. 1978–81, Gen. Man. 1981–85. *Address:* Arbedostrasse 24, CH 4059, Basle, Switzerland.

SCHLENKER, Rudolf; German tobacco executive; b. 18 June 1915, Dortmund; m. Liselotte Riesenberg 1944; two s. one d.; ed. business management studies, Cologne; Adviser Prov. Economy Office, Württemberg Baden and in Prov. Parl. after Second World War, later in Econ. Admin. Office, Frankfurt; in Fed. Ministry of Economy, Bonn 1949–51, in Washington, D.C. 1951–53; mem. Man. Bd. H. F. and Ph. F. Reemtsma 1953–75, Spokesman of Man. Bd. 1958, Chair. Man. Bd. 1962–75; fmr. Chair. Cigarette Industry Asscn.; Chair. Int. Bureau of Chambers of Commerce 1980–; Chair. Hamburger Sparkasse 1983–; Pres. Hamburg Chamber of Commerce 1975–81, Vice-Pres. 1981–; Vice-Pres. Deutscher Industrie- und Handelstag 1976–; mem. Advisory Bd. Deutsche Bank A.G., Badische Anilin & Sodafabrik A.G., Hapag-Lloyd A.G., Nord-Deutsche und Hamburg-Bremer Versicherungs-AG; mem. Advisory Council Aachener und Münchener Feuer-Versicherung AG, Gerling-Konzern, Henkel GmbH, Hermes Kreditversicherungs AG. *Address:* Parkstrasse 51, 2000 Hamburg 52, Federal Republic of Germany.

SCHLESINGER, Arthur, Jr., A.B.; American writer and educator; b. 15 Oct. 1917, Columbus, Ohio; s. of the late Arthur Meier and Elizabeth Bancroft Schlesinger; m. 1st Marian Cannon 1940 (divorced 1970), two s. two d.; m. 2nd Alexandra Emmet 1971, one s.; ed. Phillips Exeter Acad., Harvard Univ. and Peterhouse, Cambridge, England; Soc. of Fellows Harvard 1939–42; with Office of War Information 1942–43; Office of Strategic Services 1943–45; U.S. Army 1945; Assoc. Prof. of History, Harvard Univ. 1946–54, Prof. 1954–61; Special Asst. to Pres. of U.S.A. 1961–64; Schweitzer Prof. of the Humanities, City Univ. of New York 1966–; Consultant, Econ. Co-operation Admin. 1948, Mutual Security Admin. 1951–52; mem. Adlai Stevenson campaign staff 1952 and 1956; mem. American Historical Asscn., American Inst. of Arts and Letters (Pres. 1981–84, Chancellor 1984–87), Jury Cannes Film Festival 1964, Bd. of Dirs. John F. Kennedy Library, Harry S. Truman Library Inst., American Civil Liberties Union etc.; Hon. Litt.D. (Muhlenberg) 1950, (Aquinas Coll.) 1971; Hon. D.C.L. (New Brunswick) 1960; Hon. L.H.D. (Tusculum Coll.) 1966, (Rhode Island Coll.) 1969, (Oxford) 1987, (Akron) 1987; Hon. LL.D. (Bethany) 1956, (New School for Social Research) 1966, (Western New England Coll.) 1974, (Ripon Coll.) 1976, (Iona Coll.) 1977, (Utah State) 1978, (Louisville) 1978, (Northeastern Univ.) 1981, (State Univ. of New York) 1984, (New Hampshire) 1985; Parkman Prize 1957, Pulitzer Prize for History 1946, for Biography 1966; Nat. Book Award 1966, Gold Medal, Nat. Inst. of Arts and Letters 1967, Fregene Prize for Literature 1983. *Publications:* Orestes A. Brownson: A Pilgrim's Progress 1939, The Age of Jackson 1945, The Vital Center (English title The Politics of Freedom) 1949, The General and the President (with R. H. Rovere) 1951, The Age of Roosevelt: Vol. I The Crisis of the Old Order 1957, Vol. II The Coming of the New Deal 1958, Vol. III The Politics of Upheaval 1960, Kennedy or Nixon 1960, The Politics of Hope 1963, Paths of American Thought (ed. with Morton White) 1963, A Thousand Days: John F. Kennedy in the White House, 1965, The Bitter Heritage: Vietnam and American Democracy 1941–1966 1967, The Crisis of Confidence 1969, History of American Presidential Elections (ed. with F. L. Israel) 1971, The Imperial Presidency 1973, Robert Kennedy and His Times 1978, Cycles of American History 1986; articles in various magazines and newspapers. *Leisure interests:* tennis, movies. *Address:* City University of New York, 33 West 42nd Street, New York, N.Y. 10036, U.S.A. (Office). *Telephone:* (216) 642-2060.

SCHLESINGER, Helmut, DR.OEC.; German banker; b. 4 Sept. 1924, Penzberg; s. of Franz Schlesinger and Maria Schlesinger; m. Carola Mager; one s. three d.; ed. Univ. of Munich; Ifo Inst. for Econ. Research, Munich 1949–52; joined Deutsche Bundesbank 1952, Head, Research and Statistics Dept. 1964, mem. Directorate and Cen. Bank Council 1972, Deputy Gov. 1980–; mem. Supervisory Bd. DG-Bank, Frankfurt; Hon. Prof. Hochschule für Verwaltungswissenschaften, Speyer; Ludwig Erhard Prize for econ. journalism; Dr. h.c. (Frankfurt, Göttingen). *Publications:* numerous professional publs. *Leisure interests:* mountaineering, skiing. *Address:* Deutsche Bundesbank, Wilhelm-Epstein-Strasse 14, P.O.B. 10 06 02, 6000 Frankfurt am Main, Federal Republic of Germany. *Telephone:* (069) 158 2114.

SCHLESINGER, James Rodney, PH.D.; American economist and government official; b. 15 Feb. 1929, New York, N.Y.; s. of Julius and Rhea (Rogen) Schlesinger; m. Rachel Mellinger 1954; four s. four d.; ed. Harvard Univ.; Asst. and Assoc. Prof., Univ. of Va. 1955–63; Sr. Staff mem. RAND Corpn. 1963–67, Dir. Strategic Studies 1967–69; Asst. Dir., Office of Man. and Budget 1969–71; Chair. U.S. Atomic Energy Comm. 1971–73; Dir. Cen. Intelligence Agency Feb.-May 1973; Sec. of Defence 1973–75; Special Asst. to Pres. for Energy Jan.-Aug. 1977; U.S. Sec. for Energy 1977–79; Sr. Adviser Shearson Lehman Brothers Inc. 1979–, Center for Strategic and Int. Studies 1979–; Distinguished Service Medal from U.S. Intelligence Community 1976, Nat. Security Award 1979. *Address:* 1800 K Street, N.W., Suite 400, Washington, D.C. 20006, U.S.A. *Telephone:* 833-8587.

SCHLESINGER, John Richard, C.B.E.; British film and theatre director; b. 16 Feb. 1926, London; s. of Dr. Bernard Schlesinger, O.B.E., F.R.C.P.; and Winifred Henrietta Regensburg; ed. Uppingham School and Balliol Coll. Oxford; early career as actor on television and in films Singlehanded, Battle of the River Plate, Brothers in Law and numerous others; directed shorts for Tonight and Monitor; made films for BBC Television including part of The Valiant Years; joined Sapphire Films for Four Just Men; Assoc. Dir. Nat. Theatre 1973–88; Shakespeare Prize (FVS Found., Hamburg) 1981. *Major films:* Terminus 1961 (Venice Golden Lion), A Kind of Loving 1962 (Berlin Golden Bear), Billy Liar 1963, Darling 1965 (New York Film Critics' Award), Far From the Madding Crowd 1967, Midnight Cowboy 1968 (Dirs. Guild of America Award, Acad. Award for best Dir. and British Film Acad. Award), Sunday Bloody Sunday 1970 (David Donatello Award, British Film Acad. Award), Olympic Marathon in Visions of Eight 1973, The Day of the Locust 1974, Marathon Man 1976, Yanks 1978, Honky Tonk Freeway 1980, The Falcon and the Snowman 1985, The Believers 1986, Madame Sousatzka 1988. *Plays:* No Why (John Whiting), Aldwych Theatre 1964, Timon of Athens, Royal Shakespeare Theatre, Stratford 1965, Days in the Trees, Aldwych 1966, I and Albert, Piccadilly Theatre 1972, Heartbreak House, Nat. Theatre 1975, Julius Caesar, Nat. Theatre 1977, True West, Nat. Theatre 1980, Separate Tables (for TV) 1982, An Englishman Abroad (BBC) 1983 (British Acad. Award, Barcelona Film Festival and Broadcasting Press Guild Award). *Operas directed:* Les Contes d'Hoffmann, Royal Opera House, Covent Garden (Soc. of West End Theatres Award 1980), Der Rosenkavalier, Covent Garden 1984. *Leisure interests:* gardening, travel, music, antiques. *Address:* c/o Duncan Heath, 162 Wardour Street, London, W.1; 10 Victoria Road, London, W8 5RD, England. *Telephone:* 01-937 3983 (Home).

SCHLIEPHAKE, Prof. Dietrich, DR.RER.NAT.; German chemist and business executive; b. 18 April 1930; ed. Tech. Univ. Braunschweig, Tech. Hochschule Hannover; Man. Scholven-Chemie AG, Gelsenkirchen-Buer 1957–59; Head Dept., Inst. für Landwirtschaftliche Tech., Tech. Univ. Braunschweig 1959–64, lecturer 1964–70, made Prof. of Chemical Tech. 1970; Asst. to Bd. of Dirs., Scholven-Chemie AG 1964–67, Head of Production Plant 1967, mem. Bd. VEBA-CHEMIE AG (fmrly. Scholven-Chemie AG) 1971–77; Chair. Man. Bd. Dynamit Nobel AG 1977–82. *Address:* c/o Dynamit Nobel AG, 521 Troisdorf, Postfach 1209, Federal Republic of Germany.

SCHLÖNDORFF, Volker; German film director; b. 1939, Wiesbaden; m. Margarethe von Trotta; has directed numerous cinema and television films; mem. German PEN Centre; Prize of the Int. Film Critics, Cannes 1966. *Films include:* Der junge Törless, Mord und Totschlag, Michael Kohlhaas, Der plötzliche Reichtum der armen Leute von Kombach, Baal, Die Moral der Ruth Halbfass, Strohfeuer, Die Ehegattin, Übernachtung in Tirol, Die verlorene Ehre der Katharina Blum, Die Blechtrommel (The Tin Drum) (Golden Palm of Cannes) 1979, Die Fälschung 1981, Circle of Deceit 1982, Eine Liebe von Swann (Swann in Love) 1984, Death of a Salesman 1985, The Handmaid's Tale 1989. *Address:* Obermaierstrasse 1, 8000 Munich 22, Federal Republic of Germany.

SCHLUMPF, Leon; Swiss politician; b. 3 Feb. 1925, Felsberg, Canton Grisons; m. Trudi Rupp; three d.; ed. Univ. of Zürich; private practice as lawyer and notary, Chur 1951-65; mem. Grisons Cantonal Parl. 1955-74, Pres. 1964-65, Head, Cantonal Dept. of Interior and Public Econ. 1966-74; mem. Nat. Council 1966-74; mem. Council of States 1974-; Controller of Prices, Swiss Confed. 1974-78; mem. Fed. Council 1979-87; Head of Fed. Dept. of Transport, Communications and Energy 1979-87; Pres. of Switzerland Jan.-Dec. 1984; Swiss People's Party. *Address:* c/o Department of Transport, Communications and Energy, Berne, Switzerland.

SCHLÜTER, Poul Holmskov, LL.B.; Danish lawyer and politician; b. 3 April 1929, Tønder; s. of Johannes Schlüter; m. Lisbeth Schlüter 1979 (died 1988); two s. one d.; ed. Univs. of Aarhus and Copenhagen; barrister and Supreme Court Attorney; Leader of Conservative Youth Movement (KU) 1944, nat. leader 1951; del. to Int. Congress of World Assen. of Youth 1951, 1954; Chair. Young Conservatives, mem. Exec. Cttee. Conservative Party 1952-55, 1971, Nat. Chair. Jr. Chamber 1961, Vice-Pres. Jr. Chamber Int. 1962; mem. Folketing (Parl.) 1964-; Chair. Jt. Danish Consultative Council on UN 1966-68; M.P. Foreign Affairs Cttee. 1968, Chair. 1982-; mem. Council of Europe 1971-74; Chair. Conservative Party 1974-; Chair. Danish del. to Nordic Council and mem. presiding cttee. 1978-79; Prime Minister of Denmark Sept. 1982-. *Address:* Prime Minister's Office, Christiansborg, Prins Jørgens Gaard 11, 1218 Copenhagen K, Denmark. *Telephone:* 01 923300.

SCHMALENBACH, Werner, DR.PHIL.; German art museum director; b. 13 Sept. 1920, Göttingen; s. of Dr. Herman Schmalenbach and Sala (née Müntz); m. Esther Grey; two d.; ed. Basle Grammar School and Univ. of Basle; organiser of exhbns., Gewerbemuseum, Basle 1945-55; Dir. Kestner Gesellschaft, Hannover 1955-62; mem. working cttee., "Documenta II", Kassel 1959, 1964, 1968; German Commr., Venice Biennale 1960, São Paulo Biennale 1961, 1963, 1965; Dir. Kunstsammlung Nordrhein-Westfalen, Düsseldorf (Museum of Modern Art) 1962-; Grosses Bundesverdienstkreuz; Officer, Nat. Order of Southern Cross (Brazil). *Publications:* Der Film 1947, Die Kunst Afrikas 1956, Julius Bissier 1963, Kurt Schwitters 1967, Antoni Tàpies 1974, Fernand Léger 1976, Eduardo Chillida 1977, Marc Chagall 1979, Emil Schumacher 1981, Joan Miró 1982, Paul Klee 1986, African Art from the Barbier-Mueller Collection (ed.) 1989. *Address:* Poststrasse 17, 4005 Meerbusch 1, Federal Republic of Germany. *Telephone:* (02105) 3801.

SCHMAUS, Michael, DR. THEOL.; German theologian and university professor; b. 17 July 1897, Oberbaar, Bavaria; s. of Georg Schmaus and Rosina (née Pfundmair) Schmaus; ed. Gymnasium Rosenheim and Univ. Munich; ordained 1922; Lecturer Philosophische-theologische Hochschule und Seminar, Freising 1924-29; lecturer Munich Univ. 1928-29; Prof. of Dogmatic Theology, German Univ. in Prague 1929-33; f. Grabmann Institut zur Erforschung der mittelalterlichen Philosophie und Theologie 1954; Prof. Univ. Münster 1933-45, Munich 1946-65, Emer. 1965-; Visiting Prof. Chicago 1969-70; Rector Munich Univ. 1951-52; Peritus of Second Vatican Council 1960-65; Supernumerary Pronotary Apostle 1984; mem. Bavarian Acad. of Sciences; Günther Kunze Prize 1983, Commdr. of Greek Order of Phoenix, Commdr. Spanish Order of Civil Merit, Bayerischer Verdienststorden, Bayerische Maximiliansorden für Wissenschaft und Kunst 1984; Grosses Bundesverdienstkreuz, Päpstlicher Ehrenprälat; Erzbischöflicher Geistlicher Rat. *Publications include:* Die psychologische Trinitätslehre des Heiligen Augustinus 1927, Der Liber propugnatorius des Thomas Anglicus und die Lehrunterschiede zwischen Thomas von Aquin und Duns Scotus 1930, Katholische Dogmatik, 8 Vols. 1938-64, Von den letzten Dingen 1948, Handbuch der Katholischen Dogmatik 1969-70, Die Denkform Augustins in seinem Werk "De Trinitate" 1962, Wahrheit als Heilsbegegnung 1964, articles, translations and several series. *Address:* Junkerstrasse 5, 8035 Gauting bei München, Federal Republic of Germany. *Telephone:* Munich 850 2800.

SCHMELCK, Robert Marie Jean-Pierre, LIC. EN DROIT, D.E.S.; French lawyer; b. 25 Aug. 1915, Sarreguemines; s. of Pierre Schmelck and Anne (née Nicklaus); m. Thérèse Rodel 1942; two s. three d.; ed. Univs. of Strasbourg and Paris; trainee lawyer at Sarreguemines 1936-43; Judge at Beauvais 1943-44; del. to Minister of Justice 1944-45; Deputy Dir., then Dir. of Justice, French High Comm. in Germany 1945-55; Commr., Dept. of Keeper of Seals, Ministry of Justice 1955-58; Deputy Prosecutor, Court of the Seine, Adviser, Ministry of Justice 1959-60; Attorney-Gen., Algiers 1960-61; Prisons Dir. Ministry of Justice 1961-64; Advocate, Cour de Cassation (highest French Appeal Court) 1964-75; Dir. Dept. of Keeper of Seals, Ministry of Justice 1974-76; Leading Advocate, Cour de Cassation 1975-77; Attorney-Gen. Cour de Cassation 1978-80; Pres. Cour de Cassation 1980-83; retd. 1984; now French Judge, Supreme Court of Restitutions, Munich 1964-; mem. Perm. Court of Arbitration, The Hague 1981-; int. arbitrator; Pres. Perm. Govt. Comm. on Public Records and Legal History, Asscn. for Prevention of Audiovisual Piracy (ALPA); mem. Nat.

Council of Hunting and Wildlife Preservation; Grand Officier, Légion d'honneur, Grand Officier de l'Ordre nat. du mérite, and decorations from Fed. Repub. of Germany, Italy, Belgium, Luxembourg. *Publications:* Penologie et droit penitentiaire 1967, Revue de science criminelle et droit penal comparé, and numerous articles on legal questions. *Leisure interests:* shooting, tennis. *Address:* 12 rue Chauveau, 92200 Neuilly, France. *Telephone:* 1-46.37.23.34.

SCHMELZER, W. K. Norbert; Netherlands politician; b. 22 March 1921, Rotterdam; s. of Wilhelm Jakob and Maria Helena Schmelzer; m. Daphne Mary van Nieuwenhuizen 1980; two s. one d.; ed. Catholic Univ., Tilburg; with Unilever N.V., Rotterdam 1947-50; Ministry of Econ. Affairs 1950-56; State Sec. for Home Affairs 1958-59, for Gen. Affairs 1959-63; mem. Second Chamber of Parl. 1963-71; Minister of Foreign Affairs 1971-73; Industrial Adviser 1973-; Chair. European Inst. of Public Admin. 1984-; Vice-Chair. Governmental Council Peace and Security 1985-; Grand Officer Order of Orange-Nassau; Commdr. Order of Netherlands Lion; Grand Cross Ordre du Mérite de la France and others; Hon. G.C.M.G.; Christian Democratic Appeal (C.D.A.). *Leisure interests:* music, literature, sport. *Address:* Park Oud-Wassenaar 40, 2243 BX Wassenaar, Netherlands. *Telephone:* (01751) 78698.

SCHMID, Rudi, PH.D., M.D.; American (b. Swiss) professor of medicine; b. 2 May 1922, Glarus, Switzerland; s. of Rudolf Schmid and Bertha Schiesser; m. Sonja D. Wild 1949; one s. one d.; ed. gymnasium, Zurich, Univ. of Zurich, Univ. of Minnesota; intern in internal medicine Univ. of Calif., San Francisco 1948-49, Prof. of Medicine and Chief Gastroenterology Unit and Dir. of Liver Center 1966-83, Dean School of Medicine 1983-; Resident Internal Medicine, Univ. of Minn. 1949-52, Instructor in Medicine 1952-54; Resident Fellow in Biochem. Columbia Univ. Coll. of Physicians and Surgeons 1954-55; Sr. Investigator Nat. Insts. of Health, Bethesda, Md 1955-57; Assoc. in Medicine Harvard Medical School, Thorndike Memorial Lab., Boston City Hosp. 1957-59, Asst. Prof. of Medicine Harvard Medical School 1959-62; Prof. of Medicine Univ. of Chicago 1962-66; mem. N.A.S. 1974-, American Acad. of Arts and Sciences 1982-, Acad. Leopoldina (German Acad. of Sciences) 1965. *Publications:* over 200 scientific publs. in the field of porphyrin, heme and bile pigment metabolism, liver function, liver disease, muscle and blood diseases. *Leisure interests:* travel, reading, music, skiing, mountain climbing, tennis. *Address:* University of California Medical Center, San Francisco, Calif. 94143 (Office); 211 Woodland Road, Kentfield, Calif. 94904, U.S.A. (Home). *Telephone:* (415) 476-2341 (Office).

SCHMID, Wolfgang P(aul), DR.; German professor of linguistics; b. 25 Oct. 1929, Berlin; s. of Bruno Schmid and Gertrud Morgenstern; m. Anneliese Reichert 1960; two s.; ed. Kirchliche Hochschule, Berlin, Univ. of Tübingen and School of Oriental and African Studies, London; Prof. Univ. of Innsbrück 1964; Prof. of Comparative and Gen. Linguistics, Univ. of Göttingen 1965-; mem. Mainz Acad. (Vice-Pres. 1977-86); corresp. mem. Göttingen Acad.; mem. Herder-Forschungsrat, Marburg; external mem. Leipzig Acad. *Publications:* several books on linguistics and numerous papers in journals. *Leisure interest:* gardening. *Address:* Sprachwissenschaftliches Seminar der Universität, Humboldt-Allee 13, 3400 Göttingen (Office); Schladeberg 20, 3403 Friedland 5, OT. Niedernjesa, Federal Republic of Germany (Home). *Telephone:* 0551-395481/2 (Office); 05509/13 36 (Home).

SCHMIDT, Adolph William; American diplomatist; b. 1904; m. Helen Sedgeley Mellon 1936; one s. one d.; ed. Univs. of Princeton, Harvard, Dijon, Berlin and Paris; with Mellon Nat. Bank 1929-38; with A. W. Mellon Interests, Pittsburgh 1938-42; war service 1942-46; Gov. T. Mellon & Sons 1946-69; Chair. Pa. State Planning Bd. 1955-67, etc.; U.S. Del., Conf. on North Atlantic Community 1957 and Atlantic Congress 1959; mem. U.S. Citizens Comm. on NATO 1961-62; U.S. Del. Atlantic Convention of NATO nations 1962; Dir. Atlantic Council of U.S. 1962-; Adviser U.S. Del., Economic Comm. for Europe 1967; mem. Bd. of Govs. Atlantic Inst., Paris 1960-69; Amb. to Canada 1969-74; mem. Canadian-American Cttee. 1974-; Hon. LL.D. (Univs. of Pittsburgh, New Brunswick, Princeton Univ.); Hon. L.H.D. (Chatham Coll., Carnegie-Mellon Univ.). *Address:* R. D4, Ligonier, Pa. 15658, U.S.A.

SCHMIDT, Benno C., Jr.; American university president; b. 20 March 1942, Washington; s. of Benno Charles Schmidt Sr. and Martha Chastain; m. 2nd Helen Cutting Whitney 1980; one d. (one s. one d. by previous marriage); ed. Yale Coll. and Yale Law School; Clerk to Chief Justice Earl Warren 1966-67; Dept. of Justice 1967-69; mem. Faculty, Columbia Univ. Law School 1969-86, Dean 1984-86; Pres. and Prof. of Law, Yale Univ. 1986-; Hon. Master of Bench, Gray's Inn 1988. *Publications:* Freedom of the Press versus Public Access 1974, The Judiciary and Responsible Government 1910-1921 (with A. M. Bickel) 1985; papers on constitutional law, freedom of the press and first amendment issues. *Address:* Yale University, New Haven, Conn. 06520, U.S.A.

SCHMIDT, Chauncey Everett, B.S., M.B.A.; American banker; b. 7 June 1931, Oxford, Ind.; s. of Walter F. Schmidt and Vilda Saxton; m. Anne Garrett McWilliams 1954; one s. two d.; ed. U.S. Naval Acad., Harvard Graduate School of Business Admin.; with First Nat. Bank of Chicago 1959-75, Vice-Pres. 1965, Gen. Man., London 1966, Gen. Man. for Europe, Middle East and Africa 1968, Sr. Vice-Pres. 1969-72, Exec. Vice-Pres.

1972, Vice-Chair. 1973, Pres. 1974-75; Chair., Pres. and C.E.O., Bank of Calif. 1976-84; Chair., Pres., C.E.O. BanCal Tri-State Corpn. 1976-85; Dir. Amfac Ltd., Calif. Bankers Clearing House Asscn., Calif. Roundtable, Bay Area Council; Exec. Bd. San Francisco Bay Area Council of Boy Scouts of America; Bd. of Govs. San Francisco Symphony; mem. Fed. Advisory Council of Fed. Res. System, Advisory Council of Japan-U.S. Econ. Relations, SRI Int. Council, Int. Monetary Conf., American Bankers Asscn. *Address:* c/o The Bank of California, N.A., 400 California Street, San Francisco, Calif. 94104 (Office); 234 Albion Road, Woodside, Calif. 94062, U.S.A. (Home). *Telephone:* (415) 765-2525 (Office).

SCHMIDT, Gerhard, DR.PHIL.; Austrian art historian; b. 11 May 1924, Vienna; s. of Walter Schmidt and Elisabeth Trabert; m. Gunthilde Tschinkel 1959; one s. one d.; ed. Univ. of Vienna and Ecole du Louvre, Paris; Asst. Dept. of Art History, Univ. of Vienna 1953-59, Dozent 1959-65, Assoc. Prof. 1966-68, Prof. 1968-; Visiting Prof. Columbia Univ., N.Y. 1963, Univ. of Freiburg im Breisgau 1965; Visiting mem. Inst. for Advanced Study, Princeton 1964, 1970; Slade Prof. Univ. of Cambridge 1981-82; mem. Austrian Acad. of Science. *Publications:* Neue Malerei in Österreich 1956, Die Armenbibeln des XIV Jahrhunderts 1959, Die Wiener Biblia pauperum 1962, Die Malerschule von St. Florian 1962, Krumauer Bildercodex 1967; book chapters. *Address:* Department of Art History, University of Vienna, Universitätsstrasse 7, 1010 Vienna (Office); Linzerstrasse 352/8/1, A-1140 Vienna, Austria (Home). *Telephone:* 4300/2611 (Office); 94 33 45 (Home).

SCHMIDT, Helmut, German economist and politician; b. 23 Dec. 1918, Hamburg; s. of Gustav and Ludovica Schmidt; m. Hannelore Glaser 1942; one d.; ed. Lichtwarkschule and Univ. Hamburg; Man. Transport Admin. of State of Hamburg 1949-53; mem. Social Democrat Party 1946-; mem. Bundestag 1953-62, 1965-87; Chair. Social Democrat (SPD) Parl. Party in Bundestag 1967-69; Vice-Chair. SPD 1968-84; Senator (Minister) for Domestic Affairs in Hamburg 1961-65; Minister of Defence 1969-72, for Econ. and Finance July-Dec. 1972, of Finance 1972-74; Fed. Chancellor 1974-82; Sr. Ed. Die Zeit 1983-, Publr. 1985-; Adviser, Daiwa Securities Research Inst. 1986-; Dr. Iur. h.c. (Newberry Coll.) 1973, (Johns Hopkins Univ.) 1976, (Harvard Univ.) 1979, Hon. D.C.L. (Oxford) 1979, Hon. Dr. (Sorbonne Univ.) 1981, (Louvain) 1984, (Georgetown) 1986; European Prize for Statesmanship (F.U.S. Foundation) 1979; Nahum Goldmann Silver Medal 1980; Athinai Prize 1986. *Publications:* Defence or Retaliation 1962, Beiträge 1967, Strategie des Gleichgewichts 1969 (English edition "Balance of Power" 1970), Auf dem Fundament des Godesberger Programms 1973, Bundestagsreden (2nd edition) 1975, Kontinuität und Konzentration (2nd edition) 1976, Als Christ in der politischen Entscheidung 1976, Deutschland 1976—Zwei Sozialdemokraten im Gespräch (with Willy Brandt) 1976, Der Kurs heisst Frieden 1979, Pflicht zur Menschlichkeit 1981, Freiheit verantworten 1983, Weltwirtschaft ist unser Schicksal 1983, Eine Strategie für den Westen, (English ed.) A Grand Strategy for the West, (Adolphe Bentinck Prize 1986) 1985, Vom deutschen Stolz: Bekenntnisse zur Erfahrung von Kunst 1986, Von Menschen und Mächten 1987, (English ed.) Men and Power 1988. *Address:* c/o Die Zeit, Postfach 10 68 20, Speersort 1, 2000 Hamburg 1, Federal Republic of Germany.

SCHMIDT, Maarten, PH.D., SC.D.; Netherlands astronomer; b. 28 Dec. 1929, Groningen; s. of W. Schmidt and A. W. Haringhuizen; m. Cornelia J. Tom 1955; three d.; ed. Univs. of Groningen and Leiden; Scientific Officer Univ. of Leiden Observatory 1949-59; Carnegie Fellow Mt. Wilson Observatory, Pasadena 1956-58; Assoc. Prof. Calif. Inst. of Tech. 1959-64, Prof. of Astronomy 1964-; discovered large red shifts in spectra of quasi-stellar radio sources (quasars); Rumford Award, American Acad. of Arts and Sciences 1968. *Leisure interest:* classical music. *Address:* California Institute of Technology, Pasadena, Calif. 91125, U.S.A. *Telephone:* (213) 795-6841.

SCHMIDT, Werner P., DR.RER.POL.; German business executive; b. 5 July 1932, Borken, Westphalia; m. Annely Bresser 1957; one s. one d.; ed. Univ. of Münster, Kalamazoo Coll., Michigan, Univ. of Cologne; Sales Planning Man., Marketing Man., Domestic Sales Man., Ford Werke AG 1956-67; Export Man., Volkswagen Werk AG 1967-71; Pres. Volkswagen do Brasil 1971-73; Chair. Man. Bd., Audi NSU Auto Union AG 1973-75, mem. Man. Bd., Volkswagen AG 1975-. *Address:* Volkswagen AG, 3180 Wolfsburg, Federal Republic of Germany.

SCHMIDT-CLAUSEN, Kurt Hermann, DR.THEOL.; German international church official; b. 1 Oct. 1920, Hanover; m. Erika Rokahr 1943; one s. one d.; ed. Hanover Gymnasium, Univs. of Vienna and Göttingen, Christ Church Coll. Oxford, and Loccum Preachers' Seminary; Pastor City Parish, Hanover 1951-52; mem. Admin. Staff Evangelical Lutheran Church of Hanover 1952-55; Pastor Wunstorf Suburban Parish (near Hanover) 1955-60; Asst. Exec. Sec., later Acting Exec. Sec., Lutheran World Fed. 1960-61, Exec. Sec. 1961-64, Gen. Sec. 1964-65, mem. Exec. Cttee. 1970-77; Chair. Ecumenical Comm., Evangelical Lutheran Church of Hanover; Ed. Lutherische Monatshefte (monthly); Regional Bishop of Osnabrück Diocese 1970-82. *Publications:* Vorweggenommene Einheit 1964, Reformation als ökumenisches Ereignis 1970, Geschichte des Lutherischen Weltkonvents 1975. *Leisure interests:* Roman archaeology, history and liturgical music.

Address: 3000 Hanover, Lemförderstrasse 8A, Federal Republic of Germany. *Telephone:* 0511/887347.

SCHMIDT-NIELSEN, Knut, DR. PHIL.; American professor of physiology; b. 24 Sept. 1915, Norway; s. of Sigval and Signe Torborg (Sturzen-Becker) Schmidt-Nielsen; ed. Oslo and Copenhagen Univs.; Research Fellow Carlsberg Labs., Copenhagen 1941-44; Research Fellow, Univ. of Copenhagen 1944-46; Research Assoc. Swarthmore Coll. Dept. of Zoology 1946-48; Research Assoc. Stanford Univ. Dept. of Physiology 1948-49; Docent Univ. of Oslo 1947-49; Asst. Prof. Univ. of Cincinnati Coll. of Medicine 1949-52; Prof. of Physiology, Dept. of Zoology, Duke Univ. 1952-; James B. Duke Prof. of Physiology 1963-; Guggenheim Fellow, Algeria 1953-54; Brody Memorial Lecturer Univ. of Mo. 1962; Harvey Soc. Lecturer 1962 (Hon. mem. 1962); Regents' Lecturer Univ. of Calif. (Davis) 1963; Hans Gadow Lecturer Cambridge Univ. 1971; Visiting Agassiz Prof. Harvard Univ. 1972; mem. numerous scientific Cttees., including Advisory Bd. to the Physiological Research Laboratory Scripps Inst. of Oceanography 1963-69, Chair. 1968-69; U.S. Nat. Cttee. for Int. Union of Physiological Sciences 1966-78, Vice-Chair. 1969-78; Biomedical Engineering Advisory Cttee., Duke Univ. 1968-; Animal Resources Advisory Cttee., Nat. Inst. of Health 1968; mem. Organizing Cttee., First Int. Conf. Comparative Physiology 1972, Pres. 1972-80; mem. Advisory Bd., Bio-Medical Sciences, Inc. 1973-74; Chair. Interunion Comm. on Comparative Physiology 1976-80; Pres. Int. Union of Physiological Sciences 1980-86; mem. Editorial Bd. several scientific journals; mem. N.A.S., Royal Norwegian Soc. of Arts and Science 1973, Royal Danish Acad. 1975; Foreign mem. Royal Soc., London 1986; Fellow, American Acad. of Arts and Sciences, N.Y. Acad. of Science, A.A.A.S.; Foreign Assoc. Acad. des Sciences (France) 1968; Hon. D.Med. (Univ. of Lund, Sweden) 1986. *Publications:* Animal Physiology 1960 (trans. in several languages), Desert Animals, Physiological Problems of Heat and Water 1964 (Russian trans. 1972), How Animals Work 1972 (Japanese trans. 1972, German trans. 1975, Russian trans. 1976), Animal Physiology, Adaptation and Environment 1975, Scaling: Why is Animal Size so Important? 1984 (trans. into Russian 1987); numerous articles. *Address:* Department of Zoology, Duke University, Durham, N.C. 27706, U.S.A. *Telephone:* (919) 684-2687.

SCHMIDT-ROHR, Ulrich, DR.RER.NAT.; German physicist; b. 25 May 1926, Frankfurt an der Oder; s. of Georg and Ruth Schmidt-Rohr; m. Helma Wernery 1963; four s. one d.; ed. Friedrichsgymnasium, Frankfurt an der Oder, Technische Hochschule, Berlin and Brunswick, and Univ. of Heidelberg; research Lab., OSRAM 1948-49; Asst., Univ. of Heidelberg 1950-53; F.S.S.P. Fellow, M.I.T. 1954; Asst. Max-Planck-Inst. for Medical Research 1955-58, Max Planck Inst. for Nuclear Physics 1958-61; Dir. Inst. for Nuclear Physics, Kernforschungsanlage, Jülich 1962-65; Dir. Max-Planck-Inst. for Nuclear Physics 1966-. *Publications:* papers on nuclear physics and accelerators. *Address:* Max-Planck-Institut Für Kernphysik, Postfach 10 39 80, D-6900 Heidelberg 1, Federal Republic of Germany. *Telephone:* (06221) 516 202-204.

SCHMIEDER, Werner, DR.RER.OEC.; German politician; b. 1927; mem. Socialist Unity Party, G.D.R.; mem. People's Police 1945-49; with German Investbank, Dresden 1949-55; Tech. Coll. of Finance, Gotha 1953; Dir. Investbank, Cottbus 1955-62; Chair. State Planning Comm. and mem. Exec. Cttee., Cottbus Dist. 1962-67; Deputy Minister 1967-74; State Sec. Ministry of Finance 1974-80; Minister of Finance 1980-81; Vaterländischer Verdienstorden in Bronze 1965, in Silver 1969, and other decorations. *Address:* c/o Ministry of Finance, Berlin, German Democratic Republic.

SCHMIT, André, L. EN D.; French civil servant; b. 12 Feb. 1915, Geneva, Switzerland; s. of Albert and Suzanne (née Liégeois) Schmit; m. Nicole Delmas 1942; two s. one d.; ed. Ecole des Sciences Politiques, Ecole Nat. de la France d'Outre-Mer (Indo-China) and Cambridge Univ.; Colonial Admin. (Senegal and Indo-China) 1941-45; Asst. Dir. Press Relations, Ministry of Information 1946, Inspector Gen. 1946; Dir. Press Council 1947; Dir. Nouvelles Messageries de la Presse Parisienne 1949-; Chef de Cabinet, Ministry of Public Works, Transport and Tourism 1954-55, Ministry of State 1956-57, Ministry of Defence 1957-58; Chef de Cabinet of Pres. of Nat. Ass. 1958-69; Pres. Bill-posting and Advertising Admin. 1964; Dir. du Cabinet of Pres. of Nat. Ass. 1969-73; Colonel de Réserve (Troupes de Marine); mem. Conseil Econ. et Social 1979-; Officier, Légion d'honneur, Croix de guerre, Commdr., Ordre nat. du Mérite. *Address:* 48 avenue de New York, 75116 Paris, France.

SCHMITT, Francis Otto, PH.D.; American neurobiologist; b. 23 Nov. 1903, St. Louis, Mo.; s. of Otto Franz and Clara Elizabeth (Senniger) Schmitt; m. Barbara Hecker 1927 (deceased); two s. (one deceased) one d.; ed. Washington Univ. St. Louis, Univ. Coll., London, Kaiser Wilhelm Inst., Berlin-Dahlem, Washington Univ., Univ. of California, Berkeley; Asst. Prof. of Zoology, Washington Univ. 1929-34, Assoc. Prof. 1934-38, Prof. 1938-40, Head of Dept. 1940; Prof. of Biology, M.I.T. 1941, Head of Dept. 1942-55, Inst. Prof. 1955-69, Inst. Prof. Emer. 1969-, Chair. Neurosciences Research Program 1962-74, mem. 1974-; mem. N.A.S., Nat. Research Council's Cttee. on Neurobiology 1945, Cttee. on Growth 1946-50, Cttee. on Radiation Cataracts 1949-53, Cttee. on Atherosclerosis 1953-54, Biology Council 1954-56, Nat. Advisory Health Council U.S. Public Health Service 1959-63, Nat. Advisory Gen. Medical Sciences Council 1969-71; mem. Bd. of Science Consultants of Sloan-Kettering Inst. of Cancer Research 1963-

71, Cttee. for Fellowships for Basic Neuroscience Research, Sloan Foundation 1971-78, Nat. Advisory Council Marine Biomedical Inst., Univ. of Texas 1973-76, Nat. Insts. of Health 1976-; Trustee and exec. mem. of several insts.; Fellow, American Acad. of Arts and Sciences (Council mem. 1950-52, 1964-65), A.A.A.S., New York Acad. of Sciences; mem. numerous scientific socs. including Soc. of Gen. Physiologists, American Philosophical Soc. (Council mem. 1964-66, Vice-Pres. 1973-75), Soc. for Growth and Devt. (Treas. 1945-46, Pres. 1947), Biophysical Soc. (Council mem.), Electron Microscope Soc. of America (Dir. 1944-47, Pres. 1949), Swedish Royal Acad. of Sciences, Hon. D.Sc. (seven univs.), Hon. M.D. (Univ. of Gothenburg, Sweden), Hon. LL.D. (Wittenburg Univ. and Juniata Coll.); Alsop Award of American Leather Chemical Asscn. 1947, Lasker Award of American Public Health Asscn. 1956, T. Duckett Jones Memorial Award of Helen Hay Whitney Foundation 1963. *Publications:* Fundamental Transfer Processes in Aqueous Biomolecular System 1960, Macromolecular Specificity and Biological Memory 1962, Neuro-sciences—A Study Program 1967, Neurosciences—Second Study Program 1970, Neurosciences—Third Study Program 1973, Neurosciences Research Symposium Vols. I-VII 1966-74, Functional Linkage in Biomolecular Systems 1974, Neuro-sciences—Fourth Study Program 1977, Molecular Genetic Neuroscience 1982, The Unceasing Search 1989. *Leisure interest:* music. *Address:* Massachusetts Institute of Technology, R. 16-512, Department of Biology, Cambridge, Mass. 02139; 72 Byron Road, Weston, Mass. 02193, U.S.A. (Home). *Telephone:* (617) 253-5015 (Office); (617) 235-6976 (Home).

SCHMITT, Harrison H., PH.D.; American politician and fmr. astronaut; b. 3 July 1935, Santa Rita, N.M.; s. of Harrison A. and Ethel Hagan Schmitt; m. Teresa Fitzgibbons 1985; ed. Calif. Inst. of Technology, Univ. of Oslo, Norway, and Harvard Univ.; Fulbright Fellowship 1957-58, Kennecott Fellowship in Geology 1958-59, Harvard Fellowship 1959-60, Harvard Travelling Fellowship 1960, Parker Travelling Fellowship 1961-62, Nat. Science Foundation Postdoctoral Fellowship, Dept. of Geological Sciences, Harvard 1963-64; has done geological work for Norwegian Geological Survey, Oslo, for U.S. Geological Survey, N.M. and Montana, and in Alaska 1955-56; with U.S. Geological Survey Astrogeology Dept. until 1965; Project Chief on photo and telescopic mapping of moon and planets; selected as scientist-astronaut by NASA June 1965; completed flight training 1966; Lunar Module pilot Apollo XVII Dec. 1972; Chief, Astronaut Office, Science and Applications, Johnson Space Center 1974; Asst. Admin., Energy Programs, NASA, Washington, D.C. 1974-76; Senator from New Mexico 1977-83; Consultant 1983-; mem. Pres.'s Foreign Intelligence Advisory Bd. 1984-85, Army Sciences Bd. 1985-; Republican. *Address:* P.O. Box 14338, Albuquerque, N.M. 87191, U.S.A.

SCHMITZ, Wolfgang, LL.D.; Austrian economist and editor; b. 28 May 1923, Vienna; s. of Dr. Hans Schmitz and Maria Habel; m. Dr. Elisabeth Mayr-Harting 1951 (divorced 1981); one s. four d.; ed. Univs. of Vienna and Fribourg (Switzerland), Catholic Univ., Washington, D.C.; legal practice 1949-50; Austrian Fed. Econ. Chamber 1950-64, Sec. Econ. Policy Dept. and Sec. Austrian Nat. Cttee. of Int. Chamber of Commerce 1950-64; Chair. Beirat für Wirtschafts-und Sozialfragen 1963-64; Head of Econ. Policy Dept. Jan.-April 1964; Fed. Minister of Finance 1964-68; Pres. Austrian Nat. Bank 1968-73; Gov. of World Bank for Austria 1964-68, of IMF 1968-73; Hon. Pres. Austro-American Soc., Austro-Japanese Soc.; Lecturer Univ. Innsbruck; Chair. of Editorial Cttee. Europäische Rundschau, Vienna, Die Furche, Vienna; Hon. LL.D. (St. John's Univ., New York). *Publications:* Die österreichische Wirtschafts- und Sozialpolitik, Würdigung, Kritik, Ansatzpunkte 1961, Geldwertstabilität und Wirtschaftswachstum—Währungs-politik im Spannungsfeld des Konjunkturverlaufs (Ed.) 1970, Convertibility, Multilateralism and Freedom—World Economic Policy in the Seventies (Ed.) 1972, International Investment—Growth and Crisis 1975, Die antizyklische Konjunkturpolitik—eine Illusion 1976, Die Gesetzesflut: Folge und Ausdruck der Überforderung des Staates 1979, Was macht den Markt sozial? Die Grundzüge der Sozialen Marktwirtschaft (ed.) 1982, Die Währung: eine offene Flanke staatlicher Verfassungsordnung 1983, and numerous articles on economic, financial and social policy matters. *Address:* c/o Austrian Federal Economic Chamber, 63 Wiedner Hauptstrasse, Postfach 187, A-1045, Vienna; Gustav Tschermak Gasse 3/2, 1180 Vienna, Austria (Home). *Telephone:* (0222) 65054280 (Office); 343333 (Home).

SCHMÜCKER, Toni; German automobile executive (retd.); b. 23 April 1921, Frechen; mem. Bd. Ford-Werke AG 1961-68, Rheinstahl AG March-July 1968; Chair. of Bd. Rheinstahl AG 1968-75; Chair. Man. Bd. Volkswagenwerk AG 1975-81; Chair. Supervisory Bd. Audi NSU Auto Union 1975-82; fmr. Chair. Bd. of Dirs. VW of America Inc., VW Manufacturing Corpn. of America; Pres. Conselho Consultivo VW do Brasil, Consejo de Administración VW de Mexico; Deputy Chair. Bd. of Dirs. VW of South Africa Ltd.; mem. admin. bd. Deutsche Automobilgesellschaft; mem. supervisory bd. Deutschen Babcock AG, Brown, Boveri and Cie AG (BBC), Allianz Lebensversicherung AG, Thyssen Handelsunion AG, Thyssen AG, Deutsche Messe-und Austellungs AG; mem. admin. council Commerzbank AG; mem. bd. Verband der Automobilindustrie, Bundesverband der Deutschen Industrie e.V.; mem. bd. of Dirs. CCMC, Brussels. *Address:* c/o Volkswagenwerk AG, Postfach, 3180 Wolfsburg; Vittingshoffstrasse 51, 4300 Essen-Stadtwald, Federal Republic of Germany.

SCHMUDE, Dr. Jürgen; German lawyer and politician; b. 9 June 1936, Insterburg; m.; two c.; ed. Göttingen, Berlin, Bonn, Cologne Univs.; practised law, Essen; mem. Social Democratic Party 1957-; various local party functions 1957-; mem. town council and del. district council, Moers 1964-71; mem. Bundestag 1969-; Sec. of State to Fed. Minister of the Interior 1974-78; Fed. Minister of Educ. and Science 1978-81, of Justice 1981-82; Pres. Synod of Evangelical Churches (Fed. Repub. of Germany) 1985-. *Address:* Herrenhäuserstrasse 12, 3000 Hanover 21, Federal Republic of Germany.

SCHNEEMELCHER, Wilhelm; German theologian; b. 21 Aug. 1914, Berlin; s. of Wilhelm Schneemelcher and Paula Sachse; m. Eva Ackermann 1940; three s. one d.; pastor, Sülbeck, Kreis Einbeck 1947-49; teaching appt. Göttingen 1946-49, Prof. 1953; Prof. of New Testament and History of the Ancient Church, Bonn 1954, Dean Evangelical Theology Faculty 1958-59, 1963-64; Rector, Univ. of Bonn 1967-68; now Prof. Emer.; Pres. Rhineland-Westphalia Acad. of Sciences, Düsseldorf 1982-85; Grosses Bundesverdienstkreuz mit Stern; Dr. h.c. *Publications:* Gesammelte Aufsätze zum NT und zur Patristik 1974, Das Urchristentum 1981, Martin Luther, Sein Leben und sein Werk 1983, Evangelisches Staatslexikon (co-ed.) 1987, Neutestamentliche Apokryphen, (2 vols.) (ed.) 1987-89. *Address:* Böckingstrasse 1, 5340 Bad Honnef, Federal Republic of Germany. *Telephone:* 02224/5450.

SCHNEIDER, Oscar, DR.JUR.UTR.; German politician; b. 3 June 1927, Altenheideck, Bavaria; s. of Josef Schneider; m. Josefine Kampfer 1961; two d.; ed. Univs. of Erlangen and Würzburg; mem. Nuremberg City Council 1956; mem. Bundestag 1969-; Chair. Bundestag Cttee. on Regional Planning, Building and Urban Devt. 1972-82; Minister for Regional Planning, Building and Urban Devt. 1982-89; CSU. *Address:* Ganghoferstrasse 16, 8500 Nürnberg, Federal Republic of Germany. *Telephone:* 592331.

SCHNEIDER, William George, O.C., PH.D., F.R.C.S., F.R.S.; Canadian physical chemist; b. 1 June 1915, Wolseley, Saskatchewan; s. of Michael Schneider and Phillipina Kraushaar; m. Jean Purves 1940; two d.; ed. Saskatchewan, McGill and Harvard Univs.; Research Physicist Oceanographic Inst., Woods Hole, Mass., U.S. 1943-46; Research Chemist Div. of Pure Chem. Nat. Research Council of Canada, Ottawa 1946, Dir. Div. of Pure Chem. 1963-66, Vice-Pres. (Scientific) 1965-67, Pres. 1967-80; Pres. Int. Union of Pure and Applied Chemistry 1983-85; Hon. LL.D. (Alberta, Laurentian); Hon. D.Sc. (Memorial, Saskatchewan, Moncton, McMaster, Laval, York, New Brunswick, Montreal, McGill, Acadia, Regina, Ottawa); Henry Marshall Tory Medal of the Royal Soc. of Canada; Chemical Inst. of Canada Medal, Montreal Medal 1973. *Publications:* High Resolution Nuclear Magnetic Resonance (with J. A. Pople and H. J. Bernstein) 1959; over 120 scientific papers. *Leisure interests:* skiing, tennis. *Address:* National Research Council of Canada, Sussex Drive, Ottawa, Ont. K1A 0R6, Canada. *Telephone:* 613-993-9821.

SCHNEIDERHAN, Wolfgang; Austrian violinist; b. 28 May 1915; m. Irmgard Seefried (q.v.) 1948; three d.; studied under Prof. Julius Winkler and Prof. Ottokar Sevcik; solo debut in Copenhagen 1926; leader Vienna Symphonic Orchestra 1933-37, Vienna Philarmonic Orchestra 1937-49; mem. Schneiderhan Quartet 1937-51; Prof. Mozarteum, Salzburg 1936-56; Prof. Staatsakademie, Vienna 1939-50; Prof. Musik-Hochschule, Vienna 1975-; formed trio with Edwin Fischer and Enrico Mainardi 1949-55; Leader of master classes, Lucerne 1949-; f. Festival Strings, Lucerne 1956; Conductor 1965-; f. Int. Fritz Kreisler Violin Competition, Vienna 1979; f. trio with Boris Pergamenschikow and Paul Badura-Skoda 1981; mem. Royal Acad. of Music, Stockholm; Hon. mem. Verein des Beethoven-Hauses, Bonn 1964-, Österreichen-Deutschen Kulturgesellschaft 1980; Schubert Medal 1927, Musikpreis Stadt Berlin 1940, Mozart Medal 1941, 1953, Nicolai Medal (Vienna Philharmonic) 1942, Grosses Ehrenkreuz (1st class) 1961, Grosses Verdienstorden (Fed. Repub. of Germany) 1965, Ritterkreuz Daneborg-Orden (Denmark) 1963, Ehrennadel (Luzern) 1980, Grosses Silbernes Ehrenzeichen (Austria) 1980, Honour Medal of Vienna in Gold 1986, Title of Hofrat 1986. *Musical arrangements:* Beethoven Violin Concerto 1968, works by Brahms, Mozart, Haydn, Tartini, Viotti 1977. *Leisure interest:* painting. *Address:* Kaasgrabengasse 98 A, 1190 Vienna, Austria.

SCHNITTKE, Alfred; Soviet composer; b. 24 Nov. 1934, Engels, Saratov Region; s. of Harry Schnittke and Maria Vogel; m. 1st Galina Koltsina 1956 (divorced 1958), 2nd Irina Katyaeva 1961; one s.; ed. Moscow Conservatory; teacher of instrumentation, polyphony and composition, Moscow Conservatory 1961-71; mem. U.S.S.R. Composers' Union, U.S.S.R. Film Makers' Union, West Berlin Acad. of Fine Arts, Royal Swedish Music Acad.; corresp. mem. Bavarian Acad. of Fine Arts; State Prize of R.S.F.S.R. 1986. *Compositions include:* 4 symphonies, 4 violin concertos, 3 concerti grossi, concerto for viola and orchestra, concerto for cello and orchestra, Peer Gynt (ballet), choral music, chamber music, film and theatre music. *Publications:* musicological articles. *Address:* 117333 Moscow, 48 Ulitsa Vavilova, Apt. 419, U.S.S.R. *Telephone:* 137 58 94.

SCHNITZER, Moshe, M.A.; Israeli diamond exporter; b. 21 Jan. 1921; ed. Balfour High School, Tel-Aviv, Hebrew Univ. of Jerusalem; Chair. Asscn. of Diamond Instructors 1943-46; Vice-Pres. Israel Diamond Exchange 1951-66, Pres. 1966-; Pres. Israel Exporters' Asscn. of Diamonds 1962-;

World Pres. Int. Fed. of Diamond Exchanges 1968–72; partner Diamond Export Enterprise 1953–; mem. Consulting Cttee. to Minister of Commerce and Industry 1968–; Ed. The Diamond; Most Distinguished Exporter of Israel 1964. *Publication:* Diamond Book (in Hebrew) 1946. *Address:* Israel Diamond Exchange, 3 Jabotinsky Road, Ramat Gan; 78 Sharet Street, Tel-Aviv, Israel.

SCHNURRE, Wolfdietrich; German writer; b. 22 Aug. 1920, Frankfurt am Main; s. of Dr. Otto Schnurre; m. 2nd Marina Schnurre 1966; one s.; ed. Humanistisches Gymnasium; Army Service 1939–45; Freelance writer 1945–; Founder-mem. "Group 47" 1947; mem. Akademie für Sprache und Dichtung 1959, West German PEN 1958–61; Young Generation Prize, City of Berlin 1958, Immermann Prize, Düsseldorf 1959, George Mackensen Literature Prize 1962, Literaturpreis der Stadt Köln 1982, Georg-Büchner-Preis 1983; Bundesverdienstkreuz 1981. *Publications:* Die Rohrdommel ruft jeden Tag (stories) 1950, Aufzeichnungen des Pudels Ali (satire) 1951, 1962, Kassiber (poems) 1956, 1964, Abendländler (satirical poems) 1957, Protest im Parterre (fables) 1957, Eine Rechnung, die nicht aufgeht (short stories) 1958, Als Vaters Bart noch rot war (novel) 1958, Das Los unserer Stadt (novel) 1959, Man sollte dagegen sein (short stories) 1960, Die Mauer des 13 August (documentary) 1961, Berlin—eine Stadt wird geteilt (documentary) 1962, Funke im Reisig (short stories) 1963, Schreibtisch unter freiem Himmel (essays) 1964, Ohne Einsatz kein Speil (short stories) 1964, Die Erzählungen (stories) 1966, Spreezimmer möbliert (radio plays) 1967, Die Zwengel (for children) 1967, Was ich für mein Leben gern tue (collection of prose pieces) 1968, Ein Schneemann für den grossen Bruder (for children) 1969, Gocko (for children) 1970, Die Sache mit den Meerschweinchen (for children) 1970, Schnurre heiter (short stories) 1970, Die Wandlung des Hippipotamos (satire) 1970, Immer mehr Meerschweinchen (for children) 1971, Der Spatz in der Hand (tales and verse) 1971, Wie der Koalabär wieder lachen lernte (for children) 1971, Der Meerschweinchendieb (for children) 1972, Auf Tauchstation (prose pieces) 1973, Ich frag ja bloss (dialogue) 1973, Der wahre Noah (satire) 1974, Schnurren und Murren (for children) 1974, Ich brauch dich (short stories) 1976, Eine schwierige Reparatur (prose pieces) 1976, der Schattenfotograf (essay) 1978, Ein Unglücksfall (novel) 1981, Gelernt ist gelernt (essays) 1984. *Leisure interest:* drawing. *Address:* Prinz-Friedrich-Leopold-strasse 33a, 1000 Berlin 38, Federal Republic of Germany. *Telephone:* 803-53-47.

SCHOCKEMÖHLE, Alwin; German show jumper (retd.); b. 29 May 1937, Osterbrock, Kreis Meppen; s. of Aloys and Josefa (née Borgerding) Schockemöhle; m. 2nd Rita Wiltfang; two s. one d.; began riding 1946, in public events 1948–; riding 1954–55; reserve for Mil. and Showjumping, Melbourne Olympics 1956; specialized in showjumping 1956–77; first Derby win, riding "Bachus", Hamburg 1957; continually in int. showjumping events 1960–77; Showjumping Champion Fed. Repub. of Germany (four times); second in European Championship (three times); European Champion riding "Warwick" 1975, 1976; Gold Medal (Team Award) Rome Olympics 1960; Gold Medal (Individual Award) and Silver Medal (Team Award) riding "Warwick" Montreal Olympics 1976. *Publication:* Sportkamerad Pferd (A Horse for Companion in Sport). *Address:* Münsterlandstrasse, 2841 Mühlen, Federal Republic of Germany.

SCHOCKEN, Gershom Gustav; Israeli editor and publisher; b. Sept. 1912; ed. Univ. of Heidelberg and London School of Economics; joined staff of Haaretz (daily newspaper) 1937, Publr. and Ed. 1939–; Dir. Schocken Publishing House Ltd.; mem. Knesset (Parl.) 1955–59; Int. Ed. of the Year (World Press Review) 1983. *Address:* 18 Chayutman Street, Tel-Aviv, Israel.

SCHOELLER, François; French engineer; b. 25 March 1934, Nancy; m.; three c.; ed. Ecole Polytechnique and Ecole Nat. Supérieure des Télécommunications; eng. equatorial office of P.T.T., Brazzaville 1960–63; Chief Eng., regional man., Télécommunications de Strasbourg 1963–73; Operational Dir. Télécommunications de Marseille 1973–75, Regional Dir. Montpellier 1975–80, Regional Dir. with grade of engineer-general 1980; Chair. TéléDiffusion de France 1983–86; Chevalier, Ordre nat. du Mérite; Chevalier, Légion d'honneur. *Address:* c/o TéléDiffusion de France, 21–27 rue Barbes, B.P. 518, 92542 Montrouge Cedex, France.

SCHOELLER, Franz Joachim Philipp; German diplomatist; b. 24 July 1926, Düsseldorf; s. of Franz and Therese Schoeller; m. Helga Ingetraud Neul 1956; one s. one d.; ed. Univs. of Paris and Cologne; Attaché Foreign Service, Bonn 1955; Third Sec., Foreign Office, Bonn 1957–59, Second Sec. 1963–66, Minister and Deputy Chief of Protocol, 1973–75, Amb. and Chief of Protocol 1975–80; served Paris 1956–57, Rome 1959–61; Consul and chargé d'affaires, Dar-es-Salaam 1961–63; First Sec., Madrid 1966–69; Counseller, Teheran 1971–73; Amb. to Brazil 1980–83, Amb. to France 1983–87, Amb. to Poland 1987–; Order of Merit of Fed. Repub. of Germany; Commdr. Légion d'honneur. *Leisure interests:* history, philosophy, skiing, mountain climbing. *Address:* Embassy of the Federal Republic of Germany at Warsaw, Postfach 1500, 5300-D, Bonn 1, Federal Republic of Germany. *Telephone:* Warsaw 17 30 11.

SCHOEMAN, Hendrik; South African politician; b. 11 June 1927, Delmas, Transvaal; m. Christelle Loedolff; two c.; ed. Afrikaans Boys' High School, Pretoria; mem. for Standerton Nat. Party 1966–; Deputy Minister of

Agric. 1968–72, Minister 1972–80, for Transport 1980–86; fmr. Chair. Bd. Langeberg Co-operative; Chair. Delmas Agricultural Corpn., Delmas Consumer Corpn.; mem. Co-operative Council and Maize Cttee., Transvaal Agricultural Union; widespread farming interests. *Address:* c/o Ministry of Transport, Private Bag X483, Pretoria 0001, Republic of South Africa.

SCHOEN, Max Howard, D.D.S., DR.P.H.; American professor of dentistry; b. 4 Feb. 1922, New York; s. of Adolph Schoen and Ella Grossman; m. Beatrice Mildred Hoch 1950; one s. one d.; ed. DeWitt Clinton High School, City Coll. of New York, Univ. of California, Los Angeles and Univ. of Southern California; Dentist (rank of Capt.) in U.S. Army Corps 1943–46; private practice, Los Angeles 1946–54; Founder, Partner and Dental Dir., Group Practice in Los Angeles 1954–71; Visiting Prof., Univ. of Connecticut School of Dental Medicine 1972; Assoc. Clinical Prof. of Community Dentistry, Univ. of S. Calif. School of Dentistry 1972–73; Prof. of Dental Health Services, School of Dental Medicine, State Univ. of New York, Stony Brook 1973–76, Acting Dean 1974–75, Assoc. Dean of Clinical Affairs 1975–76; Chair. Section of Public Health and Preventive Dentistry, Univ. of Calif. School of Dentistry 1976–82, Prof. School of Dentistry 1976–, Prof. School of Public Health 1976–; mem. Inst. of Medicine of Nat. Acad. of Sciences. *Publications:* numerous articles and papers on the financing, delivery and quality of dental care. *Leisure interests:* reading, swimming. *Address:* 5818 Sherbourne Drive, Los Angeles, Calif. 90056 (Home); University of California at Los Angeles School of Dentistry, Section of Public Health and Preventive Dentistry, 63-025 Center for the Health Sciences, Los Angeles, Calif. 90024, U.S.A. (Office). *Telephone:* (213) 670-1847 (Home); (213) 825-6544 (Office).

SCHOLES, Gordon Glen Denton; Australian politician and fmr. engine driver; b. 7 June 1931; s. of Glen Scholes and Mary Scholes; m. Della Kathleen Robinson 1957; two d.; mem. House of Reps. 1967–; Councillor, Geelong City 1965–67; Pres. Geelong Trades Hall Council 1965–67, Chair. Cttees. House of Reps. 1965–66, Deputy Speaker and Chair. Cttees. 1973–75, Speaker 1975–76; Opposition Spokesman on Postal and Telecommunications Comms. 1976–77, on Primary Industry June–Dec. 1977, on Defence 1977–83, on A.C.T. 1980–83; Minister for Defence 1983–84, for Territories 1984–87. *Leisure interests:* golf, stamp-collecting. *Address:* 11 Lascelles Avenue, Geelong West, Vic. 3218, Australia. *Telephone:* 052 213083.

SCHOLEY, Sir David Gerald, Kt., F.R.S.A., C.B.E.; British banker; b. 28 June 1935, London; s. of Dudley and Lois Scholey; m. Alexandra Drew 1960; ed. Wellington Coll. and Christ Church, Oxford; joined S.G. Warburg & Co. Ltd. 1965, Dir. 1967–, Deputy Chair. 1977–80, Joint Chair. 1980–; Dir. Mercury Securities PLC 1969–, Deputy Chair. Mercury Securities PLC 1980–84, Chair. 1984–86; Chair. S. G. Warburg Group PLC 1985–; Dir. Orion Insurance Co. PLC 1963–, Stewart Wrightson Holdings PLC 1972–81, Union Discount Co. of London Ltd. 1976–81, Bank of England 1981–, British Telecom PLC Oct. 1985–; mem. Export Guarantees Advisory Council 1970–75, Deputy Chair. 1974–75; Chair. Construction Exports Advisory Bd. 1975–78; mem. Cttee. on Finance for Industry, Nat. Econ. Devt. Office 1980–87; Gov. Wellington Coll. 1977–; Hon. Treasurer I.I.S.S. 1984–. *Address:* S. G. Warburg & Co. Ltd., 33 King William Street, London, EC4R 9AS, England. *Telephone:* 01-280 2222.

SCHOLEY, Sir Robert, Kt., C.B.E.; British engineer and company executive; b. 8 Oct. 1921, Sheffield; s. of Harold and Eveline Scholey; m. Joan Methley 1946; two d.; ed. King Edward VII School, Sheffield Univ.; joined United Steel Co. 1947, holding various eng. and production posts within the organization until the nationalization of the steel industry; Dir. Rotherham Div., Midland Group (British Steel Corpn.) 1968, Dir. Special Steels Div., Steelworks Group 1970, Man. Dir. Operations 1972, Man. Dir. Strip Mills Div. 1972–73, Chief Exec., mem. of Bd. 1973–76, Deputy Chair. and Chief Exec. 1976–86, Chair. April 1986–; Pres. Eurofer 1985–; Dir. Eurotunnel 1987–; City Personality of the Year Award 1989. *Leisure interests:* history of the arts, reading, photography, camping, gardening. *Address:* The Coach House, Much Hadham, Herts., England (Home). *Telephone:* Much Hadham 2908 (Home).

SCHOLL, Günther; German diplomatist; b. 11 Jan. 1909, Stettin; s. of Hermann and Hertha (née Krause) Scholl; m. 1st Brunhild Meister (died 1969), two d.; m. 2nd Dr. Anna Elisabeth Wolff 1971, two d.; Scientific Asst., Foreign Office 1939–45; at Diergardt-Mevissen III coal mine 1945–50; Ministry of Interior 1950–52; rose through German Diplomatic Service, Belgrade 1954–56, Foreign Office 1956–60, Moscow 1960–63; Amb. to Pakistan 1963–70, to Denmark 1970–73; Commdr., Order of Phoenix, Grosses Bundesverdienstkreuz mit Stern, Hilal-i-Quaid-i-Azam (Pakistan), Grand Cross of Dannebrog (Denmark). *Leisure interests:* art, history, music, sport. *Address:* 8000 Munich 19, Zuccalistrasse 17a, Federal Republic of Germany. *Telephone:* 17-55-20.

SCHÖLLKOPF, Ulrich, PH.D.; German professor of chemistry; b. 10 Nov. 1927, Ebersbach; m. Edith Jennewein 1957; two s. one d.; ed. Univ. of Tübingen, Univ. of Calif., Los Angeles; lecturer in Chem., Univ. of Heidelberg 1961–63; Assoc. Prof. Univ. of Göttingen 1964–68, Prof. 1968–; Ed. Liebigs Annalen der Chemie; mem. Cttee. for the Dr. Paul-Janssen Prize, Akad. der Wissenschaften, Göttingen, Liebigs Denkmünze der GDCh; Award of the Japanese Soc. for the Promotion of Science. *Publi-*

cations: 250 articles in scientific journals. *Address:* Institut für Organische Chemie der Universität, Tammannstrasse 2, 3400 Göttingen (Office); Eichenweg 5, D-3406 Bovenden, Federal Republic of Germany (Home).

SCHOLTEN, Willem, B.L.; Netherlands politician; b. 1 June 1927, Deventer; s. of G. and W. H. (née Berends) Scholten; m. C. M. van der Eijk 1954; one s. one d.; ed. Rijksbelastingacademie, Univ. of Amsterdam; Insp. of Taxes 1950-63; mem. Second Chamber, States-Gen. (Parl.) 1963-71; Sec. of State for Finance 1971-73; mem. European Parl. 1973-76; mem. Council of State 1976-78; Minister of Defence 1978-80; Vice-Pres. Council of State 1980-. *Address:* Binnenhof 1, 2513 AA 's-Gravenhage (Office); Kievitlaan 2, 2261 ER Leidschendam, Netherlands (Home). *Telephone:* 070-624871 (Office); 070-276785 (Home).

SCHOLZ, Rupert, DR. JUR.; German politician and fmr. academic; b. 23 May 1937, Berlin; m.; ed. Free Univ. of Berlin and Univ. of Heidelberg; taught law, Berlin and Munich 1972-81; Senator for Justice, W. Berlin 1981-88, for Fed. Affairs 1983-88; Minister of Defence 1988-89; mem. CDU 1983-. *Address:* c/o Ministry of Defence, Hardhöhe, 5300 Bonn 1, Postfach 1328, Federal Republic of Germany.

SCHON, Baron (Life Peer), cr. 1976, of Whitehaven in the County of Cumbria; **Frank Schon,** Kt.; British industrialist; b. 18 May 1912, Vienna, Austria; s. of Dr. Frederick and Henriette (née Nettel) Schon; m. Gertrude Secher 1936; two d.; ed. Rainer Gymnasium, Vienna and Univs. of Prague and Vienna; co-founder Marchon Products Ltd. 1939, Solway Chemicals Ltd. 1943, Chair. and Man. Dir. of both until 1967; Dir. Albright & Wilson Ltd. 1956-67, Blue Circle Industries PLC 1967-82; mem. Nat. Research Devt. Corpn. 1967-79, Chair. 1969-79; Chair. Cumberland Devt. Council 1964-68; mem. Council, King's Coll., Newcastle, in Durham Univ. 1959-63; mem. Council, Univ. of Newcastle upon Tyne 1963-66, mem. Univ. Court 1963-78; mem. Northern Econ. Planning Council 1965-68, Industrial Reorganization Corpn. 1966-71, Advisory Council of Tech. 1968-70; Part-time mem. Northern Gas Bd. 1963-66; Hon. D.C.L. (Durham Univ.) 1961; Freeman of Whitehaven 1961. *Leisure interests:* golf, reading. *Address:* 82 Prince Albert Court, 33 Prince Albert Road, London, NW8 7LU, England. *Telephone:* 01-586 1461.

SCHONBERG, Harold C.; American music critic; b. 29 Nov. 1915, New York, N.Y.; s. of David and Minnie Schonberg; m. 1st Rosalyn Krokover 1942 (died 1973), 2nd Helene Cornell 1975; ed. Brooklyn Coll. and New York Univ.; Assoc. Ed. American Music Lover 1938-42; Music Critic New York Sun 1946-50; Contributing Ed. and Record Columnist Musical Courier 1948-52; Music and Record Critic New York Times 1950-60, Sr. Music Critic 1960-80, Cultural Correspondent 1980-85; columnist for The Gramophone (London) 1948-60; Contributing Ed. Int. Encyclopaedia of Music and Musicians; U.S. Army service 1942-46; Pulitzer Prize for Criticism 1971. *Publications:* The Guide to Long-Playing Records: Chamber and Solo Instrument Music 1955, The Collector's Chopin and Schumann 1959, The Great Pianists 1963, The Great Conductors 1967, Lives of the Great Composers 1970, Grandmasters of Chess 1973, Facing the Music 1981, The Glorious Ones: Classical Music's Legendary Performers 1985. *Leisure interests:* chess, golf, poker, backgammon. *Address:* 160 Riverside Drive, New York, N.Y. 10024, U.S.A.

SCHÖNE, Albrecht, DR.PHIL.; German philologist; b. 17 July 1925, Barby; s. of Friedrich Schöne and Agnes Moeller; m. Dagmar Haver 1952; one s. one d.; ed. Univs. of Freiburg, Basle, Göttingen and Münster; Extraordinary Prof. of German Literature, Univ. of Münster 1958; Prof. of German Philology, Univ. of Göttingen 1960-; Pres. Int. Asscn. for Germanic Studies 1980-85; mem. Akad. der Wissenschaften, Göttingen, Deutsche Akad. für Sprache und Dichtung, Bayrische Akad. der Wissenschaften, Austrian and Netherlands Acads.; Hon. mem. Modern Language Assn. of America; several prizes. *Publications:* numerous books and articles on German literature and philology. *Leisure interests:* riding, hunting, painting. *Address:* Humboldtallee 13, 3400 Göttingen, Federal Republic of Germany. *Telephone:* 0551-56449.

SCHÖNZELER, Hans-Hubert; British (b. German) musician; b. 22 June 1925, Leipzig; m. 1st 1962 (divorced), m. 2nd Helmi Preisler 1982; one s.; ed. Sydney Conservatorium, Australia, Paris Conservatoire, France, Accademia Chigiana, Italy, studied with Rafael Kubelik, Wilhelm Furtwängler; conductor and musicologist 1952-; conductor 20th Century Ensemble, London 1957-61; Resident Conductor, West Australian Symphony Orchestra 1967; Guest engagements in numerous European countries, Australia, New Zealand, Canada; now freelance; Dir. Ernst Eulenburg Ltd., London 1959-63; numerous gramophone recordings; Hon. Mem. Dvořák Soc., Prague; Hon. Prof. (Austria); Medal of Honor, Bruckner Soc. of America, Bruckner Medal Int. Bruckner Soc., Vienna. *Publications:* Bruckner 1970, Of German Music 1976, Dvořák 1984, Furtwängler; numerous articles. *Leisure interest:* sleeping. *Address:* c/o Savage Club, 9 Fitzmaurice Place, London, W.1, England.

SCHOPPER, Herwig Franz, DR. RER. NAT.; German physicist; b. 28 Feb. 1924, Landskron, Czechoslovakia; s. of Dr. Franz Schopper and Grete (née Stark) Schopper; m. Ingeborg Stieler; one s. one d.; ed. Univ. of Hamburg; Research Assoc. Tech. Univ. Stockholm 1950-51, Cavendish Lab. Cambridge 1956-57, Cornell Univ. 1960-61; Assoc. Prof. and Lecturer, Univ. of Erlangen 1954-57; Prof. and Dir. Nuclear Physics Inst. Univ. of Karlsruhe

1957-60; Research Assoc. CERN, Geneva 1966-67; Chair. Scientific Council, Nuclear Physics Centre of Karlsruhe 1967-69; Head, Particle Physics Dept. and mem. Directorate, CERN 1970-73; Chair. of Directorate, DESY Particle Physics Lab. 1973-80; Prof. Univ. of Hamburg (on leave of absence) 1973-; Dir.-Gen. CERN, Geneva 1981-88; mem. Acad. of Sciences Leopoldina, Halle; corresp. mem. Bavarian Acad. of Sciences; Dr. h.c. (Erlangen) 1982, (Moscow); several awards including Carus Medal (Acad. Leopoldina) 1959, Ritter von Gerstner Medal 1978, Golden Plate Award (American Acad. of Achievement) 1984, Grosses Verdienstkreuz. *Leisure interests:* science, philosophy, piano, gardening. *Address:* Department of Physics, University of Hamburg, 2000 Hamburg 13, Edmund-Siemers-Allee 1, Federal Republic of Germany.

SCHOTTE, Most Rev. Jan; Belgian ecclesiastic; b. 29 April 1928, Beveren-Waregem; s. of Marcel Schotte and Rhea Duhou; ed. Sacred Heart Diocesan Coll., Waregem, Belgium, C.I.C.M. Scholasticate, Scheut-Brussels and Katholieke Universiteit, Leuven; Asst. Prof. Canon Law Catholic Univ. Leuven 1955-62; Rector I.H.M. Seminary, Catholic Univ. of America, Washington D.C. 1963-66; Sec. Gen. Congregation Immaculate Heart of Mary, Rome 1967-72; Attaché for Int. Orgs. Secr. of State, Vatican 1972-80; Vice-Pres. Pontifical Comm. for Justice and Peace 1980-85; Sec. Gen. World Synod of Bishops 1985-; Titular Bishop of Silli 1984, Titular Archbishop 1985; Officier, Légion d'honneur, Ordre Leopold II (Belgium), Kt. Commdr. with Star, Order of Holy Sepulcher (U.S.A.). *Address:* Sinodo dei Vescovi, 00120 Vatican City State, Italy. *Telephone:* 0039-6-6984821.

SCHRAM, Armin; German business executive; b. 31 Jan. 1929, Prague; ed. Vienna Technical Univ.; mem. Man. Bd. Deutsche Texaco AG 1967, Vice-Chair. 1973, Chair. 1979-. *Address:* Überseering 40, 2000 Hamburg 60, Federal Republic of Germany.

SCHRANK, Ralf Gerd, DR.RER.NAT.; German public relations executive; b. 14 Feb. 1949, Celle; s. of Gerd and Irmgard Schrank; m. Karola Girth 1970; ed. Univ. of Hannover and Ruhr-Universität-Bochum; Scholarship, Max-Planck-Gesellschaft, Inst. für Strahlchemie, Mülheim/Ruhr 1977-81; Freelance Scientific Journalist 1981-; Ed. for tech. and science W. C. Heraeus GmbH, Hanau 1982-, Exec. Public Affairs Div. 1984-. *Publications:* various publications on popular science. *Leisure interests:* hiking, writing. *Address:* Heraeus Holding GmbH, Postfach 1553, 6450 Hanau 1 (Office); Kurt-Schumacher-Ring 45, 6454 Brückköbel 2, Federal Republic of Germany (Home). *Telephone:* (6181) 35858 (Office); (6181) 73238 (Home).

SCHREIER, Peter; German tenor and conductor; b. 29 July 1935, Meissen; ed. Dresden Hochschule für Musik; sang with Dresden State Opera 1959-63; joined Berlin Staatsoper 1963; has appeared at Vienna State Opera, Salzburg Festival, La Scala, Milan, Sadler's Wells, London, Metropolitan Opera, New York and Teatro Colón, Buenos Aires; recital début London 1978; début as conductor 1969; has conducted recordings of several choral works by J. S. Bach and Mozart. *Address:* c/o Norman McCann International Artists Ltd., 56 Lawrie Park Gardens, London, SE26 6XJ, England. *Telephone:* 01-659 5955.

SCHREYER, Rt. Hon. Edward Richard, P.C., C.C., C.M.M., C.D., M.A. LL.D.; Canadian politician and diplomatist; b. 21 Dec. 1935, Beausejour, Manitoba; s. of John J. Schreyer and Elizabeth Gottfried; m. Lily Schulz 1960; two s. two d.; ed. Cromwell Public School, Beausejour Collegiate, United Coll., St. John's Coll. and Univ. of Manitoba; mem. for Brokenhead, Manitoba Legislature 1958, re-elected 1959, 1962; Prof. Political Science and Int. Relations, Univ. of Manitoba 1962-65; M.P. for Springfield Constituency 1965-68, for Selkirk 1968; Leader, Manitoba New Democratic Party 1969-78; Premier of Manitoba, Pres. of the Council and Minister of Dominion-Provincial Relations 1969-77, Minister of Industry and Commerce July-Dec. 1969, of Finance 1972-76; Leader of the Opposition 1977-78; Gov.-Gen. of Canada 1979-84; High Commr. to Australia 1984-88; mem. Canadian Assn. of Univ. Teachers, Commonwealth Parl. Assn., Inter-Parl. Union; Gov.-Gen. Vanier Medal 1974. *Leisure interests:* reading, golf, carpentry. *Address:* 3069 Henderson Highway, RR3, Winnipeg MB R3C 2E7, Canada.

SCHREYER, William Allen, B.A.; American business executive; b. 13 Jan. 1928, Williamsport, Pa.; s. of late William Schreyer and Elizabeth Engel; m. Joan Legg 1953; one d.; ed. Pennsylvania State Univ.; with Merrill Lynch, Pierce, Fenner & Smith, Inc. 1948-, Vice-Pres. 1965-78, Sales Dir., New York 1969-72, Regional Dir. 1972-73, now Chair., Pres. and C.E.O.; Chair. Merrill Lynch Govt. Securities, Inc. 1973-76, 1981-; Exec. Vice-Pres. Capital Markets Activities 1976-78, fmr. Pres. and C.E.O.; Pres., C.E.O. and Dir. Merrill Lynch & Co. 1984-, Chair. 1985-; Dir. Merrill Lynch & Co. Trustee Medical Center, Princeton 1974-80; Trustee American Man. Assons. 1979-; mem. Securities Industry Assn., Gov. 1979-; Hon. D.H.; Distinguished Alumnus Award (Pa. State Univ.). *Leisure interests:* tennis, reading, swimming. *Address:* Merrill Lynch & Co. Inc., One Liberty Plaza, New York, N.Y. 10080 (Office); 117 Mercer Street, Princeton, N.J. 08540, U.S.A. (Home).

SCHRIEFFER, John Robert, PH.D.; American professor of physics; b. 31 May 1931, Oak Park, Ill.; m. Anne Grete Thomson 1960; one s. two d.; ed. Mass. Inst. of Technology and Univ. of Illinois; Nat. Science Foundation Fellow, Univ. of Birmingham, U.K., and Univ. Inst. for Theoretical Physics, Copenhagen 1957-58; Asst. Prof., Univ. of Chicago 1957-60, Univ. of Ill.

1959-60; Assoc. Prof., Univ. of Ill. 1960-62; Prof., Univ. of Pa. 1962, Mary Amanda Wood Prof. of Physics 1964-79; Prof. of Physics, Univ. of Calif., Santa Barbara 1980-84, Essan Khashoggi Prof. of Physics 1985-; Dir. Inst. for Theoretical Physics, Santa Barbara 1984-; Andrew D. White Prof. Cornell Univ. 1969-75; mem. N.A.S., American Acad. Arts and Sciences, mem. American Philosophical Soc. 1974, mem. Royal Danish Acad. of Science and Letters; Guggenheim Fellow 1967-68; hon. doctorates (Geneva, Technische Hochschule, Munich, Univs. of Pa., Ill., Cincinatti and Tel Aviv); Buckley Prize 1968; Comstock Prize (N.A.S.) 1968; Nobel Prize in Physics (with J. Bardeen (q.v.) and L. N. Cooper) 1972; John Ericsson Medal (American Soc. of Swedish Engineers) 1976, Alumni Achievement Award, Univ. of Ill. 1979, Nat. Medal of Science 1985. *Publication:* Theory of Superconductivity 1964. *Address:* Inst. for Theoretical Physics, University of California, Santa Barbara, Calif. 93106 (Office); 1009 Las Palmas Drive, Santa Barbara, Calif. 93110, U.S.A. (Home). *Telephone:* 805-961-2280 (Office).

SCHRÖDER, Ernst Augustus; German actor; b. 27 Jan. 1915, Wanne-Eickel; s. of B. Schröder and Gertrud Noël; m. Gesa Ferck 1946; one s. two d.; ed. Freie Universität, Berlin, Gastrrof. Hochschule der Künste; theatre and stage-man. Munich, Zurich, Vienna, Salzburg; acted in England, France, South America, Belgrade; acted in Galileo Galilei, Strese-mann, Tartuffe, Macbeth, Richard III, Master Builder, Mephisto, King Lear; Grosse Kunstpreis BLN, Filmband in Gold (Fed. Repub. of Germany). *Publications:* Die Besessenen 1946, Die Arbeit der Schauspielers, Das Leben Verspielt 1978. *Address:* Podere Montalto, Castellina in Ch., Siena 53011, Italy; Hinteregg im Bad, CH-8021 Zurich, Switzerland. *Telephone:* 0577 740912 (Italy).

SCHRÖDER, Dr. Gerhard; German lawyer and politician; b. 11 Sept. 1910, Saarbrücken; s. of Jan and Antina (née Duit) Schröder; m. Brigitte Landsberg 1941; three c.; ed. Kaiser-Wilhelm-Gymnasium, Trier and Univs. of Königsberg, Edinburgh, Berlin and Bonn; Asst. Law Faculty Bonn Univ. and Kaiser-Wilhelm Inst. for Foreign and Int. Private Law, Berlin 1933-36; practice in Berlin 1936-39; served 1939-45 war; served Land Govt. Nordrhein-Westfalen 1945-47; mem. post-war Comm. on Electoral Law; practice in Düsseldorf since 1947; concerned with reorganization of mining and iron and steel industries 1947-53; mem. (Christian Democratic Union) Fed. Parl. 1949-80; Minister of the Interior 1953-61, of Foreign Affairs 1961-66, of Defence 1966-69; Chair. Foreign Affairs Cttee. of Parl. 1969-80; Pres. German Photographic Soc. 1954-78; Dr. h.c. (Univ. of Md.) 1959; Hermann Ehlers Prize 1981; Grosskreuz Verdienstorden 1958. *Publications:* Für eine heile Welt-Politik in und für Deutschland 1963; Decision for Europe 1964. *Leisure interests:* photography and painting. *Address:* Pappelweg 25a, 5300 Bonn-Bad Godesberg, Federal Republic of Germany. *Telephone:* 321010.

SCHRÖDER, Gerhard; German public servant; b. 3 March 1921; ed. Marburg Univ.; Officer, Radio, Film and Press Affairs, Ministry of Education, Lower Saxony 1952-59; Head of Arts Dept., Ministry of Education, Lower Saxony 1960-61; mem. Admin. Council, North German Radio 1955-61; Dir.-Gen. Norddeutscher Rundfunk (North German Radio and TV) 1961-73; Chair. ARD (Assen. of German Broadcasting Orgs.) 1970-71; Dir.-Gen. Radio Bremen (Radio and TV) 1974-80, Chair. Bd. of Dirs. and Dir.-Gen. 1980-86. *Address:* Rondeel 5, 2000 Hamburg 60, Federal Republic of Germany.

SCHRÖDER, Werner Hermann, DR. PHIL.; German professor of philology; b. 13 March 1914, Vaethen; s. of Hermann Schröder and Hedwig Eikemeier; m. 1st Ursula Nehm 1949, 2nd Anne-Ilse Radke 1973; three s. three d.; ed. Universität Halle; archivist, Landeshauptarchiv Sachsen-Anhalt, Magdeburg 1948-52; Dozent, Martin Luther Univ. Halle-Wittenberg 1953-56, Prof. of German Philology 1956-59; Prof. of Germanic and German Philology, Univ. of Marburg 1960-82, Prof. Emer. 1982-; mem. Mainz Acad. *Publications:* seven books. *Address:* 3550 Marburg, Roter Hof 10; 7272 Altensteig, Uhlandstrasse 34, Federal Republic of Germany.

SCHROEDER, Manfred Robert, DR.RER.NAT.; American (b. German) physicist; b. 12 July 1926, Ahlen, North Rhine-Westphalia; s. of Karl and Hertha Schroeder; m. Anny Menschik 1956; two s. one d.; Head of Acoustics Research Dept., Bell Labs., U.S.A. 1958-63, Dir. of Acoustics, Speech and Mechanics Research 1963-69; Dir. Drittes Physikalisches Inst., Univ. of Göttingen 1969-; mem. Nat. Acad. of Eng. Washington, Göttingen Acad. of Sciences, Max-Planck Soc.; Fellow American Acad. of Arts and Sciences 1986-; Gold Medal, Audio Eng. Soc. 1972; Baker Prize Award, Inst. of Electrical and Electronics Engineers, New York 1977; Sr. Award, Acoustics, Speech and Signal Processing Soc. 1979; Lord Rayleigh Gold Medal, British Inst. of Acoustics. *Publications:* Speech and Speaker Recognition 1985, Number Theory in Science and Communication 1986, and about 130 articles on acoustics, speech, hearing, microwaves, computer graphics. *Leisure interests:* skiing, sailing, bicycling, photography. *Address:* Drittes Physikalisches Institut, Universität Göttingen, Bürgerstrasse 42-44, D-3400 Göttingen; Rieswartenweg 8, D-3400 Göttingen, Federal Republic of Germany (Home).

SCHROEDER, Steven Alfred, M.D.; American professor of medicine; b. 26 July 1939, New York; s. of Arthur E. Schroeder; m. Sally Ross Schroeder 1967; two s.; ed. El Cerrito High School, Stanford Univ.,

Harvard Univ.; Fellow, Harvard Community Health and Medical Care and Instructor Harvard Medical School 1970-71; Asst. Prof. of Medicine and Health Care Sciences, later Assoc. Prof., The George Washington Univ. Medical Center 1971-76; Medical Dir. The George Washington Univ. Health Plan 1971-76; Assoc. Prof. of Medicine, Univ. of Calif., San Francisco 1976-80, Prof. 1980-, Chief, Div. of Gen. Internal Medicine 1980-; Visiting Prof. Dept. of Community Medicine, St. Thomas's Hosp. Medical School, London 1982-83; Ed. Current Medical Diagnosis and Treatment 1987-. *Publications:* more than 80 articles. *Leisure interests:* climbing, hiking, tennis, gardening, literature, history. *Address:* Division of General Internal Medicine, 400 Parnassus Ave., 405, San Francisco, Calif. 94143 (Office); 10 Paseo Mirasol, Tiburon, Calif. 94920, U.S.A. *Telephone:* 415-476 4362 (Office); 415-435 2858 (Home).

SCHUBERT, Richard F.; American business executive; b. 2 Nov. 1936, Trenton, N.J.; s. of Yaro Schubert and Frances Mary Hustak; m. Sarah Jane Lockington 1957; one s. one d.; ed. Eastern Nazarene Coll., Quincy, Mass., Yale Law School; Attorney in labour relations div. of Bethlehem Steel 1961-66, Asst. Man. of Div. 1966-70; Exec. Asst. to Under-Sec. of Labor James D. Hodgson 1970-71; Solicitor, Dept. of Labor 1971-73; Asst. to Vice-Pres. Bethlehem Steel Dept. of Industrial Relations 1973; Under-Sec. of Labor 1973-75; Asst. Vice-Pres. in Public Affairs Dept., Bethlehem Steel 1975-76, Vice-Pres. 1977-79; Pres. and Dir. Bethlehem Steel Corpn. 1979-82, Vice-Chair. 1980-82; Pres. American Red Cross 1983-; Chair. Comm. on Workforce Quality and Labour Market Efficiency 1988; mem. Northampton Co. and Pennsylvania Bar Assens.; Chair. corp. environmental control cttee. 1975-78; fmr. Chair. Cttee. on Int. Trade of American Iron and Steel Inst.; Dir. Nat. Alliance of Business; mem. American Iron and Steel Inst., Council on Foreign Relations, Conference Bd.; Bd. of Dirs. of Roosevelt Centre of Public Policy Centre, American Security Bank, Weirton Steel; Chair. Dept. of Labor Transition Team 1980; Co-Chair. UN Assen. of the U.S.A. Econ. Policy Council, Panel on Productivity; mem. Nat. Productivity Advisory Council; Trustee, Nat. Safety Council, Eastern Nazarene Coll., St. Francis de Sales Coll. 1984; Hon. LL.D. (Eastern Nazarene Coll.) 1975, (St. Francis de Sales Coll.) 1985; Hon. Hum. Litt. (Muskingum Coll.) 1986, Hon. D. Hum. (Springfield Coll.) 1986. *Leisure interests:* skiing, tennis. *Address:* American Red Cross, 17th and D Streets, Washington, D.C. 20006 (Office); 7811 Old Dominion Drive, McLean, Va. 22102, U.S.A. (Home). *Telephone:* (202) 639-3292 (Office).

SCHUESSEL, Wolfgang; Austrian politician; Minister of Econ. Affairs April 1989-; mem. People's Party. *Address:* Ministry of Economic Affairs, Stubenring 1, 1010 Vienna, Austria. *Telephone:* (01) 75-0-00.

SCHULBERG, Budd, LL.D.; American novelist and scriptwriter; b. 27 March 1914, New York, N.Y.; s. of Benjamin P. and Adeline (Jaffe) Schulberg; m. 1st Virginia Ray 1936 (divorced 1942), one d.; m. 2nd Victoria Anderson 1943 (divorced 1964), two s.; m. 3rd Geraldine Brooks 1964 (died 1977); m. 4th Betsy Langman 1979, one s. one d.; ed. Deerfield Acad. and Dartmouth Coll.; short-story writer and novelist 1936-; Screenwriter for Samuel Goldwyn, David O. Selznick and Walter Wanger, Hollywood, Calif. 1936-40; Lieut. U.S. Navy 1943-46, assigned to Office of Strategic Service; taught writing courses and conducted workshops at various institutes in the U.S.; mem. Authors Guild, Dramatists Guild, American Civil Liberties Union, American Soc. Composers Authors and Publishers, Sphinx, Bd. of Trustees, Humanitas Prize, Advisory Cttee. on Black Participation John F. Kennedy Center for the Performing Arts; Founder Watts Writers Workshop, Frederick Douglass Creative Arts Center, New York; numerous awards for writings. *Publications:* novels: What Makes Sammy Run? 1941, The Harder They Fall 1947 (screen adaptation 1955), The Disenchanted 1950, Waterfront 1955, Sanctuary V 1969, Some Faces in the Crowd (short stories) 1953, From the Ashes: Voices of Watts (Ed. and author of introduction) 1967, Loser and Still Champion: Muhammad Ali 1972, The Four Seasons of Success 1972, Swan Watch (with Geraldine Brooks) 1975, Everything That Moves 1980, Moving Pictures: Memories of a Hollywood Prince 1981, Writers in America 1983; plays: Winter Carnival (with F. Scott Fitzgerald) 1939, The Pharmacist's Mate 1951, On the Waterfront (Acad. Award and Screen Writers Guild Award for the screenplay) 1954, A Face in the Crowd (German Film Critics Award) 1957, Wind Across the Everglades 1958, The Disenchanted 1958, What Makes Sammy Run (television play 1959, stage 1964); stories and articles in numerous anthologies; contrib. to Newsday Syndicate, Esquire, Saturday Review, Life, Harper's, Playboy, Intellectual Digest, The New Republic. *Leisure interests:* bird watching, boxing, fishing, Mexican archaeology, Black Arts movement. *Address:* c/o Alyss Dorese Agency, 1400 Ambassador Street, Los Angeles, Calif. 90035 (Office); Westhampton Beach, New York, N.Y. 11978, U.S.A. *Telephone:* (212) 556-0710.

SCHULLER, Gunther; American composer and conductor; b. 22 Nov. 1925, New York; s. of Arthur E. and Elsie (Bernartz) Schuller; m. Marjorie Black 1948; two s.; ed. St. Thomas Choir School, New York, N.Y. and Manhattan School of Music; Principal French horn, Cincinnati, Symphony Orchestra 1943-45, Metropolitan Opera Orchestra 1945-59; teacher, Manhattan School of Music 1950-63; Head Composition Dept., Tanglewood 1963-84; Music Dir. First Int. Jazz Festival, Washington 1962; active as conductor since mid-1960s with major orchestras in Europe and U.S.A.; reconstructed and orchestrated 1912 opera Der Gelbe Klang by De Hartmann/Kandinsky; Pres. New England Conservatory of Music 1967-77; Pres. Nat. Music Council 1979-81; Artistic Dir. Summer Activities, Boston Symphony Orchestra, Tanglewood, Berkshire Music Center 1969-84, Festival at Sandpoint 1985-; f. and Pres. Margun Music Inc. 1975, G.M. Records 1980; mem. Acad. of Arts and Letters; Creative Arts Award, Brandeis Univ. 1960; Nat. Inst. Arts and Letters Award 1960; Guggenheim Grant 1962, 1963; ASCAP Deems Taylor Award 1970; Rogers and Hammerstein Award 1971; William Schuman Award, Columbia Univ. 1989; Hon. D.Mus. (Ill. Univ.) 1966; (Northeastern Univ.) 1967, (Colby Coll.) 1969, (Ill. Univ.) 1970, (Williams Coll.) 1975. *Compositions include:* Symphony for Brass and Percussion 1950, Fantasy for Unaccompanied Cello 1951, Recitative and Rondo for Violin and Piano 1953, Dramatic Overture 1951, Music for Violin, Piano and Percussion 1957, String Quartet No. 1 1957, Woodwind Quintet 1958, Spectra 1958, Concertino for Jazz Quartet and Orchestra 1959, Seven Studies on Themes of Paul Klee 1959, Conversations 1960, Variants (ballet with choreography by Balanchine) 1961, Music for Brass Quintet 1961, String Quartet No. 2 1965, Symphony 1965, Sacred Cantata 1966, Gala Music (Concerto for Orchestra) 1966, The Visitation (opera commissioned by Hamburg State Opera) 1966, Movements for Flute and Strings, Six Renaissance Lyrics, Triplum I 1967, Shapes and Designs 1968, Fisherman and his Wife (opera) 1970, Capriccio Stravagante 1972, Tre Invenzioni 1972, Three Nocturnes 1973, Four Soundscapes 1974, Triplum II 1975, Violin Concerto 1976, Concerto No. 2 for Horn and Orchestra 1976, Diptych (for organ) 1976, Concerto No. 2 for Orchestra 1977, Concerto for Contrabasson and Orchestra 1978, Deaï (for three orchestras) 1978, Concerto for Trumpet and Orchestra 1979, Eine Kleine Posaunenmusik 1980, In Praise of Winds (symphony for large wind orchestra) 1981, Concerto No. 2 for Piano and Orchestra 1981, Symphony for Organ 1981, Concerto Quarternio 1983, On Light Wings (piano quartet) 1984, Farbenspiel (Concerto No. 3 for Orchestra) 1985, String Quartet No. 3 1986, Sextet for Bassoon, Piano and String Quartet 1986. *Publications:* Horn Technique 1962, Early Jazz, Its Roots and Musical Development, Vol. I 1968, Musings: The Musical Worlds of Gunther Schuller 1985, The Swing Era: The Development of Jazz 1930-45 1989. *Address:* c/o Margun Music Inc., 167 Dudley Road, Newton Center, Mass. 02159, U.S.A. *Telephone:* 617-332-6398.

SCHULMANN, Horst, DR.RER.POL.; German fmr. government official and international economist; b. 13 April 1933, Frankfurt am Main; m. Ulrike Wagner 1973; one s. one d.; ed. Goethe-Universität, Frankfurt am Main, Univ. des Saarlandes, Saarbrücken; Sec.-Gen. German Council of Econ. Advisers 1967-69; Programming Officer, Div. Chief, Programming Adviser, then Deputy Dir. World Bank 1970-74; Dir. Comm. of European Communities 1975-77; Dept. Head, Ministry of Finance, Bonn 1977-78, Office of the Fed. Chancellor, Bonn 1978-80, Sec. of State, Ministry of Finance, Bonn 1980-82; Deputy Man. Dir. Inst. of Int. Finance, Washington 1984-86, Man. Dir. 1987-. *Leisure interests:* cycling, skiing. *Address:* c/o The Institute of International Finance Inc., 2000 Pennsylvania Avenue, N.W., Washington, D.C., U.S.A. *Telephone:* (202) 857-3604.

SCHULTÉN, Cay Gerhard af; Finnish administrative official; b. 24 April 1938, Helsinki; s. of Marius af Schultén and Judith af Schultén; m. 1st Monica Ström 1961; one s. two d.; m. 2nd Pauliine Koskelo 1987; Counsellor Ministry of Justice 1970-78; Consumer-Ombudsman 1978-87; Sec.-Gen. Nordic Council 1987-. *Leisure interests:* music and travel. *Address:* Secretariat of the Presidium, Nordic Council, Box 19506, S-104 32, Stockholm, Sweden. *Telephone:* 08 143420.

SCHULTES, Richard Evans, PH.D.; American botanist, plant explorer, professor and museum director; b. 12 Jan. 1915, Boston, Mass.; s. of Otto Richard Schultes and Maude Beatrice (Bagley) Schultes; m. Dorothy McNeil 1959; two s. one d.; ed. Harvard Univ.; Research Fellow, Harvard Botanical Museum 1942-53, Curator, Ames Orchid Herbarium 1953-58, Curator, Econ. Botany 1958-85, Dir. Harvard Botanical Museum 1967-85; Prof. of Biology Harvard Univ. 1970-72, Mangelsdorf Prof. of Natural Sciences 1973-81, Jeffrey Prof. of Biology 1981-85, Prof. Emer. 1985-; NRC Fellow, Exploration Amazon 1941-42, Collaborator U.S. Dept. of Agriculture, Amazon 1942-43, Plant Explorer 1944-54; Adjunct Prof. of Pharmacognosy, Univ. of Ill. 1975-; Guggenheim Fellow 1942; Hon. D. Sc. (Massachusetts Coll. of Pharmacy); Orden Victoria Regia (Colombia) 1969, Cruz de Boyacá 1983; Gold Medal for Conservation (Duke of Edin. Award for World Wildlife Fund, Int.) 1984, Tyler Prize for Environmental Achievement 1987. *Publications:* Economic Botany of the Kiowa Indians (with Vestal) 1941, Native Orchids of Trinidad and Tobago, Plants and Human Affairs (with Hill) 1960, Generic Names of Orchids: their origin and meaning (with Pease) 1963, The Botany and Chemistry of Hallucinogens (with Hofmann) 1973, Plants of the Gods (with Hofmann) 1979, Hallucinogenic Plants 1976, The Glass Flowers at Harvard (with Davis) 1982, Where the Gods Reign 1988. *Leisure interests:* gardening, photography. *Address:* Botanical Museum, Harvard University, Cambridge, Mass. 02138; 78 Larchmont Road, Melrose, Mass. 02176, U.S.A. (Home). *Telephone:* (617) 449-2326 (Office); (617) NOZ-8449 (Home).

SCHULTHEISZ, Emil, M.D., PH.D.; Hungarian physician, professor of history of medicine, and politician (retd.); b. 1923, Budapest; ed. Univ. of Liberal Arts, Kolozsvár (now Cluj, Romania), and Medical Univs. of Debrecen and Budapest; practised in Budapest Hospitals 1950-54; qualified

as specialist for internal diseases 1954; Chief of Internal Dept., Cen. State Hospital 1960, Vice-Dir., later Dir. 1970-72; Deputy Minister of Health, later First Deputy Minister and Sec. of State for Health 1972; Minister of Health 1974-84; Chief Dir. Semmelweis Museum of Medical History until 1973; mem. numerous medical socs. in Hungary and abroad; Hon. M.D. (Cracow); Order of Merit of Hungary. *Publications:* two books and more than 150 medical articles. *Address:* c/o Ministry of Health, V. Arany János utca. 6-8, 1361 Budapest, Hungary.

SCHULTZ, Theodore W., M.S., PH.D.; American economist; b. 30 April 1902, Arlington, S.D.; s. of Henry Edward Schultz and Anna Elizabeth Weiss; m. Esther Florence Werth; one s. two d.; ed. South Dakota State Coll., Univ. of Wisconsin; Faculty of Econs., Iowa State Coll. 1930-43, Head of Dept. of Econs. and Sociology 1934-43; Prof. of Econs., Univ. of Chicago 1943-72, Chair. Dept. of Econs. 1946-61, Charles L. Hutchinson Distinguished Service Prof. 1952-72, Prof. Emer. 1972-; Pres. American Econ. Asscn. 1960; Hon. LL.D. (Grinell Coll., Mich. State Univ., Univs. of Ill. and Wis., Catholic Univ. of Chile, Dijon Univ., N.C. State Univ.); Francis A. Walker Medal (American Econ. Asscn.) 1972, Leonard Elmhirst Medal (IAEA) 1976, shared Nobel Prize for Econ. Science 1979 with Sir Arthur Lewis (q.v.). *Publications:* Agriculture in an Unstable Economy 1945, Transforming Traditional Agriculture 1964, Economic Growth and Agriculture 1968, Investment in Human Capital: the Role of Education and Research 1971, Human Resources 1972; ed.: Food for the World 1945, Investment in Human Beings 1962, Investment in Education: Equity-Efficiency Quandary 1972, New Economics Approaches to Fertility 1973, Marriage, Human Capital and Fertility 1974, Economics of the Family 1975, Distortion of Agricultural Incentives 1978, Investing in People: The Economics of Population Quality 1981. *Address:* Department of Economics, University of Chicago, 1126 East 59th Street, Chicago, Ill. 60637; and 5620 S. Kimbark Avenue, Chicago, Ill. 60637, U.S.A. *Telephone:* (312) 962-8250 (Office); (312) 493-6083 (Home).

SCHULTZE, Charles Louis, PH.D.; American economist and government official; b. 12 Dec. 1924, Alexandria, Va.; s. of Richard Lee and Nora Woolls (née Baggett) Schultze; m. Rita Irene Hertzog 1947; one s. five d.; ed. Georgetown Univ. and Univ. of Maryland; U.S. Army 1943-46; Admin. Asst. Democratic Nat. Cttee. 1948; Research Specialist, Army Security Agency 1948-49; Instructor, Coll. of St. Thomas (St. Paul, Minn.) 1949-51; Economist, Office of Price Stabilization 1951-52, Council of Econ. Advisers 1952-53, 1955-59, Machine and Allied Products Inst. 1953-54; Assoc. Prof. of Econs., Indiana Univ. 1959-61; Prof. of Econs., Univ. of Md. 1961-87; Asst. Dir., Bureau of the Budget 1962-65, Dir. 1965-68; Sr. Fellow, Brookings Inst., Washington 1968-76, 1981-87; Dir. Econ. Studies, Brookings Inst., Washington 1987-; Chair. Council of Econ. Advisers to Pres. 1977-81. *Publications:* National Income Analysis 1964, The Politics and Economics of Public Spending 1969 (co-author), Setting National Priorities: The 1974 Budget, The Public Use of Private Interest 1977, Other Times, Other Places 1986, American Living Standards (Co-Ed. and Co-Author) 1988, Barriers to European Growth (Co-Ed. and Co-Author) 1989. *Address:* Brookings Institution, 1775 Massachusetts Avenue, N.W., Washington, D.C. 20036; 5826 Nevada Avenue, N.W., Washington, D.C. 20015, U.S.A. (Home).

SCHULZ, Charles Monroe; American cartoonist; b. 26 Nov. 1922, Minneapolis, Minn.; s. of Carl and Dena (née Halverson) Schulz; m. Joyce Halverson 1949; two s. three d.; Cartoonist for St. Paul Pioneer Press, St. Paul, Minn., Saturday Evening Post 1948-49; created syndicated comic strip Peanuts 1950; Hon. L.H.D. (Anderson Coll., Ind.) 1963; Outstanding Cartoonist award (Nat. Cartoonist Soc.) 1956; Emmy Award (CBS children's programme A Charlie Brown Christmas 1966). *Publications:* collected cartoons published in book form: Peanuts 1952, More Peanuts 1954, Good Grief, More Peanuts 1956, Good Ol' Charlie Brown, Snoopy, You're Out of Your Mind Charlie Brown, But We Love You Charlie Brown, Peanuts Revisited, Go Fly a Kite Charlie Brown, Peanuts Every Sunday, You Can Do It Charlie Brown, Happiness is a Warm Puppy 1962, Love is Walking Hand in Hand 1965, A Charlie Brown Christmas 1965, You Need Help, Charlie Brown 1969, Charlie Brown's All-Stars 1966, You've Had It Charlie Brown 1969, The Snoopy Festival 1974, Its Your Turn Snoopy 1978; author and illustrator of Snoopy and the Red Baron 1966, Snoopy and His Sopwith Camel 1969, The Snoopy Come Home Movie Book 1972, The Charlie Brown Dictionary. *Address:* c/o Fawcett World, 1515 Broadway, New York, N.Y. 10036, U.S.A.

SCHULZ, Peter; German lawyer; b. 25 April 1930, Rostock; s. of Albert Schulz and Emmi Munck; m. Dr. Sonja Planeth 1955; one s. one d.; ed. Univ. of Hamburg; practising lawyer, Hamburg 1959-; mem. Hamburg City Council 1961-, Senator for Justice 1966-71; fmr. Deputy Regional Chair. Social Democratic Party, Hamburg-North; Second Burgomaster of Hamburg and Deputy Pres. of the Senate and Dept. of Educ. 1970-71; Chief Burgomaster of Hamburg and Pres. of Senate 1971-74; Pres. of Hamburg City Council 1978-82, Vice-Pres. 1982-83, Pres. 1983-87. *Address:* Kleine Reichenstrasse 1, 2000 Hamburg 11, Federal Republic of Germany.

SCHULZE, Rudolph; German politician; b. 18 Nov. 1918, Chemnitz (now Karl-Marx-Stadt); mem. Christlich-Demokratische Union (CDU) 1948-, CDU Presidium 1954-; mem. Volkskammer (People's Chamber), G.D.R.

1958–; Minister of Posts and Telecommunications 1963–; Deputy Chair. Council of Ministers 1971–; Vaterländischer Verdienstorden in Silver (twice), Vaterländischer Verdienstorden in Gold (twice), Ehrenspange to Vaterländischer Verdienstorden in Gold, Verdienter Werktätiger des Post und Fernmeldewesens, Held der Arbeit. *Address:* Ministerium für Post-und Fernmeldewesen, Mauerstrasse 69-75, Berlin-1066, German Democratic Republic.

SCHUMACHER, Robert Alan, B.A.; American business executive; b. 13 Jan. 1923, Marshall, Tex.; m. Dorothy Wemyss 1945; ed. Univ. of Virginia; Vice-Pres. Groveton Paper Co. 1946-56; Pres. Vanity Fair Paper Co. 1956-62; Vice-Pres. N.E. Div. Georgia-Pacific Corpn. 1963-74, Sr. Vice-Pres. N.E. Div. 1974-82, Exec. Vice-Pres. Pulp and Paper 1982-85, Pres. and C.O.O. Georgia-Pacific Corpn. 1985-88. *Address:* c/o Georgia-Pacific Corporation, 133 Peachtree Street, N.E., Atlanta, Ga. 30303, U.S.A.

SCHUMAN, William Howard, B.S., M.A.; American musician; b. 4 Aug. 1910, New York; m. Frances Prince 1936; one s. one d.; ed. Columbia Univ. and privately; lecturer and Dir. of Chorus, Sarah Lawrence Coll., Bronxville 1935-45; Dir. of Publications, G. Schirmer Inc. 1945-51; Pres. Juilliard School of Music 1945-62, Pres. Emer. 1962–; Pres. Lincoln Center for the Performing Arts 1962-69, Pres. Emer. 1969–; Chair. of Bd. Video-record Corpn. 1970-72; Chair. Norlin Foundation; Fellow, Nat. Inst. of Arts and Letters, American Acad. of Arts and Letters; Hon. mem. Royal Acad. of Music; Guggenheim Fellowships; Hon. doctorates (Chicago Musical Coll., Univ. of Wis., Philadelphia Conservatory of Music, Cincinnati Coll. of Music, Columbia Univ., Hartt Coll. of Music, Colgate Univ., Allegheny Coll., New York Univ., Brandeis Univ., Oberlin Coll., Adelphi Coll., Northwestern Univ., Bates Coll. and others); Pulitzer Prize for Music 1943; Award of Nat. Inst. of Arts and Letters, League of Composers Award, New York Critics Circle Award and Award of Merit of Nat. Assn. of American Composers and Conductors. *Compositions include:* ten symphonies, four string quartets, "Amaryllis" Variation for String Trio, American Festival Overture, Credendum, New England Triptych, Circus Overture, Concerto for Piano and Orchestra, Concerto for Violin and Orchestra, A Song of Orpheus (fantasy for 'cello and orchestra), The Witch of Endor, In Praise of Shahn, Quartettino for Four Bassoons, Variations for String Trio, The Mighty Casey (opera), secular cantatas and music for ballets, band works and piano music. *Address:* Lincoln Center for the Performing Arts, 150 W. 65th Street, New York, N.Y. 10023 (Office); Richmond Hill Road, Greenwich, Conn. 06830, U.S.A.

SCHUMANN, Horst; German politician; b. 6 Feb. 1924; ed. elementary school; fmr. piano-maker, fmr. mem. Kommunistische Partei Deutschlands; mem. SED 1945–; District Sec. Freie Deutsche Jugend (FDJ), Leipzig 1947-48; Sec. for Pioneer Questions in Saxony FDJ 1949-50; First Sec. Saxon FDJ 1950-52; First Sec. FDJ District Headquarters 1952-55; mem. Bureau of Cen. Cttee. of FDJ 1955–, Cen. Cttee. SED 1959–; First Sec. Cen. Cttee. FDJ 1959-67, Second Sec. 1969-70; mem. State Council 1960-71, Volkskammer 1963–; First Sec. SED Leipzig 1970–. *Address:* Unter den Linden 36-38, Berlin W.8, German Democratic Republic.

SCHUMANN, Maurice, L. ÈS L.; French writer and politician; b. 10 April 1911, Paris; s. of Julien Schumann and Thérèse Michel; m. Lucie Daniel 1944; three d.; ed. Lycées Janson-de-Sailly and Henri IV and Univ. of Paris; with Havas News Agency 1932-40; Chief Official Broadcaster, BBC French Service 1940-44; Liaison Officer with Allied Expeditionary Forces from D-Day until liberation of Paris; mem. of French Provisional Consultative Assembly Nov. 1944-July 1945; mem. of both Constituent Assemblies Oct. 1945-May 1946 and June-Nov. 1946; Chair Mouvement Républicain Populaire (MRP) 1945-49; elected Deputy for Nord, Nat. Ass. 1945, 1958, 1967, 1968; Sec. of State for Foreign Affairs 1951-54; Pres. Foreign Affairs Comm. of Nat. Ass. 1959; Minister of State attached to the Prime Minister's Office (Territorial Planning) April-May 1962; Minister of State for Scientific Research 1967-68; Minister of Social Affairs 1968-69, of Foreign Affairs 1969-73; Senator for Nord 1974–, Vice-Pres. Senate 1977-83; Pres. Senate Comm. on Cultural Affairs 1986; chief contrib. to L'Aube; mem. Acad. Française 1974–; Hon. LL.D. (Cantab.) 1972; Grand Prix Catholique de Littérature (for Angoise et certitude) 1978; Prix Aujourd'hui (for Un Certain 18 juin) 1980; Compagnon de la Libération; Chevalier, Légion d'honneur, Order of Léopold; Croix de guerre; Rassemblement pour la République. *Publications:* Le germanisme en marche 1938, Mussolini 1939, Les problèmes ukrainiens et la paix européenne 1939, Honneur et patrie 1946, Le vrai malaise des intellectuels de gauche 1957, Le rendezvous avec quelqu'un (novel) 1961, La voix du couvre-feu (speeches) 1964, Les flots roulant au loin (novel) 1973, La communication (novel) 1974, La mort née de leur propre vie: essai sur Péguy, Simone Weil et Gandhi 1974, Angoisse et certitude 1978, Un Certain 18 juin 1980, Le concerto en ut majeur (novel) 1982, Qui a tué le duc d'Eughien? 1984, Une grande imprudence 1986. *Address:* Palais du Luxembourg, 75291 Paris Cedex 06 (Office); 53 avenue du Maréchal-Lyautey, 75016 Paris, France (Home).

SCHÜRER, Gerhard; German politician; b. 14 April 1921, Zwickau; fmr. machine fitter; mem. SED 1948–; Dept. Head for Planning, Dept. of Planning and Finance, Central Cttee. of SED 1951; Student at CPSU Party Univ. 1955-58; Head of Dept. of Planning and Finance, SED Cen. Cttee 1960-62; Deputy Chair. G.D.R. State Planning Comm. 1962-63, First Deputy Chair. 1963-65, Chair. 1965–; mem. Council of Ministers 1965,

Deputy Chair. 1967–; mem. Cen. Cttee. of SED 1963; Vaterländischer Verdienstorden in Silver and Gold and other decorations. *Address:* State Planning Commission, Berlin, German Democratic Republic.

SCHURMANN, Ivan; Czechoslovak painter and graphic artist; b. 28 June, 1935, Bratislava; s. of Josef Schurmann and Terezia Schurmann; m. 1976; one s.; ed. Coll. of Fine Arts, Bratislava 1956-62; Chief Sec. Union of Slovak Fine Artists 1972-77; Sec., Union of Czechoslovak Fine Artists 1978-82; mem. Presidium, Union of Czechoslovak Fine Artists 1978–, Cand. Cen. Cttee. CP of Slovakia 1981–; Deputy Chair., Union of Czechoslovak Fine Artists 1982–; Artist of Merit, Médaille d'argent, Grand Prix Int. d'art de Lyon, and numerous other awards. *Works:* stamps, newspaper designs, book illustrations, collections of graphic sheets, lino-cuts and litho-print, including: on the occasion of the 20th anniversary of the Slovak Nat. Uprising 1964, on the occasion of the 61st anniversary of the Great October Socialist Revolution 1978; individual exhbns: Bratislava 1969, 1975, Kiev 1970, Berlin, Havana 1973, Vienna 1975, Warsaw 1976, Prague 1977, 1981, Baghdad 1980, Budapest 1982, Sofia 1983, Paris 1986. *Leisure interest:* music. *Address:* c/o Union of Czechoslovak Creative Artists, Gottwaldovo nábr. 250, 110 00 Prague 1, Czechoslovakia.

SCHÜRMANN, Leo, D.IUR.; Swiss jurist and banker; b. 1917, Olten; m. Cécile Baur 1943; one s. one d.; ed. Univ. of Basel; Advocate and Notary, Clerk of Court and Legal Sec., canton of Soleure 1940; engaged in banking 1947; own law office 1949; Chief Justice, canton of Soleure 1953-74; Habilitation at Fribourg Univ. 1956, Extraordinary Prof. 1964–; Chair. Swiss Cartel Comm., also of various Fed. and Cantonal Cttees. of Experts 1964-74; Cantonal Councillor 1957-69; Nat. Councillor 1959-74; mem. Governing Bd. Swiss Nat. Bank 1974-80 (Vice-Chair. 1976-80), Head Second Dept., Berne 1976; Gen.-Dir. Swiss Broadcasting Corpn. 1981-87. *Publications:* Textbook on the Economic Articles of the Federal Constitution, Handbook of Economic Administrative Law 1983, Commentary of Swiss National Bank Law 1980. Author of bills, inter alia on the laws on town and country planning and on housing devt., of the Fed. Decree on measures against abuses in the rental system, of an executive order related to the environmental protection article, of a new press article in the Fed. Constitution and a press-promoting law, of the Fed. law on investment assistance to mountain areas, of the law enacted by the canton of Soleure on admin. judicature, of the law on disaster provisions and of communal decrees 1964-74. *Address:* c/o Swiss Broadcasting Corporation, Giacometti-strasse 3, 3000 Berne 15, Switzerland. *Telephone:* (031) 439111.

SCHUSTER, Hans-Günter, D.SC.; German scientist and civil servant; b. 17 Dec. 1918, Bonn; s. of Rudolf Schuster and Sophie Schuster-Leinen; m. Helga Schuster-Kleffmann 1944; one s. one d; ed. Univs. of Göttingen and Bonn; Asst. Bonn Univ. 1948-50, Scientific Asst. Inst. of Applied Physics 1950-55, Head of Physical Studies 1956-65; Adviser, Ministry of Scientific Research 1965-67; Dir. Nuclear Research and Technical Div., Ministry of Educ. and Science 1968-71; Deputy Dir.-Gen. of Industrial, Tech. and Scientific Affairs Comm. of the European Communities 1971-73, Dir.-Gen. of Research, Science and Educ. 1973-81, Co-ordinator for bilateral co-operation, Fed. Ministry for Research and Tech., in particular for India 1981-83; Special Adviser to Senate of Berlin 1984-88. *Address:* Höhenweg 32, D-5300 Bonn 1, Federal Republic of Germany. *Telephone:* (0228) 28-33-43 (Home).

SCHÜTZ, Klaus; German politician and diplomatist; b. 17 Sept. 1926; m. Heide Seeberger 1953; three c.; ed. Paulsen-Realgymnasium, Humboldt Univ. zu Berlin and Harvard Univ., U.S.A.; war service, seriously wounded 1944-45; Asst., Inst. für Politische Wissenschaften, Freie Univ., Berlin 1951-61; mem. City Ass. 1954-57, 1963-77; mem. Bundestag 1957-61; Liaison Senator between Berlin Senate and Bonn Govt. 1961-66; mem. Bundesrat 1961-77, Pres. 1967-68; Under-Sec. Ministry of Foreign Affairs 1966-67; Governing Mayor of West Berlin 1967-77; Chair. Berlin Social Democratic Party 1968-77; Amb. to Israel 1977-81; Dir.-Gen. Deutsche Welle 1981-87; Dir. Landesanstalt für Rundfunk NRW, Düsseldorf 1987–. *Address:* Raderberggürtel 50, 5000 Cologne 51, Federal Republic of Germany.

SCHÜTZ, Paul, DR. RER. POL.; German banker; b. 27 June 1910, Tholey, Saar; s. of Nikolaus and Barbara (née Simon) Schütz; m. Christiane Waelder 1947; ed. Univs. of Würzburg, Berlin and Freiburg im Breisgau; industrial posts 1936-46; Chair. Man. Bd. of a credit house 1947-61; Pres. Saarland Asscn. of Savings and Deposit Banks 1955-61; Pres. of Landeszentralbank im Saarland 1960-80; mem. of Bd. of Deutsche Bundesbank, Frankfurt. *Leisure interest:* foreign languages. *Address:* Willi-Graf-Strasse 30, 66 Saarbrücken 3, Federal Republic of Germany.

SCHÜTZEICHEL, Rudolf, DR. PHIL.; German professor of philology; b. 20 May 1927, Rahms; s. of Matthias Schützeichel and Gertrud Schützeichel; m. Margrit Britten 1955; two d.; ed. Univ. of Mainz; Docent Univ. of Cologne 1960-63; Prof. of German Philology, Univ. of Gröningen 1963-64, Univ. of Bonn 1964-69, Univ. of Münster 1969–; Officer Order of Orange Nassau, Festschrift 1987 (Althochdeutsch 2 Bände Heidelberg). *Publications:* Mundart, Urkdsprache und Schriftsprache 1974, Grundlagen d.w. Mitteldtsch 1976, Das alem. Memento Mori 1967, Althocho. Wörterb. 1981, Codex. Pal. lat. 52 1982, Mittelrh. Passionsspiel 1978, Gottschald Namenkunde 1982, Addenda und Corrigenda (I) 1982, (II) 1985, Textgebundenheit 1981; Ed. BNF.NF. 1966–, Sprachwissenschaft 1975–. *Address:* Potstiege 16, D-4400 Münster, Federal Republic of Germany. *Telephone:* 0251 861345.

SCHWAB, John Joseph, M.D., M.S.; American professor of psychiatry; b. 10 Feb. 1923, Cumberland, Md.; s. of Joseph L. Schwab and Eleanor A. Cadden; m. Ruby E. Baxter 1985; one d.; ed. Univs. of Kentucky, Louisville and Illinois; Fellow in Psychosomatic Medicine, Duke Univ.; Resident in Medicine, Univ. of Louisville; Fellow in Cardio-Renal Physiology, Univ. of Ill.; Resident in Psychiatry, Univ. of Fla.; Internist/psychosomaticist, Holzer Clinic, Galipolis, Ohio 1954–59; Nat. Inst. of Mental Health career teacher, Univ. of Fla. 1962–64; Psychiatrist and mem. Faculty, Univ. of Fla. 1961–73; Prof. of Psychiatry and Medicine, Gainesville 1967–73; Prof., Chair. Dept. of Psychiatry and Behavioral Sciences, School of Medicine, Univ. of Louisville 1974–; Chair. Epidemiologic Studies Review Comm., Center for Epidemiologic Studies, Nat. Inst. of Medical Health 1973–75, Consultant, Psychiatry Br. 1975–. *Publications:* author or co-author of five books on psychiatry and mental health. *Leisure interest:* music. *Address:* Department of Psychiatry and Behavioral Sciences, School of Medicine, University of Louisville, Louisville, Ky. 40292 (Office); 6217 Innes Trace Road, Louisville, Ky. 40222, U.S.A. (Home). *Telephone:* 502-588-5391 (Office); 502-426-6015 (Home).

SCHWALB LÓPEZ ALDANA, Fernando; Peruvian politician; b. 26 Aug. 1916, Lima; m. Carmen Rosa Tola de Schwalb 1950; two s. one d.; ed. Pontifica Univ. Católica del Perú; entered Ministry of Foreign Affairs 1933; entered diplomatic service 1939; Second Sec., Washington, D.C. 1944–45, First Sec. 1945–48, Minister Counsellor 1948; pvt. law practice 1949–50, 1950–53, 1968–69; Alt. Exec. Dir. IBRD 1950; Senator from Lima 1962 (prevented from taking office by coup d'état); Minister of Foreign Affairs 1963–65; Chair. Council of Ministers 1963–65; Chair. Peruvian Del. to Gen. Ass. of UN 1963; First Vice-Pres. 1980–84, Prime Minister of Peru 1983–84, Minister of Foreign Affairs 1983–84; Amb. to U.S.A. 1980–82; Pres. Banco Central de Reserva del Perú 1966–68; Rep. of Pres. to Bogotá Meeting of Presidents 1966; Banco de la República, Bogotá 1969; Consultant, Cen. Banking Service, IMF 1969–82; mem. Partido Acción Popular. *Publication:* El Contrato de la Florgreen y el Pago a la I.P.C. *Address:* c/o Oficina del Primer Ministro, Lima, Peru.

SCHWARTZ, Jacob T., PH.D.; American computer scientist; b. 9 Jan. 1930, New York; s. of Harry and Hazel Schwartz; m. Frances E. Allen 1972; two d.; ed. City Coll. of New York, Yale Univ.; Instructor, Computer Science Dept., Yale Univ. 1951–53, Asst. Prof. 1953–56; Assoc. Prof. of Math. and Computer Science, New York Univ. 1957–58, Prof. 1958–; Chair. Computer Science Dept., Courant Inst. of Mathematical Sciences, New York Univ. 1969–77, now Dir.; Assoc. Ed. Journal of Programming Languages; mem. Editorial Bd., Journal of Computer and System Sciences, Communications on Pure and Applied Math., Advances in Applied Math.; mem. N.A.S.; mem. (fmr. Chair.) Computer Science Bd., Nat. Research Council; Sloane Fellow 1961–62; Distinguished Lecturer, Univ. of Calif., Santa Barbara 1978, M.I.T. 1980; Wilbur Cross Medal (Yale Univ.), Townsend Harris Medal (City Univ. of New York), Steele Prize (American Mathematical Soc.) 1981. *Publications:* numerous scientific papers; Linear Operators (3 vols.) 1958–70, Matrices and Vectors for High Schools and Colleges 1961, Relativity in Illustrations 1962, Lectures on the Mathematical Method in Analytical Economics (2 vols.) 1962, W*Algebras 1967, Lie Groups; Lie Algebras 1967, Lectures on Nonlinear Functional Analysis 1968, Lectures on Differential Geometry and Topology 1969, Programming Languages and their Compilers 1969, On Programming: an Interim Report on the SETL Project 1973, Higher Level Programming 1981. *Leisure interests:* history, music. *Address:* New York University, Courant Institute of Mathematical Sciences, 251 Mercer Street, New York, N.Y. 10012, U.S.A. *Telephone:* (212) 460-7267.

SCHWARTZ, Laurent, D. ÈS SC.; French academic (retd.); b. 5 March 1915, Paris; s. of Anselme Schwartz and Claire Debré; m. Marie-Hélène Lévy 1938; one d.; ed. Ecole Normale Supérieure; Prof. Faculté des Sciences, Univ. of Nancy 1945–52, Faculté des Sciences, Paris 1953–59, Univ. of Paris VII 1959–69, Ecole Polytechnique 1959–80; Pres. Comité Nat. d'Evaluation des Univs. 1985–89; mem. Acad. des Sciences, numerous foreign acads.; Fields Medal 1950, Grand Prix de Math. et Physique (Acad. des Sciences), Prix Cognacq-Jay (together with J. L. Lian and B. Malgrange). *Publications:* Théorie des distributions 1950–51, Méthodes mathématiques pour les sciences physiques 1961, Sous-espaces Hilbertiens et noyaux associés 1964, Cours d'Analyse 1967, Radon measures on arbitrary topological spaces and cylindrical measures 1980, Semi-martingales sur des variétés et martingales conformes 1980. *Address:* 37 rue Pierre Nicole, 75005 Paris, France. *Telephone:* 43 54 50 30.

SCHWARTZ, Maxime; French scientist and administrator; b. 1 June 1940, Blois; ed. Ecole Polytechnique; entered Inst. Pasteur 1963, Deputy Dir. 1985–87, Dir. 1987–; also mem. of the Scientific Council of the Inst. Pasteur and Head of the Dept. of Molecular Biology. *Address:* L'Institut Pasteur, 25–28 rue du Dr Roux, 75015 Paris, France.

SCHWARTZ, Robert George, M.B.A.; American insurance company executive; b. 27 March 1928, Czechoslovakia; s. of George and Frances (née Antoni) Schwartz; m. Caroline Bachurski 1952; one s. two d.; ed. Pennsyl-

vania. State Univ., New York Univ.; joined Metropolitan Life Insurance Co., New York 1949, Vice-Pres. Securities 1968–70, Vice-Pres. 1970–75, Sr. Vice-Pres. 1975–78, Exec. Vice-Pres. 1979–80, Vice-Chair. Bd. and Chair. Investments Cttee. 1980–83, Chair. 1983–; Dir. various Metropolitan subsidiaries, Potlatch Corpn., Lowe's Cos. Inc., Kaiser Cement Corpn., NL Industries Inc., R. H. Macy and Co., Greater New York Councils; Chair. Investment Advisory Cttee. of the Christophers Inc., Metropolitan Asset Man. Cttee.; mem. Pres.'s Export Council, the Urban Land Inst, Trustee Cttee. for Econ. Devt. *Leisure interest:* golf. *Address:* 1 Madison Avenue, New York, N.Y. 10010, U.S.A. (Office).

SCHWARTZENBERG, Roger-Gérard, D. EN D.; French politician and professor of law; b. 17 April 1943, Pau, Pyrénées-Atlantiques; s. of André Schwartzenberg and Simone née Gutelman; unmarried; ed. Inst. d'Etudes Politiques, Paris; Prof. Univ. de droit, d'économie et de sciences sociales de Paris II 1969–, Inst. d'Etudes Politiques 1972–; Pres. Mouvement des Radicaux de Gauche 1981–83, Hon. Pres. 1983–; mem. European Parl. 1979–83; Sec. of State, Ministry of Educ. 1983–84; Sec. of State responsible for univs., Ministry of Educ. 1984–86; Deputy for Val de Marne to Nat. Ass. 1986–. *Publications:* books on political and legal topics. *Leisure interest:* tennis. *Address:* Assemblée Nationale, 75355 Paris; Université de Droit de Paris, 12 Place du Panthéon, Paris, France.

SCHWARZ, Antoine, L. EN D.; French administrator and business executive; b. 9 Aug. 1943, Paris; s. of Willy Schwarz and Elisabeth du Brusle de Rouvroy; m. Christine Coudreau 1974; three c.; ed. Inst. d'Etudes Politiques de Paris, Ecole Nat. d'Admin.; Admin. to the Treasury, Ministry of the Economy and Finance 1971–74; Prin. Inst. d'Études Politiques 1972–74; Head Service Juridique et Technique de l'Information 1974; Head of Cabinet André Rossi 1975–76, Raymond Barre 1977; Dir. Radio Monte-Carlo 1978–81, Editions Mondiales 1982–83; Counsellor Centre Nat. de la Cinématographie 1984–85; Pres. and Dir.-Gen. Société Financière de Radiodiffusion (SOFIRAD) 1986–; Chevalier Ordre du Mérite. *Address:* 78 avenue Poincaré, 75116 Paris (Office); 150 rue de l'Université, 75007 Paris, France (Home).

SCHWARZ, Gerard; American conductor; b. 19 Aug. 1947, Weehawken, N.J.; m. Jody Greitzer 1984; one s. one d.; ed. Professional Children's School, Juilliard School; joined American Brass Quintet 1965; Co-Prin. Trumpet, New York Philharmonic 1973–74; conducting début, Aspen Festival 1974; Guest Conductor, Cosmopolitan Symphony, Aspen Festival Chamber Orchestras; has conducted many U.S. orchestras, the Hong Kong Philharmonic, Jerusalem Symphony, Israeli Chamber and English Chamber, London Symphony, Helsinki Philharmonic and Monte Carlo Philharmonic Orchestras, Ensemble Contemporain, Paris and Nat. Orchestra of Spain; Music Dir. Seattle Symphony, Y Chamber Symphony and Mostly Mozart Festival Orchestras, Music Today series, Merkin Concert Hall, New York; Prin. Conductor Waterloo Festival and Music Dir. Music School 1975–; Music Dir. New York Chamber Symphony 1977–, Los Angeles Chamber Orchestra 1978–86; operatic conducting début, Washington Opera 1982; many gramophone recordings; Dr. h.c. (Farleigh Dickenson Univ.). *Address:* 575 West End Avenue, Apt. 4B, New York, N.Y. 10024, U.S.A.

SCHWARZ, Rudolf, C.B.E.; British conductor; b. 29 April 1905, Vienna, Austria; s. of Josef Schwarz and Bertha Roth; m. Greta Ohlson 1950 (deceased); two s. one d.; ed. in Vienna; Conductor, Opera House, Düsseldorf 1923–27, Opera House, Karlsruhe 1927–33; worked for Jewish Cultural Org. in Berlin 1936–41; Conductor, Bournemouth Municipal Orchestra 1947–51, City of Birmingham Symphony Orchestra 1951–57; Conductor-in-Chief B.B.C. Symphony Orchestra 1957–62; Conductor Northern Sinfonia Orchestra, Newcastle upon Tyne 1964–73; Conductor Laureate Northern Sinfonia Orchestra; Hon. D.Mus. (Univ. Newcastle upon Tyne). *Address:* 24 Wildcroft Manor, London, S.W.15, England.

SCHWARZ, Štefan, DR.SC.; Czechoslovak mathematician; b. 18 May 1914, Nové Mesto nad Váhom; ed. Universita Karlova, Prague; Asst. Charles Univ., Prague 1937; Docent, Univ. of Bratislava 1945; Professor, Technical Univ., Bratislava 1947–; mem. Czechoslovak Acad. of Sciences 1960–, Vice-Pres. 1965–70; mem. Slovak Acad. of Sciences 1953–, Vice-Pres. 1958–65, Pres. 1965–70; mem. Cen. Cttee. of C.P. of Czechoslovakia 1966–71, and of Slovakia 1966–68; Dir. Mathematical Inst. of Slovak Acad. of Sciences 1965–87, mem. Presidium, Slovak Acad. of Sciences 1970–82; State Prize 1955; Order of Labour 1964, 1982; Hon. Gold Plaque of Czechoslovak Acad. of Sciences for Services to Science and Mankind 1969; Gold Medal, Slovak Acad. of Sciences 1974; S.S.R. Nat. Prize 1980. *Publications:* Three books and about 100 papers, mostly on algebra and number theory, in particular on theory of semi-groups. *Address:* Porubského 8, Bratislava 81106, Czechoslovakia.

SCHWARZKOPF, Elisabeth; German born singer (now Austrian/British nationality); b. 9 Dec. 1915, Jarotschin; d. of Friedrich and Elisabeth (née Fröhlich) Schwarzkopf; m. Walter Legge (died 1979); ed. privately and at Berlin Hochschule für Musik; debut in Parsifal 1938; Zerbinetta in Ariadne auf Naxos 1941; sang at inauguration of post-war Bayreuth Festival; since 1947 principal soprano at Vienna State Opera, La Scala Milan, Covent Garden, San Francisco; Metropolitan Opera, New York 1964–66; guest singer, Salzburg Festival 1947–64; created Anne Trulove in Stravinsky's

Rake's Progress; prin. roles include Contessa, Le nozze di Figaro, Marschallin, Rosenkavalier, Fiordiligi, Cosí fan Tutte, Eva, Meistersinger, Donna Elvira, Don Giovanni, Gräfin, Capriccio, etc.; producer Der Rosenkavalier, Brussels 1981; Hon. mem. Acad. di Santa Cecilia, Rome, Acad. of Arts and Letters, Stockholm, R.A.M.; throughout her career has concentrated on German Lieder; Hon. D.Mus. (Cambridge) 1976, American Univ. of Washington D.C.; mem. Ordre pour le Mérite, (Fed. Repub. of Germany) 1983; Commdr., Ordre des Arts et des Lettres, 1985; Lilli Lehmann Medal, Salzburg 1950, Grosses Verdienstkreuz 1974, Order of Dannebrog (1st Class) (Denmark), Preis Diapason d'Or 1984, etc. *Publication:* Walter Legge: On and Off the Record, A Memoir 1982. *Leisure interests:* tennis, mountain walking. *Address:* 29 Rebhusstrasse, C.H. 8126 Zumikon, Switzerland.

SCHWARZSCHILD, Martin, PH.D.; American professor of astronomy; b. 31 May 1912, Potsdam, Germany; s. of Karl and Else (Rosenbach) Schwarzschild; m. Barbara Cherry 1945; ed. Gymnasium and Univ. of Göttingen; Research Fellow, Univ. of Oslo, Norway 1936-37, Harvard Univ. 1937-40; lecturer, Asst. Prof., Columbia Univ. 1940-47; Prof., Princeton Univ. 1947-50, Higgins Prof. Astronomy 1950-79; Vice-Pres. Int. Astronomical Union 1964-70, American Astronomical Soc. 1967-69, Pres. 1970-72; Fellow, American Acad. of Arts and Sciences; mem. Akad. der Naturforscher Leopoldina, Nat. Acad. of Sciences, Norwegian Acad. of Science and Letters, American Philosophical Soc.; Life mem. Astronomical Soc. of the Pacific, Royal Astronomical Soc. of Canada; Foreign mem. Royal Netherlands Acad. of Sciences and Letters, Royal Danish Acad. of Sciences and Letters; Corresp. mem. Soc. Royale des Sciences de Liège; Assoc. Royal Astronomical Soc.; Hon. D.Sc. (Swarthmore Coll.) 1960, (Columbia Univ.) 1973; Draper Medal, Nat. Acad. of Sciences, Eddington Medal and Gold Medal, Royal Astronomical Soc., Bruce Medal, Astronomical Soc. of the Pacific, Albert A. Michelson Award, Case Western Reserve Univ., Dannie Heinemann Prize, Akad. der Wissenschaften zu Göttingen, Rittenhouse Silver Medal, Rittenhouse Astronomical Soc., Prix Janssen, Soc. Astronomique de France, Medal of Asscn. pour le Développement Int. de l'Observatoire de Nice. *Publications:* Structure and Evolution of the Stars; numerous articles on research on internal constitution and evolution of stars, and on astronomical observations with telescopes carried by balloons into stratosphere and on dynamics of galaxies. *Leisure interests:* collecting minerals and fossils, bird-photography. *Address:* 12 Ober Road, Princeton, N.J. 08540, U.S.A.

SCHWARZ-SCHILLING, Christian, DR.PHIL.; German politician; b. 19 Nov. 1930, Innsbruck, Austria; m. Marie-Luise Schwarz-Schilling; ed. Univs. of Berlin and Munich; mem. Landtag, Hesse, Fed. Repub. of Germany 1966-76; Sec.-Gen. Hesse CDU 1967-80; mem. Bundestag 1976-; Minister of Posts and Telecommunications Oct. 1982-. *Address:* Bundesministerium für Post- und Fernmeldewesen, Adenauerallee 81, 5300 Bonn, Federal Republic of Germany.

SCHWEBEL, Stephen M., B.A., LL.B.; American lawyer and judge; b. 10 March 1929, New York; s. of Victor Schwebel and Pauline Pfeffer Schwebel; m. Louise I. N. Killander 1972; two d.; ed. Harvard Coll., Univ. of Cambridge and Yale Law School; Attorney 1954-59; Asst. Prof. of Law, Harvard Univ. 1959-61; Asst. Legal Adviser, then Special Asst. to Asst. Sec. of State for Int. Org. Affairs 1961-67; Exec. Vice-Pres. and Exec. Dir. American Soc. of Int. Law 1967-73; Consultant, then Counsellor on Int. Law, Dept. of State 1967-74, Deputy Legal Adviser 1974-81; Prof. of Int. Law, then Edward B. Burling Prof. of Int. Law and Org., Johns Hopkins Univ., Washington 1967-81; Legal Adviser to U.S. Del. and Alt. Rep. in 6th Cttee., UN Gen. Ass. 1961-65; visiting lecturer or professor at Cambridge Univ. 1957, 1983, Australian Nat. Univ. 1969, Hague Acad. of Int. Law 1972, Inst. Univ. de hautes études int., Geneva 1980; Rep. in various Cttees. UN 1962-74; Assoc. Rep., Rep., Counsel or Deputy Agent in cases before Int. Court of Justice 1962-80; mem. Int. Court of Justice Jan. 1981-; mem. Int. Law Comm. 1977-81; mem. Bd. of Arbitration, British Petroleum Co. v. Iran and Nat. Iranian Oil Co. 1982-85; presiding arbitrator, Marine Devt. Drive v. Ghana Devt. Agency 1989-; mem. Bd. of Eds., American Journal of Int. Law; mem. American Law Inst. and U.S. branch of Int. Law Asscn.; mem. Inst. of Int. Law. *Publications:* The Secretary-General of the United Nations 1952, The Effectiveness of International Decisions (ed.) 1971, International Arbitration: Three Salient Problems 1987; author of some 80 articles in legal periodicals and the press on problems of international law and relations. *Leisure interests:* music, tennis. *Address:* International Court of Justice, Peace Palace, 2517 KJ, The Hague, Netherlands.

SCHWEIKER, Richard Schultz, B.A.; American businessman and fmr. politician; b. 1 June 1926, Norristown, Pa.; s. of Malcolm A. Schweiker and Blanche Schultz; m. Claire Joan Coleman 1955; two s. three d.; ed. Pennsylvania State Univ.; Business exec. 1950-60; mem. U.S. House of Reps. 1960-68; U.S. Senator from Pa. 1969-80; Sec. of Health and Human Services 1981-83; Pres. American Council of Life Insurance 1983-; mem. Bd. of Dirs. Nat. Medical Enterprises Inc. 1984-; Regular mem. Conf. Bd.; ten hon. degrees and numerous awards; Republican. *Address:* American Council of Life Insurance, 1001 Pennsylvania Avenue, N.W., Washington, D.C. 20004-2599, U.S.A. (Office). *Telephone:* (202) 624-2000.

SCHWEIKHER, Paul, B.F.A., M.A.; American architect; b. 28 July 1903, Denver, Colo.; s. of Frederick Schweikher and Elizabeth Ann Williams; m. Dorothy Mueller 1921; one s.; ed. Colorado and Yale Univs.; private architectural practice 1933-; co-founder, Chicago Workshops 1933-35; Lieut. Commdr. in U.S. Naval Reserve 1941-45; Partner, Schweikher and Elting 1945-53; Visiting Critic in Architecture, Yale Univ. 1947-51, Prof. of Architecture, Chair. Dept. of Architecture 1953-56; Prof., Head Dept. of Architecture, Carnegie Mellon Univ. 1956-69, Prof. Emer. 1969-; lecturer, panellist and juror at many educ. and professional insts.; mem. Fulbright Fellowships in Architecture selection cttee. 1953-55, interviewing cttee. for American Acad. in Rome fellowships 1955; Adviser, Memphis (Tenn.) Arts Center Competition 1956; Consultant on master planning, Yale Univ. 1953-56; mem. Arts Club of Chicago (Bd. of Dirs. 1939-56), Pittsburgh Planning Comm. 1961-63; mem. Advisory Council, Princeton Univ. School of Architecture 1960-70; Adviser, Allegheny Square Competition, Pittsburgh 1964; Visiting Prof. Princeton 1960-61; Ford Foundation research grant for theatre design 1960-61; life mem. Chicago Art Inst. 1946; Fellow, Silliman Coll., Yale 1954-55; architectural work at exhbns. New York Museum of Modern Art and several other museums and insts. 1933-; perm. collection of architectural presentation and working drawings, Northern Ariz. Univ., Flagstaff, Ariz.; perm. exhbn. Art Inst. of Chicago 1984; Distinguished Citizen Award, Denver 1958, Architect of the Year, Pittsburgh 1966, Artist of the Year, Pittsburgh 1968, and other awards. *Leisure interests:* art, travel. *Address:* 50 Tonto Road, Sedona, Ariz. 86336, U.S.A. *Telephone:* (602) 282-9251.

SCHWEITZER, Louis, L. EN D.; French administrative official; b. 8 July 1942, Geneva, Switzerland; m. Agnes Schmitz 1972; two d.; ed. Inst. d'Etudes Politiques, Paris, Faculté de Droit, Paris and Ecole Nat. d'Administration; Insp. of Finance 1970-; special assignment, later Deputy Dir., Ministry of the Budget 1974-82; Dir. du Cabinet to Minister of Budget 1981-83, of Industry and Research 1983, to Prime Minister 1984-86; Prof. Inst. d'Etudes Politiques de Paris 1982-86; Vice-Pres. for Finance and Planning 1986-; Dir. Régie Renault 1986-, Chief Finance Officier 1988-; Admin. (Desig.) Soc. Générale April 1989. *Address:* 34 quai du Point du Jour, 92100 Boulogne-Billancourt; 1 rue Dauphine, 75006 Paris, France.

SCHWEITZER, Pierre-Paul; French banker; b. 29 May 1912, Strasbourg; s. of Paul and Emma (Munch) Schweitzer; m. Catherine Hatt 1941; one s. one d.; ed. Univs. of Strasbourg and Paris; Official, French Treasury 1936-47; Alt. Exec. Dir. for France, IMF 1947-48; Sec.-Gen. Interministerial Comm. European Econ. Co-operation 1948-49; Financial Attaché, French Embassy, Washington, D.C. 1949-53; Dir. of Treasury, Ministry of Finance 1953-60; Deputy Gov. Bank of France 1960-63; Man. Dir., Chair. Exec. Bd. IMF 1963-73; Inspecteur général honoraire des finances; Chair. Bank of America Int., Luxembourg 1974-77, Banque Petrofigaz, Paris 1974-79, Cie. de Participations et d'Investissements Holding, Luxembourg 1975-84, Soc. Financière Int. de Participations 1976-84, Compagnie Monégasque de Banque de Monaco 1978-88; Advisory Dir. Unilever N.V., Rotterdam 1974-84; Dir. Robeco Group Rotterdam 1974-82; Dir. Banque Pétrofigaz 1974-; Hon. LL.D. (Yale) 1966, (Harvard) 1966, (Leeds) 1968, (New York) 1968, (George Washington Univ.) 1972, (Univ. of Wales) 1972, (Williams Univ.) 1973; Grand Croix Légion d'honneur, Croix de guerre, Médaille de la Résistance. *Address:* Route de Mon Idée 170, 1253 Vandœuvres, Switzerland. *Telephone:* (022) 50.13.13.

SCHWEITZER WALTERS, Miguel; Chilean lawyer, diplomatist and politician; b. 22 July 1940, Santiago; s. of Miguel Schweizer Speisky and Cora Walters Antognini; m. María Luisa Fernández Maynard 1964; two s. one d.; ed. The Grange School, Universidad de Chile, Santiago and Univ. of Rome; Asst. in Commercial Penal Law, lecturer in Legal Medicine and lecturer in Penal Law 1968; Amb. for Special Missions 1976; mem. Chilean del. to UN and mem. Human Rights Comm. 1975; Amb. to U.K. 1980-83; Minister of Foreign Affairs 1983. *Address:* c/o Ministry of Foreign Affairs, Palacio de la Moneda, Santiago, Chile. *Telephone:* 725613, 6980889.

SCHWINDEN, Ted, M.A.; American politician; b. 31 Aug. 1925, Wolf Point, Montana; s. of Michael James and Mary (Preble) Schwinden; m. B. Jean Christianson 1946; one s. two d.; ed. Montana School of Mines, Univ. of Montana and Univ. of Minn.; propr. grain farm, Roosevelt Co., Mont. 1954-; Land Commr., Mont. 1969-76; Lieut.-Gov. State of Mont. 1977-80, Gov. 1981-89; mem. U.S. Wheat Trade Mission to Asia 1968; Chair. Mont. Bicentennial Advisory Council 1973-76; mem. Mont. House of Reps. 1959, 1961, Legis. Council 1959-61; Combat Infantry Badge; Democrat. *Address:* 1335 Highland Street, Helena, Mont. 59601, U.S.A.

SCHWINGER, Julian Seymour, PH.D.; American physicist; b. 12 Feb. 1918, New York; s. of Benjamin and Belle (née Rosenfeld) Schwinger; m. Clarice Carrol 1947; ed. Columbia Univ.; Nat. Research Council Fellow 1939-40; Research Assoc. Univ. of Calif. (Berkeley) 1940-41; Instructor, later Asst. Prof. Purdue Univ. 1941-43; staff mem. Radiation Lab., M.I.T. 1943-46; mem. staff Metallurgy Lab., Univ. of Chicago 1943; Assoc. Prof. Harvard Univ. 1945-47, Prof. 1947-72, Higgins Prof. 1966-72; Prof. of Physics, Univ. of Calif. 1972-80, Univ. Prof. 1980-; mem. N.A.S., American Acad. of Arts and Sciences, A.A.A.S., New York Acad. Sciences, American Physical Soc., Civil Liberties Union, Royal Inst. of G.B.; Guggenheim Fellow 1970; Ed. Quantum Electrodynamics 1958; Hon. D. Sc. (Purdue Univ.) 1961, (Harvard) 1962, (Brandeis Univ.) 1973, (Gustavus Adolphus

Coll.) 1975, Hon. LL.D. (City Coll. of New York) 1972; Nobel Prize for Physics (with R. Feynman and S. Tomonaga) 1965, American Acad. of Achievement Award 1987, and other awards. *Publications:* Discontinuities in Wave Guides 1968, Particles, Sources and Fields 1970, Vol. II 1973, Quantum Kinematics and Dynamics 1970, Einstein's Legacy 1985. *Address:* Department of Physics, University of California at Los Angeles, 405 Hilgard Avenue, Calif. 90024; 10727 Stradella Court, Los Angeles, Calif. 90024, U.S.A.

SCHWYZER, Robert, DR. PHIL.; Swiss molecular biologist; b. 8 Dec. 1920, Zürich; s. of Robert Schwyzer and Rose Schätzle; m. Rose Nägeli 1948; two s. one d.; ed. primary school, Nathan Hale, Minneapolis, U.S.A., Canton High School (A), Zürich, and Dept. of Chemistry, Univ. of Zürich; Privatdozent, Univ. of Zürich 1951-59, Asst. Prof. 1960-63; initiation of Polypeptide Research, Head of Polypeptide Research Group, Ciba Ltd., Basel 1952-63, Asst. Man. 1960-63; Prof. and Head of (new) Dept. of Molecular Biology, Swiss Fed. Inst. of Tech., Zürich 1963-; Werner Award, Swiss Chemical Soc. 1957; Ruzicka Prize, Swiss Fed. Inst. of Tech. 1959; Otto Nägeli Award, Switzerland 1964; Vernon Stouffer Award, American Heart Asscn., Cleveland 1968; Ernesto Scoffone Award 1982; Alan E. Pierce Award, American Peptide Symposia 1985; Rudinger Gold Medal, European Peptide Symposia 1988. *Publications:* Scientific papers on syntheses of biologically active polypeptides; structure activity relationships; relationships between structure and biophysical interactions with lipid-bilayer membranes; molecular mechanisms of opioid receptor selection by peptides, new principles governing receptor specificity. *Leisure interests:* mountain climbing, skiing, literature. *Address:* Institut für Molekularbiologie und Biophysik, Eidgenössische Technische Hochschule, 8093 Zürich; 8180 Bülach, Switzerland (Home). *Telephone:* 01-3772461.

SCHYGULLA, Hanna; German actress; b. 1943; has made nearly 40 films; *stage appearances include:* Mother Courage 1979; *films include:* Die Ehe der Maria Braun (Silberner Bär Berlinale) 1979, Die Dritte Generation 1979, Lili Marleen 1980, Die Fälschung 1981, La Nuit de Varennes 1982, Eine Liebe in Deutschland 1983, The Story of Piera 1983; *television appearances include:* 8 Stunden sind kein Tag (series) 1972. *Leisure interests:* travel, painting. *Address:* Nymphenburger Str. 67, 8000 Munich 2, Federal Republic of Germany.

SCIAMA, Dennis William, PH.D., F.R.S.; British scientist; b. 18 Nov. 1926, Manchester; s. of Abraham Sciama and Nelly Ades; m. Lidia Dina 1959; two d.; ed. Malvern Coll. and Trinity Coll. Cambridge; Prize Fellow, Trinity Coll. Cambridge 1952-56; Lecturer in Mathematics, Cambridge Univ. 1961-70; Sr. Research Fellow, All Souls Coll. Oxford 1970-85; Prof. of Astrophysics, Int. School of Advanced Studies, Trieste, Italy 1983-; Consultant, Int. Centre for Theoretical Physics, Trieste; Foreign mem. American Philosophical Soc., American Acad. of Arts and Sciences, Accademia dei Lincei. *Publications:* The Unity of the Universe 1959, The Physical Foundations of General Relativity 1966, Modern Cosmology 1971. *Address:* International School of Advanced Studies, Strada Costiera 11, 34014 Trieste, Italy. *Telephone:* (040) 224 9330.

SCIASCIA, Leonardo; Italian writer; b. 8 Jan. 1921, Recalmuto; ed. Istituto Magistrale Caltanissetta; Deputy European Parl. for Radical Party; has won many prizes including Premio Crotone, Premio Libera Stampa Lugano, and Premio Prato. *Publications:* Le parrocchie di Regalpetra 1956, Gli zii di Sicilia 1958, Il giorno della civetta 1961 (Mafia Vendetta 1963), Pirandello e la Sicilia 1961, Il consiglio d'Egitto 1963, A ciascuno li suo 1963, Morte dell'inquisitore 1964, Feste religiose in Sicilia 1965, Recitazione della controversia liparitana 1969, Il contesto 1971, Il mare colore del vino 1973. *Address:* Viale Scaduto 10/B, 1-90144 Palermo, Italy.

SCITOVSKY, Anne A., M.A.; American economist; b. 17 April 1915, Ludwigshafen, Germany; d. of H. W. and Gertrude M. Aickelin; m. Tibor Scitovsky 1942 (divorced 1966); one d.; ed. Barnard Coll., New York, L.S.E., Columbia Univ.; Economist Legis. Reference Service, Library of Congress 1941-44; Economist Bureau of Research and Statistics, Social Security Bd. 1944-46; Sr. Research Assoc. Palo Alto Medical Research Foundation 1963-73, Chief, Health Economics Dept. 1973-; Lecturer Inst. for Health Policy Studies, School of Medicine, Univ. of Calif., San Francisco 1975-; mem. Nat. Cttee. on Vital Health Statistics 1975-79, mem. Pres.'s Comm. for the Study of Ethical Problems in Medicine and Biomedical and Behavioral Research 1979-82, Inst. of Medicine Council on Health Care Tech. Assessment 1986-; mem. N.A.S. Inst. of Medicine 1980-. *Publications:* articles in official documents and professional journals. *Leisure interests:* reading, photography, swimming. *Address:* Research Institute, Palo Alto Medical Foundation, 860 Bryant Street, Palo Alto, Calif. 94301 (Office); 161 Erica Way, Menlo Park, Calif. 94025, U.S.A. (Home). *Telephone:* (415) 326 8120 (Office); (415) 854 5767 (Home).

SCLATER, John G., PH.D., F.R.S.; British professor of geophysics; b. 17 June 1940, Edinburgh, Scotland; s. of John G. Sclater and Margaret Bennett Glen; m. 1st Fredrica R. Sclater 1968 (died 1985), two s.; m. 2nd Paula Ann Edwards 1985; ed. Stonyhurst Coll., Edinburgh Univ. and Cambridge Univ.; Postdoctoral Research Geophysicist, Scripps Inst. of Oceanography 1965-67, Asst. Research Geophysicist 1967-72; Assoc. Prof. M.I.T. 1972-77, Prof. 1977-83; M.I.T. Dir., Jt. Program in Oceanography with the Woods Hole Oceanographic Inst. 1981-83; Assoc. Dir. Inst. for

Geophysics, Univ. of Texas at Austin, Prof., Dept. of Geological Sciences and Shell Distinguished Chair. in Geophysics 1983-; Rosenstiel Award 1978; Shell Distinguished Chair in Geophysics 1983, Bucher Medal, American Geophysical Union 1985. *Leisure interests:* running, swimming, golf. *Address:* The Institute for Geophysics, University of Texas at Austin, P.O. Box 7456, Austin, Tex., 78712, U.S.A. *Telephone:* (512) 471-6156.

SCOFIELD, Paul, C.B.E.; British actor; b. 21 Jan. 1922; m. Joy Parker 1943; one s. one d.; trained London Mask Theatre Drama School; Birmingham Repertory Theatre 1941 and 1943-46; Stratford-on-Avon Shakespeare Memorial Theatre 1946-48; Arts Theatre 1946; Phoenix Theatre 1947; with H. M. Tennent 1949-56; Assoc. Dir. Nat. Theatre 1970-71; Hon. LL.D. (Glasgow Univ.), Hon. D.Lit. (Kent) 1973, (Sussex) 1985; Shakespeare Prize, Hamburg 1972; Danish Film Acad. Award; Tony Award. *Has appeared in:* Chekhov's Seagull, Anouilh's Ring Round the Moon, Charles Morgan's The River Line; Richard II, Time Remembered, A Question of Fact, Hamlet (also in Moscow), Power and the Glory, Family Reunion, A Dead Secret, Expresso Bongo, The Complaisant Lover, A Man for all Seasons, Stratford Festival, Ont., Canada 1961, Coriolanus, Don Armado New York 1961-62, A Man for All Seasons London 1962-63, King Lear 1963 (E. Europe, Helsinki, Moscow, New York 1964), Timon of Athens 1965, The Government Inspector London 1966, Staircase 1967, Macbeth 1968, The Hotel in Amsterdam 1968, Uncle Vanya 1970, The Captain of Köpenik 1971, Rules of the Game 1971, Savages 1973, The Tempest 1974, 1975, Dimetos 1976, Volpone 1977, The Madras House 1977, The Family 1978, Amadeus 1979, Othello 1980, Don Quixote 1982, A Midsummer Night's Dream 1982, I'm Not Rappaport 1986. *Films:* The Train 1963, A Man for All Seasons 1967 (Oscar and New York Film Critics Award, Moscow Film Festival and British Film Acad. Awards), King Lear 1970, Scorpio 1972, A Delicate Balance 1972, '1919', Anna Karenina 1984. *Television:* The Ambassadors 1977, The Potting Shed 1981, If Winter Comes 1981, Song at Twilight 1982, Come into the Garden Maud 1982, A Kind of Alaska 1984, Summer Lightning 1985, Only Yesterday 1986, The Attic 1987, Why the Whales Come 1988, Henry V 1989. *Address:* The Gables, Balcombe, Sussex, England.

SCOGNAMIGLIO, Carlo, D.ECON.; Italian economist and business consultant; b. 27 Nov. 1944, Varese; s. of Luigi Scognamilio and Esther (née Pasini) Scognamilio; m. Delfina Rattazzi 1980; one s. one d.; ed. L. Bocconi Univ., Landai School of Econs.; Asst. Prof. of Finance, Univ. of Padua 1973-79; Asst. Prof. of Industrial Econs. Univ. L. Bocconi, Milan 1975-84; Prof. of Industrial Econs., Libera Universita Int. degli Studi Sociali, Rome 1979-, Dean and Rector 1984-; Pres. Rizzoli Corriere della Sera 1983-84, Vice-Pres. 1984-; Bulkitalia 1984-. *Publications:* The White Book on PPSS 1981, The White Book on the Italian Financial Market 1982, Theory and Policy of Finance 1987, Industrial Economics 1987. *Leisure interests:* economics, history. *Address:* Libera Universita Int. degli Studi Sociali, Viale Pola 12, 00198 Rome; 2 Via Carducci, 20123 Milan, Italy.

SCOON, Sir Paul, G.C.M.G., G.C.V.O., O.B.E.; Grenadian public administrator; b. 4 July 1935; m. Esmai Monica Lumsden 1970; two step-s., one step-d.; ed. Inst. of Educ., Leeds, Toronto Univ.; teacher Grenada Boys' Secondary School 1953-67, Chief Ed. Officer 1967-68; with Civil Service 1968-, Vice-Pres. Civil Service Assen. 1968, Perm. Sec. 1969, Sec. to Cabinet 1970-72, Deputy Dir, Commonwealth Foundation 1973-78, Gov. Centre for Int. Briefing, Farnham Castle 1973-78, Gov.-Gen. of Grenada 1978-. *Address:* Governor-General's House, St. George's, Grenada. *Telephone:* 2401.

SCORSESE, Martin, M.A.; American film director and writer; b. 17 Nov. 1942, Flushing, N.Y.; s. of Charles and Catherine (née Cappa) Scorsese; m. 1st Laraine Marie Brennan 1965, one d.; m. 2nd Julia Cameron (divorced), one d.; m. 3rd Isabella Rossellini 1979 (divorced 1983); m. 4th Barbara DeFina 1985; ed. New York Univ.; faculty asst. and instructor, Film Dept., New York Univ. 1963-66; instructor 1968-70; dir. and writer of films: What's a Nice Girl Like You Doing in a Place Like This? 1963, It's Not Just You, Murray 1964, Who's That Knocking At My Door? 1968, The Big Shave 1968; dir. play The Act 1977-78; dir. and writer of documentaries; supervising ed. and asst. dir. Woodstock 1970; assoc. producer and post-production supervisor Medicine Ball Caravan 1971, Box Car Bertha 1972; dir. films: Mean Streets 1973, Alice Doesn't Live Here Any More 1974, Taxi Driver 1976, New York, New York 1977, King of Comedy 1981; actor and dir. The Last Waltz 1978; dir. Raging Bull 1980, After Hours 1985, The Color of Money 1986; dir. The Last Temptation of Christ 1988 (Courage in Filmmaking Award, Los Angeles Film Teachers Assen. 1989); acted in Cannonball 1976, Triple Play 1981; Edward J. Kingsley Foundation Award 1963, 1964; first prize, Rosenthal Foundation Awards of Soc. of Cinematologists 1964; named Best Dir., Cannes Film Festival 1986; first prize, Screen Producer's Guild 1965, Brown Univ. Film Festival 1965, etc. *Publication:* Scorsese on Scorsese 1989. *Address:* c/o Jay Julien and Associates, 1501 Broadway, New York, N.Y. 10036, U.S.A.

SCOTT, Alastair Ian, PH.D., F.R.S.E., F.R.S.; British professor of chemistry; b. 10 April 1928, Glasgow, Scotland; s. of William and Nell (Newton) Scott; m. Elizabeth M. Walters 1950; one s. one d.; ed. Univ. of Glasgow; Lecturer in Organic Chem. Univ. of Glasgow 1957-62; Prof. Univ. of British Columbia, Vancouver 1962-65, Univ. of Sussex 1965-68, Yale Univ. 1968-77; Distinguished Prof. Texas A & M Univ. 1977-80, Davidson Prof. of Chemistry and Biochemistry 1982-; Prof. Dept. of Chem. Univ. of Edin.

1980–82; mem. American Chem. Soc., Royal Soc. of Chem., Biochem. Soc.; Hon. mem. Pharmaceutical Soc. of Japan 1984; Hon. M.A. (Yale) 1968, Carday Morgan Medal, Royal Soc. of Chem. 1964, Guenther Award, American Chem. Soc. 1975, and other awards. *Publications:* Interpretation of Ultraviolet Spectra of Natural Products 1964; articles in professional journals. *Address:* Department of Chemistry, Texas A & M University, College Station, Tex. 77843, U.S.A. *Telephone:* (409) 845-3243.

SCOTT, Sir David Aubrey, G.C.M.G.; British diplomatist (retd.) and company director; b. 3 Aug. 1919, London; s. of the late H. S. and of Barbara E. Scott, J.P.; m. Vera Kathleen Ibbitson 1941; two s. one d.; ed. Charterhouse and Birmingham Univ.; Royal Artillery 1939–47; Chief Radar Adviser, British Mil. Mission to Egyptian Army 1945–47; Commonwealth Relations Office 1948–50, South Africa 1951–53; Cabinet Office 1954–56; Singapore 1956–58; British Deputy High Commr. in Fed. of Rhodesia and Nyasaland 1961–63; Imperial Defence Coll. 1964; Deputy High Commr. in India 1965–67; High Commr. in Uganda 1967–70; Amb. to Rwanda (non-resident) 1967–70; Asst. Under-Sec. of State, Foreign and Commonwealth Office 1970–72; High Commr. New Zealand and Gov. of Pitcairn Island 1973–75; Amb. to South Africa 1976–79; Dir. Barclays Bank Int. 1979–85, Mitchell Cotts Group 1980–86, Bradbury Wilkinson PLC 1984–86; Chair. Ellerman Lines PLC 1981–83, Nuclear Resources Ltd. 1984–88; Chair. Royal Overseas League 1981–86; Vice-Pres. U.K.-S.A. Trade Assen. 1981–85; Chair. Sadler's Wells Devt. 1984–87. *Publication:* Ambassador in Black and White 1981. *Leisure interests:* bird-watching, music, theatre. *Address:* Wayside, Moushill Lane, Milford, nr. Godalming, Surrey, GU8 5BQ, England. *Telephone:* (048 68) 21935.

SCOTT, Hon. Douglas Barr; Australian politician; b. 12 May 1920, Grenfell, N.S.W.; m. Pamela Scott 1948; one s. one d.; ed. Scotch Coll., Adelaide, St. Andrew's Coll., Sydney Univ.; Royal Australian Navy 1941–46; entered Parl. as Senator Aug.–Nov. 1970; re-elected Nat. Party Senator for N.S.W. 1974, 1975–; Deputy Leader Nat. Party Feb. 1976; mem. Senate Standing Cttee. on Foreign Affairs and Defence 1976–, Standing Orders and Privileges Cttees.; Deputy Pres. and Chair. Govt. Cttees. 1978–, including Industrial Relations Cttee., Leader Nat. Party in Senate 1980–85; Leader Parl. Del. to Commonwealth Parl. Assen. Conf. in Mauritius 1976, to S.E. Asia and Republic of Korea 1979; Minister for Special Trade Representations and Assisting Minister for Trade and Resources 1979–80; mem. Livestock and Grain Producers' Assen.; Nat. Country Party. *Leisure interests:* pasture and stock management, cereal and oil seed production. *Address:* Glenview, Grenfell, N.S.W. 2810, Australia.

SCOTT, The Most Rev. Edward Walter, C.C., B.A., L.TH.; Canadian ecclesiastic; b. 30 April 1919, Edmonton, Alberta; s. of Thomas and Kathleen Scott; m. Isabel Florence Brannan 1942; one s. three d.; ed. Univ. of British Columbia, Anglican Theological Coll., British Columbia; ordained in Anglican Church 1942; Parish Priest in Seal Cove, Prince Rupert, B.C. 1942–45; Gen. Sec. Student Christian Movement, Univ. of Manitoba 1945–50; Rector, Church of St. John the Baptist, Fort Garry 1949–55, St. Jude's Church, Winnipeg 1955–60; Dir. of Social Service and Priest in charge of Indian Work, Diocese of Rupert's Land 1960–64; Assoc. Sec., Council for Social Service, Nat. Office of Anglican Church 1964–66; Bishop of Kootenay 1966–71; Primate of Anglican Church of Canada 1971–86; Moderator, Exec. and Cen. Cttees. of WCC 1975–83; Pres. Canadian Council of Churches 1985–; mem. Commonwealth Group on S. Africa 1985–86; 14 hon. degrees; Human Relations Award, Canadian Council of Christians and Jews 1987. *Leisure interest:* carpentry. *Address:* 29 Hawthorn Avenue, Toronto, Ont. M4W 2Z1, Canada (Home). *Telephone:* (416) 920-1975.

SCOTT, George C(ampbell); American actor, producer and director; b. 18 Oct. 1927, Wise, Va.; s. of George C. Scott and late Helena Scott; m. Trish Van Devere 1972; 6 c. from previous marriages; ed. Redford High School and Univ. of Missouri; appeared in Richard III, New York Shakespeare Festival 1957; subsequent theatrical appearances included As You Like It, Children of Darkness 1957–58; Broadway appearances in Comes a Day 1958, The Andersonville Trial 1959, The Wall 1960; co-founder Theater of Mich. Company 1961; produced, directed and appeared in General Seeger 1962 and produced Great Day in the Morning 1962; Dir. Death of a Salesman, New York 1975, All God's Chillun Got Wings 1975; Dir. and acted in Present Laughter 1982. *Films include:* The Hanging Tree 1958, Anatomy of a Murder 1959, The Hustler 1962, Dr. Strangelove 1963, The List of Adrian Messenger 1963, The Yellow Rolls-Royce 1964, The Bible 1966, The Flim-Flam Man 1967, Petulia 1969, Patton: Lust for Glory 1970, Jane Eyre 1971, They Might be Giants 1971, The Hospital 1972, Precinct 1945, Oklahoma Crude, Rage (also dir.), Day of the Dolphin 1973, Bank Shot (also dir.), The Savage is Loose (also dir.), The Hindenberg, Sly Fox 1976, The Prince and The Pauper 1976, Islands in the Stream 1977, Movie Movie 1978, Hard Core 1979, The Changeling 1980, The Formula 1980, Taps 1981, Il Duce 1985; refused Acad. Award (Oscar) for Patton: Lust for Glory 1971; *TV series:* East Side, West Side 1963–64. *Address:* c/o Jane Deacy Agency, 300 East 7th Street, New York, N.Y. 10021, U.S.A.

SCOTT, Sir Ian Dixon, K.C.M.G., K.C.V.O., C.I.E.; British fmr. diplomatist; b. 6 March 1909, Inverness; s. of Thomas Henderson Scott, O.B.E., M.I.C.E., and Mary Agnes (née Dixon); m. Hon. Anna Drusilla Lindsay 1937; one s. four d.; ed. Queen's Royal Coll., Trinidad, Balliol Coll., Oxford, London School

of Econs.; entered Indian Civil Service 1932; joined Indian Political Service 1935; Asst. Commr., N.W. Frontier Province 1935; Asst. Political Officer, Chitral 1936–37; Census Supt., N.W. Frontier Province 1940–41; Asst. Dir. of Intelligence, Peshawar 1941; Principal, Islamia Coll., Peshawar 1942–45; Deputy Private Sec. to the Viceroy 1945–47; with John Lewis Partnership 1948–50; Foreign Service, London 1950, First Sec. Foreign Office 1950–51; British Legation, Helsinki 1952–53; First Sec. and Head of Chancery, Lebanon 1954, Counsellor 1956, Chargé d'Affaires 1956, 1957, 1958; Imperial Defence Coll. 1959; Consul-Gen., then Amb. to Congo 1960–61, to Sudan 1961–65, to Norway 1965–68; Dir. Clarksons Holiday Holdings Ltd. 1969, Chair. 1972–73; Chair. Davell and Rufford (Holdings) Ltd. 1970–72; mem. Bd. of Govs., Felixstowe Coll. 1971–84 (Chair. 1972–80); Chair. Bd. of Govs., Suffolk Area Health Authority 1973–77; mem. of Council, Dr. Barnardo's 1970–84, Chair. 1972–78, Vice-Pres. 1984–; Pres. Indian Civil Service Assen 1977–. *Publication:* Tumbled House 1969. *Leisure interest:* sailing. *Address:* Ash House, Alde Lane, Aldeburgh, Suffolk, England.

SCOTT, John Vivian, LL.B.; New Zealand diplomatist (retd.); b. 19 Nov. 1920 Cambridge, England; m. Marguerite Boxer 1946; three d.; ed. Victoria Univ., Wellington; joined New Zealand Dept. of External Affairs 1947; has served in Canberra, New York and London; mem. New Zealand Perm. Mission at UN 1951–55; Amb. to Japan, Repub. of Korea 1965–68, to France, Spain, Portugal, Holy See 1979–82, also Perm. Rep. to OECD –1982; Perm. Rep. to UN 1969–73; Deputy Sec. of Foreign Affairs 1973–79; Dir. N.Z. Inst. of Int. Affairs 1984–. *Leisure interests:* gardening, music, walking. *Address:* P.O.B. 214, Waikanae, New Zealand (Home). *Telephone:* Paraparaumu 87329.

SCOTT, Jonathan L.; American business executive; b. 2 Feb. 1930, Nampa, Ida.; s. of Buell Bonnie and Jewel Pearl (née Horn) Scott; four s. (one deceased); ed. Coll. of Idaho, Harvard Univ.; with Western Enterprises Inc. 1952–53; First Lieut. U.S.A.F. 1953–55; Gen. Supervisor Albertson's Inc. 1955–61, Exec. Vice-Pres. 1961–65, Pres., Dir. 1965–72, C.E.O. 1972–74; Chair., C.E.O., Dir. Great Atlantic & Pacific Tea Co. Inc. 1975–80; Chair., C.E.O., Dir. J. L. Scott Enterprises Inc., American Superstores Inc. 1987–89; Vice-Chair. and Dir. American Stores Co. 1987–, C.E.O. Jan. 1989–; Dir. Morrison-Knudsen Co., Trus Joist Corpn.; Trustee Boys Clubs of America, Cttee. for Econ. Devt. *Leisure interests:* water sports, hunting, snow skiing, tennis, reading. *Address:* American Stores Company, 5201 Amelia Earhart Drive, Salt Lake City, Utah 84116 (Office); 3898 Thousand Oaks Circle, Salt Lake City, Utah 84124 U.S.A. (Home).

SCOTT, Sir Michael, K.C.V.O., C.M.G.; British diplomatist (retd.); b. 19 May 1923; m. 1st Vivienne Sylvia Vincent Barwood 1943, three s.; m. 2nd Jennifer Smith Slawikowski (née Cameron Smith) 1971; ed. Dame Allan's School and Durham Univ.; Indian Army 1942–47; Colonial Office 1949; Commonwealth Relations Office (CRO) 1957; First Sec., Karachi 1958–59; Deputy High Commr., Peshawar 1959–62; CRO 1962; Counsellor (Information) and Dir. British Information Services, Delhi 1963–65; Head of E. Africa Dept., FCO 1965–68; Counsellor, Nicosia 1968–72; Amb. to Nepal 1974–77; High Commr. in Malawi 1977–80, in Bangladesh 1980–81; Sec. Gen. Royal Commonwealth Soc. 1983–88. *Address:* 87A Cornwall Gardens, London, SW7 4AY, England. *Telephone:* 01-589 6794.

SCOTT, Peter Lowell, B.S.; American business executive; b. 27 May 1927, Bellaire, Ohio; s. of Peter Lowell and Paula Bertha Scott; m. Clara M. Papas 1948; two s.; ed. Yale Univ., Ohio State Univ.; service U.S.N. 1945–46; Pres. and Prin. founder Hermetic Seal Transformer Co., Tex. 1952–57; Pres. Dresser Electronics Div. Dresser Industries, Tex. 1957–63; Pres. and founder Scott Electronics, Orlando, Fla. 1964–65; Pres. Electronic Communications Inc.; Vice-Pres. NCR, St. Petersburg, Fla. 1965–75; Pres. United Techs. Corpn., Pres. and C.E.O. Essex Group, Fort Wayne, Ind., Pres. Norden Systems, Norwalk 1978–79; Exec. Vice-Pres. Electronics Sector United Corpn., Hartford 1979–83; Chair. and C.E.O. Emhart Corpn., Farmington, Conn. 1987–; mem. Bd. of Dirs. Hartford Steam Boiler Inspection and Insurance Co., Owens Corning Fiberglas Corpn., Nat. Intergroup Inc., Mack Trucks Inc., Planning Research Corpn., Kaman Corpn., Dexter Corpn. Electronics Foundation, Nat. Science Center for Communications; mem. American Defense Preparedness Assen. *Address:* Emhart Corporation, 426 Colt Highway, Farmington, Conn. 06032, U.S.A.

SCOTT, Sir Peter (Markham), Kt., C.H., C.B.E., D.S.C., M.A., F.R.S.; British artist and ornithologist; b. 14 Sept. 1909, London; s. of late Capt. Robert Falcon Scott and Kathleen Bruce; m. 1st Elizabeth J. Howard 1942 (divorced 1951), one d.; m. 2nd Philippa Talbot-Ponsonby 1951, one s. one d.; ed. Oundle School, Trinity Coll., Cambridge, Munich State Acad., and Royal Acad., London; founded, now Hon. Dir., The Wildfowl Trust (now called Wildfowl and Wetlands Trust) 1946; Rep. G.B. in Olympic Games, in single-handed sailing (bronze medal) 1936; served in Navy during 1939–45 War; Pres. Int. Yacht Racing Union 1955–69; Chair. Olympic Int. Yacht Racing Jury, Melbourne 1956, Naples 1960, Tokyo 1964; 1st Vice-Pres. World Wildlife Fund 1961–84, and Hon. Chair. Council, World Wildlife Fund Int. 1985–; Int. Vice-Pres. Inland Waterways Assen.; Pres. Fauna and Flora Preservation Soc. 1981–; Hon. Dir. Survival Anglia Ltd., Wildfowl Trust; mem. Council of Winston Churchill Memorial Trust; Pres. Wildlife Youth Service –1981; Chair. Survival Service Comm. of Int. Union for the Conservation of Nature and Natural Resources 1963–80; Chair. Falkland Islands Foundation 1979–; Chancellor Birmingham Univ. 1974–83;

eight hon. degrees; Cherry Kearton Medal R.G.S. 1967; Albert Medal, R.S.A. 1970; Bernard Tucker Medal B.O.U. 1970; Arthur Allan Medal Cornell Univ. 1971; Gold Medal, N.Y. Zoological Soc. 1974; Icelandic Order of Falcon 1969, Commdr. Dutch Order of Golden Ark 1976, Int. Pahlavi Environment Prize (UN) 1977, I.U.C.N. John Phillips Medal 1981, World Wildlife Fund 20th Anniversary Special Award 1981, Philadelphia Acad. of Nat. Sciences Gold Medal 1983, Conservationist of the Year (World Wildlife News) 1988. *Publications:* Morning Flight 1935, Wild Chorus 1938, The Battle of the Narrow Seas 1945, Portrait Drawings 1949, Key to the Wild Fowl of the World 1949, Wild Geese and Eskimos 1951, A Thousand Geese (with James Fisher) 1953, The Eye of the Wind 1961, Animals in Africa 1962 (with Philippa Scott), The Swans 1972 (with the Wildfowl Trust), Fishwatchers' Guide to West Atlantic Coral Reefs 1972, Observations of Wildlife 1980, Travel Diaries of a Naturalist 1983, 1985, 1987; illustrated many books incl. Bird in the Bush (Lord Kennet), Grey Goose, and Through the Air (Michael Bratby), The Snow Goose (Paul Gallico), The Swans (with the Wildfowl Trust), etc.; Joint Ed. and Illustrator of Wildfowl Trust Annual Reports 1948–. *Leisure interests:* exploring, birdwatching. *Address:* New Grounds, Slimbridge, Glos., GL2 7BT, England.

SCOTT, Ridley; British film director; dir. of numerous award-winning TV commercials since 1970; début as feature film dir. with The Duellists 1978. *Other films include:* Alien, Blade Runner, Legend. *Address:* Hampstead Grove, London, N.W.3, England.

SCOTT, Ronald (Ronnie), O.B.E.; British musician; b. 28 Jan. 1927, E. London; s. of Jock Scott and Sylvia Rosenbloom; ed. Cen. Foundation School, London; Professional Musician 1943–; opened Ronnie Scott's Club 1959. *Publication:* Some of My Best Friends are Blues 1979. *Leisure interest:* music. *Address:* 47 Frith Street, London, W.1, England. *Telephone:* 01-439 0747.

SCOTT, Timothy; English sculptor; b. 18 April 1937, Richmond, Surrey; s. of A. C. Scott and Dorothea Scott; m. Malkanthi Wirekoon 1958; two s. three d.; ed. Lycée Jaccard, Lausanne, Architectural Assen. and St. Martin's School of Art, London; worked at Atelier Le Corbusier-Wegenscky and others, Paris 1959–61; Sr. Lecturer Canterbury Coll. of Art 1975–76; Head of Fine Art Dept., Birmingham Polytechnic 1976–78; Head Dept. of Sculpture, St. Martin's School of Art 1980–86; numerous visiting lectureships in U.S.A., Canada, Australia, Germany and U.K.; one-man exhbns. since 1964: Waddington, Kasmin Galleries, London, Rubin, Emmerich, Tibor de Nagy, Meredith Long Galleries, New York, Galerie Wentzel, Hamburg, Cologne, David Mirvish, Toronto, Klonaridis, Toronto; ; retrospectives: Whitechapel, London 1967, Museum of Fine Arts, Boston, U.S.A. 1972, Edmonton Art Gallery, Alberta 1976; touring retrospective Bielefeld, Lübeck, Ludwigshafen, Munich, Brunswick, Münster, Leverküsen, Saarbrücken, Regensburg, etc. 1979. *Leisure interests:* music, architecture, travel, Sri Lanka, Indian culture, food. *Address:* 21 Ferdinand Street, London, N.W.1 (Studio); 7 Prideaux Place, London, W.C.1; Keepers Cottage, Troutsdale, N. York Moors, N. Yorks., England; Riverdale Road, Aniewatte, Kandy, Sri Lanka. *Telephone:* 01-482 4940 (Studio); 01-837 7157 (Home).

SCOTT, William George, C.B.E.; British artist; b. 15 Feb. 1913, Scotland; s. of William John Scott and Agnes Scott; m. Hilda Mary Lucas 1937; two s.; ed. Enniskillen, Belfast School of Art and Royal Acad. Schools, London; exhbns. at Leger Gallery 1942, 1944, 1946, Leicester Gallery 1948, 1951, Hanover Gallery 1953, 1956, 1961, 1965, 1967, 1969, Tate Gallery 1963 (all in London); Martha Jackson Gallery, New York 1954, 1958, 1973, 1975; Venice Biennale 1958; São Paulo, Brazil 1953, 1961; Retrospective exhbn. Tate Gallery 1972, 1986, Ulster 1979, 1986; exhbn. Gimpel Fils, London 1974, 1976, 1978, 1980, 1985, 1987, Gallery Kasahara, Tokyo 1976, Gallery Moos, Toronto 1978, 1982, Nat. Galleries of Scotland 1986; War Paintings 1942–46, Imperial War Museum 1981; Hon. Dr. R.C.A.; Hon. D.Litt. (Queen's Univ., Belfast, and Dublin Univ.). *Leisure interest:* farming. *Address:* 13 Edith Terrace, Chelsea, London, S.W.10, England. *Telephone:* 01-352 8044.

SCOTT, William Lloyd, J.D.; American lawyer and politician; b. 1 July 1915, Williamsburg, Va.; s. of William David Scott and Nora Bell Ingram; m. Ruth Inez Huffman 1940; two s. one d.; ed. George Washington Univ.; admitted to Va. bar; Trial Attorney, Dept. of Justice 1942–60; Special Asst. to solicitor, Dept. of Interior 1960–61; private law practice, Fairfax, Va. 1961–60, Springfield, Va. 1979–; mem. House of Reps. 1966–72; Republican Senator from Va. 1973–79. *Address:* 7114 Wolf Den Road, Fairfax Station, Virginia 22039, U.S.A. (Home).

SCOTT, W. (William) Richard, PH.D.; American educator and sociologist; b. 18 Dec. 1932, Parsons, Kan.; s. of Charles H. Scott and Hildegarde Hewit; m. Joy Lee Whitney 1955; three c.; ed. Parsons Jr. Coll., Kan., Univ. of Kan., Univ. of Chicago; Asst. Prof., Dept. of Sociology, Stanford Univ. 1960–65, Assoc. Prof. 1965–69, Prof. 1969–, Chair. Dept. of Sociology 1972–75, Dir. Orgs. Research Training Program 1972–88; Dir. Stanford Center for Orgs. Research 1988–; Prof. by courtesy, Dept. of Family, Community and Preventative Medicine, School of Medicine, and of Educ., School of Educ., and of Organizational Behaviour, Graduate School of Business, Stanford Univ.; Sr. Researcher, Nat. Center for Health Services Research, Dept. of Health, Educ. and Welfare, Washington, D.C. 1975–76;

Ed. Annual Review of Sociology 1986–; Woodrow Wilson Fellow 1954–55; Social Science Research Council Fellow 1958–59; mem. Inst. of Medicine; Distinguished Scholar Award, Acad. of Man. 1988. *Publications:* Metropolis and Region (with others) 1960, Formal Organizations (with P. M. Blau) 1962, Social Processes and Social Structures 1970, Evaluation and the Exercise of Authority (with S. M. Dornbusch) 1975, Organizations: Rational, Natural and Open Systems 1981, Organizational Environments (with J. W. Meyer) 1983, Hospital Structure and Performance (with A. Flood) 1987. *Leisure interests:* reading, tennis, cross-country skiing. *Address:* Stanford University Department of Sociology, Building 120, Stanford, Calif. 94305 (Office); 940 Lathrop Place, Stanford, Calif. 94305, U.S.A. (Home). *Telephone:* (415) 857-1834 (Home).

SCOTTO, Renata; Italian soprano; b. 24 Feb. 1935, Savona; m. Lorenzo Anselmi; ed. under Ghirardini at Milan; joined La Scala Opera Company after début in La Traviata at Teatro Nuovo, Milan 1953; then studied under Merlino and Mercedes Llopart; known for roles in La Sonnambula, I Puritani, L'Elisir d'amore, Lucia di Lammermoor, Falstaff, La Bohème, Turandot, I Capuleti, Madame Butterfly, Tosca, Manon Lescant, Otello, etc. *Address:* c/o Il Teatro alla Scala, via Filodrammatici 2, Milan, Italy; c/o Robert Lombardo Associates, 61 W. 62nd Street, Suite 6F, New York, N.Y. 10023, U.S.A.

SCOWCROFT, Lieut.-Gen. Brent, PH.D.; American air force officer and government official; b. 19 March 1925, Odgen, Utah; s. of James and Lucile Balantyne Scowcroft; m. Marian Horner 1951; one d.; ed. U.S. Mil. Acad., West Point, and Columbia Univ.; Operational and Admin. positions in U.S. Air Force 1948–53; taught Russian history as Asst. Prof., Dept. of Social Sciences, U.S. Mil. Acad., W. Point 1953–57; Asst. Air Attaché, U.S. Embassy, Belgrade 1959–61; Assoc. Prof., Political Science Dept., U.S. Air Force Acad., Colorado 1962–63, Prof., Head of Dept. 1963–64; Plans and Operations Section, Air Force HQ, Washington 1964–66; various Nat. Security posts with Dept. of Defense 1968–72; Mil. Asst. to Pres., The White House 1972, Deputy Asst. to Pres. for Nat. Security Affairs 1973–75, Asst. to Pres. for Nat. Security Affairs 1975–77, 1989–; mem. Pres.' Gen. Advisory Cttee. on Arms Control 1977–81; Dir. Atlantic Council, U.S. Bd. of Visitors U.S. Air Force Acad. 1977–79, Council on Foreign Relations, Rand Corpn., Mitre Corpn.; Vice-Chair. UNA/U.S.A.; Chair. Presidential Comm. on Strategic Forces 1983–89; mem. Cttee. of Enquiry into Nat. Security Council 1986–87; Defense D.S.M., Air Force D.S.M. (with two oak leaf clusters), Legion of Merit (with oak leaf cluster), Air Force Commendation Medal, Nat. Security Medal. *Address:* National Security Council, Executive Office Bldg., Washington, D.C. 20506, U.S.A. *Telephone:* (202) 395-3440.

SCRANTON, William Warren, A.B., LL.B.; American lawyer and politician; b. 19 July 1917, Madison, Conn.; s. of Worthington and Marion Margery Warren Scranton; m. Mary Lowe Chamberlin 1942; three s. one d.; ed. Hotchkiss School, Yale Univ. and Yale Univ. Law School; U.S. Army Air Force 1941–45; Pa. bar 1946; Assoc. O'Malley, Harris, Harris and Warren 1946–47; Vice-Pres. Int. Textbook Co., Scranton, Pa. 1947–52, later Dir. and mem. Exec. Cttee.; Pres. Scranton-Lackawanna Trust Co. 1954–56; Chair. Bd. and Dir. Northeastern Pennsylvania Broadcasting Co. 1957–61; Special Asst. to U.S. Sec. of State 1959–60; mem. U.S. House of Reps. 1961–63; Gov. of Pennsylvania 1963–67; Special Envoy to Middle East on behalf of Pres.-elect Nixon Dec. 1968; Chair. President's Commission on Campus Unrest 1970; Special Consultant to the Pres. 1974; Perm. Rep. to UN 1976–77; Chair of Bd. Northeastern Bank of Pa. 1974–76; Chair. UNA; Dir. Cummins Engines Co., IBM Corpn., New York Times Co., Mobil Oil; numerous hon. degrees; Republican. *Leisure interests:* tennis, swimming, hiking. *Address:* Northeastern Bank, Scranton, Pa. 18503, U.S.A.

SCREECH, Michael Andrew, M.A., D.LITT., F.B.A.; British academic; b. 2 May 1926, Plymouth; s. of Richard John Screech, M.M. and Nellie Screech (née Maunder); m. Anne Reeve 1956; three s.; ed. Sutton High School, Plymouth and Univ. Coll. London; served Intelligence Corps, Far East; Lecturer then Sr. Lecturer, Birmingham Univ. 1951–60; Reader, then Prof. of French, Univ. of London 1960–71, Fielden Prof. of French Language and Literature 1971–84; Visiting Prof. London, Ont. 1964, Albany, N.Y. 1969; Johnson Prof. Madison, Wis. 1979; Edmund Campion Lecturer, Regina, Sask. 1985, Dorothy Ford Wiley Prof. of Renaissance Culture, Chapel Hill, N.C. 1986; Sr. Research Fellow, All Souls Coll. Oxford 1984–; Fellow Univ. Coll. London; Hon. Citizen Ville de Tours; Ordre National du Mérite. *Publications:* The Rabelaisian Marriage 1958, L'Evangélisme de Rabelais 1959, Le Tiers Livre de Pantagruel 1964, Les 52 Semaines de Lefèvre d'Etaples 1965, Les Regrets et Antiquités de Du Bellay 1966, Gargantua 1967, La Pantagrueline Prognostication 1975, Rabelais 1979, Ecstasy and the Praise of Folly 1981, 1988, Montaigne and Melancholy 1983, Erasmus' Annotations on the New Testament (with Anne Reeve) Vol. 1 1986, Vol. 2 1989, A New Rabelais Bibliography (with Stephen Rawles) 1987, Montaigne: An Apology for Raymond Sebond 1987. *Leisure interest:* walking. *Address:* 5 Swanston-Field, Whitchurch-on-Thames, Pangbourne, Reading, RG8 7HP, England.

SCRIBNER, Charles, Jr., A.B.; American publisher; b. 13 July 1921, Quogue, N.Y.; s. of Charles Scribner and Vera (Bloodgood) Scribner; m. Dorothy Joan Sunderland 1949; three s.; ed. St Paul's School and Princeton Univ.; in U.S. Navy 1943–46, 1950–52; Advertising Man., Charles Scribner's

Sons 1946–48, Production Man. 1948–50, Pres. 1952–77, Chair. 1977–79; Chair. Scribner Book Cos. Inc. 1978–; Pres. Princeton Univ. Press. 1957–68, American Book Publrs.' Council 1966–68; Trustee, Princeton Univ. 1969–79; mem. American Philosophical Soc., Editorial Advisory Cttee. of The Writings of Albert Einstein. *Publications:* The Devil's Bridge 1978, The Enduring Hemingway (Ed.) 1974; translations: Doppelfinten (Gabriel Laub) 1977, Le Jardin du Sphinx (Pierre Berloquin) 1985. *Address:* Charles Scribner's Sons, 866 3rd Avenue, New York, N.Y. 10022 (Office); 211 East 70th Street, New York, N.Y. 10021, U.S.A. (Home).

SCRIMSHAW, Nevin Stewart, PH.D., M.D., M.P.H.; American professor of nutrition; b. 20 Jan. 1918, Milwaukee, Wis.; s. of Stewart and Harriet (née Smith) Scrimshaw; m. Mary Ware Goodrich 1941; four s. one d.; ed. Ohio Wesleyan Univ., Harvard Univ. and Univ. of Rochester; Consultant in Nutrition, Pan American Sanitary Bureau, Regional Office of the Americas, WHO 1948–49, Regional Adviser in Nutrition 1949–53; Dir. Inst. of Nutrition of Cen. America and Panama (INCAP), Guatemala 1949–61, Consulting Dir. 1961–65, Consultant 1965–; Adjunct Prof., Public Health Nutrition, Columbia Univ. 1959–61, Visiting Lecturer 1961–66; Visiting Lecturer on Tropical Public Health, Harvard Univ. 1968–85; Head, Dept. of Nutrition and Food Science, M.I.T. 1961–79, Inst. Prof. 1976–, Dir. Clinical Research Centre 1962–66, 1979–85, Principal Investigator 1962–; Dir. M.I.T./Harvard Int. Food and Nutrition Program 1979–; Programme Dir. Food, Nutrition and Poverty UN Univ. 1982– (Dir. Devt. Studies Div.); Pres. Int. Union of Nutritional Scientists 1978–81; Fellow, A.A.A.S. American Acad. of Arts and Sciences; mem. N.A.S., Inst. of Medicine and numerous other nat. and foreign scientific socs. and asscns.; mem. numerous cttees. and advisory panels to UN agencies and other orgs.; Int. Award, Inst. of Food Technologists 1969, Goldberger Award in Clinical Nutrition, American Medical Asscn. 1969, First James R. Killian Jr. Faculty Achievement Award, M.I.T. 1972, McCollum Award, American Soc. for Clinical Nutrition 1975, Conrad A. Elvehjem Award, American Inst. of Nutrition 1976, 1st Bolton L. Corson Medal, Franklin Inst. 1976, Medal of Honor, Fundacion F. Cuenca Villoro 1978, etc. *Publications:* over 500 scientific articles and 11 books on various aspects of human and animal nutrition, nutrition and infection, agricultural and food chemistry, and public health. *Address:* International Food and Nutrition Program, Massachusetts Institute of Technology, E38-756, 292 Main Street, Cambridge, Mass. 02139 (Office); Sandwich Notch Farm, Thornton, N.H. 03223, U.S.A. (Home); *Telephone:* 617-253-5101 (Office).

SCRIPPS, Charles Edward; American newspaper publisher; b. 27 Jan. 1920, San Diego; s. of Robert Paine and Margaret Lou (née Culbertson) Scripps; m. Louann Copeland 1941 (divorced 1947); m. 2nd Lois Anne MacKay 1949; two s. two d.; ed. William and Mary Coll. and Pomona Coll.; Reporter, Cleveland Press, Ohio 1941; Successor-Trustee, Edward W. Scripps Trust 1945, Chair. Bd. of Trustees 1948–; Vice Pres., Dir. E.W. Scripps Co. 1946–, Chair. of Bd. 1953–; Chair. Bd. Scripps Howard, Inc. 1987–. *Address:* Scripps Howard, 1100 Central Trust Tower, Cincinnati, Ohio 45202 (Office); 10 Grandin Lane, Cincinnati, Ohio 45208, U.S.A. (Home).

SCULLEY, John, B.ARCH., M.B.A.; American business executive; b. 6 April 1939, New York; s. of John and Margaret (Blackburn) Sculley; m. Carol L. Adams 1978; one s. two d.; ed. Brown Univ. and Univ. of Pennsylvania; Asst. account exec. Marschlk Co., New York 1963–64, account exec. 1964–65, account supervisor 1965–67; Dir. of Marketing, Pepsi-Cola, Purchase, N.Y. 1967–69, Vice-Pres. Marketing 1970–71, Sr. Vice-Pres. Marketing 1971–74; Pres. PepsiCo Foods 1974–77; Pres., C.E.O. Pepsi-Cola Co. 1977–83; Pres., C.E.O. Apple Computer Inc. 1983–, Chair. 1986–. *Address:* 20525 Mariani Avenue, Cupertino, Calif. 95014, U.S.A.

SCULLY, Sean Paul, B.A.; American artist; b. 30 June 1945, Dublin; s. of John Anthony and Holly Scully; m. Catherine Lee; ed. Croydon Coll. of Art; with Fine Art Dept., Newcastle Univ. 1967–71; lecturer Harvard Univ. 1972–73; lecturer Chelsea School of Art and Goldsmiths School of Art, London 1973–75; lecturer Princeton Univ. 1978–83; lecturer in Painting Parsons School of Design, New York 1983–; one-man exhbns. in London, Los Angeles, New York, Berlin, Washington 1973–; exhibited at Carnegie Inst., Pittsburgh, Boston Museum of Fine Arts, Chicago Art Inst. 1987, Univ. Art Museum, Berkeley, Calif. 1987, Whitechapel Art Gallery, London 1989; works in public collections in U.K., U.S.A., Australia, Germany, Ireland; Stuyvesant Foundation Prize 1970, 1972 Prize, John Moore's Liverpool Exhbn. 8, 1974 Prize John Moore's Liverpool Exhbn. 9; Guggenheim Fellowship 1983. *Address:* c/o Mayor Rowan Gallery, 31A Bruton Place, London, W1X 7AB, England. *Telephone:* 01-499-3011.

SCULTHORPE, Peter Joshua, O.B.E.; Australian composer; b. 29 April 1929, Launceston, Tasmania; s. of Joshua Sculthorpe and Edna Moorhouse; ed. Launceston Grammar School, Univ. of Melbourne and Wadham Coll., Oxford; Sr. lecturer in Music, Univ. of Sydney 1963–; Visiting Fellow, Yale Univ. 1965–67; Reader in Music, Univ. of Sydney 1968–; Visiting Prof. of Music, Univ. of Sussex 1971–72; comms. from bodies including Australian Broadcasting Comm., Birmingham Chamber Music Soc., Australian Elizabethan Theatre Trust and Australian Ballet; Hon. D.Litt. (Tasmania); Fulbright Scholar-in-Residence 1980; Australian Council Composers' Award 1975–78, Australian Film Award 1980. *Compositions published include:* The Loneliness of Bunjil 1954, Sonatina 1954, Violin Sonata 1955, Irkanda

I 1955, II 1959, III 1960, IV 1961, Ulterior Motifs, a musical farce and music for various revues 1957–59, Sonata for Viola and Percussion 1960, Orchestral Suite (from film They Found a Cave) 1962, Sonata for Piano 1963, The Fifth Continent 1963, String Quartet No. 6 1965, South by Five 1965, Sun Music I 1965, Sun Music for Voices 1966, Sun Music III 1967, IV 1967, Morning Song for the Christ Child 1966, Red Landscape 1966, Tabuh Tabuhan 1968, Autumn Song 1968, Sea Chant 1968, Sun Music II 1969, Orchestral Suite (from film The Age of Consent) 1968, Sun Music Ballet 1968, Ketjak for orchestra 1969, String Quartet Music 1969, Love 200 for pop group and orchestra 1970, The Stars Turn 1970, Music for Japan 1970, Rain 1970, Dream 1970, Rain 1965–70, Snow, Moon & Flowers 1971, Landscape 1971, Stars 1971, How The Stars Were Made 1971, Ketjak 1972, Koto Music 1972, Rites of Passage 1973, Music of Early Morning 1974; various works for radio, television, theatre and film. *Address:* 91 Holdsworth Street, Woollahra, N.S.W. 2025, Australia.

SEABORG, Glenn T(heodore), PH.D.; American chemist; b. 19 April 1912, Ishpeming, Mich.; s. of H. Theodore and Selma (Erickson) Seaborg; m. Helen L. Griggs 1942; four s. two d.; ed. Univ. of California; Research Assoc., Univ. of Calif. 1937–39, Instructor 1939–41, Asst. Prof. 1941–45, Prof. of Chem. 1945–71; Dir. Nuclear Chemical Research, Lawrence Radiation Lab. 1946–58, 1972–75, Assoc. Dir. Lawrence Radiation Lab. 1954–61, 1971–; Chancellor, Univ. of Calif., Berkeley 1958–61, on leave of absence to head plutonium chem. work of Manhattan Project at Univ. of Chicago Metallurgical Laboratory 1942–46; on leave of absence to serve as Chair. U.S. Atomic Energy Comm. 1961–71; Univ. Prof. 1971, Prof. Graduate School of Educ. 1983–; Assoc. Dir. Lawrence Berkeley Laboratory 1972–; Dir. Lawrence Hall of Science, Berkeley 1982–84, Chair. 1984–; Chair. Steering Cttee., Chemical Educ. Material Study (CHEM Study), Nat. Science Foundation 1959–74; Pres. Bd. of Trustees, Science Service 1966–; mem. Bd. of Trustees, Educational Broadcasting Corpn. 1970–73; mem. Nat. Programming Council for Public Television 1970–72; Pres. A.A.A.S. 1972, Chair. of the Bd. 1973; Pres. American Chem. Soc. 1976; Trustee Swedish Council of America 1976–; Pres. Int. Org. for Chemical Sciences in Devt. (UNESCO) 1981, mem. 1980–; mem. Nat. Comm. on Excellence in Educ., U.S. Dept. of Educ. 1981–; Pres. Int. Platform Asscn. 1981–; Chair. Bd. Kevex Corpn., Burlingame, Calif.; Chair. IOCD, France 1981; mem. N.A.S.; co-discoverer of elements 94 (plutonium), 95 (americium), 96 (curium), 97 (berkelium), 98 (californium), 99 (einsteinium), 100 (fermium), 101 (mendelevium), 102 (nobelium) and 106; author of actinide concept of heavy element electronic structure; Nobel Prize in Chem. 1951; Enrico Fermi Award 1959; Franklin Medal 1963; Arches of Science Award 1968; foreign mem. ten nat. acads. of science, including U.S.S.R.; Officier Légion d'honneur 1973; other awards include 49 hon. degrees. *Publications:* The Transuranium Elements: Research Papers (ed. with J. J. Katz and W .M. Manning) 1949, Production and Separation of U²³³ (ed. with L. I. Katzin) 1951, The Actinide Elements (ed. with J. J. Katz) 1954, Comprehensive Inorganic Chemistry Vol. I (with others) 1953, The Chemistry of the Actinide Elements (with J. J. Katz) 1957, The Transuranium Elements 1958, Elements of the Universe (with E. G. Valens) 1958, Man-made Transuranium Elements 1963, Education and the Atom (with D. M. Wilkes) 1964, The Nuclear Properties of the Heavy Elements, Vol. I: Systematics of Nuclear Structure and Radioactivity, and Vol. II: Detailed Radioactivity Properties (with E. K. Hyde and I. Perlman) 1964, Man and Atom (with W. R. Corliss) 1971, Nuclear Milestones 1972, Transuranium Elements: Products of Modern Alchemy (Ed.) 1978, Kennedy, Khrushchev and the Test Ban 1981, Nuclear Chemistry (Ed. with W. Loveland) 1982; more than 300 papers on nuclear chemistry and physics, etc. *Address:* Lawrence Berkeley Laboratory, University of California, Berkeley, Calif. 94720, U.S.A. *Telephone:* (415) 486-5661.

SEAGA, Rt. Hon. Edward Philip George, B.A., P.C.; Jamaican politician; b. 28 May 1930, Boston, Mass., U.S.A.; s. of Philip and Erna (née Maxwell) Seaga; m. Marie Elizabeth Constantine 1965; two s. one d.; ed. Wolmers Boys' School, Kingston, and Harvard Univ.; Field Researcher with Inst. of Social and Econ. Research (Univ. of West Indies) on devt. of child and revival spirit cults; nominated to Upper House, Legis. Council 1959; Asst. Sec. to Jamaican Labour Party 1960, Sec. 1962; M.P. for Western Kingston 1962–; Minister of Devt. and Social Welfare 1962–67, of Finance and Planning 1967–72; Leader of Jamaican Labour Party Nov. 1974–; Leader of Opposition 1974–80; Prime Minister 1980–89; Minister of Finance and Planning, Information and Culture 1980–89, of Defence 1987–89; Managing Dir. Consulting Service Ltd., Capital Finance Co. Ltd. *Publications:* Development of the Child, Revival Spirit Cults. *Leisure interests:* classical music, reading, shooting, hockey, football, cricket, tennis, swimming. *Address:* Vale Royal, Kingston, Jamaica, West Indies (Home).

SEAMAN, Christopher, M.A., A.R.C.M.; British conductor; b. 7 March 1942, Faversham; s. of Albert Edward Seaman and Ethel Margery (née Chambers) Seaman; ed. Canterbury Cathedral Choir School, The King's School, Canterbury, King's Coll., Cambridge; prin. timpanist London Philharmonic Orchestra 1964–68; Asst. Conductor BBC Scottish Symphony Orchestra 1968–70, Chief Conductor 1971–77; Chief Conductor Northern Sinfonia Orchestra 1973–79; Prin. Conductor BBC Robert Mayer Concerts 1978–87; Conductor-in-Residence Baltimore Symphony Orchestra 1987–; Chief Guest Conductor Utrecht Symphony Orchestra 1979–83; now appears as Guest

Conductor worldwide, and has appeared in U.S.A., Germany, France, Holland, Belgium, Italy, Spain, Australia, and all parts of the U.K.; Hon. F.G.S.M. *Leisure interests:* people, reading, shopping, theology. *Address:* 2 The Paddox, Oxford, OX2 7PN, England.

SEAMAN, Rev. Sir Keith Douglas, K.C.V.O., K.ST.J., O.B.E., B.A., LL.B.; Australian state governor and ecclesiastic; b. 11 June 1920, McLaren Vale; s. of late Eli Semmens Seaman and Ethel Maud Seaman; m. Joan Isabel Birbeck 1946; one s. one d.; ed. Unley High School and Univ. of Adelaide; South Australia (S.A.) Public Service 1937-54; entered Methodist ministry 1954; Minister, Renmark 1954-58; Cen. Methodist Mission 1958-77; Dir. 5KA, 5AU, 5RM Broadcasting Cos. 1960-77 (Chair. 1971-77); Sec. Christian TV Asscn. S.A. 1959-73; mem. Exec. World Asscn. of Christian Broadcasting 1963-70; R.A.A.F. Overseas HQ, London 1941-45, Flt. Lieut.; Supt. Adelaide Cen. Methodist Mission 1971-77; mem. Australian Govt. Social Welfare Comm. 1973-76; Gov. of S. Australia 1977-82. *Leisure interests:* gardening, reading. *Address:* 31 Heggerton Street, Victor Harbor, South Australia 5211, Australia. *Telephone:* (085) 523535.

SEAMANS, Robert Channing, Jr.; American scientist and government official; b. 30 Oct. 1918, Salem Mass.; s. of Robert Channing and Pauline (Bosson) Seamans; m. Eugenia Merrill 1942; three s. two d.; ed. Harvard and Mass. Inst. of Technology; Mass. Inst. of Tech. 1941-55, teaching and project management positions, successively Assoc. Prof. Dept. of Aeronautical Eng., Chief Engineer Project Meteor 1950-53, Dir. Flight Control Lab. 1953-55; Radio Corpn. of America 1955-60, successively Man. Airborne Systems Lab., Chief Systems Engineer Airborne Systems Dept., Chief Engineer Missile Electronics and Control Div.; Assoc. Admin. and later Deputy Admin. Nat. Aeronautics and Space Admin. (NASA) 1960-68; Consultant to Admin. (NASA) 1968-69; Sec. of Air Force 1969-73; Visiting Prof. of Aeronautics and Astronautics and of Management, Mass. Inst of Tech. 1968, Jerome Clarke Hunsaker Prof. 1968-69, Henry R. Luce Prof. of Environment and Public Policy 1977-84, Dean of Eng. 1978-81; mem. Nat. Acad. of Eng. 1968-, Pres. 1973-74; Admin., Energy Research and Devt. Admin. 1974-77; mem. Scientific Advisory Board, U.S. Air Force 1957-62, Assoc. Adviser 1962-67; Nat. Del. to Advisory Group for Aerospace Research and Devt. (NATO) 1966-69; Dir. Nat. Geographic Soc., Putnam Funds; fmr. Dir. Charles Stark Draper Lab. Inc., Combustion Eng. Inc., Eli Lilly and Co., Johnny Appleseed's Inc., Aerospace Corpn.; mem. numerous scientific and other orgs.; Hon. Degrees; D.Sc. (Rollins Coll.) 1962, (New York Univ.) 1967; D. Eng. (Norwich Acad.) 1971, (Notre Dame) 1974, (Rensselaer Polytech. Inst.) 1974; LL.D. (Univ. of Wyoming) 1975, Thomas Coll. 1980; Dr. of Public Service (George Washington Univ.) 1975; *Awards include:* Naval Ordnance Devt. Award 1945; Lawrence Sperry Award, American Inst. of Aeronautics and Astronautics 1951; NASA Distinguished Service Medal 1965, 1969; General Thomas D. White U.S. Air Force Space Trophy 1973; Dept. of Defense Distinguished Public Service Medal 1973; Dept. of Air Force Exceptional Civilian Award 1973, Nat. Soc. of Professional Engineers Achievement Award, Thomas D. White Nat. Defence Award 1980. *Leisure interests:* tennis, sailing, skiing. *Address:* Massachusetts Institute of Technology, Room 33-406, 77 Massachusetts Avenue, Cambridge, Mass. 02139, U.S.A. *Telephone:* (617) 253-7383 (Office).

SEARLE, John; American professor of philosophy; b. 1932, Denver, Colo.; s. of George W. Searle and Hester Beck Searle; m. Dagmar Carboch 1958; two s.; ed. Univ. of Wisconsin, Oxford Univ.; Prof. of Philosophy Univ. of California, Berkeley 1959-; Chair. Educ. TV series in Calif. 1960-74; involved with student radical movt. 1964; Advisor to Nixon Admin. on student unrest in Univs. 1971, Reith Lecturer 1984; Rhodes Scholar 1952. *Publications:* Speech Acts 1969, The Campus War 1972, Expression and Meaning 1979, Intentionality 1983, Minds, Brains and Science 1984, The Foundations of Illocutionary Logic (with D. Vanderveken) 1985; articles on artificial intelligence and philosophy. *Address:* Department of Philosophy, University of California, Berkeley, Calif. 94720, U.S.A. *Telephone:* (415) 642 1441/3173.

SEARLE, Ronald, A.G.I.; British artist; b. 3 March 1920, Cambridge; s. late of William James and of Nellie (Hunt) Searle; m. 1st Kaye Webb (dissolved 1967), one s. one d.; m. 2nd Monica Koenig 1967; ed. Central School, Cambridge and Cambridge School of Art; first drawings published 1935-39; served with Royal Engineers 1939-46; prisoner-of-war in Japanese camps 1942-45; contributor to nat. publs. 1946-; mem. Punch 'Table' 1956-; special features artist Life magazine 1955-; Holiday 1957, The New Yorker 1966-; Designer of medals for the French Mint 1975-, British Art Medal Soc. 1983-; One-Man Exhbns. Leicester Galleries (London) 1950, 1954, 1957, Kraushaar Gallery (New York) 1959, Bianchini Gallery (New York) 1963, Kunsthalle (Bremen) 1965, in Paris 1966, 1967, 1968, 1969, 1970, 1971, Bibliothèque Nationale 1973, in Munich 1967, 1968, 1969, 1970, 1971, 1973, 1976, 1981, in London 1968, Neue Galerie Wien, Vienna 1985, 1988, Imperial War Museum 1986, Fitzwilliam Museum, Cambridge 1987, etc.; work rep. in Victoria and Albert Museum, Imperial War Museum, and British Museum (London), Bibliothèque Nationale, Paris and in several German and American museums; designer of several films including John Gilpin, On the Twelfth Day, Energetically Yours (awards at Venice, Edinburgh, San Francisco and other film festivals), Germany 1960, Toulouse-Lautrec, Dick Deadeye, or Duty Done 1975; designed animation sequences for films

Those Magnificent Men in their Flying Machines 1965, Monte-Carlo or Bust! 1969, Scrooge 1970, Dick Deadeye 1975; Los Angeles Art Dirs. Club Medal 1959, Philadelphia Art Dirs. Club Medal 1959, Nat. Cartoonists' Soc. Award 1959, 1960, Gold Medal, III Biennale, Tolentino, Italy 1965, Prix de la Critique Belge 1968, Grand Prix de l'Humour noir (France) 1971, Prix d'Humour, Festival d'Avignon 1971, Medal of French Circus 1971, Prix International "Charles Huard" 1972, La Monnaie de Paris Medal 1974. *Publications:* Forty drawings 1946, John Gilpin 1952, Souls in Torment 1953, Rake's Progress 1955, Merry England 1956, Paris Sketchbook 1957, The St. Trinian's Story (with Kaye Webb) 1959, U.S.A. For Beginners 1959, Russia for Beginners 1960, The Big City 1958 (all with Alex Atkinson), Refugees 1960 1960, Which Way did he Go? 1961, Escape from the Amazon 1963, From Frozen North to Filthy Lucre 1964, Those Magnificent Men in their Flying Machines 1965, Haven't We Met Before Somewhere? (with Heinz Huber) 1966, Searle's Cats 1967, The Square Egg 1968, Hello—Where did all the People Go? 1969, Secret Sketchbook 1970, The Second Coming of Toulouse-Lautrec 1970, The Addict 1971, More Cats 1975, Designs for Gilbert and Sullivan 1975, Paris! Paris! (with Irwin Shaw) 1977, Searle's Zoodiac 1977, Ronald Searle (monograph) 1978, The King of Beasts 1980, The Big Fat Cat Book 1982, Illustrated Winespeak 1983, Ronald Searle in Perspective (monograph) 1984, Ronald Searle's Golden Oldies: 1941-1961, 1985, Something in the Cellar 1986, To the Kwai—and Back 1986, Ah Yes, I Remember It Well . . .: Paris 1961-1975 1987, Non-Sexist Dictionary 1988, etc. *Address:* c/o Tessa Sayle Agency, 11 Jubilee Place, London, SW3 3TE, England; John Locke Studio, 15 East 76th Street, New York, N.Y. 10021, U.S.A. *Telephone:* 01-823-3883 (London); (212) 288-8010 (New York).

SEARS, Ernest Robert, PH.D.; American geneticist; b. 15 Oct. 1910, Oregon; s. of Jacob P. Sears and A. Estella McKee; m. 1st Caroline F. Eichorn 1936, 2nd Lotti M. Steinitz 1950; two s. two d.; ed. Oregon State Coll. and Harvard Univ.; Geneticist, U.S. Dept. of Agriculture 1936-80; Research Assoc. Univ. of Mo., Columbia 1937-63, Prof. 1963-80, Emer. Prof. 1980-; mem. N.A.S., American Acad. of Arts and Sciences, Genetics Soc. of America (Pres. 1978-79); Hon. D.Sc. (Göttingen); Agronomy Soc. Award 1951, Hoblitzelle Award 1958, Gamma Sigma Delta Award 1958, U.S. Dept. of Agriculture Superior Service Award 1958, Distinguished Service Award 1980, Ore. State Univ. Distinguished Service Award 1973, Genetics Soc. of Canada Award of Excellence 1977, Nat. Agri-Marketing Asscn. Award 1981, Wolf Prize in Agric. 1986. *Publications:* 100 papers and articles on wheat cytogenetics. *Address:* 108 Curtis Hall, University of Missouri, Columbia, Mo. 65211 (Office); 2009 Mob Hill, Columbia, Mo. 65201, U.S.A. (Home). *Telephone:* (314) 882-7225 (Office).

SEATON, Michael John, PH.D., F.R.S.; British professor of physics; b. 16 Jan. 1923, Bristol; s. of Arthur William Robert and Helen Amelia (née Stone) Seaton; m. 1st Olive May Singleton 1943 (died 1959), 2nd Joy Clarice Balchin 1960; two s. one d.; ed. Wallington County School, Surrey, Univ. Coll., London; Asst. Chemist British Industrial Solvents 1940-42; Navigator R.A.F. 1942-46; student Univ. Coll., London 1946-50, Asst. lecturer 1950-52, lecturer 1952-59, Reader 1959-63, Prof. 1963-; Chargé de Recherche, Inst. d'Astrophysique, Paris 1954-55; Fellow-Adjoint, Jt. Inst. Lab. Astrophysics, Boulder, Colo. 1968-; Sr. Research Fellow, Science and Eng. Research Council 1984-88; Pres. Royal Astronomical Soc. 1979-81; Hon. mem. American Astronomical Soc. 1983; Foreign Assoc. N.A.S. 1986; Gold Medal, Royal Astronomical Soc. 1983, Guthrie Medal and Prize, Inst. of Physics 1984. *Publications:* over 200 papers in various journals on theoretical atomic physics and astronomy. *Address:* Department of Physics and Astronomy, University College London, Gower Street, London, WC1E 6BT (Office); 51 Hall Drive, London, SE26 6XL, England (Home). *Telephone:* 01-380 7156 (Office); 01-778 7121 (Home).

SEAWELL, William Thomas, B.S., J.D.; American airline executive (retd.); b. 27 Jan. 1918, Pine Bluff, Ark.; s. of George M. Seawell and Harriet A. Aldridge; m. Judith T. Alexander 1941; one s. one d.; ed. U.S. Military Acad. and Harvard Law School; served U.S.A.F. 1942-63, retd. Brig-Gen.; Vice-Pres. (Operations and Engineering) Air Transport Asscn. 1963-65, Senior Vice-Pres. (Operations) American Airlines Inc. 1965-68; Pres. Rolls-Royce Aero Engines Inc. 1968-71; Pres. and C.O.O. Pan American World Airways Inc. 1971-72, Chair. Bd. and C.E.O. 1972-82; mem. Bd., McDermott Int., McGraw Hill Inc. *Address:* 340 Palmetto Point, John's Island, Vero Beach, Fla. 32963, U.S.A. *Telephone:* (305) 231-1038.

SECOMSKI, Kazimierz, DR.ECON.SC.; Polish economist and politician; b. 26 Nov. 1910, Kamieńsk, Piotrków Trybunalski District; s. of Piotr Secomski and Maria Secomski; m. 1934; one d.; ed. Main School of Commerce, Warsaw; Lecturer Univ. of Łódź 1947, Main School of Planning and Statistics, Warsaw 1948-55, Extraordinary Prof. 1955-60, Prof. 1960-81, Prof. Emer. 1981-; Corresp. mem. Polish Acad. of Sciences 1961-66, mem. 1966-, Deputy Scientific Sec. 1968-71, mem. Presidium 1972-80; Dir. of Dept. Cen. Planning Office 1945-49; Dir.-Gen. State Comm. of Econ. Planning 1953-55, Deputy Chair. 1955-56; Vice-Chair. Econ. Council, Council of Ministers 1957-62; Vice-Chair. Planning Comm., Council of Ministers 1957-68, First Vice-Chair. 1971-80; Deputy Prime Minister 1976-80; Vice-Chair. Council of State April 1980-85, mem. Council of State 1985-; mem. Consultative Council attached to Chair. Council of State 1986-; Deputy to Seym. 1980-; mem. Club of Rome 1972-; Charter mem. Polish Econ. Soc.

1946–, fmr. Chair. Chief Council; Foreign mem. Czechoslovak Acad. of Sciences 1981–; mem. Presidium, Polish Club of Int. Relations 1988–; State Prize 2nd Class 1970, 1st Class 1974; Order of Builders of People's Poland 1974; Order of Banner of Labour, 1st and 2nd class; Dr. h.c. (Higher School of Econs., Poznań) 1970, (Warsaw Univ.) 1975, Cracow Econ. Acad. 1984. *Publications:* Planowanie inwestycji 1954–55, Wstęp do teorii rozmieszczenia sił wytwórczych 1956, Studia z zakresu efektywności inwestycji 1957, Podstawy planowania perspektywicznego 1966, Elementy polityki ekonomicznej 1970, Prognostyka 1971, Polityka Społeczno-Ekonomiczna. Zarys Teorii 1977, Ekonomika regionalna 1982, Teoria regionalnego rozwoju i planowania 1987. *Leisure interest:* hunting. *Address:* Kancelaria Rady Państwa, ul. Wiejska 4/6, 00-902 Warsaw; ul. Boya 6 m. 29, 00621 Warsaw, Poland.

SEDCOLE, Cecil Frazer, F.C.A.; British business executive; b. 15 March 1927, London; s. of William J. and Georgina I. (née Moffatt) Sedcole; m. Jennifer B. Riggall 1962; one s. one d.; ed. Uppingham School; served R.A.F. 1945–48; joined Unilever group of companies 1952; Dir. Birds Eye Foods Ltd. 1960–66; Vice-Chair. Langnese-Iglo, Germany 1966–67, Frozen Products Group, Rotterdam 1967–71; mem. Overseas Cttee. 1971–75, Chair. 1979; Dir. Unilever PLC & NV 1974, Vice-Chair. Unilever PLC 1982–85; Dir. Tate & Lyle 1982–; Chair. UAC Int. 1976–79; mem. Overseas Cttee., CBI 1979–, Exec. Cttee., Canning House 1979–82, British Overseas Trade Bd. 1982–86, Bd. of Commonwealth Devt. Corpn. 1984–; Deputy Chair. Bd. of Commonwealth Devt. Corpn., Reed Int. PLC 1985–87; Trustee, Leverhulme Trust 1982–. *Leisure interest:* golf. *Address:* Beeches, Tyrrells Wood, Leatherhead, Surrey, KT22 8QH, England.

SEDKI, Atef, D.ECON.; Egyptian politician; b. 1930; ed. law school and the Sorbonne, Paris; Prof. of Gen. Finance, Cairo Univ. 1958–73; Cultural Attaché, Egyptian Embassy, Paris 1973–80; Pres. Govt. Advisory Council Comm. for Economic and Financial Affairs 1980–85; Pres. Govt. Audit Office 1985–86; Prime Minister of Egypt 1986–; Minister of Int. Co-operation 1987–. *Address:* Office of the Prime Minister, Cairo, Egypt.

SEDNEY, Jules; Suriname politician; b. 28 Sept. 1922, Paramaribo; s. of Eugene Edwin Leonard Sedney and Marie Julia Linger; m. Ina Francis Waaldyk 1951; two s. two d.; ed. Graaf van Zinzendorfschool, Mulo, and Univ. of Amsterdam; fmr. teacher; held sr. post with Cen. Bank of Suriname 1956–58, Pres. 1980–; Minister of Finance 1958–63; Dir. Industrial Devt. Corpn. of Suriname and Nat. Devt. Bank 1963; left Nationale Partij Suriname (NPS) and joined Progressieve Nationale Partij (PNP) 1967; Prime Minister and Minister of Gen. Affairs 1970–73; Prof. of Econs., Univ. of Suriname 1976–80; Chair. Nat. Planning Council 1980. *Address:* Centrale Bank van Suriname, Waterkant 20, P.O.B. 1801, Paramaribo, Suriname.

SEDOV, Leonid Ivanovich; Soviet scientist; b. 14 Nov. 1907, Rostov-on-Don; s. of Ivan and Raisa Sedov; m. Galia Tolstova 1931; one s. one d.; ed. Moscow Univ.; at the Aero-hydro-dynamics Inst. 1930–47; Prof. at Moscow Univ. 1937–; Chief, Dept. of Hydrodynamics 1941–; at the Cen. Aircraft Engine Designing Inst. 1947–53; mem. U.S.S.R. Acad. of Sciences 1953–; Chief Ed. Cosmic Research; Pres. Int. Astronautical Fed. 1959–61, Vice-Pres. 1962–80; Vice-Pres. Int. Astronautical Acad. 1980–; Hon. mem. several acads.; awarded six Orders of Lenin, two Orders of Red Banner, Chaplygin Prize 1946, State Prize 1952, Lomonosov Prize 1954, Hero of Socialist Labour 1967, Belsch Prize 1968, Légion d'honneur 1971; Liapounov Medal 1974, H. Obert Gold Ring 1976, D. and F. Guggenheim Int. Astronautics Award 1977, A.D. Emil Prize 1981; Hon. mem. of a number of foreign acads. and univs. *Publications:* Extension of Powerful Blasts, Two-Dimensional Problems in Hydrodynamics and Aerodynamics 1950, 1980, Similarity and Dimensional Methods in Mechanics 1944, Some Unsteady Movements in Compressible Liquid 1945, Introduction to Continuous Mechanics 1962, Nonlinear Mechanics of Continuous Media 1969, Mechanics of Continuous Media, Vols. I and II 1973, 1976, 1983, Thoughts about Science and Scientists 1980. *Address:* Moscow V-234, Leninskie Gory, MGU, Zona II, kv. 84, U.S.S.R.

SEDYKH, Yuriy; Soviet athlete; b. 11 May 1955, Novocherkassk, North Caucasus; m.; one s.; ed. secondary school and Kiev Inst. of Physical Culture; hammer thrower; mem. U.S.S.R. athletics team 1973–; European Junior Champion 1973; European Champion, Prague 1978; gold medallist Olympic Games, Montreal 1976, Moscow 1980; world hammer throwing record 81.80 m., Moscow 1980 (record broken 1982). *Address:* U.S.S.R. Sports Council, Sports Committee of U.S.S.R., No. 4 Skatertny pereulok, Moscow, U.S.S.R.

SEEAR, Baroness (Life Peer) cr. 1971, of Paddington in the City of Westminster, **Beatrice Nancy Seear,** P.C., B.A.; British politician, writer and lecturer; b. 7 Aug. 1913, Epsom, Surrey; d. of Herbert Charles Seear; ed. Croydon High School for Girls, Newnham Coll. Cambridge and L.S.E.; Personnel Man., C. & J. Clark Ltd. 1936–46; Lecturer in Personnel Man., then Reader, L.S.E. 1946–78; Hon. Visiting Prof. of Personnel Man. in City Univ., London 1980–89; Leader of the Liberal Peers, House of Lords 1984–; LL.D. h.c. (Leeds) 1979, D.Litt. h.c. (Bath) 1982, Dr. Iur. (Exeter) 1989. *Publications:* Married Women Working (with others) 1962, A Career for Women in Industry? (with others) 1964, The Re-Entry of Women into Employment (Report for OECD) 1971. *Leisure interests:* gardening,

travelling, reading. *Address:* The Garden Flat, 44 Blomfield Road, London, W9 2PF, England. *Telephone:* 01-286 5701.

SEEBOHM, Baron (Life Peer), cr. 1972, of Hertford; **Frederic Seebohm,** Kt., T.D., F.R.S.A.; British banker; b. 18 Jan 1909, Hitchin, Herts.; s. of Hugh Exton Seebohm and Leslie Gribble; m. Evangeline Hurst 1932; one s. two d.; ed. Leighton Park School, Reading, and Trinity Coll., Cambridge; Barclays Bank Ltd. 1929–79, Sheffield, York and Birmingham, Dir. 1947–80, Deputy Chair. 1968–74; Dir. Barclays Bank D.C.O., now Barclays Bank Int., 1951–55, Vice-Chair. 1955–59, Deputy Chair. 1959–65, Chair. 1965–72, Chair. London Cttee. 1965–72; Chair. Finance for Industry Ltd., Industrial and Commerical Finance Corpn. Ltd., Finance Corpn. for Industry Ltd. 1974–79; Chair. Ship Mortgage Finance Co. Ltd., Estate Duties Investment Trust Ltd. to 1980; Dir. Friends' Provident Life Office 1952–79; Pres. Inst. of Bankers 1966–68; Chair. Export Guarantees Advisory Council 1967–72; High Sheriff of Hertfordshire 1970–71; mem. of many commercial, social and educational orgs. *Leisure interests:* painting, golf. *Address:* 28 Marsham Court, Marsham Street, London, SW1P 4JY, England.

SEEFEHLNER, Egon Hugo, DR.IUR.; Austrian opera director; b. 3 June 1912, Vienna; s. of Dr. Egon Ewald Seefehlner and Charlotte de Kerpely-Krassó; ed. Theresianum, Univ. of Vienna, Konsularakademie; Co-founder and Gen. Sec. Austrian Cultural Assen. 1945; Chief Ed. Der Turm (cultural) magazine 1945; also in Ministry of Educ.; organized art exhbns., especially modern painting and sculpture; Gen. Sec. Wiener Konzerthausgesellschaft 1946–61; f. and organized Vienna Int. Music Festivals; Deputy Dir. Vienna State Opera 1954–61, Gen. Man. 1976–, Dir. 1976–82, 1984–86; Deputy Gen. Man. and Gen. Sec. Deutsche Oper, Berlin 1961–72, Gen. Man. 1972–76; Commdr's Cross, Papal Order of Silvester; Officier Ordre des Arts et des Lettres; Goldenes Ehrenzeichen für Verdienste um das Land Wien; Österreichisches Ehrenkreuz für Wissenschaft und Kunst (1st Class). *Address:* Staatsoper, Opernring 2, Vienna (Office); Weyrgasse 3/10, 1030 Vienna, Austria (Home).

SEEFELDER, Matthias, DR.RER.NAT.; German industrial executive; b. 1920, Boos, Kreis Memmingen, Bavaria; ed. Humanistisches Gymnasium, Univ. of Munich; joined BASF AG 1951, Deputy mem. Man. Bd. 1971, mem. Man. Bd. 1973, Chair. Man. Bd. 1974–83, Chair. Supervisory Bd. 1983–; Hon. Prof., Faculty of Chem., Univ. of Heidelberg 1974; Chair. Supervisory Bd. MAN Aktiengesellschaft 1983–, German Multiple Sclerosis Soc.; mem. Council of Admin., Fondation de la Maison de la Chimie, Paris; mem. Museum Council, German Museum, Munich, Bd. of Trustees of the Soc. of the Friends of the Haus der Kunst, Munich; corresp. mem. of the Acad. of Sciences, Mainz; hon. mem. Court of the Tech. Univ. of Munich, Univ. of Mannheim and Univ. of Heidelberg; Chair. Deutsch-Französische Gesellschaft für Wissenschaft und Tech. (DFGWT), e.v., Bonn; Chevalier de la Légion d'honneur 1979, Cross of Outstanding Merit, Grand Cross with Star, Order of Merit (Fed. Repub. of Germany); Gran Cruz de la Orden del Mérito Civil (Spain) 1982. *Address:* BASF Aktiengesellschaft, 6700 Ludwigshafen, Federal Republic of Germany. *Telephone:* 0621-604 3261.

SEEISO, Constantine Bereng (see H.M. King Moshoeshoe II).

SEEISO, Morena Mathealira; Lesotho politician; b. 1943, Matsieng; s. of late Paramount Chief Seeiso Griffith, O.B.E.; ed. Christ the King High School; installed as Prin. Chief of Mokhotlong 1967; Minister of Interior, Chieftainship Affairs and Rural Devt. 1986–, mem. Lesotho Cttee. of 'World Vision' for the handicapped and destitute; mem. Senate 1985. *Address:* The Military Council, Maseru, Lesotho.

SEELYE, Talcott Williams; American diplomatist (retd.); b. 6 March 1922, Beirut, Lebanon; s. of Laurens and Kate C. Seelye; m. Joan Hazeltine 1950; one s. three d.; ed. Deerfield Acad., Amherst Coll. and George Washington Univ.; Army service 1943–46; teacher, Deerfield Acad., Deerfield, Mass. 1947–48; speech writer, Washington 1948–49; joined State Dept. 1949; served in Germany, Jordan and Lebanon; Consul, Kuwait 1956–60; Chargé d'affaires, Saudi Arabia 1965–66, Deputy Chief of Mission 1966–68; Amb. to Tunisia 1972–76; Deputy Asst. Sec. for African Affairs 1976–77; Special Presidential Emissary to Lebanon June-Aug. 1976; Amb. to Syria 1978–81; private consultant 1981–; mem. Exec. Advisory Council Hampshire Coll.; mem. Bd. of Trustees Amherst Coll.; White House Commendation; Hon. LL.D. (Amherst Coll.) 1974. *Publications:* articles in various journals. *Leisure interests:* sport, music, archaeology. *Address:* 5510 Pembroke Road, Bethesda, Md. 20034, U.S.A. (Home).

SEFALI, Michael Malefetsane, M.SC. (ECON.), PH.D.; Lesotho university teacher and politician; b. 20 May 1939, Qacha's Nek; ed. Roma Coll., Nat. Univ. of Lesotho; joined Mohaleroe, Sello and Co. law firm; lecturer in Econs. Nat. Univ. of Lesotho (NUL) 1975, Dean Faculty of Natural Sciences 1976–78; Dir. Inst. of Southern African Studies (ISAS) until 1986; mem. Univ. Council 1981–86; Exec. Sec. Southern African Devt. Research Assen. (SADRA) 1983; Minister of Planning, Econ. and Manpower Devt. 1986–. *Address:* The Military Council, Maseru, Lesotho.

SEFRIN, Max; German politician; b. 21 Nov. 1913, Stambach/Pfalz; ed. Oberrealschule; served as pilot, Second World War; prisoner of war in U.S.S.R.; on return worked as man. of private firm; Hon. Councillor for Trade and Supply, City Council of Jüterborg 1946–; mem. Volkskammer

(People's Chamber), G.D.R. 1952-; mem. Christian Dem. Union (CDU) 1946-, and Pres. of CDU group in Volkskammer 1952-58, Deputy Gen. Sec. 1966-, now Vice-Chair.; Deputy Chair. Council of Ministers and Minister of Health 1958-71; Chair. CDU Viet-Nam Cttee. 1965-; Deputy Chair. Cttee. on Nat. Defence, Volkskammer, 1971-; Vaterländischer Verdienstorden in Bronze and Gold (twice). *Address:* Christlich-Demokratische Union, Otto-Nuschke-Strasse 59-60, 108 Berlin, German Democratic Republic.

SEGAL, George, B.A.; American film actor and producer; b. 13 Feb. 1934, New York, N.Y.; s. of George and Fanny (Bodkin) Segal; m. 1st Marion Sobol 1956 (divorced 1983); two d.; m. 2nd Linda Rogoff 1983; ed. Manhasset Bay High School, Great Neck Junior High School, The George School, Haverford Coll., Columbia Coll. *Films include:* The Young Doctors 1961, Act One 1962, The Longest Day 1962, Invitation to a Gunfighter 1964, The New Interns 1964, Ship of Fools 1965, King Rat 1965, Who's Afraid of Virginia Woolf? 1966, The Quiller Memorandum 1966, Bye Bye Braverman 1968, No Way to Treat a Lady 1968, The Bridge at Remagen 1969, She Couldn't Say No 1969, The Southern Star 1969, Loving 1970, Where's Poppa? 1970, The Owl and the Pussy Cat 1970, Born to Win 1972, The Hot Rock 1972, A Touch of Class 1972, Blume in Love 1972, The Terminal Man 1973, California Split 1973, Blackbird 1974, Russian Roulette 1975, The Duchess and the Dirtwater Fox 1976, Fun with Dick and Jane 1976, Rollercoaster 1977, Who is Killing the Great Chefs of Europe? 1978, Lost and Found 1979, The Last Married Couple in America 1980, Stick 1983, The Endless Game (TV) 1989. *Address:* c/o Wallin, Simon and Black, 1350 Avenue of the Americas, New York, N.Y. 10019, U.S.A.

SEGAL, Irving Ezra, PH.D., A.B.; American professor of mathematics; b. 13 Sept. 1918, New York; s. of Aaron Segal and Fannie (née Weinstein) Segal; ed. Princeton Univ., Yale Univ.; Instructor in Math., Harvard Univ. 1941; Research Asst., then Assoc. Princeton Univ. 1941-43, Asst. to Prof. O. Veblen and mem. Inst. for Advanced Study 1945-47; Asst. Prof., then Assoc. Prof., then Prof. of Math. Univ. of Chicago 1948-60; Prof. of Math. M.I.T. 1960-; Guggenheim Fellowship, mem. N.A.S., Royal Danish Acad. Sciences; Humboldt Award (Fed. Repub. of Germany). *Publications:* Mathematical Problems of relativistic physics 1963, Mathematical Cosmology and extragalactic astronomy 1976, more than 150 papers in scientific journals. *Leisure interests:* music, hiking. *Address:* Massachusetts Institute of Technology, Room 2-244, Cambridge, Mass. 02139 (Office); 25 Moon Hill Road, Lexington, Mass. 02173, U.S.A. (Home). *Telephone:* (617) 253-4985 (Office); (617) 862-0007 (Home).

SEGAL, Judah Benzion, M.C., D.PHIL., F.B.A.; British university professor of Semitic Languages; b. 21 June 1912, Newcastle upon Tyne; s. of Prof. Moses Hirsch Segal and Hanna Leah; m. Leah (née Seidemann) 1946; two d.; ed. Magdalen Coll. School, Oxford, St. Catharine's Coll., Cambridge and St. John's Coll., Oxford; Deputy Asst. Dir., Public Security, Anglo-Egyptian Sudan 1939-41; served in army in Middle East 1942-44, in charge of Arab Educ., Tripolitania, Libya 1945-46; Lecturer in Hebrew, Reader in Aramaic and Syriac, S.O.A.S., Univ. of London 1947-60; Prof. of Semitic Languages, Univ. of London 1961-79, Prof. Emer. 1979-; Prin. Leo Baeck Coll., London 1982-85; Hon. Fellow S.O.A.S. *Publications:* The Diacritical Point and the Accents in Syriac 1953, The Hebrew Passover 1963, Edessa, the Blessed City 1970, Aramaic Texts from North Saqqara 1983. *Leisure interests:* walking, meditation. *Address:* 17 Hillersdon Avenue, Edgware, Middx. HA8 75G, England (Home). *Telephone:* 01-958 4993.

SEGAL, Ronald Michael, B.A.; South African author; b. 14 July 1932, Cape Town; s. of Leon and Mary Segal; m. Susan Wolff 1962; one s. two d.; ed. Univ. of Cape Town and Trinity Coll., Cambridge; Dir. Faculty and Cultural Studies Nat. Union of S. African Students 1951-52; Pres. Univ. of Cape Town Council of Univ. Socs. 1951; won Philip Francis du Pont Fellowship to Univ. of Virginia (U.S.A.) 1955 but returned to S. Africa to found Africa South (quarterly) 1956; helped launch economic boycott April 1959; banned by S. African Govt. from all meetings July 1959; in England with Africa South in Exile, April 1960-61; Gen. Ed. Penguin African Library 1961-84; Pluto Crime Fiction 1983-86; Hon. Sec. S. African Freedom Asscn. 1960-61; Convenor, Int. Conf. on Econ. Sanctions against S. Africa 1964, Int. Conf. on S.W. Africa 1966; Visiting Fellow, Center for Study of Democratic Insts., Santa Barbara 1973; Founding Chair. The Walton Soc. 1975-79, Pres. 1979-. *Publications:* The Tokolosh (a fantasy) 1960, Political Africa: A Who's Who of Personalities and Parties 1961, African Profiles 1962, Into Exile 1963, Sanctions Against South Africa (Ed.) 1964, The Crisis of India 1965, The Race War 1966, South West Africa: Travesty of Trust (Ed.) 1967, America's Receding Future 1968, The Struggle against History 1971, Whose Jerusalem? The Conflicts of Israel 1973, The Decline and Fall of the American Dollar 1974, The Tragedy of Leon Trotsky 1979, The State of the World Atlas 1981, The New State of the World Atlas 1984, The Book of Business, Money and Power 1987. *Leisure interest:* day-dreaming. *Address:* The Old Manor House, Manor Road, Walton-on-Thames, Surrey, England. *Telephone:* (0932) 227766.

SEGAL, Uri; Israeli orchestral conductor; b. 7 March 1944, Jerusalem; m. 1966; one s. three d.; ed. Rubin Acad., Jerusalem and Guildhall School of Music, London; Prin. Conductor Bournemouth Symphony Orchestra 1980-82, Philharmonia Hungarica 1981-85; orchestras conducted include Berlin Philharmonic, Stockholm Philharmonic, New York Philharmonic, Concert-

gebouw, Orchestre de Paris, Vienna Symphony and Israel Philharmonic; tours have included Austria, Switzerland, Spain, Italy, France, U.K., Scandinavia and the Far East; recordings include Mahler Symphony No. 4 (with N.Z. Symphony Orchestra), music by Britten (Bournemouth Symphony), music by Stravinsky (Suisse Romande), concertos with Lupu, De Larrocha, Firkušný and Ashkenazy; First Prize Dimitri Mitropoulos Int. Competition, New York 1969. *Leisure interests:* reading, photography, cooking. *Address:* c/o Terry Harrison Artists Management, 9A Penzance Place, London, W11 4PE, England. *Telephone:* 01-221-7741.

SEGERSTEDT, Torgny, D.PHIL.; Swedish university administrator; b. 11 Aug. 1908, Mellerud; s. of Prof. Torgny and Augusta Segerstedt; m. Marie Louise Karling 1934; one s. two d.; ed. Lund Univ.; Asst. Prof. in Moral Philosophy, Lund Univ. 1934-38; Prof. of Moral Philosophy, Uppsala Univ. 1938, of Sociology 1947, Dean of Faculty of Philosophy 1947-54, Rector 1955-78; Chair. Social Science Research Council; Chair. Univ. Comm. 1957-63; Chair. Bank of Sweden Research Council 1965-74; mem. Swedish Acad.; Grand Commdr. Order of Northern Star; Commdr. of the Order of Finnish White Rose; Officier, Légion d'honneur; Dr. h.c. (Univ. of Helsinki, Finland, Uppsala Univ., Sweden, Upsala Coll., N.J., U.S.A., Univ of Aberdeen, U.K., Univ. of Florida, Gainesville, U.S.A., Cracow). *Publications:* Value and Reality in Bradley's Philosophy 1934, The Problem of Knowledge in Scottish Philosophy 1935, Common-Sense-Skolan 1937, Värde och Verklighet (Value and Reality) 1938, Demokratins Problem 1939, Ordens Makt 1944, Människan i industrisamhället 1952, 1955, The Nature of Social Reality 1966, Gesellschaftliche Herrschaft als soziologisches Konzept 1968, Den Akademiska Friheten I-III 1971-76, Ingvar Andersson en Minnesteckning 1975, Nils Rosen v. Rosenstein, a Biography 1982, Universitetet i Uppsala 1852-1977 1983. *Address:* P.O. Box 115, 75104 Uppsala, Sweden.

SEGRÈ, Emilio, PH.D.; American physicist; b. 1. Feb. 1905, Tivoli, Rome, Italy; s. of Giuseppe and Amelia (Treves) Segrè; m. 1st Elfriede Spiro 1936 (deceased), one s. two d.; m. 2nd Rosa Mines 1972; ed. Univ of Rome; Asst. Prof. Univ. of Rome 1928-35; Prof. of Physics and Dir. Physics Laboratory, Palermo Univ. 1936-38; Research Asst. and Lecturer Univ. of Calif., Berkeley 1938-42; Group Leader Los Alamos Scientific Lab. 1942-46; naturalized U.S. citizen 1944; Prof. of Physics Univ. of Calif., Berkeley 1946-, Emer. 1972; Prof. of Physics, Univ. of Rome 1974-75; mem. Nat. Acad. of Sciences, American Philosophical Soc., Accad. dei Lincei, Heidelberg Acad. of Sciences, American Acad. of Arts and Sciences, Indian Acad. of Sciences, Int. Acad. History of Sciences, Paris, etc.; Rockefeller Fellow 1931; Fulbright Fellow 1953; Guggenheim Fellow 1958; Hoffman Medal (German Chemical Soc.), Cannizzaro Medal (Accad. dei Lincei), Nobel Prize in Physics (with Owen Chamberlain) 1959; Hon. D.Sc. Palermo Univ., Gustavus Adolphus Coll., S. Marcos Univ., Lima, Tel Aviv Univ., Hon. D.Chem. (Genova Univ.), etc.; Grande Ufficiale al Merito della Repubblica (Italy); co-discoverer of the elements Technetium, Astatine and Plutonium, of the slow neutrons and the anti-proton. *Publications:* Numerous papers on atomic and nuclear physics in Physical Review, Proceedings of the Royal Society (London), Nature, Nuovo Cimento; books: Nuclei and Particles, Enrico Fermi physicist, From X-rays to Quarks: Modern Physicists and their Discoveries, From Falling Bodies to Radio Waves, Classical Physicists and their Discoveries. *Leisure interests:* hiking, fishing.
[Died 22 April 1989.]

SÉGUIN, Philippe Daniel Alain, LÉS L.; French politician; b. 21 April 1943, Tunis, Tunisia; s. of Robert Séguin and Denyse Danielle; m. 2nd Béatrice Bernascon, one d.; two s. one d. by first m.; ed. Lycée Carnot, Tunis, Lycée de Draguignan, Ecole Normale d'Instituteurs, Var, Faculté des Lettres, Aix-en-Provence and Ecole Nationale d'Administration; Auditor, Cour des Comptes 1970, Conseiller Référendaire 1977; Acad. de Nice 1971; Dir. of Studies, Inst. d'Etudes Politiques, Aix-en-Provence 1970-74; Maître de Conferences, Inst. d'Etudes Politiques, Paris 1971-77; Prof. Centre de Formation Professionelle et de Perfectionnement 1971-73; Secr.-Gen. Presidency of the Repub. 1973-74; Asst. to Dir. of Physical Educ. and Sport 1974-75; Dir. Office of Sec. of State responsible for relations with Parl. 1977; Chargé de mission, Office of Prime Minister 1977-78; Deputy to Nat. Ass. 1978-86, Vice-Pres. 1981-86; Mayor of Epinal 1983-; Nat. Sec. RPR 1984-86; Minister of Social Affairs and Employment 1986-88; Hon. D.Litt. (Loughborough Univ. of Tech.) 1987; Chevalier du Mérite Agricole. *Publication:* Réussir l'alternance 1985. *Address:* 127 rue de Grenelle, 75007 Paris, France.

SEGUY, Georges; French trade unionist; b. 16 March 1927, Toulouse; s. of André Seguy and Gabrielle Monfouga; m. Cécile Sédeillah 1949; two s. one d.; ed. Armand-Leygues school, Toulouse; apprentice typographer 1942; mem. French C.P. 1942-, mem. Cen. Cttee. 1954-, Political Bureau 1956-82; arrested by Gestapo and deported to Mauthausen Concentration Camp 1944; electrician, S.N.C.F. (French Railways) 1946-70; mem. Railway Workers' Union, Toulouse 1946-49; Sec. Fédération des cheminots C.G.T. (Confédération Générale du Travail) 1949, Sec.-Gen. 1961-65; Sec. C.G.T. 1965-67, Sec.-Gen. 1967-82; Pres. Inst. C.G.T. d'Histoire Sociale; mem. Exec. Cttee. Fédération syndicale mondiale 1970-; Chevalier, Légion d'honneur; Order of the October Revolution 1982. *Publications:* Le 1er mai de la C.G.T. 1972, Lutter (autobiog.) 1975, 100 printemps 1989. *Leisure interests:* shooting, fishing. *Address:* 263 rue de Paris, 93516 Montreuil Cedex, France (Office).

SEHGAL, Amar Nath, M.A.; Indian sculptor; b. 5 Feb. 1922, Campbellpur, West Pakistan; s. of Ram Asra Mal and Parmeshwari Devi; m. Shukla Dhawan 1954; two s.; ed. Punjab Univ., Govt. Coll., Lahore, and New York Univ.; one-man exhbns. New York 1950-51, Paris 1952, East Africa and India; Hon. Art Consultant to Ministry of Community Devt., Govt. of India 1955-66; organized sculpture exhbns. in Belgrade 1964, Musée d'Art Moderne, Paris 1965, Pauls-kirche Frankfurt 1965, Haus am Lutzoplatz West Berlin 1966, Musées Royaux D'Art et Histoire, Brussels 1966, Musée Etat Luxembourg 1966, Wiener Secession, Vienna 1966, Flemish Acad. Arts 1967, Tokyo Int. Fair 1973, etc.; retrospective exhbn. Nat. Gallery of Modern Art, New Delhi 1972, City Hall, Ottawa 1975, Aerogolf, Luxembourg 1975, India House, New York 1976, Rathaus, Fransheim, Fed. Repub. of Germany 1977, Frankfurt Airport 1977, Neustadt 1978, Brenners Park, Baden-Baden 1979, Luxembourg 1980; exhbns., Dubai, Abu Dhabi 1980, Jeddah 1981, Chaux de Fond (Switzerland) 1985; participated in Sculpture Biennale, Musée Rodin, Paris 1966 and UNESCO Conf. on role of art in contemporary soc. 1974; org. Int. Children Art Workshop UNESCO, Paris 1979; Sculpture Award, Lalit Kala Acad. 1957; President's Award, Lalit Kala Acad. 1958 (donated to Prime Minister Nehru during Chinese invasion). *Major works:* Voice of Africa (Ghana) 1959, A Cricketer 1961, Mahatma Gandhi, Amritsar, To Space Unknown (bronze; Moscow) 1963; commissioned to decorate Vigyan Bhawan (India's Int. Conferences Building) with bronze sculptural mural depicting rural life of India; bronze work Conquest of the Moon, White House Collection 1969; Anguished Cries (bronze) monument, W. Berlin 1971; Gandhi monument, Luxembourg 1971; Monument to Aviation, New Delhi Airport, 1972; Rising Spirit, White House Collection 1978; The Crushing Burden, inaugurated 2nd World Population Conf., Mexico 1984; Victims of Torture, designed for U.N.; works in Jerusalem, Vienna, Paris, West Berlin, Antwerp, Luxembourg, Connecticut, New Delhi; UN Peace Medal 1985. *Publications:* Arts and Aesthetics, Organising Exhibitions in Rural Areas, Der Innere Rhythmus (poems) 1975, Folio of Graphics 1981; folios of graphics with poetry in English, French, Arabic 1981-84. *Leisure interests:* writing poetry, photography. *Address:* J-23 Jangpura Extension, New Delhi 14, India. *Telephone:* 699206.

SEIBERT, Donald Vincent; American retail executive; b. 17 Aug. 1923, Hamilton, Ohio; s. of Carl F. Seibert and Minnie L. Wells; m. Verna S. Stone 1944; one s. two d.; ed. Univ. of Cincinnati; joined J. C. Penney Co. Inc. as shoe salesman 1947, Store Man. 1957, Dist. Man. 1959, Dir. of Planning and Research 1963, of Catalogue Operations 1964, of Int. Operations 1972, of Corp. Planning and Devt. 1973, Chair. and C.E.O. 1974-83; Dir. Continental Can Co. Inc. 1975-, Citicorp, Sperry Rand Corpn., KMI Continental Inc., Nat. Legal Center for Public Interest 1987-; Chair. Bd. of Trustees, Nyack Coll. 1972; Hon. LL.D. (Nyack Coll.) 1974, Hon. D.C.S. 1975; William Howard Taft Award, Univ. of Cincinnati 1975. *Leisure interests:* music, art, reading, tennis. *Address:* 1301 Avenue of the Americas, New York, N.Y. 10019, U.S.A. (Office).

SEIBOLD, Eugen; German professor of geology and palaeontology; b. 11 May 1918, Stuttgart; s. of Josef and Maria (née Geiger) Seibold; m. Dr. Ilse Usbeck 1952; one d.; ed. schools in Stuttgart, Univs. of Esslingen, Tübingen and Bonn; Asst. Prof. Geological Inst., Univ. of Tübingen 1949-51, Assoc. Prof. 1954-58; Asst. Prof. Geological Inst., Tech. Univ. of Karlsruhe 1951-54; Prof. and Dir. of Geological Inst., Univ. of Kiel 1958-85; Pres. German Research Council 1980-85, Int. Union of Geological Sciences 1980-84; Pres. European Science Foundation 1985-; mem. Deutsche Akad. der Naturforscher Leopoldina, Akad. der Wissenschaften und der Künste, Mainz, and geological socs. of France, U.S.A. and U.K.; Fellow, American Asscn. for Advancement of Science; Corresp. mem. Bayerische Akad. der Wissenschaften, Heidelberger Akad. der Wissenschaften; Hon. D.Sc. (Univ. of East Anglia) 1984, (Paris) 1988; Hon. Prof., Tongji Univ., Shanghai 1985, Freiborg 1986; Chevalier, Ordre du Palme académique; Medal of Albert I, Monaco; *Publications:* co-author of several books on geology and over 130 contributions to int. scientific journals. *Address:* Richard-Wagner-strasse 56, D7800 Freiburg, Federal Republic of Germany. *Telephone:* (0761) 55 33 68.

SEIDENFADEN, Erik; Danish writer and college warden; b. 24 April 1910, Hasle; s. of Aage Seidenfaden and Annelise Teilmann Harck; m. 1st Jytte Kaastrup Olsen 1935 (dissolved), 2nd Lone Knutson 1953 (died 1978); one s. two d.; university education; with Nationaltidende, Copenhagen 1931-34; London corresp. of Berlingske Tidende 1935-37; city ed. of Politiken 1937, Rome corresp. 1940; during German occupation of Denmark was head of Free Danish information services in Stockholm; Ed.-in-Chief of ind. daily Information and monthly review of foreign affairs Fremtiden 1946-66; Warden Danish Students' Coll., La Cité Int. de l'Université, Paris 1966-82; contrib. on foreign affairs to Scandinavian, English and American newspapers and periodicals; Diplomatic Columnist Berlingske Tidende 1967-79, Politiken 1980-82; Copenhagen Corresp. The Times, London; mem. Council of the Inst. for Strategic Studies, London 1966-76; Pres. Students Asscn., Copenhagen Univ. 1964-65; mem. Conseil d'Administration and Asst. Del.-Gen. de la Cité Int. de l'Université de Paris

1970-75; mem. Trilateral Comm. 1976; Hon. M.B.E. (U.K.); Knight of Dannebrog (Denmark); Chevalier, Légion d'honneur. *Publications:* Borgerkrig i Spanien (Civil War in Spain) 1936, Hitler beskyddar Danmark (Hitler Protects Denmark) 1943 (published in Stockholm), Spidser 1948, Den hellige krig om det hellige land 1956, Nuclear Arms and Foreign Policy 1960, Disengagement 1961, Disarmament 1962, Nato and Denmark 1968, The Roads Towards Europe 1970, Frederiksholm Kanal og Verdenshavet (essays) 1982. *Address:* Strandlund 5, 2920 Charlottenlund, Denmark.

SEIDENFADEN, Gunnar, D.PH. & SC.; Danish scientist and diplomatist; b. 24 Feb. 1908, Varde; s. of Aage Seidenfaden and Annalise Teilmann Harck; m. Alix Arnstedt 1939; one s. four d.; ed. Copenhagen Univ.; expeditions to Greenland 1928-34, Thailand 1934-35, Spitzbergen 1938; U.S.A., Canada, Alaska 1947-49, S. America 1950, Far East 1955-57, China and Japan 1958, Thailand 1964-80; Danish Foreign Service 1940-73, Washington 1945-50, Ministry of Foreign Affairs, Copenhagen 1950-55, Amb. S.E. Asia 1955-59, to U.S.S.R. 1959-61; Deputy Under-Sec. of State 1961-67; Chair. Nat. Security Cttee. 1968-70; Amb. for Environment Problems 1970-78; mem. Royal Danish Acad. of Sciences and Letters; Danish and foreign awards. *Publications:* Modern Arctic Exploration 1938, The Orchids of Thailand (with Tem Smitinand) 1959-65. *Leisure interest:* East-Asiatic orchids. *Address:* Borsholmgård pr. 3100 Hornbak, Denmark. *Telephone:* 42240106.

SEIDLER, Harry, A.C., O.B.E., M.ARCH.; Australian architect; b. 25 June 1923, Vienna, Austria; s. of Max and Rose Seidler; m. Penelope Evatt 1958; one s. one d.; ed. Wasagymnasium, Vienna, Austria, Cambridge Tech. School, U.K., Univ. of Manitoba, Canada, Harvard Univ. and Black Mountain Coll., U.S.A.; postgraduate work under Walter Gropius, Harvard Univ. 1946; study with painter Josef Albers, Black Mountain Coll. 1946; Chief Asst. with Marcel Breuer, New York 1946-48; Prin. Architect, Harry Seidler and Assocs., Sydney, Australia 1948-; Thomas Jefferson Prof. of Architecture, Univ. of Va. 1978-; Visiting Prof. Harvard Univ., Univ. of N.S.W. 1980; mem. Acad. d'Architecture, Paris 1982, Int Acad. of Architects, Sofia 1987; Hon. F.A.I.A. 1966; Life Fellow, Royal Australian Inst. of Architects 1970; Design Critic, Univ. of Sydney 1984; Fellow Australia Acad. of Tech. Sciences 1979; Wilkinson Award 1965, 1966, 1967; Sir John Sulman Medal 1951, 1967, 1981, 1983, Civic Design Award 1967, 1981, Pan Pacific Citation of the A.I.A. 1968, R.A.I.A. Gold Medal 1976, R.A.I.A. Nat. Award 1987. *Major works:* flats and housing units in Australia, urban redevelopment projects for McMahons Point 1957, city centre redevelopment "Australia Square", Sydney 1962-66; Commonwealth Trade Office Complex, Canberra 1970-72; High Rise Apartments, Acapulco 1970; M.L.C. Center, Martin Place, Sydney 1972-75; Australian Embassy, Paris 1974-76; Hong Kong Club and Offices 1980-84; Hilton Hotel, Brisbane 1983-86; Riverside Centre, Brisbane 1984-86. *Publications:* Houses, Interiors and Projects 1949-1954, Harry Seidler 1955-63, Architecture in the New World 1974, Australian Embassy, Paris 1979, Two Towers, Sydney 1980, Interment: The Diaries of Harry Seidler 1986. *Address:* 2 Glen Street, Milsons Point, New South Wales 2061 (Office); 13 Kalang Avenue, Killara, N.S.W. 2071, Australia (Home). *Telephone:* 9221388 (Office); 4985986 (Home).

SEIDOV, Hassan; Soviet politician; b. 1932; ed. Azerbaizhan Polytechnical Inst.; mem. CPSU 1956-, mem. Cen. Cttee. 1981-; Asst. foreman of machine-building works, later Man.; Sec. Azerbaizhan CP; mem. Supreme Soviet, Azerbaizhan S.S.R.; Chair. Council of Ministers, Azerbaizhan S.S.R. 1981-88; cand. mem. CPSU Cen. Cttee. 1986-89. *Address:* c/o Council of Ministers, Baku, Azerbaizhan S.S.R., U.S.S.R.

SEIFERT, Robin (Richard), J.P., F.R.I.B.A., F.R.S.A., DIP.ARCH.; British architect; b. 25 Nov. 1910, Switzerland; s. of William Seifert; m. Josephine Jeannette Harding 1939; two s. one d.; ed. Cen. Foundation School, London and Univ. Coll., London; commenced architectural practice 1934; Prin., R. Seifert and Partners, Architects 1934-; Corps of Royal Engineers 1940-44; Indian Army 1944-46; Hon. Lt.-Col. 1946; pvt. practice 1948-; Prin. of R. Seifert and Partners; Liveryman, City of London; fmr. mem. British Waterways Bd. 1971-74, Home Office Cttee. of Man. for Homeless Discharged Prisoners; fmr. mem. Council R.I.B.A. 1971-74; Fellow, Univ. Coll. London 1971. *Principal works include:* Centre Point, St. Giles Circus; Drapers Gardens; Nat. Provincial Bank H.Q.; Royal Garden Hotel, Kensington; Tolworth Towers, Surbiton; Woolworth House, Marylebone Rd.; I.C.T.H.Q., Putney; Kellogg House, Baker Street, The Times Newspaper Bldg., Printing House Square, Guiness Mahon Bank, Gracechurch Street, Dunlop House, King Street, St. James's, B.S.C. Research Labs., Middlesbrough, Britannia Hotel, Park Tower Hotel, London, Heathrow Hotel, Sobell Sports Centre, A.T.V. Centre Birmingham, Int. Press Centre, Metropolitan Police H.Q., Putney, Wembley Conference Centre, Princess Grace Hospital, Marylebone Road, Euston Square Station. *Leisure interests:* chess, violin. *Address:* Eleventrees, Milespit Hill, Mill Hill, London, N.W.7, England (Home). *Telephone:* 01-959 3397 (Home).

SEIGNER, Louis; French actor, b. 23 June 1903, Saint-Chef; s. of Joseph and Louise (née Monin) Seigner; m. Marie Cazaux 1927; one s. three d. (one deceased); ed. Lycée de Lyon and Conservatoires d'Art dramatique de Lyon et de Paris; actor, Théâtre des Celestins, Lyon 1919-23, Théâtre de l'Odéon, Paris 1923-39; Pensionnaire, Comédie Française 1939-43, Sociétaire 1943, Doyen 1960, Hon. Sociétaire 1971; Prof. Conservatoire Nat.

d'Art Dramatique 1962-76; Officier, Légion d'honneur, Commdr. des Arts et des Lettres, Order nat. du Mérite. *Plays acted in include:* Le Roi soleil, Madame Sans-Gêne, Cyrano de Bergerac, Pelléas et Mélisande, Le Chevalier Canepin, Le Dindon, Tristan et Iseult, Le Roi Lear, La Tempête, Le Marchand de Venise, Lorenzaccio. *Films acted in include:* La Symphonie fantastique, Nous sommes tous des assassins, La belle Otéro, Marguerite de la nuit, Le bourgeois gentilhomme, La vérité, L'eclipse, Les amitiés particulières, Le soleil noir, Prêtres interdits, La race des seigneurs, Section speciale, Bons baisers de Hong Kong 1975, Asphalte 1981, Les misérables 1982. *Television appearances:* Les rois maudits 1972, Molière pour rire et pour pleurer 1973, La femme de paille 1976. *Address:* 12 rue Pierre-et-Marie-Curie, 75005 Paris, France.

SEIGNORET, Sir Clarence (Henry Augustus), G.C.B., O.B.E.; Dominican Head of State; b. 25 Feb. 1919, Roseau; s. of Clarence A. Seignoret and Violet Seignoret, née Riviere; m. Judith Laronde 1950; two s.; ed. Convent High School and Dominica Grammar School, Roseau and Balliol Coll., Oxford; Perm. Sec. 1956-67; Sec. to the Cabinet 1967-77; apptd. Admin.'s Deputy, Gov.'s Deputy and Acting Pres. on six occasions 1966-83; apptd. Acting Pres. on two occasions 1981-83; Exec. Sec. Dominica Assen. of Industry and Commerce 1980-83; Pres. of Dominica Dec. 1983-; The Collar of the Order of the Liberator Simon Bolivar (Venezuela) 1987. *Leisure interests:* agriculture, horticulture. *Address:* The President's Office, Roseau, Commonwealth of Dominica, West Indies. *Telephone:* 82054 (Office); 82108 (Home).

SEIGNORET, Eustace Edward, B.SC.; Trinidadian diplomatist; b. 16 Feb. 1935, Curepe; m. 1954; two s. one d.; ed. Queen's Royal Coll., Trinidad, Howard Univ., Washington, D.C., and Univ. of North Wales, Bangor; Agric. Officer, Dept. of Agric. 1953; Admin. Asst., West Indies Fed. Public Service 1958, Asst. Sec. 1960; diplomatic trainee on courses in U.K. 1960-61; First Sec., Mission of Trinidad and Tobago to UN, New York 1962, Counsellor 1963; Counsellor, Mission of Trinidad and Tobago at Office of UN, Geneva 1965-68; Minister/Counsellor and Deputy High Commr., London 1968-71; Amb. and Perm. Rep. to UN, New York 1971-75, concurrently Amb. to Cuba 1973-76; Perm. Sec. Ministry of External Affairs 1975-77; High Commr. in U.K. 1977-82, in Guyana 1982-84; del. to numerous int. confs. including sessions of UN Gen. Ass., other UN meetings and Non-aligned Conf., Algiers 1973. *Address:* c/o Ministry of External Affairs, Queen's Park West, Port of Spain, Trinidad and Tobago.

SEIPP, Walter, DR.JUR.; German banker and business executive; b. 13 Dec. 1925, Langen; m. 1954; two s.; ed. Univ. of Frankfurt am Main; Jr. Barrister 1950-53; with Deutsche Bank AG 1951-74 (Exec. Vice-Pres. 1970-74); mem. Man. Bd., Westdeutsche Landesbank Girozentrale 1974-77, Vice-Chair. 1978-81; Chair. Man. Bd., Commerzbank AG 1981-; Chair. Supervisory Bd., Berliner Commerzbank AG, Rheinische Hypothekenbank AG, Frankfurt, Karstadt AG, Essen; Chair. Admin. Bd., Commerzbank Int. S.A., Luxembourg, Commerzbank (Schweiz) AG, Zürich; Chair. Supervisory Bd. Commerz Int. Capital Man. GmbH, Frankfurt; Chair. Bd. of Dirs., Commerzbank Capital Markets Corpn., N.Y., Commerz-Securities (Japan) Co. Ltd., Commerzbank, S.E. Asia Ltd., Singapore; mem. Bd. of Dirs., Int. Monetary Conf., Wash. (Pres. 1987-88), mem. Supervisory Bd., Bayer AG, Leverkusen, Daimler Benz AG, Stuttgart, Standard Elektrik Lorenz AG, Stuttgart, Vereinigte Industrie-Unternehmungen AG, Bonn, Linde AG Wiesbaden, Allianz Versicherungs AG, Munich, Hochtief AG, Essen, MAN AG, Munich, Thyssen AG, Duisburg; mem. Bd. of Man. Dirs. Bundesverband deutscher Banken e.V., Cologne; mem. advisory cttee. of three cos. *Address:* Commerzbank Aktiengesellschaft, Neue Mainzer Strasse 32-36, 6000 Frankfurt am Main, Federal Republic of Germany.

SEITZ, Frederick, A.B., PH.D.; American physicist; b. 4 July 1911, San Francisco; s. of Frederick and Emily Seitz; m. Elizabeth K. Marshall 1935; ed. Stanford and Princeton Univs.; Instructor of Physics, Univ. of Rochester 1935-36, Asst. Prof. 1936-37; on staff of Research Laboratory of Gen. Electric Co. 1937-39; Asst. Prof., Univ. of Pa. 1939-41; Assoc. Prof. 1941-42, Prof. and Head of Dept. of Physics, Carnegie Inst. of Tech. 1942-49; Prof. Physics Univ. of Ill. 1949-57, Head of Dept. 1957-64, Dean Graduate Coll. and Vice-Pres. of Research 1964-65; NATO Science Adviser 1959-60; mem. American Philosophical Soc., N.A.S. (full-time Pres. 1962-69), American Physics Soc. 1961, American Acad. of Arts and Sciences, American Inst. of Physics; Pres. Rockefeller Univ. 1968-78, Pres. Emer. 1978-; mem. numerous advisory cttees., incl. Advisory Group on Anticipated Advances in Science and Tech. (White House) 1970-76, Nat. Aeronautics and Space Admin. (SPAC) 1973- (Chair. 1976-77), Nat. Cancer Advisory Bd. 1976-82; Chair. of Bd., John Simon Guggenheim Foundation 1976-83; Dir. Texas Instruments 1971-82, Akzona Corpn. 1973-82, Ogden Corpn. 1977-; mem. Bd. of Trustees, Rockefeller Univ., Univ. Corpn. for Atmospheric Research (UCAR) 1975-82, American Museum of Natural History 1975-; Nat. Medal of Science 1973; Vannevar Bush Award 1983; numerous hon. degrees. *Publications:* The Modern Theory of Solids 1940, The Physics of Metals 1943, Solid State Physics 1955. *Address:* Rockefeller University, 1230 York Avenue, New York, N.Y. 10021, U.S.A. *Telephone:* (212) 570-8423.

SEKANINA, Karl; Austrian politician; b. 27 Oct. 1926, Vienna; m.; two c.; ed. Foreman School for Mechanical Eng.; apprenticed as toolmaker firm of Kapsch, shop steward 1951; Sec. Metal and Mine Workers Union 1958,

Gen. Sec. 1962-65, Man. Chair. 1971; Vice-Pres. Austrian Trade Union Fed. 1979; Fed. Minister for Construction and Eng. 1979-85; mem. Austrian Socialist Party (SPO).

SEKHONYANA, Evaristus Rets'elisitsoe, B.A.; Lesotho diplomatist, politician and business executive; b. 22 March 1937, Mount Moorosi, Quthing Dist.; ed. Roma Coll.; joined Civil Service as Asst. Sec., Ministry of Foreign Affairs; posted to Lesotho Mission to UN as Counsellor; Alt. Chair. and Lesotho Del. to Econ. and Social Cttee. XXV Session of UN Gen. Ass.; Minister of Finance 1970 1986-, of Commerce and Industry 1971, of Planning and Econ. Affairs 1981-86, with special responsibilities for Foreign Affairs 1983-84; Chair. of ruling Basotho Nat. Party until 1986; Leader of House in Interim Nat. Ass.; now Chair. Lesotho Bank, Lesotho Nat. Insurance Co. (Pty) Ltd., Lesotho Building Finance and Kingsway Brokers (Lesotho) (Pty) Ltd. *Address:* c/o The Military Council, Maseru, Lesotho.

SEKINE, Masao, D.THEOL.; Japanese theologian; b. 14 Aug. 1912, Tokyo; s. of Prof. Masanao Sekine; m. Yasuko Shirai 1946; three s.; ed. Tokyo High School, Univ. of Tokyo and Univ. of Halle (Germany); became a Christian 1929; evangelization 1949; monthly evangelical journal 1950; Asst. Prof. (Semitic Languages and Old Testament), Univ. of Tokyo 1954, Prof. 1964-76; Dir. Japanese Biblical Inst. 1959-88; Pres. Japanese Soc. of Old Testament Study 1970-79; mem. Japan Acad.; mem. D. Litt. (Govt. of Japan) 1962; Dr. theol. h.c. (Erlangen) 1971; Purple Prize for Christian Theology (Govt. of Japan) 1977. *Publications:* Cultural History of Israel 1952, History of Old Testament Literature, (2 vols.) 1978-80, The Thinkers of Ancient Israel 1982, Selected Works of Masao Sekine (18 vols.) 1979-88; articles in German, British and U.S. journals. *Leisure interest:* Japanese short poetry. *Address:* 5-11-14 Nishiogikita, Suginamiku, Tokyo, Japan. *Telephone:* 03-390-6538.

SEKO, Masataka, M.D.; Japanese politician; b. 6 Jan. 1923, Wakayama Pref.; ed. Nippon Univ.; Prof. Medical Faculty, Nippon Univ. 1965; Pres. Kinki Univ. 1965-; mem. House of Reps. 1967; mem. House of Councillors 1971-, Chair. Standing Cttee., on Educ. 1973-74, Special Cttee. on Prices 1979-80; Vice-Chair. Liberal-Democratic Party Policy Affairs Research Council 1981; Minister of Home Affairs and Dir.-Gen. Nat. Public Safety Comm. 1981-82. *Publications:* two collections of poems. *Address:* c/o Liberal-Democratic Party, 7, 2-chome, Hirakawacho, Chiyoda-ku, Tokyo, Japan.

SEKUŁA, Ireneusz, D. POL. SC.; Polish politician; b. 22 January 1943, Sosnowiec; m.; one d.; ed. Warsaw Univ.; mem. Polish Youth Union (ZMP) 1955-56, Polish Pathfinders' Union (ZHP) 1956-, former Instructor of ZHP Chief HQ and mem. ZHP Chief Council; Head, Dept of Technical Schools of ZHP Chief HQ 1964-68, Chief of Staff of 1001—Frombork Operation 1966-68; Sr. Inspector, Labour and Pay Dept., Ministry of Engineering Industry 1969-71; Plenipotentiary of Minister of Labour, Pay and Social Services for Employment Graduates of Warsaw Technical Univ. 1972-73; Inspector, Science and Education Dept. of PZPR Cen. Cttee. 1974-76; Dir. Dept. for Personnel Additional Training 1977-81, subsequently Dir. Employment Dept. 1981-83, Ministry of Labour, Pay and Social Services; Pres. Polish Nat. Insurance (ZUS) 1984-88; Minister of Labour and Social Policy 1988; Deputy Chair. Council of Ministers Oct. 1988-; Chair. Economic Cttee. of Council of Ministers 1988-; mem. Scientific Council, Social Policy Inst. of Warsaw Univ. 1979-83, Inst. of Labour and Social Services, Warsaw 1979-; mem. Presidium, Party-Govt. Comm. for Inspection and Modernization Organizational Structures of Economy and State, Chair. Team for Organizational Structures of Social Services; mem. Union of Professional Advancement Institutions, mem. Gen. Board 1977-; mem. Bureau of Int. Assen. of Social Security (AISS), Chair. Family Allowances Comm. 1984-; mem. Polish United Workers' Party (PZPR) 1966-, mem. Social Policy Comm. of PZPR Cen. Cttee. 1986-; Knight's Cross of Polonia Restituta Order, Nat. Education Comm. Medal, Cross for Services to ZHP and other decorations. *Publications:* numerous works on psychology, social policy, personnel pol.cy, employment, insurance and management. *Leisure interests:* yachting, travelling by car, science fiction. *Address:* Urząd Rady Ministrów, Al. Ujazdowskie 1/3, 00-583 Warsaw, Poland.

SEKYI, Henry Van Hien, B.A.; Ghanaian diplomatist; b. 15 Jan. 1928; m. Maria Joyce Tachie-Menson 1958; one s. one d.; ed. Univ. Coll. of the Gold Coast (now Univ. of Ghana), King's Coll., Cambridge Univ. and London School of Econs.; entered Foreign Service 1957; successively Third Sec., Second Sec. and First Sec., Ghana Embassy, Washington 1958-61; First Sec. and later Counsellor, Ghana Embassy, Rome 1962; Ministry of Foreign Affairs, Dir. divs. of Eastern Europe and China, Middle East and Asia, UN Affairs, Personnel and Admin. 1962-65; Acting Prin. Sec. 1965; Ghana High Commr. to Australia 1966-70; Amb. to Italy 1970-72; High Commr. to U.K. 1972-75; Supervising Dir. of the Political Dept., Ministry of Foreign Affairs, 1975-76, Sr. Prin. Sec. 1976-79, Perm. Rep. to UN 1979-81. *Leisure interests:* classics, music, Africana, gymnastics. *Address:* c/o Ministry of Foreign Affairs, Accra, Ghana.

SELA, Michael (Salomonowicz), PH.D.; Israeli chemist and immunologist; b. 6 March 1924, Tomaszow, Poland; s. of Jakob and Roza Salomonowicz; m. 1st Margalit Liebman 1948 (died 1975), two d.; m. 2nd Sara Kika 1976, one d.; ed. Hebrew Univ., Jerusalem and Geneva Univ.; joined Weizmann Inst. of Science 1950, Head Dept. of Chemical Immunology 1963–75, Vice-Pres. 1970–71, Dean Faculty of Biology 1970–73, mem. Bd. of Govs. 1970–, Pres. 1975–85, Deputy Chair. 1985–; W. Garfield Weston Prof. of Immunology 1985; Visiting Scientist, Nat. Insts. of Health, Bethesda 1956–57, 1960–61; Visiting Prof. Molecular Biology, Univ. of Calif., Berkeley 1967–68; Visiting Prof., Dept. of Medicine, Tufts Univ. School of Medicine, Boston 1986–87; Visiting Prof., Dept. of Biology, M.I.T. 1986–87; Visiting Prof. of Pathology, Harvard Univ. 1986–87; Inst. Prof. 1985; Fogarty Scholar-in-Residence, Fogarty Int. Center, Bethesda, Md. 1973–74; mem. WHO Expert Advisory Panel of Immunology 1962–; mem. Council, Int. Union of Pure and Applied Biophysics 1972–78; Chair. Council, European Molecular Biology Org. 1975–79; Pres. Int. Union Immunological Socs. 1977–80; Chair. Scientific Advisory Cttee. European Molecular Biology Lab. Heidelberg 1978–81; mem. Comité de Direction Inst. de Recherches Scientifiques sur le Cancer (France) 1977–81, Scientific and Tech. Advisory Cttee. UNDP, World Bank, WHO Advisory Cttee. on Medical Research 1979–82, mem. WHO Special Programme for Research and Training in Tropical Diseases 1979–81; mem. Scientific Council Int. Inst. of Cellular and Molecular Pathology, Brussels 1980–83; mem. Council Paul Ehrlich Foundation (Frankfurt) 1980–; mem. Scientific Bd., Institut Scientifique Roussel Italia 1986–; Nat. mem. Gen. Cttee. Int. Council of Scientific Unions 1984–(88); mem. Scientific Advisory Group of Experts, Programme for Vaccine Devt., WHO 1987–(89); mem. BARD (U.S.-Israel Binational Agric. Research and Devt. Fund), External Review Comm. 1987; mem. Int. Guidance Panel, The Israel Inst. for Gifted Children 1987; mem. other int. bodies; serves on many editorial bds., including European Journal of Immunology, Cambridge Encyclopedia of the Life Sciences, Critical Reviews of Biochemistry, Handbook of Biochemistry and Molecular Biology, Asian Pacific Journal of Allergy and Immunology, Experimental and Clinical Immunogenetics, Receptor Biology Reviews, The FASEB Journal, Encyclopedia of Human Biology; mem. Israel Acad. of Sciences and Humanities 1971, Pontifical Acad. of Sciences 1975; Hon. mem. American Soc. Biological Chemists 1968, American Asscn. of Immunologists 1973, Scandinavian Soc. for Immunology 1971, Harvey Soc. 1972, French Soc. for Immunology 1979, Chilean Soc. for Immunology 1981, Council Int. for Immunopharmacology 1982–85; Foreign mem. Max-Planck Soc., Freiburg 1967; Foreign Assoc. U.S. Nat. Acad. of Sciences 1976; mem. Advisory Bd. UCLAF, France 1980–; Foreign Hon. mem. American Acad. Arts and Sciences 1971; Dr. h.c. (Bordeaux II) 1985, (Nat. Autonomous Univ. of Mexico) 1985; awarded Nat. Insts. of Health Lectureship 1973; Israel Prize Natural Sciences 1959, Rothschild Prize for Chem. 1968, Otto Warburg Medal, German Soc. of Biological Chem. 1968, Emil von Behring Prize, Phillipps Univ. 1973, Gairdner Int. Award, Toronto 1980, Prize, Inst. de la Vie Fondation Electricité de France, Lille 1984, Prix Jaubert, Faculty of Science, Univ. of Geneva 1986; Commdr.'s Cross of Order of Merit Award, Fed. Repub. of Germany 1986; Officier, Légion d'Honneur, 1987. *Publications:* over 500 in immunology, biochemistry and molecular biology; Ed. The Antigens (6 vols. published). *Address:* Weizmann Institute of Science, Rehovot, Israel. *Telephone:* 8-483159, 8-466969.

SELANGOR, H.R.H. the Sultan of; Sultan Salahuddin Abdul Aziz Shah ibni Al-Marhum Sultan Hisamuddin Alam Shah Haji, D.K., D.M.N., S.P.M.S., S.P.D.K., D.P.; Malaysian ruler; b. 8 March 1926; ed. Sekolah Melayu Pengkalan Batu, Kelang, Malay Coll., Kuala Kangsar, London Univ.; Tengku Laksamana Selangor 1946; Regent of Selangor during father's absence 1960; succeeded his late father as Ruler of Selangor Sept. 1960; Maj. Royal Malay Regt.; Hon. Group Capt. Royal Malaysia Air Force; Chancellor Univ. of Agric., Malaysia. *Address:* Shah Alam, Selangor, Malaysia.

SELDIN, Donald Wayne, M.D., F.R.S.M.; American medical doctor and university professor; b. 24 Oct. 1920, New York; s. of Laura Ueberal and Abraham L. Seldin; m. Muriel Goldberg 1943; one s. two d.; ed. New York Univ. and Yale Univ. School of Medicine; Asst. in Medicine, Dept. of Medicine, Yale Univ. School of Medicine 1944–46, Instructor 1948–50, Asst. Prof. 1950-51; Assoc. Prof., Dept. of Medicine, Univ. of Tex. Southwestern Medical Center 1951–52, Prof. and Chair. Dept. of Internal Medicine 1952–; Fellow American Acad. of Arts and Sciences; mem. Inst. of Medicine, N.A.S.; Master, American Coll. of Physicians; Pres. American Soc. for Clinical Investigation 1966, American Soc. of Nephrology 1968, Assen. of Profs. of Medicine 1971, Assen. of American Physicians 1980, Int. Soc. of Nephrology 1984–87; Hon. D.Hum.Litt. (Southern Methodist Univ.) 1977; Hon. D.Sc. (Medical Coll. of Wis.) 1980, (Yale Univ.) 1988; Dr. h.c. (Université de Paris VI, Pierre et Marie Curie) 1983; David M. Hume Award, Nat. Kidney Foundation 1981, John P. Peters Award, American Soc. of Nephrology 1983, Ellen Browning Scripps Soc. Medal 1984, Kober Medal, Assen. of American Physicians 1985, Volhard Medal, Gesellschaft für Nephrologie (Fed. Repub. of Germany) 1986, Alexander von Humboldt Sr. U.S. Scientist Award 1988–92. *Publications:* Frontiers in Hypertension Research (Co-Ed.) 1981, The Kidney: Physiology and Pathophysiology, Vols. 1-2 (Co-Ed.) 1985; monographs and numerous contribs. to textbooks, and scientific papers. *Leisure interests:* art, literature. *Address:* UTHSCD Department of Medicine, 5323 Harry Hines blvd., Dallas, Tex. 75235, U.S.A.

SELECMAN, Charles E.; American business executive; b. 17 Sept. 1928, Dallas, Tex.; s. of Frank A. and Eloise (née Olive) Selecman; m. 1st Nan Harton Nash 1951 (divorced 1975), three d.; m. 2nd Judith Wallace Pollard 1976; ed. Southern Methodist Univ.; fmrly. employed by Gen. Motors Corpn. and Chance Vought Aircraft; Divisional Personnel Man., Axelson Div., U.S. Industries Inc. 1956, Exec. Vice-Pres., Axelson Div. 1966; Vice-Pres. U.S. Industries Inc. 1967, Exec. Vice-Pres. and Dir. 1968, Pres. 1970–73, Vice-Chair. and Chief Exec. 1973–74; owner Charles E. Selecman and Assocs. 1974–75; Pres., C.E.O. E. T. Barwick Industries Inc. 1975–78, Marshalsea Industries Inc. 1980–, Spinks Industries Inc. 1980–; partner Marshalsea Texas Partners, Dallas 1978–. *Address:* P.O. Box 40295, Fort Worth, Tex. 76140 (Office); 3433 Southwestern Boulevard, Dallas, Tex. 75225, U.S.A.

SELF, Colin Ernest, D.F.A.; British artist; b. 17 July 1941, Rackheath; s. of Ernest Walter Self and Kathleen Augustine (née Bellamy) Self; m. 1st Margaret Ann Murrell 1963; m. 2nd Jessica Prendergast 1978; one s. two d.; ed. Norwich Art School, Slade School of Fine Art, London Univ.; various one-man and group exhbns.; Drawing Prize Biennale de Paris 1967, Giles Bequest Prize Bradford Biennale 1969, Tolly Cobbold Prize 1979. *Leisure interests:* nature study: in a constant perennial dreamy but acute way, un-academically, all music. *Address:* 31 St. Andrews Avenue, Thorpe, Norwich, Norfolk, NR7 0RG, England.

SELIGMAN, Henry, O.B.E., PH.D.; British scientist; b. 25 Feb. 1909, Frankfurt-am-Main, Germany; s. of Milton Chase Seligman and Marie Gans; m. Lesley Bradley 1941; two s.; ed. Liebigschule, Frankfurt-am-Main, Univs. of Lausanne, Paris and Zürich; joined Atomic Energy Team, Cavendish Lab., Cambridge 1941; worked on atomic research with N.R.C., Canada 1943–46; f. Isotope Div., Harwell 1947, Deputy Dir.-Gen. of Research and Isotopes at the Int. Atomic Energy Agency, Vienna 1958–69, Scientific Adviser 1969–; Pres. Joint Cttee. on Applied Radioactivity, Int. Council of Scientific Unions (ICSU) 1957–69; Pres. and Dir. EXEC AG, Basel 1974–83; Cultural Medal of Monaco, Austrian Cross for Art and Science 1979, Great Silver Cross (Austria) 1986. *Leisure interests:* skiing, music, modern art. *Address:* Scherpegasse 8/VI/3, 1190 Vienna, Austria. *Telephone:* 323225.

SELKIRK, 10th Earl of; George Nigel Douglas-Hamilton, K.T., P.C., G.C.M.G., G.B.E., A.F.C., A.E., Q.C.; Scottish advocate and politician; b. 4 Jan. 1906, Dorset; m. Audrey Sale Barker 1949; ed. Eton, Balliol Coll., Oxford, and Univs. of Edinburgh, Bonn, Vienna and Paris; admitted to Faculty of Advocates 1934; commanded 603 Squadron A.A.F. 1934–38; mem. Edinburgh Town Council 1935–40; Capt. 41st Co. of the Edinburgh Boys Brigade; Commr. for Gen. Bd. of Control (Scotland) 1936–39 and for Special Areas (Scotland) 1937–39; served R.A.F. 1939–45; elected Scots Rep. Peer 1945–63; served successively in Churchill, Eden and Macmillan govts. 1951–60; Paymaster Gen. 1953–55; Chancellor of the Duchy of Lancaster (in cabinet) 1955–57; First Lord of the Admiralty 1957–59; U.K. Commr. for Singapore and Commr.-Gen. for S.E. Asia, Singapore 1959–63; U.K. Council Rep. to S.-E. Asia Treaty Org. 1960–63; Chair. Conservative Commonwealth and Overseas Council 1965–72, Victoria League 1971–77; Pres. Building Socs. Assen. 1964–82, Nat. Ski Fed. of Great Britain 1964–68, Royal Soc. for Asian Affairs 1965–76; Freeman of Hamilton 1937; Hon. Citizen City of Winnipeg 1982; Hon. Chief of the Saulteaux Indians. *Address:* Rose Lawn Coppice, Wimbourne, Dorset; 60 Eaton Place, London, S.W.1, England. *Telephone:* 01-235-6926; (0202) 883160.

SELLA, George John, Jr., B.S., M.B.A.; American business executive; b. 29 Sept. 1928, West New York, N.J.; s. of George John Sella and Angelina Dominoni; m. Janet May Auf-der Heide 1955; two s. three d.; ed. Princeton and Harvard Univs.; joined American Cyanamid Co. 1954, Pres. Europe/Mideast/Africa Div. 1976–77, Corp. Vice-Pres. 1977, Vice-Chair. 1978, Pres. 1979–, C.E.O. 1983–, Chair. 1984–; mem. NAM, Soc. of Chem. Industry, Pharmaceutical Manufacturers Assen. *Address:* American Cyanamid Co., One Cyanamid Plaza, Wayne, N.J. 07470, U.S.A. *Telephone:* (201) 831-2000.

SELLAEG, Wenche Frogn; Norwegian physician and politician; b. 12 Aug. 1937, Oslo; ed Univ. of Oslo Medical School and London Univ.; served as dist. medical officer and specialist in internal medicine; missionary physician, Bhutan 1972; Asst. Chief Physician, Namdalen Hosp., Namsos 1973; mem. Norwegian Cultural Council 1977–, State Sports Council, State Museums Council 1979–; proxy mem. Storting 1981–; Minister of Environment 1981–83. *Address:* c/o Ministry of Environment, Myntgaten 2, Pb 8013 Dep, Oslo, Norway.

SELLARS, Peter, B.A.; American theatre director; b. 27 Sept. 1957; ed. Harvard Univ.; Dir. Boston Shakespeare Co. 1983–84; Dir. and Man. American Nat. Theater at J. F. Kennedy Center, Washington 1984–; Fellow MacArthur Foundation, Chicago 1983. *Address:* American National Theater, Kennedy Center, Washington, D.C. 20566, U.S.A.

SELLECK, Tom; American actor; b. 29 Jan. 1945, Detroit, Mich.; ed. Univ. of Southern Calif.; m. 1st Jackie Ray (divorced); one s.; m. 2nd Julie Mack 1987; *Films include:* Myra Breckenridge, Midway, Coma, Seven Minutes, High Road to China, Runaway, Lassiter, Three Men and a Baby, Her Alibi 1988. *Television includes:* Returning Home, Bracken's World, The Young and the Restless, The Rockford Files, The Sacketts, played

Thomas Magnum in Magnum P.I., Divorce Wars, Countdown at the Super Bowl, Gypsy Warriors, Boston and Kilbride, The Concrete Cowboys, Murder She Wrote. *Leisure interests:* volleyball (Hon. Capt. U.S. Men's Volleyball Team for 1984 Olympic Games), outrigger canoe specialist. *Address:* McCartt, Oreck and Barrett, 10390 Santa Monica Boulevard West, Los Angeles, Calif. 90025, U.S.A.

SELLERT, Wolfgang, DR. JUR.; German professor of law; b. 3 Nov. 1935, Berlin; s. of Else Horst-Günther; m. Dr. Urte Wenger 1962; two d.; Asst. in Dept. for History of German Law, Univ. of Frankfurt 1965-72, Prof. 1972-77; Prof. History of German Law and Civil Law Georg-August Univ., Göttingen 1984-; mem. Akademie der Wissenschaften, Göttingen 1984-. *Publications:* Über die Zuständigkeitsabgrenzung von Reichshofrat und Reichskammergericht 1965, Prozessgrundsätze über Stilus Curiae am Reichshofrat 1973, Die Ordungen des Reichshofrats 1980. *Leisure interests:* collecting old manuscripts and baroque literature. *Address:* Konrad-Adenauer-Str. 25, 3400 Göttingen, Federal Republic of Germany. *Telephone:* 0551/23771.

SELLICK, Phyllis, O.B.E., F.R.A.M., F.R.C.M.; British concert pianist; b. 16 June 1911, Newbury Park, Essex; m. Cyril Smith 1937 (died 1974); one s. one d.; ed. Glenarm Coll., Ilford, Royal Acad. of Music and in Paris; Prof. Royal Coll. of Music, London; Vice-Pres. Inc. Soc. of Musicians Centenary Year 1982-83; Hon. F.R.C.M. *Leisure interests:* gardening, cooking, yoga. *Address:* Beverley House, 29A Ranelagh Avenue, Barnes, London, SW13 0BN, England.

SELLNER, Gustav Rudolf; German theatre director; b. 25 May 1905, Traunstein, Upper Bavaria; s. of Gustav and Frieda (Elliesen) Sellner; m. Ilse Pässler 1951; one s. one d.; ed. Gymnasium, Univ. of Munich, and drama training at Kammerspiele, Munich; Actor, Producer, Stage Dir. and Dir., Oldenburg, Göttingen, Hanover 1924-38; Producer at Kiel, Essen and Hamburg 1945-51; Dir. Hessisches Landestheater, Darmstadt 1951-67; Deutsche Oper, Berlin 1961-72; Hon. Pres. Int. Richard-Strauss-Gesellschaft 1967-; numerous awards and prizes. *First performances include:* Alkmene (Giselher Klebe) Berlin 1961, Dir Orestie (Darius Milhaud) Berlin 1963, Montezuma (Roger Sessions) Berlin 1964, Der junge Lord (Hans Werner Henze) Berlin 1965, Die Bassariden (Henze) Salzburg 1966, Zwischenfälle bei einer Notlandung (Boris Blacher) Hamburg 1966, Prometheus (Carl Orff) Stuttgart 1968, Odysseys (Luigi Dallapiccola) Berlin 1968, 200,000 Taler (Boris Blacher) Berlin 1969, Melusine (Aribert Reimann) Berlin/Schwetzingen 1971; leading part in film The Pedestrian 1973. *Publication:* Theatralische Landschaft (with Werner Wien) 1962. *Leisure interests:* modern arts, architecture. *Address:* 7744 Königsfeld-Burgberg, Federal Republic of Germany *Telephone:* 07725/7674.

SELLSCHOP, Jacques Pierre Friedrich, PH.D., F.INST.P.; South African professor of nuclear physics; b. 8 Jan. 1930, S.W. Africa (now Namibia); s. of Jacques Pierre François Sellschop and Millicent Emily Sellschop (née Sehnert); m. Susan Tucker 1966; two s. two d.; ed. Christian Brothers' Coll., Pretoria, Univs. of Pretoria and Stellenbosch, Cambridge Univ., U.K.; Founding Dir. Nuclear Physics Research Unit, Univ. of Witwatersrand, Johannesburg 1958, Dean Faculty of Science 1979-83, Deputy Vice-Chancellor (Research) 1984-; Fellow A.A.A.S., Inst. Nuclear Eng., Geological Soc. of S.A.; Dr. h.c. (Frankfurt); South African Medal of South African Asscn. of the Advancement of Science, Percy Fox Foundation Annual Award, John F.W. Herschel Award. *Publications:* 125 scientific publs. *Leisure interest:* woodwork. *Address:* University of the Witwatersrand, P.O. WITS 2050, South Africa. *Telephone:* (011) 716-1111.

SELVARATNAM, Viswanathan, PH.D.; Malaysian educationalist; b. 4 Dec. 1934, Ipoh; m. Sivagambikai Selvaratnam 1962; one s. two d.; ed. Univs. of Malaya, Delhi and Manchester; Assoc. Prof., Faculty of Econs. and Public Admin., Univ. of Malaya 1976-82, Chair., Div. of Rural Devt. 1978-79; Dir. Regional Inst. of Higher Educ. and Devt. 1979-. *Publications:* Labour Migration in Central Africa 1969, Indian Plantation Labour in Peninsular Malaysia 1976, Ethnic Relations in Peninsular Malaysia 1982. *Address:* Regional Institute of Higher Education and Development, 30 Orange Grove Road, 08-03, Singapore 1025; 51a Duchess Avenue, Singapore 1025.

SEMEDO, Inacio, Jr., PH.D.; Guinea-Bissau diplomatist; b. 15 June 1944, Bambadinca; s. of Tiburcio Julio Semedo and Domingas Lopes d'Oliveira; m. Alcina de Figueiredo Garcia; two s. one d.; ed. Univ. of Agricultural Sciences, Gödöllő, Hungary and Budapest Acad. of Sciences, Hungary; head of student section, African Party for Guinea-Cape Verde Independence (PAIGC); served in PAIGC secr. (foreign affairs) 1972-73; PAIGC rep. Algeria 1973-74; Dir.-Gen. of Int. Co-operation 1974-; Perm. Rep. of Guinea-Bissau to the UN 1981-86; Amb. to Sweden, Norway, Denmark and Finland 1986-. *Leisure interests:* travel, reading, sport. *Address:* Embassy of the Republic of Guinea-Bissau, Sturegatan 8-3°, Box 10141, 100 55 Stockholm, Sweden. *Telephone:* 08-109-305.

SEMEGA-JANNEH, Bocar Ousman, M.B.E.; Gambian diplomatist; b. 21 July 1910; s. of late Ousman Semega-Janneh and Koumba Tunkara; m. 1936; several c.; ed. Mohammedan Primary School and Methodist Boys' High School; joined Gambia Surveys Dept. 1931, Sr. Surveyor 1948, Dir. 1953-66; mem. Bathurst (now Banjul) City Council 1951-67, Mayor 1965-67; High Commr. to Senegal 1967-71, also accred. as Amb. to Mali, Mauritania, Guinea and Liberia and High Commr. to Sierra Leone 1969-71; High

Commr. to U.K. 1971-80, also accred. as Amb. to Fed. Repub. of Germany, France, Austria, Sweden, Switzerland, The Vatican, Rome; del. to UN Gen. Ass. and to OAU 1968-; Grand Officer, Order of Merit (Senegal, Mauritania). *Leisure interests:* football, cricket, lawn tennis, golf. *Address:* 15 Hagan Street, Banjul, The Gambia.

SEMENOV (see Semyonov).

SEMICHASTNY, Vladimir Yefimovich; Soviet politician; b. 15 Jan. 1924; m. Antonina Valerievna Semichastry; one s. one d.; ed. Kemerovo Chemical Technological Inst. and Kiev Univ.; fmr. First Sec., Communist League of Youth; fmr. sr. official, CPSU, Moscow; fmr. Sec. CP of Azerbaijan; Chair. State Security Cttee. of Council of Ministers of U.S.S.R. 1961-67; First Vice-Chair. Ukrainian Council of Ministers 1967-81; Vice-Pres. All-Union Soc. 'Znanie' 1981-; Cand. mem. Cen. Cttee. CPSU 1956-64, mem. 1964-71. *Leisure interests:* reading fiction and political works, bringing up grandchildren. *Address:* All-Union Society 'Znanie', 4 Proezd Serova, Moscow, U.S.S.R.

SEMIZOROVA, Nina Lvovna; Soviet ballerina; b. 15 Oct. 1956, Krivoi Rog; ed. Kiev Choreographic School; danced with Shevchenko Theatre of Opera and Ballet, Kiev 1975-78, with Bolshoi, Moscow 1978-; many appearances abroad. First Prize, Int. Ballet Competition, Moscow 1977, Artist of Merit of Ukrainian S.S.R. 1977. *Roles include:* Odile-Odette, Lady Macbeth (ballet-master Vasiliev). *Address:* Bolshoi Theatre, Sverdlov Square, Moscow, U.S.S.R.

SEMKOW, Jerzy (Georg), M.A.(MUS.); Polish conductor; b. 12 Oct. 1928, Radomsko; s. of Aleksander and Waleria Sienczak Semkow; ed. Jagiellonian Univ. of Cracow, Higher School of Music, Cracow and Leningrad Music Conservatoire; Asst. Conductor, Leningrad Philharmonic Orch. 1954-56; Conductor, Bolshoi Opera and Ballet Theatre, Moscow 1956-58; Artistic Dir. and Prin. Conductor, Warsaw Nat. Opera 1960-62; Perm. Conductor, Danish Royal Opera, Copenhagen 1965-68; Prin. Conductor Italian Radio and TV Orchestra (RAI), Rome 1969-73; Musical Dir. and Prin. Conductor St. Louis Symphony Orchestra 1975-; Artistic Dir and Prin. Conductor, Rochester Philharmonic Orchestra, New York 1986-; guest conductor of London Philharmonic, New York Philharmonic, Chicago Symphony, Boston Symphony and many other leading European and American orchestras; engagements at Covent Garden, La Scala, Berlin, Vienna, Madrid, Paris, Rome, etc.; Commdr. Cross of Polonia Restituta. *Leisure interests:* reading, yachting. *Address:* Ul. Dynasy 1, 00-354 Warsaw, Poland. *Telephone:* 26-37-82.

SEMPRÚN, Jorge; Spanish writer and politician; in exile in France following Spanish Civil War; fought in the French Resistance in World War II, captured by Nazis and sent to Buchenwald concentration camp; became leader of proscribed Spanish Communist Party, expelled as deviationist; Minister of Culture Aug. 1988-. *Publications:* Le Grand Voyage (novel, in French), The Autobiography of Federico Sánchez (under pseudonym); screenplays for films: Z, La Guerre est finie. *Address:* Ministry of Culture, Madrid, Spain.

SEMYAKINA, Ludmila Ivanovna; Soviet ballerina; b. 16 Jan. 1952, Leningrad; ed. Leningrad Choreographic School (under G. Ulanova); danced with Kirov 1970-72, then Bolshoi, Moscow 1972-; Prizes: All-Union, Moscow 1969, 1972, Varna 1972, Lenin Komsomol 1975, Tokyo 1976, Anna Pavlova Prize, Paris 1976, U.S.S.R. Artist of Merit 1976. *Roles include:* Aurore (Eshpai) (State Prize 1977), Odette-Odile (Giselle), Anastasia (Ivan the Terrible), Katerina (Stone Flower). *Address:* Bolshoi Academic Theatre of Opera and Ballet, Sverdlov Square, Moscow, U.S.S.R.

SEMYONOV, Julian; Soviet author; b. 1932. *Publications:* author of some 35 novels including best-selling spy-thriller Tass is Authorised to Announce . . . (translated into English 1987), Seventeen Moments of Spring 1988, Intercontinental Knot 1989. *Address:* c/o John Calder, 18 Brewer Street, London, W.1, England.

SEMYONOV, Viktor Vladimirovich, DR.TECH.SC.; Soviet cybernetics specialist; b. 1937, Moscow; ed. Bauman Higher Tech. Coll.; mem. Staff of Bauman Higher Tech. Coll. 1960-; specialist in automatic control-systems; U.S.S.R. State Prize 1972. *Publications:* co-author of series on Eng., and Tech. Cybernetics, The Theory of Automatic Control (4 vols.) 1967-69. *Address:* Moskovskoye vysheye tekhnologicheskoye uchrezhdenie im. Baumana, Moscow, U.S.S.R.

SEMYONOV, Vladilen Grigorevich; Soviet ballet-dancer and teacher; b. 1932, Leningrad; ed. Leningrad Ballet School (teacher V. I. Ponomarev); danced with Kirov Ballet 1950-72; prin. teacher with Leningrad Ballet School 1963-70; ballet-master at Kirov Ballet, Leningrad 1970-; People's Artist of the U.S.S.R. *Address:* c/o Kirov Ballet, Teatralnaya ploshchad, Leningrad, U.S.S.R.

SEMYONOV, Vladimir Semyonovich; Soviet diplomatist and politician; b. 16 Feb. 1911, Krasnoslobodskoe, Tambov Region; ed. Moscow Inst. of Philosophy, History and Literature; Counsellor in Kaunas 1939-40, Berlin 1940-41, Stockholm 1942-45; Political Adviser Berlin 1945-53; rank of Minister 1945, of Amb. 1949; High Commr. in Germany 1953-54; Deputy Foreign Minister 1955-; mem. CPSU 1938, Cand. Cen. Auditing Comm. CPSU 1952-66; Cand. mem. CPSU Cen. Cttee. 1966-; Head U.S.S.R. Del.

to Strategic Arms Limitations Talks (SALT) 1969–; Amb. to Fed. Repub. of Germany 1978–86; Order of Lenin (twice), Order of October Revolution and other decorations. *Address:* c/o The Kremlin, Moscow, U.S.S.R.

SEN, Amartya Kumar, PH.D., F.B.A.; Indian economist; b. 3 Nov. 1933, Santiniketan, Bengal; s. of Ashutosh and Amita Sen; m. 1st Nabaneeta Dev 1960 (divorced 1975), two d.; m 2nd Eva Colorni 1978 (died 1985); one s. one d.; ed. Presidency Coll., Calcutta and Trinity Coll., Cambridge; Prof. of Econs., Jadavpur Univ., Calcutta 1956–58; Fellow, Trinity Coll., Cambridge 1957–63; Prof. of Econs., Univ. of Delhi 1963–71, Chair. Dept. of Econs. 1966–68; Hon. Dir. Agricultural Econs. Research Centre, Delhi 1966–68, 1969–71; Prof. of Econs. L.S.E. 1971–77, Oxford Univ. 1977–80; Drummond Prof. of Political Economy 1980–88; Lamont Univ. Prof., Harvard Univ. 1988–; Visiting Prof., Univ. of Calif., Berkeley 1964–65, Harvard Univ. 1968–69; Andrew D. White Prof.-at-Large Cornell Univ. 1978–84; Pres. Int. Econ. Asscn. 1986–(89); Fellow, Econometric Soc., Pres. 1984; Hon. Prof. Delhi Univ.; Foreign hon. mem. American Acad. of Arts and Sciences; Hon. Fellow, Inst. of Social Studies, The Hague, Hon. Fellow L.S.E., Inst. of Devt. Studies; Hon. D.Litt. (Univ. of Saskatchewan, Canada) 1979 (Visva-Bharati Univ., India) 1983; Hon. D.Univ. (Essex) 1984, (Caen) 1987; Hon. D.Sc. (Bath) 1984, (Bologna) 1988. *Publications:* Choice of Techniques: An Aspect of Planned Economic Development 1960, Growth Economics 1970, Collective Choice and Social Welfare 1970, On Economic Inequality 1973, Employment, Technology and Development 1975, Poverty and Famines 1981, Utilitarianism and Beyond (jointly with Bernard Williams) 1982, Choice, Welfare and Measurement 1982, Resources, Values and Development 1984, Commodities and Capabilities 1985, On Ethics and Economics 1987, The Standard of Living 1988; articles in various journals in econs., philosophy and political science. *Address:* Department of Economics, Harvard University, Cambridge, Mass. 02138, U.S.A. *Telephone:* (617) 495-1871.

SEN, Mrinal; Indian film director; b. Calcutta; started making films 1956, directed 17 feature films; *Films include:* The Dawn 1956, Bhuvan Shome 1968, Calcutta trilogy—The Interview, Calcutta 71 and Guerrilla, Royal Hunt, The Outsiders, Man with an Axe, Anatomy of Famine 1980, And Quiet Rolls the Dawn 1980, The Case is Closed 1983, Genesis 1986. *Address:* 4E, Motilal Nehru Road, Calcutta 700029, India.

SEN, Samar, B.A., B.SC.(ECON.); Indian diplomatist (retd.); b. 10 Aug. 1914, Dacca (now Dhaka in Bangladesh); s. of late Surendranath and Charubula Sen; m. Sheila Lall 1950; two s. two d.; ed. Univs. of Calcutta, London and Oxford, and Lincoln's Inn; joined Indian Civil Service, London 1938; held several posts in Bengal 1939–46; joined Indian Political Service; Under-Sec., Dept. of External Affairs; Liaison Officer to UN 1946–48; Deputy Sec., Ministry of External Affairs and Commonwealth Relations; Head of Chancery, High Comm., London 1949; Deputy Sec. in charge of External Publicity, Ministry of External Affairs 1951–53; Consul-Gen. and rep. to Int. Orgs. Geneva 1953–55; Chair. Int. Comm., Laos 1955–57, 1961; Joint Sec. Ministry of External Affairs 1957–59; High Commr. to Australia and New Zealand 1959–62; Amb. to Algeria 1962–64, to Lebanon, Jordan and Kuwait and High Commr. to Cyprus 1964–66; High Commr. to Pakistan 1966–69; Perm. Rep. to UN 1969–74; High Commr. to Bangladesh 1974–76; Amb. to Sweden 1977–78; retd. from diplomatic service; mem. UN Admin. Tribunal Jan. 1980–; Kaiser-i-Hind 1943, Padma Shri 1957. *Leisure interests:* reading, chess, bridge, writing. *Address:* Krishi Bhavan, New Delhi, India.

SEN, Samar R., PH.D.; Indian economist; b. 29 June 1916, Noakhali; s. of late Satya R. Sen and of Ashalata Sen; m. Anita Sen 1948; two s.; ed. Calcutta Univ., Univ. of Dhaka and London School of Econs.; taught econs., Univ. of Dacca 1940–48; Deputy Econ. Adviser, Govt. of India 1948–51; Econ. and Statistical Adviser, Ministry of Food and Agric., Govt. of India 1951–58; Joint Sec. (Plan Co-ordination and Admin.), Planning Comm. 1959–63; Adviser (Programme Admin.) and Additional Sec., Govt. of India 1963–69; Vice-Chair. Irrigation Comm., Govt. of India 1969–70; Pres. Int. Assen. of Agricultural Economists 1970–76; Amb. and Exec. Dir. IBRD, IFC and IDA 1970–78; Chair. Int. Food Policy Research Inst., Washington, D.C. 1979, Govt. of India Comm. on Cost of Production 1979, Cttee. of Chairmen of Int. Agric. Research Centres of World Bank Group 1981–; Dir. Reserve Bank of India 1982–; mem. Comm. on Centre-State Relations, Govt. of India 1983–; has taken part in and led numerous Indian and int. agric. and devt. comms., and delegations; Pres. Int. Assen. of Agric. Economists 1970. *Publications:* Strategy for Agricultural Development, Economics of Sir James Steuart, Population and Food Supply, Planning Machinery in India, Growth and Instability in Indian Agriculture, Politics of Indian Economy, Decision Making and Agriculture, International Monetary and Financial System and Institutions. *Leisure interest:* photography. *Address:* 41 Poorvi Marg, Vasant Vihar, New Delhi, 11057, India. *Telephone:* 675861.

SEN, Satyendra Nath, M.A., PH.D.; Indian university administrator; b. 1909, Rangpur (now in Bangladesh); s. of Surendra Nath Sen and Carubala Sen; m. Santi Sen 1940; ed. London Univ.; fmr. Dean of Faculties of Arts and Commerce, Univ. of Calcutta, Prof. of Econs. 1958–76, Vice-Chancellor 1968–76; Visiting Prof. Princeton and Stanford Univs. 1962–63; Pres. Calcutta Bd. and mem. Cen. Bd. of Dirs. State Bank of India 1979–; Chair. Bd. of Govs. Indian Inst. of Tech., Kharagpur 1981–; mem. Gov. Body,

Research and Training School, Indian Statistical Inst., Calcutta; mem. Bd. of Trustees, Indian Museum, Victoria Memorial, Mahajati Sadan (all in Calcutta); Chair. Cttee. for the Review of Univ. and Coll. Teachers' Salaries; mem. various govt. advisory bodies, etc.; Hon. Fellow The Asiatic Soc. 1982, Pres. 1983–; Hon. D.Sc. (Bath) 1984. *Publications:* Central Banking in Underdeveloped Money Markets 1952, The City of Calcutta: A Socio-economic survey 1954–55 to 1957–58 1960, The Co-operative Movement in West Bengal 1966, Industrial Relations in the Jute Industry in West Bengal (with T. Piplai) 1968. *Leisure interests:* reading books, travelling. *Address:* 18c Lake View Road, Calcutta, West Bengal 70029, India. *Telephone:* 46-69-88.

SENANAYAKE, Maithripala; Sri Lankan politician; b. 1916; ed. St. Joseph's Coll., Anuradhapura, St. John's Coll., Jaffna, and Nalanda Vidyalaya, Colombo; joined Govt. Service 1940, Cultivation Officer 1940–47; M.P. 1947–; Minister of Transport and Works 1956–59; Minister of Industries, Home Affairs and Cultural Affairs 1960–63; Minister of Commerce and Industries 1963–64, of Rural and Industrial Devt. 1964–65, of Irrigation, Power and Highways 1970–77; Leader of the House of Reps. (later Nat. State Assembly) 1970–77; Sri Lanka Freedom Party, Deputy Leader –Dec. 1981. *Address:* 121 MacCarthy Road, Colombo 7, Sri Lanka.

SENARD, Comte Jacques, L. EN D.; French diplomatist; b. 21 Nov. 1919, Corgoloin, Côte d'Or; s. of Daniel Senard and Magdeleine Mistral Bernard; m. Mireille de la Croix de Chevrières de Sayve; two s. one d.; ed. Ecole Nationale d'Administration; Press Service, Ministry of Foreign Affairs 1947–49; attached to Ministry of Foreign Affairs 1950; attached to Cen. Admin. 1951; attached to Ministry of Foreign Affairs 1951–56; attached to Cen. Admin. for Europe 1956–61; attached to NATO 1961–64; attached to Cen. Admin. 1964–65; First Councillor, Cairo 1965–67; attached to Gen. Secr., Ministry of Foreign Affairs 1967–69; Head of Protocol 1969–72; Amb. to Netherlands 1972–76, to Egypt 1976–79; Gen.-Insp. for Foreign Affairs 1979–81; Amb. to Italy 1981; Conseiller Diplomatique du Gouvernement 1982–84; Commdr., Légion d'honneur, Commdr., Ordre nat. du Mérite, Croix de guerre. *Address:* 2 rue d'Andigné, 75116 Paris, France.

SENDAK, Maurice Bernard; American writer and illustrator; b. 10 June 1928, New York; s. of Philip and Sadie (Schindler) Sendak; ed. Art Students League, New York; writer and illustrator of children's books 1951–; one-man show Gallery School of Visual Arts, New York 1964, Ashmolean Museum, Oxford 1975, American Cultural Center, Paris 1978; Hans Christian Andersen Illustrators Award 1970. *Publications (writer and illustrator):* Kenny's Window 1956, Very Far Away 1957, The Sign on Rosie's Door 1960, The Nutshell Library 1963, Where Wild Things Are (Caldecott Medal 1964) 1963, On Books and Pictures 1986, Caldecott and Co. (collection of reviews and articles) 1989. *Illustrator:* A Hole is to Dig 1952, A Very Special House 1954, I'll Be You and You Be Me 1954, Charlotte and the White Horse 1955, What Do You Say, Dear? 1959, The Moonjumpers 1960, Little Bear's Visit 1962, Schoolmaster Whackwell's Wonderful Sons 1962, Mr. Rabbit and the Lovely Present 1963, The Griffin and the Minor Canon 1963, Nikolenka's Childhood 1963, The Bat-Poet 1964, Lullabies and Night Songs 1965, Hector Protector and As I Went Over the Water 1965, Zlateh the Goat 1966, Higgelty Pigglety Pop, Or There Must Be More To Life 1967, In the Night Kitchen 1970, The Animal Family 1965, In The Night Kitchen Coloring Book 1971, Pictures by Maurice Sendak 1971, The Juniper Tree and Other Tales from Grimm 1973, Outside Over There 1981, The Love for Three Oranges (with Frank Corsaro) 1984, Nutcracker (with Ralph Manheim) 1984; writer dir. and lyricist for TV animated special Really Rosie 1975. *Stage designs:* The Magic Flute 1980, The Love for Three Oranges 1984, L'enfant et les sortilèges 1987. *Address:* c/o Harper & Row, 10 E. 53rd Street, New York, N.Y. 10022, U.S.A.

SENDERENS, Alain; French chef; b. 2 Dec. 1939, Hyeres; s. of René Senderens and Lucette (née Azan) Senderens; m. Eventhia (née Pappadinas) Senderens 1974; one s.; ed. Lycée de Vic-en Bigorre; Apprentice Chef l'Hôtel des Ambassadeurs, Lourdes 1957–61, La Tour d'Argent, Paris 1963; Sauce Cook Lucas Carton 1963–65, Man. 1985–; Chief Sauce Cook Orly Hilton Hotel, Paris 1966–68; Gen. Man. l'Archestrate, Paris 1968–85; Chair. Bd. of Dirs., Auberge Franc Comtoise, Lucas Carton; Officier des Arts et des Lettres, ordre nat. du Mérite, Chevalier du Mérite Agricole. *Publications:* La Cuisine Réussie 1981, La Grande Cuisine à Petits Prix 1984. *Leisure interests:* football, jogging, classical music. *Address:* Restaurant Lucas Carton, 9 Place de la Madeleine, 75008 Paris, France. *Telephone:* 42 65 22 90.

SENDOV, Blagovest Hristov, D.SC., PH.D.; Bulgarian mathematician; b. 8 Feb. 1932, Assenovgrad; s. of Christo and Marushka Sendov; m. 1st Lilia Georgieva 1958 (divorced 1982), two d.; m. 2nd Anna Marinova 1982; one s.; ed. gymnasium in Assenovgrad, Sofia Univ., Moscow State Univ., and Imperial Coll., London; cleaner in Sofia 1949–52; teacher in Boboshevo and Elin Pelin 1956–58; Asst., Dept. of Algebra, Univ. of Sofia 1958–60, Asst. in numerical analysis and computer science 1960–63, Asst. Prof. of Computer Sciences 1963–67, Prof. of Computer Science 1967, Dean, Faculty of Math. 1970–73, Rector 1973–79; mem. Parl. 1976–; Vice-Pres. Bulgarian Acad. of Sciences 1980–82, Vice-Pres. and Scientific Sec.-Gen. 1982–88; Pres. 1988–; Pres. Comm. of Science 1986–88; Hon. Pres. Int. Assen. of Univs. 1985–; Vice-Pres. Int. Fed. for Information Processing 1985–88, Pres. 1988–; Vice-Pres. World Peace Council 1983–86, IIP—UNESCO

1986–; mem. Exec. Cttee. and Bd. of Dirs., Int. Foundation for Survival and Devt. of Humanity 1988–; awards and decorations include Dimitrov Prize for science, Honoured Scientist 1984 and two Orders of People's Repub. of Bulgaria. *Publications:* Numerical Analysis, Old and New 1973, Hausdorff Approximation 1979, Averaged Moduli of Smoothness (monograph); textbooks and articles in learned journals. *Leisure interests:* tennis, travelling. *Address:* Bulgarian Academy of Sciences, Sofia, 1 '7 Noemvri', Bulgaria. *Telephone:* 87-40-86.

SENGHAAS, Dieter, DR.PHIL.; German professor of social science; b. 27 Aug. 1940, Geislingen; m. Eva Knobloch 1968; one d.; ed Univs. of Tübingen, Mich. and Frankfurt, and Amherst Coll.; Research Fellow, Center for Int. Affairs, Harvard Univ. 1968–70; Research Dir., Peace Research Inst., Frankfurt (PRIF) 1971–78; Prof. of Int. Relations, Univ. of Frankfurt 1972–78; Prof. of Social Science, Univ. of Bremen 1978–; mem. several nat. and int. scientific orgs.; Lentz Int. Peace Research Award 1987. *Publications:* Aggressivität und kollektive Gewalt 1972, Aufrüstung durch Rüstungskontrolle 1972, Gewalt-Konflikt-Frieden 1974, Weltwirtschaftsordnung und Entwicklungspolitik (5th edn.) 1987, Abschreckung und Frieden (3rd edn.) 1981, Rüstung und Militarismus (2nd edn.) 1982, Von Europa lernen 1982, The European Experience 1985, Die Zukunft Europas 1986, Europas Entwicklung und die Dritte Welt 1986, Konfliktformationen im internationalen System 1988; Ed. and co-Ed. of 20 books related to political science, int. affairs, etc. *Leisure interest:* music. *Address:* Freiligrathstrasse 6, D-2800 Bremen 1, Federal Republic of Germany. *Telephone:* 0421-23 04 36.

SENGHOR, Léopold Sédar; Senegalese writer and politician; b. 9 Oct. 1906; m. 2nd Colette Hubert 1957; three s. (two deceased); ed. Lycée de Dakar, Lycée Louis-le-Grand, Paris and Univ. de Paris; Classics Teacher, Lycée Descartes, Tours 1935–44, Lycée Marcelin Berthelot, Paris 1944–48; mem. Constituent Assemblies 1945–46; Deputy from Senegal to Nat. Assembly 1946–58; Prof., Ecole Nat. de la France d'Outre-Mer 1948–58; Sec. of State, Présidence du Conseil 1955–56; mem. Consultative Assembly, Council of Europe; Pres. Fed. Ass., Mali Fed. of Senegal and Sudan 1959–60, Pres. Senegal Repub. 1960–80, also Minister of Defence 1968–69; Chair. OCAM 1972–74; fmr. Sec.-Gen. Union Progressiste Sénégalaise (from 1977 Parti Socialiste Sénégalais), nat. party of Parti Fédéraliste Africain (PFA); Chair. ECONAS 1978–79; Vice-Pres. Socialist Int.; Vice-Pres. Haut conseil de la francaphonie 1985–; Chair. Exec. Bureau, Socialist Inter-African Feb. 1981–; fmr. Pres. Int. Confed. of Socs. of Authors and Composers; mem. Inst. Français: Acad. des Sciences morales et politiques 1969, Acad. Française 1983 (mem. Comm. du dictionnaire 1986–), American Acad. of Arts and Letters; numerous hon. degrees; Dag Hammarskjöld Prize 1965; Peace Prize of German Book Trade, Frankfurt; Haile Sellassie African Research Prize 1973; Apollinaire Prize for Poetry 1974, Alfred de Vigny Prize, Aasan World Prize 1981, Jawaharlal Nehru Award 1984, Athinai Prize 1985; Grand-croix, Légion d'honneur, Commdr. Ordre des Palmes académiques, des Arts et des Lettres. *Publications:* Chants d'ombres (poems) 1945, Hosties noires (poems) 1948, Chants pour Naëtt (poems) 1949, Ethiopiques (poems) 1956, Nocturnes (poems) 1961, Langage et poésie négro-africaine 1954, L'apport de la poésie nègre 1953, Esthéthique négro-africain 1956, Collected Poems 1977, Liberté IV: Socialisme et planification 1983, Poèmes 1984. *Address:* 1 square de Tocqueville, 75017 Paris, France.

SENGUPTA, Arjun K., PH.D.; Indian economist; b. 10 June 1937, Calcutta; s. of J. K. Sengupta; m. Jayshree Sengupta 1966; one d.; ed. Presidency Coll., Calcutta and Massachusetts Inst. of Tech.; Econ. Adviser, Ministry of Commerce 1973–77; Minister for Econ. Affairs, High Comm. of India, London 1977–79; Visiting Fellow, Queen Elizabeth's House, Oxford Univ., England and Chr. Michelsens Inst., Bergen, Norway 1979–81; Special Sec. to Prime Minister 1981–85; Exec. Dir., IMF 1985–88, Special Adviser to Man. Dir. Nov. 1988–; has taught at L.S.E. and Delhi School of Econs. and has been consultant to several int. orgs.; Chair. IMF-IBRD Group of 24, Working Group on Reform of the Int. Monetary System 1985; Chair. Group of 24, Working Group on Role of IMF 1986–87; Consultant and mem. various Expert Groups of UNCTAD, ESCAP, UN, Commonwealth Secr. and OECD. *Publications:* International Financial Co-operation—Framework of Change (Co-author), A Review of the North-South Negotiating Process, Commodities, Finance and Trade (Ed.). *Leisure interest:* reading. *Address:* c/o IMF, 700 19th Street, N.W., Washington, D.C. 20431, U.S.A. *Telephone:* (202) 623-4997.

SENNING, Åke, M.D.; Swedish surgeon; b. 14 Dec. 1915, Rätivik; s. of D. Senning and E. Senning; m. Ulla Ronge 1942; three s. one d.; ed. Uppsala and Stockholm Medical Schools; Assoc. Prof. of Experimental Surgery, Univ. Thoracic Clinic, Kardinska Hospital, Stockholm 1956, Prof. of Surgery and Dir. Univ. Surgical Clinic, Zurich 1961–85; several medical prizes and hon. memberships. *Publications:* 380 scientific papers. *Leisure interests:* golf, sailing, skiing. *Address:* Belsitostr. 14, 8044 Zurich, Switzerland. *Telephone:* 01/47 55 11.

SENOUSSI, Badreddine, M.A., LL.M.; Moroccan diplomatist; b. 30 March 1933, Fez; s. of Ahmed and Zineb Senoussi; m. Touria Kerdoudi 1958; three s.; ed. Lycée Rabat, and Univs. of Rabat and Paris; Counsellor, High Tribunal of Rabat 1956; with Ministry of State in charge of admin.

1957; Gen. Sec. Nat. Tobacco Office 1958; Chief of Royal Cabinet 1963; Under-Sec. of State for Commerce, Industry, Mines and Merchant Marine 1964, for Admin. Affairs 1965; Minister of Post Offices and Telecommunications 1966; Minister of Youth, Sport and Social Affairs 1970; Deputy to Chamber of Reps. 1970; Amb. to U.S.A. 1971–74, to Iran 1974–76, to U.K. 1976–80; numerous foreign awards and decorations. *Leisure interests:* tennis, water skiing, hunting. *Address:* c/o Ministry of State for Foreign Affairs, Rabat; 238 boulevard Zarktouni, Casablanca, Morocco.

SENSI, H.E. Cardinal Giuseppe Maria, D.CN.L.; Italian ecclesiastic; b. 27 May 1907, Cosenza; s. of Francesco Sensi and Melania Sensi Andreotti Loria; ed. Lateran Univ., Rome; ordained 1929; diplomatic service for the Holy See 1934–76; cr. Cardinal 1976; mem. Pontifical Comm. for Vatican City State; hon. mem. Acad. Cosentina 1976. *Address:* 16 Piazza S. Calisto, 00153 Rome, Italy.

SEOW, Yit Kin; British concert pianist; b. 28 March 1955, Singapore; ed. Yehudi Menuhin School and Royal Coll. of Music, England; went to U.K. 1967; toured U.S.A. 1972; Promenade Concerts, Royal Albert Hall and Royal Festival Hall (with Philharmonia Orchestra), London 1975; appeared Beethovenfest, Bonn 1977, Hong Kong Arts Festival (with Berlin Radio Symphony Orchestra) 1977, Promenade Concerts (with Royal Philharmonic Orchestra) 1982, Poland 1984, Hongkong Asian Arts Festival 1984; toured Russia for BBC 1988; recordings of Satie, Beethoven, Schubert 1989; Gold Disc of Yellow River Concerto 1984; appeared on BBC TV 1985; winner BBC Piano Competition 1974, Rubinstein Prize 1977. *Leisure interests:* gardening, theatre, cinema. *Address:* 20a Southwood Lane, London, N6 5EE, England. *Telephone:* 01-340 4105.

SEPPALA, Richard Rafael; Finnish diplomatist and barrister; b. 15 Jan. 1905; ed. Turku Lyceum, Hamina Reserve Officers' School, Helsinki Univ.; entered Foreign Service 1930; served in Riga, Rio de Janeiro and London; Chief of Bureau, Ministry of Foreign Affairs 1942–43, Asst. Dir. and Dir. Political Dept. 1943–48; Consul Gen. and Perm. Observer, UN 1948–53; Sec.-Gen. Ministry of Foreign Affairs 1953; Sec. of State 1954–56; Amb. to France 1956–58, 1965–72, to U.S.A. 1958–65; Perm. Rep. to UNESCO 1967–72, OECD 1968–69; Grand Commdr. White Rose of Finland, Crown of Belgium, Légion d'honneur, Icelandic, Netherlands, Polish, Brazilian, Mexican and British decorations. *Address:* Lokkalantie 10E, 00330 Helsinki 33, Finland. *Telephone:* 487577.

SEPÚLVEDA, Bernardo, LL.B.; Mexican politician; b. 14 Dec. 1941, Mexico City; s. of Bernardo and Margarita Sepulveda; m. Ana Yturbe 1970; three s.; ed. Nat. Univ. of Mexico and Queens' Coll., Cambridge; fmrly. taught int. law, El Colegio de México and Centre for Research and Teaching in Econs.; Asst. Dir. of Juridical Affairs, Ministry of Presidency 1968–70; Dir.-Gen. of Int. Financial Affairs, Ministry of Finance 1976–81; Int. Adviser, Minister of Programming and Budget 1981; Amb. to U.S.A. March–Dec. 1982; Sec. of Foreign Affairs 1982–88; Amb. to U.K. 1989–; Sec. Int. Affairs Institutional Revolutionary Party (PRI) 1981–82; Pres. to UN Sixth Comm. on Transnat. Corpns. 1977–80; Hon. G.C.M.G. *Publications:* Foreign Investment in Mexico 1973, Transnational Corporations in Mexico 1974, A View of Contemporary Mexico 1979, Planning for Development 1981. *Address:* Mexican Embassy, 48 Belgrave Square, London, SW1X 7TW, England.

SEQUEIRA, Luis, PH.D.; American professor of plant pathology; b. 1 Sept. 1927, San José, Costa Rica; s. of Raul Sequeira and the late Dora Jenkins; m. Elisabeth Steinvorth 1954; one s. three d.; ed. Harvard Univ.; Teaching Fellow, Harvard Univ. 1949–52; Parker Fellow, Harvard and Instituto Biologico, São Paulo, Brazil 1952–53; Plant Pathologist, Asst. Dir., then Dir. Coto Research Station, United Fruit Co., Costa Rica 1953–60; Research Assoc., N.C. State Univ., Raleigh, N.C. 1960–61; Assoc. Prof., then Prof., Dept. of Plant Pathology, Univ. of Wis., Madison 1961–78, Prof., Depts. of Bacteriology and Plant Pathology 1978–82, J. C. Walker Prof. 1982–; Chief Scientist, Competitive Grants Office, USDA, Washington, D.C. 1987–88; research interests include physiology and biochemistry of plant-parasite interactions, identification of genes for virulence in pathogens, particularly bacteria, and breeding plants for disease resistance; Fellow American Phytopathological Soc. (Pres. 1985–86); mem. N.A.S. *Publications:* approximately 200 publs. in journals and covering plant pathology, bacteriology, biochemistry and genetics. *Leisure interests:* classical music, cross-country skiing. *Address:* Department of Plant Pathology, University of Wisconsin, Madison, Wis. 53706; 10 Appomattox Court, Madison, Wis. 53705, U.S.A. (Home). *Telephone:* (608) 262-3456 (Office); (608) 833-3440 (Home).

SEQUENS, Jiří, Czechoslovak film and television director; b. 23 April 1922, Brno; s. of Roman Sequens and Frantiska Sequens; m. Zdena Lederer 1951; one s. one d.; actor, Land Theatre Brno, Czechoslovak Radio, Brno, the E.F. Burian Theatre, Prague 1942–49; studied at Brno Conservatory Coll. of Cinematography, Moscow 1946–47; dir., State Film Theatre, Prague 1949–50, Film Studios Barrandov, Prague 1949–; head, film dept., Union of Czechoslovak Dramatic and Film Artists 1959–63; mem. Union of Czech Dramatic Artists 1971–; head, dept. of film and television directing, Film Acad. of Performing Arts, Prague 1979–; Silver Medal, World Festival of Youth and Students, Moscow 1957, title Artist of Merit 1972, Nat. Artist 1979, Order of Labour 1982. *Films include:* Road to Happiness 1951,

Escape from the Shadow 1958, Love Needs but a Few Words 1961, Assassination 1964, A Good Catch of a Handsome Dragoon 1970, Murder in the Excelsior Hotel 1971, Death of the Black King 1972, Chronicle of a Hot Summer 1973, A Hostage from Bella Vista 1979, That Instant, that Moment 1981, Bitter Autumn with the Scent of Mango 1983, Two on Horses, One on Donkey 1986; several television serials, including The Sinful People from Prague 1968-69, Thirty Cases of Major Zeman 1973-79, The Spiral of Bronze 1988; short documentary films. *Address:* Stursova 8, Prague 6, Czechoslovakia. *Telephone:* 322124.

SERAPHIM, His Beatitude Archbishop; Greek ecclesiastic; b. 1913, Artesianon, Karditsa, Thessaly; ed. Theological School, Univ. of Athens; ordained 1938; participated in Nat. Resistance against Nazi occupation; Clerk, later Sec. of Holy Synod; Metropolitan of Arta 1949, of Ioannina 1958; Archbishop of Athens and All Greece 1974-; participated in First Pan-Orthodox Conf. of Rhodes. *Address:* c/o Holy Synod of the Church of Greece, Athens, Greece.

SERAPHIN, Oliver; Dominican politician; b. 2 Aug. 1943; s. of Perry and Theotil Seraphin; m. Virginia Rabess 1978; three s.; Prime Minister of Dominica and Minister for Foreign Affairs 1979-80; Leader Democratic Labour Party 1979-85, Deputy Leader Labour Party of Dominica 1985. *Leisure interests:* table-tennis, reading, music. *Address:* 44 Green's Lane, Goodwill, Dominica.

SERE, Jouko Emil Markus, DIPL. ING.; Finnish business executive; b. 12 Feb. 1927, Uskela; s. of Emil Seren and Alina Weikkolin; m. Helena Mattila 1952; two d.; ed. Helsinki Univ. of Tech.; Planning Eng. Valmet Oy 1955-56; Dept. Man. Rauma-Repola Oy 1956-63, Shipyard Man. 1963-70, Dir. and mem. Man. Group 1970-76, Man. Dir. and mem. Bd. of Dirs. 1976-84, Vice-Chair. Bd. of Dirs. 1984-; Vice-Chair. Bd. of Dirs. Polarrakennusoy 1978; Chair. Bd. of Dirs. Pohjolan Voima 1980-; numerous other directorships. *Leisure interests:* golf, hunting. *Address:* Rauma-Repola Oy, P.O. Box 203, 00171 Helsinki (Office); Westendintie 47, 02160 Espoo, Finland (Home). *Telephone:* (358-0) 18281 (Office).

SEREBRIER, José; American (Uruguayan-born) conductor and composer; b. 3 Dec. 1938, Montevideo; m. Carole Farley 1969; one d.; started conducting at age of 12; went to U.S.A. 1950; studied composition with Vittorio Giannini, Curtis Inst., Phila. 1956-58, and conducting with Antal Dorati; guest conductor in U.S.A., S. America and Europe; conducted first performance in Poland of Charles Ives' Fourth Symphony; Composer-in-Residence with Cleveland Orchestra 1968-70; Music Dir. Cleveland Philharmonic Orchestra 1968-71; Artistic Dir. Int. Festival of Americas, Miami 1984, Miami Festival 1985-. *Compositions:* Quartet for Saxophones 1955, Pequeña música (wind quintet) 1955, Symphony No. 1 1956, Momento psicológico (string orchestra) 1957, Suite canina (wind trio) 1957, Symphony for Percussion 1960, The Star Wagon (chamber orchestra) 1967, Nueve (double bass and orchestra) 1970, Colores mágicos (variations for harp and chamber orchestra) 1971. *Address:* 270 Riverside Drive, New York, N.Y. 10025, U.S.A.

SERGEYEV, Yevgeniy Mikhailovich; Soviet geologist; b. 10 March 1914, Moscow; ed. Moscow Univ.; mem. CPSU 1939; served in Soviet Army 1941-43; mem. Faculty of Geology, Moscow Univ. 1940-41, 1943-, Prof. 1953-; Head of Dept. of Soil Science and Geological Eng. 1954-; Head of Dept. of Geology 1954-57, 1963-64; Pro-Rector of Moscow Univ. 1964-; mem. U.S.S.R. Acad. of Sciences; awards include: Hon Dr. (Bratislava Univ.) 1972, (Warsaw Univ.) 1974; Order of Lenin, Order of October Revolution, Lenin Prize 1982 etc. *Address:* Office of the Pro-Rector, Moscow M.V. Lomonosov State University, Leninskie Gory, Moscow 119808, U.S.S.R.

SERJEANT, Graham Roger, C.M.G., M.D., F.R.C.P.; British medical research scientist; b. 26 Oct. 1938, Bristol; s. of Ewart E. Serjeant and Violet E. Serjeant; m. Beryl K. King 1965; no c.; ed. Sibford School, Banbury, Bootham School, York, Clare Coll. Cambridge, London Hosp. Medical School and Makerere Coll. Kampala; House Physician, London Hosp. 1963-64; Royal United Hosp. Bath 1965-66; Royal Postgraduate Medical School 1966; Medical Registrar, Univ. Hosp. of the West Indies 1966-67; Wellcome Research Fellow, Dept. of Medicine, Univ. Hosp. of the West Indies 1967-71; mem. scientific staff, MRC Abnormal Haemoglobin Unit, Cambridge 1971-72, Epidemiology Research Unit, Jamaica 1972-74; Dir. MRC Labs., Jamaica 1974-. *Publications:* The Clinical Features of Sickle Cell Disease 1974, Sickle Cell Disease 1985; numerous papers on sickle cell disease in medical journals. *Leisure interest:* squash. *Address:* Medical Research Council Laboratories, University of the West Indies, Kingston 7, Jamaica, W.I. *Telephone:* (809) 927-2984.

SERJEANT, Robert Bertram, PH.D., F.B.A.; British Arabist and traveller; b. 23 March 1915, Edin.; s. of R. T. R. Serjeant and Agnes Beatson Serjeant (née Blair); m. Marion Keith Robertson 1941; one s. one d.; ed. Edin. and Cambridge Univs.; studentship to study South Arabian dialects, S.O.A.S., spent in Aden and Protectorate 1940-41; Gov.'s Comm. Aden Protectorate Govt. Guards and Mission 106 1940; Lecturer in Arabic, S.O.A.S., London 1941; seconded to BBC Arabic Service 1942; Ed. Arabic Listener 1943; Reader in Arabic, S.O.A.S. 1946; Colonial Research Fellow in Hadramawt 1947-48; Prof. of Arabic 1955; mem. Minister of Educ.'s commission to examine instruction in Arabic in N. Nigeria 1956, Sec. of

State for Colonies mission to examine Muslim Educ. in E. Africa 1957; Lecturer in Arabic, Cambridge Univ. 1964, Reader 1966, Sir Thomas Adams's Prof. of Arabic and Dir. Middle East Centre, Cambridge 1970-82; Adviser on customary law of irrigation in Yemen on a number of occasions; Ed. (with R. L. Bidwell) Arabian Studies 1974-; mem. Editorial Bd. Cambridge History of Arabic Literature 1983-, Acad. of the Arabic Language, Cairo; Hon. D.Litt. (Edin); T. E. Lawrence Medal, Royal Asiatic Soc. 1974, Richard Burton Memorial Medal, Royal Soc. for Asian Affairs 1981. *Publications:* Materials for a History of Islamic Textiles 1942-51, Prose and Poetry from Hadramawt 1950, Saiyids of Hadramawt 1957, Portuguese off the South Arabian Coast 1961, South Arabian Hunt 1976, San'ā': an Arabian Islamic City (with Ronald Lewcock) 1983, Studies in South Arabian History and Civilisation 1981. *Address:* Summerhill Cottage, Denhead, Nr. St. Andrews, Fife, Scotland. *Telephone:* (033) 485 211.

SERKIN, Peter Adolf; American concert pianist; b. 24 July 1947, New York; s. of Rudolf Serkin (q.v.) and Irene Busch; ed. Curtis Inst. of Music; début, New York 1959; concert appearances in recital and with orchestra worldwide including Philadelphia, Cleveland, New York, London, Zürich, Paris and Japan; has premiered works composed for him by Takemitsu, Lieberson, Berio; has given benefit performances to aid hunger and war victims; records for RCA, ProArte, CBS, New World; Premio Accademia Musicale Chigian Siena 1983. *Address:* c/o Shirley Kirshbaum & Associates, 711 West End Avenue, New York, N.Y. 10025, U.S.A.

SERKIN, Rudolf; American pianist; b. 28 March 1903, Eger, Bohemia; s. of Mordko Serkin and Augusta Schargl; m. Irene Busch 1935; two s. four d.; debut with the Vienna Symphony Orchestra 1915; with Adolf Busch in a series of sonatas for violin and piano; American debut 1933; appeared with Toscanini 1935, with Nat. Orchestral Assen. 1937; annual tours of the U.S.A. 1934-; Head Piano Dept., later Dir., Curtis Inst. of Music, resigned 1976; Artistic Dir. and Pres. Marlboro School of Music; Fellow American Acad. of Arts and Sciences; fmr. mem. Nat. Council on the Arts, Carnegie Comm. Report; Presidential Medal of Freedom 1963; Hon. mem. Philharmonic Soc. of New York 1971, Neue Bachgesellschaft, Bonn, Acad. of St. Cecilia, Rome, Verein Beethoven Haus, Bonn, Riemenschneider-Bach Inst.; Fifth annual Pa. award for Excellence in the Field of Performing Arts 1971, Kennedy Centre Award 1981, Nat. Medal of Arts 1988; Chevalier, Légion d'Honneur and numerous other awards; Dr. h.c. Curtis Inst., Temple Univ., Univ. of Vermont, Williams Coll., Oberlin Coll., Univ. of Rochester, Harvard Univ., Marlboro Coll. *Address:* R.F.D.3, Brattleboro, Vt. 05301, U.S.A.

SERLE, (Alan) Geoffrey, A.O., D.PHIL., F.A.H.A., F.A.S.S.A., F.R.A.H.S.; Australian historian; b. 10 March 1922, Melbourne; s. of Percival Serle and Dora B. Hake; m. Jessie C. Macdonald 1955; three s. one d.; ed. Scotch Coll. Melbourne and Univs. of Melbourne and Oxford; Australian Imperial Force 1942-44; Rhodes Scholar for Vic. 1947; lecturer, Sr. Lecturer in History, Univ. of Melbourne 1951-60; Sr. Lecturer and Reader in History, Monash Univ. 1961-83; Gen. Ed. Australian Dictionary of Biography, A.N.U. 1975-88; Fellow, Royal Historical Soc. of Vic., Museum of Vic. *Publications:* The Golden Age 1963, The Rush to be Rich 1971, From Deserts the Prophets Come 1973, John Monash 1982. *Leisure interests:* sport, reading. *Address:* 31 Lisson Gove, Hawthorn, Vic., 3122, Australia. *Telephone:* 03 818 4778.

SERMAN, Ilya Zakharovich; Soviet literary critic and historian; b. 1913, Vitebsk; ed. Leningrad Inst. of Literature and History; research fellow of Pushkinsky dom, Leningrad 1945-49, arrested for 'cosmopolitanism' and sentenced to 25 years of prison camp 1949; rehabilitated 1954; Dr. of Philological Studies, Prof., research fellow at Pushkinsky dom Inst. 1954-76; author of numerous books and papers on the history of Russian literature and culture; left for Israel 1976. *Publications include:* The Poetic Style of Lomonosov 1966, Russian Classicism 1973, Konstantin Batyushkov 1977, and numerous scholarly papers.

SEROTA, Nicholas Andrew, M.A.; British art gallery director; b. 27 April 1946; s. of Stanley Serota and Baroness Serota; m. Angela M. Beveridge 1973; two d.; ed. Haberdashers' Askes School, Hampstead and Elstree, Christ's Coll. Cambridge and Courtauld Inst. of Art; Regional Art Officer and Exhbn. Organizer, Arts Council of G.B. 1970-73; Dir. Museum of Modern Art, Oxford 1973-76; Dir. Whitechapel Art Gallery 1976-88; Dir. The Tate Gallery, London 1988-; Hon. Fellow, Queen Mary Coll., Univ. of London. *Address:* The Tate Gallery, Millbank, London, S.W.1, England. *Telephone:* 01-821 1313.

SERRA, Narcís, DR.ECON.; Spanish politician; b. 30 May 1943, Barcelona; ed. Barcelona Univ., London School of Econs.; worked in Chamber of Commerce, Industry and Shipping, Barcelona; mem. Moviment Febrer del 62, linked to Catalan branch of Frente de Liberación Popular; Asst. Prof. of Econ. Theory, Barcelona Univ.; opened econ. research bureau, Barcelona; mem. Convergència Socialista de Catalunya 1974, mem. Exec.; joined Office of Territorial Policy and Town Planning, Generalitat (Catalan autonomous govt.) 1977-79; Mayor of Barcelona 1979; Minister of Defence Dec. 1982-. *Address:* Ministerio de Defensa, Po. Castellana No. 109, 28071 Madrid, Spain (Office).

SERRA RAMONEDA, Antoni, PH.D.; Spanish economist and university rector; b. 20 July 1933, Barcelona; s. of Antoni Serra Riera and Enriqueta

Ramoneda Ruis; m. Magarita de la Figuera Buñuel 1958; one s. two d.; ed. Lycée Français, Barcelona and Universidad Complutense de Madrid; Sec. Faculty of Econ. Sciences, Univ. of Barcelona 1960–64; Sec.-Gen. Universidad Autónoma de Barcelona 1970–72, Dir. Inst. of Educ. Sciences 1977–78, Rector 1980–85; Pres. Comisión de Control Caja de Pensiones para la Vejez y de Ahorros 1979–82, Sec.-Gen. 1982–84; Pres. Caja de Ahorros de Cataluña 1984–. *Publications:* Libro Blanco sobre los efectos para Cataluña del ingreso de España en la CEE, La industria textil algodonera y el Mercado Común Europeo, Sistema Economico y Empresa. *Address:* Pl. Bonanova 5, Barcelona 08022, Spain (Home). *Telephone:* (93) 2478101 (Home).

SERRE, Jean-Pierre, D. ÉS SC.; French mathematician; b. 15 Sept, 1926, Bages; s. of Jean and Adèle Serre; m. Josiane Heulot 1948; one d.; ed. Lycée de Nîmes and Ecole Normale Supérieure; Prof. of Algebra and Geometry, Collège de France 1956–; mem. Acads. of Sciences of France, Sweden, U.S.A., Netherlands; Hon. F.R.S. (U.K.); Officier, Légion d'honneur, Commdr., Ordre nat. du Mérite; Fields Medal, Int. Congress of Math. 1954; Prix Balzan 1985. *Publications:* Homologie singulière des espaces fibrés 1951, Faisceaux algébriques cohérents 1955, Groupes algébriques et corps de classes 1959, Corps Locaux 1962, Cohomologie galoisienne 1964, Abelian l-adic representations 1968, Cours d'arithmétique 1970, Représentations linéaires des groupes finis 1971, Arbres, amalgames, SL2 1977. *Address:* Collège de France, place M. Berthelot, 75231 Paris Cedex 05 (Office); 6 avenue de Montespan, 75116 Paris, France (Home). *Telephone:* (1) 553 35 63 (Home).

SERRIN, James B., PH.D.; American professor of mathematics; b. 1 Nov. 1926, Chicago, Ill.; s. of Helen Wingate Serrin and James B. Serrin; m. Barbara West 1952; three d.; ed. Western Michigan Coll. and Indiana Univ.; M.I.T. 1952–54; Univ. of Minn. 1954–, Chair. 1964–65, Regents Prof. of Math. 1968–; Fellow A.A.A.S., American Acad. of Arts and Sciences; mem. N.A.S.; Hon. D.Sc. (Sussex, England); G. D. Birkhoff Award, American Math. Soc. *Publications:* Mathematical Principles of Fluid Dynamics 1958, New Perspectives on Thermodynamics 1985, The Problem of Dirichlet for Quasilinear Elliptic Differential Equations 1969. *Address:* Department of Mathematics, University of Minnesota, Minneapolis, Minn. 55455, U.S.A. *Telephone:* (612) 373-4685.

SERTOLI, Giandomenico, IUR.D.; Italian international civil servant and banker; b. 26 Sept. 1922, Vicenza; s. of Giovanni F. and Angela Maddalena Sertoli; m. Marianne Roblin 1946; two s.; ed. Univ. of Padua and Inst. des Hautes Etudes Internationales, Geneva; Asst. to the Pres. and Sec. Bd. of Dirs., ARAR, Rome 1946–54; mem. Finance Dept., European Coal and Steel Community, Luxembourg 1954–58; Deputy Man. Finance and Treasury Dept., European Investment Bank 1958–60, Man. 1960–68; Financial Adviser to Banca Commerciale Italiana 1968–, Deputy Gen. Man. 1969, Gen. Man. 1976; Vice-Chair. Banca della Svizzera Italiana 1978–83; Dir. Banca Commerciale Italiana Holding, Danieli Int. Holding, Multinvest S.A., Zambon S.P.A. *Leisure interests:* tennis, skiing, bridge. *Address:* 11 rue de Beaumont, 1206 Geneva, Switzerland (Home). *Telephone:* 022-47 02 81 (Home).

SERVAN-SCHREIBER, Jean-Claude, L. EN D.; French newspaperman; b. 11 April 1918, Paris; m. 1st Christiane Laroche 1947 (divorced); m. 2nd Jacqueline Guix de Pinos 1955 (divorced), two s. three d.; m. 3rd Paule Guinet 1983; ed. Exeter Coll., Oxford and Sorbonne; served World War II in Flanders 1940, in Resistance 1941–42, in North Africa 1943, France 1944, Germany 1945; with Les Echos 1946–65, Gen. Man. 1957, Dir. 1963–65; Deputy for Paris, Nat. Ass. 1965–67; Asst. Sec.-Gen. U.N.R.-U.D.T. 1965; Pres. Rassemblement français pour Israël May 1967; Dir.-Gen. Régie française de publicité 1968–78; mem. Haut Conseil de l'audiovisuel 1973–81; Pres. Groupe Européen des Régisseurs de Publicité Télévisée 1975–78; mem. Conseil politique, R.P.R. 1977–81; Conseiller du Groupe de Presse L'Expansion; Commdr., Légion d'honneur, Ordre nat. du Mérite, Médaille mil., Croix de guerre, Croix du Combattant volontaire de la Résistance, Legion of Merit (U.S.A.), etc. *Address:* 147 bis rue d'Alésia, 75014 Paris, France.

SERVAN-SCHREIBER, Jean-Jacques; French economist and writer; b. 13 Feb. 1924, Paris; s. of Emile and Denise (née Bresard) Servan-Schreiber; ed. Ecole Polytechnique, Paris; joined the Free French Forces of Gen. de Gaulle as fighter pilot 1943 (trained U.S. Air Force); Foreign Affairs Ed. Le Monde 1948–53; founder L'Express 1953, Ed. 1953–70; elected and re-elected Pres. Social Radical Party 1970–79; elected and re-elected Deputy for Nancy 1970–79, and Pres. Region of Lorraine 1975–78; Minister of Reform 1974; Pres. World Centre for Computer Literacy 1981–85; Chair. Int. Cttee. Carnegie Mellon Univ. 1985–; Croix de la Valeur mil. *Publications:* Lieutenant en Algérie 1957, Le défi Américain 1967, Le manifeste radical 1970, Le pouvoir régional 1971, Le défi mondial 1981, The Knowledge Revolution 1986. *Address:* Carnegie Mellon University, 5000 Forbes Avenue, Pittsburgh, Pa. 15213, U.S.A.

SERVATIUS, Bernhard, DR.JUR.; German lawyer; b. 14 April 1932, Magdeburg; s. of Rudolf Servatius and Maria Servatius; m. Ingeborg Servatius 1985; ed. Univs. of Fribourg, Hamburg and other univs.; lawyer 1959–, now Sr. Partner, Dr. Servatius & Partner (legal firm); Sole Partner, Treubesitz GmbH, Hamburg (trust co.); legal adviser to Axel Springer and

Springer Publishing Group 1970; Chair. Supervisory Bd. Rheinische Merkur GmbH; Chief Rep. of Axel Springer and Acting Chair. of Man. Admin. Verlagshaus Axel Springer 1984; Chair. Supervisory Bd. Axel Springer Verlag July 1985–; Prof. 1985–; many other professional and public appts. *Address:* Axel Springer Verlag AG, Kaiser-Wilhelm-Str., 6, 2000 Hamburg 36; Rondeel 5, 2000 Hamburg 60, Federal Republic of Germany. *Telephone:* (090) 34734047.

SERVOLINI, Luigi, D.LIT., D.F.A.; Italian xylographer, writer and art critic; b. 1 March 1906, Leghorn (Livorno), Tuscany; s. of Carlo Servolini; m. Odetta Andreoni 1930; one s. one d.; ed. Pisa Univ., Acad. of Fine Arts, Carrara; Prof. of Xylography and Lithography, R. Istituto del Libro di Urbino, and Dir. of Library, Urbino Univ. 1930–39; Dir. artistic and cultural insts. at Forlì 1939–53; First Gen. Dir. Istituto Rizzoli per l'Insegnamento delle arti grafiche, Milan 1953–56; Prof. History of Art; Headmaster; Prof. Special School for Art Historians, Istituto Storia d'Arte, Univ. of Pisa 1969–72; Pres. "Incisori d'Italia" Assen. 1955–; also painter and lithographer and has since 1923 taken part in many important exhbns.; works represented in 80 European and American Public Galleries; has won several prizes; Hon. mem. Accademico Disegno, Florence; Ed. "Comanducci" Dictionary; mem. Ordine dei Giornalisti (Rome) 1935; Ed. La Voce degli IDIT (fortnightly); Pres. of Engraving Art Acad., Rome 1974–, Nat. Assen. of Art Critics (ANCA-ECSA), Rome 1980–; Grand Officer Italian Repub. *Publications:* Ugo da Carpi 1929, La Xilografia a chiaroscuro italiana nei secoli XVI, XVII e XVIII 1930, Tecnica della Xilografia 1935, A. Bosse 1937, Problemi e aspetti dell'Incisione 1939, J. de Barbari 1943, Pittura gotica romagnola 1944, Xilografia giapponese 1949, La Xilografia 1950, Incisione italiana di cinque secoli 1951, Incidere 1952, 1961, Dizionario Incisori ital. moderni e contemporanei 1955, Mosaico di Romagna 1957, Autobiografia di Bodoni 1958, I procedimenti artistici e industriali della Grafica 1959–63, Gli Incisori d'Italia 1960, Il Comanducci: Dizionario dei Pittori (5 vols.) 4th edn. 1971–73, Acqueforti di Giovanni Fattori 1966, Athena: Storia dell' Arte classica e italiana (3 vols.) 1966–68, Dalla pietra litografica alla stampa offset 1968, L'Arte di Incidere 3rd edn. 1971, La Serigrafia Originale 1973, Gli Incisori d'Italia, Vol. II, 1974, Tecnica della Xilografia giapponese 1975, La storia e le tecniche dell' Incisione 1977, Ugo da Carpi: i chiaroscuri e le altre opere 1977. *Leisure interests:* ancient and modern prints, ex libris, hypnotism. *Address:* 00195 Rome, Via Simone de Saint Bon 25, Italy. *Telephone:* 06/385990.

SESSIONS, William S., J.D.; American judge; b. 27 May 1930, Fort Smith, Ark.; s. of Will A. Sessions and Edith A. Steele; m. Alice June Lewis 1952; three s. one d.; ed. Baylor Univ.; called to Texas Bar 1959; Partner, McGregor & Sessions, Waco, Tex. 1959–61; Assoc. Tirey, McLaughlin, Gorin & McDonald, Waco 1961–63; Partner, Haley, Fulbright, Winniford, Sessions & Bice, Waco 1963–69; Chief, Govt. Operations Section, Criminal Div. Dept. of Justice 1969–71; U.S. Attorney, U.S. Dist. Court (Western Dist.) Texas, San Antonio 1971–74, Dist. Judge 1974–80, Chief Judge 1980–87; Dir. Fed. Bureau of Investigation (FBI) Nov. 1987–; mem. A.B.A.; numerous awards. *Publications:* articles in professional journals. *Address:* Federal Bureau of Investigation, J. Edgar Hoover FBI Bldg, Washington, D.C. 20535, U.S.A.

SETCH, Terry, D.F.A.; British artist and teacher; b. 11 March 1936, Lewisham, London; s. of Frank Setch and Florence Beatskeggs; m. Dianne Shaw 1967; one d.; ed. Sutton School of Art and Slade School of Fine Art; Lecturer, Foundation Dept., Leicester Coll. of Art 1960–64; Sr. Lecturer in Fine Art, Cardiff Coll. of Art 1964–, in Art History Hayward Gallery, London 1987; works in Tate Gallery and other collections, elected to Faculty of Painting, British School at Rome 1984, Faculty of Fine Arts 1987; John Moores Exhbn. (Third Prize) 1985. *Address:* 111 Plymouth Road, Penarth, South Glamorgan, South Wales. *Telephone:* (0222) 702757.

SETCHELL, David Lloyd, M.A.; British chartered accountant; b. 16 April 1937, Anston, Yorks.; s. of Raymond Setchell and Phyllis Jane Lloyd; m. Muriel Mary Davies 1962; one s. one d.; ed. Woodhouse Grammar School and Jesus Coll. Cambridge; Peat Marwick 1960–64; Shawinigan Ltd. 1964–71; Vice-Pres. Gulf Oil Chemicals (Europe) 1971–82; Man. Dir. Gulf Oil (G.B.) Ltd. 1982–. *Leisure interests:* golf, tennis, theatre. *Address:* South Hayes, Sandy Lane Road, Cheltenham, Glos. GL53 9DE, England. *Telephone:* (0242) 571390.

SETER, Mordecai; Israeli composer; b. 1916, Russia; s. of Itzhac and Beraha Seter; m. Dina Pevsner 1939; two c.; studied Paris with Paul Dukas and Nadia Boulanger 1932–37; Full Prof. Israel Acad. of Music, Tel Aviv; Tel-Aviv Municipality Prize 1945, 1954; Prix Soc. d'Auteurs et de Compositeurs 1956; Prix Italia 1962; Israel State Prize 1965, Prix Soc. d'Auteurs et de compositeurs 1981. *Works include:* Children's Rhymes 1938, Sabbath Cantata 1940, Festivals 1947, Festive Songs 1951, Three Motets 1951, Sonata for two violins 1952, Sonata for unaccompanied violin 1954, Midnight Vigil 1962, Dithyramb 1966, Jerusalem 1966; Ricercar (for strings) 1956, Variations 1959–67, Sinfonietta 1961, Jephthah's Daughter 1965, Meditation 1967, etc. (symphonic music); The Legend of Judith 1962, Part Real, Part Dream 1964 (ballet); Fantasia 1964, Yemenite Suite 1967, Rounds 1968 (orchestral); Partita (for violin and piano) 1951, Elegy (for viola or clarinet and piano or strings) 1954, Trio ('cello, violin and piano) 1973, Chaccone and Scherzo (piano) 1954, Chamber Music '70 (six works for different instrumental combinations, for two to four instruments:

Intimo, Monodrama, Epigrams, Requiem, Quartet, Autumn) 1970; Espressivo for strings 1971; Soliloquio, Capricci, Intervals, Sine Nomine, Janus (for piano), Three Fughettas 1972–73, Piano Quartet I 1973–81, Piano Cycle 1982, Sonata for Piano 1982, Music for Piano 1982, Preludes for Piano 1982, Piano Quartet II 1982, Opposites Unified, No Dialogue (both for piano) 1984, Moto Perpetuo, Triptique I (both for piano) 1985; Concertante (for violin, oboe, horn and piano) 1973; Trio (for clarinet, 'cello and piano) 1974; Wood-Wind Trio 1974; Quintet (for violin, 'cello, flute, horn and piano) 1975; Ensemble (for six instruments) 1975; Three String Quartets 1976; Solo and Tutti (for clarinet and string quartet) 1976; Music (for string quartet) 1976; String Quartet No. IV 1977; Romantic Harmony (20 short studies) 1981, Dialogues, Improvisation (for piano) 1983; Triptique II (for piano) 1985, Triptique III (for piano) 1986, The Circle (for piano) 1986, Violin and Piano 1986, Double (for clarinet and piano) 1986, Dialogue? (for piano) 1987, Presence (for piano) 1987, Diptique (for piano) 1987, educ. music, etc. *Address:* The Rubin Academy of Music, Tel-Aviv University, Ramat Aviv; 1 Karny Street, Ramat Aviv, Tel Aviv, Israel (Home). *Telephone:* 420111 (Office); 417766 (Home).

SETHI, Prakash Chandra, B.A., LL.B.; Indian politician; b. 19 Oct. 1920, Jhalrapatan, Rajasthan; s. of Shri Bhanwarlal Sethi; m. 1939; five d.; ed. Madhav Coll., Ujjain and Holkar Coll., Indore; mem. Quit India Movement 1942; Pres. Madhav Nagar Ward Congress 1947, Ujjain Dist. Congress 1951, 1954, 1957, Textile Clerks Assen. 1948–49; Madhya Bharat Employees Assen. Vice-Pres. 1942, 1949, 1952; Treas. Madhya Bharat Congress 1954–55; mem. Ujjain Dist. and Madhya Baharat Congress Cttee. Exec. 1953–57; Dir. Ujjain Dist. Co-operative Bank 1957–59; A.I.C.C. Zonal Rep. for Karnataka, Maharashtra, Bombay and Gujarat 1955–56; observer for Bihar Dec. 1966; elected to Rajya Sabha Feb. 1961, April 1964, to Lok Sabha Feb. 1967; Deputy Minister for Steel, Heavy Industries and Mines, Cen. Govt. 1962–67, Minister of State 1967–69; Minister for Revenue and Expenditure 1969–70; Minister of Defence Production 1970–71; Minister of Petroleum and Chemicals 1971–72; Chief Minister Madhya Pradesh 1972–75; Minister of Fertilizers and Chemicals 1975–77; arrested Oct. 1977; Minister of Works and Housing Jan.–Oct. 1980, of Petroleum, Chemicals and Fertilizers 1980–81, of Railways Jan.–Sept. 1982, for Home Affairs 1982–84, of Planning and Irrigation 1984–85; suspended from Congress Oct. 1986; Rep. Govt. of India at Commonwealth Finance Ministers' Conference, Barbados 1969; leader of del. to Colombo Plan Conf., Victoria 1969; Gov. for India, Asian Devt. Bank, Manila, and Int. Bank for Reconstruction and Devt. 1969. *Leisure interests:* tennis, travel, music, reading. *Address:* 7 Safdarjang Road, New Delhi 110011, India.

SETHNESS, Charles Olin, A.B., M.B.A.; American government official, investment banker and university administrator; b. 24 Feb. 1941, Evanston, Ill.; s. of C. Olin Sethness and Alison Louise Burge; m. 2nd Geraldine Greene 1977; one s., one step.-s. two step.-d.; ed. New Trier High School, Princeton Univ. and Harvard Business School; Sr. Credit Analyst, American Nat. Bank and Trust Co. of Chicago 1963–64; Research Asst. Harvard Business School 1966–67; with Morgan Stanley & Co. 1967–73, 1975–81; Vice-Pres. 1972–73, Man. Dir. 1975–81; Man. Morgan & Cie. Int. S.A., Paris 1971–73; Exec. Dir. IBRD, IFC, IDA 1973–75; Special Asst. to Sec. of Treasury 1973–75; Assoc. Dean for External Relations, Harvard Business School, Boston 1981–85; Asst. Sec. of the Treasury for Domestic Finance 1985–. *Address:* U.S. Treasury Department, 15th and Pennsylvania Avenue, N.W., Washington, D.C. 20220; 6219 Garnett Drive, Chevy Chase, Md. 20815, U.S.A.

SETTE, Pietro, LL.D.; Italian lawyer and executive; b. 1915, Bari; m. Renata Pes 1956; two s.; ed. Univ. of Bari; practice in commercial law, corpn. law, law of commercial credit 1938–; lecturer, Univ. of Rome 1939–50; Chair. Finanziaria Breda and assoc. cos. 1951–76, Società MCS 1957–75, Nuova Iniziativa per il Sud (INSUD) 1963–76, Ente Partecipazione e Finanzia Industria Manifatturiera (EFIM) 1963–75, Ente Nazionale Idrocarburi (ENI) 1975–79, Istituto per la Ricostruzione Industriale (IRI) 1979–82; mem. Bd. ENI 1960–74; fmr. mem. del. to ECSC; fmr. Vice-Pres. Finmeccanica; fmr. Pres. Terni; now mem. European Advisory Council, CEEP; Knight, Grand Cross, Order of Merit (Italy), Cavaliere del Lavoro; Dr. of Mining Eng. h.c. (Univ. of Cagliari). *Address:* Via Puccini 9, Rome, Italy. *Telephone:* 85 72 30.

SETTE CÂMARA, José; Brazilian diplomatist; b. 14 April 1920, Alfenas, Minas Gerais; s. of José Rodrigues and Ocarlina Sette Camara; m. Elba Carvalho Sette Camara 1945; two s.; ed. Univ. de Minas Gerais and McGill Univ., Canada; Brazilian Diplomatic Service 1945–; Third Sec. Washington 1947; Vice-Consul, Montreal 1947–50; Third Sec. UN, New York 1950–52; Sec. to Civil Household of Pres. of Brazil 1952–55, Deputy Head of Civil Household 1956–59, Head 1959–60; Consul, Florence 1955–56; Provisional Gov., State of Guanabara 1960; Head Perm. Del. of Brazil to UN, Geneva 1960–61; Amb. to Canada 1961–62; Mayor of Brasília 1962–63; Amb. to Switzerland 1963–64; Perm. Rep. to UN 1964–68; Publr. Jornal do Brasil 1969–; mem. UN Int. Law Comm. 1970–79; Judge, Int. Court of Justice 1979–88, Vice-Pres. 1982. *Leisure interests:* reading, walking, swimming. *Address:* Rua Carvalho Azaredo 96, Rio de Janeiro, R.J., Brazil. *Telephone:* Rio de Janeiro 286-8475.

SEVAREID, Arnold Eric, A.B.; American news correspondent; b. 26 Nov. 1912, Velva, N.D.; s. of Alfred and Clare (née Hougen) Sevareid; m. 3rd

Suzanne St. Pierre 1979; two s. one d. from previous marriages; ed. Univ. of Minnesota; Reporter, Minneapolis Journal 1936; joined CBS 1939; war corresp., France and London 1939–40; CBS Washington Bureau 1940–43; war corresp. China 1943; subsequently covered final stages of war in Europe; returned to U.S.A. to cover founding of UN, San Francisco Conf. 1945; attached to CBS Washington Bureau 1946–59; roving European corresp., London 1959–61; returned to New York and served as moderator for various broadcasts 1961–64; Nat. Corresp., CBS News 1964–77, Consultant 1977–; War Corresp. Vietnam 1966; George Foster Peabody Award 1950, 1964, 1967; Order of the Crown (Belgium); Freedom Medal (Norway); Alfred I. Du Pont Award; George Polk Award and numerous other awards and decorations; several hon. degrees. *Publications:* several books incl. Not So Wild a Dream 1946, In One Ear 1952, Small Sounds in the Night 1956, Candidates 1960 (ed.), This is Eric Sevareid 1964, essays and articles. *Address:* CBS News, 2020 M Street, N.W., Washington, D.C. 20036, U.S.A.

SEVERIN, (Giles) Timothy, M.A., B.LITT.; British traveller and author; b. 25 Sept. 1940; s. of Maurice Watkins and Inge Severin; m. Dorothy Virginia Sherman 1966 (divorced 1979); one d.; ed. Tonbridge School, Keble Coll., Oxford; Commonwealth Fellow, U.S.A. 1964–66; expeditions: led motorcycle team along Marco Polo's route 1961, canoe and launch down River Mississippi 1965, Brendan Voyage from W. Ireland to N. America 1977, Sindbad Voyage from Oman to China 1980–81, Jason Voyage from Greece to Soviet Georgia 1984, Ulysses Voyage, Troy to Ithaca 1985; Crusade: on horseback from Belgium to Jerusalem 1987–88. *Publications:* Tracking Marco Polo 1964, Explorers of the Mississippi 1967, The Golden Antilles 1970, The African Adventure 1973, Vanishing Primitive Man 1973, The Oriental Adventure 1976, The Brendan Voyage 1978, The Sindbad Voyage 1982, The Jason Voyage 1984, The Ulysses Voyage 1987. *Address:* Courtmacsherry, Co. Cork, Ireland. *Telephone:* Bandon 46127.

SEWARD, George Chester, LL.B.; American lawyer; b. 4 Aug. 1910, Omaha; s. of George F. Seward and Ada L. Rugh; m. Carroll F. McKay 1936; two s. two d.; ed. Univ. of Virginia; admitted Va. Bar 1935, later to Bar of New York, Kentucky, Washington D.C. and U.S. Supreme Court; with Shearman & Sterling, New York 1936–53, Seward & Kissel, New York 1953–; mem. Legal Advisory Comm. New York Stock Exchange 1984–87; Fellow, American Bar Foundation; mem. Int. Bar Assen., American Law Inst. *Publications:* Basic Corporate Practice, Seward and Related Families, Model Business Corporation Act Annotated (co-author). *Address:* Seward & Kissel, Wall Street Plaza, New York, N.Y. 10005; 818 Connecticut Avenue, Washington, D.C. 20006 (Offices); 48 Greenacres Avenue, Scarsdale, N.Y. 10583, U.S.A. (Home).

SEYBOU, Brig. Ali; Niger army officer and politician; fmr. army chief of staff; mem. Supreme Mil. Council; Pres. of Niger Nov. 1987–. *Address:* Office of the President, Niamey, Niger.

SEYDOU, Amadou; Niger scholar and diplomatist; b. 1928; ed. Dakar, Inst. des Hautes Etudes, Algiers, Al Azhar Univ., Cairo and Univ. of Paris; fmr. teacher, founded Nat. School of Medersa 1960; Chargé d'affaires, Niger Embassy, Paris 1960–61, Amb. to France 1961–66, concurrently to U.K. 1964–66; Dir. Dept. of Culture, UNESCO Oct. 1967–74; Amb. to France (also accred. to Italy, Spain, Switzerland and U.K.) 1974–81; Perm Rep. to UNESCO 1981–83; Pres. Directorie du Club de Dakar Feb. 1985–; Commdr., Légion d'honneur. *Address:* c/o Ministry of Foreign Affairs, Niamey, Niger.

SEYDOU, Traoré, B.A.; Mali diplomatist; b. 1927; m.; four c.; ed. Ecole Nat. de la France d'Outre-Mer, Paris; Sec.-Gen. Ministry of Foreign Affairs, Mali 1975–79; Perm. Rep. to UN 1979–82; fmr. Amb. to U.S.A. (also accred. to Canada, Haiti, Brazil, Sweden, Fed. Repub. of Germany and the EEC); mem. Mali Del., Conf. of Heads of State of OAU, UN Conf. on Devt. 1964. *Address:* c/o Ministry of Foreign Affairs and International Co-operation, Koulouba, Bamako, Mali.

SEYERSTED, Finn, DR.IUR.; Norwegian professor of international law and diplomatist; b. 29 Dec. 1915, Oslo; s. of Fredrik Sejersted and Dakky Kiaer; m. Sölvi Gierløff 1957; two d.; ed. Oslo Univ., Faculté de Droit, Paris, Columbia Univ. Law School, New York, and Nat. Defence Coll.; Sec. Ministry of Foreign Affairs 1945–46, 1949–50, 1951–53, Chief of Div. 1955–60; Sec. Perm. Del. of Norway at UN 1946–49; UNESCO mission to Indonesia, Philippines and Laos 1953–54; Dir. Legal Div., IAEA, Vienna 1960–65; Amb. to Argentina, Paraguay and Uruguay 1968–73; Prof. of Int. Law, Univ. of Oslo 1974–. *Publications:* Objective International Personality of Intergovernmental Organizations 1963, United Nations Forces in the Law of Peace and War 1966, Applicable Law in Relations between Intergovernmental Organizations and Private Parties 1967. *Leisure interests:* forestry, languages, skiing. *Address:* Universitet, Karl Johans gt. 47, Oslo 1 (Office); Jerpefaret 23, 0393, Oslo 3 (Home); Hovda, 2656 Leirflaten, Norway (Vacation Home). *Telephone:* 42 90 10 (University); 14 65 11 (Home); 062-34935 (Vacation Home).

SEYMOUR, Lynn, C.B.E.; Canadian ballet dancer; b. 8 March 1939, Wainwright, Alberta; d. of E. V. Springett; m. 1st Colin Jones 1963 (divorced 1974), three s.; m. 2nd Philip Pace 1974; m. 3rd Vanya Hackel 1983 (divorced 1988); ed. Royal Ballet School; Graduated into Royal Ballet 1957; promoted to Soloist rank 1958, to Prin. 1958; joined Deutsche Oper, Berlin

1966; Guest Artist, Royal Ballet 1970-78; Artistic Dir. of Ballet Bayerische Staatsoper 1979-80; Guest Artist with other cos. incl. Alvin Ailey; Evening Standard Drama Award 1977. *Ballets:* The Burrow 1958, Swan Lake 1958, Giselle 1958, The Invitation 1960, The Two Pigeons 1961, Symphony 1963, Romeo and Juliet 1964, Anastasia 1966, Dances at a Gathering, The Concert, The Seven Deadly Sins, Flowers 1972, Shukumei, The Four Seasons 1975, Side Show, Rituals 1975, Manon Lescaut 1976, A Month in the Country 1976, Mayerling 1978, Manon 1978, Choreography for Rashomon 1976, The Court of Love 1977, Intimate Letters 1978, Mae and Polly, Boreas, Tattooed Lady, Wolfy, the Ballet Rambert 1987. *Publication:* Lynn: leaps and boundaries (autobiog. with Paul Gardner) 1984. *Address:* c/o Artistes in Action, 16 Balderton Street, London, W1Y 1TF, England.

SEYNES, Philippe de; French United Nations official; b. 4 Jan. 1910; ed. Ecole Libre des Sciences Politiques, Univ. de Paris; Insp. des Finances 1936-39; mobilized 1939; P.O.W. 1940-45; mem. French Mission in Germany, later Deputy Sec.-Gen. Allied Reparations Agency Brussels 1945-49; Financial Adviser to French Del. to UN 1949-54, on staff of Minister of Foreign Affairs 1954 (Adviser to M. Mendès-France); Under-Sec. for Econ. and Social Affairs, United Nations 1955-68, Under-Sec.-Gen. 1968-74; Dir. Programme for the Future, UNITAR 1975-82, Pres. 1983-, Sr. Fellow UNITAR; Pres. Asscn. Int. Futuribles 1976-79; Officier, Légion d'honneur, Croix de guerre. *Address:* c/o UNITAR, 801 United Nations Plaza, New York, N.Y. 10017, U.S.A.

SEYPIDIN AZE; Chinese (Uighur) politician; b. 1916, Artush, Xinjiang; ed. Cen. Asia Univ., Moscow; Leader of Uighur Uprisings 1933, 1944; participant in armed rebellion and establishment of E. Turkestan Repub. 1944; Minister of Educ., E. Turkistan Repub. 1945; Deputy Chair. Xinjiang Uighur People's Govt. 1949-54, Chair. 1955-68; Deputy Commdr. Xinjiang Uighur Mil. Region, People's Liberation Army 1949; Second Sec. CCP Xinjiang Uighur 1956-68; Alt. mem. 8th Cen. Cttee. of CCP 1956; Pres. Xinjiang Uighur Univ. 1964; Vice-Chair. Xinjiang Uighur Revolutionary Cttee. 1968, Chair. 1972-78; mem. 9th Cen. Cttee. of CCP 1969; Second Sec. CCP Xinjiang Uighur 1971, First Sec. 1973-78; Alt. mem. Politburo, 10th Cen. Cttee. of CCP 1973, 1975-78; First Political Commissar Xinjiang Uighur Mil. Region, PLA 1974-78; Chair. Presidium Nat. People's Congress 1975; Alt. mem. Politburo, 11th Cen. Cttee. of CCP 1976; Exec. Chair. Presidium 5th Nat. People's Congress; Vice-Chair. Standing Cttee. 5th Nat. People's Congress 1978-83; Vice-Chair. Standing Cttee. 6th Nat. People's Congress 1983-, Exec. Chair. Presidium 6th NPC 1986-; Hon. Pres. Minority Writers' Soc. 1985-, Minority Literature Foundation Dec. 1986-; mem. 12th CCP Cen. Cttee. 1982-87, 13th Cen. Cttee. 1987-. *Address:* People's Republic of China.

SFAR, Rachid; Tunisian politician; b. 11 Sept. 1933, Mahdia; ed. Lycée des Garçons, Sfax, Inst. d'Hautes Etudes, Tunis and Ecole Nat. des Impôts, Paris; Inspector of Taxes 1960; Dir.-Gen. Régie Nat. des Tabacs et Allumettes (RNTA) 1965; Dir. of Taxation, Ministry of Finance 1969; Sec.-Gen. Ministry of Educ. 1971-73, Ministry of Finance 1973-77; Minister of Mines and Energy 1977-78, of Defence 1978-80, of Health 1980-83, of Nat. Economy 1983-86, of Finance and Economy April-July 1986; Prime Minister 1986-87; Deputy to Nat. Ass. 1979-; mem. Cen. Cttee. and Politburo, Parti Socialiste Destourien 1979-; Grand Cordon, Ordre de l'Indépendence; Grand Officier, Ordre de la République. *Address:* c/o Office of the Prime Minister, Tunis, Tunisia.

SGORLON, Carlo Pietro Antonio, PH.D.; Italian novelist and journalist; b. 27 July 1930, Cassacco, Udine; s. of Antonio Sgorlon and Livia Sgorlon; m. Edda Agarinis 1961; ed. Liceo Classico di Udine, Univ. di Pisa, Univ. di Munich; Secondary School teacher 1953-79; journalist 1969-; Enna Prize 1968, Rapallo Prize 1968, Campiello Prizes 1973 and 1983, Vallombrosa Prize 1983, Soroptomist Prize 1983, Strega Prize 1985. *Publications:* Kafka narratore 1961, La Poltrona 1968, Elsa Morante 1972, Il Trono di Legno 1973, Regina di Saba 1975, Gli dei Torneranno 1977, La Luna Color Ametista 1978, La Carrozza di Rame 1979, La Contrada 1981, La Conchiglia di Anataj 1983, L'Armata dei Fiumi Perduti 1985, Sette Veli 1986, L'Ultima Valle 1987. *Leisure interests:* painting, carpentry, walking. *Address:* Via Micesio 15, Udine CAP 33100, Italy. *Telephone:* 0432 294140.

SHAALI, Mohammad Bin Hussain Al-; United Arab Emirates diplomatist; b. 1950, Ajman; m.; three c.; ed. Beirut Univ.; employee Dept. of Political Affairs Diplomatic and Consular Service 1974-77; Chargé d'Affaires Embassy, Vienna 1977-78, Tunis 1978; fmr. Acting Dir. Dept. of Political Affairs, fmr. Chief Arab and Gulf Affairs Div.; fmr. Acting Dir. Dept. of Admin. and Finance; Dir. Arab World Dept. Ministry of Foreign Affairs 1982-85; Perm. Rep. to UN 1985-, Pres. Security Council 1986; del. to several sessions and special sessions of UN Gen. Ass. 1978, 1980, 1982, Deputy Chair. of Del. 1984; Head Del. at preparatory meetings on charter of Gulf Co-operation Council. *Address:* Permanent Mission of the United Arab Emirates to the United Nations, 747 Third Avenue, 36th Floor, New York, N.Y. 10017, U.S.A. *Telephone:* (212) 371-0480.

SHABANOV, Gen. Vitaly Mikhailovich; Soviet military official; b. 1923, Lobachi, Kostroma Dist.; ed. Leningrad Air Force Acad.; mem. CPSU 1947-; served at front 1941-45; engineer and test-pilot at Air Force research Insts. 1945-49; sr. posts in U.S.S.R. Ministry of Radio Industries 1949-72; Dir. of a scientific production Assen. 1972-74; Deputy Minister of

Radio Industry 1974-78, of Defence Industry 1978-; Cand. mem. of Cen. Cttee. CPSU 1981-86, mem. 1986-; elected to Congress of People's Deputies of the U.S.S.R. 1989; Engineer, Col.-Gen., U.S.S.R. State Prize 1953, Lenin Prize 1963, Order of Lenin, Order of October Revolution, Order of Red Banner of Labour, Order of Red Star, Hero of Socialist Labour 1981. *Address:* The Kremlin, Moscow, U.S.S.R.

SHACK, William Alfred, PH.D.; American professor of anthropology; b. 19 April 1923, Chicago, Ill.; s. of William Shack and Emma McAvoy Shack; m. Dorothy C. Nash 1960; one s.; ed. School of Art, Inst. of Chicago, Univ. of Chicago, L.S.E., Univ. of London; Asst. Prof. of Sociology and Anthropology, N.E. Ill. State Coll. 1961-62; Asst. Prof. of Sociology, Haile Sellassie 1 Univ., Ethiopia 1962-65; Assoc. Prof. of Anthropology, Univ. of Ill., Chicago 1966-70; Prof. of Anthropology, Univ. of Calif., Berkeley 1970-, Dean, Grad. Div. 1970-88; Research Assoc., Dept. of Anthropology, Univ. of Chicago 1965-66; Chair., N. American Cttee., Royal Anthropological Inst., London 1983-86, Int. African Inst., London 1987-; Chevalier, ordre nat. du Mérite 1987. *Publications:* The Gurage 1966, The Central Ethiopians 1974, Gods and Heroes (co-author) 1974, Strangers in African Societies (co-ed.) 1979, Politics in Leadership (co-ed.) 1979, The Kula 1985. *Leisure interest:* vintage motor racing. *Address:* Department of Anthropology, University of California, Berkeley, Calif. 94720, U.S.A. *Telephone:* (415) 642-3391.

SHACKLETON, Baron (Life Peer), cr. 1958; **Edward Arthur Alexander Shackleton,** K.G., P.C., O.B.E., M.A.; British politician and industrialist; b. 15 July 1911; s. of the late Sir Ernest Shackleton, Antarctic explorer; m. Betty Muriel Marguerite Homan 1938; one s. (deceased) one d.; ed. Radley Coll. and Magdalen Coll., Oxford; Surveyor, Oxford Univ. Expedition to Sarawak 1932; Organizer and Surveyor, Oxford Univ. Expedition to Ellesmereland 1934-35; BBC Producer 1938-40; Royal Air Force 1940-45; M.P. 1946-55; Parl. Pvt. Sec. to Minister of Supply 1949-50, to Lord Pres. of Council 1950-51, to Foreign Sec. 1951; Minister of Defence for the R.A.F. 1964-67, Minister without Portfolio and Deputy Leader House of Lords 1967-68; mem. Cabinet 1968-70; Leader, House of Lords 1968-70; Lord Privy Seal Jan.-April 1968, 1968-70; Paymaster-Gen. April-Nov. 1968; Leader of Opposition, House of Lords 1970-74; Exec. Dir. John Lewis partnership 1955-64; Chair. Eastern European Trade Council 1977-86, RTZ Development Enterprises 1973-83, etc.; Dir. Rio Tinto-Zinc Corpn. PLC 1973-83, Deputy Chair. 1975-82, Joint Deputy Chair. 1978-82, Adviser 1982-86; Chair. Anglesey Aluminium Metal Ltd. 1981-85; Pres. Asscn. of Special Libraries and Information Bureaux (ASLIB) 1963-65; Pres. Royal Geographical Soc. 1971-74; Chair. Arctic Club 1969 and 1979; Pres. Parl. and Scientific Cttee. 1976-80; Chair. Political Hons. Scrutiny Cttee. 1976-, Council, Royal Inst. of Int. Affairs 1977-80, East European Trade Council 1977-86 (Hon. Pres. 1986-); Pres. British Standards Inst. 1977-80; Chair. Britain-Australia Soc. 1983, House of Lords Select Cttee. on Science and Tech.; Pro-Chancellor, Univ. of Southampton 1984; Hon. LL.D. (Newfoundland) 1970, Hon. D.Sc. (Warwick) 1978, (Southampton) 1986; Hon. Fellow Magdalen Coll., St. Hugh's Coll., Oxford; Hon. Elder Brother of Trinity House; Cuthbert Peek Award, Royal Geographical Soc. 1933, Ludwig Medallist, Munich Geog. Soc. 1938; Freedom of Stanley, Falkland Islands 1988; Labour. *Publications:* Arctic Journeys, Nansen the Explorer, Borneo Jungle (part author), Review of the Operation of the Prevention of Terrorism (Temporary Provisions) Acts 1974 and 1976, Economic Survey of the Falkland Islands 1976, 1982. *Address:* Cleveland House, 19 St. James's Square, London, SW1Y 4JG, England. *Telephone:* 01-930 1752.

SHACKLETON, Robert Millner, PH.D., F.R.S.; British geologist; b. 30 Dec. 1909, Purley, Surrey; s. of John Milner Shackleton and Agnes Mitford Shackleton; m. 1st Gwen Isabel Harland 1933 (divorced); m. 2nd Judith Wyndham Jeffreys 1948 (divorced); m. 3rd Peigi Wallace 1983; two s. three d.; ed. Sidcot School, Somerset, Univ. of Liverpool and Imperial Coll., London; Chief Geologist, Whitehall Explorations Ltd., Fiji 1933-34; Lecturer, Imperial Coll. 1934-40; Geologist, Geological Survey, Kenya 1940-45; Lecturer, Imperial Coll. 1945-48; Herdman Prof. of Geology, Univ. of Liverpool 1948-63; Prof. of Geology, Univ. of Leeds 1963-76, Dir. Research Inst. of African Geology 1966-76; Sr. Research Fellow, Open Univ. 1977-; Visiting Prof., Imperial Coll. 1985-; Silver Medal, Liverpool Geological Soc.; Murchison Medal, Geological Soc. of London; Clough Medal, Edinburgh Geological Soc. *Publications:* several papers in geological journals. *Leisure interests:* gardening, painting, travel. *Address:* Department of Earth Sciences, Open University, Walton Hall, Milton Keynes, MK7 6AA (University); The Croft Barn, East Hendred, Oxfordshire, England (Home). *Telephone:* (0908) 655166 (Open University); (0235) 834802 (Home).

SHAFAREVICH, Igor Rostislavovich; Soviet mathematician; b. 1923, Moscow; ed. Moscow Univ; Research Officer Moscow Mathematical Inst. 1943-44; staff mem. Faculty of Mechanics and Mathematics, Moscow Univ. 1944-52; Prof. Moscow Univ. 1953; mem. U.S.S.R. Acad. of Sciences; mem. Bd. Moscow Mathematics Soc. 1964; dissident activity 1968-; mem. U.S.S.R. Human Rights Cttee.; Heinemann Prize, Göttingen Acad. of Sciences 1975; dismissed from post at Moscow Univ. for dissident activity 1975; Hon. mem. U.S. Acad. of Sciences. *Publications* (apart from *samizdat*) *include:* Has Russia a Future? and "Socialism" in Solzhenitsyn's From Under the Rubble, Socialism as a Phenomenon in Global History 1977.

SHAFEI, Col. Hussein Mahmoud El–; Egyptian army officer and politician; b. 8 Feb. 1918, Tanta; s. of Mahmoud El-Shafei; m. Magda Gabr 1948; two s. one d.; ed. Mil. Coll., Cairo; commissioned as 2nd Lieut. 1938; took part in Palestine hostilities 1948; graduated from Staff Officers' Coll. 1953 and apptd. Officer-in-Charge Cavalry Corps; Minister of War and Marine 1954; of Social Affairs (Egypt) 1954–58; Minister of Labour and Social Affairs, U.A.R. 1958–61; Vice-Pres. of U.A.R. and Minister of Social Affairs and Waqfs 1961–62; mem. Presidency Council 1962–64; Vice-Pres. of U.A.R. (Egypt) 1964–67, 1970–75; Vice-Pres. and Minister of Religious Institutions (Waqfs) 1967–70; Pres. Egyptian del. to OAU Summit Conf. 1973–74; participated in preparing constitution of federation between Egypt, Syria and Libya. *Leisure interests:* riding, tennis, swimming, drawing. *Address:* 6 Sharai Wizaret, El Ziraä Dokki, Giza, Egypt. *Telephone:* 705844, 705222.

SHAFFER, Peter Levin, C.B.E., F.R.S.L.; British playwright; b. 15 May 1926, Liverpool; s. of Jack Shaffer and Reka (née Fredman) Shaffer; ed. St. Paul's School, London, and Trinity Coll., Cambridge; Evening Standard Drama Award 1958; New York Drama Critics Circle Award 1959–60; Antoinette Perry Award for Best Play and N.Y. Drama Critics Circle Award 1975 (Equus) and 1981 (Amadeus); Evening Standard Drama Award 1957 (Five Finger Exercise) and 1980, London Drama Critics Award; Acad. Award for Best Screenplay (Amadeus) 1984. *Plays:* Five Finger Exercise 1958, The Private Ear and The Public Eye 1962, The Royal Hunt of the Sun 1964, Black Comedy 1965, White Liars 1967, The Battle of Shrivings 1970, Equus 1973 (film 1977), Amadeus 1979 (film 1984), Yonadab 1985, Lettice and Lovage 1987 (Evening Standard Award for Best Comedy 1988); also television plays. *Leisure interests:* architecture, walking, music. *Address:* c/o McNaughton-Lowe Representation, 200 Fulham Road, London, S.W.10, England.

SHAFIE, Tan Sri Haji Mohammed Ghazali, P.M.N., S.S.A.P., S.I.M.P., S.P.D.K.; Malaysian politician; b. 22 March 1922, Kuala Lipis; m. Puan Sri Khatijah binti Abdul Majid; two s.; ed. Raffles Coll., Singapore, Univ. Coll. of Wales; fmr. civil servant; assigned to Office of Commr. for Malaya, London; later Commr. for Fed. of Malaya, New Delhi; Deputy Sec. for External Affairs 1957, Acting Perm. Sec. 1959; Senator 1970–72; Minister with Special Functions 1970–72, also of Information 1971–72; mem. Parl. 1972–; Minister of Home Affairs 1973–81, of Foreign Affairs 1981–84; Govt. Special Envoy 1984; Chair. Paremba; Visiting Prof., Nat. Univ. of Singapore. *Address:* 15 Jalan Ampang Hilir, 55000 Kuala Lumpur, Malaysia. *Telephone:* 456 24 63.

SHAFIQ, Mohammad Musa, M.A.; Afghan politician; b. 1924, Kabul; ed. Ghazi High School, Al Azhar Univ., Cairo and Columbia Univ., U.S.A.; joined Ministry of Justice 1957, later became Dir. Legis. Dept.; also taught at Faculty of Law and Political Science, Kabul Univ.; Partner, pvt. law firm, Kabul 1961; Deputy Minister of Justice 1963–66; Adviser, Ministry of Foreign Affairs 1966–68; Amb. to Egypt, also accred. to Lebanon, Sudan and Ghana 1968–71; Minister of Foreign Affairs 1971–73; Prime Minister 1972–73 (deposed by mil. coup); in detention 1973–75; arrested April 1978.

SHAGARI, Alhaji Shehu Usman Aliu; Nigerian educationist and politician; b. May 1925, Shagari; ed. Middle School, Sokoto, Barewa Coll., Kaduna, Teacher Training Coll., Zaria; Science Teacher, Sokoto Middle School 1945–50; Headmaster, Argungu Sr. Primary School 1951–52; Sr. Visiting Teacher, Sokoto Prov. 1953–58; mem. Fed. Parl. 1954–58; Parl. Sec. to the Prime Minister 1958–59; Fed. Minister of Econ. Devt. 1959–60, of Establishments 1960–62, of Internal Affairs 1962–65, of Works 1965–66; Sec. Sokoto Prov. Educ. Devt. Fund 1966–68; State Commr. for Educ., Sokoto Prov. 1968–70; Fed. Commr. for Econ. Devt. and Reconstruction 1970–71, for Finance 1971–75; fmr. Chair. Peugeot Automobile Nigeria Ltd.; mem. Constituent Assembly 1977–83; Presidential candidate for the Nat. Party of Nigeria (NPN) 1979; Pres. of Nigeria and C.-in-C. of the Armed Forces 1979–83 (deposed by mil. coup), also Minister of Defence 1982–83; under house arrest 1983–86, banned from holding public office and from political activity Aug. 1986; confined to Shagari Village 1986–88; Hon. LL.D. (Ahmadu Bello Univ.) 1976. *Publications:* Wakar Nigeria (poem), Shehu Usman Dan-Fodio: Ideas and Ideals of his Leadership.

SHAH, Eddy (Selim Jehane); British newspaper publisher; b. 1944, Cambridge; s. of Moochool Shah and Hazel Strange; m. Jennifer Shah; two s. one d.; ed. several schools including Gordonstoun; worked as Asst. Stage Man. in Repertory Theatre; also worked in TV, and later as space salesman for free newspaper once published by Manchester Evening News; launched Sale and Altrincham Messenger freesheet in 1974, Stockport Messenger 1977, also propr. of Bury Messenger; launched Today newspaper 1986, Chair., CEO 1986–88; launched The Post Oct. 1988 (folded Dec. 1988). *Leisure interest:* golf. *Address:* c/o Today, 70 Vauxhall Bridge Road, London, S.W.1, England.

SHAHA, Rishikesh; Nepalese politician and diplomatist; b. 1925, Tansen, Palpain Province; s. of Raja Tarak Bahadur Shaha and Madan Dibeshwari; m. Siddhanta Rajyalakshmi 1946; one s.; ed. Patna Univ. and Allahabad Univ., India; Lecturer in English and Nepalese Literature, Tri-Chandra Coll. 1945–48; Opposition Leader, First Advisory Assembly 1952; Gen. Sec., Nepalese Congress 1953–55; Perm. Rep. (with rank of Amb.) to UN 1956–60; Amb. to U.S.A. 1958–60; Chair. UN Int. Comm. investigating

death of Dag Hammarskjöld 1961; Minister of Finance, Planning and Economic Affairs 1961–62, of Foreign Affairs July-Sept. 1962; Amb.-at-large 1962–63; Chair. Standing Cttee., Council of State 1963–64; Visiting Prof. East-West Center, Univ. of Hawaii 1965–66; M.P. 1967–70; Solitary confinement 1969–70; Visiting Prof., School of Int. Studies of Jawaharlal Nehru Univ. 1971; Regent's Prof., Univ. of Calif. at Berkeley 1971–72; returned to Nepal, arrested Dec. 1974; Fellow, Woodrow Wilson Int. Center for Scholars, Washington, D.C. 1976–77; Alumni Fellow, East-West Centre 1984; returned to Nepal, arrested May 1977; campaigned for restoration of multi-party democracy before 1980 Referendum. *Publications:* Nepal and the World 1954, Heroes and Builders of Nepal (in U.K.) 1965, An Introduction to Nepal 1975, Nepali Politics—Retrospect and Prospect (in U.K.) 1975, Essays in the Practice of Government in Nepal (in India) 1982, Future of South Asia (in India) 1986. *Leisure interests:* reading, writing, big game hunting. *Address:* Shri Nivas, Kamal Pokhari, Kathmandu, Nepal. *Telephone:* 411766.

SHAHABUDDEEN, Mohamed, B.SC., PH.D., Q.C.; Guyana international judge; b. 7 Oct. 1931; ed. Univ. of London and Hague Acad. of Int. Law; called to the Bar, Middle Temple, London 1954; pvt. legal practice 1954–59; magistrate 1959; Crown Counsel 1959–62; Solicitor-Gen. (with rank of Justice of Appeal from 1971) 1962–73; Minister of Justice 1978–88; Vice-Pres. of Guyana 1983–88; Deputy Prime Minister 1984–85, First Deputy Prime Minister 1985–88; Chief Legal Adviser to Guyana Govt. on all maj. int. questions 1973–; mem. Guyana del. to numerous int. confs. including UN Gen. Ass., Commonwealth Heads of Govt. meetings etc.; Judge, Int. Court of Justice 1988–; Order of Roraima, Cacique's Crown of Honour. *Publications:* numerous books and articles. *Address:* International Court of Justice, Peace Palace, 2517 KJ The Hague, The Netherlands. *Telephone:* 92 44 41.

SHAHAL, Moshe; Israeli politician and lawyer; b. 1934, Iraq; m.; two c.; ed. Haifa Univ., Tel Aviv Univ.; mil. service Israeli Defence Forces; mem. Seventh Knesset (Parl.) –1974, mem. Finance Cttee., mem. Econ. Cttee., mem. Labour Cttee.; Eighth Knesset 1974–77, mem. Finance Cttee., mem. Constitution, Law and Justice Cttee.; Tenth Knesset 1983–; Deputy Speaker, mem. Knesset Cttee., mem. Constitution, Law and Justice Cttee.; Minister of Energy and Infrastructure Sept. 1984–; fmr. Chair. Israeli Consumers' Council; fmr. Perm. Observer to European Council; fmr. Perm. Rep. to Inter-Parl. Union; Labour Party. *Address:* Ministry of Energy and Infrastructure, Hakirya, Jerusalem.

SHAHAR, David; Israeli writer and novelist; b. 17 June 1926, Jerusalem; s. of Meyer and Sara Shahar; m. Shulamith Weinstock 1956; one s. one d.; ed. Hebrew Univ., Jerusalem; mem. Bd. Jerusalem Writers' House 1968–; lecturer in Hebrew Literature, Univ. of Paris, France 1971–72; mem. Bd. Mossad Bialik Publishing Co. 1975–, Council for Culture and the Arts 1982–; del. to Int. P.E.N. Congress 1971, 1973; Pres. Asscn. of Hebrew Writers 1972; Prime Minister's Award for Literature 1969, 1978, Agnon Prize of the City of Jerusalem 1973, Prix Médicis Etranger 1981, Bialik Prize, City of Tel-Aviv 1984, Newman Prize for Hebrew Literature of New York City Univ. and Bar-Ilan Univ. 1987; Commandeur, Ordre des Arts et des Lettres, France 1985. *Publications include:* The Moon of Honey and Gold 1959, The Palace of Shattered Vessels (cycle of novels including Summer in the Road of the Prophets 1969, A Voyage to Ur of the Chaldees 1971, The Day of the Countess 1976, Nin-Gal 1983, The Day of the Phantoms 1985), His Majesty's Agent 1979 (novels); The Death of the Little God 1970, The Pope's Moustache 1971, Stories from Jerusalem 1974 (short stories). *Leisure interests:* painting, music, walking. *Address:* 17 Hovevey Zion Street, Talbieh, Jerusalem, Israel.

SHAHI, Agha, M.A., LL.B.; Pakistani diplomatist; b. 25 Aug. 1920, Bangalore; s. of Agha Abdullah; ed. Madras Univ. and Allahabad Univ.; Indian Civil Service 1943; Pakistan Foreign Service 1951–82; Deputy Sec., Ministry of Foreign Affairs, in charge of UN and Int. Confs. Branch 1951–55; First Counsellor and Minister, Wash. 1955–58; Deputy Perm. Rep. to UN 1958–61; Dir.-Gen. in charge Divs. of UN and Int. Conf. Affairs, Soviet, Chinese and Arab Affairs, Ministry of Foreign Affairs 1961–64; Additional Foreign Sec. 1964–67; Perm. Rep. to UN 1967–72; Pakistan Rep. to Security Council 1968–69; Pres. UN Security Council Jan. 1968; Pres. Governing Council for UN Devt. Programme 1969; Pakistan Rep. to Conf. of the Cttee. on Disarmament 1969; Foreign Sec. 1972; Chair. Pakistan Del. UN Gen. Assembly 1973–77; Sec.-Gen. Foreign Affairs 1977–78; Minister of State, Adviser to Pres. on Foreign Affairs 1978–82; Chair. UN Advisory Bd. on Disarmament Studies Nov. 1978–; mem. Cttee. of Islamic Conf. on Afghanistan 1980–. *Leisure interests:* riding, reading. *Address:* c/o Ministry of Foreign Affairs, Islamabad, Pakistan.

SHAKAA, Riyadh al, B.A.; Jordanian lawyer and politician; b. 1941, Nablus; ed. Univ. of Cairo; Lawyer and mem. Jordanian Bar Assc.; mem. Lower House of Parl. for Nablus 1985–; Minister of Justice 1985–. *Address:* Ministry of Justice, P.O.B. 6040, Amman, Jordan. *Telephone:* 663101.

SHAKED, Shaul, PH.D.; Israeli professor of Iranian studies and comparative religion; b. 8 Feb. 1933, Debrecen, Hungary; m. Miriam Schächter 1960; one s. two d.; ed. Hebrew Univ. Jerusalem and S.O.A.S., Univ. of London; Asst. lecturer, SOAS 1964–65; lecturer, SOAS 1964–65; lecturer, Assoc. Prof., now Prof. Hebrew Univ. Jerusalem 1965–, Chair. Dept. of

Indian, Iranian and Armenian Studies 1971-72, 1974-75, Chair. Dept. of Comparative Religion 1972-74, 1977-79; Chair. Ben Zvi Inst. for Study of Jewish Communities in the East 1975-79, Inst. of Asian and African Studies 1981-85; Fellow, Israel Acad. of Sciences and Humanities; Visiting Prof. Univ. of Calif. Berkeley 1969-70, Columbia and New York Univs. 1980-81, Univ. of Heidelberg 1987-88. *Publications include:* A tentative bilbliography of Geniza documents 1964, Amulets and Magic Bowls (with J. Naveh) 1985; articles and book chapters. *Address:* Institute of Asian and African Studies, The Hebrew University, Jerusalem 91905, Israel (Office). *Telephone:* (02) 8836575 (Office); (02) 416005 (Home).

SHAKER, Field Marshal Sharif Zaid ibn; Jordanian army officer and politician; b. 4 Sept. 1934, Amman; s. of Amir Shaker; m.; one s. one d.; ed. Vic. Coll., Alexandria, Sandhurst Mil. Coll., U.K., Long Armour Course and Staff Coll., Leavenworth, U.S.A.; Asst. Mil. Attache, Embassy, U.K. 1957-58; Commdr. 1st Infantry Regiment 1963; Asst. Chief of Staff for Operations 1970, Chief of Staff 1972; C.-in-C. Jordan Armed Forces 1976-88; Minister of State, Chief of the Royal Court, Adviser to King Hussein (q.v.) on Armed Forces Affairs 1988-89; Prime Minister of Jordan April 1989-; numerous decorations, including Order of the Star of Jordan (First Class). *Address:* Office of the Prime Minister, P.O. Box 80, 35216 Amman, Jordan. *Telephone:* 641211.

SHAKESPEARE, Frank; American diplomatist and fmr. radio and television executive; b. 9 April 1925, New York; s. of Frank J. Shakespeare Sr. and Frances Hughes Shakespeare; m. Deborah Ann Spaeth Shakespeare 1954; one s. two d.; ed. Holy Cross Coll., Worcester, Mass.; Liberty Mutual Insurance Co., Washington, D.C. 1947-49; Procter and Gamble Co. 1949-50; Radio Station WOR, New York 1950, CBS 1950; Gen. Man. WXIX-TV, Milwaukee, Wis. 1957-59; Vice-Pres. and Gen. Man. WCBS-TV, New York 1959-63; Vice-Pres and Asst. to Pres. CBS-TV Network 1963-65; Exec. Vice-Pres. CBS-TV Stations 1965-67; Pres. CBS Television Service Div. 1967-69; Dir. U.S. Information Agency 1969-73; Exec. Vice-Pres. Westinghouse Electric Co. 1973-75; Pres. RKO Gen. 1975-83, Vice-Chair. 1983-85; Chair. Bd. Radio Free Europe/Radio Liberty Inc. 1982-85; Amb. to Portugal 1985-86, to the Holy See 1986-; Young Man of Year, New York 1960. *Address:* American Embassy, The Holy See, APO New York 09794, U.S.A. *Telephone:* (396) 639-0558.

SHAKKAR, Karim Ebrahim al-, B.A.; Bahraini diplomatist; b. 23 Dec. 1945; m.; three d.; ed. Univ. of New Delhi; joined Ministry of Foreign Affairs 1970; mem. Perm. Mission to the UN, rising to rank of 1st Sec.. 1972-76; Apptd. Chief Foreign Affairs and Int. Org., Bahrain 1977; Consul-Gen. to Switzerland 1982; Non-Resident Amb. Extraordinary and Plenipotentiary to Fed. Repub. of Germany and Austria 1984-; Perm Rep. to the UN Office, Vienna 1982, Non-Resident Perm. Rep. 1984-; Perm Rep. to the UN Aug. 1987-. *Address:* Permanent Mission of Bahrain to the United Nations, 2 United Nations Plaza, 25th Floor, New York, N.Y. 10017, U.S.A. *Telephone:* (212) 223-6200.

SHALAYEV, Stepan Alekseevich; Soviet trade union official; b. 1929; ed. Moscow Tech. Inst. of Forestry; mem. CPSU 1954; dir. of various forest production works 1955-62; Chair. of Cen. Cttee. of Timber, Paper and Wood-Processing Industries Workers' Union 1963-68; Sec. of All-Union Cen. Council of Trade Unions 1968-80, Pres. 1982-; Deputy to U.S.S.R. Supreme Soviet 1979-; mem. Presidium of U.S.S.R. 1982-; U.S.S.R. Minister of Timber, Paper and Wood-Processing Industries 1980-82. *Address:* All-Union Central Council of Trade Unions, 117119 Moscow, Leninsky prospekt 42, U.S.S.R.

SHAMGAR, Meir; Israeli judge; b. 13 Aug. 1925, Danzig; s. of Eliezer Shamgar and Dina Shamgar; m. Gevla Shamgar 1955 (deceased); two s. one d.; ed. Balfour Coll. Tel Aviv, Hebrew Univ. Jerusalem, Govt. Law School and London Univ.; Mil. Advocate-Gen. 1961-68; Legal Adviser, Ministry of Defence April-Aug. 1968; Attorney-Gen. of Israel 1968-75; Justice, Supreme Court 1975, Deputy Chief Justice 1982, Pres. of Supreme Court (Chief Justice of Israel) 1983-; Dr. h.c. (Weizman Inst.). *Publications:* The Military Government of the Territories Administered by Israel 1967-80: The Legal Aspects 1982; numerous articles and essays in legal publs. *Address:* 6 Heshin Street, Jerusalem (Office); 12 Shachar Street, Jerusalem, Israel (Home). *Telephone:* 02-246644.

SHAMIR, Shimon, PH.D.; Israeli professor and diplomatist; b. 15 Dec. 1933, Romania; m. Daniela (née Levin) Shamir 1958; one s. two d.; ed. Hebrew Univ. of Jerusalem and Princeton Univ.; lecturer in Modern History, Hebrew Univ. of Jerusalem 1960-66; Prof. of Modern History, Tel Aviv Univ. 1966-; Dir. Shiloah Center 1966-73, Head Graduate School of History 1973-76; Kaplan Chair in the History of Egypt and Israel 1980-; Dir. Israeli Acad. Center, Cairo 1982-84; Amb. to Egypt 1988-. *Publications:* A Modern History of the Arabs in the Middle East, 1798-1918 1965, Egypt under Sadat: The Search for a New Orientation 1978, Self-Views in Historial Perspective in Egypt and Israel 1981, The Jews of Egypt: A Mediterranean Society in Modern Times 1987. *Address:* 6 Sharia ibn el-Malek, Cairo (Giza), Egypt (Office); 10 Agron Str., Jerusalem 94265, Israel (Home). *Telephone:* (02) 729329 (Office); 223994 (Home).

SHAMIR, Yitzhak; Israeli politician; b. (as Yitzhak Jazernicki) 15 Oct. 1915, Poland; m.; one s. one d.; ed. Hebrew Secondary School, Białystok, Warsaw Univ. and Hebrew Univ. of Jerusalem; mem. Irgun Zvai Leumi (Jewish Mil. Org.) 1937, then a founder and leader of Lohamei Herut

Yisrael (Stern Gang) 1940-41; arrested by British Mandatory Authority 1941, 1946 (exiled to Eritrea); given political asylum in France, returned to Israel 1948; retd. from political activity until 1955; Sr. post Civil Service 1955-65; Man. Dir. several business concerns 1965-; mem. Herut Movt. 1970-, Chair. Exec. Cttee. 1975-; mem. Knesset 1973-, Speaker 1977-80; Minister of Foreign Affairs 1980-83, Prime Minister of Israel 1983-84, Oct. 1986-; Deputy Prime Minister Sept. 1984-86, Minister of Foreign Affairs 1984-86; Acting Minister of the Interior 1987-88. *Address:* Office of the Prime Minister, Hakirya, Ruppin Street, Jerusalem, Israel.

SHAMSHIN, Vasily Alexandrovich; Soviet politician; b. 1926; ed. Moscow Electrotech. Inst. of Communication; from 1949 engineer, senior engineer, sr. research assoc., head of lab. at Research Inst. of U.S.S.R. Ministry of Communications; deputy head of Research Inst. for Academic Studies 1965-68; Deputy Minister of Communications of U.S.S.R. 1968-75, First Deputy Minister 1975-80, Minister 1980-; mem. of CPSU 1962-; alt. mem. of CPSU Cen. Cttee. 1981-86, mem. 1986-. *Address:* Ministry of Communications, ul. Gorkogo 7, Moscow, U.S.S.R. *Telephone:* (095) 229-69-66.

SHANKAR (Shankar Pillai, K.); Indian newspaper cartoonist; b. 31 July 1902, Kayamgulam, Kerala; s. of the late Narayana Pillai and of Mrs. Kochukunjamma; m. Thankam Shankar 1931; two. s. three d.; fmr. cartoonist for Hindustan Times, New Delhi; f. Indian News Chronicle, Delhi 1947; Founder and Ed. Shankar's Weekly 1948-; initiated Shankar's Int. Children's Art Competition 1949; f. Children's Book Trust 1957 of which he is now Exec. Trustee; f. Children's World 1968, now Chief Ed.; Dir. Int. Dolls Museum; Founder and Dir. Children's Library and Reading Room; Padma Shri (India) 1954, Padma Bhushan (India) 1966, Padma Vibhushan (India) 1976, Order of Smile (Poland) 1977, UN Assen. (Hamilton Branch) Award 1979, and has written more than 50 books for children. *Leisure interests:* reading, writing for children, bridge. *Address:* Children's Book Trust, Nehru House 4, B.S.Z Marg, New Delhi 110002 (Office); 9 Purana Kila Road, New Delhi 110001, India (Home). *Telephone:* 271921-5, 273568 (Office); 386306 (Home).

SHANKAR, Ramsewak; Suriname politician and economist; fmr. Agric. Minister; Pres. of Suriname Jan. 1988-. *Address:* Office of the President, Paramaribo, Suriname.

SHANKAR, Ravi; Indian sitar player and composer; b. 7 April 1920; pupil of Ustad Allauddin Khan 1938; m. Sukanya Rajan 1989; solo sitar player; fmr. Dir. of Music All-India Radio and founder of the Nat. Orchestra; Founder Kinnara School of Music, Bombay 1962, Kinnara School of Music, Los Angeles 1967; many recordings of traditional and experimental variety in India, U.K. and the U.S.A.; Concert tours in Europe, U.S.A. and the East; Visiting Lecturer Univ. of Calif. 1965; appeared in film, Raga 1974; elected to Rajya Sabha (Upper House) 1986; Fellow Sangeet Natak Akademi 1976; Silver Bear of Berlin; Award of Indian Nat. Acad. for Music, Dance and Drama 1962; award of Padma Bhushan 1967, Padma Vibushan 1981, Deshitotlam 1982, Int. Music Council UNESCO Award 1975. *Film Scores:* Pather Panchali, The Flute and the Arrow, Nava Rasa Ranga, Charly, Gandhi, etc. and many musical compositions including Concerto for Sitar No. 1 1971, No. 2 1981, Raga Jogeshwari 1981, Homage to Mahatma Gandhi 1981. *Publication:* My Music, My Life 1969, Rag Anurag (Bengali). *Address:* c/o Basil Douglas Artists' Management, 8 St. George's Terrace, London, NW1 8XJ, England.

SHANKARANAND, B., B.A., L.L.B.; Indian politician; b. 19 Oct. 1925, Chikodi, Belgaum District, Karnataka; s. of Buburao Shankaranand; m. Kamaladevi Shankaranand; two s. six d.; ed. Govt. Law Coll., Bombay and R.L. Law Coll., Belgaum; fmrly. associated with Republican Party of India and PSP; mem. Lok Sabha; Gen. Sec. Congress Party in Parl. 1969-71, mem. Exec. Cttee.; Deputy Minister, Dept. of Parl. Affairs, Govt. of India 1971-77; Minister of Educ., Health and Family Welfare 1980-85, of Health and Family Welfare Jan.-Sept. 1985, of Water Resources 1985-87, 1988-; of Law and Justice June 1988-; mem. numerous cttees.; Del. to UNCTAD 1968, UN Gen. Assembly 1969. *Address:* Ministry of Law and Justice, Shastri Bharan, Dr Rajendra Prasad Road, New Delhi 110 001, India. *Telephone:* (11) 384777.

SHANKARDASS, Raghuvansh Kumar Prithvinath, M.A., LL.M.; Indian lawyer; b. 9 June 1930, Nairobi, Kenya; s. of P. N. Shankardass and Pushpavati Shankardass; m. Ramma Handoo 1955; ed. Trinity Coll., Cambridge, Lincoln's Inn, London; Gen. Sec. Bar Assen. of India 1975-85, Vice-Pres. 1985-; Asst. Sec.-Gen. Int. Bar Assen. 1980-82, Vice-Pres. 1984-86, Pres. 1986-88; Gen. Sec. Indian Law Foundation 1975-; Pres. Cambridge Univ. Majlis 1953. *Leisure interests:* golf, badminton, music, reading, travel. *Address:* B-12 Maharani Bag, New Delhi-110 065 (Home); 87 Lawyer's Chambers, Supreme Court of India, New Delhi-110 001, India, (Office). *Telephone:* 6830636 (Home); 383703 (Office).

SHANKER, P. Shiv, B.A., LL.B.; Indian lawyer and politician; b. 10 Aug. 1929, Mamidi Palli, Hyderabad, A.P.; m.; two s. one d.; ed. City Coll., Hyderabad and Hindu Coll., Amritsar; began legal practice 1952; Sec. Hyderabad City Civil Court Bar Assen. 1952-61; mem. Bar Council of Andhra Pradesh 1965; prin. govt. pleader, High Court of Andhra Pradesh 1972, additional judge 1974-75; latterly practiced as advocate of Supreme Court; mem. Lok Sabha 1979-84; Minister of Petroleum, Energy and Coal

1982–84, of Commerce 1986–87, of Planning, Programme Implementation, and Law and Justice 1987–88, of Planning and Programme Implementation Feb.–June 1988, of Human Resources Devt. June 1988–. *Address:* Ministry of Human Resources Devt., Shastri Bhavan, New Delhi 110 001, India. *Telephone:* (11) 381298.

SHANNON, Claude Elwood, PH.D.; American applied mathematician; b. 30 April 1916; s. of Claude Elwood and Mabel Catherine Wolf; m. Mary Elizabeth Moore 1949; two s. one d.; ed. Univ. of Michigan and M.I.T.; Research mathematician Bell Telephone Laboratories 1941–56, Consultant 1957–72; Visiting Prof. of Communication Sciences M.I.T. 1956, Prof. of Communication Sciences and Math. 1957–58, Donner Prof. of Science 1958–78, Prof. Emer. 1978–; Fellow Center for Advanced Study in the Behavioral Sciences, Stanford, Calif. 1957–58, Inst. of Radio Engineers; Visiting Fellow, All Souls Coll., Oxford 1978; mem. N.A.S., American Acad. of Arts and Sciences, I.R.E., American Mathematical Soc.; Hon. D.Sc. (Oxford) 1978, (East Anglia) 1982; Alfred Noble Prize A.I.E.E., Morris Liebman Award I.R.E., Stuart Ballantine Medal, Franklin Soc., Research Corpn. Award, Harvey Prize, Technion, Haifa, Israel; Kyoto Prize 1985. *Publications:* Mathematical Theory of Communication 1949; numerous technical papers; Ed. (with J. McCarthy) Automata Studies 1956. *Address:* 5 Cambridge Street, Winchester, Mass. 01890, U.S.A.

SHANNON, James Augustine, A.B., M.D., PH.D.; American medical research administrator; b. 9 Aug. 1904, Hollis, N.Y.; s. of James A. Shannon and Anna Margison Shannon; m. Dr. Alice Waterhouse 1934; one s. one d.; ed. Coll. of Holy Cross, Worcester, Mass. and New York Univ. Coll. of Medicine and Graduate School; Asst. Prof. of Physiology, New York Univ. 1935–41, Asst. Prof. of Medicine 1941–42, Assoc. Prof. of Medicine 1942–46; Consulting Physician N.Y. hospitals 1938–44; Dir. Squibb Inst. for Medical Research, New Brunswick, N.J. 1946–49; Chair. Malaria Study Section, Nat. Insts. of Health, Bethesda, Md. 1946–47, Assoc. Dir. Nat. Heart Inst. 1949–52, Assoc. Dir. Nat. Inst. of Health 1952–55, Dir. 1955–68; Special Consultant to Surgeon-Gen., U.S. Public Health Service 1946–49; mem. WHO Advisory Comm. on Medical Research 1959–63; Consultant, President's Science Advisory Comm. 1959–65, Advisory Comm. on Research to AID 1963–68, PAHO Advisory Comm. on Medical Research 1962–68; Prof. Biomedical Sciences Rockefeller Univ. 1969–75, Adjunct Prof. 1975–; Scholar in Human Biology Elinor Roosevelt Cancer Inst. Univ. of Colo. 1977–; mem. N.A.S. 1965–, Philosophical Soc. 1965–, American Acad. of Arts and Sciences 1965–, A.A.A.S., American Physiological Soc., American Soc. of Clinical Investigation; special adviser to Pres. Nat. Acad. Sciences 1968–70; Founder-mem. Nat. Inst. of Medicine 1970, now Sr. mem.; Presidential Medal for Merit 1948, N.A.S. Public Welfare Medal 1962, Rockefeller Public Service Award 1964, Presidential Distinguished Fed. Civilian Service Award 1966, Nat. Medal for Science 1966, Distinguished Achievement Award, Univ. of Oregon 1981, KOBER Medal, American Assen. of Physicians 1982, Fahray Medal, Franklin Inst. 1986, Centennial Award, American Assen. of Anatomists 1987; numerous hon. degrees from U.S. and foreign insts.; Chair. and mem. of numerous cttees. of Nat. Research Council. *Leisure interests:* gardening, cabinet making, electronics. *Address:* Woodcreek Apt. 1305, 3280 S.W. 170th Avenue, Beaverton, Ore. 97006, U.S.A.

SHANTARAM, V(ankudre); Indian film director, producer and actor; b. 18 Nov. 1901; ed. Kolhapur High School; worked in film industry 1920–; Founder mem. Prabhat Film Co., Poona; fmr. Chief Producer Govt. of India Films Div., mem. Censor Bd., Film Advisory Bd., Film Enquiry Cttee.; f. V. Shantaram Motion Picture Scientific Research and Cultural Foundation for devt. of film industry, for making awards, etc.; has directed and produced over 60 films 1926–, including King of Ayodhya, Chandrasena, Duniya-na-mane, Shakuntala (first Indian film released in U.S.A.), Ramjoshi, Amar Bhoopali, Jhanak Jhanak Payal Baaje and Do Ankhen Barah Haath; 11 awards including Berlin Gold Bear, Int. Catholic Award and Hollywood Foreign Press Award; Dr. h.c. (Nagpur). *Address:* Rajkamal Kalamandir Private Ltd., Parel, Bombay 12, India.

SHAO DADI: Chinese artist; b. 16 Jan. 1938, Beijing; s. of Shao Wen-Gang and Song Jun-Mei; m. Jiang Ruizhen 1968; one s. one d.; ed. Middle School attached to Cen. Art Inst., teacher training, Dept. of History of Arts and Crafts at Cen. Inst. of Arts and Crafts; Lecturer, Beijing Arts and Crafts School; mem. Beijing Branch, Chinese Assen. of Artists, Beijing Inst. of Arts and Crafts. *Works include:* Portrait of Characters (sketch), Comers from the North of Shaanxi Province (oil painting), Scenery Sketch of Xinjiang Uygur Autonomous Region, Bronze Decorative Patterns, Electrical Appliance for Family Use (book jacket design). *Publications:* A Collection of Anatomical Pictures for Artistic Use, Handbook of Literature and Art (contrib.), Picture-story Book, Beautification and Ornamentation of Environment 1987, Gouache and Watercolour Painting (textbook for arts and crafts schools in China) 1987. *Leisure interests:* literature, mountaineering, music. *Address:* Beijing Arts and Crafts School, Northern Area, He Ping Li District, Beijing, People's Republic of China.

SHAO YANXIANG: Chinese poet; b. 1933, Beijing; attached to Radio Beijing as editor and corresp. 1949. *Poems include:* China's Highway Call for More Cars, If Life Begins Anew, Silent Banana Tree, All That Time, Eyes, My Eyes. *Publications:* In Praise of Beijing, To My Comrades. *Address:* People's Republic of China.

SHAPAR, Howard Kamber, B.A., J.D.; American international official; b. 6 Nov. 1923, Boston, Mass.; m. Henriette Albertine Emilie von Gerrevink 1977; three c.; ed. Amherst Coll., Yale Univ.; Chief Counsel U.S. Atomic Energy Comm.'s Idaho Operations Office 1956–62; Asst. Gen. Counsel for Licensing and Regulation, U.S. Atomic Energy Comm. 1962–76; Exec. Legal Dir. U.S. Nuclear Regulatory Comm. 1976–82; Dir.-Gen. OECD Nuclear Energy Agency, Paris 1982–88; Counsel to Shaw, Pittman, Potts and Trowbridge 1988–; Past Pres. Int. Nuclear Law Assen.; mem. Bars of State of New Mexico, Court of Appeals for Dist. of Columbia, Dist. of Columbia Bar Assen., U.S. Supreme Court; Distinguished Service Award, U.S. Nuclear Regulatory Comm. 1980; Presidential Award of Meritorious Exec. 1981. *Publications:* articles in legal journals and periodicals; papers on atomic energy law. *Address:* 2300 N. Street, N.W., Washington, D.C. 20037 (Office); 4610 Langdrum Lane, Chevy Chase, Md. 20815, U.S.A.

SHAPIRO, Ascher H(erman), S.B., SC.D.; American mechanical engineering educator and consultant; b. 20 May 1916, New York City; s. of Bernard Shapiro and Jennie (Kaplan) Shapiro; m. 1st Sylvia Helen Charm 1939, 2nd Regina Julia Lee 1961, 3rd Kathleen Larke Crawford 1985; one s. two d.; ed. Massachusetts Inst. of Technology; mem. Teaching Faculty M.I.T. 1938–, Ford Prof. of Eng. 1962–75, Chair. of Faculty 1964–65, Head of Dept. of Mechanical Eng. 1965–74, Inst. Prof. 1975–; Visiting Prof., Cambridge Univ. 1955–56; Founder and Chair. Nat. Cttee. for Fluid Mechanics Films 1962–; mem. U.S.A.F. Scientific Advisory Bd. 1964–66; Councillor, American Acad. of Arts and Sciences 1966–69; mem. Editorial Bd. Journal Applied Mech. 1955–56, Editorial Cttee. Annual Review of Fluid Mech. 1967–71, Editorial Bd. M.I.T. Press 1977–, Chair. 1982–87; Consultant to Govt. and Industry in propulsion, compressors and turbines, fluid dynamics; Patentee: fluid metering equipment, combustion chamber, propulsion apparatus and gas turbines, magnetic disc storage devices, vacuum pump, low density wind tunnels, recipe-conversion calculators; mem. Bd. of Govs., Israel Inst. of Tech.; Fellow, American Acad. of Arts and Sciences, A.S.M.E., A.I.A.A.; mem. N.A.S., Nat. Acad. of Eng.; Dr Sc. h.c. (Salford, U.K.) 1978, (Technion-Israel Inst. of Tech.) 1985; Naval Ordnance Devt. Award 1945, Joint Certificate for Outstanding Contribution, War and Navy Depts. 1947, Richards Memorial Award of A.S.M.E. 1960, Worcester Reed Warner Medal of A.S.M.E. 1965, Lamme Medal of American Soc. for Eng. Educ. 1977, Townsend Harris Medal (Coll. of the City of New York) 1978; Fluids Eng. Award (A.S.M.E.) 1981, J. P. Den Hartog Distinguished Educator Award of M.I.T. 1984. *Publications:* The Dynamics and Thermodynamics of Compressible Fluid Flow Vol. I 1953, Vol. II 1954, Physical Measurements in Gas Dynamics and Combustion (Contrib. to) 1954, Shape and Flow: The Fluid Dynamics of Drag 1961, Handbook of Fluid Dynamics (Contrib. to) 1961; and numerous tech. articles in fields of thermodynamics, propulsion, gas dynamics, fluid mechanics, educational films (The Fluid Dynamics of Drag 1958, Vorticity 1961, Pressure Fields and Fluid Acceleration 1964), biomedical engineering; 39 videotape lecture series, Fluid Dynamics (with text notes) 1984. *Address:* Mechanical Engineering Department, Massachusetts Institute of Technology, 77 Massachusetts Avenue, Cambridge, Mass. 02139; 111 Perkins Street, Jamaica Plain, Mass. 02174, U.S.A. (Home). *Telephone:* (617) 253-2009 (Office); (617) 522-4418 (Home).

SHAPIRO, Eli, PH.D.; American economist and business consultant; b. 13 June 1916, New York; s. of Samuel Shapiro and Pauline Kushel Shapiro; m. Beatrice Ferbend 1946; one s. one d.; ed. Brooklyn Coll., Columbia Univ.; Prof. of Finance, Univ. of Chicago 1946–51; Prof. of Finance and Assoc. Dean M.I.T. 1952–61; Sylvan C. Coleman Prof. of Financial Man., Harvard Univ. 1962–70; Alfred P. Sloan Prof. of Man. M.I.T. 1976–84, Emer. 1984–; Dir. Norlin Corpn. 1966–83, Dexter Corpn. 1976–84, REECE Corpn. 1986–; Commonwealth Mortgage Corpn. 1986–; Dir. and Chair. Finance Cttee., The Travelers Corpn. 1971–76, Vice-Chair. The Travelers Corpn. 1976–78, Dir. 1978–83; Chair. Bd. Fed. Home Loan Bank of Boston 1978–; Pres. Nat. Bureau of Econ. Research 1982–84; Trustee, Wells Fargo Mortgage and Equity Trust 1981–, Putnam Funds 1983–. *Publications:* Personal Finance Industry and its Credit Standards (with others) 1939, Money and Banking (with Steiner) 1941, Development of Wisconsin Credit Union Movement 1947, Money and Banking (with Steiner and Solomon) 1958, Corporate Sources and Uses of Funds (with Meiselman) 1963, Money and Banking (with Solomon and White) 1968, The Role of Private Placements in Corporate Finance (with Wolf) 1972, Capital for Productivity and Growth (Ed. with White) 1977. *Address:* Massachusetts Institute of Technology, Cambridge, Mass. 02139; 180 Beacon Street, Boston, Mass. 02116, U.S.A. (Home).

SHAPIRO, Harry L(ionel), A.B., A.M., PH.D.; American anthropologist; b. 19 March 1902, Boston, Mass.: s. of Jacob Shapiro and Rose Clemens Shapiro; m. Janice Sandler Shapiro 1938 (died 1962); two s. one d.; ed. Harvard Univ.; Tutor, Harvard Univ. 1925–26; Asst. Curator, American Museum of Natural History 1926–31, Assoc. Curator 1931–42, Chair. of Dept. of Anthropology and Curator 1942–70, Curator Emer. 1970; Research Prof., Hawaii 1930–35; Prof., Columbia Univ., New York City 1938–73; Scientific Resident Lehman Coll. New York 1979–; Prof., Univ. of Pittsburgh 1970; Assoc., Bishop Museum, Honolulu; mem. Bd. of Dirs. Louise Wise Services 1958–; Sec. American Soc. of Physical Anthropology 1935–39, Vice-Pres. 1941–42; Pres. American Anthropological Assen. 1948, American Ethnological Soc. 1942–43, American Eugenics Soc. 1956–63; Dir. Louise Wise Services 1985–; Fellow, N.A.S., American Acad. of Arts and Sciences;

mem. Social Science Research Council, American Eugenics Soc.; Hon. mem. Die Anthropologische Gesellschaft, Vienna; Theodore Roosevelt Distinguished Service Medal 1964; New York Acad. of Sciences Award for Scientific Achievement 1977; Forensic Anthropology Award, American Acad. of Forensic Sciences 1983. *Publications:* Heritage of the Bounty 1936, Migration and Environment 1939, Aspects of Culture 1956, Man, Culture and Society (Ed.) 1956, The Jewish People 1960, Peking Man 1975. *Leisure interests:* music, literature, gardening. *Address:* American Museum of Natural History, Central Park West at 79th Street, New York, N.Y. 10024; 26 East 91st Street, New York, N.Y., U.S.A. (Home).

SHAPIRO, Irving S., LL.B.; American lawyer and business executive; b. 15 July 1916, Minneapolis, Minn.; s. of Samuel and Frieda Shapiro; m. Charlotte Farsht 1942; one s. one d.; ed. Univ. of Minnesota; with U.S. Office of Price Admin. 1942–43; U.S. Justice Dept. 1943–51; E. I. du Pont de Nemours & Co. 1951–81, Legal Dept. 1951–65, Asst. Gen. Counsel 1965, Vice-Pres., Dir., mem. Exec. Cttee. 1970, Sr. Vice-Pres. 1972, Vice-Chair. Bd. of Dirs. 1973–74, Chair., C.E.O. 1974–81; Dir. Continental American Co., Hospital Corp. of America; Sr. Partner, Skadden, Arps, Slate, Meagher and Flom 1981–. *Address:* Skadden, Arps, Slate, Meagher and Flom, 1 Rodney Square, P.O. Box 636, Wilmington, Del. 19899, U.S.A. *Telephone:* (302) 651-3000.

SHAPIRO, Irwin I., PH.D.; American physicist; b. 29 Oct. 1929, New York; s. of Esther Feinberg and Samuel Shapiro; m. Marian Helen Kaplun 1959; one s. one d.; ed. Cornell and Harvard Univs.; mem. staff., M.I.T. Lincoln Lab. 1954–70, Prof. of Geophysics and Physics 1967–80; Redman Lecturer, McMaster Univ. 1969; Sherman Fairchild Distinguished Scholar, Calif. Inst. of Tech. 1974; Schlumberger Prof., M.I.T. 1980–86, Prof. Emer. 1986–; Sr. Scientist Smithsonian Astrophysical Observatory 1982–; Paine Prof. of Practical Astronomy and Prof. of Physics, Harvard Univ. 1982–; Dir. Harvard-Smithsonian Center for Astrophysics 1983–; John C. Lindsay Lecturer, NASA Goddard Space Flight Center 1986; current research is on radio and radar techniques, applications to astrometry, astrophysics, geophysics, planetary physics and tests of theories of gravitation; mem. Editorial Bd. Celestial Mechanics 1969–75, Annals of Physics 1977–82; Assoc. Ed. Icarus 1969–75; Fellow A.A.A.S., American Geophysical Union, American Physical Soc.; mem. Int. Astronomical Union, N.A.S.; mem. Radio Science Teams, Mariner Venus-Mercury, Viking, and Pioneer Venus Missions 1970–79, Space Science Bd. (N.A.S.) 1977–82, NSF Astronomy Advisory Cttee. 1983–86, Task Group on Astronomy and Astrophysics of Nat. Research Council Space Science Bd. Study "Major Directions for Space Science: 1995–2015" 1984–86, Tech. Oversight Cttee. of Nat. Earth Orientation Service 1986–; Albert A. Michelson Medal of Franklin Inst. 1975, Benjamin Apthorp Gould Prize of N.A.S. 1979, John Simon Guggenheim Fellowship 1982, New York Acad. of Sciences Award in Physical and Math. Sciences 1982, Dannie Heineman Award of American Astronomical Soc. 1983. *Publications:* Prediction of Ballistic Missile Trajectories from Radar Observations 1958; Ed. of trans. of Mathematical Foundations of Quantum Statistics (Khinchin) 1960; numerous scientific articles and tech. reports. *Address:* 60 Garden Street, Cambridge, Mass. 02138 (Office); 17 Lantern Lane, Lexington, Mass. 02173, U.S.A. (Home). *Telephone:* (617) 495-7100; (617) 495-1490.

SHAPIRO, Joel, M.A.; American sculptor; b. 27 Sept. 1941, New York; s. of Dr. Joseph Shapiro and Dr. Anna Shapiro; m. Ellen Phelan; one d.; ed. N.Y. Univ.; teacher Princeton Univ. 1974–75, 1975–76, School of Visual Arts 1977–82; One-man exhbns. at Whitney Museum of Art, New York Stedelijk Museum, Amsterdam 1985, Hirshorn Museum and Sculpture Garden, Washington, D.C. 1987; Nat. Endowment for the Arts 1975; Brandeis Award 1984; Skowhegan Medal for Sculpture 1986. *Publications:* Chicago Museum of Contemporary Art 1976, The Whitney Museum of American Art 1982. *Address:* 280-90 Lafayette Street, Apt. 3D, New York, N.Y. 10012, U.S.A. *Telephone:* (212) 477-6958.

SHAPIRO, Karl Jay; American poet and fmr. university teacher; b. 10 Nov. 1913; s. of Joseph and Sara Shapiro; m. 1st Evalyn Katz 1945 (divorced 1967), one s. two d.; m. 2nd Teri Kovach 1967 (died 1982);m. 3rd Sophie Wilkins 1985; ed. Johns Hopkins Univ.; served with U.S. Army 1941–45; Consultant in poetry, Library of Congress 1946–47; Assoc. Prof. of Writing, Johns Hopkins Univ. 1947–50; Ed. Poetry 1950–55; Prof. of Writing, Univ. of Nebraska 1956–66; Prof. of English, Univ. of Ill. at Chicago Circle 1966–68; Prof. of English Univ. of Calif. at Davis 1955–56, 1968–85; Ed. Prairie Schooner 1956–63; Guggenheim Fellowship 1945–46, 1953–54; mem. Nat. Inst. of Arts and Letters, American Acad. of Arts and Sciences, PEN; Fellow in American Letters, Library of Congress; Hon. D.H.L. (Wayne State) 1960, Hon. D. Litt. (Bucknell) 1972; Jeanette S. Davis Prize 1942; Levinson Prize 1943; Contemporary Poetry Prize 1943; American Acad. of Arts and Letters Grant 1944; Pulitzer Prize (Poetry) 1945; Shelley Memorial Prize 1945; Bollingen Prize for Poetry 1969. *Publications:* Poems 1935, Person, Place and Thing 1942, The Place of Love 1942, V-Letter and Other Poems 1944, Essay on Rime 1945, Trial of a Poet 1947, Bibliography of Modern Prosody 1948, Poems 1942–53 1953, Beyond Criticism 1953, Poems of a Jew 1958; Ed. Newberry Library Bulletin 1953–, In Defence of Ignorance 1960, American Poetry Anthology 1960, The Bourgeois Poet 1964, A Prosody Handbook (with Robert Beum) 1965, To Abolish Children 1968, White-haired Lover 1968, Selected Poems

1968, Edsel (novel) 1971, The Poetry Wreck (selected essays) 1975, Adult Bookstore (poems) 1976, Collected Poems 1940–1978, Love and War, Art and God 1984, New and Selected Poems 1940–86, The Younger Son (autobiog., vol.1) 1988. *Leisure interest:* painting. *Address:* 904 Radcliffe Drive, Davis, Calif. 95616, U.S.A. *Telephone:* 666-7401 (Home).

SHAPLEIGH, Warren McKinney; American business executive; b. 27 Oct. 1920, St. Louis, Mo.; m. Jane Smith 1945; two d.; ed. St. Louis Country Day School, Yale Univ.; U.S.N. 1942–46; Vice-Pres. Buying & Merchandising, Shapleigh Hardware Co. 1946–56; Pres. Washington Land & Mining Co. 1956–63; Pres. Hipolite Co. 1956–59; Vice-Pres. Sterling Aluminium Products 1959–61; Man. Diversification Planning, Ralston Purina Co. 1961–63, Vice-Pres. Consumer Products Div. 1963–70, Dir. 1966–, Exec. Vice-Pres. 1968–72, Pres. Consumer Products Group 1970–72, Pres. 1972–79, Vice-Chair. 1978–; Dir. Brown Group Inc., St. Louis 1969–, St. Louis Union Trust Co. 1972–, First Nat. Bank, St. Louis 1972–, J. P. Morgan & Co. 1974–, Morgan Guaranty Trust 1974–, Union Pacific Corpn. 1983–, Union Pacific Railroad 1983–, and other cos.; mem. Grocery Mfrs. of America 1961–, Exec. Cttee. Cereal Inst. 1962–72, Bd. of Dirs., Pet Food Inst. 1962–72; mem. Bd. of Trustees, Washington Univ. 1966–, Yale Univ. Devt. Bd. 1971–, Govt. Research Inst., St. Louis 1972–, The Brookings Inst., Washington, D.C. 1972–, and many other civic orgs. *Leisure interests:* skiing, tennis, sailing, gardening. *Address:* 1310 Mason Road, St. Louis, Mo. 63131, U.S.A. (Home).

SHAPLEY, Lloyd Stowell, PH.D.; American professor of mathematics and economics; b. 2 June 1923, Cambridge, Mass.; s. of Harlow Shapley and Matha Betz Shapley; m. Marian Ludolph 1955; two s.; ed. Belmont Hill School, Phillips Exeter Acad., Harvard Coll. and Princeton Univ.; served in U.S. Army, working in meteorology and cryptanalysis 1943–45; research mathematician, Rand Corpn. 1948–49, 1954–81; Calif. Inst. of Tech. 1955–56; Hebrew Univ. of Jerusalem 1979–80; Catholic Univ. of Louvain, Belgium 1982; intermittent teaching, Rand Graduate Inst. 1970–; Prof. of Math. and Econs. U.C.L.A. 1981–; main research interest: theory of games; Fellow, Econometric Soc., American Acad. of Arts and Sciences; mem. N.A.S.; Hon. Ph.D. (Hebrew Univ. of Jerusalem) 1986; Bronze Star, U.S. Army 1943; Von Neumann Theory Prize, ORSA/TIMS 1981. *Publications:* Geometry of Moment Spaces (with S. Karlin) 1953, Values of Non-Atomic Games (with R. Aumann) 1974. *Leisure interest:* Kriegsspiel. *Address:* Department of Mathematics and Department of Economics, University of California at Los Angeles, Los Angeles, Calif., 90024, U.S.A. *Telephone:* (213) 825-4418.

SHARARI, Hisham; Jordanian civil servant and politician; b. 1939, Ma'an; ed. Univ. of Ankara, Turkey; fmr. Gen. Dir. Shoubok Agricultural Station, Mayor of Ma'an, Deputy Dir. Aqaba Railway Corpn., Dir. Agricultural Prosperity Org., Agricultural Devt. Org.; mem. Agricultural Corpn. Org., mem. Nat. Consultative Council 1982–84; Minister of Youth 1985–86. *Address:* c/o Ministry of Youth, P.O.B. 1794, Amman, Jordan.

SHARIF, Omar (Michael Chalhoub); Egyptian actor; b. 10 April 1932, Cairo; s. of Claire and Joseph Chalhoub; m. Faten Hamama 1955; one s.; ed. Victoria Coll., Cairo; Salesman, lumber-import firm; made first film The Blazing Sun 1953; starred in 24 Egyptian films and two French co-production films during following five years; commenced int. film career with Lawrence of Arabia; appeared in play The Sleeping Prince, England 1983. *Films include:* Lawrence of Arabia, The Fall of the Roman Empire, Behold a Pale Horse, Genghis Khan, The Yellow Rolls-Royce, Doctor Zhivago, Night of the Generals, Mackenna's Gold, Funny Girl, Cinderella-Italian Style, Mayerling, The Appointment, Che, The Last Valley, The Horsemen, The Burglars, The Island, The Tamarind Seed, Juggernaut, Funny Lady, Ace Up My Sleeve, Crime and Passion, Bloodline, Green Ice, Top Secret, Peter the Great (TV), The Possessed. *Publication:* The Eternal Male (autobiog.) 1978. *Leisure interests:* bridge and horse racing. *Address:* c/o William Morris Agency, 147 Wardour Street, London, W.1, England.

SHARIF-EMAMI, Jafar, G.C.M.G.; Iranian engineer and politician; b. 8 Sept. 1910, Teheran; s. of Haji Mohamed Hossein and Banu Kobra Sharif-Emami; m. Mrs. Eshrat Moazami 1946; one s. two d.; ed. Secondary Schoo. Teheran, German Cen. Railway School and Borǎs Tech. School, Sweden; joined Iranian State Railways 1931, Tech. Deputy Gen. Dir. 1942, Gen. Dir. 1950–51; Chair. and Man. Dir. Ind. Irrigation Corpn. 1946–50; Under-Sec. of State to Ministry of Roads and Communications, Minister of Roads and Communications 1950–51; mem. High Council, Plan Org. 1951–52, Man. Dir. and Chair. High Council Plan Org. 1953–54; Senator from Teheran 1955–57, 1963–78, Pres. of Senate 1963–78; Minister of Industry and Mines 1957–60; Prime Minister 1960–61, Aug-Nov 1978; Deputy Custodian Pahlavi's Foundation 1962–78; mem. Bd. of Trustees Queen Pahlavi's Foundation 1966–78; Chair. Industrial and Mining Devt. Bank 1963–78, Pres. Chamber of Industries and Mines 1962–67; Pres. Iranian Asscn. of World Federalists 1963–73; Pres. Iranian Engineers Asscn. 1966–78; Pres. Third Constituent Assembly 1967; Pres. of 22nd Int. Conf. of the Red Cross 1973; Pres. Int. Bankers Asscn. 1975; Dir. Red Lion and Sun 1963, Vice-Pres. 1963, Deputy Pres. 1966–78; mem. American Soc. of Civil Engineers 1946– (Fellow 1979), Bd. of Dirs. Royal Org. of Social Services 1962–78, Bd. of Trustees, Pahlavi Univ. 1962–78, Nat. Univ. Teheran

1962–78, Aria Mehr Tech. Univ., Teheran 1965–78; mem. of Bd. of Founders of Soc. for Preservation of Nat. Monuments 1966–78; Dr. h.c. (Seoul Univ.) 1978; Iranian decorations: Order of Homayoun (1st Grade), Order of Taj (1st Class) and eight others; foreign decorations incl. Grosses Kreuz Verdienstorden (Germany), Grand Croix, Légion d'honneur (France), Order of Rising Sun, 1st Class (Japan), Order of St. Michael and St. George (U.K.) and 23 others. *Leisure interests:* literature, philosophy, history.

SHARIR, Abraham; Israeli politician and lawyer; b. 1932, Tel Aviv; m.; four c.; ed. law faculty, Hebrew Univ., Jerusalem; mil. service with Israeli Air Force; mem. Ninth Knesset (Parl.) –1981, mem. Finance Cttee., Chair. Likud Faction; mem. Tenth Knesset; Minister of Tourism 1981, 1984–86, of Tourism and Justice 1986–88; mem. High Court of Labour Relations, of Govt. Cttee. on Pensions; Likud Party. *Address:* c/o Ministry of Tourism, P.O. Box 1018, Jerusalem, Israel.

SHARMA, Anant Prasad; Indian politician and trade unionist; b. 25 Dec. 1919, Gandarh Village, Bihar; s. of Shri Ram Naresh Sharma and Smt. Manrakhan Devi; m. Smt. Tara Devi; two s. four d.; ed. Bihar Nat. Coll.; active in Nat. Movt.; mem. Lok Sabha 1962, 1971–77, Rajya Sabha 1968–71, 1978–; Minister of State for Industry and Civil Supplies 1974–77; Minister of Shipping and Transport Jan.-Oct. 1980, of Tourism and Civil Aviation June–Oct. 1980; Minister for Communications 1982–83; Gov. of Punjab Feb.–Oct. 1983, of West Bengal 1983–84; Gen. Sec. Nat. Fed. of Indian Railwaymen 1949, Pres. 1969; Pres. Indian Nat. Trade Union Congress 1978; Vice Pres. ICFTU 1978; mem. Indian del. to UN 1970; rep. at ILO 1969; mem. of numerous other dels. to int. confs. etc.; mem. Congress (I). *Leisure activities:* trade union activities and reading literature on trade unionism especially Gandhian trade unionism. *Address:* c/o Rajya Sabha, New Delhi, India.

SHARMA, Arun Kumar, D.SC., F.N.A., F.A.SC., F.N.A.SC.; Indian botanist; b. 31 Dec. 1924, Calcutta; s. of late Charu Chandra Sharma and of Shovamoyee Sharma; m. Archana Mookerjea 1955; ed. Univ. of Calcutta; Research Scholar, Botanical Survey of India 1946–48; Asst. Lecturer, Univ. of Calcutta 1948–52, Lecturer 1952–62, Reader 1962–69, Prof. and Head, Dept. of Botany 1969–80, Programme Co-ordinator, Centre of Advanced Study, Dept. of Botany 1980–; Pres. Indian Nat. Science Acad. 1983–85, Golden Jubilee Prof. 1985–; Gen. Pres. Indian Science Congress Assen. 1981; Pres. Fed. of Asian Scientific Acads. and Socs. 1984–; Padma Bhusan and numerous other awards. *Publications:* Chromosome Techniques: Theory and Practice (with Archana Sharma) 1965; book chapters, articles in journals etc. *Address:* Centre of Advanced Study (Cell & Chromosome Research), Department of Botany, University of Calcutta, 35 Ballygunge Circular Road, Calcutta 700 019 (Office); Flat No. 2F2, 18/3 Gariahat Road, Calcutta, 700 019, India (Home). *Telephone:* 47-3681 (Office); 46-1802 (Home).

SHARMA, Krishna Dayal, M.A.; Indian diplomatist; b. 6 Sept. 1931, Pratapgarh; s. of Mr. Justice P. D. Sharma and Prakash Kumari Sharma; m. Veena Sharma 1962; two s.; with Ministry of External Affairs, New Delhi 1956–58; Third Sec. Embassy, Belgrade 1958–60; Under-Sec. Ministry of External Affairs 1960–63; First Sec. Embassy, Teheran 1963–66, Counsellor, Washington 1966–69; Dir. Ministry of External Affairs 1969–71; High Commr. in Mauritius 1971–74, in Tanzania 1974–78; Joint Sec. Ministry of External Affairs 1978–80; High Commr. in Australia 1980–82; Amb. to Pakistan 1982–84, to Spain 1985–. *Address:* c/o Ministry of Foreign Affairs, South Block, New Delhi 110 011, India.

SHARMA, Shanker Dayal, M.A., LL.M., PH.D.; Indian barrister and politician; b. 19 Aug. 1918; ed. Lucknow Univ., Cambridge Univ. and Lincoln's Inn; lawyer 1942–; mem. All India Congress Cttee. 1950–; Pres. Bhopal State Congress Cttee. 1950–52; Chief Minister of Bhopal 1952–56; mem. Cen. Advisory Bd. of Educ. 1952–64; mem. Consultative Cttees. on Legislation, Bhopal and Madhya Pradesh Legis. Assemblies 1952–64; Minister, Madhya Pradesh Govt. 1956–67; Gen. Sec. Indian Nat. Congress 1968–72; Pres. All India Congress Cttee. 1972–74; mem. Lok Sabha (Parl.) 1971–77; Minister of Communications 1974–77; fmr. Gov. of Andhra Pradesh –1985, Gov. of Punjab 1985–86; Vice-Pres. of India Sept. 1987–; served as Chair. and mem. of numerous parl. cttees.; suspended from Congress (I) Party 1986; Ed.-in-Chief Light and Learning, Ilm-au-Noor; Ed. Lucknow Law Journal; Hon. D.P.A. (London), LL.D. (Vikram and Bhopal Univs.) *Publication:* Congress Approach to International Affairs. *Leisure interests:* travel, reading, swimming. *Address:* 135/1 Professor's Colony, Bhopal, Madhya Pradesh, India.

SHAROEV, Ioakim Georgevich; Soviet theatre and film director; b. 19 Aug. 1930, Baku; s. of Georg Georgeevich Sharoev and Valentina Nikolaevna (née Rizkova) Sharoeva; m. Irene Nikolaevna Agafonova 1965; one s. one d.; ed. Lunacharsky State Inst. of Dramatic Art; Dir. of State Academic Bolshoi Theatre 1954–59; Artistic Dir. of Kremlin Theatre 1959–60; prin. dir. of All-Russian Visiting Concert Admin. and Moscow Variety Theatre 1960–64; artistic dir. of musical film org. Ekran 1969–73; teacher Lunacharsky Inst. of Theatre Studies, 1964–77, Prof. 1977–; Prin. Dir. of Moscow Stanislavsky-Nemirovich-Danchenko Musical Theatre 1982–; U.S.S.R People's Artist 1984. *Leisure interest:* collecting semi-precious stones.

Address: c/o State Institute of Theatre Art, Sobinovsky pezeulok 6, Moscow, U.S.S.R. *Telephone:* 297-7-417.

SHARON, Major-Gen. Ariel; Israeli army officer (retd.) and politician; b. 1928; m.; two s.; active in Hagana since early youth; Instructor, Jewish Police units 1947; Platoon Commdr. Alexandroni Brigade; Regimental Intelligence Officer 1948; Co. Commdr. 1949; Commdr. Brigade Reconnaissance Unit 1949–50; Intelligence Officer, Cen. Command and Northern Command 1951–52; studies at Hebrew Univ. 1952–53; in charge of Unit 101, on numerous reprisal operations until 1957, Commdr. Paratroopers Brigade, Sinai Campaign 1956; studies Staff Coll., Camberley, U.K. 1957–58; Training Commdr., Gen. Staff 1958; Commdr. Infantry School 1958–69; Commdr. Armoured Brigade 1962; Head of Staff, Northern Command 1964; Head, Training Dept. of Defence Forces 1966; Head Brigade Group during Six-Day War 1967; resigned from Army July 1973; recalled as Commdr. Cen. Section of Sinai Front during Yom Kippur War Oct. 1973, forged bridgehead across Suez Canal; with others formed Likud Front Sept. 1973; mem. Knesset (Parl.) 1973–74, 1977–; Adviser to Prime Minister 1975–77; Minister of Agric. in charge of Settlements 1977–81, of Defence 1981–83, without Portfolio 1983–84, of Trade and Industry Sept. 1984–. *Address:* c/o Knesset, Jerusalem, Israel.

SHARP, Margery, B.A.; British writer; m. Major G. L. Castle 1938; ed. London Univ. *Publications:* The Flowering Thorn, Four Gardens 1935, The Nutmeg Tree 1937 (play, U.S.A. 1940, England 1941), Cluny Brown 1944, Britannia Mews 1946, The Foolish Gentlewoman 1948 (play, England 1949), Lise Lillywhite 1951, The Gypsy in the Parlour 1954, The Eye of Love 1957, The Rescuers 1959, Something Light 1960, Martha in Paris 1962, Miss Bianca (for children) 1962, The Turret 1963, Martha, Eric and George 1964, The Sun in Scorpio 1965, Miss Bianca in the Salt Mines (for children) 1966, Lost at the Fair (for children) 1967, In Pious Memory 1968, Rosa 1969, Miss Bianca in the Orient (for children) 1970, Miss Bianca in the Antarctic (for children) 1971, The Innocents 1971, Miss Bianca and the Bridesmaid (for children) 1972, The Lost Chapel Picnic (short stories) 1973, The Faithful Servants 1975, Bernard the Brave (for children) 1976, Summer Visits 1977, Bernard into Battle (for children) 1978. *Address:* c/o William Heinemann Ltd., 10 Upper Grosvenor Street, London, W1X 9PA; 32 Crag Path, Aldeburgh, Suffolk, England.

SHARP, Phillip Allen, PH.D.; American scientist and professor of biology; b. 6 June 1944; s. of Joseph W. Sharp and Katherin A. Sharp; m. Ann H. Holcombe 1964; three d.; ed. Union Coll., Ky., Univ. of Illinois and California Inst. of Tech. and Cold Spring Harbor, New York; Research Asst., Dept. of Chem., Univ. of Ill. 1966–69; Postdoctoral Fellow, Lab. of Prof. Norman Davidson, Calif. Inst. of Tech. 1969–71; Cold Spring Harbor Lab. 1971–72, Sr. Research Investigator 1972–74; Assoc. Prof., Center for Cancer Research and Dept. of Biology, M.I.T. 1974–79, Prof. 1979–, Assoc. Dir. Center for Cancer Research 1982–85, Dir. 1985–; mem. N.A.S., American Acad. of Arts and Sciences; Howard Ricketts Award, Eli Lilly Award, N.A.S. U.S. Steel Foundation Award, Gen. Motors Research Foundation Alfred P. Sloan, Jr. Prize for Cancer Research, Gairdner Foundation Int.-Award, New York Acad. of Sciences Award in Biological and Medical Sciences, Louisa Gross Horwitz Prize, Albert Lasler Basic Medical Research Award. *Publications:* numerous papers in scientific journals. *Leisure interests:* family, reading, sports. *Address:* Center for Cancer Research, Room E17-529B, Massachusetts Institute of Technology, 77 Massachusetts Avenue, Cambridge, Mass. 02139, U.S.A. *Telephone:* (617) 253-6421.

SHARP, Robert Phillip, PH.D.; American geologist; b. 24 June 1911, Calif.; s. of Julian Hebner Sharp and Alice Darling; m. Jean Prescott Todd 1938; one s. one d. (both adopted); ed. Oxnard Union High School, Calif., California Inst. of Tech., Harvard Univ.; Asst. Prof., Univ. of Ill. 1938–43; Capt., U.S.A.A.F. 1943–46; Prof. of Univ. of Minn. 1946–47; Prof., Calif. Inst. of Tech. 1947–79, Robert P. Sharp Emer. Prof. of Geology 1979–, Chair. Div. of Geological Sciences 1952–68; mem. N.A.S.; Kirk Bryan Award, Penrose Medal, Geological Soc. of America, NASA Exceptional Scientific Achievement Medal. *Publications:* Living Ice: understanding glaciers and glaciation 1989, 100 papers on geomorphology, glaciers, glaciation, dunes and related subjects in scientific journals, and several books. *Leisure interests:* fly fishing, snorkelling, skiing. *Address:* Division of Geological and Planetary Sciences, California Institute of Technology, Pasadena, Calif. 91125; 1901 Gibraltar Road, Santa Barbara, Calif. 93105, U.S.A. (Home). *Telephone:* (818) 356-6124 (Office); (805) 962-6675 (Home).

SHARP, Hon. Mitchell (William), P.C., O.C., B.A.; Canadian government official; b. 11 May 1911, Winnipeg, Manitoba; s. of Thomas and Elizabeth (Little) Sharp; m 1st Daisy Boyd 1938 (deceased), one s.; m. 2nd Jeannette Dugal 1976; Director Econ. Policy Div. of Dept. of Finance 1947; M.P. 1963–78 (resigned); fmr. Deputy Minister of Trade and Commerce; fmr. Vice-Pres. Brazilian Traction Co.; Minister of Trade and Commerce 1963–65, of Finance 1965–68; Sec. of State for External Affairs 1968–74; Pres. of Privy Council; Leader of Govt. in House of Commons 1974–76; resigned as MP 1978; Commr. Northern Pipeline Agency 1978–88, Co. Chair. Task Force on Conflict of Interest 1983–84. *Address:* 3rd Floor, 50 O'Connor Street, Ottawa, Ont., K1P 6L2, Canada.

SHARPE, Kevin Michael, M.A., D.PHIL., F.R.HIST.S.; British historian; b. 26 Jan. 1949, Kent; s. of Thomas H. Sharpe and Nell D. Sharpe; unmarried;

ed. Sir Joseph Williamson's Mathematical School, Rochester and St. Catherine's Coll. Oxford; Sr. Scholar, St. Catherine's Coll. Oxford 1971–74; Fellow, Oriel Coll. Oxford 1974–78; lecturer, Christ Church, Oxford 1976–78; lecturer in Early Modern History, Univ. of Southampton 1978–; Visiting Fellow, Inst. for Advanced Study, Princeton 1981, Huntington Library, San Marino, Calif. 1982; Visiting Prof. Stanford Univ. Humanities Center 1985–86; Wolfson Award 1980; Fulbright Fellow 1981; Royal Historical Soc. Whitfield Prize 1987. *Publications:* Faction and Parliament 1978, Sir Robert Cotton: History and Politics in Early Modern England 1979, Criticism and Complaint: The Politics of Literature in the England of Charles I 1987, Politics of Discourse 1987; articles and reviews in The Sunday Times, Times Literary Supplement, Spectator, History Today and other journals. *Leisure interests:* cycling, travel, conversation. *Address:* Department of History, University of Southampton, SO9 5NH (Office); 97 Livingstone Road, Portswood, Southampton, SO2 1DG, England. *Telephone:* 0703 559122 (Office); 0703 553303 (Home).

SHARPE, Tom (Thomas Ridley), M.A. (CANTAB.); British novelist; b. 30 March 1928, London; s. of Rev. George Coverdale Sharpe and Grace Egerton Sharpe; m. Nancy Anne Cooper 1969; three d.; ed. Lancing Coll., Pembroke Coll., Univ. of Cambridge; Social Worker 1952; Teacher 1952–56; Photographer 1956–61; Lecturer in History at Cambridge Coll. of Arts and Tech. 1963–71; full-time novelist 1971–. *Publications:* Riotous Assembly 1971, Indecent Exposure 1973, Porterhouse Blue 1974, Blott on the Landscape 1975, Wilt 1976, The Great Pursuit 1977, The Throwback 1978, The Wilt Alternative 1979, Ancestral Vices 1980, Vintage Stuff 1982, Wilt on High 1984. *Leisure interests:* photography, gardening. *Address:* c/o Richard Scott Simon Ltd., 43 Doughty Street, London, WC1N 2LF, England.

SHATKIN, Aaron Jeffrey, PH.D.; American scientist; b. 18 July 1934, R.I.; s. of Morris and Doris Shatkin; m. Joan Arlene Lynch 1957; one s.; ed. Bowdoin Coll. and Rockefeller Univ.; Research Chemist Nat. Inst. of Health, Bethesda, Md. 1961–68; Visiting Scientist Salk Inst., La Jolla, Calif. 1968–69; mem. Roche Inst. of Molecular Biology, Nutley, N.J. 1968–, Head Lab. of Molecular Biology 1977–83, Head Dept. of Cell Biology 1983–86; Adjunct Prof. Rockefeller Univ. 1978–, N.J. Univ. of Medicine 1981–, Princeton Univ. 1984–; Dir. and Prof., N. J. Center for Advanced Biotechnology and Medicine 1986–; Visiting Prof. Georgetown Univ. Medical School, Washington, D.C. 1968; Instructor Cold Spring Harbor Lab. 1972, 1973, 1974, Univ. of Puerto Rico 1978, 1980; Ed.-in-Chief Molecular and Cellular Biology 1980–; mem. N.A.S. 1981–; Hon. D.Sc. (Bowdoin Coll.) 1979; U.S. Steel Award in Molecular Biolology 1977. *Publications:* more than 150 publs. in scientific journals including original reports and review articles. *Leisure interests:* travel, birds, running. *Address:* New Jersey Center for Advanced Biotechnology and Medicine, c/o Waksman Institute, P.O. Box 759, Piscataway, N.J. 08854 (Office); 1381 Rahway Road, Scotch Plains, N.J. 07060, U.S.A. (Home). *Telephone:* (201) 932-3143/3144 (Office).

SHATLA, Mohamed Nagui, M.A., PH.D.; Egyptian politician; b. Dec. 1939; m.; three c.; ed. Cairo and Louisiana Univs.; fmr. mem. teaching staff, High Agricultural Inst., Shebin-el-Kom; Asst. teacher, Faculty of Agric. Assiut Univ.; Vice-Dean, Faculty of Agric., Shebin-el-Kom 1975–80; Vice-Rector, Menufia Univ. 1980; Asst. Sec.-Gen. Nat. Democratic Party 1979; mem. Shura Council; Gov. of Kafr-el-Sheikh 1981; Minister of State for Supply 1982; Minister of Supply and Internal Commerce 1985–86.

SHATROV (Marshak), Mikhail Filippovich; Soviet dramatist and script-writer; b. 3 March 1932; ed. Moscow Mining Inst.; began writing plays in 1955; U.S.S.R. State Prize 1983. *Plays include:* In the Name of Lenin 1966, The Sixth of July 1968, Trust 1976, Przevalsky's Horse 1976, The Dictatorship of Conscience 1986, The Peace of Brest Litovsk 1982; Scripts for films include: Two Lines of Tiny Handwriting 1981, Tehran -43 1981. *Address:* U.S.S.R. Union of Writers, ul. Vorovskogo 52, Moscow, U.S.S.R.

SHATTOCK, Francis Mario Mackenzie, F.F.C.M., M.P.H., D.T.P.H., M.R.C.G.P., M.B., B.S., M.R.C.S., L.R.C.P.; British physician; b. 22 June 1922, London; s. of Clement Shattock and Fede Shattock; m. Julie I. Fuery 1957; two s. one d.; ed. Beaumont Coll., Windsor, St. Bartholomew's Hosp., London, London School of Hygiene and Tropical Medicine and Univ. of Calif. Berkeley; various surgical appts. London and Oxford 1949–59; Surgeon and Physician-in-charge, Wingfoot Hosp., Goodyear Sumatra Plantations Co. 1959–64, Kilembe Mines Hosp. Uganda 1964–66; Medical Officer, Pusan City, Save the Children Fund, S. Korea 1966–69; Maternal and Child Health Specialist, Ministry of Health, Zambia 1969–72; Sr. Lecturer in Int. Community Health, Liverpool School of Tropical Medicine 1973–82, Head, Dept. of Int. Community Health 1982–84; Assoc. Prof. Family and Community Medicine, King Faisal Univ. Dammam, Saudi Arabia 1984–87; Visiting Assoc. Prof. of Public Health, Boston Univ. 1984–; Prof. and Head, Dept. of Social Medicine, Univ. of Zambia 1987–. *Publications:* author and co-author of ten books; various papers on maternal and child health, community health and use of paraprofessionals. *Leisure interests:* photography, travel. *Address:* School of Medicine, University of Zambia, Department of Community Health, P.O. Box 50110, Lusaka, Zambia.

SHAUB, Harold A.; American business executive; b. 28 Nov. 1915, Lancaster County, Pa.; s. of Arthur and Clara Cramer Shaub; m. Eileen Bair 1939; one s. two d.; ed. Drexel Univ.; Asst. Plant Man., Campbell Soup Co., Chicago 1956–57; Vice-Pres.-Gen. Man., Campbell Soup Co., Ltd., Toronto 1957–60; Pres. 1960–66; Sr. Vice-Pres. Campbell Soup Co., Camden, N.J. 1968–70, Exec. Vice-Pres. and Dir. 1970–72, Pres. and C.E.O. 1972–80; Pres. Pepperidge Farm Inc., Norwalk, Conn. 1966–68; Chair. Penjerdel Corpn.; Bd. of Trustees Drexel Univ.; Regional Vice-Pres. and Dir. Nat. Assen. of Mfrs.; Dir. Exxon Corpn., R. H. Macy & Co. Inc. *Leisure interests:* golf, curling, fishing, hunting. *Address:* 1250 Country Club Road, Gladwyne, Pa. 19035, U.S.A. (Home).

SHAURO, Vasiliy Filimonovich; Soviet official; b. 1912, Byelorussia; ed. Mogilev Pedagogical Inst. and Party Higher School of Cen. Cttee. of CPSU; teacher and dir. of a secondary school in Vitebsk Dist. 1930–36, 1937–40; served in Soviet Army 1936–37; various posts in Cen. Cttee. of Byelorussian CP 1942–48; Sec. Minsk Dist. Cttee. of Byelorussian CP 1948–56, First Sec. 1956–60; mem. Supreme Soviet of Byelorussian S.S.R. 1955–61, 1963–67; Deputy to Budget Comm. of U.S.S.R. 1958–62, mem. 1962–66; mem., then Sec. Cen. Cttee. of Byelorussian CP 1960–65; Chair. Supreme Soviet of Byelorussian S.S.R. 1963–65; cand. mem. Cen. Cttee. of CPSU 1966–80, mem. 1980–; Head of Cultural Dept. of Cen. Cttee. of CPSU 1966–; Order of Red Banner. *Address:* The Kremlin, Moscow, U.S.S.R.

SHAW, Bernard Leslie, PH.D.; British professor of chemistry; b. 28 March 1930, Springhead, Yorks.; s. of Tom Shaw and Vera Shaw; m. Mary Elizabeth Neild 1951; two s.; ed. Hulme Grammar School, Oldham and Manchester Univ.; Sr. DSIR Fellow, Torry Research Station, Aberdeen 1953–55; Research Scientist, ICI Ltd. 1956–61; Lecturer, School of Chem., Univ. of Leeds 1962–65, Reader 1965–71, Prof. 1971–; Tilden Lecturer, Chemical Soc. 1975; Visiting Prof. Univ. of Western Ont., Carnegie Mellon Univ. 1969, ANU 1983, Univ. of Auckland 1986; mem. Science and Eng. Research Council Chemistry Cttee. 1975–78, 1981–84; Chemical Soc. Award in Transition Metal Chem. 1975. *Publications:* Inorganic Hydrides, Organo-Transition Metal Compounds and Related Aspects of Homogeneous Catalysis and about 300 research papers. *Leisure interests:* walking, pottery, gardening, tennis. *Address:* School of Chemistry, University of Leeds, Leeds, LS2 9JT (Office); 14 Monkbridge Road, Leeds, LS6 4DX, England (Home). *Telephone:* (0532) 431751 (Office); (0532) 755895 (Home).

SHAW, Neil McGowan; Canadian business executive; b. 31 May 1929, Montreal; s. of Harold LeRoy Shaw and Fabiola Shaw (née McGowan); m. 1st Frances Audrey Robinson 1952 (divorced 1980), two s. three d.; m. 2nd Elizabeth Fern Mudge 1985; ed. Knowlton High School, Lower Canada Coll.; Trust Officer Crown Trust Co. 1947–54; with Canada Dominion Sugar (now Redpath Industries) 1954–, Merchandising Man. 1954–66, Vice-Pres. 1967–72, Pres. 1972–80, Vice-Chair. 1981–; Group Man. Dir. Tate and Lyle PLC, England 1980–, Chair. and C.E.O. 1986–; Dir. Tunnel Refineries Ltd., England, United Biscuits (Holdings) PLC 1988–; Chair. Tate and Lyle Holdings Ltd., England; Chair. Tate and Lyle Industries Ltd., England, Tate and Lyle Inc., New York; Dir. G. R. Amylum N.V., Brussels, Texaco Canada Inc., Toronto, Americare Corpn. Alcantara, Lisbon, Smiths Industries PLC, England 1986–, Canadian Imperial Bank of Commerce, Toronto 1986–, World Sugar Research Org., Scottish and Newcastle PLC 1986; Vice-Chair. A. E. Staley Manufacturing Co., Ill. 1988; Gov. Montreal Gen. Hospital, Reddy Memorial Hospital; mem. Advisory Council of Youth Enterprise School 1986–, of London Enterprise Agency 1986–. *Leisure interests:* sailing, skiing, golf. *Address:* Fairfield, London Road, Sunninghill, Ascot, Berks. SL5 0PN, England *Telephone:* 01-626 6525.

SHAW YU-MING, PH.D.; Chinese public servant and academic; b. 1938, Harbin; m. Shirley Shiow-jyu Lu; one s. one d.; ed. Nat. Chengchi Univ., Tufts Univ. and Univ. of Chicago, U.S.A.; Asst. Prof. of History, Newberry Coll., S.C. 1967–68, 1972–73; lecturer in History, Univ. of Notre Dame, Ind. 1973–82; held various research posts in Asian studies in U.S.A.; Dir. Asia and World Inst., Taiwan 1983–84; Dean, Graduate School of Int. Law and Diplomacy, Nat. Chengchi Univ. 1984–, Dir. Inst. of Int. Relations 1984–; Dir.-Gen. Govt. Information Office and Govt. spokesman 1987–; awards from American Council of Learned Socs., Asia Foundation, Inst. of Chinese Culture, U.S.A. and others. *Publications include:* China and Christianity 1979, Problems in Twentieth Century Chinese Christianity 1980, Twentieth Century Sino-American Relations 1980, History and Politics in Modern China 1982, International Politics and China's Future 1987. *Address:* Government Information Office, 3, Sec.1, Chung Hsiao E. Road, Taipei, Taiwan.

SHAWA, Lol Mohammed; Chad politician and fmr. resistance leader; b. 15 June 1939, Mao (Kanem); s. of Mohammed Shawa and Amy Shawa; m. Fatimé Adouly Lol 1970; four s. two d.; ed. Int. Inst. of Public Admin. and Inst. for the Study of Int. Relations, Paris; Leader of Mouvement populaire pour la libération du Tchad (the Third Army) 1979; Prime Minister and Head of State April–Aug. 1979; studied in Paris 1979–82; Minister of Transport 1982–85. *Address:* B.P. 1104, N'Djamena, Chad. *Telephone:* 36.65.

SHAWCROSS, Baron (Life Peer), cr. 1959, of Friston; **Hartley William Shawcross,** Kt., P.C., G.B.E., Q.C., LL.D.; British jurist, politician and businessman; b. 4 Feb. 1902, Giessen, Germany; s. of John and Hilda Shawcross; m. Joan Winifred Mather (died 1974); two s. one d.; ed. Dulwich Coll. and abroad; called to Bar 1925; Sr. Law Lecturer Liverpool Univ. 1927–34;

SHA

Deputy Regional Commr. S.E. Region 1941; Regional Commr. N.W. Region 1942–45; Recorder of Salford 1941–45; Chair. Catering Wages Comm. 1943–45; Asst. Chair. E. Sussex Quarter Sessions 1941; Labour M.P. for St. Helens 1945–58; Attorney-Gen. 1945–51; Pres. Bd. of Trade April-Nov. 1951; Judge of Int. Court of Arbitration, The Hague; Chair. Royal Comm. on the Press 1961–62; Chair. British Medical Research Council 1962–65; Chair. "Justice" (British branch of Int. Comm. of Jurists) 1956–73; Chief Prosecutor, Nuremberg Trials 1945–46; U.K. del. UN 1945–49; withdrew from Labour Party 1958, joined SDP 1983; mem. Monckton Comm. 1959–60 (resigned); Pres. Rainer Foundation until 1972; Chair. Int. Chamber of Commerce Special Comm. of Eminent Persons on Ethical Practices; Chair. Dominion Lincoln Assurance Co. Ltd., Thames Television Co. Ltd. 1969–74, Upjohn and Co. Ltd. to 1977, City of London Panel on Takeovers and Mergers 1969–80, Press Council 1974–78, London and Continental Bankers 1974–80; Dir. Shell Transport and Trading Co. Ltd. until 1973, EMI Ltd. until 1980, European Enterprises Devt. Co. S.A. (Luxembourg), Times Newspapers Ltd. 1967–74, Ranks, Hovis Macdougall Ltd. until 1977 (consultant 1977–), Caffyns Ltd. (now Deputy Chair.), Morgan et Cie. S.A., Morgan et Cie. International S.A. until 1976, The Observer 1981–; Special Adviser to Morgan Guaranty Trust Co. of New York; mem. Court of London Univ. until 1978; Sussex Univ. Exec. Council, Pro-Chancellor 1962–65, Chancellor 1965–85; mem. Int. Cttee. of Jurists, Bd. of Trustees, American Univ. of Beirut until 1975, Council of Int. Chambers of Commerce; Hon. mem. New York and American Bar Assens.; Hon. F.R.C.O.G. 1979, Royal Coll. of Surgeons 1981; Hon. D.Litt.(Loughborough) 1980; Hon. LL.D. (Columbia, Bristol, Michigan, Lehigh, Liverpool, Hull Univs.); Hon. D.C.L. (New Brunswick Univ. and London). *Leisure interest:* yachting. *Address:* Morganbank, Angel Court, London, EC2R 7AE (Office); Friston Place, Sussex; 12 Grays Inn Square, London, W.C.1, England. *Telephone:* East Dean 2206; 01-242 5500; 600 2300 (Office).

SHAWE-TAYLOR, Desmond Christopher, C.B.E.; British music critic; b. 29 May 1907; s. of Frank and Agnes Shawe-Taylor (née Ussher); ed. Shrewsbury School, Oriel Coll., Oxford; music critic, New Statesman 1945–58, Sunday Times 1958–; Guest music critic, New Yorker 1973–74; served in R.A. 1939–45. *Publications:* Covent Garden 1948, The Record Guide (with Edward Sackville-West, later Lord Sackville) 1951–56. *Leisure interests:* travel, croquet, gramophone. *Address:* Long Crichel House, Wimborne, Dorset; 15 Furlong Road, London, N7 8LS, England. *Telephone:* Tarrant Hinton 250; 01-607 4854.

SHAWN, William; American editor; b. 31 Aug. 1907, Chicago; s. of Benjamin and Anna (née Bransky) Chon; m. Cecille Lyon 1928; two s. one d.; ed. Univ. of Michigan; Reporter, Las Vegas (N.M.) Optic 1928; Midwest Ed. Int. Illustrated News, Chicago 1929; reporter The New Yorker 1933–35, Assoc. Ed. 1935–39, Man. Ed. 1939–52, Ed. The New Yorker 1952–87; Ed. Farrar, Strauss and Giroux 1987–. *Address:* Farrar, Strauss and Giroux, 19 Union Square, W., New York, N.Y. 10003 (Office).

SHAZLY, Lt.-Gen. Saad Mohamed el-Husseiny el-, M.POL.SC.; Egyptian army officer and diplomatist; b. 1 April 1922, Cairo; s. of Mohamed el-Husseiny el-Shazly and Tafida Ibrahim el-Shazly; m. Zeinat Mohamed Metwally 1942; ed. Khedive Ismail Secondary School, Cairo, Cairo Univ., Mil. Coll., and in U.S.S.R; Officer of the Guards 1943–48; Platoon Commdr. Arab-Israeli War 1948; Commdr. of Parachute School 1954–56; Commdr. of Parachute Battalion 1956–58; Commdr. United Arab Repub. Contingent, UN, Congo 1960–61; Defence Attaché, London 1961–63; Brigade Commdr. in Yemen Civil War 1965–66; Commdr. Shazly Task Force Group, Egyptian-Israeli War 1967; Commdr. of Special Forces, Paratroopers and Rangers 1967–69; Commdr. Red Sea District 1970–71; Chief of Staff of Egyptian Armed Forces 1971–73; Amb. to U.K. 1974–75, to Portugal 1975–78; founder and Sec.-Gen. Nat. Front Party March 1980–; Chief Ed. Algabha, Alger 1980–; mem. Int. Inst. for Strategic Studies; mem. Bd. of Dirs. Islamic Inst. of Defence Tech.; holder of 23 decorations including Mil. Medal of Courage 1949, Médaille de Congo 1961, Medal of Yemen 1966, Medal of Distinguished Mil. Duty 1972, Order of the Repub. (1st Class) 1974, Honour Star 1974, Syrian Honour Star (Knight) 1974, Palestinian Honour Star 1974. *Publications:* How an Infantry Division can Cross a Water Barrier 1973, Fonética Arabe Com Letras Portuguesas 1978, Kuraaunnn Kariim 1978, The Crossing of the Suez 1980, Four Years in the Diplomatic Service 1983, Arab Military Option 1984; contributes to numerous journals. *Leisure interests:* gliding, shooting, fencing, golf, camping, chess. *Address:* P.O. Box 778, Alger-Gare, Algeria. *Telephone:* (213) 260 9493 (Office); (213) 260 4759 (Home).

SHCHADOV, Mikhail Ivanovich, CAND. TECH. SC.; Soviet politician; b. 1927; ed. Tomsk Polytechnic, CPSU Cen. Cttee. Higher Party School, All-Union Inst. of Finance and Economy; collective farm worker 1943–48; mem. CPSU 1947–; mechanic with coal-mining trust 1948–53; chief mining engineer 1953–60; man. of coal-mining trust 1960–66, Deputy Chief 1964–75; Gen. Dir. of Eastern Siberian coal-mining production unit 1975–77; U.S.S.R. Deputy, First Deputy Minister of Coal Mining 1977–85, Minister 1985–; mem. of CPSU Cen. Cttee. 1986–; Deputy to U.S.S.R. Supreme Soviet; State Prize 1984. *Address:* The Kremlin, Moscow, U.S.S.R.

SHCHARANSKY, Anatoly (see Scharansky, Natan).

SHCHEDRIN, Rodion Konstantinovich; Soviet composer; b. 16 Dec. 1932, Moscow; s. of Konstantin Mikhailovich Shchedrin and Konkordia Ivanovna Shchedrin; m. Maya Plisetskaya 1958; ed. Moscow Conservatoire; mem. Supreme Soviet of U.S.S.R., Soviet Cttee. for World Defence; U.S.S.R. State Prizes, U.S.S.R. Order of Merit. *Compositions include:* Not Only Love (opera) 1961, Dead Souls (operatic scenes in three acts) 1976, Humpbacked Horse (ballet) 1960, The Twenty-Eight; Burokratiada (cantatas) 1953, 1963, two symphonies 1958, 25 Preludes 1965, Concerto for Orchestra 1963, Concerto for Piano & Orchestra 1954, Chamber Suite 1961, Lenin in the Heart of the People (oratorio) 1969, Piano quintet, twelve preludes & fugues, songs, The Carmen Suite (opera) 1967, Anna Karenina (opera) 1972, The Seagull (ballet) 1980, Stykhira 1988, The Sealed Angel (Slavonic Mass) 1988, music for theatre and cinema. *Address:* Union of Soviet Composers, ul, Nezhdanovoi 8/10, Moscow, U.S.S.R.

SHCHERBINA, Boris Yevdokinovich; Soviet politician; b. 5 Oct. 1919, Debaltzevo, Ukraine; ed. Kharkov Inst. of Railway Engs.; mem. CPSU 1939–; railway station engineer 1942; Sec. Kharkov regional Cttee., Young Communist League, and Chief of Dept., CPSU regional Cttee. 1942–48; Second Sec. CPSU Dist. Cttee., Kharkov, and Sec. Kharkov city Cttee., CP of Ukraine 1948–51; Sec. Irkutsk Regional Cttee., CPSU 1951–61; First Sec. Tumen Regional Cttee., CPSU 1961–73; Minister for Construction of Oil and Gas Industry Enterprises 1973–84; Deputy Chair. U.S.S.R. Council of Ministers Jan. 1984–; Head Comm. to Investigate Chernobyl 1986–; mem. CPSU Cen. Cttee. 1976–; Deputy to Supreme Soviet of the U.S.S.R. (6th-10th sessions); State decorations. *Address:* Ministry for the Construction of Oil and Gas Industry Enterprises, The Kremlin, Moscow, U.S.S.R.

SHCHERBITSKY, Vladimir Vasiliyevich; Soviet politician; b. 17 Feb. 1918, Verkhnedneprovsk; ed. Dnepropetrovsk Chemical Eng. Inst.; Instructor, Young Communist League Dist. Cttee. 1934–35; served Soviet Army 1941–45; mem. CPSU 1941–, Ukraine Supreme Soviet 1935; mem. Presidium Ukraine CP 1957; Sec. Cen. Cttee. 1957–61; Prime Minister of Ukraine 1961–63 and 1965–72; Cand. mem. of Presidium of the Cen. Cttee. of CPSU 1961–63, 1965–66, Cand. mem. Politburo 1966–71, mem. 1971–; First Sec. Dnepropetrovsk Industrial Regional Cttee. CP of Ukraine 1963–65; First Sec. Dnepropetrovsk Regional Cttee. CP of Ukraine 1964–65; mem. Cen. Cttee. of CPSU 1961–; First Sec., Cen. Cttee. CP of Ukraine 1972–; Deputy to U.S.S.R. Supreme Soviet 1958–; mem. Presidium of U.S.S.R. Supreme Soviet 1972; elected to Congress of People's Deputies of the U.S.S.R. 1989; Order of Lenin (6 times), Order of October Revolution, Hero of Socialist Labour (twice) and other decorations. *Address:* Central Committee of the Communist Party of the Ukraine, Kiev, U.S.S.R.

SHEA, Joseph Francis; American scientist; b. 5 Sept. 1926, New York; s. of Joseph Anthony and Mary Veronica (née Tully) Shea; m. Carol Dowd Manion; four d. (from previous marriage); ed. Univ. of Michigan; Instructor, Eng. Mechanics, Univ. of Mich. 1948–50, 1953–55; Research Mathematician, Bell Telephone Lab. 1950–53, Devt. Engineer 1955–59; Dir., Advanced System R. and D., and Man. Titan Inertial Guidance Program, A.C. Spark Plug 1959–61; Space Program Dir. Space Tech. Lab. 1961–62; Deputy Dir., Manned Space Flight (Systems), Nat. Aeronautics and Space Admin. 1962–63, Program Man. Apollo Spacecraft, Manned Spacecraft Center 1963–67; Deputy Assoc. Man. for Manned Space Flight April-July 1967; Vice-Pres. Polaroid Corpn. 1967–68; Sr. Vice-Pres. and Gen. Man. equipment division, Waltham, Mass., Raytheon Co. 1968–; Sr. Vice-Pres. and Group Exec. Lexington, Mass. 1975–81, Sr. Vice-Pres. Eng. 1981–. *Address:* 141 Spring Street, Lexington, Mass. 02173 (Office); 53 Autumn Road, Weston, Mass. 02193, U.S.A. (Home).

SHEARER, Rt. Hon. Hugh Lawson; Jamaican politician; b. 18 May 1923, Martha Brae, Trelawny; ed. St. Simon's Coll.; journalist Jamaica Worker 1941–47; mem. Kingston and St. Andrew Corpn. 1947–51; mem. House of Reps. 1955–59; mem. Legis. Council (now Senate) 1961–66; Minister without Portfolio and Leader of Govt. Business in the Senate 1962–67; Deputy Leader Jamaica Labour Party 1967–74; Jamaican del. to UN 1962–72; Prime Minister, Minister of Defence and Minister of External Affairs 1967–72; Leader of the Opposition 1972–74; M.P. for South-East Clarendon 1976–; Deputy Prime Minister and Minister of Foreign Affairs 1980–89, Minister of Foreign Trade 1980–86, of Industry 1986–89; Island Supervisor, Bustamante Industrial Trade Union 1953, Vice-Pres. 1960–79, Pres. 1979–; Hon. LL.D. (Howard Univ.). *Address:* c/o Ministry of Foreign Affairs, 85 Knutsford Boulevard, Kingston 5, Jamaica.

SHEARMAN, John Kinder Gowran, M.A., PH.D., F.B.A.; British professor of history of art; b. 24 June 1931, Aldershot; s. of Brig. C. E. G. Shearman and Evelyn W. Shearman; m. 1st Jane D. Smith 1957 (deceased), 2nd Deirdre Roskill 1983; one s. three d.; ed. Felsted School, Courtauld Inst.; Lecturer to Prof., Courtauld Inst., Univ. of London 1957–79, Deputy Dir. 1974–78; Dept. of Art and Archaeology, Princeton Univ., U.S.A. 1979–, Chair. 1979–85, Class of 1926 Prof. 1986–87, Prof. of Fine Art, Harvard Univ. 1987–, William Door Boardman Prof. 1988–; Serena Medal, British Acad.; mem. Accademia del Disegno, Florence. *Publications:* Andrea del Sarto 1965, Mannerism 1967, Raphael's Cartoons 1972, Catalogue, Earlier Italian Paintings in the Royal Collection 1983, Funzione e Illusione 1983. *Leisure interests:* sailing, music, travel. *Address:* 3 Clement Circle, Cambridge, Mass. 02138, U.S.A.

SHEED, Wilfrid John Joseph, M.A.; American author; b. 27 Dec. 1930, London, England; s. of Francis Joseph and Maisie (Ward) Sheed; m. 1st

Maria Bullitt Dartington 1957 (divorced); three c.; m. 2nd Maria Ungerer; one s. two d.; ed. Lincoln Coll., Oxford Univ.; film reviewer Jubilee magazine 1959-61, Assoc. Ed. 1959-66; drama critic and fmr. book ed. Commonweal magazine, New York; film critic Esquire magazine 1967-69; Visiting Prof. Princeton Univ. 1970-71; judge and mem. editorial bd. Book of the Month Club 1972-; Guggenheim Fellow 1971-72; mem. P.E.N. Club. *Publications:* A Middle Class Education 1961, The Hack 1963, Square's Progress 1965, Office Politics 1966, The Blacking Factory 1968, Max Jamison 1970, The Morning After 1971, People Will Always Be Kind 1973, Three Mobs: Labor, Church, and Mafia 1974, Transatlantic Blues 1978, The Good Word 1979, Clare Boothe Luce 1982, Frank and Maisie 1985, The Boys of Winter 1987; ed. of G. K. Chesterton's Essays and Poems 1957, 16 Short Novels 1986; contributes articles to popular magazines. *Address:* Sag Harbor, New York, N.Y. 11963, U.S.A.

SHEEHAN, John Clark, PH.D.; American professor of organic chemistry; b. 23 Sept. 1915, Battle Creek, Mich.; m. Marion M. Jennings 1941; two s. one d.; ed. Univ. of Michigan; Research Assoc., Nat. Defense Research Cttee. Project Michigan 1941; Sr. Research Chemist Merck and Co., N.J. 1941-46; Asst. Prof. of Chemistry, M.I.T. 1946-49, Assoc. Prof. 1949-52, Prof. of Organic Chemistry 1952-77, Prof. Emer. and Sr. lecturer 1977-; fmr. mem. Editorial Bd. Journal of Organic Chem., Ed.-in-Chief Organic Syntheses 1958; Scientific Liaison Officer, U.S. Embassy, London 1953-54; Consultant to the President's Scientific Advisory Cttee. (Office of Science and Tech.) 1961-65; Consultant to Arms Control and Disarmament Agency, U.S. State Dept. 1962-64; Chair. Bd. John C. Sheehan Inst. for Research, Inc., SISA Inc., Cambridge, Mass.; Reilly Lecturer Univ. of Notre Dame 1953, Swiss-American Foundation Lecturer 1958, McGregory Lecturer 1958, A. H. Robins Lecturer 1975, Bachmann Memorial Lecturer, Univ. of Mich. 1959; fmr. mem. and Chair. of numerous scientific cttees.; mem. A.C.S. (Chair. Div. of Organic Chemistry 1959-60), N.A.S., American Acad. of Arts and Sciences, New York Acad. of Arts and Sciences, American Inst. of Chemists, Chemical Soc., London; Hon. D.Sc. (Notre Dame); A.C.S. Award in Pure Chemistry 1951, A.C.S. Award for Creative Work in Synthetic Organic Chemistry 1959, John Scott Award and Medal of City of Philadelphia 1964, Synthetic Organic Chemical Mfrs. Asscn. Medal 1969, Outstanding Achievement Award 1971. *Leisure interests:* tennis, boating, colour photography. *Address:* 10 Moon Hill Road, Lexington, Mass. 02173; and 166 Harbor Drive, Key Biscayne, Florida 33149, U.S.A.

SHEEHY, Patrick; British business executive; b. 2 Sept. 1930; s. of Sir John Francis Sheehy and Jean (née Newton) Sheehy; m. Jill Patricia Tindall 1964; one s. one d.; ed. Ampleforth Coll., Yorks; Irish Guards 1948-50; joined British-American Tobacco Co. 1950, first appointment, Nigeria, Ghana 1951, Regional Sales Man., Nigeria 1953, Ethiopian Tobacco Monopoly 1954, Marketing Dir., Jamaica 1957, Gen. Man., Barbados 1961, Netherlands 1967; Dir. British-American Tobacco 1970-82, mem. Chair.'s Policy Cttee. and Chair. Tobacco Division Bd. 1975; Deputy Chair. BAT Industries 1976-81, Vice-Chair. 1981-82, Chair. Oct. 1982-; Chair. British-American Tobacco Co. 1976-81; Dir. Eagle Star Holdings 1984-87, British Petroleum 1983-; Chair. BAT Financial Services 1985-, Batus 1986-; mem. Pres.'s Cttee., CBI 1986-; mem. Trade Policy Research Centre, Action Cttee. for Europe; mem. CBI Task Force on Urban Regeneration. *Leisure interests:* golf, reading. *Address:* BAT Industries PLC, Windsor House, 50 Victoria Street, London, SW1H 0NL, England. *Telephone:* 01-222 7979.

SHEEN, Martin (b. Ramon Estevez); American actor; b. 3 Aug. 1940, Dayton, Ohio; m. Janet Sheen; three s. one d.; worked as shipping clerk, American Express Co., New York. *Stage appearances:* The Connection (début, New York and European tour), Never Live Over A Pretzel Factory, The Subject Was Roses. *Films:* The Incident, Catch-22, Rage, Badlands, Apocalypse Now, Enigma, Gandhi, The King of Prussia, That Championship Season, Man, Woman and Child, The Dead Zone, Final Countdown, Loophole, Wall Street, Nightbreaker, Da 1988. *TV appearances include:* The Defenders, East Side/West Side, My Three Sons, Mod Squad, Cannon, That Certain Summer, Missiles of October, The Last Survivors. *Address:* Jeff Ballard, 4814 Lemona Avenue, Sherman Oaks, Calif. 91403, U.S.A.

SHELBOURNE, Sir Philip, Kt., M.A.; British business executive; b. 15 June 1924, London; s. of the late Leslie John Shelbourne and Phyllis Mary Stoodley; ed. Radley Coll., Corpus Christi Coll., Oxford, and Harvard Univ. Law School; barrister 1951-62; partner N. M. Rothschild & Sons 1962-70; C.E.O. Drayton Corpn. 1971-72; Chair. Drayton Group and Drayton Corpn. 1973-74; Chair. Samuel Montagu & Co. Ltd. 1974-80; Chair. BNOC 1980-82; Chair. Britoil PLC 1982-88; Chair. Henry Ansbacher Holdings 1988-; Deputy Chair. Mergers and Take-overs Panel 1987-; Dir. IBM World Trade Europe/Middle East/Africa Corpn. 1983-; Hon. Master of the Bench of the Inner Temple 1984-. *Leisure interest:* music. *Address:* Henry Ansbacher Holdings, Priory House, 1 Mitre Square, London, EC3A 5AN, England.

SHELBY, Richard Craig, A.B., LL.B.; American politician; b. 6 May 1934, Birmingham, Ala.; s. of O. H. Shelby and Alice L. Skinner; m. Annette Nevin 1960; two s.; ed. Alabama Univ.; Law Clerk, Supreme Court of Ala. 1961-62; law practice, Tuscaloosa, Ala. 1963-79; Prosecutor, City of Tuscaloosa 1964-70; U.S. Magistrate, Northern Dist. of Ala. 1966-70; Special Asst. Attorney Gen., State of Ala. 1969-70; Pres. Tuscaloosa Co.

Mental Health Asscn. 1969-70; mem. Ala. State Senate 1970-78; mem. 96th-99th Congresses, 7th Ala. Dist. 1979-87; Senator from Alabama Jan. 1987-; mem. Exec. Cttee. Ala. State Democratic Party; mem. American Bar Asscn.; Democrat. *Address:* U.S. Senate, Washington, D.C. 20510 (Office); 1414 High Forest Drive, N. Tuscaloosa, Ala. 35406, U.S.A. (Home).

SHELLEY, Howard Gordon; British concert pianist and conductor; b. 9 March 1950, London; s. of Frederick Gordon Shelley and Anne Taylor; m. Hilary MacNamara 1975; one s. one step s.; professional début Wigmore Hall, London 1971; regular soloist with all London and provincial British orchestras; regular tours to U.S.A. and Canada, Australia, Hong Kong, U.S.S.R. and Europe; repertoire from Mozart through Liszt to Gershwin; three piano concertos written for him (Cowie, Chapple, Dickinson); recordings include Rachmaninov's complete piano music, Vaughan Williams Piano Concerto, Schubert Sonatas, Chopin Preludes, Mozart Piano Concertos 21 and 24, Peter Dickinson's Piano Concerto and Howard Ferguson Sonata; conducting début with London Symphony Orchestra 1985; Dannreuther Concerto Prize 1971. *Address:* c/o Intermusica, Grafton House, 2/3 Golden Square, London, W1R 3AD; and 38 Cholmeley Park, Highgate, London, N6 5ER, England. *Telephone:* 01-434 1836 (Intermusica); 01-341 2811 (Home).

SHELLEY, Rulon Gene, M.S.; American business executive; b. 10 June 1924, Pasadena, Calif.; m. Theora Whiting 1946; three s. one d.; ed. Univ. of Arizona and Mass. Inst. of Technology; graduate work at Univ. of S. Calif., U.C.L.A. and Northwestern Univ.; rose from Engineer B to Chief Engineer, Armament and Flight Control Div., North American Aviation 1949-61; Vice-Pres. Tamar Electronics 1961-64; Man., Santa Barbara Operation, Space & Information Systems Div., Raytheon Co. 1964, Gen. Man. Electromagnetic Systems 1969, Vice-Pres. 1973, Gen. Man. Equipment Div. 1975, Group Exec., Electromagnetic Systems Div. and Kuras Alterman 1978, Sr. Vice-Pres. 1979, Sr. Vice-Pres. & Group Exec., Submarine Signal Div. and Raytheon Service Co. 1981, Pres. Raytheon Co. 1986-. *Address:* Raytheon Company, 141 Spring St., Lexington, Mass. 02173, U.S.A.

SHEMIN, David, B.S., A.M., PH.D.; American professor of biochemistry; b. 18 March 1911, New York; s. of Louis Shemin and Mary Bushkoff Shemin; m. 1st Mildred Sumpter (died 1962), 2nd Charlotte Norton 1963; two d.; ed. Coll. of City of New York and Columbia Univ.; Asst. Prof. of Biochem., Columbia Univ. 1945-49, Assoc. Prof. 1949-53, Prof. 1953-68; Prof. of Biochem. and Molecular Biology, Northwestern Univ. 1968-, Chair. Dept. of Biochem. and Molecular Biology 1974-79; Deputy Dir. Basic Sciences Cancer Center of Northwestern Univ. 1975-; mem. Nat. Acad. of Sciences; Fellow, American Acad. of Arts and Sciences; Guggenheim Fellowship, Commonwealth Fund Fellow, Fogarty International Scholar 1979; Pasteur Medal; Townsend Harris Medal. *Publications:* Biosynthesis of Porphyrins (Harvey Lecture) 1955; Ed. Biochemical Preparations Vol. 5 1957; about 100 publs. in scientific journals dealing with amino acid metabolism, porphyrin and B12 synthesis, enzymology. *Leisure interests:* reading, music, photography, gardening, tennis, swimming, snorkling and jogging. *Address:* Northwestern University, Evanston, Ill. 60201; 33 Lawrence Farm Road, Woods Hole, Mass. 02543, U.S.A. *Telephone:* 617-548-4199 (Home).

SHEMYAKIN, Yevgeniy Ivanovich, DR. TECH. SC.; Soviet mining specialist; b. 9 Dec. 1929, Novosibirsk; m. L.T. Petrova 1952; one s. one d.; ed. Leningrad Univ.; sr. research asst. at U.S.S.R. Acad. of Sciences Inst. of Chemico-Physics 1955-60; mem. CPSU 1963; Prof. 1968; head of lab. of U.S.S.R. Acad. of Sciences Inst. of Theoretical and Applied Mechanics 1960-71; Dir. of U.S.S.R. Acad. of Sciences Inst. of Mining (Siberian Div.) 1971-87; Vice-Pres. of Presidium of Siberian Div. of Acad. of Sciences 1980-85; mem. of U.S.S.R. Acad. of Sciences 1984, Royal Swedish Acad. of Eng. Sciences 1987. *Leisure interest:* ancient history. *Address:* ul. Griboedova 12, Moscow, U.S.S.R. *Telephone:* (095) 2 2081119.

SHEN, James C.H., M.A.; Chinese diplomatist; b. 15 June 1909; m. Winifred Wei; one s. two d.; ed. Yenching Univ., Peking (now Beijing), Univ. of Missouri, Columbia, U.S.A.; Ed. Cen. News Agency, Nanjing 1936-37; Chief Editorial Section, Int. Dept., Ministry of Information, Chongqing 1938-43; Dir. Pacific Coast Bureau, Ministry of Information 1943-47; Dir. of Int. Dept., Govt. Information Office 1947-48, Sec. to Pres. of Repub. of China, Taipei 1956-59; Dir. of Information Dept., Ministry of Foreign Affairs, Taipei 1959-61; Dir.-Gen. 1961-66; Amb. to Australia 1966-68; Vice-Minister of Foreign Affairs 1968-71; Amb. to U.S.A. 1971-79; Nat. Policy Adviser to the Pres. 1979-; Ed. China News, Taipei 1983-85; Faculty-Alumni Gold Medal (Univ. of Missouri) 1972. *Publication:* The US and Free China—How the US Sold Out Its Ally. *Address:* 7th Floor, 11 Lansui Bldg., Garden City, Hsintien, Taipei Co., Taiwan.

SHEN BAOQING; Chinese broadcaster and educationalist; ed. St. John's Univ., Shanghai; English teacher Beijing Univ. 1950-; host for English language programmes English on Sunday and Learning English with Lanlan; Hon. Pres. Yanjing Coll. of Foreign Languages. *Address:* Beijing University, Hai Dian, Beijing 100871, People's Republic of China.

SHEN BEIYAN; Chinese artist; b. 1942, Chongqing, Sichuan Prov.; m.; one d.; teacher, Beijing Cinema Coll.; specialises in line drawings. *Publication:* An Introduction to Nude Art 1988. *Address:* Beijing Cinema College, Beijing, People's Republic of China.

SHEN DALI; Chinese writer, translator and historian; b. 4 Sept. 1938, Yanan; s. of Shen Xiu and Song Ying; m. Liu Fongyun 1962; one s. one d.; ed. Beijing Foreign Languages Inst.; Lecturer, French Dept. Beijing Foreign Languages Inst. 1957–; translator at UNESCO, Paris 1979–81, réviseur 1985–; awarded title "Membre d'honneur" by L'Association des Amis de la Commune de Paris, 1981; mem. Chinese Writers' Asscn. *Publications:* The Children of Yenan (novel, also in French and Italian) 1985, Les Lys rouges (novel) 1987, La Flûte des Titans 1987, The Humble Violet, The Meteor. *Translations include:* Le Temps des cerises, Montserrat, Selected Poems of Eugene Pottier (additional transls.): Les Fleurs jumelles (play) 1982, L'Epreuve (novel) 1985, Les Trésors de la cité interdite 1986, Poésies choisies de la Commune de Paris 1986. *Leisure interest:* music. *Address:* Beijing Foreign Languages Institute, Beijing, People's Republic of China.

SHEN DAREN; Chinese party official; b. 1928, Jiangsu Prov.; Deputy Sec. Jiangsu Prov. CCP Cttee. 1983–86; Sec. Changzhou Municipal CCP Cttee.; Sec. Ningxia Hui Autonomous Regional Cttee. Jan. 1988–; mem. CCP Cen. Cttee. 1987–. *Address:* Central Committee of the Chinese Communist Party, Zhongnanhai, Beijing, People's Republic of China.

SHEN GUANGWEI; Chinese artist; b. 1950, Weifang, Shandong. *Address:* Weifang Popular Art Centre, Shandong, People's Republic of China.

SHEN JIAN; Chinese diplomatist; b. 1915, Hebei Prov.; m. Xiong You-Zhen 1946; three s. one d.; ed. Beijing Teachers' Coll., Western Reserve Univ.; Dir. Secr., Gen. Office, Mil. Council, Cen. People's Govt. 1949; Counsellor, Embassy, India 1950–55; Deputy Dir. America and Australia Dept., Ministry of Foreign Affairs 1956–59, Dir. 1959–60; Amb. to Cuba 1960–64; Deputy Minister, Int. Liaison Dept. CCP Cen. Cttee. 1965–79; Amb. to India 1980–84; Vice-Chair. Inst. of Foreign Affairs, Beijing, Prof. 1985–; Sr. mem. Research Council, Inst. of Contemporary Int. Relations, Beijing 1985–; Chair. China-Cuba Friendship Asscn.; Vice-Chair. China-Latin American Friendship Asscn.; Perm. Council mem., Chinese People's Asscn. for Friendship with Foreign Countries; mem. Standing Cttee., 5th CPPCC 1978–82; mem. 6th CPPCC 1982–87. *Address:* c/o Ministry of Foreign Affairs, Beijing, China.

SHEN RONG; Chinese writer; b. Oct. 1936, Hupei; d. of Shen Zutao and Yang Shufang; m. Fan Rongkang 1956; two s. one d.; salesgirl in bookshop 1951; worked for Radio Beijing as translator and ed.; later taught in a middle school; mem. Beijing Br., Chinese Writers' Asscn. China PEN, Chinese Int. Exchange Asscn. *Publications:* Forever Green (novel), No Way Out, Light and Dark. *Address:* Beijing Writers' Association, Beijing, People's Republic of China.

SHEN TU; Chinese aviation administrator; Deputy Dir. Bureau of Civil Aviation in Ministry of Communications 1959–62; Vice-Chair. Civil Aviation Admin. under State Council 1962; disappeared during Cultural Revolution 1967–73; Deputy Dir.-Gen. Civil Aviation Admin. 1973, Dir.-Gen. 1978; mem. of Cen. Greening Cttee. 1982; mem. 12th CCP Cen. Cttee. 1982–87; Vice-Pres. China Asscn. for Promotion of Int. Friendship 1985–. *Address:* c/o Chinese Civil Aviation Administration, State Council, Beijing, People's Republic of China.

SHEN YINLUO; Chinese party official; Sec. CCP Cttee., Wuhan Iron and Steel Co. –1981; mem. 12th CCP Cen. Cttee. 1982–87; Sec. CCP Prov. Hubei Prov. 1982–83, Deputy Sec. 1983–86; Chair. Hubei Prov. Cttee. May 1988–. *Address:* Hubei Provincial Chinese Communist Party, Wuhan, Hubei, People's Republic of China.

SHEN ZULUN; Chinese party and government official; Vice-Gov. Zhejiang Prov. 1983–86; Gov. Zhejiiang Prov. People's Govt. Feb. 1988–; mem. CCP Cen. Cttee. 1987–. *Address:* Central Committee of the Chinese Communist Party, Zhongnanhai, Beijing, People's Republic of China.

SHENOUDA III, Anba, B.A., B.D.; Egyptian ecclesiastic; b. 3 Aug. 1923; ed. Cairo Univ. and Coptic Orthodox Theological Coll.; theological teacher and writer; fmr. Bishop and Prof. of Theology, Orthodox Clerical Coll., Cairo; 1st Chair., Asscn. of Theological Colls. in the Near East; 117th Pope of Alexandria and Patriarch of the See of St. Mark of Egypt, the Near East and All Africa (Coptic Orthodox Church) 1971–81, 1985–; removed from post by Pres. Sadat and banished to desert monastery Wadi Natroun Sept. 1981, released Jan. 1985. *Address:* Coptic Orthodox Patriarchate, Anba Ruess Building, Ramses Street, Abbasiya, Cairo; St. Bishoi Monastery, Wadi Natrun, Egypt.

SHEPARD, Alan B., Jr.; American astronaut; b. 18 Nov. 1923, E. Derry, N.H.; m. Louise Brewer; two d.; ed. U.S. Naval Acad.; destroyer service in Pacific, U.S.N., Second World War; naval flight experience 1947–58; graduated from Naval War Coll., Newport, R.I. 1958; Air Readiness Officer, Staff of C.-in-C. Atlantic Fleet 1958–59; selected by NASA as astronaut April 1959; pilot of Mercury-Redstone III (sub-orbital flight, and first American in space) 1961; Chief, Astronaut Office 1965–74; Commdr. Apollo XIV Jan.-Feb. 1971; partner, Marathon Construction Co., Houston 1974–77; Pres. Windward Distributing Co., Houston 1974, Partner 1976–; Pres. Seven Fourteen Enterprises 1986–; fifth man to walk on the moon; NASA Distinguished Service Medal 1961; U.S. Nat. Space Hall of Fame Award 1969, Langley Medal 1969, Congressional Medal of Honor (Space) 1978.

SHEPARD, Roger Newland, M.S., PH.D.; American professor of psychology; b. 30 Jan. 1929, Palo Alto, Calif.; s. of Orson C. Shepard and Grace N. Shepard; m. Barbaranne Bradley 1952; two s. one d.; ed. Stanford and Yale Univs.; N.A.S.-N.R.C. Postdoctoral Research Assoc. Naval Research Lab. Washington, D.C. 1955–56; Research Fellow, Harvard Univ. 1956–58; mem. tech. staff, Bell Telephone Labs. 1958–66, Head of Dept. 1963–66; Prof. of Psychology, Harvard Univ. 1966–68, Dir. Psychological Labs. 1967–68; Prof. of Psychology, Stanford Univ. 1968–; Pres. Psychometric Soc. 1973–74, Div. of Experimental Psychology, American Psychological Asscn. 1980–81; Guggenheim Fellow 1971–72; Fowler Hamilton Fellow, Christ Church, Oxford 1987–; mem. N.A.S., American Acad. of Arts and Sciences; Distinguished Scientific Contribution Award, American Psychological Asscn. 1976; Howard Crosby Warren Medal, Soc. of Experimental Psychologists 1981. *Publications:* Multidimensional Scaling: Theory and Applications in the Behavioral Sciences (with A. K. Romney and S. B. Nerlove) 1972, Mental Images and their Transformations (with L. A. Cooper) 1982. *Leisure interests:* art, music, theoretical physics. *Address:* Building 420, Stanford University, Stanford, Calif. 94305, U.S.A.

SHEPARD, Sam; American playwright and actor; b. 5 Nov. 1943, Fort Sheriden, Ill.; s. of Samuel Shepard Rogers and Jane Schook Rogers; divorced; one s.; two c. with Jessica Lange (q.v.); ed. Duarte High School, Mount San Antonio Jr. Coll. *Plays include:* Cowboys—Rock Garden (double bill), Chicago—Icarus' Mother—Red Cross (triple bill) 1966, Obie Award), La Turista (1967 Obie Award), Forensic and the Navigators (1968 Obie Award), Melodrama Play, Tooth of Crime (1973 Obie Award), Back Dog Beast Bait, Operation Sidewinder, 4-H Club, The Unseen Hand, Mad Dog Blues, Shaved Splits, Rock Garden (included in Oh! Calcutta!), Curse of the Starving Class (1978 Obie Award), True West, Fool for Love. *Film appearances include:* Days of Heaven, Frances, The Right Stuff, Country, Crimes of the Heart, Baby Boom. *Screenplay:* Paris, Texas (Palme d'Or, Cannes Film Festival 1984).

SHEPHEARD, Sir Peter Faulkner, Kt., C.B.E., B.ARCH.; British architect, town planner and landscape architect; b. 11 Nov. 1913, Birkenhead; s. of Thomas Faulkner Shepheard, and Catherine Emily Shepheard; m. Mary Bailey 1943; one s. one d.; ed. Birkenhead School; Liverpool School of Architecture; Asst. to Derek Bridgwater 1937–40; Royal Ordinance Factories, Ministry of Supply 1940–43; Tech. Officer on Greater London Plan, later on Research and Master Plan, Stevenage New Town, Ministry of Town and Country Planning 1943–47; Deputy Chief Architect and Planner, Stevenage Devt. Corpn. 1947–48; pvt. practice (Shepheard Epstein & Hunter) 1948–; Visiting Prof. of Landscape Architecture, Graduate School of Fine Arts, Univ. of Pennsylvania 1959–70, Prof. of Architecture and Environmental Design 1971–, Dean 1971–78, Dean Emer. 1979–; Pres. R.I.B.A. 1969–71; Pres. Architectural Asscn. 1954–55, Inst. of Landscape Architects 1965–66; Master, Art Workers Guild 1984; mem. Royal Fine Art Comm. 1968–71, Countryside Comm. 1968–71; Artistic Advisor, Commonwealth War Graves Comm. 1977–; RIBA Distinction in Town Planning 1956; Hon. Fellow, Royal Architectural Inst. of Canada 1972, A.I.A. 1973. *Publications:* Modern Gardens 1953, Gardens 1969, Illustrator A Book of Ducks and Woodland Birds. *Leisure interests:* music, poetry, drawing, gardening. *Address:* 21 Well Road, London, NW3 1LH, England; 723A Wolcott Drive, Philadelphia, Pa. 19118, U.S.A. *Telephone:* 01-435 3019.

SHEPHERD, 2nd Baron, cr. 1946, of Spalding; Malcolm Newton Shepherd, P.C.; British politician; b. 27 Sept. 1918, Blackburn; s. of George Robert and Ada Shepherd; m. Allison Redmond 1941; two s.; ed. Friends' School, Saffron Walden; Opposition Chief Whip, House of Lords 1963–64, Govt. Chief Whip 1964–67, Minister of State, Commonwealth Office 1967–68, FCO 1968–70; Deputy Leader of House of Lords 1967–70, Deputy Leader of the Opposition, House of Lords 1970–74; Lord Privy Seal, Leader of House of Lords 1974–76 (resgnd.); Deputy Chair. Sterling Group of Cos. 1976–86; Chair. Packaging Council, Civil Service Pay Research Unit 1978–81, Nat. Bus Co. 1979–84; Chair. Medical Research Council 1978–82; Adviser, Sun Hung Kai Securities, Hong Kong 1978–; Pres., Centre Européen de l'Entreprise Publique 1985–, Inst. of Road Transport Engineers 1987–. *Leisure interest:* golf. *Address:* 29 Kennington Palace Court, Sancroft Street, London, S.E.11, England. *Telephone:* 01-582 6772.

SHEPPARD, Rt. Rev. David Stuart, M.A.; British ecclesiastic and former test cricketer; b. 6 March 1929, Reigate, Surrey; m. Grace Isaac 1957; one d.; ed. Sherborne School, Trinity Hall, Cambridge and Ridley Hall Theological Coll. Cambridge; Asst. Curate, St. Mary's Islington 1955–57; Warden, Mayflower Family Centre, Canning Town 1957–69; Bishop Suffragan of Woolwich 1969–75; Bishop of Liverpool 1975–; Chair. BBC and IBA Cen. Religious Advisory Cttee. May 1989–; played cricket for Cambridge 1950–52 (Capt. 1952), Sussex 1947–62 (Capt. 1953), England 22 times 1950–63 (Capt. 1954); Hon. LL.D. (Liverpool Univ.) 1983, Hon. D. Tech. (Liverpool Polytechnic) 1987. *Publications:* Parson's Pitch 1964, Built as a City 1974, Bias to the Poor 1983, The Other Britain (Dimbleby Lecture) 1984, Better Together (with Archbishop Worlock q.v.) 1988. *Leisure interests:* family, reading, music, painting, theatre. *Address:* Bishop's Lodge, Woolton Park, Woolton, Liverpool, L25 6DT, England.

SHEPPERD, Sir Alfred Joseph, Kt., B.SC. (ECON.); British business executive; b. 19 Dec. 1925, London; s. of Alfred C. Shepperd and Mary A. Williams; m. Gabrielle Bouloux 1950; two d.; ed. Archbishop Tenison's

School and Univ. Coll., London; with Rank Org. 1949, Selincourt & Sons, Ltd. 1963, Chamberlain Group 1965; Man. Dir. Keyser Ullmann Industries, Ltd. 1967; Dir. Keyser Ullman Ltd. 1967; Laporte Industries, Ltd. 1971; Finance Dir. Wellcome Foundation, Ltd. 1972, Chair. and Chief Exec. 1977–; Chair. and Chief. Exec. Wellcome PLC 1986–; Chair. Burroughs Wellcome Co. 1986–; Dir. Anglia Maltings (Holdings) Ltd. 1972-, Mercury Asset Man. Group PLC 1987-, Mercury Asset Man. Holdings Ltd. 1987-. *Address:* The Wellcome Foundation Ltd., P.O. Box 129, 183 Euston Road, London, NW1 2BP, England. *Telephone:* 01-387 4477.

SHEPS, Cecil George, M.D., M.P.H.; American professor of social medicine; b. 24 July 1913, Winnipeg, Canada; s. of George Sheps and Polly Sheps; m. 1st Hindel Cherniack 1937 (died 1973), 2nd Ann S. Mann; one s.; ed. Univ. of Manitoba and Yale Univ.; Asst. Deputy Minister, Dept. of Health, Prov. of Sask. 1944–46; Assoc. Prof. of Public Health, Univ. of N.C. 1947–53; Gen. Dir. Beth Israel Hosp. and Clinical Prof. of Preventive Medicine, Harvard Medical School 1953-60; Prof. of Medical and Hosp. Admin. Grad. School of Public Health, Univ. of Pittsburgh 1960-65; Gen. Dir. Beth Israel Medical Center and Prof. of Community Medicine, Mt. Sinai Medical School, New York 1965–68; Dir. Health Services Research Center, Univ. of N.C. at Chapel Hill 1968–72, Vice-Chancellor of Health Services 1971–76, Prof. of Social Medicine 1968–79, Taylor Grandy Distinguished Prof. of Social Medicine 1980–86, Prof. of Epidemiology 1981–86, Prof. Emer. 1986–; Hon. D.Sc. (Chicago Medical School) 1970, (Manitoba) 1985; Hon. Ph.D. (Ben Gurion Univ. of the Negev) 1983. *Publications:* author of six books; co-ed of three books. *Address:* Health Services Research Center, CB 7490, Chase Hall, University of North Carolina-CH, Chapel Hill, N.C. 27599-7490, U.S.A.

SHER, Antony; British actor; b. 14 June 1949, Cape Town, South Africa; numerous appearances at Liverpool Playhouse, Nottingham Playhouse, Royal Court Theatre, Nat. Theatre, RSC at Stratford, etc.; for performance of Richard III received Best Actor Awards from Drama Magazine and The London Standard Awards 1985 and for performance of Richard III (with RSC) and as Arnold in Torchsong Trilogy received Olivier Award for Best Actor from Soc. of West End Theatres 1985. *Plays include:* The Good Woman of Setzuan, John, Paul, George, Ringo and Bert, The Government Inspector, Travesties, Knickers, Twelfth Night, A Flea in her Ear, The Cherry Orchard, Teeth and Smiles, Ziggomania, Cloud Nine, King Lear, Molière, Astonish Me, Red Noses, Richard III, Torchsong Trilogy, Goosepimples, Tartuffe, Maydays, True West, Merchant of Venice, The Revenger's Tragedy, Hello and Goodbye (R.S.C.). *Films:* Yanks, Superman II, Shadey, Erik the Viking; several TV appearances including The History Man, Collision Course, Cold Harbour. *Publications:* The Year of the King 1986, Middlepost 1988. *Address:* c/o Hope & Lyne, 108 Leonard Street, London, EC2A 4RH, England. *Telephone:* 01-739-6200.

SHERFIELD, 1st Baron, cr. 1964; **Roger Mellor Makins**, G.C.B., G.C.M.G., D.L., F.R.S.; British diplomatist, public servant and business executive; b. 3 Feb. 1904; s. of Brig.-Gen. Sir Ernest Makins, K.B.E., D.S.O. and Florence Mellor; m. Alice Davis 1934 (died 1985); two s. four d.; ed. Winchester and Christ Church, Oxford; Barrister 1927; Foreign Service 1928, Washington and Oslo; mem. Staff of Resident Minister in W. Africa 1942, of Resident Minister, Allied Force H.Q. Mediterranean 1943-44; Minister in Washington 1945-47; Asst. Under-Sec. of State for Foreign Affairs 1947-48, Deputy Under-Sec. 1948-52; Amb. to U.S.A. 1952-56; Joint Perm. Sec. to Treasury 1956-59; Chair. U.K. Atomic Energy Authority 1960-64; Chair. Industrial and Commercial Finance Corpn. 1964-74, Estate Duties Investment Trust 1966-73, Ship Mortgage Finance Co. 1966-74, Hill Samuel Group Ltd. 1966-70, Tech. Devt. Capital Ltd. 1966-74, A. C. Cossor Ltd. 1968-82, Raytheon Europe Int. Co. 1970-82, Wells Fargo Ltd. 1972-84, Finance for Industry Ltd. 1973-74, Badger Ltd. 1981-83; Fellow, All Souls Coll., Oxford; Fellow, Winchester Coll. 1964-79, also Warden 1974-79; Chair. Governing Body Imperial Coll. of Science and Tech. 1962-74; Chair. Marshall Aid Commemoration Comm. 1966-73; Trustee, Kennedy Memorial Trust 1964-74; Chancellor, Univ. of Reading 1970-; Pres. Parl. and Scientific Cttee. 1969-73; Pres. British Standards Inst. 1970-73; Chair. House of Lords Select Cttee. on Science and Tech. 1984-87; Hon. D.C.L. (Oxford), Hon. F.I.C.E., Hon. D.Litt. (Reading), Hon. LL.D. (London); Hon. Student, Christ Church (Oxford), D.L. (Hants); Benjamin Franklin Medal 1982. *Leisure interests:* shooting, gardening. *Address:* 81 Onslow Square, London, S.W.7; Ham Farm House, Ramsdell, Basingstoke, Hants., England.

SHERLOCK, Alexander, C.B.E., F.R.S.A., M.B., B.S., M.E.P.; British doctor and politician; b. 14 Feb. 1922, Coventry; s. of Thomas Sherlock and Evelyn Alexander; m. 1st Clarice C. Scarff 1945, m. 2nd Eileen Hall 1971; one s. three d.; ed. Magdalen Coll. School, Oxford, Stowmarket Grammar School, London Hosp. Medical School and Gray's Inn; House Physician, House Surgeon, London Hosp. 1945; R.A.F. 1946-48; medical practitioner 1948-79; mem. European Parl. 1979- (Spokesman on Environment, Health and Consumer Protection); Vice-Pres. Inst. of Trading Officers, Asscn. of Environmental Health Officers, Asscn. of District Councils; Officer, Order of St. John of Jerusalem. *Leisure interest:* gardening. *Address:* 54 Orwell Road, Felixstowe, Suffolk, IP11 7PS, England; A.4. Rue du Grand Duc, 1040 Brussels, Belgium. *Telephone:* (0394) 284503 (England); 640 49 30 (Belgium).

SHERMAN, Sir Alfred, Kt., B.SC.; British journalist and public affairs adviser; b. 11 Nov. 1919; s. of Jacob Vladimir Sherman and Eva Sherman (née Goldental); m. Zahava (née Levin) Sherman 1958; one s.; ed. Hackney Downs County Secondary School, London and L.S.E.; served in Int. Brigade, Spanish Civil War 1937–38 and in field security and occupied enemy territory admin., war of 1939–45; leader writer, Jewish Chronicle; various positions on Daily Telegraph 1965-86, leader writer 1977-86; Public Affairs Adviser in private practice as Interthought; Co-Founder Centre for Policy Studies 1974, Dir. of Studies –1984; Consultant, Nat. Bus Co.; mem. economic advisory staff, Israeli Govt. in 1950s; Councillor, RBK&C 1971–78; mem. West End Synagogue, Council, Anglo-Jewish Asscn. *Publications:* Local Government Reorganisation and Industry 1970, Councils, Councillors and Public Relations 1973, Local Government Reorganization and the Salary Bill 1974, Waste in Wandsworth (with D. Mallam) 1976, Crisis Calls for a Minister for Denationalization 1980, The Scott Report 1981, Communism and Arab Nationalism: a reappraisal, Capitalism and Liberty, Our Complacent Satirists: an encounter; contribs. to newspapers and periodicals. *Address:* 10 Gerald Road, London, S.W.1 (Office); 16 Great College Street, London, S.W.1, England (Home). *Telephone:* 01-730 2838 (Office); 01-222 1019 (Home).

SHERMAN, Frank (Howard); Canadian iron and steel executive; b. 4 Oct. 1916, Bellevue, Pa., U.S.A.; s. of Frank A. Sherman and Anna Mary Howard; m. Catherine Audrey Carpenter 1941 (died 1972); two s.; ed. Westdale Secondary School, Hamilton, Ont. and Queen's Univ.; Metallurgical Asst. Dofasco Inc. 1939-40, in Devt. and Operation of Armaments Dept. 1940-44, Asst. Works Man. 1945-47, Works Man. 1947-49, Vice-Pres. and Works Man. 1949-52, Exec. Vice-Pres. 1952-57, Gen. Man. 1957-59, Pres. and Gen. Man. 1959-64, Chair. and C.E.O. 1964-87, Chair. 1987-; Dir. American Iron and Steel Inst., Arnaud Railway Co., Bank of Nova Scotia, Canadian Pacific Ltd., Canron Ltd., Crown Life Insurance Co., Dofasco Inc., Great Lakes Waterways Devt. Asscn., Knoll Lakes Minerals Ltd., Nat. Steel Car Corpn., Ltd., Wabush Lake Railway Co. Ltd.; mem. Bd. of Govs. McMaster Univ., Hamilton Philharmonic Orchestra, Art Gallery of Hamilton; mem. Nat. Exec. Council, Canadian Manufacturers' Asscn. *Leisure interests:* golf, photography, boating, fishing, skeet shooting, hunting, horse-racing, tennis. *Address:* P.O. Box 460, Hamilton, Ont., L8N 3J5 (Office); 9 Turner Avenue, Hamilton, Ont., L8P 3K4, Canada (Home).

SHERROD, Robert Lee, A.B.; American writer; b. 8 Feb. 1909; s. of Joseph Arnold and Victoria Evers Sherrod; m. 1st Elizabeth Hudson 1936 (died 1958), two s.; m. 2nd Margaret Carson Ruff 1961 (divorced 1972); m. 3rd Mary Gay Labrot Leonhardt 1972 (died 1978); ed. Univ. of Georgia; Newspaper reporter 1929–35; Corresp. Time and Life 1935–52; Far East Corresp. Saturday Evening Post 1952–55, Man. Ed. 1955–62, Ed. 1962–63, Ed.-at-Large 1963–65; Vice-Pres. and Editorial Co-ordinator, Curtis Publishing Co. 1965–66; contract writer, Life 1966–68; Historical Adviser to U.S. Marine Corps 1973–76, 1979–; mem. President's Advisory Cttee. Univ. Ga. 1975–78; mem. Bd. of Judges, Nat. Magazine Awards 1979–86; Benjamin Franklin Award 1955. *Publications:* Tarawa, The Story of a Battle 1944, On to Westward 1945, 'Life's' Picture History of World War II 1950, History of Marine Corps Aviation 1952, Kobunsha's History of the Pacific War 1950, Apollo Expeditions to the Moon (co-author) 1975. *Address:* 4000 Cathedral Avenue, N.W., Washington, D.C. 20016, U.S.A. (Home).

SHERWOOD, David J.; American business executive; b. 1922; ed. Rutgers Univ., Boston Univ., Stanford Univ.; served with U.S. army 1942-46; Vice-Pres. Fireman's Fund and Insurance Co. 1946-70; with Prudential Insurance Co. of America 1970-, Exec. Vice-Pres. 1977-78, Pres. and Dir. 1978-84; Gov. New York Insurance Corpn. 1984-. *Address:* c/o Prudential Insurance Co., Prudential Plaza, Newark, N.J. 07101, U.S.A.

SHEVARDNADZE, Eduard Amvrosiyevich; Soviet politician; b. 25 Jan. 1928, Mamati Lanchkhutsky raion, Georgia; ed. Party School of the Cen. Cttee., CP of Georgia, and Kutaisi Pedagogical Inst.; mem. CPSU 1948–; Komsomol and party work 1946-56; Second Sec. 1956-57, First Sec. Komsomol in Georgia 1957-61; First Sec. Mtskheti raion 1961-63, Pervomaisky raion, Tbilisi, CP of Georgia 1963-64; First Deputy Minister 1964-65, Minister of Public Order (renamed Ministry of Internal Affairs 1968) 1965-72; First Sec. Tbilisi City Cttee. of Cen. Cttee., CP of Georgia 1972; mem. Cen. Cttee., CP of Georgia 1958-64, 1966-, mem. Politburo 1972-, First Sec. 1972-85; mem. Cen. Cttee. of CPSU 1976-, Cand. mem. Politburo 1978-85, mem. July 1985-; Deputy to U.S.S.R. Supreme Soviet 1978-; Minister of Foreign Affairs July 1985-; Order of Lenin (five times), Order of Red Banner of Labour, Hero of Socialist Labour (twice) and various other decorations. *Address:* Ministry of Foreign Affairs, Smolenskaya-Sennaya pl. 32/34, Moscow, U.S.S.R.

SHEVCHENKO, Arkadiy Nikolayevich, D.JUR.; Soviet diplomatist; b. 11 Oct. 1930, Gorlovka, Ukraine; m. Lenguina Iosifovna Shevchenko 1951; one s. one d.; ed. Moscow State Inst. of Int. Relations; joined Ministry of Foreign Affairs 1956, held sr. diplomatic posts in Dept. of Int. Orgs. 1956-63; Counsellor, then Sr. Counsellor, Perm. Mission to UN 1963-70; Adviser to Minister of Foreign Affairs, with rank of Amb. 1970-73; part-time Sr. Research Fellow, Inst. of U.S. Studies, U.S.S.R. Acad. of Sciences 1970-73; UN Under Sec.-Gen. for Political and Security Council Affairs 1973-78; defected to U.S.A. 1978; several U.S.S.R. decorations. *Publi-*

cations: Struggle of the Soviet Union for Disarmament 1961, Current Problems of Disarmament 1965, Breaking with Moscow 1985, and other books and various articles on the problems in int. relations and int. law. *Leisure interests:* research, journalism.

SHEVCHENKO, Valentina Semionovna; Soviet politician; b. 1935, Krivoy Rog, Ukraine; trained as teacher; worked in schools and in Komsomol (Young Communist League); was Minister of Educ., Ukrainian S.S.R. and Chair. Presidium of the Ukrainian Soc. of Friendship and Cultural Relations with Foreign Countries; Deputy Chair. Presidium of the Ukrainian S.S.R. Supreme Soviet 1975-85, Chair. 1985-; a Vice-Chair. Presidium of Supreme Soviet of U.S.S.R. 1985-; elected to Congress of People's Deputies of the U.S.S.R. 1989; Order of the Oct. Revolution, of the Red Banner of Labour and of Peoples' Friendship. *Address:* Supreme Soviet of the Ukrainian S.S.R., Kiev, Ukraine, U.S.S.R.

SHEVELEVA, Yekaterina; Soviet writer, poetess and essayist; b. 31 Dec. 1916, Moscow; m. 1st Lev Soloveichik 1946, 2nd Alexandr Latsis 1950, 3rd Ergeny Nikolskis 1989; two d.; worked as lathe-mechanic 1931-37; ed. Gorky Literary Inst; first collection of lyric poetry Lirika 1940; Sec. of Moscow Br. of U.S.S.R. Union of Writers; V. Vorovsky Prize for int. journalism. *Publications include: Poetry:* Steppe-Poppy 1944, Youth 1946, Friends 1950, Encounters on the Planet 1962, The Eight Colours of the Rainbow 1971, A Frank Conversation 1973, Selected Poetry 1974, A Russian Girl 1980, Joy in Grief 1982, The Fire on the Snow 1985. *Stories and novellas:* Exclusively about Women 1966, Selected Works 1979, The Thirty-First Step 1980, Princesses, Sprites and Paths 1981. *Novels:* The Alexandrovsky Garden 1977, The Domestic Hearth 1983. *Essays:* In the Japanese Capital 1958, People Need Peace 1962, Weekdays in India 1965. *Leisure interests:* tennis, jogging. *Address:* Cherniakovskogo str., Flat No 1, 125319 Moscow; U.S.S.R. Union of Writers, ulitsa Vorovskogo 52, Moscow, U.S.S.R.

SHI HONGMO; Chinese artist; b. 4 May 1937, Yangquan, Shanxi; s. of Shi Jingnu and Liu Shuxan; m. Liu Meiyun 1968; one s.; Art Ed. Beijing Publishing House 1984-. *Publications:* The Great Wall (illustration), The Stories About Chinese Calligraphy (illustration), All Nobel's Life (picture-story book), A Penguin's Stories (picture-story book). *Leisure interests:* travelling, swimming, singing, reading. *Address:* Art Department, Beijing Publishing House, Beijing, People's Republic of China. *Telephone:* (201) 6699-249.

SHI LIMING; Chinese biologist; b. 18 Dec. 1939; m.; two d.; ed. Fudan Univ., Shanghai; Dir. Kunming Inst. of Zoology. *Address:* Kunming Institute of Zoology, Yunnan Province, People's Republic of China.

SHI LU; Chinese artist; b. 1919, Penshou Co., Sichuan; graphic artist, N. Shaanxi 1940s; Chair. Xian branch Chinese Artists' Asscn.

SHI MEIYING; Chinese sculptor; b. 1933, Beijing; two s. one d.; lecturer at Beijing Cen. Acad. of Fine Arts. *Address:* Beijing Central Academy of Fine Arts, Beijing, People's Republic of China.

SHI XIAOJIE; Chinese comedian, satirist, writer and performer of humorous singing routines. *Address:* Chinese Artists' Association, Beijing, People's Republic of China.

SHIBAEV, Aleksey Ivanovich; Soviet politician; b. 21 Feb. 1915, Maslovka, Gorky oblast; ed. Gorky State Univ.; mem. CPSU 1940-; apprentice, tech. draftsman, designer at Krasnoe Sormovo Works, Gorky 1933-43, party organiser at works, Dir. of works, Rostov and Saratov oblasts 1943-55, Second Sec., 1955-59; First Sec. Saratov oblast Cttee. CPSU 1959-76, Saratov Industrial oblast Cttee. CPSU 1963-64; mem. Cen. Cttee., CPSU 1962-; Deputy to U.S.S.R. Supreme Soviet 1962-, mem. Presidium 1977-82; Chair. of All-Union Cen. Council of Trade Unions 1976-82; Deputy Minister of Instrument-making, Automation Equipment and Control Systems March 1982-; Hero of Socialist Labour 1973, Order of Lenin (four times); various decorations. *Address:* c/o Ministry of Instrument-making, Automation Equipment and Control Systems, ulitsa Ogareva 5, Moscow, U.S.S.R.

SHIELDS, Hon. Margaret Kerslake, B.A., M.P.; New Zealand politician; b. 1941, Wellington; m. Patrick John Shields 1960; two d.; ed. Victoria Univ., Wellington; researcher Consumers' Inst. and Dept. of Statistics; M.P. for Kapiti 1981-; Minister of Customs and of Consumer Affairs 1984-87, of Women's Affairs, Consumer Affairs and Statistics 1987-88, of Customs Dec. 1988-; mem. Wellington Hosp. Bd. 1977-80; co-founder, Pres. and Nat. Sec. of Soc. for Research on Women; Co-convenor of Second UN Womens' Convention 1975; Govt. Del. to UN Int. Womens' Year Conf. Mexico 1975, participated in Inter-Parl. Union Conf. Seoul 1983; Labour. *Leisure interests:* tennis, hiking, skiing, music, drama. *Address:* House of Representatives, Parliament Bldgs., Wellington, New Zealand.

SHIELDS, Robert, M.D., CH.B., F.R.C.S., F.R.C.S. (E.); British surgeon and professor of surgery; b. 8 Nov. 1930, Paisley, Scotland; s. of Robert Alexander Shields and Isobel Dougall Shields; m. Grace Marianne Swinburn 1957; one s. two d.; ed. John Neilson Inst., Paisley, Univ. of Glasgow; House Officer posts at Western Infirmary, Glasgow 1953-54; served R.A.M.C. 1954-56, R.A.M.C. (T.A.), Surgeon Specialist 1956-61; Lecturer, Univ. of Glasgow 1960-63; Sr. Lecturer, then Reader in Surgery, Welsh

Nat. School of Medicine 1963-69; Prof. of Surgery, Univ. of Liverpool, Hon. Consultant Surgeon, Liverpool Health Authority 1969-; Dean Faculty of Medicine, Univ. of Liverpool 1980-84; mem. Gen. Medical Council 1982-, MRC 1987-; Moynihan Medal, Asscn. of Surgeons of G.B. and Ireland 1965; Bellahouston Medal (Univ. of Glasgow) 1966. *Publications:* Surgical Emergencies II 1979, Textbook of Surgery 1983. *Leisure interests:* sailing, walking. *Address:* Strathmore, 81 Meols Drive, West Kirby, Merseyside, L48 5DF, England. *Telephone:* (051) 632 3588.

SHIH CHI-YANG, LL.M., D.JUR.; Chinese politician; b. 5 May 1935, Taichung City; m. Jeanne Tchong-koei Li 1969; ed. Nat. Taiwan Univ. and Univ. of Heidelberg; Asst. Dept. of Law, Nat. Taiwan Univ. 1959-62, Assoc. Prof. 1967-71, Prof. (part-time) 1971-84; Research Asst. Inst. of Int. Relations, Nat. Chengchi Univ. 1967-69, Research Fellow 1969-71; Deputy Dir. 5th Section, Cen. Cttee., Kuomintang 1969-72, Deputy Dir. Dept. of Youth Activities 1972-76; Admin. Vice-Minister, Ministry of Educ. 1976-79; Political Vice-Minister, Ministry of Educ. 1979-80, Ministry of Justice 1980-84; Minister of Justice 1984-88; Vice-Premier 1988-. *Address:* Executive Yuan, 1 Chung-hsiao E. Road, Sec. 1, Taipei, Taiwan. *Telephone:* 3217039.

SHIHABI, Samir, B.A.; Saudi Arabian diplomatist; b. 1925, Jerusalem; ed. American Univ., Beirut, Lebanon and Cairo, Egypt, Yale Univ., U.S.A. and Fitzwilliam Coll., Cambridge Univ., England; joined Saudi Arabian Foreign Service 1949; later served as First Sec. in Berne, Switzerland; Chargé d'Affaires in Italy 1959-61; Dir. UN and Int. Orgs. Dept., Ministry of Foreign Affairs 1961-64; Amb. to Turkey 1964-73, to Somalia 1973-74, to Pakistan 1980-83; Perm. Rep. to UN 1983-. *Address:* Permanent Mission of Saudi Arabia to the United Nations, 405 Lexington Ave., 56th Floor, New York, N.Y. 10017, U.S.A.

SHIHATA, Ibrahim F. I., L. EN D., S.J.D.; Egyptian lawyer and administrator; b. 19 Aug. 1937, Damietta; s. of Ibrahim Shihata and Neamat El Ashmawy; m. Samia S. Farid 1967; one s. two d.; ed. Cairo Univ., Harvard Univ., U.S.A.; mem. of the Council of State of Egypt 1957-60; lecturer, Faculty of Law, Ain Shams Univ. 1964-66, Assoc. Prof. 1970-72; Legal Adviser to Kuwait Fund for Arab Econ. Devt. 1966-70, Gen. Counsel 1972-76; also adviser and consultant to Arab Govts. and Int. Orgs. 1965-; Dir.-Gen. OPEC Fund for Int. Devt. (frmly. OPEC Special Fund) 1976-83; mem. Exec. Bd., IFAD 1977-83; Vice-Pres. and Gen. Counsellor, IBRD 1983-; Sec.-Gen. Int. Centre for Settlement of Investment Disputes (ICSID) 1983; Chair. of Bd. Int. Devt. Law Inst. 1983-; mem. Bd. Int. Law Inst. 1975-; mem. Exec. Council, American Soc. Int. Law 1984-; Founding Advisory Dir. Inst. of Transnat. Arbitration 1986-; mem. Advisory Cttee. Research Centre for Int. Law 1985-. *Publications:* eleven books and more than 100 essays on different aspects of international law and finance. *Address:* The World Bank, 1818 H Street, N.W., Washington D.C. 20433, U.S.A.

SHIKANAI, Nobutaka; Japanese businessman; b. 17 Nov. 1911, Hokkaido; m. Eiko Shikanai 1941; one s. two d.; ed. Waseda Univ., Tokyo; Man. Dir., Japan Fed. of Employers' Asscns. 1948; Pres. Nippon Broadcasting System Inc. 1961, Fuji TV Network Inc. 1964, Hakone Open-Air Museum 1968-, Sankei Shimbun 1968, Ueno Royal Museum 1972-, Utsukushi-ga-hara Open-Air Museum 1981-; Grande Ufficiale Ordine Al Merito della Repubblica Italiana 1976, Commdr., Légion d'honneur (France) 1978, First Class Order of the Sacred Treasure (Japan) 1982. *Publications:* Labor-Management Relations in the U.S.A. 1952, Television Broadcasting in Europe and the U.S.A. 1957. *Address:* The Sankei Shimbun, 7-2, 1-chome, Ohtemachi, Chiyoda-ku, Tokyo, 100 Japan. *Telephone:* 231-0658.

SHILLINGFORD, (Romeo) Arden Coleridge, M.B.E.; Dominican diplomatist; b. 11 Feb. 1936; s. of Stafford Shillingford and Ophelia Thomas; m. 1st Evelyn Blanche Hart, one s. one d.; m. 2nd Maudline Joan Green, three s.; ed. Wesley High School, Roseau Boys' School, Dominica, grammar school, School of Law; joined Dominican Civil Service 1957; jr. clerk various Govt. Depts. 1957-59; Clerk of Court, then Chief Clerk, Magistrates Office 1960-61; joined staff Eastern Caribbean Comm., London, on secondment from Dominican Civil Service 1965; served as Migrants' Welfare Officer, Students' Offices, Asst. Trade Sec. and Personal Asst. to Commr. 1968-71; Admin. Asst. Consular and Protocol Affairs 1973-78; Acting Commr. on several occasions 1975-78; High Commr. in U.K. 1978-85, also accred. as Amb. to France, Spain, Belgium, EEC and UNESCO; Perm. Sec., Ministry of Community Devt. and Social Affairs 1985-; Deputy Chair. Bd. of Govs., W. Indian Student's Centre 1970-75, Chair. 1976-79; mem. W. Indian Cttee., Vice-Pres. 1979-; Founder-mem. and Vice-Chair. Jaycees (Dominican Jr. Chamber of Commerce); fmr. mem. numerous cttees. and other bodies for W. Indian immigrant welfare and educ. *Leisure interests:* cricket, collecting authentic folk music, swimming. *Address:* Ministry of Community Development, Housing and Social Affairs, Government Headquarters, Roseau, Dominica.

SHILOV, Aleksandr Maksovich; Soviet artist; b. 1943; ed. Surikov Inst. of Arts, Moscow; painted series of portraits of Soviet celebrities including cosmonauts, Arkhipova, M. Ulyanov; Lenin Komsomol Prize 1977; People's Artist of U.S.S.R. 1985. *Address:* U.S.S.R. Academy of Artists, Universitetskaya naberezhnaya, Leningrad, U.S.S.R.

SHIMA, Shigenobu; Japanese fmr. diplomatist; b. 1907, Inchon, Korea; s. of Shigeharu and Sada (Nishimura) Shima; m. Sanaye Shimasuye 1935;

two d.; ed. Univ. of Tokyo; entered diplomatic service 1930; served London 1931–35; Pvt. Sec. to Foreign Minister 1936–37; Beijing, Tianjin and Qingdao 1937–41; Foreign Ministry 1942–47; Dir. Osaka Liaison Office 1948–51; Counsellor (European Affairs), Foreign Ministry 1951–53; Minister in Washington 1954–57; Amb. to Sweden 1957–59; Deputy Vice-Minister for Foreign Affairs 1959–62, Vice-Minister 1963–64; Amb. to U.K. 1964–68; Grand Master of Ceremonies, Imperial Japanese Court 1968–73; Adviser to Foreign Minister 1977–86. *Address:* Shiroganedai 1-1-21-405, Minato-ku, Tokyo 108, Japan. *Telephone:* (03) 444-3679.

SHIMASAKI, Hitoshi; Japanese politician; b. 28 March 1923, Komatsu City; s. of Yosobei Shimasaki and Maki Shimasaki; m. Tsukiko Shimasaki 1973; one s. one d.; ed. Tokyo Univ.; with Ministry of Finance; mem. House of Councillors 1971–; Parl. Vice-Minister for Int. Trade and Industry; Minister for Justice 1984–85; Chair. of House of Councillors Rules and Admin. Cttee. 1986–; Liberal Democratic Party. *Leisure interests:* Go playing, reading, golf. *Address:* c/o House of Councillors, 2-1-1-438, Nagatachou, Chiyoda-ku, Tokyo 100, Japan. *Telephone:* 03-508-8438.

SHIMODA, Takeso; Japanese diplomatist and lawyer; b. 3 April 1907, Tokyo; s. of Dr. Jiro and Iku (Kitagawa) Shimoda; m. Mitsue Suzuki 1938; one s. two d.; ed. Tokyo Imperial Univ.; entered Japanese Diplomatic Service 1931, served Nanking, Moscow, The Hague; Dir. Treaties Bureau, Ministry of Foreign Affairs 1952–57; Minister to U.S.A. 1957–60; Adviser to Minister of Foreign Affairs 1960–61; Amb. to Belgium and Chief of Japanese Del. to European Communities 1960–63; Amb. to U.S.S.R. 1963–65; Vice-Minister of Foreign Affairs 1965–67; Amb. to U.S.A. 1967–70; Justice of the Supreme Court 1970–77; Judge, Perm. Court of Arbitration 1972–; admitted to Tokyo Bar; Adviser to Minister of Foreign Affairs 1977–86; Pres. Honda Foundation 1978–; Commr. of Baseball 1979–85; Dir. Japanese Asscn. of Int. Law, Japanese Asscn. of Maritime Law; Hon. mem. American Bar Asscn.; Hon. LL.D. (Univ. of Nebraska); numerous foreign decorations. *Leisure interests:* golf, fishing. *Address:* 4-16, Nishikata 1-chome, Bunkyo-ku, Tokyo, Japan. *Telephone:* 03-811-2660.

SHINEFIELD, Henry Robert, B.A., M.D.; American paediatrician; b. 11 Oct. 1925, Paterson, N.J.; s. of Louis Shinefield and Sarah (Kaplan) Shinefield; m. Jacqueline Walker 1983; one s. three d.; ed. Columbia Univ.; Asst. Resident Paediatrician New York Hosp. (Cornell) 1950–51, Paediatrician Outpatients 1953–59, Instructor in Paediatrics 1959–60, Asst. Prof. 1960–64, Assoc. Prof. 1964–65; Chief of Paediatrics, Kaiser-Permanente Medical Center, San Francisco 1965–; Assoc. Clinical Prof. of Paediatrics, Univ. of Calif. 1966–68, Clinical Prof. of Paediatrics 1968–, Clinical Prof. of Dermatology 1970–; mem. Inst. of Medicine, N.A.S., American Bd. of Pediatrics; Fellow American Acad. of Pediatrics. *Leisure interests:* skiing, tennis, travel. *Address:* 2200 O'Farrell Street, San Francisco, Calif. 94115 (Office); 2705 Larkin Street, San Franciso, Calif. 94109, U.S.A. (Home). *Telephone:* (415) 929-5054 (Office); (415) 771-5372 (Home).

SHINGU, Yasuo; Japanese business executive; b. 1926, Hyogo Pref.; m.; one s. one d.; ed. Univ. of Tokyo; Gen. Man. Treasury Dept. Sumitomo Metal Industries Ltd. 1971, Gen. Man. Controlling Dept. 1974, Dir. 1977, Man. Dir. 1981, Sr. Man. Dir. 1983, Exec. Vice-Pres. 1984, Pres. 1986–; Chair. Bd. of Dirs. Iron and Steel Educ. Inst.; Exec. Dir. Japan Fed. of Econ. Orgs., Japan Fed. of Employers' Asscns., Kansai Econ. Fed.; Man. Dir. Kansai Cttee. for Econ. Devt.; Dir. Int. Iron and Steel Inst., Japan Iron and Steel Fed. *Leisure interests:* golf, visiting historic sites. *Address:* Sumitomo Metal Industries Ltd., 15 Kitahama, 5-chome, Higashi-ku, Osaka 541, Japan.

SHINTO, Hisashi, D.ENG.; Japanese industrial executive; b. 2 July 1910, Fukuoka Prefecture; s. of Yasuhide Shinto and Michiyo Shinto; m. Michiko Kushiro 1936; three s. one d.; ed. Saga Sr. High School and Kyushu Imperial Univ.; entered Harima Shipbuilding & Eng. Co. Ltd. 1934; entered Nat. Bulk Carriers Corpn., Kure Yard 1951; Man. Dir. Ishikawajima-Harima Heavy Industries Ltd. (IHI), Gen. Man. of Shipbuilding Div. 1960, Exec. Vice-Pres. IHI 1964, Pres. IHI 1972–79, Counsellor 1979–80; Dir. Japan Line Ltd. 1977–80; Man. Dir. Japan Ship Exporters' Asscn. 1979–80; Counsellor, Transportation Technics, Ministry of Transportation 1979–81; Pres. and Commr. Man. Cttee. Nippon Telegraph and Telephone Public Corpn. (NTT) Jan. 1981–85; Pres. and C.E.O. Nippon Telegraph and Telephone Corpn. 1985–88; arrested on charges of accepting bribes in Recruit Shares Scandal March 1989; Medal of Honour with Blue Ribbon. *Leisure interests:* golf, photography. *Address:* NTT, Head Office, 1-6 Uchisawai-cho, 1-chome, Chiyodaku, Tokyo 100 (Office); 9-15, Zenpukuji 1-chome, Suginami-ku, Tokyo 167, Japan (Home). *Telephone:* 03-509-3000 (Office); 03-390-0219 (Home).

SHIOKAWA, Masajuro; Japanese politician; b. 13 Oct. 1921, Osaka; ed. Keio Univ.; mem. House of Reps. 1967–; Parl. Vice-Minister of Int. Trade and Industry 1972; Deputy Chief Cabinet Sec. 1976; Chair. Standing Cttee. on Commerce and Industry, House of Reps. 1979–80; Minister of Transport 1980–81, of Educ., Science and Culture 1986–87. *Address:* c/o Ministry of Education, 3-2, Kasumigaseki, Chiyoda-ku, Tokyo, Japan.

SHIPLEY, Walter Vincent, B.S.; American banker; b. 2 Nov. 1935, Newark; s. of L. Parks and Emily (née Herzog) Shipley; m. Judith Ann Lyman 1957, four d. one s.; ed. Williams Coll., New York Univ.; with

Chemical Bank 1956–, Exec. Vice-Pres. Int. Div., New York 1978–79, Sr. Exec. Vice-Pres. –1981, Pres. 1982–83, Chair. Bd. 1983–; Dir. Champion Int. Corpn., NYNEX Corpn.; mem. Bd. Dirs. Japan Soc., Lincoln Center for the Performing Arts Inc., N.Y. City Partnership Inc., New York Chamber of Commerce and Industry, Goodwill Industries of Greater N.Y. Inc., United Way of Tri-State; mem. The Business Council, Business Roundtable, Council for Foreign Relations, Pilgrims of U.S., English-Speaking Union; mem. Bd. of Trustees, Cen. Park Conservancy. *Address:* 277 Park Avenue, New York, N.Y. 10172, U.S.A. (Office).

SHIRAISHI, Takashi, PH.D.; Japanese professor of economics; b. 1921, Tokyo; m. Toshiko Shiraishi; one d.; ed. Keio Univ., Harvard Business School; lecturer Keio Univ. 1947–49, Asst. Prof. 1949–58, Prof. 1958–, Vice-Pres. 1965–77, Dean, Faculty of Business and Commerce 1975–77; Prin. Keio High School 1964–65; Dean Faculty of Social Sciences, Kyori Univ. 1984–; Dir. Japan Soc. of Int. Econs. 1974–; Dir. and Sec.-Gen. of Union of Nat. Econ. Assens. in Japan 1975–; mem. Int. Exchange Program Cttee. of Japan Soc. for the Promotion of Science 1982–84; mem. Exec. Cttee., Int. Econ. Assen. 1984–. *Publications:* Economic Development and Direct Investment 1978, History of Economic Growth and Policy of Japan since the Second World War 1983. *Address:* 1-19-10, Jiyugaoka, Meguroku, Tokyo, Japan. *Telephone:* 03-717-7118.

SHIRAYANAGI, Mgr. Peter Seiichi; D.CN.L.; Japanese ecclesiastic; b. 17 June 1928, Tokyo; ed. Gyosei Stella Maris School, Major Seminary, Tokyo and Urban Univ., Rome; ordained priest 1954; Sec. Archbishop's House 1954–66, in Rome 1957–60; Auxiliary Bishop of Tokyo 1966; Coadjutor with right of succession 1969; Archbishop of Tokyo 1970–; Vice-Pres. Bishops' Conf. of Japan 1975, Pres. 1983; Pres. Episcopal Comm. for Social Action 1975. *Address:* Archbishop's House, 16-15 Sekiguchi, 3-Chôme, Bunkyo-ku, Tokyo 112, Japan. *Telephone:* (03)-943-2301.

SHIRENDEV, Badzaryn, DR.HIST.; Mongolian historian and politician; b. 15 May 1912; ed. School of Agric. at Tsetserleg, Mongolian Workers' Faculty at Ulan-Ude, U.S.S.R., Teacher Training Inst., Irkutsk, Inst. of Oriental Studies, Moscow; Man. of a commune 1930–31; Rector of Mongolian State Univ. 1933–52, Minister of Educ. 1951–54; Chair. Mongolian Peace Cttee. 1950–57; First Deputy Chair. Council of Ministers 1954–57; mem. Acad. of Sciences 1951–82, Pres. 1958–82; Chair. Perm. Cttee. of Int. Congress of Mongolists 1970–; Chair. Mongolian Assen. of Graduates from Soviet Educ. Insts. 1972–; fmr. Deputy Chair. of People's Great Hural (Assembly); Deputy to People's Great Hural; mem. Political Bureau of Mongolian People's Revolutionary Party (MPRP) Cen. Cttee, 1953–58; mem. MPRP Cen. Cttee. 1966–; Hon. mem. Acad. of Sciences of Bulgaria, Czechoslovakia, German Democratic Repub., Hungary, Poland, U.S.S.R.; Hon. Dr. Litt. (Leeds); Order of Sühbaatar and other awards. *Publications:* numerous books on Mongolian history. *Address:* c/o Academy of Sciences, Ulan Bator, Mongolia.

SHIRER, William Lawrence, B.A., LITT.D.; American author and journalist; b. 23 Feb. 1904, Chicago, Illinois; m. Theresa Stiberitz 1931 (divorced 1970); two d.; ed. Coe Coll.; Foreign corresp. various American newspapers, Europe, Near East and India 1925–45; Pres. Authors' Guild 1956–57; contrib. various publs.; Légion d'honneur. *Publications:* Berlin Diary 1941, End of a Berlin Diary 1947, The Traitor (novel) 1950, Midcentury Journey 1952, Stranger Come Home (novel) 1954, The Challenge of Scandinavia 1955, The Consul's Wife (novel) 1956, The Rise and Fall of the Third Reich 1960, The Rise and Fall of Adolf Hitler 1961, The Sinking of the Bismarck 1962, The Collapse of the Third Republic 1969, 20th Century Journey, A Memoir of a Life and the Times 1976, (Vol. 2 1984), Gandhi–A Memoir 1979, 20th Century Journey (Vol. 2), The Nightmare Years 1984, A Memoir of a Life and Times 1985. *Leisure interests:* music, gardening, sailing, hiking. *Address:* Box 487, 34 Sunset Avenue, Lenox, Mass. 01240, U.S.A.

SHIRIASHI, Kazuko; Japanese poet; b. 1931, Vancouver, B.C.; m.; one d.; mem. VOU avant-garde literary group 1948–53; with Kazuo Ono has mounted series of poetry/dance spectaculars. *Publications:* poetic works include Seasons of Sacred Lust (in English) 1978.

SHIRKOV, Dmitriy Vasilevich, PH.D.; Soviet physicist; b. 3 March 1928, Moscow; s. of Vasili Vas Shirkov and Elizaveta Makushina; m. Svetlana Rastopchina 1950; two s. one d.; ed. Physics Dept., Lomonosov State Univ.; attached to Steklov Math. Inst. of Acad. of Sciences, in Moscow 1950–58 and Jt. Inst. for Nuclear Research, Dubna 1958–60; worked at Inst. of Math., Siberian Div. of Acad. of Sciences, Novosibirsk 1960–69; Prof., Univ. of Novosibirsk 1963–69; Nobel Guest Prof., Lund Univ., Sweden 1969–70; at Jt. Inst. of Nuclear Research, Dubna, Prof., Moscow State Univ. 1970–; Corresp. mem. U.S.S.R. Acad. of Sciences; Foreign mem. Saxonian Acad. of Sciences; Lenin and State Prize. *Publications:* Co-author: Introduction to the Theory of Quantized Fields 1957, A New Method in the Theory of Superconductivity 1958, Dispersion Theories of Strong Interactions at Low Energies 1967, Quantum Fields 1980, Theory of Particle Interactions 1986; numerous published papers mainly on the theory of elementary particles. *Address:* Laboratory of Theoretical Physics, Joint Institute for Nuclear Research, 101000 Moscow, Head Post Office, P.O. Box 79; Department of Nuclear Physics, U.S.S.R. Academy of Sciences, 117901 Moscow B-71, Lenin Prospect 14, U.S.S.R. *Telephone:* 9262255 (Inst.); 2342286 (Acad.).

SHIRLEY, George; American tenor; b. 18 April 1934, Indianapolis, Ind.; s. of Irving E. and Daisy (née Bell) Shirley; m. Gladys Lee Ishop 1956; one s. one d.; ed. Wayne State Univ.; debuts with Metropolitan Opera, New York Opera, Festival of Two Worlds (Spoleto, Italy), Santa Fé Opera 1961, Teatro Colón, Buenos Aires 1965, La Scala, Milan 1965, Glyndebourne Festival 1966, Royal Opera, Covent Garden, Scottish Opera 1967, Vienna Festival 1972, San Francisco Opera 1977, Chicago Lyric Opera 1977, Théâtre Municipal d'Angers 1979, Edinburgh Festival 1979, Nat. Opera Ebony, Philadelphia 1980, Spoleto Festival, Charleston, S.C. 1980, Tulsa Opera, Oklahoma 1980, Ottawa Festival 1981, Deutsche Oper 1983, Guelph Spring Festival 1983; Prof. of Voice, Univ. of Md.; Artistic Dir. New School for the Arts, Montclair; Hon. H.D.H. (Wilberforce Univ.); Hon. LL.D. (Montclair State Coll.); Nat. Arts Club Award 1960, Concorso di Musica e Danza (Italy) 1960; Distinguished Scholar-Teacher Award, Univ. of Md. 1985–86. *Leisure interests:* tennis, sketching and cartoons, writing. *Address:* c/o Ann Summers International, Box 188, Sta. A, Toronto M5W 1B2, Canada; University of Michigan School of Music, Ann Arbor, Mich. 48109-7821, U.S.A. *Telephone:* 416 362-1422 (Canada); 665-7821 (Mich.).

SHIRLEY-QUIRK, John, C.B.E., B.SC.; British concert and opera singer; b. 28 Aug. 1931, Liverpool; s. of Joseph Stanley and Amelia Shirley-Quirk; m. 1st Dr. Patricia Hastie 1952 (died 1981), one s. one d.; m. 2nd Sara Watkins 1981, one s. two d.; ed. Holt School, Liverpool, and Liverpool Univ.; Flying Officer, R.A.F. (Educ. Branch) 1952–55; Asst. lecturer, Acton Tech. Coll. 1956–60; Vicar Choral, St. Paul's Cathedral 1960–61; professional singer 1961–; Joint Artistic Dir. Aldeburgh Festival 1981–; mem., Court, Brunel Univ. 1977–; Hon. R.A.M. 1972; D.Mus. h.c. (Liverpool) 1976; Hon. D.Univ. (Brunel) 1981; many recordings and first performances, particularly works of Benjamin Britten. *Leisure interests:* clocks, canals, trees. *Address:* c/o Harrison/Parrott Ltd., 12 Penzance Place, London, W11 4PA; 51 Wellesley Road, Twickenham, Middx., TW2 5RX, England.

SHITIKOV, Aleksey Pavlovich; Soviet politician; b. 14 March 1912, Gorka, Kostroma oblast; ed. Gorki Agricultural Inst. and Higher Party School; Member CPSU 1939–; party work, Soviet army 1941–45; Apparatus, Khabarovsk Krai Cttee. CPSU 1945–48, 1950–52; Sec. Kamchatka oblast Cttee. CPSU 1948–50, The First Sec. Jewish Autonomous Region 1952–55; Sec. Khabarovsk Krai Cttee. CPSU 1955–57, First Sec. 1957–70; Chair. Soviet of Union, U.S.S.R. Supreme Soviet 1970–, U.S.S.R. Parl. Group of Inter-Parl. Union 1970–; mem. Central Cttee. CPSU 1961–; Deputy to U.S.S.R. Supreme Soviet 1954–; mem. Cttee. for Foreign Affairs, Soviet of Union 1970–; Chair. Soviet Cttee. for European Security and Co-operation 1971–84, Chair. of Soviet Soc. for Cultural Relations with Compatriots Abroad 1984–; Order of Lenin (three times), Order of the October Revolution 1982, and other decorations. *Address:* Presidium of the U.S.S.R. Supreme Soviet, The Kremlin, Moscow.

SHKABARDNYA, Mikhail Sergeyevich; Soviet official; b. 1930; ed. Novocherkassk Polytech. Inst.; mem. CPSU 1960–; engineer, tech. Lab. Chief, Chief engineer in an electrical measuring instruments plant, Krasnodar 1954–68; Head of 'Soyuzelektropribor' Assoc. of U.S.S.R. Ministry of Instrument-Making, Automation Equipment and Control Systems 1968–74; Deputy Minister 1974–80, Minister 1980–; Deputy to U.S.S.R. Supreme Soviet 1979–; Cand. mem. of Cen. Cttee. CPSU 1981–86; mem. 1986–; State Prize 1976. *Address:* Ministry of Instrument-Making, Automation Equipment and Control Systems, Moscow, U.S.S.R.

SHKADOV, Ivan Nikolaevich; Soviet army general and politician; b. 2 May 1913, Naumovo, Kaluga Dist.; komsomol posts in Kaluga Dist. 1931–35; ed. School for Tank Troops, Kharkov; mem. CPSU 1938–; commdr. of a tank platoon, asst. to chief of staff, chief of staff, special tank bn. 1938–41; asst. to chief of staff, reconnaissance tank regt., commdr. of a tank regt. bn. 1941–42; commdr. of a special tank regt. 1942–45; commdr. of special tank brigades 1945–50; Deputy Commdr. of a mechanized div. 1950–53; attended Mil. Acad. for Tank and Mechanized Troops until 1953; attended Mil. Acad. of Gen. Staff, Moscow until 1959; commdr. of a tank div. 1953–59; sr. ranks in Soviet Army 1959–61; Deputy Commdr. of Carpathian Mil. Dist. 1961–64; sr. mem. of a group of mil. specialists and chief consultant to Ministry of Revolutionary Armed Forces, Cuba 1964–66; Commdr. of Northern Group of Forces (Poland) 1967–68; First Deputy Chief of Mil. Acad. of Staff 1968–; Head of Main Directorate of Mil. Training Facilities, U.S.S.R. Ministry of Defence 1969–72; Head of Main Directorate of Cadres, U.S.S.R. Ministry of Defence 1972–82; Deputy to Council of the Union, U.S.S.R. Supreme Soviet 1977–; rank of Army Gen. 1975; U.S.S.R. Deputy Minister of Defence for Personnel 1982–; Orders of Red Banner (five times), Suvorov Order (3rd class), Order of Red Star (twice), Order of October Revolution 1973, Hero of the Soviet Union 1978, Order of Lenin 1978, 1983. *Address:* Ministry of Defence, Moscow, U.S.S.R.

SHKOLNIKOV, Aleksey Mikhailovich; Soviet politician; b. 1914; ed. Industrial Acad. and Party Higher School of Cen. Cttee. of CPSU, Moscow; foreman and later chief power technician at plant in Perm Dist. 1933–43; mem. CPSU 1940–; party work 1943–45; Rep. for Voronezh Dist. Party Control Cttee. of Cen. Cttee. of All-Union CP 1945–47; Second Sec. Kaluga Dist. of All-Union CP 1947–49; First Sec. Tambov Dist. Cttee. of CPSU 1952–55; cand. mem., later mem. Cen. Cttee. of CPSU 1956–89; Deputy to Foreign Affairs Comm. 1954–66; mem. of Draft Bills Comm., U.S.S.R.

Supreme Soviet 1966–74; First Deputy Chair. Council of Ministers of R.S.F.S.R. 1965–74; Chair. U.S.S.R. Cttee. on People's Control 1974–87; numerous Soviet decorations. *Address:* The Kremlin, Moscow, U.S.S.R.

SHLAUDEMAN, Harry Walter, B.A.; American diplomatist; b. 17 May 1926, Los Angeles, Calif.; s. of Karl Whitman and Florence Pixley Shlaudeman; m. Carol Jean Dickey 1948; two s. one d.; ed. Stanford Univ., Calif.; served U.S. Marine Corps. 1944–46; joined U.S. Foreign Service 1955; Vice-Consul, Barranquilla, Colombia 1955–56; Political Officer, Bogotá, Colombia 1956–58; assigned language training, Washington, D.C. 1958–59; Consul, Sofia, Bulgaria 1960–62; Chief of Political Section, Santo Domingo, Dominican Repub. 1962–64; Officer in Charge of Dominican Affairs, Dept. of State, Washington, D.C. 1964–65, Asst. Dir. Office of Caribbean Affairs 1965–66, Sr. Seminar Foreign Policy 1966–67, Special Asst. to Sec. of State 1967–69, Dir. INR RAR, Dept. of State 1969; Deputy Chief of Mission, Counsellor of Embassy, Santiago, Chile 1969–73; Deputy Asst. Sec. of State for Inter-American Affairs 1973–75; Amb. to Venezuela 1975–76; Asst. Sec. of State for Inter-American Affairs 1976–77; Amb. to Peru 1977–80, to Argentina 1980–83; Exec. Dir. Nat. Bipartisan Cttee. on Cen. America 1983–84; Pres.'s Special Amb. to Cen. America 1984–86; Amb. to Brazil 1986–. *Leisure interest:* golf. *Address:* American Embassy, SES, Av. das Naçoẽs Lote 3, 70.403 Brasilia, D.F., Brazil; 3531 Winfield Lane, N.W., Washington, D.C. 20007, U.S.A. (Home).

SHLYAPNIKOV, German Evlampevich; Soviet diplomatist; b. 1929; diplomatic service 1960–; various posts in U.S.S.R. Embassies in China and Mongolia; embassy counsellor in New Zealand and Bolivia 1970–75; Amb. to Ecuador 1975–80, to Nicaragua 1980–86. *Address:* c/o Ministry of Foreign Affairs, Smolenskaya-Sennaya pl. 32-34, Moscow, U.S.S.R.

SHOCK, Maurice, M.A.; British academic; b. 15 April 1926; s. of Alfred Shock and Ellen Shock; m. Dorothy Donald 1947; one s. three d.; ed. King Edward's School, Birmingham and Balliol and St. Antony's Colls. Oxford; served Intelligence Corps. 1945–48; Lecturer in Politics, Christ Church and Trinity Coll. Oxford 1955–56; Fellow and Praelector in Politics, Univ. Coll. Oxford 1956–77; Estates Bursar 1959–74; Vice-Chancellor, Univ. of Leicester 1977–87; Rector, Lincoln Coll. Oxford 1987–; mem. Franks Comm. of Inquiry into Univ. of Oxford 1964–66; Hebdomadal Council, Oxford Univ. 1969–75; Chair. Univ. Authorities Panel 1980–85. *Publications:* The Liberal Tradition; articles on politics and recent history. *Leisure interests:* gardening, theatre. *Address:* Lincoln College, Oxford, England.

SHOCKLEY, William (Bradford), B.SC., PH.D.; American scientist; b. 13 Feb. 1910, London, England; s. of William Hillman and May (née Bradford) Shockley; m. 1st Jean Alberta Bailey 1933, two s. one d.; m. 2nd Emmy Lanning 1955; ed. California Inst. of Tech., M.I.T.; mem. Tech. Staff 1936–42, Dir. Solid State Physics Research Program 1945–54 and Dir. Transistor Physics Research 1954–55, Bell Telephone Laboratories; Dir. of Research, anti-submarine Warfare Operations Research Group U.S.N. 1942–44; Expert Consultant, Office of the Sec. of War 1944–45; Visiting lecturer Princeton Univ. 1946; Scientific Adviser, Policy Council, Joint Research and Devt. Bd. 1947–49; Scientific Advisory Panel, U.S. Army 1951–63; Visiting Prof. California Inst. of Tech. 1954–55; Deputy Dir. and Dir. of Research, Weapons Systems Evaluation Group, Dept. of Defence 1954–55; Dir. Semi-conductor Laboratory of Beckman Instruments Inc. 1955–58; Pres. Shockley Transistor Corpn. 1958–60; Dir. Shockley Transistor (unit of Clevite Transistor) 1960–63; Mem. of President's Science Advisory Comm. on Scientific and Tech. Manpower 1962; Alexander M. Poniatoff Prof. of Eng. and Applied Science, Stanford Univ. 1963–75, Emer. Prof. 1975–; mem. Air Force Scientific Advisory Bd. 1958–62; Exec. Consultant to Bell Labs. 1965–75; Sr. Consultant to Army Scientific Advisory Panel; inventor of junction transistor; research on energy bands of solids, ferromagnetic domains, plastic properties of metals, semi-conductor theory applied to devices and device defects such as dislocations, fundamentals of electro-magnetic energy and momentum, mental tools for scientific thinking; operations research on human quality problems; holder of over 90 U.S. patents; mem. Scientific and Tech. Advisory Comm. to NASA, Nat. Acad. of Sciences, American Inst. of Physics, Inventors Hall of Fame of Nat. Council of Patent Law Asscn.; Fellow I.E.E.E.; Hon. Dr. (Univ. of Pa.) 1955, (Rutgers) 1956, (Gustavus Adolphus Coll.) 1963; numerous awards 1946–69 including Medal for Merit 1946, Morris Liebman Prize (I.E.E.E.) 1952, O.E. Buckley Prize (American Physics Soc.) 1953, Nobel Prize for Physics 1956; Comstock Prize (Nat. Acad. of Sciences), Holley Medal (American Soc. of Mechanical Engineers) Wilhelm Exner Medal (Österreichischer Gewerbeverein) 1963, NASA Certificate of Appreciation 1969 and NASA Public Service Group Achievement Award 1969, I.E.E.E. Gold.Medal, 25th anniversary of Transistor 1972; Nat. Inventors Hall of Fame 1974; I.E.E.E. Medal of Honour 1980, Calif. Inventors' Hall of Fame 1983. *Publications:* Electrons and Holes in Semi-conductors 1950, Imperfections of Nearly Perfect Crystals 1952; Mechanics (co-author) 1966, and many articles. *Leisure interests:* swimming, gardening. *Address:* 797 Esplanada Way, Stanford, Calif. 94305, U.S.A. (Home). *Telephone:* (415) 857-1378.

SHOEMAKER, Eugene Merle, M.S., M.A., PH.D.; American geologist; b. 28 April 1928, Los Angeles; s. of George Shoemaker and Muriel M. Scott Shoemaker; m. Carolyn J. Spellmann 1951; one s. two d.; ed. Calif. Inst. of Tech. and Princeton Univ.; Geologist, U.S. Geological Survey 1948–,

Chief, Br. of Astrogeology 1961–66, Chief Scientist, Center of Astrogeology 1966–68, Research Geologist 1976–; Visiting Prof. Calif. Inst. of Tech. 1962, Research Assoc. 1964–68, Prof. of Geology 1969–85; Acting Dir. NASA Manned Space Sciences Div. 1963; Co-Investigator, Television experiment, Project Ranger 1961–65; Prin. Investigator, TV experiment, Project Surveyor 1963–68; Prin. Investigator, Geological field investigations in Apollo lunar landings 1965–70; Co-Investigator, TV experiment, Project Voyager 1978–; mem. N.A.S. and other professional socs.; numerous awards and hon. degrees. *Address:* U.S. Geological Survey, 2255 North Gemini Drive, Flagstaff, Ariz. 86001 (Office); P.O. Box 984, Flagstaff, Ariz. 86002, U.S.A. (Home). *Telephone:* 602-774-4350 (Home).

SHOEMAKER, Willie (William Lee); American jockey; b. 19 Aug. 1931, Fabens, Tex.; s. of Bebe and Ruby (Call) Shoemaker; m. Cynthia Barnes 1978; one d.; jockey since 1949; Winner Ky. Derby 1955, 1959, 1965, 1986, Belmont Stakes 1957, 1959, 1962, 1967, 1985, Preakness Stakes 1963, 1967; has won more than 810 Stakes races; first jockey to have 8,000 wins. *Address:* c/o Vincent Andrews Management, 315 S. Beverly Drive, Suite 216, Beverly Hills, Calif. 90212, U.S.A.

SHOEMATE, C. Richard, M.B.A.; American business executive; b. 10 Dec. 1939, LaHarpe, Ill.; s. of Richard Osborne Shoemate and Mary Jane (née Gillette) Shoemate; m. Nancy Lee Gordon 1962; three s.; ed. Western Ill. Univ. and Univ. of Chicago; Comptroller Corn Products Unit, CPC Int. 1972–74, Plant Man. 1974–76, Vice-Pres. Operations 1976–81; Corpn. Vice-Pres. CPC Int. 1983–88, Pres. 1988–; Pres. Canada Starch Co. 1981–83, mem., Bd. of Dirs. 1981–88; Bd. of Dirs. Corn Refiners Asscn. 1985–88. *Address:* CPC International Inc., International Plaza, P.O.Box 8000, Englewood Cliffs, N.J. 07632, U.S.A. (Office). *Telephone:* (201) 894-2797 (Office).

SHOENBERG, David, M.B.E., F.R.S., PH.D.; British physicist (retd.); b. 4 Jan. 1911, St. Petersburg, Russia; s. of Sir Isaac Shoenberg and Esther Shoenberg (née Aisenstein); m. Catherine Félicitée Fischmann 1940; one s. two d.; ed. Latymer Upper School, London and Trinity Coll. Cambridge; Exhbn. of 1851 Sr. Student 1936–39; Research in Low Temperature Physics 1932–; in charge of Royal Soc. Mond. Lab. 1947–73; Lecturer in Physics 1944–52, Reader 1952–73, UNESCO Adviser on Low Temperature Physics, Nat. Physical Lab. of India 1953–54; Prof. of Physics Cambridge Univ. and Head of Low Temperature Physics Group, Cavendish Lab. 1973–78, Prof. Emer. 1978–; Life Fellow Gonville and Caius Coll. Cambridge; Hon. Foreign mem. American Acad. of Arts and Sciences; Dr. h.c. (Lausanne) 1973; Fritz London Award for Low Temperature Physics 1964. *Publications:* Superconductivity 1938, 1952, Magnetism 1949, Magnetic Oscillations in Metals 1984; scientific papers on low temperature physics and magnetism. *Address:* c/o Cavendish Laboratory, Madingley Road, Cambridge, CB3 0HE (Office); 2 Long Road, Cambridge, England (Home). *Telephone:* Cambridge 337389 (Office).

SHOGO, Watanabe; Japanese executive; b. 31 Aug. 1915; m. Murako Tajima 1943; two s. one d.; ed. Tokyo Univ.; with the Industrial Bank of Japan Ltd. 1938–62; Man. Dir. Nikko Securities Co. 1962, Sr. Man. Dir. 1963, Vice-Pres. 1966, Pres. 1970–, Chair. 1973–; Pres. Nikko Research Centre Ltd. 1970–88, Japan Fund Inc. 1973– (Vice-Chair. 1974–), Dir. Pvt. Investment Co. for Asia (PICA) 1975–, Tokyo Stock Exchange 1973–; Exec. Dir. Japan Fed. of Employers' Asscn. 1970–; Trustee, Japan Cttee. for Econ. Devt. 1971–; Man. Dir. Fed. of Econ. Orgs. (Keidanren) 1970–; Pres. Bond Underwriters Asscn. of Japan 1972–73; mem. Trilateral Comm. 1973–; Chair. Securities Dealers Asscn. of Japan 1975–; mem. Securities and Exchange Council 1976–, Financial System Council 1976–, Taxation System Council of Govt. *Leisure interest:* oil painting. *Address:* Nikko Securities Company Ltd., 3-1, Marunouchi 3-chome, Chiyoda-ku, Tokyo (Office); 6-2, Eifuku 3-chome, Suginami-ku, Tokyo, Japan (Home). *Telephone:* (03) 283-2211 (Office); (03) 328-4205 (Home).

SHONE, Sir Robert Minshull, C.B.E., M.A., M.ENG.; British economist; b. 1906, Birkenhead; ed. Sedbergh School, Liverpool Univ. and Univ. of Chicago; Industrial work 1928–32; Commonwealth Fellow (U.S.A.) 1932–34; Lecturer, L.S.E. 1935–36; Gen. Dir. Ministry of Supply, Iron and Steel Control 1942–45; Dir. British Iron and Steel Fed. 1950–53; exec. mem. Iron and Steel Bd. 1953–61; Dir.-Gen. Nat. Econ. Devt. Council 1962–66; Dir. M. and G. Group PLC 1966–84; Visiting Prof. of Applied Econs., City Univ. (London) 1967–84; Dir. Rank Org. Ltd. 1968–78, A.P.V. Holdings Ltd. 1970–76; Special Prof. Nottingham Univ. 1971–73. *Publications:* Problems of Investment 1971, Price and Investment Relationships 1975, and numerous articles in journals. *Leisure interest:* golf. *Address:* 7 Windmill Hill, London, N.W.3, England. *Telephone:* 01-435 1930.

SHONO, Senkichi, LL.B.; Japanese banker; b. 22 Sept. 1913, Tokyo; s. of Danroku and Shige Shono; m. Yuki Minoda 1943; one s. two d.; ed. Tokyo Univ.; joined The Mitsui Trust and Banking Co., Ltd. 1937, Dir. and Man., Security Dept. 1959, Dir. and Man. Nagoya Branch 1962, Man. Dir. and Man., Head Office Business Dept. 1965, Sr. Man. Dir. 1968, Pres. 1971–79, Dir. and Counsellor 1979–81, Counsellor 1981–; Dir. Mitsui Memorial Hosp. 1972–; Counsellor, Mitsui Petrochemical Industries Ltd. 1987. *Leisure interests:* listening to music, reading, golf. *Address:* Mitsui Trust & Banking Co. Ltd., 1-1 Nihonbashi-Muromachi, 2-chome, Chuo-ku, 103 Tokyo (Office); 1605 Fueda, 17-3 Kamakurayama 1-chome, Kamakura-shi, Kanagawa Pref., 248 Japan (Home). *Telephone:* 03-270-9511 (Office); 0467-31-1647 (Home).

SHOPPEE, Charles William, M.A., D.PHIL., PH.D., D.SC., F.R.S.; British university professor; b. 24 Feb. 1904, London; elder s. of J. W. and Elizabeth Shoppee; m. Eileen Alice West 1929; one d.; ed. Stationers' Company School, London, and Univs. of London, Leeds and Basel; Sr. Student of Royal Comm. for Exhbn. of 1851 1926–28; Asst. Lecturer and Lecturer in Organic Chem., Univ. of Leeds 1929–39; Rockefeller Research Fellow, Univ. of Basel 1939–45; Reader in Chem., Univ. of London, at Royal Cancer Hospital 1945–48; Prof. of Chem., Univ. of Wales, at Univ. Coll., Swansea 1948–56; Prof. of Organic Chem., Univ. of Sydney 1956–69, now Emer.; Robert A. Welch Foundation Prof. of Chem., Tex. Technological Univ. 1970–75; Reilly Lecturer, Univ. of Notre Dame 1951; Visiting Prof. of Organic Chem., Duke Univ. 1963, Univ. of Georgia 1966, Univ. of Miss. 1968, Fellow, Australian Acad. of Science 1958–; Hon. Prof. Fellow Macquarie Univ. 1975–79; Hon. Visiting Prof. (La Trobe Univ.) 1980–. *Publications:* some 250 scientific papers in Journal of Chemical Society (London), Journal of American Chemical Society, Helvetica Chimica Acta and Australian Journal of Chemistry. *Leisure interests:* bridge, music. *Address:* 1/75 Normanby Road, Kew, Vic. 3101, Australia. *Telephone:* (03) 8172644.

SHORE, Rt. Hon. Peter (David), P.C., M.P.; British politician; b. 20 May 1924; m. Elizabeth Catherine Wrong 1948; two s. (one deceased) two d.; ed. Quarry Bank High School, Liverpool, and King's Coll., Cambridge; mem. Labour Party 1948–; Head of Research Dept., Labour Party 1959–64; M.P. for Stepney 1964–74, for Tower Hamlets, Stepney and Poplar 1974–83, Bethnal Green and Stepney 1983–87; Parl. Pvt. Sec. to Prime Minister 1965–66; Joint Parl. Sec. Ministry of Tech. 1966–67; Sec. of State for Econ. Affairs 1967–69; Minister without Portfolio 1969–70; Labour Party Spokesman on European Affairs 1971–74; Sec. of State for Trade 1974–76, for the Environment 1976–79; Pres. British Overseas Trade Bd. 1974–76; Opposition Spokesman for Foreign Affairs 1979–80, for Treasury and Econ. Affairs Dec. 1980–83, for Trade and Industry 1983–84; Shadow Leader of the House of Commons 1983–87; mem. Select Cttee. On Foreign Affairs 1987–; Hon. Fellow, Queen Mary Coll., London. *Publication:* Entitled to Know 1966. *Leisure interest:* swimming. *Address:* House of Commons, London, S.W.1; 23 Dryburgh Road, London, S.W.15, England.

SHORT, Rt. Hon. Edward Watson (see Glenamara, Baron).

SHORTER, Wayne, B.A.; American musician; b. 25 Aug. 1933, Newark; ed. New York Univ.; played saxophone with Art Blakey 1959–63, Miles Davis 1964–70, Weather Report 1970–86; served U.S. Army 1956–58; winner numerous Down Beat Magazine Awards, Best Soprano Sax 1984, 1985. *Solo albums include:* Native Dancer, Soothsayer, Etcetera 1981, Atlantis 1986, Phantom Navigator 1987. *Address:* c/o Brighton Agency, 9615 Brighton Way, Beverly Hills, Calif. 90201, U.S.A.

SHOSTAKOVICH, Maksim Dmitriyevich; Russian pianist and conductor; b. 1938, Leningrad; s. of the late Dmitriy Shostakovich; m.; one s.; ed. Cen. Music School, Moscow Conservatory; studied conducting under Rabinovich, Gauk, Rozhdestvensky (q.v.); Asst. Conductor, Moscow Symphony Orchestra; Conductor, Govt. Academic Symphony Orchestra; piano debut age 19 in father's Second Piano Concerto; Prin. Conductor and Artistic Dir. U.S.S.R. Radio and TV Symphony Orchestra, touring Western Europe, Japan, U.S.A. 1971–81; requested and granted political asylum in U.S.A. while on tour with U.S.S.R. Radio and TV Symphony Orchestra, Nuremberg April 1981; conducted Nat. Symphony Orchestra, Capitol steps, Washington, D.C., U.S.A. May 1981; Prin. Guest Conductor Hong Kong Philharmonic 1982–; Musical Adviser Hartford Symphony Orchestra, Conn. 1985–; conducted premiere of father's 15th Symphony and recorded virtually all father's symphonies in U.S.S.R.; has performed with leading soloists, incl. Emil Gilels, Oistrakh, Rostropovich. *Address:* c/o Columbia Artists Inc., 165 W. 57th Street, New York, N.Y. 10019, U.S.A.

SHOTTON, Frederick William, M.B.E., F.R.S., D.SC., F.ENG.; British geologist; b. 8 Oct. 1906, Coventry; s. of Frederick John Shotton and Ada Shotton (née Brookes); m. 1st Alice L. Linnett 1930 (deceased 1979); m. 2nd Lucille F. Bailey 1983; two d.; ed. Bablake School, Coventry and Sidney Sussex Coll. Cambridge; Geologist/Lecturer, Birmingham Univ. 1928–36; Geologist/Lecturer, Cambridge Univ. 1936–45; Prof., Sheffield Univ. 1945–49; Prof., Birmingham Univ. 1949–74, Prof. Emer., continuing Quaternary research, writing and work as consultant 1975–; Dean of Faculty of Science, Birmingham Univ. 1957–60; Pro-Vice-Chancellor and Vice-Principal, Birmingham Univ. 1965–71; Pres. Geological Soc. of London 1964–66, Birmingham Archaeological Soc. 1982–85, Warwickshire Nature Conservation Trust 1980–83; mem. Natural Environment Research Council 1969–72; Chair. X INQUA Congress, Birmingham 1977; Gov., The Coventry School; served as Maj. in Royal Engineers Middle East and Europe 1940–45; M.B.E. (mil.) and three times mentioned in despatches; Hon. mem. Int. Union for Quaternary Research, Royal Irish Acad., Société belge de Géologie; Prestwich Medal, Geological Soc. of London; Stopes Medal, Geological Asscn. *Publications:* The Pleistocene deposits of the area between Coventry, Rugby and Leamington, 1953, British Quaternary Studies (ed. and contrib.) 1977; approx. 150 scientific papers. *Leisure interests:* natural history, nature conservation, archaeology. *Address:* 111 Dorridge Road, Dorridge, West Midlands, B93 8BP, England. *Telephone:* Knowle 2820.

SHOUKRY, Mohammed Anwar; Egyptian egyptologist; b. 1905; ed. Cairo Univ. Inst. of Egyptology and Univ. of Göttingen; Asst. Prof. of Egyptology Cairo Univ. 1948-52, Prof. 1952; Chief Archaeologist Centre of Documentation of Egyptian Art and Civilisation 1956-59; Dir.-Gen. Dept. of Egyptian Antiquities 1959-66; Asst. Under-Sec. of State, Ministry of Culture and Nat. Guidance 1961-70; Resident Archaeologist in Nubia 1964. *Publications:* Die Grabstatue im Alten Reich, Egyptian Art from the Beginning till the End of the Ancient Kingdom (in Arabic). *Address:* c/o Ministry of Culture, Cairo, Egypt.

SHPEDKO, Ivan Fedeyevich; Soviet diplomatist; b. 1918, Ukraine; ed. Kharkov Pedagogic Inst.; diplomatic service 1941-; Counsellor, Embassy in Afghanistan 1949-53; sr. posts in U.S.S.R. Ministry of Foreign Affairs 1953-56; Amb. to Pakistan 1956-60; Deputy Head of S. Asia Dept., Ministry of Foreign Affairs 1960-63; Amb. to Canada 1963-69; Deputy Head of Second European Dept. 1969-70; Head of Second Far East Dept., Ministry of Foreign Affairs 1970-76; Amb. to Indonesia 1976-83. *Address:* c/o Ministry of Foreign Affairs, Moscow, U.S.S.R.

SHRESTHA, Marich Man Singh; Nepali politician; fmr. high school headmaster; fmr. Chair. Rashtriya Panchayat (Nat. Ass.); Prime Minister of Nepal, Minister of Royal Palace Affairs and Defence June 1986-. *Address:* Office of the Prime Minister, Kathmandu, Nepal.

SHRIMALI, Kalu Lal, M.A., PH.D., LL.D., D.LITT.; Indian educationist and politician; b. 30 Dec. 1909, Udaipur, Rajasthan; s. of R. L. and K. Shrimali; m. Gangabai Shrimali 1926; two s. three d.; ed. Banaras Hindu Univ., Calcutta Univ. and Columbia Univ., New York; Dean, Faculty of Educ. Univ. of Rajputana 1951-54; Parl. Sec. Ministry of Educ. New Delhi 1953-55, Deputy Minister for Educ. 1955-57, Minister of State in Ministry of Educ. and Scientific Research 1957-58, Minister of Educ. 1958-63; Vice-Chancellor Univ. of Mysore 1964-69; Vice-Chancellor, Banaras Hindu Univ. 1969-77; Chair. Assen. of Commonwealth Univs. 1969-70; mem. Admin. Bd., Int. Assen. of Univs. 1970-74, Vice-Pres. 1975-80; Chair. Inter-Univ. Bd. of India 1972-73; Pres. All-India Fed. of Educ. Assens.; Leader Indian Del. to U.S.S.R. (sponsored by Nat. Cttee., Indo-Soviet Cultural Soc.) June 1973; Admin. Vidya Bhawan Soc. 1980-85, Pres. 1985-; life mem. Vidya Bhawan Soc. 1931; Chair. Bd. of Trustees, Intercultural Co-operation (India) 1987-; Hon. D.Litt. (Banaras Hindu Univ. and Mysore Univ.), Hon. LL.D. (Vikram Univ.), Hon. D.Sc. (Kiev Univ.); Padma Vibhushan 1976. *Publications:* Bachon Ki Kuch Samasyayen (Hindi), Shiksha aur Bhartiya Loktantra (Hindi), The Wardha Scheme, Adventures in Education, Problems of Education in India, Education in Changing India, The Prospects for Democracy in India, A Search for Values in Indian Education, The Myth of University Autonomy. *Leisure interest:* gardening. *Address:* 310 Fatehpura, Udaipur, Rajasthan, India. *Telephone:* 24311 (Office); 23992 (Home).

SHRIVER, (Robert) Sargent, Jr., A.B., LL.D.; American executive and public servant; b. 9 Nov. 1915, Westminster, Md.; s. of Robert Sargent and Hilda Shriver; m. Eunice Kennedy 1953; four s. one d.; ed. Yale Univ.; admitted to N.Y. Bar 1941; served U.S.N. (Lieut. Commdr.) 1941-45; Asst. Ed. Newsweek 1945-46; Adviser The Joseph P. Kennedy, Jr. Foundation 1955-; Asst. Gen. Man. The Merchandise Mart 1948-61; mem. Chicago Bd. of Educ. 1955-60, Pres. 1956-60; Dir. The Peace Corps 1961-66, Office of Econ. Opportunity 1964-68; Special Asst. to the Pres. 1964-68; Amb. to France 1968-70; Democratic Vice-Presidential Cand. 1972; Partner, Fried, Frank, Harris, Shriver & Jacobson 1971-86, of counsel 1986-; mem. American Comm. on East-West Accord 1978-, Americans for SALT 1979-; Dir. The Arms Control Assen. 1983-; mem. Bd. of Arms Control Assen.; Pres. Special Olympics Int. 1984-; official of numerous educational bodies; Hon. LL.D., Hon. L.H.D., Hon. D.C.L., etc. from numerous univs.; Golden Heart Presidential Award (Philippines), Médaille de Vermeil (City of Paris) and many national awards. *Publication:* Point of the Lance 1964. *Address:* c/o Fried, Frank, Harris, Shriver & Jacobson, 1350 New York Avenue, N.W., Washington, D.C. 20005; 600 New Hampshire Avenue, N.W., Washington, D.C., U.S.A. *Telephone:* (202) 342-3555.

SHRONTZ, Frank Anderson, LL.B., M.B.A.; American business executive; b. 14 Dec. 1931, Boise, Ida.; s. of Thurlyn Howard Shrontz and Florence Elizabeth Anderson; m. Harriet Ann Houghton 1954; three s.; ed. Univ. of Idaho, Harvard Graduate School and Stanford Graduate School (Sloan Fellow); Asst. Sec. of the Air Force 1973-75; Asst. Sec. of Defense 1976; Corpn. Vice-Pres., Contract Admin. and Planning 1977; Vice-Pres., Gen. Man. Boeing Commercial Airplane Co. 1978-82, Vice-Pres., Sales, Boeing Commercial Airplane Co. (Div. of Boeing Co.) 1982-84, Pres. 1984-85, Pres., C.E.O. and mem. of Bd. of Dirs., The Boeing Co. 1986-88, Chair. and C.E.O. Jan. 1988-; mem. Bd. of Dirs. Citicorp 1986-; Distinguished Service Award, Dept. of Defense. *Leisure interests:* hunting, skiing, golf. *Address:* The Boeing Company, P.O. Box 3707, Seattle, Wash. 98124 (Office); Mercer Island, Wash. 98040, U.S.A. (Home). *Telephone:* (206) 655-2121 (Office).

SHTOKOLOV, Boris; Soviet opera singer; b. 19 March 1930, Kuznetsk; soloist with Sverdlovsk Opera 1954-59; with Kirov Opera 1959-; bass; People's Artist of U.S.S.R. 1965. *Address:* Kirov Opera, Teatralnaya ploshchad, Leningrad, U.S.S.R.

SHU TING; Chinese poet; b. June 1952, Xiamen (Amoy), Fujian Prov.; m. Chen Zhongyi; ed. Xiamen middle school; was sent to Southern Fujian 1969-72; worker, bulb factory, Xiamen 1977-; mem. Writers' Assen., Fujian 1981-; mem. a Writers Del. to Horizonte Festival in West Berlin 1985-. *Publications:* Shuangweichuan (Two-masts) 1982. Shuqing Shixuan (Collection of Poems) 1984. *Address:* 13 Zhonghua Road, Gulangyu, Xiamen City, People's Republic of China.

SHU TONG; Chinese politician and calligrapher; b. 14 Dec. 1906, Jiangxi Prov.; s. of Renxin and Mrs. (née Lè) Shu; m. 1st M. Wei 1924 (died 1928); m. 2nd Wang Yunfei; two s. two d.; ed. Shangzhi School and 3rd Prov. Normal School, Jiangxi; joined CCP 1926, Red Army 1930 and took part in the Long March 1935; held many important Army posts; Chair. of Culture and Educ. Comm. of East China Civil and Mil. Comm.; Pres. East China People's Revolutionary Univ., East China Party School; First Political Commissar Jinan Mil. Region, Party Sec. Shandong Prov. Party Comm. 1954; mem. Cen. Comm. of 8th Party Congress 1956; Sec. of Shanxi Prov. Party Comm. 1963; suffered political persecution 1966-67; Vice-Pres. and mem. Party Standing Comm. of the Acad. of Mil. Science of Chinese People's Liberation Army 1978-83; mem. Gen. Advisory Comm. of 12th Party Congress; Rep. to 1st, 2nd and 3rd Nat. People's Congress; mem. Standing Comm. to 5th Congress of CCP; Hon. Prof. Hunan Univ. of Science and Tech.; first Pres. Chinese Calligraphers Assen. 1981-85, Hon. Pres. 1985-; created the Shu Style of calligraphy, which has spread throughout world; Inst. of Shu Tong Calligraphy founded in Jiangxi and Shandong Provs. *Publications:* Copybooks of Chinese Calligraphy in regular script, running hands and cursive hands; numerous articles on subjects combining theory of Marxism and its practice in China. *Leisure interests:* Chinese painting, poetry and art history of calligraphy. *Address:* c/o Academy of Military Science, The Chinese People's Liberation Army, Beijing, People's Republic of China.

SHUCKBURGH, Sir Evelyn, G.C.M.G., C.B.; British fmr. diplomatist; b. 26 May 1909, London; s. of Sir John Shuckburgh, K.C.M.G., C.B.; m. Hon. Nancy Brett 1937; two s. one d.; ed. Winchester Coll. and King's Coll., Cambridge; joined Foreign Office 1933; served Cairo 1937-39, Ottawa 1940-42, Buenos Aires 1942-45, Prague 1945-47; Head of S. American Dept., Foreign Office 1947-48, Western Dept., Western Orgs. Dept. 1949-51; Pvt. Sec. to Sec. of State for Foreign Affairs 1951-54; Asst. Under-Sec. of State, Foreign Office 1954-56; seconded to Imperial Defence Coll. as civilian instructor 1956-58; Asst. Sec.-Gen. (Political Affairs) NATO 1958-60; Deputy Under-Sec. Foreign Office, responsible for NATO, Western European Union, Council of Europe and W. European Countries 1960-62; Perm. Rep. to NATO 1962-66; Amb. to Italy 1966-69; Chair. Exec. Cttee., British Red Cross Soc. 1970-80, Chair. Council 1976-80, Vice-Chair. 1980-81; mem. Standing Comm. Int. Red Cross 1974-81, Chair. 1977-81; Dir. Commercial Union Assurance 1971-80. *Leisure interests:* music, cabinet making. *Address:* High Wood, Watlington, Oxford, England. *Telephone:* Watlington 2433.

SHUKLA, Vidya Charan, B.A.; Indian politician; b. 2 Aug. 1929, Raipur; s. of Ravi Shanker and Bhawani Shukla; m. Sarala Shukla 1951; three d.; ed. Morris Coll., and Univ. Coll. of Law, Nagpur; mem., Lok Sabha 1957-62, 1962-67, 1967-70, 1971-77; Deputy Minister of Communications and Parl. Affairs Jan.-Feb. 1966; Deputy Minister for Home Affairs 1966-67; Minister of State in Ministry of Home Affairs 1967-70; Minister of Revenue and Expenditure in Ministry of Finance 1970-71; Minister of Defence Production 1971-74, Minister of State for Planning 1974-75, for Information and Broadcasting 1975-77, for Civil Supplies 1980-81; Pres. Special Organising Cttee., 9th Asian Games, Delhi; Pres. All-India Council of Sports 1981-83; Chair. Nat. Insts. of Physical Educ. and Sports 1981-85; Pres. Indian Olympic Assen. 1984-88; expelled from Congress (1) Party 1987; f. Jan Monha (People's Front) Oct. 1987. *Leisure interests:* hunting, tracking and photography. *Address:* 1 Willingdon Crescent, New Delhi 110004, India. *Telephone:* 301-3883.

SHUKRY, Ibrahim; Egyptian politician; b. 22 Sept. 1916; joined Misr al-Fatat (Young Egypt) party 1935; shot in Cairo strike 1935; managed family estate, Sharbeen; Sec.-Gen. Misr al-Fatat 1946; elected Vice-Pres., then Pres. Socialist Party (fmrly. Misr al-Fatat) 1947-53; mem. for Kahaliyya, People's Assembly 1949-52; imprisoned for opposing the monarchy 1952; released after revolution 1952; returned to estate; joined Arab Socialist Union on its formation 1962, elected to Exec. Cttee. 1964; re-elected mem. for Kahaliyya 1964-68; Pres. Farmers' Union and Gen. Professional Assen. 1965-66; Gov. Wadi al-Gadeed 1968-76; elected to People's Ass. 1976; Minister of Agric. and Agrarian Reform Feb. 1977-May 1978, of Land Improvement May-Oct. 1978; Chair. Socialist Labour Party and Man. Ed. Al-Sha'b (party newspaper) Oct. 1978-; Leader of the Opposition, People's Assembly 1979-86. *Address:* Socialist Labour Party, People's Assembly Street, Cairo, Egypt.

SHULL, Harrison, PH.D.; American professor of chemistry; b. 17 Aug. 1923, Princeton, N.J.; s. of Prof. George H. Shull and Mary J. Nicholl; m. 1st Jeanne L. Johnson 1948 (dissolved 1962); m. 2nd Wil J. Bentley 1962; five s. three d.; ed. Princeton Univ. and Univ. of California (Berkeley); Nat. Research Council post-doctoral Fellow, Univ. of Chicago 1948-49; Asst. Prof., Iowa State Univ., Ames, Iowa 1949-54; Assoc. Prof., Indiana Univ. 1955-58, Prof. 1958-61, Research Prof. 1961-79, Dir. Research

Computing Center 1959-63, Dean Graduate School 1965-72; founder, supervisory Quantum Chemistry Program Exchange 1962-87; Vice-Chancellor for Research and Devt., Indiana Univ. 1972-76; Provost, Rensselaer Polytechnic Inst. 1979-82; Chancellor, Univ. of Colorado at Boulder 1982-85, Prof. of Chem. 1985-; Nat. Science Foundation Sr. post-doctoral Fellow 1968-69; Guggenheim Fellow 1954-55; Alfred P. Sloan Research Fellow 1956-58; mem. N.A.S.; Fellow, American Acad. of Arts and Sciences. *Publications:* numerous articles in Journal of Chemical Physics, Physical Review, Journal of Physical Chemistry etc. *Address:* University of Colorado at Boulder, Campus Box B17, Boulder, Colo. 80309; 1490 Patton Street, Boulder, Colo. 80303, U.S.A. (Home).

SHULMAN, Lawrence Edward, M.D., PH.D., F.A.C.P.; American biomedical research administrator and rheumatologist; b. 25 July 1919, Boston, Mass.; s. of David Herman Shulman and Belle (Tishler) Shulman; m. 1st Pauline K. Flint 1946, m. 2nd Reni Trudinger 1959; one s. two d.; ed. Harvard and Yale Univs.; Research Assoc. John B. Pierce Foundation, New Haven, Conn. 1942-45; Intern, Resident and Fellow in Internal Medicine, Johns Hopkins Hospital and Univ. of Baltimore 1949-53; Dir. Connective Tissue Div. Johns Hopkins Univ. Medical School 1955-75; Assoc. Prof. of Medicine, Johns Hopkins Univ. 1964-; Assoc. Dir. for Arthritis, Musculoskeletal and Skin Diseases, NIH 1976-82, Dir. 1982-86; Dir. Nat. Inst. of Arthritis and Musculoskeletal and Skin Diseases 1986-; several awards. *Publications:* over 100 scientific publications. *Address:* NIAMS, National Institutes of Health, Building 31, Room 4C-32, Bethesda, Md. 20892; 6302 Swords Way, Bethesda, Md. 20817, U.S.A. *Telephone:* 301-530-1019; 301-496-4353.

SHULMAN, Robert Gerson, M.A., PH.D.; American biophysicist; b. 3 March 1924, New York; s. of Joshua S. Shulman and Freda (Lipshay) Shulman; m. 1st Saralee Deutsch 1952 (died 1983), three s.; m. 2nd Stephanie S. Spangler 1986; ed. Columbia Univ.; Research Assoc. Columbia Univ. Radiation Lab., New York 1949; AEC Fellow in Chem Calif. Inst. of Tech. 1949-50; Head, Semiconductor Research Section, Hughes Aircraft Co. Culver City, Calif. 1950-53; mem. technical staff, Bell Labs., Murray Hill, N.J. 1953-66, Head, Biophysics Research Dept. 1966-79; Prof. of Molecular Biophysics, Yale Univ. 1979-; numerous visiting professorships, lectureships etc.; mem. N.A.S., Inst. of Medicine; Guggenheim Fellow, Cambridge 1961-62. *Address:* J. W. Gibbs Research Laboratories, Yale University, New Haven, Conn.; 401 Saint Ronan Street, New Haven, Conn. 06511, U.S.A. (Home).

SHULTZ, George Pratt, B.A., PH.D.; American economist, educator and government official; b. 13 Dec. 1920, New York; s. of Birl E. and Margaret Lennox Pratt Shultz; m. Helena M. O'Brien 1946; two s. three d.; ed. Princeton Univ. and M.I.T.; Assoc. Prof. of Industrial Relations, M.I.T. 1955-57; Senior Staff Economist, President's Council of Econ. Advisers 1955-56; Prof. of Industrial Relations, Graduate School of Business, Univ. of Chicago 1957-68; Dean, Graduate School of Business, Univ. of Chicago 1962-68; Pres. Industrial Research Asscn. 1968; U.S. Sec. of Labor 1969-70; Dir. Office of Man. and Budget, Exec. Office of the Pres. 1970-72; U.S. Sec. of Treasury 1972-74; Chair. Council on Econ. Policy 1973-74; Sec. of State 1982-89; Exec. Vice-Pres. Bechtel Corpn. 1974-75, Pres. 1975-80, Pres. Bechtel Group Inc. 1981-82; Prof. of Man. and Public Policy, Graduate School of Business, Stanford Univ. 1974-82, of Int. Economy Jan. 1989-; Chair. Int. Council, Morgan Guaranty Trust 1989-; Dir. Gen. Motors 1989-, Boeing Corpn. 1989-; mem. Treasury Advisory Cttee. on Reform of Int. Monetary System 1975-; mem. Cttee. to Fight Inflation; Dir. Gen. Motors Corpn. 1981-82, Dillon, Read & Co. Inc. 1981-82; Chair. Pres. Reagan's Econ. Policy Advisory Bd. 1981-; mem. Bd. of Trustees, Center for Advancement of Study in the Behavioral Sciences, Stanford, Calif.; Jefferson Award 1986. *Publications:* The Dynamics of a Labor Market, Management Organization and the Computer, Strategies for the Displaced Worker, Guidelines, Informal Controls and the Market Place, Economic Policy beyond the Headlines (co-author). *Leisure interests:* golf, tennis. *Address:* Graduate School of Business, Stanford University, Stanford, Calif. 94305; Falmouth Road, Bethesda, Md., U.S.A. *Telephone:* (202) 647-4910.

SHUMWAY, Forrest Nelson; American business executive; b. 21 March 1927, Skowhegan, Me.; s. of Sherman Nelson and Agnes Brooks Mosher; m. Patricia Ann Kelly 1950; one s. one d.; ed. Stanford Univ.; in U.S. Marine Corps; Sr. Law Clerk and Deputy County Counsel, Los Angeles until 1957; joined Legal Dept., Signal Oil and Gas Co. (now Signal Cos. Inc.) 1957, Sec. 1959-60, Asst. Gen. Counsel 1960-61, Vice-Pres. and Gen. Counsel 1961-64, Dir. 1958-, Pres. 1964-80, of Signal Co. Inc., C.E.O. 1968-80, Chair. of Bd. 1980-85; Vice-Chair. Allied Signal Inc. 1985-; Dir. Aluminium Co. of America, First Interstate Bancorp, Transamerica Corpn., The Clorox Co.; official of civic orgs. *Address:* 11255 North Torrey Pines Road, La Jolla, Calif. 92037, U.S.A.

SHUMWAY, Norman Edward, M.D., PH.D.; American surgeon; b. 1923, Kalamazoo, Mich.; m. Mary Lou Sturman; one s. three d.; ed. Vanderbilt Univ. and Univ. of Minnesota; Intern, Univ. of Minnesota Hospitals 1949-50, Medical Fellow in Surgery 1950-51, 1953, 1954; Nat. Heart Inst. Research Fellow 1954-56, Special Trainee 1956-57; mem. Surgical Staff, Stanford Univ. Hospitals 1958-, Asst. Prof. of Surgery 1959-61, Assoc. Prof. 1961-65, Head of Div. of Cardiovascular Surgery 1964-74, Prof. of Surgery 1965-74, Prof. Cardiovascular Surgery 1974-, Francis and Charles

D. Field Prof. 1976-; Chair. Dept. of Cardiovascular Surgery, Stanford Univ. Medical Center 1974-; has performed heart transplant operations. *Address:* Department of Cardiovascular Surgery, Stanford University Medical Center, Stanford, Calif. 94305, U.S.A. *Telephone:* (415) 497-5771.

SIAD BARRE, Maj.-Gen. Mohamed; Somali army officer and politician; b. 1921, Garbaharrey, Gedo Region; m. Khadija Siad Barre; twenty c.; ed. private schools in Mogadishu, Mil. Acad. (Italy), School of Admin. and Politics (Somalia); Chief Insp., Somali Police Force, Benadir, Upper Juba Region, during British admin. and from 1950, Italian trusteeship; attended Mil. Acad. (Italy) 1952; held various high posts in Police force 1954-60; Col., Vice-Commdt. Somali Nat. Army 1960, Commdr. 1962, Brigadier-Gen., Maj.-Gen. 1966, C.-in-C. of the Armed Forces; led successful coup against govt. Oct. 1969; Head of State Oct. 1969-; Pres. Supreme Revolutionary Council 1969-76; Sec.-Gen. Somali Revolutionary Socialist Party (SRP) July 1976-; Chair. Council of Ministers 1976-87; Pres. Somali Democratic Repub. Jan. 1980-, Prime Minister 1980-87; Chair. OAU 1974-75. *Publication:* The Philosophy of the Somali Revolution 1978. *Address:* Office of the Head of State, Mogadishu, Somalia.

SIBLEY, Antoinette, C.B.E.; British ballerina; b. 27 Feb. 1939, Bromley, Kent; d. of Edward G. Sibley and Winifred Smith; m. 1st Michael Somes 1964 (dissolved); m. 2nd Panton Corbett 1974, one s. one d.; joined the Royal Ballet 1956, Soloist 1959, Prin. Ballerina 1960-; dances leading roles in: Swan Lake, Sleeping Beauty, Coppelia, The Nutcracker, La Fille Mal Gardée, Romeo and Juliet, Jabez and the Devil (cr. role of Mary), The Dream (cr. Titania), Jazz Calendar (cr. Friday's Child), Enigma Variations (cr. Dorabella), Thais (cr. Thais), Triad (cr. the Girl), Manon (cr. Manon), Soupirs (cr. pas de deux), Symphonic Variations, Daphnis and Chloe, Varii Capricci, The Good-Humoured Ladies, A Month in the Country, etc.; L'Invitation au Voyage; made film The Turning Point 1978; mem. Arts Council Dance Advisory Panel 1980-. *Publications:* Sibley and Dowell 1976, Antoinette Sibley 1981, Reflections of a Ballerina 1985. *Leisure interests:* doing nothing, opera, cinema, reading. *Address:* c/o The Royal Ballet, Covent Garden, London, W.C.2, England.

SIBTHORP, Mary Margaret, O.B.E.; British organization official (retd.); b. 24 Dec. 1905, London; d. of Shurmer Llewellyn Sibthorp and Mildred Amalie Lane; ed. Henrietta Barnet High School, Hampstead, London; co-founder and Sec. Refugee Aliens Protection Cttee., subsequently Nat. Cttee. for Rescue from Nazi Terror 1940-46; Asst. Sec. New Commonwealth Soc. 1946-69; Dir. and Ed. David Davies Memorial Inst. of Int. Studies 1969-84. *Publication:* Jurisprudence of the World Court (collaborated with J.H.W. Verzitl). *Leisure interests:* reading, gardening, international affairs and conservation. *Address:* Charlton House, 173 Lower Addiscombe Road, Croydon, CR0 6PZ, Surrey, England. *Telephone:* 654-1512.

SICAT, Gerardo P., M.A., PH.D.; Philippine economist and government official; b. 7 Oct. 1935; s. of Eloy S. Sicat and Flora C. Pasión; m. Loretta S. Makasiar 1958; two s. three d.; ed. Univ. of the Philippines and M.I.T.; Prof. of Econ., Univ. of the Philippines 1969-72, Regent 1972-; Chair. Nat. Econ. Council 1970-72; Dir.-Gen. Nat. Econ. and Devt. Authority, Govt. of the Philippines 1972-78, Minister for Econ. Planning 1974-80; Chair. Philippines Inst. of Devt. Studies 1978-, Population Comm. 1978-; mem. Monetary Bd.; mem. Batasang Pambansa (Nat. Ass.) 1978-86. *Publications:* Production Functions in Philippine Manufacturing 1964, Regional Economic Development in the Philippines 1970, Philippine Development and Economic Policy 1972, Taxation and Progress 1972, New Economic Directions in the Philippines 1974, and several other works. *Leisure interests:* tennis, swimming, running. *Address:* c/o National Economic and Development Authority, Padre Faura Street, Ermita, Manila, Philippines. *Telephone:* 59-48-75; 58-56-14.

SICILIANO, Enzo, PH.D.; Italian novelist, playwright and journalist; b. 27 May 1934, Rome; s. of Natale Siciliano and Giuseppina Jenzi; m. Flaminia Petrucci 1963; two s.; literary critic, La Stampa, Turin 1969-77; Jt. Ed., with Alberto Moravia (q.v.) and Leonardo Sciascia (q.v.), Nuovi Argomenti 1972-; Literary Critic, Corriere della Sera, Milan 1977-; Theatre Critic, Epoca, Milan 1982-85; Literary Critic, L'Espresso, Rome 1985-; Premio Viareggio 1981. *Publications:* Racconti ambigui 1963, Autobiografia letteraria 1971, Rosa (pazza e disperata) 1973, La notte matrigna 1975, Puccini 1977, Vita di Pasolini 1978, La voce di Otello 1982, Diamante 1984, La Letteratura Italiana (Vols. 1, 2) 1986, 1987. *Address:* Nuovi Argomenti, via Sicilia 136, 00187 Rome (Office); via Caroncini 53, 00197 Rome, Italy (Home). *Telephone:* 06 474971 (Office).

SICKINGHE, Jonkheer Feyo Onno Joost, LL.D.; Netherlands business executive; b. 1 May 1926, The Hague; s. of Jonkheer D. W. Sickinghe and Jonkvrouwe W. J. M. E. Radermacher Schorer; m. M. C. van Eeghen 1952; two s. two d.; ed. Univ. of Utrecht; Solicitor 1952-55; various functions within VMF Stork 1955-63; Man. Dir. Koninklijke Machinefabriek Stork N.V. 1963-69; mem. Bd. of Man., Verenigde Machinefabrieken Stork N.V. 1969, Chair. 1971; mem. Bd. of Dirs. De Nederlandsche Bank N.V., Hagemeijer N.V., European Assets Trust N.V., Parenco B.V., Pechiney Nederland N.V.; Exec. mem. Fed. of Netherlands Industry. *Leisure interests:* sailing, theatre. *Address:* Oud Blaricummerweg 7, Naarden, Netherlands. *Telephone:* 02159-43728.

SIDDALL, Sir Norman, Kt., C.B.E., B.ENG., D.SC., F.ENG., F.I.MIN.E., C.B.I.M., F.R.S.A.; British mining engineer; b. 1918; m.; two s. one d.; ed. King Edward VII School, Sheffield, Sheffield Univ.; with B.A. Collieries Ltd. as Undermanager, then Asst. Man. of Gedling Colliery, later as Man. of Bestwood Colliery, Nottingham 1936–47; Area Gen. Man. of No. 5 Area in East Midlands Div.; Area Gen. Man. of No. 1 (Bolsover) Area 1957; Chief Mining Eng., H.Q. Production Dept. 1966; Dir.-Gen. of Production 1967; mem. Nat. Coal Bd. 1971–83, Deputy Chair. 1973–82, Chair. 1982–83; Vice-Chair. Int. Organizing Cttee. World Mining Congress 1977; mem. A.I.M.E.; Dir. British Mining Consultants Ltd., CIN Management Ltd.; Hon. D.Sc. (Nottingham) 1982; Krupinski Medal 1982, D.L. (Notts.). *Address:* Brentwood, High Oakham Road, Mansfield, Notts, NG18 5AJ, England.

SIDDHI SAVETSILA, Air Chief Marshal; Thai air force officer and politician; b. 7 Jan. 1919; ed. Ghulalongkorn Univ. and M.I.T.; fmr. pilot officer, Royal Thai Air Force and Adviser to Royal Thai Air Force; mem. Nat. Ass. 1973, Nat. Reform Council 1976; Minister, Prime Minister's Office, Second Kriangsak Govt.; Sec.-Gen. Nat. Security Council 1974–80; Minister of Foreign Affairs Feb. 1980–; Leader Social Action Party. *Address:* Ministry of Foreign Affairs, Saranromya Palace, Bangkok 2, Thailand.

SIDDIKY, B. A., B.L.; Bangladesh diplomatist; b. 4 Jan. 1915, Dhaka; m. (wife deceased); nine c.; ed. Calcutta and Dhaka Univs.; Advocate, Calcutta High Court 1946, Advocate-Gen. of East Pakistan 1957–60, served on Bench of Dhaka High Court 1960–67, Chief Justice of East Pakistan 1967–72; mem. Exec. Cttee. of World Judges Conf., Geneva and ex-officio mem. Supreme Judicial Council of Pakistan; past Chair. of Pakistan and Bangladesh Red Cross Socs.; past Pres. of Bangladesh Muslim League; Cabinet Minister and Adviser to Pres. of Bangladesh 1985–86; Perm. Rep. of Bangladesh to the UN 1986–. *Address:* Permanent Mission of the People's Republic of Bangladesh to the UN, 821 United Nations Plaza, 8th Floor, New York, N.Y. 10017, U.S.A. *Telephone:* 867-3434.

SIDDIQI, M. Raziuddin, M.A., PH.D.; Pakistani educationist and scientist; b. 2 Jan. 1908, Hyderabad (Deccan): s. of M. Muzaffaruddin Siddiqi and Amatullah Begum; m. Khurshid Jahan Kazim Yar Jung 1933; one s. three d.; ed. Osmania, Cambridge, Berlin, Göttingen, Leipzig, Paris Univs.; Prof. of Mathematics, Dir. of Research and Vice-Chancellor, Osmania Univ. 1931–50; Dir. of Research and Vice-Chancellor, Peshawar Univ. 1950–58; Vice-Chancellor, Univ. of Sind 1959–64; Pres. Pakistan Acad. of Sciences 1961–67, 1984–86, Sec. 1953–61, 1969–78, Sec.-Gen. 1978–84; Vice-Chancellor, Univ. of Islamabad 1965–73; Prof. Emer. Quaid-i-Azam Univ. 1980–; Joint Sec. (in charge) Scientific and Technological Research Div., President's Secr.; Hon. D.Sc. *Publications:* Lectures on Quantum Mechanics 1937, Boundary Problems in Non-linear Partial Differential Equations 1938, Theory of Relativity 1940, Problems of Education 1943, Iqbal's Concept of Time and Space 1973, Establishing a New University: Policies and Procedures; numerous research papers. *Leisure interests:* educational, scientific, literary studies and writings. *Address:* Pakistan Academy of Sciences, G5, 5 Constitution Avenue, Islamabad; House No. 2, Hill Road, F-7/3, Islamabad, Pakistan (Home). *Telephone:* 827789 (Office); 823541 (Home).

SIDDIQUI, Maj.-Gen. Abdul Mannan; Bangladesh army officer and government official; b. 3 April 1935, Jessore; s. of the late Moulvi Abdul Latif Siddiqui; m.; one s. two d.; ed. Jessore Zilla School, Dhaka Coll., Pakistan Mil. Acad., Army Eng. School, U.S.A.; commissioned 1955, served Gen. HQ, Rawalpindi 1967–70, achieved rank of Lieut.-Col. 1970, Commdr. Cen. Ordnance Dept. Dhaka 1973–75, apptd. Dir. Ordnance Services Army HQ 1975, rank of Brig. 1976, of Maj.-Gen. 1978, Quartermaster-Gen. Army HQ 1981–82; served UN Forces Congo 1964; Adviser-in-Charge Ministry of Public Works and Urban Devt. 1982, Minister of Home Affairs 1984–85, of Fisheries and Oceans 1985–86, of Relief and Rehabilitation, of Food, of Fisheries and Livestock 1985–86. *Address:* c/o Ministry of Relief and Rehabilitation, Dhaka, Bangladesh.

SIDDON, Thomas Edward, PH.D.; Canadian politician and engineer; b. 9 Nov. 1941, Drumheller, Alb.; m. Patricia Audrey Yackimetz; five c.; ed. Univs. of Alberta and Toronto; professional engineer 1965; faculty mem. and Assoc. Prof. Mechanical Eng. Univ. of B.C. 1968–; f. acoustical eng. firm, audio-metrical testing business, has worked as acoustic consultant throughout Canada and U.S.A.; fmr. alderman, Richmond, B.C.; first elected M.P. 1978, Parl. Sec. to Minister of Fisheries and Oceans 1979; Minister of State for Science and Tech. 1984–85, Minister for Fisheries and Oceans 1985–; Progressive Conservative Party. *Address:* House of Commons, Ottawa, Ont., K1A 0A6, Canada.

SIDENBLADH, Göran; Swedish architect and town planner; b. 19 March 1912, Stockholm; s. of Karl E. Sidenbladh and Gertrud Bernström; m. Suzanne Hedenlund 1944; two d.; ed. Royal Inst. of Polytechnics, Stockholm; Asst. Planner, Stockholm Co. Council; Consultant with Göteborg City Planning Dept. 1936–43; Sr. Planner, Stockholm Planning Dept. 1944–55, Dir. 1955–73; Consultant, Prof., Nordic Inst. for Planning, Stockholm 1973–77; mem. Royal Swedish Acad. of Eng. Sciences 1962–; corresp. mem. RIBA 1963; mem. Swedish Tech. Science Acad. 1988. *Publications:* articles and books on town planning. *Leisure interests:* dendrology, roses. *Address:* Narvägen 23, 11460 Stockholm, Sweden. *Telephone:* (08) 6616631.

SIDHU, Gurbachan Singh, M.SC., PH.D.; Indian research scientist; b. 4 July 1920, Patiala; s. of late Gopal Singh Sidhu and Jai Kur; m. Mahijit Kaur Sidhu 1954; one s. one d.; ed. Lucknow Univ. and Univ. of Heidelberg; teacher of Organic Chem., Lucknow Univ.; Scientific Officer, Regional Research Lab. (RRL), Hyderabad, Dir. 1962–81; Dir.-Gen. Council of Scientific and Industrial Research and Sec. to Govt. of India May 1981–; Chair., Nat. Research Devt. Corpn., New Delhi 1980–82; K. G. Naik Gold Medal; Fed. of Indian Chambers of Commerce and Industry Award; Padmashri. *Publications:* more than 150 research papers. *Leisure interests:* reading, concerts, bridge. *Address:* Council of Scientific and Industrial Research, Rafi Marg, New Delhi-110001, India (Office). *Telephone:* 383652 (Office); 698813 (Home).

SIDI BABA, Dey Ould; Moroccan diplomatist; b. 1921, Atar, Mauritania; m.; five c.; Counsellor, Ministry of Foreign Affairs, Morocco 1958–59; Head of African Div. 1959–61; mem. Moroccan Dels. to UN Gen. Assembly 1959–64; Amb. to Guinea 1961–62; Acting Perm. Rep. of Morocco to UN 1963–65, Perm. Rep. 1965–67; Vice-Pres. of Gen. Assembly of UN 1966; Minister of Royal Cabinet 1967–71, Dir. 1972–73; Amb. to Saudi Arabia 1971–72; Minister of Educ. 1973–74, of Waqfs and Islamic Affairs 1974–77; Pres. Chamber of Reps. and Deputies 1977–84; mem. Nat. Defence Council March 1979–; Commdr. du Trône alaonite 1965, Niger Grand Order of Merit, Officer of Libyan Order of Independence, Commdr. of Syrian Order of Merit. *Address:* c/o Chamber of Representatives, Rabat, Morocco.

SIDKI, Aziz, B.ENG., M.A., PH.D.; Egyptian politician; b. 1 July 1920, Cairo; ed. Cairo Univ., Univ. of Oregon and Harvard Univ.; taught Cairo Univ.; Tech. Counsellor to the President 1953; Ministry for Industry 1956–63, Deputy Prime Minister and Minister for Industry and Mineral Wealth 1964–65; Minister for Industry, Petroleum and Mineral Wealth 1968–71; Deputy Prime Minister 1971–72; Prime Minister 1972–73; Acting Gen. Sec. Arab Socialist Union 1971–73; Personal Asst. to Pres. Sadat 1973–75; has participated in various int. confs. on industrial affairs. *Address:* c/o The Presidency, Cairo, Egypt.

SIDLIN, Murry, M.M.; American conductor; b. 6 May 1940, Baltimore, Md.; ed. Academia Chigiana, Siena, Cornell Univ.; Asst. Conductor, Baltimore Symphony Orchestra 1971–73; Dir. of Md. Ballet Co. 1971–73; Prin. Conductor Baltimore Chamber Players 1971–73; Resident Conductor Nat. Symphony Orchestra under Dorati 1973–77, Wolf Trap American Univ. Music Acad. 1974; Host and Conductor Children's TV series Music is . . . . 1977; Music Dir. Tulsa Philharmonic Orchestra 1978–80; Music Dir. Hew Haven Symphony 1977–, Long Beach Symphony 1980–, Resident Conductor Aspen Music Festival 1978–; Guest Conductor with numerous orchestras in N. America, also performances in Europe and at the Festival Casals in Puerto Rico; Carnegie Hall Début 1975; winner of Baltimore Symphony Orchestra Young Conductor's Competition 1962. *Address:* c/o J.B. Keller, 250 West 57th Street 1130, New York, N.Y. 10107, U.S.A. *Telephone:* (212)315-2430.

SIDOROV, Veniamin Aleksandrovich; Soviet physicist; b. 19 Oct. 1930, Babarino, Suzdal Dist., Vladimir Region; s. of Alexandr Mikhailovich Sidorov and Maria Vasilievna Sidorova; m. 1st Gendlina Larisa Semenovna 1962, one s. one d.; m. 2nd Lupashina Irina Sergeevna 1975, one s.; ed. Moscow State Univ.; attached to Inst. of Atomic Energy, then Inst. of Nuclear Physics, Siberian Div. of U.S.S.R. Acad. of Sciences 1962–, Deputy Dir. of Inst. 1977–; Corresp. mem. U.S.S.R. Acad. of Sciences 1968–. *Publications:* numerous works, mainly on colliding beam experiments in elementary particle physics. *Address:* Institute of Nuclear Physics, Lavrentiev prospect 11, 630090 Novosibirsk, U.S.S.R. *Telephone:* 35-60-31.

SIDOROV, Adm. Vladimir Vasilevich; Soviet naval officer; b. 1924; ed. Pacific Ocean Higher Mil.-Naval School, and Mil.-Naval Acad.; service in U.S.S.R. Navy 1942–; command posts in navy 1946–; commdr. of a flotilla, First Deputy Commdr. of Pacific Ocean and Baltic fleets 1967–78; mem. CPSU 1959–; Commdr. of Pacific Fleet 1978–81, Baltic Fleet 1981–86; Deputy Chief Commdr. of Navy 1986–, now Chief Commdr.; cand. mem. of U.S.S.R. Supreme Soviet 1981–; Deputy to U.S.S.R. Supreme Soviet. *Address:* The Kremlin, Moscow, U.S.S.R.

SIEBER, Günter; German politician and diplomatist; b. 11 March 1930, Ilmenau; fmr. forestry worker; mem. Socialist Unity Party (SED) 1948–; with Deutsche Wirtschaftskommission 1948–49, G.D.R. Ministry of Planning 1949–51, State Planning Comm. 1951–52; First Sec. SED org. in State Planning Comm. 1954–62; Deputy Chair. Zentrale Kommission für Staatliche Kontrolle 1962–63; mem. Zentrale Revisionskommission der SED 1963–67; Cand. mem. SED Cen. Cttee. 1976–; Minister for Trade 1965–72; Amb. to Poland 1973–80; Head Int. Relations Dept. of Cen. Cttee. 1980–; mem. SED Cen. Cttee. 1981, People's Chamber 1981–; Vaterländischer Verdienstorden in Bronze, Silver and Gold, Orden Banner der Arbeit and other decorations. *Address:* Haus des Zentralkomitees, 1020 Berlin, Am Marx-Engels-Platz, German Democratic Republic.

SIEBER, Rolf, DR.RER.OEC., DR.SC.OEC.; German diplomatist; b. 10 Dec. 1929, Lunzenau, Kreis Rochlitz; ed. Hochschule für Ökonomie, Berlin, Univ. of Moscow; Lecturer, Hochschule für Ökonomie, Berlin 1956–74, Rector 1978–; Prof. of Political Economy 1969–; Official of G.D.R. Ministry of Foreign Affairs 1973–, Amb. to U.S.A. 1974–78; mem. Volkskammer 1967–76, Chair. of Interparl. Group of Volkskammer 1967–74; mem. Communist Party (KPD) 1945, Socialist Unity Party (SED) 1946–; Vaterländischer Verdienstorden in Gold, Verdienstmedaille der DDR and other decorations. *Address:* c/o Hochschule für Ökonomie Bruno Leuschner, Hermann-Duncker-Strasse 8, Berlin 1157, German Democratic Republic.

SIEBERT, Manfred Fritz Eduard Walter, DR.RER.NAT.; German professor of geophysics; b. 2 June 1925, Ribbeck, Templin; s. of Walter Siebert and Lisbeth Rosner; m. Barbara Gassmann 1962; two d.; ed. Univ. of Göttingen; Research Asst. and Chief Asst. Inst. of Geophysics, Univ. of Göttingen 1955–68, Acting Dir. Inst. of Geophysics 1964–68, Prof. of Geophysics and Dir. Inst. of Geophysics 1968–; Fellow, Göttingen Acad. of Sciences. *Publications:* contribs. to textbooks and journals. *Address:* Hohler Graben 4, 3400 Göttingen, Federal Republic of Germany. *Telephone:* (0551) 21330.

SIEBERT HELD, Brig.-Gen. Bruno; Chilean army officer and politician; m. Gesa Charlotte Wendi Zichermann; three c.; ed. Mil. School; Regimental Commdr. Arauco, Prov. Gov. Osorno, mem. Presidential Staff, mem. Junta's Assessorial Cttee., Deputy Chief of Presidential Staff, Mil. Attaché, Embassy Fed. Repub. of Germany, Commdt. Army Engineers; Minister of Public Works 1982–. *Address:* Ministry of Public Works, Enrique MacIver 541, 1°, Santiago, Chile. *Telephone:* 394001.

SIEBOLD, Klaus; German mining engineer and politician; b. 12 Sept. 1930; Head of Coal Industry in G.D.R. State Planning Comm. Econ. Council 1959–63; Deputy Chair. Econ. Council (Coal and Energy) 1963–65; Minister of Raw Materials Industry 1965–71; Minister for Coal and Energy 1971–79; Vaterländischer Verdienstorden in Bronze and Silver. *Address:* c/o Ministerrat, Berlin, German Democratic Republic.

SIEFEIN, William Naguib, B.SC.; Egyptian politician; b. April 1939, Aswan; ed. Univ. of Cairo; mem. People's Ass. and Deputy Chair. Agric. and Irrigation Cttee.; fmr. First Under-Sec. Ministry of Irrigation; Minister of State for Immigration and Egyptian Expatriates 1985–86. *Address:* c/o Ministry for Immigration and Egyptian Expatriates, Cairo, Egypt.

SIEFF OF BRIMPTON, Baron (Life Peer), cr. 1980, of Brimpton in the Royal County of Berkshire; **Marcus Joseph Sieff,** O.B.E., M.A.; British business executive (retd.); b. 2 July 1913; s. of late Lord Sieff; m. 1st Rosalie Fromson 1937 (dissolved 1947), one s.; m. 2nd Elsa Gosen 1951 (dissolved 1953); m. 3rd Brenda Beith 1956 (dissolved 1962), one d; m. 4th Mrs. Pauline L. Moretzki (née Spatz) 1963, one d.; ed. Manchester Grammar School, St. Paul's, and Corpus Christi Coll., Cambridge; served War 1939–45, R.A.; joined Marks and Spencer Ltd., 1935, Dir. 1954, Asst Man.-Dir. 1963, Vice-Chair. 1965, Jt. Man. Dir 1967–83, Deputy Chair. 1971, Chair, Marks and Spencer PLC 1972–84, Pres. 1984–85; Hon. Pres. 1985; mem. British Nat. Export Council 1965–71 (Chair. Export Cttee. for Israel 1965–68); Hon. Pres., Jt. Israel Appeal; Vice Pres., Policy Studies Inst., mem. Exec. 1975–; Pres., Anglo-Israeli Chamber of Commerce, 1975–; Chair. First Int. Bank of Israel Trust Oct. 1983–; Dir. N. M. Rothschild & Sons 1983–; Chair. Newspaper Publishing Oct. 1986–; Trustee, Nat. Portrait Gallery 1986–; Hon. F.R.C.S. 1984; Hon. LL.D. (St. Andrews) 1983, (Reading) 1985, Hon. Dr. (Babson Coll., Mass.) 1984; Hambro Award, Businessman of the Year, 1977; Hon. Master of Bench of Inner Temple 1987; Aims Nat. Free Enterprise Award, 1978; B'nai B'rith Int. Gold Medallion for Humanitarianism 1982; Retailer of the Year Award, Nat. Retail Merchants' Asscn. 1982, British Inst. of Management Gold Medal 1983; Hon. LL.D. (Leicester) 1987. *Address:* c/o Marks and Spencer PLC, Michael House, Baker Street, London, WIA IDN, England.

SIEGBAHN, Kai Manne Börje, B.SC., D.PHIL.; Swedish physicist; b. 20 April 1918, Lund; s. of Dr. Manne Siegbahn (winner of 1924 Nobel Prize for Physics) and of Karin (née Högbom) Siegbahn; m. Anna-Brita Rhedin 1944; three s.; Prof. of Physics, Royal Inst. of Tech., Stockholm 1951–54, Univ. of Uppsala 1954–; mem. Royal Swedish Acad. of Science, Royal Swedish Acad. of Eng. Sciences, Royal Soc. of Science, Royal Acad. of Arts and Science of Uppsala, Royal Physiographical Soc. of Lund, Societas Scientiarum Fennica, Norwegian Acad. of Science, Royal Norwegian Soc. of Sciences and Letters, Papal Acad. of Science 1986–; Hon. mem. American Acad. of Arts and Sciences, Comité Int. des Poids et Mesures, Paris; Pres. Int. Union of Pure and Applied Physics; Hon. D.Sc. (Univ. of Durham) 1972, (Univ. of Basel) 1980, (Univ. of Liège) 1980, (Upsala Coll., N.J.) 1982, (Sussex) 1983; Lindblom Prize 1945, Björkén Prize 1955, 1977, half-share of Nobel Prize for Physics 1981 for work on atomic spectroscopy; Celsius Medal 1962, Sixten Heyman Award 1971, Harrison Howe Award 1973, Maurice F. Hasler Award 1975, Charles Frederick Chandler Medal 1976, Torbern Bergman Medal 1979, Pittsburgh Award of Spectroscopy 1982, Röntgen Medal 1985, Finggi Award 1986, Humboldt Award 1986. *Publications:* Beta- and Gamma-Ray Spectroscopy 1955, Alpha-, Beta- and Gamma-Ray Spectroscopy 1965, ESCA-Atomic Molecular and Solid Structure Studied by Means of Electron Spectroscopy 1967, ESCA Applied to Free Molecules 1969 and 450 scientific papers. *Address:* c/o Institute of Physics, University of Uppsala, Box 530, S-751 21, Uppsala, Sweden (Office).

SIEGEL, Milton P.; American fmr. international official, educationist and management consultant; b. 23 July, 1911, Des Moines, Ia.; s. of Barney and Silvy (Levinson) Siegel; m. Rosalie Rosenberg 1934; one s. (deceased) two d. (one deceased); ed. Drake Univ., Des Moines; Dir. of Finance and Statistics, Ia. Emergency Relief Admin., Treas., Ia. Rural Rehabilitation Admin. 1933–35; Regional Finance and Business Man., Farm Security Admin., U.S. Dept. of Agriculture 1935–41, Chief Fiscal Officer 1942–44; Asst. Treas., Dir. Office for Far East, UNRRA 1944–45; Asst. Dir., Fiscal Branch, Production and Marketing Admin., U.S. Dept. of Agric. 1945–47; Asst. Dir.-Gen. WHO 1947–71; Health Man. Consultant, to Govt. of Iran 1975–76; Visiting Prof. Univ. of Michigan 1967; mem. Perm. Scale of Contributions Comm. LRCS 1967–81; Visiting Prof., Univ. of N.C. 1970; Consultant to Carolina Population Center 1970; Prof. of Int. Health, Health Science Center, Univ. of Tex. at Houston 1971–75; Pres. and C.E.O., Fed. of World Health Foundations 1978–; Chair. Bd. of Dirs., C.E.O., Man. Planning Systems Int. Inc. 1977–; Man. Consultant, UN Devt. Programme 1976–77; Sr. Man. Scientist, Childrens Nutrition Research Center, Baylor Coll. of Medicine, Houston, Tex. 1979–80; mem. American Public Health Asscn. *Publications:* articles and papers. *Address:* 1 rue Viollier, 1207 Geneva, Switzerland; 2833 Sackett, Houston, Tex. 77098, U.S.A. *Telephone:* (022) 36-36-09 (Geneva); (713) 526-2583 (Houston).

SIEKEVITZ, Philip, PH.D.; American professor of cell biology; b. 25 Feb. 1918, Philadelphia; s. of Joseph and Tilly Siekevitz; m. Rebecca Burstein 1949; two d.; ed. Philadelphia Coll. of Pharmacy and Science and Univ. of Calif., Berkeley; United States Public Health Service Fellow Harvard Univ. 1949–51; Fellow in Oncology Univ. of Wis. 1951–54; Asst. Prof. Rockefeller Univ. 1954–59, Assoc. Prof. 1959–66, Prof. of Cell Biology 1966–; Pres. American Soc. of Cell Biology 1966–67; Ed. Journal of Cellular Physiology 1970–; mem. New York Acad. of Sciences (Pres. 1976), N.A.S., American Acad. of Arts and Sciences; Hon. Ph.D. (Philadelphia Coll. of Pharmacy and Science) 1971, (Univ. of Stockholm) 1974. *Publications:* Cell Structure and Function (with A. Loewy) 1963, New Directions (short stories); numerous scientific journals. *Leisure interests:* piano, literature, writer of short stories and essays. *Address:* Rockefeller University, 1230 York Avenue, New York, N.Y. 10021 (Office); 290 West End Avenue, New York, N.Y. 10023, U.S.A. (Home). *Telephone:* (212) 570-8119 (Office); (212) 362-2539 (Home).

SIEVERS WICKE, Hugo K.; Chilean veterinary physician and politician; b. 1903, Rengo; m. Elena Kutz Schroer 1931; ed. Colegio Alemán, Santiago and Univs. de Chile, Buenos Aires, La Plata, Rio de Janeiro, Inst. Pasteur and Inst. Curie, Paris, Inst. of Tropical Medicine, Hamburg; Asst. at Inst. for Veterinary Research 1924–27; Prof. School of Agric. 1927–28; Mil. Veterinary Physician 1926–32; Dir. Inst. of Veterinary Research, Ministry of Agriculture 1930–42; Dean School Veterinary Medicine, Univ. de Chile 1936–61; Vice-Rector Univ. de Chile 1953–61, now Prof. Emer.; Minister of Agric., Lands and Colonization 1955; Perm. Del. Int. Congress of Veterinary Medicine 1936–59; Pres. Chilean Soc. of Sciences 1964; Founder mem. Soc. of Veterinary Physicians of Chile (and fmr. Pres.), Chilean Natural History Soc., Anatomical Soc.; mem. Chilean Acad. Natural Sciences; Hon. mem. Soc. of Veterinary Science, Peru; Hon. Prof. Cen. Univ. de Quito, and Univ. Nacional de San Marcos, Lima; Dr. h.c. Univ. Austral de Chile; Decoration of the Rising Sun, Japan 1959; Decoration Eloy Alfaro Int. Foundation, Gold Medal Camara di Commercio, Industria e Agricultura, Trento, Italy. *Publications:* La vuelta del Mundo con 10 Estudiantes, Rutas Patagónicas, Chilenos en la Amazonia, Max Westenhöfer 1871-1951 (biography), Domingo Amunátegui Solar (biography), Teliatría, Nosotros y la Comunidad, Proteinas y Alimentación. *Address:* Las Trinitarias 6881, Las Condes, Santiago 10, Chile. *Telephone:* 480717.

SIEVERTS, Thomas C. W., DIPL.ING.; German architect and town planner; b. 8 June 1934, Hamburg; s. of Prof. Dr. Rudolf Sieverts and Elisabeth (née Ronnefeldt; m. Heide Pawelzick 1965; one s. two d.; ed. in Stuttgart, Liverpool and Berlin; with Kossak and Zimmermann founded Freie Plannungsgruppe Berlin 1965; Prof. of Town Planning Dept. of Architecture, Hochschule der Künste, Berlin 1967–70; Guest Prof., Graduate School of Design, Harvard Univ. 1970–71; Prof. of Town Planning, Dept. of Architecture, Technische Hochschule, Darmstadt 1971–; Special Prof. of Urban Design, Inst. of Planning Studies, Univ. of Nottingham 1978–; in practice as architect and town planner, Bonn 1978–; town planning consultant to the City of Vienna, planning Danubia area 1973–78, the Gürtel area 1984–. Deubau Prize (Essen) 1969. *Publications:* many contributions to periodicals and books; co-ed. Stadtbauwelt. *Leisure interest:* drawing. *Address:* Buschstrasse 20, D-53 Bonn 1, Federal Republic of Germany. *Telephone:* 0228/218706 (Office); 0228/214682 (Home).

SIGNORILE, Claudio; Italian politician; b. 9 Sept. 1937, Bari; Lecturer in Modern History, Univs. of Rome and Sassari, in Contemporary History, Univ. of Lecce until 1972; mem. Italian Socialist party (PSI) 1956–; Nat. Sec. Young Socialist Fed. 1964–66; M.P. for Lecce-Brindisi-Taranto 1972–; mem. party Nat. Exec. 1970–, mem. Nat. Secr., in charge of econ. policies 1976–, Deputy Nat. Sec. 1978–80; Minister for Extraordinary Aid to Mezzogiorno (South) in first and second Spadolini Govts. and Fanfani Govt.; Minister of Transport 1983–87. *Address:* c/o Ministry of Transport, Piazza della Croce Rossa 1, 00100 Rome, Italy.

SIGRIST, Helmut, DR. RER. POL.; German diplomatist; b. 8 Sept. 1919, Frankfurt/Main; s. of Friedrich and Gertrude (née Oslender) Sigrist; m. Berthild Klein 1951; two s. two d.; ed. Humanistisches Gymnasium, Leipzig, Erfurt, Gelsenkirchen-Schalke, Philosophisch-theologische Hochschule, Bamberg, and Univs. of Heidelberg and Denver, Colo., U.S.A.; Nat. Labour Service 1937; Mil. Service and P.O.W. 1937–45; univ. studies 1945–50; entered Diplomatic Service 1951; Second Sec., later Sec., Washington 1953–55, Sec., Rome 1957–62, New Delhi 1962–64; Dir. Training Centre for Senior Foreign Service Officials, Bonn 1955–57; Deputy Exec. Sec. EEC Comm. 1964–67; Deputy Sec.-Gen. Comm. of European Communities, Brussels 1967; Dir.-Gen. External Relations, Comm. of European Communities 1968–72; in charge of Int. Trade Negotiations for the Fed. Repub. of Germany 1973–75; Asst. Dir. Foreign Trade Policy, Devt. Policy and European Econ. Integration 1974–77; Perm. Rep. (Amb.) of the Fed. Repub. of Germany with the European Communities 1977; Amb. to Greece 1979–84. *Address:* Donatusstr. 21, D-5300 Bonn 2, Federal Republic of Germany. *Telephone:* 0228-374495.

SIGURÐARDÓTTIR, Jóhanna; Icelandic politician; b. 4 Oct. 1942; m. Thorvaldur Steiner Jóhannesson; ed. Commercial Coll. of Iceland; stewardess Loftleider (Icelandic Airways) 1962–71; clerk Kassagerd Reykjavíkur 1971–78; M.P. for Reykjavík 1978–; Deputy Leader SDP; Minister of Social Affairs 1987–; Chair. Govt. Cttee. on Handicapped 1979–83; mem. Social Security Bd. 1978- (Chair. 1979–80); leadership cttee. Icelandic Air Hostesses' Union 1966–69 (Chair. 1966, 1961); Reykjavík Shop and Office Workers' Union 1976–83. *Address:* Ministry of Social Affairs, Hafnarhúsinu við Tryggvagötu, 150 Reykjavík, Iceland.

SIGURDSEN, Gertrud; Swedish politician; b. 11 Jan. 1923, Nävekvarn; two s.; Sec. at Swedish Confed. of Trade Unions 1949–64; Information Sec., Information Div. 1964–68; mem. Exec. Bd. Social Democratic Party 1968–; M.P. 1969–; Minister for Int. Devt. Assistance 1973–76; mem. Parl. Standing Cttee. on Foreign Affairs 1976, Vice-Chair. 1979–82; Chair. Social Democratic Jr. League 1977–80; Minister for Public Health and Medical Services 1982–85; Minister for Health and Social Affairs 1985–89. *Address:* c/o Ministry of Health and Social Affairs, S-103 33 Stockholm, Sweden.

SIGURDSSON, Jón; Icelandic lawyer and industrial executive; b. 29 Oct. 1934, Reykjavík; s. of Sigurdur Jonsson and Ingibjörg Pálsdóttir; m. Bergljot Jonatansdottir 1955; one s. two d.; ed. Univ. of Iceland and Univ. of Southern California School of Public Admin.; Asst. to Sec.-Gen., Ministry of Fisheries and Agric. 1958–62, Chief of Div. 1962–66; Adviser to Minister of Finance 1965–66; Budget Dir., Ministry of Finance 1966–67, Sec.-Gen. 1967–74, 1976–77; Exec. Dir. for Denmark, Finland, Iceland, Norway, Sweden, IBRD 1974–76; Man. Dir. Icelandic Alloys Ltd. 1977-. *Address:* Mörk, Skilmannahreppi, 301 Akranes, Iceland. *Telephone:* (3) 13346.

SIGURDSSON, Jón, M.SC.ECON.; Icelandic politician and economist; b. 14 April 1941, Ísafjördur; m. Laufey Thorbjarnardóttir; four c.; ed. Akureyn Coll., Univ. of Stockholm and L. S. E.; Economist Inst. of Iceland 1964–71 (Dir. Econ. Research 1970–71); Chief Econ. Research Div. Econ. Devt. Inst. 1972–74; Man. Dir. Nat. Econ. Inst. 1974–86; Econ. Adviser to govt.; Exec. Dir. for Nordic countries IMF 1980–83, Alt. Gov. IMF for Iceland and Assoc. jt. IBRD/IMF Devt. Cttee. 1974–87, Gov. 1987–; mem. Althing (SDP) 1987–; Minister of Justice and Ecclesiastical Affairs 1987–88, of Commerce, Industry and Nordic Co-operation Sept. 1988–; mem. Salaries Arbitration Court 1970–80; Rep. for Iceland Econ. and Devt. Review Cttee. OECD 1970; Bd. Nordic Investment Bank 1976–87 (Chair. 1984–86). *Address:* Ministry of Commerce, Arnarhváli, 150 Reykjavík, Iceland.

SIGURDSSON, Niels P.; Icelandic diplomatist; b. 1926, Reykjavík; s. of Sigurdur B. Sigurdsson and Karitas Einarsdóttir; m. Olafia Rafnsdóttir; two s. one d.; ed. Univ. of Iceland; joined Diplomatic Service 1952; First Sec. Paris Embassy 1956–60; Deputy Perm. Rep. to NATO and OECD 1957–60; Dir. Int. Policy Div. Ministry of Foreign Affairs, Reykjavík 1961; Del. to the UN Gen. Assembly 1965; Amb. and Perm. Rep. of Iceland to North Atlantic Council; Amb. to Belgium and the EEC 1968; Amb. to UK. 1971–76, to Fed. Repub. of Germany 1976–78, Amb. at Large 1979–84, to Norway 1985–; Chair. Icelandic Del. to Madrid Conf. 1980–83. *Leisure interests:* swimming, riding. *Address:* Icelandic Embassy, 30 Stortingsgt., Oslo, Norway.

SIHANOUK, Prince Norodom (see Norodom Sihanouk, Prince).

SIIG, Arvi; Soviet Estonian poet; b. 8 Nov. 1938, Tallinn, Estonia; s. of Karl Siig and Helene Siig; m. Valentine Siig 1974; one s. one d.; ed. Tallinn Teacher Training College, and Tartu Univ.; first works published 1958; author of at least ten books of poetry, translated into several foreign languages. *Leisure interests:* travelling, gardening. *Address:* Union of Writers of Estonian S.S.R., Tallinn; Harju 1, 200001 Estonia, U.S.S.R. *Telephone:* 44-68-32.

SIILASVUO, Lieut.-Gen. Ensio; Finnish army officer; b. 1 Jan. 1922, Helsinki; s. of Lieut.-Gen. Hjalmar Siilasvuo and Salli Kolsi; m. Salli Paldanius 1947; three s.; ed. Lycée of Oulu, Finnish Mil. Acad., Finnish Command and Staff Coll.; Platoon Commdr., Infantry Co. Commdr. and Chief of Staff, Infantry Regiment 11 1941–44; Company Commdr., Infantry Regt. 1 1945–50; attended Command and Staff Coll. 1951–52; various staff appointments in mil. districts of N. Finland 1953–57; Commdr. Finnish Contingent, UN Emergency Force 1957; Mil. Observer, UN Observation Group in Lebanon 1958; Finnish Defence Attaché in Warsaw 1959–61; Staff Officer Third Div. 1962–64; Commdr. Finnish Contingent, UN Force in Cyprus 1964–65; Instructor, Nat. Defence Coll. 1965–67; Chief, Foreign Dept. GHQ 1967; Sr. Staff Officer, UN Truce Supervision Org. in Palestine

1967–70; Chief of Staff, UN Truce Supervision Org. in Palestine 1970–73, Commdr. UN Emergency Force 1973–75; Chief Co-ordinator of UN Peace-Keeping Missions in Middle East 1975–80, retd. from UN Service 1980; Grand Cross of the Order of the Lion of Finland; Finnish Cross of Freedom 3rd and 4th Class; Knight of the Order of the White Rose of Finland 1st Class; Grand Cross of the Egyptian Order of Merit; Grand Cross of the Belgian Order of Leopold II, Commdr., Légion d'Honneur, Commdr., Lebanese Order of the Cedar, Commdr., U.S. Legion of Merit, Grand Cross of the Order of the Pole Star (Sweden). *Leisure interests:* UN peacekeeping affairs, history of the Middle East. *Address:* Castrenikatu 6A18, 00530 Helsinki 53, Finland.

SIJPESTEIJN, Pieter Johannes, PH.D.; Netherlands professor of ancient history; b. 16 Sept. 1934, Rotterdam; s. of J.P. Sijpesteijn and M.R. Sijpesteijn; m. Etty Anna Sijpesteijn-Moen 1966; one s. one d.; ed. High School at Eindhoven and Rotterdam, Univ. of Leiden and abroad (Vienna, Madison); schoolteacher, Arnhem and Rotterdam 1961–64; Sr. Lecturer, Univ. of Amsterdam 1964–80, Prof. of Papyrology and Ancient History 1980–; mem. Nederlandse Akad. van Wetenschappen. *Publications:* P. Mich XIII 1977, P. Mich XV 1982, Customs Dues in Graeco-Roman Egypt 1987; numerous articles in various periodicals. *Leisure interests:* travel, walking, swimming. *Address:* Oude Turfmarkt 129, 1012 GC Amsterdam (Office); Wilhelminalaan 10, 3743 DC Baarn, Netherlands (Home). *Telephone:* 020-5252588 (Office); 02154-12839 (Home).

SIJTHOFF, Hendrik Albert Henri; Netherlands publisher; b. 1915; ed. Univs. of Leipzig and Lausanne; Chair. Bd. of Het Financieele Dagblad; C.E.O. Sijthoff Holding N.V. *Address:* Weesperstraat 85, 1018 VN, Amsterdam, Netherlands (Office); Ch. de Cyrano, 1009 Pully, Switzerland (Home).

SIK, Ota, DR.SC.; Swiss (b. Czechoslovak) economist; b. 11 Sept. 1919, Plzeň; s. of Oswald and Marie Šik; m. Lilli Grünfeld 1947; two s.; deprived of Czech citizenship 1970, naturalized Swiss 1983; Dir., Econ. Inst. of Czechoslovak Acad. of Sciences 1963–68; Chair. of Scientific Collegium of Econ. Czechoslovak Acad. of Sciences 1963–69; Corresp. mem. Czechoslovak Acad. of Sciences 1960; mem. Cen. Cttee. of CP of Czechoslovakia 1962–69; mem. Econ. Comm., Cen. Cttee. of CP of Czechoslovakia 1962–69; mem. State Comm. for Man. and Org. 1963–68; mem. State Planning Comm.; Deputy Prime Minister 1968; mem. Econ. Council 1968–69; Deputy to Czech Nat. Council 1968–69; now Prof., Univ. of St. Gallen; Order of 25th February 1948; Klement Gottwald State Prize 1966; Dr. h.c. (Univ. of Lancaster); granted political asylum in Switzerland April 1970. *Publications include:* Economics, Interests, Politics, On the Question of Socialist Commodity Relations, Plan and Market under Socialism, Facts about the Czechoslovakian Economy, Democratic and Socialist Economy, Structural Changes of the Economic Systems in East-Europe, The Bureaucratic Economy 1972, Argumente für den dritten Weg 1973, The Third Way 1976, The Communist Power System 1981, Humane Wirtschaftsdemokratie 1979, For a Humane Economic Democracy 1985, Wirtschaftssysteme, Vergleiche-Theorie-Kritik 1987, Wachstum und Krisen 1988, Prager Frühlingserwachen 1988. *Leisure interests:* sport, painting pictures. *Address:* Gatterstrasse 1, 9000 St. Gallen, Switzerland. *Telephone:* (071) 302-566.

SIKIVOU, Semesa Koroikilai, C.B.E., M.A.; Fijian diplomatist and politician; b. 13 Feb. 1917, Rewa, Fiji; s. of Navitalai Tubuna and Ateca Canavusa; m. 1st Seini Ratuvou 1944 (deceased); m. 2nd Salote Tabuanitoga 1957; five s. one d.; ed. schools in Fiji, Auckland Training Coll. and Auckland Univ., and London Univ. Inst. of Educ.; Teacher 1935–42; Mil. Service 1942–46; Asst. Master, Queen Victoria School, 1949, 1951–59; Educ. Officer 1960–62; Asst. Dir. of Educ., Fiji 1963–66, Deputy Dir. 1966–70; Perm. Rep. to UN 1970–76; Vice-Pres. of 28th Session of UN Gen. Assembly 1973; High Commr. to Canada 1971–76; Amb. to U.S.A. 1971–76; M.P. 1977–, Minister of Educ. 1977–82, of Communications and Works 1982–84, of Communications, Transport and Works 1984–85, of Foreign Affairs and Civil Aviation 1985–86; mem. Fiji Broadcasting Comm. 1955–62, 1966–70; mem. Fiji Legis. Council 1956–66; mem. Fijian Affairs Bd. 1955–66, 1969–70, Fijian Devt. Fund Bd. 1956–66, Native Land Trust Bd. 1965–70; mem. Advisory Council on Educ. 1954–70; mem. Council of Chiefs 1952–70; mem. many other govt. and civic bodies. *Leisure interests:* reading, walking. *Address:* c/o Ministry of Foreign Affairs and Civil Aviation, Ganilau House, Suva (Office); P.O. Box 2311, Suva, Fiji (Home).

SIKLAR, Osman; Turkish banker; b. 1929; ed. Acad. of Econ. and Commercial Sciences, Istanbul; Foreign Exchange Dept., Central Bank 1954–59; trained at Société Générale, Paris 1960–61; Deputy Rep. Cen. Bank of Turkey, Zürich 1962–64, Gen. Man. Foreign Exchange Dept., Turkey 1965–75, Vice-Gov. 1976–78; retd. from Cen. Bank, then Chair. several export cos.; mem. Bd. Anadolu Bankası Bank, Istanbul; returned to Central Bank as Gov. 1981–83; Financial Consultant, Embassy, Bonn 1983–. *Address:* c/o Turkish Embassy, 5300 Bonn 2, Ute Strasse 47, Federal Republic of Germany.

SILAS, Cecil Jesse, B.S.; American business executive; b. 15 April 1932, Miami; s. of David Edward and Hilda Videll (née Carver) Silas; m. Theodosea Hejda 1965; three s. one d.; ed. Miami Sr. High School, Georgia Inst. of Tech.; joined Phillips Petroleum Co. 1953–; Pres. Phillips Petroleum

Co. Europe-Africa, Brussels and London 1968–74; Man. Dir. NRG Europe-Africa, London 1974–76; Vice-Pres. Gas and Gas Liquids, NRG, Bartlesville, Okla. 1976–78; Sr. Vice-Pres. Natural Resources Group, Bartlesville 1978–80, Exec. Vice-Pres. 1980–82; Pres. and C.O.O. (also Dir. and Chair. Exec. Cttee.) Phillips Petroleum Co. 1982–85, Chair. and C.E.O. April 1985–; Dir. First Nat. Bank, Bartlesville, First Nat. Bank and Trust Co., Tulsa, American Petroleum Inst., Inst. of Gas Tech.; mem. Georgia Inst. of Tech. Nat. Advisory Bd. (Chair. 1982–83); Commdr., Royal Order of St. Olav, Norway 1976; NCAA Silver Anniversary Award 1978. *Leisure interests:* golf, fishing, hunting. *Address:* Phillips Petroleum Co., Bartlesville, Okla. 74004; 2400 Terrace Drive, Bartlesville, Okla. 74003, U.S.A. (Home). *Telephone:* 918-661-6600 (Office); 918-333-8577 (Home).

SILAYEV, Ivan Stepanovich; Soviet politician; b. 1930; ed. Kazan Aviation Inst.; mem. CPSU 1959; foreman, shop Supt., deputy chief engineer, chief engineer, plant dir. in Gorky 1954–74; Deputy Minister of Aircraft Industry of U.S.S.R. 1974–77, First Deputy Minister 1977–80, Minister 1981–85; Minister of Machine Tool and Instrument-Making Industry of U.S.S.R. 1980–81; mem. of CPSU Cen. Cttee. 1981–; Deputy Pres. of Council of Ministers of the U.S.S.R. 1985–; Hero of Socialist Labour 1975; Lenin Prize winner 1972; Deputy to U.S.S.R. Supreme Soviet (10th convocation). *Address:* c/o Ministry of Aircraft Industry, Moscow, U.S.S.R.

SILBER, John Robert, PH.D., L.H.D., LL.D. ED.D., LITT.D., F.R.S.A.; American professor of philosophy and university administrator; b. 15 Aug. 1926, San Antonio, Tex.; s. of Paul G. Silber and Jewell Joslin; m. Kathryn Underwood 1947; one s. six d.; ed. Trinity, Yale and Evansville Univs.; Instructor of Philosophy, Yale Univ. 1952–55; Asst. Prof., Univ. of Texas 1955–59, Assoc. Prof. 1959–62, Prof. of Philosophy 1962–70, Chair. Dept. of Philosophy 1962–67, Univ. Prof. of Arts and Letters 1967–70, Dean, Coll. of Arts and Sciences 1967–70; Prof. of Philosophy and Law, Boston Univ. 1971–; Bd. of Dirs., Nat. Humanities Faculty 1968–72; Exec. Bd., Nat. Humanities Inst. 1975–78; mem. Pres. Advisory Bd., Radio Broadcasting to Cuba 1985–; Wilbur Lucius Cross Medal, Yale 1971; Fullbright Research Fellow 1959–60; Guggenheim Fellow 1963–64; Pres. Southwestern Philosophy Soc. 1966–67. *Publications:* The Ethical Significance of Kant's "Religion" 1960, Democracy: Its Counterfeits and Its Promise 1967, The Tuition Dilemma 1978; Ed. Religion Within the Limits of Reason Alone 1960, Works in Continental Philosophy 1967; Assoc. Ed. Kant-Studien 1968–. *Address:* Office of the President, Boston University, 147 Bay State Road, Boston, Mass. 02215; 132 Carlton Street, Brookline, Mass. 02146, U.S.A. *Telephone:* (617) 353-2208 (Office).

SILBERMAN, Laurence Hirsch, LL.B.; American lawyer, banker and diplomatist; b. 12 Oct. 1935, York, Pa.; s. of William and Anna Hirsch; m. Rosalie Gaull 1957; one s. two d.; ed. Dartmouth Coll., Harvard Law School; with Moore, Torkildson & Rice, Quinn & Moore, law firm 1961–64; Partner Moore, Silberman & Schulze 1964–67; Lawyer Nat. Labor Relations Bd. 1967–69; Solicitor, Labor Dept. 1969–70, Under-Sec. for Labor Affairs 1970–73; Partner Steptoe & Johnson 1973–74; Deputy Attorney-Gen., Dept. of Justice 1974–75; Amb. to Yugoslavia 1975–77 (withdrawn); Man. Partner Morrison and Foerster (Washington, D.C.) 1978–79, 1983–85; Exec. Vice-Pres. Legal and Govt. Affairs Div., Crocker Nat. Bank 1979–83; Sr. Fellow, American Enterprise Inst. for Public Policy Research, Washington, D.C. 1977–78, Visiting Fellow 1978–85; Vice-Chair. Advisory Council on Gen. Govt., Republican Nat. Comm. 1977–80; mem. U.S. Gen. Advisory Cttee. on Arms Control and Disarmament 1981–85; U.S. Circuit Judge 1985–. *Address:* U.S. Court of Appeals, D.C. Circuit, U.S. Courthouse, Washington, D.C. 20001, U.S.A.

SILES ZUAZO, Hernán, D.IUR.; Bolivian lawyer, politician and diplomatist; b. 1914; ed. Univ. de San Andres; Sergeant in Chaco War 1932; legal practice in La Paz 1939; M.P. for La Paz 1943–46; in exile in Argentina and Chile, where he worked as translator for U.S. news agencies 1946–51; Vice-Presidential cand. 1951; a leader of the revolution of 1952; Vice-Pres. of Bolivia 1952–56, Pres. 1956–60, 1982–85; Amb. to Uruguay 1960–63, to Spain 1963–64; in exile 1964–78; Pres. Movimiento Nacionalista Revolucionario-Izquierdo (MNRI) 1978–; leading Presidential cand. July 1979, June 1980. *Address:* c/o Presidential Palace, La Paz, Bolivia.

SILJA, Anja; German opera singer; b. 17 April 1940, Berlin; m. Christoph von Dohnanyi (q.v.); one s. two d.; appearances in Salome, Lulu, Fidelio, Elektra, and the complete Wagner repertoire, also as Marie (Wozzeck), Hana Glawari (The Merry Widow), Carmen, Tosca, Katya Kabanová, Die Frau (Erwartung), Elena (The Makropoulos Case), Minnie (The Girl of the Golden West), Luise (Kabale und Liebe), Jenny (Rise and Fall of the City of Mahagonny), Katerina (Lady Macbeth of Mtsensk); guest appearances in Vienna, New York, San Francisco, Chicago, Salzburg Festivals, Stuttgart, Cologne, Budapest, Brussels, London, Tokyo, Geneva, Paris, Rome, Barcelona, Copenhagen, Hamburg, Frankfurt, Bayreuth. *Leisure interests:* driving, tennis, ice-skating. *Address:* Severence Hall, Cleveland, Ohio, 44106, U.S.A.

SILKIN, Jon, B.A.; British writer and editor; b. 2 Dec. 1930, London; s. of Joseph and Doris (née Rubenstein) Silkin; m. Lorna Tracy 1974; three s. one d.; ed. Wycliffe and Dulwich Colls., Leeds Univ.; journalist 1947; Nat. Service as teacher in Educ. Corps 1948–49; worked as manual labourer 1950–55; taught English to foreign students 1956–58; Gregory Fellowship

in Poetry (non-academic fellowship given to a practising poet), Univ. of Leeds 1958–60, graduated 1962, research 1962–65; Ed. Stand Magazine, Newcastle-upon-Tyne 1952; visited U.S.A., giving poetry reading tours; Visiting Lecturer, Denison Univ., Ohio; taught at Writers' Workshop, Univ. of Ia. 1968–69; Visiting Writer, Australian Arts Council and Univ. of Sydney 1974, Coll. of Idaho 1978; Mishkenot Sha'ananim (Israel) 1980; Bingham Visiting Poet, Univ. of Louisville 1981; Elliston Poet in Residence, Univ. of Cincinnati 1983; Visiting Poet, American Univ., Wash., D.C. 1989; Visiting Speaker, World Congress of Poets, Korea 1979, Madrid 1982, Corfu 1985, Florence 1986; C. Day Lewis Fellowship 1976–77; Geoffrey Faber Memorial Prize for Nature with Man 1966. *Publications:* The Peaceable Kingdom 1954 (reissued 1976), The Two Freedoms 1958, The Re-ordering of the Stones 1961, Nature With Man 1965, Penguin Modern Poets 7 (with Richard Murphy and Nathaniel Tarn) 1965, Poems New and Selected 1966, Killhope Wheel 1970, Amana Grass 1971, Out of Battle (criticism) 1972, Poetry of the Committed Individual (Co-editor) 1973, The Principle of Water 1974, The Little Time-Keeper 1976, Penguin Book of First World War Poetry (Ed.) 1979, The Psalms with their Spoils 1980, Selected Poems 1980, 1988, Autobiographical Stanzas 1983, Gurney (play) 1985, The 'War' Poems of Wilfred Owen 1985, The Ship's Pasture 1986, Penguin Book of First World War Prose (with Jon Glover) 1989. *Leisure interest:* travelling. *Address:* 19 Haldane Terrace, Newcastle-upon-Tyne, NE2 3AN, England. *Telephone:* 091-281 2614.

SILLARD, Yves; French aerospace engineer; b. 5 Jan. 1936, Coutances, Manche; s. of Roger and Madeleine (Guerrand) Sillard; m. Annick Legrand 1966 (divorced); ed. Ecole Massillon, Ecole Polytechnique, Ecole nat. Supérieure de l'Aéronautique; Test. Eng. and then Head of Colomb-Béchard unit of Centre d'Essais en Vol 1960–62, Tech. Dir. of Cazeaux annex 1963–64; Head of Concorde Programme at Secrétariat général à l'Aviation civile 1965; Head of Div. setting up French Guiana Space Centre, Kourou 1966–68; Tech. Dir. and then Dir. Space Centre, Kourou 1968–72; Dir. of Launchers, Centre Nat. des Etudes Spatiales 1973–76, Man. Dir. 1976–82; Chair. and Man. Dir. Centre nat. pour l'exploitation des océans 1982–; Chair. Conseil d'administration de l'institut français de recherche pour l'exploitation de la mer 1985–; French Nat. Co-ordinator for EUREKA Programme 1986–; Officier, Légion d'honneur, Chevalier, Ordre nat. du Mérite, Médaille de l'Aéronautique. *Address:* 66 avenue d'Iéna, 75116 Paris (Office); 26 rue Liancourt, 75014 Paris, France (Home).

SILLITOE, Alan; British author; b. 4 March 1928, Nottingham; s. of Christopher Archibald Sillitoe and Sylvina Burton; m. Ruth Esther Fainlight 1959; one s. one d. (adopted); ed. elementary school, Radford, Nottingham; worked in various factories, Nottingham 1942–46; served as wireless operator, R.A.F., Malaya 1946–49; lived six years in France and Spain; Fellow, Royal Geographical Soc.; Hon. Fellow, Manchester Polytechnic; Hawthornden Prize 1960. *Publications:* (novels) Saturday Night and Sunday Morning 1958, The General 1960, Key to the Door 1961, The Death of William Posters 1965, A Tree on Fire 1967, A Start in Life 1970, Travels in Nihilon 1971, Raw Materials 1972, The Flame of Life 1974, The Widower's Son 1976, The Storyteller 1979, Her Victory 1982, The Lost Flying Boat 1983, Down From The Hill 1984, Life Goes On 1985, Out of the Whirlpool 1987; (stories) The Loneliness of the Long Distance Runner 1959, The Ragman's Daughter 1963, Guzman, Go Home 1968, Men, Women and Children 1973, The Second Chance 1981, (essays) Mountains and Caverns 1975; (poems) The Rats and Other Poems 1960, A Falling Out of Love 1964, Love in the Environs of Voronezh 1968, Barbarians and Other Poems 1974, Storm and Other Poems 1974, Snow on the North Side of Lucifer 1979, Sun Before Departure 1984, Tides and Stone Walls (with Victor Bowley) 1986; (travel) Road to Volgograd 1964; The Saxon Shore Way (with Fay Godwin) 1983, Nottinghamshire (with David Sillitoe) 1986; (plays) Three Plays 1978; All Citizens are Soldiers 1969 (trans. of Lope de Vega play Fuenteovejuna, with Ruth Fainlight); (children's books) The City Adventures of Marmalade Jim 1967, Big John and the Stars 1977, The Incredible Fencing Fleas 1978, Marmalade Jim on the Farm 1980, Marmalade Jim and the Fox 1985, The Far Side of the Street (short stories) 1988, The Open Door (novel) 1989. *Leisure interests:* geography, navigation, travel. *Address:* c/o Savage Club, 9 Fitzmaurice Place, London, W.1, England.

SILLS, Beverly; American coloratura soprano; b. (as Belle Silverman) 26 May 1929, Brooklyn, New York; d. of the late Morris Silverman and of Sonia Bahn; m. Peter Bulkeley Greenough 1956; one s. one d. three step-c.; ed. pupil of Estelle Liebling; debut at San Francisco Opera as Helen of Troy in Mefistofele 1953, at New York City Opera as Rosalinda in Die Fledermaus 1955; with New York City Opera 1955–80, Gen. Dir. 1979–88, Pres. New York City Opera Bd. 1989–; debut at the Vienna State Opera as Queen of the Night (The Magic Flute) 1967, at La Scala, Milan in The Siege of Corinth 1969, at Royal Opera House, Covent Garden in title role of Lucia di Lammermoor 1970, Metropolitan Opera, New York as Pamira in Siege of Corinth 1975; other best known roles include Cleopatra (Julius Caesar), Queen Elizabeth I (Roberto Devereux), all three heroines in The Tales of Hoffmann, Manon (Manon), Violetta (La Traviata), Marie (Daughter of the Regiment), Rosina (Barber of Seville); title roles in Anna Bolena and Maria Stuarda, Norma, Lucrezia Borgia; recordings for Columbia, RCA, Angel, ABC—Audio Treasury; has appeared at most of the major opera houses of Europe and Latin America and given numerous recitals with leading orchestras throughout U.S.A.; retd. 1980; Dir. Warner Communications Inc., New York 1982–. *Publications:* Bubbles: a self-portrait 1976, Beverly (autobiog.) 1987. *Address:* New York City Opera, New York State Theatre, Lincoln Center, New York, N.Y. 10023, U.S.A.

SILUNGWE, Annel Musenga, LL.M.; Zambian lawyer; b. 10 Jan. 1936, Mbala, Zambia; s. of Solo Musenga Silungwe and Janet Nakafunda Silungwe; m. Abigail Nanyangwe Silungwe 1960; two s. four d.; ed. Univ. of Zambia, Inner Temple, London; Resident Magistrate 1967, Sr. Resident Magistrate (Class II) 1968, (Class I) 1970; Judge of the High Court 1971; nominated M.P. and apptd. Minister of Legal Affairs and Attorney-Gen. 1973; State Counsel 1974; Chief Justice 1975–; Chair. Judicial Services Comm. 1975, Council of Legal Educ. 1975, Council of Law Reporting 1975. *Leisure interests:* music, golf, photography. *Address:* Supreme Court of Zambia, P.O. Box 50067, Lusaka, Zambia. *Telephone:* 253249, 251743 (Office); 253918 (Home).

SILVA-CONCHA, Mario; Chilean diplomatist; b. 22 Oct. 1924, Santiago; m. Marta Vidaurre 1950; two s.; ed. Instituto Nacional and Univ. of Chile, Santiago; entered Foreign Service 1948; served Japan 1953–57, Netherlands 1960–61, France 1961–66, Czechoslovakia 1968–70, Argentina 1970–71, Denmark 1971–73, Austria 1977–78; Amb. to Romania 1978–80, Canada 1981–84, U.K. 1985–87; Sub-Dir. of Diplomatic Acad. 1966; Dir. of Cen. Services 1967; Deputy Dir.-Gen. Admin. Affairs 1967–68; Dir. of Protocol 1974–76; Prof. Diplomatic Acad. 1976; Dir. of Protocol 1980; decorations from several countries. *Leisure interests:* reading, arts, music. *Address:* c/o Ministry of Foreign Affairs, Palacio de la Moneda, Santiago de Chile, Chile.

SILVA HENRÍQUEZ, H.E. Cardinal Raúl; Chilean ecclesiastic; b. 3 July 1907, Talca; ed. Universidad Católica de Chile and Ateneo Salesiano, Turin; fmr. Prof. Canon and Moral Law, Salesian Study Centre, La Cisterna and Pres. Fed. of Catholic Colls., Chile; Pres. Caritas, Chile, Caritas Internacional and organizer of other social welfare projects; Diocesan Bishop, Valparaíso 1959–61; Archbishop of Santiago 1961–83, Archbishop Emer. 1983–; cr. Cardinal 1962; fmr. Chancellor, Universidad Católica de Chile; Hon. LL.D. (Univ. of Notre Dame); Latin America Jewish Conf. Human Rights Prize 1972, UN Prize 1978, Bruno Kreisky Foundation 1979. *Publication:* La Misión Social del Cristianismo: Conflicto de Clases o Solidaridad Cristiana. *Address:* c/o Palacio Arzobispal, Casilla 30-D, Santiago, Chile.

SILVA HERZOG, Jesús, M.A.; Mexican politician; b. Mexico; m.; ed. Nat. Univ. of Mexico and Yale Univ.; Dept. of Econ. Studies, Banco de Mexico 1962; Dir. of Tech. Studies, Office of Dir. of Banco de Mexico 1964; Dir.-Gen. of Credit, Ministry of Finance and Public Credit 1970; Dir.-Gen. Nat. Fund for Workers' Housing 1972, Banco de Mexico 1977; Dir.-Gen. of Public Credit, Ministry of Finance and Public Credit 1978, Under-Sec. 1979; Sec. of Finance and Public Credit 1982–86; has lectured at many univs. in Mexico and abroad; fmr. mem. of admin. bds. of main financial orgs. of Mexican public sector. *Publications:* co-author of several books on econ. and financial matters and numerous articles in specialized journals. *Address:* c/o Secretaria de Hacienda y Credito Publico, Palacio Nacional, Mexico, D.F., Mexico.

SILVER, Robert Simpson, C.B.E., M.A., B.SC., PH.D., D.SC.; British mechanical engineer; b. 13 March 1913, Montrose, Scotland; s. of Alexander Clark Silver and Isabella Simpson; m. Jean MacIntyre Bruce 1937; two s.; ed. Montrose Acad. and Glasgow Univ.; Research Physicist, ICI Ltd. 1936–39; Head of Research Dept., G. & J. Weir Ltd. 1939–46; Asst. Dir. of Research, Gas Research Bd. 1946–48; Dir. of Research, Federated Foundries Ltd. 1948–54; Chief Designer, John Brown Land Boilers Ltd. 1954–56; Tech. Dir. G. & J. Weir Ltd. 1956–62; Prof. of Mechanical Eng., Heriot-Watt Univ., Edinburgh 1962–66; James Watt Prof. of Mechanical Eng., Univ. of Glasgow 1967–79, now Prof. Emer.; Foreign Assoc., U.S. Acad. of Eng. 1979–; Inst. of Mechanical Engineers Prizes: George Stephenson Prize 1945, Thomas Lowe Gray Prize 1964, James Clayton Prize 1965; Memorial Award, American Soc. of Mechanical Engineers 1963; UNESCO Science Prize 1968. *Publications:* An Introduction to Thermodynamics 1971; many papers on thermodynamics and mechanical engineering of power and process plant with particular reference to desalination in later work; The Bruce, Robert I King O'Scots (play in 3 acts) 1986. *Leisure interest:* fly fishing. *Address:* Oakbank, Breadalbane Street, Tobermory, Isle of Mull, Scotland. *Telephone:* (0688) 2024.

SILVERMAN, Fred, M.A.; American broadcasting executive; b. 13 Sept. 1937, New York; m. Cathy Kihn; one s. one d.; ed. Syracuse Univ., Ohio State Univ.; with WGN-TV Chicago; exec. position WP1X-TV New York; Dir. Daytime Programmes CBS-TV New York, Vice-Pres. Programmes 1970–75; Pres. ABC Entertainment 1975–78; Pres. NBC 1978–81; ind. film producer 1981–; Pres. The Fred Silverman Co. 1986–. *Address:* The Fred Silverman Co., 12400 Wilshire Boulevard, Los Angeles, Calif. 90025, U.S.A.

SILVESTRINI, H.E. Cardinal Achille; Italian ecclesiastic; b. 25 Oct. 1923, Brisighella; ordained Catholic priest 1946, elected Archbishop of Novaliciana, Mauritania 1979, consecrated bishop 1979, cr. Cardinal 1988; Sec. for the Council for Public Affairs of the Church. *Address:* c/o The Vatican, Vatican City, Rome, Italy.

SIMAI, Mihály; Hungarian economist; b. 4 April 1930, Budapest; s. of Mátyás Simai and Jolán Rosenberg; m. Vera Bence; one d.; Prof. of World Economy, Karl Marx Univ. of Econ., Budapest 1971–; Dir. Research Inst. of World Econ., Budapest 1974–; Pres. Editorial Cttee. Acta Oeconomica; editorial board mem. Valóság; mem. Hungarian Acad. of Sciences 1979–; Pres. Hungarian UNO Soc., Hungarian Cttee. for UNICEF, World Fed. of UNO Socs.; mem. Council UN Univ.; Dir. Inst. for World Econs.; Co-Chair. British-Hungarian Round Table; Labour Order of Merit (Golden Degree), Order of the Star of Hungary (Golden Degree). *Publications:* Tőkekivitel a jelenkori kapitalizmusban (Capital Export in the Contemporary Capitalist System) 1962; A kapitalizmus világgazdasági rendszere (The World Economic System of Capitalism) 1965, Kilátás a 26. emeletről (View from Floor 26) 1969, A harmadik évezred felé (Towards the Third Millennium) 1969, Közös vállalkozás külföldi partnerekkel (Joint Ventures with Foreign Partners) 1971, Az Egyesült Államok a 200. évforduló előtt (The United States before the 200th Anniversary) 1974, Tervezés és tervvégrehajtás a fejlődő országokban (Planning and Plan Implementation in the Developing Countries) 1975, Az ENSZ és a Világproblémák (The United Nations and the Global Problems) 1977, Interdependence and Conflicts in the World Economy 1981, A fejlődő országok és a gazdasági dekolonizáció (Economic Decolonization and the Developing Countries) 1981, Power and Technology in the World Economy 1985, The United Nations Today and Tomorrow 1985; numerous articles on int. econ. and political issues. *Leisure interests:* hiking, skiing, rowing. *Address:* Világgazdasági Kutatóintézet, 1124 Budapest, Kálló esperes utca 15, Hungary. *Telephone:* (1) 664-572.

SIMATUPANG, Lieut.-Gen. Tahi Bonar; Indonesian international church official and retd. army officer; b. 28 Jan. 1920, Sidikalang; s. of late Simon Mangaraja Soaduon and of Mina Boru Sibuea; m. Sumarti Budiardjo 1949; two s. one d.; ed. Mil. Acad.; Dir. of Org., Gen. Staff of Indonesian Nat. Army 1945–48; Deputy Chief of Staff, Armed Forces of Repub. of Indonesia 1948–49, Acting Chief of Staff 1949–51, Chief of Staff 1951–54; Mil. Adviser to Govt. of Indonesia 1954–59; retd. from mil. service 1959; Pres. Council of Churches in Indonesia 1967–, Christian Conf. in Asia 1973–77; mem. Presidium World Council of Churches 1975–83; mem. Supreme Advisory Council, Republic of Indonesia 1973–78; D.Hum. Litt. (Tulsa) 1969. *Publications:* Pioneer in War, Pioneer in Peace (Role of the Armed Forces in Indonesia) 1954, Report from Banaran—Experiences during the People's War 1959, Christian Task in Revolution 1966, National Resilience in the New Situation in Southeast Asia 1980, From Revolution to Development 1984, Christian Faith and Pancasile (the Indonesian State Ideology) 1984, Hope, Fear and Determination 1985, Christian Presence in War, Revolution and Development 1986, Indonesia: Leadership and National Security Perceptions 1987. *Leisure interest:* reading. *Address:* Jalan Diponegoro 55, Jakarta, Indonesia. *Telephone:* 337800.

SIMBA, Iddi, B.SC., C.E.R.; Tanzanian banking official; b. 8 Oct. 1935, Usumbura; m. Khadija Simba; one s. two d.; ed. Punjab Univ., Pakistan, and Univ. of Toulouse, France; Agricultural Field Officer, Ministry of Agric. 1961–62; Asst. Dir. of Planning, Ministry of Econ. Affairs and Planning; Alt. Exec. Dir. IBRD 1966–68; Chair. and Dir.-Gen. E. African Devt. Bank 1968–78; Resident Dir. African Devt. Bank 1978–80; Fellow Int. Bankers' Assen., and Econ. Devt. Inst. (IBRD). *Publications:* Planning of a Typical Peasant Farm to Meet Complete Dietary and Cash Needs of a Five-Member Peasant Family 1962, The Use of a National Centre for the Collection of Agricultural Statistics in the Planning of Peasant Agriculture in Tanzania 1964. *Leisure interests:* music, light reading. *Address:* c/o Ministry of Foreign Affairs, Dar-es-Salaam, Tanzania.

SIMBANAIYE, Artémon; Burundi diplomatist and government official; b. 1935, Rubonwa, Bururi Province; ed. Univ. of Louvain, Belgium and Law Faculty of Paris Univ.; Gen. Counsellor in Ministry of Justice, Information, Public Safety and Immigration 1965, concurrently Tech. Adviser to Supreme Court and Court of Appeals 1965; Sec. of State (Minister) of Justice 1965–66; Minister of Justice, Public Safety and Immigration, concurrently State Prosecutor 1966–67; Dir.-Gen. Ministry of Foreign Affairs and Co-operation 1969; Cabinet Minister Attached to the Office of the Pres., concurrently Minister for Planning 1969–71; Pres. Gov. Council, Bujumbura Univ. 1970–73; Minister for Foreign Affairs, Co-operation and Planning 1971–72; Amb. without Portfolio May-July 1972; Minister for Foreign Affairs, Co-operation and Planning 1972–74; Minister for Nat. Educ. and Culture 1974–76; Perm. Rep. to UN 1977–81; Amb. to Ethiopia 1981–; Pres. UNDP 1978; mem. Del. to Gen. Assembly 1969, leader of Del. 1971–74. *Address:* Embassy of Burundi, P.O. Box 3641, Addis Ababa, Ethiopia.

SIMBOMANA, Adrien; Burundi politician; fmr. Deputy Speaker Nat. Ass.; Gov. of Muramvya Prov. –1988; fmr. Vice-Pres. of Comm. on Nat. Unity; Prime Minister of Burundi Oct. 1988–. *Address:* Office of the Prime Minister, Bujumbura, Burundi.

SIMENON, Georges; Belgian novelist; b. 13 Feb. 1903, Liège; s. of Désiré and Henriette (née Brull) Simenon; m. Denise Ouimet 1950; three s. one d. (deceased); ed. Coll. St. Servais, Liège; mem. Acad. Royale de Langue et de Littérature Française, Brussels; abandoned novel writing 1973 to write daily journal and Letter to my Mother. *Publications:* 212 novels, including 80 in the Maigret series, and 21 vols. of daily notations; books translated into 57 languages and published in 40 countries; memoirs: Mémoires intimes 1981. *Address:* Secretariat de Georges Simenon, avenue du Temple 19B, 1012 Lausanne (Office); 12 avenue des Figuiers, 1007 Lausanne, Switzerland (Home).

SIMEÓN NEGRÍN, Rosa Elena; Cuban professor of veterinary medicine; b. 17 June 1943, Havana; m.; one d.; ed. Marianao High School and Univ. of Havana; Chief, Dept. of Virology, Nat. Center of Scientific Research (CENIC) 1968–73, Chief, Microbiological Div. 1974–76; Prof. School of Veterinary Medicine 1969–73, Nat. Hosp. and Nat. Center of Scientific Investigations 1975, Nat. Inst. of Veterinary Medicine 1977–78, 1981; Dir. Nat. Center of Agric. Health (CENSA) 1985; Pres. Acad. of Sciences of Cuba 1985–; many other professional appts.; awards and decorations from Cuba, Czechoslovakia and France. *Publications:* articles in professional journals. *Address:* Academia de Ciencias de Cuba, Industria y San José, Zona 2, Havana, Cuba.

SIMINOVITCH, Louis, O.C., PH.D., F.R.S., F.R.S.C.; Canadian scientist; b. 1 May 1920, Montreal; s. of Nathan and Golda (Watchman) Siminovitch; m. Elinore Esther Faierman 1944; three d.; ed. McGill Univ., Montreal, Memorial Univ., St. John's Newfoundland and McMaster Univ., Hamilton, Ont.; Prof., Dept. of Medical Biophysics, Univ. of Toronto, Ont. 1960–, Prof., Dept. of Medical Cell Biology (now Medical Genetics) 1966–; Geneticist-in-Chief, The Hosp. for Sick Children, Toronto 1970–85; Univ. Prof., Univ. of Toronto 1976–, Prof., Dept. of Pediatrics 1978–; Dir. of Research, Mount Sinai Hosp., Toronto 1983–; Dir. Canadian Weizmann Inst. of Science 1972–; Nat. Cancer Inst. of Canada Fellowship 1953–55; Centennial Medal, Canada 1967; Queen Elizabeth II Jubilee Silver Medal 1977; Flavelle Gold Medal, Royal Soc. of Canada 1978; Izaak Walton Killam Memorial Prize 1981; Gairdner Foundation Wightman Award 1981, Environmental Mutagen Soc. Award, Baltimore 1986, R.P. Taylor Award of Canadian Cancer Soc.-Nat. Cancer Inst. 1986. *Publications:* 190 scientific papers. *Leisure interests:* reading, theatre, swimming. *Address:* Mount Sinai Hospital, 600 University Avenue, Toronto, Ont., M5G 1X5, Canada. *Telephone:* (416) 586-8224.

SIMION, Eugen I., PH.D.; Romanian literary critic; b. 25 May 1933, Chiojdeanca, Prahova County; s. of Dragomir Simion and Sultana Simion; m. Adriana Manea 1957; one d.; ed. Coll. of Philology, Bucharest Univ.; scientific researcher Romanian Acad. 1957–62; Ed. Gazeta literară 1962–68; Asst. Lecturer 1964, Lecturer 1971, Prof. of Romanian Literature, Bucharest Univ. 1969–; visiting Prof. Sorbonne, Paris 1970–73; mem. leading Bd. of the Romanian Writers' Union; prizes of the Romanian Writers' Union; Prize of the Romanian Acad.; mem. of the Int. Union of Literary Critics. *Works include:* Eminescu's Fiction 1964, Trends in Today's Literature 1965, E. Lovinescu the Skeptic Saved 1971, The Romanian Writers Today (Vol. I) 1974, (Vol. II) 1975, (Vol. III) 1983; A Time to Live, a Time to Confess (Paris Diary), The Morning of Poets 1980, Defying Rhetoric 1985. *Address:* Edgar Quinet 7, Bucharest, Romania.

SIMITIS, Constantine, DR.JUR.; Greek lawyer and politician; b. 1936, Athens; m.; two c.; ed. Univ. of Marburg and London School of Econs.; Supreme Court lawyer 1961–; taught in W. German univs. 1971–75; Prof. of Commercial Law, Univ. of Athens 1975–; active in politics 1965–, mem. Nat. Council of Panhellenic Liberation Movt. (PAK) during colonels' dictatorship, mem. Pasok 1974–, mem. Cen. Cttee. of Pasok; Minister of Agric. 1981–85, of Nat. Economy 1985–87. *Publications:* several books and numerous articles in Greek and German on legal and econ. matters. *Address:* c/o Ministry of National Economy, Syntagma Square, Athens, Greece.

SIMKIN, William E.; American labour arbitrator and mediator; b. 13 Jan. 1907, Merrifield, N.Y.; s. of Alfred E. Simkin and Florence Manchester; m. Ruth Commons 1929; two s.; ed. Earlham Coll. and Univ. of Pennsylvania; Prin. Cen. High School, Sherwood 1928–30; Teacher Brooklyn Friends School 1930–32; Rep. in W. Virginia, American Friends Service Cttee. 1932–37; Instructor Wharton School of Finance and Commerce, Pa. Univ. 1937–39; Labor Arbitrator 1939–61, 1969–89; Assoc. Impartial Chair. Philadelphia Men's Clothing Industry 1940–61, Philadelphia Dress Industry 1947–61; Arbitrator, American Viscose Corpn. 1947–61, Sun Shipbuilding Co. 1945–49, and for many other firms; Pres. Nat. Acad. of Arbitrators 1950; Dir. Fed. Mediation and Conciliation Service 1961–69; Chair. Basic Steel Industry Incentive Study Group 1969–70; Chair. Labor Relations Panel, Fed. Reserve System 1970–79; Chair. Foreign Service Grievance Bd. 1971–76; Lecturer and Fellow, Harvard Univ. 1969–73. *Publication:* Mediation and the Dynamics of Labor Relations 1986. *Leisure interests:* woodwork, golf. *Address:* 5210 N. Nina Drive, Tucson, Arizona 85704, U.S.A. *Telephone:* (602) 888-4091.

SIMMONDS, Rt. Hon. Dr. Kennedy Alphonse, P.C.; St. Christopher-Nevis politician; b. 12 April 1936; s. of the late Arthur Simmonds and of Bronte Clarke; ed. Basseterre Boys' School, St. Kitts-Nevis Grammar School and Univ. of the West Indies; Intern, Kingston Public Hosp., Jamaica 1963; Registrar in Internal Medicine, Princess Margaret Hosp., Bahamas 1966–68; Resident in Anaesthesiology, Pittsburgh 1968–69; medical practice in St. Kitts and Anguilla 1964–66, in St. Kitts 1969–80; founder mem. People's Action Movt. 1965, Pres. 1976, unsuccessfully contested elections 1966, 1971, 1975; elected to Parl. 1979; Premier 1980–83; Minister

of Home and External Affairs, Trade, Devt. and Industry 1980–84, of Finance, Home and Foreign Affairs 1984–; Prime Minister Sept. 1983–; Fellow American Coll. of Anaesthesiologists. *Address:* Office of the Prime Minister, Basseterre, St. Kitts, West Indies. *Telephone:* 809-465 2103.

SIMMONDS, Wilfred John, M.B., B.S., D.PHIL., F.R.A.C.P., F.A.A.; Australian professor of physiology; b. 29 Nov. 1918, Brisbane; s. of Dr John Lloyd Simmonds and Dorothy G. Dawson; m. Natalie Baker 1946; one s. one d.; ed. Ipswich Grammar School, Queensland, and Univs. of Queensland and Oxford; lecturer, Univ. of Queensland 1946; demonstrator, Physiology, Univ. of Oxford 1947–50; Sr. Research Fellow, Kanematsu Memorial Inst. of Pathology, Sydney Hosp. 1950–57; Foundation Prof. of Physiology, Univ. of W. Australia 1957–83, Prof. Emer. and Hon. Research Fellow 1983–; Visiting Faculty mem. Mayo Foundation, Grad. School of Medicine 1972; Visiting Prof. Univ. of Calif. at San Diego 1977; Pres. Australian Physiological Soc. 1986–(89); mem. various nat. scientific advisory cttees.; Fulbright Fellow 1965; Commonwealth Fund of New York Fellow 1965; Hon. D.Sc. (Univ. of W. Australia) 1986. *Publications:* about 60 research papers and reviews. *Leisure interests:* tennis, reading, research. *Address:* Department of Physiology, University of Western Australia, Nedlands, Western Australia 6009; Unit 2, 32 Strickland Street, South Perth, Western Australia 6151. *Telephone:* 380 3394.

SIMMONS, Adele Smith, PH.D. (OXON.); American college administrator; b. 21 June 1941, Lake Forest, Ill.; d. of Hermon D. and Ellen T. (née Thorne) Smith; m. John L. Simmons; two s. one d.; ed. Radcliffe Coll., Oxford Univ.; Dean, Jackson Coll., Tufts Univ., Medford, Mass. 1970–72; Asst. Prof. History, Dean Student Affairs, Princeton Univ. 1972–77; Pres. Hampshire Coll., Amherst, Mass. 1977–; Dir. Affiliated Publs., Boston, Marsh & McLennan, N.Y., Boston Globe, Zayre Corpn.; Trustee, Chair. Bd. Carnegie Foundation for Advancement of Teaching; Trustee Union of Concerned Scientists, World Policy Inst.; mem. American Assen. Higher Educ., Pres.'s Comm. on World Hunger 1978–80; Hon. L.H.D. (Lake Forest Coll.) 1976, (Amherst Coll.) 1977, (Franklin Pierce Coll.) 1978, (Univ. Massachusetts) 1982, (Alverno Coll.) 1986, (Marlboro Coll.) 1987. *Publications:* Modern Mauritius 1980; articles to professional journals. *Address:* Hampshire College, Amherst, Mass. 01002, U.S.A.

SIMMONS, Jean; British actress; b. 31 Jan. 1929, London; d. of Charles Simmons and Winifred Ada (née Loveland) Simmons; m. 1st Stewart Granger 1950 (divorced 1960), one d.; m. 2nd Richard Brooks (q.v.) 1960, one d.; ed. Orange Hill School, Burnt Oak, London; in films from 1943; stage appearance, Philadelphia, and on tour in A Little Night Music 1974–75; appeared in TV series The Dain Curse 1978, Down at the Hydro 1982. *Films include:* Great Expectations 1946, Black Narcissus 1946, Hamlet 1948, Adam and Evelyne 1949, So Long at the Fair 1950, Young Bess 1953, The Robe 1953, The Actress 1953, Guys and Dolls 1956, The Big Country 1958, Home Before Dark 1958, Elmer Gantry 1960, Spartacus 1960, The Grass is Greener 1961, All the Way Home 1963, Life at the Top 1965, Tough Night in Jericho 1967, Divorce American Style 1967, The Happy Ending 1969, Dominique 1979, The Thornbirds (TV) 1982, The Dawning 1988. *Address:* c/o Morgan Maree, 6363 Wilshire Boulevard, Los Angeles, Calif. 90048, U.S.A.

SIMMONS, Neville Keith; Barbados lawyer and politician; b. 16 Sept. 1938; m. Lucille Ianthe; two c.; ed. Combermere School and Inns of Court School of Law, London; civil servant 1958–61; R.A.F. 1961–66; pvt. practice 1970–73, 1981–86; magistrate 1973–81; mem. of Parl. for St. James South; Second Vice-Pres. Democratic Labour Party; Minister of Health 1986–88, of Employment, Labour Relations and Community Devt. Oct. 1988–. *Address:* Ministry of Employment, Labour Relations and Community Development, Marine House, Hastings, St. Michael 29 (Office); Far Horizons, Gibbs Hill, St. Peter, Barbados (Home).

SIMMONS, Richard D., A.B., LL.B.; American newspaper publisher; b. 30 Dec. 1934, Cambridge, Mass.; m. Mary DeWitt Bleecker 1961; two s.; ed. Harvard and Columbia Univs.; admitted to New York bar; Assoc. Satterlee, Warfield & Stephens 1958–62; Gen. Counsel Giannini Science Corpn. 1962–64; Vice-Pres. and Gen. Counsel Southeastern Publishing Service Corpn. 1964–69; Counsel Dun & Bradstreet Inc., New York 1969–70, Vice-Pres. and Gen. Counsel 1970–72; Pres. Moody's Investors Service 1973–76, Dun & Bradstreet Inc. 1975–76; Exec. Vice-Pres. Dun & Bradstreet Corpn., New York 1976–78, Dir. and Vice-Chair. Bd. 1979–81; Pres. and C.O.O. The Washington Post Co. 1981–; Pres. Int. Herald Tribune May 1989–; Dir. Union Pacific Corpn.; Trustee The Children's Aid Soc., Int. House, Rockefeller Univ. Council, Cttee. for Econ. Devt. *Address:* 1150 15th Street, N.W., Washington, D.C. 20071, U.S.A. (Office).

SIMMONS, Richard S., B.A., LL.B.; American banker; b. 28 Sept. 1928, New York; s. of William Simmons and Mary Simmons; m. Margaret P. Casey 1955; one s.; ed. Princeton Univ. and Yale Law School; Deputy Supt. and Counsel, New York State Banking Dept. 1959–60; Partner, Cravath, Swaine & Moore 1963–85; Vice-Chair. Chemical New York Corpn. and Chemical Bank 1985–. *Leisure interests:* golf, reading, swimming. *Address:* 277 Park Avenue, New York, N.Y. 10172, U.S.A. *Telephone:* (212) 310-4803.

SIMMS, Most Rev. George Otto, PH.D., D.D.; Irish ecclesiastic; b. 4 July 1910, Dublin; s. of John Francis Arthur and Ottilie Simms; m. Mercy

Felicia 1941; three s. two d.; ed. Cheltenham Coll. and Trinity Coll., Dublin; ordained Deacon 1935, Priest 1936; Curate-Asst., St. Bartholomew's, Dublin 1935-38; Chaplain, Lincoln Theological Coll. 1938-39; Dean of Residence, Trinity Coll., Dublin 1939-52; Chaplain, Church of Ireland Training Coll. 1943-52; Dean of Cork 1952; Bishop of Cork 1952-56; Archbishop of Dublin, Bishop of Glendalough and Kildare, Primate of Ireland 1956-69; Archbishop of Armagh and Primate of All Ireland 1969-80; Pres. The Leprosy Mission 1964-; Chair. Irish Council of Churches 1972-74; Co-Chair. Anglican-Roman Catholic Int. Comm. on the Theology of Marriage 1968-75; Pres. Asscn. for Promoting Christian Knowledge 1983-; mem. Royal Irish Acad. 1957; D.D. h.c. (Huron, Canada) 1963, Hon. D.C.L. (Kent) 1978, D.Litt. h.c. (New Univ. of Ulster) 1981; Hon. Fellow Trinity Coll., Dublin 1978; Hon. Life mem. Royal Dublin Soc. 1984. *Publications:* Joint Ed. Facsimile Edition of the Book of Kells 1951, Facsimile Edition of the Book of Durrow 1960; For Better, For Worse 1945, The Book of Kells: a short description 1950, The Bible in Perspective 1953, Memoir of Michael Lloyd Ferrar 1962, Christ within Me 1975, Irish Illuminated Manuscripts 1980, contributor to Irish Spirituality 1981, In My Understanding 1982, Tullow's Story 1983, contrib. to Ireland: A Cultural Encyclopedia 1983, Pioneers and Partners (with R. G. F. Jenkins) 1985; contrib. to Treasures of the Library, Trinity College, Dublin 1986; Rathmichael: A Parish History by Kathleen Turner (Ed.) 1987, Angels and Saints 1988, Exploring the Book of Kells 1988. *Address:* 62 Cypress Grove Road, Dublin 6, Ireland. *Telephone:* Dublin 905594.

SIMON, Claude; French writer; b. 10 Oct. 1913, Tananarive, Madagascar; s. of Antoine Simon and Suzanne (née Denamiel) Simon; ed. Collège Stanislas, Paris; Prix de l'Express for La Route des Flandres 1960; Prix Médicis for Histoire 1967, Nobel Prize for Literature 1985; Grand Officier, Ordre nat. du Mérite. *Publications:* Le tricheur 1945, La corde raide 1947, Gulliver 1952, Le sacre du printemps 1954, Le vent 1957, L'herbe 1958, La route des Flandres 1960, Le palace 1962, Histoire 1967, La bataille de Pharsale 1969, Orion aveugle 1970, Les corps conducteurs 1971, Tryptique 1973, Leçon de choses 1975, Les Géorgiques 1981, La chevelure de Bérénice 1985, Discours de Stockholm 1986, L'Invitation 1988. *Address:* Editions de Minuit, 7 rue Bernard-Palissy, 75006 Paris; 3 place Monge, 75005 Paris; place Vieille, Salses, 66600 Rivesaltes, France.

SIMON, David Alec Gwyn, M.A., M.B.A.; British business executive; b. 24 July 1939, London; s. of Roger Simon and Barbara Hudd; m. Hanne Mohn 1964; two s.; ed. Gonville and Caius Coll., Cambridge; joined B.P. 1961, Supply Dept. 1966-72, Marketing Dir., Holland 1972-75, Govt. Affairs Dept. 1975, Marketing Co-ordinator, European Region 1975-80, Marketing Dir., Oil U.K. 1980-82, Man. Dir., Oil Int. Ltd. 1982-85, Man. Dir. B.P. Co. PLC 1986-; Non-Exec. Dir. The Plessey Co. 1986-. *Leisure interests:* golf, tennis, books, music. *Address:* The British Petroleum Co. PLC, Britannic House, Moor Lane, London, EC2Y 9BU, England. *Telephone:* 01-920 8000.

SIMON, Herbert A., PH.D.; American social scientist and professor; b. 15 June 1916, Milwaukee, Wis.; s. of Arthur Simon and Edna Merkel Simon; m. Dorothea Pye 1937; one s. two d.; ed. Univ. of Chicago; Research Asst., Univ. of Chicago 1936-38; Staff mem. Int. City Managers' Asscn. 1938-39; Dir. of Admin. Measurement Studies, Bureau of Public Admin. Univ. of Calif. at Berkeley 1939-42; Asst. Prof., later Prof., Ill. Inst. of Tech. 1942-49, Chair. of Dept. 1946-49; Prof. of Admin., Carnegie-Mellon Univ. 1949-65, Richard King Mellon Prof. of Computer Sciences and Psychology 1965-; Chair. Bd. of Dirs. Social Science Research Council 1961-66, Div. of Behavioral Sciences of Nat. Research Council 1968-70; Ford Lecturer, New York Univ. 1960, Vanuxem Lecturer, Princeton Univ. 1961, William James Lecturer, Harvard Univ. 1963, Harris Lecturer, Northwestern Univ. 1967, Compton Lecturer, M.I.T. 1968, Katz-Newcomb Lecturer, Univ. of Michigan 1976, Hovland Lecturer, Yale Univ. 1976, Gaither Lecturer, Univ. of Calif. (Berkeley) 1980, Camp Lecturer, Stanford Univ. 1982, Lecturer, Univ. of Calif. (Los Angeles) 1983, Univ. of Michigan 1983; mem. President's Science Advisory Cttee. 1968-72, Nat. Acad. of Sciences, American Philosophical Soc., Bd. of Trustees, Carnegie-Mellon Univ. 1972-; Distinguished Fellow, American Econ. Asscn. 1976; Hon. mem. Inst. of Electrical and Electronic Engineers; Foreign mem. Yugoslav Acad. of Sciences; Hon. Prof., Tianjin Univ., Beijing Univ.; Hon. mem. Inst. of Psychology, Chinese Acad. of Sciences; Distinguished Scientific Contributions Award, American Psychological Asscn. 1969; A. M. Turing Award, Asscn. for Computing Machinery 1975; Nobel Prize for Econs. 1978; Procter Prize 1980; James Madison Award, American Political Science Asscn. 1984; Nat. Medal of Science 1986; Hon. D.Sc. (Yale Univ., Case Inst. of Tech., Marquette Univ., Columbia Univ., Gustavus Adolphus Univ.), Hon. LL.D. (Univ. of Chicago, McGill Univ., Univ. of Mich., Univ. of Pittsburgh), Hon. Fil.D. (Lund Univ.), Hon. D.Phil. (Paul Valery Univ. of Montpellier) 1984; Hon. Dr. Econ.Sc. (Erasmus Univ.). *Publications:* Administrative Behavior 1947, 1957, 1976, Public Administration 1950, Models of Man 1957, Organizations 1958, The Shape of Automation 1960, 1965, The Sciences of the Artificial 1969, 1981, Human Problem-Solving 1972, Models of Discovery 1977, Models of Thought 1979, Models of Bounded Rationality (2 vols.) 1982, Reason in Human Affairs 1983, Protocol Analysis 1984, Scientific Discovery 1986. *Leisure interests:* hiking, music. *Address:* Department of Psychology, Carnegie-Mellon University, Pittsburgh, Pa. 15213, U.S.A. *Telephone:* (412) 578-2787.

SIMON, Josef, Ing.; Czechoslovak economist, diplomatist and politician; b. 10 March 1921, Medlešice; m. Eliska Backovská 1947; one s. one d.; Head of Dept., Regional Cttee. CP of Czechoslovakia 1948-50; Dir. nat. enterprise Tatra, Kopřivnice 1951-52; Head of Dept., Ministry of Eng. 1953-57; Dir. Skoda enterprise, V.I. Lenin Works, Pilsen 1958-62; Head of Dept., Ministry of Heavy Eng. 1962-66; Dir. AZNP Motor Car Works, Mladá Boleslav 1966-69; fmr. Minister of Industry, Czech S.R.; Deputy to Czech Nat. Council and Fed. Assembly 1969-71, to House of Nations, Fed. Assembly 1969-81; mem. Cen. Cttee. of CP of Czechoslovakia 1971-81; Minister of Metallurgy and Eng. 1971-73, of Metallurgy and Heavy Eng. 1973-74; Vice-Premier of Czechoslovakia 1974-81; Chair. CMEA Standing Cttee. for Eng. 1974-, Czechoslovak section of Czechoslovak-Bulgarian Cttee. for Econ. Co-operation 1974-81, Inter-governmental Czechoslovak-Mongolian Comm. for Econ. and Scientific Tech. Co-operation 1974-81, Czechoslovak section of Inter-governmental Comm. for Co-operation in the Construction of the Gas Pipeline Orenburg-Western Border of U.S.S.R. 1975-, Czechoslovak section of Mixed Czechoslovak-Romanian Governmental Comm. for Econ. and Scientific Tech. Co-operation 1976-81; Amb. to Romania 1981-84; Order of Labour 1971, Order of Labour, Order of Friendship between Nations (U.S.S.R.) 1974, Order of Iraq (Gold) 1974, Order of the Repub. 1981, Order of Tudor Vladimirescu (Gold) 1983. *Address:* Na Ostrohu 6, 160 00 Prague 6, Czechoslovakia.

SIMON, Neil; American playwright; b. 4 July 1927, New York; s. of Irving and Mamie Simon; m. 1st. Joan Baim 1953 (deceased), two d.; m. 2nd Marsha Mason 1973 (divorced); m. 3rd Diane Lander 1987, one step-d.; wrote for various television programmes, including The Tallulah Bankhead Show 1951, The Phil Silvers Show 1958-59, NBC Special, The Trouble with People 1972. *Plays:* Come Blow Your Horn 1961, Little Me (musical) 1962, Barefoot in the Park 1963, The Odd Couple 1965, Sweet Charity (musical) 1966, The Star-Spangled Girl 1966, Plaza Suite 1968, Promises, Promises 1968, The Last of the Red Hot Lovers 1969, The Gingerbread Lady 1970, The Good Doctor 1973, The Prisoner of Second Avenue 1971, The Sunshine Boys 1972, God's Favorite 1974, California Suite 1976, I Ought to be in Pictures 1980, They're Playing Our Song 1980, Fools 1981, Little Me (revised version) 1982, Brighton Beach Memoirs 1983, Biloxi Blues 1984, The Odd Couple Female Version 1985, Broadway Bound 1986; wrote screenplay for films After the Fox 1966, Barefoot in the Park 1967, The Odd Couple 1968, The Out-of-Towners 1970, Plaza Suite 1971, Last of the Red Hot Lovers 1972, The Heartbreak Kid 1973, The Prisoner of Second Avenue 1975, The Sunshine Boys 1975, Murder By Death 1976, The Goodbye Girl 1977, The Cheap Detective 1978, Chapter Two 1979, California Suite 1979, Seems Like Old Times 1980, Only When I Laugh 1981, I Ought to Be in Pictures 1982, Max Dugan Returns 1983, The Slugger's Wife 1984, Brighton Beach Memoirs 1986, Rumours 1988, Biloxi Blues 1988; mem. Dramatists Guild; Emmy Award 1957, 1959; Antoinette Perry (Tony) Award Best Playwright 1965, 1985; Hon. D.Hum.Litt. (Hofstra Univ. 1981, Williams Coll.) 1984. *Address:* A. DaSilva, 502 Park Avenue, New York, N.Y. 10022, U.S.A.

SIMON, Paul; American politician, educationalist, and writer; b. 29 Nov. 1928, Eugene, Ore.; s. of Martin Paul Simon and Ruth (née Troemel) Simon; m. Jeanne Hurley 1960; one s. one d.; ed. Univ. of Oregon, Dana Coll., Blair, Neb.; publisher Troy (Ill.) Tribune 1948-66, and weeklies; mem. Ill. House of Reps. 1955-63, Ill. Senate 1963-69, Lieut. Gov. Ill. 1969-73; Fellow John F. Kennedy Inst. of Politics, Harvard 1972-73; Prof. of Public Affairs Reporting Sangamon State Univ., Springfield 1973; mem. 94th-98th Congresses, Ill.; U.S. Senator from Illinois 1985-; mem. Bd. of Dirs. Dana Coll.; recipient American Political Science Asscn. Award 1957; holds 27 hon. degrees; Democrat. *Publications:* Lovejoy: Martyr to Freedom 1964, Lincoln's Preparation for Greatness 1965, a Hungry World 1966, You Want to Change the World, So Change It 1971, The Tongue-Tied American 1980, The Once and Future Democrats 1982, The Glass House, Politics and Morality in the Nation's Capitol 1984, Beginnings 1986, Let's Put America Back to Work 1986 (with Jeanne Hurley Simon) Protestant-Catholic Marriages Can Succeed 1967, (with Arthur Simon) The Politics of World Hunger 1973. *Address:* 462 Dirksen Senate Building, Washington, D.C. 20510, U.S.A.

SIMON, Paul, B.A.; American composer and musician; b. Newark; s. of Louis and Belle Simon; m. 1st Peggy Harper; one s.; m 2nd Carrie Fisher 1983; ed. Queens Coll., Brooklyn Law School; fmrly. mem. singing duo Simon and Garfunkel (q.v.) 1964-71; solo performer 1972-; *songs with Garfunkel include:* The Sounds of Silence, Dangling Conversation, Homeward Bound, I Am a Rock, At the Zoo, 7 O'Clock News, 59th Street Bridge Song, Scarborough Fair, Mrs. Robinson, The Boxer, Bridge Over Troubled Water; *albums with Garfunkel:* Wednesday Morning 3 A.M. 1964, Sounds of Silence 1966, Parsley, Sage, Rosemary and Thyme 1966, The Graduate 1968. Bookends 1968, Bridge Over Troubled Water 1970, Concert in Central Park 1982; *solo albums:* Paul Simon 1972, There goes Rhymin' Simon 1973, Live Rhymin' 1975, Still Crazy After All These Years 1975, Greatest Hits, etc. 1977, One-Trick Pony 1980, Hearts and Bones 1983; Graceland 1986; wrote score, author screenplay One-Trick Pony; appeared in film Annie Hall 1977; Grammy Award for Mrs Robinson (song), Bridge Over Troubled Water (album), The Graduate (soundtrack), Still Crazy After All These Years (album), Graceland (album) 1986; Emmy Award for NBC Paul Simon Special.

SIMON, William Edward, B.A.; American financier and government official; b. 27 Nov. 1927, Paterson, N.J.; s. of Charles Simon and Eleanor Kearns; m. Carol Girard 1950; two s. five d.; ed. Lafayette Coll., Easton, Pennsylvania; joined Union Securities, N.Y. 1952, Asst. Vice-Pres., Man. Municipal Trading Dept. 1955; Vice-Pres. Weedon & Co. 1957–64; joined Salomon Bros. 1964, later Partner; Deputy Sec. U.S. Treasury Dept. 1973–74, Head of Federal Energy Office 1973–74; Sec. of the Treasury 1974–77; Chair. Econ. Policy Bd. 1974–77; Chair. Council on Wage and Price Stability 1975–77; Chair. Wesray Corpn., Morristown 1981–86, Wesray Capital Corpn. 1984–86, WSGP Int. Inc., William E. Simon Foundation Inc.; partner WS GP Int.; mem. Bd. of Govs., Exec. Cttee. Investment Bankers' Assen. of America until 1972; mem. Bd. of Dirs., Exec. Cttee. Securities Industry Assen. 1972; Chair. Public Finance Council; Founder, Past Pres. Assen. of Primary Dealers in U.S. Govt. Securities; mem. Cttee. to Fight Inflation 1980; mem. Econ. Policy Advisory Bd. 1981–; Nat. Chair. Fund Raising, U.S. Olympic Cttee.; Chair. Debt Man. Cttee. of N.Y.; Trustee, Lafayette Coll., Mannes Coll. of Music, Newark Acad.; Hon. LL.D. (Lafayette Coll.) 1973, (Pepperdine Univ.) 1975, Hon. D.C.L. (Jacksonville Univ.) 1976, Hon. D.Sc. (New England Coll.) 1977, Hon. Dr. Phil. (Tel Aviv Univ.) 1976; Jefferson Award 1976; now consultant in Wall Street. *Publications:* A Time for Truth 1978, A Time for Action 1980. *Address:* William E. Simon and Sons Inc., 310 South Street, P.O. Box 1913, Morristown, N.J. 07962-1913, U.S.A.

SIMON OF GLAISDALE, Baron (Life Peer), cr. 1970; **Jocelyn Edward Salis Simon,** Kt., P.C.; British judge; b. 15 Jan. 1911, London; s. of Frank Cecil Simon and Claire Evelyn Simon, M.B.E.; m. 1st Gwendolen Helen Evans 1934 (died 1937); m. 2nd Fay Elizabeth Leicester Pearson 1948, three s.; ed. Gresham's School, Holt and Trinity Hall, Cambridge; M.P. (Conservative) 1951–62; Joint Parl. Under-Sec. of State, Home Office 1957–58; Financial Sec. to Treasury 1958–59; Solicitor-Gen. 1959–62; Pres. of Probate, Divorce and Admiralty Div. of High Court 1962–71; Lord of Appeal in Ordinary 1971–77; Hon. Fellow Trinity Hall, Cambridge 1963; Elder Brother Trinity House. *Publications:* Co-author of Change is Our Ally 1954, Rule of Law 1955, The Church and the Law of Nullity 1955. *Address:* Midge Hall, Glaisdale Head, nr. Whitby, Yorkshire, England (Home).

SIMONARD, André, D. EN D.; French lawyer; b. 11 Feb. 1917, Boulogne-sur-Mer; s. of Georges Simonard and Jeanne Husson; m. Monique Wahl 1962; two s.; lawyer, Court of Paris 1937–; Prof., Ecole des Hautes Etudes Commerciales 1949–69, Hon. Prof. 1970–; Tech. Adviser to Minister of Public Works 1953–54; Head of Staff to Sec. of State for Youth 1954–55, to Sec. of State for Foreign Affairs 1957, to Minister of Information 1957–58; Prof., Univ. of Paris VIII 1968–78, Pres. Dept. of Law 1970, later Dean, Hon. Dean 1980–; mem. Harvard Club of France; Commdr., Légion d'honneur; Chevalier du mérite maritime; Officier des Palmes académiques, Officier des Arts et des Lettres, Officier de l'Ordre de Léopold (Belgium). *Leisure interest:* hunting. *Address:* 21 boulevard Richard Wallace, 92200 Neuilly-sur-Seine, France. *Telephone:* 722-11-22.

SIMONE, Nina (b. Eunice Wayman); American singer; b. 21 Feb. 1933, Tryon, N.C.; ed. Juilliard School of Music, N.Y.; sang in clubs in Philadelphia; signed contract with Bethlehem Records 1959, Colpix 1960, Phillips 1965, RCA 1967; active in civil rights movt. in early 60's; moved to Paris, now lives in the Netherlands; *recordings include:* I Loves You Porgy, Don't Let Me Be Misunderstood, I Put a Spell on You, Ain't Got No . . . I Got Life, Young, Gifted and Black, Baltimore, My Baby Just Cares For Me, etc.; Dr. h.c. (Chicago, Univ. of Mass., Amherst).

SIMONET, Henri François, D. EN D., D. ÉS SC.; Belgian politician; b. 10 May 1931, Brussels; m. Marie-Louise Angenent 1960; one s. one d.; ed. Univ. Libre de Bruxelles and Columbia Univ., U.S.A.; Asst., Univ. Libre de Bruxelles 1956–58, now Prof.; Financial Adviser, Inst. National d'Etudes pour le Développement du Bas-Congo 1958–59; Legal Adviser, Comm. of Brussels Stock Exchange 1959–60; Deputy Dir. Office of Econ. Programming 1961; Dir. of Cabinet of Ministry of Econ. Affairs and Power 1961–65; Dir. of Cabinet of Deputy Prime Minister responsible for Co-ordination of Econ. Policy 1965; Mayor of Anderlecht 1966–84; M.P. for Brussels 1966–84, 1985–; Minister of Econ. Affairs 1972–73; mem., Vice-Pres. Comm. of European Communities 1973–77; Minister of Foreign Affairs 1977–80; Sec. of State for Brussels Econ. Affairs 1977–79; Financial Consultant and Corp. Dir. *Publications:* various books and articles on economics, financial and political topics. *Address:* 34 avenue Franklin Roosevelt, 1050 Brussels, Belgium.

SIMONETTA; Italian fashion designer; b. Duchess Colonna di Cesarò; d. of Duke Giovanni Colonna di Cesarò and Countess Barbara Antonelli; m. 1st Count Galeazzo Visconti di Modrone 1944, one d.; m. 2nd Alberto Fabiani (fashion designer) 1952, one s.; separated Feb. 1970 and has taken back her maiden name of Duchess Colonna di Cesarò; opened fashion Atelier, Rome 1946; transferred fashion business to Paris 1962; Philadelphia Fashion Group Award 1953, Davison Paxon Award, Atlanta 1959, Fashion Oscar from Filene's of Boston 1960; after five consecutive years in list of world's best dressed women is in "Hall of Fame"; Hon. citizen of Austin, New Orleans and Las Vegas. *Publication:* A Snob in the Kitchen 1967. *Address:* 40 rue François 1er, 75008 Paris, France (Office). *Telephone:* 359-5671 (Office).

SIMONIS, H.E. Cardinal Adrianus J.; Netherlands ecclesiastic; b. 26 Nov. 1931, Lisse, Rotterdam; ordained 1957; consecrated Bishop of Rotterdam 1971; Archbishop of Utrecht 1983–; cr. Cardinal 1985. *Address:* Aartsbisdom, B.P. 14019, 3508 SB Utrecht, Netherlands. *Telephone:* (030) 316956.

SIMONNET, Maurice-René; French lawyer and politician; b. 4 Oct. 1919, Lyons; s. of René and Paule (née Reynaud) Simonnet; m. Jeanne-Marie Montagne 1948; five s. three d.; ed. Ecole des Sciences Politiques, Paris, Faculty of Law, Lyons; Dir. Les cahiers de notre jeunesse 1941–46; Deputy for Drôme, Nat. Assembly 1946–62; Sec. of State for the Merchant Marine 1957–58; Sec.-Gen. Mouvement Républicain Populaire (MRP) 1955–62; mem. European Parl. 1979–84; Dir. de la Revue France-Forum; mem. Constitutional Council 1984–; Hon. Dean, Faculty of Law, Univ. of Lyons; Officier, Légion d'honneur, Croix de guerre (1939–45), Croix de Combattant Volontaire de la Résistance. *Address:* 2 rue de la Roche, 26290 Donzère, France. *Telephone:* (75) 51-61-30.

SIMONOV, Yevgeniy Rubenovich; Soviet theatrical producer; b. 21 June 1925; ed. Maly Theatre School; Art Dir. worker theatre club Kauchuk 1948–54; Producer, E. Vakhtangov Theatre 1955–62, Chief Stage Dir. 1968–; Chief Stage Dir. Maly Theatre 1962–68; Teacher B. Schukin Theatre School 1954–; Honoured Artist of the R.S.F.S.R.; People's Artist of the U.S.S.R. 1975; Order of Red Banner, and other decorations. *Main productions:* Maly Theatre: Two Gentlemen of Verona (Shakespeare) 1952, Filumena Marturano (De Filippo) 1956, Town at Daybreak (Arbuzov) 1957, Irkutsk Story (Arbuzov) 1959, Little Tragedies (Pushkin) 1959; E. Vakhtangov Theatre: Misfortune from Intellect (Griboedov) 1963, They are Waiting for Us Somewhere (Arbuzov) 1963, Clever Things (Marshak) 1965, Antony and Cleopatra (Shakespeare) 1971, Veitslera and Misharina 1974, Front (Korneichuk) 1975. *Publications:* Plays: Aleksei Berezhnoi 1962, John Reed 1967. *Address:* E. Vakhtangov Theatre, 26 Arbat, Moscow, U.S.S.R.

SIMONOV, Yuriy Ivanovich; Soviet conductor; b. 4 March 1941, Saratov; ed. Leningrad Conservatoire; Conductor, Kislovodsk Philharmonic Soc. 1967–69; Conductor, State Bolshoi Opera and Ballet Theatre, Moscow 1969–70, Chief Conductor 1970–87; Maly Symphony Orchestra 1987–; conducts: The Marriage of Figaro, Aida, Boris Godunov, Prince Igor, Pskovityanka; has toured solo and with Theatre in France, Italy and German Democratic Repub.; Laureate of 2nd U.S.S.R. Competition of Conductors, Moscow 1966; First Prize, 5th Int. Competition of Conductors, Santa Cecilia Acad., Rome 1968. *Address:* 1 ploshchad Sverdlova, Moscow, U.S.S.R.

SIMONS, Elwyn LaVerne, M.A., PH.D., D.PHIL.; American professor of anthropology and anatomy; b. 14 July 1930, Lawrence, Kan.; s. of Verne F. Simons and Verna I. (Cuddeback) Simons; m. 2nd Friderun A. Ankel 1972; one s. one d.; one d. by previous marriage; ed. Rice, Princeton and Oxford Univs.; Lecturer in Geology, Princeton Univ. 1958–59; Asst. Prof. of Zoology, Univ. of Pennsylvania 1959–61; Visiting Assoc. Prof. of Geology and Curator of Vertebrate Paleontology, Yale Univ. 1960–61, Assoc. Prof. and Head Curator 1961–65; Prof. of Geology and Curator in charge, Div. of Vertebrate Paleontology, Peabody Museum 1965–77; Prof. of Anthropology and Anatomy, Dir. Duke Univ. Primate Center 1977–82, James B. Duke Prof. and Dir. Primate Center 1982–; has directed over 40 expeditions to Wyoming, Iran, India and Madagascar, including 17 to the Egyptian Fayum in search of fossil primates and associated fauna; mem. N.A.S.; numerous awards; Hon. M.A. (Yale) 1967. *Publications:* over 150 scientific articles, abstracts and books. *Leisure interests:* drawing and painting, folk singing, genealogy. *Address:* Duke University Primate Center, 3705 Erwin Road, Durham, N.C. 27706 (Office); 2621 W. Cornwallis Road, Durham, N.C. 27706, U.S.A. (Home). *Telephone:* (919) 684-2535 (Office); (919) 489-5079 (Home).

SIMONSEN, Mário Henrique; Brazilian engineer and economist; b. 19 Feb. 1935, Guanabara; s. of Mário Simonsen and Carmen Roxo Simonsen; m. Iluska Pereira da Cunha Simonsen; ed. Univ. do Brazil, Univ. do Rio de Janeiro; Lecturer Instituto de Matemática Pura e Aplicada 1958, Escola Nacional de Engenharia 1958–60; Dir. Crédito, Financiamento e Investimento S.A. 1962–63; Dir. Econs. Dept. Confederação Nacional da Indústria 1961–65; Dir. Post-Graduate School of Econs., Fundação Getúlio Vargas 1965–; mem. Bd. Banco Nacional de Habitação 1965–; mem. Bd. Mercedes Benz do Brasil 1968–; Vice-Pres. Banco Bozano, Simonsen de Investimentos 1969–; Pres. Fundação MOBRAL—Movimento Brasileiro de Alfabetização 1970–; Minister of Finance 1974–79, of Planning 1979–80. *Publications:* Ensaios sobre Economia e Política Econômica 1961, Teoría Microeconômica 1967–69, Brasil 2001 1969, Brasil 2002 1972, and various essays and monographs. *Address:* c/o Banco Bozano, Simonsen de Investimento, S.A., Avenue Rio Branco 138, Rio de Janeiro, R.J., Brazil.

SIMONSEN, Palle; Danish politician; b. 1933; m. Kirsten Krog 1960; three d.; ed. Commercial Coll., Aarhus; employed in private enterprises 1963–70; Gen. Man. DCK Int. A/S 1968–70; Dir. Civil Defence Assen. 1970–82; Minister for Social Affairs 1982–84, for Finance 1984–; mem. Folketing (Parl.); Deputy Chair. Conservative Party 1975–81; fmr. chair. and mem. several parl. cttees.; Commdr. Order of the Dannebrog. *Address:* Christiansborg Slotsplads 1, DK-1218 Copenhagen K (Office); L.E. Bruunsvej

17A, DK-2920 Charlottenlund, Denmark (Home). *Telephone:* 45-1-11 11 41 (Office).

SIMPSON, Alan, M.A., D.PHIL.; American (b. British) educator and administrator; b. 23 July 1912, Gateshead; s. of George and Isabella Graham Simpson; m. Mary M. McEldowney 1938; one s. two d.; ed. Dame Allan's School, Newcastle-upon-Tyne, Worcester Coll. and Merton Coll., Oxford, and Harvard Univ.; Sr. Lecturer in Modern British History and American History, Univ. of St. Andrews, Scotland 1938-46; Lecturer in Constitutional Law, Univ. Coll., Dundee, Scotland 1938-46; R.A. 1941-45; Asst. Prof. of History, Univ. of Chicago 1946-54, Assoc. Prof. 1954-59, Thomas E. Donnelley Prof. of History, and Dean of Coll., Univ. of Chicago 1959-64; Pres. of Vassar Coll. 1964-77; L.H.D. (Nat. Coll. of Educ., Evanston, Univ. of Rochester); LL.D. (Knox Coll.). *Publications:* The People Shall Judge: Readings in the Formation of American Policy (2 vols.) (co-author) 1949, Puritanism in Old and New England 1955, The Wealth of the Gentry 1540-1660: East Anglian Studies 1961, Diary of King Philip's War (1675-76) by Colonel Benjamin Church (with Mary Simpson) 1975, I Too am Here: a Selection of Letters of Jane Welsh Carlyle (with Mary Simpson) 1976, Jean Webster Storyteller (with Mary Simpson) 1984, The Mysteries of the 'Frenchman's Map' of Williamsburg, Virginia 1984. *Leisure interest:* planting trees. *Address:* Yellow Gate Farm, Little Compton, R.I. 02837, U.S.A.

SIMPSON, Alan Kooi, B.S., J.D.; American politician; b. 2 Sept. 1931, Cody, Wyo.; s. of Milward Lee Simpson and Lorna (née Kooi) Simpson; m. Ann Schroll 1954; two s. one d.; ed. Univ. of Wyoming; called to Wyo. Bar 1958, U.S. Supreme Court 1964; Asst. Attorney Gen. Wyo. State 1959; Attorney for Cody 1959-69; Partner Simpson, Kepler, Simpson & Cozzens, Cody 1959-78; mem. Wyo. House of Reps. 1964-77, U.S. Senate from Wyoming 1978-, Asst. Majority Leader 1985-87, Asst. Minority Leader 1987-; Trustee Buffalo Bill Historical Center, Cody, Gottsche Foundation Rehabilitation Center; mem. Wyo. Bar Asscn., American Bar Asscn., Asscn. of Trial Lawyers of America; Hon. LL.D. (Calif. Western School of Law) 1983, (Colo. Coll.) 1986, (Notre Dame Univ.) 1987; recipient Centennial Alum Award (Wyoming Univ.) 1987. *Address:* U.S. Senate, 261 Dirksen Senate Building, Washington, D.C. 20510, U.S.A.

SIMPSON, (Alfred William) Brian, J.P., M.A., D.C.L., F.B.A.; British professor of law; b. 17 August 1931, Kendal; s. of Rev. B. W. Simpson and M. E. Simpson; m. 1st Kathleen Seston 1954 (divorced 1968), one s. one d.; m. 2nd Caroline E. A. Brown 1969, one s. two d.; ed. Oakham School, Rutland and Queen's Coll., Oxford; Jr. Research Fellow, St. Edmund Hall, Oxford 1954-55; Fellow Lincoln Coll., Oxford 1955-73, Jr. Proctor 1967-68; Dean Faculty of Law, Univ. of Ghana 1968-69; Prof. of Law, Univ. of Kent 1973-85, Prof. Emer. 1985-; Prof. of Law, Univ. of Chicago, U.S.A. 1983-86; Prof. of Law, Univ. of Mich. 1987-. *Publications:* A History of the Common Law of Contract 1975, Cannibalism and the Common Law 1984, A Biographical Dictionary of the Common Law (Ed.) 1984, A History of the Land Law 1986, Legal Theory and Legal History 1987, Invitation to Law 1988. *Leisure interests:* sailing, flying. *Address:* University of Michigan Law School, Hutchins Hall, Ann Arbor, Mich. 48109, U.S.A.; 36 High Street, Wingham, Kent, CT3 1AB, England. *Telephone:* (313) 763-0413 (U.S.A.); (227) 720 979 (England).

SIMPSON, Louis Aston Marantz, PH.D.; American writer and teacher; b. 27 March 1923, Jamaica, West Indies; s. of Aston and Rosalind (Marantz) Simpson; m. 1st Jeanne Rogers 1949 (divorced 1954), one s.; m. 2nd Dorothy Roochvarg 1955 (divorced 1979), two s. one d.; m. 3rd Miriam Bachner 1985; ed. Munro Coll., Jamaica, Columbia Univ., New York; Assoc. Ed. Bobbs-Merrill Publishing Co., New York 1950-55; Instructor, Asst. Prof. Columbia Univ. 1955-59; Prof. Univ. of Calif. at Berkeley 1959-67; Prof. State Univ. of New York at Stony Brook 1967-; Hon. D.H.L. (Eastern Michigan Univ.) 1977; Pulitzer Prize for Poetry 1964; Columbia Univ. Medal for Excellence 1965; Elmer Holmes Bobst Award for poetry 1987. *Publications:* poetry: The Arrivistes: Poems 1940-49 1949, Good News of Death and other Poems 1955, The New Poets of England and America (Ed.) 1957, A Dream of Governors 1959, At the End of the Open Road 1963, Selected Poems 1965, Adventures of the Letter I 1971, Searching for the Ox 1976, Caviare at the Funeral 1980, People Live Here: Selected Poems 1949-83; The Best Hour of the Night 1983; Collected Poems 1989; prose: James Hogg: a Critical Study 1962, Riverside Drive 1962, An Introduction to Poetry (Ed.) 1967, North of Jamaica 1971, Three on the Tower: the Lives and Works of Ezra Pound, T. S. Eliot and William Carlos Williams 1975, A Revolution in Taste 1978, A Company of Poets 1981, The Character of the Poet 1986, Selected Prose 1989. *Leisure interests:* dogs, fishing. *Address:* 1 Highview Avenue, Setauket, New York, N.Y. 11733, U.S.A. *Telephone:* (516) 751-2727.

SIMPSON, Norman Frederick; British playwright; b. 29 Jan. 1919, London; s. of George Frederick Simpson; m. Joyce Bartlett 1944; one d.; ed. Emanuel School, London, and Birkbeck Coll., Univ. of London; teacher in adult educ. until 1963; full-time playwright 1963-. *Publications:* plays: A Resounding Tinkle 1958, The Hole 1958, One Way Pendulum (also film) 1959, The Form 1961, The Cresta Run 1965, Some Tall Tinkles 1968; Co-Author Diamonds for Breakfast (film) 1968, Was He Anyone? 1973; novel: Harry Bleachbaker 1976. *Leisure interests:* reading, walking. *Address:* c/o Deborah Rogers Ltd., 5-11 Mortimer Street, London, W.1, England.

SIMPSON, Robert Wilfrid Levick, D.MUS., F.R.A.S.; British composer; b. 2 March 1921, Leamington, Warwickshire; s. of Robert Warren Simpson and Helena Hendrika Govaars; m. 1st Bessie Fraser 1946 (died 1981); m. 2nd Angela Musgrave 1982; ed. Westminster City School, studied also with Herbert Howells; mem. of BBC Music Div. 1951-80; Fellow Royal Astronomical Asscn.; mem. British Astronomical Asscn.; Carl Nielsen Gold Medal (Denmark) 1956, Medal of Honour of Bruckner Soc. of America 1962; chief musical interest: Beethoven. *Main compositions:* Symphonies Nos. 1-10 1951, 1956, 1962, 1972, 1972, 1977, 1977, 1981, 1986, 1988; String Quartets Nos. 1-12 1952, 1953, 1954, 1973, 1974, 1975, 1977, 1979, 1982, 1983, 1984, 1987; Concerto for Violin 1959, for Piano 1967; Piano Sonata 1946; Variations and Finale on a Theme of Haydn, for piano 1948; Allegro Deciso, for string orchestra; Canzona for Brass 1958; Variations and Fugue for recorder and string quartet 1959; Trio for clarinet, cello and piano 1967; Quintet for clarinet and strings 1968; Quartet for horn, violin, cello and piano 1975-76; Media morte in vita sumus (Motet for choir, brass and timpani) 1975, Volcano (Symphonic Study for brass band) 1978; Incidental Music to Ibsen's The Pretenders 1965, to Milton's Samson Agonistes 1974; Energy (Symphonic Study for brass band) 1971; Sonata for two pianos 1980; Quintet for clarinet, bass clarinet and three double basses (also for clarinet, bass clarinet and string trio) 1980-81, The Four Temperaments: Suite for brass band 1982, Variations on a Theme of Carl Nielsen for orchestra 1983, Trio for horn, violin and piano 1984, Sonata for violin and piano 1984, Eppur si muove, for organ 1985, Introduction and Allegro on a Bass by Max Reger for brass band 1986, String Quintet 1987, String Trio 1987, Piano Trio 1988-89. *Publications:* Carl Nielsen, Symphonist 1952, 1979, The Essence of Bruckner 1966, The Proms and Natural Justice 1981, numerous articles in journals; BBC booklets: Bruckner and the Symphony, Sibelius and Nielsen, The Beethoven Symphonies; Contributor: Encyclopaedia Britannica, Musik in Geschichte und Gegenwart; Ed.: The Symphony 1966. *Leisure interest:* astronomy. *Address:* Síochán, Killelton, Camp, near Tralee, Co. Kerry, Ireland. *Telephone:* Tralee 30213.

SIMSON, Otto von, PH.D.; German scholar; b. 17 July 1912, Berlin; m. 1st Louise von Schönburg-Hartenstein 1936 (died 1976), two s.; m. 2nd M. A. zu Salm-Reifferscheidt-Dyck; ed. Arndt Gymnasium, Berlin, and Munich Univ.; Prof. of the History of Art, Chicago Univ. 1945-57; Perm. Del. of the Fed. Repub. of Germany to UNESCO 1959-64; mem. Exec. Bd. UNESCO 1960-64; Prof. Inst. History of Art, Freie Univ. Berlin; Foreign hon. mem. American Acad. of Arts and Sciences; Pres. German Nat. Comm. for UNESCO 1975-86; Officier, Légion d'honneur, Grosses Bundesverdienstkreuz, Commdr. Ordre national du Mérite, Verdienstorden des Landes Berlin. *Publications:* Zur Genealogie der weltlichen Apotheose im Barock 1936, Sacred Fortress: Byzantine Art and Statecraft in Ravenna 1948, 1987, The Gothic Cathedral 1956, 1962, Die Kunst des Hohen Mittelalters 1972, Der Blick nach Innen 1986; numerous contributions to newspapers and scholarly publs. *Address:* 1000 Berlin 33, Max-Eyth-Strasse 26, Federal Republic of Germany. *Telephone:* 8312082.

SIN, H.E. Cardinal Jaime L., B.SC.ED., D.D.; Philippine ecclesiastic; b. 31 Aug. 1928, New Washington, Aklan; s. of Juan Sin and Maxima Reyes Lachica de Sin; ed. New Washington Elementary School, St. Vincent Ferrer Seminary; ordained Roman Catholic Priest 1954; Missionary Priest 1954-57; First Rector, St. Pius X Seminary, Roxas City 1957-67; Domestic Prelate to Pope John XXIII 1960; Auxiliary Bishop of Jaro, Iloilo 1967; Archbishop of Jaro 1972, of Manila 1974-; cr. Cardinal 1976; Chair. Comm. on Seminaries and Priestly Vocations 1969-73, Comm. on Clergy 1974-77; mem. Pontifical Comm. on Social Communications 1975-; mem. Admin. Council, Catholic Bishops' Conf. of the Philippines (CBCP) 1968-72, Vice-Pres. CBCP 1970-74; Perm. mem. of the Synod of Bishops in Rome 1977-; mem. Pontifical Comm. on the Evangelization of Peoples 1978; mem. Sacred Congregation for Catholic Educ. 1978; mem. Secr. for Non-Christians 1978; Royal Acad. of Spanish Language 1978; Pres. Catholic Bishops' Conf. of the Philippines 1978, 1980; Hon. LL.D. 1975, Hon. D.H.L. 1975, Hon. D.S.T. (Santo Tomas Univ. Manila) 1977, Hon. LL.D. (Angeles Univ.) 1978, Hon. D.Hum.Litt. (Univ. of Iloilo City) 1980, Hon. D.Phil. (Manila) 1980, Hon. D.Phil. (Fu Jen Univ. Taipei) 1980, Dr. h.c. (Yale) 1986; over 100 citations; Distinguished Son of Iloilo Award 1974, Honoured Don of Capiz Award 1976, Outstanding Aklanon Award 1979, Grand Cross, Knights of the Holy Sepulchre of Jerusalem 1976, Distinguished Son of Manila 1976, Rajah Soliman Award for Distinguished Citizenry 1976, Gran Cruz de Isabel la Catolica of the King of Spain 1977, Outstanding Citizen Award for Religion, Manila 1979, Bailiff Grand Cross of Honour and Devotion, Sovereign Military Order of Malta, Rome 1979. *Publications:* Ratio Fundamentalis for Philippine Seminaries 1972, The Revolution of Love 1972, The Church Above Political Systems 1973, A Song of Salvation 1974, Unity in Diversity 1974, La Iglesia Renueva Sus Medios de Evangelicación y Adapta a la Idiosincracia de los Pueblos 1978, The Future of Catholicism in Asia 1978, Christian Basis of Human Rights 1978, Separation, Not Isolation 1978, Slaughter of the Innocents '79, 1979, Discipline, Discipleship and Discerning Service, The Making of "Men for Others" 1980; over 200 papers, articles in periodicals. *Leisure interests:* music: Bach, Chopin, Wagner, Strauss; reading, writing. *Address:* Villa San Miguel, Shaw Boulevard, Mandaluyong, Metro Manila, Philippines. *Telephone:* 79-26-71.

SINATRA, Frank; American singer, actor and composer; b. (as Francis Albert Sinatra) 12 Dec. 1915, Hoboken, N.J.; s. of Anthony Sinatra and

Natalie Garaventi; m. 1st Nancy Barbato 1939 (divorced), one s. two d.; m. 2nd Ava Gardner (q.v.) 1951 (divorced); m. 3rd Mia Farrow (q.v.) 1966 (divorced 1968); m. 4th Barbara Marx 1976; ed. Drake Inst.; sang with Harry James and Tommy Dorsey Bands; film debut as singer 1941, as actor 1943; mem. Pres.'s Cttee. on Arts and Humanities 1982–; Jean Hersholt Humanitarian Award, Motion Picture Acad. 1971; Hon. citizen of Chicago 1975; Hon. Chief, Bophuthatswana 1981; Hon. D.Hum.Litt. (Nebraska) 1976; Cultural Award (Israel) 1977, Pied Piper Award (U.S.A. Soc. of Composers, Authors and Publrs.) 1980; Cross of Honour of Science and the Arts (Austria) 1984, Pres. Medal of Freedom 1985, Life Achievement Award, Nat. Assen. for Advancement of Colored People 1987. *Films include:* Higher and Higher 1943, Step Lively 1944, Anchors Aweigh 1945, Take Me Out to the Ball Game 1948, On the Town 1949, Double Dynamite 1950, From Here to Eternity (Acad. Award for Best Supporting Actor) 1953, Young at Heart 1954, The Tender Trap 1955, Not as a Stranger 1955, The Man with the Golden Arm 1956, Johnny Concho 1956, The Pride and the Passion 1956, Around the World in Eighty Days 1956, Guys and Dolls 1956, High Society 1956, Pal Joey 1957, The Joker is Wild 1957, Kings Go Forth 1958, Some Came Running 1958, A Hole in the Head 1959, Can Can 1959, Never So Few 1959, Ocean's Eleven 1960, The Devil at Four O'Clock 1961, Sergeants Three 1962, The Manchurian Candidate 1962, Four for Texas 1963, The List of Adrian Messenger 1963, Come Blow Your Horn 1963, Robin and the Seven Hoods 1964, None But the Brave (also dir.) 1964, Von Ryan's Express 1965, Marriage on the Rocks 1965, Cast a Giant Shadow 1966, Assault on a Queen 1966, The Naked Runner 1967, Tony Rome 1967, The Detective 1968, Lady in Cement 1968, Dirty Dingus Magee 1970, The First Deadly Sin 1981. *Address:* Sinatra Enterprises, Goldwyn Studios, 1041 N. Formosa, Los Angeles, Calif. 90046, U.S.A.

SINCLAIR, Sir Clive Marles, Kt.; British inventor and business executive; b. 30 July 1940, London; s. of George William Carter Sinclair and Thora Edith Ella (née Marles) Sinclair; m. Ann Trevor-Briscoe 1962 (divorced); two s. two d.; ed. St. George's Coll., Weybridge; Ed. Bernards Publrs. Ltd. 1958–61; Chair. Sinclair Radionics Ltd. 1962–79, Sinclair Research Ltd. 1979–, Sinclair Browne Ltd. 1981–; Chair. British Mensa 1980–; Visiting Fellow, Robinson Coll., Cambridge 1982–; Visiting Prof. Imperial Coll., London 1984–; Hon. D.Sc. (Bath Univ.) 1983, (Warwick Univ., Heriot Watt) 1983, (UMIST) 1984; Hon. Fellow, Imperial Coll., London 1984; Royal Soc. Mullard Award 1984. *Publications:* Practical Transistor Receivers 1959, British Semiconductor Survey 1963. *Address:* 18 Shepherd House, London, W1Y 7LD, England. *Telephone:* 01-408 0199.

SINCLAIR, Ernest Keith, C.M.G., O.B.E., D.F.C.; Australian journalist; b. 13 Nov. 1914, Hawthorn, Victoria; s. of J. E. and F. Sinclair; m. Jill Nelder 1949; one s.; ed. Melbourne High School; served R.A.F., Second World War; C.O. 97 Pathfinder Squadron 1945, mentioned in despatches; Foreign Corresp., Europe 1938, 1946; Ed. The Age 1959–66; Chair. Australian Assoc. Press 1965–66; Dir.-Gen. Television Corpn. 1959–66; Consultant to Prime Minister 1967–74, Consultant to Dept. of Prime Minister and Cabinet 1977–79; Dir. Australian Paper Manufacturers 1966–85; Deputy Chair. Australian Tourist Comm. 1969–75; Vice-Pres. Library Council of Victoria 1973–78; Assoc. Commr. Industries Comm. 1974–80; Commr. Australian Heritage Comm. 1976–81; Hon. Ed. R.H.S.V. Journal 1982–86; Councillor Royal Historical Soc. of Victoria 1981–86. *Leisure interests:* gardening, reading. *Address:* 138 Toorak Road West, South Yarra, Victoria 3141, Australia. *Telephone:* (03) 267-1405 (Melbourne).

SINCLAIR, Hon. Ian David, O.C., Q.C., B.A., LL.B.; Canadian politician, lawyer, business executive (retd.); b. 27 Dec. 1913, Winnipeg, Manitoba; s. of John David and Lillian Sinclair; m. Ruth Beatrice Drennan 1942; two s. two d.; ed. public schools, Winnipeg and Univ. of Manitoba; Asst. Solicitor, Canadian Pacific Railway Co. 1942, Solicitor 1946, Asst. to Gen. Counsel 1951, Gen. Solicitor 1953, Vice-Pres. Gen. Counsel 1960, Vice-Pres. Law 1960–61, Vice-Pres. 1961–66, Pres. 1966–69, Pres. and C.E.O. 1969–72; Chair. and C.E.O. Canadian Pacific Ltd. 1972–81, mem. Exec. Cttee. 1961–82, Dir. 1961–84; Chair. and C.E.O. Canadian Pacific Enterprises Ltd. 1972–82, Chair. 1982–84, Dir. 1962–84; Dir. numerous cos.; mem. Int. Advisory Cttee., Chase Manhattan Bank, N.A.; Senator 1983–88; Hon. LL.D. (Manitoba) 1967; Hon. D.B.A. (Laval) 1981; Hon. D.C.L. (Acadia) 1982. *Leisure interests:* reading, motoring. *Address:* Suite 1100, University Place, 123 Front Street West, Toronto, Ont. M5J 2M2, Canada. *Telephone:* (416) 860-0144.

SINCLAIR, Rt. Hon. Ian McCahon, P.C., B.A., LL.B.; Australian politician; b. June 1929, Sydney; s. of George and Hazel Sinclair; m. 1st Margaret Tarrant 1956 (died 1967), 2nd Rosemary Edna Fenton 1970; two s. two d.; ed. Knox Grammar School, Wahroonga and Sydney Univ.; barrister 1952–; mem. Legis. Council in N.S.W. Parl. 1961–63, House of Reps. 1963–; Minister for Social Services 1965–68; Minister Assisting Minister for Trade and Industry 1966–71; Minister for Shipping and Transport 1968–71, for Primary Industry 1971–72; Deputy Leader Country Party (now Nat. Party) 1971–84, Fed. Parl. Leader 1984–89, Party Spokesman on Defence, Foreign Affairs, Law and Agric. 1973–75, Opposition Spokesman on Agric., Leader of Opposition in House of Reps. 1974–75; Minister for Agric. and Northern Australia Nov.-Dec. 1975, for Primary Industry 1975–79, for Communications 1980–82, for Defence 1982–83; Leader of Govt. in House of Reps. 1975–82; Leader of Opposition in House of Reps. 1983, Opposition Spokesman for Defence 1983–; Dir. Farmers' and Graziers' Co-operative Co. Ltd. 1962–65; Nat. Party. *Leisure interests:* squash, sailing, surfing. *Address:* Parliament House, Canberra, A.C.T. 2600; Glenclair, Bendemeer, N.S.W., Australia (Home).

SINCLAIR, Keith Val, A.O., M.A., LIT.D., D.PHIL., D.LITT.; Australian professor of French; b. 8 Nov. 1926, Auckland N.Z.; s. of late Valentine L. Sinclair and Coral D. Keith; unmarried; ed. Univ. of N.Z., Victoria Univ. of Wellington, Univs. of Paris and Oxford; part-time tutor, Univ. of Oxford 1952–55; Lecturer, Sr. Lecturer, Australian Nat. Univ. 1955–62; Assoc. Prof. Univ. of Calif. (Davis) 1963–64; Sr. Lecturer, Assoc. Prof. Univ. of Sydney 1964–71; Visiting Prof. Northwestern Univ. Evanston, Ill. 1971; Prof. of French, Univ. of Conn., Storrs 1972–79; Prof. of French and Head, Dept. of Modern Languages, James Cook Univ., Townsville 1979–, Dir. Inst. of Modern Languages 1982–, mem. Council 1982–85; mem. various professional socs. etc.; K.St.J.; decorations from Belgium, France, Italy etc. *Publications:* eight books. *Leisure interests:* swimming, tennis. *Address:* Department of Modern Languages, James Cook University of North Queensland, Townsville, Queensland 4811 (Office); 7 Kennedy Street, Townsville, Queensland 4810, Australia (Home). *Telephone:* 077 814241 (Office); 077 724419 (Home).

SINCLAIR, Sir Ronald Ormiston, K.B.E., LL.M.; British lawyer (retd.); b. 2 May 1903, Dunedin, New Zealand; s. of W. A. Sinclair; m. Ellen Isabel Entrican 1935; two s.; ed. Auckland Univ. Coll. and Balliol Coll., Oxford; joined Nigerian Admin. Service 1931, Magistrate 1936; Resident Magistrate, Northern Rhodesia 1938; Puisne Judge, Tanganyika 1948–53; Chief Justice, Nyasaland 1953–56; Vice-Pres. East African Court of Appeal 1956–57; Chief Justice of Kenya 1957–62; Pres. H.M. Court of Appeal for Eastern Africa 1962–64; Pres. Court of Appeal for the Bahamas Islands 1965–70, Court of Appeal for Bermuda 1965–70, Court of Appeal for British Honduras 1968–70; Chair. Industrial Tribunals, England and Wales 1965–69. *Leisure interest:* bird watching. *Address:* 158 Victoria Avenue, Remuera, Auckland, 5, New Zealand. *Telephone:* 546-391.

SINCLAIR OYANEDER, Brig.-Gen. Santiago; Chilean army officer and politician; b. 29 Dec. 1927, Santiago; m. Doris Manley Ramirez; three s. one d.; ed. Cavalry School, Acad. of War; Sec. of Studies, Mil. School 1963; Adjutant, Army C.-in-C. 1966; Head of Army Public Relations 1967; mem. UN Observers Group, Suez Canal 1968; Lecturer, Acad. of War 1970, Vice-Dir. 1973; Commdr. 2nd Cazadores Cavalry Regt. 1973; Mil. Attaché, Chilean Embassy, South Korea 1975; Sec., Deputy C.-in-C. of Army 1976; Dir. of Army Operations 1977; Chief Min. of Presidential Staff 1979; Head Pres.'s Consultative Cttee. 1982–; numerous mil. decorations. *Address:* Edif. Diego Portales, Santiago, Chile.

SINDEN, Donald Alfred, C.B.E., F.R.S.A.; British actor and author; b. 9 Oct. 1923, Plymouth; s. of Alfred E. and Mabel A. (née Fuller) Sinden; m. Diana Mahony 1948; two s.; entered theatrical profession 1942; mem. British Theatre Museum Assen. 1960, Chair. 1971–77; Vice-Pres. London Appreciation Soc. 1960–; mem. Council, British Actors Equity Assen. 1966–77; Assoc. Artist, Royal Shakespeare Co. 1967–; Pres. Fed. of Playgoers Socs. 1968–, Royal General Theatrical Fund 1982–; Chair. Theatre Museum Advisory Council 1973–80; mem. Arts Council Drama Panel 1973–77, Arts Council 1982–86; mem. Council, London Acad. of Music and Dramatic Art 1976–. *Publications:* A Touch of the Memoirs 1982, Laughter in the Second Act 1985, The Everyman Book of Theatrical Anecdotes 1987, The English Country Church 1988. *Leisure interest:* serendipity. *Address:* c/o Garrick Club, Garrick Street, London, W.C.2, England.

SINDERMANN, Horst; German politician; b. 5 Sept. 1915, Dresden; m.; two c.; mem. Communist Union of Youth, Saxony 1929; political imprisonment 1934–45 (including Sachsenhausen concentration camp); later Chief Ed. Volksstimme (Voice of the People), Chemnitz (now Karl-Marx-Stadt); later Chief Ed., Press Service of SED; Chief Ed. SED District paper Freiheit (Freedom), Halle/Saale; staff of Cen. Cttee. SED 1954–63, Cand. mem. Cen. Cttee. SED 1959–63, First Sec. Dist. Council of SED 1963–71; mem. 1963–; Cand. mem. Politbüro 1963–67, mem. 1967–; First Deputy Chair. G.D.R. Council of Ministers 1971–73, Chair. 1973–76; Vice-Chair. Council of State 1976–; mem. Volkskammer (People's Chamber) 1963–, Pres. 1976–; Karl Marx Order (twice), Vaterländischer Verdienstorden in silver and gold (twice), Fransisco de Meranda Order (Venezuela), and other decorations. *Address:* Volkskammer, Berlin, German Democratic Republic.

SINDI, Sheikh Kamil; Saudi Arabian airline executive; b. 3 Jan. 1932, Mecca; s. of Abdul Rasool Sindi and Asma Mitwalli; m. Wafiga al-Sadat 1954; three s.; joined Saudi Arabian Airlines (SAUDIA) and Civil Aviation Org., Operations and Maintenance Dept. 1947, Sec. to Dir.-Gen. until 1960, Deputy Dir.-Gen. 1960; Dir.-Gen. of Civil Aviation 1961–66; Dir.-Gen. SAUDIA 1967–79, Asst. Minister of Defence and for Civil Aviation Affairs 1980–; Pres. Arab. Air Carriers Org. (AACO) 1971; mem. Exec. Cttee. IATA 1974–; Chevalier de l'Ordre d'Orange-Nassau. *Address:* Ministry of Defence, Jeddah, Saudi Arabia.

SINFELT, John Henry, PH.D.; American chemist; b. 18 Feb. 1931, Munson, Pa; s. of Henry Gustave Sinfelt and June Lillian McDonald; m. Muriel Jean Vadersen 1956; one s.; ed. Pennsylvania State Univ. and Univ. of Illinois; Scientist Exxon Research and Eng. Co. 1954–, Sr. Research Assoc.

1968-72, Scientific Adviser 1972-79, Sr. Scientific Adviser 1979-; active in catalysis research, formulated and developed the concept of bimetallic clusters as catalysts, applied the concept in petroleum refining for production of lead-free petrol; mem. Nat. Acad. of Sciences, Nat. Acad. of Eng.; Fellow American Acad. of Arts and Sciences; Hon. Sc.D. (Univ. of Ill.) 1981; Nat. Medal of Science 1979, Perkin Medal in Chem. 1984 and many other awards and prizes. *Publications:* Bimetallic Catalysts: Discoveries, Concepts and Applications 1983; more than 100 articles in scientific journals; 45 patents. *Address:* Corporate Research Science Laboratories, Exxon Research and Engineering Company, Clinton Township, Route 22 East, Annandale, N.J. 08801, U.S.A.

SINGER, Isaac Bashevis, D.H.L.; American journalist and author; b. 14 July 1904, Radzymin, Poland; s. of Pinchos Menachem and Bathsheba Zylberman; m. Alma Haimann 1940; one s.; ed. Rabbinical Seminary, Warsaw; came to U.S.A. 1935; on staff of Jewish Daily Forward 1935-; Nat. Inst. of Arts and Letters grant 1959, Nat. Council on the Arts grant 1966; Fellow Jewish Acad. of Arts and Sciences, American Acad. and Inst. of Arts and Letters, New York; mem. American Acad. of Arts and Sciences; Louis Lamed Prize (twice), Creative Arts Award of Brandeis Univ. 1970, Nat. Book Award 1970, 1974; Nobel Prize for Literature 1978; Hon. DHL (Hebrew Union Coll., Los Angeles) 1963; Handel Medallion 1986. *Publications include:* The Family Moskat 1950, Satan in Goray 1955, Gimpel the Fool and other Stories 1957, The Magician of Lublin 1959, The Spinoza of Market Street 1961, The Slave 1962, Short Friday 1964, Zlateh the Goat and Other Stories 1966, In My Father's Court 1966, The Manor 1967, The Séance 1968, The Estate 1969, A Friend of Kafka and Other Stories 1970, Enemies, A Love Story 1972, Crown of Feathers 1974, Why Noah Chose the Dove 1974, Passions 1975, A Little Boy in Search of God (memoirs) 1976, A Young Man in Search of Love (memoirs) 1978, Shosha 1978, Old Love 1980, The Family Moskat 1980, The Collected Stories 1982, The Golem 1982, Yentl, The Yeshiva Boy 1983, Love and Exile 1984, The Image and Other Stories 1985, Stories for Children 1987, The Death of Methuselah and Other Stories 1988, The King of the Fields 1988; Play: Teibele and her Demon (with Eve Friedman) 1979. *Leisure interest:* walking in the bad air of New York City. *Address:* c/o Farrar, Straus and Giroux Inc., 19 Union Square W., New York, N.Y. 10003; 209 West 86th Street, New York, N.Y. 10024, U.S.A. *Telephone:* (212) 877-5968.

SINGER, Isadore Manuel, PH.D.; American mathematician; b. 4 May 1924, Detroit, Mich.; s. of Simon Singer and Freda Rose; m. Sheila Ruff 1961; two s. one d.; ed. Univs. of Michigan and Chicago; C.L.E. Moore Instructor at M.I.T. 1950-52; Asst. Prof. Univ. of Calif. (Los Angeles) 1952-54; Visiting Asst. Prof. Columbia Univ. 1954-55; Visiting mem. Inst. for Advanced Study, Princeton 1955-56; Asst. Prof. M.I.T. 1956, Assoc. Prof. 1958, Prof. of Math. 1959, Norbert Wiener Prof. of Math. 1970-79; Visiting Prof. of Math., Univ. of Calif., Berkeley 1977-79, Prof. 1979-83; Miller Prof. Univ. of Calif., Berkeley 1982-83; John T. MacArthur Prof. of Math., M.I.T. 1983-; mem. N.A.S., American Math. Soc., Math. Asscn. of America, American Acad. of Arts and Sciences, American Philosophical Soc., American Physical Soc.; Sloan Fellow 1959-62, Guggenheim Fellow 1968-69, 1975-76; Bôcher Memorial Prize 1969, 1975-76; Nat. Medal of Science 1985. *Publications:* Lecture Notes on Elementary Topology and Geometry; author of research articles in functional analysis, differential geometry and topology. *Leisure interests:* literature, hiking, tennis. *Address:* Department of Mathematics, Massachusetts Institute of Technology, Cambridge, Mass. 02139, U.S.A.

SINGER, Maxine, PH.D.; American biochemist; b. 15 Feb. 1931, New York; d. of Henrietta Perlowitz Frank and Hyman Frank; m. Daniel M. Singer 1952; one s. three d.; ed. Swarthmore Coll. and Yale Univ.; Research Chemist, Enzymes and Cellular Biochemistry Section, Nat. Inst. of Arthritis and Metabolic Diseases, Nat. Insts. of Health, Bethesda, Md. 1958-74, Chief, Nucleic Acid Enzymology Section, Lab. of Biochemistry, Div. of Cancer Biology and Diagnosis, Nat. Cancer Inst. 1974-79, Chief, Lab. of Biochemistry 1979-87, research chemist 1987-88; Pres. Carnegie Inst., Wash. 1988-; Visiting Scientist, Dept. of Genetics, Weizmann Inst. of Science, Rehovot, Israel 1971-72; Dir. Foundation for Advanced Educ. in Sciences 1972-78, 1985-86; mem. Scientific Council Int. Inst. of Genetics and Biophysics, Naples 1982-86; mem. N.A.S., Yale Corpn., Bd. of Govs. of Weizmann Inst., American Soc. of Biological Chemists, American Soc. of Microbiologists, American Chemical Soc., American Acad. of Arts and Sciences, Inst. of Medicine of N.A.S.; Hon. D.Sc. (Wesleyan Univ.) 1977, (Swarthmore Coll.) 1978; Dir.'s Award, Nat. Insts. of Health 1977 and other awards. *Publications:* numerous, in major scientific journals. *Leisure interests:* scuba diving, cooking, literature. *Address:* Carnegie Institution of Washington, 1530 P St. N.W., Washington, D.C. 20005 (Office); 5410 39th Street, N.W., Washington, D.C. 20015, U.S.A. (Home). *Telephone:* (202)-387-6404.

SINGER, Peter Albert David, M.A., B.PHIL.; Australian professor and author; b. 6 July 1946, Melbourne; s. of Ernest Singer and Cora Oppenheim; m. Renata Diamond 1968; three d.; ed. Scotch Coll., Univ. of Melbourne and Univ. Coll. Oxford; Radcliffe Lecturer, Univ. Coll. Oxford 1971-73; Visiting Asst. Prof. Dept. of Philosophy, New York Univ. 1973-74; Sr. Lecturer, Dept. of Philosophy, La Trobe Univ. 1975-76; Prof. Dept. of Philosophy, Monash Univ. 1977-, Dir. Centre for Human Bioethics, Part-

time 1983-87, Full-time 1987-; various visiting positions in U.S.A. and Canada. *Publications:* author, co-author and ed. of numerous books. *Leisure interests:* bushwalking, gardening, swimming. *Address:* Centre for Human Bioethics, Monash University, Clayton, Vic. 3168, Australia. *Telephone:* (03) 565 4270.

SINGH, Bhishma Narain, B.A.; Indian politician; b. 13 July 1933, Palamau, Bihar; m. Ram Kumari Devi 1950; two s. two d.; ed. Takeya High School, Sasaram, Bihar and Banaras Hindu Univ.; active Congress worker 1953-; mem. All Indian Congress Cttee.; mem. Bihar Legis. Assembly 1967-69, 1969-72, 1972-76; Minister of State, Govt. of Bihar 1971, 1972-73, 1973-74; mem. Rajya Sabha 1976-, Deputy Chief Whip, Congress Parl. Party 1977, later Chief Whip; Minister of Parl. Affairs 1980-83, of Communications Jan.-March 1980, of Works and Housing 1980-83; fmr. Gov. of Sikkim -1985; Deputy Chair. Cen. Cooperative Bank, Daltonganj 1964; Dir. Bihar State Co-operative Mktg. Union 1967; Chair. Bihar State Co-operative Housing Construction Finance Soc. 1974-75, Bihar State Credit and Investment Corpn. 1974-, Gov. *Leisure interests:* horse riding, marksman, music, dance and drama, especially tribal folk dances. *Address:* P.O. Udigarh, P.S. Chhatarpur, District Palamau, Bihar; Hamidaganj, P.O. Daltonganj, District Palamau, Bihar, India.

SINGH, Birendra Bahadur, M.A.; Indian public official; b. 1 March 1928; ed. Allahabad Univ.; Indian Defence Accounts Service 1953; Controller of Accounts, Int. Comm. for Supervision and Control for Viet-Nam, Laos and Cambodia 1960-62; Asst. Financial Adviser, Ministry of Irrigation and Power 1962-63; Deputy Sec. Ministry of Finance 1963-66, Deputy Sec. Ministry of Finance on deputation to Harvard Univ. as Public Service Fellow 1966-67; Deputy Financial Adviser, Ministry of Food and Agric., Dept. of Food 1967-68; Financial Adviser and Chief Accounts Officer Hindustan Copper Ltd. (Govt. of India undertaking) 1968-70, Acting Chair. and Man. Dir. 1969-70; Financial Adviser, Indian Farmers Fertilizers Co-operative Ltd. 1970-72, Finance Dir. 1972-75; Chair. and Man. Dir. Nat. Fertilisers Ltd., New Delhi 1975-79; Chair. Industrial Finance Corpn. of India 1979-84, Madhya Pradesh Consultancy Org. Ltd., Bhopal; Sec., Minister of Fertilisers 1985-88; Minister of Communications June 1988-; Dir. on Bd. of Dirs. Industrial Devt. Bank of India, Industrial Reconstruction Corpn. of India Ltd. and Delhi Stock Exchange Asscn. Ltd.; mem. of Gen. Council Nat. Co-operative Devt. Corpn.; mem of Bd. of Govs. of Man. Devt. Inst., Bd. of Trustees of Risk Capital Foundation and Unit Trust of India; mem. Exec. Bd. Standing Conf. of Public Enterprises; Fellow Kennedy School of Govt., Harvard Univ. *Address:* Ministry of Communications, Sanchar Bharan, 20 Asoka Road, New Delhi 110 001, India. *Telephone:* (11) 381209 (Office).

SINGH, Bipin; Indian dancer and choreographer; b. 23 Aug. 1918, Vill-Singari-Cachar; s. of Laikhomsana Singha and Indubala Devi; m. 1st Manorama Sinha; m. 2nd Kalavati Devi; five s. three d.; Manipuri dance teacher, Calcutta 1936; joined Madam Menaka Troup 1938, toured India and abroad; dir. dance dramas, Bombay 1943; collected and recorded the oral traditions of Manipuri dance and music; toured world with routines; founded Manipuri Nartanalaya in Bombay, Manipur and Calcutta 1972. *Publications:* Vaisnav Sangeet Damodar (Ed.) 1985, Panchamsarsanhita and Sangeet Damodar (Ed.) 1986. *Leisure interests:* walking, listening to news. *Address:* Manipuri Nartanalaya, 15A Bipin Pal Road, Calcutta 700026, India. *Telephone:* 465 922.

SINGH, Buta; Indian politician; b. 21 March 1934, Jalandhar Punjab; s. of Sardar Bir Singh; ed. Lyallpur Khalsa Coll., Jalandhar and Guru Nanak Khalsa Coll., Bombay; elected for Lok Sabha 1962, 1967, 1971, 1980, 1984; Union Deputy Minister for Railways 1974-76, for Commerce 1976-77; Minister of State in Ministry of Shipping and Transport 1980-81; Minister of Supply and Rehabilitation 1981-82, of Sport 1982-83, Cabinet Minister in charge of several ministries 1983-84, Minister of Agric. 1984-86, of Home Affairs May 1986-; mem. Planning Comm. 1985, Gen. Sec. Indian Nat. Congress 1978-80; Pres. Amateur Athletic Fed. of India 1976-84. *Address:* Ministry of Home Affairs, North Block, New Delhi 110001, India. *Telephone:* (11) 3011989.

SINGH, Dinesh, B.A., M.P.; Indian politician; b. 19 July 1925, Kalakankar, Uttar Pradesh; s. of Raja Avadhesh Singh and Rani Lakshami Kumari; m. Rani Neelima Kumari Singh 1944; six d.; ed. Doon School, Dehra Doon, and Colvin Coll., Lucknow Univ.; mem. Lok Sabha (Lower House Parl.) 1957-77, Rajya Sabha (Upper House) 1977-; fmr. Pvt. Sec. to Prime Minister; fmr. Sec. to the High Commr. for India in London, to the Embassy in Paris; leader Indian Dels. to FAO, ECAFE, ECOSOC, UNCTAD and UN; Deputy Minister for External Affairs 1962-66; Minister of State for External Affairs 1966-67; Minister of Commerce 1967-69; Pres. of UNCTAD II 1968-72; Minister for External Affairs 1969-70, of Industrial Devt. and Internal Trade 1970-71, of Water Resources Feb.-June 1988, of Commerce June 1988-; Pres. of Indian Council for South Asian Cooperation. *Publications:* Towards New Horizons 1971, India and the Changing Asian Scene 1973. *Leisure interest:* photography. *Address:* Ministry of Commerce, Udyog Bhavan, New Delhi 110 001, India. *Telephone:* (11) 3016664.

SINGH Giani Zail; Indian politician; b. 5 May 1916, Sandhwan, Faridkot district, Punjab; s. of Kishan Singh and Ind Kaur; m. Pardan Kaur; one s.

three d.; took leading part in movement against autocratic rule in Punjab states; arrested at Faridkot 1938; f. Faridkot State Congress and launched Nat. Flag Movement 1946; formed parallel Govt. in Faridkot State 1948; Pres. State Union (PEPSU) Govt. 1948–49, Minister for Public Works and Agric 1951–52; Pres. PEPSU PCC 1955–56; mem. Rajya Sabha 1956–62, Punjab Assembly 1962; Minister of State and Pres. Punjab PCC 1966–72; Chief Minister of Punjab 1972–77; Pres. Punjab Co-operative Union; Minister of Home Affairs 1980–82; Pres. of India 1982–87. *Address:* c/o Raj Bhavan, Chandigarh, Punjab, India.

SINGH, Gopal, PH.D.; Indian poet, writer and statesman; b. 29 Nov. 1919, Serai Niamat Khan, N.W. Frontier Prov.; s. of Atma Singh and Nanaki Devi; m. 1950; one d.; nominated M.P. 1962–68; Amb. to Bulgaria and Caribbean countries 1970–76; Chair. High Power Comm. of Minorities, Scheduled Castes, Scheduled Tribes and other Weaker Sections 1980–84; Gov. Goa, Daman and Diu 1984–; has lectured at univs. in U.K., U.S.A., Thailand, Egypt, Iran and India; fmr. Sec.-Gen. Indian Council for Africa; Chair. Presidium, World Punjabi Congress; many awards and decorations. *Publications:* first free-verse English translation of the Sikh Scripture; five books of Punjabi verse; A History of the Sikh People 1469–1978, The Religion of the Sikhs, A History of Punjabi Literature; The Unstruck Melody (poetry), The Man Who Never Died (poetry); collection of short stories, children's books, an English-Punjabi lexicon, several biographies and books of literary criticism. *Leisure interests:* reading, walking. *Address:* Raj Bhavan, Goa, India. *Telephone:* 3445.

SINGH, Karan, M.A., PH.D.; Indian politician; b. 9 March 1931, Cannes, France; s. of Lieut.-Gen. H.H. Maharaja Sir Hari Singh, G.C.S.I., G.C.I.E., G.C.V.O., and Maharani Tara Devi, C.I.; m. Princess Yasho Rajya Lakshmi of Nepal 1950; two s. one d.; ed. Doon School, Univ. of Jammu and Kashmir, and Delhi Univ.; appointed Regent of Jammu and Kashmir 1949; elected Sadar-i-Riyasat (Head of State) by Jammu and Kashmir Legislative Assembly Nov. 1952, recognized by Pres. of India and assumed office 17 Nov. 1952, re-elected 1957 and 1962, Gov. 1965–67; Union Minister for Tourism and Civil Aviation 1967–73, for Health and Family Planning 1973–75, 1976–77, for Educ. 1979–80; re-elected mem. of Parl. 1977, 1980; Vice-Pres. Indian Council for Cultural Relations; Pres. Delhi Music Soc.; led Indian Del. to World Population Conf., Bucharest; Vice-Pres. World Health Assembly 1975–76; fmr. Chancellor Jammu and Kashmir Univ., Banaras Hindu Univ.; fmr. Sec. Jawaharlal Nehru Memorial Fund; fmr. Chair. Indian Bd. for Wild Life, Life Trustee of the India Int. Centre; Hon. Maj.-Gen. Indian Army; Hon. Col. Jammu and Kashmir Regt. 1962; Dr. h.c. (Aligarh Muslim Univ.) 1963. *Publications:* Prophet of Indian Nationalism: The Political Thought of Sri Aurobindo Ghosh 1893–1910 1963, Heir Apparent 1983, One Man's World 1986, Religions of India, and several books on political science, philosophical essays, travelogues, translations of Dogra-Pahari folksongs and poems in English. *Leisure interests:* travel, music (particularly Indian classical music), tennis, badminton, golf, bridge, chess, reading. *Address:* 3 Nyaya Marg, Chanakyapuri, New Delhi 110011, India. *Telephone:* 301 5291; 301 1744.

SINGH, Kewal, B.A., LL.B.; Indian diplomatist; b. 1 June 1915, Lyallpur (West Pakistan); s. of late S. Mihan Singh and Ganga Devi; m. Shamie Grewal 1942; one d.; ed. Forman Christian Coll., Lahore, Law Coll., Lahore, and Balliol Coll., Oxford; joined ICS 1938; ICS appointments 1940–48; First Sec. Indian Embassy, Ankara 1948–49; Indian Military Mission, Berlin 1949–51; Chargé d'affaires, Lisbon 1951–53; Consul-General, Pondicherry 1953–54; Chief Commr., State of Pondicherry, Karaikal, Mahe and Yanam 1955–57; Amb. to Cambodia 1957–58, to Sweden (concurrently accred. to Denmark and Finland from 1960) 1958–62; Deputy High Commr. in U.K. 1962–65; High Commr. in Pakistan 1965–66; Amb. to U.S.S.R. 1966–68; Sec. Ministry of External Affairs 1968–70; Amb. to Fed. Repub. of Germany 1970–72; Foreign Sec., Ministry of External Affairs 1972–76; Amb. to U.S.A. 1976–77; Distinguished Visiting Prof., Calif. State Univ., Northridge, Los Angeles and San Francisco 1978–79, Univ. of Ky. 1983–87; Lexington 1983–85; Visiting Prof., Univ. of Ky. 1980–83; Regent Lectureship, Univ. of Calif. at Los Angeles May 1980–; Hon. LL.D. (Kentucky) 1987; awarded Padma Shri for distinguished services leading to merger of French Possessions with India; Padma Sri Award. *Leisure interests:* reading and writing, attending seminars on int. relations, golf, travelling. *Address:* c/o Ministry of Foreign Affairs, New Delhi (Office); 1/31 A. Shanti Niketan, New Delhi 110021, India (Home). *Telephone:* 670 663 (Home).

SINGH, Khushwant, LL.B.; Indian author; b. Feb. 1915; m. Kaval Malik; one s. one d.; ed. Government Coll., Lahore, King's Coll. and Inner Temple, London; practised, High Court, Lahore 1939–47; joined Indian Ministry of External Affairs 1947; Press Attaché, Canada and then Public Relations Officer, London 1948–51; Ministry of Information and Broadcasting; edited Yojana; Dept. of Mass Communication, UNESCO 1954–56; commissioned by Rockefeller Foundation and Muslim Univ., Aligarh, to write a history of the Sikhs 1958; M.P. 1980–; Ed.-in-Chief The Hindustan Times, New Delhi 1980–83; Visiting lecturer Hawaii, Oxford, Princeton, Rochester, Swarthmore; numerous TV and radio appearances; Grove Press Award; Mohan Singh award; Padma Bhushan 1974; Ed. The Illustrated Weekly of India 1969–78. *Publications:* Mark of Vishnu 1949, The Sikhs 1951, Train to Pakistan 1954, Sacred Writings of the Sikhs 1960, I shall not hear the Nightingale 1961, Umrao Jan Ada—Courtesan of Lucknow (trans.) 1961,

History of the Sikhs (1769–1839) Vol. I 1962, Ranjit Singh: Maharaja of the Punjab 1962, Fall of the Sikh Kingdom 1962, The Skeleton (trans.) 1963, Land of the Five Rivers (trans.) 1964, History of the Sikhs (1839-Present Day) Vol. II 1965, Khushwant Singh's India 1969, Indira Gandhi Returns 1979, Editor's Page 1980, Iqbal's Dialogue with Allah (trans.) 1981, Punjab Tragedy (with Kuldip Noyar) 1984, and others. *Address:* 49E Sujan Singh Park, New Delhi 110003, India. *Telephone:* 690159.

SINGH, Raja Roy; Indian educationist; b. 5 April 1918, Pithoragarh; s. of Th. Durg Singh; m. Zorine Bonifacius 1943; two s. three d.; ed. Univ. of Allahabad; entered Indian Admin. Service 1943; fmr. Dir. of Educ., Uttar Pradesh; fmr. Joint Sec., Fed. Ministry of Educ., New Delhi; fmr. Joint Dir. Indian Council of Educ. Research and Training, Nat. Inst. of Educ.; at Office of Educ. Planning, UNESCO Headquarters, Paris 1964–65; Dir. UNESCO Regional Office for Educ. in Asia 1965–, Asst. Dir.-Gen. UNESCO. *Publication:* Education in the Soviet Union. *Leisure interests:* art, theatre, music. *Address:* UNESCO Regional Office for Educ. in Asia, P.O. Box 1425, Darakarn Building, 920 Sukhumvit Road, Bangkok, Thailand. *Telephone:* 391-8474.

SINGH, Sardar Swaran, M.SC., LL.B.; Indian politician; b. 19 Aug. 1907; ed. Govt. Coll., Lahore, and Lahore Law Coll.; elected Punjab Legis. Ass. 1946; Minister of Devt., Food, Civil Supplies 1946–47; mem. Gov's. Security Council, then Partition Cttee. 1947; Minister of Home, Gen. Admin., Revenue, Irrigation and Electricity in first Punjab Congress Ministry 1947–49; resigned to resume legal practice; Minister of Capital Projects and Electricity 1952; Minister for Works, Housing and Supply (Cen. Govt.) 1952–57; fmr. mem. Rajya Sabha; initiated Subsidized Industrial Housing Scheme; mem. Lok Sabha 1957–77; Minister for Steel, Mines and Fuel 1957–62; Minister for Railways 1962–63, of Food and Agric. 1963–64, of Industry, Eng. and Tech. Devt. June-July 1964, of External Affairs 1964–66, 1970–74, of Defence 1966–70, 1974–75; Pres. Indian Nat. Congress March-May 1977, 1978–79; Pres. Indian Council of World Affairs; led Indian Del. to UN Gen. Ass. 1964–66, 1970–73, ECOSOC 1954, 1955; Rep. to Commonwealth Prime Ministers' Conf. 1971, 1973; mem. Commonwealth Group on S. Africa 1985. *Address:* 7 Hastings Road, New Delhi, India.

SINGH, Virbhadra, M.A.; Indian politician and agriculturalist; b. 23 June 1934, Sarahan, Simla Dist.; m. Ratan Kumari 1954; ed. Bishop Cotton School, Simla, St. Stephen's Coll., Delhi, Delhi Univ.; has been mem. various Himachal Pradesh Govt. cttees. and bds. and mem. Himachal Pradesh Congress Cttee.; fmr. ADC to Pres. of India with hon. rank of Col. in Indian Army; mem. third Lok Sabha 1962–67, Estimate Cttee. of third Lok Sabha, fourth Lok Sabha 1967–72 and fifth Lok Sabha 1972–77; Union Deputy Minister for Tourism and Civil Aviation 1976–77; re-elected to Parl. 1980; Union Minister of State for Industries 1982; Chief Minister of Himachal Pradesh 1983–; won by-election to Himachal Pradesh Vidhan Sabha from Jubbal-Kotkhai Constituency 1985. *Leisure interests:* reading, gardening (especially growing of apples), travelling and long walks in rural surroundings. *Address:* P.O. Rampur, District Shimla, Himachal Pradesh, India.

SINGH, Vishwanath Pratap, LL.B.; Indian politician; b. 25 June 1931, Allahabad; s. of Raja Bahadur Ram Gopal Singh; m. Sita Kumari 1955; two s.; ed. Poona and Allahabad Univs.; Pres. Students Union, Udai Pratap Coll., Varanasi 1947–48; mem. Exec. Body, Allahabad Univ. 1969–71; mem. Legis. Ass., Uttar Pradesh 1969–71; Whip, Congress Legis. Party 1970–71; mem. Lok Sabha 1971–74, Rajya Sabha 1983; Union Deputy Minister for Commerce 1974–76, Union State Minister for Commerce 1976–77, 1983; Minister of Finance 1984–86, of Defence 1986–87; Chief Minister of Uttar Pradesh 1980–82, mem. Legis. Council 1980–81, Legis. Ass. 1981–83, Pres. Uttar Pradesh Congress Cttee. 1984; Additional Charge of Dept. of Supply 1983; expelled from Congress (1) Party 1987; f. and Leader Jan Morcha Party Oct. 1987–; Pres. Samajwadi Janata Dal (Coalition) 1988–. *Leisure interests:* painting, photography. *Address:* 4 Ashok Road, Allahabad, India.

SINGHANIA, D.C., B.A., LL.B.; Indian lawyer; b. 15 Oct. 1932, Pacheri Bari; s. of M.L. and Narmada (née Devi) Singhania; m. Tarawati Singhania 1954; two s. three d.; ed. Ramgarhia Coll., Phagwara, Punjab Univ.; business lawyer with Singhania & Co., specializing in overseas collaboration, tech. transfer and licensing arrangements, co. law and exchange control regulations; Consultant to a number of multinational corpns. active in India; bd. mem. some Jt. Venture Cos.; mem. Governing Body Indian Council of Arbitration, Chartered Inst. of Arbitrators, London, Int. Law Asscns., World Peace Through Law Center; rep. for India at int. conferences Vienna, Mexico City, London, Washington, São Paulo, Paris, Lausanne, Berlin; lecturer in India and abroad. *Publications:* (reviser) Sethna's Company Law, chapter on India in Enforcement of Judgments Abroad (Mathew Bender) 1988. *Leisure interests:* travel, reading philosophy and religious books, meeting people. *Address:* B-92 Himalaya House, 23 Kasturba Gandhi Marg, New Delhi-110 001, India. *Telephone:* 91 (011) 3318300 (Office); 667925, 660439 (Home).

SINGHASANEH, Suthee; Thai politician; b. 22 July 1928, Bangkok; m. Dr. Pyom Singhasaneh; one s. one d.; ed. Sarasit Pitthayalai School, Ratchaburi, Thammasat Univ., Univ. of Illinois, U.S.A.; joined Audit

Council of Thailand 1958; mem. Audit Council 1963; Dir. Co-operative Auditing Div., Dept. of Co-operative Auditing 1966; Dir.-Gen. Co-operative Auditing Dept., Ministry of Agric. and Co-operatives 1967–76; Dir. of Budget Bureau, Office of Prime Minister 1976–86; Deputy Minister of Finance 1979–86, Minister 1986–88. *Address:* c/o Ministry of Finance, Grand Palace, Na Phra Lau Road, Bangkok 10200, Thailand.

SINGHUBER, Dr. Kurt; German engineer and politician; b. 20 April 1932, Vienna, Austria; ed. Metallurgical Inst., Dnepropetrovsk, U.S.S.R.; Deputy Minister of Ore Mining, Metallurgy and Potash, G.D.R. 1966–67, Minister 1967–; mem. G.D.R. Research Council 1966–; mem. SED 1951–; Orden Banner der Arbeit. *Address:* Ministry of Ore Mining, Metallurgy and Potash, Karl-Liebknecht-Strasse, 102 Berlin, German Democratic Republic.

SINGHVI, Laxmi Mall, LL.D., S.J.D.; Indian jurist; b. 9 Nov. 1931, Jodhpur; s. of Dashrathmal Singhvi and Akal Kaur Singhvi; m. Kamla Singhvi 1957; one s. one d.; ed. Jodhpur, Allahabad, Harvard and Cornell Univs.; Dir. Indian Law Inst. 1957–58; Sr. Standing Counsel for Govt. of India and State of Uttar Pradesh; Sr. Advocate, Supreme Court of India 1967–; independent mem. for Jodhpur, Lok Sabha 1962–67; Tagore Law Prof.; Dir. Benett Coleman & Co. Ltd. (owners of the Times of India Publications) and Punjab Nat. Bank Ltd.; Founder and Chair. Inst. of Constitutional and Parl. Studies 1965; Chair. Commonwealth Legal Educ. Asscn. 1972–77; Chair. Nat. Legal Aid Asscn. of India; Chair. Nat. Fed. of UNESCO Assens. in India 1974–; Chair. Indian Nat. Cttee. for Abolition of Death Penalty 1977–, Govt. of India Cttee. on Local Self Govt. 1986–87; fmr. Pres., now Pres. Emer. Supreme Court of India Bar Assen., Pres. Asian Human Rights Conf. 1985, Indian Human Rights Trust, Indian Centre for the Independence of Judges and Lawyers; mem. UN Sub-Comm. on Protection of Minorities, UN Working Group for Protection of All Persons under any Form of Imprisonment or Detention; Chair. Samachar Bharati news agency; Life Trustee India Int. Centre; Hon. Prof. of Law (Delhi, Andhra), Calcutta); Hon. LL.D. (Jabalpur Univ.) 1983, (Banaras Hindu Univ.) 1984; Hon. Patron, Commonwealth Legal Educ. Assoc., London. *Leisure interests:* performing arts, poetry, gardening. *Address:* B-8, South Extension Pt. II, New Delhi 110049, India. *Telephone:* New Delhi 661308 and 664831.

SINGLETON, William Dean; America newspaper proprietor; b. 1951; Pres. Gloucester County Times Inc., N.J.; owner of 29 daily newspapers including Dallas Times Herald, Denver Post, Houston Post. *Address:* c/o Houston Post, 4747 Southwest Freeway, Houston, Tex. 77001, U.S.A.

SINHA, Satya Narayan; Indian politician; b. 9 July 1900, Shambhupath, Bihar; s. of Beni Prasad; m. Sansarwati Devi; one s. three d.; ed. Patna Univ.; joined Non-Violence Movement and imprisoned 1920; mem. Bihar Legislature 1926–30; Pres. Darbhanga District Congress Cttee. 1930–47; mem. Indian Constituent Ass. 1926–47, of Lok Sabha 1947; Minister of State for Parl. Affairs 1949–52; Minister for Parl. Affairs 1952–67, of Information and Broadcasting 1963–64, of Civil Aviation 1964, of Communications 1964–67; Minister without Portfolio 1967; Minister of Health, Family Planning and Urban Devt. 1967–69; Minister of Information, Broadcasting and Communications 1969–71; Gov. Madhya Pradesh 1971–77, Kerala Feb. 1988–; Pres. Indian Council of Medical Research; Chief Whip Congress Party in Cen. Ass. and Constituent Ass. *Address:* c/o Raj Bhavan, Bhopal, India.

SINNER, George Albert, B.A.; American politician; b. 29 May 1928, Fargo, N.D.; s. of Albert Sinner and Katherine (née Wild) Sinner; m. Elizabeth Jane Baute 1951; seven s. four d.; ed. St. Johns Univ. Minn.; farmer Sinner Bros. and Bresnahan, N.D. 1952–; mem. N.D. Senate 1962–66, N.D. House of Reps. 1982–84, Gov. of North Dakota 1985–; founder N.D. Crops Council 1978–83, Interstate Oil Compact Comm. 1986–; mem. N.D. Broadcasting Council 1968–73, N.D. Bd. of Higher Educ. 1966–75, Chair. 1970; co-founder bd. of Dirs. Tri-Coll. Univ. Bd. Fargo/Moorhead, N.D. 1970–84; mem. numerous N.D. farming assens.; Democrat. *Address:* Governor's Office, State Capitol, Bismarck, N.D. 58505, U.S.A.

SINOPOLI, Giuseppe; Italian conductor and composer; b. 2 Nov. 1946, Venice; ed. Benedetto Marcello Conservatoire, Venice and Medical School of Univ. of Padua; practised as surgeon and psychiatrist; studied conducting with Swarowsky, Vienna 1972; f. Bruno Maderna Ensemble, Venice, to play contemporary music 1975; début Covent Garden, London (Puccini's Manon Lescaut) 1983; U.S. début with New York Philharmonic Orchestra 1983; Prin. Conductor Philharmonia Orchestra, London 1983–. *Compositions include:* 25 studi su tre parametri 1969, Musica per calcolatori analogici 1969, Numquid et unum (cembalo and flute) 1970, Opus Ghimal (orchestra) 1971, Sunyata (string quintet and soprano) 1972, Piano Sonata 1974, String Quartet 1977, Lou Salome (opera) 1981. *Address:* c/o Philharmonia Orchestra, 76 Great Portland Street, London, W1N 5AL, England. *Telephone:* 01-580 9961.

SINOWATZ, Dr. Fred; Austrian politician, b. 5 Feb. 1929, Neufeld an der Leitha, Burgenland; m. Hermine Sinowatz 1954; one s. one d.; ed. Univ. of Vienna; joined Burgenland provincial govt. service 1953; mem. Burgenland Prov. Legis. 1961–71, Pres. 1964; Party Sec. Burgenland Austrian Socialist Party (SPÖ) Org. 1961–78, Deputy Chair. 1978, Chair. -1988; mem. Nat. Exec. SPÖ 1981, Chair. 1983–88; mem. Nationalrat 1971; Fed. Minister of Educ. and Arts 1971–83; Fed. Vice-Chancellor 1981,

Chancellor 1983–86; charged with committing perjury in 1987 libel case May 1989. *Address:* Loewelstrasse 18, 1010 Vienna, Austria.

SINSHEIMER, Robert Louis, S.B., S.M., PH.D.; American biologist; b. 5 Feb. 1920, Washington, D.C.; s. of Allen and Rose Davidson Sinsheimer; m. 1st Flora Joan Hirsch 1943 (divorced 1972), 2nd Kathleen Mae Reynolds 1972, 3rd Karen B. Keeton 1981; one s. two d.; ed. M.I.T.; Research Assoc., Biology, M.I.T. 1948–49; Assoc. Prof. of Biophysics, Iowa State Coll. 1949–55, Prof. 1955–57; Prof. of Biophysics, Calif. Inst. of Tech. 1957–77, Chair. Div. of Biology 1968–77, Visiting Prof. of Biology 1987–88; Prof. Dept. of Biological Sciences, Univ. of Calif. at Santa Barbara 1988–; Chancellor, Univ. of Calif. at Santa Cruz 1977–87; mem. N.A.S., mem. Council 1970–73; Calif. Scientist of the Year Award 1968, Beijerinck Medal of the Royal Netherlands Acad. of Sciences 1969; Pres. Biophysical Soc. 1970–71; Chair. Bd. of Editors, N.A.S. Proceedings 1972–80. *Publications:* More than 200 scientific papers 1946–78. *Leisure interests:* camping, hiking and photography. *Address:* Department of Biological Sciences, University of California at Santa Barbara, Santa Barbara, Calif. 93106 (Office); 4606 Via Cavente, Santa Barbara, Calif. 931110, U.S.A. (Home). *Telephone:* (805) 961-3511 (Office); (805) 683-2247 (Home).

SINT, Marjanne; Netherlands politician; b. 24 July 1949, Amsterdam; m. H. G. van Noordenburg 1985; no c.; ed. Univ. of Amsterdam and IMEDE Business School; mem. Staff, Ministry of Econ. Affairs 1974–77, Ministry of Culture, Health and Social Affairs 1977–79; Econ. Ed., Intermediair 1979–80, Chief Ed. 1980–81; Publisher, VNU Business Publs. 1981–87; Pres. Dutch Labour Party (PvdA) 1987–, Chair. 1988–. *Publications:* Tussen wal en schip, etnische minderheden in Nederland 1980, Economen over crisis 1982. *Leisure interests:* literature, poetry, music, modern art and architecture. *Address:* Partij van de Arbeid, Nic. Witsenkade 30, 1017 ZT Amsterdam, Netherlands. *Telephone:* (31)-020 55.121.55.

SINYAVSKAYA, Tamara Ilyinichna; Soviet opera-singer (mezzo-soprano); b. 1943, Moscow; ed. Moscow Conservatoire 1964; soloist with U.S.S.R. Bolshoi Theatre 1964–; studied at La Scala 1973–74; *Roles include:* Olga in Tchaikovsky's Eugene Onegin; Carmen; Blanche and Frosya in Prokofiev's Gambler and Semyon Kotko; First Prize Int. Singing Competition, Sofia 1968, First Prize at Int. Tchaikovsky Competition, Moscow 1970, People's Artist of R.S.F.S.R. 1976, People's Artist of U.S.S.R. 1982. *Address:* c/o Bolshoi Theatre, Ploshchad Sverdlova, Moscow, U.S.S.R.

SINYAVSKY, Andrey Donatovich (pseudonym Abram Tertz); Soviet writer; b. 1925, Moscow; m. M. Rozanova; ed. Moscow Univ.; mem., Gorky Inst. of World Literature -1965; taught and wrote articles for Novy Mir - 1965; arrested for "distributing anti-Soviet propaganda" (allowing his works to be published in West) 1965; convicted with Yuli Daniel and sentenced to hard labour 1966; held in a succession of forced labour camps 1966–71; left Soviet Union and settled in Paris 1973; now teaches at Paris Univ. 1973–; one of chief contribs. to Sintaksis (Ed. M. Rozanova-Sinyavskaya). *Publications:* Chapters on Gorky and Bagritsky in History of Soviet Russian Literature 1958, On Socialist Realism (in French, Esprit, Feb. 1959), The Trial Begins (in Russian, in Polish Kultura, Paris, later in English in Encounter) 1960, The Icicle and Other Stories (Paris) 1961, (English trans. 1962), The Poetry of the Revolutionary Era (Moscow) 1964, Introduction to Pasternak's Poetry (Moscow) 1965; novel: Lyubimov (Paris) 1964, (English trans. The Makepeace Experiment 1965), Unguarded Thoughts (New York 1965), Pkhentz (short-story) in Encounter 1966, The Fantastic World of Abram Tertz (New York) 1967, introductory essay to Anna Akhmatova (Penguin) 1969, A Voice from the Chorus 1974 (English trans. 1976), Strolling with Pushkin 1975, In The Shadow of Gogol 1975. *Address:* c/o Sintaksis, 8 rue Boris Vilde, 92260 Fontenay-aux-Roses, France.

SIPILÄ, Helvi Linnea; Finnish lawyer and United Nations official; b. 5 May 1915, Helsinki; d. of Vilho Sipilä and Sanni Maukola; m. Sauli (Sipilä) 1939; three s. one d.; ed. Univ. of Helsinki; acting judge, rural district courts 1941–42; Sec. Ministry of Supply 1942–43; held various legal posts in Supreme Court and Supreme Admin. Court 1941–51; Dir. and founder of law office 1943–72; mem. various Finnish govt. cttees. on matrimonial leg., protection of children, social benefits for children, citizenship educ. and int. devt. aid 1950–; mem. World Cttee. of World Assen. of Girl Guides and Girl Scouts 1957–66; Chief Commr. of Finnish Girl Guides 1952–69; mem. Council, Human Rights Inst., Strasbourg 1969–; Pres. Int. Fed. of Women Lawyers 1954–56, ZONTA Int. 1968–70; Vice-Pres. Int. Council of Women 1970–; Chair. Finnish Refugee Council 1965–72; Rep. of Finland, UN Comm. on Status of Women 1960–68, 1971–72, Vice-Chair. 1963–66, Chair. 1967; mem. Finnish del. to UN Gen. Ass. 1966–72, Chair. Third Cttee. 1971; Asst. Sec.-Gen. (for social and humanitarian matters), UN 1972–83; Gen. Sec. UN Int. Women's Year 1975. *Address:* c/o International Council of Women, c/o 13 rue Caumartin, 75009 Paris, France.

SIPPEL, Heinz, DR.RER.POL.; German banker; b. 7 Nov. 1922, Leverkusen; m. Christa Dausel 1953; one d.; ed. Carl Duisberg Gymnasium, Leverkusen, Cologne Univ.; Kreditanstalt für Wiederaufbau 1951–56; Man. Regional Credit Dept., Commerzbank AG, Düsseldorf 1957–61; Head of Credit Dept., Bankhaus Friedrich Simon, Düsseldorf 1961–62; joined Rheinische Girozentrale und Provinzialbank as Head of Essen Branch 1962, Alt. mem. Man. Bd. 1967, mem. Man. Bd. 1968; mem. Man. Bd., Westdeutsche

Landesbank Girozentrale 1969; Chair. Man. Bd., Hessische Landesbank Girozentrale 1975-85; Dir. LHB Internationale Handelsbank AG, Frankfurt (AR-Vors), MHB Mitteleuropäische Handelsbank AG, Deutsche Westminster Bank (AR-Vors); Neue Heimat Hamburg (AR-Vors); Trustee for the Neue Heimat Group; Erster Staatskommissar für die Frankfurter Westpapierbörse 1989; Bundesverdienstkreuz 1982. *Leisure interests:* hiking, gardening, classical music. *Address:* 6242 Kronberg, Parkstrasse 38, Federal Republic of Germany.

SIRADZE, Viktoria Moiseyevna; Soviet politician; b. 1929, Georgia; ed. Georgian Polytechnical Inst.; Sec. of Komsomol Cttee. of Polytechnic 1949-52; mem. CPSU 1951-; First Sec. Tbilisi Regional Cttee., Georgian Komsomol; Second Sec., then First Sec. Tbilisi City Cttee., Georgian Komsomol; Sec. Tbilisi Regional Cttee., Georgian CP; Sec. Tbilisi City Cttee., Georgian CP 1952-61; mem. Auditing Cttee., Georgian CP 1956-58, cand. mem. Cen. Cttee. of Georgian CP 1958-60, mem. 1960-; Sec. Politburo, Cen. Cttee. of Georgian CP 1961-62; Deputy Chair. Council of Ministers of Georgian S.S.R. 1962-73; Sec. Cen. Cttee. of Georgian CP 1973-86; Party Sec. for Ideology and Propaganda 1975-79; Deputy Chair. Presidium, Supreme Soviet of Georgian S.S.R. 1979-. *Address:* Supreme Soviet of the Georgian S.S.R., Tbilisi, Georgian S.S.R., U.S.S.R.

SIRAT, René-Samuel; French rabbi; b. 13 Nov. 1930, Bône (now Annaba), Algeria; s. of Ichoua Sirat and Oureida Atlan; m. 1st Colette Salamon 1952; one s. two d.; m. 2nd Nicole Holzman 1978; ed. Lycée St. Augustin, Bône, Univs. of Strasbourg, Paris (Sorbonne) and Jerusalem, Ecole Nat. des Langues Orientales (ENLOV); Rabbi, Toulouse 1952-55; Chaplain, Jeunesse juive 1955-63; Prof., Institut Nat. des Langues et Civilisations orientales (ENLOV), Dir. of Hebrew Studies 1965-; Prof., Ecole Rabbinique de France 1965-70, 1977-; Insp.-Gen. of Hebrew, Ministry of Educ. 1972-80; Pres. Hebrew Examining Bd., Certificate of Professional Aptitude and Higher Studies 1973-78; Dir. Centre de Documentation et Recherches des Etudes Juives modernes et contemporaines 1974; Pres. Hebrew Examining Bd., Agrégation 1978-80; Dir. Ecole Hautes Etudes de Judaisme 1985-; Pres. Centre Universitaire Rachi, Troyes 1989; Chief Rabbi of France 1981-87; Chief Rabbi, Consistoire Centrale 1988; Chevalier, Légion d'honneur, Officier, Ordre nat. du Mérite, Officier des Palmes Académiques, Prix de Jérusalem, Commdr. des Arts et des Lettres. *Publications:* Omer Hasikha (co-ed.) 1973, Mélanges A. Neher (co-ed.) 1974, Mélanges Vajda 1974-80 (co-ed.). *Address:* 51 rue de Rochechouart, 75009 Paris, France. *Telephone:* 401 69 555.

SIREGAR, Melanchton; Indonesian teacher and politician; b. 7 Aug. 1913, Pea-Arung Numbang, N. Tapanuli; m. 1st Bertha Ramian Siburian 1940 (died 1947), 2nd Setjawan Siburian 1948; ed. Christian Teachers' Training Coll. (H.I.K.), Solo, and Coll. for Headmasters' Degree, Bandung; teacher and Headmaster in various schools 1938-45; Dir. Higher Tech. School, Pematang Siantar 1945-47; Head of Gen. and Vocational Training Divs. of Service of Educ., Instruction and Culture, Pematang Siantar, Sumatra 1947, similar sr. appts. in Educ. Service and Insp. of Secondary Schools in N. Sumatra 1947-51; Co-ordinator of Office for Inspection of Educ. of N. Sumatra Region, Medan 1952-56; mem. of Exec., N. Sumatra Rep. Council 1948-50; M.P. 1956-71; Gen. Chair. in N. Sumatra and Co-ordinator in Sumatra, PARKINDO 1950-60, Vice-Chair. Man. Bd. 1960-64, Gen. Chair. of Exec. Bd. 1964-67, Gen. Chair. 1967-73; Vice-Chair. Peoples' Congress of Repub. of Indonesia (MPRS) 1966-72; Minister of Trade March 1988-; mem. of Indonesian Dels. to UN 1957, 1967. *Leisure interest:* reading about politics, literature and theology. *Address:* Ministry of Trade, Jalan Mohd Ikhwan Ridwan Rais 5, Jakarta, Indonesia.

SIREN, Heikki; Finnish architect; b. 5 Oct. 1918, Helsinki; s. of Prof. J. S. and Sirkka Siren; m. Kaija Siren (q.v.) 1944; two s. two d.; started private practice with Kaija Siren, Siren Architects Ltd. 1949-; mem. Finnish Acad. of Tech. Sciences 1971-; Foreign mem. Académie d'Architecture, Paris 1983; Hon. F.A.I.A.; Hon. Citation and Medal São Paulo Biennal 1957, Medal São Paulo Biennal 1961, Hon. Citation "Auguste Perret", Union Int. des Architectes 1965; Prof. h.c. 1970, Hon. D.Tech. 1982; Officier Ordre nat. du Mérite 1971, SLK (Finland) 1974, Grand Silver Order of Austria 1977, Camillo Sitte Prize, Vienna 1979, Grande Médaille d'Or d'Académie d'Architecture, Paris 1980, Architectural Prize of the State of Finland 1980, Grand Golden Order of the City of Vienna 1982, Prize of Finnish Cultural Foundation 1984. *Major works include:* Little Stage of Nat. Theatre, Helsinki 1954, Concert House, Lahti 1954, Chapel in Otaniemi 1957, Church in Orivesi 1960, Office Buildings, Helsinki 1965, Housing Area in Boussy St. Antoine, Paris 1970, "Round Bank" Kop, Helsinki, schools, sports centres, offices, industrial bldgs., housing, holiday centres, etc., Brucknerhaus Concert Hall, Linz, Austria 1974, Golf complex, Karuizawa, Japan 1974, Golf Club, Onuma, Hokkaido, Japan 1976, Reichsbrücke, Vienna, Austria, Conference Palace, Baghdad, Iraq. *Publications:* Kaija and Heikki Siren, Architects 1978. *Leisure interests:* boat planning, theatre. *Address:* Lounaisväylä 8A, 00200 Helsinki, Finland. *Telephone:* 673032 (Office).

SIREN, Katri (Kaija) Anna-Maija Helena; Finnish architect; b. 23 Oct. 1920, Kotka; d. of Gottlieb and Lydia Tuominen; m. Heikki Siren (q.v.) 1944; two s. two d.; private practice in partnership with Heikki Siren, Siren Architects Ltd. 1949-; Hon. F.A.I.A.; Hon. Citation and Medal São Paulo Biennal 1957, Medal São Paulo Biennal 1961, Hon. Citation "Auguste

Perret", Union Int. des Architectes 1965; Grand Silver Order of Austria (with star) 1977, Grande Médaille d'Or d'Académie d'Architecture, Paris 1980, Architectural Prize of the State of Finland 1980, SVR 1 rit. (Finland) 1981; Foreign mem. Académie d'Architecture, Paris 1983; Prize of Finnish Cultural Foundation 1984. *Publications:* selected works published in Kaija and Heikki Siren, Architects 1976. *Leisure interests:* fine arts and nature. *Address:* Lounaisväylä 8, Helsinki 20, Finland. *Telephone:* 673032 (Office).

SIRI, H.E. Cardinal Giuseppe; Italian ecclesiastic; b. 20 May 1906, Genoa; s. of Nicolò Siri and Giulia Bellavista; ed. Episcopal Seminary, Genoa, and Pontifical Gregorian Univ., Rome; ordained priest 1928; Titular Bishop of Livias 1944; Archbishop of Genoa 1946-87; cr. Cardinal by Pope Pius XII 1953; Pres. Episcopal Dir. Comm., Italian Catholic Action, Episcopal Conf. of Italy (C.E.I.) 1959-61; Chair. Italian Episcopal Conf. 1955-65; Apostolic Admin. of Bobbio 1983-; mem. Sacred Congregations of Sacraments of the Council and of Seminaries and Univs. of Study. *Publications:* Corso di Teologia per Laici 1942, La Strada passa per Cristo 1956, Riflessioni sul movimento teologico contemporaneo 1975, Ortodossia, Lettere Pastorali, Setsemani 1980, La giovinezza della Chiesa 1983, Il primato della ven'ta 1984.

[Died 2 May 1989.]

SIRICA, John Joseph; American judge; b. 19 March 1904, Waterbury, Conn.; s. of Fred and Rose (Zinno) Sirica; m. Lucille M. Camalier 1952; one s. two d.; ed. Georgetown Univ.; fmr. practising lawyer; Asst. U.S. Attorney for District of Columbia 1930-34; trial lawyer for Hogan & Hartson (law firm), Washington 1949-57; Judge, U.S. District Court for District of Columbia 1957-, Chief Judge 1971-74; tried "Watergate" wiretapping and conspiracy cases 1973-74; Adjunct Prof. of Law, Georgetown Univ. Law Center; mem. American Bar Assocn.; Award of Merit, American Judges Assocn. *Publication:* To Set the Record Straight 1979. *Address:* U.S. Court House, Washington, D.C. 20001, U.S.A.

SISCO, Joseph John, PH.D.; American government official; b. 31 Oct. 1919; m. Jean Churchill Head 1946; two d.; ed. Knox Coll. and Univ. of Chicago; U.S. Army 1941-45; CIA 1950-51; Dept. of State 1951-76, Officer-in-Charge, UN Political Affairs 1951-58; Deputy Dir. Office of UN Political and Security Affairs 1958-60, Dir. 1960-62; Deputy Asst. Sec. 1962-65; Asst. Sec. of State for Int. Org. Affairs, Dept. of State July 1965-69; Asst. Sec. State, Middle East-S. Asia 1969-74; Under-Sec. of State for Political Affairs 1974-76; mem. U.S. dels. to UN Gen. Ass. 1952-68; Pres. American Univ. in Washington 1976-80, Chancellor 1980-81; Foreign Affairs Analyst, Castle TV news; Partner Sisco Assocs., Man. Consultants, Washington; Dir. Geico, Raytheon, Gilette, Tenneco, Inter Public Group Inc.; Rockefeller Public Service Award 1971. *Address:* 1730 M Street, Washington, D.C. 20036 (Office); 2517 Massachusetts Avenue, N.W., Washington, D.C. 20008, U.S.A (Home).

SISSON, Charles Hubert, B.A., F.R.S.L.; British writer; b. 22 April 1914, Bristol; s. of R. P. and E. M. (née Worlock) Sisson; m. Nora Gilbertson 1937; two d.; ed. Univ. of Bristol, postgraduate studies in Berlin and Paris; various posts in Ministry of Labour, later Dept. of Employment 1936-, Under-Sec. 1962-73; served in army, in the ranks 1942-45; Simon Senior Research Fellow, Univ. of Manchester 1956-57; Joint Ed. PN Review (fmrly. Poetry Nation) 1976-84; Hon. D.Litt. (Bristol) 1980. *Publications:* An Asiatic Romance 1953, Versions and Perversions of Heine 1955, The Spirit of British Administration 1959, The London Zoo (poems) 1961, Christopher Homm 1965, Art and Action 1965, Numbers (poems) 1965, Catullus (trans.) 1966, Metamorphoses (poems) 1968, English Poetry 1900-1950 1971, The Case of Walter Bagehot 1972, In the Trojan Ditch (collected poems and selected trans.) 1974, The Poetic Art 1975, Lucretius (trans.) 1976, Anchises (poems) 1976, David Hume 1976, The Avoidance of Literature (collected essays) 1978, Some Tales of La Fontaine (trans.) 1979, Exactions (poems) 1980, The Divine Comedy of Dante (trans.) 1980, Philip Mairet: Autobiographical and Other Papers (ed.) 1981, Selected Poems 1981, Anglican Essays 1983, The Song of Roland (trans.) 1983, The Regrets of Joachim du Bellay (trans.) 1984, Collected Poems 1984, The Aeneid (trans.) 1986, Britannicus 1987, Phaedra 1987, Athalia of Racine (trans.) 1987, God Bless Karl Marx (poems) 1987, On the Look-Out (autobiog.) 1989. *Address:* Moorfield Cottage, The Hill, Langport, Somerset, TA10 9PU, England. *Telephone:* (0458) 250845.

SITHOLE, Rev. Ndabaningi; Zimbabwean clergyman and politician; b. 1920; ed. Waddilove Inst., Marandellas and Newton Theological Coll., U.S.A.; teacher 1941-55; U.S.A. 1955-58; ordained at Mount Silinda Congregationalist Church 1958; Principal, Chikore Cen. Primary School; Pres. African Teachers Assocn. 1959-60; Treas. Nat. Dem. Party (NDP) 1960; Del. to Fed. Review Conf. London Dec. 1960; fmr. Chair. Zimbabwe African People's Union (ZAPU) S. Rhodesia, Pres. July-Aug. 1963; Leader Zimbabwe African Nat. Union (ZANU) Rhodesia 1963, incorporated in African Nat. Council Dec. 1974, formed ANC (Sithole), contested March 1980 elections as leader of ZANU (Sithole) Party; sentenced to 12 months imprisonment Dec. 1963, sent to Wha Wha Restriction Camp May 1965; tried and sentenced to six years hard labour for incitement to murder Ian Smith Feb. 1969, released Dec. 1974; then in exile in Zambia with section of the African Nat. Council (ANC) led by Bishop Muzorewa; withdrew faction of ZANU from ANC Sept. 1976; attended Rhodesian Constitutional Conf., Geneva 1976; mem. Transitional Exec. Council to prepare for transfer of power in Rhodesia 1978-79; M.P. 1979; seeking political asylum in U.S.A. 1987. *Publications:* African Nationalism 1969, 1967, The Polygamist 1973, Roots of a Revolution: Scenes from Zimbabwe's Struggle 1977.

SITKOVETSKY, Dmitry; American (fmrly. Soviet) violinist; b. 27 Sept. 1954, Baku, U.S.S.R.; son of Julian Sitkovetsky and Bella Davidovich; m. Susan Roberts; ed. Moscow Conservatory, The Juilliard School of Music; début with Berlin Philharmonic 1980; appearances with Vienna Symphony, Orchestre de Paris, and the Amsterdam, Rotterdam, Munich and Royal Philharmonics in Europe and the Chicago, Cincinnati, Detroit, Montreal and Toronto Symphonies in North America, Carnegie Hall début 1986; Artistic Dir. Kuhmo Festival, Finland 1983-; First Prize Fritz Kreisler Competition, Vienna 1979, Avery Fisher Career Grant 1983. *Address:* c/o J. B. Keller, 250 West 57th Street, 1130 New York, N.Y. 10107, U.S.A. *Telephone:* (212) 315-2430.

SITNIKOV, Vasiliy Ivanovich; Soviet politician; b. 13 Dec. 1927; ed. Tomsk Polytech. Inst.; mem. CPSU 1948-; lecturer in eng. 1948-54; party work for Kemerovo Regional Cttee., CPSU 1954-68; mem. All-Union Cen. Council of Trade Unions 1968-77; Chair. Trade Union Council, Kemerovo Dist. 1968-74; Sec. of Kemerovo Dist. Cttee. CPSU 1974-83; Deputy to R.S.F.S.R. Supreme Soviet 1980-84; First Sec., Irkutsk Dist. Cttee. CPSU and mem. Mil. Council, Transbaikal Mil. Dist. 1983-; Deputy to Council of the Union, U.S.S.R. Supreme Soviet 1984-; mem. Cen. Cttee. CPSU 1986-. *Address:* The Kremlin, Moscow, U.S.S.R.

SITRUK, Jo; French rabbi; b. 16 Oct. 1944, Tunis; m. 1965; nine c.; ed. Seminary rue Vauquelin, Paris; Asst. to Rabbi Max Warsharski, Lower Rhine region 1970-75; Rabbi, Marseilles 1975-87; Chief Rabbi of France 1988-. *Address:* Consistoire Central Israélite de France et d'Algérie, 17 rue Saint Georges, 75009 Paris, France.

SITU HUIMIN; Chinese civil servant; b. 1909; ed. Art Academy of Tokyo; went to U.S.A. and U.S.S.R. to study studio management 1946; Deputy Dir., Film Industry Admin., Ministry of Culture 1959; Deputy Dir., Cinema Bureau 1961-65; in disgrace during Cultural Revolution 1966-77; Vice-Minister of Culture 1978-82; Pres., Society of Motion Pictures and TV Eng. 1982-. *Address:* Ministry of Culture, Shatan Street, Beijing, People's Republic of China.

SITU ZHAOGUANG; Chinese sculptor; b. 1940, Hong Kong. *Address:* Beijing Central Academy of Fine Arts, Beijing, People's Republic of China.

SIVADON, Paul Daniel; French psychiatrist; b. 10 Jan. 1907, Moncoutant; s. of Daniel Sivadon and Leïla de Verbizier; m. Renée Nodot 1930; three c.; ed. Lycée Blaise Pascal, Clermont Ferrand, and Univ. de Paris; Head, Clinic for Mental Illness, Faculté de Paris 1935-36; Dir. Colonie Familiale, Seine 1936-43; Head Dr. Psychiatric Hospital, Ville-Evrard 1943-58; Prof. of Psychiatry and Medical Psychology, Univ. of Brussels 1959-77; Dir. Psychiatric Services for Nat. Educ. 1958-72; Consultant WHO 1951-65; fmr. Pres. World Fed. for Mental Health 1960-61; Pres. French League for Mental Hygiene 1961-66; Soc. Médico-Psychologique 1975; Officier Légion d'honneur, Officier de la Santé publique, Commdr. Ordre de la Couronne, Grand Officier Ordre Léopold II (Belgium). *Publications include:* Psychoses puerpérales 1933, Rééducation Corporelle des Fonctions Mentales 1965, Psychopathologie du Travail 1969, Traité de Psychologie Médicale (three vols.) 1973, Santé Mentale 1979, Tempo del Hombre, Tempo de Trabajo 1982, Temps de travail; temps de vivre 1984, Corps et thérapeutique 1986, and over 400 scientific articles. *Address:* 8 rue de L'Alboni, 75016 Paris, France. *Telephone:* 45-20-64-87.

SIVAN, Amiram; Israeli business executive; b. 1938, Israel; m. Aliza Sivan 1960; two s. one d.; ed. Hebrew Univ., Jerusalem; Econ. Research Dept. of State Revenue Authority 1962-65, Co-ordinator of social budgets, Budget Dept. 1965-69, Deputy Dir. of Budgets 1969-73; Dir. Gen. of Nat. Insurance Inst. 1974-76; Dir. Gen. of Ministry of Finance 1976-79; Chair. Bd. of Dirs. and C.E.O. of TEUS (Devt. Areas Industrialization Ltd.) 1980-86; Chair. Bd. of Man. of Bank Hapoalim B.M. 1986-. *Leisure interest:* music. *Address:* 50 Rothschild Blvd., Tel-Aviv (Office); 33 Mishol Ha'ya'ara, Ramot 02, Jerusalem, Israel (Home). *Telephone:* 611677.

SIVASITHAMPARAM, Murgugesu; Ceylonese (Tamil) lawyer and politician; b. 20 July 1923, Jaffna; s. of Cittampalam and Maheswari Murugesu; m. Sarathadevi (Sivasitthamparan) 1949; one s. one d., ed. Vigresmara Coll., St. Joseph's Coll., Univ. Coll., Law Coll.; Sec. of Union Soc., Univ. Coll. 1947-48; Pres. Law Students' Union, Law Coll. 1949-50; mem. House of Reps. for Uduppiddi 1960-70; Gen. Sec. All Ceylon Tamil Congress 1966-77, then Pres.; Joint Sec.-Gen. Tamil United Liberation Front (TULF) 1976-78, Pres. 1978-; M.P. for Nallur 1977-83. *Address:* Head Office, Tamil United Liberation Front, 238 Main Street, Jaffna (Office); 100 Norris Canal Road, Colombo 10, Sri Lanka (Home). *Telephone:* 7176 (Office); 91017 (Home).

SIWICKI, Gen. Florian; Polish army officer and politician; b. 10 Jan. 1925, Łuck; ed. Polish Officers' School, Ryazan, and Gen. Staff Acad. of U.S.S.R.; worked in U.S.S.R. 1940-43; in Red Army 1943; volunteer, Tadeusz Kościuszko First Infantry Div. 1943; Commdr. of sub-unit, subsequently lecturer Tadeusz Kościuszko Infantry Officers' School, worked in cen. insts. of Ministry of Nat. Defence, commdr. different tactical units; Mil., Air and Naval Attaché of Embassy in People's Repub. of China

1961-63; Chief of Staff, Silesian Mil. Dist. 1963-68, Dist. Commdr. 1968-71; 1st Deputy Chief of Gen. Staff of Polish Armed Forces 1971-73; Chief of Gen. Staff, Deputy Minister of Nat. Defence 1973-83, Minister of Nat. Defence 1983-; mem. Mil. Council of Nat. Salvation 1981-83; Gen. of Army 1984; mem. Polish Workers' Party 1945-48; mem. Polish United Workers' Party (PZPR) 1948-, deputy mem. PZPR Cen. Cttee. 1969-75, mem. 1975-; alt. mem. Political Bureau of PZPR Cen. Cttee. 1981-86, mem. Political Bureau 1986-; Deputy to Seym 1976-; Order of Builders of People's Poland, Order of Grunwald Cross (1st Class), Order of Banner of Labour (1st and 2nd Class), Order of Lenin 1984, other Polish and foreign mil. decorations. *Leisure interests:* reading, sport, hunting. *Address:* Ministerstwo Obrony Narodowej, 00-909 Warsaw 60, Poland.

SIYAD BARRE, Muhammad (see Siad Barre).

SIZENKO, Yevgeny Ivanovich, CAND.ECON.SC.; Soviet politician; b. 1931; mem. CPSU 1953-; started career as agronomist; Vice-Chair., then First Vice-Chair. of Moscow Regional Exec. Cttee., Sec. Moscow Regional Cttee. of CPSU; First Sec. of Bryansk Regional Party Cttee. 1978-; mem. CPSU Cen. Cttee., 26th Party Congress; Minister of Meat and Dairy Industry of U.S.S.R. 1984-85; First Deputy Pres. of State Agro Industries 1985-; Deputy to U.S.S.R. Supreme Soviet *Address:* c/o Ministry of Meat and Dairy Industry, Moscow, U.S.S.R.

SIZOVA, Alla Ivanovna; Soviet ballet dancer; b. 22 Sept. 1939, Moscow; d. of Ivan Sizov and Ekaterina Sizova; m. Mikhail Serebrennikov 1965; one s.; ed. Leningrad School of Ballet; joined Leningrad Kirov Theatre of Opera and Ballet 1958-; teacher A. Vagnova Choreography School 1987-; honoured artist of the R.S.F.S.R. *Major roles:* Masha (Nutcracker), Mirta (Giselle), Pas de trois (Corsair), Katerina (Stone Flower), Waltz and Mazurka (Chopiniana), Pas de trois (Swan Lake), Aurora (Sleeping Beauty), Maria (Fountain of Bakhchisarai), Juliet (Romeo and Juliet), Cinderella (Cinderella), Kitri (Don Quixote), Girl (Leningrad Symphony); Gold Medals Youth Festival, Vienna 1959, 1st Int. Ballet Contest, Varna; Anna Pavlova Diploma, Paris 1964; People's Artist of the U.S.S.R. 1983. *Address:* State Kirov Academic Theatre of Opera and Ballet, ploshchad Iskusstv 1, Leningrad, U.S.S.R.

SJAASTAD, Anders Christian, PH.D.; Norwegian politician; b. 21 Feb. 1942, Oslo; s. of Andreas and Ingrid Sjaastad; m. Torill Oftedal Sjaastad 1969; one d.; ed. Univ. of Oslo; Pres. Norwegian Students' Asscn., Univ. of Oslo 1967; Research Asst., Inst. of Political Science, Univ. of Oslo 1968-70; Research at Norwegian Inst. of Int. Affairs 1970-, Dir. of Information 1973-; mem. Hoyre (Conservative Party), Vice-Chair. Oslo Høyre 1977-88; Deputy mem. Storting (Parl.) 1981-85; mem. Storting (Parl.) 1985-; Minister of Defence 1981-86; mem. Norwegian Nat. Defence Comm. 1974-78; Norwegian Cttee. on Arms Control and Disarmament 1976-81. *Publications:* Departmental Decision Making (Co-author) 1972, Politikk og Sikkerhet i Norskehavsområdet (with J. K. Skogan) 1975, Norsk Utenrikspolitisk Arbok (Ed.) 1975, Deterrence and Defence in the North (Co-Ed. and contrib.). *Address:* Stortinget, Karl Johans gt. 22, 00 26 Oslo 1, Norway. *Telephone:* (2) 313050.

SJADZALI, Munawir, M.A.; Indonesian politician; b. 7 Nov. 1924, Klaten, Cen. Java; ed. Univ. of Exeter and Georgetown Univ.; Instr. Islamic Religious Training Centre (Madrasah), Ungaran, Cen. Java 1943; joined Dept. of Foreign Affairs 1950, served Washington, Colombo, London; Amb. to Kuwait, concurrently to Bahrain and Qatar; Minister of Religious Affairs 1983-. *Address:* Ministry of Religious Affairs, Jln. Thamrin 6, Jakarta Pusat, Indonesia.

SKAK-NIELSEN, Niels Verner, CAND. POL.; Danish international civil servant; b. 18 Feb. 1922, Århus; s. of Jens and Thora Skak-Nielsen; m. Birthe Reinwald 1947; two s. two d.; ed. Univ. of Copenhagen; joined Foreign Service 1947; Econ. Sec. of Danish Govt. 1949-51; Deputy Chief of Section, Ministry of Foreign Affairs 1951-53; Sec., Del. to NATO 1953-56; Chief of Section, Ministry of Foreign Affairs 1956-59; Counsellor, Del. to OEEC 1959-60; Minister and Perm. Rep. to EFTA and European Office of UN 1960-66, Amb. 1963-66; Asst. Under-Sec. of State for Econ. Affairs, Ministry of Foreign Affairs 1966; Chief Statistician of Denmark 1966-; mem. of Bd. of Chairmen of Econ. Council 1967-73. *Address:* Danmarks Statistik, Sejerøgade 11, Copenhagen Ø, Denmark. *Telephone:* 01-298222.

SKÁLA, Ivan; (b. as Karel Hell); Czechoslovak poet; b. 6 Oct. 1922, Brandýs nad Labem; ed. Commercial School, Prague, -1941; forced to work in Germany 1942-45; Cen. Cttee. Czechoslovak Union of Youth 1945-46; cultural ed., Rudé Právo, Prague 1946-59; First Sec., Union of Czechoslovak Writers, Prague 1959-64; mem. Cen. Cttee. Union of Czechoslovak-Soviet Friendship 1959-68; mem. of Presidium and Chair. of Cultural Cttee., Nat. Ass. 1960-64; Deputy to Nat. Ass. 1960-69; mem. Cen. Cttee., CP of Czechoslovakia 1962-71, mem., Ideological Comm. 1963-69; Ed. Rudé Právo, Prague 1964-67; Dir. Mladá Fronta publishing house, Prague 1967-68; Deputy to House of the People, Fed. Ass. of ČSSR 1969-71; dir., Československý spisovatel publishing house, Prague 1970-82; mem. of preparatory Cttee., Union of Czech Writers 1977-; Deputy Chair., Union of Czech Writers 1977-82, Chair. 1982-, mem. of Presidium, Union of Czechoslovak Writers, 1982-, Deputy Chair. 1982-; Klement Gottwald State Prize 1959, 1983, Artist of Merit 1974, National Artist 1979, Order of Labour 1982, World Peace Council Medal 1982. *Works: collections of poems:* Křesadlo 1946, Přes práh 1948, Máj země 1950, Fronja je všude 1951, A cokoliv se stane 1957, Ranní vlak naděje 1958, Zdravím vás, okna 1962, Blankytný kalendář 1963, Posel přichází pěšky 1968, Čtyři básně o smrti a strom 1969, Co si beru na cestu 1975 Žízeň, Čí je jaru 1976, Osudová 1978, Oheň spěchá 1979, Okno dokořán 1981; selection from his works as a publicist: Kontinuita 1, 2 1980. *Address:* Svaz čs. spisovatelů, Národní tř. 11, Prague 1, Czechoslovakia.

SKALWEIT, Stephan, D.PHIL.; German professor of modern history; b. 5 May 1914, Giessen; s. of August Skalweit; m. Else Messing 1950; ed. Univs. of Kiel, Vienna, Paris and Frankfurt; archivist Pr. G. Staats-archiv 1939-45; lecturer Univ. of Bonn 1951-57; Prof. of Modern History, Univ. of Saarbrucken 1957-63, Free Univ. of Berlin 1963-64, Univ. of Bonn 1964-, Prof. Emer. 1982-; Chair. Anglo-German Group of Historians 1975-77; Pres. Comm. int. pour l'edition des sources de l'Histoire européene 1978-88; Officier Ordre des Palmes académiques, Bundesverdienstkreuz (1st Class). *Publications:* Die Berliner Wirtschaftskriese v. 1763 1937, Frankreich und Friedrich d.Gr. 1952, Edmund Burke und Frankreich 1956, Reich u. Reformation 1967, Der Beginn der Neuzeit 1982. *Address:* Haager Weg 31, 5300 Bonn 1, Federal Republic of Germany (Home); Konviktstr. 11, Federal Republic of Germany (Univ.). *Telephone:* 0228-735971 (Office); 0228-28 11 18 (Home).

SKÅNLAND, Hermod, M.A.; Norwegian banker; b. 15 June 1925, Tromsø; s. of Peder Skånland and Margit (née Maurstad) Skånland; m. Jorid Henden 1972; one d.; ed. Univ. of Oslo; Asst. Bureau of Statistics 1949-52, Consultant 1952-58, Head of Section 1958-71; Dir.-Gen. Ministry of Finance 1960-; Deputy Gov. Bank of Norway 1971-85, Gov. 1985-; Commdr. Order of St. Olav 1987. *Publications:* The Dilemma of Income Policies 1981, The Central Bank and Political Authorities 1984, The Norwegian Credit Market since 1900 1987. *Address:* Norge Bank, Bankplassen 2, 0107 Oslo 1 (Office); Solveien 1B, 1177 Oslo 11, Norway (Home).

SKAUGE, Arne; Norwegian politician; b. 27 Jan. 1948, Bergen; ed. Norwegian School of Econs. and Business Admin; auditing dept.; municipality of Bergen 1966-67; consultant, private consulting firm for social planning 1971-76; Dir. of personnel, Bergen municipality 1976-; proxy mem. Storting 1973-77, mem. 1977-; Minister of Trade and Shipping 1981-83; Conservative Party. *Address:* c/o Ministry of Trade and Shipping, Oslo, Norway.

SKEAT, Theodore Cressy, B.A.; British papyrologist; b. 15 Feb. 1907, St. Albans, Herts.; s. of Walter William Skeat and Theodora Duckworth; m. Olive Martin 1942; one s.; ed. Whitgift School, Christ's Coll., Cambridge, and British School of Archaeology, Athens; Assistant Keeper, Dept. of Manuscripts, British Museum 1931-48, Deputy Keeper 1948-61, Keeper 1961-72; Cromer Greek Prize 1932. *Publications:* Fragments of an Unknown Gospel (with H. I. Bell) 1935, Scribes and Correctors of the Codex Sinaiticus (with H. J. M. Milne) 1938, The Reigns of the Ptolemies 1954, Papyri from Panopolis 1964, Catalogue of Greek Papyri in the British Museum, Vol. VIII 1974, The Birth of the Codex (with C. H. Roberts) 1983. *Address:* 63 Ashbourne Road, London, W5 3DH, England. *Telephone:* 01-998 1246.

SKEGGS, Leonard Tucker, Jr., A.B., M.S., PH.D.; American research biochemist; b. 9 June 1918, Fremont, Ohio; s. of late Leonard T. Skeggs, Sr. and Frances E. Wolfe; m. Jean Hossel 1941; one s.; ed. Youngstown State Univ. and Case Western Reserve Univ. (now Case Western Reserve Univ.); U.S. Navy 1943-46; Research Fellow in Clinical Biochem., Western Reserve Univ. 1948-49, Instructor in Biochem. 1950-51, Sr. Instructor in Biochem. (Dept. of Pathology) 1951-52, Asst. Prof. 1952-59, Assoc. Prof. 1959-69, Prof. 1969-; Chief of Biochem. Section and Co-Dir. Hypertension Research Lab., Veterans' Admin. Hosp., Cleveland, Ohio 1947-68, Dir., Prin. Investigator 1968-83; Medical Investigator in Hypertension, Veterans' Admin. 1976-85; mem. American Soc. of Biological Chemists, American Chemical Soc., Bd. of Editors Circulation Research; Fellow, American Assen. of Clinical Chemists, New York Acad. of Sciences, American Heart Assen. Council on High Blood Pressure; mem. American Heart Assen. Council on Basic Sciences; Hon. D.Sc. (Youngstown) 1960, Hon. D.Hum.-Litt. (Baldwin-Wallace Coll.) 1980; Arthur S. Flemming Award 1957, Van Slyke Medal 1963, American Chemical Soc. Award for Chemical Instrumentation 1966, Ames Award 1966, Middleton Award 1968, Career Service Award (Greater Cleveland Growth Assen.) 1968, Stouffer Award 1968; Bendetti-Pichler Award in microchem. 1971; John Scott Award for invention of the Auto Analyzer 1972, Cleveland Award, Int. Soc. for Artificial Organs 1978; Edward Longstreth Medal (Franklin Inst.) 1980, Pittsburgh Analytical Chemistry Award (Soc. for Analytical Chemists of Pittsburgh) 1982. *Major fields of work include:* Hypertension, automatic chemical analysis, multiple automatic analysis; 85 publs. and 20 patents. *Leisure interests:* competitive distance riding, fishing, backpacking, breeding Arabian horses. *Address:* Department of Pathology, Case Western Reserve University, 2040 Adelbert, Cleveland, Ohio 44106 (Office); 10212 Blair Lane, Kirtland, Ohio 44094, U.S.A. (Home). *Telephone:* (216) 942-4527 (Home).

SKEMPTON, Alec Westley, D.SC., F.I.C.E., F.G.S., F.R.S.; British professor of engineering; b. 4 June 1914, Northampton; s. of A. W. Skempton and

Beatrice Edridge Payne; m. Mary Wood 1940; two d.; ed. Northampton Grammar School and Univ. of London; at Building Research Station 1936-46; Univ. Reader in Soil Mechanics, Imperial Coll., Univ. of London 1946-54, Prof. of Soil Mechanics 1955-57, Prof. of Civil Eng. 1957-81, Prof. Emer. 1981-, Sr. Research Fellow 1981-; Lecturer in Copenhagen, Paris, Harvard Univ., Univs. of Illinois, Stockholm, Madrid, Florence, Tokyo, Berkeley; Special Lecturer, Architectural Assen. 1948-57; Visiting Lecturer, Cambridge Univ. School of Architecture 1962-66, Edinburgh Univ. School of Architecture 1968; Hitchcock Foundation Prof. at Univ. of Calif., Berkeley 1978; Chair. Joint Cttee. on Soils, Ministry of Supply and Road Research Bd. 1954-59; Pres. Int. Soc. Soil Mechanics and Foundation Eng. 1957-61; mem. Council Inst. of Civil Eng. 1949-54, Vice-Pres. Inst. of Civil Eng. 1974-76; mem. Cathedrals Advisory Cttee. 1964-69, Council N.E.R.C. 1973-76; Consultant to Binnie & Partners, John Mowlem & Co. Ltd.; Pres. Newcomen Soc. 1977-79, Pres. Smeatonian Soc. 1981; Fellow, Royal Soc. 1961; Foreign Assoc. U.S. Nat. Acad. of Eng. 1976; Hon. D.Sc. (Durham) 1968, (Aston) 1980, (Chalmers, Gothenburg) 1982; James Alfred Ewing Medal 1968, Lyell Medal 1972, Dickinson Medal 1974, Inst. Structural Eng. Gold Medal 1981. *Publications:* Over 100 papers on soil mechanics, geology and history of civil engineering; William Jessop, Engineer (Co-author), John Smeaton, F.R.S., Selected Papers on Soil Mechanics 1984. *Address:* Department of Civil Engineering, Imperial College, London, S.W.7; 16 The Boltons, London, S.W.10, England. *Telephone:* 01-589 5111 (Office); 01-370 3457 (Home).

SKIBNIEWSKA, Halina, D.ENG.; Polish architect and town planner; b. 10 Jan. 1921, Warsaw; d. of Wacław and Ewelina (Kuczkowska) Erentz; m. Zygmunt Skibniewski 1951; ed. Warsaw Technical Univ.; worked at Bureau for Rebuilding of the Capital, Warsaw 1945-47; Asst. Warsaw Technical Univ. 1945-54, Lecturer 1954-62, Acting Prof. 1962-71, Asst. Prof. 1971-75, Prof. Extraordinary 1975-; Chief Architect, Design Office 1953-; Deputy to Seym 1965-85, Vice-Marshal of Seym 1971-85; Chair. Cen. Bd. of Soc. for Polish-French Friendship 1972-; Deputy Chair. Council for Family Affairs attached to Council of Ministers 1978-; mem. Consultative Council attached to Chair. of Council of State 1986-; chief works include schools, housing estates and Nat. Theatre, Warsaw; mem. Assen. of Architects of Polish Republic 1951-, Assen. of Polish Urban Planners, Centro Internazionale di studio e documentazione dell' abitare, Bologna 1978-; Corresp. mem. Acad. d'Architecture (France) 1981-; Hon. Prize of Polish Architects Assen. 1978; Commdr. and Knight's Cross, Order of Polonia Restituta, Grand Officier Légion d'honneur 1972, State Prize 1st Class 1972, 1976, Medal of 30th Anniversary of People's Poland 1974, Lenin Prize for Peace 1979, Order of Banner of Labour (1st Class) 1984 and other decorations. *Publications:* Dziecko w mieszkaniu i osiedlu 1969, Wyniki badań w zakresie budownictwa w Polsce dla ludzi z ciężkim uszkodzeniem narządów ruchu 1968, Rodzina a mieszkanie 1974, Tereny otwarte w miejskim środowisku mieszkalnym (co-author) 1979. *Leisure interests:* ecology, music. *Address:* Wydziat Architektury Politechniki Warszawskiej, Ul. Koszykowa 55, 00-659 Warsaw; Ul. Frascati 4, 00-483 Warsaw, Poland. *Telephone:* 215755 (Office); 291686 (Home).

SKINNER, Burrhus Frederic, PH.D., SC.D., LITT.D., L.H.D., L.L.D., D.SC.S.; American professor of psychology; b. 20 March 1904, Susquehanna, Pa.; s. of William and Grace Burrhus Skinner; m. Yvonne Blue 1936; two d.; ed. Hamilton Coll. and Harvard Univ.; with Nat. Research Council, Harvard 1931-33; Jr. Fellow, Harvard 1933-36; Instructor, Minnesota Univ. 1936-37, Asst. Prof. 1937-39, Assoc. Prof. 1939-45 (war research 1942-43); Prof. and Chair. Dept. of Psychology, Indiana Univ. 1945-48; Prof., Harvard Univ. 1948-57, Edgar Pierce Prof. 1958-74, Prof. Emer. 1975-; Fellow, American Psychological Assen., American Philosophical Soc., N.A.S., A.A.A.S., American Acad. of Arts and Sciences, Swedish Psychological Soc., British Psychological Soc., Spanish Psychological Soc., Royal Soc. of Arts; numerous hon. degrees; Nat. Science Medal 1968, Gold Medal, American Psychological Assen. 1971, Joseph Kennedy Award 1971. *Publications:* Behavior of Organisms 1938, Walden Two 1948, Science and Human Behavior 1953, Verbal Behavior 1957, Schedules of Reinforcement 1957 (with C. B. Ferster), Cumulative Record 1959, 1961, Analysis of Behavior (with James G. Holland) 1961, The Technology of Teaching 1967, Contingencies of Reinforcement: A Theoretical Analysis 1969, Beyond Freedom and Dignity 1971, About Behaviorism 1974, Particulars of My Life 1976, Reflections on Behaviorism and Society 1978, The Shaping of a Behaviorist 1979, Notebooks 1980, Skinner for the Classroom 1982, A Matter of Consequences 1983, Enjoy Old Age 1983; *autobiographies:* Particulars of my Life 1976, The Shaping of a Behaviorist 1979, A Matter of Consequences 1983, Upon Further Reflection 1987, Current Issues In The Analysis of Behaviour 1989. *Leisure interest:* music. *Address:* 13 Old Dee Road, Cambridge, Mass. 02138, U.S.A. (Home). *Telephone:* 864-0848 (Home).

SKINNER, Hon. James John, Q.C.; Irish-born lawyer; b. 24 July 1923; s. of late William Skinner; m. Regina Brigitte Reiss 1950; three s. two d.; ed. Trinity Coll., Dublin and King's Inns, Dublin; called to the Irish Bar 1946, joined Leinster Circuit; called to the English Bar, Gray's Inn 1950, to the Northern Rhodesia Bar 1951; Q.C., N. Rhodesia 1964; M.P. for Lusaka E. 1964-68; Minister of Justice, Lusaka 1964-65; Attorney-Gen. 1965-69; Minister of Legal Affairs 1967-68; Chief Justice of Zambia March-Sept. 1969; Chief Justice of Malawi 1970-85; Social Security Commr.

1986–; Grand Commdr., Order of Menelik II (Ethiopia) 1965. *Address:* 65 Castelnau, London, S.W.13, England. *Telephone:* 01-748 1228.

SKINNER, Quentin Robert Duthie, M.A., F.B.A.; British professor of political science; b. 26 Nov. 1940, Oldham; s. of Alexander Skinner and Winifred (née Duthie) Skinner; m. Susan James 1979; one s. one d.; ed. Bedford Coll., Gonville and Caius Coll., Cambridge; Fellow Christ's Coll., Cambridge 1962–; Lecturer in History, Univ. of Cambridge 1967-78, Prof. of Political Science 1978–; mem. of the Inst. of Advanced Study, Princeton, N.J. 1974-75, 1976-79; Wolfson Literary Award 1979, Hon. Foreign mem. American Acad. of Arts and Sciences 1986. *Publications:* The Foundations of Modern Political Thought, Vol. I The Renaissance 1978, Vol. II The Age of Reformation 1978, Machiavelli 1981, Philosophy in History (ed. jtly. and contrib.) 1984, The Return of Grand Theory in the Human Sciences (ed. and contrib.) 1985, The Cambridge History of Renaissance Philosophy (ed. jtly. and contrib.) 1987, Machiavelli: The Prince (ed. and introduction) 1988. *Address:* Christ's College, Cambridge, CB2 3BU, England.

SKLYAROV, Yuri Aleksandrovich; Soviet journalist; b. 1925; served in Soviet Army 1943-45; ed. Kharkov Univ.; mem. CPSU 1944–; sr. posts in Kharkov City and Dist. Cttee. of Ukrainian CP 1955-63; lecturer at Kharkov Univ. 1963-64; Asst. Prof. 1964; Sec. of Kharkov Dist. Cttee. 1964-69; Deputy Chief of Propaganda Dept. of Cen. Cttee. of CPSU 1969-76; First Deputy Ed.-in-Chief of Pravda 1976–; Cand. mem. Cen. Cttee. CPSU 1981-89. *Address:* Pravda, Ul. "Pravdy" 24, Moscow A-137, U.S.S.R.

SKOLIMOWSKI, Jerzy; Polish film director; b. 5 May 1938, Warsaw; m. Joanna Szczerbic; ed. Warsaw Univ. and State Superior Film School, Łódź; wrote scripts for Wajda's Innocent Sorcerers, Polanski's Knife in the Water and Łomnicki's Poślizg; dir., designer, author, ed., actor Rysopis 1964, author, dir., actor, Walkover 1965; author, dir., Barrier 1966; dir. Le Départ 1967; author, dir., actor Hands Up 1967; dir. Adventures of Gerard 1969; Grand Prix for Barrier Int. Film Festival, Bergamo 1966, Silver Palm for Scream, Cannes Film Festival 1978, British Film Award (for Moonlighting) 1982, Special Prize, Venice Film Festival 1985. *Films:* Rysopis (Identification Marks: None) 1964, Walkover 1965, Bariera (Barrier) 1966, Le Départ 1967, Ręce do góry (Hands Up) 1967, Dialogue 20-40-60 1968, Adventures of Gerard 1969, The Deep End 1971, King, Queen, Knave 1972, Lady Frankenstein (or Terminus) 1976, The Shout 1978, Moonlighting 1982, Success is the Best Revenge 1984, The Lightship 1985, Torrents of Spring 1988. *Publications:* Poetry: Gdzieś blisko siebie (Somewhere Close to Oneself), Play: Ktoś się utopił (Somebody Got Drowned). *Address:* c/o Film Polski, ul. Mazowiecka 6/8, 00-048 Warsaw, Poland.

SKOOG, Folke (Karl), PH.D.; American plant physiologist; b. 15 July 1908, Sweden; s. of Karl (G.) Skoog and Sigrid (Person) Skoog; m. Birgit Anna Lisa Bergner 1947; one d.; ed. California Inst. of Technology and Univ. of California; Instructor and Research Assoc., Harvard Univ. 1937-41; Asst. Prof., Assoc. Prof. of Biology, Johns Hopkins Univ. 1941-44; Tech. Rep. (Chemist), U.S. Army 1944-46; Assoc. Prof. of Botany, Univ. of Wis. 1947-49, Prof. of Botany 1949–; mem. American Soc. of Plant Physiologists (Vice-Pres. 1956-57, Pres. 1957-58), Botanical Soc. of America (Chair. Physiology Section 1954-55), N.A.S., American Acad. of Arts and Sciences, Soc. of Gen. Physiologists (Pres. 1957-58), Soc. of Devt. Biology (Pres. 1970-71), Int. Plant Growth Substances Asscn. (Vice-Pres. 1976-79, Pres. 1979-82), Royal Soc. of Sciences, Sweden, Royal Acad. of Sciences, Sweden, Akad. Leopoldina, Germany; mem. of editorial bd. Journal of Plant Growth Regulation 1982–, Plant Cell Reports 1981–, Archives of Biochem. and Biophysics 1980-85; Hon. Ph.D. (Lund, Sweden); Hon. D.Sc. (Univ. of Ill.) Stephen Hales Medal of American Soc. of Plant Physiologists 1955, Certificate of Merit of Botanical Soc. of America 1956, Reid Barnes Award, American Soc. of Plant Physiologists 1970. *Publications:* Plant Growth Substances (Editor) 1951 and 1980; author and co-author of many scientific articles on plant growth, auxins and cytokinins 1933-87. *Leisure interests:* farming, sport. *Address:* Institute of Plant Development, Birge Hall, University of Wisconsin, Madison, Wis. 53706 (Office); 2248 Branson Road, Oregon, Wis. 53575, U.S.A. (Home). *Telephone:* (608) 262-2790 (Office); (608) 835 3264 (Home).

SKOU, Jens Christian, M.D.; Danish professor of biophysics; b. 8 Oct. 1918, Lemvig; s. of Magnus Martinus Skou and Ane Margrethe Skou; m. Ellen Margrethe Nielsen 1947; two d.; ed. Univ. of Copenhagen; Asst. Prof. Inst. of Physiology, Univ. of Aarhus 1946, Assoc. Prof. 1954, Prof. and Chair. of Dept. 1963, Prof. of Biophysics 1978–; mem. Royal Danish Acad. of Sciences, Deutsche Akad. der Naturforscher, Leopoldina, European Molecular Biology Org.; Foreign Assoc. N.A.S. (U.S.A.); Hon. mem. Japanese Biochemical Soc.; Dr. medicinae h.c. (Copenhagen) 1986; Leo Prize 1959, Novo Prize 1964, Consul Carlsen Prize 1973, Anders Retzius Gold Medal 1977, Erik K. Fernström's Nordic Prize 1985. *Publications:* scientific papers on the mechanism of action of local anaesthetics 1946-57; scientific pubs. on structure and function of the Na, K-pump, the transport system in the cell membrane responsible for the exchange of cations across membranes 1957–. *Leisure interests:* classical music, yachting, skiing. *Address:* Rislundvej 9, Risskov, 8240, Denmark. *Telephone:* 06-177918.

SKOULARIKIS, Ioannis P.; Greek lawyer and politician; b. 1929, Smyla, Ileia Pref.; m. Koula Poulos; one s. one d.; ed. Athens Univ. Law School;

specialist in labour law; former Counsel, Supreme Court and State Council; Legal Counsel, Greek Gen. Confed. of Labour 1964-65; active in dissident politics from student days and helped set up several anti-regime orgs. including Panhellenic Liberation Movt. (PAK) during colonel's dictatorship; Minister of Public Order 1981-85, of Justice March 1989–. *Address:* Ministry of Justice, Odos Zinonos 12, Athens, Greece. *Telephone:* (01) 5225903.

SKRINSKY, Aleksandr Nikolayevich, D.SC.; Soviet physicist; b. 15 Jan. 1936, Orenburg; s. of Nikolay Alexandrovich Skrinsky and Galina Stepanovna Skrinskaya; m. Lydia Borisovna Golovanova; one s. one d.; ed. Moscow State Univ.; Research Worker, Inst. of Nuclear Physics, Siberian Dept., U.S.S.R. Acad. of Sciences Head of Laboratory 1959–, Dir. of Inst. 1977–; Prof. Novosibirsk Univ. 1967–; corresp. mem. U.S.S.R. Acad. of Sciences 1968-70, mem. 1970–; mem. Int. Cttee. for Future Accelerators (ICFA) 1983–, CERN Scientific Policy Cttee. 1985–; Lenin Prize 1967; Order of Red Banner and other decorations. *Publications:* more than 200 scientific works in the field of accelerator physics and technology, elementary particle physics. *Leisure interests:* ski-running, swimming. *Address:* Institute of Nuclear Physics, Siberian Department of the U.S.S.R. Academy of Sciences, 630090 Novosibirsk, U.S.S.R. *Telephone:* 35-60-31.

SKROWACZEWSKI, Stanisław; Polish conductor and composer; b. 3 Oct. 1923, Lwów (now Lvov, U.S.S.R.); s. of Paweł and Zofia (Karszniewicz) Skrowaczewski; m. Krystyna Jarosz 1956; two s. one d.; ed. Lwów Conservatoire and State Higher School of Music, Cracow; Conductor, Wrocław Philharmonic Orchestra 1946-47; further composition studies with Nadia Boulanger and P. Klecki, Paris 1947-49; Artistic Dir. and First Conductor, Silesian Philharmonic Orch., Katowice 1949-54; First Conductor, Cracow Philharmonic Orch. 1955-56; Dir. Nat. Philharmonic Orch., Warsaw 1957-59; Musical Dir. Minnesota Orchestra 1960-79; tours in Europe, N. and S. America, Israel; Prin. Conductor and Musical Adviser, Hallé Orchestra Sept. 1984–; Musical Adviser St. Paul Chamber Orchestra 1986–; D.H.L. h.c. (Hamline Univ., St. Paul, Minnesota) 1961; D.Mus. h.c. (Macalester Coll., St. Paul, Minn.) 1977; Dr. h.c. (Univ. of Minnesota) 1979; State Prize (3rd class) 1956, First Prize, Int. Conductor's Competition, Rome 1956, Conductor's Award of Columbia Univ., New York 1973, Third Prize, Kennedy Center Friedheim Award Competition (for Ricercari Notturni) 1978; Commdr. Cross of Order Polonia Restituta. *Compositions include:* Symphony for String Orchestra, three other symphonies, Muzyka Nocą (Music by Night, suite of nocturnes), four string quartets, two overtures, Cantique des Cantiques (voice and orch.), Prelude, Fugue, Post-Ludium (orch.), English Horn Concerto 1969, Ricercari Notturni (orchestral), Clarinet Concerto, Violin Concerto 1985, Concerto for Orchestra 1985, Fanfare for Orchestra 1987, Trio for piano, clarinet and bassoon; also music for opera, ballet, film and theatre. *Leisure interests:* alpinism, skiing, books, film, theatre. *Address:* 1111 Nicollett Mall, Minneapolis, Minn. 55403 (Office); P.O. Box 700, Wayzata, Minn. 55391, U.S.A. (Home).

SLABBERT, Frederik van Zyl, D.PHIL.; South African politician; b. 2 March 1940, Pretoria; m. 1st Mana Jordaan; one s. one d.; m. 2nd Jane Stephens 1984; ed. Pietersburg High School, Univs. of Witwatersrand and Stellenbosch; Lecturer in Sociology, Univ. of Stellenbosch 1964-68, Sr. Lecturer 1970-71; Sr. Lecturer and Acting Head, Dept. of Sociology, Rhodes Univ., Grahamstown 1969, Univ. of Cape Town 1972-73; Prof. and Head Dept. of Sociology, Univ. of Witwatersrand 1973-74; M.P. for Rondebosch 1974-86; Nat. Leader Progressive Fed. Party and Leader of the Opposition 1979-86; work with Inst. for Democratic Alternatives 1988–. *Publications:* South Africa's Options; Strategies for Sharing Power (with David Welsh) 1979, The Last White Parliament 1986 and various articles on S.A. politics. *Leisure interests:* squash, tennis, swimming. *Address:* P.O. Box 98, Wits 2050, South Africa. *Telephone:* (011) 6436641.

SLADE, Rt. Hon. Sir Christopher John; British judge; b. 2 June 1927, London; s. of late George Penkivil Slade, K.C., and Mary A. A. Slade; m. Jane G. A. Buckley 1958; one s. three d.; ed. Eton and New Coll., Oxford; called to bar 1951, Q.C. 1965; in practice at Chancery Bar 1951-75; Judge, High Court of Justice, Chancery Div. 1975-82; Judge of Restrictive Practices Court 1980-82, Pres. 1981-82; Lord Justice of Appeal 1982–; mem. Gen. Council of Bar 1958-62, 1965-69; mem. Senate of Four Inns of Court 1966-69; Bencher, Lincoln's Inn 1973; mem. Lord Chancellor's Legal Educ. Cttee. 1969-71. *Leisure interests:* multifarious. *Address:* Royal Courts of Justice, Strand, London, W.C.2, England.

SLADKEVIČIUS, H.E. Cardinal Vincentas; Soviet ecclesiastic; b. 20 Aug. 1920, Kaišiadorys; ordained 1944, elected bishop of Abora 1957, consecrated 1957; cr. Cardinal 1988; Apostolic Admin. Sanctae Sedis of Kaišiadorys. *Address:* R. Čarno 31, 234230 Kaišiadorys, Lietuva, Lithuanian S.S.R., U.S.S.R. *Telephone:* 51. 873.

SLANEY, Sir Geoffrey, K.B.E., M.SC., CH.M., F.R.C.S., F.R.A.C.S., F.C.S.S.L., F.A.C.S.; British professor of surgery; b. 19 Sept. 1922, West Hallam; s. of Richard and Gladys L. Slaney; m. Josephine M. Davy 1956; one s. two d.; ed. Univs. of Birmingham, London and Illinois; House Surgeon and Surgical Registrar, Gen. Hosp., Birmingham 1947-48; Capt. R.A.M.C. 1948-50; Surgical Registrar, Coventry, London and Hackney Hosps. 1950-53; Surgical Registrar, Lecturer in Surgery and Surgical Research Fellow, Queen Elizabeth Hosp., Birmingham 1953-59; Hunterian Prof. Royal Coll. of Surgeons 1961-62; Prof. of Surgery, Univ. of Birmingham 1966-87; Barling

Prof., Head Dept. of Surgery, Queen Elizabeth Hosp., Birmingham 1971–86; Pres. Royal Coll. of Surgeons of England 1982–86, James IV Asscn. Surgeons 1984–87, Int. Surgical Group 1985–86, Vascular Surgical Soc. 1974–75; Chair. Asscn. Profs. of Surgery 1979–81, Confed. of Royal Colls. and Faculties in the U.K. 1984–86; Hon. Consulting Surgeon Emer. City of London and Hackney Health Authority; Fellow, Asscn. of Surgeons of G.B. and Ireland, American Surgical Asscn.; Hon. F.R.C.S.I., F.R.A.C.S., F.C.S.S.L., F.A.C.S., F.R.C.S.C., F.C.S.S.A.; Jacksonian Prize and Medal (Royal Coll. of Surgeons) 1959, Pybus Memorial Medal 1978, Miles Memorial Medal 1984, Vanderbilt Univ. Medal 1987. *Publications:* metabolic derangements in gastrointestinal surgery (with B. N. Brooke) 1967; numerous contributions to medical and surgical journals. *Leisure interests:* family, fishing. *Address:* 23 Aston Bury, Edgbaston, Birmingham, B15 3QB, England. *Telephone:* 021-454 0261.

SLATER, Edward Charles, F.R.S., M.SC., PH.D., SC.D.; Australian emeritus professor of physiological chemistry; b. 16 Jan. 1917, Melbourne; s. of Edward Brunton Slater and Violet Podmore; m. Marion Winifred Hutley 1940; one d.; ed. Univs. of Melbourne and Cambridge, U.K.; Biochemist, Australian Inst. of Anatomy, Canberra 1939–46; Research Fellow, Molteno Inst., Cambridge Univ. 1946–55; Prof. of Physiological Chem., Dir. Lab. of Biochem., Univ. of Amsterdam, Netherlands 1955–85; Hon. Prof. Univ. of Southampton 1985–; mem. Royal Netherlands Acad. of Science and Letters, Hollandsche Maatschappij van Wetenschappen; Corresp. mem. Australian Acad. of Science; Hon. mem. American Soc. of Biological Chemists, Acad. Nacional de Ciencias Exactas, Fisicas y Naturales, Argentina, Japanese Biochem. Soc.; Foreign mem. Acad. Royale de Médecine, Belgium; Royal Swedish Acad. of Sciences; Kt. Order of the Netherlands Lion. *Publications:* about 450 contributions to learned journals. *Leisure interests:* yachting, skiing. *Address:* 9 Oaklands, Lymington, Hants., SO41 9TH. *Telephone:* (0703) 559000 (Office); (0590) 79455 (Home).

SLATER, Gordon James Augustus; British diplomatist (retd.); b. 8 July 1922; s. of William Augustus Slater and Edith Garden; m. 1st Beryl Oliver 1952 (divorced 1968), one s. one d.; m. 2nd Gina Lambert 1976 (dissolved 1988), one d.; ed. Sydney Australia; Commonwealth Relations Office 1958; First Sec. (Information), Karachi, Dacca 1958, Vancouver 1961, Kuala Lumpur 1964; First Sec. and Head of Information Section, Lagos 1967; FCO 1970; Consul and First Sec., Port Moresby 1973; seconded to Dept. of Industry 1975; Deputy Gov., Falkland Islands 1976; High Commr. in Solomon Islands 1978–82; Sec. to Gov. and Adviser to Foreign Affairs Dept., Tuvalu 1985–86. *Address:* 5 Ordak Avenue, Gymea, N.S.W. 2227, Australia.

SLATER, James Derrick, F.C.A.; British company director; b. 13 March 1929, Wirral, Cheshire; s. of Hubert and Jessie Slater; m. Helen Wyndham Goodwyn 1965; two s. two d.; ed. Preston Manor County School; Dir., A.E.C. Ltd. 1959; Deputy Sales Dir., Leyland Motor Corpn. 1963; acquired with associates, H. Lotery and Co., Ltd., which was then renamed Slater, Walker Securities Ltd., and appointed Chair. and Man. Dir. 1964–72, Chair., C.E.O. 1972–75. *Publications:* Return to Go (autobiog.) 1977, Goldenrod, Goldenrod and the Kidnappers, Grasshopper and the Unwise Owl, The Boy Who Saved Earth, A. Mazing Monsters, Grasshopper and the Pickle Factory 1979, Roger the Robot Series 1980 (children's books). *Leisure interests:* chess, backgammon, reading, bridge, salmon fishing. *Address:* Combe Court, Combe Lane, Chiddingfold, Surrey, England. (Home).

SLATER, Joseph Elliott; American administrator; b. 17 Aug. 1922, Salt Lake City, Utah; m.; two c.; ed. Univ. of California; Naval Reserve Officer, Mil. Govt. Planning Officer, Berlin, London and Paris 1943–46; U.S. Sec. of Econ. Directorate, Allied Control Comm. for Germany; Asst. U.S. Sec. of Allied Control Council Econ. and Financial Affairs 1945–48; mem. UN Affairs Planning Staff, Dept. of State, Washington 1949; Sec.-Gen. Allied High Comm. for Germany, Bonn 1949–52; Exec. Sec. Office of U.S. Special Rep. in Europe, U.S. Sec. to NATO and mem. U.S. Del. to OEEC 1952; Chief Economist, Creole Petroleum Corpn., Caracas 1954–57; Sec. to President's Comm. on Foreign Assistance 1959; Assoc. Dir., Int. Affairs Program, Program Officer (Office of Int. Relations), Ford Foundation 1957–67; Asst. Man. Dir. Devt. Loan Fund 1960–61, and Deputy Asst. Sec. of State for Educ. and Cultural Affairs 1961–62; Pres. Salk Inst. 1967–72; Pres. Aspen Inst. for Humanistic Studies 1969–86; Pres. Emer., Trustee, Sr. Fellow 1986–; Pres. Anderson Foundation 1969–72; Pres. Emer. Salk Inst.; Chair. John J. McCloy Int. Center 1986–; mem. Council on Foreign Relations, New York, UN Policy Studies Group, Dir. AMIDEAST, Centre for Public Resources; Trustee, Acad. for Educ. Devt., Int. Inst. for Environmental Affairs, American Council on Germany, Carnegie Hall, Eisenhower Exchange Fellowships, Trustee and Special Fellow, Salk Inst.; mem. of bd. Volvo N. America; Hon. LL.D. (Univ. of Denver, Colorado Coll., Kyung Hee Univ., Korea, Univ. of N.H.); Commander's Cross, German Order of Merit. *Address:* John J. McCloy International Centre, 680 5th Avenue, 9th Floor, New York, N.Y. 10019 (Office); 870 UN Plaza, New York, N.Y. 10017, U.S.A. (Home).

SLATKIN, Leonard; American conductor; s. of Felix Slatkin and Eleanor Aller; studied violin, piano, viola, composition, conducting; ed. Indiana Univ., Los Angeles City Coll., Juilliard School of Music; Founder, Music Dir. and Conductor St. Louis Symphony Youth Orchestra 1979–80, 1980–81; Guest Conductor, orchestras in most countries; Asst. Conductor Youth Symphony of New York, Carnegie Hall 1966, Juilliard Opera, Theatre and Dance Dept. 1967, St. Louis Symphony Orchestra 1968–71, Assoc. Conductor 1971–74, Assoc. Prin. Conductor 1979–; Prin. Guest Conductor Minn. Orchestra 1974–, summer artistic dir. 1979–80; Music Dir. New Orleans Philharmonic Symphony Orchestra 1977–78. *Address:* St. Louis Symphony Orchestra, Powell Symphony Hall, 718 N. Grand Blvd., Saint Louis, Mo. 63103, U.S.A.

SLATTERY, Rear-Admiral Sir Matthew Sausse, K.B.E., C.B., F.R.AE.S.; British naval officer (retd.) and company director; b. 12 May 1902, Chislehurst, Kent; s. of H. F. Slattery and Agnes Cuddon; m. Mica Mary Swain 1925; two s. one d.; ed. Stonyhurst Coll., and R.N. Colls. of Osborne and Dartmouth; joined R.N. 1916; Dir. of Air Material, Admiralty 1939–41; in command H.M.S. Cleopatra and Danae 1941–42; Dir.-Gen. Naval Aircraft Devt. and Production (Ministry of Aircraft Production) 1941, and Chief Naval Rep. 1943; Vice-Controller (Air) and Chief of Naval Air Equipment (Admiralty) and Chief Naval Rep. Supply Council (Ministry of Supply) 1945–48; retd. from R.N. with war service rank of Rear Adm. 1948; Man. Dir. Short Bros. & Harland Ltd. 1948–52, Chair. and Man. Dir. 1952–60; Chair. S.B. Realisations Ltd. 1952–60, Bristol Aircraft Ltd. 1957–60; Dir. Bristol Aeroplane Co. Ltd. 1957–60; Special Adviser to Prime Minister on Transport of Middle East Oil 1957–59; Chair. BOAC 1960–63, BOAC/Cunard 1962–63; Dir. (fmr. Chair.) R. & W. Hawthorn, Leslie & Co. Ltd. 1964–80; Hon. D.Sc.; Legion of Merit (U.S.A.). *Leisure interests:* living in the country, gardening. *Address:* Harvey's Farm, Warninglid, Sussex, England. *Telephone:* (044 485) 291.

SLICHTER, Charles Pence, B.A., M.A., PH.D.; American professor of physics; b. 21 Jan. 1924, Ithaca, N.Y.; s. of Sumner Huber Slichter and Ada Pence Slichter; m. 1st Gertrude Thayer Almy 1952 (divorced 1977), m. 2nd Anne FitzGerald 1980; five s. one d.; ed. Browne and Nichols School, Cambridge, Mass. and Harvard Univ.; Instructor, Univ. of Ill. 1949–51, Asst. Prof. of Physics 1951–54, Assoc. Prof. 1954–55, Prof. of Physics 1955–, mem. Center for Advanced Study, Univ. of Ill. 1968–, Prof. of Chemistry 1986–; Morris Loeb Lecturer, Harvard Univ. 1961; mem. President's Science Advisory Cttee. 1965–69, Cttee. on the Nat. Medal of Science 1969–74, President's Cttee. on Science and Tech. 1976; Alfred Sloan Fellow 1957–63; mem. Nat. Acad. of Sciences, American Acad. of Arts and Sciences, Corpn. of Harvard Univ., American Philosophical Soc., Nat. Science Bd. 1975–84; mem. Int. Soc. of Magnetic Resonance (ISMAR), Vice-Pres. 1983–86, Pres. 1987–(90); mem. Bd. of Dirs. Polaroid Corpn. 1975–; Langmuir Prize of American Physical Soc. 1969; ISMAR Award 1986. *Publications:* Principles of Magnetic Resonance 1963, 1978; articles on solid state physics, chemical physics and magnetic resonance. *Address:* Dept. of Physics, Univ. of Illinois at Urbana-Champaign, 1110 W. Green Street, Urbana, Ill. 61801 (Office); 61 Chestnut Court, Champaign, Ill. 61821, U.S.A. (Home). *Telephone:* (217) 333-3834 (Office); (217) 352-8255 (Home).

SLIM, Taieb; Tunisian politician and diplomatist; b. 19 Jan. 1919, Tunis; s. of Abed Slim and Habiba Beyram; m. Leyla Zaouche 1959; two d.; ed. Tunis Lycée and Univ. of Paris; mem. Néo-Destour Party, detained 1941–43; Arab Maghreb Bureau, Cairo 1946–49; Head, Tunisian Office, Cairo 1949, established Tunisian offices, New Delhi, Jakarta, Karachi; Head, Foreign Affairs, Presidency of Council of Ministers 1955–56; Amb. to U.K. 1956–62, also accred. to Denmark, Norway and Sweden 1960–62; Perm. Rep. to UN 1962–67, concurrently Amb. to Canada; Sec. of State, Personal Rep. of Pres. 1967–70; mem. Nat. Ass. 1969; Amb. to Morocco 1970–71; Minister of State 1971–73; mem. Political Bureau Destour Socialist Party 1970–74; Amb. and Perm. Rep. to UN, Geneva 1973–74; Amb. to Canada 1974–76; Minister of State 1976–77; Perm. Rep to UN 1981–84. *Leisure interest:* sailing. *Address:* c/o Ministry of Foreign Affairs, Tunis, Tunisia.

ŚLIWIŃSKI, Marian, M.D.; Polish physician and politician; b. 2 Feb. 1932, Strzelce Wielkie; ed. Medical Acad., Łódź; mem. of PZPR (Polish United Workers Party) 1948–; fmr. mem. of youth orgs.; Asst. Physiological Inst. Med. Acad., Łódź 1952–55; Asst., later lecturer II Surgical Clinic, Medical Acad. Łódź 1955–65; Dir. Clinical Hosp., Łódź 1960–64; doctorate 1963; Asst. Prof. 1965; Deputy mem. Cen. Cttee. PZPR 1971–80, mem. 1980–81; Dir. Educ. and Scientific Dept., Ministry of Health and Social Welfare 1964–70, Vice-Minister 1970–72, Minister 1972–80; Head of Cardio-Surgical Clinic, Inst. of Cardiology, Warsaw 1980–; Nat. Cardiosurgery Expert 1987–; Pres. Polish Cardiosurgeons' Club 1985–; scientific prize of Łódź City; mem. of nat. and int. medical socs.; several Polish decorations, including Commdr.'s and Knight's Crosses of Order of Polonia Restituta, Hon. Meritous Physician of People's Poland 1979. *Publications:* numerous papers on surgery of the thorax and cardiosurgery. *Address:* c/o Instytut Kardiologii, Alpejska 42, 04-628 Warsaw (Office); Polna 24 m. 7, 00-630 Warsaw, Poland (Home). *Telephone:* 15 36 07 (Office); 25 70 76 (Home).

SLOMAN, Sir Albert Edward, Kt., C.B.E., M.A., D.PHIL.; British university administrator; b. 14 Feb. 1921, Launceston, Cornwall; s. of Albert Sloman and L. F. Brewer; m. Marie B. Bergeron 1948; three d.; ed. Launceston Coll. and Wadham Coll., Oxford; lecturer, Univ. of Calif. (Berkeley) 1946–47; Reader in Spanish, Univ. of Dublin 1947–53; Fellow, Trinity Coll., Dublin 1950–53; Prof. of Spanish, Univ. of Liverpool 1953–62; Vice-Chancellor, Univ. of Essex 1962–87; Pres. Conf. of European Rectors and Vice-Chancellors 1969–74; Vice-Pres. Int. Asscn. of Univs. 1970–75; Chair. Cttee.

of Vice-Chancellors and Principals 1981–83; Chair. Bd. of Govs. Centre for Information on Language Teaching and Research 1979–86; Chair. British Acad. Studentship Selection Cttee. (Humanities) 1965–87, Overseas Research Students Fees Support Scheme 1980–87, Univs. Council for Adult and Continuing Educ. 1984–, Selection Cttee. Commonwealth Scholarships Comm. 1985–; Chair. Int. Bd. United World Colls. 1988–; Vice-Chair. Council of Asscn. of Commonwealth Univs. 1984–; mem. Econ. and Social Cttee. EEC 1973–82; mem. Cttee. for Int. Co-operation in Higher Educ. 1981– (Chair. 1985–); mem. Cttee. of Man., British Inst. in Paris 1982–; mem. Bd. of Govs. Univ. of Guyana 1966–. *Publications:* The Sources of Calderón's El Príncipe Constante 1950, The Dramatic Craftsmanship of Calderón 1958, Calderón, La Vida Es Sueño (Editor) 1960, Bulletin of Hispanic Studies (Editor) 1953–62, A University in the Making 1964. *Leisure interest:* travel. *Address:* 19 Inglis Road, Colchester, Essex, C03 3HU, England.

SLONIMSKI, Piotr, D.SC., M.D.; French biologist; b. 9 Nov. 1922, Warsaw; s. of Piotr Slonimski; m. Hanna Kulagowska 1951; one d.; ed. Lycée Stephane Batory, underground Univ. of Warsaw, Jagellonian Univ. of Cracow and Faculté des Sciences, Paris; Polish underground army 1939–45; Asst. Univ. of Cracow 1945–47; Attaché, CNRS 1947, Chargé 1952, Maître 1956, Dir. 1962; Prof. of Genetics, Faculté des Sciences and Univ. P. et M. Curie 1965–; Dir. Centre de Génétique Moléculaire, CNRS 1971–; Visiting Prof. Univs. of Calif. and Chicago; mem. Acad. des Sciences (Inst. de France), Bavarian, Polish and Belgian Acads. etc.; Chevalier, Légion d'Honneur, Mil. Cross (Poland), CNRS Gold Medal 1985, Hansen Gold Medal 1987 and other awards. *Publications:* scientific publs. on cellular respiration, genetics and biogenesis of mitochondria, structure and function of genes. *Leisure interest:* mushroom hunting. *Address:* Centre de Génétique Moléculaire du CNRS, avenue de la Terrasse, 91198 Gif-sur-Yvette Cedex; Institut de France, 23 Quai Conti, 75006 Paris, France. *Telephone:* 1 69 82 32 08.

SLONIMSKY, Nicolas; American musician and author; b. 27 April 1894, St. Petersburg, Russia; s. of Leonid Slonimsky and Faina Slonimsky; m. Dorothy Adlow 1931; one d.; ed. St. Petersburg Conservatory of Music; Conductor, Pierian Sodality, Harvard Univ. 1928–30; Instr. Eastman School of Music, New York 1923–25; Boston Conservatory of Music 1925–45; Instr. Slavic Languages and Literature, Harvard Univ. 1946–47; Lecturer in Music, Peabody Conservatory 1956–57; Univ. of Calif. Los Angeles 1964–67, Regents Lecturer 1985; Guest Conductor, Paris, Berlin, Budapest, Havana, San Francisco, Hollywood 1931–33; Hon. D.F.A. (Northwestern) 1980. *Musical compositions:* Studies in Black and White (piano) 1928, My Toy Balloon (orchestra) 1945, Suite for Cello and Piano 1950; songs. *Publications:* Music Since 1900, Music of Latin America, Lexicon of Musical Invective, Baker's Biographical Dictionary of Musicians, Perfect Pitch: A Life Story 1988. *Leisure interests:* chess, mathematics, languages, travel. *Address:* 2630 Midvale Avenue, Los Angeles, Calif. 90064, U.S.A. *Telephone:* (213) 474-0117.

SLONIMSKY, Sergey Mikhailovich; Soviet composer, pianist and musicologist; b. 12 Aug. 1932, Leningrad; s. of Mikhail Slonimsky and Olga Kaplan; m. Raisa Zankisova; one d.;ed. Leningrad Conservatoire; Teacher of composition at Leningrad Conservatoire 1958–; works include Virineya (opera) 1967, The Master and Margarita 1970–72, Icarus (ballet) 1975, Mary Stuart (opera) 1980 and nine symphonies. *Leisure interest:* telling funny stories. *Address:* Leningrad Conservatoire of Music, Teatralnaya ploshchad, Leningrad; 9 Kanal Griboedova, Kv. 97, Leningrad, U.S.S.R.

ŚLOPEK, Stefan, M.D.; Polish microbiologist and immunologist; b. 1 Dec. 1914, Skawa, near Cracow; s. of Stanisław and Kunegunda Ślopek; m. 1st Kazimiera Dobrowolska 1942; one s. one d.; m. 2nd Lucyna Karasiewicz 1974; ed. Medical Faculty, Lvov Univ.; Doctor Jagiellonian Univ. 1945–48, Docent 1948, Assoc. Prof. 1948–50, Extraordinary Prof. 1950–57, Prof. 1957–; Dir. Inst. of Immunology and Experimental Therapy, Polish Acad. of Sciences (PAN), Wrocław 1954–85, Corresp. mem. PAN 1965–73, mem. 1973–, mem. Presidium 1972–80, 1984–, Chair. Cttee. of Immunology 1972–78, Microbiology 1966–72; Prof. of Medical Microbiology, Medical Acad., Wrocław 1954–73; Hon. mem. Polish Soc. of Microbiologists 1975–, Polish Immunological Soc. 1977–; Pres. Polish Immunological Soc. 1969–72, Dr. h.c. Silesian, Wrocław and Poznań Medical Acads.; State Prize, 2nd Class 1952, 1st Class 1970, Knight's and Officer's Crosses and Commdr. Cross with Star, Order of Polonia Restituta, Order of Banner of Labour, 1st Class 1969, The Armed Forces in the Service of the Fatherland Gold Medal 1971, Copernicus Medal of Polish Acad. of Sciences 1979. *Publications:* Immunologia 1963, Schorzenia ropne skóry (Suppurant Diseases of the Skin) (co-author) 1967, Mikrobiologia lekarska. Podręcznik dla studentów Akademii Medycznych (Medical Microbiology. Handbook for Medical Acad. Students) (five edns.), Mikrobiologia kliniczna (Clinical Microbiology) 1974; Ed. Archivum Immunologiae et Therapiae Experimentalis 1956–, Immunologia praktyczna (Practical Immunology) 1970, Słownik Immunologiczny (Illustrated Immunological Dictionary) 1977, 2nd ed. 1983; numerous articles in Polish and foreign languages. *Address:* Pl. Muzealny 5 m.1, 50-035 Wrocław, Poland. *Telephone:* 352 39.

SLYNN, Sir Gordon, Kt., M.A., LL.B.; British lawyer; b. 17 Feb. 1930; s. of late John and Edith Slynn; m. Odile M. H. Boutin 1962; ed. Sandbach School, Goldsmith's Coll. and Trinity Coll., Cambridge; called to bar, Gray's

Inn 1956, Bencher 1970, Vice-Treas. 1987, Treas. 1988; Q.C. 1974; Lecturer in Air Law, London School of Econs. 1958–61; Junior Counsel, Ministry of Labour 1967–68, Treasury (Common Law) 1968–74; Leading Counsel to Treasury 1974–76; Recorder of Hereford 1971, a Recorder and Hon. Recorder 1972–76; Judge, High Court of Justice, Queen's Bench Div. 1976–81; Pres. Employment Appeal Tribunal 1978–81; Chief Steward of Hereford 1978–; Advocate-Gen., Court of Justice of the European Communities 1981–88, Judge 1988–; Visiting Prof. in Law, Univ. of Durham 1981–88, Cornell 1983 (Irvine Lecturer 1984, Kings Coll., London 1988–); Hon. Vice-Pres. Union Int. des Avocats 1976–;Vice-Chair. Exec. Council Int. Law Asscn. 1986–88, Chair. 1988–; Treasurer Gray's Inn 1988; hon. mem. Canadian Bar Asscn., Georgia Trial Lawyers' Asscn., Fla. Defense Lawyers Asscn., Indian Soc. of Int. Law, Fellow Int. Soc. of Barristers (U.S.A.); Hon. Fellow, Univ. Coll. at Buckingham 1981; Hon. LL.D. (Birmingham) 1983, (Buckingham) 1983, (Exeter) 1985; Hon. D.Jur (Mercer) 1986. *Publications:* contributions to Halsbury's Laws of England and Atkins' Court Forms. *Address:* Court of Justice of the European Communities, Kirchberg, L-2925, Luxembourg. *Telephone:* 4303-1.

SLYUNKOV, Nikolay Nikitovich; Soviet official; b. 1929, Garadzets, Gomel Dist., Byelorussia; ed. Byelorussian Inst. of Mechanisation of Agric.; mem. CPSU 1954–; various posts, including Deputy Chair. and Chair. of the Minsk Tractor Plant 1950–60; Dir. of Minsk Spare Parts Plant 1960–65; Dir. of Minsk Tractor Plant 1965–72; mem. Cen. Cttee. of Byelorussian CP 1966–76; First Sec. Minsk City Cttee. of Byelorussian CP 1972–74; Deputy Chair. of U.S.S.R. State Planning Cttee. (GOSPLAN) 1974–83; First Sec. and mem. of Politburo of Cen. Cttee. of Byelorussian CP 1983–; Cand. mem. Politburo CPSU 1986–87, mem. June 1987–; Sec. Cen. Cttee. CPSU 1987; Head Socio-Econ. Comm. 1988–; elected to Congress of People's Deputies of the U.S.S.R. March 1989. *Address:* Central Committee of Byelorussian Communist Party, Minsk, Byelorussian S.S.R., U.S.S.R.

SMALE, John G., B.S.; American business executive; b. 1 Aug. 1927, Listowel, Ont., Canada; s. of Vera G. and Peter J. Smale; m. Phyllis Anne Weaver 1950; two s. two d.; ed. Miami Univ. (Ohio); worked for Vick Chemical Co., New York 1949–50; with Bio-Research Inc., New York 1950–52; with Procter and Gamble Co. 1952–, Dir. 1972–, Pres. 1974–86, C.E.O. 1981–, Chair. 1986–; Hon. LL.D. (Kenyon Coll.) 1974, Hon. LL.D. (Miami Univ.) 1979, Hon. D.Sc. (DePauw Univ.) 1983, Hon. D.Iur (St. Augustine's Coll.) 1985. *Address:* The Procter and Gamble Company, 1 Procter and Gamble Plaza, Cincinnati, Ohio 45202, U.S.A. *Telephone:* (513) 983-1100.

SMALE, Stephen, M.S., PH.D.; American professor of mathematics; b. 15 July 1930, Michigan; s. of Lawrence and Helen Smale; m. Clara Davis 1955; two c.; ed. Univ. of Mich.; Prof., Columbia Univ. 1961–64; Prof., Univ. of Calif., Berkeley 1964–; mem. N.A.S.; Veblen Prize; Field Medal, Int. Union of Mathematicians. *Publications:* Differential Equations, Dynamical Systems and Linear Algebra (with M. Hirsch) 1974, various articles on topology and global analysis. *Leisure interests:* mineral collecting, skin diving. *Address:* Department of Mathematics, University of California, Berkeley, Calif. 94720 (Office); 68 Highgate Road, Berkeley, Calif., U.S.A. (Home). *Telephone:* 642-4367 (Office).

SMALL, Charles John, B.A., B.S.A.; Canadian economist; b. 19 Dec. 1919, Chengdu, Sichuan, China; s. of Rev. and Mrs. Walter Small; m. Jean McNeel 1946; four d.; ed. Ontario Agricultural Coll. and Univ. of Toronto; Royal Canadian Navy serving in North Atlantic, Mediterranean, Normandy and Australia 1941–46; mem. Dept. of Trade and Commerce 1949, serving in The Hague 1950–55; Dept. of External Affairs 1955–84; studied Chinese language at Univ. of Toronto 1956–57, seconded to Dept. of Trade and Commerce and apptd. Canadian Govt. Trade Commr., Hong Kong 1958–61, Ottawa 1961–63; Counsellor, Karachi 1963–65; Perm. Rep. to OECD, concurrently observer to Council of Europe 1965–69; Amb. to Pakistan 1969–72, concurrently to Afghanistan; Amb. to People's Repub. of China 1972–76, concurrently to Democratic Repub. of Viet-Nam 1975–76; Canadian Del. to 2nd Cttee., UN Gen. Ass. 32nd session 1977, Deputy Sec.-Gen. (Econ.) of Commonwealth Secr. 1978–83, Canadian High Commr. in Malaysia and Brunei 1983–84; Admin., Code of Conduct Concerning the Employment Practices of Canadian Cos. Operating in S. Africa 1986–89; Devt. Consultant; LL.D. h.c. (Univ. of Guelph) 1975. *Publication:* Code of Conduct: Canadian Companies in South Africa 1986. *Leisure interests:* tennis, golf, swimming, sinology. *Address:* 34 Arundel Avenue, Ottawa, Ont., K1K 0B6, Canada.

SMALL, William Jack, M.A.; American broadcasting company executive; b. 20 Sept. 1926, Chicago; s. of Louis and Libby (Mell) Small; m. Gish Rubin 1947; two d.; ed. Univ. of Chicago; served with U.S. Army 1944–45; News Dir. Station WLS, Chicago 1951–56, dir. Station WHAS-AM and T.V., Louisville 1956–62; Dir. of News and Washington Bureau Chief CBS 1962–74; Sr. Vice-Pres. CBS News, New York 1974–78, Vice-Pres. CBS, Inc., Washington 1978–79; Pres. NBC News, New York 1979–82, UPI 1982–84; Felix Larkin Prof. of Communications, Fordham Univ. 1986–, Dir. Center for Communications 1986–; mem. Radio-TV News Dirs. Assn. (fmr. Pres.), Nat. Assn. Broadcasters (Exec. Bd.), Nat. Journalism Center (Dir.); Paul White Award (Radio T.V. News Dirs. Assn.) 1974, James Madison Award (Nat. Broadcast Editorial Assn.) 1983. *Publications:* To Kill a Messenger: Television and the Real World 1970, Political Power and the Press 1972. *Address:* Graduate School of Business Administration, Fordham University, Lincoln Center, New York, N.Y. 10023, U.S.A.

SMALLMAN, Barry Granger, C.M.G., C.V.O., M.A.; British diplomatist and consultant (retd.); b. 22 Feb. 1924, Ealing; s. of the late C. Stanley Smallman and Ruby M. Granger; m. Sheila M. Knight 1952; two s. one d.; ed. St. Paul's School, London, and Trinity Coll., Cambridge; entered Colonial Office 1947; Asst. Private Sec. to Sec. of State 1951–52; attached to U.K. del. to UN, New York, 1956–57, 1958, 1961, 1962; seconded to Govt. of W. Nigeria as Senior Asst. Sec., Gov.'s Office 1959–60; transferred to Commonwealth Relations Office 1961; Deputy High Commr. in Sierra Leone 1963–64, in N.Z. 1964–67; Imperial Defence Coll. 1968; Counsellor and Consul Gen., Bangkok 1971–74; High Commr. in Bangladesh 1975–78; resident diplomatic service chair. Civil Service Selection Bd. 1978–81; High Commr. in Jamaica (also Amb. to Haiti) 1982–84; Propr. Granger Consultancies; Chair. of Council Benenden School 1986–; mem. of Council St. Lawrence Coll. 1984–, Leprosy Mission 1984–, SPCK 1984–. *Leisure interests:* reading, music, tennis, golf, bird watching. *Address:* Beacon Shaw, Benenden, Kent, England (Home). *Telephone:* (0580) 240625 (Home).

SMALLMAN, Raymond Edward, PH.D., D.SC., F.R.S.; British professor of metallurgy and materials science; b. 4 Aug. 1929, Wolverhampton; s. of David Smallman and Edith French; m. Joan D. Faulkner 1952; one s. one d.; ed. Rugeley Grammar School and Univ. of Birmingham; Sr. Scientific Officer, A.E.R.E. Harwell 1953–58; Lecturer, Dept. of Physical Metallurgy, Univ. of Birmingham 1958–63, Sr. Lecturer 1963–64, Prof. of Physical Metallurgy 1964–69, Head, Dept. of Physical Metallurgy and Science of Materials 1969–81, Head, Dept. of Metallurgy and Materials 1981–, Deputy Dean, Faculty of Science and Eng. 1981–84, Dean 1984–85, Dean of Eng. 1985–87, Vice-Prin. Univ. of Birmingham 1987–; Sir George Beilby Gold Medal, Inst. of Metals and Chem Soc. 1969; Rosenhain Medal Inst. of Metals 1972; Elegant Work Prize, Metals Soc. 1979. *Publications:* Modern Physical Metallurgy 1962, Modern Metallurgy (jtly.) 1968, Structure of Metals and Alloys (jtly.) 1969, Defect Analysis in Electron Microscopy (jtly.) 1975. *Leisure interests:* writing, travel, painting, friendly golf, bridge. *Address:* Department of Metallurgy and Materials, University of Birmingham, P.O. Box 363, Birmingham, B15 2TT (Office); 59 Woodthorne Road South, Tettenhall, Wolverhampton, WV6 8SN, England (Home). *Telephone:* 021-472 1301 Ext. 3235 (Office); (0902) 752545 (Home).

SMALLPEICE, Sir Basil, K.C.V.O., F.C.A., B.COM.; British businessman; b. 18 Sept. 1906, Rio de Janeiro, Brazil; s. of Herbert Charles Smallpeice and Georgina Ruth (née Rust); m. 1st Kathleen Ivey Singleton Brame 1931 (died 1973); m. 2nd Rita Barbara Mary Burns 1973; with Bullimore and Co., chartered accountants 1925–30; Accountant, Hoover Ltd. 1930–37; Chief Accountant and Sec. Doulton & Co. 1937–48; Dir. of Costs and Statistics, British Transport Comm. 1948–50; Financial Comptroller, BOAC 1950–56, mem. Bd. 1953–63, Deputy Chief Exec. 1954–56, Man. Dir. 1956–63; Man. Dir. BOAC-Cunard Ltd. 1962–63; Dir. Cunard Steamship Co. 1964–71, Chair. 1965–71; Chair. Assoc. Container Transportation (Australia) 1971–79, ACT (Australia)/Australian Nat. Line Co-ordinating Bd. 1969–79; Admin. Adviser, Queen's Household 1964–80; mem. Cttee. for Exports to U.S.A. 1964–66; Dir. Charterhouse Group 1965–69; Chair. English-Speaking Union of the Commonwealth 1965–68; Chair. B.I.M. 1970–72, Vice-Pres. 1972–; Dir. Barclays Bank, London Local Bd. (fmr. Martins Bank) 1966–74; Deputy Chair. Lonrho Ltd. 1972–73; Pres. Inst. of Freight Forwarders 1977–78. *Publication:* Of Comets and Queens 1981. *Leisure interests:* golf, gardening. *Address:* Bridge House, Leigh Hill Road, Cobham, Surrey, England (Home).

SMART, (Alexander Basil) Peter; British diplomatist; b. 19 Feb. 1932, Durham; s. of Henry P. Smart and Mary G. Todd; m. Joan M. Cumming 1955; three s.; ed. Ryhope Grammar School, Durham; mem. H. M. Diplomatic Service; served Douala 1956, Cyprus 1956, Seoul 1959, Rangoon 1968; Head of Communications, Tech. Services Dept. FCO 1975; Deputy High Commr., Canberra 1978; Head of Chancery, Prague 1983; High Commr. to the Seychelles 1986–. *Leisure interest:* enjoying the excellent in any sphere. *Address:* c/o Foreign and Commonwealth Office (Victoria, Seychelles), King Charles Street, London, SW1A 2AH, England.

SMART, John Jamieson Carswell, M.A., B.PHIL., F.A.H.A.; Australian professor of philosophy; b. 16 Sept. 1920, Cambridge, England; s. of William M. Smart and Isabel M. Carswell; m. 1st Janet Paine 1956 (died 1967), 2nd Elizabeth Warner 1968; one s. one d.; ed. King's Coll. Choir School, Cambridge, The Leys School, Cambridge, Univ. of Glasgow and Queen's Coll. Oxford; Lieut. Royal Signals 1940–45; Jr. Research Fellow, Corpus Christi Coll. Oxford 1948–50; Hughes Prof. of Philosophy, Univ. of Adelaide 1950–72, Prof. Emer. 1972–; Reader in Philosophy, La Trobe Univ. 1972–76; Prof. of Philosophy, Research School of Social Sciences, A.N.U. 1976–85, Prof. Emer. 1986–; Fellow, Center for Advanced Study in the Behavioral Sciences, Stanford 1979; Visiting Prof. Princeton 1957, Harvard 1963, Yale 1964, Stanford 1982; G.D. Young lecturer, Univ. of Adelaide 1987; Hon. D.Litt. (St. Andrews) 1983. *Publications:* An Outline of a System of Utilitarian Ethics 1961, Philosophy and Scientific Realism 1963, Between Science and Philosophy 1968, Ethics, Persuasion and Truth 1984, Essays Metaphysical and Moral 1987. *Leisure interest:* walking. *Address:* 74 Mackenzie Street, Hackett, A.C.T. 2602, Australia. *Telephone:* (062) 488171.

SMART, Louis Edwin, A.B., J.D.; American lawyer and business executive; b. 17 Nov. 1923, Columbus, Ohio; s. of Louis Edwin and Esther (née Guthery) Smart; m. 1st Virginia Alice Knouff 1944 (divorced 1958), one s. one d.; m. 2nd Jeanie Alberta Milone 1964, one s.; ed. Harvard Coll., Harvard Law School; admitted to N.Y. State Bar 1950; Assoc. Hughes, Hubbard and Ewing, New York 1949–56; Partner, Hughes, Hubbard and Reed, New York 1957–64; Pres. Bendix Int., Dir. Bendix Corpn. and foreign subsidiaries 1964–67; Sr. Vice-Pres. Trans World Airlines Inc. 1967–71, Corpn. Affairs 1971–75, Vice-Chair. 1976, Chair. of Bd. and C.E.O. 1977–80, Chair. 1979–85; Chair., C.E.O., Trans World Corpn. (now TW Services Inc.) 1977–78, Chair. of Bd. 1979–85, Chair. of Bd. and C.E.O. 1978–85, Chair. Exec. Cttee. 1987–; Dir. Hilton Int. Co. 1967– (Exec. Officer 1968–73, Chair. 1978–86, Chair. Exec. Cttee. 1986–), SONAT Inc., ACF Industries Inc., Canteen Corpn. (now Chair.), Continental Corpn., Century 21 Real Estate, Spartan Food Systems 1979– (now Chair.); mem. American Bar Asscn., New York County Lawyers' Asscn.; Trustee Cttee. for Econ. Devt. 1977–, Conf. Bd. 1977–; U.S.N.R. 1943–46. *Address:* TW Services Inc., 605 Third Avenue, New York, N.Y. 10158 (Office); 535 East 86th Street, New York, N.Y. 10028, U.S.A.; Coakley Bay, Christiansted, St. Croix, U.S. Virgin Islands 00820.

SMART, (Roderick) Ninian, M.A., B.PHIL.; British professor of religious studies; b. 6 May 1927, Cambridge; s. of William Marshall Smart and Isabel Macquarrie Carswell; m. Libushka Bariffaldi 1954; two s. two d.; ed. Glasgow Acad. and Oxford Univ.; army service, Intelligence Corps. 1945–48, rank of Capt. 1947; Lecturer in Philosophy Univ. Coll., Wales 1952–56, in History and Philosophy of Religion King's Coll., London 1956–61; H.G. Wood Prof. of Theology Birmingham Univ. 1961–67; founding Prof. of Religious Studies Lancaster Univ. 1967–82, Hon. Prof. 1982–; Prof. of Religious Studies Univ. of Calif., Santa Barbara 1976–, J.F. Rowny Prof. of Religious Studies 1988–; editorial consultant BBC TV series The Long Search 1974–77; Visiting Lecturer Yale Univ. 1955–56, Banaras Hindu Univ. 1960; Visiting Prof. in Philosophy and History, Univ. of Wis. 1965, of Religious Studies, Princeton Univ. 1971, Univ. of Otago 1971, Univ. of Qd. 1980, 1985, Univ. of Cape Town 1982, Harvard Univ. 1983; Gifford Lecturer Edin. Univ. 1979–80; Hon. D.H.L. (Loyola Chicago) 1968, Hon. D.Litt. (Glasgow) 1984, Hon. D. Univ. (Stirling) 1986. *Publications:* Reasons and Faiths 1958, Doctrine and Argument in Indian Philosophy 1964, Philosophers and Religious Truth 1964, The Philosophy of Religion 1968, The Religious Experience of Mankind 1969, The Phenomenon of Religion 1973, The Science of Religion and the Sociology of Knowledge 1974, Beyond Ideology 1981, Concept and Empathy 1986, Religion and the Western Mind 1987, World Religions 1989. *Leisure interests:* painting, poetry, cricket and tennis. *Address:* Department of Religious Studies, Univ. of California at Santa Barbara, Calif. 93106, U.S.A.; Religious Studies, University of Lancaster, LA1 4YG, England. *Telephone:* (0524) 65201.

SMART, Stephen Bruce, Jr., A.B., S.M.; American government official and fmr. business executive; b. 7 Feb. 1923, New York; s. of Stephen Bruce Smart and Beatrice Cobb; m. Edith Minturn Merrill 1949; one s. three d.; ed. Harvard Coll., and Mass. Inst. of Tech.; U.S. Army 1943–46, 1951–53; Sales Engineer, Permutit Co., New York 1947–51; joined Continental Group (fmrly. Continental Can Co.) 1951, various sales and gen. man. posts 1951–62, Vice-Pres. Cen. Div. 1962–65, Marketing and Corpn. Planning 1965–68, Exec. Vice-Pres. Paper Operations 1969–73, Vice-Chair. 1973–75, Pres. and C.O.O. 1975–81; Chair. and C.E.O. Continental Group 1981–85; Under-Sec. for Int. Trade U.S. Dept. of Commerce 1985–; Dir. several cos.; Vice-Chair. Bd. and Trustee Smith Coll. *Address:* U.S. Commerce Department, Room 3850, 15th and Constitution Avenue, N.W., Washington, D.C. 20230 (Office); 4375 Congress Street, Fairfield, Conn. 06430, U.S.A. (Home).

SMEDLEY, Geoffrey; British sculptor and professor of fine art; b. 24 Feb. 1927, London; s. of Clifford Lawson Smedley and Dorothy Louise Smedley; m. 1st Sylvia Collett 1948 (divorced 1979), 2nd Brigid Simpson 1979; one s. one d.; ed. Wilson's Grammar School, Camberwell School of Art and Slade School of Fine Art; army service 1945–48; Head of Sculpture, Portsmouth Polytechnic 1964; Prof. of Sculpture Univ. of B.C., Vancouver 1978–; one-man exhibits. at Artist Int. Asscn., London 1965, St. Pauls School Gallery, London 1969, Vancouver Art Gallery 1982; sculptures include: Flange with hollow spaces 1965, Evidence of the Manifold 1966, Rotation and Reflection 1966, Proposition 1972, Concerning Canto 1976, White Pleasure 1983. *Publication:* Gambier Island, Gibson, B.C. 1986. *Leisure interests:* reading mathematics, history of philosophy. *Address:* route 3, Gambier Island, Gibsons, B.C., Canada. *Telephone:* (604) 886-9469.

SMEDLEY, Sir Harold, K.C.M.G., M.B.E.; British diplomatist (retd.); b. 19 June 1920, Hove, Sussex; s. of late Ralph Davies Smedley, M.D.; m. Beryl Harley Brown 1950; two s. two d.; ed. Aldenham School and Pembroke Coll., Cambridge; Royal Marine Commandos, Second World War; Dominions Office 1946, British High Comm. in New Zealand 1948–50, S. Rhodesia 1951–53, India 1957–60; Pvt. Sec. to Commonwealth Sec. 1954–57; High Commr. in Ghana 1964–65 and 1966–67; Amb. to Laos 1967–70; Asst. Under-Sec. of State, FCO 1970–72; Sec.-Gen. Comm. on Rhodesian Opinion 1971–72; High Commr. in Sri Lanka and Amb. (non-resident) to the Repub. of Maldives 1973–75, High Commr. in New Zealand 1976–80, concurrently to Western Samoa 1977–80, and fmr. Gov. of Pitcairn Islands; Chair. Bank of New Zealand London Bd. 1983–; Vice-Chair. Victoria League for Commonwealth Friendship, London 1981–; Pres. Hakluyt Soc. 1987–. *Leisure interest:* gardening. *Address:* 11a Beehive Lane, Ferring, West Sussex, BN12 5NN, England. *Telephone:* Worthing 506302.

SMEDT, Rt. Rev. Bishop Aemilius Josephus de, D.PHIL., D.THEOL.; Belgian ecclesiastic; b. 30 Oct. 1909, Opwijk; ed. Univ. Gregorianum, Rome; Auxiliary Bishop, Malines 1950; Bishop of Bruges 1952–85; mem. Secr. for Christian Unity, Rome; Kt. Order of Leopold. *Publications:* Le mariage, Le grand Mystère, Le Christ dans le quartier, Le sacerdoce des fidèles, L'amour conjugal, Pour un dialogue "Parents-Adolescents", Pour un climat de Liberté, Il les fit Homme et Femme, Orientations éthiques pour une éducation sexuelle, Rencontrer. *Address:* c/o 4 H. Geeststraat, 8000 Bruges, Belgium. *Telephone:* 050-335906.

SMETS, Georges Joseph G. R., PH.D.; Belgian professor of chemistry; b. 11 Aug. 1915, Louvain; s. of Guillaume Smets and Marguerite van Marsenille; m. Elisabeth Maria A. Stas 1941; one s. four d.; ed. Catholic Univ. of Louvain; Research Fellow, Nat. Research Council 1940–42; Officer for Research and Devt., Gevaert NV 1942–44; Assoc. Prof. Catholic Univ. of Louvain 1944–48, Prof. 1948–84, Prof. Emer. 1984–, Dean of Faculty of Sciences 1970–73; Exchange Prof., U.K. 1956, France 1959, 1961, U.S.S.R. 1964, 1978, Poland 1967, 1975, Japan 1972, Visiting Prof. Univ. of Massachusetts 1981, Univ. of Notre-Dame, Ind. 1981; mem. Koninklijke Acad. van België 1953–, Pres. 1962, 1986; Fellow, New York Acad. of Sciences; mem. Bureau, IUPAC 1969, Exec. Cttee. 1973, Pres. 1977–79; Pres. Nat. Cttee. for Chemistry (Belgium) 1979–88; mem. Exec. Bd. ICSU 1980–84; Hon. mem. Real Sociedad Española Física y Química, Soc. of Polymer Science, Japan, Chemical Soc. of Japan; Dr. h.c. (Aberdeen), Dr. h.c. rer.nat. (Mainz); Polymer Chem. Award, American Chem. Soc.; Decennial Award in Chem. (Belgium) 1968; Centennial Fellow American Chem. Soc. 1976. *Publications:* about 280 papers in int. scientific journals incl. Journal of Polymer Science, Makromolekulare Chemie, Pure and Applied Chemistry, Journal of Organic Chemistry. *Address:* Katholieke Universiteit te Leuven, Department of Chemistry, Celestijnenlaan 200 F, 3030 Heverlee, Louvain (Office); 5 Beukelaan, 3030 Heverlee, Louvain, Belgium (Home). *Telephone:* 016 20-06-56 (Office); 016 22-48-36.

SMIRNOV, Georgiy Lukich, DR.PHIL.SC.; Soviet politician; b. 14 Nov. 1922; m.; two s. one d.; ed. Volgograd Pedagogical Inst.; mem. CPSU 1943–; Asst. Prof.; Komsomol Worker 1942–44; various party posts 1948–57; posts in Cen. Cttee. of CPSU 1957–62; mem. of editorial staff of Kommunist 1962–65; posts in Cen. Cttee. of CPSU 1965–69; Deputy Chief of Propaganda Dept. of Cen. Cttee. of CPSU 1969–74, First Deputy Chief 1974–; cand. mem. of Cen. Cttee. CPSU 1976–; personal asst. to Mikhail Gorbachev (q.v. 1985–87); Dir. of Inst. of Marxism-Leninism 1987–. *Address:* U.S.S.R. Institute of Marxism-Leninism, 129256 Moscow, U.S.S.R.

SMIRNOV, Igor Pavlovich, DR.PHIL.SC.; Soviet literary scholar; b. 19 May 1941, Leningrad; s. of Valentina Lomakina and Pavel Smirnov; m. Johanna Renate Döring 1979; ed. Leningrad Univ.; Research Assoc. Leningrad Inst. of Russian Literature; left U.S.S.R. 1981; Prof. Univ. of Konstanz, Fed. Germany. *Publications include:* Meaning in Art and the Evolution of Poetic Systems 1977, Diachronic Transformations of Literary Genres and Motifs 1981, Essays on the History of the Typology of Culture (with Johanna Smirnov) 1982, The Emergence of the Inter-text 1985, Towards a Theory of Literature 1987. *Address:* Department of Russian, University of Konstanz, 7750 Konstanz, Postfach 5560; Cosimastrasse 228, 8 München 81, Federal Republic of Germany. *Telephone:* (089) 95 2831 (Home).

SMIRNOV, Leonid Vasiliyevich; Soviet politician; b. 16 March 1916; ed. Novocherkassk Industrial Inst.; Engineer, Foreman, Head of Electrical Dept., Factory Dir. 1939–61; Deputy Chair., later Chair. State Cttee. for Defence Equipment, U.S.S.R. Ministry of Armaments, U.S.S.R. Ministry of Defence Equipment 1961–63; mem. Cen. Cttee. of CPSU 1961–; Vice-Chair. Council of Ministers 1963–85; Deputy to U.S.S.R. Supreme Soviet 1962–; Hero of Socialist Labour 1961, Orders of Lenin (three), Hammer and Sickle Gold Medal, Lenin Prize 1960 and other decorations. *Address:* Council of Ministers, The Kremlin, Moscow, U.S.S.R.

SMIRNOV, Adm. Nikolay Ivanovich; Soviet naval officer; b. 5 Oct. 1917, Robtsovo, Kostroma Oblast; joined CPSU 1942; served in navy 1937–; graduated from Frunze Naval Coll. 1939, Mil. Acad. of Gen. Staff 1959; served in Pacific Fleet as navigation officer, submarine Commdr. 1939–44; submarine Commdr. in Black Sea Fleet 1944, then Chief of Staff and Commdr. of submarine Div., then Deputy Commdr. of Staff Dept. 1950–53, submarine Commdr. 1953–56, Commdr. of submarine forces 1956–57; Commdr. of submarine forces, Baltic Fleet 1959–60; Chief of Staff, First Deputy Commdr., Black Sea Fleet 1960–64; head of Dept., Deputy Chief of Main Staff of Soviet navy 1964–69; Commdr. of Pacific Fleet 1969–74; rank of Adm. 1973; First Deputy C.-in-C.-Sept. 1974–; Cand. mem. Cen. Cttee., CPSU 1971–76; Deputy to Supreme Soviet of the U.S.S.R. 1972–; Order of Lenin, Order of the Red Banner, Order of Red Banner of Labour and other decorations. *Address:* c/o Ministry of Defence, Moscow, U.S.S.R.

SMIRNOV, Vitaliy Stepanovich; Soviet diplomatist; b. 1930, Vitebsk; ed. Inst. of Philosophy and Law, Minsk; Komsomol posts 1953–57; Second Sec. and mem. of Politburo of Cen. Cttee. of Byelorussian S.S.R. 1957–61; mem.

Auditing Comm. of Cen. Cttee. of Byelorussian CP 1966–71, 1976–81; Perm. Rep. of Byelorussian S.S.R. to UN 1969–74; Amb. to Pakistan 1980–85. *Address:* The Kremlin, Moscow, U.S.S.R.

SMIRNOV, Vladimir Nikolaevich; Soviet biochemist; b. 1937; ed. Leningrad Univ.; mem. CPSU 1976–; post-graduate 1959–64; Jr., Sr. Research Fellow at U.S.S.R. Acad. of Med. Science Inst. of Medical Radiology 1964–68; Head of Biochemical Section, Ministry of Health 1968–72; Corresp. mem. of U.S.S.R. Acad. of Sciences 1981, now mem.; Prof. of Biological Science 1977; Head of Lab. at All-Union Scientific Centre for Cardiology (br. of U.S.S.R. Acad. of Medical Science) 1973–76, Dir. 1976–82; Dir. of Inst. of Experimental Cardiography of Acad. of Medical Science 1982–; corresp. mem. Acad. of Medical Sciences; U.S.S.R. State Prize 1978. *Address:* Institute of Experimental Cardiography, U.S.S.R. Academy of Medical Science, Ul. Solyanka, 14, Moscow 109801, U.S.S.R.

SMIRNOVSKY, Mikhail Nikolayevich; Soviet engineer and diplomatist; b. 7 Aug. 1921, Tver (now Kalinin); ed. secondary school, Kalinin, and Moscow Aviation Inst.; fmr. engineer, Moscow; Diplomatic Service 1948–; joined staff of U.S.S.R. Representation in Far East Comm. 1949; later Third and First Sec., Washington; Asst., later Deputy Head, U.S. Dept., Ministry of Foreign Affairs 1955–58; Counsellor, later Counsellor-Minister, Washington 1958–62; Head of U.S. Dept., Ministry of Foreign Affairs 1962–66; Amb. to U.K. 1966–73, concurrently to Malta 1967–73; mem. Cen. Auditing Comm. of CPSU 1966–76; numerous awards. *Address:* Ministry of Foreign Affairs, 32-34 Smolenskaya Sennaya ploshchad, Moscow, U.S.S.R.

SMIT, Hendrik Hanekom, B.COM.; South African politician; b. 31 Oct. 1925, Moorreesburg, Cape Prov.; m. Elsabé Lambrechts 1953; two s. two d.; ed. Dirkie Uys High School, Moorreesburg, Univ. of Stellenbosch; joined editorial staff Die Burger 1947–48; Chair. Nasionale Jeugbond (Junior Nat. Party) 1950–55; farmer, Darling 1957–; M.P. for Stellenbosch 1958–82; Chief Information Officer Nat. Party 1969–74; Chair. several Parl. select cttees.; Deputy Minister of Social Welfare and Pensions and Coloured, Rehoboth and Nama Relations 1974, later Minister; Minister of Coloured Relations and Statistics 1976–79, of Posts and Telecommunications 1979–82; Chair. Planning Cttee., Pres.'s Council; Decoration for Meritorious Service (D.M.S.) 1981. *Address:* Planning Committee, President's Council, P.O. Box 3601, Cape Town, South Africa.

SMIT-KROES, Neelie, B.ECONS.; Netherlands politician; b. 19 July 1941; m. Wouter-Jan Smit; one s.; ed. Netherlands School of Econs., Rotterdam Univ.; mem. academic staff Netherlands School of Econs., Rotterdam Chamber of Commerce, Rotterdam Municipal Council; M.P. 1971–77, 1981–82; Sec. of State, Transport and Public Works 1977–81, Minister of Transport and Public Works 1982–; Hon. D.Sc. (Hull) 1989. *Address:* c/o Ministry of Transport and Public Works, Plesmanweg 1, P.O. Box 20901, 2500 EX The Hague, Netherlands. *Telephone:* (070) 51.61.71.

SMITH, Albert Charles, PH.D.; American biologist; b. 5 April 1906, Springfield, Mass.; s. of Henry J. and Jeanette R. (Machol) Smith; m. 1st Nina Grönstrand 1935, one s. one d.; m. 2nd Emma van Ginneken 1966; ed. Columbia Univ.; Asst. Curator, N.Y. Botanical Garden 1928–31, Assoc. Curator 1931–40; Curator, Herbarium Arnold Arboretum, Harvard Univ. 1940–48; Curator, Div. of phanerogams, U.S. Nat. Museum, Smithsonian Inst. 1948–56; Program Dir. Systematic Biology, Nat. Science Foundation 1956–58; Dir. Museum of Nat. History, Smithsonian Inst. 1958–62, Asst. Sec. 1962–63; Prof. of Botany and Dir. of Research, Univ. of Hawaii 1963–65, Gerrit Parmile Wilder Prof. of Botany 1965–70, Prof. Emeritus 1970–; Ray Ethan Torrey Prof. of Botany, Univ. of Mass. 1970–76, Prof. Emer. 1976–; Editorial Consultant, Pacific Tropical Botanical Garden 1977–; mem. N.A.S.; Fellow, American Acad. of Arts and Sciences, Linnean Soc. of London, etc.; Robert Allerton Award for excellence in Tropical Botany 1979. *Publications:* Flora Vitiensis Nova: A New Flora of Fiji (Vol. I of six) 1979, (Vol. II) 1981, (Vol. III) 1985, (Vol. IV) 1988, and articles on plant taxonomy, evolutionary biology and phytogeography. *Address:* Department of Botany, University of Hawaii, Honolulu, Hawaii 96822, U.S.A.

SMITH, Anthony David, C.B.E., B.A.; British administrator; b. 14 March 1938; s. of Henry and Esther Smith; unmarried; ed. Brasenose Coll., Oxford; Current Affairs Producer, B.B.C. 1960–71; Fellow, St. Antony's Coll., Oxford 1971–76; Dir. British Film Inst. 1979–88; Pres. Magdalen Coll., Oxford 1988–; mem. Bd. of Dirs. Channel Four TV 1980–84; mem. Acton Soc. Trust 1978–, Writers and Scholars Educational Trust 1982–. *Publications:* The Shadow in the Cave: the broadcaster, the audience and the state 1973, British Broadcasting 1974, The British Press since the War 1976, Subsidies and the Press in Europe 1977, The Politics of Information 1978, Television and Political Life 1979, The Newspaper: an international history 1979, Newspapers and Democracy 1980, Goodbye Gutenberg—the newspaper revolution of the 1980s, The Geopolitics of Information 1980. *Address:* Magdalen College, Oxford; Bridge Cottage, Old Minster Lovell, Oxford, OX9A 5RN, England. *Telephone:* (0993) 75629.

SMITH, Anthony Felstead, LL.B.; Australian lawyer; b. 12 April 1936, Newcastle, N.S.W.; s. of late Thomas W.F. Smith and Zara M. Wells; m. Beverley J. Green 1960; three s.; ed. Newcastle and Melbourne High Schools and Univ. of Melbourne; practising solicitor 1960–; partner Gillotts 1966; now Sr. Partner, Minter Ellison, Melbourne; mem. Int. Bar Assen.

1976-, Sec.-Gen. 1988-(90). *Publication:* Defamation in Civil Precedents and Pleadings (co-author) 1989. *Address:* 40 Market Street, Melbourne, Vic. 3000 (Office); 30 Ferdinand Avenue, North Balwyn, Vic. 3104, Australia (Home). *Telephone:* (03) 617 4605 (Office); (03) 857 7110.

SMITH, Arnold Cantwell, C.H., O.C., M.A., D.C.L., LL.D.; Canadian diplomatist, international official and university professor (retd.); b. 18 Jan. 1915, Toronto; s. of Victor Arnold and Sarah Cory (Cantwell) Smith; m. Evelyn Hardwick Stewart 1938 (died 1987); two s. one d.; ed. Upper Canada Coll., Toronto, Lycée Champoléon, Grenoble, Univs. of Toronto, Oxford (Christ Church) and Gray's Inn, London; Asst. Prof. of Econs., Tartu (Estonia) Univ. 1939-40; Ed. Baltic Times, Tallin, Estonia 1939-40; Attaché, British Embassy, Cairo 1940-43; Sec. Canadian Embassy Kuibyshev 1943, Moscow 1943-45; Assoc. Dir. Nat. Defence Coll. of Canada 1947-49; Alt. Rep. of Canada on UN Security Council and Atomic Energy Comm., and Principal Adviser to Canadian Del., Lake Success 1949-50; Counsellor, Canadian Embassy, Brussels 1950-53; Special Asst. to Sec. of State for External Affairs, Ottawa 1953-55; Commr. Int. Truce Comm., Cambodia 1955-56; Canadian Minister, London 1956-58; Amb. to U.A.R. 1958-61, U.S.S.R. 1961-63; Asst. Under-Sec. of State for External Affairs, Ottawa 1963-65; elected First Sec.-Gen. of the Commonwealth 1965-75; Visiting Centenary Prof., Toronto Univ. 1967; Lester B. Pearson Prof. of Int. Affairs, Carleton Univ., Ottawa 1975-81, now Adjunct Prof.; Ida Green Visiting Prof., Univ. of B.C. Feb.-March 1978; Chair. North-South Inst., Hudson Inst. of Canada, Int. Peace Acad.; Hon. Pres. Canadian Bureau for Int. Educ.; Hon. Pres. Canadian Mediterranean Inst. 1981-; Life Vice-Pres. Royal Commonwealth Soc.; Trustee Hudson Inst., N.J. 1976-81; Cambridge Univ. Commonwealth Trust 1982-; Gov. Newsconcern Int. Foundation 1983-; mem. Univ. Coll. Cttee., Univ. of Toronto 1982-; Hon. Fellow Lady Eaton Coll., Trent Univ.; Hon. D.C.L. (Univ. of Mich., Oxon., Bishop's Univ.), Hon. LL.D. (Ricker Coll. of North-East, Queen's Univ., Toronto Univ., N.B. Univ., B.C. Univ., Leeds Univ., Trent Univ.); Zimbabwe Independence Medal 1980. *Publications:* Stitches in Time: The Commonwealth in World Politics 1981, The We-They Frontier: from International Relations to World Politics 1983, International Negotiation and Mediation: Instruments and Methods (with Arthur Lall) 1985, Tisserands de l'Histoire 1987; numerous articles. *Leisure interests:* fishing, reading, farming in France, travelling. *Address:* 260 Metcalfe Street, Apartment 4-B, Ottawa, Ont., K2P 1R6, Canada (Home); Aux Anjeaux, Gavaudun, 47150 Montflanquin, France (Summer). *Telephone:* (613) 235 3073; (53) 711316 (France).

SMITH, Bernard William, PH.D.; Australian academic; b. 3 Oct. 1916, Sydney; s. of Charles Smith and Rose Anne (née Tierney) Smith; m. Ruth C. Adeney 1941; one s. one d.; ed. Univ. of Sydney, Warburg Inst., London and A.N.U., Canberra; school teacher N.S.W. 1935-44, Educ. Officer, Art Gallery, N.S.W. 1944-52; lecturer, Sr. Lecturer Univ. of Melbourne 1955-63, Reader 1964-66; Art critic The Age, Melbourne 1963-66; Prof. of Contemporary Art and Dir. Power Inst. of Fine Arts, Univ. of Sydney 1967-77, Sr. Assoc., Dept. of Fine Arts; Pres. Australian Acad of Fine Arts 1977-80; Chevalier, Ordre des Arts et des Lettres. *Publications:* Place, Taste and Tradition 1945, European Vision and the South Pacific 1960, Australian Painting 1962, The Boy Adeodatus 1985, The Art of Captain Cook's Voyages (Jt. author) 1985-87, The Death of the Artist as Hero. *Leisure interests:* swimming, walking, reading. *Address:* 168 Nicholson Street, Fitzroy, Vic. 3065, Australia. *Telephone:* (03) 419-7470.

SMITH, Charles Edward Gordon, C.B., M.D., F.R.C.P., F.R.C.PATH.; British physician; b. 12 May 1924, Edinburgh; s. of late John Alexander Smith and Margaret Inglis (née Fletcher) Smith; m. Elsie McClellan 1948; one s. two d.; ed. Forfar Acad., St. Andrews Univ.; H.M. Colonial Medical Service, Malaysia 1948-57; Sr. Lecturer/Reader, London School of Hygiene and Tropical Medicine 1957-64; Dir. Microbiological Research Establishment, Ministry of Defence 1964-70; Dean, London School of Hygiene and Tropical Medicine 1971-; Chair. Public Health Lab. Service 1972-; Wellcome Trustee 1972- (Deputy Chair. 1983-); Hon. D.Sc. (St. Andrews) 1975, Stewart Prize, B.M.A. 1973, Tulloch Award, Dundee, 1982. *Publications:* articles on tropical diseases and third world development. *Leisure interests:* golf, gardening. *Address:* Wild Close, Woodgreen, Fordingbridge, Hants., SP6 2QZ, England. *Telephone:* (072 522) 349 (Hants.).

SMITH, Cyril Stanley, D.SC., D.LITT., SC.D.; American (naturalized) metallurgist and historian of technology; b. 4 Oct. 1903, Birmingham, England; s. of Joseph Seymour Smith and Frances (Norton) Smith; m. Alice Marchant Kimball 1931; one s. one d.; ed. Univ. of Birmingham and M.I.T.; Research Assoc. M.I.T. 1926-27; Research Metallurgist American Brass Co. 1927-42; Research Supervisor Nat. Defense Research Cttee. 1942-43; Assoc. Div. Leader (Metallurgy) Los Alamos Scientific Lab. 1943-46; Dir. Inst. for the Study of Metals, Chicago Univ. 1946-57, Prof. of Metallurgy 1946-61; Inst. Prof. M.I.T. 1961-69; Prof. Emer. 1969-; mem. Gen. Advisory Cttee., U.S. Atomic Energy Comm. 1946-52; mem. Materials Advisory Bd. 1954-56, President's Science Advisory Cttee. 1959, Cttee. on Science and Public Policy of Nat. Acad. of Sciences 1965-67, Smithsonian Inst. Council 1966-75; Visiting Fellow, St. Catherine's Coll. Oxford 1968; Pres. Soc. for the History of Tech. 1963-64; mem. Akad. der Wissenschaften, Göttingen, American Philosophical Soc., N.A.S., American Acad. of Arts and Sciences; Medal for Merit 1946, Clamer Medal (Franklin Inst.) 1952, American Soc. of Metals Gold Medal 1962, American Inst. Mining and Metallurgical

Engineers Douglas Medal 1963, Leonardo da Vinci Medal 1966, Inst. of Metals (London) Platinum Medal 1970, Dexter Award, American Chemical Soc. 1980, Pomerance Award, American Inst. of Archaeology 1982; Hon. mem. Japan Inst. of Metals; Hon. mem. Inst. of Metals (London); Hon. mem. Indian Inst. of Metals. *Publications:* A History of Metallography 1960, Sources for the History of the Science of Steel 1968, From Art to Science 1980, A Search for Structure 1981; translations (in collaboration) of Pirotechnia (Biringuccio) 1942, 1959, 1966, Treatise on Ores and Assaying (Lazarus Ercker) 1951, On Divers Arts (Theophilus) 1963, Mappae Clavicula 1974; Ed. Sorby Centennial Symposium on the History of Metallurgy 1965, Kodó Zuroku 1983; many papers in scientific and learned journals. *Leisure interest:* Oriental art. *Address:* Room 14N-238, Massachusetts Institute of Technology, Cambridge, Mass. 02139 (Office); 31 Madison Street, Cambridge, Mass. 02138, U.S.A. (Home). *Telephone:* (617) 253-3722 (Office); (617) 491-1916 (Home).

SMITH, Darwin Eatna, B.S., LL.B.; American business executive; b. 16 April 1926, Garrett, Ind.; s. of Kay B. Smith and Hazel R. Sherman; m. Lois Claire Archbold 1950; twin s. and d. and one s. one d.; ed. Indiana Univ. and Harvard Law School; employee, Sidley & Austin (law firm), Chicago 1955-58; joined Kimberly Clark Corpn. 1958-, Gen. Attorney 1959-, Vice-Pres. 1962, Vice-Pres. (Finance and Law) 1967, Exec. Vice-Pres. 1969, Pres. 1970-, Chair. of Bd. and C.E.O. 1971-. *Address:* Kimberly-Clark Corporation, P.O. Box 619100, DFW Airport Station, Dallas, Tex. 75261-9100 (Office); P.O. Box 612547, Dallas, Tex. 75261-2547, U.S.A. (Home).

SMITH, David Collville; Zimbabwe politician and farmer; b. 1922, Argyllshire, U.K.; came to S. Rhodesia as farm asst. 1946; later set up farming partnership in Mazoe Valley; appointed to various agricultural cttees.; Minister of Agric. 1968-76, Deputy Prime Minister and Minister of Finance 1976-79; Minister of Commerce and Industry 1980-81; fmr. mem. Rhodesian Front. *Address:* c/o Ministry of Commerce and Industry, Harare, Zimbabwe.

SMITH, Dodie (pseudonym C. L. Anthony); British dramatist and novelist; b. 3 May 1896, Bury, Lancs.; d. of late Ernest Smith and Ella Furber; m. Alec Macbeth Beesley 1939; ed. St. Paul's School for Girls and Royal Acad. of Dramatic Art; fmr. actress; buyer at Heal and Son until 1931. *Plays:* As C. L. Anthony: Autumn Crocus 1931, Service 1932, Touch Wood 1934; As Dodie Smith: Call It a Day 1935, Bonnet Over the Windmill 1937, Dear Octopus 1938 (revived 1967), Lovers and Friends 1943, Letter from Paris 1952, I Capture the Castle 1954, These People—Those Books 1958; Novels: I Capture the Castle 1948, The New Moon with the Old 1963, The Town in Bloom 1965, It Ends with Revelations 1967, A Tale of Two Families 1970, The Girl from the Candle-Lit Bath 1978; Children's Books: The Hundred and One Dalmatians 1956, The Starlight Barking 1967, The Midnight Kittens 1978; Autobiography: Look Back With Love 1974, Look Back With Mixed Feelings 1978, Look Back With Astonishment 1979, Look Back With Gratitude 1985. *Leisure interests:* reading, music, Dalmatian dogs. *Address:* The Barretts, Finchingfield, Essex, England. *Telephone:* (0371) 810260.

SMITH, Emil L., B.S., PH.D.; American biochemist and biophysicist; b. 5 July 1911, New York City; s. of Abraham and Esther Smith; m. Esther Press 1934; two s.; ed. Columbia, Cambridge and Yale Univs.; Instructor, Columbia Univ. 1936-38; Fellow, Rockefeller Inst. 1940-42; Senior Biochemist and Biophysicist, E. R. Squibb & Sons 1942-46; Assoc. Prof. and Prof., Univ. of Utah 1946-63; Prof. and Chair. Dept. of Biological Chem., Univ. of Calif., Los Angeles 1963-79; Prof. Emer. 1979-; mem. N.A.S., American Acad. of Arts and Sciences, American Philosophical Soc., etc.; Guggenheim Fellow (Cambridge and Yale) 1938-40. *Publications:* Principles of Biochemistry (co-author) 1954; many articles in biochemistry and biophysics. *Leisure interests:* music, literature, art. *Address:* Department of Biological Chemistry, University of California, School of Medicine, Los Angeles, Calif. 90024, U.S.A. *Telephone:* (213) 825-6494.

SMITH, Francis Barrymore, PH.D., F.A.H.A.; Australian historian; b. 16 May 1932, Hughesdale; s. of Francis John Smith and Bertha Smith; m. Ann Stokes 1965; two s. two d.; ed. Univ. of Melbourne and Cambridge Univ.; lecturer in History, Univ. of Melbourne 1962-66; Prof. Fellow in History, Inst. of Advanced Studies, A.N.U. 1974-; Ed. Historical Studies 1963-67; Pres. Australian Historical Asscn. 1978-80. *Publications:* Making of the Second Reform Bill 1966, Radical Artisan: William James Linton 1973, The People's Health 1830-1910 1979, Florence Nightingale Reputation and Power 1982, Retreat of Tuberculosis 1987. *Address:* Department of History, Institute of Advanced Studies, Australian National University, Canberra 2601, Australia. *Telephone:* (062) 492354.

SMITH, Sir Francis Graham, Kt., PH.D., F.R.S., F.R.A.S.; British professor of radio astronomy; b. 25 April 1923, Roehampton, Surrey; m. Elizabeth Palmer 1946; three s. one d.; ed. Rossall School, Epsom Coll., Downing Coll., Cambridge; with Telecommunications Research Lab. 1943-46; Cavendish Lab. 1947-64; 1851 Exhbn. 1951-52; Warren Research Fellow, Royal Soc. 1959-64; Prof. of Radio Astronomy, Univ. of Manchester 1964-74, 1981-87, Pro-Vice-Chancellor 1987, Dir. Nuffield Radio Astronomy Labs. 1981-, Langworthy Prof. of Physics 1987-; Deputy Dir. Royal Greenwich Observatory 1974-75, Dir. 1976-81; Astronomer Royal 1982-;

Visiting Prof. of Astronomy, Univ. of Sussex 1975–81; Sec. Royal Astronomical Soc. 1964–71, Pres. 1975–77; Fellow, Downing Coll. 1953–64, Hon. Fellow 1970–; Chair. of Govs., Manchester Grammar School 1987–; Hon. D.Sc. (Keele) 1987; Royal Medal, Royal Soc. 1987. *Publications:* Radio Astronomy 1960, Optics (with J. H. Thomson) 1971, Pulsars 1977, Pathways to the Universe (with Sir Bernard Lovell) 1988. *Leisure interests:* badminton, gardening, t'ai chi. *Address:* Old School House, Henbury, Macclesfield, Cheshire, SK11 9PH, England. *Telephone:* (0625) 612657.

SMITH, Sir Frederick Gladstone, Kt., Q.C., B.A.; Barbadian lawyer; b. 6 July 1924; s. of the late Cecil Gladstone Smith and Lillian Angelique Smith; m. Lois Ernesta Douglas Smith 1958; one s. one d.; ed. Combermere School, Harrison Coll., Codrington Coll., Univ. of Durham 1946–48; Classics master, Combermere School 1934–36; Gray's Inn, London 1949–52; Barrister-at-Law (England) 1952; Pvt. Law practice, Barbados 1952–58; Deputy Barbados House Ass. 1956–58; Crown Counsel, Jamaica 1958–62, 1971–64; Asst. Attorney General Federal Repub. of Cameroon 1962; Acting Attorney Gen. W. Cameroon 1962; Acting Deputy Dir. of Public Prosecutions, Jamaica 1965–66; Resident Magistrate 1966; Attorney General 1966–71; Queen's Counsel 1966; Privy Councillor (Barbados) 1966–68; Senator, Barbados 1966–70, 1986–87; Cabinet Minister 1966–76, Minister of Communication and Works 1971–75, of Educ. and Sports 1975–76; Leader of the Opposition 1976–78, Sr. Counsel Repub. of Guyana 1971; private practice 1976–; non-resident Chief Justice, Turks and Caicos Islands 1987; mem. Exec. Council, House Ass., House of Chiefs, W. Cameroon 1962; Vice-Pres. Bar Asscn. 1978–79, Pres. 1979–80; Vice-Pres. Org. of Caribbean Bar Asscn. *Leisure interests:* cricket, football, gardening, reading. *Address:* 45 Wanstead Heights, Cave Hill, St. Michael, Barbados, W. Indies. *Telephone:* 4243806 (Home); 427568 (Office).

SMITH, George Ivan, M.A.; Australian United Nations administrator (retd.); b. 1915; ed. Sydney Univ.; Ed. of Talks, Australian Broadcasting Comm. 1937–39; Dir. Australian Short-Wave Service 1939–41; Dir. BBC Pacific Service 1941–45; Int. Affairs Films 1945–47; UN Information Services, Lake Success 1947–49; Dir. UN Information Centre, London 1949–58; Dir. External Relations, UN, New York; Sr. Dir. of Public Information, UN 1961–62; UN Rep. Katanga 1961–62; Personal Rep. of UN Sec.-Gen. in E. and Cen. Africa; Regional Dir. UN Tech. Assistance Programmes in Cen. Africa 1962–66; Visiting Prof. Princeton Univ. and Fletcher School of Law and Diplomacy Boston (on special leave from UN) 1966–68; Dir. UN Office, London 1968–74; Sr. Consultant, Int. Inst. for Environment and Devt., London 1974–. *Publication:* Ghosts of Kampala—The Rise and Fall of Idi Amin 1980. *Address:* Elm Cottage, Butterow West, Stroud, Glos., GL5 3TZ, England. *Telephone:* (045 36) 6696.

SMITH, Gerard Coad, LL.B.; American government official and lawyer; b. 4 May 1914, New York City; s. of John T. Smith and Mary A. (Smith) Smith; m. Bernice Latrobe Maguire 1941; three s. one d.; ed. Canterbury School, New Milford, Yale Coll. and Yale Law School; Lawyer, New York 1939–50; U.S. Navy 1941–45; Special Asst., U.S. Atomic Energy Comm. 1950–54, to Sec. of State for Atomic Affairs 1954–57; Deputy Chief, U.S. Del. negotiating IAEA Treaty 1955–56; Chief U.S. Political Adviser to first Atoms-for-Peace Conf. and to talks with U.S.S.R. on safeguards against diversion of nuclear materials to weaponry 1955; State Dept. Liaison Officer to Senate Foreign Relations Cttee. on Disarmament Affairs 1957; Chief Aide to Sec. of State, London Disarmament Conf. 1957; originated nuclear test restraint concept agreed upon at Bermuda Heads of Govts. meeting 1957; Asst. Sec. of State and Dir. Policy Planning Staff Dept. of State 1957–61; originated Washington-Moscow "Hot Line" concept 1959; Consultant, State Dept. Policy Planning Council 1961–68; Foreign Policy Consultant, Washington Centre Foreign Policy Research 1961–69; Special Adviser to Sec. of State for Multilateral Force Negotiations 1962, 1964; Founder Interplay magazine 1967–68; Dir., U.S. Arms Control and Disarmament Agency 1968–72; Head, U.S. Del. to SALT, Helsinki and Vienna 1969–72; American Chair. Trilateral Comm. 1973–77; Counsel Wilmer, Cutler and Pickering, Washington 1973–77; U.S. Special Rep. for Non-proliferation Matters 1977–81; U.S. Rep. to IAEA 1977–80; Amb. at Large 1977– (responsible for negotiations regarding the supply of uranium); mem. Council on Foreign Relations 1961–. *Leisure interests:* golf, reading, walking. *Address:* 2425 Tracy Place, N.W., Washington, D.C. 20008, U.S.A.

SMITH, Gordon Scott, PH.D.; Canadian diplomatist; b. 19 July 1914, Montreal, P.Q.; s. of Gerald M. Smith and Marjorie H. Scott; m. Lise G. Lacroix; three s. one d.; ed. Lower Canada Coll. Montreal, McGill Univ., Univ. of Chicago and M.I.T.; joined Defence Research Bd. 1966; transferred to Dept. of External Affairs 1967; mem. Canadian Del. to NATO 1968–70; Special Adviser to Minister of Nat. Defence 1970–72; joined Privy Council Office 1972; Deputy Sec. to Cabinet (Plans) 1978–79; Deputy Under-Sec. Dept. of External Affairs 1979; Assoc. Sec. to Cabinet, Privy Council Office 1980–81; Sec. Ministry of State for Social Devt. 1981–84; Assoc. Sec. to Cabinet and Deputy Clerk of Privy Council 1984; Deputy Minister for Political Affairs, Dept. of External Affairs 1985; Amb. and Perm. Rep. of Canada to NATO 1985–. *Leisure interests:* squash, tennis, sailing, skiing, antiques. *Address:* NATO Headquarters, boulevard Léopold III, Brussels 1110, Belgium. *Telephone:* 216-0346.

SMITH, Hamilton O., M.D.; American university professor and research scientist; b. 23 Aug. 1931, New York; s. of Tommie Harkey and Bunnie

Othanel Smith; m. Elizabeth Anne Bolton 1957; four s. one d.; ed. Univ. of Illinois, Univ. of California at Berkeley, Johns Hopkins Univ. School of Medicine, Baltimore, Md.; Internship, Barnes Hosp., St. Louis, Mo. 1956–57; Lieut. in U.S.N.R., Sr. Medical Officer 1957–59; Resident, Henry Ford Hosp., Detroit, Mich. 1960–62; Postdoctoral Fellow, Dept. of Human Genetics, Univ. of Mich. 1962–64, Research Assoc. 1964–67; Asst. Prof. of Microbiology, Johns Hopkins Univ. School of Medicine 1967–69, Assoc. Prof. 1969–73, Prof. of Microbiology 1973–81, Prof. of Molecular Biology & Genetics 1981–; sabbatical year with Inst. für Molekular-Biologie, Zürich Univ. 1975–76; Guggenheim Fellow 1975–76; shared Nobel Prize for Physiology and Medicine 1978 with Prof. Werner Arber and Dr. Daniel Nathans (qq.v.) for work on restriction enzymes; mem. N.A.S. 1980. *Leisure interests:* piano, classical music. *Address:* Department of Molecular Biology & Genetics, Johns Hopkins University School of Medicine, Baltimore, Md. 21205 (Office); 8222 Carrbridge Circle, Baltimore, Md. 21204, U.S.A. (Home). *Telephone:* (301) 955-3650 (Office); (301) 821-5409 (Home).

SMITH, Harvey (see Smith, Robert Harvey).

SMITH, Henry Sidney, M.A., F.B.A., D.LITT.; British professor of Egyptology; b. 14 June 1928, London; s. of Sidney Smith and Mary W. Smith (née Parker); m. Hazel Flory Leeper 1961; ed. Merchant Taylors School, Sandy Lodge, Middx. and Christ's Coll., Cambridge; Asst. Lecturer in Egyptology, Faculty of Oriental Studies, Cambridge 1954–59, Lecturer 1959–63; Wallis Budge Fellow in Egyptology, Christ's Coll., Cambridge 1955–63; Field Dir. Egypt Exploration Soc. Archaeological Survey of Nubia, Epigraphist at Nubian sites 1959–65; Reader in Egyptian Archaeology, Univ. Coll. London 1963–70, Edwards Prof. of Egyptology 1970–86, Emer. Prof. 1986–; Prin. Epigraphist and Site Supervisor, Egypt Exploration Soc., Saqqara, Egypt 1964–70, Field Dir., Sacred Animal Necropolis 1971–76, Anubieion 1976–81, Dir. Memphis Project in Egypt 1981–88; Corresp. mem. Deutsches Archäologisches Institut; Medallist, Collège de France, Paris 1984. *Publications:* Preliminary Reports of the EES Archaeological Survey of Egyptian Nubia 1961, A Visit to Ancient Egypt: Memphis and Saqqara, c. 600–30 B.C. 1974, The Fortress of Buhen, II: The Inscriptions 1976, II: The Archaeological Report (with W. B. Emery and A. Millard) 1979, Saqqara Demotic Papyri I (with W. J. Tait) 1984, The Anubieion at Saqqara: The Settlement and The Temple Precinct (with D. G. Jeffreys) 1988; excavation reports, text publications and historical articles in int. journals. *Leisure interests:* varied. *Address:* Department of Egyptology, University College London, Gower Street, London, WC1E 6BT; Ailwyn House, High Street, Upwood, Huntingdon, Cambridgeshire, PE17 1QE, England (Home). *Telephone:* 01-380 7236 (Univ.); (0487) 812196 (Home).

SMITH, Sir Howard Frank Trayton, G.C.M.G.; British diplomatist (retd); b. 15 Oct. 1919, Brighton, Sussex; s. of the late Frank Howard Smith; m. 1st Mary Cropper 1943 (died 1982); one d.; m. 2nd Mary Penney 1983; ed. Polytechnic Secondary School, London, and Sidney Sussex Coll., Cambridge; Foreign Office 1939–47; Second Sec., Oslo 1947–50; First Sec., Washington 1950–53, Caracas 1953–56; Foreign Office 1956–61; Counsellor, Moscow 1961–63; Head of N. Dept., Foreign Office 1964–68; Amb. to Czechoslovakia 1968–71; Special Rep. of British Govt. in Ulster 1971–72; Deputy Sec. to Cabinet Office 1972–75; Amb. to U.S.S.R. 1976–78. *Address:* Coromandel, Cross in Hand, Heathfield, East Sussex, England. *Telephone:* (043 52) 4420.

SMITH, Ian Douglas; Zimbabwean politician; b. 8 April 1919; m. Janet Watt; two s. one d.; ed. Chaplin School, Gwelo, S. Rhodesia (now Gweru, Zimbabwe), and Rhodes Univ., Grahamstown, S. Africa; R.A.F. 1941–46; farmer; M.P. S. Rhodesia Legis. Ass. 1948–53, Parl. of Fed. of Rhodesia and Nyasaland 1953–61; fmr. Chief Whip United Fed. Party, resgnd. 1961; foundation mem. and Vice-Pres. Rhodesian Front (renamed Republican Front 1981) 1962, Pres. 1964–87; Deputy Prime Minister and Minister of Treasury S. Rhodesia 1962–64; Prime Minister of Rhodesia 1964–79, proclaimed Rhodesia's Unilateral Declaration of Independence, Nov. 1965; Minister without Portfolio in Bishop Muzorewa's Govt. 1979; mem. Transitional Exec. Council to prepare for transfer of power in Rhodesia 1978–79; M.P. for Republican Front (now Conservative Alliance) 1980–, suspended from Parl. 1987–88; Independence Decoration 1970, Grand Commdr., Order of the Legion of Merit 1979. *Address:* House of Assembly, Harare; Gwenoro Farm, Shurugwi, Zimbabwe.

SMITH, Jack; British artist; b. 18 June 1928, Sheffield; s. of John Edward Smith and Laura Smith; m. Susan Craigie Halkett 1956; ed. Sheffield Coll. of Art, St. Martin's School of Art and Royal Coll. of Art; one-man exhbns. Beaux Arts Gallery 1952–54, 1956, 1958, Catherine Viviano, New York 1958, 1962–63, Whitechapel Gallery, London 1959, Matthiesen Gallery, London 1960–63, Midland Group Gallery, Nottingham 1961, Grosvenor Gallery, London 1965, Marlborough Fine Art, London 1968, Gothenberg Museum, Sweden 1968, Whitechapel Gallery, London 1971, Redfern Gallery, London 1974, 1976, 1977, Fischer Fine Art, London 1981–83; sets and costumes for Ballet Rambert's Carmen Arcadiae Mechanicae Perpetuum 1985, Royal Ballet's Pursuit 1987; 1st Prize, John Moores, Liverpool 1957; Nat. Prize, Guggenheim Int. 1960. *Address:* 29 Seafield Road, Hove, Sussex, BN3 2TP, England. *Telephone:* (0273) 738312.

SMITH, Sir James Eric, Kt., C.B.E., M.A., SC.D., PH.D., F.R.S.; British zoologist; b. 23 Feb. 1909, Hull, Yorks.; s. of Walter Smith and Elsie K. Pickett; m.

Thelma A. Cornish; one s. one d.; ed. Hull Grammar School and King's Coll., London; Asst. lecturer, Manchester Univ. 1932–35; lecturer, Sheffield Univ. 1935–38, Cambridge Univ. 1938–50; Prof. of Zoology, Queen Mary Coll., London 1950–65; Dir. Plymouth Lab. and Sec., Marine Biological Asscn. of U.K. 1965–74; mem. Science Research Council 1963–66; Chair. Trustees of British Museum (Natural History) 1969–74; Chair. Special Cttee. on Problems of the Environment, ICSU 1970–73; mem. Advisory Bd. for Research Councils 1974–77; Pres. Soc. for History of Nat. History 1984–87; Fellow, Queen Mary Coll., London, King's Coll., London, Plymouth Polytechnic; Hon. Assoc. Natural History Museum 1981; Hon. D.Sc. (Exeter) 1968. *Publications:* various papers on the ecology, nervous system and behaviour of echinoderms and other marine invertebrates. *Leisure interests:* travel, gardening. *Address:* Wellesley House, 7 Coombe Road, Saltash, Cornwall, PL12 4ER, England. *Telephone:* (075 55) 2495.

SMITH, James Hamilton, F.C.A., B.COM.; Canadian business executive; b. 14 July 1931, Montreal, Quebec; s. of Alexander Laidlaw Smith; m. Lois M. Smith; one s. two d.; with Price Waterhouse & Co. (Chartered Accountants), Montreal 1953–66, London 1966; Asst. Controller, Domtar Inc., Montreal 1966–68, Controller 1968–71, Vice-Pres. Domtar Pulp & Paper Products 1971–74, Vice-Pres. Finance, Domtar Inc. 1974–78, Exec. Vice-Pres. 1978, Pres. Domtar Packaging 1979, Pres. Domtar Inc. 1981, Pres., Dir. and C.E.O. 1982-. *Leisure interests:* golf, skiing, baseball, swimming. *Address:* P.O. Box 7210, Station A, Montreal, Que. H3C 3M1, Canada. *Telephone:* (514) 848-5400.

SMITH, James Herbert, M.A.(ECON.); Bahamian banker; b. 26 Oct. 1947, Nassau; s. of late Bertram A. Smith and of Rosalie B. Smith; m. Portia M. Campbell 1973; two s. one d.; ed. Ryerson Polytechnical Coll., Toronto and Univs. of Windsor and Alberta, Canada; Deputy Perm. Sec. Ministry of Econ. Affairs 1977–79; Under-Sec. Cabinet Office 1980–84; Sec. for Revenue, Ministry of Finance 1984–85, Perm. Sec. 1985–86; Chair. Bahamas Devt. Bank; Gov. Cen. Bank of the Bahamas 1987-. *Leisure interests:* reading, golf. *Address:* P.O. Box 4868, Nassau (Office); P.O. Box 2327, Nassau, Bahamas (Home). *Telephone:* (809) 322-2193 (Office); (809) 326-66339 (Home).

SMITH, Rt. Hon. John, P.C., Q.C., M.A., LL.B.; British politician; b. 13 Sept. 1938, Dalmally, Argyll; s. of the late A. L. Smith; m. Elizabeth Margaret Bennett 1967; three d.; ed. Dunoon Grammar School, Univ. of Glasgow; called to Scottish Bar 1967; M.P. for Lanarkshire (North) 1970–83, Monklands East 1983-; Parl. Under-Sec. of State for Energy 1974–75, Minister of State for Energy 1975–76, Minister of State, Privy Council Office 1976–78; Sec. of State for Trade 1978–79; mem. Shadow Cabinet, Opposition Spokesman on Trade 1979–82, on Energy 1982–83, on Employment 1983–84, on Trade and Industry 1984–87, on Treasury and Econ. Affairs 1987-; Labour. *Leisure interests:* tennis, hill walking. *Address:* 21 Cluny Drive, Edinburgh, EH10 6DW, Scotland.

SMITH, John Derek, PH.D., F.R.S.; British scientist; b. 8 Dec. 1924, Southampton; s. of Richard Ernest Smith and Winifred Strickland Smith (née Davis); m. Ruth Irwin Aney 1955 (divorced 1968); ed. King James' Grammar School, Knaresborough and Clare Coll. Cambridge; Scientific Staff, Agricultural Research Council, Virus Research Unit, Cambridge 1945–59; Sr. Research Fellow, Calif. Inst. of Tech. 1959–62; mem. of Scientific Staff, MRC Lab. of Molecular Biology, Cambridge 1962–88; Research Fellow, Clare Coll. 1949–52; Visiting Scientist, Institut Pasteur, Paris 1952–53; Rockefeller Foundation Fellow, Univ. of Calif., Berkeley 1955–57; Sherman Fairchild Distinguished Scholar, Calif. Inst. of Tech. 1974–75. *Publications:* numerous papers in scientific journals on biochemistry and molecular biology and in particular on the biochemistry of nucleic acids. *Leisure interests:* travel, cuisine. *Address:* Medical Research Council Laboratory of Molecular Biology, Hills Road, Cambridge, CB2 2QH (Office); 12 Stansgate Avenue, Cambridge, England (Home). *Telephone:* (0223) 247841 (Home).

SMITH, John Francis, Jr., M.B.A.; American business executive; b. 6 April 1938, Worcester, Mass.; s. of John Francis Smith Sr. and Eleanor C. Sullivan; m. Marie Roberta Halloway 1962; two s.; ed. Boston and Massachusetts Univs.; Divisional Man., Gen. Motors Corpn., Framingham, Mass. 1961–73, Asst. Treas., New York 1973–80, Comptroller, Detroit 1980–81, Dir. Worldwide Planning 1981–84, Pres. and Gen. Man., Gen. Motors Canada, Oshawa 1984–86, Vice-Pres. Gen. Motors Corpn. and Pres. Gen. Motors Europe 1986–88; mem. Bd. Govs. Jr. Achievement Canada, Ltd. 1984. *Address:* c/o General Motors Corporation, 3044 Grand Boulevard, Detroit, Mich. 48202; 767 Fifth Avenue, New York, N.Y. 10153, U.S.A.

SMITH, John Herbert, C.B.E., F.C.A., I.P.F.A., C.I.GAS.E., F.R.S.A.; British accountant and executive; b. 30 April 1918, Shipley, Yorkshire; s. of Thomas A. Smith and Pattie Smith; m. Phyllis Mary Baxter 1945; two s. three d.; ed. Salt High School, Shipley, Yorkshire; Articled Clerk, Bradford & Otley 1934–39; served R.A.M.C. 1940–46; Deputy Clerk and Chief Financial Officer, Littleborough, Lancashire 1946–49; various posts in West Midlands Gas Board, to Asst. Chief Accountant 1949–61; Chief Accountant, Southern Gas Bd. 1961–65; Dir. of Finance and Admin., East Midland Gas Bd. 1965–68; full-time mem. East Midland Gas Board, also Deputy Chair. 1968–72; mem. for Finance, Gas Council 1972, British Gas Corpn. 1973–76; Deputy Chair. and C.E.O. British Gas Corpn. 1976–83; Chair. Moracrest Investments Ltd. 1977–85; mem. Pension Funds Property Unit Trust

1975- (Deputy Chair. 1984-); Lazards American Exempt Fund 1976-, British American Property Unit Trust 1982-; mem. United Property Unit Trust 1983- (Chair. 1985-), Council of the Inst. of Chartered Accountants in England and Wales, London 1977–81. *Leisure interests:* music, piano playing, choral activities. *Address:* 81 Albany, Manor Road, East Cliff, Bournemouth, Dorset, BH1 3EJ, England. *Telephone:* (0202) 298 157.

SMITH, Sir Leslie Edward, Kt., F.C.A.; British business executive; b. 15 April 1919, London; s. of Edward V. Smith and Doris E. Browning; m. 1st Lorna Pickworth 1943, two d.; m. 2nd Cynthia Holmes 1964; one s. one d.; ed. Christ's Hospital; Chief Exec., Finance, The British Oxygen Co. Ltd. (now The BOC Group) 1961–65, Dir. (Commercial) 1965–67, Jt. Man. Dir. 1967–69, Group Man. Dir. 1969–72, Chair. and Chief Exec. 1972–79, Chair. 1979–85; Chair. BOC Group Inc. (U.S.A.); Dir. Cadbury Schweppes 1977–85; mem. Foundation Bd. of Int. Man. Inst., Geneva; non-exec. Dir. British Gas PLC 1982-; Chair. British Cttee. on S.A. Ltd. 1989-. *Leisure interest:* reading. *Address:* Cookley House, Cookley Green, Swyncombe, nr. Henley-on-Thames, Oxon., RG9 6EN, England. *Telephone:* (0491) 641258.

SMITH, Lloyd Bruce; American business executive (retd.); b. 13 Oct. 1920, Milwaukee, Wis.; s. of Lloyd Raymond and Agnes (Gram) Smith; m. Lucy Anne Woodhull 1945; three s. one d.; ed. Sheffield Science School, Yale; with A. O. Smith Corpn., Milwaukee 1942-, successively Asst. to Pres., then Vice-Pres., Dir., Man. Home Appliances div., Asst. Gen. Man., Pres. 1951–67, Chair. and C.E.O. 1967–84, Chair. 1984-, also Dir.; Dir. First Wis. Corpn., Goodyear Tire and Rubber Co., Medical Coll. of Wis., Deere and Co.; mem. Business Council; Distinguished Life mem. American Soc. for Metals. *Address:* P.O. Box 23971, Milwaukee, Wis. 53223, U.S.A. *Telephone:* (414) 359-4040.

SMITH, Maggie Natalie, C.B.E.; British actress; b. 28 Dec. 1934, Ilford, Essex; d. of Nathaniel Smith and Margaret Little; m. 1st Robert Stephens (q.v.) 1967 (dissolved 1975), two s.; m. 2nd Beverley Cross 1975; ed. Oxford High School for Girls; first appeared with Oxford Univ. Dramatic Soc. (O.U.D.S.) in Twelfth Night 1952; appeared in revue New Faces N.Y. 1956, Share My Lettuce 1957, The Stepmother 1958; with Old Vic Co. 1959–60 playing in The Double Dealer, As You Like It, Richard II, The Merry Wives of Windsor, What Every Woman Knows; other appearances include Rhinoceros 1960, Strip the Willow 1960, The Rehearsal 1961, The Private Ear and The Public Eye 1962, Mary, Mary 1963; with Nat. Theatre played in The Recruiting Officer 1963, Othello (Desdemona) 1964, The Master Builder 1964, Hay Fever 1964, Much Ado About Nothing 1965, Miss Julie 1965, A Bond Honoured 1966, The Beaux' Stratagem 1970, Hedda Gabler 1970, Three Sisters, Design for Living (Los Angeles) 1971, Private Lives London 1972, U.S.A. 1974–75, Peter Pan 1973, Snap 1974; played 1976, 1977, 1978 and 1980 seasons, Stratford, Ont., Canada, Night and Day 1979, Virginia, London 1981, The Way of the World, Chichester Festival and London 1984–85, Interpreters, London 1985, The Infernal Machine 1986, Coming in to Land 1987, Lettice and Lovage, London 1987; Hon. D.Lit. (St. Andrews, Univ. of Leicester 1982). *Films include:* The V.I.P.s 1963, The Pumpkin Eater 1964, Young Cassidy 1965, Othello 1966, The Honey Pot 1967, Hot Millions 1968, The Prime of Miss Jean Brodie 1969, Travels with My Aunt 1972, Love and Pain and the Whole Damn Thing 1973, Murder by Death 1975, Death on the Nile 1978, California Suite 1978, Quartet 1980, Clash of the Titans 1981, Evil under the Sun 1982, Ménage à Trois 1982, The Missionary 1982, A Private Function 1984, A Room with a View 1986, The Lonely Passion of Judith Hearn 1987, Paris by Night 1988; Dir. United British Artists 1983-; Awards: Evening Standard Best Actress Award 1962, 1970, 1982, 1985; Variety Club Actress of the Year 1963; L.A. Critics Award Best Actress 1970; Variety Club Award Best Stage Actress 1972 (plays); Acad. Award for Best Actress 1969, for Best Supporting Actress 1979; Best Actress Award from Soc. of Film and Television Arts (U.K.) 1969; Best Actress Award from Film Critics' Guild (U.S.A.) 1969 (films), BAFTA Award for Best Actress 1984, 1987, 1989; Hon. D.Litt. (Bath) 1986. *Leisure interest:* reading. *Address:* c/o ICM Ltd., 388 Oxford Street, London, W1N 9HE, England.

SMITH, Margaret Chase; American politician; b. 14 Dec. 1897, Skowhegan, Maine; d. of George Emery and Carrie (née Murray) Chase; m. Clyde H. Smith 1930 (died 1940); ed. Skowhegan High School; began career as teacher; with Independent Reporter 1919–28, Daniel E. Cummings Co. 1928–30; Treas., New England Process Co. 1928–30; mem. House of Reps. 1940–48; Senator from Me. 1948–72; Republican; Chair. Freedom House (New York) 1970–77, Northwood Inst. Nat. Women's Bd. 1978–81, Trustee 1980-; Dir. Lilly Endowment, Inc. 1976-; Visiting Prof. Woodrow Wilson Nat. Fellowship Foundation 1973–76; numerous awards; 90 hon. degrees. *Publications:* numerous papers and articles; syndicated newspaper and magazine columns; Gallant Women 1968, Declaration of Conscience 1972. *Address:* Norridgewock Avenue, Skowhegan, Maine 04976, U.S.A.

SMITH, Michael, PH.D., F.R.S., F.R.S.C.; Canadian professor of biochemistry; b. 26 April 1932, Blackpool, England; s. of Rowland Smith and Mary Agnes Smith (née Armstead); m. Helen Wood Christie 1960; two s. one d.; ed. Arnold School, Blackpool, Univ. of Manchester; Postdoctoral Fellow, B.C. Research Council, Univ. of B.C., Vancouver, B.C., Canada 1956–60; Research Assoc., Inst. for Enzyme Research, Univ. of Wis., U.S.A. 1960-

61; Head, Chem. Div., Vancouver Lab., Fisheries Research Bd. of Canada, Vancouver 1961-66; Assoc. Prof., Dept. of Biochemistry, Univ. of B.C., Vancouver 1966-70, Prof., Dept. of Biochemistry 1970-, Dir. of Biotechnology Lab.; Career Investigator (fmrly. entitled Research Assoc.), M.R.C. of Canada 1966-; Boehringer-Mannheim Prize, Canadian Biochemical Soc. *Publications:* numerous publs. in scientific literature. *Leisure interests:* classical music, sailing, skiing. *Address:* Biotechnology Laboratory, Room 237, Westbrook Building, 6174 University Boulevard, University of British Columbia, Vancouver, B.C. V6T 1WF; 303-2466 West 3rd Avenue, Vancouver, B.C. V6K 1L8, Canada (Home). *Telephone:* (604) 732-8691 (Home).

SMITH, Murray Robert, A.C.A.; New Zealand business executive; b. 6 June 1941, Hamilton; s. of Robert P. Smith and Helen J. Painter; m. Miette Bennett 1962; four s. one d.; ed. Hamilton Tech. Coll.; br. accountant, N.Z. Public Trust Office 1959-72; mem. Parl. for Whangarei 1972-75; Man. Hamilton br. office, Devt. Finance Corpn. 1976-77, Man. Small Business Agency 1978-80, Asst. Gen. Man., Deputy Gen. Man. 1980-86, Group Man. Dir. DFC N.Z. Ltd. 1986-; Chair. N.Z. Railways Corpn. 1985-88, Agricola Ltd. 1987-; mem. N.Z. Tourism Council. *Leisure interests:* squash, cricket, table tennis, music. *Address:* DFC New Zealand Ltd., P.O. Box 3090, Wellington (Office); 77 Churton Drive, Johnsonville, Wellington, New Zealand (Home).

SMITH, Norman Brian, C.B.E., PH.D., M.SC.; British business executive; b. 10 Sept. 1928, Winton; s. of Vincent Smith and Louise Smith; m. Phyllis Smith 1955; one s. one d.; ed. Sir John Deanes Grammar School, Northwich and Univ. of Manchester; joined ICI 1954, Deputy Chair. Fibres Div. 1972, Chair. Fibres Div. 1975-78, Dir. ICI 1978-85, Chair. ICI Americas 1981-85; Deputy Chair. Metal Box PLC (now MB Group PLC) 1985-86, Chair. 1986-; Dir. Lister & Co., Davy Corpn.; Pres. British Textile Confed. 1977-79; mem. British Overseas Trade Bd. 1980-81, 1983-87; Chair. Priorities Bd. for R and D into Agric. and Food 1987-; Dir. Cable and Wireless PLC 1988-; Fellow Textile Inst. *Leisure interests:* cricket, sailing, tennis, gardening. *Address:* MB Group PLC, Caversham Bridge House, Waterman Place, Reading, Berks., RG1 8DN, England. *Telephone:* (0734) 581177.

SMITH, Norman Henry, F.C.C.A.; British business executive; b. 16 May 1925, London; s. of Henry Smith and Ada Priestley; m. Margaret de Casagrande 1954; two s. five d.; ed. St. Ignatius Grammar School, London; joined Courtaulds Group 1952, Chief Accountant 1968, Finance Dir. 1970, Deputy Chair. 1976-86; Chair. Delta & Pine Land Co., Miss. 1972-78, Courtaulds Fabric Group 1977-82, Courtaulds Pensions Investment Cttee. 1976-; Dir. Svenska Rayon and AB Celloplast 1971-81, Courtaulds North America Inc. 1971-86, Courtaulds Canada Inc. 1972-86; Chair. Orion Insurance Co. PLC. *Leisure interests:* music, (opera), photography, golf, gardening. *Address:* 2 Coombehurst Close, Hadley Wood, Barnet, Herts., EN4 0JU, England. *Telephone:* 01-440 4776.

SMITH, Oliver, B.A.; American theatrical designer; b. 13 Feb. 1918, Waupun, Wis.; s. of Larue F. and Nina (née Kincaid) Smith; ed. Pa. State Univ.; Co-Dir. American Ballet Theatre (now Ballet Theatre Foundation) 1945-; Master Teacher, New York Univ.; mem. Nat. Council for the Arts; Hon. dr. (Bucknell Univ.); Donaldson Award 1946, 1947, 1949, 1953; Antoinette Perry (Tony) Award 1957, 1958, 1960, 1961, 1964, 1965; Schubert Award 1960; Distinguished Alumni Award, Pa. State Univ. 1962; New York Handel Medallion 1975. *Co-produced and designed plays:* On the Town 1945, Billion Dollar Baby 1945, No Exit 1946, Me and Molly 1947, Gentlemen Prefer Blondes 1949, Bless You All 1950, In The Summer House 1952, Clearing in the Woods 1957, Time Remembered, Romulus 1961, The Night of the Iguana, Lord Pengo 1962, Barefoot in the Park 1963, 110 in the Shade 1963, The Girl Who Came to Supper 1963, Dylan 1963, The Chinese Prime Minister 1964, Ben Franklin in Paris 1964, Luv 1964, Poor Richard 1964, The Odd Couple 1965. *Designed musicals:* Brigadoon 1946, High Button Shoes 1946, Miss Liberty 1949, Paint Your Wagon 1952, Pal Joey 1952, On Your Toes 1955, Candide 1955, My Fair Lady 1956, Auntie Mame 1956, West Side Story 1958, Jamaica, Destry, Flower Drum Song, Camelot, Beckett, Broadway, First Monday in October, Martha 1961, Hello Dolly (Tony Award) 1963, I Was Dancing 1964, Candide 1971, The Little Black Book 1972, The Time of Your Life 1972, Lost in the Stars 1972, Naughty Marietta (New York Opera) 1978; *ballets:* Rodeo 1942, Fancy Free 1943, Fall River Legend 1946, Swan Lake, Les Noces; La Traviata (Metropolitan Opera) 1958; *films:* Band Wagon 1952, Oklahoma 1955, Guys and Dolls 1955, Porgy and Bess, The Sound of Music, The Unsinkable Molly Brown 1960. *Exhbns.:* Pa. State Coll., Museum of Modern Art, Brooklyn Museum, Chicago Art Inst., Cocoran Gallery, Yale Univ. *Address:* c/o Ballet Theatre Foundation, 890 Broadway, New York, N.Y. 10003, U.S.A.

SMITH, Orin Robert, B.A. (ECONS.), M.B.A.; American business executive; b. 13 Aug. 1935, Newark, N.J.; s. of Sydney R. Smith and Gladys DeGroff Smith; m. Ann Raymond 1964; two d.; ed. Brown and Seton Hall Univs.; on staff of Allied Corpn. 1959-69; Marketing Man., Dir. of Marketing, Dir. Sales and Marketing, J. T. Baker 1969-72; Dir. Sales and Marketing M & T Chemicals 1972-75, Pres. 1975-77; Sr. Vice-Pres. New Business and Research and Devt., Engelhard Minerals & Chemicals Corpn. 1977-78, Pres. Minerals and Chemicals Div. and Sr. Vice-Pres. of the Corpn. 1978-81, Dir. 1979-81; Pres. Engelhard Corpn. Minerals and Chemicals

Div. 1981-84, Corpn. Exec. Vice-Pres. and Dir. 1981-84; Sr. Exec. Vice-Pres. and Acting C.E.O. Engelhard Corpn. Feb.-May 1984, Pres. and C.E.O. May 1984-; Dir. Vulcan Materials Co., Summit Bancorporation, Summit Trust Co. and Re-Insurance Co.; Vice-Chair. Bd. of Trustees Centenary Coll.; mem. Bd. Overseers, N.J. Inst. of Tech.; Dir. Research Corpn.; Dir. N.J. State Chamber of Commerce; mem. Exec. Cttee. Machinery and Allied Products Inst. *Leisure interests:* classic and racing automobiles. *Address:* Engelhard Corporation, Menlo Park CN 40, Edison, N.J. 08818 (Office); Fox Chase Farm, Gladstone, N.J. 07934, U.S.A. (Home).

SMITH, Ray Fred, PH.D.; American entomologist and educator; b. 20 Jan. 1919, Los Angeles, Calif.; s. of Ray M. and Elsie E. (Weisheit) Smith; m. Elizabeth J. McClure; two s. one d.; ed. Univ. of California at Berkeley; Technician, Lab. Asst., Univ. of Calif. at Berkeley 1941-45, Assoc., Experimental Station 1945-46, Instructor in Entomology and Jnr. Entomologist 1946-48, Asst. Prof., Asst. Entomologist 1948-54, Assoc. Prof. Assoc. Entomologist 1960-67, Prof. and Entomologist 1967-82, Prof. Emer. 1982-; Chair. Dept. of Entomology and Parasitology, Berkeley-Davis 1959-63; Chair. Dept. of Entomological Sciences, Berkeley 1963-73; Exec. Dir. Consortium for Int. Crop Protection 1979-87; Chair. and mem. Panel of Experts on Integrated Pest Control, FAO 1966-83; Consultant to FAO 1965-, to USAID 1969-; mem. Governing Bd. Int. Centre for Insect Physiology and Ecology 1974-78; Chair. Council for Int. Congress of Entomology 1984-, N.A.S. World Food and Nutrition Study, Crop Protection Study Team 1975; Pres. and Chair. Governing Bd. Entomology Soc. of America 1976; Ed. Annual Review of Entomology 1960-75; Guggenheim Fellow; Fellow American Acad. of Arts and Sciences; mem. N.A.S.; Berkeley Citation 1983. *Publications:* over 300 publs. on insect ecology, systematics of Diabrotica, and integrated control of agricultural pests, with emphasis on Third World. *Leisure interests:* shell collecting, wines. *Address:* 3092 Hedaro Court, Lafayette, Calif. 94549, U.S.A. (Home).

SMITH, Richard, C.B.E.; British artist; b. 1931, Letchworth, Herts.; m. Betsy Scherman; two s.; ed. Luton School of Art, St. Albans School of Art and Royal Coll. of Art; lived in New York 1963-65; teacher St. Martin's School of Art, London 1961-63; Artist-in-Residence, Univ. of Virginia 1967; Grand Prix São Paulo Bienal 1967; one-man exhbns. at the Kasmin Gallery 1963, 1967, Whitechapel Gallery 1966; participated in the Pittsburgh Int. 1961, New Shapes in Colour, Amsterdam, Berne and Stuttgart 1966-67 and in exhbns. at Guggenheim Museum, Tate Gallery, etc.; works represented in Tate Gallery, Stuyvesant Foundation, Contemporary Art Soc., the Ulster Museum, Belfast, the Walker Art Center, etc.

SMITH, Sir Robert Courtney, Kt., C.B.E., F.R.S.E., M.A., C.A.; British business executive; b. 10 Sept. 1927; s. of late John Smith and Agnes Smith; m. Moira R. Macdougall 1954; one s. two d. (and one s. deceased); ed. Kelvinside Acad. Glasgow, Sedbergh School and Trinity Coll. Cambridge; served R.M. 1945-47 and Royal Marine Forces Volunteer Reserve 1951-57; Partner, Arthur Young McClelland Moores & Co. (chartered accountants) 1957-78; Chair. Sidlaw Group 1980-88, Standard Life Assurance 1982-88, Alliance and Second Alliance Trust 1984-; Dir. William Collins (Vice-Chair. 1979-), Volvo Trucks (GB), Edinburgh Investment Trust, British Alcan Aluminium, Bank of Scotland; Chair. Scottish Industrial Devt. Bd.; Chancellor's Assessor, Glasgow Univ. 1984-; Hon. LL.D. (Glasgow) 1978; mem. Order of St. John. *Leisure interests:* racing, gardening. *Address:* 64 Reform Street, Dundee, DD1 1TJ; North Lodge, Dunkeld, Perthshire, PH8 0AR, Scotland.

SMITH, (Robert) Harvey; British farmer and show jumper; b. 29 Dec. 1938; m. 1st Irene Shuttleworth (divorced 1986); two s.; m. 2nd Susan Dye 1987; winner of numerous int. show jumping competitions including John Player Trophy (7 times), King George V Gold Cup, British Jumping Derby (4 times); Grand Prix and Prix des Nations wins in UK, Ireland, Europe and U.S.A.; participated in Olympic Games 1968, 1972; BBC TV commentator, Olympic Games, Los Angeles 1984. *Publications:* Show Jumping with Harvey Smith 1979, Bedside Jumping 1985.

SMITH, Robert Powell, M.A.; American diplomatist (retd.); b. 5 March 1929, Joplin, Mo.; s. of Powell Augusta and Estella (Farris) Smith; m. Alice Irene Rountree 1953; three s. one d.; ed. Texas Christian Univ.; Foreign Service Officer, Dept. of State 1955; Press Officer, Washington 1955; Vice-Consul, Lahore, West Pakistan 1956-58; Second Sec., Beirut, Lebanon 1959-61; Consul and Prin. Officer, Enugu, Nigeria 1963-65; Officer-in-Charge Ghanaian Affairs 1966; Officer-in-Charge Nigerian Affairs, Deputy Dir. Office of West African Affairs 1967-69; Deputy Chief of Mission, Counsellor, Pretoria, S.A.; Amb. to Malta 1974-76, to Ghana 1976-79, to Liberia 1979-81; Pres. African Wildlife Foundation 1981-85; Air Medal; Meritorious Honor Award, Dept. of State. *Leisure interests:* tennis, music, reading. *Address:* c/o African Wildlife Foundation, 1717 Massachusetts Avenue, N.W. 602, Washington, D.C. 20036 (U.S.A.).

SMITH, Roger B., M.B.A.; American business executive; b. 12 July 1925, Columbus, Ohio; s. of Emmet Quimby and Bess (née Obetz) Smith; m. Barbara Ann Rasch 1954; two s. two d.; ed. Detroit Univ. School and Univ. of Mich.; served in U.S. Navy 1944-46; with Gen. Motors, Detroit 1949-, Dir. Financial Analysis Section, Asst. Treas., New York 1960-68, Gen. Asst. Treas., Detroit 1968, Treas. 1970-71, Vice-Pres. Financial Staff 1971-72, Vice-Pres. and Group Exec., Nonautomotive and Defense Group

1972-74, Dir. Dec. 1974-, Exec. Vice-Pres. 1974-81, Vice-Chair. Finance Cttee. 1975-80, Chair. and C.E.O. Gen. Motors Jan. 1981-; Vice-Chair. Gen. Motors Cancer Research Foundation 1978-; mem. U.S. Corp. Council on S. Africa 1985-; Chair. Business Roundtable 1986-; Trustee Cranbrook Schools and Michigan Colls. Foundation; mem. Bd. of Dirs. Council for Financial Aid to Educ., Motor Vehicle Mfrs. Asscn.; Dr. h.c. (DePauw Univ.) 1979. *Address:* 3044 West Grand Boulevard, Detroit, Mich. 48202 (Office); Bloomfield Hills, Mich. 48013, U.S.A. (Home).

SMITH, Roland, B.A., PH.D.(ECON.); British professor and business executive; b. 1 Oct. 1928; s. of late Joshua Smith and of Hannah Smith; m. Joan Shaw 1954; ed. Univs. of Birmingham and Manchester; flying officer R.A.F. 1953; Asst. Dir. Footwear Mfrs. Fed. 1955; lecturer in Econs., Univ. of Liverpool 1960, Dir. Business School 1963; part-time Prof. of Marketing, Univ. of Manchester 1966-88, Prof. Emer. 1988-; Chair. Temple Bar Investment Trust Ltd. 1980-, House of Fraser 1981-86 (Deputy Chair. 1980-81), Readicut Int. 1984- (Deputy Chair. 1982-84), Hepworth Ceramic Holdings 1986-, Phoenix Properties and Finance 1986-87, Kingston Oil and Gas 1987-, British Aerospace 1987-, P & P PLC 1988-; non-exec. Chair. Sr. Eng. Ltd. 1973-; Dir.-Consultant to numerous cos. *Leisure interest:* walking. *Address:* British Aerospace, 11 Strand, London, W.C.2, England.

SMITH, Wilbur Addison, B.COMM.; British (naturalized) author; b. 9 Jan. 1933, Zambia; m. Danielle Antoinette Smith 1971; two s. one d.; ed. Michaelhouse, Natal and Rhodes Univ.; business exec. 1954-58; factory owner 1958-64; professional author 1961-. *Publications:* When the Lion Feeds 1961, The Sound of Thunder 1962, The Dark of the Sun 1964, Shout at the Devil 1966, Gold Mine 1968, The Diamond Hunters 1969, The Sunbird 1971, Eagle in the Sky 1972, The Eye of the Tiger 1973, Cry Wolf 1975, A Sparrow Falls 1976, Hungry as the Sea 1978, Wild Justice 1979, A Falcon Flies 1980, Men of Men 1981, The Angels Weep 1982, The Leopard Hunts in Darkness 1984, The Burning Shore 1985, Power of the Sword 1986, Rage 1987, The Courtneys 1987, A Time to Die 1989. *Leisure interests:* fishing, wildlife. *Address:* c/o Charles Pick Consultancy, Flat 3, 3 Bryanston Place, London, W1H 7FN, England.

SMITH, Wilfred Cantwell, M.A., PH.D., D.D., LL.D., D.LITT., D.H.L.; Canadian university professor; b. 21 July 1916, Toronto; s. of Victor Arnold Smith and Sarah Cantwell; m. Dr. Muriel Struthers 1939; three s. two d.; ed. Upper Canada Coll., Univ. of Grenoble, Univ. of Madrid, American Univ., Cairo, Univ. of Toronto, Cambridge and Princeton Univs.; served as rep. among Muslims of the Canadian Overseas Missions Council, chiefly in Lahore 1940-49; lecturer in Indian and Islamic History, Forman Christian Coll., Lahore 1941-45; Prof. of Comparative Religion 1949-63, and Dir. Inst. of Islamic Studies, McGill Univ. 1951-63; Visiting Prof., London Univ. 1960, Princeton Univ. 1965, Univ. of Toronto 1968, Univ. of Washington 1978; Prof. of World Religions and Dir. Center for the Study of World Religions, Harvard Univ. 1964-73; McCulloch Prof. of Religion, Dalhousie Univ., Halifax, Canada 1973-78; Prof. of Comparative History of Religion and Chair., The Study of Religion, Harvard Univ. 1978-84; Sr. Killam Fellow, Univ. of Toronto, Visiting Prof. of Religion, Trinity Coll., Toronto 1985-86; Pres. American Soc. for the Study of Religion 1966-69; Fellow, Royal Soc. of Canada (Pres. Humanities and Social Sciences Section 1972-73), American Acad. of Arts and Sciences; Pres. Middle East Studies Asscn. of N. America 1977-78, Pres. Canadian Theological Soc. 1979-80, Pres. American Acad. of Religion 1982-83; Chauveau Medal, Royal Soc. of Canada 1974. *Publications:* Modern Islam in India 1943, Islam in Modern History 1957, Meaning and End of Religion 1963, Faith of Other Men 1963, Questions of Religious Truth 1967, Religious Diversity 1976, Belief and History 1977, Faith and Belief 1979, Towards a World Theology 1981, On Understanding Islam 1981. *Address:* 476 Brunswick Avenue, Toronto, Ont., M5R 2Z5, Canada (Home). *Telephone:* 416-968-5913 (Home).

SMITH, William French, A.B., LL.B.; American lawyer; b. 26 Aug. 1917, Wilton, N.H.; s. of William French and Margaret (Dawson) Smith; m. Jean Webb 1964; four s. two d.; ed. Univ. of Calif. and Harvard Univ.; admitted to Calif. bar 1942; Attorney, Sr. Partner Gibson, Dunn and Crutcher, Los Angeles 1946-80, Partner 1985-; U.S. Attorney-Gen. 1981-85; mem. U.S. Advisory Comm. on Int. Educational and Cultural Affairs, Washington 1971-78; U.S. Del. East-West Cen. Cultural and Tech. Interchange, Hawaii 1975-77; Dir. Los Angeles World Affairs Council 1970-81, Pres. 1975-76; mem. Stanton Panel on Int. Information, Educ. and Cultural Relations, Washington 1974-75; mem. Bd. of Dirs., RCA Corpn. 1985-86, NBC 1985-, Pacific Lighting Corpn. 1985-, Earle M. Jorgensen Co. 1974-81, 1985-, Pacific Telesis Group, Pacific Bell 1985-, H. F. Ahmanson Co. 1985-, American Int. Group Inc. 1985-, Gen. Electric Co. 1986-; mem. Pres.'s Foreign Intelligence Advisory Bd. 1985-, Bd. of Regents, Univ. of Calif. 1968-, Advisory Council, Harvard Univ. School of Govt. 1977-, Advisory Bd., Centre for Strategic and Int. Studies, Georgetown Univ. 1978-82, 1985-; Trustee, The Ronald Reagan Presidential Foundation 1985-, Chair. 1985-; Chair. The Huntington Library and Art Gallery 1971-; Fellow A.B.A.; mem. American and Los Angeles Co. Bar Assens., State Bar. Calif., American Judicature Soc., American Law Inst., Calif. Chamber of Commerce (Dir. 1963-, Pres. 1974-75). *Leisure interests:* tennis, golf. *Address:* Gibson, Dunn and Crutcher, 333 South Grand Avenue, Los Angeles, Calif. 90071, U.S.A. (Office). *Telephone:* (213) 229-7560.

SMITH, William Reece, Jr., B.S., J.D., LL.D., D.C.L., D.H.L.; American lawyer; b. 19 Sept. 1925, Athens, Tenn.; s. of William Reece Smith and Gladys Moody Smith; m. 1st Marlene Medina 1963 (divorced), 2nd Gay Culverhouse 1987; one s.; ed. Univs. of S.C. and Fla. and Univ. of Oxford (Rhodes Scholar); U.S.N.R. 1943-46; mem. Faculties of Law, Univ. of Fla. and Stetson Univ. 1952-57; mem. Carlton, Fields, Ward, Emmanuel, Smith & Cutler, Tampa, Fla. 1953-, Chair. 1976-; Pres. Fla. Bar. 1972-73; Acting Pres. Univ. of S. Fla. 1976-77; Pres. A.B.A. 1980-81, Int. Bar Assen. 1988-; Fellow, American Coll. of Trial Lawyers, American Law Inst.; Herbert Harley Award (American Judicature Soc.); Medal of Honor, Fla. Bar. Foundation, Distinguished Alumnus award (Univ. of Fla.), Algernon S. Sullivan award (Univ. of S.C.). *Publications:* numerous articles in American and int. legal periodicals. *Leisure interests:* fishing, riding, tennis. *Address:* One Harbour Place, P.O. Box 3239, Tampa, Fla. 33601 (Office); 1002 Frankland Road, Tampa, Fla. 33629, U.S.A. (Home). *Telephone:* (813) 223-7000 (Office); (813) 254-0007 (Home).

SMITHERS, Sir Peter Henry Berry Otway, Kt., D.PHIL.; British politician and international civil servant; b. 9 Dec. 1913, Moor Allerton, Yorks.; s. of the late Lt.-Col. H. Otway Smithers, J.P. and Ethel M. M. Berry; m. Dorothy Jean Sayman 1943; two d.; ed. Harrow School and Magdalen Coll., Oxford; called to Bar, Inner Temple 1936, joined Lincoln's Inn 1937; Naval Service 1939-45; M.P. 1950-64; Parl. Pvt. Sec. to Minister of State for Colonies 1952-56, to Sec. of State for Colonies 1956-59; Vice-Chair. Conservative Parl. Foreign Affairs Cttee. 1958-62; Parl. Under-Sec. of State, Foreign Office 1962-64; U.K. Del. to UN Gen. Assembly 1960-63; Consultative Assembly, Council of Europe 1952-56, 1960; Vice-Pres. European Assembly of Local Authorities 1959-62; Sec.-Gen. Council of Europe 1964-69; Senior Fellow, UNITAR, New York 1969-73; Gen. Rapporteur, the European Conf. of Parliamentarians and Scientists 1971-76; one-man exhbns. of photography at Oklohoma Art Center 1984, Musée Cernuschi, Paris 1985, Minneapolis 1986, Oklohoma City 1987, St Louis 1987, New York 1987; Chevalier, Légion d'honneur; Orden Mexicana de la Aguila Azteca; Humboldt Gold Medal (for int. work on conservation of nature and natural resources) 1970; Royal Horticultural Soc. Gold Medals for Photography of Plants 1981, 1983, 1985; Grenfell Medal 1984; Medal of Honour of the Parl. Ass., Strasbourg 1984; Hon. Dr.jur. (Zürich) 1970; Conservative. *Publication:* Life of Joseph Addison 1954. *Leisure interest:* horticulture. *Address:* 6921 Vico Morcote, Switzerland.

SMITHSON, Alison Margaret; British architect; b. 22 June 1928, Sheffield; d. of Ernest Gill and Alison Jessie Malcolm; m. Peter Denham Smithson (q.v.) 1949; one s. two d.; ed. South Shields, Sunderland, George Watson's Ladies Coll., Edinburgh and Univ. of Durham; Asst. with London County Council 1949-50; in private practice as architect with Peter Smithson 1950-. *Principal works:* Hunstanton School; Economist Bldg., London; Robin Hood Gardens, G.L.C. Housing in Tower Hamlets; Garden Bldg. St. Hilda's Coll., Oxford; Upper Lawn, Solar Pavilion, Folly. *Exhibitions:* Twenty-four Doors to Christmas 1979, Christmas and Hogmanay, 1980-81. *Publications:* Young Urbit (novel), Urban Structuring Studies (with P. Smithson), Team 10 Primer (Ed.), Euston Arch, Ordinariness and Light, Without Rhetoric, The Heroic Period of Modern Architecture, The Shift: Monograph (all with P. Smithson), The Tram Rats, The Christmas Tree, Calendar of Christmas, Places Worth Inheriting, An Anthology of Christmas, An Anthology of Scottish Christmas and Hogmanay, AS in DS: An Eye on the Road, The 1930s (with P. Smithson). *Address:* Cato Lodge, 24 Gilston Road, London, SW10 9SR, England. *Telephone:* 01-373 7423 and 01-373 3838.

SMITHSON, Peter Denham; British architect; b. 18 Sept. 1923, Stockton-on-Tees; s. of William Blenkiron Smithson and Elizabeth Denham; m. Alison Margaret Gill (Smithson, q.v.) 1949; one s. two d.; ed. Stockton-on-Tees Grammar School, Univ. of Durham and Royal Acad. Schools, London; Asst. at L.C.C. 1949-50; in private practice as architect with Alison Smithson 1950-; Visiting Prof. of Architecture, Bath Univ. 1978-. *Principal works:* Hunstanton School; Economist Bldg., London; Robin Hood Gardens, G.L.C. Housing in Tower Hamlets; Garden Bldg. St. Hilda's Coll., Oxford; Amenity Building, Univ. of Bath; Second Arts Building, Univ. of Bath; 6E, Univ. of Bath. *Exhibitions:* Milan Triennale 1968, Venice Biennale 1976. *Publications:* Urban Structuring Studies, Euston Arch, Ordinariness and Light, Without Rhetoric, The Heroic Period of Modern Architecture, The Shift: Monograph (all with A. Smithson), Walks Within the Walls, Bath, Oxford and Cambridge Walks, The 1930s (with A. Smithson). *Address:* Cato Lodge, 24 Gilston Road, London SW10 9SR, England. *Telephone:* 01-373 7423 and 01-373 3838.

SMITSENDONK, Anton G. O., D.IUR.; Netherlands diplomatist; b. 1928, Utrecht; ed. Univ. of Utrecht; joined Ministry of Foreign Affairs 1955, posted to Belgrade 1955-56, Rome 1958-61, São Paulo 1961-64, Washington 1964-69; Counsellor for Dev. Assistance Jakarta 1969-72; Deputy Chief of Mission Ankara 1973-77; Econ. Minister Washington 1977-81; Chargé d' Affaires Peking 1981; Amb. to People's Repub. of China 1981-86; Perm. Rep. of Netherlands to OECD 1986-. *Publications:* Trade and Labor: two American Policies, Meridian Gate, thoughts about China. *Address:* c/o Netherlands Delegation to OECD, 14 rue Octave Feuillet, Paris 73116, France. *Telephone:* 45 24 99 31.

SMOKTUNOVSKY, Innokenty Mikhailovich; Soviet actor; b. 28 March 1925, Tatyanovka, Tomsk Region; ed. Pushkin Dramatic Theatre Studio, Krasnoyarsk; Army 1943-45; Leningrad Gorky Bolshoi State Drama Theatre 1957-; worked in cinema 1960-; Honoured Artist of R.S.F.S.R., Lenin Prize 1965, People's Artist of the U.S.S.R. 1974 and other decorations. *Principal stage roles:* Prince Myshkin in The Idiot, Sergei in Irkutsk Story, Fyodor in Tsar Fyodor Ioannovich (A. N. Tolstoy), Gaev In Cherry Orchard, Ivanov in Ivanov. *Films include:* 9 Days in One Year, Hamlet 1964, Be Aware of a Car 1966, Tchaikovsky 1969, Crime and Punishment 1970, Uncle Vanya 1971, The Legend of Tila 1979, The Seagull 1980. *Address:* c/o Bolshoi State Drama Theatre, Leningrad, U.S.S.R.

SMOLDEREN, Luc Hippolyte Marie, LL.D.; Belgian diplomatist; b. 7 Feb. 1924, Antwerp; m. Baroness Fiorella de Vinck de Winnezeele 1954; one s. three d.; ed. Catholic Univ., Louvain; Attorney, Brussels 1950-53; joined Ministry of Foreign Affairs 1953; mem. Del. to UN, New York 1956-58, to NATO, Paris 1959-64; Inspector of Diplomatic Posts, Ministry of Foriegn Affairs, Brussels 1965-71; Amb. to Syria 1972-76; Perm. Rep. to IAEA, Vienna 1976-80; Amb. to Morocco 1981-85, to France 1986-; mem. Soc. Royale de Numismatique de Belgique (Vice-Pres.), Acad. Royale d'Archéologie de Belgique; Grand Officer, Ordre de la Couronne de Belgique, de la Couronne de Chêne (Luxembourg); Commdr., Ordre de Léopold, de Léopold II, Ordine al Merito (Italy); Grand Cordon, Order of Merit (Syria). *Publications:* Jonghelinck waradin de la Monnaie d'Anvers 1969, Quentin Metsys médailleur d'Erasme 1969, La Statue du duc d'Albe à Anvers 1972, Le Tombeau de Charles le Téméraire 1980; more than 20 studies on Flemish sculpture and medals in the 16th century. *Address:* Ambassade de Belgique, 9 rue de Tilsitt, 75017 Paris (Office); 25 rue de Surène, 750908 Paris, France (Home).

SMOLICH, Dmitri Nikolaevich; Soviet opera director; b. 1919; ed. Stanislavsky Opera and Drama Studio; mem. CPSU 1956-; Dir. and Chief Dir. of Chelyabinsk, Odessa, Minsk and Kiev opera-houses 1941-70; Chief Dir. of Shevchenko Opera, Kiev 1970-; People's Artist of U.S.S.R. 1979. *Productions include:* Ivan Susanin, Queen of Spades, Prince Igor, La Traviata, Macbeth, Otello, Barber of Seville, Carmen, Bogdan Khmelnitsky, Yaroslav the Wise and many others. *Address:* Shevchenko Opera House, Kiev, U.S.S.R.

SMOLIŃSKI, Adam Karol; Polish radio electronic specialist; b. 1 Oct. 1910, Radziechów; s. of Antoni Smoliński and Helena Brüch; m. Wanda Zaruska 1934; one d.; ed. Warsaw Tech. Univ. ; constructor, Tech. Man. State Plant of Tele- and Radio Engineering, Warsaw 1933-48; head of section State Inst. of Telecommunications 1949-51; head of section, then head of dept., then Vice-Dir. Inst. of Fundamental Tech. Research, Polish Acad. of Sciences 1952-65; Prof., then head of section, then head of dept. Inst. of Elements of Electronics, Dean, Faculty of Electronics, Warsaw Tech. Univ. 1945-81, Extraordinary Prof. 1949, Ordinary Prof. 1956; Corresp. mem. Polish Acad. of Sciences 1962, mem. 1973; Hon. mem. Polish Assen. of Electrical Engineers 1987; mem. numerous eng. socs.; Copernicus Medal, Polish Acad. of Sciences 1985; numerous Polish decorations including Commdr.'s Cross of Polonia Restituta Order, Order of Banner of Labour (1st and 2nd Class). *Publications:* monographs: Zasady wzmacniania (przebiegów elektrycznych) vol. I 1947, vol. II 1952, vol. III 1956, vol. IV 1964, Mikrofalowa elementa ciała stałego 1973, Światłowody i ich zastosowania 1979, Optoelektronika światłowodowa 1985 and numerous articles in scientific journals. *Address:* ul. Polna 54 m. 48, 00-644 Warsaw, Poland. *Telephone:* 25-18-81.

SMOUT, Thomas Christopher, M.A., PH.D., F.R.S.E., F.B.A.; British historian; b. 19 Dec. 1933, Birmingham; s. of Sir Arthur J. G. Smout and Lady Smout (Hilda Smout, née Follows); m. Anne-Marie Schøning 1959; one s. one d.; ed. Leys School, Cambridge, Clare Coll. Cambridge; joined staff Edin. Univ. 1959, Prof. of Econ. History 1970-79; Prof. of Scottish History, Univ. of St. Andrews 1980-. *Publications:* Scottish Trade on the Eve of the Union 1963, History of the Scottish People, 1560-1830 1969, State of the Scottish Working Class in 1843 (with Ian Levitt) 1979, Scottish Population History from the 17th Century to the 1930s (with M. W. Flinn) 1976, Century of the Scottish People, 1830-1950 1986. *Leisure interests:* birdwatching, conservation. *Address:* Chesterhill, Shore Road, Anstruther, Fife, KY10 3DZ, Scotland. *Telephone:* 0333-310330.

SMYTH, Craig Hugh, A.B., M.F.A., PH.D.; American art historian and educationist; b. 28 July 1915, New York; s. of George Hugh Smyth and Lucy Salome Humeston; m. Barbara Linforth 1941; one s. one d.; ed. Hotchkiss School, Princeton Univ.; Research Asst. Nat. Gallery of Art, Wash., D.C. 1941-42; served in U.S. N.R. 1942-46; Officer-in-Charge, Dir. Cen. Art Collecting Point, Munich 1945-46; lecturer Frick Collection, New York 1946-50; Asst. Prof. of Fine Arts, Inst. of Fine Arts, New York Univ. 1950-53, Assoc. Prof. 1953-57, Prof. 1957-73, Acting Dir. 1951-53, Dir. 1953-73; Visiting Scholar, Inst. for Advanced Study, Princeton 1971, Bibliotheca Hertziana, Rome 1972, 1973; Prof. of Fine Arts, Harvard Univ. 1973-85, Prof. Emer. 1985-; Kress Prof. Center for Advanced Study in the Visual Arts, Nat. Gallery of Art, Washington 1987-88; Dir. Harvard Univ. Center of Italian Renaissance Studies, Florence 1974-85; mem. American Acad. of Arts and Sciences 1978-, Inst. for Advanced Study, Princeton 1978, American Philosophical Soc. 1979-, Advisory Cttee. for the Getty Center for Advanced Study 1982-, Comm. for the Conf. celebrat-

ing the 400th Anniversary of the Uffizi Gallery 1982; Academician, Acc. Fiorentina delle Arti del Disegno 1978-; Alt. mem. Comité Int. d'Histoire d'Art 1970-73, mem. 1982-85; Trustee, The Burlington Magazine 1987-; Hon. Trustee, Metropolitan Museum of Art; Chevalier Légion d'honneur. *Publications:* Mannerism and Maniera 1963, Bronzino as Draughtsman 1971, Michelangelo Architect (with H.A. Milton) 1988, Repatriation of Art from the Collecting Point in Munich after World War II 1988, series of articles on Michelangelo and St. Peter's (with H. A. Millon) 1969-, articles on relations between Venice and Florence in painting and sculpture during 15th and 16th centuries 1979. *Address:* P.O. Box 39, Cresskill, N.J. 07626, U.S.A.

SNEAD, Samuel Jackson; American golfer; b. 27 May 1912, Hot Springs, Va.; m. Audrey Snead; two s.; professional 1934-; Canadian Open Champion 1938, 1940, 1941; U.S. P.G.A. Champion 1942, 1949, 1951; British Open Champion 1946; four times runner-up U.S. Open; World Sr. Professional Champion 1964, 1965, 1970, 1972, 1973; played in seven Ryder Cup matches, twice as capt.; eight times in World Cup, four times in winning team; oldest professional to win a major tournament 1965; at age 62 tied for third place in U.S. P.G.A. Championship; 135 tournament wins (164 unofficially, with 84 official U.S. P.G.A. tournaments); U.S. P.G.A. Player of the Year 1949. *Publications:* How to Hit a Golf Ball 1940, How to Play Golf 1946, Education of a Golfer (with Al Stump) 1962, The Driver 1974, Golf begins at Forty 1978. *Address:* c/o Professional Golf Association of America, Box 12458, Palm Beach Gardens, Fla. 33410, U.S.A.

SNEATH, William S., M.B.A.; American business executive; b. 29 March 1926, Buffalo, N.Y.; s. of William and Cyrena (née Kean) Sneath; ed. Williams Coll. and Harvard Graduate School of Business Admin.; joined Union Carbide Corpn. 1950, Treas. 1961, Vice-Pres., Treas. and Chief Financial Officer 1965, Dir. 1969-, Pres. 1971-76, Chair. 1977-82; Dir. Barclays Bank Int. June 1982-, Chair. Advisory Bd. 1983-. *Leisure interests:* skiing, golf, sailing. *Address:* c/o Union Carbide Corporation, 270 Park Avenue, New York, N.Y. 10017, U.S.A.

SNEDDON, Ian Naismith, M.A., D.SC., F.R.S.E., F.R.S., F.R.S.A., F.I.M.A.; British professor of mathematics (retd.); b. 8 Dec. 1919, Glasgow; s. of Naismith and Mary Sneddon; m. Mary C. Macgregor 1943; two s. one d.; ed. Hyndland School, Glasgow, and Univ. of Glasgow; Jr. Scientific Officer, Ministry of Supply 1942-45; Bryce Fellow in Math. Univ. of Glasgow 1945-46, lecturer in Natural Philosophy 1946-50, Simson Prof. of Math. 1956-85, Prof. Emer. 1985-; Prof. of Math. Univ. Coll. of North Staffs. (now Univ. of Keele) 1950-56; Visiting Prof. of Math., Univ. of Strathclyde 1985-; Foreign mem. Polish Acad. of Sciences, Accad. delle Scienze di Torino; Eringen Prize (Soc. of Eng. Science, U.S.A.). *Publications:* Wave Mechanics and its Applications (with N. F. Mott) 1947, The Elements of Partial Differential Equations 1957, Mixed Boundary Value Problems in Potential Theory 1966, Crack Problems in the Mathematical Theory of Elasticity (with M. Lowengrub) 1969, An Introduction to the Use of Integral Transforms 1972, The Linear Theory of Themoelasticity 1974, The Solution of Ordinary Differential Equations (with E. L. Ince) 1987. *Leisure interests:* music, painting in oils. *Address:* 19 Crown Terrace, Glasgow, G12 9ES, Scotland. *Telephone:* (041-339) 4114.

SNEGIREV, Vladimir Vsevolodovich; Soviet diplomatist; b. 1923; mem. of Diplomatic Service 1955-; various posts at Ministry of Foreign Affairs, Moscow, 1955-61 and 1968-78; Embassy Counsellor, France 1961-63; Deputy Chief of First European Countries Dept., Ministry of Foreign Affairs 1963-64; Amb. to Cameroon 1964-68, to Nigeria 1978-86. *Address:* c/o Ministry of Foreign Affairs, Smolenskaya-Sennaya pl. 32-34, Moscow, U.S.S.R.

SNELL, Esmond Emerson, B.A., M.A., PH.D.; American professor of biochemistry; b. 22 Sept. 1914, Salt Lake City, Utah; s. of Heber C. Snell and Hedwig Ludwig; m. Mary Caroline Terrill 1941; two s. one d.; ed. Brigham Young Univ. and Univ. of Wis.; Asst. Prof. of Chem., Univ. of Texas 1941-42, Assoc. Prof. 1943-45, Prof. 1951-56, Assoc. Dir. Clayton Foundation, Biochemical Inst. of Univ. of Texas 1954-56; Assoc. Prof. of Biochem., Univ. of Wis. 1945-47, Prof. 1947-51; Prof. of Biochem., Univ. of Calif. at Berkeley 1956-76, Chair. Dept. of Biochem. 1956-62; Prof. and Chair. Dept. of Microbiology, Univ. of Texas at Austin 1976-80, Ashbel Smith Prof. of Chemistry and Microbiology 1980-; Ed. Annual Review of Biochemistry 1962-64, 1968-83; Walker-Ames Visiting Prof. of Biochem., Univ. of Wash., Seattle 1953; Guggenheim Fellow, Univs. of Cambridge, Copenhagen and Zürich 1954-55, Max-Planck Inst. für Zellchemie, Munich 1962-63, Rockefeller Univ., New York, Hebrew Univ., Jerusalem, and Univs. of Freiburg and Würzburg 1970; mem. N.A.S., American Soc. of Biological Chemists (Pres. 1961-62); Hon. D.Sc. (Wisconsin) 1982; Eli Lilly Award in Bacteriology and Immunology 1945, Meade-Johnson Vitamin B Complex Award 1946, Osborn Mendel Award 1951, Kenneth A. Spencer Award in Agricultural Chem. (American Chemical Soc.) 1973, U.S. Sr. Scientist Award, Humboldt Fund 1978, W. C. Rose Award (American Soc. of Biological Chemists) 1985. *Publications:* over 300 research papers in scientific journals, including Journal of Biological Chemistry, Journal of Bacteriology, Biochemistry, Proceedings of Nat. Acad. of Sciences, Journal of American Chemical Soc.; Biochemical Preparations, Vol. III (Ed.) 1953, Methods in Enzymology (Contributor) 1957, 1967, Comprehensive Biochemistry (Contributor) 1963, 1964, 1971, International Union of Biochemistry

Symposium Series, Vol. 30 1963, Vol. 35 1968 (Co-Ed.), Annual Review of Biochemistry (vols. 38 to 52) (Ed.). *Leisure interests:* travel, gardening. *Address:* Department of Microbiology, University of Texas at Austin, Austin, Tex. 78712, U.S.A. *Telephone:* (512) 471-5543.

SNELL, George Davis, D.SC.; American research geneticist; b. 19 Dec. 1903, Bradford, Mass.; s. of Cullen Bryant and Katherine Davis Snell; m. Rhoda Carson 1937; three s.; ed. Dartmouth Coll. and Harvard Univ.; Instructor in Zoology, Dartmouth Coll. 1929-30, Brown Univ. 1930-31; Nat. Research Council Fellow, Univ. of Texas 1931-33; Asst. Prof., Washington Univ., St. Louis 1933-34; Research Assoc., The Jackson Laboratory 1935-56; Science Admin. 1949-50; Guggenheim Fellow, Univ. of Texas 1953-54; Sr. Staff Scientist, The Jackson Laboratory 1957-69, Sr. Staff Scientist Emer. 1969-; mem. Nat. Inst. of Health Allergy and Immunology Study Section 1958-62; mem. American Acad. of Arts and Sciences, N.A.S.; Foreign Assoc. French Acad. of Sciences; Assoc. American Philosophy Soc.; Bertner Foundation Award 1962; Gregor Mendel Medal, Czechoslovak Acad. of Sciences 1967; Gairdner Foundation Award 1976; Wolf Prize in Medicine 1978; shared Nobel Prize for Physiology or Medicine 1980; Hon. M.D. (Charles Univ., Prague) 1967, Hon. Sc.D. (Dartmouth Coll. 1974, Univ. of Maine 1981, Gustavus Adolphus Coll. 1981, Bates Coll. 1982, Ohio State Univ. 1984), Hon. LL.D. (Colby Coll.) 1982; Hon. mem. British Transplantation Soc. *Publications:* The Biology of the Laboratory Mouse (Ed.) 1941, Histocompatibility 1976, Search for a Rational Ethic 1988, and numerous papers in technical journals and books. *Leisure interest:* gardening. *Address:* The Jackson Laboratory, Bar Harbor, Maine 04609 (Office); 21 Atlantic Avenue, Bar Harbor, Me. 04609, U.S.A. (Home). *Telephone:* (207) 288-3624.

SNELLGROVE, David Llewelyn, LITT.D., PH.D., F.B.A.; British professor of Tibetan and author; b. 29 June 1920, Portsmouth; s. of Lieut.-Commdr. Clifford Snellgrove, R.N. and Eleanor M. Snellgrove; unmarried; ed. Christ's Hospital, Horsham, Southampton Univ. and Queen's Coll., Cambridge; war service in India until 1946; Lecturer in Tibetan, School of Oriental & African Studies, Univ. of London 1950-60, Reader in Tibetan, Univ. of London 1960-74, Prof. of Tibetan 1974-82, Prof. Emer. 1982-; has undertaken numerous expeditions to India and the Himalayas; co-founder, Inst. of Tibetan Studies (now Inst. of Buddhist Studies), Tring, Herts. 1966, fmr. Chair. of Trustees; numerous overseas visits as visiting Prof. or consultant; Rockefeller Grant 1961-64; Leverhulme Grant 1978-81. *Publications:* Buddhist Himalaya 1957, Himalayan Pilgrimage 1961, The Hevajra Tantra (2 vols.) 1959, The Nine Ways of Bon 1967, Four Lamas of Dolpo (2 vols.) 1967, A Cultural History of Tibet (with H. E. Richardson) 1968, The Cultural Heritage of Ladakh (with T. Skorupski) (2 vols.) 1979-80, Indo-Tibetan Buddhism, Indian Buddhists and their Tibetan successors 1986; gen. ed. and maj. contrib. The Image of the Buddha 1978. *Leisure interests:* mountain climbing, reading. *Address:* Via Matteo Gay 26/7, 10066 Torre Pellice, Italy.

SNELLING, Richard A., B.A.; American politician and company executive; b. 18 Feb. 1927, Allentown, Pa.; s. of Walter Otheman and Marjorie (née Gahring) Snelling; m. Barbara Weil 1947; two s. two d.; ed. public schools in Allentown, Pa., Univ. of Havana, Cuba, Lehigh Univ., Pa., Harvard Univ., Mass.; served U.S. Army in Europe 1944-46; fmr. Chair. Shelburne Industries Inc.; fmr. mem. Vt. Republican State Cttee., Republican Nat. Finance Cttee.; fmr. Chair. Vt. Republican Finance Cttee.; mem. Vt. House of Reps. from Shelburne 1959-60, from Dist. 30 1973-74, from Chittenden Dist. 7 1975-76; Majority Leader in Vt. House 1975-76; Republican Nominee for Gov. of Vt. 1966, Gov. of Vt. 1977-84, mem. Advisory Cttee. on Intergovernmental Relations 1977-83; mem. Presidential Advisory Cttee. on Federalism 1981-85; Pres. Snelling Capital Corpn. 1985-; fmr. Pres. Greater Burlington Industrial Corpn.; fmr. Chair. United Way Fund Drive, Vt. Aeronautics Bd., Shelburne Town Planning and Zoning Bds., Chittenden County Planning Cttee.; fmr. Dir. United Community Services of Chittenden County; fmr. mem. Vt. Devt. Comm., Gov.'s Comm. on the Status of Women. *Address:* 201 Harbor Road, Shelburne, Vt. 05482, U.S.A. (Office).

SNETKOV, Gen. Boris Vasilevich; Soviet army officer; b. 1925; ed. Tank Forces Div. of Mil. Acad. and GHQ Mil. Acad.; served in Soviet Army 1943-; mem. CPSU 1945-; various command posts; Commdr. Siberian Div. of Armed Forces 1979-81; Leningrad Dist. 1981-; Gen. 1986; cand. mem. of CPSU Cen. Cttee.; Deputy to U.S.S.R. Supreme Soviet. *Address:* The Kremlin, Moscow, U.S.S.R.

SNIJDERS, Wouter, LL.D.; Netherlands lawyer; b. 26 May 1928, Hilversum; s. of Emilius Paulus Snijders and Aleida Augustus Berendina Eskes; m. Henderika Borst 1952; four c.; ed. Gymnasium Hilversum and Univ. of Amsterdam; lawyer Rotterdam 1954-58, Court's Clerk 1958-61, Judge Dist. Court 1961-70; Judge Raadsheer Supreme Court 1970-86, Vice-Pres. 1986-; Govt. Commr. New Civil Code 1971-; Hon. Dr. (Univ. of Leiden); mem. Koninklijke Med. Akad. van Weterschappen. *Address:* Schiefbaanstraat 25, The Hague, The Netherlands.

SNODGRASS, Anthony McElrea, D.PHIL., F.B.A., F.S.A.; British professor of archaeology; b. 7 July 1934, London; s. of Maj. W. M. Snodgrass and Kathleen M. Snodgrass; m. 1st Ann Vaughan 1959 (divorced 1978), 2nd Annemarie Künzl 1983; one s. three d.; ed. Marlborough Coll. and Worces-

ter Coll., Oxford; nat. service R.A.F. 1953-55; Lecturer in Classical Archaeology, Univ. of Edin. 1961-68, Reader 1968-75, Prof. 1975-76; Laurence Prof. of Classical Archaeology, Univ. of Cambridge 1976-; Sather Prof. in Classics, Univ. of Calif. at Berkeley 1984-85; Fellow, Clare Coll., Cambridge 1977-. *Publications:* Early Greek Armour and Weapons 1964, Arms and Armour of the Greeks 1967, The Dark Age of Greece 1971, Archaeology and the Rise of the Greek State 1977, Archaic Greece: the Age of Experiment 1980, An Archaeology of Greece 1987. *Leisure interests:* mountaineering, skiing. *Address:* Museum of Classical Archaeology, Sidgwick Avenue, Cambridge, CB3 9DA; Clare College, Cambridge, CB2 1TL, England. *Telephone:* (0223) 335153 (Museum).

SNODGRASS, William DeWitt, B.A., M.A., M.F.A.; American poet, critic and teacher; b. 5 Jan. 1926, Wilkinsburg, Pa.; s. of Bruce DeWitt Snodgrass and Helen J. Murchie; m. 1st Lila Jean Hank 1946 (divorced 1953), one d.; m. 2nd Janice Marie Wilson 1954 (divorced 1966), one s. one d.; m. 3rd Camille Rykowski 1967 (divorced 1978), one d.; m. 4th Kathleen Brown 1985; ed. State Univ. of Iowa; Instructor, English Dept., Cornell Univ., Ithaca 1955-57, Univ. of Rochester 1957-58; Prof. English Dept., Wayne State Univ. 1959-68; Prof. English and Speech, Syracuse Univ. 1968-76; Distinguished Prof. of Creative Writing and Contemporary Poetry, Univ. of Delaware 1979-; Visiting Prof., Old Dominion Univ., Norfolk, Va. 1978; Leader, Poetry Workshop, Morehead, Kentucky 1955, Yellow Springs, Ohio 1958, 1959; mem. Nat. Inst. of Arts and Letters 1972-, Acad. American Poets 1973-; Guggenheim Fellow 1972-73; Pulitzer Prize for Poetry 1960, Coll. of William and Mary Bicentennial Medal 1976, and other awards. *Publications:* Heart's Needle 1959, After Experience 1968, In Radical Pursuit (critical essays) 1975, The Fuhrer Bunker (poems) 1977, Six Troubadour Songs (trans. with music) 1977, Traditional Hungarian Songs (trans. with music) 1978, If Birds Build with your Hair 1979, The Boy Made of Meat 1983, Six Minnesinger Songs (trans. with music) 1983, Magda Goebbels (poems) 1983, D.D. Byrde Callyng Jennie Wrenn (poem) 1984, The Four Seasons 1984, Remains 1985, The Death of Cock Robin 1987, Selected Poems, 1957-1987 1987. *Leisure interests:* translating medieval music to be sung, playing the lute, woodcarving, owl-watching. *Address:* Department of English, University of Delaware, Newark, Del. 19711 (Office); R.D.1, Erieville, N.Y. 13061, U.S.A. (Home).

SNOWDON, 1st Earl of, cr. 1961; Antony Charles Robert Armstrong-Jones, G.C.V.O., F.R.S.A., R.D.I.; British photographer; b. 7 March 1930, London; s. of late Ronald Owen Lloyd Armstrong-Jones, M.B.E., Q.C., D.L., and the Countess of Rosse; m. 1st H.R.H. The Princess Margaret (q.v.) 1960 (divorced 1978), one s. one d.; m. 2nd Lucy Lindsay-Hogg 1979, one d.; ed. Eton Coll. and Jesus Coll., Cambridge; Consultant, Council of Industrial Design 1962-; in charge of design of Investiture of H. R. H. the Prince of Wales, Caernarfon 1969; Editorial Adviser, Design Magazine 1961-87; Artistic Adviser to The Sunday Times and Sunday Times Publs. Ltd. 1962-; Constable of Caernarvon Castle 1963-; Pres. Civic Trust for Wales, Contemporary Art Soc. for Wales, Welsh Theatre Co.; Vice-Pres. Univ. of Bristol Photographic Soc.; Sr. Fellow, Royal Coll. of Art 1986; Fellow, Inst. of British Photographers, Soc. of Industrial Artists and Designers, Royal Photographic Soc., Royal Soc. of Arts, Manchester Coll. of Art and Design; mem. Faculty Royal Designers for Industry; Hon. mem. North Wales Soc. of Architects, South Wales Inst. of Architects; mem. Council, Nat. Fund for Research for the Crippled Child; Founder Snowdon Award Scheme for Disabled Students 1980; Pres. (England) Int. Year of the Disabled; Chair. Snowdon Report on Integrating the Disabled 1972; Metropolitan Union of YMCA's, British Water Ski Fed., Welsh Nat. Rowing Club, Circle of Guide Dog Owners; designed Snowdon Aviary, London Zoo 1965, Chairmobile 1972; Art Dirs. Club of New York Certificate of Merit 1969, Soc. of Publication Designers Certificate of Merit 1970, The Wilson Hicks Certificate of Merit for Photocommunication 1971, Soc. of Publication Designers' Award of Excellence 1973, Design and Art Dirs. Award 1978, Royal Photographic Soc. Hood Award 1979, Silver Progress Medal, Royal Photographic Soc. 1986. *Television documentaries:* Don't Count the Candles (six awards, including two Emmys) 1968, Love of a Kind 1970, Born to be Small 1971, Happy being Happy 1973, Mary Kingsley 1975, Burke and Wills 1975, Peter, Tina and Steve 1977, Snowdon on Camera (presenter) 1981; exhbns. Photocall, London 1958, Assignments, Cologne, London, Brussels 1974, U.S.A., Canada, Japan, Australia, Denmark, France, Holland, Serendipity, Brighton 1989. *Publications:* London 1958, Malta (in collaboration with Sacheverell Sitwell, q.v.) 1958, Private View (with John Russell and Bryan Robertson) 1965, Assignments 1972, A View of Venice (with Derek Hart) 1972, Inchcape Review 1977, Pride of the Shires (jointly) 1979, Personal View 1979, Tasmania Essay 1981, Sittings: 1979-83 1983, Israel: A First View 1986, My Wales (with Viscount Tonypandy) 1986, Stills 1983-87, 1987. *Leisure interest:* photography. *Address:* 22 Launceston Place, London, W8 5RL, England. *Telephone:* 01-937 1524.

SNOWMAN, A. Kenneth; British antique dealer; b. 26 July 1919, London; s. of Emanuel Snowman, M.V.O., O.B.E. and Harriette Snowman (née Wartski); m. Sallie Moghilevkine 1942; one s.; ed. University College School, London, St. Martin's School of Art, Byam Shaw School of Art (under F. Ernest Jackson); War Painter, mem. Civil Defence during Second World War; exhibits sporadically at Royal Acad.; also exhibited at Salon, Paris, Leicester Galleries, London; has illustrated several children's books; joined family firm Wartski 1940, now Chair.; organized Fabergé Exhbn., Victoria and

Albert Museum, London 1977; Guest Curator, Cooper Hewitt Museum, New York 1983; Pres. British Antique Dealers Asscn. 1976–77; Chair. Burlington House Fair, Royal Acad. (original Antique Dealers' Fair); Liveryman, Goldsmiths Co. and Painter Stainers Co. *Publications:* The Art of Carl Fabergé 1953, Eighteenth Century Gold Boxes of Europe 1966, Eighteenth Century Gold Boxes of Paris 1974, Carl Fabergé, goldsmith to the Imperial Court of Russia 1979; catalogue Fabergé Exhbn., Victoria and Albert Museum 1977, Fabergé Exhbn., Cooper Hewitt Museum 1983; contrib. to catalogue Munich Fabergé Exhbn. 1986–87, Helsinki Fabergé Exhbn. 1980, Connoisseur Dictionary of Antiques 1955, Great Houses of Europe 1961, Great Private Collections 1963, Masterpieces from the House of Fabergé 1984; contrib. for many years to Connoisseur, Apollo and Antique Collector magazines and to Antiques Magazine, New York. *Leisure interests:* painting, writing. *Address:* 3 North End Avenue, London, NW3, England.

SNOY ET D'OPPUERS, Count Jean-Charles; Belgian economist; b. 2 July 1907, Bois-Seigneur-Isaac, Brabant; s. of Baron Thierry Snoy et d'Oppuers and Viscountess Claire de Beughem de Houtem; m. Countess Nathalie d'Alcantara 1935; two s. five d.; ed. Univ. of Louvain and Harvard Univ.; entered banking business in Belgium 1931; became Attaché to Minister for Economic Affairs 1934, Dir., Int. Treaty Section, Ministry of Econ. Affairs 1936, Sec.-Gen. of the Ministry 1939; dismissed from post by the Germans and active in Resistance Movement during Second World War; re-assumed duties after Liberation and became Pres. Four Party Supply Cttee. of Belgium; played prominent part in creation of Benelux Econ. Union and was Chair. Council for Econ. Union; also contributed to work leading to creation of OEEC in 1948; Chair. OEEC Council 1948–50, Steering Bd. for Trade OEEC 1952, 1960; Chief Belgian del. 1955 to Int. Cttee. set up at Messina Conf., which later became Int. Conf. for European Common Market and Euratom; Pres. Interim Cttee. for European Common Market and Euratom 1957; Sec.-Gen. Ministry of Econ. Affairs until 1960; Perm. Rep. to European Econ. Community 1958–59; Man. Dir. Cie. Lambert pour l'Industrie et la Finance 1960–68; Partner Banque Lambert 1965–68; mem. Lower House of Parl. 1968–71; Minister of Finance 1968–72; several Belgian and foreign decorations including Grand Officer, Order of Leopold and Grand Officer Order of the Crown (Belgium); Grand Cross Order of Crown of Oak (Luxembourg), Royal Order George I (Greece), Order of Merit (Italy), Grand Cross Order of Orange-Nassau (Netherlands), Hon. K.B.E. (U.K.), Grand Cross Order of Merit (Fed. Repub. of Germany); Schuman Prize 1984. *Leisure interests:* shooting, alpinism, tennis. *Address:* Château de Bois-Seigneur-Isaac, 1421 Braine L'Alleud, Belgium.

SOARES, Mário Alberto Nobre Lopes, L. ÈS L., D. EN D.; Portuguese lawyer, historian and politician; b. 7 Dec. 1924, Lisbon; s. of João Lopes Soares and Elisa Nobre Soares; m. Maria Barroso Soares 1949; one s. one d.; ed. Univ. of Lisbon and Faculty of Law, Sorbonne, Paris; Leader MUD Juvenil (United Democratic Youth Movement), mem. MUD Cen. Cttee. 1946–48; Sec. presidential cand. of Gen. Norton de Mattos 1949; mem. Exec. of Social Democratic Action 1952–60; mem. Campaign Cttee. for Delgado in presidential elections 1958; Democratic Opposition cand. for Lisbon in legis. elections 1965, 1969; deported to São Tomé March–Nov. 1968; rep. of Portuguese socialists at various European socialist congresses and 11th Congress of Socialist Int., Eastbourne 1969; Portuguese rep. Int. League of Human Rights; imprisoned 12 times on political grounds; in exile in Paris 1970–74, returned to Portugal after coup April 1974; Minister of Foreign Affairs 1974–75; in charge of negotiations leading to independence of Guinea-Bissau, Mozambique, Angola, São Tomé and Cape Verde; Minister without Portfolio March–Aug. 1975; Deputy, Constituent Ass. 1975, Legis. Assembly 1976; Prime Minister of Portugal for three periods 1976–85; initiated negotiations in 1977 leading to Portugal's accession to the European Communities in 1985; Pres. of Portugal March 1986–; f. Partido Socialista 1973, Sec.-Gen. 1973–86; mem. Council of State; participant in all major int. Socialist summits since 1973; Vice-Pres. Socialist Int. 1976–; mem. Co-ordination and Solidarity between Europe and Latin America; Head of the Socialist Int. Comm. on Latin America, then on the Socialist Int. Comm. on Middle East; corresp. República (Lisbon), Ibéria (New York), Seara Nova (Lisbon), Neuva Socieadad (Latin America) etc.; Corresp. mem. Academia Brasileira de Letras; numerous Portuguese and foreign decorations; Dr. h.c. (Rennes, Hankuk, Lancaster, São Paulo, Brown, Salamanca, Princeton Univs., Univ-Libre Bruxelles); Joseph Lemaire Prize 1975, Int. Prize of Human Rights 1977, Robert Schuman Prize 1987. *Publications:* As ideias político-sociais de Teófilo Braga 1950, Escritos Políticos 1969, Le Portugal Baillonne 1972, Destruir o Sistema, Construir uma Vida Nova 1973, Caminho Difícil, do Salazarismo ao Caetanismo 1974, Escritos do Exílio 1975, Liberdade para Portugal (with Willy Brandt and Bruno Kreisky) 1975, Portugal, quelle Révolution? 1976, O Futuro será o Socialismo Democrático 1979, Resposta Socialista para o Mundo em Crise 1983, Persistir 1983, A Árvore e a Floresta 1985, Intervenções 1987. *Leisure interests:* bibliophile and collector of contemporary Portuguese paintings. *Address:* Presidência da República, Palácio de Belém, 1300 Lisbon (Office); Rua Dr. João Soares, 2-3, 1600 Lisbon, Portugal (Home).

SOARES ALVES, Francisco José, M.A.; Portuguese archaeologist; b. 18 April 1942, Lisbon; s. of José Augusto Ferreira Alves and Margaret Hellen Libbie Mason Soares; m. (divorced); ed. D.João de Castro High School,

Lisbon, Univ. of Paris, DEA–Inst. d'Art et d'Archéologie, Paris; Dir. archaeological campus, Braga (Bracara Augusta) 1976–80; Dir. Portuguese Dept. of Archaeology 1980–82; Dir. Nat. Museum of Archaeology 1980–; Dir. of underwater archaeology on the site of "L'Océan" (French flagship sunk in 1759) 1984–. *Leisure interest:* diving. *Address:* Museu Nacional de Arqueologia e Etnologia, Praça do Império, 1400 Lisbon, Portugal. *Telephone:* 616241/2/3/4.

SOBELL, Sir Michael, Kt.; British business executive; b. 1 Nov. 1892, Borislaw, Austria; s. of Lewis and Esther Sobell; m. Anne Rakusen 1917; two d.; ed. Cen. London Foundation School; Dir., Gen. Electric Co. 1960–67; Chair. Gen. Electric (Radio & Television) Ltd. 1968–, Radio and Allied Holdings Ltd.; Pres. British Technion Soc. 1958–66, Nat. Soc. for Cancer Relief 1964–; Freeman and Liveryman, Carmen Company; Hon. Fellow, Jew's Coll., Bar Ilan Univ., Royal Coll. of Pathologists; Hon. Dr. (Bar Ilan Univ., Technion, Israel). *Leisure interests:* racing, charitable work. *Address:* Bakeham House, Englefield Green, Surrey, TW20 9TX, England.

SOBERS, Sir Garfield (Garry) St. Auburn, Kt.; Barbadian cricketer; b. 28 July 1936, Bridgetown; s. of Thelma and John Sobers; m. Prudence Kirby 1969; two s. one d.; ed. Bay St. School, Barbados; left-hand batsman, left-arm bowler, using all kinds of bowling; debut for Barbados v. India 1953; rep. West Indies in 86 Test Matches, 39 as Capt. 1953–74; made world record Test Match score of 365 not out, West Indies v. Pakistan, Kingston, Jamaica 1958; hit 6 sixes in an over, Notts. v. Glamorgan 1968; Capt. of West Indies and Barbados 1965–74, Nottinghamshire 1968–74; on retirement from Test cricket (1974) held following Test records: 365 not out, 26 centuries, 235 wickets, 110 catches; Hon. Life mem. M.C.C. 1981. *Publications:* Cricket Advance 1965, Cricket Crusader 1966, King Cricket 1967 (with J. S. Barker), Cricket in the Sun (with J.S. Barker) 1967, Bonaventure and the Flashing Blade 1967, Sobers: Twenty Years at the Top 1988. *Address:* c/o West Indies Cricket Board of Control, 9 Appleblossom Avenue, Petit Valley, Diego Martin, Trinidad, West Indies.

SOBHI, Mohamed Ibrahim, B.SC.; Egyptian international official (retd.); b. 28 March 1925, Alexandria; s. of Gen. Ibrahim Sobhi; m. Laila Ahmed Sobhi 1950; two s. one d.; ed. Cairo Univ.; served Egyptian Engineer Corps 1950–54; Tech. Sec., Communications Comm., Perm. Council for Devt. and Nat. Production 1954; Tech. Dir. Office of Minister of Communications for Posts, Railways and Coordination 1956–61; Dir.-Gen. Sea Transport Authority 1961–64; Under-Sec. of State for Communications 1964–68; Chair. Postal Org. of Egypt 1968–74; Sec.-Gen. African Postal Union 1968–74; Dir.-Gen. Int. Bureau of Universal Postal Union 1975–84; Order of Merit, 1st Class (Egypt) 1974, Heinrich von Stephan Medal (Fed. Repub. of Germany) 1979, Order of Postal Merit, Gran Placa (Spain) 1979. *Leisure interests:* reading, philately, music. *Address:* 4 Sheik Zakaria El-Ansary Street, Heliopolis, Cairo, Egypt.

SOBOLEV, Viktor Viktorovich; Soviet astronomer; b. 1915; ed. Univ. of Leningrad, Chair. of Dept. of Astrophysics, Univ. of Leningrad 1948–, Prof. 1949–; corresp. mem. U.S.S.R. Acad. of Sciences 1958–81, mem. 1981–; Dir. Leningrad Univ. Observatory 1961–62; Hero of Socialist Labour, Order of Lenin, Hammer and Sickle Gold Medal. *Publications:* Moving Envelopes of Stars 1960, A Treatise on Radioactive Transfer 1968, Light Scattering in Planetary Atmospheres 1975, etc. *Address:* Leningrad State University, Universiterskay a nab 7/9, 199164 Leningrad, U.S.S.R.

SOBOLEV, Vladimir Mikhailovich; Soviet diplomatist; b. 1 Oct. 1924; m. Julia Dmitrievna; one s. one d.; diplomatic service 1964–; U.S.S.R. Ministry of Foreign Affairs 1964–65, 1970–71; Counsellor, Embassy, Algiers 1965–68, Counsellor Envoy 1968–70; Amb. to Belgium 1971–75, to Finland 1980–88; Ministry of Foreign Affairs 1975–80. *Leisure interests:* cross-country walking, fishing. *Address:* c/o Ministry of Foreign Economic Relations, Smolenskaya-Sennaya Pl., 32/34, U.S.S.R.

SÖDER, Karin A. M.; Swedish politician; b. 30 Nov. 1928, Frykerud; d. of Yngve and Lilly Bergenfur; m. Gunnar Söder 1952; two s. one d.; Vocational Guidance Teacher 1965; Co. Councillor, Stockholm 1968–73; mem. Riksdag (Parl.) 1971–; Minister for Foreign Affairs 1976–78, for Health and Social Affairs 1979–82; Pres. Nordic Council 1984–85, Vice-Pres. 1985–86; Second Vice-Chair. Centre Party 1971, Chair. 1986–87; fmr. Chair. Stockholm Int. Peace Research Inst.; mem. Nat. Bd. of Health and Welfare 1972–76, Nat. Courts Admin. Bd. 1975–76; mem. Board, Royal Dramatic Theatre 1973–76, Rädda Barnen. *Leisure interests:* music, mountain trekking. *Address:* Vretvägen 11, 183 63 Täby, Sweden (Home). *Telephone:* 08-756-52-23.

SÖDERBERG, Erik Axel Olof R:son, M.SC.; Swedish business executive; b. 17 Nov. 1926, Stockholm; s. of Ragnar O. Söderberg and Ingegerd A. Wallenberg; m. 1st Helene M. Schultz 1948; two s. two d.; m. 2nd Sonja Blichfeldt 1980; ed. Univ. of Commerce, Göteborg and Columbia Univ., New York; Dir. Söderberg & Haak AB, Stockholm 1952, Vice-Pres. 1954–66; Man. Dir. Förvaltnings AB Ratos, Stockholm (investment co.) 1958–69, Chair. 1974–; Man. Dir. AB Nordiska Kompaniet 1966–76; mem. of Bd., Esselte AB, Stockholm, Esselte Business System New York, Dahl Invest Int. A/S, Köpenhamm, AB Export Invest, Stockholm, Welbond AB, Smedjebacken; Hon. R.V.O., Hon. C.B.E. 1969. *Leisure interests:* golf, yachting, skiing, reading, racehorse owner. *Address:* Villavägen 27, S-182 75, Stocksund, Sweden. *Telephone:* 46-8700-1700 (Office).

SÖDERSTROM, Elisabeth Anna, C.B.E.; Swedish soprano opera singer; b. 7 May 1927; m. Sverker Olow 1950; three s.; studied singing under Andrejewa de Skilonz and Opera School, Stockholm; engaged at Royal Opera, Stockholm 1950–; appearances at Salzburg 1955, Glyndebourne 1957, 1959, 1961, 1963, 1964, 1979, Metropolitan Opera, New York 1959, 1960, 1962, 1963, 1983, 1984, 1986, 1987; frequent concert and TV appearances in Europe and U.S.A.; toured U.S.S.R. 1966; mem. Royal Acad. of Music, Hon. R.A.M.; Singer of the Court (Sweden) 1959; Order of Vasa; Stelle della Solidarietà dell'Italia; Prize for Best Acting, Royal Swedish Acad. 1965, "Literis et Artibus" award 1969, Commdr. of the Order of Vasa 1973, Commandeur des Arts et des Lettres 1986. *Roles include:* Fiordiligi (Così Fan Tutte), Countess and Susanna (Figaro), Countess (Capriccio), Christine (Intermezzo); sang three leading roles in Der Rosenkavalier 1959. *Publications:* I Min Tonart 1978, Sjung ut Elisabeth 1986. *Leisure interests:* sailing, literature, embroidery. *Address:* c/o Royal Opera House, Stockholm, Sweden.

SODNOM, Dumaagiyn; Mongolian politician; b. 1933; ed. School of Finance and Econs., Ulaanbaatar, Higher School of Finance and Econs., U.S.S.R.; Expert, Ministry of Finance 1950–54, Dir. of Dept. in Ministry 1958–63; Minister of Finance 1963–69; First Deputy Chair. State Planning Comm. with rank of Minister 1969–72, Chair. State Planning Comm. 1972–74; Deputy Chair. Council of Ministers 1974–84, Chair. Dec. 1984–; mem. Cen. Cttee. Mongolian People's Revolutionary Party (MPRP) 1966–, mem. Political Bureau 1984–; Deputy, Great People's Hural (Assembly) 1966–. *Address:* Government Palace, Ulaanbaatar, Mongolia.

SOEDARSONO, Nani; Indonesian politician; b. 28 March 1928, Purwodadi, Cen. Java; ed. Faculty of Law, Gajah Mada Univ., Yogyakarta; schoolteacher 1950–58; mem. Soc. Research Bd., Dept. of Social Affairs, Yogyakarta 1958–63; Dept. of Communications 1964–70; Vice-Chair. Exec. Bd. of Functional Group (GOLKAR) 1978; Chair. Functional Women Asscn. 1981; Minister of Social Affairs 1983–88. *Address:* c/o Ministry of Social Affairs, Jln. Ir. H. Juanda 36, Jakarta Pusat, Indonesia.

SOEDJARWO; Indonesian politician; b. 15 April 1922, Wonogiri, Cen. Java; ed. Jr. High School of Forestry and Forestry Acad., Bogor; various posts in regional forestry 1953–64; Minister of Forestry 1964–66, 1983–88; Dir.-Gen. of Forestry, Dept. of Agric. 1966–82; Hon. Ph.D. (S. Korea) 1980. *Address:* c/o Ministry of Forestry, Jln. S. Parman, Jakarta Selatan, Indonesia.

SOEDJATMOKO; Indonesian social scientist and retd. public official; b. 10 Jan. 1922, Sawahlunto, Sumatra; s. of K.R.T. Saleh Mangundiningrat and Isnadikin Citrokusumo; m. R. Adjeng Ratmini Subranti Gandasubrata 1957; three d.; ed. Medical Coll., Jakarta, and Littauer Graduate School of Public Admin., Harvard Univ.; Deputy Head of Foreign Press Dept., Ministry of Information 1945; Chief Ed. Het Inzicht, Ministry of Information 1946; Deputy Chief Ed. Siasat magazine 1947; Del., later Alt. Perm. Rep. to UN 1947–51; mem. Indonesian Constituent Assembly 1956–59; Assoc. Ed. Pedoman (daily) 1952–60; Dir. P.T. Pembangunan (publishing co.) 1953–61; Vice-Chair. Del. to 21st UN Gen. Assembly 1966; Personal Adviser to Minister of Foreign Affairs 1967–77; Amb. to U.S.A. 1968–71; Special Adviser on Social and Cultural Affairs to Chair. Nat. Devt. Planning Agency 1971–80; Rector UN Univ., Tokyo 1980–87; Magsasay Award for Int. Understanding 1978; Hon. doctorates from Yale Univ., Cedar Crest Coll., Penn., Williams Coll. Williamstown, Georgetown, Washington D.C., U.S.A., Asian Inst. of Tech., Bangkok, Thailand and Kwansei Gakuin Univ., Japan. *Publications:* An Introduction to Indonesian Historiography (co-editor) 1965, The Re-emergence of Southeast Asia: An Indonesian Perspective, Southeast Asia in World Politics (published jointly as Southeast Asia Today and Tomorrow 1969), Development and Freedom 1980, The Primacy of Freedom in Development 1986; also articles in periodicals and reviews. *Address:* 18 Jalan Tanjung, Jakarta 10350, Indonesia. *Telephone:* 327-014.

SOFAER, Abraham David, LL.D.; American lawyer; b. 6 May 1938, Bombay, India; m. Marian Bea Scheuer 1977; four s. one d.; ed. Yeshiva Coll. and New York Univ.; called to New York Bar 1965; law clerk, U.S. Court of Appeals 1965–66, to Hon. William J. Brennan, Jr., U.S. Supreme Court 1966–67; Asst. U.S. Attorney, South Dist., New York 1967–69; Prof. of Law, Columbia Univ. 1969–79; Meyer Prof. of Law and Social Research 1974–75; Adjunct Prof. of Law 1979–80; Judge, U.S. Dist. Court for South Dist., New York 1979–85; Legal Adviser, State Dept., Washington, D.C. 1985–. *Publications:* War, Foreign Affairs and Constitutional Power: The Origins 1976; articles in legal journals. *Address:* Office of the Legal Adviser, Department of State, Washington, D.C. 20520, U.S.A.

SOFOLA, Idowu; Nigerian lawyer; b. 29 Sept. 1934, Ikenne, Olgun State; s. of late Chief Sanni Sofola and Chief Salamotu Sofola; m. Olusola Sofola 1963; four s. one d.; ed. Eke Boys High School, Westminster Coll. of Commerce and Holborn Coll. of Law, London; Gen. Sec. Nigerian Bar Asscn. 1979–81; Asst. Sec.-Gen. Int. Bar. Asscn. 1980–82, Sec.-Gen. 1986–88; mem. Gen. Council of the Bar 1978–83; mem. Body of Benchers 1983; Distinguished Citizen of Ogun State. *Leisure interest:* table tennis. *Address:* 132 Broad Street, P.O. Box 5854, Lagos, Nigeria. *Telephone:* 66425; 772702; 664449.

SØGAARD, Poul; Danish politician; b. 12 Nov. 1923, Dalum, Fyn; s. of the late Johannes Christian and Anna Søgaard; m. Rita Ruth Nielsen 1946; one d.; ed. elementary and high school; mem. of local exec. of Social Democratic Party (DsU), Odense 1951; Chair. of a Constituency, mem. Nat. Exec. and Nat. Secr. of DsU 1953, mem. Nat. Exec. 1953–61; mem. Odense City Council 1954–63; temp. mem. Folketing (Parl.) 1959, mem. Folketing 1960–; mem. various parl. cttees. dealing with Ministry of Defence affairs 1964–; mem. Cttee. on Finance 1966–72, 1973–; mem. del to UN 1967; party spokesman on Defence 1971; mem. Standing Defence Cttee. 1972–77; Commr. for Home Guard 1972–; Deputy Chair. Social Democratic Group and Chair. Parl. Cttee. on Educ. 1977; Minister of Defence 1977–82; fmr. Chair. Odense Tech. School, Rågelund Skolehjem (boarding school); fmr. mem. and Chair. Danish NATO Parl. Group. *Publication:* Fra landsoldat til 70'ernes værnepligtige (From the Soldier of Former Times to the Conscript of the 1970s) as contribution to book Forsvaret til debat (Defence up for Debate). *Leisure interests:* reading, fishing, football. *Address:* Medlem af Folketinget, Christiansborg, 1240 Copenhagen K, Denmark. *Telephone:* 01-11-66-00.

SOISSON, Jean-Pierre Henri Robert, L. EN D.; French politician; b. 9 Nov. 1934, Auxerre; s. of Jacques and Denise (Silve) Soisson; m. Catherine Lacaisse 1961; one s.; ed. Lycée Jacques-Amyot, Auxerre, Faculté de Droit, Paris, Ecole nationale d'administration; Auditor, Audit Office 1961; with del. to Algeria 1961–62; lecturer, Institute d'études politiques de Paris 1962–68; tech. adviser to Sec.-Gen. of Merchant Navy 1964–65, to Sec. of State for Information, later for Foreign Affairs 1966–67, to Minister of Agric. 1967–68; Conseiller referendaire, Audit Office 1968–; Deputy to Nat. Assembly for Yonne 1968–74; Deputy Sec.-Gen. Fédération nationale des républicains indépendants 1969–75, Vice-Pres. 1975–78; fmr. Sec.-Gen. Parti Republicain; Co. Councillor, Auxerre sud-ouest 1970–76, Mayor 1971–; Pres. Caisse d'Aide à l'équipement des collectivités locales 1973–74; fmr. Pres. parl. group for rural devt.; Sec. of State for Univs. 1974–76, for Professional Training 1976, to Minister of the Quality of Life (Youth and Sport) 1976–78; Minister for Youth, Sport and Leisure 1978–81, of Labour, Employment and Professional Training May 1988–; Conseiller Général for Canton of Auxerre Sud-Ouest 1982–; Vice-Pres. Regional Council for Bourgogne 1983–, 1st Vice-Pres., Yonne 1982–; Pres. Comm. de surveillance de la Caisse des dépots et consignations; Croix de la valeur militaire, Chevalier du Mérite agricole, Officier de l'ordre nat. (Madagascar), Chevalier de l'ordre nat. (Senegal, Benin and Niger); Union pour la démocratie française. *Publications:* Le Piège (with Bernard Stasi and Olivier Stirn) 1973, La victoire sur l'hiver 1978, L'enjeu de la formation professionnelle 1987. *Leisure interests:* tennis, skiing. *Address:* Mairie, 89000 Auxerre; 22 rue Philibert Roux, 89000 Auxerre, France.

SOKOLOFF, Louis, M.D.; American research scientist; b. 14 Oct. 1921, Philadelphia; s. of Morris and Goldie Sokoloff; m. Betty Jane Kaiser 1947; one s. one d.; ed. Univ. of Pennsylvania; Research Fellow, Instructor and Assoc. in Physiology and Pharmacology, Graduate School of Medicine, Univ. of Pa. 1949–53; Assoc. Chief, Section on Cerebral Metabolism, Lab. of Neurochemistry, Nat. Inst. of Mental Health, Bethesda, Md. 1953–56, Assoc. Chief, Section on Cerebral Metabolism, Lab. of Clinical Science 1956–57, Chief 1957–68, Chief Lab. of Cerebral Metabolism 1968–; F. O. Schmitt Medal in Neuroscience 1980, Albert Lasker Clinical Medical Research Award 1981. *Publications:* The Action of Drugs on the Cerebral Circulation (Pharmacological Review 11) 1959, The Relationship Between Function and Energy Metabolism: Its Use in the Localization of Functional Activity in the Nervous System (Neurosciences Research Program Bulletin 19 (2)) 1981, Metabolic Probes of Central Nervous System Activity in Experimental Animals and Man (Magnes Lecture Series, Vol. I) 1984. *Leisure interests:* music, tennis, literature, history. *Address:* Laboratory of Cerebral Metabolism, National Institute of Mental Health, Building 36, Room 1A05, 9000 Rockville Pike, Bethesda, Md. 20892, U.S.A.

SOKOLOV, Boris Sergeyevich, D.SC.; Soviet paleontologist and geologist; b. 9 April 1914, Vyshny Volochek, Tver (now Kalinin) Region; ed. Leningrad State Univ.; Laboratory State Asst., Asst. Lecturer, Leningrad State Univ. 1937–41, lecturer 1945–60, Prof. 1964–; Chief of Geological search party, Sr. Research Worker, Head of Dept., All-Union Oil Research Geological Inst. 1943–60; Head of Dept., Inst. of Geology and Geophysics, Siberian Dept. of U.S.S.R. Acad. of Sciences 1960–; Vice-Pres. Int. Palaeontological Asscn. 1972–; Pres. All-Union Palaeontological Soc. of U.S.S.R. Acad. of Sciences 1974–; Acad. Sec., section of Geology, Geophysics and Geochemistry and mem. of Presidium of U.S.S.R. Acad. of Sciences 1975–; mem. French Geological Soc. 1963; Corresp. mem. U.S.S.R. Acad. of Sciences 1958–68, Academician 1968–; Hon. mem. Swedish Geological Soc. 1968–; Lenin Prize 1967; Order of Lenin (twice) and other decorations. *Address:* Akademgorodok, Novosibirsk, U.S.S.R.

SOKOLOV, Marshal Sergey Leonidovich; Soviet army officer; b. 1 July 1911, Yevtpatoriya, Sebastopol; ed. Mil. Acad. for Armoured and Mechanized Troops, Gen. Staff Mil. Acad.; food packer; then joined Army 1932, Tank Corps Far East 1934, then Europe, apptd. Chief of Staff 32nd Army, Karelia 1941, Chief Commdr. (rank of Col.) 1944, regimental Commdr., then Chief-of-Staff of Div., then Commdr. of Div., then Chief-of-Staff, then First Deputy Commdr. Moscow Mil. Dist. 1960–64, of Leningrad Mil. Dist. 1964, Commdr. (rank of Col.-Gen.) 1965–67, First Deputy

Minister of Defence (rank of Gen.) 1967–84, Minister of Defence (rank of Marshal) 1984–87; mem. CPSU 1937–, cand. mem. Cen. Cttee. 1965–67, mem. 1968–89, cand. mem. Politburo 1985–87; Order of Red Banner, Order of Red Star (twice). *Address:* The Kremlin, Moscow, U.S.S.R.

SOKOLOV, Yefrem Yevseevich; Soviet politician; b. 25 April 1926, Byelorussia; ed. Byelorussian Agricultural Academy and Higher Party School of Cen. Cttee. of CPSU; served in Soviet Army 1944–50; Chief Agronomist, Dir. machine and tractor station, Chief of Agric. Inspectorate for Exec. Cttee. of Ivanovo Dist. People's Deputies' Soviet 1956–58; 2nd Sec. Ivanovo Dist. Cttee., Byelorussian CP 1958–61; 1st Sec. Urliutiub Dist. Cttee., Kazakhstan and other party work 1961–65; Chair. Brest Regional Cttee., Agricultural Trade Union; First Sec. Ivanovo Dist. Cttee., C.P. of Byelorussia; Deputy Chief, then Chief, Agric. Dept., Cen. Cttee., C.P. of Byelorussia 1965–77; First Sec. Brest Regional Cttee., C.P. of Byelorussia 1977–87, First Sec. Cen. Cttee. 1987–; Cand. mem., Cen. Cttee. CPSU 1981–86, mem. 1986–; mem. Cen. Cttee. C.P. of Byelorussia 1976–; Deputy to U.S.S.R. Supreme Soviet 1979–, mem. Presidium 1987–; Deputy to Byelorussian S.S.R. Supreme Soviet 1976–80, 1987–, mem. Presidium 1987–; elected to Congress of People's Deputies 1989; Hero of Socialist Labour, Order of Lenin, Order of October Revolution, Order of Red Banner of Labour (three times) and other decorations. *Address:* Central Committee of the Communist Party of Byelorussia, Minsk, U.S.S.R.

SOKOMANU, George (b. George Kalkoa); Vanuatu politician; fmr. Deputy Chief Minister and Minister of the Interior of New Hebrides; Pres. of Vanuatu 1980–88; arrested Dec. 1988; sentenced to six years imprisonment March 1989, released April 1989.

SOKORSKI, Włodzimierz; Polish writer and journalist; b. 2 July 1908, Aleksandrowsk; m.; four c.; ed. Univ. of Warsaw; General Sec. Polish Socialist Party "Left Wing" 1929–31; Col., Polish Army Second World War; Vice-Minister 1948–53, Minister of Culture and Art 1953–56; Pres., Cttee. for Radio and Television 1956–72; Ed.-in-Chief monthly Miesięcznik Literacki 1966–; Vice-Pres. Polish UNESCO Cttee.; fmr. mem. Bd. Warsaw Branch, Polish Writers' Assen., Deputy Chair. 1979–80; mem. Nat. Council of Culture 1982–; Deputy mem. Cen. Cttee. Polish United Workers' Party 1948–75; Deputy to Seym 1947–55, 1965–76; Chair. Gen. Bd. of Union of Fighters for Freedom and Democracy (ZBoWiD) 1981–82, Presidium mem. 1983–; numerous Govt. and Army awards including Virtuti Militari, Order of Lenin (U.S.S.R.), Order of Banner of Labour, 1st Class, Commdr. Cross and Commdr. Cross with Star of Order of Polonia Restituta, Order of Builders of People's Poland 1979. *Publications:* Rozdarty bruk (The Torn Pavement—novel) 1936, Problemy polityki kulturalnej (Problems of Cultural Policy) 1947, Sztuka w walce o socjalizm (Arts for Socialism) 1950, Dziennik podróży (The Journey Diary) 1954, Grubą kreską (Drawing Thick Lines—essay) 1958, Zakręty (Curves—essay) 1959, Okruchy (Crumbs—short stories) 1961, Escapes (play) 1961, Współczesność i młodzież (The Present Day and Youth) 1963, Współczesna kultura masowa (The Modern Mass Culture) 1967, Spotkania (The Meeting—play), Milczenie (Silence—play), Polacy pod Lenino (Poles of Lenino—war memoirs) 1971, Notatki (Notes—Memoirs) 1975, Nie ma powrotów tych samych (Returning is Never the Same—play) 1975, Piotr (Peter—novel) 1976, Ludzie i sprawy (People and Affairs—memoirs) 1977, Ludzie stamtąd (history) 1978, Leon Schiller, Xawery Dunikowski 1978; Kroki (novel) 1978, Tamte lata 1979, Refleksje o kulturze: literatura i sztuka trzydziestopięciolecia 1980, Czas, który nie mija (memoirs) 1980, Umarli przychodzą nad ranem 1980, Zostać sobą 1982, Każda rzeka ma swój nurt 1983, Nie można powtórzyć 1984, Skazani na siebie (novel) 1986, Znaki zapytania (novel) 1987; Wspomnienia (Reminiscences) in Miesięcznik Literacki 1984–; numerous radio and television plays. *Leisure interests:* swimming, skiing, flowers. *Address:* Aleja Róż 6 m.5, 00-556 Warsaw, Poland. *Telephone:* 29-55-20.

SOLANA MADARIAGA, Javier (brother of Solana Madariaga, Luis, q.v.); Spanish politician; b. 1942, Madrid; m. Concepción Jiménez; two c.; ed. Colegio del Pilar, Universidad Complutense de Madrid; won Fulbright scholarship to study physical sciences in U.S.A. until 1968; Asst. to Prof. Nicolas Cabrera, Univ. of Va. 1968–71, then at Universidad Autónoma de Madrid (where contract was cancelled for political reasons); mem. Exec., Federación Socialista Madrileña and Federación de Trabajadores de la Enseñanza, Unión General de Trabajadores; Prof. of Physical Sciences, Universidad Complutense de Madrid; mem. Congress of Deputies for Madrid; mem. Fed. Exec. Comm., Partido Socialista Obrero Español, former Press Sec. and Sec. for Research and Programmes; Minister of Culture and Govt. Spokesman 1982–88; Minister of Educ. July 1988–. *Address:* Ministry of Education, Alcala 34, 28070 Madrid, Spain (Office).

SOLANA MADARIAGA, Luis (brother of Javier Solana Madariaga, q.v.); Spanish business executive; b. 1935, Madrid; m. Leonor Perez Pita; two c.; ed. Univ. of Madrid; joined Banco Urquijo, rising to Gen. Deputy Dir.; opened pvt. law office; Deputy for Segovia 1977; Pres. Nat. Telephone Co. of Spain 1982–89; Chair. R.T.V.E. 1989–; mem. Bd. of Dirs C.E.O.E., Regional Cttee., Madrid Socialist Fed.; Vice-Pres. Spanish Mastiff Assen. *Publications:* Rota ha entrado en guerra (novel), numerous articles in newspapers and magazines. *Address:* Casa de la Radio, Prado del Rey, 28023 Madrid, Spain (Office).

SOLANA MORALES, Fernando; Mexican politician; Sec. of Commerce 1976–77, of Educ. 1977–82, of Foreign Affairs Dec. 1988–; Pres. Banco Nacional de Mexico 1982–88. *Address:* Secretariat of State for Foreign Affairs, Ricardo Flores Magon 1, Tlatelolco, 06995 Mexico, D.F., Mexico. *Telephone:* 2775470.

SOLANDT, Omond McKillop, O.B.E., C.C., M.D., D.SC., LL.D., F.R.C.P., F.R.S.C., F.A.A.A.S., D.ENG.; Canadian physiologist; b. 2 Sept. 1909, Winnipeg, Man.; s. of Donald McKillop and Edith (Young) Solandt; m. 1st Elizabeth McPhedran 1941 (died 1971), one s. two d.; m. 2nd Vaire Pringle 1972; ed. Univ. of Toronto; Lecturer in Physio-logy, Univ. of Cambridge 1939; Dir. S.W. London Blood Supply Depot 1940; Dir. Physiological Laboratory, Armoured Fighting Vehicle School 1941; Dir. Tank Section, Army Operational Research Group 1942; Deputy Supt. Army Operational Research Group 1943, Supt. 1944; Chair. Defence Research Bd. 1946–56; Asst. Vice-Pres., Research and Devt., Canadian Nat. Railways 1956, Vice-Pres. 1957–63; Vice-Pres. Research and Devt. and Dir. de Havilland Aircraft of Canada Ltd. 1963; Vice-Chair. Bd. of Electric Reduction Co. of Canada Ltd. 1966–70; Dir. Mitchell, Plummer and Co. Ltd. 1971–75, Huyck Corpn. 1966–80; Chancellor Univ. of Toronto 1965–71; Chair. Science Council of Canada 1966–72; Chair. Science Advisory Bd. Northwest Territories 1976–82; Dir. Expo 67; Public Gov. Toronto Stock Exchange 1971–76; Trustee, Int. Maize and Wheat Improvement Centre 1976–86, Int. Centre for Agricultural Research in Dry Areas 1976–81, Int. Centre for Insect Physiology and Ecology, Nairobi 1977–83, Int. Centre for Diarrhoeal Diseases Research, Dhaka 1979–82; Research Adviser, Royal Comm. on the Ocean Ranger Marine Disaster, St. John's, Newfoundland 1981–85; Fellow Royal Soc. of Canada, Royal Coll. of Physicians (London) 1948; Hon. mem. Eng. Inst. of Canada; Hon. D.Sc. (British Columbia, Manitoba, Laval, McGill and St. Francis Xavier, Royal Mil. Coll., Univ. of Montreal), Hon. LL.D. (Toronto, Dalhousie, Sir George Williams Univ., Saskatchewan), Hon. D.Eng. (Waterloo); Medal of Freedom (with Bronze Palm). *Leisure interests:* skiing and canoeing. *Address:* The Wolfe Den, R.R.1, Bolton, Ont. L7E 5R7, Canada (Home). *Telephone:* (416) 880-4981.

SOLCHAGA CATALÁN, Carlos; Spanish politician; b. 1944, Tafalla; m.; two c.; ed. Escolapios de Tafalla, Instituto de Pamplona; worked in Research Dept., later Head of Balance of Payments and Int. Econ. Section, Banco de España 1967–74, 1974–76; Research Dept., Instituto Nacional de Industria 1974; joined Partido Socialista Obrero Español 1974, mem. Exec., Basque Country section 1978; Research Dept., Banco de Vizcaya, Bilbao 1976–79; Head of Trade Section, Consejo Gen. Vasco; mem. Congress of Deputies April 1980–; Minister of Industry 1982–85, of Econs., Finance and Trade July 1985–. *Address:* Ministerio de Economia, Alcalá 11, Madrid 1, Spain (Office).

SOLERI, Paolo, D.ARCH.; American (b. Italian) architect and urban planner; b. 21 June 1919, Turin, Italy; m. Corolyn Woods 1951 (deceased); two d.; ed. Torino Polytechnico, Frank Lloyd Wright Fellowship, Taliesin, Ariz.; went to U.S.A. 1947 to study; returned to Italy 1949; commissioned to design and build ceramics factory, Ceramica Artistica Solimene; resident in U.S.A 1955–; Pres. Cosanti Foundation (for research into urban planning); Prin. Paolo Soleri Assocs. Inc., Architects; since 1970 developing Arcosanti as an Urban Lab. in Cen. Ariz.; exbhns. of work have appeared in over 70 public and private museums, colls. and univs., U.S.A.; Distinguished Visiting Lecturer, Coll. of Architecture, Ariz. State Univ.; Gold Medal, World Biennale of Architecture, Sofia, Bulgaria 1981; Gold Medal, American Inst. of Architects; Hon. Dr. (Dickinson Coll., Carlisle, Pa., Moore Coll. of Art, Phila., Ariz. State Univ.). *Publications:* Sketchbooks of Paolo Soleri 1970, Arcology: City in the Image of Man 1970, Matter becoming Spirit 1971, Fragments 1981, Omega Seed 1981, Arcosanti: an Urban Laboratory? 1983, Paolo Soleri's Earth Casting (with Scott M. Davis) 1984, Space for Peace 1984, Technology and Cosmogenesis 1986. *Address:* 6433 Doubletree Road, Scottsdale, Ariz. 85253, U.S.A. *Telephone:* (602) 948-6145.

SOLESBY, Tessa Audrey Hilda, C.M.G., M.A.; British diplomatist; b. 5 April 1932; d. of Charles Solesby and Hilda Solesby; ed. Clifton High School and St. Hugh's Coll., Oxford; joined H. M. Diplomatic Service 1956; served Manila 1957–59, Lisbon 1959–62, U.K. Mission at UN, Geneva 1964–68, U.K. Mission at UN, New York 1970–72; on secondment to NATO Int. Staff, Brussels 1975–78; Counsellor, East Berlin 1978–81; temporary Minister, U.K. Mission to UN, New York 1981–82; Minister, Pretoria 1986–87; Leader, U.K. Del to Conf. on Disarmament 1987–; Hon. Fellow, St. Hugh's Coll., Oxford 1988. *Leisure interests:* music, hill walking. *Address:* c/o Foreign and Commonwealth Office, King Charles Street, London, S.W.1, England.

SOLH, Rashid; Lebanese lawyer and politician; b. 1926, Beirut; ed. Coll. des Frères des Ecoles Chrétiennes, Coll. Al Makassed, Faculty of Law; Beirut; successively Judge, Pres. of the Labour Arbitration Council, Examining Magistrate, Attorney-Gen. of the Charéi Tribunal; Ind. mem. Chamber of Deputies for Beirut 1964, 1972; Prime Minister 1974–75. *Address:* Chambre des Députés, Place de l'Etoile, Beirut, Lebanon.

SOLIMAN, Mohammed Sidky; Egyptian engineer and politician; b. 1919; ed. Fuad I Univ., Cairo; studied eng. and mil. science; Col. in Egyptian Army -1962; Minister of Aswan High Dam 1962–66; Prime Minister 1966–

67; Deputy Prime Minister and Minister of Industry, Electricity and the Aswan Dam June 1967-70, 1971; Order of Lenin. *Address:* Cairo, Egypt.

SOLIS PALMA, Manuel; Panamanian politician; Minister of Educ. 1984-88; Prime Minister of Panama Feb. 1988-; First Vice-Pres. of Panama 1988-; Minister in Charge of the Presidency of the Repub. Feb. 1988-. *Address:* Office of the Prime Minister, Panama City, Panama.

SOLIS RUIZ, José; Spanish politician and trade unionist; b. 1913; Barrister and mil. lawyer; fmr. mem. Falange labour and trade union org., organized First Nat. Congress of Workers 1946; fmr. Civil Gov., Pontevedra and Guipuzcoa; Nat. Del. of Syndicates 1951-57; Minister and Sec.-Gen. of Falange 1957-69, Minister of Labour 1975-76. *Address:* Alcalá 44, Madrid, Spain.

SÖLLE, Horst; German politician; b. 3 June 1924, Leipzig; ed. Karl Marx Univ., Leipzig; Official, Ministry of Transport of G.D.R.; mem. staff Cen. Cttee. of Socialist Unity Party (SED) 1952-62, Cand. mem. 1963-76, mem. 1976-; Sec. of State, Ministry of Foreign and Inter-German Trade of G.D.R. 1962-65; Minister of Foreign Trade, G.D.R. 1965-86; mem. Presidium, Council of Ministers 1976-, First Deputy Chair. 1986-88; Perm. Rep. to CMEA Nov. 1988-; Medal of Merit of G.D.R.; Patriotic Order of Merit in Silver and Gold, Order Banner of Labour. *Address:* CMEA, Prospekt Kalinina 56, Moscow 121205, U.S.S.R.

SOLLERO, Lauro; Brazilian pharmacologist; b. 23 Jan. 1916; ed. Ginásio Raul Soares, Ubá, Minas Gerais, and Universidade do Brasil; Prof. in Dept. of Pharmacology, School of Medicine and Surgery, Rio de Janeiro 1953-, Faculty of Medicine, Univ. do Brasil 1963-; Fellow, Guggenheim Foundation, Rockefeller Foundation. *Publications include:* Curarização, Orgão elétrico do Electrophorus electricus, Serotonina, Bloqueadores A-drenérgicos. *Address:* Laboratório de Farmacologia, Faculdade Nacional de Medicina, Avenida Pasteur 458, Rio de Janeiro, RJ, Brazil.

SOLOMENKO, Nikolai Stepanovich; Soviet construction-mechanics specialist; b. 5 Dec. 1923, Minsk; s. of Stepan Alexandrovich Solomenko and Anastasia Konstantinora Solomenko; m. Raisa Savelierna Solomenko 1947; one s.; ed. Dzerzhinsky Higher Mil. Naval Eng. School; mem. CPSU 1944-; served in Red Army; researcher Cen. Inst. of Eng. 1946-59, Deputy Head, Head of Dept. 1959-70, Deputy Dir. 1971-84; First Deputy Dir. of Presidium of Leningrad Scientific Centre of U.S.S.R. Acad. of Sciences 1984-88; concurrently teacher Leningrad Univ. 1951-53, Dept. Head 1988-; mem. of U.S.S.R. Acad. of Sciences 1984-; specialises in naval constructional mechanics; U.S.S.R. State Prize 1984, Order of the Patriotic War 1985. *Publications:* Construction Mechanics of Ships, and numerous other publs. on naval construction mechanics. *Leisure interests:* chess, symphonic music. *Address:* U.S.S.R. Academy of Sciences, Moscow V-71, Leninsky Pr. 14; 9 Frunze Street, Kv. 112, 196135 Leningrad, U.S.S.R.

SOLOMENTSEV, Mikhail Sergeyevich; Soviet politician; b. 7 Nov. 1913; ed. Leningrad Polytechnic Inst.; mem. CPSU 1940-; Engineer, Workshop Foreman, Chief Engineer, Factory Dir., Lipetsk and Chelyabinsk Regions 1940-54; Sec., later Second Sec. Chel-yabinsk Regional Cttee. of CPSU 1954-57; Chair. Chelyabinsk Nat. Econ. Council 1957-59; First Sec. Karaganda Regional Cttee. CP of Kazakhstan 1959-62, Second Sec. Cen. Cttee., CP of Kazakhstan 1962-64; First Sec. Rostov District Cttee. of CPSU 1964-66; Sec. CPSU Central Cttee. 1966-67; Head of Dept. of Heavy Industry, CPSU Central Cttee. 1967-71; Chair. Council of Ministers of R.S.F.S.R. 1971-83, mem. 1983; Chair. CP Control Comm. 1983-88; Chair. Cen. Auditing Comm. 1984-86; Chair. State Comm. to investigate crimes of Stalin 1988-; mem. Cen. Cttee. of CPSU 1961-89; Cand. mem. Politburo 1971-83, mem. 1983-88; Deputy to U.S.S.R. Supreme Soviet 1958-; Order of Lenin (six times), Sixty Years of Armed Forces of U.S.S.R. Medal and other decorations. *Address:* R.S.F.S.R. Council of Ministers, 3 Delegatskaya ulitsa, Moscow, U.S.S.R.

SOLOMON, Anthony Morton, M.A., PH.D.; American economist and banker; b. 27 Dec. 1919, Arlington, N.J.; s. of Jacob and Edna (née Yudin) Solomon; m. Constance Beverly Kaufman 1950; one s. one d.; ed. Univ. of Chicago, Harvard Univ.; mem. American Financial Mission to Iran 1942-46; Securities Analyst, Bache & Co. 1950-51; Publr. Nat. Industrial Directory, Mexico 1951-53; Pres. Rosa Blanca Products Corpn., Mexico 1953-61; Deputy Asst. Sec. of State for Latin America and Deputy Asst., Agency for Int. Devt. (AID) 1963-65; Asst. Sec. of State for Econ. Affairs 1965-69; Pres. Int. Investment Corpn. for Yugoslavia, London 1969-72; Adviser to Chair., Ways and Means Cttee., House of Reps. 1972-73; Under-Sec. for Monetary Affairs, Treasury Dept. 1977-80; Pres. and C.E.O. New York Federal Reserve Bank 1980-84; Lecturer, Harvard Business School 1961-63; Chair. AID Mission to Bolivia 1963; Chair., as Special Consultant to Pres. Kennedy on Mission of U.S. Trust Territory, Pacific Islands 1963; Dir. Syntex Corpn., Mercury Int. Group PLC, S. G. Warburg (U.S.A.) Inc. (Chair. 1985-); Adviser, Man. Bd. Banca Commerciale Italiana 1985-; Chair. Exec. Cttee. Inst. for Int. Econs.; Chair. of Bd. Bellevue Hosp. *Leisure interest:* sculpture. *Address:* S.G. Warburg U.S.A. Inc., Equitable Tower, 787 7th Avenue, New York, N.Y. 10019, U.S.A. (Office).

SOLOMON, Arthur Kaskel, PH.D., D.PHIL., SC.D.; American professor of biophysics; b. 26 Nov. 1912, Pittsburgh, Pa.; s. of Mark K. Solomon and Hortense Nattans; m. Mariot Fraser Mathews 1972; one s. one d. from

previous m.; ed. Univs. of Princeton, Harvard and Cambridge; Research Fellow, Cavendish Lab., Cambridge 1937-39; Research Assoc., Physics and Chem., Harvard Univ. 1939-41; Research Fellow, Biological Chem., Harvard Medical School 1940-42, Asst. Prof. of Physiological Chem. 1946-57, Assoc. Prof. Biophysics 1957-68, Prof. Biophysics 1968-; Chair. Comm. on Higher Degrees in Biophysics, Harvard 1959-80, Council on the Arts, Harvard 1973-76; Fellow, American Acad. of Arts and Sciences; Sec.-Gen. Int. Union for Pure and Applied Biophysics 1961-72; mem. Exec. Cttee., Int. Council of Scientific Unions 1966-72; mem. U.S. Nat. Comm. for UNESCO 1969-74; Science Policy Adviser to Thai Govt. 1969-72; mem. Editorial Bd. Journal of General Physiology 1958-; mem. Bd. of Int. Orgs. and Programs, N.A.S. 1973-80; Chair. ICSU-UNESCO Distinguished Fellowship Cttee. 1982-85; Chair. 1977-79; mem. American Chem. Soc., American Physiol. Soc., Biophysics Soc., Soc. Gen. Physiology; Pres. Read's Inc. 1961-77; mem. U.S. Del to Gen. Ass. of UNESCO, Paris 1978; U.S. Del. to 17th Gen. Assembly of Int. Council of Scientific Unions, Athens 1978; Fellow American Acad. of Arts and Sciences; Trustee, Inst. of Contemporary Art, Boston 1946-84, Pres. 1965-71; Overseer, Museum of Fine Arts, Boston 1978-84; mem. Collectors Cttee., Nat. Gallery of Art, Washington, D.C. 1985-; Order Andres Bello, Venezuela 1974. *Publications:* Why Smash Atoms 1940, and over four hundred scientific articles. *Leisure interests:* art, travel. *Address:* Biophysical Laboratory, Harvard Medical School, 25 Shattuck Street, Boston, Mass. (Office); 27 Craigie Street, Cambridge, Mass., U.S.A. (Home). *Telephone:* (617) 732-1953 (Office); (617) 876-0149 (Home).

SOLOMON, David H., M.D.; American professor of medicine; b. 7 March 1923, Cambridge, Mass.; s. of Frank Solomon and Rose Roud Solomon; m. Ronda Markson 1946; two d.; ed. Brown Univ. and Harvard Medical School; Medical House Officer, Peter Bent Brigham Hospital 1946-47; Research Fellow in Medicine, Peter Bent Brigham Hospital and Harvard Medical School 1947-48; Sr. Asst. Surgeon, U.S. Public Health Service and Investigator, Gerontology Section, Nat. Heart Inst. 1948-50; Sr. Asst. Resident Physician, Peter Bent Brigham Hospital 1950-51; Fellow in Endocrinology, New England Center Hospital 1951-52; Instr. School of Medicine, Univ. of Calif. Los Angeles (UCLA) 1952-54, Asst. Prof. 1954-60, Assoc. Prof. 1960-66, Prof. of Medicine 1966-, Assoc. Dir. Multicampus Div. of Geriatric Medicine 1982-; Consultant, Wadsworth Hosp., Los Angeles 1952-, Sepulveda Hosp. 1971-; several awards. *Publications:* co-author of three books, author of 148 scientific papers, 29 book chapters, 11 review articles and 122 published abstracts. *Leisure interests:* tennis, running, reading, hiking, bridge. *Address:* University of California (Los Angeles), Department of Medicine, 10833 Le Conte Avenue, 32-144 CHS, Los Angeles, Calif. 90024 (Office); 863 Woodacres Road, Santa Monica, Calif. 90402, U.S.A. (Home). *Telephone:* 213-825-8255 (Office).

SOLOMON, David Henry, D.SC., PH.D., F.A.A., F.R.A.C.I., F.T.S.; Australian research scientist; b. 19 Nov. 1929, Adelaide; s. of H. J. Solomon and M. Mead; m. Valerie Newport 1954; three d.; ed. N.S.W. Univ. of Tech. and Univ. of N.S.W.; Balm Paints Pty. Ltd. (now Dulux Australia Ltd.), Sydney 1946-53, 1955-63; demonstrator/teacher Fellow, N.S.W. Univ. of Tech. 1953-55; seconded to ICI Paints Div., Slough 1959-60; Sr. Research Scientist, Sr. Prin. Research Scientist, CSIRO Div. of Applied Mineralogy 1963-70; at Georgia Kaolin Co., Elizabeth, N.J., U.S.A. 1968-69; Chief Research Scientist/Chief of Div. CSIRO Div. of Applied Organic Chem. 1970-86; Acting Dir. CSIRO Inst. of Industrial Technology 1986-87; Chief, CSIRO Div. of Chemicals & Polymers 1988-; Fellow, Australian Acad. of Technological Sciences and Eng.; David Syme Research Medal 1976, Polymer Medal 1977, Leighton Memorial Medal 1985, CSIRO Medal (with D. Addison) 1987 and other awards. *Publications:* five books, 23 patents and 139 scientific papers. *Leisure interests:* farming, squash. *Address:* CSIRO Division of Chemicals & Polymers, Private Bag 10, Clayton, Vic. 3168, Australia. *Telephone:* (03) 542 2244.

SOLOMON, Ezra, PH.D.; American professor of finance and government official; b. 20 March 1920, Rangoon, Burma; s. of Ezra and Emily Rose Solomon; m. Janet Cameron 1949; three d.; ed. Univs. of Rangoon and Chicago; Faculty mem., Univ. of Chicago 1948-60; Dean William Prof. of Finance, Stanford Univ. 1961-71, 1973-; Dir. Int. Cen. for Advancement of Man. Educ., Stanford Univ. 1961-64; mem. Council of Econ. Advisers to Pres. Nixon 1971-73 (resigned); Dir. Encyclopaedia Britannica Inc., First Nationwide Financial Corpn., McKesson Corpn. Inc., Capital Preservation Funds, Benham Man. Funds; served in RNVR 1942-47; mem. American Econ. Asscn., American Finance Asscn. *Publications:* The Management of Corporate Capital 1960, Metropolitan Chicago—An Economic Analysis 1960, The Theory of Financial Management 1963, Money and Banking (5th edn.) 1968, Wall Street in Transition 1974, The Anxious Economy 1975, An Introduction to Financial Management 1977, Beyond the Turning Point 1981, International Patterns of Inflation: A Study in Contrasts 1984. *Leisure interest:* reading. *Address:* 775 Santa Ynez, Stanford, Calif. 94305, U.S.A. *Telephone:* (415) 323-6925.

SOLOMON, Patrick Vincent Joseph; Trinidadian diplomatist (retd.), politician and physician; b. 12 April 1910; s. of the late Charles and Euphemia (née Payne) Solomon; m. 2nd Leslie Richardson 1974; two s. from previous m.; ed. St. Mary's Coll., Trinidad, Queen's Univ., Belfast; practised medicine in Scotland, Ireland, Wales, Leeward Islands 1934-43;

medical practice in Trinidad 1943-; mem. Legis. Council, Trinidad 1946-50, 1956-61; Deputy Pol. Leader, People's Nat. Movement 1956-66; Minister of Educ. and Culture 1956-60; Minister of Home Affairs 1960-64; Deputy Prime Minister 1962-66; Minister of Foreign Affairs 1964-66; Perm. Rep. of Trinidad and Tobago to UN 1966-71, Vice-Pres. Gen. Assembly 1966, Chair. Fourth Cttee. of Gen. Assembly 1968, Vice-Chair. Sea-Bed Cttee. 1971; High Commr. to U.K. and Amb. to Norway, Finland, Denmark, Switzerland, Fed. Repub. of Germany, France, Netherlands, Italy, Luxembourg 1971-75, EEC and Belgium 1971-73; Pres. of Ass., IMCO (UN) 1976-77; Chair. Crown Life (Caribbean) Ltd. 1977-. *Publication:* Solomon: An Autobiography 1981. *Leisure interests:* bridge, fishing. *Address:* 8 Woodlands Road, Valsayn Park, Trinidad and Tobago.

SOLOMON, Richard L., A.B., M.SC., PH.D.; American professor of psychology; b. 2 Oct. 1918, Boston; s. of Frank Solomon and Rose Roud; divorced; two d.; ed. Brown Univ.; Instructor, Brown Univ. 1946; Asst. Prof. Harvard Univ. 1947-50, Assoc. Prof. 1950-57, Prof. of Social Psychology 1957-60; Prof. of Psychology, Univ. of Pa. 1960-74, James M. Skinner Prof. of Science 1975-85, Emer. 1985-; Prof., Princeton Univ. 1974-75; mem. American Acad. of Arts and Sciences, N.A.S. *Leisure interests:* hiking, mountaineering, summer camp counselling. *Address:* P.O. Box 2075, Conway, N.H. 03818, U.S.A. *Telephone:* (603) 447-5708.

SOLOMON, Robert, PH.D.; American econo mist; b. 2 May 1921, New York; s. of late Sol Solomon and of Betty Brownstone Solomon; m. Fern Rice Solomon 1946; three d.; ed. Univ. of Michigan and Harvard Univ.; Economist, Fed. Reserve Bd. 1947-65, Adviser 1965-76, Dir. Div. of Int. Finance 1966-72; Sr. Staff Economist, Council of Econ. Advisers 1963-64; Vice-Chair. Deputies of Cttee. of Twenty 1972-74; Adjunct Prof., American Univ., Washington, D.C. 1962-67; Sr. Fellow, Brookings Inst. Washington, D.C. 1976-80, Guest Scholar 1980-, publr. Int. Econ. Letter 1981-; Pres. RS Assocs. 1980-; Columnist, Journal of Commerce 1977-; Rockefeller Public Service Award 1971; Officier, Légion d'honneur 1977. *Publications:* The Interdependence of Nations: An Agenda for Research 1977, The International Monetary System, 1945-81 1982, The International Co-ordination of Economic Policies 1989; numerous articles. *Leisure interests:* cycling, hiking, photography, music. *Address:* 8502 West Howell Road, Bethesda, Md. 20817, U.S.A. (Home). *Telephone:* (301) 365-8623 (Home).

SOLOMON, Yonty, B.MUS.; British (b. South African) concert pianist; b. 6 May 1938, Cape Town, South Africa; s. of David and Chaze Riva Solomon; ed. Univ. of Cape Town; studied with Dame Myra Hess in London, Guido Agosti in Rome, Charles Rosen (q.v.) in U.S.A.; Concert début in Wigmore Hall, London 1963; recitals and concertos in U.K., Netherlands, U.S.A., Canada, Romania, South Africa; gave first performances of works dedicated to him by Richard Rodney Bennett (q.v.), Wilfred Mellers, Merilaainen, Wilfred Josephs; given solo performing rights by composer Kaikhosru Sorabji 1976-77 for all his works; panel of judges of Royal Overseas League Commonwealth Music Competition 1974-; many TV and radio engagements; many recitals devoted to Charles Ives, J. S. Bach (The Well-Tempered Klavier and Klavierübung), Janáček, Boulez, Granados, Albéniz and much rarely performed piano music; first performance of unpublished scores by K. S. Sorabji 1978; Prof. of Piano, Royal Coll. of Music, London 1978-; Visiting Artist-in-Res., Nottingham Univ. 1980-; Hon. mem. Royal Philharmonic Soc.; Hon. F.R.C.M. (1981), Hon. R.C.M. (London) 1982; Master classes in piano and chamber music at Int. Musicians Seminar (Cornwall) 1982; Scholarships from Univ. of Cape Town; Harriet Cohen Beethoven Medal 1962, Commonwealth Award. *Publications:* Schumann Symposium 1973, Bach's "48", Analysis and Historical Survey 1972. *Leisure interests:* collecting botanical books, growing camellias. *Address:* 43 Belsize Park Gardens, London, NW3 4JJ, England. *Telephone:* 01-586 3983.

SOLONITSYN, Anatoliy; Soviet film actor; b. 1928; trained at studios in Sverdlovsk Drama Theatre; first screen appearance in The Kurt Klausewitz Affair 1964. *Roles include:* Rublev (Andrei Rublev) 1965, Commissar Yevstryukov (No Ford Through Fire) 1968, Kalmykov (To Love a Man) 1968, Sartorius (Solaris) 1973.

SOLOUKHIN, Vladimir Alekseyevich; Soviet writer; b. 14 June 1924, Alepino Stavrovsky; ed. Gorky Inst. of Literature; mem. CP 1952-; Order of Red Banner of Labour, Badge of Honour. *Publications:* (first publs. 1945); verse: Rain in the Steppes 1953, Saxifrage, Streamlets on the Asphalt 1959, Tale of the Steppes 1960, How to Drink the Sun 1961, Postcards from Viet-Nam 1962; novels: Birth of Zernograd 1955, The Goldmine 1956, Beyond the Blue Seas 1957, Country Roads of Vladimir (lyrical diary) 1958, The Drop of Dew 1963, A Lyrical Story 1964, Mother—Stepmother 1971; short stories: The Loaf of Bread 1965, A Slavonic Notebook 1965, The Third Hunt 1968, Kukushkin's Son 1969, White Grass 1971, The Rule of the Tocsin 1972, The Ponds of Olepin 1973, The Straw Cordon 1974, Selected Works 1974; poetry: Don't Seek Shelter from the Rain 1967, The Steppe 1968, A Winter's Day 1969, Selected Lyrics 1970, Argument—(Verse) 1972, The Straw Cordon (stories) 1974. *Address:* Union of U.S.S.R. Writers, 52 Ulitsa Vorovskogo, Moscow, U.S.S.R.

SOLOVEY, Yelena Yakovlevna; Soviet actress; b. 24 Feb. 1947; ed. VGIK. *Roles include:* Klarich in King Stag 1970, Rimma in The Seven Brides of Zbruyev 1971, Dostigaeva in Yegor Bulychov and Others 1973, Lyuba in An Old-Style Drama 1972, Lenochka in Vanyushin's Kids 1974,

Olga Voznesenskaya in Slave of Love 1976, Sofia in An Unfinished Piece for Mechanical Piano 1977, Olga Ilyinskaya in A Few Days in the Life of I. I. Oblomov 1980, Nadezhda Antonovna in Crazy Money 1982, The Fact 1982 (1981 Cannes Prize), There Was No Sorrow 1983.

SOLOVIČ, Ján; Czechoslovak dramatist, writer and script editor; b. 8 March 1934, Pliešovce, Zvolen Dist.; ed. Coll. of Musical Arts, Bratislava 1953-58; script ed. 1957-63, artistic chief 1963-70, Czechoslovak Radio, Bratislava; mem. Cttee., Union of Slovak Dramatic Artists, 1963-69; mem. of Municipal Cttee., CP of Slovakia, Bratislava 1964-70; mem. of Presidium, Municipal Cttee. of CP of Slovakia, Bratislava, 1966-70; Chair. Union of Slovak Writers 1984-86; mem. Bds. numerous theatrical and literary bodies, numerous Czechoslovak decorations, World Peace Council Medal 1980, Order of Labour 1984. *Works: dramas:* Posledná hrmavica 1955, Nepokojná mladosť 1957, Súhvezdie draka 1958, U nás taká obyčaj 1960, Strašne ošemetná situácia 1968, Žebrácke dobrodružstvo 1970, Veža nádeje 1972, Meridián 1974, Strieborný jaguár 1975, Zlatý dážď 1976, Pozor na anjelov 1978, Právo na omyl 1981; *TV plays:* Polnoc bude o päť minút 1958, Kar na konci roku 1963, Kde leží naša bieda 1967, Zhasnuté svetlá 1967, Traja z deviateho poschodia 1969, Rekomando 1970, Straty a nálezy 1976. *radio plays:* Torunský génius 1953, Ako Budeme žiť 1960, Ruky pre Luciu 1962, Dialóg s vami 1965.

SOLOVYOV, Gleb Mikhailovich; Soviet surgeon; b. 1928; ed. First Medical Inst. Moscow; mem. CPSU 1950-; postgraduate studies 1952-55; attached to Acad. of Medical Sciences 1955-60; Head of Lab. of Research Inst. of Clinical and Experimental Surgery 1960-69, Deputy Dir. 1963-69; Dir. of Inst. for Organ and Tissue Transplants, Acad. of Sciences 1969; State Prize (for part in developing kidney transplants) 1971. *Address:* Academy of Sciences of U.S.S.R., Leninsky Pr. 14, Moscow V-71, U.S.S.R.

SOLOVYOV, Yuri Filippovich; Soviet official; b. 1925, Leningrad; ed. Leningrad Inst. of Railway Engineers; mem. C.P.S.U. 1955-; served in Soviet Army 1943-44; engineer 1944-67; Head Man. Construction of Leningrad Underground 1967-73; Deputy Pres. Leningrad City Exec. Cttee. 1973-76; Second Sec. of Leningrad Dist. Cttee. CPSU 1976-85, First Sec. 1985-; mem. Cen. Cttee. CPSU 1976-; cand. mem. Politburo of Cen. Cttee. CPSU 1986-. *Address:* The Kremlin, Moscow, U.S.S.R.

SOLOW, Robert Merton, PH.D.; American economist; b. 23 Aug. 1924, Brooklyn, N.Y.; s. of Milton and Hannah Solow; m. Barbara Lewis 1945; two s. one d.; ed. Harvard Univ.; Asst. Prof. of Statistics, Massachusetts Inst. of Technology 1949-53, Assoc. Prof. of Econs. 1954-57, Prof. of Econs. 1958-73, Inst. Prof. 1973-; Sr. Economist, Council of Econ. Advisers 1961-62; Marshall Lecturer, Cambridge Univ. 1963-64; De Vries Lecturer, Rotterdam 1963, Wicksell Lecturer, Stockholm 1964; Eastman Visiting Prof., Oxford Univ. 1968-69; Killian Prize Lecturer, M.I.T. 1978; Geary Lecturer, Dublin 1980; Overseas Fellow, Churchill Coll., Cambridge 1984; Mitsui Lecturer, Birmingham 1985; mem. Nat. Comm. on Tech., Automation and Econ. Progress 1964-65, Presidential Comm. on Income Maintenance 1968-69; mem. Bd. of Dirs. Fed. Reserve Bank of Boston 1975-81, Chair. 1979-81; Fellow, Center for Advanced Study in Behavioral Sciences 1957-58, Trustee 1982-; Vice-Pres. American Econ. Asscn. 1968, Pres. 1979, Vice-Pres. A.A.A.S. 1970; Pres. Econometric Soc. 1964; mem. American Acad. of Arts and Sciences, mem. of Council Nat. Acad. of Sciences 1977-80; corresp. mem. British Acad., mem. American Philosophical Soc.; Foreign mem. Acad. dei Lincei (Rome); Hon. LL.D. (Chicago) 1967, (Lehigh) 1977, (Brown) 1972, (Wesleyan) 1982, Hon. Litt.D. (Williams Coll.) 1974, Dr. h.c. (Paris) 1975, (Geneva) 1982, Hon. D.Litt. (Warwick) 1976, Hon. Sc.D. (Tulane) 1983, Hon. Dr. Soc. Sc. (Yale) 1986, Hon. D.Sc. in Business Admin. (Bryant Coll.) 1987; David A. Wells Prize, Harvard Univ. 1951, John Bates Clark Medal, American Econ. Asscn. 1961, Seidman Award in Political Econ. 1983, Nobel Prize for Econs. 1987. *Publications:* Linear Programming and Economic Analysis 1958, Capital Theory and the Rate of Return 1963, Sources of Unemployment in the United States 1964, Price Expectations and the Behavior of the Price Level 1970, Growth Theory: An Exposition 1970. *Leisure interest:* sailing. *Address:* Department of Economics, Massachusetts Institute of Technology, Cambridge, Mass.; 528 Lewis Wharf, Boston, Mass., U.S.A. (Home). *Telephone:* 617-253-5268; 617-227-4436.

SOŁTAN, Jerzy, M.ARCH. & ENG.; American (b. Polish) architect; b. 6 March 1913, Prezma, Latvia; s. of Wladyslaw Soltan and Helena Soltan; m. Hanna Boruciński 1944; one s. one d.; ed. Warsaw Polytechnic Inst.; prisoner-of-war, Germany 1939-45; worked with Le Corbusier, France 1945-49; Prof. Acad. of Fine Arts, Warsaw 1949-65; Prof. Grad. School of Design, Harvard Univ. 1961-78, Prof. Emer. 1978-; architectural practice in Warsaw 1938-39, 1950-65; design practice (with A. Szabo) in Cambridge, Mass. 1967-69, with several architects in U.S.A. 1969-; Hon. Prof. of Architecture, Univ. F. Villareal, Lima, Peru; mem. Akad. der Künste, Berlin; Medal (Pedagogy), Acad. d'Architecture, Paris, A.C.S.A. Medal (Pedagogy), U.S.A.; several architectural prizes. *Leisure interest:* mountains. *Address:* 6 Shady Hill Square, Cambridge, Mass. 02138, U.S.A. *Telephone:* 617-876-2924.

SOLTÉSZ, István; Hungarian engineer and politician; b. 1927, Hámor, County Borsod; s. of Ernő Soltész and Teréz Offenthaler; m. Kovács Borbála 1952; one s. two d.; ed. Tech. Univ. of Sopron; joined Communist Party (now HSWP) 1947; taught as asst. at Miskolc Univ. of Heavy

Industry; held positions in Ministry of Educ. and Ministry of Metallurgy and Machine Industry; Dir. Fémthermia Co. of Apc 1954 and Metallochemia Co. 1955–64; Dir. Metal Dept. Csepel Iron and Metal Works 1964–72, Deputy Dir.-Gen. 1972–74, Dir.-Gen. 1974–78; Minister of Metallurgy and Machine Industry 1978–80; Deputy Minister of Industry 1980–; mem. standing CMEA Cttee. for metal foundry; mem. Soviet-Hungarian Cttee. for Tech. and Scientific Co-operation; Hon. mem. Hungarian Chamber of Commerce; Pres. Hungarian Soc. of Mining and Metallurgy; Labour Order of Merit. *Leisure interests:* gardening, touring. *Address:* c/o Ministry of Industry, 1024 Budapest, Martirok utja 85, and 1111 Budapest Lágymányosi utca 15, Hungary. *Telephone:* 665-874.

SOLTI, Sir Georg, K.B.E.; British (naturalized) musician; b. 21 Oct. 1912, Budapest, Hungary; s. of Mor Stern Solti and Teresa Rosenbaum; m. 1st Hedwig Oeschli 1946; m. 2nd Anne Valerie Pitts 1967; two d.; ed. High School of Music, Budapest, and studied with Zoltán Kodály, Béla Bartók and Ernst von Dohnányi; Conductor and Pianist, State Opera, Budapest 1930–39; General Music Dir., Munich State Opera 1946–52; Gen. Music Dir., Frankfurt Opera, Perm. Conductor of Museum Concerts, Frankfurt 1952–61; Music Dir., Royal Opera House, Covent Garden 1961–71, Principal Guest Conductor 1971–; Principal Conductor and Artistic Dir. London Philharmonic Orchestra 1979–83, Conductor Emer. 1983–; Music Dir., Orchestre de Paris 1971–75, Chicago Symphony Orchestra 1969–(91); has also appeared as Guest Conductor with numerous symphony orchestras and opera cos. in Europe and the U.S.A.; First Prize as a pianist, Concours International, Geneva 1942; Grand Prix Mondiale du Disque 1959, awarded 12 times; 29 Grammy Awards and numerous other record awards; Hon. C.B.E. 1968, Hon. K.B.E. 1971; Hon. Prof. Baden-Württemberg 1985; Hon. D.Mus. (Leeds 1971, Oxford 1972, Yale 1974, Harvard 1980, de Paul 1975, Surrey 1983, London 1986, Rochester 1987); Hon. F.R.C.M. 1980; Commdr. Légion d'honneur 1974, Silver Medal of Paris 1984, Order of the Flag (Hungary) 1987. *Address:* Chalet Haut Pré, Villars sur Ollons, Vaud, Switzerland.

SOLVAY, Jacques Ernest; Belgian business executive; b. 4 Dec. 1920, Ixelles; s. of Ernest-John Solvay and Marie Graux; m. Marie-Claude Boulin 1949; one s. three d.; ed. Univ. of Brussels; joined Solvay Cie. 1950, mem. Bd. 1955, Chair. June 1971–; Dir. Société Générale de Banque 1965–; Chair. Soltex Polymer Corpn. 1974–; Hon. Pres. Fédération des Industries Chimiques de Belgique; Pres. Belgo-British Union; mem. European Advisory Council, Tenneco Inc. 1986–; Chevalier de l'Ordre de Leopold; Hon. K.B.E. *Leisure interest:* orchid growing. *Address:* Solvay Cie. S.A., rue de Prince Albert 33, B-1050 Brussels.

SOLZHENITSYN, Aleksandr Isayevich; Soviet writer; b. 11 Dec. 1918, Rostov-on-Don; m. 1st Natalya Reshetovskaya (separated 1970), 2nd Natalya Svetlova; three s.; ed. Rostov Univ. and Correspondence Course in Literature, Moscow Univ.; joined Army 1941, attended artillery school, commissioned 1942, served at front as Commdr. of Artillery Battery, and twice decorated for bravery; sentenced to eight years in a forced labour camp 1945–53; contracted, later cured of cancer; in exile in Siberia 1953–57; officially rehabilitated 1957; taught mathematics at secondary school, Ryazan; expelled from Writers' Union of U.S.S.R. Nov 1969; mem. American Acad. of Arts and Sciences 1969–; expelled from U.S.S.R. Feb. 1974, now living in U.S.A.; Prix du Meilleur Livre Etranger (France) for The First Circle and Cancer Ward 1969; Nobel Prize for Literature 1970; Templeton Prize 1983; Hon. U.S. Citizen 1974; Hon. Fellow, Hoover Inst. on War, Revolution and Peace 1975. *Publications:* One Day in the Life of Ivan Denisovich 1962 (film 1971), Matryona's Home and An Incident at Krechetovka Station 1963 (short stories), For the Good of the Cause 1964 (short story), The First Circle (publ. U.S.A. and U.K. 1968), Cancer Ward (U.S.A. and U.K. 1968), The Easter Procession (short story), The Love Girl and the Innocent (play, U.K.) 1969, Collected Works (6 vols.) 1969, 1970, Stories and Prose Poems 1971, August 1914 1971, The Gulag Archipelago Vol. I 1973, Vol. II 1974, Vol. III 1976, Letter to Soviet Leaders 1974, Peace and Aggression 1974, Quiet Flows the Don: The Enigma of a Novel 1974, Candle in the Wind (play), The Oak and the Calf: Sketches of Literary Life in the Soviet Union 1975, The Nobel Prize Lecture 1975, Lenin in Zürich 1975, Détente (with others) 1976, Prussian Nights (poem trans. by Robert Conquest) 1977, Collected Works 1978–, Victory Celebrations, Prisoners (play) 1983, October 1916 1985. *Address:* c/o Harper and Row Inc., 10 East 53rd Street, New York, N.Y. 10022, U.S.A.

SOMARE, the Rt. Hon. Michael Thomas, P.C., C.H.; Papua New Guinea politician; b. 9 April 1936; m. Veronica Somare 1965; three s. two d.; ed. Sogeri Secondary School, Admin. Coll.; Teacher various schools 1956–62; Asst. Area Educ. Officer, Madang 1962–63; Broadcasts Officer, Dept. of Information and Extension Services, Wewak 1963–66, Journalist 1966–68; mem. House of Assembly for East Sepik Regional 1968–; Parl. Leader Pangu Party 1968–88; Deputy Chair. Exec. Council 1972–73, Chair. 1973–75; Chief Minister Papua New Guinea 1972–75, Prime Minister 1975–80, 1982–85; Minister for Nat. Resources 1976–77, for Public Service Comm. and Nat. Planning 1977–80; Acting Minister for Police 1978–80; Minister of Foreign Affairs 1988–; Leader of the Opposition 1980–82; Chair. Bd. of Trustees, P.N.G.; mem. Second Select Cttee. on Constitutional Devt. 1968–72, Australian Broadcasting Comm. Advisory Cttee.; Hon. Dr. of Laws (Australian Nat. Univ.) 1979; Pacific Man of the Year Award 1983.

Address: Minister of Foreign Affairs, Central Government Offices, Kumul Avenue, Wards Strip, Waigani, Papua New Guinea.

SOMLYÓ, György; Hungarian poet, novelist, critic and translator of poetry; b. 28 Nov. 1920, Balatonboglár; s. of Zoltán Somlyó and Margit Bolgár; one s.; ed. Budapest Univ. and the Sorbonne, Paris; lecturer in Modern Poetry Budapest Univ. 1975–78; ed. Arion 1966–; organizer Int. Meeting of Poets, Budapest 1966, 1970; corresp. PO&SIE poetry magazine, Paris 1976–; corresp. mem. Académie Mallarmé, Paris 1977–; József Attila prize (four times), Tibor Déry Prize 1987; Officier, Ordre des Arts et Lettres (France) 1984. *Publications include:* Collected Works: Vol. 1: A költészet vérszerződése (The Blood Covenant of Poetry) 1977, Vols 2, 3: Collected Poems 1978, Vol. 4: Másutt (Elsewhere) 1979, Vol. 5: Szerelőszőnyeg (Catwalk) 1981, Vol. 6: Megiratlan könyvek (Unwritten Books) 1982, Vol. 7: Miért hal meg az ember? (Why the Man Dies?) 1984, Philoktetész sebe (Philoctetes' Wound) 1980, Árnyjáték (Shadow Play) 1977, Rámpa (Ramp) 1984, Picasso 1981, Parisiens (poems in French) 1987, Selected Poems 1988, A Költészet ötö dik évada (The Fifth Season of Poetry) 1988; *translations:* Szélrózsa I/II (Compass Card) 1973, Az utazás (The Journey), French Poetry from Baudelaire to our days 1984. *Address:* 1111 Budapest, Irinyi J.u. 39, Hungary. *Telephone:* 296-737.

SOMMARUGA, Cornelio, LL.D.; Swiss diplomatist; b. 29 Dec. 1932, Rome, Italy; s. of Carlo Sommaruga and Anna-Maria Valagussa; m. Ornella Marzorati 1957; two s. four d.; ed. Rome, Paris, Univ. of Zürich; bank trainee, Zürich 1957–59; joined Diplomatic Service 1960; Attaché, Swiss Embassy, The Hague 1961; Sec. Swiss Embassy, Bonn 1962–64, Geneva 1965–68; Deputy Head of Del. to EFTA, GATT and UNCTAD, Geneva 1969–73; Asst. Sec.-Gen. EFTA July 1973–75; Minister plenipotentiary, Div. of Commerce, Fed. Dept. of Public Economy, Berne 1976, Amb. 1977; del. Fed. Council for Trade Agreements 1980–84; State Sec. for External Econ. Affairs 1984–87; Pres. Int. Cttee. Red Cross 1987–; Pres., UN Econ. Comm. for Europe 1977–78. *Publications:* La posizione costituzionale del Capo dello Stato nelle Costituzioni francese ed italiana del dopoguerra 1957, and numerous articles in journals and periodicals. *Address:* International Committee of the Red Cross, 19 avenue de la Paix, 1202 Geneva, Switzerland (Office). *Telephone:* (022) 346001.

SOMMER, Theo, DR.PHIL.; German journalist; b. 10 June 1930, Constance; s. of Theo and Else Sommer; m. 1st Elda Tsilenis 1952; two s. one d.; m. 2nd Heide Grenz 1976; ed. Schwäbisch-Gmünd, Tübingen, Chicago and Harvard Univs.; Local Ed. Schwäbisch-Gmünd 1952–54; Political Ed. Die Zeit 1958, Deputy Ed.-in-Chief 1968, Ed.-in-Chief and Joint Publr. 1973–; Lecturer in Int. Relations, Univ. of Hamburg 1967–70; Head of Planning Staff, Ministry of Defence 1969–70; mem. Deutsche Gesellschaft für Auswärtige Politik, mem. Council Int. Inst. for Strategic Studies; Contrib. Ed. Newsweek; Commentator German TV, Radio; Theodor-Wolff-Preis 1966; Hon. Dr. Univ. of Md., U.S.A. *Publications:* Deutschland und Japan zwischen den Mächten 1935–40, Vom Antikominternpakt zum Dreimächtepakt 1962, Reise in ein fernes Land 1964, Ed. Denken an Deutschland 1966, Ed. Schweden-Report 1974, Die chinesische Karte 1979, Allianz in Umbruch 1982, Blick zurück in die Zukunft 1984, Reise ins andere Deutschland 1986. *Address:* Die Zeit, Pressehaus, Speersort, 2000 Hamburg 1 (Office); Zabelweg 17, 2000 Hamburg 67, Federal Republic of Germany (Home). *Telephone:* 3280-210 (Office); 603-73-00 (Home).

SOMMERFELT, Søren Christian; Norwegian diplomatist; b. 9 May 1916, Oslo; s. of Søren Christian Sommerfelt and Sigrid Nicolaysen; m. Frances Bull Ely 1947; one d.; ed. Oslo Economic High School and Oslo Univ.; entered Norwegian Foreign Service 1941; UN Secr. Div. for Refugees and Displaced Persons 1946–48; First Sec., Copenhagen 1948–50; Counsellor, Norwegian Perm. Del. to NATO 1951–52; Deputy Head, Politico-Econ. Dept., Norwegian Ministry of Foreign Affairs 1953–56, Head 1956–60; Amb., Head, Norwegian Perm. Del. to EFTA, European Office of UN and other int. orgs. at Geneva 1960–68, to Fed. Repub. of Germany 1968–73, to U.S.A. 1973–79, to Italy 1979–81; counsel to Arent, Fox, Kintner, Plotkin and Kahn 1982–84; Assoc. of Washington Resources Inc., Washington, D.C. 1985; Chair. Bd., Nordic Enterprises Inc. 1986–; leader numerous trade dels., leader Norwegian Del. to negotiations establishing EFTA 1959; Chair. EFTA Perm. Council 1962, 1966; Chair. GATT Perm. Council 1963–64, leader Norwegian del. to GATT Tariff negotiations (Kennedy Round) 1964–67; Chair. GATT Contracting Parties 1968; Norwegian Rep. CERN Council 1960–68; Chair. Norwegian Del. in membership negotiations with EEC 1970–72; Order of St. Olav (Norway), Grosses Verdienstkreuz (Fed. Repub. of Germany), Grand Cross of the Order of Merit (Italy), North Star (Sweden), Dannebrog (Denmark), Falcon (Iceland), Leopold II (Belgium), Ethiopian Star. *Leisure interests:* skiing, tennis. *Address:* 2700 Calvert Street, N.W., Washington, D.C. 20008, U.S.A. *Telephone:* (202) 462-6829.

SOMOGYI, József; Hungarian sculptor; b. 9 June 1916, Félszerfalva (now Hirm, Austria); s. of János Somogyi and Borbála Diósy; m. Mária Miske 1945; two d.; ed. Budapest Coll. of Fine Arts 1942; gymnasium teacher of visual arts 1945–63; Prof., Budapest Coll. of Visual Arts 1963–74, Rector and Leading Prof., Sculpture Section 1974–87; Pres. Hungarian Fed. of Visual Artists 1968–77; fmr. bd. mem. Nat. Council of Patriotic People's Front; fmr. mem. Nat. Assembly; fmr. mem. Presidential Council; Secular Chair. Calvinist Church of Hungary 1984–; designs figural compositions, monuments, sculptural decoration, animals, figurines, medals; Kossuth Prize 1954; Munkácsy Prize 1956; Eminent Artist title 1970; Labour Order of Merit, Golden Degree 1976; Grand Prize, shared with Jenő Kerényi, for Dancers at World Exhibition of Brussels 1958; exhibitor, Venice Biennial 1971. *Works include:* Lion, in front of Nat. Assembly Bldg., Budapest 1948, Bruin 1950, Smelter 1954, Mother 1962, Family 1964, Girl with Colt 1965; Miklós Zrinyi 1968, Bartók bust, Musikverein, Vienna 1981, Three-Nude Fountain 1981; monuments: Dózsa, Cegléd 1958, Dózsa, Kiskunfélegy-háza, Szántó-Kovács, Hódmezővásárhely 1965, Liberation, Salgótarján 1967, Liberation, Miskolc 1975, Bartók, Budapest 1981; Prince Ferenc Rákóczi II sepulchres: Mednyánszky, Mihályfi; sculptured ornaments, Radio Budapest HQ and Television Transmitter bldg., Mt. Széchenyi; The Crucified, parish church of Hollóháza, The Crucified, church of Cserépvá-ralja. *Leisure interests:* gardening, pets. *Address:* 1038 Budapest, Márton ut 3/5, Hungary. *Telephone:* 671-953.

SOMOGYI, László; Hungarian engineer and politician, b. 1932, Székes-fehérvár; m. Maria Csatáry 1958; ed. Tech. Univ., Budapest; various eng. posts, chief engineer 1963, later deputy tech. man. with County Fejér State Bldg. Co. (now ALBA REGIA Bldg. Co.); Dir. Co. for Public Bldg. Construction 1978-84; Minister of Bldg. and Town Planning 1984-88; Govt. Commr. for Vienna-Budapest World Exhbn. Jan. 1989-. *Leisure interests:* tennis, cooking. *Address:* 1022 Budapest, Bimbó u. 45, Hungary (Home). *Telephone:* 112-200, 123-420 (Office).

SOMORJAI, Gabor Arpad, PH.D.; American (b. Hungarian) professor of chemistry; b. 4 May 1935, Budapest; s. of Charles Somorjai and Livia Ormos; m. Judith Kaldor 1957; one s. one d.; ed. Univ. of Tech. Sciences, Budapest, Univ. of Calif., Berkeley; mem. Research Staff IBM, New York 1960-64; at Faculty of Dept. of Chem., Univ. of Calif., Berkeley 1964-, Asst. Prof. 1964-67, Assoc. Prof. 1967-72, Prof. 1972-; Faculty Sr. Scientist, Materials and Molecular Research Div., Lawrence Berkeley Lab., Berkeley, Calif. 1964-; numerous awards and visiting professorships in U.S.A. and U.K. including Visiting Fellow Emmanuel Coll., Univ. of Cambridge 1969; Centenary Lecturer Royal Soc. of Chem., U.K. 1983; mem. N.A.S. 1979-, Fellow A.A.A.S. 1982-, American Physical Soc., mem. American Acad. of Arts and Sciences 1983, American Chem. Soc.; Emmett Award American Catalysis Soc. 1977, Colloid and Surface Chem. Award American Chem. Soc. 1981. *Publications:* serves Editorial Bds. of numerous scientific publs., three textbooks on chem., nearly 400 publs. in major scientific journals. *Leisure interest:* swimming. *Address:* Department of Chemistry, University of California, Berkeley, Calif. 94720, U.S.A. *Telephone:* (415) 642-4053.

SON SANN; Kampuchean financial administrator and politician; b. 1911, Phnom-Penh; m. Nema Machhwa 1940; five s. two d.; ed. Ecole des Hautes Etudes Commerciales de Paris; Deputy Gov. Provinces of Battambang and Prey-Veng 1935-39; Head of Yuvan Kampuchearath (Youth Movement); Minister of Finance 1946-47; Vice-Pres. Council of Ministers 1949; Minister of Foreign Affairs 1950; Mem. of Parl. for Phnom-Penh and Pres. Cambodian Nat. Assembly 1951-52; Gov. of Nat. Bank of Cambodia 1954-68; Minister of State (Finance and Nat. Economy) 1961-62; Vice-Pres., in charge of Economy, Finance and Planning 1965-67, Pres. Council of Ministers May-Dec. 1967; First Vice-Pres. in charge of Econ. and Financial Affairs 1968; Leader Khmer People's Nat. Front (1986) reported overthrown; involved in help for Khmer refugees 1979; involved in anti-Vietnamese guerrilla war 1979-; Prime Minister, Coalition Govt. of Demo-cratic Kampuchea June 1982-; Grand Croix de l'Ordre Royal du Cambodge, Séna yayasedth, Commdr. du Sowathara (Mérite économique), Grand Offic-ier Légion d'honneur, Commdr. du Monisaraphon, Médaille d'or du Règne, Grand Officier du Million d'Eléphants (Laos). *Leisure interest:* Buddhist books.

SON SEN; Kampuchean politician; b. c. 1930; ed. Univ. in France; exile in Hanoi 1963; mem. Cen. Cttee. Pracheachan (Cambodian Communist Party); liaison officer between Khmers Rouges and exiled Royal Govt. of Nat. Union in Beijing 1970; Chief of Gen. Staff, Khmer Rouge armed forces 1971-79; Third Deputy Prime Minister, Minister of Defence 1975-79, Deputy Premier in guerrilla forces after Vietnamese invasion 1979; mem. Co-ordination Cttee. for Defence, Coalition Govt. of Democratic Kampuchea June 1982-; Vice-Pres. Khmer Rouge Sept. 1985-; Commdr.-in-Chief Demo-cratic Kampuchean Nat. Army Sept. 1985-.

SONDHEIM, Stephen Joshua; American song writer; b. 22 March 1930, New York City; s. of Herbert Sondheim and Janet Fox; ed. George School, Newtown, Pa., Williams Coll., Williamstown, Mass., private instruction; Pres. Dramatists' Guild 1973-81, Council mem. 1981-; mem. American Acad. and Inst. of Arts and Letters 1983-; Antoinette Perry Award for Company 1971, Follies 1972, A Little Night Music 1973, Sweeney Todd 1979; Drama Critics' Award 1971, 1972, 1973, 1976, 1979; Grammy Award 1984, 1986; television: Topper (co-author) 1953, Evening Primrose (music and lyrics) 1967; lyrics: West Side Story 1957, Gypsy 1959, Do I Hear a Waltz? 1965, Candide 1974; music and lyrics: A Funny Thing Happened on the Way to the Forum 1962, Anyone Can Whistle 1964, Company 1970, Follies 1971, A Little Night Music 1973, The Frogs 1974, Pacific Overtures 1976, Sweeney Todd 1978, Merrily We Roll Along 1981, Sunday in the Park with George 1984, Into the Woods (Drama Critic's Circle Award 1988) 1986, Follies 1987; anthologies: Side by Side by Sondheim 1977,

Marry Me a Little 1980; screenplay: (with Anthony Perkins) The Last of Sheila 1973; film scores: Stavisky 1975, Reds 1981. *Address:* c/o Flora Roberts, 65 East 55th Street, Suite 702, New York, N.Y. 10022, U.S.A.

SONG CHENGZHI, Maj.-Gen.; Chinese army officer; service with 4th Field Army, Korean War 1950; Deputy Commdr. Artillery Command, N.E. Mil. Region 1951; Commdr. Artillery Command, Shenyang Mil. Region 1957; Deputy Commdr. PLA Artillery 1965, Commdr. 1978-; mem. Stand-ing Cttee. 6th NPC 1983-, Law Cttee. NPC 1986-; Deputy Head China-Turkey Friendship Group 1985-. *Address:* People's Liberation Army Head-quarters, Beijing, People's Republic of China.

SONG HANLIANG; Chinese geologist and party official; b. 1934, Shaoxing, Zhejiang Prov.; ed. Xibei Univ.; geologist, head of geological prospecting team and Dir. of Prospecting Research Inst., Xinjiang Petroleum Admin. Bureau; Vice-Chair. Xinjiang Autonomous Region CCP Cttee. 1983-85, Sec. Oct. 1985-; mem. Standing Cttee. of Xinjiang Prov. CCP Cttee. 1985-, Sec. 1985-86; First Political Commissar, Xinjiang Production and Construction Corps 1987-; mem. CCP Cen. Cttee. 1987-. *Address:* Central Committee of the Chinese Communist Party, Zhongnanhai, Beijing, People's Republic of China.

SONG HONG-ZHAO, B.S., M.D.; b. 13 Aug. 1915, Suzhou, Jiangsu; m.; three s. one d.; ed. Peiping Union Medical Coll.; Prof. of Obstetrics and Gynaecology, Chinese Union Medical Coll., Chinese Acad. of Medical Sciences, Beijing; Hon. Prof., Chi-nan Univ. School of Medicine, Guang-dong, W. China Medical Univ., Sichuan, Xian Medical Univ., Shaanxi; mem. Chinese People's Political Consultation Conf., Nat. Cttee.; special interests: gynaecological oncology, especially trophoblastic diseases; Chair. Soc. of Obstetrics and Gynaecology; Chief Ed. Chinese Journal of Obstetrics and Gynaecology; Pres. Int. Soc. on Study of Trophoblastic Diseases. *Publications:* Trophoblastic Neoplasms: Diagnosis and Treatment (in Chinese) 1981, Studies of Trophoblastic Diseases in China 1988; 50-60 papers in Chinese and foreign scientific journals. *Address:* Department of Obstetrics and Gynaecology, Peking Union Medical College Hospital, Beij-ing 100730, People's Republic of China.

SONG JIAN; Chinese state official; b. 29 Dec. 1931, Shandong; Pres. Automation Soc. 1980; Vice-Minister, Space Industry 1982-84, Minister of State Scientific and Technological Comm. Sept. 1984-; alt. mem. 12th CCP Cen. Cttee. 1982, mem. 1985, mem. 13th Cen. Cttee. 1987-; State Councillor 1986-; Sec. Party Group, State Scientific and Tech. Comm. 1986-; mem. Leading Group for Scientific Work, State Council 1985-; Deputy Head, Leading Group for Devt. of Electronics Industry 1984-; Pres. Soc. of Automation 1980-; Head Nat. Group in Charge of Professional Job Desig-nation 1986-; Head Nat. Group on Protection and Devt. of Marine Resources 1987-; Chair. State Environmental Protection Cttee. 1988-; mem. State Planning Comm. 1988-. *Address:* State Scientific and Technological Com-mission, 52 Sanlihe, Fuxingmenwai, Beijing, People's Republic of China.

SONG JIWEN; Chinese politician; b. 1920, Dingyuan, Anhui Prov.; Dir. Financial Bureau, Nanjing People's Govt. 1949; mem. Financial and Econ. Cttee., East China Mil. and Admin. Council (reorganized into East China Admin. Council 1953) 1949-54; Dir. Tax Bureau, Shanghai People's Govt. 1953; Office of Finance, Food and Trade 1955; Deputy Mayor, Shanghai 1957-83 Cultural Revolution; mem. Standing Cttee., Shanghai Municipality CCP Cttee. 1962-83 Cultural Revolution; Pres. Shanghai Higher People's Court 1977; Vice-Minister of Light Industry 1978-81, Acting Minister May-Sept. 1981, Minister 1981-82, Pres. Light Industry Asscn. 1982-; mem. Presidium CPPCC 1983-, CPPCC Standing Cttee. 1985-; Deputy Head Work Group for Econ. Construction CPPCC 1983-; Pres. Quality Control Comm. 1984-. *Address:* c/o State Council, Beijing, People's Repub-lic of China.

SONG PING; b. 1917; Chinese party official; Vice-Minister, Labour 1953; Vice-Chair. State Planning Comm. 1957-63; Sec. CCP Gansu, and Vice-Chair. Gansu Revolutionary Cttee. 1972, First Sec. CCP Gansu, Chair. Gansu Revolutionary Cttee., Second Political Commissar, PLA Lanzhou Mil. Region and First Political Commissar Gansu Mil. District, PLA 1977-80; mem. 11th Cen. Cttee. 1977; First Vice-Chair. State Planning Comm. 1981-83; Minister in charge of State Planning Comm. 1983-87; mem. 12th Cen. Cttee. CCP 1982-, Political Bureau 1987-; Deputy Sec.-Gen., First Session of the 7th NPC March 1988-; Deputy Dir. Leading Group for Co-ordinating Nat. Scientific Work 1983-; State Councillor 1983-88; Vice-Chair. Environmental Protection Cttee. State Council 1984-, Nat. Agric. Zoning Cttee. 1983-; Deputy Head Leading Group for Scientific Work, State Council 1983-; Head Leading Group for Econ. Information Man., State Council 1986-. *Address:* State Planning Commission, Beijing, People's Republic of China.

SONG RENQIONG; Chinese politician; b. 1903, Hunan; ed. Whampoa Mil. Acad.; joined CCP 1926, on Long March 1934-35; Alt. mem. 7th Cen. Cttee. CCP 1945; Cadre in S.W. China 1949-54; Minister of 3rd Ministry of Machine Building 1954, 2nd Ministry of Machine Building 1959-60, 7th Ministry of Machine Building 1977-79; mem. 8th Cen. Cttee. CCP 1956, First Sec. N.E. Bureau 1961-67; Dir. Org. Dept. CCP 1979-; Chair. Credentials Cttee. 5th NPC 1980-83; mem. Secr. 11th Cen. Cttee. CCP; mem. Politburo 12th Cen. Cttee. CCP 1982-85, Chair. Credentials Cttee. 1982; Vice-Chair. Cen. Advisory Comm. 1985; Adviser Cen. Party Consolidation Guidance Comm. 1983-. *Address:* Zongguo Gongchan Dang, Beijing, People's Republic of China.

SONG WENZHI; Chinese artist; b. 5 Sept. 1919, Taicang Co., Jiangsu; s. of Mong Chou and Ma Xingmei, m. 1944; two s. two d.; ed. Suzhou Art School; worked at Jiangsu Art Acad. 1957; Dir. Jiangsu Art Acad.; Vice-Pres. Jiangsu branch, Chinese Artists' Asscn.; Prof. of Nanjing Univ.; Vice-Chair. Jiangsu Int. Cultural Exchange Centre; exhbn. of works in Japan, Singapore, Hong Kong and Beijing 1979-83. *Works include:* Rafting Along the Xiangjiang River, Great Changes of Mountains and Rivers, On the Jialing River, Mount Hua, plus published collections of his traditional Chinese paintings. *Leisure interests:* studying Chinese opera, collecting modern Chinese art. *Address:* No. 19-5-20 Wenchang Lane, Nanjing, People's Republic of China.

SONG ZHENMING; Chinese politician; Sec. CCP, Daqing Oilfield 1976; Vice-Minister, Petroleum and Chemical Industries 1976; Minister of the Petroleum Industry 1978-80; Head of Group for Construction and Devt. of Zhongyuan Oilfield 1983-; Pres. China Nat. Oil Devt. Corpn. 1985-. *Address:* China National Oil Development Corporation, Liupukang, Beijing, People's Republic of China. *Telephone:* 444313.

SONG ZHIGUANG; Chinese diplomatist; b. April 1916, Guangdong Province; ed. univ.; Counsellor, Embassy in German Democratic Repub.; Deputy Dir. Dept. of W. European Affairs, Ministry of Foreign Affairs; Counsellor, Embassy to France; Amb. to German Democratic Repub. 1970-72, to U.K. 1972-77, to Japan 1982-86; Vice-Pres. China-Japan Friendship Asscn. Dec. 1986-; Asst. to Minister of Foreign Affairs 1977-81; Adviser Foreign Affairs Cttee. NPC 1986. *Address:* China-Japan Friendship Asscn., Beijing, People's Republic of China.

SONNENFELDT, Helmut, M.A.; American international business consultant and fmr. government official; b. 13 Sept. 1926, Berlin, Germany; s. of Dr. Walther H. Sonnenfeldt and Dr. Gertrud L. Sonnenfeldt; m. Marjorie Hecht 1953; two s. one d.; ed. Univ. of Manchester, Johns Hopkins Univ.; went to U.S.A. 1944; mem. Counterintelligence Corps, U.S. Army, Pacific and European Theaters; with Dept. of State 1952-69, Policy Officer, U.S. Disarmament Admin. 1960-61, Director Office of Research and Analysis for the U.S.S.R. and E. Europe 1966-69; Senior Staff mem. for Europe and East-West Relations, Nat. Security Council 1969-74; Counsellor of Dept. of State 1974-77; Trustee, Johns Hopkins Univ. 1974-, Visiting Scholar, School of Advanced Int. Studies, Johns Hopkins Univ. 1977-78; Guest Scholar, Brookings Inst. 1978-; Lecturer on Soviet Affairs, Johns Hopkins Univ. School of Advanced Int. Studies; Consultant Washington Center for Foreign Policy Research; Gov. and Dir. UN Asscn. of U.S.A. 1980-; Dir. Atlantic Council of U.S.A. 1978, Corning Int. Corpn., N.Y. 1978-; mem. Int. Inst. of Strategic Studies, London 1977-, (mem. Exec. Cttee. 1986-), Council of Foreign Relations, Royal Inst. of Int. Affairs, Int. Advisory Council, Credit-Anstalt-Bankverein, Vienna 1983-; Editorial Bd. Politique Internationale (Paris) 1978-, Foreign Policy 1980-; govt. rep. to numerous confs. and meetings abroad; Consultant to int. investments firms and banks. *Publications:* Soviet Policy in the 1980s 1985, articles on int. issues in American and European journals. *Address:* Brookings Institution, Washington, D.C. 20036; 4105 Thornapple Street, Chevy Chase, Md. 20815, U.S.A. *Telephone:* (301) 656-6731 (Home).

SONODA, Kiyomitsu; Japanese politician; b. 6 Oct. 1929; ed. Hosei Univ.; Chair. Kumamoto Prefectural Ass.; mem. House of Councillors 1965-; Parl. Vice-Minister for Agric. and Forestry 1972; Chair. Liberal-Democratic Party Policy Bd., House of Councillors 1978-79; Minister of State and Dir.-Gen. Nat. Land Agency 1979-80. *Publication:* Asu no aru Nogyo (Agriculture for Tomorrow) 1974. *Leisure interests:* go, golf.

SONTAG, Susan, M.A.; American author and film director; b. 16 Jan. 1933; one s.; ed. Univ. of Chicago and Harvard Univ.; mem. American Inst. of Arts and Letters, PEN (Pres. American Centre 1987-89); Officier, Ordre des Arts et des Lettres (France); Guggenheim Fellow 1966, 1975, Rockefeller Foundation Fellow 1965, 1974; recipient Ingram Merrill Foundation Award in Literature in the Field of American Letters 1976, Creative Arts Award, Brandeis Univ. 1976, Arts and Letters Award, American Acad. of Arts and Letters 1976, Nat. Book Critics Circle Prize 1978. *Films include:* Duet for Cannibals 1969, Brother Carl 1971, Promised Lands 1974, Unguided Tour 1983. *Publications:* The Benefactor (novel) 1963, Death Kit (novel) 1967, Against Interpretation (essays) 1966, Styles of Radical Will 1969, On Photography 1977, Illness as Metaphor 1978, I, Etcetera (stories) 1978, Under the Sign of Saturn 1980, A Susan Sontag Reader (anthology) 1982, A Barthes Reader (introduction) 1982, AIDS and Its Metaphors 1989. *Address:* c/o Farràr, Straus and Giroux, 19 Union Square West, New York, N.Y. 10003, U.S.A.

SOONG, James Chu-yul, PH.D.; Chinese politician; b. 16 March 1942, Hunan; m. Viola Chen; one s. one d.; ed. Nat. Chengchi Univ., Taipei, Univ. of California, Berkeley, Catholic Univ. of America, Georgetown Univ., Washington D.C.; Sec. Exec. Yuan, Taiwan 1974-77; Deputy Dir.-Gen. Govt. Information Office 1977-79; Assoc. Prof., Nat. Taiwan Univ. 1975-79; Research Fellow, Inst. of Int. Relations, Nat. Chengchi Univ. 1974-; Personal Sec. to the Pres. 1978-; Dir.-Gen. Govt. Information Office, Govt. Spokesman 1979-84; Dir.-Gen. Dept. of Cultural Affairs, Kuomintang 1984-87; Deputy Sec.-Gen., Cen. Cttee. Kuomintang 1987-, mem. Standing

Cttee. 1988-; Man. Dir. China TV Co. 1984-, Taiwan TV Enterprise 1984-; Chair. Hua-hsia Investment Corpn.; Eisenhower Fellowship 1982, and several decorations. *Publications:* A Manual for Academic Writers, How to Write Academic Papers, Politics and Public Opinions in the United States, Keep Free China Free. *Address:* 11 Chungshan South Road, Taipei 10040, Taiwan.

SOONG CHANG-CHIH; Chinese naval officer and politician; b. 10 June 1916, Liaochung County; m.; three s. one d.; ed. Chinese Naval Acad., Royal Naval Coll., Greenwich, Armed Forces Univ. and Nat. War Coll.; Commdg. Officer, Rating Training School 1946-52; Commdr. Landing Ship Squadron 1954-55; Supt. Chinese Naval Acad. 1955-62; Chief of Staff, Naval H.Q. 1965-67; Deputy C.-in-C. Navy 1967-70; C.-in-C. Navy 1970-76; Chief of Gen. Staff, Ministry of Nat. Defence 1976-81; Minister of Nat. Defence 1981-86; Strategic Adviser to the Pres. 1986-; Amb. to Panama 1988-; Hon. Ph.D. (Konkuk) 1982. *Address:* 538 Lei-An Road, Taipei 10493, Taiwan; Apartado 4285, Panama 5, Panama. *Telephone:* 505-2908.

SOPER, Baron (Life Peer), cr. 1965, of Kingsway; **Rev. Donald Oliver Soper,** M.A., PH.D.; British Methodist minister; b. 31 Jan 1903, London; s. of late Ernest Frankham and Caroline Amelia (Pilcher) Soper; m. Marie Gertrude Dean 1929; four d.; ed. St. Catharine's Coll., Cambridge; Wesley House, Cambridge and London Univ.; Minister to the South London Mission 1926-29, to the Cen. London Mission 1929-36; Superintendent of the West London Mission, Kingsway Hall 1936-78; Pres. of the Methodist Conf. 1953; Alderman, London County Council 1958-65; Chair. Shelter 1974-78; Pres. League Against Cruel Sports; Hon. Fellow, St. Catharine's Coll., Cambridge 1966; World Methodist Council's Peace Award 1981-82; Hon: D.D. (Cambridge) 1988. *Publications:* Christ and Tower Hill, Question Time on Tower Hill, Answer Time on Tower Hill, Christianity and its Critics, Popular Fallacies about the Christian Faith, Will Christianity Work?, Practical Christianity To-Day, Questions and Answers in Ceylon, Children's Prayer Time, All His Grace, It is Hard to Work for God, The Advocacy of the Gospel, Tower Hill, 12.30, Aflame with Faith, Christian Politics, Calling for Action. *Leisure interests:* music, most games. *Address:* 19 Thayer Street, London, W1M 5LJ, England.

SOPHUSSON, Fridrik; Icelandic politician; b. 18 Oct. 1943, Reykjavík; m. (separated); five c.; ed. Reykjavík Higher Secondary Grammar School and Univ. of Iceland; part-time teacher Hlídaskóli School, Reykjavík 1963-67; Man. Icelandic Man. Asscn. 1972-78; mem. Radio Council Icelandic State Broadcasting Service 1975-78; Nat. Research Council and Exec. Cttee. of State Hosps. 1984-87; Cen. Cttee. Independence Party 1969-77, Vice-Chair. 1981-, Pres. Independence Party's Youth Fed. 1973-77; M.P. for Reykjavík 1978-; Minister of Industry and Energy 1987-88. *Address:* Ministry of Industry, Arnarhváli, 150 Reykjavík, Iceland.

SORATO, Dr. Bruno, D.ECON.; Italian business executive; b. 7 May 1922, Venice; m. Giovanna Coin 1949; one d.; ed. in Rome; Exec. SAVA, Venice 1947-64; Exec. AISA São Paulo 1965-66; Man. Dir. NABALCO Pty. Ltd., Sydney 1967-72; mem. Exec. Cttee. Swiss Aluminium Ltd. 1972-74, Deputy Chair. Exec. Cttee. 1975-83, Pres. and C.E.O. 1983-85; Dir. Union Bank of Switzerland 1981-. *Address:* Union Bank of Switzerland, Bahnhofstrasse 45, 8000 Zürich, Switzerland.

SØRENSEN, Bengt Algot, DR.PHIL.; Danish professor of German Literature; b. 24 Nov. 1927, Aarhus; s. of Christian Sørensen and Selma Mellquist; m. Agnes M. Pedersen 1954; one s. two d.; ed. Aarhus, Hamburg and Tübingen Univs.; lecturer in Scandinavian Languages and Literature, Bonn, Germany 1955-60; lecturer in German Literature, Aarhus Univ. 1962-66; Prof. of German Literature, Odense Univ. 1966-; Visiting Prof. Univ. of Calif. at Irvine 1980, Univ. of Kiel 1983; Pres. Danish Research Council for the Humanities 1971-73; mem. Exec. Council European Science Foundation; mem. Royal Danish Acad.; Gold Medal, Univ. of Aarhus 1953. *Publications:* Symbol und Symbolismus 1963, Allegorie und Symbol 1972, Herrschaft und Zärtlichkeit 1984, Jens Peter Jacobsen 1989; numerous articles about Danish and German literature. *Leisure interests:* fishing, gardening. *Address:* University of Odense, 5230 Odense (Office); Hjelmbjegvej 4, 5900 Rudkøbing, Denmark. *Telephone:* 09-158600 (Office); 09-501620 (Home).

SØRENSEN, John Kousgård, M.A., DR.PHIL.; Danish academic; b. 6 Dec. 1925, Copenhagen; s. of Erik Sørensen and Astrid Sørensen; m. Solveig Baastrup 1951; one s.; ed. Univ. of Copenhagen; Asst. Prof. Inst. for Name-Research, Univ. of Copenhagen 1951, Assoc. Prof. 1965, Prof. of Danish Language 1969-; Hon. Vice-Pres. English Place-Name Soc. 1969; mem. Royal Danish Acad.; Sahlgren Prize 1981; Dr. h.c. (Uppsala) 1981. *Publications:* Danske bebyggelsesnavne på-sted 1958, Svendborg amts bebyggelsesnavne 1958, Danske sø- og ånavne 1-7 1968-89, Odense amts bebyggelsesnavne 1969, Stadnavneforskning 1-2 (with V. Dalberg) 1972-79, Danmarks gamle Ordsprog 2, 6, 7 1977-88, Patronymer i Danmark I 1984; articles on onomastics, lexicography, proverbs etc. *Leisure interest:* music. *Address:* Nivåvaenge 12-3, 2990 Nivå, Denmark. *Telephone:* 02 247543.

SØRENSEN, Knud, D.PHIL.; Danish professor of philology; b. 2 Feb. 1928, Aarhus; s. of late Oscar Sørensen and Ingeborg Petersen; m. 1st Gerda Riisberg 1955 (died 1973), 2nd Margit Riisberg 1975; two s. one d.; ed. Copenhagen Univ.; lecturer, Handelshøjskolen i Kobenhavn 1955-62; Prof. Danmarks Lærerhøjskole 1962-67; Prof. of English Philology, Aarhus

Univ. 1967–; Assoc. Ed. English Studies 1970–; Visiting Prof. State Univ. of New York, Binghamton; mem. Vetenskapssocieteten i Lund, Royal Danish Acad. *Publications:* Thomas Lodge's Translation of Seneca's De Beneficiis 1960, Engelsk grammatik (with P. Steller) 1966, Engelske lån i dansk 1973, Aspects of Modern English Prose Style 1975, English Influence on Contemporary Danish 1982, Charles Dickens: Linguistic Innovator 1985. *Leisure interest:* classical music. *Address:* Department of English, Aarhus University, 8000 Aarhus C (Office); Råhøj Allé 12, 8270 Højbjerg, Denmark (Home). *Telephone:* 06 27 21 06.

SORENSEN, Theodore Chaikin, B.S.L., LL.B.; American lawyer and government official; b. 8 May 1928, Lincoln, Nebraska; s. of Christian A. Sorensen and Annis Chaikin; m. Gillian Martin 1969; three s. one d.; ed. Univ. of Nebraska; Attorney, Fed. Security Agency 1951–52; Staff Researcher, Joint Cttee. on Railroad Retirement 1952–53; Asst. to Senator John F. Kennedy 1953–61; Special Counsel to Presidents Kennedy and Johnson 1961–64; with law firm Paul, Weiss, Rifkind, Wharton & Garrison, New York 1966–; Ed.-at-Large Saturday Review 1966–69; Commentator Nat. Affairs Metromedia Channel 5, 1971–73; mem. Advisory Cttee. for Trade Negotiations March 1979–81; Chair. Task Force on Political Action Cttees.; mem. Task Force on Foreign Policy 1986, Int. Trade Round Table 1986, Democratic Nat. Cttee. 1981–82; Chair. N.Y.S. Democratic Cttee. on Ethical Conduct 1986; mem. Task Force on Foreign Policy 1986; Democrat. *Publications:* Decision-Making in the White House 1963, Kennedy 1964, The Kennedy Legacy 1970, Watchmen in the Night: Presidential Accountability After Watergate 1975, A Different Kind of Presidency 1984, A Widening Atlantic? Domestic Change and Foreign Policy (co-author Ralf Dahrendorf) 1986, Let the World go Forth: The Speeches, Statements and Writings of John F. Kennedy (Ed.) 1988. *Address:* 1285 Avenue of the Americas, New York, N.Y. 10019-6064, U.S.A. *Telephone:* (212) 373-3000.

SORESCU, Marin; Romanian poet, dramatist and essayist; b. 19 Feb. 1936, Bulzeşti, Dolj; s. of Stefan and Nicoliţa Sorescu; m. 1981; ed. Univ. of Iaşi; literary critic with Bucharest review Luceafărul; Ed.-in-Chief literary journal Ramuri 1970–; mem. Acad. Mallarmé, Paris; Union of Romanian Writers Prize (several times), Romanian Acad. Prize (several times), Fernando Riello Prize (Madrid) 1983. *Publications include:* Tinereţea lui Don Quijote 1968, Iona 1968, Tuşiţi 1970, O aripă şi un picior 1971, Suflete bun la toate 1972; Astfel 1973, La lilieci 1973, 1986, Setea muntelui de sare (play) 1974, Norii 1975, Descîntoteca 1976, Trei dinţi din faţa 1977, Paracliserul 1978, Viziunea vizuinii (novel) 1981, Gedichten 1981, La Juventud de Don Quijote 1981, Selected Poems 1982, Symmetries 1982, Fîntîni in mare 1982, Ieşirea prin cer (plays) 1984, Ceramique 1984, El huracan del papel 1985, Let's Talk about the Weather 1985, The Thirst of the Salt Mountain (plays) 1985, Tratat de inspiraţie (essays) 1985, Abendrot Nr. 15 (poems) 1985, Uşor cu pianul pe scări (essays), La lilieci (poems) 1987, The Biggest Egg in the World 1987, Vlad Dracula the Impaler (play) 1987, The Youth of Don Quijote 1987, Apă vie, apă moartă (poems) 1987. *Leisure interest:* painting. *Address:* Strada Grigore Alexandrescu 43, Bucharest 71128, Romania. *Telephone:* 504788.

SORGENICHT, Klaus, DR.RER.POL.; German politician; b. 24 Aug. 1923, Wuppertal-Elberfeld; m.; one c.; ed. Volksschule and Akad. für Staats- und Rechtswissenschaft; Mayor of Güstrow 1946, Chair. local council 1946–49; Head of Dept., Mecklenburg Ministry of Interior 1949–51; Head of Dept., Ministry of Interior of G.D.R. 1951–52; Head of Dept. for Co-ordination and Control of Labour in admin. service of G.D.R. 1952–54; Head of Dept., Cen. Cttee. of Sozialistische Einheitspartei Deutschlands (SED) 1954–; mem. KPD 1945, SED 1946, Volkskammer 1958–; mem. Comm. on Law and Constitution 1963–; mem. State Council 1963–; Vaterländischer Verdienstorden, in Bronze, Silver and Gold, Orden Banner der Arbeit and other decorations. *Address:* Staatsrat der Deutschen Demokratischen Republik, 1020 Berlin, Marx-Engels-Platz, German Democratic Republic.

SOROKIN, Adm. Aleksey Ivanovich; Soviet naval official; b. 1922; ed. V.I. Lenin. Mil. Political Acad.; mem. CPSU 1943–; served in Soviet Armed Forces 1949–; posts of mil.-political responsibility in Soviet Navy in recent years 1949–79; mem. of Mil. Council, Head of Political Div. of Soviet Naval Forces 1979–; First Deputy of Political Div. of U.S.S.R. Army and Navy 1981–; rank of Adm. 1979; cand. mem. of CPSU Cen. Cttee. 1986–; Deputy to U.S.S.R. Supreme Soviet. *Address:* The Kremlin, Moscow, U.S.S.R.

SORSA, (Taisto) Kalevi; Finnish politician; b. 21 Dec. 1930, Keuruu; s. of Kaarlo O. Sorsa and Elsa S. (née Leinonen); m. Elli Irene Lääkäri 1953; ed. School of Social Science (now Univ. of Tampere); Chief Ed., Vihuri 1954–56; Literary Ed. Tammi (publishing house) 1956–59; Programme Asst. Specialist UNESCO 1959–65; Sec.-Gen. of Finnish UNESCO Cttee. 1965–69; Deputy Dir. Ministry of Educ. 1967–69; Sec.-Gen. Social Democratic Party 1969–75, Pres. 1975–; mem. Parl. 1970–; Minister for Foreign Affairs Feb.-Sept. 1972, 1975–76; Prime Minister 1972–75, 1977–79, 1982–87; Deputy Prime Minister and Minister of Foreign Affairs 1987–89; Speaker of Parl. 1989–; Chair. Foreign Affairs Cttee. 1970–72, 1977, 1979–82, Socialist Int. Study Group on Disarmament 1978–80, Chair. Socialist Int. Advisory Council 1980–, Vice-Pres. 1980–; Chair. Bd. of Admin. Finnair 1981–; Nat. Defence Council 1982–, Soviet-Finnish Comm. on Econ. Co-operation 1983–; Dir. Bank of Finland; Commdr. Grand Cross, Order of the White Rose of Finland, Grand Cross, Order of Orange-Nassau,

Grand Cross, Order of the Icelandic Falcon, Great Golden Decoration with Ribbon, Order of Merit of Austria, Grand Cross of the Order of Merit, People's Repub. of Poland, Grand Cross, Order of the North Star of Sweden, Grand Star, Order of the Star of Friendship between Peoples (G.D.R.), Grand Cross, Order of San Marino, Grand Cross, Order of Merit of the Repub. of Senegal, Grand Cross, Order of Dannebrog (Denmark), Order of the Banner of Hungary (Second Class), Grand Cross of the Order of Merit (Federal Repub. of Germany); Hon. G.C.M.G. *Leisure interests:* the arts, social and international questions, outdoor life. *Address:* Finnish Parliament, 00102 Helsinki, Finland. *Telephone:* 4321.

SOSRODARSONO, Suyono; Indonesian politician; b. 3 March 1926, Madiun, E. Java; ed. Inst. of Tech., Bandung; employed by People's Housing Service 1955–60, Head 1958–60; Head, Public Works Service, Province of S. Sumatra 1960–63; Head, Directorate of Construction Layout and Project Supervisor for Prevention of Floods 1963–65; First Asst. to Minister of Basic Irrigation 1965–66; Dir.-Gen. of Irrigation, Dept. of Public Works 1966–82; Sec.-Gen. Dept. of Public Works 1982–83; Minister of Public Works 1983–88. *Address:* c/o Ministry of Public Works, Jln. Pattimura 20, Jakarta Selatan, Indonesia.

SOTIN, Hans; German opera and concert singer; b. 10 Sept. 1939, Dortmund; m. Regina Elsner 1964; three c.; with Opera House, Essen 1962–64; State Opera, Hamburg 1964–, State Opera, Vienna 1970–; perm. mem. Bayreuth Festival 1971–; guest appearances worldwide; private singing teacher. *Address:* 2106 Bendestorf, Schulheide 10, Federal Republic of Germany. *Telephone:* 04183/6614.

SOTIRHOS, Michael; American diplomatist; b. 12 Nov. 1928, New York; m. Estelle Manos 1968; two c.; ed. Bernard M. Baruch School of Business and Civic Admin., City Coll. of New York; founder and Chair. Ariston Interior Designers, Inc. New York 1948–85; partner, Cortina Valley Assocs., Haines Valley, New York, Marla Realty, New York, Hampton Properties, Hampton, Va.; mem. Bd. of Dirs. The Rainbow Fund; active service in Republican Party since 1960; Nat. Chair.. Ethnic Voters for Reagan-Bush '84; fmr. Nat. Chair. Nat. Republican Heritage Groups Council; fmr. mem. Exec. Cttee. Republican Nat. Cttee.; has held numerous Govt. and public appts.; Amb. to Jamaica 1985–; awards include Dwight D. Eisenhower Award (Republican Nat. Cttee.) 1985; Order of St. Mark (Patriarchate of Jerusalem), Order of St. Andrew (Greek Orthodox Church). *Address:* Department of State, Washington, D.C. 20520-3210, U.S.A. (Office); 8 Long Lane, Kingston, Jamaica (Residence). *Telephone:* (809) 929-4850 Ext. 201/2 (Office); (809) 942-2629 (Residence).

SOTO, Jesús-Rafael; Venezuelan artist; b. 5 June 1923, Ciudad Bolívar; ed. School of Fine Arts, Caracas; Dir., School of Fine Arts, Maracaibo, Venezuela 1947–50; in Paris since 1950; early exponent of "optical art"; various films made on works in field of kinetic art and vibrations since 1958; one-man exhbns. at Caracas 1957, 1961, Paris 1956, 1959, 1962, 1965, 1967, 1969, 1970, 1979, Brussels 1957, Essen 1961, Antwerp 1962, Stuttgart 1964, New York 1965, 1966, 1971, 1974, Retrospective Exhbn., Signals, London 1965; represented in perm. collections including: Tate Gallery, London, Museum of Fine Arts, Caracas, Albright-Knox Art Gallery, Buffalo, Cali Inst. of Fine Arts, Cali, Colombia, Stedelijk Museum, Amsterdam, Museum of Contemporary Arts, São Paulo, Moderna Museet, Stockholm, Kaiser Foundation, Cordoba, Argentina, Palace of Fine Arts, Brussels, Kröller-Müller Museum, Otterloo, Holland, Museum of Modern Art, Jerusalem; numerous prizes including Wolf Prize, São Paulo Bienal 1963, David Bright Foundation Prize, Venice Biennale 1964. *Major works include:* sculpture for garden of School of Architecture, Univ. City of Caracas, two murals and sculpture for Venezuelan pavilion, Brussels Exhbn. 1958. *Address:* 10 rue Villehardouin, 75003 Paris, France. *Telephone:* (1) 277 75 33.

SOTOMAYOR, Antonio; Bolivian painter; b. 1904, Chulumani; s. of Carmen Celina Meza and Juan Sotomayor; m. Grace La Mora Andrews 1926; ed. La Paz School of Applied Arts; awarded first prize of Nat. Exposition of Painting 1921; F.R.S.A. *Works include:* El Crucifijo, Copacabana, Lavanderas, Funeral Aimara, Alacitas, Madre, Rezando Reposo, Historical Murals Palace Hotel and Sharon Building, San Francisco, Murals at Sonoma Mission Inn, Calif., Mural El Tigero, Hillsborough, Calif.; murals Peruvian Pavilion and terra cotta fountain Pacific Area, Theme Building, Golden Gate, Int. Exposition 1939–40, Murals, San Francisco; Art Faculty, Mills Coll. and Calif. School of Fine Arts; Mural Altarpiece, St. Augustine Church, Pleasanton, Calif., Glass Mosaic Facade, Hillsdale Methodist Church, Calif.; Mural, Matson Navigation Co., San Francisco, Calif.; Murals, Grace Cathedral, San Francisco, Calif.; backdrop for San Francisco Civic Auditorium Concerts; Altarpiece, Church of St. Francis, Nuevo Progresso, Guatemala; Mural, Peruvian Embassy, Washington, D.C.; Chapel Altarpiece, La Casa de los Pobres, Tihuana, Mexico; Award of Honor (City and County of San Francisco) 1978. *Publications:* Pinturas interpretativas de indígenas de Bolivia 1929, Pinturas con motivos mejicanos 1930, Khasa Goes to the Fiesta 1967, Balloons 1972. *Leisure interests:* music, travel. *Address:* 3 Le Roy Place, San Francisco, Calif. 94109, U.S.A. *Telephone:* (415) 673-6193.

SOULAGES, Pierre; French painter; b. 24 Dec. 1919, Rodez; m. Colette Llaurens 1942; ed. Lycée de Rodez; exhibited abstract painting since 1947

in Salon des Surindépendants, Salon de Mai et Réalités Nouvelles; one-man exhbn., Lydia Conti Gallery, Paris 1949, Birch Gallery, Copenhagen 1951, Stangl Gallery, Munich 1952, Kootz Gallery, New York 1954-65, Gimpel Gallery, London 1955, Galerie de France, Paris 1956-77, Knoedler Gallery 1968; exhibited in int. festivals including Biennales of Venice and São Paulo, and the itinerary of the Guggenheim Collection, the Carnegie Inst., Pittsburgh, The New Decade at the Museum of Modern Art, New York, Tate Gallery, London, etc.; also décors for theatres and ballet; and lithographs and engravings. Works in Museums of Modern Art, Paris, and N.Y., Tate Gallery, London, Guggenheim Museum, N.Y., Phillips Gallery, Washington, Museum of Modern Art, Rio de Janeiro, museums in many American cities, in Europe, Australia and Japan; retrospective exhbns. Hanover, Essen, The Hague, Zürich 1960-61, Ljubljana 1961, Massachusetts Inst. of Tech. 1962, Copenhagen Glyptothek 1963, Fine Arts Museum, Houston 1966, Musée Nat. d'Art Moderne, Paris 1967; Carnegie Inst., Pittsburgh, Albright Knox Art Gallery, Buffalo, Musée de Québec, Musée d'Art Contemporain, Montreal 1968, Oslo, Aalborg, Neuchâtel, Charleroi 1973, Musée Dynamique, Dakar 1974, Gulbenkian Foundation, Lisbon, Museo de arte contemporaneo, Madrid, Musée Fabre, Montpellier, Museo de Arte Moderno, Mexico City 1975, Museu de Arte Moderna, Rio de Janeiro, Museo de Arte Moderno, Caracas 1976, Museu de Arte Contemporaneo, São Paulo 1976, Centre Georges Pompidou, Paris 1979, Museé du Parc de la Boverie, Liège 1980, Kunstlerhaus, Salzburg 1980, Kunstbygning, Århus; Kunstpavillon, Esbjerg; Palais de Charlottenborg, Copenhagen 1982; Musée d'Unterlinden, Colmar 1983; Museum Seibu, Tokyo 1984; Pulchri Studio, Gemeentemuseum, The Hague 1985, Galerie de France 1986; Hon. mem. American Acad. of Arts and Letters; Officier Légion d'honneur; Grand Prix, Tokyo Biennale 1957, Carnegie Prize 1964, Grand Prix des Arts de la Ville de Paris 1975, Rembrandt Prize 1976. *Address:* 18 rue des Trois-Portes, 75005 Paris, France.

SOULIOTI, Stella; Cypriot lawyer and politician; b. 13 Feb. 1920, Limassol; sister of Michael Cacoyannis (q.v.); d. of Panayiotis and Angeliki Cacoyannis; m. Demetrios Soulioti 1949; one d.; ed. Cyprus, Egypt and Gray's Inn, London; joined Women's Auxiliary Air Force, Nicosia and served in Middle East 1943-46; called to the Bar, London 1951; law practice, Limassol 1952-60; Minister of Justice 1960-70, concurrently Minister of Health 1964-66; Law Commr. 1971-84; Attorney-Gen. 1984; Co-ordinator of Foreign Aid to Cyprus Refugees 1974-; Adviser to Greek Cypriot Negotiator on Cyprus Intercommunal Talks 1976-; Chair. Cyprus Overseas Relief Fund 1977-82; Visiting Fellow Wolfson Coll., Cambridge 1982-83; Pres. Cyprus Red Cross 1961-, Cyprus Scholarship Board 1962-; Chair. Cyprus Town and Country Planning Cttee. 1967-70; Vice-Pres. Cyprus Anti-Cancer Soc. 1971-; Hon. Vice-Pres. Int. Fed. of Women Lawyers 1967-; Trustee Cambridge Commonwealth Scholarship Trust for Cyprus 1983-; mem. Exec. Bd. UNESCO 1987-; LL.D. h.c. (Nottingham) 1972. *Leisure interests:* reading, writing, music, theatre. *Address:* P.O. Box 4102, Nicosia, Cyprus. *Telephone:* 224648.

SOUPAULT, Philippe; French writer; b. 2 Aug. 1897, Chaville; s. of Maurice Soupault and Cécile Dancongnée; m. 3rd Renée Niemeyer 1936; two d.; ed. Univ. de Paris à la Sorbonne; Co-founder Littérature (review) 1919; fmr. Prof. Swarthmore Coll., Pa., U.S.A.; Strassburger Prize 1932, Prix Italia 1958, 1963, Grand Prix de Poésie (Acad. Française) 1972, Grand Prix de la Soc. des Gens de Lettres 1972, Grand Prix national des Lettres 1977, Prix Saint-Simon 1981. *Publications:* Poetry: Les champs magnétiques 1919, Westwego 1922, Georgia 1926, Poésies complètes 1937, L'arme secrète 1947, Message de l'île déserte 1948, Chansons 1950, Sans phrases 1953, Poèmes et Poésies 1973; novels: Le bon apôtre 1923, Les frères Durandeau 1925, En joue! 1925, Le coeur d'or 1927, Le Nègre 1927, Les dernières nuits de Paris 1928, Les moribonds 1934, biographies of Henri Rousseau, Charles Baudelaire 1927, Paolo Uccello 1928, William Blake 1929, Lautréamont 1931, Souvenirs de James Joyce 1943; plays: La fille qui faisait des miracles 1951, Comment dresser une garce 1954, Tous ensemble au bout du monde 1955, Rendezvous 1957, La nuit de temps 1962, Alibis 1969, Etranger dans la nuit 1978; essays: Profils perdus 1963, Eugène Labiche 1964, Le sixième coup de minuit 1972, Ecrits sur la peinture (essays) 1980, Mémoires de l'oubli 1981. *Leisure interest:* reading. *Address:* 11 rue Chanez, 75016 Paris, France. *Telephone:* 743-96-90.

SOUPHANOUVONG; Laotian politician; b. (as Prince Souphanouvong) 1902; half-brother of Prince Souvanna Phouma; ed. Lycée Saint-Louis (Paris), Ecole Nationale des Ponts et Chaussées; studied eng. in France; returned to Laos 1938 and became active in the Nationalist Movement; joined Pathet Lao and fought against the French; formed Nationalist Party (Neo Lao Hak Sat) in Bangkok 1950; Leader of the Patriotic Front; Minister of Planning, Reconstruction and Urbanism 1958; arrested 1959, escaped May 1960, rejoined Pathet Lao Forces, became Leader; Pathet Lao del., Geneva Conf. on Laos 1961-62; Vice-Premier and Minister of Econ. Planning 1962, absent, returned 1974; Chair. Joint Nat. Political Council 1974-75; Pres. of Lao People's Democratic Repub. 1975-86; Chair. Cen. Cttee., Lao Front for Nat. Reconstruction 1979-; fmr. mem. Nat. Ass.; mem. Politburo; Order of the October Revolution (U.S.S.R.) 1979, and other awards. *Address:* c/o Office of the President, Vientiane, Laos.

SOURROUILLE, Juan Vital; Argentine economist; b. 13 Aug. 1940, Adrogue; m. Susana Romero Escobar; three s.; ed. Public Accountant Nat.

Univ. of Buenos Aires; consultant Latin American Econ. Comm., Latin American Inst. for Econ. and Social Planning; Prof. of Macroeconomy for Econ. and Social Devt. Inst.; consultant ILO and IBRD; Under-Sec. of Economy and Labour 1971; Sec. of Planning 1983; Minister of Economy 1985-89. *Address:* c/o Ministerio de Economia, Hipolito Yrigoyen 250, C.P. 1310, Buenos Aires, Argentina.

SOUSTELLE, Jacques, D. ÉS L.; French scientist and politician; b. 3 Feb. 1912, Montpellier; s. of Jean Soustelle and Germaine (Blatière) Soustelle; m. Georgette Fagot 1931; ed. Ecole normale supérieure; various scientific missions to Mexico 1932-34, 1935-36, 1939; Asst. Dir. Musée de l'Homme, Paris 1937; joined Gen. de Gaulle in London 1940; French Nat. Cttee. Del. in Central America, Mexico and West Indies 1941-42; Nat. Commr. for Information 1942-43; Dir.-Gen. Special Services, Algiers 1943-44; Commissaire de Repub., Bordeaux 1944; Minister of Information 1945; Minister for the Colonies 1945; mem. Constituent Assembly 1945-46; Sec.-Gen. of Rassemblement du Peuple Français 1947-51; elected Deputy for Rhône, Nat. Assembly 1951, 1958, 1973; Gov.-Gen. of Algeria 1955-56; leader, Gaullist group in Nat. Assembly 1956-58; Del. to UN, New York 1957; returned to Algeria May 1958; Minister of Information July 1958-Jan. 1959; Minister attached to Prime Minister as Minister for Sahara and Atomic Questions 1959-60; mem. Cen. Cttee. U.N.R. 1958-60; Del.-Gen. Org. commune des régions sahariennes 1959-60; Pres. Information centre on Problems of Algeria and Sahara 1960; Political Dir. Voici Pourquoi 1960; warrant issued for arrest for subversion 1962; in exile, mainly in Italy and Switzerland 1961-68; returned to France after case dismissed Oct. 1968; Dir. of Studies, Ecole des Hautes Etudes en sciences sociales 1969-85; Founder-Pres. Mouvement Nat. Progrès et Liberté 1970; mem. Nat. Council of Scientific Research 1971-79; mem. Lyon City Council 1971-77; joined Reformist group in Nat. Assembly 1974; French rep. to Council of Europe 1973; in charge of Special Mission to Prime Minister 1975; Chair. European Univ. Centre, Ravello (Italy); mem. Académie Française 1983; Commdr., Légion d'honneur; Hon. C.B.E.; Commdr. Aguila Azteca (Mexico); Commdr. Polonia Restituta; Order of Grand Officer Nat. Order of Merit (Paraguay). *Publications:* Envers et contre tout 1946, La vie quotidienne des Aztèques 1955, 1962, Aimée et souffrante Algérie 1956, L'espérance trahie 1962, Sur une route nouvelle 1964, La page n'est pas tournée 1965, L'art du Mexique ancien 1966, Les quatre soleils 1967, Vingt-huit ans de Gaullisme 1968, la longue Marche d'Israël 1968, Les Aztèques 1970, Lettre ouverte aux victimes de la décolonisation 1973, Archéologie et Anthropologie 1976, L'Univers des Aztèques 1979, Les Olmèques 1980, Les Maya 1982, La Civilisation de Teotihuacán. *Address:* 85 avenue Henri Martin, 75116 Paris, France (Home). *Telephone:* 45-04-05-18 (Home).

SOUTHALL, Ivan Francis, A.M., D.F.C.; Australian author; b. 8 June 1921, Melbourne; s. of Francis and Rachel (née Voutier) Southall; m. 1st Joyce Blackburn 1945 (divorced), one s. three d.; m. 2nd Susan W. Stanton 1976; ed. Box Hill Grammar School; RAAF 1942-47; self-employed writer 1947-; Whitall Poetry and Literature Lecturer, Library of Congress 1973; May Hill Arbuthnot Honor Lecturer 1974; Australian Children's Book of the Year Award 1966, 1968, 1971, 1976, Australian Picture Book of the Year Award 1969, Carnegie Medal 1972, Nat. Children's Book Award 1986. *Publications:* over 50 works translated into 22 languages including They Shall Not Pass Unseen 1956, Softly Tread the Brave 1960, Hills End 1962, Ash Road 1965, To the Wild Sky 1967, The Fox Hole 1967, Let the Balloon Go 1968, Bread and Honey 1970, Josh 1971, Fly West 1974, Matt and Jo 1974, What About Tomorrow 1976, King of the Sticks 1979, The Golden Goose 1981, The Long Night Watch 1983, A City out of Sight 1984, Christmas in the Tree 1985, Rachel 1986, Blackbird 1988. *Leisure interests:* house and garden. *Address:* P.O. Box 25, Healesville, Vic. 3777, Australia.

SOUTHAM, Gordon Hamilton, O.C., B.A.; Canadian civil servant (retd.); b. 19 Dec. 1916, Ottawa; s. of Wilson Mills Southam and Henrietta Alberta (née Cargill); m. 1st Jacqueline Lambert-David 1940 (dissolved 1968), three s. one d.; m. 2nd Gro Mortensen 1968 (dissolved 1978), one s. one d.; m. 3rd Marion Charpentier 1981; ed. Ashbury Coll., Trinity Coll., Toronto and Christ Church, Oxford; Officer, Second World War, British and Canadian Armies; Reporter The Times, London 1945-46; Editorial Writer Ottawa Citizen 1946-47; joined Dept. of External Affairs 1948; Second Sec., Stockholm 1949-53, Ottawa 1953-59; Chargé d'affaires, Warsaw Mar. 1959-60, Amb. 1960-62; Head Information Div., Dept. of External Affairs 1962-64; Dir. Southam Inc. 1964-87; Co-ordinator, Nat. Arts Centre 1964-67, Dir.-Gen. 1967-77; Chair. Festival Canada Cttee. 1978-79, Nat. Theatre School, Montreal 1979-81; Pres. Canadian Mediterranean Inst. 1980-86, Chair. 1986-; Chair. Official Residences Council 1985-; Chancellor Univ. of King's Coll. 1988; Hon. LL.D. (Univ. of Trent, Carleton Univ.) 1978, Hon. D.C.L. (King's Coll.)., Dr. h.c. (Ottawa). *Leisure interests:* the arts, sailing, tennis. *Address:* 9 Rideau Gate, Ottawa K1M 1M6, Canada. *Telephone:* 749-0124.

SOUTHERN, Sir Richard (William), Kt., F.B.A.; British historian; b. 8 Feb. 1912; s. of Matthew Henry Southern; m. Sheila (née Cobley) 1944; two.s.; ed. Royal Grammar School, Newcastle upon Tyne and Balliol Coll., Oxford; Jr. Research Fellow, Exeter Coll., Oxford 1933-37; studied in Paris 1933-34 and Munich 1935; Fellow and Tutor, Balliol Coll. 1937-61; served with Oxford and Bucks. Light Infantry 1940, Second Lieut. Durham Light Infantry 1941, 155th Regiment R.A.C. 1942, rank of Capt. 1943,

Maj. 1944; Political Intelligence Dept. Foreign Office 1943-45; Jr. Proctor Oxford Univ. 1948-49; Birkbeck Lecturer in Ecclesiastical History Trinity Coll., Cambridge 1959-60; Chichele Prof. of Modern History, Oxford 1961-69; Pres. Royal Historical Soc. 1968-72, Selden Soc. 1973-76, St. John's Coll., Oxford 1969-81; Raleigh Lecture, British Acad. 1962, David Murray Lecture, Glasgow Univ. 1963, Gifford Lecture, Glasgow Univ. 1970-72, G. M. Trevelyan Lecture Cambridge Univ. 1980-81; Corresponding Fellow Medieval Acad. of America 1965, Monumenta Germaniae Historica 1982; Foreign Hon. mem. American Acad. of Arts and Sciences 1972; Hon. Fellow, Balliol Coll., Oxford 1968, Sidney Sussex Coll., Cambridge 1971, St. John's Coll., Oxford 1981; Hon. D.Litt. (Glasgow) 1964, (Durham) 1969, (Cantab) 1971, (Bristol) 1974, (Newcastle) 1977, (Warwick) 1978, (St. Anselm's Coll.) 1981, (Columbia) 1982, (Univ. of the South) 1985; Hon. LL.D. (Harvard) 1977; Int. Balzan Foundation Prize 1987. *Publications:* The Making of the Middle Ages 1953, Western Views of Islam in the Middle Ages 1962, Eadmer's Vita Anselmi (ed.) 1963, St Anselm and his Biographer 1963, Memorials of St. Anselm (co-ed.) 1969, Medieval Humanism and other studies 1970 (R.S.L. award), Western Society and the Church in the Middle Ages 1970, Robert Grosseteste 1986; articles in English Historical Review, Medieval and Renaissance Studies, etc. *Address:* 40 St. John Street, Oxford, 0X1 2LH, England.

SOUTHWOOD, Sir (Thomas) Richard Edmund, Kt., F.R.S., A.R.C.S., PH.D., D.SC.; British professor of zoology; b. 20 June 1931, Kent; s. of Edmund W. Southwood and Ada Mary (née Regg) Southwood; m. Alison Langley (Harden) 1955; two s.; ed. Gravesend Grammar School and Imperial Coll., Univ. of London; ARC Research Scholar, Rothamsted Experimental Station 1952-55; Research Asst. and Lecturer, Zoology Dept., Imperial Coll. 1955-64; Visiting Prof., Escuela Nacional de Agricultura, Mexico 1964; Visiting Prof., Dept. of Entomology, Univ. of Calif. at Berkeley 1964-65; Reader in Insect Ecology, Univ. of London 1964-67, Prof. of Zoology and Applied Entomology 1967-79; Linacre Prof. of Zoology, Univ. of Oxford 1979-; Fellow of Merton Coll. Oxford; Vice-Chancellor, Univ. of Oxford 1989-; A. D. White Prof.-at-Large, Cornell Univ., U.S.A. 1985-; Fellow of Imperial Coll., London 1984; Dean of Royal Coll. of Science 1971-72; Trustee British Museum (Natural History) 1974-83, Chair. 1980-83; Mem. Royal Comm. on Environmental Pollution 1974-85, Chair. 1981-85; Pres. British Ecological Soc. 1976-78, Hon. mem. 1988; Vice Pres. Royal Soc. 1982-84; Chair. Nat. Radiological Protection Bd. 1985-; Rhodes Trustee 1985-; East Malling Trustee 1986-; Lawes Trustee 1987-; Hon. Foreign mem. American Acad. of Arts and Sciences; Foreign mem. Norwegian Acad. of Science and Letters; Foreign Assoc. N.A.S.; Hon. mem. Ecological Soc. of America; Fellow Entomological Soc. of America; Hon. D.Sc. (Griffith Univ., East Anglia, McGill, Warwick); Fil. Dr. h.c. (Lund, Sweden); Scientific Medal, Zoological Soc. *Publications:* Land and Water Bugs of the British Isles 1959, Life of the Wayside and Woodland 1963, Ecological Methods 1966, Insects on Plants (with D. R. Strong and J. H. Lawton) 1984, Insects and the Plant Surfaces (with B. Juniper) 1986, Radiation and Health (with R.R. Jones) 1987. *Leisure interests:* gardening, natural history, reading. *Address:* Merton College, Oxford, England.

SOUTOU, Jean-Marie Léon; French diplomatist; b. 18 Sept. 1912, Bruges; s. of Antoine and Marie (née Matocq-Massey) Soutou; m. Maria Isabel de Semprun y Maura 1942; one s.; ed. Univ. de Paris à la Sorbonne; entered Ministry of Foreign Affairs 1943, served Switzerland 1943-44, Yugoslavia 1945; Admin., Ministry of Foreign Affairs 1950; Sec. of Foreign Affairs 1951; Asst. Dir. Cabinet of M. Mendès-France 1954-55; E. European Sub-Dir. to Minister of Foreign Affairs 1955-56; Minister-Counsellor, Moscow 1956-58; Consul-Gen., Milan 1958-61; Dir. European Affairs, Ministry of Foreign Affairs 1961-62, Dir. African and Middle East Affairs 1962-66; Insp.-Gen. Diplomatic and Consular Corps 1966-71; Amb. to Algeria 1971-75; Perm. Rep. to the European Communities 1975-76; Sec.-Gen. Ministry of Foreign Affairs 1976-83; Pres. French Red Cross 1978-83; Ambassadeur de France 1976; Commdr., Légion d'honneur, Grand Officier, Ordre nat. du Mérite. *Address:* Croix-Rouge Française, 17 rue Quentin Bauchart, 75008 Paris, France. *Telephone:* 723 9201.

SOUZA, Francis Newton; Indian painter; b. 12 April 1924, Goa; s. of Joseph Newton Souza and Lily Mary Antunes; m. 1st Maria Figueredo 1947 (divorced); one d.; m. 2nd Liselotte Kristian (in common law); three d.; m. 3rd Barbara Zinkant 1965 (divorced 1977); one s.; ed. St. Xavier's Coll. and Sir Jamsetjee Jeejeebhoy School of Art, Bombay, Central School of Art, London, École des Beaux Arts, Paris; f. Progressive Artists' Group; one-man exhbns. in London and major cities of England, in Paris, Stockholm, Copenhagen, Johannesburg and principal cities of Germany and U.S.A., Switzerland and U.A.E.; retrospective exhbns. in London 1951, New Delhi 1965, Leicester 1967, Detroit 1968, Minneapolis Int. Art Festival 1972, New Delhi and Bombay 1987; festival of Indian exhibits, Museum of Modern Art, Oxford and R.A. 1982; East-West Visual Arts Encounter 1985 (organized by Fed. Repub. of Germany), Bombay; represented in Baroda Museum, Nat. Gallery, New Delhi, Tate Gallery, London, Wakefield Gallery, Haifa Museum, Nat. Gallery, Melbourne, etc.; several awards. *Publications:* Nirvana of a Maggot in Encounter, Words and Lines (autobiog.) 1959, Statements 1977, The White Flag Revolution 1982, New Poems 1985. *Address:* 148 West 67 Street, New York City, N.Y., U.S.A. *Telephone:* (212) 874-2181.

SOUZAY, Gérard (Gérard Marcel Tisserand); French singer; b. 8 Dec. 1920, Angers; s. of Georges and Madeleine (née Hennique) Tisserand; ed. Coll. de Chinon, Lycée Hoche (Versailles), Lycée Carnot (Paris); debut 1945; since then numerous tours and appearances in Europe, N. and S. America, S. Africa, Australia and Japan. *Appeared in:* The Marriage of Figaro, Metropolitan Opera, New York 1965, in Pelléas et Mélisande, La Scala, Milan 1973; radio and television performances; Premier Prix d'Excellence, Paris Conservatoire; Chevalier, Légion d'honneur, Chevalier des Arts et des Lettres, Officier, Ordre nat. du Mérite. *Leisure interest:* painting. *Address:* 26 rue Freycinet, 75116 Paris, France.

SOVERN, Michael Ira, B.A., LL.B.; American professor of law and university president; b. 1 Dec. 1931, New York; m. Joan Wit 1974; two s. two d., one step-s. one step-d.; ed. Columbia Coll., Columbia School of Law; called to the Bar 1956; mem. Faculty, Columbia Law School 1957-, Prof. of Law 1960-, Dean, Law School 1970-79, Chancellor Kent Prof. in Law 1977-, Univ. Provost 1979-80, Pres. 1980-; Dir. Chemical Bank, AT and T, GNY Insurance Group, Orion Pictures Corpn., Asian Cultural Corpn.; Fellow, American Acad. of Arts and Sciences; mem. American Law Inst.; Hon. D.Phil (Tel Aviv), Hon. LL.D (Columbia) 1980. *Address:* Columbia University, 202 Law Library, New York, N.Y. 10027, U.S.A. *Telephone:* (212) 854-2825.

SOWIŃSKI, Mieczysław; Polish physicist and politician; b. 1930, Piel-aszów; ed. Kazan Univ., Asst. Warsaw Univ. 1955-59; Lecturer Inst. for Nuclear Research, Swierk nr. Warsaw 1959-73; Scientific practice Inst. of Atomic Energy, Moscow 1958-59; Scholarship of Joliot-Curie Found. Inst. of Nuclear Physics, Orsay, France 1967-69; Vice-Pres. Atomic Energy Office 1973-76; Vice-Dir. United Inst. for Nuclear Research, Dubna 1977-82; Pres. State Atomic Energy Agency 1982-; mem. PZPR; Prize of State Council for Peaceful Uses of Atomic Energy. *Publications:* many scientific works on nuclear physics and its application. *Address:* Państwowa Agencja Atomistyki, ul. Krucza 36, 00-921 Warsaw, Poland.

SOYINKA, Wole, B.A.; Nigerian playwright and lecturer; b. 13 July 1934, Abeokuta; s. of Ayo and Eniola Soyinka; m.; c.; ed. Univ. of Ibadan, Nigeria, and Univ. of Leeds, England; worked at Royal Court Theatre, London; Research Fellow in Drama, Univ. of Ibadan 1960-61; Lecturer in English, Univ. of Ife 1962-63; Sr. Lecturer in English, Univ. of Lagos 1965-67; political prisoner 1967-69; Artistic Dir. and Head Dept of Theatre Arts, Univ. of Ibadan 1969-72; Research Prof. in Dramatic Literature, Univ. of Ife 1972, Prof. of Comparative Literature and Head of Dept. of Dramatic Arts 1976-; Ed. Ch'Indaba (fmrly. Transition) Accra; Artistic Dir. Orisun Theatre, 1960 Masks; Literary Ed. Orisun Acting Editions; Pres. Int. Theatre Inst. 1986-; Fellow, Churchill Coll., Cambridge 1973-74; Hon. D.Litt. (Leeds) 1973, (Yale) 1981; Prisoner of Conscience Award, Amnesty Int., Jock Campbell-New Statesman Literary Award 1969; Nobel Prize for Literature 1986; mem. American Acad. of Arts and Letters; Pres. Nigeria Road Safety Service 1988-. *Publications:* plays: The Lion and the Jewel 1959, The Swamp Dwellers 1959, A Dance of the Forests 1960, The Trials of Brother Jero 1961, The Strong Breed 1962, The Road 1964, Kongi's Harvest 1965, Madmen and Specialists 1971, Before the Blackout 1971, Jero's Metamorphosis 1973, Camwood on the Leaves 1973, The Bacchae of Euripides 1974, Death and the King's Horsemen 1975, Opera Wonyosi 1978; novels: The Interpreters 1964, The Forest of a Thousand Demons (trans.), Season of Anomy 1973; non-fiction: The Man Died (prison memoirs) 1972; poetry: Idanre and Other Poems 1967, A Shuttle in the Crypt 1972, Poems of Black Africa (editor) 1975, Ogun Abibman 1977, Mandela's Earth and Other Poems 1988; lectures: Myths, Literature and the African World 1972; Aké, The Years of Childhood (autobiog.) 1982, Art, Dialogue and Outrage 1988; film: Blues for a Prodigal 1985; *Address:* c/o Department of Dramatic Arts, University of Ife, Ile-Ife, Nigeria.

SPACEK, Mary Elizabeth (Sissy); American actress; b. 25 Dec. 1949, Quitman, Tex.; d. of Edwin A. and Virginia Spacek; m. Jack Fisk 1974; one d.; ed. Lee Strasberg Theater Inst. *films:* Prime Cut 1972, Ginger in the Morning 1972, Badlands 1974, Carrie 1976, Three Women 1977, Welcome to L.A. 1977, Heart Beat 1980, Coal Miner's Daughter 1980, Raggedy Man 1981, Missing 1982, The River 1984, Marie 1985, Violets are Blue 1986, Crimes of the Heart 1986, 'night Mother 1986. *TV films:* The Girls of Huntington House 1973, The Migrants 1973, Katherine 1975, Verna, USO Girl 1978; Best Actress (Nat. Soc. Film Critics) for Carrie 1976, Best Supporting Actress (New York Film Critics) for Three Women 1977, Best Actress (New York and Los Angeles Film Critics, Foreign Press Asscn., Nat. Soc. Film Critics) 1980; Album of the Year Award (Country Music Asscn.) for Coal Miner's Daughter 1980. *Address:* Creative Artists Agency, 1888 Century Park East, Los Angeles, Calif. 90067, U.S.A.

SPADOLINI, Giovanni, LL.D.; Italian journalist and politician; b. 21 June 1925, Florence; writer for Il Messaggero; Political Ed. Gazzetta del Popolo 1950-52, of Corriere della Sera 1953-55; Ed. Resto del Carlino 1955-68; Ed. Corriere della Sera and Corriere d'Informazione 1968-72; Teacher of Contemporary History, Faculty of Political Science, Florence; Minister of the Environment 1974-76, of Educ. March-Aug. 1979; Senator, Republican Party (PRI) 1972-; Political Sec. Republican Party 1979-87; Pres. Council of Ministers (Prime Minister) 1981-82; Minister of Defence 1983-87; Pres. of the Senate 1987-; Uff. della Legion d'Onore; Cavaliere di Gran Croce dell'Ordine al Merito della Repubblica. *Publications:* Sorel 1947, Il 1848 realtà e leggenda di una rivoluzione 1948, Ritratto dell'Italia moderna 1949, Lotta sociale in Italia 1949, Il papato socialista 1950, L'opposizione cattolica da Porta Pia al '98 1954, Giolitti e i cattolici 1960, I radicali dell'Ottocento 1962, I repubblicani dopo l'Unità 1962, Un dissidente del Risorgimento 1962, Firenze Capitale 1967, Il Tevere più largo 1967, Storia Fiorentina, Carducci nella storia d'Italia, Il Mondo di Giolitti 1969, Il 20 Settembre nella storia d'Italia 1970, Autunno del Risorgimento 1971, L'Italia della ragione 1979, L'Italia dei Laici 1980, Giolitti: Un época (articles) 1985. *Address:* c/o Partito Repubblicano Italiano, Piazza dei Caprettari 70, Rome, Italy.

SPAGHT, Monroe Edward, PH.D.; American oil executive; b. 9 Dec. 1909, Eureka, Calif.; s. of Frederick E. and Alpha (Light) Spaght; three c.; ed. Humboldt State Univ., Univ. of Leipzig, Stanford Univ.; Research Scientist and Technologist, Shell Oil Co., (Calif.) 1933–40, Man. (Devt. and Mfg.) 1940–44; mem. U.S. Naval Tech. Mission to Europe 1944–45; Dir. U.S. Strategic Bombing Survey, Japan 1945–46; Vice-Pres. Shell Devt. Co., New York 1946–48; Pres. Shell Devt. Co., San Francisco 1949–53; Exec. Vice-Pres. Shell Oil Co., New York 1953–60, Pres. 1961–65; Man. Dir. Royal Dutch-Shell Group, London 1965–70; Dir. Shell Cos. U.S.A. 1953–80 (Chair. 1965–70), Royal Dutch Petroleum Co. 1965–80, Shell Petroleum N.V. 1965–80, Shell Petroleum Co. Ltd. 1965–80; Dir. numerous other cos. and orgs., including Inst. of Int. Educ. 1953– (Chair. 1971–74), American Petroleum Inst. 1953–, Wells Fargo Ltd. 1972–76, Inst. of Int. Educ. 1953–74, Stanford Research Inst. 1953–70, Princeton Advisory Council 1953–60, American Chamber of Commerce (U.K.) 1965–72, The Ditchley Foundation (U.K.) 1965–77, English Nat. Opera Ltd. 1984–; Hon. D.Sc. (Rensselaer Polytechnic Inst.) 1958, (Drexel Inst. of Tech.) 1962; Hon. LL.D. (Univ. of Manchester) 1964, (Calif. State Colls.) 1965, (Millikin Univ., Ill.) 1967, (Wesleyan Univ., Conn.) 1968; Hon. D. Eng. (Colorado School of Mines) 1971; Axel Johnson Medal, Sweden 1966, Order of Francisco de Miranda, Venezuela 1968, Commdr. Order of Oranje Nassau (Netherlands) 1970. *Publications:* Minding My Own Business 1971, The Multinational Corporation—Its Manners, Methods and Myths 1978, The Long Road from Eureka 1986. *Address:* 2 Lyall Mews, Belgravia, London, SW1X 8DJ, England.

SPAHR, Charles Eugene, B.S.; American oil executive; b. 8 Oct. 1913; s. of Charles T. Spahr and Imogene (Hedrick) Spahr; m. Mary Jane Bruckmiller 1937; one s. four d.; ed. Univ. of Kansas and Harvard Univ. Business School; joined Standard Oil Co. (Ohio) 1939, Vice-Pres. (Transportation) 1951, Exec. Vice-Pres. and Dir. 1955, Pres. 1957–69, Chair. 1970–78; Major in Army Corps of Engineers 1942–45; Dir. Supply and Transportation Div. Petroleum Admin. for Defense 1952; fmr. Dir. Air Products and Chemicals Inc., Ohio Bell, Lincoln Inst. of Land Policy, Repub. Steel Corpn., Harco Corpn., TRW Inc., Cleveland Electric Illuminating Co. (now part of Centerior Energy); Hon. Dir. and fmr. Chair. American Petroleum Inst.; Hon. Trustee Lutheran Hospital; Hon. Trustee Colgate Rochester Divinity School; mem. Bd. of Trustees Baldwin-Wallace Coll., Chair. 1964–78; Bd. of Trustees and First Chair., Int. Center for Artificial Organs and Transplantation; fmr. mem. Nat. Petroleum Council; fmr. Chair. Plans for Progress Advisory Council; Hon. Dr. Eng. (Cleveland State Univ.), Hon. LL.D. (Baldwin-Wallace Coll.), Citation for Distinguished Service (Univ. of Kansas); Gold Medal for Distinguished Achievement, American Petroleum Inst. 1980, NERO Distinguished Service Award 1984. *Leisure interests:* hunting, fishing, golfing. *Address:* 3615 Euclid Avenue, Cleveland, Ohio 44115 (Office); 24075 Lyman Boulevard, Shaker Heights, Ohio 44122; 800 Beach Road, 174 Vero Beach, Fla 32963, U.S.A.

SPAIN, James W., M.A., PH.D.; American diplomatist; b. 22 July 1926, Chicago; s. of Patrick Spain and Mary Ellen Forristal; m. Edith Burke James; three s. one d.; ed. Univ. of Chicago, Columbia Univ.; Consultant to Sec. of the Army, Tokyo 1949–50; Cultural Officer, Dept. of State, Karachi, Pakistan 1951–53; Research Fellow, Ford Foundation 1953–55; Research Lecturer, Columbia Univ. 1955–63; mem. Policy Planning Staff, Dept. of State 1963–64; Dir. Office of Research and Analysis for Near E.-S. Asian Affairs 1964–66; Country Dir. for Pakistan and Afghanistan 1966–69; Chargé d'affaires, Islamabad 1969; Consul-Gen., Istanbul 1970–72; Deputy Chief of Mission, Ankara 1972–74; Diplomat in Residence, Florida State Univ., Tallahassee 1974–75, Amb. to Tanzania 1975–79, to Turkey 1980–81, to Sri Lanka 1985–; Foreign Affairs Fellow, Carnegie Endowment for Int. Peace and Rand Corpn., Washington 1982–84. *Publications:* The Way of the Pathans 1962, The Pathan Borderland 1963, American Diplomacy in Turkey 1984. *Address:* U.S. Embassy, 210 Galle Road, Colombo, Sri Lanka. *Telephone:* 548007.

SPALDING, D. Brian, SC.D., PH.D., F.I.MECH.E., F.INST.F., F.R.S.; British professor of heat transfer and business executive; b. 9 Jan. 1923, New Malden, Surrey; s. of Harold and Kathleen Spalding; m. 1st Eda Ilse-Lotte Goericke, two s. two d.; m. 2nd Colleen King, two s.; ed. King's Coll. School, Wimbledon, The Queen's Coll. Oxford and Pembroke Coll. Cambridge; Bataafsche Petroleum Matschapij 1944–45; Ministry of Supply 1945–47; ICI Research Fellow at Cambridge Univ. 1948–50, Demonstrator in Eng. 1950–54; Reader in Applied Heat, Imperial Coll. of Science and Tech., London 1954–58, Prof. of Heat Transfer 1958–, Head of Computational Fluid Dynamics Unit 1981–; Man. Dir. Conduction Heat and Mass Transfer

Ltd. 1970–, Concentration, Heat and Momentum Ltd. 1975–; Chair. CHAM of N. America Ltd. 1977–; Bernar Lewis Combustion Medal 1982, Medaille d'Or 1980; mem. Royal Norwegian Soc. *Publications:* Numerical Prediction of Flow, Heat Transfer Turbulence and Combustion (selected works) 1983, Heat Exchanger Design Handbook (jtly.) 1982, Combustion and Mass Transfer 1979, GENMIX: A General Computer Program 1978, Mathematical Models of Turbulence (jtly.) 1972, Heat and Mass Transfer in Recirculating Flows (Co-Author) 1969, Convective Mass Transfer (Co-Author) 1963, Engineering Thermodynamics (Co-Author) 1958, Some Fundamentals of Combustion 1955; numerous scientific papers. *Leisure interests:* poetry and reading. *Address:* Computational Fluid Dynamics Unit, Imperial College of Science and Technology, Room 440 ME Building, Exhibition Road, London, SW7 2AZ, England. *Telephone:* 01-589 5111.

SPALVINS, Janis Gunars, B.ECON., F.C.I.S.; Australian business executive; b. 26 May 1936, Riga, Latvia (now U.S.S.R.); s. of Mr. and Mrs. P. Spalvins; m. Cecily Westall Rymill 1961; two s.; ed. Concordia Coll., Univ. of Adelaide; Group Sec. and Dir. Subsidiary cos., Camelec Group of cos. 1955–73; Asst. Gen. Man. Adelaide Steamship Co. Ltd. 1973–77, Gen. Man. 1977–79, Chief Gen. Man. and Dir. 1979–81, Man. Dir. Aug. 1981–; Chief Exec. David Jones Ltd. 1980–; Chair. David Jones (Australia) Pty. Ltd. 1980–; Chair. Tooth & Co. Ltd. 1981–, H. C. Sleigh Ltd. (now Petersville Sleigh Ltd.) 1982–, Nat. Consolidated Ltd. 1982–, Natcorp Investments Ltd., John Martin Retailers Ltd.; Dir. Sidney Cooke Ltd., Epstein & Co. Ltd.; Fellow, Inst. of Secretaries and Administrators 1961, Australian Soc. of Accountants 1967. *Leisure interests:* snow skiing, sailing, tennis, water skiing. *Address:* The Adelaide Steamship Company Ltd., 123 Greenhill Road, Unley, South Australia 5061; 2 Brookside Road, Springfield, South Australia 5062, Australia. *Telephone:* 08 272 3077 (Office).

SPANG-HANSSEN, Ebbe, D.PHIL.; Danish professor of romance philology; b. 14 Sept. 1928, Copenhagen; m. Gerda Friese Jensen 1952; two s. one d.; ed. Univ. of Copenhagen and Paris-Sorbonne; lecturer Paris-Sorbonne 1961–64; Prof. of Romance Philology, Univ. of Copenhagen 1966–; mem. Royal Danish Acad. of Sciences. *Publications:* Les Prépositions incolores du Français moderne 1963, La Segmentation automatique du Français écrit (with Bente Maegaard) 1978, Grammaire Française (ed. and co-author) (5 vols.) 1980–85. *Leisure interest:* music. *Address:* Lindevej 28, 3500 Vaerlose, Denmark.

SPANGENBERG, Christa; German publisher; b. 1928, Munich; d. of Edgar J. Spangenberg and Minni Jung; m. Berthold Spangenberg 1946 (died 1986); two s.; ed. music and language studies; Assoc. and Collaborator, Nymphenburger Verlagshandlung (founded by Berthold Spangenberg in 1946) 1960; Publr. and owner, Ellermann Verlag 1967–; honorary work for Börsenverein des Deutschen Buchhandels; lecturer, Univ. of Munich 1987–. *Publications:* Elly Petersens praktisches Gartenlexikon, Praktisches Balkon- und Zimmerpflanzen-lexikon, Grüne Uhr, Garten Uhr. *Leisure interests:* gardening, music. *Address:* Bäumlstrasse 6, 8000 Munich 19; Romanstrasse 16, 8000 Munich 19, Federal Republic of Germany. *Telephone:* 17 14 23; 13 37 37.

SPANOS, Marcos; Cypriot politician; b. 6 Aug. 1932, Lefkonico; s. of P. M. Spanos and Anna P. Spanou; m. 1960; one s. one d.; ed. Famagusta Greek Gymnasium, American Acad., Larnaca, Gray's Inn, London; called to the Bar 1956; practised law in Nicosia 1957; Dir.-Gen. Office of the Pancyprian Cttee. of Human Rights 1958, resident corresp. Int. League for the Rights of Man 1959, Rapporteur, Supreme Constitutional Court 1962–64, Counsel of the Repub., Legal Dept. 1964–67; seconded to Ministry of Labour to establish Arbitration Tribunal 1967, Chair. Arbitration Tribunal 1968; Minister of Labour and Social Insurance 1972–74, 1975–78; now practising lawyer in Nicosia; founder mem. UN Asscn. of Cyprus; Hon. Consul for Oman in Cyprus; Hon. Sec. Consular Corps of Cyprus; mem. Bd. of Dirs. Int. Fed. of Consular Corps and Asscns.; Chair. Consultative Cttee. to Cyprus Athletic Org. 1969; fmr. Pres. Anti-Cancer Soc. of Cyprus, Pres. Friends of the Paraplegic Soc. of Cyprus. *Leisure interests:* sports, reading, music. *Address:* Menandrou Street 1E, 4th Floor, Flat 3, P.O. Box 4670, Nicosia, Cyprus. *Telephone:* 453311/2; 453321.

SPARGO, Peter Ernest, F.R.S.S.A.; South African educator; b. 7 June 1927, Johannesburg; s. of Alfred Hugh Spargo and Lilias (née Fisher) McCall Spargo; m. Celia Rosamunde Key 1964; four d.; ed. Jeppe High School, Univ. of Witwatersrand, Johannesburg and Magdalene Coll., Cambridge; Science Teacher Jeppe High School 1961–63; Lecturer in Science Educ. Johannesburg Coll. of Educ. 1964–71; Science Educ. Planner, Pretoria 1972–75; School of Educ., Univ. of Cape Town 1976–, Dir. Science Educ. Unit 1980–; Nat. Chair. S.A. Asscn. of Teachers of Physical Science 1975–82; Nat. Pres. Fed. of Science and Math. Teachers Asscns. of S.A. 1977–79, 1984–85; Gen. Sec. Royal Soc. of S. Africa 1986–; Medal of Honour 1981. *Publications:* numerous publs. in the fields of science education, history of science and history of physics and chemistry, author of science textbooks. *Leisure interests:* walking, reading, gardening. *Address:* Science Education Unit, University of Cape Town, Rondebosch 7700, South Africa. *Telephone:* (47) 21 650 2778 (Office); (47) 21 686 4289 (Home).

SPARK, Muriel Sarah, O.B.E., F.R.S.L.; British author; b. Edinburgh; d. of Bernard Camberg and Sarah Elizabeth Maud (Uezzell); m. S. O. Spark 1937 (dissolved); one s.; ed. James Gillespie's High School for Girls,

Edinburgh; Foreign Office 1944–45; Ed. The Poetry Review 1947–49; Gen. Sec. Poetry Soc., London; Hon. mem. American Acad. of Arts and Letters; Hon. D.Litt. (Strathclyde) 1971, (Edinburgh) 1989; The Observer Story Prize 1951, Italia Prize 1962, James Tait Black Memorial Prize 1965. *Publications:* The Fanfarlo and Other Verse 1952, John Masefield (a critical study) 1953, The Comforters 1957, Robinson 1958, The Go-Away Bird and Other Stories 1958, Memento Mori 1959 (play 1964), The Bachelors 1960, The Ballad of Peckham Rye 1960, The Prime of Miss Jean Brodie 1961 (play 1966, film 1969), Voices at Play 1961, Doctors of Philosophy (play) 1963, The Girls of Slender Means 1963, The Mandelbaum Gate 1965, Collected Stories I. 1967, Collected Poems I. 1967, The Public Image 1968, The Very Fine Clock 1968, The Driver's Seat 1970 (film 1974), Not to Disturb 1971, The Hothouse by The East River 1973, The Abbess of Crewe 1974 (film 1977), The Takeover 1976, Territorial Rights 1979, Loitering with Intent 1981, Bang-Bang You're Dead 1982, Going Up to Sotheby's (poems) 1982, The Only Problem 1984, The Stories of Muriel Spark 1985, Mary Shelley 1987, A Far Cry from Kensington 1988. *Address:* c/o David Higham Assocs. Ltd., 5–8 Lower John Street, Golden Square, London, W1R 4HA, England.

SPASSKY, Boris Vasiliyevich; Soviet journalist and chess-player; b. 30 Jan. 1937, Leningrad; m. Marina Shcherbacheva 1975; ed. Faculty of Journalism, Leningrad State Univ.; in Leningrad Section of Voluntary Sport Soc., Trud 1959–61; Trainer, Leningrad Section of Voluntary Sport Soc., Locomotiv 1964–; played in numerous individual and command int. chess tournaments; U.S.S.R. Grand Master, Int. Grand Master and World Chess Student Champion 1956, U.S.S.R. Chess Champion 1962, World Chess Champion 1969–72; several decorations. *Address:* State Committee for Sports and Physical Culture of U.S.S.R. Council of Ministers, Skatertny pereulok 4, Moscow, U.S.S.R.

SPÄTH, Lothar; German politician; b. 16 Nov. 1937, Sigmaringen; s. of Friedrich and Helene (née Lillich) Späth; m. Ursula Heinle 1962; one s. one d.; ed. Gymnasium, Heilbronn, State School of Man., Stuttgart; mem. Landtag 1968–; Chair. of CDU group in Stuttgart Landtag 1972; Rep. of CDU for Baden-Württemberg 1977; Sec. of Interior Feb. 1978, Minister-Pres. of Baden-Württemberg Aug. 1978–; Pres. Bundesrat 1985–86; Dr. h.c. (Karlsruhe) 1984. *Publications:* Politische Mobilmachung, Partnerschaft statt Klassenkampf 1976. *Leisure interests:* modern painting and graphics, skating, tennis. *Address:* Staatsministerium Baden-Württemberg, Richard-Wagner-Strasse 15, 7000 Stuttgart 1, Federal Republic of Germany. *Telephone:* 0711-2153-1.

SPAULDING, Winston, Q.C.; Jamaican lawyer and politician; called to the Bar, Inner Temple, London 1966; subsequently practised law in the Bahamas and later established legal practice in Jamaica; Senator 1977; Attorney-General of Jamaica 1980–86, subsequently also Minister of Nat. Security and Justice. *Address:* c/o Office of the Attorney-General, Kingston, Jamaica.

SPEAR, Ruskin, C.B.E., R.A., A.R.C.A.; British artist; b. 30 June 1911, London; s. of Augustus and Jane (née Lemon) Spear; m. Hilda Mary Hill 1935; one s. one d.; ed. Royal Coll. of Art; elected London Group 1942, Pres. 1950; Visiting Teacher of Painting, Royal Coll. of Art (retd. 1976); paintings exhibited in many English and Australian art galleries; travelling exhbns. U.S.A.; exhbn. Pushkin Museum, Moscow 1957, also exhibited Europe, S. Africa, New Zealand; retrospective exhbn. at Royal Acad., London 1980; works purchased by The Chantrey Trustees, The British Council, The Arts Council, Stratford Memorial Theatre, St. Clement Dane's R.A.F. Memorial Church; murals for liner Canberra; numerous portraits incl. Duke of Westminster, Lord Goodman, Sir Harold Wilson, Chief Justice Dalton-Wells of Toronto, Lord Adrian, Lord Rothermere, Archbishop of Canterbury, Dowager Duchess of Devonshire, Sir Aubrey Lewis, Sir Ian Jacob, Lord Olivier, Barbara Castle, Sir Hugh Carleton Greene, Lord Netherthorpe, Sir Maurice Bridgeman, Lord Redcliffe-Maude, Lord Butler, Francis Showering, Sir Cyril Clarke, Sir David Willcocks, Prof. Dame Sheila Sherlock, Sir John Kendrew; portraits in Nat. Portrait Gallery, London: Lord Wilson, Lord Redcliffe-Maude, Self Portrait, Francis Bacon, Sir Alan Herbert, Lord Hailsham. *Leisure interest:* music. *Address:* 60 British Grove, London, W4 2PV, England.

SPEAR, Walter Eric, PH.D., F.R.S., F.R.S.E., F.INST.P.; British physicist; b. 20 Jan. 1921, Frankfurt/Main, Germany; s. of David and Eva (née Reineck) Spear; m. Hilda D. King 1952; two d.; ed. Univ. of London; lecturer in Physics, Univ. of Leicester 1953, Reader 1967; Visiting Prof., Univ. of Purdue and Univ. of N.C. 1957–58, 1965–66; Prof. of Physics, Univ. of Dundee 1968–; Max Born Prize 1977, Europhysics Prize 1977, MakDougal-Brisbane Medal (R.S.E.) 1981, Rank Prize for Optoelectronics 1988. *Publications:* numerous papers in scientific journals and contributions to books on electronic, optical and transport properties in crystalline and amorphous solids and liquids. *Leisure interests:* music, languages, literature. *Address:* Carnegie Laboratory of Physics, University of Dundee, Dundee, DD1 4HN (Office); 323 Blackness Road, Dundee, DD1 1SH, Scotland (Home). *Telephone:* (0382) 23181 Ext. 4563/4564 (Office); (0382) 67649 (Home).

SPECTER, Arlen; American politician; b. 12 Feb. 1930, Wichita, Kan.; s. of Harry and Lillie Shanin Specter; m. Joan Lois Levy 1953; one s. one d.; ed. Univ. of Okla., Univ. of Pa., Yale Univ.; served U.S.A.F. 1951–53;

Asst. Dist. Attorney, Phila., Pa. 1959–63, Dist. Attorney 1966–74; Asst. Counsel, Warren Comm., Washington, D.C. 1964; Special Asst. Attorney-Gen., Pa. Dept. of Justice 1964–65; Del. Republican Nat. Convention 1968, 1972, Alt. Del. 1976; Republican Senator from Pennsylvania Jan. 1981–; mem. Nat. Advisory Cttee. on Peace Corps 1969–; Lecturer in Law, Univ. of Pa. Law School 1969–72, Temple Univ. Law School 1972–76; mem. White House Conf. on Youth 1971, Gov. Justice Comm., Regional Planning Council, Nat. Advisory Comm. on Criminal Justice Standards and Goals, Criminal Rules Cttee. of Pa. Supreme Court and Judicial Council of Phila.; mem. American, Pa. and Phila. Bar Assens., Nat. Council on Alcoholism; Hon. LL.B (Phila. Coll. of Textiles and Science) 1968; Sons of Italy Award, Alessandroni Lodge. *Publications:* articles in law reviews. *Address:* 331 Hart Senate Building, Washington, D.C. 20510 (Office); 3417 Warden Drive, Philadelphia, Pa. 19129, U.S.A. (Home).

SPEDEN, Ian Gordon, PH.D.; New Zealand geologist; b. 4 March 1937, Gore; s. of Gordon Speden and Emaria F. M. Speden; m. Erica Tarlton 1958; one s. one d.; ed. Univ. of Otago and Yale Univ.; geologist, N.Z. Geological Survey, DSIR 1956–61, 1965–78, Regional Geologist 1978–84, Dir. 1984–; Nat. Research Advisory Council Fellowship, Yale Univ. 1961–64. *Publications:* five geological and paleontological bulletins, two geological maps and more than 100 scientific papers; co-compiler of Natural Hazards in New Zealand (Unesco) 1984, and contributor to Land Alone Endures 1980. *Leisure interests:* travelling, tramping, landforms, plants, animals and people, furniture restoration. *Address:* New Zealand Geological Survey, P.O. Box 30368, Lower Hutt, New Zealand. *Telephone:* (04) 699 059, 691 479.

SPEKREIJSE, Henk; Netherlands professor of visual systems analysis; m. Y.J.M. van der Heijden; two d.; ed. Tech. Univ. Delft and Univ. of Amsterdam; Prof. of Visual Systems Analysis, Netherlands Opthalmic Research Inst., Lab. of Medical Physics and Informatics 1977–; Dir. of Research Netherlands Opthalmic Research Inst. 1985–; mem. Royal Netherlands Acad. of Arts and Sciences 1985–; AKZO Award 1985. *Publications:* Analysis of EEG responses in man, evoked by sine wave modulated light 1966, Spatial Contrast (with L.H. van der Tweel) 1977, Visual Pathways, Electrophysiology and Pathology (with P.A. Apkarian) 1981, Systems Approach in Vision (with D. Regan and D.M. Shapley) 1986. *Address:* The Netherlands Ophthalmic Research Institute and the Laboratory of Medical Physics, P.O. Box 12141, 1100 AC Amsterdam-Zuidoost (Office); Voorstraat 11, 1394 CS Nederhorst den Berg, Netherlands (Home).

SPELLING, Aaron, B.A.; American television producer and writer; b. 22 April 1928, Dallas, Tex.; s. of David Spelling and Pearl Wall; m. Carole Gene Marer 1968; one s. one d.; ed. Univ. de Paris (Sorbonne), Southern Methodist Univ.; served U.S.A.A.F. 1942–45; Co-owner Thomas-Spelling Productions 1969–72; Co-Pres. Spelling-Goldberg Productions 1972–76; Pres. Aaron Spelling Productions Inc., Los Angeles 1977–86, Chair. and C.E.O. 1986–; mem. Bd. of Dirs. American Film Inst.; mem. Writers' Guild of America, Producers' Guild of America, The Caucus, Hollywood Radio and TV Soc., Hollywood TV Acad. of Arts and Sciences; Bronze Star Medal; Purple Heart with oak leaf cluster; Eugene O'Neill Award 1947, 1948; Nat. Assen. for Advancement of Colored People Image Award 1970, 1971, 1973, 1975; Man of the Year Award (Publicists' Guild of America) 1971; B'nai B'rith Man of the Year Award 1985, N.A.A.C.P. Humanitarian of the Year 1983; producer of numerous TV programmes, including Dynasty and Hotel and about 100 Movies of the Week for American Broadcasting Corpn.; films produced include Mr. Mom, 'Night, Mother and Second Surrender; author of numerous TV plays and films. *Address:* 1041 North Formosa Avenue, Los Angeles, Calif. 90046, U.S.A. (Office).

SPELLMAN, John D., B.S.S., J.D.; American lawyer and politician; b. 29 Dec. 1926, Seattle, Washington; s. of Sterling B. Spellman and Lela A. Cushman; m. Lois Murphy 1954; three s. three d.; ed. Seattle Univ. and Georgetown Univ. Law School; King Co. Commr. 1967–69, First Exec. 1969, 1973, 1977; First Vice-Pres. Nat. Assen. of Counties; Chair. Nat. Agric. Lands Advisory Cttee.; Vice-Chair. U.S. Coastal Zone Man. Advisory Cttee.; Chair. King-Snohomish Manpower Consortium; Gov. of Washington State 1981–85; mem. firm Carney, Stephenson, Bradley, Smith, Mueller and Spellman, Seattle 1985–; Hon. LL.D. (Seattle) 1981; Republican. *Leisure interests:* fishing, listening to jazz. *Address:* c/o Carney, Stephenson, Bradley, Smith, Mueller and Spellman, 2300 Columbia Center, 701 5th Avenue, Suite 2300, Seattle, Wash. 98104 U.S.A.

SPENCER, Anthony James Merrill, M.A., PH.D., F.R.S.; British professor and atomic scientist; b. 23 Aug. 1929, Birmingham; s. of James L. Spencer and Gladys Merrill; m. Margaret Bosker 1955; three s.; ed. Queen Mary's Grammar School, Walsall and Queens' Coll. Cambridge, Univs. of Keele and Birmingham; Research Assoc., Div. of Applied Math., Brown Univ., U.S.A. 1955–57; Sr. Scientific Officer UKAEA 1957–60; lecturer Dept. of Theoretical Mechanics Nottingham Univ. 1960–63, Reader 1963–65, Prof. 1965–; Visiting Prof. Brown Univ. 1966, 1971, Lehigh Univ. 1978, Univ. of Queensland 1982. *Publications:* Deformation of Fibre-Reinforced Materials 1972, Engineering Mathematics (2 vols.) 1975, Continuum Mechanics 1980, Ed.: Continuum Theory of the Mechanics of Fibre-Reinforced Composites 1984, Continuum Models of Discrete Systems 1987. *Address:* Department of Theoretical Mechanics, University of Nottingham, Nottingham, NG7 2RD (Office); 43 Stanton Lane, Stanton-on-the-Wolds, Keyworth, Nottingham, England (Home). *Telephone:* (0602) 484848 (Office); 06077-3134 (Home).

SPENCER, Donald Clayton, PH.D., SC.D.; American professor of mathematics; b. 25 April 1912, Boulder, Colo.; s. of Frank Robert Spencer and Edith (Clayton) Spencer; m. 1st Mary J. Halley 1936, 2nd Natalie Robertson Sanborn 1951; one s. two d.; ed. Univ. of Colorado, M.I.T. and Univ. of Cambridge; Instructor, M.I.T. 1939–42; Assoc. Prof., Stanford Univ. 1942–46, Prof. 1946–50, 1963–68; Assoc. Prof. Princeton Univ. 1950–53, Prof. 1953–63, 1968–78, Henry Burchard Fine Prof. 1972–78, Emer. 1978–; mem. Applied Mathematics Group, Nat. Defense Research Cttee., New York Univ. 1944–45; mem. N.A.S., American Acad. of Arts and Sciences; Bocher Prize of American Mathematical Soc. (joint recipient) 1948; Sc.D. h.c. (Purdue), 1971. *Publications:* (Monographs): Coefficient Regions for Schlicht Functions (with A. C. Schaeffer), American Mathematical Society Colloquium Publications Vol. 35 1950, Functionals of Finite Riemann Surfaces (with M. Schiffer) 1954, Advanced Calculus (with H. K. Nickerson and N. E. Steenrod) 1959, Lie Equations Vol. I: General Theory (with A. Kumpera) 1972; Selecta (3 vols.) 1985; articles in mathematical journals. *Leisure interests:* conservation, hiking. *Address:* 943 County Road 204, Durango, Colo., 81301, U.S.A. *Telephone:* (303) 247-9714.

SPENCER, Elizabeth, M.A.; American author; b. Carollton, Miss.; d. of James L. Spencer and Mary James McCain; m. John A. B. Rusher 1956; ed. Belhaven Coll. and Vanderbilt Univ.; Writer-in-residence, Univ. of N. Carolina 1969, Hollins Coll. 1973, Concordia Univ. 1977–78, Adjunct Prof. 1981–; mem. American Inst. of Arts and Letters; Guggenheim Foundation Fellow 1953; Rosenthal Foundation Award, American Acad. of Arts and Letters 1957; McGraw-Hill Fiction Award 1960, Award of Merit for short story, American Acad. of Arts and Letters 1983, and other awards; Hon. Litt. D. (Southwestern Univ., Memphis) 1968. *Publications:* Fire in the Morning 1948, This Crooked Way 1952, The Voice at the Back Door 1956, The Light in the Piazza 1960, Knights and Dragons 1965, No Place for an Angel 1967, Ship Island and other stories 1968, The Snare 1972, The Stories of Elizabeth Spencer 1981, Marilee 1981, The Salt Line 1984; short stories in magazines and collections. *Address:* 2300 Saint Mathieu, Apt. 610, Montréal, P.Q., Canada (Home).

SPENCER, Michael Clifford, M.A., D.PHIL., F.A.H.A.; British professor of French; b. 3 Feb. 1936, Peterborough; s. of Stephen C. Spencer and Elsie M. Spencer; m. Isobel M. C. King 1965; one s. one d.; ed. Chislehurst and Sidcup Co. Grammar School for Boys and Univs. of Sheffield and Oxford; Fellow in Modern Languages, Sidney Sussex Coll. Cambridge 1962–68; Sr. Lecturer in French, Univ. of Adelaide 1969–70; Sr. Lecturer in French, and Warden, Richardson Hall, Monash Univ. Melbourne 1971–73; Prof. of French, Univ. of Queensland 1974–, Head Dept. 1974–87. *Publications:* The Art Criticism of Théophile Gautier 1969, Michel Butor 1974, Charles Fourier 1980, Michel Butor, Letters from the Antipodes 1981. *Leisure interests:* travel, model railways, gardening. *Address:* Department of French, University of Queensland, Brisbane 4067 (Office); 24 Thorpe Street, Indooroopilly, Queensland 4068, Australia (Home). *Telephone:* 64 (7) 3772270 (Office); 64 (7) 378141.

SPENCER, William I.; American banker; b. 24 July 1917, Mesa County, Colo.; s. of Eugene W. Spencer and Nellie Haviland; m. Kathryn M. Cope 1953; ed. Mesa Coll., Colorado Coll., Colorado Springs and Columbia Univ.; Vice-Pres., Special Industries Div., First National City Corpn. 1954; Senior Vice-Pres. in charge of Special Industries Group 1959; Exec. Vice-Pres. in charge of Specialized Industries Div. 1965, in charge of Operating Group 1968; Pres. First National City Bank (Citibank 1976–82) 1970–82; Pres. CITICORP 1970–82; Chair. New York Blood Center Inc., Investment Comm., Bridge Capital Investors; Hon. Chair. Berkshire Farm Center and Services for Youth; Dir. United Techs. Corpn., Capital Cities Comm. Inc., Amerada Hess Corpn., Trust Co. of the West, Odyssey Inst. Inc.; Bd. of Govs. The Nature Conservancy; mem. Nat. Advisory Cttee. on Banking Policies and Practices, Trust Admin. Comm. of Eastern Air Lines; Trustee Colorado Coll., New York Univ. Medical Center, Corporate Property Investors, Hudson Inst. *Leisure interests:* hunting, golf, photography. *Address:* 12 Beekman Place, New York, N.Y. 10022, U.S.A.

SPENDER, Sir Stephen, Kt., C.B.E.; British writer; b. 28 Feb. 1909; s. of Edward and Violet (née Shuster) Spender; m. 1st Agnes Marie Inez 1936; m. 2nd Natasha Litvin 1941, one s. one d.; ed. Univ. Coll. School, London, and Univ. Coll., Oxford; poet and critic; Co-editor Horizon 1939–41; Counsellor, Section of Letters UNESCO 1947; Co-ed. Encounter 1953–66, Corresp. Ed. 1966–67; Consultant in Poetry in English to U.S. Library of Congress 1965; Visiting Prof., Univ. of Connecticut 1969, Vanderbilt Univ. 1979; Mellon Lecturer, Washington 1965, Northcliffe Lecturer, London 1969; Prof. of English, Univ. Coll., London 1970–77, Prof. Emer. 1977–; Pres. English PEN Centre 1975–; Hon. mem. American Acad. Arts and Letters; Hon. D.Litt. (Montpellier Univ., Cornell Coll., Loyola Univ.); C.Lit. (R.S.L.) 1977; Queen's Gold Medal for Poetry 1971. *Publications:* Poems in New Signatures 1933, Poems (2 editions), The Destructive Element 1934, The Burning Cactus (stories), Forward From Liberalism 1936, The Trial of a Judge 1937, The Still Centre 1939, trans. Ernst Toller's Pastor Hall 1939, The Backward Son 1940, Ruins and Visions 1942, Life and the Poet 1942, Citizens in War and After 1944, European Witness 1946, Poems of Dedication 1946, The Edge of Being 1949, World Within

World (autobiog.) 1951, The Creative Element 1953, Collected Poems 1955, Engaged in Writing 1957; translation of Schiller's Maria Stuart 1959; The Struggle for the Modern 1962, Selected Poems 1964, The Year of the Young Rebels 1969, The Concise Encyclopedia of English and American Poets and Poetry (edited with Donald Hall) 1970, The Generous Days 1971, Ed. A Choice of Shelley's Verse 1971, Ed. D. H. Lawrence: Novelist, Poet, Prophet 1973, Love-Hate Relations: A Study of Anglo-American Sensibilities 1974, T. S. Eliot 1975, Ed. W. H. Auden: A Tribute 1975, Memoirs: The Thirties and After, Poetry, Politics, People 1978, Letters to Christopher 1981, China Diary (with David Hockney, q.v.) 1982, Oedipus Trilogy (trans.) 1983 (staged 1983), Journals 1939–1982 1985, Collected Poems 1930–1985 1985, The Temple (novel) 1988. *Address:* 15 Loudoun Road, London, NW8, England.

SPERLICH, Harold K., M.B.A., B.S.; American business executive; b. 1 Dec. 1929, Detroit; s. of Harold Christ Sperlich and Elva Margaret Stoker; m. Polly A. Berryman 1976; two s. one d., three step-s. one step-d.; ed. Arthur Hill High School, Univ. of Mich.; with American Aluminium Co. 1951–54; served as Lieut. U.S. Navy 1954–57; with Ford Motor Co. 1957–77, Vice-Pres. 1970–77, Gen. Man. Truck Operations 1970, Asst. to Pres. for European Automotive Operations 1971, Product Planning and Research 1972–75, Car Operations 1975, Special Asst. to Exec. Vice-Pres. 1976; joined Chrysler Corpn. 1977–, Exec. Asst. to Exec. Vice-Pres. Eng. 1977, Vice-Pres. Product Planning and Design 1977, Group Vice-Pres. Eng. and Product Devt. 1978, Exec. Vice-Pres. 1979, Dir. 1980–, Pres. N. American Automotive Operations 1981, Pres. Chrysler Motors 1985–88. *Address:* 3333 West Shore Drive, Orchard Lake, Mich. 48033, U.S.A. (Home).

SPERLICH, Peter Werner, P.H.D.; American political scientist; b. 27 June 1934, Breslau, Germany (now Wrocław, Poland); s. of Max Otto and Anneliese Gertrud (née Greulich) Sperlich; arrived in U.S.A. 1956, naturalized 1961; ed. Mankato State Univ., Univ. of Mich.; faculty mem. Univ. of Calif., Berkeley 1963–, Prof. of Political Science 1980–, Prof. Law School 1963–; consultant, court and law firms; Social Science Research Council Fellow 1966, Ford Foundation Fellow 1968; mem. American Legal Studies Asscn., Law and Soc. Asscn., Nat. Asscn. for Dispute Resolution, Int. Soc. of Political Psychology, Soc. for Psychological Study of Social Issues, American, Int. and Western Political Science Asscns., Conf. Group on German Politics; research on law and politics in U.S., G.D.R., Fed. Repub. of Germany, Austria, Denmark, the Netherlands, Switzerland, the U.K., Canada, the U.S.S.R., Japan. *Publications:* Conflict and Harmony in Human Affairs 1971, Single Family Defaults and Foreclosures 1975, Trade Rules and Industry Practices 1976, Over-the-Counter Drug Advertisements 1977, Residing in a Mobile Home 1977, An Evaluation of the Emergency School Aid Act Nonprofit Organisation 1978, also numerous articles. *Address:* University of California, 210 Barrows Hall, Berkeley, Calif. 94720 (Office); 39 Adeline Drive, Walnut Creek, Calif. 94596, U.S.A. (Home).

SPERRY, Roger Wolcott, A.B., M.A., PH.D.; American professor of psychobiology; b. 20 Aug. 1913, Hartford, Conn.; s. of Frances Bushnell Sperry and Florence Kramer; m. Norma Deupree 1949; one s. one d.; ed. Oberlin Coll., Univ. of Chicago and Harvard Univ.; Research Assoc., Yerkes Laboratories Primate Biology 1942–46; Asst. Prof. of Anatomy, then Assoc. Prof. of Psychology, Univ. of Chicago 1946–52; Section Chief Developmental Neurology, Nat. Insts. of Health 1952–53; Hixon Prof. of Psychobiology, Calif. Inst. of Tech. 1954–84; Prof. Emer. 1984–; mem. Nat. Acad. of Sciences 1960–, American Acad. of Arts and Sciences 1963–, American Philosophical Soc. 1974–, The Royal Soc. 1976–, Pontifical Acad. of Sciences 1978–; Hon. D.Sc. (Cambridge) 1972, (Univ. of Chicago) 1976, (Kenyon Coll.) 1979, (Rockefeller Univ.) 1979, (Oberlin Coll.) 1982; awards include: Warren Medal of Experimental Psychology 1969, DSC Award of American Psychological Assoc. 1971, Calif. Scientist of Year Award 1972, Wakeman Research Award of the Nat. Paraplegic Foundation 1972, Passano Award for Medical Research 1973, Karl Lashley Award of American Philosophical Soc. 1976, Wolf Foundation Prize in Medicine 1979, Albert Lasker Basic Medical Research Award 1979, Ralph Gerard Prize for Distinguished Contributions to Neuroscience 1979, Nobel Prize for Medicine or Physiology 1981, Realia Award, Inst. for Advanced Philosophical Research 1986. *Publications:* Science and Moral Priority 1983, Nobel Prize Conversations (with Eccles, Josephson and Prigogine) 1985; numerous scientific and philosophic publications in professional journals and textbooks. *Leisure interests:* sculpture, natural history, palaeontology. *Address:* California Institute of Technology, 1201 East California Boulevard, Pasadena, Calif. 91125; 3625 Lombardy Road, Pasadena, Calif. 91107 U.S.A. (Home). *Telephone:* (818) 356-4962 (Office); (818) 793-0117 (Home).

SPERTI, George Speri, E.E., SC.D.; American scientist; b. 17 Jan. 1900, Covington, Ky.; s. of George and Caroline (Speri) Sperti; ed. Univ. of Cincinnati; Asst. Chief Meter Laboratories U.G. & E., Cincinnati 1922; Asst. Research Dir. Duncan Electrical and Manufacturing Co., Lafayette 1923; Research Asst. Univ. of Cincinnati 1924–25; Research Prof. and Dir. of Research (also co-founder) Basic Science Research Laboratory, Univ. of Cincinnati 1925–35; mem. Bd. of Dirs. Gen. Devt. Laboratories Inc., New York 1930–35, Sperti Lamp Corpn. 1930–40, Sperti Drug Products Inc.; Dir. Sperti Lamp. Corpn. 1935–; Research Prof., Dir. of Research, mem. Bd. of Trustees, mem. Bd. of Regents and Pres. St. Thomas Inst.; Principal

Consultant War Production Bd. 1942; mem. Pontifical Acad. Science, American Asscn. for Advancement of Science, American Physical Society; mem. Royal Soc. of Arts, London, Founding mem. American Soc. for the Aged and mem. of its Medical & Scientific Cttee.; Bd. of Dirs. American Council for Int. Promotion of Democracy under God Inc. 1959; Dir. Franklin Corpn.; mem. Emeritus Hall; Hon. mem. Società Italiana de Fisica; mem. Académie Internationale de Philosophie des Sciences, Brussels; mem. Engineering Soc. of Cincinnati; mem. Academia de Doctores, Madrid; Hon. D.Sc. (Dayton) 1934, (Duquesne) 1936, (Bryant Coll.) 1957, (Thomas More Coll.) 1975, (Xavier) 1978; Hon. L.H.D. (Caldwell Coll.) 1974; Catholic Action Medal 1942, Mendel Medal 1943, Christian Culture Award 1947; Star of Solidarity Third Class of the Italian Repub. 1956; Gold Medal Univ. Int. degli Studi Sociali "Pro Deo" 1958, William Howard Taft Award 1970, Cincinnati Scientist Engineer-of-the-Year Award 1970; developed type of therapeutic lamp; other developments with selective irradiation and on fluorescent lighting; discovered biological substances Biodynes; specialist in cancer research. *Publications:* Probiotics; co-author Quantum Theory in Biology 1927, and Correlated Investigations in the Basic Sciences; Ed. Studies Inst. Divi Thomae. *Leisure interests:* farming, horseback riding. *Address:* St. Thomas Institute, 1842, Madison Road, Cincinnati, Ohio 45206, U.S.A. *Telephone:* (513) 861-3460.

SPICER, Warwick Charles Richard; New Zealand journalist; b. 10 Dec. 1929, Christchurch; s. of Albert Spicer and Florence Ditford; m. Elizabeth F. Medlin 1963; three s.; ed. Christchurch Boys High School and N.Z. Inst. of Management; Asst. Ed., The Star, Christchurch 1981–82; Ed., Auckland Star 1983; Ed. and Man. Auckland Star Ltd. 1984–. *Leisure interests:* fishing, reading, sports spectator. *Address:* Auckland Star Ltd., P.O. Box 1407, Auckland (Office); 76 Mayfair Crescent, Mairangi Bay, Auckland, New Zealand (Home). *Telephone:* 797.626 (Office); 478.7307 (Home).

SPIELBERG, Steven, B.A.; American film director; b. 18 Dec. 1947, Cincinnatti, Ohio; s. of Arnold and Leah (née Posner) Spielberg; m. Amy Irving 1985 (divorced 1989); one s.; ed. Calif. State Coll., Long Beach; won film contest with war film Escape to Nowhere 1961; dir. episodes of TV series, including Night Gallery, Marcus Welby, M.D., Columbo; directed 20-minute short Amblin'; Dir. TV films Duel 1971, Something Evil 1972; Dirs. Guild of America Award Fellowship 1986; Irving G. Thalberg Award 1987. *Films directed:* The Sugarland Express 1974, Jaws 1975, Close Encounters of the Third Kind 1977, 1941 1979, Raiders of the Lost Ark 1981, E.T. (The Extra Terrestrial) 1982, Indiana Jones and the Temple of Doom 1984, The Colour Purple (also produced) 1985, Empire of the Sun 1988; I Wanna Hold Your Hand (produced) 1978, Poltergeist (co-wrote and produced) 1982, Gremlins (produced) 1984, Young Sherlock Holmes 1985 (exec. producer), Back to the Future (co-exec. producer), The Goonies (writer and exec. producer) 1986, Batteries Not Included (exec. producer) 1986, The Money Pit (co-produced) 1986, An American Tail (co-exec. produced) 1986, Always 1989. *Publication:* Close Encounters of the Third Kind (with Patrick Mann). *Address:* c/o Amblin Entertainment, 100 Universal Plaza, Bungalow 477, Universal City, Calif. 91608, U.S.A.

SPIERS, Ronald Ian, B.A., M.A.; American diplomatist; b. 9 July 1925, Orange, N.J.; s. of Thomas Hoskins and Blanca (née De Ponthier) Spiers; m. Patience Baker 1949; one s. three d.; ed. Dartmouth Coll., Princeton Univ.; mem. U.S. Del. to UN 1955–58; Dir. Disarmament Affairs, State Dept., Washington 1958–62, NATO Affairs 1962–66; Political Counsellor, U.S. Embassy in London 1966–69, Minister 1974–77; Asst. Sec. of State for Political-Mil. Affairs 1969–73; Amb. to the Bahamas 1973–74, to Turkey 1977–80; Dir. Bureau of Intelligence and Research, Dept. of State 1980–81; Amb. to Pakistan 1981–83; Under-Sec. for Man., Dept. of State 1983–. *Address:* c/o Department of State, 2201 C Street, N.W., Washington, D.C. 20520 (Office); 2315 Kimbro Street, Alexandria, Va. 22307, U.S.A. (Home).

SPIES von BÜLLESHEIM, Freiherr Adolf Wilhelm, DR.JUR.; German lawyer and farmer; b. 4 June 1929, Hückelhoven; s. of Egon Freiherr von Büllesheim and Maria Freiin von Oer; m. Maria Gräfin von Mirbach-Harff 1961; one s. four d.; ed. Univs. of Bonn and Munich; solicitor, Düsseldorf and Mönchengladbach 1960–; farmer on family estate in Hückelhoven 1961–; Mayor of Hückelhoven 1969–73; mem. Bundestag 1972–87; mem. WEU 1977–87, Council of Europe 1977–87; Chair. Eschweiler Bergwerks Verein AG, Herzogenrath 1987–; mem. bd. of several cos.; Bundesverdienstkreuz. *Leisure interests:* hunting, skiing. *Address:* Haus Hall bei Ratheim, P.O. Box 6209, 5142 Hückelhoven, Federal Republic of Germany. *Telephone:* 02433-5067.

SPILHAUS, Athelstan Frederick, M.S., D.SC.; American (naturalized) meteorologist and oceanographer; b. 25 Nov. 1911, Cape Town, South Africa; s. of Karl Antonio and Nellie (Muir) Spilhaus; m. 1st Mary Atkins 1934, two s. three d.; m. 2nd Gail Griffin 1964; m. 3rd Kathleen Fitzgerald 1978; ed. Univ. of Cape Town and M.I.T.; went to America 1931, naturalized 1946; research Asst. M.I.T. 1933–35; Asst. Dir. of Technical Services, Union of South Africa Defense Forces 1935–36, Woods Hole Oceanographic Inst. 1936–37, Investigator in Physical Oceanography 1938–60, Assoc. 1960, now Hon. Staff mem.; Asst. Prof. New York Univ. 1937–38, Assoc. Prof. 1939–41, Prof. of Meteorology 1942–48, started Dept. of Meteorology and Oceanography, Chair. 1938–47; Capt. U.S.A.F. 1943, Major 1944, Lieut.-Col. 1946; Dir. of Research, New York Univ. 1946–48; Meteorological

Adviser to Govt. of Union of South Africa 1947; Dean and Prof. Inst. of Technology, Univ. of Minnesota 1949–66, Prof. School of Physics 1966; mem. Nat. Science Bd. 1966–72; Pres. Franklin Inst. 1967–69, Aqua Int. Inc. 1969–70, Pan Geo, Inc. 1983–; Fellow Woodrow Wilson Int. Center for Scholars 1971–74; with Nat. Oceanic and Atmospheric Admin., Dept. of Commerce 1974–80; Royal Meteorological Soc., A.I.A.A., A.A.A.S.; mem. American Meteorological Soc., Royal Soc. of S. Africa, American Geophysical Union, American Soc. of Limnology and Oceanography, American Phil. Soc.; mem. U.S. Nat. Cttee. Int. Geophysical Year, Cttee. on Oceanography and Polar Research of Nat. Acad. of Sciences; Trustee Woods Hole Oceanographic Inst., Int. Oceanographic Foundation, Science Service Inc., Aerospace Corpn. 1963–; mem. Bd., Nat. Maritime Center 1988–; Dir. Donaldson Co. Inc., American Dynamics Corpn.; U.S. Rep. UNESCO Exec. Bd. 1954–58; U.S. Commr. Seattle World's Fair 1961–63; inventor of bathythermograph 1938; Distinguished Scholar, Cen. for the American Experience, Annenberg School of Communications, Univ. of S. Calif. 1981; Visiting Fellow, Inst. for Marine and Coastal Studies, Univ. of Southern Calif. 1981; Legion of Merit 1946; Exceptional Civilian Service Medal, U.S.A.F. 1952; Patriotic Civilian Service Award, Dept. of the Army 1959; Berzelius Medal 1962; Proctor Prize, Scientific Research Soc. of America 1968, 15th Anniversary Award, Marine Tech. Soc. 1977; Compass Award, Marine Tech. Soc. 1981; 16 hon. degrees from U.S.A. and U.K. *Publications:* Workbook in Meteorology (textbook) 1942, Weathercraft (for children) 1951, Meteorological Instruments (with W.E.K. Middleton) 1953, Satellite of the Sun 1958, Turn to the Sea 1959, The Ocean Laboratory 1966, Experimental Cities 1966, Waste Management, The Next Industrial Revolution 1966, Mechanical Toys: How Old Toys Work (with Kathleen Spilhaus) 1989; Our New Age (daily and Sunday feature); more than 200 articles in journals and magazines. *Address:* Pan Geo, Inc., P.O. Box 2000, Middleburg, Va. 21117, U.S.A. (Office). *Telephone:* (703) 687-6579.

SPÍNOLA, Marshal António Sebastião Ribeiro de; Portuguese army officer (retd.) and fmr. Head of State; b. 11 April 1910, Estremoz; m. Maria Helena Martin Monteiro de Barros 1932; ed. Mil. Schools, Lisbon, Univ. of Lisbon; promoted to rank of Capt. 1944, Maj. 1956, Lt.-Col. 1961, Col. 1963, Brig. 1966, Gen. 1969; held various posts in Portuguese Army; Deputy Commdr., later Commdr. 2nd Lancers Regt. 1961; Commdr. 345th Cavalry Group, Angola 1961–64; Provost Marshal 1964–65; High Command Course 1965–66; Cavalry Insp. 1966–67; Deputy Commdr. Nat. Republican Guard 1967–68; Gov., C.-in-C. of the Armed Forces of Portuguese Guinea 1968–73; Deputy Chief of Staff of the Armed Forces 1973–74; Head Junta Nacional de Salvação 1974; Pres. of Portugal May–Sept. 1974; retd. from Army Nov. 1974; implicated in attempted coup d'état March 1975, in exile in Brazil and Switzerland 1975; returned to Portugal, arrested, freed and returned to exile Aug. 1976; restored to rank of Gen. 1978, Marshal 1981; Dir. Sociedade Hípica Portuguesa (Equestrian Soc.) 1940–44, Pres. 1967; mem. Bd. of Dirs. Siderurgia Nacional (Nat. Steel Works Co.) 1955–64; Commdr., Order of Aviz 1959, Gold Medal for Exemplary Conduct 1965, of Mil. Merit with Laurels 1972, Tower and Sword with Palms 1973, and many other mil. decorations. *Publications:* Por Uma Guiné Melhor (For a Better Guinea) 1970, Linha de Accão (Line of Action) 1971, Portugal e o Futuro (Portugal and its Future) 1974, País sem Rumo 1978. *Address:* c/o Ministério da Defesa, Lisbon, Portugal.

SPIRIDONOV, Lev Nikolayevich, CAND.PHIL.SC.; Soviet politician, diplomatist and journalist; b. 1931; ed. Moscow Univ.; Komsomol work 1955–60; mem. CPSU 1956–; instructor, Head of Section, Sec. of Moscow Komsomol City Cttee.; diplomatic work 1960–65; Deputy Pres. of U.S.S.R. Cttee. of Youth Orgs. 1965–68; Deputy Head of Section of Moscow City Cttee. 1968–71; work for CPSU Cen. Cttee. 1971–72; Ed. Moskovskaya pravda 1972–83; Head of Section of CPSU Cen. Cttee. 1983–85; Sec., Head of Section of int. links, Moscow City Cttee. 1985–; First Deputy Ed.-in-Chief Pravda 1986–; cand. mem. of CPSU Cen. Cttee. 1986–. *Address:* Pravda, ul. Pravdy 24, Moscow, U.S.S.R.

SPIRIN, Aleksandr Sergeyevich; Soviet biochemist; b. 4 Sept. 1931, Kaliningrad, Moscow Region; m. Lydia Pavlovna Gavrilova; one s.; ed. Moscow State Univ.; mem. Staff, Bakh Inst. of Biochem. 1958–62, Head of Lab. 1962–73; Prof. Moscow State Univ. 1964–, Head of Chair. of Molecular Biology 1973–; Head of Lab. and Dir. Inst. of Protein Research 1967–; Corresp. mem. U.S.S.R. Acad. of Sciences 1966–70, Academician 1970–; mem. Deutsche Akad. der Naturforscher Leopoldina 1974; Dr. h.c. (Univ. of Granada) 1972; Lenin Prize 1976; Sir Hans Krebs Medal 1969; Order of Lenin and other decorations. *Publications:* Macromolecular Structure of Ribonucleic Acids 1964, The Ribosome 1969, Ribosome Structure and Protein Biosynthesis 1986. *Leisure interest:* hunting. *Address:* Institute of Protein Research, U.S.S.R. Academy of Sciences, 142292 Poushchino, Moscow Region, U.S.S.R. *Telephone:* 923-48-11.

SPIRO, Sidney, M.C.; business executive; b. 1914, South Africa; s. of Marcus and Clara Spiro; m. Diana D. M. Susskind; two d.; ed. Grey Coll., Bloemfontein and Cape Town Univ.; joined Anglo-American Corpn. S.A. Ltd. 1953, Exec. Dir. 1961–77; Consultant to Anglo American Group 1977–; Vice-Chair. and Man. Dir. Charter Consolidated Ltd 1969–71, Chair. and Man. Dir. 1971–72, Chair 1972–76, Dir. (non-exec.) 1976–; Chair. Landor Assocs. (Europe) Ltd. 1985–; Dir. De Beers Consolidated Mines Ltd., Minerals and Resources Corpn. Ltd., First Security Group Ltd.; Consultant, Hambros Bank Ltd. *Leisure interests:* shooting, golf, tennis. *Address:* 41 Tower Hill, London, EC3N 4HA, England. *Telephone:* 01-480-5000.

SPITAL, Hermann Josef Silvester, DR.THEOL.; German ecclesiastic; b. 31 Dec. 1925, Münster; ed. Gymnasium Paulinum, Münster, and theological studies in Münster; ordained 1952; Generalvikar, Münster 1973; consecrated bishop 1980; Bishop of Trier 1981-. *Address:* Liebfrauenstrasse 1, 5500 Trier, Federal Republic of Germany. *Telephone:* 0651-7105209.

SPITERI, Lino, M.A.; Maltese politician and consultant; b. 21 Sept. 1938, Qormi; m. Vivienne Azzopardi 1964; two s. two d.; ed. Lyceum, Plater Coll. and St. Peter's Coll., Oxford; emergency teacher 1956-57; Clerk U.K. Mil. Establishment 1957-62; Deputy Ed. Il-Helsien (daily) 1962-64, It-Torca (weekly) 1964-66; Ed. Malta News 1967-68; Research Officer Malta Chamber of Commerce 1968-70; with Cen. Bank of Malta as Sr. Research officer, then Asst. Head of Research 1971, Acting Head of Research 1972, Deputy Gov. 1974-81; Minister of Finance 1981-83, of Econ. Planning and Trade 1983-87; mem. Malta Labour Party Gen. Exec. 1958-66; Gen. Sec. Labour League of Youth 1961-62; M.P. 1962-66; Malta Corresp. for Observer, Observer Foreign News Service, Guardian 1967-71; mem. Malta Broadcasting Authority 1968-70; mem. Comm. on Higher Educ. 1977-79; Chair. Students Selection Bd. 1978-79; Pres. Qormi Football Club 1977-79. *Publications:* Studies: The Development of Tourism in Malta 1968, The Development of Industry in Malta 1969; *Fiction:* Tad-Demm u L-Laham u stejjer ohra (short stories) 1968, Hala taz-Zghozija u stejjer ohra (short stories) 1970, Anatomija (short stories) 1978, Iz-Zewgt Ihbieb u stejjer ohra (short stories) 1979, Stqarrija (verses) 1979, Rivoluzzjoni do minori (novel), Il-Halliel u stejjer ohra (short stories), Jien Nimxi Wandi (verses). *Leisure interests:* reading, writing. *Address:* Dar iz-Zerniq, Notary Zarb Street, Attard, Malta. *Telephone:* 442705.

SPITZER, Lyman, Jr., B.A., PH.D.; American astronomer; b. 26 June 1914; s. of Lyman Spitzer and Blanche Brumback Spitzer; m. Doreen D. Canaday 1940; one s. three d.; ed. Phillips Acad., Andover, Mass., and Yale, Cambridge, Princeton and Harvard Univs.; Instructor in Physics and Astronomy Yale Univ. 1939; Scientist Special Studies Group 1942, and Dir. Sonar Analysis Group 1944, Columbia Univ., Division of War Research; Assoc. Prof. of Astrophysics Yale Univ. 1946; Prof. of Astronomy, Chair. of Dept. and Dir. of Observatory, Princeton Univ. 1947-79, Charles A. Young Prof. of Astronomy 1952-82; Dir. Project Matterhorn 1953-61; Chair. Exec. Cttee. Plasma Physics Laboratory 1961-66; Chair. Univ. Research Bd. 1967-72, Space Telescope Inst. Council 1981-; mem. N.A.S. 1952-, Royal Astronomical Soc. (Assoc. 1973-), American Astronomical Soc. (Pres. 1960-62), Physical Soc., American Acad. of Arts and Sciences, American Philosophical Soc., American Alpine Club, Alpine Club (London); Hon. D.Sc. (Yale Univ., Case Inst., Harvard Univ., Princeton), Hon. LL.D. (Toledo Univ.); NASA Medal 1972, Bruce Medal 1973, Henry Draper Medal, U.S. Nat. Acad. of Sciences 1974, James Clerk Maxwell Prize, American Physical Soc. 1975, Distinguished Public Service Medal, NASA 1976; Gold Medal of Royal Astronomical Soc. 1978, Nat. Medal of Science 1980, Jules Janssen Medal, Soc. Astron. de France 1980, Franklin Medal, Franklin Inst. 1980, Craoford Prize, Royal Swedish Acad. of Sciences 1985, James Madison Medal, Princeton Univ. 1989. *Publications:* Physics of Sound in the Sea (Editor) 1946, Physics of Fully Ionized Gases 1956, 1962, Diffuse Matter in Space 1968, Physical Processes in the Interstellar Medium 1978, Searching Between the Stars 1982, Dynamical Evolution of Globular Clusters 1987, and many articles. *Leisure interests:* mountain climbing, skiing. *Address:* Princeton University Observatory, Peyton Hall, Princeton, N.J. 08544, U.S.A. *Telephone:* (609) 452-3809.

SPIVAKOVSKY, Tossy; American (b. Russian) violinist; b. 4 Feb. 1907, Odessa, U.S.S.R.; s. of David and Rahel Spivakovsky; m. Erika Lipsker 1934; one d.; ed. Hochschule für Musik, Berlin; brought to Berlin 1909; concert debut 1917; recitals and solo performances in Europe 1917-33; concert tour, Australia and New Zealand 1933; settled in Melbourne, taught at Melbourne Univ. Conservatory Master Class; settled in U.S.A. 1943-; mem. Violin Faculty, Juilliard School, New York; yearly concert tours, U.S.A., Canada and Europe; apart from classical and romantic repertoire, is well known for his introductory performances of concertos by Bartok, Stravinsky, Menotti, Miklos Rozsa, Leonard Bernstein, Roger Sessions, Carl Nielsen, William Schuman, Leroy Robertson, Frank Martin and others; numerous recordings. *Publications:* cadenzas to Beethoven's Violin Concerto and to all of Mozart's Violin Concerti; Hon. D.Hum.Litt. (Fairfield Univ.) 1970, Hon. D.Mus. (Cleveland Inst. of Music) 1975. *Leisure interest:* reading. *Address:* 29 Burnham Hill, Westport, Conn. 06880, U.S.A. *Telephone:* (203) 227-9057 (Home).

SPOCK, Benjamin McLane, B.A., M.D.; American paediatrician; b. 2 May 1903, New Haven, Conn.; s. of Benjamin Ives Spock and Mildred Stoughton Spock; m. 1st Jane Cheney 1927 (divorced 1976), two s.; m. 2nd Mary Morgan Wright 1976; ed. Phillips Acad., Yale Coll., Coll. of Physicians and Surgeons, Columbia Univ.; paediatric practice, Cornell Medical Coll., New York Hosp. and New York City Health Department 1933-47; served in U.S. Navy 1944-46; mem. staff, Rochester (Minn.) Child Health Inst., Mayo Clinic and Univ. of Minnesota 1947-51; organized teaching programme in child psychiatry and development, Pittsburgh Univ. Medical School 1951-55; Prof. of Child Development, Western Reserve Univ. 1955-67; specializes in application of psychoanalytic principles to paediatric practice; mem.

Nat. Cttee. for Sane Nuclear Policy (SANE) 1962-, later Co-Chair. and Spokesman; Candidate for U.S. Presidency, People's Party, 1972, for Vice-Pres. 1976. *Publications:* Baby and Child Care 1946, revised edns. 1957, 1968, 1976, 1985, A Baby's First Year (with John Reinhart and Wayne Miller) 1955, Feeding Your Baby and Child (with Miriam E. Lowenberg) 1955, Dr. Spock Talks with Mothers 1961, Problems of Parents 1962, Caring for your Disabled Child (in collaboration) 1965, Dr. Spock on Vietnam (with Mitchell Zimmermann) 1968, Decent and Indecent: Our Personal and Political Behaviour 1970, A Teenager's Guide to Life and Love 1970 (U.K.: A Young Person's Guide to Life and Love 1971), Raising Children in a Difficult Time 1974, Dr. Spock on Parenting 1987. *Leisure interest:* sailing. *Address:* P.O. Box 1890, St. Thomas, U.S. Virgin Islands 00803.

SPOEHR, Alexander, PH.D.; American anthropologist; b. 23 Aug. 1913, Tucson, Ariz.; s. of Herman A. and Florence M. Spoehr; m. Anne D. Harding 1941; one s. one d.; ed. Stanford Univ. and Univ. of Chicago; Asst. Curator, Field Museum of Natural History 1940-44, Curator 1945-52; Dir. Bernice P. Bishop Museum 1953-61; Prof. of Anthropology, Yale Univ. 1953-61; Chancellor, East-West Center, Hawaii 1962-63; U.S. Commr. South Pacific Comm. 1957-60; Prof. of Anthropology, then Prof. Emer. Univ. of Pittsburgh 1964-; mem. N.A.S.; Guggenheim Fellow 1952. *Publications:* Majuro 1949, Saipan 1954, Marianas Prehistory 1957, Zamboanga and Sulu: An Archaeological Approach to Ethnic Diversity 1973, Protein from the Sea 1980 and numerous articles on ethnology and archaeology. *Leisure interests:* gardening, swimming. *Address:* 2548 Makiki Heights Drive, Honolulu, H.I. 96822, U.S.A. *Telephone:* (808) 528-1478.

SPOHR, Arnold Theodore, O.C.; Canadian ballet director, teacher and choreographer; b. 26 Dec. 1927, Rhein, Canada; ed. St. John's High School and Winnipeg Teachers' Coll.; Piano Teacher 1946-51; Prin. Dancer Royal Winnipeg Ballet 1947-54; CBC Television Choreographer and performer 1955-57; Choreographer Rainbow Stage 1957-60; Artistic Dir. Royal Winnipeg Ballet 1958-; Dir.-Teacher Royal Winnipeg Ballet School 1958-; Dir. Nelson School of Fine Arts Dance Dept. 1964-67; Artistic Dir. Dance Dept. Banff School of Fine Arts 1967-; mem. Bd. of Dirs. Canadian Theatre Centre; Hon. LL.D. (Univ. of Manitoba) 1970, many awards including Molson Prize, Canada Council 1970, Order of Canada 1970, Centennial Medal, Gov. of Canada 1967. *Choreography:* Ballet Premier 1950, Intermed 1951, E Minor 1959, Hansel and Gretel 1960, and 18 musicals for Rainbow State. *Leisure interests:* sports, piano, travel-research for study of every type of dancing. *Address:* Royal Winnipeg Ballet, 289 Portage Avenue, 2nd Floor, Winnipeg, Manitoba R3B 2B4, Canada.

SPONG, Rt. Rev. John Shelby, A.B., D.D.; American ecclesiastic; b. 16 June 1931, Charlotte, N.C.; s. of John Shelby Spong and Doolie Griffith Spong; m. Joan Lydia Ketner 1952 (died 1988); three d.; ed. Univ. of North Carolina, Chapel Hill, Virginia Theological Seminary, Alexandria, Va. and St. Paul's Coll.; Rector St. Joseph's, Durham, N.C. 1955-57, Calvary Church, Tarboro, N.C. 1957-65, St. John's Church, Lynchburg, Va. 1965-69, St. Paul's Church, Richmond, Va. 1969-76, Bishop, Diocese of Newark, N.J. 1976-; Pres. N.J. Council of Churches; Roger Baldwin Award. *Publications:* Honest Prayer 1973, This Hebrew Lord 1974, 1988, Dialogue: In Search of Jewish-Christian Understanding 1975, Christpower 1975, Life Approaches Death. A Dialogue on Medical Ethics 1976, The Living Commandments 1977, The Easter Moment 1980, Into the Whirlwind 1983, Beyond Moralism 1986, Survival and Consciousness 1987, Living in Sin? *Address:* 24 Rector Street, Newark, N.J. 07102; 42 Ogden Road, Morristown, N.J. 07960, U.S.A. *Telephone:* (201) 622-3876 (Newark); (201) 538-9825 (Morristown).

SPOONER, Sir James Douglas, Kt.; British accountant and business executive; b. 11 July 1932, London; s. of the late Vice-Adml. E. J. Spooner, D.S.O., and Megan (née Foster) Spooner; m. Jane A. Glover 1958; two s. one d.; ed. Eton and Christ Church, Oxford; served in R.N.V.R. 1951-52; with Shell Int. Petroleum 1955-59; Deloitte Plender Griffiths & Co. 1959-62; Partner, Dixon Wilson & Co. (chartered accountants) 1963-72; Chair. Coats Viyella PLC 1969-; Chair. Morgan Crucible Co. PLC 1983-, King's Coll., London 1986; Dir. John Swire & Sons Ltd. 1970-, Abingworth PLC 1973-, J. Sainsbury PLC 1981-, Barclays Bank PLC 1983-, Royal Opera House, Covent Garden Ltd. 1986-. *Leisure interests:* music, reading, shooting. *Address:* Swire House, 59 Buckingham Gate, London, S.W.1, England.

SPORBORG, Christopher Henry; British banker; b. 17 April 1939; s. of Henry Nathan Sporborg and Mary Rowlands; m. Lucinda Jane Hanbury 1961; two s. two d.; ed. Rugby School, Emmanuel Coll., Cambridge; served as officer, Coldstream Guards; joined Hambros Bank PLC 1962-, Dir. 1970, Exec. Dir. Corp. Finance Dept. 1975, Deputy Chair. 1983-, C.E.O. Non-Banking Activities; Vice-Chair. Hambros PLC 1986-; Dir. Hambro Pacific and various other Hambro Group Cos.; Chair. Stal-Laval Ltd. *Leisure interests:* riding, racing. *Address:* Walker Farm House, Farnham, Nr. Bishops Stortford, Herts., England.

SPOTSWOOD, Marshal of the Royal Air Force Sir Denis, G.C.B., C.B.E., D.S.O., D.F.C., F.R.A.E.S.; British air force officer; b. 26 Sept. 1916, England; s. of F. H. and M. C. Spotswood; m. Ann Child 1942; one s.; joined Royal Air Force 1936; service in Squadrons U.K. and N. Africa 1937-43; Dir. of Plans, H.Q. Supreme Allied Commdr., S.E. Asia 1944-46; Stations (Fighter)

1948–50, 1954–56; Commdt. and Air Officer Commdg. (A.O.C.) R.A.F. Coll. Cranwell, 1958–61; Asst. Chief of Staff (Air Defence) SHAPE 1961–63; C.-in-C. R.A.F. Germany and Commdr. 2nd Allied Tactical Air Force 1965–68; C.-in-C. Strike Command 1968–71; Chief of Air Staff 1971–74; Vice-Chair. Rolls-Royce Ltd. 1974–81; Chair. Rolls-Royce (India) 1979–80; Pres. Soc. of British Aerospace Cos. 1978–79; Chair. Smiths Industries Int. Aerospace and Defence Cos. 1980–82, Dir. 1982–; Chair. Turbo Union Ltd.; Dir. Rolls Royce/Turbomeca Ltd.; Chair. Trustees, Royal Air Force Museum 1974–80; Chair. Royal Star and Garter Home 1979–84; A.D.C. to H.M. The Queen 1957–61, Air A.D.C. to H.M. The Queen 1970–74; U.S. Legion of Merit. *Leisure interests:* shooting, bridge, rugby (spectator), golf. *Address:* Coombe Cottage, Hambleden, Oxon, RG9 6SD, England.

SPRAGUE, George F., PH.D., D.SC.; American research agronomist; b. 3 Sept. 1902, Crete, Neb.; s. of E. E. Sprague and Lucy K. Manville; m. 1st Mary S. Whitworth 1926, 2nd Amy M. Millang 1945; two s. two d.; ed. Univ. of Nebraska and Cornell Univ.; Jr. Agronomist, U.S. Dept. of Agric. 1924–28, Asst. Agronomist 1928–34, Assoc. Agronomist 1934–39, Agronomist 1939–42, Sr. Agronomist 1942–58, Prin. Agronomist 1958, Leader of Corn and Sorghum Investigations 1958–72; Prof. Univ. of Ill., Urbana 1973; Fellow A.A.A.S., American Soc. of Agronomy; mem. N.A.S., Washington Acad. of Sciences; Crop Science Award, Superior Service Award of Dept. of Agric. 1960, Distinguished Service Award 1970. *Publications:* Corn and Corn Improvement 1956, Quantitative Genetics in Plant Improvement 1966; and over 100 research papers in scientific journals. *Address:* c/o Department of Agronomy, University of Illinois at Urbana, Ill. 61801; 2212 S. Lynn Street, Urbana, Ill. 61801, U.S.A. (Home). *Telephone:* 344-6685 (Home).

SPRATT, Sir Greville Douglas, G.B.E., T.D., D.L., F.R.S.A., J.P.; British business executive; b. 1 May 1927, Westcliff-on-Sea; s. of Hugh D. Spratt and Sheelah I. Stace; m. Sheila F. Wade 1954; three d.; ed. Leighton Park and Charterhouse; served Coldstream Guards 1945–46; Command Oxfordshire and Bucks Light Infantry 1946; seconded to Arab Legion 1946–48; joined HAC Infantry Bn. 1950, C.O. 1962–65, Regimental Col. 1966–70, mem. Court of Assistants 1960–70, 1978–; ADC to H.M. The Queen 1973–70; Lloyds of London 1948–61; Man. Dir. J. & N. Wade group of cos. 1972–76; Liveryman, Ironmongers' Co. 1977–; Alderman, City of London 1978–; Sheriff of City of London 1984–85; Lord Mayor of London 1987–88; Chancellor, City Univ. 1987–88; holder of numerous civic and charitable positions; Hon. D.Litt. (City Univ.) 1988; Chevalier, Ordre Nat. du Mérite (France); Commdr. Order of Lion (Malawi), Order of Aztec Eagle (Mexico), Order of Olav (Norway), Order of Merit (Senegal). *Leisure interests:* tennis, music, mil. history, forestry, stamp, coin and bank-note collecting. *Address:* Grayswood Place, Three Gates Lane, Haslemere, Surrey, GU27 2ET, England. *Telephone:* 0428 4367.

SPRECKLEY, John Nicholas Teague, B.A., C.M.G.; British diplomatist; b. 6 Dec. 1934, Great Malvern; s. of Air Marshal Sir Herbert Spreckley and Winifred Emery Teague; m. Margaret Stewart 1958; one s. one d.; ed. Winchester Coll. and Magdalene Coll., Cambridge; British Embassy, Tokyo 1957–62; FCO, London 1962–66, Head of Chancery, Dakar 1966–70, Paris 1970–75, Head of Referendum Unit FCO, London 1975, Head of Chancery, Tokyo 1976–78; Fellow, Centre for Int. Affairs, Harvard 1978–79; Head of European Community Dept. FCO, London 1979–83; Amb. to Repub. of Korea 1983–86; High Commr. in Malaysia 1986–. *Address:* c/o Foreign and Commonwealth Office, London, SW1A 2AH, England.

SPRENT, John Frederick Adrian, C.B.E., PH.D., F.R.C.V.S., F.A.A.; British university professor (retd.); b. 23 July 1915, London; s. of late Frederick F. Sprent and Violet A. Sprent; m. Muriel F. Hines 1937; two s. one d.; ed. Shrewsbury School, Royal Veterinary Coll. London and Univ. of London; Veterinary Research Officer, Colonial Service, Nigeria 1942–44; Research Fellow, Univ. of Chicago 1946–48; Sr. Research Fellow, Ontario Research Foundation, Toronto 1948–52; Research Prof. Univ. of Queensland, Brisbane 1952–56, Prof. 1956–83, Prof. Emer. 1983–, Dean, Faculty of Veterinary Science 1960–63; consultant, WHO 1963–83; Ed.-in-Chief, Int. Journal for Parasitology 1974–. *Publications:* Parasitism 1963; 105 scientific papers in refereed journals. *Leisure interests:* gardening, natural history. *Address:* Department of Parasitology, University of Queensland, St. Lucia, Brisbane 4067; 120 Livesay Road, Moggill, Brisbane 4070, Australia (Home).

SPRING, Richard, B.A., B.L.; Irish politician; b. 29 Aug. 1950, Tralee, Co. Kerry; s. of Dan Spring and Anna Laide; m. Kristi Lee Hutcheson 1977; two s. one d.; ed. Mount St. Joseph Coll., Roscrea, Co. Tipperary, Trinity Coll., Dublin, King's Inns, Dublin; mem. Dáil Éireann (House of Reps.) for Kerry North June 1981–; Leader of Labour Party Nov. 1982–; Deputy Prime Minister 1982–87, and Minister for the Environment 1982–83, for Energy 1983–87; fmr. Irish rugby union int. *Leisure interests:* sport, reading, swimming. *Address:* Dáil Éireann, Dublin 2; Dunroamin, Cloonanorig, Tralee, Co. Kerry, Ireland (Home). *Telephone:* 789911, ext. 244 (Office).

SPRINGER, Sir Hugh Worrell, G.C.M.G., G.C.V.O., K.A., C.B.E., M.A.; Barbadian barrister and educationist; b. 22 June 1913, Barbados; s. of Charles Wilkinson Springer and Florence Springer; m. Dorothy Drinan Gittens 1942; three s. one d.; ed. Harrison Coll., Barbados, Hertford Coll., Oxford and Inner Temple, London; practised at Bar of Barbados 1939–47; mem. House of Assembly, Barbados 1940–47; mem. Exec. Cttee., Barbados 1944–47; mem. Educ. Board, Barbados 1944–47; Gen. Sec. Barbados Labour Party 1940–47; Organizer and first Gen. Sec. Barbados Workers' Union 1940–47; Registrar, Univ. of West Indies 1947–63; mem. Educ. Authority of Jamaica 1950–56, ILO Cttee. of Experts on Social Policy in Non-Metropolitan Territories 1953–58, W. Indies Trade and Tariff Comm. 1957–58, Univ. Grants Cttee., Ghana 1959, Jamaica Public Service Comm. 1959–63, W. Indies Fed. Service Comm. 1960–61; Guggenheim Fellow and Fellow Harvard Centre for Int. Affairs 1961–62; Sr. Visiting Fellow, All Souls Coll., Oxford 1962–63, Hon. Fellow 1988–; Acting Gov. of Barbados 1964, Gov. Gen. Feb. 1984–; Dir. Inst. of Educ. of Univ. of W. Indies 1963–66; Chair. Commonwealth Caribbean Medical Research Council 1965–84; Sec. Commonwealth Educ. Liaison Cttee. and Commonwealth Asst. Sec.-Gen. (Educ.) 1966–70; mem. Council of Bernard van Leer Foundation 1967–78; Fellow, Royal Soc. of Arts 1968–; mem. of Bermuda Civil Disorders Comm. 1968; Sec.-Gen. Assen. of Commonwealth Univs. 1970–80; Chair. Commonwealth Human Ecology Council 1971–80 (Hon. Pres. 1981–), Commonwealth Foundation 1974–77, Trustee 1967–80; Chair. Joint Commonwealth Societies Council 1978–80, Tenth Anniversary Review Cttee., Univ. of the South Pacific 1979; Chair. Nat. Training Bd. of Barbados 1982–84, Income Tax Appeals Bd. 1983–84; Pres. Educ. Section of British Assen. 1974–75; Vice-Pres. British Caribbean Assen. 1974–80; mem. Bd. of Dirs., United World Colls. 1978–(92), Bd. of Trustees, Sir Ernest Cassell Educ. Trust 1978–80; Hon. Fellow, Hertford Coll., Oxford 1974; Hon. D.Sc. Soc. (Laval Univ., Quebec) 1958; Hon. LL.D. (Victoria Univ., British Columbia, Univs. of West Indies, St. Andrew's, Manchester, Univ. of New Brunswick, Univ. of York, Ont., Univ. of Zimbabwe, Univ. of Bristol, Univ. of Birmingham), Hon. D.Litt. (Warwick, Ulster, Heriot-Watt, Hong Kong, City (London) Univs.), D.C.L. (Oxford, Univ. of East Anglia) 1980; Hon. Prof. of Educ. (Mauritius) 1981; Silver Medal of Royal Soc. of Arts 1970; Kt. of St. Andrew in the Order of Barbados. *Publications:* Reflections on the Failure of the First West Indian Federation 1962, Problems of National Development in the West Indies 1965, Barbados as a Sovereign State, University Government Relations in the West Indies 1967, Relevance or Respectability in Education—The Rural Problem 1970, Educational Aspects of Human Ecology and Development 1971, and articles in journals. *Leisure interests:* walking, reading and conversation. *Address:* Government House, Bridgetown, Barbados (Office); Gibbes, St. Peter, Barbados, West Indies (Home). *Telephone:* 4292646 (Office); 4222591 (Home).

SPRINGER, Konrad Ferdinand, DR.PHIL.; German publisher; b. 23 Sept. 1925, Berlin; s. of Ferdinand Springer and Elisabeth Kalvín; m.; one s. three d.; ed. Staatliches Kaiserin-Augusta-Gymnasium, Berlin, Staatliches Kant-Gymnasium, Berlin, and Univ. of Zürich; Partner Springer Verlag, Berlin, Heidelberg and New York 1963–, J. F. Bergmanns Verlagsbuchhandlung, Munich 1963–, Lange and Springer Scientific Bookshop, Berlin 1963–, Springer-Verlag, Minerva Wissenschaftliche Buchhandlung, Vienna 1965; Hon. Senator Univ. of Salzburg. *Leisure interest:* minerals. *Address:* Tiergartenstrasse, 17, 69 Heidelberg 1, Federal Republic of Germany.

SPRINGSTEEN, Bruce; American singer and songwriter; b. 23 Sept. 1949, Freehold, N.J.; s. of Douglas and Adele Springsteen; m. Julianne Phillips 1985 (divorced 1989); attended community coll.; performed in New York and N.J. nightclubs; signed with Columbia Records 1972; first LP record Greetings from Asbury Park, New Jersey 1973; tours of U.S.A. and Europe with E-Street Band 1974–. *Albums include:* The Wild, The Innocent and the E-Street Shuffle 1974, Born to Run 1975, Darkness on the Edge of Town 1978, The River 1981, Nebraska 1982, Born in the U.S.A. 1984, Bruce Springsteen and the E. Street Band Live 1975–85 1986, Tunnel of Love 1987; Grammy Award, Best Male Vocalist 1984, 1987. *Address:* c/o Premier Talent Agency, 3 E. 54th Street, New York, N.Y. 10022, U.S.A.

SPRINKEL, Beryl Wayne, PH.D.; American economist and government official; b. 20 Nov. 1923, Richmond, Mo.; s. of Clarence and Emma (née Schooley) Sprinkel; m. Barbara Angus Pipher; two s. two d.; ed. N.W. Missouri State Univ., Oregon, Chicago and De Paul Univs.; served with U.S. army 1943–45; Instructor in Econs. and Finance, Univ. of Missouri, Columbia 1948–49, Univ. of Chicago 1950–52; with Harris Trust and Savings Bank, Chicago 1952–81, Vice-Pres., economist 1966–68, Dir. Research 1968–81, Exec. Vice-Pres. 1974–81; Under-Sec. for Monetary Affairs, Dept. of the Treasury 1981–85; Chair. Pres.'s Council of Econ. Advisors 1985–87; mem. Pres.'s Cabinet 1987–89; consultant, Fed. Reserve Bd. 1955–59, Bureau of Census 1962–70, Jt. Econ. Comm. U.S. Congress 1958, 1962, 1967, 1971, House of Reps. Banking and Currency Comm. 1963, Senate Banking Comm. 1975; mem. Econ. Advisory Bd. to Sec. Commerce 1967–68, Bd. Economists Time Magazine, Editorial Advisory Bd. Financial Analysts Journal 1964–; Pres. Homewood-Flossmoor (Ill.) Community High School 1959–60. *Publications:* Money and Stock Prices 1964, Money and Markets—A Monetarist View 1971, Winning with Money (co-author) 1977. *Address:* 6612 Madison of McLean Drive, McLean, Va. 22101, U.S.A. (Home).

SPÜHLER, Willy; Swiss economist and politician; b. 31 Jan. 1902; ed. Gymnasium of Zürich and Univs. of Zürich and Paris; Statistician, Zürich 1931–34; Head of Employment Bureau, Zürich 1935–42; Head, Cen. Office of War Economy 1939–48; mem. Zürich Town Council 1942–59; Pres. Swiss Radio and TV Corpn. 1957–58; mem. Bd., Fed. Inst. of Tech. (ETH) 1949–59; mem. Nat. Council 1938–55; mem. Council of States, Fed. Ass. 1956–59; mem. Fed. Council 1959–70, Pres. Jan.-Dec. 1963, Jan.-Dec. 1968, Vice-Pres. Jan.-Dec. 1967; Head of Transport, Communications and Power Dept. 1959–65; Head of Fed. Political (Foreign Affairs) Dept. 1966–70; Pres. of Foundations "Pro Helvetia" 1971–78. *Address:* Hirschengraben 20, 8001 Zürich, Switzerland.

SPULER, Bertold, DR. PHIL.; German orientalist (retd.); b. 5 Dec. 1911, Karlsruhe, Baden; s. of Dr. Rudolf and Natalena (née Lindner) Spuler; m. Gerda Roehrig 1937; two s. one d.; ed. Univs. of Heidelberg, Munich, Hamburg and Breslau; Collaborator Soc. for Silesian History 1934–35; Asst. Dept. of East European History, Univ. of Berlin and Co-editor Jahrbücher für Geschichte Osteuropas 1935–37; Asst. Dept. of Near Eastern Studies, Univ. of Göttingen 1937–38, Dozent 1938–42; Full Prof. Univ. of Munich 1942, Göttingen 1945, Hamburg 1948–80; Ed. Der Islam 1949–, Handbuch der Orientalistik 1952–, Studien zur Sprache, Geschichte und Kultur des Islamischen Orients, 1965–; Co-editor Das Historische-Politische Buch 1953–79; Hon. Dr. Theol. (Berne), Hon. D. ès Lettres (Bordeaux). *Publications include:* Die europäische Diplomatie in Konstantinopel bis 1739 1935, Die Minderheitenschulen der europäischen Türkei von der Reformzeit bis zum Weltkriege 1936, Die Mongolen in Iran: Politik, Verwaltung und Kultur der Ilchanzeit 1220–1350 1939, 1985 (Turkish edn. 1956, Persian edn. 1972), Die Goldene Horde, Die Mongolen in Russland, 1223–1302 1943, 1965, Die Gegenwartslage der Ostkirchen in ihrer staatlichen und völklichen Umwelt 1948, Geschichte der islamischen Länder im Überblick I: Chalifenzeit; II: Mongolenzeit 1952–53, Iran in frühislamischer Zeit: Politik, Kultur, Verwaltung und öffentliches Leben 633-1055 1952 (Persian edn. 1970), Regenten und Regierungen der Welt 1953, 1962–66, 1971 (English edn. 1977), Wissenschaftlicher Forschungsbericht: Der vordere Orient in islamischer Zeit 1954, The Age of the Caliphs 1960, 1968, The Age of the Mongols 1960, 1968, Geschichte der morgenländischen Kirchen 1961, Innerasien seit dem Aufkommen der Türken 1966, Les Mongols dans l'histoire 1961 (Spanish edn. 1966, English edn. 1971), Wüstenfeld-Mahlersche Vergleichungstabellen der muslimischen, iranischen und orientchristlichen Zeitrechnung 1961, Die islamische Welt (Saeculum Weltgeschichte III-VII, 1967–75), Die orthodoxen Kirchen Nos. 1–99 1939–89, Geschichte der Mongolen nach östlichen und europäischen Zeugnissen 1968 (English edn. 1970), Die historische und geographische Literatur in persischer Sprache 1968, Kulturgeschichte des Islams (östlicher Teil) 1971, Die Kunst der Islam (with J. Sourdel-Thomine) 1973, Wirtschafts Geschichte Irans und Mittelasiens im Mittelalter 1977, Krimgeschichte 1977, Gesammelte Aufsätze 1980, Studien zur Geschichte und Kultur des Vorderen Orients 1981. *Leisure interests:* participation in church music, hiking. *Address:* Mittelweg 90, 2 Hamburg 13; Rothenbaumchaussee 1936, 2 Hamburg 13, Federal Republic of Germany. *Telephone:* (040) 4123-3181.

SPYROPOULOS, Jannis; Greek artist; b. 12 March 1912, Pylos, Peloponnese; s. of Georges J. Spyropoulos and Phigalia G. J. Spyropoulos; m. Zoe Margaritis 1954; ed. School of Fine Arts, Athens, and Ecole des Beaux Arts, Paris; numerous one-man exhbns. in Europe, U.S.A. and Australia 1950–; on touring exhbns. of Greek Art, Rome 1953, Belgrade 1954, Malmö and Gothenburg 1959, Canada 1959, Cyprus 1960, Helsinki 1961; participated in Alexandria Biennale 1955, São Paulo Bienal 1957, Venice Biennale 1960, Carnegie Internationals 1961, 1964; Documenta III (Kassel) 1964, etc.; represented in Guggenheim Museum, New York, Museum of Contemporary Art, Dallas, Bezallel Nat. Museum, Jerusalem, Museum of Contemporary Art, Belgrade, Museum of Fine Arts, Ostend, Toronto Art Gallery, Nat. Art Gallery of Athens, Museum of Modern Art, Paris, Israel Museum, Jerusalem, Museum of Modern Art, Brussels, in galleries Nebraska, Rochester, Vermont, New Jersey, Washington, D.C. (U.S.A.), Nuremburg, Mainz (Fed. Republic. of Germany), Sydney (Australia), Auckland (New Zealand), and at Expo 1967 (Montreal) and 1970 (Osaka); Commdr., Royal Order of Phoenix; UNESCO Prize 1960. *Leisure interest:* photography. *Address:* 11 Sarantaporou Street, Athens 905, Greece. *Telephone:* 281-182.

SQUIRE, Clifford William, PH.D.; British diplomatist (retd.); b. 7 Oct. 1928; s. of Clifford J. Squire and Eleanor E. Harpley; m. 1st Marie J. Carlier 1959 (died 1973), 2nd Sara L. Hutchison 1976; two s. three d.; ed. St. John's Coll. Oxford, Coll. of Europe, Bruges and School of Oriental & African Studies, Univ. of London; Second Sec. Bucharest 1959–65; First Sec. U.K. Mission at UN, New York 1965–69; First Sec. Bangkok 1969–72; Counsellor, Washington 1976; Amb. to Senegal, Mauritania, Guinea, Guinea-Bissau, Mali, Cape Verde 1979–82; Amb. to Israel 1984–88; Devt. Dir. Univ. of Cambridge 1988–. *Address:* Wolfson College, Cambridge, CB3 9BB, England.

SRB, Adrian Morris, M.S., PH.D.; American professor of genetics; b. 4 March 1917, Howells, Neb.; s. of Jerome Ve. Srb and Viola Morris; m. Jozetta Marie Helfrich 1940; one s. two d.; ed. Howells High School, Univ. of Nebraska, Stanford Univ. and California Inst. of Tech.; Civilian, Office of Scientific Research and Devt. 1944; Asst. Prof. of Biology, Stanford Univ. and Research Fellow, Calif. Inst. of Tech. 1946–47; Assoc. Prof. Plant Breeding, Cornell Univ. 1947–51; Research Assoc., Calif. Inst. of Technology 1949; Prof. of Plant Breeding, Cornell Univ. 1951–63, Prof. of Genetics,

Devt. and Physiology, Biological Sciences 1965; Jacob Gould Schurman Prof. 1976; Fulbright Research Scholar and Guggenheim Fellow, Univ. of Paris 1953–54; Nat. Science Foundation Sr. Post-doctoral Research Fellow, Centre Nat. de la Recherche Scientifique, Gif-sur-Yvette, France 1960–61, Univ. of Edinburgh, Scotland 1967–68; mem. N.A.S.; Educ. Advisory Bd., John Simon Guggenheim Memorial Foundation; Hon. mem. Chilean Genetics Soc.; Fellow, American Acad. of Arts and Sciences; Hon. Foreign Fellow, Edinburgh Botanical Soc.; Fellow, New York Acad. of Sciences, A.A.A.S.; Trustee, Cornell Univ. 1975–; Hon. D.Sc. (Univ. of Nebraska) 1969; Distinguished Teacher Award 1967. *Publications:* General Genetics (with R. D. Owen) 1952, Pathways to the Understanding of Genetics 1953, Adaptation (with B. Wallace) 1961, 1964, General Genetics (with R. D. Owen and R. S. Edgar) 1965, 2nd. Edn. Genes, Enzymes, and Population 1973; over 100 research papers in scientific journals. *Leisure interests:* music, collecting juvenile books, gardening. *Address:* c/o Section of Genetics and Development, Cornell University, Ithaca, N.Y. 14850 (Office); 411 Cayuga Heights Road, Ithaca, N.Y. 14850, U.S.A. (Home). *Telephone:* 256-3145 (Office); 272-8492 (Home).

SREEKANTAN, Badanaval Venkata, PH.D.; Indian scientist; b. 30 June 1925, Nanjangud; s. of B. V. Pandit; m. Ratna Sreekantan 1953; two s.; ed. Univs. of Mysore and Bombay; Assoc. Prof., Tata Inst. of Fundamental Research, Bombay 1961, Prof. 1967, Sr. Prof. 1974, Dir. 1975–88; Homi Bhabha Medal, Indian Nat. Science Acad.; C. V. Raman Award, Univ. Grants Comm.; R. D. Birla Award, Indian Physics Asscn. *Publications:* 130 papers concerning cosmic rays, elementary particles, X-ray and gamma ray astronomy in int. journals. *Leisure interest:* philosophy. *Address:* 1010 Bhaskera, Homi Bhabha Road, Colaba, Bombay 5, India.

SRITHIRATH, Soubanh; Laotian diplomatist; b. 9 Sept. 1936, Khong, Lower Laos; m.; four c.; participated in revolution, Laos 1961–74; Chef de Cabinet, Ministry of Foreign Affairs 1974–78, Sec.-Gen. 1978–82; Perm. Rep. of Laos to the UN 1982–83. *Address:* c/o Ministry of Foreign Affairs, Vientiane, Laos.

SRIVASTAVA, Chandrika Prasad, LL.B., M.A.; Indian international civil servant; b. 8 July 1920, Unnao; s. of B. B. Srivastava and Mataji Srivastava; m. Nirmala Salve 1947; two d.; ed. Univ. of Lucknow, Bhopal Univ. and Univ. of Wales; Deputy Dir.-Gen. of Shipping, Govt. of India 1954–57; Man. Dir. Shipping Corpn. of India Ltd., Bombay 1961–64; Chair. 1966–73; Jt. Sec. to Prime Minister 1964–66; Pres. Indian Nat. Shipowners' Asscn. 1971–73; Dir. Reserve Bank of India 1972–73; Pres. UN Diplomatic Conf. of Plenipotentiaries on a Code of Conduct for Liner Confs. 1973–74; Sec.-Gen. IMO 1974–88; Chancellor, World Maritime Univ. 1983–; Pres. Int. Maritime Lecturers' Asscn. 1980–; mem. Advisory Bd. Seatrade Acad., Bd. Int. Maritime Bureau of ICC, Bd. of Dirs., ICC Centre for Maritime Co-operation; Hon. Fellow, The Nautical Inst. (U.K.); Hon. mem. Int. Fed. of Shipmasters' Asscns.; Hon. LL.D. (Bhopal) 1984, (Univ. of Wales, Univ. of Malta) 1987; Gold Medals for English Literature and Political Science (Univ. of Lucknow); Padma Bhushan 1972, Admiral Padilla Award (Colombia) 1978, Commdr. du Mérite maritime 1982, Commdr. of the Order of St. Olav (Norway) 1982, Hon. mem. Royal Inst. of Navigation 1984, Gold Mercury Int. Award 1984, Orden de Manuel Amador Guerrero, Gran Cruz, Panama 1985, and other decorations. *Publications:* contributions to maritime journals. *Leisure interests:* music, tennis, reading. *Address:* c/o International Maritime Organization, 4 Albert Embankment, London, SE1 7SR, England.

SSEMOGERERE, Paul Kawanga; Ugandan politician; Leader Democratic Party (DP); fmr. leader of Opposition in Nat. Ass.; Minister of Internal Affairs 1986–88, Second Deputy Prime Minister and Minister of Foreign Affairs Feb. 1988–, of Regional Co-operation 1989–. *Address:* Ministry of Foreign Affairs, P.O. Box 7048, Kampala, Uganda.

STAAB, Heinz A., DR.RER.NAT., DR.MED.; German professor of chemistry; b. 26 March 1926, Darmstadt; m. Dr. Ruth Müller 1953; one s. one d.; ed. Univs. of Marburg, Tübingen and Heidelberg; research assoc., Max Planck Inst., Heidelberg 1953–59; Asst. Prof. of Chem., Univ. of Heidelberg 1959–61, Assoc. Prof. 1961–62, Prof. 1963–; Dir. Inst. of Organic Chem., Univ. of Heidelberg 1964–74; Dir. Max Planck Inst. for Medical Research 1974; Pres. Max Planck Soc. for the Advancement of Science, Munich 1984–; mem. German Science Council 1976–79; Senator, Deutsche Forschungsgemeinschaft 1976–82 and 1984–; Pres. Gesellschaft Deutscher Naturforscher und Ärzte 1981–82; Pres. German Chem. Soc. 1984–85; mem. Heidelberg Acad. of Sciences, Acad. Leopoldina (G.D.R.); Ph.D. h.c. (Weizmann Inst. of Science) 1984; Adolf von Baeyer Award (German Chem. Soc.) 1979. *Publications:* Einführung in die theoretische organische Chemie 1959 (translations) and about 250 publications in professional journals. *Leisure interests:* travel, history, classical music. *Address:* Rezidenstrasse 1-A, 8000 Munich 2; Schlosswolfsbrunnenweg 43, D-6900 Heidelberg, Federal Republic of Germany (Home). *Telephone:* (06221) 803330 (Home).

STAATS, Elmer Boyd, PH.D.; American economist and government official; b. 6 June 1914, Richfield, Kansas; s. of Wesley F. and Maude (Goodall) Staats; m. Margaret S. Rich 1940; one s. two d.; ed. McPherson Coll., and Univs. of Kansas and Minnesota; Research Asst., Kansas Legis. Council 1936; mem. Staff, Public Admin. Service, Chicago 1937–38; Fellow, Brookings Inst. 1938–39; Staff mem. Bureau of the Budget 1939–47, Asst. to

Dir. 1947, Asst. Dir. (Legis. Reference) 1947-49, Exec. Asst. Dir. 1949-50, Asst. Dir. 1958-59, Deputy Dir. 1950-53, 1959-66; Research Dir., Marshall Field & Co., Chicago 1953; Exec. Officer Operations Co-ordinating Bd., Nat. Security Council 1953-58; Comptroller Gen. of the United States 1966-81; mem. Bd. of Dirs. of several corpns.; mem. numerous public orgs. including Pres. American Soc. for Public Admin. 1961-62; Pres. Harry S. Truman Scholarship Foundation 1981-84, Chair. Bd. of Trustees 1984-; Chair. Govt. Procurement Round Table 1984-; mem. Bd. of Dirs. of American Acad. of Political and Social Science 1966, Bd. of Govs. Int. Org. of Supreme Audit Insts. 1969-81, Visiting Cttee. John F. Kennedy School of Govt., Harvard Univ. 1974-80, Visiting Cttee., Graduate School of Man., Univ. of Calif. at Los Angeles 1976-, Visiting Cttee. to the Cttee. in Public Policy Studies, Univ. of Chicago 1976-; President's Comm. on Budget Concepts 1967-68; mem. Bd. of Govs. Int. Center on Election Law and Admin. 1985-87; Dir. George C. Marshall Foundation 1985-; mem. Bd. of Visitors, Nat. Defense Univ. 1981-; Hon. mem. Soc. of Mfg. Engineers 1978-; Hon. Life mem. Municipal Finance Officers Asscn. of U.S.A. and Canada 1980; Dr. Publ. Service (George Washington Univ.) 1971, Dr. Admin. (Univ. of S. Dak.) 1973, Hon. Certified Internal Auditor (Inst. of Internal Auditors) 1973; Hon. LL.D. (McPherson Coll.) 1966, (Duke Univ.) 1975, (Nova Univ.) 1976, (Lycoming Coll.) 1982, (Univ. of Penn.); Hon. D.Hum.Litt. (Ohio State Univ.) 1982; Rockefeller Public Service Award 1961; Productivity Award, American Productivity Cen. 1980; Medal of Honor AICPA 1980, Accounting Hall of Fame 1981, Inst. of Internal Auditors Thurston Award 1988, and other medals and awards. *Publication:* Personnel Standards in the Social Security Program 1939. *Address:* 712 Jackson Place, N.W., Washington, D.C. 20006; 5011 Overlook Road, N.W., Washington, D.C. 20016, U.S.A. *Telephone:* (202) 395-3530/4831 (Office).

STACEY, Col. Charles Perry, O.C., O.B.E., C.D., A.M., PH.D., LL.D., D.LITT., D.SC.MIL., F.R.S.C.; Canadian army officer and university professor (retd.); b. 30 July 1906, Toronto; s. of Dr. C. E. Stacey and Pearl Perry; m. Doris Newton Shiell 1939 (died 1969); m. 2nd Helen Kathleen Allen 1980; ed. Univs. of Toronto, Oxford and Princeton; on Canadian Army Reserve 1929-40; mem. Princeton Univ. History Dept. 1934-40; Historical Officer, Canadian Mil. HQ, London 1940-45; Pres. Canadian Historical Asscn. 1952-53; Pres. Canadian Writers' Foundation 1958-59; Dir. Historical Section, Canadian Army Gen. Staff 1945-59; Hon. Sec. Royal Soc. of Canada 1957-59, Hon. Ed. 1964-68; Pres. Section II Royal Soc. of Canada 1968-69; Special Lecturer in History, Univ. of Toronto 1959-60, Univ. Prof. 1973-76; on leave while acting as Dir. of History, Canadian Forces HQ, Ottawa 1965-66. *Publications:* Canada and the British Army 1846-1871 1936 (2nd edn. 1963), The Military Problems of Canada 1940, The Canadian Army 1939-1945: an Official Historical Summary 1948, Introduction to the Study of Military History for Canadian Students 1955, Six Years of War 1955, Quebec 1759: The Siege and the Battle 1959, Records of the Nile Voyageurs 1884-1885 1959, The Victory Campaign 1960, Arms, Men and Governments: The War Policies of Canada 1939-1945 1970, The Arts of War and Peace 1914-45 (Historical Documents of Canada, Vol. V) 1972, A Very Double Life: The Private World of Mackenzie King 1976, Mackenzie King and the Atlantic Triangle 1977, Canada and the Age of Conflict Vol. 1 1977, Vol. 2 1981, 100 Years: The Royal Canadian Regiment 1883-1983 (with Ken Bell) 1983, A Date with History 1983, The Half-Million: The Canadians in Britain 1939-1946 (with Barbara M. Wilson) 1987. *Address:* 21 Dale Avenue, Apartment 706, Toronto, Ont. M4W 1K3, Canada (Home). *Telephone:* (416) 961-4147 (Home).

STACEY, Frank Donald, PH.D., D.SC., F.A.A.; British professor of applied physics; b. 21 Aug. 1929, London; s. of the late Herbert Wilkie Stacey and of Daisy Winifred née Parkins; m. Joyce Winter 1953; three s. one d.; ed. Leyton County High School and Queen Mary Coll., London; Research Fellow in Physics, Univ. of British Columbia 1953-56; Research Fellow in Geophysics, Australian Nat. Univ. 1956-61; Royal Soc. Gassiot Fellow in Geomagnetism, Meteorological Office, U.K. 1961-64; Reader in Physics, Univ. of Queensland 1964-71, Prof. of Applied Physics 1971-; Vice-Pres. Australian Acad. of Science 1983-84. *Publications:* Physics of the Earth 1969, The Physical Principles of Rock Magnetism (with S. K. Banerjee) 1974. *Leisure interests:* tropical fruit cultivation, children's music. *Address:* Department of Physics, University of Queensland, Brisbane, Queensland, 4067 (Office); 46 Edson Street, Kenmore, Queensland, 4069, Australia (Home).

STACEY, Maurice, C.B.E., PH.D., D.SC., F.R.S.; British professor of chemistry; b. 8 April 1907, Newport, Shropshire; s. of J. H. and Ellen Stacey; m. Constance Mary Pugh 1937; two s. two d.; ed. Adams School, Shropshire, Birmingham Univ., London Univ. and Columbia Univ., New York; Beit Memorial Research Fellow, London Univ. 1933-37; Lecturer, Birmingham Univ. 1937-46, Prof. of Chem. 1946-56, Mason Prof. of Chem. 1956-74, Emer. Prof. 1974-, Head of Dept. 1956-74, Jubilee Memorial Lecturer Soc. of Chemical Industry 1972; Vice-Pres. Chemical Soc. 1950-53, 1955-58, 1960-63, 1968-71, Edgbaston High School for Girls 1984-; Assoc. Ed. Advances in Carbohydrate Chemistry 1950-; Ed. Advances in Fluorine Chemistry 1960-73; Founder Ed. European Polymer Journal; mem. Home Office Science Council 1966-76; Hon. Sr. Research Fellow 1974-76, Fellow, Royal Soc. of Chem., Royal Soc. of Arts and Science; Hon. Fellow, Mark Twain Soc.; Hon. D.Sc. (Univs. of San Marcos, Peru and Keele, U.K.); Meldola Medal 1933; Virtanen Medal; Tilden Medal 1946; U.S. Nat. Acad.

Sciences Award 1950; John Scott Medal and Award 1969, Haworth Medal 1970, Médaille d'Honneur (Biochem. Soc. France) 1972. *Publications:* 400 publs. on chemical and biochemical topics, two books (with S. A. Barker) on Polysaccharides. *Leisure interests:* collector of antiques, travel, horticulture, athletics. *Address:* 12 Bryony Road, Weoley Hill, Birmingham, B29 4BU, England. *Telephone:* 021-475 2065.

STADEN, Berndt von; German diplomatist; b. 24 June 1919, Rostock; s. of Richard von Staden and Camille von Voigt; m. Wendelgard von Neurath 1961; three c.; ed. Bonn Univ., Hamburg Univ.; Mil. service 1940-45; studied law, Hamburg Univ. 1946-48; Jr. Barrister 1948-51; with Foreign Ministry 1951-; Third Sec., Embassy, Brussels 1953-55; Dir. Desk of Soviet Affairs, Foreign Office, Bonn 1955-58; Staff mem. EEC Comm., Brussels, Head of Office of Pres. of Comm. 1958-63; Counsellor, First Class, Embassy, Washington 1963-68; Deputy Asst. State Sec., Foreign Office 1968-70, Asst. State Sec., Head of Political Dept. 1970-73; Amb. to U.S.A. 1973-79; Head of Dept. for Foreign Relations and Security, Fed. Chancery 1979-81; State Sec. Foreign Office 1981-83; Co-ordinator for German-American Co-operation in the field of Inter-social Relations, Cultural and Information Policy 1982-86; William Fulbright Prof. of Diplomacy, Georgetown Univ., Washington, D.C. 1985-88; Order of Merit (Fed. Repub. of Germany). *Leisure interests:* music, horseback riding. *Address:* Leinfelderhof, D-7143 Vaihingen/Enz, Federal Republic of Germany. *Telephone:* (0049) 7042-5440.

STADINGER, István; Hungarian politician, b. 1927, Keszthely; fmr. air mechanic; party worker 1951-; factory leader with several cos.; Gen. Dir. Metropolitan Gas Works, Budapest 1962; Deputy Chair. Metropolitan Council 1978-88; mem. of Parl. 1980; Sec. Parl. Cttee. for Industry 1980-85; Chair Parl. Cttee. for Bldg. and Communication 1985-; First Speaker of Parl. 1988-89.

STADNYUK, Ivan Fotievich; Soviet author; b. 1920, Kordyshevka, Vinnitsa Dist.; m. 2nd Natalya Stadnyka; ed. Editors' Dept., Moscow Polygraphic Inst.; mem. CPSU 1940-; first works published 1940-; worked for various army newspapers 1941-45. *Publications include:* Maksim Perepelitsa 1952, People with Guns 1956, The Heart Remembers 1962, War Stories 1967, People Are Not Angels 1962-65, War (3 vols.) 1970-82, The Bitter Bread of Truth 1971, Moscow 41 1985, Sword over Moscow 1989. *Address:* U.S.S.R. Union of Writers, Ul. Vorovskogo 52, Moscow, U.S.S.R.

STADTMAN, Earl R., PH.D.; American biochemist; b. 15 Nov. 1919, Carrizozo, N.M.; s. of Walter W. Stadtman and Minnie Ethyl Stadtman; m. Theresa Campbell Stadtman 1943; ed. Univ. of California; Research Asst. Dept. of Food Technology, Univ. of Calif. 1943-46, Research Asst., Div. of Plant Nutrition 1948-49; Atomic Energy Comm. Fellow, Biochemical Research Lab., Mass. Gen. Hospital 1949-50; Chemist (Biochem.) GS-15-Lab. for Cellular Physiology and Metabolism Nat. Insts. of Health (NIH) 1950-58, Chief of Enzyme Section, Lab. of Cellular Physiology and Metabolis, NIH 1958-62, Chief, Lab. of Biochem., Nat. Heart Inst., NIH 1962-; mem. N.A.S., American Acad. of Arts and Sciences, U.S. Cttee. for Int. Union of Biochemistry (mem. Council 1977-80), Exec. Cttee. 1982-85, Council of American Soc. of Biological Chemists, Pres. 1983-84; Hon. D.Sc. (Michigan) 1987; Paul Lewis Award in Enzyme Chem. 1952, Washington Acad. of Sciences Annual Award in Biological Chem. 1957, Superior Service Award of Dept. of Health, Educ. and Welfare 1968, Distinguished Service Award 1970, Hillebrand Award of American Chemical Soc. 1969, Award in Microbiology, N.A.S. 1970, Nat. Medal of Science 1980, Meritorious Rank Award, Sr. Exec. Service 1981, Presidential Rank Award, Distinguished Sr. Exec. 1982, ASBC-Merck Award in Biochemistry 1983. *Publications:* numerous scientific articles 1953-. *Leisure interests:* gardening, bowling, badminton, travelling. *Address:* National Heart and Lung Institute, Bethesda, Md. 20014 (Office); 16907 Redland-Derwood Road, Derwood, Md. 20855, U.S.A. (Home). *Telephone:* (301) 869-1747 (Home).

STADTMAN, Thressa Campbell, PH.D.; American biochemist; b. 12 Feb. 1920, Sterling, New York; d. of Earl and Bessie (Waldron) Campbell; m. Earl R. Stadtman 1943; ed. Cornell Univ. and Univ. of California (Berkeley); Research Assoc., Univ. of Calif. (Berkeley) 1942-47; Research Assoc., Harvard Medical School, Boston 1949-50; Biochemist, Nat. Heart, Lung and Blood Inst., Nat. Insts. of Health 1950-, Section Head, Lab. of Biochemistry 1974-; Ed.-in-Chief Bio Factors (IUB-sponsored journal) 1987-; Helen Haye Whitney Fellow, Oxford Univ., England 1954-55; Rockefeller Foundation Grantee, Univ. of Munich, Fed. Repub. of Germany 1959-60; mem. N.A.S., American Acad. of Arts and Sciences; Hillebrand Award, Chemical Soc. of Washington 1979, Rose Award, American Soc. of Biological Chemists 1987. *Publications:* original research papers in fields of Methane Biosynthesis, Amino Acid Metabolism, Vitamin B12 biochemistry, selenium biochemistry. *Leisure interests:* travel, gardening, skiing. *Address:* National Heart, Lung and Blood Institute, HHS Building 3, Room 108, Bethesda, Md. 20892; 16907 Redland Road, Derwood, Md. 20855, U.S.A. (Home). *Telephone:* (301) 496-3002 (Office).

STAFFORD, Godfrey Harry, C.B.E., M.SC., PH.D., F.R.S.; British physicist; b. 15 April 1920, Sheffield; s. of Henry and Sarah Stafford; m. Helen Goldthorp 1950; one s. twin d.; ed. Rondebosch Boys' High School, Univ. of Cape Town, Gonville and Caius Coll., Cambridge; South-African Naval

Forces 1941–46; A.E.R.E., Harwell 1949–51; Head of Biophysics Subdivision, Council for Scientific and Industrial Research, Pretoria 1951–54; Cyclotron Group, AERE 1954–57; Head of Proton Linear Accelerator Group, Rutherford Laboratory 1957, Head of High Energy Physics Div. 1963, Deputy Dir. 1966, Dir. 1969–79; Dir. of Atlas and Rutherford Laboratory 1975–79, Dir.-Gen. 1979–81; U.K. del IUPAP Comm. on Particles and Fields 1975–81; Vice-Pres. Inst. of Physics Meetings Cttee. 1976–79; Chair. CERN Scientific Policy Cttee. 1978–81; Master of St. Cross Coll., Oxford 1979–87; Pres. European Physical Soc. 1984–86, Inst. of Physics 1986–88; Vice-Pres. European Physical Soc. 1982; Gov. Westminster Coll., Oxford Centre for Postgraduate Hebrew Studies; Ebden Scholar, Univ. of Cape Town; Hon. Scientist Rutherford Appleton Lab. 1986; Hon. D.Sc. (Birmingham) 1980; Glazebrook Prize and Medal, Inst. of Physics 1981. *Publications:* papers and articles in learned journals on biophysics, nuclear physics and high energy physics. *Leisure interests:* music, foreign travel, walking. *Address:* Ferry Cottage, North Hinksey Village, Oxford, OX2 0NA, England. *Telephone:* (0865) 247621 (Home).

STAFFORD, John Rogers, A.B., J.D.; American business executive and lawyer; b. 24 Oct. 1937, Harrisburg, Pa.; s. of Paul Henry Stafford and Gladys Lee Sharp; m. Inge Paul 1959; four d.; ed. Montgomery Blair High School, Dickinson Coll., George Washington Univ. Law School; Assoc., Steptoe and Johnson 1962–66; Gen. Attorney, Hoffman-LaRoche 1966–67, Group Attorney 1967–70; Gen. Counsel, American Home Products Corpn. 1970–74, Vice-Pres. 1974–77, Sr. Vice-Pres. 1977–80, Exec. Vice-Pres. 1980–81, Pres. 1981–, Chair., Pres. and C.E.O. 1986–; Dir. Mfrs. Hanover Corpn., Metropolitan Life Insurance Co., Cen. Park Conservancy, Pharmaceutical Mfrs. Asscn.; mem. Bd. of Trustees U.S. Council for Int. Business; mem. American Bar Asscn., Dist. of Columbia Bar Asscn.; Order of the Coif; Outstanding Achievement Alumnus Award 1981. *Leisure interests:* boating, golf. *Address:* American Home Products Corporation, 685 Third Avenue, New York, N.Y. 10017, U.S.A.

STAFLEU, Frans Antonie; Netherlands professor of systematic botany; b. 8 Sept. 1921, Velsen; s. of Frans J. Stafleu and Elisabeth S. Ladan; m. Charlotte A. M. Corporaal 1947; two s.; ed. Univ. of Utrecht; Geneticist Java Sugar Experiment Station 1948–50; Scientific Officer, Univ. of Utrecht 1950–66, Prof. of Botany 1966–86, Emer. 1986–; Sec.-Gen. Int. Asscn. for Plant Taxonomy 1953–87, Pres. 1987–; Treas. Int. Union of Biological Sciences 1964–67, Sec.-Gen. 1967–70; Sec.-Gen. Int. Council of Scientific Unions 1970–74; mem. and Sec.-Treas.-Gen. Royal Netherlands Acad. of Sciences; Foreign mem. Linnean Soc. of London, Finnish Acad. of Sciences, Helsinki; Dr. h.c. (Bergen, Norway). *Publications:* A Monograph of the Vochysiaceae 1-5 1948–53, Index nominum genericorum (editor and part author) 1955–79, Taxonomic Literature 1967, 1976–88, Linnaeus and the Linnaeans 1971; series Taxon and Regnum vegetabile (editor and author). *Leisure interests:* walking, book-collecting. *Address:* Department of Botany, Room 1904, Tweede Transitorium, Uithof, Utrecht; 33 Weg naar Rhynauwen Utrecht, Netherlands (Home). *Telephone:* 030-517955 (Home).

STÅHLE, Anders Oscar Kåse, LL.B.; Swedish diplomatist and public servant; b. 12 July 1901, Helsingborg; s. of Isaac W. Ståhle and Karin Trapp; m. Birgit Olsson Falkenskiold 1926; one s. three d.; ed. Univ. of Lund; entered Swedish Foreign Service 1927; served home and abroad until 1948; Exec. Dir. and mem. Bd. Nobel Foundation 1948–72; Chair. Swedish del. several post-war bilateral trade negotiations and represented Sweden in post-war int. confs. on shipping and trade; Del. Maritime Transport Cttee., OEEC Paris 1947–59; Chair. Int. Fed. of Insts. for Advanced Study 1972–74 (Chair. Panel of Special Advisers 1974–84), Swedish Racing Asscn. 1973–76, Swedish Jockey Club 1972–77 (Vice-Chair. 1955), Assembly Int. Inventor Award 1976–88; board mem. several banking and industrial cos. 1948–75; mem. Bd. Scandinavia Japan Sasakawa Foundation 1984–86; holds Swedish and foreign decorations; Dr. Iur. h.c. *Leisure interest:* riding. *Address:* Nobel House, Sturegatan 14, 11436 Stockholm; Stora vägen 45, 26043 Arild, Sweden (Summer). *Telephone:* 08-633787 (Stockholm); 042-463 69 (Arild).

STAHLE, Hans, M.A.; Swedish business executive; b. 8 Aug. 1923; ed. Uppsala Univ., Stockholm School of Econs. and IMEDE Management Devt. Inst., Lausanne; Deputy Man. Dir. Alfa-Laval AB (machinery) until 1960, Managing Dir. 1960–82, Chair. 1982–; Hon. M.B.E. *Address:* Office of the Chairman, Alfa Laval AB, Postfack, 14700, Tumba, Sweden.

STAHR, Elvis J., Jr., M.A., B.C.L.; American conservationist, lawyer and university official; b. 9 March 1916, Hickman, Ky.; s. of Elvis J. and Mary A. (McDaniel) Stahr; m. Dorothy Howland Berkfield 1946; two s. one d.; ed. Univ. of Kentucky, Oxford Univ. (Rhodes Scholar), Yale Univ.; with New York law firm; served U.S. Army, Second World War; Assoc. Prof. of Law, Univ. of Ky. 1947–48, Prof. and Dean of Law Coll. 1948–54; served Dept. of Army in Korean War; Provost, Univ. of Ky. 1954–56; Exec. Dir. President's Cttee. on Educ. Beyond Secondary School Level 1956–57; Vice-Chancellor, Univ. of Pittsburgh 1957–59; Pres. W. Va. Univ. 1959–61; Sec. of the Army 1961–62; Pres. Indiana Univ. 1962–68; Pres. Nat. Audubon Soc. 1968–79, Senior Counsellor 1979–81, Pres. Emer. 1981–; Pres. Univ. Associates Inc. 1981–; Special Partner, law firm of Chickering and Gregory 1982–; Exec. Vice-Pres. Public Resource Foundation 1982–; mem. U.S. Del. to UN Conf. on Human Environment, Stockholm 1972 and to Int.

Whaling Comm., London 1975 and 1978; mem. Joint U.S.-U.S.S.R. Cttee. on Co-operation for Protection of the Environment, Washington 1973, Nat. Cttee. for World Population Year 1974, Nat. Petroleum Council 1974–79; Bd. of Dirs. Environmental and Energy Study Inst., Nat. Parks and Conservation Asscn.; fmr. Dir. Alliance to Save Energy, Nat. Water Alliance, Acacia Mutual Life Insurance Co., Chase Manhattan Bank; fmr. Pres. Asscn. of the U.S. Army, fmr. Nat. Chair. United Service Orgs., fmr. Deputy Chair. of Bd. Fed. Reserve Bank of Chicago; mem. Presidential Aviation Advisory Comm. 1970–73, Bd. of Advisers, Nat. Exec. Service Corps, The Population Inst., Fed. for American Immigration Reform; Chair. Washington Conservation Roundtable 1986–87; Senior Assoc. Cassidy and Assocs. Inc. 1984–; Hon. Trustee, C.E.D.; Hon. LL.D. (Univ. of Maryland, Univ. of Pittsburgh, Louisiana State Univ., Texas Christian Univ., Univ. of Kentucky, Univ. of Notre Dame, Brown Univ., Northwestern Univ., Indiana Univ., Univ. of Florida and 8 others); Hon. D.Mil.Sc. (Northeastern Univ.), Hon. D.Pub.Admin. (Bethany Coll.), Hon. D.H.L. (De Pauw Univ., Transylvania Univ.), Hon. D. Env. Sci (Rollins Coll.), Hon. Litt. D. (Univs. of Maine, Cincinnati), Hon. Ph.D (Culver Stockton Coll.), Hon. D.Sc. (Norwich Univ., Hanover Coll.); numerous decorations and awards, etc. *Leisure interests:* tennis, books, travel. *Address:* Chickering and Gregory, 1815 H. Street, N.W., Washington, D.C. 20006 (Office); Martin Dale, Greenwich, Conn. 06830, U.S.A. (Home). *Telephone:* (202) 463-7456 (Office).

STALLONE, Sylvester Enzio; American actor and film director; b. 6 July 1946, New York; s. of Frank Stallone and Jacquline Labofish; m. 1st Sasha Czach 1974 (dissolved), two c.; m. 2nd Brigitte Nielsen 1985 (divorced 1987); ed. American Coll. of Switzerland, Univ. of Miami; has had many jobs including usher, bouncer, horse trainer, store detective, physical education teacher; now, actor, and producer and dir. of own films; Oscar for best film 1976, Golden Circle Award for best film 1976, Donatello Award 1976, Christopher Religious Award 1976; Dir. Carolco Pictures Inc. 1987–; mem. Screen Actors Guild, Writers Guild, Dirs. Guild; Hon. mem. Stuntmans' Asscn. *Film appearances include:* Lords of Flatbush 1973, Capone 1974, Rocky 1976, F.I.S.T. 1978, Paradise Alley 1978, Rocky II 1979, Nighthawks 1980, Escape to Victory 1980, Rocky III 1981, First Blood, Rambo 1984, Rocky IV 1985, Cobra 1986, Over the Top 1986, Rambo III 1986, Rambo III 1988; producer, dir. film Staying Alive 1983. *Address:* c/o Ron Meyer Creative Artists Agency, 1888 Central Park, E. Suite, 1400 Los Angeles, Calif. 90067, U.S.A.

STALLONES, Reuel, M.D.; American professor of epidemiology; b. 10 Oct. 1923, N. Little Rock, Ark.; s. of Wilner Leroy Stallones and Jet (Wilson) Stallones; m. Joyce Graves 1945 (divorced 1977); one s. two d.; ed. Visalia Jr. and Ripon Colls., Univ. of Michigan, Western Reserve Univ. and Univ. of California, Berkeley; Intern, Letterman Hosp., San Francisco 1949–50; Asst. Chief, Dept. of Epidemiology, Walter Reed Army Inst. of Research 1954–56; Lecturer, then Prof., Univ. of Calif., Berkeley 1956–68; Dean and Prof. of Epidemiology, School of Public Health, Univ. of Texas Health Science Center, Houston 1968–. *Publications:* To Advance Epidemiology (in Annual Review of Public Health) 1980, Epidemiology and Public Policy: Pro and Anti-Biotic (in American Journal of Epidemiology) Vol. 115 (4) 1982, Ischemic Heart Disease and Lipids in Blood and Diet (in Annual Review of Nutrition) 1983. *Address:* 7447 Cambridge No. 32, Houston, Tex. 77054; 12414 Modena Tr., Austin, Tex. 78729, U.S.A.

STAMBOLIĆ, Petar; Yugoslav politician; b. 12 July 1912; ed. Univ. of Belgrade; mem. Young Communist League 1933, CP of Yugoslavia 1935–; organized resistance in Serbia 1941; Sec. Cen. Cttee. of Nat. Liberation Army and partisan units for Serbia 1943; Deputy and mem. Presidium Antifascist Council of Nat. Liberation of Yugoslavia 1943; mem. Cen. Cttee. of CP of Serbia 1945, Sec. 1948–57; First Vice-Chair. Council of Ministers, Serbia 1945–47; Pres. Exec. Council, Serbia 1948–53, Pres. Serbian Assembly 1953–57; Minister of Agric. and Forests, Yugoslavia 1947–48; Pres. Fed. People's Assembly 1957–63; Pres. Fed. Exec. Council 1963–67; mem. Collective Presidency of Yugoslavia 1974–84, Vice-Pres. 1974–75, 1981–82, Pres. 1982–83; mem. Cen. Cttee. of CP of Yugoslavia 1948–, mem. Politbureau 1951–68, and Exec. Cttee. 1952–68, Cen. Cttee. League of Communists of Yugoslavia, Chair. Ideological Comm. 1948–63; mem. Presidium of Cen. Cttee. of League of Communists of Yugoslavia 1966–; mem. Council of Fed. 1963–; Pres. Cen. Cttee. League of Communists of Serbia 1968–88; Order of Hero of the People and other decorations. *Address:* c/o Collective Presidency of Yugoslavia, Belgrade, Yugoslavia.

STAMO, Yevgeniy Nikolayevich; Soviet architect; b. 1912, Kiev; ed. Moscow Architectural School; numerous important bldgs., including Kremlin Palace of Congresses 1959–61 (Lenin Prize 1962); Matveyevsky residential dist. 1966–, Hungarian Embassy, Moscow 1967, Progress Publishing House 1976; Order of Lenin, Honoured Architect of R.S.F.S.R. 1969.

STAMP, Terence; British actor; b. 22 July 1938, London; s. of Thomas Stamp and Ethel Esther Perrott; theatre work before film debut in Billy Budd 1962. *Other films include:* Term of Trial 1962, The Collector 1965, Modesty Blaise 1966, Far From the Madding Crowd 1967, Poor Cow 1967, Blue 1968, Theorem 1968, Tales of Mystery 1968, The Mind of Mr. Soames 1969, A Season in Hell 1971, Hu-man 1975, The Divine Creature 1976, Striptease 1977, Meetings With Remarkable Men 1978, Superman 1978, Superman II 1979, Death in the Vatican 1980, The Bloody Chamber 1982,

The Hit 1984, Link 1985, Legal Eagles 1986, The Sicilian 1986, Wall Street 1988, Alien Nation 1988, Young Guns 1988. *Theatre:* Dracula, The Lady from the Sea. *Publications:* Stamp Album (memoirs, Vol. 1) 1988, Coming Attractions (memoirs, Vol. 2) 1988, Double Feature (memoirs, Vol. 3) 1989. *Address:* c/o Plant and Froggatt, 4 Windmill Street, London, W.1, England.

STAMPER, Malcolm T.; American aviation executive; b. 4 April 1925, Detroit; s. of Fred Theodore and Lucille (née Cayce) Stamper; m. Mari Guinan; four s. two d.; ed. Univ. of Michigan, Georgia Tech. Coll.; with Gen. Motors 1948-62; joined Boeing Co. 1962, Vice-Pres., Gen. Man. fmr. Boeing Turbine Div. 1965, Man. Boeing Everett Branch (now 747 Div.) 1966, in charge of 747 programme 1966-69, Gen. Man. Commercial Airplane Group 1969-71, Sr. Vice-Pres. Operations 1971-72, Pres. 1972-86, Vice-Chair. 1986-. *Address:* The Boeing Co., P.O. Box 3707, Seattle, Washington 98124, U.S.A.

STANBURY, Hon. Robert Douglas George, P.C., Q.C.; Canadian executive, lawyer and fmr. politician; b. 26 Oct. 1929, Exeter, Ont.; s. of James George Stuart Stanbury and Elizabeth Jean (Hardy); m. Miriam Voelker 1952; two s. two d.; ed. Exeter and St. Catharines public schools, St. Catharines Coll. Inst., Univ. of Western Ontario and Osgoode Hall Law School; Pres. Canadian Univ. Liberal Fed. 1954; Partner Hollingworth & Stanbury, Barristers and Solicitors, Toronto 1955-65; mem. North York Bd. of Educ. 1961-64, Vice-Chair. 1962, Chair. 1963-64; mem. Metropolitan School Bd., Toronto 1963-64 and Metropolitan Toronto Planning Bd. 1963; M.P. 1965-77; Chair. House of Commons Standing Cttee. on Broadcasting, Films and Assistance to the Arts 1966-68; Parl. Sec. to Sec. of State of Canada 1968-69; Minister without Portfolio responsible for Citizenship 1969-71, for Information Canada 1970-71; Minister of Communications 1971-72; Minister of Nat. Revenue 1972-74; Del. to UN Gen. Assembly 1974, 1975, 1976, to UNESCO Conf., Paris 1969, UN Conf. on Crime, Kyoto 1970, UN Conf. on Apartheid, Lagos 1977, Inter-American Devt. Bank meeting, Kingston 1977; Chair. Canadian Group Inter-Parliamentary Union 1974-77; Founding Chair. Canadian Parl. Helsinki Group 1977; Pres. Hamilton Foundation 1982-83; Vice-Pres. Gen. Counsel and Dir., Firestone Canada Inc. 1977-83, Chair. and C.E.O. 1983-85; Dir. Art Gallery of Hamilton (Vice-Pres. 1982-86, Pres. 1986-87); Dir. Hamilton and Dist. Chamber of Commerce 1980-85 (Pres. 1983-84), Dayton Tire Canada Ltd. 1977-85, Canadian Chamber of Commerce 1982-86, Chedoke-McMaster Hospitals 1983- (Vice-Chair. 1987-), Workers' Compensation Bd. of Ont. 1985-; Pres. Inst. of Corporate Dirs. in Canada 1987-88; Chair. McMaster Univ. Business Advisory Council 1987-88; Pres. and C.E.O. Canadian Council for Native Business 1989-; Chair. and C.E.O. Globescope Inc. 1986-; Counsel Inch Easterbrook & Shaker 1986-; mem. Queen's Privy Council for Canada 1969-; Queen's Counsel 1974-; F. Inst. Dir. 1985-; mem. Int. Bar Asscn., Canadian Bar Asscn., Int. Comm. of Jurists, UNA in Canada. *Address:* Box 783, Hamilton, Ont. L8N 3M8 (Office); 607 Edgewater Crescent, Burlington, Ont., L7T 3L8, Canada (Home). *Telephone:* (416) 525-4481 (Office); (416) 632-9394 (Home).

STĂNESCU, Ion; Romanian politician; b. 23 Jan. 1929, Ghercești, Dolj County; s. of Hariton and Lenuța Stănescu; m. Ecaterina Stănescu 1953; ed. Faculty of Law, Bucharest; mem. Union of Communist Youth 1944, leading functions 1948-51; mem. Romanian Communist Party (RCP) 1947-; served as officer in Ministry of Internal Affairs; Chair. Council of State Security 1967-72; Minister of Internal Affairs 1972-73; Minister, Sec. of State of Ministry of Industrial Bldg. 1978-81, of Ministry of the Chemical Industry 1981, Minister of Sports and Tourism 1984-; Deputy Chair. of Council of Ministers 1977-78; mem. Grand Nat. Ass. 1965-; Deputy Head of Section, RCP Cen. Cttee. 1962-64, First Sec. Regional Cttee. Oltenia 1964-67, First Sec. County Cttee., Dimbovita and Chair. County People's Council 1974-77; mem. RCP Cen. Cttee. 1969-79, mem. 1984-; alt. mem. Exec. Political Cttee. 1969-74; Sec. of Cen. Cttee 1977-78; Chief Dept. for Overseas Construction 1981-84; mem. Nat. Council of Socialist Unity Front 1968-. *Leisure interests:* hunting, fishing. *Address:* Ministry of Tourism, Bd. Magheru 7, Bucharest, Romania.

STANFIELD, Hon. Robert Lorne, B.A., LL.B., Q.C., LL.D.; Canadian politician; b. 11 April 1914, Truro, Nova Scotia; s. of Frank Stanfield and Sarah Emma (Thomas) Stanfield; m. 1st Nora Joyce Stanfield (died 1954), 2nd Mary Stanfield (died 1977), 3rd Anne Stanfield 1978; one s. three d.; ed. Ashbury Coll., Ottawa, Dalhousie and Harvard Univs.; Gov. Dalhousie Univ. 1949-56; Premier, Minister of Educ., Nova Scotia 1956-67; M.P. for Halifax, Nova Scotia 1968-79; fmr. Leader Progressive Conservatives Nova Scotia; Leader of Opposition, Leader Nat. Progressive Conservative Party of Canada 1967-76; Leader Govt. Mission to Middle East 1979-80; Chair. Inst. for Research on Public Policy 1981-87; Chair. Commonwealth Foundation 1986-; Hon. LL.D. (New Brunswick) 1958, (Mc Gill) 1967, (St. Dunstan's) 1967, (St. Mary's) 1968, (Dalhousie), (McMaster) 1985. *Leisure interest:* gardening. *Address:* 136 Acacia Avenue, Rockcliffe Park, Ottawa, Ont., Canada.

STANIER (COHEN-BAZIRE), Germaine, PH.D.; French research scientist; b. 2 Sept. 1920, Thonon, Haute-Savoie; d. of M. and Mme. Gabriel Bazire; m. 1st Mr Cohen 1945, 2nd Mr Stanier 1956; two c.; Research Asst. C.N.R.S. 1945-53, Research Fellow 1953-55; Research Assoc. Univ. of Calif., Berkeley 1955-71; Dir. of Research, C.N.R.S. 1971-; Prof. Inst. Pasteur 1985-; Guggenheim Fellow. *Publications:* 90 scientific publications

in biochemistry and structure function in micro-organisms. *Leisure interests:* other people's scientific discoveries, reading, music, walking. *Address:* Institut Pasteur, 28 rue du Dr. Roux, 75724 Paris Cedex 15; 143 rue de Videlles, 78830 Les Carneaux, Bullion, France.

STANIER, Field Marshal Sir John Wilfred, G.C.B., M.B.E., M.B.I.M., F.R.G.S.; British army officer; b. 6 Oct. 1925, Essex; s. of the late Harold Allan and Penelope Rose (née Price) Stanier; m. Cicely Constance Lambert 1955; four d.; ed. Marlborough Coll., Merton Coll., Oxford, Imperial Defence Coll., Staff Coll.; commissioned into 7th Queen's Hussars 1946; served North Italy, Germany and Hong Kong; commanded Royal Scots Greys 1966-68, 20 Armoured Brigade 1969-70; G.O.C. 1st Armoured Div. 1973-75; Commdt. Staff Coll., Camberley 1975-78; Vice-Chief of Gen. Staff 1978-80; C.-in-C. U.K. Land Forces 1981-82; Chief of Gen. Staff 1982-85; rank of Field Marshal 1985; Aide-de-Camp to the Queen 1981-85; Chair. Royal United Services Inst. for Defence Studies 1986-; Col. Royal Scots Dragoon Guards 1979-85; Col. Commdt. Royal Armoured Corps 1982-85; Chair. Control Risks (GS) Ltd. 1985-; Dir. Royal Ordnance PLC 1986-. *Leisure interests:* hunting, fishing, sailing, talking. *Address:* c/o Coutts & Co., 440 The Strand, London, WC2R 0QS, England.

STANISLAUS, Lamuel A., D.D.S.; Grenada diplomatist; b. 22 April 1921, Petite Martinique; m.; five c.; ed. Howard Univ., Washington, D.C.; Asst. Teacher, Petite Martinique and St. Patrick's R.C. Schools 1939-41; Statistical Clerk, Harbour and Wharves Dept., Port-of-Spain 1941-45; mem. New Nat. Party and founding mem. Grenada Nat. Party; mem. Mayor of New York's Advisory Council; practised dentistry in New York 1956-; Perm. Rep. of Grenada to the UN 1985-. *Address:* Permanent Mission of Grenada to the United Nations, 141 East 44th Street, Suite 905, New York, N.Y. 10017, U.S.A. *Telephone:* (212) 599-0301.

STANISZEWSKI, Stefan, M.A.; Polish diplomatist; b. 11 Feb. 1931, Bukowa; s. of Andrzej and Katarzyna Staniszewski; m. Wanda Szuszkiewicz 1953; one d.; ed. Warsaw Univ. and Jagellonian Univ., Cracow; fmr. active mem. of student and social org. 1951-58; Head of Dept., Iskry Publrs., Warsaw 1958-60; in Ministry of Foreign Affairs 1960-; official, Office of Minister 1960-63, Second Sec., then First Sec. and Counsellor, Polish Embassy, Paris 1963-69; Dir. Dept. for West Europe, Ministry of Foreign Affairs; mem. Governing Council of Ministry 1969-72; Amb. to Sweden 1972-77, to U.K. 1981-86; Dir. Dept. of Press, Cultural and Scientific Co-operation, Ministry of Foreign Affairs 1977-81, Dir. Dept. of Press and Information 1987-, Press Spokesman of Ministry 1988-; mem. Polish United Workers' Party (PZPR) 1949-; Commdr. and Officer's Cross, of Order of Polonia Restituta, Commdr., Légion d'Honneur, Commdr., First Class, Order of Polar Star (Sweden), Commdr., Aztec Eagle Order (Mexico). *Leisure interests:* swimming, modern painting. *Address:* ul. Okrąg 1 m. 51, 00-415 Warsaw, Poland (Home). *Telephone:* 212755.

STANKIEWICZ, Witold, DR.HABIL.; Polish librarian, editor, and historian; b. 30 Aug. 1919, Kargoszynek; ed. Warsaw Univ.; official in co-operative societies; mem. Scientific Council, Co-operative Research Inst.; mem. History Inst., Polish Acad. of Sciences, Extraordinary Prof. 1977-; Chief Dir. Nat. Library 1962-82; Chief Ed. The National Library Yearbook 1965-82; Vice-Chair. Nat. Library Council 1969-80; Chair. Polish Librarians Asscn. 1972-81; mem. Supreme Council and Chair. Scientific Comm., Soc. for Relations with Poles Abroad "Polonia" 1973; mem. Ed. Bd. Roczniki Dziejów Ruchu Ludowego 1959-, Dzieje Najnowsze 1969-, Kwartalnik Historyczny 1975-, Polish Links 1985-; Assoc. Ed. Libri: International Library Review (Copenhagen) 1987-; Commdr., Cross of Order Polonia Restituta 1980 and other decorations. *Publications:* People's Newspaper Publications in the Polish Kingdom 1905-1914 1957, History of the Polish People's Movement in Outline (co-author) 1963, 1970, Social Conflicts in Rural Poland 1918-20 1963, Source Materials to the History of the Peasant Movement (co-author) 1966, Programmes of the People's Parties (co-author) 1969, The Political Archives of Ignace Jan Paderewski, Vols. 1-4 (co-ed.) 1973-74 and numerous articles on Polish history and libraries. *Address:* History Institute, Polish Academy of Sciences, Rynek Starego Miasta 29/31, 00-272 Warsaw, Poland.

STANLEY, Eric Gerald, PH.D., F.B.A.; British academic; b. 19 Oct. 1923; m. Mary Bateman, M.D., F.R.C.P. 1959; one d.; ed. Queen Elizabeth's Grammar School, Blackburn, Univ. Coll., Oxford; lecturer in English Language and Literature, Univ. of Birmingham 1951-62; Reader in English Language and Literature, Univ. of London, Queen Mary Coll. 1962-64, Prof. 1964-75; Prof. of English, Yale Univ. 1975-76; Rawlinson and Bosworth Prof. of Anglo-Saxon, Univ. of Oxford Jan. 1977-; mem. Mediaeval Acad. of America 1975-; mem. Connecticut Acad. of Arts and Sciences 1976-; Sir Israel Gollancz Memorial lecturer, The British Acad. 1984. *Publications:* books and academic articles, some of them in A Collection of Papers with Emphasis on Old English Literature 1987. *Leisure interests:* travel, photography. *Address:* Pembroke College, Oxford, OX1 1DF, England.

STANLEY, Henry Sydney Herbert Cloete, C.M.G.; British diplomatist (retd.); b. 5 March 1920; s. of Sir Herbert Stanley and Reniera Cloete; m. Margaret Dixon 1941; three s.; ed. Eton and Balliol Coll., Oxford; Commonwealth Relations Office 1947; served in Pakistan 1950-52, Swaziland and S. Africa 1954-57, U.S.A. 1959-61, Tanganyika 1961-63, Kenya 1963-65; Inspector, H.M. Diplomatic Service 1966-68, Chief Inspector

1968–70; High Commr. to Ghana 1970–75, to Trinidad and Tobago 1977–80. *Address:* Silver How, 7 Harberton Mead, Oxford, OX3 0DB, England.

STANLEY, Julian Cecil, Jr., B.S., ED.D.; American professor of psychology; b. 9 July 1918, Macon, Ga.; s. of Julian C. Stanley and Ethel May Cheney Stanley; m. 1st Rose Roberta Sanders 1946 (died 1978); m. 2nd Barbara Sprague Kerr 1980; one d. one step-s. one step-d.; ed. Georgia Southern Coll. and Harvard Univ.; postdoctoral studies at Univs. of Mich., Chicago, Catholic Univ. of Louvain, Belgium (Fulbright Act Research Scholar), Center for Advanced Study in the Behavioral Sciences, Stanford Univ., Calif.; taught science and math., Atlanta, Ga. 1937–42; Instructor in Psychology, Newton (Mass.) Jr. Coll. 1946–48; Instructor in Educ., Harvard Univ. 1948–49; Assoc. Prof. of Educational Psychology, George Peabody Coll. for Teachers 1949–53; Assoc. Prof. of Educ., Univ. of Wis. 1953–57, Prof. 1957–62, Prof. of Educational Psychology 1962–67, Chair. Dept. 1962–64, Dir. Lab. of Experimental Design 1961–67; Prof. of Educ. and Psychology, Johns Hopkins Univ. 1967–71, Prof. of Psychology 1971–, Dir. of Study of Mathematically Precocious Youth 1971–; Fellow A.A.A.S., American Statistical Asscn., American Psychological Asscn. *Publications:* author, co-author or ed. of 13 books and approx. 400 articles, book chapters and reviews; books (co-author) include Experimental and Quasi-Experimental Designs for Research 1966, Mathematical Talent 1974, The Gifted and the Creative 1977, Educating the Gifted 1979, Academic Precocity 1983. *Leisure interests:* cinema, hiking, travelling. *Address:* Study of Mathematically Precocious Youth (SMPY), 430 Gilman Hall, Johns Hopkins University, Baltimore, Md. 21218, U.S.A. *Telephone:* (301) 338-6179, 7087.

STANOVNIK, Janez; Yugoslav politician, economist and international official; b. 4 Aug. 1922, Ljubljana; s. of Ivan Stanovnik and Ana Jeglich; m. Dragica Dragovich 1953; four s.; ed. Faculty of Law, Ljubljana Univ., and Inst. for Social Sciences, Belgrade; took part in Nat. Liberation Struggle 1941–45; fmr. Dir. of Exec. Office of Vice-Pres. and Foreign Minister 1945–52; Econ. Counsellor to Yugoslav Perm. Mission in New York 1952–55; Dir. of Inst. for Int. Econs. and Policy in Belgrade 1955–61; Prof. of Econs. Ljubljana Univ. 1961–65; special adviser Sec.-Gen. UNCTAD 1965–67; mem. of Yugoslav Fed. Parl. and Govt. mem. (in charge of foreign trade) 1967–68; leader of del. to UNCTAD II (Delhi) 1968–82; Exec. Sec. of UN Econ. Comm. for Europe 1968–82; UN Under Sec.-Gen. *Publications:* dealing with problems of the world economy from point of view of developing countries. *Address:* Economic Commission for Europe, Palais des Nations, Geneva; 9 avenue Krieg, 1208 Geneva, Switzerland (Home). *Telephone:* 34-60-11 (Office); 47-83-10 (Home).

STANS, Maurice Hubert, C.P.A., LL.D.; American investment banker and government official (retd.); b. 22 March 1908, Shakopee, Minn.; s. of J. Hubert Stans and Mathilda Nyssen; m. Kathleen Carmody 1933 (died 1984); two s. two d.; ed. Northwestern Univ., Columbia Univ.; joined Alexander Grant and Co., Chicago 1928; exec. partner 1940–55; Dir. 10 maj. business corpns. 1935–55; Financial Consultant to U.S. Postmaster Gen. 1953–55; Deputy Postmaster Gen. 1955–57; Dir. Bureau of the Budget, U.S. Govt. 1958–61; Pres. Western Bancorporation 1961–62; Vice-Chair. United Calif. Bank 1961–62; Sr. partner, William R. Staats & Co. 1963–65; Pres. Glore Forgan, Wm. R. Staats Inc. 1965–69; Finance Chair. Nixon for President Cttee. 1968–69; Chair. Republican Nat. Finance Cttee. 1968–69, 1972–73, Finance Cttee. to Re-elect the President 1972–73; U.S. Sec. of Commerce 1969–72; fmr. Pres. American Inst. of Certified Public Accountants 1954; Outstanding Service citation, American Inst. of C.P.A.'s and American Accounting Asscn. 1952; elected Accounting Hall of Fame 1960–62; Republican; 13 hon. degrees; Tax Foundation Public Service Award 1959, Great Living American Award of U.S. Chamber of Commerce 1961. *Publications:* The Terrors of Justice 1978; numerous articles on govt. and business; syndicated columnist Los Angeles Times 1961–62. *Leisure interests:* fishing, hunting. *Address:* 211 So. Orange Grove Avenue, Pasadena, Calif. 91105, U.S.A. *Telephone:* 795-2318.

STANSFIELD, George Norman, C.B.E.; British diplomatist (retd.); b. 28 Feb. 1926, Salford; s. of George and Alice Stansfield; m. Elizabeth Margaret Williams 1947; in civil service, Ministries of Food and Supply 1948–60; Personal Asst. to Dir.-Gen. Armaments Production, War Office 1960–61; Commonwealth Office 1961–62; Second Sec., Calcutta 1962–66, Port of Spain 1966–68; First Sec. FCO 1968–71, Singapore 1971–74; Consul, Durban 1974–78; FCO 1978–82 (First Sec., then Counsellor 1980–82, Head of Overseas Estate Dept.); High Commr. in Solomon Islands 1982–86. *Leisure interests:* sailing, cine-photography, wildlife. *Address:* Deryn's Wood, 80 Westfield Road, Woking, Surrey, GU22 9QA, England.

STANTON, Frank (Nicholas), PH.D.; American administrator; b. 20 March 1908, Muskegon, Mich.; s. of Frank Cooper Stanton and Helen Josephine Schmidt; m. Ruth Stephenson 1931; ed. Ohio Wesleyan Univ., Ohio State Univ.; Dir. CBS Inc. 1945–78, Pres. 1946–71, Vice-Chair. 1971–73, Pres. Emer. 1973–; Chair. American Red Cross 1973–79, Vice-Pres. League of Red Cross Socs., Geneva; Licensed Psychologist, N.Y.; Diplomate, American Bd. of Professional Psychology; Dir. New York Life Insurance Co. 1956–81, Atlantic Richfield Co. 1973–81, Pan American World Airways Inc. 1967–81, American Electric Power Co. Inc. 1969–80, New Perspective Fund, Inc., Interpublic Group of Cos. Inc., EuroPacific Growth Fund, Thinking Machines Corpn., Capital Income Builder Fund, CBS Records, Vision Hardware Group; Chair. Broadcast Int.; Co-owner Access Press

Ltd., New York; Trustee American Crafts Council 1957–75, Inst. for Architecture and Urban Studies 1970–75, Rockefeller Foundation 1961–73, The Rand Corpn. 1956–78, Int. Herald Tribune 1983–; Chair. Carnegie Inst. of Washington; Founding Chair. and Trustee, Center for Advanced Study in the Behavioural Sciences 1953–71; Chair. U.S. Advisory Comm. on Information 1964–73; Co-Founder, Office of Radio Research, Princeton Univ. 1937; Chair., Panel on Int. Information, Educ. and Cultural Relations, Georgetown Univ. 1974–75; Dir.-Trustee, Educational Broadcasting Corpn., Int. Design Conf. in Aspen, Lincoln Center Inst., Museum of Broadcasting, etc.; Dir. Recorded Anthology of American Music Inc., Lincoln Center for the Performing Arts 1960, Business Cttee. for the Arts 1967–77, Chair. 1972–74, Municipal Art Soc. of New York 1974–77; mem. The Business Council 1956–, N.Y. Council on the Arts 1965–70, Advisory Council, Rockefeller Archive Centre 1974–78; Rockefeller Univ., Nat. Portrait Gallery Comm. 1977–, Bd. of Overseers Harvard 1978–84; Pres.'s Cttee. on the Arts and the Humanities; Fellow, A.A.A.S., American Psychological Asscn., American Acad. of Arts and Sciences, New York Acad. of Science; mem. Architectural League of N.Y., Council on Foreign Relations Inc., Inst. of Electrical and Electronic Engineers, Nat. Acad. of Television Arts and Sciences (elected to Hall of Fame 1986), Radio-Television News Dirs. Asscn., Int. Radio and Television Soc.; numerous medals, awards, and hon. degrees. *Publications:* Students' Guide—The Study of Psychology (co-author) 1935, Radio Research 1941, Radio Research 1942–43, Communications Research 1948–49 (co-ed.), International Information, Education and Cultural Relations—Recommendations for the Future 1975. *Address:* 10 East 56 Street, New York, N.Y. 10022, U.S.A. (Office). *Telephone:* (212) 752-4445.

STANWYCK, Barbara (Ruby Stevens); American actress; b. 16 July 1907, Brooklyn, New York; d. of Byron and Catherine (née McGee) Stevens; m. 1st Frank Fay 1928 (divorced 1935); one s.; 2nd Robert Taylor 1939 (divorced 1951); appeared in several Ziegfeld Follies and George White Scandals; also appeared on Broadway in Burlesque 1927 and Tattle Tales 1933; Special Acad. Award 1982; film début in The Locked Door 1929; other films include Ladies of Leisure 1930, Miracle Woman 1931, Night Nurse 1931, Forbidden 1932, The Bitter Tea of General Yen 1933, Baby Face 1933, The Secret Bride 1935, Annie Oakley 1935, His Brother's Wife 1936, Stella Dallas 1937, Always Goodbye 1938, Golden Boy 1939, The Lady Eve 1941, Meet John Doe 1941, Ball of Fire 1941, Flesh and Fantasy 1943, Double Indemnity 1944, My Reputation 1945, The Strange Love of Martha Ivers 1946, Two Mrs. Carrolls 1947, Sorry Wrong Number 1948, The Furies 1949, Clash by Night 1953, Titanic 1953, Executive Suite 1954, Witness to Murder 1954, Escape to Burma 1955, Crime of Passion 1957, Forty Guns 1957, Roustabout 1964, The Night Walker 1965; television includes guest appearances on Jack Benny, Ford Theater, Zane Grey and Alcoa Goodyear; Barbara Stanwyck Show (series) 1960–61, The Big Valley (series) 1965–69; The House That Would Not Die 1970, A Taste of Evil 1971, The Letters 1973, The Thornbirds 1983, The Colbys 1985–87; Emmy Award for Best Actress 1983, Lifetime Achievement Award American Film Inst. 1987. *Address:* c/o A. Morgan Maree & Assocs. Inc., 6363 Wilshire Boulevard, Suite 600, Los Angeles, Calif. 90048, U.S.A.

STANZEL, Franz Karl, D.PHIL.; Austrian professor of English; b. 4 Aug. 1923, Molln; s. of Franz and Luise Stanzel; m. Traude Mühlbacher 1955; one d.; ed. Univ. of Graz and Harvard Univ.; lecturer in English, Univ. of Graz 1949–50, 1951–57; Asst. Prof. Univ. of Göttingen 1957–59; Prof. Univ. of Erlangen 1959–62; Prof. of English, Univ. of Graz 1962–, Dean, Faculty of Arts and Sciences 1967–68, Head Dept. of English 1962–78; mem. Austrian Acad.; Dr. h.c. (Fribourg). *Publications include:* Typische Erzählsituationen im Roman 1959, Typische Formen des Romans 1964, Narrative Situations in the Novel 1969, Aspekt unserer Vorstellungen vom Charakter fremder Völker 1974, Theorie des Erzählens 1979, Englische und deutsche Kriegsdichtung, Sprachkunst 1987. *Leisure interests:* skiing, mountaineering, travel. *Address:* Moserhofgasse 24d 8010 Graz, Austria. *Telephone:* (0316) 80 22 59.

STAPP, Col. John Paul; PH.D., M.D., SC.D.; American fmr. air force officer and aerospace scientist; b. 11 July 1910, Bahia, Brazil; s. of late Rev. Charles F. and Mary Louise (née Shannon) Stapp; m. Lillian Lanese 1957; ed. Baylor Univ. (Texas), Univs. of Texas and Minnesota and School of Aviation Medicine; joined U.S.A.F. Medical Corps 1944; pioneer of research on effects of mechanical force on living tissues, especially with regard to high-speed flight and space flight; conducted rocket sled deceleration tests on himself; planned and directed high-altitude (102,000 feet) manned balloon flights 1957; organized Aeromedical Facility (Edwards Air Force Base, Calif.) and Aeromedical Field Lab. (Holloman Air Force Base, N.M.); Chief Aerospace Medical Lab., Wright Air Devt. Div. (Wright-Patterson Air Force Base, Ohio) 1958–60; Special Asst. Advanced Studies, Aerospace Medical Center (Brooks Air Force Base, Tex.) 1960–61, Chief Scientist 1961–65; Chief of Impact Injury, Armed Forces Inst. of Pathology 1965–67; retd from U.S.A.F. 1970; Chief Scientist (Medicine) Nat. Highway Safety Traffic Admin. 1967–70; Vice-Pres. Int. Astronautical Fed. 1960; Perm. Chair. Annual Stapp Car Crash Conf. 1955–; Pres. Civil Aviation Medical Assen. 1968; Consultant Dept. of Transport 1970–, Science Lab., New Mexico State Univ. 1972; Adjunct Prof. Univ. Southern Calif. Systems Man. Center 1972–; Adviser Los Angeles Safety and Systems Man. Center 1973–; Fellow, American Inst. Aeronautics and Astronautics, British Inter-

STA INTERNATIONAL WHO'S WHO STA

planetary Soc., Soc. of Automotive Engineers 1983; mem. Int. Acad. Astronautics, Int. Acad. Aviation and Space Medicine, American Medical Asscn., Nat. Research Council Int. Acad. Aviation Medicine, etc.; many awards include: John Jefferies Award 1953, Cheney Award 1955, Liljenkrantz Award 1957, Gorgas Medal 1957, Commdr., Legion of Merit 1955, Distinguished Service Medal (U.S.A.F.) 1971, Elliot Cresson Medal of Franklin Inst. 1973, Excalibur Award, Nat. Motor Vehicle Safety Council 1975, Certificate of Achievement, Nat. Space Club 1976; elected to Int. Space Hall of Fame 1979, Lovelace Award (NASA Asscn. of Flight Surgeons) 1982, Outstanding Award (Aviation and Service), Honda Medal, American Soc. of Mechanical Engineers 1984, Nat. Aviation Hall of Fame 1985. *Publications:* Human Exposure to Linear Deceleration (Journal of Aviation Medicine) 1950, Crash Protection in Air Force Transports (Aeronautical Engineering Review) 1953, Effects of Mechanical Force on Living Tissue (Journal of Aviation Medicine) 1955, 1956 and 1958, Space Cabin Landing Impact Vector Effects on Human Physiology 1964, Biomechanics of Injury in the Prevention of Highway Injury 1967, Voluntary Human Tolerance Levels in Impact Injury and Crash Protection 1970, Biodynamics of Deceleration, Impact and Blast in Aerospace Medicine 1971. *Leisure interests:* travel, writing, music, teaching. *Address:* P.O. Box 553, Alamogordo, N.M. 88310, U.S.A. (Home). *Telephone:* (505) 437-3645 (Home).

STARCK, Christian, DR.IUR.; German professor of law; b. 9 Jan. 1937, Breslau; s. of Walter Starck and Ruth Hubrich; m. Brigitte Edelmann 1965; one s. two d.; ed. Univs. of Kiel, Freiburg and Würzburg; Clerk, Fed. Constitutional Court 1964–67; govt. official 1968–69; lecturer, Univ. of Würzburg 1969–71; Prof. of Public Law, Univ. of Göttingen 1971–; Rector, Univ. of Göttingen 1976–77; Vicarius Judge, Constitutional Court of Lower Saxony 1977–; mem. TV Bd. Zweites Deutsches Fernsehen 1978–; mem. Exec. Cttee. Int. Asscn. of Constitutional Law 1981–; mem. Exec. Cttee. German Asscn. of Comparative Law 1985–; Visiting Prof. Paris I (Panthéon-Sorbonne) 1987; mem. Acad. of Sciences of Göttingen 1982–. *Publications include:* Der Gesetzesbegriff des Grundgesetzes 1970, Rundfunkfreiheit als Organisationsproblem 1973, Das Bundesverfassungsgericht im politischen Prozess 1976, Vom Grund des Grundgesetzes 1979, Das Bonner Grundgesetz 1985. *Leisure interests:* architecture, literature, walking. *Address:* Platz der Göttinger Sieben 6, 3400 Göttingen (Office); Schlegelweg 10, 3400 Göttingen, Federal Republic of Germany (Home). *Telephone:* 0551/397412 (Office).

STARCK, Philippe-Patrick; French designer; b. 18 Jan. 1949, Paris; s. of André Starck and Jacqueline Lanourisse; m. Brigitte Laurent 1977; one d.; ed. Institution Notre-Dame de Sainte-Croix, Neuilly-sur-Seine, Ecole Nissim de Camondo, Paris; f. Starck Product 1979; Interior Architect, La Main-Bleue 1976, Les Baines-Douches 1978, pvt. apartments in Palais de l'Elysée 1982, Le Café Costes 1984, La Cigale, Paris 1987; restaurants, housing and offices in Tokyo 1987–88, hotels in New York 1988; created furniture for Pres. of the Repub. 1982, Minister of Culture, for French, Italian, Spanish and Japanese cos.; designed boats for Beneteau, vases for Daum, luggage for Vuitton, etc.; Admin. Centre Culturel des Arts Plastiques, Ministry of Culture 1986–; Prof., Domus Acad., Milan, Italy, Ecole des Arts Décoratifs de Paris; Artistic Dir. Int. Design Yearbook (U.K.), Société française d'édition de mobilier XO; exhbns. include Nouveaux plaisirs d'architecture 1985, Créer dans le Créé (Musée Georges Pompidou, Paris) 1986, Arts et Industrie (Musée des Monuments Français, Paris) 1985, Starck Mobilier (Marseille) 1987; also Villa Medici, Italy, Deutsch Museum, Munich, Kunstmuseum, Düsseldorf, Museum of Modern Art, Kyoto, Japan and in U.S.A.; numerous prizes, including Oscar du Luminaire 1980, three 1st prizes at Neocone, Chicago 1986, Delta de Plata, Barcelona 1986, Platinum Circle Award, Chicago 1987; Chevalier des arts et des lettres. *Leisure interest:* sailing. *Address:* 4 rue de Dion, 78 490 Montfort L'Amaury, France.

STARFIELD, Barbara, M.D., M.P.H.; American physician; b. 18 Dec. 1932; d. of Martin and Eva (née Illions) Starfield; m. Neil A. Holtzman 1955; three s. one d.; ed. Swarthmore Coll., State Univ. of New York, The Johns Hopkins Univ.; teaching·asst. (anatomy), Downstate Med. Center, New York 1955–57; intern. and resident in Pediatrics, Johns Hopkins Univ. Hosp. 1959–62, Dir., Pediatric Medical Care Clinic 1963–66; Dir. Pediatric Clinical Scholars Program, Johns Hopkins Univ. 1971–76, Asst. Prof., Assoc. Prof. 1967–76, Prof. and Div. Head, Health Policy, The Johns Hopkins Univ. School of Hygiene and Public Health 1976–; Dave Luckman Memorial Award 1958, Career Devt. Award 1970–75, Armstrong Award (Ambulatory Pediatric Asscn.) 1983, mem. Inst. of Medicine, N.A.S. *Publications:* Effectiveness of Medical Care 1985, over 100 learned articles. *Address:* The Johns Hopkins Univ. School of Hygiene and Public Health, 624 N. Broadway, Baltimore, Md. 21205, U.S.A. *Telephone:* (301) 955 3737.

STARIBACHER, Josef, DR.RER.POL.; Austrian politician; b. 25 March 1921, Vienna; s. of Josef and Marianne (née Ine) Staribacher; m. Gertrude Mayerhofer 1943; two s.; ed. Univ. of Vienna; joined Vienna Chamber of Labour 1945, Deputy Dir. 1961–68, Dir. 1968; Chair. Food, Beverage and Tobacco Workers' Union 1961–; mem. Nationalrat 1961–; Minister for Trade, Commerce and Industry 1970–83; Chair. Supervisory Bd. ÖIAG; Socialist Party. *Leisure interests:* sports (walking, cycling). *Address:* Gewerkschaft der Lebens und Genussmittelarbeiter, Albertgasse 35, 1080 Vienna, Austria.

STARK, Sir Andrew Alexander Steel, K.C.M.G., C.V.O., M.A., D.L.; British diplomatist (retd.); b. 30 Dec. 1916, Fauldhouse, Scotland; s. of Thomas Bow Stark, and Barbara Black Stark; m. Rosemary Helen Oxley Parker 1944; three s. (one deceased); ed. Bathgate Acad. and Univ. of Edinburgh; British Army 1940–46; entered Diplomatic Service 1946, First Sec., British Embassy, Vienna 1951–53; Asst. Pvt. Sec. to Sec. of State 1953–56; First Sec., British Embassy, Belgrade 1956–58, Rome 1958–60; Counsellor, Foreign Office 1960–63; Counsellor British Embassy, Bonn 1964–68; Amb. British Mission to UN 1968; UN Under-Sec.-Gen. 1968–71; Amb. to Denmark 1971–76; Deputy Under-Sec. of State, FCO 1976–78; Dir. Maersk Co. Ltd. 1978– (Chair. 1978–87), Scandinavian Bank Ltd. 1978–88, Carlsberg Brewery Ltd. 1980–87; Adviser on European Affairs to Soc. of Motor Manufacturers and Traders Ltd. 1978–; Chair. Anglo-Danish Trade Advisory Bd. 1983–, Anglo-Danish Soc. 1983–; Pro-Chancellor and Chair. Council of Univ. of Essex 1983–89; Grosses Verdienstkreuz, Fed. Repub. of Germany 1965, Kt. Grand Cross, Order of the Dannebrog 1974. *Leisure interests:* reading, music, shooting, skiing, tennis, golf. *Address:* Fambridge Hall, White Notley, Witham, Essex, England. *Telephone:* (0376) 83117.

STARK, Dame Freya Madeline, D.B.E.; British explorer and writer; b. 31 Jan. 1893, Paris, France; d. of Robert Stark and Flora (née Stark); m. Stewart Perowne 1947 (separated); ed. School of Oriental Studies and privately; travelled in Middle East and Iran 1927–31 and in S. Arabia 1934–35, 1937–38; joined Ministry of Information Sept. 1939, sent to Aden 1939, Cairo 1940, Baghdad 1944, U.S.A. and Canada 1943; Hon. LL.D. (Glasgow Univ.) 1952, Hon. D.Litt. (Durham Univ.) 1970; Founder's Medal, Royal Geographical Soc., Mungo Park Medal, Royal Scottish Geographical Soc., Sir Percy Sykes Medal, Royal Cen. Asian Soc., Burton Medal, Royal Asiatic Soc.; Sister C.St.J. 1981. *Publications:* The Valleys of the Assassins 1934, The Southern Gates of Arabia 1936, Baghdad Sketches 1937, Seen in the Hadhramaut 1938, A Winter in Arabia 1940, Letters from Syria 1942, East is West 1945, Perseus in the Wind 1948, Traveller's Prelude 1950, Beyond Euphrates 1951, The Coast of Incense 1953, Ionia: A Quest 1954, The Lycian Shore 1956, Alexander's Path 1958, Riding to the Tigris 1959, Dust in the Lion's Paw 1961, The Journey's Echo 1963, Rome on the Euphrates 1966, The Zodiac Arch 1968, Space, Time and Movement in Landscape 1969, The Minaret of Djam 1970, Turkey: Sketch of Turkish History 1971, Selected Letters (6 vols.) 1974, 1975, 1976, 1977, 1978, 1981; A Peak in Darien 1976, Rivers of Time 1982. *Leisure interests:* reading, mountaineering, embroidery. *Address:* Via Canova, Asolo, Treviso, Italy; and c/o John Murray, 50 Albemarle Street, London, W.1, England. *Telephone:* Treviso 52732.

STARK, Nathan J., B.S., J.D.; American lawyer; b. 9 Nov. 1920, Minn.; s. of Harold and Anna Stark; m. Lucile Seidler 1943; three s. one d.; ed. U.S. Merchant Marine Acad. and Illinois Inst. of Tech., Chicago Kent Coll. of Law; Man., Vice-Pres. Rivac Mfg. Co. 1952–58; Partner, Downey, Abrams, Stark & Sullivan, law firm 1958–59; Sr. Vice-Pres. Hallmark Cards Inc. 1959–74; Pres., Chair. of Bd., Crown Center Redevt. Corpn. 1970–74; Sr. Vice-Chancellor, Health Sciences, Univ. of Pittsburgh, also Prof. of Health Services Admin. 1974–84; Under-Sec., U.S. Dept. of Health and Human Services 1979–80; Sr. Vice-Chancellor Emer., Univ. of Pittsburgh 1984–; partner, law firm of Kominers, Fort, Schlefer & Boyer 1984–; mem. Nat. Bd. of Medical Examiners, N.A.S. Inst. of Medicine; Hon. mem. American Hosp. Asscn.; Hon. Fellow American Coll. of Hosp. Admins.; numerous awards including Citation of a Layman for Distinguished Service, American Medical Asscn.; Hon. LL.D. (Park Coll.) (Univ. of Missouri); Hon. D.Hum.Litt. (Scholl Coll. of Pediatric Medicine, Hahnemann Univ.). *Publications:* numerous papers on health admin. and contribs. to professional journals. *Address:* Kominers, Fort, Schlefer & Boyer, 1401 New York Avenue, N.W., Washington, D.C. 20005, U.S.A.

STARKE, H. F. Gerhard, DR. PHIL.; German newspaper editor; b. 16 Aug. 1916, Berbersdorf; s. of Richard and Elsbeth (née Burghaus) Starke; m. Ingeborg Bechmann-Baumgarten 1941; ed. Univs. of Leipzig and Geneva; Ed. Deutsche Allgemeine Zeitung, Berlin 1939–45; Ed. Prisma and Thema (cultural periodicals), Munich and Gauting 1946–49; Chief Ed. and Chief Political Dept., Nordwestdeutscher Rundfunk (NWDR) and Norddeutscher Rundfunk (NDR), Hamburg 1949–61; Dir. Deutschlandfunk, Cologne 1961–66; Chief Ed. Die Welt, Hamburg 1966–68; agent in Bonn for Axel Springer publishing group 1969. *Leisure interests:* philosophy and political sciences. *Address:* 5300 Bonn-Bad Godesberg, Deutschherrenstrasse 7, Federal Republic of Germany. *Telephone:* 33-00-31.

STARKE, Dr. Heinz; German politician; b. 27 Feb. 1911, Schweidnitz; s. of Fritz Starke and Margarete Dorn; m. Madeleine Nuel 1958; ed. Univs. of Berlin, Breslau and Jena; worked for Econ. Admin. Body of British Zone of Occupation; fmr. Dir. Bayreuth Chamber of Commerce; mem. European Assembly 1958–79; mem. Bundestag 1953–80; Minister of Finance 1961–62; mem. Free Democratic Party until 1970, Christian Social Union 1970–. *Leisure interests:* history and history of the arts. *Address:* Europastrasse 6, 53 Bonn 2, Federal Republic of Germany. *Telephone:* Bonn 375049.

STARKER, Janos; American (b. Hungarian) cellist and educator; b. 5 July 1924, Budapest; s. of Margit and Sandor Starker; m. 1st Eva Uranyi 1944 (divorced), one d.; m. 2nd Rae Busch 1960; one d.; ed. Franz Liszt Acad. of Music, Budapest; solo cellist, Budapest Opera House and Philharmonic

1479

Orchestra 1945–46; solo cellist Dallas Symphony Orchestra 1948–49, Metropolitan Opera Orchestra 1949–53, Chicago Symphony Orchestra 1953–58; Resident cellist, Indiana Univ. 1958–, Prof. of Music 1961, now Distinguished Prof. of Music; inventor of Starker bridge for orchestral string instruments; Hon. D.Mus. (Chicago Conservatory) 1961, (Cornell Coll.) 1978, (East West Univ.) 1982, (Williams Coll.) 1983; Grand Prix du Disque 1948, George Washington Award 1972, Sanford Fellowship Award, Yale 1974, Herzl Award 1978, Ed Press Award 1983, Kodály Commemorative Medallion, New York 1983; Arturo Toscanini Award 1986, Indiana Univ. Tracy Sonneborn Award 1986; Hon. mem. Royal Acad. of London 1981; mem. American Fed. of Musicians; world-wide concert tours, over 90 recordings. *Publications:* Method 1964, Bach Suites 1971, Concerto Cadenzas, Schubert-Starker Sonatina, Bottermund-Starker Variations, Beethoven Sonatas, Beethoven Variations, Dvořák Concerto; numerous magazine articles. *Leisure interests:* writing, swimming and staying alive. *Address:* Department of Music, Indiana University, Bloomington, Ind. 47401, U.S.A.

STAROBINSKI, Jean, PH.D., M.D.; Swiss academic; b. 17 Nov. 1920, Geneva; s. of Aron Starobinski and Szayndla Frydman; m. Jacqueline H. Sirman 1954; three s.; ed. Univs. of Geneva and Lausanne; Asst. Prof. Johns Hopkins Univ. 1953–56, Prof. of French Literature, History of Ideas 1958–85; Pres. Rencontres Int. de Genève 1965–; mem. Acad. Lincei, British Acad., American Acad. of Arts and Sciences, Deutsche Akad.; Assoc. mem. Acad. des Sciences Morales et Politiques (France); Hon. degrees from Univs. of Lille 1973, Brussels, Lausanne 1979, Chicago 1986, Columbia (New York) 1987, Montreal 1988, Strasbourg 1988; Chevalier, Legion d'honneur; Balzan Prize 1984, Monaco Prize 1988. *Publications:* Rousseau 1958, The Invention of Liberty 1964, Words Upon Words 1971, 1789: The Emblems of Reason 1973, Montaigne In Motion 1983, Le Remède Dans Le Mal 1989. *Leisure interest:* music. *Address:* 12, Rue de Candolle, 1205 Geneva, Switzerland. *Telephone:* (22) 209864; (22) 298003.

STARR, Ringo (Richard Starkey), M.B.E.; British entertainer; b. 7 July 1940, Dingle, Liverpool; m. 1st Maureen Cox 1965 (divorced 1975), two s. one d.; m. 2nd Barbara Bach 1981; ed. Dingle Vale Secondary Modern School; plays drums; formerly an apprentice engineer; played with Rory Storme's Hurricanes 1959–62; joined The Beatles Aug. 1962; appeared with The Beatles in the following activities: performances in Hamburg 1962; toured Scotland, Sweden, U.K. 1963, Paris, Denmark, Hong Kong, Australia, New Zealand, U.S.A., Canada 1964, France, Italy, Spain, U.S.A. 1965, Canada, Spain, Philippines, U.S.A. 1966; attended Transcendental Meditation Course at Maharishi's Acad., Rishikesh, India Feb. 1968; formed Apple Corps Ltd., parent org. of The Beatles Group of Companies 1968; following break-up of group, now records solo. *Recordings by the Beatles include:* Please, Please Me 1963, With the Beatles 1963, A Hard Day's Night 1964, Beatles for Sale 1965, Help! 1965, Rubber Soul 1966, Revolver 1966, Sergeant Pepper's Lonely Hearts Club Band 1967, The Beatles (White Album) 1968, Yellow Submarine 1969, Abbey Road 1969, Let It Be 1970. *Films by The Beatles:* A Hard Day's Night 1964, Help! 1965, Yellow Submarine (animated colour cartoon film) 1968, Let it Be 1970; TV film Magical Mystery Tour 1967. *Individual appearances in films:* Candy 1968, The Magic Christian 1969, 200 Motels 1971, Blindman 1971, That'll be the Day 1973, Born to Boogie (also directed and produced) 1974, Son of Dracula (also produced) 1975, Lisztomania 1975, Ringo Stars 1976, Caveman 1981, The Cooler 1982, Give My Regards to Broad Street 1984.

STASHENKOV, Nikolai Alekseevich; Soviet official; b. 15 March 1934, Dryageli, Smolensk Dist., Byelorussia; ed. Inst. of Econs., Minsk; worked in trade sector, Vitebsk Dist. 1957–71; mem. CPSU 1960–; Head of Dept. of Trade and Consumer Services, Cen Cttee. of Byelorussian CP 1971–78; cand. mem. Cen. Cttee. of Byelorussian CP 1971–81, mem. 1981–86; Deputy to Byelorussian Supreme Soviet 1971–85; Byelorussian Minister of Trade 1980–81; U.S.S.R. Deputy Minister of Trade and Chair. of Council for Consumer Research, U.S.S.R. Ministry of Trade 1981–83; Deputy Head of Dept. for Trade and Consumer Services, Cen. Cttee. CPSU 1984–85, Head 1985–; cand. mem. Cen. Cttee. CPSU 1986–. *Address:* The Kremlin, Moscow, U.S.S.R.

STASI, Bernard, L. EN D.; French politician; b. 4 July 1930, Reims; s. of Mario and Mercédès (née Camps) Stasi; m. Danielle Beaugier 1979; ed. Institut d'Etudes Politiques, Paris and Ecole Nat. d'Admin.; attached to the Cabinet of the Pres. of the Nat. Assembly 1955; served in army 1955–57; Civil Admin., Ministry of Interior 1959; Chef de Cabinet to the Prefect of Algiers 1959–60; Head of Section, Directorate-Gen. of Political Affairs and Territorial Admin., Ministry of Interior 1960–62; Tech. Adviser, Cabinet of the Sec. of State for Youth and Sports 1963–65; Directeur de Cabinet to the Sec. of Overseas Depts. 1966–68; Deputy for Marne, Nat. Assembly 1968–73, 1978–; charged with missions to Israel, G.B., Cuba and Chile; Mayor of Epernay 1970–77, 1983–; Vice-Pres. Centre Démocratie et Progrès 1969–75, Centre des Démocrates Sociaux 1976–84 (first Vice-Pres. 1984–); Minister for Overseas Depts. and Territories 1973–74; Fed. Sec. Féd. des Réformateurs 1975–; mem. Regional Council of Champagne-Ardenne 1976–, Pres. 1981–; Pres. Fédération française de course d'orientation 1970–; Pres. Nat. Council for Regional Econ. and Productivity 1986–; Mayor of Epernay 1970–77, 1983–; Founder, Groupe d'études parlementaires pour l'aménagement rural 1970; Bd. of Dirs. Association des Maires

de France; mem. various municipal orgs.; fmrly. active mem. of youth movements; Officier de Réserve, Chevalier, Grand' Croix de l'Ordre du Croissant vert (Comoros), ier du Mérite sportif, Grand' Croix de l'Ordre de l'Etoile d'Anjouan. *Publication:* Le Piège (with J. P. Soisson and O. Stirn) 1973, Vie associative et démocratie nouvelle 1979, l'Immigration: une chance pour la France 1984. *Leisure interests:* football, tennis, skiing, sailing. *Address:* Hôtel de Ville, 51200 Epernay, France. *Telephone:* 51-34-30 (Epernay).

STASSEN, Hendrik Gerard, D.SC.; Netherlands academic; b. 29 Sept. 1935, Goes; s. of J. W. Stassen and E. G. Palm; m. M.W.P. van Zutphen; two s. one d.; ed. Tech. Coll. Utrecht and Delft Univ. of Tech. (DUT); air traffic controller, Air Base New Amsterdam 1958–59; Asst. Prof. in Control Eng. DUT 1963–67, Assoc. Prof. 1967–76, Prof. in Man-Machine Systems 1977–; lecturer in Man-Machine Systems, M.I.T. 1967–68; Visiting Prof. Stanford Univ. 1987–88; Sr. mem. I.E.E.E.; mem. Royal Netherlands Acad. of Sciences. *Publications:* 105 articles, chapters etc., on man-machine systems and rehabilitation of physically-handicapped. *Leisure interests:* man-machine systems, rehabilitation, bio-engineering. *Address:* Faculty of Mechanical Engineering, Delft University of Technology, Mekelweg 2, 2628 CD Delft, The Netherlands. *Telephone:* (015) 78 36 07.

STASSINOPOULOS, Michael; Greek politician, university professor and judge; b. 27 July 1905, Calamata; s. of Demetrios Stassinopoulos and Catherine Scopetou; m. Stamatia Ritsoni 1942; one d.; ed. Athens Univ.; Lecturer in Admin. Law, Athens Univ. 1937–68; Prof. Admin. Law, High School of Political Sciences, Athens 1939–68, Dean 1951–58; State Council Adviser 1943–58; Political Adviser to Dodecanese Gov. 1947; Chair. Cttee. for the Civil Servants Code 1948; Minister of the Press and subsequently Minister of Labour 1952; Chair. Hellenic Nat. Broadcasting Inst. Admin. Bd. 1953; Chair. Nat. Opera Admin. Bd. 1953–63; Minister of the Press 1958; Vice-Pres. State Council 1963, Pres. 1966–69; M.P. Nov.–Dec. 1974; Pres. of Greece Dec. 1974–June 1975; Judge ad hoc, Int. Court of Justice, The Hague 1976–78; mem. Acad. of Athens 1968, Pres. 1978; Chief Justice until 1974; Dr. h.c. (Univ. of Bordeaux) 1957, (Univ. of Paris) 1974, Order of St. George (First Class). *Publications:* The States' Civil Responsibility 1949, Administrative Acts Law 1950 (in French), Civil Service Laws 1951, Administrative Disputes Laws 1953, Principles of Administrative Law 1954, Principles of Public Finance 1956, Traité des actes administratifs (in French), Poems 1949, The Land of the Blue Lakes 1950, Harmonia (poems) 1956, Thought and Life (essays) 1970, The Wolf's Law (essays) 1972, Le droit de la défense (in French) 1977, Political History of Greece 1978, Two Seasons (poems) 1979. *Leisure interests:* poetry, cinema, gardening. *Address:* Taygetoy Street 7, (Psichicon), Athens, Greece. *Telephone:* 6713-197.

STĂTESCU, Constantin, LL.D.; Romanian lawyer and politician; b. 27 Nov. 1927, Curtea de Argeş; ed. Faculty of Law, Univ. of Bucharest; mem. of Staff, Faculty of Law, Bucharest 1950–66, Prof. 1967–; Justice, Supreme Court of Romanian S.R. 1964–67, Vice-Pres. 1967–75, Pres. 1975–77; mem. Grand Nat. Ass. 1965–; Sec. State Council 1967–75; mem. Romanian CP, of Cen. Cttee. 1974–84; Minister of Justice 1977–79; mem. Acad. of Social and Political Sciences 1970–; Dean, Law Coll., Bucharest Univ. *Publications:* works and textbooks on Common Law, State Arbitration and Arbitration Practice 1962, Civil Law 1967, 1970, 1973, 1981, Amb. to Holland 1984–. *Address:* c/o Ministry of Foreign Affairs, Piaţa Victoriei 1, Bucharest, Romania.

STAUDINGER, Ulrich; German publisher; b. 30 May 1935, Berlin; s. of Wilhelm Staudinger and Elfriede Poth; m. Irmengard Ehrenwirth 1960; one s. two d.; ed. Volksschule and Realgymnasium; publishing training 1954–57; Lingenbrinck Barsortiment, Hamburg 1957–58; Publicity and Sales, Ensslin & Laiblin, Jugendbuchverlag, Reutlingen 1958–59; Production, Carl Hanser Verlag, Munich 1959–60; Dawson & Sons, London 1960; Franz Ehrenwirth Verlag, Munich 1960; partner, Ehrenwirth Verlag, Munich 1964; responsible for purchase of Franz Schneekluth Verlag KG, Darmstadt by Ehrenwirth Verlag 1967 and following purchase of all parts of Franz Schneekluth Verlag the cos. were amalgamated into a single firm in 1976; purchased parts of Philosophia Verlag G.m.b.H., Düsseldorf 1978; various professional appts. *Address:* Franz Schneekluth Verlag, Widenmayerstrasse 34, 8000 Munich 22 (Office); Asgardstrasse 34, 8000 Munich 81, Federal Republic of Germany (Home). *Telephone:* 089/22 13 91 (Office); 089/98 63 67 (Home).

STAVELEY, Adm. Sir William (Doveton Minet), G.C.B., A.D.C.; British naval officer; b. 10 Nov. 1928, Marnhull, Dorset; s. of the late Adm. Cecil Minet Staveley, C.B., C.M.G., and Margaret Adela (née Sturdee); m. Bettina Kirstine Shuter 1954; one s. one d.; ed. West Downs, Winchester, Royal Naval Colls., Dartmouth and Greenwich; entered R.N. as cadet 1942, R.N. Staff Coll. 1959, Commdr. H.M.S. Zulu, Intrepid, Albion 1967–72, Royal Coll. of Defence Studies 1973, Dir. of Naval Plans, Naval Staff 1974–76, Flag Officer, 2nd Flotilla 1976–77, Flag Officer, Carriers and Amphibious ships, NATO Commdr., Carrier Striking Group Two 1977–78, Chief of Staff to C.-in-C. Fleet 1978–80, Vice-Chief of Naval Staff 1980–82, rank of Adm. Oct. 1982–, C.-in-C. Fleet and Allied C.-in-C. Channel and E. Atlantic 1982–85; First Sea Lord and Chief of Naval Staff 1985–89; First and Prin. A.D.C. to H.M. the Queen 1985–; mem. Chatham Historic Dockyard Trust 1988–. *Leisure interests:* gardening, shooting, fishing, riding, sailing, restoring antiques. *Address:* Old Graingers, Plaxtol, Nr. Sevenoaks, Kent, TN15 0P2, England.

STAWSKI, Henryk Tadeusz; Polish politician; b. 21 Oct. 1929, Troyes, France; m.; one s. one d.; ed. Adam Mickiewicz Univ., Poznań; Head Planning Dept. Voivodship Bd. of State Local Industry, Zielona Góra 1950–54; Head, Dept. of Industry and Service Voivodship Econ. Planning Comm. Zielona Góra 1954–60; Pres. Chamber of Crafts, Zielona Góra 1957–63; councillor Voivodship Nat. Council, Zielona Góra 1958–, mem. Presidium 1965–69, Vice-Chair. 1972–76, Chair. 1980–84; Deputy to Seym 1972–85; Vice-Chair. Deputies' Club of Democratic Party 1981–85; mem. State Council 1983–85; mem. Democratic Party 1956–, Vice-Pres. Voivodship Cttee. 1959–63, Sec. Voivodship Cttee. 1963–80, Chair. Voivodship Cttee., Zielona Góra 1980–; mem. Cen. Cttee. 1965–; decorations including Officer's and Knight's Cross of Polonia Restituta Order, Order of Banner of Labour, 2nd Class. *Publications:* Ziemia Lubuska 1960, Aktualne problemy społeczno-ekonomiczne Polski 1976. *Leisure interest:* work on allotment. *Address:* ul. Moniuszki 37 m. 2, 65-409 Zielona Góra, Poland (Home).

STEAD, Eugene A., Jr., B.S., M.D.; American professor of medicine; b. 6 Oct. 1908, Atlanta; m. Evelyn Selby 1940; one s. two d.; Prof. of Medicine and Chair. Dept. of Medicine, Emory Univ. 1942–46; Dean, Emory Univ. School of Medicine 1945–46; Florence McAlister Prof. of Medicine, Chair. Dept. of Medicine, Duke Univ., Physician-in-Chief, Duke Hosp. 1947–67; Florence McAlister Prof. Emer. of Medicine, Duke Univ. 1967; Distinguished Physician of the Veterans' Admin. 1978–85; Ed. N. Carolina Medical Journal 1983–; Abraham Flexner Award for Distinguished Service to Medical Educ., Asscn. of American Medical Colls. 1970; Golden Heart Award, American Heart Asscn. 1976; Kober Medal, Asscn. of American Physicians 1980. *Publications:* contribs. to the field of cardiovascular research. *Leisure interest:* building houses. *Address:* Rt. 1, Box 194, Bullock, N.C. 27507; P.O. Box 3910, Duke University Medical Center, Durham, N.C. 27710, U.S.A.

STEAD, Rev. (George) Christopher, LITT.D., F.B.A.; British professor of divinity (retd.); b. 9 April 1913, Wimbledon; s. of Francis B. Stead and Rachel E. née Bell; m. D. Elizabeth Odom 1958; two s. one d.; ed. Marlborough Coll., King's Coll., Cambridge, New Coll., Oxford and Cuddesdon Coll., Oxford; ordained 1938; Curate, St. John's Newcastle-upon-Tyne 1939; Fellow and Lecturer in Divinity, King's Coll., Cambridge 1938–48; Asst. Master, Eton Coll. 1940–44; Fellow and Chaplain, Keble Coll., Oxford 1949–71; Ely Prof. of Divinity, Cambridge and Canon Residentiary of Ely Cathedral 1971–80, Canon Emer. 1981–; Fellow, King's Coll., Cambridge 1971–85, Professorial Fellow 1971–80; Emer. Fellow, Keble Coll., Oxford 1981–. *Publications:* Divine Substance 1977, Substance and Illusion in the Christian Fathers 1985, Philosophie und Theologie I, Alte Kirche 1989; contrib. to books, journals, etc. *Leisure interests:* walking, sailing, music. *Address:* 13 Station Road, Haddenham, Ely, Cambs., England. *Telephone:* (0353) 740575.

STEADMAN, Ralph Idris; British cartoonist, writer and illustrator; b. 15 May 1936; s. of Raphael Steadman and Gwendoline Steadman; m. 1st Sheila Thwaite 1959 (dissolved 1971); two s. two d.; m. 2nd Anna Deverson 1972; one d.; ed. London School of Printing and Graphic Arts; with de Havilland Aircraft Co. 1952; Cartoonist Kemsley (Thomson) Newspapers 1956–59; freelance for Punch, Private Eye, Daily Telegraph during 1960s; political cartoonist New Statesman 1978–80; restrospective exhbns.: Nat. Theatre 1977, Royal Festival Hall 1984; designed set of stamps Halley's Comet 1986; recipient Designers and Art Dirs. Asscn. Gold Award 1977, Silver Award 1977. *Publications:* Jelly Book 1968, Still Life with Raspberry: collected drawings 1969, The Little Red Computer 1970, Dogs Bodies 1971, Bumper to Bumper Book 1973, Two Donkeys and the Bridge 1974, Flowers for the Moon 1974, The Watchdog and the Lazy Dog 1974, America: drawings 1975, America: collected drawings 1977 (r.e. Star Strangled Banger 1987), I, Leonardo 1983, Between the Eyes 1984, Paranoids 1986; *written and illustrated:* Sigmund Freud 1979, A Leg in the Wind and Other Canine Curses 1982, That's My Dad 1986, The Big I Am 1988; *illustrator:* many books from 1961. *Leisure interests:* gardening, sheep husbandry, fishing, trumpet.

STEBBINS, George Ledyard, PH.D.; American professor of genetics; b. 6 Jan. 1906, Lawrence, N.Y.; s. of George Ledyard and Edith Candler; m. 1st Margaret Chamberlaine 1931 (divorced 1958), 2nd Barbara Jean Brumley 1958; two s. (one deceased) one d.; ed. Cate School, Carpinteria, Calif., and Harvard Univ.; Instructor in Biology, Colgate Univ. 1931–35; Jr. Geneticist, Univ. of Calif., Berkeley 1935–39, Asst. Prof. 1939–40, Assoc. Prof. 1940–47, Prof. of Genetics 1947–50, Prof. of Genetics, Univ. of Calif., Davis 1950–73, Prof. Emer. 1973–; mem. N.A.S., American Acad. of Arts and Sciences, American Philosophical Soc., Linnean Soc. London, Royal Swedish Acad. of Sciences, Deutsche Akad. Leopoldina; Jesup Lecturer, Columbia Univ. 1946; Prather Lecturer, Harvard Univ. 1958; Hon. D.Sc. (Paris) 1962; Verrill Medal, Yale Univ. 1968, Gold Medal, Linnean Soc., London 1973, Nat. Medal of Science 1980. *Publications:* The Human Organism and the World of Life (with C. W. Young) 1938, Variation and Evolution in Plants 1950, Processes of Organic Evolution 1966, The Basis of Progressive Evolution 1969, Chromosomal Evolution in Higher Plants 1971, Flowering Plants: Evolution above the Species Level 1974, Evolution (with T. Dobzhansky, F. Ayala, and J. Valentine) 1977, Darwin to DNA:

Molecules to Humanity 1982. *Leisure interests:* hiking, mountain climbing, plant collecting, music as listener. *Address:* Department of Genetics, University of California, Davis, Calif. 95616 (Office); 216 F Street No. 165, Davis, Calif. 95616, U.S.A. (Home). *Telephone:* (916) 752-7574 (Office); (916) 753-2665 (Home).

STEEL, Sir David (Edward Charles), Kt., D.S.O., M.C., T.D.; British company director; b. 29 Nov. 1916; s. of late Gerald Arthur Steel; m. Ann Price 1956; one s. two d.; ed. Rugby School and Univ. Coll., Oxford; Officer, Q.R. Lancers, serving in France, the Middle East, N. Africa and Italy 1940–45; admitted as Solicitor 1948; worked for Linklaters and Paines 1948–50; in Legal Dept., British Petroleum Co. Ltd. 1950–56; Pres. British Petroleum (N. America) Ltd. 1959–61, Regional Co-ordinator, Western Hemisphere, B.P. Co. Ltd. 1961–62; Man. Dir. Kuwait Oil Co. Ltd. 1962–65, Dir. 1965–; a Man. Dir. British Petroleum Co. Ltd. 1965–72, Deputy Chair. 1972–75, Chair. 1975–81; Dir. B.P. Oil 1976–77; Dir. Bank of England 1978–84, Kleinwort, Benson, Lonsdale 1985–; Trustee, The Economist 1979–; Chair. Wellcome Trust 1982–89; Deputy Chair. Governing Body, Rugby School 1982, Chair. 1984–; Pres. London Chamber of Commerce and Industry 1982–85; Hon. Fellow, Univ. Coll., Oxford 1982; Hon. D.C.L. (City) 1983. *Address:* c/o Britannic House, Moor Lane, London, EC2Y 9BV, England.

STEEL, Rt. Hon. David Martin Scott, P.C., M.A., LL.B.; British (Scottish) politician, journalist and broadcaster; b. 31 March 1938, Kirkcaldy; s. of Very Rev. Dr. David Steel; m. Judith Mary MacGregor 1962; three s. one d.; ed. Prince of Wales School, Nairobi, Kenya, George Watson's Coll. and Edinburgh Univ.; Pres. Edinburgh Univ. Liberals 1959; mem. Students' Rep. Council 1960; Asst. Sec., Scottish Liberal Party 1962–64; M.P. for Roxburgh, Selkirk and Peebles 1965–83, for Tweeddale, Ettrick and Lauderdale June 1983–; Scottish Liberal Whip 1967–70, Liberal Chief Whip 1970–75; Leader of Liberal Party 1976–88; co-founder Social and Liberal Democrats 1988; mem. Parl. del. to UN Gen. Ass. 1967; fmr. Liberal spokesman on Commonwealth Affairs; Sponsor, Pvt. Member's Bill to reform law on abortion 1966–67; Pres. Anti-Apartheid Movement of U.K. 1966–69; Chair. Shelter, Scotland 1969–73; BBC TV Interviewer in Scotland 1964–65; Presenter of weekly religious programme for Scottish TV 1966–67, for Granada 1969, for BBC 1971–76; Rector Univ. of Edinburgh 1982–85; Chubb Fellow, Yale Univ., U.S.A. 1987. *Publications:* Boost for the Borders 1964, No Entry 1969, A House Divided 1980, Border Country 1985, Partners in One Nation 1985, The Time Has Come (with David Owen) 1987, Mary Stuart's Scotland (with Judy Steel) 1987. *Leisure interests:* angling, vintage motoring. *Address:* House of Commons, London, SW1A 0AA, England; Cherry Dene, Ettrick Bridge, Selkirkshire, Scotland (Home).

STEEL, Dawn; American film company executive; b. 19 Aug. 1946, New York; m. Charles Roven; one d.; ed. Boston and New York Univs.; sportswriter, Maj. League Baseball Digest, Nat. Football League, New York 1968–69; Ed. Penthouse magazine, New York 1969–74; Pres. O. Dawn, Inc., New York 1975–78; consultant, Playboy magazine 1978–79; Vice-Pres. Paramount Pictures, New York 1979–80, Sr. Vice-Pres. (Production) Los Angeles 1980–85, Pres. (Production) 1985–87; Pres. Columbia Pictures Int. 1987–. *Address:* c/o Columbia Pictures, Columbia Plaza, Burbank, Calif. 91505, U.S.A.

STEELE, Dr. John Hyslop, D.SC., F.R.S., F.R.S.E.; British scientist; b. 15 Nov. 1926, Edinburgh, Scotland; s. of Adam Steele and Annie Hyslop Steele; m. Margaret Evelyn Travis 1956; one s.; ed. George Watson's Boys' Coll., Edin., Univ. Coll., Univ. of London; Marine Lab., Aberdeen, Scotland 1951–77, Marine Scientist 1951–66, Sr. Prin. Scientific Officer 1966–73, Dir. 1973–77; Dir. Woods Hole Oceanographic Inst., Mass. 1977–, Pres. 1986; Fellow N.A.S. 1980; Agassiz Medal 1973. *Publications:* Structure of Marine Ecosystems 1974, over 80 articles in oceanographic and ecological journals. *Leisure interest:* sailing. *Address:* Woods Hole Oceanographic Institution, Woods Hole, Mass. 02543, U.S.A. *Telephone:* (617) 548-1400.

STEELE, John Roderic, C.B., M.A., F.C.I.T.; British civil servant; b. 22 Feb. 1929, Wakefield; s. of late Harold Graham Steele and Doris (née Hall) Steele; m. Margaret Marie Stevens 1956; two s. two d.; ed. Queen Elizabeth Grammar School, Wakefield, Queen's Coll., Oxford; Asst. Prin., Ministry of Civil Aviation 1951–54, Private Sec. to Parl. Sec. 1954–57; Prin., Rd. Transport Div. 1957–60, Sea Transport Div. 1960–62, Shipping Policy 1962–64; Asst. Sec. (Shipping Policy) Bd. of Trade 1964–67; Counsellor (Shipping), British Embassy, Washington 1967–71; Asst. Sec. (Civil Aviation Div.), Dept. of Trade and Industry 1971–73, Under-Sec., Space Div. 1973–74, Shipping Policy Div. 1974–75, Gen. Div., Dept. of Trade, Deputy Sec. 1976–80; Deputy Sec., Dept. of Industry 1980–81; Dir.-Gen., Directorate-Gen. for Transport, Comm. of the European Communities 1981–86; Transport Consultant 1986–. *Leisure interests:* cricket, tennis, opera. *Address:* 7 Kemerton Road, Beckenham, Kent, England; 30 Square Ambiorix, Bte 30, 1040 Brussels, Belgium.

STEELE, Tommy, O.B.E.; British actor and singer; b. (as Thomas Hicks) 17 Dec. 1936, Bermondsey, London; s. of Thomas Walter Hicks and Elizabeth Ellen Bennett; m. Ann Donoughue 1960; one d.; ed. Bacon's School for Boys, Bermondsey; entered Merchant Navy 1952; first stage appearance Empire Theatre, Sunderland 1956, London début 1957; roles include Buttons (Cinderella) London 1958/59, Tony Lumpkin (She Stoops to Conquer) 1960, Arthur Kipps (Half A Sixpence) 1963/64, New York 1965/66, Truffaldino (The Servant of Two Masters) 1968, title role in Hans Andersen, London 1974/75, 1977/78, 1981, Don Lockwood (Singin' in the Rain), London 1983-85 (also dir.); film debut in Kill Me Tomorrow 1956; sculpted tribute to the Beatles' Eleanor Rigby 1982. *Films include:* The Tommy Steele Story, The Duke Wore Jeans 1957, Tommy the Toreador 1959, Light Up the Sky 1963, Its All Happening 1966, The Happiest Millionaire 1967, Half A Sixpence, Finian's Rainbow 1968, Where's Jack 1971; TV début in Off the Record 1956, cabaret début, Caesar's Palace, Las Vegas 1974; composed and recorded musical autobiog. My Life, My Song 1974; An Evening with Tommy Steele (stage) 1979; Quincy's Quest (TV) 1979. *Publications:* Hans Andersen (co-author, stage version), Quincy 1981, The Final Run 1983. *Leisure interests:* squash, painting. *Address:* c/o Isobel Davie, 37 Hill Street, London, W1X 8JY, England.

STEEN, Reiulf; Norwegian politician; b. 16 Aug. 1933, Saetre, Hurum; s. of Nils and Astrid Steen; factory worker 1951; joined Fremtiden as journalist 1955; Sec. AUF (Labour Party Jr. Org.) 1958, Chair. 1961-64; Sec. Labour Party Parl. Group 1964, Vice-Chair. Labour Party 1965-75, Chair. 1975-81; Deputy mem. Storting 1961-65, mem. 1977-; Minister of Communications 1971-72; Chair. Foreign Relations Cttee., Stortinget 1977-. *Leisure interests:* literature, politics. *Address:* Arbeiderpartiet, Youngstorget 2, Oslo 1, 330180; Stortinget, Oslo 1, 413810, Norway.

STEENSBERG, Axel, DR.PHIL.; Danish academic; b. 1 June 1906, Sinding; s. of Jens Steensberg and Maren Steensberg; m. Frida Sillesen 1934 (died 1964); two s. one d.; working farmer until 1928; Asst. to Gudmund Hatt surveying prehistoric fields and excavating villages of the Iron Age 1934-37; Head, Third Dept. Nat. Museum 1946-59; Chair. Int. Secr. for Research on History of Agricultural Implements 1954-; Prof. of Material Culture, Copenhagen 1959-70; consultant, UNESCO, S. Pacific 1970-71; Ed. Tools and Tillage 1968-; Patron Techniques et Culture 1982-; excavations of deserted Danish villages 1937-82; research in Papua New Guinea, 1968, 1971, 1975, 1983; Hon. mem. Gustav Acad. Uppsala, Asscn. Int. des Musées d'Agriculture, Ethnographic Soc. Budapest. *Publications include:* Ancient Harvesting Implements 1943, Atlas of Borup Fields 1968, Store Valby I-III 1974, Draved, an experiment in Stone Age agriculture, burning, sowing and harvesting 1979, New Guinea Gardens 1980, Borup A.D. 700-1400 I-II 1983, Man the Manipulator 1986, Hard Grains, Irrigation, Numerals and Script in the Rise of Civilizations 1989. *Address:* Cæciliavej 30, Copenhagen-Valby, Denmark.

STEENSGARD, Niels Palle, D.PHIL.; Danish academic; b. 7 March, 1932, Rødovre; s. of Knud Steensgard and Kirstine (née Knop) Steensgard; m. Illa Frilis 1954; two d.; ed. Univ. of Copenhagen, S.O.A.S., London; Assoc. Prof. Inst. of History, Univ. of Copenhagen 1962, Dean, Faculty of Humanities 1974-76, Prof. 1977-; mem. Danish Research Council for the Humanities 1980-88, Chair. 1985-87; mem. Nordic Cttee. Humanities Research Councils 1983-88, Chair. 1985-87; Danish Rep., Standing Cttee. for the Humanities, European Science Foundation 1983-88; Chair. Nat. Cttee. of Danish Historians 1989; mem. Royal Danish Acad. of Sciences and Letters 1982. *Publications:* The Asian Trade Revolution of the Seventeenth Century 1973, Verden På Øpdagelsernes tid 1984, Verdensmarked og kulturmøter 1985. *Leisure interests:* losing my way in large books or towns. *Address:* Institute of History, University of Copenhagen, Njalsgade 102, Copenhagen 2300 S (Office); Lemnosvej 19, Copenhagen 2300 S, Denmark (Home).

STEFANESCU, I. Stefan, PH.D.; Romanian historian; b. 24 May 1929, Goicea, Dolj City; ed. Coll. of History, Bucharest Univ. Lomonosov Univ. Moscow; researcher in history 1951-65; Head Romanian Medieval History Dept. of the N. Iorga Inst. of History of the Romanian Acad. 1965-66, Deputy Dir. 1966-70, dir. 1970-; Dean of the Coll. of History and Philosophy, Bucharest Univ. 1977-85; mem. Romanian Acad. of Social and Political Sciences 1970-; corresp. mem. Romanian Academy 1974-; mem. Romanian Soc. for Historical Sciences (on main bd.), Int. Comm. for Hist. of State Ass., Comm. int. des études slaves; Vice-Chair. of the Nat. Cttee. of Historical Sciences; Chair. of the Dept. of History and Archaeology, Romanian Acad. of Social and Political Sciences 1970-; mem. European Acad. of History 1981-; Prize of the Romanian Acad. 1967; Order of Scientific Merit 1966, Star of the Repub. 1971; Deputy Nat. Ass. 1975-80, 1985-(90). *Works include:* The History of the Romanian People 1970, Medieval Wallachia from Basarab I the Founder until Michael the Brave, 1970, History of Dobrudja, Vol. III (with I. Barnea), Demography—a Dimension of History, 1974. *Address:* Bucharest University, Edgar Quinet St. 7, Bucharest (Office); Bd. Aviatorilor 1, Bucharest (Office); Calea Victorie 214, Apt. 44, Bucharest I, Romania (Home).

STEFANOPOULOS, Constantine; Greek lawyer; b. 1926, Patras; s. of Demetrius and Vrisiis Stefanopoulos; m. Eugenia El. Stounopoulou 1959; two s. one d.; pvt. law practice; M.P. for Achaia (Nat. Radical Union) 1964, (New Democracy) 1974, 1977, 1981-; Under-Sec. of Commerce July-Oct. 1974; Minister of the Interior 1974-76, of Social Services 1976-77; in Prime Minister's Office 1977-81; Parl. Rep., New Democracy Party 1981-85; Pres. Party of Democratic Renewal 1985-. *Address:* Dafnis 9, P. Psychicho, Athens, Greece. *Telephone:* 6723580, 6723530.

STEFANOWICZ, Janusz, HH.D.; Polish journalist and diplomatist; b. 24 Nov. 1932, Włocławek; s. of Jozef Stefanowicz and Julia Stefanowicz; m. 1957; ed. Faculty of Law, Warsaw Univ.; publicist, newspaper Słowo Powszechne, Warsaw 1955-80, Ed.-in-Chief 1972-80; Deputy Ed.-in-Chief daily Życie Warszawy 1981-82; Dir. PAX Publishing Inst., Warsaw 1982-84; mem. PAX Asscn. 1959-, Deputy Chair. PAX Gen. Bd. 1976-80, 1982-; Deputy to Seym (Parl.) 1979-85; Amb. to France 1984-88; mem. Polish Journalists' Assn. 1955-82, Deputy Pres. Polish Club of Int. Commentators 1972-84; Kt.'s Cross of Order of Polonia Restituta, Order of Banner of Labour (2nd Class), Gold Cross of Merit and others. *Publications:* some 20 books, including Chrześcijańska Demokracja (Christian Democracy) 1963, Watykan i Włochy (Vatican City and Italy) 1966, Świat w trzydziestu odsłonach (A World in Thirty Scenes) 1966, Włochy współczesne (Contemporary Italy) 1976, Europa powojenna (Post-war Europe) 1978, Stary nowy świat (Old New World) 1978, Co-author: Tożsamość Europy (European Identity) 1979, Bezpieczeństwo państw współczesnych (Security of Contemporary States) 1984. *Leisure interests:* historical literature, hiking, cycling and car trips. *Address:* ul. Tamka 49 m.7, 00-355 Warsaw, Poland (Home). *Telephone:* 27-15-55 (Home).

STEFAŃSKI, Piotr, M.A.; Polish politician and journalist; b. 6 April 1931, Warsaw; s. of Henryk and Julianna Stefański; m. Alina Stefańska 1950; two c.; ed. Higher School of Social Sciences, Warsaw; fmr. active mem. of Youth Orgs.; mem. Democratic Party (SD) 1948-; Ed. Tygodnik Demokratyczny, SD weekly newspaper 1956-59; Chair. Press, Information and Educ. Team of SD Cen. Cttee. 1962-69, Sec. SD Cen. Cttee 1969-76, mem. Presidium 1969-, Deputy Chair. SD Cen. Cttee. 1976-81; Deputy to Seym 1972-, Chair. SD Seym Deputies' Club 1972-80; Vice-Marshal of Seym 1976-85; Chair. Seym Comm. of Culture 1985-; mem. Council of State 1985-; mem. Presidium and Sec. All-Poland Cttee. of Nat. Unity Front (OK FJN)1971-83; Deputy Chair. of Gen. Council, Polish-Soviet Friendship Soc. 1979-; Chair. Poland-Latin America Soc.; mem. Presidium, Polish Cttee. for Security and Co-operation in Europe; Kt.'s Cross and Commdr.'s Cross, Order of Polonia Restituta, Order of Banner of Labour (1st and 2nd Class), Gold Cross of Merit. *Leisure interest:* electronics. *Address:* Asfaltowa 3m. 4, 02-570 Warsaw, Poland. *Telephone:* 49-11-21.

STEFÁNSSON, Alexander; Icelandic politician; b. 6 Oct. 1922; m. Björg H. Finnbogadóttir; six c.; ed. Cooperative's Commercial Coll.; Office Man. Ólafsvíkurhreppur 1962-66, Commercial Man. 1964-79; Chair. Commercial Council 1964-; Deputy mem. of Parl. 1972-74, mem. 1978-; Deputy Speaker, Lower House of Parl. 1979-; mem. Bd. Union of Local Authorities 1974, Union of Harbour Authorities 1969-; Deputy Chair. of Bd. Fisheries Bank of Iceland 1976-; Minister of Social Affairs 1983-87; Progressive Party. *Address:* Althingi, Reykjavík, Iceland.

STEFFE, Horst-Otto, D.ECON.; German economist and financial executive; b. 27 Aug. 1919, Berlin; m. Margareta Spangl; three c.; ed. Leipzig and Vienna Univs.; mil. service 1937-45; Economist, Austrian Inst. for Econ. Research 1948; Asst., then Deputy Section Head, Fed. Ministry of Econ. Affairs 1952; Man. Dir. Gemeinschaft zum Schutz der deutschen Sparer 1957; Dir. Nat. Econ. and Econ. Trends, EEC Comm., Brussels 1960, also Chair. EEC Cttee. of Experts for Business Cycle Analysis and of Working Parties on Econ. Budgets, Cyclical Statistics and Econ. Tendency Surveys 1960; mem. Short Term Econ. Policy and Budgetary Policy Cttees.; alt. mem. Monetary Cttee.; Man. Econ. and Research Dept., European Investment Bank (EIB) 1967-72, Vice-Pres., Vice-Chair. Bd. of Dirs. 1972-84, Hon. Vice-Pres. Aug. 1984-. *Publications:* numerous works on econs. investment and related subjects. *Address:* c/o European Investment Bank, 100 Boulevard Konrad Adenauer, L-2950, Luxembourg.

STEGER, Dr. Norbert; Austrian lawyer and politician; b. 6 March 1944, Vienna; s. of Karl and Anna Steger; m. Margarete Steger 1970; ed. Univ. of Vienna; started private law office, Vienna 1975; mem. FPÖ (Austrian Freedom Party) Fed. Exec. 1974, Deputy Chair. 1978, Chair. 1980; mem. Nationalrat 1979-; Vice-Chancellor and Fed. Minister of Commerce, Trade and Industry 1983-86. *Leisure interests:* music, skiing, basketball. *Address:* Alserstrasse 47/33, A-1080 Vienna, Austria.

STEGER, Otfried; German civil engineer and politician; b. 25 Sept. 1926, Wechselberg, Saxony; Gen. Dir. Electrical Enterprise 1959-63; Head of Elec. Eng. Industry in Econ. Council 1963-65; Cand. mem., Cen. Cttee. SED 1967-71, mem. 1971-; Minister for Electrical Eng. and Electronics 1965-82; mem. Volkskammer 1976-; Vaterländischer Verdiensterden in Gold, and other decorations. *Address:* c/o Ministerrat, Berlin, German Democratic Republic.

STEGMANN, Johannes Augustus, D.SC., D.COMM.; South African business executive; b. 15 Oct. 1926, Bloemfontein; s. of late J. A. Stegmann; m. Myra de Villiers 1955; two s. two d.; ed. Cen. High School, Bloemfontein, Witwatersrand Univ. and Univ. of Pretoria; Pretoria Municipality 1948-52; Gen. Electric, U.S.A. 1949-50; joined Sasol Ltd. 1952, C.E.O. 1976, Chair. 1987-; Fellow Inst. of Marketing Man. 1987-; Hon. Prof. Dept. of Business Econs., Univ. of Pretoria 1982-; several hon degrees; one of Business Times Top Five Businessmen of 1979. *Leisure interests:* music, arts, *Address:* Sasol Ltd., P.O. Box 5486, Johannesburg 2000, South Africa.

STEGMUELLER, Wolfgang, D.PHIL., DR. RER. POL.; Austrian/German professor of philosophy, logic and theory of science; b. 3 June 1923, Natters,

Austria; s. of Dr. Alfred Stegmueller and Antonia Stegmueller; m. 1987; Lecturer in Philosophy, Univ. of Innsbruck 1949-56, Titular Prof. 1956-57; Visiting Prof., Univ. of Kiel 1957-58, Univ. of Bonn 1958; Prof., Munich Univ. 1958-; Visiting Prof., Univ. of Pa. 1962-63, 1964; Corresp. mem. Austrian Acad. of Sciences 1966; mem. Bayer Acad. of Sciences 1967-; mem. Int. Inst. of Philosophy 1973-. *Publications:* Metaphysik, Wissenschaft, Skepsis 1969, Wahrheitsproblem 1970, Unvollständigkeit und Unentscheidbarkeit 1970, Theorienstrukturen und Dynamik 1973, Personelle Wahrscheinlichkeit und Rationale Entscheidung 1973, Statistisches Schliessen und Statistische Begründung 1973, Hauptströmungen der Gegenwartsphilosophie 1979, The Structuralist View of Theories 1979, Rationale Rekonstruktion von Wissenschaftsphilosophie 1979, Neue Wege der Wissenschaftsphilosophie 1980, Strukturtypen der Logik 1984, Die Entwicklung des Strukturalismus seit 1973 1986, Hauptströmungen der Gegenwartsphilosophie 1987. *Leisure interest:* classical music. *Address:* Seminar für Philosophie, Logik und Wissenschaftstheorie, Ludwigstrasse 31, 8000 Munich 22 (Office); Hügelstrasse 4, D-8032 Gräfelfing, Federal Republic of Germany (Home). *Telephone:* 2180 3469 (Office).

STEIGER, Rod; American actor; b. 14 April 1925, W. Hampton, N.Y.; s. of Frederick Steiger and Lorraine Driver; m. 1st Sally Gracie 1952; m. 2nd Claire Bloom (q.v.) 1959 (divorced), one d.; m. 3rd Sherry Nelson 1973 (divorced 1979); m. 4th Paula Ellis 1986; ed. public schools; Berlin Film Festival Award 1964; British Film Acad. Award; Acad. Award (Oscar) Best Actor 1967. *Stage appearances include:* Night Music 1951, An Enemy of the People 1953, Rashomon 1959. *Numerous film appearances include:* On the Waterfront 1953, Big Knife 1955, Oklahoma 1956, Jubal 1957, Across the Bridge 1958, Al Capone 1959, Seven Thieves 1959, The Mark 1960, The World in my Pocket 1960, The Tiger Among Us 1961, The Longest Day 1961, Convicts 4 1961, The Time of Indifference 1962, Hands on the City 1963, The Pawnbroker 1964, The Loved One 1964, Doctor Zhivago 1966, In the Heat of the Night 1967, No Way to Treat a Lady 1968, The Illustrated Man 1968, The Sergeant 1968, Three into Two Won't Go 1969, Waterloo 1970, The Lolly Madonna War, Lucky Luciano 1973, The Heroes 1974, Les innocents aux mains sales 1975, Hennessy 1975, W.C. Fields and Me 1976, Jesus of Nazareth (TV) 1977, F.I.S.T. 1978, The Amityville Horror 1979, The Chosen 1980, Lion of the Desert 1981, The Magic Mountain 1982, Portrait of a Hitman 1984, The Naked Face 1985, The January Man 1988, American Gothic 1988. *Address:* c/o The Gersh Agency, 222 North Canon Drive, Beverly Hills, Calif. 90210, U.S.A.

STEIN, Elias M., M.A., PH.D.; American professor of mathematics; b. 13 Jan. 1931, Antwerp, Belgium; s. of Elkan Stein and Chana Goldman Stein; m. Elly Intrator 1959; one s. one d.; ed. Univ. of Chicago; Instr. M.I.T. 1956-58; Asst. Prof. Univ. of Chicago 1958-61, Assoc. Prof. 1961-63; mem. Inst. for Advanced Study, Princeton 1962-63, 1984-85; Prof. Princeton Univ. 1963-, Chair. of Dept. of Math. 1968-70, 1985-; mem. American Acad. of Arts and Sciences, N.A.S., American Mathematical Soc.; A.M.S. Steele Prize 1984; Guggenheim Fellow 1976-77, 1984-85. *Publications:* Singular Integrals and Differentiability Properties of Functions 1970, Topics in Harmonic Analysis Related to the Littlewood-Paley Theory 1970, Introduction to Fourier Analysis on Euclidean Spaces (with G. Weiss) 1971. *Address:* Department of Mathematics, Princeton University, Fine Hall, Washington Road, Princeton, N.J. 08544 (Office); 132 Dodds Lane, Princeton, N.J. 08544, U.S.A. (Home). *Telephone:* (609) 452-3497 (Office); (609) 924-9335 (Home).

STEIN, Herbert, PH.D.; American economist; b. 27 Aug. 1916, Detroit; s. of David and Jessie Stein; m. Mildred Fishman 1937; one s. one d.; ed. Williams Coll. and Univ. of Chicago; Economist, U.S. Govt. 1938-45; Economist, Cttee. for Econ. Devt. 1945-48, Assoc. Dir. of Research 1948-56, Dir. of Research 1956-66, Vice-Pres. and Chief Economist 1966-67; Sr. Fellow, Brookings Inst. 1967-69; mem. President's Council of Econ. Advisers 1969-, Chair. 1972-74; A. Willis Robertson Prof. of Econs., Univ. of Va. 1971-84; Sr. Fellow American Enterprise Inst. 1977-87; mem. Bd. of Contributors Wall Street Journal 1974-; mem. Econ. Advisory Panel Congressional Budget Office 1976-; mem. Pres.'s Econ. Policy Advisory Bd. 1981-, Blue Ribbon Comm. on Defence Man. 1985-86; mem. American Acad. of Arts and Sciences 1983-; Pres. Southern Econ. Asscn. 1983-84; Co-Chair. Comm. to Fight Inflation 1982; mem. Exec. Cttee., Cttee. on the Present Danger; fmr. Columnist Scripps-Howard Newspapers; frequent contrib. to Fortune Magazine; Ed. AEI Economist 1977-; Dir. Reynolds Metals Co.; Hon. LL.D. (Rider Coll.) 1971, (Hartford Univ.) 1973, (Williams Coll.) 1980, (Roanoke Coll.) 1984. *Publications:* The Fiscal Revolution in America 1969, On the Brink (with Benjamin Stein) 1977, Moneypower (with Benjamin Stein) 1980, Presidential Economics 1984, Washington Bedtime Stories 1986. *Address:* 1704 Yorktown Drive, Charlottesville, Va. 22901, U.S.A. (Home).

STEIN, Peter Gonville, F.B.A.; British professor of law; b. 29 May 1926, Liverpool; s. of Walter O. Stein and Effie D. Walker; m. 1st Janet Chamberlain 1953, three d.; m. 2nd Anne Howard 1978, one step-s.; ed. Liverpool Coll., Gonville and Caius Coll. Cambridge and Univ. of Pavia, Italy; served R.N. 1944-47; admitted solicitor 1951; Prof. of Jurisprudence, Univ. of Aberdeen 1956-68; Regius Prof. of Civil Law, Univ. of Cambridge and Fellow of Queens' Coll. Cambridge 1968-; mem. Univ. Grants Cttee. 1971-76; J.P., Cambridge 1970-; Fellow, Winchester Coll. 1976-; Pres. Soc.

of Public Teachers of Law 1980-81; mem. U.S.-U.K. Educational Comm. 1985-; Foreign Fellow, Accademia Nazionale dei Lincei, Accademia di Scienze Morali e Politiche di Napoli, Accad. degli Intronati di Siena; Dr. Juris h.c. (Göttingen) 1980. *Publications:* Regulae Iuris: from juristic rules to legal maxims 1966, Legal Values in Western Society (with J. Shand) 1974, Legal Evolution 1980, Legal Institutions 1984, The Character and Influence of the Roman Civil Law: essays 1988. *Leisure interest:* hill walking. *Address:* Queens' College, Cambridge, CB3 9ET; Wimpole Cottage, Wimpole Road, Great Eversden, Cambridge, CB3 7HR, England (Home). *Telephone:* (0223) 335569 (Coll.); (0223) 262349 (Home).

STEINBERG, Saul; American (b. Romanian) artist and architect; b. 15 June 1914, Romanic-Sarat, Romania; s. of Maurice and Rosa (née Jacobson) Steinberg; m. Hedda Lindenberg Sterne 1944; ed. Milan Polytechnic School; Cartoonist 1936-39; practising architect 1939-41; moved to U.S. 1942; illustrator for the New Yorker 1942-; represented in Museum of Modern Art N.Y.; numerous one-man exhbns. 1953-; Gold Medal, American Acad. of Arts and Sciences 1974. *Publications:* All in Line 1945, The Art of Living 1949, The Passport 1954, The Labyrinth 1960, The Inspector 1973. *Address:* c/o Sidney Janis Gallery, 110 W. 57th Street, New York, N.Y. 10019, U.S.A.

STEINBERGER, Jack, PH.D.; American physicist; b. 25 May 1921, Germany; s. of Ludwig Steinberger and Bertha (May) Steinberger; m. 1st Joan Beauregard 1943, 2nd Cynthia Eve Alff 1961; three s. one d.; ed. Univ. of Chicago; Visiting mem. Inst. of Advanced Study, Princeton 1948-49; Research Asst., Univ. of Calif. (Berkeley) 1949-50; Prof. Columbia Univ., New York 1950-71, Higgins Prof. 1967-71; Staff mem. Centre Européen pour la Recherche Nucléaire 1968-; mem. N.A.S. 1967-, Heidelberg Acad. of Sciences 1967-, American Acad. of Arts and Sciences 1969-; Hon. Prof., Heidelberg 1968; Pres.'s Science Medal, U.S. 1988, Nobel Prize in Physics (jtly.) 1988. *Publications:* Muon Decay 1949, Pi Zero Meson 1950, Spin of Pion 1951, Parity of Pion 1954, 1959, Z° Hyperon 1957, Properties of "Strange Particles" 1957-64, Two Neutrinos 1962, CP Violating Effects in K° Decay 1966-74, High Energy Neutrino Physics 1975-83, Preparation of Lep Detector 1981. *Leisure interests:* mountaineering, flute, cruising. *Address:* CERN, Geneva 23; 25 Chemin des Merles, 1213 Onex, Geneva, Switzerland (Home). *Telephone:* 934612 (Home).

STEINEM, Gloria, B.A.; American writer, journalist and feminist activist; b. 25 March, 1934, Toledo; d. of Leo and Ruth (Nuneviller) Steinem; ed. Smith Coll.; Chester Bowles Asian Fellow, India 1957-58; Co-Dir., Dir. Ind. Research Service, Cambridge, Mass. and New York 1959-60; editorial asst., contributing ed., ed., freelance writer various nat. and New York publs. 1960-; Co-Founder New York Magazine 1968, Ms Magazine 1971 (Ed. 1971-87, columnist 1980-); active various civil rights and peace campaigns including United Farmworkers, Vietnam War Tax Protest, Cttee. for the Legal Defense of Angela Davis and political campaigns of Adlai Stevenson, Robert Kennedy, Eugene McCarthy, Shirley Chisholm, George McGovern; Co-Founder and Chair Bd. Women's Action Alliance 1970-; Convenor, mem. Nat. Advisory Cttee. Nat. Women's Political Caucus 1971-; Co-Founder, mem. Bd. Ms. Foundation for Women; founding mem. Coalition of Labor Union Women; Penney-Missouri Journalism Award 1970; Ohio Gov.'s Award for Journalism 1972; named Woman of the Year, McCall's Magazine 1972; Woodrow Wilson Int. Center for Scholars Fellow 1977. *Publications:* The Thousand Indias 1957, The Beach Book 1963, Marilyn 1986; contribs. to various anthologies. *Address:* c/o Ms Magazine, 119 W. 40th Street, New York, N.Y. 10018, U.S.A.

STEINER, George, D.PHIL., F.R.S.L.; American writer and scholar; b. 23 April 1929, Paris, France; s. of Dr. and Mrs. F. G. Steiner; m. Zara Shakow 1955; one s. one d.; ed. Univs. of Paris and Chicago, Harvard Univ. and Balliol Coll., Oxford; Editorial Staff The Economist, London 1952-56; Fellow, Inst. for Advanced Study, Princeton 1956-58; Gauss Lecturer, Princeton Univ. 1959-60; Fellow and Dir. of English Studies, Churchill Coll., Cambridge 1961-69, Extraordinary Fellow 1969-; Albert Schweitzer Visiting Prof., New York Univ. 1966-67; Visiting Prof. Yale Univ. 1970-71; Prof. of English and Comparative Literature, Univ. of Geneva 1974-; delivered Massey Lectures 1974, Ransom Memorial Lectures 1976, F. D. Maurice Lectures, Univ. of London 1984; Leslie Stephen Lecturer, Cambridge Univ. 1985; W. P. Ker Lecturer, Univ. of Glasgow 1986; Robertson Lecturer, Courtauld Inst., London 1985; Page-Barbour Lectures, Univ. of Va. 1987; Pres. The English Assen. 1975-76; Corresp. mem. German Acad.; Hon. D.Litt. (Univ. of East Anglia) 1976, (Univ. of Louvain) 1979, (Bristol) 1989; O. Henry Award 1958, Jewish Chronical Book Award 1968, Zabel Prize of Nat. Inst. of Arts and Letters 1970, Le Prix du Souvenir 1974, King Albert Medal of the Royal Belgian Acad. 1982; Chevalier, Légion d'honneur. *Publications:* Tolstoy or Dostoevsky 1959, The Death of Tragedy 1961, Anno Domini: Three Stories 1964, Language and Silence 1967, Extraterritorial 1971, In Bluebeard's Castle 1971, The Sporting Scene: White Knights in Reykjavík 1973, Fields of Force 1974, A Nostalgia for the Absolute (Massey Lectures) 1974, After Babel 1975, Heidegger 1978, On Difficulty and Other Essays 1978, The Portage of A.H. to San Cristobal 1981; Ed. Penguin Book of Modern Verse Translation 1967, Antigones 1984, George Steiner: A Reader 1984, Real Presences: Is there anything in what we say? 1989. *Leisure interests:* chess, music, mountain walking. *Address:* 32 Barrow Road, Cambridge, England; Harvard Club, New York, N.Y., U.S.A.

STEINKÜHLER, Franz; German trade union executive; b. 20 May 1937, Würzburg; m.; one c.; trained as toolmaker and became Chief of Production Planning 1951-60; joined IG Metall 1951, mem. Youth Group 1952, Chair. Youth Del. 1953, numerous local exec. positions 1953-63, Sec. Regional Exec. Bd., Stuttgart 1963-72, Dir. Stuttgart Region 1972-83, Vice-Pres. IG Metall 1983-86, Pres. Oct. 1986-; mem. Int. Metalworkers' Fed. June 1987-; mem. SPD 1951-, Vice-Pres. in Baden-Württemberg 1975-83, mem. Programme Cttee. of Exec. Bd. 1984; Workers' Rep. VW-AG, Wolfsburg Mannesmann AG, Supervisory Bd., Daimler Benz AG Supervisory Bd.; mem. State Tribunal of Baden-Württemberg 1983; Hon. Senator Univ. of Konstanz 1983. *Address:* Industriegewerkschaft Metall, Postfach 11 1031, 6000 Frankfurt 11, Federal Republic of Germany.

STEJSKAL, Jan; Czechoslovak politician; b. 1933, Mokrosuky, Klatovy Dist.; mem. CP of Czechoslovakia (CPCZ) 1953-, mem. Cen. Cttee. Econ. Comm., Cen. Control and Auditing Comm.; worked at Int. Bank for Int. Co-operation, Moscow 1971-75; political worker for CPCZ Cen. Cttee. 1975-79; Chair. Czechoslovak State Bank 1981-88; Minister of Finance Oct. 1988-; mem. State Planning Comm., Czechoslovak People's Control Cttee. *Address:* Ministry of Finance, Prague, Czechoslovakia.

STEMPEL, Robert C., M.B.A.; American engineer; b. 15 July 1933, Trenton, N.J.; ed. Worcester Polytechnic Inst., Mass., Mich. State Univ.; joined Oldsmobile 1958, Constructor, undercarriage devt., Driving Track Engineer 1964, Engineer 1969, Deputy Chief Engineer 1972; Asst. to Pres. Gen. Motors 1973-74; Chief Engineer for Engines and Components, Chevrolet 1974; Dir. Construction Dept. 1975; Gen. Dir. Pontiac 1978-80; Vice-Pres. Gen. Motors 1978-87, Pres. and C.O.O. Sept. 1987-; Chair. Bd. and Gen. Dir. Adam Opel AG, Fed. Repub. of Germany 1980-82; Head of Chevrolet Div., Gen. Motors 1982-, Head of Buick-Oldsmobile-Cadillac Group 1984-; mem. Soc. of Automotive Engineers, American Soc. of Mechanical Engineers. *Address:* General Motors Corporation, 3044 West Grand Boulevard, Detroit, Mich. 48202, U.S.A. (Office).

STENBÄCK, Pär Olav Mikael, M.A.; Finnish international administrator and fmr. politician; b. 12 Aug. 1941, Porvoo (Borgå); s. of Arne Mikael and Rakel Stenbäck; m. Liv Sissel Lund 1970; two s.; Ed. with Finnish Broadcasting Co. 1964-69; Chair. Svensk Ungdom (youth org. of Swedish People's Party of Finland) 1967-70; Chair. Swedish People's Party 1977-85; Minister of Educ. 1979-82, of Foreign Affairs 1982-83; Dir. Hanaholmen Swedish-Finnish Culture Centre 1974-85; Sec.-Gen. Finnish Red Cross 1985-88; Sec. Gen. League of Red Cross and Red Crescent Socs., Geneva 1988-; Grand Cross, Royal Order of Northern Star (Sweden), Grand Cross of the Falcon (Iceland), Grand Cross St. Olav (Norway), Grand Cross of Dannebrog (Denmark), Commdr. of the Order of the Lion (Finland). *Leisure interests:* literature, fishing, stamps. *Address:* 17 chemin des Crêts, Petit-Saconnex, P.O. Box 372, CH-1211 Geneva 19, Switzerland. *Telephone:* 41-22-345580 (Office).

STENLUND, Bengt Gustav Verner, D.TECH.; Finnish professor of polymer technology; b. 17 Aug. 1939, Kristinestad; s. of Gustav Stenlund and Linda Hofman; m. Kerstin Ottosson 1964; one s.; Research Assoc. The Finnish Pulp and Paper Research Inst. 1965-77; Acting Prof. of Polymer Tech., Åbo Akad. 1977-79, Prof. 1979-, Dean. Dept. of Chemical Eng. 1982-85, Vice-Rector 1985-88, Rector 1988-; Chair. Council of Tech., Finnish Acad. of Sciences 1986-88; mem. Bd. Nordic Foundation of Tech. 1987-88; mem. Scientific Del. of Finnish Chemical Industry 1985-; mem. Finnish Acad. of Eng., Royal Swedish Acad. of Eng. *Publications:* Gel Chromatography of Liguosulfonates 1970; about 50 publs. about natural and synthetic polymers. *Leisure interests:* art, archipelago. *Address:* University Åbo Akademi, 20500 Åbo, Finland. *Telephone:* 358-21-654100.

STENNIS, John Cornelius, B.S., LL.B.; American politician; b. 3 Aug. 1901, Kemper Co., Miss.; s. of Hampton Howell and Cornelia Adams Stennis; m. Coy H. Stennis 1929; one s. one d.; ed. Mississippi State Coll. and Univ. of Virginia Law School; mem. Miss. House of Reps. from Kemper County 1928-32; Dist. Prosecuting Attorney, Sixteenth Judicial Dist. 1931 and 1935; appt. Circuit Judge, Sixteenth Judicial District 1937 and elected 1938, 1946; U.S. Senator from Mississippi 1947-89, Pres. U.S. Senate protempore 1987-88; Chair. Armed Services Cttee. (Senate) -1980; Hon. LL.D. (Miltsaps Coll.) 1957, (Wyoming Univ.) 1962, (Miss. Coll.) 1969, (Bellhaven Coll.) 1972, (William Carey Coll.) 1975; Democrat. *Leisure interests:* hunting, fishing, reading, sporting events. *Address:* Dekalb, Miss. 39328, U.S.A.

STENT, Gunther Siegmund, PH.D.; American professor of molecular biology; b. 28 March 1924, Berlin, Germany; s. of George and Elizabeth Stensch; m. Inga Loftsdottir 1951; one s.; ed. Hyde Park School, Chicago and Univ. of Illinois; Research Asst. U.S. War Production Bd., Synthetic Rubber Research Programme 1944-48; Document Analyst, Field Intelligence Agency, Occupied Germany 1946-47; Merck Postdoctoral Fellow Calif. Inst. of Tech. 1948-50; American Cancer Soc. Postdoctoral Fellow Univ. of Copenhagen and Inst. Pasteur, Paris 1950-52; Asst. Research Biochemist Univ. of Calif., Berkeley 1952-56, Assoc. Prof. of Bacteriology 1956-59, Prof. of Molecular Biology 1959-, Chair. Molecular Biology and Dir. Virus Lab. 1980-86; Natural Science Foundation Sr. Fellow Univs. of Kyoto and Cambridge 1960-61; Guggenheim Fellow Harvard Medical School 1969-70; mem. N.A.S., American Acad. of Arts and Sciences,

American Philosophical Soc.; External mem. Max Planck Inst. for Molecular Genetics, Berlin 1966-; Fellow, Inst. for Advanced Studies, Berlin 1985-; Hon. D.Sc. (York, Toronto Univs.) 1984. *Publications:* Molecular Biology of Bacterial Viruses 1963, Phage and the Origins of Molecular Biology 1966, The Coming of the Golden Age 1969, Molecular Genetics 1970, Function and Formation of Neural Systems 1977, Paradoxes of Progress 1978, Morality as a Biological Phenomenon 1978, Shinri to Satori 1981. *Leisure interest:* car repairs. *Address:* Department of Molecular Biology, University of California, Berkeley, Calif. 94720 (Office); 145 Purdue Avenue, Berkeley, Calif. 94708, U.S.A. (Home). *Telephone:* (415) 642-5214 (Office).

ŠTĚPÁN, Miroslav; Czechoslovak politician; b. 5 Aug. 1945, Louny, N. Bohemia; ed. agricultural coll.; fmr. technician, Research Inst. of Agricultural Tech., Prague; joined Communist Party of Czechoslovakia (CPCZ) 1965, mem. Presidium Cen. Cttee. CPCZ 1988-; Chair. Socialist Youth Union's Prague City Cttee. 1974; Deputy to House of the People 1981-, Chair. Foreign Relations Cttee. 1986-. *Address:* Central Committee of Communist Party of Czechoslovakia, Nábř Ludvíka, Svobody 12, 125 11 Prague, Czechoslovakia.

STEPANOV, Vladimir Sevastyanovich, CAND.HIST.SC.; Soviet politician and diplomatist; b. 1927; ed. Moscow Inst. of Int. Relations; Head of Section, Sec. of Komsomol Cen. Cttee. of Karelo-Finnish S.S.R. 1951-55; mem. CPSU 1952-; Pres. of 'Lenin's Path' Collective farm, Karelia 1955-58; Sec. of Karelian CPSU Dist. Ctte. 1961-63; diplomatic work 1963-73; Amb. to Finland 1973-79; First Deputy Pres. of Council of Ministers of Karelian A.S.S.R. 1979-84; First Sec. of CPSU Karelian Dist. 1984-; mem. of CPSU Cen. Cttee. 1986-; Deputy to U.S.S.R. Supreme Soviet. *Address:* The Kremlin, Moscow, U.S.S.R.

STEPHANI, Christakis, B.COMM., F.C.A.; Cypriot banker; b. 28 Sept. 1926, Cyprus; m. Vera Halliday 1951; one s. two d.; ed. London School of Econs.; Accountant-Gen. of the Repub. of Cyprus 1960-65; Gov. Cen. Bank of Cyprus 1965-82; Area Exec., Arab Bank Ltd., Cyprus. *Address:* 7 P. Nirvana Street, Nicosia, Cyprus.

STEPHANOPOULOS, Constantine (see Stefanopoulos).

STEPHEN, Rt. Hon. Sir Ninian Martin, A.K., G.C.M.G., G.C.V.O., K.B.E.; Australian lawyer and administrator; b. 15 June 1923; s. of the late Frederick and Barbara (née Cruickshank) Stephen; m. Valery Mary Sinclair 1949; five d.; ed. George Watson's School, Edinburgh Acad., St. Paul's School, London, Chillon Coll., Switzerland, Scotch Coll., Melbourne, Melbourne Univ.; served World War II, Australian Army; admitted as barrister and solicitor, Victoria 1949; Q.C. 1966; Judge, Supreme Court, Victoria 1970; Justice, High Court, Australia 1972-82; Gov.-Gen. of Australia 1982-89; Hon. Bencher Gray's Inn 1981; K.St.J. 1982. *Address:* Flat 1, 193 Domain Road, South Yarra, Vic., Australia.

STEPHENS, Olin James II; American naval architect and yacht designer; b. 13 April 1908, New York City; s. of Roderick Stephens and Marguerite Dulon; m. Florence Reynolds 1930; two s.; ed. M.I.T.; Partner, Sparkman & Stephens 1928; Chief Designer, Vice-Pres. and Dir., Sparkman & Stephens Inc. 1929-64, Chief Designer, Pres. and Dir. 1964-78, Chair and Dir. Jan. 1979-85, Dir. Emer. 1987-; Chair. Int. Tech. Cttee. of Offshore Racing Council 1967-74, 1977-79, Councillor of honour 1979; Chair. of Research Cttee. of Offshore Racing Council 1980; mem. Jt. Cttee. of Soc. of Naval Architects and U.S. Yacht Racing Union on Yacht Capsize 1980-85; mem. Royal Designers for Industry, London; Hon. mem. and Fellow, Soc. of Naval Architects and Marine Engineers; Hon. M.S. (Stevens Inst. of Tech.) 1945; Hon. M.A. (Brown Univ.) 1959; some yachts designed: Dorade 1930, Stormy Weather 1934, (with W. Starling Burgess) Ranger 1937, Vim, Goose, Bolero 1938, Finisterre 1954, Columbia 1958, Constellation 1964, Intrepid 1967, Morning Cloud 1969, 1971, 1973, 1975, Courageous 1974, Flyer 1977, Freedom 1979. *Leisure interest:* computer studies. *Address:* Sparkman and Stephens Inc., 79 Madison Avenue, New York, N.Y. 10016; P.O. Box 346, Putney, Vt., 05346, U.S.A.

STEPHENS, Robert; British actor; b. 14 July 1931; m. Maggie Smith (q.v.) 1967 (dissolved 1975); two s.; mem. English Stage Co., Royal Court 1956-62; Nat. Theatre Co. 1963, 1978-. *Stage appearances include:* Hay Fever 1964, The Royal Hunt of the Sun 1964, Much Ado About Nothing 1965, Lindsay in Armstrongs' Last Goodnight 1965, Tom Wrench (Trelawney of the Well's) 1965, Leonido (A Bond Honoured) 1966, Harold Goringe (Black Comedy) 1966, Kurt (The Dance of Death) 1967, Vershinin (Three Sisters) 1967, Jacques (As You Like It) 1967, Tartuffe (Tartuffe) 1967, Frederick (Home and Beauty) 1968, Beaux Stratagem 1970, Design for Living 1970, Private Lives 1972, The Seagull, Ghosts, Hamlet 1974, Murderer, Zoo Story, Sherlock Holmes 1975, Othello, Private Lives 1976, The Cherry Orchard 1978, Brand 1978, The Double Dealer 1978, Has "Washington" Legs 1978, Pygmalion 1979, Othello (S. Africa) 1982, W.C.P.C. 1982, A Midsummer Night's Dream 1983, Inner Voices 1983, Cinderella 1983, Three Passion Plays 1985, Light Up the Sky 1985; directed one of a triple bill A Most Unwarrantable Intrusion 1968; appeared in and co-directed Macrune's Guevara 1969; directed and appeared in Apropos the Falling Sleet. *Films:* The Prime of Miss Jean Brodie 1969, The Private Life of Sherlock Holmes 1970, The Asphyx 1972, Travels with my Aunt 1972, Luther 1972, The Duellists 1977, La nuit tous les chats sont gris

1977, The Holocaust 1978, The Shout 1978, Alexander the Great 1980, Les jeux de la comtesse 1980, Dolingen de Gratz 1980, Year of the French 1982, Ill Fares the Land 1982, Puccini 1984, Comrades 1985, High Season 1986, Empire of the Sun 1987, The Fruit Machine 1988, Henry V 1989; numerous TV and radio plays including series Hells Bells (BBC TV) and Three Passion Plays (Channel 4 TV) 1984-85, Lizzie's Pictures (BBC TV series) 1986, Fortunes of War (BBC TV series) 1987, Shostakovich 1987. *Address:* c/o Film Rights Ltd., 4 New Burlington Place, Regent Street, London, W1X 2AS, England. *Telephone:* 01-437 7151.

STEPHENSON, Gordon, C.B.E., M.C.P., B.ARCH., L.F.R.A.I.A., L.F.R.A.P.I., F.R.I.B.A., F.L.I., F.R.T.P.I.; British architect and town planner; b. 6 June 1908, Liverpool; s. of Francis Edwin and Eva Eliza Stephenson; m. Flora Bartlett Crockett 1938 (died 1979); three d.; ed. Liverpool Inst., Univs. of Liverpool and Paris, M.I.T.; with Le Corbusier and Pierre Jeanneret 1930-32; Lecturer, Univ. of Liverpool 1932-36; Commonwealth Fellow, M.I.T. 1936-38; Master, Architectural Assen. School of Architecture 1939-40; Div. Architect, Royal Ordinance Factory and War Hostels 1940-42; Sr. Research Officer and Chief Planning Officer, Ministry of Town and Country Planning 1942-47; Prof. of Civic Design and Ed. Town Planning Review, Univ. of Liverpool 1948-53; Consultant to Govt. of W. Australia, City of Perth and Univ. of W. Australia 1954-55; consultant to cities of Toronto, Ottawa and Kingston, Ontario, and Halifax, Nova Scotia 1955-60; Prof. of Town and Regional Planning, Univ. of Toronto 1955-60; Consultant Architect and Prof. of Architecture, Univ. of W. Australia 1960-72; Emer. Prof. 1972-; mem. Nat. Capital Planning Cttee., Canberra 1967-73; Hon. LL.D. (Univ. of W. Australia), Hon. D.Arch. (Univ. of Melbourne), Hon. D.Sc. (Flinders Univ.); Hon. D. Univ. (Murdoch). *Publications:* (with Flora C. Stephenson) Community Centres 1940, (with J. A. Hepburn) Plan for the Metropolitan Region of Perth and Fremantle 1955, A Redevelopment Study of Halifax, Nova Scotia 1957, (with G. G. Muirhead) A Planning Study of Kingston, Ontario 1959, (with R. J. Ferguson) Physical Planning Report, Murdoch University 1973, The Design of Central Perth 1975, Joondalup Regional Centre 1977, Planning for the University of Western Australia: 1914-1970 1986. *Address:* 55/14 Albert Street, Claremont, Western Australia 6010. *Telephone:* 09-385-2309.

STEPHENSON, Hugh; British journalist; b. 18 July 1938, Simla, India; s. of late Sir Hugh Stephenson G.B.E., K.C.M.G., C.I.E., C.V.O. and Lady Stephenson; m. Auriol Stevens 1962; two s. one d.; ed. New Coll., Oxford, Univ. of California, Berkeley; served diplomatic service, London and Bonn 1964-68; with The Times, London 1969-81, Ed., The Times Business News 1971-81; Ed. The New Statesman 1982-86; Prof. of Journalism, The City Univ. 1986-. *Publications:* The Coming Clash 1972, Mrs. Thatcher's First Year 1980, Claret and Chips 1982. *Address:* Graduate Centre for Journalism, 223-227 St. John Street, London, E.C.1, England.

STĘPIEŃ, Zofia; Polish politician; b. 1 Aug. 1939, Częstochowa; warping machine operator, Stradom Flax Industry Works, Częstochowa 1963-; mem. Polish United Workers' Party (PZPR) 1965-; fmr. First Sec. Basal Party Org., mem. Exec. PZPR Plant Cttee., Stradom Flax Industry Works; mem. PZPR Town Cttee., Częstochowa; alt. mem. PZPR Cen. Cttee. 1981-84, mem. 1984-, mem. Political Bureau of PZPR Cen. Cttee. 1986-89; Head, Comm. for Family Matters of PZPR Cen. Cttee. 1987-; Sec. PZPR Cen. Cttee. 1989-; Knight's Cross Order of Polonia Restituta and other awards. *Address:* Komitet Centralny PZPR, ul. Nowy Świat 6, 00-497 Warsaw, Poland.

STERCKEN, Hans, DR.PHIL.; German politician; b. 2 Sept. 1923, Aachen; s. of Josef Stercken and Johanna Jeuckens; m. Annemaire Wittelsberger 1953; one s. four d.; ed. Kaiser-Karl-Gymnasium, Aachen and Univ. of Bonn; Ed. Bonner Rundschau 1952-54; Head of Div. Press and Information Office of Fed. Govt. 1954-68; Adviser to Govt. of Turkey 1957-58, to Govts. of Cameroon, Guinea, Mauritania and Senegal 1965; Man. Dir. Fed. Centre for Political Educ. 1969-76; mem. Bundestag (for Aachen) 1976-, Chair. Cttee. on Foreign Affairs 1985-; Pres. German Africa Foundation 1978-86; mem. Exec. Cttee. IPU 1983-88; Pres. Inter-Parl. Council of IPU 1983-88; Pres. Inter-Parl. Council of IPU 1985-88; decorations from Fed. Repub. of Germany, Austria, Belgium, Cameroon, France, Greece, Guinea, Italy, Portugal, Spain, Order of Malta, German Red Cross; Christian Democrat. *Publications:* De Gaulle hat gesagt 1968, Vive l'Europe 1969, Zurück zum Leben 1980. *Address:* Heinrich-Lübke Strasse 9, 5300 Bonn 1, Federal Republic of Germany. *Telephone:* (0228) 231833.

STERKY, Håkan Karl August, DR. TECH.; Swedish electrical engineer; b. 7 April 1900, Stockholm; s. of Carl Edvard Sterky and Hilma Almén; m. Kerstin Tottie 1927; two s. one d.; ed. Royal Inst. of Tech., Stockholm, and Harvard Univ., Cambridge, Mass., U.S.A.; Radio engineer, ASEA 1923-24; Transmission engineer, Royal Bd. of Swedish Waterfalls 1926-27, Svenska Radio AB 1927-31, and L. M. Ericsson Telephone Co. 1931-33; Head of Design Dept., L. M. Ericsson Telephone Co. 1933-37; Asst. Prof. of Telegraphy and Telephony 1934-37; Prof. pro tem. 1937-39, Ord. Prof. 1939-42, and Vice-Prin. 1942, of Royal Inst. of Tech., Stockholm; Dir.-Gen. Royal Bd. of Swedish Telecommunications 1942-65; Pres. Swedish Nat. Comm. Int. Scientific Radio Union 1946-69, Bd. of Trustees, Swedish Nat. Comm. of Int. Electro-technical Comm. 1948-71; mem. Bd. Nat. Museum of Science and Tech. 1942-76, Atomic Energy Co. 1947-69, Pripp Breweries Co. 1950-69, Scania Vabis Co. 1966-72, IBM Swedish Co. 1966-71, Inter-

Union Cttee. on Frequency Allocations for Radio Astronomy and Space Sciences (I.C.S.U.) 1960-72; mem. Royal Swedish Acad. of Eng. Sciences, Royal Swedish Acad. of Sciences, Royal Swedish Acad. of Mil. Sciences, Science Soc. of Uppsala and Danish Acad. of Tech. Sciences; Polhem Gold Medal and Hon. mem. Swedish Assen. of Engineers and Architects; I.V.A. Gold Medal 1969 and First Hon. mem. 1981. *Publications:* The Use of Thermionic Valves for Generating Multiple Frequencies 1930, Methods of Computing and Improving the Complex Effective Attenuation, Load Impedances and Reflexion Coefficients of Electric Wave Filters 1933, Frequency Multiplication and Divison 1937, Puissance et affaiblissement dans les circuits électriques 1940, Fernwirkbetrieb in Stromversorgungs-netzen 1941, Uebertragungsverhältnisse auf bespülten und wahlrufsbetrie-benen Fernsprechleitungen 1943, Telecommunications in Sweden, Present and Future 1950, Past, Present and Future Telecommunication Standardiz-ation 1954, The First Century of Swedish Telecommunications and what we can learn from it 1956, The Foundation of Agriculture and Industry in Modern Sweden 1957, Trends of Development in the Swedish Telecommun-ication Services 1960, Swedish Telecommunications 1965, A Tele-Vision: Community Planning and Telecommunications 1972, A Tele-vision Comes True 1977. *Leisure interests:* skiing, handicraft. *Address:* Larsbergsvägen 46, 18138 Lidingö, Stockholm, Sweden. *Telephone:* 08-7678200.

STERLING, Sir Jeffrey Maurice, Kt., C.B.E.; British business executive; b. 27 Dec. 1934; s. of Harry Sterling and Alice Sterling; m. Dorothy Ann Smith 1985; one d.; ed. Reigate Grammar School, Preston Manor County School and Guildhall School of Music, London; Paul Schweder & Co. (Stock Exchange) 1957-63; Financial Dir. General Guarantee Corpn. 1963-64; Man. Dir. Gula Investments Ltd. 1964-69; Chair. Sterling Guarantee Trust PLC 1969-85, P & O Steam Navigation Co. 1983-, European Ferries Group PLC 1987-; Special Adviser to Sec. of State for Industry 1982-83, to Sec. of State for Trade and Industry 1983-; mem. British Airways Bd. 1979-82; mem. Exec., World ORT Union 1966-, Chair. Org. Cttee. 1969-73; Chair. ORT Tech. Services 1974-; Vice-Pres. British ORT 1973-; Deputy Chair. and Hon. Treasurer London Celebrations Cttee. Queen's Silver Jubilee 1975-83; Chair. Young Vic Co. 1975-83; Chair. of the Govs. Royal Ballet School 1983-; Gov. Royal Ballet 1986-; Vice-Chair. and Chair. of Exec. Motability 1977-. *Leisure interests:* music, swimming, tennis. *Address:* The Peninsular & Oriental Steam Navigation Company, 79 Pall Mall, London, SW1Y 5EJ, England.

STERN, Ernest, M.A., PH.D.; American international official; b. 25 Aug. 1933, Frankfurt, Germany; s. of Henry Stern; m. Zina Gold 1957; ed. Queens Coll., New York, and Fletcher School of Law and Diplomacy; Economist, U.S. Dept. of Commerce 1957-59; Program Economist, U.S. Agency for Int. Devt. (USAID) 1959-63; Instructor, Middle East Tech. Univ. 1960-61; Economist, Office of Pakistan Affairs, USAID 1963-64, Officer in Charge of Pakistan Affairs 1964-64, Asst. Dir. for Devt. Policy USAID India 1965-67, Deputy Dir. USAID Pakistan 1967-68, Deputy Staff Dir. Comm. on Int. Devt. (Pearson Comm.) 1968-69; Lecturer, Woodrow Wilson School of Public and Int. Affairs, Princeton 1971; Sr. Staff mem. Council on Int. Econ. Policy, White House 1971; joined Int. Bank for Reconstruction and Devt. (World Bank) 1972, various posts incl. Deputy Chair. Econ. Cttee., Sr. Adviser on Devt. Policy, Dir. Devt. Policy, then Vice-Pres. S. Asia until 1978; Vice-Pres. Operations, World Bank July 1978-, Sr. Vice-Pres., Operations 1980-87, Sr. Vice-Pres., Finance 1987-; mem. Bd. Advisors Inst. for Int. Econs., Washington D.C.; mem. Advisory Bd. Woodrow Wilson School, Princeton Univ.; William A. Jump Memorial Foundation Meritorious Award 1964, 1966. *Address:* International Bank for Reconstruction and Development, 1818 H Street, N.W., Washington, D.C. 20433; 2323 Wyoming Avenue, N.W., Washington, D.C. 20008, U.S.A. (Home). *Telephone:* (202) 234-7040 (Home).

STERN, Fritz, PH.D.; American historian and professor; b. 2 Feb. 1926, Breslau, Germany; s. of Rudolf A. Stern and Catherine B. Stern; m. Margaret J. Bassett 1947; one s., one d.; ed. Bentley School, New York, Columbia Univ.; Lecturer and Inst. Columbia Univ. 1946-51; Acting Asst. Prof. Cornell Univ. 1951-53; Asst. Prof. Columbia Univ. 1953-57, Assoc. Prof. 1957-63, Full Prof. 1963-67, Seth Low Prof. 1967-; Provost Columbia Univ. 1980-83; Visiting Prof. Free Univ. of Berlin 1954, Yale Univ. 1963, Fondation Nationale des Sciences Politiques, Paris 1979; Consultant U.S. State Dept. 1966-67; mem. OECD team on German Educ. 1971-72; mem. bd. of dirs. German Marshall Fund 1981-, Trilateral Comm. 1983-, Aspen Inst. Berlin 1983-; mem. American Acad. of Arts and Sciences 1969-; Hon. D.Litt. (Oxford) 1985, Lucas Prize (Tübingen) 1984, Lionel Trilling Book Award 1977. *Publications:* The Politics of Cultural Despair: A Study in the Rise of the Germanic Ideology 1961, Gold and Iron: Bismarck, Bleich-roeder, and the Building of the German Empire 1977, The Failure of Illiberalism: Essays in the Political Culture of Modern Germany 1972, Dreams and Delusions: The Drama of German History 1987, ed. The Varieties of History from Voltaire to the Present 1956, Der Nationalsozial-ismus als Versuchung, in Reflexionen Finsterer Zeit 1984. *Leisure inter-ests:* reading, hiking, cross-country skiing. *Address:* 501 Fayerweather Hall, Columbia University, New York, N.Y. 10027 (Office); 15 Claremont Avenue, New York, N.Y. 10027, U.S.A. *Telephone:* (212) 666-2891 (Home).

STERN, Isaac; American violinist; b. 21 July 1920, Russia; s. of Solomon and Clara Stern; m. 1st Nora Kaye 1948; m. 2nd Vera Lindenblit 1951;

two s. one d.; studied San Francisco, notably with Naoum Blinder; début, San Francisco Symphony 1935; New York début 1937; world tours every year 1947–; Hon. Chair. Marian Anderson Celebration Cttee. 1988–; appearances with major orchestras; extensive recordings; frequent appearances major festivals—Edinburgh Casals, Berkshire, etc.; Pres. Carnegie Hall; Chair. Bd. of Dirs., American Israel Cultural Foundation; fmr. mem. Nat. Arts Council; f. Jerusalem Music Centre 1973; awarded first Albert Schweitzer Music Award 1975, Grammy Award 1971, Acad. Award 1981 (for documentary From Mao to Mozart), 1973, Kennedy Center Award 1984, Wolf Foundation Prize in Arts 1987, Grammy Lifetime Achievement Award 1987, Acad. Award (Carnegie Hall Re-opening) 1987; Commdr., Ordre de la Couronne, Officier, Légion d'honneur. *Address:* ICM Artists Ltd., 40 West 57th Street, New York, N.Y. 10019, U.S.A.

STERN, Klaus, DR.IUR.; German professor of law and judge; b. 11 Jan. 1932, Nuremberg; m. Helga Stern 1976; ed. Humanistisches Gymnasium, Nuremberg and Univs. of Erlangen and Munich; Dozent, Univ. of Munich 1961; Prof. Berlin Univ. 1962; Prof. and Dir. Inst. für öffentliches Recht und Verwaltungslehre, Univ. of Cologne 1966–; Judge, Constitutional Court, Nordrhein-Westfalen 1976–. *Publications:* Staatsrecht der Bundesrepublik Deutschland (3 vols.); many other books and articles on constitutional and admin. law. *Address:* Universität Köln, Institut für öffentliches Recht und Verwaltungslehre, Albertus-Magnus-Platz, 5000 Cologne 1, Federal Republic of Germany.

STERNBERG, Eli, PH.D.; American university professor; b. 13 Nov. 1917, Vienna, Austria; s. of Philip Sternberg and Eva Sternberg; m. Rae S. Shifrin 1956; one s. one d.; ed. Technische Hochschule, Vienna, Univ. of London, Univ. of North Carolina and Illinois Inst. of Technology; Instructor, Ill. Inst. of Tech. 1943–45, Asst. Prof. 1945–47, Assoc. Prof. 1947–51, Prof. of Mechanics 1951–56; Prof. of Mechanics, Brown Univ. 1957–64; Prof. of Mechanics, Calif. Inst. of Tech. 1964–; Visiting Prof., Tech. Hogeschool, Delft, Netherlands 1956–57; Visiting Prof., Keio Univ., Tokyo 1963–64; Sr. Research Fellow, Univ. of Glasgow, Scotland 1968; Visiting Prof., Univ. of Chile 1970–71; Visiting Prof., Univ. of Calif., Berkeley 1979; Fulbright Award; Guggenheim Fellow; Hon. D.Sc. (North Carolina), Hon. D.Sc. (Technion); Fellow, American Acad. Arts and Sciences; mem. Nat. Acad. Eng., N.A.S. *Publications:* papers on continuum mechanics, elasticity theory, viscoelasticity theory. *Leisure interests:* art, music. *Address:* Division of Engineering and Applied Science, California Institute of Technology, Pasadena, Calif. 91125 (Office); 2052 Pinecrest Drive, Altadena, Calif. 91001, U.S.A. (Home). *Telephone:* (818) 356-4178 (Office); (818) 798-6830 (Home).

STERNBERGER, Dolf, DR. PHIL.; German writer and professor of political science; b. 28 July 1907, Wiesbaden; s. of Georg Sternberger and Luise Schauss; m. Ilse Rothschild 1931; Prof. Emer. of Political Science, Heidelberg Univ.; fmr. Chair. German Assen. of Political Science; fmr.Pres. German PEN Club; Hon. Pres. German Acad. of Language and Literature; Dr. h.c. (Sorbonne); Dr. phil. h.c. (Trier) 1981, Great Cross of Order of Merit, Johannes-Reuchlin Prize, Award for Literature, Bavarian Acad. of Fine Arts and other awards. *Publications:* Der verstandene Tod, eine Untersuchung zu Martin Heideggers Existential-Ontologie 1934, Panorama oder Ansichten vom 19. Jahrhundert 1938, 1955, 13 Politische Radioreden 1947, Figuren der Fabel 1950, Aus dem Wörterbuch des Unmenschen 1955, 1968, Lebende Verfassung, Studien über Koalition und Opposition 1956, Über den Jugendstil und andere Essays 1956, Indische Miniaturen 1957, Begriff des Politischen 1961, Grund und Abgrund der Macht 1962, Ekel an der Freiheit? 1964, Die grosse Wahlreform 1964, Kriterien-Ein Lesebuch 1965, Ich wünschte, ein Bürger zu sein 1967, Heinrich Heine und die Abschaffung der Sünde 1972, Schriften I Ubёr den Tod 1977, Schriften II Drei Wurzeln der Politik 1978, Schriften III Herrschaft und Vereinbarung 1980, Schriften IV Staatsfreundschaft 1980, Schriften V Panorama, Schriften VI Vexierbilder des Menschen 1981, Die Politik und der Friede 1986, Schriften VII Grund und Abgrund der Macht (new edn.) 1986, Schriften VIII Gang zwischen Meistern 1987. *Address:* Park Rosenhöhe 35, 6100 Darmstadt, Federal Republic of Germany. *Telephone:* 06151-75943.

STERNFELD, Reuben; American international financial official; b. 5 May 1924, New York; s. of Morris A. and Ethel (née Kaplan) Sternfeld; m. Marcia Katz 1967; ed. Univs. of Maryland and Michigan; held various positions with Bureau of the Budget 1949–60; Special Asst. to Under-Sec. of State and Exec. Sec. Pres.'s Task Force on Foreign Econ. Assistance 1960–61; Officer, Bureau of Latin-American Affairs, Agency for Int. Devt. 1961–65; Assoc. U.S. Co-ordinator, Alliance for Progress 1965; Alt. Exec. Dir. IDB 1966–73; Asst. Dir. Council on Econ. Policy, Office of Pres. of U.S.A. 1973–74; Exec. Vice-Pres. IDB 1975–82, Special Rep. in Europe 1982–86, Adviser to Pres. 1986–. *Address:* Inter-American Development Bank, 1300 New York Avenue, N.W., Washington, D.C. 20577 (Office); 2800 Battery Place, Washington, D.C. 20016, U.S.A. (Home).

STETTEN, DeWitt, Jr., M.D., PH.D.; American professor of biochemistry; b. 31 May. 1909, New York; s. of DeWitt Stetten, Sr. and Magdalen Ernst Stetten; m. 1st Marjorie R. Stetten 1941, 2nd Jane Lazarow Stetton 1984; one s. three d.; ed. Columbia Univ.; Asst. Prof., Dept. of Biochemistry, Columbia Univ. 1940–47; Dept. of Physiological Chem., Harvard Medical School 1947; Chief, Lab. of Physiology and Nutrition, Public Health Inst.,

New York 1948; Scientific Dir. NIAMD, Nat. Insts. of Health 1948; Founding Dean of Rutgers Medical School 1960; Dir. NIGMS, Nat. Insts. of Health 1970, Deputy Director for Science 1973, Deputy Dir. Emer. 1986–; Sr. Scientific Adviser 1979; Smith Prize; Alvarenga Prize; Banting Medal. *Publications:* Principle of Biochemistry (Co-Author) 1954, National Institutes of Health: An Account in its Laboratories and Clinics 1984, How My Light Was Spent 1984; 192 publs. in scientific journals. *Leisure interests:* cabinet work, sailing. *Address:* National Institutes of Health, Building 16, Room 118, 9000 Rockville Pike, Bethesda, Md. 20892 (Office); 2 West Drive, Bethesda, Md. 20814, U.S.A. (Home). *Telephone:* (301) 496-1932 (Office); (301) 656-5471 (Home).

STETTER, Ib; Danish businessman and politician; b. 1 March 1917, Odense; s. of Egon Madsen; ed. Copenhagen School of Business Admin.; Man. Dir. of large co. in Ålborg, Pres. of North Jutland Econ. Council; M.P. 1964–; Cttee. Chair. Parl. Group of Conservative Party, Nat. Chair. 1977–81; fmr. Pres. of Nordic Council; Minister for Industry 1986–87; Conservative. *Address:* c/o Ministry of Industry, Slotsholmsgade 12, 1216 Copenhagen K, Denmark.

STEVENS, Denis William, C.B.E., M.A., D.H.L.; British musicologist and conductor; b. 2 March 1922, High Wycombe, Bucks.; s. of William James Stevens and Edith Ruby Driver; m. 1st Sheila Holloway 1949 (divorced 1975), m. 2nd Lillian Kwasny 1975 (divorced 1984); two s. one d.; ed. Royal Grammar School, High Wycombe and Jesus Coll. Oxford; R.A.F. Intelligence, India and Burma 1942–46; Producer, BBC Music Div. 1949–54; Visiting Prof. of Musicology, Cornell Univ., U.S.A. 1955, Columbia Univ., U.S.A. 1956; Sec. Plainsong and Medieval Music Soc. 1958–63; Ed. Grove's Dictionary of Music and Musicians 1959–63; Prof. R.A.M. 1960; Visiting Prof. of Musicology, Univ. of Calif. (Berkeley), U.S.A. 1962; Distinguished Visiting Prof., Penn. State Univ. 1962–63; Prof. of Musicology, Columbia Univ. 1964–76; Visiting Prof. of Musicology, Univ. of Calif. (Santa Barbara) 1974–75; Distinguished Visiting Prof. of Musicology, Univ. of Wash., Seattle 1976; Visiting Prof., Univ. of Mich., Ann Arbor 1977; Pres. and Artistic Dir. Accad. Monteverdiana 1961–; Consultant in Musicology, St. Thomas Church, New York City 1985–. *Publications:* The Mulliner Book 1952, Thomas Tomkins 1957, A History of Song 1960, Tudor Church Music 1961, Musicology 1980, Letters of Claudio Monteverdi 1980, Musicology in Practice 1987; numerous articles, reviews, edns. and recordings. *Leisure interests:* travel, photography. *Address:* 146 West 73rd Street, Apt. 2B, New York, N.Y. 10023, U.S.A. *Telephone:* (212) 724-9898.

STEVENS, Graeme Roy, M.SC., PH.D., D.SC., F.R.S.N.Z.; New Zealand palaeontologist; b. 17 July 1932, Lower Hutt; m. Diane L. M. Qllivier 1962; two s. one d.; ed. Waterloo School, Hutt Valley High School, Victoria Univ. and Cambridge Univ.; Jr. Lecturer in Geology, Vic. Univ., Wellington 1954–56; Palaeontologist, N.Z. Geological Survey 1956–, now Chief Palaeontologist; demonstrator, Cambridge Univ. 1956–59; Hamilton Award (Royal Soc. of N.Z.) 1959 and other awards. *Publications:* six books and 135 scientific papers. *Leisure interests:* cross-country running, walking, local history, popularization of science. *Address:* N.Z. Geological Survey, P.O. Box 30368, Lower Hutt (Office); 2 Christina Grove, Normandale, Lower Hutt, New Zealand (Home). *Telephone:* 699059 (Office); 697543 (Home).

STEVENS, John Edgar, C.B.E., M.A., PH.D., F.B.A.; British university professor (retd.); b. 8 Oct. 1921, London; s. of William C. J. Stevens and Fanny Stevens; m. Charlotte E. M. Somner 1946; two s. two d.; ed. Christ's Hospital, Horsham and Magdalene Coll., Cambridge; served R.N.; Bye Fellow, 1948, Research Fellow 1950, Fellow, Magdalene Coll., Cambridge 1950, Tutor 1958–74, Pres. Magdalene Coll. 1983–88; Univ. Lecturer in English 1954–74, Reader in English and Musical History 1974–78, Prof. of Medieval and Renaissance English 1978–88; Hon. D. Mus. (Exeter) 1989. *Publications:* Medieval Carols 1952, Music and Poetry in the Early Tudor Court 1961, Music at the Court of Henry VIII 1962, Medieval French Plays (with R. Axton) 1971, Medieval Romance 1973, Early Tudor Songs & Carols 1975, Words and Music in the Early Middle Ages 1986. *Leisure interests:* viol-playing, sailing, bricklaying. *Address:* 4 & 5 Bell's Court, Cambridge, England.

STEVENS, John Paul, J.D.; American judge; b. 20 April 1920, Chicago, Ill.; m. 1st Elizabeth Jane Sheeren, four c.; m. 2nd Maryan Mulholland Simon 1979; ed. Univ. of Chicago, Northwestern Univ. School of Law; served U.S.N. (Bronze Star Medal) 1942–45; Co-Ed. of Law Review at Northwestern Univ. School of Law 1947; Law Clerk to Supreme Court Justice Wiley Rutledge 1947; worked with Poppenhusen, Johnston, Thompson and Raymond law practice 1948–51, 1952; Partner, Rothschild, Stevens, Barry and Myers 1952–70; Circuit Judge, Seventh Circuit Court of Appeals 1970–75; Assoc. Justice, U.S. Supreme Court Dec. 1975–; Assoc. Counsel, Monopoly Power Sub-Cttee. of House of Reps. Judiciary Cttee. 1951; mem. Attorney Gen.'s Nat. Cttee. on Antitrust Laws 1953–55; part-time teacher, Northwestern Univ. School of Law, later Univ. of Chicago Law School 1952–56; admitted to Ill. Bar 1949, to U.S. Supreme Court 1954. *Publications:* numerous articles on commercial monopoly affairs. *Address:* United States Supreme Court, 1 First Street, N.E., Washington, D.C. 20543, U.S.A.

STEVENS, Rosemary Anne, PH.D.; American university professor; b. 18 March 1935, U.K.; d. of William E. Wallace and Mary A. Wallace; m.

Robert B. Stevens 1961 (divorced 1983); one s. one d.; ed. Oxford and Manchester Univs., U.K. and Yale Univ., U.S.A.; trained in hosp. admin. and worked as hosp. admin. Nat. Health Service, U.K.; mem. Faculty, Prof. of Public Health, Prof. in Inst. of Policy Studies, Yale Univ., U.S.A. 1962–76; Prof., Dept. of Health Systems Man. (Chair. 1977-78) and Adjunct Prof. of Political Science, Tulane Univ. 1976–79; Prof. of History and Sociology of Science, Univ. of Pa. 1979–, Chair. 1980–83, 1986–; mem. Inst. of Medicine of N.A.S., American Bd. of Pediatrics; Rockefeller Humanities Award 1983–84; Guggenheim Award 1984–85. *Publications:* Medical Practice in Modern England 1966, American Medicine and the Public Interest 1971, Foreign Trained Physicians and American Medicine 1972, Welfare Medicine in America 1974, The Alien Doctors: Foreign Medical Graduates in American Hospitals 1978; various articles. *Leisure interests:* painting, reading, flea markets. *Address:* Department of History and Sociology of Science, University of Pennsylvania, HSS D-6, 215 S. 34th Street, Philadelphia, Pa. 19194, U.S.A. *Telephone:* (215) 898-4225.

STEVENS, Sinclair McKnight, P.C., Q.C.; Canadian lawyer and politician; b. 11 Feb. 1927, Milton, Ont.; s. of Robert M. Stevens and Anna B. McKnight; m. Noreen M. T. Charlebois 1958; ed. Purpleville Public School, Weston Collegiate and Vocational School, Univ. of W. Ontario and Osgoode Hall Law School; fmr. lawyer with Fraser & Beatty, Stevens & Stevens; M.P. 1972–; Pres. Treasury Bd. of Canada 1979–80; Minister of Regional Industrial Expansion 1984–86; Progressive Conservative. *Leisure interest:* farming. *Address:* House of Commons, Ottawa, Ont., K1A 0A6; R.R. No. 3, King City, Ontario, L0G 1K0, Canada.

STEVENS, Theodore Fulton, LL.B.; American lawyer and politician; b. 18 Nov. 1923, Indianapolis, Ind.; s. of George A. and Gertrude (née Chancellor) Stevens; m. 1st Ann Cherrington 1952 (deceased), three s. two d.; m. 2nd Catherine Chandler 1980, one d.; ed. High School, Redondo Beach, Calif., Univ. of Calif. at L.A., and Harvard Law School; U.S. Attorney, Fairbanks, Alaska 1953–56; Legis. Counsel, Dept. of Interior, Washington, D.C. 1956–58; Asst. to Sec. of Interior 1958–60; Solicitor of Interior Dept. 1960; pvt. law practice, Anchorage, Alaska 1961–68; Senator from Alaska 1968–; Asst. Minority Leader U.S. Senate 1977–80, Asst. Majority Leader 1981–85; U.S. Senate del. to Int. Law of the Sea Conf., to Canadian-U.S. Interparl. Conf.; Republican. *Address:* Room 522, Hart Senate Office Building, Washington, D.C. 20510, U.S.A. (Office). *Telephone:* (202) 224-3004.

STEVENS, Thomas Stevens, F.R.S., F.R.S.E., D.PHIL.; British professor of chemistry (retd.); b. 8 Oct. 1900, Renfrew, Scotland; s. of John Stevens and Jane Elliot Stevens (née Irving); m. Janet Wilson Forsyth 1949; ed. Paisley Grammar School, Glasgow Acad., Glasgow Univ. and Oxford Univ.; Asst., Glasgow Univ. 1921–23, 1925–26, Lecturer 1926–47; Sr. Lecturer, Sheffield Univ. 1947–48, Reader 1948–63, Personal Chair 1963–66; Visiting Prof., Univ. of Strathclyde 1966–67, Research Fellow 1967–70; Hon. D.Sc. (Glasgow) 1985. *Publications:* Selected Molecular Rearrangements (with W. E. Watts) 1973, extensive contribs. to Chem. of Carbon Compounds 1957–60 and to Chem. Soc. Annual Reports 1941–43, Karl Freudenberg, biographical memoir 1984; numerous scientific papers. *Leisure interest:* unsophisticated bridge. *Address:* 313 Albert Drive, Glasgow, G41 5RP, Scotland. *Telephone:* 041-432 6928.

STEVENS OF LUDGATE, Baron (Life Peer), cr. 1987, of Ludgate in the City of London; **David Robert Stevens,** M.A.; British business executive; b. 26 May 1936; s. of (Arthur) Edwin Stevens; m. Melissa, Countess Andrassy 1977 (died 1989); one s. one d.; ed. Stowe School and Sidney Sussex Coll. Cambridge; man. trainee, Elliott Automation 1959; Dir. Hill Samuel Securities 1959-68, Drayton Group 1968–74; Chair. City & Foreign (now Alexander Proudfoot Holdings) 1976–, Drayton Far East 1976–, English & Int. 1976–, Dualvest 1979–, Consolidated Venture (formerly Montagu Boston) 1979–, Triplevest 1979–, Drayton Consolidated 1980–, Drayton Japan 1980–, Econ. Devt. Cttee. for Civil Eng. 1984–; Dir. United Newspapers PLC 1974–, Chair. 1981–; Chair. MIM Britannia Ltd. (fmrly. Montagu Man. Ltd.) 1980–, C.E.O. 1980–87; Chair. Express Newspapers 1985–; Deputy Chair. Britannia Arrow Holdings PLC 1987–. *Leisure interest:* golf. *Address:* 11 Devonshire Square, London, EC2M 4YR, England.

STEVENSON, Adlai E., III; American senator; b. 10 Oct. 1930, Chicago, Ill.; s. of late Adlai Stevenson II (fmr. Gov. of Illinois, presidential candidate and Amb. to UN); great-grandson of Adlai E. Stevenson (Vice-Pres. of U.S.A. 1893-97); m. Nancy Anderson 1955; two s. two d.; ed. Milton Acad., Mass., and Harvard Univ.; law clerk to a justice of Ill. Supreme Court 1957; joined Chicago law firm of Mayer, Brown and Platt 1958–66, partner 1966–67, 1981–; elected to Ill. House of Reps. 1964; State Treas. of Ill. 1966–70; Senator from Illinois 1970–81; Democratic Cand. for Gov. of Ill. 1982, 1986; numerous awards, hon. degrees and directorships; Democrat. *Address:* 190 S. La Salle Street, Chicago, Ill. 60603, U.S.A. (Office).

STEVENSON, Robert Wilfrid, M.A., A.C.C.A.; British film executive; b. 19 April 1947, Lochalsh; s. of James Stevenson and Elizabeth Macrae; m. Jennifer Grace Antonio 1972 (divorced 1979); ed. Edinburgh Acad. and Univ. Coll., Oxford; Research Officer Univ. of Edinburgh Students Assen. 1970–74; Sec. and Acad. Registrar, Napier Polytechnic, Edinburgh 1974–87;

Deputy Dir. B.F.I. 1987-88, Dir. 1988–. *Leisure interests:* cinema, hill walking, squash, bridge, choral singing. *Address:* 21 Stephen Street, London, W1P 1PL, England. *Telephone:* (01) 255 1444.

STEVER, Horton Guyford, PH.D.; American scientist and company director; b. 24 Oct. 1916, Corning, N.Y.; s. of Ralph Raymond Stever and Alma Matt; m. Louise Risley 1946; two s. two d.; ed. Colgate Univ. and Calif. Inst. of Tech.; mem. Staff Radiation Lab. and Instructor, Officers' Radar School, M.I.T. 1941–42; Science Liaison Officer, London Mission, Office of Scientific Research and Devt. 1942–45; Asst. Prof. of Aeronautical Eng. Mass. Inst. of Tech. 1946–51, Assoc. Prof. 1951–56, Prof. 1956–65; Chief Scientist, U.S.A.F. 1955–56; Assoc. Dean of Eng., Mass. Inst. of Tech. 1956–59, Head Depts. of Mechanical Eng. Naval Architecture and Marine Eng. 1961–65; Pres. Carnegie-Mellon Univ. 1965–72; Chair. U.S.A.F. Scientific Advisory Bd. 1962–69; mem. Exec. Cttee. Defense Science Bd., Dept. of Defense 1962-69; mem. Panel on Science and Tech. U.S. House of Reps. Comm. on Science and Tech., 1959–72, Science and Tech. Adviser to Pres. 1976–77; Science Consultant 1977–; Trustee, Colgate Univ. 1962–72, Sarah Mellon Scaife Foundation 1965–72, Shady Side Acad. 1967–72, Univ. Research Assen. 1977– (Pres. 1982–84); Dir. Fisher Scientific Co. 1965–72, Koppers Co. 1965–72, System Devt. Corpn. 1965–70, United Aircraft Corpn. 1966–72, TRW 1977–88, Saudi Arabian Nat. Center for Science and Tech. 1978–80, Schering Plough 1980–89, Goodyear 1981–86; mem. Nat. Acad. of Eng., Chair. Aeronautics and Space Eng. Bd. 1967–69, Foreign Sec. 1984–; mem. Nat. Science Bd. 1970–72; Dir. Nat. Science Foundation 1972–76; Science Adviser and Chair. Fed. Council for Science and Tech., Exec. Cttee. Nat. Science Bd., Energy R & D Advisory Council; U.S. Chair. U.S.-U.S.S.R. Joint Comm. on Scientific and Tech. Co-operation; mem. U.S.-Japan Cttee. on Scientific Co-operation, Fed. Council on the Arts and Humanities, Nat. Council on Educational Research, and many other Govt. bodies; 18 hon. degrees; President's Certificate of Merit 1948, Exceptional Civilian Service Award, U.S.A.F. 1956, Scott Gold Medal of American Ordnance Assen. 1960, Alumni Distinguished Service Award Calif. Inst. of Technology 1966, Distinguished Public Service Medal, Dept. of Defense 1969, Commdr., Order of Merit, Poland 1976, Distinguished Public Service Medal, NASA 1988. *Publication:* Flight (with J. J. Haggerty) 1965. *Leisure interests:* skiing, fishing, golf, hiking. *Address:* 1528 33rd Street, N.W., Washington, D.C. 20007, U.S.A. *Telephone:* (202) 338-5537.

STEWART, (Bernard Harold) Ian (Halley), M.P., LITT.D., R.D., C.ST.J., F.B.A., F.R.S.E.; British politician; b. 10 Aug. 1935, London; s. of Prof. H. C. Stewart; m. Deborah C. Buchan 1966; one s. two d.; ed. Haileybury Coll. and Jesus Coll. Cambridge; R.N.V.R. 1954–56; Brown, Shipley & Co., Ltd. (Merchant Bankers) 1960–83; mem. Parl. for Hitchin 1974–83, for N. Herts. 1983–; Parl. Under-Sec. of State for Defence Procurement Jan.–Oct. 1983; Econ. Sec. to H.M. Treasury 1983–87; Minister of State for the Armed Forces 1987–88, Northern Ireland Office 1988–; Conservative. *Publications:* The Scottish Coinage 1955, Studies in Numismatic Method (Ed. with C. N. L. Brooke and others) 1983. *Leisure interests:* history, tennis. *Address:* House of Commons, London, S.W.1, England. *Telephone:* 01-219 4138.

STEWART, Rt. Hon. Donald James, P.C.; British politician; b. 17 Oct. 1920, Stornoway, Scotland; s. of Neil and Jessie Stewart; m. Christina Macaulay 1955; no c.; ed. Nicolson Inst., Stornoway; Co. Dir. until 1970; M.P. for the Western Isles 1970–87; Leader Parl. Scottish Nat. Party 1974–87, Pres. 1982–87; three terms as Provost of Stornoway; Hon. Sheriff 1960. *Leisure interests:* gardening, fishing, photography. *Address:* Hillcrest, 41 Goathill Road, Stornoway, Isle of Lewis, Scotland. *Telephone:* (0851) 2672.

STEWART, Frederick Henry, K.B., B.SC., PH.D., D.SC., F.R.S., F.R.S.E.; British geologist; b. 16 Jan. 1916, Aberdeen; s. of Frederick R. Stewart and Hester Alexander; m. Mary Florence Elinor Rainbow 1945; ed. Fettes Coll., Edinburgh, Univ. of Aberdeen, Emmanuel Coll., Cambridge; Mineralogist in Research Dept., ICI Ltd. 1941–43; Lecturer in Geology, Durham Univ. 1943–56; Regius Prof. of Geology, Edinburgh Univ. 1956–82; Chair. Natural Environment Research Council 1971–73, Advisory Bd. for the Research Councils 1973–79; mem. Advisory Council for Applied Research and Devt. 1977–79; Trustee British Museum (Natural History) 1983–88; Lyell Fund Award, J. B. Tyrrell Fund, Lyell Medal, Geological Soc. of London; Mineralogical Soc. of America Award; Clough Medal, Geological Soc. of Edinburgh; Sorby Medal, Yorkshire Geological Soc. 1975. *Publications:* papers in Mineralogical Magazine, Journal of Geological Soc. of London and other journals dealing with igneous and metamorphic petrology and salt deposits. *Address:* 79 Morningside Park, Edinburgh, EH10 5EZ, Scotland (Home).

STEWART, James (Maitland), D.F.C., B.S.; American actor; b. 20 May 1908, Indiana, Pa.; s. of Alexander and Elizabeth (Jackson) Stewart; m. Gloria McLean 1949; two s. (one deceased) twin d.; ed. Mercersburg Acad. and Princeton Univ.; stage debut in New York 1932; film debut 1935; in U.S. Air Force 1943-45, entering Air Force reserves 1945, rising to Lt.-Col., retd. as Brigadier Gen. 1968; American Motion Picture Acad. Award for Philadelphia Story 1940, New York Film Critics' Award for Mr. Smith Goes to Washington 1939, Volpi Cup, Venice 1959, for performance in Anatomy of a Murder; Special Acad. Award 1985; Croix de guerre (with palm); Presidential Medal of Freedom 1985, Master Screen Artist Award 1989. Stage Performances: Harvey, New York 1947, London 1975. *Films include:*

Seventh Heaven 1937, Vivacious Lady 1938, You Can't Take It with You 1938, Mr. Smith Goes to Washington 1939, Destry Rides Again 1939, The Shop Around the Corner 1939, The Philadelphia Story (Acad. Award) 1940, Ziegfeld Girl 1941, It's a Wonderful Life 1946, Call Northside 777 1947, Rope 1948, Winchester 73 1950, Broken Arrow 1950, Harvey 1950, The Greatest Show on Earth 1951, Bend of the River (British title Where the River Bends) 1952, The Naked Spur 1953, Thunder Bay 1953, The Glenn Miller Story 1953, Rear Window 1954, The Far Country 1954, The Man from Laramie 1955, The Man Who Knew Too Much 1956, The Spirit of St. Louis 1957, Vertigo 1958, Bell, Book and Candle 1958, Anatomy of a Murder 1959, Two Rode Together 1961, The Man Who Shot Liberty Valance 1962, Mr. Hobbs Takes a Vacation 1962, How the West Was Won 1962, Cheyenne Autumn 1964, Shenandoah 1965, The Flight of the Phoenix 1965, The Rare Breed 1966, Firecreek 1967, Bandolero 1968, The Cheyenne Social Club 1970, Fool's Parade 1971, Dynamite Man from Glory Jail 1971, The Shootist 1976, Airport 77 1977, The Big Sleep 1977, The Magic of Lassie 1978, Right of Way 1982. TV series: The Jimmy Stewart Show 1971-72, Hawkins on Murder 1973-74. *Address:* c/o 8899 Beverly Boulevard, 402 A Chasin, Los Angeles, Calif. 90048; P.O. Box 90, Beverly Hills, Calif., U.S.A.

STEWART, John Anthony Benedict, C.M.G., O.B.E., M.A., B.SC.; British diplomatist (retd.); b. 24 May 1927, Cardiff; s. of the late Edward V. Stewart and Emily Veronica (née Jones); m. Geraldine Margaret Clifton 1960; one s. one d.; ed. St. Illtyd's Coll., Univ. of Wales, Cambridge Univ., Imperial Coll., Royal Coll. of Defence Studies; Midshipman, R.N.V.R. 1944-47; Geologist, Geological Survey of British Somaliland 1952-57; Liaison Officer (later Sr. Liaison Officer), Anglo-Ethiopian Agreement Territories 1957-60; Dist. Commr., Northern Rhodesia 1960-66; FCO 1966-70; Deputy High Commr., Barbados 1970-72; Head of Chancery, Kampala, Uganda 1972-73; Amb. to Viet-Nam 1974-76, to Laos 1978-80, to Mozambique 1980-84; High Commr. to Sri Lanka 1984-87; A. H. Cox Gold Medal of Geology. *Publications:* The Geology of the Mait Area 1958. *Leisure interests:* fly fishing, bridge. *Address:* c/o National Westminster Bank, 135 High Street, Guildford, Surrey, 6U1 1UT, England.

STEWART, John Young (Jackie), O.B.E.; Scottish racing driver (retd.); b. 11 June 1939, Milton, Scotland; s. of the late Robert Paul Stewart and Jean Clark Young; m. Helen McGregor 1962; two s.; ed. Dumbarton Acad.; first raced 1961; competed in 4 meetings driving for Barry Filer, Glasgow 1961-62; drove for Ecurie Ecosse and Barry Filer, winning 14 out of 23 starts 1963, 28 wins out of 53 starts 1964; drove formula 1 for British Racing Motors (BRM) 1965-67, for Ken Tyrrell 1968-73; has won Australian, New Zealand, Swedish, Mediterranean, Japanese and many other non-championship major int. motor races; set new world record by winning his 26th World Championship Grand Prix (Zandvoort) 1973, 27th (Nürburgring) 1973; Third in World Championship 1965, 2nd in 1968 and 1972, World Champion 1969, 1971, 1973; British Automobile Racing Club Gold Medal 1971, 1973, Daily Express Sportsman of the Year 1971, 1973, BBC Sports Personality of the Year 1973, Scottish Sportsman of the Year 1973, U.S. Sportsman of the Year 1973, Segrave Trophy 1973; film: Weekend of a Champion 1972. *Publications:* World Champion (with Eric Dymock) 1970, Faster! (with Peter Manso) 1972, On the Road 1983, Jackie Stewart's Principles of Performance Driving 1986. *Leisure interests:* shooting (clay pigeon champion), golf, tennis. *Address:* 24 route de Divonne, 1260 Nyon, Vaud, Switzerland. *Telephone:* Geneva 61-01-52.

STEWART, Rt. Hon. Michael (see Stewart of Fulham).

STEWART, Robert W., O.C., M.SC., PH.D., F.R.S.C., F.R.S.; Canadian oceanographer, b. 21 Aug. 1923, Smoky Lake, Alberta; m. 1st V. Brande 1948 (dissolved 1972), two s. one d.; m. 2nd Anne-Marie Robert 1973, one s.; ed. Queen's Univ., Kingston, Ont., Cambridge Univ.; research scientist, Canadian Defence Research Bd., Victoria, B.C. 1950-61; Prof. of Physics and Oceanography, Univ. of British Columbia, Vancouver 1961-70, Hon. Prof. 1971-; Dir.-Gen., Pacific Region, Ocean and Aquatic Sciences, Dept. of the Environment, Victoria, B.C. 1970; Asst. Deputy Minister, Science and Tech., Ministry of Educ., Science and Tech. 1979, Deputy Minister, Ministry of Univs., Science and Communications, Victoria, B.C. 1979-84; Pres. Alberta Research Council 1984-87; Dir. Centre for Earth and Ocean Research, Univ. of Vic. 1987-; Visiting Prof., Dalhousie Univ. 1960-61, Harvard Univ. 1964, Pa. State Univ. 1964, Cambridge Univ. 1967-68; mem. Jt. Organizing Cttee., Global Atmospheric Research Programme 1967-80, Vice-Chair. 1968-72, Chair. 1972-76; mem. Council, American Meteorological Soc. 1977-81; mem. Cttee. on Climate Change and the Ocean 1980-, Chair. 1983-87; Hon. D.Sc. (McGill) 1972. LL.D. (Dalhousie) 1974; Patterson Medal, Canadian Meteorological Soc. 1973; IMO Lecturer 1975; Sverdrup Gold Medal, American Meteorological Soc. 1976. *Publications:* approx. 60 publs. on turbulence, oceanography and meteorology. *Address:* Centre for Earth and Ocean Research, University of Victoria, P.O. Box 1700, Victoria, B.C. V8W 2Y2, Canada. *Telephone:* (604) 721-8848.

STEWART, Rod (Roderick David); British pop singer; b. 10 Jan. 1945, London; m. Alana Collins 1979 (divorced 1984); one s. one d.; d. with Kelly Emberg; singer with Jeff Beck Group 1968-69, Faces 1969-75; *solo albums include:* Rod Stewart, Gasoline Alley, Every Picture Tells a Story, Never a Dull Moment, A Night on the Town, Atlantic Crossing, Smiler, Footloose

and Fancy Free, Blondes Have More Fun, Foolish Behaviour, Body Wishes, Out of Order; Rock Star of the Year, Rolling Stone Magazine 1971. *Address:* c/o Bill Gaff, Gaff Management, Riva Records, Hotel Navarro, Suite 705, 112 Central Park S., New York, N.Y. 10019, U.S.A.

STEWART, Thomas, MUS.B.; American opera singer; b. 29 Aug. 1928, San Saba, Tex.; s. of Thomas James Stewart and Gladys Naomi (Reavis) Stewart; m. Evelyn Lear (q.v.) 1955; one s. one d.; ed. Baylor Univ., Juilliard School of Music; joined Berlin Opera 1958; first performance at Bayreuth Festival 1960; has performed at Metropolitan Opera, New York, Royal Opera House, Covent Garden, London, La Scala, Milan, Vienna State Opera, Grand Opera, Paris, Bavarian State Opera, San Francisco Opera, Chicago Opera, Hamburg Opera; appears with all major orchestras of the world; gives recitals internationally with Evelyn Lear. *Major roles include:* Hans Sachs (The Mastersingers of Nuremberg), Falstaff, Wotan (The Ring cycle), The Flying Dutchman, Scarpia (Tosca), Iago (Otello), Golaud (Pelléas et Mélisande), Amfortas (Parsifal); Fellow, American Univ. 1967; Berlin Kammersänger 1963, Richard Wagner Medal 1963, Grammy Awards 1969, 1971. *Leisure interests:* theatre, tennis, golf. *Address:* c/o Columbia Artists Management Incorporated, 165 West 57th Street, New York, N.Y. 10019, U.S.A.

STEWART, William D. P., PH.D., D.SC., F.R.S., F.R.S.E.; British university professor; b. 7 June 1935, Glasgow; s. of John Stewart and Margaret Stewart; m. Catherine Macleod 1958; one s.; ed. Univ. of Glasgow; Asst. Lecturer, Univ. of Nottingham 1961-63; Lecturer, Westfield Coll., Univ. of London 1963-68; Visiting Research Worker, Univ. of Wis., U.S.A. 1966, 1968; Boyd-Baxter Prof. of Biology, Univ. of Dundee 1968-, Vice-Prin. 1985-87; Sec. and Deputy Chair. to Agricultural and Food Research Council 1988-; Visiting Prof., Univ. of Kuwait 1980, Univ. of Otago, N.Z. 1984; Chair. Royal Soc. Educ. Cttee. 1977-80; Vice-Pres. British Phycological Soc. 1973-75, Pres. 1975-77; Trustee, Estuarine and Brackish-Water Sciences Assoc. 1978-88; Sec. Int. Cttee. on Microbiological Ecology (ICOME) 1980-83, Chair. 1984-86; mem. of Council, Royal Soc. of Edinburgh 1976-79, of Royal Soc. 1984-86; Chair. Council, Scottish Marine Biological Assocn. 1985-87; Chair. Royal Soc. Study Group on the Nitrogen Cycle 1979-83, on Educ. and Training for Biotech. Leeuwenhoek Lecturer, Royal Soc. 1984; Distinguished Lecturer, Phycological Soc. of America 1977. *Publications:* The Blue-Green Algae (co-author) 1973, Algal Physiology and Biochemistry (ed.) 1974, Nitrogen Fixation (ed.) 1976 and 1980, The Nitrogen Cycle of the United Kingdom (ed.) 1984; more than 200 scientific papers. *Leisure interests:* music, house-renovation. *Address:* Agricultural and Food Research Council, Wiltshire Court, Farnsby Street, Swindon, SN1 5AT, England; 45 Fairfield Road, Broughty Ferry, Dundee, Scotland. *Telephone:* (0382) 76702 (Home).

STEWART OF FULHAM, Baron (Life Peer), cr. 1979, of Fulham in Greater London; **(Robert) Michael Maitland Stewart,** P.C., C.H.; British politician and author; b. 6 Nov. 1906, Bromley, Kent; s. of Robert and Eva Stewart; m. Elizabeth Birkinshaw (Baroness Stewart of Alvechurch) 1941; ed. Brownhill Road LCC School, Christ's Hospital and St. John's Coll., Oxford; M.P. 1945-79, Govt. Whip 1945-47, Under-Sec. of State for War 1947-51, Parl. Sec. Ministry of Supply 1951; Sec. of State for Educ. and Science 1964-65, for Foreign Affairs 1965-66; First Sec. of State 1966-68; Sec. of State for Econ. Affairs 1966-67, for Foreign and Commonwealth Affairs 1968-70; Leader, British Labour Del. to European Parl. 1975-76; Labour. *Publications:* The Forty Hour Week 1936, Bias and Education for Democracy 1937, The British Approach to Politics 1938, Modern Forms of Government 1959, Life and Labour (autobiog.) 1980, European Security: the case against unilateral nuclear disarmament 1981, Apocalypse 2000 (with Peter Jay) 1987. *Leisure interests:* chess, painting. *Address:* 11 Felden Street, London, S.W.6, England. *Telephone:* 01-736 5194.

STEYN, Daniel Wynand, M.COMM.; South African engineer and politician; b. 12 May 1923, Heilbron Dist., O.F.S.; m. Hermana Rossouw; two s. three d.; ed. Univs. of Stellenbosch and Pretoria; temporary town engineer, Senekal, O.F.S. 1948-49; planning engineer, GPO, Pretoria 1949-52; engineer, Pretoria City Council 1953-66; Man. Telecommunications Dept., later Radar and Computer Depts., Armscor 1967-74; M.P. 1974-; Deputy Minister of Finance and of Industries, Commerce and Tourism 1980-82; Minister of Educ. and Training 1982-83, of Mineral and Energy Affairs 1983-86, of Econ. Affairs and Tech. 1986-; mem. S.A. Council for Professional Engineers, Engineers Asscn. of S.A.; Pres. S.A. Soc. of Engineers 1981; mem. several official cttees. *Leisure interests:* woodwork, photography, sport. *Address:* House of Assembly, Cape Town 8000, South Africa.

STEYN, S. J. Marais, B.A., LL.B.; South African politician and diplomatist (retd.); b. 25 Dec. 1914, Cape Prov.; s. of M. H. Steyn; m. Susan E. Moolman 1940; two s. two d.; ed. Univ. of Cape Town, Univ. of Witwatersrand; Journalist 1938-40; Govt. Information Services 1940-42; Political Sec. 1942-48; M.P. 1948-80 (United Party to 1974); joined Nat. Party 1974; Minister of Tourism 1975-78, of Indian Affairs 1975-80, of Coloured Relations 1979-80, of Community Devt. 1976-80; Amb. to U.K. 1980-84, to Transkei 1984-87; Decoration for Meritorious Service 1983. *Leisure interests:* bowls, sound recordings. *Address:* P.O. Box 6077, Uniedal, 7612 South Africa.

STEYRER, Kurt, DR.MED.; Austrian politician, b. 3 June 1920, Linz; m. 1946; two s.; ed. medical studies in Vienna and Prague; dermatologist, Vienna Rudolfspital; opened own medical practice, Vienna 1951; on staff of Vienna Health Insurance Agency 1951-58; medical officer, Simmering-Graz-Pauker A.G. 1952-81; joined Austrian Socialist Party (SPÖ) 1946; mem. Nationalrat 1975-; Fed. Minister for Health and Environmental Protection 1981-86. *Leisure interests:* hiking, tennis, skiing. *Address:* c/o Federal Ministry of Health and Environment, 1010 Vienna, Stubenring 1, Austria.

STICH, Otto, D.ECON.; Swiss politician; b. 10 Jan. 1927, Dornach, Canton Solothurn; m.; two c.; ed. Basle; teacher -1971; mem. Dornach Accounts Audit Comm. 1953; Communal Councillor and part-time Mayor of Dornach 1953-65; Prefect of Dornach-Thierstein 1961-70; mem. Nat. Council (Fed. Parl.) 1963-83, mem. External Trade Cttee. 1965-71 (Chair. 1969-71), Finance Cttee. 1971-77, 1982-83, Econ. Affairs Cttee. 1978-81, fmr. mem. other cttees.; Fed. Councillor Dec. 1983-, Head Fed. Dept. of Finance Jan. 1984-, Vice-Pres. Fed. Council 1987, Pres. of Swiss Confed. Jan.-Dec. 1988; Chair. of Ministers, IMF Group of 10; joined Swiss SDP 1947, Chair. Solothurn cantonal party 1968-72, mem. Man. Cttee. of Swiss SDP 1970-75, Vice-Chair. parl. party 1980; Chair. Trade Union Group of Assen. of Staffs of Pvt. Transport Firms and Swiss Railwaymen's Assen.; Man. Cen. Personnel Dept., Co-op Switzerland 1971-80, Deputy Dir. and Head of Personnel and Training Dept. 1980. *Address:* Federal Department of Finance, Bundesgasse, 3003 Berne, Switzerland.

STICHT, J. Paul; American business executive; b. 3 Oct. 1917, Clairton, Pa.; s. of Joseph P. and Adah M. Sticht; m. A. Ferne Cozad 1940; two s.; ed. Grove City Coll. and Univ. of Pittsburgh Graduate School; started as shipping clerk, U.S. Steel Co. 1939, industrial engineer 1941-44; Air Transport Command, TWA airlines div. 1944-48; Vice-Pres. Campbell Soup Co. 1949-57, Int. Pres. 1957-60; Exec. Vice-Pres. Federated Dept. Stores 1960-65, Vice-Chair. 1965-67, Pres. 1967-72; Chair Exec. Cttee. and Dir. R. J. Reynolds Industries Inc. 1972-73, Pres., C.O.O. and Dir. 1973-78, Pres., C.E.O. and Dir. 1978-79, Chair. 1979-84, C.E.O. 1979-83; Chair. R. J. R. Nabisco March-Oct. 1987, Feb. 1989-, Nat. Chamber Foundation; Dir. Textron Inc., Caribbean Cen. American Action McKesson Inc., Chrysler Corpn.; sr. mem. The Conference Bd. Inc., Visitor, Bowman Gray School of Medicine, Fuqua School of Business of Duke Univ.; Trustee, Grove City Coll. *Leisure interests:* golf, boating, fishing. *Address:* 11732 Lake House Court, North Palm Beach, Fla., U.S.A. (Home).

STICKLER, H.E. Cardinal Alfons, S.D.B.; Austrian ecclesiastic; b. 23 Aug. 1910, Neunkirchen, Vienna; ordained 1937; consecrated Archbishop (Titular See of Volsinium) 1983; cr. Cardinal 1985; fmr. Chief Vatican Librarian and Archivist; Deacon of S. Giorgio of Velabro. *Address:* Biblioteca Apostolica Vaticana, Città del Vaticano, Rome, Italy.

STIGLER, George Joseph; American professor of economics; b. 17 Jan 1911, Renton, Wash., U.S.A.; s. of Joseph Stigler and Elizabeth Hungler; m. Margaret Mack 1936 (deceased); three s.; ed. Univs. of Washington, Chicago and Northwestern Univ.; Asst. Prof. Iowa State Univ. 1936-38, Univ. of Minn. 1938-41, Assoc. Prof. 1941-44, Prof. 1944-46; Prof. Brown Univ. 1946-47; Prof. Columbia Univ. 1947-57, Center for Advanced Study in Behavioral Sciences 1957-58, Univ. of Chicago 1958-; Pres. American Econ. Assen. 1964; Vice-Chair. Securities Investor Protection Corpn. 1971-74; Ed. Journal of Political Economy 1973-; Alumnus Summa Laude Dignatus (Univ. of Washington) 1969; Hon. Dr. Sc. (Carnegie-Mellon Univ.) 1973, (Rochester Univ.) 1974, (Helsinki School of Economics) 1976, (Northwestern Univ.) 1979; Hon. LL.D. (Brown Univ.) 1980, (Carleton Coll.) 1984; Nobel Prize for Econs. 1982, Nat. Medal of Science 1987. *Publications:* many books and papers. *Leisure interests:* golf, photography. *Address:* University of Chicago, Chicago, Ill. 60637; 5825 Dorchester Avenue, Chicago, Ill. 60637, U.S.A. (Home). *Telephone:* (312) 702-7519 (Office); (312) 947-0118 (Home).

STIGWOOD, Robert Colin; Australian business executive; b. 16 April 1934, Adelaide; s. of Gordon and Gwendolyn (née Burrows) Stigwood; ed. Sacred Heart Coll., Adelaide; est. Robert Stigwood Orgn. (RSO) 1967; formed RSO Records 1973; founder, Music for UNICEF; *Producer of films:* Jesus Christ Superstar, Bugsy Malone, Gallipoli, Tommy, Saturday Night Fever, Grease, Sergeant Pepper's Lonely Hearts Club Band, Moment by Moment, Times Square, The Fan, Grease 2, Staying Alive; *Producer of stage musicals:* Hair, Oh! Calcutta, The Dirtiest Show in Town, Pippin, Jesus Christ Superstar, Evita; TV Producer in England and U.S.A. of The Entertainer and The Prime of Miss Jean Brodie; Chair. of Bd. Stigwood group of companies; Key to cities of Los Angeles and Adelaide; Tony Award 1980 for Evita; Int. Producer of the Year, ABC Interstate Theatres Inc. *Leisure interests:* tennis, swimming, sailing, reading. *Address:* 21st Floor, 1775 Broadway, New York, N.Y. 10019, U.S.A.

STILL, Ray; American professor of oboe; b. 12 March 1920, Elwood, Ind.; s. of Roy R. Still and Lillian Taylor; m. Mary Powell Brock 1940; two s. two d.; ed. Juilliard School of Music and privately under Phillip Memoli and Robert Bloom; oboist, Kansas City Philharmonic Orchestra 1939-41; mil. service 1941-46; Buffalo Philharmonic Orchestra 1947-49; Prof. of Oboe and mem. Baltimore Symphony 1949-53; solo oboist, Chicago Symphony Orchestra 1953-; Prof. of Oboe, Northwestern Univ. 1960-; Conductor,

Stratford Music Festival, Canada 1964-69; mem. of a Quintet for 100th anniversary of Yamaha Co., recordings, Tour of Japan, judge int. oboe competition, Japan 1988; has undertaken coaching of many symphony orchestra wind and brass sections; numerous recordings, including Oboe Quartettes (with Perlman, Zuckermann, Harrel) and Mozart Oboe Concerto with Chicago Symphony Orchestra, conducted by Claudio Abbado. *Leisure interests:* collecting classical comedy films, listening to great jazz artists of '20s, '30s and '40s, records of great lieder singers. *Address:* c/o Chicago Symphony Orchestra, 220 South Michigan Avenue, Chicago, Ill. 60604; 585 Hawthorne Place, Chicago, Ill. 60657, U.S.A.

STILWELL, Richard Dale, MUS.B.; American baritone; b. 6 May 1942, St. Louis; s. of Otho John Clifton and Tressie (née Parrish) Stilwell; m. 1st Elizabeth Louise Jencks 1967 (divorced); m. 2nd Kerry M. McCarthy 1983; ed. Anderson Coll., Univ. of Indiana; with Metropolitan Opera Co., New York 1970-; appearances in maj. roles Washington Opera Soc., Marseilles Opera Co., Santa Fe Opera, San Francisco Opera Co., Paris Opera Co., La Scala, Covent Garden, Hamburg State Opera, Glyndebourne Opera Festival, Van. Opera Co., Chicago Opera Co., Tanglewood Festival, Israel Philharmonic, etc.; soloist with Nat. Symphony, Washington, Chicago Symphony, American Symphony, Carnegie Hall, Boston Symphony, Los Angeles Philharmonic, etc.; Nat. Soc. of Arts and Letters award 1963, Fisher Foundation award Metropolitan Opera Auditions 1965; mem. American Guild Musical Artists. *Address:* c/o Harrison/Parrott Ltd., 12 Penzance Place, London, W11 4PA, England.

STILWELL, Richard Giles; American government official and fmr. army officer; b. 24 Feb. 1917, Buffalo; s. of William Stilwell and Mina Frazer; m. Alice K. Simpson 1938; two s. three d.; ed. Brown Univ. and U.S. Mil. Acad.; commissioned U.S. Army 1938; Asst. Mil. Adviser to Sec. of State, Europe 1945-47; Special Mil. Adviser to U.S. Amb., Italy 1947-49; C.I.A. 1949-52; served in Korea 1952-53; Instructor Army War Coll. 1954-56; SHAPE 1956-58; Commdr. Western Area, Germany 1958-59; Commdr. Cadet Regt. U.S. Mil. Acad 1959-61, Commdt. of Cadets 1961-63; Chief, Operations, U.S. Mil. Assistance Command, Vietnam 1963; Chief of Staff 1964-65; Chief, Joint U.S. Mil. Advisory Group, Thailand 1965-67; Commdg. Gen 1st Armored Div. Fort Hood, Tex. 1967-68; Commdg. Gen. Vietnam 1968-69; Deputy Chief of Staff, Mil. Operations, U.S. Army and sr. army mem. U.S. del. Mil. Staff Comm. UN 1969-72; Commdg. Gen. 6th U.S. Army, San Francisco 1972-73; Commdr-in-Chief, UN Command, Commdr. U.S. Force, Korea and Commdg. Gen. 8th U.S. Army 1973-76; retd. 1976; Deputy Under-Sec. for Policy, Defense Dept., Washington, D.C. 1981-85; numerous mil. decorations and honours awarded by U.S.A., France, Belgium, Luxembourg, U.S.S.R. etc. *Address:* 8417 Weller Avenue, McLean, Va. 22102, U.S.A.

STING (see Sumner, Gordon Matthew).

STINGL, Josef; German administrator; b. 19 March 1919, Maria-Kulmiegerland; s. of Georg and Amalie (née Hüttl) Stingl; m. 1st Dorothea Behmke 1943 (died 1986); one s. two d. (and two adopted d.); m. 2nd Elvira Lougear Stingl 1988; ed. Deutsche Hochschule für Politik, Berlin; in air force 1938-45; building worker, Berlin 1946-47; employee in a building soc. 1947-52; employee, Industrie- und Handelskammer, Berlin 1952-68; mem. Bundestag 1953-68; Instructor, Otto Suhr Inst., Freie Univ., Berlin 1955-70; Chair. Social Policy Working Party, CDU/CSU-Fraktion 1963-68; Pres. Bundesanstalt für Arbeit 1968-84; Hon. Senator Univ. of Mannheim, Hon. Prof. Univ. of Bamberg; several decorations, including Grosses Bundesverdienstkreuz mit Stern und Schulterband, Bayerischer Verdiensttorden, Grosskreuz des Gregorius Ordens, etc.; Dr.rer.pol. h.c. (Hochschule für Verwaltungswissenschaften, Speyer) 1979. *Publications:* numerous articles in professional journals. *Leisure interests:* family, music, theatre. *Address:* Delmondstrasse 32, 5456 Rheinbrohl, Federal Republic of Germany. *Telephone:* 02635-5333.

STINSON, George Arthur, A.B., LL.B.; American lawyer and business executive; b. 11 Feb. 1915 ; s. of John McCollum Stinson and Alice Loving; m. Betty Millsop 1947; three s. one d.; ed. Northwestern Univ. and Columbia Univ.; admitted to New York Bar 1939; U.S.A.F. 1941-45; Partner in law firm Cleary, Gottlieb, Friendly and Hamilton, New York, 1946-61; Act. Asst. Attorney-Gen., Washington, D.C. 1947-48; Nat. Steel Corpn., Pittsburgh, Vice-Pres. and Sec. 1961-63, Dir. 1963-86, Hon. Dir. 1986-, Pres. 1963-75, C.O.O. 1963-75, C.E.O. 1963-79, Chair. of Bd. of Dirs. 1972-81, Chair. Exec. Cttee. 1981-83; Chair. American Iron and Steel Inst. 1969-71; Dir. Int. Iron and Steel Inst., Vice-Chair. 1974, Chair. 1975-77; mem. of Bd. Hanna Mining Co., Iron Ore Co. of Canada, Ralston Purina Co., Allegheny Int. Inc.; Trustee, Mutual Life Insurance Co. of New York, Univ. of Pittsburgh, Presbyterian Univ. Hosp., Pittsburgh; mem. American Law Inst., Bd. of Regents, Northwestern Univ., Pres.'s Cttee. on Int. Trade and Investment Policy 1970-71; Hon. LL.D. (West Virginia Univ.) 1968, (Bethany Coll.) 1972; Hon. L.H.D. (Thiel Coll.) 1974; Legion of Merit. *Address:* 20 Stanwix Street, Pittsburgh, Pa. 15219 (Office); Hunting, Country Road, Tryon, N.C. 28782, U.S.A. (Home).

STIRLING, Charles James Matthew, PH.D., D.SC., C.CHEM., F.R.S.C., F.R.S.; British professor of organic chemistry; b. 8 Dec. 1930, Croydon; s. of Brigadier A. D. Stirling, and Isobel M. Matthew; m. Eileen G. Powell 1956; three d.; ed. Edinburgh Acad., Univ. of St. Andrews and King's Coll.

London; Civil Service Research Fellow Chemical Defence Experimental Establishment 1955-57; ICI Fellow, Univ. of Edinburgh 1957-59; Lecturer in Organic Chem. Queen's Univ. Belfast 1959-65; Reader in Organic Chem. King's Coll. London 1965-69; Prof. of Organic Chem. Univ. Coll. of N. Wales, Bangor 1969-; mem. various int. scientific cttees. etc. *Publications:* 150 scientific articles and papers. *Leisure interests:* Christianity, choral music, travel, furniture restoration. *Address:* Department of Chemistry, University College of North Wales, Bangor, Gwynedd, LL57 2UW, Wales. *Telephone:* (0248) 351151 (Ext. 2375).

STIRLING, Duncan Alexander; British banker (retd.); b. 6 Oct. 1899; s. of Major William Stirling, D.L., J.P. and Charlotte Eva Mackintosh; m. Lady Marjorie Murray 1926; two s.; ed. Harrow and New Coll., Oxford; Partner with H. S. Lefevre and Co. 1929-49; Dir. Westminster Bank (now Nat. Westminster Bank Ltd.) 1935-74, Deputy Chair. 1948-61, Chair. 1962-69; Chair. Cttee. of London Clearing Bankers 1966-68; Dir. London Life Assoc. 1935-80, Pres. 1952-66; Pres. Inst. of Bankers 1964-66. *Address:* 20 Kingston House South, Ennismore Gardens, London, SW7 1NF, England.

STIRLING, James, DIP.ARCH., A.R.I.B.A., F.R.S.A.; British architect and town planner; b. 1926, Glasgow; s. of Joseph Stirling and Louisa Frazer; m. Mary Shand 1966; one s. two d.; ed. Liverpool School of Art, Liverpool Univ. School of Architecture; with Assen. of Town Planning and Regional Research, London 1950-52; Asst. Lyons, Israel and Ellis 1953-56; mem. Inst. of Contemporary Art Ind. Group 1952-56; pvt. practice 1956-, with James Gowan 1956-63, with Michael Wilford 1971-; exhbns. New York 1969, London 1974; Charles Davenport Visiting Prof., Yale Univ. 1970; has lectured in Europe, U.S.A. 1960-; Hon. mem. Akad. der Kunst, Berlin 1969, A.I.A. 1975, Florence Acad. of Arts 1979; Hon. Dr. R.C.A. 1979; Alvar Aalto Mem. Award 1978, Royal Gold Medal (R.I.B.A.) 1980, Pritzker Prize 1981. *Major works:* Flats, Ham Common 1955-58, Leicester Univ. Engineering Building (U.S.A. Reynolds Award) 1959-63, Cambridge Univ. History Faculty 1964-67, Andrew Melville Hall, St. Andrews Univ. 1964-68, Dorman Long Steel Co. Head Office 1965, Runcorn New Town Housing 1968-, Florey Building, Queen's Coll., Oxford 1967-71, Redevt. Plan of West Mid-Town Manhattan for New York Planning Comm. 1968-69, Olivetti Training School 1969-72, Olivetti Head Office, U.K. 1970-, Regional Centre 1976, State Art Gallery, Stuttgart, Bayer Agrochemical Research Centre, Fed. Repub. of Germany 1978, Chandler North, Columbia Univ., U.S.A. 1979, Fogg Museum, Harvard Univ. 1979, School of Architecture, Rice Univ., U.S.A. 1979, Turner Museum Extension, Tate Gallery, London 1982, Tate Gallery, Liverpool 1983, Performing Arts Centre, Cornell Univ. 1983, Science Centre, Berlin 1984, Music and Theatre Acad., Stuttgart 1985, Brera Museum Extension, Milan 1986, Science Library, Univ. of Calif. at Irvine 1987. *Publications:* include James Stirling: Buildings and Projects 1950-74, R.I.B.A. Drawings Catalogue. *Address:* 8 Fitzroy Square, London, W.1., England. *Telephone:* 01-388 6188.

STIRN, Olivier, L. EN D.; French civil servant; b. 24 Feb. 1936, Boulogne-Billancourt; s. of Alexandre Stirn and Geneviève Dreyfus; two s.; ed. Univ. of Paris; Deputy for Calvados 1968-86, for Manche 1986-; Councillor Gen., Mayor of Vire 1970-; Sec. of State for Parl. Relations 1973, for Overseas Territories 1974-78, for Foreign Affairs 1978-81, for Defence 1980-81; Minister Del. for Overseas Territories May-June 1988, Minister Del. attached to Minister of Industry and Territorial Devt. June 1988-. *Publications:* Le Piège (with Bernard Stasi and J. P. Soisson) 1973, Une certaine idée du centre 1985. *Address:* 29 quai d'Anjou, 75004 Paris, France. *Telephone:* 46.33.17.78.

STOCKHAUSEN, Karlheinz; German composer; b. 22 Aug. 1928, Moedrath bei Köln; s. of Simon Stockhausen and Gertrud Stupp; m. 1st Doris Andreae 1951, 2nd Mary Bauermeister 1967; two s. four d.; ed. Cologne State Music Conservatory, Univs. of Cologne and Bonn; worked with Olivier Messiaen and with the "Musique Concrète" Group in Paris 1952-53; with Westdeutscher Rundfunk Electronic Music Studio, Cologne 1953-, Artistic Dir. 1963-; first composition of purely electronic music (Studie 1 for sinewaves) 1953; Co-ed. Die Reihe (Universal Edn.) 1954-59; Dozent for composition and analysis at the Int. Summer School for New Music, Darmstadt 1955-74; concert tours throughout the world since 1958; Founder, composition classes in Kölner Kurse für Neue Musik 1963-68; f. ensemble for live electronic music 1964-; exclusive contract with Deutsche Grammophon for interpretation of own works 1968-; Int. World Fair Expo 70, Osaka; Prof. for Composition Staatliche Hochschule für Musik, Cologne 1971-77; mem. Royal Swedish Acad., Akademie der Künste, Berlin, American Acad. and Inst. of Arts and Letters and others; Hon. mem. Royal Acad. of Music, London; many prizes including Preis der deutschen Schallplattenkritik 1964, Grand Prix du Disque 1968, Diapason d'Or 1983; Bundesverdienstkreuz (1st Class), Commdr., Ordre des Arts et des Lettres (France). *Compositions:* Chöre für Doris 1950, Drei Lieder (alto voice and chamber orchestra) 1950, Choral (chorus) 1950, Sonatine (violin and piano) 1951, Kreuzspiel 1951, Formel (orchestra) 1951, Etude (musique concrète) 1952, Schlagtrio 1952, Spiel (orchestra) 1952, Punkte (orchestra) 1952 (new version 1962), Klavierstücke I-IV 1952-53, Kontra-Punkte (ten instruments) 1952-53, Elektronische Studien 1953-54, Klavierstücke V-X 1954-61, Zeitmasze (five woodwind) 1955-56, Gruppen (three orchestras) 1955-57, Klavierstück XI 1956, Gesang der Jünglinge (electronic) 1955-56, Zyklus (percussionist) 1959, Refrain (three players) 1959, Carré (four orchestras

and four choruses) 1959-60, Kontakte (piano, percussion and/or electronic sounds) 1959-60, Originale (musical theatre) 1961, Momente (soprano, four choral groups and 13 instrumentalists) 1962-64, Plus Minus 1963, Mikrophonie 1 (tam-tam, two microphones, two filters and potentiometers) 1964, Mixtur (orchestra, four sine-generators and ring-modulators) 1964, Mikrophonie II (choir, Hammond organ and four ring-modulators) 1965, Stop (orchestra) 1965, Telemusik (electronic music) 1966, Solo (melodic instrument and feed-back) 1966, Adieu (wind quintet) 1966, Hymnen (electronic and concrete music with or without soloists) 1966-67, Prozession (tam-tam, viola, electronium, piano, filters and potentiometers) 1967, Ensemble (process planning) 1967, Kurzwellen (six players) 1968, Stimmung (six vocalists) 1968, Aus den sieben Tagen (fifteen compositions of intuitive music) 1968, Musik für ein Haus (process planning) 1968, Spiral (soloist) 1968, Dr. K-Sextett 1969, Fresco (four orchestral groups) 1969, Hymnen Dritte Region (hymns with orchestra) 1969, Pole (two players/singers) 1970, Expo (three players/singers) 1970, Mantra (two pianists) 1970, Sternklang (park music for 5 groups instrumentalists/singers), Trans (orchestra) 1971, Für kommende Zeiten (17 texts of intuitive music) 1968-70, Alphabet for Liège (13 musical pictures for soloists and duos) 1972, "Am Himmel wandre ich" (12 American Indian songs) 1972, Ylem (19 or more players) 1972, "Atmen gibt das Leben" (choir with orchestra or tape) 1974, Inori (Adorations for soloists and orchestra) 1973-74, Herbstmusik (4 players) 1974, Musik im Bauch (six percussionists and music boxes) 1975, Tierkreis (12 melodies of the star-signs) 1975, Harlekin (clarinet) 1975, The Little Harlequin (clarinet) 1975, Sirius (electronic music and trumpet, bass-clarinet, soprano and bass) 1975-77, Amour (5 pieces for clarinet or flute) 1976, Jubiläum (for orchestra) 1977, In Freundschaft 1977, Licht, die sieben Tage der Woche (for solo voices/instruments, dancers, choir, orchestra, ballet, electronic and concrete music) 1977-, an operatic cycle that includes Donnerstag 1981, Samstag 1984, Montag 1988, and other scenes for a combination of forces; over 90 records. *Publications:* Texte (6 vols.) 1952-62, 1963-70, 1970-77, 1977-84, Stockhausen on Music-Lectures and Interviews 1989. *Address:* Studio für Elektronische Musik, Westdeutscher Rundfunk, Wallrafplatz 5, Cologne; Stockhausen-Verlag, 5067 Kürten, Federal Republic of Germany.

STOCKMAN, David Allen, B.A.; American politician and administrator; b. 10 Nov. 1946, Fort Hood, Tex.; s. of Allen and Carol (Bartz) Stockman; m. Jennifer Blei 1983; one d.; ed. Michigan State Univ., East Lansing, and Harvard Univ. Divinity School; Special Asst. to Congressman John Anderson 1970-73; Exec. Dir. Republican Conf., House of Reps. 1972-75; mem. House of Reps. from 4th Dist. of Mich. 1977-79, mem. Interstate and Foreign Commerce Cttee., Admin. Cttee.; Chair. Republican Econ. Policy Task Force 1977-81; Dir. U.S. Office of Man. and Budget 1981-85; with Salomon Bros. 1985-88; Partner Blackstone Group 1988-; mem. Nat. Comm. on Air Quality 1978; Jefferson Award 1981. *Publication:* The Triumph of Politics: Why the Reagan Revolution Failed 1986. *Address:* c/o Salomon Brothers, 1 New York Plaza, New York, N.Y. 10004, U.S.A.

STOCKTON, 2nd Earl of; Alexander Daniel Alan Macmillan, F.B.I.M., F.R.S.A., B.A.; British publisher; b. 10 Oct. 1943, Oswestry; s. of the late Maurice Victor Macmillan (Viscount Macmillan of Ovenden) and of Dame Katherine Macmillan (Viscountess Macmillan of Ovenden), D.B.E.; grandson of the late 1st Earl of Stockton (formerly, as Harold Macmillan, Prime Minister of U.K. 1957-63); m. Hélène Birgitte Hamilton 1970; one s. two d.; ed. Eton Coll. and Paris and Strathclyde Univs.; Sub.-Ed. Glasgow Herald 1963-65; Reporter, Daily Telegraph 1965-67, Foreign Corresp. 1967-68, Chief European Corresp., Sunday Telegraph 1968-70; Dir. Birch Grove Estates Ltd. 1969-86, Chair. 1983-; Dir. Macmillan and Co. Ltd. 1970-76, Deputy Chair. 1976-80, Chair. 1984-; Chair. Macmillan Publrs. Ltd. 1980-, St. Martin's Press, New York 1983-88 (Dir. 1974-), Sidgwick and Jackson 1989-; Dir. Book Trade Benevolent Soc. 1976-88, Chair. Bookrest Appeal 1978-86; Dir. United British Artists Ltd. 1985- (Chair. 1985-); mem. Lindemann Fellowship Cttee. 1979- (Chair. 1983-), British Inst. of Man. 1981-, Council of Publrs. Assen. 1985-88, Carlton Club Political Cttee. 1975-88 (Chair. 1984); Gov. Archbishop Tenison's School 1979-86, Merchant Taylor's School 1980-82, English Speaking Union 1980-84, 1986-; Liveryman Worshipful Co. of Merchant Taylors 1972, Court Asst. 1986, of Stationers 1973. *Leisure interests:* shooting, fishing, motor racing, aviation. *Address:* Macmillan Publishers Ltd., 4 Little Essex Street, London, WC2R 3LF (Office); 8 Little Boltons, Kensington, London, SW10 9LP, England (Home). *Telephone:* 01-836 6633 (Office); 01-373-6379.

STOCKWOOD, Rt. Rev. (Arthur) Mervyn, M.A.; British ecclesiastic; b. 27 May 1913; s. of late Arthur and Beatrice Ethel Stockwood; ed. Kelly Coll., Christ's Coll. and Westcott House, Cambridge; ordained 1936; Curate, St. Matthew Moorfields, Bristol, and Blundell's School Missioner 1936-41, Vicar 1941-45; Hon. Canon, Bristol 1953-55; Vicar, St. Mary the Great, Cambridge 1955-59; Bishop of Southwark 1959-80; Church Comm. 1972-79; Labour mem. Bristol City Council 1946-55, Cambridge City Council 1956-59; mem. Council Bath Univ. 1980-; Freedom of City of London 1976; Hon. D.D. (Lambeth Univ.) 1959, D.Litt. (Sussex Univ.) 1963, D.D. (Bucharest Univ.) 1977. *Publications:* There is a Tide 1946, Whom They Pierced 1948, I Went to Moscow 1955, The Faith Today 1959, Cambridge Sermons 1959, Bishop's Journal 1965, The Cross and the Sickle 1978, From Strength to Strength 1980, Chanctonbury Ring (autobiog.) 1982. *Leisure interests:*

fishing, walking. *Address:* 15 Sydney Buildings, Bath, Avon, BA2 6BZ, England. *Telephone:* (0225) 63978.

STOECKER, Dietrich, DR.JUR.; German lawyer and diplomatist (retd.); b. 11 Nov. 1915, Cologne; s. of Otto Stoecker and Ina Rottenburg; m. Ingrid Bergemann 1942; four s.; ed. Marburg/Lahn and Lausanne Univs.; Asst. Judge Hanseatic Court of Appeals, Hamburg 1946-48; Official, High Court for Combined Econ. Area, Cologne 1948-49; Official, Fed. Ministry of Justice 1949-52; Diplomatic Service 1953-; Counsellor, German Embassy, Luxembourg 1954-57, Vatican 1957-61; Consul-Gen., Gothenburg 1961-68; Head Admin. Dept., Foreign Office, Berlin 1968-72; Amb. to Sweden 1972-76, to Bulgaria 1976-79. *Publications:* Kommentar zum Gesetz über Ordnungswidrigkeiten 1952, Das Deutsche Obergericht für das Vereinigte Wirtschaftsgebiet in Gedächtnisschrift für Herbert Ruscheweyh 1966. *Address:* Hobsweg 45, 5300 Bonn-Röttgen, Federal Republic of Germany.

STOICHEFF, Boris Peter, O.C., PH.D., F.R.S., F.R.S.C.; Canadian professor of physics; b. 1 June 1924, Bitol, Yugoslavia; s. of Peter Stoicheff and Vasilka (née Tonna) Stoicheff; m. Lillian Joan Ambridge 1954; one s.; ed. Jarvis Collegiate Inst., Toronto, Canada and Univ. of Toronto; Postdoctoral Fellow, Physics, Nat. Research Council, Ottawa 1951-53, Research Officer 1953-64; Visiting Scientist, M.I.T., U.S.A. 1963-64; Prof. of Physics, Univ. of Toronto 1964-, Univ. Prof. 1977-; Chair., Eng. Science 1972-77; I.W. Killam Scholar 1977-79; Visiting Scientist, Stanford Univ., U.S.A. 1978; Exec. Dir., Ontario Laser and Lightwave Research Centre 1988-; professional interests include lasers, atomic and molecular spectroscopy and structure, light scattering and two-photon processes, nonlinear optics and generation of ultraviolet radiation; determined structures of many molecules by light scattering, and discovered inverse Raman effect and stimulated Brillouin scattering (or the generation of sound by light); mem. Gov. Council of Nat. Research Council, Ottawa 1977-83; Hon. Fellow, Indian Acad. of Sciences, Macedonian Acad. of Science and Arts, Yugoslavia, Hon. D.Sc. (Skopje) 1982, (York Univ., Canada) 1982, (Univ. of Windsor, Canada) 1989; Medal of Achievement in Physics, Canadian Assen. of Physicists 1974 (Pres. 1983), William F. Meggers Medal 1981, Frederic Ives Medal, Optical Soc. of America 1983 (Pres. 1976), Henry Marshall Tory Medal, Royal Soc. of Canada 1989. *Publications:* over 150 scientific publs. in int. journals. *Leisure interests:* travel, art, music. *Address:* Department of Physics, University of Toronto, Toronto, Ont., M5S 1A7 (Office); 66 Collier Street, Apt. 6B, Toronto, Ont., M4W 1L9, Canada (Home). *Telephone:* (416) 978-2948 (Office); (416) 923-9622 (Home).

STOKER, Sir Michael George Parke, Kt., C.B.E., M.A., M.D., F.R.S., F.R.S.E., F.R.C.P.; British medical researcher; b. 4 July 1918, Taunton, Somerset; s. of Dr. S. P. Stoker and Mrs. D. (née Nazer) Stoker; m. Veronica Mary English 1942; three s. two d.; ed. Sidney Sussex Coll., Cambridge, and St. Thomas's Hosp., London; Capt. R.A.M.C. 1942-47; lecturer in Pathology, Univ. of Cambridge 1947-58, Fellow of Clare Coll., Cambridge 1948-58; Prof. of Virology, Univ. of Glasgow 1959-68; Dir. Imperial Cancer Research Fund Labs., London 1968-79; Visiting Prof., Univ. Coll., London 1968-79; Fellow of Clare Hall, Cambridge 1978, Pres. 1980-87; Foreign Sec., Vice-Pres. Royal Soc. 1976-81; Gen. Cttee. Int. Council of Scientific Unions 1977-82; Foreign mem. Czech. Acad. of Sciences; Hon. Foreign mem. American Acad. of Arts and Sciences; Hon. D.Sc. (Glasgow) 1982. *Publications:* over 200 articles and reviews on virology, oncology and cell biology. *Address:* 12 Willow Walk, Cambridge, CB1 1LA, England.

STOKES, Baron (Life Peer), cr. 1969, of Leyland in the County Palatine of Lancaster; **Donald Gresham Stokes,** Kt., T.D., D.L., F.ENG., F.I.MECH.E.; British engineer and business executive; b. 22 March 1914, London; s. of Harry Potts Stokes; m. Laura Lamb 1939; one s.; ed. Blundell's School and Harris Inst. of Tech., Preston; student engineer Leyland Motors 1930-33; Tech. Asst. 1933-39; mil. service 1939-45; Export Man. Leyland Motors 1946-50, Gen. Sales and Service Man. 1950, Dir. 1954; Man. Dir. Leyland Motors Corpn. 1963, Chair. 1967; Man. Dir. British Leyland Motors Corpn. 1968-73, Chair. 1968-75, Chief Exec. 1973-75, Pres. British Leyland Ltd. 1975-80, Consultant 1980-81; fmr. Chair. British Leyland U.K. Ltd., NV Leyland Industries Belgium S.A., NV British Leyland (Belgium) S.A., British Leyland Motors Inc. U.S.A.; Chair. British Arabian Advisory Co. Ltd 1977-85, Two Counties Radio Ltd. 1979-84 (Pres. 1984-); Chair. Jack Barclay Ltd. and Jack Barclay (Service) Ltd. 1980-; fmr. Dir. British Leyland Motor Corpn. of Australia Ltd., Leyland Motor Corpn. of S. Africa Ltd., N.Z. Motor Corpn., Ashok Leyland Ltd. India, Ennore Foundries Ltd. India, British Leyland Motors Canada Inc., Automóviles de Turismo Hispano Ingleses S.A., Metalúrgica de Santa Ana, British Leyland France S.A., Leyland Motor Corpn. (Malawi) Ltd.; Dir. Nat. Westminster Bank Ltd. 1969-81, OPUS Public Relations Ltd. 1979-85, Scottish and Universal Investments Ltd. 1980-, The Dutton-Forshaw Motor Group Ltd. 1980- (Chair. 1981-), KBH Communications Ltd. 1985-, Beherman Auto-Transports N.V. 1982-, The Dovercourt Motor Co. 1982-; Vice-Pres. Empresa Nacional de Auto-camiones S.A. (Spain) 1969-73; mem. Council of Soc. of Motor Mfs. and Traders 1953, Vice-Pres. 1961, Pres. 1962, Deputy Pres. 1963; mem. Worshipful Co. of Carmen 1964, North West Econ. Planning Council 1967-70, E.D.C. for the Motor Mfg. Industry 1967, Nat. Advisory Council for the Motor Mfg. Industry 1967; Vice-Pres. Eng. Employers Fed. 1967-75, Inst. of Motor Industry 1967-; Vice-Pres. U.M.I.S.T. 1968, Pres. 1972; Deputy Lieut. for the Lancashire County

Palatine 1968-; Deputy Chair. Ind. Reorganization Corpn. 1968-71; Vice-Pres. I.Mech.E. 1971, Pres. 1972; Cdre. Royal Motor Yacht Club, Poole 1979-81; Hon. Fellow, Keble Coll., Oxford 1968; Fellow, Inst. of Road Transport Engineers 1968, Pres. 1982-; Officer, Ordre de La Couronne (Belgium); Commdr., Ordre de Léopold II (Belgium) 1972; Hon. LL.D. (Lancaster Univ.) Hon. D.Tech. (Loughborough), Hon. D.Sc. (Southampton and Salford); U.K. Marketing Award 1964. *Leisure interest:* yachting. *Address:* Branksome Cliff, Westminster Road, Poole, Dorset, BH13 6JW; Jack Barclay Ltd., 18 Berkeley Square, London, W1X 6AE, England.

STOLLEY, Paul David, M.D., M.P.H.; American professor of medicine; b. 17 June 1937, Pawling, New York; s. of Herman Stolley and Rosalie Chertock; m. Jo Ann Goldenberg 1959; one s. two d.; ed. Lafayette Coll., Cornell Univ. Medical School and Johns Hopkins School of Public Health; Medical Officer, U.S. Public Health Service 1964-67; Asst. and Assoc. Prof. of Epidemiology, Johns Hopkins School of Public Health 1968-76; Herbert C. Rorer Prof. of Medical Science, Univ. of Pennsylvania School of Medicine 1976-; Pres. American Coll. of Epidemiology 1987-88; mem. Inst. of Medicine, N.A.S., Soc. for Epidemiologic Research (Pres. 1984), Int. Epidemiology Assen. (fmr Treasurer), Johns Hopkins Soc. of Scholars; Hon. M.A. (Pennsylvania) 1976. *Publications:* Case Control Studies (co-author) 1982 and numerous articles on epidemiological subjects. *Leisure interests:* classical music, history, literature, jogging. *Address:* University of Pennsylvania School of Medicine, 420 Service Drive, Philadelphia, Pa. 19104 (Office); 138 Montrose Avenue, 9 Rosemount, Pa. 19010, U.S.A. (Home).

STOLTE, Dieter; German television administrator and professor; b. 18 Sept. 1934, Cologne; ed. Univs. of Tübingen and Mainz; Head of Science Dept., Saarländischer Rundfunk 1961; Personal adviser to Dir.-Gen. of Zweites Deutsches Fernsehen (ZDF) 1962, Controller, Programme Planning Dept. 1967, Programming Dir. 1976-, Dir.-Gen. ZDF March 1982-; Dir. and Deputy Dir. Gen., Südwestfunk 1973; Prof. Univ. of Music and Presentation Arts, Hamburg 1980-; mem. Admin. Council, German Press Agency (dpa), Hamburg, European Broadcasting Union (EBU); Chair. Admin. Council TransTel, Cologne; mem. Int. Broadcast Inst., London; mem. Council, Nat. Acad. of TV Arts, New York, Int. Acad. of Arts and Sciences, New York; Cross of Order of Merit, Officer's Cross, Golden Order of Merit (Austria), Bavarian Order of Merit, Hon. Citizen of State of Tenn., U.S.A. *Publications:* ed. and co-author of several books on programme concepts and function of television, etc.; several essays on subjects relating to the philosophy of culture and the science of communication. *Address:* Essenheimer strasse, P.O. Box 40 40, D-6500 Mainz, Federal Republic of Germany. *Telephone:* (0 61 31) 70-2000.

STOLTENBERG, Gerhard, DR.PHIL.; German scientist and politician; b. 29 Sept. 1928, Kiel; m. Margot Rann 1958; one s. one d.; ed. Grammar School, Bad Oldesloe, and Kiel Univ.; Scientific Asst., Kiel Univ. 1954-60, lecturer 1960-65; Deputy Chair. CDU, Schleswig-Holstein 1955, Chair. 1971; Fed. Chair. "Junge Union" 1955-61; mem. Schleswig-Holstein Parl. 1954-57, 1971-82; mem. Bundestag 1957-71, 1983-; Fed. Minister for Scientific Research 1965-69; Fed. Vice-Chair. CDU 1969-; Minister-Pres. Land Schleswig-Holstein 1971-82; Minister of Finance 1982-89 of Defence April 1989-; Chair. Kreditanstaltfür Wiederaufbau 1983-; mem. Bd. of Man. Fried. Krupp, Essen 1965, 1969-70; Grosses Bundesverdienstkreuz. *Publications:* Der Deutsche Reichstag 1871-73, Politische Strömungen im schleswig-holsteiner Landvolk 1919-33. *Address:* Hardthöhe, P.O. Box 1328, 5300 Bonn 1, Federal Republic of Germany.

STOLTENBERG, Thorvald; Norwegian politician; b. 8 July 1931, Oslo; m. Karin Stoltenberg; three c.; joined Foreign Service 1959; served in San Francisco, Belgrade, Lagos and Foreign Ministry; Int. Sec. Norwegian Fed. of Trade Unions 1970-71; Under-Sec. of State, Foreign Ministry 1971-72, 1976-79; Under-Sec. of State, Ministry of Defence 1973-74, Ministry of Commerce 1974-76; Minister of Defence 1979-81, of Foreign Affairs March 1987-; Deputy Mayor of Oslo 1985-87; Municipal Councillor, Oslo 1984-; mem. Finance and Planning Cttees. *Address:* Ministry of Foreign Affairs, P.O.B. 8114, Dep., 0032 Oslo 1, Norway. *Telephone;* (2) 20-41-70.

STONE, Donald Crawford, LL.D.; American government official and educator; b. 17 June 1903, Cleveland, Ohio; s. of Alfred W. and Mary R. Stone; m. Alice Kathryn Biermann 1928; one s. three d.; ed. Colgate, Syracuse, Cincinnati and Columbia Univs.; Staff mem. Cincinnati Bureau of Governmental Research 1927-28, Inst. of Public Admin., New York 1929-30; Dir. of Research, Int. City Man. Assen., Chicago 1930-33; Exec. Dir., Public Admin. Service, Chicago 1933-39; Asst. Dir. Bureau of the Budget, Exec. Office of the Pres., Washington 1939-48; Dir. of Admin., E.C.A. (Marshall Plan), Washington D.C. 1948-51, Mutual Security Agency 1951-53; Pres. Springfield Coll. 1953-57; Adviser to U.S. Del., to UN Conf., San Francisco 1945, to U.S. Del. to UNESCO Organizing Conf., London 1945, to Gen. Ass. of UN, London 1946, and New York 1947, to U.S. Rep. to Econ. and Social Council New York 1946; U.S. Rep. to UNESCO Preparatory Comm., London 1946; mem. UN Standing Cttee. on Admin. and Budgetary Affairs 1946-48; Dean, Graduate School of Public and Int. Affairs, Pittsburgh Univ. 1957-69, now Distinguished Public Service Prof. School of Urban and Public Affairs, Carnegie-Mellon Univ.; Advisory assignments or studies in approx. 25 countries; Consultant to OAS 1958-60, to UN 1970-74, 1981; Chair. Cttee. on Leaders and Specialists and mem. Comm. on Educ. and Int Affairs, American Council on

Educ. 1955–61; Pres. Int. Asscn. of Schools and Insts. of Admin. 1961–82, Cttee. on Int. Admin., Nat. Acad. of Public Admin. 1974–; Chair. American Consortium for Int. Public Admin. 1978–80, Int. Conf. on Improving Public Man. and Performance, Washington, D.C. 1979, Int. Round Table on Public Admin., Canberra, Australia 1981; Dir. Coalition to Improve Man. in State and Local Govt. *Publications:* numerous articles, monographs and books on government, international development and education. *Leisure interests:* sports, music, religious activities. *Address:* School of Urban and Public Affairs, Carnegie-Mellon Univ., Pittsburgh, Pa. 15213, U.S.A. *Telephone:* (412) 268-2179.

STONE, Francis Gordon Albert, SC.D., F.R.S.; British professor of chemistry; b. 19 May 1925, Exeter; s. of Sidney Charles and Florence Stone; m. Judith M. Hislop 1956; three s.; ed. Christ's Coll., Univ. of Cambridge; Fulbright Scholarship, Univ. of Southern Calif. 1952–54; Instructor and Asst. Prof., Harvard Univ. 1954–62; Reader, Queen Mary Coll., Univ. of London 1962–63; Head, Dept. of Inorganic Chem. and Prof., Univ. of Bristol 1963–; Visiting Prof., numerous univs.; Pres. Dalton Div., Royal Soc. of Chem. 1981–83; Guggenheim Fellow 1961; Sr. Visiting Fellow, Australian Acad. of Sciences 1966; mem. Council, Royal Soc. of Chem. 1968–70, 1981–83, Chem. Cttee., Science and Eng. Research Council 1971–74, 1982–85; mem. Council of Royal Soc. 1986–88 (Vice-Pres. 1987–88); Royal Soc. of Chem. Medals for Organometallic Chemistry 1972, Transition Metal Chemistry 1979; Chugaev Medal and Diploma, Kurnakov Inst., U.S.S.R. Acad. of Sciences 1978; American Chem. Soc. Award in Inorganic Chem. 1985. *Publications:* over 500 articles in scientific journals and books; Advances in Organometallic Chemistry, Vols. 1–27 (Ed.); Comprehensive Organometallic Chemistry, Vols. 1–9 (Co-Ed.) 1982. *Leisure interest:* travel. *Address:* School of Chemistry, University of Bristol, Bristol, BS8 1TS, England. *Telephone:* (0272) 303674.

STONE, Irving, M.A., CAND. PH.D.; American writer; b. 14 July 1903, San Francisco, Calif.; s. of Charles and Pauline (Rosenberg) Tennenbaum (took step-father's name 1911); m. Jean Factor 1934; one s. one d.; ed. Univ. of California, Univ. of Southern Calif.; Teaching Fellow, Univ. of Southern Calif. 1923–24, Univ. of Calif. 1924–26; Lecturer in Creative Writing, Indiana 1948, Washington 1961, Univ. of Southern Calif. 1966, Calif. State Colleges 1966, Univ. of Pacific, New York Univ., Johns Hopkins Univ. 1985; Regents Prof., Univ. of Calif. (Los Angeles) 1984–85; book reviews, magazine contributions; mem. numerous cultural, literary socs.; numerous awards, including McGovern Award for Literature 1988; founder Irving and Jean Stone prizes for biog. and historical novels 1968–; Fellow, Historical Soc. of Southern Calif.; Hon. D.Lit. (Univ. of S. Calif., Coe Coll., Calif. State Colls.), Hon. LL.D. (Univ. of Calif. at Berkeley), D.Hum.Litt. (Hebrew Union Coll.) 1978; Commdr. dans l'Ordre des Arts et des Lettres (France) 1984; Commendatore (Italy) 1965; Grande Ufficiale (Italy) 1982. *Publications:* Pageant of Youth 1933, Lust for Life 1934, Dear Theo 1937, Sailor on Horseback 1938, False Witness 1940, Clarence Darrow for the Defense 1941, They also Ran 1943, Immortal Wife 1944, Adversary in the House 1947, Earl Warren 1948, The Passionate Journey 1949, We Speak for Ourselves 1950, The President's Lady 1951, Love is Eternal 1954, Men to Match My Mountains 1956, The Biographical Novel 1957, The Agony and the Ecstasy 1961, Lincoln, A Contemporary Portrait (Ed.) 1962, I, Michelangelo, Sculptor 1962, The Irving Stone Reader 1963, Story of Michelangelo's Pietà 1964, The Great Adventures of Michelangelo 1965, Those Who Love 1965, There Was Light: Autobiography of University, Berkeley, 1868-1968 1970, The Passions of the Mind 1971, Mary Todd Lincoln: A Final Judgment? 1974, The Greek Treasure 1975, Irving Stone's Jack London, A Biography, with 28 Jack London Stories 1977, The Origin 1980, Darwin's Legacy 1982, Depths of Glory (biographical novel about Camille Pissarro) 1985, The Science, and the Art, of Biography 1986. *Address:* c/o Doubleday, 666 Fifth Avenue, New York, N.Y. 10103, U.S.A.

STONE, John O., B.A., B.SC.; Australian financial executive and politician; b. 31 Jan. 1929, Perth; s. of Horace and Eva Stone (née Hunt); m. Nancy Hardwick 1954; four s. one d.; ed. Univ. of Western Australia and New Coll., Oxford; Asst. to Australian Treasury Rep. in London 1954–56, Australian Treasury Rep. in London 1958–61; in Research and Information Div., Gen. Financial and Econ. Policy Branch, Dept. of Treasury, Canberra 1956–57, in Home Finance Div. 1961–62, Asst. Sec. Econ. and Financial Surveys Div. 1962–66; Exec. Dir. for Australia, New Zealand and S. Africa, Int. Monetary Fund (IMF) and IBRD—World Bank 1967–70; First Asst. Sec., Revenue, Loans and Investment Div., Treasury 1971; Sec. Australian Loan Council, Sec. Australian Nat. Debt Comm. 1971; Deputy Sec. (Econ.) Treasury 1971–76, Deputy Sec. Treasury 1976–78, Sec. 1979–84; Visiting Prof. Centre of Policy Studies, Monash Univ., Melbourne 1984; Consultant, Potter Partners, Stockbrokers 1985–; weekly columnist, Sydney Morning Herald, etc. 1985–; Dir. Sperry (Australia) Ltd. 1985–, Peko-Wallsend Ltd. 1986; Senator for Queensland 1987–; Leader of Nat. Party in the Senate, Shadow Minister for Finance; Sr. Fellow, Inst. of Public Affairs, Melbourne 1985–. *Leisure interests:* reading, tennis, wine and food. *Address:* Potter Partners, 325 Collins Street, Melbourne, Vic. 3000, Australia.

STONE, Sir (John) Richard (Nicholas), Kt., C.B.E., SC.D., F.B.A.; British economist (retd.); b. 30 Aug. 1913; s. of the late Sir Gilbert Stone; m. 1st Winifred Jenkins 1936 (dissolved); m. 2nd Feodora Leontinoff 1941 (died 1956), one d.; m. 3rd Mrs. Giovanna Croft-Murray 1960; ed. Westminster

School and Gonville and Caius Coll., Cambridge; with C. E. Heath and Co. (Lloyd's Brokers) 1936–39; Ministry of Econ. Warfare 1939–40; offices of War Cabinet, Cen. Statistical Office 1940–45; Dir. Dept. of Applied Econs., Cambridge 1945–55; Leake Prof. of Finance and Accounting, Cambridge 1955–80; Fellow, King's Coll., Cambridge 1945–, Econometric Soc. (Pres. 1955); mem. Int. Statistical Inst.; Foreign Hon. mem. American Acad. of Arts and Sciences 1968, American Econ. Asscn. 1976; Hon. Fellow Gonville and Caius Coll., Cambridge 1976; Pres. Royal Econ. Soc. 1978–80; Sc.D. 1957, Dr. h.c. (Oslo and Brussels Univ.) 1965, (Geneva Univ.) 1971, (Warwick Univ.) 1975, (Paris) 1977, (Bristol Univ.) 1978; Nobel Prize for Econs. 1984; Foreign mem. Acad. dei Lincei 1987. *Publications:* The Role of Measurement in Economics 1951, The Measurement of Consumers' Expenditure and Behaviour in the United Kingdom 1920–1938 Vol. I (with others) 1954, Vol. II (with D. A. Rowe) 1966, Quantity and Price Indexes in National Accounts 1956, Social Accounting and Economic Models (with Giovanna Croft-Murray) 1959, Input-Output and Nat. Accounts 1961, National Income and Expenditure (with Giovanna Stone) 1961, A Programme for Growth (gen. ed., series with others) 1962–74, Mathematics in the Social Sciences and Other Essays 1966, Mathematical Models of the Economy and Other Essays 1970, Demographic Accounting and Model Building 1971, Aspects of Economic and Social Modelling 1980; numerous articles in learned journals. *Address:* 13 Millington Road, Cambridge, England.

STONE, Lawrence; American (b. British) professor of history; b. 4 Dec. 1919, Epsom, Surrey; s. of Lawrence Frederick and Mabel Annie Julia Stone; m. Jeanne Caecilia Fawtier 1943; one s. one d.; ed. Charterhouse School, Sorbonne, Paris, Christ Church, Oxford; Lieut. R.N.V.R. 1940–45; Bryce Research Student, Univ. of Oxford 1946–47, Jt. Lecturer, Univ. and Corpus Christi Colls., Oxford 1947–50, Fellow of Wadham Coll., Oxford 1950–63; mem. Inst. for Advanced Study, Princeton, N.J. 1960–61, Dodge Prof. of History, Princeton Univ. 1963–, Chair. of History Dept. 1967–69, Dir. Shelby Cullom Davis Center for Historical Studies 1969–; mem. American Philosophical Soc. 1970; Fellow of American Acad. of Arts and Sciences 1968; Hon. D.Hum.Litt. (Chicago) 1979, (Pennsylvania) 1986; Hon. D.Litt. (Edin.) 1983. *Publications:* Sculpture in Britain: The Middle Ages 1955, An Elizabethan: Sir Horatio Palavicino 1956, The Crisis of the Aristocracy, 1558-1641 1965, Social Change and Revolution in England, 1540-1642 1965, The Causes of the English Revolution 1529-1642 1972, Family and Fortune: Studies in Aristocratic Finance in the 16th and 17th Centuries 1973, The Family, Sex and Marriage in England 1500-1800 1977, The Past and Present 1981, An Open Elite? England 1540-1880 1984. *Leisure interest:* travel. *Address:* 266 Moore Street, Princeton, N.J. 08540, U.S.A.; 231A Woodstock Road, Oxford, England. *Telephone:* (609) 921-2717 (U.S.A.); (0865) 59174 (England).

STONE, Norman, M.A.; British historian; b. 8 March 1941, Glasgow; s. of late Norman Stone and of Mary Robertson Stone (née Pettigrew); m. 1st Marie-Nicole Aubry 1966 (dissolved 1977), two s.; m. 2nd Christine Booker (née Verity) 1982, one s.; ed. Glasgow Acad. and Gonville & Caius Coll., Cambridge; research student, Christ's Coll., Cambridge attached to Austrian and Hungarian insts. 1962–65; Research Fellow, Gonville & Caius Coll. 1965–67; Asst. Lecturer, Faculty of History, Univ. of Cambridge 1967–72, lecturer in History (Russian) 1973–84; Fellow, Jesus Coll., Cambridge and Dir. of Studies in History 1971–79; Fellow, Trinity Coll., Cambridge 1979–84; Prof. of Modern History, Univ. of Oxford and Fellow, Worcester Coll., Oxford 1984–; Wolfson Prize 1976. *Publications:* The Eastern Front 1914–17 1976, Hitler 1980, Europe Transformed 1878–1919 1982, articles in the Sunday Times and learned journals. *Leisure interests:* music, Eastern Europe, languages. *Address:* Worcester College, Oxford; The Grey Barn, Queen Street, Bampton, Oxon.; 18 Thorncliffe Road, Oxford, England. *Telephone:* (0865) 242571 (College); (0993) 850214 (Bampton); (0865) 511334 (Oxford, Home).

STONE, Oliver, B.F.A.; American film director and screenwriter; b. 15 Sept. 1946, New York; s. of Louis Stone and Jacqueline Goddet; ed. Yale Univ. and New York Univ. Film School; Teacher, Cholon, Vietnam 1965–66; U.S. Merchant Marine 1966, U.S. Army, Vietnam 1967–68; taxi driver, New York 1971. Wrote screenplay for films Midnight Express (Acad. Award for best screenplay adapted from another medium) 1978, Conan the Barbarian (co-wrote) 1982, Scarface 1983. Directed and wrote films: Seizure 1973, The Hand 1981, Year of the Dragon (with Michael Cimino) 1985, Salvador (co-wrote) 1986, Platoon (Acad. Award for Best Film, Best Dir.) 1986, Wall Street 1987, Talk Radio (co-wrote) 1988, Evita, Born on the Fourth of July. *Address:* 9100 Sunset Blvd., Suite 355, Los Angeles, Calif. 90069 (Office); P.O. Box 43, Sagaponack, New York, N.Y. 11962, U.S.A. (Home).

STONE, Sir Richard (see Stone, Sir J. R. N.).

STONER, Oliver Gerald, B.A. (ECONS.); Canadian government official; b. 21 Aug. 1922, London, Ont.; s. of Oliver C. and Ethel Stoner; m. Elizabeth M. Allen 1951; one. s. one d.; ed. Univ. of Western Ontario and Queen's Univ.; joined Dept. of External Affairs 1947, served Paris 1950–54, Brussels 1958–59; Sr. Asst. Sec. of Cabinet and Asst. Clerk of Privy Council 1964–67, Acting Sec. to Cabinet and Acting Clerk of Privy Council 1967–68, Deputy Clerk of Privy Council and Deputy Sec. to Cabinet 1968–69; Deputy Minister of Transport 1969–75; Deputy Minister, Dept. of Industry, Trade and Commerce 1975-77; mem. Bd. of Dirs. Canadian Devt. Corpn. 1975-77; Vice-Chair. DeHavilland Aircraft 1975-77, Export Devt. Corpn. 1975-77; Commr. Fed. Royal Comm. on Financial Man. and Accountability 1977-79; Chair. Restrictive Trade Practices Comm. 1979-; Hon. LL.D. (W. Ont.) 1980. *Leisure interests:* tennis, music, reading. *Address:* 161 Maple Lane, Rockcliffe Park, Ottawa, Ont., K1M 1G4, Canada. *Telephone:* 992-0217.

STOOKEY, John Hoyt; American business executive; b. 29 Jan. 1930, New York City; s. of Byron Stookey and Helen Stookey; m. Katherine Elizabeth Emory 1954; two s. two d.; ed. Amherst Coll. and Columbia School of Eng.; mem. of bd. of Nat. Distillers and Chemical Corpn. 1970, Pres. 1975-86, Dir. 1970-, Chair. and C.E.O. April 1986-; fmr. Pres. Wallace Clark, Inc., New York; fmr. U.S. Rep. Banco Nacional de Obras y Servicios Publicos S.A. and Financiera Metropolitana S.A.; Dir. Riegel Textile Corpn., Rexham Corpn.; Chair. Bio-Energy Council; Pres. Berks. Choral Inst.; Trustee Boston Symphony Orchestra and Coll. for Human Services; mem. of Council on Foreign Relations and Advisory Council of Nat. Public Radio. *Address:* National Distillers and Chemical Corpn., 99 Park Avenue, New York, N.Y. 10016, U.S.A.

STOPH, Willi; German politician; b. 9 July 1914, Berlin; m.; four c.; worked as a mason and foreman bricklayer, later as a tech. architect, following extra-mural studies; mem. CP of Germany 1931; Head of Econ. Policy Section, SED 1948-50; mem. SED Cen. Cttee. 1950-, mem. Politburo of SED Cen. Cttee. 1953-; mem. Volkskammer (People's Chamber) 1950-; mem. Council of State 1963-, Deputy Chair. 1964-73, 1976-, Chair. (Head of State) 1973-76; Minister of the Interior 1952-55; Minister of Nat. Defence (rank of Gen. of Army) 1956-60; Deputy Chair. Council of Ministers 1954-64, Chair. Council of Ministers 1964-73, 1976-; Vaterländischer Verdienstorden in Gold (twice), Order of Lenin (twice), Order of October Revolution (U.S.S.R.), Jose Marti Order (G.D.R.) 1984 and other decorations. *Address:* Kolsterstrasse 47, 102 Berlin, German Democratic Republic.

STOPPARD, Tom, C.B.E., F.R.S.L.; British writer; b. (as Thomas Straussler) 3 July 1937, Zlin, Czechoslovakia; s. of the late Dr. Eugene and Martha Straussler; stepson of Kenneth Stoppard; m. 1st Jose Ingle 1965 (divorced 1972), two s.; m. 2nd Dr. Miriam Moore-Robinson 1972, two s.; ed. Pocklington Grammar School, Yorks.; Journalist, Bristol 1954-60; freelance journalist, London 1960-64; mem. Cttee. of the Free World 1981-; John Whiting Award, Arts Council 1967, New York Drama Critics Best Play Award 1968, Antoinette Perry Award 1968, 1976, Evening Standard Awards 1967, 1972, 1974, 1978, 1982; Italia Prize (radio drama) 1968; Hon. M.Litt. (Bristol, Brunel Univs.), Hon. Litt.D. (Leeds Univ.) 1979, (Sussex) 1980, (Warwick) 1981, (London) 1982. *Publications:* plays: Rosencrantz and Guildenstern are Dead 1967, The Real Inspector Hound 1968, Enter a Free Man 1968, After Magritte 1970, Dogg's Our Pet 1972, Jumpers 1972, Travesties 1975, Dirty Linen 1976, New-Found-Land 1976, Every Good Boy Deserves Favour (with music by André Previn, q.v.)) 1978, Night and Day 1978, Dogg's Hamlet, Cahoots Macbeth 1979, Undiscovered Country 1980, On the Razzle 1981, The Real Thing 1982, Rough Crossing 1984, Hapgood 1988; Dalliance (adaption of Schmitzler's Liebelei) 1986; radio plays: The Dissolution of Dominic Boot 1964, M is for Moon among other things 1964, Albert's Bridge 1967, If You're Glad I'll be Frank 1968, Where Are They Now? 1970, Artist Descending a Staircase 1972, The Dog it was that Died 1983; short stories: Introduction 2 1963; novel: Lord Malquist and Mr. Moon 1966; screenplays: The Romantic Englishwoman (co-author) 1975, Despair 1977, film scripts: The Human Factor 1979, Brazil (with Terry Gilliam, q.v. and Charles McKeown) 1984, Empire of the Sun 1987, Rosencrantz and Guildenstern are Dead 1989; television plays: Professional Foul 1977, Squaring the Circle 1984. *Address:* c/o Fraser & Dunlop Scripts Ltd., 91 Regent Street, London, W.1; Iver Grove, Iver, Bucks., England.

STORCH, Marcus, M.SC.; Swedish business executive; b. 28 July 1942, Stockholm; s. of Hilel Storch and Anna Storch; m. Gunilla Berglund 1972; one s. one d.; ed. Royal Inst. of Tech., Stockholm; Dept. Head, Welding 1968-72; Pres. Welding Div. AGA AB 1972-75, Pres. Gas Div. 1975-81, Exec. Vice-Pres. AGA AB 1978-81, Pres. and C.E.O. 1981-88, Man. Dir. 1988-; mem. Bd. Esselte, Inter Innovation, Swedish Employers' Confed. *Address:* Grevgatan 65, S-114 59 Stockholm, Sweden. *Telephone:* 08/617195.

STOREY, David Malcolm; British author and playwright, b. 13 July 1933, Wakefield, Yorkshire; s. of Frank Richmond and Lily (née Cartwright) Storey; m. Barbara Hamilton 1956; two s. two d.; ed. Wakefield Grammar School, Wakefield Coll. of Art and Slade School of Art; Fellow, Univ. Coll. London 1974. *Publications:* novels: This Sporting Life (MacMillan Award) 1960, Flight into Camden (John Llewellyn Rhys Memorial Prize 1961, Somerset Maugham Award 1963) 1960, Radcliffe 1963, Pasmore (Faber Memorial Prize 1972) 1972, A Temporary Life 1973, Saville (Booker Prize 1976) 1976, A Prodigal Child 1982, Present Times 1984; plays: The Restoration of Arnold Middleton (Evening Standard Award 1967), In Celebration 1969 (also film), The Contractor (New York Critics' Prize 1974) 1969, Home (Evening Standard Award, New York Critics' Prize) 1970, The Changing Room (New York Critics' Prize) 1971, Cromwell 1973, The Farm 1973, Life Class 1974, Night 1976, Mother's Day 1976, Sisters 1978, Dreams of Leaving 1979, Early Days 1980, The March on Russia 1989. *Address:* c/o Jonathan Cape Ltd., 32 Bedford Square, London, WC1B 3EL, England.

STORK, Gilbert, PH.D.; American professor of chemistry; b. 31 Dec. 1921, Brussels, Belgium; s. of Jacques Stork and Simone Weil; m. Winifred Elizabeth Stewart 1944; one s. three d.; ed. Univ. of Wisconsin; Instructor, Harvard Univ. 1946-48, Asst. Prof. 1948-53; Assoc. Prof., Columbia Univ. 1953-55, Prof. 1955-67, Eugene Higgins Prof. of Chem. 1967-, Chair. of Dept. 1973-76; mem. N.A.S., American Acad. of Arts and Sciences; Hon. Fellow, Royal Soc. of Chemistry; Hon. Fellow Pharmaceutical Soc. of Japan; Hon. D.Sc. (Lawrence Coll.) 1961, (Univ. of Paris) 1979, (Univ. of Rochester) 1982; Award in Pure Chemistry of A.C.S. 1957, Baekeland Medal of N. Jersey Section of A.C.S. 1961, Harrison Howe Award 1962, Edward Curtis Franklin Memorial Award of Stanford Univ. 1966, A.C.S. Award in Synthetic Organic Chemistry 1967, Nebraska Award 1973, Roussel Prize 1978, Nichols Medal 1980, Arthur C. Cope Award, A.C.S. 1980, N.A.S. Award in Chemical Sciences 1982, Netherlands Medal of Science 1983, Cliff S. Hamilton Award 1986, and numerous other awards and medals. *Address:* Columbia University, New York, N.Y. 10027 (Office); 459 Next Day Hill Drive, Englewood, N.J. 07631, U.S.A. (Home). *Telephone:* (201) 871-4032.

STOVE, David Charles, B.A., F.A.H.A.; Australian philosopher; b. 15 Sept. 1927, Moree, N.S.W.; m. Jessie A. Leahy 1959; one s. one d.; ed. Newcastle Boys' High School and Univ. of Sydney; Assoc. Prof. Dept. of Traditional and Modern Philosophy, Univ. of Sydney 1960-87. *Publications:* Probability and Hume's Inductive Scepticism 1973, Popper and After 1982, The Rationality of Induction 1986. *Leisure interests:* growing trees, camping. *Address:* Nepean Gorge Drive, Mulgoa 2750, N.S.W., Australia (Home). *Telephone:* (047) 738258 (Home).

STOWE, Leland, M.A.; American journalist; b. 10 Nov. 1899, Southbury, Conn.; s. of Frank Philip and Eva Sarah (née Noe) Stowe; m. 1st Ruth F. Bernot 1924, one. s.; m. 2nd Theodora F. Calauz 1952; ed. Wesleyan Univ.; mem. staff Worcester Telegram 1921; Foreign Ed. Pathé News 1924; Paris corresp. New York Herald Tribune 1926-35; Pres. Anglo-American Press Club of Paris 1935-35; reporter in N. and S. America for New York Herald Tribune 1935-38; war corresp. Chicago Daily News Scandinavia, U.S.S.R. Balkans, Egypt and Far East 1939-42, Europe 1944-45; News Analyst, American Broadcasting Co. 1944-45; Greek Mil. Cross 1945; Lecturer-Writer New York Post Syndicate; Foreign Ed. The Reporter Magazine 1948-50; Dir. News and Information Service, Radio Free Europe, Munich 1952-54; Roving Ed. The Reader's Digest 1955-76; Prof. of Journalism, Univ. of Michigan 1956-70; Hon. D.Litt. (Wesleyan Univ., Hobart Coll.); Pulitzer Prize for best foreign corresp. 1930. *Publications:* Nazi Means War 1933, No Other Road to Freedom 1941, They Shall Not Sleep 1944, While Time Remains 1946, Target: You 1949, Conquest by Terror: The Story of Satellite Europe 1952, Crusoe of Lonesome Lake 1957, The Last Great Frontiersman 1982. *Address:* 801 Greenhills Drive, Ann Arbor, Mich. 48105, U.S.A.

STRADLING, Rt. Rev. Leslie Edward, M.A., D.C.L.; British ecclesiastic (retd.); b. 11 Feb. 1908; ed. Oxford Univ., Westcott House, Cambridge; Curate in London 1933-38, Vicar 1938-45; Bishop of Masasi 1945-52, of S.W. Tanganyika 1952-61, of Johannesburg, S.A. 1961-74. *Publications:* A Bishop on Safari 1960, The Acts through Modern Eyes 1963, An Open Door 1966, A Bishop at Prayer 1971, Praying Now 1976, Praying the Psalms 1977. *Address:* Braehead House, Auburn Road, 7700 Kenilworth, South Africa. *Telephone:* 71-6251.

STRANZ, Benon, DR.TECH.SC.; Polish mining engineer and economic administrator (retd.); b. 30 Aug. 1918, Drensteinfurt, Germany; ed. Mining Acad., Cracow; works in coal-mining 1948-; Dir. coal-mine Klimontów, subsequently Deputy Dir. for tech. matters in Dąbrowa Górnicza Dist. Coal Industry Union; Dir. coal-mine Sosnowiec 1949-56, Dir. for tech. matters, then Gen. Dir. of Katowice Union of Coal Industry 1956-72; Gen. Dir. of Main Mining Inst., Katowice 1972-74; Under-Sec. of State, Ministry of Mining 1974-78; Extraordinary Prof. 1976; Chair. State Mining Council 1979-87; mem. Polish United Workers' Party (PZPR) 1956-; Chair. Int. Organizational Cttee. of World Mining Congress 1976-88; Hon. mem. Eng. Asscn. of Yugoslavia, Asscn. of Mining and Metallurgy Engs. of U.K., Asscn. of Mining Engs. of N. Italy; Commdr. Cross with Star, Officer's and Knight's Cross of Polonia Restituta Order, Order of Banner of Labour (1st Class), and other decorations. *Publications:* some 50 theoretical and practical studies on exploitation of mines, and on surface protection against mining damages. *Address:* ul. Gilów 3, 40-563 Katowice, Poland. *Telephone:* 28-59-80 (Office).

STRASSER, Daniel Charles Joachim; French civil servant; b. 10 June 1929, Paris; s. of Charles and Renée Strasser; m. Princess Anneliese Radziwill 1963; one s.; ed. Univ. of Paris; mem. Cabinet of Gen. Sec. of French Govt. 1953-58; mem. Gen. Secr. Comm. of European Communities 1958-59, Asst. Dir.-Gen., Personnel and Admin. 1959-63, Dir. for Admin. 1963-70, for Personnel 1970-73, for Budgets 1977-86; Conseilleur Maître, Cour des Comptes; Prime Minister's del., Cttee. on Air Space 1986-; mem. Exec. Cttee. Int. Inst. of Admin. Sciences; Prof. of European Law, Strasbourg; Dr. h.c. (Oviedo, Spain); Lauréat de l'Inst. de France; Chevalier, Légion d'honneur, Grand Croix Order of Merit (Fed. Repub. of Germany), Commdr. de l'Ordre du mérite civil d'Espagne. *Publications:* Réalités et promesses sahariennes 1956, Les Finances de l'Europe 1975, 1980, 1984 (English trans. 1977, 1981, Spanish

1978, 1982, German 1979, 1982, Italian 1979, 1982, Greek 1980, Portuguese 1981, Danish 1982, Dutch 1982). *Leisure interests:* photography. *Address:* 15 rue Chalgrin 75116, Paris, France. *Telephone:* 4500-4509.

STRASSER, Hans; Swiss banker; b. 19 July 1919, Bienne; m. Liliane Lambelet 1949; joined Schweizerische Bankverein (Swiss Bank Corpn.) 1938; Man. Bienne Branch Office 1956–60, Berne Branch Office 1960–63, Gen. Man. Head Office, Basel 1963–78, Chair. Bd. of Dirs. 1978–84; mem. Bd. of Dirs. Nestlé S.A., Vevey. *Leisure interests:* golf, skiing. *Address:* c/o Schweizerische Bankverein, Aeschenvorstadt 1, 4002 Basel, Switzerland. *Telephone:* 061-20 20 20.

STRATAS, Teresa, O.C.; Canadian opera singer; b. 26 May 1938, Toronto, Ont.; began singing career in nightclubs in Toronto; début at Toronto Opera Festival 1958; noted opera performances at Metropolitan Opera, New York include Berg's Lulu and Jenny in Brecht and Weill's Mahagonny; appeared as Violetta in Zeffirelli's film of La Traviata 1983; appeared in Broadway musical Rags 1986.

STRATTON, Julius A., SC.D., S.M., S.B.; American physicist; b. 18 May 1901, Seattle, Wash.; s. of Julius and Laura Stratton; m. Catherine Coffman 1935; three d.; ed. Univ. of Washington, Mass. Inst. of Tech., Eidgenössische Technische Hochschule, Zürich; with Mass. Inst. of Tech. 1924–; Asst. Prof. Dept. of Electrical Eng. 1928–30, Asst. Prof. of Physics 1930–35, Assoc. Prof. 1935–41, Prof. 1941–51, Dir. Research Lab. of Electronics 1944–49, Provost, M.I.T. 1949–56, Vice-Pres. 1951–56, Chancellor 1956–59, Acting Pres. 1957–59, Pres. 1959–66, Pres. Emer. 1966–; Expert Consultant, Sec. of War 1942–46; mem. Defense Science Bd. 1956–57, Gov. Bd. Nat. Research Council 1961–65, Nat. Science Bd. 1956–62, 1964–67, Naval Research Advisory Cttee. 1954–59 (Chair. 1956–57); Chair. of Bd., The Ford Foundation 1966–71; Dir. Standard Oil Co. of N.J. (now Exxon) 1966–70, Westinghouse Electric Corpn. 1965–73; Trustee Boston Museum of Fine Arts 1955–66, Ford Foundation 1955–71, Pine Manor Coll. 1962–71, RAND Corpn. 1955–65, Vassar Coll. 1962–70; Life Trustee, Boston Museum of Science; Chair. Comm. on Marine Science, Eng. and Resources 1967–69; Life mem. Corpn., M.I.T.; mem. Nat. Advisory Cttee. on Oceans and Atmosphere 1971–73, American Philosophical Soc., N.A.S. (Vice-Pres. 1961–65); mem. emer. of Corpn., Charles Stark Draper Lab. (Dir. and mem. 1973–79); founding mem. Nat. Acad. of Eng.; Life Fellow, Inst. of Electrical and Electronics Engineers; Fellow, American Acad. of Arts and Sciences, A.A.A.S., American Physical Soc.; numerous hon. degrees and awards and decorations, including Officier, Légion d'Honneur 1961, Kt. Commdr., Order of Merit (Fed. Repub. of Germany) 1966. *Publications:* Electromagnetic Theory 1941, Science and the Educated Man 1966, also numerous papers. *Address:* Massachusetts Institute of Technology, Cambridge, Mass. 02139; 100 Memorial Drive, Cambridge, Mass. 02142, U.S.A. (Home).

STRAUB, F. Bruno; Hungarian biochemist and politician; b. 5 Jan. 1914; s. of Ferenc Straub and Teréz Krén; m. 1st Erzsébet Lichtneckert 1940 (died 1967), m. 2nd Gertrud Szabolcsi 1972; two d.; Univ. Prof.; mem. Bd. of Govs. IAEA 1969–71, Vice-Chair. Safeguards Cttee. 1970–71; Dir. Biology Centre of Hungarian Acad. of Sciences 1970–78; Pres. Nat. Council for Environment and Nature Protection 1978; Dir. Inst. of Enzymology 1979–; work mainly concerns studies on muscle proteins, respiration and enzymology; Pres. of Hungary June 1988–; Vice-Pres. Nat. Peace Council 1958–62; mem. Hungarian Acad. of Sciences, Vice-Pres. 1967–72, 1985–; Vice-Pres. Int. Council of Scientific Unions (ICSU) 1974–76, Pres. 1976–78; foreign mem. Polish Acad. of Sciences, Czechoslovak Acad. of Sciences, G.D.R. Acad of Sciences; Dr. h.c. (Lublin Univ.), (Humboldt Univ. Berlin) 1975; Kossuth Prize 1948, 1958; Banner Order of Hungary, 2nd degree 1974. *Publications:* Inorganic and Analytical Chemistry 1950, Organic Chemistry 1952, Biochemistry 1958. *Address:* Office of the President, Kossuth Lajos tér 1/3, 1055 Budapest; Inst. of Enzymology, Biological Research Centre, Hungarian Academy of Sciences, 1113 Budapest; Ábrányi Emil u. 3, 1026 Budapest II, Hungary (Home). *Telephone:* 668-858 (Office); 168-666 (Home).

STRAUS, Robert, PH.D.; American professor of behavioural science, sociology and pharmacy; b. 9 Jan. 1923, New Haven; s. of Samuel H. Straus and Alma Fleischner; m. Ruth E. Dawson 1945; two s. two d.; ed. Yale Univ.; Instructor, Dept. of Applied Physiology, Yale Univ. 1947–48, Asst. Prof. 1948–51, Research Assoc. 1951–53; Asst. Prof., Dept. of Public Health and Preventive Medicine, State Univ. of New York 1953–55, Assoc. Prof. 1955–56; mem. Medical Center Planning Staff, Ky. Univ. 1956–60, Prof. of Sociology 1956–, Prof. Dept. of Behavioral Science 1959–, Chair. 1959–87, Prof. of Pharmacy 1975–; Visiting Prof., Calif. Univ. (Berkeley) 1978, Visiting Scholar 1986; Scientific Achievement Award, Ky. Medical Assen., 1966; mem. Inst. of Medicine, N.A.S. 1975. *Publications:* Medical Care for Seamen 1950, Drinking in College (co-author) 1953, Medicine and Society (co-ed.) 1963, Alcohol and Society 1973, Escape from Custody 1974. *Leisure interests:* music, theatre. *Address:* Department of Behavioral Science, University of Kentucky, Lexington, Ky. 40536-0086; 656 Raintree Road, Lexington, Ky. 40502, U.S.A. *Telephone:* (606) 233-5390; (606) 268-0873 (Home).

STRAUSS, Botho; German playwright and novelist; b. 2 Dec. 1944, Naumburg; moved with family to Remscheid, Ruhr region; on staff of Theater heute, West Berlin; Dramaturg at Schaubühne Theater, West Berlin 1970–75; Mülheimer Drama Prize 1982. *Plays include:* Die Hypochonder (first play, 1971, winner Hannover Dramaturgie Award), Trilogie des Wiedersehens, Gross und Klein and Der Park; *novels include:* Die Widmung 1979, Rumor 1980, Paare, Passanten 1981–, Der Junge Mann 1984, Niemand Anderes 1987. *Address:* Keithstr. 8, 1000 Berlin 30, Federal Republic of Germany.

STRAUSS, Paul; German carpenter and politician; b. 27 April, 1923, Vipernitz, Kreis Güstrow; joined SED 1954; mem. Presidium of Trade Union Orgs. (FDGB) 1959–; Cand. mem. Cen. Cttee. SED 1963–67, mem. 1967–; mem. G.D.R. Volkskammer 1963–, Council of State 1963–; Hero of Labour (twice), Vaterländischer Verdienstorden in Silver and other decorations. *Address:* Staatsrat, Berlin, German Democratic Republic.

STRAUSS, Robert Schwarz, LL.B.; American politician and trade negotiator; b. 19 Oct. 1918, South Central Texas; s. of Charles H. and Edith V. (née Schwarz) Strauss; m. Helen Jacobs 1941; two s. one d.; ed. Univ. of Texas Law School; Special Agent for Fed. Bureau of Investigation (FBI) in Ia., Ohio and Dallas, Tex. 1941–45; admitted to Texas Bar 1941; co-founder of law firm Akin, Gump, Strauss, Hauer and Feld 1945; Pres. Strauss Broadcasting Co. 1965; Dir. Archer Daniels Midland, Lone Star Industries, MCA, Pepsico, Xerox Corpn.; mem. Texas State Banking Bd. 1963–68; mem. Democratic Nat. Cttee. 1968–70, Treas. 1970–72; Chair. 1972–77; U.S. Prin. Trade Negotiator (rank of Amb.) 1977–79; Special Envoy of Pres. to Middle East April–Nov. 1979; Chair. Pres. Carter's Campaign Cttee. 1979–80; mem. Nat. Bipartisan Comm. of Cen. America 1983–84; Chair. Nat. Econ. Comm. 1988–; partner Akin, Gump, Strauss, Hauer and Feld, Dallas 1945–77, 1981–; Presidential Medal of Freedom 1981. *Leisure interests:* golf, horse racing. *Address:* Akin, Gump, Strauss, Hauer and Feld, 4100 First City Center, Dallas, Tex. 75201, U.S.A. (Office).

STRAUSZ-HUPE, Robert, A.M., PH.D.; American diplomatist; b. 25 March 1903, Vienna, Austria; s. of Rudolph and Doris (née Hedwig) Strausz-Hupe; m. 1st Eleanor de Graff Cuyler (died 1976); m. 2nd Mayrose Ferreira 1979; ed. Univ. of Pennsylvania; engaged in investment banking 1927–37; Assoc. Ed., Current History 1939–41; Assoc. Prof. of Political Science, Univ. of Pa. 1946–52, Prof. 1952–; Dir. Foreign Policy Research Inst. 1955–69; Amb. to Ceylon and Repub. of Maldives 1970–72, to Belgium 1972–74, to Sweden 1974–75, to Turkey 1981–89; Perm. Rep. to N. Atlantic Council 1976–77; fmr. Dir. Atlantic Council of U.S.A.; Diplomat-in-Residence Foreign Policy Research Inst., Philadelphia 1977; Guest Prof. Geschwister Scholl Inst. Ludwig-Maximilians Univ., Munich 1978–79; mem. Council on Foreign Relations, American Political Science Assen.; F.R.G.S., Fellow, Bd. of Visitors Nat. Defense Univ. 1977–78; Distinguished Public Service Medal (U.S. Dept. of Defense), Marilla Ricker Award (U.S. Dept. of State) 1975, Ehrenkreuz für Wissenschaft und Kunst (Austria) 1982, and other awards. *Publications:* The Russian-German Riddle 1940, Axis-America 1941, Geopolitics 1942, The Balance of Tomorrow 1945, International Relations 1950, The Zone of Indifference 1952, Power and Community 1956, Protracted Conflict (co-author) 1959, A Forward Strategy for America 1961 (co-author), Building the Atlantic World (co-author) 1963, In My Time 1967, Dilemmas Facing the Nation 1979; over 40 articles on int. affairs. *Address:* Goshen and Grubb Mill Roads, Newton Square, Pa. 19073, U.S.A.

STRAWSON, Sir Peter Frederick, Kt., F.B.A., M.A.; British professor of metaphysical philosophy; b. 23 Nov. 1919, London; s. of Cyril Walter Strawson and Nellie Dora Strawson; m. Grace Hall Martin 1945; two s. two d.; ed. Christ's Coll., Finchley, St. John's Coll., Oxford; served in the army with rank of Capt. 1940–46; Asst. Lecturer in Philosophy, Univ. Coll. of N. Wales 1946–47, Lecturer in Philosophy, Univ. Coll., Oxford 1947–48, Fellow and Praelector 1948–68, Univ. Reader in Philosophy 1966–68, Waynflete Prof. of Metaphysical Philosophy and Fellow of Magdalen Coll., Oxford 1968–87; Woodbridge Lecturer, Columbia Univ., U.S.A. 1983; Visiting Prof., Collège de France, Paris 1985; Immanuel Kant Lecturer, Munich Univ. 1985; John Locke Prize 1946; Hon. Fellow of St. John's and Univ. Colls. *Publications:* Introduction to Logical Theory 1952, Individuals 1959, The Bounds of Sense 1966, Logico-Linguistic Papers 1971, Freedom and Resentment 1974, Subject and Predicate in Logic and Grammar 1974, Naturalism and Skepticism 1985, Analyse et Métaphysique 1985. *Leisure interests:* reading, travel. *Address:* Magdalen College, Oxford; 25 Farndon Road, Oxford, OX2 6RT, England (Home). *Telephone:* 515026 (Home).

STRAY, Svenn Thorkild; Norwegian lawyer and politician; b. 11 Feb. 1922, Arendal; s. of Gudmund and Anne Johanne Marie Stray; m. Gwynneth Enoch 1954; one d.; ed. Law School, Univ. of Oslo; Deputy Judge, Oslo, later Moss (county of Østfold) 1947–49; started own law firm, Moss 1950; mem. Moss City Council 1956; mem. Cen. Exec. Hoyre (Conservative Party) 1946–54, 1958–82, Chair. Nat. Union of Young Conservatives 1950–54; Proxy mem. Storting (Parl.) 1950–53, full mem. 1957–85, Parl. Leader of Conservatives 1965–70; Vice-Pres. Storting 1973–81, mem. Standing Cttee. of Foreign Affairs and Constitution; Minister of Foreign Affairs 1970–71, 1981–86; mem. Nordic Council, Parl. Ass. of Council of Europe; fmr. Chair. European Movt. in Norway, Org. of People and Defence; Grand Cross, Order of Icelandic Falcon, Grand Cross (First Class), Order of Merit (Fed. Repub. of Germany), Grand Cross, Order of Isabel la Católica (Spain), Grand Decoration of Honour in Gold with Sash for Service (Austria), Ordre du Mérite (France), Order of the Rising Sun (Japan). *Address:* Bergstien 10, 1500 Moss, Norway (Home).

STREEP, Meryl (Mary Louise), A.B., M.F.A.; American actress; b. 22 June 1949, Summit, N.J.; d. of Harry Streep, Jr. and Mary W. Streep; m. Donald Gummer 1978; one s. two d.; ed. singing studies with Estelle Liebling; studied drama at Vassar, Yale School of Drama; stage début in New York in Trelawny of the Wells; 27 Wagons Full of Cotton, New York; New York Shakespeare Festival 1976 in Henry V, Measure for Measure; also acted in Happy End (musical), The Taming of the Shrew, Wonderland (musical), Taken in Marriage and numerous other plays; Acad. Award for Best Supporting Actress for Kramer vs. Kramer 1980; Best Supporting Actress awards from Nat. Soc. of Film Critics for The Deer Hunter, New York Film Critics Circle for Kramer vs. Kramer, The Seduction of Joe Tynan and Sophie's Choice; Emmy Award for Holocaust, British Acad. Award 1982, Acad. Award for Best Actress, for Sophie's Choice 1982; Hon. Dr. (Yale) 1983, (Dartmouth) 1981, (Lafayette) 1985. *Films acted in include:* Julia 1976, The Deer Hunter 1978, Manhattan 1979, The Seduction of Joe Tynan 1979, The Senator 1979, Kramer vs. Kramer 1979, The French Lieutenant's Woman 1980, Sophie's Choice 1982, Still of the Night 1982, Silkwood 1983, Plenty 1984, Falling in Love 1984, Out of Africa 1985, Heartburn 1985, Ironweed 1987, A Cry in the Dark (Best Actress Award, New York Critics 1988) 1988, Evita 1989, The Lives and Loves of a She Devil. *TV appearances include:* The Deadliest Season, Uncommon Women, Holocaust, Velveteen Rabbit. *Leisure interests:* peace and anti-nuclear causes, gardening, skiing, raising family, visiting art galleries and museums. *Address:* c/o International Creative Management, 40 West 57th Street, New York, N.Y. 10019, U.S.A.

STREET, Anthony Austin; Australian fmr. politician and business executive; b. 8 Feb. 1926, Victoria; s. of Brig. the Hon. G.A. Street, M.C.; m. V.E. Rickard 1951; three s.; ed. Melbourne Grammar; Royal Australian Navy; primary producer; mem. for Corangamite, House of Reps. 1966–84; Sec. Govt. Mems. Defence and Wool Cttees. 1967–71; mem. Joint Parl. Cttee. on Foreign Affairs 1969; Chair. Fed. Rural Cttee. of Liberal Party 1970–74; mem. Fed. Exec. Council 1971–; Asst. Minister for Labour and Nat. Service 1971–72; mem. Liberal Party Shadow Cabinet for Social Security, Health and Welfare 1973, for Primary Industry, Shipping and Transport 1973, for Science and Tech. and A.C.T. 1974, for Labour 1975; Minister for Labour and Immigration Nov.–Dec. 1975; Minister Assisting the Prime Minister in Public Service Matters 1975–77; Minister for Employment and Industrial Relations 1975–78, for Industrial Relations 1979–80, for Foreign Affairs 1980–83; resgnd. from Parl. Jan. 1984; now Man. and Co. Dir. *Leisure interests:* flying, cricket, golf, tennis. *Address:* 153 The Terrace, Ocean Grove, Vic. 3226, Australia (Home).

STREET, Sir Laurence Whistler, LL.B., K.C.M.G.; Australian lawyer; b. 3 July 1926, Sydney, N.S.W.; s. of late Sir Kenneth Street; m. Susan Gai Watt 1952; two s. two d.; ed. Cranbrook School, Sydney, Univ. of Sydney; served in Royal Australian Navy 1943–47; mem. Bar, N.S.W. 1951–; Q.C. 1963; Judge Supreme Court, N.S.W. 1965–74, Judge of Appeal 1972–74, Chief Judge in Equity 1972–74, Chief Justice N.S.W. 1974–88; Lieut.-Gov. N.S.W. 1974–; Hon. Col., 1st/15th Royal N.S.W. Lancers 1986–; mem. London Court of Int. Arbitration 1988–; Hon. LL.D. (Sydney) 1984; K.St.J. 1976; Grand Officer of Merit of Sovereign Mil. Order of Malta 1977. *Address:* G.P.O. Box 5341, Sydney, N.S.W. 2001, Australia. *Telephone:* (02) 228-5987.

STREET, Robert, A.O., PH.D., D.SC., F.A.A.; Australian academic and physicist; b. 16 Dec. 1920, Wakefield, England; m. Joan Marjorie Bere 1943; one s. one d.; ed. Univ. of London; Scientific Officer, Dept. of Supply, U.K. 1942–45; Lecturer Dept. of Physics, Univ. of Nottingham 1945–54; Sr. Lecturer, Dept. of Physics, Univ. of Sheffield 1954–60; Foundation Prof. of Physics, Monash Univ., Melbourne, Victoria 1960–74; Dir. Research School of Physical Sciences, Australian Nat. Univ. 1974–77; Vice-Chancellor Univ. of Western Australia 1978–86; fmr. Pres. Australian Inst. of Nuclear Science and Eng.; mem. and Chair. Australian Research Grants Cttee. 1970–76; Chair. Nat. Standards Comm. 1967–78; F.A.A. 1973, Treas. 1976–77; Pres. Int. Inst. of Business and Tech., Perth, W.A. 1987–. *Address:* The University of Western Australia, Nedlands, Western Australia 6009; 60 Temby Avenue, Kalamunda, Western Australia 6076, Australia (Home).

STREETON, Terence George, C.M.G., M.B.E.; British diplomatist; b. 12 Jan. 1930, Wellingborough, Northants.; s. of Alfred Victor Streeton and Edith Streeton (née Deiton); m. Molly Horsburgh 1962; two s. two d.; ed. Wellingborough Grammar School; Govt. Service 1946–52; Foreign Office 1953–65, with Diplomatic Service 1965–, First Sec., Bonn 1966–70, First Sec. Foreign Office 1970–72, First Sec. and Head of Chancery, Bombay 1972–75, Counsellor, Brussels 1975–78, Head of Finance Dept. Foreign Office 1979–81, Asst. Under-Sec. of State and Principal Finance Officer 1982–83, High Commr. in Bangladesh 1983–. *Leisure interests:* private flying, walking. *Address:* British High Commission, Abu Bakr House, Plot 7, Road No. 84, Gulshan, Dhaka, Bangladesh. *Telephone:* 600133/7.

STREIBL, Max; German politician; b. 6 Jan. 1932, Oberammergau; s. of Max and Irene (née Oswald) Streibl; m. Irmingard Junghans 1960; two s. one d.; ed. Univ. of Munich; worked for Bavarian State Chancellery 1960; mem. Bavarian State Parl. 1962–; Bavarian State Minister for Land Devt.

and Environment 1970–77, for Finance 1977–88; Minister-Pres. of Bavaria Oct. 1988–; Gen. Sec. CSU 1967–71; Chair. Supervisory bd. Bayernwerke AG, Messerschmitt–Bölkow–Blohm GmbH, Energieversorgung Ostbayern AG, Bayerische Wasserkraft AG; Deputy Chair. Admin. Bd. ZDF (Second German TV Channel); Chair. Admin. Bd. Bayerische Landesbank, Flughafen München GmbH; mem. Supervisory Bd. Rhein-Main-Donau AG, Industrieverwaltungsgesellschaft AG, Fernsehstudio München GmbH (TV-centre Munich), Deutsche Genossenschaftsbank; Grosses Bundesverdienstkreuz mit Stern und Schulterband, Bayerischer Verdienstorden and other decorations. *Publications:* Verantwortung für Alle, Die Freiheit fordert jeden 1980, Verantwortung und Augenmass—Finanzpolitik in schwerer Zeit 1980, Staatliche Schlösser in Bayern 1982, Sparen und Investieren 1983, Solide in Bayerns Zukunft 1984, Gesunde Finanzen-Gesicherte Zukunft 1985. *Address:* Bayerisches Staatsministerium der Finanzen, Odeonsplatz 5, 8000 Munich 22, Federal Republic of Germany. *Telephone:* 089/23061.

STREISAND, Barbra Joan; American actress and singer: b. 24 April 1942, Brooklyn, N.Y.; d. of Emanuel and Diana (née Rosen) Streisand; m. Elliot Gould 1963 (divorced 1971); one s.; ed. Erasmus Hall High School; nightclub debut at Bon Soir 1961; appeared in off-Broadway revue Another Evening with Harry Stoones 1961; appeared at Caucus Club, Detroit and Blue Angel New York 1961; played in musical comedy I Can Get It for You Wholesale 1962; began recording career with Columbia records 1963; appeared in musical play Funny Girl, New York 1964, London 1966; television programme My Name is Barbra shown in England, Holland, Australia, Sweden, Bermuda and the Philippines, winning five Emmy awards; second programme Color Me Barbra also shown abroad; numerous concert and nightclub appearances; New York, Critics Best Supporting Actress Award 1962; Grammy awards for Best Female Pop Vocalist 1963, 1964, 1965, 1977, 1986; London Critics' Musical Award 1966; Academy Award (Oscar) for film Funny Girl 1968; American Guild of Variety Artists' Entertainer of the Year Award 1970, Commdr. des Arts et Lettres 1984. *Films:* Funny Girl 1968, Hello Dolly 1969, On a Clear Day you can see Forever 1969, The Owl and the Pussycat 1971, What's up Doc? 1972 Up the Sandbox 1973, The Way We Were 1973, For Pete's Sake 1974, Funny Lady 1975, A Star is Born 1977, Yentl 1983 (also dir. and produced), Nuts 1987. *Address:* c/o I.C.M., 8899 Beverly Boulevard, Hollywood, Calif., U.S.A.

STREITWIESER, Andrew, Jr., M.A., PH.D.; American professor of chemistry; b. 23 June 1927, Buffalo, N.Y.; s. of Andrew Streitwieser and Sophie Morlock; m. 1st Mary Ann Good 1950 (died 1965), 2nd Suzanne Cope 1967; one s. one d.; ed. Stuyvesant High School and Columbia Univ.; Atomic Energy Comm. Postdoctoral Fellow, M.I.T. 1951–52; Instructor in Chem. Univ. of Calif. at Berkeley 1952–54, Asst. Prof. 1954–59, Assoc. Prof. 1959–63, Prof. of Chem. 1963–; Consultant to Industry 1957–; Guggenheim Fellow 1969; mem. N.A.S., American Acad. of Arts and Sciences; A.C.S. awards: Calif. Section 1964, Award in Petroleum Chem. 1967; Humboldt Sr. Scientist Award (Bonn) 1976, Humboldt Award (Bonn) 1979, Norris Award in Physical Organic Chemistry 1982. *Publications:* Molecular Orbital Theory for Organic Chemists 1961, Solvolytic Displacement Reactions 1962, Supplemental Tables of Molecular Orbital Calculations (with J. I. Brauman) Vols. I and II 1965, Progress in Physical Organic Chemistry (co-ed.) Vols I-XI 1963–74, Dictionary of π-Electron Calculations (with C. A. Coulson) 1965, Orbital and Electron Density Diagrams (with P. H. Owens) 1973, Introduction to Organic Chemistry (with C. H. Heathcock) 1976, 1981, 1985, Solutions Manual and Study Guide for Introduction to Organic Chemistry (with C. H. Heathcock and P. A. Bartlett) 1985 (3rd edn.). *Leisure interests:* music (especially opera), wine, photography. *Address:* Department of Chemistry, University of California, Berkeley, Calif. 94720, U.S.A. *Telephone:* (415) 642-2204.

STRENGER, Hermann Josef; German business executive; b. 26 Sept. 1928, Cologne; m. Gisela Buchholtz 1956; two s. two d.; joined Bayer AG as commercial trainee 1949; Chemical Sales Dept. –1954; assigned to subsidiary, Brazil 1954–57, to Bayer subsidiary, A.B. Anilin Kemi, Sweden 1958–61; Head, Sales Dept. for raw materials for surface coatings, Leverkusen 1961–65; Head, Polyurethanes Dept. 1965–69, Dir. 1969–70; Commercial Head, Polyurethanes Div. 1970–72; mem. Bd. of Man. 1972–; Deputy Chair. Man. Bd. Bayer AG 1978–84, Chair. 1984, also Chief Exec. 1984; Chair. Carl Duisberg Gesellschaft 1987–; mem. Supervisory Bd. Hapag-Lloyd AG 1983, Karstadt AG 1983. *Address:* 5674 Bergisch Neukirchen, Domblick 3, Federal Republic of Germany (Home). *Telephone:* 0214/308774.

STRENGERS, Jan; Netherlands diplomatist; b. 22 April 1914, Utrecht; s. of Theodoor Strengers; m. Marie A. de Beaufort 1946; ed. Utrecht State Univ.; worked at banking inst. 1940–48; Ministry of Econ. Affairs 1948–52; Directorate-Gen. for Econ. Co-operation, Ministry of Foreign Affairs 1952–58; Minister Plenipotentiary, Head of OECD Section of Netherlands Perm. Del. to OECD and NATO 1958–67; Amb. Perm. Del. to OECD 1967–69; Consul-Gen. to Istanbul 1969–74; Amb. to Morocco 1974–79; mem. Bd., Netherlands Inst. for Near-East, Leiden, Netherlands Historical Archeological Inst., Istanbul. *Address:* Les Oliviers de St. Jean, 82 Avenue de Saint-Exupéry, Grasse 06130, France. *Telephone:* 93 363360.

STRITCH, Elaine; American singer and actress; b. 2 Feb. 1925, Detroit; d. of George J. Stritch and Mildred (née Tobe) Stritch; m. John Bay 1973 (died 1982); ed. Sacred Heart Convent, Detroit, Drama Workshop, New School for Social Research; Broadway début as Pamela Brewster in Loco 1946; other performances include, Three Indelicate Ladies 1947, Yes M'Lord 1949, Melba Snyder in revival of Pal Joey 1952, Bus Stop 1955, Mimi Paragon in Sail Away, New York 1961, London 1962, Martha in Who's Afraid of Virginia Woolf? 1962 and 1965, Joanne in Company, New York 1970, London 1971; films include, The Scarlet Hour 1956, Three Violent People 1956, A Farewell to Arms 1957, The Perfect Furlough 1958, Who Killed Teddy Bear 1965, Pigeons 1971, September 1988; numerous television appearances, including My Sister Eileen 1962, Two's Company (British Series) 1975–76 and 1979. Address: c/o Actors Equity, 165 West 46th Street, New York, N.Y. 10036, U.S.A.

STROBEL, Käte; German politician (retd.); b. 23 July 1907, Nuremberg; d. of Friedrich Müller and Anna (née Breit) Müller; m. Hans Strobel 1928; two d.; ed. primary and tech. schools, Nuremberg; mem. SPD 1925–; State Chair. of SPD youth org. in Bavaria; mem. Bundestag 1949–72; mem. European Parl. 1958–66, Vice-Pres. 1962–64, Chair. Social Democratic Group 1964–66; Fed. Minister of Health 1966–72, Fed. Minister of Youth, Family and Health 1969–72; mem. Econ. and Social Cttee., EEC 1974–86, mem. Presidium 1976–80, Grosses Bundesverdienstkreuz mit Stern und Schulterband 1972. Address: Erlachweiherstrasse 3, 8500 Nürnberg 60, Federal Republic of Germany.

STROBL, Gottlieb Maximilian; German motor manufacturing executive (retd.); b. 14 Oct. 1916, Munich; m. Hildegard Regel 1943; two d.; ed. Kronprinz Ruprecht Oberrealschule, Munich; joined Auto Union AG, Chemnitz (now Karl-Marx-Stadt) as trainee clerk 1938; Nat. Service 1940–45; Purchasing Man. of reconstituted Auto Union GmbH, mem. Bd. with responsibility for Materials Planning Div. 1950–71; mem. Bd. Dirs., Audi NSU Auto Union AG with responsibility for purchasing and materials 1971–73, Chair. Bd. 1975–78 (retd.); mem. Bd. of Dirs. Volkswagenwerk AG 1973–78; mem. Bd. of Trustees, Deutsche Bank AG; Grosses Bundesverdienstkreuz 1980. Leisure interest: classical music. Address: Gärtnerstrasse 12, 8070 Ingolstadt, Federal Republic of Germany. Telephone: 0841-34239.

STROESSNER, Gen. Alfredo; Paraguayan army officer and politician; b. 3 Nov. 1912; ed. Military Coll., Asunción; entered Paraguayan army; commissioned 1932, served through all ranks to Gen; C.-in-C. of Armed Forces 1951; Pres. of Paraguay 1954–89; overthrown in coup Feb. 1989; flown to exile in Brazil 1989; mem. Partido Colorado; Cruz del Chaco, Cruz del Defensor, decorations from Argentina and Brazil.

STROMINGER, Jack L.; American professor of biochemistry; b. 7 Aug. 1925, New York; m.; four c.; ed. Harvard and Yale Univs.; Intern, Barnes Hosp., St. Louis 1948–49; Research Fellow, American Coll. of Physicians, Dept. of Pharmacology, Washington Univ. School of Medicine, St. Louis 1949–50, Research Asst. 1950–51; Sr. Asst. Surgeon, U.S. Public Health Service, Nat. Inst. of Arthritis and Metabolic Diseases, Bethesda 1951–54; leave of absence, Carlsberg Lab., Copenhagen, Denmark and Molteno Inst., Cambridge Univ., England, Commonwealth Fund Fellow 1955; Asst. Prof. of Pharmacology, Dept. of Pharmacology, Washington Univ. School of Medicine, Markel Scholar in Medical Science 1958–60, Prof., 1960–61, Forsyth Faculty Fellow 1960, Prof. of Pharmacology and Microbiology, Depts. of Pharmacology and Microbiology 1961–64; Prof. of Pharmacology and Chemical Microbiology, Univ. of Wis. Medical School, Madison, Chair. Dept. of Pharmacology, mem. Univ. Cttee. on Molecular Biology 1964–68; Prof. of Biochemistry, Dept. of Biochemistry and Molecular Biology, Harvard Univ., Cambridge, Mass. 1968–, Chair. Dept. of Biochemistry and Molecular Biology 1970–73, Dir. of Basic Sciences, Sidney Farber Cancer Center 1974–77, mem. Tumor Virology Div. 1977–, Higgins Prof. of Biochemistry 1983–; mem. Steering Cttee. Biomedical Sciences Scientific Working Group, WHO; mem. N.A.S., American Acad. of Arts and Sciences, Nat. Inst. of Medicine, A.A.A.S., American Soc. of Biological Chemists, of Microbiologists, of Pharmacology and Experimental Therapeutics, American Assen. of Immunologists, American Chemical Soc.; Hon. D.Sc. (Trinity Coll., Dublin) 1975; Guggenheim Fellowship1974–75; John J. Abel Award in Pharmacology 1960, Paul-Lewis Labs. Award in Enzyme Chem. 1962, N.A.S. Award in Microbiology in Honour of Selman Waxman 1968, Rose Payne Award, American Soc. for Histocompatibility and Immunogenetics 1986. Address: Department of Biochemistry and Molecular Biology, Harvard University, Cambridge, Mass. 02138, U.S.A.

STRONG, Maurice F., O.C., F.R.S.A., F.R.S.C.; Canadian environmentalist, international official and business executive; b. 29 April 1929, Oak Lake, Manitoba; s. of Frederick Milton Strong and Mary Fyfe Strong (deceased); m. 1st Pauline Olivette Williams 1950 (divorced), two s. two d.; m. 2nd Hanne Marstrand 1981; one foster d.; served in UN Secr. 1947; Pres. or Dir. of various Canadian and int. corpns. 1954–66; also involved in leadership of various pvt. orgs. in field of devt. and int. affairs; Dir.-Gen. External Aid Office of Canadian Govt. 1966 (now Canadian Int. Devt. Agency); Chair. Canadian Int. Devt. Bd.; Alt. Gov. IBRD, ADB, Caribbean Devt. Bank; UN Under-Sec. Gen. with responsiblity for environmental affairs 1970–72, Chief Exec. for 1972 Conf. on Human Environment, Stockholm, June 1972; Exec. Dir. UN Environment Programme 1973–75; Chair. Petro Canada

1976–78; Pres. Stronat Investments Ltd. 1976–80; Chair. Bd. of Govs. Int. Devt. Research Centre 1977–78; Pres. Strouest Holdings Inc.; Chair. Procor Inc. 1978–79, AZL Resources Inc. 1978–83, Int. Energy Devt. Corpn. 1980–83, N.S. Round Table Soc. for Int. Devt., Canadian Devt. Investment Corpn., 1982–84, and dir. or mem. numerous business and conservation groups in Canada and internationally; Under Sec.-Gen., U.N. 1985–87; Pres. World Fed. UNA 1987–, Better World Soc. 1988–; Chair., Pres. American Water Devt. Inc., Denver 1986–; several hon. degrees. Publications: various articles in journals. Address: Suite 2950, 1099 18th Street, Denver, Col. 80202, U.S.A.

STRONG, Sir Roy Colin, Kt., PH.D.; British museum director; b. 23 Aug. 1935, London; s. of George Edward Clement Strong and Mabel Ada Smart; m. Julia Trevelyan Oman (q.v.) 1971; ed. Queen Mary Coll., Univ. of London and Warburg Inst.; Asst. Keeper, Nat. Portrait Gallery, London 1959–67, Dir. 1967–73; Dir. Victoria and Albert Museum, London 1974–87; Vice-Chair. South Bank Bd. (now S. Bank Centre) 1985–; Patron, Pallant House, Chichester 1986–; Organizer of Exhbns. incl. The Elizabethan Image (Tate Gallery) 1969, The Destruction of the Country House (Victoria and Albert Museum) 1974, Artists of the Tudor Court (Victoria and Albert Museum) 1983; mem. Arts Council of G.B. 1983–87 (Chair. Arts Panel 1983–87), Council, R.C.A. 1979–87; Dir. Oman Productions Ltd.; Fellow, Royal Soc. of Antiquaries, Queen Mary Coll., Univ. of London; Hon. D.Litt. (Leeds) 1983, (Keele) 1984; Shakespeare Prize 1980 (F.V.S. Foundation, Hamburg). Publications: Portraits of Queen Elizabeth I 1963, Leicester's Triumph (with J. A. Van Dorsten) 1964, Holbein and Henry VIII 1967, Tudor and Jacobean Portraits 1969, The English Icon: Tudor and Jacobean Portraiture 1969, Van Dyck: Charles I on Horseback 1972, Inigo Jones: The Theatre of the Stuart Court 1972 (with S. Orgel), Elizabeth R (with Julia Trevelyan Oman (q.v.)) 1971, Mary Queen of Scots (with Julia Trevelyan Oman) 1972, Splendour at Court: Renaissance Spectacle and The Theatre of Power 1973, Nicholas Hilliard 1975, An Early Victorian Album (with Colin Ford) 1974, The Cult of Elizabeth: Elizabethan Portraiture and Pageantry 1977, And When Did You Last See Your Father? The Victorian Painter and British History 1978, The Renaissance Garden in England 1979, Britannia Triumphans, Inigo Jones, Rubens and Whitehall Palace 1980, Holbein 1980, The English Miniature (with J. Murdoch, J. Murrell and P. Noon) 1981, The English Year (with Julia Trevelyan Oman) 1982, The English Renaissance Miniature 1983, Artists of the Tudor Court (with J. Murrell) 1983, Glyndebourne, A Celebration (Contrib.) 1984, Art and Power, Renaissance Festivals 1450–1650 1984, Strong Points 1985, Henry Prince of Wales and England's Lost Renaissance 1986, C. V. Wedgwood Festschrift (Contrib.) 1986, Creating Small Gardens 1986, Gloriana, Portraits of Queen Elizabeth I 1987, The Small Garden Designers Handbook 1987, Cecil Beaton: the Royal portraits 1988 and numerous articles in newspapers and periodicals. Leisure interests: gardening, cooking, country life. Address: 3CC Morpeth Terrace, London, SW1P 1EW, England.

STROUGAL, Lubomír, J.U.DR.; Czechoslovak politician; b. 19 Oct. 1924, Veselí nad Lužnicí; ed. Charles Univ., Prague; mem. CP of Czechoslovakia 1945–; Sec. České Budějovice Regional Cttee., CP of Czechoslovakia 1955–57, Chief. Sec. 1957–59; mem. Cen. Cttee., CP of Czechoslovakia 1958–; Minister of Agric. and Forestry 1959–61, of the Interior 1961–65; Deputy Nat. Ass. 1960–69; Sec. Cen. Cttee., CP of Czechoslovakia 1965–68; Deputy Prime Minister 1968; mem. Comm. for Questions of Living Standards, Cen. Cttee. 1966–69, Chair. 1967–69; Chair. Econ. Council 1968–69; mem. Presidium, Cen. Cttee. of CP of Czechoslovakia 1968–88, Sec. and mem. Secr. 1968–70, mem. Exec. Cttee. 1968–69; Chair. Bureau for directing Party work in the Czech lands, Cen. Cttee. CP of Czechoslovakia 1968–70; Deputy to Czech Nat. Council 1968–71; Deputy to House of the People Fed. Ass. 1969–; Prime Minister of Czechoslovak Socialist Repub. 1970–88; Chair. Govt. Comm. for Physical Culture and Sports 1978–81; Commdr. Czech People's Militia 1969; Order of Merit for Construction 1958, Dimitrov Order (Bulgaria) 1970, Order Stara Planina (1st Class) (Bulgaria) 1972, Order of Victorious Feb. 1973, Order of Sukhe Bator (Mongolia) 1973, Order of State Banner (1st Class) (Democratic People's Republic of Korea) 1973, Order of May Revolution (Argentina) 1974, Order of the Republic 1974, Order of the Crown (1st Class) (Iran) 1976, Golden Medal of FAO (UN), Order of Oct. Revolution 1984. Address: Government Presidium of C.S.S.R., Prague 1, nábř. kpt. Jaroše 4, Czechoslovakia.

STROWGER, Gaston Jack, C.B.E., F.B.I.M.; British business executive (retd.); b. 8 Feb. 1916, Kessingland, Suffolk; s. of A. H. Strowger and Lily Ellen Tripp; m. Katherine Ellen Gilbert; two s. one d.; ed. Lowestoft Grammar School; joined London Electricity Supply Co. 1934; served with 24th Lancers, Eighth Army 1939–43; Accountant, Thorn Electrical Industries Ltd. 1943, Group Chief Accountant 1952, Exec. Dir. 1961, mem. Bd. 1966, Financial Dir. 1967, Man. Dir. 1970–79, Chair. Eng. Div. 1972–79 (retd.); Chair. Thorn Ericsson Telecommunications Ltd. 1974–81; Non-exec. Chair. Gen. Telephone Systems Ltd., The Birmingham Telephone Co. Ltd., Harland & Simon (Group) PLC; Chair. Hornby Hobbies 1981–, Wiltminser Ltd. 1981–. Leisure interests: gardening, fishing, bowls. Address: 46 Maplin Close, Eversley Park Road, London, N21 1NB, England.

STRUCHKOVA, Raisa Stepanovna; Soviet ballerina; b. 5 Oct. 1925, Moscow; ed. Bolshoi Theatre Ballet School; Soloist, Bolshoi Theatre Ballet

Group 1944-; lecturer in classical dancing Lunacharsky State Inst. of Theatrical Art 1968-; mem. CPSU 1962; People's Artist of U.S.S.R. 1958; Order of the Red Banner and other decorations. *Principal roles include:* Cinderella (Cinderella, Prokofiev), Juliet (Romeo and Juliet, Prokofiev), Giselle (Giselle, Adan), Princess Aurora (Sleeping Beauty, Tchaikovsky), Odette-Odile (Swan Lake, Tchaikovsky), Kitri (Don Quixote), Parasha (Copper Rider, Glier), Tao Khoa (Red Poppy, Glier), Maria (Fountain of Bakshisarai, Asafyev), Janne, also Diana de Mirrel (Flames of Paris, Asafyev), Gayane (Gayane, Khachaturyan), Vakchanka (Walpurgisnacht, Gounod); films: Crystal Slipper, Your Name. *Address:* State Academic Bolshoi Theatre, 1 ploshad Sverdlova, Moscow, U.S.S.R.

STRUGATSKY, Arkadiy Natanovich; Soviet science-fiction writer and translator; b. 28 Aug. 1925, Batumi; s. of Natan Strugatsky; brother of B. N. Strugatsky (q.v.); ed. Mil. Inst. of Foreign Languages, Moscow; trans. from and lecturer in Japanese, Moscow; publ. first work (with brother) 1957. *Publications with B. N. Strugatsky include:* The Land of Purple Clouds 1959, The Return 1962, Escape Attempt 1962, The Far-Away Rainbow 1964, Rapacious Things of the Century 1965, The Inhabited Island 1971, The Ugly Swans 1972, Stories 1975, The Forest 1982.

STRUGATSKY, Boris Natanovich; Soviet astronomer and science-fiction writer; b. 15 April 1933, Leningrad; s. of Natan Strugatsky; brother of A. N. Strugatsky (q.v.); ed. Leningrad Univ.; astronomer's post in Pulkovo Observatory, Leningrad 1955-65; started publishing science-fiction (with his brother) 1957. *Publications (with A. N. Strugatsky) include:* The Land of Purple Clouds 1959, The Return 1962, Escape Attempt 1962, The Far-Away Rainbow 1964, Rapacious Things of the Century 1965, The Inhabited Island 1971, The Ugly Swans 1972, Stories 1975, The Forest 1982.

STRUMINSKY, Vladimir Vasiliyevich, D.SC.(ENG.); Soviet scientist (Mechanics); b. 29 April 1914, Orenburg; ed. Moscow State Univ.; scientific work in Cen. Inst. of Aerohydrodynamics 1941-66; Prof. Moscow Physical-Tech. Inst. 1947-66; Prof., Novosibirsk State Univ. and Dir. U.S.S.R. Acad. of Sciences Siberian Dept. Inst. of Theoretical and Applied Mechanics 1966-71; Head of Physical Aerodynamics Section, Inst. of Mechanical Problems, U.S.S.R. Acad. of Sciences 1971-77; Holder of Chair. of Mechanics of Heterogeneous Media, Moscow Physical-Tech. Inst. 1974-; Chief, Dept. of Mechanics of Inhomogeneous Media, U.S.S.R. Acad. of Sciences 1977-89; Corresp. mem. U.S.S.R. Acad. of Sciences 1958-66, mem. 1966-; State Prize (twice), Zhukovsky Gold Medal, Lenin Prize, Order of Lenin and other decorations. *Address:* Department of Mechanics of Inhomogeneous Media, U.S.S.R. Academy of Sciences, 7 Leningradsky Prospekt, A-40, Moscow 125040, U.S.S.R. *Telephone:* 251-52-08.

STRUŻEK, Bolesław, D.AGRIC.SC.; Polish agricultural economist and politician; b. 26 August 1920, Kolonia Sobolew; m.; six c.; ed. Łódź Univ., Lublin Catholic Univ.; worked in rural co-operative movt. during German occupation, then active in youth movt.; mem. Peasants' Party (SL) 1948-49, United Peasants' Party (ZSL) 1949-, Deputy Head, Agric. Dept. of ZSL Chief Cttee. 1950-52; on staff, Main School of Farming (now Agric. Acad.), Warsaw 1950-, lecturer, Agrarian Policy Dept. 1950-65, Asst. Prof. 1962, Head, Dept. of Co-operative Movt. and Trade Turnover 1965-76, Extraordinary Prof. 1969, Ordinary Prof. 1976-, Head, World Agric. Research Centre 1976-79, Head, Inst. of Agricultural Econs. and Agrarian Policy, Econs. and Agricultural Faculty 1979-81, 1983-84; Head, Agric. Policy and Co-operation Research Centre 1985-; Deputy to Seym (Parl.) 1952-56, 1972-; mem. ZSL Chief Cttee. 1956-; Sec. for Econ. and Agricultural matters of ZSL Chief Cttee. 1971-76, mem. Pres. ZSL Chief Cttee. 1972-; mem. Chief Co-operative Council 1960-; Deputy Chair. Council of State 1984-85; mem. Extraordinary Comm. for Initiation of Econ. Reform 1988-; numerous awards and decorations including Order of Builders of People's Poland, Commdr.'s and Knight's Cross of Order of Polonia Restituta, Order of Banner of Labour (First and Second Class). *Publications:* numerous works on agricultural economy, agrarian policy and rural co-operative movt. *Leisure interests:* collecting and reading books, farm work during holidays. *Address:* Al. Przyjaciół 8 m. 12, 00-565 Warsaw, Poland (Home). *Telephone:* 21-42-94 (Home).

STRZELCHIK, Vladislav Ignatevich; Soviet actor; b. 31 Jan. 1921; ed. Babochkin's Theatre Studio, Leningrad Gorky Theatre; worked at Babochkin's Theatre Studio 1940-; R.S.F.S.R. State Prize 1971, U.S.S.R. People's Artist 1974; small roles in Mashenka 1942, Enemies 1953, Resurrection 1960. *Major roles in:* What's Your Name Now? 1965, Major Vikhr 1967, War and Peace (Napoleon) 1966-67, Tchaikovsky 1970, His Excellency's Adjutant 1970, The End of the Ataman 1971, A Star of Beguiling Happiness 1975, Always With Me 1977, Marriage 1978, Father Sergius 1978, The Front Behind the Lines 1978, Wings 1980, My Dad's an Idealist 1981, A Time for Desires 1984. *Address:* c/o Gosudarstvennyi akademicheskii bolshoi teatr im. M. Gorkogo, Leningrad, U.S.S.R.

STUART, Francis; Irish novelist and poet; b. 29 April 1902, Australia; s. of Henry Irwin Stuart and Elizabeth Montgomery; m. 1st Iseult Gonne 1920, one s. one d.; m. 2nd Gertrude Meissner 1954; ed. Rugby School; born of Northern Irish parents and brought up in Co. Antrim, ed. at English schools; Irish republican 1922-23, interned by Free State Govt.; Lecturer Berlin Univ., Germany during 2nd World War, subsequently imprisoned in French-occupied Germany, lived in Paris 1949-51, London

1951-58, settled in Ireland 1958. *Publications:* two vols. of poetry and 22 novels, including We Have Kept the Faith (poems) 1923, Women and God 1931, Pigeon Irish 1931, The Pillar of Cloud 1948, Redemption 1949, Black List, Section H. 1971, The High Consistory 1981, Faillandia 1985, The Abandoned Snail Shell 1987. *Address:* 2 Highfield Park, Dublin 14, Ireland.

STUART, Sir Kenneth Lamonte, Kt., M.D., F.R.C.P., F.A.C.P.; Barbadian medical adviser and fmr. professor of medicine; b. 16 June 1920, Barbados; s. of Egbert Stuart and Louise Stuart; m. Barbara Cecille Ashby 1958; one s. two d.; ed. Harrison Coll., Barbados, Queen's Univ., Belfast, Northern Ireland; Rockefeller Foundation Fellow in Cardiology, Mass. Gen. Hosp., Boston, U.S.A. 1956-57; Wellcome Research Fellow, Harvard Univ., U.S.A. 1960-61; Prof. of Medicine, Univ. of W. Indies 1966-76, Dean Medical School 1969-73, Head Dept. of Medicine 1972-76; Commonwealth Medical Adviser 1976-85; Consultant Adviser, Wellcome Tropical Inst. 1985-; mem. Bd. of Govs., Int. Research Centre of Canada 1985-; Chair. Court of Govs., London School of Hygiene and Tropical Medicine 1983-86; Hon. D.Sc. (Queen's, Belfast) 1986. *Leisure interests:* tennis, music, literature. *Address:* The Wellcome Tropical Institute, 24 Stephenson Way, London, NW1 2BQ (Office); Red Oak, 31 Fairmile Avenue, Cobham, Surrey, KT11 2JA, England (Home). *Telephone:* 01-387 4477 (Office); (0932) 63826 (Home).

STUART, Robert Douglas, Jr., J.D.; American diplomatist and business executive; b. 26 April 1916, Hubbard Woods, Ill.; s. of Robert Douglas and Harriet (McClure); m. Barbara McMath Edwards 1938; three s. one d.; ed. Princeton and Yale Univs.; with Quaker Oats Co., Chicago 1947-84; Chair. and C.E.O. 1966-82; fmr. Dir. Molson Cos. of Canada, United Airlines, Inc., First Nat. Bank of Chicago, Deere & Co.; mem. Business Council 1972-; Amb. to Norway 1984-. *Address:* American Embassy, Drammensveien 18, 0225 Oslo 2, Norway; 1601 Conway Road, Lake Forest, Ill. 60045, U.S.A. (Home).

STUBBE, Hans, DR. AGR.; German geneticist; b. 7 March 1902, Berlin; ed. Landwirtschaftliche Hochschule, Berlin, and Univ. of Göttingen; agricultural employment 1922-25; asst. at Inst. für Vererbungsforschung, Berlin-Dahlem 1927-28; asst. and departmental dir. Kaiser-Wilhelm-Inst. für Züchtungsforschung, Müncheberg 1929-36; Kaiser-Wilhelm-Inst. für Biologie 1936-43; Dir. Kaiser-Wilhelm-Inst. für Kulturpflanzenforschung, Vienna 1943-45, Inst. für Kulturpflanzenforschung der Deutschen Akad. der Wissenschaften, Gatersleben 1945-68; Prof. of Gen. and Special Genetics and Dir. Inst. of Genetics, Univ. of Halle 1946-67; Pres. Deutsche Akad. der Landwirtschaftswissenschaften, Berlin 1951-68; mem. Agric. Council of Ministers 1963-72; Hon. Pres. Akad. der Landwirtschaftswissenschaften der D.D.R., Berlin; mem. Akad. der Wissenschaften der D.D.R. and Emer. Dir. of its Zentral Inst. für Genetik- und Kulturpflanzenforschung, Gatersleben; mem. other acads. and research bodies; several hon. doctorates; Nat. Prize 1949, 1960; Vaterländischer Verdienstorden (silver) 1954, (gold) 1961, Helmholtz-Medaille (Akad. d. Wissenschaften der D.D.R.) 1970, Stern d. Völkerfreundschaft 1982 and other decorations. *Publications:* books on genetics. *Address:* Schmiedestrasse 1, Gatersleben, 4325, German Democratic Republic. *Telephone:* Gatersleben 50.

STÜCKLEN, Richard; German electrical engineer and politician; b. 20 Aug. 1916; s. of Georg S. and Mathilde (née Bach) Stücklen; m. Ruth Geissler 1943; one s. one d.; ed. vocational school, tech. coll.; fmr. Industrial Dept. Man.; Army Service 1940-44; then Man. in family business; mem. Bundestag 1949-; Deputy Chair. Christian Democratic Union/Christian Social Union (CSU) Group and Chair. CSU in Bundestag 1953-57, 1966-76; Fed. Minister of Posts and Telegraphs 1957-66; Vice-Pres. Bundestag 1976-79, 1983-, Pres. 1979-83; awards include Grosskreuz des Verdienstordens der Bundesrepublik Deutschland, Bayerische Verdienstorden. *Leisure interests:* tennis, football, chess. *Address:* Bundeshaus, 53 Bonn; Eichstätter Strasse 27, 8832 Weissenburg, Federal Republic of Germany (Home). *Telephone:* 27-20.

STUKALIN, Boris Ivanovich; Soviet official; b. 4 May 1923, Voronezh; m. Olga Jakovlevna 1949; one s. one d.; journalist and Ed. of Voronezh Komsomol newspaper 1952-56; Ed. of Voronezh CPSU Cttee. newspaper Kommuna 1956-60; Head of R.S.F.S.R. Div. of Dept. of Propaganda and Agitation of Cen. Cttee. CPSU 1960-63; Chair. of State Cttee. on Printing and Publishing, R.S.F.S.R. Council of Ministers 1963-65; Deputy Ed. Pravda 1965-70; Chair. of Cttee. on Printing and Publishing 1970-83; mem. Cen. Cttee. CPSU 1976-; Head of CPSU Propaganda Dept. 1983-85; Amb. to Hungary 1985-. *Address:* Soviet Embassy, Bajza u. 35, Budapest, Hungary.

STUKALIN, Viktor Fyodorovich; Soviet diplomatist; b. 1927; mem. diplomatic service 1964-; Counsellor at Embassy, Pakistan 1964-66, Consul-General 1966-69; work for Ministry of Foreign Affairs 1969-80; U.S.S.R. Deputy Minister of Foreign Affairs 1980-; Chair U.S.S.R. Cttee. for UNESCO Affairs 1982-. *Address:* Ministry of Foreign Affairs, Moscow, U.S.S.R.

STUMPF, Paul Karl, PH.D., F.L.S.; American professor of biochemistry; b. 23 February 1919, New York; s. of Karl Stumpf and Annette Shreyer; m. Ruth Rodenbeck 1947; two s. three d.; ed. Harvard and Columbia Univs.; Instructor, School of Public Health, Univ. of Mich. 1946-48; Asst. Prof. of Plant Nutrition, Univ. of Calif., Berkeley 1948-52, Assoc. Prof. of Plant

Biochemistry 1952–57, Prof. 1957–58; Prof. of Biochemistry, Univ. of Calif., Davis 1958–84, Emer. Prof. 1984–; Consultant, Palm Oil Research Inst., Malaysia 1982–; Stephens Hales Award 1974, Lipid Chem. Award 1974, Guggenheim Fellow 1962, 1969, Alexander von Humboldt Fellow 1976; mem. Royal Danish Acad. of Sciences, N.A.S., American Soc. of Plant Physiologists (Chair., Bd. of Trustees 1986–89). *Publications:* Outlines of Enzyme Chemistry (with J. B. Nielands), Outlines of Biochemistry (with E. E. Conn); Ed.-in-Chief Biochemistry of Plants (12 vols.), Exec. Ed. Archives of Biochemistry 1965–88; over 250 scientific publs. *Address:* Department of Biochemistry and Biophysics, University of California, Davis, Calif. 95616; 764 Elmwood Drive, Davis, Calif. 95616, U.S.A. (Home). *Telephone:* (916) 752-3523 (Office); (916) 753-5022 (Home).

STURÉN, Olle; Swedish retd. civil engineer and administrator; b. 20 Feb. 1919, Stockholm; m. Solveig Winqvist 1943; ed. Royal Inst. of Tech., Stockholm; worked for Stockholm Bldg. Bd. 1944–47; Tech. Officer, Bldgs. Div., Swedish Standards Inst. 1947–49, Deputy Dir. 1949–57, Dir. 1957–68; UN expert on industrial standardization, Turkey 1953–54, 1955–56; Officer-in-Charge UN Office, Ankara Turkey, 1954; Town Council, Danderyd 1962–68; Chair. European Cttee. for Standardization 1966–68; Sec.-Gen. Int. Org. for Standardization (ISO) 1968–86, Emer. Sec.-Gen. 1986–; Exec. Cttee. Swedish Tennis Assen. 1947–60; Hon. Fellow Turkish Standards Inst., Standards Eng. Soc., U.S.A., Standards Assen. of N.Z., Swedish Tennis Assen. *Leisure interest:* sport. *Address:* 10 avenue de Champel, 1206 Geneva, Switzerland.

STURTEVANT, Julian Munson, PH.D.; American professor of chemistry and research scientist; b. 9 Aug. 1908, Edgewater, N.J.; s. of Edgar Howard Sturtevant and Bessie Fitch Sturtevant; m. Elizabeth Caroline Reihl 1929; one s. one d.; ed. Columbia and Yale Univs.; Instructor, Asst. Prof., Assoc. Prof., Prof. of Chemistry Yale Univ. 1931–77, Prof. of Molecular Biophysics and Biochemistry 1965–77, Prof. Emer. and Sr. Research Scientist 1977–; Staff mem., Radiation Lab., M.I.T. 1943–46; Guggenheim Fellow, Fulbright Scholar, Cambridge Univ. 1955–56; Fulbright Scholar, Univ. of Adelaide, Australia 1962–63; Alexander von Humboldt Sr. Scientist Award, Univ. of Regensburg, Fed. Repub. of Germany 1978–79; Fellow American Acad. of Arts and Sciences; mem. N.A.S.; Hon. D.Sc. (Illinois Coll.) 1962, Hon. D.Sc. (Regensburg) 1978; William Clyde DeVane Medal (Yale Univ.) 1978; Innovator in Biochemistry Award, Medical Coll. of Va. 1984, Wilbur Cross Medal, Yale Univ. 1986. *Publications:* 240 scientific papers etc. *Leisure interests:* hiking, camping, mountains, chemistry. *Address:* Department of Chemistry, Yale University, P.O. Box 6666, New Haven, Conn. 06511 (Office); 28 Wakefield Road, Branford, Conn. 06405, U.S.A. (Home). *Telephone:* (203) 432-3997 (Office); (203) 432-5206 (Laboratory); (203) 488-2894 (Home).

STURUA, Robert; Soviet (Georgian) theatrical director; b. 1938, Tbilisi; trained at Georgian Theatre Inst. 1956–61; Dir. Rustaveli Theatre, Tbilisi 1961–, Artistic Dir. 1978–; has directed over 30 productions, including The Crucible (Miller), Italian Straw Hat (Labiche), Good Woman of Szechuan (Brecht), Caucasian Chalk Circle, Medea (Anouilh), and many Russian and Georgian plays; also Richard III at Düsseldorf and Roundhouse, London; first guest Dir. at Saarbrücken State Theatre.

STÜTZLE, Walther K. A., DR. RER. POL.; German research director; b. 29 Nov. 1941, Westerland-Sylt; s. of the late Moritz Stützle and of Annemarie Ruge; m. Dr. H. Kauper 1966; two s. two d.; ed. Westerland High School and Univs. of Berlin, Bordeaux and Hamburg; researcher, Inst. for Strategic Studies, London 1967–68, Foreign Policy Inst. Bonn 1968–69; Desk Officer, Ministry of Defence, Planning Staff, Bonn 1969–72, Pvt. Sec. and Chef de Cabinet, 1973–76, Head, Planning Staff, Under-Sec. of Defence, Plans and Policy 1976–82; editorial staff, Stuttgarter Zeitung 1983–86; Dir. Stockholm Int. Peace Research Inst. (SIPRI) 1986–. *Publications:* Adenauer und Kennedy in der Berlinkrise 1961–62 1972, Politik und Kräfteverhältnis 1983; co-author: Europe's Future—Europe's Choices 1967, ABM Treaty—To Defend or Not to Defend 1987. *Leisure interests:* history, reading, sailing, mountain walking. *Address:* Pipers väg 28, S 17173 Solna (Office); Stockholmsvägen 104, S 18261 Djursholm, Sweden (Home). *Telephone:* 08-559700 (Office); 08-7531464 (Home).

STUYCK, Guy, D.JUR.; Belgian diplomatist; b. 1921, Antwerp; ed. Louvain Univ.; joined Foreign Service 1947; served Rome 1951–53; Deputy Head, Belgian del. to GATT negotiations 1953–58; Econ. Counsellor, Rome 1958–60; Counsellor, Cairo 1960–61; Chargé d'Affaires, Bucharest 1961–62; Counsellor, London 1962–65; Consul-Gen. Geneva and Perm. Rep. to GATT 1967–70; Head, Foreign Multilateral External Relations Dept., Ministry of Foreign Affairs 1970–75; Amb. to Finland 1975–79, to Italy (also accred. to Multilateral Orgs.) 1979–83; Deputy Dir.-Gen. for Policy, Ministry of Foreign Affairs 1983–86; Perm. Rep. to OECD 1986–88.

STUYT, L. B. J., M.D., F.R.C.P.(LOND.); Netherlands politican; b. 16 June 1914, Amsterdam; m. Jkvr. E. van Ryckevorsel van Kessel 1956; three s.; ed. medical studies in Amsterdam and Leiden; fmr. consultant physician, The Hague; mem. Bd. Catholic Univ. Nijmegen; mem. Nat. Health Council; Pres. Netherlands Soc. of Internal Med.; Minister of Public Health and Environment 1971–73; Pres. Netherlands Cen. Org. for Applied Scientific Research TNO, The Hague 1974–80; mem. Council of State 1980–86; Chair. Health Council 1983–87; Chair. Bd., Inst. of Bioethics, Maastricht 1984–;

mem. Advisory Bd., Kansai Research Inst., Japan 1987–. *Leisure interests:* music, tennis, gardening. *Address:* Parkflat Marlot, Flat 1A, Offenberglaan 1, 2594 BM The Hague, Netherlands. *Telephone:* (070) 476055.

STYLES, Margretta, ED.D.; American professor of nursing; b. 19 March 1930, Mt. Union, Pa.; d. of Russell B. and Agnes Wilson Madden; m. Douglas F. Styles 1954; two s. one d.; ed. Juniata Coll., Yale Univ., Univ. of Florida; Prof. and Dean, School of Nursing, Univ. of Texas, San Antonio 1969–73, Wayne State Univ., Detroit 1973–77, Univ. of Calif., San Francisco 1977–87, Prof. and Livingston Chair. in Nursing 1987–; mem. Nat. Comm. on Nursing 1980–; First Distinguished Scholar, American Nurses' Foundation; mem. N.A.S., Inst. of Medicine; American Nurses' Assen. Hon. Recognition Award (Pres. 1986–88). *Publications:* On Nursing: Toward a New Endowment, Project on the Regulation of Nursing, Int. Council of Nurses 1985. *Leisure interest:* skydiving. *Address:* School of Nursing, Box 0608, University of California (San Francisco), San Francisco, Calif. 94143 (Office); 12 Commons Lane, Foster City, Calif. 94404, U.S.A. (Home). *Telephone:* (415) 476 6701 (Office), (415) 754 3870 (Home).

STYLES, Richard Geoffrey Pentland, B.COMM.; Canadian banker; b. 3 Dec. 1930, Regina, Sask.; s. of Alfred G. Styles and C. Ila (Pentland) Styles; m. Jacqueline Joyce Frith 1959; one s. one d.; ed. Univ. of Saskatchewan; joined The Royal Bank of Canada, Victoria, B.C. 1951, served in various posts, B.C. 1951–57, Asst. Rep., Chicago 1957–59, Credit Officer, Dist. HQ, Toronto 1959–60, Asst. Man., London Main Br., Ont. 1960–61, Toronto Main Br. 1961–64, Asst. Supervisor, Int. Div., Montreal 1964–66, Supervisor 1966–68, Asst. Gen. Man. 1968–70, Sr. Rep. and Dir., seconded to Orion Royal Banking Group, London, England 1970–73, Deputy Gen. Man., Int. Div., Montreal 1973–74, Gen. Man., Metropolitan Toronto Dist. 1974–79, Chair. Bd. of Supervisory Dirs. of RBC Holdings B.V. and RBC Houdstermaatschappij B.V., holding cos. for 22 Royal Bank int. subsidiaries, London, England 1979–80, Exec. Vice-Pres., World Trade and Merchant Banking, Toronto 1980–83, Sr. Exec. Vice-Pres., Int. and Corp. Banking, Toronto 1983–86, Vice-Chair., Royal Bank of Canada 1986–88, also Dir.; Chair. Exec. Cttee., Orion Royal Bank Ltd., Advisory Bd., Centre for Int. Business Studies, Univ. of W. Ont.; mem. Advisory Council, Faculty of Admin. Studies, York Univ., Advisory Bd., Int. Council, The Asia Soc.; Dir. The Canadian Club of Toronto, Niagara Inst.; Dir. and Trustee Toronto Symphony.

STYLIANOU, Petros Savva, PH.D.; Cypriot politician, journalist and writer; b. 8 June 1933, Kythrea; s. of Savvas and Evanthia Stylianou; m. Voula Tzanetatou 1960; two d.; ed. Pancyprian Gymnasium, Univs. of Athens and Salonika; served with Panhellenic Cttee. of the Cyprus Struggle (PEKA) and Nat. Union of Cypriot Univ. Students (EFEK), Pres. EFEK 1953–54; co-founder Dauntless Leaders of the Cypriot Fighters Org. (KARI); joined liberation movement of Cyprus 1955; imprisoned in Kyrenia Castle 1955, escaped; leader, Nat. Striking Group; sentenced to 15 years imprisonment 1956, transferred to U.K. prison, released 1959; mem. Cen. Cttee. United Democratic Reconstruction Front (EDMA) 1959; Deputy Sec.-Gen. Cyprus Labour Confed. (SEK) 1959, Sec.-Gen. 1960–62; f. Cyprus Democratic Labour Fed. (DEOK) 1962, Sec.-Gen. 1962–73, Hon. Pres. 1974–; mem. House of Reps. 1960–70, 1982–, Sec. 1960–62, promoted Parl. legislation for establishment of cultural, educ. and scientific insts.; Man. Ed. Ergatiki Foni (Voice of the Working Class) newspaper 1960–62, Ergatikos Agonas (The Workers' Struggle) DEOK newspaper 1962–63, Allaghi (Change) 1963; mem. co-ordination cttee. of 28 assoc. vocational and scientific orgs. 1964–66; Founder and Pres. Pancyprian Org. for Rehabilitation of the Disabled 1967; Founder, Pancyprian Olive Produce Org. 1967; Founder, Man. Dir. Kypriakos Logos magazine 1969–, Anaperikon Vima (The Step of the Disabled) 1970–; Founder, Pres. Cyprus Historical Museum and Archive 1974–; Founder, Pres. Pancyprian Cttee. for the Enclaved Greek Population 1974–; Founder and Pres., Political Cttee. for the Cyprus Struggle (PEKA) 1976–; mem. Int. Council on Archives 1975–, Admin. Bd. of Hellenic Inst. for Research in Rehabilitation 1976–; Dir. Museum of Nat. Struggle 1979–80; Deputy Minister of Interior 1980–82; Special Adviser to Pres. on Cultural Affairs April 1982–Dec. 1985; Founder Pancyprian Orgs. for Rehabilitation of Spastics, Rehabilitation from Kidney Disease, from Haemophilia and from Myopathy; Pres. Cyprus Historical Museum and Archives; numerous awards and prizes from Cyprus, Greece and U.S.A. *Publications:* numerous works on poetry, history, etc. *Address:* Stasicratous 16, Nicosia (Office); Kimononos 10 Engomi, Nicosia, Cyprus (Home). *Telephone:* 472002 (Office); 445972 (Home).

STYNE, Jule; American (b. English) composer and producer; b. 31 Dec. 1905, London, England; s. of Isadore Styne and Anna (Kertman) Styne; m. Margaret Brown; three s. one d.; ed. Chicago Music Coll. and Northwestern Univ.; composed music for stage productions including Sugar, Funny Girl and Gypsy, for films including Living It Up, songs including People; Producer (with George Abbott) of Say, Darling and Show Stoppers; Acad. Award (with Sammy Cahn) for song Three Coins in the Fountain, Donaldson Award and Critics' Award for Production Pal Joey 1954, Tony Award for Co-Writer Best Score, Music and Lyrics, Best Musical, Hallelujah Baby 1968. *Address:* 237 West 51st Street, New York, N.Y. 10019, U.S.A.

STYRON, William, A.B.; American writer; b. 11 June 1925, Newport News, Va.; s. of William Styron and Pauline Abraham; m. Rose Burgunder

1953; one s. three d.; ed. Davidson Coll., Duke Univ.; Advisory Ed., Paris Revue 1953–; Hon. Consultant, Library of Congress; Pres. Cannes Film Festival 1983; mem. Signet Soc. Harvard Univ.; Fellow, Silliman Coll., Yale Univ.; Fellow, American Acad. of Arts and Sciences; mem. American Acad. of Arts and Letters 1987–; Pulitzer Prize for best novel 1968; Howells Medal for Fiction 1970, Commdr., Ordre des Arts et des Lettres, Conn. Arts Award 1984, Prix Mondial Cino del Duca 1985; Commandeur, Légion d'honneur. *Publications:* Lie Down in Darkness 1951, The Long March 1955, Set this House on Fire 1960, The Confessions of Nat Turner 1967, In the Clap Shack (play) 1973, Sophie's Choice 1979 (American Book Award 1980), This Quiet Dust (Essays) 1982. *Leisure interests:* tennis, sailing. *Address:* R.F.D., Roxbury, Conn. 06783; Vineyard Haven, Mass. 02568, U.S.A. (Summer). *Telephone:* (617) 693-2535.

SU BUQING; Chinese mathematician; b. 23 Sept. 1902, Pingyang Co., Zhejiang Prov.; ed. Tokyo Industrial School, Imperial Tohoku Univ.; lecturer, Zhejiang Univ. 1931–; Dir. Dept. of Math. 1946–; Dean, Shanghai Fudan Univ. 1954–57; mem., Dept. of Physics, Math. and Chemistry, Acad. Sinica 1955; in disgrace during Cultural Revolution 1966–77; mem. Standing Cttee. 5th NPC 1978–83; Vice-Pres. Math. Society of China 1978–; Vice-Chair. Cen. Cttee. of China Democratic League 1979–; mem., Standing Cttee. 6th NPC 1983–88; Hon. Pres. Shanghai Fudan Univ. 1983–; mem. Standing Cttee. 7th NPC 1988–. *Address:* Room 61, Bldg. 9, Fudan University, Shanghai, People's Republic of China. *Telephone:* 480080.

SU GANG; Chinese politician; mem. Standing Cttee., CCP Prov. Cttee., Hunan 1960–65, alt. mem. Secr. 1965–Cultural Revolution; disappeared during Cultural Revolution; cadre, Hunan 1977; Deputy Sec. CCP Prov. Cttee., Guizhou 1977–78, Sec. 1978–85; Vice-Chair. Prov. Revolutionary Cttee., Guizhou 1977–79; Gov. Guizhou 1980–83; Deputy for Guizhou, 5th NPC 1980; mem. 12th Cen. Cttee. CCP 1982–87; Chair. Advisory Cttee. CCP Provincial Cttee., Guichow 1985–. *Address:* Office of the Provincial Governor, Guiyang, Guizhou Province, People's Republic of China.

SU SHAOZHI, M.A.; Chinese research professor; b. 25 Jan. 1923, Peking; s. of Su Xiyi and Jin Yunquan; m. Hu Jianmei; two d.; ed. Chongqing Univ. and Nankai Inst. of Econs.; Assoc. Prof. Fudan Univ. 1949–63; ed. Theoretical Dept. Renmin Ribao (People's Daily) 1963–79; Deputy Dir. Inst. of Marxism-Leninism-Mao Zedong Thought (MLMT) 1979–82, Dir. 1982–87; Research Prof. Chinese Acad. of Social Sciences (CASS) 1982–87, mem. Acad. Cttee. of CASS 1982–85, Prof. Graduate School of CASS 1982–; Ed. Studies of Marxism (quarterly) 1983–. *Publications:* Democracy and Socialism in China 1982, Marxism in China 1983, Democratization and Reform 1988; books and articles on politics and economics. *Leisure interests:* calligraphy and paintings, classical music. *Address:* Institute of Marxism-Leninism-Mao Zedong Thought, The Chinese Academy of Social Sciences, 5 Jianguomen Nei Dajie, Beijing 100732 (Office); 5-3 Building 28, Guang Hua Li, Jianguomen Wai, Beijing 100020, People's Republic of China (Home). *Telephone:* 507744-3149 (Office); 594552 (Home).

SU YIRAN; Chinese politician; Council mem., S. Anhui Admin. Region 1950, Dir. Public Security Bureau 1952; mem. People's Council, Anhui Prov. 1955; Vice-Gov. Anhui 1957–63; mem. Standing Cttee., CCP Cttee., Anhui 1957–63, alt. mem. Secr. 1959–63; transferred to Shandong Prov. 1963; Sec. CCP Prov. Cttee., Shandong 1964; disappeared during Cultural Revolution; Vice-Chair. Provincial Revolutionary Cttee., Shandong 1971; Deputy Sec. CCP Prov. Cttee., Anhui 1971–77; Sec. CCP Prov. Cttee., Shandong 1977–82; mem. 11th Cen. Cttee., CCP 1977; First Political Commissar, Shandong Mil. Dist. 1978–86; mem. 12th Cen. Cttee. CCP 1982–87; mem. Cen. Advisory Comm. 1987–; Vice-Gov. Shandong 1979, Gov. 1979–82, First Sec. 1982–83, Leading Sec. 1983–85. *Address:* Office of the First Secretary, Jinan, Shandong Province, People's Republic of China.

SUÁREZ, The Duke of; Adolfo Suárez González; Spanish lawyer and politician; b. 25 Sept. 1932, Cebreros, Avila Province; m. Amparo Illana; five c.; ed. Univs. of Salamanca and Madrid; Civil Gov. of Segovia 1969, then Dir.-Gen. Radio and TV; Pres. Empresa Nacional de Turismo; Pres. Unión del Pueblo Español; Vice-Sec.-Gen. Falange until 1975; Sec.-Gen. 1975–76; Prime Minister and Pres. of Council of Ministers 1976–81; named Duke of Suarez 1981; Leader Unión Centro Democrático (UCD) 1977–81, Hon. Pres. Jan.–Dec. 1981, resigned July 1982; f. and Leader Centro Democratico y Social (CDS) Aug. 1982–, Pres. 1982–; M.P. for Madrid 1982–; Pres. Int. Liberals 1988–; Pres. Inst. of European-Latin American Relations (IRELA). *Address:* c/o Antonio Maura 4, 1°, 28014 Madrid, Spain. *Telephone:* 222.10.06.

SUBANDRIO, Dr.; Indonesian politician, diplomatist and surgeon; b. 1914; ed. Medical Univ., Jakarta; active in Nat. Movement as student and gen. practitioner; worked with underground anti-Japanese Forces during Second World War; forced to leave post at Jakarta Gen. Hosp. and then established a pvt. practice at Semarang; following declaration of independence abandoned practice to become Sec.-Gen., Ministry of Information and was later sent by Indonesian Govt. as special envoy to Europe; est. Information Office, London 1947; Chargé d'affaires, London 1949, Amb. to U.K. 1950–54, to U.S.S.R. 1954–56; Foreign Minister 1957–66; Second Deputy First Minister 1960–66, concurrently Minister for Foreign Econ. Relations 1962–66; convicted of complicity in attempted communist coup and sentenced to

death Oct. 1966; sentence commuted to life imprisonment 1970. *Address:* Jakarta, Indonesia.

SUBBA RAO, K.; Indian judge; b. 1902, Rajahmundry; s. of Subrahmaneswara Rao; m. Parijatham 1925; one s. one d.; ed. Govt. Arts Coll., Rajahmundry and Madras Law Coll.; practice at Madras Bar 1926–48; Judge, Madras High Court 1948–54; Chief Justice, Andhra High Court 1954–56, Andhra Pradesh High Court 1956–58; Justice, Supreme Court of India 1958–67, Chief Justice of India 1966–67; Chancellor, Venkateswara Univ. 1954, Pro-Chancellor Delhi Univ. 1966–67; Hon. LL.D. (Univs. of Osmania and Bangalore). *Publications:* Fundamental Rights, Philosophy of Indian Constitution, Some Constitutional Problems, Man and Society, The Conflicts in Indian Polity, The Centre and State Relations, The Indian Democracy. *Address:* 7 Rest House Crescent, Bangalore 1, India. *Telephone:* 51774.

SUBBULAKSHMI, Madurai Shanmugavadivu; Indian classical Karnatic musician; b. 16 Sept. 1916, Madurai; m. Sri T. Sadasivam 1940; ed. privately; recitals with her mother, Guru Veena Shanmugavadivu 1928–32; gave solo performances and became a leading musician before age 18; acted title role in Hindi film Meera; numerous benefit performances, donated royalties from many of her records to social and religious causes; rep. Karnatic music at Edinburgh Festival 1963; concerts in London, Frankfurt, Geneva, Cairo; 7-week tour of U.S.A. 1966; performed in Tokyo, Bangkok, Hong Kong, Manila, Singapore, Malaysia, New York, Pittsburgh; Pres. Madras Music Acad. Conf. 1968; Life mem. Int. Music Council 1981; Hon. D.Litt. (Ravindra Bharati Univ.) 1967, (Shri Venkateswara Univ.) 1971, (Delhi Univ.) 1973, (Banaras Hindu Univ.), (Madhya Pradesh Univ.) 1979; Padma Bhushan 1954; President's Award for Karnatic Music 1956, Ramon Magsaysay Award for Public Service (Philippines) 1974; Sangeet Natak Acad. Fellowship 1974; Padma Vibhushan 1975; hon. title Sangeetha Khalanidhi; hon. title Sapthagiri Sangeetha Vidwanmani 1975. *Address:* c/o 4 Tank Road, Nungambakkam, Madras 600034, India. *Telephone:* 472288; 479366.

SUBOTNICK, Morton Leon, M.A.; American composer; b. 14 April 1933, Los Angeles; s. of Jack Jacob Subotnick and Rose Luckerman; m. 1st Linn Pottle 1953 (divorced 1971), one s. one d.; m. 2nd Doreen Nelson 1976 (divorced 1977); m. 3rd Joan La Barbara 1979, one s.; ed. Univ. of Denver, Mills Coll.; Co-Founder, San Francisco Tape Music Center 1961–65; fmr. Music Dir., Ann Halprin's Dance Co. and San Francisco Actors' Workshop; fmr. Music Dir. of Lincoln Center Repertory Theatre; Dir. of electronic music at original Electric Circus, St. Mark's Place, New York 1967–68; Artist-in-Residence at New York Univ. School of the Arts 1966–69; Visiting Prof. in Composition, Univ. of Maryland 1968, Univ. of Pittsburgh 1969, Yale Univ. 1982, 1983; has toured extensively as a lecturer and Composer/Performer; currently mem. Faculty of the California Inst. of the Arts 1969–; Composer-in-Residence DAAD, West Berlin 1981, M.I.T. 1986; Brandeis Award for Music 1983, and numerous other grants and awards. *Compositions include:* Silver Apples of the Moon, The Wild Bull, Trembling, The Double Life of Amphibians, Jacobs Room, The Key to Songs; Return: The Triumph of Reason (electronic composition in honour of the return of Halley's Comet) 1986, In Two Worlds 1987–88, And The Butterflies Began to Sing 1988. *Address:* c/o Theodore Presser, Presser Place, Bryn Mawr, Pa. 19010; P.O. Box 1004, Pecos, New Mexico 87552, U.S.A. (Home). *Telephone:* (215) 525 3636 (Publr's. office); (505) 757 6742 (Home).

SUBRAMANIAM, Chidambaram, B.A., B.L.; Indian politician; b. 30 Jan. 1910, Pollachi, Coimbatore District of Tamil Nadu; ed. Madras Univ.; joined Satyagraha Movement and imprisoned 1932; started legal practice Coimbatore 1936; political imprisonment 1941, 1942; Pres. Coimbatore Dist. Congress Cttee. and mem. Working Cttee. of All-India Congress Cttee.; mem. Constituent Ass. of India 1946–51, Madras Legis. Ass. 1952–62; Minister of Finance, Educ. and Law, Madras State 1952–62; mem. Lok Sabha 1962–67, 1971–; Minister of Steel 1962–63, of Steel, Mines and Heavy Eng. 1963–64, of Food and Agriculture 1964–66, of Food, Agriculture, Community Devt. and Co-operation 1966–67, of Planning, Science and Tech. 1971–72, of Industrial Devt., Science and Tech. 1972–74, of Finance 1974–77, of Defence 1979–80; Chair. Nat. Comm. on Agric. 1970; Chair. Rajaji Int. Inst. of Public Affairs and Admin. 1980–; Pres. Madras Voluntary Health Services 1987–; Deputy Chair. Nat. Planning Comm. 1971; Hon. Pres. Int. Centre for Public Enterprises in Developing Countries, Ljubljana, Yugoslavia 1985–87; Sr. Vice-Pres. Bharativa Vidyabhavan, Bombay 1985–; mem. Governing Council of Int. Wheat and Maize Improvement Centre, Mexico; mem. Bd. of Govs. Int. Rice Research Inst., Manila; Pres. All-India Tennis Asscn. *Publications:* Travelogues in Tamil: Countries I Visited, Around the World, India of my Dreams, War on Poverty, New Agricultural Strategy. *Address:* River View, Guindy, Madras 85; and Bharatiya Vidyabhavan, Kasturba Gandhi Marg, New Delhi, India.

SUBRAMANYAN, Kalpathi Ganapathi; Indian artist and professor of art; b. 5 Feb. 1924, Kerala; s. of K. P. Ganapathi and Alamelu Ammal; m. Susheela Jasra 1951; one d.; ed. Univ. of Madras, Kalabhavana, Visvabharati and Slade School of Art, London; Lecturer in Painting, Faculty of Fine Arts, M. G. Univ., Baroda 1951–59, Reader 1961–66, Prof. 1966–80, Dean, Faculty of Fine Arts 1968–74; Prof. of Painting, Kalabhavana, Visvbharati, Santiniketan 1980–; Deputy Dir. (Designs), All India Handloom Bd., Bombay 1959–61, Design Consultant 1961–65; Visiting Lecturer, Canada 1976;

Visiting Fellow, Visvabharati, Santiniketan 1977-78; UDR III Fund Fellowship, New York 1967-68; Hon. Mention (Sao Paolo Biennale) 1961; Nat. Award 1965; Gold Medal, 1st Indian Triennale 1968; Padma Shri (India) 1975; Kalidas Samman 1981. *Publications:* Moving Focus (essays on art) 1978, Living Tradition 1985. *Leisure interests:* reading, handicraft. *Address:* Kalabhavana, Santiniketan, 731235, West Bengal (Office); Kailas, 13 Purvapalli, Santiniketan, 731235, West Bengal, India (Home).

SUBROTO, M.A., PH.D.; Indonesian politician; b. 19 Sept. 1928, Surakarta; ed. Univ. of Indonesia, McGill, Stanford and Harvard Univs.; fmr. Dir.-Gen. of Research and Devt., Ministry of Trade; Prof. in Int. Econs., Univ. of Indonesia; Minister of Manpower, Transmigration and Co-operatives 1971-78, of Mining and Energy 1978-87; Chair., Pres. Pertamina; Sec.-Gen. OPEC July 1988-. *Publications:* numerous books on econ. topics. *Address:* OPEC, Obere Donaustrasse 93, 1020 Vienna, Austria.

SUCHARITKUL, Sompong, M.A., D.PHIL., LL.M.; Thai diplomatist and international lawyer; b. 4 Dec. 1931, Bangkok; s. of Phra Phibul Aisawan and Khun Sopha Sucharitkul; m. Thaithow Sucharitkul 1952, one s. two d.; ed. Univs. of Oxford and Paris, Harvard Law School, Middle Temple, London and Int. Law Acad., The Hague; lecturer in Int. Law and Relations, Chulalongkorn Univ. 1956, also lecturer in Int. Econ. Law, Thammasat Univ.; mem. Nat. Research Council 1959-70; joined Ministry of Foreign Affairs 1959, Sec. to Minister 1964-67, Dir.-Gen. Econ. Dept. 1968-70; Amb. to Netherlands (also accred. to Belgium and Luxembourg) 1970-73, to Japan 1974-77, to France and Portugal 1977-78, to Italy and Greece 1980; Rep. to UN Comm. on Int. Trade Law (UNCITRAL) 1967, Perm. Del. to UNESCO 1977-78, mem. UN Int. Law Comm. 1977- (Special Rapporteur on Jurisdictional Immunities of States and their Property 1978-); mem. Thai Nat. Group, Perm. Court of Arbitration 1979-; Dir.-Gen. Treaty and Legal Dept. Ministry of Foreign Affairs; elected Assoc. l'Inst. de Droit Int. 1973, mem. 1979; mem. Civil Aviation Bd. of Thailand; del. to various int. confs., etc. *Publications:* various books and articles on int. law. *Leisure interest:* golf. *Address:* c/o Ministry of Foreign Affairs, Bangkok, Thailand.

SUCHODOLSKI, Bogdan, PH.D.; Polish educator and philosopher; b. 27 Dec. 1903, Sosnowiec; s. of Kazimierz and Helena (Sułowska) Suchodolski; m. Maria Bartczak 1946; ed. Univs. of Warsaw, Cracow, Berlin and Paris; Prof. of Educ., Warsaw Univ. 1946-68; Dir. Inst. of Pedagogical Sciences, Warsaw Univ. 1958-68; Head, Inst. of History of Science and Tech., Polish Acad. of Sciences 1958-73; mem. Polish Acad. of Science, mem. Presidium 1969-80; mem. Int. Asscn. for Advancement of Educ. Research, Pres. 1969-73; mem. European Asscn. of Comparative Educ., Vice-Pres. 1964-71; mem. Int. Acad. for History of Science, Vice-Pres. 1968-71; mem. World Future Studies Fed., Vice-Pres. 1977-86; mem. Soc. Européenne de Culture; Prof. Emer. 1974-; Chair. Comm. of Science, Culture and Educ. in Cttee. "Poland 2000" 1970-; Chair. Nat. Council of Culture 1983-; Dr. h.c. (Silesian Univ., Katowice) 1978, (Univ. of Padua) 1983, (Warsaw) 1983, (High Pedagogical School, Opole) 1985, (Lomonosov Univ. Moscow) 1988; Order of Builders of People's Poland, Order of Banner of Labour 1st Class (twice), Commdr. Cross of Order Polonia Restituta, Nat. Educ. Comm. Medal, and others. *Publications:* Uspołecznienie kultury (Dissemination of Culture) 1937, 1947, Wychowanie dla przyszłości (Education for the Future) 1947, 1959, 1968 (trans. into Hungarian, Italian and Spanish), U podstaw materialistycznej teorii wychowania (Foundations of the Materialist Theory of Education) (trans. into German, Spanish, Portuguese, and Italian) 1957, La Pédagogie et les grands courants philosophiques 1960 (trans. into Italian and Romanian), Narodziny nowożytnej filozofii człowieka (Origins of Modern Philosophy of Man) 1963, 1968 (trans. into Serbian and French), Rozwój nowożytnej filozofii człowieka (Development of Modern Philosophy of Man) 1967 (trans. into French), Podstawy wychowania socjalistycznego (Foundations of Socialist Education) 1967 (trans. into Italian and Czech), Trzy pedagogiki (Three Pedagogies) 1970 (trans. into Serbian), Edukacja narodu 1918-1968 (National Education 1918-1968) 1970, La Scuola Polacca 1971, Labirynty współczesności Niewola i wolność człowieka (Labyrinths of the Present Time) 1972, 1974, Nasza współczesność a wychowanie (Our Present Time and Education) with Irena Wojnar 1972, Oświata i człowiek przyszłości (Education and Man of the Future) 1974, Kim jest człowiek? (Who is man?) 1974, 1976, 1980, 1986, Theorie der sozialistischen Bildung 1974, Kształt życia (Shape of Life) 1979, Dzieje kultury polskiej (History of Polish Culture) 1980, 1986, Polska i Polacy (Poland and Polish People) 1981, Wychowanie i strategia życia (Education and Strategy of Life) 1983, 1987, Polska-Naród i Sztuka (Poland—Nation and Arts) (with Maria Suchodolska) 1988, Humanizm i edukacja humanistyczna (Humanism and Humanistic Education) (Anthology with Irene Wojnar) 1988; ed. Wielka Encyklopedia Powszechna (Great Encyclopaedia, 13 vols.) 1962-70, Historia Nauki Polskiej (History of Polish Science, 5 vols.) 1970-. *Leisure interests:* cars, travel, dogs. *Address:* Ul. Śmiała 63 A, 01-526 Warsaw, Poland. *Telephone:* 39-20-27.

SUCHOŇ, Eugen, DR.SC.; Czechoslovak composer; b. 25 Sept. 1908, Pezinok; s. of Ladislav Suchoň and Serafína Suchoňová Balga; m. Herta Schischitz 1940; two c.; ed. Acad. of Music and Drama, Bratislava and Prague Conservatoire; Prof. of Composition Acad. of Music and Drama, Bratislava 1933-41; Prof. at the Dept. of Musicology and Music Pedagogy, Bratislava Univ. 1949-60, Prof. Philosophical Faculty 1960-74; mem. Presi-

dium, Union of Slovak Composers 1970-, Chair. 1972-82; mem. Cttee. Union of Czechoslovak Composers, Chair. 1973-81; Deputy to Slovak Nat. Council 1968-78, Vice-Chair. 1978-82; founder of the Slovak Nat. Opera; Corresp. mem., Acad. of Arts of D.D.R.; Dr. h.c. Univ. of Bratislava 1969; Czechoslovak State Prize (3 times), Nat. Artist 1958, Order of Labour 1968; Kl. Gottwald State Prize 1973; Order of Victorious February 1978, Laureate of Int. Herder's Prize 1981, Talich Medal 1983. *Works include:* Sonata for Violin and Piano 1930, String Quartet 1931, Serenade for Wind Quintet 1931, Serenade for String. Orchestra 1932, Nox et Solitudo (mezzo-soprano and orchestra) 1932, Little Suite with Passacaglia (orchestra or piano) 1932, Piano Quartet 1933, Fantasy and Burlesque for Violin and Orchestra 1933, 1948, King Svätopluk (overture) 1934, Ballad Suite 1936, Sonatina for Violin and Piano 1937, Psalm of Carpathian Country (chorus and orchestra) 1938, music to Stodola's drama King Svätopluk 1937, From the Hills (four male-voice choirs a capella) 1940, Krútňava (opera, The Vortex) 1941-49, Three Slovak Folk Songs (male choir) 1950, Metamorphoses (orchestra) 1951-52, Pictures of Slovakia (six cycles for piano or various instrumental and vocal ensembles) 1955-56, Sinfonietta Rustica (orchestra) 1956, Svätopluk (musical drama in three acts) 1952-59, Ad Astra (soprano and orchestra) 1961, Five Songs of Men (mixed chorus a capella) 1962, Six Pieces for String Orchestra 1963, Poème Macabre (violin and piano) 1963, Contemplazioni (reciter and piano) 1964, Partita Rapsodica (piano and orchestra) 1965, Kaleidoskop (six cycles for string orchestra and piano or organ and percussion) 1968, Toccata for Piano 1973, Symphonic Fantasy on B-A-C-H for Organ, String Orchestra and Percussion 1972, Slovak Song (mixed choir) 1975, Concertino for Clarinet and Orchestra 1977, Prielom Symphony 1976, Elegie (for piano) 1978, Look to the Unknown (cycle of songs for treble voice and piano or orchestra) 1977, Echoes (cycle for mixed choir) 1980, Three songs for bass and orchestra 1985. *Address:* Bradlanská ul., 11 Bratislava, 81103 Czechoslovakia. *Telephone:* Bratislava 313233.

SUCKLING, Charles W., C.B.E., D.SC., PH.D., F.R.S.C., F.R.S.; British chemist; b. 24 July 1920, Teddington; s. of Edward Ernest and Barbara Suckling (née Thomson); m. Eleanor Margaret Watterson 1946; two s. one d.; ed. Oldershaw Grammar School, Wallasey, Univ. of Liverpool; with Imperial Chemical Industries PLC 1942-82, Deputy Chair. Mond Div. 1969-72, Chair. Paints Div. 1972-77, Gen. Man. Research and Tech. 1977-82; Chair. Bradbury, Suckling and Partners Ltd. 1981-; Dir. (non-exec.) Albright and Wilson 1982-; Visiting Prof. Stirling Univ. 1969-; mem. Science Consultative Group, BBC 1979-82; mem. Royal Comm. on Environmental Pollution 1981-; Treas. Royal Coll. of Art, London 1984-; mem. Electricity Supply Research Council 1983-; John Scott Medal of City of Philadelphia for invention of anaesthetic halothane 1973; Leverhulme Prize Soc. Chem. Industrialists 1942; Hon. D.Sc. (Liverpool) 1980, Hon. (D. Univ.) Stirling 1985. *Publications:* Research in the Chemical Industry 1969, Chemistry Through Models (with C. J. and K. E. Suckling) 1978. *Leisure interests:* music, writing, horticulture. *Address:* Willowhay, Shoppenhangers Road, Maidenhead, SL6 2QA, England. *Telephone:* (0628) 27502.

SUCKSDORFF, Arne Edvard; Swedish film producer; b. 3 Feb. 1917; ed. Stockholm. *Films include:* documentaries: Shadow over the Snow, Cliff Face, The Open Road, Rhythm of a City, Summer Interlude, Indian Village, and The Divided World; feature films: The Great Adventure, The Flute and the Arrow, The Boy in the Tree.

SUCRE-FIGARELLA, José Francisco; Venezuelan diplomatist; b. 6 April 1931, Tumeremo; ed. Central Univ. of Caracas, Univ. of Chile amd L.S.E., London; after joining diplomatic service, held numerous posts in Venezuela's embassies, including that of First Sec. in France, Fed. Repub. of Germany and Denmark, Counsellor in U.S.A., Consul-Gen. in France, Minister-Counsellor in Italy, Amb. to Fed. Repub. of Germany; Amb. to Poland 1981-84; Perm. Rep. to UN 1984-85; Minister of State and Minister of Culture 1988-89; Pres. Venezuelan Office for Guayanan Devt. March 1989-.

SUDEARY, Abdelmuhsin M. Al-, M.AGR.; Saudi Arabian diplomatist; b. 7 Feb. 1936, Riyadh; s. of Mohammed and Lululua Al-Sudeary; m. Hissa Al-Sudeary; one s. two d.; ed. Colorado State Univ. and Arizona Univ.; worked at Ministry of Agric. and Waters; Amb. to FAO 1972, Chair. N.E. Group; Chair. OPEC during UN Conf. on the Establishment of Int. Fund for Agric. Devt. (IFAD) June 1975; Chair. World Food Programme Cttee. on Food Aid Policies and Programmes 1976, Preparatory Comm. for IFAD 1976-77; Pres. IFAD 1977-84, Middle East Magazine Dec. 1984-; Gold Medal Award (Pio Manzu Centre, Italy) 1978, Int. Prize of the Italian Agricultural Press Assen. 1978; Order Francisco de Miranda (Venezuela) 1979. *Address:* c/o International Fund for Agricultural Development, 107 Via del Serafico, 00142 Rome, Italy.

SUDHARMONO, Gen.; Indonesian politician; b. 12 March 1927, Gresik; ed. Mil. Law Acad., Mil. Law Inst., Army Staff and Command Coll.; Commdr. Reserve Troops, Ronggolawe Div., E. and Cen. Java 1945-49; army officer, Bandung Educ. Centre 1950-52; Staff Officer, Cen. War Authority 1957-61; Alternate Mil. Attorney/Staff Officer, Supreme War Authority Office 1962-63; Asst. to Special Affairs Dir. of Consultative Team to Leadership of the Revolution 1963-66; Sec. Econ. Stabilisation Council 1966; Cabinet Sec. 1966; Chair., Co-ordinator, Cttee. for Int. Tech. Co-operation 1966; Sec. Audit Team 1971; became Major-Gen. 1971; State

Sec. (and Cabinet Sec.) 1972; Minister, State Sec. 1973-88; Vice-Pres. of Indonesia March 1988-. *Address:* Office of the Vice-President, Jalan Merdeka Selatan 6, Jakarta, Indonesia. *Telephone:* (021) 363539.

SUDOMO; Indonesian politician; b. 20 Sept. 1926, Malang, E. Java; ed. Navigation High School, Cilacap, Cen. Java, Artillerie School Koninklijke Marine Den Helder, Netherlands, Inst. for Nat. Defence (LEMHANAS), School for Marine Commdrs., Surabaya and Naval Staff and Command Coll., Jakarta; Battalion III Base IX 1945-50; Commdr. Flores and First Officer Gajah Madah 1950-56; Head, Directorate of Operations and Training Credits, Naval H.Q., Commdr. Special Fighting Unit, promoted Vice-Adm. 1956-62; Theatre Naval Commdr. for liberation of W. Irian 1962-64; Asst. to Minister of Sea Communications 1964-66; Insp.-Gen. of Navy 1966-68; Commdr. Cen. Maritime Territory 1968-69; Chief of Staff of Indonesian Navy, promoted Admiral 1969-73; Deputy Chief of Command for Restoration of Security and Order 1973-74; Chief of Staff 1974-78; Deputy Commdr. in charge of Armed Forces 1978-83; Minister of Manpower 1983-88, Co-ordinating Minister of Political Affairs and Security March 1988-. *Address:* Jalan Merdeka Barat 15, Jakarta, Indonesia.

SUDREAU, Pierre Robert, L. EN D.; French politician; b. 13 May 1919; m. France Brun 1939; two s. one d.; ed. Ecole des Sciences Politiques, Law and Letters Faculties, Paris Univ.; served 2nd World War, prisoner in Buchenwald; Dir. de Cabinet, Sec. d'Etat à la Présidence du Conseil 1946; Jt. Dir. Gen., Dir. of Admin. and Gen. Affairs, Sûreté Nationale 1947; Dir. Financial Services, Ministry of the Interior 1949; Prefect, Loir-et-Cher 1951-55; Commr. for Reconstruction and Town Planning, Paris Region 1955-58; Minister of Housing (De Gaulle cabinet) 1958-59; Minister of Construction (Debré cabinet) 1959-62, of Educ. (Pompidou cabinet) 1962; Deputy for Loir-et-Cher, Nat. Ass. 1967-; mem. Union Centriste group in Nat. Ass.; Pres. Féd. des Industries Ferroviaires 1963-; Pres. Conseil français du mouvement européen 1968-72, Hon. Pres. 1972-; Pres. Comité Nat. pour l'aménagement du territoire français 1970-, Group to Promote Industrial Co-operation between France and Japan 1969-; Mayor of Blois 1971-; Pres. Cttee. on Industrial Reform 1974, Région Centre 1976; Hon. Pres., Asscn. Mer du Nord-Méditerranée 1985-; Chair. French Foreign Trade Cttee.; mem. du Conseil, Ordre de la Légion d'honneur; Grand Officier Légion d'honneur, Croix de guerre, Médaille de la Résistance, Commdr. des Palmes académiques and numerous other foreign awards. *Publications:* L'Enchaînement 1967, La stratégie de l'absurde 1980, De l'inertie politique 1985. *Address:* 12 rue Bixio, Paris 75007, France.

SUENENS, H.E. Cardinal Leo Jozef, D.D., PH.D., B.C.L.; Belgian ecclesiastic; b. 16 July 1904, Ixelles; ed. Pontifical Gregorian Univ., Rome; ordained Priest 1927; Teacher, Inst. Sainte-Marie, Brussels 1929; lecturer in Philosophy, Malines Seminary 1930-40; Vice-Rector, Louvain Univ. 1940-45; Pvt. Chamberlain to Pope 1941; Auxiliary Bishop and Vicar-Gen. of Archdiocese of Malines 1945-61; Archbishop of Malines-Brussels and Primate of Belgium 1961-79, now Archbishop Emer.; cr. Cardinal 1962; Moderator of Vatican Council 1962-65; mem. Pontifical Comm. for Revision of Canon Law 1962-; Pres. Belgian Bishops' Conf.; Templeton Foundation Prize 1976. *Publications:* Theology of the Apostolate of the Legion of Mary, Edel-Mary Quinn, The Right View on Moral Rearmament, The Gospel to Every Creature, Mary the Mother of God, Love and Control, The Nun in the World, Christian Life Day by Day, Co-responsibility in the Church, The Future of the Christian Church, A New Pentecost? Ecumenism and Charismatic Renewal, Charismatic Renewal and Social Action: A Dialogue (with H. Camara), Rene-wal and the Powers of Darkness. *Address:* Boulevard de Smet de Mayer 570, 1020 Brussels, Belgium. *Telephone:* (02) 4791950.

SUESS, Hans Eduard, PH.D.; American professor of geochemistry; b. 16 Dec. 1909, Vienna, Austria; s. of Franz Eduard Suess and Olga Frenzl; m. Ruth V. Teuteberg 1940; one s. one d.; ed. Univ. of Vienna; Instructor Univ. of Vienna 1933-35; Research Asst., Fed. Tech. High School, Zürich, Switzerland 1935-36, Univ. of Hamburg, Germany 1937-39; Asst. Prof. 1940-47, Assoc. Prof. 1948-50; Research Fellow, Univ. of Chicago, U.S. 1950-51; Physical Chemist, U.S. Geological Survey, Washington, D.C. 1951-55; Research Chemist, Scripps Inst. of Oceanography, La Jolla, Calif. 1955-58; Prof. of Chem., Univ. of Calif., San Diego 1958-, now Emer.; Guggenheim Fellow 1966; mem. American Acad. of Arts and Science, N.A.S., Austrian and Heidelberg Acads. of Sciences, Max Planck Soc.; Hon. D.Sc.; Gold Medal of American Geochem. Soc. (Goldschmidt Medal) 1974, Meteoritical Soc. Medal 1977. *Publications:* 158 on geochemistry, oceanography, nuclear physics and cosmochemistry; book: Chemistry of the Solar System 1987. *Address:* Department of Chemistry, B-017, University of California, San Diego, La Jolla, Calif. 92093, U.S.A. *Telephone:* (619) 453-0183.

SUGAÏ, Kumi; Japanese painter; b. 1919; ed. Osaka School of Fine Arts; one-man shows, Galerie Cruen, Paris, Palais des Beaux Arts, Brussels 1954, St. George's Gallery, London 1955, Galerie Legendre, Paris 1957; rep. at Pittsburgh Carnegie Int. Exhbn. 1955, and Salon des Réalités Nouvelles 1956, 1957, Salon de Mai 1957, 1958, Salon Biennale 1957 (all Paris) and Dunn Int. Exhbn., London 1963; Int. Painting Prize, São Paulo Bienal 1965. *Publication:* La quête sans fin. *Address:* Paris, France.

SUGAR, Alan Michael; British business executive; b. 24 March 1947; s. of Nathan Sugar and Fay Sugar; m. Ann Simons 1968; two s. one d.; ed.

Brooke House School, London; Chair. and owner Amstrad PLC 1968-. *Leisure interest:* tennis. *Address:* 169 King's Road, Brentwood, Essex, England. *Telephone:* 228888.

SUGIURA, Binsuke; Japanese banker; b. 13 Nov. 1911, Tokyo; s. of Kenichi and Toshi Sugiura; m. Chizuko Hayashida 1939; three d.; ed. Tokyo Univ.; Dir. The Long-Term Credit Bank of Japan Ltd. 1958-61, Man. Dir. 1961-68, Sr. Man. Dir. 1968-69, Deputy Pres. 1969-71, Pres. 1971-78, Chair. June 1978-; Medal with Blue Ribbon. *Leisure interest:* golf. *Address:* The Long-Term Credit Bank of Japan Ltd., 2-4, Ohtemachi 1-chome, Chiyoda-ku, Tokyo 100; 31-5, Kami-Meguro 3-chome, Meguro-ku, Tokyo 153, Japan (Home). *Telephone:* 211-5111 (Office); 719-5505 (Home).

SUHARTO, Gen., T.N.I.; Indonesian army officer and politician; b. 8 June 1921, Kemusu, Yogjakarta; m. Siti Hartinah 1947; six c.; ed. mil. schools and Indonesian Army Staff and Command Coll.; Officer in Japanese-sponsored Indonesian Army 1943; Battalion, later Regimental Commdr., Yogjakarta 1945-50; Regimental Commdr., Cen. Java 1953; Brig.-Gen. 1960, Maj.-Gen. 1962; Deputy Chief of Army Staff 1960-65; Chief of Army Staff 1965-68, Supreme Commdr. 1968-73; Minister of Army 1965; assumed emergency exec. powers March 1966; Deputy Prime Minister for Defence and Security 1966; Chair. of Presidium of Cabinet, in charge of Defence and Security, also Minister of Army 1966-67; Full Gen. 1966; Acting Pres. of Indonesia 1967-68; Prime Minister 1967, concurrently Minister for Defence and Security 1967-73; Pres. of Indonesia March 1968-; UN Population Award 1989. *Publication:* Suharto, My Thoughts, Words and Deeds 1989. *Address:* Office of the President, 15 Jalan Merdeka Utara, Jakarta; 8 Jalan Cendana, Jakarta, Indonesia (Home).

SUHL, Harry, PH.D.; American professor of physics; b. 18 Oct. 1922, Leipzig, Germany; s. of Bernhard Suhl and Klara Bergwerk; m. 1949 (deceased); no c.; ed. Univ. Coll., Cardiff and Oriel Coll., Oxford; Temp. Experimental Officer, Admiralty, London 1943-46; Tech. Staff, Bell Labs., N.J. 1948-60; Prof. of Physics, Univ. of Calif. (San Diego) 1961-; Consultant, Aerospace Corpn. 1961-, Exxon Research and Eng., N.J. 1977-; Fellow, American Physics Soc., N.A.S.; Guggenheim Fellow 1968-69; Nat. Science Foundation Fellow 1971; Co-Ed. Magnetism 1961-74; ed. Solid State Communications 1961-. *Publication:* Magnetism—a Treatise on Modern Theory and Materials (with G.T. Rado) 1966. *Address:* Physics Department, University of California, San Diego, La Jolla, Calif. 92093, U.S.A. *Telephone:* (619) 534-4748.

SUICH, Maxwell Victor; Australian journalist; b. 1 April 1938, Sydney; s. of Henry John Suich and Catherine McDonell; m. Jennifer Mary Sorrell 1963; two d.; ed. Canterbury High School; Tokyo Corresp. Australian Financial Review, Sydney Morning Herald, The Age 1968-71; Deputy Ed. Australian Financial Review 1971-72; Ed. The National Times 1972-78; Man. Ed. The Sun-Herald 1979; Exec. Dir. Radio Station 2GB 1979-80; Chief Editorial Exec. John Fairfax and Sons Ltd. 1980-. *Publications:* Crisis in Resources Diplomacy 1972, The Tax Club 1978, The Leo Port Story (with Anne Summers) 1978. *Leisure interest:* travelling to Melbourne. *Address:* John Fairfax and Sons Ltd., GPO Box 506, Sydney 2001, N.S.W., Australia.

SUITNER, Otmar; Austrian conductor; b. 16 May 1922, Innsbruck; s. of Karl Suitner and Maria Rizzi; m. Marita Wilckens 1948; ed. Pädagogium Innsbrück, Mozarteum Salzburg; Music Dir. in Remscheid 1952-57; Gen. Dir. of Pfalzorchester in Ludwigshafen/Rh. 1957-60; Gen. Dir. of State Opera Dresden 1960-64; Gen. Dir. German State Opera Berlin 1964-; Hon. Conductor Nippon Hoso Kyokai Orchestra, Tokyo 1973; Guest Conductor San Francisco, Tokyo, Vienna, Bayreuth Festival, etc.; many recordings; led course for conductors, Int. Summer Acad. Univ. Mozarteum, Salzburg 1975, 1976; Prof. 1968; Prof. in Conducting, Hochschule für Musik, Vienna 1977-88; Commendatore, Gregorian Order 1973. *Address:* Berlin-Niederschönhausen, Platanenstr. 13, German Democratic Republic; Widerhoferplatz 4/48, A-1090 Vienna, Austria.

SUITS, Chauncey Guy, B.A., D.SC.; American physicist; b. 12 March 1905; ed. Univ. of Wisconsin and Swiss Fed. Inst. of Tech.; Physics Consultant, U.S. Forest Products Lab., Madison, Wis. 1929-30; Research Physicist, Gen. Electric Co., Research Lab., Schenectady, N.Y. 1930-40, Asst. to Dir. 1940-45; Vice-Pres. and Dir. of Research 1945-66; Chief, Div. 15 and mem. Div. 14 of Nat. Defence Research Cttee. of Office of Scientific Research and Devt., Govt. 1942-46; mem. Naval Research Advisory Cttee. 1956-64, Chair. 1958-61; mem. N.Y. State Science and Tech. Foundation 1965-, Vice-Chair. 1968-; Consultant Industrial Research Man.; founding mem. Nat. Acad. of Eng.; mem. N.A.S., American Philosophical Soc., American Acad. of Arts and Sciences; Silliman Lecturer, Yale Univ. 1952; Hon. D.Sc. (Union and Hamilton Colls., Drexel Inst. of Tech., Marquette Univ.), Hon. D.Eng. (Rensselaer Polytechnic Inst.) 1959; H.M. Medal for Service in the Cause of Freedom 1948; US Medal for Merit 1948; Procter Prize Award-RESA 1958; Medal of Industrial Research Inst. 1962; Medal of American Soc. for Metals 1966; Frederik Philips Award I.E.E.E. 1974. *Publications:* Suits: Speaking of Research, Applied Physics: Electroptics, Metallurgy (with Harrison and Jordan); 80 U.S. and foreign patents, numerous scientific papers. *Address:* Crosswinds, Pilot Knob, N.Y. 12844, U.S.A. (Home).

SUJA, Stanislav, D.JUR.; Czechoslovak diplomatist; b. 13 Nov. 1940, Viglaš; s. of Jan and Zlata Suja; m. Sárka Balušková 1970; two s. one d.; ed. Moscow Inst. for Int. Relations, Charles Univ., Prague; with Fed. Ministry for Foreign Affairs 1968, with depts. for Latin America, Africa, Int. Orgs., Western Europe: del. to UN Gen. Ass. 1968-75, 1977-80; Vice-Chair. 4th Cttee. (Decolonization) 1974; Counsellor, Czechoslovak Embassy, Portugal 1975-77; Chef de Cabinet of Minister for Foreign Affairs 1977-81; Amb. and Perm. Rep. of Czechoslovakia to UN 1981-83; Amb. to U.S.A. 1983-85; Head Gen. Secr. Ministry of Foreign Affairs 1986-87; Prin. Pvt. Sec., Minister of Foreign Affairs 1987-88, Dir. Dept. for Int. Orgs.; Czechoslovak State Decoration "For Outstanding Work". Publications: The Blue Helmets 1981, Operation Blue Berets 1981, Czechoslovak Foreign Policy After World War II 1982 (co-author), Foreign Policy of Czechoslovakia 1976-81 1982 (co-author), Washington, D.C. 1989. Address: c/o Ministry of Foreign Affairs, Prague, Czechoslovakia.

SUK, Josef; Czechoslovak violinist; b. 8 Aug. 1929, Prague; great-grandson of Antonin Dvořak; grandson of Josef Suk; m. Maria Poiakova 1951; ed. Prague Conservatory and studied with Jaroslav Kocian; First violinist, Prague String Quartet 1950; f. Suk Trio 1952; Prof., Vienna Conservatoire 1979-; has performed as a soloist or with trio throughout the world; Grand Prix du Disque 1960, 1966, 1968, 1974, 1978, Czechoslovak State Prize 1964, Edison Prize 1972, Wiener Flötenuhr 1974, Honoured Artist 1970, National Artist 1977. Address: Karlovo Namesti 5, 12000 Prague 2, Czechoslovakia. Telephone: 299407.

ŠUKRIJA, Ali; Yugoslavian (b. Albanian) politician; b. 12 Sept. 1919, Kosovska Mitrovica; ed. Kosovska Mitrovica, Peć, Vranje, Prizren, Belgrade; mem. League of Communist Youth of Yugoslavia 1937; mem. CP of Yugoslavia 1939-; fmr. Party Inst. of Local Cttee. of CP, Belgrade; fmr. Sec. of local Cttee. for Kosovska Mitrovica; mem. regional and Prov. Cttees. for Kosovo and Metohija; Del. 8th Prov. Conf. for Montenegro, Boka, Sandžak, Kosovo and Metohija; with Nat. Liberation Struggle 1941-45; Commissar of Head of Operating Zone of Kosovo; mem. Presidency of Regional Nat. Liberation Cttee. of Kosovo and Metohija 1943-45; mem. Third Session of Anti-Fascist Council of Nat. Liberation of Yugoslavia; Public Prosecutor for Kosovo and Metohija 1945; Pres. Cttee. for Public Utilities and Town Planning, Sec. of Cen. Cttee. for Public Health and Social Policy of Serbia; fmr. Deputy to Repub. and Prov. Ass.; Vice-Pres., Pres. of Exec. Council of Ass. of Kosovo; mem. Fed. Exec. Council, Sec.-Gen. of Fed. Conf. of Socialist Alliance of Yugoslavia; mem. Cen. Cttee. of League of Communists of Serbia and Yugoslavia -1989, mem. of Presidency 1974, 1978, Pres. of Presidium of Cen. Cttee. of League of Communists of Yugoslavia 1984-85; Pres. of Presidency of Prov. of Kosovo 1981-82; numerous medals. Address: c/o Savez komunista Jugoslavije, Novi Beograd, bul. Lenjina 6, Yugoslavia.

SUKSELAINEN, Vieno Johannes; Finnish economist and politician; b. 12 Oct. 1906, Paimio; m. Elma Bonden 1938; three s. one d.; Lecturer School of Social Sciences, Helsinki 1939; Sec. to Prime Minister 1941-45; teacher of political econs., Univ. of Turku 1945-47; Prof. School of Social Sciences, Univ. of Tampere 1947-54, Rector 1953-54, Chancellor 1969-78; Pres. of the Agrarian Union 1945-64; mem. Finnish Parl. 1948-70, 1972-79, Speaker 1956-57, 1958-59, 1968-70, 1972-75; Minister of Finance 1950-51 and 1954; Minister of Interior 1951-53; Gen. Dir. People's Pension Inst. 1954-71; Prime Minister May-Nov. 1957, 1959-61; fmr. mem. Nordic Council, Pres. 1972, 1977. Leisure interest: agriculture. Address: Tapiola, Finland. Telephone: Helsinki 462189.

SULIOTIS, Elena; Greek soprano opera singer; b. 28 May 1943, Athens; d. of Constantino Souliotis and Gallia Cavalengo; m. Marcello Guerrini 1970; one d.; ed. Buenos Aires and Milan; grew up in Argentina; went to Milan and was introduced to Gianandrea Gavazzeni 1962; studied singing with Mercedes Llopart; debut in Cavalleria Rusticana, Teatro San Carlo, Naples 1964; sang Amelia in Un Ballo in Maschera, Trieste 1965 and has since sung frequently throughout Italy; debut at La Scala as Abigail in Nabucco 1966; U.S. debut as Helen of Troy in Mefistofele, Chicago 1966; debut at Covent Garden as Lady Macbeth 1969; has also appeared at Teatro Colon, Buenos Aires and in Rio de Janeiro, São Paulo, Mexico City, New York, Dallas, Philadelphia, San Antonio, Montreal, Paris, Kiel, Lübeck, Höchst, Tokyo, Lisbon, Athens and Madrid; repertoire includes: Manon Lescaut, La Giaconda, Macbeth, Norma, Otello, Aida, Luisa Miller, Il Trovatore, Tosca, Loreley, La Forza del Destino, etc.; has recorded Norma, Cavalleria Rusticana, Nabucco, Anna Bolena, Macbeth and arias for Decca; recipient of several prizes. Leisure interests: country life, looking after plants and animals. Address: Villa il Poderino, Via Incontri 38, Florence, Italy.

SULLIVAN, Barry F., M.B.A.; American business executive; b. 21 Dec. 1930, Bronx, N.Y.; m.; four s. one d.; ed. Georgetown and Columbia Univs. and Univ. of Chicago; with Chase Manhattan Bank 1957-80, mem. Man. Cttee. 1974-80; Chair. of Bd. and C.E.O. First Chicago Corpn., First Nat. Bank of Chicago July 1980-; mem. Econ. Devt. Comm. of Chicago, Assn. of Reserve City Bankers, Mayor's Airport Study Comm., Chicago Clearing House Cttee., World's Fair Finance Cttee.; Vice-Pres. Exec. Cttee., Chicago Assn. of Commerce and Industry; Dir. United Way—Crusade of Mercy Chicago, Campaign Dir. 1985; Trustee and mem. Exec. Cttee., Univ. of Chicago, also Chair. of Council of Graduate School of Business;

Trustee, Art Inst. of Chicago. Address: First National Bank of Chicago, One First National Plaza, Chicago, Ill. 60670, U.S.A.

SULLIVAN, Dennis P., PH.D.; American mathematician; b. 12 Feb. 1941, Fort Huron, Mich.; one s. two d.; ed. Rice and Princeton Univs.; NATO Fellow, Univ. of Warwick, England 1966; Miller Fellow, Univ. of Berkeley 1967-69; Sloan Fellow of Mathematics, M.I.T. 1969-72, Prof. of Mathematics 1972-73; Prof. Permanent, Institut des Hautes Etudes Scientifiques, Paris, France 1974-; Einstein Prof. of Sciences, Queens Coll. and Cuny Graduate School, Cuny, New York 1981-; mem. N.A.S.; Dr. hon. (Warwick) 1984; Oswald Veblen Prize in Geometry 1971; Elie Cartan Prix en Géométrie, French Acad. of Sciences 1981. Publications: several papers in mathematical journals. Leisure interest: people. Address: Department of Mathematics, 33 West 42nd Street, Room 708, New York, N.Y. 10036, U.S.A. Telephone: (212) 790-4569.

SULLIVAN, Eugene John, B.S., M.B.A.; American business executive (retd.); b. 28 Nov. 1920, New York; s. of Cornelius and Margaret Sullivan; m. Gloria Roesch; three s. one d.; ed. St. John's Univ. and New York Univ.; with Borden Chemical Co. 1946-, Vice-Pres. Sales 1957, Exec. Vice-Pres. 1958-64, Pres. 1964, Vice-Pres. Borden Inc. 1964-67, Exec. Vice-Pres. 1967-73, Dir. 1967-, Pres. 1973-85, Chair. 1979-87, C.E.O. 1979-86, Chair. Exec. Cttee. 1987-; Dir. Bank of N.Y., Warner Lambert Co., F. W. Woolworth Co.; Dir., Sec. Grolery Manufacturers of America; Adjunct Prof. St. John's Univ. Business School 1974-87, Prof. 1987-; Trustee Emigrant Savings Bank, Atlantic Mutual Insurance Co., N.Y. Medical Coll.; Trustee, Sec. St. John's Univ.; Hon. Ph.D. (St. John's Univ.) 1973. Address: c/o Borden, Inc., 277 Park Avenue, New York, N.Y. 10017, U.S.A.

SULLIVAN, Fred R., B.S., M.B.A.; American business executive; b. 22 Aug. 1914, Fort Wayne, Ind.; s. of Walter H. and Grace P. Sullivan; m. Judith O. Omanoff 1967; one s. two d.; ed. Rutgers and New York Univs.; joined Monroe Calculating Machine Co. 1934, Pres. 1953; Monroe merged with and became Div. of Litton Industries Inc. 1958, Sr. Vice-Pres. and Dir. Litton Industries 1958-64; C.E.O., Dir. Walter Kidde & Company, Inc. 1963-, Pres. 1964-, Chair. Bd. 1966-; dir. numerous cos; Hon. LL.D. (Washington, Jefferson Colls.) 1974. Address: Park 80, West Plaza 2, Box 5555, Saddle Brook, N.J. 07662, U.S.A.

SULLIVAN, Louis Wade, M.D.; American physician and politician; b. 16 Oct. 1933, Atlanta; s. of Walter Wade Sullivan and Lubirda Elizabeth (née Priester) Sullivan; m. Eve Williamson 1955; three c.; ed. Morehouse Coll., Atlanta, Boston Univ.; Intern New York Hosp.-Cornell Medical Centre, New York 1958-59, resident in internal medicine 1959-60; Fellow in Pathology, Mass. Gen. Hosp., Boston 1960-61; Research Fellow Thorndike Memorial Lab., Harvard Medical School, Boston 1961-63, Instructor of Medicine 1963-64; Asst. Prof. Medicine N.J. Coll. Medicine 1964-66; Co-Dir. Haematology, Boston Univ. Medical Centre 1966, Assoc.-Prof. 1968-74, Prof. of Medicine and Physiology 1974-75; Dir. Hematology, Boston City Hosp.; Dean School of Medicine, Morehouse Coll. 1975-, Pres.; Sec. of State for Health and Human Services March 1989-; mem. sickle cell anemia Advisory Cttee., Nat. Insts. of Health 1974-75, Medical Advisory Bd., Nat. Leukemia Assn. 1968-70, (Chair. 1970); mem. American Soc. of Hematology, American Soc. of Clinical Investigation, Inst. of Medicine. Publications: numerous papers on medical matters. Address: Office of the Secretary of Health and Human Services, 200 Independence Avenue, S.W., Washington, D.C. 20201; 223 Chestnut Street, Atlanta, Georgia 30314, U.S.A.

SULLIVAN, Michael J., J.D.; American lawyer and state governor; b. 23 Sept. 1939, Omaha; s. of Joseph B. Sullivan and Margaret Hamilton; m. Jane Metzler 1961; one s. two d.; ed. Univ. of Wyoming; Assoc. Brown, Drew, Apostolos, Barton & Massey, Casper, Wyoming 1964-67; partner, Brown, Drew, Apostolos, Massey & Sullivan, Casper 1967-; Gov. of Wyoming 1987-; mem. A.B.A.; Democrat. Address: Office of the Governor, State Capitol, Cheyenne, Wyo. 82002-0010; 5001 Central Avenue, Cheyenne, Wyo. 82002, U.S.A. (Home).

SULLIVAN, Walter Seager, B.A.; American journalist and author; b. 12 Jan. 1918, New York; s. of Walter S. and Jeanet E. L. Sullivan; m. Mary E. Barrett 1950; one s. two d.; ed. Groton School and Yale Univ.; Field Work, Alaska, American Museum of Natural History 1935; New York Times 1940-67; U.S.N. 1940-46; Foreign Corresp., Far East, New York Times 1948-50, UN 1950-52, Germany and Berlin 1952-56, U.S. Antarctic Expeditions 1946-47, 1954-55, 1956-57, 1976, Science News Ed. 1960-63, Science Ed. 1964-67; Gov. Arctic Inst. of N. America 1959-66; Councillor, American Geographical Soc. 1959-81; Fellow, A.A.A.S.; Hon. H.L.D. (Yale), (Newark Coll. of Eng.) 1973; Hon. D.Sc. (Hofstra Univ.) 1975, (Ohio State) 1977; Westinghouse Award of A.A.A.S. 1963, 1968, 1972; George Polk Memorial Award, New York 1959; Int. Non-Fiction Book Prize, Frankfurt 1965, Grady Award, A.C.S. 1969, American Inst. Physics U.S. Steel Foundation Award in Physics and Astronomy 1969, Washburn Medal, Boston Museum of Science 1972, Daly Medal, American Geographical Soc. 1973, Ralph Coats Roe Medal, A.S.M.E. 1975, Science-in-Society Journalism Award, Nat. Assn. of Science Writers 1976, Distinguished Public Service Award, Nat. Science Foundation 1978, Public Welfare Medal, Nat. Acad. of Sciences 1980. Publications: Quest for a Continent 1957, White Land of Adventure 1957, Assault on the Unknown 1961, We Are Not Alone 1964,

Continents in Motion 1974, Black Holes—The Edge of Space, The End of Time 1979, Landprints 1984. *Leisure interest:* chamber music. *Address:* New York Times, Times Square, New York, N.Y. 10036 (Office); 66 Indian Head Road, Riverside, Conn., U.S.A. (Home). *Telephone:* (203) 637-3318.

SULLIVAN, William Healy; American diplomatist; b. 12 Oct. 1922; ed. Brown Univ. and Fletcher School of Law and Diplomacy; U.S. Navy 1943–46; Foreign Service 1947–, served Bangkok 1947–49, Calcutta 1949–50, Tokyo 1950–52, Rome 1952–55, The Hague 1955–58; Officer-in-Charge, Burma Affairs, Dept. of State 1958–59; Foreign Affairs Officer 1959; UN Adviser, Bureau of Far Eastern Affairs 1960–63; Special Asst. to Under-Sec. for Political Affairs 1963–64; Amb. to Laos 1964–69; Deputy Asst. Sec. of State for E. Asia (with special responsibility for Viet-Nam); Amb. to the Philippines 1973–77, to Iran 1977–79. *Address:* American Assembly, Columbia University, New York, N.Y. 10027, U.S.A. *Telephone:* (212) 280-3456.

SULLO, Fiorentino; Italian politician; b. 29 March 1921, Paternopoli, Avellino; s. of Clorindo and Guilia Emilia (née Calienno) Sullo; m. Elvira de Laurentiis 1961; one d.; mem. Constituent Ass. 1946–48, Chamber of Deputies 1948–; fmr. Under-Sec. for Defence, Under-Sec. for Industry and Commerce, Under-Sec. for State Participation; Minister of Transport 1960, of Labour and Social Insurance 1960–62, of Public Works 1962–63, of Educ. 1968–69; Minister without portfolio for scientific and tech. research 1972–73, for Regions 1973; Pres. Interior Comm., Chamber of Deputies 1966–68; Pres. Public Works Comm. 1979–81; now State Councillor; Ed. Le Discussione 1966–69; editorial contrib. Roma di Napoli; Contributor to Il Punto, Politica and Mattino 1977–79, to Roma 1979–; Pres. Christian Democrat group in Parl. 1968; resigned from Christian Democrat Party 1974; mem. Social Democrat Party 1974–82; returned to Christian Democrat Party Aug. 1982, to Chamber of Deputies 1983–87; mem. Majority of Regulation, Constitutional Affairs Comm., Regional Questions Comm., Chamber of Deputies, Admin. Law Council in Sicilian Region 1988, Second Section of State Council 1989; Co-Pres. Italy-U.S.S.R. Cultural Assen.; Grand Officier, Légion d'honneur, Grand Cross Kt. of Italian Repub. *Publication:* Lo Scandalo Ubanistico 1964. *Leisure interest:* tennis. *Address:* Via Venanzio Fortunato 54, 00136 Rome, Italy. *Telephone:* 345 10 31.

SULMAN AL-KHALIFA, H.H. Shaikh Isa bin (see Khalifa, H. H. Shaikh Isa bin Sulman al-).

SULSTON, John Edward, PH.D., F.R.S.; British scientist; b. 27 March 1942, Fulmer; s. of the late Rev. Canon Arthur Edward Aubrey Sulston and of Josephine Muriel Frearson Blocksidge; m. Daphne Edith Bate 1966; one s. one d.; ed. Merchant Taylor's School and Pembroke Coll., Cambridge; Postdoctoral Fellowship at the Salk Inst., Calif. 1966–69; Staff scientist, MRC Lab. of Molecular Biology, Cambridge 1969–. *Publications:* papers in scientific journals. *Leisure interests:* gardening, walking, avoiding people. *Address:* Medical Research Laboratory of Molecular Biology, Hills Road, Cambridge, CB2 2QH; 39 Mingle Lane, Stapleford, Cambridge, CB2 5BG, England (Home). *Telephone:* (0223) 248011; (0223) 842248 (Home).

SULTAN IBN ABDUL AZIZ, H.R.H. Prince; Saudi Arabian politician; b. 1922; s. of the late King Abdul Aziz ibn Saud and Hassa Bint Sudairi; brother of King Fahd and of the late King Khalid; fmr. Pres. of Royal Guard, Minister of Communications; Minister of Defence and Aviation and Insp. Gen. 1962–. *Address:* Ministry of Defence, Airport Road, Riyadh, Saudi Arabia. *Telephone:* (1) 478-5900.

SULTAN, Fouad, B.SC.; Egyptian politician; b. Jan. 1931; ed. Univ. of Cairo; worked for 21 years with Cen. Bank of Egypt; seconded to IMF, North Yemen 1971–74; Head of Misr-Iran Bank 1974; head of several cttees. in Fed. of Egyptian Banks; Minister of Tourism and Civil Aviation 1985–. *Address:* Ministry of Tourism, 110 Sharia Kasr El-Eini, Tahrir Square, Cairo, Egypt. *Telephone:* 31921.

SULZBERGER, Arthur Ochs; American newspaper executive; b. 5 Feb. 1926, New York; s. of Arthur Hays and Iphigene (née Ochs) Sulzberger; m. 1st Barbara Grant 1948 (divorced 1956), one s. one d.; m. 2nd Carol Fox 1956, one d.; ed. Columbia Univ.; U.S. Marine Corps, Second World War and Korean War; The New York Times Co., New York 1951–, Asst. Treas. 1958–63, Pres. and Publr. 1963–; Co-Chair. Bd. Int. Herald Tribune 1983–; Chair. Newspaper Pres. Assen. 1988–; Dir., Times Printing Co., Chattanooga, Gapesia Pulp and Paper Co. Ltd. of Canada; Trustee Columbia Univ., mem. Coll. Council; Trustee Metropolitan Museum of Art; Hon. L.H.D. (Montclair State Coll.), (Tufts Univ.) 1984; Alexander Hamilton Medal 1982. *Address:* New York Times Co., 229 West 43rd Street, New York, N.Y. 10036, U.S.A. *Telephone:* 556-1234.

SULZBERGER, Cyrus Leo, B.S.; American author; b. 27 Oct. 1912, New York; s. of Leo and Beatrice Sulzberger; m. Marina Lada 1942 (died 1976); one s. one d.; ed. Harvard Univ.; fmr. columnist for New York Times; Pulitzer Citation 1951; Overseas Press Club of America awards 1957, 1970, 1973. *Publications:* Sit Down with John L. Lewis 1938, The Big Thaw 1956, What's Wrong with U.S. Foreign Policy 1959, My Brother Death 1961, The Test: de Gaulle and Algeria 1962, Unfinished Revolution 1965, History of World War II 1966, A Long Row of Candles, Memoirs and Diaries 1934–54 1969, The Last of the Giants 1970, The Tooth Merchant 1973, Unconquered Souls—The Resistentialists 1973, An Age of Mediocrity 1973, The Coldest War—Russia's Game in China 1974, Postscript with a Chinese Accent 1974, Go Gentle Into the Night 1976, The Fall of Eagles 1977, Seven Continents and Forty Years 1977, The Tallest Liar 1977, Marina 1979, How I Committed Suicide 1982, Such a Peace: The Roots and Ashes of Yalta 1982, The World and Richard Nixon 1987, Fathers and Children 1987. *Leisure interests:* fly fishing, walking. *Address:* 25 boulevard du Montparnasse, 75006 Paris, France.

SUMMER, Donna; American singer and actress; b. 31 Dec. 1948, Boston; d. of Andrew Gaines and Mary Gaines; m. 1st Helmut Sommer (divorced), one d.; m. 2nd Bruce Sudano, one s. one d.; singer 1967–; appeared in German stage production Hair; in Europe 1967–75, appearing in Vienna Folk productions of Porgy and Bess, and German productions of The Me Nobody Knows; Best Rhythm and Blues Female Vocalist, Nat. Acad. of Recording Arts and Sciences 1978, Best Female Rock Vocalist 1979, Favourite Female Pop Vocalist, American Music Awards 1979, Favourite Female Vocalist of Soul Music 1979, Ampex Golden Reel Award for single and album On the Radio 1979, album Bad Girls, Soul Artist of Year, Rolling Stone Magazine 1979, Best Rock Performance, Best of Las Vegas Jimmy Award 1980, Grammy Award for Best Inspirational Performance 1984; several awards for best-selling records; has sold over 20 million records. *Albums:* The Wanderer, Star Collection, Love to Love You Baby, Love Trilogy, Four Seasons of Love, I Remember Yesterday, The Deep, Shut Out, Once upon a Time, Bad Girls, On the Radio, Walk Away, She Works Hard for the Money, Cats without Claws. *Address:* c/o Munao Management, 1224 North Vine Street, Los Angeles, Calif. 90038, U.S.A.

SUMMERFIELD, Arthur, B.SC.TECH., B.SC., F.B.P.S.S.; British psychologist and university teacher; b. 31 March 1923, Wilmslow; s. of the late Arthur Summerfield and Dora Gertrude (née Perman Smith) Summerfield; m. 1st Aline Whalley 1946, one s. one d.; m. 2nd Angela Barbara Steer 1974; ed. Manchester Grammar School, Victoria Univ. of Manchester, Univ. Coll., London; Electrical Officer, R.N.V.R. (Naval Air Stations 1943–46, Dept. of Sr. Psychologist to Admiralty 1946); Asst. Lecturer in Psychology, Univ. Coll., London 1949–51, Lecturer 1951–61, Hon. Research Assoc. 1961–70, Hon. Research Fellow 1970–; Prof. of Psychology, Univ. of London, and Head, Dept. of Psychology, Birkbeck Coll. 1961–88, Prof. Emer. 1988–, Gov. 1982–86; Pres. British Psychological Soc. 1963–64, Int. Union of Psychological Science 1976–80, Section J (Psychology), British Assen. for the Advancement of Science 1976–77, Int. Social Science Council (UNESCO) 1977–81, mem. Exec. Cttee. 1981–83; mem. Cttee. on Int. Relations in Psychology, American Psychological Assen. 1977–79; mem. Bd. of Dirs., European Co-ordination Centre for Research and Documentation in Social Sciences 1977–81; mem. Social Science Research Council (G.B.) 1979–81; mem. Int. Council of Scientific Unions Study Group on the Biological, Medical and Physical Effects of the Large-scale Use of Nuclear Weapons 1983–; Asst. Ed. British Journal of Psychology (Statistical Section) 1950–54, Ed. British Journal of Psychology 1964–67; Scientific Ed. British Medical Bulletin (experimental psychology) 1964, (cognitive psychology) 1971, (psychobiology) 1981. *Address:* Department of Psychology, Birkbeck College, University of London, Malet Street, London, WC1E 7HX (Office); 14 Colonels Walk, The Ridgeway, Enfield, Middx., England (Home). *Telephone:* 01-631 6312 (Office); 01-367 1771 (Home).

SUMMERSON, Sir John Newenham, C.H., C.B.E., F.B.A., F.S.A., A.R.I.B.A.; British architectural historian; b. 25 Nov. 1904, Darlington; s. of Samuel Summerson and Dorothea Newenham; m. Elizabeth Hepworth 1938; three s.; ed. Univ. Coll., London; served in architects' offices and taught Edinburgh Coll. of Art 1929–30, took up architectural journalism; on staff Architect and Building News 1934–40; Deputy Dir. Nat. Bldgs. Record 1940–45; Curator Sir John Soane's Museum 1945–84; mem. Royal Comm. on Historical Monuments, Historic Bldgs. Council (Dept. of Environment); Chair. Nat. Council for Diplomas in Art and Design 1960–69; Lecturer in History of Architecture, Birkbeck Coll. 1961–70; Slade Prof. of Fine Art, Oxford 1958–59; Ferens Prof. of Fine Art, Hull 1960–61, 1970–71, Slade Prof. of Fine Art, Cambridge 1966–67; Trustee, Nat. Portrait Gallery 1966–73; Bampton Lecturer, Columbia 1967–68; Hon. mem. American Acad. of Arts and Sciences; Hon. D.Litt. (Univs. of Leicester, Oxford, Hull and Newcastle), Hon. D.Sc. (Univ. of Edinburgh); Royal Gold Medal for Architecture 1976. *Publications:* John Nash 1934, Georgian London 1945, Heavenly Mansions 1949, Sir John Soane 1952, Sir Christopher Wren 1953, Architecture in Britain 1530–1830 (Pelican History of Art) 1953, The Classical Language of Architecture 1964, Book of John Thorpe (Walpole Soc., Vol. XL) 1966, Inigo Jones 1966, Victorian Architecture 1970, The Life and Work of John Nash 1980, Architecture of the Eighteenth Century 1986, The Unromantic Castle (essays) 1989. *Address:* 1 Eton Villas, London, N.W.3, England. *Telephone:* 01-722 6247.

SUMNER, Gordon Matthew ("Sting"); British singer, bass-player, songwriter and film actor; b. 2 Oct. 1951, Northumberland; m. Frances Tomelty (divorced 1984); four c.; fmr. primary school teacher, Cramlington, Newcastle; singer, bass-player and songwriter for The Police (rock group) 1977–; first solo album The Dream of the Blue Turtles 1985, Nothing Like the Sun 1987; has undertaken major tours in U.K., Europe and U.S.A.; *film appearances include:* Brimstone and Treacle 1984, Quadrophenia, The Bride of Frankenstein, Plenty, Dune 1985, The Adventures of Baron von Munchausen 1989, Stormy Monday 1989, Rosencrantz and Guildenstern are Dead; Ivor Novello Award for Best Song 'They Dance Alone' 1989. *Publication:* Jungle Stories: The Fight for the Amazon 1989. *Address:* IRL, The Bugle House, Noel Street, London, W1, England; c/o Frontier Booking International, 1776 Broadway, New York, N.Y. 10019, U.S.A.

SUN DAGUANG; Chinese politician; Dir. N.E. Gen. Bureau of Navigation 1949; Dir. Planning Dept., Ministry of Communications 1953–54; Pres. N.E. Navigation Coll. 1954–; Asst. to Minister of Communications 1955–58; Vice-Minister of Communications 1958–64; mem. Cttee. for Receiving and Resettling Returned Overseas Chinese, State Council 1960; Minister of Communications 1964; Deputy to 3rd NPC 1964; mem. Nat. Defence Council 1965-Cultural Revolution; disappeared during Cultural Revolution; rehabilitated 1974; Dir. Nat. Geological Bureau, State Council 1978; deputy to 5th NPC 1978; Minister of Geology 1979–82, of Geology and Minerals 1982–85; mem. 12th Cen. Cttee. CCP 1982–87, mem. Cen. Advisory Comm. 1987–; Chair. Nat. Cttee. on Mineral Reserves 1984. *Address:* c/o State Council, Beijing, People's Republic of China.

SUN GUOZHI; Chinese politician; Deputy Dir. Transport Dept., CCP Prov. Cttee., Hunan 1958, Dir. Communications and Transport Dept. 1959; Dir. Bureau of Irrigation, Agric. and Forestry, Hunan People's Council 1964; Sec. CCP Prov. Cttee., Hunan 1966; disappeared during Cultural Revolution; mem. Standing Cttee., CCP Prov. Cttee., Hunan 1973–77; Chair. Planning Cttee., Prov. Revolutionary Cttee., Hunan 1977, Vice-Chair. Prov. Revolutionary Cttee. 1977–79; Sec. CCP Prov. Cttee., Hunan 1977–; Deputy for Hunan to 5th NPC 1978, 6th NPC 1983; mem. Credentials Cttee., 2nd Session, 5th NPC 1979; Gov. Hunan Prov. 1979–83; Chair. Prov. People's Congress, Hunan 1983–85, People's Congress, Hebei 1985; alt. mem. 12th Cen. Cttee. CCP 1982–85; mem. Presidium, 6th NPC 1986. *Address:* c/o Office of the Chairman of the People's Congress, 25921 Shijiazhuang City, Hebei Province, People's Republic of China.

SUN JIABO; Chinese woodcarver; b. 11 Dec. 1939, Beijing; s. of Sun Zengpei and Jiang Jingchun; m. Gu Ziaoyun 1980; one s.; ed. Middle School at Cen. Inst. of Fine Arts; researched folk wood sculpture and lacquer painting, Research Inst. of Arts and Crafts, Fujian Prov. 1965–70; forced to become farmworker, Qingliu Co. 1970; became radio announcer, photographer and purchasing agent for Fujian Vinylon Factory 1971; postgraduate studies, Sculpture Dept., Cen. Inst. of Fine Arts 1978–80, Teacher at Inst. 1980–, now Assoc. Prof.; taught at Fine Arts Dept., Yarmouk Univ., Jordan; many works exhibited Chinese Art Gallery and in Paris, Tokyo, Hong Kong, including Qu Yuan and Haw; other works include Sanitation Worker (bronze) in front of Beijing Municipal People's Govt. Offices, Driving Herds Homeward, Sculpture Garden, Shijingshan, Old Beijing Man (in yellow cypress), Mother (in pine). *Leisure interests:* sports, music. *Address:* 3 Shuaifuyuan, Sculpture Department, Central Institute of Fine Arts, Beijing, People's Republic of China. *Telephone:* 554731 Ext. 258.

SUN JINGWEN; Chinese politician; b. Hebei Province; Mayor of Zhangjiakou 1950; Dir. Urban Construction Bureau, Ministry of Building 1954–55; mem. State Construction Comm., State Council 1954–58; Deputy Dir., Urban Construction Bureau, State Council 1955–56; Vice-Minister Urban Construction 1957–58, of Building 1958–59, of Petroleum 1959; Vice-Chair. State Capital Construction Comm., State Council 1965; Minister of Chemical Industry 1978–82; mem. NPC Standing Cttee. 1983–, Credentials Cttee. 1983–, Financial and Econ. Cttee. 1986; Deputy Head China-European Parl. Friendship Group 1985–; Vice-Chair. Nat. Petro-Chemical Corpn. 1983–. *Address:* China National Petro-Chemical Corporation, 2-5 Hepinglu, Beijing, People's Republic of China. *Telephone:* 464785, 446531.

SUN QI; Chinese party and government official; Vice-Gov. Liaoning Prov. 1983–84; mem. Standing Cttee. and Deputy Sec. Liaoning Prov. CCP Cttee. 1985–86; alt. mem. CCP Cen. Cttee. 1987–. *Address:* Central Committee of the Chinese Communist Party, Zhongnanhai, Beijing, People's Republic of China.

SUN QIMENG; Chinese politician; b. 1908, Xiuning Co., Anhui Prov.; ed. Suzhou Univ.; Ed., Shenbao Daily, Shanghai 1932–33; Sec.-Gen., Assen. for Vocational Training, Shanghai 1934–37; Head Yunnan Br. of Assen. for Vocational Training, Kunming 1937–45; Ed.-in-Chief Wenhui Bao, Hong Kong 1948–49; Deputy Sec.-Gen. Govt. Admin. Council 1949–54; Deputy Sec.-Gen. 1st NPC 1954–59; mem., Standing Cttee., CPPCC 1974–79; Vice-Chair. Cen. Cttee., CPPCC of China Democratic Nat. Construction Assen. 1979–; Deputy Sec.-Gen., 6th CPPCC 1984–88; Vice-Chair. 7th NPC 1988–. *Address:* Standing Committee of National People's Congress, Beijing, People's Republic of China.

SUN WEIBEN; Chinese party official; alt. mem. 12th CCP Cen. Cttee. 1982, mem. 1985, mem. 13th Cen. Cttee. 1987–; Sec. CCP Cttee., Liaoning Prov. 1983–85, CCP Cttee., Heilongjiang Prov. 1985–; 1st Sec. Party Cttee., PLA Heilongjiang Provincial Command 1985. *Address:* Heilongjiang Provincial Chinese Communist Party, Heilongjiang, People's Republic of China.

SUN XIAOCUN; Chinese banking official; Vice-Chair. Nat. Resources Comm. 1930; mem. Govt. Admin. Cttee., Finance and Econ. Cttee. 1949–54; Man. China Vegetable Oil Co. 1949; mem. Nat. Cttee. of CPPCC 1949, Vice-Chair. 1988–; Dir. Beijing Agricultural Coll. 1951–60; in political disgrace 1967–72; Man. Dir. Bank of China 1979; Pres. Cen. Socialist Acad.

1983, mem. Presidium CPPCC 1983–, Standing Cttee., CPPCC Nat. Cttee. 1983–; Vice-Chair. China Democratic Nat. Construction Assen. 1979–87, Chair. Cen. Consultative Cttee. 1987–; Vice-Chair. Bd. of Dirs., China Industry, Commerce and Econ. Devt. Corpn. 1987–. *Address:* China Democratic National Construction Association, Beijing, People's Republic of China.

SUN YUN-SUAN, B.S.; Chinese politician and engineer; b. 11 Nov. 1913, Penglai, Shantung; m. Yu Hui-hsuan 1947; two s. two d.; ed. Harbin Polytechnic Inst.; engineer with Nat. Resource Comm. 1937–40; Supt. Tienshui Electric Power Plant 1940–43; Training Engineer Tenn. Valley Authority, U.S.A. 1943–45; Head Engineer, Electrical and Mechanical Dept., Taiwan Power Co. 1946–50, Chief Engineer 1950–62, Vice-Pres. 1953–62, Pres. 1962–64; C.E.O. and Gen. Man. Electricity Corpn. of Nigeria 1964–67; Minister of Communications 1967–69, of Econ. Affairs 1969–78; Premier of Taiwan 1978–84; Sr. Adviser to the Pres. 1984–; Fellow Int. Acad. of Man. 1983; Cravat of the Order of Brilliant Star 1952; Eng. Award of the Chinese Inst. of Engineers 1954. *Leisure interests:* reading, classical music, sports. *Address:* 10, Lane 6, Chungking S. Road, Sec. 2, Taipei 100, Taiwan. *Telephone:* (02) 3915231.

SUNDBY, (Carl) Olof (Werner), B.A., D.D.; Swedish ecclesiastic (retd.); b. 6 Dec. 1917, Karlskoga; s. of Josef Sundby and Gerda Gustafson; m. Birgitta Nordfors 1944; one s. three d.; ed. Univ. of Lund; ordained 1943; Parish Curate; Mil. Chaplain; Prison Chaplain; Diocesan Youth Pastor, Karlstad 1944; Sr. Lecturer on Theological Ethics, Univ. of Lund 1959; Rector of St. Peter, Lund 1960; Bishop of Växjö 1970; Archbishop of Uppsala 1972–83 (retd.); Pres. Swedish Ecumenical Council; mem. Cen. Cttee., mem. Exec. Cttee., World Council of Churches; mem. Presidium 1975–83; Chair. Swedish Cttee. for the Life-and-Peace Inst., Uppsala 1984–; Chair. of Bd. Kyrkans Tidning 1982–88. *Publications:* Lutheran Conception of Marriage 1959, Pastoral Letter to the Diocese of Växjö 1970. *Leisure interests:* tennis, skiing. *Address:* Gilleskroken 8, S-222 47, Lund, Sweden. *Telephone:* (0) 46-136505.

SUNDERLAND, Sir Sydney, Kt., C.M.G., D.SC., M.D., B.S., F.R.A.C.P., F.R.A.C.S., F.A.A.; Australian anatomist; b. 31 Dec. 1910, Brisbane; m. Nina Johnston 1939; one s.; ed. Melbourne Univ.; Sr. Lecturer in Anatomy, Melbourne Univ. 1936–37; Asst. Neurologist Alfred Hospital Melbourne 1936–37; Demonstrator Dept. of Human Anatomy, Oxford 1938–39; Prof. of Anatomy and Histology, Melbourne Univ. 1939–61, of Experimental Neurology 1961–75, Dean Medical Faculty 1953–71, Prof. Emer. 1976–; Visiting Specialist, injuries of the peripheral nervous system, Australian Gen. Mil. Hosp. 1941–45; Visiting Prof. of Anatomy, Johns Hopkins Univ. 1953–54; mem. Nat. Health and Medical Research Council of Australia 1953–69; Foundation Fellow and Sec. for Biological Sciences, Australian Acad. of Sciences 1955–58; Trustee, Nat. Museum of Vic. 1954–82, Van Cleef Foundation 1971; mem. Zool. Bd. of Vic. 1944–65; Deputy Chair. Advisory Cttee. of Victorian Mental Hygiene Authority 1952–63; rep. Pacific Science Council 1957–69; mem. Defence Research and Devt. Policy Cttee. 1957–75, Medical Services Cttee. 1957–78, Commonwealth Dept. of Defence; mem. Nat. Radiation Advisory Cttee. 1957–64, Chair. 1959–64; Chair. Safety Review Cttee. 1961–74, Australian Atomic Energy Comm.; Medical Research Advisory Cttee. of Nat. Health and Medical Research Council 1953–69, Chair. 1964–69; Chair. Protective Chemistry Research Advisory Cttee., Dept. of Supply 1964–73; Vice-Pres. Int. Assen. for Study of Pain 1975–78; mem. Scientific Advisory Cttee. Australian Atomic Energy Comm. 1962–63, Australian Univs. Comm. 1962–75, Cttee. of Man. Royal Melbourne Hosp. 1963–71, Victorian Medical Advisory Cttee. 1962–71, Advisory Medical Council of Australia 1970–71; Foreign mem. Soc. Française de Neurologie; Hon. mem. American Neurological Assen., Australian Assen. of Neurologists, Neuro-Surgical Soc. of Australasia, American Soc. for Surgery of the Hand; Fogarty Scholar-in-Residence, Nat. Insts. of Health, Bethesda, U.S.A. 1972, Sterling Bunnell Lecturer and Visiting Prof. of Orthopedic Surgery, Univ. of Calif. 1977; Gov. Ian Potter Foundation 1964–; mem. Bd., Walter and Eliza Hall Inst. 1968–75; Hon. M.D. (Tasmania) 1970, (Queensland) 1975; Hon. LL.D. (Melbourne) 1975, (Monash) 1977. *Publication:* Nerves and Nerve Injuries 1968, 1978. *Leisure interest:* tennis. *Address:* Department of Experimental Neurology, University of Melbourne, Parkville 3052, Victoria (Office); 72 Kingstoun, 461 St. Kilda Road, Melbourne, Vic. 3004, Australia (Home). *Telephone:* 203431 (Office); 266 5858 (Home).

SUNDERLAND, Thomas Elbert, A.B., LL.B., J.D.; American lawyer and business executive; b. 28 April 1907, Ann Arbor, Mich.; s. of Prof. Edson R. and Hannah Dell Read Sunderland; m. Mary Louise Allyn 1946; three d.; ed. Sorbonne, Univs. of Michigan, California and Harvard; legal practice, Detroit 1930–31, New York 1931–48, Chicago 1948–59, Phoenix and Scottsdale (Ariz.) 1969–; Lieut.-Col. U.S.A.F. 1942–46; Gen. Counsel Pan American Petroleum and Transport Co., American Oil Co. 1940–48; Dir., mem. Exec. Cttee. Pan American Petroleum and Transport Co. 1947–54; Gen. Counsel, Dir. Standard Oil Co. (Ind.) 1948–60; Vice-Pres., mem. Exec. Cttee. 1954–60; Pres. and Dir. United Fruit Co. 1960–65, Chair. of Bd. and Dir. 1965–69; Dir. Nat. Cash Register Co., Johns-Manville Corpn., Liberty Mutual Insurance Co., First Nat. Bank of Boston; Trustee Laurence Hall of Science, Univ. of Calif. at Berkeley, Phoenix Symphony Orch. (Pres. 1979–81); Univ. of Mich. Nat. Business Leadership Award 1966, Univ. of

Mich. Outstanding Achievement Award 1970. *Address:* Suite A-201, 6991 East Camelback Road, Scottsdale, Ariz. 85251-2466 (Office); 5840 East Starlight Way, Paradise Valley, Scottsdale, Ariz. 85253 (Home: winter); 66 Fernwood Road, Brookline, Mass. 02167, U.S.A. (Home: summer). *Telephone:* (602) 941-5440 (Office).

SUNDQVIST, Ulf Lundvig, M.POL.SC.; Finnish politician; b. 22 Feb. 1945, Sipoo; s. of Karl Eric Sundqvist and Helga Linnea Lönnkvist; m. Eine Kristiina Joki 1969; one s. one d.; ed. Univ. of Helsinki; mem. Exec. Bd., Nat. Union of Finnish Students 1966-67, Chair. 1968; mem. Party Council, Finnish Social Democratic Party 1969-75, Party Sec. 1975; mem. Municipal Council of Sipoo 1969-76, Vice-Chair. 1976-; mem. Finnish Parl. 1970-; Minister of Educ. 1972-75, of Trade and Industry 1979-81; Pres. Finnish UNA 1968-70; mem. Bd. of Supervisors, Neste Ltd. (state-owned oil-refining Co.) 1970-, Chair. 1976-. *Leisure interests:* music, literature. *Address:* c/o Suomen Sosialidemokraattinen Puolue, Saariniemenkatu 6, 00530 Helsinki, Finland.

SUNTRANGKOON, Gen. Prachuab; Thai army officer and politician; b. 4 April 1920, Sukhothai; m. Khunying Pimpa; one s. one d.; ed. Mil. Acad. (now Chulachomklao Royal Mil. Acad.), Bangkok Metropolis and Cavalry School, Royal Thai Army, Ground Gen. School, Fort Riley and Armour School, Fort Knox, U.S.A., Nat. Defence Coll.; rank of Col. 1957; Dir. Port Authority of Thailand 1959-72; Maj.-Gen., Chief Cavalry Div. 1962-69; Lieut.-Gen., Army Adviser 1969-72; Deputy Dir.-Gen. Police Dept., with rank of Police Lieut.-Gen. 1972, Dir.-Gen., then Police Gen.; Deputy Minister of Communications 1973-74; Deputy Minister of Interior 1974-75; attached to Office of Supreme Commdr. of Armed Forces, with rank of Army Gen.; Deputy Prime Minister 1981-86; Minister of Interior 1986-88. *Address:* c/o Ministry of the Interior, Atasadang Road, Bangkok 10200, Thailand.

SUNUNU, John H., PH.D.; American politician; b. 2 July 1939, Havana, Cuba; m. Nancy Hayes 1958; five s. three d.; founder, Chief Engineer Astro Dynamics 1960-65; Pres. J.H.S. Eng. Co. and Thermal Research Inc., Salem, N.H. 1965-82; Assoc. Prof. Mechanical Eng., Tufts Univ. 1966-82, Assoc. Dean Coll. of Eng. 1968-73; mem. N.H. House of Reps. 1973-74, Govt. Energy Council; Chair. Govt. Council on N.H. Future 1977-78; mem. Govt. Advisory Cttee. on Science and Tech. 1977-78; Gov. State of N.H. Concord 1983-; Chair. coalition of N.E. Govs. 1985-86; White House Chief of Staff Jan. 1989-; Chair. Task force on Tech.; Vice-Chair. Alliance for Acid Rain Control; Chair. Republican Gov.'s Asscn., New England Gov.'s Asscn.; Vice-Chair. Advisory Comm. on Intergovt. Relations. *Address:* The White House, 1600 Pennsylvania Avenue, Washington, D.C. 20500, U.S.A.

SUOMINEN, Ilkka Olavi, M.POL.SC.; Finnish politician; b. 8 April 1939, Nakkila; s. of Leo Suominen and Anna Suominen; m. Riitta Suhonen 1977; one s. two d.; Dept. Head, J. W. Suominen Oy 1960-72, Deputy Man. Dir. 1972-74, Man. Dir. 1975-79, mem. Man. Bd. 1980-; Chair. Admin. Bd. Oy Alko Ab 1980-88; Dir. of Finnish Industries 1978-79; Chair. Admin. Bd. Oy Alko Ab 1980-88; Dir. 1989-; mem. Parl. 1970-75, 1983-; Speaker of Parl. 1987; Minister of Trade and Industry 1987-; Leader Nat. Coalition Party 1979-. *Leisure interests:* hunting, fishing. *Address:* Ministry of Trade and Industry, Aleksanterin-katu 10, 10070 Helsinki, Finland. *Telephone:* (90) 1601.

SUONIO, Kaarina Elisabet; Finnish psychologist, lawyer and politician; b. 7 Feb. 1941, Helsinki; d. of Prof. Karl Otto Brusiin and Ulla Helena Raassina; m. 1st Reino Kalevi 1961; m. 2nd Kyösti Kullervi Suonio 1967; one s. one d.; psychologist, Inst. of Occupational Health 1963-71; Researcher, Ministry of Justice 1971-75; mem. Helsinki City Council 1973-; M.P. 1975-86; Alt. mem. SDP Exec. 1981-84; Second Minister of Educ. (Minister of Culture and Science) 1982-83, Minister of Educ. 1983-86; Deputy Mayor of Tampere 1986-. *Address:* c/o City of Tampere, PL 87, 33211 Tampere, Finland.

SUORTTANEN, Sulo, BARR.-AT-LAW; Finnish politician; b. 13 Feb. 1921, Valkeala; s. of Elias Suorttanen and Amánda Askola; m. Lea Annikki Laakso 1949; one s.; Asst. Police-Insp., Kymi Admin. District 1958-62; M.P. 1962-70, 1972-; held numerous high positions in local govt. and in co-operative orgs.; Minister of Defence 1966-70. *Leisure interests:* horse racing, motoring.

SUPPES, Patrick, B.S., PH.D.; American educationist; b. 17 March 1922, Tulsa, Okla.; m. 1st Joan Farmer 1946 (divorced 1970), one s. two d.; m. 2nd Joan Elizabeth Sieber 1970 (divorced 1973); m. 3rd Christine Johnson 1979, one d.; ed. Univ. of Chicago and Columbia Univ.; mem. faculty Stanford Univ. 1950-, Prof. of Phil., Statistics Educ. and Psychology, Dir. Inst. for Mathematical Studies in the Social Sciences 1959-; Pres. Computer Curriculum Corpn. 1967-; Fellow A.A.A.S., American Psychological Asscn.; mem. Nat. Acad. of Educ. 1965- (Pres. 1973-77), American Acad. of Arts and Sciences 1968-, Finnish Acad. of Science and Letters 1974-, N.A.S. 1978-; Dr. h.c. (Social Sciences) (Nijmegen) 1979; Palmer O. Johnson Memorial Award, American Educational Research Asscn. 1967; Distinguished Scientific Contribution Award, American Psychological Asscn. 1972; Columbia Univ. Teachers College Medal for Distinguished Service 1978, E. L. Thorndike Award for Distinguished Psychological Contribution to Educ., American Psychological Asscn. 1979; Dr. h.c., Acad. de Paris,

Univ. René Descartes 1982. *Publications:* Introduction to Logic 1957, Decision Making: An Experimental Approach (with D. Davidson and S. Siegel) 1957, Axiomatic Set Theory 1960, Markov Learning Models for Multiperson Interactions (with R. C. Atkinson) 1960, First Course in Mathematical Logic 1964, Experiments in Second-Language Acquisition (with E. Crothers) 1967, Computer Assisted Instruction: Stanford's 1965-66 Arithmetic Program (with M. Jerman and D. Brian) 1968, Studies in the Methodology and Foundations of Science 1970, A Probabilistic Theory of Causality 1970, Foundations of Measurement (with D. Krantz, R. D. Luce, A. Tversky) Vol. I 1971, Computer-assisted Instruction at Stanford, 1966-68 (with M. Morningstar); Probabilistic Metaphysics 1974, The Radio Mathematics Project: Nicaragua 1974-1975 (with B. Searle and J. Friend) 1976, Logique du Probable 1981, and over 200 articles in professional journals. *Address:* 678 Mirada Avenue, Stanford, Calif. 94305, U.S.A.

SUPPLE, Barry Emanuel, PH.D., F.R.HIST.S., F.B.A.; British professor of economic history; b. 27 Oct. 1930; s. of Solomon Supple and Rose Supple; m. Sonia (née Caller) Supple; two s. one d.; ed. Hackney Downs Grammar School, L.S.E. and Christ's Coll. Cambridge; Asst. Prof. of Business History, Grad. School of Business Admin., Harvard Univ., U.S.A. 1955-60; Assoc. Prof. of Econ. History, McGill Univ. 1960-62; Lecturer in Econ. and Social History, Univ. of Sussex, Reader, then Prof. 1962-78, Dean, School of Social Sciences 1965-68, Pro-Vice-Chancellor (Arts and Social Studies) 1968-72, Pro-Vice-Chancellor 1978; Reader in Recent Social and Econ. History, Univ. of Oxford 1978-81, Professorial Fellow, Nuffield Coll. 1978-81; Prof. of Econ. History Univ. of Cambridge 1981-, Professorial Fellow, Christ's Coll. 1981-83, Hon. Fellow 1984; Master of St. Catharine's Coll., Cambridge 1984-; mem. Social Science Fellowship Cttee., Nuffield Foundation 1974-; Hon. Fellow Worcester Coll., Oxford 1986; Co-Ed. Econ. History Review 1973-82. *Publications:* Commercial Crisis and Change in England, 1600-42, 1959, The Experience of Economic Growth (Ed.) 1963, Boston Capitalists and Western Railroads 1967, The Royal Exchange Assurance: a history of British insurance 1720-1970, 1970, Essays in Business History (Ed.) 1977, History of the British Coal Industry, Vol. IV (1914-46), The Political Economy of Decline 1987, articles and reviews in learned journals. *Leisure interests:* tennis, photography. *Address:* The Master's Lodge, St. Catharine's College, Cambridge, England. *Telephone:* (0223) 359445.

SUQUÍA GOICOECHEA, H.E. Cardinal Angel; Spanish ecclesiastic; b. 2 Oct. 1916, Zaldivia, San Sebastián; ordained 1940; consecrated Bishop of Almeria 1966, of Málaga 1969; Archbishop of Santiago de Compostela 1973, of Madrid 1983; cr. Cardinal 1985; mem. Congregation for Catholic Educ., Congregation for the Bishops, and several others. *Address:* Arzobispado, Bailén 8, 28013 Madrid, Spain. *Telephone:* (91) 24.14.804.

SUREAU, Claude, M.D.; French obstetrician and gynaecologist; b. 27 Sept. 1927, Paris; s. of Maurice Sureau and Rita Jullian; m. Janine Murset 1956; three c.; ed. Paris Univ.; Visiting Fellow, Columbia Presbyterian Medical Center 1955-56; Asst. Prof., Paris Univ. 1956-61, Assoc. Prof. 1961-74; Prof. and Chair., Dept. of Obstetrics and Gynaecology, St. Vincent de Paul Hosp., Paris 1974-76; Pres., Int. Fed. of Obstetricians and Gynaecologists 1982-85, Pres., Standing Cttee. on Ethical Aspects of Human Reproduction 1985-; Prof. and Chair., Dept. of Obstetrics and Gynaecology, Univ. Clinique Baudelocque 1976-; Dir. Unit 262, Physiology and Physiopathology of Reproduction, Nat. Inst. of Health and Medical Research 1983-; mem. Nat. Acad. of Medicine of France 1978-; Chevalier, Légion d'Honneur 1977. *Publications:* Le Danger de Naitre 1978; Co-Ed.: Clinical Perinatology 1980, Immunologie de la Réproduction Humaine 1983. *Address:* Clinique Universitaire Baudelocque, 123 Boulevard de Port Royal, 75674 Paris, Cedex 14, France. *Telephone:* (16-1) 42 34 11 38.

SÜREN, Choynoryn; Mongolian politician; b. 1932; ed. Teacher Training School, Higher School of Eng. and Econs., U.S.S.R.; teacher in various provinces 1949-52; technician in State Construction Directorate 1955-56; expert of State Construction Cttee., Deputy Chair. State Construction Comm. 1959-61; Deputy Minister of Construction and Construction Materials Industry 1961-64; lecturer at Mongolian State Univ., Dir. of Dept. at Construction Research Inst. 1964-67; Deputy Chair. and later Chair. Exec. Cttee. of Darhan City People's Deputies' Hural (Assembly) 1967-72; Counsellor, Embassy in Moscow 1972-74; Deputy Chair. Council of Ministers 1974-; Minister of Light Industry 1987-, of Food Industry 1987-88; Chair. State Cttee. for Construction, Architecture and Tech. Control 1982-84; mem. Mongolian People's Revolutionary Party (MPRP) Cen. Cttee. 1976-; Deputy to People's Great Hural (Assembly) 1977-. *Address:* c/o Government Palace, Ulan Bator, Mongolia.

SURJANINGRAT, Suwardjono, M.D.; Indonesian politician (retd.); b. 3 May 1923, Purwodadi, Cen. Java; ed. Faculty of Medicine, Univ. of Indonesia and Columbia and Harvard Univs. Obstetric and Gynaecological Clinics; army medical officer 1945-76; Maj.-Gen. 1976; Minister of Health 1978-88. *Address:* c/o Ministry of Health, Jln. Prapatan 10, Jakarta Pusat, Indonesia.

SURLYK, Finn C., PH.D.; Danish professor of geology; b. 17 March 1943, Copenhagen; s. of C. Surlyk and K. Surlyk; m. Nanna Noe-Nygaard; two c.; Adjunct Prof. Univ. of Copenhagen 1968-69, Assoc. Prof. 1969-80, Research Prof. 1984-; Head Dept. of Oil Geology, Geological Survey of

Greenland, Copenhagen 1981–84; Gold Medal, Univ. of Copenhagen 1969. *Publications:* over 90 papers on the geology of Greenland. *Leisure interests:* jazz, bass-playing, outdoor life. *Address:* Islandsvej 11, 2800 Lyngby, Denmark. *Telephone:* (02) 877209.

SUROWIEC, Zygmunt, M.A.; Polish politician; b. 3 Dec. 1920, Podlesice, Częstochowa Voivodship; ed. Wrocław Univ.; during Nazi occupation co-organizer Peasant Bns. (BCh), Olkusz Dist. platoon commdr. of BCh Partisans Detachment, Włoszczowa Dist. 1942–45; mem. Peasant Party (SL) 1940–49; after liberation, organizer SL in Włoszczowa Dist.; worked at Voivodship Information and Propaganda Office, Koszalin 1945; Deputy Head, Szczecin Office 1946–47; Deputy Pres. SL Voivodship Board, Koszalin 1945, Sec. SL Voivodship Board, Szczecin 1946; mem. SL Chief Council 1946–49; Sec. Voivodship Bd. of Wici Rural Youth Union, Szczecin 1947; Sec. SL Voivodship Bd., Wrocław 1948; mem. United Peasant Party (ZSL) 1949–; Sec. ZSL Voivodship Exec. Cttee., Wrocław 1949–51; worked at Bldg. of Workers' Housing Estates Head Office, Wrocław 1951–56; Deputy Chair. Presidium of Voivodship Nat. Council and Deputy Pres. ZSL Voivodship Cttee., Wrocław 1956–69; alt. mem. ZSL Chief Cttee. 1964–88, Head, Propaganda Dept. 1969, Sec. 1969–72, mem. Secr. 1972–81; Deputy to Seym 1969–, Chair. Parl. Comm. of Internal Affairs and Jurisdiction 1980–85; Deputy Chair. ZSL Deputies' Club 1983–85; Pres. Bd. of LSW Publishing Co-operative 1972–76; Sec. All-Poland Cttee. of Nat. Unity Front 1976–83; Vice-Pres. Gen. Bd. of Country's Defence League; mem. Chief Council and Gen. Bd. of Union of Fighters for Freedom and Democracy; Sec. Council of State Nov. 1985–; Commdr.'s Cross of Order of Polonia Restituta, Order of Banner of Labour (1st and 2nd Classes); Cross of Valour, Partisan Cross and other decorations. *Address:* Kancelaria Rady Państwa, ul. Wiejska 2/6, 00-902 Warsaw, Poland.

SURTEES, John, M.B.E.; British racing motorcyclist and driver; b. 11 Feb. 1934, Tatsfield, Surrey; s. of Jack Surtees; m. Jane Sparrow 1987; one d.; ed. Ashburton Secondary School, London; began motorcycle road racing 1949, 350 c.c. World Champion 1958, 1959 and 1960, 500 c.c. World Champion 1956, 1958, 1959 and 1960; began car racing 1960, World Champion 1964, runner-up 1966, CanAm Champion 1966. *Grand Prix wins:* 1963 German (Ferrari), 1964 German (Ferrari), 1964 Italian (Ferrari), 1966 Belgian (Ferrari), 1966 Mexican (Cooper-Maserati), 1967 Italian (Honda); retd. 1972. *Leisure interests:* restoration of period property, Grand Prix motor cycles and cars, antiques, food and wine. *Address:* Team Surtees Ltd., Station Road, Edenbridge, Kent, TN8 6HL, England. *Telephone:* (0732) 863773.

SUSLOV, Vladimir Pavlovich; Soviet diplomatist; b. 1923, Moscow; mem. of Diplomatic Service 1948–; Adviser to UN Soviet Del. 1957–61; mem. of staff of Ministry of Foreign Affairs 1961–63; Deputy Sec.-Gen. for Political Questions and World Security Council Affairs 1963–65; Sr. posts at Ministry of Foreign Affairs 1965–73; Head of Second European Dept. of U.S.S.R. Ministry of Foreign Affairs 1973–. *Address:* The Kremlin, Moscow, U.S.S.R.

SÜSSENGUTH, Hans, DIPL.ING.; German aviation executive; b. 8 Sept. 1913, Neustadt/Coburg; s. of Franz H. and Rosalie Süssenguth; m. Christa Reischel 1942; one s. one d.; ed. Oberrealschule, Coburg and Tech. Hochschule, Darmstadt; Technician in Research and Devt. and Maintenance and Operations Depts. Deutsche Lufthansa A.G., Berlin 1939–45; Engineer in father-in-law's business 1945–50; Engineer at Gummi-Werke Fulda 1950–52; rejoined Lufthansa in Eng. Div., Hamburg 1952, Tech. Dir. 1954, Head of Traffic Division 1958, Deputy mem. Exec. Bd. 1959, mem. 1963–, responsible for sales, worldwide field org., in-flight services and marketing, retd. June 1978, mem. Bd. Deutsche Lufthansa AG June 1978–; Chair. Advisory Bd., Berlin Penta Hotelgesellschaft, DSG-Deutsche Schlafwagen- und Speisewagen GmbH Frankfurt, AMK-Ausstellungs-Messe-Kongress GmbH, Berlin; mem. Exec. Bd. and Vice-Pres., German Tourist Bd.; mem. Advisory Bd., Hansa Luftbild GmbH, Münster, Deutscher Aerokurier, Cologne; mem. Bd. of Trustees, Hessian Inst. for Aviation; mem. Chartered Inst. of Air Transport, London; Dir. START-Datentechnik für Reise und Touristik GmbH, Frankfurt; Hon. Consul Repub. of Togo; Hon. Prof. Technische Univ., Berlin; Grosses Bundesverdienstkreuz 1978. *Address:* 6420 Kronberg/Taunus, Taunusstrasse 2, Federal Republic of Germany (Home). *Telephone:* (06173) 79538 (Home).

SUTCLIFFE, Reginald Cockcroft, C.B., O.B.E., F.R.S., B.SC., PH.D.; British meteorologist; b. 1904, Wrexham, North Wales; s. of late O. G. Sutcliffe and late Jessie Sutcliffe (née Cockcroft); m. Evelyn Williams 1929; two d.; ed. Whitcliffe Mount Grammar School, Cleckheaton, Leeds Univ. and Univ. Coll., Bangor; Professional Asst., Meteorological Office 1927, Met. Office appts. in Malta 1928–32, Felixstowe 1932–35, Air Ministry 1935–37, Thorney Island 1937–39; Sqdn.-Ldr. R.A.F.V.R., France 1939–40; Sr. Met. Officer No. 3 Bomber Group, R.A.F. 1941–44; Group Capt.; Chief Met. Officer Allied Expeditionary Air Force (later British Air Forces of Occupation), Germany 1944–46; Research, Met. Office 1946–, Dir. of Research 1957–65; Prof. of Meteorology Reading Univ. 1965–70, Prof. Emer. 1970–; Hon. mem. American Meteorological Soc. 1975; Hon. F.R.Met.Soc. 1976; Symons Gold Medal 1955, Buchan Prize 1950, Charles Chree Medal of Physical Soc. 1959, Int. Met. Org. Prize 1963. *Publications:* Meteorology for Aviators 1938, Weather and Climate 1966, meteorological papers in

journals. *Leisure interests:* swimming, gardening. *Address:* Pound Farm, Cadmore End, High Wycombe, Bucks., HP14 3PF, England. *Telephone:* (0494) 883007.

SUTER, Albert Edward, B.M.E., M.B.A.; American business executive; b. 18 Sept. 1935, New Jersey; s. of Joseph V. Suter and Catherine Clay; m. Michaela S. Suter 1966; two s. one d.; ed. Cornell Univ.; Knight & Assocs., Chicago 1959–79, fmr. Pres. and C.E.O.; Vice-Chair. Emerson Electric Co., St. Louis, Mo. 1979–87; Pres. and C.O.O. Firestone Tire & Rubber Co., Akron, Ohio 1987–; Pres. and C.O.O. Whirlpool Co. Aug. 1988–. *Address:* Whirlpool Co., Benton Harbour, Michigan 49022, Chicago, Ill. 60601-5965, U.S.A. *Telephone:* (312) 819-8580.

SUTERMEISTER, Heinrich; Swiss composer; b. 12 Aug. 1910, Feuerthalen; m. Verena-Maria Renker 1948; one d.; studied philology at Paris and Munich, and music at the Acad. of Music at Munich; Prof. Hochschule für Musik, Hanover 1963–; Pres. Schweizerische Mechanlizenz; mem. Bayerische Akad. der Schönen Künste 1977; Salzburg Opera Prize 1965, Asscn. of Swiss Composers' Prize 1967. *Operas include:* L'araignée noire, Romeo and Juliet, The Tempest, Niobe, Raskolnikoff (Stockholm and Scala, Milan), Botte Rouge, Titus Feuerfuchs (opera burlesque) (Basel and Brussels) 1958, Seraphine, The Canterville Ghost (for television), Madame Bovary (Zürich), König Bereuger I 1985; *other works:* Missa da Requiem 1953, three piano concertos 1954, two cello concertos 1953, 1971, 1 concerto for clarinet and orchestra 1974, La Croisade des Enfants 1969 (for television), The Bottle Imp (for television), two divertimenti, eight cantatas, Te Deum 1975, Quadrifoglio (Concerto for four wind instruments and orchestra) 1977, Consolatio Philosophiae (Cantata for high voice and orchestra), 6 Lettres d'amour (for soprano and orchestra) 1979. *Leisure interest:* dog breeding (Belgian shepherd dogs). *Address:* Vaux-sur-Morges, Switzerland. *Telephone:* 021-801 1126.

SUTHERLAND, Donald McNichol, O.C.; Canadian actor; b. 17 July 1935, St. John, N.B.; s. of Frederick McLae and Dorothy Isabel (McNichol) Sutherland; m. 1st Lois May Hardwick 1959, 2nd Shirley Jean Douglas 1966 (divorced), 3rd Francine Racette 1971; four s. one d.; ed. Bridgewater, N.S., High School, Univ. of Toronto; TV Hallmark Hall of Fame; appeared on television (BBC and ITV) in Hamlet, Man in the Suitcase, The Saint, Gideon's Way, The Avengers, Flight into Danger, Rose Tattoo, March to the Sea, Lee Harvey Oswald, Court Martial, Death of Bessie Smith, Max Dugan Returns, Crackers, Louis Malle, The Disappearance. *Films include:* The World Ten Times Over 1963, Castle of the Living Dead 1964, Dr. Terror's House of Horrors 1965, Fanatic 1965, The Bedford Incident 1965, Promise Her Anything 1966, The Dirty Dozen 1967, Billion Dollar Brain 1967, Oedipus Rex 1968, Interlude 1968, Joanna 1968, The Split 1968, Start the Revolution Without Me 1969, Act of the Heart 1970, M*A*S*H* 1970, Kelly's Heroes 1970, Little Murders 1970, Alex in Wonderland 1971, Klute 1971, Johnny Got His Gun (as Christ) 1971, Steelyard Blues 1972, Lady Ice 1972, Alien Thunder 1973, Don't Look Now 1973, S*P*Y*S* 1974, The Day of the Locust 1975, 1900 1976, Casanova (Fellini) 1976, The Eagle Has Landed 1977, The Great Train Robbery 1978, Blood Relatives 1978, Bear Island 1979, Ordinary People 1980, Lolita 1981, Eye of the Needle 1981, Threshold 1982, Winter of Our Discontent, Ordeal by Innocence 1984, Revolution 1985, Gauguin 1986, The Wolf at the Door 1987, A Dry White Season 1988, Bethune: The Making of a Hero 1989. *Play:* Lolita (Broadway) 1981; Pres. McNichol Pictures Inc.; Hon. Ph.D. *Leisure interests:* sailing, baseball, Montreal. *Address:* c/o Creative Artists Agency Inc., 1888 Century Park East, (Suite 1400), Los Angeles, Calif.; 760 N. La Cienega Boulevard, Los Angeles, Calif. 90069, U.S.A. *Telephone:* (213) 306-1633.

SUTHERLAND, Dame Joan, A.C., D.B.E.; Australian opera singer; b. 7 Nov. 1926, Sydney; d. of William McDonald Sutherland and Muriel Beatrice (née Alston); m. Richard Bonynge (q.v.) 1954; one s.; ed. St. Catherine's School, Waverley, Sydney; début as Dido in Purcell's Dido and Aeneas, Sydney 1947; Royal Opera Co., Covent Garden, London 1952–. *Has sung leading soprano roles at:* the Vienna State Opera, La Scala, Milan, Teatro Fenice, Venice, the Paris Opera, Glyndebourne, San Francisco and Chicago Operas, The Metropolitan, New York, the Australian Opera, Hamburg, the Canadian Opera, etc.; leading roles in Lucia di Lammermoor, La Traviata, Adriana Lecouvreur, Les Contes D'Hoffmann, Lucrezia Borgia, Semiramide, Don Giovanni, Faust, Die Zauberflote, Dido and Aeneas, etc.; Hon. life mem. Australia Opera Co. 1974; Hon. D.Mus. (Sydney) 1984; F.R.C.M. 1981. *Publication:* The Joan Sutherland Album (autobiography, with Richard Bonynge) 1986. *Leisure interests:* reading, needlepoint. *Address:* c/o Ingpen and Williams, 14 Kensington Court, London, W.8, England.

SUTHERLAND, James, C.B.E., M.A.; British lawyer; b. 15 Feb. 1920, Glasgow; s. of James Sutherland and Agnes Walker; m. 1st Elizabeth Kelly Barr 1948, 2nd Grace Williamson Dawson 1984; two s.; ed. Queens Park Secondary School, Glasgow and Glasgow Univ.; war service in Royal Signals 1940–46; partner McClure Naismith Anderson & Gardiner 1951–88, Consultant 1988–; examiner, Glasgow Univ. 1951–55, 1968–69; Dean Royal Faculty of Procurators in Glasgow 1977–80; mem. Bd. of Man., Glasgow Maternity and Women's Hosps. 1964–74, Chair. 1966–74; mem. Council Law Soc. of Scotland 1959–77, Vice-Pres. 1969–70, Pres. 1972–74; mem. Council Int. Bar Asscn. 1972–88, Hon. mem. 1988–; mem. Gen. Dental

Council 1975-, Court Univ. of Strathclyde 1977-, Scottish Dental Estimates Bd. 1982-87. *Leisure interest:* golf. *Address:* Greenacres, Easter Belmont Road, Edinburgh, EH12 6EX, Scotland. *Telephone:* 031-337 1888.

SUTHERLAND, Peter D., S.C., B.C.L.; Irish lawyer and politician; b. 25 April 1946; s. of W. G. Sutherland and Barbara Sutherland; m. Maruja Cabria 1971; two s. one d.; ed. Gonzaga Coll., Univ. Coll., Dublin and King's Inns; called to Irish Bar (King's Inns), English Bar (Middle Temple) and New York Bar; admitted to Bar of the Supreme Court of the United States; practising mem. of Irish Bar 1968-81; Tutor in Law, Univ. Coll., Dublin 1968-71; apptd. Sr. Counsel 1980; Attorney-Gen. June 1981-Aug. 1982, 1982-85; mem. Strategy Cttee. Fine Gael Party 1978-81, Dir. Policy Programme, 1981 General Election; mem. Comm. of the European Communities (responsible for Competition and Relations with the European Parliament) 1986-89; Dir. (non-exec.) Allied Irish Banks Feb. 1989-, Chair. April 1989-; Bencher of the Hon. Soc. of the King's Inns; mem. Bar Council of Ireland; Hon. LL.D. (St. Louis). *Publications:* numerous articles in law journals. *Leisure interests:* reading, sport. *Address:* Allied Irish Banks, 12 Old Jewry,, London, EC2R 8DP, England.

SÜTŐ, András; Hungarian writer (of Romanian nationality); b. 17 June 1927, Pusztakamarás, Transylvania; m. Éva Szabó 1949; two s.; ed. Bethlen Gábor Coll., Nagyenyed, and Reformed Coll., Kolozsvár (now Cluj, Romania); started as journalist with daily newspaper Világosság, Kolozsvár; contrib., later Ed.-in-Chief, Falvak Népe 1949-54; Deputy Chief Ed. literary monthly Igaz Szó, Marosvásárhely (Tirgu Mures) 1955-57; Chief Ed. pictorial Uj Élet, Marosvásárhely 1957-; Vice-Pres. Writers' Fed. of Socialist Repub. of Romania 1973-81; State Prize for Literature Romania 1953, 1954; Herder Prize, Vienna 1979. *Publications include:* Emberek indulnak (short stories) 1953, Félrejáró Salamon (short novel) 1956, Anyám könnyü álmot igér (novel) 1970, Rigó és apostol (essays, travelogue) 1973, Engedjétek hozzám jönni a szavakat (novel) 1977, Az Idő Markában (essays) 1984; A lóttlábu madár nyomában 1988; dramatic works: Tékozló szerelem (play) 1963, Pompás Gedeon (play) 1968, Egy lócsiszár virágvasárnapja 1978, Csillag a máglyán 1978, Cain and Abel 1978, A szuzai menyegző 1979, Advent a Hargitán 1985, Álomkommandó; books translated into Romanian, German, Russian, Bulgarian, Slovak and Ukrainian; plays performed in Budapest, Bucharest, Cluj, Novi-Sad, Zagreb, Bratislava and New York. *Address:* Tirgu Mures (Marosvásárhely), Str. Mărăşti Nr. 36, Romania. *Telephone:* 14-176.

SUTRISNO, Gen. Tri; Indonesian army officer; mil. engineer; Aide-de-Camp to Pres. 1974-78; Army Chief of Staff 1986-88; Commdr. of the Armed Forces Feb. 1988-. *Address:* Ministry of Defence, Jalan Merdeka Barat 13, Jakarta Pusat, Indonesia.

SUTTON, Leslie Ernest, M.A., D.PHIL., F.R.S.; British chemist; b. 22 June 1906, London; s. of Edgar W. Sutton and Margaret L. W. (Heard) Sutton; m. 1st Catharine V. Stock 1932 (died 1962), two s.; one d.; m. 2nd Rachel A. Long (née Batten) (died 1987) 1963, two s.; ed. Watford Grammar School, Lincoln Coll., Oxford, Leipzig Univ., and Calif. Inst. of Tech.; Fellow, Magdalen Coll., Oxford 1932-36, Fellow and Tutor 1936-73, Vice-Pres. 1947-48, Fellow Emer. 1973-; Univ. Lecturer, Oxford 1945-62, Reader in Physical Chem. 1962-73; Sec. Chemical Soc. 1951-57, Vice-Pres. 1957-60; Treas. Lawes Agric. Trust Cttee. 1978-82, Chair. 1982-; Visiting Prof. Heidelberg Univ. 1960, 1964, 1967; Baggesgaard Rasmussen Lecturer, Copenhagen 1974; Rockefeller Fellow 1933-34; Hon. D.Sc. (Salford Univ.) 1973; Meldola Medal (Royal Inst. of Chem.) 1932, Harrison Prize (Chem. Soc.) 1935, Tilden Lecturer (Chem. Soc.) 1940. *Publications:* books and papers in scientific and chemical journals. *Leisure interests:* music, photography. *Address:* 62 Osler Road, Headington, Oxford, OX3 9BN, England. *Telephone:* (0865) 66456.

SUTTON, Philip John, A.R.A., F.R.A.; British artist; b. 20 Oct. 1928, Poole, Dorset; s. of L. L. Sutton and Anne Sutton; m. Heather Cooke 1953; one s. three d.; ed. Slade School of Fine Art and Univ. Coll., London; Lecturer, Slade School of Fine Art, Univ. Coll. 1954-; one-man exhbns. bi-annually at Roland Browse & Delbanco and Browse & Darby 1956-84; Leeds City Art Gallery retrospective 1960; travelled in Australia and Fiji painting landscapes 1963-64; retrospective exhbn. Diploma Gallery, Royal Acad. 1977; toured Israel with ten British artists 1979; visited Australia 1980; exhibited six paintings of Great Barrier Reef at Royal Acad. 1983; exhbns. of drawings, watercolours and paintings in London, Bath and Litchfield 1985; exhbn. of 'Shell' tapestry at Royal Acad. 1985; exhbns. of ceramics, paintings, tapestries at Poole, I.O.W. 1986; ceramic wall, NMB Bank HQ, Amsterdam 1987; ceramic exhbn. Odette Gilbert Gallery, London 1987; painting exhbn., Paris 1988, Mowbray Gallery, London 1988. *Leisure interests:* swimming, running. *Address:* 10 Soudan Road, London, SW11 4HH, England. *Telephone:* 01-622 2647.

SUVIRANTA, Antti Johannes, LL.M., S.J.D.; Finnish judge; professor of law and legal administrator; b. 30 Nov. 1923, Helsinki; s. of Bruno and Aino (née Tarjanne) Suviranta; m. Dr. Annikki Elosuo 1953; three d.; ed. Helsinki Experimental High School, Univ. of Helsinki and Harvard Law School; clerk, Rector's office, Univ. of Helsinki 1949-55; dist. judge's clerk and deputy, dist. of Janakkala 1951; civil servant, Ministry of Finance 1956-59; teaching fellow, Faculty of Law, Univ. of Helsinki 1958-62, Acting Prof. of Labour Law 1962-67, Prof. of Labour Law (on leave of absence

1968, 1971-82) 1967-82; Auxiliary Justice, Supreme Admin. Court of Finland 1968; Pres. The Finnish Labour Court 1970-82; part-time lecturer on Fiscal Law, Univ. of Turku 1963-70; Chair. Finnish Labour Council 1973-79, Finnish Labour Law Soc. 1974-82, Finnish Lawyers' Assen. 1977-79; mem. Exec. Cttee., Int. Soc. for Labour and Social Security 1970-85; Pres. Supreme Admin. Court of Finland 1982-; mem. Int. Labour Org. Cttee. of Experts for Application of Conventions and Recommendations 1984-; Chair. Finnish Branch Int. Assen. of Legal Science 1986-; Pres. Int. Assen. of Supreme Admin. Jurisdictions 1986-89; mem. Finnish Acad. of Sciences; Hon. LL.D. (Univ. of Stockholm) 1984; Grand Cross Order of Finnish White Rose; Grand Cross, Order of Judiciary Merit of Labour (Brazil); Grand Cross, Royal Order of the North Star (Sweden). *Publications:* The notion of employment in tax law 1961, Joint taxation of spouses 1962, The role of the member states in the unification work of the ILO 1966, Direct taxation in Finland 1972, Labour Law and Industrial Relations in Finland 1987, also learned articles. *Leisure interest:* gardening. *Address:* Unioninkatu 16, SF-00130 Helsinki (Office); Teinintie 11B, SF-00640 Helsinki 64, Finland (Home). *Telephone:* 185 3200 (Office); 728 7884 (Home).

SUY, Erik, DR.IUR., DR.SC. POL.; Belgian international lawyer; b. 15 Aug. 1933, Ghent; m. Ute Stenzel 1962; one d.; ed. Univs. of Ghent, Geneva and Vienna; mem. UN Conf. on Diplomatic Intercourse 1961, on Law of Treaties 1968-69; Adviser to Ministry for Foreign Affairs 1967-73; mem. del. to UN Gen. Ass. 1969-72; Chair. Sixth Cttee. Gen. Ass. 1972; Under-Sec.-Gen. Legal Counsel, UN 1974-83; Dir.-Gen. UN Office, Geneva 1983-87; Prin. Pvt. Sec., Ministry of Foreign Affairs 1987-; Prof. Int. Law, Univ. of Leuven; mem. Int. Law Assen., American, Belgian, French and German Socs. of Int. Law; Mexican Acad. of Int. Law, Inst. of Int. Law, Perm. Court of Arbitration; Chevalier, Leopold Order, Officier, Crown Order, Officier, Order of Merit (Austria); Dr. h.c. (Montpelier). *Publications:* Les actes juridiques unilatéraux en droit international public 1962, The Concept of Jus Cogens in International Law 1967, and over 60 articles on int. and European law. *Address:* c/o Ministry of Foreign Affairs, 2 rue des Quatres Bras, 1000 Brussels; School of Law, 41 Tiense Straat, B-3000 Leuven, Belgium.

SUZMAN, Helen, B.COM., M.P.; South African politician; b. Germiston, Transvaal; m. Dr. M. M. Suzman 1937; two d.; ed. Parktown Convent, Univ. of Witwatersrand; Asst. statistician, War Supplies Bd. 1941-44; part-time lecturer, Dept. of Econs. and Econ. History, Univ. of Witwatersrand 1944-52; M.P. Houghton 1953-; (United Party) 1953-61, Progressive Party (now Progressive Fed. Party) 1961- (merged with Democratic Party 1989); mem. S. African Inst. of Race Relations; Hon. Fellow St. Hugh's Coll., Oxford 1973, L.S.E. 1975; Hon. D.C.L. (Oxford) 1973, Hon. LL.D. (Harvard and Witwatersrand Univs.) 1976, (Columbia Univ. and Smith Coll.) 1977, (Brandeis Univ.) 1981, (Cape Town) 1986; Hon. D.Hum. Litt. (Denison Univ., Ohio) 1982, (Sacred Heart Univ., U.S.A.) 1984, (New School for Social Research, New York) 1984, (Jewish Theological Seminary of New York) 1986; recipient Human Rights Award UN 1978; Medallion of Heroism (New York) 1980; American Liberties Medallion (American Jewish Cttee.) 1984; recipient Moses Mendelssohn Award, Berlin Senate 1988. *Leisure interests:* golf, bridge. *Address:* c/o The House of Assembly, Cape Town, Cape Province; 49 Melville Road, Hyde Park, Sandton, 2196 Transvaal, South Africa (Home).

SUZMAN, Janet, B.A.; actress; b. 9 Feb. 1939, Johannesburg, South Africa; d. of Saul Suzman and Betty Sonnenberg; m. Trevor Nunn (q.v.) 1969 (divorced 1986); one s.; ed. Kingsmead Coll., Univ. of the Witwatersrand, London Acad. of Music and Dramatic Art; moved to Britain 1960; Best Actress, Evening Standard Drama Award 1973, 1976, Plays and Players Award 1976; *roles for Royal Shakespeare Co. include:* Lady Anne, La Pucelle, Lady Percy, Luciana, Lulu in The Birthday Party 1963-64, Portia, Rosaline 1965, Carmen in The Balcony, She Stoops to Conquer 1966, Katharina, Celia and Berinthia in The Relapse 1967, Beatrice, Rosalind 1968-69, Cleopatra and Lavinia 1972-73, Hester in Hello and Goodbye (Kings Head) 1973, Masha in Three Sisters (Cambridge Theatre) 1976; Shen Te in The Good Woman of Setzuan (Tyneside Theatre Co.) 1976, at Royal Court Theatre 1977; Hedda Gabler (Duke of York's Theatre) 1977, Duchess of Malfi 1978, The Greeks (Aldwych) 1980, Cowardice (Ambassadors Theatre) 1983, Boesman and Lena (Hampstead) 1984, Vassa (Greenwich Theatre) 1985; dir. Othello, (Market Theatre, Johannesburg) 1987, Andromache (Old Vic) 1987; *films:* A Day in the Death of Joe Egg 1970, Nicholas and Alexandra 1971, Nijinsky 1978, Priest of Love 1981, The Draughtsman's Contract 1981, E la Nave Va 1982, A Dry White Season 1988; *television plays since 1966 include:* The Family Reunion 1967, Saint Joan 1968, The Three Sisters 1969, Macbeth 1970, Hedda Gabler 1972, Twelfth Night 1973, Antony and Cleopatra 1974, Miss Nightingale, Clayhanger (serial) 1975-76, Robin Hood (CBS TV) 1983, Mountbatten: The Last Viceroy 1985, The Singing Detective 1986, The Miser 1987; directed Othello for television 1988; Hon. Dr. (Open Univ.) 1984. *Address:* William Morris Agency (U.K.) Ltd., 31/32 Soho Square, London, W.1, England. *Telephone:* 01-434 2191.

SUZUKI, Gengo; Japanese banker; b. 11 Feb. 1904, Mino-Kamo City; s. of Seijiro Suzuki and Sumi Kani; m. 1st Hide Motoda 1929 (died 1975), two s.; m. 2nd Toshi Toki 1976; ed. Taihoku Coll. of Commerce and Univ.

of Wisconsin; Instructor, then Prof. Econs. Taihoku Coll. of Commerce, Taihoku, Taiwan 1930–45; Prof. Econs. Taiwan Nat. Univ. 1945–48; Deputy Financial Commr. Ministry of Finance 1949–51, Financial Commr. 1951–57; Financial Minister, Embassy of Japan, Washington, D.C. 1957–60; Special Asst. to Minister of Foreign Affairs and to Minister of Finance 1960–66; Exec. Dir. IMF and IBRD 1960–66; Japan's Rep. to Group of Ten Deputies and Working Party 3 of OECD 1963–66; Auditor, Bank of Japan, Tokyo 1966–70; mem. Advisory Bd. Mekong Comm. ESCAP 1968–75; Chief Finance Mission on Ryukyu Islands 1968–69; mem. World Bank's Investment Dispute Conciliation Panel 1968–74; Trustee, Int. Christian Univ., Tokyo 1968–, ICU Cambridge House (Charitable Trust), Cambridge 1981–; Chair. Bd. Rikkyo School in England (Charitable Trust), Rudgwick, Surrey 1972–85, Associated Japanese Bank (Int.) Ltd., London 1970–79, Bd. Counsellor 1979–87; Publisher Int. Devt. Journal Ltd., Tokyo 1970–85; Editorial Adviser 1985–; Gov. and mem. Steering Cttee., Atlantic Inst. for Int. Affairs, Paris 1971–85; Gov. 1986–; mem. European Atlantic Group, London 1971–79; mem. Council of Int. Chamber of Commerce, Paris 1974–85; mem. Comm. on Unethical Practices (ICC) 1976–77; Councillor Atlantic Council of the U.S., Washington, D.C. 1986–. *Leisure interest:* golf. *Address:* Apartment 717, The Olympus, 6301 Stevenson Avenue, Alexandria, Va. 22304, U.S.A. (Home); 2-5-13 Nukuikitamachi, Koganei-shi, Tokyo, Japan (Home). *Telephone:* (703) 370-8649 (Washington); 0423-83-5751 (Tokyo).

SUZUKI, Haruo, LL.B.; Japanese business executive; b. 31 March 1913, Hayama, Kanagawa Pref.; s. of Chuji and Masu Suzuki; m. Itoko Hibiya 1941; two d.; ed. Tokyo Univ.; with Nomura Securities Co. Ltd. 1936–39; joined Showa Denko K.K. 1939, Exec. Vice-Pres. 1959–71, Pres. 1971–81, Chair. 1981–87, Hon. Chair. 1987–; Chair. Abrasive Industry Assen. 1972–81, Council on Basic Material Industries 1978–, Japan Carbon Assen. 1979–81; Pres. Japan Chemical Industry Assen. 1976–78; Vice-Pres. Japan Inst. of Invention and Innovation 1980–; Dir. Japan Cttee. for Econ. Devt. 1946–, Int. Primary Aluminium Inst. 1974–76; Exec. Dir. Fed. of Econ. Orgs. 1972–; Chair. Japan-Southern U.S. Assen. 1984–; mem. Industrial Structure Council of Ministry of Int. Trade and Industry 1972–, Legis. Council, Ministry of Justice 1982–; mem. Industrial Property Council 1983, Japan-China Cttee. for Friendship in the 21st Century 1984–. *Publications:* Chemical Industry 1968, What the Classics Have Taught Me 1979. *Leisure interests:* reading, art appreciation, painting, swimming. *Address:* Showa Denko K.K., 13-9, Shiba Daimon 1-chome, Minato-ku, Tokyo 1-810; 7 Mita 2-chome, Minato-ku, Tokyo, Japan (Home). *Telephone:* 432-5111 (Office).

SUZUKI, Hideo; Japanese investment banker; b. 4 June 1917, Hayama, Kanagawa Pref.; m.; two c.; ed. Univ. of Tokyo; entered Ministry of Finance 1940; Deputy Supt. of Kobe Customs, Ministry of Finance 1953–55; Head, Treasury Div., Financial Bureau, Ministry of Finance 1955–57; Head Govt., Investment Div., Financial Bureau, Ministry of Finance 1957–58, Co-ordinating Div., Foreign Exchange Bureau 1958–59; Financial Counsellor, Japanese Embassy, Consul in New York and Rep. of Ministry of Finance in New York 1959–62; Deputy Dir. Int. Finance Bureau Ministry of Finance 1962–64; mem. Policy Bd., Bank of Japan, concurrently Deputy Dir. Int. Finance Bureau, Ministry of Finance 1964–65; Dir. Int. Finance Bureau 65-66; Special Adviser to Minister of Finance and Special Asst. to Minister of Foreign Affairs 1966–74; Exec. Dir. IMF, IBRD 1966–72; Vice-Chair., Deputies of Cttee. of 20, IMF 1972–74; Adviser, Nomura Securities 1974–, Goldman, Sachs and Co. 1989–; Chair. Nomura Europe, N.V. 1974–88, and Nomura Int. Finance PLC 1986–88. *Address:* The Nomura Securities Co., 1-9-1, Nohonbashi, Chuo-ku, Tokyo 103; 11-10 Nampeidaicho, Shibuyaku, Tokyo 150, Japan (Home).

SUZUKI, Osamu; Japanese business executive; b. 30 Jan. 1930, Gero, Gifu; s. of Shunzo and Toshiko Suzuki; m. Shoko Suzuki 1958; two s. one d.; ed. Chuo Univ.; joined Suzuki Motor Co. Ltd. 1958, Dir. 1963–66, Jr. Man. Dir. 1967–71, Sr. Man. Dir. 1972–77, Pres. 1978–; Award 'Sitara-i-Pakistan' (Pakistan) 1984. *Leisure interest:* golf. *Address:* Suzuki Motor Co. Ltd., Hamamatsu-Nishi, P.O. Box 1, 432-91, Hamamatsu, Japan. *Telephone:* (0534) 40-2027.

SUZUKI, Shunichi, LL.D.; Japanese politician; b. 6 Nov. 1910, Tokyo; s. of Toshio and Kii Suzuki; m. Atsu Suzuki 1935; two s. one d.; ed. Tokyo Imperial Univ.; joined Ministry of Home Affairs; lecturer on public admin. law at Komazawa Univ. 1941–46; lecturer on local autonomy system at Waseda Univ. 1945–57; Vice-Minister, Ministry of Home Affairs 1950–58; Deputy Chief Cabinet Sec. 1958; Vice-Gov. of Tokyo 1959–67, Gov. April 1979–; Sec.-Gen., Expo '70 in Osaka 1967–70; Pres., Tokyo Expressway Public Corpn. 1971–77; Gov. Finance Corpn. of Local Public Enterprise 1978–79; Conservative. *Leisure interest:* golf. *Address:* 3-5-1. Marunouchi, Chiyoda-ku, Tokyo, Japan. *Telephone:* (03) 212-5111.

SUZUKI, Zenko; Japanese politician; b. 11 Jan. 1911, Iwate Pref.; ed. Ministry of Agric. Acad. of Fisheries; elected 12 times to House of Reps.; Chair. Standing Cttee. on Local Admin. 1958–60; Minister of Post and Telecommunications 1960–64; Chief Cabinet Sec. 1964–65; Minister of Health and Welfare 1965–68, of Agric., Forestry and Fisheries 1976–77; various posts in Liberal-Democratic Party (LDP) incl. Chair. of Exec. Council 1968–80, Pres. –Oct. 1982; Prime Minister of Japan 1980–82. *Address:* c/o Office of the Prime Minister, 1-6-1, Nagata-cho, Chiyoda-ku, Tokyo, Japan. *Telephone:* 01-581-2361.

SVART, Anker; Danish diplomatist; b. 15 Sept. 1918, Taps; s. of Jakob and Helene (née Olsen) Svart; m. Nina Jonsson 1949; no c.; ed. Aarhus Univ., Denmark and Univ. of Sheffield, England; Attaché, Danish Legation, Iceland 1944–45; Ministry of Foreign Affairs, Copenhagen 1945–52; Sec. Danish Legation, Canada 1952–55; Counsellor, Moscow 1956–60, Bonn 1960–62; Amb. to the People's Repub. of China (Beijing) 1962–65; Head of Dept., Econ. Div., Ministry of Foreign Affairs 1965–66; Amb. to U.S.S.R. (also accred. to Mongolia) 1966–73; Amb. to NATO 1973–83, also accred. to Belgium and Luxembourg 1973–81, to Sweden 1983–88.

SVEDBERG, Bjoern, M.SC.; Swedish business executive; b. 4 July 1937, Stockholm; s. of Inge and Anna-Lisa Svedberg; m. Gunnel Nilsson 1960; four c.; ed. Royal Inst. of Tech., Stockholm and Man. Devt. Inst. (IMEDE), Univ. of Lausanne; Man. Eng. Telephone Exchange Div., L. M. Ericsson Telephone Co. 1972–76, Sr. Vice-Pres. Research and Devt. 1976–77, Pres. 1977–; mem. Bd. Fed. of Swedish Industry, L. M. Ericsson and several other cos.; mem. Royal Swedish Acad. of Eng. Sciences. *Address:* Telefonaktiebolaget L. M. Ericsson, S 126 25 Stockholm, Sweden. *Telephone:* 719 00 00.

SVEJGAARD, Arne, D.SC.; Danish hospital administrator; b. 13 March 1937, Odense; m. Else Lyngsoe 1960; two s. one d.; ed. Univ. of Aarhus Medical School and Univ. Hosp. of Aarhus; Dir. Tissue Typing Lab., Univ. Hosp. of Copenhagen 1970–87, Dept. of Clinical Immunology 1987–; Councillor Int. Histocompatibility Workshops 1975–; Chair. Danish Cttee. for Immunology 1985–; mem. Royal Danish Acad. of Sciences and Letters 1981–; Gaardon Prize 1980, Novo Prize 1981. *Publications:* Iso-antigenic Systems of Human Blood Platelets 1969, The HLA System (with others) 1975, HLA and Disease (with J. Dausset) 1977, numerous scientific articles. *Address:* Department of Clinical Immunology, University Hospital, Tagensvej 20, 2200 Copenhagen; Skovvang 67, 3450 Allerod, Denmark. *Telephone:* (45-1) 386633, ext. 7630; (45-2) 273211.

SVERČINA, Otakar, RS.DR.; Czechoslovak journalist and politician; b. 10 Dec. 1925, Petřvald, Karviná Dist.; ed. Coll. of Political and Social Sciences, Prague, Political Coll. of CP Cen. Cttee.; Ed. Czechoslovak News Agency (ČTK), corresp. in several European countries and the Middle East 1948–69; Deputy Chief Ed. Rudé právo (CP daily newspaper) 1969; Dir.-Gen. ČTK Prague 1969–89; mem. Ideological Comm. CP Cen. Cttee. 1971–; mem. House of the People, Fed. Assembly 1971–; mem. Presidium, Czechoslovak group of Interparl. Union 1972–; Chair. Bd., Assen. of Socialist Agencies Photo Int. 1970–74, 1981–; Chair.-Co-ordinator, Conf. of Gen. Dirs. of Socialist Press Agencies 1972–73, 1984–85; Vice-Pres. European Alliance of Press Agencies 1973–75, Pres. 1975–76, 1986–87, Vice-Pres. 1983–86; mem. Czech Peace Cttee. 1981–; Award for Merits in Construction 1971; Order of Labour 1975; Czechoslovak Prize for Journalism 1984; Order of Victorious February 1985. *Address:* Československá tisková kancelář, Opletalova 5-7, 111 44 Prague, Czechoslovakia.

SVETLANOV, Yevgeniy Fyodorovich; Soviet composer and conductor; b. 6 Sept. 1928, Moscow; ed. Gnesiny Music Educ. Inst. and Moscow Conservatoire; Asst. Conductor, Moscow Radio 1954; Conductor, Bolshoi Theatre, Moscow 1955–63, Chief Conductor 1963–65; Prin. Conductor, U.S.S.R. State Symphony Orchestra 1965–; Prin. Guest Conductor, London Symphony Orchestra 1979–; People's Artist of R.S.F.S.R., of U.S.S.R. 1968; Lenin Prize 1972, Grand Prix (France); Order of Lenin, State Glinka Prize 1975, Order of Red Banner (twice), State Prize in Music 1983, and other decorations. *Compositions include:* Symphony, Tone-Poems Festival 1950, Daugava 1953, Siberian Fantasy 1953, Rhapsody 1954, Cantata Home Fields 1949, Concerto 1951, five Sonatas 1946–52, five Sonatinas 1946–51, Preludes 1945–51, Symphony 1957, Beautiful Kalina (symphonic poem) 1975; about 50 Romances and Songs. *Has conducted:* Rusalka (Dargomyshski), Pskovityanka, The Czar's Bride, Sadko, Snow-Maiden (Rimsky-Korsakov), Prince Igor (Borodin), The Sorceress (Tchaikovsky), Not Only Love (Schchedrin), Boris Godunov (Mussorgsky), October (Muradelya), Storm Along the Path (Karayev), Paganini (Rachmaninov), Swan Lake (Tchaikovsky), Night Town (Bartok), Pages of Life (Belanchivadze), Chopiniana (Chopin). *Address:* U.S.S.R. State Symphony Orchestra, 31 Ulitsa Gorkogo, Moscow, U.S.S.R.

SVIRIDOV, Georgiy Vasilevich; Soviet composer; b. 3 Dec. 1915, Fatezh, Kursk Dist.; ed. Leningrad Conservatory studied under P. R. Ryazanov and D. D. Shostakovich; Sec. of Bd. of U.S.S.R. Composers' Union 1962–74; Sec. of Board of R.S.F.S.R. Composers' Union 1968–73; *Works include:* Kursk Songs 1964, Snow 1965, Spring Cantata 1972. *Address:* c/o U.S.S.R. Union of Composers, Moscow, U.S.S.R.

SVIRSKY, Grigoriy Tsezarevich; Soviet writer; b. 1921; m.; one c.; served in Soviet Army 1941–45 in Arctic; mem. CPSU –1968; began publishing novels 1947; dissident activity 1965–72; expelled from U.S.S.R. Writers' Union 1971; nine awards and medals. *Publications:* Hostages 1967, The Arctic Tragedy 1971, On Lobnoye Mesto 1979, A History of Post-War Soviet Writing: The Literature of Moral Opposition 1981.

SVOBODA, Josef; Czechoslovak architect and stage designer; b. 10 May 1920, Čáslav; s. of Růžena and Josef Svoboda; m. Libuše Hrubešová 1948; one d.; ed. Special School for Interior Architecture, Prague and School of Fine and Applied Arts, Prague; Stage designer, Nat. Theatre, Prague 1947, Head Designer 1951–; Prof. Acad. of Applied Arts 1968–; mem.

Union of Czech Dramatic Artists 1975–, Union of Czech Designers, Union of Czech Architects, Union of United Scenic Artists, U.S.A.; Gen. Sec. Int. Org. of Scenographers and Theatre Technicians 1971–; Artistic Dir. of Laterna Magica 1973; created over 500 stage sets in Czechoslovakia and for theatres in Belgium, France, Italy, Germany, U.S.S.R., U.K., U.S.A., etc.; Hon. Degree, R.C.A. 1969, Denison Univ., Ohio 1977; State Prize 1954, Order of Labour 1963, Honoured Artist 1966; Best Stage Designer Art Biennale São Paulo 1961, London Theatre Critics' Award for the Best Stage Set (The Insect Comedy, Čapek and Tempest, Ostrovsky) 1966, Nat. Artist 1968, Nederlands Sikkenprijs 1969, L.A. Drama Critics Circle Award for Distinguished Set Design (The Three Sisters) 1970, Kulturpreis, German Photographic Soc. 1971, Int. Theatre Award, American Theatre Assen. 1976; Chevalier, Ordre des Arts et des Lettres 1976. *Leisure interest:* motoring. *Address:* National Theatre, Anenské nám. 2, Prague 1; Filmářská 535/17, 15200 Prague 5, Czechoslovakia (Home). *Telephone:* 27-72-69 (Office); 53-75-37 (Home).

SWAELEN, Frank, LL.D.; Belgian politician; b. 23 March 1930, Antwerp; m. M. J. Gobin 1958; one s. two d.; ed. Coll. of St.-Lievens, Antwerp, Catholic Univ. of Louvain, Harvard Int. Seminar; Sec.-Gen. Nat. Confed. of Parents' Assens. 1956–66; Nat. Chair. Young Christelijke Volks Partij (CVP) 1964–66; Gen. Sec. Political CVP-PSC (Christian Democrats) 1966–76; mem. Chamber of Reps. 1968–84, Senator 1984–; Polit. Bureau of European Union of Christian Democrats, Nat. Bureau CVP 1971–; Vice-Chair. CVP group in Chamber of Reps. 1979–80; Chair. CVP group in Council of the Flemish Cultural Community 1979–80; Minister of Defence 1980–81; Nat. Pres. CVP 1981–; Mayor of Hove 1971–; Commdr. Order of Leopold. *Leisure interests:* tennis, reading. *Address:* Tweekerkenstraat 41, 1040 Brussels (Office); Mortselsesteenweg 69, 2540 Hove, Belgium (Home). *Telephone:* 02-238-38-11 (Office); 03-455 26 12 (Home).

SWAFFIELD, Sir James, Kt., C.B.E., R.D., D.L., M.A., LL.B.; British local government official; b. 16 Feb. 1924, Cheltenham; s. of Frederick and Kate Elizabeth Swaffield; m. Elizabeth Margaret Ellen Maunder 1950; two s. two d.; ed. Cheltenham Grammar School, Haberdashers' Aske's Hampstead School, Univ. of London; Articled Town Clerk, Lincoln 1946–49; Asst. Solicitor, Norwich Corpn. 1949–52, Cheltenham Corpn. 1952–53, Southend-on-Sea Corpn. 1953–56; Deputy Town Clerk, then Town Clerk and Clerk of Peace, Blackpool 1956–62; Sec. Assen. of Municipal Corpns. 1962–72; Dir.-Gen. GLC 1972–84; Clerk to ILEA and of Lieutenancy for Greater London 1973–84; Chair. British Rail Property Bd. 1984–; fmr. Pres. Soc. of Local Authority Chief Execs., Standing Technological Conf. of European Local Authorities; fmr. Gov. Henley, the Admin. Coll. and Govt. Policy Studies Inst.; mem. Council of Law Soc.; Hon. Fellow, Inst. of Local Govt. Studies, Univ. of Birmingham; Order of St. John. *Address:* 10 Kelsey Way, Beckenham, Kent, England. *Telephone:* 01-650 2002.

SWALES, William Edward, M.S.; American oil company executive; b. 15 May 1925, Parkersburg, W. Va.; s. of John Richard Swales and Ellen (South) Swales; m. Lydia Eugena Mills 1948; two s. one d.; ed. West Virginia Univ.; Geologist, Marathon Oil Co., Terre Haute, Ind. 1954, Advanced Geologist, Evansville, Ind. 1956–57, various positions, Guatemala, Ireland, England and Australia 1957–66, Man., Western Hemisphere and Australia Div., Findlay, Ohio 1967–70; Exec. Vice-Pres., Oasis Oil Co. of Libya Inc. 1970–72, Pres. 1972–74; Special Asst. to Sr. Vice-Pres., Production Int., Marathon Oil Co. 1974, Vice-Pres. 1974–77, mem. Bd. of Dirs. 1975–, Sr. Vice-Pres. 1977–82, Pres. Marathon Petroleum Co. 1982–83, Sr. Vice-Pres., Exploration and Production, Marathon Oil Co. and Chair. Marathon Int. Oil Co. 1984; Pres. and Dir. Marathon Oil Co. 1985–87; Vice-Chair. Energy USX Corpn., Pittsburgh 1987–; mem. Bd. of Dirs. U.S. Steel Corpn. and Vice-Chair., Oil and Gas and Related Resources 1985–; Dir. First Nat. Bank of Findlay, American Petroleum Inst. *Leisure interests:* golf and bowling. *Address:* USX Corporation, 600 Grant Street, Pittsburgh, Pa. 15230, U.S.A. (Office).

SWALLOW, John Crossley, PH.D., F.R.S.; British oceanographer (retd.); b. 11 Oct. 1923, Huddersfield, Yorks.; s. of Alfred Swallow and Elizabeth Swallow (née Crossley); m. Mary Morgan (née McKenzie) 1958; one step-d.; ed. Holme Valley Grammar School, Yorks. and St. John's Coll., Cambridge; Admiralty Signal and Radar Establishment 1943–46; Geophysical Surveys in H.M.S. Challenger 1949–53; Nat. Inst. of Oceanography (subsequently Inst. of Oceanographic Sciences), concerned mainly with ocean circulation, especially measurement of deep currents 1954–83; Bigelow Medal and Award, Woods Hole Oceanographic Inst. 1962; Murchison Grant, Royal Geographical Soc. 1965; Sverdrup Medal, American Meteorological Soc. 1978; Prince Albert I of Monaco Medal, Institut Océanographique 1982. *Publications:* various papers on oceanographic topics. *Leisure interests:* oceanography, gardening. *Address:* Heath Cottage, Drakewalls, Gunnislake, Cornwall, PL18 9EA, England. *Telephone:* (0822) 832 100.

SWAMINATHAN, Jagdish; Indian painter; b. 21 June 1928, Simla; m. Bhavani 1955; two s.; ed. Delhi Polytechnic and Acad. of Fine Arts, Warsaw; early career of freedom fighter, trade unionist, journalist, and writer of children's books; mem. Delhi State Cttee. of Congress Socialist Party and Ed. of its weekly organ, Mazdoor Awaz; Sr. Art Teacher, Cambridge School, New Delhi; Founder-mem. Group 1890 (avant-garde group of India artists); mem., Nat. Cttee., Int. Assen. of the Arts 1967, Exec. Cttee. Delhi Slipi Chakra 1967–, also Founder-Ed. monthly journal,

Contra 1966 and full-time painter; one-man exhbns. in New Delhi 1962, 1963, 1964, 1965, 1966, in Bombay 1966; in group shows Warsaw 1961, Saigon 1963, Tokyo Biennale 1965, Art Now in India, London, Newcastle and Brussels 1965–66, Seven Indian Painters, London 1967; Jawaharlal Nehru Research Fellow; represented in various public and pvt. collections in India and abroad. *Address:* c/o Gallery Chemould, Jahangir Art Gallery, Mahatma Gandhi Road, Bombay 1; 6/17 W.E.A., New Delhi 5, India.

SWAMINATHAN, Monkombu Sambasivan, PH.D., F.R.S., F.R.S.A.; Indian geneticist and international administrator; b. 7 Aug. 1925, Tamil Nadu; m. Mina Bhoothalingam Swaminathan; three d.; ed. Travancore and Madras Univs., Indian Agric. Research Inst., New Delhi and Univ. of Cambridge; UNESCO Fellow in Genetics, Agric. Univ., Wageningen, Netherlands 1949–50; Research Assoc. in Genetics, Univ. of Wis., U.S.A. 1952–53; Asst. Botanist, Cen. Rice Research Inst., Cuttack 1954; Asst. Cytogeneticist, Indian Agric. Research Inst. 1954–56, Cytogeneticist 1956–51, Dir. 1966–72; Dir.-Gen. Indian Council of Agric. Research and Sec. to Govt. of India, Dept. of Agric. Research and Educ. 1972–79, Ministry of Agric. 1979–80; mem. (Agric.) Planning Comm. 1980–82; Dir.-Gen. Int. Rice Research Inst., Los Baños, Philippines 1982–88; Pres. Int. Union for the Conservation of Nature and Natural Resources 1988–, Nat. Acad. of Sciences; Ind. Chair. FAO Council; Chair. UN Advisory Cttee. on Science and Tech. for Dev. (ACSTD); Pres. Int. Fed. of Agric. Research Systems for Dev. (IFARD), Soc. for Breeding Research in Asia and Oceania (SABRAO), Int. Bee Research Assen., XV Int. Congress of Genetics, Int. Union for Conservation of Nature and Natural Resources (IUCN); fmr. Pres. Indian Soc. of Genetics and Plant Breeding, Indian Soc. of Nuclear Techniques in Agric. and Biology, Indian Soc. of Agric. Statistics, Nutrition Soc. of India, Indian Soc. of Agric. Econs., Indian Soc. for Cotton Improvement; has held many nat. and int. consultative positions, etc.; Fellow, Indian Nat. Acad., Indian Acad. of Sciences; Foreign mem. Royal Swedish Acad. of Agric. and Forestry 1983–; Foreign Assoc. U.S. Nat. Acad. of Sciences, All Union Acad. of Agric. Sciences of U.S.S.R.; numerous awards and decorations, including Nobel Peace Prize 1970 for contributions to the green revolution, Albert Einstein World Science Award 1986, World Food Prize 1987, Golden Heart Presidential Award 1987; 30 hon. degrees. *Publications:* over 200 research papers in nat. and int. journals. *Address:* 11 Rathana Nagar Teynampet, Madras 600018, India. *Telephone:* (044) 455339.

SWAN, John William David, B.A.; Bermudian politician; b. 3 July 1935, Bermuda; s. of John Nicholas and Margaret Swan; m. Jacqueline Roberts 1965; one s. two d.; ed. Cen. School and Howard Acad., Bermuda and W. Virginia Wesleyan Coll.; Real-Estate Salesman with Rego Ltd. 1960–62; Founder, C.E.O. and Chair. of John W. Swan Ltd. 1962–; mem. Parl. 1972–, Minister for Marine and Air Services, Labour and Immigration 1977–78, Home Affairs 1978–82, Premier of Bermuda 1982–; fmr. Parl. Sec. for Finance, Chair. Bermuda Hosp. Bd., Chair. Dept. of Civil Aviation; mem. Chief. Execs. Org. and World Business Council; Hon. LL.D. (Tampa Univ.) 1986, (W. Va. Wesleyan Coll.) 1987; St. Paul's A.M.E. Anniversary Citation 1969, Outstanding Young Man of the Year 1969; Hon. Citizen City of London 1985; Int. Medal of Excellence, Poor Richard Club of Pa. 1987. *Leisure interests:* tennis, sailing. *Address:* The Cabinet Office, 105 Front Street, Hamilton, HM12, Bermuda. *Telephone:* 809 292 5501.

SWAN, Richard Gordon, PH.D.; American professor of mathematics; b. 21 Dec. 1933, New York; s. of A. Gordon Swan and Rose Nespor Swan; m. Erdmuthe Plesch-Ritz; one s. one d.; ed. Phillips Exeter Acad. and Princeton Univ.; Nat. Science Foundation Postdoctoral Fellow, Oxford 1957–58; Faculty mem. Univ. of Chicago 1958–, Prof. 1965–, Louis Block Prof. 1982–; Alfred P. Sloan Fellow 1961–65; Cole Prize in Algebra (American Math. Soc.) 1969. *Publications:* The Theory of Sheaves 1964, Algebraic K-Theory 1968, K-Theory of Finite Groups and Orders 1970; papers include: Induced Representations and Projective Modules 1960, Groups of Cohomological Dimension one 1969, Vector Bundles over Affine Surfaces (with M. P. Murthy) 1976, Projective Modules over Binary Polyhedral Groups 1983, K-Theory of Quadric Hypersurfaces 1985. *Leisure interest:* music. *Address:* Department of Mathematics, University of Chicago, 5734 University Avenue, Chicago, Ill. 60637 (Office); 475 Oakdale Avenue, Glencoe, Ill. 60022, U.S.A. (Home). *Telephone:* (312) 962-7347 (Office).

SWANK, Emory Coblentz, M.A.; American diplomatist (retd.); b. 29 Jan. 1922, Frederick, Md.; s. of late George P. Swank and Ruth Coblentz McCollough; m. Margaret K. Whiting; ed. Franklin and Marshall Coll., Harvard Univ. and Nat. War Coll., Washington, D.C.; served in U.S. Army 1943–46; Instructor in English, Franklin and Marshall Coll. 1946; joined foreign service 1946; appointments in China, Indonesia and U.S.S.R.; Deputy Chief, U.S. Embassy, Bucharest 1958–60; Special Asst. to Sec. of State 1960–63; Deputy Chief, U.S. Embassy, Vientiane, Laos 1964–67; Minister, Moscow 1967–69; Deputy Asst. Sec. for European Affairs, Dept. of State 1969–70; Amb. to Khmer Repub. 1970–73; Political Adviser to C.-in-C., Atlantic, and Supreme Allied Commdr., NATO Atlantic Forces 1973–75; Pres. and C.E.O. Cleveland Council on World Affairs 1977–87; Bronze Star. *Leisure interests:* swimming, golf, music, literature. *Address:* 2 Deerfield Lane, Beachwood, Ohio 44122, U.S.A. *Telephone:* (216) 831-4124.

SWANN, Baron (Life Peer), cr. 1981, of Coln St. Denys in the County of Gloucestershire, Michael Meredith Swann, Kt., M.A., PH.D., F.R.S., F.R.S.E.;

British university teacher and administrator; b. 1 March 1920; s. of M. B. R. Swann; m. Tess Gleadowe 1942; two s. two d.; ed. Winchester and Gonville and Caius Coll., Cambridge; Army Service 1940;46; Demonstrator, Dept. of Zoology, Univ. of Cambridge 1946–52; Prof. of Natural History, Univ. of Edinburgh 1952–62, Dean of Faculty of Science 1962–65, Prin. and Vice-Chancellor, Univ. of Edinburgh 1965–73; mem. Medical Research Council 1962–65; mem. Cttee. on Manpower Resources 1965–68; mem. Council for Scientific Policy 1965–69, Science Research Council 1970–73; Chair. BBC 1973–80; Chair. Council for Science and Society 1973–78, Council for Applied Science in Scotland 1978–80, Tech. Change Centre 1980–87; Chair. Cttee. of Inquiry into the Educ. of Children from Ethnic Minority Groups 1981–85; Provost Oriel Coll. Oxford 1980–81; Chancellor, York Univ. 1979–; Pres. ASLIB 1980–82; Dir. New Court Natural Resources Ltd. 1973–85, M & G Group PLC 1981–89; Chair. R.A.M.; Trustee Wellcome Trust 1973–, British Museum of Natural History 1982–87, Gov. Ditchley Foundation 1975–; Queen's Lecture, Berlin 1975; F.I.Biol.; Hon. F.R.C.S.E. 1967; Hon. F.R.C.P.E. 1972; Hon. A.R.C.V.S. 1976; Hon. Assoc. British Veterinary Assoc. 1984; Hon. LL.D. (Aberdeen) 1967; Hon. D.Sc. (Leicester) 1968; Hon. D.Univ. (York) 1970, (Edinburgh) 1983; Hon. D.Litt. (Heriot Watt) 1971. *Publications:* papers in scientific journals. *Leisure interests:* gardening, sailing. *Address:* Tallat Steps, Coln St. Denys, near Cheltenham, England (Home). *Telephone:* (0285) 72533 (Home).

SWANN, Donald Ibrahim, M.A.; British composer, pianist and entertainer; b. 30 Sept. 1923, Llanelli, Wales; s. of Herbert Swann and Naguimé Piszóva; m. Janet Oxborrow 1955 (dissolved); two d.; ed. Westminster School and Christ Church, Oxford; musical contrib. to London revues, including Airs on a Shoestring (Jt. leader writer) 1953–54; musical play Wild Thyme 1955, Hilda Tablet Series (with Henry Reed) for BBC Radio; with Michael Flanders in two-man revues, At the Drop of a Hat, and At the Drop of Another Hat (singer and accompanist of own songs); toured U.K., Australia, New Zealand, S.A., U.S.A. and Canada. *Other works include:* London Sketches 1958, Festival Matins 1962, Perelandra (opera by David Marsh based on book of C. S. Lewis) 1961–62, settings of John Betjeman's poems 1964; since 1966 has appeared in own concert/entertainments Set by Swann (setting of poetry by Tolkien and others), An Evening in Crete (Greek songs), Soundings by Swann (church music), Between the Bars (musical autobiog.) 1970, A Crack in Time (a concert in search of peace) 1973, The Five Scrolls, Seasons of the Jewish Year, (cantata with Albert Friedlander) 1975, Swann in Jazz in collaboration with Digby Fairweather 1986; *recordings include:* Flanders and Swann material (EMI Encore), Tolkien Songs (Caedmon). *Publications and Major Compositions:* Sing Round the Year (carols for children) 1965, The Road Goes Ever On (with J. R. R. Tolkien), The Space between the Bars 1967, Reflections, Requiem for the Living (choral work, with C. Day Lewis) 1970, Song of Caedmon (narration with songs) 1971, The Rope of Love (more carols) 1973, Swann's Way Out 1975, A Posthumous Adventure, The Songs of Michael Flanders and Donald Swann 1977, Singalive, Wacky and His Fuddlejig, and Baboushka (three joint works with Arthur Scholey) 1978 and 1979, The Yeast Factory (music drama, with Alec Davison) 1979, Round the Piano with Donald Swann (children's songs) 1979, Candle Tree (opera with Arthur Scholey about St. Boniface) 1980, The Visitors (opera, with Scholey, from a Tolstoy story) 1983, Swann with Topping (Multimedia) 1983, Voyage of Brendan (with Scholey), Cantata for children and adults 1984, World Service of BBC, third series of Reflections 1984–85, Mamahuhu (musical with Evelyn Kirkhart and Mary Morgan) 1986, South African Song Cycle (to S. African poets) 1986, Music to Richard Crane's play Envy 1986; Alphabetor: Essays (with illustrations by Natasha Swann Etheridge, designed by Robert Poulter) 1987, Victorian Song Cycle, Tennyson and Christina Rosetti 1987, Brighton Festival 1988. *Leisure interest:* going to the launderette. *Address:* 13 Albert Bridge, London, SW11 4PX, England. *Telephone:* 01-622 4281.

SWANSON, August George, M.D.; American physician; b. 25 Aug. 1925, Kearny; s. of Oscar V. Swanson and Elnora Block; m. Ellyn C. Weinel 1947; two s. four d.; ed. Harvard Medical School and Washington Univ.; Instructor in Medicine and Paediatrics for Neurology, Washington Univ. School of Medicine 1958–64, Dir. Div. of Neurology 1964–67, Assoc. Dean for Academics and Student Affairs 1967–71; Vice-Pres. for Academic Affairs, Asscn. of American Medical Colls. 1971–; Hon. D.Sc. (Nebraska); John and Mary R. Markle Scholar in Medical Sciences; mem. Inst. of Medicine of N.A.S. *Publication:* Medical Education in the U.S. and Canada (Chapter) 1986. *Leisure interest:* yacht racing. *Address:* Association of American Medical Colleges, Suite 200, 1 Dupont Circle, N.W., Washington, D.C. 20036, U.S.A. *Telephone:* (202) 828-0475.

SWANSON, David Heath, M.A.; American business executive; b. 3 Nov. 1942, Illinois; s. of Neil H. Swanson and Helen M. Swanson; m. Elizabeth Farwell 1963; two s.; ed. Harvard Coll. and Univ. of Chicago; Account Exec. First Nat. Bank of Chicago 1966–69; Deputy Man. Brown Brokers Harriman 1969–72; Treas. Borden Int. 1972–75; Chief Financial and Admin. Officer, Continental Grain, then Sr. Vice-Pres. and Group Pres., Sr. Vice-Pres. and Gen. Man. World Grain Div. 1975–86; Pres. and C.E.O. Central Soya Co. Inc. 1986–; mem. Council on Foreign Relations; mem. Advisory Bd. Export-Import Bank of U.S. *Publications:* articles on mountaineering and exploration. *Address:* Central Soya Co., Inc., 1300 Fort Wayne

National Bank Building, P.O. Box 1400, Fort Wayne, Ind. 46801 (Office); 1207 Three Rivers East, Fort Wayne, Ind. 46802, U.S.A. (Home). *Telephone:* (219) 425-5138 (Office); (219) 422-8521 (Home).

SWANWICK, Betty, R.A.; British artist, book illustrator and mural painter; b. 22 May 1915; d. of Henry Gerad Swanwick; ed. Lewisham Prendergast School, Goldsmiths' Coll. School of Art and Royal Coll. of Art; murals for various orgs.; has designed posters and press advertisements; now painting in watercolours; mem. Royal Soc. of Painters in Water Colours. *Publications:* The Cross Purposes 1945, Hoodwinked 1957, Beauty and the Burglar 1958. *Leisure interest:* gardening. *Address:* Caxton Cottage, Frog Lane, Tunbridge Wells, Kent, England.

SWAR AL-DAHAB, Gen. (see Dahab, Gen. Swar al-).

SWART, Karel, B.CHEM.ENG.; Netherlands oil company executive; b. 26 May 1921, Singapore; m. Wilhelmina A. Bruinsma 1950; ed. Delft Univ.; with Royal Dutch Shell-Laboratory, Amsterdam 1948; Refinery Start-up Team, Shell Berre 1953; Bombay 1954, Geelong 1955; Cen. Office, The Hague 1956; various tech. and managerial posts at Cardón Refinery, Compañía Shell de Venezuela Ltd. 1958–65; Gen. Man. Curaçao 1965; Dir. Mfg. and Supply, Venezuela 1967; Special Assignment, Cen. Office, The Hague 1968; Man. Dir. N.V. Koninklijke Nederlandsche Petroleum Maatschappij (Royal Dutch) 1979, The Shell Petroleum Co. Ltd. 1979, Prin. Dir. Shell Petroleum N.V. 1970–79; Chair. Supervisory Bd., Royal Boskalis Westminster NV (Papendrecht) 1980–; Kt. Order of Netherlands Lion. *Address:* Brouwerlaan 6, Voorschoten, The Netherlands (Home).

SWARTZ, Col. the Hon. Sir Reginald William Colin, K.B.E., M.B.E., E.D., F.B.I.M., F.A.I.M.; Australian fmr. politician and company director; b. 14 April 1911; ed. Toowoomba and Brisbane Grammar Schools; Parl. Under-Sec. Ministry of Commerce and Agric. 1952–56; Parl. Sec. Ministry of Trade 1956–61; Minister for Repatriation 1961–64; Minister for Health 1964–66; Minister for Social Services 1965–, for Civil Aviation 1966–69, for Nat. Devt. 1969–72; Leader of House of Reps. 1971–72; (retd.); fmr. Dir. eight Australian cos.; fmr. Councillor, Inst. of Dirs.; life mem. Liberal Party. *Address:* 32 Leawarra Crescent, Doncaster East, 3109, Melbourne, Victoria, Australia. *Telephone:* 842-1439.

SWARTZ, William John, J.D., M.S.; American business executive; b. 6 Nov. 1934, Hutchinson, Kan.; s. of George G. Swartz and Helen M. Prather; m. Dorothy J. Parshall 1956; two s.; ed. Duke Univ., George Washington Univ. and Mass. Inst. of Technology; served U.S. Marine Corps. 1956–59; joined AT & SF Railway 1961, Asst. Vice-Pres. Exec. Dept. 1973–77, Vice-Pres. Admin. 1977–78, Exec. Vice-Pres. 1979–83; Exec. Vice-Pres. Santa Fe Industries, Chicago 1978–79, Pres. 1983–, Vice-Chair. 1988–. *Address:* 223 E. Walton Place, Chicago, Ill. 60661, U.S.A. (Home).

SWE, U Ba; Burmese politician; b. 19 April 1915, Tavoy; s. of U Tun Hlaing and Daw Pe Lay Swe; m. Daw Nu Nu Swe 1944; six s. four d.; ed. Rangoon Univ.; Pres. Rangoon Univ. Students' Union 1940–41; one of the founders of People's Revolutionary Party 1939; Chief of Civil Defence in the "Kebotai" 1942–45; one of leaders of Anti-Japanese Resistance Movement, in charge of Rangoon, Hanthawaddy and Insein Dists. 1944–45, arrested and detained by Japanese; Pres. Socialist Party (originally People's Revolutionary Party) 1945, later Sec.-Gen.; Pres. Asia Socialist Conf. 1952–56, 1956–60; Sec.-Gen. Anti-Fascist People's Freedom League 1947–58; Leader of "Stable" Group 1958; fmr. M.P. from Taikkyi; Minister of Defence 1952–58, concurrently Prime Minister 1956; Deputy Prime Minister 1957–59; Leader of Opposition 1958; under political arrest 1963–66; Yugoslav Banner, First Class, Noble Order of the White Elephant (Thailand), Star of Revolution, First Degree, Naing-Ngani Gon Yi, Title Class 1 1980. *Leisure interests:* gardening, billiards, writing. *Address:* 84 Innes Road, Rangoon, Burma. *Telephone:* 21355.

SWEARINGEN, John Eldred, M.S.; American businessman; b. 7 Sept. 1918, Columbia, S.C.; s. of John E. Swearingen and Mary Hough; m. 1st Rolly A. Ostberger 1942, three d.; m. 2nd Bonnie Bolding 1969; ed. Univ. of South Carolina and Carnegie Mellon Univ.; Chemical Engineer, Standard Oil Co. (Indiana) 1939–47; various positions Stanolind Oil and Gas Co. (now Amoco Production Co.) 1947–51 and Dir. 1951; Gen. Man. Production, Standard Oil Co. (Indiana) 1951, Dir. 1952, Vice-Pres. 1954, Exec. Vice-Pres. 1956, Pres. 1958–65, C.E.O. 1960–83, Chair. of Bd. 1965–83; Chair., C.E.O. Continental Illinois Nat. Bank of Trust Co. of Chicago 1984–87; Dir. Chase Manhattan Corpn., First Nat. Bank, Chicago, American Nat. Bank and Trust Co., American Petroleum Inst. (Chair. 1978–79), Northwestern Memorial Hosp. 1965–, Chicago; Trustee, Carnegie Mellon Univ. 1960–83, DePauw Univ., Orchestral Asscn., Chicago; mem. Nat. Petroleum Council (Chair 1974–76), Advisory Bd. Hoover Inst. for War, Revolution and Peace, Int. Advisory Bd., Morgan Stanley 1984–; mem. Nat. Acad. of Eng., A.C.S., American Inst. of Mining and Metallurgical Engineers; Fellow, A.I.Ch.E.; Hon. D.Eng. (S.D. School of Mines and Tech.), Hon. LL.D. (DePauw Univ., Univ. of S. C., Knox Coll., Butler Univ., Ill. Coll, Stamford Univ., Calumet Coll.), Hon. D.L.H. (Nat. Coll. of Educ.), Hon. D.Bus.-Mgt. (Indiana Inst. of Tech.). *Leisure interests:* reading, fishing, hunting, golf. *Address:* 1420 Lake Shore Drive, Chicago, Ill. 60610, U.S.A. (Home).

SWEDEN, King of (see Carl XVI Gustaf).

SWEETING, William Hart, C.M.G., C.B.E.; British banker (retd.); b. 18 Dec. 1909, Nassau, Bahamas; s. of Charles C. and Clara M. Sweeting; m. Isabel J. Woodall 1950; ed. Queen's Coll., Nassau and Univ. of London; Asst. Receiver-Gen. and Treas., Bahamas 1946; Financial Sec., Dominica 1950–52; Receiver-Gen. and Treas., Bahamas 1955; Chair. Bahamas Currency Commrs. 1955–63; Chair. Bahamas Broadcasting and TV Comm. 1956–62; mem. Legis. Council, Bahamas 1960–64; Chief Sec., Bahamas 1964, Deputy Gov. 1969; Chair. Bank of London and Montreal (BOLAM) 1970–79; Chair. Bahamas Public Disclosure Comm. 1978–84. *Leisure interests:* swimming, painting, music, bird-watching. *Address:* Ryswick, P.O. Box N573, Nassau, Bahamas (Home). *Telephone:* 829-39-3518.

SWIFT, Hewson Hoyt, PH.D.; American biologist; b. 8 Nov. 1920, Auburn, New York; s. of Arthur L. Swift Jr. and Hildegarde Hoyt Swift; m. Joan Woodcock 1942; two d.; ed. Swarthmore Coll., State Univ. of Iowa and Columbia Univ.; Curator of Spiders, U.S. Nat. Museum, Washington, D.C. 1945–46; Instr. in Zoology, Univ. of Chicago 1949–51, Asst. Prof. 1951–55, Assoc. Prof. 1955–58, Prof. of Zoology 1958–68, Prof. of Biology 1968–71, Distinguished Service Prof. of Biology and Pathology and Chair. Dept. of Biology 1973–77, George Wells Beadle Distinguished Service Prof. of Biology and Pathology 1977–84, of Molecular Genetics and Cell Biology and of Pathology 1984–; Visiting Prof. Harvard Univ. 1970–71; Sr. Visiting Research Fellow, CSIRO, Canberra 1977–78; mem. N.A.S., N.A.S. (India), American Acad. of Arts and Sciences; various awards. *Publications:* about 130 scientific research articles. *Leisure interests:* wildlife study, photography. *Address:* Department of Molecular Genetics and Cell Biology, 1103 East 57th Street, Chicago, Ill. 60637, U.S.A. *Telephone:* (312) 702-8041.

SWING, William Lacy, M.TH.; American diplomatist; b. 11 Sept. 1934, North Carolina; s. of Baxter D. and Mary F. (née Barbee) Swing; one s.; ed. Catawba Coll. and Yale Univ.; Vice-Consul, Port Elizabeth, S. Africa 1963–66; int. economist, Bureau of Econ. Affairs, Dept. of State 1966–68; Consul, Hamburg 1968–72; Dept. of State 1972–74; Deputy Chief of Mission, U.S. Embassy, Bangui, Cen. African Repub. 1974–76; Sr. Fellow, Center for Int. Affairs, Harvard Univ. 1976–77; Deputy Dir., Office of Cen. African Affairs, Dept. of State 1977–79; Amb. to People's Repub. of Congo 1979–81, to Liberia 1981–85; Dir. Office of Foreign Service Assignments and Career Devt. 1985–87; Deputy Asst. Sec. for Personnel 1987–; Hon. LL.D. (Catawba Coll.); Presidential Distinguished Service Award 1985. *Publication:* U.S. Policy Towards South Africa: Dilemmas and Priorities 1977. *Leisure interests:* tennis, squash. *Address:* U.S. Department of State (DGPIPER), Washington, D.C. 20520 (Office); 3416 N. Street, N.W., Washington, D.C. 20007, U.S.A. (Home).

SWINNERTON-DYER, Sir (Henry) Peter Francis, Bt., K.B.E., M.A., F.R.S.; British mathematician and university professor; b. 2 Aug. 1927, Ponteland; s. of the late Sir Leonard Dyer; m. Dr. Harriet Crawford 1983; ed. Eton and Trinity Coll., Cambridge; Research Fellow, Trinity Coll. 1950–54; Commonwealth Fund Fellow, Univ. of Chicago 1954–55; Coll. Lecturer in Math., Trinity Coll. 1955–71, Dean 1963–70; Lecturer in Math., Cambridge Univ. 1960–71, Prof. of Math. 1971–88, Master of St. Catharine's Coll. 1973–83; Vice-Chancellor, Cambridge Univ. 1979–81; Chair. Univ. Grants Cttee. 1983–89, Chief Exec. Univs. Funding Council 1989–; mem. Advisory Bd. for Research Councils 1977–; Vice-Pres. Inst. of Manpower Studies 1983–; Visiting Prof. Harvard Univ. 1970–71; Chair. Cttee. on Acad. Org., Univ. of London 1980–81; mem. Advisory Council on Science and Tech. 1987–; Hon. Fellow, Worcester Coll., Oxford 1980, St. Catharine's Coll., Cambridge 1983, Trinity Coll., Cambridge 1983; Hon. D.Sc. (Bath) 1981. *Publications:* Analytic Theory of Abelian Varieties 1974, and papers in learned journals. *Leisure interests:* tennis, squash, chess. *Address:* University Grants Committee, 14 Park Crescent, London, W1N 4DH, England. *Telephone:* 01-636 7799.

ŚWIRGOŃ, Waldemar, M.A.; Polish journalist and politician; b. 15 March 1953, Dobryniów, Chełm Voivodship; ed. Warsaw Univ.; Asst., later Sr. Asst. Warsaw Univ. 1976–; mem. Rural Youth Union 1970–73, Socialist Youth Union 1971–72, Polish Students' Asscn., subsequently Polish Socialist Students' Union 1972–80; Chair. Nat. Bd. of reactivated Rural Youth Union 1980–82; Chair. Gen. Council Peasant Sports Clubs Assen. 1981–; Ed.-in-Chief Chłopska Droga (daily), Warsaw Dec. 1986–; mem. Polish United Workers' Party (PZPR), deputy mem. PZPR Cen. Cttee. 1981–82, mem. PZPR Cen. Cttee. 1982–, and Sec. Cen. Cttee. Oct. 1982–86. *Address:* Redakga "Chfopskiej Drogi", Pl. Starynkiewicza 7/9, 00-973 Warsaw, Poland. *Telephone:* 28-25-58 (Office).

ŚWITAŁA, Kazimierz, LL.M.; Polish lawyer and politician (retd.); b. 21 April 1923, Rakoniewice, Wolsztyn Dist.; s. of Wacław and Maria Świtała; m. Urszula Świtała 1949; one s.; ed. Teodor Duracz Higher School of Law, Warsaw and Univ. of Poznań; Officer, Second Polish Army 1944–46; Judge, Poznań 1951–55; Chief Justice, Voivodship Court of Justice, Katowice 1955–58; Deputy Chief Justice, then Chief Justice, Voivodship Court of Justice, Warsaw, and Dir. of Dept., Ministry of Justice 1958–61; Deputy Prosecutor-Gen. 1961–65; Under-Sec. of State, Ministry of Justice 1965–67; Deputy Minister, then Minister of Internal Affairs 1967–71; Head of Office of Seym (Parl.) 1972–86; mem. Cen. Cttee. Polish United Workers' Party (PZPR) 1968–71; mem. Polish Lawyers' Assen., Supreme Bd., Union of Fighters for Freedom and Democracy; numerous decorations including Commdr. Cross and Commdr. Cross with Star, Order of Polonia Restituta, Order of Banner of Labour 1st Class, Order of Builders of People's Poland.

SWOBODA, Peter, D.B.A.; Austrian professor of finance; b. 13 April 1937, Bad-Deutsch Altenburg; s. of Gottfires Swoboda and Maria Magdalena Swoboda; m. 1st Eva Swoboda 1959; m. 2nd Birgit Swoboda 1978 (divorced 1988); one s. three d.; ed. Hochschule für Welthandel, Vienna; Asst. Prof. Hochschule für Welthandel, 1959–64; Visiting Assoc. Prof. in Accountancy, Univ. of Ill. (Urbana-Champaign) 1965–66; Full Prof. in Accountancy and Finance, Johann Wolfgang Goethe Univ., Frankfurt 1966–70; Full Prof. in Industrial Operations and Finance, Karl Franzens Univ., Graz 1970–; Pres. European Finance Assen. 1980–81; Assoc. mem. Australian Acad. of Sciences 1980, Full mem. 1983. *Publications:* Investition und Finanzierung, Betriebliche Finanzierung 1981. *Address:* Hans-Sachs-Gasse 3/III, A-8010 Graz, Austria. *Telephone:* 0316/380-3511.

SYBERBERG, Hans-Jürgen; German film producer; b. 8 Dec. 1935, Pomerania; ed. studies in literature and history of art at Munich; produced over 80 short TV films 1963–65. *Films:* Fritz Kortner Rehearses Schiller's Intrigue and Love 1965, Shylock Monolog 1966, The Count Pocci 1967, How Much Earth Does a Man Need 1968, Sexbusiness Made in Passing 1969, San Domingo 1970, After My Last Removal 1971, Ludwig - Requiem for a Virgin King 1972, Ludwig's Cook 1972, Karl May - In Search of Paradise Lost 1974, The Confessions of Winifred Wagner 1975, Hitler, A Film from Germany 1977, Parsifal (Kritiker Preis, Berlin 1983) 1982. *Publications:* The Film as the Music of the Future 1975, Filmbuch 1976, Die Kunst als Rettung aus der deutschen Misere (essay) 1978. *Address:* Center Strasse 15a, 8000 München 23, Federal Republic of Germany.

SYDOW, Erik von. B.L.; Swedish diplomatist; b. 2 Sept. 1912, Göteborg; s. of Oscar von Sydow and Mary (née Wijk) von Sydow; m. Lia Akel 1940; one s. one d.; ed. Uppsala Univ.; Ministry of Foreign Affairs 1936; early service Germany and Baltic States; Sec. Legation to Japan 1940, Chargé d'affaires 1945–46; Head of Div., Ministry of Foreign Affairs 1947–49; Perm. Rep. to OEEC 1949–53; Counsellor, U.S.A. 1954–56; Asst. Under-Sec. Commercial and Econ. Affairs, Ministry of Foreign Affairs 1959–63; Amb. and Perm. Rep. to EFTA and other int. orgs. in Geneva 1964–71; Amb. to the EEC, Brussels 1972–78; Chair. Museum of E. Asiatic Art and numerous bilateral and multilateral trade negotiations. *Address:* Hazeliusbacken 18, S-115 21 Stockholm, Sweden.

SYDOW, Max von; Swedish actor; b. 10 April 1929, Lund, Sweden; s. of Carl W. von Sydow and Greta Rappe; m. Christina Olin 1951; two s.; ed. Royal Dramatic Theatre School, Stockholm; Norrköping-Linköping Theatre 1951–53, Hälsingborg Theatre 1953–55, Malmö Theatre 1955–60, Royal Dramatic Theatre, Stockholm 1960–; Sorrento Prize 1968; Litteris et Artibus 1978, Best Actor, European Film Award, Berlin 1988. *Plays acted in include:* Peer Gynt, Henry IV (Pirandello), The Tempest, Le misanthrope, Faust, Ett Drömspel, La valse des toréadors, Les sequestrés d'Altona, After the Fall, The Wild Duck, The Night of the Tribades 1977, Duet for One 1981, The Tempest 1988. *Films acted in include:* Bara en mor 1949, Miss Julie 1950, Det sjunde inseglet (The Seventh Seal) 1957, Ansiktet (The Face) 1958, The Virgin Spring 1960, Såsom i en spegel (Through a Glass Darkly) 1961, Nattvardsgästerna (Winter Light) 1963, The Greatest Story Ever Told 1963, 4×4 1965, Hawaii 1965, Quiller Memorandum 1966, The Hour of the Wolf 1966, The Shame 1967, A Passion 1968, The Emigrants 1969, The New Land 1969, The Exorcist 1973, Steppenwolf 1973, Heart of a Dog 1975, Three Days of the Condor 1975, The Voyage of the Damned 1976, The Desert of the Tartars 1976, Cadaveri Eccelenti 1976, Deathwatch 1976, Flash Gordon 1979, Victory 1980, The Flight of the Eagle 1981, Emerald 1984, Hannah and Her Sisters 1985, The Second Victory 1985, Duet for One 1986, Pelle the Conqueror 1986, Katinka 1987, The Wolf at the Door 1987; Dir. Katinka 1989. *Television:* The Last Civilian, Christopher Columbus, Samson and Delilah 1983, The Last Place on Earth 1984, The Belarus File 1984, Gosta Berling's Saga 1985, The Wisdom and the Dream 1989. *Leisure interest:* nautical history. *Address:* c/o Filmhuset, Box 27126, 102 52 Stockholm 27, Sweden; c/o Paul Kohner Inc., 9169 Sunset Blvd., Los Angeles, Calif. 90069, U.S.A.

SYED PUTRA BIN SYED HASSAN JAMALULLAIL (see Perlis).

SYED ZAHIRUDDIN BIN SYED HASSAN, Tun, S.M.N., D.U.N.M., P.S.M., G.C.V.O., J.M.N., S.P.M.P., P.J.K.; Malaysian government official; b. 11 Oct. 1918, Perak; s. of Syed Hassan bin Syed Ibrahim and Raja Halimah binti Raja Abdullah; m. Halimah Binti Haji Mohd Noh 1944; five s. five d.; ed. Raffles Coll., Singapore; Malay Officer 1945–47; Deputy Asst. Dist. Officer, Krian 1948, Asst. Dist. Officer 1951; Asst. Dist. Officer, Tanjong Malim 1953; Ipoh 1954; Second Asst. State Sec., Perak 1955, Registrar of Titles and Asst. State Sec. (Lands) 1956; Dist. Officer, Batang Padang, Tapah 1957; Deputy Sec. Public Services Comm. 1958; Prin. Asst. Sec., Fed. Establishment Officer 1960; State Sec. Perak 1961; Perm. Sec. Ministry of Agric. and Cooperatives 1963, Ministry of Educ. 1966; Dir.-Gen. Public Services Comm. 1969; retd. 1972; High Commr. in U.K. 1974–75; Gov. of Malacca 1975–85; Chair. Railways Services Comm. 1972–73, Special Cttee. on Superannuation 1973–74, Bd. of Govs. Malay Coll., 1970–74, Cen. Bd. for Teachers 1972–73. *Leisure interest:* golf. *Address:* c/o Office of the Governor, Malacca, Malaysia.

SYEDUZZAMAN, M., M.A., M.SC.; Bangladesh administrator and economist; b. 1 Jan. 1934, Dhaka; s. of Moulvi Shaikh Muhammad Syeduzzaman and Khojesta Akhtar Khatoon; m. Hafeeza Zaman 1957; one s. one d.; ed. Dhaka Univ., St. John's Coll., Cambridge and Williams Coll., Mass.; Deputy Sec. of Finance, East Pakistan 1961–66, Jt. Sec. 1966–67; Deputy Sec., Econ. Affairs Div., Pres. Secr. 1967–69, Deputy Sec., Ministry of Commerce 1969–70, Jt. Sec., Ministry of Finance 1970–72; Sec. Ministry of Planning, Bangladesh Govt. 1973–76, Sec. Ministry of Finance 1976–77, 1982–84, Prin. Finance Sec. and Financial Adviser, Ministry of Finance and Planning 1984–85, Adviser, Ministry of Finance (with rank of Minister) 1985–86; Minister of Finance 1986–87; Alt. Gov., IMF 1970–71, Gov. 1976–77, 1982–84; Alt. Exec. Dir., World Bank 1977–82; participated Tidewater Group meeting 1986; mem. Bd. of Trustees, Int. Food Policy Research Inst., Washington, D.C. 1987–; Nuffield Foundation Fellow, U.K. 1969. *Leisure interests:* literature, music, collecting books. *Address:* c/o Ministry of Finance, Bhaban 7, 3rd Floor, 1st 9-Storey Bldg., Dhaka; House No. 405E, Road No. 16 (Old 27), Dhanmandi Residential Area, Dhaka, Bangladesh (Home).

SYKES, Lynn R., PH.D.; American professor of geological sciences; b. 16 April 1937, Pittsburgh, Pa.; s. of Lloyd A. Sykes and Margaret Woodburn Sykes; m. (divorced); ed. Massachusetts Inst. of Tech. and Columbia Univ.; Research Asst., Lamont-Doherty Geological Observatory, Columbia Univ. 1961–64, Research Assoc. 1964–66, Adjunct Asst. Prof. of Geology 1966–68, Head of Seismology Group 1973–83, Higgins Prof. of Geological Sciences 1978–; main areas of interest are seismology, tectonics and arms control, earthquake prediction and the detection and identification of underground atomic tests; Chair. Nat. Earthquake Prediction Evaluation Council; Fellow American Geophysical Union, Geological Soc. of America, Royal Astronomical Soc., A.A.A.S.; mem. N.A.S., American Acad. of Arts and Sciences, Geological Soc. of London, Arms Control Assen.; Walter H. Bucher Medal of American Geophysical Union for original contribs. to basic knowledge of earth's crust 1975. *Publications:* numerous articles in scientific journals. *Leisure interests:* hiking, canoeing, opera, travel. *Address:* Lamont-Doherty Geological Observatory, Palisades, New York, N.Y. 10964, U.S.A. *Telephone:* (914) 359-2900.

SYKES, Peter, B.SC., M.SC., PH.D., F.R.S.C.; British chemistry teacher; b. 19 Feb. 1923, Manchester; s. of Charles Hyde Sykes and Alice Booth; m. Joyce Tyler 1946; two s. one d.; ed. Rydal School, Colwyn Bay, Univ. Manchester, Clare Coll., Cambridge; Research Fellow, St. John's Coll., Cambridge 1947–50, Univ. Demonstrator in Organic Chem. 1947–55, Lecturer 1955–82, Fellow, Christ's Coll. 1956–, Vice-Master 1984–88; Visiting Research Prof., Coll. of William and Mary, Williamsburg, Va. 1970–71, 1977–78; Visiting Prof., Univ. of Cape Town 1974, 1980, Univs. of São Paulo and Campinas, Brazil 1976, Univ. of Melbourne 1983–84; Mellor Medal, Univ. of N.S.W. 1984. *Publications:* The Search for Organic Reaction Pathways 1972, A Guidebook to Mechanism in Organic Chemistry 1986 (both trans. in numerous languages), and numerous papers on organic reaction mechanisms. *Leisure interests:* chamber music, church architecture, talking, wine. *Address:* University Chemical Laboratory, Lensfield Road, Cambridge, CB2 1EW; Christ's Coll., Cambridge, CB2 3BU, England. *Telephone:* (0223) 336367 (Laboratory); (0223) 334917 (College).

SYLVESTRE, (Joseph Jean) Guy, O.C., M.A.; Canadian librarian and author; b. 17 May 1918, Sorel, Quebec; s. of Maxime A. Sylvestre and Yvonne Lapierre; m. Françoise Poitevin 1943; two s. one d.; ed. Univ. of Ottawa; Private Sec. to Prime Minister 1948–50; Assoc. Parl. Librarian 1953–68; Nat. Librarian of Canada 1968–83; Pres. Canadian Inst. for Historical Microreproductions 1983–86; Commdr. Ordre int. du Bien public, Order of Merit of Poland; numerous hon. degrees; Fellow (past Pres.), Royal Soc. of Canada, Hon. Librarian 1975–. *Publications:* Louis Francoeur, journaliste 1941, Situation de la poésie canadienne 1942, Anthologie de la poésie canadienne d'expression française 1943, Poètes catholiques de la France contemporaine 1944, Jules Laforgue 1945, Sondages 1945, Impressions de théâtre 1950, Panorama des lettres canadiennes-françaises 1964, Canadian Writers/Écrivains canadiens 1964, Un siècle de littérature canadienne 1967, Guidelines for National Libraries 1987. *Leisure interests:* golf, reading. *Address:* 2286 Bowman Road, Ottawa, Ont., KIH 6V6, Canada.

SYME, Sir Ronald, Kt., O.M., F.B.A.; British university professor (retd.); b. 11 March 1903, Eltham, New Zealand; ed. New Zealand and Oriel Coll. Oxford; Fellow and Tutor, Trinity Coll., Oxford 1929–49; Press Attaché, British Legation, Belgrade 1940–41, Ankara, 1941–42; Prof. of Classical Philology Univ. of Istanbul 1942–45; Camden Prof. of Ancient History Univ. of Oxford 1949–70; Pres. Int. Fed. Classical Societies 1951; Pres. Soc. for the Promotion of Roman Studies 1948–52; Sec.-Gen. Int. Council for Philosophy and the Humanities 1952, Pres. 1971–75; Prof. of Ancient History, Royal Acad. of Arts 1976–; Foreign mem. Royal Danish Acad., American Phil. Soc., American Acad. of Arts and Sciences, American Historical Soc.; Assoc. mem. Inst. de France; mem. Lund Soc. of Letters, etc.; Fellow, Wolfson Coll. 1970; Hon. Fellow, Oriel Coll., Oxford 1958, Trinity Coll., Oxford 1970; Emer. Fellow, Brasenose Coll., Oxford 1970; Foreign mem. Orden für Wissenschaften und Künste 1975; Hon. D.Litt. (N.Z. 1949, Durham 1952, Belfast 1959, Emory 1962, Graz 1962, Ohio 1970, Boston Coll, 1974, Ball State Univ. 1981, Cambridge 1984, Pavia 1986, Köln 1988), Hon. D. ès L. (Liège 1952, Paris 1962, Lyon 1967, Louvain

1976), Hon. Ph.D. (Tel-Aviv 1975), Hon. D.Litt. (N.Y.) 1984, (Cambridge) 1985, (Pavia) 1986, (Athens) 1987, (Wisconsin) 1988; Hon. LL.D. (Harvard) 1988; Commdr., Ordre des Arts et des Lettres 1975, Kenyon Medal, British Acad. 1975. *Publications:* The Roman Revolution 1939, Tacitus 1958, Colonial Elites 1958, Sallust 1964, Ammianus and the Historia Augusta 1968, Ten Studies in Tacitus 1970, Emperors and Biography 1971, The Historia Augusta; a Call for Clarity 1971, Danubian Papers 1971, History in Ovid 1978, Roman Papers 1979, Some Arval Brethren 1980, Historia Augusta Papers 1983, Roman Papers, vol. 3 1984, vols. 4 and 5 1988, The Augustan Aristocracy 1986, Roman Papers, (vols. 4 and 5) 1988. *Address:* Wolfson College, Oxford, England. *Telephone:* 57093.

SYMMONDS, Algernon Washington; Barbadian lawyer and diplomatist (retd.); b. 19 Nov. 1926; s. of late Algernon French Symmonds and Olga (née Harper) Symmonds; m. Gladwyn Ward 1954; one s. one d.; ed. Codrington Coll.; solicitor, Barbados 1953, U.K. 1958; Deputy Registrar 1955–59; Crown Solicitor 1959–66; Perm. Sec. Ministry of Home Affairs 1966–72, of Educ. and Youth Affairs, Community Devt. and Sports 1972–76, of External Affairs 1976–79; apptd. Amb. 1977; High Commr. in U.K. 1979–83, also non-resident Amb. to Denmark, Sweden, Norway, Finland and Iceland 1981–83, to the Holy See 1982–83; Perm. Sec. to Prime Minister 1983–86; Head of Civil Service 1986; Dir. Sandy Bay Hotel Ltd., Roybar Investment Corpn.; Gold Crown of Merit (Barbados). *Leisure interests:* lawn tennis, cricket, football. *Address:* Margaret Terrace, Pine Gardens, St. Michael, Barbados.

SYMMS, Steven Douglas, B.S.; American politician; b. 23 April 1938, Nampa, Idaho; s. of Darwin and Irene (Knowlton) Symms; m. Frances E. Stockdale 1959; one s. three d.; ed. Idaho Univ.; with Symms Fruit Ranch, Inc., Caldwell, Idaho 1963–72; mem. House of Reps. 1973–81 from 1st Dist., Idaho; mem. House of Reps. Interior and Insular Affairs and Agric. Cttees. and Vice-Chair. Republican Study Cttee.; Senator from Idaho 1981–; mem. Task Force on Foreign Policy, Republican Research Cttee.; many awards and prizes. *Publications:* articles and chapters for journals and books. *Leisure interests:* jogging, hunting. *Address:* 509 Hart Senate Office Building, Washington, D.C. 20510, U.S.A.

SYMONS, Patrick Stewart, A.R.A.; British artist; b. 24 Oct. 1925, Bromley; s. of Norman Holding Symons and Nora (née Westlake) Symons; ed. Bryanston School, Blandford, Camberwell School of Arts and Crafts; teacher at Camberwell and St. Albans Schools of Art 1953–59; ran Foundation Course at Chelsea School of Art 1959–77, Visiting Teacher 1977–86; individual exhbns.: New Art Centre 1960, William Darby Gallery 1975–76, Browse and Darby 1982; Tolly Cobbold Award 1981, New English Art Club 1986. *Leisure interests:* botany and mathematics. *Address:* 20 Grove Hill Road, Camberwell, London, SE5 8DG, England. *Telephone:* 01-274 2373.

SYNGE, Henry Millington; British stockbroker; b. 3 April 1921, Liverpool; s. of Richard Millington Synge and Eileen B. N. Hall; m. Joyce Helen Topping 1947; two s. one d.; ed. Shrewsbury School; with Merchant Navy 1939–46; Partner, Sing White and Co. (Stockbrokers) 1947; Dir. Union Int. Co. Ltd. 1956, Chair. 1969–88; Man. Liverpool Trustee Savings Bank 1956–71, Chair. 1968–69; Gen. Commr. of Income Tax 1980; Consultant, Tilney & Co. Stockbrokers, Liverpool, London and Shrewsbury; mem. Bd. Trustee Savings Bank of Wales and Border Counties 1970–85. *Leisure interests:* fishing, aviation, amateur radio. *Address:* Lake Cottage, Llynclys Hill, Oswestry, Salop, SY10 8LL, England. *Telephone:* (0691) 830845.

SYNGE, John Lighton, M.A., SC.D., F.R.S., M.R.I.A.; Irish mathematician; b. 23 March 1897, Dublin; s. of Edward and Ellen Synge (née Price); m. Elizabeth Allen 1918 (died 1985); three d.; ed. St. Andrew's Coll., Dublin, and Trinity Coll., Dublin; Lecturer in Math. Trinity Coll., Dublin 1920; Asst. Prof. of Math. Univ. Toronto 1920–25; Fellow and Univ. Prof. of Natural Philosophy, Trinity Coll., Dublin 1925–30; Prof. of Applied Math., Toronto Univ. 1930–43; Prof. of Math. Ohio State Univ. 1943–46; Prof. of Math. Carnegie Inst. of Tech. 1946–48; Prof. Inst. for Advanced Studies, Dublin 1948–72, Emer. Prof. 1972–; Visiting Lecturer Princeton Univ. 1939, Visiting Prof. Brown Univ. 1941, Univ. of Md. 1951; Pres. Royal Irish Acad. 1961–64; Hon. Fellow, Trinity Coll., Dublin; Hon. LL.D. (St. Andrews) 1966; Hon. D.Sc. (Belfast) 1969, (Nat. Univ. of Ireland) 1970; Tory Medal (Royal Soc. of Canada) 1943, Boyle Medal (Royal Dublin Soc.) 1972. *Publications:* Mathematical Papers of Sir W. R. Hamilton, Vol. I (Editor, with A. W. Conway) 1931, Geometrical Optics 1937, Principles of Mechanics (with B. A. Griffith) 1942, Tensor Calculus (with A. Schild) 1949, Science: Sense and Nonsense 1951, Geometrical Mechanics and de Broglie Waves 1954, Relativity: the Special Theory 1956, The Relativistic Gas, Kandelman's Krim, The Hypercircle in Mathematical Physics 1957, Relativity: The General Theory 1960, Talking About Relativity 1971. *Leisure interests:* reading, motoring. *Address:* Torfan, 8 Stillorgan Park, Blackrock, Co. Dublin, Ireland. *Telephone:* 881251.

SYNGE, Richard Laurence Millington, PH.D., F.R.S.C., F.R.S.E., F.R.S.; British biochemist; b. 28 Oct. 1914, Liverpool; ed. Winchester Coll. and Trinity Coll., Cambridge; Int. Wool Secr. Student in Biochem., Univ. of Cambridge 1938 (transferred to Wool Industries Research Assen., Leeds 1939); Biochemist, Wool Industries Research Assen., Leeds 1941–43; Staff Biochemist, Lister Inst. of Preventive Medicine, London 1943–48 (studied at Inst.

of Physical Chem., Uppsala 1946–47); Head of Dept. of Protein Chem., Rowett Research Inst., Bucksburn, Aberdeen, Scotland 1948–67; Biochemist, Food Research Inst., Norwich 1967–76; Hon. Prof. School of Biological Sciences, Univ. of East Anglia 1968–84; mem. Editorial Bd. Biochemical Journal 1949–55; Visiting biochemist Ruakura Animal Research Station, Hamilton, N.Z. 1958–59; Hon. mem. Royal Irish Acad., Royal Soc. N.Z., American Soc. of Biological Chemists, Phytochem. Soc. Europe; Nobel Prize for Chemistry (with A. J. P. Martin) 1952 for invention of partition chromatography 1941; John Price Wetherill Medal, Franklin Inst. U.S.A. 1959. *Address:* 19 Meadow Rise Road, Norwich, NR2 3QE, England.

SYQUIA, Enrique, LL.D.; Philippines practising lawyer and professor of law; b. 22 May 1930, Manila; s. of late Vicente A. Syquia and Consolacion P. Syquia; m. Leticia Corpus Syquia 1964; five s.; ed. Univ. of Santo Tomas, Univ. of Madrid and Hague Acad. of Int. Law; Head Syquia Law Offices, Manila 1954–; Prof. of Law 1956–; Publr. The Lawyers Review 1986–; Dir. Philippine Bar Asscn. 1971–, Pres. 1981–84; mem. Exec. Council, Int. Bar Asscn. 1974–, Vice-Pres. 1982–84; Acting Pres. Philipines Council for Foreign Relations 1986–; mem. and/or officer of numerous nat. and int. law orgs. including A.B.A., American Judicature Soc., American Soc. of Int. Law, Inst. Hispanao-Luso-Americano de Derercho Internacional; Hon. Consul-Gen. of Kingdom of Jordan in the Philippines 1987–; del. to numerous law confs. at home and abroad since 1953; various hon. trusteeships etc.; Sovereign Mil. Order of Malta. *Publications:* The Tokyo Trial 1955, A Manual on International Law 1957; articles in legal journals. *Leisure interests:* reading, heraldry, stamp-collection. *Address:* 6th Floor, Cattleya Condominium, 235 Salcedo Street, Legaspi Village, Makati, Manila (Office); 127 Cambridge Circle, North Forbes, Makati, Manila, Philippines (Home). *Telephone:* 817-1089; 817-1095/1098 (Office); 810-7975; 810-7977 (Home).

SYRIMIS, George; Cypriot politician and accountant; b. Oct. 1921; m. Barbara Petropoulou; four c.; ed. Pancyprian Gymnasium, London Univ.; worked in father's shop, Nicosia until 1945; studied econs. and qualified as certified accountant in U.K.; worked as accountant until 1988; Minister of Finance 1988–. *Address:* Ministry of Finance, Nicosia, Cyprus.

SYSTSOV, Apollon Sergeyevich; Soviet politician; b. 1929; ed. Tashkent Polytechnic Inst.; chief engineer aviation works 1948–75; mem. CPSU 1961–; gen. dir. of Ulyanov Aviation Industrial Complex 1975–81; U.S.S.R. First Deputy Minister of Aviation 1981–85; Minister 1985–; mem. of CPSU Cen. Cttee. 1986–; Deputy to U.S.S.R. Supreme Soviet; State Prize 1973. *Address:* The Kremlin, Moscow, U.S.S.R.

SYTENKO, Mikhail Dmitrievich; Soviet diplomatist; b. 8 Nov. 1918, Troitskoye, Lugansk (now Voroshilovgrad) Region; ed. First Moscow State Inst. for Foreign Languages, Higher Diplomatic School of Ministry of Foreign Affairs; Diplomatic Service 1942–78, Amb. to Ghana 1959-62; Head of Second African Dept. of Ministry of Foreign Affairs 1962–65; Amb. to Indonesia 1965–69; Head of Near Eastern Countries Dept. of Ministry 1969–78; mem. del. to several sessions of UN Gen. Ass., to Geneva Peace Conf. on Middle East; UN Under-Sec.-Gen. for Political and Security Council Affairs 1978–81; Perm. Rep. of U.S.S.R. at UN European Office, Geneva 1983–88; Official, Ministry of Foreign Affairs 1988–. *Address:* c/o Ministry of Foreign Affairs, Smolenskaya-Sennaya pl. 32-34, Moscow, U.S.S.R.

SZABLOWSKI, Jerzy Jan, PH.D.; Polish historian of art and museologist; b. 30 Jan. 1906, Cracow; s. of Mieczysław Szablowski and Stanisława Pawlica; m. Wanda Henneberg 1951; ed. Jagiellonian Univ., Cracow ; Asst. Jagiellonian Univ., Cracow 1929–35; custodian Royal Park and Palace, Łazienki, Warsaw 1935–38; Head State Art Collections, Warsaw 1938–39; organizer of cataloguing of monuments of art in Poland; Head Cen. Office for Cataloguing Monuments of Art, Warsaw 1935–39, 1945–46; during German occupation participated in salvage of Polish cultural and artistic possessions; Dir. Wawel Museum, Cracow 1949–51; Dir. State Art Collections at Wawel, Cracow 1952–; participated in regaining historical Wawel treasures stored in Canada for the war period 1959, 1961; Extraordinary Prof. 1954, Ordinary Prof. 1966; Corresp. mem. Polish Acad. of Sciences 1969–80, mem. 1980–; mem. Soc. Européenne de Culture, Venice 1983–, Polish Art and Culture Foundation, San Francisco 1980–; numerous decorations including Great Cross, Order of Polonia Restituta, Kt.'s Cross, Order of Coroana Romaniei, Commdr.'s Cross, Order of the Crown (Belgium), Commdr.'s Cross with Star, Commdr.'s and Officer's Cross, Order of Polonia Restituta, Order of Banner of Labour (First Class). *Publications:* Architektura Kalwarii Zebrzydowskiej 1600–1702 1933, Ze studiów nad związkami artystycznymi polsko-czeskimi w epoce renesansu i renesansem zachodniosłowiańskim 1948, Zabytki sztuki w Polsce, Powiat Żywiecki 1948, Domniemana rola Sabbionety w sztuce polskiej okresu manieryzmu 1962, Architektura renesansowa i manierystyczna w Polsce 1965, Arrasy flamandzkie w zamku królewskim na Wawelu (co-author and scientific Ed.) 1972, Zbiory Zamku Królewskiego na Wawelu (co-author and scientific Ed.) 1975. *Leisure interests:* touring, unprofessional painting and drawing, artistic photography. *Address:* ul. Syrokomli 19A m. 4, 30-102 Cracow, Poland. *Telephone:* 22-23-25 (Home); 22-19-50 (Office).

SZABO, Denis, O.C., D. ÈS SC., F.R.S.C.; Canadian/Belgian professor of criminology; b. 4 June 1929, Budapest, Hungary; s. of Jenö Denes and Catherine Zsiga; m. Sylvie Grotard 1956; two d.; ed. Univs. of Budapest, Louvain

and Paris; Asst. Univ. of Louvain 1952–56; lecturer in Sociology, Catholic Univ. of Paris and Lyon 1956–58; Asst. Prof. Univ. of Montreal 1958–59, Assoc. Prof. 1959–66, Prof. of Criminology 1966–; founder and Dir. School of Criminology, Univ. of Montreal 1960–70; founder and Dir. Int. Center for Comparative Criminology, Univ. of Montreal 1969–84, now Chair. of Bd.; consultant to Canadian, U.S., French and UN comms. and bodies on crime prevention; Hon. Pres. Int. Soc. of Criminology; Dr. h.c. (Siena, Budapest); Commdr. Ordre Nat. du Merit, Côte d'Ivoire. *Publications:* Crimes et Villes 1960, Criminologie et Politique Criminelle 1978, The Canadian Criminal Justice System (with A. Parizeau), Science et Crimes 1986, Criminologie Empirique au Québec (ed. with M. Leblanc). *Leisure interest:* gardening, swimming. *Address:* University of Montreal, C.P. 6128, Montreal, H3C 3J7 (Office); C.P. 26, Georgeville, JÕB 1TO, Canada (Home). *Telephone:* 514-343-7065 (Office); 819-843-4343 (Home).

SZABÓ, István; Hungarian farmer and politician; b. 30 Oct. 1924, Nádudvar; Pres. Red Star Agric. Co-operative of Nádudvar 1952–; Pres. Nat. Council of Co-operatives 1967, 1972, 1975, 1978, 1981, 1984–; M.P. 1958–; Pres. Maize and Industrial Crop Producers Union 1976–; mem. Hungarian Socialist Workers Party (HSWP) Political Cttee. 1985–89; Kossuth Prize 1958, State Prize 1980. *Address:* National Council of Agricultural Co-operatives (TOT), 1054 Budapest, Akadémia utca 1/3, Hungary. *Telephone:* 325-515.

SZABÓ, István; Hungarian film director and scenario author; b. 18 Feb. 1938; s. of Dr. István Szabó and Mária Vita; m. Vera Gyürey; ed. Budapest Acad. of Theatre and Film Arts; started as mem. Balázs B. Studio, Budapest; leading mem. Hungarian Film Studios; awarded Béla Balázs Prize 1967, Kossuth Prize 1975; Tutor, Coll. of Theatre and Film Arts, Budapest and Deutsche Film- und Fernsehakademie, West Berlin; mem. Acad. of Motion Picture Arts and Sciences, Akademie der Künste, Berlin; Hon. Citizen of New Orleans. *Productions:* short films: Concert 1961, Variations upon a Theme 1961, Te (You) 1963 (Grand Prix de Tours), Budapest, amiért szeretem (Budapest, Why I Love It), 1971; a series including: Álom a házról (Dream about the House) 1971 (Main Prize of Oberhausen); documentaries: Kegyelet (Piety) 1967, Várostérkép (City Map) 1977 (Grand Prix of Oberhausen); *TV plays:* Ösbemutató (Première) 1974, Katzenspiel (Cat Play) 1982, Bali 1983; *full-length films:* Álmodozások kora (The Age of Day-Dreaming) 1964, Apa (Father) 1966, Szerelmesfilm (A Film of Love) 1970, Tüzoltó utca 25 (No. 25 Fireman's Street) 1973 (Grand Prix of Locarno), Budapesti mesék (Budapest Tales) 1976, Bizalom (Confidence) 1979 (Silver Bear of Berlin, Acad. Award Nomination 1981), Der grüne Vogel (The Green Bird) 1979 (Silver Bear of Berlin), Mephisto 1981 (Acad. Award 1982, David di Donatello Prize (Italy), Prize of Italian Critics, Prize of Critics, U.K.), Colonel Redl 1985 (Acad. Award Nomination 1986, BAFTA Award 1986, Best W. German Film—Golden Band), Hanussen 1988. *Address:* Objektiv Film Studió—MAFILM, 1149 Budapest, Lumumba utca 174, Hungary. *Telephone:* 632-482.

SZABÓ, Magda; Hungarian author; b. 5 Oct. 1917, Debrecen; d. of Alex Szabó and Madeleine Jablonczay; m. Tibor Szobotka 1948; graduated as a teacher 1940; worked in secondary schools 1940–44, 1950–59; started literary career as poet and has since written novels, plays, radio dramas, essays and film scripts; works have been translated into 28 languages including English, French, German, Italian, Russian, Polish, Swedish; mem. Acad. of Sciences of Europe; József Attila Prize 1959 and 1972, Kossuth Prize 1978. *Publications:* poems: Neszek (Noises); autobiog.: Ókut (Old Well); novels for children: Szigetkék (Island-Blue), Tündér Lala (Lala the Fairy), Abigél (Abigail); novels: Az öz (The Fawn), Fresko (Fresco), Disznótor (Night of Pig-Killing), Pilatus (Pilate), A Danaida (The Danaid), Mózes 1.22 (Genesis 1.22), Katalin utca (Kathleen Street), A szemlélök (The Onlookers), Régimódi történet (Old-Fashioned Story), Az ajtó (The Door); plays: Az a szép fényes nap (That Bright Beautiful Day), A meráni fiu (The Boy of Meran), A csata (The Battle) 1982, Béla Király (King Béla), A Macskák Szerdája (The Wednesday of the Cats) 1985. *Leisure interest:* pets. *Address:* H-1026 Budapest II, Julia-utca 3, Hungary.

SZABÓ, Zoltán, M.D.; Hungarian physician and politician; b. 17 Feb. 1914, Patalom; s. of Béla Szabó and Mária Klapp; m. Erzsébet Nagy 1948; one s. one d.; ed. Pécs Univ.; Asst. Lecturer, Univ. Medical School, Pécs 1945, Univ. Medical Clinic, Budapest 1957, Asst. Prof. 1963; Pres. Physicians and Health Workers Union 1952, Gen. Sec. 1963; First Deputy Minister of Health 1963; Minister of Health 1964–74; mem. Cen. Cttee. Hungarian Socialist Workers' Party 1962–75; Gen. Sec. World Fed. of Hungarians 1974–80; Pres. Union of Medical Practitioners and Health Workers 1985; Red Banner Order of Merit 1974; Standard Order of the Hungarian People's Repub. 1984. *Address:* II. Sarolta-u. 12, H-1028 Budapest, Hungary. *Telephone:* 150-627.

SZABOLCSI, Miklós; Hungarian literary critic and historian; b. 3 March 1921, Budapest; s. of Lajos Szabolcsi and Erzsébet Mészáros; m. Hedvig Margulesz 1948; one s.; ed. Budapest Univ.; Gymnasium teacher 1945–48, 1950–53; Prof., Kossuth Lajos Univ., Debrecen 1964–70; Prof., Eötvös Loránd Univ., Budapest 1979–; Visiting Prof., Univ. of Paris 1965–66; Corresp. mem. Hungarian Acad. of Sciences 1965, mem. 1976–; Dept. Head, Hungarian Acad. of Sciences Inst. for History of Literature 1957, Man. Dir. 1967–81; Pres. Section I (Language and Literature), Hungarian Acad. of Sciences 1970–85; Gen. Dir. Nat. Inst. of Pedagogy 1981–88; Pres.

Féd. Int. des Langues et Littératures Modernes 1981–84; Vice-Pres. Asscn. Int. des Critiques Littéraires 1972–; Ed. literary periodicals: Csillag 1953–56, Élet és Irodalom 1959–61; Neohelicon, Látóhatár; State Prize 1980. *Publications:* Költészet és korszerűség 1959, Kis Magyar Irodalomtörténet 1960, Elődök és Kortársak 1962, József Attila 1962, A verselemzés kérdéseihez 1969, Jel és kiáltás 1971, Szocialista irodalom—változó világ 1973, A clown mint a művész önarcképe a modern művészetben 1979, A neo-avantgarde 1981, Biography of Attila József Vol. I–II, A XX. század világirodalmi áramlatai (20th Century World Literature Trends) 1987; about 80 studies on comparative and Hungarian literature and theory of literature in Hungarian and foreign scientific papers. *Address:* XII. Németvölgyi u. 75/a, 1124 Budapest, Hungary. *Telephone:* 758-921.

SZAJNA, József; Polish theatre director, scenographer and painter; b. 13 March 1922, Rzeszów; s. of Julian Szajna and Karolina Pieniążek; m. Bożena Sierosławska 1953; one s.; ed. Cracow Acad. of Fine Arts; mem. Anti-Nazi Resistance, in Auschwitz and Buchenwald 1939–45; Lecturer, Acad. of Arts, Cracow 1954–65; Co-founder and scenographer Teatr Ludowy, Nowa Huta 1955–63, Man. Dir. 1963–66; Dir. and Scenographer, Teatr Stary, Cracow 1966–70; Man. Dir. Teatr Klasyczny, now Art Gallery and experimental theatre called Teatr Studio, Warsaw 1971–82; Extraordinary Prof. Acad. of Arts, Warsaw 1972–, and Dir. School for Stage Designers 1972–78; Dir. Acropolis 1962, Inspector 1963, Puste Pole 1965, Zamek 1965; Dir. and Scenario Faust 1971, Replika I, Göteborg 1971, Replika II, Edin. Festival 1972, Replika III, Nancy Festival 1973, Replika IV, Poland 1973, Replika V, France, Théâtre des Nations 1980, Replika VI, Istanbul Festival 1984, Replika VII, Tel-Aviv 1986, Witkacy 1972, Gulgutiera 1973, Dante, Int. Theatre Festival, Florence 1974, Cervantes 1976, (Special Prize, XIII Kalisz Theatre Encounters 1977), Majakowski 1978, Śmierć na gruszy 1978, Dante żywy (Dante Alive) 1981, Dante III 1985; one-man exhbn. Reminiscence, XXXV Venice Biennale 1970, Gegenwart einer Vergangenheit (Present of the Past), Frankfurt-am-Main 1978, Silhouettes, São Paulo 1979, Pictures of Man, West Berlin 1980, Essen 1984, Tel-Aviv, Jerusalem 1986, Cracow 1986, Warsaw 1987, Moscow 1987, Biennial Sao Paulo 1989; contrib. to many int. exhbns. and theatre festivals, including Quebec Festival 1986 (award winner); works of art in galleries and museums in Poland and abroad; Hon. mem. Int. Asscn. of Art; Reviewers Award 1957, ITI Distinction Award for decorations and costumes, Paris 1958; Nowa Huta Artistic Award 1959, First Prize of All-Poland Short-Feature Film Festival, Cracow 1962, Prize of Minister of Culture and Art (3rd Class) 1963, (2nd Class) 1971, Annual Award of Arkady Gallery, Cracow 1968, Gold Medal of "Quadriennale", Prague 1971, First Prize and Gold Medal, IV Art Festival, Warsaw 1972, Prize of Chair. of Council of Ministers (1st Class) 1979, Gold Centaur Award of Accademia Italia delle Arti et del Lavoro 1981, 1987, European Art Banner, Italian Accad. d'Europa, Statue of Victory, Centro Studi e Richerche delle Nazioni in Salsomaggiore 1984, Oscar d'Italia 1985, Accad. Italia in Calvatone 1985, Artistic Award of Warsaw 1987; numerous decorations including Kt.'s and Commdr.'s Cross of Order of Polonia Restituta 1959, 1979, Order of Banner of Labour (1st Class); Gold Centaur Award 1982, Meritorious Award for Nat. Culture 1986, Gold Medal, 40th Anniversary of War Veteran's, U.S.S.R. 1987. *Publications:* Teatr Organiczny (Organic Theatre), On the New Function of Scenography, The Open Theatre, The Matter of Spectacle, Visual Narrative. *Address:* Spasowskiego 14 m.8, 00-389 Warsaw, Poland. *Telephone:* 26-47-52.

SZAŁAJDA, Zbigniew, M.ENG.; Polish politician; b. 11 May 1934, Vilnius, Lithuania (now part of U.S.S.R.); ed. Mechanical Faculty of Silesian Tech. Univ., Gliwice; foreman in Florian Steelworks, Świętochłowice 1956–67; Deputy Dir., then Chief Engineer, F. Dzierżyński Steelworks, Dąbrowa Górnicza 1967–70; Dir.-Gen. Kościuszko Steelworks, Chorzów 1970–74, Katowice Steelworks 1974–80; Minister of Metallurgy 1980–81, Metallurgy and Eng. Industry 1981–82; Vice-Chair. Council of Ministers 1982–88; mem. PZPR 1960–, deputy mem. PZPR Cen. Cttee. 1980–81, mem. 1986–; Chair. Science and Tech. Progress Cttee. attached to Council of Ministers 1984–; Order of Banner of Labour (1st class), Commdr.'s Cross with Star, Order of Polonia Restituta. *Address:* c/o Urząd Rady Ministrów, Aleje Ujazdowskie 1/3, 00-583 Warsaw, Poland.

SZARKA, Károly; Hungarian diplomatist; b. 1923, Budapest; m.; two c.; entered foreign service 1948; served in Hungarian embassies in London 1949–50, New Delhi 1951–53, Washington, D.C. 1953–56; Deputy Minister for Foreign Affairs 1956–68; Amb. to Egypt (also accred. to Libya, Sudan, Yemen Arab Repub. and People's Democratic Repub. of Yemen) 1968–70; Perm. Rep. to UN 1970–74; Deputy Minister of Foreign Affairs 1974–83; Amb. to Japan 1983–85; Order of Merit, and several other Hungarian and foreign decorations. *Address:* c/o Ministry of Foreign Affairs, Bem rkp. 47, 1027 Budapest, Hungary.

SZASZ, Thomas Stephen, M.D.; American psychiatrist, psychoanalyst, author and lecturer; b. 15 April 1920, Budapest, Hungary; s. of Julius Szasz and Lily Wellisch; m. (divorced); two d.; ed. Cincinnati Univ. and Medical Coll.; staff mem., Chicago Inst. for Psychoanalysis 1951–56; mil. service with U.S. Naval Hosp., Bethesda (attained rank of Commdr.) 1954–56; Prof. of Psychiatry, State Univ. of N.Y., Upstate Medical Center 1956–; Co-founder and Chair. Bd. of Dirs., American Asscn. for the Abolition of Involuntary Mental Hospitalization Inc.; mem. Bd. of Dirs.,

Nat. Council on Crime and Delinquency; Consultant, Cttee. on Mental Hygiene, N.Y. State Bar Assch. and other advisory positions; mem. A.A.A.S. and other assens., Int. Editorial Bd. The International Journal of the Addictions, Contemporary Psychoanalysis, Editorial Bd. Journal of Humanistic Psychology, The Humanist, also consulting positions with journals; Hon. Pres. Int. Comm. for Human Rights 1974; D.Sc. h.c. (Allegheny Coll.) 1975, (Univ. Francisco Marroquin, Guatemala) 1979. *Publications:* Pain and Pleasure 1957, The Myth of Mental Illness 1961, 1974, Law, Liberty and Psychiatry 1963, Psychiatric Justice 1965, The Ethics of Psychoanalysis 1965, Ideology and Insanity 1970, The Manufacture of Madness 1970, The Age of Madness 1973, The Second Sin 1973, Ceremonial Chemistry 1974, Heresies 1976, Schizophrenia: The Sacred Symbol of Psychiatry 1976, Karl Kraus and the Soul-Doctors 1976, Psychiatric Slavery 1977, The Theology of Medicine 1977, The Myth of Psychotherapy 1978, Sex By Prescription 1980, Sex: Facts, Frauds and Follies 1981, The Therapeutic State 1984, Insanity: The Idea and its Consequences 1987. *Address:* Department of Psychiatry, State University of New York, Upstate Medical Center, 750 East Adams Street, Syracuse, N.Y. 13210 (Office); 4739 Limberlost Lane, Manlius, N.Y. 13104, U.S.A. (Home). *Telephone:* (315) 473-8105 (Office); (315) 637-8918 (Home).

SZCZEPAŃSKI, Jan, PH.D.; Polish sociologist; b. 14 Sept. 1913, Ustroń, Cieszyn dist.; s. of Paweł and Ewa Szczepański (née Cholewa); m. Eleonora Poczobut 1937; one s. one d.; ed. Univ. of Poznań; Asst. Poznań Univ. 1935–39; during Nazi occupation forced labour in Germany; Asst. Łódź Univ. 1945–52, Extraordinary Prof. 1952–63, Prof. 1963–70, Rector 1952–56; Chief Sociological Dept. Inst. of Philosophy and Sociology, Polish Acad. of Sciences 1957–58, Deputy Dir. 1961–68, Dir. 1968–75; mem. Polish Acad. of Sciences 1964–, Vice-Pres. 1971–80; Pres. Int. Sociological Assch. 1966–70; Vice-Chair. All-Poland Cttee. of Nat. Unity Front 1971–83; Deputy to Sejm 1957–60, 1972–85, Chair. Sejm Socio-Econ. Council 1982–85; Chair. Chief Council of Science, Higher Educ. and Tech., Ministry of Science, Higher Educ., and Tech. 1973–82; Chair. Scientific Council of Intercollegiate Inst. for Research on Higher Educ. 1973–; mem. Council of State 1977–82; Chair., Seym Extraordinary Comm. for Control the Realisation of Gdansk, Szczecin and Jastrzębie-Zdrój Agreements 1981; mem. Consultative Council attached to Chair. of State Council 1986–; mem. Bd. UNRISD, Assch. Int. de Sociologie (AIS); mem. Nat. Acad. of Educ., U.S.A.; Foreign mem. Finnish Acad. of Science and Literature; Hon. mem. American Acad. of Arts and Sciences 1972; Dr. h.c. (Brno Univ.) 1969, (Łódź Univ.) 1973, (Warsaw Univ.) 1979, (Sorbonne) 1980; Hon. C.B.E. 1978; Commdr.'s Cross with Star, Commdr.'s and Knight's Cross, Order Polonia Restituta 1969, Order of the Builders of People's Poland 1974, State Prize (1st Class) 1974, Commdr. of O.B.E., and others. *Publications:* Structure of Intelligentsia in Poland (in Polish) 1960, History of Sociology (in Polish) 1961, Sociological Problems of Higher Education (in Polish, French, Hungarian) 1963, edited Studies in Polish Class Structure (28 vols.), Introduction to Sociology (in Polish, Czech, Russian, Hungarian and Finnish) 1963, Problems of Contemporary Sociology (in Polish) 1965, Industry and Society in Poland (in Polish) 1969, Sociology and Society (in Bulgarian) 1970, Changes of the Present Time (in Polish) 1970, Co-editor Social Problems of Work Production (in Polish, Russian) 1970, Considerations on the Republic (in Polish) 1971, Reflections on Education (in Polish) 1973, Changes of Polish Community in the Process of Industrialization 1973, Essays on Higher Education 1976, Sprawy ludzkie (Res Humanae) 1979, Konsumpcja a rozwój człowieka (Consumption and Development of Man) 1981, Zapytaj samego siebie 1983, Korzeniami wrosłem w ziemię 1985, O indywidualności 1985. *Address:* Mokotowska 46a m.23, 00-543 Warsaw, Poland. *Telephone:* 28-21-93.

SZCZEPAŃSKI, Maciej, M.A.; Polish journalist; b. 7 July 1928, Sosnowiec; s. of Maria and Aleksander Szczepański; m. Ewa Wiland-Szczepańska; one s.; ed. journalistic studies; Editorial Sec. Nowiny Rzeszowskie daily newspaper 1951–55; Deputy Ed.-in-C. Polskie Radio broadcasting station, then Head of Propaganda Dept., Katowice Voivodship Cttee. of Polish United Workers' Party (PZPR) 1955–66; Ed.-in-C. Trybuna Robotnicza daily newspaper, Katowice 1966–72; Chair. Cttee. for Radio and TV, Polskie Radio i Telewizja 1972–80; Deputy to Sejm 1969–80; indicted and tried on charges of embezzlement and bribe taking Nov. 1981–Jan. 1984; sentenced to eight years imprisonment for misappropriation of state funds, accepting bribes and involvement in illegal currency transactions Jan. 1984; mem. PZPR 1954–80, Deputy mem. Cen. Cttee. until 1975, mem. PZPR Cen. Cttee. 1975–80; Commdr., Cross with Star of Order of Polonia Restituta 1978 and other decorations.

SZEKÉR, Gyula; Hungarian engineer and politician; b. 24 Sept. 1925, Szombathely; s. of János Szekér and Karolina Ferenczi; m. Éva Apró; two s.; ed. Tech. Univ.; joined CP 1948; mem. Cen. Cttee. Hungarian Socialist Workers Party; important posts in Ministry of Heavy Industry 1954–75, First Deputy Minister 1963, Minister 1971–75; Deputy Prime Minister, Council of Ministers 1975–80; Chair. State Office for Tech. Devt. 1980–84; Pres. Hungarian Office for Standardization 1984–. *Leisure interests:* tennis, hunting. *Address:* Hungarian Office for Standardization, Üllői ut 25, Budapest, Hungary. *Telephone:* 184-807.

SZELACHOWSKI, Tadeusz; Polish physician and politician; b. 7 April 1932, Sielachowskie; s. of Konstanty Szelachowski and Eugenia Szelachowski; m. 1954; two s.; ed. Medical Acad., Białystok; Head of Dept. of Health and Social Welfare, Presidium of Dist. Nat. Council, Białystok 1956-63; Deputy Head, Dept. of Health and Social Welfare, Presidium of Voivodship Nat. Council, Białystok 1963-69, Head 1970-73, Dir. of Dept. 1973-75; Białystok Voivodship Physician 1975-77; Under-Sec. of State, Ministry of Health and Social Welfare 1977-80, Head of Ministry 1980-81, Minister of Health and Social Welfare 1981-85; Deputy to Sejm 1985-; Deputy Chair. Council of State 1985-; mem. Polish Youth Union 1949-56, Polish Peasant Party (ZSL) 1958-; mem. ZSL Chief Cttee. 1980-, mem. Presidium Chief Cttee. 1983-, Vice-Pres. ZSL Chief Cttee. 1988-, Chair. ZSL Deputies' Club 1985-; Chief Ed. monthly Zdrowie Publiczne (Public Health) 1983-; Commdr.'s and Kt.'s Cross of Order of Polonia Restituta, and other decorations. *Leisure interests:* tourism, history. *Address:* Kancelaria Rady Państwa, ul. Wiejska 4/8, 00-902 Warsaw (Office); ul. Bonifraterska 6 m. 16, 00-213 Warsaw, Poland (Home). *Telephone:* 29-48-42 (Home).

SZENTÁGOTHAI, János, M.D.; Hungarian professor of anatomy; b. 31 Oct. 1912, Budapest; s. of Gustav and Margaret (Antal) Schimert; m. Alice Biberauer 1938; three d.; ed. Univ. of Budapest; Research Asst., Dept. of Anatomy, Univ. of Budapest 1935-37, Lecturer 1937-40, Reader 1940-47; Prof. and Head, Dept. of Anatomy, Univ. of Pécs 1947-63, Univ. of Budapest 1963-77; Ed. Journal Hirnforschung 1963; mem. Hungarian Acad. of Sciences 1948 (Vice-Pres. 1976-77, Pres. 1977-85, mem. Presidium 1985-), Presidential Council Hungarian People's Repub., Deutsche Akad. der Naturforscher Leopoldina 1964, Akad. der Wissenschaften und der Natur, Mainz 1969, Acad. Royale de Médecine de Belgique 1970, Nat. Acad. of Sciences, Washington 1972, American Acad. of Arts and Sciences 1973, Norwegian Acad. of Science and Letters 1976, Royal Soc. of London 1978, Royal Swedish Acad. of Sciences 1978, Bulgarian Acad. of Sciences 1979, Polish Acad. of Sciences, Czechoslovak Acad. of Sciences 1980, Pontifical Acad., Vatican City, Acad. of Arts and Sciences of Slovenia, Ljubljana 1981, U.S.S.R. Acad. of Sciences 1982, Indian Nat. Science Acad. 1984, Acad. of Sciences of G.D.R., Acad. of Finland 1985; Hon. D.Sc. (Oxford) 1978, Hon. D.M. (Turku Univ.) 1980; Kossuth State Prize 1950, Hufeland Memorial Medal 1969, State Award (1st Class) 1970, Karl Spencer Lashley Prize 1973, Gold Medal of Milan 1973, Order of Friendship of Nations (Hungary) 1982. *Publications:* Die Rolle der einzelnen Labyrinthrezeptoren bei der Orientation von Augen und Kopf im Raume 1952, Hypothalamic Control Anterior Pituitary (with others) 1962, The Cerebellum as a Neuronal Machine (with others) 1967, Functional Anatomy 1971, Atlas of Human Anatomy 1946-75; author numerous articles. *Leisure interests:* water colour sketching, scientific illustration, gardening. *Address:* Tüzoltó u. 58, Budapest 1450, Hungary. *Telephone:* 138-806; 567-280.

SZIJÁRTÓ, Károly, DR.; Hungarian lawyer; b. 26 Jan. 1927, Székesfehérvár; s. of Károly Szijártó and Magdolna Langmár; m. Magdolna Gerber 1949; one s. one d.; ed. Budapest Univ. of Political and Legal Sciences; joined Hungarian CP 1945; Pres. Budapest Mil. Court of Law 1965-71; Vice-Pres. Hungarian Supreme Court 1971-75; Chief Public Prosecutor 1975-. *Address:* Office of the Chief Public Prosecutor, Budapest, V. Markó utca 16, P.O. Box 438, Hungary. *Telephone:* 316-150.

SZILBEREKY, Jenő; Hungarian lawyer; b. 1917, Lugos; ed. Szeged Univ. of Legal and Political Sciences; junior law practitioner, Dist. courts of Tiszafüred and Szeged; apptd. judge at Szeged court 1948; staff mem. Ministry of Justice 1950; helped to set up Chief Public Prosecutor's Office 1953; apptd. group leader, Deputy Chief of Attorney's Dept.; rejoined Ministry of Justice, apptd. Deputy Minister 1962; Sec. of State 1978; Pres. Hungarian Supreme Court of Justice 1980-; Univ. Prof. 1960-; Pres. Hungarian Soc. for the Aid of Industrial Rights 1968-80; Co-Pres. Fed. of Tech. and Natural Science Socs.; foundation mem. Hungarian Civil Servants' Trade Union; Order of Merit of Socialist Hungary, Gold Medal of Labour Order of Merit (twice). *Address:* Supreme Court of the Hungarian People's Republic, Budapest, V., Markó utca 16. 1363, Hungary. *Telephone:* 324-934.

SZLACHCIC, Franciszek, M.ENG.; Polish politician; b. 5 Feb. 1920, Byczyno, near Chrzanów; m. Bronisława Wałach 1945; one s. one d.; ed. Acad. of Mining and Metallurgy, Cracow; fmr. miner; mem. People's Guard and People's Army during occupation; mem. Polish Workers' Party 1943-48; mem. Polish United Workers' Party (PZPR) 1948-, deputy mem. Cen. Cttee. 1964-68, mem. 1968-75, Sec. Cen. Cttee. 1971-74, mem. Political Bureau 1971-75; Deputy Minister of Home Affairs 1962-71, Minister Feb.-Dec. 1971; mem. Council of State 1972-74; Deputy Chair. Council of Ministers 1974-76; Deputy to Sejm 1972-76; Pres. Polish Cttee. for Standardization, Measures and Quality Control 1976-86; Order of Banner of Labour (1st and 2nd Class), Grunwald Cross (3rd Class), Cross of Valour, Medal of 30th Anniversary of People's Poland 1974, Order of October Revolution (U.S.S.R.), Order of Red Banner (U.S.S.R.), and others. *Leisure interests:* hunting, reading, tennis. *Address:* c/o ul. Szarotki 11A, 02-609, Poland.

SZLACHTA, Jan, M.ENG.; Polish politician; b. 1940, Siersza, Katowice Voivodship; ed. Acad. of Mining and Metallurgy, Cracow; worked at Wujek Colliery, Katowice 1963-65; mining supervisor, then Chief Eng., Makoszowy Colliery, Zabrze 1965-75; Gen. Dir., Knurów Colliery, Knurów 1975-82; Dir., Coal-Mines Union, Zabrze 1982-84; Gen. Dir., Zabrze Miners' Guild, Zabrze 1984-86; Under-Sec. of State, Ministry of Mining and Power

Industry May-Sept. 1986, Minister of Mining and Power Industry 1986-87; mem. Polish United Workers' Party (PZPR); Kt's Cross of Order of Polonia Restituta, Order of Banner of Labour (2nd Class) and other decorations.

SZLETYŃSKI, Henryk; Polish theatre actor and director; b. 27 Feb. 1903, Homel; s. of Zofia Szletyński and Maksymilian Szletyński; m. Zofia Tymowska 1928; ed. Philosophical Faculty of Warsaw Univ.; actor in Rozmaitości Theatre, Warsaw 1923-24; actor and literary Man. Stefan Jaracz Ateneum Theatre, Warsaw 1930-31; actor and dir., Miejski Theatre, Łódź 1931-37, municipal theatres, Lvov 1937-38, Polish Army Theatre, Łódź 1945-49, Narodowy (Nat.) Theatre, Warsaw 1959-73; Man. Dir. and Artistic Man., State Lower Silesian Theatres, Wrocław 1949-50, drama theatres, Cracow 1950-54, Juliusz Słowacki Theatre, Cracow 1954-55, Powszechny Theatre, Warsaw 1955-56; Lecturer, Faculty of Acting and Faculty of Directing of State Higher School of Drama, Warsaw 1946-49, 1955-73, Ordinary Prof. 1957, Dean, Faculty of Acting 1947-48, mem. Senate 1965-70, Prof. Emer. 1973; Head, Theatre History and Theory Research Centre and mem. Scientific Council of Art Inst. of Polish Acad. of Sciences (fmrly. State Art Inst.), Warsaw 1955-61; mem. Art Sciences Cttee. of Polish Acad. of Sciences 1955-61; mem. Comité Executif FIA 1963-65; Chair. Theatre Section and mem. Presidium Higher Artistic Educational Council of Ministry of Culture and Art 1967-73; founder mem. SPATiF-ZASP Polish Theatre and Film Artists Assçn. 1950-82, Pres. Gen. Bd. 1959-61, 1963-65; Pres. Gen. Bd., Union of Polish Stage Artists (ZASP) 1983-85, Hon. Pres. 1985-; mem. Société Européenne de Culture (SEC) 1986-; mem. Polish Workers' Party (PPR) 1943-48, Polish United Workers' Party (PZPR) 1948-; Deputy Chair. Culture and Art Comm. of PZPR Warsaw Cttee. 1958-64, Nat. Council of Culture, Cttee. of Nat. Prizes; City of Warsaw Prize 1985; Commdr.'s Cross with Star, Officer's Cross of Order of Polonia Restituta, Order of Banner of Labour (2nd Class), (1st Class) 1988, Medal of 40th Anniversary of People's Poland and other decorations. *Theatre roles include:* Chamberlain in Pan Jowialski (Fredro), Grabiec in Balladyna (Słowacki), President in Wolves at Night (Rittner), Wilkosz in Little Quail Has Flown (Żeromski), Euripides in The Frogs, Polonius in Hamlet, Malvolio in Twelfth Night, Engstrand in Ghosts; *has directed* Vengeance (Fredro), Fantazy (Słowacki), Legenda (Wyspiański), Rose (Żecromski), Summer at Nohant (Iwaszkiewicz) and Antigone, Richard II, Mizantrop, Yegor Bulichev, Port Royal and others; *Publications include:* Szkice o aktorach (Essays on Actors) 1975, Prawidłowe mówienie (Correct Speaking) (co-author) 1975, Szkice o teatrze (Essays on Theatre) 1979, Gawędy z czasów młodości (Tales from Young Days) 1979, Kształtowanie się nowoczesnej sztuki aktorskiej w Polsce (Formation of Modern Acting in Poland) 1981, Sylwety i wspominki 1984, Stefana Jaracza wzloty i zabłądzenia 1984, Opowiesc o Leonie Schillere (Story about Leon Schiller) 1987. *Leisure interests:* reading, travel. *Address:* ul. Poznańska 23 m.5, 00-685 Warsaw, Poland. *Telephone:* 21-84-74 (Home).

SZMAJDZIŃSKI, Jerzy, M.ECON.SCI; Polish youth leader; b. 9 April 1952; s. of Henryk and Helena Szmajdziński; ed. Econ. Acad., Wrocław; mem. of school org. of Socialist Youth Union (ZMS) 1968; during studies held managerial posts in Socialist Union of Polish Students, including Chair. of Acad. Council, Econ. Acad., Wrocław; mem. Polish Socialist Youth Union (ZSMP), Deputy Chair. of ZSMP Voivodship Bd., Wrocław 1977-81, Sec. and mem. of Presidium of ZSMP Gen. Bd. Feb. 1981-, Chair. ZSMP Gen. Bd. 1984-; mem. Polish United Workers' Party (PZPR) 1973-, mem. PZPR Cen. Cttee. 1986-; Deputy to Sejm 1985-; Chair. Cttee. of Young Deputies to Sejm; mem. Presidium Polish Olympic Cttee., Presidium of State Cttee. for Physical Culture and Sports. *Leisure interests:* sports, basketball, football. *Address:* Zarząd Główny ZSMP, ul. Smolna 40, 00-920 Warsaw, Poland. *Telephone:* 26-28-17.

SZOKA, H.E. Cardinal Edmund Casimir; American ecclesiastic; b. 14 Sept. 1927, Grand Rapids; ordained 1954, elected to Gaylord 1971, consecrated bishop of Detroit 1971, prefect 1981; cr. Cardinal 1988. *Address:* 1234 Washington Boulevard, Detroit, Mich. 48226, U.S.A. *Telephone:* (313) 237-5816.

SZOKOLAY, Sándor; Hungarian composer; b. 30 March 1931, Kunágota; s. of Bálint Szokolay and Erzsébet Holecska; m. 1st Sári Szesztay 1952, 2nd Maja Weltler 1970; four s. one d.; ed. Bekestharos Music High School, Budapest Music Acad.; currently musical adviser Hungarian TV; Chair. Hungarian Kodály Soc.; has won prizes in Warsaw, Moscow, Vienna, Merited Artist Distinction 1976, Honoured Artist Distinction 1986, Bartok-Pasztory Prize 1987. *Works include:* Blood Wedding (opera) 1963, Hamlet (opera) 1968, Az iszonyat balladája (The Ballad of Horror), Tetemrehivás (Ordeal of the Bier), Samson (opera) 1973, Csalóka Péter (children's opera, text by Sándor Weöres q.v.) 1985, Ecce Homo (opera) 1986, Ecce Hamo (passion-opera) 1987; Oratorios: A tüz márciusa (March Fire), Istár pokoljárása (Ishtar's Descent to Hell); has also written cantatas, songs, chamber music and choral works. *Leisure interests:* car driving, mountaineering. *Address:* 1112 Budapest, Hegyalja ut 70, Hungary. *Telephone:* 846-328.

SZŐLLŐSY, András, D.PH.; Hungarian composer and music historian; b. 27 Feb. 1921, Szászváros; s. of János Szőllősy and Julia Tóth; m. Éva Keményfy 1944; ed. Univ. of Budapest; studied composition, Music Acad., Budapest, under Zoltán Kodály, Accademia di Santa Cecilia, Rome, under Goffredo Petrassi; Prof. of History and Theory of Music, Liszt Ferenc Music Acad., Budapest 1950-; top qualifier, UNESCO Prize, Tribune Int.

des Compositeurs, Paris 1970, Merited Artist title 1974, Outstanding Artist 1982, Kossuth Prize 1985, Bartok-Pasztory Prize 1986; Commandeur, Ordre des Arts et Lettres 1987. *Compositions include:* Oly korban éltem (Improvisation of Fear) (ballet) 1963; orchestral works: five Concertos, Musica per Orchestra 1972, Trasfigurazioni 1972, Musica Concertante 1973, Preludio, Adagio e Fuga 1973, Sonorita 1974, Musiche Per Ottoni 1975, Concerto for Harpsichord and Strings 1979, Pro Somno Igoris Stravinsky Quieto 1979, Fabula Phaedri for vocal ensemble 1982 (composed for the King's Singers), In Phariseos (for choir) 1982, Tristia (for strings) 1983, Planctus Mariae (for female choir) 1983, Suoni di tromba 1984, Miserere (composed for the King's Singers) 1985, Fragments 1985, Quartetto di Tombau 1986, Paesaggio Con Morti (for piano), Canto d'autunno (for orchestra) 1986; Due Paesaggi (for piano) 1987, String Quartet 1988; songs; incidental music for plays and films. *Publications:* Kodály művészete 1943, Honegger 1960, 1980; Ed. writings of Kodály and Bartók. *Address:* 1118 Budapest, Somlói ut 12, Hungary. *Telephone:* 660-035.

SZŐNYI, Erzsébet; Hungarian musician; b. 25 April 1924; d. of Jenő Szőnyi and Erzsébet Piszanoff; m. Dr. Lajos Gémes 1948; two s.; ed. Music Acad. Budapest and Paris Conservatoire; Teacher of music at a Budapest grammar school 1945-48, Music Acad. Budapest 1948-; leading Prof. Music Acad. 1960-81; Vice-Pres. Int. Soc. for Music Educ. 1970-74; Co-Chair. Hungarian Kodály Soc. 1978-; Gen. adviser of methodology, Int. Kodály Soc. 1979-; mem. Chopin Soc. of Warsaw, Liszt Soc. of Hungary; Erkel Prize 1959. *Works:* Concerto for Organ and Orchestra; symphonic works: Musica Festiva, Divertimento 1 and 2, Prelude and Fugue, Three Ideas in Four Movements; operas: Tragedy of Firenze, A Gay Lament, Break of Transmission, Elfrida (madrigal opera) 1987-, several children's operas; chamber music, oratorios, vocal compositions, etc. *Publications:* Methods of Musical Reading and Writing, Kodály's Principles in Practice, Travels on Five Continents, Twentieth Century Music Methods. *Leisure interests:* gardening, cooking. *Address:* Ormódi-utca 13, 1124 Budapest XII, Hungary. *Telephone:* 567-329.

SZOPA, Jerzy, M.SC.; Polish engineer and politician; b. 29 Jan. 1930, Piotrków Trybunalski; s. of Stefan and Genowefa Szopa; m. Zofia Szopa 1952; one s. one d.; ed. State Nautical School and Gdańsk Technical Univ.; Stoker, then Officer, on cargo ships; Chief Mechanic, then Tech. Man., Polish Ocean Lines; Under-Sec. of State, Ministry of Shipping 1965-69; Minister of Shipping 1969-73; mem. Polish United Workers' Party (PZPR); mem. Cen. Cttee. 1971-75; Deputy Sec.-Gen. COMECON, Moscow 1974-82; Vice-Chair. Polish Chamber of Foreign Trade (PIHZ) 1983-; Order of Banner of Labour (2nd Class) 1969. *Address:* Polska Izba Handlu Zagranicznego, ul. Trębacka 4, 00-074 Warsaw, Poland. *Telephone:* 26-00-17.

SZOSLAND, Janusz, D.TECH.SC.; Polish textile engineer; b. 16 Jan. 1925, Łódź; s. of Wacław Szosland and Halina (née Szmidt) Szosland; m. 1st 1950 (wife deceased); m. 2nd 1986; two s.; ed. Łódź Polytechnic; mem. staff Łódź Tech. Univ. 1950-, Asst., Lecturer, then Asst. Prof. 1950-73, Extraordinary Prof. 1973-86, Ordinary Prof. 1986-, Dean, Textile Faculty 1969-75, Head, Weaving Dept. 1967-70, Dir., Inst. of Mechanical Tech. of Fibres 1970-; lecturer, Częstochowa Tech. Univ. 1952-55, Higher State School of Fine Arts, Łódź 1957-60; mem. Presidium Seym Socio-Econ. Council 1986-; mem. Consultative Council attached to Chair. of State Council 1986-; Vice-Pres. Polish Textile Assen. 1956-74, Pres. 1974-; Chair., Main Council of Polish Fed. of Eng. Assen. 1982-; Dr. h.c., Moscow Textile Inst. 1979; Chair. numerous scientific councils; Hon. mem. Textilipari Muszaki es Tudomanyos Egyesulet 1978; Commdr.'s Knight's and Officer's Cross Order of Polonia Restituta, Nat. Educ. Comm. Medal, Meritorius Teacher of Polish People's Repub. and numerous other Polish awards. *Publications:* numerous books and articles in Polish and foreign professional journals. *Leisure interests:* long-distance running, photography, technical vocabulary. *Address:* ul. Harcerska 5 m. 25, 91-710 Łódź, Poland. *Telephone:* 36-32-74 (Office); 57-80-05 (Home).

SZÜRÖS, Mátyás; Hungarian politician; b. 11 Sept. 1933, Püspökladány; studied at Moscow Univ. Inst. of Int. Relations 1953-59; on staff of Foreign Ministry 1959-65; staff mem. 1965-74; Deputy Leader Foreign Dept. of HSWP Cen. Cttee. 1974-75, Head 1982-83; Amb. to G.D.R. 1975-78, to U.S.S.R. 1978-82; mem. Cen. Cttee. HSWP 1978-, Secr. 1983-89; Chair.

Foreign Relations Parl. Cttee. 1985-; Pres. of Parl. March 1989-; Labour Order of Merit 1975, People's Friendship Order (U.S.S.R.) 1982. *Publication:* Hazánk és a nagyvilág (Homeland and World) 1985, Hazánk és Európa (Homeland and Europe) 1987. *Address:* Hungarian Socialist Workers' Party, Central Committee, 1358 Budapest, Széchenyi rakpart 19, Hungary. *Telephone:* 111-400.

SZYDLAK, Jan; Polish politician; b. 24 Nov. 1925, Siemianowice, Silesia; ed. Party School, Cen. Cttee., Polish United Workers' Party (PZPR), Warsaw; mem. Katowice Voivodship Cttee., Polish Workers' Party (PPR) 1947-48; Vice-Chair. Voivodship Bd., Polish Youth Union, Kielce 1948, subsequently in Szczecin; mem. Polish Socialist Workers' Party (PZPR) 1948-81; Head, Propaganda Dept., PZPR Voivodship Cttee., Katowice 1951, Sec. 1952-54; Sec. Cen. Bd. of Polish Youth Union 1954-56; Sec. PZPR Voivodship Cttee., Katowice 1957-60; First Sec. PZPR Voivodship Cttee., Poznań 1960-68; mem. Cen. Cttee. PZPR 1964-80, Sec. Cen. Cttee. PZPR 1968-77; deputy mem. Politburo 1968-70, mem. Politburo 1970-80; Deputy to Sejm 1961-80; mem. Presidium All-Poland Cttee. of Nat. Unity Front 1970-81; Chair. Cen. Bd. of Polish-Soviet Friendship Soc. 1971-80, Party-State Comm. on Econ. Modernization 1971-80; Deputy Chair. Council of Ministers 1976-80; Deputy Chair. Council for Family Affairs attached to the Council of Ministers 1978-80; Chair. Cen. Council of Trade Unions Feb.-Aug. 1980; interned Dec. 1981-Dec. 1982; Order of Banner of Labour (1st and 2nd Class), Commdr., Cross of Polonia Restituta.

SZYMAŃSKI, Władysław, D.ECON. SCI.; Polish economist and politician; b. 18 March 1941, Gorlice, Nowy Sącz Voivodship; ed. Main School of Planning and Statistics, Warsaw; during studies active in Rural Youth Union 1960-63; mem. United Peasant Party (ZSL) 1963-; fmr. Pres. ZSL Circle of Main School of Planning and Statistics, Warsaw; scientific worker of Main School of Planning and Statistics, Warsaw 1964-, Asst., Sr. Asst., then Lecturer 1964-79, Asst. Prof. 1979-, Pro-Dean 1980-87, Dean 1987-, Faculty of Production Econs.; Ed. monthly "Wieś Współczesna" 1974-77; Adviser to Pres. of ZSL Chief Cttee. 1977-, subsequently Head Advisers' Team attached to Presidium of ZSL Chief Cttee.; alt. mem. ZSL Chief Cttee. April-Dec. 1980, mem. 1980-88; mem. Presidium of ZSL Chief Cttee. 1980-81, mem. Secr. of ZSL Chief Cttee. 1980-84; Deputy to Sejm (Parl.) 1985-; mem. Council of State Nov. 1985-; Kt.'s Cross of Order of Polonia Restituta, Gold Cross of Merit and other decorations. *Publications:* numerous works on econs., mainly on econs. of agric. *Address:* Kancelaria Rady Państwa, ul. Wiejska 4/6, 00-902 Warsaw, Poland (Office).

SZYMBORSKA, Wisława; Polish poet, translator and literary critic; b. 2 July 1923, Prowent-Bnin near Poznań; m.; ed. Jagiellonian Univ., Cracow; first work published 1945; mem. Polish Writers' Assen. 1952-83, mem. Gen. Bd. 1978-83; mem. Editorial Staff Życie Literackie (weekly) 1953-; Gold Cross of Merit 1955, Kt.'s Cross, Order of Polonia Restituta 1974. *Publications:* poetry: Dlatego żyjemy 1952, Wołanie do Yeti 1957, Sól 1962, Sto pociech 1967, Poezje 1970, Wszelki wypadek 1972, Wybór wierszy (Selected Poems) 1973, Wielka liczba 1976. *Address:* Ul. 18 Stycznia 82/89, 30-079 Cracow, Poland.

SZYR, Eugeniusz; Polish economist and politician (retd.); b. 16 April 1915, Łodygowice, Żywiec Dist.; m.; one d.; mem. Union of Polish Communist Youth 1930-34, later Polish CP 1934-36; Spanish Civil War 1937-39; prisoner in concentration camps in France and Algeria 1940-43; Polish Army, U.S.S.R. 1944; Under-Sec. of State in Ministry of Industry and Commerce 1946-49; Deputy Chair. State Comm. for Econ. Planning 1949-53, Chair. 1954-56; Sec. of Econ. Cttee., Council of Ministers 1957-59, Vice-Chair. 1959-69; Vice-Pres. Council of Ministers 1959-72; Chair. Cttee. of Science and Tech. 1963-68; Chair. Polish Cttee. for Solidarity with Nations of Africa and Asia 1965-; mem. Cen. Cttee. Polish United Workers' Party 1948-81; mem. Politburo 1964-68; Deputy to Seym 1952-56, 1961-68, 1972-76; Vice-Chair. Chief Council of Union of Fighters for Freedom and Democracy (ZBoWiD) 1948-; Chair. State Council of Economy of Materials 1972-76; Minister of Economy of Materials 1976-81; Vice-Chair. Cttee. for Research on Asia, Africa and Latin America of Polish Acad. of Sciences 1985-; Chair. Polish-African Soc. for Friendship 1982-; Grunwald Cross (2nd Class) 1949, Order of Banner of Labour (1st Class) 1950 and 1964, Order of Builders of People's Poland 1974. *Address:* Polski Kamitet Solidarnósci z Narodami Azji i Afryki, ul. Rajcow 10, 00-220 Warsaw, Poland.

T

TABAI, The Hon. Ieremia T., C.M.G.; Kiribati politician; b. 1950, Nonouti; m.; two c.; ed. King George V School, Tarawa, St. Andrew's Coll., Christchurch, N.Z., Victoria Univ., Wellington, N.Z.; mem. Gilbert Islands House of Ass. 1974–; fmr. Leader of the Opposition; Chief Minister of the Gilbert Islands 1978–79, also Minister of Local Govt.; Pres. of Kiribati and Minister of Foreign Affairs (fmrly. Gilbert Islands) July 1979–. *Address:* Office of the President, Tarawa, Kiribati.

TABAKOV, Oleg Pavlovich; Soviet stage and film actor; b. 17 Aug. 1935; ed. Moscow Arts Theatre Studio-School; acted with Sovremennik Theatre 1957–83; with Moscow Arts Theatre 1983–; film debut 1957; mem. CPSU 1965; U.S.S.R. State Prize for acting 1967. *Film roles include:* Viktor Bulygin in People on the Bridge 1960, Kolya Babushkin in Greenhorn 1963, Krutikov in the Living and the Dead 1964, Usievich in The Heart of Russia 1971, Komarovsky's father in Decline 1977, Nikolai Pavlovich in Flights of Fancy 1983. *Address:* Moscow Arts Theatre (MXAT), Proezd Khadozhestvennogo teatra, Moscow, U.S.S.R.

TABARLY, Eric Marcel Guy; French marine officer and competitive sailor; b. 24 July 1931, Nantes; s. of Guy Tabarly and Yvonne Pogam; ed. Coll. St.-Charles, St. Brieuc, Ecole Navale; served to rank of Lieut. 1966; at Ministry of Youth and Sport 1964–71; Insp. of Sailing Ecole des Sports Interarmes, Fontainebleau 1971–; winner of numerous races in his yachts Pen Duick I–VI ('Blue Tit with Black Head') including Transatlantic Plymouth–Newport race 1964, Morgan Cup 1967, Gotland Round, Channel Race, Fastnet, Plymouth–La Rochelle 1967, Solo Transpacific 1969, Los Angeles–Tahiti 1972, Solo Plymouth–Newport Transatlantic 1976; Transatlantic Speed Record 1980; Solo Transatlantic, fourth place 1984; Captain, Frégate 1982; Officier, Légion d'honneur, Ordre nat. du Mérite, du Mérite maritime. *Publications include:* Victoire en solitaire 1964, De Pen Duick en Pen Duick 1970, Du Tour du monde à la Transat 1976, Guide Pratique de manoeuvre 1978, Histoire d'un record, l'Atlantique en 10 jours 1981, Embarqué avec Eric Tabarly (jtly.) 1982. *Leisure interest:* tennis. *Address:* 5 boulevard de Lesseps, 78000 Versailles (Office); Boite Postale 13, 29118 Benodet, France (Home).

TABATONI, Pierre, DR.ECON.; French academic; b. 9 Feb. 1923, Cannes; s. of Joseph and Rose (née Altavelle) Tabatoni; m. Jacqueline Ferrat 1949; two s.; ed. Lycée de Cannes, Faculties of Letters and Law, Aix-en-Provence, London School of Econs., Harvard Univ.; Assoc. Prof. Univs. of Algiers and Aix-en-Provence 1950–54; Prof. Aix-Marseilles Univ., Dir. of Inst. of Business Admin. 1954–61; Prof. Univ. of Paris 1961–, Pres. Univ. Paris IX 1968; Counsellor for Highr Educ., Ministry of Educ. 1969–73; Dir. of Cultural Affairs, French Embassy, Washington, D.C. 1973–75; Dir. CAB; Minister of Univs.; Dir. for Int. Univ. Relations, Ministry of Univs. 1975–79; Rector of Acad. 1980–82; Chancellor of Paris Univs.; Pres. CERPEM (Center for Man. Process); Vice-Pres. European Inst. for Man. Research, Partner Semametra–Strategie Financière; Dr. h.c. (Brussels, Waseda Univ. (Tokyo); Chevalier, Légion d'honneur, Commdr., Palmes académiques, Commdr., Ordre Nat. (Ivory Coast), Commdr., Ordre Mérite (Fed. Repub. of Germany); Commdr. Ordre de Léopold (Belgium). *Publications:* Etudes sur l'incidence des impôts 1950, Economics of Financial Institutions (co-author) 1963, Policy and Structures in Management Systems (co-author) 1975, Problems of European Management of Enterprises (Platt Report, OECD) 1960, The Enterprise in Financial Revolution 1988. *Leisure interest:* sailing. *Address:* 33 rue Lhomond, 75005 Paris, France. *Telephone:* 43314196.

TABEYEV, Fikhryat Akhmedzhanovich, CAND.ECON.SC.; Soviet official and diplomatist; b. 1928, Kazan; ed. Kazan Univ.; mem. CPSU 1951–; kolkhoz worker and student 1945–51; Lecturer, Asst. Prof. of Political Econ., Kazan Univ. 1951–57; Deputy head of Tartar Dist. CPSU 1957–59; Deputy to Presidium of U.S.S.R. Supreme Soviet 1958–62, mem. 1962–80; First Sec. of Tartar Dist. CPSU Cttee. 1960–79; mem. of Cen. Cttee. of CPSU 1961–; Amb. to Afghanistan 1979–86; First Deputy-Pres. of RSFSR Council of Ministers 1986–. *Address:* c/o Ministry of Foreign Affairs, Smolenskaya-Sennaya 32-34, Moscow, U.S.S.R.

TABONE, Anton, M.P.; Maltese politician; b. 1937; m. Margerite Stivala; three s.; ed. St. Aloysius Coll.; employee, Nat. Bank of Malta 1955–66; mem. Parl. for Gozo 1966–; mem. Gozo Civic Council 1966–73; Minister for Gozo 1987–; Nationalist Party. *Address:* House of Representatives, Valletta, Malta.

TABONE, Vincent, M.D., D.O., D.O.M.S., D.M.J., F.R.C.S., M.P.; Maltese ophthalmic specialist and politician; b. 30 March 1913, Victoria, Gozo; m. Maria Wirth 1941; three s. five d.; ed. St. Aloysius Coll., Univ. of Malta and Univ. of Oxford; served Royal Malta Artillery during World War II; has held sr. ophthalmic posts in various hosps. in Malta; mem. Exec. Cttee. Nationalist Party 1961, Sec.-Gen. 1962–72, First Deputy Leader 1972–77, Pres. 1978–85; mem. Parl. 1966–; Minister of Labour, Employment and Welfare 1966, of Foreign Affairs 1987–89; Pres. of Repub. of Malta April 1989–. *Address:* Office of the President, The Palace, Valletta, Malta. *Telephone:* 221221.

TABOR, David, B.SC., PH.D., SC.D., F.R.S., F.INST.P.; British physicist; b. 23 Oct. 1913, London; s. of Charles Tabor and Rebecca Weinstein; m. Hannalene Stillschweig 1943; two s.; ed. Royal Coll. of Science, London, Cambridge Univ.; Tribophysics, CSIRO, Melbourne, Australia 1940–46; Asst. Dir. of Research, Cambridge Univ. 1946–61, Lecturer in Physics 1961–64, Reader 1964–73, Prof. 1973–81, Emer. Prof. 1981–, Head of Physics and Chem. of Solids, Cavendish Lab. 1969–81; Visiting Prof. Imperial Coll., London 1981–; Fellow of Gonville and Caius Coll., Cambridge 1957–; Int. Fellow, Stanford Research Inst. 1956; UNESCO Visiting Prof., Israel 1961; Russell Springer Visiting Prof. Univ. of Calif., Berkeley 1970; Hon. D.Sc. (Bath Univ.) 1985; Nat. Award, American Soc. for Lubrication Engineers 1955, Wilson Award, American Soc. of Metals 1969, Inaugural Gold Medal for Tribology, Inst. of Mechanical Engineers 1972, Mayo D. Hersey Award, American Soc. of Mechanical Engineers 1974, Guthrie Medal, Inst. of Physics 1974. *Publications:* Hardness of Metals 1951, Gases, Liquids and Solids 1969 (new edn. 1979); (with F. P. Bowden) Friction and Lubrication of Solids, Part I 1950, 1986, Part II 1964, Friction—an Introduction to Tribology 1973; contributions to learned journals on friction and adhesion. *Address:* 8 Rutherford Road, Cambridge, CB2 2HH, England. *Telephone:* (0223) 337200 (Office); (0223) 841336 (Home).

TABOR, Hans, DR.RER.POL.; Danish diplomatist; b. 25 April 1922, Copenhagen; s. of S. Rasmussen; m. Inger Petersen 1945; two d.; ed. Birkerød Statsskole and Univ. of Copenhagen; Sec., Gen. Secr. OEEC, Paris 1948–50; Sec. Ministry of Foreign Affairs, Copenhagen 1950–52; Asst. Head Danish del. to OEEC 1952–56; Branch Head Ministry of Foreign Affairs 1956, 1957–59; Deputy Sec.-Gen. Suez Canal Users' Asscn., London 1957; Econ. Counsellor, Asst. Head Danish Mission to the European Communities 1959–61, Minister and Head 1961–64, Amb. 1963–64; Perm. Rep. to the UN 1964–67; Minister of Foreign Affairs 1967–68; Rep. of Denmark on the UN Security Council 1967–68; Amb. to Italy (also accred. to Malta) 1968–74, to Norway Feb. 1986–; Perm. Rep. to UN 1974; Amb. to Canada 1975–79; Amb. and Perm. Rep. at OECD 1979–86; Chair. OECD Exec. Cttee. 1983. *Publications:* Danmark og Marshallplanen (Denmark and the Marshall Plan) 1961, De Seks og det økonomiske samarbejde i Vesten (The Six and Economic Co-operation in the Western World) Krig og Krise—Trods FN (War and Crisis—in spite of the United Nations). *Leisure interests:* tennis, swimming, reading. *Address:* Embassy of Denmark, Villaveien 31, N-0371, Oslo, Norway.

TACHI, Ryuichiro; Japanese professor of economics; b. 11 Sept. 1921, Yokohama; m. Yoko Shinmei 1951; two s.; ed. Univ. of Tokyo; Assoc. Prof. of Econs., Univ. of Tokyo 1950–61, Prof. 1961–82, Emer. Prof. 1982–, Dean Faculty of Econs. 1972, Vice-Pres. 1979–81; Prof. of Econs., Aoyama Gakuin Univ. 1984–; Chief Counsellor Inst. for Monetary and Econ. Studies, Bank of Japan 1982–; Dir. Inst. of Public Finance 1982–84; Pres. Japan Soc. of Monetary Econs. 1982–88, Inst. of Fiscal and Monetary Policy, Ministry of Finance 1985–; mem. Japan Acad. 1986–. *Address:* 2-6-20 Kamiosaki, Shinagawa-ku, Tokyo 141, Japan. *Telephone:* (03) 441 0558.

TADESSE, Tesfaye, M.A.; Ethiopian diplomatist; b. 11 Nov. 1943, Kaffa Region; s. of G. Hiywot Tadesse and Adera Boyalech; m. Zewditu Tesfuye 1974; one s. one d.; ed. Ithaca Coll., New York and Michigan State Univ.; Producer and Programmer, Lutheran World Broadcasting Service 1963–64; Founder and Pres. Ethiopian Journalists' Asscn.; Man. Asst., Head of Public Relations, Agricultural and Industrial Devt. Bank 1971–74; Dept. Head, Radio Ethiopia 1974–75; Perm. Sec., Ministry of Information and Nat. Guidance 1975–76; mem. Cen. Cttee. Worker's Party of Ethiopia 1984–86; Ed.-in-Chief Sertoader 1984–86; Perm. Rep. of Ethiopia to the UN 1986–; Amb. to Canada 1988–; Chair. UN Special Cttee. on Decolonization Feb. 1987–; mem. UN Security Council Jan 1989–. *Leisure interests:* swimming, tennis, travel, hiking. *Address:* Permanent Mission of Ethiopia to the United Nations, 866 United Nations Plaza, Room 560, New York 10017, U.S.A. *Telephone:* 421-1830.

TAFT, Robert, Jr.; American politician; b. 26 Feb. 1917, Cincinnati; s. of Robert A. Taft and Martha Bowers; m. 1st Blanca Noel 1939 (deceased), two s. two d.; m. 2nd Joan McKelvy 1978; ed. Yale and Harvard Univs.; U.S.N.R. 1942–46; partner, Taft, Stettinius & Hollister, Cincinnati 1951–56, 1977–87, of Counsel 1987–; mem. Ohio House of Reps. 1955–62, Majority Floor Leader 1961–62; mem. U.S. House of Reps. 1963–64, 1967–70, mem. Cttees. on Banking and Currency, Educ. and Labor, Foreign Affairs; House Republican Leadership 1969–70; Senator from Ohio 1971–76, mem. Cttees. on Labor and Public Welfare, Armed Services, Banking and Currency, Jt. Econ. Cttee.; mem. American, Ohio, Federal, Cincinnati Bar Asscns.; Trustee, Population Crisis Cttee., The Draper Fund; Republican. *Address:* 1620 I Street, N.W., Washington, D.C. 20006 (Office); 1800 First National Bank Center, Cincinnati, Ohio 45202 (Office); 4300 Drake Road, Cincinnati, Ohio 45243, U.S.A. (Home).

TAFT, William Howard, IV; American lawyer and government official; b. 13 Sept. 1945, Washington; s. of William Howard and Barbara Hoult Bradfield; m. Julia Vadala 1974; one s. two d.; ed. Yale and Harvard

Univs.; Assoc. Winthrop, Stimson, Putnam & Roberts, New York City 1969-70; Adviser to Chair. FTC, Washington 1970; Prin. Asst. to Deputy Dir. of The Office of Man. and The Budget, Washington 1970-72, Exec. Asst. to Dir. 1972-73; Exec. Asst. to Sec. HEW 1973-76, Gen. Counsel 1976-77; Partner Leva, Hawes, Symington, Martin & Oppenheimer 1977-81; Gen. Counsel, The Pentagon 1984-89; Perm. Rep. (desig.) to NATO March 1989-. *Address:* Permanent Representative of the United States, North Atlantic Treaty Organisation, 1110 Brussels, Belgium.

TAGAWA, Seiichi, Japanese journalist and politician; b. 1919; fmrly. worked for Asahi Shimbun (newspaper); fmr. mem. Liberal Democratic Party; elected Deputy to House of Reps. from second constituency of Kanagawa Pref. (nine times); fmr. Parl. Vice-Minister of Science and Tech., of Health and Welfare, fmr. Chair. House of Reps. Social and Labour Cttee.; later joined New Liberal Club Party; Minister of Home Affairs Jan.-Nov. 1984; f. and Leader Progressive Party Jan. 1989-. *Address:* Progressive Party, Shinpoto, 2-2-1, Marunouchi, Chiyoda-ku, Tokyo, Japan.

TAHA, Mohammed Fathi; Egyptian meteorologist; b. 15 Jan. 1914, Cairo; m. 1948; ed. Cairo Univ. and Imperial Coll. of Science and Tech., London; Under-Sec. of State and Chair. Bd. of Dirs. Egyptian Meteorological Authority 1953-76; Meteorological Counsellor to Ministry of Civil Aviation 1976-83; Vice-Pres. Int. Meteorological Org. (IMO) Cttee. for Africa 1947, Int. Aeronautical Fed. (IAF) 1965; mem. WMO Exec. Cttee. 1955-81, Second Vice-Pres. 1959-69, Pres. 1971-79; Pres. Perm. Meteorological Cttee. of Arab League Org. 1971-77; Chair. Nat. Cttee. on Geodesy and Geophysics 1967-75; mem. Outer Space Exploration Cttee. for Peaceful Uses; mem. Nat. Cttee. Int. Council of Scientific Unions, Cttee. of High-level Policy on Civil Aviation and many other nat. cttees. dealing with scientific research in Egypt; First Order of Merit 1977, First Order of Science and Arts 1981, IMO Prize 1983. *Address:* 64 Elkalifa el Maamoun Street, Cairo, Egypt. *Telephone:* 2574788.

TAHER, Abdul Hadi, PH.D.; Saudi Arabian government official; b. 1930, Medina; ed. Ain Shams Univ., Cairo, and Univ. of Calif.; entered Saudi Arabian Govt. service 1955; Dir.-Gen. Ministry of Petroleum and Mineral Resources 1960; Gov., Gen. Petroleum and Mineral Org. (PETROMIN), Riyadh 1962-86; Man. Dir. Saudi Arabian Fertilizers Co. (SAFCO) 1966-76, Jeddah Oil Refinery 1970-; Chair. Arab Maritime Petroleum Transport Co. -1981; Dir. Arabian American Oil Co. (ARAMCO), Saudi Govt. Railways Corpn.; Trustee, Coll. of Petroleum and Minerals; mem. Industrial Research and Devt. Center, Saudi Arabia; Hon. mem. American Soc. of Petroleum Engineers. *Publications:* Income Determination in the International Petroleum Industry 1966, Development and Petroleum Strategies in Saudi Arabia (Arabic) 1970, Energy—A Global Outlook 1981; lectures and papers on economic and petroleum affairs. *Address:* c/o General Petroleum and Mineral Organization (PETROMIN), P.O. Box 757, Riyadh, Saudi Arabia.

TAHIR, Achmad; Indonesian politician; b. 27 June 1924, Kisaran, N. Sumatra Prov.; s. of Achmad Tahir and Siti Kalsum; m. Rooslila Achmad Tahir 1947; four s. two d.; ed. Jayabaya Univ. and mil. training courses in Indonesia and U.S.A.; various army command and staff appts. 1943-56; Mil. Attaché, Rome 1956-60; Instr. Army Staff and Command Coll. 1960-62; joined Theatre Army Commdr. for liberation of W. Irian 1962-63; Chief of Staff of Mil. Gov. of E. Indonesia 1962-63; Acting Chair. Telecommunications Council and mem. Auxiliary Conf. on Nat. Planning 1963-66; Gov. Armed Forces Acad. Magelang 1966-68; Dept. of Defence and Security 1968-69; Commdr. Defence Territory 1/Sumatra 1969-73; Amb. to France 1973-76, to Spain 1973-75; Sec.-Gen. Dept. of Communications 1976-83; Minister of Tourism, Posts and Telecommunications 1983-88; Chair. Nat. Telecommunication Council 1983-; Chair. Indonesian Tourism Devt. Bd. 1983-; mem. Consultative People's Congress 1983-; Vice-Chair. Int. Independent Comm. for Worldwide Telecommunication Devt., ITU 1983-: Chair. Indonesian Veterans Legion 1979-. *Leisure interests:* sports, swimming, football, golf, tennis, bowling. *Address:* 3 Jalan Gondangdia Lama, Jakarta Pusat, Indonesia (Home). *Telephone:* (021) 344342 (Home).

TÄHKÄMAA, Taisto Toivo Johannes; Finnish politician and agrologist; b. 11 Dec. 1924, Parainen; s. of Toivo Oskar Rudolf Tähkämaa and Laina Siviä Engblom; m. Riita-Leena Kokolahti 1961; two d.; Consultant, Dist. beet growing 1954-56; State Office, Turku 1956-64; Head, Primary Production Devt. Dept., S.W. Finland Co-operative Abattoir 1964-70; M.P. 1970-; Minister of Defence 1977-79, of Agric. and Forestry 1979-83; mem. Centre Party. *Address:* c/o Ministry of Agriculture and Forestry, Hallituskatu 3, 00170 Helsinki 17, Finland. *Telephone:* 1601.

TAILLARD, Willy Francis, M.D., PH.D.; Swiss orthopaedic surgeon; b. 15 March 1924, Geneva; s. of Emile Taillard and Marthe Girardin; m. Claude Labruhe 1952; four s. one d.; ed. Coll. of Calvin, Geneva, Univ. of Geneva; surgeon, Univ. Hosp., Geneva 1948-50, French Hosp., London, U.K. 1950-51, Balgrist Univ. Clinic 1952-57; Chief, Univ. Orthopaedic Clinic, Basle 1957-63; Prof. of Orthopaedic Surgery, Univ. of Basle 1960-63, Univ. of Geneva 1963-; Dir. Orthopaedic Clinic, Univ. Hosp., Geneva 1963-; hon. mem. various scientific socs. *Publications:* Les Spondylousthesis 1958, Beinl Ängenunterschiede 1965; numerous articles in scientific and medical journals. *Leisure interests:* mountaineering, aeronautics. *Address:* Ortho-

paedic Clinic, Hopital Cantonal Universitaire, Boulevard de la Cluse, Geneva, Switzerland. *Telephone:* 22.71.00.

TAILLIBERT, Roger René; French architect; b. 21 Jan. 1926, Châtres-sur-Cher; s. of Gaston Taillibert and Melina Benoit; m. Béatrice Pfister 1965; one d.; ed. Schools in Toulouse, Castres, Dreux, Argenton-sur-Creuse, Tours and Ecole Nat. des Beaux-Arts, Paris; own practice 1963-; Curator Grand Palais des Champs-Elysées 1977-82, of Palais de Chaillot 1982-. *Main works:* Olympic Complex (Parc des Sports, indoor sports hall, swimming pool), Montreal, Canada; Olympic swimming pool, Luxembourg; Nat. Geographic Centre, Amman, Jordan; Officers' Club, Abu Dhabi, U.A.E.; sports complex, Baghdad, Guest's Palace, Bahrain, univ. bldgs., Sousse, Gabès, Tunisia, sports facilities, Cameroon, sports and golf club houses, Yamoussoukro and Abidjan, Côte d'Ivoire; in France: School of Pharmacy, Toulouse, Coca Cola plant, Grigny, pharmaceutical lab. P. Fabre, Castres, DAF plant, Survilliers, skiing and mountaineering nat. school, Chamonix, Parc des Princes stadium, Paris, Nat. Inst. for Sports and Physical Educ., Paris, pre-Olympic centre, Font-Romeu, nuclear plants Penly and Civaux; studies for projects in Iraq and Lebanon; feasibility studies for projects in Argentina and Uruguay (hotels, sports facilities, leisure parks, etc.).; mem. Acad. d'architecture 1974-; mem. Acad. des Beaux-Arts, Inst. de France, Académie des Sports, Royal Soc. of Arts; Officier, Légion d'honneur, Commdr., ordre nat. du Mérite, Officier des Palmes Académiques, Officier des Arts et des Lettres. *Publications:* Montreal—Jeux Olympiques 1976, Construire l'avenir 1977, Roger Taillibert (autobiog.) 1978. *Leisure interests:* photography, music, painting. *Address:* 163 rue de la Pompe, 75116 Paris, France. *Telephone:* 47.04.29.92.

TAIPALE, Mrs. Vappu Tuulikki, D.M.; Finnish psychiatrist and politician; b. 1 May 1940, Vaasa; m.; two s. two d.; Psychiatrist, Aurora Youth Polyclinic 1970-74; Pediatric Clinic 1975-79; Asst. Prof. of Child Psychiatry, Kuopio Univ. 1980-83, Tampere Univ. 1983-; First Minister of Social Affairs and Health July 1982-May 1983, Second Minister 1983-84; Dir.-Gen. Nat. Bd. of Social Welfare Nov. 1984-; mem. SDP. *Address:* National Board of Social Welfare, Siltsaarenkatu 18, 00530 Helsinki 53, Finland. *Telephone:* 7319202

TAIT, James Francis, PH.D., F.R.S.; British-American scientist; b. 1 Dec. 1925, Stockton-on-Tees; s. of H. Tait and C. L. Brotherton; m. Sylvia A. S. Wardropper 1956; ed. Univ. of Leeds; lecturer in Medical Physics, Middx. Hospital Medical School 1947-57, Joel Prof. of Medical Physics 1970-82, Dir. Biophysical Endocrinology Unit 1970-85; External Scientific Staff, MRC 1955-58; Prof. Emer., Univ. of London 1982-; Sr. Scientist, Worcester Foundation, U.S.A. 1958-70; Reichstein Award, Int. Soc. of Endocrinology 1976; Hon. D.Sc. (Hull) 1979; CIBA Award, American Heart Assoc. for Hypertension Research 1977, Dale Medal, Soc. for Endocrinology 1979. *Publications:* numerous papers on medical physics and endocrinology. *Leisure interests:* gardening, walking. *Address:* Moorlands, Main Road, East Boldre, nr. Brockenhurst, Hants., SO42 7WT, England. *Telephone:* (059) 065-312.

TAITT, Branford Mayhew, LL.B., M.P.A.; Barbados politician; b. 15 May 1938; m. Marjorie C. Taitt; one s. two d.; ed. Univ. of West Indies, New York Univ. and Brooklyn Coll., New York; Cable and Wireless 1954-62; Conf. Officer, UN Secr. 1962-65; U.S. Rep. Barbados Industrial Devt. Corpn. 1965-67; mem. Barbados del. to UN 1966-71; Consul-Gen. of Barbados, New York 1967-71; mem. Barbados Senate 1971-76; fmr. Minister of Trade, Industry and Commerce, of Tourism and Industry 1986-88, of Health Oct. 1988-; Pres. Democratic Labour Party 1978-84; fmr. part-time Lecturer in Law, Univ. of W. Indies, Cave Hill, Barbados and visiting or guest lecturer and univs. and colls in U.S.A. *Publications:* over 200 articles in newspapers and periodicals. *Address:* Ministry of Health, Jemmott's Lane, St. Michael, Barbados (Office); 10 Stanmore Crescent, Black Rock, St. Michael, Barbados (Home). *Telephone:* 426-5080.

TAITTINGER, Jean; French vintner and politician; b. 25 Jan. 1923, Paris; s. of Pierre Taittinger; m. Marie Corinne Deville 1948; three s. two d.; Deputy for Marne, Nat. Assembly 1958-73; Mayor of Rheims 1959-77; Nat. Sec. UNR-UDT (Union Démocratique du Travail) 1967; mem. Exec. Office and Nat. Treas. UDR Feb.-Oct. 1968, Deputy Sec.-Gen. 1974-76; Vice-Pres. Finance Comm. of Nat. Assembly 1967-68, Pres. 1968-71; Sec. of State, Ministry of Finance and Econ. Affairs 1971-73; Minister of Justice 1973-74; Minister of State for Justice March-May 1974; Chair Imprimerie Union Républicaine 1960-, Soc. du Louvre 1977, Soc. des Hôtels Concorde 1978, Cofidev 1979, Société Deville 1979, Société Hôtelière Martinez 1981, Banque Privée de Dépôt et de Crédit 1987; Vice-Chair. Société Taittinger 1947-, Société Hôtelière Lutetia Concorde 1980; Dir. Banque de l'Union Occidentale 1976-85, Banque Worms 1978-82, Establissements V.Q. Petersen 1979-84; Pres. Dir.-Gen. Banque du Louvre 1989-; Dir. Gen. Compagnie Financière Taittinger 1989-. *Address:* 58 boulevard Gouvion, Saint-Cyr, 75017 Paris, France. *Telephone:* 47.58.11.60.

TAKATORI, Osamu; Japanese politician; b. June 1929, Niigata Pref.; m.; two s. one d.; ed. Univ. of Tokyo; mem. House of Reps. 1969-; Parl. Vice-Chair. of Finance 1976; Minister of State, Dir.-Gen. Man. and Co-ordination Agency 1987-88; fmr. Chair. House Standing Cttee. on Judical Affairs and Local Admin.; Liberal-Democratic Party. *Leisure interests:* sport, music. *Address:* Kudan Shukusha, 2-14-3 Fujimi, Chiyoda-ku, Tokyo 102, Japan.

TAKEDA, Yutaka; Japanese steel industry executive; b. 6 Jan. 1914, Tokyo; s. of Tadashi Takeda and Yuriya Takeda; m. Teruyo Ito 1948; one s.; ed. Univ. of Tokyo; joined Japan Iron and Steel Co. Ltd. 1939; Dir. Fuji Iron and Steel Co. Ltd. 1965, Man. Dir. 1967, Sr. Man. Dir. 1970; Sr. Man. Dir. Nippon Steel Corpn. 1970, Exec. Vice-Pres. 1977, Rep. Dir. and Pres. 1981–87, Chair. 1987; Chair. The Japan Iron and Steel Fed. 1984–, Int. Iron and Steel Inst. 1983–85; Vice-Chair. Japan Fed. of Econ. Orgs. 1986; Order of the Sacred Treasure (First Class). *Leisure interests:* Kyudo, Go and fishing. *Address:* 31-8, Hanegi 1-chome, Setagaya-ku, Tokyo, Japan.

TAKEIRI, Yoshikatsu; Japanese politician; b. 10 Jan. 1926, Nagano Prefecture; m. Kiku Takeiri 1951; one s. two d.; ed. Inst. of Politics (Seiji Daigakko); with Japan Nat. Railways 1948–59; Bunkyo Ward Assembly, Tokyo 1959; Tokyo Metropolitan Ass. 1963–67; Vice-Sec.-Gen. Komeito (Clean Govt.) Party 1964–67, Chair. 1967–86, Supreme Adviser 1986–; mem. House of Reps. 1967–. *Leisure interests:* movies, fishing. *Address:* 17 Minami-Motomachi, Shinjuku-ku, Tokyo 160, Japan. *Telephone:* 353-0111.

TAKEMI, Taro; Japanese physician; b. 7 March 1904, Kyoto; m. Eiko Akizuki 1941; two s. two d.; ed. Keio Univ. School of Medicine; Pioneer in study of medical application of nuclear physics; mem. team measuring radioactivity of atomic bomb, Hiroshima 1945; built the first portable electro-cardiograph 1937; invented the vectorcardiograph 1939; also patented the method of extracting chlorophyll and the mfg. process for pentose nucleotide; Asst., Keio Univ. Hosp. 1930–37; Inst. of Physical and Chemical Research 1938–50; Takemi Clinic 1939–; now also Visiting Prof. at Keio, Kitasato and Tokai Univs.; Vice-Pres. Japan Medical Asscn. 1950, Pres. 1957–82; Pres. World Medical Asscn. 1975–76; also of Japan-Latin America Medical Asscn. and Japan-Italy Medical Asscn.; Vice-Pres. Japan-WHO Asscn.; Adviser, Nat. Cancer Centre; Trustee, Japan Cancer Soc., Princess Takamatsu Cancer Research Fund; Auditor, Nishina Memorial Foundation, Waksman Foundation; Pres. Keio Univ. Medical School Alumni Asscn.; Commdr., Order of Merit (Italy) 1963, Cultural Gold Medal (Italy) 1964, Award for Cultural Merit (Italy) 1964, Silver Medal from Pope Paul VI 1966, Diploma from Lisbon Univ. 1968, Gold Medal from Milan Univ. 1967, from Italian Tuberculosis Soc. 1968, Medal of Grand Distinction from Brazilian Acad. of Mil. Medicine 1972, Grand Cross of Honour of Fed. German Order of Merit 1974, Order of Rising Sun (First Class) 1975, Special Cravat of Order of Brilliant Star (Taiwan) 1976, Nat. Order of Southern Cross (Brazil) 1976, Hon. K.B.E. 1977, Grande Ufficiale nell'Ordine (Italy), Civil Merit Mu Gung Hua Medal (Repub. of Korea), The Golden Heart Presidential Award (Philippines). *Publications:* An Epigram on Medical Affairs, My Memoirs, numerous papers. *Address:* c/o Seishokan 2, Ginza 4-chome, Chuo-ku, Tokyo 106; 48-8, Moto-Azabu 3-chome, Minato-ku, Tokyo 104, Japan (Home). *Telephone:* 03-401 2439 (Home).

TAKESHITA, Noboru; Japanese politician; b. 26 Feb. 1924; m.; three d.; ed. School of Commerce, Waseda Univ.; Jr. High School Teacher; elected to Shimane Prefectural Ass. (two terms) 1951; mem. House of Reps. 1958–, Parl. Vice-Minister for Int. Trade and Industry 1963–64; Deputy Chief Cabinet Sec. 1964–65, Chief Cabinet Sec. 1971–72, Nov.–Dec. 1974; Minister of Construction 1976; Chair. Budget Cttee. of House of Reps. 1978–79; Minister of Finance 1979–80, 1982–86; Chair. Diet Policy Cttee., Nat. Org. Cttee. of Liberal Democratic Party (LDP), Standing Cttee. on Budget, House of Reps. 1978; Sec.-Gen. LDP 1986–87; Pres. 1987–; Prime Minister of Japan 1987–89; Chair. B. of Govs. IMF and World Bank 1984, Group of Ten 1985; Hon. LL.D. (Columbia) 1986. *Publications:* six books including Waga michi o yuku (Seeking after the path) 1979, Magokoro no seiji (Honest Politics) 1983, Subarashi kuni Nihon (Wonderful Japan) 1987. *Leisure interests:* judo (holds 5th dan), golf, reading, fine arts (especially Japanese-style painting), yachting. *Address:* Liberal Democratic Party, 11-23 Nagata-cho, 1-chome, Chiyoda-ku, Tokyo; 3-5-9 Daisawa, Setagaya-ku, Tokyo, Japan (Home).

TAKLA, Philippe; Lebanese politician and banker; b. 3 Feb. 1915; ed. Univ. Law School, Beirut; Law practice, Beirut 1935–45; M.P. 1945, 1947–; Minister of Nat. Economy and Communications 1945–46; Minister of Foreign Affairs 1949, 1961–63, 1964–65, 1966; Gov. Bank of Lebanon 1963–66, 1966–67; Perm. Rep. to UN 1967–68; Amb. to France 1968–71; Minister of Foreign Affairs 1974–76, also of Educ. and Planning 1975–76. *Address:* Rue Maarad, Beirut, Lebanon.

TAKRITI, Saddam Hussein (see Hussein, Saddam).

TALAAT, Ahmed Samih, M.L.; Egyptian lawyer and politician; b. 23 Nov. 1920, Cairo; s. of Abd-el-Wahab Pacha Talaat and Hamida Hilmy; m. Nazly el-Chourbagy 1955; two s.; ed. Elsaideyha Secondary School, Faculty of Law; began career as Asst. Prosecutor 1942–51; Judge 1951–58; Deputy of Court 1958–59; Chief of Court 1959–63; Counsellor at Appeal Court 1963–67; Gen. Lawyer 1967–69; expelled from office 1969; reinstated as counsellor for Court of Cassation (Supreme Court) 1972; Supreme Counsel, Union Supreme Court, United Arab Emirates 1973–76; Minister of Justice, Egypt 1976–78; resgnd. 1978; mem. Shoura Ass. Oct. 1980; lawyer and law consultant, farmer 1978–; decorations include Kuwait Badge of Honour (First Class) 1977. *Leisure interests:* rowing, reading, farming. *Address:* 321 El-Ahram Street, Guiza, Cairo, Egypt. *Telephone:* 851730, 853116.

TALAL IBN ABDUL AZIZ, H.R.H. Prince; Saudi Arabian politician and international official; b. 1934; s. of the late King Abdul Aziz ibn Saud; ed. Prince's School, Royal Palace, Riyadh; positions held in his early 20s include responsibility for the Royal Palaces, Minister of Communications; fmr. Minister of Economy and Finance; fmr. Amb. to France; f. Riyadh's first girls' school, first pvt. hosp. and Mecca's first coll. for boys; passport cancelled 1962; exile in Egypt; returned to Saudi Arabia 1964; fmr. Special Envoy, UNICEF; now Pres. Arab Gulf Programme for UN Devt. Orgs. "AGFUND". *Leisure interests:* history, amateur radio, swimming. *Address:* 26 Avenue de Friedland, 75008 Paris, France. *Telephone:* 43 80 22 97.

TALBOT, Frederick Hilborn, S.T.M.; Guyanese diplomatist; b. 13 Oct. 1927, Mahaicony, East Coast Demerara; m. Sylvia Ross; ed. Allen Univ., South Carolina, Yale Univ. and Pacific School of Religion, Calif.; Pastor, St. Peter's A.M.E. Church, Georgetown 1961–71; Caribbean Consultant of Church World Service; Chair. Guyana Council of Churches; mem. World Methodist Org., Bd. of Poor Law Commrs. of Guyana, Govt. Hospitals Cttee., etc.; Perm. Rep. to UN 1971–73; Amb. to U.S.A. 1973–75; High Commr. to Canada 1973–74, to Jamaica (also accred. to Barbados, the Dominican Republic and Grenada) 1975–82; hon. degrees from Wilberforce Univ., Payne, Edward Waters and Monrovia Colls. *Address:* c/o Ministry of Foreign Affairs, Georgetown, Guyana.

TALBOT, Godfrey Walker, L.V.O., O.B.E.; British author and broadcaster; b. 8 Oct. 1908; s. of Frank Talbot and Kate Bertha Talbot; m. Bess Owen 1933; one s.; ed. Leeds Grammar School; with Yorkshire Post 1928; ed. Manchester City News 1932–34; editorial staff Daily Dispatch 1934–37; joined BBC 1937; war correspondent for BBC 1941–45 (despatches); Chief Reporter, BBC Home Reporting Unit; Sr. News Reporter and Commentator on staff of BBC 1946–69; official BBC observer accred. to Buckingham Palace 1948–69; Pres. Queen's English Soc.; Deputy Chair. Royal Overseas League. *Publications:* Speaking from the Desert 1944, Ten Seconds from Now 1973; Queen Elizabeth the Queen Mother 1973, Permission to Speak 1976, Royal Heritage 1977, The Country Life Book of Queen Elizabeth the Queen Mother 1978, The Country Life Book of the Royal Family 1980, and numerous articles on the British Monarchy. *Leisure interest:* keeping quiet. *Address:* Holmwell, Hook Hill, Sanderstead, Surrey, England.

TALBOYS, Rt. Hon. Brian Edward, P.C., C.H.; New Zealand farmer and former politician; b. 7 June 1921, Wanganui; s. of F. P. Talboys; m. P. F. Adamson 1950; two s.; ed. Wanganui Collegiate School, Univ. of Manitoba, Canada, Victoria Univ., Wellington; served R.N.Z.A.F. in Second World War; joined N.Z. Dairy Exporter 1950, later Asst. Ed.; has 500-acre farm, Heddon Bush, Southland; M.P. 1957–81; Parl. Under-Sec. to Minister of Trade and Industry 1960–62; Minister of Agric. 1962–69, of Educ. 1969–72, of Science 1964–72; Minister of Trade and Industry and Minister of Overseas Trade Feb.-Dec. 1972; Deputy Prime Minister, Minister of Foreign Affairs and Minister of Overseas Trade 1975–81, of Nat. Devt. 1975–77; mem. Nat. Party, Deputy Leader 1974–81; Chair. Bd. Indosuez New Zealand Ltd. 1982–, Genestock N.Z. 1983–, Ericsson Communications 1983–; Dir. Sedgwick Group N.Z. 1984–; Hon. D.Sc. (Massey Univ.) 1980, Hon. D.Litt. (Chung-Ang Univ., Seoul) 1981; Hon. A.C. 1982. *Address:* Parliament House, Wellington; 1 Hamilton Avenue, Winton, New Zealand (Home). *Telephone:* 533 (Home).

TALEYARKHAN, Homi J. H., B.A.; Indian politician; b. 9 Feb. 1917, Bombay; s. of Jehangir and Tehmina Taleyarkhan; m. Padma Sri Thrity Rustomjee Lichmore; one s.; ed. Univ. of Bombay, King's Coll., London, Lincoln's Inn, London; mem. Bombay Municipal Corpn. and Chair. Works Cttee. 1948–52; mem. Maharashtra State Legis. Ass. 1952–71; Gen. Sec. Congress Legis. Party, Chief Whip and Cabinet Minister, Maharashtra 1952–67 (consecutively Minister of Health, Family Planning, Food, Civil Supplies, Housing, Tourism, Nat. Savings, Fisheries and Printing Presses); Amb. to Libya 1971–77; Chair. Maharashtra State Financial Corpn.; Gov. Sikkim State 1981–84; Amb. to Italy 1984–85; mem. Minorities Comm., Govt. of India 1985–; del. to UNCTAD II, Delhi; Chair. Nat. Savings Re-organization Cttee., Land Re-organization Cttee., Govt. of India; mem. Small Family Norms Cttee., All India Congress Cttee.; Vice-Pres. Maharashtra State Congress Cttee.; Dir. Shipping Corpn. of India; Vice-Pres. Indian Council of Foreign Trade; mem. Working Cttee., All India Mfrs. Org., Exec. Cttee., Asscn. of Industries, Eng. Asscn., Nat. Productivity Council, Maharashtra State Industries Advisory Cttee., State High-Power Co-ordination Cttee.; Chair. Maharashtra branch, World Ass. of Small and Medium Enterprises (Delhi). *Publications:* I Have It from Gandhiji, They Told Me So, Hyderabad and Her Destiny, United India in Australia, In the Land of the Blue Hills, Three Graces of Kashmir, Roads to Beauty around Bombay, Village Welfare on the Way, Community Projects in India, Escape from the City, Splendour of Sikkim, Environment and Forestry in Economic Development, numerous papers and pamphlets. *Leisure interests:* reading, writing, riding, tennis, dogs, walking, trekking, driving. *Address:* Minorities Commission, Lok Nayak Bharan, Khan Market, New Delhi 110003, India. *Telephone:* 623710 (Delhi Office); 697142 (Delhi Home); 4928667 (Bombay).

TALHOUNI, Bahjat, LL.B.; Jordanian politician; b. 1913, Ma'an; ed. Damascus Univ.; Lawyer 1936–38; Judge, Kerak 1938–52; Pres. Court of

Appeals 1952–53; Minister of Interior 1953, of Justice 1953–54; Chief Royal Cabinet 1954–60, 1963–64, June–Aug. 1969, 1973–74; Prime Minister 1960–62, 1964–65, 1967–70, concurrently Minister of Foreign Affairs 1967–68, of Defence 1968–69, of Interior April–Sept. 1968; mem. Senate 1962–, Pres. of Senate Dec. 1974–83; Personal Rep. of H.M. King Hussein 1967–69; mem. Consultative Council 1967; Pres. Cttee. for Preparation of Civil Law 1971; Trustee, Jordan Univ. 1962–. *Address:* P.O. Box 72, Amman, Jordan.

TALIB, Maj.-Gen. Naji; Iraqi soldier and politician; b. 1917; ed. Iraqi Staff Coll., and Sandhurst, England; Mil. Attaché, London 1954–55; Commdr. Basra Garrison 1957–58; Minister of Social Affairs 1958–59; lived abroad 1959–62; Minister of Industry 1963–64; mem. U.A.R.-Iraq Jt. Presidency Council 1964–65; Minister of Foreign Affairs 1964–65; Prime Minister and Minister of Petroleum Affairs 1966–67. *Address:* Baghdad, Iraq.

TALLBOYS, Richard Gilbert, C.M.G., O.B.E., LL.B.; Australian business executive; b. 25 April 1931, England; s. of H. Tallboys; m. Margaret Evelyn Strutt 1954; two s. two d.; ed. Palmers School, Univ. of Tasmania, Univ.of London; Apprentice to 2nd Mate British and Australasian Ships 1947–55; accountant 1955–62; Dir. Nat. Heart Foundation, Australia 1959–62; Govt. Trade Commr. 1962–68; joined British Diplomatic Service 1968; Consul Gen., Houston 1980–85; Amb. to Vietnam 1985–87; C.E.O. World Coal Inst. Oct. 1988–; Freeman City of London 1985; Assoc. Fellow Australian Inst. of Export 1988. *Publication:* Doing Business with Indonesia 1968. *Leisure interests:* skiing, opera, ballet. *Address:* 7 Chapel Side, Bayswater, London, W1 4LG, England; 5/14 Henrietta Street, Double Bay, Sydney 2028, Australia. *Telephone:* 01-727 2441; 327 6834.

TALLCHIEF, Marjorie; American ballerina; b. 1927; m. George Skibine 1947 (died 1981); two s.; ed. Beverly Hills High School, Calif.; daughter of the Chief of the Osages Indians; studied with Bronislava Nijinska; joined American Ballet Theatre; *created role of:* Medusa in Undertow; Prima Ballerina, Ballet de Monte Carlo 1948, American Ballet Theater 1960; *created leading roles in:* Somnambula, Concerto Barrocco, Les Biches, Boléro, Idylle, Prisoner of the Caucasus and Annabel Lee; Première Danseuse Etoile, Paris Opera 1957–; *leading roles in:* The Firebird, Les Noces Fantastiques, Giselle, Conte Cruel, Concerto and numerous other ballets; Prima Ballerina, Hamburg State Opera 1965–; Chevalier du Nicham-Iftikar.

TALLING, John Francis, PH.D., F.R.S.; British freshwater biologist; b. 23 March 1929, Grange Town; s. of Frank and Miriam Talling; m. Ida Bjornsson 1959; two c; ed. Sir William Turner's School, Coatham, Yorks., Univ. of Leeds and Univ. of London; Lecturer in Botany, Univ. of Khartoum 1953–56; Postdoctoral Fellow, Univ. of Calif. 1957; Biologist, Freshwater Biological Assocn., England 1958–. *Publications:* about 60 scientific papers. *Leisure interests:* walking, archaeology. *Address:* Freshwater Biological Association, Ambleside, Cumbria, England. *Telephone:* (09662) dr.sc.nat.2468.

TALMI, Igal, DR.SC.NAT.; Israeli professor of physics; b. 31 Jan. 1925, Kiev, U.S.S.R.; s. of Moshe Talmi and Lea (née Weinstein) Talmi; m. Chana (née Kivelewitz) Talmi 1949; one s. one d.; ed. Herzlia High School, Hebrew Univ. of Jerusalem and Swiss Fed. Inst. of Tech.; served in Israeli Defence Forces 1947–49; Research Fellow Princeton Univ. 1952–54, Visiting Assoc. Prof. 1956–57, Visiting Prof. 1961–62, 1966–67; Prof. of Physics, Weizmann Inst. of Science 1958–, Head Dept. of Nuclear Physics 1967–76, Dean Faculty of Physics 1970–84; mem. Israel Acad. of Sciences and Humanities 1963–, Chair. Div. of Sciences 1974–80; Weizmann Prize of the Tel Aviv Municipality 1962, Israel Prize (with A. de Shalit) 1965, Rothschild Prize 1971. *Publications:* Nuclear Shell Theory (with A. de Shalit) 1963, numerous publs. on theoretical nuclear physics. *Leisure interest:* bird watching. *Address:* Department of Nuclear Physics, The Weizmann Institute of Science, Rehovot 76100, Israel (Work). *Telephone:* (8) 482060 (Work); (8) 483521 (Home).

TALÜ, Naim; Turkish banker and politician; b. 22 July 1919, Istanbul; s. of Havva Mirat and Mehmet Nizamettin; m. Gevher Erdoğan 1946; two d.; ed. Faculty of Economics, Istanbul Univ.; joined Türkiye Cumhuriyet Merkez Bankasi (Cen. Bank of Repub. of Turkey) 1946, Chief 1952, Asst. Dir. of Ankara Branch 1955–58, Dir. of Exchange Dept. 1958–62, Asst. Gen. Dir. 1962–66, Acting Pres. and Gen. Dir. 1966–67, Pres. and Gen. Dir. 1967–70, Chair. Bd. and Gov. 1970–71; Chair. Foreign Investment Encouragement Cttee. 1967–68; Chair. Banks Assocn. of Turkey 1967–71; Sec.-Gen. Cttee. for Regulation of Bank Credits 1967–70; Minister of Commerce 1971–73; Prime Minister April 1973–Jan. 1974; mem. Senate 1972–76; Chair. Akbank T.A.S., Akçimento Ticaret A.S., Olmuk Mukvva San. ve Tic. A.S., April 1976–; mem. Political and Social Studies Foundation 1980–. *Leisure interests:* playing bridge, sailing, swimming, tennis. *Address:* Akbank T.A.S., Fındıklı, Istanbul, Turkey. *Telephone:* 1494122.

TALVELA, Martti Olavi; Finnish opera and concert singer; b. 4 Feb. 1935, Hiitola; s. of Toivo and Nelly Talvela; m. Anna Kääriäinen 1957; one s. two d.; teacher Lahti Music High School 1958; Royal Opera House, Stockholm 1961–62; performances at Deutsche Oper, Berlin 1962–, Staatsoper, Hamburg, Vienna, Munich, Royal Opera, Covent Garden, Metropolitan Opera, New York, La Scala, Milan, also in Rome, San Francisco, Tokyo, Bayreuth, Salzburg 1962–; Artistic Dir. Savonlinna Opera Festival, Finland 1972–; has made numerous recordings, television appearances; Pro

Finlandia 1973; Finnish State Prize 1973. *Leisure interests:* music, books, fishing. *Address:* Herbert H. Breslin Inc., 119 W. 57th Street, New York, N.Y. 10019, U.S.A.

TALYZIN, Nikolai Vladimirovich; Soviet politician; b. 28 Jan. 1929, Moscow; ed. Moscow Electrotechnical Inst. of Communications; electrician and technician-constructor 1944; engineer, chief constructor, Sr. scientist and Deputy Dir. of Scientific Research Inst. 1955–65; Deputy Minister for Communications 1965–75, Minister 1975–80; a Vice-Chair. Council of Ministers 1980–85, Oct. 1988–, First Deputy Chair. 1985–88, Deputy Chair., responsible for Relations with Comecon Oct. 1988–; Chair. State Planning Cttee. 1985–88; Cand. mem. Cen. Cttee. of CPSU, mem. 1986–; Deputy to the Supreme Soviet of the U.S.S.R. (10th session); Chair. Cen. Bd. U.S.S.R.-Finland Soc.; Dr. and Prof. of Tech. Sciences; Laureate of State. *Address:* c/o Council of Ministers, The Kremlin, Moscow, U.S.S.R.

TAMAGNINI, Giulio; Italian diplomatist; b. 24 July 1921, Milan; s. of Egidio and Giulia Girogetti; m. Maria R. Torrealba 1950 (separated 1980); wife died 1987); one s. two d.; ed. Beccaria Classical High School, Milan, Coll. Ghisleri, Pavia and Univs. of Pavia and Paris; joined Italian foreign service 1948; served in Egypt, U.K., Yugoslavia and Rome 1950–64; Counsellor, Italian Del. to NATO 1964–69; Minister-Counsellor, Moscow 1969–73, Washington, D.C. 1974–77; Amb. to Iran 1978–80, to People's Repub. of China 1980–83; Head, Italian Dels. to CSCE conferences in Ottawa, Budapest, Berne 1984–86; Prof. of Diplomacy, School of Political Science, Univ. of Pavia 1987–88; Croce di guerra (twice); Cavaliere di Gran Croce. *Leisure interests:* tennis, bridge. *Address:* Via Minucio Felice 1, 00136 Rome, Italy. *Telephone:* 358 6777.

TAMAMES GOMEZ, Ramón, LL.D., D.ECON.; Spanish professor of economics; b. 1 Nov. 1933, Madrid; s. of Manuel Tamames, M.D. and Carmen Tamames; m. Carmen Prieto 1960; one s. two d.; ed. French Lycée, Madrid, Univ. of Madrid, London School of Econs.; Services Dir., Ministry of Commerce 1957–59; Full Prof., Univ. of Granada 1968, Univ. Autónoma de Madrid 1975–; lectures and courses at Univs. of Mexico, Venezuela, Santo Domingo, Bologna, Rome, Marseilles, Berlin (Free Univ.), Brussels (Free Univ.), Sydney, Harvard; mem. Communist Party of Spain 1956–81; mem. Exec. Comm. July 1976–; M.P. for Madrid prov. 1977–; Deputy Mayor of Madrid 1979–81; founder, Progressive Fed. 1981; imprisoned several times for political opinions; United Left M.P. 1986–. *Publications:* 30 books incl. Introduction to the Economy of Spain, Economic Structure of Spain 1960, International Economic Structure 1971, The Spanish Republic and the Era of Franco 1973, Ecology and Development 1977, The Future and the Nation 1981, The European Common Market: A Guide 1986, The Spanish Economy: An Introduction 1986. *Leisure interests:* painting, swimming. *Address:* Santísima Trinidad 5, 28010 Madrid, Spain. *Telephone:* (91) 4461100.

TAMBO, Oliver; South African politician; b. 1917; ed. Anglican mission schools and Univ. Coll. of Fort Hare, Cape Province; Teacher, Secondary School; Solicitor, Johannesburg, 1951–60; banned from attending meetings 1954–56 and for five years 1959–64; arrested on treason charges 1956, charges withdrawn 1957; Deputy Pres. African Nat. Congress 1958–67, Acting Pres. 1967, Pres. 1977–; escaped to London 1960; mem. del. of exiled reps. of S. African parties to Third Conf. of Ind. African States, Addis Ababa 1960; attended UN Gen. Ass. (15th Session) 1960; Head, External Mission of African Nat. Congress of South Africa. *Publication:* Preparing for Power (speeches) 1987. *Address:* African National Congress of South Africa, P.O. Box 2239, Dar es Salaam, Tanzania; 28 Penton Street, London N.1, England. *Telephone:* 28031 (Tanzania); 01-837 2012 (England).

TAMM, Ditlev, DR.JUR., DR.PHIL.; Danish professor of legal history; b. 7 March 1946, Copenhagen; s. of Henrik Tamm and Lizzie Knutzen; m. Maria Pilar Lorenzo 1973 (separated 1987); two d.; ed. Univ. of Copenhagen and in Germany and France; Prof. of Legal History, Univ. of Copenhagen 1978–; mem. Royal Danish Acad.. and several other Danish and int. scientific bds. and cttees.; A.S. Orsted Award 1974. *Publications:* Fra lovkyndighed til retsvidenskab 1976, Retsopgøret efter besaettelsen 1984; several minor books and articles on Danish and European legal history. *Address:* 13 Svanemøllevej, 2100 Copenhagen Ø, Denmark. *Telephone:* 01-299392; 01-912166.

TAMM, Igor, M.D.; American professor and physician; b. 27 April 1922, Tapa, Estonia; s. of Alexander Tamm and Olga Tamm; m. Olive E. Pitkin 1953; one s. two d.; ed. Tartu Univ., Estonia, Karolinska Inst., Stockholm, Sweden and Yale Univ. School of Medicine; Intern and Asst. Resident, Grace-New Haven Community Hosp. Univ. Service 1947–49; Asst. in Medicine, Yale Univ. School of Medicine, New Haven, Conn. 1947–49; Asst. and Asst. Physician, The Rockefeller Inst., New York 1949–53, Assoc. and Assoc. Physician 1953–56, Assoc. Prof. and Assoc. Physician 1956–58, Assoc. Prof. and Physician 1958–64; Prof. and Sr. Physician, The Rockefeller Univ., New York 1964–86, Abby Rockefeller Mauzé Prof. and Sr. Physician 1986–; Alfred Benzon Prize 1967, Sarah L. Poiley Award, New York Acad. of Sciences 1977. *Publications:* scientific papers on biology of viruses and cells, Symposium on Viruses, American Journal of Medicine 1965 (Ed.), Viral and Rickettsial Infections of Man 1964 (Co-Ed.). *Address:* The Rockefeller University, 1230 York Avenue, New York, N.Y. 10021 (Office); 450 East 63rd Street, New York, N.Y. 10021, U.S.A. (Home).

TAMM, Peter; German publisher; b. 12 May 1928, Hamburg; s. of Emil Tamm; m. Ursula Weisshun 1958; one s. four d.; ed. Univ. of Hamburg; Shipping Ed., Hamburger Abendblatt 1948-58; Man. Dir. Ullstein GmbH (Publr.) 1960-62, 1984; Man. Dir. BILDzeitung 1962-64; Dir., Verlagshaus Axel Springer, Berlin 1964-70, mem. Exec. Bd. 1970-82, Chair. Man. Bd. 1982-; Vice-Pres. Bundesverband Deutscher Zeitungsverleger 1980-; Bayerischer Verdienstorden. *Publication:* Maler der See 1980. *Leisure interests:* model ships, marine books. *Address:* Kochstrasse 50, 1000 Berlin 61, Federal Republic of Germany. *Telephone:* (030) 2591-0.

TAMURA, Hajime; Japanese politician; b. May 1924, Mie Pref.; m.; one d.; elected to House of Reps. 12 times 1955-; Parl. Vice-Minister of Construction 1960, of Labour 1962; Chair., House of Reps. Cttee. on Construction 1966, Cttee. on Finance 1968; Chair. Liberal Democratic Party (LDP) Public Relations Cttee. 1971; Minister of Labour 1972, of Transport 1976; Chair. House of Reps. Cttee. on Budget 1980; Chair. LDP Nat. Org. Cttee. 1980, LDP Diet Policy Cttee. 1981, Research Comm. on Party's Fundamental Policy and Operation 1984, LDP Party Presidential Election Control Cttee. 1986; Minister of Int. Trade and Industry 1986-88. *Leisure interests:* sumo, reading, go, gardening, photography. *Address:* 1-16-10 Shoto, Shibuya-ku, Tokyo, Japan.

TAN DUN; Chinese composer; b. 8 Aug. 1957, Hunan; s. of Tan Xiang Qiou and Hwang Quin Yin; ed. Cen. Conservatory of Music, Beijing, Columbia Univ., U.S.A.; fmr. violinist, Beijing Opera; Vice-Pres. Cen. Conservatory of Music 1978-; Second place, Weber Int. Chamber Music Composition Competition, Dresden 1983; numerous awards in China; works performed by maj. orchestras in China and at Aspen Music Festival, U.S.A. 1982, Dresden Music Festival 1983, Contemporary Chinese Composers' Festival, Hong Kong 1986, and by Cen. Philharmonic of China during U.S. tour 1987; four recordings of his maj. orchestral works, oriental instrumental music, chamber music and electronic music issued by China Nat. Recording Co.; works also include 14 film scores for U.S. and Chinese films, six modern ballet scores, music for several stage plays; Nine Songs (opera) to be premiered New York 1989; orchestral piece commissioned by Inst. for Devt. of Intercultural Relations Through the Arts, U.S.A. for Beijing Int. Music Festival July 1988. *Leisure interests:* painting in ink, calligraphy. *Address:* School of the Arts, Music Division, Dodge Hall, Columbia Univ., New York, N.Y. 10027, U.S.A. *Telephone:* (212) 662 7437.

TAN JIAZHEN; Chinese biologist; b. 1910; ed. California Inst. of Tech. U.S.A.; Prof. of Genetics, Shanghai Fudan Univ. 1961-; in disgrace during Cultural Revolution 1966-77; mem. Standing Cttee. 5th CPPCC 1978-83; Vice-Pres. Shanghai Fudan Univ. 1978-; mem. Dept. of Biology, Acad. Sinica 1980; Vice-Chair. China Democratic League 1983-; Dir. Genetics Inst. of Fudan Univ 1984-; Foreign Assoc., U.S. Nat. Acad. of Science 1985; Pres., Genetics Soc. of China 1985-. *Address:* Genetics Institute, Fudan University, Siping Road, Shanghai, People's Republic of China.

TAN KENG YAM, Tony, PH.D.; Singapore politician; b. 7 Feb. 1940, Singapore; ed. St. Patrick's School, St. Joseph's Inst., Univ. of Singapore, Mass. Inst. of Tech. and Univ. of Adelaide; lecturer in Maths. Univ. of Singapore 1967-69; Sub-Man. Overseas Chinese Banking Corpn. 1969, Gen. Man. 1978; M.P. 1979-; Sr. Minister of State (Educ.) 1979; Minister of Educ. 1980, concurrently Vice-Chancellor, Nat. Univ. of Singapore; Minister for Trade and Industry, concurrently Minister in charge of Nat. Univ. of Singapore and Nanyang Tech. Inst. 1981-83; Minister of Finance 1983-85, of Educ. and Health Jan.-April 1985, for Trade and Industry 1985-86, of Educ. 1985-88; Vice-Chair. People's Action Party Cen. Exec. Cttee. 1984-. *Address:* c/o Ministry of Education, Kay Siang Road, 1024 Singapore.

TAN LIANGDE; Chinese diver; b. 1965, Guangdon Prov.; Gold Medallist World Univ. Games 1987. *Address:* China Sports Federation, Beijing, People's Republic of China.

TAN QILONG; Chinese party official; b. 1912, Jiangxi; Dir. Political Dept., Hunan-Hubei-Jiangxi Border Region 1937; Political Commissar Guerilla Force 1943, People's Liberation Army 1944-49; Deputy Sec. CCP Zhejiang 1949-52, Sec. 1952-55; Political Commissar Zhejiang Mil. District, PLA 1952-55; Gov. of Zhejiang 1952-55; Acting Gov. of Shandong 1954; Alt. mem. 8th Cen. Cttee. of CCP 1956; Sec. CCP Shandong 1955-56, Second Sec. 1956-61, First Sec. 1961-67; Gov. of Shandong 1958-63; First Political Commissar Jinan Mil. Region, PLA 1963; Sec. E. China Bureau, CCP 1965-67; criticized and removed from office during Cultural Revolution 1967; Alt. mem. 9th Cen. Cttee. of CCP 1969; Vice-Chair. Fujian Revolutionary Cttee. 1970; Sec. CCP Fujian 1971; Sec. CCP Zhejiang 1972, First Sec. 1973-77; Vice-Chair. Zhejiang Revolutionary Cttee. 1973, then Chair. until 1977; Chair. Qinghai Revolutionary Cttee. 1977; First Sec. CCP Qinghai 1977; First Political Commissar Qinghai Mil. Dist.; First Sec. CCP Sichuan 1980-83; First Political Commissar, PLA Sichuan Mil. Dist. 1981; Chair. Advisory Cttee. of CCP, Sichuan 1983-; mem. 10th Cttee. of CCP 1973, 11th Cen. Cttee. 1977, 12th Cttee. 1982-85; mem. Cen. Advisory Comm. 1987-; Hon. Dir. China Welfare Fund for the Handicapped 1986-.

TAN QIXIANG: Chinese historian; b. 25 Feb. 1911, Shenyang; m. Li Yongfan 1936; two s. two d.; Chief Ed. Chinese Historical Atlas. *Publication:* Changshui Ji 1987. *Address:* Chinese Historical Geography Institute, Fudan University, Shanghai (Office); 1753 Huaihaizhong Road, Room 102, Shanghai, People's Republic of China (Home). *Telephone:* 374244 (Home).

TAN QUANSHU; Chinese artist and woodcutter; b. 31 Aug. 1936, Bao Tou City, Inner Mongolia; s. of the late Tan Qi and Wang Xueying; m. Jin Yurui 1963; one d.; ed. Beijing Sixth Middle School, Cen. Inst. of Fine Arts, Beijing; taught at Middle School, attached to Cen. Inst. of Fine Arts 1962-73, Lecturer, Engraving Dept., Cen. Inst. of Fine Arts 1973-86; Assoc. Prof., Chair. of Teaching and Research Section,and Chair. Woodcut Studio 1986-; exhbns. since 1959 in France, Japan, Switzerland, U.S.S.R. and S. America; mem. Chinese Artists' Asscn. 1979-, Chinese Engraving Asscn. 1980-; mem. Council of Chinese Engravers' Asscn. 1986-; mem. and Sec.-Gen. Standing Cttee. Chinese Woodcut EX-LIBRIS 1986-; Head of Engraving Section, Beijing Artists' Asscn. 1986-; EX-LIBRIS works displayed 81st and 82nd Int. EX-LIBRIS Exhbn. *Publications:* The new course of studying Xylography 1984, Album of Woodcuts 1985. *Leisure interests:* music, ball games. *Address:* Central Institute of Fine Arts, Dong Cheng District, Beijing, People's Republic of China.

TAN SHANHE, Maj.-Gen.; Chinese army officer; b. 1915, Chaling Co., Anhui Prov.; joined CCP 1931, Red Army 1934; Commdr. Eng. Corps, Chinese People's Volunteers, Korea 1951; Deputy Commdr. Beijing Mil. Region 1954-76; disappeared during Cultural Revolution; mil. leader, Beijing 1975; Commdr. PLA Eng. Corps 1977-; alt. mem. 11th Cen. Cttee., CCP 1977-82; Deputy for PLA, 5th NPC 1978; mem. 12th Cen. Cttee., CCP 1982-85; mem. Cen. Advisory Comm. 1985-. *Address:* People's Liberation Army Headquarters, Beijing, People's Republic of China.

TAN YOULIN; Chinese army officer; b. Nov. 1916, Jiangling, Hubei Prov.; s. of Tan Lianggong and Tan Chenshi; m. Lu Fang 1944; four s. three d.; Political Commissar Xijang Mil. Region 1980-83; mem. 12th Cen. Cttee. CCP 1982-85; Political Commissar Lanzhou Mil. Region 1983-85; mem. Cen. Advisory Comm. 1985-. *Address:* No. 35 Yuqun Hutong, East District, Beijing, People's Republic of China.

TANAKA, Kakuei; Japanese politician; b. 4 May 1918, Niigata Pref.; s. of Kazuki Tanaka and Fume Tanaka; m. Hanako Sakamoto 1942; one d.; ed. Chuo Tech. High School, Tokyo; est. own construction business 1937; building contractor in Tokyo 1940-47; mem. Lower House of Parl. 1947-; Parl. Vice-Minister of Justice Oct.-Nov. 1948; Minister of Posts and Telecommunications (Kishi Cabinet) 1957-58; Chair. Policy Research Council of Liberal Dem. Party 1961-62; Sec.-Gen. Liberal Democratic Party 1965-66, 1968-71; Minister of Finance 1962-65; Chair. Research Comm. on Municipal Policy, Liberal Dem. Party 1967-68; Minister of Int. Trade and Industry 1971-72; Pres. Liberal Democratic Party and Prime Minister 1972-74; Chair. Bd. of Dirs., Echigo Traffic Co. Ltd. 1960; arrested on corruption charges July 1976, resgnd. from party leadership July 1976, sentenced to four years' imprisonment 1983. *Publication:* A Proposal for Remodelling the Japanese Archipelago. *Leisure interest:* golf. *Address:* 12-19-12, Mezirodai, Bunkyo-ku, Tokyo, Japan. *Telephone:* 03-943-0111.

TANAKA, Shoji, PH.D.; Japanese professor of applied physics; b. 19 Sept. 1927, Kanagawa; s. of Hiroshi Tanaka and Sai Tanaka; m. Kimiko Tanaka 1959; one s.; ed. Univ. of Tokyo; lecturer, Dept. of Applied Physics, Univ. of Tokyo 1955-57, Assoc. Prof. 1958-68, Prof. 1968-; mem. Cttee. on Industrial Tech., Ministry of Int. Trade and Industry 1979-. *Leisure interest:* golf.

TANAKA, Tatsuo; Japanese politician; b. 20 Sept. 1910, Yamaguchi Pref.; s. of late Gen. Giichi Tanaka, fmr. Prime Minister; ed. Tokyo Univ.; worked with Manchuria Railway Co.; elected Gov. of Yamaguchi after World War II; mem. House of Reps. 1953-; Parl. Vice-Minister of Econ. Planning 1955; Deputy Chief Cabinet Sec. 1957-58; Vice-Chair. Policy Affairs Research Council, Liberal-Democratic Party (LDP) 1960; Deputy Sec.-Gen. LDP 1961-62; State Minister, Dir.-Gen. Prime Minister's Office 1967-70; Minister of Int. Trade and Industry 1976-77, of Educ. 1980-81; Chair. LDP Research Council on Petroleum 1977-80; fmr. Chair. LDP Exec. Council. *Publications:* Yearning South America 1954, A Historical View on the Relationships between Japan and Korea 1963.

TANANAYEV, Ivan Vladimirovich; Soviet inorganic and analytical chemist; b. 4 June 1904, Serpovoe, Tambov Region; s. of Vladimir Aleksandrovich and Maria Ivanovna Tananayev; m. Galina Semionovna 1929; two d.; ed. Dept. of Chemistry, Polytech. Inst., Kiev; Asst. in Analytical Chem., Kiev Polytech. Inst. 1925-30, Docent 1930-34; Chief of Analytical Chem. Lab., Acad. of Sciences of Georgian S.S.R., Tbilisi 1934-35; Science worker, Inst. of Gen. and Inorganic Chem. of Acad. of Sciences of U.S.S.R., Moscow 1935-39, Dr. and Prof. 1939, Head, Analytical Lab. and Rare Elements Lab. 1939-48, Deputy Dir. 1948-54; mem. CPSU 1942; lecturer, Inst. of Chemical Tech. 1962-; Ed.-in-C. Inorganic Materials 1965-; Corresp. mem. U.S.S.R. Acad. of Sciences 1946-58, mem. 1958-; mem. Inorganic Chem. Section of IUPAC 1959-63; Kurnakov Premium 1948; State Prizes 1949, 1951, 1971; Mendeleev Gold Medal 1973, Order of Lenin (three times), Hero of Socialist Labour, Hammer and Sickle Gold Medal and other decorations. *Publications:* The Physico-Chemical Analysis Method in Analytical Chemistry 1950, 1956, 1959, 1961, The Chemistry of Metal Fluorides 1938, Ferrocyanides of Metals 1938, Rare Elements Chemistry 1954, 1955, 1957, 1959, 1962-78, Phosphates of Metals 1962, The Chemistry of Fluorine

Compounds of Actinides 1963, The Chemistry of Germanium 1967, The Chemistry of Ferrocyanides of four valent metals 1972; more than 400 articles. *Leisure interests:* playing and composing music. *Address:* Institute of General and Inorganic Chemistry of U.S.S.R. Academy of Sciences, 31 Leninsky Prospekt, 117071 Moscow, U.S.S.R.

TANASIE, Petre, D.ECON.; Romanian diplomatist; b. 9 Oct. 1927, Slaticara; m. Silvia Iliescu; one s. one d.; ed. Bucharest Acad. of Econ. Studies; Prof. of World Econ. Bucharest Acad. of Econ. Studies 1951–; joined Foreign Service 1960; Dir. Ministry of Foreign Affairs 1967–69, 1978–87; Amb. to India, Sri Lanka and Nepal 1969–77; Perm. Rep. of Romania to UN 1987–; fmr. Head dels. at numerous int. confs., meetings, etc.; mem. Romanian Asscn. for Int. Law and Int. Relations. *Publications:* numerous works and papers on int. econ. relations. *Address:* Permanent Mission of Romania to the United Nations, 573–577 Third Avenue, New York, N.Y. 10016, U.S.A. *Telephone:* (212) 682-3273.

TANFORD, Charles, PH.D.; American professor of physiology; b. 29 Dec. 1921, Halle, Germany; s. of Max and Charlotte Tanford; m. Lucia Brown 1948 (divorced 1969); two s. one d.; ed. New York and Princeton Univs.; Lalor Fellow, Harvard Univ. 1947–49; Asst. Prof., Univ. of Iowa 1949–54, Assoc. Prof. 1954–59, Prof. 1959–60; Prof. Duke Univ. 1960–70, James B. Duke Prof. of Physical Biochem. 1970–80, James B. Duke Prof. of Physiology 1980–; mem. Whitehead Medical Research Inst. 1977–83; George Eastman Visiting Prof., Oxford Univ. 1977–78; Pres. Biophysical Soc. 1979; Walker-Ames Prof. Univ. of Washington 1979, Reilly Lecturer, Univ. of Notre Dame 1979; Guggenheim Fellow 1956–57; mem. N.A.S., American Acad. of Arts and Sciences; Alexander von Humboldt Prize 1984. *Publications:* Physical Chemistry of Macromolecules 1961, The Hydrophobic Effect 1973 (new edn. 1980); 200 scientific articles in various journals. *Leisure interests:* photography, hiking, travel. *Address:* Department of Physiology, Duke University, Durham, N.C. 27710 (Office); 1430 North Mangum Street, Durham, N.C. 27701, U.S.A. (Home). *Telephone:* (919) 684-5805 (Office); (919) 688-8912 (Home).

TANG, Bishop Dominic; Chinese ecclesiastic; b. 13 May 1908, Hong Kong; ordained May 1941; Apostolic Administrator, Canton 1951–57; imprisoned China 1957; released 1980; apptd. Archbishop of Canton by Pope John Paul II June 1981; appointment rejected by Chinese Catholics. *Address:* Catholic Mission, She-Se, Guangzhou, Guangdong, People's Republic of China.

TANG AOQING, PH.D.; Chinese professor of chemistry; b. 18 Nov. 1915, Yixing Co., Jiangsu Prov.; s. of Tang Linking and Chu Yongmei; m. Shi Guangxia 1943; three s. three d.; ed. Beijing and Colombia Univs.; taught at Nat. South-West Associated Univ., Kunming, after graduation; now Dir. Inst. of Theoretical Chem., Jilin Univ., Pres. 1978–; Chair. State Natural Science Foundation 1986; Vice-Pres. China Asscn. for Science and Tech. 1986–; Pres. Soc. of Chem. 1986–; Vice-Pres. China Asscn. for Int. Exchange of Personnel 1986–; a leading researcher in quantum chemistry and in the physical chemistry of macromolecules; announced irreducible tensorial method of Ligand field theory, Beijing symposium on physics 1966; developed the graph theory of molecular orbitals, the theory of symmetry conservation and the statistical theory of polymer reactions; Third Class Award, Chinese Acad. of Sciences, Nat. Science Award (First Class) 1982. *Leisure interest:* literature. *Address:* Institute of Theoretical Chemistry, Jilin University, Changchun; National Natural Science Foundation of China, 43 Baojia Street, Xicheng District, Beijing, People's Republic of China. *Telephone:* 23189; (Science Foundation) 654695.

TANG KE; Chinese politician; Vice-Minister, Petroleum Industry 1966–67; criticized and removed from office during Cultural Revolution 1967; Vice-Minister of Fuel and Chemical Industries 1971, 1975; Minister of Metallurgy Industry 1977–82, of Petroleum Industry 1982–86; First Vice-Chair. China Int. Trust and Investment Corpn. 1985–; Chair. Bd. of Dirs., China Kanghua Devt. Corpn. May 1988–; mem. 11th Cen. Cttee. and Presidium, 11th Nat. Congress CCP 1977; mem. 12th Cen. Cttee., 12th Nat. Congress CCP 1982. *Address:* China Kanghua Devt. Corporation, Beijing, People's Republic of China.

TANG MINGZHAO; Chinese university professor and United Nations official; b. 1910, Guangdong Prov.; ed. Qinghua Univ. and Univ. of California; fmr. mem. Council, Chinese People's Inst. on Foreign Affairs, Chinese People's Asscn. for Friendship with Foreign Countries; Deputy to Nat. Congress, People's Repub. of China; Adviser, Int. Liaison Dept. 1981–; Under-Sec.-Gen. for Political Affairs, Trusteeship and Decolonization, UN 1972–79; mem. del. to UN Gen. Ass. 1971; mem. Chinese People's Political Consultative Conf.; Vice-Pres. Chinese Asscn. for Int. Understanding; Prof. Dept. of Political Science, Nankai Univ. *Address:* Nankai University, Balitai, Tianjin, People's Republic of China.

TANG PEISONG, B.A., PH.D.; Chinese plant physiologist and biochemist; b. 12 Nov. 1903, Xishui Co., Hupeh Prov.; m. 1st Violet Wong (deceased); three s. one d.; m. 2nd Zheng Xiang 1949; one d.; Dir. Inst. of Plant Physiology 1959; in political disgrace 1967–77; Prof. and Emer. Dir. Inst. of Botany, Chinese Acad. of Sciences; Pres. Chinese Botanical Soc. Oct. 1978–; mem. Academia Sinica; Corresp. mem. American Soc. of Plant Physiology, American Botanical Soc. *Publication:* Green Thraldom 1949. *Leisure interest:* bridge playing. *Address:* Institute of Botany, Academia

Sinica, Beijing (Office); Apt. 303, Building 810, Huang Zhang, Beijing 100080, People's Republic of China (Home). *Telephone:* 28-4536.

TANG ZHONGWEN; Chinese state official; cadre of the 5th Ministry of Machine Bldg. 1975–78; Vice-Minister of Ordnance Industry 1982–88, of Machine Bldg. and Electronics Industry May 1988–; Vice-Chair. China Northern Industrial Corpn. Sept. 1986–; alt. mem. 12th CCP Cen. Cttee. 1982–87. *Address:* Ministry of Ordnance Industry, Beijing, People's Republic of China.

TANGAROA, Hon. Sir Tangoroa, Kt., M.B.E.; Cook Islands administrator; b. 6 May 1921; s. of Tangaroa and Mihiau; m. 1941; two s. seven d.; ed. Avarua Primary Schoo, Rarotonga; radio operator 1939–54; shipping clerk, Donald and Ingram Ltd. 1955–63; M.P. for Penrhyn 1958–84; Minister of Educ., Works, Survey, Printing and Electric Power Supply, then Minister of Internal Affairs 1978–80; Queen's Rep. Cook Islands 1984–; Pres. Crippled Children's Soc. 1966–; Deacon Cook Islands Christian Church; fmr. Pres. Cook Islands Boys Brigade; Del. Islands Sports Asscn. *Address:* Government House, Rarotonga, Cook Islands. *Telephone:* 23499.

TANGE, Sir Arthur Harold, Kt., A.C., C.B.E., B.A.; Australian diplomatist (retd.); b. 18 Aug. 1914, Sydney; s. of Charles Tange and Maud Kingsmill; m. Marjorie Shann 1940; one s. one d.; ed. Univ. of W. Australia; Economist, Econ. Dept. Bank of N.S.W. 1938–40; various Australian Govt. Depts., Canberra 1942–45; First Sec., Dept. of External Affairs 1945; First. Sec., Australian Mission to UN, New York 1946–48; Counsellor, UN Div., Canberra 1948–50; Asst. Sec. Dept. of External Affairs 1951–53, Sec. 1954–65; Minister, Australian Embassy, Washington, D.C. 1953–54; High Commr. to India and Amb. to Nepal 1965–70; Sec. Dept. of Defence 1970–79; mem. Australian del. Bretton Woods Monetary Conf., UN Preparatory Conf. UN Gen. Ass. 1946, 1947, 1950, 1951, and Econ. and Social Council, Reparations Conf., Paris, ILO, Paris, Montreal and San Francisco; Commonwealth Confs., London, Colombo, Sydney 1949–78, etc. *Leisure interests:* music, stream fishing. *Publications:* various articles on defence and public administration. *Address:* 32 La Perouse Street, Canberra, A.C.T. 2603, Australia. *Telephone:* 062-958879.

TANGE, Kenzo, DR.ENG.; Japanese architect; b. 4 Sept. 1913, Osaka; s. of Tokiyo and Tei (Komaki) Tange; m. 1st Toshiko Kato 1949; m. 2nd Takako Iwata 1973; one s. one d.; ed. Tokyo Univ.; Prof. Univ. of Tokyo 1946–74, Emer. 1974–; Pres. Japanese Architects Asscn. 1986–; Hon. mem. American Acad. of Arts and Letters, Akad. der Künste, West Berlin, Colegio de Arquitectos de Venezuela 1978; Hon. Fellow American Inst. of Architects; Royal Gold Medal, R.I.B.A. 1965; Founding mem. Foundation Arquitectura y Urbanismo, Argentina 1978; Assoc. mem. Paris Acad. of Fine Arts 1984; Foreign corresp. l'Acad. d'Architecture pour Japon, France 1979; Academic corresp. in Japan of Nat. Acad. of Fine Arts, Argentina 1978; Hon. Prof. (Univ. Nacional Federico Villarreal, Peru) 1977, (Univ. Buenos Aires) 1978; Hon. Dr. Arts (Harvard); Hon. doctorate (Sheffield Univ.); Hon. Dr. Fine Arts (Univ. of Buffalo); Hon. Dr.-Ing. (Technische Hochschule, Stuttgart); Hon. Dr. Arch. (Politecnico di Milano, Italy); Hon. D.Sc. (Univ. of Hong Kong); AIA Gold Medal, American Inst. of Architects 1966; Medal of Honour, Danish Royal Acad. of Fine Arts, Grand Prix, Architectural Inst. of Japan 1986, Pritzker Architecture Prize 1987, and several other awards; Grande Médaille d'Or, Acad. française 1973, Ordre pour le Mérite (Fed. Repub. of Germany) 1976, Commdr., Ordre nat. du Mérite 1977, Mexican Order of the Aguila Azteca (Grade Encomienda) 1978, Commendatore nell' Ordine al Merito della Repubblica Italiana 1979, Person of Cultural Merit, Japan 1979, Order of Culture, Japan 1980, Commdr., Ordre des Arts et des Lettres 1984, Grande Ufficiale nell'Ordine al Merito, Italy 1984, Pritzker Architecture Prize 1987. *Buildings include:* Peace Memorial Park and Buildings, Hiroshima, Tokyo City Hall, Tokyo, Kurashiki City Hall, Kurashiki, Kagawa Prefectural Govt. Office, Takamatsu, Roman Catholic Cathedral, Tokyo, Nat. Gymnasiums for 1964 Olympic Games, Tokyo, Kuwait Int. Air Terminal Bldg., Skopje City Centre Reconstruction Project, Skopje, Yugoslavia, Yamanashi Press and Broadcasting Centre, Yamahashi, Master Plan for Expo 1970, Osaka, Int. Fairs' Fiera Dist. Centre, Bologna, Italy, Univ. Hospital and Dormitory, Oran, Algeria, Baltimore Inner Harbour Project, residential redevt., Royal State Palace, Jeddah, Saudi Arabia 1977–82, Royal Palace for H.M. the King, Jeddah, Saudi Arabia 1977–82, new capital of Nigeria 'Abuja' Urban Design for Cen. Civic Axis 1979, Overseas Union Bank Centre Bldg., Singapore 1980, Naples Admin. Centre, Italy 1980, Int. Tech. Centre, Singapore 1982, Ekime Culture Centre, Japan 1982, Yokohama City Museum, Japan 1983, Singapore Indoor Stadium 1985–, Ohutsu Prince Hotel, Japan 1985–, The UN Univ., Tokyo 1986–, New Tokyo City Hall Complex, Tokyo 1986–, Mil. Acad. Complex, Singapore 1986–. *Publications:* Katsura, Tradition and Creation in Japanese Architecture 1960, A Plan for Tokyo, 1960 1961, Ise 1962, Japan in the Future 1966, Kenzo Tange, 1946–1958 1966, Kenzo Tange, 1958–1964 1966, Kenzo Tange 1964–1969 1970, Japan in the 21st Century 1971. *Address:* 7-2-21 Akasaka, Minato-ku, Tokyo (Office); 1702, 2-3-34 Mita, Minato-ku, Tokyo 108, Japan (Home). *Telephone:* 408-7121/4 (Office); 455-2787 and 453-7301/3 (Home).

TANIKAWA, Kazuo; Japanese politician; b. 1930, Hiroshima Pref.; ed. Keio Univ.; mem. House of Reps. from Hiroshima 1958–; fmrly. Parl. Vice-Minister of Educ., Chair. Judicial Affairs and Educational Affairs Cttees., House of Reps.; Deputy Sec.-Gen. Liberal-Democratic Party 1981–82;

Minister of State, Dir.-Gen. Defence Agency 1982–83. *Leisure interests:* skin-diving, yachting. *Address:* Liberal-Democratic Party, 7, 2-chome, Hirakawacho, Chiyoda-ku, Tokyo, Japan.

TANIMURA, Hiroshi, B.A.; Japanese financial official; b. 26 May 1916, Tokyo; m. Kyoko Saito 1943; two s.; ed. Tokyo Imperial Univ.; Ministry of Finance 1938–68, Chief Sec. to Minister 1963–65, Dir. of Budget Bureau 1965–67, Vice-Minister 1967–68; Chair. Fair Trade Comm. 1969–72; Pres. Tokyo Stock Exchange 1974–82; Chair. Securities and Exchange Council 1983–. *Publications:* four essays 1970, 1974, 1980, 1982. *Leisure interests:* painting, travelling. *Address:* 4-8-3, Sanno, Ohta-ku, Tokyo 143, Japan. *Telephone:* Tokyo 771-6971.

TANK, Maksim (pseudonym of Yevgeniy Ivanovich Skurko); Soviet (Byelorussian) writer and poet; b. 1912, Pilkovshchina, Minsk Region; s. of Ivan Fyodorovich Skurko and Dumna Ivanovna Skurko; m.; one s. two d.; Underground Komsomol, Poland 1927; arrested and sentenced to six yrs. imprisonment 1932; mem. CPSU 1936–; contrib. to front and partisan newspapers 1941–45; literary work 1945–; Deputy to Supreme Soviet, Byelorussian S.S.R. 1947–59, 1963–; Chair. of Byelorussian section of Soviet-Polish Friendship Soc. 1958–; Cand. mem. Cen. Cttee. Byelorussian CP 1961–66, mem. 1966–; Sec. U.S.S.R. Writers' Union 1966–; Order of Lenin (four times); Order of the Red Banner of Labour (twice); Stalin Prize; Hero of Socialist Labour 1974; Order of October Revolution; Golden Peace Medal; State Prize 1980. *Publications:* In Stages 1936, Before the Mast 1938, Prepare to Fire 1945, That They May Not Know 1948, En Route 1954, Trace of Lightning 1957, My Daily Bread 1962, Lyrics 1963, Selected Works (2 vols.), 1952–54, Flower Garden of Happiness 1965, Toward the Sun 1965, Herring with Verse (humorous verse) 1966, Collected Works (4 vols.) 1966–67, Pages of the Calendar 1970, Let There Be Light 1972, Behind My Table 1984. *Leisure interest:* nature. *Address:* U.S.S.R. Union of Writers, Ul. Vorovskogo 52, Moscow, U.S.S.R.

TANNER, Alain; Swiss film director; b. 1933, Geneva; ed. in London; made numerous documentaries before directing feature films. *Films include:* Charles Dead or Alive 1969; The Salamander, The Middle of the World, Jonah Who Will be 25 in the Year 2000, Light Years Away (Special Jury Prize, Cannes Film Festival 1985) 1981, No Man's Land 1985, Une Flamme Dans Mon Coeur 1987.

TANNER, Champ Bean, PH.D.; American professor of soil science and of meteorology; b. 16 Nov. 1920, Idaho Falls, Ida.; s. of Bertrand M. Tanner and Orea B. Tanner; m. Catherine C. Cox 1941; three s. two d.; ed. Provo High School, Brigham Young Univ., Univ. of Wisconsin; served U.S. Army 1942–46; Instructor, Univ. of Wis. 1950–51, Asst. Prof. of Soil Science 1951–55, Assoc. Prof. 1955–60, Prof. 1960–79, Prof. of Meteorology 1965–79, Emil Truog Prof. of Soil Science 1979–, Chair. Dept. of Soil Science 1984–; Fellow A.A.A.S., American Soc. of Agronomy; mem. N.A.S., American Meteorological Soc.; Soil Science Society of American Research Award 1978, Emil Truog Professorship 1979, American Meteorological Soc. Biometeorological Award 1980. *Publications:* numerous articles in scientific journals. *Leisure interest:* reading. *Address:* Department of Soil Science, 1525 Observatory Drive, University of Wisconsin, Madison, Wis. 53706; 6404 Cooper Court, Middleton, Wis. 53562, U.S.A. (Home).

TANNER, Roger Ian, PH.D.; British professor of mechanical engineering; b. 25 July 1933, Wells, Somerset; s. of R. J. Tanner and E. Tanner; m. Elizabeth Bogen 1957; two s. three d.; ed. Univs. of Bristol, Calif. (Berkeley) and Manchester; eng. apprentice, Bristol Aero Engines 1950–53; lecturer in Mechanical Eng. Univ. of Manchester 1958–61; Sr. Lecturer, Reader, Univ. of Sydney 1961–66; Prof. Brown Univ. Providence, R.I. 1966–75; P.N. Russell Prof. of Mechanical Eng. Univ. of Sydney 1975–; Edgeworth David Medal 1966. *Publication:* Engineering Rheology 1985. *Leisure interests:* tennis, opera. *Address:* Department of Mechanical Engineering, University of Sydney, 2006 (Office); Marlowe, Sixth Mile Lane, Roseville, 2069, Australia (Home). *Telephone:* (02) 692-2285 (Office); (02) 467-2863 (Home).

TANNERY, Jean-Paul; French business executive; b. 11 May 1911, Colmar; s. of Jacques and Suzanne (née Molk) Tannery; m. Yvonne Pilliard 1933; three s. one d.; ed. Lycées Montaigne and Louis-le-Grand, and Ecole Nat. Supérieure des Mines, Paris; Engineer, Soc. des Aciéries de Longwy 1934–53, Dir. Longwy works 1945; Asst. Dir.-Gen. Soc. Lorraine-Escaut (merger of Aciéries de Longwy, Senelle-Maubeuge and Escaut-et-Meuse) 1953–62, Dir.-Gen. 1962–66; Dir.-Gen. Soc. Usinor (merger of Usinor and Lorraine-Escaut) 1966; Dir.-Gen. Vallourec 1967–73, Dir. 1968–73, Pres.-Dir.-Gen. 1973–77; Hon. Pres. 1977; Officier, Légion d'honneur; Chevalier des Palmes académiques; Croix de guerre. *Address:* 48 rue du Docteur-Blanche, 75016 Paris, France (Home). *Telephone:* 42-885627 (Home).

TANNOUS, Afif I., M.A., PH.D.; American government official (retd.) and social scientist; b. 25 Sept. 1905, Bishmizzeen, Koura, Lebanon; s. of Ishak and Theodora Tannous; m. Josephine Milkey 1941; two s.; ed. American Univ. of Beirut, St. Lawrence Univ., Canton, N.Y., and Cornell Univ.; admin. position with British Govt. in Sudan 1929–31; with Educ. Dept., Govt. of Palestine and Rural Improvement Programme 1931–33; taught Social Science at American Univ. of Beirut and directed rural improvement work 1933–37; taught Social Science at Univ. of Minn., U.S.A. 1940–43; joined U.S. Dept. of Agric. as Middle East specialist, later Head of Middle East Div.; Advisory Ed., Middle East Journal 1947–81; lecturer on Middle

East, School of Advanced Int. Studies, Washington, D.C. 1948–51; Deputy Dir. U.S. Tech. Co-operation Service for Lebanon 1951–54; Co-ordinator, Dept. of Agric. Services to Tech. Co-operation Admin. 1954–61; mem. U.S. Agricultural Mission to Middle East 1946; FAO Agricultural Mission, Greece 1946, UN Econ. Survey Mission, Middle East 1949; Chief Africa and Middle East Branch, Foreign Agric. Service 1956–61; Area Officer, Near East and Africa 1961–71; retd. Jan. 1971; mem. Bd. of Dirs. Int. Centre for Dynamics of Devt., Washington, D.C. 1972–88; researcher and writer on Middle East Devt.; Deputy Dir. U.S. Exhibit, Cairo Int. Agricultural Exhbn. 1961; Founder mem. Soc. for Int. Devt.; mem. U.S. Dept. of Agric. Team for Appraisal of Agricultural Devt. in Egypt Oct.-Nov 1975; mem. American Acad. of Political and Social Science, A.A.A.S., American Sociological Asscn., American Agricultural Econ. Asscn., Soc. for Applied Anthropology, Rural Sociological Soc., Middle East Inst. *Publications:* numerous articles, reports and chapters in books on Middle East Affairs. *Leisure interests:* hunting, hiking, gardening, reading and writing, and synthesis of science and humanities. *Address:* 6912 Oak Court, Annandale, Va. 22003, U.S.A. *Telephone:* (703) 256-0767.

TAO DAYONG; Chinese academic; b. 1918; Dean, Dept. of Political Science, Beijing Univ. 1953–57; branded a rightist opportunist and purged 1957; rehabilitated 1978; Vice-Pres., World Econs. Soc. of China 1980–; Dir. Econs. Dept., Beijing Normal Univ. 1982–; mem., Standing Cttee. 6th CPPCC 1983–88; Ed.-in-Chief, magazine Qunyan (Opinion) 1985–. *Address:* Economics Department, Beijing Normal Univeristy, Bei Taiping Zhuang, Beijing, People's Republic of China.

TAO DUN; Chinese ballad singer; Vice-Chair. Fed. of Literature and Art 1979–. *Address:* Chinese Association of Ballad Singers, Beijing, People's Republic of China.

TAOFINU'U, H.E. Cardinal Pio; Samoan ecclesiastic; b. 8 Dec. 1923, Falealupo, Savaii; s. of Solomona Taofinu'u and Mau Solia; ordained priest 1954; Archbishop of Samoa-Apia and Tokelau 1968–; cr. Cardinal by Pope Paul VI March 1973. *Publication:* The Kava Ceremony is a Prophecy 1973. *Leisure interests:* gardening, music, art. *Address:* Cardinal's Office, P.O. Box 532, Apia, Western Samoa. *Telephone:* Apia 20 400.

TAPE, Gerald Frederick, M.S., PH.D.; American physicist and scientific administrator; b. 29 May 1915, Ann Arbor, Mich.; s. of Henry A. Tape and Flora Simmons Tape; m. Josephine Waffen 1939; three s.; ed. Eastern Michigan Univ., and Univ. of Michigan; Asst. in Physics, Eastern Mich. Univ. 1933–35, Univ. of Mich. 1936–39; Instructor in Physics, Cornell Univ. 1939–42; Staff mem. Radiation Lab. M.I.T. 1942–46; Asst., later Assoc. Prof. of Physics Univ. of Ill. 1946–50; Asst. to Dir. 1950–51, Deputy Dir., Brookhaven Nat. Lab. 1951–62; Vice-Pres. Associated Univs. Inc. 1962, Pres. 1962–63, 1969–80, Special Asst. to Pres. 1980–82; U.S. Atomic Energy Commr. 1963–69; U.S. Rep. to IAEA with rank of Amb. 1973–77; mem. Pres.'s Science Advisory Cttee. 1969–73; mem. Defense Science Bd. 1970–74, Chair. 1970–73; mem. AEC High Energy Physics Advisory Panel 1969–74, IAEA Scientific Advisory Panel 1972–74, Energy Research and Devt. Admin. Gen. Advisory Cttee. 1975–77, Nat. Science Foundation Advisory Group on Science Programs 1975–76, Dept. of Energy Advisory Cttee. on Nuclear Facility Safety 1988–; Dir. Atomic Industrial Forum Inc. 1970–73, Science Service Inc. 1971–, Electric Power Research Inst. Advisory Council 1978–85; Univ. Chicago, Bd. of Govs. for Argonne Nat. Lab. 1982–85; mem. Nat. Acad. of Eng., American Astronomical Soc.; Fellow, American Physical Soc., American Nuclear Soc., A.A.A.S.; Hon. D.Sc. (E. Mich. Univ. 1964); Army-Navy Certificate of Appreciation 1947; Dept. of State Tribute of Appreciation 1969; Sec. of Defense Meritorious Civilian Service Medal 1969; Dept. of Defense Distinguished Public Service Medal 1973; Henry DeWolf Smyth Nuclear Statesman Award, Atomic Industrial Forum, American Nuclear Soc. 1978; Commdr., Order of Leopold II (Belgium) 1978; Nat. Science Foundation Distinguished Public Service Award 1980; Distinguished Assoc. Award, Dept. of Energy 1980, Enrico Fermi Award 1987. *Publications:* co-author with L. J. Haworth Relay Radar Chapter of M.I.T. Radiation Laboratory Technical Series; co-author with Dr. F. K. Pittman and M. F. Searl Future Energy Needs and the Role of Nuclear Power 1964, Proceedings of Third International Conference on Peaceful Uses of Atomic Energy 1964, Proceedings of the Thermionic Electrical Power Generation Symposium, Stresa 1968, Why We Test 1968, National Policy on Peaceful Uses of Nuclear Explosives 1969, The Next Twenty Years—IAEA's Role 1977. *Address:* 6717 Tulip Hill Terrace, Bethesda, Md. 20816, U.S.A. *Telephone:* (301) 229-6264.

TÀPIES PUIG, Antoni; Spanish painter; b. 13 Dec. 1923, Barcelona; m. Teresa Barba; three c.; ed. Inst. Menéndez Pelayo and Univ. of Barcelona; first one-man exhbn., Barcelona 1948, later in Paris, New York, London, Zürich, Rome, Milan, Munich, Stockholm, Hanover, Washington, Pasadena, Buenos Aires, Caracas, Düsseldorf, Bilbao, Madrid and Barcelona; cr. Mural for Saint Gallen Theatre, Switzerland 1971; French Govt. Scholarship 1950; Officier des Arts et des Lettres; UNESCO Prize, Venice Biennale and Pittsburgh Int. Prize 1958, Guggenheim Prize 1964, Rubens Prize 1972, City of Barcelona Prize 1979, Rembrandt Prize, Goethe Foundation, Basle 1984, French Nat. Grand Prize for Painting 1985. *Publications:* La pràctica de l'art, L'art contra l'estètica, Memòria personal (autobiog.) 1978, La realitat com a art 1983. *Address:* C. Zatagoza 57, 08006 Barcelona, Spain. *Telephone:* (93) 2173398.

TAPSELL, Peter, M.B.E., M.B., CH.B., F.R.C.S.(E.), F.R.C.S.; New Zealand politician; b. 1930, Rotorua; s. of May Sheehan and Peter Tapsell; m. 1951; two s. two d.; ed. Ngarimu and Otago Univs., Medical School, Dunedin; House Surgeon, Waikato Hosp., Hamilton, demonstrator in Anatomy, School of Medicine, Dunedin; Resident Surgical Officer, Dunedin Public Hosp.; orthopaedic surgeon to Rotorua and Queen Elizabeth Hosps. 1971–84; M.P. for Eastern Maori 1984–; Minister of Internal Affairs, Civil Defence and the Arts, and Assoc. Minister of Local Govt. and Tourism 1984–87, of Police, Forestry, Lands, Recreation and Sport, of Survey and Land Information, of Valuation Dept. Aug. 1987–; Deputy Mayor Roturua City; Chair. N.Z. Maori Arts and Crafts Inst., Ngati Whakane Lands Corpn.; mem. Cabinet Select Cttee. of Maori Affairs; Vice-Capt. Maori All Blacks Fiji Tour 1954; Labour. *Leisure interests:* rugby, hunting, fishing, skiing. *Address:* 2 Ngahu Street, Rotorua, New Zealand. *Telephone:* Rotorua 85432.

TĂRANU, Cornel, D.MUS.; Romanian composer and conductor; b. 20 June 1934, Cluj; s. of Francisc Tăranu and Elisabeta Tăranu; m. Daniela Mărgineanu 1960; one d.; ed. Cluj Conservatory; Prof. of Composition, Cluj Conservatory; Conductor of Ars Nova, contemporary music ensemble; Prize of the Romanian Composers' Union 1972, 1978, 1981, 1982, Prize of the Romanian Acad. 1973, The Koussewitsky Prize 1982; mem. of the Romanian Composers' Union of Société des Auteurs, Compositeurs et Editeurs de Musique, Paris. *Works include:* sonatas for flute, piano, clarinet and percussion, sonata for double bass solo, one piano concerto, cantatas, four symphonies, Don Giovanni's Secret (Chamber opera), Chansons nomades (an oratorio), Chansons sans amour, lieder, Sempre Ostinato, Chansons sans réponse, Hommage à Paul Célan, also film music. *Address:* Str. Nicolae Iorga 7, Cluj-Napoca 3400, Romania. *Telephone:* (951) 47-331.

TARASSOV, Nikolai Konstantinovich; Soviet diplomatist; b. 2 Oct. 1923; s. of K. N. Tarassov and E. A. Tarassova; m. Marianna A. Zinovieva 1955; two d.; ed. Moscow State Univ.; Head of Section, Presidium of U.S.S.R. Supreme Soviet 1949–56; Counsellor, Iran Embassy 1956–61; sr. posts, Ministry of Foreign Affairs 1961–68; Deputy Perm. Rep. at UN 1968–72; Amb. to Mexico 1972–76; Chief Counsellor Ministry of Foreign Affairs 1976–85; Head of U.S.S.R. Del. for Mutual Force and Armament Reductions in Cen. Europe negotiations, Vienna 1976–81; mem. Int. Court of Justice, The Hague 1985–. *Leisure interests:* painting, coin collecting. *Address:* International Court of Justice, Peace Palace, Carnegieplein 2, 2517-KJ, The Hague, Netherlands. *Telephone:* (070) 924441.

TARATUTA, Vasily Nikolaevich; Soviet official and diplomatist; b. 1930, Ukraine; ed. Agric. Inst. of Ukraine; mem. CPSU 1957–; worked in agronomy and forestry, Vinnitsa Dist., Ukrainian S.S.R. 1955–57; party work 1957–; Sec. of Vinnitsa Dist. Cttee. of Ukrainian CP 1966–67, First Sec. 1970–84, Pres. of Vinnitsa Dist. Exec. Cttee. 1967–70, Cand. mem. of Cen. Cttee. CPSU 1971–76, mem. 1976–; Deputy to Supreme Soviet; Amb. to Algeria 1984–. *Address:* Embassy of U.S.S.R., Impasse Boukhandoura, El-Biar, Algiers, Algeria.

TARAZEVICH, Georgiy Stanislavovich; Soviet politician; b. 17 July 1937, Sloboda, Minsk, Byelorussia; ed. Lvov Polytechnic Inst.; engineer in an aerial survey enterprise 1959–66; Prof., Byelorussian Inst. of Engineers of Railway Transport 1966–69; joined CPSU 1967; Second, then First Sec. Dist. CP Cttee., Minsk, then Second Sec. Minsk City Cttee. of CP of Byelorussia; Chair. Exec. Cttee., Minsk City Soviet of People's Deputies 1980–83, First Sec. 1983–85; Chair. Presidium, Supreme Soviet of Byelorussian S.S.R. 1985–; Deputy Chair., Presidium of Supreme Soviet of U.S.S.R. 1986–; mem. CPSU Cen. Cttee., Cen. Cttee. CP of Byelorussia; Order of the Red Banner of Labour, Order of Friendship among the Peoples, two Orders of Honour. *Address:* Presidium of the Supreme Soviet of the Byelorussian S.S.R., Minsk, Byelorussian S.S.R., U.S.S.R.

TARBELL, Dean Stanley, A.M., PH.D.; American professor of chemistry; b. 19 Oct. 1913, Hancock, New Hampshire; s. of Sanford M. Tarbell and Ethel L. Millikan; m. Ann Tracy 1942; two s. one d.; ed. Thayer High School, Winchester, N.H., and Harvard Univ.; Postdoctoral Fellow, Univ. of Ill. 1937–38; Instructor, rising to Houghton Prof. of Chem. and Chair. of Dept., Univ. of Rochester 1938–67; Distinguished Prof. of Chem., Vanderbilt Univ. 1967–, Branscom Distinguished Prof. 1975–76, Distinguished Prof. Emer. 1981–; R. C. Fuson Lecturer, Nevada 1972; Consultant, U.S. Public Health Service; mem. N.A.S., American Acad. of Arts and Sciences, American Chemical Soc., Chemical Soc. of London; Herty Medallist 1973. *Publications:* Roger Adams, Scientist and Statesman (with Ann Tarbell) 1981, Essays on the History of Organic Chemistry in the United States, 1875–1955 (with Ann Tarbell) 1986, and about 215 research papers in organic chemistry and history of chemistry 1936–. *Leisure interests:* history, out of doors, music. *Address:* Department of Chemistry, Vanderbilt University, Nashville, Tenn. 37235 (Office); 6033 Sherwood Drive, Nashville, Tenn. 37215, U.S.A. (Home).

TARCHER, Jeremy Phillip, B.A.; American publisher; b. 2 Jan. 1932, New York; s. of Jack D. Tarcher and Mary Bregor Tarcher; m. Shari Lewis 1958; one d.; ed. St. John's Coll., Annapolis, Md.; Founder and Pres. Jeremy P. Tarcher Inc., L.A. 1964–; Vice-Pres. Houghton Mifflin, Boston 1980–83; Chair. Bd. Audio Renaissance Tapes, L. A. 1985–; mem. Bd. Trustees The Esalen Inst., Big Sur, Calif. 1986–; Producer Shari Lewis

Show, NBC Network 1959–62; Exec. Producer A Picture of U.S. (Emmy Award for Children's Programming 1976) 1976. *Leisure interests:* entheogenic research, travel, reading, primitive oceanic art. *Address:* Jeremy P. Tarcher Inc., 9110 Sunset Boulevard, Los Angeles, Calif. 90069; 603 North Alta Drive, Beverly Hills, Calif. 90210, U.S.A. *Telephone:* (213) 273-3274; (213) 274-7207.

TARDIEU, Jean; French writer; b. 1 Nov. 1903, Saint-Germain-de-Joux; s. of Victor and Caroline (née Luigini) Tardieu; m. Marie-Laure Tardieu-Blot 1932; one d.; ed. Lycée Condorcet and Univ. de Paris; with Radiodiffusion Télévision Française (O.R.T.F.), Head Drama Section 1944–45, Dir. Club d'essai-centre d'Etudes 1945–60, Dir. France musique O.R.T.F. 1954–64, Admin. Counsellor 1964–74; Officier, Légion d'honneur; Commdr. des Arts et des Lettres; Grand Prix de Poésie (Acad. française) 1972, Prix de la Critique 1976, Grand Prix de Poésie (Ville de Paris) 1981, Prix de la Langue de France 1986. *Publications:* Accents, Le témoin invisible, Figures, Monsieur Monsieur, Un mot pour un autre, La première personne du singulier, Une voix sans personne, Théâtre de chambre, L'espace et la flûte, Poèmes à jouer, De la peinture abstraite, Choix de poèmes, Histoires obscures, Il était une fois, deux fois, trois fois (children's book), Pages d'écriture, Le fleuve caché, Les portes de toile, La part de l'ombre, Formeries, Obscurité du jour, Comme ceci comme cela, Les tours de Trébizonde, La cité sans sommeil, Des idées et des ombres, L'accent grave et l'accent aigu, Poèmes à voir, Margeries; trans. of German poems and plays (Goethe, Hölderlin). *Address:* 72 boulevard Arago, 75013 Paris, France.

TARIKI, Abdallah; Saudi Arabian oil executive; b. 19 March 1919; s. of Houmoud and Lolwa Tariki; m. 1st Eleanore Nicholas 1948, 2nd Maha Jumblatt 1969; two c.; ed. Univs. of Cairo and Texas; studied at Univ. of Texas and worked as trainee with Texaco Inc. in W. Texas and Calif. 1945–49; Dir. Oil Supervision Office, Eastern Prov., Saudi Arabia (under Ministry of Finance) 1949–55; Dir.-Gen. of Oil and Mineral Affairs (Saudi Arabia) 1955–60; Minister of Oil and Mineral Resources 1960; Dir. Arabian American Oil Co. 1959–62; Leader Saudi Arabian del. at Arab Oil Congresses 1959, 1960; Ind. Petroleum Consultant 1962–; Chair. Arab Petroleum Consultants; co-founder of OPEC; publr. of monthly petroleum magazine Naft El-Arab; adviser to Algerian, Libyan, Emirates (Abu Dhabi) and Kuwait govts. on oil matters. *Leisure interest:* breeding Arab horses. *Address:* KAC Building, Floor 10, Apt. 3, Al-Sharie Al-Hilali, Kuwait (Office); P.O. Box 22699, Safat, Kuwait (Home). *Telephone:* 415860, 412561 (Office); 443466.

TARJÁN, Imre; Hungarian physicist; b. 26 July 1912, Szabadka (now in Yugoslavia); s. of József Tarján and Erzsébet Tomasics; m. Margit Kardos; three d.; ed. Budapest Univ. of Sciences; Prof. Budapest Coll. of Pedagogy 1949; Prof. Budapest Univ. of Medicine and Dir. of Univ. Inst. of Biophysics 1950–82, including Research Group for Crystal Physics of Hungarian Acad. of Science 1961–76, research advisor 1982–; Dean Budapest Medical Univ. Faculty of General Medicine 1959–63, Univ. Vice-Rector 1970–73; Corresp. mem. Hungarian Acad. of Sciences 1970, Section III (Mathematics and Physical Sciences) mem. 1970–; Deputy Pres. 1964–76, Pres. 1976–; mem. of Presidium; mem Bd. Eötvös Loránd Physical Soc., Biophysical Soc.; Medal of Merit (Korean People's Repub.) 1953; Labour Order of Merit 1960, 1964; Kossuth Prize 1961; Inventor's Silver Degree 1970; Hungarian Order of Merit 1982; State Prize 1985; specialized in crystal defects and growth, biological macromolecular structure and function. *Publications:* Fizika orvosok és biológusok számára (Physics for Physicians and Biologists) textbook 1964, 1968, 1971, Laboratory Manual on Crystal Growth (UNESCO) 1972, A biofizika alapjai (An Introduction to Biophysics) 1977, 1981, 1987; 160 contribs. to science magazines and books in Hungarian and other languages. *Address:* Semmelweis University of Medicine, Institute of Biophysics, 1088 Budapest, Puskin utca 9, Hungary. *Telephone:* 339-599.

TARKKA, Asko, LL.M.; Finnish lawyer; b. 24 May 1929, Tampere; s. of Kaarlo and Helmi (née Hellberg) Tarkka; m. Pirjo Kourula 1957; two s. one d.; ed. Helsinki Univ.; Commercial Lawyer, Sec. of the Bd., Staff Man., Admin. Dir. and Exec. Vice-Pres. at Huhtamäki Oy 1958–76, Pres. 1976–, Chair. and C.E.O. 1982–; Chair. Bd. of Finnish Employers' Confed. 1980–85. *Address:* Huhtamäki Oy, Ratavartijankatu 2, SF-00520 Helsinki 52, Finland. *Telephone:* 140611 (Office).

TARNOPOLSKY, Walter Surma, A.M., LL.M., F.R.S.C.; Canadian professor and judge; b. 1 Aug. 1932, Gronlid, Sask.; s. of Harry Tarnopolsky and Mary Surma; m. 1st Helen Rempel 1960, one s. two d.; m. 2nd Joanne Kramer 1973, one s. one d.; ed. Univ. of Sask., Columbia Univ., L.S.E., Univ. of London; Asst. and Assoc. Prof. of Law, Univ. of Sask. 1963–67; Prof. and Dean of Law, Univ. of Windsor 1968–72; Vice-Pres., York Univ. 1972, Prof., Osgoode Hall Law School 1972–80; Dir., Human Rights Research and Educ. Centre, Univ. of Ottawa 1980–83; Justice, Ont. Court of Appeal 1983–; Pres., Nat. Fed. of Canadian Univ. Students 1957–58; Pres., Canadian Civil Liberties Asscn. 1977–81; mem. Human Rights Cttee., UN 1977–83; mem. (part-time), Canadian Human Rights Comm. 1978–83; mem. Cttee. on Freedom of Science and Scholarship of the Royal Soc. of Canada; Hon. LL.D. (St. Thomas Univ., Fredericton, N.B.) 1982, (Alberta, Trent) 1986. *Publications:* Canadian Bill of Rights 1966, Some Civil Liberties Issues of the Seventies (Ed.) 1975, Discrimination and the

Law in Canada 1982, 1985, Canadian Charter of Rights: Commentary (Co-ed.) 1982. *Leisure interests:* history, human rights. *Address:* Ontario Court of Appeal, Osgoode Hall, 130 Queen Street West, Toronto, Ont. M5H 2N5 (Office); 608 Shenandoah Drive, Mississauga, Ont. L5H 1V9, Canada (Home). *Telephone:* (416) 363-4101 (Office); (416) 274-3745 (Home).

TASCHEREAU, Pierre, Q.C., LL.L.; Canadian airline administrator; b. 13 Jan. 1920, Quebec, Que.; s. of the late Edouard and Juliette (Carroll) Taschereau; m. Yseult Beaudry 1945; two s. one d.; ed. Garnier Coll., Que., Laval Univ., Que., Univ. of Western Ontario; called to Bar of Quebec 1941; Sec. Advisory Cttees., Dept. of Justice, Ottawa 1941–42; Attorney, Canadian Nat. Railways, Montreal 1946–63; Sr. mem. Geoffrion & Prud'homme, barristers and solicitors, Montreal 1963–67; Vice-Pres. Canadian Transport Comm., Ottawa 1967–71; Vice-Pres. Law, Canadian Nat. Railways 1971–72, Exec. Vice-Pres., Corporate Affairs 1972–74, Chair. Bd. 1974–77; Chair. Bd. Air Canada 1976–81; Dir. The Royal Trustco Ltd., Commercial Union of Canada Holdings Ltd.; Gov. Montreal General Hosp., Hôpital Marie Enfant, Montreal. *Leisure interests:* tennis, bridge. *Address:* 3788 Grey Avenue, Montreal, Que., H4A 3N7, Canada (Home). *Telephone:* (514) 488-4549.

TAŞÇIOĞLU, Mükerrem; Turkish politician; b. 1926, Zine; ed. Galatasaray Lycée, Istanbul Tech. Univ., Liège State Univ. and Faculty of Political Science, Paris; fmr. admin. in student orgs. and founding mem. World Asscn. of Youth; Asst. Prof. Istanbul Technical Univ.; Planning Dir. Ministry of Transport; later worked for Dept. of Highways and Ministries of Public Works and Transport; fmr. Minister of Culture and Tourism; Minister of Labour and Social Security 1986–87. *Address:* c/o Ministry of Labour and Social Security, Calisma ve Sosyal Guvenlik Bakanliği, Mithad Pasa Cad., Ankara, Turkey.

TASHIRO, Kikuo; Japanese newspaper and television executive; b. 22 April 1917; ed. Waseda Univ.; joined Asahi Shimbun 1940; City Ed. 1959; Man. Ed. 1966; Exec. Dir. in charge of Editorial Affairs 1969; Pres. Asahi Nat. Broadcasting Co. Ltd. (TV Asahi) 1983–. *Address:* c/o Asahi Shimbun, 6-1, 2-chome, Yuraku-cho, Chiyoda-ku, Tokyo (Office); 6-4-10 Roppongi, Minato-ku, Tokyo 106, Japan (Home). *Telephone:* 03-405-3211 (Home).

TASWELL, Harold Langmead Taylor, M.COM.; South African business consultant and fmr. diplomatist; b. 14 Feb. 1910, Cape Town; s. of Stephen Taswell and Helen Simkins; m. Vera Blytt 1940; three d.; ed. Christian Brothers Coll., Pretoria, and Univ. of Cape Town; Dept. of External Affairs 1937–, Berlin 1937–39, London 1939, The Hague 1940, New York 1940–46; Consul, Elisabethville 1946–49; Int. Trade and Econ. Section, Dept. of External Affairs, Pretoria 1949–51; First Sec., Washington 1951–56; Consul-Gen., Luanda, Angola 1956–59; High Commr. of S. Africa in Fed. of Rhodesia and Nyasaland 1959–61, Accred. Diplomatic Rep. 1961–63, Accred. Diplomatic Rep. in S. Rhodesia 1963–64; Head, Africa Div., Dept. of Foreign Affairs, Pretoria 1964; Amb. to U.S.A. 1965–71, to UN Geneva 1971–75 (retd.); mem. Council Africa Inst. of S. Africa 1975–84. *Leisure interest:* walking. *Address:* 39 Simonstown Road, 7975 Fish Hoek, South Africa.

TATA, Jamshed Rustom, D.SC., F.R.S.; British medical research scientist; b. 13 April 1930, Bombay, India; s. of Dr. Rustom J. Tata and Gool (née Contractor); m. Renée S. Zanetto 1954; two s. one d.; ed. Univ. of Bombay, Indian Inst. of Science, Bangalore, Coll. de France, Paris and Univ. de Paris, Sorbonne; Postdoctoral Fellow, Sloan-Kettering Inst., New York 1954–55; Beit Memorial Fellow, Nat. Inst. for Medical Research, London 1956–60; Visiting Scientist, Wenner-Gren Inst., Univ. of Stockholm 1960–62; mem. Scientific Staff, MRC, Nat. Inst. for Medical Research, London 1962–73, Head, Lab. of Developmental Biochem. 1973–; Visiting Prof., Univ. of Calif. (Berkeley) 1969–70; Fogarty Int. Scholar, Nat. Insts. of Health, Bethesda, Md. 1983–86; mem. Indian Nat. Acad. of Sciences; corresp. mem. Soc. de Biologie, France; Fellow Third World Acad. of Sciences; various awards. *Publications:* The Thyroid Hormones 1959, Chemistry of Thyroid Diseases 1960, Metamorphosis 1972, The Action of Growth and Developmental Hormones 1983. *Leisure interests:* gardening, reading, travel, tennis. *Address:* Laboratory of Developmental Biochemistry, National Institute for Medical Research, Mill Hill, London, NW7 1AA (Office); 15 Bittacy Park Avenue, Mill Hill, London, NW7 2HA, England (Home). *Telephone:* 01-959 3666 (Office); 01-346 6291 (Home).

TATA, Jehangir Ratanji Dadabhoy; Indian industrialist (retd.); b. 29 July 1904; joined Tata Sons Ltd. 1926; Chair. Tata Sons Ltd., Tata Ltd., London, Tata Inc., New York, Tata Inst. of Fundamental Research, Indian Hotels Co. Ltd., Tata Burroughs Ltd., Tata A.G. (Switzerland), Tata Int. A.G. (Switzerland), Air-India 1953–78; fmr. Chair., now Chair. Emer. and Dir. Tata Industries Ltd., Tata Oil Mills Co. Ltd.; Chair. Emer. Tata Chemicals Ltd.; Pres. Court of Indian Inst. of Science; Pres. of Honour for Life, Aero Club of India; mem. Bd. Man. Leslie Sawhny Prog. for Training in Democracy; Gov. Bd. Family Planning Foundation; Dir. Tata Eng. and Locomotive Co. Ltd., Air India; hon. patron mem. Indo-French Chamber of Commerce and Industry; Trustee, Gandhi Smarak Nidhi, Kasturba Gandhi Nat. Memorial Trust, Jawaharlal Nehru Memorial Fund, N. R. Tata Family Trust, Bai Navajbai Tata Zoroastrian Girls' School, N. R. Tata Poor Relations Trust; Chair. Sir Dorabj Tata Trust, Family Planning Foundation, J.N. Tata Endowment for the Higher Educ. of

Indians, Lady Tata Memorial Trust, Homi Bhabha Fellowships Council, J.R.D. Tata Trust, Jamsetji Tata Trust, Governing Council Tata Inst. of Fundamental Research, Man. Council Nat. Centre for the Performing Arts and mem. numerous exec. cttees.; Fellow Indian Nat. Science Acad.; first pilot to qualify in India holding a private licence 1929; solo flight India–England 1930; Hon. Air Vice-Marshal Indian Air Force; Padma Vibhushan 1955; Commdr., Légion d'honneur; Kt. Commdr., Order of St. Gregory the Great 1964; Kt. Commdr.'s Cross of the Order of Merit (Fed. Repub. of Germany) 1978; Hon. D.Sc. (Allahabad) 1947, (Banaras Hindu Univ.) 1980; LL.D. (Bombay Univ.) 1981; Tony Jannus Award 1979; Edward Warner Prize 1986. *Address:* Bombay House, 24 Homi Mody Street, Bombay 400 023 (Office); The Cairn, Altamount Road, Bombay 400 026, India (Home).

TATAI, Ilona, D.TECH.SC.; Hungarian chemical engineer and politician; b. 1935, Budapest; asst. People's Army lab. 1952–59, then in Hungarian Transmitter Tube Works; asst., later works leader, rubber factory (now Nat. Rubber Works), Dept. Head. Tech. Adviser, Production Man.; Gen. Dir. TAURUS Hungarian rubber Works 1975–; joined HSWP 1965, Cen. Cttee. 1987–; mem. CC Econ. Cttee. 1987; mem. Party Political Cttee. 1988–. *Address:* TAURUS Hungarian Rubber Works, Budapest VIII, Kerepesi ut 17, Hungary. *Telephone:* 130-830.

TATARINOV, Leonid Petrovich; Soviet palaeontologist and zoologist; b. 12 Nov. 1926, Tula; s. of Piotr Lukich Tatarinov and Anna Nikolaevna Tatatrinova; two d.; ed. Moscow Univ.; mem. CPSU 1964–; served in Soviet Army 1943–44; sr. scientific ed. of Foreign Language Publishing House 1953–54; mem. of staff of U.S.S.R. Acad. of Sciences' Inst. of Palaeontology (jr. research fellow, then head of lab. and sr. research fellow) 1955–73, Dir. 1975; Corresp. mem. of U.S.S.R. Acad. of Sciences 1974, mem. 1981–; Foreign mem. Linnean Soc., London; sr. mem. of staff of U.S.S.R. Acad. of Sciences' Inst. of Evolutionary Morphology and Ecology of Animals 1973–75; U.S.S.R. State Prize 1978. *Leisure interests:* music, history. *Address:* Palaeontological Institute, Academy of Sciences, Profsoyuznaya Street 123, Moscow V-321, U.S.S.R.

TATARINTSEV, Vladimir Mikhailovich; Soviet engineer, chemist and technologist; b. 24 Sept. 1941; ed. Mendeleyev Chemical-Tech. Inst., Moscow; on staff of Inst. of Physics of U.S.S.R. Acad. of Sciences 1966–, sr. post 1975; mem. CPSU 1970; Lenin Prize 1980 for work on creation of and research into a new class of micro-crystals and fianites. *Address:* Institute of Physics, U.S.S.R. Academy of Sciences, Vavilov Str. 38, 117333 Moscow, U.S.S.R.

TATAY, Sándor; Hungarian writer; b. 6 May 1910, Bakonytamási; s. of Lajos Tatay and Teréz Varga, m. Maria Takács 1944; one d.; ed. Sopron, Pécs; Journalist Kelet Népe 1937–. *Publications:* Thunderstorm 1941, The Simeon Family (5 vols.) 1955–59, White Carriage 1960; The House under the Rocks (film) 1958; Lyuk a tetőn (novel) 1980; children's books and short stories. *Leisure interest:* vineyard. *Address:* Gyöngyösi, u. 53, H-1131 Budapest XIII, Hungary. *Telephone:* 409-523.

TATE, Jeffrey Philip, M.A., M.B., B.CHIR.; British conductor; b. 28 April 1943; s. of Cyril H. Tate and Ivy Ellen Naylor (nee Evans); ed. Farnham Grammar School, Christ's Coll. Cambridge and St. Thomas' Hosp. London; trained as medical dr. 1961–67; joined London Opera Centre 1969; joined staff of Royal Opera House, Covent Garden 1970; made recordings as harpsichordist 1973–77; Asst. to Pierre Boulez (q.v.) for the Ring, Bayreuth 1976–81; Asst. to Sir John Pritchard, Cologne Opera 1977; conducted Gothenburg Opera, Sweden 1978–80; Metropolitan Opera début 1979; Covent Garden début 1982; Chief Guest Conductor, Geneva Opera 1983–; Prin. Conductor, English Chamber Orchestra 1985–, Royal Opera House, Covent Garden 1986–; appears with maj. orchestras in Europe and America; numerous recordings with English Chamber orchestra. *Leisure interests:* church-crawling, with gastronomic interludes. *Address:* c/o Royal Opera House, London, WC2E 7QA, England.

TATE, Robert Brian, PH.D., F.B.A.; British professor of Hispanic studies; b. 27 Dec. 1921, Belfast, Northern Ireland; s. of Robert Tate and Jane Grantie Tate; m. Beth Ida Lewis 1951; one s. one d.; ed. Royal Belfast Academical Inst., The Queen's Univ., Belfast; Asst. Lecturer, Manchester Univ. 1949–52; Lecturer, The Queen's Univ., Belfast 1952–56; Reader in Hispanic Studies, Nottingham Univ. 1956–58, Prof. 1958–83, Emer. Prof. 1983–; Corresp. Fellow of Institut d'Estudis Catalans, of Real Acad. de Buenas Letras, Barcelona, of Real Acad. de Historia, Madrid. *Publications:* numerous publications on Hispanic topics. *Leisure interests:* art, architecture, jazz, walking. *Address:* 11 Hope Street, Beeston, Nottingham, England. *Telephone:* (0602) 256919.

TATISHVILI, Tsisana Bezhanovna; Soviet opera-singer (soprano); b. 1939, Tbilisi, Georgia; ed. Sarandzhishvili Conservatoire, Tbilisi; soloist with Tbilisi State Opera 1963–; has toured in Germany, Poland, Czechoslovakia and other countries; People's Artist of Georgian S.S.R. 1973, Paliashvili Prize 1979 (for concert season 1977-78), People's Artist of U.S.S.R. 1979. *Roles include:* Tatiana in Eugene Onegin, Liza in Queen of Spades, Aida, Leonora in Il Trovatore, Donna Anna in Don Giovanni, Ortrud in Lohengrin, Tamar in Taktakishvili's Abduction of the Moon. *Address:* c/o Tbilisi State Opera, Tbilisi, Georgian S.S.R., U.S.S.R.

TATLIEV, Suleyman Bayram ogly; Soviet party official and politician; b. 1925, Azerbaijan; Red Army 1943–45; ed. Azerbaijan Univ.; technologist in oil refinery plant 1951–56; mem. CPSU 1959; deputy chief engineer of synthetic rubber works and head of section of Azerbaijan S.S.R. Sovnarkhoz (Econ. Planning Org.) 1956–63; deputy head of section of Cen. Cttee. of Azerbaijan CP 1963–65; organizational head of Council of Ministers of Azerbaijan S.S.R. 1965–78; First Deputy Pres. of Council of Ministers of Azerbaijan S.S.R. 1978–85; Pres. of Presidium of Supreme Soviet of Azerbaijan S.S.R. 1985–; a Deputy Chair. Presidium of the Supreme Soviet of the U.S.S.R. 1985–; Deputy to Supreme Soviet of U.S.S.R. 1986–. *Address:* Presidium of Supreme Soviet of Azerbaijan S.S.R., Baku, U.S.S.R.

TATON, (André) René, D. ÉS L.; French historian; b. 4 April 1915, L'Echelle (Ardennes); s. of André and Marie-Thérèse (née Launoy) Taton; m. Juliette Battesti 1945; two d.; ed. Faculté des Sciences, Nancy and Paris, Ecole Normale Supérieure de St. Cloud; Research Asst., Centre Nat. de la Recherche Scientifique 1946, rising to Research Dir. 1952–83; Prof. Ecole pratique des Hautes Etudes 1964–, Dir. Centre Alexandre-Koyré for Research into History of Science; mem. Acad. Int. d'Histoire des Sciences; Sec.-Gen. of Int. Union of the History and Philosophy of Sciences 1955–71, Vice-Pres. 1972–74, Pres. 1975–78; Lauréat Acad. des Sciences and George Sarton Medal 1975; Chevalier, Légion d'honneur, Commdr. des Palmes académiques. *Publications:* L'oeuvre scientifique de Gaspard Monge 1951, L'oeuvre mathématique de G. Desargues 1951, Causalités et accidents de la découverte scientifique 1958 (translated into English, Spanish, Japanese), ed. Histoire générale des sciences (4 vols.) (translated into English, Italian, Spanish, Portuguese), numerous articles on the history of mathematics and the history of sciences in general. *Address:* 12 rue Colbert, 75002 Paris; 64 rue Gay-Lussac, 75005 Paris, France (Home).

TÁTRAI, Vilmos; Hungarian violinist; b. 7 Oct. 1912, Kispest; s. of Vilmos Tátrai and Maria Obernauer; m. Zsuzsa Kreismann 1938; one s. one d.; ed. National Conservatoire, Budapest; Teacher 1946–53; First Violinist, Budapest Symphony Orchestra 1933; mem. Radio Orchestra 1938; Leading Violinist Metropolitan State Concert Orchestra 1940–; Founder-Leader Tátrai String Quartet 1946, tours throughout Europe 1952–; Founder-Leader Hungarian Chamber Orchestra 1957–; Prof. of Music, Budapest Acad. of Music 1965–; First Violin, Béla Bartók Competition 1948, Liszt Prize 1952, 1972, Kossuth Prize 1958, Eminent Artist of Hungarian People's Republic, Labour Order of Merit (golden degree). *Leisure interests:* walking, photography. *Address:* Raoul Wallenberg u. 4; Zeneművészeti Főiskola, Liszt Ferenc tér. 2, H-1136 Budapest XIII, Hungary. *Telephone:* 110-529.

TATSUMI, Sotoo, LL.B.; Japanese banking executive; b. 7 Oct. 1923, Fukui; s. of Kennosuke Nakano and Hisa Nakano; m. Tomoko Araki 1949; one s. one d.; ed. Kyoto Univ.; joined Sumitomo Bank Ltd. 1947, Dir. 1972, Man. Dir. 1975–79, Sr. Man. Dir. 1979–82, Deputy Pres. 1982–87, Pres. Oct 1987–; Co-Chair. Kansai Community for Econ. Devt. 1987–; Vice-Chair. Osaka Bankers' Asscn. 1987–. *Leisure interests:* driving, literature, music. *Address:* 3-2, Marunouchi 1-chome, Chiyoda-ku, Tokyo 100 (Office); 12-3, NishiOkamoto 7-chome, HigashiNada-ku, Kobe 658, Japan (Home). *Telephone:* (03) 282-5111 (Office); (078) 452-0678 (Home).

TAUBE, Henry, B.S., M.S., PH.D.; American professor of chemistry; b. 30 Nov. 1915, Saskatchewan, Canada; s. of Samuel Taube and Albertina Tiledetzki Taube; m. Mary Alice (née Wesche) 1952; two s. two d.; ed. Univs. of Sask. and Calif. (Berkeley); Instructor Univ. of Calif. at Berkeley 1940–41; Instructor-Asst. Prof. Cornell Univ. 1941–46; Asst. Prof., Prof. Univ. of Chicago 1946–61; Prof. of Chem., Stanford Univ., Calif. 1962–; Guggenheim Fellow 1949–55; mem. N.A.S., Royal Physiographical Soc. of Lund, American Philosophical Soc.; foreign mem. Royal Soc. 1988; Hon. mem. Hungarian Acad. of Science 1988; Hon. LL.D. (Univ. of Sask.) 1973, Ph.D. h.c. (Hebrew Univ. of Jerusalem) 1979, Hon. Dr. Sc. (Univ. of Chicago) 1983, (Lajos Kossuth Univ. of Debrecen) 1988, (Seton Hall Univ.) 1988; Baker Lecture, Cornell Univ. 1965, Priestley Lecture, Pa. State 1976; American Chem. Soc. Awards 1955, 1960, Chandler Medal of Columbia Univ., Kirkwood Award, Harrison Howe Award, Rochester Section, ACS, 1960, Nichols Medal, New York Section, ACS 1971; Willard Gibbs Medal, Chicago Section, ACS 1971; F. P. Dwyer Medal, Univ. of N.S.W. 1973; Nat. Medal of Science 1977; Allied Chemical Award for Excellence in Graduate Teaching and Innovative Science 1979; T. W. Richards Medal, Northeastern Sec. ACS 1980, ACS Award in Inorganic Chem. of the Monsanto Co. 1981, Linus Pauling Award, Puget Sound Section ACS 1981, N.A.S. Award in Chemical Sciences 1983, Baillar Medal, Univ. of Ill. 1983, Robert A. Welch Foundation Award in Chem. 1983, Nobel Prize for Chem. 1983, Priestley Medal 1984, Distinguished Achievement Award, Precious Metals Inst. 1986, Oesper Award 1986. *Publications:* Approx. 330 scientific articles in chemical journals. *Leisure interests:* record-collecting, gardening. *Address:* Department of Chemistry, Stanford University, Stanford, Calif. 94305 (Office); 441 Gerona Road, Stanford, Calif. 94305, U.S.A. (Home). *Telephone:* (415) 723-1736 (Office), (415) 328-2759 (Home).

TAUBMAN, Alfred; American entrepreneur; b. 31 Jan. 1925, Pontiac, Mich.; s. of Philip Taubman and Fannie Taubman; m. 1st Reva Kolodney 1949 (divorced 1977), one s. one d.; m. 2nd Judith Mazor 1982; ed. Univ. of Michigan, Lawrence Inst. of Tech.; Chair. and C.E.O. The Taubman Co.,

Troy, Michigan (specializing in shopping-centre design, planning and devt.) 1950–; Chair. A & W Restaurants (restaurant franchising operation) 1982–, R.H. Macy Inc. 1986–, Sothebys Holdings 1983; owner Woodward and Lothrop Inc. 1984–; has a controlling stake in Michigan Panthers' Football team; non-exec. Dir. Core Industries, Mfrs. Nat. Corpn., United Brands; owner of Sotheby's (art auctioneers) 1983–. *Address:* The Taubman Co. Inc., 200 E. Long Lake Road, Bloomfield Hills, Mich. 48303, U.S.A.

TAUBMAN, (Hyman) Howard, A.B.; American journalist, author and critic; b. 4 July 1907; ed. Cornell Univ.; Journalist 1929–; with New York Times 1930–, Music Critic 1956–60, Drama Critic 1960–65, Critic-at-Large 1965–72; mem. Philadelphia Music Acad. 1959–; Hon. Mus.D. (Cornell Univ. and Oberlin Coll.). *Publications:* Opera Front and Back 1938, Music as a Profession 1939, Music on My Beat 1943, The Maestro, The Life of Arturo Toscanini 1951, How to Build a Record Library 1953, How to Bring up Your Child to Enjoy Music 1958, The Making of the American Theatre 1965.

TAUFA'AHAU Tupou IV, G.C.V.O., G.C.M.G., K.B.E., B.A., LL.B.; H.M. the King of Tonga; b. 4 July 1918; eldest son of the late Queen Salote Tupou III of Tonga and the late Hon. Uiliami Tungi, C.B.E., Premier of Tonga; brother of Prince Fatafehi Tu'ipelahake (q.v.); m. H.R.H. Princess Halaevalu Mata'aho 1947; three s. one d., of whom the eldest, H.R.H. Crown Prince Tupoutoa, is heir to the throne; ed. Newington Coll. and Sydney Univ., N.S.W.; Minister of Educ. 1943, of Health 1944–49, Premier of Tonga, also Minister of Foreign Affairs and Agric. 1949–65; King of Tonga 1965–; est. Teachers' Training Coll. and revised Tonga alphabet 1944; f. Tonga High School 1947, Broadcasting Station 1961, Govt. newspaper 1964; Chancellor Univ. of the S. Pacific 1970–73; Hon. LL.D.; Kt. Commdr., Order of Merit (Fed. Repub. of Germany) 1978; numerous citations and awards. *Address:* The Palace, P.O. Box 6, Nuku'alofa, Tonga. *Telephone:* Nuku'alofa 21-000.

TAUFER, Jiří; Czechoslovak writer; b. 5 July 1911, Boskovice, Blansko Dist.; ed. Faculty of Law, Brno; co-operation with left-wing periodicals, Rudé právo, Tvorba, Haló-noviny 1931–39; prison sentence for co-operation in the publ. of underground periodicals Rovnost and Antifašista, 1934; in Poland and U.S.S.R. 1939–45; Ed., Tvorba, Dir., Svoboda publishing house 1945–48; mem., Cen. Cttee., CP of Czechoslovakia 1946–54; Amb. to Yugoslavia 1948–49; Deputy Minister of Foreign Affairs 1949, of Finance 1950–53, of Culture 1954–56; Chair. State Cttee. for Art Affairs 1953–54; professional writer and trans. 1956–; Cen. Cttee. Presidium mem., Left Front 1969–71; Presidium mem. Union of Czech Writers 1972–82. *Collection of poems:* Evening Eyes 1928, Shadow Plays 1931, Checkmate, Europe 1933, See You Again, CCCP 1935, Roentgenograms 1938, Annals 1958, Clinkstone 1961, The Memory Theme 1966, Seven 1972, Annual Rings 1972, Dialogue with Vladimir Mayakovsky 1977, To Be Continued 1979; *studies:* N.V. Gogol 1952, Maxim Gorky, Master of Soviet Culture 1952, Vítězslav Nezval, Monograph 1957, Bedřich Václavek 1957, Portraits and Silhouettes 1980; *translations:* Mehring: In Defiance of Them … 1938, Mayakovsky: From His Work 1950, Eisenstein 1959, Hikmet: 5 plays 1959; Order of February 25, 1948 1949, State Prize 1951, Order of the Republic 1960, Order of the Red Banner of Labour (U.S.S.R.) 1971, State Prize of Klement Gottwald 1974, Nat. Artist 1975, Maxim Gorky Prize (U.S.S.R.) 1979, Antonín Zápotocký Prize 1980.

TAUS, Josef, LL.D.; Austrian banker, industrialist and politician; b. 8 Feb. 1933, Vienna; s. of Josef Taus and G. Schinko; m. Martha Loibl 1960; ed. Univ. of Vienna, Hochschule für Welthandel; Journalist; law practice; with Austrian Inst. of Econ. Research; Sec. and Head of Econ. Div., Girozentrale und Bank der Österreichischen Sparkassen AG 1958, mem. Man. Bd. 1967–68, Chair. and Man. Dir. 1968–75; fmr. Man. Sparinvest-Kapitalanlage GmbH; mem. Parl. 1975–; State Sec. Fed. Ministry of Communications and Nationalized Enterprises 1966–67; Fed. Chair. Austrian People's Party (ÖVP) 1975–79; Man. Partner Constantia IndustrieverwaltungsgesmbH. 1979–86; mem. Bd. Constantia Industrieholding AG 1986–89; mem. Bd. ECO TRUST Holding AG 1989; Chair. GZ TRUST Holding AG 1989; Managing Dir. Fremdenverkehrsbetriebe Gmbh and Co. OHG. *Leisure interests:* skiing, music, reading, swimming. *Address:* Opernring 19, 1010 Vienna (Office); Zahnradbahnstrasse 17, A-1190 Vienna, Austria (Home). *Telephone:* 222/588 45-0 (Office).

TAVARD, Rev. Georges Henri, S.T.D.; American ecclesiastic; b. 6 Nov. 1922, Nancy, France; s. of Ernest Henri Tavard and Marguerite Wasser; ed. Ecole St. Sigisbert, Nancy, Grand Séminaire, Nancy and Facultés Catholiques, Lyon; mem. Order of Austinians of the Assumption; ordained 1947; lecturer in Theology, Capenor House, Surrey, U.K. 1949–51; Assoc. Ed. Documentation Catholique Paris 1951–52; lecturer in Theol. Assumption Coll., Worcester, Mass. 1953–58; Chair. and Prof. Dept. of Theology, Carlow Coll. Pittsburgh, Pa. 1959–66; Prof. of Religious Studies, Penn. State Univ. 1966–69; Prof. of Theology, Methodist Theological School, Ohio 1970–87, Prof. Emer. 1987–; Medal of St. Augustine of Canterbury; Hon. D.D. (Kenyon Coll.). *Publications:* Holy Writ or Holy Church 1959, The Quest for Catholicity 1963, Woman in Christian Tradition 1973, The Seventeenth Century Tradition 1978, Poetry & Contemplation in St. John of the Cross 1988; under pseudonym Henri Wasser: Song for Avalokita, Poems 1979. *Address:* Methodist Theological School, Delaware, Ohio 43015 (Office); 2151 Waldorf Road, Columbus, Ohio 43229, U.S.A. (Home). *Telephone:* 614-548-4824 (Office); 614-475-6811 (Home).

TAVENER, John; British composer; b. 28 Jan. 1944, London; s. of Kenneth Tavener and Muriel Tavener; m. Victoria Marangopoulou 1974 (divorced 1986); ed. Highgate School and R.A.M.; Organist St. John's Church, London 1960; Prof. of Composition, Trinity Coll. of Music, London 1968–; youngest composer ever performed at Promenade Concert, London 1969, at Royal Opera House, Covent Garden (Thérèse) 1979; works performed in U.K., U.S.A., U.S.S.R., Greece, Poland, Australia, Fed. Repub. of Germany, Scandinavia, S. America and elsewhere; converted to Russian Orthodox Church 1974; lives and works Aegina, Greece for half year; works include The Whale, Celtic Requiem, Ultimos Ritos, Palintropos, Antigone, Thérèse, Akhmatova-Rekviem, Liturgy of St. John Chrysostom, 16 Haiku of Seferis, Sappho—Lyrical Fragments, Great Canon of St. Andrew of Crete, Prayer for the World, Kyklike Kinesis, Ikon of Light, The Gentle Spirit, All-Night Vigil Service of the Orthodox Church (commissioned by Orthodox and Anglican Churches, for Christ Church Cathedral, Oxford 1985), Two Hymns to the Mother of God, Trisāgion, Mandelion; Eis Thanaton (a ritual), Ikon of St. Cuthbert, God is with Us, Acclamation for Patriarch Demetrios, Akathist of Thanksgiving, Meditation on the Light, Panikhida, Ikon of Saint Seraphim, The Protecting Veil; Hon. A.R.A.M.; Hon. F.T.C.L.; Prince Rainier Int. Prize 1965; First Prize Sacred Music Int. Composition Contest 1972. *Leisure interests:* iconography, love of Greece. *Address:* c/o Chester Music, 8–9 Frith Street, London, England.

TAVERNAS-GUZMÁN, Juan Aristides, B.A., D.JUR.; Dominican Republic diplomatist; b. 24 Nov. 1936, Moca; m.; three c.; ed. Univ. Autonoma de Santo Domingo; practised law 1966–69; Sec. of State for Interior and Police 1969–71; Attorney-Gen. 1971–73; Sec. of State without Portfolio 1973–78, for Labour 1978–87; Perm. Rep. to UN 1987–; founding mem. and preliminary cand. for Pres. Partido Reformista. *Publications:* La IV República, la de Balaguer, Por los Fueros de Cibao and over 800 newspaper articles. *Address:* Permanent Mission of the Dominican Republic to the United Nations, 144 East 44th Street, 4th Floor, New York, N.Y. 10017, U.S.A. *Telephone:* (212) 867-0833.

TAVERNER, Sonia; Canadian ballerina; b. 18 May 1936, Byfleet, Surrey; d. of H. J. Taverner; ed. Elmhurst Ballet School and Royal Ballet School, London, and ballet school in New York; joined Royal Ballet 1955, toured U.S.A. and Canada; joined Royal Winnipeg Ballet 1956, leading dancer 1957, ballerina 1962–66; appeared with Royal Winnipeg Ballet, Commonwealth Arts Festival, London 1964; joined "Les Grands Ballets Canadiens" as prin. dancer 1966–74; appeared as guest artist with the Boston Ballet Co., in Swan Lake 1967; Guest teacher Les Grands Ballets Canadiens Summer School 1970; prin. artist with The Pa. Ballet 1971–72; Head of Ballet Div., Grant MacEwan Community Coll. 1975–80; Dir. Professional Program Devt., Alberta Ballet School, Alberta Sept. 1981–; f. School of Classical Ballet, Alberta Sept. 1982; Producer own concert variations 1977; guest artist with Vancouver Opera 1977, Les Grands Ballets Canadiens in Giselle and The Nutcracker 1977, 1978, Alberta Ballet Co. in The Nutcracker and Raymonda 1978, 1979; guest teacher with Alberta Ballet Summer School 1975, 1976, Pacific Ballet Theatre Summer School 1979; guest artist with Toronto, Winnipeg and Vancouver Symphony Orchestras; guest teaching in Penticton, B.C. 1984–85; has toured extensively over North America, Jamaica and U.K.; mem. Royal Acad. of Dancing, Actors Equity Asscn., American Guild of Musical Artists. *Leisure interests:* cooking, books. *Address:* P.O. Box 129, Stony Plain, Alberta, Canada.

TAVERNIER, Bertrand René Maurice; French film director; b. 25 April 1941, Lyon; s. of René Tavernier and Geneviève Dumond; m. Claudine O'Hagen 1965; one s. one d.; ed. Ecole St.-Martin de Pontoise, Lycées Henri-IV, Fénelon, Paris, Univ. de Paris (Sorbonne); press attaché and journalist, then film dir. *Films include:* Le baiser de Judas, Une charge explosive, La chance et l'amour; jt. screenplay and Dir. L'horloger de Saint-Paul (Louis Delluc prize 1973), Que la fête commence (César Best Screenplay, Best Direction), Le juge et l'assassin (César Best Screenplay 1976), Coup de torchon 1981, La Passion Béatrice 1987; jt. Screenplay, Dir. and Co-Producer Les enfants gâtés 1977, La mort en direct (foreign press award 1979), Une semaine de vacances 1980, Un dimanche à la campagne, Round Midnight 1986; jt. screenplay La trace 1983. *Publication:* 30 ans de cinéma américain (jtly.).

TAVIANI, Paolo; Italian film director; b. 1931, San Miniato; brother of Vittorio Taviani (q.v.); co-dir. with Vittorio Taviani of the following films: Un uomo da Bruciare 1963, I fuorilegge del metraimonio 1963, Sovversivi 1967, Sotto il segno dello scorpione 1969, San Michele aveva un gallo 1971, Allonsanfan 1974, Padre Padrone 1977, The Meadow 1979, La notte di San Lorenzo (The Night of the Shooting Stars) 1981, Xaos 1984, Good Morning, Babylon 1988. *Address:* c/o Ministry of Culture and Education, Via Della Ferratella 51, 00184 Rome, Italy.

TAVIANI, Paolo Emilio; Italian politician; b. 6 Nov. 1912; s. of Ferdinando and Elide (née Banchelli) Taviani; m. Vittoria Festa; seven c.; ed. Univ. of Genoa; Prof. History of Econ. Theory at Genoa Univ.; leader Partisan War 1943–45; organizer of Christian Democratic Party (in Genoa area) 1943; mem. Constituent Ass. 1946–48; M.P. 1948–; Deputy Sec. Christian Democratic Party 1946–49, Sec. 1949–50; Ed. and Dir. Civitas, monthly magazine of political studies, 1950–; Italian Rep. to Schuman Plan Conf. 1951 and to later E.D.C. Confs.; Under-Sec. for Foreign Affairs 1951–53; Minister of Defence 1953–58, of Finance 1959–60, of Treasury 1960–62, of

Interior 1962–68, for interventions in Southern Italy 1968–73, of the Interior 1973–74; Pres. of F.I.V.L. (Nat. Fed. of Partisans War 1943–45) 1972, Pres. of Foreign Affairs Cttee. of Senate 1979–87; Vice-Pres. of Senate 1987–. *Publications include:* Social Reformers of the Italian Risorgimento 1940, Social Prospects 1945, Ownership 1946, The Schuman Plan 1952, Atlantic Solidarity and European Community 1957, Defence of Peace 1958, Christian Principles and Democratic Systems 1965, The Concept of Utility in Economic Theory Vol. I 1968, Vol. II 1970, Utility, Economics and Morals 1970, The Problem of Development and the "Cassa del Mezzogiorno" Experience 1972, Christopher Columbus: The Genesis of the Great Discovery 1974, Ligurian Lands 1976, The Voyages of Columbus 1984, Christopher Columbus: The Grand Design 1985. *Address:* Via di Fontanegli 33, Bavari, Genoa, Italy.

TAVIANI, Vittorio; Italian film director; b. 1929, San Miniato; brother of Paolo Taviani (q.v.); co-dir. with Paolo Taviani of the following films: Un uomo da Bruciare 1963, I fuorilegge del metraimonio 1963, Sovversivi 1967, Sotto il segno dello scorpione 1969, San Michele aveva un gallo 1971, Allonsanfan 1974, Padre Padrone 1977, The Meadow (Italian-French) 1979, La nottte di San Lorenzo (The Night of the Shooting Stars) 1981, Xaos 1984, Good Morning, Babylon 1988. *Address:* c/o Ministry of Culture and Education, Via Della Ferratella 51, 00184 Rome, Italy.

TAX, Sol, PH.D., PH.B.; American university professor; b. 30 Oct. 1907, Chicago, Ill.; s. of Morris Paul Tax and Kate (Hanowitz) Tax; m. Gertrude Jospe Katz 1933; two d.; ed. Univs. of Wisconsin and Chicago; mem. Logan Museum N. Africa Expedition 1930; field research, Apache Indians 1931, Fox Indians 1932–34; Investigator, and later Ethnologist, Carnegie Inst. 1934–48; field research in Guatemala and Chiapas (Mexico) 1934–43; Research Assoc. in Anthropology, Univ. of Chicago 1940–44, Assoc. Prof. 1944–48, Prof. of Anthropology 1948–, Assoc. Dean Social Sciences Div. 1948–53, Chair. Anthropology Dept. 1955–58, Dean Univ. Extension 1963–68; Assoc. Ed. American Anthropologist 1948–52, Ed. 1953–56; Ed. Current Anthropology 1957–74, Viking Fund Publs. in Anthropology 1959–68; Gen. Ed. World Anthropology 1975–80, Proceedings IX Int. Congress of Anthropological and Ethnological Sciences; Fellow American Anthropological Assn. (Pres. 1958–59), Center for Advanced Study in the Behavioral Sciences 1969–70; Man-Nature Project in Chiapas, Mexico 1956–59; Chair. Cttee. on Darwin Centenary (1859-1959) 1956–59; U.S. Nat. Comm. for UNESCO 1959–65, Exec. Cttee. 1963–65; Consultant, U.S. Office of Educ. 1965–70; Special Adviser, Smithsonian Inst. 1965–, and Dir., Center for Study of Man 1968–76; mem. Bd. of Advisers, Council on Int. Communication 1966–; Pres. Int. Union of Anthropological and Ethnological Sciences 1968–73; Dir. Council, Study of Mankind 1963–79; mem. Advisory Council, Nat. Anthropological Film Center 1976– (Chair. 1978–); Founding Chair. Library-Anthropology Resource Group 1973–; Trustee; Native American Educational Services (NAES Coll.) 1977–; Hon. Fellow, Royal Anthropological Inst., Slovakian Anthropological Soc. of Slovak Acad. of Sciences, Chilean Anthropological Soc., Ethnological Soc. of Hungary; D. Hum. Litt. (Wis. Univ.) 1969, Hon. LL.D. (Wilmington College) 1974, Hon. D.Sc. (Univ. del Valle de Guatemala) 1974, (Beloit Coll.) 1975; Viking Medallist 1961; Medal of Govt. of Czechoslovakia 1969; Bronislaw Malinowski Award of Soc. for Applied Anthropology 1977; Distinguished Service Award of the American Anthropological Asscn. 1977, Thomas Jefferson Award in Int. Anthropology 1983. *Publications:* Heritage of Conquest: The Ethnology of Middle America 1952, Penny Capitalism, A Guatemalan Indian Economy 1953, 1963; Ed. for 29th Int. Congress of Americanists Proceedings 1949–52, Civilizations of Ancient America 1951, Acculturation in the Americas 1952, Indian Tribes of Aboriginal America 1952, Evolution After Darwin (3 vols.) 1960, Anthropology Today—Selections 1962, Horizons of Anthropology 1963, 1977, The Draft: A Handbook of Facts and Alternatives 1967, Ed.: The People Versus the System 1968. *Address:* 1700 East 56th Street, Chicago, Ill. 60637, U.S.A. *Telephone:* (312) DO3-0990.

TAXELL, (Lars Evald) Christoffer, LL.M.; Finnish politician; b. 14 Feb. 1948, Turku; s. of Lars Erik Taxell and Elna Hillevi Brunberg; m. Rachel Margreta Nygård 1974; Chair. Youth Org., Swedish People's Party 1970–72, mem. Party Exec. 1970–72, 1973–, Chair. 1985–; Political Sec. 1970–71; Asst., School of Econ., Åbo Akademi, Turku 1973–75; M.P. 1975–; Minister of Justice 1979–87, of Educ. and Science 1987–. *Address:* Ministry of Education and Science, Meritullinkatu 10, 00170 Helsinki, Finland. *Telephone:* 134171.

TAYA, Col. Maawiya Ould Sid'Ahmed; Mauritanian army officer and politician; b. 1943; served in Saharan War 1976–78, Chief of Mil. Operations, then Commdr. garrison at Bir Mogkrein; Minister of Defence 1978–79; Commdr. nat. gendarmerie 1979–80; Minister in charge of Perm. Secr., Mil. Cttee. for Nat. Recovery 1979–81; Army Chief of Staff 1980–81, March-Dec. 1984; Prime Minister and Minister of Defence 1981–84, Dec. 1984–; Pres. of Mauritania and Chair. Mil. Cttee. for Nat. Salvation Dec. 1984–. *Address:* Présidence de la République, B.P. 184, Nouackchott, Mauritania.

TAYLOR, Alan John Percivale, M.A.; British historian; b. 25 March 1906, Southport; s. of Percy Lees Taylor and Constance Thompson; m. Éva Haraszti 1976; four s. two d.; ed. Oriel Coll. Oxford; Rockefeller Fellow in Social Sciences 1929–30; Lecturer in History, Univ. of Manchester 1930–38;

Lecturer in Int. History, Oxford Univ. 1953–63, Tutor in Modern History, Magdalen Coll., Oxford 1938–63, Fellow 1938–76, Hon. Fellow 1976, of Oriel Coll., Oxford 1980; Pres. City Music Soc., London; Hon. Fellow Zagreb Univ. 1984, Hungarian Acad. of Sciences 1986; Hon. D.C.L. (Univ. of New Brunswick), Hon. D.Univ. (York Univ.), Hon. D.Litt. (Bristol, East Anglia, Warwick, Manchester). *Publications:* The Italian Problem in European Diplomacy 1847-49 1934, Germany's First Bid for Colonies 1938, The Course of German History 1945, The Habsburg Monarchy 1809-1918 1948, From Napoleon to Stalin 1950, Rumours of Wars 1952, The Struggle for Mastery in Europe 1848-1914 1954, Bismarck 1955, Englishmen and Others 1956, The Trouble-Makers 1957, The Russian Revolution of 1917 (TV lectures) 1958, The Origins of the Second World War 1961, The First World War 1963, Politics in Wartime 1964, English History 1914-1945 1965, From Sarajevo to Potsdam 1966, Europe: Grandeur and Decline 1967, War by Timetable 1969, Churchill: Four Faces and the Man (with others) 1969, Beaverbrook 1972, The Second World War 1975, Essays in English History 1976, The Last of Old Europe 1976, The Russian War 1941-45 1978, The War Lords 1978, How Wars Begin 1979, Revolutions and Revolutionaries 1980, Politicians, Socialism and Historians 1980, A Personal History 1983, An Old Man's Diary 1984, How Wars End 1985, A Life with Alan. The Diary of A. J. P. Taylor's wife Eva from 1978 to 1985 1987. *Leisure interests:* walking, churches. *Address:* 32 Twisden Road, London, NW5 1DN, England. *Telephone:* 01-485 1507.

TAYLOR, Allan Richard; Canadian banker; b. 14 Sept. 1932, Prince Albert, Saskatchewan; s. of Norman Taylor and Anna Lydia Norbeck Taylor; m. Shirley Irene Ruston 1957; one s. one d.; Chair. and C.E.O. The Royal Bank of Canada 1986–; Dir. Canadian Pacific Ltd., Montreal, TransCanada Pipelines Ltd., Toronto, Ont., General Motors of Canada Ltd., Int. Monetary Conf.; Founding Dir. Corp. Higher Educ. Forum; mem. Bd. ot Trustees, Queen's Univ., Kingston, Ont., Advisory Cttee., School of Business Admin., Univ. of Western Ontario. *Address:* The Royal Bank of Canada, Royal Bank Plaza, Toronto, Ont., M5J 2J5, Canada.

TAYLOR, Arnold Joseph, C.B.E., M.A., D.LITT., F.B.A., F.S.A., F.R.HIST.S.; British government official (retd.); b. 24 July 1911, Battersea; s. of John G. Taylor and Mary M. (née Riley) Taylor; m. Patricia K. Guilbride 1940; one s. one d.; ed. Merchant Taylors' School and St. John's Coll., Oxford; schoolmaster 1934–35; Inspectorate of Ancient Monuments and Bldgs. 1935–72, Chief Inspector 1961–72; R.A.F. (Intelligence) 1942–46; Pres. Soc. of Antiquaries of London 1975–78; Hon. D.Litt. (Wales) 1970; Dr. h.c. (Caen) 1980. *Publications:* Records of the Barony of Lewes 1940, History of the King's Works (part author) 1963, Four Great Castles 1983; many guides to historical monuments and contrib. to archaeological and historical journals. *Leisure interests:* research in archives, travel, music. *Address:* Rose Cottage, Lincoln's Hill, Chiddingfold, Surrey, England. *Telephone:* (042 879) 2069.

TAYLOR, Arthur Robert, M.A.; American business executive; b. 6 July 1935, Elizabeth, N.J.; s. of Arthur Earl Taylor and Marion Hilda Scott; m. Marion McFarland 1959 (divorced); three d.; m. 2nd Kathryn Pelgrift; ed. Brown Univ.; Asst. Dir. of Admissions, Brown Univ. 1957–60; with The First Boston Corpn. 1961–70, Vice-Pres. Underwriting Dept. 1966–70, Dir. 1970–; Vice-Pres. (Finance), Int. Paper Co. 1970–71, Exec. Vice-Pres. 1971–72, Dir. 1971–72; Pres. and Dir. CBS Inc. 1972–76; Dir. Arthur Taylor & Co., New York 1977- (Chair. 1977-), Travelers Corpn., Rockefeller Centre Inc., American Friends of Bilderberg, Pitney Bowes Inc., Louisiana Land and Exploration, Eastern Airlines, Namura Pacific Basin Fund, etc.; Vice-Chair. Forum Corpn., Boston, Mass 1988-; Dean, Faculty of Business, Fordham Univ. 1985–; mem. Council on Foreign Relations, Nat. Cttee. on American Foreign Policy, Center for Inter-American Relations, Japan Soc.; Trustee, Brown Univ., Franklin Savings Bank, N.Y. Hospital, William H. Donner Foundation; Commr. Trilateral Comm. *Publications:* article in Harvard Review of Business History 1971, chapter in The Other Side of Profit 1975. *Address:* 1095 Park Avenue, New York, N.Y. 10128; Main Street, Salisbury, Conn. 06068, U.S.A. (Home).

TAYLOR, Bernard David, B.SC., C.B.I.M.; British business executive; b. 17 Oct. 1935, Coventry; s. of Thomas Taylor and Winifred (Smith) Taylor; m. Nadine B. Taylor 1959; two s. two d.; ed. Univ. of Wales and London Business School; science teacher, Coventry Educ. Authority until 1958; Sales and Marketing, SKF 1960–64; Sales and Marketing Man. Glaxo New Zealand 1964–67; New Products Man. Glaxo U.K. 1967–72; Man. Dir. Glaxo Australia 1972–84; Dir. Glaxo Holdings PLC and Man. Dir. Glaxo Pharmaceuticals U.K. 1984–86; Chief Exec. Glaxo Holdings PLC 1986–89; mem. CBI Europe Cttee. 1987–, British Overseas Trade Bd. 1987–. *Address:* Clarges House, 6-12 Clarges Street, London, W1Y 8DH, England. *Telephone:* 01-493 4060.

TAYLOR, Carl Ernest, M.D., M.P.H., DR.P.H., D.SC.; American physician; b. 26 July 1916, Landour, U.P., India; s. of Dr. John C. Taylor and Dr. Elizabeth Siehl Taylor; m. Mary Daniels Taylor 1943; two s. one d.; ed. Muskingum Coll., Ohio and Harvard Univ.; Chief of Medical Service, Marine Hosp., Pittsburgh 1945–47; Supt. Mission Hosp., Fategarh, India 1947–49; Prof. of Preventive and Social Medicine, Christian Medical Coll., Ludhiana, India 1952–56; Asst. Prof., Assoc. Prof. Epidemiology, Harvard School of Public Health 1956–60, Prof. of Int. Health and Chair. of Dept., Johns Hopkins Univ. 1961–83, Prof. Emer. 1984–; UNICEF Country Rep. for China 1984–;

many awards from int. agencies and appts. to special bds.; F.R.C.P. (Canada); Hon. Dr.Sc. (Muskingum Coll.); Hon. D.Hum.Litt. (Towson State Univ.). *Publications:* 10 books and over 150 journal publications and chapters. *Leisure interests:* mountain climbing, photography, swimming. *Address:* UNICEF, 12 Sanlitun Lu, Beijing, China (Office); 1106 Bellemore Road, Baltimore, Md. 21210, U.S.A. (Home). *Telephone:* 52-3131 (Office).

TAYLOR, Charles, D.PHIL. F.B.A.; Canadian professor of philosophy; b. 5 Nov. 1931, Montreal; s. of Walter Margrave Taylor and Simone Beaubien; m. Alba Romer 1956; five d.; ed. McGill and Oxford Univs., Fellow of All Souls Coll., Oxford 1956–61; Prof. of Political Science and Philosophy, McGill Univ. 1961–; Prof. of Philosophy, Univ. of Montreal 1962–71; Chichele Prof. of Social and Political Theory, Oxford Univ. and Fellow of All Souls Coll. 1976–81; mem. Royal Soc. of Canada; John Locke Prize, Oxford 1955. *Publications:* The Explanation of Behaviour 1964, Hegel 1975, Hegel and Modern Society 1979, Human Agency and Language 1985, Philosophy and the Human Sciences 1985. *Leisure interests:* skiing, swimming, hiking. *Address:* Department of Political Science, McGill University, 855 Sherbrooke Street W., Montreal H3A 2T7; 344 Metcalfe Avenue, Montreal, H32 2J3, Canada (Home).

TAYLOR, Edward Plunket, C.M.G., B.SC., LL.D.; Canadian industrialist; b. 29 Jan. 1901, Ottawa; s. of Lt.-Col. P. B. Taylor and Florence Magee; m. Winifred Thornton Duguid 1927; one s. two d.; ed. Ashbury Coll., Ottawa Collegiate Inst., and McGill Univ., Montreal; Joint Dir.-Gen. Munitions Production 1940; Exec. Asst. to Ministry of Munitions and Supply 1941; Pres. War Supplies Ltd., Washington, D.C. 1941; Pres. and Vice-Chair. British Supply Council in N. America Sept. 1941; Dir.-Gen. British Ministry of Supply Mission Feb. 1942; Canadian Deputy mem. on Combined Production and Resources Bd. Nov. 1942; Canadian Chair. Jt. War Aid Cttee. U.S. Canada Sept. 1943; Pres. Lyford Cay Co. Ltd., Windfields Farm Ltd.; Chair. New Providence Devt. Co., Nassau, Int. Housing (Cayman) Ltd., Int. Housing Ltd.; Chair. and Chief Steward Jockey Club of Canada; Hon. Chair. Ontario Jockey Club. *Address:* The Cay House, Lyford Cay, Nassau, Bahamas.

TAYLOR, Elizabeth; British film actress; b. 27 Feb. 1932, London; m. 1st Conrad Nicholas Hilton, Jr. 1950 (divorced); m. 2nd Michael Wilding 1952 (divorced), two s.; m. 3rd Mike Todd 1957 (died 1958), one d.; m. 4th Eddie Fisher 1959 (divorced); m. 5th Richard Burton 1964 (divorced 1974, remarried 1975, divorced 1976), one adopted d.; m. 7th Senator John Warner (q.v.) 1976 (divorced 1982); ed. Byron House, Hawthorne School, and Metro-Goldwyn-Mayer School; Chair. American Foundation for AIDS Research 1987–; Acad. Award (Oscar) for Best Actress for Butterfield 8 1960, for Who's Afraid of Virginia Woolf? 1967; Silver Bear Award for Hammersmith is Out, Berlin 1972, Cecil B. De Mille Award 1984; Commdr. des Arts et des Lettres 1985; Légion d'honneur 1987; Onassis Prize 1988. *Plays include:* The Little Foxes (New York) 1979–80, (Los Angeles) 1981, (London) 1982, Private Lives (New York) 1983. *Films include:* Lassie Come Home 1943, Jane Eyre 1943, National Velvet 1944, The Rich Full Life 1944, Courage of Lassie 1945, A Date With Judy 1948, Little Women 1949, Father of the Bride 1950, A Place in the Sun 1951, Ivanhoe 1952, The Girl Who Had Everything 1953, Elephant Walk 1954, Beau Brummel 1954, The Last Time I Saw Paris 1955, Giant 1956, Raintree Country 1957, Cat on a Hot Tin Roof 1958, Suddenly Last Summer 1959, Butterfield 8 1960, Cleopatra 1962, The VIPs 1963, The Sandpiper 1965, Who's Afraid of Virginia Woolf? 1966, The Taming of the Shrew 1967, Doctor Faustus 1967, The Comedians 1967, Reflections in a Golden Eye 1967, Boom 1968, Secret Ceremony 1968, The Only Game in Town 1969, Under Milk Wood 1971, Zee & Co. 1971, Hammersmith is Out 1972, Night Watch 1973, Ash Wednesday 1974, Identikit 1974, Blue Bird 1975, A Little Night Music 1976, The Mirror Crack'd 1981, Winter Kills 1985, The Young Toscanini 1987. *Publication:* Elizabeth Takes Off 1987. *Address:* c/o Chen Sam and Associates, 315 East 72nd Street, New York, N.Y. 10021, U.S.A. *Telephone:* (212) 628-5915.

TAYLOR, Sir George, Kt., D.SC., F.R.S., F.R.S.E., F.L.S.; British botanist; b. 15 Feb. 1904; s. of George W. and Jane (Sloan) Taylor; m. 1st Alice H. Pendrich 1929 (died 1977), two c.; m. 2nd Norah English (died 1967); m. 3rd Beryl, Lady Colwyn (died 1981); mem. botanical expedition to Southern Africa 1927–28; jt. leader, British Museum expedition to Ruwenzori and mountains of E. Africa 1934–35; expedition to Tibet and Bhutan 1938; Prin., Air Ministry 1940–45; Deputy Keeper of Botany, British Museum 1945–50, Keeper 1950–56; Dir. Royal Botanical Gdns., Kew 1956–71; Dir. Stanley Smith Horticultural Trust 1970–; mem. Council, Nat. Trust 1961–72 and fmr. holder of many other professional appts.; mem. or hon. mem. many nat. and int. scientific socs.; Veitch Gold Medal, Royal Horticultural Soc. 1963, Scottish Horticultural Medal 1983; Hon. LL.D. (Dundee); Hon. Dr.Phil. (Gothenburg). *Publications:* An Account of the Genus Meconopsis 1934; articles on flowering plants in various periodicals. *Leisure interests:* gardening, music, angling. *Address:* Belhaven House, Dunbar, East Lothian, EH42 1NS, Scotland. *Telephone:* (0368) 63546.

TAYLOR, Harold McCarter, C.B.E., T.D., M.SC.(NZ), M.A., PH.D.; British retd. university official; b. 13 May 1907, Dunedin, New Zealand; s. of James and Louisa (née McCarter) Taylor; m. 1st Joan Sills 1933 (died 1965), 2nd Judith Samuel 1966; two s. two d.; ed. Otago Boys' High School, Dunedin, N.Z., Univ. of Otago and Clare Coll., Cambridge; Univ. Lecturer in

Mathematics, Univ. of Cambridge 1933–45, Treas., Univ. of Cambridge 1945–53, Sec.-Gen. of the Faculties 1953–61; Vice-Chancellor Univ. of Keele 1961–67, retd.; Rede Lecturer, Univ. of Cambridge 1966; Fellow, Soc. of Antiquaries 1961, Vice-Pres. 1974–77; mem. Royal Comm. on Historical Monuments 1972–78; Lt.-Col. Royal Artillery 1939–45; Smith's Prize, Univ. of Cambridge 1932, John Henry Lefroy Medal, Royal Artillery 1946, Alice Davis Hitchcock Medallion, Soc. of Architectural Historians 1965, William Frend Medal, Soc. of Antiquaries 1982. *Publications:* Anglo-Saxon Architecture Vols. I and II (with Joan Taylor) 1965, Vol. III 1978, Why Should We Study The Anglo-Saxons? 1966, numerous archaeological articles in nat. journals. *Leisure interests:* ski-mountaineering, history of architecture. *Address:* 192 Huntingdon Road, Cambridge, CB3 0LB, England. *Telephone:* (0223) 276324.

TAYLOR, Sir James, Kt., M.B.E., D.SC., PH.D., C.CHEM., F.R.S.C., H.F.I.MIN.E., F.R.S.A.; British industrial consultant; b. 16 Aug. 1902, Sunderland; s. of James and Alice Taylor; m. Margaret Lennox Stewart 1929; two s. one d.; ed. Bede Coll., Sunderland, Rutherford Coll., Newcastle upon Tyne, Univs. of Durham, Utrecht, Cambridge and the Sorbonne; joined Nobel Div., ICI Ltd. 1928, Research Dir. 1946, Jt. Man. Dir. 1951, Dir. 1952–64; Chair. Yorkshire Imperial Metals Ltd. 1958–64, Imperial Aluminium Co. Ltd. 1959–64, Imperial Metal Industries Ltd. 1962–64; Deputy Chair. Royal Ordnance Factories Bd. 1959–72 (mem. 1952–72); Pres. Inst. of Physics and Physical Soc. 1966–68; Chair. Fulmer Research Inst. Ltd. 1976–78, Chloride Silent Power Ltd. 1974–81; Dir. Oldham Int. Ltd. 1965–71, Surrey Independent Hosp. PLC 1981–86; Pres. Research and Devt. Soc. 1970–76; Hon. mem. Newcomen Soc. (U.S.A.) 1970; mem. Council of R.S.A. 1964, Chair. 1969–71, Vice-Pres. 1969, Hon. Vice-Pres. 1986; mem. Court of Brunel Univ. 1967–81; Hon. D.Sc. (Bradford), Hon. D.C.L. (Newcastle); Medal of the Soc. of the Chemical Industry 1965, Silver Medal, Royal Soc. of Arts 1969, Silver Medal for Service to the Chemical Soc. 1972; Hon. F.Inst.P. 1972. *Publications include:* On the Sparking Potentials of Electric Discharge Tubes 1927, Detonation in Condensed Explosives 1952, British Coal Mining Explosives 1958, Solid Propellent and Exothermic Compositions 1959, The Modern Chemical Industry in Great Britain 1961, Arts, Crafts and Technology 1969, New Horizons in Research and Development 1971, The Scientific Community 1973, lectures and numerous articles in learned journals. *Leisure interests:* gardening, writing, cooking. *Address:* Culvers, Seale, near Farnham, Surrey, GU10 1JN, England. *Telephone:* (02518) 2210.

TAYLOR, J(ames) Herbert, PH.D.; American university professor; b. 14 Jan. 1916, Texas; s. of Charles Aaron Taylor and Delia May (McCain); m. Shirley C. Hoover 1946; one s. two d.; ed. Southeastern Oklahoma State, Univ. of Oklahoma, Univ. of Virginia; Asst. Prof. of Plant Science, Univ. of Okla. 1946–47; Assoc. Prof. of Botany, Univ. of Tenn. 1947–51; Asst. Prof. of Botany, Columbia Univ. 1951–54, Assoc. Prof. 1954–58, Prof. of Cell Biology 1958–64; Prof. of Biological Science and Assoc. Dir. Inst. of Molecular Biophysics, Florida State Univ. 1964–80, Dir. 1980–85, Robert O. Lawton Distinguished Prof. of Biological Science 1983–; mem. N.A.S.; Guggenheim Fellow at Calif. Inst. of Tech. 1958–59; Pres. American Soc. of Cell Biology 1969. *Publications:* Selected Papers on Molecular Genetics 1965, Molecular Genetics (3 vols.) 1963, 1967 and 1979, DNA Methylation and Cellular Differentiation 1984. *Leisure interests:* canoeing and hiking in wilderness areas, travel to wild areas of the world. *Address:* Institute of Molecular Biophysics, Florida State University, Tallahassee, Fla. 32306-3015 (Office); 1414 Hilltop Drive, Tallahassee, Fla. 32303, U.S.A. (Home). *Telephone:* (904) 644-1421 (Office); (904) 385-7862 (Home).

TAYLOR, John Bryan, PH.D., F.R.S.; British physicist; b. 26 Dec. 1928, Birmingham; s. of Frank H. Taylor and Ada Taylor (née Stinton); m. Joan M. Hargest 1951; one s. one d.; ed. Oldbury Co. High School and Birmingham Univ.; served R.A.F. 1950–52; Physicist, Atomic Weapons Research Establishment, Aldermaston 1955–59, 1961–62; Harkness Fellow, Univ. of Calif. 1959–60; on staff of UKAEA, Culham Lab. 1962–, Head of Theory Div. 1963–81, Chief Physicist Culham Lab. 1981–; mem. Inst. for Advanced Study, Princeton, N.J. 1969, 1980 and 1981; Fellow American Physical Soc.; Maxwell Medal (Inst. of Physics) 1971, Max Born Prize and Medal (German Physical Soc.) 1979, Award for Excellence in Plasma Research (American Physical Soc.) 1986. *Publications:* contribs. to scientific learned journals. *Leisure interests:* gliding, model engineering. *Address:* Culham Laboratory, Abingdon, Oxon., OX14 3DB, England. *Telephone:* (0235) 463344 or (0235) 21840 Ext. 3344.

TAYLOR, John Clayton, PH.D., F.R.S.; British professor of mathematical physics; b. 4 Aug. 1930, London; s. of Leonard and Edith Taylor; m. Gillian M. Schofield 1959; two s.; ed. Selhurst Grammar School, Croydon and Peterhouse, Cambridge; Lecturer, Imperial Coll., London 1956–60; lecturer, Cambridge Univ. and Fellow of Peterhouse 1960–64; Reader in Theoretical Physics, Oxford Univ. and Fellow of Univ. Coll. 1964–80; Prof. of Mathematical Physics, Cambridge Univ. and Fellow of Robinson Coll. 1980–. *Publication:* Gauge Theory of Weak Interactions 1976. *Address:* 9 Bowers Croft, Cambridge, CB1 4RP, England.

TAYLOR, John Russell, M.A.; British writer and professor of cinema studies; b. 19 June 1935, Dover, Kent; s. of Arthur Russell Taylor and Kathleen Mary (née Picker) Taylor; ed. Dover Grammar School, Jesus Coll., Cambridge, Courtauld Inst. of Art; Sub Ed., Times Educ. Supplement 1959–60; Editorial Asst., Times Literary Supplement 1960–62; Film Critic, The Times 1962–73; Prof., Div. of Cinema, Univ. of Southern Calif., U.S.A. 1972–78; Art Critic, The Times 1978–; Ed. Films and Filming 1983–. *Publications:* Anger and After 1962, Anatomy of a Television Play 1962, Cinema Eye, Cinema Ear 1964, Penguin Dictionary of the Theatre 1966, The Art Nouveau Book in Britain 1966, The Rise and Fall of the Well-Made Play 1967, The Art Dealers 1969, The Hollywood Musical 1971, The Second Wave 1971, Directors and Directions 1975, Hitch 1978, Impressionism 1981, Strangers in Paradise 1983, Ingrid Bergman 1983, Alec Guinness 1984, Vivien Leigh 1984, Hollywood 1940s 1985, Portraits of the British Cinema (with John Kobal) 1986, Orson Welles 1986, Edward Wolfe 1986, Great Movie Moments 1987; edited: Look Back in Anger: A Casebook 1968, The Pleasure Dome (Graham Greene on Film) 1972, Masterworks of British Cinema 1974. *Leisure interest:* book collecting. *Address:* c/o The Times, 1 Pennington Street, London, E1 9BD, England. *Telephone:* 01-782-5000.

TAYLOR, Ken; British screenwriter; b. 1922, Bolton, Lancs.; has written numerous original plays for TV including: One of Us, Special Occasion, The Tin Whistle Man, China Doll, Into the Dark, Parkin's Primitives, The Long Distance Blue, The Slaughtermen, The Devil and John Brown, The Seeker, The Magicians, The Edwardians: E. Nesbit, Death or Liberty (Churchill's People), The Pankhursts, Christabel Pankhurst, Sylvia Pankhurst (3 plays for BBC's Shoulder to Shoulder), The Poisoning of Charles Bravo, The Devil's Crown (5 plays on Henry II); many adaptations for TV of works by Somerset Maugham, D.H. Lawrence, H.G. Wells etc. also The Jewel in the Crown from Paul Scott's The Raj Quartet 1982–83 (Royal Television Soc.'s Writers' Award). *Address:* c/o Peters Fraser and Dunlop, 5th Floor, The Chambers, Chelsea Harbour, Lots Road, London, SW10 0XF, England. *Telephone:* 01-376-7676.

TAYLOR, Kenneth D., O.C., M.B.A.; Canadian diplomatist; b. 5 Oct. 1934, Calgary, Alberta; s. of Richard and Nancy (née Wiggins) Taylor; m. Patricia E. Lee 1960; one s.; ed. Univs. of Toronto and Calif. (Berkeley); joined Canadian foreign service 1959; served Guatemala 1960–63, Detroit 1963–66, Karachi 1966–67, London 1967–71, Ottawa 1971–77; Amb. to Iran 1977–80; Consul-Gen. in New York, concurrently Commr. to Bermuda 1981–84; joined Nabisco Brands, Inc. 1984, Sr. Vice-Pres. RJR Nabisco, Inc. 1987–; U.S. Congressional Gold Medal; Hon. LL.D. (Laurentian Univ., State Univ. of New York and St. Francis Xavier Univ. (Antigonish)) and other awards. *Address:* RJR Nabisco Inc., 9 West 57th Street, New York, N.Y. 10019, U.S.A. (Office). *Telephone:* (212) 872-9441 (Office); (212) 757-0921 (Home).

TAYLOR, Lauriston Sale, A.B., D.SC.; American physicist; b. 1 June 1902, Brooklyn, N.Y.; s. of Charles Taylor and Nancy Sale; m. Azulah Walker 1925 (deceased 1972), two s.; m. 2nd Robena Harper Taylor 1973, four d.; ed. Stevens Inst. of Tech., Cornell, Columbia Univs.; Bell Telephone Labs., New York City 1922–; Nat. Bureau of Standards (N.B.S.) 1927–64, Chair. Nat. Comm. Radiation, Protection and Measurements 1929–64, Pres. Nat. Council 1964–77, Hon. Pres. 1977–; mem. Int. Comm. on Radiological Protection 1928–69, mem. Emer. 1970; Chief, Operations Research, Eighth Fighter Command, Ninth U.S. Air Force, Europe 1943–45; Chief Biophysics Branch A.E.C. 1947–48; Chief Atomic and Radiation Physics Div. 1950–62, Assoc. Dir. N.B.S. 1962–64; mem. Int. Comm. on Radiation Units and Measurements 1928–34, Sec. 1934–50, Chair. 1953–69, Hon. Chair. and mem. Emer. 1969–; Special Asst. to Pres., N.A.S. 1965–70; Exec. Dir. Advisory Comm. to Office of Emergency Preparedness 1965–71; Hon. D.Sc. (Univ. of Pa. and St. Procopius Coll.); numerous awards and honours. *Publications:* Organization for Radiation—The Operations of the ICRP & NCRP, 1928–1974 (1980), X-Ray measurements and Protection—The Role of the National Bureau of Standards and the National Radiological Organizations 1913–1964 (1981), Vignettes of Early Radiation Workers (1982), The Tri-partite Conferences on Radiation Protection Standards (U.K., Canada, U.S.A.) 1949–53 1983, 21 books and about 185 papers principally on X-radiation measurement and protection. *Leisure interests:* cabinet making, plumbing, electrical work. *Address:* 7407 Denton Road, Bethesda, Md. 20814, U.S.A. *Telephone:* (301) 652-5096.

TAYLOR, Rev. Michael Hugh, M.A., B.D.; British minister of religion and charity administrator; b. 8 Sept. 1936, Northampton; s. of Albert Taylor and Gwendolen Taylor; m. Adele May Dixon 1960; two s. one d.; ed. Northampton Grammar School, Manchester Univ., Union Theological Seminary, New York; Baptist Minister, North Shields, Northumberland and Hall Green, Birmingham 1964–69; Prin. Northern Baptist Coll., Manchester 1970–85; lecturer in Theology and Ethics, Univ. of Manchester 1970–85; Examining Chaplain to Bishop of Manchester 1975–85; Dir. Christian Aid Oct. 1985–; mem. Comm. on Theological Educ., WCC 1972, Vice-Moderator 1985; Fulbright Travel Award 1969. *Publications:* Variations on a Theme 1971, Learning to Care 1983. *Leisure interests:* walking, theatre, cooking. *Address:* 53 Woodland Rise, London, N10 3UN, England. *Telephone:* 01-883 7217.

TAYLOR, Paul B.; American modern dancer and choreographer; b. 29 July 1930, Allegheny Co., Pa.; s. of Paul B. Taylor and Elizabeth P. Rust; ed. Virginia Episcopal School, Syracuse Univ., Juilliard School of Music, Metropolitan School of Ballet and Martha Graham School of Contemporary Dance; fmr. dancer with the cos. of Martha Graham, George Balanchine, Charles Weidman, Anna Sokolow, Merce Cunningham, Katherine Litz,

James Waring and Pearl Lang; Dancer-Choreographer-dir. The Paul Taylor Dance Co. 1955-; since 1956 has undertaken 42 foreign tours, more than 90 tours throughout U.S.A. and 10 seasons on Broadway; Hon. Dr. Fine Arts (Connecticut Coll., Duke Univ.) 1983, (Syracuse Univ.) 1986; Guggenheim Fellowship 1961, 1965, 1983; Commdr., Ordre des Arts et des Lettres; Centennial Achievement Award (Ohio State Univ.), 1970; Brandeis Univ. Creative Arts Award gold medal 1978, Dance Magazine Award 1980, Samuel H. Scripps/American Dance Festival Award 1983, MacArthur 'Genius' Award 1985, New York State Governor's Award 1987; several int. awards for choreography. *Choreography includes:* Three Epitaphs 1956, Rebus 1958, Tablet 1960, Junction 1961, Fibers 1961, Insects and Heroes 1961, Tracer 1962, Piece Period 1962, Aureole 1962, Party Mix 1963, Scudorama 1963, Duet 1964, From Sea to Shining Sea 1965, Post Meridian 1965, Orbs 1966, Agathes' Tale 1967, Lento 1967, Public Domain 1968, Private Domain 1969, Churchyard 1969, Foreign Exchange 1970, Big Bertha 1970, Fêtes 1971, Book of Beasts 1971, Guests of May 1972, So Long Eden 1972, Noah's Minstrels 1973, American Genesis 1973, Untitled Quartet 1974, Sports and Follies 1974, Esplanade 1975, Runes 1975, Cloven Kingdom 1976, Polaris 1976, Images 1976, Dust 1977, Aphrodisiamania 1977, Airs 1978, Diggity 1978, Nightshade 1979, Profiles 1979, Le Sacre du Printemps (subtitled The Rehearsal) 1980, Arden Court 1981, Lost, Found and Lost 1982, Mercuric Tidings 1982, Sunset 1983, Snow White 1983, Musette 1983, Equinox 1983, Byzantium 1984, Roses 1985, Last Look 1985, A Musical Offering 1986, Ab Ovo Usted Mala 1986, Syzygy 1987, Kith and Kin 1987, Minikin Fair 1989, Speaking in Tongues 1989. *Publication:* Private Domain (autobiog.) 1987. *Leisure interests:* gardening, snorkeling. *Address:* 550 Broadway, New York, N.Y. 10012, U.S.A.

TAYLOR, Most Rev. Robert Selby, C.B.E., M.A.; British ecclesiastic; b. 1 March 1909, Cumberland; s. of late Robert Taylor; unmarried; ed. Harrow School, St. Catharine's Coll., Cambridge and Cuddesdon Coll.; ordained Deacon 1932, Priest 1933; Mission Priest, Diocese of Northern Rhodesia 1935, Principal Diocesan Theological Coll. 1939; Bishop of Northern Rhodesia 1941-51, of Pretoria 1951-59, of Grahamstown 1959-64; Archbishop of Cape Town 1964-74; Bishop of Cen. Zambia 1979-84; Hon. Fellow, St. Catharine's Coll., Cambridge 1964; Hon. D.D. (Rhodes Univ.) 1966. *Leisure interest:* mountain climbing. *Address:* 36 Alexandra Road, Wynberg 7700, South Africa. *Telephone:* 77 1440.

TAYLOR, Stuart Ross, M.A., PH.D., D.SC., F.A.A.; Australian geochemist; b. 26 Nov. 1925; s. of late T.S. Taylor; m. Noel White 1958; three d.; ed. Ashburton High School, N.Z., Canterbury Univ. Coll., Univ. of N.Z. and Indiana Univ.; lecturer in Mineralogy, Univ. of Oxford 1954-58; Sr. Lecturer in Geochemistry, Univ. of Cape Town 1958-60; Professorial Fellow, Research School of Earth Science, Australian Nat. Univ. (ANU) 1961-; mem. Council, ANU 1971-76; mem. Lunar Sample Preliminary Examination Team, Houston, Tex. 1969-70, Prin. Investigator, Lunar Sample Analysis Program 1970-; Hon. Fellow, U.K. and Indian Geological Socs. *Publications include:* Spectrochemical Analysis (jtly.) 1961, Moon Rocks and Minerals (jtly.) 1971, Lunar Science: A Post-Apollo View 1975, Planetary Science: A Lunar Perspective 1982, The Continental Crust: Its Composition and Evolution (jtly.) 1985. *Leisure interests:* reading history, gardening, classical music. *Address:* 18 Sheehan Street, Pearce, A.C.T. 2607, Australia.

TAYLOR, Wendy Ann, C.B.E., L.D.A.D.; British sculptor; b. 29 July 1945, Stanford, Lincs.; d. of Edward P. Taylor and Lilian M. Wright; m. Bruce Robertson 1982; one s.; ed. St. Martin's School of Art; one-man exhbns. at Axiom Gallery, London 1970, Angela Flowers Gallery, London 1972, King's Lynn Festival and World Trade Centre, London 1974, Annely Juda Fine Art, London 1975, Oxford Gallery, Oxford 1976, Oliver Dowling Gallery, Dublin 1976, 1979, Bldg. Centre Gallery 1986; participated in more than 100 group exhbns. 1964-82; work represented in collections in U.K., Europe, U.S.A. etc.; numerous maj. commissions in towns and cities throughout U.K.; mem. Fine Art Bd. Council of Acad. Awards 1980-85, specialist adviser 1985-; mem. Cttee. for Art and Design, Council of Nat. Acad. Awards; mem. Royal Fine Art Comm.; mem. Council, Morley Coll.; mem. Court R.C.A.; Design consultant, New Towns Comm. (Basildon) 1985-; Walter Neurath Award 1964, Pratt Award 1965, Sainsbury Award 1966, Arts Council Award 1977, Duais Na Riochta Gold Medal, Eire 1977. *Leisure interest:* gardening. *Address:* 73 Bow Road, London, E3 2AN, England. *Telephone:* 01-981 2037.

TAZAWA, Kichiro; Japanese politician; b. 1 Jan. 1918, Aomori Pref.; ed. Waseda Univ.; mem. House of Reps. 1960-; Parl. Vice-Minister of Posts and Telecommunications 1966; Chair. Standing Cttee. on Rules and Admin., House of Reps. 1971-72, 1975; Deputy Sec.-Gen. Liberal-Democratic Party 1973; Minister of State, Dir.-Gen. Nat. Land Agency 1976-77, Defence Agency Sept. 1988-; Minister of Agric., Forestry and Fisheries 1981-82. *Address:* Defence Agency, 9-7, Akasaka, Minato-ku, Tokyo, Japan.

TAZIEFF, Haroun; French vulcanologist; b. 11 May 1914, Warsaw, Poland; m. 1st Pauline de Ways-Ruart d'Elzius 1952; m. 2nd France Depierre 1958; ed. Institute Agronomique de Gembloux, Univ. de Liège; engineer, tin mines, Mitwaba, Katanga, Belgian Congo (now Zaire) 1945-47; geologist, geological survey, Belgian Congo 1948-49; Asst. Prof. of Mining Geology, Univ. of Brussels 1950-52; Head of Research, Centre Nat. de la Recherche Scientifique (CNRS), France 1967-70, Dir. 1971-81; Commr. à

la prévention des risques naturels majeurs 1981-84, Del. April-July 1984; Sec. of State in the Prime Minister's Office for Prevention of Natural Disasters 1974-86; Mayor of Mirmande 1977-; Dr. h.c. (Bradford, Gembloux). *Publications:* about 20 books on volcanoes and world tectonics, including Forecasting Volcanic Events 1983, Sur L'Etna 1984. *Leisure interests:* rugby, mountaineering, volcanological movie filming. *Address:* Mairie, Mirmande, 26270 Loriol-sur-Drome (Office); 15 quai Bourbon, 75004 Paris, France (Home). *Telephone:* 1-550-7172 (Office).

TCHERINA, Ludmila (Tchemerzine, Monika); French actress, dancer, painter, sculptor and writer; b. 10 Oct. 1924, Paris; d. of Prince Avenir Tchemerzine and Stéphane Finette; m. 1st Edmond Audran (deceased), 2nd Raymond Roi 1953; ed. privately and studied under Yvan Clustine; First dancer and choreographer, Grands Ballets de Monte Carlo (youngest-ever primer ballerina) 1940-44, Ballets de Paris 1951-58; f. Compagnie de Ballet Ludmila Tcherina 1958. *Chief appearances include:* Ballets: Romeo and Juliet (with Serge Lifar) Paris 1942, Giselle La Scala, Milan 1954, Bolshoi Theatre, Moscow 1959, Le martyre de Saint Sébastien Paris Opera 1957, Buenos Aires 1967, Les amants de Teruel Théâtre Sarah Bernhardt, Paris 1959, Gala (by Salvador Dali and Maurice Béjart) Venice 1961, Brussels and Paris 1962, La muette de Portici Florence 1968, Anna Karénine Versailles 1975, etc. *Films include:* The Red Shoes, The Tales of Hoffmann, Clara de Montargis, La légende de Parsifal, La nuit s'achève, Oh! Rosalinda, A la mémoire d'un héros, La fille de Mata-Hari, Honeymoon, Les amants de Téruel (Cannes Film Festival, French Entry 1962; New York Critics Award), Jeanne au bûcher, etc. *TV appearances include:* Le Mandarin marveilleux, Bonaparte (title role), Salomé, Bonaparte, La possédée, La dame aux camélias, La passion d'Anna Karénine, La création de la Féminine (based on her career), La Reine de Saba, Portrait de Ludmila Tcherina. *Works:* exhibited Sully Museum and Centre Georges Pompidou, Paris, and in many capital cities worldwide; Prize for Best Feminine Performance, Vichy Film Festival for La nuit s'achève 1950, First Prize Dance Film Festival, Buenos Aires for A la mémoire d'un héros 1952, "Oscar" for Best Performance by a Foreign Actress in Tales of Hoffmann 1952, Paris Gold Medal 1959, Oscar Italien de la Popularité 1959, Prix Michel Ange 1973, Prix d'honneur Gemail-1973, Grande Médaille de Vermeil de la Ville de Paris 1978, Prix d'interpretation (Monte Carlo); Officier, Légion d'honneur 1980, Chevalier des Arts et des Lettres. *Publication:* L'amour au miroir (novel) 1983, La Femme à l'envers (novel) 1986. *Address:* 42 cours Albert 1er, 75008 Paris, France. *Telephone:* 43-59-18-33.

TCHOUNGI, Simon Pierre; Cameroonian doctor and politician; b. 28 Oct. 1916; ed. Ecole Primaire Supérieure, Centre Médicale, Ayos, Ecole de Médecine, Dakar, and Univ. de Paris à la Sorbonne; former Dir. of Office, Ministry of Public Health and Population, then of Ministry of Public Works; Dir. Int. Relations, Ministry of Public Health and Population 1959-60; Dir. of Public Health for Cameroon 1961; Minister of Public Health and Population 1961-64; Minister of Nat. Economy 1964-65; Sec. of State to the Presidency 1965; Prime Minister of East Cameroon 1965-72; numerous decorations. *Address:* Boite Postale 1057, Yaoundé, Cameroon.

TEAR, Robert, C.B.E., M.A., F.R.S.A., R.C.M.; British opera and concert singer; b. 8 March 1939, Barry, Wales; s. of Thomas Arthur and Edith Tear; m. Hilary Thomas 1961; two d.; ed. Barry Grammar School, King's Coll., Cambridge; embarked on solo career as tenor after singing as member of King's Coll. Choir 1957-60, and St. Paul's Cathedral Choir; joined English Opera Group 1964; worked with leading conductors (including Karajan, Giulini, Bernstein, Solti), and appeared in numerous operas by Benjamin Britten 1964-68; first appearance at Covent Garden in The Knot Garden, other appearances: Eugene Onegin, Die Fledermaus 1977, Peter Grimes 1978, The Rake's Progress 1979, Thérèse 1979, Rheingold 1980, Alceste 1981, Die Meistersinger 1982, Billy Budd 1982, Turn of the Screw 1989; début with Scottish Opera in works including La Traviata, Alceste, Don Giovanni, Peter Grimes 1974; Paris Opera 1976, Lulu 1979; appearances in all major festivals; close asscn. with Sir Michael Tippett (q.v.) 1970-. *Publications:* Victorian Songs and Duets and numerous recordings including premier recording of Tippett's opera King Priam 1981. *Leisure interests:* sport, television, digging, 18th- and 19th-century English water colours. *Address:* 11 Ravenscourt Square, London, W.6, England. *Telephone:* 01-748 6130.

TEBALDI, Renata; Italian soprano; b. 1 Feb. 1922, Pesaro; d. of Teobaldo Tebaldi and Guisseppina (née Barbieri) Tabaldi; ed. Arrigo Boito Conservatory, Parma, Gioacchino Rossini Conservatory, Pesaro, then pupil of Carmen Melis and Giuseppe Pais.; début as Elena in Mefistofele, Rovigo 1944; has sung the principal soprano operatic roles in America and Europe. *Address:* c/o S.A. Gorlinsky Ltd., 33 Dover Street, London, W1X 4NJ, England; 1 Piazza Guastella, Milan, Italy. *Telephone:* 01-493 9158 (London).

TEBBIT, Sir Donald Claude, G.C.M.G., M.A.; British diplomatist (retd.); b. 4 May 1920, Cambridge; m. Barbara Margaret Olson Matheson 1947; one s. three d.; ed. Perse School, Cambridge, Trinity Hall, Cambridge Univ.; Royal Naval Volunteer Reserve 1941-46; Foreign Office 1946-48; Second Sec. British Embassy, Washington, D.C. 1948-51; Foreign Office 1951-54; First Sec. (Commercial), Bonn 1954-58; Private Sec. to Minister of State, Foreign Office 1958-61, Counsellor 1962, Sec. Cttee. on Representational Services Overseas 1962-64; Counsellor and Head of Chancery, Copenhagen 1964-67; Head of W. and Cen. Africa Dept., Commonwealth Office 1967;

Asst. Under-Sec. of State, FCO 1968; Commercial Minister, Washington, D.C. 1970-71, Minister 1971-72; Deputy Under-Sec. of State, FCO 1973-76; High Commr. in Australia 1976-80; Pres. (U.K.) Australia-British Chamber of Commerce 1980-; Dir.-Gen. British Property Fed. 1980-85; Dir. Rio Tinto Zinc Corpn. Ltd. 1980-; Chair. English-Speaking Union of the Commonwealth 1983-87; Gov. (Deputy Chair.) Nuffield Hospitals 1980-; Chair. Diplomatic Service Appeals Bd. 1980-87, Marshall Aid Commemoration Comm. 1985-; mem. Appeals Bd. Council of Europe 1981-. *Address:* Priory Cottage, Toft, Cambridge, England.

TEBBIT, Rt. Hon. Norman Beresford, P.C., C.H., M.P.; British politician; b. 29 March 1931, Enfield; s. of Leonard and Edith Tebbit; m. Margaret Elizabeth Daines 1956; two s. one d.; ed. State Primary Schools, Edmonton Co. Grammar School; R.A.F. Officer 1949-51; Commercial Pilot and holder of various posts, British Air Line Pilots' Asscn. 1953-70; M.P. for Epping 1970-74, for Chingford 1974-; Parl. Pvt. Sec. Dept. of Employment 1972-73; Under-Sec. of State, Dept. of Trade 1979-81; Minister of State, Dept. of Industry Jan.-Sept. 1981; Sec. of State for Employment 1981-83, for Trade and Industry 1983-85; Chancellor of the Duchy of Lancaster 1985-87; Chair. Conservative Party 1985-87; Dir. B.E.T. PLC, Blue Arrow PLC, British Telecom PLC, Sears PLC, JCB Excavators PLC. *Publication:* Upwardly Mobile 1988. *Leisure interests:* peace and quiet. *Address:* House of Commons, Westminster, London, SW1A 0AA, England.

TEDDER, 2nd Baron, cr. 1946, of Glenguin; **John Michael Tedder,** M.A., SC.D., PH.D., D.SC., F.R.S.E.; British professor of chemistry; b. 4 July 1926, London; s. of the late Marshal of the R.A.F. the 1st Lord Tedder, G.C.B., and of Rosalinde Wilhelmina Tedder (née Maclardy); m. Peggy Eileen Growcott 1952; two s. one d.; ed. Dauntsey's School, Wilts., Magdalene Coll., Cambridge, Univ. of Birmingham; Lecturer in Chem., Sheffield Univ. 1954-62, Reader in Organic Chem. 1962-64; Roscoe Prof. of Chem., Queens Coll., Dundee 1964-69; Purdie Prof. of Chem., St. Salvator's Coll., St. Andrews Univ. 1969-; mem. Court of St. Andrews Univ. 1971-75; Vice-Pres. Perkin Div., Chemical Soc. 1978-81. *Publications:* Basic Organic Chemistry (Parts I-V) 1966-73, Valence Theory 1966, The Chemical Bond 1978; original papers in Journal of the Chemical Society, Transactions of the Faraday Society and other learned journals. *Address:* Department of Chemistry, University of St. Andrews, St. Andrews, Fife, KY16 9ST (Office); Little Rathmore, Kennedy Gardens, St. Andrews, Fife, Scotland (Home).

TEER, Kees, F.I.E.E.E.; Netherlands university professor; b. 6 June 1925, Haarlem; m. Jozina A. Kas 1951; four c.; ed. Tech. Univ. Delft; joined Philips Research Labs., Eindhoven 1950, Sr. Researcher, Deputy Head of Acoustics, 1958, Deputy Dir. 1966, Man. Dir. 1968, Chair. Man. Cttee. 1982-85; Prof. Tech. Univ. Delft 1987; mem. Netherlands Scientific Council for Govt. 1985; mem. Royal Netherlands Acad. of Sciences. *Publications:* several publs. on electro-acoustics, television systems, electronic principles, science and tech. etc. *Address:* Hoge Dwinlaan 3, 5582 KD Waalre, The Netherlands. *Telephone:* 4904-16861.

TEETS, John William; American businessman; b. 15 Sept. 1933, Elgin, Ill.; s. of John William Teets and Maudie Teets; m. Nancy Teets 1965; four d.; ed. Elgin High School and Univ. of Illinois; Pres. and partner, Winter Garden Restaurant, Carpentersville 1957-63; Vice-Pres. Greyhound Food Man., Pres. Post Houses and Horne Enterprises 1964-68; Pres. John R. Thompson 1968-71; Pres. Canteen Corpn. 1971-74; Exec. Vice-Pres. Bonanza Int. 1974-76; Chair. and C.E.O. Greyhound Food Man. 1976-; Vice-Pres. Greyhound Food Services Group 1980-82; Vice-Pres. Pres.'s Conf. on Foodservice Industry; Vice-Chair. Greyhound Corpn. 1980-82, Chair. Jan. 1982-, also Pres. and C.E.O.; Chair. and Pres. Armour & Co. 1981-; Bd. mem. U.S. Chamber of Commerce, UCLA Bd. of Visitors, School of Business Admin., Univ. of Southern Calif.; Hon. LL.D. (Trinity Coll., Deerfield, Ill.) 1982; Golden Plate Award (foodservice) 1980, Nat. Human Relations Award, American Jewish Cttee. 1986. *Leisure interests:* golf, running, weightlifting. *Address:* The Greyhound Corporation, Greyhound Tower—1918, Phoenix, Ariz. 85077 (Office); 5303 Desert Park Lane, Scottsdale, Ariz. 85253, U.S.A. (Home).

TEITELBAUM, Philip, PH.D.; American professor of psychology; b. 9 Oct. 1928, Brooklyn, New York; s. of Bernard Teitelbaum and Betty Schechter; m. 1st Anita Stawski 1955, m. 2nd Evelyn Satinoff 1963, m. 3rd Osnat Boné 1985; five s.; ed. Johns Hopkins Univ.; Instructor and Asst. Prof. in Psychology, Harvard Univ. 1954-59; Assoc., Full Prof., Univ. of Pa. 1959-73; Prof., Univ. of Ill. 1973-85, Emer. Prof. 1985-; Fellow in Center for Advanced Studies, Univ. of Ill. 1979-85; Grad. Research Prof. in Psychology, Univ. of Fla. 1984-; mem. N.A.S.; Guggenheim Fellow; Fulbright Fellow; American Psychology Asscn. Scientific Contrib. Award. *Publications:* Fundamental Principles of Physiological Psychology 1967, Vol. on Motivation, Handbook of Behavioral Neurobiology (with Evelyn Satinoff) 1983. *Address:* Psychology Department, University of Florida, Gainesville, Fla. 32611, U.S.A. *Telephone:* (904) 392-0615 and (904) 372-5714.

TEJADA, Marquis de (see Coronel de Palma, Luis).

TEJCHMA, Józef; Polish politician; b. 14 July 1927, Markowa; ed. Acad. of Political Sciences, Warsaw and Higher School of Social Sciences, Warsaw; active leader of Rural Youth Union (Wici Z.M.W.) 1945-48; instructor

for school youth problems, Cen. Bd. of Polish Youth Union (Z.M.P.) 1948; plenipotentiary, Cen. Bd. of Z.M.P. at Nowa Huta 1951-54; Deputy Head of the Organizational Dept. Cen. Bd. of Z.M.P. 1954-55; Co-organizer Rural Youth Union Z.M.W., Chair. Organizational Cttee., Provisional Bd. and later Cen. Bd. 1956-63; Head of Agric. Dept. Polish United Workers' Party (P.Z.P.R.) Cen. Cttee. 1963-64; mem. P.Z.P.R. 1952-; Deputy mem. Cen. Cttee. 1959-64, mem. 1964-71, Sec. Cen. Cttee. 1964-72; mem. Politburo 1968-80; deputy to Seym 1958-80; Vice-Chair. of Presidium of All-Poland Cttee. of Nat. Unity Front 1971-83; Deputy Chair. Council of Ministers 1972-79; Minister of Culture and Art 1974-78, 1980-82, of Educ. and Pedagogy 1979-80; Consultant, Minister of Foreign Affairs 1983-84; Amb. to Switzerland May-Oct. 1980, to Greece and Cyprus 1984-; Chair. Presidium, Council of Higher Artistic Educ.; Deputy Chair. Cttee. of Nat. Prizes; Order of the Banner of Labour (1st Class) 1964, Medal of 30th Anniversary of People's Poland, Order of Builders of People's Poland 1977, and others. *Address:* Polish Embassy, 22 Chrissanthemon, Athenes-Paleo Psychico, Greece. *Telephone:* 6716917.

TE KAAT, Erich Heinz; German professor of physics; b. 27 Dec. 1937, Hamminkeln; s. of Wilhelm and Brigitta te Kaat; m. Antje Witte 1964; two s. one d.; ed. Staatliches Gymnasium Wesel and Univs. of Munich and Münster; teaching asst. Univ. of Münster 1968; consultant, IBM, U.S.A. 1970-72; research fellow, Kernforschungsanlage Jülich (KFA) 1972; Prof. of Experimental Physics, Univ. of Dortmund 1972-, Rektor 1976-78. *Leisure interests:* music, violin, string quartet and orchestra. *Address:* Forstbann 9, D-4600 Dortmund 50, Federal Republic of Germany. *Telephone:* 0231-736045.

TE KANAWA, Dame Kiri, D.B.E.; New Zealand opera singer (soprano); b. 6 March 1944, Gisborne; m. Desmond Park 1967; one s. one d.; ed. St. Mary's Coll., Auckland, London Opera Centre; first appearance at Royal Opera, Covent Garden, London, 1970, Santa Fe Opera, U.S.A. 1971, Lyons Opera, France 1972, Metropolitan Opera, New York, U.S.A. 1974; appeared at Australian Opera, Royal Opera House Covent Garden, Paris Opera during 1976-77 season; appeared at Houston Opera, U.S.A., and Munich Opera 1977; début La Scala, Milan 1978, Salzburg Festival 1979; San Francisco Opera Co. 1980; Edin. Festival, Helsinki Festival 1980. *Operas:* Boris Godunov 1970-71, Parsifal 1971, The Marriage of Figaro 1971, 1972, 1973, 1976, 1979, Otello 1972, 1973, 1974, Simon Boccanegra 1973, 1974, 1975, 1976, 1977, 1979, 1980, Carmen 1973, Don Giovanni 1974, 1975, 1976, 1979, 1981, Faust 1974, The Magic Flute 1975, 1980, La Bohème 1975, 1976, 1977, 1979, 1980, Eugene Onegin 1975, 1976, Così fan tutte 1976, 1981, Arabella 1977, 1980, 1981, Die Fledermaus 1978, La Traviata 1978, 1980, Der Rosenkavalier 1981, Manon Lescaut 1983, Don Giovanni (film) 1979; sang at Wedding of H.R.H. the Prince of Wales (q.v.) July 1981; Hon. Fellow (Somerville Coll., Oxford) 1983, Hon. LL.D. (Dundee) 1982, Hon. D.Mus. (Durham) 1982, (Oxford) 1983. *Recordings include:* Don Giovanni (as Elvira), Così fan tutti (as Fiordiligi), Carmen (as Michela), Mozart Vespers, Mozart C Minor Mass, The Magic Flute (Pamina), The Marriage of Figaro, Hansel and Gretel, Strauss Songs with Orchestra, recital records. *Leisure interests:* golf, swimming, cooking. *Address:* c/o Basil Horsfield, Estoril 3, 31 avenue Princess Grace, Monte Carlo, Monaco.

TEKOAH, Yosef, L. EN D., M.A.; Israeli diplomatist; b. 4 March 1925; s. of Saul and Dvora; m. Ruth Weidenfeld 1952; two s. one d.; ed. Univ. L'Aurore, Shanghai and Harvard Univ.; Instructor in Int. Relations, Harvard Univ. 1947-48; Deputy Legal Adviser, Ministry of Foreign Affairs 1949-53; Dir. Armistice Affairs, and Head Israeli dels. to Armistice Comms. with Egypt, Jordan, Syria and Lebanon 1953-58; Deputy Perm. Rep. to UN 1958, Acting Perm. Rep. 1959-60; Amb. to Brazil 1960-62, to U.S.S.R. 1962-65; Asst. Dir.-Gen. Ministry of Foreign Affairs 1966-68; Perm. Rep. to UN 1968-75; Pres. Ben-Gurion Univ. of the Negev 1975-80, Chancellor 1981; Pres. B.R.I.G. Int. Inc. 1982-. *Publication:* In the Face of the Nations: Israel's Struggle for Peace 1976.

TELEGDI, Valentine L., M.SC., PH.D.; American physicist; b. 11 Jan. 1922, Budapest; s. of late George Telegdi and of Ella Telegdi (née Csillag); m. Lidia Leonardi 1950; ed. Lausanne Univ. and Swiss Fed. Inst. of Tech.; Asst., Swiss Fed. Inst. of Tech. 1947-50; Instructor, Univ. of Chicago 1951-53, Asst. Prof. 1953-56, Assoc. Prof. 1956-58, 1958-71, Enrico Fermi Distinguished Service Prof. 1971-78; Prof. of Physics, Swiss Fed. Inst. of Tech., Zürich 1976-; Nat. Science Foundation Sr. Postdoctoral Fellow CERN, Geneva 1959, guest Prof. 1970-74, mem. CERN Scientific Policy Cttee. 1977-, Chair. 1980-83; mem. N.A.S., American Acad. of Arts and Sciences; American Physical Soc.; Loeb Lecturer, Harvard Univ. 1966. *Publications:* numerous articles in professional journals. *Leisure interests:* travel, gastronomy, jazz. *Address:* Eidgenössische Technische Hochschule, Höuggerberg, Zürich, Switzerland. *Telephone:* 1-3772040 (Office).

TELLENBACH, Gerd, PH.D.; German university professor; b. 17 Sept. 1903, Berlin-Lichterfelde; s. of Leo Tellenbach and Margarete Eberty; m. Marie-Elisabeth Gerken 1945; two s. one d.; ed. Univs. of Freiburg and Munich; Asst., Prussian Historical Inst. in Rome 1928-33; Lecturer, Heidelberg, Giessen and Würzburg Univs. 1933-38; Prof., Giessen 1938-42, Münster 1942-44; Prof. of Medieval and Modern History, Univ. of Freiburg, and Dir. Historical School 1944-63; Dir. German Historical Inst., Rome 1962-72; Prof. Univ. of Freiburg 1972; D. h.c. Ph. et Litt. (Louvain), Hon. D.Litt. (Glasgow). *Publications include:* Die bischöfliche passauischen

Eigenklöster und ihre Vogteien 1928, Römischer und christlicher Reichsgedanke in der Liturgie des früheren Mittelalters 1934, Libertas, Kirche und Weltordnung im Zeitalter des Investiturstreites 1936, Königtum and Stämme in der Werdezeit des deutschen Reiches 1939, Church, State and Christian Society 1940, Die Entstehung des deutschen Reiches 1940, Goethes geschichtlicher Sinn 1949, Europa im Zeitalter der Karolinger, Historia Mundi V 1956, Studien und Vorarbeiten zur Geschichte des grossfränkischen und frühdeutschen Adels 1957, Zur Bedeutung der Personenforschung für die Erkenntnis des früheren Mittelalters 1957, Kaisertum, Papsttum und Europa im hohen Mittelalter, Historia Mundi VI 1958, Neue Forschungen über Cluny und die Cluniacenser 1959, Repertorium Germanicum II 1933-61, Der Sybyllinische Preis, Schriften und Reden zur Hochschulpolitik 1946-1963 1963, Empfehlungen zur Neuordnung des Studiums in den Philosophischen Fakultäten 1966, Saeculum Weltgeschichte III und IV 1967, V 1970, Aus erinnerter Zeitgeschichte 1981; Ed.: Monumenta Germaniae historica: Liber memorialis Romaricensis (with E. Hlawitschka and K. Schmid) 1970. *Address:* Hintere Steige 4, 78 Freiburg/Br., Federal Republic of Germany (Home). *Telephone:* 56497.

TELLER, Edward, PH.D.; Hungarian-born American scientist; b. 15 Jan. 1908, Budapest, Hungary; s. of Ilona and Max Teller; m. Augusta Maria Harkanyi 1934; one s. one d.; ed. Karlsruhe Technical Inst., and Univs. of Munich and Leipzig; Research Assoc., Leipzig 1929-31, Göttingen 1931-33; Rockefeller Fellow, Copenhagen 1934; Lecturer, Univ. of London 1934-35; Prof. of Physics, George Washington Univ. 1935-41, Columbia Univ. 1941-42; Physicist, Manhattan Engineer Dist. 1942-46; Prof. of Physics, Univ. of Chicago 1946-52; Physicist, and Asst. Dir. Los Alamos Scientific Lab. 1949-52; Consultant, Univ. of Calif. Radiation Lab. Livermore 1952-53, Assoc. Dir. Lawrence Livermore Radiation Lab. 1954-75, Dir. 1958-60, Dir. Emer. 1975-; Prof. of Physics Univ. of Calif. 1953-60, Prof. of Physics-at-Large 1960-70, Univ. Prof. 1970-, Prof. Emer. 1975-; Chair. Dept. of Applied Science, Univ. of Calif. 1963-66; Visiting Prof., Arthur Spitzer Chair of Science, Pepperdine Univ. 1975-77; mem. N.A.S., American Acad. of Arts and Sciences, U.S.A.F. Scientific Advisory Bd., etc.; Fellow, American Nuclear Soc.; Sr. Research Fellow, Hoover Inst. for War, Revolution and Peace 1975-; Joseph Priestley Memorial Award 1957, Albert Einstein Award 1958, Mid-West Research Inst. Award, Living History Award 1960, Enrico Fermi Award 1962, Robins Award of America 1963, Harvey Prize 1975, Nat. Medal of Science 1983, Sylvanus Thayer Award 1986; Hon. D.Sc. (Yale, Alaska, Fordham, George Washington, S. Calif., St. Louis, Clarkson Coll. Clemson Univ., Maryland); Hon. LL.D. (Mount Mary). *Publications:* The Structure of Matter (with F. O. Rice) 1949, Magneto-Hydrodynamic Shocks (with F. de Hoffmann) 1950, Theory of Origin of Cosmic Rays 1954, Our Nuclear Future (with A. Latter) 1958, Legacy of Hiroshima (with Allen Brown) 1962. The Reluctant Revolutionary 1964, Constructive Uses of Nuclear Explosives (with Talley, Higgins & Johnson) 1968, Great Men of Physics (with others) 1969, General Remarks on Electronic Structure 1970, The Hydrogen Molecular Ion 1970, General Theory of Electron Structure 1970, Energy from Heaven and Earth 1979, The Pursuit of Simplicity 1980, Better a Shield than a Sword 1987. *Leisure interests:* chess, swimming, piano. *Address:* Hoover Institution, Stanford, Calif. 94305, U.S.A. (Office).

TEMBO, John Zenas Ungapake; Malawi politician; b. Sept. 1932; ed. senior primary school, Kongwe, Mlanda School, Ncheu, Blantyre Secondary School and Roma Univ. Coll., Basutoland; worked for Colonial Audit Dept. Zomba 1949-55; studied at Roma Univ. Coll. 1955-58; fmr. mem. African Students' Rep. Council; attended course for educational diploma, Salisbury, S. Rhodesia 1958-59; teacher Kongwe Secondary School 1959-61; mem. Legis. Council for Dedza 1961-62; Parl. Sec. for Finance 1962-64; M.P. for Dedza North 1964, resgnd. May 1970; Minister of Finance 1964-68, concurrently Minister of Trade, Industry, Devt. and Planning 1964-68; Minister of Trade and Finance 1968-70; Gov. Reserve Bank of Malawi 1970-84; mem. Nat. Cttee. Malawi Congress Party 1987-. *Address:* Malawi Congress Party, Lilongwe, Malawi.

TEMIN, Howard M., PH.D.; American professor and virologist; b. 10 Dec. 1934, Philadelphia, Pa.; s. of Henry and Annette (née Lehman) Temin; m. Rayla G. Greenberg 1962; two d.; ed. Swarthmore Coll., Calif. Inst. of Tech.; Postdoctoral Fellow, Calif. Inst. of Tech. 1959-60; Asst. Prof. of Oncology, Univ. of Wis., Madison 1960-64, Assoc. Prof. 1964-69, Prof. 1969-, Wis. Alumni Research Foundation Prof. of Cancer Research 1971-80; American Cancer Soc. Prof. of Viral Oncology and Cell Biology 1974-, Harold P. Rusch Prof. of Cancer Research 1980-, Steenbock Prof. of Biological Sciences 1982-; mem. NAS/IOM Comm. for a Nat. Strategy for AIDS 1986; mem. Editorial Bd. Annual Review Genetics 1983-, Molecular Biology-Evolution 1983-, Rapid Communications Section 1984-, Journal of Virology 1971-; Herz Memorial Lecturer Tel-Aviv Univ. 1985, Amoroso Memorial Lecturer, Univ. of the West Indies 1986; mem., American Acad. of Arts and Sciences 1973, N.A.S. 1974, American Philosophical Soc. 1978, American Soc. of Microbiology, American Asscn. of Cancer Research, American Soc. of Virology; foreign mem. Royal Soc.; U.S. Steel Foundation Award in Molecular Biology, N.A.S. 1972, Griffuel Prize, Asscn. for Research against Cancer, Villejuif 1973, American Chem. Soc. Award in Enzyme Chem. 1973, G. H. A. Clowes Award and Lectureship, American Asscn. for Cancer Research 1974, Gairdner Foundation Int. Award (shared) 1974, Albert Lasker Award in Basic Medical Science 1974, Nobel Prize in

Physiology or Medicine (shared) 1975, Lucy Wortham James Award in Basic Research, Soc. of Surgical Oncologists 1976, Alumni Distinguished Service Award, Calif. Inst. of Tech. 1976, Lila Gruber Research Award, American Acad. of Dermatology 1981, First Hilldale Award in the Biological Sciences 1986, and other awards; Hon. D.Sc. (Swarthmore Coll., Univ. of Pa., Lawrence Univ., New York Medical Coll., Hahnemann Medical Coll., Temple Univ., Medical Coll., Wis., Colorado State Univ.). *Publications:* author and co-author of over 180 articles and contributions to books. *Address:* McArdle Laboratory for Cancer Research, University of Wisconsin, 450 North Randall Avenue, Madison, Wis. 53706, U.S.A. *Telephone:* (608) 262-1209.

TEMIRKANOV, Yuriy Khatuyevich; Soviet conductor; b. 10 Dec. 1938, Nalchik; s. of Khatu Sagidovich Temirkanov and Polina Petrovne Temirkanova; m. Irina Guseva; one s.; ed. Leningrad Conservatoire; first violinist with Leningrad Philharmonic Orchestra 1961-66; Conductor for Maly Theatre and Opera Studio, Leningrad 1965-68; Chief Conductor, Leningrad Philharmonic Orchestra and Kirov Theatre 1968-76; Kirov Opera and Ballet Co. 1976-88; Artistic Dir. Leningrad Symphony Orchestra 1988-; Prof. Leningrad Conservatory 1979-; guest conductor in a number of countries, including Scandinavia (Sweden 1968), U.S.A. and G.B. (Royal Philharmonic Orchestra 1981-); Soviet People's Artist 1974, Glinka Prize 1975; *Operas:* Porgy and Bess (at Maly), Peter the Great (at Kirov), Shchedrin's Dead Souls (at Bolshoi), Tchaikovsky's Queen of Spades 1979. *Address:* Leningrad Symphony Orchestra, ul. Brodskogo 2, Leningrad, U.S.S.R.

TEMPLE, George, C.B.E., F.R.S., D.SC., M.A.; British mathematician; b. 2 Sept. 1901, London; s. of James Temple and Frances Compton; m. Dorothy Carson 1930; ed. Birkbeck Coll., and Trinity Coll., Cambridge; Asst. at Birkbeck Coll. 1922-24; Asst. Lecturer in Mathematics City and Guilds Coll. 1924-28; Asst. Prof. Royal Coll. of Science 1930-32; Prof. of Math. King's Coll. London 1932-53; Chief Scientific Adviser to Minister of Civil Aviation 1947-49; Sedleian Prof. of Natural Philosophy, Oxford Univ. 1953-68, now Prof. Emer.; Hon. Fellow, Queen's Coll., Oxford 1966; Chair. Aeronautical Research Council 1961-64; Leverhulme Emer. Fellowship 1971-73; became Benedictine monk 1982, ordained 1983; Hon. D.Sc. (Dublin, Louvain, Reading Univs.) 1966; Hon. D.Lit. (Western Ont.) 1969. *Publications:* Introduction to Quantum Theory 1931, Rayleigh's Principle 1933, General Principles of Quantum Theory 1934, An Introduction to Fluid Dynamics 1958, Cartesian Tensors 1960, The Structure of Lebesgue Integration Theory 1971, 100 Years of Mathematics 1981. *Address:* Quarr Abbey, Ryde, Isle of Wight, England.

TEMPLE, Joseph George, Jr., B.S. (CHEM. ENG.); American business executive; b. 29 Aug. 1929, Brooklyn, New York; s. of Joseph George Temple and Helen Frances (Beney) Temple; m. Ann Elizabeth McFerran 1952; two s. one d.; ed. Purdue Univ.; joined Dow Chem. U.S.A. 1951, Vice-Pres. 1976-78, Dir. Dow Chemical Co. 1979-, Group Vice-Pres. for Human Health 1980-83, Exec. Vice-Pres. May 1983-; Pres. Dow Chemical Latin America 1978-80; Pres. Merrell Dow Pharmaceuticals Inc. 1983-88, Chair., C.E.O. Jan. 1988-; Distinguished Alumni Award, Purdue Univ. 1978, Silver Kt. Award, Nat. Man. Asscn. 1976, Gold Kt. Award 1982. *Address:* The Dow Chemical Company, 2030 W.H. Dow Center, Midland, Mich. 48674 (Office); 3612 White Pine Way, Midland, Mich. 48640, U.S.A. (Home).

TEMPLE, Shirley (see Black, Shirley Temple).

TEMPLEMAN, Baron (Life Peer), cr. 1982, of White Lackington in the County of Somerset; **Sydney William Templeman,** P.C., Q.C., M.B.E., M.A.; British judge; b. 3 March 1920, London; s. of Herbert W. and Lilian (née Pheasant) Templeman; m. Margaret Rowles 1946 (died 1988); two s.; ed. Southall Grammar School and St. John's Coll., Cambridge; served 4/1st Gurkha Rifles 1941-46; mem. Middle Temple 1946-, Treas. 1987-; mem. Bar Council 1961-65, 1970-72; Q.C. 1964; Attorney-Gen., Duchy of Lancaster 1970; Judge, Chancery Div., 1972; Pres. Senate of Inns of Court and Bar 1974; mem. Royal Comm. on Legal Services 1976; Lord Justice of Appeal 1978-82; Lord of Appeal in Ordinary 1982-; Hon. Fellow, St. John's Coll., Cambridge 1982; Hon. mem. Canadian Bar Asscn. 1976, American Bar Asscn. 1976, Newfoundland Law Soc. 1984; Hon. D.Litt. (Reading) 1980, Hon. L.L.D. (Birmingham) 1986. *Address:* Manor Heath, Knowl Hill, Woking, Surrey, GU22 7HL, England. *Telephone:* (04862) 61930.

TEMPLETON, Hugh Campbell, B.A.; New Zealand politician; b. 1929, Wyndham; m.; two c.; ed. Univ. of Otago, Dunedin and Oxford Univ.; joined Ministry of Foreign Affairs 1954, served London, Western Samoa 1960-62, N.Z. Mission to UN 1962-64, and at Ministries of Foreign Affairs and Defence 1965-69; M.P. 1969-; Minister of Broadcasting, Minister in charge of Public Trust Office and Postmaster-Gen. 1975-77; Minister of Broadcasting, Assoc. Minister of Finance, Minister of Statistics and Minister in charge of Inland Revenue Dept. and Friendly Socs. 1977-81, also Minister for Customs 1978-82, Minister of Trade and Industry 1981-84; National Party. *Leisure interests:* cultural affairs, history and literature. *Address:* 96 Bolton Street, Wellington, New Zealand.

TEMPLETON, Sir John M., Kt., M.A.; British investment counsellor; b. 29 Nov. 1912, Winchester, Tenn., U.S.A.; s. of Harvey Maxwell and Vella Handly Templeton; m. 1st Judith Dudley Folk 1937 (died 1951), two s. one d.; m. 2nd Irene Reynolds Butler 1958; ed. Yale Univ., Balliol Coll., Oxford

Univ. (Rhodes Scholar); Sec.-Treas., Vice-Pres. and Dir. Nat. Geophysical Co., Dallas and New York 1937–41; Pres. and Dir. Templeton, Dobbrow and Vance, Inc., New York 1941–65, Templeton Growth Fund Canada Ltd., Toronto 1954–85, Templeton Funds, Inc. 1977–86; Templeton Global Funds, Inc. 1981–86; Chair. Templeton Damroth Corpn. 1959–62; Vice-Pres. and Dir. First Trust Bank Ltd., Bahamas 1963–; Dir. Magic Chef, Inc., Cleveland, Tenn. 1965–86; Chase Manhattan Trust Co. 1972–82, British-American Insurance Co. 1973–82; Chair. Templeton, Galbraith and Hansberger Ltd. 1986–; Chair. Bd. of Trustees Princeton Theological Seminary 1967–73, 1979–85; Pres. and Trustee Templeton Theological Seminary 1985–; Trustee Templeton Foundation Inc. 1952–, Wilson Coll. 1951–73, Englewood Hosp. 1953–56, Center of Theological Inquiry, Princeton 1967–, Buena Vista Coll. 1981–, Soc. for Promoting Christian Knowledge (U.S.A.) 1984–, Balliol Coll. Oxford Endowments Fund 1984–, Templeton Project Trust (England) 1984–, America European Community Asscn.; mem. Bd. of Visitors Harvard Divinity School, Advisory Bd. Harvard Center for Study of World Religions, Council on Theological Seminaries, United Presbyterian Church of the U.S.A. 1959–84, Bd. Corporators Presbyterian Ministers' Fund Inc. 1960–, Comm. on Ecumenical Mission 1961–70; Bd. of Mans. American Bible Soc.; Man. Council Templeton Coll. (Oxford); mem. New York Soc. of Security Analysts 1942–; Hon. Rector Dubuque Univ.; Hon. LL.D. (Beaver Coll., Marquette Univ., Jamestown Coll., Maryville Coll.), Hon. D.Litt. (Wilson Coll.), Hon. D.C.L. (Univ. of the South), Hon. D.D. (Buena Vista Coll.). *Publications:* The Humble Approach 1981, The Templeton Touch (co-author) 1985, The Templeton Plan 1987, and articles in financial and religious journals. *Address:* Box N-7776, Nassau, Bahamas (Office); Lyford Cay Club, Nassau, Bahamas (Home).

TENGBOM, Anders, D.ARCH.; Swedish architect; b. 10 Nov. 1911, Stockholm; s. of Ivar and Hjördis Tengbom; m. Margareta Brambeck 1937; two s. two d.; ed. Royal Inst. of Tech. and Royal Acad. of Fine Arts, Stockholm, Cranbrook Acad., Mich., U.S.A.; travelled in Europe, U.S.A., Japan, China and the U.S.S.R. 1935–36; architectural practice in Stockholm 1938–, designed bldgs. for many different functions in Sweden, Belgium, Venezuela and Saudi Arabia; Acting Prof. of Architecture, Royal Inst. of Tech., Stockholm 1947; Pres. Nat. Asscn. of Swedish Architects (SAR) 1963–65; mem. Bd. Swedish Hospitals Fed. 1962–70; Pres. Swedish Assen. of Consulting Architects (SPA) 1972–75; mem. Royal Acad. of Fine Arts, Stockholm 1973–, Pres. 1980–86; Hon. corresp. mem. R.I.B.A. 1963: Hon. Fellow, American Inst. of Architects 1978. *Leisure interests:* skiing, sailing. *Address:* Kornhamnstorg 6, 111 27 Stockholm (Office); Canton 2, 170 11 Drottningholm, Sweden (Home). *Telephone:* 08-24 24 60 (Office); 08-759 01 75 (Home).

TEN HOLT, Friso; Netherlands painter and etcher; b. 6 April 1921, Argelès-Gazost, France; m. A. Taselaar 1946; two s. one d.; ed. Rijksakademie van Beeldende Kunsten, Amsterdam; paintings mainly of swimmers, landscapes and nudes, portraits and figures; Prof. of painting, Rijksakademie van Beeldende Kunsten, Amsterdam 1969–83; one-man exhibitions in Netherlands since 1952, London 1959, 1962, 1963, 1965, 1969; Group exhbns. at Beaverbrook Art Gallery, Canada, and Tate Gallery, London 1963, Biennale Salzburg 1964, Carnegie Inst., Pittsbugh 1964, Netherlands travelling exhbn. 1957–58; works in collections in Netherlands, Sweden, U.K., France and America. *Major works:* stained-glass windows for churches in Amsterdam and The Hague and for Haarlem cathedral. *Leisure interest:* reading. *Address:* Keizersgracht 614, Amsterdam, Netherlands. *Telephone:* 02248-1727 (Studio); 230736 (Home).

TENNANT, Sir Peter Frank Dalrymple, Kt., C.M.G., O.B.E., M.A.; British company director and industrial adviser; b. 29 Nov. 1910, Hoddesdon; s. of George F.D. and Barbara (née Beck) Tennant; m. 1st Hellis Fellenius 1934, 2nd Galina Bosley 1953; one s. two d. and one step-s.; ed. Marlborough Coll. and Trinity Coll., Cambridge; Fellow, Queens' Coll., Cambridge 1933–47, Lecturer in Scandinavian languages 1933–39; diplomatic service 1939–52, served in Stockholm, Paris and Berlin; Overseas Dir., later Deputy Dir.-Gen. Fed. of British Industries 1952–65; Dir.-Gen. British Nat. Export Council 1965–71; Industrial Adviser, Barclays Bank Int. 1972–81; Dir. C. Tennant Sons & Co. Ltd., London 1972–80, Prudential Corpn. 1979–86, Prudential Assurance Co. Ltd. 1972–81, Anglo-Romanian Bank (until 1981), Northern Eng. Industries (Int.) Ltd. (until 1982), Int. Energy Bank 1980–83; Visiting Fellow St. Cross Coll., Oxford 1982–; fmr. Chair. Gabbitas Thring Educ. Trust; fmr. Chair. London Chamber of Commerce (Pres. 1978–79); Chair. U.K. Cttee. European Cultural Foundation; Vice-Chair. Academic Council Wilton Park, fmr. mem. Gov. Body Int. Briefing Centre, Farnham Castle; fmr. mem. Design Council, BBC Advisory Council. *Publications:* Ibsen's Dramatic Technique, The Scandinavian Book, Touchlines of War—Revolution of Sweden in World War II 1989. *Leisure interests:* country pursuits, painting, writing, travel, languages. *Address:* Blue Anchor House, Linchmere Road, Haslemere, Surrey, GU27 3QF, England. *Telephone:* (0428) 3124.

TENNEKES, Hendrik, D.S. (ENG.); Netherlands meteorologist; b. 13 Dec. 1936, Kampen; s. of late Cornelis Tennekes and of Harmpje Noordman; m. Olga Vanderpot 1964; one s. one d.; ed. Delft Tech. Univ.; Asst. Prof., Assoc. Prof., Prof. of Aerospace Eng., Pennsylvania State Univ. 1965–77; Dir. of Research, Royal Netherlands Meteorological Inst. 1977–; Prof.

of Meteorology, Free Univ., Amsterdam 1977–; Visiting Prof. Univ. of Washington, Seattle 1976–77; Visiting Sr. Scientist, Nat. Center for Atmospheric Research, Boulder, Colo. 1987; mem. Royal Netherlands Acad. of Sciences. *Publication:* A First Course in Turbulence (with J. L. Lumley) 1972. *Leisure interests:* poetry, painting, model trains. *Address:* P.O. Box 201, 3730 AE De Bilt (Office); Acacialaan 18-B, 3707 EV Zeist, Netherlands (Home).

TENNSTEDT, Klaus; German conductor; b. 6 June 1926, Merseburg; m. Ingeborg Fischer 1960; studied, Leipzig; leader, then Conductor, Municipal Theatre Orchestra, Hall an der Saale 1948; Conductor, Dresden Opera 1958–62; Musical Dir. Mecklenburg State Theatre and Orchestra, Schwerin; frequently conducted Leipzig Gewandhaus and Dresden Philharmonic Orchestras during 1960s; left G.D.R. 1971; went to Sweden, then Fed. Repub. of Germany; Gen. Music Dir. Kiel Opera; conducted Toronto and Boston Symphony Orchestras 1974; Leader N. German Radio Symphony Orchestra 1979–81; Guest Conductor, London Philharmonic Orchestra 1977–80, Prin. Guest Conductor 1980–83, Prin. Conductor 1983–87, Conductor Laureate 1987–; has also conducted and recorded with Berlin Philharmonic Orchestra; appearances in Amsterdam, Paris, Hamburg, Berlin, Tel-Aviv; notable performances and recordings of works of Bruckner and Mahler; Hon. D.Mus. (Colgate Hamilton, N.Y.) 1984. *Address:* c/o London Philharmonic Orchestra, 35 Doughty Street, London, W.C.1, England; Rothenbaumchaussee 132-134, 2000 Hamburg 13, Federal Republic of Germany.

TEREBILOV, Vladimir Ivanovich, CAND.JUR.SC.; Soviet lawyer; b. 18 March 1916, Petrograd (now Leningrad); ed. Leningrad Inst. of Law; Regional Public Procurator 1939–49; Sr. Scientific Worker and Scientific Sec., Inst. of Criminology 1949–57; Deputy Head of Bd. of Public Procurators, U.S.S.R. 1957–61; mem. U.S.S.R. Coll. of Public Procurators 1961–62; Vice-Chair. of U.S.S.R. Supreme Court 1962–70; U.S.S.R. Minister of Justice 1970–84; Deputy to U.S.S.R. Supreme Soviet 1970–; mem. CPSU 1940; mem. Cen. Auditing Cttee of CPSU 1971–76; Pres. U.S.S.R. Supreme Court 1984–89; Cand. mem. Cen. Cttee. CPSU 1976–86, mem. 1986–89; Order of Lenin 1976, and other decorations. *Address:* c/o U.S.S.R. Ministry of Justice, 15 Ulitsa Vorovskogo, Moscow, U.S.S.R.

TEREKHOVA, Margarita Borisovna; Soviet actress; b. 25 Aug. 1942; ed. Tashkent Univ. and Mossoviet Studio School with Mossoviet Theatre 1964–83; film début 1966; R.S.F.S.R. Artist of Merit 1976. *Films include:* Hi! It's Me! 1966, Byelorussian Station 1971, My Life 1972, Monologue 1973, Mirror 1975, Day Train 1976, Who'll go to Truskovets? 1977, Dog in a Manger 1977, Kids, Kids, Kids 1978, Let's get Married 1983.

TERENZIO, Pio-Carlo, LL.D.; Italian international civil servant; b. 4 Sept. 1921, Lausanne, Switzerland; s. of Rodolfo Arnoldo Terenzio and Katherine Agopian; m. Luisa de Notaristefani 1950; two s.; ed. Univs. of Rome and Geneva; joined Int. Labour Office (ILO) 1948; Officer in charge of Relations with Int. Orgs, UNESCO 1948–60, Dir. in charge of Congo Operations 1960–63, Dir. Bureau of Relations with Member States 1963–69, Dir. Bureau of Personnel 1969–70; Sec.-Gen. Inter-Parl. Union (IPU) 1970–86. *Publications:* La rivalité anglo-russe en Perse et en Afghanistan 1947. *Address:* Villa della Minerva, 12, 00186 Rome, Italy. *Telephone:* (396) 6791714.

TERESA, Mother (Agnes Gonxha Bojaxhiu); Albanian-born Roman Catholic missionary; b. 27 Aug. 1910, Skopje, now Yugoslavia; joined Sisters of Loretto 1928; worked at Loretto insts. in Ireland and India; Principal St. Mary's High School, Calcutta; founded the Missionaries of Charity 1950; through the Missionaries of Charity has set up over fifty schools, orphanages and houses for the poor in India and other countries; opened Nirmal Hriday (Pure Heart) Home for Dying Destitutes 1952; started a leper colony in West Bengal 1964; Padma Shri 1962, Pope John XXIII Peace Prize 1971, Templeton Foundation Prize 1973, Nobel Peace Prize 1979, Bharat Ratna (Star of India) 1980; Hon. D.D. (Cambridge) 1977, Hon. O.B.E. 1978, Star of India 1980, Hon. Dr.Med. (Catholic Univ. of Sacred Heart, Rome) 1981, (Catholic Univ. of Louvain) 1982, Hon. Citizen of Assisi 1982, Hon. O.M. 1983, Presidential Medal of Freedom 1985, Woman of the Year Award 1989. *Publication:* Gift for God 1975. *Address:* 54A Acharya Jagadish Chandra Bose Road, Calcutta 700016, India. *Telephone:* 24-741150.

TERESHKOVA, Valentina Vladimirovna Nikolayeva-; Soviet cosmonaut; b. 6 March 1937, Tutayev, Yaroslavl Region; d. of late Vladimir Tereshkova and of Elena Fyodorovna Tereshkova; m. Andriyan Nikolayev 1963; one d.; ed. Yaroslavl Textile Coll. and Zhukovsky Air Force Engineering Acad.; former textile worker, Krasny Perekop textile mill, Yaroslavl, and textile mill Sec., Young Communist League; mem. CPSU 1962–, Cen. Cttee. CPSU 1971–; cosmonaut training March 1962–; made 48 orbital flights of the earth in spaceship Vostok VI 16th–19th June 1963; first woman in world to enter space; Deputy to U.S.S.R. Supreme Soviet 1962–; Chair. Soviet Women's Cttee. 1968–; mem. Supreme Soviet Presidium 1974–; Head U.S.S.R. Int. Cultural and Friendship Union 1988–; Visit to U.K. 1977; Pilot-Cosmonaut of U.S.S.R., Hero of Soviet Union, Order of Lenin (twice), Gold Star Medal, Joliot-Curie Gold Medal, World Peace Council 1966, Order of the Nile (Egypt) 1971, Order of the Red Banner of Labour 1986. *Address:* Soviet Women's Committee, 6 Nemirovich-Danchenko Street, 103009 Moscow; Zvezdny Gorodok, Moscow, U.S.S.R.

TERKEL, Studs Louis, PH.B., J.D.; American actor, interviewer and author; b. 16 May 1912, New York; s. of Samuel and Anna (née Finkel) Terkel; m. Ida Goldberg 1939; one s.; ed. Chicago Univ.; stage appearances include: Detective Story 1950, A View from the Bridge 1958, Light up the Sky 1959, The Cave Dwellers 1960; star TV programme Studs Place 1950–53, radio programme Wax Museum 1945–, Studs Terkel Almanac 1952–, Studs Terkel Show (station WFMT-FM Chicago); master of ceremonies, Newport Folk Festival 1959, 1960, Ravinia Musical Festival 1959, Chicago Univ. Folk Festival 1961 and others; lecturer and film narrator; Prix Italia, UNESCO Award for best Radio Programme (East-West Values) 1962; Communicator of the Year Award (Chicago Univ. Alumni Asscn.) 1969. *Publications:* Giants of Jazz 1956, Division Street America 1966, Amazing Grace (play) 1959, Hard Times 1970, Working 1974, Talking to Myself 1977, American Dreams: Lost and Found 1980, The Good War: An Oral History of World War Two 1985, Talking to Myself: A Memoir of My Times 1986, Chicago 1986, The Great Divide: Second Thoughts on the American Dream 1988 and short stories. *Address:* 850 West Castlewood Terrace, Chicago, Ill. 60640, U.S.A. (Home).

TERLOUW, Jan-Cornelis, PH.D.; Netherlands physicist, politician and international civil servant; b. 15 Nov. 1931, Kamperveen; s. of J. C. and Gré (née Stein) Terlouw; m. Alexandra Van Hulst; one s. three d.; ed. Univ. of Utrecht; Head of Research Group, Inst. for Plasma Physics, Univ. of Utrecht 1958–71; with M.I.T. 1960–62; in Stockholm 1965–66; mem. Netherlands Parl. 1971–81, Leader of Parl. Group 1973, Vice-Prime Minister and Minister of Econ. 1981–82; Sec.-Gen., European Conf. of Ministers of Transport (ECMT) Sept. 1983–; Commdr., Order of Orange-Nassau. *Publications:* several books, including novels for children. *Address:* European Conference of Ministers of Transport, 19 rue de Franqueville, 75775 Paris, Cedex 16, France. *Telephone:* (1) 45-24-97-10.

TERRAGNO, Rodolfo H., D.JUR.; Argentinian politician; b. 16 Nov. 1945, Buenos Aires; m. Sonía Pascual Sánchez; two s.; ed. Univ. de Buenos Aires; Asst. Prof. Univ. de Buenos Aries 1973–80; researcher Inst. of Latin American Studies, London 1980–82, L.S.E. 1980–82; Pres. Terragno S.A. de Industrias Químicas 1970–76; Exec. Vice-Pres. El Diario de Caracas S.A. 1976–80; Vice-Pres. Alas Enterprises Inc., N.Y. 1982–86; Dir. Letters S.A.R., Luxembourg 1982–86, Latin American Newsletters Ltd., London and Paris 1982–86; also columnist on several newspapers; rep. at int. conferences, including Dispute with U.K. over Falkland Islands 1983–85; Sec. to Cabinet 1987–, Minister of Works and Public Services 1987–; Pres. Fundación Argentina Siglo 21 1986–87. *Publications:* Los dueños del poder 1972, Los 400 días de Perón 1974–75, Contratapas 1976, Muerte y resurrección de los políticos 1981, La Argentina del Siglo 21 1985–87, also numerous research papers. *Address:* Ministerio de Obras y Servicios Publicos, Buenos Aires, Argentina.

TERRAINE, John Alfred, F.R.HIST.S.; British writer; b. 15 Jan. 1921, London; s. of Charles William Terraine and Evelyn Holmes; m. Joyce Elizabeth Waite 1945; one d.; ed. Stamford School, Keble Coll., Oxford; Recorded Programmes Section, BBC 1943, Radio Newsreel 1945, Russian Section 1947, Pacific and S. African Programme Organizer 1953; free-lance writer 1963–; f. and Pres. Western Front Assen. 1980–; Screenwriters' Guild Documentary Award 1964, Soc. of Film and TV Arts Script Award 1969. *Publications:* Mons 1960, Douglas Haig: The Educated Soldier 1963, The Great War (TV series) 1964, The Western Front 1964, General Jack's Diary (Ed.) 1964, The Life and Times of Lord Mountbatten 1968 (TV series), Impacts of War, 1914 and 1918 1970, The Mighty Continent 1974 (TV series), Trafalgar 1976, The Road to Passchendaele 1977, To Win a War: 1918 The Year of Victory 1978, The Smoke and the Fire 1980, White Heat: the New Warfare 1914–18 1982, The First World War 1914–18 1983, The Right of the Line: The Royal Air Force in the European War 1939–45 1985; Chesney Gold Medal, Royal United Service Inst. 1982, Yorkshire Post Book of the Year 1985, C. P. Robertson Memorial Trophy, Air Public Relations Assen. 1985. *Address:* 74 Kensington Park Road, London, W11 2PL, England. *Telephone:* 01-229 8152.

TERRENOIRE, Louis; French journalist and politician; b. 10 Nov. 1908, Lyon; m. Elisabeth Gay 1935; two s. two d.; former trade union Sec.; Ed. La Voix Sociale, Nouveau Journal de Lyon 1930–31, Editorial Sec. L'Aube 1932–39, later Ed.; Sec. Conseil Nat. de la Résistance 1944; captured and deported; elected Deputy for Orne, Nat. Ass. 1945, 1958, 1962, 1967, 1968; Sec.-Gen. Rassemblement du Peuple français (R.P.F.) 1951–54; Dir. News and Information, Radiodiffusion-Télévision Française July-Nov. 1958; Minister of Information Feb. 1960-Aug. 1961; Minister attached to Office of Prime Minister Aug. 1961-Apr. 1962; Sec.-Gen. Union pour la Nouvelle République 1962; mem. European Parl. 1963–73, Vice-Pres. 1967–73; Pres. Assen. de solidarité Franco-arabe 1967–78; Pres. Union pour la Nouvelle République Group in Ass. 1959–60; Commdr., Légion d'honneur, Croix de guerre, Rosette de la Résistance. *Publications:* De Gaulle et l'Algérie 1964, De Gaulle vivant 1971, Sursitaires de la mort lente 1976, De Gaulle 1947–54 1981. *Address:* 6 rue de Rémusat, 75016 Paris; Le Moulin de Soucé, 53300 Ambrières-les-Vallées, France. *Telephone:* 525 23 43 (Paris).

TERRY, John Quinlan, A.A.DIP., F.R.I.B.A.; British architect; b. 24 July 1937, London; s. of Philip and Phyllis Terry; m. Christina de Ruttié 1961; one s. four d.; ed. Bryanston School, Architectural Assen.; joined late Raymond Erith R.A. 1962–73, work includes Kingswalden Bury, the Gibson Square Ventilation Shaft, the New Common Room Bldg. at Gray's Inn, the restoration of St. Mary's Church on Paddington Green, "Le Pavillon" at Little Horkesley, first design for the new Bahai Temple; Partner Erith and Terry 1967–; in pvt. practice 1973–, work includes second design for Bahai Temple, Waverton House at Moreton-in-Marsh, Newfield at Ripon, The Ass. Hall, St. Mary's Church, Paddington Green, much restoration and extension work including Queen's Coll., Oxford; Prix Internationale de la Reconstruction 1983. *Address:* Higham Hall, Higham, Colchester, Essex, England. *Telephone:* (020 637) 209.

TERRY-THOMAS (Thomas Terry Hoar Stevens); British actor; b. 14 July 1911; s. of Ernest Frederick Stevens and Ellen Elizabeth Hoar; m. 1st Ida Patlanskey 1938; m. 2nd Belinda Cunningham 1963, two s.; ed. Ardingley Coll., Sussex; served World War II; appeared in Piccadilly Hayride, Prince of Wales Theatre, London 1946–47; radio series To Town With Terry 1948–49, Top of the Town 1951–52; TV series How Do You View 1951–52. *Films:* Private's Progress, Green Man 1956; Brothers-in-Law, Blue Murder at St. Trinians, Lucky Jim, Naked Truth 1957; Tom Thumb, Happy is the Bride 1958; Carlton Browne of the FO, I'm All Right Jack, Too Many Crooks 1959; Make Mine Mink, School for Scoundrels, His and Hers 1960; A Matter of Who, Bachelor Flat, Operation Snatch, The Wonderful World of the Brothers Grimm 1961; Kill or Cure, It's a Mad, Mad, Mad, Mad World 1962, Wild Affair 1963, How to Murder Your Wife 1964, Those Magnificent Men in their Flying Machines 1965, Jules Verne's Rocket to the Moon 1967; Don't Look Now, Where Were You When the Lights Went Out? 1968; Monte Carlo or Bust! 1969; Thirteen, Seven Times Seven, Arthur, Arthur, Atlantic Wall, Dr. Phibes 1970; Lei, Lui, Loro, la Legge 1971, Dr. Phibes Rises Again, The Heros 1972; Side By Side, Spanish Fly 1975, The Last Remake of Beau Geste 1976, The Hound of the Baskervilles 1978. *Publication:* Filling the Gap 1959. *Leisure interests:* horse riding, water skiing. *Address:* Juan de Saridakis 83, Genova Palma, Mallorca.

TESCH, Emmanuel Camille Georges Victor; Luxembourg iron and steel company executive and engineer; b. 9 Dec. 1920, Hespérange; s. of Georges Tesch and Marie-Laure Weckbecker; m. Thérèse Laval 1949; one s.; ed. Technische Hochschule, Aachen and Eidgenössische Technische Hochschule, Zürich; Engineer, Manufacture de Tabacs Heintz van Landewyck 1948–51; fmr. Man. Dir. Soc. Générale pour le Commerce de Produits Industriels (SOGECO); joined ARBED as auditor 1958, Dir. 1968–69, Dir. delegated to Chair. 1969–72, Chair. Bd. of Man. 1972–86, Chair. Bd. of Dirs. 1972–; Chair. Bd. of Dirs. ARBED Finance S.A., Electro Holding Co., S.A. Luxembourgeoise d'Exploitations Minières; Dir. S.A. Accumulateurs TUDOR; Dir. SIDMAR S.A., Compagnie Maritime Belge, SOGECO S.A., LE FOYER S.A., Banque Générale du Luxembourg S.A., FININCO (Financial and Investment Co.); Adviser Société Générale de Belgique, Companhia Siderurgica Belgo-Mineira; mem. Supervisory Bd. Dresdner Bank; mem. Internationaler Beraterkreis der Allianz-Versicherungs-Gesellschaft, Conseil Economique et Social (Luxembourg); Pres. Chambre de Commerce du Grand-Duché de Luxembourg, Médaille de la Résistance (France); Grand Officier Ordre de la Couronne de Chêne (Luxembourg); Commdr. avec Couronne dans l'Ordre de mérite civil et militaire d'Adolphe de Nassau (Luxembourg); Ordre de la Couronne (Belgium); Commdr. Order of Orange-Nassau (Netherlands); Cavaliere di Gran Croce (Italy); Order of Tudor Vladimirescu (Romania); Hon. K.B.E.; Grosses Goldenes Ehrenzeichen mit Stern des Verdienstordens der Republik Österreich; Grosses Verdienstkreuz mit Stern des Verdienstordens der Bundesrepublik Deutschland; Encomienda de numero, Merito Civil, Spain. *Leisure interests:* shooting, fishing, gardening, literature. *Address:* Administration Centrale de l'ARBED, avenue de la Liberté, L-2930 Luxembourg (Office); La Cléchère, L-1899 Kockelscheuer, Luxembourg (Home). *Telephone:* 47921 (Office); 36-81-68 (Home).

TESAURO, Guiseppe; Italian professor of international law; b. 15 Nov. 1942, Naples; m. Paola Borrelli 1967; three c.; ed. Liceo Umberto, Naples, Univ. of Naples, Max Planck Inst. Volkerrecht-Heidelberg; Asst. Prof. of Int. Law, Univ. of Naples 1965–71; Prof. of Int. Law and Int. Org., Univs. of Catania, Messina, Naples, Rome 1971–88; Dir. EEC Law School, Univ. of Rome 1982–88; mem. Council Legal Affairs, Ministry of Foreign Affairs 1986–; mem. EEC Court of Justice, Advocate Gen. 1988–. *Publications:* Financing International Institutions 1968, Pollution of the Sea and International Law 1971, Nationalizations and International Law 1976, Movements of Capitals in the EEC 1984, Course of EEC Law 1988. *Leisure interests:* tennis, football, sailing. *Address:* Cour de Justice CEE, Plateau Kirchberg, Luxembourg; Via A. Falcone 249, Naples, Italy. *Telephone:* (00352) 43032220; (081) 663543.

TESSON, Philippe, D. ÈS L.; French journalist; b. 1 March 1928, Wassigny (Aisne); m. Dr. Marie-Claude Millet; one s. two d.; Sec. of Parl. Debates 1957–60; Ed.-in-Chief, Combat 1960–74; candidate in legis. elections 1968; Diarist and Drama Critic, Canard Enchaîné 1970–83; Co-Man. and Dir. Société d'Editions Scientifiques et Culturelles 1971, Pres. 1980–; Dir. and Ed.-in-Chief, Quotidien de Paris 1974–; Dir. Nouvelles Littéraires 1975–83; Drama Critic, L'Express Paris 1986; Dir. and Co-Man. Quotidien du Maire 1987–; Chevalier, Légion d'honneur. *Publication:* de Gaulle 1er 1965. *Address:* Quotidien de Paris, 2 rue Ancelle, 92200 Neuilly/Seine (Office); 9 rue La Fontaine, 78400 Chatou, France (Home). *Telephone:* 47.47.12.32 (Office).

TETLEY, Glen; American ballet director and choreographer; b. 3 Feb. 1926, Cleveland, Ohio; s. of Glenford Andrew Tetley and Mary Eleanor Byrne; ed. Franklin and Marshall Coll., Lancaster, Pa. and New York Univ.; performed with Hanya Holm, José Limon, Pearl Lang, John Butler modern dance cos.; prin. dancer, New York City Opera 1951–54; leading soloist, Robert Joffrey Ballet 1955–56, Martha Graham Dance Co. 1957–59, American Ballet Theater 1959–61, Jerome Robbins' Ballet U.S.A. 1961–62; f. own co. 1962–69; dancer and choreographer, Nederlands Dans Theater, Co-Artistic Dir. 1969; guest choreographer Royal Danish, Swedish, Norwegian Ballets, Hamburg State Opera; choreographer Royal Ballet, Covent Garden, American Ballet Theatre, Ballet Rambert; Dir. Stuttgart Ballet 1974–76; Artistic Assoc. Nat. Ballet of Canada 1987–; German Critics Award (for Die Feder) 1969, Queen Elizabeth II Coronation Award 1981, Prix Italia 1982, RAI Prize 1982, Tennant Caledonian Award 1983, Ohioana Career Medal for 1986, N.Y. Univ. Achievement Award 1988. *Performances:* Kiss me Kate, Out of this World, Amahl and the Night Visitors; choreography: Pierrot Lunaire, Sargasso, The Anatomy Lesson, Circles, Imaginary Film, Arena, Small Parades, Mutations, Embrace Tiger and Return to Mountain, Ziggurat, Rag Dances, Ricercare, Field Figures, Laborintus, Mythical Hunters, Gemini, Chronocromie, Threshold, Moveable Garden, Voluntaries, Le sacre du printemps, Greening, Nocturne, Sphinx, Praeludium, Contredances, The Tempest, Summer's End, Dances of Albion, Dark Night: Glad Day, Fire Bird, Murderer Hope of Women, Revelation and Fall, Pulcinella, Dream Walk of the Shaman, Alice, Orpheus, La Ronde. *Address:* 15 West 9th Street, New York, N.Y., U.S.A. *Telephone:* (212) 4754604.

TETSUO, Yamanaka; Japanese banker; b. 24 May 1921, Nagasaki; ed. Tokyo Imperial Univ.; Chief Rep., Bank of Japan, New York 1967; Adviser to Gov. Bank of Japan on Foreign Affairs 1970; Man. Management Service and Computer Dept. 1970, Personnel Dept. 1971, Foreign Dept. 1974, Exec. Div. 1975; Sr. Adviser to Gov. 1979; Deputy Pres. The Kyowa Bank Ltd. 1979, Pres. 1980–86, Chair. 1986–. *Address:* The Kyowa Bank Ltd., 1-2 Otemachi 1-chome, Chiyoda-ku, Tokyo; 4-1-11-702 Hiroo, Shibuya-ku, Tokyo, Japan (Home). *Telephone:* (03) 486-3773 (Home).

TETT, Sir Hugh Charles, Kt., A.R.C.S., B.SC., D.I.C.; British businessman; b. 28 Oct. 1906, Exeter, Devon; s. of late James Charles Tett and of Florence Tett (née Lihou); m. 1st Katie Sargent 1931 (died 1948), 2nd Joyce Lilian (née Mansell) 1949 (died 1979), 3rd Barbara Mary Riley 1980; two d.; ed. Univ. Coll., Exeter, and Royal Coll. of Science, London; Esso Petroleum Co. 1928–67, Chair. 1959–67; Chair. Addis Ltd. 1973–76; Dir. Esso-Europe 1966–68, Pirelli Gen. Cable Works Ltd. 1970–80, Black and Decker Ltd. 1970–77, Bristol Composite Materials Ltd. 1972, Chair. 1974–79; Pro-Chancellor Univ. of Southampton 1967–79; Fellow Imperial Coll., London 1964; Hon. D.Sc. (Southampton 1965, Exeter 1970). *Leisure interest:* travel. *Address:* Primrose Cottage, Bosham, Chichester, West Sussex, PO18 8HZ, England. *Telephone:* (0243) 572705.

TÉVOÉDJRÈ, Albert, D. ès SC.ECON. et SOC., L. ès L.; Benin politician and international civil servant; b. 10 Nov. 1929, Porto Novo; s. of Joseph Tévoédjrè and Jeanne Singbo Tévoédjrè; m. Isabelle Ekué 1953; three s.; ed. Toulouse Univ., Fribourg Univ., Institut Universitaire de Hautes Etudes Internationales, Geneva, Sloan School of Management and M.I.T. (Advanced Programme for Sr. Executives); teaching assignments include: Lycée Delafosse, Dakar, Senegal 1952–54, Ecole Normale d'Institutrices, Cahors, France 1957–58, Lycée Victor Ballot, Porto Novo 1959–61, Geneva Africa Inst. 1963–64, Georgetown Univ., Washington D.C. 1964; Sec. of State for Information 1961–62; Sec.-Gen. Union Africaine et Malgache (U.A.M.) 1962–63; Research Assoc. Harvard Univ., Centre for Int. Affairs 1964–65; Int. Labour Office 1965–, Regional Dir. for Africa March 1966, Asst. Dir.-Gen. 1969–75, Deputy Dir.-Gen. 1975–; Dir. Int. Inst. for Labour Studies 1975–84; Sec.-Gen. World Social Prospects Asscn. (AMPS) 1980–; fmr. Chief Ed. L'Etudiant d'Afrique Noire; founder mem. Promotion Africaine (society to combat poverty in Africa); founder-mem. Nat. Liberation Movt. and mem. Cttee. 1958–60; Deputy Sec.-Gen. of Nat. Syndicate of Teachers, Dahomey 1959–60; Visiting Prof. Sorbonne 1979–, Univ. des Mutants, Dakar 1979–, Nat. Univ. of Ivory Coast 1979–, Northwestern Univ., Ill. 1980; Int. Humanitarian Medal 1987. *Publications:* L'Afrique revoltée 1958, La formation des cadres africains en vue de la croissance économique 1965, Pan-Africanism in Action 1965, L'Afrique face aux problèmes du socialisme et de l'aide étrangère 1966, Une stratégie du progrès social en Afrique et la contribution de l'OIT 1969, Pour un contrat de solidarité 1976, La pauvreté—richesse des peuples 1978, etc. *Address:* 15 Chemin du Pommier, Le Grand Saconnex, Geneva, Switzerland. *Telephone:* 985157 (Office); 989105 (Home).

THAHANE, Timothy Thahane, B.COMM., M.A.; Lesotho government official and diplomatist; b. 2 Nov. 1940, Leribe; s. of Nicodemus and Beatrice Thahane; m. Dr. Edith Mohapi 1972; one s. one d.; ed. Lesotho High School, Univs. of Newfoundland and Toronto, Canada; Asst. Sec., Prin. Asst. Sec., Cen. Planning Office 1968–70, Dir. of Planning 1970–73; Amb. to EEC for Negotiations of Lomé Convention 1973–74; Alt. Dir. World Bank 1974–76, Exec. Dir. 1976–78, representing 17 African countries and Trinidad and Tobago; Vice-Chair. and Chair., Jt. Audit Cttee. of World Bank Group 1976–78; Amb. to the U.S.A. 1979–80; Vice-Pres. and Sec., IBRD April 1980–; mem. Bd. of Lesotho Bank (Vice-Chair. 1972–73), Third

World Foundation. *Publications:* articles on econ. planning and investment in Lesotho, Southern Africa and Africa in general. *Leisure interests;* reading, music. *Address:* c/o International Bank for Reconstruction and Development, 1818 H Street, N.W., Washington, D.C. 20433, U.S.A.

THAILAND, King of (see Bhumibol Adulyadej).

THAJEB, Sjarif, M.D.; Indonesian physician, diplomatist and politician; b. 7 Aug. 1920, Peureula, Atjeh; s. of Tueku Tjhi Hadji Mohamad Thajeb, Ulubalang of Peureula and Raden Aju Nurhamidah Thajeb; m. Nunijati Hidajat Prawirodiprodjo; one s. three d.; ed. Jakarta Medical Coll., Harvard Medical School, Temple Univ. School of Medicine, Philadelphia, Pa. and Army Staff and Command School, Jakarta; former army doctor; fmr. lecturer, Children's Div., Dept. of Medicine, Univ. of Indonesia; fmr. Pres. Univ. of Indonesia; fmr. Minister of Higher Educ. and Sciences; fmr. Vice-Chair. of Parl.; Amb. to U.S.A. 1971–74; Minister of Educ. and Culture 1974–77, Acting Minister of Foreign Affairs 1977–78; mem. Exec. Bd. UNESCO 1976–; participant in several int. paediatric confs.; Hon. Dr., Univ. of Mindanao (Philippines); several medals and decorations. *Publications:* papers and articles on various subjects published in numerous paediatric magazines and journals. *Leisure interests:* music, theatre, golf, bowling. *Address:* c/o Ministry of Foreign Affairs, Jakarta, Indonesia.

THALMANN, Ernesto A., DR. IUR.; Swiss diplomatist (retd.); b. 14 Jan. 1914, Bellinzona; s. of Fritz Thalmann and Clara Good; m. Paula Degen 1943; two s. one d.; ed. Univ. of Zürich; Lawyer, Dist. Court of Zürich 1940; Fed. Dept. of Public Economy 1941; Attaché, Swiss Fed. Political Dept. 1945; Sec. Extraordinary Powers Cttee. and the Cttee. of Foreign Affairs of the Nat. Council 1946; Second Sec. of Legation 1947; Deputy Chief, Press and Information Service, Swiss Fed. Political Dept. 1947; Sec. Swiss del. UN Conf. for Freedom of Press and Information, Geneva 1948; Swiss Legation, Paris 1949, First Sec. 1951; Swiss Legation, Prague 1952; Deputy Chief, Div. of Org. and Admin. Affairs, Swiss Political Dept. 1954–57; Counsellor and Deputy Chief of Mission, Swiss Embassy in U.S.A. 1957–60, Minister-Counsellor 1960–61; Perm. Observer to UN with rank of Amb. 1961–66; Chief, Div. for Int. Orgs., Fed. Political Dept. 1966–71; Special Mission in Jerusalem after Six-Day War, as Personal Rep. of UN Sec.-Gen. 1967; Sec.-Gen. of Fed. Political Dept. and Dir. of Political Affairs 1971–75; Amb. to U.K. 1976–79; Pres. Nat. Swiss UNESCO Cttee. 1981–85. *Leisure interest:* gardening. *Address:* Anshelmstrasse 8, 3005 Berne, Switzerland.

THANI, Sheikh Abdul Aziz ibn Khalifa al-, B.S.; Qatar politician; b. 12 Dec. 1948, Doha; one s. three d.; ed. Northern Indiana Univ., U.S.A.; Deputy Minister of Finance and Petroleum June-Dec. 1972, Minister of Finance and Petroleum, State of Qatar 1972–; Chair. State of Qatar Investment Bd. 1972–, Qatar Nat. Bank 1972–, Qatar Gen. Petroleum Corpn. 1973–; Gov. IMF and IBRD (World Bank) 1972–; rep. at numerous int. confs. including OPEC, OAPEC, and Arab, Islamic and Non-Aligned summit confs. *Leisure interest:* scuba diving. *Address:* Ministry of Finance and Petroleum, P.O. Box 36, Doha; Qatar General Petroleum Corporation, P.O. Box 3212, Doha, Qatar.

THANI, Sheikh Khalifa bin Hamad al-; Emir of Qatar; b. 1932, Doha; s. of the late Heir Apparent Sheikh Hamad bin Abdullah bin Jassim al-Thani; ed. Royal Mil. Coll., Sandhurst, U.K.; appointed Heir-Apparent 1948; served successively as Chief of Security Forces, Chief of Civil Courts, Minister of Educ., Finance and Petroleum; Deputy Ruler 1960–72, also Minister of Educ. 1960–70; Prime Minister 1970–72, Minister of Finance 1970–72; Chair. Investment Bd. for State Reserves 1972; deposed his cousin Sheikh Ahmad and took office as Emir of Qatar Feb. 1972–. *Address:* The Royal Palace, Doha; Ministry of the Interior, P.O. Box 2433, Doha, Qatar.

THANIN KRAIVICHIEN (see Kraivichien, Thanin).

THAPA, Ganesh Bahadur; Nepalese banker; b. 7 July 1936, Doti; s. of Sanad Bahadur Thapa and Laxmi Devi Thapa; m. Sabitri Thapa 1957; three s. one d.; ed. Jt. Sec. Ministry of Industry and Commerce 1967; Gen. Man. Nepal Industrial Devt. Corpn. 1971; Deputy Gov. Nepal Rashtra Bank 1974, Gov. 1985–; UNDP Adviser to Indonesian Govt. 1981–85; Trishakti Patta (3rd Class), Gorakha Dakshinbahu Medal. *Leisure interests:* reading, jogging. *Address:* Nepal Rastra Bank, Central Office, Kathmandu, Nepal. *Telephone:* 410386.

THAPA, Surya Bahadur; Nepalese politician; b. 20 March 1928, Muga, East Nepal; s. of Bahadur Thapa; m. 1953; one s. two d.; ed. Allahabad Univ., India; House Speaker, Advisory Ass. to King of Nepal 1958; mem. Upper House of Parl. 1959; Minister of Forests, Agric., Commerce and Industry 1960; Minister of Finance and Econ. Affairs 1962; Vice-Chair. Council of Ministers, Minister of Finance, Econ. Planning, Law and Justice 1963; Vice-Chair. Council of Ministers, Minister of Finance, Law and Gen. Admin. 1964–65; Chair. Council of Ministers, Minister of Palace Affairs, 1965–69; Prime Minister of Nepal and Minister of Palace Affairs 1979–83; Minister of Finance 1979–80, of Defence 1980–81, 1982–83, of Foreign Affairs 1982; mem. Royal Advisory Cttee. 1969–72; arrested 1972, 1975; Tri-Sahkti-Patta 1963, Gorkha Dakshinbahu I 1965, Om Rama Patta 1980; several Nepalese and foreign awards. *Address:* Tangal, Katmandu, Nepal.

THARP, Twyla; American dancer and choreographer; b. 1 July 1941, Portland, Ind.; m. Robert Huot (divorced); one s.; ed. Pomona Coll., American Ballet Theatre School, Barnard Coll.; studied with Richard Thomas, Merce Cunningham, Igor Schwezoff, Louis Mattox, Paul Taylor, Margaret Craske, Erick Hawkins; with Paul Taylor Dance Co. 1963-65; freelance choreographer with own modern dance troupe and various other cos., including Joffrey Ballet and American Ballet Theatre 1965-; Artistic Assoc. Choreographer American Ballet Theatre, New York 1988-; maj. works choreographed Tank Dive 1965, Re-Moves 1966, Forevermore 1967, Generation 1968, Medley 1969, Fugue 1970, Eight Jelly Rolls 1971, The Raggedy Dances 1972, As Time Goes By 1974, Sue's Leg 1975, Push Comes to Shove 1976, Once More Frank 1976, Mud 1977, Baker's Dozen 1979, When We Were Very Young 1980, Amadeus 1984, White Nights 1985, Rules of the Game 1989; film Hair 1979; videotape Making Television Dance 1977, CBS Cable Confessions of a Corner Maker 1980; Hon. D. Performing Arts (Brown) 1981 and others; Dance Magazine Annual Award 1981. *Address:* c/o Twyla Tharp Dance Foundation, 38 Walker Street, New York, N.Y. 10013, U.S.A.

THATCHER, Rt. Hon. Margaret Hilda, P.C., M.P., M.A., B.SC., F.R.S.; British barrister and politician; b. 13 Oct. 1925; d. of the late Alfred Roberts; m. Denis Thatcher 1951; one s. one d. (twins); ed. Grantham High School and Somerville Coll., Oxford; Research chemist 1947-51; called to the Bar, Lincoln's Inn 1953; M.P. for Barnet, Finchley 1959-; Parl. Sec. Ministry of Pensions and Nat. Insurance 1961-64; Chief Opposition Spokesman on Educ. 1969-70; Sec. of State for Educ. and Science 1970-74; Leader of Conservative Party Feb. 1975-; Leader of H.M. Opposition 1975-79; Prime Minister May 1979-; First Lord of the Treasury and Minister for the Civil Service May 1979-; Hon. Bencher, Lincoln's Inn 1975; Hon. Master of the Bench of Gray's Inn 1983; Hon. Fellow Royal Inst. of Chem. 1979; Freedom of Royal Borough of Kensington and Chelsea 1979, of London Borough of Barnet 1980, of Falkland Is. 1983, of City of London 1989; mem. Worshipful Co. of Glovers 1983-; Hon. LL.D. (Univ. of Buckingham) 1986; Conservative. *Publication:* In Defence of Freedom 1986. *Address:* 10 Downing Street, London, S.W.1, England.

THÉ, Guy Blaudin de (see de Thé, Guy Blaudin).

THEBERGE, James Daniel, M.A., M.P.A.; American diplomatist; b. 28 Dec. 1930, Oceanside, N.Y.; s. of Lionel J. and Antoinette M. Theberge; m. Giselle Fages 1964; three s.; ed. Columbia, Oxford, Harvard and Heidelberg Univs.; Econ. Adviser, U.S. Embassy, Argentina 1961-64; Special Adviser, U.S. Sec. of Treasury 1966; Adviser, Sr. Economist IDB 1966-69; Visiting Lecturer 1968; Research Assoc. St. Antony's Coll., Oxford 1969-70; Dir. Latin-American and Hispanic Studies, Center for Strategic and Int. Studies, Georgetown Univ. 1970-75; Dir. Latin American Project, Rockefeller Comm. on Critical Choices for Americas 1974-75; Amb. to Nicaragua 1975-77; Pres. Inst. for Conflict and Policy Studies, Washington, D.C. 1977-79; Sr. Devt. Adviser, Planning Research Corpn., New York 1979-80; Special Asst. to Dept. of Defense, Inter-American Affairs 1980-81; Amb. to Chile 1982-85; Chair. Nat. Cttee. on Cen. America 1985-; Pres. Core Int. 1986-; Sr. Consultant Atlantic Inst. 1986-; mem. Pres.'s Int. Narcotics Control Comm. 1986-. *Publications:* Economics of Trade and Development 1968, The Western Mediterranean 1972, Soviet Sea Power in the Caribbean 1972, Russia in the Caribbean 1973, Soviet Presence in Latin America 1975, Latin America in the World System 1975, Spain in the Seventies 1976, Latin America: Struggle for Progress 1977, Reflections of a Diplomat: United States and Latin America 1985. *Leisure interests:* tennis, riding, sailing, swimming. *Address:* 4462 Cathedral Avenue, N.W., Washington, D.C. 20016, U.S.A.

THEIS, Adolf; German university president; b. 24 March 1933, Karlsruhe; s. of Ludwig and Maria Theis; m. H. Genzmer; two s.; ed. Univs. of Marburg, Heidelberg, Freiburg and Munich; asst. judge 1960-61; legal adviser in a state ministry 1961-65; Head of Admin. Univ. of Hohenheim 1965-68; Fed. Ministry for Scientific Research, Bonn 1968; mem. Fed. Ministry of Interior's Project Group for Govt. and Admin. Reform for Ministry of Science and Research 1969, Deputy Chair. 1971; Ministerial Adviser, Fed. Chancellery 1970; consultant for planning methods and techniques 1971; Pres. Univ. of Tübingen 1972-; Bundesverdienstkreuz; Hon. LL.D. (Temple Univ.). *Publications:* articles on political planning and university organization. *Address:* 7400 Tübingen, Wilhelmstrasse 5, Federal Republic of Germany. *Telephone:* (07071) 292512.

THEOBALD, Thomas C.; American business executive; b. 1937, Cincinnati, Ohio; m. Gigi Mahon 1987; ed. Holy Cross Coll. and Harvard Grad. School of Business Admin.; various man. posts with Citicorp/Citibank 1960-87, latterly Vice-Chair. with responsibility for worldwide investment banking activities; Chair. and C.E.O. Continental Bank Corpn. 1987-; Dir. Xerox Corpn. *Address:* c/o Corporate Affairs, Continental Bank Corporation, 231 S. LaSalle Street, Chicago Ill. 60697, U.S.A. *Telephone:* (312) 828-2345.

THEOCHARIS, Reghinos D., PH.D.; Cypriot economist; b. 10 Feb. 1929, Larnaca; s. of Demetrios and Florentia Theocharis; m. Madeleine Loumbou 1954; one s. one d.; ed. Graduate School of Economics, Athens, Univ. of Aberdeen, and L.S.E.; Insp. of Commercial Educ., Cyprus 1953-56; at L.S.E. 1956-58; Bank of Greece, Athens 1958-59; Minister of Finance in

Cyprus Provisional Govt. March 1959-Aug. 1960; Minister of Finance 1960-62; Gov. of Bank of Cyprus 1962-75; Prof. Athens School of Econs. and Commercial Sciences, Athens 1975-; Dir.-Gen. Center of Planning and Econ. Research (KEPE), Athens 1978-81; Hon. Fellow, L.S.E. 1971. *Publication:* On the Stability of the Cournot Solution on the Oligopoly Problem 1960, Early Developments in Mathematical Economics 1983. *Leisure interests:* chess, gardening. *Address:* c/o Anotati Scholi Economikon kai Emborikon Epistimon, Odos Patission 76, Athens 104; 2 Raidestou Street, Kessariani, Athens, 16122, Greece (Home). *Telephone:* 7214531.

THEODORAKIS, Mikis; Greek composer; b. 29 July 1925, Chios (Greek Island); s. of Georges Michel Theodorakis and Aspasia Poulaki; m. Myrto Altinoglou 1953; one s. one d.; ed. secondary and high school, Greece, Athens Conservatoire and Paris Conservatoire; joined resistance against German occupation of Greece 1943; arrested and deported during civil war 1947-52; moved to Paris 1953 and studied under Olivier Messiaen (q.v.); first public concert Sonatina (for pianoforte), Paris 1954; set to bouzouki music the poem Epitaphios by Iannis Ritsos 1958-59 and subsequently wrote numerous other successful songs; Ballet music for Antigone (first performed in London by Dame Margot Fonteyn) and Les amants de Teruel; returned to Greece 1961; leader Lambrakis youth movement; M.P. 1963; arrested for political activities 1967, released April 1970; resgnd. from CP March 1972; United Left cand., parl. election Nov. 1974; fmr. M.P. (CP) 1981, 1985-1986 (resgnd.); Gold Medal, Moscow Shostakovitch Festival 1957; Copley Prize, U.S.A. 1957; First Prize Athens Popular Song Festival 1961; Sibelius Award, London 1963, Lenin Int. Peace Prize 1982. *Works include:* Sinfonia (oratorio) 1944, Love and Death (voice, strings) 1945-48, Assi-Gonia (orchestra) 1945-50, Sextet for Flute 1946, Oedipus Tyrannus (strings) 1946, Greek Carnaval (ballet suite) 1947, First Symphony (orchestra) 1948-50, Five Cretan Songs (chorus, orchestra) 1950, Orpheus and Eurydice (ballet) 1952, Barefoot Battalion (film) 1953, Suite No. 1 (four movements, piano and orchestra) 1954, Poèmes d'Eluard (Cycle 1 and Cycle 2) 1955, Suite No. 2 (chorus, orchestra) 1956, Suite No. 3 (five movements, soprano, chorus, orchestra) 1956, Ill Met by Moonlight (film) 1957, Sonatina No. 1 (violin, piano) 1957, Les amants de Teruel (ballet) 1958, Piano Concerto 1958, Sonatina No. 2 (violin, piano) 1958, Antigone (ballet) 1958, Epitaphios (song cycle) 1959, Deserters (song cycle) 1958, Epiphania (song cycle) 1959, Honeymoon (film) 1960, Phoenician Women—Euripides (theatre music) 1960, Axion Esti (pop oratorio) 1960, Electra—Euripides (film), Phaedra (film) 1962, The Hostage (song cycle) 1962, The Ballad of the Dead Brother (musical tragedy) 1962, Zorba the Greek (film), The Ballad of Mathausen (song cycle) 1965, Romiossini (song cycle) 1966, Lusistrata—Aristophanes (theatre music) 1966, Romancero Gitano (Lorca) (song cycle) 1967, Sun and Time (song cycle) 1967, Arcadias Nos. 1-10 (song cycles) 1968-69, Canto General (Pablo Neruda) (pop oratorio) 1972, Z (film), Etat de Siège (film) 1973, Ballads (song cycle) 1975, Symphony No. 2 (orchestra and piano) 1981, Messe Byzantine (Litourgia) 1982, Symphony No. 3 (orchestra, chorus, soprano) 1982, Sadoukeon Passion (cantata for orchestra, chorus, soloists) 1983, Litourgie No. 2 1983, Symphony No. 7 (orchestra, chorus, soloists) 1984, Requiem 1985, Kostas Kariotakis (opera in two acts) 1985. *Publications:* Journals of Resistance 1972, Culture et dimensions politiques 1973, Culture Combattante 1980, Anatomy of Music 1983, Les chemins de l'Archange (autobiog.) 1986, The Faces of the Sun (song cycle) 1987, The Memory of Stone (song cycle) 1987, Like Ancient Wind (song cycle) 1987; Symphony No. 4 1987. *Address:* 42 rue Notre Dame des Champs, 75006 Paris, France; Epifanous 1, Akropolis, Athens, Greece. *Telephone:* 45.48.14.77 (Paris); 92 24 690 (Athens).

THEROUX, Paul Edward, B.A., F.R.S.L., F.R.G.S.; writer; b. 10 April 1941, Medford, Mass.; s. of Albert Eugene Theroux and Anne Dittami Theroux; m. Anne Castle 1967; two s.; ed. Univ. of Massachusetts, U.S.A.; lecturer, Univ. of Urbino, Italy 1963, Soche Hill Coll., Malawi 1963-65, Makerere Univ., Kampala, Uganda 1965-68, Univ. of Singapore 1968-71; Writer-in-Residence, Univ. of Va. 1972; Hon. D.Litt. (Tufts Univ.) 1983, (Univ. of Mass.) 1988. *Publications:* (novels) Waldo 1967, Fong and the Indians 1968, Girls at Play 1969, Murder in Mount Holly 1969, Jungle Lovers 1971, Sinning with Annie 1972, Saint Jack 1973 (filmed 1979), The Black House 1974, The Family Arsenal 1976, The Consul's File 1977, Picture Palace 1978 (Whitbread Award 1978), A Christmas Card 1978, London Snow 1980, World's End 1980, The Mosquito Coast 1981, The London Embassy 1982, Doctor Slaughter 1984 (filmed as Half Moon Street 1987), O-Zone 1986, The Black House 1986; (play) The White Man's Burden 1987; (criticism) V.S. Naipaul 1972; (travel) The Great Railway Bazaar 1975, The Old Patagonian Express 1979, The Kingdom by the Sea 1983, Sailing through China 1983, Riding the Iron Rooster: By Train Through China (Thomas Cook Prize for Best Literary Travel Book 1989) 1988, My Secret Life 1989; (screenplay) Saint Jack 1979; reviews in The Sunday Times, New York Times, etc. *Leisure interest:* rowing. *Address:* c/o Hamish Hamilton Ltd., 77 Wrights Lane, London, W8 5TZ, England.

THESIGER, Wilfred, C.B.E., D.S.O., M.A., F.R.S.L.; British traveller; b. 3 June 1910, Addis Ababa, Ethiopia; s. of the Hon. Wilfred Thesiger, D.S.O., and Kathleen Mary Vigors, C.B.E.; ed. Eton and Magdalen Coll., Oxford; explored Danakil country of Abyssinia 1933-34; Sudan Political Service, Darfur and Upper Nile Provinces 1935-39; served in Ethiopia, Syria and Western Desert with Sudan Defence Force and Special Air Service, Second World War; explored the Empty Quarter of Arabia 1945-50; lived with the Madan in the Marshes of Southern Iraq 1950–58; awarded Back Grant, Royal Geographical Soc. 1936, Founders Medal 1948; Lawrence of Arabia Medal, Royal Central Asian Soc. 1955; David Livingstone Medal, Royal Scottish Geographical Soc. 1961; W. H. Heinemann Bequest, Royal Soc. of Literature 1964; Burton Medal, Royal Asiatic Soc. 1966; Hon. D.Litt. (Leicester); Hon. Fellow, British Acad. 1982, Magdalen Coll., Oxford 1982. *Publications:* Arabian Sands 1958, The Marsh Arabs 1964, Desert, Marsh and Mountain: The World of a Nomad 1979, The Life of My Choice (autobiog.) 1987, Visions of a Nomad (photographs) 1987. *Leisure interests:* photography, travel in remote places. *Address:* 15 Shelley Court, Tite Street, London, S.W.3, England. *Telephone:* 01-352 7213.

THEWS, Gerhard, DR. RER. NAT., DR. MED.; German professor of physiology; b. 22 July 1926, Königsberg; m. Dr. Gisela Bahling 1958; three s. one d.; ed. Univ. of Kiel; Research Fellow Univ. of Kiel 1957–61, Asst. Prof. 1961–62, Assoc. Prof. 1962–63, Prof. 1964–, Dir. Physiological Inst. 1964–, Dean Faculty Medicine 1968–69; Vice-Pres. Acad. Science and Literature 1977–85, Pres. 1985–; Pres. German Physiological Soc. 1968–69; mem. German Scientific Council 1970–72; Pres. Int. Soc. for Oxygen Transport 1973–75; Wolfgang Heubner Prize (Berlin) 1961; Feldberg Prize (London) 1964; Carl Diem Prize 1964; Adolf Fick Prize (Würzburg) 1969; Ernst von Bergmann Medal (Germany) 1986. *Publications:* Human Physiology 1983, Human Anatomy, Physiology and Pathophysiology 1985, Autonomic Functions in Human Physiology 1985. *Address:* Department of Physiology, University of Mainz, Saarstrasse 21, D-6500 Mainz, Federal Republic of Germany.

THIAM, Habib, L. EN D.; Senegalese politician; b. 21 Jan. 1933, Dakar; ed. Brevet Ecole Nat. de la France d'Outre-mer; Sec. of State for the Devt. Plan 1963; Minister for the Plan and Devt. 1964–67, of Rural Econ. 1968–73; mem. Nat. Ass. 1973–, Pres. 1983–84; Prime Minister 1981–83; Press Sec. Union progressiste sénégalaise (now Parti socialiste sénégalaise-PS); Pres. Parl. Group PS April 1978–; now Chair. Bd. Banque Int. pour le Commerce et l'Industrie du Sénégal; Dir. Ethiopique 1976–, L'Unité Africaine 1976–. *Address:* 2 avenue Roume, B.P. 392, Dakar, Senegal (Office).

THIANDOUM, H.E. Cardinal Hyacinthe; Senegalese ecclesiastic; b. 2 Feb. 1921, Popoguine; s. of François Fari Thiandoum and Anne Ndiémé Sène; ed. Univ. de la Propagande and Gregorian Univ., Rome; ordained Priest at Dakar Cathedral 1949; Archbishop of Dakar 1962–, cr. Cardinal 1976; fmrly. mem. Congregation for the Doctrine of the Faith; fmr. Pres. Episcopal Conf. of Senegal and Mauritania; fmrly. mem. Perm. Cttee. Episcopal Conf. of Francophone West Africa (CERAO); fmrly. Pres. Symposium of Episcopal Confs. of Africa and Madagascar (SECAM); mem. Pontifical Comm. for Social Communications; mem. Congregation for the Religious and for Secular Insts.; mem. Sacred Congregation for the Clergy; mem. Council of Secr. Gen. of the Rome Synod of Bishops (Deputy Pres. 1977); Gen. Reporter to the Synod 1987; mem. Episcopal Comm. for Mass Media, CERAO; Hon. Chaplain with Grand Cross, Order of Malta 1972; Grand Cross, Order of Lion 1976; Commdr., Légion d'honneur 1980. *Address:* Archevêché, B.P. 1908, Dakar, Senegal. *Telephone:* 22 59 18.

THIBAU, Jacques Henri; French diplomatist; b. 26 Oct. 1928, Marseilles, France; s. of Henri Thibau and Catherine (née Lagrave) Thibau; four c.; ed. Lycée Thiers, Marseille, Facultés de droit et des lettres, Aix-en-Provence, Ecole nat. d'admin., Paris; overseas admin., Cambodia 1951–55; Sec., F.O. 1958–60, French Embassy, London 1961–62; Prin. Private Sec., Alain Peyrefitte 1962–65; Counsellor, Foreign Office 1964, Berne 1969–72, Foreign Office for cen. admin. 1974–; Asst. Dir., Office de Radiodiffusion-Television Francaise, Dir., Second Channel 1965–68; lecturer, Ecole Nat. d'admin. 1963–67; Dir.-Gen. Cultural Relations Ministry of Foreign Affairs 1981–82; Minister 1982; Amb. to Belgium 1983–86, to Nigeria 1986–; Officier, ordre nat. du Merite, de l'ordre royal du Cambodge. *Publications:* Une télévision pour tous les Français 1970, la Télévision, le Pouvoir et l'Argent 1972, le Monde: histoire d'un journal, un journal dans l'histoire 1978, la France colonisée 1980. *Address:* c/o Ministère des Affaires étrangères, 37 quai d'Orsay, 75007 Paris, France.

THIEBAUD, Wayne; American artist; b. 15 Nov. 1920, Mesa, Ariz.; m. 1st Patricia Patterson 1945 (divorced 1959), two d.; m. 2nd Betty Jean Carr 1959; one s. one step s.; ed. Frank Wiggins Trade School, Long Beach Jr. Coll., San. José State Coll. (now San José State Univ.), Calif. State Coll. (now Calif. State Univ.); worked as commercial artist and freelance cartoonist from 1938; served U.S.A.A.F. 1942–45; started career as painter 1947; Asst. Prof., Dept. of Art, Univ. of Calif. at Davis 1960, Assoc. Prof. 1963–67, Prof. 1967–; Co-founder Artists Co-operative Gallery (now Artists Contemporary Gallery), Sacramento 1958; numerous one-man exhbns. in U.S.A. since 1950; one-man exhbn. Galleria Schwarz, Milan, Italy 1963; represented U.S.A. at São Paulo Bienal, Brazil 1968; commissioned to do paintings of Wimbledon tennis tournament, England 1968; selected as Nat. Juror for the Arts, Washington, D.C. 1972; commissioned by U.S. Dept. of Interior to paint Yosemite Ridge Line for Bicentennial Exhbn., America 1976; mem. American Acad., Inst. of Arts and Letters, New York City 1985, Nat. Acad. of Design, New York City; Award of Distinction, Nat. Art Schools Asscn. and Special Citation Award, Nat. Asscn. of Schools of Art and Design 1984. *Publication:* Wayne Thiebaud: Private Drawings—The Artist's Sketchbook 1987. *Address:* c/o Department of Art, University of California (Davis), Calif. 95616, U.S.A.

THIELE, Ilse (Neukrantz); German politician; b. 4 Nov. 1920, Berlin; ed. secondary school; shorthand typist; mem. C.P. 1945, SED 1946; Chair. DFD (Democratic Women's League) 1953–; mem. Cen. Cttee. SED 1954; mem. Volkskammer 1954–; mem. Council of State 1971–; Vaterländischer Verdienstorden in Gold; Orden "Banner der Arbeit", and other decorations. *Address:* Demokratischer Frauenbund Deutschlands (DFD), 1080 Berlin, Clara-Zetkin-Strasse 16, German Democratic Republic.

THIEMANN, Bernd, D.JUR.; German banking executive; b. 5 July 1943, Münster; m.; one c.; ed. schools in Münster and Münster Univ.; mem. Bd. of Man. Kreissparkasse Meppen 1971–73, Chair. Bd. 1974–76; Dir. Norddeutsche Landesbank, Head Cen. Dept., Savings Bank Credit Business, Savings Bank Asscn. 1976, Deputy mem. Bd. of Man. Norddeutsche Landesbank 1976–78, mem. 1978–, Chair. Bd. 1981–; Hon. Consul-Gen., British Consulate-Gen. *Address:* Norddeutsche Landesbank, Georgsplatz 1, 3000 Hanover 1; Habichtshorststrasse 22, 3000 Hanover 51, Federal Republic of Germany. *Telephone:* (0511) 103-2200.

THIEMELE, Amoakon-Edjampan; Côte d'Ivoire diplomatist; b. 7 April 1941, Abengourou; s. of Boa Thiemele and Eugénie Dacoua; m. Joséphine Vallée 1968; four s. two d.; ed. Centre d'Enseignement supérieur, Abidjan, Univ. of Paris; Admin. in Dept. of Finance 1967; First Counsellor for Econ. and Commercial questions, Ivory Coast del. in Geneva 1968–72; Direction of Int. Co-operation, Ministry of Foreign Affairs 1973; Amb. to Fed. Repub. of Germany 1974–77; Perm. Rep. to the UN 1977–80; Minister of Commerce 1981–83; Amb. to People's Repub. of China 1984–; mem. Bd. of Dirs. of PDCI-RDA (Parti démocratique de la Côte d'Ivoire); Officier, Légion d'honneur and Nat. Orders of Côte d'Ivoire, Morocco, Netherlands, Tunisia and Fed. Repub. of Germany. *Leisure interests:* music, reading, tennis, football. *Address:* Embassy of Côte d'Ivoire, Beijing, People's Republic of China. *Telephone:* 5321223.

THIER, Samuel Osiah, M.D.; American physician; b. 23 June 1937, Brooklyn, New York; s. of Sidney Thier and May H. Kanner Thier; m. Paula Dell Finkelstein 1958; three d.; ed. Cornell Univ., State Univ. of New York, Syracuse; Intern, Mass. Gen. Hosp. 1960–61, Asst. Resident 1961–62, 1964–65, Postdoctoral Fellow 1965; Clinical Assoc. Nat. Inst. of Arthritis and Metabolic Diseases 1962–64; Chief Resident in Medicine, Mass. Gen. Hosp. 1966; Instr. to Asst. Prof. Harvard Medical School 1967–69; Assoc. Prof. then Prof. of Medicine, Univ. of Pa. Medical School 1969–74; Prof. and Chair. Dept. of Medicine, Yale Univ. School of Medicine and Chief of Medicine, Yale-New Haven Hosp. 1975–85; Pres. Inst. of Medicine, N.A.S. 1985–. *Publications:* numerous articles and chapters in medical journals and textbooks. *Address:* Institute of Medicine, National Academy of Sciences, 2101 Constitution Avenue, Washington, D.C. 20418, U.S.A. *Telephone:* (202) 334-3300.

THIEU, Lt.-Gen. Nguyen Van (see Nguyen Van Thieu).

THIMANN, Kenneth Vivian, B.SC., A.R.C.S., D.I.C., PH.D.; American biologist and educationalist; b. 5 Aug. 1904, Ashford, Kent, England; s. of Phoebus and Muriel (Harding) Thimann; m. Ann Mary Bateman 1929 (died 1987); three d.; ed. Caterham School, and Imperial Coll., London; Instructor in Biochem., Calif. Inst. of Technology 1930–35; Lecturer, Harvard Univ. 1935–36, Asst. Prof. 1936–39, Assoc. Prof. 1939–46, Prof. of Biology 1946–62, Higgins Prof. of Biology 1962–65; Prof. of Biology and Provost Crown Coll., Univ. of Calif. at Santa Cruz 1965–72, Prof. Emer. 1972–, Chair. Bd. of Studies in Biology 1973–74; Acting Dean of Natural Sciences 1965–66; Visiting Prof. Univ. of Paris 1954–55, Univ. of Mass. 1974, Univ. of Texas 1976; Pres. Soc. of Gen. Physiologists 1949–50, American Soc. of Plant Physiologists 1950, American Soc. of Naturalists 1955, Botanical Soc. of America 1960, American Inst. of Biological Sciences 1965; Pres. XI Int. Botanical Congress, Seattle 1969, Pres. VIII Int. Congress. on Plant Growth Substances, Tokyo 1973; Frank Hatton Prize for Chemistry 1924, Stephen Hales Prize, American Soc. of Plant Physiologists 1936 and Barnes hon. life membership; Silver Medallist IX Int. Congress on Plant Growth Substances, Lausanne 1976, Balzan Prize 1982; mem. Nat. Acad. of Sciences (Councillor 1968–71), Philosophical Soc. (Councillor 1972–75), American Acad. of Arts and Sciences; Foreign mem. Royal Soc. (London) 1969, Accad. Nazionale dei Lincei (Rome), Acad. Nat. Roumaine des Arts et Sciences, Akad. Leopoldina, Acad. des sciences (Paris), Acad. d'Agric. (Paris), Botanical Socs. of Japan and the Netherlands; Dr. h.c. (Univs. of Basel and Clermont-Ferrand). *Publications:* Phytohormones (with F. W. Went) 1937, Les Auxines 1955, The Action of Hormones in Plants and Invertebrates (with B. Scharrer and F. Brown) 1948, The Life of Bacteria 1955, 1963 (German trans. 1964), The Natural Plant Hormones 1972, Hormones in the Life of Plants 1977, Senescence in Plants 1980, and about 300 papers in scientific journals; Ed. Vitamins and Hormones vols. 1–17, 1943–60, Consulting Ed. 1961–, The Hormones vols. 1-5, 1948–63; Editorial Bd.: Plant Physiology. *Leisure interests:* music, garden. *Address:* Thimann Laboratories, Division of Natural Sciences, University of California, Santa Cruz, Calif. 95064, U.S.A. *Telephone:* (408) 429-2418.

THIN, U Tun, PH.D.; Burmese economist; ed. Rangoon, Michigan and Harvard Univs.; Chair. Econ. Dept., Univ. of Rangoon; Dir. Cen. Statistics and Econs. Dept., Ministry of Planning, Burma; Alt. Exec. Dir. IMF for Burma, Ceylon, Japan and Thailand; Asst. Dir. IMF Asian Dept. 1959–66, Deputy Dir. 1966–72, Dir. 1972–86; Special Adviser to the Rector, UN

Univ. 1986-. *Publication:* Theory of Markets 1970. *Address:* 2212 South Lynn Street, Arlington, Va. 22202, U.S.A. *Telephone:* (703) 892-5348.

THIRRING, Walter E., PH.D.; Austrian professor of physics; b. 29 April 1927, Vienna; s. of Hans Thirring and Antonia Thirring; m. Helga Georgiades 1952; two s.; ed. Univ. of Vienna and Dublin Inst. of Advanced Studies; Fellow, Univ. of Glasgow 1950; Asst. Max-Planck-Inst. Göttingen 1950-51; UNESCO Fellow, Fed. Inst. of Tech. Zürich 1951-52; Asst. Univ. of Berne 1952-53; mem. Inst. of Advanced Study, Princeton 1953-54; Docent, Univ. of Berne 1954-56, Prof. 1958; Prof. Univ. of Vienna 1959-; mem. CERN Directorate 1968-71; Visiting Prof. M.I.T. 1956-57, Univ. of Washington, Seattle 1957-58; mem. Austrian Acad., Pontifical Acad. of Sciences, Akad. der Naturforscher Leopoldina (G.D.R.); Hon. mem. Hungarian Physical Eötvös Soc. *Publications:* A Course in Mathematical Physics, 4 vols.; more than 120 scientific papers. *Leisure interest:* music. *Address:* Nussberggasse 7a/5/7, 1190 Vienna, Austria. *Telephone:* 34 26 30 410.

THIRSK, (Irene) Joan, PH.D., F.B.A., F.R.HIST.S.; British historian and academic; b. 19 June 1922, London; d. of William Henry Watkins and Daisy Watkins (née Frayer); m. James Wood Thirsk 1945; one s. one d.; ed. Camden School for Girls, London and Westfield Coll., Univ. of London; war service in Auxiliary Territorial Service (ATS) 1942-45; Asst. Lecturer in Sociology, L.S.E. 1950-51; Sr. Research Fellow in Agrarian History, Dept. of English Local History, Leicester Univ. 1951-65; Reader in Econ. History, Oxford Univ. 1965-83, Professorial Fellow of St. Hilda's Coll. 1965-83, Hon. Fellow 1983-; mem. Royal Comm. on Historical Monuments of England 1977-86; Pres. British Asscn. for Local History 1986-; Gen. Ed. Agrarian History of England and Wales 1975-; Mellon Sr. Fellow, Nat. Humanities Center, N.C., U.S.A. 1986-87; Foreign mem. American Philosophical Soc.; Corresp. mem. Colonial Soc. of Massachusetts; Hon. D.Litt. (Leicester) 1985. *Publications:* Ed. and Contrib., The Agrarian History of England and Wales, IV 1500-1640 1967, V 1640-1750 1985; Seventeenth-Century Economic Documents (with J. P. Cooper) 1972, The Restoration 1976, Economic Policy and Projects: The Development of a Consumer Society in early modern England 1978, The Rural Economy of England: Collected Essays 1984, England's Agricultural Regions and Agrarian History 1500-1750 1987. *Leisure interests:* gardening, sewing and machine knitting. *Address:* 1 Hadlow Castle, Hadlow, Tonbridge, Kent, TN11 0EG, England.

THO, Le Duc (see Le Duc Tho).

THODE, Henry George, C.C., M.B.E., M.SC., PH.D., D.SC., LL.D., F.R.S., F.R.S.C., F.C.I.C.; Canadian chemist and university administrator; b. 10 Sept. 1910, Dundurn, Sask.; s. of Charles H. and Zelma Thode; m. Sadie Alicia Patrick 1935; three s.; ed. Univs. of Saskatchewan and Chicago, and Columbia Univ.; Instructor, Pa. Coll. for Women 1935-36; Research Asst., Columbia Univ. 1936-38; Research Chemist U.S. Rubber Co., N.J. 1938-39; Asst. Prof. of Chem., McMaster Univ. 1939-42, Assoc. Prof. 1942-44, Prof. of Chem. 1944-79; Head Dept. of Chem. 1948-52, Vice-Pres. 1957-61, Dir. of Research 1947-61, Pres. 1961-72, Vice-Chancellor 1961-72; Principal Hamilton Coll., McMaster Univ. 1944-63, Prof. Emer. 1979-; Research Chemist, Atomic Energy Project 1943-46, Consultant 1945-51; Visiting Prof. and Sr. Foreign Scientist, Nat. Science Foundation, Calif. Inst. of Tech. 1970; Dir. Hamilton Health Assn. 1948-68, Western New York Nuclear Research Centre 1965-73, Atomic Energy of Canada Ltd. 1966-81, Stelco Inc. 1969-85; mem. Royal Soc. of Canada (Pres. Section III 1950-51), Pres. 1959-60; Pres. Chemical Inst. of Canada 1951-52; mem. Nat. Research Council 1955-61, Defence Research Bd. 1955-61, Bd. of Govs., Ontario Research Foundation 1955-82, Comm. on Atomic Weights, Inorganic Chem. Div., Int. Union of Pure and Applied Chem. 1963-79, Canadian Nat. Cttee. for Int. Union of Pure and Applied Chem. 1975-79; Hon. LL.D. (Saskatchewan, Regina); Hon. D.Sc. from nine univs.; Chemical Inst. of Canada Medal 1957; Royal Soc. of Canada Tory Medal 1959, Centenary Medal 1982; Geological Soc. of America Day Medal 1980. *Publications:* numerous papers on nuclear chemistry, isotope chemistry, isotope abundances in terrestrial and extraterrestrial material, separation of isotopes, magnetic susceptibilities, electrical discharges in gases, sulphur concentrations and isotope ratios in lunar materials. *Leisure interests:* swimming, farming, golf. *Address:* Nuclear Research Building, McMaster University, 1280 Main Street West, Hamilton, Ont., L8S 4K1, Canada. *Telephone:* (416) 525-9140, Ext. 4249 (Office).

THOM, Ronald James; Canadian architect; b. 15 May 1923, Penticton, B.C.; ed. Vancouver School of Art; began career as concert pianist; studied art; taught in Vancouver School of Art and at School of Architecture, Univ. of B.C.; Partner, Thompson, Berwick, Pratt, Vancouver 1958; R. J. Thom Architects, Toronto 1963-; has lectured at univs. throughout Canada; Fellow, Royal Architectural Inst. of Canada; mem. Royal Canadian Acad. of Arts, Ontario Asscn. of Architects, Architectural Inst. of B.C.; Hon. LL.D. (Trent Univ.) 1971, Hon. D.Eng. (Nova Scotia Tech. Coll.) 1973. *Publications:* many articles on architecture in arts journals. *Address:* The Thom Partnership, 47 Colborne Street, Toronto, Ont. (Office); 95 Meadowcliffe Drive, Scarborough, Ont., Canada (Home).

THOMAS, André Jean, D. EN MED., D. ÉS SC.; French biologist; b. 4 April 1905, Besançon; s. of Albert Thomas and Marie-Louise Sulter; m. Suzanne

Anne-Marie Dautremant 1940; one s. two d.; ed. Lycée de Besançon, Faculté de Médecine and Faculté des Sciences, Paris; Prof., Faculté des Sciences, Paris 1943-, Titular Prof. of Cellular Biology 1951-77, Dir. Centre for Cellular Physiology 1955-77, Prof. Emer. 1986-; Deputy Dir. Ecole des Hautes Etudes 1942-45, Dir. 1946-77; mem. Inst. Pasteur 1929-68, Head of Cellular Biology Science 1951-68; mem. Acad. des Sciences (Inst. de France), Acad. nat. de Médecine (Pres. 1988), and many other scientific socs.; Hon. Fellow, Int. Coll. of Surgeons, New York Acad. of Science; Officier, Légion d'honneur, Ordre de Léopold (Belgium); Médaille de la Résistance. *Address:* Université Pierre et Marie Curie, Centre de Physiologie cellulaire, 7 quai Saint-Bernard, 75005 Paris (Office); 8 rue Pierre et Marie Curie, 75005 Paris, France (Home). *Telephone:* 336-25-25, Ext. 34-20 (Office); 326-59-04 (Home).

THOMAS, David; British singer; b. 26 Feb. 1943, Orpington; m. Veronica Joan Dean 1982; three d.; ed. St. Paul's Cathedral Choir School, London, King's School, Canterbury, King's Coll., Cambridge; has performed all over the world in most of the major concert halls with leading conductors, particularly works of the Baroque and Classical period; Chair. Artistic Advisory Cttee.; mem. Bd. Blackheath Concert Halls. *Works include:* more than 50 records, including Handel's Messiah, Semele, Esther, Athalia, La Resurrectione; Bach's B Minor Mass and Cantata "Ich habe genug"; Mozart's Requiem. *Leisure interest:* woodwork. *Address:* 74 Hyde Vale, Greenwich, London, SE10 8HP, England.

THOMAS, Sir Derek Morison David, K.C.M.G., M.A.; British diplomatist; b. 31 Oct. 1929, London; s. of K. P. D. Thomas and Mali Thomas; m. Lineke Van der Mast; one s. one d.; ed. Radley Coll. and Trinity Hall, Cambridge; articled apprentice, Dolphin Industrial Devts. Ltd. 1947; entered H.M. Foreign Service 1953; R.N.V.R. 1953-55; Third, later Second Sec. Moscow 1957-59; Second Sec. Manila 1959-61; First Sec. Sofia 1964-67, Ottawa 1967-69; seconded to H.M. Treasury 1969-70; Financial Counsellor, Paris 1971-75; Head, North American Dept. FCO 1975-76; Asst. Under-Sec. of State, FCO 1976-79; Minister Commercial, later Minister, Washington, D.C. 1979-84; Deputy Under-Sec. of State for Europe and Political Dir. FCO 1984-87; Amb. to Italy 1987-. *Leisure interests:* exploring the past and present, music, theatre, wines, reading when there is time, water. *Address:* c/o Foreign and Commonwealth Office, London, S.W.1, England.

THOMAS, Donald Michael, M.A.; British novelist and poet; b. 27 Jan. 1935, Redruth, Cornwall; s. of Harold Redvers Thomas and Amy Thomas (née Moyle); two s. one d.; ed. Redruth Grammar School, Univ. High School, Melbourne, New Coll., Oxford; English teacher, Teignmouth, Devon 1959-63; lecturer, Hereford Coll. of Educ. 1963-78; full-time author 1978-; Gollancz/Pan Fantasy Prize, PEN Fiction Prize, Cheltenham Prize, Los Angeles Times Fiction Prize. *Publications:* Two Voices 1968, Logan Stone 1971, Love and Other Deaths 1975, Honeymoon Voyage 1978, The Flute-Player 1978, Birthstone 1980, The White Hotel 1981, Dreaming in Bronze 1981, Ararat 1983, Selected Poems 1983, Swallow 1984, Sphinx 1986, Summit 1987, Memories and Hallucinations 1988. *Address:* The Coach House, Rashleigh Vale, Tregolls Road, Truro, Cornwall, TR1 1TJ, England. *Telephone:* (0872) 78885.

THOMAS, Franklin; American lawyer and foundation official; b. 27 May, 1934, Brooklyn; s. of James Thomas and Viola Atherley; m. (divorced); two s. two d.; served with U.S.A.F. 1956-60; called to bar, N.Y. 1964; Attorney, Housing and Home Finance Agency, New York 1963-64; Asst. U.S. Attorney for Southern Dist., New York 1964-65; Deputy Police Commr. for legal affairs, New York 1965-67; Community Devt. Pres. and C.E.O. Bedford Stuyvesant Restoration Corpn. 1967-77; Consultant and Lawyer 1977-79; Dir. ALCOA, CBS Inc., AT & T, Cummins Engine Co., CITICORP; Trustee, Ford Foundation (Pres. 1979-); Medal of Excellence, Colombia Univ. 1976, Alexander Hamilton Award 1983. *Address:* Ford Foundation, 320 East 43rd Street, New York, N.Y. 10017, U.S.A. (Office). *Telephone:* (212) 573-5383.

THOMAS, Gareth, PH.D.; American professor of science; b. 1932, England; m.; one s.; ed. Univ. of Wales, Cambridge Univ. with Univ. of Calif., Berkeley 1960-, Prof. 1966, Assoc. Dean, Graduate Div. 1968-69, Asst. to Chancellor 1969-72, Acting Vice-Chancellor, Acad. Affairs 1971-72, Chair. Faculty of Coll. of Eng. 1977-78, Sr. Faculty Scientist, Materials and Molecular Research Div., Scientific Dir., Nat. Center for Electron Microscopy, Prof. Dept. of Materials and Mineral Eng. 1982-; mem. N.A.S., Nat. Acad. of Eng. and numerous cttees.; Hon. Sc.D. (Cambridge) 1969 and numerous other awards. *Publications:* several books and 475 research papers 1985. *Leisure interests:* squash, skiing, cricket. *Address:* Department of Materials Science and Mineral Engineering, University of California, 284 Hearst Mining Building, Berkeley, Calif. 94720, U.S.A. *Telephone:* (415) 642 1441.

THOMAS, Rt. Hon. George (see Tonypandy, Viscount).

THOMAS, Henri, L. ÈS L.; French writer and poet; b. 7 Dec. 1912, Anglemont (Vosges); s. of Joseph and Mathilde Thomas; m. 2nd. Jacqueline Le Beguec 1957; one d.; ed. Lycée Henri IV, Paris and Strasbourg Univ.; Teacher until 1939; armed forces 1940-47; Programme Asst. B.B.C. French Section 1947-58; lecturer in French, Brandeis Univ., Mass., U.S.A. 1956-60; in charge German Dept. Gallimard's Publishing House 1960-; Prix Sainte-Beuve 1956, Prix Médicis 1960; Prix Fémina 1961; Prix Valéry Larbaud

1970; Chevalier, Légion d'honneur; Officier, Ordre nat. du Mérite. *Publications:* Verse: Travaux d'aveugle, Signe de vie, Le monde absent, Nul désordre, Poésies complètes 1970, A quoi tu penses 1980, Joueur surpris 1982, Le migrateur, le tableau d'avancement 1983, Le croc des chiffonniers 1985, Une saison volée 1986; Novels: Le seau à charbon, Le précepteur, La vie ensemble, Les déserteurs, Le porte-à-faux, La nuit de Londres, La dernière année, John Perkins (Prix Médicis 1960), Le promontoire (Prix Fémina 1961), La chasse aux trésors, Le parjure, Sous le lien du temps, La relique, Tristan le dépussédé, Les tours de Notre Dame (Prix des Sept); Short stories: La cible, Histoire de Pierrot, Sainte Jeunesse; Trans.: Goethe, Stifter, Jünger, Shakespeare, Pushkin. *Address:* Editions Gallimard, 5 rue Sébastien-Bottin, 75007 Paris; 14 rue Paul Fort, 75014 Paris, France.

THOMAS, Ivor Bulmer-, C.B.E., M.A.; British writer and politician; b. 30 Nov. 1905, Cwmbran, Mon.; s. of Alfred Ernest and Zipporah Thomas; m. 1st Dilys Llewelyn Jones 1932 (died 1938), one s.; 2nd Margaret Joan Bulmer 1940, one s. two d.; ed. St. John's and Magdalen Colls., Oxford; Editorial staff of The Times 1930–37; Chief Leader writer News Chronicle 1937–39, on staff Daily Telegraph 1952–56; served R. Fusiliers 1939–40, Royal Norfolk Regt. 1940–42, 1945; Labour M.P. for Keighley 1942–48, Ind., later Cons. 1948–50; Parl. Sec. Ministry of Civil Aviation 1945–46; Parl. Under-Sec. of State Colonial Office 1946–47; mem. Gen. Synod of Church of England (Church Ass.) 1950–85; Chair. Exec. Cttee. Historic Churches Preservation Trust 1952–56; Sec. Ancient Monuments Soc. 1957–75, Chair. 1975–; Hon. Dir. Friends of Friendless Churches 1957–; Convener British Group Inst. Int. des Civilisations Différentes 1959–; Joint Hon. Sec. Friends of St. John's 1962–75 (Hon. Treas. 1969–75); Chair. Redundant Churches Fund 1969–76; Fellow, Soc. of Antiquaries of London 1970–; Hon. Fellow St. John's, Oxford; Hon. D.Sc. *Publications:* Coal in the New Era 1934, Gladstone of Hawarden 1936, Top Sawyer 1938, Greek Mathematics 1939–42, The Problem of Italy 1946, The Socialist Tragedy 1949, The Party System in Great Britain 1953, Growth of the British Party System 1965, Ciò che è originale e ciò che è derivato negli Elementi di Euclide 1973, St. Paul: Teacher and Traveller (ed.) 1975, East Shefford Church 1978, Dilysia: A Threnody 1987. *Leisure interest:* athletics. *Address:* 12 Edwardes Square, London, W8 6HG, England. *Telephone:* 01-602 6267.

THOMAS, Jean Olwen, SC.D., F.R.S., M.I.S.C., M.R.C.; British reader in biochemistry of macromolecules; b. 1 Oct. 1942; d. of John Robert Thomas and Lorna Prunella (née Harris) Thomas; ed. Llwyn-y-Bryn High School for Girls, Swansea, Univ. Coll., Swansea, Univ. of Wales; demonstrator in Biochem., Univ. of Cambridge 1969–73, lecturer 1973–87, reader in the Biochem. of Macromolecules 1987–; tutor, New Hall, Cambridge 1970–76, Vice-Pres. 1983–87; mem. European Molecular Biology Org.; Beit Memorial Fellow; Hon. Fellow, U.C.W., Swansea 1987. *Awards include:* Ayling Prize 1964, Hinkel Research Prize 1967, K. M. Stott Research Prize, Newnham Coll., Cambridge 1976. *Publications:* numerous papers in scientific journals. *Leisure interests:* reading, music, walking. *Address:* Department of Biochemistry, Tennis Court Road, Cambridge, CB2 1QW (Office); New Hall, Huntingdon Road, Cambridge, CB3 0DF, England (Home). *Telephone:* (0223) 333670 (Office); (0223) 351721 (Home).

THOMAS, Sir Jeremy (Cashel), K.C.M.G.; British diplomatist; b. 1 June 1931; s. of Rev. H. C. Thomas and Margaret Betty (née Humby) Thomas; m. Diana Mary Summerhayes 1957; three s.; ed. Eton and Merton Coll., Oxford; H.M. Forces 1949–51, entered Foreign Office 1954, served in Singapore, Rome and Belgrade; Deputy Head Personnel Operations Dept., FCO 1970–74, Counsellor and Head of Chancery, U.K. Mission to UN New York 1974–76, Head Perm. Under-Sec.'s Dept., FCO 1977–79, Asst. Under-Sec. of State 1982–85; Amb. to Luxembourg 1979–82, to Greece 1985–. *Leisure interests:* sailing, fishing. *Address:* c/o Foreign and Commonwealth Office, London, S.W.1, England.

THOMAS, John Meurig, M.A., D.SC., LL.D., F.R.S.; British scientist; b. 15 Dec. 1932, Llanelli, Wales; s. of David J. Thomas and Edyth Thomas; m. Margaret Edwards 1959; two c.; ed. Gwendraeth Grammar School, Univ. Coll., Swansea, Queen Mary Coll., London; Scientific Officer, UKAEA 1957–58; Asst. Lecturer, Lecturer, Sr. Lecturer then Reader, Dept. of Chem., Univ. Coll. of N. Wales, Bangor 1958–69; Prof. and Head Dept. of Chem., Univ. Coll. of Wales, Aberystwyth 1969–78; Head of Dept. of Physical Chem., Cambridge Univ., Professorial Fellow of King's Coll. 1978–86; Dir. Royal Inst. of G.B. 1986–, Resident Prof. 1986–88, Fullerian Prof. of Chem. 1988–; Dir. Davy Faraday Labs. 1986–; Chair. Chem. Research Applied to World Needs, IOPAC 1987–; Pres. Chem. Section, B.A.A.S. 1988–89; Hon. Visiting Prof. of Physical Chem., Queen Mary Coll., London 1986–; of Chem., Imperial Coll., London 1986–; Trustee British Museum (Natural History) 1986–; Hon. Professorial Fellow Academia Sinica (Shanghai), Imperial Coll. London, Queen Mary Coll. London 1986; Hon. Fellow Indian Acad. (Bangalore), Indian Acad. (Delhi), UMIST 1985, Univ. Coll. Swansea 1985; Hon. Bencher, Gray's Inn 1986. *Publications:* Principles of Heterogeneous Catalysis 1967, Characterization of Catalysts 1980, Heterogeneous Catalysis: Theory and Practice 1988; Pan Edrychwyf ar y Nefoedd (Welsh Radio Lecture) 1978; over 500 articles on solid-state and surface science. *Leisure interests:* walking, birdwatching, Welsh literature, ancient civilizations. *Address:* The Royal Institution, 21 Albemarle Street, London, W1X 4BS, England. *Telephone:* 01-409 2992.

THOMAS, Sir Keith Vivian, Kt., M.A., F.B.A.; British historian; b. 2 Jan. 1933, Wick, Glamorgan, Wales; s. of Vivian and Hilda Thomas; m. Valerie June Little 1961; one s. one d.; ed. Barry County Grammar School and Balliol Coll. Oxford (Brackenbury Scholar); nat. service in Royal Welch Fusiliers 1950–52; Fellow of All Souls Coll. Oxford 1955–57; Fellow of St. John's Coll. Oxford 1957–86, Tutor 1957–85; Reader in Modern History, Univ. of Oxford 1978–85, Prof. 1986, Pres. Corpus Christi Coll. 1986–; G. M. Trevelyan Lecturer, Univ. of Cambridge 1979; mem. Econ. and Social Research Council 1985–; Hon. D.Litt. (Kent) 1983, (Wales) 1987, (Williams) 1988; Hon. Fellow, Balliol Coll. Oxford 1984, St. John's Coll., Oxford 1986; Wolfson Literary Award for History 1971; Foreign Hon. mem. American Acad. of Arts and Sciences 1983. *Publications:* Religion and the Decline of Magic 1971, Puritans and Revolutionaries (Ed., with Donald Pennington) 1978, Man and the Natural World 1983. *Leisure interest:* visiting secondhand bookshops. *Address:* Corpus Christi College, Oxford, OX1 4JF (Office); The President's Lodgings, 3 Merton Street, Oxford, OX1 4JE, England (Home). *Telephone:* (0865) 249431 (Office).

THOMAS, Lewis, B.A., M.S., M.D.; American cancer research administrator and professor; b. 25 Nov. 1913, Flushing, N.Y.; s. of late Joseph S. Thomas and late Grace Emma Peck; m. Beryl Dawson 1941; three d.; ed. Princeton Univ., Harvard Medical School, Yale Medical School; Prof. of Medicine, Tulane Univ. School of Medicine 1949–50; Prof. of Paediatrics and Internal Medicine (American Legion Heart Research Prof.), Univ. of Minn. Medical School 1950–54; Prof. and Chair., Dept. of Pathology, New York Univ. Medical School 1954–58, Prof. and Chair., Dept. of Medicine 1958–66, Dean of Medical School 1966–69; Prof. and Chair., Dept. of Pathology, Yale Medical School 1969–73, Dean of Medical School 1972–73; Prof. of Medicine and Pathology, Cornell Univ. Medical Coll. 1973–; Pres. and Chief Exec. Officer, Memorial Sloan-Kettering Cancer Center 1973–80, Chancellor 1980–83, Pres. Emer. 1984–; Prof. SUNY Stony Brook 1983–; Prof. of Biology, Graduate School Medical Sciences 1973–, Co-dir. 1974–80; Adjunct Prof. Rockefeller Univ. 1975–; mem. Scientific Advisory Cttee., Inst. for Cancer Research 1974–, and numerous advisory bds. and cttees.; mem. Nat. Acad. of Sciences, New York Acad. Sciences, American Public Health Asscn., Int. Acad. Pathology, American Asscn. of Univ. Profs. etc.; Dir.-at-Large American Cancer Soc. 1974–; mem. Pres.'s Comm. on Agenda for the 1980s; Overseer, Harvard Univ.; Trustee, Rockefeller Univ. 1975–, Draper Lab. 1975–81, John Simon Guggenheim Memorial Foundation 1975–; numerous honorary degrees; Nat. Book Award in Arts and Letters 1974, Modern Medicine's Award for Distinguished Achievement 1975, American Acad. and Inst. of Arts and Letters Award 1980, American Book Award (for Medusa and the Snail) 1981, Richard Hopper Day Award 1985, Lewis Thomas Award for Communications 1986, Milton Helpern Memorial Award 1986, Encyclopaedia Britannica Award 1986. *Publications:* The Lives of a Cell 1974, Medusa and the Snail 1979, The Youngest Science 1983, Late Night Thoughts Listening to Mahler's Ninth Symphony 1983. *Leisure interests:* music, literature, science. *Address:* Memorial Sloan-Kettering Cancer Center, 1275 York Avenue, New York, N.Y. 10021 (Office); 333 East 68th Street, New York, N.Y. 10021, U.S.A. (Home).

THOMAS, Llewellyn Hilleth, PH.D., D.SC.; American professor of theoretical physics; b. 21 Oct. 1903, London, England; s. of Charles James Thomas and Winifred May Thomas fmrly. Lewis; m. Naomi Estelle (née Frech) Thomas 1933; one s. two d.; ed. Merchant Taylors School, Trinity Coll. Cambridge and Inst. of Theoretical Physics, Copenhagen; Prof. of Physics, Ohio State Univ. 1929–43, 1945–46; Physicist and Ballistician, Ballistic Research Lab., Aberdeen Proving Ground, Md. 1943–45; mem. of Sr. Staff, Watson Scientific Computing Lab., and Prof. of Physics, Columbia Univ. New York 1946–68, Prof. Emer., 1976–; Univ. Prof. N.C. State Univ., Raleigh 1968–76, Emer. 1976–; mem. N.A.S. 1958; D.Sc. (Cantab.) 1965; Smith Prize 1925, Davisson-Germer Prize 1982. *Publications:* over 100 papers in scientific journals. *Leisure interests:* mountain-walking, chess. *Address:* 3012 Wycliff Road, Raleigh, N.C. 27607, U.S.A. *Telephone:* (919) 781-2222 (Home).

THOMAS, Michael Tilson; American conductor; b. 1944, Los Angeles; s. of Ted and Roberta Thomas; studied under Ingolf Dahl; Asst. Conductor, Boston Symphony Orch. 1969, Assoc. Conductor 1970–72, Principal Guest Conductor 1972-74; Music Dir., Conductor, Buffalo Philharmonic Orch. 1971–79; Conductor, Dir. New York Philharmonic Young People's Concerts, CBS-TV 1971–77; Dir. Ojai Festival 1972–77; Prin. Guest Conductor, Los Angeles Philharmonic 1981–85; Prin. Conductor Great Woods Center for the Performing Arts 1985; visiting conductor with numerous orchestras in U.S.A., Europe and Japan; Grammy Awards 1976, 1983; Hon. L.H.D. (D'Youville Coll.), Hon. LL.D. (Hamilton Coll.); Musician of the Year, Musical America 1970. *Address:* c/o Carson Office, 1414 Avenue of the Americas, New York, N.Y. 10019, U.S.A.

THOMAS, René François, L. EN D.; French administrator; b. 13 Jan. 1929, Brest; s. of François Thomas and Jeanne Milbéo; m. Nicole Larrousse 1956 (deceased); one s. one d.; ed. Voltaire High School and Univ. of Paris; Inspecteur Général des finances 1955; del. in Morocco for Moroccan Ministry of Finance 1959; mem. Comm. of Enquiry into public cos'. accounting 1960; Sec.-Gen. Banque Nat. de Paris 1961–62, Deputy Dir. 1962–65, Dir. 1965–72, Cen. Dir. 1972–79, Deputy Dir.-Gen. 1979–82, Admin.-Gen. 1982–, Chair. July 1982–, also C.E.O.; Vice-Pres. French Asscn. of Banks 1982–86;

Dir. BMCI, Casablanca, UBCI, Tunis, BNP PLC, London, BNP (Suisse), Basle, BNP España, Madrid, FABC, New York, BANEXI, Paris, Crédit Nat., Thomson-CSF, Société Nationale Elf Aquitaine, Compagnie Générale des Eaux; Chair. BNP "I"; mem. Advisory Bd. Compagnie Bancaire; Chevalier, Légion d'honneur, Officier, Ordre nat. du Mérite. *Address:* 16 boulevard des Italiens, 75450 Paris (Office); 59 boulevard d'Inkermann, 92200 Neuilly-sur-Seine, France.

THOMAS, Richard Lee, M.B.A.; American banker; b. 11 Jan. 1931, Marion, Ohio; s. of Marvin C. and Irene (Harruff) Thomas; m. Helen Moore 1953; two s. one d.; ed. Kenyon Coll., Univ. of Copenhagen, Denmark, Harvard Business School; served army 1954–56; joined First Nat. Bank of Chicago 1958, Vice-Pres. 1963, Sr. Vice-Pres. 1969, Exec. Vice-Pres. 1972, Dir. 1973, Vice-Chair. Bd. 1973, Pres. 1975–; Sr. Vice-Pres., Gen. Man. First Chicago Corpn. 1969–72, Exec. Vice-Pres. 1972–73, Vice-Chair. 1973–74, Pres. 1974–; Dir. CNA Financial Corpn. 1970, Sara Lee Corpn. 1976, Chicago Bd. Options Exchange 1979; Trustee Northwestern Univ., Rush-Presbyterian-St. Luke's Medical Centre 1971, Kenyon Coll. 1971; Chair. Bd. of Trustees Chicago Symphony Orchestra, Orchestral Asscn. 1976; Hon. LL.D. (Kenyon Coll.). *Leisure interests:* golf, tennis, various outdoor sports, travel, reading. *Address:* First National Bank of Chicago, One First National Plaza, Suite 0518, Chicago, Ill. 60670, U.S.A. *Telephone:* (312) 732-6480 (Office).

THOMAS, Ronald Stuart; Welsh clergyman and poet; b. 29 March 1913, Caerdydd; m. Mildred E. Eldridge; one s.; ed. Univ. of Wales and St. Michael's Coll., Llandaff; ordained Deacon 1936, Priest 1937; Curate of Chirk 1936–40, of Hammer 1940–42; Rector of Manafon 1942–54; Vicar of St. Michael's Eglwysfach 1954–68, of St. Hywyn, Aberdaron 1968–78; Rector of Rhiw with Llanfaelrhys 1973–78; Heinemann Award of Royal Soc. of Literature 1956 for Song at the Year's Turning; Sovereign's Gold Medal for Poetry 1964, Cholmondeley Award 1978. *Publications:* Stones of the Field (privately published) 1947, Song at the Year's Turning 1955, Poetry for Supper 1958, Tares 1961, The Bread of Truth 1963, Pieta 1966, Not That He Brought Flowers 1968, H'm 1972, Selected Poems 1946–1968 1974, Laboratories of the Spirit 1975, Frequencies 1978, Between Here and Now 1981, Later Poems 1972–1982 1983, Experimenting with an Amen 1986, The Echoes Return Slow 1988. *Address:* Sarn y-Plas, Y Rhiw, Pwllheli, Wales.

THOMAS, Rt. Hon. (Thomas) George (see Tonypandy, Viscount).

THOMAS OF SWYNNERTON, Baron (Life Peer), cr. 1981, of Notting Hill in Greater London; **Hugh Swynnerton Thomas**, M.A.; British historian; b. 21 Oct. 1931, Windsor; s. of Hugh Whitelegge and Margery (née Swynnerton) Thomas; m. Vanessa Jebb 1962; two s. one d.; ed. Sherborne School, Queens' Coll., Cambridge, and Sorbonne, Paris; Foreign Office 1954–57; Sec. U.K. Del. to UN Disarmament Sub-Cttee. 1955–56; worked for UNA 1959–61; Prof. of History, Univ. of Reading 1966–76; Chair. Graduate School of European Studies 1973–76, Centre for Policy Studies 1979–; mem. Acad. Advisory Bd., Conservative Research Dept. 1982–; Fellow, Royal Historical Soc.; Somerset Maugham Prize 1962, Arts Council Nat. Book Award for History 1980; Commdr., Order of Isabel la Católica, Spain 1986. *Publications include:* The Spanish Civil War 1961, The Suez Affair 1966, Cuba or the Pursuit of Freedom 1971, Goya and the Third of May 1808 1973, John Strachey 1973, An Unfinished History of the World 1979, A Case for the Round Reading Room 1983, Havannah! (novel) 1984, Armed Truce: the beginnings of the Cold War 1945–46 1986, Klara (novel) 1988, Madrid: A Traveller's Companion (Ed.) 1988. *Address:* 29 Ladbroke Grove, London, W.11; Well House, Sudbourne, Suffolk, England. *Telephone:* 01-727 2288.

THOMASEN, Ole; Danish central banker; b. 9 Feb. 1934, Randers; m. Charlotte Ingwersen 1965; Asst. Prin. Ministry of Commerce 1961–63; Asst. Head of Div. Jt. Council of Danish Commercial Banks 1963, Head Dept. 1965–68; Asst. Man. Amagerbanken A/S 1969, Deputy Man. 1972, Man. 1975, Man. Dir. 1978–79; mem. Bd. of Govs. Danmarks Nationalbank 1980–; mem. Bd. Danish Inter-Bank Transfer Centre 1971–79, Regional Banks 1974–79, Housing Mortgage Fund 1979, Finance Corpn. for Industry and Crafts 1980–, Mortgage Fund for Danish Agric. 1981–, Ship Credit Fund of Denmark (Deputy Chair. 1982–), Danish Air Lines 1986–. *Address:* Danmarks Nationalbank, Havnegade 5, 1093 Copenhagen K, Denmark. *Telephone:* 01-14-14-11.

THOMPSON, Alan Eric, PH.D., F.R.S.A.; British professor of economics; b. 16 Sept. 1924; s. of Eric and Florence Thompson; m. Mary Heather Long 1960; three s. one d.; ed. Univ. of Edinburgh; Lecturer in Econs., Univ. of Edinburgh 1953–59, 1964–71; Parl. Adviser to Scottish TV 1966–76; Visiting Prof., Graduate School of Business, Stanford Univ., Calif. 1966, 1968; Labour M.P. for Dunfermline 1959–64; Econ. Consultant, Scotch Whisky Asscn. 1965–70; A. J. Balfour Prof. of Econs. of Govt., Heriot-Watt Univ., Edinburgh 1972–87, Prof. of Econs., School of Business and Financial Studies 1987–; mem. Scottish Council for Adult Educ. in H.M. Forces 1973–; mem. Local Govt. Boundaries Comm. for Scotland 1975–82; mem. Joint Mil. Educ. Cttee., Edinburgh and Heriot-Watt Univs. 1975–; mem. Court, Heriot-Watt Univ. 1980; Chair. Northern Offshore Maritime Resources Study 1974–, Newbattle Abbey Coll. 1980–82; BBC Nat. Gov. for Scotland 1976–79; Royal Fine Art Comm. for Scotland 1975–80, Scottish-

Soviet Co-ordinating Cttee. for Trade and Industry 1985–; Parl. Adviser Pharmaceutical Gen. Council (Scotland) 1985–; Chair. Bd. of Govs., Newbattle Abbey Coll. 1980; Hon. Vice-Pres. Asscn. of Nazi War Camp Survivors 1960–. *Publications:* The Development of Economic Doctrine (with Alexander Gray) 1980; contributions to learned journals. *Leisure interest:* writing children's stories and plays. *Address:* Department of Economics, Heriot-Watt University, 31–35 Grassmarket, Edinburgh, EH1 2HT (Office); 11 Upper Gray Street, Edinburgh, EH9 1SN, Scotland (Home). *Telephone:* 031-225 8432 (Office); 031-667 2140 (Home).

THOMPSON, Charles; British diplomatist; b. 20 March 1930, Liverpool; s. of Walter Thompson and Irene (née Davies) Thompson; m. 1st Claudia Hilpern 1956 (dissolved), 2nd Maria Anna Kalderimis 1977; ed. Harrison Jones School, Liverpool; employed at GPO 1944–55; entered Foreign (later Diplomatic) Service 1955; served in Rome, Washington, Tokyo, Leopoldville (later Kinshasa) 1956–68; Second Sec., Rangoon 1972–74; Second Sec. (Commercial), Wellington 1974–79; then First Sec. FCO 1980–83; High Commr. in Kiribati 1983–. *Leisure interests:* music, reading, travel and real ale. *Address:* British High Commission, P.O. Box 61, Bairiki, Tarawa, Kiribati. *Telephone:* 21327.

THOMPSON, Daley (Francis Morgan), M.B.E.; British athlete; b. 30 July 1958, Notting Hill, London; m. Tisha Quinlan 1987; Sussex Schools 200m. title 1974; first competitive decathlon, Welsh Open Championship June 1975; European Junior Decathlon Champion 1977; European Decathlon Silver Medallist 1978, Gold Medallist 1982 and 1986; Commonwealth Decathlon Gold Medallist 1978, 1982 and 1986; Olympic Decathlon Gold Medallist 1980 (Moscow) and 1984 (L.A.); World Decathlon Champion 1983; established new world record for decathlon (at Olympic Games, L.A.). *Publication:* Going for Gold 1987.

THOMPSON, Sir Edward Hugh Dudley, Kt., M.B.E., T.D., D.L.; British company executive; b. 12 May 1907; s. of Neale Dudley Thompson and Mary Gwendoline Scutt; m. 1st Ruth Monica Wainwright; two s.; m. 2nd Doreen Maud Tibbitt; one s. one d.; ed. Uppingham and Lincoln Coll., Oxford; Solicitor 1931–36; Asst. Man. Dir. Ind. Coope and Allsopp Ltd. 1936–39, Man. Dir. 1939; Army Service 1939–45; Man. Dir. Ind Coope Ltd. 1945–55, Chair. 1955–62; Chair. Brewers' Soc. 1959–61; Dir. Allied Breweries Ltd. 1961–78 (Chair. and Chief Exec. 1961–68); High Sheriff of Derbyshire 1964, Deputy Lieut. of Derbyshire 1978; mem. Council Nottingham Univ. 1968, Council of Royal Agricultural Soc. 1972, (Hon. Vice-Pres. 1985); Hon. LL.D. (Nottingham) 1984. *Leisure interest:* farming. *Address:* Culland Hall, Brailsford, Derbyshire, England. *Telephone:* (0335) 60247.

THOMPSON, Edward K(ramer), A.B., D.HUM.LITT.; American editor; b. 17 Sept. 1907, Minneapolis; s. of Edward T. Thompson and Bertha K. Thompson; m. 1st Marguerite Maxam 1927 (divorced); two s.; m. 2nd Lee Eitingon 1963; ed. Univ. of North Dakota; Ed. Foster Co. Independent, Carrington, N.D. 1927; City Ed. Fargo (N.D.) Morning Forum 1927; Picture Ed., Asst. News Ed. Milwaukee Journal 1927–37; Assoc. Ed. Life 1937–42, Asst. Man. Ed. 1945–49, Man. Ed., later Ed. 1949–67; Ed. and Publr. Smithsonian Inst. magazine 1969–81, Consultant to Sec. 1981–83, to Ed., Publr. 1983–; served with U.S. Armed Forces 1942–45; decorated Legion of Merit, Hon. O.B.E., Joseph Henry Medal, Smithsonian Inst. 1973; Lifetime Achievement Award, Int. Inst. of Photography 1986, Publishing Hall of Fame. *Address:* Smithsonian Institution, Washington, D.C. 20560; Rock Ledge Farm, Union Valley Road, RD 8 Box 350, Mahopac, N.Y. 10541, U.S.A. (Home).

THOMPSON, Francis Michael Longstreth, D.PHIL., F.B.A.; British professor of history; b. 13 Aug. 1925, Purley, Surrey; s. of Francis Longstreth-Thompson; m. Anne Challoner 1951; two s. one d.; ed. Bootham School, York and The Queen's Coll., Oxford; Lecturer in History, Univ. Coll. London 1951–63, Reader in Econ. History 1963–68; Prof. of Modern History, Univ. of London and Head of Dept. of History, Bedford Coll. London 1968–77, Prof. of History and Dir. of Inst. of Historical Research 1977–; Pres. Econ. History Soc. 1983–86, Hon. Vice-Pres. 1986–; British mem. Standing Cttee. for Humanities, European Science Foundation 1983–; Pres. Royal Historical Soc. 1988–. *Publications:* English Landed Society in the 19th century 1963, Chartered Surveyors: the growth of a profession 1968, Victorian England: the horse-drawn society 1970, Hampstead: building a borough, 1650–1964 1974, Countrysides (in The Nineteenth Century, ed. Asa Briggs) 1970, Britain (in European Landed Elites in the Nineteenth Century, ed. David Spring) 1977, Landowners and Farmers (in The Faces of Europe, ed. Alan Bullock) 1980, The Rise of Suburbia (Ed.) 1982, Horses in European Economic History (Ed.) 1983, The Rise of Respectable Society: A Social History of Victorian Britain 1988. *Leisure interests:* gardening, walking, carpentry, tennis. *Address:* Institute of Historical Research, University of London, Senate House, London, WC1E 7HU; Holly Cottage, Sheepcote Lane, Wheathampstead, Herts., England. *Telephone:* 01-636 0272; (058 283) 3129 (Home).

THOMPSON, Harold Lindsay, M.B., B.S., F.R.A.C.G.P.; Australian medical practitioner; b. 23 April 1929, Aberdeen, Scotland; s. of Harold and Johan D. Thompson; m. Audrey J. Harpur 1957; three s. two d.; ed. Aberdeen, Melbourne and Sydney Grammar Schools and postgrad. training in U.K.; Surgeon-Lieut. Royal Australian Navy 1956–60; now in gen. practice in

Lakemba, N.S.W.; Fellow Australian Medical Asscn. 1973, Pres. 1982–85; Pres. Confed. of Med. Asscns. of Asia and Oceania 1985–87, Immediate Past Pres. 1987–(89); Vice-Chair. Australian Council on Hospital Standards 1985–; Vice-Pres. Australian Council of Professions 1985–; mem. Council, World Medical Asscn. 1984–, Pres. 1988–(89); mem. numerous advisory bds., cttees., etc.; Gold Medal, Australian Medical Asscn. 1986. *Leisure interests:* golf, skiing, fishing. *Address:* 53 Railway Parade, Lakemba, N.S.W. 2195 (Surgery); 7 Strathfield Avenue, Strathfield, N.S.W. 2135, Australia (Home). *Telephone:* (02) 7591244 (Surgery); (02) 766200 (Home).

THOMPSON, Homer Armstrong, B.A., M.A., PH.D.; Canadian-born American classical archaeologist; b. 7 Sept. 1906, Devlin, Ont.; s. of William J. and Gertrude Thompson; m. Dorothy Burr 1933; three d.; ed. Univs. of British Columbia and Michigan; Staff mem., American School of Classical Studies excavations of the Athenian Agora 1929–, Field Dir. 1945–67; Prof. of Classical Archaeology, Toronto Univ. 1933–47, Head of Dept. of Art and Archaeology 1946–47; Prof., Princeton Inst. for Advanced Study 1947–77, Emer. 1977–; Asst. Dir., Curator of Classical Collection, Royal Ont. Museum, Toronto 1933–47; George Eastman Visiting Prof., Oxford Univ. 1959–60; Geddes-Harrower Prof. of Greek Archaeology and Art, Aberdeen Univ. 1964–65; Distinguished Visitor Australian-American Educ. Foundation; Corresp. Fellow British Acad.; Hon. mem. German Archaeological Inst., Soc. for Promotion of Hellenic Studies, Greek Archaeological Soc. (Hon. Vice-Pres.), Royal Soc. of Arts and Letters (Gothenburg), Acad. of Sciences (Heidelberg), Royal Swedish Acad., Soc. of Antiquaries (London); mem. American Philosophical Soc., American Acad. of Arts and Sciences; Hon. LL.D. (Toronto and British Columbia); Litt.D. (Michigan); L.H.D. (Dartmouth Coll., Univs. of Athens, Lyons, Freiburg, New York, Wooster Coll., Paris, Queen's); Commdr. Order of the Phoenix (Greece); Gold Medal Archaeological Inst. of America 1972; Drexel Medal, Univ. of Pa. 1978. *Publications:* studies in topography, architecture, sculpture and ceramics of ancient Athens (chiefly in Hesperia) 1934–; The Agora of Athens (with R. E. Wycherley) 1972. *Leisure interest:* gardening. *Address:* Institute for Advanced Study, Princeton, N.J. (Office); Meadow Lakes, Apt. 30-06 Hightstown, N.J. 08520, U.S.A. (Home). *Telephone:* (609) 734-8304.

THOMPSON, James Burleigh, Jr., PH.D.; American geologist; b. 20 Nov. 1921, Calais, Maine; s. of James B. and Edith (Peabody) Thompson; m. Eleanora Mairs 1957; one s.; ed. Dartmouth Coll. and Mass. Inst. of Tech.; Instructor in Geology, Dartmouth Coll. 1942–46; Research Asst. in Geology, M.I.T. 1946–47; Instructor in Petrology, Harvard Univ. 1949–50, Asst. Prof. in Petrography 1950–55, Assoc. Prof. of Mineralogy 1955–60, Prof. 1960–77, Sturgis Hooper Prof. of Geology 1977–; Sherman Fairfield Distinguished Scholar, Calif. Inst. of Tech. 1976; mem. American Asscn. for the Advancement of Science, American Geophysical Union, American Acad. of Arts and Sciences, N.A.S., Geochemical Soc. (Pres. 1968–69); Fellow, Geological Soc. of America, Mineralogical Soc. of America (Pres. 1967–68); Faculty Fellowship, Fund for Advancement of Educ. (Ford Foundation) 1952–53, Guggenheim Fellowship 1963; Hon. D.Sc. (Dartmouth) 1975; Arthur L. Day Medal, Geological Soc. of America 1964, Roebling Medal, Mineralogical Soc. of America 1978, Victor M. Goldschmidt Medal, Geochemical Soc. 1985. *Publications:* articles on metamorphic petrology and geology of the Northern Appalachians in professional journals. *Leisure interests:* skiing, mountain climbing. *Address:* Department of Geological Sciences, Harvard University, Cambridge, Mass. 02138 (Office); 20 Richmond Road, Belmont, Mass., U.S.A. (Home). *Telephone:* (617) 495-1672 (Office); (617) 484-9525 (Home).

THOMPSON, James R., LL.D.; American lawyer and politician; b. 1936, Chicago, Ill.; s. of Dr. J. Robert Thompson and Agnes Thompson; m. Jayne Carr 1976; one d.; ed. Univ. of Illinois, Washington Univ., St. Louis, Mo., Northwestern Univ. Law School; admitted to Illinois Bar 1959; Prosecutor, State Attorney's Office, Cook County, Ill. 1959–64; Assoc. Prof. North Western Univ. Law School, Ill. 1964–69; Chief, Dept. of Law Enforcement and Public Protection, Office of Ill. Attorney-Gen. 1969–70, First Asst. U.S. Attorney 1970–71, U.S. Attorney for Northern Dist. of Ill. 1971–75; Counsel, Winston and Strong law firm, Chicago 1975–77; Gov. of Ill. Jan. 1977–; mem. Exec. Cttee. Nat. Govs.' Asscn. (NGA) 1980–82, Chair. 1983–84; Co-Chair. Attorney Gen.'s Task Force on Violent Crime 1981; mem. Presidential Advisory Cttee. on Federalism 1981; Chair. Republican Govs.' Asscn., Midwestern Govs.' Conf., NGA Task Force on Job Creation and Infrastructure 1982–; Chair. Council of Great Lakes Govs. 1985; Vice-Chair. Martin Luther King Jr. Nat. Holiday Cttee. 1985; Hon. LL.D. (Lincoln Coll.) 1975, Hon. D.Hum.Litt. (Roosevelt Univ.) 1979, Hon. D.Jur. (Northwestern Univ. and Illinois Coll.) 1979, Hon. LL.D. (Monmouth Coll.) 1981, (Marshall Law School) 1984, (Elmhurst Coll.) 1985, Dr. h.c. (Pratt Inst.) 1984; Justice in Legislation Award, American Jewish Congress 1984; Distinguished Public Service Award, Anti-Defamation League 1984, Swedish-American of the Year, Vasa Order of America 1985; Republican. *Publications:* Co-author of four textbooks incl. Cases and Comments on Criminal Procedure; numerous articles in professional journals. *Address:* Office of the Governor, State Capitol, Springfield, Ill. 62706, U.S.A.

THOMPSON, J(ay) Lee; British writer, stage actor, film director and producer; b. 1914, Perth, Scotland; m. Lucille Steiner 1967; one s. one d.; ed. Dover Coll.; stage actor and playwright 1931–34; film scriptwriter 1934–50; film dir. 1950–; living in U.S.A. 1959–; Cannes Film Festival

Special Award for Yield to the Night; Silver Bear for Best Picture, Berlin Film Festival, Int. Critics Award, Golden Globe for Best Picture for Woman in a Dressing-Gown; Int. Critics Award for Tiger Bay; Int. Critics Award for Ice Cold in Alex; Int. Critics Award for I Aim at the Stars; numerous awards for The Guns of Navarone; San Sebastian Film Award for Return from the Ashes; Best Science Thriller Award (Paris) for Eye of the Devil; European Best Thriller Award for Reincarnation of Peter Proud. *Films directed include:* Yield to the Night 1956, Woman in a Dressing-Gown 1957, Ice Cold in Alex (U.S. title Desert Attack) 1958, Tiger Bay 1959, Northwest Frontier 1959, I Aim at the Stars 1960, The Guns of Navarone 1961, Cape Fear 1961, Taras Bulba 1962, Kings of the Sun 1963, What a Way to Go 1964, John Goldfarb, Please Come Home! 1965, Return from the Ashes 1965, Mackenna's Gold 1968, Before Winter Comes 1968, The Chairman 1969, Country Dance (U.S. title Brotherly Love) 1970, Conquest of the Planet of the Apes 1972, The Reincarnation of Peter Proud 1975, St. Ives 1976, The White Buffalo 1976, The Greek Tycoon 1978, The Passage 1978, Cabo Blanco, Happy Birthday to Me. *Publications.* plays: Murder Happens, Double Error, Murder Without Crime, The Human Touch, Getting Away with Murder, The Curious Dr. Robson.

THOMPSON, Robert Henry Stewart, C.B.E., M.A., D.SC., D.M., B.CH., F.R.C.P., F.R.C.PATH., F.R.S.; British chemical pathologist; b. 2 Feb. 1912, Croydon; s. of Dr. Joseph H. Thompson and Mary E. Rutherford; m. Inge V. A. Gebert 1938; one s. two d.; ed. Trinity Coll., Oxford, and Guy's Hospital Medical School, London; Adrian Stokes Travelling Fellowship to Hospital of Rockefeller Inst. for Medical Research, New York 1937–38, Gillson Research Scholar in Pathology, Soc. of Apothecaries, London 1938; Fellow and Tutor, Univ. Coll., Oxford 1938–47, now Hon. Fellow; Demonstrator in Biochem., Oxford Univ. 1938–47; served as Major in R.A.M.C. 1944–46; Dean of Medical School, Oxford 1946–47; Prof. of Chemical Pathology, Guy's Hosp. Medical School, Univ. of London, and Consulting Chemical Pathologist to Guy's Hosp. 1947–65; Courtauld Prof. of Biochemistry, Middlesex Hosp. Medical School, Univ. of London 1965–75; Hon. Fellow, Univ. Coll., Oxford 1983; Trustee, Wellcome Trust 1963–82; awarded Radcliffe Prize for Medical Research, Oxford 1943; Hon. mem. Biochemical Soc. 1986; Fellow, Royal Soc. of Medicine; Sec.-Gen. Int. Union of Biochem. 1955–65; mem. British Nat. Cttee. for Biochemistry 1967–70. *Publications:* Biochemistry in Relation to Medicine (with C. W. Carter) 1953, Biochemical Disorders in Human Disease (with I. D. P. Wootton) 1970; numerous papers in medical and scientific journals. *Leisure interest:* gardening. *Address:* 1 Church Way, Hurst Green, Oxted, Surrey RH8 9EA, England. *Telephone:* (0883) 713526.

THOMPSON, Robert Norman, B.SC., D.C., LL.D.; Canadian politician and educator; b. 17 May 1914, Duluth, Minn.; s. of Theodore Olaf Thompson and Hannah Olafson Thompson; m. Hazel Maxine Kurth 1939; five s. three d.; ed. Provincial Normal School, Calgary, Garbutt's Business Coll., Calgary, Bob Jones Univ., Greenville, Univ. of British Columbia, Palmer Coll. of Chiropractic and Wheaton Coll.; Public school teacher, Alberta 1934–36; chiropractor 1939–40; service in Second World War, R.C.A.F. (Flight Lieut.) 1940–43; Colonel and Officer Commanding Imperial Ethiopian Air Force Acad. 1943–44; fmr. Lieut.-Col. Officer commanding 78th Fraser Highlanders, Fort Fraser Garrison, Vancouver; Asst. Headmaster Haile Selassie Secondary School, Ethiopia 1944–46; Dir. of Educ. Kaffa Province, Ethiopia 1946; Dir. of Provincial Educ. Ministry of Educ., Ethiopia 1947–51; Headmaster Haile Selassie Secondary School, Addis Ababa 1947–51; diplomatic missions for Ethiopian Govt. 1946–58; Educ. Dir. Sudan Interior Mission 1952–58; Pres. Social Credit Asscn. Canada 1960–61; Nat. Leader, Social Credit Party 1961–67; Conservative M.P. 1968–72; Prof. of Political Science, Wilfred Laurier Univ. 1968–72; Nat. Co-ordinator of Organization, Canadian Conservative Party 1968–72; Chair. of Bd. World Vision of Canada 1966–76; Pres. Gospel Recording of Canada 1971–73, Int. Co-ordinator 1975–79; C.E.O. Mardel Int. Trading Corpn. 1988–; Pres. Evangelical Fellowship of Canada 1971–73; Pres. Thompson Assocs. Ltd.; Dir. Mission Aviation Fellowship, Roman Corpn., Toronto; Prof. of Political Science, Trinity Western Univ., Vancouver 1972–84, Vice-Pres. Samaritans' Purse; mem. Fed. Bd. of Parole 1985–86, B.C. Bd. of Parole 84–88; Publications Ed., Vanguard Inst., Vancouver; Fellow, Canadian Guild of Authors, Royal Geographical Soc., London; mem. Inter-Parl. Union, Commonwealth Parl. Asscn., Canadian Inst. of Strategic Studies, NATO Parl. Asscn., Gideons Int.; Knight Commdr. Order of St. Lazarus of Jerusalem; Commdr. of Merit; Sovereign Order of St. John; Commdr. Ethiopian Star of Honour; Centennial Medal; Royal Jubilee Medal; Lifestyle Award, Govt. of Canada 1985. *Publications:* Common Sense for Canadians, Canadians, It's Time You Knew, Canadians Face Facts, Social Economics, A Model Constitution for Canada 1982, Liberation: The First to be Freed 1987. *Leisure interests:* reading, hiking. *Address:* Box 430, Fort Langley, B.C. (Home); 9064 Church Street, Fort Langley, B.C. V0X 1J0, Canada (Office). *Telephone:* (604) 888-7511 (Office); (604) 533-1780 (Home).

THOMPSON, (Rupert) Julian (de la Mare), M.A.; British business executive; b. 23 July 1941; s. of Rupert Spens and Florence Elizabeth (de la Mare) Thompson; m. Jacqueline Julie Ivimy 1965; three d.; ed. Eton Coll. and King's Coll., Cambridge; joined Sotheby's 1963, Dir. 1969–, Chair.

1982-86, Chair. Sotheby's Int. 1982-85, Deputy Chair. 1987-. *Address:* 43 Clarendon Road, London, W11 4JD, England. *Telephone:* 01-727 6039.

THOMPSON, Tommy George, J.D.; American state governor; b. 19 Nov. 1941, Elroy, Wis.; s. of Allan Thompson and Julie Dutton; m. Sue A. Mashak 1969; two s. one d.; ed. Univ. of Wisconsin; political intern, U.S. Rep. Thomson 1963; legis. messenger, Wis. State Senate 1964-66; sole practice, Elroy and Mauston, Wis. 1966-87; mem. Dist. 87 Wis. State Ass. 1966-87, Asst. Minority Leader 1972-81, Floor Leader 1981-87; Gov. of Wisconsin 1987-; self-employed real estate broker, Mauston 1970-; mem. American Bar Asscn.; Republican. *Address:* Office of the Governor, Room 115 E, State Capitol, P.O. Box 7863, Madison, Wis. 53707-7863, U.S.A.

THOMPSON, Winston; Fijian diplomatist; b. 8 July 1940, Yasawas; m.; three c.; ed. Imperial Coll. of Tropical Agric., Trinidad and Queensland Univ., Australia; Agricultural Officer, Fiji Govt. 1962, later Chief Agricultural Officer, Deputy Dir. of Agric. and Dir. of Agric., Perm. Sec. in Ministry of Agriculture and Fisheries 1973-78, in Ministry of Finance 1978-83; Sec. Public Service Comm. of Fiji 1983-85; Perm. Rep. of Fiji to the UN 1985-. *Address:* Permanent Mission of Fiji to the United Nations, 1 United Nations Plaza, 26th Floor, New York, N.Y. 10017, U.S.A. *Telephone:* 355-7316.

THOMSEN, Ib; American business executive; b. 8 Oct. 1925, Copenhagen, Denmark; s. of Niels Thomas and Magda Marie Thomsen; m. Lisa Edith Voss 1947; two s. one d.; ed. Harvard Univ. Graduate School of Business Admin.; joined Goodyear Int. Corpn. 1952; Treas. Goodyear-India 1957-58; Treas. Goodyear-U.K. 1958, Financial Dir. and Sec. 1961, Asst. to Man. Dir. 1964, Deputy Man. Dir. 1964, Man. Dir. 1966; Vice-Pres. Goodyear Int. Corpn. 1971, Pres. 1972; Dir. and Exec. Vice-Pres. Goodyear Tire & Rubber Co. 1973-81, Dir. and Group Exec. Vice-Chair. 1981-87. *Address:* 630 Hampton Ridge Drive, Akron, Ohio 44313, U.S.A. (Home).

THOMSEN, Niels Jørgen, DR.PHIL.; Danish university professor; b. 21 April 1930; s. of late Sigurd Thomsen and Gudrun Kirkegaard; m. Birgit Nüchel Petersen 1953; two s.; ed. Univ. of Copenhagen; Dir. Danish Press Museum, Aarhus 1958-65; lecturer, School of Journalism, Aarhus 1962-65; Asst. Prof. of Econ. History, Univ. of Copenhagen 1965-71, Asst. Prof. of Political Science 1971-73, Prof. of Modern History 1973-; Danish Ed. Pressens Årbog 1968-; Chair. Soc. for History and Econs., Copenhagen 1980-; mem. Royal Danish Acad. of Science and Letters. *Publications:* Partipressen 1965, Dagbladskonkurrencen 1870-1970 I-II 1972, Københavns Universitet 1936-66 1986; about 80 articles on political and media history in professional journals. *Address:* Institute of Economic History, University of Copenhagen, Njalsgade 102, 2300 Copenhagen S (Office); Christiansholms parallelvej 1, 2930 Klampenborg, Denmark (Home). *Telephone:* 01 54 22 11 (Office); 01 64 33 16 (Home).

THOMSON, Sir Adam, Kt., C.B.E.; Scottish businessman; b. 7 July 1926, Glasgow; s. of Frank Thomson and Jemina Rodgers; m. Dawn Elizabeth Burt 1948; two s.; ed. Rutherglen Acad., Coatbridge Coll., Royal Tech. Coll. Glasgow; pilot Fleet Air Arm 1944-47; Flying Inst. British European Airways (BEA) 1947-50, pilot with BEA and Britavia 1951-59; founded Caledonian Airways Ltd. 1961, Chair., C.E.O. British Caledonian Airways Ltd. 1970-88; Chair., C.E.O. The Caledonian Aviation Group PLC 1970-88 (fmrly. Airways Interests (Thomson) Ltd., Chair. and Man. Dir. 1964-70); Chair. Asscn. of European Airlines 1977-78, Caledonian Airmotive Ltd. 1978-87; Chair. Gold Stag 1988-; Deputy Chair. Martin Currie Pacific Trust PLC 1985-, Inst of Dirs. 1988-; Dir. Royal Bank of Scotland Group 1982-, MEPC PLC 1982-; Hambro Award Businessman of the Year 1970; Hon. LL.D. (Glasgow) 1979, (Sussex) 1984, (Strathclyde) 1986. *Leisure interests:* golf, sailing. *Address:* 154 Buckswood Drive, Crawley, West Sussex, England.

THOMSON, Bryden, B.MUS., F.R.S.A.M.D., DIP.MUS.ED., L.R.A.M., A.R.C.M.; Scottish orchestral conductor; b. Ayr; m. Mary Ellison; ed. Ayr Acad., Royal Scottish Acad. of Music and Dance, Staatliche Hochschule für Musik, Hamburg; Asst. Conductor BBC Scottish Symphony Orchestra 1958-60; Assoc. Conductor, Scottish Nat. Orchestra 1964-67; Prin. Conductor BBC Philharmonic Orchestra 1968-73, BBC Welsh Symphony Orchestra 1978-82; Prin. Dir. Ulster Orchestra 1977-85, Conductor Emer. 1985-, Artistic Dir. 1977-; Conductor for the Norwegian Opera, Oslo 1964-66, for the Royal Opera, Stockholm 1966-69; Prin. Conductor Radio Telefis Eireann Symphony Orchestra, Dublin, Eire 1984-87; Hon. D.Litt. *Leisure interests:* golf, gardening, reading. *Address:* 2 Leeson Village, Dublin 4, Ireland.

THOMSON, David Spence, P.C., M.C., E.D., M.P.; New Zealand dairy farmer and politician; b. 14 Nov. 1915, Stratford; m. June Grace Adams 1942; one s. three d.; ed. Stratford Primary and High School; Territorial Army 1931-59, served Middle East 1939-42, Prisoner of war 1942-45, Brigadier (Reserve of Officers); Chair. Federated Farmers Sub-provincial Exec. 1959-63; M.P. for Stratford 1963-84; Minister of Defence, Minister in charge of Tourism, Minister in charge of Publicity 1966-67; Minister of Defence, Minister Asst. to Prime Minister, Minister in charge of War Pensions, Minister in charge of Rehabilitation Feb.-March 1967; Minister of Defence, Minister of Tourism, Minister Asst. to Prime Minister, Minister in charge of Publicity, Minister in charge of War Pensions, Minister in charge of Rehabilitation 1967-69; Minister of Defence, of Police, in charge of War Pensions, in charge of Rehabilitation 1969-72; Assoc. Minister of

Labour and Immigration 1971-72, Minister Feb.-Dec. 1972; Minister of Justice 1975-78; Minister of State, of State Services, Leader of the House Dec. 1978-84; also Minister of Defence and Minister in Charge of War Pensions and Rehabilitation Aug. 1980-84; National Party. *Leisure interests:* fishing, golf, music. *Address:* 22 Bird Road, Stratford, New Zealand (Home).

THOMSON, Sir John, K.B.E., T.D., M.A.; British banker; b. 3 April 1908, Oxfordshire; s. of Guy and Evelyn Vera (Hughes) Thomson; m. 1st Elizabeth Brotherhood 1935 (died 1977); m. 2nd Eva Elizabeth Dreaper 1979; ed. Winchester Coll. and Magdalen Coll., Oxford; High Sheriff of Oxon. 1957; Vice-Chair. Barclays Bank Ltd. 1956-58, Deputy Chair. 1958-62, Chair. 1962-73, Dir. 1978; Chair. Nuffield Medical Trustees 1951-82, Nuffield Orthopaedic Trust (until 1982); Pres. British Bankers Asscn. 1964-66; Dir. Union Discount Co. of London 1960-74; Chair. Morland and Co. Ltd. 1979-83; Lord Lieut. of Oxfordshire 1963-79; mem. Royal Comm. on Trade Unions and Employers Assens. 1965-68; Steward, Jockey Club 1974-77; Deputy High Steward, Oxford Univ.; Curator, Oxford Univ. Chest 1949-74; Hon. Fellow St. Catherine's Coll., Oxford; Hon. D.C.L. (Oxon.); Knight of the Order of St. John. *Address:* Manor Farm House, Spelsbury, Oxford, England. *Telephone:* 0608-810266.

THOMSON, Sir John Adam, G.C.M.G., M.A.; British diplomatist (retd.); b. 27 April 1927, Aberdeenshire; s. of the late Sir George Thomson, Kt., F.R.S. and Kathleen Smith; m. Elizabeth Anne McClure 1953; three s. one d.; ed. Philips Exeter Acad., N.H., U.S.A., Aberdeen Univ., Trinity Coll., Cambridge; Third Secretary, Embassy in Jeddah 1951, in Damascus 1954; Foreign Office 1955; Private Sec. to Perm. Under-Sec. 1958; First Sec., Embassy in Washington, D.C. 1960; Foreign Office 1964; Acting Head of Planning Staff 1966; Counsellor, Head of Planning Staff 1967; seconded to Cabinet Office as Chief of Assessment Staff 1968; Minister, Deputy Perm. Rep. to NATO 1972; Asst. Under-Sec. of State, Foreign and Commonwealth Office 1973; High Commr. in India 1977-82; Perm. Rep. to UN 1982-87; Co-Dir., 21st Century Trust 1987-; Dir. Grindlays Bank 1987-; mem. Council Int. Inst. of Strategic Studies; mem. Governing Body Inst. of Devt. Studies, Sussex; mem. Council Overseas Devt. Inst., London; Assoc. mem. Nuffield Coll., Oxford; Hon. LL.D. (Ursinus Coll., Penn.) 1984, (Aberdeen) 1986. *Publication:* Crusader Castles (with Robin Fedden). *Leisure interests:* castles, oriental carpets. *Address:* 21st Century Trust, Church House, Westminster, London, SW1, England (Office).

THOMSON, Peter Alexander Bremner, C.V.O., M.PHIL.; British diplomatist; b. 16 Jan. 1938, Orpington, Kent; s. of Alexander Thomson and Dorothy Scurr; m. Lucinda Sellar 1965; three s.; ed. Canford School, Royal Naval Coll. Dartmouth and S.O.A.S., London; serving officer, R.N. 1958-66; Lieut.-Commdr. ashore in Taiwan and Hong Kong 1970-74; First Sec. H.M. Diplomatic Service, London, Lagos and Hong Kong 1975-84; Counsellor, Peking 1984-87; High Commr. in Belize 1987-. *Leisure interests:* sailing, walking. *Address:* c/o Foreign & Commonwealth Office, London, S.W.1; The Red House, Charlton Horethorne, Sherborne, Dorset, England (Home).

THOMSON, Peter William, C.B.E.; Australian golfer; b. 23 Aug. 1929, Melbourne; m. Stella Mary 1960; one s. three d.; turned professional 1949; British Open Champion 1954, 1955, 1956, 1958, 1965 (only player to win three successively since Open became 72-hole event 1892); won British P.G.A. Match-Play Championship four times and 16 major tournaments in Britain; Australian Open Champion 1951, 1967, 1972, N.Z. Open Champion nine times; won open titles of Italy, Spain, Hong Kong, Philippines, India and Germany; played 11 times for Australia in World Cup (won twice); won World Seniors Championship 1984, PGA Seniors Championship of America 1984; Pres. Professional Golfers' Assen. of Australia; mem. James McGrath Foundation, Vic. *Leisure interests:* classical music, literature. *Address:* 44 Mathoura Road, Toorak, Vic. 3142, Australia.

THOMSON, Richard Murray, B.A.SC.(ENG.), M.B.A.; Canadian banker; b. 14 Aug. 1933, Winnipeg, Man.; s. of H. W. Thomson; m. Heather Lorimer 1959; ed. Univ. of Toronto, Harvard Business School, Queen's Univ., Kingston, Ont.; joined Toronto-Dominion Bank, Head Office 1957, Senior Asst. Man., St. James & McGill, Montreal 1961, Asst. to Pres., Head Office 1963, Asst. Gen. Man. 1965, Chief Gen. Man. 1968, Vice-Pres., Chief Gen. Man., Dir. 1971, Pres. 1972-79, Pres. and C.E.O. 1977-79, Chair. and C.E.O. May 1978-; Dir. Eaton's of Canada, Canadian Gypsum Co., S. C. Johnson & Co. Ltd., Cadillac Fairview Corpn. Ltd., Union Carbide of Canada, The Prudential Insurance Co. of America, Toronto Dominion Bank, Inco Ltd., Int. Thomson Org. Ltd.; Trustee, Hospital for Sick Children. *Leisure interests:* golf, tennis, skiing. *Address:* Toronto-Dominion Bank, P.O. Box 1, Toronto-Dominion Centre, 55 King Street West, Toronto, Ont. M5K 1A2, Canada.

THOMSON, Thomas Harold, B.A.SC., M.B.A.; Canadian business executive; b. 12 Feb. 1935, Winnipeg; s. of Harold W. Thomson and Mary H. Lees; m. Nancy Fockler 1958; one s. two d.; ed. Univ. of Toronto and Harvard Business School; various positions, Imperial Marketing Dept., Imperial Oil 1959-73, Man. Automotive Div. 1973-74, Exec. Vice-Pres. Home Oil Distributors, Vancouver 1974-75; Adviser, Production Dept.-Strategic Planning Dept., Exxon Inc., New York 1975-76; Vice-Pres. and Gen. Man., Marketing, Imperial Oil 1976-80, Sr. Vice-Pres., Dir. and mem. Man.

Comm. 1980–84; Pres. and C.O.O. Suncor Inc. 1985–86, Pres. and C.E.O. 1986–. *Leisure interests:* tennis, skiing, golf. *Address:* Suncor Inc., 36 York Mills Road, North York, Ont. M2P 2C5, Canada.

THOMSON, Thomas James, C.B.E., M.B., CH.B., F.R.C.P.; British consultant physician and gastroenterologist (retd.); b. 8 April 1923, Airdrie; s. of Thomas Thomson and Annie Jane Grant; m. Jessie Smith Shotbolt 1948; two s. one d.; ed. Airdrie Acad. and Univ. of Glasgow; posts in clinical medicine continuously 1945–87, teacher 1948–87; posts as Lecturer in Dept. Materia Medica, Univ. of Glasgow 1953–87, Hon. Lecturer 1961–87; Consultant Physician and Gastroenterologist Stobhill Gen. Hosp., Glasgow 1961–87; Postgraduate Clinical Tutor to Glasgow Northern Hosps. 1961–87; Chair., Greater Glasgow Health Bd. 1987–; Hon. Fellow American Coll. of Physicians. *Publications:* Dilling's Pharmacology (joint ed.) 1969, Gastroenterology—an integrated course 1972. *Leisure interests:* swimming and golfing. *Address:* 1 Varna Road, Glasgow, G14 9NE, Scotland. *Telephone:* 041-959 5930.

THOMSON, Virgil, A.B.; American composer and critic; b. 25 Nov. 1896, Kansas City, Mo.; s. of Quincy A. and May Gaines Thomson; ed. Harvard Univ., and studied under Nadia Boulanger and Rosario Scalero; Asst. Instructor in Music, Harvard Univ. 1921–25; Organist, King's Chapel, Boston 1922–23; lived in Paris 1925–40; Music Critic N.Y. Herald Tribune 1940–54; Pulitzer Prize in Music 1949; Gold Medal Nat. Inst. of Arts and Letters 1966; Brandeis Award 1968, Kennedy Centre Honours 1983, Henry Elias Howland Memorial Prize, Yale Univ. 1986, Nat. Medal of Arts 1988; mem. American Acad. of Arts and Letters, American Acad. Arts and Sciences, Academia Nacional de Bellas Artes, Argentina, Académie des Beaux Arts, France; Hon. D.F.A. (Syracuse, Roosevelt, Missouri), Hon. Litt.D. (Rutgers Univ., Emerson Coll., Boston) 1981, (Bard Coll.) 1982, (Univ. of Conn.) 1985, Litt. Hum. Doc. (Park Coll.), Johns Hopkins Univ., Brooklyn Coll.) 1981, (Manhattanville Coll.) 1983, (New School for Social Research), (William Jewell Coll.), D.Mus. (Fairfield Univ., N.Y. Univ., Columbia, Univ. of Windsor, Ont.) 1981, (Harvard Univ.) 1982, (New England Conservatory of Music) 1986; Officier, Légion d'honneur. *Publications:* The State of Music 1939, The Musical Scene 1945, The Art of Judging Music 1948, Music Right and Left 1951, Virgil Thomson (memoirs) 1966, Music Reviewed 1940–54 1967, American Music since 1910 1971, A Virgil Thomson Reader 1982, Selected Letters of Virgil Thompson 1988, Words With Music 1989. *Compositions include:* three operas: Four Saints in Three Acts 1928, The Mother of Us All 1947, Lord Byron 1968; ballets: Filling Station 1938, Parson Weems and the Cherry Tree 1975; incidental music for plays and films, including: The Plow that Broke the Plains 1936, The River 1937, Louisiana Story 1948, The Goddess 1957, Power Among Men 1957, Journey to America 1964, The Day After 1983; three Symphonies and many shorter works for orchestra (incl. 25 Portraits and eight Suites), a Cello Concerto, a Flute Concerto, a Concertino for Harp, two String Quartets, and other chamber music; four Piano Sonatas and many short piano pieces, songs and choruses; Missa pro Defunctis for men's and women's choirs and orchestra; Cantata on Poems of Edward Lear (for soprano and baritone soloists, chorus and orchestra) 1973. *Leisure interest:* cooking. *Address:* 222 West 23rd Street, New York, N.Y. 10011, U.S.A. *Telephone:* (212) 243-3700.

THOMSON, William Cran, C.A., C.B.I.M.; British business executive; b. 11 Feb. 1926, Glasgow; s. of William Thomson and Helen Cran; m. Jessie Wallace 1951; four s.; ed. Hutcheons (Boys) Grammar School; joined Royal Dutch/Shell Group 1951, Shell Co. of Egypt 1951–54, of Sudan 1954–56, of Aden 1956–58, Finance Dir. P.T. Shell Indonesia 1961–64, Finance Co-ordinator Shell Int. Chemical Co. 1966–70, Chemical Co-ordinator Shell Int. Chemical Co. 1970–79, Chair. Shell Chemicals U.K. 1974–79, Finance Dir. Shell Petroleum Co. 1979–86, Man. Dir. Royal Dutch/Shell Group 1979–86, Man. Dir. Shell Transport and Trading 1979–86 (Dir. 1986–), Chair. Shell Holdings (U.K.) 1981–86; Dir. Coats Viyella PLC 1986–, The Nickerson Group 1986–, Mafatlal Finance Co. Private Ltd. 1987–. *Leisure interests:* golf, shooting. *Address:* Royal Dutch/Shell Group, Shell Centre, London, SE1 7NA, England.

THOMSON OF FLEET, 2nd Baron (cr.1964), of Northbridge in the City of Edinburgh; **Kenneth Roy Thomson,** M.A.; Canadian newspaper proprietor; b. 1 Sept. 1923, Toronto; s. of the late Roy Thomson, the 1st Lord Thomson of Fleet, and Edna Anna Irvine; m. Nora Marilyn Lavis 1956; two s. one d.; ed. Upper Canada Coll. and Cambridge Univ.; served with Canadian Air Force during Second World War; in Editorial Dept., Timmins Daily Press, Timmins, Ont. 1947; Advertising Dept. Galt Reporter 1948–50, Gen. Man. 1950–53; directed U.S. and Canadian Operations of Thomson Newspapers in Toronto 1953–68; Deputy Chair. Times Newspapers Ltd. 1966–67, Chair. 1968–70, Co-Pres. 1971–81; Chair. of Bd., Pres., C.E.O. and Dir. Thomson Newspapers Ltd. (owners of 39 newspapers in Canada); Chair. of Bd. and Dir. Int. Thomson Org. PLC, Thomson Corpn. Ltd., Thomson Int. Corpn. Ltd., Thomson Org. PLC, Woodbridge Co. Ltd., Ontario Newspapers Ltd., TECL Holdings Ltd., Thomson Equitable Corpn. Ltd., Thomson Investments Ltd., Thomson Newspapers Inc. (owners of 93 newspapers in U.S.A.); The Standard St. Lawrence Co. Ltd.; Pres. and Dir. Dominion-Consolidated Holdings Ltd., Fleet Street Publrs. Ltd., Kenthom Holdings Ltd., Thomfleet Holdings Ltd., Thomson Mississauga Properties Ltd., Thomson Works of Art Ltd.; Vice-Pres. and Dir.

Cablevue (Quinte) Ltd., Veribest Products Ltd.; Dir. Abitibi-Price Inc., The Advocate Co. Ltd., Caribbean Trust Ltd., Cen. Canada Insurance Service Ltd., IBM (Canada) Ltd., Hudson's Bay Co., Victoria Insurance Co. of Canada, Scottish and York Insurance Ltd., Load & Go Transport Inc., McCallum Transport Inc., Nipa Lodge Co. Ltd., Orchid Lodge Co. Ltd., Scottish & York Holdings Ltd., Simpsons Ltd., Thomson Scottish Assocs. Ltd., Thomson Television Ltd., The Toronto-Dominion Bank. *Leisure interests:* collecting antiques and paintings, art and golf. *Address:* Thomson Newspapers Ltd., Thomson Building, 65 Queen Street West, Toronto, Ontario M5H 2M8, Canada; The Int. Thomson Org. PLC, P.O. Box 4YG, 4 Stratford Place, London WIN 4YG, England; 8 Castle Frank Road, Toronto 5, Ontario M4W 2Z4, Canada; 8 Kensington Palace Gardens, London, W.8, England (Homes). *Telephone:* 864-1710 (Thomson Newspapers); 01-492 0321 (Thomson Organisation).

THOMSON OF MONIFIETH, Baron (Life Peer), cr. 1977, of Monifieth in the District of the City of Dundee; **George Morgan Thomson,** K.T., P.C.; British journalist and politician; b. 16 Jan. 1921, Stirling, Scotland; s. of James Thomson; m. Grace Jenkins 1948; two d.; ed. Grove Acad., Dundee; Royal Air Force 1940–45; Ed. Forward 1946–53; M.P. 1952–72; Chair. Commonwealth Educ. Council 1959–64; Chair. Parl. Group for World Govt. 1962–64; Minister of State, Foreign Office 1964–66, Jan.-Aug. 1967; Chancellor of Duchy of Lancaster 1966–67; Sec. of State for Commonwealth Affairs 1967–68; Minister without Portfolio 1968–69; Chancellor of Duchy of Lancaster and Deputy Foreign Sec. (with special responsibility for European Affairs and Common Market negotiations) 1969–70; Opposition Spokesman on Defence 1970–72; Chair. Standing Conf. of British Refugee Orgs. 1971–72; Chair. David Davies Memorial Inst. 1971–77; Chair. Labour Cttee. for Europe 1972–73, European Movement 1977–79; mem. Comm. of European Communities, with special responsibility for Regional Policy 1973–76; First Crown Estate Commr. 1977–80; Chair. Advertising Standards Authority 1977–80; Deputy Chair. Ind. Broadcasting Authority 1980–81, Chair. 1981–88; Vice-Pres. Royal Television Soc. 1982–; Chair. Franco-British Council 1979–81, Anglo-Romanian Round Table 1979–81; Chancellor, Heriot-Watt Univ. 1977–; Pres. History of Advertising Trust 1985–; Dir. ICI, Royal Bank of Scotland, Woolwich Equitable Bldg. Soc. (Sr. Vice-Chair. 1988–); Trustee Thomson Foundation; Hon. LL.D. (Dundee) 1967, D.Litt. (Heriot-Watt) 1973, (New Univ. of Ulster) 1984; Hon. D.Sc. (Aston) 1976, (Loughborough) 1980; Labour. *Leisure interests:* swimming, hill walking. *Address:* Independent Broadcasting Authority, 70 Brompton Road, London, SW3 1EY, England. *Telephone:* 01-584 7011.

THONE, Charles, LL.B.; American lawyer and politician; b. 4 Jan. 1924, Hartington, Neb.; m. Ruth Raymond 1953; three d.; ed. Univ. of Nebraska Coll. of Law; Pvt., then Officer, U.S. Army; Deputy Sec. of State, Neb. 1950–51; Asst. Attorney Gen., Neb. and mem. of staff, Senator Dwight Griswold 1951–52; Asst. Dist. Attorney, Lincoln 1952–54; Admin. Asst. to Senator Roman L. Hruska 1954–59; pvt. law practice, Lincoln 1959–70; mem. House of Reps. for 1st Dist. of Neb. 1971–79; Asst. Republican (minority) Whip, mem. various Cttees.; Gov. of Neb. 1979–83; Pres. Univ. of Neb. Young Republicans 1949; State Chair. Neb. Young Republicans 1952; State Chair. Neb. Republican Party 1959–62; Del. Republican Nat. Convention 1952 and 1960, Chair. Neb. Del. 1972 and 1980; Pres. Neb. Jaycees 1953–54; Nat. Pres. Univ. of Neb. Alumni Assocn. 1961–62; Chair. Lincoln Human Rights Comm. 1967–69; mem. Bd. of Govs., John G. Neihardt Foundation 1968–; Univ. of Neb. Alumni Achievement Award 1974. *Address:* c/o Office of the Governor, State Capitol, Lincoln, Neb. 68509, U.S.A.

THONEMANN, Peter Clive, M.SC., D.PHIL.; British physicist and emeritus professor; b. 3 June 1917, Melbourne, Australia; s. of Frederick Emil and Mabel Jessie Thonemann; one s. one d.; ed. Univs. of Melbourne and Sydney and Trinity Coll., Oxford; Commonwealth Research Scholar (Sydney Univ.) 1944–46; ICI Fellow, Clarendon Lab., Oxford (proposed principles and initiated research for a fusion reactor) 1946–49; Head of Research on Controlled Thermonuclear Reactions, A.E.R.E., Harwell 1949–60, Deputy Dir., Culham Lab. of the Atomic Energy Authority 1965–66; Prof. of Physics and Head of Dept., Univ. Coll. of Swansea 1968–84. *Leisure interests:* physics, musical composition. *Address:* 130 Bishopston Road, Swansea, SA3 3EU, Wales. *Telephone:* (044128) 2669 (Swansea).

THORENS, Justin Pierre, D. EN D.; Swiss professor of law; b. 15 Sept. 1931, Geneva; s. of Paul L. Thorens and Germaine Falquet; m. Colette F. Vecchio 1963; one s. one d.; ed. Univ. of Geneva, Freie Univ. Berlin and Univ. Coll. London; attorney-at-law, Geneva Bar 1956–; Alt. Pres. Jurisdictional Court, Geneva 1971–78; lecturer, Faculty of Law, Univ. of Geneva 1967, Assoc. Prof. 1970, Prof. 1973–, Dean 1974–77; Rector, Univ. of Geneva 1977–83; Visiting Scholar, Stanford and Calif. (Berkeley) Univs. 1983–84; Guest Prof. Univ. of Munich 1984; mem. Cttee. European Center for Higher Educ. (CEPES), Bucharest 1981–, Pres. 1986–88; Pres. Bd. Int. Assocn. of Univs. (AIU), Paris 1985–; Chair. Council, UN Univ. Tokyo 1988–; other professional appts.; Prix Huet du Pavillon 1957; Prix Bellot 1963. *Publications:* publs. on pvt. law, civil procedure, Anglo-American property law, univ. politics, cultural questions. *Leisure interests:* history and all its aspects, both European and the rest of the world; interaction of cultures of various times and regions. *Address:* 7 rue de la Fontaine, 1204 Geneva (Office); 18 chemin du Nant d'Aisy, 1246 Corsier, Switzerland (Home). *Telephone:* 21.87.66 (Office); 51.12.62. (Home).

THORN, Gaston, D. EN D.; Luxembourg politician; b. 3 Sept. 1928, Luxembourg; s. of Edouard Thorn and Suzanne Weber; m. Liliane Petit 1957; one s.; ed. Univs. of Montpellier, Lausanne and Paris; admitted to Luxembourg Bar; Pres. Nat. Union of Students, Luxembourg; mem. Legis. 1959–; mem. European Parl. 1959–69, Vice-Pres. Liberal Group; Pres. Democratic Party, Luxembourg 1961; Minister of Foreign Affairs and Minister of Foreign Trade 1969–80, also Minister of Physical Educ. and Sport 1969–77, Prime Minister and Minister of State 1974–79, Minister of Nat. Econ. and Middle Classes 1977–80, of Justice 1979–80; Deputy Prime Minister 1979–80; Pres. Comm. of the European Communities 1981–84, also responsible for Secr. Gen., Legal Service, Spokesman's Group, Security and Cultural Affairs; Pres. Liberal Int. 1970–82; Pres. of 30th Session of the UN Gen. Ass. 1975–76; Pres. Fed. of Liberal and Democratic Parties of European Community 1976–80; Pres. Banque Int., Luxembourg 1985–, Mouvement Européen Int. 1985–; Vice-Pres., Dir.-Gen. RTL Luxembourg 1985–, Pres. 1987–; numerous decorations. *Leisure interests:* lecturing, tennis, golf. *Address:* RTL, Villa Louvigny, Luxembourg-Ville (Office); 1 rue de la Forge, Luxembourg (Home). *Telephone:* 47-66-1 (Office); 420-77 (Home).

THORN, George Widmer, M.D.; American physician; b. 15 Jan. 1906, Buffalo, N.Y.; s. of George W. and Fanny (Widmer) Thorn; m. 1st Doris Weston 1931 (died 1984); one s.; m. 2nd Claire Steinert 1985; ed. Coll. of Wooster, Ohio; House Officer, Millard Fillmore Hosp., Buffalo (N.Y.) 1929–30; Asst. Univ. of Buffalo 1931–34; Rockefeller Fellow in Medicine, Harvard Medical School and Mass. Gen. Hosp. 1934–35; Asst. Prof. Dept. of Physiology, Ohio State Univ. 1935–36; Assoc. Prof. of Medicine, Johns Hopkins Medical School, Assoc. Physician Johns Hopkins Hosp. 1936–42; Physician-in-Chief, Peter Bent Brigham Hosp., Hersey Prof. of Theory and Practice of Physic, Harvard Univ. 1942–72, Emer. 1972–; Samuel A. Levine Prof. of Medicine, Harvard Medical School 1967–72, Emer. 1972–; Dir. of Research, Howard Hughes Medical Inst. 1956–78, mem. Exec. Cttee. 1978–, Chair. Medical Advisory Bd. 1978–; mem. Corpn. and of Exec. Cttee. of Corpn. of M.I.T. 1965–; First Wingate Johnson Visiting Prof., Bowman Gray School of Medicine, Wake Forest Univ. 1972; Pres. Howard Hughes Medical Inst., Boston 1981–84, Chair. Bd. and Trustee 1984–; Consultant U.S. Public Health Service, etc.; Fellow, Royal College of Physicians, London; mem. Nat. Advisory Cttee. on Radiation; Trustee, Diabetic Fund; numerous awards including John Philips Memorial Award (American Coll. of Physicians) 1955, Modern Medicine Award 1961, George Minot Award (American Medical Asscn.) 1963, Robert H. Williams Award (Asscn. of Profs. of Medicine) 1972; Hon. mem. Soc. Columbiana de Endocrinología (Bogotá), Royal Soc. of Medicine (Great Britain); mem. Royal Acad. of Medicine (Belgium), Norwegian Medical Soc., Swedish Medical Soc.; First Lilly Lecturer, Royal Coll. of Physicians, London 1966; Commdr. Order of Hipólito Unanue (Peru). *Leisure interests:* tennis, music, arboriculture. *Address:* Howard Hughes Medical Institute, 350, Longwood Avenue, Longwood Galleria, Boston, Mass. 02115, U.S.A.

THORN, Niels Anker, M.D.; Danish professor of physiology; b. 1 Aug. 1924; s. of Niels Johan Thorn and Dagny Thorn; m. Dr. Ingrid Thorn 1954; two s.; ed. Univ. of Copenhagen 1951; Fellow Rockefeller Univ., N.Y. 1953–56; Resident Assoc. Univ. of Copenhagen 1956, Assoc. Prof. of Physiology 1957, Prof. 1967–; Chair. Danish Nat. Cttee. for US Public Health Service 1970–85; Ed. Acta Physiologica Scandinavia 1981–; leader Danish Govt. Biotech. Center for Neuropeptide research 1988; mem. Danish Medical Research Council 1973–77, European Medical Research Council 1975–79, Royal Danish Acad. of Sciences 1982; Sec.-Gen. Scandinavian Physiology Soc. 1973–82; Alfred Benson Prize 1959; Thorvald Madsen Prize 1967. *Publications:* Antidiuretic Hormones and Their Analogues (thesis) 1960, The Alkalai Metal Ions in Biology 1960, Neurohypophysical Hormones and Similar Polypeptides 1968, Transport Mechanism in Epithelia 1973, Secretory Mechanism of Exocrine Glands 1974, Calcium Transport in Contraction and Secretion 1975, the Secretory Granule 1982, Molecular Mechanisms in Secretion 1988. *Leisure interests:* travel, sailing, skating. *Address:* Institute of Medical Physiology C, University of Copenhagen, 3c Blegdamcvej, DK-2200 Copenhagen N, Denmark. *Telephone:* 31-357900 (Office).

THORNBURGH, Dick, B.ENG., LL.B.; American lawyer; b. 16 July 1932, Pittsburgh; s. of Charles G. Thornburgh and Alice Sanborn; m. Virginia W. Judson 1963; four s.; ed. Yale Univ. and Univ. of Pittsburgh; admitted to Pa. Bar 1958, U.S. Supreme Court Bar 1965; attorney, Kirkpatrick & Lockhart, Pittsburgh 1959–79, 1977–79, 1987–; U.S. attorney for Western Pa., Pittsburgh 1969–75; Asst. Attorney-Gen. Criminal Div. U.S. Justice Dept. 1975–77; Gov. of Pennsylvania 1979–87; now Dir. Inst. of Politics, J.F. Kennedy School of Govt., Harvard Univ.; mem. Bd. of Dirs. Rite Aid Corpn., ARCO Chemical Co., Merrill Lynch & Co. Inc.; Fellow, American Bar Foundation; mem. American Judicature Soc.; 20 hon. degrees; Republican. *Publications:* articles in professional journals. *Address:* Kirkpatrick & Lockhart, 1500 Oliver Building, Pittsburgh, Pa. 15222, (Office); Gateway Towers, Apt. 12B, Fort Duquesne Boulevard, Pittsburgh, Pa. 15222, U.S.A. (Home).

THORNE, Kip Stephen, PH.D.; American university professor, research physicist and writer; b. 1 June 1940, Logan, Utah; s. of David Wynne Thorne and Alison Comish; m. 1st Linda Jeanne Peterson 1960 (divorced 1977), 2nd Carolee Joyce Winstein 1984; one s. one d.; ed. Calif. Inst. of Tech. and Princeton Univ.; Postdoctoral Fellow, Princeton Univ. 1965–66; Research Fellow in Physics, Calif. Inst. of Tech. 1966–67, Assoc. Prof. of Theoretical Physics 1967–70, Prof. 1970–, William R. Kenan Jr. Prof. 1981–; Adjunct Prof. of Physics, Univ. of Utah 1971–; Fulbright Lecturer, France 1966; Visiting Prof., Moscow Univ. 1969, 1975, 1978, 1981, 1982, 1986, 1988; Andrew D. White Prof.-at-Large, Cornell Univ. 1986–; Guggenheim Fellow 1967; mem. Int. Cttee. on Gen. Relativity and Gravitation 1971–80, Cttee. on U.S.-U.S.S.R. Co-operation in Physics 1978–79, Space Science Bd., NASA 1980–83; Hon. D.Sc. (Ill. Coll.) 1979, Dr. h.c. (Moscow State Univ.) 1981; Fellow American Acad. of Arts and Sciences; mem. N.A.S.; American Inst. of Physics—US Steel Foundation Science Writing Award in Physics and Astronomy 1967. *Publications:* (co-author) Gravitation Theory and Gravitational Collapse 1965, High Energy Astrophysics, Vol. 3 1967, Gravitation 1973, Black Holes: The Membrane Paradigm 1986. *Address:* California Institute of Technology 130-33, Pasadena, Calif. 91125, U.S.A. *Address:* (818) 346-4598.

THORNEYCROFT, Baron (Life Peer), cr. 1967, of Dunston in the County of Stafford; **(George Edward) Peter Thorneycroft,** P.C., C.H.; British barrister and politician; b. 26 July 1909; ed. Eton and Royal Military Acad., Woolwich; commissioned service in Royal Artillery 1930–33; called to Bar, Inner Temple 1935; practised in Birmingham; served R.A. in Second World War; Conservative M.P. for Stafford 1938–45, for Monmouth 1945–66; Parl. Sec., Ministry of War Transport 1945; Pres. of the Bd. of Trade 1951–57, Chancellor of the Exchequer 1957–58; Minister of Aviation 1960–62, of Defence 1962–64; Sec. of State for Defence April–Oct. 1964; Dir. Securicor Ltd. 1969–85, British Reserve Insurance Co. 1979–87 (Chair. 1980–87), Gil, Carvajal & Partners Ltd. 1980– (Chair. 1981), Riunione Adriatica di Sicurta 1981–, Banca Nazionale del Lavoro 1984–; Chair. Pirelli Gen. PLC (fmrly. Pirelli Gen. Cable Works Ltd.) 1967–87 (Pres. 1987–), Pirelli PLC 1969–87 (Pres. 1987–), Pirelli U.K. PLC 1987–, Pye of Cambridge Ltd. 1967–79, Pye Holdings Ltd. 1967–79, SITPRO (Simplification of Int. Trade Procedures) 1968–75, Pirelli PLC 1969–, British Overseas Trade Bd. 1972–75, Cinzano (U.K.) Ltd. 1982–85; Chair. Trust Houses Forte Ltd. 1971–81, Pres. 1982–; Chair. of Conservative Party 1975–81. *Publication:* The Amateur: a companion to watercolour 1985. *Address:* House of Lords, London, S.W.1, England. *Telephone:* 01-219 4093; (Personal Sec.) 01-748 5843.

THORNHILL, Arthur Horace, Jr., B.A.; American book publisher; b. 1 Jan. 1924, Boston, Mass.; s. of Arthur Horace Thornhill and Mary J. Peterson; m. Dorothy M. Matheis 1944; one s. one d.; ed. Englewood School for Boys and Princeton Univ.; joined Little, Brown & Co. 1948, Vice-Pres. 1955–58, Exec. Vice Pres. 1958–62, Pres. and C.E.O. 1962–86, Chair. of Bd. 1987–; Vice-Pres. Time Inc. 1968–87; Dir. Conrac Corpn. 1972–87; Treas. and Trustee, Princeton Univ. Press. 1971–86; Air Medal (U.S.A.F.); Princeton Univ. Press Medal. *Leisure interests:* American history, tennis. *Address:* Little, Brown & Co., 34 Beacon Street, Boston, Mass. 02108 (Office); 200 Cliff Road, Wellesley Hills, Mass. 02181, U.S.A. (Home). *Telephone:* 617-227-0730 (Office); 617-235-7675 (Home).

THORNTON, Clive Edward Ian, C.B.E., LL.B., C.B.I.M.; British business executive; b. 12 Dec. 1929, Newcastle upon Tyne; s. of Albert and Margaret Thornton; m. Maureen née Crane 1956; one s. one d.; ed. St Anthony's School and Coll. of Commerce, Newcastle-upon-Tyne and Coll. of Law, London; articled, Kenneth Hudson, Solicitor, London 1959; Solicitor to Cassel Arenz (merchant bankers), London 1964; Chief Solicitor, Abbey Nat. Bldg. Soc. 1967, Deputy Chief Gen. Man. 1978, Chief Gen. Man. 1979–83, Dir. 1980–83; Chair. Commerce and Industry Group, The Law Soc. 1974–75; mem. Council, Bldg. Socs. Assocn. 1979–83, Housing Corpn. 1980–86; Chair. Shelter Housing Aid Centre 1983–86, Mirror Group of Newspapers Jan.–July 1984, Thorndale Farm 1984–, Financial Weekly Ltd. 1984–87, Thamesmead Town Ltd. 1986–, Universe Publs. 1986–; Dir. Investment Data Services 1986–, Melton Mowbray Building Soc. 1986–; Council mem., St. Mary's Hosp. Medical School 1986–; Partner, Stoneham Langton and Passmore (int. lawyers) 1984–88. *Publication:* Building Society Law: Cases and Materials 1975. *Leisure interests:* antique collecting, music, reading, breeding Devon cattle. *Address:* The Old Rectory, Creeton, nr. Grantham, Lincs.; Flat 11, Irvine Court, Whitfield Street, London, W.1, England. *Telephone:* (078 081) 401 (Grantham); 01-387 5437 (London).

THORNTON, Valerie Genestra Marion; British artist and printmaker; b. 13 April 1931, London; d. of Nigel Heber Thornton and Margaret M. G. Thornton; m. Oliver Michael Chase 1966; ed. West Heath Girls' School, Byam Shaw School of Drawing and Painting, Regent Street Polytechnic and Atelier 17 (S. W. Hayter); Asst. Art Teacher, Charterhouse School 1955–56; one-woman exhbns. in Colchester, Oxford, Philadelphia, U.S.A., London and Farnham; group exhbns. at R.A. and Royal Soc. of Painter-Etchers and Engravers; etchings in many collections including British Museum, Victoria and Albert Museum, London, Albertina Museum, Vienna, Bibliothèque Nationale, Paris, Staedlijk Museum, Amsterdam, Metropolitan Museum, New York, Museum of Fine Art, Boston, U.S.A., Museum of Modern Art, New York, Nat. Gallery, Ottawa; Fellow of Royal Soc. of Painter-Etchers and Engravers; Nat. Diploma in Design. *Leisure interests:* looking at and drawing romanesque architecture. *Address:* Lower Common Farmhouse, Chelsworth, Ipswich, Suffolk, IP7 7HY, England. *Telephone:* (0449) 740639.

THOROGOOD, Rev. Bernard George, M.A.; British minister of religion; b. 21 July 1927; s. of Frederick Thorogood and Winifred Thorogood; m. Jannett Lindsay Paton 1952 (died 1988); two s.; ed. Glasgow Univ., Scottish Congregational Coll.; ordained in Congregational Church 1952; missionary appt. under London Missionary Soc. in S. Pacific Islands 1953-70; Gen. Sec. Council for World Mission 1971-80; Gen. Sec. The United Reformed Church 1980-; Moderator British Council of Churches Exec. Cttee. 1984; mem. WCC Cen. Cttee. 1984. *Publications:* Not Quite Paradise 1960, Guide to the Book of Amos 1971, Our Father's House 1983, Risen Today 1987, The Flag and the Cross 1988, No Abiding City 1989. *Leisure interest:* sketching. *Address:* 86 Tavistock Place, London, WC1H 9RT, England. *Telephone:* 01-837 7661.

THOROGOOD, Kenneth Alfred Charles; British international trade financier; b. 1924, London; s. of Albert Jesse and Alice Lucy Thorogood; m. 1st José Patricia Smith 1947; two d.; m. 2nd Gaye Lambourne 1979; ed. Highbury County Grammar School; Flight Lieut., R.A.F. 1942-46; Chair. British Export Houses Asscn. 1968-70, Vice-Pres. 1973-76; mem. Cttee. of Invisible Exports 1968-70; Exec. Chair., Tozer Kemsley & Millbourn (Holdings) PLC (int. finance and investment group) 1971-81; Chair. Ardil (Holdings) UK Ltd. 1984-; Dir. Alexanders Discount Co. Ltd. 1973-83, Royal Insurance Co. Ltd. 1973-83, Liverpool & London & Globe Insurance Co. Ltd. 1973-78, London & Lancashire Insurance Co. Ltd. 1973-78, Welbeck Finance Ltd. Jan. 1980-, Dir. Welbeck Finance PLC 1984-; Trade and Industry Acceptance Corpn. (London) Ltd. 1984-. *Leisure interests:* aviation, music. *Address:* 71 Chester Square, London, SW1W 9DU, England.

THORP, Willard Long, A.M., PH.D.; American economist; b. 24 May 1899, Oswego, N.Y.; s. of Rev. Charles N. Thorp and Susan Long (Thorp); m. Clarice F. Brows; one s. two d.; ed. Amherst Coll., Univ. of Michigan, and Columbia Univ.; taught Econs. at Univ. of Michigan and Amherst Coll. 1926-34; Research Staff of the Nat. Bureau of Econ. Research 1923-33; Chief Statistician N.Y. State Bd. of Housing 1925-26; Dir. U.S. Bureau of Foreign and Domestic Commerce 1933-34; Dir. Econ. Research, Dun & Bradstreet Inc. and Ed. of Dun's Review 1935-40; Econ. Adviser to Sec. of Commerce 1939-40; Chair. of Bd. of Gen. Public Utilities Corpn. 1940-46, Deputy to Asst. Sec. of State for Econ. Affairs 1945-46, Asst. Sec. of State for Econ. Affairs 1946-52; U.S. rep. UN Econ. and Social Council 1946-50; Prof. of Econs., Amherst Coll. and Dir. Merrill Center for Econs. 1952-65; Fellow American Acad. of Arts and Sciences; Dir. Nat. Bureau Econ. Research 1956-; Trustee Associated Gas and Electric Corpn. 1940-46, Brandeis Univ. 1956-62; American Asscn. Univ. Profs. Council 1957-60; Foreign Bondholders Protective Council 1958-63; Nat. Comm. on Money and Credit 1958-61; Acting Pres. Amherst Coll. 1957; Chief UN Econ. Survey Mission to Cyprus 1960; Chief, President's Special Econ. Mission to Bolivia 1961; Chair. Devt. Assistance Cttee. OECD 1963-67; mem. UN Mission to Philippines 1974; Chair. Finance Cttee., Pelham, Mass. 1975-84, Chair. 1978-84, Treas. 1987-; Sr. Fellow, Council on Foreign Relations, N.Y.C. 1968-69; Consultant, Admin. Man., UN 1970-72; Distinguished Visiting Prof. Univ. of Florida 1971; Hon. LL.D. (Marietta, Amherst, Allbright Colls., Univs. of Mass., Michigan); Claremont Medal for Public Service 1985. *Publications:* The Integration of Industrial Operation 1924, Business Annals 1926, Economic Institutions 1928, The Structure of Industry (co-author) 1941, Trade, Aid or What? 1954, The New Inflation (co-author) 1959; contrib. to Recent Economic Changes, Cyprus: Suggestions for a Development Program 1961; Ed.: Economic Problems in a Changing World 1939, The United States and the Far East (American Assembly series 1956), 1962, Development Assistance Efforts and Policies 1963, 1964, 1965, 1967, The Reality of Foreign Aid 1971. *Address:* 9 Harkness Road, Pelham, Mass. 01002, U.S.A. *Telephone:* (413) 256-8019.

THORPE, James, M.A., PH.D., LITT.D., L.H.D., LL.D., H.H.D.; American literary scholar; b. 17 Aug. 1915, Aiken, S.C.; s. of J. Ernest Thorpe and Ruby E. Holloway; m. Elizabeth M. Daniells 1941; two s. one d.; ed. The Citadel, Charleston, S.C., Univ. of N. Carolina and Harvard Univ.; Col., U.S.A.F. 1941-46; Prof. of English, Princeton Univ. 1946-66; Dir. Huntington Library, Art Gallery and Botanical Gardens 1966-83, Sr. Research Assoc. 1966-; Guggenheim Fellow 1949-50, 1965-66; Fellow, American Philosophical Soc., A.A.A.S., American Antiquarian Soc. *Publications:* Rochester's Poems 1950, Etherege's Poems 1963, Literary Scholarship 1964, Principles of Textual Criticism 1972, Use of Manuscripts in Literary Research 1974, Gifts of Genius 1980, A Word to the Wise 1982, John Milton: The Inner Life 1983, The Sense of Style: Reading English Prose 1987. *Leisure interest:* gardening. *Address:* Huntington Library, Art Gallery and Botanical Gardens, San Marino, Calif. 91108 (Office); 1199 Arden Road, Pasadena, Calif. 91106, U.S.A. (Home). *Telephone:* (818) 405-2121 (Office); (818) 405-0938 (Home).

THORPE, Rt. Hon. (John) Jeremy, P.C.; British politician; b. 29 April 1929; m. 1st Caroline Allpass 1968 (died 1970), one s.; m. 2nd Maria (Marion) Stein, fmr. Countess of Harewood, 1973; ed. Rectory School, Conn., Eton Coll. and Trinity Coll., Oxford; Barrister, Inner Temple 1954; M.P. for N. Devon 1959-79; Treas. UN Parl. Group 1962-67; Hon. Treas. Liberal Party 1965-67, Leader 1967-76; Pres. N. Devon Liberal Assen. 1987-; Consultant, Stramit; Chair. Jeremy Thorpe Assocs. Ltd.; Hon. Fellow, Trinity Coll. Oxford Univ.; Hon. DCL, Exeter Univ. *Publications:* To All Who Are

Interested in Democracy 1951, Europe: The Case for Going In 1971. *Address:* No. 2 Orme Square, Bayswater, London, W2, England.

THORSTEINSSON, Pétur; Icelandic diplomatist (retd.); b. 1917, Reykjavík; m. Oddny Stefansson 1948; three s.; ed. Univ. of Iceland; entered Ministry of Foreign Affairs 1944; served Moscow 1944, Ministry of Foreign Affairs 1947; del. to FAO Assembly, Washington 1949; Sec. Icelandic FAO Cttee. 1948-51; Chief of Div., Ministry of Foreign Affairs 1951, Head, Commercial Div. 1950-53; Chair. Inter-Bank Cttee. on Foreign Exchange 1952-53; Minister to U.S.S.R. 1953-56, Amb. 1956-61 (concurrently Minister to Hungary 1955-61 and to Romania 1956-61); Amb. to Fed. Repub. of Germany (concurrently Amb. to Greece and Minister to Switzerland and Yugoslavia) 1961-62, to France (concurrently Perm. Rep. to NATO and OECD) 1962-65, concurrently Amb. to Belgium 1962-65, to Luxembourg 1962-65, to EEC 1963-65; Amb. to U.S.A. 1965-69, concurrently accred. to Argentina, Brazil, Canada and Mexico and Minister to Cuba; Sec.-Gen. Ministry of Foreign Affairs 1969-76; Amb. to Distant Countries (Asia and Africa) with residence in Reykjavík 1976-, also accred. to People's Repub. of China, Japan and Iran 1976-, to India and Pakistan 1976-84, to Thailand 1977, to Bangladesh 1978-84, to Iraq 1980-84, to Tunisia 1980-84, to Repub. of Korea and Democratic Repub. of Korea 1982-, to Australia 1984-, to Indonesia 1985-; Commdr. with Star, Order of the Icelandic Falcon; Belgian, French, Luxembourg, Norwegian, Danish, Swedish, Finnish, Japanese and Korean decorations. *Address:* Ministry of Foreign Affairs, Reykjavík, Iceland. *Telephone:* 25-000.

THOULESS, David James, PH.D., F.R.S.; British physicist; b. 21 Sept. 1934, Bearsden, Scotland; s. of Robert and Priscilla (née Gorton) Thouless; m. Margaret Scrase 1958; two s. one d.; ed. Winchester Coll., Trinity Hall, Cambridge, Cornell Univ.; Physicist, Lawrence Radiation Lab., Berkeley 1958-59; ICI Research Fellow, Birmingham Univ. 1959-61, Prof. of Mathematical Physics 1965-79; Lecturer at Cambridge and Fellow of Churchill Coll. 1961-65, Royal Soc. Research Prof. and Fellow of Clare Hall, Cambridge 1983-86; Prof. of Applied Science, Yale Univ. 1979-80; Prof. of Physics Univ. of Washington 1980-; Maxwell Prize 1973, Holweck Medal 1980, Fritz London Award 1984, Fellow American Acad. of Arts and Sciences 1980, American Physical Soc. 1987. *Publication:* Quantum Mechanics of Many-Body Systems 1961. *Address:* Department of Physics FM-15, University of Washington, Seattle, Wash. 98195, U.S.A. *Telephone:* (206) 545-2393.

THRANE, Hans Erik, M.ECON.; Danish diplomatist; b. 14 April 1918, Copenhagen; s. of Julius Peter Thrane and Frieda Jensen; m. Gerda Boye 1941; two s.; ed. Københavns Universitet; Danish Foreign Service 1945-; Econ. Attaché, Paris 1948-52; Ministry of Foreign Affairs, Copenhagen 1952-56; Econ. Counsellor, Washington 1956-59; Alt. Exec. Dir., IBRD (World Bank) 1958-59; Ministry of Foreign Affairs, Copenhagen 1959-66, Minister 1962, Asst. Undersec. of State for Econ. Affairs 1964; Amb. and Perm. Rep. EFTA, and Perm. Rep. to UN Office and other int. orgs. in Geneva 1966-74; Chair. Council, GATT 1968-71; Amb. to Norway 1974-79, to Switzerland 1980-86, to the Holy See 1982-86; Ministry of Foreign Affairs 1986-; mem. Bd. of Dirs., Nordic Investment Bank 1986-, (Chair. 1988-), Nordic Devt. Fund for the Western North 1987-. *Leisure interests:* sailing, skiing, mountaineering, modern art. *Address:* Ministry of Foreign Affairs, Copenhagen, Denmark. *Telephone:* 920000.

THRUSH, Brian Arthur, M.A., SC.D., F.R.S.; British professor of physical chemistry; b. 23 July 1928, London; s. of late Arthur and Dorothy Thrush; m. Rosemary C. Terry 1958; one s. one d.; ed. Haberdashers' Aske's Hampstead School and Emmanuel Coll., Cambridge; Univ. Demonstrator, Asst. Dir. of Research, Lecturer, Reader in Physical Chem. Univ. of Cambridge 1953-78, Prof. of Physical Chem. 1978-; Head Dept. of Chem., Univ. of Cambridge 1988-; mem. Natural Environment Research Council 1985-; Fellow, Emmanuel Coll., Cambridge 1960-, Vice-Master 1986-; Visiting Prof. Chinese Acad. of Sciences 1980-; Tilden Lecturer 1965 and M. Polanyi Medal 1980 of Royal Soc. of Chem. *Publications:* papers on spectroscopy, gas reactions and atmospheric chem. in learned journals. *Leisure interests:* wine, walking, gardens. *Address:* Department of Physical Chemistry, University of Cambridge, Lensfield Road, Cambridge, CB2 1EP (Office); Brook Cottage, Pemberton Terrace, Cambridge, CB2 1JA, England (Home). *Telephone:* (0223) 336537 (Office); (0223) 357637 (Home).

THULIN, Ingrid; Swedish actress and director; b. 27 Jan. 1929, Sollefteå; d. of Adam Thulin and Nanna Larsson; m. 1st Claes Sylwander 1951, 2nd Harry Schein 1956; ed. Royal Dramatic Theatre School, Stockholm; has appeared in many modern and classical plays for Royal Dramatic Theatre, Stockholm, and for municipal theatres of Malmo and Stockholm until 1962; has also appeared on Broadway, the Italian stage and U.S. T.V.; many nat. and int. awards. *Films include:* When Love Comes to the Village 1950, Wild Strawberries 1957, So Close to Life 1958, The Face 1958, The Judge 1960, The Four Horsemen of the Apocalypse 1961, Winter Light 1962, The Silence 1963, La guerre est finie 1968, The Damned 1970, Cries and Whispers 1973, A Handful of Love 1974, La cage 1975, Cassandra Crossing 1976, Agnes Will Die 1977, One and One 1978, The Rehearsal, Il Corsario 1983; wrote and dir. feature film Broken Skies 1983. *Address:* Kevingestrand 7B, 18231 Danderyd, Sweden; 00060 Sacrofano, Rome, Italy. *Telephone:* 08-755-68-98 (Sweden); 06-9084171 (Italy).

THUNBORG, Anders; Swedish diplomatist; b. 9 June 1934, Stockholm; m. Ingalill Thunborg; three s. two d.; Organizing Sec. of Stockholm Branch, Social Democratic Party 1958, transferred to party Exec. 1960, later Information Sec. and then Int. Sec.; Asst. Party Sec. 1967-69; Under-Sec. of State, Ministry of Defence 1969-74, Ministry of Foreign Affairs 1974-76; Perm. Rep. to UN 1977-83; Chair. UN Trust Fund S.A. 1977-82; Vice-Chair. UN Comm. on Decolonisation 1978-79; Chair. UN Study Group on Nuclear Weapons 1979-82; Minister of Defence 1983-85; Amb. to U.S:.S.R. and Mongolia 1986-89, to U.S.A. 1989-. *Publications:* a number of books, handbooks and essays mainly on int. affairs and defence policy. *Address:* Swedish Embassy, 600 New Hampshire Avenue, N.W., Washington, D.C. 20008, U.S.A.; c/o Ministry of Foreign Affairs, 103 35 Stockholm, Sweden.

THUNHOLM, Lars-Erik, K.B.E.; Swedish business executive; b. 2 Nov. 1914, Stockholm; s. of Nils Thunholm and Ebba Olsson; m. May Bruzelli 1939; ed. Stockholm School of Economics, Univ. of Stockholm; joined Svenska Handelsbanken 1938, Econ. Adviser and Man. of Econ. Dept. 1948-55, Dir. 1951-55; Head of Fed. of Swedish Industries 1955-57; Man. Dir. Skandinaviska Banken, Stockholm (now Skandinaviska Enskilda Banken) 1957-65, Chief Man. Dir. 1965-76, Chair. of Bd. 1976-84; Chair. Nobel Industrier Sverige AB; Chair. Bd., Banque Scandinave en Suisse, Scandinavian Bank Ltd. -1984, Swedish Match -1985, Billerud, Hon. Chair. 1982-84, AB, Svenska Dagbladet, AB Bofors -1984; Hon. Ph.D.; Kt. Commdr. of the Royal Order of Vasa; Grand Cross, Order of the North Star. *Publications:* Svenskt Kreditvasen 1969, Bankvasendet i utlandet 1969, Bankerna och penningpolitiken 1964, Bankerna och samhället 1974. *Address:* Skeppsbron 24, S-111 30 Stockholm, Sweden (Home).

THURAU, Klaus Walther Christian, M.D.; German physiologist; b. 14 June 1928, Bautzen; s. of Walther Thurau and Helene Engel; m. Antje Wiese 1957; two s.; ed. High School, Berlin, and Univs. of Erlangen and Kiel; Lecturer in Physiology, Univ. of Göttingen 1955-65; Chair. Dept. of Physiology, Univ. of Munich 1968-; Visiting Prof. American Heart Assen. 1964; Gilman Prof., Dartmouth Medical School 1968; Visiting Prof., American Kidney Foundation 1980; Pres. Int. Soc. of Nephrology; Treas. and Councillor Int. Union of Physiological Science; Nat. Rep. and Treas. Int. Council of Scientific Unions; Chair. Research Council on Smoking and Health, German UNESCO Comm. on Natural Sciences; mem. German Physiological Soc., Soc. for Clinical Investigation, American Soc. of Physiology, Int. Soc. for Hypertension, Int. Soc. of Nephrology; Hon. mem. Australian Soc. of Nephrology, S. African Soc. of Nephrology; Chief Ed. European Journal of Physiology (Pflingers Archiv.). *Publications:* various papers on renal function (in medical journals). *Leisure interest:* music. *Address:* Josef-Vötterstrasse 6, 8000 Munich 90, Federal Republic of Germany. *Telephone:* 64 89 32.

THURLOW, 8th Baron, cr. 1792; Francis Edward Hovell-Thurlow-Cumming-Bruce, K.C.M.G.; British diplomatist; b. 9 March 1912, London; s. of 6th Baron Thurlow and Grace Catherine Trotter; m. Yvonne Diana Wilson 1949; two s. (one deceased) one d.; ed. Shrewsbury School and Trinity Coll., Cambridge; Asst. Prin., Dept. of Agric. for Scotland 1935-37, Dominions Office 1937; Asst. Sec. Office of U.K. High Commr. in New Zealand 1939-44, in Canada 1944-46; Prin. Pvt. Sec. to Sec. of State 1946-48; Asst. Sec. Commonwealth Relations Office (C.R.O.) 1948; Head of Political Div., Office of U.K. High Commr. in India 1949-52; Establishment Officer, C.R.O. 1952-54, Head of Commodities Dept. 1954-55; Adviser on External Affairs to Gov. of Gold Coast 1955-57, Deputy High Commr. for U.K. in Ghana 1957-58; Asst. Under-Sec. of State, C.R.O. 1958; Deputy High Commr. for U.K. in Canada 1958-59, High Commr. in New Zealand 1959-63, High Commr. in Nigeria 1964-66; Gov. and C.-in-C. Bahamas 1968-72; Chair. Inst. for Comparative Study of History, Philosophy and the Sciences 1974-80, Alexandria Foundation 1980-83; K.St.J. 1969. *Leisure interest:* nature study. *Address:* 102 Leith Mansions, Grantully Road, London, W9 1LJ, England. *Telephone:* 01-289 9664.

THURMOND, Strom; American lawyer, farmer and politician; b. 5 Dec. 1902, Edgefield, S.C.; s. of J. William and Eleanor Gertrude (née Strom) Thurmond; m. 1st Jean Crouch 1947 (died 1960), 2nd Nancy Moore 1968; two s. two d.; ed. Clemson Coll.; Teacher, S. Carolina Schools 1923-29, Supt. 1929-33; admitted to the Bar 1930, served as City and County Attorney; State Senator 1933-38; Circuit Judge 1938-46; active service in Europe and Pacific 1942-46; Maj.-Gen. in U.S. Army Reserve (retd.); Gov. of South Carolina 1947-51; U.S. Senator from S. Carolina 1954-; Chair. Senate Judiciary Cttee. 1981-87, Ranking Minority mem. 1987-; Pres. U.S. Senate protempore 1981-87; Trustee, Bob Jones Univ.; Chair. S.C. Democratic del. and mem. Nat. Exec. Cttee. 1948; mem. American Bar Assen., Clemson Alumni Assen.; 14 hon. degrees; decorations include Legion of Merit with Oak Leaf Cluster, Bronze Star with "V", Purple Heart, Croix de guerre, Croix de la Couronne, Army Commendation Ribbon, Congressional Medal, Honor Soc. Nat. Patriot's Award 1974, American Legion Distinguished Public Service Award 1975, American Judges Distinguished Service Award 1981 and numerous other awards; Republican 1964-. *Address:* Senate Office Building, Washington, D.C. 20510; Aiken, S.C. 29801, U.S.A. (Home). *Telephone:* (202) 224-5972.

THURN UND TAXIS, Johannes, Prince von; German landowner, industrialist and banker; b. 5 June 1926, Höfling/Regensburg; s. of Prince Karl August von Thurn and Taxis and Princess Maria Anna, Princess of Braganza; m. Princess Gloria, Countess von Schönburg-Glauchau 1980; one s. two d.; ed. high school and training in banking; Head of the House of Thurn and Taxis; Malteser Orden, Orden der Rautenkrone. *Leisure interests:* sport, travel, conversation, music, art. *Address:* Emmeramsplatz 5, Schloss, D-8400 Regensburg, Federal Republic of Germany. *Telephone:* 0941-50 480.

THYGESEN, Jacob Christoffer, M.A.; Danish industrialist; b. 11 April 1901, Kolding, Jutland; s. of S. Thygesen; m. Rigmor Thygesen 1932; one s.; ed. Copenhagen Univ.; worked in Danish Foreign Service 1926-30; joined The Danish Distilleries Ltd. 1930, Man. Dir. 1953-71; Barrister, High Court 1939; Chair. Fed. of Danish Industries 1961-66; Pres. Nat. Cttee. Int. Chamber of Commerce 1959-66; mem. Acad. of Tech. Science 1956-, Atomic Energy Comm. 1964-68; Vice-Pres. Business and Industry Advisory Comm. to OECD (BIAC), Paris 1966-68; Chair. Danish Section, European League for Econ. Co-operation, Hon. mem. 1980; Chair. The Nat. Bank of Denmark 1966-77, Superfos Ltd., The Royal Chartered Fire Insurance Co. Ltd; Dir. Scandinavian Tobacco Co. Ltd., Synthetic Ltd., and other industrial cos. and foundations; Commdr. 1st Grade Order of Dannebrog; Knight, Order of Orange-Nassau (Netherlands), Grand Officer, Order of the Crown (Belgium). *Leisure interest:* golf. *Address:* Amaliegade 22, 1256 Copenhagen K, Denmark.

THYSSEN-BORNEMISZA DE KASZON, Baron Hans Heinrich; Swiss industrialist and administrator; b. 13 April 1921, Gröningen; m. 1st Princess Theresa Von Lippe 1939, 2nd Nina Ryer, 3rd Fiona Campbell-Walker, 4th Denise Short, 5th Carmen Barker; ed. Realgymnasium, The Hague, Fribourg Univ.; positions held: Chair. Supervisory Bd. Thyssen-Bornemisa Group NV, Advisory Bd. BHF-Bank, Frankfurt; Pres. Bremer Vulkan Schiffbau- und Maschinenfabrik, Bremen, Thyssengas GmbH, Duisburg; Dir. Heineken NV, Heineken Holding NV, Nederlandse Credietbank NV, Amsterdam; picture collection housed and exhibited in Villa Favorita. *Address:* 56 Chester Square, London, SW1W 9AE, England; Villa Favorita, 6976 Castagnola di Lugano, Switzerland.

TIAN JIYUN; Chinese politician; Deputy Sec.-Gen. State Council 1981-83, Sec.-Gen. 1983-85; mem. 12th Cen. Cttee. CCP 1982, elected to Political Bureau Sept. 1985; Vice-Premier, State Council June 1983-; Head, Commodity Prices Group, State Council 1984-; mem. Secr. CCP Cen. Cttee. 1985-87; mem. Politburo of CCP Cen. Cttee. 1987-; Head State Flood Control HQ 1988-, Cen. Forest Fire Prevention HQ 1987-. *Address:* State Council, Beijing, People's Republic of China.

TIAN SHIXING; Chinese army officer; Deputy for PLA to 5th NPC 1978; Deputy Commdr., Fuzhou Mil. Region 1982-; alt. mem. 12th CCP Cen. Cttee. 1982-87. *Address:* Fuzhou Military Region Headquarters, Fuzhou, Fujian, People's Republic of China.

TIAN YIMIN; Chinese diplomatist; concurrently Amb. to Gabon also accred. to São Tomé and Príncipe) 1985-. *Address:* Embassy of the People's Republic of China, B.P. 3914, Libreville, Gabon.

TICKELL, Sir Crispin (Charles Cervantes), G.C.M.G., K.C.V.O., F.R.G.S., F.Z.S.; British diplomatist; b. 25 Aug. 1930; s. of late Jerrard Tickell and Renée Haynes; m. 1st Chloë Gunn 1954 (divorced 1976), two s. one d.; m. 2nd Penelope Thorne 1977; ed. Westminster School and Christ Church, Oxford; entered H.M. Diplomatic Service 1954; served at The Hague 1955-58, Mexico 1958-61, Paris 1964-70; Pvt. Sec. to Chancellor of Duchy of Lancaster 1970-72; Head, Western Orgs. Dept. FCO 1972-75; Fellow, Center for Int. Affairs Harvard Univ. 1975-76; Chef de Cabinet to Pres. of Comm. of European Communities 1977-81; Visiting Fellow, All Souls Coll. Oxford 1981; Amb. to Mexico 1981-83; Deputy Under-Sec. of State FCO 1983-84; Perm. Sec. Overseas Devt. Admin. FCO 1984-87; Perm. Rep. of U.K. to UN 1987-; mem. Mexican Acad. of Int. Law; Officer, Order of Orange-Nassau. *Publication:* Climatic Change and World Affairs 1977. *Leisure interests:* climatology, palaeohistory, art, mountains. *Address:* c/o Foreign and Commonwealth Office, London, S.W.1, England.

TIDBURY, Charles Henderson; British company director; b. 26 Jan. 1926, Camberley; s. of the late Brig. O. H. Tidbury, M.C. and of Beryl (née Pearce) Tidbury; m. Anne Russell 1950; two s. three d.; ed. Eton Coll.; King's Royal Rifle Corps 1943-52; joined Whitbread & Co. Ltd. 1952, a Man. Dir. 1959, Chief Exec. 1974, Deputy Chair. 1977, Chair. 1978-84; Chair. Brickwoods Brewery Ltd. 1966-71; Dir. Whitbread & Co. PLC, Whitbread Investment Co. PLC, Barclays PLC, Barclays Bank PLC, Barclays Bank UK Ltd., Mercantile Credit Co. Ltd. 1985-, Nabisco Group Ltd. 1985-, Pearl Assurance PLC 1985-, Vaux Group PLC 1985-, ICL (UK) 1985-; Pres. Inst. of Brewing 1976-78; Chair. Brewers' Soc. 1982-84, Vice-Pres. 1985-; Pres. Shire Horse Soc. 1985-87 (Jt. Vice-Pres. 1988-), British Inst. of Innkeeping 1985-; Chair. Mary Rose Devt. Trust 1980-86, William and Mary Tercentenary Trust Ltd. 1986-, Brewing Research Foundation 1985-; Trustee, Nat. Maritime Museum 1984-; Gov. Nat. Heart and Chest Hosps. 1988-, Portsmouth Polytechnic 1988-. *Leisure interests:* family, countryside, sailing, shooting. *Address:* 20 Queen Anne's Gate, London, SW1H 9AA (Office); Crocker Hill Farm, Forest Lane, Wickham, Hants., PO17 5DW (Home); 22 Ursula Street, London, SW11 3DW, England (Home). *Telephone:* 01-222 7060 (Office).

TIE YING; Chinese party official; b. 1916, Jiangxi; Divisional Political Commissar, East China Field Army 1948; Deputy Dir. Mil. Tribunal, Nanjing Mil. Region, PLA 1955; Sec. CCP Zhejiang 1972–77; Vice-Chair. Zhejiang Revolutionary Cttee. 1972–77; Political Commissar, Zhejiang Mil. District, PLA 1972; Alt. mem. 10th Cen. Cttee. CCP 1973; First Sec. CCP Zhejiang 1977–83; 1st Political Commr. Zhejiang Mil. Dist. 1977–85; Chair. Zhejiang Provincial Revolutionary Cttee. 1977–79; Chair. Zhejiang Provincial People's Congress 1979–83; Chair. Advisory Cttee. CCP Zhejiang 1983–; mem. 11th Cen. Cttee. CCP 1977, 12th Cen. Cttee. 1982–85; mem. Cen. Advisory Cttee. 1987–. *Address:* Office of the First Secretary, Chinese Communist Party, Hangzhou, Zhejiang Province, People's Republic of China.

TIEMANN, Norbert Theodore; American businessman, administrator and former governor; b. 18 July 1924, Minden, Neb.; s. of Martin William Tiemann and Alvina T. Rathert; m. Lorna Lou Bornholdt 1950; one s. three d.; ed. Univ. of Nebraska, Midland Lutheran Coll., Neb.; Asst. County Agent, Lexington 1949–50; Asst. Man. Neb. Hereford Asscn. 1950; army service 1943–46, 1950–52; Exec. Sec. Nat. Livestock Feeders Asscn., Omaha 1952; Dir. of Industry Relations Nat. Livestock and Meat Bd., Chicago 1952–54; Mayor of Wausa 1957–70; Pres. Commercial State Bank, Wausa 1957–70; Republican Gov. of Nebraska 1967–71; Fed. Highway Admin. 1973–77; Vice-Pres. Henningon, Curham and Richardson, Va. 1977–; mem. Bd. of Dirs. Lutheran Church of America; mem. American Legion. *Address:* 5902 Mount Eagle Road, 1504 Alexandria, Va. 22303, U.S.A. (Home).

TIEN, Ping-King, M.S., PH.D.; Chinese research engineer; b. 2 Aug. 1919, Checking Prov., China; s. of N. S. Tien and C. S. (Yun) Tien; m. Nancy Chen 1952; two d.; ed. Nat. Cen. Univ., China and Stanford Univ.; Vice-Pres. Tien-Sun Industrial Co. 1942–47; Research Assoc. Stanford Univ. 1948–52; mem. Tech. Staff, AT & T Bell Labs. 1952–61, Head, Electronics Physics Research 1961–80, Head, Microelectronics Research 1980–84, Head, High Speed Electronics Research 1984–; Fellow, AT & T Bell Labs. 1984, I.E.E.E., Optical Soc. of America; mem. Nat. Acad. of Eng., N.A.S.; Chinese Inst. of Eng. Achievement Award. *Publications:* numerous technical publs. *Address:* AT & T Bell Laboratories, Crawfords Corner Road, Holmdel, N.J. 07733 (Office); 9 Carolyn Court, Holmdel, N.J. 07733, U.S.A. (Home). *Telephone:* 201-949-6925 (Office).

TIETMEYER, Hans, DR.RER.POL.; German economist and civil servant; b. 18 Aug. 1931, Metelen; s. of Bernhard and Helene Tietmeyer; m. 1st Marie-Luise Tietmeyer (died 1978), 2nd Maria-Therese Tietmeyer 1980; two c.; ed. Univs. of Münster, Bonn and Cologne; Sec. Bischöfliche Studienforderung Cusanuswerk 1959–62; Fed. Ministry of Econs. 1962–82, Head of Div. of Gen. Econ. Policy 1973–82; mem. Econ. Policy Cttee. of European Community and OECD 1972–82; Sec. of State, Ministry of Finance 1982–89; mem. Bd. of Dirs., Bundesbank. *Publications:* more than 100 articles on economics. *Leisure interests:* sport, literature. *Address:* 5300 Bonn-Bad Godesberg, Federal Republic of Germany.

TIGYI, József; Hungarian biophysicist; b. 19 March 1926, Kaposvár; s. of András Tigyi and Julianna Mátrai; m. Anna Sebes; two s.; ed. Medical Univ. of Pécs; Prof. and Dir. of Biophysical Inst. Medical Univ. Pécs 1971–, Vice-Rector 1967–73, Rector 1973–; corresp. mem. Hungarian Acad. of Sciences 1967–76, mem. 1976–, Vice-Pres. 1988–; Pres. Acad. Section No. 8 (Biological sciences) 1980–; Pres. Hungarian Biophysical Soc. 1972–; Pres. UNESCO European Collaboration in Biophysics 1976–86; Chief Ed. Acta Biochimica et Biophysica 1981–; mem. Royal Soc. of Medicine, New York Acad. of Sciences 1980–; WHO Exec. Bd. 1972–75; Int. Council of Scientific Unions (ICSU) Gen. Cttee.; Cttee. on the Teaching of Science 1986–; Gesellschaft für mathematische u. physikalische Biologie (G.D.R.), Biophysical Soc. of Romania, of India; Gen. Sec. Int. Union of Pure and Applied Biophysics (IUPAB) 1984–; Labour Order of Merit (Silver) 1966, (Gold) 1970, 1979. *Publications:* Application of Radioactive Isotope in Experimental Medicine 1965; Biophysics—Theory of bioelectric phenomena, Biological semi-conductors; Energetics of cross-striated muscle 1977. *Address:* Biophysical Institute of the Medical University, 7643 Pécs, Szigeti ut 12, Hungary. *Telephone:* 36/72/ 14-017.

TIHELI, Moeketsi Mackenzie, B.A.(HONS.); Lesotho educationalist and poltician; b. 21 June 1931, Mohalinyane, Mohale's Hoek; ed. Siloe Intermediate School, Basutoland Training Coll.; teacher, then Deputy Educational Sec. 1968–69, Educational Sec. 1970–86; Minister of Employment, Social Security and Pensions 1986–; has served on many cttees. and comms., including Nat. Comm. for UNESCO, Teaching Service Comm., Tech. and Vocational Educ. Bd.; fmr. mem. Bd. of Govs. Nat. Teacher Training Coll. and Lerotholi Tech. Inst. *Address:* c/o The Military Council, Maseru, Lesotho.

TIKHONOV, Andrey Nikolayevich; Soviet mathematician and geophysicist; b. 30 Oct. 1906, Gzhatsk (now Gagarin), Smolensk Region; m. N. V. Golubkova 1934; two s. two d.; ed. Moscow State Univ.; Postgraduate, Jr. Scientific Worker, Moscow State Univ. 1927–35; Sr. Scientific Worker, U.S.S.R. Acad. of Sciences Inst. of Theoretical Geophysics 1935–58; Deputy Dir. U.S.S.R. Acad. of Sciences Inst. of Applied Maths. 1953–79; Dir. U.S.S.R. Acad. of Sciences Keldysh Inst. of Applied Maths 1979–; Dean of Faculty of Computer Maths. and Cybernetics 1969–; Prof. Moscow State

Univ. 1936–; Corresp. mem. U.S.S.R. Acad. of Sciences 1939–66, mem. 1966–; Lenin Prize 1966, State Prizes 1953, 1976, Hero of Socialist Labour 1954, 1986, Order of Lenin (five times), and other decorations. *Publications:* Works on theoretical pluralistic topology, on mathematical physics, on geophysics and computational maths; foundation works on the solution methods for ill-posed problems (regularization method). *Address:* The Keldysh Institute of Applied Mathematics, Miusskaya Sq. 4, 125047 Moscow, U.S.S.R. *Telephone:* 2581314.

TIKHVINSKY, Sergej Leonidovich; Soviet historian and academician; b. 1918; ed. Oriental Inst., Moscow; mem. CPSU 1941–; diplomatic service in China, U.K. and Japan 1939–57; Head of Asian Dept., U.S.S.R. State Cttee. with Council of Ministers for Foreign Cultural Relations 1957–60; Prof. Moscow Univ. 1959; Dir U.S.S.R Acad. of Sciences Inst. of Sinology 1960–61; Deputy Dir. of Acad. of Sciences Inst. of the Peoples of Asia 1961–63; Dir. of Acad. of Sciences Inst. of World Socialist Economies 1963–65; Corresp. mem. of Acad. of Sciences 1968–81, mem. 1981–; Chief of Dept., then Head of Asia Section in U.S.S.R. Ministry of Foreign Affairs 1965–80; Rector of Diplomatic Acad. of U.S.S.R. Ministry of Foreign Affairs 1980–86; Academician-Sec. of Historical Section of U.S.S.R. Acad. of Sciences 1982–88; Pres. Nat. Cttee. of Soviet Historians 1989–. *Address:* Dmitri Ulianov 19, Moscow 117036, U.S.S.R.

TILLETT, Kenneth Erroll, M.S.C.; Belize diplomatist; b. 19 Dec. 1940, Crooked Tree; m.; four c.; ed. Bethany Coll., Oklahoma and Georgetown Univ.; Prin. at Nazarene Primary School, San Ignacio Cayo Dist. 1960; Prin. at Nazarene High School, Belize City 1972–75; Teacher at Wesley Coll., Belize City 1975–80; City Councillor, Belize City 1974–80, served in Belize Senate 1975–79; fmrly. salesman for Schering Corpn., Kansas; Perm. Rep. of Belize to UN 1985–. *Address:* Permanent Mission of Belize to the United Nations, 801 Second Avenue, Suite 401-02, New York, N.Y. 10017, U.S.A. *Telephone:* 599-0233, 0286.

TILLINGHAST, Charles C., Jr., PH.B., J.D.; American lawyer and corporation executive; b. 30 Jan. 1911, Saxton's River, Vt.; s. of Charles C. and Adelaide Barrows (Shaw) Tillinghast; m. Lisette Micoleau 1935; one s. three d.; ed. Brown and Columbia Univs.; admitted N.Y. Bar 1935; Deputy Asst. Dist. Attorney N.Y. County 1938–40; partner, Hughes, Hubbard & Ewing and successor firm of Hughes, Hubbard, Blair & Reed 1942–57; Vice-Pres. and Dir. Bendix Corpn. and various subsidiaries and affiliates 1957–61; Pres., C.E.O. and Dir. Trans World Airlines Inc. 1961–69, Chair. and C.E.O. and Dir. 1969–76, Dir. 1976–81; mem. Conference Bd. Midwest Research Inst. 1965–76; mem. Cttee. for Econ. Devt. 1967–; Vice-Chair. White, Weld and Co. Inc. 1977–78; Vice-Pres. Merrill Lynch, Pierce, Fenner Smith Inc. 1978–82; Chancellor Brown Univ. 1968–79, Fellow 1979–; Hon. L.H.D. (S. Dakota School of Mines and Tech. 1959); Hon. LL.D. (Franklin Coll. 1963, Redlands Univ. 1964, Brown Univ. 1967, Drury Coll. 1967, William Jewel Coll. 1973). *Leisure interests:* golfing, shooting, gardening, woodworking. *Address:* 25 John Street, Providence, R.I. 02906, U.S.A. (Home).

TILSON, Joseph (Joe), A.R.C.A., A.R.A.; British artist; b. 24 Aug. 1928, London; m. Joslyn Morton 1955; one s. two d.; ed. St. Martin's School of Art, Royal Coll. of Art, British School, Rome; Visiting Lecturer Slade School, Univ. of London, 1962–63, King's Coll., Univ. of Durham 1962–63, exhibited at Venice Biennale 1964; Lecturer School of Visual Arts, New York 1966, Staatliche Hochschule, Hamburg 1971–72; retrospective Exhbn. Boymans van Beuningen Museum, Rotterdam 1978; Rome Prize 1955, Grand Prix Fifth Biennale, Cracow 1974, Henry Moore Prize, Bradford 1984, Grand Prix, 15th Biennale, Ljubljana 1985. *Address:* The Old Rectory, Christian Malford, Wiltshire, SN15 4BW, England. *Telephone:* (0249) 720223.

TIMAKATA, Fred; Vanuatu politician; b. 1936, Shepard Islands; Speaker of Parl. 1985–88; Minister of Health 1988–89; Pres. of Vanuatu Jan. 1989–. *Address:* Office of the President, Port Vila, Vanuatu.

TIMÁR, Dr. Mátyás; Hungarian politician; b. 1923, Mohács; m. Éva Vágó; two d.; ed. Univ. of Law; former leather worker; Hungarian CP 1943–; fmr. teacher Faculty of State and Legal Sciences, Loránd Eötvös Univ. of Sciences; afterwards Head Finance Faculty, Karl Marx Univ. of Econs., Budapest; Ministry of Finance 1949–, Deputy Minister of Finance 1955–57, 1960–62, Minister of Finance 1962–67; Deputy Chair. Council of Ministers 1967–75; mem. Central Cttee. Hungarian Socialist Workers' Party 1966–88, mem. Political Econ. Bd. attached to HSWP Cen. Cttee. 1967–; mem. State Planning Cttee. 1973–; Pres. Nat. Bank of Hungary 1975–88. *Publications:* Economic Development and Directive Systems in Hungary 1968, Economic Policy in Hungary 1967-1973 1973. *Leisure interests:* tennis, hunting, gardening. *Address:* c/o National Bank of Hungary, Szabadság-tér 8, H-1850, Budapest, Hungary. *Telephone:* 112-600.

TIMOFEYEVA, Nina Vladimirovna; Soviet ballet dancer; b. 11 June 1935, Leningrad; one d.; ed. Leningrad Ballet School; with Ballet Company of the Leningrad Kirov State Academic Theatre of Opera and Ballet 1953–56; Deputy to Supreme Soviet of the U.S.S.R. (7th Convocation); mem. Bolshoi Theatre 1956–; has toured with Bolshoi Ballet in U.S.A., Fed. Repub. of Germany and other countries; People's Artist of the R.S.F.S.R. 1963; People's Artist of U.S.S.R. 1969; prizewinner at three int. classic dance competitions; various decorations. *Principal roles:* Odette-

Odile (Swan Lake), Marta (Giselle), Laurensia (Laurensia), Yegina (Spartacus), Kitri (Don Quixote), Mistress of the Copper Mountain (Stone Flower), Diane Mireille (Flames of Paris), Gayane (Gayane), Raymonda (Raymonda), Princess Aurora (Sleeping Beauty), Leili (Leili and Medjnun), Mekhmene Banu (Legend of Love), Giselle (Giselle), Asel (Asel), Bacchante (Faust), Masha (Nutcracker), Shopeniana, Beatrice (Much Ado About Nothing), Juliet (Romeo and Juliet) 1976, Lady Macbeth (Macbeth) 1980. *Films:* White Nights (Dostoevsky), Phaedra (Euripides), The Way the Heart Reveals Itself, Raymonda, Classic Duets, Spartacus, Macbeth, This Wonderful World, Improvisations, The Three Cards, Allegro, Something More About Ballet, Grand Pas, Five Corners 1988. *Leisure interests:* autosports, music. *Address:* State Academic Bolshoi Theatre of the U.S.S.R., ploshchad Sverdlova 1, Moscow, U.S.S.R.

TINBERGEN, Jan; Netherlands economist; b. 12 April 1903, The Hague; s. of Dr. D. C. Tinbergen and Jeannette van Eek; m. Tine Johanna De Wit 1929; four d.; ed. Leiden Univ. (Dr. of Physics); Staff of Cen. Bureau of Statistics, The Hague 1929-36, 1938-45; Business cycle research expert, League of Nations, Geneva 1936-38; Dir. Cen. Planning Bureau, The Hague 1945-55; Prof. of Devt. Planning, Univ. of Rotterdam 1933-73, Leiden 1973-75; mem. Netherlands Acad. of Sciences; Erasmus Prize 1967; Nobel Prize for Econs. 1969. *Publications:* Business Cycles in the U.S.A. 1919-1932 1939, On the Theory of Economic Policy 1952, Economic Policy: Principles and Design 1956, Selected Papers 1959, Shaping the World Economy 1962, Development Planning 1968, Income Distribution 1975, Warfare and Welfare 1987. *Leisure interests:* grandchildren, languages, drawing. *Address:* Haviklaan 31, 2566XD The Hague, Netherlands. *Telephone:* 070-644630.

TINDALE, Lawrence Victor Dolman, C.B.E., C.A.; British chartered accountant; b. 24 April 1921, Moorsley, Durham; s. of John S. Tindale and Alice L. (Dolman) Tindale; m. Beatrice M. Barton 1946; ones. one d.; ed. Upper Latymer School, London; articled clerk, McClelland Ker 1938-39, Man. 1946-50, Partner 1951-59; joined Investors in Industry 1959, Deputy Chair. 1974-; Dir. Industrial Devt. Dept. of Trade and Industry 1972-74; Deputy Chair. Consumers' Assen. 1982-84; Chair. British Inst. of Management 1982-84; Chair. C. & J. Clark Ltd., Edbro PLC; Dir. NEI PLC, BTG, Polly Peck Int. PLC etc. *Leisure interest:* opera. *Address:* 91 Waterloo Road, London, SE1 8XP (Office); 3 Amyand Park Gardens, Twickenham, Middx., TW1 3HS, England (Home). *Telephone:* 01-928-7822.

TINDEMANS, Leo; Belgian politician; b. 16 April 1922, Zwijndrecht; m. Rosa Naesens 1960; two s. two d.; ed. State Univ. of Ghent, Catholic Univ. of Louvain; mem. Chamber of Deputies 1961-; Mayor of Edegem 1965-76; Minister of Community Affairs 1968-71; Minister of Agric. and Middle Class Affairs 1972-73; Deputy Prime Minister and Minister for the Budget and Institutional Problems 1973-74; Prime Minister 1974-78; Minister of Foreign Affairs Dec. 1981-; Vice-Pres. European Union of Christian Democrats; Pres. European People's Party; mem. European Parl. 1979-81; Pres. Belgian Christian People's Party (CVP) 1979-81; Visiting Prof., Faculty of Social Sciences, Catholic Univ., Louvain; Hon. D.Litt. (City Univ., London) 1976; Dr. h.c. (Heriot-Watt Univ., Edinburgh) 1978, (Georgetown Univ.) 1984; Charlemagne Prize 1976; St.-Liborius-Medaille für Einheit und Frieden 1977; Stresemann Medal 1979; Robert Schuman Prize 1980; Christian Democrat. *Publications:* Ontwikkeling van de Benelux 1958, L'autonomie culturelle 1971, Regionalized Belgium, Transition from the Nation State to the Multinational State 1972, Een handvest voor woelig België 1972, Dagboek van de werkgroep Eyskens 1973, European Union 1975, Europe, Ideal of Our Generation 1976, Open Brief aan Gaston Eyskens 1978, Atlantisch Europa 1980. *Leisure interests:* reading, writing, walking. *Address:* rue Quatre Bras 2, Brussels; Jan Verbertlei 24, B-2520 Edegem, Belgium (Home). *Telephone:* 02/516-82-11 (Office).

TINDLE, David, R.A.; British artist; b. 29 April 1932, Huddersfield, Yorks.; m. Janet Trollope 1969; one s. two d.; ed. Coventry School of Art; numerous exhbns. in London and provinces since 1952; first one-man exhbn. London 1953, regular one-man shows, Piccadilly Gallery 1954-83, Hamburg Gallerie XX 1974-85, Los Angeles and San Francisco 1964, Bologna and Milan 1968; one-man show, Fischer Fine Art 1985, 1989; has participated in numerous group exhbns. and int. biennales in Europe; works in many public and private collections including the Tate Gallery, Nat. Portrait Gallery; designed and painted set for Iolanta (Tchaikovsky), Aldeburgh Festival 1988; Visiting Tutor, Royal Coll. of Art 1973-83, Fellow 1981, Hon. Fellow 1984; Ruskin Master of Drawing, St. Edmund Hall, Oxford 1985-87, Hon. Fellow 1988-; Hon. M.A. (St. Edmund Hall, Oxford) 1985; R.A. Johnson Wax Award 1983. *Leisure interests:* music, cats and dogs. *Address:* Flat 1, 61 Holly Walk, Leamington Spa, Warwicks, CV32 4JG, England.

TINÉ, Jacques Wilfrid Jean Francis, L. EN D.; French diplomatist (retd.); b. 24 May 1914, Algiers; s. of Edouard Tiné and René Pittaluga; m. Helena Terry 1948; one s. one d.; ed. Lycée d'Alger, Faculté des Lettres and Ecole Libre des Sciences Politiques, Paris; entered diplomatic service 1938; Counsellor French Embassy, Copénhagen 1949-50, UN 1950-55, London 1955-61; Minister Plenipotentiary, Rabat, Morocco 1961; Deputy Perm. Rep. to UN 1963-67; Dir. for Europe, Ministry for Foreign Affairs 1967-69; Amb. to Portugal 1969-73; Diplomatic Counsellor to the Govt. 1973-75; Perm. Rep. to NATO 1975-79; Ambassadeur de France 1977; Chair. Office

Nat. de Diffusion Artistique 1975-82, Cie. européenne de Radio et de Télévision 1980-86; Officier de la Légion d'honneur, Croix de guerre, Commdr de l'Ordre nat. du Mérite, Commdr. des Arts et Lettres. *Address:* 120 rue de Bac, 75007 Paris, France. *Telephone:* 4548-0876.

TING, Samuel Chao Chung, B.S.E., PH.D.; American physicist; b. 27 Jan. 1936, Ann Arbor, Mich.; s. of Prof. Kuan Hai Ting and Prof. Tsun-Ying Wang; m. 1st Kay Louise Kuhne 1960, two d.; m. 2nd Susan Carol Marks 1985; one s.; ed. primary and secondary schools in China, Univ. of Michigan; Ford Foundation Fellow, European Org. for Nuclear Research (CERN), Geneva 1963; Instructor, Columbia Univ., N.Y. 1964, Asst. Prof. 1965-67; Group Leader, Deutsches Elektronen Synchrotron (DESY), Hamburg, Fed. Repub. of Germany 1966; Assoc. Prof. of Physics, M.I.T., Cambridge 1967-68, Prof. 1969-, Thomas Dudley Cabot Inst. Prof. 1977-; Programme Consultant, Div. of Particles and Fields, American Physical Soc. 1970; Hon. Prof. Beijing Normal Coll., China 1984, Jiatong Univ., Shanghai, China 1987; Assoc. Ed. Nuclear Physics B 1970; mem. Editorial Bd. Nuclear Instruments and Methods 1977, Mathematical Modelling, Chinese Physics; worked chiefly on physics of electron or muon pairs, investigating quantum electro-dynamics, production and decay of photon-like particles, searching for new particles which decay to electron or muon pairs; Fellow, American Acad. of Arts and Sciences 1975; mem. American, Italian and European Physical Socs.; Foreign mem. Academia Sinica, Taiwan 1975, Pakistani Acad. of Science 1984, Acad. of Science, U.S.S.R. 1988; mem. N.A.S. 1977-; Hon. Sc.D. (Michigan) 1978, (Chinese Univ. of Hong Kong) 1987, (Bologna) 1988; Ernest Orlando Lawrence Award 1976, Nobel Prize for Physics, jointly with Burton Richter (q.v.), for discovery of the heavy, long-lived 'J' (or 'psi') particle 1976, Eringen Medal, Soc. of Eng. Scientists 1977, De Gasperi Gold Medal for Science, Italy 1988, Gold Medal for Science, City of Brescia, Italy 1988. *Address:* Department of Physics, Massachusetts Institute of Technology, 51 Vassar Street, Cambridge, Mass. 02139, U.S.A.

TING MAO; Chinese party official; b. 1913, Liaoning; joined CCP 1936; Bn. Instructor Daqingshan Detachment, Shanxi-Suiyuan Mil. Dist. 1943; Deputy Dir. Political Dept., Nei Monggol (Inner Mongolia) Mil. Dist. 1947, Dir. 1952; Deputy Political Commissar, Nei Monggol Mil. Region 1955; identified as Maj.-Gen. 1956; disappeared during Cultural Revolution; Second Political Commissar, Nei Monggol Mil. Dist. 1979: Second Sec. CCP Cttee., Nei Monggol Autonomous Region 1979; Chair. Autonomous Regional People's Congress, Nei Monggol 1979-83; mem. Cen. Advisory Comm. 1987-. *Address:* Office of the Chairman, People's Congress, Nei Monggol Autonomous Region, People's Republic of China.

TINKHAM, Michael, M.S., PH.D.; American professor of physics; b. 23 Feb. 1928, near Ripon, Wis.; s. of Clayton H. and Laverna Krause Tinkham; m. Mary S. Merin 1961; two s.; ed. Ripon Coll., Ripon, Wis., M.I.T. and Univ. of Oxford; Research Asst., Univ. of Calif. (Berkeley) 1955-57, Asst. Prof. of Physics 1957-59, Assoc. Prof. of Physics 1959-61, Prof. of Physics 1961-66; Gordon McKay Prof. of Applied Physics and Prof. of Physics, Harvard Univ. 1966-80, Rumford Prof. of Physics and Gordon McKay Prof. of Applied Physics 1980-, Chair. Dept. of Physics 1975-78; Richtmyer Lecturer (of American Physical Soc. and American Assen. of Physics Teachers) 1977; Visiting Miller Research Prof., Univ. of Calif. (Berkeley) 1987; mem. N.A.S.; Fellow, American Acad. of Arts and Sciences; Guggenheim Fellow 1963-64; Buckley Prize 1974; Awardee, Alexander von Humboldt Foundation 1978-79. *Publications:* Group Theory and Quantum Mechanics 1964, Superconductivity 1965, Introduction to Superconductivity 1975; numerous articles in journals. *Address:* Department of Physics, Harvard University, Cambridge, Mass. 02138 (Office); 98 Rutledge Road, Belmont, Mass. 02178, U.S.A. (Home). *Telephone:* 617-495-3735 (Office).

TINSLEY, Right Rev. Ernest John, M.A., B.D.; British ecclesiastic; b. 22 March 1919, Maghull, Lancashire; s. of Ernest William and Esther Tinsley; m. Marjorie Dixon 1947 (died 1977); two d.; ed. Univ. of Durham and Westcott House, Cambridge; Lecturer in Theology, Univ. Coll., Hull 1946-54, Lecturer in charge of Dept. of Theology 1954-61, Sr. Lecturer and Head of Dept. 1961-62; Prof. of Theology and Head of Dept., Leeds Univ. 1962-75; Anglican Bishop of Bristol 1976-85; Special Lecturer, Bristol Univ. 1976-84; Chair. Gen. Synod Bd. of Educ. 1979-82. *Publications:* The Imitation of God in Christ 1960, The Gospel According to Luke 1964, Modern Theology 1969, Art and Religion as Communication 1974, Dictionary of Christian Spirituality 1983. *Leisure interests:* gardening, travel. *Address:* 100 Acre End Street, Eynsham, Oxford, OX9A 1PD, England. *Telephone:* (0865) 880 822.

TIPPETT, Sir Michael Kemp, Kt., O.M., C.H., C.B.E.; British composer; b. 2 Jan. 1905, London; s. of Henry William and Isabel (Kemp) Tippett; ed. Royal Coll. of Music; taught at Hazelwood School until 1932; Dir. of Music, Morley Coll. 1940-51; Dir. Bath Festival 1969-74; Pres. Kent Opera 1978-; Pres. London Coll. of Music 1983-; Hon. mem. American Acad. of Arts and Letters 1973; Hon. Fellow Royal Northern Coll. of Music 1984; Hon. D.Mus.(Cantab.) 1964, (Dublin) 1964, (Leeds) 1965, (Oxford) 1967, (Leicester) 1968, (Wales) 1968, (Bristol) 1970, (Bath) 1972, (London) 1975, (Sheffield) 1976, (Birmingham) 1976, (Lancaster) 1977, (Liverpool) 1981, (Keele) 1986, (Aberdeen) 1987; Hon. Dr. Univ. (York) 1966; Hon. D.Litt.(Warwick) 1974; Gold Medal of Royal Philharmonic Soc. 1976, Foundation Prince Pierre Monaco Competition Prize 1984. *Works include:* String Quartet No. 1 1935,

Piano Sonata No. 1 1937, Concerto for Double String Orchestra 1939, A Child of Our Time 1941, Fantasia on a Theme of Handel for Piano and Orchestra 1941, String Quartet No. 2 1942, Symphony No. 1 1945, String Quartet No. 3 1946, Little Music for Strings 1946, Suite for the Birthday of Prince Charles (Suite in D) 1948, The Heart's Assurance 1951, The Midsummer Marriage 1952, Fantasia Concertante on a Theme of Corelli for String Orchestra 1953, Divertimento on "Sellinger's Round", for Chamber Orchestra 1953–54, Concerto for Piano and Orchestra 1955, Sonata for Four Horns 1955, Symphony No. 2 1957, Crown of the Year 1958, King Priam (opera) 1961, Magnificat and Nunc Dimittis 1961, Piano Sonata No. 2 1962, Incidental Music to The Tempest 1962, Praeludium for Brass, Bells and Percussion 1962, Concerto for Orchestra 1963, The Vision of St. Augustine 1965, The Knot Garden (opera) 1970, The Shires Suite 1965–70, Songs for Dov 1970, Symphony No. 3 1972, Piano Sonata No. 3 1973, The Ice Break (opera) 1976, Symphony No. 4 1977, String Quartet No. 4 1978, Triple Concerto 1979, Wolftrap Fanfare 1980, The Blue Guitar 1983, The Mask of Time 1983, Festal Brass with Blues 1983, Piano Sonata No. 4 1984, New Year (opera) 1988. *Publications:* Moving into Aquarius 1959, Music of the Angels 1980. *Address:* c/o Schott & Co., 48 Great Marlborough Street, London, W1V 2BN, England. *Telephone:* 01-437 1246; 01-439 2640.

TIPPETT, Willis Paul, Jr., A.B.; American business executive; b. 27 Dec. 1932, Cincinnati, Ohio; s. of Willis Paul and Edna Marie (née Conn) Tippett; m. Carlotta Prichard 1959; one s. one d.; ed. Wabash Coll.; Brand Man., Advertising Supervisor, Procter & Gamble, Cincinnati 1958–64; Advertising and Sales Promotion Man. Ford Motor Co., Dearborn, Mich. 1964–65, Gen. Marketing Man. 1965–69; Advertising Man. Ford Div. 1969–70, Advertising and Sales Promotion Man. 1970–72; Vice-Pres. Product and Marketing Philco-Ford Corpn., Philadelphia 1972–73; Dir. Sales and Marketing Ford (Europe) Inc., Brentwood, Essex, England 1973–75; Pres. and Dir. STP Corpn., Fort Lauderdale, Fla. 1975–76; Exec. Vice-Pres. and Dir. Singer Co., New York 1976–78; Pres., C.O.O. and Dir. American Motors Corpn., Southfield, Mich. 1978–82, Chair. and C.E.O. 1982–85; Pres. and Dir. Springs Industries 1985–; Dir. Barry Wright Corpn. *Address:* Springs Industries, Inc., P.O. Box 70, Fort Mill, S.C. 29715, U.S.A. *Telephone:* (803) 547-3777.

TIRIKATENE-SULLIVAN, The Hon. Tini Whetu Marama, B.A., DIP.SOC.-SCI., F.R.A.I.; New Zealand social worker and politician; b. 9 Jan. 1932, Ratana Pa, Via Wanganui; d. of the late Hon. Sir Eruera Tirikatene and of Lady Tirikatene; m. Dr. Denis Sullivan; one s. one d.; ed. Rangiora High School, Victoria Univ. of Wellington, Nat. Univ. of Australia; Sec. N.Z. Labour Party's Maori Policy Cttee. 1949–60, Jt. Sec. 1960–63, 1963–65, Exec. mem. 1967–, Chair. 1979–86; Sec., Royal Tour Staff for visit of H.M. Queen Elizabeth II and H.R.H. The Duke of Edinburgh 1953–54; fmr. Social Worker, Depts. of Maori Affairs, Social Security and Child Welfare; mem. for Southern Maori House of Reps. 1967–; Minister of Tourism 1972–75; Assoc. Minister of Social Welfare 1972–74; Minister for the Environment 1974–75; Diploma in Social Sciences. *Leisure interests:* research (historical, political, social and scriptural), tutoring Christian youth leaders. *Address:* Parliament House, Wellington, New Zealand. *Telephone:* 749-199.

TIRIMO, Martino, DIP. R.A.M., F.R.A.M.; British (b. Greek/British) concert pianist and conductor; b. 19 Dec. 1942, Larnaca, Cyprus; s. of Dimitri Tirimo and Marina Tirimo; m. Mione J. Teakle 1973; one s. one d.; ed. Bedales School, England (Cyprus Govt. Scholarship), Royal Acad. of Music, London (Liszt Scholarship, etc.), Vienna State Acad. (Boise Foundation Scholarship); first public recital, Cyprus 1949; conducted 7 performances of La Traviata with singers and musicians from La Scala, Milan, at Cyprus Opera Festival 1955; Fifth Prize Beethoven Competition, Vienna 1965; London début 1965; Jt. Winner Munich Int. Piano Competition 1971; Winner Geneva Int. Piano Competition 1972; gave first public performance of Schubert complete piano sonatas cycle, London 1975 and 1985; first public performance of Beethoven complete piano concertos cycle directed from keyboard in two consecutive evenings, Dresden 1985, London 1986; first performance Tippett Piano Concerto in Denmark 1986, in G.D.R. 1987; concerts and recitals, radio and TV appearances U.S.A., Canada, U.K. and many E. and W. European countries 1965–; recordings include Enjoying Chopin, Early Schubert Sonatas, Brahms 1st and 2nd Piano Concertos, Rachmaninov 2nd Concerto and Paganini Rhapsody; Gulbenkian Foundation Fellowship 1967–69. *Leisure interests:* chess, reading, philosophy, theatre, badminton. *Address:* 2 Combemartin Road, London, SW18 5PR, England. *Telephone:* 01-788 2710.

TISCH, Laurence Alan, M.A.; American business executive; b. 15 March 1923, New York; s. of Al Tisch and Sadye Brenner; m. Wilma Stein 1948; four s.; ed. New York Univ., Univ. of Pa. and Harvard Law School; Pres. Tisch Hotels Inc., New York 1946–; Chair. Exec. Cttee. Loews Theaters Inc. (now Loews Corpn.), New York 1959–65, Chair. of Bd. 1960–, Pres. 1965–69, C.E.O. 1969–; Chair. and C.E.O. CBS Inc. New York 1986–; Chair. CNA Finance Corpn. (subsidiary of Loews Corpn.), Chicago; Chair. Bd. CNA; Dir. Automatic Data Processing Corpn., CBS. *Address:* Loews Corporation, 666 Fifth Avenue, New York, N.Y. 10103 (Office); Island Drive, North Manursing Island, Rye, N.Y. 10580, U.S.A. (Home).

TISHCHENKO, Boris Ivanovich; Soviet composer; b. 23 March 1939, Leningrad; s. of Ivan I. and Zinaida A. Tischenko; m. Irina A. Donskaya

1977; three s.; ed. Leningrad Conservatory, with post-grad. course under D. D. Shostakovich; Prof. at Leningrad Conservatory; Sec. R.S.F.S.R. Composers Union; 1st Prize, Int. Contest of Young Composers, Prague 1966, Winner State Award M.I. Glinka 1978, People's Artist of R.S.F.S.R. 1986; *Compositions include:* The Stolen Sun (opera) 1968, The Twelve (ballet) 1963, Jaroslavna (The Eclipse) 1974, Lenin Lives (cantata) 1959, Requiem (words by A. Akhmatova) 1966; *symphonies:* French Symphony 1958, Sinfonia Robusta 1970, Violin Symphony (2nd Violin Concerto) 1981, The Siege Chronicle 1984; also Concertos for violin, piano, cello, flute and harp 1962–77, Piano Quintet 1985, String Quartets 1957–84, orchestral and instrumental suites and pieces, song cycles, choral works, music for drama productions and films. *Address:* Korablestroitelj Street, 37-1-573, Leningrad, 199397, U.S.S.R. *Telephone:* 351-23-41.

TISHLER, Max, M.S., PH.D.; American organic and medicinal chemist and university professor; b. 30 Oct. 1906, Boston, Mass.; s. of Samuel and Anna Gray Tishler; m. Elizabeth M. Verveer 1934; two s.; ed. Tufts Coll. and Harvard Univ.; Research Assoc. Harvard Univ. 1934–36, Instructor in Chem. 1936–37; Research Chemist Merck & Co., Inc. 1937–41, Section Head in charge of Process Devt. 1941–44, Dir. of Devt. Research 1944–53, Vice-Pres. for Scientific Activities 1954–56; Vice-Pres. and Exec. Dir. Merck Sharp & Dohme Research Labs. Div. 1956–57, Pres. 1957–69; mem. Bd. of Dirs. Merck & Co. Inc. 1962–70, Sr. Vice-Pres. Research and Devt. 1969–70; Prof. of Sciences, Wesleyan Univ. Middletown, Conn. 1970–72, Univ. Prof. 1972–75, Prof. Emer. 1975–, Chair. Dept. of Chem. 1973–75; Co-Ed. Chemistry and the Economy, American Chemical Soc.; mem. Editorial Bd. Separation Science, Clinical Pharmacology and Therapeutics; mem. Science Bd. of Govs. Weizmann Inst.; Trustee Tufts Univ., Union Coll.; mem. numerous advisory councils and cttees. of various educational orgs.; fmr. mem. Bd. of Dirs. and Awards Cttee. Industrial Research Inst., Asscn. Harvard Chemists (Pres. 1946); mem. Council for Analysis and Projections, American Cancer Soc. 1973–, Bd. Scientific Advisers, Sloan Kettering Inst. 1974–80, Research and Devt. Section Pharmaceutical Manufacturers Asscn., etc.; mem. N.A.S., American Acad. of Arts and Sciences, A.A.A.S., American Chem. Soc. (Chair. Organic Chem. Div. 1951, Pres. 1972), Soc. of Chemical Industry (Chair. American Section 1966–67, Hon. Vice-Pres. 1968), American Inst. of Chemists, N.Y. Acad. of Sciences, Chem. Soc. (London), Chem. Soc. of Japan, Swiss Chem. Soc., Conn. Acad. of Arts and Sciences, hon. mem. Soc. Chimique de France, American Pharmaceutical Asscn., Chemist Club, New York; Fellow, Acad. of Pharmaceutical Sciences and Eng., Conn. Acad. of Science and Eng.; Life Fellow, American Inst. of Chemists 1977; Hon. Fellow, Royal Soc. of Chem. 1981; Dir. Royal Soc. of Medicine Foundation; Hon. D.Sc. (Tufts, Bucknell, Philadelphia Coll. of Pharmacy and Science, Upsala Coll., Univ. of Strathclyde, Rider Coll., Fairfield Univ., Wesleyan Univ.); Hon. D.Eng. (Stevens Inst. of Tech.); numerous honours and awards including Industrial Research Inst. Award 1961, Chem. Industry Medal of Soc. of Chem. Industry 1963, Chem. Pioneer Award of American Inst. of Chemists 1968, Priestley Medal of American Chem. Soc. 1970, Gold Medal of American Inst. of Chemists 1977, C. Chester Stock Award of Sloan Kettering Inst. 1984, Nat. Medal of Science 1987. *Publications:* Co-author: Chemistry of Organic Compounds 1937; Streptomycin 1949; Editor-in-Chief, Organic Syntheses Vol. 39; over 100 scientific publs. in the fields of vitamins, steroids, antibiotics, sulfonamides. *Leisure interest:* horticulture.
[*Died 18 March 1989.*]

TITHERIDGE, John Edward, PH.D., F.R.S.N.Z.; New Zealand research scientist; b. 12 June 1932, Auckland; s. of Leslie Edward Titheridge and Clarice Muriel Barnes; m. Patricia Joy Brooker 1970; one s. one d.; ed. Avondale Coll., Univ. of Auckland and Univ. of Cambridge; Research Fellow Univ. of Auckland 1960–, Sr. Research Fellow 1961, Assoc. Prof. 1967–; Cheeseman-Pond Memorial Prize 1962, Mechaelis Memorial Prize 1972, N.Z. Geophysics Prize, Wellington Branch Royal Soc. of N.Z. 1977. *Publications:* 90 refereed scientific papers 1959–87. *Leisure interests:* music, photography, reading. *Address:* Physics Department, University of Auckland, Auckland (Office); 1500 Dominion Road, Auckland 4, New Zealand (Home). *Telephone:* (64-09) 737-999 Ext. 8866 (Office); (64-09) 696-231 (Home).

TITOV, Lieut.-Gen. Herman Stepanovich; Soviet air force officer and cosmonaut; b. 11 Sept. 1935, Attaiski Krai; s. of Stepan Pavlovich Titov and Alexandra Mikhailovna Titova; m. Tamara Vasilevna; two d.; ed. secondary school, Stalingrad (now Volgograd) Pilots' School and Zhukovsky Air Force Eng. Acad.; training for space flight 1960–61; in space-ship Vostok II circled earth 17 times during a journey of 25 hours 11 minutes 6-7 Aug. 1961; mem. Young Communists' League; Cand. mem. CP until 1961, mem. 1961–; graduate, Zhukovsky Air Force Eng. Acad. 1968; K.E. Voroshilov Acad. of Gen. Staff 1972–; Deputy, Supreme Soviet of U.S.S.R. 1962–70; Major-Gen. of Air Force 1975–79, Lieut.-Gen. 1979–; Pres. Viet-Nam-Soviet Friendship Soc., Fed. of Aerial Views of Sport; Hon. Master of Sport of U.S.S.R.; Hero Soviet Union 1961, Order of Lenin (twice), Gold Star Medal, Order of the Workers' Red Flag, Hero of Mongolian People's Repub., Hero of Labour of Viet-Nam, Hero of Socialist Labour of Bulgaria and other awards. *Publications:* 700,000 km. in Space 1961, Seventeen Cosmic Dawns 1963, Aviation and Cosmonautics 1963, My Sky-blue Planet

1973. *Leisure interests:* hunting, fishing, theatre. *Address:* Zvezdny Gorodok, Moscow, U.S.S.R.

TITOV, Yuriy Evlampevich; Soviet gymnast; b. 27 Nov. 1935, Omsk; all-round champion of U.S.S.R. 1958, 1961, of Europe 1959 and the world 1962; Honoured Master of Sports 1956; Olympic gymnastics champion 1956; won 13 gold medals at European, world championships and Olympic Games; int. class judge 1968; mem. CPSU 1969; Pres. World Gymnastic Fed. 1976–; three orders and various medals. *Publication:* Summa Ballov 1971.

TITS, Jacques Léon, DR.SC.; French professor of group theory; b. 12 Aug. 1930, Uccle, Belgium; s. of Léon Tits and Louisa (née André) Tits; m. Marie-Jeanne Dieuaide 1956; ed. Univ. of Brussels; Asst. Univ. of Brussels 1956–57, in-charge of course 1957–62, Prof. 1962–64; Prof. Univ. of Bonn 1964–74; Assoc. Prof. Coll. de France, Paris 1973–74, Titular Prof. of Theory of Groups 1975–; Visiting Teacher and Prof. Eidgenössische Technische Hochschule, Zürich 1950, 1951, 1953, Inst. of Advanced Study, Princeton 1951–52, 1963, 1969, 1971–72, Univ. of Rome 1955, 1956, Univ. of Chicago 1963, Univ. of Calif., Berkeley 1963, Univs. of Tokyo and Kyoto 1971, Yale Univ. 1966–67, 1976, 1980, 1984; mem. Cttee. for editing of periodicals and scientific works; Ed.-in-Chief Math. Publs. of IHES 1980–; attended Int. Congresses of Mathematicians, Stockholm 1962, Nice 1970, Vancouver 1974; lecture tours in U.S.A., U.K., Israel, etc.; mem. Deutsche Akad. der Naturforscher Leopoldina 1977; Corresp. mem. Acad. des Sciences, Paris 1977, mem. 1979; Foreign mem. Royal Netherlands Acad. of Arts and Sciences 1988; Dr. h.c. (Utrecht) 1970, (Ghent) 1979, (Bonn) 1987; Prix scientifique Interfacultaire L. Empain 1955, Prix Wettrems, Acad. de Belgique 1958, Grand Prix des Sciences mathématiques et physiques, Acad. des Sciences 1976. *Publications:* c. 150 scientific papers. *Leisure interests:* languages, literature, arts. *Address:* Collège de France, 11 Place Marcélin-Bertholdt, 75231 Paris, Cedex 05 (Office); 12 rue de Moulin des Prés, 75013 Paris, France (Home). *Telephone:* 43291211 (Office); 45889603 (Home).

TITTERTON, Sir Ernest William, Kt., C.M.G., M.SC., PH.D., F.A.A., F.R.S.A.; British nuclear physicist; b. 4 March 1916, Tamworth; s. of William A. and Elizabeth Titterton; m. Peggy E. Johnson 1942; one s. two d.; ed. Queen Elizabeth's Grammar School, Tamworth and Univ. of Birmingham; Research Officer, Admiralty 1939–43; mem. U.K. team developing nuclear weapon, Los Alamos, U.S.A. 1943–47, Head, Electronics Div., Los Alamos Lab. 1946; Research Group Leader, Atomic Energy Research Lab., Harwell 1947–50; Foundation Prof. of Nuclear Physics, A.N.U. 1950–81, Dean Research School of Physical Sciences 1965–68, Dir. 1968–73, Prof. Emer. and Hon. Research Fellow 1982–. *Publications:* Facing the Atomic Future 1955, Uranium: Energy Source of the Future? 1979; 231 papers in international scientific journals on nuclear physics, accelerators and electronics. *Leisure interests:* piano and classical organ playing, gardening. *Address:* 21 Gilmore Crescent, Garran, Canberra, A.C.T. 2605, Australia. *Telephone:* (062) 812164.

TIWARI, Narayan Datt, M.A.; Indian politician; b. 18 Oct. 1925, Balyuti, Nainital Dist., U.P.; s. of Poorna Nand Tiwari; m. Sushila Tiwari 1954; ed. Allahabad Univ.; joined Indian Freedom Movt. aged 13; joined "Quit India Movt." 1942; imprisoned for 15 months; Pres. Allahabad Univ. Students' Union 1947; Sec. Political Sufferers' Distress Relief Soc.; Ed. Hindi monthly Prabhat; mem. U.P. Ass. 1952–; Leader of Opposition and Chair. Public Accounts Cttee. 1957; mem. U.P. Vidhan Sabha 1969; Minister for Planning, Labour and Panchayats, also Deputy Chair. State Planning Comm., Govt. of U.P. 1969, Minister for Finance and Parl. Affairs 1970–76, for Heavy Industries and Cane Devt. 1973–76; Chief Minister of U.P. 1976–77, 1984–85, June 1988–; Leader of Opposition (U.P. Congress (I) Legis. Party) 1977–80; mem. Lok Sabha 1980–; Minister of Planning, Govt. of India 1980–81, of Labour 1980–82, of Industry 1981–84, 1985–86, of External Affairs 1986–87, of Finance and Commerce 1987–88, of Steel and Mines 1982–83. *Publication:* European Miscellany. *Address:* 2 Jantar Mantar Road, New Delhi 11001, India.

TIXIER, Claude, L. ÉS L., D. ÉS D.; French economist; b. 22 Nov. 1913, Paris; m. Simone Lamy 1939; two s. three d.; ed. Arts and Law Faculties and Ecole des Sciences Politiques, Univ. of Paris; Deputy Insp. of Finances 1939, Insp. of Finances 1942; Deputy Dir. to Ministry of Nat. Economy 1945; Chief, Service of Econ. Survey 1946; Dir. Cabinet of Sec. of State for the Budget 1947; Deputy Dir. Cabinet of Minister of Finances 1948; Dir. Cabinet of Prime Minister (Finances) 1948; Dir. Cabinet of Minister of Finances 1949; Dir.-Gen. of Finances to the Algerian Ministry, Algiers 1949–58; Vice-Pres. EIB 1958–62; Pres. and Dir.-Gen. Banque Industrielle de Financement et Crédit 1962–67; Vice-Pres. Banque Worms 1967–82; Pres. Unibail 1974–81, Hon. Pres. 1981–; Pres. Foncière 1978–81; Chevalier, Légion d'honneur. *Leisure interests:* theory of numbers, cosmology. *Address:* 5 square des Ecrivains Combattants, 75016 Paris, France (Home). *Telephone:* 4224-62-55.

TIZARD, Rt. Hon. Robert James, P.C., M.A.; New Zealand teacher and politician; b. 7 June 1924, Auckland; s. of Henry James and Jessie May Tizard (née Phillips); m. 1st Catherine Anne Maclean 1951 (dissolved 1983), one s. three d.; m. 2nd Mary Nacey 1983, one s.; ed. Auckland Grammar School, Auckland Univ.; served in R.N.Z.A.F., Canada, U.K. 1943–46; Jr. Lecturer in History, Auckland Univ. 1949–53, teaching posts 1955–57, 1961–62; M.P. 1957–60, 1963–; Minister of Health and State Services

1972–74; in charge of State Advances Corpn. 1972–73; Deputy Prime Minister, Minister of Finance 1974–75; Deputy Leader of Opposition 1975–79; Minister of Energy, Statistics, Science and Tech., Minister in Charge of Audit Dept. 1984–87, Minister of Defence, Science and Tech. 1987–. *Leisure interests:* golf, squash. *Address:* Parliament Buildings, Wellington; 8 Glendowie Road, Glendowie, Auckland, New Zealand (Home).

TJEKNAVORIAN, Loris-Zare; American (Armenian) composer and conductor; b. 13 Oct. 1937; s. of Haikaz and Adriné Tjeknavorian; m. Linda Pierce 1964 (divorced 1979); one s.; ed. Vienna Acad. of Music, Salzburg Mozarteum; studied with the late Carl Orff 1963–64; worked in U.S.A. until 1970; fmr. Teaching Fellow, Univ. of Michigan; fmr. Composer-in-Residence, Concordia Coll., Minnesota; Composer-in-Residence, Ministry of Culture and Fine Arts; Prin. Conductor, Teheran Opera 1972–79; artist with RCA 1976–; Composer-in-Residence American-Armenian Int. Coll., La Verne Univ., Calif. 1979–; principally associated with London Symphony Orchestra with whom he has recorded; Chair. Bd. of Trustees, Inst. of Armenian Music, London 1976–80; Order of Homayoun; several int. tours as a conductor. *Works include:* Requiem for the Massacred 1975, Simorgh (ballet music), Lake Van Suite, Erebouni for 12 strings 1978, a piano concerto, several operas, several chamber works, Credo Symphony Life of Christ (after medieval Armenian chants) 1976, Liturgical Mass, Violin Concerto, oratorios Lucifer's Fall and Book of Revelation, Mass in Memoriam 1985, Othello (ballet), ballet suites for orchestra, five symphonies. *Address:* c/o Thea Dispeker Artist Representative, 59 East 54th Street, New York, N.Y. 10022 (Agent); 347 West 57th Street, Apt. 37C, New York, N.Y. 10019, U.S.A. (Home). *Telephone:* (212) 421-7676 (Agent); (212) 397 0803 (Home).

TJIBAOU, Jean-Marie; Melanesian separatist leader; Leader Front de libération nat. Kanake Socialiste 1984–; Pres. N. Region.
[Died 4 May 1989.]

TLASS, Maj.-Gen. Mustapha el–; Syrian army officer and politician; b. 11 May 1932, Rastan City, Mouhafazat Homs; m. Lamyaa al-Jabri 1958; two s. two d.; ed. Mil. and Law Colls. and Voroshilov Acad., Moscow; active mem. Baath Arab Socialist Party 1947–, Sec. of Rastan Section 1951; Sports teacher, Al-Kraya School, Mouhafazat al-Soueda 1950–52; attended Mil. Coll. 1952–54; deputed to Egyptian army 1959–61; Insp. Ministry of Supply 1962; mem. Free Officers' Movement 1962–63, detained 1962–63; Commdr. Tank Bn. and Chief of Cen. Region of Nat. Security Court 1963; Chief of Staff, 5th Armoured Brigade 1964–66; mem. Regional Command, Regional Congress of Baath Arab Socialist Party 1965, 1968, 1969, 1975, of Politbureau 1969–, of Nat. Council of Revolution 1965–71; participated in movement of 23 Feb., promoted to Commdr. of Cen. Region and of 5th Armoured Brigade; rank of Lieut.-Gen. Feb. 1968, Chief of Staff of Armed Forces 1968–70, First Deputy Minister of Defence 1968–72; participated in correctional movement installing Pres. Hafez Al-Assad Nov. 1970; First Deputy C.-in-C. Armed Forces 1970–72, Deputy C.-in-C. 1972–; mem. People's Council 1971–; Minister of Defence 1972–, now also Deputy Prime Minister; Deputy Chief of Joint Supreme Mil. Council of Syrian and Egyptian Armed Forces 1973; 26 orders and medals. *Publications:* Guerilla War, Military Studies, An Introduction to Zionist Strategy, The Arab Prophet and Technique of War, The Armoured Brigade as an Advanced Guard, Bitter Memories in the Military Prison of Mezzah, The Fourth War between Arabs and Israel, The Second Chapter of the October Liberation War, Selections of Arab Poetry, The Steadfastness Front in confrontation with Camp David, The Algerian Revolution, Art of Soviet War, American Policy under the Carter Regime, The Technological Revolution and Development of the Armed Forces. *Leisure interests:* reading and writing books, military and historical studies. *Address:* Ministry of Defence, Damascus, Syria.

TLOU, Thomas, M.A.T., M.A., PH.D.; Botswana diplomatist and professor of history; b. 1 June 1932, Gwanda, S. Rhodesia (now Zimbabwe); s. of Malapela Tlou and Moloko Nare; m. Sheila Dinotshe 1977; two s. one d.; ed. schools in Rhodesia, Luther Coll., Decorah, Iowa, Johns Hopkins Univ., Baltimore and Univ. of Wisconsin; primary school teacher, Rhodesia 1957–62; lecturer in history, Luther Coll. 1969, Univ. of Wis. 1970–71; lecturer in history, Univ. of Botswana, Lesotho and Vice-Swaziland 1971, later Prof., Dean of Faculty of Humanities and Head of History; mem. Bd. Nat. Museum and Art Gallery of Botswana 1974–76, 1981–, mem. Univ. Senate and Council of UBLS 1974–76; Acting Dir. Nat. Research Inst. 1976; Perm. Rep. to UN 1977–80; Deputy Vice-Chancellor Univ. of Botswana 1980–, Vice-Chancellor 1984–, mem. Senate and Council of Univ. of Botswana and Swaziland (now Univ. of Botswana) 1980–, mem. Nat. Archives Advisory Council; mem. American-African Studies Asscn., life mem. Botswana Soc.; Hon. D.Litt. (Luther Coll.) 1978; Hon. LL.D. (Ohio) 1986; Chevalier, Ordre des Palmes Académiques 1982. *Publications:* History of Botswana (co-author), A Political History of North West Botswana 1750–1906, and several articles and book chapters on history of Botswana and Ngamiland. *Leisure interest:* swimming. *Address:* University of Botswana, P/B 0022, Gaborone, Botswana. *Telephone:* 52252.

TO HUU; Vietnamese poet and politician; b. 1920, Central Viet-Nam; poet and leading intellectual; in charge of propaganda and ideological training in Lao Dong Party (now CP of Viet-Nam); alt. mem. Politburo, CP of Viet-Nam 1976; Vice-Premier, Council of Ministers 1980–86; mem. Nat. Defence

Council 1981. *Address:* Central Committee of the Communist Party of Viet-Nam, No. 1-C, rue Hoang Van Thu, Hanoi, Viet-Nam.

TOBAR ZALDUMBIDE, Carlos; Ecuadorian diplomatist; b. 29 Dec. 1912, Quito; s. of Carlos Manuel Tobar-Borgoño and Rasorion Zaldumbide; m. Adela Eastmann 1939; one s. two d.; ed. Univ. of Paris-Sorbonne; diplomatic posts in Spain, Portugal, Brazil and Peru 1939–43, Under-Sec., Ministry of Foreign Affairs 1944–45, 1948–49, 1951, Sec.-Gen. of Public Admin. 1950, del. to UN conferences 1945, 1949; Minister of Foreign Affairs 1956–60; Amb. to France and mem. Consultative Cttee. for Foreign Affairs 1963–64; Perm. Rep. of Ecuador to UN 1986–; engaged in business in pvt. sector 1964–86; fmrly. Prof. of Diplomatic Theory and Practice, Cen. Univ. of Quito; Cross of Merit (Fed. Repub. of Germany), Great Gross San Lorenzo. *Address:* Permanent Mission of Ecuador to the United Nations, 820 Second Avenue, 15th Floor, New York, N.Y. 10017 U.S.A. *Telephone:* 986-6670, 6671.

TOBIAS, Phillip Vallentine, PH.D., D.SC., M.B.B.CH., F.R.S.S.AF., F.L.S.; South African professor of anatomy; b. 14 Oct. 1925, Durban; s. of the late Joseph Newman Tobias and Fanny Norden (née Rosendorff); ed. St. Andrew's School, Bloemfontein, Durban High School, Univ. of the Witwatersrand and Emmanuel Coll., Cambridge; Lecturer in Anatomy, Univ. of Witwatersrand 1951–52, Sr. Lecturer 1953, Prof. and Head of Anatomy Dept. 1959–, Dean of Faculty of Medicine 1980–82; Visiting Prof. Cambridge Univ.; founder Pres. Inst. for the Study of Man in Africa, Anatomical Soc. of Southern Africa, S. African Soc. for Quaternary Research; hon. mem. and mem. numerous int. asscns.; Fellow, Royal Anthropological Inst. of Great Britain and Ireland, Royal Soc. of S. Africa, Linnean Soc. of London; sometime Vice-Pres. and acting Exec. Pres. S. African Assen. for the Advancement of Science; Pres. Royal Soc. of S. Africa 1970–72; Perm. Council mem. Int. Union of Prehistoric and Protohistoric Sciences, Pan-African Congress of Prehistory and Quaternary Studies, Int. Asscn. of Human Biologists; Trustee, Leakey Foundation, Pasadena, Calif.; Hon. Prof. of Palaeo-anthropology, Bernard Price Inst. for Palaeontological Research; Hon. Prof. of Zoology; Hon. D.Sc. (Natal) 1980, (Cambridge) 1988, (Univ. of Western Ont.) 1986; Overseas Fellow, Austrian Acad. of Sciences 1978; Paul Harris Fellow of Rotary Int. 1981; British Asscn. Medal 1952; Simon Biesheuvel Medal 1966; South Africa Medal 1967; Sr. Captain Scott Medal 1973; Rivers Memorial Medal 1978, Anisfield-Wolf Award for Race Relations 1978, Percy Fox Foundation Award 1983, Phillip Tobias Medal 1983, Certificate of Honour, Univ. of Calif. 1983, Int. Balzan Foundation Prize 1987. *Publications:* Chromosomes, Sex-cells and Evolution 1956, Olduvai Gorge Vol. II 1967, Man's Anatomy (with M. Arnold) 1968, The Brain in Hominid Evolution 1971, The Meaning of Race 1972, The Bushmen 1978, Dart, Taung and the Missing Link 1984, Hominid Evolution: Past, Present and Future 1985; about 700 scientific and other publs. *Leisure interests:* archaeology, philately, music, books, people. *Address:* Department of Anatomy, University of the Witwatersrand Medical School, York Road, Parktown, 2193 Johannesburg (Office); 602 Marble Arch, 36 Goldreich Street, Hillbrow, Johannesburg, South Africa (Home). *Telephone:* 647-2405 (Office); 642-9176 (Home).

TOBIN, James, PH.D.; American economist; b. 5 March 1918, Champaign, Ill.; s. of late Louis Michael and of Margaret Edgerton; m. Elizabeth Ringo 1946; three s. one d.; ed. Harvard Univ.; U.S. Navy 1942–46; Teaching Fellow in Econs., Harvard Univ. 1946–47, Junior Fellow 1947–50; Assoc. Prof. of Econs., Yale Univ. 1950–55, Prof. 1955–, Dir. Cowles Foundation for Research in Econs., Yale Univ. 1955–61, Sterling Prof. of Econs., Yale Univ. 1957–88, Chair. Dept. of Econs. 1974–76, Prof. Emer. 1988–; Visiting Prof. Univ. of Nairobi, Kenya 1972–73; Ford Visiting Prof. Univ. of California, Berkeley Jan.–June 1983; mem. Pres.'s Council of Econ. Advisers 1961–62; Fellow American Acad. of Arts and Sciences, Econometric Soc.; mem. N.A.S. 1972–; Foreign Assoc. mem. Acad. das Ciències de Lisboa; Nobel Prize in Econs. 1981; numerous hon. degrees. *Publications:* National Economic Policy 1966, Essays in Economics Vol. I Macroeconomics 1972, Vol. II Consumption and Econometrics 1975, Vol. III Theory and Policy 1982, The New Economics One Decade Older 1974, Asset Accumulation and Economic Activity 1980, Policies for Prosperity: Essays in a Keynesian Mode 1987. *Leisure interests:* skiing, sailing, tennis. *Address:* Department of Economics, Yale University, Box 2125 Yale Station, New Haven, Conn. 06520 (Office); 117 Alden Avenue, New Haven, Conn. 06515 (Home). *Telephone:* 203-432-3720 (Office); 203-436-2330 (Home).

TODD, Baron (Life Peer), cr. 1962, of Trumpington in the County of Cambridge; **Alexander Robertus Todd,** O.M., D.SC., D.PHIL., F.R.S.; British chemist; b. 2 Oct. 1907, Glasgow; s. of Alexander Todd, J.P.; m. Alison Sarah Dale 1937 (deceased 1987); one s. two d.; ed. Glasgow, Frankfurt-am-Main and Oxford Univs.; Asst. in Medical Chem. 1934–35, Beit Memorial Research Fellow 1935–36, Edinburgh Univ.; mem. staff Lister Inst. Preventive Medicine, London 1936–38; Sir Samuel Hall Prof. of Chem. and Dir. Chemical Labs. Manchester Univ. 1938–44; Prof. Organic Chem. Cambridge Univ. 1944–71, Master, Christ's Coll. 1963–78; Man. Trustee, Nuffield Foundation 1950–73, Chair. 1973–79; Chair. Advisory Council on Scientific Policy 1952–64; Pres. Chemical Soc. 1960–62, 1981–82; Master, Salters' Co. 1961–62; Chancellor, Univ. of Strathclyde 1965–; Chair. Royal Comm. on Medical Educ. 1965–68; Chair. Govs. United Cambs. Hosps. 1969–74; Pres. Royal Soc. 1975–80; Chair. Croucher Foundation, Hong Kong 1980–89,

Pres. 1989–; Trustee, Ciba Foundation 1963–82; mem. Nat. Acad. of Sciences; Hon. mem. numerous insts. and acad. of sciences; Hon. LL.D. (Glasgow, Calif., Chinese Univ. of Hong Kong, Edinburgh and Manchester); Hon. D.Litt. (Sydney Univ., Widener Coll., Pa.); Hon. Dr.rer.nat. (Kiel); Hon. D.Sc. (Durham, London, Madrid, Exeter, Leicester, Melbourne, Aligarth, Wales, Yale, Sheffield, Harvard, Adelaide, Australian Nat. Univ. Liverpool, Oxford, Warwick, Paris, Michigan, Strasbourg, Strathclyde, Hokkaido, Philippines, Tufts, Hong Kong); Hon. Sc.D. (Cambridge); awarded Meldola Medal 1936; Lavoisier Medal, French Chemical Soc. 1948; Davy Medal of Royal Soc. 1949; Royal Medal 1955; Nobel Prize for Chem. 1957; Cannizzaro Medal, Italian Chemical Soc. 1958; Longstaff Medal, Chemical Soc. of London 1963; Copley Medal, Royal Soc. 1970, Hanbury Medal, Pharmacological Soc. of G.B. 1986; Ordre pour le Mérite (Fed. Repub. of Germany); Second Class Order of Rising Sun (Japan); Lomonosov Gold Medal (U.S.S.R.) 1979. *Address:* Christ's College, Cambridge, CB2 3BU, England.

TODD, Olivier, M.A.; French writer; b. 19 June 1929, Neuilly; s. of Julius Oblatt and Helen Todd; m. 1st Anne-Marie Nizan 1948, 2nd France Huser 1982; two s. two d.; ed. Sorbonne, Corpus Christi Coll., Cambridge; teacher Lycée Int. du Shape 1956–62; Univ. Asst. Saint-Cloud 1962–64; reporter Nouvel Observateur 1964–69; Ed. TV Programme Panorama 1969–70; Asst. Ed. Nouvel Observateur 1970–77; columnist and Man. Ed. L'Express 1977–81; worked for BBC (Europa, 24 Hours) 1964–69; Prix Cazes 1981. *Publications:* Une demi-campagne 1957, La traversée de la Manche 1960, Des trous dans le Jardin 1969, L'année du Crabe 1972, Les Paumes 1973, Les Canards de Ca Mao 1975, La marelle de Giscard 1977, Portraits 1979, Un fils rebelle 1981, Un cannibale très convenable 1982, Une légère gueule de Bois 1983, La balade du chômeur 1986, Cruel Avril 1987. *Leisure interest:* walking. *Address:* 12, Rue de Tournon, 75006 Paris; 8, Rue du Pin, 83310 La Garde Freinet, France. *Telephone:* (43) 25-98-65; (94) 43-63-34.

TODD, Hon. Sir (Reginald Stephen) Garfield, Kt., D.D.; Zimbabwean rancher and politician; b. 13 July 1908, Invercargill, New Zealand; s. of Thomas and Edith Todd; m. Jean Grace Wilson; three d.; ed. Otago Univ., Glen Leith Theological Coll. and Univ. of Witwatersrand, S.A.; worked with Thomas Todd & Sons Ltd., Invercargill, N.Z.; Supt. Dadaya Mission, Southern Rhodesia 1934–53, Chair. Governing Bd. 1963–85; M.P. for Shabani 1946–58; Pres. United Rhodesia Party 1953–58; Prime Minister 1953–58; Minister of Labour 1954–58, of Native Educ. 1955–57, of Labour and Social Welfare 1958; f. (with Sir John Moffat) Cen. Africa Party 1959, Pres. 1959–60; f. New African Party, July 1961; Dir. Hokonui Ranching Co. Ltd.; restricted to his ranch for 12 months Oct. 1965; imprisoned Jan. 1972, under house arrest 1972–76; Adviser to Joshua Nkomo (q.v.) at Constitutional Conf. on Rhodesia, Geneva 1976; mem. Senate 1980–85; Hon. LL.D.; received medal from Pope Paul for efforts for peace and justice in Southern Rhodesia 1973. *Leisure interest:* ranching. *Address:* P.O. Dadaya, Zimbabwe. *Telephone:* 231722 Zvishavane.

TODD, Richard Andrew Palethorpe; British actor and producer; b. 11 June 1919, Dublin, Ireland; s. of Major A. W. and Marvilla Palethorpe Todd (née Agar-Daly); m. 1st Catherine Stewart Crawford Grant-Bogle 1949 (divorced 1970), one s. one d.; m. 2nd Virginia Anne Rollo Mailer 1970, two s.; ed. Shrewsbury, privately; began theatrical career, London 1937; founder-mem. Dundee Repertory Co. 1938–39, rejoined 1947; served in King's Own Yorkshire Light Infantry and Parachute Regt. 1940–46; entered film industry in For Them That Trespass 1948. *Other films include:* The Hasty Heart 1949, Stage Fright 1950, Lightning Strikes Twice (U.S.A.) 1951, Robin Hood 1952, Twenty-Four Hours of a Woman's Life, The Venetian Bird 1953, Rob Roy 1954, The Sword and the Rose 1954, The Dam Busters 1955, A Man Called Peter 1955, The Virgin Queen (U.S.A.) 1955, The Sixth of June, Yangtse Incident 1956, Saint Joan, Chase a Crooked Shadow 1957, The Naked Earth, Danger Within 1958, The Long, the Short and the Tall 1959, Don't Bother to Knock (for own film co. Haileywood Films Ltd.) 1960, The Hellions 1960, Never Let Go 1961, The Longest Day 1962, The Boys 1962, Sanders 1963, Operation Crossbow 1965, Coast of Skeletons 1965, The Last of the Long-Haired Boys 1968, Dorian Gray 1970, Asylum 1972; returned to London stage as Lord Goring (An Ideal Husband), tour of S.A. 1965, Nicholas Randolph (Dear Octopus), Haymarket 1967; formed Triumph Theatre Production 1970, appeared in numerous productions in Britain, as the Comte (The Marquise), U.S.A. 1972, as Andrew Wyke (Sleuth), Australia and New Zealand 1972–73, English tour 1976, R.S.C. productions of The Hollow Crown and Pleasure and Repentance, Canada and U.S.A. 1974, as Martin Dysart (Equus) for Australian Nat. Theatre Co., Perth Festival 1975, toured as John (Miss Adams Will Be Waiting) 1975, toured S.A. in On Approval 1976, in Quadrille 1977, The Heat of the Moment 1977, appeared in Double Edge in U.K. and Canada 1978, in Nightfall, South Africa 1979, in This Happy Breed, U.K. 1980; The Business of Murder (Duchess Theatre 1981, Mayfair Theatre 1981–88). *TV appearances include:* Wuthering Heights, Dr. Who; nominated for Best Actor Award, Acad. Awards 1950, won British Nat. Film Award, Picturegoer Award, Hollywood Golden Globe; Past Grand Steward, Grand Lodge of England, Past Master Lodge of Emulation No. 21. *Publications:* Caught in the Act (Vol. I of autobiog.) 1986, In Camera (Vol. II of autobiog.) 1989. *Leisure interests:* game shooting, fishing, gardening. *Address:* Chinham Farm, Faringdon, Oxon., SN7 8E2, England. *Telephone:* 03677 284.

TODD, Ronald (Ron); British trade union official; b. 11 March 1927, Walthamstow; s. of George and Emily Todd; m. Josephine Tarrant 1945; one s. two d.; ed. St. Patrick's School, Walthamstow; served Royal Marine Commandos; joined Transport and Gen. Workers' Union (T&GWU) while employee of Ford Motor Co., Deputy Convenor 1954–62, full-time Union Officer, Metal, Eng. and Chemical Sections 1962–69, Regional Officer 1969–75, Regional Secretary, Region No. 1 1976–78, Nat. Organiser 1978–84, Gen. Sec. 1985–; mem. TUC Gen. Council, TUC Econ. Cttee., Equal Rights, Health Service Cttees., TUC Gen. Council mem. of NEDC, TUC/Labour Party Liaison Cttee.; Chair. TUC Int. Cttee.; Commr. on Manpower Services Comm.; Pres. Unity Trust; Hon. Vice-Pres. Campaign for Nuclear Disarmament, Nat. Cttee. World Disarmament Campaign; Trades Union rep. Anti-Apartheid Cttee., T&GWU rep. on Nat. Union of Mineworkers Dispute Co-ordinating Cttee. *Leisure interests:* palaeontology and collecting Victorian music covers. *Address:* Transport and General Workers' Union, Transport House, Smith Square, London, SW1P 3JB; 20 Manor Road, Walthamstow, London, E.17, England. *Telephone:* 01-828 7788 (Office); 01-527 0274 (Home).

TODOROV, Stanko; Bulgarian politician; b. 10 Dec. 1920, Pernik Region; m. Sonya Todorova 1947; two s.; active in Resistance Movement 1941–44; mem. Nat. Ass.; Minister of Agric. 1952–58; Sec. Central Cttee. Bulgarian C.P. 1958–59, 1966–71; Full mem. Politburo 1961–88; Deputy Prime Minister 1959–66; Perm. Bulgarian Representative to Council for Mutual Econ. Assistance (COMECON) 1962–66; Chair. Council of Ministers 1971–81; Chair. Nat. Ass. 1981–; Order of the October Revolution 1981. *Address:* Narodno Sobranie, Sofia, Bulgaria.

TOENNIES, Jan Peter, PH.D.; American physicist; b. 3 May 1930, Philadelphia, Pa.; s. of Dr. Gerrit Toennies and Dita Jebens; m. Monika Zelesnick 1966; two d.; ed. Amherst Coll., Brown Univ.; Asst., Bonn Univ., Fed. Repub. of Germany 1962–65, Privat dozent 1965–67, Dozent 1967–69; Scientific mem. and Dir. Max-Planck-Inst. für Strömungsforschung (Fluid Dynamics) 1969; Assoc. Prof. Göttingen Univ. 1971–; Hon. Prof. Bonn Univ. 1971; Physics Prize, Göttingen Acad. of Sciences 1964. *Publications:* Chemical Reactions in Shock Waves (with E.F. Greene) 1964, A Study of Intermolecular Potentials with Molecular Beams at Thermal Energies (with H. Pauly) in Advances in Atomic and Molecular Physics 1965, Molecular Beam Scattering Experiments, contribution in Physical Chemistry, an Advanced Treatise 1974, Rotationally and Vibrationally Inelastic Scattering of Molecules 1974, Scattering Studies of Rotational and Vibrational Excitation of Molecules (with M. Faubel) 1977, Advances in Atomic and Molecular Physics 1977. *Leisure interest:* sailing. *Address:* Max-Planck-Institut für Strömungsforschung, Bunsenstrasse 10, 3400 Göttingen (Office); Ewaldstrasse 7, 3400 Göttingen, Federal Republic of Germany (Home). *Telephone:* 0551-7092600 (Office); 0551-57172 (Home).

TOEPLITZ, Jerzy, O.A., LL.B., PH.D.; Polish film critic and historian; b. 24 Nov. 1909, Kharkov, U.S.S.R.; s. of Teodor and Helena Toeplitz; m. Izabella Stanisława Górnicka 1943; three d.; ed. Warsaw Univ.; co-founder "Start" (film asscn.) 1929, Sec. and Vice-Pres. 1930–34; film work in England and Italy 1934–37; mem. Cen. Council for Film Industry 1938; Rector and Prof. State Theatrical and Film Higher School, Łódź 1949–52, 1957–68; Pres. Int. Fed. of Film Archives (FIAF) 1948–72, Hon. mem. 1972–; Vice-Pres. Int. Film and Television Council 1966–72; mem. Int. Bureau of Historical Research 1952–; mem. Jury, Int. Film Festival, Karlovy Vary 1951, 1952, and 1956, Venice Documentary Film Festival 1957, 1962, Cannes 1958, 1965, Venice 1960, 1964, Mar del Plata 1961, Moscow 1959, 1961, Bergamo 1963, 1964, Florence 1965, Cracow 1964, 1965, San Sebastian 1966, New Delhi 1969; Dir. Inst. of Art, Polish Academy of Sciences 1961–68; Visiting Prof. Univ. of Calif. 1967; Head of Cinema Dept., Inst. of Art 1968–72, Prof. Emer. 1973–; Vice-Pres. CILECT (Centre Int. de Liaison des Ecoles et de Télévision) 1976–79, Hon. mem. 1981–; Dir. Australian Film and Television School, Sydney (retd. 1979); decorations include Commdr. Cross of Order Polonia Restituta, Raymond Langford Award 1979; Hon. Officer, Order of Australia 1986. *Publications:* Historia Sztuki Filmowej (History of Cinematographic Art) Vol. I 1955, Vol. II 1956, Vol. III 1959, Vol. IV 1969, Vol. V 1971, Vol. VI 1989, Film i telewizja w U.S.A. (Film and T.V. in U.S.A.) 1963, Nowy Film Amerykański 1973, Hollywood and After 1974. *Leisure interests:* music, walking, lectures. *Address:* Al. Armii Ludowej 6 m. 165, 00-571 Warsaw, Poland (Home). *Telephone:* 21-63-65.

TOH CHIN CHYE, PH.D.; Singapore physiologist and politician; b. 10 Dec. 1921, Malaya; s. of Toh Kim Poh and Tan Chuan Bee; m. Yeapp Sui Phek; one d.; ed. Raffles Coll., Singapore, Univ. Coll., London Univ., and National Inst. for Medical Research, London; Founder, People's Action Party, Chair. 1954–; Reader in Physiology, Univ. of Singapore 1958–64; Research Assoc., Univ. of Singapore 1964; Deputy Prime Minister of Singapore 1959–68; Minister for Science and Tech. 1968–75, for Health 1975–81; M.P. Singapore 1959–88; Chair. Bd. of Govs., Singapore Polytechnic 1959–75; Vice-Chancellor, Univ. of Singapore 1968–75; Chair. of Bd. of Govs. Regional Inst. for Higher Educ. and Devt. 1970–75; Chair. Applied Research Corpn. 1973–75; Hon. D.Litt. (Univ. of Singapore) 1976. *Publi-*

cations: papers in journals of physiology, etc. *Leisure interests:* golf, reading. *Address:* 23 Greenview Crescent, Singapore 1128, Singapore.

TOIVO, Andimba (Herman) Toivo ja; Namibian politician; b. 22 Aug. 1924, Omungundu, Ovamboland; four c.; ed. St. Mary's Mission School, Odanga; taught at St. Mary's Mission School, Odanga; served in S.A. Army 1942–45; worked in S.A. gold mines and on railways; mem. Modern Youth Soc.; deported to Ovamboland 1958; f. (with Sam Nujoma) S.W. African People's Org. (SWAPO); arrested 1966; sentenced to 20 years' imprisonment, Robben Island 1968; released in Windhoek, Namibia 1984; mem. Politburo and Sec.-Gen. SWAPO 1984–; leader SWAPO del. to UN 1984.

TOKAREV, Aleksandr Maksimovich; Soviet politician; b. 27 Nov. 1921; ed. Kuibyshev Inst. of Construction Engineers; mem. CPSU 1942–; Soviet Army service 1940–45; Komsomol Leader 1949–51; Sec. Stavropol, later First Sec. Novo Kuibyshev City Cttees. of CPSU 1951–55; Sec. Kuibyshev Regional Cttee. of CPSU 1958–59; Chair. Exec. Cttee. Kuibyshev Regional Soviet of Working People's Deputies 1959–63; First Sec. Kuibyshev Regional Cttee. of CPSU 1963–67; Minister of Industrial Construction, U.S.S.R. 1967–84; mem. Cen. Cttee. CPSU 1966–; Deputy to U.S.S.R. Supreme Soviet 1962–; Order of Lenin (four times), Order of Red Banner and other decorations. *Address:* U.S.S.R. Ministry of Industrial Construction, Moscow, U.S.S.R.

TŐKEI, Ferenc, M.A., D.LITT.SC.; Hungarian philosopher and sinologue; b. 3 Oct. 1930, Budapest; s. of Ferenc Tőkei and Irma Kiss; m. Margit Egry; two s. one d.; ed. Eötvös Loránd Univ. Budapest; on staff Hopp Ferenc Museum of East-Asian Arts, Budapest 1956–57; Ed. Europa Publishing House, Budapest 1957–67; acad. researcher 1967–69; Dir. Inst. of Philosophy, Hungarian Acad. of Sciences 1969–73; corresp. mem. of Acad. 1971–; Head of Orientalistic Research Group 1972–; Chair. Hungarian Philosophical Asscn. 1987–; mem. Bd. Kőrösi Csoma Soc., ed. Acta Orient.; Pres. Cttee. for Orientalistic Studies, Hungarian Acad. of Sciences 1976–86; Prof. of Philosophy Eötvös L. Univ. Budapest 1970–; mem. Cen. Cttee. H.S.W.P. 1988–; State Prize Award 1986. *Publications:* A kinai elégia születése 1959, Naissance de l'élégie chinoise 1967, Áz ázsiai termelési mód kérdéséhez 1965, Zur Frage der asiatischen Produktionsweise 1969, Műfajelmélet Kinában a III-VI. században 1967, Kinai filozófia, Ókor 1962–67, 1980, Vázlatok a kinai irodalomról 1970, A szépség szive 1973, Sinológiai mühley 1973, A társadalmi formák marxista elméletének néhány kérdése 1977, Kortársunk-e Marx? 1984–. *Leisure interests:* travelling, tourism. *Address:* 1022 Budapest, Fenvinci ut 22, Hungary. *Telephone:* 36/1/ 356-244.

TOKOMBAYEVA, Aysylu Asanbekovna; Soviet ballerina; b. 1947, Kirghizia; ed. Vaganova Dancing School, Leningrad; soloist with Theatre of Kirghizia 1966–; mem. CPSU 1973–; *major roles include:* Odette-Odile (Swan Lake); Aurore (Sleeping Beauty); Giselle; Bayadère: Frigia (Spartacus); Lady Macbeth (by K. Molchanov); U.S.S.R. State Prize 1976; People's Artist of Kirghizia 1976; U.S.S.R. People's Artist 1981.

TOL SAUT (see Pol Pot).

TOLBA, Mostafa Kamal, D.I.C., PH.D.; Egyptian scientist, administrator and international official; b. 8 Dec. 1922, Gharbiah; s. of Kamel Tolba and Shafika Abu Samra; m. Saneya Tolba (née Zaki Labib); ed. Cairo Univ., Imperial Coll., London; Asst. Lecturer, later Lecturer and Prof. of Microbiology, Cairo Univ., Egyptian Nat. Research Centre and Baghdad Univ., Iraq 1943–59; Asst. Sec.-Gen., later Sec.-Gen. Supreme Science Council, Egypt 1959–63; Cultural Counsellor and Dir. Egyptian Educ. Bureau, Washington, D.C., U.S.A. 1963–65; Under-Sec. of State for Higher Educ. 1965–71; Minister of Youth 1971; Pres. Acad. of Scientific Research and Tech. 1971–73; Deputy Exec. Dir. UNEP 1973–75, Exec. Dir. 1975–; State Prize in Biology 1959; decorations from 12 countries; Hon. Dr. (Moscow Univ.), Hon. Dr. Sc. (Seoul), Hon. Prof. Beijing Univ. *Publications:* Development without Destruction 1982; 95 scientific papers in journals of seven countries. *Address:* United Nations Environment Programme, P.O. Box 30552, Nairobi, Kenya. *Telephone:* 520600.

TOLKACHEV, Vitaly Antonovich; Soviet physicist; b. 1934, Byelorussia; ed. Byelorussian Univ. of Minsk; work at U.S.S.R. Acad. of Sciences Inst. of Physics 1958–, where now occupies sr. post; mem. CPSU 1972–; Lenin Prize 1980 for work on spectroscopy of free complex molecules. *Address:* Institute of Physics, U.S.S.R. Academy of Sciences, Leninsky Pr. 53, Moscow, U.S.S.R.

TOLKUNOV, Lev Nikolayevich; Soviet politician and fmr. journalist; b. 22 Jan. 1919, Bukreyevka, Kursk Region; ed. Gorky Inst. of Literature, Moscow and Higher Party School of CPSU; Sub-Ed. and Military Correspondent Pravda 1938–44; Deputy Exec. Sec. and Head of Dept. For a Lasting Peace, For a People's Democracy 1947–51; Deputy Ed., later Ed., People's Democracies Dept. Pravda 1951–57; Employee of apparatus of Cen. Cttee. CPSU 1957–65, Deputy Chief of Cen. Cttee. of CPSU Dept. for Liaison with Communist and Workers' Parties in other Communist Countries 1961–65; Ed.-in-Chief Izvestia 1965–75, 1983–84; Chair. of Bd. of Novosti Press Agency 1976–83; mem. CPSU 1943–, Cand. mem. CPSU Cen. Cttee. 1966–76, mem. 1976–; Deputy to U.S.S.R. Supreme Soviet 1966–; Chair., Soviet of the Union of U.S.S.R. Supreme Soviet 1984–88,

Soviet Cttee. for European Security 1984–, U.S.S.R. Parl. Group; Order of Lenin (twice), Red Banner of Labour (three times), Red Star, Order of October Revolution, Order of People's Friendship, Order of the Patriotic War, and medals. *Address:* The Kremlin, Moscow, U.S.S.R.

TOLSTYKH, B.L.; Soviet politician; Chair. of U.S.S.R. State Cttee. on Science and Tech.; Deputy Chair. U.S.S.R. Council of Ministers 1986–; Deputy Prime Minister of U.S.S.R. 1986–. *Address:* The Kremlin, Moscow, U.S.S.R.

TOMA, Maiava Iulai; Western Samoan diplomatist; b. 5 July 1940; ed. Marist Brothers School, Apia, Scots Coll. Wellington, N.Z., Victoria Univ., Wellington; joined W. Samoan Public Service, Prime Minister's Dept. 1964; Sr. Commr. to S. Pacific Comm. 1973–74; Sec. to Govt. of W. Samoa 1975–77; Perm. Rep. to UN and concurrently Amb. to U.S.A. and High Commr. in Canada 1977–. *Address:* Permanent Mission of Western Samoa to the United Nations, 820 Second Avenue, New York, N.Y. 10017, U.S.A.

TOMÁŠEK, H.E. Cardinal František, D.D.; Czechoslovak ecclesiastic; b. 30 June 1899, Studénka; ed. Seminary in Olomouc; Asst. lecturer in Educ. and Catechetics, Theol. Faculty of Olomouc Univ. 1934, lecturer in Educ. 1945, Ordinary Prof. 1947; Auxiliary Bishop in Olomouc 1949; Apostolic Admin. in Prague 1965; cr. Cardinal June 1977; Archbishop of Prague, Metropolitan and Primate of Bohemia March 1977–. *Publications:* (Ed.) Letters on Education, (author) 25 monographs on theol., educ. and catechism of the Catholic religion. *Leisure interests:* education, catechism. *Address:* Hradčanské náměstí 16, 119 02 Prague 1, Czechoslovakia. *Telephone:* 53 45 83.

TOMASINI, Roberto Jorge, PH.D.; Argentine engineer and politician; b. 15 April 1929, Buenos Aires; m. Haydee Lacreuse; three s.; ed. Nat. Univ. of Buenos Aires; consultant for the bi-national project of the High Uruguay River Hydroelectrical Devt. 1975; regional consultant United Nations Devt. Program 1972–74; Minister of Economy of Buenos Aires Prov. 1983–85; Minister of Public Works & Services 1985–86. *Address:* c/o Ministerio de Obras y Servicios Publicos, Avenida 9 de Julio 1925, C.P. 1332, Buenos Aires, Argentina.

TÓMASSON, Tómas Ármann, M.A.; Icelandic diplomatist; b. 1 Jan. 1929, Reykjavík; s. of Tómas Tómasson and Gudrun Thorgrimsdottir; m. Heba Jónsdóttir 1957 (divorced); three s. one d.; ed. Reykjavík Grammar School, Univ. of Illinois, Fletcher School of Law and Diplomacy and Columbia Univ.; entered Icelandic foreign service 1954; Sec. Moscow 1954–58; Ministry for Foreign Affairs 1958–60; Deputy Perm. Rep. to NATO and OECD 1960–66; Chief of Div., Ministry for Foreign Affairs 1966–69, Deputy Sec.-Gen. of Ministry 1970–71; Amb. to Belgium and EEC and Perm. Rep. on N. Atlantic Council 1971–77, 1984–86, also accred. to Luxembourg 1976–77, 1984–86; Perm. Rep. to UN 1977–82; Amb. to France (also accred. to Portugal, Spain, Cape Verde) 1982–84; Amb. to U.S.S.R. (also accred. to Bulgaria, G.D.R., Hungary, Mongolia and Romania) 1987–; Order of the Falcon (Iceland), and decorations from France, Belgium, Luxembourg, Portugal and Sweden. *Address:* Icelandic Embassy, Khlebnyi pereulok 28, Moscow, U.S.S.R. *Telephone:* 2904742, 2904653.

TOMASZEWSKI, Henryk; Polish choreographer, ballet master and mime; b. 20 Nov. 1919, Poznań; ed. Ballet School, Ivo Gall's Studio; mem. F. Parnell Ballet Ensemble, then of Wrocław Opera Ballet 1949–56; organized Mime Studio 1956 (now Mime Theatre); now Artistic Man. Wrocław Mime Theatre; won 1st Prize, World Festival of Youth, Moscow with his first programme 1957; Medal of French Critics, Festival of Nations 1962, Gold Medal, Swedish Soc. of Dance 1963, Gold Star, VIII Int. Festival of Dance 1971, Venezuelan Theatre Critics' Prize (for Przyjeżdżam jutro) 1978), Officer's Cross, Order of Polonia Restituta 1976, Commdr.'s Cross 1986, Press Prize, Wrocław, Minister of Culture and Arts Prize, 2nd Class 1962; performances in Europe, America and Africa; *ballets:* Process (from Kafka) 1966, Gilgamesh 1968, Kłatwa (by Wyspiański) 1969, Odejście Fausta 1970, Menażeria Cesarzowej Filissy (with F. Wedekinda), Peer Gynt 1974, Księżniczka Turandot (by C. Gozzi) 1974, Przyjeżdżam jutro 1974, Gra w zabijanego (by Ionesco) 1975, Sceny fantastyczne z legendy o Panu Twardowskim 1976, Spór (by Pierre de Marivaux) 1978, dir. Hammerman and Baker (film for Norwegian TV) 1978, Equus 1978, Hamlet Ironia i Żałoba 1979, Historia konia 1981, Rycerze Króla Artura 1981, Pericles (Shakespeare) 1982, Syn marnotrawny (based on Hogarth's A Rake's Progress) 1984, Action—A Midsummer Night's Dream 1986. *Address:* Al. Dębowa 16, 53-121 Wrocław, Poland. *Telephone:* 67-52-80 (Office).

TOMBAUGH, Clyde William, M.A.; American astronomer; b. 4 Feb. 1906, Streator, Ill.; s. of Muron and Adella Tombaugh (née Chritton); m. Patricia Edson 1934; one s. one d.; ed. Univ. of Kansas; Asst. Astronomer, Lowell Observatory, Flagstaff, Ariz. 1929–43; Science Instructor, Ariz. State Coll. 1943–45; Optical Physicist and Astronomer, White Sands Missile Range 1946–55; Astronomer, N.M. State Univ. 1955–61; Assoc. Prof. Dept. of Earth Sciences and Astronomy, N.M. State Univ. 1961–65, Prof. 1965–73; Emer. 1973–; planetary searches and observations, including the Moon, Mars, Venus, Jupiter and Saturn; discovered ninth planet, Pluto 1930, and five new galactic star clusters and one globular star cluster; mem. American Astronomical Soc. 1931–; Meteoritical Soc. 1932–; mem. Int. Astronomical Union Comm. on Planets and Satellites; Fellow, American Int. of Aeronautics and Astronautics; Hon. D.Sc. (Northern Ariz. Univ.); numerous awards.

Publications: The Search for Small Natural Earth Satellites 1959 (co-author), Lectures in Aerospace Medicine 1960, 1961, The Trans-Neptunian Planet Search 1961, Geology of Mars, Out of the Darkness: The Planet Pluto (with Dr. Patrick Moore) 1980 and over 35 other papers. *Leisure interest:* grinding, polishing and figuring telescope mirrors. *Address:* Dept. of Astronomy, Box 4500, New Mexico State University, University Park, New Mexico; and P.O. Box 306, Mesilla Park, N.M. 88047, U.S.A. *Telephone:* 646-2107 (Office); 505-526-9274 (Home).

TOMBS, Sir Francis Leonard, B.SC., LL.D., D.SC., F.ENG., F.I.E.E.; British business executive; b. 17 May 1924, Walsall; s. of Joseph and Jane Tombs; m. Marjorie Evans 1949; three d.; ed. Elmore Green School, Walsall and Birmingham Coll. of Tech.; with British Electricity Authority 1948–57; Gen. Man., Gen. Electric Co. Ltd. 1958–67; Dir. and Gen. Man. James Howden and Co. 1967–68; Dir. of Eng., S. of Scotland Electricity Bd. 1969–73, Deputy Chair. 1973–74, Chair. 1974–77; Chair. Electricity Council for England and Wales 1977–80; Dir. N. M. Rothschild and Sons Ltd. 1981–; Chair. The Weir Group Ltd. 1981–83; Dir. Rolls-Royce Ltd., Chair. Feb. 1985–; Dir. Shell (U.K.) Ltd. 1982–, Celltech Ltd. 1982–; Chair. Turner and Newall PLC 1982–; Chair. Eng. Council 1985–88; Hon. Fellow, Inst. of Civil Engineers 1986; Hon. D.Eng. (Bradford) 1986, Dr. h.c. (Council for Nat. Acad. Awards) 1988. *Publications:* Nuclear Energy Past, Present and Future—Electronics and Power 1981. *Leisure interests:* music and golf. *Address:* Honington Lodge, Honington, Shipston-upon-Stour, Warwicks., CV36 5AA, England.

TOMIC, Romero Radomiro; Chilean lawyer, politician and diplomatist; b. 7 May 1914; ed. Universidad Católica de Chile; Newspaper Ed. 1937–41; mem. Chamber of Deputies 1941–45, 1945–49, Senate 1950–53, 1961–65; founded Partido Demócrata Cristiano (PDC) 1935, Chair. of Youth Movement 1935–37, Nat. Chair. of PDC 1946–47, 1952–53; Amb. to U.S.A. 1965–68; Leader of PDC (now suspended by junta) 1969; Presidential cand. 1970. *Publications:* numerous political essays and The Inter-American System and the Regional Market 1958.

TOMINOMORI, Eiji, M.A.; Japanese journalist; b. 20 Sept. 1928, Kyoto; s. of Kyoji and Matsue Tominomori; m. Satoko Iwamatsu 1958; two s.; ed. Doshisha and Columbia Univs.; Washington Corresp. Asahi Shimbun 1966–69, Political Ed. 1976–78, Deputy Man. Ed. 1978–83, Man. Ed. 1983–. *Publications:* Seven Sins of Japanese Bureaucracy 1974, A History of Conservative Parties in Post-War Japan 1977. *Leisure interest:* golf. *Address:* 6-16-3 Ohizumi-gakuen-cho, Nerima-ku, Tokyo, Japan. *Telephone:* (03) 924-2070.

TOMKINS, Rt. Rev. Oliver Stratford, M.A., D.D.; British theologian; b. 9 June 1908, Hankow, China; s. of Rev. Leopold Charles Fellows Tomkins and Mary Katie Stratford; m. Ursula Mary Dunn 1939; one s. three d.; ed. Trent Coll., Christ's Coll., and Westcott House, Cambridge; Asst. Gen. Sec. Student Christian Movement 1933–36; Ed. Student Movement Magazine 1936–40; Vicar Holy Trinity Church, Millhouses, Sheffield 1940–45; Assoc. Gen. Sec. World Council of Churches and Sec. of its Comm. on Faith and Order 1945–52; Warden of Theological Coll., Lincoln 1953–59; Bishop of Bristol 1959–75; mem. World Council of Churches Cen. Cttee. 1968–74; Hon. D.D. (Edinburgh Univ.) 1953, Hon. LL.D. (Bristol Univ.) 1975. *Publications:* The Wholeness of the Church 1949, The Church in the Purpose of God 1950, Lund 1952: The Report of the Third World Conference on Faith and Order (ed.), The Life of Edward Woods 1957, A Time for Unity 1964, Guarded by Faith 1971, A Fully Human Priesthood 1985, Prayer for Unity 1987. *Leisure interests:* gardening and grandchildren. *Address:* 14 St. George's Square, Worcester, WR1 1HX, England. *Telephone:* (0905) 25330.

TOMKINSON, John Stanley, C.B.E., M.B., CH.B., F.R.C.S., F.R.C.O.G.; British gynaecologist and obstetrician; b. 8 March 1916, Stafford; s. of Harry Tomkinson and Katie Tomkinson; m. Barbara Marie Pilkington 1954; two s. (one deceased) one d.; ed. Rydal School, N. Wales, Birmingham Univ. Medical School, St. Thomas' Medical School, London; Surgeon-Lieut., R.N.V.R. in Atlantic and Indian Oceans 1942–46; Consultant Surgeon in Gynaecology and Obstetrics, Guy's Hosp. and Queen Charlotte's Maternity Hosp. and Chelsea Hosp. for Women, London 1953–81; Consultant Adviser in Gynaecology and Obstetrics to Dept. of Health for England and Wales 1966–81; Sec.-Gen. Int. Fed. of Gynaecology and Obstetrics 1976–85, Hon. Sec.-Gen. 1985–; Consultant Adviser WHO 1972, 1981, 1985; frmly. Examiner to Univs. of Oxford, Cambridge, London, Queen's (Belfast), Birmingham, E. Africa, Haile Selassie (Addis Ababa, Ethiopia), Al Fateh (Tripoli, Libya), Singapore and to Royal Coll. of Obstetricians and Gynaecologists, to Conjoint Examining Bd. in England and Cen. Midwives Bd.; William Hawksworth Memorial Lecturer 1971; Winston Churchill Memorial Lecturer 1972; Edward Sharp Memorial Lecturer 1977; Foundation Lecturer, American Asscn. of Obstetricians and Gynaecologists 1977; Charter Day Lecturer, Nat. Maternity Hosp., Dublin 1979; John Figgis Jewett Lecturer (First), Boston, Mass., U.S.A. 1988; Bert B. Hershenon Lecturer, Boston 1988; Hon. mem. of socs. of obstetrics and gynaecology of Cali (Colombia), Nigeria, Italy, Romania, S. Africa, Spain, Canada, Poland, Jordan, Yugoslavia, Brazil, Korea; Surgical Prize, Univ. of Birmingham 1939, Priestly-Smith Prize 1941. *Publications:* Queen Charlotte's Textbook of Obstetrics, 12th edn. (Ed.) 1970, Report on Confidential Enquiries into Maternal Deaths in England and Wales 1964–66; 1967–69; 1970–72; 1973–75;

1976–78, Inversion of the Appendix, in Acta. Obstet. Scand. 1977. *Leisure interests:* fly fishing for salmon and trout, fly tying, painting. *Address:* Keats House, Guy's Hospital, London, SE1 GRT; 3 Downside, St. John's Avenue, London, SW15 2AE (Home); Rose Cottage, Up Somborne, Nr. Stockbridge, Hants., SO20 6QY, England (Home). *Telephone:* 01-407 7600 Ext. 3090 (Hosp.); 01-789 9422 (Home, London); 0794-388-837 (Home, Hants.)

TOMKO, H.E. Cardinal Jozef; Czechoslovak ecclesiastic; b. 11 March 1924, Udavaké, Košice; ordained 1949; consecrated Bishop (Titular See of Doclea) 1979; cr. Cardinal 1985; Sec.-Gen. of Synod of Bishops; Pro-Prefect of the Congregation for the Evangelization of Peoples. *Address:* Villa Betania, Via Urbano VIII 16, 00165 Rome, Italy. *Telephone:* (06) 656.03.31.

TOMLINSON, John; British (bass) opera singer; b. 22 Sept. 1946, Accrington, Lancs.; s. of Rowland Tomlinson and Ellen Greenwood; m. Moya Joel 1969; one s. two d.; ed. Accrington Grammar School, Manchester Univ. and Royal Manchester Coll. of Music; debut at Glyndebourne Festival 1972, English Nat. Opera 1974, Royal Opera House, Covent Garden 1976; since then has appeared in many operatic roles throughout Europe and N. America; numerous broadcasts, recordings, opera videos and concert performances. *Address:* c/o Music International, 13 Ardilaun Road, Highbury, London, N5 2QR, England.

TOMLINSON, Mel Alexander, B.F.A.; American professional dance artist; b. 3 Jan. 1954, Raleigh, N.C.; s. of Tommy W. A. Tomlinson and Marjorie-line Henry Tomlinson; ed. F. J. Carnage Jr. High School, J. W. Ligon High School, N.C. Gov.'s School and N.C. School of the Arts; Prin., Agnes DeMille's Heritage Dance Theater 1973, Dance Theatre of Harlem Inc. 1974–77, Alvin Ailey American Dance Theatre 1977–78, Dance Theatre of Harlem Inc. 1978–81; mem. corps de ballet, New York City Ballet 1981, soloist 1982–; guest appearance, DeMille Tribute, Jofferey Ballet. *Leisure interests:* knitting, swimming, gymnastics, reading, sewing, games. *Address:* New York City Ballet, Lincoln State Theater, New York, N.Y. 10023; 790 Riverside Drive, Apt. 6B, New York, N.Y. 10032; 1216 Bunche Drive, Raleigh, N.C. 27610, U.S.A. *Telephone:* (212) 234-3320; (919) 834-7010.

TOMOS; Chinese artist; b. 26 Nov. 1932, Tumed Banner, Inner Mongolia (Nei Monggol); s. of Yun Yao and Xing Yu; m. Xiahe-xiou 1967; two s.; ed. Cen. Inst. of Fine Arts, Beijing; Assoc. Prof. of Fine Arts, Inner Mongolia Normal Coll.; Dean of Fine Arts, Inner Mongolia Teachers' Training Coll. 1984–; Adviser on Fine Arts to Children's Palace, Huhehot, Inner Mongolia; Vice-Chair. Inner Mongolian Branch of Chinese Artists' Asscn. 1980–; Dir. Standing Cttee., Chinese Artists' Asscn. May 1985–, mem. Oil Art Cttee. Oct. 1985–; mem. Selection Cttee. for Sixth Nat. Art Exhbn. of oil paintings; mem. Art Educ. Cttee. of Nat. Educ. 1986–; Dir. Inner Mongolia branch of China External Culture Exchange Assn.; First Prize for Art, Inner Mongolia; exhbns. include: oil paintings and sketches, Huhehot 1979, oil paintings Exhbn. Hall of Cen. Inst. of Fine Arts, Cultural Palace of minority nationalities, Beijing 1981, oil paintings and sketches, Changsha, Hunan Prov. 1984; Modern Oil Painting Exhbn., China Art Gallery; China Modern Oil Painting Exhbn., U.S.A. 1987. *Works include:* Mine, Wind on the Grasslands, Having a Break, Dawn, Milkmaid, A Woman Hay-making (Nat. Silver Medal 1985), At Dusk, Polo (Nat. Copper Medal 1985), Spring Wind, White Horse and Wind, At Dark and many others. *Publication:* Selection of oil-paintings. *Leisure interests:* Chinese Gongfu, Peking opera, Chinese medicine. *Address:* Art Department, Normal College, Nei Monggol Autonomous Region, People's Republic of China.

TOMOWA-SINTOW, Anna; Austrian (Bulgarian-born) opera singer; b. 22 Sept. 1941, Stara Zagora, Bulgaria; m. Albert Sintow 1963; one d.; ed. Nat. Conservatory of Sofia; début Leipzig Opera 1967; joined Deutsche Staatsoper, Berlin 1969; guest engagements at most leading European and U.S. opera houses, including La Scala, Milan, Vienna, Covent Garden, London, Paris, Bavarian State Opera and Bolshoi, Moscow; début N. America at Metropolitan Opera, New York 1978; has toured Japan with Scala di Milano and Berlin Philharmonic under von Karajan; regular guest at Salzburg Festival since 1973; major roles include Arabella, Ariadne, Madelaine (in Capriccio), Countess Almaviva, Elsa (in Lohengrin), Elisabeth (in Tannhäuser), Aida, Tosca, Butterfly, Traviata, Manon Lescaut, Maddalena (in Andrea Chenier), Leonora (in La Forza del Destino), etc.; has sung in several TV productions; recordings include Lohengrin, Le nozze di Figaro, Don Giovanni, Die Zauberflöte, Mozart Coronation Mass, Mozart Requiem, Brahms German Requiem, Strauss Four Last Songs and Capriccio monologue, Beethoven Missa Solemnis, Ariadne auf Naxos (in preparation), recitals of Verdi arias and of Italian and German arias; winner Kammersängerin Prize. *Leisure interests:* nature, reading books, singing. *Address:* c/o S. A. Gorlinsky Ltd., 33 Dover Street, London, W1X 4NJ, England. *Telephone:* 01-493 9158.

TOMPKINS, Frederick Clifford, PH.D., F.R.S.; British professor of physical chemistry (retd.); b. 29 Aug. 1910, Yeovil, Somerset; s. of Frederick W. and Maud Tompkins; m. Catherine L. Macdougall 1936; one d.; ed. Yeovil School, Univ. of Bristol and King's Coll., London; lecturer, King's Coll., London 1935, Univ. of Natal, Pietermaritzburg 1937, Sr. Lecturer 1943; ICI Fellowship, King's Coll., London 1946; Reader, Imperial Coll., London 1947, Prof. of Chem. 1956–77, Prof. Emer. 1977–; Hon. A.R.C.S. (Imperial Coll.); Hon. D.Sc. (Bradford). *Publications:* Chemisorption of Gases on

Metals 1969; about 120 papers in scientific journals. *Leisure interests:* gardening, music, writing. *Address:* 9 St. Helen's Close, Southsea, Portsmouth, Hants., PO4 0NN, England. *Telephone:* (0705) 731901.

TOMUR DAWAMAT; Chinese (Uygur) party official; b. 1927, Uyhur; m. Gulzirahan 1932; five s. two d.; ed. Cen. Nationalities Coll., Beijing; village chief 1950; joined CCP 1952; Sec. CCP Cttee., Toksun Cttee., Tunpan Basin 1956, First Sec. 1960; Vice-Chair. Xinjiang Autonomous Region 1964; Deputy for Xinjiang, 3rd NPC; mem. Standing Cttee., Autonomous Regional Revolutionary Cttee., Xinjiang 1968; disappeared until 1976; Deputy for Xinjiang, 5th NPC 1978; mem. Standing Cttee., 5th NPC 1978; Deputy Sec. CCP Cttee. Xinjiang 1978–; Vice-Minister of State Nationalities Affairs Comm., State Council 1979; Chair. Autonomous Regional People's Congress, Xinjiang 1979–85; mem. 12th Cen. Cttee., CCP 1982; Chair. Xinjiang Autonomous Region 1985–; Vice-Sec. Xinjiang Autonomous Region CCP Cttee. 1985; mem. 13th Cen. Cttee., CCP 1987. *Address:* People's Government, Xinjiang Uygur Autonomous Region, People's Republic of China. *Telephone:* 24681-232.

TONČIĆ-SORINJ, Lujo, LL.D.; Austrian landowner and politician; b. 12 April 1915, Vienna; s. of Dušan Tončić-Sorinj and Mabel Plason de la Woesthyne; m. Renate Trenker 1956; one s. four d.; ed. Grammar School, Salzburg, and Univs. of Vienna and Zagreb; Asst. to Chair. S.E. Europe Dept., Berlin Univ. 1940–44; Mil. Service 1941–44; Head of Political Dept., Austrian Research Inst. for Econs. and Politics 1946–49, Ed. Berichte und Informationen 1946–49; M.P. for Land Salzburg 1949–66; Chair. Legal Cttee. of Austrian Parl. 1953–56, Foreign Affairs Cttee. 1956–59; in charge of Foreign Affairs questions, Austrian People's Party 1959–66; Austrian mem. Consultative Ass. of Council of Europe 1953–66, Vice-Chair. Political Cttee.; Vice-Pres. Council of Europe 1961–62; Minister of Foreign Affairs 1966–68; Sec.-Gen. Council of Europe 1969–74; Pres. Austrian Asscn. of UN 1977–; Perm. Rep. Austrian People's Party to Christian-Democratic Group in European Parl. 1980–; Pres. Union Int. de la Propriété Immobilière 1987–; Grosses Goldenes Ehrenzeichen am Bande (Austria) and other decorations. *Publications:* Erfüllte Träume (autobiog.) 1982, Vorbei am Abgrund 1988, and about 350 articles and essays on history and int. politics. *Leisure interests:* history, geography, swimming, diving. *Address:* 5020 Salzburg, Schloss Fürberg, Pausingerstrasse 11, Austria. *Telephone:* 0662-73437.

TONEGAWA, Susumu, PH.D.; Japanese immunologist; b. 5 Sept. 1939, Nagoya; s. of Tsutomu Tonegawa and Miyuko Tonegawa; m. Mayumi Yoshinari 1985; one c.; ed. Kyoto Univ. and Univ. of Calif. San Diego; postgraduate work at Dept. of Biology, Univ. of Calif. San Diego 1968–69, The Salk Inst. San Diego 1969–70; mem. Basle Inst. for Immunology, Basle, Switzerland 1971–81; Prof. of Biology, Center for Cancer Research and Dept. of Biology, M.I.T. 1981–; mem. American Acad. of Arts and Sciences; Foreign Assoc. mem. N.A.S.; Hon. mem. American Asscn. of Immunologists, Scandinavian Soc. for Immunology; numerous awards and prizes including Avery Landsteiner Prize 1981, Gairdner Foundation Int. Award 1983, Robert Koch Prize 1986, Lasker Prize 1987, Nobel Prize for Medicine 1987; Bunkakunsho Order of Culture 1984. *Address:* Department of Biology, Massachusetts Institute of Technology, 77 Massachusetts Avenue, Cambridge, Mass. 02139, U.S.A.

TONGA, King of (see Taufa'ahau Tupou IV).

TONKIN, Hon. David Oliver, M.B., B.S., D.O., F.R.A.C.O.; Australian politician and ophthalmologist; b. 20 July 1929, S. Australia; s. of Oliver Athelstone Prisk Tonkin and Bertha Ida Louise Kennett; m. Prudence Anne Juttner 1954; three s. three d.; ed. St. Peter's Coll., Adelaide, Univ. of Adelaide, Inst of Ophthalmology, London; Private ophthalmic practice and visiting staff Royal Adelaide Hosp. 1958–68; mem. Social Welfare Advisory Council, Govt. of S. Australia 1968–70; Liberal M.P. for Bragg, S. Australia Parl. 1970–83, Leader of the Opposition 1975–79; Premier, Treas., Minister for State Devt., Minister for Ethnic Affairs, Govt. of S. Australia 1979–82; Sec.-Gen. Commonwealth Parl. Asscn. 1986–; Freeman City of London 1981. *Publication:* Patient Care Review—Quality Assurance in Health Care 1986. *Leisure interests:* family, music and theatre. *Address:* Palace of Westminster, 7 Old Palace Yard, London, SW1P 3JY, England. *Telephone:* 01-219 4666.

TONYPANDY, 1st Viscount (cr. 1983), of Rhondda in the County of Mid-Glamorgan, **Thomas George Thomas,** P.C.; British politician; b. 29 Jan. 1909, Wales; s. of Zachariah and Emma Jane Thomas; ed. Tonypandy Grammar School and Univ. Coll. of Southampton; M.P. for Central Cardiff 1945–50, W. Cardiff 1950–83 (Labour until 1976); Parl. Under-Sec. of State, Home Office 1964–66; Minister of State, Welsh Office 1966–67, Commonwealth Office 1967–68; Sec. of State for Wales 1968–70; Deputy Speaker, House of Commons, Chair. Ways and Means Cttee. 1974–76, Speaker 1976–83; Vice-Pres. Methodist Conf. 1960–61; Pres. Community Projects Foundation 1981–, Coll. of Preceptors 1983–87; British Heart Foundation 1984; Chair. Nat. Children's Home 1982–, Jt. Commonwealth Soc. Council 1984–87, Bank of Wales 1985–; Hon. mem. Livery of the Worshipful Co. of Blacksmiths 1980; Freeman of the Borough of Rhondda 1970, City of Cardiff 1975; Hon. Fellow, Univ. Coll. Cardiff 1972, Polytechnic of Wales 1984; Hon. Master of the Bench of Gray's Inn 1982; Hon. LL.D. (Asbury Coll., Kentucky) 1976, (Wales, Southampton) 1977, (Birmingham) 1978, (Oklahoma) 1981, (Leeds, Liverpool) 1982, (Keele, Warwick) 1984; Hon. D.C.L. (Oxford) 1983; Dr. h.c. (Open Univ.) 1983; Dato Setia Negara, Brunei 1971. *Publications:* The Christian Heritage in Politics, Memoirs of Viscount Tonypandy 1985, My Wales (with Earl of Snowdon, q.v.) 1986. *Leisure interest:* travel. *Address:* House of Lords, Westminster, London, S.W.1, England; Tilbury, 173 King George V Drive East, Cardiff, Wales (Home).

TOOLEY, Sir John, Kt., M.A.; British administrator; b. 1 June 1924, Rochester, Kent; s. of late H. R. Tooley; m. 1st Judith Craig Morris (dissolved 1965), three d.; m. 2nd Patricia J. N. Bagshawe 1968, one s.; ed. Repton School and Magdalene Coll., Cambridge; Sec. Guildhall School of Music and Drama 1952-55; Asst. to Gen. Admin., Royal Opera House, Covent Garden 1955-60, Asst. Gen. Admin. 1960-70, Gen. Admin. 1970-80, Gen. Dir. 1980-88; Commendatore of Italian Repub.; Hon. F.R.A.M., Hon. G.S.M.; Hon. mem. Royal Northern Coll. of Music. *Leisure interests:* walking, theatre. *Address:* Avon Farmhouse, Stratford-sub-Castle, Salisbury, Wiltshire; and 2 Mart Street, London, W.C.2, England. *Telephone:* 01-836 1404.

TOON, Malcolm, M.A.; American diplomatist; b. 4 July 1916, Troy, N.Y.; s. of George Toon and Margaret Broadfoot; m. Elizabeth J. Taylor 1943; one s. two d.; ed. Tufts Univ., Fletcher School of Law and Diplomacy, and Harvard Univ.; Research Technician, Nat. Resources Planning Bd. 1939-41; Ensign, Lt.-Commdr., U.S. Naval Reserve 1942-46; in U.S. Foreign Service 1946-79; Amb. to Czechoslovakia 1969-71, to Yugoslavia 1971-75, to Israel 1975-76, to U.S.S.R. 1976-79; Dir. McKesson Corpn., San Francisco; mem. Bd. of Trustees Tufts Univ., Bd. of Visitors Fletcher School; Hon. LL.D. (Tufts Univ.) 1977, (Middlebury Coll.) 1978, (Drexel Univ.) 1980, (American Coll. of Switzerland) 1985; Superior Honor Award, Dept. of State 1965; Distinguished Honor Award, Dept. of State 1979; Freedom Leadership Award Hillsdale Coll., Mich. 1980, Freedom Award 1981, Wallace Award 1984, Gold Medal, Nat. Inst. of Social Sciences 1987. *Leisure interests:* golf, tennis, hunting, fishing. *Address:* 375 PeeDee Road, Southern Pines, N.C. 28387, U.S.A. (Home).

TOPCHEYEV, Yuriy Ivanovich; DR. TECH. SC.; Soviet cyberneticist; b. 1920; ed. Moscow Aviation Inst.; mem. CPSU 1948-; Prof. 1968-; Sr. scientist with a research inst. 1943-68; mem. of staff of Inst. of Physical Eng., Moscow 1968-; Prof. 1972-; State Prize 1972. *Publications:* co-author of Technical Cybernetics (4 vols.) 1967-69. *Address:* Institute of Physical Engineering, Moscow, U.S.S.R.

TOPE, Trimbak Krishna, M.A., LL.B.; Indian lawyer and teacher; b. 28 Feb. 1914, Yeola, Naskit District; s. of Krishnaji Trimbak and Satyabhama K. Tope; one s. three d.; ed. Bombay Univ.; Prof. of Sanskrit, Ramnarain Ruia Coll. 1939-47; Advocate, Bombay High Court 1946; Prof. of Law, Govt. Law Coll. 1947, Principal and Perry Prof. of Jurisprudence 1958; Vice-Chancellor, Univ. of Bombay 1971-78; Pres. Maharashtra Samajik Parishad, Bombay Social Reform Asscn.; Sheriff of Bombay 1985-86. *Publications:* Why Hindu Code?, A Modern Sage, Bombay and Congress Presidents, Bombay and Congress Movement, A Constitutional Law of India 1982, A Shorter Constitution of India, Union State Relations in India. *Leisure interests:* music, reading, gardening. *Address:* Q7 Prathamesh, Veer Sauarkar Road, Prabha Devi, Bombay 400025, India. *Telephone:* 4225565.

TOPOL, Chaim; Israeli actor, producer and director; b. 9 Sept. 1935, Tel Aviv; s. of Jacob Topol and Rela Goldman; m. Galia Finkelstein 1956; one s. two d.; joined entertainment unit during army service 1953; f. The Green Onion satirical theatre 1956, Municipal Theatre of Haifa 1959; starred in London stage productions of Fiddler on the Roof, Ziegfeld 1988; currently Actor, Producer, Director for the Genesis Project, filming the Bible, New York, N.Y.; Golden Globe Award, San Francisco Film Festival Winner. *Films include:* Cast A Giant Shadow 1965, Sallah 1966, Before Winter Comes 1969, A Time for Loving, Fiddler on the Roof 1971, The Public Eye, Galileo 1974, Flash Gordon, For Your Eyes Only 1980, The Winds of War 1981. *Publication:* Topol by Topol (autobiog.) 1981. *Address:* 108 Dizengoff Street, Tel Aviv, Israel.

TOPOLSKI, Feliks; British painter; b. 14 Aug. 1907, Warsaw, Poland; s. of Edward Topolski and Stanisława Drutowska; m. 1st Marion Everall 1944 (divorced 1975), one s. one d.; m. 2nd Caryl Stanley 1975; ed. Acad. of Art, Warsaw, Paris and Italy; came to England 1935; official war artist from 1940 to 1945; works in British Museum, Victoria and Albert Museum, Tate Gallery, Imperial War Museum, South Bank Art Centre (mural-environment Memoir of the Century) 1975, Glasgow, Nottingham, Edinburgh, Theatre Museum (London), Toronto, Brooklyn, Texas Univ., Melbourne, Tel-Aviv, Delhi, Warsaw, Singapore and in Buckingham Palace, London; exhbns. in Europe, Canada, U.S., India and Australia; Dr. h.c. (Jagiellonian Univ. of Cracow). *Publications:* The London Spectacle 1935, illustrated Bernard Shaw's Geneva 1939, In Good King Charles' Golden Days 1939, Pygmalion 1941; Penguin Prints 1941, Britain in Peace and War 1941, Russia in War 1942, Three Continents 1944-45, Portrait of G. B. S. 1946, Confessions of a Congress Delegate 1949, 88 Pictures 1951, Topolski's Chronicle 1953-79, Sketches of Gandhi 1954, The Blue Conventions 1956, Topolski's Chronicle for Students of World Events 1958, Topolski's Legal London 1961, Face to Face 1964, The United Nations:

Sacred Drama (with Conor Cruise O'Brien (q.v.)) 1968, Holy China 1968, Shem Ham Japheth Inc. U.S.A. 1969, Paris Lost 1973, Topolski's Buckingham Palace Panoramas 1977, Sua Sanctitas Johannes Paulus Papa II 1978, The London Symphony Orchestra 75th Anniversary Prints, Topolski's Panoramas 1980, Topolski's Theatre 1981, Fathers and Sons: South American Journey (with Daniel Topolski) 1982, Topolski's Chronicle 1953-79, 1982, Fourteen Letters (autobiog.) 1987. *Films:* Topolski's Moscow (for CBS TV) 1969, Paris Lost 1980. *Address:* Bridge Arch 158, opposite Artists' Entrance, Royal Festival Hall, London, S.E.1, England.

TOPOLSKI, Jerzy; Polish historian; b. 20 Sept. 1928, Poznań; s. of Władysław and Halina (née Pietrzyńska) Topolski; m. 1st Zofia Kulejewska 1954; m. 2nd Maria Barbara Antczak 1961; m. 3rd Maria Danuta Łabędzka 1978; one s. one d.; ed. Univ. of Poznań; Doctor 1951-56, Docent 1959-61, Extraordinary Prof. 1961-68, Prof. 1968-; with Inst. of Social Sciences of Cen. Cttee., Polish United Workers' Party (PZPR) 1951-54; with Inst. of History, Polish Acad. of Sciences (PAN) 1954-61, Pres. Polish Cttee. of Historical Sciences 1984-; Corresp. mem. PAN 1971-76, mem. 1977-; with Inst. of History, Poznań Univ. 1954-, Deputy Head of Dept. of Methodology of History 1973-81, Dir. Inst. of History 1981-87; Chair. Scientific Council, Inst. of History of Material Culture; mem. Scientific Cttee. of History of Historiography Int. Review, Studia Metodologiczne, Studia Historiae Oeconomicae; mem. Cen. Board, Int. Asscn. of Econ. History, State Tribunal 1982-; State Prize, 2nd Class 1970, 1st Class 1978, Knight's and Commdr.'s Cross, Commdr.'s Cross with Star, Order of Polonia Restituta, Award of Pomeranian Griffin, Medal of 30th and 40th anniversary of People's Poland, Nat. Educ. Comm. Medal. *Publications:* Methodology of History 1968, 1973, 1975, 1976, Narodziny kapitalizmu w Europie XIV-XVIII wieku 1965, Świat bez historii 1972, Wielkopolska poprzez wieki 1973, Zarys dziejów Poznania 1973, co-author Dzieje Wielkopolski 1969, Dzieje Polski 1975, 1976, 1977 (ed. and co-author), Marksizm i Historia 1977, Gospodarka Polska a Europejska 1977, Rozumienie Historii 1978, Theory of Historical Knowledge 1983, Truth and Models in History (1982), O nowy model historii Jan Rutowski (1886-1949) 1986. *Leisure interest:* travels. *Address:* Bastionowa 45, 61-663, Poznań, Poland. *Telephone:* 22-25-32 (Home); 51191 (Office), Ext. 12.

TOPOROV, Vladimir Nikolayevich; Soviet writer, literary historian and linguist; b. 1928, Moscow; ed. Moscow Univ.; first articles published 1958; Sr. Research Fellow at Inst. of Slavic and Balkan Studies, U.S.S.R. Acad. of Sciences; Specialist in Indo. European and semiotician; author of articles both in Soviet and int. professional publs., some in collaboration with Mikhail Meilakh; some works published outside U.S.S.R. *Publications include:* Akhmatova and Blok 1981; Gospodin Prokharchin 1982.

TORALDO DI FRANCIA, Giuliano; Italian physicist; b. 17 Sept. 1916, Florence; Prof. of Physics, Univ. of Florence 1958-; Pres. Int. Comm. of Optics 1966-69, Soc. Italiana di Fisica 1967-73; Thomas Young Medal, Inst. of Physics and Physical Soc.; C. E. K. Mees Medal, Optical Soc. of America. *Publications:* Electromagnetic Waves 1956, La Diffrazione della Luce 1958, L'indagine del mondo Fisico 1976. *Address:* Via Panciatichi 56-27, Florence, Italy.

TÖRMÄLÄ, Pertti, DR.PHIL.; Finnish professor of plastics technology; b. 26 Nov. 1945, Tampere; s. of Matti Törmälä and Elma Vitanen; m. Kirsti Miettinen 1967; two d.; Assoc. Prof. of Non-Metallic Materials, Tampere Univ. of Tech. 1975, Prof. of Fibre Raw Materials, Prof. of Plastics Tech. and Head Inst. of Plastics Tech. 1985-; Research Prof. Acad. of Finland; Nat. Inventor Prize 1986; Nordic Tech. Prize 1988. *Publications:* eight textbooks, 20 patents, over 300 scientific papers. *Leisure interests:* exercise, music. *Address:* Tampere University of Technology, Institute of Plastics Technology, P.O. Box 527, 33101 Tampere, Finland. *Telephone:* 358-31-162111.

TØRNAES, Laurits; Danish politician; b. 17 July 1936, Stenderup, Jutland; fmr. owner fishing vessel Vidar, fmr. Pres. Danmarks Havfiskeriforeining (Danish Fishermen's Asscn.); took part in negotiations for common fisheries policy in EEC; mem. Folketing (Parl.) 1981-; Liberal Party Spokesman 1982-; Minister of Agric. 1988-. *Address:* Ministry of Agriculture, Slotsholmsgade 10, 1216 Copenhagen K, Denmark. *Telephone:* (01) 92-33-01.

TORRANCE, Very Rev. Prof. Thomas Forsyth, M.B.E., M.A., DR.THEOL., D.LITT., F.B.A., F.R.S.E.; British minister of religion and university professor; b. 30 Aug. 1913, Chengtu, China; s. of Rev. Thomas and Annie Elizabeth (Sharp) Torrance; m. Margaret Edith Spear 1946; two s. one d.; ed. Bellshill Acad., Univs. of Edinburgh, Basel and Oxford; war service with Church of Scotland Huts and Canteens, Middle East and Italy 1943-45; Prof. of Systematic Theol., Auburn Theol. Seminary, U.S.A. 1938-39; Minister, Alyth Barony Parish, Church of Scotland 1940-47, Beechgrove Parish Aberdeen 1947-50; Prof. of Church History, Univ. of Edinburgh 1950-52, of Christian Dogmatics, also Head of Dept. 1952-79; Cross of St. Mark, Cross of Aksum, Protopresbyter of Greek Orthodox Church; Collins Prize, Templeton Prize; Hon. D.D. (Montreal, St. Andrews), Hon. D.Theol. (Geneva, Faculté Libre Paris), Hon. Dr.Teol. (Oslo), Hon. D.Sc. (Heriot Watt Univ.) 1983, Hon. D.Theol. (Debrecen). *Publications:* The Doctrine of Grace in the Apostolic Fathers 1948, Calvin's Doctrine of Man 1949, Royal Priesthood 1955, Kingdom and Church 1956, Conflict and Agreement in the Church (two vols.) 1959, 1960, Karl Barth: Introduction to his Early

Theology 1962, Theology in Reconstruction 1965, Theological Science 1969, Space, Time and Incarnation 1969, God and Rationality 1971, Theology in Reconciliation 1975, Space, Time and Resurrection 1976, The Ground and Grammar of Theology 1980, The Incarnation (ed.) 1980, Belief in Science and in Christian Life (ed.) 1980, Christian Theology and Scientific Culture 1980, Divine and Contingent Order 1981, Reality and Evangelical Theology 1981, Juridical Law and Physical Law 1982, Transformation and Convergence in the Frame of Knowledge 1984, James Clerk Maxwell. A Dynamical Theory of the Electromagnetic Field (ed.) 1982, Reality and Scientific Theology 1985, The Mediation of Christ 1983, The Christian Frame of Mind 1985, The Trinitarian Faith 1988, The Hermeneutics of John Calvin 1988. *Leisure interests:* walking, occasional fishing, golf, travel. *Address:* 37 Braid Farm Road, Edinburgh, EH10 6LE, and Sea Spray, Canty Bay, North Berwick, East Lothian, Scotland (Homes). *Telephone:* (031) 447 3224 (Home); (0620) 2508 (Home).

TORRELIO VILLA, Gen. Celso; Bolivian army officer and politician; b. 3 June 1933, Sucre; m. Teresa Toledo; ed. School of Arms Application, School of Motors, Panama, School of Command; Head, 6th EMGE Dept.; Commandant, Mil. Coll.; Chief Div. Commdr., 5th Army Div.; Head, 4th Logistical Dept., EMGE; Commdt., Mil. and Army Coll.; Minister of the Interior Feb.–June 1981; C.-in-C. of Army 1981–82; mem. ruling mil. junta June–Sept. 1981; Pres. of Bolivia 1981–82; Guerrilleros Lanza; Constancia Militar (second class). *Address:* c/o Oficina del Presidente, La Paz, Bolivia.

TORRES BERNÁRDEZ, Santiago, LL.D.; Spanish lawyer and international civil servant; b. 18 Nov. 1929, Vigo; s. of Apolinar Torres and Soledad Bernárdez; m. Maria del Rosario Camprubi Pardo de Figueroa 1984; ed. Miguel de Unamuno High School, Bilbao, Univs. of Valladolid, Saarland and Würzburg, Fed. Repub. of Germany; mem. Codification Div. of the Office of Legal Affairs of the UN 1959–75, Deputy Dir. 1975–80; mem. in various capacities of the Secr. of UN Int. Law Comm. 1960–80, Sixth Cttee. of UN Gen. Ass. 1959–79, UN Special Cttee. on the question of Defining Aggression, Friendly Relations, Sea-bed and Ocean Floor beyond Nat. Jurisdiction 1960–72, UN Confs. on Diplomatic Intercourse and Immunities, Elimination or Reduction of Statelessness 1961, Consular Relations 1963, Law of Treaties 1968–69, Rep. of States in their Relations with Int. Orgs. 1975, Territorial Asylum 1977, Succession of States in respect of Treaties 1977–78; UN observer at Diplomatic Conf. on Reaffirmation and Devt. of Int. Humanitarian Law 1974–76; UN expert at meetings on the problem of the use of certain conventional weapons convened by Int. Cttee. of Red Cross 1973; mem. UN mission to monitor plebiscite on Panama Canal Treaties 1977; Visiting Lecturer, Acad. of Int. Law, The Hague 1970, 1972; Registrar, Int. Court of Justice 1980–; mem. Inst. of Int. Law, Soc. française pour le droit international, Spanish branch of Int. Law Asscn., American Soc. of Int. Law, Hispano-Luso-Americano Inst. of Int. Law. *Publications:* Codification Methods and International Judicial Procedures; articles and papers on int. law. *Leisure interests:* history, literature, arts, sport.

TORRES YRIBAR, Dr. Wilfredo; Cuban doctor and professor of medicine; b. 19 June 1933, Guantánamo; s. of Elpidio Torres Torres and Dulce María Yribar Olivares; m. Marianna Rivera Heredia 1956; two s. one d.; ed. Univ. of Havana; Haemotology Tech. 1951–60; Dir. Mayarí Arriba de Oriente Rural Hosp. 1961; Dir. Clinical Lab. William Soler Paediatric Hosp. 1962–65; Dir. Clinical Haemotology and Clinical Lab. Enrique Cabrera Nat. Hosp. 1963–65, Consulting Prof. Hnos. Ameijeiras Hosp., Havana; Nat. Dir. Clinical Lab., Ministry of Public Health; Gen. Vice-Dir. Nat. Centre of Scientific Research 1965–66, Gen. Dir. 1966–76, Pres. Gen. Scientific Council 1966–76; Vice-Dir. and mem. Cen. Scientific Council Univ. of Havana until 1976; Pres. Acad. of Sciences 1976–86; rank of Cabinet Minister; Pres. Cuban Section, Sub-Comm. of Soviet-Cuban Scientific and Tech. Collaboration; mem. Acad. of Science, Czechoslovakia, U.S.S.R. Acad. of Sciences; Foreign mem. Hungarian Acad. of Science; Hon. mem. New York Acad. of Science; founder-mem. Soc. of Haemotology; mem. Int. Soc. of Haemotology; various decorations including Commdr. Orden del Sol (Peru) 1973. *Publications:* numerous specialist articles in Cuba and overseas. *Address:* Avenida Primera numero 2403, entre 24 y 26, Miramar, Cuba (Home).

TORROJA MENENDEZ, José María, DR.SC.; Spanish professor of astronomy and geodesy; b. 29 Aug. 1916, Madrid; s. of José María and Isabel Torroja; m. Aurora Torroja 1962; two s.; ed. Univ. of Madrid; Geographical Engineer, Instituto Geográfico, Madrid 1942–52; Astronomer, Observatory of Madrid 1952–67; Prof. of Astronomy and Geodesy, Univ. of Madrid 1945–83; Vice-Rector, Univ. of Madrid 1971–76; Sec.-Gen. Real Academia de Ciencias Exactas, Físicas y Naturales, Pres. Real Sociadad Geográfica. *Publications:* several publications on astronomy and geodesy. *Address:* Islas Filipinas 50, 28003 Madrid, Spain. *Telephone:* 2544721.

TORTELIER, Paul; French cellist and composer; b. 21 March 1914, Paris; s. of Joseph Tortelier and Marguerite Boura; m. Maud Martin 1946; one s. three d.; ed. Conservatoire Nat. de Musique de Paris; First Cellist Monte Carlo 1935–37; 3rd Cellist Boston Symphony Orchestra 1937–40; 1st Cellist Soc. des Concerts du Conservatoire de Paris 1946–47; solo cellist with leading orchestras (Europe, U.S.A., Israel, etc.) 1947–56; Prof. Conservatoire Nat. Supérieur de Musique de Paris 1956–69, Folkwang Musikhochschule, Essen, Conservatoire National de Region, Nice, 1978–80; mem.

Soc. des Auteurs compositeurs et éditeurs de musique; Hon. mem. R.A.M., London, F.R.C.M. (London) 1979; Hon. Prof. Cen. Conservatory, Beijing 1980; Hon. D.Mus. (Leicester Univ.) 1972, (Oxford Univ.) 1975; Dr. h.c. (Univ. of Aston, Birmingham) 1979. *Works published:* Concerto for Two Cellos, Symphonie Israélienne, Cello Sonata, Suite for Unaccompanied Cello, Trois Petits Tours (cello and piano), Spirales (cello and piano), Elegie, Toccata (cello and piano), duos for two cellos; Cadenzas for Haydn, Schumann, Boccherini and C. P. E. Bach concertos; edition of Sammartini Sonata; Concerto for Violin and Orchestra; Concerto for Piano and Orchestra; Offrande; The Great Flag for UN 1960, Sonata Breve, Variations on "May Music save Peace", Mon Cirque (for unaccompanied cello), Romance and Dance Variations (for flute and piano). *Publication:* How I Play, How I Teach 1973, Self Portrait: in conversation with David Blum 1984. *Leisure interest:* flute and piano playing. *Address:* c/o Ibbs and Tillett, 450-452 Edgware Road, London W2 1EG, England; or c/o M. A. de Valmalète, Building Gaveau, 11 avenue Delcassé, 75635 Paris, France.

TORTELIER, Yan Pascal; French conductor and violinist; b. 19 April 1947, Paris; s. of Paul Tortelier (q.v.) and Maud Tortelier; m. Sylvie Brunet-Moret 1970; two s.; ed. Paris Conservatoire and Berks. Music Centre; début as concert violinist, Royal Albert Hall 1962; has since toured extensively all over the world; Konzertmeister, Assoc. Conductor of Orchestre du Capitole de Toulouse 1974–82; has conducted operas and concerts in Europe, Japan and U.S.A. *Leisure interests:* skiing, windsurfing, scuba diving, nature. *Address:* Le Garagaï, Camps-La-Source, 83170, France.

TORUMTAY, Gen. Necip; Turkish army officer; b. 1926, Vakfikebir, Trabzon; s. of Nihat Torumtay and Edibe Toruntay; m. Mrs. Türkân 1949; one s. one d.; ed. Army War Coll., Artillery School, War Acads. Unit Commdr. at platoon, battery and bn. levels; Deputy Attaché Turkish Embassy, Tokyo; Turkish Mil. Rep. Planning Officer NATO Mil. Cttee., Washington; Regt. Commdr. and Br. Chief Turkish Gen. Staff H.Q.; promoted Brig.-Gen. 1970; Deputy Div. Commdr., Brigade Commdr., Br. Chief at SHAPE and T.G.S. H.Q., Army Corps. C.-in-C, Operations, then Plan and Policy; promoted to Gen. 1982; Deputy Sec.-Gen. to the Presidency, Sec.-Gen. to the Presidency and Nat. Security Council; Deputy Chief of T.G.S. and First Army Commdr.; Commdr. Turkish Land Forces; Chief of Gen. Staff 1987–. *Leisure interest:* aviation. *Address:* Ministry of Defence, Savunma Bakantig 1, Ankara, Turkey. *Telephone:* 118 77 94.

TOSAR, Héctor A.; Uruguayan composer and pianist; b. 1923; ed. Montevideo, and Conservatoire Nationale de Musique, Paris, and Ecole Normale de Musique, Paris (under D. Milhaud, J. Rivier and A. Honegger); Prof. of History of Music and Musical Analysis, Conservatorio de Música, Montevideo 1951–60; Prof. of Harmony, Composition and Analysis, and Head of Theory Dept., Conservatorio de Música de Puerto Rico 1961; Guggenheim Fellowships, U.S.A. 1946–47, 1960–61. *Principal works:* Symphony for Strings 1959, Te Deum for bass, chorus and orchestra 1959, Sinfonia Concertante for piano and orchestra 1961.

TOTT, Konrad, D.SC.TECH.; Polish electromechanical engineer and politician; b. 31 Jan. 1936, Brusno Nowe, Przemyśl Voivodship; ed. Aircraft Faculty of Mil. Tech. Acad., Warsaw; scientific worker in Air Forces Tech. Inst. and other mil. research insts. 1959–82; Asst. Prof. 1979–; Man. Dir. Aviation Inst., Warsaw 1982–84, 1989–; Minister, State Office for Scientific and Tech. Devt. 1984–88; mem. Transport Cttee. of Polish Acad. of Sciences and numerous other Polish and foreign Cttees.; mem. Polish United Workers' Party (PZPR) 1962–; Order of Banner of Labour, (2nd Class), Kt.'s Cross of Order of Polonia Restituta, Gold Cross of Merit and other decorations. *Publications:* numerous scientific works. *Address:* Instytut Lotnictwa, Al. Krakowska 110/114, 02-256 Warsaw, Poland. *Telephone:* 46-09-93.

TÖTTERMAN, Richard Evert Björnson, LL.M., D.PHIL.; Finnish diplomatist; b. 10 Oct 1926, Helsinki; s. of B. Björn Tötterman and Katharine Clare Wimpenny; m. Camilla S. Veronica Huber 1953; one s. one d.; ed. Univ. of Helsinki and Brasenose Coll., Oxford; entered Ministry for Foreign Affairs 1952; diplomatic posts in Stockholm 1954–56, Moscow 1956–58, at Ministry of Foreign Affairs 1958–62, Berne 1962–63, Paris 1963–66; Deputy Dir. Ministry of Foreign Affairs 1966; Sec.-Gen. Office of Pres. of Finland 1966–70; Sec. of State Ministry of Foreign Affairs 1970–75; Amb. to U.K. 1975–83, to Switzerland 1983–, concurrently to the Holy See 1988–; Chair. Multilateral Consultations preparing Conf. on Security and Co-operation in Europe 1972–73; Hon. Fellow, Brasenose Coll. 1982; Hon. G.C.V.O., Hon. O.B.E; Kt. Commdr. Order of the White Rose (Finland); Grand Cross, Order of Dannebrog (Denmark), Order of Merit (Austria), Order of Orange-Nassau (Netherlands), Order of the Pole Star (Sweden), Order of the Falcon (Iceland); Grand Officier Ordre de la Couronne (Belgium), Order of St. Olav (Norway), Order of Merit (Poland), Order of Lion (Senegal), Order of the Banner (Hungary), Commandeur, Ordre Nat. du Mérite (France). *Address:* Ahornweg 8, 3074 Muri/Berne, Switzerland. *Telephone:* 43-30-31.

TOTTIE, Thomas, FIL.LIC.; Swedish librarian; b. 3 July 1930, Waxholm; s. of the late John Tottie and Gerda (née Willers) Tottie; two d. (by previous m.); m. Marianne Sandels 1972; two s. ed. Stockholm Univ.; Asst. Librarian, Royal Library, Stockholm 1961; Sec. Swedish Council of

Research Libraries 1966–73; Deputy Dir. Stockholm Univ. Library 1975–76; Dir. Library of Royal Carolingian Medico-Chirurgical Inst., Stockholm 1977; Librarian, Uppsala Univ. 1978–; mem. and official of various professional orgs. *Publications:* 2 books and numerous articles and reports on librarianship. *Leisure interests:* biography, sailing. *Address:* Kyrkogardsgatan 5A, 752 20 Uppsala, Sweden. *Telephone:* 18 39 10 (Office); 018-14 36 55 (Home).

TOUBON, Jacques, L. EN D.; French politician; b. 29 June 1941, Nice; s. of Pierre-Constant and Yolande (Molinas) Toubon; m. 2nd Lise Weiler 1982; ed. Lycée Masséna, Nice, Lycée Jean Perrin, Lyon, Faculté de Droit, Lyon, Inst. d'Etudes Politiques, Lyon, and Ecole Nat. d'Admin.; civil servant 1965–76, Chef de Cabinet, to Minister of Agric. 1972–74, to Minister of Interior 1974, Tech. Adviser, Office of Prime Minister 1974–76; Dir. Fondation Claude Pompidou 1970–77; Asst. Sec.-Gen. Rassemblement pour la République (RPR) 1977–81, Sec.-Gen. 1984–88; Deputy to Nat. Ass. 1981–; Mayor 13th Arrondissement, Paris 1983–, Asst. to Mayor of Paris 1983–; Chevalier du Mérite Agricole. *Publication:* Pour en finir avec la peur 1984. *Address:* Assemblée nationale, 75355 Paris (Office); 86 rue Notre-Dame des Champs, 75006 Paris, France (Home).

TOUGAS, Gérard Raymond, M.A., PH.D., F.R.S.C.; Canadian professor and writer; b. 5 Aug. 1921, Edmonton; s. of Alfred Tougas and Alphonsine Chouinard; m. Doris Kirk 1949; one s. one d.; ed. Univ. of Alberta, McGill Univ., Sorbonne, Paris and Stanford Univ., Calif.; interpreter (French and English) Int. Labour Office, WHO, Geneva 1947–50; instructor in French Stanford Univ., Calif. 1951–53; Asst., Assoc. then Full Prof. (specializing in language and cultures of French-speaking countries) Univ. of B.C., Vancouver 1954–84, Prof. Emer. 1984–; Fellow Carnegie Corpn., New York; Prix Halphen, Acad. Française. *Publications:* Littérature romande et culture française 1963, History of French Canadian Literature 1966, La francophonie en péril 1967, Les écrivains d'expression française et la France 1973, Puissance littéraire des Etats-Unis 1979, Destin littéraire du Québec 1982. *Leisure interest:* piano. *Address:* 1727 West 16th Avenue, Vancouver, V6J 2L9, Canada. *Telephone:* (604) 734-4244.

TOULEMON, Robert, L. EN D.; French civil servant; b. 2 July 1927, Montagnac-le-Crempse (Dordogne); s. of Henri Toulemon and Henriette Chaussade; m. Madeleine Fargeot 1951; three s.; ed. Univs. of Toulouse and Paris, Institut d'Etudes Politiques de Paris and Ecole nat. d'Admin.; Insp. of Finance 1954–57; lecturer, Inst. d'Etudes Politiques de Paris 1958–60; Tech. Adviser, Office of Sec. of State for Econ. Affairs 1959–60; Special Mission, Foreign Econ. Affairs 1958–62; Head, Export Credit Section, Ministry of Finance and Econ. Affairs 1960–62; Chef de Cabinet to Vice-Pres. of Comm. of EEC 1962–63; Dir. of Section in External Relations Directorate, Comm. of EEC 1963–67, Gen. Dir. of Industrial Affairs 1968–70, of Industrial, Tech. and Scientific Affairs 1970–73; Prof. Inst. d'Etudes politiques, Paris 1974–80; Dir. of Cabinet of Minister of Co-operation 1974–76, mem. Cabinet of Minister of Quality of Life Jan.-Aug. 1976; Insp.-Gen. of Finance 1977; Dir. Usinor-Châtillon 1979–; Pres. Asscn. française d'études pour l'union européenne 1974–; Chair. Comm. interministerielle des comptes du patrimoine naturel 1978–; Chair. Groupe d'Etudes et de Mobilisation Environnement, Ministry of European Affairs 1988–; Treas. Asscn. of Old French Bldgs. 1978–; mem. Bd. of Dirs. Radio France Overseas 1983–, Nat. Museum of Natural History 1986–; Officier, Légion d'honneur. *Leisure interests:* tennis, chess. *Address:* 41 rue d'Assas, 75006 Paris, France (Home). *Telephone:* 42 22-16-59.

TOUMPAS, Vice-Admiral John N., D.S.O.; Greek naval officer and politician; b. 24 Feb. 1901; m. Yvonne-Agnes Bondi 1944; ed. naval and mil. schools; Distinguished Naval service, Second World War; Commdr. Salamis Dockyard 1945; Naval Attaché Washington 1946; Commdr., Naval Cadet School 1946–47; Dir. of Personnel, Admiralty 1947–49; Supreme Commdr. Coastal Defence Forces 1949–51; C.-in-C. Coastal Defences 1950–52; Nat. Mil. Rep., NATO Command HQ, Paris 1952; C.-in-C. of the Fleet 1952–53; Liberal M.P. 1956, Centre Union 1958–64; Minister of State Nov.–Dec. 1963; Minister of the Interior 1964–65, of the Interior and Public Order (Security) July-Aug. 1965, of Industry 1965–66, of Foreign Affairs May-Dec. 1966; M.P. (New Democracy Party) 1974–; mem. Acad. of Athens (Positive Sciences) 1979–; f. and Pres. Liberal Party. *Address:* c/o Ministry of Athens. *Grand Commdr.* of Phoenix; War Cross (four awards), U.S.A. Legion of Merit, Romanian Grand Cross of August 23rd Order, Yugoslavian Grand Cross of the Star Order, Grand Cross of the Holy Tomb Order, Grand Commdr. of Danish Order. *Publication:* Enemy in Sight (memories of World War II) 1954 (Academy Award). *Leisure interests:* athletics, motoring, swimming. *Address:* 10 Alopekis Street, Athens 139, Greece. *Telephone:* 714-048.

TOURAINE, Alain Louis Jules François, D. ÈS L.; French sociologist; b. 3 Aug. 1925, Hermanville; s. of Albert Touraine and Odette Cleret; m. Adrianna Arenas 1957; one s. one d.; ed. Lycées Montaigne and Louis-le-Grand, Paris and Ecole Normale Supérieure; Dir. of Studies, Ecole Pratique des Hautes Etudes (now Ecole des Hautes Etudes en Sciences Sociales) 1960–; Prof. Faculté des Lettres de Paris-Nanterre 1966–69; f. Lab. de Sociologie Industrielle (now Centre d'Etude des Mouvements Sociaux) 1958–80; f. and Dir. Centre d'Analyse et d'Intervention Sociologiques 1980–; Chevalier, Légion d'honneur, Officier des Arts et Lettres. *Publications:* Sociologie de l'Action 1965, La Société post-industrielle 1969, Production de la société 1973, Pour la sociologie 1974, La voix et le regard

1978, Mort d'une gauche 1979, L'après-socialisme 1980, Solidarité 1982, Le mouvement ouvrier (with Dubet and Wieviorka) 1984, Le retour de l'acteur 1984, La parole et le sang? Politique et société en Amérique Latine 1988. *Leisure interest:* Latin America. *Address:* CADIS, 54, blvd Raspail, 75006 Paris (Office); Le Dôme, 32, blvd de Vaugirard, 75015 Paris, France (Home). *Telephone:* 45 44 39 79 (Office); 43 20 61 06 (Home).

TOURÉ, Ismaël; Guinean politician; b. 1925; ed. in France; Head, Kankan Meteorological Station; mem. Kankan Muncipal Council 1956; mem. Faranah Territorial Ass.; Minister of Works 1957–59, of Posts, Telegraphs and Transport 1959–61; Minister of Public Works and Transport 1961–62; Minister of Econ. Devt. 1963–68; Minister of Finance 1968–72, of the Economy and Finance Domain 1972–79, of Mining and Geology 1979–84; under arrest April 1984; led Guinea del. to All-African People's Conf. 1960; del. to UN 1960, 1961; fmr. mem. Political Bureau Parti Démocratique de Guinée.

TOURÉ, Mamoudou, PH.D.; Senegalese civil servant; b. 1928; ed. Univs. of Dakar and Paris and Ecole Nat. de la France d'Outre Mer; served in Office of High Commr. in Paris of del. of French W. Africa 1957–58; Counsellor and Head of Assoc. Overseas Countries and Territories in Secr. of European Community, Brussels 1958–61; Amb. Extraordinary and Plenipotentiary of Mauritania to W. Europe 1961–62; Sec.-Gen. Tech. Co-operation Comm. in Africa 1962–63; Consultant and Expert, UN Int. Children's Emergency Fund, New York and Paris 1963–65; Dir. UN African Inst. for Econ. Devt. and Planning, Dakar 1965–67; Dir. African Dept., IMF, Washington, U.S.A. 1967–76; Special Adviser, Office of Pres. of Senegal and Adviser, Gov. of Cen. Bank of W. African States (BCEAO) 1976–81; Minister of Planning and Co-operation 1981–83; Minister of Economy and Finance 1983–88, Minister-Del. for Finance and Economy April 1988–; Senegal's Gov. for IMF and World Bank, Chair. 40th Annual Meetings. *Address:* c/o Ministry of Economy and Finance, Centre Peytavin, rue Charles Laisné et ave. Carde, B.P. 462, Dakar, Senegal. *Telephone:* 21-06-99.

TOURNIER, Michel, L. ÈS L., L. EN D., D.PHIL.; French author; b. 19 Dec. 1924, Paris; s. of Alphonse and Marie-Madeleine (née Fournier) Tournier; ed. Saint-Germain-en-Laye, and Univs. of Paris (Sorbonne) and Tübingen; radio and television production 1949–54; press attaché, Europe No. 1 1955–58; head of literary services, Editions Plon 1958–68; Officier, Légion d'honneur; Grand Prix du Roman, Acad. Française 1967, Prix Goncourt 1970; mem. Acad. Goncourt 1972–. *Publications:* Vendredi ou les limbes du Pacifique 1967, Le Roi des Aulnes 1970, Les météores 1975, Le vent paraclet 1977, Le coq de bruyère 1978, Des clefs et des serrures 1979, Gaspard, Melchior et Balthazar 1980, Le vol du Vampire 1981, Gilles et Jeanne 1983, La Goutte d'Or 1986, The Wind Spirit (autobiog.) 1988. *Leisure interest:* photography. *Address:* Le presbytère, Choisel, 78460 Chevreuse, France. *Telephone:* 3052-05-29.

TOUSEY, Richard, PH.D.; American physicist; b. 18 May 1908, Somerville, Mass.; s. of Coleman Tousey and Adella R. H. (Hill) Tousey; m. Ruth Lowe 1932; one d.; ed. Tufts and Harvard Univs.; Instructor Harvard Univ. 1933–36; Research Instructor Tufts Univ. 1936–41; Physicist in Optics Div., Naval Research Lab. 1941–58, Head of Rocket Spectroscopy Branch, Space Science Div. (fmrly. Atmosphere and Astrophysics Div.) 1958–78, Consultant 1978–; Henry Norris Russell Lecturer, American Astronomical Soc. 1966; Whiting Fellow, Harvard Univ. 1929–31, Bayard Cutting Fellow 1935–36; Fellow American Acad. of Arts and Sciences, American Physical Soc., Optical Soc. of America, American Geophysical Union; mem. N.A.S., American Astronomical Soc. (Vice-Pres. 1964–66), A.A.A.S., and numerous other U.S. and int. socs.; Hon. D.Sc. (Tufts Univ.); several awards, including Prix Ançel Award of Soc. Française de Photographie 1962, Henry Draper Medal of Nat. Acad. of Sciences 1965, Navy Award for Distinguished Achievement in Science 1963, Eddington Medal of Royal Astronomical Soc. 1964, NASA Exceptional Scientific Achievement Medal 1974. *Publications:* Numerous articles in various technical journals. *Leisure interests:* music, ornithology. *Address:* Code 4107, U.S. Naval Research Laboratory, Washington, D.C. 20375; 7725 Oxon Hill Road, Oxon Hill, Md. 20745, U.S.A. (Home). *Telephone:* (202) 767-3441 (Office).

TOVSTONOGOV, Georgiy Aleksandrovich; Soviet theatrical director and teacher; b. 28 Sept. 1915, Tbilisi, Georgia; s. of Aleksandr Tovstonogov and Tamara Papitashvili; m.; two s.; ed. Lunacharsky Inst. of Theatrical Art; began as actor and Asst. Dir. at Junior Theatre, Tbilisi 1931; Dir. Griboyedov Russian Drama Theatre, Tbilisi 1938–46; Dir. Cen. Children's Theatre Moscow 1946–49; Dir. Leningrad Komsomol Theatre 1950–56, also a number of others; Chief Dir. Leningrad State Drama Theatre 1956–; Chair. of Directing at Leningrad Inst. of Theatre, Music and Cinema 1962–; Co-Ed. Theatre (monthly); awards include State Prizes 1950, 1952, 1968; People's Artist of U.S.S.R. 1957, Order of Lenin (twice), Order of Red Banner. *Productions include:* Kremlin Chimes 1940, School for Scandal 1942, Pompadours (Shchedrin) 1954, Irkutsk Story (Arbuzov) 1960, Woe from Wit (Griboyedov) 1962, Virgin Soil Upturned (Sholokhov) 1964, Three Sisters (Chekhov) 1964, The Idiot (Dostoyevsky), 1966, Merchants (Gorky) 1966, Khanuma (Tsagareli) 1973. *Publications include:* Notes on the Theatre 1960, Talking about Directing 1962, On Being a Director 1965, My Thoughts at Large 1972. *Leisure interest:* collecting masks. *Address:*

Leningrad State Academic Bolshoi Drama Theatre, 65 Fontanka, Leningrad, U.S.S.R.

TOWE, Peter Milburn, M.A.; Canadian diplomatist; b. 1 Nov. 1922, London, Ont.; s. of Allen M. and Clare (Durdle) Towe; m. Carol Krumm 1953; one s. two d.; ed. Univ. of W. Ontario and Queen's Univ.; joined Royal Canadian Air Force 1942, served in Europe, discharged 1945; joined Dept. of External Affairs 1947, served in Washington, Bonn, Beirut, Paris; Deputy Dir. Gen., External Aid Office 1962-67; Minister, Canadian Embassy, Washington 1967-72; Amb. and Perm. Rep. to OECD 1972-75; Asst. Under-Sec. of State for External Affairs 1975-77; Amb. to U.S.A. 1977-81; Chair. Petro-Canada Int. Assistance Corpn. 1981-; Hon. LL.D. (Univ. of W. Ont.) 1981. *Leisure interests:* golf, fishing. *Address:* Suite 1601, 360 Albert Street, Ottawa, Ont. K1R 7X7, Canada. *Telephone:* (613) 990-6000.

TOWEETT, Taaitta, PH.D.; Kenyan politician; b. 5 May 1925, Kericho; s. of Toweett and Tapaasee Maera; m.; two s. one d.; ed. Alliance High School and Makerere Coll., Uganda, and Univs. of S. Africa and Nairobi; mem. Legis. Council 1958-59; Asst. Minister of Agric. 1960-61; Minister of Labour and Housing 1961-62, of Lands, Survey and Town Planning 1962-63, of Educ. 1969-74, of Housing and Social Services 1974-76, of Educ. 1976-79; Pres. 19th Session of Gen. Conf. of UNESCO; Chair. Kenya Literature Bureau 1980-. *Publication:* Tears over a Dead Cow (short stories), Epitaph on Colonialism (poems) 1979, Traditional History of Kipsigis 1979, English-Swahili-Kalenjin Nouns Pocket Dictionary 1979, Study of Kalenjin Linguistics 1979. *Leisure interest:* study of origins of personal names. *Address:* P.O. Box 46055, Nairobi, Kenya. *Telephone:* 23030 (Office); 891-386 (Home).

TOWER, John Goodwin; American politician (retd.); b. 29 Sept. 1925, Houston; s. of Joe Z. and Beryl (née Goodwin) Tower; three d.; ed. Southwestern Univ., Texas, Southern Methodist Univ., and London School of Econs.; Radio Announcer, Beaumont, Texas 1948, Taylor, Texas 1948-49; Insurance Agent, Dallas 1950-51; Asst. Prof. of Political Science, Midwestern Univ. Texas 1951-61; U.S. Senator from Texas (elected to fill vacancy caused by election of Lyndon Johnson as Vice-Pres. of U.S.A. 1961-85), re-elected 1966, 1972, 1978; Chair. Senate Armed Services Cttee. 1981-85; U.S. Negotiator on Strategic Nuclear Arms (SALT talks) and mem. U.S. Del. to Negotiations on Nuclear and Space Arms 1985-86; Chair. Comm. of Inquiry into Nat. Security Council 1986-87; Distinguished Lecturer in Political Science S. Methodist Univ., Dallas 1986-; mem. Tower, Eggers and Greene Consultants Inc. 1987-; mem. Bd. of Dirs., Macmillan 1989-; nominated as Sec. for Defense Dec. 1988, rejected by Senate March 1989; fmr. mem. Banking, Housing and Urban Affairs Comm., Budget Comm.; Dir. Astrotech Int., Inc., British Aerospace, Gray & Co.; Chair. Pergamon-Brassey's Int. Defense Publs., Inc., Navy Memorial Foundation; Hon. Fellow L.S.E. 1984; Kt. Commdr.'s Cross of Order of Merit, Fed. Repub. of Germany, Order of Merit, Tunisia; Republican. *Address:* 710 Turtle Creek Centre, 3811 Turtle Creek Boulevard, Dallas, Tex. 75219; c/o Dickstein, Shapiro & Morin, 2101 L Street, N.W., 10th Floor, Washington, D.C. 20037, U.S.A. (Offices). *Telephone:* (214) 526-5997 (Dallas); (202) 775-4789 (Washington).

TOWNES, Charles Hard, PH.D.; American physicist; b. 28 July 1915, Greenville, S. Carolina; s. of Henry Keith and Ellen Sumter Hard; m. Frances H. Brown 1941; four d.; ed. Furman and Duke Univs., California Inst. of Technology; Asst. Calif. Inst. of Tech. 1937-39; mem. Tech. staff, Bell Telephone Labs. 1939-47; Assoc. Prof. of Physics, Columbia Univ. 1948-50, Prof. 1950-61; Exec. Dir. Radiation Lab. 1950-52, Chair. Dept. of Physics 1952-55; Vice-Pres. and Dir. of Research, Inst. for Defense Analyses 1959-61; Provost and Prof. of Physics, M.I.T. 1961-66, Inst. Prof. 1966-67; Univ. Prof., Univ. of Calif. 1967-86, Prof. Emer. 1986-; Trustee Carnegie Inst. of Washington 1965-, Bd. of Dirs. Perkin-Elmer Corpn. 1966-85, Gen. Motors 1973-86, Bulletin of the Atomic Scientists 1964-69; Chair. Science and Tech. Advisory Comm. for Manned Space Flight, Nat. Aeronautics and Space Admin. 1964-69; Chair. Space Science Bd., N.A.S. 1970-73; Guggenheim Fellow 1955-56; Fulbright Lecturer, Paris 1955-56, Tokyo 1956; Richtmyer Lecturer, American Physical Soc. 1959; Scott Lecturer, Cambridge 1963; Jansky Lecturer, Nat. Radio Astronomy Observatory 1971; Lincoln Lecturer 1972-73; Halley Lecturer, Oxford 1976; Schiff Memorial Lecturer, Stanford 1982, Michelson Memorial Lecturer, U.S. Naval Acad. 1982; mem. Pres.'s Science Advisory Cttee. 1966-70, Vice-Chair. 1967-69; Dir. British Aerospace Inc. 1986-; Centennial Lecturer, Univ. of Toronto 1967; mem. Editorial Bd. Review of Scientific Instruments 1950-52, Physical Review 1951-53, Journal of Molecular Spectroscopy 1957-60, etc.; Fellow, American Physical Soc. (Council mem. 1959-62, 1965-71, Pres. 1967), Inst. of Electrical and Electronics Engineers; mem. American Acad. of Arts and Sciences, American Philosophical Soc., American Astronomical Soc., Space Program Advisory Council, NASA, N.A.S. (council mem. 1967-72, 1978-81); Hon. mem. Optical Soc. of America; Foreign mem. Royal Soc. 1976; mem. Pontifical Acad. of Science 1983; mem. Bd. of Trustees Rand Corpn. 1965-70; Trustee, Calif. Inst. of Tech. 1979-; Fellow of Calif. Acad. of Sciences; awards include Comstock Award (N.A.S.) 1959, Stuart Ballantine Medal (Franklin Inst.) 1959, 1962, Rumford Premium (American Acad. of Arts and Sciences) 1961, David Sarnoff Award in Electronics (American Inst. of Electrical Engineers) 1961, John A. Carty Medal (N.A.S.) 1962, Thomas Young Medal and Prize (Inst. of

Physics and Physical Soc., England) 1963, Nobel Prize for Physics 1964, Distinguished Public Service Medal (NASA) 1969, Medal of Honor, Inst. of Electrical and Electronics Engineers 1967, Wilmer Exner Award 1970, Plyler Prize American Physical Soc. 1977, Niels Bohr Int. Gold Medal 1979, LeConte Medal 1980, Nat. Medal of Science 1982; hon. degrees include D.Litt., Sc.D., Dott.Ing., LL.D., L.H.D., D. Med Sc.; Nat. Inventors' Hall of Fame 1976, Eng. and Science Hall of Fame 1983; holder of patents in electronics, including fundamental patents on masers and lasers, etc. *Publications:* Microwave Spectroscopy 1955, Quantum Electronics 1960, Quantum Electronics and Coherent Light 1964; other scientific papers on microwave spectroscopy, molecular and nuclear structures, radio and infra-red astronomy, masers and lasers, etc. *Leisure interest:* natural history. *Address:* University of California, Department of Physics, Berkeley, Calif. 94720, U.S.A.

TOWNSHEND, Peter Dennis Blandford; British composer, performer of rock music, publisher and author; b. 19 May 1945, London; s. of Clifford and Betty Townshend; m. Karen Astley 1968; two d.; ed. Acton County Grammar School and Ealing Art Coll.; record contracts with The Who with Fontana Records 1964, M.C.A. records 1965, W.E.A. Records 1979; retd. from The Who 1984; solo contract with Atlantic Records 1979-; owner, Eel Pie Recording Ltd. 1972-; est. Eel Pie (book publishing co.) 1976; E., Faber & Faber (publrs.) 1983-; Ivor Novello Award 1981, British Phonographic Industry Award 1983. *Recordings include:* with The Who: Can't Explain 1965, My Generation, Tommy (rock opera), Quadrophenia (rock opera); solo: Empty Glass 1980, All the Best Cowboys Have Chinese Eyes 1982, White City 1985. *Publication:* Horse's Neck: Lyrical Prose 1985. *Leisure interests:* sailing, Indian mysticism and Sufism. *Address:* The Boathouse, Ranelagh Drive, Twickenham, TW1 1QZ, England. *Telephone:* 01-891 1266.

TOY, Sam, M.A.; British business executive; b. 21 Aug. 1923, Mabe, Cornwall; s. of Edward and Lilian Toy; m. 1st Jean Balls 1944, one s.; m. 2nd Joan Franklin Rook 1950, two s. one d.; m. 3rd Janetta McMorrow 1984; ed. Falmouth Grammar School and Univ. of Cambridge; R.A.F. pilot 1942-48; joined Ford Motor Co. Ltd. 1948, Chair. and Man. Dir. 1980-86; Vice-Pres. Soc. Motor Mfrs. and Traders Ltd. 1982-86, Pres. 1986-87. *Leisure interests:* trout and salmon fishing, golf. *Address:* 35 Stanhope Terrace, Lancaster Gate, London, W2 2UA, England.

TOYE, Wendy; British theatrical producer, film director, choreographer, actress and dancer; b. 1 May 1917; d. of Ernest W. and Jessie Crichton (Ramsay) Toye; ed. privately, trained with Euphen MacLaren, Tamara Karsavina, Anton Dolin, Morosoff, Legat, Marie Rambert; first performance aged 3 years, Albert Hall; first professional appearance as Cobweb (Midsummer Night's Dream), Old Vic 1929; prin. dancer Hiawatha, Albert Hall 1931; played Marigold and Phoebe, and produced dances, Toad of Toad Hall, Royalty 1931-32; masked dancer Ballerina, Gaiety 1933; danced and choreographed for Carmargo Soc. of Ballet; mem. Ninette de Valois' original Vic Wells Ballet, danced in C. B. Cochran's The Miracle, Lyceum 1932, prin. dancer The Golden Toy, Coliseum 1934; toured with Anton Dolin's Ballet (choreographer for divertissements and short ballets) 1934-35; Tulip Time, Alhambra, then prin. dancer and choreographer, Markova-Dolin Ballet 1935; arranged dances and ballets for many shows and films 1935-42, including most of George Black's productions notably Black Velvet (also prin. dancer) 1939; Shakespearean season, Open Air Theatre 1939; *Theatre productions:* Big Ben, Bless the Bride, Tough at the Top (for C. B. Cochran), Adelphi, The Shepherd Show, Prince's, Peter Pan (co-dir. and choreographer), New York, And So To Bed, New Theatre, Feu d'Artifice (co-dir. and choreographer), Paris, Night of Masquerade, Queen, Second Threshold, Vaudeville, Three's Company (choreographer) in Joyce Grenfell Requests the Pleasure, Fortune, Wild Thyme, Duke of York's, Lady at the Wheel and Robert and Elizabeth, Lyric, Hammersmith, Majority of One, Phoenix, Magic Lantern and On the Level, Saville, As You Like It, Old Vic, Virtue in Danger, Mermaid and Strand, A Midsummer Night's Dream, Shakespeare quatercentenary, Latin American tour 1964, Soldier's Tale, Edinburgh Festival 1967, Boots and Strawberry Jam, Nottingham Playhouse 1968, The Great Waltz, Drury Lane 1970, Showboat, Adelphi 1971, She Stoops to Conquer, Young Vic 1972, Cowardy Custard, Mermaid 1972, Stand and Deliver, Roundhouse 1972; at Chicester R. Loves J 1973, The Confederacy 1974, Follow The Star 1974, Made in Heaven 1975, Make Me a World 1976, Once More with Music 1976, Oh Mr. Porter, Mermaid 1977, Gingerbread Man, Watermill Theatre 1981, This Thing Called Love, Watermill Theatre 1982, Ambassadors Theatre 1983, Singing in the Rain (Assoc. Producer), Palladium 1983, Noel and Gertie, Monte Carlo 1983, Birds of A Feather 1984, Barnum (Assoc. Producer) 1985, Madwoman of Chaillot, Torville and Dean World Tour (Assoc. Producer) 1985, Once Upon A Mattress, Water Mill Theatre 1985, Kiss Me Kate, Copenhagen 1986, Laburnham Grove, Palace Theatre, Watford 1987, Miranda, Chichester Festival Theatre 1987, Get the Message, Molecule 1987, Songbook, Watermill 1988; *opera productions:* Bluebeard's Castle (Bartók), Sadler's Wells and Brussels, The Telephone (Menotti), Rusalka (Dvořák), and La Vie Parisienne, Sadler's Wells, Die Fledermaus, Coliseum and Sadler's Wells, Orpheus in the Underworld, Sadler's Wells and Australia, The Abduction from the Seraglio, Bath Festival 1967, The Impresario, Don Pasquale (for Phoenix Opera Group) 1968, The Italian Girl in Algiers, Coliseum 1968, Orpheus 1978, Merry Widow 1979-80, Orpheus 1981,

Mikado (Turkey) 1982, The Italian Girl in Algiers 1982; *films directed:* The Stranger Left No Card 1952, The Teckman Mystery, Raising a Riot, The Twelfth Day of Christmas, Three Cases of Murder 1954, All for Mary 1955, True as a Turtle 1956, We Joined the Navy 1962, The King's Breakfast, Cliff in Scotland, A Goodly Manor for a Song, Girls Wanted—Istanbul; productions for TV, Follow the Star 1979, Tales of the Unexpected 1981, Trial By Jury 1982, Di Ballo 1982; musicals, variety, cabaret; Guest Artist with Sadler's Wells Ballet and Mme. Rambert's Ballet Club; prin. dancer with British Ballet organized by Adeline Genée, Denmark 1932, lectured in Australia 1977; Adviser, Arts Council Training Scheme 1978–; The Queen's Silver Jubilee Medal. *Leisure interests:* embroidery, gardening. *Address:* c/o David Watson, Simpson Fox, 52 Shaftesbury Avenue, London, W1V 7DE, England. *Telephone:* (01) 434-9167.

TRABUCCHI, Alberto, LL.D.; Italian lawyer; b. 26 July 1907, Verona; s. of Marco Trabucchi and Maria Zamboni; m. Nanda Nanni Sparavieri 1945; five c.; ed. Liceo Maffei, Verona, Univ. of Padua; Asst., Istituto di Filosofia del Diritto, Padua 1929–35; Lecturer in Civil Law, Univ. of Ferrara 1936–40; Prof. of Private Law, Univ. of Venice 1938–52; Prof. of Civil Law, Univ. of Padua 1942–82, of Roman Law 1943–45, of Private Comparative Law 1949–60; Mayor of Illási (Verona) 1950–; Judge, Court of Justice of European Communities 1962–72; Advocate-Gen., Court of Justice of European Communities 1972–76; Doyen Padua Faculty of Jurisprudence; Dir. of Giurisprudenza Italiana and Rivista diritto civile. *Publications:* Il Matrimonio putativo 1936, Il Dolo nella teoria dei vizi del volere 1937, Codice delle Comunità Europea 1962, Commentario Trattato C.E.E. 1965, Commentario Trattato C.E.C.A. 1970, Istituzioni di Diritto civile 1978–89; Commentario alla riforma del diritto di famiglia (3 vols) 1977, Commentario breve al Codice Civile 1988. *Address:* Via Rudena 39, Padua, Italy. *Telephone:* 049 650428.

TRACY, Honor Lilbush Wingfield; British writer; b. 19 Oct. 1913, Bury St. Edmunds, Suffolk; d. of Humphry Tracy and Christabel May Clare Miller; ed. Grove School, Highgate, London; Foreign Corresp. The Observer 1947–50; Daily Telegraph columnist 1973–88. *Publications:* Travel: Kakemono: A Sketchbook of Postwar Japan 1950, Mind You, I've Said Nothing 1953, Silk Hats and No Breakfast 1957, Spanish Leaves 1964, Winter in Castille 1973, The Heart of England 1983; Fiction: The Deserters 1954, The Straight and Narrow Path 1956, The Prospects are Pleasing 1958, A Number of Things 1959, A Season of Mists 1961, The First Day of Friday 1963, Men at Work 1966, The Beauty of the World 1967, Settled in Chambers 1968, The Butterflies of the Province 1970, The Quiet End of Evening 1972, In a Year of Grace 1975, The Man From Next Door 1977, The Ballad of Castle Reef 1979. *Leisure interests:* travelling, gardening, botany and wild life. *Address:* 1 Mead House, Heathfield Lane, Chislehurst, Kent, England. *Telephone:* 01-467 1438.

TRAGER, William, PH.D.; American professor of parasitology; b. 20 March 1910, Newark, N.J.; m. Ida Sosnow 1935; one s. two d.; ed. Rutgers and Harvard Univs.; Fellow Nat. Research Council 1933–34; with Rockefeller Inst. for Medical Research and Rockefeller Univ. 1934–, Prof. and Head of Lab. of Parasitology 1964–80, Prof. Emer. 1980–; Capt. of Sanitary Corps, Malaria Research, U.S. Army, S.W. Pacific 1943–45; Hon. Sc.D. (Rutgers Univ.) 1965, (Rockefeller Univ.) 1987; Guggenheim Found. Fellow 1973–74; Fellow A.A.A.S.; mem. N.A.S.; numerous awards and mem. of numerous cttees. *Publications:* Living Together: The Biology of Animal Parasitism 1986; numerous scientific papers. *Address:* The Rockefeller University, 1230 York Avenue, New York, N.Y. 10021, U.S.A. *Telephone:* (212) 570-8630.

TRAILL, Sir Alan, G.B.E., M.A., D.MUS.; British insurance broker; b. 7 May 1935, London; s. of George and Margaret (Matthews) Traill; m. Sarah Jane Hutt 1964; one s.; ed. Charterhouse and Jesus Coll., Cambridge; Dir. Morice Tozer Beck (insurance brokers) 1960; Founder Dir. Traill Attenborough (Lloyds brokers) 1973, Chair. 1980; Chair. PWS Marine Ltd.; Dir. PWS Holdings PLC 1986, Aegis Insurance Brokers 1987–; Dir. City Arts Trust Ltd., City of London Sinfonia Ltd.; mem. London Court of Int. Arbitration, Council of Man., Royal Shakespeare Theatre Trust; mem. Court of Common Council (of City of London) 1970, Alderman 1975, Sheriff 1982–83, Lord Mayor of London 1984–85; K. St. J. 1985. *Leisure interests:* shooting, skiing, DIY, travel, opera, music, assisting education. *Address:* Thrale House, 44-46 Southwark Street, London, SE1 1UN, England. *Telephone:* 01-929 239.

TRAIN, Russell Errol, LL.B.; American conservationist; b. 4 June 1920, Washington, D.C.; s. of Rear Admiral Charles R. Train and Errol C. (Brown) Train; m. Aileen Bowdoin 1954; one s. three d.; ed. St. Albans School, Washington, D.C., Princeton and Columbia Univs.; Attorney, Congressional Jt. Cttee. on Internal Revenue Taxation 1948; Clerk (Chief Counsel), House Cttee. on Ways and Means 1953, Minority Adviser 1955; Treasury Dept. 1956; Judge, Tax Court of U.S.A. 1957–65; Pres. Conservation Foundation 1965–69; mem. Nat. Water Comm. 1968–69; Under-Sec. of the Interior 1969–70; Chair. Council on Environmental Quality 1970–73; Dir. Environmental Protection Agency 1973–78; Sr. Assoc. Conservation Fund 1977–; Pres. and C.E.O. World Wildlife Fund US 1978–85, Chair. of Bd. 1985–; fmr. Dir. American Cttee. for Int. Wildlife Protection; mem. Exec. Cttee., Int. Union for Conservation of Nature and Natural Resources; several hon. degrees; Albert Schweitzer Medal, Animal Welfare Inst. 1972, Aldo Leopold Medal, Wildlife Soc. 1975; Conservationist of the Year, Nat. Wildlife Fed. 1974. *Address:* c/o World Wildlife Fund-U.S., 1601 Connecticut Avenue, N.W., Washington, D.C., 20009, U.S.A. (Office).

TRAN BUU KIEM; Vietnamese politician; b. 1921, Can Tho; ed. Faculty of Law, Hanoi Univ.; mem. Indo-Chinese Student Org.; organized a popular uprising in Saigon 1945; Sec.-Gen. Admin. and Resistance Cttee. for Southern Region of Viet-Nam, Indo-Chinese Student Org., Deputy Dir. for Econ. Services in Southern Region 1950; Deputy Sec.-Gen. Cen. Cttee. of Democratic Party 1960; mem. Cen. Cttee. NLF; Pres. Student Union of South Viet-Nam; head of NLF Del. to Paris Conf. on Viet-Nam; Minister to Presidency, Provisional Revolutionary Govt. of South Viet-Nam 1975–76. *Address:* c/o Office of the President, Hanoi, Viet-Nam.

TRAN NAM TRUNG (see Tran Van Tra, Gen.).

TRAN TAM TINH, Rev., PH.D., F.R.S.C.; Vietnamese/Canadian professor of classical archaeology; b. 16 April 1929, Nam Dinh; ed. Séminaire Pontifical, Università Laterano, Université de Fribourg, Ecole Pratique des Hautes Etudes, Paris, C.N.R.S.; ordained Priest 1956; excavations at Soli, Cyprus 1965–74, Pompeii and Herculaneum 1969–76; Co-f. Fraternité Vietnam 1976; Prof. of Classical Archaeology, Laval Univ. 1964–, Sr. Prof. 1971–; Tatiana Warscher Award for Archaeology (American Acad. at Rome) 1973, Prix G. Mendel (Académie des Inscriptions et Belles-Lettres, France) 1978. *Publications:* Le culte d'Isis à Pompéi 1964, Le culte des divinités orientales à Herculanum 1971, Le culte des divinités orientales en Campanie 1972, Isis lactans 1973, Catalogue des peintures romaines au musée du Louvre 1974, I cattolici nella storia del Vietnam 1975, Dieu et César 1978, Sérapis debout 1983, Soloi I, La Basilique 1985, La casa dei Cervi à Herculanum 1988, Tôi vê Hanoi 1974, Tro vê nguôn 1974. *Address:* Faculté des Lettres, Université Laval, Québec, P.Q., G1K 7P4, Canada. *Telephone:* (418) 656-3159.

TRÂN THIEN KHIEM, Gen.; Vietnamese army officer and politician; b. 15 Dec. 1925; Army service 1947–75; held off attempted coup against Pres. Diem 1960, took part in coup against him 1963; with Gen. Nguyen Khan led coup removing Gen. Duong Van Minh 1964; Defence Minister and C.-in-C. 1964; Amb. to U.S.A. 1964–65, to Repub. of China 1965–68; Minister of the Interior 1968–73, Deputy Prime Minister March-Aug. 1969, Prime Minister 1969–75, Minister of Defence 1972–75; fled to Taiwan April 1975.

TRAN VAN HUONG; Vietnamese politician; b. 1 Dec. 1903; fmr. schoolteacher; participated in Viet-Minh resistance against French; Prefect of Saigon 1954 and 1964; Prime Minister Repub. of Viet-Nam 1964–65, 1968–69; Vice-Pres. of Repub. of Viet-Nam 1971–75, Pres. 21-28 April 1975.

TRAN VAN TRA, Gen.; Vietnamese army officer and politician (also known by other names Tu Chi and Tran Nam Trung); b. 1918, Quang Ngai Province, S. Viet-Nam; Alt. mem. Cen. Cttee. Lao Dong Party; Deputy Chief of Staff, N. Vietnamese Army; Chair. Mil. Affairs Cttee., Cen. Office of S. Viet-Nam (COSVN) 1964–76; rose to rank of three-star general May 1975; Minister of Defence, Provisional Revolutionary Govt. of S. Viet-Nam 1969–76 (in Saigon 1975–76); head of mil. cttee. controlling Saigon and District May 1975–Jan. 1976; Chair. Inspectorate, Council of Ministers, Socialist Repub. of Viet-Nam 1976–81. *Address:* c/o Council of Ministers, Hanoi, Viet-Nam.

TRAORÉ, Col. Diara; Guinean army officer and politician; Prime Minister of Guinea April–Dec. 1984, Minister of Nat. Educ. 1984–85; mem. Comité militaire de redressement nat. (CMRN) 1984–85; staged abortive coup d'état July 1985; arrested and sentenced to death; sentence commuted to life imprisonment; released Dec. 1988.

TRAORE, Mohamed; Guinean diplomatist; b. 1940, Forecariah; m.; five c.; ed. Mil. Coll., Tashkent and Army Acad. of Civil and Mil. Eng., Moscow; fmr. Dir. Subregional Office Liberation Cttee. of OAU, Conakry; mem. Cttee. for Nat. Recovery; fmr. Dir. Office of Research, Ministry of Nat. Defence; fmr. Minister of Communication and Tourism, and of Information; Perm. Rep. to UN 1986–. *Address:* Permanent Mission of Guinea to the United Nations, 1 United Nations Plaza, 26th Floor, New York, N.Y. 10017, U.S.A. *Telephone:* (212) 486-9170.

TRAORÉ, Gen. Moussa; Mali army officer and politician; b. 25 Sept. 1936, Kayes; ed. Training Coll., Fréjus, Cadets Coll., Kati; became N.C.O. in French Army; returned to Mali 1960; promoted Lieut. 1964, Col. 1971, Brig.-Gen. 1978; at Armed Forces Coll., Kati until 1968; led coup to depose Pres. Modibo Keita Nov. 1968; Pres. Mil. Cttee. for Nat. Liberation (Head of State) and C.-in-C. of the Armed Forces Nov. 1968–, also Prime Minister 1969–80; Pres. of Mali 1979–; Minister of Defence and Security 1978–86, of the Interior 1978–79, of Nat. Defence June 1988–; Sec.-Gen. Nat. Council Union Démocratique du Peuple Malien 1979–80, fmr. mem. Cen. Exec. Bureau; Pres. Conf. of Heads of State, Union Douanière des Etats de l'Afrique de l'Ouest 1970. *Address:* c/o Cabinet du Président, Comité militaire de libération nationale, Bamako, Mali.

TRAPEZNIKOV, Vadim Aleksandrovich, D.SC.; Soviet power engineer; b. 28 Nov. 1905, Moscow; m. Sofia Trapeznikova 1946; ed. Moscow Higher Tech. School; Power Engineer, All-Union Electrotechnical Inst. 1928–33; Instructor, Moscow Power Eng. Inst. 1930–39, Prof. of Automation and Electrical Machine Bldg. 1939–41; Inst. of Control Sciences 1941–, Dir.

1951–87, Hon. Dir. 1987–; Corresp. mem. U.S.S.R. Acad. of Sciences 1953–60, mem. 1960–; mem. CPSU 1951–; Chief Ed. Automation and Telemechanics, U.S.S.R. Acad. of Sciences 1955–88; mem. State Cttee. for Science and Tech. 1965–; Chair. Nat. Comm. on Automatic Control 1957–; mem. Hungarian Acad. of Sciences, Serbian Acad. of Sciences, Czechoslovak Acad. of Sciences; Order of Red Banner of Labour, State Prize 1946, 1953, 1971, Order of Lenin 1965, Hero of Socialist Labour 1965, Grand Gold Medal of U.S.S.R. Acad. of Science 1975. *Publications:* Design Principles for a Series of Asynchronous Machines 1937, Automatic Checking of Linear Dimensions in Manufactured Articles 1947, Generalized Conditions of Proportionality and Optimum Geometry of Transformers 1948, Cybernetics and Automatic Control 1962, Problems of Technical Cybernetics in Institute of Automation and Telemechanics 1964, Control and Scientific Technical Progress 1983; and over 60 other works 1929–74. *Address:* Institute of Control Sciences, 65 Profsoyuznaya ulitsa, GSP-312 Moscow, U.S.S.R. *Telephone:* 334-89-11.

TRAPP, Joseph Burney, M.A., F.B.A., F.S.A.; British (b. New Zealand) administrator; b. 16 July 1925, Carterton, N.Z.; s. of H. M. B. Trapp and Frances M. Trapp (née Wolters); m. Elayne Margaret Falla 1953; two s.; ed. Dannevirke High School and Victoria Univ. Coll., Wellington, N.Z.; Asst. Librarian, Alexander Turnbull Library, Wellington 1946–50; Jr. Lecturer, Victoria Univ. Coll. 1950–51; Asst. Lecturer, Univ. of Reading, England 1951–53; Asst. Librarian, then Librarian, Warburg Inst., London 1953–76, Dir. and Prof. of the History of the Classical Tradition 1976–(90); Vice-Pres. British Acad. 1983–85. *Publications:* Ed. Apology of Sir Thomas More 1979; articles in learned journals. *Address:* Warburg Institute, Woburn Square, London, WC1H 0AB, England. *Telephone:* 01-580 9663.

TRAUTLEIN, Donald Henry; American business executive; b. 19 Aug. 1926, Sandusky, Ohio; s. of Henry Francis and Lillian Amelia (née Russell) Trautlein; m. Mary Rankin 1956; two s. one d.; ed. Bowling Green State Univ., Miami Univ., Ohio; served with U.S.N. 1945–46; business trainee, Gen. Electric Corpn. 1950–51; partner Price Waterhouse and Co., New York 1951–76; Comptroller, Sr. Vice-Pres. Accounting, Dir. Bethlehem Steel Corpn., Pa. 1977–78, Exec. Vice-Pres. 1978–80, Chair. and C.E.O. 1980–86, Chair. March–June 1986; Dir. Chase Manhattan Bank, New York Bd., Exec. Cttee. American Iron and Steel Inst., Int. Iron and Steel Inst. *Address:* RFD, 1 Coopersburg, Pa. 18036, U.S.A. (Home).

TRAUTMAN, Andrzej, Polish theoretical physicist; b. 4 Jan. 1933, Warsaw; s. of Mieczysław and Eliza Trautman; m. Róża Michalska 1962; two s.; ed. Warsaw Tech. Univ., Warsaw Univ.; Asst. Inst. of Radiolocation, Tech. Univ., Warsaw 1952–53, Inst. of Applied Math. 1953–55; postgraduate studies, Inst. of Physics, Polish Acad. of Sciences 1955–58, Doctorate 1959; Lecturer 1959; scientific training, Imperial Coll., King's Coll., London, Univ. of Syracuse, U.S.A. 1959–61; Scientist, Inst. of Theoretical Physics, Warsaw Univ. 1961–, Asst. Prof. and Head of Dept. Electrodynamics and Theory of Relativity 1962–68, Extraordinary Prof. 1964–71, Ordinary Prof. 1971–; Deputy Dir. Inst. of Theoretical Physics 1968–74, Dir. 1975–85; Corresp. mem. Polish Acad. of Sciences 1969–76, mem. 1977–, mem. Presidium 1972–83, Vice Pres. 1978–80, Chair. Cttee. of Physics, Polish Acad. of Sciences; Deputy Chair. Gen. Bd. of Polish Physics Asscn. 1970–73, Foreign mem. Czechoslovak Acad. of Sciences 1980–; mem. Int. Cttee. of Theory of Relativity and Gravitation 1965–80, Editorial Staff Annales de l'Inst. H. Poincaré, Reports on Mathematical Physics, Int. Journal of Theoretical Physics; Visiting Prof., American Math. Soc., Santa Barbara 1962, Coll. de France, Paris 1963 and 1981, Brandeis Univ., U.S.A. 1964, Univ. of Chicago 1971, Univ. of Pisa, Italy 1972, The Schrödinger Professorship, Univ. of Vienna 1972, State Univ. of N.Y. at Stony Brook 1976–77, Univ. of Montreal 1982, Univ. of Tex. at Dallas 1985, 1986; State Prize 1st Class 1976, Alfred Jurzykowski Foundation Award in Physics 1984, Gold Cross of Merit, Cross of Order of Polonia Restituta. *Publications:* The Spinorial Chessboard (with P. Budinich) 1988, and numerous works on theory of gravitation waves, energy of gravitation field, modern methods of differential geometry and their application in physics, Einstein-Cartan's Theory. *Leisure interest:* chess. *Address:* Instytut Fizyki Teoretycznej UW, ul. Hoża 69, 00-681 Warsaw (Office); ul. Słupecka 4 m.87, 02-309 Warsaw, Poland (Home). *Telephone:* 283031, Ext. 295 (Office); 229048 (Home).

TRAUTMANN, Rezső; Hungarian politician; b. 1907; Structural engineer; Chair. Nat. Office of Building Construction 1953; Deputy Minister of Building Industry 1951–53, Minister 1957–68; mem. Pres. Council, Vice-Pres. 1980–; Pres. Scientific Soc. of Bldg.; Order of Merit 1977. *Address:* Presidential Council, Kossuth Lajos tér 1/3, H-1357 Budapest V, Hungary.

TRAVELL, Janet G., M.D.; American physician; b. 17 Dec. 1901, New York, N.Y.; d. of J. Willard Travell and Janet E. Davidson; m. John William Gordon Powell 1929 (died 1973); two d.; ed. Wellesley Coll. and Cornell Univ. Medical Coll.; fmr. medical practice in New York; Assoc. Prof. of Clinical Pharmacology, Cornell Univ. Medical Coll. 1951–63; Official Physician to the White House 1961–65; Assoc. Clinical Prof. of Medicine, George Washington Univ. School of Medicine 1961–70, Prof. Emer. 1970–; Special Consultant to Surgeon-Gen., U.S.A.F. 1962–64; Chair. Inaugural Medical Care and Public Health Cttee., Washington, D.C. 1965; Consultant to Veterans Admin. Hosp., Long Beach, Calif., Dept. of Rehabilitation Medicine 1974–86; Fellow, New York Acad. of Medicine, Royal Soc. of

Medicine, Int. Asscn. for the Study of Pain, etc.; Pres. N. American Acad. of Manipulative Medicine 1968–69; Hon. Dr. of Medical Sciences (Women's Medical Coll. of Pa.) 1961; Hon. D.Sc. (Wilson Coll.) 1962, (Hahnemann Univ.) 1983; mem. many professional insts. *Publications:* Office Hours: Day and Night (autobiog.) 1969, Myofascial Pain and Dysfunction: The Trigger Point Manual (with others) 1983, and many scientific papers. *Leisure interests:* home, gardening, reading. *Address:* 4525 Cathedral Avenue, N. W., Washington, D.C. 20016, U.S.A. *Telephone:* (202) 363-9090.

TRAVOLTA, John; American actor; b. 18 Feb. 1954, Englewood, N.J.; s. of Salvatore Travolta and Helen (née Burke) Travolta. *Films:* Carrie 1976, The Boy in the Plastic Bubble (for TV) 1976, Saturday Night Fever 1977, Grease 1978, Moment by Moment 1978, Urban Cowboy 1980, Blow-Out 1981, Staying Alive 1983, Two of a Kind 1983, Perfect 1985, Daddy Wanted 1989; TV series Welcome Back Kotter 1975–77; l.p. records 1976, 1977; Billboard Magazine Best New Male Vocalist Award 1976; Best Actor Award, Nat. Bd. of Review 1978; Acad. Award nomination for Best Actor 1978; Male Star of the Year, Nat. Asscn. of Theatre Owners 1983. *Publication:* Staying Fit 1984. *Leisure interest:* flying. *Address:* c/o Edwards, 4810 Woodley Avenue, Encino, Calif. 91436, U.S.A.

TREADWELL, (Charles) James, C.M.G., C.V.O., LL.B.; British diplomatist (retd.); b. 10 Feb. 1920, Wellington, New Zealand; s. of the late C. A. L. Treadwell; ed. Wellington Coll., N.Z., Univ. of N.Z.; mil. service 1939–45; Sudan Political Service and Judiciary 1945–55; at Foreign Office 1955–57; with High Comm., Lahore 1957–60, Embassy, Ankara 1960–62, Embassy, Jeddah 1962–64; Deputy High Commr. for Eastern Nigeria 1964–66; Head of Jt. Information Services Dept., FCO 1966–68; Political Agent, Abu Dhabi 1968–71; Amb. to U.A.E. 1971–73; High Commr. in Bahamas 1973–75; Amb. to Oman 1975–79; Adviser to Hill Samuel Investment Man. Ltd. 1981–; Consultant to Abu Dhabi Investment Authority 1983–. *Address:* Cherry Orchard Cottage, Buddington Lane, Midhurst, West Sussex, GU29 0QP, England.

TREBICI, Vladimir, PH.D.; Romanian demographer (retd.); b. 28 Feb. 1916, Chernovtsy-Bukovina; s. of Atanasie Trebici and Ana I. Trebici; m. Margareta Gabrovschi 1948; one d.; ed. Chernovtsy Univ.; Cavalry Lieut. 1939–45; Statistician, Dir., Councillor and Deputy Dir.-Gen. of Romania's Cen. Statistical Bd. 1946–72; Prof. (part-time) in Statistics and Demography, Acad. of Econ. Studies 1948–72, Prof. 1972–77, Assoc. Prof. of CEDOR (Centre démographique ONU—Roumanie); Order of Labour 1969; Prize of the Romanian Acad. 1961; mem. Nat. Comm. of Demography 1971; mem. Int. Union for the Scientific Study of Population, Liège 1971–; mem. Int. Statistical Inst., Netherlands, Asscn. Internationale des Démographes de Langue Française, Paris, European Asscn. for Population Studies, The Hague, European Soc. for Population Econs., Univ. of Mannheim; Hon. mem. Československá Demografická Společnost Přičsav, Prague; Hon. Pres., Lab. of Historical Demography, Bucharest Univ. 1981. *Publications include:* The World Population 1974, A Concise Encyclopaedia of Demography 1975, Romania's Population and Demographic Trends 1976, Demography 1979, A Concise Encyclopaedia of Statistics 1985, Demography and Ethnography 1986, Regional Demography of Romania 1986, World Demography 1989. *Leisure interests:* history, music. *Address:* Str. Pompiliu Eliade 4, 70752 Bucharest, Romania. *Telephone:* 153907.

TRECHSEL, Stefan, D.IUR.; Swiss lawyer; b. 25 June 1937, Berne; s. of Manfred F. Trechsel and Steffi Friedlaender; m. Franca Julia Kinsbergen 1967; two d.; ed. Univ. of Berne and Georgetown Univ., Washington; Asst. and Main Asst. for Criminal Law, Univ. of Berne 1964–71; Swiss Fed. Dept. for Tech. Cooperation 1966–67; Public Prosecutor, Dist. of Bern-Mittelland 1971–75; Guest Prof. of Criminal Law and Procedure, Univ. of Fribourg 1977–79; Prof., Hochschule St. Gallen 1979–; mem. European Comm. of Human Rights 1975–, 2nd Vice-Pres. 1975–; Hon. Dr. New York Law School 1975. *Publications:* Der Strafgrund der Teilnahme 1967, Die Europäische Menschenrechtskonvention, ihr Schutz der persönlichen Freiheit und die Schweizerischen Strafprozessrechte 1974, Strafrecht Allgemeiner Teil I (2nd ed. of textbook by Peter Noll) 1986, Schweizerisches Strafgesetzbuch, Kurzkommentar 1989. *Leisure interests:* skiing, windsurfing, music, literature, psychology, chamber music ('cello). *Address:* Tigerbergstrasse 21, CH 9000, St. Gallen, Switzerland. *Telephone:* (071) 22 34 30.

TREDE, Michael, M.B., B.CHIR., M.D.; German surgeon; b. 10 Oct. 1928, Hamburg; s. of Hilmar Trede and Gertrud (Daus) Trede; m. Ursula Boettcher 1956; one s. four d.; ed. The Leys School, Cambridge and Univ. of Cambridge; Surgeon-in-training, Freie Universität Berlin 1957–62, Heidelberg Univ. 1962–72; now Prof. and Chair. Dept. of Surgery, Klinikum Mannheim, Univ. of Heidelberg; Hon. mem. Greek and Yugoslav Surgical Asscns.; Hon. F.R.C.S. *Publications:* 200 articles on surgery in scientific journals. *Leisure interests:* painting, violin-playing, mountaineering, skiing. *Address:* Nadlerstrasse 1A, 6800 Mannheim 51, Federal Republic of Germany. *Telephone:* (0621) 796301.

TREEN, David Conner, B.A., LL.B.; American lawyer and politician; b. 16 July 1928, Baton Rouge, La.; s. of Joseph Paul and Elizabeth Speir Treen; m. Dolores Brisbi 1951; one s. two d.; ed. Fortier High School, New Orleans, La., Tulane Univ., Tulane Univ. Law School; U.S.A.F. legal corps 1951–52; Vice.-Pres. and legal counsel, Simplex Manufacturing Corpn.

1952-57; Assoc. Attorney with law firm Beard, Blue and Schmitt, then partner Beard, Blue, Schmitt and Treen 1957-72; mem. House of Reps. for 3rd Dist. of La. 1973-80; Gov. of Louisiana 1980-84. *Publication:* Can You Afford This House? *Address:* c/o Deutsch, Kerrigan & Stiles, 755 Magazine Street, New Orleans, La. 70130, U.S.A.

TREGLOWN, Jeremy Dickinson, M.A., B.LITT., PH.D.; British writer and journalist; b. 24 May 1946, Anglesey, N. Wales; s. of Rev. G. L. Treglown; m. 1st Rona Bower 1970 (divorced 1982); one s. two d.; m. 2nd Holly Eley (née Urquhart) 1984; ed. Bristol Grammar School, St. Peter's Coll., Oxford; Lecturer in English Literature, Lincoln Coll., Oxford 1973-76, Univ. Coll., London 1976-79; Asst. Ed. The Times Literary Supplement 1979-81, Ed. 1982-; contrib. The Guardian, Plays and Players 1973-76, New Statesman, The Times 1976-79, The Sunday Times, etc. 1979-; Visiting Fellow, All Souls Coll., Oxford 1986, Mellon Visiting Assoc., Calif. Inst. of Tech.; Fellow Huntington Library 1988. *Publications:* The Letters of John Wilmot, Earl of Rochester 1980, Spirit of Wit 1982, The Lantern-Bearers and Other Essays by R. L. Stevenson 1988; various articles on poetry, drama and literary history. *Address:* 102 Savernake Road, London, N.W.3, England.

TREICHL, Dr. Heinrich; Austrian banker; b. 31 July 1913, Vienna; s. of Dr. Alfred and Dorothea (née Baroness Ferstel) Treichl; m. Helga Ross 1946; two s.; ed. Univs. of Frankfurt, Germany and Vienna; Dir. Banque des Pays de l'Europe Centrale, Paris, Mercur Bank AG and Länderbank Wien AG, Vienna 1936-39; Partner, Ullstein and Co., Vienna 1946-55; Dir. Österreichische Industrie- und Bergbauverwaltungs GmbH, Vienna 1956-58; Dir. Creditanstalt-Bankverein, Vienna 1958-, Chair. of Man. Bd. 1970-81; Chair. Supervisory Bd. Bank für Kärnten und Steiermark 1986-, Bank für Oberösterreich und Salzburg AG, Bank für Tirol und Vorarlberg AG, Alcatel Austria AG; Pres. Austrian Red Cross Soc.; mem. Bd. of Govs. Österreichische Nationalbank; mem. Verwaltungsrates der Assicurazioni Generali, Trieste; Grosses Goldenes Ehrenzeichen Republik Österreich; Commdr., Order Homayoun; Commdr., Légion d'honneur; Kt. Commdr., Order of St. Gregory, Grand Decoration of Honour in Gold for Services to Repub. of Austria, Grand Decoration in Silver with Star for Services to Repub. of Austria. *Leisure interests:* literature, hunting, skiing. *Address:* 1030 Vienna, Salmgasse 2, Austria. *Telephone:* 713 31 50.

TREIKI, Ali A., PH.D.; Libyan diplomatist and politician; b. 1938, Misrata; m. Aisha Dihoum; two s. two d.; ed. Univ. of Benghazi, Libya, and Toulouse Univ., France; joined Foreign Ministry 1970; Minister Plenipotentiary 1970, Dir. of Political Admin. 1970-73, Dir. of African Admin. 1973-74, Asst. Deputy for Political Affairs 1974-76; Sec. of State for Foreign Affairs 1971-77, Foreign Sec. 1977-81, Sec. of Liaison for Foreign Affairs 1981-86; Head of Libyan del. to UN Gen. Ass. 1977-80; Perm. Rep. of Libya to the UN 1982-84, 1986-. *Address:* Permanent Mission of Libya to the United Nations, 309-315 East 48th Street, New York, N.Y. 10017, U.S.A.

TREIMAN, Sam Bard, PH.D.; American professor of physics; b. 27 May 1925, Chicago, Ill.; s. of Abraham Treiman and Sarah (Bard) Treiman; m. Joan Little 1952; one s. two d.; ed. Northwestern Univ. and Univ. of Chicago; joined Princeton Univ. 1952, Prof. of Physics 1963-, Eugene Higgins Prof. 1976-, Head of Dept. 1981-; Sloan Fellow; Guggenheim Fellow; mem. N.A.S., American Acad. of Arts and Sciences. *Publications:* Formal Scattering Theory (with M. Grossjean), Lectures on Current Algebra (with R. Jackiw and D. Gross) 1972; and numerous papers in professional journals. *Leisure interests:* tennis, reading. *Address:* Joseph Henry Laboratories, Jaduin Hall, P.O. Box 708, Princeton University, Princeton, N.J. 08540 (Office); 60 McCosh Circle, Princeton, N.J. 08540, U.S.A. (Home). *Telephone:* 452-4350 (Office); 924-0592 (Home).

TREITEL, Guenter Heinz, Q.C., M.A., D.C.L., F.B.A.; British (naturalized 1947) professor of law; b. 26 Oct. 1928, Berlin, Germany; s. of Dr. Theodor and Hanna (née Levy) Treitel; m. Phyllis M. Cook 1957; two s.; ed. Kilburn Grammar School and Magdalen Coll., Oxford; came to U.K. 1939; Fellow of Magdalen Coll., Oxford 1954-79, Emer. Fellow 1979-; All Souls Reader in English Law 1964-79; Vinerian Prof. of English Law, Univ. of Oxford, and Fellow of All Souls Coll. 1979-; Visiting Lecturer, Univ. of Chicago 1963-64, Visiting Prof. 1968-69, 1971-72; Visiting Prof., Univ. of W. Australia 1976, Univ. of Houston 1977, Southern Methodist Univ. 1978, 1988-89, Univ. of Va. 1978-79, 1983-84, Univ. of Santa Clara 1981; Consultant to Law Comm. on law of contract 1972-84; Trustee, British Museum 1983-; mem. Council Nat. Trust 1984-, British Acad. 1987-; Hon. Bencher, Gray's Inn. *Publications:* The Law of Contract 1962, An Outline of the Law of Contract 1975, Remedies for Breach of Contract: a comparative account 1988; (co-author) Benjamin's Sale of Goods 1974; ed. of other law books. *Leisure interests:* reading, music. *Address:* All Souls College, Oxford, OX1 4AL, England. *Telephone:* (0865) 279379.

TREJOS FERNÁNDEZ, José Joaquín; Costa Rican university professor and politician; b. 18 April 1916, San José; s. of Juan Trejos and Emilia F. de Trejos; m. Clara F. de Trejos 1936; five s.; ed. Univ. of Chicago; Prof. of Statistical Theory and Dean, Faculty of Econ., Univ. de Costa Rica 1952-56, Dean, Faculty of Sciences and Letters 1957-62, Prof. Emer. School of Statistics 1979-; Pres. of Costa Rica 1966-70; Partido Unidad Social Cristiana. *Publications:* Reflexiones sobre la Educación, 2nd edn. 1968, Ocho Años en la Política Nacional—Ideales Políticos y Realidad Nacional, Vol. I 1973, Vol. III 1973, Vol. IV 1973, Vol. II 1974, Ideas Politicas Elementales 1985. *Leisure interests:* music, history. *Address:* Apartado 10.096, San José, Costa Rica. *Telephone:* 24-24-11.

TRELFORD, Donald Gilchrist, M.A.; British journalist; b. 9 Nov. 1937, Coventry; s. of T. S. Trelford; m. 1st Janice Ingram 1963; two s. one d.; m. 2nd Katherine Louise Mark 1978; one d.; ed. Bablake School, Coventry, Selwyn Coll., Cambridge; Pilot Officer, R.A.F. 1956-58; worked on newspapers in Coventry and Sheffield 1961-63; Ed. Times of Malawi and Corresp. in Africa, The Times, Observer, BBC 1963-66; joined Observer as Deputy News Ed. 1966, Asst. Man. Ed. 1968, Deputy Ed. 1969-75, Dir. and Ed. 1985-; Dir. Optomen Television 1988-; mem. Editorial Advisory Group, Bloomsbury Publishing 1987-; mem. British Exec. Cttee., Int. Press Inst. 1976-, British Cttee., Journalists in Europe 1980-, Asscn. of British Eds. 1984-, Guild of British Newspaper Eds. 1985- (mem. Parl. and Legal Cttee. 1987-); Patron, Milton Keynes Civic Forum 1977-, Int. Centre for Child Studies 1984-; Sponsor Educ. for Capability 1983-, Educational Trust for Southern Africa 1986-; Trustee British Sports Trust 1988-; mem. Council, Media Soc. 1981-, Judging Panel, British Press Awards 1981-, Scottish Press Awards 1985, Olivier Awards Cttee., SWET 1984-, Communications Cttee., Inter Action Council 1985-, Defence, Press and Broadcasting Cttee. 1986-; Granada Newspaper of the Year Award 1983; commended, Int. Ed. of the Year (World Press Review) 1984. *Publications:* Siege 1980, Snookered 1986, Child of Change (with Garry Kasparov q.v.) 1987; (Contrib.) County Champions 1982, The Queen Observed 1986; (Ed.) Sunday Best 1981, 1982, 1983. *Leisure interests:* golf, cricket, snooker. *Address:* The Observer, Chelsea Bridge House, Queenstown Road, London, SW8 4NN, England. *Telephone:* 01-627 0700.

TRELLES MONTES, Dr. Oscar; Peruvian physician and politician; b. 23 Aug. 1904, Lima; s. of Juan Antonio Trelles Cáceres and María Antonia Montes Cano; m. Estela Orihuela 1964; three s.; Dir. Hosp. Neurológico Santo Toribio de Mogrovejo 1944-74; Head Dept. of Neurology Univ. Cayetano Heredia 1961-74; Minister of Public Health 1945-46; Prime Minister and Minister of Interior 1963-64; Amb. to France 1964-65; Sec.-Gen. Partido Acción Popular 1965-67; Pres. of Senate 1980-81; Dir. Revista de Neuro-Psiquiatría; mem. Editorial Bd. Review of Neurological Sciences, La Revue de Neuro-Psychologie, Handbook of Clinical Neurology; Senator-Pres. Comm. Defensa Nacional y Orden Interno; Hon. Prof. Santiago (Chile) 1959; Hon. Prof. John F. Kennedy Univ. (Argentina) 1976; Hon. Prof. Sorbonne (Paris) 1977; mem. American Acad. of Neurology 1956, Acad. de Médecine (Paris) 1963; Dr. h.c. (Aix-en-Provence); numerous prizes and awards. *Publications:* about 350 books, including Les Ramollissements Protubérantiels 1935, Précis d'Anatomo-Phisiologie Normale et Pathologique du Système Nerveux Central (with F. Masquin) 1937, La Cisticercosis Cerebral (with J. Lazarte) 1941, Traumatismos craneo-encefálicos (with M. Davila) 1942, Oliva Bulbar, Estructura, Función, Patología 1944, Jean Lhermitte, Vida y Obra 1959, and articles on medicine and the Neurological Sciences. *Address:* Av. Salaverry 1971, Lince, Lima 14 and Quilca 499, Lima 1, Peru. *Telephone:* 711881 and 238564.

TREMBLAY, Marc-Adélard, O.C., M.A., L.S.A., PH.D.; Canadian professor of social anthropology; b. 24 April 1922, Les Eboulements; s. of Wellie and Lauretta Tremblay; m. Jacqueline Cyr 1949; one s. five d.; ed. Montreal, Laval and Cornell Univs.; research assoc., Cornell Univ. 1953-56; Asst. Prof., Dept. of Sociology and Anthropology, Laval Univ. 1956, Prof. of Social Anthropology 1963-87; Founding Pres., Canadian Sociology and Anthropology Asscn. 1965-67; Pres. Canadian Ethnology Soc. 1976-77, Royal Soc. of Canada 1981-84, Asscn. of Canadian Univs. for Northern Studies 1985-87, Quebec Council for Social Research 1987; mem. many other professional and scientific orgs.; Dr. h.c. (Ottawa) 1982, (Guelph) 1984; Prix de la Province de Québec 1964; Innis-Gérin Medal, Royal Soc. of Canada; Molson Prize, The Canada Council 1987, Marcel Vincent Prize, French Canadian Asscn. for the Advancement of Science 1988. *Publications:* People of Cove and Woodlot: communities from the viewpoint of social psychiatry 1960, Les comportements économiques de la famille salariée 1964, Initiation à la recherche dans les sciences humaines 1968, Famille et Parenté en Acadie 1971, Communities and culture in French Canada 1973, Patterns of Amerindian Identity 1976, L'identité québécoise en péril 1983, Conscience et Enquête 1983; twelve books and some monographs and some 150 articles. *Leisure interests:* gardening, cross-country skiing, classical music. *Address:* Département d'Anthropologie, Université Laval, Cité Universitaire, Sainte Foy, Quebec; 835 rue Nouvelle Orléans, Sainte-Foy, Quebec, Canada (Home). *Telephone:* (418) 656-3775 (Office); (418) 653-5411 (Home).

TREMLETT, David Rex; British artist; b. 13 Feb. 1945, Cornwall; s. of Rex and Dinah Tremlett; m. (divorced); m. Laure Florence 1987; one d.; ed. St. Austell Grammar School, Falmouth Art Coll. and Royal Coll. of Art; travelled by land to Australia twice 1970, 1971; travelled extensively in Africa, N. and Cen. America 1975-84; after journeys exhibited widely in U.K., U.S.A., Europe, Africa, Australia, Mexico etc. *Publications:* Some Places to Visit 1974, On the Waterfront 1978, Scrub 1978, On the Border 1979, Restless 1983, Rough Ride 1985, Ruin 1987, Dates/Differents 1987, Sometimes We All Do 1988. *Leisure interests:* pole vaulting, African music, Saharan architecture. *Address:* Broadlawns, Chipperfield Road, Bovingdon, Herts., England. *Telephone:* (0442) 832214.

TRENGGANU, H.R.H. The Sultan of; Mahmud Al Muktafi Billah Shah, D.K.T., D.K., D.M.N., S.S.M.T., S.P.M.T.; ruler of Trengganu State; b. 29 April 1930; s. of the late Sultan Ismail Nasiruddin Shah; m. Tengku Banah 1951; ed. Grammar Crown English School; mil. training 1955, officer Territorial Army; Yang-di-Pertuan Muda 1951, Regent of Trengganu 1954, 1965, Sultan Sept. 1979–. *Leisure interests:* golf, tennis, riding. *Address:* Istana Badariah, Kuala Trengganu, Malaysia.

TRENTHAM, David R., F.R.S., PH.D.; British medical research scientist; b. 22 Sept. 1938, Solihull; s. of John A. and Julia A. M. Trentham; m. Kamalini Bhargava 1966; two s.; ed. Uppingham School and Cambridge Univ.; Faculty mem., Biochemistry Dept., Bristol Univ. 1972–77; Chair. and Edwin M. Chance Prof., Dept. of Biochemistry and Biophysics, School of Medicine, Univ. of Pa., Philadelphia, U.S.A. 1977–83; Head, Physiological and Neural Mechanisms Group and Physical Biochemistry Div., Nat. Inst. for Medical Research, London 1984–; Colworth Medal, Biochemistry Soc. 1974. *Publications:* numerous articles in biochemical and academic journals. *Address:* National Institute for Medical Research, The Ridgeway, Mill Hill, London, NW7 1AA, England (Office). *Telephone:* 01-959 3666.

TRETHON, Dr. Ferenc; Hungarian economist and politician; b. 9 Sept. 1923, Eger; s. of Árpád Trethon and Erzsébet Soós; m. Maria Szarka 1963; one s. one d.; started career in coal mines of Komló; served in Ministry of Mining and Energy, later in Ministry of Coal Mining; Head of Econ. Dept., Ministry of Heavy Industry 1957–74; Deputy Minister of Finance 1974–77; Minister of Labour 1977–81; Vice-Pres. of Fed. of Tech. and Scientific Socs.; Prof. and Head of Dept. Univ. of Chemical Eng., Veszprém; mem. Cttee. for Man. and Org. Sciences, Hungarian Acad. of Sciences; Chair. Soc. for Org. and Man. Sciences (SZVT); mem. Hungarian Assen. of Econ. Bd., Hungarian Communist (now Socialist Workers') Party 1948–; Labour Order of Merit (golden degree) 1965, Lóránd Eötvös Prize 1974, Order of Merit for Socialist Hungary. *Leisure interests:* music, literature, sports. *Address:* Federation of Technical and Scientific Societies, Fő utca 68, 1371 Budapest, Hungary. *Telephone:* 154-603.

TRETHOWAN, Sir (James) Ian (Raley), Kt., F.B.I.M.; British broadcasting executive; b. 20 Oct. 1922, High Wycombe; s. of the late Major J. J. R. Trethowan, M.B.E. and Mrs. Roy Trethowan; m. 1st Patricia Nelson 1951 (dissolved), 2nd Carolyn Reynolds 1963; three d.; Newspaper Reporter, Norwich and York; Observer, Fleet Air Arm during Second World War; Political Corresp. Yorkshire Post 1947; Political Corresp. News Chronicle 1955; Newscaster and Diplomatic Corresp., Ind. Television News (ITN), then Deputy Ed. 1958, and later Political Ed.; Commentator on politics and current affairs, BBC 1963–70, Man. Dir. Radio 1970–75, Man. Dir. BBC TV 1976–77, Dir.-Gen. 1977–82; Political Contrib., Economist 1950–58, 1965–67, The Times 1967–69; Ind. Dir. The Times 1982–; Chair. British Museum Soc. 1982–, Horserace Betting Levy Bd. 1982–; Dir. Barclays Bank 1982–87, Thorn EMI 1986– (Consultant 1982–), Thames TV 1986– (Chair. 1987–); Pres. Cinema and Television Group of the European Comm. Nov. 1988–; mem. Cttee. on Official Secrets Acts 1971–72; mem. Bd. British Council 1980–87; Trustee, Glyndebourne Arts Trust 1982–, British Museum 1984–; Hon. D.C.L. (Univ. of East Anglia) 1979; Univ. of Calif. Award for programme about U.S.A. 1961. *Publication:* Split Screen (autobiog.) 1984. *Address:* Horserace Betting Levy Board, 17–23 Southampton Row, London, WC1B 5HH, England. *Telephone:* 01-405 5346.

TRETYAK, Gen. Ivan Moiseyevich; Soviet army officer; b. 1923, Poltava Dist., Ukraine; ed. Frunze Mil. Acad. and Acad. of Gen. Staff; served in Soviet Army 1939–; Co. Commdr., Deputy Commdr. of a Regt., then Commdr. of a Regt. on Western and Second Baltic Front 1941–45; mem. CPSU 1943–; Commdr. of a Regt., Chief-of-Staff, Commdr. of a unit 1949–67; Deputy to U.S.S.R. Supreme Soviet 1966–; mem. Cen. Cttee. of Azerbaizhan CP 1966–67; Commdr. Byelorussian Mil. Dist. 1967–76; mem. Cen. Cttee. of Byelorussian CP, cand. mem. Politburo 1971–76, mem. 1976–78; cand. mem. Cen. Cttee. of CPSU 1971–76, mem. 1976–; Gen. of the Army 1976–; Commdr. Far Eastern Mil. Dist. 1976–; mem. staff Ministry of Defence 1984–, Chief Inspector 1981–87; C.-in-C. 1987–; Deputy Minister of Defence; Hero of Soviet Union Order of Lenin (twice), Order of Red Banner (three times), Aleksandr Nevsky Order, Order of Kutuzov (third class) and many others, including foreign decorations.

TREURNICHT, Andries Petrus, M.A., PH.D., M.P.; South African politician; b. 19 Feb. 1921, Piketberg; s. of Andries Petrus Treurnicht and Hester Johanna E. Albertyn; m. Engela Dreyer 1949; four d.; ed. Piketberg High School, Univ. of Stellenbosch, Theological Seminary, Stellenbosch and Univ. of Cape Town; Minister, Dutch Reformed Church 1946–60; Ed. Die Kerkbode 1960–67, Hoofstad 1967–71; M.P. for Waterberg 1971–; Leader of Nat. Party in Transvaal 1978–82; Deputy Minister of Educ. and Training 1976–78, of Plural Relations and Devt. 1978–79; Minister of Public Works, Statistics and Tourism 1979–80, for State Admin. and Statistics 1980–82; mem. Volkswag 1984–; Leader Conservative Party 1982–; Decoration for Meritorial Service 1982. *Publications:* thirteen publications on various religious and political subjects. *Address:* P.O. Box 1842, Pretoria 0001, South Africa. *Telephone:* 012 872888.

TREVINO, Lee Buck; American golfer; b. 1 Dec. 1939, Dallas, Tex.; s. of Joe Trevino and Juanita Barrett; m. Claudia Ann Fenley 1964; three s. one d.; professional 1961–; U.S. Open Champion 1968, 1971; British Open

Champion 1971, 1972; Canadian Open Champion 1971 and numerous other championships 1965–80; U.S. P.G.A. Champion 1974, 1984; has won over $2m. in prize money in U.S.A.; returned to competitive golf following back surgery as result of being struck by lightning during tournament 1976; Chair. Bd. Lee Trevino Enterprises, Inc. 1967–; U.S. P.G.A. Player of the Year 1971. *Publication:* Super Mex (autobiog.) 1983. *Address:* 14901 Quorum Drive, Suite 170, Dallas, Tex. 75240 (Office); Santa Teresa Country Club, Santa Teresa, N.M. 88063, U.S.A. (Home).

TREVOR, William, C.B.E.; Irish author; b. 24 May 1928, Co. Cork; s. of James William Cox and Gertrude Cox; m. Jane Ryan 1952; two s.; ed. St. Columba's, Dublin, Trinity Coll., Dublin; Hawthornden Prize 1965, Royal Soc. of Literature Prize 1978, Whitbread Prize for Fiction 1978, Allied Irish Banks Award for Services to Literature 1978, Whitbread Prize 1983; Hon. D.Litt. (Exeter) 1984, (Dublin) 1986. *Publications:* The Old Boys 1964, The Boarding House 1965, The Love Department 1966, The Day We Got Drunk on Cake 1967, Mrs Eckdorf in O'Neill's Hotel 1968, Miss Gomez and the Brethren 1969, The Ballroom of Romance 1970, Elizabeth Alone 1972, Angels at the Ritz 1973, The Children of Dynmouth 1977, Lovers of Their Time 1979, Other People's Worlds 1980, Beyond the Pale 1981, Fools of Fortune 1983, A Writer's Ireland: Landscape in Literature 1984, The News from Ireland 1986, Nights at the Alexandra 1987, The Silence in the Garden 1988. *Address:* c/o The Bodley Head, 30 Bedford Square, London, W.C.1, England.

TREVOR-ROPER, Hugh Redwald (see Dacre of Glanton).

TREW, Francis Sidney Edward, C.M.G.; British diplomatist (retd.); b. 22 Feb. 1931, Peshawar, India (now Pakistan); s. of Harry Francis and Alice Mary (née Sewell) Trew; m. Marlene Laurette Regnery 1958; three d.; ed. Taunton's School, Southampton; served H.M. forces 1949–51; Foreign Office 1951; posts in: Lebanon 1952, Amman 1953, Bahrain 1953–54, Jeddah 1954–56; Vice-Consul, Philadelphia, U.S.A. 1956–59; Second Sec., Kuwait 1959–62; FCO 1962; seconded as Sec., European Conf. on Satellite Communications 1963–65; Consul, Guatemala City 1965–70; First Sec., Mexico 1971–74; FCO 1974–77; Consul, Algeciras, Spain 1977–79; FCO 1979–81; High Commr. in Belize 1981–84, Amb. to Bahrain 1984–88. *Leisure interests:* fishing, carpentry. *Address:* c/o Lloyds Bank, 6 Pall Mall, London, S.W.1, England.

TRIANTAFYLLIDES, Michalakis Antoniou; Cypriot judge; b. 12 May 1927, Nicosia; ed. Gray's Inn, London; practised as a lawyer in Cyprus 1948–60, serving for three years as Sec. of Human Rights Cttee. of Bar; mem. Greek Cypriot del. to Joint Constitutional Comm. which drafted Cyprus Constitution 1959–60; Greek Cypriot Judge, Supreme Constitutional Court 1960–86, Pres. 1985–86; mem. European Comm. of Human Rights 1963–86.

TRIBE, Laurence Henry, J.D.; American professor of law; b. 10 Oct. 1941, Shanghai, China; s. of George I. Tribe and Paulina Diatlovitsky; m. Carolyn R. Kreye 1965; one s. one d.; ed. Harvard Univ.; admitted Calif. Bar 1966, U.S. Supreme Court Bar 1966; law clerk, Calif. Supreme Court 1966–67, U.S. Supreme Court 1967–68; Exec. Dir. Tech. Assessment Panel, N.A.S. 1968–69; Asst. Prof. of Law, Harvard Univ. 1969–72, Prof. 1972–82, Ralph S. Tyler Jr. Prof. of Constitutional Law 1982–; Chair. Marshall Islands Judicial Service Comm. 1979–80; Chief Appellate Counsel, Calif. Nuclear Litigation 1978–83; Special Deputy Attorney-Gen. Hawaii 1983–84; various consultancies; Fellow, American Acad. of Arts and Sciences; mem. A.B.A.; Triennial Coif Award 1978–84, Scribe Award 1980, etc.; Hon. LL.D. (Gonzaga) 1980, (Pacific) 1987. *Publications:* American Constitutional law 1978, Constitutional Choice 1985, God Save this Honorable Court 1985; articles in professional journals. *Address:* Griswold 307, Harvard Law School, Cambridge, Mass. 02138, U.S.A.

TRIBLE, Paul Seward, Jr., J.D.; American politician; b. 29 Dec. 1946, Baltimore; s. of Paul and Katherine (née Schilpp) Trible; m. Rosemary Dunaway; one s. one d.; ed. Hampden-Sydney Coll., Washington and Lee Univ.; admitted to Va. bar 1971; Law Clerk to Dist. Judge Albert V. Bryan 1971–72; Asst. Attorney, Eastern Dist., Va. 1972–74; Commonwealth's Attorney Essex Co., Va. 1974–76; mem. House of Reps. 1977–81; Senator from Va. 1983–87; Republican. *Address:* c/o The Senate, Washington, D.C. 20510, U.S.A.

TRIBOULET, Raymond, L. EN DR., L. ÈS L.; French politician; b. 3 Oct. 1906, Paris; s. of Maurice Triboulet and Josèphe Wagner; m. Luce Chauveau 1928; three s. (one deceased) three d.; ed. Univ. of Paris; active in French Resistance 1943–44; Sous-Préfet for Bayeux region 1944–46; Regional Insp. for Rhine-Palatinate 1946; M.P. 1946–; founder of Federalist group in French Parl.; Pres. of Gaullist Parl. Group (Social Republicans) 1954–58; Minister of War Veterans Jan.-Oct. 1955; mem. ECSC Common Ass. 1957; Pres. Union of New Republic (UNR) Parl. Group 1958; Minister of War Veterans 1959–63, of Co-operation 1963–66; re-elected Deputy 1958, 1962, 1967 and 1968; mem. European Parl. 1967–73; Pres. UDE group 1968–73; Pres. and founder D-Day Commemoration Cttee.; mem. Inst. (Acad. des Sciences morales et politiques) 1979; Commdr. Légion d'honneur; Croix de guerre; Médaille de la Résistance; Hon. O.B.E., and other decorations. *Publications:* Les Billets du Négus 1939, Sens dessus dessous 1951, Des Vessies pour des Lanternes 1958, Halte au Massacre 1966, Correspondance de Gaston de Renty (1611-1649) 1978, A tous ceux qui sont mal dans leur peau 1980, Un gaulliste de la IVe 1985, Un Ministre du général 1986. *Address:* 119 rue Brancas, 92310 Sèvres, France.

TRICART, Jean Léon François; French university professor; b. 16 Sept. 1920, Montmorency; s. of François Tricart and Lea Cordonnier; m. Denise Casimir 1944; four s.; ed. Lycée Rollin, Paris, and Univ. de Paris à la Sorbonne; Asst. Lecturer, Univ. de Paris 1945–48; Lecturer Univ. of Strasbourg 1948–49, Asst. Prof. 1949–55, Prof. 1955–; Vice-Dean, mem. of Univ. Senate 1967–70; Prin. Asst., Geological Map of France 1960; Founder-Dir. Centre of Applied Geography, Strasbourg 1956–; Pres. Applied Geomorphology Comm. of Int. Geographical Union 1960–68; Head of numerous tech. co-operation missions in Senegal, Mauritania, Ivory Coast, Guinea, Togo, Mali, Argentina, Brazil, Chile, Venezuela, Peru, Panama, El Salvador, Colombia, Uruguay, Mexico; FAO, UNDP, WMO and UNESCO Sr. Consultant 1968–; scientific assessor of Inst. de Recherche Agronomique Tropicale; Chair. French Nat. Cttee. of INQUA 1976–79; Dr. h.c. (Univ. of Łódź, Poland); mem. Colombian Acad. of Science 1986–; Busk Medal (Royal Geographical Soc.) 1985, medals and prizes in Argentina, Belgium, France, Hungary, Italy. *Publications:* include numerous scientific articles and Principes et méthodes de la Géomorphologie 1965, Traité de Géomorphologie (with A. Cailleux), 5 vols., La terre, Planète vivante, Eco-géographie et Aménagement rural (with J. Kilian). *Leisure interest:* philately. *Address:* Centre de Géographie Appliquée, Université Louis-Pasteur, Strasbourg, 3 rue de l'Argonne, 67083 Strasbourg-CEDEX; and 85 route de la Meinau, 67100 Strasbourg-Meinau, France. *Telephone:* 88.35.82.00 (Office); 8839-09-86 (Home).

TRIER, Peter Eugene, C.B.E., M.A., F.ENG., F.I.E.E., F.INST.P., F.I.M.A.; British research director and consultant; b. 12 Sept. 1919, Darmstadt, Germany; s. of Ernst J. Trier and Nellie M. (née Bender) Trier; m. Margaret N. Holloway 1946; three s.; ed. Mill Hill School, London and Trinity Hall, Cambridge; Royal Naval Scientific Service 1941–50; Mullard Research Labs. (now Philips Research Labs.), Redhill 1950–69, Dir. 1953–69; Dir. of Research and Devt. Philips Electronics 1969–81, mem. Bd. 1969–85; Chair. of Council, Brunel Univ. 1973–79, Pro-Chancellor 1980–; Chair. Electronics Research Council 1976–80, Defence Scientific Advisory Council 1981–85; Glazebrook Prize and Medal, Inst. of Physics 1984; Hon.D.Tech. (Brunel) 1975. *Publications:* Strategic Implications of Micro-Electronics 1982, Mathematics & Information 1983; papers in scientific and technical journals. *Leisure interests:* travel, sailing, railway history, Trier family history. *Address:* Yew Tree House, Bredon, Tewkesbury, Glos., GL20 7HF, England. *Telephone:* (0684) 72200.

TRIFFIN, Robert, LL.D., PH.D.ECON.; American economist; b. 5 Oct. 1911, Flobecq, Belgium; s. of François Triffin and Céline van Hooland; m. Lois Brandt 1940; three s.; ed. Kain-lez Tournai, Louvain Univ., Harvard Univ.; Instructor, Harvard 1939–42; Chief Latin American Div., Bd. of Govs. Fed. Reserve System 1942–46; IMF, Chief Exchange Control Div. 1946–48, Chief Rep. in Europe 1948–49; Special Policy Adviser, Econ. Co-operation Admin. and Alternate U.S. Rep. European Payments Union 1949–51; Frederick William Beinecke Prof. of Econs. Master of Berkeley Coll., Yale Univ. 1951–77; headed numerous monetary and banking reorganization missions to Latin American countries, Iran, etc.; Consultant to UN 1952; Council of Econ. Advisers (U.S.) 1953–54, 1961; Consultant OEEC 1957–58, EEC 1958–; Vice-Pres. American Econ. Asscn. 1966–67; Guest Prof. Univ. Coll. de Louvain la Neuve 1977–78; mem. Council of Econ. Advisers, Société d'Econ. Pol. (Paris); mem. American Acad. of Arts and Sciences, World Acad. of Art and Science; Assoc. Acad. Royale de Belgique; Wells Prize, Harvard 1939, San Paolo Prize for Econs., Turin 1987, Frank E. Seidman Distinguished Award in Political Econ., Rhodes Coll., Memphis, Tenn. 1988; Commdr. Ordre de la Couronne (Belgium) 1973. *Publications:* Monopolistic Competition and General Equilibrium Theory 1940, Monetary and Banking Reform in Paraguay 1946, Europe and the Money Muddle 1957, Gold and the Dollar Crisis 1960, The Evolution of the International Monetary System: Historical Reappraisal and Future Perspectives 1964, The World Money Maze: National Currencies in International Payments 1966, Our International Monetary System: Yesterday, Today and Tomorrow 1968, How to Arrest a Threatening Relapse into the 1930's? 1971, Europe's Money: Problems of European Monetary Co-ordination and Integration (Ed. with Rainer S. Masera) 1984; numerous articles in specialist journals. *Leisure interests:* reading, bridge, tourism. *Address:* IRES, Place Montesquieu, 1348 Louvain La Neuve (Office); 10 Avenue Hennebel, 1348 Louvain La Neuve, Belgium (Home). *Telephone:* (010) 47.41.38 (Office); (010) 45.10.89 (Home).

TRIGANO, Gilbert; French business executive; b. 28 July 1920, St. Maurice, Val-de-Marne; s. of Raymond Trigano and Félicie Bensaïd; m. Simone Sabah 1945; one s. three d.; Man. Dir. Soc. des villages de vacances 1959–, en Guadeloupe 1973–; Man. Dir. Club Méditerranée 1963–; Bureau Suisse S.A., Culip S.A., Spain; mem. supervisory Bd. holding co. 1969–; Admin. Tourisme France Int. 1973–; Pres. Soc. Island-Properties, Man. Dir. Soc. nouvelle Victoria, Switzerland, Cie. int. des wagons-lits 1984–; mem. Conseil économique et social 1983–; Deputy to Prime Minister, in charge of training 1985–86; Chevalier, Légion d'honneur, Officier, ordre nat. du Mérite. *Address:* Club Méditerranée, 25 rue Vilvienne, 75002 Paris, France.

TRIGONA, Alex Sceberras, LL.D., M.A., M.P.; Maltese politician; b. 3 March 1950; s. of Alexander and Connie Trigona; m. Joanna Borg 1985; ed. St. Joseph's High School, the Lyceum, Univs. of Malta and Oxford; Pres. Univ. Students' Rep. Council 1971–72; Lecturer in Int. Politics and Econ., Univ. of Malta; Int. Sec. of Ghaqda Zghazagh Socjalisti (Young Socialists Org.) 1976–79, Malta Labour Party 1977–82; Counsellor American Univ. Cairo 1978–79; Dir. Bank of Valletta 1978–81; Ed. magazine Il-Hsieb 1978, Dir. Mediterranean Conf. Centre 1980–81, Minister of Foreign Affairs and Culture 1981–87; Labour; founder and Hon. Pres. Tigne' Sports Assen. *Address:* c/o Ministry of Foreign Affairs, Palazzo Parisio, Valletta; 43 Paola Road, Tarxien, Malta.

TRINH VAN-CAN, H.E. Cardinal Joseph-Marie; Vietnamese ecclesiastic; b. 19 March 1921, Trác Bút, Hanoi; ordained priest 1949; acting Titular Archbishop of Ela 1963–78; Archbishop of Hanoi 1978–; cr. Cardinal 1979; mem. Sacred Congregation for the Evangelization of Peoples; entitled S. Maria in Via; restorer of two churches; constructed three chapels 1953–60. *Publications:* The New Testament (in Vietnamese) 1975, three books of liturgical songs 1976, book of sacraments and benedictions for priests 1979, book of consolation for the sick 1981, book of four manners of meditating The Way of the Cross 1983, book of four ways of Adoration before The Blessed Sacrament 1985, Fourth Book of Liturgical Songs, The Bible (Old and New Testaments in Vietnamese) 1987, The Prayer of the Faithful for the Whole Year 1988, Study method for Music, Harmonium and Songs 1988. *Address:* Archevêché, Hanoi, 40 Phô Nhà Chung, Viet-Nam.

TRINTIGNANT, Jean-Louis (Xavier); French actor; b. 11 Dec. 1930, Piolenc (Vaucluse); s. of Raoul Trintignant and Claire Tourtin; m. 1st Colette Dacheville (the actress Stéphane Audran, q.v.) 1954 (divorced); m. 2nd Nadine Marquand, one s. two d. (one deceased); ed. Faculté de Droit, Aix-en-Provence; theatre début 1951; film roles 1955–; Prix d'interprétation de l'Acad. du Cinéma (for Mata Hari, Agent H21) 1965; Prize, Cannes Festival (for Z) 1969; Prix David de Donatello, Taormina Festival 1972; Officier des Arts et des Lettres. *Plays include:* Macbeth, Jacques ou la Soumission (Ionesco), Hamlet, Bonheur, impaire et passe (Sagan), Deux sur la balançoire, etc. *Films include:* Et Dieu créa la femme 1956, Club de femmes 1956, Les liaisons dangereuses 1959, L'été violent 1959, Austerlitz 1959, La millième fenêtre 1959, Pleins feux sur l'assassin 1960, Coeur battant 1960, Le jeu de la vérité 1961, Horace 62 1961, Les sept péchés capitaux 1961, Il sorpasso 1962, Il successo 1962, Chateau en Suède 1963, La bonne occase 1964, Mata Hari, Agent H21 1964, Angélique marquise des anges 1964, Meurtre à l'italienne 1965, La longue marche 1965, Le 17e ciel 1965, Paris brûle-t-il? 1965, Un homme et une femme 1966, Safari diamants 1966, Trans-Europ-Express 1966, Mon amour, mon amour 1967, L'homme qui ment 1967, Les biches 1968, Le voleur de crimes 1968, Z 1969, Ma nuit chez Maud 1969, Disons un soir à dîner 1969, L'Américain 1969, La mort a pondu un oeuf 1969, Le conformiste 1970, Si douces, si perverses 1970, Le grand silence 1971, Une journée bien remplie (author and dir.) 1973, Le train 1973, Les violins du bal 1973, Le mouton enragé 1974, Le secret 1974, Le jeu avec le feu 1975, Shattering 1977, Le désert des Tartares 1977, The French Way 1978, L'argent des autres 1978, Le maitre nageur 1979 (also Dir.), La terrasse 1980, Je vous aime 1980, La femme d'à côté 1981, Un assassin qui passe 1981, Malevil 1981, Passion d'amour 1981, Une affaire d'hommes 1981, Eaux profondes 1981, Le grand-pardon 1982, Boulevard des assassins 1982, Le bon plaisir 1983, Vivement dimanche! 1983, La crime 1983, Le bon plaisir, Femmes de personne 1984, Under Fire, Viva la vie 1984, L'été prochain, Partir, revenir 1985, Rendez-vous, David, Thomas et les autres 1985, L'homme aux yeux d'argent 1985, Un homme et une femme: vingt ans déja 1986, La femme de ma vie 1986. *Address:* c/o Artmedia, 10 avenue Georges V, 75008 Paris; 30 rue des Francs-Bourgeois, 75003 Paris, France (Home).

TRIPATHI, Kamalapaṭi; Indian politician; mem., Legislative Ass. of Uttar Pradesh 1936–; Minister for Irrigation and Information and later for Home Affairs, Educ. and Information, U.P.; Deputy Chief Minister of Uttar Pradesh 1969–71, Chief Minister 1971–73; Minister of Shipping and Transport 1973–75, of Railways 1975–77, Jan.–Oct. 1980; mem. Rajya Sabha 1973–. *Address:* 9 Akbar Road, New Delhi 110011, India.

TRIPP, (John) Peter, C.M.G.; British diplomatist (retd.); b. 27 March 1921; s. of Charles Howard Tripp and Constance Tripp; m. Rosemary Rees Jones 1948; one s. one d.; ed. Sutton Valence School, Inst. de Touraine; Royal Marines 1941–46; Sudan Political Service 1946–54; H.M. Foreign Service (later Diplomatic Service) 1954–81; Amb. to Libya 1970–74; High Commr. in Singapore 1974–78; Amb. to Thailand 1978–81; Political Adviser Inchcape Group 1981–84; Dir. Gray Mackenzie & Co. Ltd., 1981–84; Chair. P.I.C.A. (U.K.) Ltd., 1981–84; Consultant Al-Tajir Bank 1986–; Chair. Anglo-Thai Soc. 1983–. *Leisure interests:* theatre, gardening. *Address:* 30 Ormonde Gate, London, S.W.3, England.

TRITSIS, Antonis, PH.D.; Greek town planner and politician; b. 1937, Argostoli, Kephallenia; m.; two d.; ed. Athens Polytechnic Univ. and Illinois Inst. of Tech.; Prof. of Planning, Athens Panteios Univ., Illinois Inst. of Tech.; Gen. Sec. Greek Cttee. for Solidarity with Peoples of Africa, Asia and Latin America; helped found Panhellenic Liberation Movement during colonel's dictatorship; mem. Panhellenic Socialist Movement (PASOK) 1974–; M.P. 1981–; Minister for Planning, Housing and the Environment 1981–84, of Educ. and Religion 1987–88; Pres. Council of

EEC Environment Ministers. *Address:* c/o Ministry of Education and Religion, Odos Metropoleos 15, Athens, Greece. *Telephone:* 3230461.

TROCCOLI, Antonio Americo, DR.; Argentine lawyer and politician; b. 21 Feb. 1925, Tres Arroyos; m. Dolores Cecilia Bustos; ed. Nat. Univ. of La Plata; mem. Chamber of Deputies 1963-66, and in 1972; Minister of the Interior 1983-87. *Address:* c/o Ministerio del Interior, Balcarce 24 C.P. 1004, Buenos Aires, Argentina.

TROFIMENKO, Genrikh Aleksandrovich; Soviet political historian; consultant adviser to U.S.S.R. Govt. and specialist on U.S.A.; formerly researcher and teacher at U.S.S.R.-U.S.A. Inst.; Head of Political Policy Div. of History Section, U.S.S.R. Acad. of Sciences. *Publications include:* The Strategy of Global War 1987. *Address:* U.S.S.R. Academy of Sciences, Leningrad, U.S.S.R.

TROFIMUK, Andrey Alekseyevich; Soviet petroleum geologist; b. 16 Aug. 1911, Khvetkovichi, Byelorussia; s. of Aleksey Ustinovich Trofimuk and Yelizaveta Onisimovna; m. Amina Taufikovna 1931; three s. one d.; ed. State Univ. of Kazan; Head Geologist and Scientific Leader of Central Research Lab. of the "Vostokneft" Trust 1934-40; Chief Geologist "Ishimbaineft" Trust 1940-42, "Bashneft" Soc. 1942-50; Chief Geologist, Main Oil and Gas Exploration Dept., Ministry of Oil Industry of U.S.S.R. 1950-53; Deputy Dir. All-Union Oil and Gas Scientific Research Inst. 1953-55, Dir. 1955-58; Dir. Inst. of Geology and Geophysics, Siberian Branch, U.S.S.R. Acad. of Sciences 1958-; Deputy to U.S.S.R. Supreme Soviet 1962-74, Deputy to R.S.F.S.R. Supreme Soviet 1980-85; mem. U.S.S.R. Acad. of Sciences 1958-; mem. Presidium U.S.S.R. Acad. of Sciences, First Vice-Chair. Siberian Branch; Ed. Geology and Geophysics; Hero of Socialist Labour 1944, State Prizes 1946, 1950, Hon. Scientist of R.S.F.S.R. 1957, Order of Lenin (six), Order of Red Banner of Labour 1959, 1961, Order of October Revolution. *Publications:* On the Nature of Ishimbaevo Oil-Bearing Limestone Massifs 1936, An Outline of Tectonics and Oil Content of Volga-Ural Region 1939, Oil Content of Paleozoic Beds of Bashkiria 1950, Conditions of Formation of Oil Deposits of Ural-Volga Oil-Bearing Region 1955, Gas Resources of the U.S.S.R. 1959, Oil and Gas Content of Siberian Platform 1960, Gas-Bearing Prospects of the U.S.S.R. 1963, Geology and Oil and Gas Content of West Siberian Lowland, a New Oil-Bearing Province of the U.S.S.R. 1960, Oil- and Gas-Bearing Basins of the U.S.S.R. 1964, Tectonics and Oil and Gas-Bearing prospects of Platform Regions of Siberia (with Yu. A. Kosygin) 1965, Some Questions on the Theory of Organic Origin of Oil and the problem of Diagnostics of Oil-Source Beds (with A. E. Kontorovich) 1965, On the Methods of Calculation of Prognostic Reserves of Oil 1966, Geology of Oil and Gas of Western Siberia (co-author) 1975, Oil and Gas Geology of Siberian Platform 1981, The Ways of Gas Hydrate Deposits Exploration 1982 (co-author), Nature Factor of Fossil Organic Matter Transformation (co-author) 1982, Nepsko-Botubinskaya arch (new perspective on oil and gas output in the E. of U.S.S.R.—co-author) 1986. *Leisure interests:* fishing, hunting. *Address:* Institute of Geology and Geophysics, Novosibirsk, Universitetsky Pr. 3, U.S.S.R. *Telephone:* 35-46-50.

TROST, Barry Martin, PH.D.; American professor of chemistry; b. 13 June 1941, Philadelphia, Pa.; s. of Joseph and Esther Trost; m. Susan Paula Shapiro 1967; two s.; ed. Univ. of Pennsylvania and M.I.T.; Asst. Prof. of Chem., Dept. of Chem., Univ. of Wis. 1965-68, Assoc. Prof. 1968-69, Prof. 1969-76, Helfaer Prof. 1976-82, Vilas Prof. 1982-87; Prof. of Chemistry, Stanford Univ. 1987-; Consultant E.I. du Pont de Nemours and Merck, Sharp & Dohme; mem. ARCO Science Bd.; mem. Cttee. on Chemical Sciences, N.A.S. 1980-83; mem. and Chair. NIH Medicinal Chem. Study Section 1982-; A.C.S. Award in Pure Chem. 1977, for Creative Work in Synthetic Organic Chem. 1981; Backland Award 1981; Chemical Pioneer Award of A.I.C. 1983; Alexander von Humboldt Award (Fed. Repub. of Germany) 1984, Cope Scholar Award of A.C.S. 1989. *Publications:* Problems in Spectroscopy 1967, Sulfur Ylides 1974, Organic Synthesis Today and Tomorrow (Ed.) 1981, Selectivity: a Goal for Synthetic Efficiency (Ed.) 1984, 395 scientific articles in leading chemical journals. *Address:* Department of Chemistry, Stanford University, Stanford, Calif. 94305 (Office); 24510 Amigos Court, Los Altos Hills, Calif. 94022, U.S.A. (Home). *Telephone:* (415) 723-3385 (Office); (415) 948-1109 (Home).

TROTTER, Sir Ronald Ramsay, Kt., B.COM., F.C.A.; New Zealand business executive; b. 9 Oct. 1927, Hawera; s. of Clement G. and Annie E. (née Young) Trotter; m. Margaret P. Rainey 1955; three s. one d.; ed. Collegiate School, Wanganui, Victoria Univ. of Wellington and Lincoln Coll., Canterbury; Dir. Wright Stephenson & Co. Ltd. 1962-68, Man. Dir. 1968-70, Chair. 1970-72; Chair. and Man. Dir. Challenge Corpn. Ltd. 1972-82; Chair. Fletcher Challenge Ltd. 1981-, C.E.O. 1981-87; Chair. N.Z. Business Roundtable 1985-; Dir. Reserve Bank of N.Z. 1986-88; Chair. Telecom Corpn. of N.Z. Ltd. 1987-; Trustee, N.Z. Inst. of Econ. Research (Inc.) 1973-86; mem. and Chair. Overseas Investment Comm. 1974-77; Int. Deputy Pres., Pacific Basin Econ. Council 1985-86, Int. Pres. 1986-88; Silver Jubilee Medal; Hon. LL.D. (Victoria Univ. of Wellington) 1983. *Address:* 16 Welsey Road, Wellington 1, New Zealand. *Telephone:* (4) 726-628.

TROUGHTON, Sir Charles Hugh Willis, Kt., C.B.E., M.C., T.D., B.A.; British administrator and business executive; b. 27 Aug. 1916, Chalfont St. Giles,

Bucks.; s. of late Charles Vivian and Constance Scylla Troughton; m. Constance Gillean Mitford 1947; three s. one d.; ed. Haileybury Coll., Trinity Coll., Cambridge; joined Territorial Army 1938, Oxford and Bucks. Light Infantry 1939, prisoner of war 1940-45; called to the Bar 1945; Dir. W. H. Smith and Son (Holdings) Ltd. 1949-77, Chair. 1972-77; Dir. Electric and Gen. Investment Co. Ltd. 1967-87, Chair. 1977-80; Chair. Open Univ. Educational Enterprises Ltd. 1977-79; Chair. British Council 1977-84, Pres. 1985-; Chair. British Kidney Patient Asscn. Investment Trust PLC 1982-87, Ranfurly Library Service 1985-; Pres. Nat. Book League 1984-; Dir. Equity and Law Life Assurance Soc. Ltd. 1965-77, Barclays Bank U.K. Ltd. 1973-81, Barclays Bank Int. Ltd. 1977-82, Thomas Tilling Ltd. 1973-79, William Collins and Sons (Holding) Ltd. 1977-89 (Deputy Chair. 1985-89), Whitbread and Co. Ltd. 1978-85, Times Newspapers Holdings Ltd. 1983-88; Whitbread Investment Co. Ltd. 1981-; mem. Court of Govs., L.S.E. 1975-, Standing Cttee. 1977-80; mem. Design Council 1975-78, Royal Coll. of Art Council 1976-79, Royal Literary Fund Gen. Cttee. 1976-, London Library Cttee. 1976-79, Bd. of Man. Navy, Army and Air Force Insts. 1953-73. *Leisure interests:* reading, country pursuits. *Address:* Little Leckmelm House, Lochbroom, Ross and Cromarty, IV23 2RH, Scotland.

TROUVOADA, Miguel Anjos da Cunha Lisboa; São Tomé politician; fmrly. in charge of foreign relations for the São Tomé and Príncipe Liberation Movement (MLSTR), fmr. mem. Political Bureau; Prime Minister of São Tomé and Príncipe 1975-78, also Minister of Defence and Foreign Affairs July-Dec. 1975, of Econ. Co-ordination, Co-operation and Tourism 1975-78, of Trade, Industry and Fisheries 1978-79; arrested and imprisoned 1979, released 1981; living in exile in Lisbon.

TROWBRIDGE, Alexander B, Jr.; American business executive; b. 12 Dec. 1929, Englewood, N.J.; s. of Alexander Buel Trowbridge and Julie Chamberlain; m. 1st Nancey Horst 1955; two s. one d.; m. 2nd Eleanor Hutzler 1981; ed. Phillips Acad., Andover, Mass., and Princeton Univ.; U.S. Marine Corps during Korean War; with overseas operations of several petroleum cos. in Cuba, El Salvador, Panama and Philippines; Pres. and Div. Man. Esso Standard Oil Co. of Puerto Rico 1963-65; Asst. Sec. of Commerce for Domestic and Int. Business 1965-67; Acting Sec. of Commerce Feb.-May 1967, Sec. of Commerce 1967-68; Pres. American Man. Asscn. 1968-70, Conf. Bd. Inc. 1970-76; Dir. Allied Chemical Corpn., then Vice-Chair. of Bd. 1976-79; mem. Bd. Dirs. Nat. Asscn. of Mfrs. 1978-, Pres. 1980-; Dir. New Jersey Chamber of Commerce, Inst. for Int. Educ., mem. Visiting Cttee. Harvard Graduate School of Business; Trustee Outward Bound Inc., World Wildlife Fund, Phillips Acad., Andover, Mass. *Leisure interests:* tennis, skiing. *Address:* 1331 Pennsylvania Avenue, N.W. Suite 1500, Washington, D.C. 20004 (Office); 1823 23rd Street, N.W., Washington, D.C. 20008, U.S.A. (Home).

TROWBRIDGE, Rear-Adm. Sir Richard (John), K.C.V.O., K.ST.J.; British naval officer and administrator; b. 21 Jan. 1920, Andover; s. of A. G. Trowbridge; m. Anne Mildred Perceval 1955; two s.; ed. Andover Grammar School; joined R.N. 1935; Commissioned as Sub-Lieut. Dec. 1940 (mentioned in despatches Aug. 1945), Commdr. 1953; Commdr. Destroyer Carysfort 1956-58; Exec. Officer H.M.S. Bermuda 1958-59, H.M.S. Excellent 1959-60; Capt. 1960; Commdr. Fishery Protection Squadron 1962-64; completed course at Imperial Defence Coll. 1966; Commdr. H.M.S. Hampshire 1967-69; Rear-Adm. 1970-, Flag Officer, Royal Yachts 1970-75; Younger Brother of Trinity House 1972; Extra Equerry to the Queen 1970-; Gov. of Western Australia 1980-83. *Leisure interests:* tennis, fishing, sailing, golf. *Address:* Old Idsworth Garden, Finchdean, Portsmouth, Hampshire, England. *Telephone:* (0705) 412714.

TROYANOVSKY, Oleg Aleksandrovich; Soviet diplomatist; b. 24 Nov. 1919, Moscow; s. of Aleksandr and Nina, Troyanovskiy; m. Tatyana Troyanovskaya 1953; one d.; ed. Moscow Foreign Languages Inst., Moscow Inst. of Philosophy, Literature and History; Diplomatic service 1944; took part in many important confs.; Amb. to Japan 1968-76, to People's Repub. of China April 1986-; Perm. Rep. to UN 1977-86; mem. CPSU Cen. Auditing Comm. 1981-86; Lenin Prize 1960. *Leisure interests:* tennis, chess. *Address:* Embassy of the Soviet Union, 4 Dong Zhi Men Wai Zhong Jie, Beijing, People's Republic of China.

TROYAT, Henri (pseudonym of Tarasoff); French writer; b. 1 Nov. 1911, Moscow, U.S.S.R.; m. Marguerite Saintagne 1948; one s. one d.; ed. Lycée Pasteur, and Law Faculty, Univ. of Paris; mem. Acad. Française 1959-; Légion d'honneur. *Publications:* Faux-jour (Prix Populiste) 1935, L'araigne (Prix Goncourt) 1938, La neige en deuil (Grand prix littéraire de Monaco) 1952, Tant que la terre durera (three vols.) 1947-50, Les semailles et les moissons (five vols.) 1953-58, La lumière des justes (five vols.) 1960-, Les Éyglretère (three vols.) 1965-67, Les héritiers de l'avenir 1968, Anne Predaille 1973, Le Moscovite 1974, La dérision 1983, Le bruit solitaire du coeur 1985, etc.; biographies: Dostoïevsky, Pouchkine, Tolstoi, Gogol, Catherine la Grande, Pierre le Grand, Alexandre Ier, Ivan le Terrible, Tchekhov, Turgenev, Gorki, Flaubert. *Address:* Académie Française, quai de Conti, 75006 Paris, France.

TRUBILIN, Nikolay Timofeyevich, DR. MED. SC.; Soviet health official; b. 1929; ed. Medical Inst., Rostov-on-Don; mem. CPSU 1959-; work with health insurance inst. Rostov Dist. 1953-77; Deputy of Rostov Dist. Health Section 1977-78; R.S.F.S.R. Deputy, First Deputy Minister of Health

1978–83, Minister 1983–; Deputy Pres. of R.S.F.S.R. Council of Ministers 1986–; mem. of CPSU Cen. Auditing Comm. 1986–. *Address:* The Kremlin, Moscow, U.S.S.R.

TRUDEAU, Garry B.; American cartoonist; b. 1948, New York; m. Jane Pauley; one s. one d.; ed. Yale Univ. School of Art and Architecture; created comic strip Doonesbury syndicated nationwide, Pinhead: selected cartoons from You Ask for Many; conceived (with Robert Altman, q.v.) Tanner '88 (TV) 1988, *Publications:* Any Grooming Hints for Your Fans, Rollie, But the Pension Fund was Just Sitting There, The Doonesbury Chronicles, Guilty, Guilty, Guilty, We Who are about to Fry, Salute You: selected cartoons from In Search of Reagan's Brain, Vol. 2, Is This Your First Purge, Miss ?, Vol. 2, It's Supposed to be Yellow, Pinhead: selected cartoons from You Ask for Many, Seetle for June, Vol. 1, The Wreck of the Rusty Nail, Dressed for Failure 1984, Confirmed Bachelors are Just So Fascinating 1984, Sir I'm Worried About Your Mood Swings 1984: contribs. to The People's Doonesbury and many others; *plays include:* Doonesbury 1983, Rapmaster Ronnie, A Partisan Review (with Elizabeth Swados) 1984. *Address:* c/o Universal Press Syndicate, 4400 Johnson Drive, Fairway, Kan. 66205, U.S.A.

TRUDEAU, Rt. Hon. Pierre Elliott, C.H., C.C., P.C.; Canadian lawyer and politician; b. 18 Oct. 1919, Montreal, Quebec; s. of Charles-Emile Trudeau and Grace Elliott; m. Margaret Sinclair 1971 (divorced 1984); three s.; ed. Collège Jean-de-Brébeuf, Montreal, Univ. of Montreal, Harvard Univ., Univ. of Paris, and L.S.E.; called to Bar, Prov. of Quebec 1943, then studied at Harvard, Paris and London; subsequently employed with Cabinet Secr., Ottawa; later practised law, Prov. of Que.; one of founders of Cité Libre (Quebec review); Assoc. Prof. of Law, Univ. of Montreal 1961; mem. House of Commons 1965–84; Parl. Sec. to Prime Minister 1966–67; Minister of Justice and Attorney-Gen. 1967–68; Leader of Liberal Party 1968–84; Prime Minister of Canada 1968–79, 1980–84; Sr. Consultant Heenan, Blaikie 1984–; mem. InterAction Council 1985; numerous hon. degrees; Freedom of City of London 1975; Albert Einstein Int. Peace Prize 1984. *Publications:* La grève de l'amiante 1956, Canadian Dualism/La dualité Canadienne 1960, Deux innocents en Chine rouge 1961, Federalism and the French Canadians 1968, Réponses 1968; and numerous articles in Canadian and foreign journals. *Address:* c/o Heenan, Blaikie, John, Potvin, Trepanier and Cobbett, Suite 1400, 1001 Maisonneuve Boulevard W., Montreal, Quebec H3A 3C8, Canada.

TRUHAUT, René Charles, D. ÈS SC.; French toxicologist; b. 23 May 1909, Pouzauges (Vendée); s. of Jules Truhaut and Sidonie Lucas; ed. Lycée de La Roche-sur-Yon, Facultés de pharmacie et des sciences de Paris; Chief Pharmacist psychiatric hospitals (Seine) 1937–82; Head of Lab., Inst. of Cancer 1930–41, Head of Chemical Research 1941–48; Head of Research Inst. Gustave Roussy 1941–74; Prof. of Toxicology and Industrial Hygiene, Faculté de Pharmacie, Paris 1949–60, Titular Prof. 1960–78; Head of teaching of industrial toxicology, Inst. of Industrial Medicine, Paris 1955–79; Sec.-Gen. European Cttee. for the Study of the Protection of Populations against the long-term effects of Toxicity (EUROTOX); Adviser to numerous int. orgs. including WHO, FAO, ILO, Perm. Int. Comm. of Occupational Medicine, Int. Union Against Cancer 1954–66, Council of Europe, EEC, Int. Union of Pure and Applied Chemistry; Perm. Consultant, Conseil supérieur d'Hygiène publique de France 1955–, and mem. of numerous nat. comms. on public health; mem. Acad. des Sciences (Inst. de France), Acad. Nat. de Médecine, Acad. de Pharmacie, Acad. d'Agric., Acad. Vétérinaire and numerous foreign socs. and acads.; Great Medal of WHO (Health for All in the year 2000), Gold Medal of European Merit 1988; Commdr., Légion d'honneur, Grand Officier, Ordre nat. du Mérite, Croix de guerre, Médaille de la Résistance, Commdr. des Palmes académiques and other awards. *Publications:* Les facteurs chimiques de cancérisation 1948, Les fluoroses 1948, Les dérivés organiques halogénés doués d'activité insecticide 1948, Toxicologie des produits phytopharmaceutiques 1952, Traitement d'urgence des intoxications 1957, La toxicologie du thallium 1958, Précis de toxicologie 1960, Compendio de toxicologia 1962, Potential Carcinogenic Hazards from Drugs 1967, Précis de médecine du travail 1975, 1978, Tratado de Toxicologia 1976. *Address:* Centre de recherches toxicologiques de la Faculté des Sciences Pharmaceutiques et Biologiques de l'Université René Descartes, 4 avenue de l'Observatoire, 75006 Paris, France. *Telephone:* 329-12-08, ext. 358.

TRUJILLO MOLINA, General Héctor Bienvenido; Dominican army officer and politician; b. 1908; ed. Univ. Autónoma de Santo Domingo; entered Army 1926; Chief of Staff of Army 1936; Supervisor-Gen. of Nat. Police 1938–43; Secretary of War, C.-in-C. of Army and Navy 1944; succeeded his brother as Pres. of the Dominican Republic 1952–60; Prof. American Int. Acad., Washington; corresp. mem. Nat. Athenaeum Arts and Sciences, Mexico; holds numerous military and other decorations of his own and foreign countries. *Address:* Living abroad.

TRULY, Rear Adm. Richard H.; American astronaut and government official; b. 12 Nov. 1937, Fayette, Miss.; s. of James B. Truly; m. Colleen Hanner; four s. one d.; ed. Georgia Inst. of Tech.; Commdr. Ensign U.S. Navy 1959, assigned Fighter Squadron 33 1960–63; Astronaut Manned Orbiting Lab. Program USAF 1959–69; Astronaut NASA 1969–; Commdr. Columbia Flight 2 1981, Columbia Flight 2, Challenger Flight 3 1983; Dir.

Space Shuttle Program 1986–; Admin. (desig.) NASA April 1989. *Address:* Lyndon B. Johnson Space Center, NASA, Houston, Tex. 77508, U.S.A.

TRUMKA, Richard Louis, J.D.; American lawyer and industrialist; b. 24 July 1949, Waynesburg, Pa.; s. of Frank Richard Trumka and Eola Elizabeth Bertugli; m. Barbara Vidovich 1982; ed. Philadelphia State Univ., Villanova Univ.; served at bar U.S. Dist. Court 1974, U.S. Court of Appeals 1975, U.S. Supreme Court 1979; Attorney United Mine Workers of America, Washington 1974–77, 1978–79, mem. Int. Exec. Bd. Dist. 4, Masontown, Pa. 1981–83, Int. Pres., Washington 1982–; Miner-Operator Jone and Loughlin Steel, Nemacolin, Pa. 1977–78, 1979–81; Dir. Nat. Bank, Washington 1983–85, Dinamo Corpn. 1983–; mem. Bd. Dirs. American Coal Fund 1983–; Trustee Philadelphia State Univ. *Address:* United Mine Workers of America, 900 15th Street, N.W., Washington, D.C. 20005, U.S.A.

TRUMP, Donald John, B.A.; American business executive; b. 1946, New York; s. of Fred C. Trump and Mary Trump; m. Ivana Winkelmayr 1977; three c.; ed. Fordham Univ., Univ. of Pennsylvania; Pres. Trump Org.; Pres., owner New Jersey Gens. U.S. Football League; owner Trump Enterprises Inc., The Trump Corpn., Trump Devt. Co., Wembley Realty Inc., Park South Co., Land Corpn. of Calif.; Business and Boxing Man. to Mike Tyson (q.v.) 1988; appeared in Ghosts Can't Do It (film) 1989. *Publication:* Trump: The Art of the Deal 1988. *Address:* Trump Organization, 725 5th Avenue, New York, N.Y. 10022, U.S.A.

TRÜMPY, D. Rudolf, DR.SC.NAT.; Swiss professor of geology (retd.); b. 16 Aug. 1921, Glarus; s. of Daniel and Maria Magdalena (née Dürst) Trümpy; m. Marianne M. Landry 1948; one s. one d.; ed. Swiss Fed. Inst. of Tech., Zürich; Tutor, Univ. of Lausanne 1947–53; Prof., Swiss Fed. Inst. of Tech. (E.T.H.) 1953–86, Univ. of Zürich 1956–86; Dean, Science Section, E.T.H. 1964–68; Treas. Int. Union of Geological Sciences 1964–68, Pres. 1976–80; mem. Acad. Leopoldina; Foreign Assoc. Royal Belgian Acad., U.S. Nat. Acad. of Sciences, American Acad. of Arts and Sciences, Acad. des Sciences (Paris); Dr. h.c. (Paris, Lausanne); Penrose Medal (Geological Soc. of America) 1985. *Publications:* Paleotectonic Evolution of the Central and Western Alps 1960, Die helvetischen Decken der Ostschweiz 1969, The Timing of Orogenic Events in the Central Alps 1973, An Outline of the Geology of Switzerland 1980, and about 100 papers, mainly on Alpine geology. *Leisure interest:* history. *Address:* Allmendboden 19, 8700 Küsnacht, Switzerland. *Telephone:* (01) 910 4520.

TRUONG NHU TANG; Vietnamese lawyer and politician; b. 1923, Cholon; ed. Univ. of Paris; Controller-General, Viet-Nam Bank for Industry and Commerce; Dir.-Gen. Viet-Nam Sugar Co., Saigon; Sec.-Gen. People's Movement for Self-Determination 1964–65; mem. Saigon Cttee. for Restoration of Peace; Pres. Viet-Nam Youth Union 1966–67; imprisoned 1967–68; joined Nat. Liberation Front 1968; Minister of Justice, Provisional Revolutionary Govt. of S. Viet-Nam 1969–76 (in Saigon 1975–76). *Address:* c/o Council of Ministers, Hanoi, Viet-Nam.

TRYOSHNIKOV, Aleksey Fedorovich, D.SC.; Soviet Polar explorer; b. 14 April 1914, Pavlovka Village, Simbirsk (now Ulyanovsk) Region; s. of Theodore Tryoshnikov and Anastasya Tryoshnikova; m. Tatyana Makarevich 1939; two d.; ed. Leningrad Univ.; Head of the Soviet drifting station SP-3 in the Arctic 1954–55; Head Soviet Int. Geophysical Year Antarctic Expedition to Mirny 1956–58; Dir. Arctic and Antarctic Scientific Research Inst., Leningrad 1960–80; Head, Oceanology Dept., Leningrad Univ. 1980–; Dir. Limnological Inst., U.S.S.R. Acad. of Sciences, Leningrad 1982–; mem. second and thirteenth Soviet Antarctic Expeditions of U.S.S.R. Acad. of Sciences 1956–58, 1967–68; Deputy Pres. U.S.S.R. Geographical Asscn. 1964–77, Pres. 1977–79; mem. U.S.S.R. Acad. of Sciences; mem. CPSU 1944–; Hero of Socialist Labour 1949; State Prize 1971, Order of Lenin (four times), Order of October Revolution, Order of Labour Red Banner. *Publications:* The History of the Discovery and Study of the Antarctic 1963, The Structure of the Currents of the Antarctic Basin 1972, My Polar Explorations 1985, Arctic Atlas (Chief Ed.) 1985; numerous articles on geography of polar regions, general geography, oceanology, lake nature conservation. *Leisure interest:* travelling. *Address:* Institute of Limnology, Sevastyanory Str. 9, ¹196199 Leningrad; Geographical Society, Grivtzeva Str. 10, 190000 Leningrad, U.S.S.R. *Telephone:* 297-22-97 (Inst. of Limnology); 315-85-35 (Geographical Soc.).

TRYPANIS, Constantine Athanasius, D.PHIL., LITT.D., F.R.S.L.; Greek university professor; b. 22 Jan. 1909, Chios; s. of Athanasius G. Trypanis and Maria Zolota; m. Aliki Macris 1942; one d.; ed. Univs. of Athens, Berlin and Munich; Lecturer in Classical Literature Athens Univ. 1939; Bywater and Sotheby Prof. of Byzantine and Modern Greek, Univ. of Oxford 1947–68; Univ. Prof. of Classics, Univ. of Chicago 1968–74; Minister of Culture and Science 1974–77; Emer. Fellow, Exeter Coll., Oxford; Fellow Int. Inst. of Arts and Letters; Archon Hieromnemon of the Oecumenical Patriarchate, Megas Archon Hieromnemon 1972; Visiting Prof., U.S. univs. 1963, 1964, 1965, 1966; Visiting mem. Inst. for Advanced Study, Princeton 1959–60; Corresp. mem. of Inst. for Balkan Studies, Salonica, Center for Neo-Hellenic Studies, Austin, Texas; mem. Acad. of Athens 1974 (Sec.-Gen. 1982–84, Vice-Pres. 1985, Pres. 1986–), Medieval Acad. of America; Hon. Fellow Int. Poetry Soc. 1976, British Acad. 1978, Soc. for Promotion of Hellenic Studies 1979; D.Hum.Litt. (MacMurray Coll., U.S.A.) 1974,

(Assumption Coll., U.S.A.) 1977; Gottfried von Herder Prize, Univ. of Vienna 1983. *Publications:* The Influence of Hesiod upon the Homeric Hymn to Hermes 1939, Alexandrian Poetry 1943, Tartessos, Phanagorea, Alexandria eschate 1945, Medieval and Modern Greek Poetry 1951, Pedasus 1955, The Stones of Troy 1957, Callimachus 1958, The Cocks of Hades 1958, Sancti Romani Melodi Cantica 1963, Pompeian Dog 1964, Fourteen Early Byzantine Cantica 1968, Sancti Romani Melodi Cantica II 1970, The Penguin Book of Greek Verse 1972, The Glass Adonis 1973, The Homeric Epics 1975, Greek Poetry, from Homer to Seferis 1981, The Refugees (play) 1983, Atticism and the Greek Language Question, Skias Onar 1986, Sophocles, Three Theban Plays (transl.) 1986. *Leisure interests:* tennis, painting, walking. *Address:* 3 George Nikolaou, Kifisia, Athens, Greece. *Telephone:* 8081018.

TSAI, Gerald, M.A.; American (naturalized) business executive; b. 10 March 1928, Shanghai, China; s. of Gerald and Ruth (Lea); m. Marlyn K. F. Chase 1969; two s. one d.; ed. Boston Univ.; Security Analyst, Bache & Co., New York 1951–52; with Fidelity Man. Research Co., Boston 1952–65, Vice-Pres. 1960–63, Dir. 1961–65, Exec. Vice-Pres. 1963–65; Chair. Tsai Man. & Research Corpn., New York 1965–68; Exec. Vice-Pres. and Dir. CNA Financial Corpn., New York 1968–86; Chair. and C.E.O. Associated Madison Cos. Inc. 1978–86, Nat. Benefit Life Insurance Co. 1979–82; Exec. Vice-Pres. American Can Co. (now Primerica Corpn.) 1982–83, Vice-Chair. 1983–87, C.E.O. 1986–, Chair. 1987–. *Address:* Primerica Corpn., American Lane, Greenwich, Conn. 06836, U.S.A.

TSCHUDI, Hans-Peter, LL.D.; Swiss politician; b. 22 Oct. 1913; ed. Basle Univ.; Prof. of Labour Law, Basle Univ. 1952–59; Head of Home Dept. Govt. of Basle 1953–59; mem. Council of States, Fed. Ass. 1956–59; mem. Fed. Council 1960–73, Vice-Pres. Jan.-Dec. 1964, Jan.-Dec. 1969, Pres. Jan.-Dec. 1965, Jan.-Dec. 1970; Head of Dept. of the Interior 1960–73; mem. Ass., Int. Red Cross; Socialist. *Publications:* Die Ferien im schweizerischen Arbeitsrecht 1948, Koalitionsfreiheit und Koalitionszwang 1948, Die Sicherung des Arbeitsfriedens durch das schweizerische Recht 1952, Gesamtarbeitsvertrag und Aussenseiter 1953. *Address:* c/o Comité International de la Croix-Rouge, avenue de la Paix 17, 1211 Geneva, Switzerland.

TSCHUDI-MADSEN, Stephan, PH.D.; Norwegian art historian; b. 25 Aug. 1923, Bergen; s. of Dr. Stephan and Aagot (née Stoltz) Tschudi-Madsen; m. Elizabeth Kverndal 1954; two s. one d.; ed. Univ. of Oslo; Keeper, Nat. Gallery, Oslo 1950–51, Vigelands Museum, Oslo 1951–52; Asst. Prof. Univ. of Oslo 1953–58; Chief Antiquarian, Cen. Office of Historic Monuments, Oslo 1959–78, Dir.-Gen. 1978–; Keeper, Akershus Castle 1961–79; Prof. Univ. of Calif. 1968–69, 1973; Sec. Gen. The Architectural Heritage Year 1974–76; Pres. Advisory Cttee. of Int. Council on Monuments and Sites 1981–88, Vice-Pres. 1988–; Vice-Pres. World Heritage Comm. 1984–87; mem. Norwegian Acad.; Hon. mem. Norwegian Soc. of Preservation; Cultural Prize of Science and Letters of Oslo City; Kt. of the Order of St. Olav, Commdr. of Order of Oranje-Nassau, Kt. of Order of King Leopold. *Publications:* To kongeslott 1952, Vigelands Fontenerelieffer 1953, Sources of Art Nouveau 1957, 1976, Rosendal 1965, Art Nouveau 1967 (translated in 11 languages), Chateauneuf's Works in London and Oslo 1968, Restoration and Anti-Restoration 1976, 1980, Henrik Bull 1983. *Leisure interest:* skiing. *Address:* Bjørn Farmannsgt. 8, Oslo 2, Norway. *Telephone:* (02) 419600.

TSEDENBAL, Yumjaagiyn; Mongolian politician; b. 17 Sept. 1916; m.; one s.; ed. Inst. of Finance and Econs. in U.S.S.R.; teacher at Ulan Bator Financial Coll.; Deputy Minister, then Minister of Finance 1939–40; Deputy C.-in-C. Mongolian People's Army, Dir. of Political Directorate 1941–45; Chair. State Planning Comm. 1945–48; Deputy Chair. Council of Ministers 1948–52, Chair. 1952–74; Deputy to People's Great Hural (Ass.) 1940–, Chair. of Presidium of People's Great Hural (Head of State) 1974–84; mem. Cen. Cttee. of Mongolian People's Revolutionary Party (MPRP) 1940–84, mem. Presidium and Gen. Sec. of Cen. Cttee. 1940–54, First Sec. of Cen. Cttee. 1958–81, Gen. Sec. of Cen. Cttee. 1981–84; Marshal of the Mongolian People's Republic; Hon. mem. Acad. of Sciences; Order of Sühbaatar, Hero of the Mongolian People's Repub., Order of Lenin. *Address:* c/o Government Palace, Ulan Bator, Mongolia.

TSELKOV, Oleg; Soviet artist; b. 1934, Moscow; ed. Moscow secondary school, Minsk Inst. of Theatre Art and Leningrad Acad. of Art; expelled from both for 'formalism'; later graduated from Leningrad Theatre Inst. as stage-designer 1958; designed numerous productions; mem. of Artists' Union. *Exhibitions:* Moscow 1965, 1970, 1975, Austria 1975, Fed. Germany, France 1976.

TSENG KWANG-SHUN, LL.B.; Chinese politician; b. 24 Dec. 1924, Haifeng County, Kwangtung, China; m. Wan Yee-mui; one s. two d.; ed. Coll. of Law and Commerce, Kwangtung and Advanced Research Inst., Kuomintang; Assoc. Prof. Chu Hai Coll., Hwa Chiao Coll., Hong Kong 1950–57; Deputy Dir. and Dir. Dept. of Culture and Youth Corps 1958–69; Deputy Dir. 3rd Section, Cen. Cttee. Kuomintang 1969–77; Deputy Dir., Acting Dir. Dept. of Overseas Affairs, Kuomintang 1969–77, Dir. 1978–84; Publr. Overseas Digest (semimonthly) 1978–84, Overseas News Service 1978–84; Chair. Overseas Chinese Affairs Comm. 1984–. *Address:* Overseas Chinese Affairs Commission, 1 Chungshan North Road, Sec. 1, Taipei 100; 30, Kungyuan Road, Taipei, Taiwan. *Telephone:* 3915231.

TSEVEGMID, Dondogiyn; Mongolian biologist and politician; b. 26 March 1915, Dornod Aimag; s. of Dondog Tsevegmid and Regzedmaa Tsevegmid; m. Dolgorsuren Tsevegmid 1950; two s. two d.; ed. Teacher Training School, Ulan Bator, and Moscow Univ.; Teacher 1930–45; Rector, Mongolian State Univ. 1951–59, Chair. Cttee. of Sciences 1959–60; Deputy Minister of Foreign Affairs 1960–62; Amb. to China 1962–67; Rector, Mongolian State Univ. 1967–72; Deputy to People's Great Hural (Ass.) 1951–, Chair. (Speaker of Parl.) 1969–72; Deputy Chair. Council of Ministers 1972, Minister of Culture 1980–84; Chair. Exec. Cttee. of Parl. Group; Chair. Atomic Energy Comm.; Chair. Cttee. for Higher and Special Secondary, Technical-Vocational Educ. 1973–80; cand. mem. Mongolian People's Revolutionary Party Cen. Cttee. 1958–66, mem. Cen. Cttee. 1966–; corresp. mem. Acad. of Sciences; Dr. h.c. (Lomonosov Univ., Moscow, Humboldt Univ., Berlin). *Publications:* The Ecological and Morphological Analysis of the Duplicidentate 1950, Fauna of the Transaltai 1963, Selected Works 1946, 1956, 1974, The Teacher (novel) 1982. *Leisure interest:* hunting. *Address:* Government Palace, Ulan Bator, Mongolia.

TSHERING, Dago; Bhutan diplomatist and politician; b. 17 July 1941, Paro; ed. Univ. of Bombay, Indian Admin. Service Training, Mussoorie and Indian Audit and Accounts Service Training, Simla, India, Univ. of Manchester, England; Asst., Ministry of Devt. 1961–62; Asst., Office of the Chief Sec., Royal Secretariat 1962–63; returned to Ministry of Devt. 1963, Sec. 1965–70; mem. Nat. Ass., Royal Advisory Council 1968–70; First Sec. Bhutan Embassy in India 1971–73; Deputy Perm. Rep. to UN 1973–74, Perm. Rep. 1974–80, 1984–85; Amb. to Bangladesh 1980–84; Deputy Minister of Home Affairs 1985–; Orange Scarf. *Address:* Ministry of Home Affairs, Tashichho Dzong, Thimphu, Bhutan.

TSINTSADZE, Sulkhan Fyodorovich; Soviet (Georgian) composer; b. 23 Aug. 1925, Gori, Georgian S.S.R.; ed. Moscow Conservatory; Rector of Tbilisi Conservatory 1965; State Prize 1950, People's Artist of the Georgian S.S.R. 1961, two other orders and various medals. *Compositions include:* operas: The Golden Fleece 1952, The Hermit 1972; ballets: The Treasure of the Blue Mountain 1957, The Demon 1961, Sketches of Antiquity 1974; three symphonies; works for piano and violin; an oratorio, Immortality, 1970; eight string quartets; much film music. *Address:* The Conservatory, Tbilisi, Georgian S.S.R., U.S.S.R.

TSOHATZOPOULOS, Apostolos Athanasios; Greek politician; b. 1939, Athens; m. Gudrun Moldenhauer; two c.; ed. Tech. Univ. of Munich, Fed. Repub. of Germany; deprived of citizenship by mil. dictatorship 1969; active in Panhellenic Liberation Movt., mem. Nat. Council during dictatorship; returned to Greece 1974; mem. Cen. Cttee. and Exec. Office PASOK 1974–; Minister to the Prime Minister 1986–87, of the Interior Sept. 1987–. *Address:* Ministry of the Interior, Odos Stadiou 27, Athens, Greece.

TSOLOV, Tano; Bulgarian politician; b. 27 June 1918; ed. High Commercial School, Commercial Acad. and Higher School for Finance and Admin.; Young Communist League 1934–40; mem. Communist Party 1940–; student, political prisoner and partisan, Young Communist League and Party functionary 1940–44; First Sec. of the Regional Cttee. of the CP and Chair. Regional Cttee. of the Fatherland Front, Byala Slatina 1944–50; Industry, Bldg. and Transport Dept., Cen. Cttee. of the CP 1950–52; mem. Cen. Cttee. of the CP 1957; Minister Heavy Industry 1952–59; Chair. Cttee. for Industry and Tech. Progress 1959; Sec. Cen. Cttee. of the CP 1959–62; Cand. mem. of Political Bureau 1962; mem. of Political Bureau 1966; Deputy Chair. Council of Ministers 1962–71; Chair. Council for Industry and Construction at Council of Ministers 1962–66; Chair. State Planning Cttee. 1968–71; Perm. Rep. of the People's Repub. of Bulgaria in the Council for Mutual Econ. Assistance (SIV) 1966–74, Chair. Exec. Cttee. 1973–74; Chair. Comm. for Econ., Scientific and Tech. Co-operation at Council of Ministers 1966; First Deputy Chair. Council of Ministers 1971–79. *Address:* c/o Council of Ministers, Sofia, Bulgaria.

TSONGAS, Paul E., M.A.; American lawyer and politician; b. 14 Feb. 1941, Lowell, Mass.; m. Nicola Sauvage 1969; three d.; ed. Lowell High School, Mass., Dartmouth Coll., Hanover, N.H., Yale Law School, New Haven, Conn., John F. Kennedy School of Govt., Harvard Univ.; Peace Corps Volunteer, Ethiopia 1962–64, Peace Corps Training Co-ordinator, West Indies 1967–68; mem. Governor's Cttee. on Law Enforcement 1968–69; Deputy Asst. Attorney-Gen. 1969–71; Lowell City Councillor 1970–72; private legal practice 1971–74; Middlesex Co. Commr. 1973–74; mem. House of Reps. for 5th Dist. of Mass., serving on Cttee. on Banking, Finance and Urban Affairs, Cttee. on Interior and Insular Affairs, and others 1975–78; Senator from Mass., serving on Cttee. on Foreign Relations, Cttee. on Energy and Natural Resources, and others 1979–84; partner in Foley, Hoag & Eliot 1985–. *Publications:* The Road From Here: Liberalism and Realities in the 1980s 1981.

TSOTETSI, Col. Michael Nkhahle; Lesotho police officer and politician; b. 12 Dec. 1938, Thupa-Buka Ha Thafeng, Berea Dist.; s. of Raphael Lejone Tsotetsi; ed. Roma Coll., subsequent law studies; joined Lesotho Mounted Police (LMP) 1964, then police investigator; joined Protective Security Unit of Police Mobile Unit 1966, becoming Lieut.-Col. 1978; P.R.O. for PMU and public; responsible for Ministries of Agric., Co-operatives and Marketing; Minister for Trade and Indsutry, Water, Energy and Mining, Youth and Women's Affairs 1986–87; mem. Mil. Council 1987–; also a progressive farmer; Medal for Meritorious Service 1980, Medal for Gallantry 1983. *Leisure interests:* agricultural modernization, soccer. *Address:* The Military Council, Maseru, Lesotho.

TSOVOLAS, Dimitris; Greek politician; b. 1942, Melissourgi, Arta; ed. Salonika Univ.; practised law at Arta until 1977; elected PASOK M.P. 1977; mem. Parl. Working Cttees. on Labour, Public Order and Premiership 1977–81; elected Sec. of Presidium of Parl.; Minister of Finance 1986–. *Address:* Ministry of Finance, Odos Karageorgi Servias 10, Athens, Greece. *Telephone:* (21) 322 4071.

TSUCHIYA, Yoshihiko; Japanese politician; b. 31 May 1926; ed. Chuo Univ.; mem. Saitama Prefectural Assembly; mem. House of Councillors 1965, returned to House of Councillors three times: Parl. Vice-Minister for Defence 1970–71; Minister of State and Dir.-Gen. Environment Agency 1979–80; Chair. Standing Cttee. on Finance, House of Councillors 1973–74; Vice-Chair. Public Relations Cttee., Liberal-Democratic Party (LDP); Deputy Sec.-Gen. LDP. *Address:* House of Councillors, Tokyo, Japan. *Telephone:* 03-581-3351.

TSUR, Yaacov; Israeli diplomatist; b. 18 Oct. 1906, Vilno; s. of Samuel and Bella Tsur; m. Vera Gotlib 1928; one s. one d.; ed. Hebrew Coll., Jerusalem, Univs. of Florence and Sorbonne; mem. staff daily newspaper Haaretz, Tel-Aviv 1929; Dir. French Dept. and later Co-Dir. Propaganda Dept. Jewish Nat. Fund, Jerusalem 1930; special Zionist missions, Belgium, Greece, France 1934–35, Bulgaria and Greece 1940; Liaison officer with G.H.Q. British Troops in Egypt 1943–45; Head del. to Greece 1945; Pres. Israeli Army Recruiting Cttee. Jerusalem 1948; Minister to Argentina 1949–53, Uruguay 1949–53, Chile 1950–53, and Paraguay 1950–53, Amb. to France 1953–59; Chair. Jewish Nat. Fund 1960–76; Chair. Zionist Gen. Council 1961–68; Minister of Immigration and Absorption 1984–88, of Health Dec. 1988–; Pres. Central Inst. for Relations with Ibero-America, Bialik Inst. Publication Soc.; Grand Officier, Légion d'honneur. *Publications:* Juifs en guerre 1947, The Birth of Israel 1949, Shacharit Shel Etmol (Autobiography) 1965, Ambassador's Diary 1967, La révolte juive 1970, Portrait of the Diaspora 1975, The Saga of Zionism 1976, The Day is Near 1979, Credentials No. 4 1981. *Address:* Ministry of Health, 2 Ben Tabai Street, Jerusalem; Mevó Yoram 5, Jerusalem, Israel. *Telephone:* 633811.

TSVETKOV, Aleksey, PH.D.; Russian poet and critic; b. 2 Feb. 1947, Stanislaw (now Ivano-Frankivsk), Ukraine; s. of Petr Tsvetkov and Bella Tsvetkov (née Tsyganov); m. Olga Samilenko 1978; ed. Odessa and Moscow Univs., Univ. of Mich., U.S.A.; journalist in Siberia and Kazakhstan; poetry recitals and participant in Volgin's Moscow Univ. literary soc. Luch 1970–75; emigrated to U.S.A. 1976; co-ed. of Russkaya zhizn', San Francisco 1976–77; Prof. of Russian Language and Literature, Dickinson Coll., Pa. 1981–85; broadcaster, Voice of America; poetry has appeared in Kontinent, Ekho, Vremya i my, Apollon, Glagol and elsewhere; Dr. h.c. (Univ. of Mich.) 1977. *Publications include:* A Collection of Pieces for Life Solo 1978, Three Poets: Kuzminsky, Tsvetkov, Limonov, 1981, Dream State 1981, Eden 1985. *Leisure interest:* collecting baroque opera records. *Address:* 1225 North Meade Street No. 25, Arlington, Va. 22209, U.S.A.

TUBMAN, Robert Colden, B.SC. (ECON.), J.D.; Liberian economist and lawyer; b. 15 June 1939, Cape Palmas; s. of the late William A. Tubman and Grace (née Puate) Tubman; brother of Winston A. Tubman (q.v.); m. Maria Helmz 1961; four s. one d.; ed. London School of Econs., Univ. of Edinburgh and Harvard Law School; Law Assoc., Ropes & Gray, Boston, U.S.A. 1968, Sullivan & Cromwell, New York 1969; Econ. Adviser, Ministry of Finance, Liberia 1970; Legal Adviser to U.K. Amb., Liberia 1970–76; Man. Dir. Tubman, Tubman & Tubman, Monrovia 1970–76; Chair. Liberian Del. to Law of Sea Conf. 1976–79; Deputy Minister of Justice 1976–79, Minister of Justice a.i. 1979; Minister of Finance 1986–87, of Labour March-Nov. 1987; Man. Dir. Econ. Community of West African States (ECOWAS) Fund, Lomé, Togo 1979–85. *Leisure interests:* swimming, table tennis, flying, photography, music. *Address:* c/o Ministry of Labour, Monrovia, Liberia.

TUBMAN, Winston A., LL.M.; Liberian lawyer and diplomatist; b. 26 Jan. 1941, Cape Palmas; s. of the late William Alfred and Grace (née Puate) Tubman; brother of Robert Colden Tubman (q.v.); m. Nehsee Lducia Gorgla 1965; one s. three d.; ed. L.S.E., St. Catharine's Coll., Cambridge, Harvard Law School; Legal Adviser to Ministry of Planning and Econ. Affairs 1966–71; lecturer in Public Int. Law, Univ. of Liberia 1967–72; Legal Counsellor to Ministry of Foreign Affairs 1971–73; Legal Officer, Office of Legal Affairs, UN, New York 1973–75; Legal Adviser to UNEP, Nairobi 1975–76; Man. Dir. Liberia Sugar Corpn. 1976–79; Perm. Rep. to UN 1979–81; Amb. to Cuba 1979–81; Minister for Justice 1982–83; mem. Panel of Experts apptd. by UN to study the Relationship between Int. Security and Disarmament 1980–82; Chair. Liberian Del. and African Group to UN Conf. on Law of the Sea 1979–81; Rep. of Liberia to Franco-African Summit, Kinshasa 1982; returned to private practice 1983–. *Leisure interests:* classical music, photography, painting, jogging. *Address:* The Tubman Law Firm, P.O. Box 1597, Pan African Plaza, Suite 305, Monrovia, Liberia.

TUCHKEVICH, Vladimir Maksimovich, D.SC.; Soviet physicist; b. 29 Dec. 1904, Yanoutsi, Chernovitsk Region; ed. Kiev State Univ.; Head of Lab., All-Ukrainian Radiological Inst. 1931–35; Head of Lab., Leningrad Radiological Inst. 1935–36, A. F. Joffe physical-technological Inst., U.S.S.R. Acad. of Sciences 1936–, Dir. 1968–; mem. CPSU 1952–; corresp. mem. U.S.S.R. Acad. of Sciences 1968–70, mem. 1970–, mem. Presidium 1971–; Honoured Scientist of R.S.F.S.R. 1966; Lenin Prize 1966; U.S.S.R. State Prize 1942, Order of Lenin (three times), Order of the Red Banner, Hammer and Sickle Gold Medal, and other decorations. *Address:* A. F. Ioffe Physical-Technological Institute, U.S.S.R. Academy of Sciences, Politekhnicheskaya ulitsa 26, Leningrad, U.S.S.R.

TUCKWELL, Barry Emmanuel, O.B.E.; British musician; b. 5 March 1931, Melbourne, Australia; s. of Charles Tuckwell and Elizabeth Hill; m. Hilary Warburton 1971; two s. one d.; ed. Sydney Conservatorium; French Horn player with Melbourne Symphony Orchestra 1947, Sydney Symphony Orchestra 1947–50, Hallé Orchestra 1951–53, Scottish Nat. Orchestra 1954–55, London Symphony Orchestra 1955–68; Horn Prof., R.A.M. 1963–74; f. Tuckwell Wind Quintet 1968; int. soloist and recording artist; Conductor of Tasmanian Symphony Orchestra 1980–83; Music Dir. and Conductor Md. Symphony Orchestra 1982–; Pres. Int. Horn Soc. 1969–76; mem. Bd. of Dirs., London Symphony Orchestra 1957–, Chair. 1961–68; mem. Chamber Music Soc. of Lincoln Center 1974–81; Hon. degrees from R.A.M., Guildhall School of Music and Drama; Harriet Cohen Int. Award for Solo Instruments 1968. *Publications:* Playing the Horn, 50 1st Exercises 1978, The Horn (Yehudi Menuhin Music Guides) 1981, entire horn repertoire of G. Schirmer Inc. (editor). *Leisure interest:* photography. *Address:* Athenaeum Club, Pall Mall, London, S.W.1, England.

TUDOR, Sir James Cameron, K.C.M.G., M.A.; Barbadian politician and diplomatist; b. 18 Oct. 1919, St. Michael; s. of James A. Tudor; unmarried; ed. Harrison Coll., Barbados, Keble Coll., Oxford; Pres. Oxford Union 1942; Broadcaster, BBC 1942–44; lecturer, Reading Univ. 1944–45; taught History at Combermere School, Barbados 1946–48, Civics and History at Queens Coll., British Guiana 1948–51; Sixth Form Master, Modern High School, Barbados 1952–61; freelance journalist, lecturer and broadcaster 1952–61; mem. Barbados Labour Party 1951–52; mem. Legislature 1954–72; Gen. Sec. Democratic Labour Party 1955–63, Third Vice-Chair. 1964–66; Minister of Educ. 1961–67; Minister of State for Caribbean and Latin American Affairs 1967–71; Leader of House of Reps. 1965–71; Minister of External Affairs 1971–72; Leader of Senate 1971–72, 1986–; High Commr. in U.K. 1972–76; Perm. Rep. to UN 1976–79; Minister of Foreign Affairs 1986–; mem. Council, Univ. of the West Indies 1962–65; Silver Star, Order of Christopher Columbus (Dominican Repub.). *Leisure interests:* reading, lecturing, Masonic and other fraternities. *Address:* Ministry of Foreign Affairs, 1 Culloden Road, St. Michael; Lemon Grove, Westbury New Road, St. Michael, Barbados (Home).

TUENI, Ghassan, M.A.; Lebanese newspaper editor; b. 5 Jan. 1926, Beirut; s. of Gebran Tueni and Adile (née Salem) Tueni; m. Nadia Hamadeh (deceased); one s.; ed. American Univ. of Beirut and Harvard Univ.; lecturer in Political Science, American Univ. of Beirut 1947–48; Ed.-in-Chief, An-Nahar (daily newspaper) 1948–; Man.-Dir. An-Nahar Publishing Co. 1963–; Co-founder Lebanese Acad. of Law and Political Science 1951, lecturer 1951–54; M.P. for Beirut 1953–57; mem. Lebanese del. to UN Gen. Assembly 1957; founded Middle East Business Services and Research Corpn. 1958, Chair. 1958–70; founder, Chair. and Man.-Dir. of Press Cooperative, S.A.L. 1960–; Deputy Prime Minister and Minister of Information and Nat. Educ. 1970–71; arrested Dec. 1973, appeared before mil. tribunal and then released in accordance with press laws; Minister for Social Affairs and Labour, Tourism, Industry and Oil 1975–76; Perm. Rep. to UN 1977–82; mem. Nat. Dialogue Cttee. 1975. *Address:* An-Nahar, P.O. Box 226, Beirut (Office); Ras Kafra, Beit Mery, Lebanon (Home).

TUFARELLI, Nicola; Italian industrial executive; b. 31 March 1923, S. Giorgio Lucano; s. of Davide Tufarelli and Maria Torchitti; m. Germana Chiantore 1959; one s. one d.; ed. Naval Acad., Livorno; Man. foreign industrial subsidiaries div., domestic and foreign production, Olivetti (Ivrea-Turin) 1952–71; joined FIAT SpA 1972, Gen. Man. 1972–74, Man. Automobile Sector 1975–79, Man. Dir. 1980–81, mem. Bd. 1980–82; Man. Dir. NTP s.r.l. 1981–; Pres. Italian-Soviet Chamber of Commerce 1979–82, CTIP SpA 1981–82, Società Mineraria e Metallurgica di Pertusola SpA 1982–. *Leisure interests:* reading, art. *Address:* NTP s.r.l., Via Giulia 147, 00186 Rome; Società Mineraria e Metallurgica di Pertusola, Piazzale Flaminio 9, 00196 Rome (Offices); Via dei Riari 5, 00186 Rome, Italy (Home). *Telephone:* 06-657835; 06-3689214 (Offices); 06-657528 (Home).

TUGENDHAT, Christopher Samuel, M.A.; British international official and politician; b. 23 Feb. 1937, London; s. of late Dr. Georg Tugendhat; m. Julia Lissant Dobson 1967; two s.; ed. Ampleforth Coll., Gonville and Caius Coll., Cambridge; Pres. Cambridge Union; Mil. Service, Commissioned in The Essex Regt. 1955–57; Leader and Feature Writer, The Financial Times 1960–70; Consultant to Wood Mackenzie & Co. Ltd., stockbrokers 1968–77; Conservative M.P. for Cities of London and Westminster 1970–74, for City of London and Westminster South 1974–77; Dir. Sunningdale Oils 1971–77, Phillips Petroleum Int. (U.K.) Ltd. 1972–77, Nat. Westminster Bank PLC 1985–, BOC Group 1985–; Chair. Civil Aviation Authority June 1986–; mem. Comm. of EEC with responsibility for Budget and Financial Control, Financial Institutions, Personnel and Admin. 1977–81; Vice-Pres. of Comm. of EEC with responsibility for

Budget and Financial Control, Financial Institutions and Taxation 1981-85; Chair. Royal Inst. of Int. Affairs (Chatham House) 1986-; Council mem. Centre for European Policy Studies, Brussels 1985-; McKinsey Foundation Book Award 1971. *Publications:* Oil: the Biggest Business 1968, The Multinationals 1971, Making Sense of Europe 1986. *Leisure interests:* reading, family, conversation. *Address:* 35 Westbourne Park Road, London, W.2, England.

TU'IPELAHAKE, H.R.H. Prince Fatafehi, K.B.E.; Tongan politician; b. 7 Jan. 1922; second son of the late Queen Salote Tupou III and the late Prince Uiliami Tungi, C.B.E., Prime Minister of Tonga; brother of King Taufa'ahau Tupou IV (q.v.); married H.R.H. Princess Melenaite 1947; six children; ed. Newington Coll., Sydney, N.S.W., and Gatton Agricultural Coll., Queensland; Gov. of Vava'u 1952-65; Prime Minister of Tonga 1965-, also Minister for Agric. and Marine Affairs, Forestry and Fisheries; Chair. Commodities Bd.; 'Uluafi Medal 1982. *Address:* Office of the Prime Minister, Nuku'alofa, Tonga.

TUITA, Baron Siosaia Aleamotu'a Laufilitonga Tuita, C.B.E.; Tongan civil servant and government official; b. 29 Aug. 1920, Lapaha, Tongatapu; s. of 'Isileli Tupou Tuita and Luseane Halaevalu Fotofili; m. Fatafehi Lapaha Tupou 1949; two s. two d.; ed. Tupou Coll., Wesley Coll., Auckland, New Zealand, Oxford Univ.; Lieut. Officer, Tonga Defence Service 1942-43; Court Interpreter and Registrar, Supreme Court 1945; Asst. Sec. Prime Minister's Office 1954; Acting Gov. of Vava'u 1956, Gov. 1957; Acting Minister of Lands 1962, of Police 1964-65; Chair. Niuafo'ou evacuation 1965; Minister of Lands and Survey and Minister of Health 1965; assumed title of Tuita 1972, conferred with title of Baron Tuita of 'Utungake 1980; Deputy Prime Minister and Minister of Lands, Survey and Natural Resources 1972-; mem. Privy Council; Chair. Town Planning Cttee., Energy Standing Cttee., Royal Land Comm., Tonga Broadcasting Comm.; mem. numerous socs. *Leisure interests:* rugby, cricket, driving, fishing. *Address:* Ministry of Lands, Survey and Natural Resources, P.O. Box 5, Nuku'alofa (Office); Mahinafekite, Nuku'alofa, Tonga (Home). *Telephone:* 22655 (Office); 22451 (Home).

TUIVAGA, Hon. Sir Timoci (Uluiburotu), Kt., B.A.; b. 21 Oct. 1931; s. of Isimeili Siga Tuivaga and Jessie Hill; m. Vilimaina Leba Parrott Tuivaga 1958; three s. one d.; ed. Univ. of Auckland; native magistrate 1958-61, called to the Bar, Gray's Inn 1964, N.S.W. 1968; Crown Counsel 1965-68, Prin. Legal Officer 1968-70, Puisne Judge 1972, Acting Chief Justice 1974, Chief Justice of Fiji 1980-; sometime Acting Gov.-Gen. 1983-87. *Leisure interests:* golf, gardening. *Address:* 228 Ratu Sukuna Road, Suva, Fiji. *Telephone:* 313-782.

TUKE, Sir Anthony Favill, Kt.; British banker; b. 22 Aug. 1920, Berkhamsted, Herts.; s. of late Anthony William Tuke and Agnes Edna Tuke (née Gannaway); m. Emilia Mila Antic 1946; one s. one d.; ed. Winchester Coll., Magdalene Coll., Cambridge; Scots Guards 1940-46; joined Barclays Bank Ltd. 1946; various appts. in Barclays Bank Ltd. including Chair. Birmingham Bd. 1964-68; Dir. Barclays Bank Ltd. 1965-, Barclays Bank U.K. 1971-81, Barclays Bank Int. 1966-87; Vice-Chair. Barclays Bank Int. Ltd. (fmrly. Barclays Bank D.C.O.) 1968-72, Chair. 1972-79; Vice-Chair. Barclays Bank Ltd. 1972-73, Chair. 1973-81; Dir. Rio Tinto-Zinc Corpn. Ltd. 1980-, Chair. 1981-85; Dir. Royal Insurance PLC Jan. 1978, Deputy Chair. 1985-; Dir. Merchants Trust PLC 1969-, Whitbread Investment Co. PLC 1984-; mem. Int. Advisory Bd. Republicbank of Dallas 1982 and Bd. various subsidiary cos. in Barclays Group; Deputy Chair. Cttee. of London Clearing Bankers 1974-76, Chair. 1976-78; fmr. Vice-Pres. Inst. of Bankers; Pres. MCC 1982-83; Dir. Savoy Hotel 1982-, Chair. 1984-. *Leisure interests:* lawn tennis, gardening. *Address:* Freelands, Wherwell, nr. Andover, Hants., England.

TUKEY, John W(ilder), PH.D., SC.D.; American statistician; b. 16 June 1915, New Bedford, Mass.; s. of Ralph H. Tukey and Adah M. Tasker; m. Elizabeth Louise Rapp 1950; ed. Brown Univ. and Princeton Univ.; Fine Instructor, Mathematics, Princeton Univ. 1939-41, Asst. Prof. 1941-48, Assoc. Prof. 1948-50, Prof. 1950-66, Prof. of Statistics 1965, Donner Prof. of Science 1976; mem. Tech. Staff, Bell Telephone Labs. 1945-58, Asst. Dir. of Research 1958-61, Assoc. Exec. Dir. Research 1961-; mem. Pres.'s Science Advisory Cttee. 1960-63, Nat. Advisory Cttee. for Oceans and Atmosphere 1975-; mem. N.A.S. 1967, American Acad. of Arts and Sciences, American Philosophical Soc.; Hon. mem. Royal Statistical Soc.; Guggenheim Fellow 1949-50; Fellow, Inst. of Mathematical Statistics (Pres. 60), American Statistical Asscn. (Vice-Pres. 1955-57), American Soc. of Quality Control, American Assen. for the Advancement of Science (Chair. 1972, 1974); Samuel Wilks Medal, American Statistical Assen. 1965; Nat. Medal of Science 1973; Hon. Sc.D. (Brown Univ., Yale Univ., Case Inst. of Technology, Univ. of Chicago). *Publications:* Convergence and Uniformity in Topology, Statistical Problems of the Kinsey Report (with W. G. Cochran and F. Mosteller), The Measurement of Power Spectra from the Point of View of Communications Engineering (with R. B. Blackman) 1959, Exploratory Data Analysis, Vols. I-III 1970-71, Robust Estimates of Location: Survey and Advances (with others) 1972, The Statistics Cum Index, Vol. I (with T. L. Dolby) 1973, Index to Statistics and Probability, Vols. II-V (with others) 1973-75; more than 150 technical papers. *Leisure interest:* table tennis. *Address:* 1A-219 Bell Telephone Laboratories, Murray Hill, N.J. 07974 (Office); 115 Arreton Road, Princeton, N.J. 08540;

Summer: P.O. Box 304, Westport Point, Mass. 02791, U.S.A. (Home). *Telephone:* (201) 582-4507 (Bell Telephone); (609) 924-5095 (Home); (617) 636-2612 (Summer).

TULL, Louis Randall, Q.C., B.A., M.A.; Barbadian politician; b. 27 Jan. 1938, Lears, St. Michael, Barbados; m. Ordene Haynes; one s. two d.; ed. St. John's Coll., Univ. of Manitoba, and St. John's Coll., Oxford; Hon. Fellow St. John's Coll., Univ. of Manitoba; barrister, Inner Temple; mem. Senate, Barbados 1971-76, House of Ass. 1976-; Minister of Educ. and Culture 1976-81; Attorney-Gen., Minister of Foreign Affairs 1981-85, of Culture 1981-83, of Commerce, Industry and Consumer Affairs 1985-87; Labour Party. *Address:* c/o Ministry of Commerce, Industry and Consumer Affairs, Reef Road, Fontabelle, St. Michael, Barbados, West Indies. *Telephone:* (809) 426 4452.

TUMANISHVILI, Mikhail Ivanovich; Soviet conductor; b. 1921, Georgia; ed. Conducting School, Georgian Theatrical Inst., Tbilisi; taught by G. A. Tovstonogov; mem. CPSU 1943-; conductor Rustaveli Theatre, Tbilisi 1949-73, and teacher at Rustaveli Theatrical Inst. 1949-; Artistic Dir. Georgian Film Studios 1978; numerous productions. *Address:* Rustaveli Theatrical Institute, Tbilisi, Georgian S.S.R., U.S.S.R.

TUMI, H.E. Cardinal Christian Wiyghan; Cameroon ecclesiastic; b. 15 Oct. 1930, Kikaikelaki; ordained 1966, elected to Yagoua 1979, consecrated bishop 1980, coadjutor bishop 1982, diocesan bishop 1984; cr. Cardinal 1988. *Address:* Archvêché, B.P. 272, Garoua, Cameroon. *Telephone:* 271.353.

TUNE, Tommy (Thomas James); American theatrical performer, director and choreographer; b. 28 Feb. 1939, Witchita Falls, Tex.; s. of Jim Tune and Eva Tune; ed. Lamar High School, Houston, Lon Morris Junior Coll., Univ. of Tex. at Austin and Univ. of Houston; began professional career as chorus dancer on Broadway; appeared in films Hello, Dolly! and The Boyfriend; appeared on Broadway in Seesaw (Tony Award, Best Supporting Actor); Off-Broadway Dir. The Club, Cloud 9 (Obie and Drama Desk Awards), Stepping Out 1987; Choreographer, A Day in Hollywood/A Night in the Ukraine (Tony Award); Dir. The Best Little Whorehouse in Texas, Nine (Tony Award 1982); actor and choreographer, My One and Only (Tony Award 1983); recipient of many other awards. *Leisure interests:* cooking, yoga, reading, drawing. *Address:* c/o Jnt. Creative Management, 40 W. 57th Street, New York, N.Y. 10019; 1501 Broadway, 1312, New York, N.Y. 10036, U.S.A. *Telephone:* (212) 719-2166.

TUNG SHU-FANG, LL.M.; Chinese politician; b. 6 July 1932, Salachi County, Suiyuan; m.; two s. two d.; ed. Chinese Mil. Acad., Nat. Chung Hsing Univ. and Nat. Chengchi Univ.; Editing Staff, Secr., Kuomintang H.Q. 1964-67, Sr. Staff, Secr. 1968-69; Lecturer, Assoc. Prof. then Prof., Chinese Culture Univ., Tamkang Univ., Nat. Chung Hsing Univ. 1969-; Ed.-in-Chief, Cen. Monthly (magazine) 1970-77; Dir. Kuomintang Documentary and Publication Center 1977-81, 1981-83; mem. Evaluation and Discipline Cttee., Cen. Cttee., Kuomintang 1981-83, Vice-Chair. 1983-84; Chair. Mongolian and Tibetan Affairs Comm. 1984-86.

TUNLEY, David Evatt, A.M., D.LITT., D.MUS., F.A.A.H.; Australian professor of music; b. 3 May 1930, Sydney; s. of Dr. Leslie Tunley and Dr. Marjorie Tunley; m. Paula Patricia Laurantus 1959; one s. two d.; ed. The Scots Coll., Sydney, State Conservatorium of Music, Sydney; music master, Fort Street Boys' High School, Sydney 1952-57; joined staff of Dept. of Music, Univ. of Western Australia 1958, Personal Chair. of Music 1980-, Head Dept. of Music 1985-; studied under Nadia Boulanger with French Govt. Scholarship 1964-65; Founder/Conductor Univ. Collegium Musicum, 1976-; Founder/Chair. York Winter Music Festival, 1982-; Nat. Press. Musicological Soc. of Australia 1980-81; Chair. Music Bd., Australia Council 1984-85; Chevalier dans l'ordre des Palmes Académiques. *Publications:* The 18th Century French Cantata 1974, Couperin 1982, Harmony in Action 1984; contribs. to the New Grove Dictionary of Music and Musicians, The New Oxford History of Music. *Leisure interests:* reading, travel, tennis. *Address:* Department of Music, University of Western Australia, Nedlands 6009, Western Australia (Office); 100 Dalkeith Road, Nedlands 6009, Western Australia, Australia (Home). *Telephone:* (09) 380 2053 (Office); (09) 386 1934 (Home).

TUNNEY, John V., B.A., LL.B.; American politician; b. 26 June 1934, New York City; s. of Gene Tunney and Mary Lauder Tunney; m. 2nd Kathinka Osborne 1977; two s. two d.; ed. Westminster School, Simsbury, Conn., Yale Univ., Univ. of Virginia School of Law and Acad. of Int. Law, The Hague; practised law, New York City 1959-60; Judge Advocate, U.S. Air Force 1960-63; taught Business Law at Univ. of Calif., Riverside; mem. U.S. House of Representatives 1964-70; Senator from California 1971-77; mem. Manatt, Phelps, Rothenberg and Tunney, Los Angeles 1977-86; Chair., Bd. of Dirs. Cloverleaf Group Inc., Los Angeles 1986-; Democrat. *Leisure interests:* tennis, sailing, skiing, handball. *Address:* Cloverleaf Group Inc., 1801 Century Park East, Suite 1000, Los Angeles, Calif. 40067, U.S.A.

TUPOLEV, Aleksey Andreyevich, DR. OF TECH. SCIENCE; Soviet aircraft designer; b. 20 May 1925, Moscow; s. of A. N. Tupolev; ed. Moscow Aviation Inst.; mem. CPSU 1959; Prof. 1964-; developed with father various supersonic jets (among which TU-144, in 1968); State Prize 1967;

Order of Lenin (three times), other orders and medals. *Address:* Moscow Aviation Institute, Moscow, U.S.S.R.

TURAY, Abdhul Rahman, M.SC., M.A.; Sierra Leonean economist; b. 6 Oct. 1938, Makeni; s. of the late Muctarr Turay and Fudiya Turay; m. Ellen Turay 1960; ed. Govt. Secondary School, Bo, Sierra Leone, Cambridge and London Univs.; joined Royal W. African Frontier Force (now Royal Sierra Leone Mil. Forces), Lieut. Col. 1958; Minister of Educ., Nat. Redemption Council (NRC), Sierra Leone 1967; Sr. Economist, Corp. Planning Dept., Fison's PLC, U.K. 1971-73; Asst. Man. Group Econs. Dept., Barclays Bank Int. Ltd., London 1973-77, Head Econs. Dept., Nigeria 1977-79, Man. Int. Banking Group, London 1982-87; Gov. Bank of Sierra Leone 1987-. *Leisure interests:* music, reading. *Address:* Bank of Sierra Leone, P.O. Box 30, Freetown, Sierra Leone. *Telephone:* 26501; 26490.

TURBAY AYALA, Julio César: Colombian diplomatist and politician; b. 18 June 1916, Bogotá; m.; one s. three d.; mem. House of Reps. 1943-53; Minister of Mines and Energy 1957-58, of Foreign Affairs 1958-61; Senator 1962-70; twice elected Vice-Pres. of Colombia, Pres. of Colombia 1978-82; Perm. Rep. to UN 1967; Amb. to U.K. 1970, to U.S.A. 1974-76; Hon. LL.D. (Univ. of Cauca) 1957. *Address:* c/o Oficina del Presidente, Bogotá, Colombia.

TURECK, Rosalyn; American concert artist, conductor and professor; b. 14 Dec. 1914, Chicago; d. of Samuel Tureck and Monya Lipson; ed. Juilliard School of Music, New York; debut in Chicago 1924; first New York appearance 1932; concert tours U.S.A.and Canada 1937-, Europe 1947-, South Africa 1959, South America 1963, Israel 1963, World Tour (Far East and India) 1971, Europe, Israel, S. America, N. American Bach Festivals 1985/86; repeated appearances at major int. festivals; specializes in the keyboard works of J. S. Bach, played on the piano, harpsichord, clavichord, organ, antique and electronic instruments; conductor 1956-; Conductor-soloist, London Philharmonic 1958, New York Philharmonic 1958, Israel Philharmonic 1963, Kol Israel Orchestra 1963, Int. Bach Soc. Orchestra 1967, 1968, 1970, Madrid Chamber Orchestra 1972, Washington Nat. Symphony 1972, Tureck Bach Players (Carnegie Hall) 1981, Bach Triennial Celebration Series (solo recitals and orchestral concerts conducting Tureck Bach Players), Carnegie Hall 1984/85; Visiting Prof. of Music, Washington Univ., St. Louis 1963-64; Prof. of Music, Univ. of Calif., San Diego 1966-72, Regents Lecturer 1966, Visiting Prof., Univ. of Md. 1982-84; Lecturer numerous univs. and colls. of music; Visiting Fellow, St. Hilda's Coll., Oxford 1974, Hon. Life Fellow 1974-; Visiting Fellow, Wolfson Coll., Oxford 1975; Founder-dir. of Composers of Today 1951-55, Tureck Bach Players 1957, Int. Bach Soc. 1966 (now Tureck Bach Inst.), Int. Bach Soc. Orchestra 1967, Inst. for Bach Studies 1968; mem. many musical socs.; Hon. D.Mus., (Colby Coll. 1964, Roosevelt Univ. 1968, Wilson Coll. 1968, Oxford Univ. 1977, etc.); First Prize, Greater Chicago Piano Playing Tournament 1928, Winner Schubert Memorial Contest, Nat. Fed. of Music Clubs 1935; Officer's Cross of Order of Merit, Fed. Repub. of Germany 1979. *Recordings:* The Well-tempered Clavier (Books I and II), Goldberg Variations, Six Partitas, Italian Concerto, French Overture, Introduction to Bach, A Bach Recital, A Harpsichord Recital, Goldberg Variations and Aria and Ten Variations in the Italian Style (harpsichord), Italian Concerto, Chromatic Fantasia and Fugue, Four Duets (piano). *Publications:* An Introduction to the Performance of Bach (3 vols.) 1959-60 (trans. into Japanese 1966, Spanish 1972), A Critical and Performance Edition of J. S. Bach's Chromatic Fantasia and Fugue; numerous articles in various periodicals; Editor: Paganini, Niccolo—Perpetuum Mobile 1950, J. S. Bach—Sarabande, C Minor 1960, Scarlatti, Alessandro—Sarabande and Gavotte; Ed. Tureck Bach Urtext Series, Publr. Italian Concerto 1983, Lute Suite, E Minor 1984, Lute Suite C Minor 1985. *Films:* Fantasy and Fugue: Rosalyn Tureck plays Bach 1972, Rosalyn Tureck plays Bach on Harpsichord and Organ 1977, Joy of Bach (Rosalyn Tureck Soloist and Consultant) 1979, Bach on the Frontier of The Future 1980, Rosalyn Tureck Plays Bach in Ephesus, Turkey 1985. *Address:* c/o Columbia Artists Management Inc., 165 West 57th Street, New York, N.Y. 10019, U.S.A.

TÜREL, Sudi Nese; Turkish politician; b. 1929, Antalya; m.; two c.; ed. Ankara Land Appropriation Lycee and Yildiz Univ.; fmr. land appropriation and maps engineer; Minister of Energy and Natural Resources 1986-87. *Address:* c/o Ministry of Energy and Natural Resources, Enerji ve Tabii Kaynaklar Bakanlıgı, Ankara, Turkey.

TURKEVICH, Anthony Leonid, PH.D.; American professor of chemistry; b. 23 July 1916, New York; s. of Rev. L. J. Turkevich and Anna (Chervinsky) Turkevich; m. Ireene T. Podlesak 1948; one s. one d.; ed. Columbia Grammar School, Curtis High School, Dartmouth Coll., Hanover N.H., Princeton Univ.; Research Assoc. Physics Dept. Univ. of Chicago 1940-41; Research Assoc. Manhattan Project, Columbia Univ., Univ. of Chicago, Los Alamos Scientific Lab. 1942-46; participant in test of first nuclear bomb, Almagordo, N.M. 1945, in theoretical work on and test of thermonuclear reactions 1945-, calculations on the production of helium during the first minutes of the Big Bang Universe 1949, chemical analysis of the moon 1967-; Asst. Prof. Enrico Fermi Inst. and Chemistry Dept. Univ. of Chicago 1946-48, Assoc. Prof. 1948-54, Prof. 1954-86, James Franck Prof. of Chemistry 1965-70, Distinguished Service Prof. 1970-86, Prof. Emer. 1986-; Consultant to U.S. Atomic Energy Comm. Labs. 1946-; Del. to Geneva Conf. on Nuclear Test Suspension 1958, 1959; Fellow Los Alamos

Science Lab. 1972-; mem. of N.A.S., American Chem. Soc., American Physical Soc., Royal Soc. of Arts (London), A.A.A.S., American Acad. of Arts and Sciences; Hon. D.Sc. (Dartmouth Coll.) 1971; E. O. Lawrence Award of U.S. Atomic Energy Comm. 1962, Atoms for Peace Prize 1969, Nuclear Applications Award (American Chemical Soc.) 1972. *Publications:* articles on intra-nuclear cascades, on chemical analysis of the moon and on high energy nuclear reactions. *Leisure interests:* hiking, reading. *Address:* 175 Briarwood Loop, Briarwood Lakes, Oak Brook, Ill. 60521, U.S.A. (Home). *Telephone:* (312) 962-7110.

TÜRKMEN, Ilter; Turkish diplomatist and politician; b. 1927, Istanbul; s. of Behçet Türkmen and Nuriye Türkmen; m. Mina Türkmen 1953; one s. one d.; ed. Galatasaray Lycée, Istanbul, Faculty of Political Sciences, Ankara; Dir.-Gen. of Policy Planning Dept., Ministry of Foreign Affairs 1964, Asst. Sec.-Gen. for Political Affairs 1967, Amb. to Greece 1968, to U.S.S.R. 1972, to France Aug. 1988-; Perm. Rep. to UN 1975-77 in Geneva 1984, in New York 1985-88; Minister of Foreign Affairs 1980-83. *Address:* Ambassade de Turquie, 16, avenue de Lambralle, 15016 Paris, France.

TURNBULL, David, PH.D.; American professor of applied physics; b. 18 Feb. 1915, Elmira, Ill.; s. of David Turnbull and Luzetta A. Murray; m. Carol M. Cornell 1946; two s. one d.; ed. Monmouth Coll., Ill., and Univ. of Illinois; Faculty, Case School of Applied Science, Cleveland, Ohio 1939-46; Scientist, Research Lab., Gen. Electric Co., Schenectady, N.Y. 1946-62; Man. Chemical Metallurgy Section, Gen. Electric Research Lab., Schenectady 1950-58; Gordon McKay Prof. of Applied Physics, Harvard Univ. 1962-86, Emer. 1986-; mem. N.A.S.; Fellow, American Acad. of Arts and Sciences; Inst. of Metals Lecturer, American Inst. of Metallurgical Engineers 1961; Campbell Memorial Lecturer (American Soc. for Metals) 1980; Hon. Sc.D. (Monmouth (Ill.) Coll.); Acta Metallurgica Gold Medal 1979; Von Hippel Prize (Materials Research Soc.) 1979, American Physics Soc. Prize for New Materials 1983, Japan Prize for Materials Science and Tech. 1986. *Publications:* Co-editor (with Ehrenreich) Solid State Physics Series; Co-Ed. (with Doremus and Roberts) Growth and Perfection of Crystals 1958; scientific publs. and reviews on nucleation, crystal growth, diffusion, liquids, glass state. *Leisure interests:* history, hiking. *Address:* Pierce Hall, Harvard University, Cambridge, Mass. 02138; 77 Summer Street, Weston, Mass. 02193, U.S.A. (Home). *Telephone:* (617) 495-2838 (Univ.).

TURNBULL, George Henry, B.SC., F.I.MECH.E., F.I.P.E., F.I.M.I., F.I.M., F.INST.D.; British business executive; b. 17 Oct. 1926, London; s. of Bartholomew and Pauline A. Turnbull; m. Marion Wing 1950; one s. two d.; ed. Bablake and Henry VIII Schools, Coventry Tech. Coll., and Birmingham Univ.; Personal Asst. to Tech. Dir. Standard Motor Co. 1950-51; Liaison Officer between Standard Motor Co. and Rolls-Royce 1951-53; Exec. in charge Experimental Div., Standard Motor Co. 1954-55; Works Man. Petters Ltd. 1955-56; Div. Man. Car Production, Standard Motor Co. 1956-59, Gen. Man. 1959-62; Dir. and Gen. Man. Standard Triumph Int. Ltd. 1962-68; Man. Dir. British Leyland Austin Morris 1968; Deputy Man. Dir. British Leyland Motor Corpn. 1968-73, Man. Dir. May-Sept. 1973; Man. Dir. Austin Morris British Leyland U.K. 1968-73; Vice-Pres., Dir. Hyundai Corpn., Seoul 1974-77; Chair., Man. Dir. and Chief Exec. Chrysler U.K. (now Talbot U.K.) 1979-84; Group Man. Dir. Inchcape PLC 1984-85, Group Chief Exec. 1985-, Chair. and C.E.O. 1986-; Vice-Pres. Soc. of Motor Mfrs. and Traders 1980-82, Pres. 1982-83; Chair. Industrial Soc. 1987-, Korea-Europe Fund Ltd. 1987-; Dir. Euro-Asia Centre 1987-, Kleinwort Benson Group PLC 1988-, Bank in Liechtenstein (UK) 1988-; mem. Man. Bd., Eng. Employers' Fed.; mem. Birmingham Chamber of Commerce and Industry. *Leisure interests:* golf, tennis. *Address:* Inchcape PLC, St. James's House, 23 King Street, London, SW1Y 6QY, England. *Telephone:* 01-321 0110.

TURNBULL, Lyle E. J. L., A.O.; Australian journalist; b. 13 April 1928, Geelong; s. of H. W. Turnbull; m. 1st Jeanette Mashado 1953 (died 1982), one s. one d.; m. 2nd Jennifer Malone 1984; ed. Geelong Coll.; joined The Herald and Weekly Times Ltd. 1946; journalist The Sun News-Pictorial 1946-67, New York Bureau 1950-51, London 1956-58, Asst. Ed. 1958-62, Ed. 1965-67; Deputy Ed.-in-Chief Herald and Weekly Times Ltd. 1962-65, 1967-70, Ed.-in-Chief 1970-75, Man. Ed. 1975-84, Dir. 1972-, Exec. Dir. 1984-; Jt. Man. Dir. Australian Associated Press 1971-, Chair. 1971-73, 1983-85; mem. Australian Newspapers Council 1972-; Chair. Australian Section Commonwealth Press Union 1974-86, London Council of the Commonwealth Press Union 1986-; Dir. Reuters Ltd., London 1974-, Reuters Holdings U.K. 1984-; mem. State Advisory Cttee. CSIRO; Astor Award (U.K.) 1984. *Address:* The Herald and Weekly Times Ltd., 44 Flinders Street, Melbourne, Vic. 3000, Australia. *Telephone:* 652 1101.

TURNBULL, Malcolm Bligh, B.A., LL.B., B.C.L.; Australian banker and lawyer; b. 24 Oct. 1954, Sydney; s. of Bruce B. Turnbull and Coral Lansbury; m. Lucinda M. F. Hughes 1980; one s. one d.; ed. Sydney Grammar School, Univ. of Sydney and Univ. of Oxford (Rhodes Scholar); State Parl. Corresp. for Nation Review 1976; journalist, The Bulletin 1977-78; Exec. Asst. to Chair. Consolidated Press Holdings Ltd. 1978; journalist, The Sunday Times, London 1978-79; barrister, Sydney 1980-82; Gen. Counsel and Sec. Consolidated Press Holdings Ltd. 1983-85; solicitor in pvt. practice, Turnbull McWilliam, Sydney 1986-87; Joint Man. Dir. Whitlam Turnbull & Co., Ltd. (Investment Bankers), Sydney 1987-; Henry

Lawson Prize for Poetry 1975. *Publication:* The Spycatcher Trial 1988. *Leisure interests:* reading, walking, riding, gardening. *Address:* Whitlam Turnbull & Co. Ltd., Level 8, 1 Chifley Square, Sydney 2000, Australia. *Telephone:* (02) 2235899.

TURNBULL, William; British sculptor, painter and print-maker; b. 11 Jan. 1922, Dundee, Scotland; m. Cheng Kim Lim 1960; two s.; ed. Slade School of Fine Art, London; one-man exhbns. in London, New York, San Francisco, Berlin, Stuttgart, Latin America, Toronto, Luxembourg, Singapore etc. since 1950 including IX Bienal, São Paolo and tour of S. American countries (sculpture and painting) 1967, Hayward Gallery, London (painting) 1968, Tate Gallery Retrospective (sculpture and painting) 1973 and exhbns. at Waddington Galleries, London 1967, 1969, 1970, 1976, 1978, 1981, 1985, 1987; has participated in numerous group exhbns. around the world since 1950; works in public collections in U.K., U.S.A., Australia and Germany. *Leisure interests:* reading, music, chess, swimming. *Address:* c/o Waddington Galleries, 11 Cork Street, London, W.1, England.

TURNBULL, William, Jr., B.A., M.F.A.; American architect and designer; b. 1 April 1935, New York; s. of William Turnbull Sr. and Elizabeth Howe; m.; one s. two d.; ed. Princeton Univ. and Ecole des Beaux Arts de Fontainebleau; with Skidmore, Owings and Merrill, San Francisco 1960–63; South Coast Master Plan, Big Sur, Monterey Co., Calif. 1961; mem. design group for Pres. Kennedy's Advisory Council, Pennsylvania Ave., Washington, D.C. 1963; Founding Partner in Moore, Lyndon, Turnbull, Whitaker (MLTW) 1962–65; Partner, MLTW-Moore Turnbull 1965–69; Dir. William Turnbull Assocs. 1970–; Design Consultant Formica Corpn. 1978–85, World Savings and Loan 1976–; lecturer, Coll. of Environmental Design, Univ. of Calif., Berkeley 1965–69, Stanford Univ. 1974–77; Visiting Prof. Univ. of Oregon 1966–68; Visiting Critic, M.I.T. 1975, Yale 1977, 1981, 1986; Architectural Critic, Univ. of Calif., Berkeley 1978–81; Fellow, American Inst. of Architects, American Acad. in Rome; mem. Soc. of Architectural Historians; work includes institutional, commercial, residential and recreational projects; numerous awards for design. *Publications:* MLTW/Sea Ranch and Sea Ranch Details in Global Architecture series; illustrator, The Place of Houses, Moore Lyndon Allen; contributions to architectural magazines and several books on architecture. *Address:* Pier 1, 1/2 The Embarcadero, San Francisco, Calif. 94111, U.S.A. (Office)

TURNER, George, DR.IUR.; German academic; b. 28 May 1935, Insterburg; s. of Albert and Martha Turner; m. Edda Horstmann 1963; three s.; law clerk 1959–63; Legal Asst. 1963–66; Docent 1966–68; legal counsel and Prof. 1968–70; Pres. Univ. of Hohenheim 1970–86; Senator for Science and Research in W. Berlin 1986–; Pres. West German Rectors' Conf. 1979–83. *Publications:* three books and numerous essays and articles on legal topics, and university management. *Leisure interests:* sport, literature. *Address:* Bredtschneiderstr. 5, 1000 Berlin 19, Federal Republic of Germany. *Telephone:* 030/3032316.

TURNER, George William, M.A.; Australian reader in English (retd.); b. 26 Oct. 1921, Dannevirke, N.Z.; s. of Albert George Turner and Elinor Jessie Turner; m. Beryl Constance Barbara Horrobin 1949; two s.; ed. Univ. Coll. London, and N.Z. Library School; secondary school teacher, N.Z. 1944–46; librarian, Christchurch 1949–54; English Dept., Univ. of Canterbury 1955–64; Reader in English, Univ. of Adelaide, Australia 1965–86; Festschrift: Lexicographical and Linguistic Studies: Essays in honour of G. W. Turner (Ed. T. L. and Jill Burton) 1988. *Publications:* The English Language in Australia and New Zealand 1966, Stylistics 1973, The Australian Pocket Oxford Dictionary (Ed.), The Australian Concise Oxford Dictionary (Ed.) 1987. *Address:* 3 Marola Avenue, Rostrevor, South Australia, 5073 Australia. *Telephone:* (08) 3372257.

TURNER, Grenville, D.PHIL., F.R.S.; British professor of isotope geochemistry; b. 1 Nov. 1936, Todmorden; s. of Arnold Turner and Florence Turner; m. Kathleen Morris 1961; one s. one d.; ed. St. John's Coll., Cambridge and Balliol Coll., Oxford; Asst. Prof., Univ. of Calif., Berkeley 1962–64; Lecturer, Sheffield Univ. 1964–74, Sr. Lecturer 1974–79, Reader 1979–80, Prof. of Physics 1980–88; Prof. of Isotope Geochem., Manchester Univ. 1988–; Visiting Assoc. in Nuclear Geophysics, Calif. Inst. of Tech. 1970–71. *Publications:* numerous scientific papers. *Leisure interests:* photography, walking, theatre. *Address:* The Royd, Todmorden, Lancs., OL14 8DW, England. *Telephone:* (0706) 818621.

TURNER, Rt. Hon. John Napier, P.C., Q.C., M.P., M.A., B.C.L.; Canadian politician and lawyer; b. 7 June 1929, Richmond, Surrey, England; s. of Leonard and Phyllis (née Gregory) Turner; m. Geills McCrae Kilgour 1963; three s. one d.; ed. schools in Ottawa, and Univs. of British Columbia, Oxford and Paris; M.P. 1962–76, 1984–; Minister without Portfolio 1965; Registrar-Gen. 1967–68; Minister of Consumer and Corp. Affairs Jan.-July 1968; Solicitor-Gen. April-July 1968; Minister of Justice and Attorney-Gen. 1968–72; Minister of Finance 1972–75; Leader Liberal Party of Canada 1984–89; Prime Minister of Canada June–Sept. 1984, Leader of Opposition 1984–89; joined law firm of McMillan, Binch Toronto 1976; Dir. Bechtel Canada Ltd., Canadian Pacific Ltd., Canadian Investment Fund Ltd., Crédit Foncier, Holt, Renfrew & Co. Ltd., MacMillan Bloedel Ltd., Marathon Realty Ltd., Massey-Ferguson Ltd., The Seagram Co. Ltd., Sandoz Canada Inc., Toronto Symphony Orchestra, Canadian Council of Christians and Jews; mem. Bd. of Govs. Ashbury Coll., Toronto School of Theology,

Advisory Bd. Salvation Army-Metro Toronto, Collegium St. Michael's Coll., Inst. for Int. Econ., Washington, Inst. for Cancer Research, Toronto; Liberal. *Publications:* The Senate of Canada 1961, Politics of Purpose 1968. *Leisure interests:* tennis, canoeing, skiing. *Address:* House of Commons, Room 409-S, Centre Block, Ottawa, Ont., K1A 0A6 (Office); Stornoway, 541 Acacia Avenue, Ottawa, Ont., K1M 0M5, Canada.

TURNER, Kathleen, M.F.A.; American actress; b. 19 June 1954, Springfield, Mo.; m. Jay Weiss 1984; one d.; ed. Cen. School of Speech and Drama, London, S.W. Mo. State Univ., Univ. of Md.; various theatre roles including Broadway debut, Gemini 1978; *TV Series include:* The Doctors 1977. *Films include:* Body Heat 1981, The Man With Two Brains 1983, Crimes of Passion 1984, Romancing the Stone 1984, Prizzi's Honour 1985, The Jewel of the Nile 1985, Peggy Sue Got Married 1986, Julia and Julia 1988, Switching Channels 1988, An Accidental Tourist 1989. *Address:* c/o The Gersch Agency Inc., 222 N. Canon Drive, Beverly Hills, Calif. 90210, U.S.A.

TURNER, Admiral Stansfield, M.A.; American naval officer (retd.) and lecturer and author; b. 1 Dec. 1923, Chicago, Ill.; s. of Oliver Stansfield and Wilhelmina Josephine (née Wagner) Turner; m. Karin Gilbert 1985; ed. Amherst Coll., U.S. Naval Acad., Annapolis, Oxford Univ., U.K.; Rhodes Scholar, Oxford Univ. 1947; active duty, U.S. Navy, serving minesweeper, destroyers, U.S.S. Horne (guided missile cruiser in action in Vietnamese conflict); served in Office of Chief of Naval Operations, then in Office of Asst. Sec. of Defence for Systems Analysis; Advanced Man. Program, Harvard Business School; Exec. Asst. and Naval Aide to Sec. of the Navy 1968–70; Rear Admiral 1970; C.O. Carrier Task Group on board U.S.S. Independence, U.S. Sixth Fleet 70; Dir. Systems Analysis Div. of Office of Chief of Naval Operations, Dept. of the Navy 1971–72; Vice-Admiral 1972; Pres. U.S. Naval War Coll., Newport, R.I. 1972–74; Commdr. U.S. Second Fleet and NATO Striking Fleet Atlantic 1974–75; Admiral 1975; C.-in-C. Allied Forces Southern Europe, NATO 1975–77; Dir. Cen. Intelligence (CIA) 1977–81; mem. Advisory Council, Univ. of Rhode Island Graduate School of Oceanography; mem. Bd. Dirs. Monsanto Co., Nat. Life Insurance Co. 1983; Hon. Fellow, Exeter Coll., Oxford 1979–; Nat. Security Medal, Legion of Merit, Bronze Star. *Publication:* Secrecy and Democracy: The CIA in Transition 1985. *Leisure interests:* tennis, reading. *Address:* 1320 Skipwith Road, McLean, Va. 22101, U.S.A. *Telephone:* (703) 528-2023.

TURNER, Tina (Annie Mae Bullock); American singer; b. 25 Nov. 1940, Brownsville, Tenn.; m. Ike Turner 1956 (divorced 1978); four s.; singer with Ike Turner Kings of Rhythm, Ike and Tina Turner Revue; concert tours of Europe 1966, 1983–84, Japan and Africa 1971; Grammy Award 1972, 1985 (three), 1986. *Films:* Gimme Shelter 1970, Soul to Soul 1971, Tommy 1975, Mad Max Beyond Thunderdome 1985. *Recordings include:* River Deep, Mountain High 1966, Proud Mary 1970, Blues Roots 1972, Nutbush City Limits 1973, The Gospel According to Ike and Tina 1974; solo albums: Let Me Touch Your Mind 1972, Tina Turns the Country On 1974, Acid Queen 1975, Rough 1978, Private Dancer 1984, Break Every Rule 1986. *Address:* c/o Roger Davies Management, 3575 Cahuenga Boulevard West, Los Angeles, Calif. 90068, U.S.A.

TURNER, Wilfred, B.SC., C.M.G., C.V.O.; former British civil servant and diplomatist; b. 10 Oct. 1921, Littleborough, Lancs.; s. of Allen and Eliza (née Leach) Turner; m. June Gladys Tite 1947; two s. one d.; ed. Heywood Grammar School and London Univ.; Ministry of Labour and Nat. Service 1938–42, 1947–55; served in British army 1942–47; Asst. Labour Adviser, British High Comm. in India 1955–59; Sr. Wages Insp., Ministry of Labour 1959–60; at Ministry of Health 1960–66; joined Foreign and Commonwealth Office 1966; First Sec. Kaduna, N. Nigeria 1966–69, Kuala Lumpur, Malaysia 1969–73; Deputy High Commr. in Ghana 1973–77; High Commr. in Botswana 1977–81; Dir. Southern Africa Assen. 1983–88, Transportation Systems and Market Research Ltd., British Rail 1987–. *Leisure interest:* hill-walking. *Address:* 44 Tower Road, Twickenham, Middx., TW1 4PE, England. *Telephone:* 01-892 1593.

TURNER, William Cochrane, B.S.; American diplomatist and business executive; b. 27 May 1929, Red Oak, Iowa; s. of James Lyman Turner and Josephine Cochrane Turner; m. Cynthia Dunbar 1955; two s.; ed. Northwestern Univ.; Vice-Pres. and Dir., Western Man. Consultants Inc. 1955–60, Pres., C.E.O. and Dir. 1960–74, Chair. and Dir. Western Man. Consultants Europe S.A. 1969–74; Dir. Ryan-Evans Drug Stores Inc. 1964–68, First Nat. Bank of Arizona 1970–74; Vice-Chair. and Dir. American Graduate School of Int. Man. 1972–85, Chair. 1986–; mem. Advisory Cttee. for Trade Negotiations 1982–84; Amb. and U.S. Rep. to OECD 1974–77; mem. U.S. Advisory Comm. on Int. Educ. and Cultural Affairs 1969–74, Nat. Review Bd., Center for Cultural and Tech. Interchange between East and West 1970–74, Panel on Int. Information, Educ. and Cultural Relations, Center for Strategic and Int. Studies, Georgetown Univ. 1973–75, Western Int. Trade Group, U.S. Dept. of Commerce 1972–74; Pres. and Dir. Phoenix Symphony Assen. 1957–72; Gov. Atlantic Inst. for Int. Affairs, Paris 1977–88, Joseph H. Lauder Inst. of Man. and Int. Studies, Univ. of Pa. 1983–; Chair. Argyle Atlantic Corpn. 1977–; Dir. Pullman Inc. 1977–80; Nabisco Brands Inc. 1977–85, Goodyear Tire and Rubber Co. 1978–, Salomon Inc. 1980–, Energy Transition Corpn. (also Vice-Chair.) 1979–86, The Atlantic Council of the U.S. 1977–, AT & T Int. 1980–84, Swensen's Inc. 1981–84, World Wildlife Fund (U.S.)/Conservation

Foundation 1983–, Atlantic Inst. Foundation Inc. 1984–; Chair. numerous advisory councils including AT & T Int. European Advisory Council 1981–88; Chair. AT & T Int. Asian Pacific Advisory Council 1981–88; Co-Chair. Int. Advisory Bd., Univ. of Nations and Pacific & Asia Christian Univ., Hawaii 1985–; mem. Avon Products Inc. Int. Advisory Council 1985–; mem. American Can Co. Asia Pacific Advisory Council 1981–85; Dir. and mem. Exec. Cttee. Sunbelt Holdings S.A., Luxembourg 1982–84; mem. IBM European Advisory Council, IBM World Trade Europe–Middle East–Africa Corpn., Paris 1977–80; mem. Gen. Electric of Brazil Advisory Council, Gen. Electric Co., Fla. 1979–81, Caterpillar of Brazil Advisory Council 1979–84; mem. Caterpillar Tractor Co. Asia Pacific Advisory Council 1984–, Spencer Stuart Advisory Council 1984–; mem. Advisory Bd., Center for Strategic and Int. Studies, Georgetown Univ. 1977–81; mem. Nat. Councils, The Salk Inst. 1978–82, Council of American Ambs. 1984–, Council on Foreign Relations 1980–, US-Japan Business Council 1987–, Nat. Advisory Council on Business Educ., Council on Int. Educ. Exchange, New York City 1987–; Chair. and mem. ASM Int. Advisory Council, Advanced Semi-conductor Materials Int. NV, Bilthoven 1985–88; Trustee and mem. Exec. Cttee., U.S. Council for Int. Business 1977–, Heard Museum, Phoenix 1983–85 (mem. Nat. Advisory Bd. 1985–); Nat. Trustee, Nat. Symphony Orchestra Asscn. 1973–84; mem. Bd. of Govs. American Hosp. of Paris 1974–77, Bd. of Trustees, American School of Paris, Saint-Cloud 1975–77, Phoenix 40 1979–. *Leisure interests:* tennis, symphony, opera, international political and economic relations. *Address:* 4350 East Camelback Road, Suite 240B, Phoenix, Ariz. 85018 (Office); 5710 North Yucca Road, Paradise Valley, Ariz. 85253, U.S.A. (Home).

TUROWICZ, Jerzy, M.A.; Polish journalist; b. 10 Dec. 1912, Cracow; s. of August and Klotylda Turowicz; m. Anna Gasiorowska 1938; three d.; ed. Jagellonian Univ., Cracow; Ed.-in-Chief, Głos Narodu (daily), Cracow 1939; Ed.-in-Chief, Tygodnik Powszechny (weekly), Cracow 1945–53, 1956–; mem. Editorial Bd., Znak (monthly), Cracow 1946–; Pres., Znak Social Publishing Inst., Cracow 1960–; mem. Polish Journalists' Asscn. 1945–82, Polish Writers' Union 1948–83, PEN Club 1975–; mem. Catholic Intelligentsia Clubs, Warsaw and Cracow 1957–; mem. Polish Episcopate Comm. for Lay Apostolate 1960–; mem. Cttee. of World Conference on Religion and Peace; Dr. h.c. (Yale) 1985; mem. Alfred Jurzykowski Foundation Award, New York 1978, Bolesław Prus Award of Polish Journalists' Asscn. 1981, Int. Gandhi Award 1988; Officer's and Kt.'s Cross of Order of Polonia Restituta, Commdr., St. Gregory the Great Order with Star. *Publications:* Chrześcijanin w dzisiejszym świecie (A Christian in the Contemporary World) 1964; numerous contributions to monthly Znak, weekly Tygodnik Powszechny and other Polish and foreign periodicals. *Address:* ul. Lenartowicza 3 m. 10, 31-138 Cracow, Poland. *Telephone:* 33-53-07.

TURPIN, Raymond Alexandre; French professor of medicine; b. 5 Nov. 1895, Pontoise (Val d'Oise); m. Simone Gaillochet 1931 (deceased); six c.; ed. Faculty of Medicine, Paris; served in First World War as Auxiliary Doctor in 9th Infantry Regt., Verdun 1916; Hosp. Intern as part of medical training 1921; Prof., Faculty of Medicine, Paris 1947; created Inst. of Progenesis, attached to the Faculty of Medicine 1959; made first BCG vaccinations against tuberculosis with Calmette and Weil-Hallé 1921; discovered the electromyographic anomalies of tetany 1942; initiated the study of human genetics in France 1941–44, and discovered in 1958 first chromosome irregularities of number (mongolism: an extra chromosome 21), then of structure (translocation) 1959; mem. Acad. de Médecine, Acad. des Sciences and numerous other learned socs. in France and abroad; Commdr. de la Légion d'honneur, Médaille militaire, Médaille de Verdun, Croix de guerre; many awards. *Publications:* include Tétanie de l'enfant, Hérédité des prédispositions morbides, La progenèse (with colleagues), Les chromosomes humains, Caryotypes normaux et variations pathologiques (with pupil). *Leisure interest:* bibliophilism. *Address:* 94 avenue Victor Hugo, 75116 Paris, France. *Telephone:* 553-05-61.

TURRO, Nicholas John, PH.D.; American professor of chemistry; b. 18 May 1938, Middletown, Conn.; s. of Nicholas J. Turro and Philomena Russo; m. Sandra J. Misenti 1960; two d.; ed. Wesleyan Univ. and Calif. Inst. of Tech.; Instr. Columbia Univ. 1964–65, Asst. Prof. 1965–67, Assoc. Prof. 1967–69, Prof. of Chem. 1969–81, William P. Schweitzer Prof. of Chem. 1981–, Chair. Dept. of Chem. 1981–84; Sloan Fellowship 1966–70; Guggenheim Fellowship, Univ. of Oxford 1984; mem. N.A.S., American Acad. of Arts and Sciences; Fellow, New York Acad. of Science; several awards and distinctions; Hon. D.Sc. (Wesleyan Univ.) 1984. *Publications:* Molecular Photochemistry 1965, Modern Molecular Photochemistry 1978. *Leisure interests:* tennis, handball, reading. *Address:* Box 610, Havemeyer Hall, Columbia University, New York, N.Y. 10027 (Office); 125 Downey Drive, Tenafly, N.J. 07670, U.S.A. (Home).

TUSA, John, M.A.; British broadcaster; b. 2 March 1936, Zlin, Czechoslovakia; s. of Jan Tusa and Lydie Sklenarova; m. Ann Hilary Dowson 1960; two s.; ed. Gresham's School, Holt, Trinity Coll., Cambridge; joined BBC as general trainee 1960; Producer, Talks and Features, BBC World Service 1964–66; Ed., Forum World Features 1966–67; Presenter, The World Tonight, Radio 4 1970–78, 24 Hours, BBC World Service 1972–78, Newsweek, BBC2 1978–79, Newsnight, BBC2 1979–86, Timewatch, BBC2 1982–84; Man. Dir., External Broadcasting, BBC 1986–; Royal TV Soc. TV Journalist of the Year 1984; BAFTA Richard Dimbleby Award 1984.

Publications: The Nuremburg Trial 1983 (with Ann Tusa), The Berlin Blockade (with Ann Tusa) 1988. *Leisure interests:* squash, tennis, opera. *Address:* 21 Christchurch Hill, London, NW3 1JY, England. *Telephone:* 01-435 9495.

TUTIN, Dorothy, C.B.E.; British actress; b. 8 April 1930, London; d. of late Dr. John Tutin and of A. E. Fryers; m. Derek Waring 1963; one s. one d.; ed. St. Catherine's Bramley, Surrey, and Royal Acad. of Dramatic Art, London; appeared at Stratford Festival 1958, 1960; took part in Shakespeare Memorial Theatre tour of Russia 1958; Shakespeare recital before Pope, Vatican 1964; Evening Standard Award as Best Actress 1960, Variety Club of Great Britain Award for Best Film Actress 1972; Soc. of the West End Theatre Award for Actress of the Year in a Revival 1976. *Principal roles:* Rose (The Living Room), Katherine (Henry V), Sally Bowles (I am a Camera), St. Joan (The Lark), Catherine (The Gates of Summer), Hedwig (The Wild Duck), Viola (Twelfth Night), Ophelia (Hamlet), Dolly (Once More, With Feeling), Portia (The Merchant of Venice), Cressida (Troilus and Cressida), Sister Jeanne (The Devils) 1961, 1962, Juliet (Romeo and Juliet) and Desdemona (Othello), Stratford-on-Avon 1961, Varya (The Cherry Orchard) 1961, Prioress (The Devils), Edinburgh 1962, Polly Peachum (The Beggar's Opera) 1963, Queen Victoria (Portrait of a Queen) 1965 and in New York 1968, Rosalind (As You Like It), Stratford-on-Avon 1967, Los Angeles 1968; Cleopatra (Antony and Cleopatra) 1977, Madame Ravanskaya (The Cherry Orchard); has also played in The Hollow Crown, New York 1963, Old Times 1971, Peter Pan 1971, 1972, What Every Woman Knows 1973, 1975, A Month in the Country 1974, 1976, Macbeth 1976, The Cherry Orchard 1978, The Double Dealer 1978, Undiscovered Country 1979, Reflections 1980, The Provok'd Wife 1980, The Deep Blue Sea 1981, After The Lions 1982, Ballerina 1984, Other Places, London 1985, Are You Sitting Comfortably 1986, Brighton Beach Memoirs 1986, Chalk Garden 1986, Thursdays Ladies 1987, Harlequinade and The Browning Version 1988. *Films include:* The Beggar's Opera, The Importance of Being Earnest, A Tale of Two Cities, Cromwell, Savage Messiah, South Riding 1978, The Shooting Party 1984. *Television appearances include:* The Double Dealer 1980, The Eavesdropper 1981, The Combination 1981, Life After Death 1981, La Ronde 1982, King Lear 1982, Landscape 1982, A Kind of Alaska, Murder with Mirrors, The Demon Lover, The Father 1985, Evensong 1986. *Leisure interest:* music. *Address:* Suite 42–43, Grafton House, 2–3 Golden Square, London, W.1, England.

TUTU, Most Rev. Desmond Mpilo, L.TH., M.TH.; South African ecclesiastic; b. 7 Oct. 1931, Klerksdorp; m. Leah Nomalizo Tutu 1955; four c.; ed. Bantu High School, Bantu Normal Coll., Univ. of South Africa, St. Peter's Theological Coll., Rosettenville, King's Coll., Univ. of London; Schoolmaster 1954–57; Parish Priest 1960–; Theological Seminary Lecturer 1967–69; Univ. Lecturer 1970–71; Assoc. Dir. Theological Educ. Fund, World Council of Churches 1972–75; Dean of Johannesburg 1975–76; Bishop of Lesotho 1977–78, of Johannesburg 1984–86; Archbishop of Cape Town, Metropolitan of the Church of the Prov. of Southern Africa 1986–; Chancellor Univ. of Western Cape 1988–; Pres. All Africa Conf. of Churches 1987–; Sec.-Gen. South African Council of Churches 1979–84; Visiting Prof. of Anglican Studies New York Gen. Theological Seminary 1984; Dir. Coca-Cola 1986–; Hon. D.D., D.C.L., LL.D., Th.D. (Gen. Theol. Sem. New York, Kent Univ., Harvard Univ., Ruhr Bochum Univ.); Hon. D.Div. (Aberdeen) 1981; S.T.D. (Columbia) 1982; Dr. h.c. (Mount Allison Univ., Sackville, N.B., Strasbourg) 1988; F.K.C. (Fellow of King's Coll. London); Onassis Award, Family of Man Gold Medallion 1983, Nobel Peace Prize 1984, Carter–Menil Human Rights Prize 1986, Martin Luther King, Jr. Peace Award 1986; Order of Jamaica; Freedom of City of Merthyr Tydfil (Wales). *Publications:* Crying in the Wilderness 1982, Hope and Suffering 1983 (both collections of sermons and addresses). *Address:* Bishopscourt, Claremont 7700, South Africa. *Telephone:* (021) 761 25 31.

TUTUOLA, Amos; Nigerian writer; b. 1920, Abeokuta, W. Nigeria; s. of Charles and Esther Tutuola; m. Victoria Tutuola 1947; four s. four d.; ed. Mission Schools; worked on father's farm; trained as coppersmith; served with R.A.F. Second World War; Nigerian Broadcasting Corpn., Ibadan 1945–; Visiting Fellow, Univ. of Ife, Nigeria 1979; took part in writing programme, Iowa, U.S.A. 1983; Hon. Citizen New Orleans 1983. *Publications:* The Palm-Wine Drinkard 1952, My Life in the Bush of Ghosts 1954, Simbi and the Satyr of the Jungle 1955, The Brave African Huntress' 1958, The Feather Woman of the Jungle 1962, Ajaiyi and His Inherited Poverty 1967, The Witch Herbalist of the Remote Town 1980, Pauper, Brawler and Slanderer 1987. *Leisure interests:* farming, writing. *Address:* P.O. Box 2251, Ibadan, Nigeria.

TUXWORTH, Ian Lindsay; Australian politician; b. 18 June 1942, Wollongong; s. of Lindsay J. Tuxworth and Hilda E. Tuxworth; m. Ruth Pease 1966; one s. two d.; ed. Rostrevor Coll. Adelaide; Chair. Tennant Creek Town Man. 1969–74; mem. Legis. Ass. for Barkly, N.T. 1974–; Exec mem. Legis. Council for Mines, Fisheries, Water Resources, Tourism, Health, Community Devt. 1974–78; Minister for Health, Mines and Energy 1978–83; Chief Minister, N.T. 1984–87; M.P. for Barkly N.T. 1987–; Country-Liberal Party. *Leisure interests:* squash, tennis, running. *Address:* Legislative Assembly of the Northern Territory, P.O. Box 796, Tennant Creek, N.T. 5760, Australia. *Telephone:* 62 2205.

TUZO, Gen. Sir Harry Craufurd, G.C.B., O.B.E., M.C., M.A.; British army officer (retd.); b. 26 Aug. 1917, Bangalore, India; s. of John A. Tuzo and Annie K. Craufurd; m. Monica P. Salter 1943; one d.; ed. Wellington Coll. and Oriel Coll., Oxford; Regimental Service, Royal Artillery 1939–45; staff appts. Far East 1946–49; Royal Horse Artillery 1950–51, 1954–58; mem. Staff, School of Infantry 1951–53; Gen. Staff Officer, War Office 1958–60; Commdg. Officer, 3rd Regt. Royal Horse Artillery 1960–62; Asst. Commdt., Sandhurst 1962–63; Commdr. 51 Gurkha Infantry Brigade 1963–65; Imperial Defence Coll. 1966; Chief of Staff, British Army of the Rhine 1967–69; Dir. Royal Artillery 1969–71; Gen. Officer Commanding, Northern Ireland 1971–73; C.-in-C. BAOR and Commdr., Northern Army Group, NATO 1973–76; Deputy Supreme Allied Commdr. Europe 1976–78; Chair. Marconi Space and Defence Systems Ltd. 1979–83; Dir. Oceonics PLC 1988–; mem. Bd. Govs. Corps. of Commrs.; Chair. Royal United Services Inst. for Defence Studies 1980–83, King's Lynn Festival, Imperial War Museum Redevt. Appeal 1985–; D.L. for County of Norfolk; Master Gunner, St. James's Park 1977–83; Hon. Fellow, Oriel Coll., Oxford. *Publications:* articles in professional publications. *Leisure interests:* music, sailing, shooting. *Address:* Heath Farmhouse, Fakenham, Norfolk, NR21 8LZ, England.

TVEDT, John; Norwegian economist and banker; b. 1938; ed. Univ. of Oslo; with Norges Bank 1963–83, Economist 1963–65, Division Chief Monetary Policy Dept. 1968–74, Dir. Monetary Policy Dept. 1974–76, Dir. Banking and Loan Dept. 1976–77, Dir. Credit Policy Dept. 1977–83, Acting Dir. Econ. Intelligence Dept. 1977–79; Economist IMF European Dept., Washington, D.C. 1965–68, Exec. Dir. IMF for Denmark, Finland, Iceland, Norway and Sweden 1983–85.

TWIGGY (see Lawson, Leslie).

TWISLETON-WYKEHAM-FIENNES, Sir Maurice Alberic, Kt., C.ENG., F.I.MECH.E.; British company director (retd.); b. 1 March 1907, London; s. of Alberic Arthur Twisleton-Wykeham-Fiennes and Gertrude Theodosia Pomeroy-Colley; m. 1st Sylvia Mabel Joan Finlay 1932, 2nd Erika Hueller von Huellenried 1967; two s. three d. (by 1st marriage); ed. Repton School, Derbyshire, and Armstrong Coll., Newcastle; Eng. Apprentice Ransomes and Rapier Ltd., Ipswich; Man. Pneumatic Tool Dept., Sir. W. G. Armstrong Whitworth and Co. 1930–37; Commercial Asst. to Man. Dir. United Steel Companies Ltd.; Gen. Works Dir. Brush Electrical Eng. Co. Ltd. 1942–45; Managing Dir. Davy and United Engineering Co. Ltd., Sheffield 1945–60; Man. Dir. Davy-Ashmore Group 1960–69, Chair. 1961–69; Dir. Continuous Casting Co. Ltd. 1957–69; Clyde Crane and Booth Ltd. 1961–68, Simon Eng. Ltd. 1962–69, North Sea Marine Eng. Construction Co. Ltd. 1964–69, Metallurgical Equipment Export Co. Ltd. 1964–67; Pres. Iron and Steel Inst. 1962–63; Steel Industry Adviser (UN) to Govt. of Peru 1974–75; Eng. Adviser (IBRD) to Venezuelan Investment Fund 1976–77; Assoc. Consultant, L. H. Manderstam and Partners Ltd. 1977–80; Hon. Vice-Pres. Indian Inst. of Metals; Hon. mem. American Iron and Steel Inst.; Verein Deutscher Eisenhüttenleute; Chair. CBI Overseas Scholarships Bd., Gov. 1970–76; Gov. Yehudi Menuhin School 1969–84. *Leisure interest:* music. *Address:* 11 Heath Rise, Kersfield Road, Putney Hill, London, SW15 3HF, England. *Telephone:* 01-785 7489.

TWITCHETT, Denis Crispin, F.B.A.; British professor of Chinese studies; b. 23 Sept. 1925, London; m. Umeko Ichikawa 1956; two s.; ed. St. Catharine's Coll., Cambridge and Inst. of Far Eastern Culture, Tokyo Univ.; Lecturer in Far Eastern History, S.O.A.S., London Univ. 1954–56; Lecturer in Classical Chinese, Cambridge Univ. 1956–60; Prof. of Chinese and Head of Dept. of Far East, S.O.A.S. 1960–68; Prof. of Chinese, Cambridge Univ. 1968–80, Professorial Fellow of St. Catharine's Coll. 1973–74; Visiting Fellow, Inst. for Advanced Study, Princeton, U.S.A. 1973–74, Visiting Prof. 1978–79, Gordon Wu Prof. of Chinese Studies 1980–. *Publications:* Financial Administration of the T'ang Dynasty 1963, Confucian Personalities (with A. F. Wright) 1963, Perspectives on the T'ang (with A. F. Wright) 1973, Times Atlas of China 1974, Printing and Publishing in Medieval China 1984, Reader T'ang History 1986; Gen. Ed. of Cambridge History of China 1977–. *Leisure interests:* music, fine arts. *Address:* 14 College Road, Princeton, N.J. 08540, U.S.A.; 24 Arbury Road, Cambridge, CB4 2JE, England.

TYAZHELNIKOV, Yevgeniy Mikhailovich; Soviet party official; b. 7 Jan. 1928, Chelyabinsk; ed. Chelyabinsk Pedagogical Inst.; mem. CPSU 1951–; post-graduate student teacher, Sec. CPSU Org. at Chelyabinsk Pedagogical Inst. 1950–61, Rector 1961–64; Sec. Chelyabinsk Dist. Cttee. of CPSU 1964–68; First Sec., mem. Cen. Cttee. U.S.S.R. Komsomol 1968–77; mem. Cen. Cttee. of CPSU 1971–, Head of Dept. of Propaganda 1977–82; Amb. to Romania Dec. 1982–; awards include Order of Red Banner, Order of Lenin. *Address:* Soviet Embassy, Şoseana Kiseleff 6, Bucharest, Romania.

TYNDALE-BISCOE, Cecil Hugh, PH.D.; Australian university teacher and research scientist; b. 16 Oct. 1929, Kashmir, India; s. of Eric Dallas Tyndale-Biscoe and Phyllis Mary (née Long) Tyndale-Biscoe; m. Marina Szokoloczi 1960; two s. one d.; ed. Wycliffe Coll., England, Canterbury Univ., N.Z., Univ. of Western Australia and Washington Univ., St. Louis, U.S.A.; Animal Ecology, Dept. of Scientific and Industrial Research, N.Z. 1951–55; lecturer Edwardes Coll., Peshawar, Pakistan 1955–58, Univ. of W.A., Perth 1961; Deputy Leader, Biologist, N.Z. Alpine Club Antarctic Expedition 1959–60; lecturer, Sr. Lecturer, Reader in Zoology, Australian Nat. Univ., Canberra 1962–75; Sr. Prin. Research Scientist Div. of Wildlife Research, CSIRO, Canberra 1976–78, Chief Research Scientist Div. of Wildlife and Ecology 1978–; mountaineering in N.Z., including first north-south traverse of Mt. Cook, first ascent of Torres from the Balfour; in the Karakorum, including first ascents of Falak Sar, Barteen and Buni Zom; Fellow Australian Inst. of Biologists; Hon. mem. R.S.N.Z.; Clarke Medal, Royal Soc. of N.S.W., Troughton Medal, Aitken Medal, CSIRO Medal. *Publications:* Life of Marsupials 1973, Reproduction and Evolution (Ed.) 1977, Reproductive Physiology of Marsupials (with M. B. Renfree) 1987, Developing Marsupials (Ed. with P. A. Janssens) 1988; about 80 papers in scientific journals of reproduction, ecology and endocrinology. *Leisure interests:* mountaineering, agroforestry, earth houses, woodwork, history of N. India. *Address:* Division of Wildlife and Ecology, CSIRO, P.O. Box 84, Lyneham, A.C.T. 2602 (Office); 4 Steele Street, Hackett, A.C.T. 2602, Australia (Home). *Telephone:* 062-421 728 (Office); 062-498 612 (Home).

TYRRELL, David Arthur John, C.B.E., M.D., D.SC., F.R.S., F.R.C.P.; British physician; b. 19 June 1925, Ashford, Middx.; s. of Sidney Charles Tyrrell and Agnes Kate Blewett; m. Betty Moyra Wylie 1950; one s. (deceased) two d.; ed. King Edward VII School, Sheffield and Sheffield Univ.; Research Registrar, Sheffield Univ. Hosps. 1950–51; Asst. Physician and Research Asst., Rockefeller Inst. Hosp., New York 1951–54; Common Cold Unit, MRC 1957–, Dir. 1962–; Dir. WHO Virus Reference Lab. 1962–; Head, Div. of Communicable Diseases, Clinical Research Centre 1967–84, Deputy Dir. 1970–84; Hon. Consultant Physician of West Hendon Hosp. 1967–70, of Northwick Park Hosp., Harrow 1970–85, of Wessex Regional Health Authority 1985–; Stewart, Ambuj Nath Bose and Conway Evans prizes. *Publications:* Common Colds and Related Diseases 1965, Inferferon and its Clinical Potential 1976, The Abolition of Infection: hope or illusion? 1982; Co-author: Microbial Diseases 1979; numerous articles in scientific and medical journals. *Leisure interests:* walking, gardening, music. *Address:* Medical Research Council, Common Cold Unit, Harvard Hospital, Coombe Road, Salisbury SP2 8BW; Ash Lodge, Dean Lane, Whiteparish, Salisbury, Wilts, SP5 2RN, England. *Telephone:* (0722) 22485; (07948) 352 (Home).

TYSON, Alan Walker, C.B.E., M.A., M.B., B.S., F.B.A.; British musicologist and psychoanalyst; b. 27 Oct. 1926, Glasgow; s. of Henry Alan M. Tyson and Dorothy (Walker) Tyson; ed. Rugby School, Magdalen Coll. Oxford, Inst. of Psychoanalysis, London and Univ. Coll. Hospital, London; Fellow, All Souls Coll. Oxford 1952–, Sr. Research Fellow 1971–; Lecturer in Psychopathology and Developmental Psychology, Oxford Univ. 1968–70, James P. R. Lyell Reader in Bibliography 1973–74; Visiting Lecturer in Psychiatry, Montefiore Hospital, New York 1967–68; Visiting Prof. of Music, Columbia Univ., New York 1969; Ernest Bloch Prof. of Music, Univ. of Calif. (Berkeley) 1977–78; mem. Inst. for Advanced Study, Princeton 1983–84; Visiting Prof. of Music, Graduate Center, City Univ., New York 1985. *Publications:* The Authentic English Editions of Beethoven 1963, Thematic Catalogue of the Works of Muzio Clementi 1967, The Beethoven Sketchbooks: History, Reconstruction, Inventory (with Douglas Johnson and Robert Winter) 1985, Mozart: Studies of the Autograph Scores 1987; ed. Beethoven Studies 1 1973, 2 1977, 3 1982. *Address:* All Souls College, Oxford, OX1 4AL; 7 Southcote Road, London, N19 5BJ, England (Home). *Telephone:* (0865) 279363 (Oxford); 01-609 2981 (Home).

TYSON, Harvey Wood; South African journalist; b. 27 Sept. 1928, Johannesburg; two s. one d.; ed. Kingswood Coll., Rhodes Univ., Grahamstown; Ed. The Star, Johannesburg 1974–. *Address:* The Star, 47 Sauer Street, P.O. Box 1014, Johannesburg 2000, South Africa.

TYSON, Mike G.; American boxer; b. 30 June 1966, New York City; s. of John Kilpatrick Tyson and Lorna Tyson; m. Robin Givens 1988 (divorced 1989); defeated Trevor Berbick to win WBC Heavyweight Title 1986; winner WBA Heavyweight Title March 1987, IBF Heavyweight Title Aug. 1987; undefeated World Champion, winner all 32 bouts; Hon. Chair. Cystic Fibrosis Assen. 1987–, Young Adult Inst. 1987–. *Address:* c/o Reel Sports Inc., East 40th Street, New York, N.Y. 10016, U.S.A.

U

ÜBLEIS, Heinrich, DR.IUR.; Austrian politician; b. 3 Feb. 1933, Edt bei Lambach; m. Eva Müller 1960 (died 1987); one s.; ed. Realgymnasium, Wels; worked in post-office in Scharnstein 1953, Vienna 1955; Budget Dept. 1965; Sec. to Minister of Transport 1971; Dir. Dept. of Cen. Planning and Co-ordination 1974; Gen. Dir. for Post and Telegraph Admin. 1979; Section Head 1980; Minister for Bldgs. and Tech. 1985–87; Dir. Gen. Österreichische Bundesbahnen (Austrian Fed. Railways) 1987–; numerous decorations. *Leisure interests:* tennis, fishing, running, skiing. *Address:* Österreichische Bundesbahnen, Elisabethstrasse 9, 1010 Vienna, Austria.

UBUKATA, Taiji; Japanese business executive; b. 23 Jan. 1916, Tokyo; s. of Teiichi and Hama Ubukata; m. Kyoko Ubukata 1949; one s. two d.; ed. Tokyo Imperial Univ.; joined Ishikawajima Shipyard Co. Ltd. 1939; Man. Accounting and Budgeting Dept., Ishikawajima-Harima Heavy Industries Co. Ltd. (IHI) 1958; Dir. Ishikawajima do Brasil Estaleiros S.A. (ISH-IBRAS) 1959; Dir. and Man. of Finance Dept., IHI 1964; Man. Dir. IHI 1968; Exec. Vice-Pres. ISHIBRAS 1973; Pres. IHI 1979–86, Chair. June 1983–; Vice-Pres. Japan Soc. of Industrial Machinery Mfrs., Japan Overseas Educational Services, Shipbuilders Assen. of Japan; Exec. Dir. Japan Fed. of Econ. Orgs.; Chair. Japan Aero Engines Corpn.; mem. Aircraft and Machineries Industries Council, Immigration Council; Ordem de Rio Branco (Brazil), Blue Ribbon Medal (Japan). *Leisure interests:* reading, travelling. *Address:* Higashi-Yukigaya 4-20-2, Ohta-ku, Tokyo 145, Japan (Home). *Telephone:* 03-720-2205 (Home).

UCHIDA, Mitsuko; Japanese pianist; b. 20 Dec. 1948, Tokyo; d. of Fujio Uchida and Yasuko Uchida; ed. Vienna Acad. of Music; recitals and concerto performances with all maj. London orchestras, Chicago Symphony, Boston Symphony, Berlin Philharmonic, and others; played and directed the cycle of 21 Mozart piano concertos with the English Chamber Orchestra in London 1985–86; recordings include Mozart Piano Sonatas and Concertos (for Philips), Chopin Piano Sonatas; First Prize Beethoven Competition Vienna 1969, Second Prize Chopin Competition Warsaw 1970, Second Prize Leeds Competition 1975. *Leisure interest:* bicycling (preferably on the flat). *Address:* c/o Van Walsum Management, 40 St. Peter's Road, London, W6 9BH, England. *Telephone:* 01-741 5881.

UDALL, Morris, LL.B.; American politician; b. 15 June 1922, St. Johns, Ariz.; s. of Levi S. and Louise (née Lee) Udall; brother of Stewart Udall (q.v.); m. 2nd Ella Royston 1968 (died 1988); three s. three d. (all by previous marriage); ed. Arizona Univ. and Law School; mem. Arizona Bar 1949–; Partner, Udall and Udall law firm, Tucson, Ariz. 1949–61; Chief Deputy County Attorney, Pima County 1953–54; Lecturer in Labour Law, Univ. of Ariz. 1955–56; mem. U.S. House of Reps. 1961–; Chair. Interior and Insular Affairs Cttee.; mem. Post Office and Civil Service Cttee.; Cand. for Democratic Presidential Nomination 1976; Legislative Conservation Award, Nat. Wildlife Fed. *Publications:* Arizona Law of Evidence 1960, The Job of the Congressman (jointly) 1966, Education of a Congressman 1972. *Address:* 235 Cannon House Office Building, Washington, D.C. 20515, U.S.A.

UDALL, Stewart Lee; American politician; b. 31 Jan. 1920, St. Johns, Ariz.; s. of Levi S. and Louise (née Lee) Udell; brother of Morris Udall (q.v.); m. Ermalee Webb 1947; four s. two d.; ed. Univ. of Arizona; served U.S. Air Force, Second World War; admitted to Arizona Bar 1948, practised law, Tucson 1948–54, Washington 1969–; of Counsel, Hill, Christopher and Phillips, Washington; mem. House of Reps. 1955–61, mem. Interior and Insular Affairs Cttee., Labor and Education Cttee.; Sec. of the Interior 1961–69; Chair. of Bd., Overview Group (int. consulting firm working to create a better environment for mankind) 1969–; writer syndicated column Udall on the Environment 1970–; Writer Visiting Prof. in Environmental Humanism, Yale School of Forestry; Democrat. *Publications:* The Quiet Crisis 1963, Agenda For Tomorrow 1968, America's Natural Treasures 1971, The National Parks of America (with others) 1972, The Energy Balloon (co-author) 1974. *Address:* 1900 M Street, Washington, D.C. 20036, U.S.A.

UDENFRIEND, Sidney, PH.D.; American biologist; b. 5 April 1918, New York; s. of Max Udenfriend and Esther Tabak; m. Shirley Frances Reidel 1943; one s. one d.; ed. Coll. of the City of New York and New York Univ.; Lab. Asst., New York City Dept. of Health 1940–42; Jr. Chemist, New York Univ. Research Service 1942–43, Asst. Chemist 1943–44, Research Chemist 1944–46; Research Asst., New York Univ. Medical School 1946–47, Instructor 1947–48; Instructor, Washington Univ. Medical School 1948–50; Biochemist, Lab. of Chemical Pharmacology, Nat. Heart Inst., Nat. Inst. of Health 1950–53, Head, Section on Cellular Pharmacology 1953–56, Chief, Lab. of Clinical Biochemistry 1956–68; Dir. Roche Inst. of Molecular Biology 1968–83, Head, Lab. of Molecular Neurobiology 1983–; Adjunct Prof., Columbia Uni. 1969–, City Univ. New York 1968–, Cornell Univ. Medical School 1982–; mem. N.A.S., American Acad. of Arts and Sciences and numerous scientific socs.; Fellow New York Acad. of Sciences; Gairdner Foundation Award 1967, Rudolph Virchow Gold Medal 1979, and others. *Publications:* Fluorescence Assay in Biology and Medicine, Vol. I

1962, Vol. II 1969, The Peptides, Analysis, Synthesis, Biology: Opioid Peptides (ed., with Johannes Meienhofer) 1984; 437 publs. on peptide chem. and neurochemistry. *Leisure interests:* reading, music. *Address:* Roche Institute of Molecular Biology, Nutley, N.J. 07110, U.S.A. *Telephone:* (201) 235-3731.

UDOMA, Sir (Egbert) Udo, M.A., PH.D.; Nigerian lawyer and legal administrator; b. 21 June 1917, Ibekwe Ntanaran Akama, Ikot Abasi, Cross River State; s. of Chief Udoma Inam and Adiaha Edem; m. Grace Bassey 1950; six s. one d.; ed. Methodist Coll., Uzuakoli, Trinity Coll., Dublin, Ireland, St. Catherine's Coll., Oxford; called to the Bar, Gray's Inn, London 1945; practised as barrister and solicitor, Supreme Court, Nigeria 1946–61; mem. House of Reps. 1952–59; Judge, Lagos High Court 1961–63; Gov.-Gen. 1963; Chief Justice of Uganda 1963–69; Justice Supreme Court of Nigeria 1969–82; Vice-Pres. Conf. Methodist Church of Nigeria 1971–75; Chair. Constituent Assembly Nigerian Constitution 1977–78; Dir. and Presiding Justice, Seminar for Judges, Nigeria 1980 and 1981; Chair. Law Reform Comm. for Cross River State 1985–; fmr. Chancellor Ahmadu Bello Univ.; Nat. Pres. Ibibio State Union 1947–61; mem. Nigeria Marketing Co. 1952–54; Man. Cttee. West Africa Inst. for Oil Palm Research 1953–63; Vice-Pres. Nigeria Bar Asscn. 1957–61; mem. Int. Comm. of Jurists, World Asscn. of Judges; Chair. Bd. of Trustees King George V Memorial Fund 1964–69; Patron Nigeria Soc. of Int. Law 1968–; awarded title of Obong Ikpa Isong Ibibio 1961; Hon. LL.D. Ibadan Univ. 1967, Ahmadu Bello Univ. 1972, Trinity Coll., Dublin 1973; C.F.R. (Nigeria) 1979. *Publications:* The Lion and the Oil Palm and Other Essays 1943, The Human Right to Individual Freedom: A Symposium on World Habeas Corpus (jt. contrib.) 1970, The Story of Ibibio Union 1987. *Leisure interests:* billiards, gardening, walking. *Address:* Mfut Itiat Enin, 8 Dr. Udoma Street, Ikot Abasi, Akwa Ibom State, Nigeria.

UEBERROTH, Peter; American sports administrator; b. 2 Sept. 1937, Evanston, Ill.; s. of Victor Ueberroth and Laura Larson; m. Ginny Nicolaus; one s. three d.; ed. San Jose Univ.; Operations Man., Trans Int. Airlines 1959, later part owner; f. Transportation Consultants (later First Travel); Head, Los Angeles Olympic Games Organizing Cttee. 1984; Major League Baseball Commr. 1984–89; mem. Young Presidents' Org.; Scopus Award 1985. *Publication:* Made in America (autobiog.) 1986. *Leisure interests:* reading (especially historical non-fiction), golf.

UEKI, Dr. Shigeaki; Brazilian lawyer and politician; b. 15 Aug. 1935, São Paulo; s. of Torizi and Masako Ueki; m. Lúcia Akico Ueki; two s.; ed. Pontifícia Univ. Católica de São Paulo; with private cos. until 1967; Adviser to Minister of Trade and Industry 1967–68; later Commercial Dir. PETROBRAS, and mem. Council of Banco Nacional do Desenvolvimento Econômico; Minister of Mines and Energy 1974–79; Pres. PETROBRAS 1979–84. *Address:* c/o PETROBRAS, Avenida República do Chile, 65-24th Floor, Rio de Janeiro, Brazil.

UEMATSU, Kunihiko, D.ENG.; Japanese engineer; b. 1931, Kochi; m.; three c.; ed. Kyoto Univ. and M.I.T.; Head, Fuel and Materials Devt. for Fast Breeder Reactor Project, Japanese Power Reactor and Nuclear Fuel Devt. Corpn. (PNC) 1968, Dir. Fuel Devt. Div. 1982, Exec. Dir. 1983–88; Dir.-Gen. OECD Nuclear Energy Agency (NEA) 1988–. *Publications:* numerous papers on tech. and policy issues in field of nuclear energy. *Address:* Nuclear Energy Agency, Organisation for Economic Cooperation and Development, 2 rue André Pascal, 75775 Paris Cedex 16, France.

UENO, Taichi; Japanese business executive; b. 10 June 1924, Ooita Pref.; s. of Tsutomu and Ayako Ueno; m. Kyoko Hikida 1951; one s. two d.; ed. Kyushu Univ.; entered Industrial Bank of Japan Ltd. 1946, Dir. 1972, Man. Dir. 1975–78; Sr. Man. Dir. Kuraray Co., Ltd. 1978, Vice-Pres. 1981, Pres. 1982–, Chair. 1985–; Pres. Kyowa Gas Chemical Co. Ltd. 1983–; Pres. Japan Chemical Fibres Asscn. *Leisure interest:* golf. *Address:* Kuraray Co. Ltd., 1-12-39 Umeda, Kita-ku, Osaka, Japan.

UFFEN, Kenneth James, C.M.G., M.A.; British diplomatist (retd); b. 29 Sept. 1925, Chiswick; s. of late Percival J. Uffen, M.B.E. and late Gladys E. James; m. Nancy E. Winbolt 1954; one s. two d.; ed. Latymer Upper School and St. Catharine's Coll., Cambridge; served R.A.F.V.R. 1943–48; Third Sec. Foreign Office 1950–52, Paris 1952–55; Second Sec. Buenos Aires 1955–58; First Sec. Foreign Office 1958–61, Moscow 1961–63; seconded to H.M. Treasury 1963–65; F.C.O. 1965–68; Counsellor, Mexico City 1968–70; Econ. Counsellor, Washington 1970–72; Commercial Counsellor, Moscow 1972–76; Resident Assoc. Inst. of Strategic Studies 1976–77; Amb. to Colombia 1977–82; Amb. and U.K. Perm. Rep. to OECD, Paris 1982–85. *Leisure interests:* music, photography. *Address:* 40 Winchester Road, Walton-on-Thames, Surrey, KT12 2RH, England. *Telephone:* (0932) 225049.

UFFEN, Robert James, O.C., PH.D., D.SC., P.ENG., F.R.S.C., F.G.S.A.; Canadian geophysicist; b. 21 Sept. 1923, Toronto, Ont.; s. of James Frederick Uffen and Elsie May (Harris) Uffen; m. Mary Ruth Paterson 1949; one s. one d.; ed. Univ. of Toronto, Western Ontario; war service 1942–45; Lecturer, Univ. of Western Ont. 1951–53, Asst. Prof. of Physics and Geology 1953–57,

Assoc. Prof. of Geophysics 1957–58, Prof. and Head of Dept. of Geophysics 1958–61, Acting Head Dept. Physics 1960–61; Prin. Univ. Coll. of Arts and Science, London, Ont. 1961–65; Dean, Coll. of Science, Univ. of Western Ont. 1965–66; Vice-Chair. Defence Research Bd., Ottawa 1966–67, Chair. 1967–69; Chief Science Adviser to the Cabinet 1969–71; Dean, Faculty of Applied Science, Queen's Univ., Kingston, Ont. 1971–80, Prof. of Geophysics 1971–; Commr. Ont. Royal Comm. on Asbestos 1980–84, on Truck Safety 1981–83; Research Fellowship, Inst. of Geophysics, Univ. of Calif., Los Angeles 1953; mem. Council of Regents Colls. of Applied Arts and Tech. 1966–69, 1973–76, Nat. Research Council of Canada 1963–66, Science Council of Canada 1967–71; Dir. Canadian Patents and Devt. Ltd. 1965–70; mem. Club of Rome 1969–83; Chair. Canadian Eng. Manpower Council 1973–74; Dir. Centre for Resource Studies 1973–76, 1980–, Ont. Hydro 1974–, (Vice-Chair. 1975–79); Councillor, Asscn. of Professional Engineers of Ont. 1975–78; Chair. Ont. Exploration Tech. Devt. Fund 1981–84; mem. Fisheries Research Bd. of Canada 1974–78; Visiting Fellow, Univ. of Sussex 1976–77; Fellow American Asscn. for the Advancement of Science 1986; Hon. D.Sc. (Queen's Univ.), (Univ. of Western Ontario), (Royal Mil. Coll. of Canada) 1978, Hon. D.Sc. (McMaster Univ.) 1983; Centennial Medal, Canada 1967, A.P.E.O. Public Service Award 1985. *Publications:* papers on geophysics, operations research, evolution, science policy and radioactive waste management. *Leisure interests:* painting, skiing, boating, old bottles. *Address:* 185 Ontario Street, No. 1504, Kingston, Ont., K7L 2Y7, Canada. *Telephone:* (613) 546-4981.

UGAROV, Boris Sergeevich; Soviet artist; b. 6 Feb. 1922, Leningrad; m. Marianna Ugarova; one s. one d.; ed. I. E. Repin Inst. of Painting, Sculpture and Architecture, Leningrad; student, post-graduate, Asst. Prof. I. E. Repin Inst. 1945–71, Prof. 1977, Rector 1977–83; Pres. Acad. of Arts of U.S.S.R. 1983–; corresp. mem. Union of Artists of Austria; Order of Red Star, Order of the Great Patriotic War, State Prize of U.S.S.R. etc. *Major Works include:* portraits, landscapes and other paintings. *Publications:* articles in Soviet periodicals. *Address:* Ul. Kropotkinskaya 21, Moscow 119034, U.S.S.R.

UGHI, Uto; Italian violinist; b. 21 Jan. 1944, Busto Arsizio; s. of Bruno Ughi and Miana Mimma; ed. Conservatoria di Geneve, Acad. Santa Cecilia, Rome; began to study the violin 1948; first public performance, Teatro Lirico, Milan 1951; became pupil of George Enescu 1954; performed Mendelssohn's Violin Concerto 1954; first European tour 1959; organizer, "Omaggio a Venezia" festival. *Leisure interests:* walking, tennis, skiing, swimming, reading. *Address:* Cannareggio 4990/E, 30121 Venice, Italy. *Telephone:* 041 5226071.

UGLOW, Euan; British artist and lecturer; b. 10 March 1932, London; s. of Ernest R. Uglow and Elizabeth J. Williams; ed. Strand Grammar School for Boys, Camberwell School of Arts and Crafts and Slade School of Fine Art, Univ. Coll., London; Spanish State Scholarship, Spain 1952; Abbey Minor (Prix de Rome) Scholar 1953; Teacher St. Albans School of Art, Herts. 1958–62, Camberwell School 1959–77, Slade School of Fine Art, Univ. Coll. London 1961–; Fellow Univ. Coll. London; work exhibited at John Moores, Liverpool, Beaux Arts Gallery, Arts Council, Camden Arts Centre, Marlborough Fine Art, London, Univ. of Stirling, Whitechapel Art Gallery, Browse & Darby, London, Hayward Annual, Tate Gallery, Corner House, Manchester, British Council. *Address:* Slade School of Fine Art, University College London, Gower Street, London, WC1E 6BT, England. *Telephone:* 01-387 7050.

UGUETO, Luis; Venezuelan international finance official; b. 24 Aug. 1936, Caracas; s. of Angel Ugueto and Maria Cristina Arismendi; m. Maria Otánez 1959; three s. one d.; ed. Universidad Católica "Andrés Bello", Caracas and London School of Econs.; Resident Inspection Engineer, Ministry of Public Works 1958–62; Adviser Banco Central de Venezuela and Ministry of Finance, Caracas 1962–63; Exec. Aerovías Venezolanas, S.A., Caracas 1962–67; Exec. Dir. Banco de Comercio, Caracas 1966–69; mem. Bd. Public Admin. Comm., Caracas 1969–70; Dir.-Gen. Ministry of Finance 1969–70; Exec. Dir. IMF 1970–72; Sec. Caucus of Latin American and Philippines Govs. to the IMF and IBRD 1970–72; Minister Counsellor for Econ. Affairs, Venezuelan Embassy in Wash. D.C. 1971–74, Deputy Chief of Mission 1972–74; Exec. Dir. IBRD 1972–74, Deputy Cttee. of Twenty 1972–73; Pres. Banco Hipotecario de Aragua 1974–76; Adviser and mem. Bd. Banco de Venezuela 1974–82; Counsellor, Andean Zone, Soc. Générale 1975–; Chair. Devt. Cttee. Universidad Metropolitana 1977–; Gen. Man. Seguros Orinoco 1978–79; Minister of Finance 1979–83. *Address:* c/o Ministerio de Hacienda, Centro Simón Bolívar, Edif. Norte, 3er Piso, Caracas, Venezuela. *Telephone:* 4831770.

UJFALUSSY, József, PH.D.; Hungarian musicologist; b. 13 Feb. 1920, Debrecen; s. of Dr. Géza Ujfalussy and Margit Mándy; ed. Debrecen Univ., Music Academy, Budapest; Secondary school teacher 1943–46; education organizer, Budapest 1946–48; Section Head, then Chief Dept. Leader Ministry of Culture 1949–55; Prof. of Aesthetics of Music and Theory of Music, Budapest Acad. of Music 1955–, Rector 1980–88; Fellow Inst. of Musicology 1969, Dir. 1973–80; Fellow Hungarian Acad. of Sciences Bartók Archives 1961, Dir. 1973–80; Corresp. mem. Hungarian Acad. of Sciences 1973–85, ordinary mem. and Vice-Pres. 1985–; mem. Hungarian UNESCO Cttee.; mem. Bd. Fed. of Hungarian Musical Artists; Erkel Prize 1961, Kossuth Prize 1966, Herder Prize 1987. *Publications:* Bartók breviárium

1958, (2nd edn. (with Vera Lamperth) 1974), Debussy 1959, A valóság zenei képe (The Musical Image of Reality) 1962, Béla Bartók Vols. I-II 1965 (3rd edn. 1976), On Music, on Aesthetics 1981. *Address:* Csévi-utca 13b, H-1025 Budapest II, Hungary. *Telephone:* 762-159.

ULANOVA, Galina Sergeyevna; Soviet ballerina; b. 10 Jan. 1910; ed. Leningrad Choreographic School; debut in Kirov Theatre 1928, dancing the Chopin Suite (produced as Les Sylphides by Diaghilev Ballet); became star at the Kirov Theatre and then of the Bolshoi Ballet and danced many leading parts; has also made musical films including Etoiles du Ballet Russe shown at Int. Film Festival, Cannes 1954; now retd. from stage and teaches ballet at Bolshoi Choreographic School; People's Artist of the U.S.S.R.; four State Prizes, Lenin Prize 1957; Order of Lenin 1980. *Principal roles:* Odette-Odile (Swan Lake), Aurora (Sleeping Beauty), Masha (The Nutcracker), Giselle (Giselle), Maria (Bakhchisarai Fountain), Cinderella (Cinderella), Juliet (Romeo and Juliet), Parasha (The Copper Horseman), Tao Khoa (The Red Flower). *Publication:* Ballets soviétiques (The making of a ballerina). *Address:* State Academic Bolshoi Theatre, 1 Ploshchad Sverdlova, Moscow, U.S.S.R.

ULLENDORFF, Edward, M.A., D.PHIL., F.B.A.; British university professor; b. 25 Jan. 1920; s. of Frederic and Cilli Ullendorff; m. Dina Noack 1943; ed. Univs. of Jerusalem and Oxford; war service in Eritrea and Ethiopia 1941–46; Asst. Sec., Govt. of Palestine 1946–47; Research Officer, Oxford Univ. Inst. of Colonial Studies 1948–49; Lecturer, later Reader, in Semitic Languages, St. Andrews Univ. 1950–59; Prof. of Semitic Languages, Manchester Univ. 1959–64; Prof. of Ethiopian Studies, London Univ. 1964–79, of Semitic Languages 1979–82, Prof. Emer. 1982–; Head of Africa Dept., School of Oriental and African Studies (SOAS) 1972–77; Chair. Asscn. of British Orientalists 1963–64, Anglo-Ethiopian Soc. 1965–68, Editorial Bd. of Bulletin of SOAS 1968–78; Schweich Lecturer, British Acad. 1967; Pres. Soc. for Old Testament Study 1971; Vice-Pres. Royal Asiatic Soc. 1975–79, 1981–85; Fellow, British Acad. 1965–, Vice-Pres. 1980–82; Haile Sellassie Prize for Ethiopian Studies 1972; Hon. D.Litt. (St. Andrews Univ.). *Publications:* Exploration and Study of Abyssinia 1945, Catalogues of Ethiopic MSS in the Bodleian Library 1951, The Royal Library, Windsor Castle 1953, Cambridge Univ. Library 1961; The Semitic Languages of Ethiopia 1955, The Ethiopians 1960, 3rd edn. 1973, Comparative Grammar of the Semitic Languages 1964, An Amharic Chrestomathy 1965, Ethiopia and the Bible 1968, Solomon and Sheba 1974, translated and annotated Emperor Haile Sellassie's autobiography 1976, Studies in Semitic Languages and Civilizations 1977, The Ethiopic Enoch (with M. A. Knibb, 2 vols.) 1978, The Amharic Letters of Emperor Theodore to Queen Victoria 1979, The Bawdy Bible, The Hebrew Letters of Prester John 1982, A Tigrinya Chrestomathy 1985, Studia Aethiopica et Semitica 1987, The Two Zions 1988, Ethiopia and the Bible 1988 and others; articles and reviews in journals of learned socs. *Leisure interests:* music, motoring in Scotland. *Address:* 4 Bladon Close, Oxford, OX2 8AD, England.

ULLMANN, Liv Johanne; Norwegian actress; b. 16 Dec. 1938, Tokyo, Japan; d. of late Viggo Ullmann and of Janna (Lund) Ullmann; m. 1st Dr. Gappe Stang 1960 (dissolved 1965), one d.; m. 2nd Donald Saunders 1985; worked in repertory company, Stavanger 1956–59; has appeared at Nat. Theatre and Norwegian State Theatre, Oslo; work for UNICEF as Goodwill Amb. 1980–; Best Actress of the Year, Nat. Soc. of Critics in America 1969, 1970, 1974; N.Y. Film Critics Award 1973, 1974; Hollywood Foreign Press Asscn.'s Golden Globe 1973; Best Actress of the Year, Swedish T.V. 1973, 1974; Donatello Award (Italy) 1975; Bambi Award (Fed. Repub. of Germany) 1975; nominated for Tony Award as Best Stage Actress, debut on Broadway in The Doll's House 1975; Los Angeles Film Critics' Award (Face to Face) 1976; New York Film Critics' Award (Face to Face) 1977; Nat. Bd. of Review of Motion Pictures Award (Face to Face) 1977; Peer Gynt Award (Norway), Eleanor Roosevelt Award 1982, Roosevelt Freedom Medal 1984, Dag Hammarskjold Award 1986. *Films include:* Pan 1965, Persona 1966, The Hour of the Wolf 1968, Shame 1968, The Passion of Anna 1969, The Night Visitor 1971, The Emigrants 1972, Cries and Whispers 1972, Pope Joan 1972, Lost Horizon 1973, 40 Carats 1973, The New Land 1973, Zandy's Bride 1973, Scenes from a Marriage 1974, The Abdication 1974, Face to Face 1975, The Serpent's Egg 1978, Sonate d'automne 1978, Richard's Things 1980, The Wild Duck 1983, Love Streams 1983, Let's Hope It's a Girl 1985, Baby Boy 1984, Dangerous Moves 1985, Gaby Brimmer 1986, Moscow Adieu 1986, Time of Indifference 1987, La Amiga 1987. *Plays include:* Brand 1973, The Doll's House 1975, Anna Christie 1977, I Remember Mama 1979, Ghosts 1982, Old Times 1985, The Six Faces of Women (TV), Mother Courage. *Publication:* Changing (autobiog.) 1976, Choices (autobiog.) 1984. *Leisure interest:* reading. *Address:* c/o London Management, 235 Regent Street, London, W.1, England.

ULLOA ELÍAS, Dr. Manuel, LL.B; Peruvian politician; b. 12 Nov. 1922, Lima; ed. Universidad Nacional de San Marcos; qualified lawyer 1947–; various posts in New York dealing with Latin American int. and industrial interests 1962–65; f. Peruvian nat. publishing co. which published Expreso and Extra 1965; Minister of Finance 1968; in exile in Spain 1968–77; f. Agencia de Noticias Latín 1969; mem. Exec. Cttee., Acción Popular, and in charge of govt. planning 1977–80; Prime Minister of Peru and Minister of Economy and Finance 1980–82; Pres. of Senate 1985. *Address:* El Senado, Lima, Peru.

ULLSTEN, Ola; Swedish politician and diplomatist; b. 23 June 1931, Umeå; s. of C. A. and Ştina Ullsten; graduated in social sciences 1956; Sec. Parl. Group Liberal Party 1957–61; journalist Dagens Nyheter 1962–64; mem. Riksdag (Parl.) 1965–; Chair. Liberal Party Stockholm County 1972–76; Minister of Int. Devt. Co-operation 1976–78; Deputy Prime Minister March-Oct. 1978, Prime Minister 1978–79; Minister for Foreign Affairs 1979–82, Deputy Prime Minister 1980–82; Chair. Liberal Party 1978–83; Amb. to Canada 1983–; mem. Interaction Council of Former Heads of Govt. *Address:* Swedish Embassy, 441 MacLaren Street, 4th Floor, Ottawa, Ont. K1N 8J6, Canada. *Telephone:* (613) 236-8553.

ULRICHSEN, Wilhelm, M.SC.; Danish diplomatist; b. 10 Feb. 1924, Copenhagen; s. of Rudolph and Carla Ulrichsen; m. Ellen Margrethe Knudsen 1948; one s. two d.; ed. Univ. of Copenhagen; Sec. Ministry of Foreign Affairs, Copenhagen 1948–54; Danish Embassy, Madrid 1954–58; Head of Section, Ministry of Foreign Affairs 1958–60; Counsellor, Chargé d'Affaires, Danish Embassy, Caracas, Venezuela 1960–61; Consul and Commercial Counsellor, Danish Consulate Gen., New York 1961–64; Head of Div., Dept. for Econ.-Political Relations, Ministry of Foreign Affairs 1964–69; Head of Danish Del. to UN Conf. on Trade and Devt., New Delhi, India 1968; Deputy Under-Sec. Danish Int. Devt. Agency (DANIDA) 1969–72, Under-Sec. 1972–77; Perm. Rep. to UN, New York 1977–84; Amb. to Spain 1984–; Gov. Asian Devt. Bank 1973–77, African Devt. Fund 1973–77, Inter-American Devt. Bank 1976–77; Order of the Icelandic Falcon, Order of Isabel la Católica (Spain). *Address:* c/o Ministry of Foreign Affairs, Asiatisk Plads 2, 1448 Copenhagen K, Denmark.

ULUSU, Adm. Bülent; Turkish naval officer and politician; b. 1923, Istanbul; s. of M. Salih Ulusu and Seniye Ulusu; m. Mizat Erensoy 1951; one d.; ed. Naval Acad.; various command posts in navy; rank of Rear-Adm. 1967, Vice-Adm. 1970, Adm. 1974; fmr. Commdr. of War Fleet; Commdr. of Turkish Naval Forces until 1980; fmr. Under-Sec., Ministry of Defence; Prime Minister of Turkey 1980–83; M.P. 1983–.

ULVESETH, Ingvald Johan; Norwegian politician; b. 25 Aug. 1924, Fjell, Hordaland; ed. Norwegian Inst. of Tech.; Consultant Construction Engineer, Bergen 1949–52; Municipal Engineer, Fjell 1952–61; mem. Fjell Municipal Council and Exec. Cttee. 1956–67, Mayor 1958–65; with Brodrene Ulveseth, Bergen 1961–65; Under-Sec. of State, Ministry of Local Govt. and Labour 1964–65; mem. Storting (Parl.) 1965–73; Chair. Man. Bd. Bergens Arbeiderblad 1968–; Deputy Chair. Standing Cttee. on Industry 1969–73; mem. Bd. Norsk Hydro 1970–73; Gov. Sogn and Fjordane 1971–73; Minister of Industry 1973–76; Dir. and fmr. Dir. of numerous cos.; Labour.

ULYANOV, Mikhail Aleksandrovich; Soviet actor and director; b. 20 Nov. 1927, Bergamak; s. of Aleksandr Andreevich Ulyanov and Elizaveta Mikhailovna Ulyanova; m. Alla Petrovna Parfanyak 1959; one d.; ed. Shchukin Theatre School; worked with Vakhtangov Theatre 1950–, Chief Theatre Dir. 1987–; mem. CPSU 1951–; with Soviet TV; début as dir. 1973; Chair. Union of Theatre Workers 1986–; elected to Congress of People's Deputies of the U.S.S.R. 1989; U.S.S.R. People's Artist 1969, R.S.F.S.R. State Prize 1975 for work in theatre. *Roles in films include:* They Were The First 1956, The Volunteers 1958, A Simple Story 1960, The Battle on the Way 1961, The Chairman 1964 (Lenin Prize 1966), Brothers Karamazov 1969, Escape 1971, Egor Bulychev and Co. 1973, Liberation 1970–72, The Blockade 1975–78, Soldiers of Freedom 1977, Unless the Enemy Surrenders 1983, No Witnesses 1983, Tevie the Milkman 1985, Choice 1987. *Films directed include:* The Very Last Day 1973, Call Me To the Bright Distant Horizon 1978, The Last Escape 1981, Private Life 1982 (Venice Film Festival Prize 1982, U.S.S.R. State Prize 1983). *Leisure interest:* reading. *Address:* c/o Gosudarstvennyi Teatr im. Vakhtangova, Moscow; 29 Bolshaya Bronnaya, Apt. 56, 103104 Moscow, U.S.S.R.

UMBA DI LUTETE, L. EN D.; Zairian diplomatist and former government official; b. (as Jean-Théodore Umba-di-Lutete) 30 June 1939, Kangu; s. of late Umba Julien and Mdbuilu Matsumba; m. Diomi Kiese 1967; three s. three d.; ed. Univ. of Lovanium, Univ. Libre de Bruxelles, Belgium; training with U.S. Agency for Int. Devt. and with Belgian Parl. and Foreign Ministry; taught at Univ. of Lovanium; at Nat. Univ. of Zaire; Minister at the Presidency 1969–70, of Energy 1970–71, of Mining 1971–74, for Foreign Affairs 1974–75, for Politics 1975–76, for State Affairs, Foreign Affairs and Int. Co-operation 1977–79, for Nat. Guidance, Culture and the Arts 1979–80; mem. Political Bureau of Mouvement populaire de la révolution (MPR), also MPR Perm. Cttee.; Perm. Rep. to UN 1976–77, 1982–84; State Commr. for Foreign and Int. Affairs 1984–85; fmr. leader of dels. to UN Gen. Ass. and Security Council, to OAU, OCAM, UNCTAD. *Address:* c/o Ministry of Foreign Affairs, Kinshasa, Zaire.

UMBA KYAMITALA, M.SC.; Zairian mining executive; b. 20 Feb. 1937, Elisabethville (now Lubumbashi); s. of Ngoie Mbuluku and Mwamba Kima; m. Ngoie Ya Kachina 1961; two s. one d.; ed. Nat. Univ. of Zaire and U.S.A.; employed in mine at Kipushi, La Générale des Carrières et Mines du Zaïre (Gécamines) 1967, Planning and Admin. of Mines and Quarries 1969, Dir. of Mines and Quarries 1972, Gen. Man. 1973, Pres. Gécamines Holdings 1978–; State Commr. for Mines and Energy 1984–85, for Foreign Trade 1985–86; Pres. Nat. Assen. of Zairian Enterprises 1977–80; mem. American Assen. of Mining Engineers and Metallurgists; major projects: sub-level excavation in Northwest Massif 1967; application of machinery

to opencast mining. *Leisure interest:* swimming. *Address:* c/o Gécamines, B.P. 450, Lubumbashi, Zaire. *Telephone:* 91-105.

UMEDA, Zenji; Japanese shipbuilder; b. 13 Sept. 1913, Wakayama; s. of Zenichi Umeda; m. Fusako Hirota 1935; two s. two d.; ed. Kyoto Univ.; joined Kawasaki Dockyard Co. Ltd. (now Kawasaki Heavy Industries) 1939, Dir. 1964, Man. Dir. 1969, Sr. Man. Dir. 1975, Exec. Vice-Pres. and Dir. 1976, Pres. and Dir. 1977–81, Chair. 1981–87; Vice-Pres. Shipbuilders' Assen. of Japan 1978; Pres. Japan Ship Exporters' Assen. 1979; Blue Ribbon Medal 1971; Award of Minister of Int. Trade and Industry 1974. *Leisure interests:* photography, sports. *Address:* 3-25-8 Kami Meguro, Meguro-ku, Tokyo, Japan.

UMRI, Gen. Hassan; Yemen politician; took part in revolution against Imamate 1962; Minister of Transport Sept.-Oct. 1962, of Communications 1962–63; mem. Council of Revolutionary Command 1962–63; Vice-Pres. of Yemen 1963–66; mem. Political Bureau 1963–66; Prime Minister Jan.-April 1965, 1965–66, 1967–68; Mil. Gov.-Gen. of Yemen 1968–69; also C.-in-C. of Army; Prime Minister Aug.-Sept. 1971; in exile in Lebanon until Jan. 1975; returned to Yemen Arab Repub. Jan. 1975.

UNDERWOOD, Cecil H., LL.D.; American politician and businessman; b. 5 Nov. 1922; ed. Salem Coll., West Virginia Univ.; U.S. Army Reserve Corps 1942–43; high-school teacher 1943–46; mem. staff Marietta Coll. 1946–50; Vice-Pres. Salem Coll. 1950–56; mem. West Virginia House of Delegates 1944–56 and Minority Floor Leader 1949–54; Gov. of West Virginia 1957–61; Temporary Chair. Republican Nat. Convention 1960; Vice-Pres. Island Creek Coal Co. 1961–64; Dir. Civic Affairs, Northeastern Region, Monsanto Co. 1965–66; Vice-Pres. Govt. and Civic Affairs, Monsanto Co., Washington, D.C. 1967; Pres. Fanswood Inc., Huntington 1968–75; Pres. Cecil H. Underwood Assens. 1965–80; field underwriter New York Life Insurance Co. 1976–78; Pres. Bethany Coll. 1972–75, Princess Coals Inc. 1978–81, Chair. Bd. 1981–83; Chair. Bd. Morgantown Industrial Park Inc. 1983–; Pres. Software Valley Corpn. 1985–; Bd. of Dirs. Huntington Fed. Savings and Loan Assen. 1960–, American Cancer Soc. 1973; mem. Governing Council, Nat. Municipal League 1966–; Chair. Bd. Salem Coll.; nine hon. degrees. *Address:* 609 13th Avenue, Huntington, West Va. 25701, U.S.A. (Home).

UNGER, Michael Ronald; British newspaper editor and executive; b. 8 Dec. 1943, Surrey; s. of Ronald Unger and Joan Stanbridge; m. Eunice Dickens 1966; one s. one d. (deceased); ed. Wirral Grammar School, Liverpool Polytechnic, trainee journalist, Stockport 1963–65; Production Ed., Reading Evening Post 1965–67; News Ed., Perth, Australia 1967–71; Deputy Ed. Daily Post, Liverpool 1971–79, Ed. 1979–82; Ed. Liverpool Echo 1982–83; Ed. Manchester Evening News 1983–; Dir. Guardian & Manchester Evening News PLC 1983–; Trustee Scott Trust 1986–; various newspaper awards including Newspaper Design 1980, 1981 and 1982, Ed. of the Year 1988. *Publication:* The Memoirs of Bridget Hitler 1979. *Leisure interests:* books, theatre. *Address:* Manchester Evening News, 164 Deansgate, Manchester, M60 2RD, (Office); The Moorings, Lees Lane, Little Neston, South Wirral, Cheshire, England (Home).

UNGERER, Werner, DR. RER. POL.; German diplomatist; b. 22 April 1927, Stuttgart; s. of Max Ungerer and Elisabeth (Mezger) Ungerer; m. Irmgard Drenckhahn 1959; one s. two d.; ed. Dillman Gymnasium, Stuttgart, Technical Univ. Stuttgart, Univ. of Tübingen and Coll. of Europe, Bruges; Attaché, diplomatic service 1952–54; Vice-Consul, Boston 1954–56; Consul, Bombay 1956–58; Head of Div. Euratom Comm. Brussels 1958–64; Ministry of Foreign Affairs 1964–70; Resident Lecturer on Diplomacy and European Integration, Univ. of Bonn 1965–66; rep. to int. orgs. in Vienna 1970–75; Consul-Gen. New York 1975–79; Ministry of Foreign Affairs 1979–85; Dir.-Gen. Dept. of Econ. Affairs 1984–85; Perm. Rep. to EEC Brussels 1985–; Order of Merit of Fed. Repub. of Germany. *Publications:* numerous articles on European integration, energy problems and int. orgs. in reviews. *Leisure interests:* pianist and composer. *Address:* 64 rue Royale, B-1000 Brussels, Belgium. *Telephone:* 513.45.00.

UNGERS, Oswald Mathias, DIPL.ENG.; German architect and university professor; b. 12 July 1926, Kaisersesch; s. of Anton and Maria (née Mitchels) Ungers; m. Liselotte Gabler 1956; one s. two d.; ed. Technical Univ., Karlsruhe; architectural practice, Cologne 1950–62, Berlin 1962–69, Ithaca, N.Y. 1969–; Prof. of Architecture, Technische Universität, Berlin 1963–73, Dean, Faculty of Architecture 1965–67; Prof. of Architecture, Cornell Univ. 1968–, Chair. of Dept. 1968–74; Visiting Prof., Harvard Univ. 1972, 1977, Univ. of Calif. (Los Angeles) 1973. *Publications:* Optimization Models for Housing, New York State Pattern Development, Settlements of the 20th Century, The Urban Block, The Urban Villa, The Urban Garden, O. M. Ungers 1951–84: Bauten und Projekte. *Address:* Belvederestrasse 60, 5000 Cologne 41, Federal Republic of Germany. *Telephone:* 0221-49 23 43.

UNO, Osamu, B.L.; Japanese business executive; b. 29 May 1917, Kyoto; s. of Kenichiro and Tami Uno; m. Yoshie Uno 1945; one s. two d.; ed. Tokyo Univ.; Dir. Toyobo Co. Ltd. 1971, Man. Dir. 1974–76, Sr. Man. Dir. 1976–77, Deputy Pres. 1977–78, Pres. 1978–83, Chair. 1983–; Vice-Pres. Japan Chemical Fibres Assen. 1980–81, Pres. 1981–82; Vice-Pres. Japanese Spinners' Assen. 1982–83, Pres. 1983–84; Vice-Chair. Kansai Econs. Fed. 1983–87, Chair. 1987–; Blue Ribbon Medal 1982. *Leisure interest:* golf. *Address:* 2-8 Dojima Hama 2-chome Kita-ku, Osaka 530 (Office); 1-46 Showa-cho, Hamadera Sakai, Osaka 592, Japan (Home). *Telephone:* (06) 348-3252 (Office).

UNO, Sosuke; Japanese politician; b. 27 Aug. 1922, Shiga Pref.; m.; two d.; ed. Kobe Univ. of Commerce; elected eight times to House of Reps.; Parl. Vice-Minister of Int. Trade and Industry 1966-69; Deputy Sec.-Gen. of Liberal Democratic Party (LDP); Minister of State, Dir.-Gen. of Defence Agency Nov.-Dec. 1974; Chair. Diet Policy Cttee. of LDP 1974-76, Public Relations Cttee. LDP 1978-79; assoc. of Yasuhiro Nakasone (q.v.); fmr. Minister of State, Dir.-Gen. of Science and Tech. Agency 1976, Chair. Atomic Energy Comm. 1976-77; Minister of State, Dir.-Gen. of Admin. Man. Agency 1979-80; Minister of Int. Trade and Industry 1983, for Foreign Affairs 1987-; Chair. LDP Special Cttee. for the Introduction of Pvt. Sector Vitality into Public Works 1984. *Publications:* Dome Tokyo (Home to Tokyo), 2 vols. haiku poetry. *Leisure interests:* painting, poetry, music, kendo. *Address:* House of Representatives, Tokyo (Office); 304 High Trio Akasaka Hatchome, 8-7-18 Akasaka, Minato-ku, Tokyo 107, Japan (Home).

UNSELD, Siegfried, DR.PHIL.; German editor and publisher; b. 28 Sept. 1924, Ulm; s. of Ludwig and Lina (née Kögel) Unseld; m. Hildegard Schmid 1951; one s.; ed. Univ. of Tübingen; joined Suhrkamp Verlag 1952, Pres. 1959-; Pres. Insel Verlag 1963-; Pres. Nomos Verlag 1963-; Guest Prof., Univ. of Texas, Austin 1976; Regents-Lecturer, Univ. of Southern Calif., San Diego-La Jolla 1978; Hermann Hesse Medal 1967; Heinrich Merck Award 1975; Goethe Medal (City of Frankfurt) 1977; Wilhelm Leuschner Medal of Hessen 1981; Ricarda Huch Prize 1984; Grosses Bundesverdienst-kreuz; Order of Merit of Poland; Dr.h.c. (Washington Univ., St. Louis, Mo., Goethe Univ., Frankfurt). *Publications:* Encounters with Hermann Hesse 1974, Hermann Hesse: A History of His Works 1973, Peter Suhrkamp—A Biography 1975, Goethe's 'The Diary' and Rilke's 'Seven Poems' 1978, The Author and his Publisher 1978; ed. of numerous works. *Address:* Suhrkamp Verlag -Insel Verlag, Suhrkamp Haus, Lindenstrasse 29, 6000 Frankfurt 1, Federal Republic of Germany. *Telephone:* 756010.

UNSÖLD, Albrecht Otto Johannes, DR.PHIL.; German physicist; b. 20 April 1905, Bolheim, Württemberg; s. of Johannes Unsöld and Clara Müller; m. Dr. Liselotte Kühnert 1934; three s. one d.; ed. Univs. of Tübingen and Munich; Asst. Inst. of Theoretical Physics, Univ. of Munich 1927; Fellow, Int. Educ. Bd. 1928; Lecturer, Univ. of Munich 1929, Univ. of Hamburg 1930; Prof. of Theoretical Physics, Dir. Inst. of Theoretical Physics and Observatory, Univ. of Kiel 1932-73; Corresp. mem. Bavarian Acad. of Sciences, Göttingen Acad. of Sciences; Assoc. Royal Astronomical Soc., London; Hon. mem. Royal Astronomical Soc. of Canada; Foreign mem. Provinciaal Utrechts Genootschap van Kunsten en Wetenschappen, Utrecht 1961; mem. Int. Acad. of Astronautics, Paris 1961, Deutsche Akademie der Naturforscher Leopoldina, Halle 1962, Kungliga Fysiograf-iska Sällskapet i Lund 1965; Fellow, A.A.A.S. 1968; Hon. Senator (Univ. of Kiel) 1983; Dr.Rer.Nat. h.c. (Utrecht State Univ.) 1961, (Univ. of Munich) 1972; (Univ. Medal Liège) 1969; Hon. D.Sc. (Edinburgh) 1970; Copernicus Prize 1943, Catherine Wolfe Bruce Gold Medal Astronomical Soc. of the Pacific 1956; Gold Medal of Royal Astronomical Soc. 1957, Cothenius Gold Medal, Deutsche Akad. der Naturforscher Leopoldina 1973. *Publications:* Physik der Sternatmosphären 1938, Der neue Kosmos 1967, (with B. Baschek), Sterne und Menschen (essays and lectures) 1972, Evolution kosmischer, biologischer und geistiger Strukturen 1981. *Leisure interests:* painting, music. *Address:* Sternwartenweg 17, D-2300 Kiel, Federal Republic of Germany. *Telephone:* 0431-84205.

UNSWORTH, Barrie John; Australian politician; b. 16 April 1934, Dubbo, N.S.W.; m. Pauline Unsworth 1955; three s. (one deceased) one d.; organizer Electrical Trades Union 1961-67; organizer Labor Council of N.S.W. 1967-75, Asst. Sec. 1975-79, Sec. 1979-84; Minister for Transport, N.S.W. 1984-86, for Health 1986; Premier of N.S.W., Minister for State Devt., Minister for Ethnic Affairs 1986-; M.P. for Rockdale 1986-; mem. Public Transport Comm. of N.S.W. 1972-75, Pipeline Authority 1973-78. *Address:* 8th Floor, Premier's Wing, State Office Block, Sydney, N.S.W. 2000, Australia. *Telephone:* (02) 228-5239.

UNTERMANN, Jürgen, DR.PHIL.; German professor of linguistics; b. 24 Oct. 1928, Rheinfelden; ed. Univs. of Frankfurt and Tübingen; Asst. Prof. Univ. of Tübingen 1953-58, Pvt. Tutor 1962-65; project on Pre-Roman inscriptions in the Iberic Peninsula 1958-62; Full Prof. Comparative Linguistics, Univ. of Cologne 1965-, Dean, Faculty of Letters 1971-72. *Publications:* Die Venetischen Personennamen 1961, Monumenta Lingu-arum Hispanicarum, Vol. I 1975, Vol. II 1980, vol. III (forthcoming), Einführung in die Sprache Homers 1987. *Address:* Institut für Sprachwis-senschaft, Universität Köln, 5000, Cologne 41 (Office); Pfalzgrafenstrasse 11, D-5024 Pulheim-2, Federal Republic of Germany (Home). *Telephone:* 0221-4702282 (Office); 02234-82274 (Home).

UNWIN, Peter William, C.M.G., M.A.; British diplomatist; b. 20 May 1932, Middlesbrough; s. of the late Arnold Unwin and Norah Unwin; m. Monica Steven 1955; two s. two d.; ed. Ampleforth Coll., York, Christ Church, Oxford; joined H.M. Foreign Service 1956, British Legation, Budapest 1958, British Embassy, Tokyo 1961, FCO 1963, British Information Ser-vices, New York, 1967, FCO 1970, British Embassy, Bonn 1973, Head of Personnel Policy Dept., FCO 1976, Harvard Univ., U.S.A. 1979, Minister

(Econ.), British Embassy, Bonn 1980, Amb. to Hungary 1983, to Denmark 1986-88; Deputy Sec.-Gen. of Econ. Affairs for the Commonwealth 1989-. *Address:* Commonwealth Secretariat, Marlborough House, Pall Mall, London, SW1; 2 Coleherne Road, London, S.W.10, England. *Telephone:* 01-373 5250 (London).

UPADHYAY, Shailendra Kumar; Nepalese diplomatist; b. 13 Sept. 1929, India; s. of Gopal Prasad Upadhyay and Uma Devi Upadhyay; m. 1st Sharmistha Upadhyay, 2nd Beena Sharma; three s. one d.; ed. Benares Hindu Univ.; Founder mem. Communist Party of Nepal 1950, mem. Cen. Cttee. and Political Bureau 1950-56; Founder Progressive Communist Party of Nepal 1958; Asst. Minister for Forests, Food and Agric. 1962-64; Minister in charge of Panchayat 1965, of Land Reform 1986-88, of Foreign Affairs July 1986-; mem. Nat. Panchayat 1963-71; Vice-Chair. Nat. Plan-ning Comm. 1969; Minister for Home and Panchayat and Minister for Land Reforms and Information 1970-71; Perm. Rep. to UN 1972-78; Amb. to Argentina, Chile, Peru and Brazil 1977-78; Exec. Chair. Inst. of Third World Econ. Studies, Nepal 1982-; decorated with Prabal Gorkha Dakshin Bahu (Order of the Right Hand of Gurkha) first class, Trishakti Patt (Second Class) 1988. *Leisure interests:* reading, riding, trekking, painting, golf. *Address:* Ministry of Foreign Affairs, Kathmandu; 5/108 Jawala Khel, Lalitpur, Kathmandu, Nepal (Home). *Telephone:* 21587 (Home).

UPDIKE, John Hoyer, A.B.; American writer; b. 18 March 1932, Shilling-ton, Penn.; s. of Wesley R. and Linda Grace Hoyer Updike; m. 1st Mary Pennington 1953; m. 2nd Martha Ruggles 1977; two s. two d.; ed. Shillington High School, Pennsylvania, and Harvard Coll.; Reporter on the magazine New Yorker 1955-57; mem. Nat. Inst. of Arts and Letters, American Acad. of Arts and Sciences; Rosenthal Award, Nat. Inst. of Arts and Letters 1960; O'Henry Story Award 1967, U.S. Nat. Book Critics Circle Award 1982, Pulitzer Prize 1982. *Publications:* The Carpentered Hen (poems) 1958, The Poorhouse Fair (novel) 1959, The Same Door (short stories) 1959, Rabbit, Run (novel) 1960, Pigeon Feathers and Other Stories 1962, The Centaur (novel) 1963, Telephone Poles and Other Poems 1963, Assorted Prose 1965, Of the Farm (novel) 1965, The Music School (short stories) 1966, Couples (novel), Midpoint and other poems 1969, Bech: A Book 1970, Rabbit Redux (novel) 1972, Museums and Women and Other Stories 1972, Buchanan Dying (play) 1974, A Month of Sundays (novel) 1975, Picked-up Pieces 1976, Marry Me (novel) 1976, The Coup (novel) 1978, Tossing and Turning (poems) 1978, Problems (short stories) 1979, Your Lover Just Called 1980, Rabbit is Rich (novel) 1981, Bech is Back 1982, Hugging the Shore (essays and criticism) 1984, The Witches of Eastwick (novel) 1984, Facing Nature 1984, The Year's Best American Short Stories (ed.) 1985, Roger's Version (novel) 1986, Trust Me (short stories) 1987, S (novel) 1988, The Broken Bubble 1989, Self-Consciousness (autobiog.) 1989. *Leisure interest:* golf. *Address:* Beverly Farms, Mass. 01915, U.S.A.

UPTON, Arthur Canfield, M.D.; American professor of environmental medicine; b. 27 Feb. 1923, Ann Arbor, Mich.; s. of Herbert Hawkes Upton and Ellen Canfield Upton; m. Elizabeth Bache Perry 1946; one s. two d.; ed. Phillips Acad., Andover, Univ. of Michigan, Ann Arbor; Chief, Pathology-Physiology Section, Oak Ridge Nat. Lab. 1954-69; Prof. of Pathology, State Univ. of New York at Stony Brook 1969-77, Chair. Dept. of Patho-logy 1969-70, Dean, School of Basic Health Sciences 1970-75; Dir. Nat. Cancer Inst., Bethesda, Md. 1977-79; Prof. and Chair. Dept. of Environ-mental Medicine and Dir. Inst. of Environmental Medicine, New York Univ. School of Medicine, New York 1980-; mem. Editorial Bd. Cancer, Risk Analysis, Environmental Research, Experimental Gerontology, Ger-ontology and Geriatrics Educ., Health and Environmental Digest; Corresp. mem. Int. Comm. for Protection Against Environmental Mutagens and Carcinogens; Chair. Biology Div. Advisory Cttee., Oak Ridge Nat. Lab. 1984-; mem. Inst. of Medicine of N.A.S., A.A.A.S., American Asscn. for Cancer Research (fmr. Pres.), American Asscn. of Pathologists and Bacteriologists, American Coll. of Toxicology, American Soc. for Experi-mental Pathology (fmr. Pres.), Int. Acad. of Pathology, Int. Asscn. for Radiation Research (Pres. 1983-), Radiation Research Soc. (fmr. Pres.) and many other professional and scientific orgs.; E. O. Lawrence Award 1965, Comfort Crookshank Award for Cancer Research 1978, Claude M. Fuess Award 1980, Sarah L. Poilley Award 1983, CHUMS Physician of the Year Award 1985, Basic Cell Research in Cytology Lectureship Award 1985. *Leisure interests:* theatre and museums. *Address:* Institute of Environmen-tal Medicine, New York University Medical Center, 550 First Avenue, New York, N.Y. 10016; 3 Washington Square Village, New York, N.Y. 10012, U.S.A. (Home). *Telephone:* (212) 340-5280 (Office); (212) 254-1246 (Home).

UQUAILI, Nabi Baksh Mohammed Sidiq, F.C.A.; Pakistani chartered accountant and banker; b. 11 Aug. 1913, Karachi; m. 1947; one s. one d.; over 35 years' experience in commercial banking, central banking, indus-trial and investment banking; Minister of Finance of Pakistan 1966-69; Chair. Bd. of Dirs. of several industrial and financial enterprises in Pakistan (1977-80); Chair. and mem. several Fed. Govt. Comms. and Cttees.; awards from Pakistan and Fed. Repub. of Germany. *Leisure interests:* reading, gardening. *Address:* 22-F Dawood Colony, Stadium Road, Karachi-5, Pakistan. *Telephone:* 516001 (Office); 411013 (Home).

URABE, Shizutaro; Japanese architect; b. 31 March 1909, Kurashiki, Okayama; m.; three s.; ed. Kyoto Univ.; Engineer Kurashiki Rayon Co. Ltd. 1934-62; Lecturer (part-time) in Architecture, Osaka Univ. Technical Course 1954-55; Lecturer (part-time) in Architecture, Kyoto Univ. Technical Course 1962-69; Pres. K.K., S. Urabe & Assoc. Architects 1962-81, Chair. 1981-85, Corp. Adviser 1985-87; Corp. Adviser Urabesekkei 1987-; Urabesekkei 1987-; Prize of Mainichi Shuppan Bunka Sho (publication) 1961, Osaka Prefecture Architectural Contest Prize 1962, Annual of Architecture Prize 1963, Architectural Inst. of Japan Prize 1964, Mainichi Art Award 1972, Architectural Asscn. Prize 1974; AIJ Grand Prize 1986; Osaka Prefecture Order of Merit 1965. *Buildings include:* Ohara Museum (Annex) 1961, Suita Service Area 1963 and other offices of Japan Road Corpn. 1965, Kurashiki Int. Hotel 1963, Aizenbashi Hospital and Nursery School etc. 1965, Asahi Broadcasting Co. Ltd. (consultant) 1966, Tokyo Zokei Univ. 1966, Tokyo Women's Christian Coll., Research Inst. 1967, Nishitetsu Grand Hotel 1969, Kurashiki Ivy Square 1974, Jiro Osaragi Memorial Hall 1978, Kurashiki Station Forecourt 1980, Kurashiki City Hall 1980, Kurashiki Cen. Hosp. 1983, Kanagawa Prefectural Archives of Modern Literature 1984. *Address:* Urabesekkei, Shinhankyu Building, 12-39 Umeda 1-chome, Kita-ku, Osaka (Office); Annex Building, 5-10 Kojimachi 4-chome, Chiyoda-ku, Tokyo (Office); 7-8, Kotoen, 1-chome, Nishinomiya Hyogo, Japan (Home).

URBACH, Ephraim Elimelech, PH.D.; Israeli professor of theology; b. 25 May 1912, Wloclawek, Poland; s. of Israel Joseph and Esther née Szpigel; m. Hanna née Pinczower 1944; two s. three d.; ed. Jewish Theological Seminary, Breslau, Univs. of Breslau and Rome; ordained as rabbi 1934; Sr. Lecturer, Jewish Theological Seminary Breslau 1938; emigrated to Israel 1938; Teacher, Rehavia Gymnasium, Jerusalem 1938-41; served in British Army 1941-45; Dir. Ma'aleh Sec. School, Jerusalem 1945-50; Supervisor Sec. Schools, Ministry of Educ. 1950-53; Lecturer in Talmud and Midrash, Hebrew Univ. of Jerusalem 1953-58, Prof. 1958-80, Prof. Emer. 1980-; Pres. Israel Acad. of Sciences and Humanities 1980-86; mem. several learned socs.; Hon. Ph.D. (Weizman Inst. of Science) 1982, (Ben-Gurion Univ.) 1984, (Tel-Aviv Univ.) 1985, (Jewish Theological Seminary, New York) 1986, and other awards and prizes. *Publications:* The Tossaphists: Their History, Writings and Methods 1955, The Sages: Concepts and Beliefs 1979, The Halakha: The Sources and Development 1984. *Address:* 22 Hativonim Street, Jerusalem, Israel.

URBAIN, Robert; Belgian politician; b. 24 Nov. 1930, Hornu; ed. Ecole Normale, Mons; fmr. teacher; Deputy for Mons 1971-; Sec. of State for Planning and Housing 1973, for Econ. Affairs (French region) 1977-79; Minister of Posts and Telephones 1979-80, of Foreign Trade 1980-81, of Health and Educ. (French sector) 1981-85, of Social Affairs and Health Feb.-May 1988, of Foreign Trade May 1988-. *Address:* Ministry of Foreign Trade, 65 rue de la Loi, 1040 Brussels, Belgium. *Telephone:* (02) 237-67-11.

URBAN, Bohumil, C.SC.; Czechoslovak politician; b. 29 June 1934, Rájov, Český Krumlov; ed. Secondary Vocational School of Papermaking, Pardubice; Technologist and Head Dept. of Production Severočeské papírny (paper-making factory), Štětí; worked for CP of Czechoslovakia 1961-68; Deputy Dir. Production, Severočeské papírny, Štětí 1969-71; Gen. Dir. Průmysl celulózy a papíru (paper-making and cellulose factory), Prague 1971-77; Deputy Minister of Industry, Czech Socialist Repub. 1978-81; Minister of Foreign Trade, Czechoslovakia 1981-87; Chair. Czech Planning Comm. 1987-; First Deputy Premier Oct. 1988-; Deputy to Czech Nat. Council 1980-; Outstanding Work Medal, Order of Labour 1984. *Address:* Ministerstvo zahraničniho obchodu, třída Politických vězňů 20, Prague 1, Czechoslavakia.

URBAN, Horst W.; German business executive; b. 1 June 1936, Lauban, Silesia; trained as tax inspector, Stuttgart 1953-56; IBM Deutschland GmbH, Stuttgart 1957-61; Ford-Werke AG, Cologne 1962-70; Vice-Pres. Bayerische Motoren Werke AG (BMW), Munich 1971-74; mem. Exec. Bd. Continental AG, Hannover 1974-87, Chair. Exec. Bd. 1987-; mem. Admin. and Advisory Bd. BHF-Bank, Allianz (N. Germany), Commerzbank (N. Germany), NORD/LB; mem. Supervisory Bd. Friedrich Deckel AG, Puma AG. *Address:* Continental Aktiengesellschaft, P.O. Box 169, 3000 Hannover 1, Federal Republic of Germany. *Telephone:* (05 11) 765 2485.

URBAN, Jerzy; Polish journalist; b. 3 Aug. 1933, Łódź; s. of Jan and Maria Urban; m. 1st 1957, one d.; m. 3rd Małgorzata Daniszewska 1986; ed. Warsaw Univ.; staff writer, weekly Po Prostu, Warsaw 1955-57; Head of home section, weekly Polityka, Warsaw 1961-81; columnist of satirical weekly Szpilki, articles written under pen-name Jan Rem; Govt. Press Spokesman 1981-89; Minister-Head Cttee. for Radio and Television April 1989-; mem. Journalists' Asscn. of Polish People's Repub. 1982-; mem. Polish Writers' Union; Prize of Pres. of Workers' Publishing Co-operative RSW Prasa 1976. *Publications:* Kolekcja Jerzego Kibica 1972, Impertynencje: Felietony z lat 1969-72 1974, Wszystkie nasze ciemne sprawy 1974, Grzechy chodzą po ludziach 1975, Gorączka 1981, Romanse 1981, Robak w jabłku 1982, Na odlew 1983, Samosądy 1 1984, Felietony dla cudzych żon 1984, Samosądy 2 1984, Z pieprzem i solą 1986. *Leisure interest:* social life. *Address:* Urząd Rady Ministrów, Aleje Ujazdowskie 1/3, 00-583 Warsaw, Poland.

URBÁN, Lajos; Hungarian engineer and politician; b. 1934; ed. Tech. Univ., Budapest; various posts with Hungarian State Railways 1955-62;

chief engineer in Ministry of Posts and Communications 1963; sr. staff mem. Nat. Planning Office 1963-67; sr. mem. Hungarian Socialist Workers Party Cen. Comm. Dept. for Political Economy 1967-73; deputy, later Gen. Dir. Hungarian State Railways 1973-76; Sec. of State, Ministry for Posts and Communications 1976-84, Minister 1984-87, of Transport 1987-88. *Address:* c/o Ministry of Transport, 1400 Budapest, Dob. U. 75/81, P.O.B. 87, Hungary.

URBANEK, Adam; Polish palaeozoologist and evolutionist; b. 15 April 1928, Krosno; s. of Izydor Urbanek and Maria Urbanek; m. 1st Barbara Luszcz 1950; two d.; m. 2nd Irina Bagajeva 1973; Prof., Primary Geology Inst. of Warsaw Univ. and Palaeobiology Research Centre of Polish Acad. of Sciences, Warsaw; Corresp. mem. Polish Acad. of Sciences 1973, mem. 1983-; mem. Presidium of Polish Acad. of Sciences, fmr. Deputy Sec., then Scientific Sec. of Biological Sciences Dept. of Polish Acad. of Sciences; Deputy Pres. of Polish Acad. of Sciences 1987-; Deputy Pres., Copernicus Polish Naturalists' Soc.; fmr. Chair. Evolutionary and Theoretical Biology Cttee. and Polar Research Cttee. of Polish Acad. of Sciences; mem. Exec. Cttee. of Int. Union of Biological Sciences; State Prize 1976, Copernicus Medal for Scientific Merit 1987. *Publications:* numerous works on structure, evolution and stratigraphy of graptolites. *Leisure interest:* history of science. *Address:* Palace of Culture, 00-901 Warsaw (Office); ul. Bruna 12 m. 11, 02-594 Warsaw, Poland (Home). *Telephone:* 20-41-68 (Office).

URBÁNEK, Karel; Czechoslovak politician; b. 1941, Bojkovice Uherske, Hradiste Dist.; fmrly. worked in railways; mem. CP of Czechoslovakia (CPCZ) 1962-; holder of various Party posts; Leading Sec. CP City Cttee. Brno 1984; Dir. Political Org. Dept. CPCZ 1988; mem. Presidium of CPCZ Cen. Cttee. Oct. 1988-; State Awards for Services to the Homeland. *Address:* Central Committee of the Communist Party, Prague, Czechoslovakia.

URBANIK, Kazimierz, D.SC.; Polish mathematician; b. 5 Feb. 1930, Krzemieniec; s. of Augustyn and Rozalia Urbanik; m. Stefania Przyborowska-Urbanik 1952; two c.; ed. Wrocław Univ.; Docent 1957-60, Assoc. Prof. 1960-64, Prof. 1964-; Corresp. mem. Polish Acad. of Sciences (PAN) 1965-73, mem. 1973-, Deputy Pres. 1984-86, mem. Presidium of PAN 1987-; fmr. mem. Presidium of PAN, fmr. Chair. Wrocław branch of PAN and mem. Scientific Council of Mathematical Inst.; Dir. Mathematical Inst. of Wrocław Univ. 1967-79, 1981-; Rector Wrocław Univ. 1975-82; mem. Editorial Staff, Studia Mathematica, Zeitschrift für Wahrscheinlichkeitstheorie und verwandte Gebiete, Journal of Multivariant Analysis; mem. many Polish and foreign socs.; Kt.'s, Officer's Crosses and Commdr.'s Cross with Star, Order of Polonia Restituta, Prize of Polish Mathematical Soc., State Prize, 2nd Class 1964, City of Wrocław Prize 1970, Order of Banner of Labour, 2nd Class 1974, Medal of 30th Anniversary of People's Poland 1974, State Prize (1st class) 1978, Meritorious Teacher of People's Poland. *Publications:* over 130, mainly concerned with the theory of probability, achievements in prediction theory, generalized processes and universal algebras. *Leisure interests:* tourism, motoring, cooking secrets of various nations. *Address:* Ul. Stefczyka 8, 51-662 Wrocław, Poland. *Telephone:* 22-97-17 (Office).

URE, Sir John Burns, K.C.M.G., L.V.O., M.A.; British diplomatist; b. 5 July 1931, London; s. of the late Tam Ure; m. Caroline Allan 1972; one s. one d.; ed. Uppingham School, Magdalene Coll., Cambridge, Harvard Business School, U.S.A.; served in Scottish Rifles, Malaya 1950-51; appointments in British Embassies Moscow, Léopoldville, Santiago and Lisbon, and at Foreign Office, London 1956-79; Amb. to Cuba 1979-81, to Brazil 1984-87, to Sweden 1987-. *Publications:* Cucumber Sandwiches in the Andes 1973, Prince Henry the Navigator 1977, The Trail of Tamerlane 1980, The Quest for Captain Morgan 1983, Trespassers on the Amazon 1986. *Leisure interests:* travel, writing. *Address:* c/o Outward Bag Room (Stockholm), Foreign and Commonwealth Office, King Charles Street, London, SW1A 2AH, England.

UREN, Thomas; Australian politician; b. 28 May 1921, Balmain, N.S.W.; m. (wife deceased); two c.; served with Royal Australian Artillery 1939, 2nd Australian Imperial Force 1941, in Japanese prisoner-of-war camp 1942-45 (Burma-Siam Railway); M.P. for Reid 1958-; mem. Opposition cabinet 1969-72; mem. Fed. Parl. Labor Party Exec. 1969-72, Deputy Leader 1976-77; First Minister of Urban and Regional Devt. 1972-75; Fed. Labor Spokesman, Urban and Regional Devt. 1976-77, on Urban and Regional Affairs, Decentralization, Local Govt., Housing and Construction 1977-80, on Urban and Regional Affairs 1980-83; Minister for the Territories and Local Govt. and Minister assisting Prime Minister for Community Devt. and Regional Affairs 1983-84, Minister for Local Govt. and Admin Services 1984-87; del. to Australasian Area Conf. of Commonwealth Parl. Asscn., Darwin 1968, to Australian Parl. Mission to Europe 1968, to Commonwealth Parl. Asscn. Conf., Canberra 1970; Labor Party. *Leisure interests:* landscape gardening, arts, photography, environmental protection. *Address:* Parliament House, Canberra, A.C.T., Australia.

URI, Pierre Emmanuel; French professor and economic consultant; b. 20 Nov. 1911, Paris; s. of Isaac Uri and Hélène Kahn; m. Monique Blanchetière 1939; two s. two d.; ed. Lycée Henri IV, Ecole Normale Supérieure and Princeton Univ.; Prof. of Philosophy 1936-40; Research Economist 1944-47; Econ. and Financial Adviser to French Planning Comm. 1947-52; Prof.

Nat. School of Public Admin. 1947-51; Econ. Dir. European Coal and Steel Community (ECSC) 1952-59, Econ. Adviser, Common Market 1958-59; European Rep., Lehman Brothers 1959-61; Econ. Consultant, particularly Counsellor for Studies, Atlantic Inst. 1962-77; Chair. Experts' Group on Long Term Development in European Economic Community 1960-64; Chair. Experts' Group on Competitive Capacity of the European Community 1968-70; Prof., Univ. Paris IX 1969-76; Vice-Chair. UN Group on Multinational Corpns. 1973-74; mem. French Econ. and Social Council 1974-79; mem. Bd. Paribas 1982-86; Pres. Univ. et entreprise 1986-; Robert Schuman Prize 1981; Officier de la Légion d'honneur, Croix de guerre, Grand Officier Ordre nat. du Mérite, etc. *Publications:* La réforme de l'enseignement 1937, Le fonds monétaire international 1945, French National Economic Budgets 1947-48, Report of French Delegation on Treaty of Paris Instituting the Coal and Steel Community 1951, Report of the Inter-Governmental Committee on the Common Market and Euratom 1956, Report on the Economic Situation of the European Community Countries 1958, Dialogue des Continents 1963, Une politique monétaire pour L'Amérique Latine 1965, Pour gouverner 1967, From Commonwealth to Common Market 1968, Un avenir pour L'Europe agricole 1971, Trade and Investment Policies for the '70's 1971, Plan quinquennal pour une révolution 1973, L'Europe se gaspille 1973, Développement sans dépendance 1974, Report on the Introduction of a Capital Gains Tax in France 1975, Aider le Tiers Monde à se nourrir lui-même 1980, Changer l'Impôt (pour changer La France) 1981, Réduire les inégalités 1983. *Leisure interests:* theatre-going, travelling. *Address:* 1 avenue du Président Wilson, 75116 Paris, France (Home). *Telephone:* 47-23-97-42 (Home).

URIS, Leon Marcus; American writer; b. 3 Aug. 1924, Baltimore; s. of Wolf William and Anna (Blumberg) Uris; ed. Baltimore City Coll.; m. 1st Betty Beck 1945, two s. one d.; m. 2nd Jill Peabody 1971; ed. High School; served with the U.S. Marine Corps 1942-45. *Publications:* Battle Cry 1953 (novel and screenplay), The Angry Hills 1955, Exodus 1957, Mila 18 1960, Gunfight at the OK Corral (screenplay), Armageddon 1964, Topaz 1967, QB VII 1970, Trinity 1976, Ireland: A Terrible Beauty (with Jill Uris) 1976, The Haj 1984, Mitla Pass 1989; with others Exodus Revisited (Photo essay) 1959. *Address:* c/o Doubleday Publishing Co., Inc., 245 Park Avenue, N.Y. 11530, U.S.A.

URQUHART, Sir Brian, K.C.M.G., M.B.E.; British United Nations official (retd.); b. 28 Feb. 1919, Bridport, Dorset; s. of Murray Urquhart and Bertha (née Rendall); m. 1st Alfreda Huntington 1944 (dissolved 1963), two s. one d.; m. 2nd Sidney Howard 1963, one s. one d.; ed. Westminster School and Christ Church, Oxford; Army service 1939-45; Personal Asst. to Exec. Sec. of Preparatory Comm. of UN. London 1945-46; Personal Asst. to Trygve Lie, First Sec.-Gen. of UN 1946-49; has served in Office of UN Sec.-Gen. since 1949; served in various capacities relating to peace-keeping operations in Office of UN Under-Sec.-Gen for Special Political Affairs 1954-71; Exec. Sec. 1st and 2nd UN Int. Confs. on Peaceful Uses of Atomic Energy 1955, 1958; Deputy Exec. Sec. Preparatory Comm. of IAEA 1957; Asst. to Sec.-Gen.'s Special Rep. in the Congo July-Oct. 1960; UN Rep. in Katanga, Congo, 1961-62; Asst. Sec.-Gen. UN 1972-74; Under-Sec.-Gen. for Special Political Affairs UN 1974-86; Scholar in residence, Ford Foundation; Hon. LL.D. (Yale Univ.) 1981, (Tufts Univ.) 1985; Dr. h.c. (Essex Univ.) 1981; Hon. D.C.L. (Oxford Univ.) 1986, Hon. degrees (City Univ. of New York, Grinnell Coll., State Univ. of New York—Binghamton) 1986, (Univ. of Colorado, Keele) 1987; Roosevelt Freedom Medal 1984, Int. Peace Acad. Prize 1985. *Publications:* Hammarskjöld 1973, A Life in Peace and War 1987. *Address:* 131 East 66th Street, New York, N.Y. 10021, U.S.A.

URSI, H.E. Cardinal Corrado; Italian ecclesiastic; b. 26 July 1908, Andria, Bari; s. of Riccardo Ursi and Apollonia Sterlicchio; ordained Priest 1931; Bishop of Nardo 1951, Archbishop of Acorensa 1961, Archbishop of Naples 1966-87; created Cardinal by Pope Paul VI 1967; mem. Congregation for Catholic Educ. *Address:* Largo Donnaregina 23, 80134 Naples, Italy. *Telephone:* 449118.

URSU, Ioan, PH.D.; Romanian physicist; b. 5 April 1928, Mânăstireni, Cluj; s. of Ioan Ursu and Ana Abrudan; m. Lucia Flămându 1930; two s. one d.; ed. Univ. of Cluj and Univ. of Princeton, U.S.A.; Asst. Prof., Univ. of Cluj 1949, Prof. and Head of Dept. 1960, Vice-Rector 1961; Prof. and Head of Dept., Univ. of Bucharest 1968-; Dir.-Gen., Inst. for Atomic Physics 1968-76; Pres. State Cttee. for Nuclear Energy 1969-76; Pres. Nat. Council for Science and Tech. 1972-79, First Vice-Chair. 1979-86, First Vice-Chair. Nat. Cttee. for Science and Tech. 1986-; Corresp. mem. Romanian Acad. 1963, mem. 1974, Pres. Physics Section 1988-; mem. Scientific Council of the Jt. Inst. for Nuclear Research, Dubna; mem. Bd. of Govs. IAEA 1971, Vice-Pres. 1972; mem. Scientific Advisory Cttee., IAEA 1979-; mem. Exec. Council, European Physical Soc. 1968, Vice-Pres. 1975, Pres. 1976-78; Pres. Balkan Physical Union 1987; Ed. two Romanian journals of physics 1985-; mem. Romanian Soc. of Physics and Chem., Physical Socs. of U.S.A., Belgium, France; mem. Bd. of Int. Soc. of Magnetic Resonance; mem. Cttee. Atomes et Molécules par Etudes Radioélectriques (AMPERE); mem. American Nuclear Assn. 1976, Canadian Nuclear Assn. 1976; Corresp. mem. Equadorian Inst. of Natural Sciences 1976, Centre for Scientific Culture "Ettore Majorana" (Erice, Italy) 1977; mem. European Acad. of Sciences, Arts and Humanities 1980, New York Acad. of Sciences

1981; Order of Labour, Order of Star of the Socialist Republic of Romania, Order of Tudor Vladimirescu, Order of 23rd August, Orders of U.S.S.R., Fed. Repub. of Germany, Netherlands and others. *Publications:* Rezonanța Electronică de Spin 1965, La résonance paramagnétique electronique 1968, Magnetic Resonance and Related Phenomena (Ed.) 1971, Energia atomică 1973, Magnetic Resonance in Uranium Compounds 1979, Magnitny Rezonans v Soedynenyah Urana 1982, Fizica și Tehnologia Materialelor Nucleare 1982, Physics and Technology of Nuclear Materials 1985, Interactiunea Radiației Laser cu Metalele (with others) 1986, Fizika i technologyia iadernyh materialov 1988, Vzaimodeistwie lazernovo izluchenyia s metallami 1988 and about 130 papers on atomic and nuclear physics, nuclear materials, nuclear technologies, solid state physics, interaction of radiation with matter. *Address:* National Committee for Science and Technology, 1 Piata Victoriei, 71202 Bucharest; Str. Iuliu Tetrat 26, Bucharest 1, Romania (Home). *Telephone:* 33-43-01 (Office).

URWICK, Sir Alan Bedford, K.C.V.O., C.M.G., M.A.; British diplomatist; b. 2 May 1930, London; s. of the late Lyndall Fownes Urwick and Joan Saunders; m. Marta Yolanda (née Montagne) 1960; three s.; ed. Dragon School, Rugby, New Coll. Oxford; joined Foreign Service 1952; served in Embassies in Belgium 1954-56, U.S.S.R. 1958-59, Iraq 1960-61, Jordan 1965-67, U.S.A. 1967-70, Egypt 1971-73; seconded to Cabinet Office as Asst. Sec., Cen. Policy Review Staff 1973-75; Head of Near East and North Africa Dept., Foreign and Commonwealth Office 1975-76; Minister, British Embassy in Madrid 1977-79; Amb. to Jordan 1979-84, to Egypt 1984-87; High Commr. in Canada 1987-. *Leisure interests:* reading, gardening. *Address:* c/o Foreign and Commonwealth Office, King Charles Street, London, S.W.1, England.

USAMI, Tadanobu; Japanese trade unionist; b. 31 Oct. 1925, Tokyo; m. 1948; two d.; ed. Takachiho Coll. of Econs.; joined Fuji Cotton Spinning Co. 1946; joined staff of Japanese Fed. of Textile, Garment, Chemical, Distributive and Allied Industry Workers' Unions (ZENSEN) 1946, successively held posts of Treas., Sec., Dir. of Gen. Affairs, mem. Cen. Exec. Cttee. ZENSEN 1947-55, Asst. Gen. Sec. 1955-61, Gen. Sec. 1961-71, Pres. 1971-; mem. Exec. Bd. ICFTU Asian Regional Org. 1960-65, Pres. 1981-; Vice-Pres. Japanese Confed. of Labour (DOMEI) 1972-80, Pres. 1981-. *Leisure interest:* golf. *Address:* 4-8-16, Kudan-Minami, Chiyoda-ku, Tokyo (Office); 4-16-19, Wakabayashi, Setagaya-ku, Tokyo, Japan (Home).

USERY, William J.; American industrial relations executive; b. 21 Dec. 1923, Hardwick, Ga.; ed. Georgia Mil. Coll., Mercer Univ.; served U.S. Navy 1943-46; Maintenance Machinist, Armstrong Cork Co. 1949-55; Grand Lodge Rep., Int. Assen. of Machinists and Aerospace Workers (IAM), AFL-CIO 1956, IAM Special Rep., Cape Canaveral Air Force Test Facilities 1956, IAM Rep. to President's Missile Sites Labor Cttee. 1961-67; Co-ordinator for Union Activities, Manned Spacecraft Center, Houston, Tex.; Co-founder, Cape Kennedy Labor-Management Relations Council 1967, Chair. 1968; Asst. Sec. of Labor for Labor-Management Relations 1969-73, Sec. of Labor 1976-77; Dir. of Fed. Mediation and Conciliation Service 1973-76; Special Asst. to the Pres. 1974-75, for Labor-Management Negotiations 1975-76; Pres. Bill Useng Assocs., Washington 1977-; Democrat.

USHAKOV, Nikolay Aleksandrovich, D.SC.; Soviet international lawyer; b. 19 Nov. 1918, Moscow; Research Prof., Inst. of State and Law, U.S.S.R. Acad. of Sciences 1948-; Chief of Editorial Board, International Law (annual); mem. Perm. Court of Arbitration, The Hague; mem. UN Int. Law Comm. 1967-; Exec. Sec. UN Assen. in U.S.S.R.; mem. Soviet Law Assen.; Vice-Pres. Soviet Int. Law Assen.; lectures in int. public law at Moscow, Kiev and Leningrad Univs.; has participated in various confs. on questions of int. law. *Publications:* over 40 learned publications in the field of int. law. *Address:* Institute of State and Law of U.S.S.R. Academy of Sciences, ul. Frunze 10, Moscow, U.S.S.R.

USHER ARSÉNE, Assouan, M.A.; Côte d'Ivoire lawyer and politician; b. 24 Oct. 1930; ed. Dakar, Bordeaux and Poitiers Univ.; Lawyer, Court of Appeals, Poitiers 1955-56; Cabinet attaché of M. Houphouet-Boigny 1956; Asst. Dir. Caisse des Allocations Familiales 1957-59; Conseiller Général 1957-59; Deputy Vice-Pres. Nat. Assembly 1959-60; Lawyer, Court of Appeals, Abidjan 1959; Head, Ivory Coast (now Côte d'Ivoire) Perm. Mission to UN 1961-67; Minister of Foreign Affairs 1967-77; mem. UN Security Council 1964-67, Polit. Bureau Parti Démocratique de Côte d'Ivoire responsible for Mass Educ. 1970-; Pres. Société des Ananas de la Côte d'Ivoire 1987-; Nat. Order of Côte d'Ivoire. *Address:* 01 B.P. 1191, Abidjan, Côte d'Ivoire.

USLAR-PIETRI, Arturo; Venezuelan writer and politician; b. 16 May 1906, Caracas; s. of Arturo Uslar and Helena Pietri de Uslar; m. Isabel Braun 1939; two s.; ed. Univ. Central de Venezuela; Prof. of Political Economy, Univ. Cen. de Venezuela 1937-41; Sec. to Pres. of Venezuela 1941-43; Minister of Nat. Educ. 1939-41, of Finance 1943, of Foreign Affairs 1945; Prof. of Latin American Literature, Columbia Univ., New York 1947, of Venezuelan Literature, Univ. Central de Venezuela; mem. Acad. Venezolana de la Lengua, Acad. of Social and Political Sciences, Acad. of History, Venezuela; Senator, Nat. Congress 1958; Nat. Candidate for Pres. Dec. 1963; Perm. Del. and mem. Exec. Bd. UNESCO; holds numerous int. awards. *Publications:* novels: Las lanzas coloradas 1931, El camino de El Dorado 1947, El laberinto de fortuna 2 vols., Oficio de Difuntos 1976, La Isla de Robinson 1981; stories: Barrabás y otros relatos 1926, Red 1936, Treinta hombres y sus sombras 1949, Pasos y Pasajeros 1965, Los Ganadores 1980; essays: Las Nubes 1951, Del hacer y deshacer de Venezuela 1963, La ciudad de nadie 1960, Oraciones para despertar, La Otra América 1974, Fantasmas de dos mundos 1979, Godos, Insurgentes y Visionarios 1986; poems: Manoa 1972; plays: Teatro 1958, Chúo Gil y las tejedoras 1960, and several monographs. *Address:* Avenida Los Pinos 49, La Florida, Caracas, Venezuela. *Telephone:* 74-40-61.

USMANI, Ishrat Husain, M.SC., PH.D., D.I.C.; Pakistani scientist and administrator; b. 15 April 1917, Delhi; s. of F. H. Usmani and Akbar Sultana; m. Nishat Usmani 1944; two s. two d.; ed. Aligarh Univ., Bombay Univ. and Imp. Coll. of Science and Tech., London; Madras Cadre of Indian Civil Service 1942–47; Civil Service of Pakistan 1947–73; fmr. Chief Controller of Imports and Exports, Pakistan; fmr. Chair. W. Pakistan Mineral Devt. Corpn., Nat. Science Council, Pakistan; mem.-Sec. Scientific Comm. 1959–61; Chair. Pakistan Atomic Energy Comm. 1960–71; Chair. Pakistan Power Comm. 1961–62; Chair. Bd. of Govs., IAEA Vienna 1962–63; Pres. UN Atoms for Peace Confs. (Geneva) 1964 and 1971; Sec. Ministry of Educ. 1968, of Science and Tech. 1972–73; Sr. Energy Adviser UNEP 1974–78; Sr. Energy Adviser CNRET 1979; Inter-Regional Adviser UN Dept. of Tech. Co-operation for Devt. 1980–85; Sec.-Gen. BCCI Int. Foundation for the Promotion of New and Emerging Sciences and Tech. (NEST), London 1985–; Hon. Consultant to UN Sec.-Gen. on Nuclear Non-proliferation Treaty; Hon. Vice-Pres. U.K. Inst. of Nuclear Engineers; awarded S.Pk. 1971. *Publications:* Rural Electrification: An Alternative for the Third World (UN Natural Resources Forum 2), Challenge of Energy (Alternative Energy Sources), Energy Bank for Small Villages (The Bulletin of the Atomic Scientist 1979), An Energy Option (Chemtech 1980). *Leisure interests:* tennis, photography. *Address:* 31 Bury Street, London, EC3A 5NQ, England. *Telephone:* 01-929 2992.

USMANKHODJAYEV, Inamdjon Buzrukovich; Soviet (Uzbek) architect and politician; b. 1930, Bagdad Village, Bagdad Dist., Ferghana Region; ed. Higher Tashkent Polytechnic Inst.; worked as engineer and Section Chief, Ferghanavodstroi Trust, then Chief Architect, Margelan 1955–60; Instructor, Ferghana Regional Party Cttee. and Head Ferghana Regional Collective Farm Construction Bd. 1960; Chair. Exec. Cttee. Ferghana City Council 1962–65; nominated Sec. Syr Darya Regional Party Cttee. 1965; Instructor, Central Cttee. of CPSU 1969–72; Chair. Namangan Regional Exec. Cttee. 1972–74; First Sec. Andidjan Regional Party Cttee. 1975; Chair. of Presidium of Supreme Soviet, Uzbek S.S.R. Dec. 1979–83; First Sec. Uzbek CP 1983–88; mem. Presidium of Supreme Soviet of U.S.S.R. 1984–; Order of Lenin, Order of the Red Banner of Labour (twice), Badge of Honour and medals. *Address:* c/o Central Committee of Communist Party of Uzbekistan, Tashkent, U.S.S.R.

USPENSKY, Boris Andreyevich; Soviet structuralist critic and semiotician; b. 1937; ed. Moscow Univ.; dissertation on structural typology of languages published 1965 and translated into English 1968 (The Principles of Structural Typology); studied under Hjelmslev at Univ. of Copenhagen 1961; research at U.S.S.R. Acad. of Sciences Inst. of African Languages 1965–; research mem. of Lab. of Computational Linguistics, Moscow Univ. 1965–; major structuralist publications 1962–. *Publications include:* The Archaic System of Old Church Slavonic Pronunciation 1968, A Poetics of Composition 1970 (English translation 1973), The First Russian Grammar 1975, The Semiotics of the Russian Icon 1976, and numerous articles. *Address:* c/o Academy of Sciences of the U.S.S.R., Leninsky Pr. 14, Moscow V-71, U.S.S.R.

USTINOV, Peter Alexander, C.B.E., F.R.S.A.; British dramatist and actor; b. 16 April 1921; s. of late Iona Ustinov and Nadia Benois; m. 1st Isolde Denham 1940 (divorced 1950), one d.; m. 2nd Suzanne Cloutier 1954 (divorced 1971), one s. two d.; m. 3rd Hélène du Lau d'Allemans 1972; ed. Westminster School and London Theatre Studio; entered theatre as actor 1939; first appearance in revue writing own material Ambassador's Theatre, London 1940; served in army 1942–46; UNICEF Amb. of Goodwill; appeared in plays: Crime and Punishment 1946, Frenzy 1948, Love in Albania 1949, The Love of Four Colonels 1951, Romanoff and Juliet 1956 (British Critics' Best Play Award), Photo Finish 1962, The Unknown Soldier and his Wife 1973, King Lear 1979–80, Beethoven's Tenth 1983, (in Berlin) 1987–88; appeared in films: The Way Ahead (collaborated on screenplay) 1944, Odette 1950, Hotel Sahara 1951, Quo Vadis 1951, Beau Brummel 1954, The Egyptian 1954, We're no Angels 1955, Lola Montes 1955, Spartacus 1961 (Acad. Award for Best Supporting Actor, Golden Globe Award), Billy Budd 1962, Topkapi 1963 (Acad. Award for Best Supporting Actor), John Goldfarb 1964, Lady L 1965, Blackbeard's Ghost 1966, The Comedians 1967, Viva Max! 1970, Hot Millions (part-author and star) 1968, Hammersmith is Out (also dir.) 1971, One of Our Dinosaurs is Missing 1975, Treasure of Matcumbe 1977, The Last Remake of Beau Geste 1977, The Thief of Baghdad 1978, Death on the Nile 1978, Ashanti 1978, Charlie Chan and the Curse of the Dragon Queen 1981, Evil Under the Sun 1981, Memed My Hawk (wrote and dir.) 1984, Appointment with Death 1988, The French Revolution 1989; has appeared in numerous TV productions; dir. operas Magic Flute, Hamburg 1968, Don Quichotte, Paris 1973 (also designed and produced), Don Giovanni, Edinburgh 1973 (also

designed), Les Brigands, Berlin 1978, Mavra, Milan 1982, Katja Kabanowa, Hamburg 1985, The Marriage of Figaro (Salzburg and Hamburg) 1987; recorded Peter and the Wolf (Grammy Award); Rector Univ. of Dundee 1968, 1971–73, Hon. D.Mus. (Cleveland Inst. of Music) 1967, Hon. LL.D. (Univ. of Dundee) 1969, (La Salle Coll., Philadelphia) 1971, Hon. D.Litt. (Univ. of Lancaster) 1972, Hon. Dr. (Univ. of Toronto) 1984; UNICEF Award 1978, Variety Club Award 1979; Benjamin Franklin Medal, R.S.A.; Commdr. Ordre des Arts et des Lettres; Foreign Assoc. mem. Acad. of Fine Arts, Paris 1988. *Publications:* plays: House of Regrets 1942, Blow Your Own Trumpet 1943, The Banbury Nose 1944, The Tragedy of Good Intentions 1945, The Indifferent Shepherd 1948, The Man in the Raincoat 1949, The Love of Four Colonels 1951, The Moment of Truth 1951, No Sign of the Dove 1953, Romanoff and Juliet 1956, Photo Finish 1962, The Life in My Hands 1963, Half Way up the Tree 1967, The Unknown Soldier and his Wife 1967, Who's Who in Hell 1974, Overheard 1981, Beethoven's Tenth 1983; short stories: Add a Dash of Pity 1959, The Frontiers of the Sea 1966; novels: The Loser 1960, Krumnagel 1971; autobiogs.: Dear Me 1977, My Russia 1983. *Leisure interests:* sailing, travel. *Address:* 11 rue de Silly, 92100 Boulogne, France.

USTINOV, Vyacheslav Aleksandrovich; Soviet diplomatist; b. 27 June 1925, Moscow; m.; ed. Moscow State Inst. of Int. Relations, Moscow State Univ., Diplomatic Acad.; joined Ministry of Foreign Affairs 1950; Counsellor at Embassy, Dar es Salaam 1962–66; Counsellor (dealing with disarmament), Dept. of Foreign Policy Planning 1966–69; Amb. to Tanzania 1969–72; Head of Third African Dept., Ministry of Foreign Affairs 1972–81; UN Under-Sec.-Gen. for Political and Security Council Affairs 1981–87. *Publications:* various articles in the field of int. affairs and history, particularly regarding Far Eastern and African affairs. *Address:* c/o Ministry of Foreign Affairs, Moscow, U.S.S.R.

USTOR, Dr. Endre, Hungarian lawyer; b. 1 Sept. 1909, Budapest; m. Lili Havas; no c.; Head, Int. Law Dept., Ministry of Foreign Affairs 1957–75, then Amb.; Hon. Prof. Karl Marx Univ. of Econs., Budapest 1968–; mem. Perm. Court of Arbitration, The Hague 1961–; mem. UN Int. Law Comm. 1967–76. Chair. 1974; mem. UN Admin. Tribunal 1976–, Vice-Pres. 1979–81, Pres. 1981–84, mem. 1985–87; mem. Inst. of Int. Law, 1967. *Publications:* The Law of Diplomatic Relations (in Hungarian) 1965, Reports on the Most Favoured Nation Clause (in Yearbooks of the UN Int. Law Comm. 1968–70, 1972–76); and several articles on int. law. *Address:* Fodor utca 73, 1124 Budapest, Hungary. *Telephone:* 857-169.

UTIGER, Ronald Ernest, C.B.E., M.A.; British business executive; b. 5 May 1926, Wallasey, Cheshire; s. of Ernest F. and Kathleen (née Cram) Utiger; m. Barbara A. von Mohl 1953; one s. one d.; ed. Shrewsbury School and Univ. of Oxford; Economist, Courtaulds Ltd. 1950–61; Financial Controller, The British Aluminium Co. Ltd. 1961–64, Commercial Dir. 1965–68, Man. Dir. 1968–79, Chair. 1979–82; Dir. British Nat. Oil Corpn. (BNOC) 1976–80, Chair. and Chief Exec. 1979–80; Dir. Tube Investments Ltd. 1979–, Man. Dir. 1980–86, Deputy Chair. 1982–84; Chair. 1984–, Dir. British Alcan Group 1983–, Ultramar PLC 1983–; Chair. Int. Primary Aluminium Asscn. 1976–78, European Primary Aluminium Asscn. 1976–77; Pres. Nat. Inst. of Econ. and Social Research 1983–; mem. NEDC 1980–84; mem. British Library Bd. 1987–. *Leisure interests:* music, reading, gardening. *Address:* 9 Ailsa Road, St. Margarets-on-Thames, Twickenham, Middx., TW1 1QJ, England. *Telephone:* 01-892 5810.

UTSUMI, Hideo; Japanese politician; b. 1922; ed. Chuo Univ.; elected to House of Reps. six times from Miyagi No. 2 constituency; fmr. Parl. Vice-Minister of Educ., Chair. Diet Rules Cttee., House of Reps.; Minister of Construction 1982–83; Minister of State and Dir.-Gen. Nat. Land Agency Nov. 1988–. *Address:* National Land Agency, 1-2-2, Kasumigaseki, Chiyoda-ku, Tokyo 100, Japan.

UTZERATH, Hansjörg; German theatre director; b. 20 March 1926; m. Renate Ziegfeld 1957; three c.; ed. Kepler Oberschule, Tübingen; began as actor, later in theatre man. in Düsseldorf, and then in production; Chief Stage Man., Düsseldorfer Kammerspiele 1955–59; Dir. 1959–66; Intendant, Freie Volksbühne, Berlin 1967–73; Dir. Städtische Bühnen, Nuremberg 1977–; Guest Producer at Staatstheater Stuttgart, Münchener Kammerspiele and Schiller-Theater, Berlin 1959–. *Productions include:* Tango 1971, Der Vater 1972, Viele heissen Kain (TV). *Address:* Städtische Bühnen Schauspiel, Richard-Wagner-Platz 2-10, 8500 Nuremberg, Federal Republic of Germany.

UTZON, Jørn; Danish architect; b. 9 April 1918, Copenhagen; ed. Royal Acad. of Fine Arts, Copenhagen; joined Helsinki Office of Alvar Aalto (q.v.) after Second World War; won travelling scholarships to Morocco and U.S.A.; designer of furniture and glassware; won competition for design of Sydney Opera House 1957, worked on project in Denmark 1957–63, in Sydney 1963–66 (resgnd. as architect); won competition for design of Zürich Schauspielhaus 1966; architect of a housing scheme near Fredensborg, his own house, Bank Melli Iran, Teheran, etc.; Fellow, Royal Australian Inst. of Architects 1965, R.I.B.A. 1978–; Ehrenpreis, Bund Deutscher Architekten 1966, Gold Metal, Royal Australian Inst. of Architects 1973, R.I.B.A. 1978, and other awards. *Address:* 3150 Hellebaek, Denmark.

UYEDA, Seiya, D.SC.; Japanese geophysicist; b. 28 Nov. 1929, Tokyo; s. of the late Seiichi and Hatsuo Uyeda; m. Mutsuko Kosaka 1952; one s.

two d.; ed. Univ. of Tokyo; Research Fellow Earthquake Research Inst., Univ. of Tokyo 1955–63, Assoc. Prof. Geophysical Inst. 1963–69, Prof. Earthquake Research Inst. 1969–; Tanakadate Prize, Soc. of Terrestrial Electricity and Magnetism 1955; Okada Prize, Oceanographical Soc. of Japan 1968; Alexander Agassiz Medal, Nat. Acad. of Sciences 1972. *Publications:* Debate about the Earth 1967, Island Arcs 1973, The New View of the Earth 1977; 250 scientific papers. *Leisure interest:* skiing. *Address:* Earthquake Research Institute, University of Tokyo, Tokyo; 2-39-6 Daizawa, Setagaya-ku, Tokyo, Japan (Home). *Telephone:* 03-812-2111 (ext. 5740) (Office).

UYS, ('Jamie') Jacobus Johannes, B.SC.; South African film maker; b. 30 May 1921, Boksburg; s. of Victor and Maria Uys (née Jacobs); m. Hester Jacoba van Rooyen 1945; one s. two d.; ed. Voortrekker High School, Boksburg, Univ. of Pretoria; worked as miner, teacher, farmer and trader; started one-man film making unit 1950; produced, wrote, directed and acted in first film; formed public co. 1954; maker of documentary and feature films; Dir. Mimosa Films 1968–; Schlesinger Drum 1953; Gold Medal, Chicago 1968; Gold Scissors Award 1974; Golden Globe Award 1974; Rapport Oscar 1975; Grand Prix, Vevey 1981; Haugesund Grand Prix 1981; London Film Festival Prize 1981; Chamrousse Grand Prix 1982. *Films include:* Daar Doer in die Bosveld 1950, Fifty-Fifty 1952, Daar Doer in die Stad 1953, Money to Burn 1954, Jabulani Africa 1954, Die Bosvelder 1955, Satan's Coral 1956, Sidney and the Boer 1957, Rip van Wyk 1958, Dingaka 1959, Doodkry is Min 1960, Lord Oom Piet 1962, All the Way to Paris 1964, The Professor and the Beauty Queen 1967, Lost in the Desert 1971, Beautiful People 1973, Funny People 1976, The Gods must be Crazy 1980, Funny People II 1983. *Leisure interests:* reading, chess, scrabble, flying model aeroplanes. *Address:* P.O. Box 50019, Randburg, Transvaal 2125, South Africa (Office). *Telephone:* (011) 787-1026 (Office); (011) 787-1026 (Home).

UYTTENBROECK, Frans, PH.D.; Belgian medical doctor, gynaecologist and oncologist; b. 11 July 1921, Lier; s. of Jozef Uyttenbroeck and Augusta Verstreken; m. Elisabeth Switters 1946; five d.; ed. Univ. of Leuven, Univ. of Amsterdam, Netherlands; Prof. of Obstetrics and Gynaecology, Univ. of Antwerp, Head of Dept. of Obstetrics and Gynaecology, St. Camille and St. Augustin Clinics 1972–; Active mem. Koninklijke Academie voor geneeskunde van België (Pres. 1987–); Foreign mem. Académie Nat. de Médecine, France, Académie de chirurgie, Paris; mem. Soc. of Pelvic Surgeons, Int. Soc. for Study of Vulvar Disease and many other nat. and int. gynaecological socs.; Founding mem. Int. Gynaecologic Cancer Soc.; Commdr. Order of Léopold; Grand Officer, Crown Order. *Publications:* 16 medical books in Dutch, English and French; many articles in nat. and int. gynaecological and medical journals. *Leisure interest:* travelling. *Address:* 12 avenue Jan Van Rijswijck, 2018 Antwerp, Belgium. *Telephone:* 32 3238 11 52.

UZAWA, Hirofumi, PH.D.; Japanese professor of economics; b. 21 July 1928, Tottori Province; s. of Tokio and Toshiko Uzawa; m. Hiroko Aoyoshi 1957; two s. one d.; ed. Univ. of Tokyo; Research Assoc., Lecturer, Asst. Prof., Dept. of Econs., Stanford Univ., Calif. 1956–60, Assoc. Prof. of Econs. and Statistics 1961–64; Asst. Prof. of Econs. and Math., Univ. of Calif., Berkeley 1960–61; Prof. of Econs. Univ. of Chicago 1964–68, Univ. of Tokyo 1969–; Matsunaga Memorial Prize 1969, Yoshino Prize 1971, Mainichi Prize 1974, desig. as Person of Cultural Merits 1983. *Publications:* in English: Studies in Linear and Nonlinear Programming (co-author) 1958; in Japanese: Economic Development and Fluctuations (co-author) 1972, Social Costs of the Automobile 1974, A Re-examination of Modern Economic Theory 1977, Transformation of Modern Economics 1986, A Critique of Japanese Economy 1987, Towards a Theory of Public Economics 1987. *Leisure interest:* walking. *Address:* University of Tokyo, Hongo, Bunkyo-ku, Tokyo; Higashi 1-3-6, Hoya, Tokyo, Japan.

UZIEMBŁO, Jerzy Zygmunt; Polish politician; b. 1942, Drohiczyn; ed. State Naval School, Gdynia; active in youth movt., mem. Socialist Youth Union 1957–76; worked at PLO Polish Ocean Lines, rank in merchant navy, from sr. sailor to Sea Capt. 1964–84; active in trades union movt., Chair. Fed. of Trade Unions of Sea Sailors and Fishermen 1984–87; mem. Presidium of All-Poland Agreement of Trade Unions (OPZZ), Deputy Chair. 1986–; alt. mem. Bureau and Gen. Council of World Fed. of Trade Unions 1985–; Deputy to Seym 1985–; mem. Council of State July 1986–; mem. Polish United Workers' Party (PZPR); Vice-Chair. Cttee. for Solidarity with Nations of Africa, Asia and Latin America 1987–; Silver Cross of Merit, Medal of 40th Anniversary of People's Poland and other decorations. *Address:* Kancelaria Rady Państwa, ul. Wiejska 2/6, 00-902 Warsaw, Poland.

V

VACHON, H.E. Cardinal Louis-Albert, C.C., D.PH., D.TH.; Canadian ecclesiastic; b. 4 Feb. 1912, St. Frédéric, Beauce Co., Quebec; s. of Napoléon Vachon and Alexandrine Gilbert; ed. Laval Univ. and St. Thomas Aquinas Univ., Rome; ordained priest 1938; Prof. of Philosophy, Laval Univ. 1941–47, of Theology 1949–55; Superior, Grand Seminaire de Quebec 1955–59, Gen. Superior 1960–77; Domestic Prelate 1958; Vice-Rector Laval Univ. 1960–72; Vicar-Gen., Diocese of Quebec 1960–81; Protonotary Apostolic 1963–77; Auxiliary Bishop of Quebec 1977–81; Archbishop of Quebec and Primate of Canada 1981–; cr. Cardinal 1985; mem. Canadian Soc. of Theology, Canadian Soc. of Authors, Admin. Bd. of English Speaking Union of Commonwealth in Canada, Royal Soc. of Canada, Admin. Bd. of Canadian Conf. Catholic Bishops, and many other bodies; Kt. Great Cross, Equestre du Saint-Sépulchre de Jérusalem 1985–, Officier, Légion d'honneur (France) 1988; Hon. degrees from several univs. *Publications:* Espérance et présomption 1958, Vérité et liberté 1962, Unité de l'université 1962, Apostolat de l'universitaire catholique 1963, Mémorial 1963, Communauté universitaire 1963, Progrès de l'université et consentement populaire 1964, Responsabilité collective des universitaires 1964, Les humanités d'aujourd'hui 1966, Excellence et loyauté des universitaires 1969. *Leisure interests:* reading, fine art. *Address:* 1073 boulevard St.-Cyrille ouest, Sillery, Quebec, G1S 4R5 (Office); 2 Port-Dauphin, C.P. 459, Haute-Ville, Quebec, G1R 4R6, Canada (Home). *Telephone:* (418) 688-1211 (Office); (418) 692-3935 (Home).

VADIM, Roger (Plemiannikov); French film director; b. 26 Jan. 1928, Paris; s. of Igor Plemiannikov and Marie-Antoinette Ardilouze; m. 1st Brigitte Bardot (q.v.) 1952 (divorced), 2nd Annette Stroyberg 1958 (divorced), 3rd Jane Fonda (q.v.) 1967 (divorced), 4th Catherine Schneider 1975 (divorced); four c.; actor; script-writer and Asst. Dir. with Marc Allegret; reporter Paris-Match 1952–54; ind. film dir. 1955–; scriptwriter Futures vedettes, Cette sacrée gamine, En effeuillant la marguerite; dir. and scriptwriter Et Dieu créa la femme, Sait-on jamais, Les bijoutiers du Clair de Lune, Les liaisons dangereuses, Et mourir de plaisir, Le repos du guerrier, Le vice et la vertu, La ronde, La curée, Histoires extraordinaires, Barbarella, Metzengerstein 1969, Pretty Maids in a Row, Hellé, Don Juan 1973, La jeune fille assassinée 1974, La femme fidèle 1976, Night Games 1979, Surprise Party 1983. *Publications:* Memoirs of the Devil 1976, The Hungry Angel 1984, Bardot, Deneuve and Fonda 1986. *Address:* 5 rue Turbigo, 75001 Paris, France (Office); 24–29 Beverly Avenue, Santa Monica, Calif., U.S.A. (Home).

VAES, Baron Robert, cr. 1985, LL.D.; Belgian diplomatist; b. 9 Jan. 1919, Antwerp; s. of Louis Vaes; m. Anne Albers 1947; one d.; Parl. Pvt. Sec. to Minister of Foreign Trade 1958–60; Dir.-Gen of Political Affairs 1964–66; Perm. Under-Sec. of State, Ministry of Foreign Affairs, Foreign Trade and Devt. Co-operation 1966–72; fmr. Chair. Council of Benelux Union; postings to Washington, Paris, Hong Kong, London, Rome, Madrid 1972–76; Amb. to U.K. 1976–84; Dir. Banque Belge (London) 1984–, Sotheby's 1984–, Contibel 1987–; decorations include Grand Officer of the Order of Léopold, Grand Officer of the Order of the Crown, Hon. K.C.M.G. *Address:* 34-35 New Bond Street, London, W1A 2AA, England.

VAGELOS, Pindaros Roy, M.D.; American pharmaceutical industry executive; b. 8 Oct. 1929, Westfield, N.J.; s. of Roy John Vagelos and Marianthi Lambrinides; m. Diana Touliatos 1955; two s. two d.; ed. Univ. of Pennsylvania and Columbia Univ. Coll. of Physicians and Surgeons; Intern in Medicine, Mass. Gen. Hosp. 1954–55, Asst. Res. in Medicine 1955–56; Surgeon, Lab. of Cellular Physiology, Nat. Insts. of Health 1956–59, Surgeon, Lab. of Biochemistry 1959–64, Head, Section on Comparative Biochemistry 1964–66; Prof. of Biochemistry, Chair. Dept. of Biological Chem., Washington Univ. School of Medicine, St. Louis, Mo. 1966–75, Dir. Div. of Biology and Biomedical Sciences 1973–75; Sr. Vice-Pres. Research, Merck Sharp & Dohme Research Labs., Rahway, N.J. 1975–76, Pres. 1976–84, Corporate Sr. Vice-Pres. Merck & Co., Inc. 1982–84, Exec. Vice-Pres. 1984–85. Pres. and C.E.O. 1985–86, Pres., Chair. and C.E.O. 1986–; Enzyme Chem. Award, American Chemical Soc. 1967, N.J. Science/Tech. Medal 1983; discoverer of acyl-carrier protein. *Leisure interests:* jogging, tennis. *Address:* Merck & Co. Inc., P.O. Box 2000, Rahway, N.J., U.S.A. *Telephone:* (201) 574-6776.

VAGO, Constant, PH.D., D.SC.; French pathologist and university professor; b. 2 May 1921, Debrecen, Hungary; s. of Vincent Vago and Françoise Schibl; m. Catherine Sary 1944; one s. one d.; ed. Lycée of Debrecen, Univ. of Marseilles; Dir. Lab. of Cytopathology, Nat. Inst. for Agron. Research, Saint-Christol 1958–; Research Dir. Nat. Inst. of Agron. Research of France 1962; Prof. of Pathology and Microbiology, Univ. of Science, Montpellier 1964–; Dir. Res. Centre of Comparative Pathology, Univ. of Montpellier 1970–; mem. Acad. of Sciences of France, Acad. of Agric. of France, New York Acad. of Sciences, Nat. Acad. of Sciences of India; Past Pres. Int. Soc. for Invertebrate Pathology; Pres. Nat. Cttee. of Biological Sciences of France; Hon. Prof. Univ. of Cen. China; mem.

numerous scientific socs.; Légion d'honneur, Ordre nat. du Mérite, and other decorations. *Publications:* Invertebrate Tissue Culture 1972, and about 400 publications on comparative pathology, tissue culture, molecular virology, chlamydial diseases, comparative oncology. *Leisure interests:* sculpture, swimming. *Address:* University of Sciences, Place Eugène Bataillon, 34060 Montpellier, France. *Telephone:* 67639144.

VAGO, Pierre; French architect and town planner; b. 30 Aug. 1910, Budapest, Hungary; s. of Joseph and Ghita (Lenart) Vago; remarried Nicole Cormier 1968; two s. two d.; ed. Ecole spéciale d'Architecture, Paris; Ed.-in-Chief Architecture d'Aujourd'hui 1932–48, Pres. of Cttee. 1948–75; Founder and Sec.-Gen. Int. Reunions of Architects 1932–48 and Int. Union of Architects 1948–69, Hon. Pres. 1969–; Head Architect for Reconstruction 1948–56; Pres. Int. Council, Soc. of Industrial Design 1963–65; fmr. Vice-Pres. Confed. of French Architects; Council mem., Comité Int. Critiques d'Architecture 1979–; Chair. Co-ordinating Group NGO's in Man-Made Environment 1981–; mem. Acad. Council, Int. Acad. of Architecture 1987–; mem. jury of many int. competitions; architect and town planner in Belgium, Austria, France, Germany, Tunisia, Mexico, Luxembourg, Israel and Italy; Prof. and Dir. of Studies Ecole Supérieure d'Architecture St. Luc de Belgique; Prof. Int. Sommerakadamie, Salzburg 1972–78; honours include Hon. mem. of R.I.B.A., American Inst. of Architects, Bund Deutscher Architekten, Acad. d'Architecture (Paris), Akad. der Künste, W. Berlin and mem. of numerous architectural socs.; Dr. h.c. (Univ. of Stuttgart), Prof. h.c. (Tech. Univ., Budapest); Chevalier, Légion d'honneur, Commdr. Grégoire le Grand, Officier Ordre des Arts et des Lettres, Medal Résistance. *Major works include:* Basilica St. Pius X, Lourdes and other churches, Cen. Bank of Tunis, Library of Univ. of Bonn, Univ. of Lille, several buildings in France, Fed. Republic of Germany, N. Africa, Mexico and Israel. *Leisure interest:* history. *Address:* Le Valparon, 77123 Noisy-sur-Ecole, France (Home). *Telephone:* (1) 64 24 56 00.

VAGRIS, Jan Janovich; Soviet politician; b. 1930, Latvia; ed. Univ. of Latvia, Higher Party School of CPSU Cen. Cttee.; technologist, boss of office for precision tools in machine-construction works 1955–58; Deputy Pres. of Eglau City Exec. Cttee. 1958–61; construction engineer on machine construciton works 1961–62; Second Sec. of Eglau City Cttee. of Latvian CP 1966–73; Head of Section of Cen. Cttee. of Latvian CP 1973–78; First Sec. of Riga City Cttee. 1978–85; Pres. of Presidium of Supreme Soviet of Latvian S.S.R. 1985–89; Deputy Pres. of U.S.S.R. Supreme Soviet –1989; mem. of CPSU Cen. Auditing Comm. *Address:* c/o Presidium of Supreme Soviet of Latvian S.S.R., Riga, Latvia, U.S.S.R.

VAILLAUD, Michel L.; French business executive; b. 23 Dec. 1931, Paris; m. Françoise Gaillard 1958; three d.; ed. Ecole Polytechnique, Paris, Paris School of Mines and Petroleum School of Paris; Civil Service 1955–73, Head of Oil and Gas Directorate 1969–73, Dir. Nat. Centre for Oceanic Exploration 1969–73, Chair. Nat. Office for Aerospace Study and Research 1972–73; joined Schlumberger Ltd. 1973, Vice-Pres., U.S. Electronics 1973–75, Exec. Vice-Pres., Measurement and Control (Europe) 1975–81, Exec. Vice-Pres., (Operations), Oilfield Services and Dir. 1981–82, Pres., C.O.O. and Dir. 1982–85, Chair. of Bd., Pres. and C.E.O. 1985–86; Admin. Cie Gen. des Eaux 1985–, RTL 1985–. *Address:* RTL, Villa Louvigny, Luxembourg-Ville, Luxembourg (Office); 60 East End Avenue, New York, N.Y. 10028, U.S.A.

VAINO, Karl Genrikhovich; Soviet politician; mem. Cen. Cttee. of Estonian CP 1956–, Chair. Dept. of Industry and Transport 1956–57; Deputy Chair. of Econ. Council of Estonian S.S.R. 1957–60; Sec. and mem. Politburo, Cen. Cttee. of Estonian CP 1960–, First Sec. of Cen. Cttee. of Estonian CP –1988; Chair. of Politburo for Industry and Construction of Estonian CP 1962–64; mem. Presidium of Supreme Soviet of Estonian S.S.R.; mem. CPSU Cen. Cttee. 1986–; Order of Lenin 1983. *Address:* Supreme Soviet of Estonian S.S.R., Tallinn, Estonian S.S.R., U.S.S.R.

VAINSHTEIN, Boris Konstantinovich; Soviet physicist; b. 6 Dec. 1920, Moscow; ed. Moscow Univ.; corresp. mem. U.S.S.R. Acad. of Sciences 1962–, Dir. U.S.S.R. Acad. of Sciences, Inst. of Crystallography 1962–, (Chief of Laboratories 1958); major research in field of radio-physics; Acad. Prize 1958, Order of the Red Banner of Labour. *Address:* Institute of Crystallography of U.S.S.R. Academy of Sciences, Pyzhevsky Pereulok, 3, Moscow, U.S.S.R.

VAINSHTEIN, Lev Al'bertovich; Soviet physicist; b. 6 Dec. 1920, Moscow; s. of Albert Vainshtein and Maria Andreevna Balashova; m. Raïsa Mash; two s. two d.; ed. Moscow State Univ.; worked at Inst. of Physical Problems, U.S.S.R. Acad. of Sciences 1957–, corresp. mem.; prin. scientific work in area of radiophysics. *Publications:* Electromagnetic Waves 1957, Extraction of Signals from Noise (with V. Zubakov) 1960, The Theory of Diffraction and the Factorization Method 1966, Open Resonators and Open Waveguides 1966, Lectures on Hyperhigh frequency Electronics (with V. A. Solntzev) 1973, Separation of Frequencies in the Theory of Oscillations and Waves (with D. Vakman) 1983. *Leisure interest:* poetry. *Address:*

Institute for Physical Problems, Kosygin str. 2, 117973, GSP 1 Moscow, U.S.S.R. *Telephone:* 137-18-66.

VAIVODS, H.E. Cardinal Julijans; Soviet ecclesiastic; b. 18 Aug. 1895, Vorkova, Latvia; ordained priest 1918; consecrated Bishop 1964; Apostolic Admin. of Metropolitan See of Riga and Liepaja; Titular Bishop of Greater Macriana; Pres. Episcopal Conference of Lestonia; Consultant to Pontifical Comm. for the Revision of the Code of Canon Law; cr. Cardinal 1983; hon. medal Soviet Peace Fund 1984. *Address:* Pils Iela 2, Riga 226047, Latvia, U.S.S.R. *Telephone:* 227266.

VAJDA, Dr. György; Hungarian engineer; b. 18 June 1927, Budapest; s. of László Vajda and Mária Daróczi; m. 1st Magdolna Krasznai (died 1987), one s. one d., 2nd Dr. Klára Berei 1988; ed. Tech. Univ., Budapest; Asst. Lecturer 1949–50; on staff of Hungarian Acad. of Sciences 1950–52; Deputy Dir. Inst. of Measurements 1952–57, Research Inst. of Electric Energetics 1957–63; Deputy Section Leader, Ministry of Heavy Industry 1963–70; Dir. Inst. for Electrical Power Research 1970–; Co-Pres. Hungarian Electrotech. Soc.; Vice-Pres. Nat. Atomic Energy Comm. 1979–; mem. Hungarian Nat. Comm. for Tech. Devt.; Corresp. mem. Hungarian Acad. of Sciences 1976–81, mem. and Section Pres. 1982–; mem. Conference Int. des Grands Reseaux Électriques, Paris, mem. World Energy Conference, London; Chair. ECE Electric Power Comm. 1972–76; State Prize 1975. *Leisure interest:* gardening. *Publications:* A szigetelések romlása (Deterioration of Insulations) 1964, Szigetelések villamos erőterei (Electric Power Fields of Insulation) 1970, Energia és Társadalom (Energy and Society) 1975, Energetika (Energetics), Vol. I–II; 150 papers in int. trade journals. *Address:* Villamosenergiaipari Kutató Intézet, Budapest V. Zrinyi utca 1, Hungary. *Telephone:* 172-319.

VAJNAR, Vratislav. JUDR., CSC.; Czechoslovak politician; b. 17 Sept. 1930, Stražice, Rokycany Dist.; ed. Acad. of Commerce, Coll. of Political and Econ. Sciences Charles Univ. Prague; teacher, Mil. Political Acad. 1956–58; official, Ministry of Foreign Affairs 1958–72; political worker, Int. Politics Dept., CP Cen. Cttee. 1972–74, aide to Gen. Sec. 1974–77, mem. 1981–; head Sec. of CP Gen. Sec. 1977–83; Minister of the Interior 1983–88. *Publication:* The Right of Nations to Self-Determination in United Nations Practice 1958; award "For service in Construction" 1971, Order of Labour 1980. *Address:* Communist Party of Czechoslovakia Central Committee, Nábř Ludvíka Svobdy 12, 125 11 Prague 1, Czechoslovakia.

VAJPAYEE, Atal Bihari, M.A.; Indian politician; b. 25 Dec. 1926, Gwalior, Madhya Pradesh; ed. Victoria Coll., Gwalior, D.A.V. Coll., Kanpur; mem. Rashtriya Swayamsewak Sangh 1941, Indian Nat. Congress 1942–46; mem. Lok Sabha 1957–62, 1967–84 (for New Delhi March 1977–84), Rajya Sabha 1962–67; founder mem. Bharatiya Jana Sangh 1951, Pres. 1968–74, Parl. Leader 1974–77; Chair. Public Accounts Cttee. Lok Sabha 1969–70; Leader Jan Sangh Party 1957–75; detained during Emergency 1975–77; mem. Janata Party 1977–, Leader until Feb. 1983; Pres. Bharatiya Janata Party 1983–86, 1986–88; Minister of External Affairs March 1977–79; mem. Nat. Integration Council 1962, IPU Conf., Tokyo 1975, Railway Convention Cttee. 1971–72. *Publications:* Amar Balidan, Mrityuya Hatya, Jana Sangh our Musalman, Kaidi Kavirai ki Kundaliya, New Dimensions of India's Foreign Policy. *Address:* 7 Safdaring Road, New Delhi 110011, India. *Telephone:* 375141.

VAKHROMEYEV, Kyril Varfolomeyevich (see Philaret).

VALCOURT, Bernard, B.A., LL.B.; Canadian lawyer and politician; b. 18 Feb. 1952, St. Quentin de Restigouche, N.B.; s. of Bertin Valcourt and Geraldine Allain; m.; two d.; ed. Académie St. Joseph, Collège St. Louis–Maillet, Univ. of New Brunswick; practised law, mem. Canadian Bar Asscn. and N.B. Lawyers Asscn.; M.P. 1984–, Parl. Sec. to Minister of State for Science and Tech., Minister of Revenue 1985–86; Minister of State for Small Business and Tourism July 1986–89, Minister of State for Indian Affairs and Northern Devt. 1987–89; Minister for Consumer and Corp. Affairs Jan. 1989–; Progressive Conservative. *Address:* House of Commons, Ottawa K1A, Canada.

VÁLEK, Miroslav, Czechoslovak poet and politician; b. 17 July 1927, Trnava; ed. College of Econs., Bratislava; official, press dept., Union of Slovak Farmers, ed., chief ed. of periodicals: Slovenský rolník (Slovak Farmer), Týždeň (Week), Družstevný obzor (Cooperative Horizon), Mladá tvorba (Youth Art) 1948–63; mem. of the Cttee., Union of Slovak Writers (SSS) 1963–68, mem. Cen. Cttee. Union of Czechoslovak Writers (SČSS), 1963–69, Sec. SSS 1965–66; chief ed., literary monthly Rhomboid, 1966–67; mem. of the Pres. and Chair., SSS 1967–68; Deputy Chair., SČSS 1968–69, Chair. 1989–; Minister of Culture of Slovak Socialist Repub. 1969–; mem. of the Cttee. SSS 1969–; mem. Cen. Cttee, CP of Slovakia, 1969–; mem. of the Pres., 1969–; Deputy Chair., Slovak Cen. Cttee., Czechoslovak-Soviet Friendship Soc. 1969–82; mem. of the Cen. Cttee. Pres., Nat. Front 1971–76; mem. Cen. Cttee. of the CP of Czechoslovakia, 1971–; Deputy, Slovak Nat. Council, 1976; Klement Gottwald State Prize 1966, Bedřich Smetana Medal 1974, title Artist of Merit 1975, Nat. Artist 1977, Order of Labour 1977, literary prize Sofia 1983 Bulgaria, 1984, *Works:* collections of poems, selected articles and interviews, translations of Russian, French and Polish poetry. *Address:* Communist Party of Czechoslovakia, Nábř. Ludvíka Svobody 12, Prague, Czechoslovakia.

VALENCIA-IBÁÑEZ, Gen. Edmundo; Bolivian army officer and diplomatist; b. 8 March 1925, La Paz; s. of Juan de Dios Valencia and Sara Ibáñez de Valencia; m. Violeta Collazos de Valencia 1950; three s. one d.; ed. various military colls., Bolivia and U.S.A.; fmr. Mil. Attaché, Paris; Chief of Staff of 3rd and 7th Div.; Commdr. of 7th Div.; fmr. Minister of Nat. Economy, of Industry and Commerce and of Finance (a.i.); fmr. Gov. IDB; Amb. to U.S.A. 1971–74, also accred. to Canada 1972; Perm. Rep. of Bolivia to OAS 1971–74; Pres. Sugar-Cane and Sugar Bd. (CNECA), Fábrica Nacional de Fósforos, Inst. for Promotion of Investments in Bolivia (INPIBOL), Nat. Council for Electricity; Pres. of Rowe Fund in OAS; Exec. Dir. Inter-American Devt. Bank 1974–77; Amb. Extraordinary and Plenipotentiary to Canada 1977–80; Special Consultant to IDB, Washington 1980–81; Rep. of IDB in Honduras 1982–, Adviser to IDB, Washington 1984–86; decorations from Bolivia, Argentina, China and Honduras. *Leisure interest:* reading. *Address:* 9821 Singleton Drive, Bethesda, Md., U.S.A. *Telephone:* (301) 530-7666.

VALENCIA-RODRÍGUEZ, Luis, LL.D.; Ecuadorean professor of law and diplomatist; b. 5 March 1926, Quito; s. of Pedro Valencia and María Rodríguez; m. Cleopatra Moreno 1952; two s. three d.; ed. Cen. Univ., Quito; entered Ecuadorean Foreign Service 1944; Counsellor, Buenos Aires 1957–59; Minister-Counsellor, UN, New York 1959–64; Minister of Foreign Affairs 1965–66, 1981–84; legal adviser on foreign affairs 1964–65, 1966–69, 1980–81; Amb. to Bolivia 1969–71, to Brazil 1971–74, to Peru 1974–78, to Venezuela 1978–79; now in private legal practice and Prof. Cen. Univ., Quito 1984–; special citation of Ecuadorean Nat. Ass. 1966 and decorations from Ecuador, Italy, Nicaragua, Bolivia, Brazil, Peru, Venezuela, Colombia, Argentina, El Salvador and Dominican Republic. *Publications:* books on legal matters, foreign affairs etc. *Leisure interests:* swimming, reading. *Address:* Calle Agustín Mentoso 273 (Urb. Mexterior), Quito, Ecuador. *Telephone:* 45-8765; 45-3510.

VALENTI, Jack; American film executive and fmr. government official; b. 5 Sept. 1921, Houston, Tex.; s. of late Mr. and Mrs. Joseph Valenti; m. Mary Margaret Wiley 1962; one s. two d.; ed. High School, Houston, Univ. of Houston and Harvard Business School; fmr. office boy, oil company; U.S.A.F., Second World War; co-f. Weekly & Valenti Advertising 1951; Special Asst. to Pres. Johnson 1963–66; Pres. and C.E.O. Motion Picture Asscn. of America 1966–; Chair. Alliance of Motion Picture and Television Producers Inc. 1966–; Dir. American Film Inst. 1967–; mem. Bd. Dirs. TW Services, Inc., Riggs Nat. Bank; mem. Bd. of Trustees, J.F.K. Center for the Performing Arts, American Film Inst. *Publications:* The Bitter Taste of Glory 1971, A Very Human President 1976, Speak Up with Confidence 1982. *Address:* 1600 I Street, N.W., Washington, D.C. 20006, U.S.A.

VALENTINE, William Newton, M.D.; American professor of medicine; b. 29 Sept. 1917, Kansas City, Mo.; s. of Herbert S. Valentine and Mabel W. Valentine; m. Martha Hickman Winfree Valentine 1950; three s.; ed. Univs. of Michigan and Missouri and Tulane Univ. School of Medicine; Intern, Asst. Resident, Chief Resident, Univ. of Rochester School of Medicine 1942–44, Instr. in Medicine 1947–48, Section Chief, Haematology, Atomic Energy Project 1947–48; Asst. Prof., Assoc. Prof. Univ. of Calif. at Los Angeles 1950–57, Prof. of Medicine 1957–88, Prof. Emer. 1988–, Chair. Dept. of Medicine 1963–71; mem. N.A.S. and various professional asscns. etc.; several awards. *Publications:* more than 200 publs. in the fields of haematology, red cell metabolism and inherited anaemias. *Address:* University of California, Center for the Health Sciences, Los Angeles, Calif. 90024 (Office); 403 North Orange Drive, Los Angeles, Calif. 90036, U.S.A. (Home). *Telephone:* 213-825-5513 (Office); 213-939-4203 (Home).

VALENTINI TERRANI, Lucia; Italian mezzo-soprano; b. 29 Aug. 1946, Padua; m. Alberto Terrani 1973; won Voci Rossiniane int. competition 1972; début La Scala, Milan in Rossini's Cenerentola (title role) 1973; has sung in the world's maj. opera houses under many famous conductors; many prizes for recordings and TV appearances. *Leisure interest:* skiing. *Address:* Via XX Settembre 72, 35100 Padova, Italy. *Telephone:* 049-655-271.

VALLANCE, Iain David Thomas, M.SC.; British business executive; b. 20 May 1943; s. of Edmund Thomas Vallance and Janet Wright Bell Ross Davidson; m. Elizabeth Mary McGonnigill 1967; one s. one d.; ed. Edinburgh Acad., Dulwich Coll., Glasgow Acad., Brasenose Coll., Oxford, London Grad. School of Business Studies; Asst. Postal Controller, Post Office 1966, Personal Asst. to Chair. 1973–75, Head of Finance Planning Div. 1975–76, Dir. Cen. Finance 1976–78, Telecommunications Finance 1978–79, Materials Dept. 1979–81; mem. Bd. for Org. and Business Systems, British Telecommunications 1981–83, Man. Dir., Local Communications Services Div. 1983–85, Chief of Operations 1985–86, Chief Exec. 1986–87, Chair. 1987–; Dir. Postel Investment Man. Ltd., 1983–85; Trustee, British Telecom Staff Superannuation Fund 1983–85; Fellow, London Business School 1989–. *Address:* 81 Newgate Street, London, EC1A 7AJ, England.

VALLANCE-OWEN, John, M.A., M.D., F.R.C.P., F.R.C.P.I., F.R.C.PATH.; British professor of medicine and physician; b. 31 Oct. 1920, London; s. of Edwin Augustine Vallance-Owen and Julia May; m. Renee Thornton 1950; two s. two d.; ed. Friars School, Bangor, Epsom Coll., Surrey, Cambridge Univ.; various appts. including Pathology Asst. and Medical First Asst., London Hosp. 1946–51; Medical Tutor, Royal Postgraduate Medical School, Hammersmith Hosp., London 1952–55, 1956–58; Consultant Physician and Lecturer in Medicine, Univ. of Durham 1958–64; Consultant Physician and Reader in Medicine, Univ. of Newcastle upon Tyne 1964–66; Prof. and Chair., Dept. of Medicine, Queen's Univ. of Belfast, and Consultant Physician to Royal Victoria Hosp., Belfast City Hosp. and Foster Gran Hosp., Belfast 1966–82; Dir. of Medical Services, The Maltese Islands 1981–82; Foundation Prof. and Chair. Dept. of Medicine, The Chinese Univ. of Hong Kong 1983–87, Assoc. Dean 1984–87; Consultant in Medicine to Hong Kong Govt. 1984–, to British Army in Hong Kong 1985–; Visiting Prof. Royal Postgraduate Medical School, Hammersmith Hosp.; Consultant Physician London Ind. Hosp.; Rockefeller Travelling Fellowship, held at Univ. of Pa., U.S.A. 1955–56; Oliver-Sharpey Prize, Royal Coll. of Physicians 1976. *Publications:* Essentials of Cardiology 1961, Diabetes: Its Physiological and Biochemical Basis 1974; numerous papers in scientific journals on carbohydrates and fat metabolism and the aetiology of diabetes mellitus, with special reference to insulin antagonism. *Leisure interests:* music, tennis, golf, trees. *Address:* 17 St Matthews Lodge, Oakley Square, London, NW1 1NB; 10 Spinney Drive, Great Shelford, Cambridge, England. *Telephone:* 01-388 3644; Cambridge 842767.

VALLEE, Bert Lester, M.D.; American (b. German) biochemist, physician and university professor; b. 1 June 1919, Hemer, Westphalia, Germany; s. of Joseph Vallee and Rosa (Kronenberger) Vallee; m. Natalie Kugris 1947; ed. Univ. of Berne, Switzerland and New York Univ. Coll. of Medicine; went to U.S.A. 1938, naturalized 1948; Research Fellow, Harvard Medical School, Boston 1946–49, Research Assoc. 1949–51, Assoc. 1951–56, Asst. Prof. of Medicine 1956–60, Assoc. Prof. 1960–64, Prof. of Biological Chem. 1964–65, Paul C. Cabot Prof. of Biological Chem. 1965–80, Paul C. Cabot Prof. of Biochemical Sciences 1980–; Research Assoc., Dept. of Biology, M.I.T. 1948–; Physician Peter Bent Brigham Hosp., Boston 1961–80; Biochemist-in-Chief, Brigham and Women's Hosp., Boston 1980–; Scientific Dir. Biophysics Research Lab., Harvard Medical School, Peter Bent Brigham Hosp. 1954–80; Head, Center for Biochemical and Biophysical Sciences and Medicine, Harvard Medical School and Brigham and Women's Hosp. 1980–; Founder and Trustee Boston Biophysics Foundation 1957–; Founder Endowment for Research in Human Biology, Inc. 1980–; Fellow A.A.A.S., N.A.S., American Acad. of Arts and Sciences, N.Y. Acad. of Sciences; mem. American Chemical Soc., Hon. Foreign mem. Royal Danish Acad. of Sciences and Letters; Hon. A.M. (Harvard) 1960, Hon. M.D. (Karolinska Inst.) 1987; Linderstrøm-Lang Award and Gold Medal 1980, Willard Gibbs' Gold Medal 1981, William C. Rose Award in Biochemistry 1982. *Publications:* over 500 publs. on zinc and other metalloenzymes; their structure, function and mechanism of action; emission, absorption, CD and MCD spectroscopy; organic chemical modification of proteins; organogenesis. *Leisure interest:* riding. *Address:* Center for Biochemical and Biophysical Sciences and Medicine, Harvard Medical School, Seeley G. Mudd Building, 1st Floor, 250 Longwood Avenue, Boston, Mass. 02115, U.S.A.

VALOV, Yuriy Nikolayevich; Soviet politician; b. 1934; ed. Moscow Inst. of Energetics; engineer, dir. of Moscow cable network Mosenergo, 1958–66; mem. CPSU 1961–; Deputy Head of Section of CPSU Moscow City Cttee. 1966–72; Pres. of Mosvoretsky regional exec. cttee., Moscow 1972–77; Head of Section of CPSU Moscow City Cttee. 1977–81; Deputy Pres. of Moscow City Exec. Cttee. 1981–83; First Deputy Man. of CPSU Cen. Cttee. 1983–; cand. mem. of CPSU Cen. Cttee. 1986–. *Address:* Central Committee of Communist Party of Soviet Union, Kremlin, Moscow, U.S.S.R.

VALTICOS, Nicholas, D. EN D.; Greek judge; b. 1918; ed. Univ. of Paris; barrister at law in Athens 1941–42; Chief of section Comm. administering Relief in Greece 1942–45; joined ILO 1949, Chief of Application of Conf. Decisions Div. 1955–64, Chief Int. Labour Standards Dept. 1964–76, Asst. Dir.-Gen. and Adviser for Int. Labour Standards 1976–81; Assoc. Prof. at Faculty of Law, Univ. of Geneva 1972–81; ad hoc Judge at Int. Court of Justice 1984–85 (case concerning Continental Shelf, Libya/Malta), 1987– (case-frontier dispute, El Salavador/Honduras); Judge at the European Court of Human Rights 1986–; Henri Rolin Professor of Int. Law, Belgium 1979–80; Corresp. mem. Acad of Athens; mem. Perm. Court of Arbitration; Council of Int. Inst. of Human Rights; American Soc. of Int. Law; Société francaise de droit int.; Int. Law Asscn.; Greek Soc. of Int. Law; mem. and Chair. of various int. arbitral tribunals and comms. of inquiry; Prix de la Faculté and Prix Dupin Aîné, Paris; Dr. h.c. Univs. of Athens, Leuven, Utrecht; Officier, Légion d'honneur, Commdr. of the Order of Honour (Greece) 1981, of Isabella la Catolica (Spain) 1986. *Address:* International Court of Justice, Peace Palace, The Hague 2517 KJ, Netherlands.

VÁMOS, Tibor, PH.D., D.SC.; Hungarian electrical engineer; b. 1 June 1926, Budapest; s. of Miklós Vámos and Ilona Rausnitz; m. Mária Fekete; one s. one d.; ed. Tech. Univ. Budapest; started in process control automation of power plants and systems, worked later in computer control of processes, robot vision, artificial intelligence; Chief Eng. Research Inst. of Power System Eng. Co. 1950–54, Automation Dept. Head 1954–64; Dir. Computer and Automation Inst. of the Hungarian Acad. of Sciences 1964–85, Chairman 1986–; Prof. Budapest Tech. Univ. 1969–; Dr. h.c. (Tallinn Univ., U.S.S.R.); Corresp. mem. Hungarian Acad. of Sciences 1973, mem. 1979–, mem. Presidium 1986–; mem. State Cttee. of Tech. Devt; Chair. Ministry of Industry Scientific Council 1986–; Pres. IFAC Int. Fed. of Automatic

Control 1981–84; Fellow IEEE Inc. 1986–; Hon. Pres. John Neumann Soc. of Computer Science; Labour Medal of Merit 1951, Labour Order of Merit 1967, 1980, State Prize 1983; specializes in expert systems combined with pattern recognition and conceptual modelling. *Publications:* Nagy ipari folyamatok irányítása (Control of Large-Scale Processes) 1970; Co-author: Applications of Syntactic Pattern Recognition 1977, Progress in Pattern Recognition 1981; about 120 contribs. to scientific journals. *Leisure interests:* fine arts, mountaineering. *Address:* Magyar Tudományos Akadémia Számítástechnikai és Automatizálási Kutatóintézet, Budapest XIII, Victor Hugo utca 18/22, Hungary. *Telephone:* 36/1/496-935.

VAN AARDENNE, Gijs M. C.; Netherlands politician; b. 18 March 1930, Rotterdam; ed. Leiden Univ.; Deputy Man. Dir. Koninklijke Fabriek Penn en Bauduin N.V., Dordrecht 1957–67, Dir. 1967–70; Councillor, Dordrecht, and two years as alderman 1964–77; Minister of Econ. Affairs 1977–81; Deputy Prime Minister and Minister of Econ. Affairs 1982–86; mem. People's Party for Freedom and Democracy. *Address:* c/o Ministry of Economic Affairs, Bezuidenhoutseweg 30, P.O. Box 20101, 2500 EG, The Hague, Netherlands.

VAN AGT, Andries A. M. (see Agt, Andries A. M. van).

VAN ALLAN, Richard; British opera singer; b. 28 May 1935, Clipstone, Notts.; s. of Joseph Arthur and Irene Hannah Jones; m. Rosemary Pickering 1976 (divorced 1987); two s. one d.; ed. Brunt's Grammar School, Mansfield, Worcester Teaching Training Coll., Birmingham School of Music; studied singing under David Franklin and Jani Strasser; first appearance with Glyndebourne Festival Opera 1964; with Welsh Nat. Opera 1967, with Sadler's Wells Opera (now English Nat. Opera) 1968, as principal bass, Royal Opera House, Covent Garden 1971–, with Paris Opera 1975, with Boston Opera, Mass., and San Diego Opera, Calif. 1976; debut Colón Theatre, Buenos Aires 1978, Le Monnaie, Brussels 1982, Miami 1985, Seattle 1987, Metropolitan, New York 1987; Dir. Nat. Opera Studio, London 1986–; John Christie award, Glyndebourne 1967, Grammy Award (The Nat. Acad. of Performing Arts and Sciences) for Don Alfonso (Così fan tutte), Grammy Nomination for Leporello (Don Giovanni); Hon. mem. R.A.M. 1987. *Leisure interests:* cricket, tennis, shooting. *Address:* 18 Octavia Street, London, SW11 3DN, England. *Telephone:* 01-228 8462.

VAN ALLEN, James Alfred PH.D.; American physicist; b. 7 Sept. 1914, Mount Pleasant, Iowa; s. of Alfred Morris and Alma (Olney) Van Allen; m. Abigail Fithian Halsey II 1945; two s. three d.; ed. Iowa Wesleyan Coll. and State Univ. of Iowa; Research Fellow, Carnegie Inst., Washington 1939–41, Physicist (Dept. of Terrestrial Magnetism) 1941–42; Applied Physics Lab., Johns Hopkins Univ. 1942, 1946–50; Lieut.-Commdr. in U.S. Navy 1942–46; Head of Dept. and Carver Prof. of Physics, Univ. of Iowa 1951–85, Emer. 1985–; now Prin. Investigator, Pioneers 10 and 11, and Interdisciplinary Scientist, Galileo project; Guggenheim Research Fellow at Brookhaven Nat. Lab. 1951; Research Assoc. Princeton Univ. Project Matterhorn 1953–54; Dir. expeditions to study cosmic radiation, Cen. Pacific 1949, Alaska 1950, Arctic 1952, 1957, Antarctic 1957; mem. Rocket and Satellite Research Panel 1946, Chair. 1947–58, Exec. Cttee. 1958–; mem. Advisory Cttee. on Nuclear Physics, Office of Naval Research 1957–60; mem. Space Science Bd., N.A.S. 1958–70, Foreign mem. The Royal Swedish Acad. of Sciences 1981; Consultant, Pres.'s Science Advisory Cttee.; mem. Cosmic Radiation, Rocket Research and Earth Satellite Panel, Int. Geophysical Year; Fellow, American Physical Soc., American Geophysical Union, American Rocket Soc., Inst. of Electrical and Electronics Engineers, American Astronautical Soc., American Acad. of Arts and Sciences, A.A.A.S., Regents' Fellow, Smithsonian Inst. 1981; Pres.-elect American Geophysical Union 1980–82, Pres. 1982–84; mem. N.A.S., Royal Astronomical Soc. (U.K.) (Gold Medal 1978); founder mem. Int. Acad. of Astronautics; Assoc. Ed. Physics of Fluids 1958–62, Journal of Geophysical Research 1959–67; mem. Editorial Bd. Space Science Reviews 1962–; Distinguished Civilian Service Medal (U.S. Army) 1959, NASA Medal for Exceptional Scientific Achievement 1974, Distinguished Public Service Award (U.S. Navy) 1976, Award of Merit, American Consulting Engineers Council 1978, Space Science Award, American Inst. of Aeronautics and Astronautics 1982, Crawford Prize, Swedish Royal Acad. of Sciences 1989; numerous Hon. D.Scs.; discoverer of the "Van Allen Belt" of radiation around the earth and a pioneer of high-altitude rocket research. *Publications:* Physics and Medicine of the Upper Atmosphere, Rocket Exploration of the Upper Atmosphere, Origins of Magnetospheric Physics 1983, and 225 scientific papers; Ed. Scientific Use of Earth Satellites. *Address:* Department of Physics and Astronomy, 701 Van Allen Hall, University of Iowa, Iowa City, Iowa 52242 (Office); 5 Woodland Mounds Road, R.F.D. 6, Iowa City, Iowa 52240, U.S.A. (Home).

VAN BELLINGHEN, Jean-Paul; Belgian diplomatist; b. 21 Oct. 1925, Mechelen; s. of Albert van Bellinghen and Fernande Clavareau; m. Martine Vander Elst 1954; one s. one d., one s. deceased; ed. Catholic Univ. of Leuven; posts in Cairo 1956, Washington 1959, New York 1962, Geneva 1968; Spokesman for Minister of Foreign Affairs 1963, Asst. Perm. Pvt. Sec. to Minister of Foreign Affairs 1967, Perm. Pvt. Sec. to Minister of Foreign Affairs 1974, to Minister of Foreign Trade 1977; Amb. to Zaire 1980–83, to U.K. 1984–; Fellow of the Harvard Center for Int. Affairs 1967. *Leisure interests:* skiing, golf. *Address:* 103 Eaton Square, London, SW1W 9AB, England. *Telephone:* 01-235 5422.

VAN CITTERS, Robert L., M.D.; American professor of medicine, physiology and biophysics; b. 20 Jan. 1926, Alton, Ia.; s. of Charles J. Van Citters and Weilhelmina T. Van Citters; m. Mary E. Barker 1949; two s. two d.; ed. Univ. of Kansas; Intern, Univ. of Kansas Medical Center 1953–54; Medical Officer, Air Research and Devt. Command, Kirtland AFB, N.M. 1954–55; Resident, Internal Medicine, Univ. of Kansas Medical Center 1957–58; Research Fellow Cardiovascular Physiology, Univ. of Washington 1958–62; Research Assoc. Cardiopulmonary Inst., Scripps Clinic and Research Foundation, La Jolla, Calif. 1962; Exchange Scientist, Jt. U.S.-U.S.S.R. Scientific Exchange Agreement 1962; Asst. Prof. of Physiology and Biophysics School of Medicine, Univ. of Washington 1963–65, Assoc. Prof. 1965–68, Assoc. Dean for Research and Grad. Programs 1968–70, Chair. Bd. of Health Sciences 1970, Dean, School of Medicine 1970–81, Dean Emer. 1981–, Prof. of Medicine (Cardiology), Prof. of Physiology and Biophysics 1981–; mem. Inst. of Medicine, N.A.S.; Hon. D.Sc. (Northwestern) 1978. *Publications:* 150 publications in scientific journals. *Leisure interests:* fishing, gardening. *Address:* Division of Cardiology, RG-22, Department of Medicine, School of Medicine, University of Washington, Seattle, Wash. 98195, U.S.A. *Telephone:* (206) 543-9952.

VAN CULIN, Rev. Samuel, B.D.; American ecclesiastic; b. 20 Sept. 1930, Hawaii; s. of Samuel Van Culin and Susie Mossman; ed. Virginia Theological Seminary; curate, St. Andrew's Cathedral, Honolulu 1955–56; Canon Precentor and Rector, Hawaiian Congregation, Honolulu 1956–58; Asst. Rector, St. John's, Washington, D.C. 1958–60; Gen. Sec. Lyman Int. 1960–61; Asst. Sec. Overseas Dept., Exec. Council of the Episcopal Church 1962–68; Sec. Africa and the Middle East 1968–76, Exec. World Mission 1976–83; Sec.-Gen. Anglican Consultative Council 1983–; Hon. Canon (Canterbury, Jerusalem, Ibadan). *Leisure interests:* music, travelling. *Address:* Anglican Consultative Council, Partnership House, 157 Waterloo Road, London, SE1 8UT, England. *Telephone:* 01-620 1110.

VAN DAM, José; Luxembourg opera singer; b. 25 Aug. 1940, Brussels, Belgium, m.; ed. Académie de Musique, Brussels, Conservatoire Royal, Brussels; début in Paris in Carmen (Escamillo) 1961, with Grand Théâtre, Geneva 1965–67, Deutsche Oper, Berlin 1967–, Salzburg Festival, opera and concerts 1966–, Festival d'Aix en Provence 1966–, title role in St-François d'Assise (Messiaen) Paris 1983–84, Wozzeck at Royal Opera House, Covent Garden 1983–84, début in Meistersinger (Hans Sachs), Brussels 1985; awards include Grand Prix de l'Académie Française du Disque 1979, Orphée d'Or, Académie Lyrique Française 1980, Prix Européen des Critiques 1985. *Address:* c/o Artist's Management Zürich, Frau Rita Schütz, Rütistrasse 52, CH-8044 Zürich-Gockhausen, Switzerland.

VAN DE VEN, Johannes Adrianus; Netherlands lawyer; b. 15 Nov. 1930, Arnhem; m. Maria A. E. Oudemans 1960; four d.; ed. Univ. of Utrecht; Assoc., Jr. Partner, Sr. Partner, Blom, Dutilh, Briët, Rotterdam 1954–70; Sr. Partner Dutilh, van der Hoeven & Slager, Rotterdam 1970–, Chair. 1982–88; Treas. Int. Bar Asscn. 1986–; Chair. Synod, Old Catholic Church of the Netherlands 1980–87; Dir. of several corpns. and other professional appts. *Leisure interests:* historic studies, walking. *Address:* Dutilh, van der Hoeven & Slager, P.O. Box 1110, 3000 BC Rotterdam (Office); 42 Oranjelaan, 3062 BT Rotterdam, Netherlands (Home). *Telephone:* 10-4020600.

VAN DEN BERGH, Gen. Hendrik Johannes; South African government official and police officer; b. 1915, Orange Free State; m. J. J. ("Kotie") van den Bergh; two s. three d.; ed. Vredefort High School, Orange Free State; joined police as constable 1934; interned for three years at Koffiefontein for opposition to S.A. mobilization in World War II; Lieut. 1950, Capt. 1953, Major 1959, Lieut.-Col. 1962; Col. and Head of Security Branch 1963; organized Rivonia raid, Poqo and Umkhonto we Sizwe arrests 1964; Brig.-Gen. 1964; African Resistance Movement and S.A. CP arrests 1964; Maj.-Gen. 1966, Lieut.-Gen. and Deputy Commr. of Police 1968; Security Adviser to Prime Minister 1968; Sec. for Security and Intelligence (head of Bureau for State Security) 1968–78 (resgnd.); passport seized 1979; rank of Gen. 1968; S.A. Police Star for Distinguished Service 1967. *Publications:* Foreword in W. G. Pretorius: Communism—Fact and Fable 1968, Chapter in (Ed.) G. Kronjé: Kommunisme: Teorie en Praktyk 1969, Article in Journal of Racial Affairs 1972, in The Public Servant 1976. *Leisure interests:* farming, listening to light classical music.

VAN DEN BROEK, Hans; Netherlands politician; b. 11 Dec. 1936, Paris, France; m.; two c.; ed. Alberdingk Thym Grammar School, Hilversum, Univ. of Utrecht; attended Sr. Man. training, De Baak, Noordwijk; solicitor in Rotterdam 1965–68; Sec. Man. Bd. ENKA B.V., Arnhem 1969–73, Commercial Man., 1973–76; City Councillor, Rheden 1970–74; mem. Second Chamber, States-Gen. (Parl.) 1976–81; served on Standing Cttees. on Foreign Affairs, Devt. Co-operation and Justice; Sec. of State for Foreign Affairs 1981–82, Minister Nov. 1982–. *Address:* Ministry of Foreign Affairs, Bezuidenhoutseweg 67, Postbus 20061, 2500 EB, The Hague, Netherlands.

VAN DEN HAAG, Ernest, PH.D.; American professor of law; b. 15 Sept. 1914, The Hague, Netherlands; s. of Max and Flora van den Haag; ed. Univs. of Florence, Naples, Iowa and the Sorbonne, Paris; Adjunct Prof. of Law, New York Law School; Lecturer in Sociology and Psychology, New School for Social Research; Adjunct Prof. of Social Philosophy, New York Univ.; John M. Olin Prof. of Jurisprudence and Public Policy,

Fordham Univ., New York 1982–88; Distinguished Scholar, Heritage Foundation 1981–; mem. Council on Foreign Relations; Guggenheim Fellow 1966; Fellow, American Sociological Asscn., Royal Econ. Soc. *Publications:* Education as an Industry 1956, The Fabric of Society (with R. Ross) 1957, Passion and Social Constraint 1969, The Jewish Mystique 1969, Political Violence and Civil Disobedience 1972, The Balancing Act (with G. Roche and A. Reynolds) 1974, Punishing Criminals 1975, Capitalism: Sources of Hostility 1979, The Death Penalty (with J. P. Conrad) 1983, The U.N.: In or Out? (with J. P. Conrad) 1987, U.S. Ends and Means in Central America: A Debate (with Tom J. Farer) 1988; numerous articles in learned journals. *Address:* 118 West 79th Street, New York, N.Y. 10024, U.S.A. *Telephone:* (212) 787 8512.

VAN DEN HOVEN, Helmert Frans; Netherlands business executive; b. 25 April 1923, IJsselmonde; m. 1st Dorothy Ida Bevan 1950 (dissolved 1981), one s.; m. 2nd Cocksy van As 1981; joined Unilever NV, Rotterdam 1938, at London Office 1948–50, at Unilever Office, Turkey 1951–62, Chair. 1958–62; Chair. Van den Bergh en Jurgens BV 1962; Dir. Unilever 1970; Vice-Chair. Unilever Ltd. (now PLC), Chair. Unilever NV 1975–83; Vice-Pres. ICC 1982–84, Pres. 1985–86, Immediate Past Pres. Jan. 1987–; mem. Supervisory Bd. Royal Boskalis Westminster; Kt. of Order of Netherlands Lion 1978, Hon. K.B.E. 1980. *Address:* c/o International Chamber of Commerce, 38 Cours Albert 1er, 75008 Paris, France.

VAN DER AVOIRD, Ad, PH.D.; Dutch professor of theoretical chemistry; b. 19 April 1943, Eindhoven; s. of H. J. van der Avoird and M. A. (née Kerkofs) van der Avoird; m. T. G. M. Lange 1964; two s.; ed. Tech. Univ., Eindhoven; Research Fellow, Inst. Batelle, Geneva, Switzerland 1965–67; Section Man. Unilever Research Lab., Vlaardingen 1967–71; Assoc. Prof., Univ. of Nijmegen, Nijmegen 1968–71, Prof. 1971–; mem. Netherlands Acad. of Sciences 1979–. *Publications:* articles in scientific journals. *Leisure interests:* sailing, windsurfing, tennis. *Address:* Institute of Theoretical Chemistry, University of Nijmegen, Toernooiveld, 6525 ED Nijmegen, The Netherlands. *Telephone:* (080) 613037.

VAN DER BEUGEL, Ernst H. (see Beugel, Ernst H. van der).

VAN DER BIEST, Alain; Belgian politician; b. 4 May 1943, Liège; ed. Univ. of Liège; taught French and Italian 1966–71; tutor, Univ. of Liège 1971–75; Deputy for Liege 1977–; Minister of Pensions 1988–. *Address:* Ministry of Pensions, Brussels, Belgium.

VAN DER BYL, The Hon. Pieter Kenyon Fleming-Voltelyn, B.A.; Zimbabwean politician; b. 11 Nov. 1923, Cape Town, S. Africa; s. of the late Major the Hon. P. V. G. and Mrs. Joy Clare Fleming van der Byl; m. Princess Charlotte of Liechtenstein 1979; one s.; ed. Cape Town, Cambridge and Harvard Univs.; Officer 7th Queen's Hussars (served in Middle East, Italy and Austria) 1943–46; tobacco farmer in Zimbabwe 1946–; M.P. 1962; Jr. Govt. Whip 1963; Deputy Minister of Information 1964–68; Minister of Information, Immigration and Tourism 1968–74, of Foreign Affairs 1974–79, of Defence 1974–76, of Public Service 1976–77, of Information, Immigration and Tourism 1977–79, Co-Minister 1978–79; Minister of Transport, Power and Posts in Bishop Muzorewa's Govt. 1979–80; mem. Senate –1987; Deputy Leader of Rhodesian Govt. Del. at Geneva Conf. on future of Rhodesia 1976; mem. Rhodesia Tobacco Asscn. Council 1956–62; Deputy Chair. Selous Farmers' Asscn. 1957. *Leisure interests:* big game hunting, shooting and fishing. *Address:* 4 Bath Road, Harare, Zimbabwe 22320; Fairfield, Caledon, Cape, South Africa. *Telephone:* Napier 1304.

VAN DER KEMP, Gerald, M.V.O.; French museum curator (retd.); b. 5 May 1912, Charenton-le-Pont; m. Florence Harris; two s. two d.; ed. Institut d'Art et d'Archéologie, Sorbonne; with Musée du Louvre 1936–41; Asst. Musée Nat. d'Art Moderne 1941–45; Curator of the Museums of Versailles, Trianons and Jeu de Paume 1945–53, Chief Curator 1953–80, Insp.-Gen. Nat. Museums 1972–80; Curator, Claude Monet Foundation at Giverny 1977–80; Hon. Pres. Christie's Europe 1980–; mem. Inst. de France (Acad. des Beaux-Arts) 1985–; Commdr., Légion d'honneur, Ordre des Arts et des Lettres, Grand Officier du Mérite de l'Ordre Souverain de Malte. *Address:* c/o Fondation Claude Monet, Giverny, 27620 Gasny-Sur-Eure, France.

VAN DER KLAAUW, Dr. Christoph Albert; Netherlands politician and diplomatist; b. 13 Aug. 1924, Leyden; m. 1st Henriette van Everdingen (deceased); five c.; m. 2nd Leontine van Noort 1989; ed. Leyden Municipal Gymnasium, State Univ. of Leyden; entered Ministry of Foreign Affairs as trainee 1952; Legation Attaché, Budapest 1952–53; Staff mem., Western Co-operation Dept. (NATO and European Defence Affairs Section), Ministry of Foreign Affairs; Second Sec., Oslo 1956–59; First Sec., Combined Perm. Netherlands Del. to N. Atlantic Council and OEEC, Paris 1959–63; Head of NATO and WEU Political Affairs Section, Ministry of Foreign Affairs, and Sec. of dels. to ministerial NATO and WEU Council sessions 1963–66; Counsellor, Rio de Janeiro 1966–70; Deputy Perm. Rep. to UN, New York 1970–74; Amb. serving as Perm. Rep. at UN and other int. orgs., Geneva 1975–77; Dir.-Gen. for European Co-operation 1977; Minister for Foreign Affairs 1977–81; Amb. to Belgium 1981–86, to Portugal 1986–; mem. People's Party for Freedom and Democracy (VVD), Advisory Cttee. on Foreign Policy 1964–66; mem. Telders Foundation 1964–66; fmr. Corresp. mem. Univ. Alumni Fund and advisory mem. Student Asscn., State Univ. of Leyden; Vice-Chair., Dutch Protestant League, Paris 1961–63,

Chair. Asscn. of Liberal Reformed Protestants of The Hague and Scheveningen 1964–66; Officer of Order of Orange-Nassau, Kt. of the Order of the Netherlands Lion, Grand Cross of the Order of Leopold (Belgium), Grand Cross of the Order of the Crown (Belgium) and other foreign decorations. *Publications:* Political Relations between the Netherlands and Belgium 1919–1939 1953, Integration at the Ministry of Foreign Affairs (article in Internationale Spectator) March 1977. *Leisure interests:* family, water sports, reading, contemporary and 19th century history. *Address:* Rua do Sacramento a Lapa 40, 1200 Lisbon, Portugal. *Telephone:* 01-607675.

VAN DER MEER, Jan, M.D.; Netherlands physician; b. 30 Aug. 1935, Leeuwarden; s. of L. van der Meer and G. Bakker; m. Joan Alkema 1962; one d.; ed. Univ. of Amsterdam; intern 1968; Sr. Registrar in Internal Medicine, Binnengasthuis, Amsterdam 1970–76; Head of Coagulation Lab., Cen. Lab. of Bloodtransfusion Service of Dutch Red Cross 1969–76; Prof. of Internal Medicine, Chair. of Dept., Acad. Hosp. of Free Univ. Amsterdam 1976–. *Publications:* Meting van de plasma renine-activiteit met behulp van een radioimmunologische bepaling van angiotensine I 1969. *Leisure interests:* music, skating, sailing. *Address:* Academic Hospital Free University, Department of Internal Medicine, P.O. Box 7057, 1007 MB Amsterdam, Netherlands. *Telephone:* (020) 548 2376.

VAN DER MEER, Simon; Netherlands engineer and physicist; b. 24 Nov. 1925, The Hague; m. Catharina M. Koopman 1966; one s. one d.; ed. gymnasium, The Hague and Univ. of Tech., Delft; Philips Physical Lab., Eindhoven 1952–56; Sr. Engineer European Org. for Nuclear Research (CERN) 1956–; Foreign Hon. mem. American Acad. of Arts and Sciences; corresp. Royal Netherlands Acad. of Sciences; Nobel Prize for Physics 1984; Hon. Dr. (Amsterdam, Geneva, Genoa). *Publications:* scientific papers. *Leisure interest:* reading. *Address:* 4 Chemin des Corbillettes, 1218 GD-Saconnex, Switzerland. *Telephone:* 984305.

VAN DER MERWE, Stoffel, D.PHIL; South African diplomatist and politician; b. 18 Dec. 1939, South Africa; s. of Rev. J. L. van der Merwe and C. M. E. Pretorius; m. Fransie Joubert 1964; three d.; ed. Pretoria and Stellenbosch Univs.; Dept. of Foreign Affairs 1962–71, Vice-Consul, Milan 1964–68, mem. del. to UN 1970; Head, Dept. of Political Science, Rand Afrikaans Univ. 1971–81; M.P. 1981–; Deputy Minister of Information 1986–88; Minister in Office of State Pres. in Charge of Information 1988–; Nat. Party. *Publications:* numerous articles on political subjects. *Leisure interests:* flying, small boat sailing. *Address:* Private Bag X745, Pretoria 0001; Private Bag X9007, Cape Town 8000, South Africa. *Telephone:* (012) 323-6162; (021) 46-8143.

VAN DER POST, Sir Laurens Jan, Kt., C.B.E.; British writer and explorer; b. 13 Dec. 1906, Philippolis, S. Africa; s. of late C. W. H. Van der Post and Marie Lubbe; m. 1st Marjorie Wendt 1929 (divorced 1947), one s. (deceased) one d.; m. 2nd Ingaret Giffard 1949; war service in Syria, Africa and the Far East 1939–45; prisoner of war 1943–45; Asst. to British Minister, Batavia 1945–47; leader of several expeditions in Africa for British Govt. and on his own account; Trustee, World Wilderness Foundation 1974–; produced films The Lost World of the Kalahari 1956, A Region of Shadow 1971, The Story of C. G. Jung 1971, All Africa Within Us 1975, Zulu Wilderness: Black Umfolozi Rediscovered 1979; hon. degrees from Univs. of Natal, Surrey, Liverpool, Rhodes, St. Andrews, Dundee. *Publications:* In a Province 1934, Venture to the Interior, A Bar of Shadow 1952, The Face Beside the Fire 1953, Flamingo Feather, The Dark Eye in Africa 1955, The Lost World of the Kalahari 1958, The Heart of the Hunter 1961, The Seed and the Sower 1962, Journey into Russia 1964, A Portrait of All the Russias 1967, The Hunter and the Whale 1967, A Portrait of Japan 1968, The Night of the New Moon 1970, A Story like the Wind 1972, A Far Off Place 1974, A Mantis Carol 1975, Jung and the Story of our Time 1976, First Catch your Eland: a Taste of Africa 1977, Yet Being Someone Other 1982, Testament to the Bushmen (with Jane Taylor) 1984, A Walk with a White Bushman: Laurens van der Post in Conversation with Jean-Marc Pottiez 1986. *Leisure interests:* walking, skiing, tennis. *Address:* 27 Chelsea Towers, Chelsea Manor Gardens, London, S.W.3; Turnstones, Aldeburgh, Suffolk, England; Wolwekop, Philippolis, South Africa.

VAN DER STEE, Alphons Petrus Johannes Mathildus Maria; Netherlands politician; b. 30 July 1928, Terheyden, N. Brabant; ed. Catholic Univ., Nijmegen; joined Begeijn, van Arkel and Co. 1956, Partner 1960; Chair. Arnhem section, Catholic People's Party 1959–63, mem. Exec. Cttee. and Treas. Catholic People's Party 1965, Chair. 1968; Sec. of State for Finance 1971–73; Minister of Agric. and Fisheries 1973–80, of Finance 1980–82, for Netherlands Antillean Affairs 1977–80; Dir. AGB Nederland 1983–; Christian Democratic Appeal Party. *Address:* c/o Ministry of Finance, Korte Voorhout 7, The Hague, Netherlands.

VAN DER STOEL, Max, LL.M., M.A.; Netherlands politician; b. 3 Aug. 1924, Voorschoten; one s. four d.; ed. Univ. of Leiden; Int. Sec. Labour Party (Partij van de Arbeid) 1958–65; mem. Exec. Bd. Socialist Int. 1958–65; mem. First Chamber of States-Gen. (Parl.) 1960–63, Second Chamber 1963–65, 1967–73, 1978–; State Sec. of Foreign Affairs 1965–66; mem. Ass. Council of Europe 1967–72; N. Atlantic Ass., European Parl. 1972–73; Minister of Foreign Affairs 1973–77, 1981–82; Perm. Rep. to the UN 1983–86; mem. Council of State 1986–; Grand Cross, Order of Merit

(Italy), Order of Repub. (Tunisia), Order of the White Rose (Finland) and other decorations. *Address:* Lubeckstraat 138, 2517 5V, The Hague, Netherlands. *Telephone:* (070) 459982.

VAN DER WAALS, J. Henri; Netherlands professor of experimental physics; b. 2 May 1920, Amsterdam; s. of Dr. H. G. van der Waals and Clara E. (née Nachenius) van der Waals; m. Elisabeth van Heek 1946; one s. two d.; ed. Montessori Lyceum, Univ. of Amsterdam, Univ. of Gröningen, King's Coll., Univ. of London; research physicist, Royal Dutch Shell labs., Amsterdam 1946–59; Assoc. Dir. for Gen. and Fundamental Research 1959–66; mem. Council, Faraday Soc. 1966–71, later Vice-Pres.; Visiting Prof. Univ. of Tokyo 1975; Chair. Div. of Natural Sciences, Royal Netherlands Acad. of Arts and Sciences 1984–87; Hon. Research Prof. Inst. of Molecular Biophysics, Fla. State Univ. 1966–67; Bourke Lecturer, Faraday Soc. 1962; Snellius Medal; Kristiakowski Lecturer, Chemical Dept., Harvard Univ. *Publications:* various articles in scientific journals. *Leisure interest:* sailing. *Address:* Huygens Laboratory, Leiden Univ., Niels Bohrweg 2, 2333 CA Leiden, Netherlands. *Telephone:* (71) 275910.

VAN DER WERFF, Terry, J., S.M., D.PHIL., F.R.S.A.; American engineering educator; b. 16 May 1944, Hammond, Ind.; s. of Sidney van der Werff and Johanna (née Oostman) van der Werff; m. Renee Marie Leet 1968; one s. four d.; ed. M.I.T., Oxford Univ.; staff engineer, ARO Inc., Tullahoma, Tenn. 1967–68; Asst. Prof. Mechanical Eng., Physiology and Biophysics, and Clinical Sciences, Colo. State Univ. 1970–73; Visiting Asst. Prof. of Medicine, Univ. of Colo. Medical Centre 1973–74; Chief Biomedical Engineer and Head, Biomedical Eng., Dept., Groote Schuur Hosp. and Univ. of Cape Town, S.A. 1974–80; Dean of Science and Eng., Seattle Univ. 1981–; Fellow, Biomedical Eng. Soc. of S.A. 1976. *Publications:* Mathematical Models of the Dynamics of the Human Eye (with R. Collins); 39 research papers, 70 book reviews and 24 newspaper articles. *Leisure interests:* book collecting. sport. *Address:* School of Science and Engineering, Seattle Univeristy, Seattle, Washington 98122, U.S.A. *Telephone:* (206) 296-5500.

VAN DER WOUDE, Adam Simon, D.D.; Netherlands professor of theology; b. 16 Oct. 1927, Oosterlittens; s. of Dirk van der Woude and Feikje (née Stremler) van der Woude; m. Frederika Catharina Sanders 1954; ed. Univ. of Gröningen; Minister Dutch Reformed Church, Noordlaren-Glimmen 1957–60; Prof. of the Old Testament, Univ. of Gröningen 1960–; Chair. Cttee. for Theological Higher Educ., Dutch Reformed Church 1987–, Governing Body Deaconess Nursing Home, Gröningen 1988–; mem. Royal Netherlands Acad. of Arts and Sciences 1974 (Chair. Arts Section 1987–); Hon. D.Theol. (Munich) 1972, Hon. D.D. (St. Andrews) 1985. *Publications:* Die messianischen Vorstellungen der Gemeinde von Qumrân 1957, (with J. P. M. van der Ploeg) Le Targum de Job de la grotte XI de Qumrân 1971, Commentaries on Micah 1974, Jonah-Nahum, Habakkuk-Sefaniah 1978, Haggai-Malachy 1982, Zefaniah 1984. *Leisure interest:* gardening. *Address:* 57 Domela Nieuwenhuislaan, 9722 LJ Gröningen, Netherlands. *Telephone:* 050-251417.

VAN DER ZALM, William N.; Canadian (b. Netherlands) politician; b. 29 May 1934, Noordwykerhout, Holland; s. of Wilhelmus Nicholaas van der Zalm and Agatha C. Warmerdam; m.; two s. two d.; ed. Phillip Sheffield High School, Abbotsford, B.C., Canada; emigrated to Canada 1947, became Canadian citizen; purchased Art Knapp Nurseries Ltd., became Co. Pres. 1956; elected to Surrey Municipal Council as Alderman 1965, as Mayor 1969; elected to Prov. Legis. for Social Credit Party, Minister of Human Resources 1975; Minister of Municipal Affairs and Minister responsible for Urban Transit Authority (now B.C. Transit) 1978; Minister of Educ. and Minister responsible for B.C. Transit 1982; est. Fantasy Garden World, major tourist attraction in Richmond 1983; Leader B.C. Social Credit Party July 1986–; Premier of B.C. July 1986–. *Address:* Office of the Premier, Victoria, British Columbia, Canada.

Van DEURSEN, Arie Theodorus; Netherlands professor of modern history; b. 23 June 1931, Gröningen; s. of Arie van Deursen and Trijntje Smilde; m. Else Ruth Junkers 1962; two s. two d.; ed. Gröningen Grammar School and Gröningen State Univ.; research asst. Univ. of Gröningen 1957; staff mem. Bureau, Royal Comm. of Dutch History 1958–67; Prof. of Modern History, Free Univ. Amsterdam 1967–; mem. Royal Acad. of Science 1978, Wijnaends Francken Award 1983. *Publications:* Professions et métiers interdits 1960, Honi soit qui mal y pense 1965, Jacobius de Rhoer 1970, Bavianen en slijkgeuzen 1974, Het kopergeld van de gouden eeuw (4 vols.) 1978–80, Willem van Oranje (with H. C. de Schepper) 1984. *Address:* Maluslaan 11, 1185 KZ Amstelveen; Vrije Universiteit, De Boelelaan 1105, P.O. Box 7161, MC Amsterdam, Netherlands.

VAN DIJK, Cornelis Pieter, B.ECONS., B.LL.; Netherlands politician; b. 25 July 1931, Rotterdam; m.; three c.; ed. Netherlands School of Econs. (now Erasmus Univ.); joined Nederlandse Bank van Suid-Afrika and ICI 1956–60; Admin. Officer Netherlands New Guinea 1960–62; with Ministry of Home Affairs, The Hague 1962–63; Consultant with OECD, Paris 1963–66; Head of a Div., World Bank, Washington 1966–73; ind. consultant on devt. co-operation; mem. Christian Democratic Alliance, Rotterdam Mun. Council; M.P. 1977–81, 1982–86; Minister for Devt. Co-operation 1981–82, for Home Affairs July 1986–; Christian Democratic Alliance. *Address:* c/o Ministry of Home Affairs, Schedeldoekshaven 200, P.O. Box 20011, 2500 EA The Hague, Netherlands. *Telephone:* (070) 71-79-11.

Van DIJK, Petrus, LL.M., S.J.D.; Netherlands professor of international law; b. 21 Feb. 1943, De Lier; s. of A. A. M. van Dijk and J. H. van Straelen; m. Francisca G. M. Lammerts 1969; one s. one d.; ed. Utrecht and Leyden Univs.; lecturer in Int. Law, Utrecht Univ. 1967-76, Prof. 1976-; Fullbright-Hays Scholar, Univ. of Mich. Law School 1970-71; Visiting Prof. Wayne State Univ. Law School 1978; Chair. Netherlands Inst. of Human Rights 1982-, Netherlands Inst. of Social and Econ. Law 1986-; mem. Court of Appeal of The Hague 1986; mem. various advisory cttees.; mem. Royal Netherlands Acad. of Arts and Sciences; mem. Netherlands Del. to UN Gen. Ass. 1981, 1983, 1986. *Publications include:* Theory and Practice of the European Convention on Human Rights (with G. J. H. van Hoof) 1979, The Final Act of Helsinki: Basis for a Pan-European System? 1980, Contents and Function of the Principle of Equity in International Economic Law; book chapters and ed. of numerous legal publs. *Address:* Gregoriuslaan 16, 3723 KR Bilthoven, Netherlands.

VAN EEKELEN, Willem Frederik, D.LL.; Netherlands diplomatist and politician; b. 5 Feb. 1931, Utrecht; m. Johanna Wentink; two c.; ed. Utrecht and Princeton Univs.; diplomatic service 1957-77; mem. Consultative Ass. Council of Europe and WEU 1981-82; Sec. of State for Defence 1978-81, for Foreign Affairs 1982-86; Minister of Defence 1986-88. *Address:* c/o Ministry of Defence, Plein 4, P.O. Box 20701, 2500 ES The Hague, Netherlands. *Telephone:* (070) 188 188.

VAN GERVEN, Walter M., DR.JUR.; Belgian lawyer; b. 11 May 1935, St. Niklaas; s. of Willy van Gerven and Germaine van Bel; m. Frieda Sintobin 1959; four s.; ed. Catholic Univ. of Louvain; Teaching Fellow, Univ. of Chicago Law School 1959-60; Assoc. Prof. of Law, Catholic Univ. of Louvain 1962-67, Prof. of Law 1967-82, Extraordinary Prof. 1982-, Vice-Rector 1970-76; Extraordinary Prof. Univ. of Amsterdam 1981-86; mem. Brussels Bar. 1970-80; Pres. Banking Comm. of Belgium 1982-88; mem. Bd. of Dirs. of several commercial cos.; Advocate-Gen. Court of Justice of European Communities 1988-; Visiting Prof. Univ. of Chicago 1968-69; mem. Royal Belgian Acad., Royal Netherlands Acad. *Publications:* Principles of Belgian Private Law 1968, Commercial and Economic Law (3 vols.) 1973-86, The Policy of the Judge 1973, In Law and Equity 1987. *Leisure interests:* modern art, music, golf. *Address:* Courts of Justice of the European Communities, Plateau de Kirschberg, 2925 Luxembourg (Office); Demarsinstraat 42, 3010 Wilsele, Belgium (Home). *Telephone:* 4303.22.61 (Office); 061/22.91.54 (Home).

VAN HOOVEN, Eckart, DR.JUR.; German company executive; b. 11 Dec. 1925; Chair. Supervisory Bd. Deutsche Kreditbank für Baufinanzierung AG, Cologne, Giesecke & Devrient GmbH, Munich, Handelsbank in Lübeck AG, Lübeck, Gebr. Happich GmbH, Wuppertal, Lübecker Hypothekbank AG, Lübeck, Mobil Oil AG, Hamburg; Deputy Chair. Supervisory Bd. Deutsche Schiffahrtsbank AG, Bremen, Hapag-Lloyd AG, Hamburg, Harpener AG, Dortmund; mem. Supervisory Bd. Kaufhof AG, Cologne, Reemtsma Cigarettenfabriken GmbH, Hamburg; mem. Bd. of Man. Dirs., Deutsche Bank AG, Frankfurt. *Address:* Deutsche Bank AG, 6000 Frankfurt am Main, Taunusanlage 12, Federal Republic of Germany.

VAN HOUTTE, Jan A(rthur Edmund), PH.D.; Belgian economic historian; b. 10 March 1913, Bruges; s. of Philibert and Marie (née de Cort) van Houtte; m. Annie van Herck 1938; three s. three d.; ed. St. Louis Coll., Bruges and Univ. of Louvain; Prof. Commercial High School, Univ. of Louvain 1936, Lecturer, Faculty of Letters 1937, Reader 1939, Prof. 1942, Prof. Emer. 1976; Dir. Acad. Belgica, Rome 1977-83; mem. Royal Belgian Acad. of Sciences 1957; Foreign mem. Royal Dutch Acad. of Sciences 1975; Corresp. mem. British Acad. 1970; Overseas Fellow, Churchill Coll., Cambridge 1974. *Publications:* Esquisse d'une histoire économique de la Belgique 1943 (also Dutch), Géopolitique 1946 (also Dutch 1945); Ed. Algemene Geschiedenis der Nederlanden (12 Vols.) 1949-58, 2nd edn. (15 vols.) 1977-83, Economische en Sociale Geschiedenis der Lage Landen 1964, Bruges, esquisse d'histoire urbaine 1967, Economic History of the Low Countries 800-1800 1977, Economische Geschiedenis der Lage Landen 1979, De Geschiedenis van Brugge 1982. *Leisure interests:* walking, sightseeing, art collecting. *Address:* "Termunkveld", Groeneweg 51, B-3030 Heverlee, Belgium (Home). *Telephone:* 016-22 15 42 (Home).

VAN ITTERSUM, Baron Boudewijn F.; Netherlands financial official; b. 1939; ed. Univ. of Amsterdam; joined Ministry of Finance; seconded to IMF, IBRD, Washington, D.C. 1970-72; subsequently Dir. of Int. Affairs, Ministry of Finance; Chair. Amsterdam Stock Exchange 1981-. *Address:* Vereniging voor de Effectenhandel Beursplein 5, 1012 JW, Amsterdam, Netherlands.

VAN LAETHEM, Gabriel, M.A., LL.M.; French international official; b. 4 Jan. 1918, Paris; s. of Henri van Laethem and Marguerite Honoré; m. Janine Burck; one s. two d.; ed. Ecole des Sciences Politiques, Paris; fought with French Forces in N. Africa and Italy during World War II; joined diplomatic service; Asst. Consul, Shanghai 1945-48; First Sec., Washington, D.C. 1949-54; First Counsellor to Gen. Commr. for Indo-China 1954-55; Head of Bilateral Tech. Assistance, Paris 1956; Dir.-Gen. of Office of High Commr. of France in Morocco 1957; Sec.-Gen. French Co. of the Sahara 1958-64; Counsellor 1964-66; Gen. Man., Dir. of Office of Industrial Co-operation in Algiers 1966-70; Minister Plenipotentiary 1969; Amb. to Australia 1971-74; Under-Sec.-Gen. for Econ. and Social

Affairs, UN 1975-78; Sr. Adviser Int. Affairs Banque Nat. de Paris 1978-; Officier, Légion d'honneur. *Address:* 96 rue de Longchamp, 92200 Neuilly-sur-Seine; La Safranette, Villefranche-sur-Mer 06230, France.

VAN LINT, Jacobus Hendricks, PH.D.; Netherlands professor of mathematics; b. 1 Sept. 1932, Bandung, Indonesia; s. of J. H. van Lint and P. C. E. Minkman; m. Elisabeth Barbara Janna Teunissen 1961; one s. one d.; ed. Univs. of Utrecht, Gottingen and Munster; Prof. of Math., Eindhoven Univ. of Tech. 1959-; mem. Tech. Staff, Bell Labs. 1966, 1971, 1977; Visiting Prof. Calif. Inst. of Tech. 1970-71, 1988-89; Pres. Wiskundig Genootschap 1968-70; mem. Royal Netherlands Acad. of Arts and Sciences 1973-. *Publications:* Coding Theory 1971, Algebra en Analyse (with S. T. M. Ackerman) 1974, Combinatorial Theory Seminar 1973, Graphs, Codes and Designs (with P. J. Cameron) 1980, Introduction to Coding Theory 1983. *Leisure interests:* philately, swimming, bridge. *Address:* Department of Mathematics, Eindhoven University of Technology, P.O. Box 513, 5600 MB Eindhoven; Beukenlaan 15, Nuenen 5671, Netherlands. *Telephone:* (31) 40 831466; (31) 40 472800.

VAN MANEN, Jan Dirk, D.SC.; Netherlands scientific adviser; b. 27 Feb. 1923, Hilversum; m. Alida A. W. Van Seters 1949; two d.; ed. Dalton High School, Tech. Univ. Delft; Head Dept. Scientific Research Netherlands Ship Model Basin (N.S.M.B.) 1952-57, Asst. Dir. 1957-62, Man. Dir. 1966-72, Pres. 1972-82; Extraordinary Prof. Resistance and Propulsion, Univ. of Delft 1962-66; Chair. Council of West European Conf. on Marine Tech. 1971-86, WEGEMT-Council 1975-81, Exec. Cttee. Int. Towing Tank Conference 1975-78, Advisory Council of ITTC 1978-84, Supervisory Bd. IHC-Inter 1982-84; Gen. Man. Maritime Research Inst. Netherlands 1982-86; Vice-Chair. Supervisory Bd. IHC-Caland 1984-; Scientific Adviser TNO 1986-; Exec. Ed. ISP 1966-86; Pres. 15th ITTC; mem. Dutch Soc. of Science, Royal Netherlands Acad. of Science; Fellow Royal Inst. of Navigation, London; Hon. mem.-Fellow The Soc. of Naval Architects and Marine Engineers; Hon. mem. Soc. of Naval Students 'William Froude'; Hon. Chair. West European Grad. Educ. in Maritime Tech. (WEGMT); Kt. of Order of the Netherlands Lion; Pres.'s Award Soc. of Naval Architects and Marine Engineers, and others. *Publications:* numerous articles and scientific papers on marine and naval architecture and marine research. *Address:* Nassau Zuilensteinstraat 12B, 2596 CB The Hague, Netherlands. *Telephone:* 31 70 246220.

van MUNSTER, Hans, DR.PHIL.; Netherlands ecclesiastic; b. 17 Nov. 1925, Gouda; s. of J. M. van Munster and A. C. B. Faay; ed. Univ. of Louvain; entered Order of St. Francis of Assisi 1944; ordained priest 1951; lecturer in Logic and Methodology, Philosophical Inst., Venray 1955-67; Regent, R.C. Lycee, Venray 1963-67; Prof. of Philosophy, Catholic Theological Faculty of Utrecht 1967-71, Rector 1968-71; Vicar-Gen. of Archdiocese of Utrecht 1970-81; Sec.-Gen. Dutch Bishops' Conf. 1981-; Officier Order of Oranje-Nassau. *Publications include:* De filosofische gedachten van de jonge Kierkegaard 1958, Kierkegaards redevoeringen 1959, Sören Aabye Kierkegaard 1963, Vanwaar? Waarheen? 1982, Drie prioriteiten voor de kerk van Europa 1983. *Leisure interests:* cycling, literature. *Address:* Jan van Scorelstraat 75, 3583 CL Utrecht, Netherlands. *Telephone:* 030-510153.

VAN NIEKERK, Willem Abraham, M.D., F.R.C.O.G., F.C.O.G. (S.A.); South African government official and gynaecologist; b. 29 June 1937, Pretoria, Transvaal; s. of Barend Johannes van Niekerk and Martha Maria Prinsloo; m. Magriet Myburgh 1960; one s.; ed. Univ. of Pretoria, Univ. of London; Research Fellow Roswell Park Memorial Inst., N.Y. 1960-66; Sr. lecturer Dept. of Obstetrics and Gynaecology, Univ. of Pretoria 1966-69; Prof. and Chair. Dept. of Obstetrics and Gynaecology, Univ. of Stellenbosch and Tygerberg Hosp., Cape Prov. 1970-82; Visiting Prof. New York Univ. 1975; Chair. Cttee. for Community Relations of the Pres.'s Council 1982-83; Admin. Gen. of S.W. Africa/Namibia 1983-85; Minister of Health and Population Devt. and Minister of Health, Ministers' Council of the House of Ass. 1985-; Daubenton Gold Medal 1969. *Publications:* Clinical, Morphological and Cytogenetic Agents 1979; seven chapters and 27 articles in medical books and journals. *Leisure interests:* fishing, tennis, performing arts, classical music. *Address:* Private Bag 9070, Cape Town 8000, South Africa.

VAN PALLANDT, Baron Wilprand, LL.D.; Netherlands diplomatist; b. 2 May 1926, Arnhem; m. Wilhelmina P. Ruys; three d.; ed. Univ. of Utrecht; Volunteer, Royal Netherlands Army 1945-49; entered Diplomatic Service 1955, Third Sec., Singapore 1955-57, Second Sec., Bonn 1957-59, Directorate NATO and WEU Affairs, Ministry of Foreign Affairs 1959-62, First Sec., Rome 1962-65, First Sec., Addis Ababa 1965-68, Counsellor, Bonn 1968-71, Directorate African and Middle Eastern Affairs, Ministry of Foreign Affairs 1971-72, (Minister) Counsellor, Madrid 1973-78; Amb. to Uruguay 1978-82, to Tunisia 1982-85, to Italy 1985-; Star for Order and Peace, Officer, Order of Orange-Nassau, Officer, Order of Merit (Italy), Commdr., Order of Merit (Fed. Repub. of Germany), Commdr. (First Class), Order of Isabel la Católica (Spain). *Leisure interests:* hunting, golf, reading. *Address:* Via della Camilluccia 750, Rome, Italy. *Telephone:* (06) 32.84.392.

VAN PRAAGH, Dame Margaret (Peggy), D.B.E.; British ballet director and teacher; b. 1 Sept. 1910, London; d. of Harold John Van Praagh and Ethel Louise Shanks; ed. King Alfred School, London; dancer with Dame

Marie Rambert 1933; examiner for Cechetti Soc. 1935; dancer, Sadler's Wells Ballet 1941–46; Ballet Mistress Sadler's Wells Theatre Ballet 1946–51; Asst. Dir. to Dame Ninette de Valois 1951–56; Artistic Dir., Borovansky Ballet, Australia 1960–61; Artistic Dir., The Australian Ballet 1962–74, 1978–79; examiner, cttee. mem. Cecchetti Soc. 1937–; Hon. D.Litt. (Univ. of New England, N.S.W.) 1974, Hon. LL.D. (Melbourne) 1981; Queen's Coronation Award, Royal Acad. of Dancing 1965; Distinguished Artist Award, Australia Council 1975. *Publications:* How I became a Ballet Dancer, The Choreographic Art (with Peter Brinson). *Address:* Flat 5, 248 The Avenue, Parkville, Victoria 3052, Australia. *Telephone:* 380-5773.

VAN RAFELGHEM, Carlos H.J.; Belgian government official; b. 8 Dec. 1925, Bruges; sr. public servant with Finance Ministry, Corpns. and Fiscal Co-ordination Directorate; has served in several ministerial depts. since 1968; Prof. of Corpn. Tax and Taxation Econs., Hogere Fiskale Leergangen and Economische Hogeschool Sint Aloysius, Brussels; Chair. SABENA (Belgian World Airlines) June 1978–. *Address:* S.A. SABENA N.V., rue Cardinal Mercier 35, 1000 Brussels, Belgium. *Telephone:* (02) 511 90 60.

VAN ROYEN, Olivier Henri Aurel; Netherlands engineer and business executive; b. 11 Feb. 1930, Budapest; m.; three s. one d.; ed. Montessori Lyceum, Amsterdam and Univ. of Delft; joined Koninklijke Nederlandsche Hoogovens en Staalfabrieken 1954; Man. Dir. NV Verenigde Buizenfabrieken VBF, Oosterhout (wholly-owned subsidiary of Hoogovens) 1970; Gen. Man. Hoogovens 1972; mem. Bd. of Man. Dirs. Hoogovens IJmuiden BV and Estel NV 1973–82; mem. Bd. of Man. Dirs. Hoogovens Groep BV 1982; Chair. Bd. of Man. Dirs. KNHS NV and Hoogovens Groep BV 1988–; mem. Supervisory Bd. AKZO Nederland BV, Arnhem, Koninklijke Nedlloyd Groep NV, Rotterdam; mem. Advisory Bd. AMRO-bank. *Address:* Hoogovens Groep BV, P.O. Box 10.000, 1970 CA IJmuiden, Netherlands. *Telephone:* 02514-99111.

VAN SWAAIJ, Willibrordus Petrus Maria, PH.D.; Netherlands professor of chemical engineering; b. 18 Jan. 1942, Nijmegen; s. of Christian van Swaaij and C. Bosman; m. J. J. T. van den Berk 1966; one s. four d.; ed. Tech. Univ. of Eindhoven, Univ. of Nancy, France; joined Shell Research 1965, worked in lab. Shell Research B.V. (KSLA), Amsterdam 1966–72, Section Chief, Gasification 1971–72; Prof. of Chemical Eng. Science, Twente Univ.; Consultant to DSM, AKZO, Unilever, Netherlands Govt., EEC; mem. Royal Netherlands Acad. of Sciences; Australian European Fellowship Award 1984; Dow Energy Prize 1985. *Publications:* Chemical Reactor Design and Operation (with Westerterp and Beenackers); about 200 scientific papers, contribs. to books etc. *Leisure interests:* sailing, surfing, model-building, gardening. *Address:* University of Twente, Department of Chemical Technology, P.O. Box 217, 7500 AE Enschede; Sportlaan 60, 7581 BZ Losser, Netherlands (Home).

VAN TAMELEN, Eugene Earle, PH.D.; American professor of chemistry; b. 20 July 1925, Zeeland, Mich.; s. of Gerrit van Tamelen and Henrietta (Vanden Bosch) van Tamelen; m. Mary Ruth Houtman 1951; one s. two d.; ed. Hope Coll. and Harvard Univ.; Instructor, Univ. of Wis. 1950–52, Asst. Prof. 1952–56, Assoc. Prof. 1956–59, Prof. 1959–61, Homer Adkins Prof. 1961–62; Prof. of Chem. Stanford Univ. 1962–87, Prof. Emer. 1987–, Chair. Dept. of Chem. 1974–78; Prof.-Extraordinarius Univ. of Groningen, Netherlands 1967–74; Ed. Bio-organic Chemistry 1971–82; G. Haight Travelling Fellow 1957, Guggenheim Fellow 1965, 1973; Research Stereochem., Biochem., Photochem. and Organic and Inorganic Chem.; mem. N.A.S., American Acad. of Arts and Sciences, Harvard Club, etc.; Hon. D.Sc. (Bucknell Univ., Hope Coll.); Pure Chemistry Award, American Chemical Soc. 1961, Leo Hendrick Baekeland Award 1965, A.C.S. Award for Creative Work in Synthetic Organic Chem. 1970. *Leisure interests:* architecture and building, theatre, travel, gardening. *Address:* Stanford University, Stanford, Calif. 94305 (Office); 23570 Camino Hermoso, Los Altos Hills, Calif. 94022, U.S.A.; Marigot des Roseaux, P.O. Box 101, Castries, St. Lucia, West Indies. *Telephone:* (415) 941-2356.

van THIJN, Eduard; Netherlands civic official; b. 16 Aug. 1934, Amsterdam; m. E. L. Herfkens; two d.; ed. Amsterdam Lyceum, Univ. of Amsterdam and Institut d'Etudes Politiques, Paris; mem. staff Wiardi Beckman Foundation (research inst. of Dutch Labour Party) 1961–67; Amsterdam City Councillor 1962–71, Chair. Labour Group 1973–78; M.P. 1967–83; Minister of the Interior 1981–82; Burgomaster of Amsterdam June 1983–; Commdr. Order of Orange-Nassau. *Publication:* Dagboek van een onderhandelaar (A Negotiator's Diary) 1978. *Leisure interests:* basketball, chess. *Address:* City Hall, Amstel 1, 1001 PN Amsterdam, Netherlands. *Telephone:* 020-552 2000.

VAN VEELEN, Evert; Netherlands business executive; b. 13 Nov. 1911, IJmuiden; m. 1st M. Habermehl (died 1977); six s. three d.; m. 2nd P. J. Farquhart; with Admin. Dept. Hoogovens 1927–31, Commercial Dept. 1931–49, Man. 1949–53; Man. Dir. Wm. H. Müller en Co. NV 1953–65; mem. Man. Bd. Estel NV Hoesch Hoogovens 1972–75, Chair. Bd. of Man. 1975, mem. Supervisory Bd. 1977; mem. Man. Bd. Hoogovens IJmuiden BV 1972–75, Chair. 1975–77, mem. Supervisory Bd. 1977; Chair. Man. Bd. Koninklijke Nederlandsche Hoogovens en Staalfabriken NV 1975–, NV DSM, Delta Lloyd NV; Chair. Supervisory Bd. Vredestein NV; Knight, Order of Netherlands Lion.

VAN VEEN, Christian (see Veen, Christian van).

VAN WACHEM, Lodewijk Christiaan; Netherlands mechanical engineer and business executive; b. 31 July 1931, Pangkalan Brandan, Netherlands E. Indies (now Indonesia); m. Elisabeth G. Cristofoli 1958; two s. one d.; ed. Technological Univ., Delft; joined Bataafsche Petroleum Maatschappij, The Hague 1953; Mech. Engineer, Cía Shell de Venezuela 1954–63; Chief Engineer, Shell-BP Petroleum Devt. Co. of Nigeria 1963–66, Eng. Man. 1966–67, Chair. and Man. Dir. 1972–76; Head Tech. Admin. Brunei Shell Petroleum Co. Ltd. 1967–69, Tech. Dir. 1969–71; Head of Production Div. Shell Int. Petroleum Maatschappij, The Hague 1971–72, Co-ordinator Exploration and Production 1976–79; Man. Dir. Royal Dutch Petroleum Co. until 1982, Pres. 1982–; mem. Presidium of Bd. of Dirs., Shell Petroleum N.V.; Man. Dir. Shell Petroleum Co. Ltd. 1977–, Chair. Shell Oil Co. U.S.A. 1982–, Dir. Shell Canada Ltd. 1982–; Chair. Jt. Cttee. of Man. Dirs. of the Royal Dutch/Shell Group 1985–; Hon. K.B.E. 1989, Kt. Order of Netherlands Lion 1981. *Address:* Carel van Bylandtlaan 30, 2596 HR The Hague, Netherlands. *Telephone:* 070-772118 (Office).

VAN WINDEN, Jacobus Cornelis Maria; Netherlands ecclesiastic and professor of Greek; b. 10 Nov. 1922, Schipluiden; ed. in Franciscan convents and Leiden Univ.; mem. Franciscan Order (OFM) 1941; ordained priest 1948; Asst. to J. H. Waszink, Prof. of Latin, Leiden 1954–56; teacher of Greek and Latin, Rotterdam 1956–66; Reader, Leiden Univ. 1966–80, Prof. of Greek of Late Antiquity 1980–87, Prof. Emer. 1987–; mem. Royal Netherlands Acad. *Publications:* Calcidius on Matter: His Doctrine and Sources 1959, An Early Christian Philosopher: Justin Martyr's Dialogue with Trypho (contrib.) 1971, Tertullianus, De idolatria (critical text, translation and commentary with J. H. Waszink) 1987. *Address:* Haarlemerstraat 106, 2312 GD Leiden, Netherlands.

VAN WYK, Willem, B.SC.; South African business executive; b. 24 July 1933, Rustenburg; m. Elizabeth Bets 1960; three d.; Engineer Vanderbijlpark Works 1958–69, Project Man. Newcastle Works 1970, Corp. Planning Man. 1974; Works Man. Pretoria Works 1976; Gen. Man. Operations 1980; Man. Dir. ISCOR, The Union Steel Corpn. Ltd., Metkor Group Ltd., Dorbyl Ltd.; Vice-Pres. SEIFSA. *Leisure interest:* golf. *Address:* P.O. Box 450, Pretoria 0001, South Africa.

VAN ZYL SLABBERT, Dr. F. (see Slabbert, F. Van Zyl).

VAN-CULIN, Rev. Canon Samuel, A.B., B.D.; American ecclesiastic; b. 20 Sept. 1930, Honolulu; s. of Samuel Van-Culin and Susie Mossman; ed. Princeton Univ. and Virginia Theological Seminary; Curate St. Andrew's Cathedral, Honolulu 1955–56; Canon Precentor and Rector Hawaiian Congregation, Honolulu 1956–58; Asst. Rector St. John's, Washington D.C. 1958–60; Gen. Sec. Lyman Int., Washington D.C. 1960–61; Asst. Sec. Overseas Dept., Exec. Council of the Episcopal Church U.S.A. 1962–68, Sec. for Africa and Middle E. 1968–76, Exec. for World Mission 1976–83; Sec. Gen. Anglican Consultative Council 1983–; Sec. to Lambeth Conf. 1988; Hon. D.D. (Virginia Theological Seminary); Hon. Canon Canterbury, Jerusalem and Ibadan. *Leisure interests:* music and travel. *Address:* Anglican Consultative Council, Partnership House, 157 Waterloo Road, London, SE1 8UT, England. *Telephone:* 620-1110.

VANAMO, Jorma Jaakko, L. en D.; Finnish diplomatist; b. 30 Oct. 1913, Mouhijärvi; s. of Eino Jaakko Vanamo and Sigrid Emilia Strunck; m. Hanna Hongisto 1938; two s. one d.; ed. Univ. of Helsinki; Diplomatic Service 1939–, Moscow 1940–41, Ministry of Foreign Affairs 1941–45, Moscow 1945–48, Ministry of Foreign Affairs 1949–51; Counsellor, Stockholm 1951–53, Washington 1954–56; Dir. of Admin. Div., Ministry of Foreign Affairs 1956–58; Amb. to Poland 1958–62, Minister to Romania 1958–60, to Bulgaria 1958–62; Amb. to U.S.S.R., also accred. to Afghanistan and Mongolia 1963–67; Sec. of State, Ministry of Foreign Affairs 1967–70; Amb. to Italy, also accred. to Cyprus and Malta 1970–75; Amb. to Sweden 1975–80; Vice-Chancellor Order of White Rose of Finland, Lion of Finland 1983–. *Leisure interests:* music, photography. *Address:* Ritarikatu 9 B 12, 00170 Helsinki 17, Finland (Home).

VANCE, Cyrus Roberts, B.A., LL.B.; American lawyer and former government official; b. 27 March 1917, Clarksburg, W. Va.; s. of John Carl and Amy (Roberts) Vance; m. Grace Elsie Sloane 1947; one s. four d.; ed. Kent School, Yale Law School and Yale Univ.; Lieut., U.S. Navy 1942–46; Asst. to Pres. The Mead Corpn. 1946–47; Simpson, Thacher and Bartlett, New York (law firm) 1947–, Partner 1956–61, 1967–76, 1980–; Chair. Bd. of Dirs., Fed. Reserve Bank, New York, Jan. 1989–; Special Counsel, Preparedness Investigating Subcttee., Cttee. on Armed Services of the U.S. Senate 1957–60; Consulting Counsel to Special Cttee. on Space and Astronautics, U.S. Senate 1958; Gen. Counsel, Dept. of Defense 1961–62; Chair. Cttee. Adjudication of Claims of the Admin. Conf. of the U.S. 1961–62; Sec. of the Army 1962–64; Deputy Sec. of Defense 1964–67; Pres. Johnson's Special Envoy on Cyprus Situation 1967, on Korean Situation 1968; negotiator at Paris talks on Viet-Nam 1968–69; mem. Cttee. investigating Alleged Police Corruption, New York 1970–72, Ind. Comm. on Disarmament and Security 1980–; Pres. Bar Asscn. of City of New York 1974–76; Chair. UN Devt. Corpn. 1976; Sec. of State Jan. 1977–80 (resgnd.); Dir. Mfrs. Hanover Corpn., Mfrs. Hanover Trust 1981–, General Dynamics Corpn., U.S. Steel Co., New York Times Co.; Chair. Bd. of Rockefeller Foundation 1975–77; mem. U.S. Supreme Court, American Bar Asscn., N.Y. State Bar Asscn., Council of Foreign Relations; Fellow, American Coll. Trial Lawyers;

numerous hon.degrees; Medal of Freedom 1969. *Publication:* Hard Choices (autobiog.) 1983. *Address:* Simpson, Thacher and Bartlett, 425 Lexington Avenue, New York, N.Y. 10017-3909, U.S.A. *Telephone:* (212) 455-7190.

VÁNCSA, Jenő; Hungarian politician; b. 1928, Brassó (now Brasov, Romania); s. of György Váncsa and Julianna Beredekk; m. Vilma Vajda 1951; one s. two d.; ed. Gödöllő Univ. of Agronomy; joined Hungarian Socialist Workers' Party 1954 and finished Party Acad.; started 1954 as Dept. Leader in State Farm of Környe; apptd. leading agronomist 1957 and Dir. State Farm of Agárd 1958; Deputy Minister of Agric. and Food 1972–80, Minister 1980–89; Pres. Hungarian Soc. for Agricultural Sciences; mem. Nat. Ass. for Fejér County 1968–75, Cen. Cttee. of Hungarian Socialist Workers' Party, Econ. Comm., Comm. for State Prizes, Comm. for Science Policies; Labour Order of Merit, Red Banner Order of Labour 1988. *Leisure interests:* hunting, gardening. *Address:* c/o Ministry of Agriculture and Food, Budapest V, Kossuth Lajos tér 11, Hungary.

VANDEBOSCH, Jacques; Belgian politician and business executive; b. 13 Aug. 1941, Liège; ed. Univ. of Liège; Asst., Calculation Dept., Univ. of Liège 1963–68; Univ. of Liège 1970–71; Head of Secr., Nat. Council of Scientific Policy 1971–78; Deputy Prin. Pvt. Sec. to Minister of Econ. Affairs 1972–73; Vice-Pres. S.A. Cockerill 1979–81; Pres. S.A. Cockerill-Sambre 1981–83; Pres. Soc. Coopérative de Production d'électricité (S.P.E.), INTER-REGIES; Deputy Mayor, Seraing. *Publications:* papers on political and economic topics and on public sector energy problems. *Leisure interests:* reading, various sports including football and tennis. *Address:* rue Royale 55, 1000 Brussels, Belgium. *Telephone:* (02) 2178117.

VANDEPUTTE, Robert M. A. C., D. EN D., D. EN SC., POL. ET SOC.; Belgian banker and university professor; b. 1908, Antwerp; m. Marie-Louise Cauwe 1938; three c.; ed. Univs. of Louvain, Nijmegen, Paris, Berlin and Berne; called to Antwerp Bar 1930–40; Prof. Univ. of Louvain 1936–78; Chef de Cabinet, Ministry of Econ. Affairs 1939–40; Sec.-Gen. Asscn. Belge des Banques 1940–42; Dir. Banque Nat. de Belgique 1943–44, Regent 1954–71, Gov. 1971–75; Man. Dir. Soc. Nat. de Crédit à l'Industrie 1944–48, Pres. 1948–71; mem. Caisse Gén. d'Epargne et de Retraite 1958–75; Dir. and mem. Directing Cttee. Société Nat. d'Investissement 1962–71; Pres. Inst. de Réescompte et de Garantie 1973–78; Minister of Finance April–Dec. 1981; Administrateur, Palais des Beaux-Arts de Belgique 1966–84; mem. Conseil Supérieur des Finances 1969–71; Pres. Administratieve en Economische Hogeschool 1959; Pres. Faculty Univ. Saint-Louis 1982–; Commdr., Order of the Crown and Knight, Order of Léopold (Belgium); Officer, Order of Merit (Italian Repub.); Commdr., Order of St. Gregory the Great (Holy See); Grand Officer, Order of Léopold II (Belgium), and other awards. *Publications:* Beginselen van Nijverheidsrecht, Handboek voor Verzekeringen en Verzekeringsrecht, Wat ik rondom mij zag, De Overeenkomst, Een Machteloos Minister, De harde strijd—Beknopte geschiedenis van het A.C.V., Economische geschiedenis van Belgie 1944–84, Het Aquilaans foutbegrip, Verbintenissen en Overeenkomsten in Kort bestek, Sociale geschiedenis van België 1944–85, Economie in België in Kort Bestek; in French: Quelques aspects de l'activité de la Société Nationale de Crédit à l'industrie, Le statut de l'entreprise, Ministre sans pouvoir, Les institutions financières belges. *Address:* Institut de Réescompte et de Garantie, rue du Commerce 78, 1040 Brussels (Office); rue au Bois 376 Bte. 21, 1150 Brussels, Belgium (Home). *Telephone:* 511-73-30 (Office).

VANDERPOORTEN, Herman, LL.D.; Belgian politician; b. 25 Aug. 1922; ed. Atheneum Berchem-Antwerp and Rijksuniversiteit te Gent; Attorney 1945; Co. Councillor, Antwerp 1949–58; Town Councillor and Deputy Justice of the Peace, Lier 1959; mem. Chamber of Reps. 1961–65; Senator 1965; Minister of Interior 1966–68, of Justice 1973–77; Deputy Prime Minister and Minister of Justice and Institutional Reforms May–Oct. 1980; Pres. Liberal Flemish Asscn. 1957–66; mem. European Parl. 1979–80; Govt. Councillor to the King 1981–. *Address:* Antwerpsesteenweg 2, Lier, Belgium.

VANDERVEKEN, John; Belgian international trade union official; b. 4 Feb. 1930, Antwerp; m.; two c.; ed. Ghent Univ.; joined ICFTU Educ. Dept. 1951; Asst., Econ., Social and Political Dept., ICFTU 1960; Geneva Office ICFTU 1971–74; Asst. Gen. Sec. ICFTU, Brussels 1974, Gen. Sec. Nov. 1982–. *Address:* International Confederation of Free Trade Unions, 37–41 rue Montagne aux Herbes Potagères, 1000 Brussels, Belgium. *Telephone:* (02) 217 80 85.

VANDROSS, Luther; American singer, songwriter and producer; b. New York; started career by singing advertising jingles and with backing groups; featured on David Bowie's record Young Americans 1975; signed contract with Epic Records 1981; has produced albums by Aretha Franklin and Cheryl Lynn. *Recordings include:* Never Too Much, Forever, for Always, for Love, A House is not a Home, Any Time.

VANE, Sir John Robert, D.SC., D.PHIL., F.R.S.; British pharmacologist; b. 29 March 1927, Tardebigg, Worcs.; s. of Maurice and Frances Florence Vane; m. Elizabeth D. Page 1948; two d.; ed. King Edward VI High School, Birmingham, and Univs. of Birmingham and Oxford; Therapeutic Research Council Fellow, Oxford 1946–48; research worker, Sheffield and Nuffield Inst. for Medical Research, Oxford 1948–51; Stothert Research Fellow, Royal Soc. 1951–53; Instructor in Pharmacology, Yale Univ. 1953–54, Asst. Prof. 1954–55; Sr. lecturer in Pharmacology, Inst. of Basic Medical Sciences

of Univ. of London at Royal Coll. of Surgeons of England 1955–61, Reader 1961–65, Prof. of Experimental Pharmacology 1966–73; Group Research and Devt. Dir., The Wellcome Foundation Ltd. 1973–85; Dir. The William Harvey Research Inst., St. Bartholomew's Hosp. Medical Coll. 1986–; mem. British Pharmacological Soc. (Foreign Sec. 1979–85), Physiological Soc., Soc. for Drug Research, Royal Acad. of Medicine of Belgium; Fellow, Inst. of Biology; Hon. Fellow, Royal Coll. of Physicians, American Coll. of Physicians, Swedish Soc. of Medical Sciences, St. Catherine's Coll., Oxford, American Physiological Soc., Council on Clinical Cardiology, American Heart Asscn., British Pharmacological Soc., Physiological Soc.; Foreign mem. N.A.S., Polish Acad. of Sciences, A.A.A.S., Royal Netherlands Acad. of Arts and Sciences, Nat. Acad. of Medicine, Buenos Aires; numerous memorial lectures in U.K. and abroad, especially U.S.A.; hon. doctorates from Copernicus Acad. of Medicine, Cracow, René Descartes Univ., Paris, Aberdeen Univ., Mount Sinai Medical School, New York, New York Medical Coll. and Birmingham, Surrey, Camerino, Louvain and Buenos Aires Univs.; shared Nobel Prize for Physiology or Medicine for discoveries concerning prostaglandins and related substances 1982; numerous other awards, prizes and distinctions. *Publications:* numerous review articles and over 400 papers on pharmacology and related topics; jt. ed. of five books. *Leisure interests:* photography, travel, underwater swimming. *Address:* The William Harvey Research Institute, St. Bartholomew's Hospital Medical College, Charterhouse Square, London, EC1M 6BQ, England. *Telephone:* 01-251 1683.

VANNECK, Air Commodore The Hon. Sir Peter Beckford Rutgers, G.B.E., C.B., A.F.C., A.E., M.A., D.SC., J.P., D.L.; British air force officer and fmr. Lord Mayor of London; b. 7 Jan. 1922; s. of Baron Huntingfield and Margaret Eleanor Crosby; m. 1st Cordelia Errington 1943 (divorced 1984); one d. (one d. deceased); m. 2nd Elizabeth Forbes 1984; ed. Geelong Grammar School, Stowe School, Trinity Coll., Cambridge and Harvard; Cadet, R.N. 1939; served in Nelson, King George V, Eskimo, 55th LCA Flot., Wren, MTB 696; in command 771 Sqdn., 807 Sqdn. FAA, resigned 1949; Cambridge Univ. Air Sqdn. 1949; 601 (Co. of London) Sqdn. R.Aux.A.F. 1950–57; 3619 (Co. of Suffolk) Fighter Control Unit 1958–59, in command 1959–61; No. 1 Maritime HQ Unit 1961–63; Group Capt. 1963; Insp. R.Aux.A.F. 1963–73, Hon. Insp.-Gen. 1974–83; Hon. Air Cdre. No. 1 (Co. Hertford) Maritime HQ Unit, 1973–87; ADC to the Queen 1963–73, Gentleman Usher 1967–79; Conservative mem. European Parl. for Cleveland 1979–84, for Cleveland and Yorkshire North 1984–; Alderman of Cordwainer Ward, City of London 1969–79; DL Greater London 1970; Sheriff, City of London 1974–75; Lord Mayor of London 1977–78; Warden, Fishmongers' Co., Prime Warden 1981; Master, Gunmakers' Co. 1977; Past Master, Guild of Air Pilots and Air Navigators; mem. Bd., Ipswich Group Hosps. 1956–62, Gov. Body British Post Graduate Medical Fed., Univ. of London 1963–71, St. Bartholomew's Hosp. Bd. of Govs. 1971–73, City and E. London Area Health Authority 1973–77; Hon. Trustee, St. Bartholomew's Hosp. 1974–82; Trustee, R.A.F. Museum 1976–87, Royal Acad. Trust 1981–87; Gov. Royal Shakespeare Theatre 1974–87; Churchwarden of St. Mary-le-Bow; K.St.J. (mem. Chapter Gen.). *Leisure interests:* sailing, shooting, skiing, bad bridge. *Address:* 2/10 Brompton Square, London, SW3 2AA, England. *Telephone:* 01-606 1066.

VARDA, Agnès; French film writer and director; b. 30 May 1928, Ixelles, Belgium; d. of Eugène Jean Varda and Christiane Pasquet; m. Jacques Demy (q.v.) 1962; one s. one d.; ed. Sète, Herault, and Univ. de Paris à la Sorbonne and Ecole du Louvre; Official Photographer, Théâtre Nat. Populaire 1951–61; reporter and photographer, film-maker 1954–; Prix Méliès 1962 (Cleo de 5 à 7), Prix Louis Delluc 1965 (Le Bonheur), David Selznick Award 1965 (Le Bonheur), Bronze Lion, Venice Festival 1964 (Salut les Cubains), Silver Bear, Berlin Festival 1965 (Le Bonheur); 1st Prize, Oberhausen (Black Panthers), Popular Univs. jury (Lions Love) 1970, Grand Prix, Taormina, Sicily 1977 (L'une chante, l'autre pas), Firenze 1981 (Mur Murs); César Award 1984 (Ulysse); Golden Lion, Best Film Venice Film Festival (Sans toit ni loi) 1985; Prix Méliès (Sans toit ni loi) 1985; L.A. Critics Best Foreign Film (Sans toit ni loi) 1985; Officier des Arts et des Lettres, Chevalier, Légion d'honneur. *Full-length films:* La pointe-courte 1954, Cleo de 5 à 7 1961, Le bonheur 1964, Les créatures 1965, Loin du Vietnam 1967, Lions Love 1969, Nausicaa 1970, Daguerreotypes 1975, L'une chante, l'autre pas 1976, Mur Murs 1980, Documenteur: An Emotion Picture 1981, Sans toit ni loi (Vagabond) 1985, Jane B par Agnès V 1987, Kung Fu Master 1987. *Short-length films:* O saisons, O châteaux 1957, L'opéra-Mouffe 1958, Du côté de la côte 1958, Salut les cubains 1963, Uncle Yanco 1967, Black Panthers 1968, Réponse de femmes 1975, Plaisir d'amour en Iran 1975, Ulysse 1982, Les dites Cariatides 1984, Les dites Curiotides 1984, T'as de beaux escaliers . . . tu sais 1986. *Address:* 86 rue Daguerre, 75014 Paris, France. *Telephone:* 43.22.66.00.

VARDANIAN, Yurik; Soviet weightlifter; b. 18 June 1956, Leninakan, Armenia; ed. Physical Culture Inst., Leninikan; fmr. volleyball player and mem. Armenian volleyball team; took up weightlifting 1972; three times European and World Champion; has set 19 world records and six jr. world records; gold medal in 82.5 kg. category, Olympic Games, Moscow 1980; set world records for snatch and total weight in 75 kg. category, also for snatch, jerk and total weight (400 kg. set in Moscow Olympic Games) in 82.5 kg. category. *Address:* Soviet Sports Council, Sports Committee of U.S.S.R., No. 4 Skatertny, Per eu lok, Moscow, U.S.S.R.

VARENNIKOV, Gen. Valentin Ivanovich; Soviet army officer; b. 1923, R.S.F.S.R.; ed. Frunze Mil. Acad.; mem. CPSU 1944-; joined army 1941; active service 1941-45; Commdr. of a corps 1967-69, of a unit 1969-71; First Deputy Supreme Commdr. Soviet Forces in Germany 1971-73; Commdr. Carpathian Mil. Dist. 1973-82; First Deputy Chief of Gen. Staff 1982-; First Deputy Head of HQ of U.S.S.R. Armed Forces 1984-; elected to Congress of People's Deputies of the U.S.S.R. 1989; Gen. 1978. *Address:* Ministry of Defence, Moscow, U.S.S.R.

VAREY, John Earl, PH.D., LITT.D., F.B.A.; British university professor and principal; b. 26 Aug. 1922, Blackburn; s. of Harold Varey and Dorothy Halstead Varey; m. Cicely Rainford Virgo 1948; three s. (one deceased) one d.; ed. Blackburn Grammar School and Emmanuel Coll., Cambridge; served Bomber and Transport Commands, R.A.F. 1942-45; Lecturer in Spanish, Westfield Coll., London Univ. 1952-57, Reader 1957-63, Prof. 1963-, Acting Prin. 1983, Prin. 1984-89; Chair. of Dirs. and Gen. Ed., Tamesis Books Ltd. 1963-, Tamesis Texts Ltd. 1979-85; Corresp. mem., Spanish Royal Acad.; Hijo ilustre de Madrid 1980. *Publications:* Historia de los títeres en España 1957, Los autos sacramentales en Madrid en la época de Calderón 1637-1681 (with N. D. Shergold) 1961, Galdós Studies (Ed.) 1970, Juan Vélez de Guevara: Los celos hacen estrellas (Co-Ed.) 1970, Pérez Galdós: Doña Perfecta 1971 (Spanish transl. 1988), Fuentes para la historia del teatro en España, 10 vols. (Co-author) 1971-, The Comedias of Calderón, 19 vols. (with D. W. Cruickshank) 1973, Lope de Vega: Peribáñez y el Comendador de Ocaña (Co-Ed.) 1980, Cosmovisión y escenografía: el teatro clásico español 1987; contrib. to Bulletin of Hispanic Studies etc. *Leisure interest:* publishing. *Address:* 38 Platts Lane, London, NW3 7NT, England. *Telephone:* 01-435 1764.

VARFIS, Grigorios; Greek politician; b. 1927, Athens; ed. Univs. of Athens and Paris; journalist in Paris, 1952-58; on staff of OECD 1953-62; Econ. Adviser to perm. Greek del. to the EEC, Brussels 1963-74; apptd. Gen. Dir., Co-ordination Ministry, with jurisdiction over Directorate of Relations with the European Communities 1974, resgnd. Jan. 1977; contributed to econ. programme of Panhellenic Socialist Movt. (PASOK) 1979-; Co-ordination Under-Sec. and Under-Sec. at Foreign Affairs Ministry, responsible for EEC Affairs 1981-83; mem. European Parl. 1984-; mem. Comm. of the European Communities (responsible for Regional Policy and Relations with European Parl.) 1985-86, for Structural Funds and Consumer Protection 1986-89. *Address:* Spefsipou 35, 10676 Athens, Greece.

VARGA, Imre; Hungarian sculptor; b. 1 Nov. 1923, Budapest; s. of Mátyás Varga and Margit Csepeli; m. Ildikó Szabó 1944; two s.; ed. Budapest Coll. of Visual Arts; Munkácsy Prize 1969, Kossuth Prize 1973, Merited Artist 1975, Eminent Artist 1980; Vice-Pres. Patriotic People's Front; mem. Nat. Ass.; Pres. FÉSZEK Artists Club; Herder Prize 1981, Order of the Flag 1983. *Works:* Prometheus 1965 and The Professor 1969 in Middelheim, Belgium, Madách Memorial 1968, Radnóti Memorial 1970, Partisans Memorial 1970, Derkovits Memorial 1971, Lenin Memorial, Heroes Monument 1974, Oslo, plurifigural St. Steven composition 1980, St. Peter's Basilica, Vatican; Bartók Memorial, Paris 1983; Kun Béla memorial, Budapest 1986; Raoul Wallenberg memorial 1987; perm. collection of work in Budapest; smaller sculptures: Erőltetett menet (Forced March), À la Recherche, Baudelaire kedvese (Baudelaire's Sweetheart), Páholy (Theatre box). *Address:* Budapest XII, Bartha-utca 1, Hungary. *Telephone:* 560-278.

VARGAS LLOSA, Mario; Peruvian writer; b. 28 March 1936; ed. Cochabamba (Bolivia), Univ. Nacional Mayor de San Marcos, Lima, and Universidad de Madrid, Spain; fmr. journalist La Crónica, Lima, La Industria, Piura, and La Radio Panamericana, Lima, Agence-France Presse, Paris; broadcaster on Latin American services of Radiodiffusion Télévision Française; lecturer in Latin American Literature, Queen Mary Coll., London Univ. (Hon. Fellow 1988), series of lectures, Cambridge 1978; f. Freedom Party; Cand. for Pres. 1989; mem. Acad. Peruana de la Lengua; Pres. PEN Club 1976-79; Prix Leopoldo Alas 1958, Prix Biblioteca Breve 1962, Critica Española Prize 1963, Rómulo Gallegos Prize 1967, Ritz Paris Hemingway Award 1984. *Publications include:* Los Jefes 1958, La Ciudad y los perros 1962, La Casa Verde 1965, Los Cachorros 1966, Conversación en la Catedral 1970, Pantaleón y las Visitadoras, Captain Pantoja and the Special Service 1978, La Tía Julia y el escribidor 1978, The War of the End of the World 1984, The Real Life of Alejandro Mayta 1986, The Perpetual Orgy: Flaubert and Madame Bovary 1986, Who Killed Palomino Molero? 1988. *Address:* c/o P.E.N., 62-63 Glebe Place, London, S.W.3, England.

VÁRKONYI, Péter, PH.D.; Hungarian politician and journalist; b. 3 April 1931, Budapest; m. Júlianna Kozák 1951; two s.; ed. Foreign Acad.; joined Hungarian CP 1948; mem. Hungarian Socialist Workers' Party (HSWP) Cen. Cttee. 1975-; diplomatic missions in U.S.A. 1951, U.K. 1951, Egypt 1957-58; head of Foreign Ministry press dept. 1958-61; Private Sec. to Prime Minister 1961-65; deputy dept. head, HSWP Cen. Cttee. 1965-69; Sec. of State as Pres. Council of Ministers' Information Office 1969-80; Ed.-in-chief daily Népszabadság 1980-82; Sec. HSWP Cen. Cttee. 1982-83; Minister of Foreign Affairs 1983-89. *Publication:* A magyar-amerikai államközi kapcsolatok története 1945-1948 (The History of Hungarian-American Inter-state Relations 1945-48) 1970. *Address:* c/o Ministry of Foreign Affairs, Bem rakpart 47, 1027 Budapest, Hungary.

VARLEY, Rt. Hon. Eric Graham, P.C., M.P.; British politician; b. 11 Aug. 1932, Poolsbrook, Derbys.; s. of Frank and Eva Varley; m. Marjorie Turner 1955; one s.; ed. Secondary Modern and Tech. Schools, and Ruskin Coll., Oxford; apprentice engineer's turner 1947-52; engineer's turner 1952-55; mining industry craftsman 1955-64; Nat. Union of Miners' Branch Sec. 1955-64; mem. Area Exec. Cttee., Derbys. 1956-64; M.P. for Chesterfield 1964-84; Asst. Govt. Whip 1967-68; Parl. Private Sec. to Prime Minister 1968-69; Minister of State, Ministry of Tech. 1969-70; Chair. Trade Union Group of Labour M.P.'s 1971-74; Sec. of State for Energy 1974-75, for Industry 1975-79; Opposition Spokesman for Employment 1979-83; Treas. Labour Party 1981-83; mem. Nat. Exec. Cttee. Labour Party 1981-83; Exec. Deputy Chair. Coalite Group Jan.-Nov. 1984, Chair. and C.E.O. June 1984-; North and East Midlands Regional Dir. Lloyds Bank Group 1987-. *Leisure interests:* gardening, reading, music, sport. *Address:* Coalite Group, Buttermilk Lane, Bolsover, Derbyshire, S44 6AB, England.

VARLOOT, Denis; French engineer; b. 25 Oct. 1937, Lille; s. of Jean and Madeleine (née Boutron) Varloot; m. Marie J. Kennel 1963; two s.; ed. Lycées in Paris, Ecole Polytechnique and Ecole Nat. Supérieure des Télécommunications; Centre Nat. d'Études des Télécommunications 1962-68; with Direction Gén. des Télécommunications, Service des Programmes et des Etudes Economiques 1968-73, deputized for head of service 1973-75; Dir. of Telecommunications, Orléans 1975-76; Head of Telecommunications Personnel 1976-81; Dir. of Scientific and Tech. Information, Ministry of Educ. 1981-82; Dir. Libraries, Museums and Scientific and Tech. Information, Ministry of Educ. 1982-87; Sr. Adviser to Chair. of France-Telecom 1987-; Chevalier, Légion d'honneur, Arts et Lettres, Ordre des Palmes Académiques, Officier, Ordre nat. du Mérite. *Leisure interest:* sailing. *Address:* 208 rue Raymond Losserand, 75014 Paris (Office); 14 rue Campagne Première, 75014 Paris, France (Home). *Telephone:* 45 64 79 44 (Office); 43 22 31 31 (Home).

VARMA, Ravindra; Indian politician; b. 18 April 1925, Mavelikkara, Kerala; ed. Maharaja's Coll. of Arts, Trivandrum, Christian Coll., Madras; mem. Madras State United Nat. Students' Org. 1944; took active part in State Congress movement for responsible govt. in Travancore and Mysore states; mem. Quit India Movement; Pres. All-India Students' Congress 1946-49; mem. Int. Exec. of Int. Students' Service—World Univ. Service 1949; Sec. and later Pres., Indian Youth Congress; Sec. Indian Cttee. of World Ass. of Youth 1958, Int. Pres. 1958-62; mem. UNESCO Int. Perm. Cttee. for Educ.; mem. third Lok Sabha 1962-67; mem. Janata Party 1977-; mem. Lok Sabha from Ranchi March 1977-; Minister of Parl. Affairs and Labour 1977-79; Pres. ILO 1979-80. *Address:* c/o Ministry of Foreign Affairs, New Delhi, India.

VARNACHEV, Yevgeniy Andreyevich; Soviet politician; b. 1932; ed. Kirov Polytechnic Inst. of Urals; various posts of responsibility at heavy construction machinery plant in Urals 1956-73; mem. CPSU 1963-; Deputy Gen. Dir., Sr. engineer 1973-78; Gen. Dir., of Uralmash 1978-85; U.S.S.R. Minister of Construction Industry 1985-; Deputy to U.S.S.R. Supreme Soviet; cand. mem. of CPSU Cen. Cttee. 1986-; U.S.S.R. State Prize 1983; Honoured Machine Construction Worker of R.S.F.S.R. 1983. *Address:* The Kremlin, Moscow, U.S.S.R.

VARTY, Keith, M.A.; British couturier and business executive; b. 9 Jan. 1952, Darlington; s. of Thomas Varty and Dorothy Craggs; ed. Hurworth Co. School, Queen Elizabeth Grammar School, Middlesbrough School of Art, St. Martins Coll. of Art and R.C.A.; Asst. Designer Dorothy Bis, Paris 1975-79, Design Consultant Geoffrey Beene, New York 1975-79; Designer 'Complice' Collection 1979-80, Byblos, Ancona, Italy and U.S.A. 1980-; Chair. and Founder United S.R.L., Milan 1986-; Visiting Lecturer R.C.A. 1986-. *Leisure interests:* travel, bull terrier breeding, Italian opera, collecting antiques. *Address:* Piazza Plebscito 55, Ancona; Bosco di San Francesco N°6, Sirolo; Via Vallone, Monte Conero, Sirolo, Italy. *Telephone:* (071) 203790; (071) 936 225; (071) 936 203.

VÅRVIK, Dagfinn; Norwegian politician; b. 8 June 1924, Leinstrand; s. of Kristian and Helga Vårvik; m. Bjørg Presttrø 1951; one s. two d.; ed. Univ. of Oslo; Sec. to Parl. Group, Centre Party 1952-61; mem. editorial staff, Nationen 1961-63, Chief Ed. 1963-; Minister of Finance Aug.-Sept. 1963, of Prices and Wages 1965-71, of Foreign Affairs 1972-73; Chair. Centre Party 1973-77. *Address:* Nationen, Arbeidergatan 4, Oslo; Theodor Løvstads vei 38, Oslo 2, Norway (Home). *Telephone:* 42.50.50 (Office); 43.81.06 (Home).

VAS, István; Hungarian poet; b. 24 Sept. 1910, Budapest; s. of Pál Vas and Erzsébet Augenstein; m. 1st Etel Nagy 1936, 2nd Maria Kutny 1945, 3rd Piroska Szántó 1951; Publr.'s Reader 1946, wrote poems and essays for the Press; noted as transl. of plays by Shakespeare, Racine, Schiller, Molière, O'Neill, poems by Apollinaire and Eliot, and novels from French, German and English; Kossuth Prize 1962, 1985, Order of Labour 1970, Pro Arte Medal 1972, Chevalier Palmes académiques 1973, Order of Banner 1980. *Publications:* Collected Poems I-III: Ki mást se tud, Rapszódia a hűségről, A tüzlopó; autobiog. novels: Nehéz szerelem (Hard Love), Collected Essays I-III: Tengerin nélkül, Vonzások és választások, Körülbelül, Ráérunk (No Hurry) (poems), Mégis (However), Igen is, nem is (Yes and No) (essays) 1987. *Address:* H-1013 Budapest, Gróza Péter rakpart 17, Hungary (Home).

VASARELY, Victor; French (b. Hungarian) artist; b. 9 April 1908, Pécs, Hungary; s. of Victor Vasarhelyi and Anna Csiszar; m. Claire Spinner 1931; two s.; ed. Budapest Bauhaus; studied medicine; settled in Paris 1930; one-man exhbns. Budapest 1929-33, and in centres throughout Europe, N. and S. America 1945-; group exhbns. in Paris, Stedelijk Museum, Amsterdam, Documenta III, Kassel, Gallery Chalette, N.Y., Sidney Janis Gallery, N.Y., Solomon R. Guggenheim Museum, N.Y., and in São Paulo, Rio de Janeiro and Montevideo, Tate Gallery, London etc.; perm. exhibits in Museum of Modern Art, New York, Musée St. Etienne, Paris, Albright Knox Gallery, Harvard, Tate Gallery, London, Stedelijk Museum, Amsterdam, and in Buenos Aires, Montevideo, Brussels, Reykjavik, São Paulo, Helsinki, etc.; Musée Vasarely at Château de Gordes, Vaucluse, opened 1970; Foundation Vasarely at Aix-en-Provence inaugurated 1976; Musée Vasarely opened in the house where he was born in Pécs, Hungary 1976; Vasarely Centre opened in New York 1978; Vasarely Centre opened in Oslo, Norway 1982; Hon. Pres. French-Hungarian Asscn. 1977, Hon. mem. Nuclear Haematology Dept. Inst. Nuclear Engineers (London) 1979; Int. Nomenclature Cttee. 1982; Hon. Life Adviser Asscn. des Arts Plastiques UNESCO 1977-; Dr. Sc. Hum. (Cleveland Univ.) 1977; Prix de Critique (Brussels) 1955, Guggenheim Int. Award for Merit 1964, Guggenheim Prize (New York) 1964, Ljubljana Award 1965, São Paulo Biennale Award 1965, Grand Prix de la VIIIème Biennale de São Paulo 1965, Carnegie Award 1967, Ministry of Foreign Affairs Prize Tokyo Biennale 1967, Painting Prize of Carnegie Inst. 1967, First Prize of Premier Biennale de la Gravure Cracovie (Poland) 1968, Première Palette d'Or Festivale Internationale de Peinture Cagnes-sur-Mer (France) 1969, Int. Art Book Prize for Vasarely II 1971, Int. Diano Marina Prize, Italy, for Discours de la Méthode—Descartes-Vasarely, 1971, Silver Medal for Vasarely II, Int. Book Fair, Leipzig 1971 Cert. of Distinction for Contribution to Aesthetic Philosophy (Univ. of New York) 1978, Der Kaiserring artistic prize (Goslar, Fed. Repub. of Germany) 1978; Hon. citizen of New Orleans 1966, Pécs 1976, Cleveland (Ohio) 1977, Aix-en-Provence 1979, Hon. Prof. in Applied Arts, Budapest 1969; Officier, Légion d'honneur, Ordre des Arts et des Lettres; Commdr. Ordre nat. du Mérite; Médaille de l'Ordre du Drapeau de la République Populaire Hongroise (with laurels) 1978, Officier du mérite culturel (Monaco) 1980, Officer, Order of Rio Branco (Brazil) 1980, Médaille du Cinquantenaire des Meilleurs Ouvriers de France 1980, Hon. Citizen New York 1984, and many others. *Publications:* Gea 1982, numerous contribs. to various periodicals. *Address:* 83 rue Aux Reliques, Annet-sur-Marne, 77410 Claye Souilly, France.

VÁSÁRY, Tamás; Hungarian concert pianist and conductor; b. 11 Aug. 1933; s. of Jozsef and Elizabeth (Baltazàr) Vasary; m. Ildiko Kovacs 1967; ed. Franz Liszt Univ. of Music, Budapest under Lajos Hernadi, Jozsef Gat and Zoltan Kodály; first solo performance at eight years; studied at Franz Liszt Acad. until 1954; remained at Franz Liszt Acad. to teach theory; recitals in Leningrad, Moscow and Warsaw; settled in Switzerland 1958; London début 1961, New York 1962; début as conductor in Menton Festival of Music 1971; has since appeared in Europe, S. Africa, S. America, U.S.A., Canada, India, Thailand, Hong Kong, Australia, Japan and Mexico; Jt. Music Dir. Northern Sinfonia, Newcastle 1979-; records for Deutsche Grammophon; Liszt Prizes: Queen Elizabeth (Belgium), Marguerite Longue (Paris); Chopin Prizes: Int. Competition, Warsaw, Int. Competition, Brazil; Bach and Paderewski Medals (London). *Principal recordings:* three records of works of F. Liszt; eight of works of Chopin, three of works of Rachmaninoff, one each of works of Debussy and Mozart. *Leisure interest:* writing fiction. *Address:* 9 Village Road, London, N.3, England. *Telephone:* 01-346 2381.

VASILIEV, Boris; Soviet author; b. 21 May 1924, Voronezh; served in Red Army in World War II, seriously wounded; mil. engineer with Acad. of Armoured Troops 1943-54. *Publications include:* Dawns 1969, My Horses are Flying 1983, The Burning Bush 1987; scripts for many films. *Address:* U.S.S.R. Union of Writers, Ul. Vorovskogo 52, Moscow, U.S.S.R.

VASILIEV, Ivan Afanasivevich; Soviet writer; b. 1924; served in Red Army; ed. Velikolug Teachers' Training College; Leningrad Higher Party School; mem. CPSU 1942-. *Publications include:* This Earth I love 1977, In the Land of My Roots (Reflections on the Russian Countryside) 1981, Permit for Initiative 1983, Return to Earth 1984; Lenin Prize 1986. *Address:* U.S.S.R. Union of Writers, Ul. Vorovskogo 52, Moscow, U.S.S.R.

VASILIEV, Lev Borisovich; Soviet politician; b. 1925; ed. Moscow Automechanical Inst.; Soviet Army 1943-44; mem. CPSU 1951-; foreman in charge of production in factory 1948-63; Dir. of Moscow Automobile works 1963-68; U.S.S.R. Deputy Minister of Automobile Industry 1968-83; Gen. Dir. of KAMAZ 1969-81; Gen. Dir. of AZLK 1981-83; Deputy Pres. of Gosplan 1983-84; U.S.S.R. Minister of Machine Construction for Light Industry, Food and Domestic Appliance Industries 1984-88; cand. mem. of CPSU Cen. Cttee. 1986-; Deputy to U.S.S.R. Supreme Soviet; Hero of Socialist Labour 1977. *Address:* The Kremlin, Moscow, U.S.S.R.

VASILIU, Emanuel, PH.D.; Romanian linguist; b. 7 Sept. 1929, Chişinău (now Kishinev, U.S.S.R.); s. of Nicolae and Gabriela Vasiliu; m. Maria-Laura Vasiliu 1952; ed. Univ. of Bucharest; Assoc. Prof. Univ. of Bucharest 1962, Prof. 1970; Visiting Prof. Univ. of Chicago 1964-65, 1970-71, of Boston 1971; mem. Soc. Linguistica Europaea, Soc. européenne de Culture, Romanian Linguistic Soc., Romanian Soc. of Romance Linguistics (SRLR),

Int. Cttee. of Linguists 1977-; mem. editorial bd. Studii şi cercetări lingvistice (Linguistic Studies and Researches), Cahiers de linguistique théorique et appliquée. *Publications:* Fonologia limbii române (Romanian Phonology) 1965; Fonologia istorică a dialectelor dacoromâne (Historical Phonology of Daco-Romanian Dialects) 1968; Elemente de teorie semantică a limbilor naturale (Some Principles of a Semantic Theory of Natural Languages) 1970; Outline of a Semantic Theory of Kernel Sentences 1972; Preliminarii logice la semantica frazei (Logic Preliminaries to a Compound Sentence Semantics) 1978; Sens, adevăr analitic, cunoaştere (Meaning, Analytic Truth and Knowledge) 1984; contrib. to Transformational Syntax of Romanian 1972, Limba română contemporană (Contemporary Romanian) vol. I 1974. *Address:* Facultatea de Filologie, Str. Edgar Quinet 7, Bucharest (Office); Intrarea Lucaci 3, 74111 Bucharest, Romania (Home). *Telephone:* 21-57-94 (Home).

VASILIYEV, German Konstantinovich, DR. PHYS. MATH. SC.; Soviet physicist; b. 1936; ed. Moscow Physical-Tech. Inst.; work for Acad. of Sciences Inst. of Chemical Physics 1963-; Head of Lab. 1977-; Lenin Prize 1984 for collaboration on series entitled Fundamental Research on Chain Reactions in Chemical Lasers. *Address:* Academy of Sciences of the U.S.S.R., Moscow V-71, Leninsky Pr. 14, U.S.S.R.

VASILIYEV, Vladimir Viktorovich; Soviet ballet dancer; b. 18 April 1940, Moscow; m. Yekaterina Maksimova (divorced 1980); ed. Bolshoi Theatre Ballet School; with Bolshoi Theatre Ballet 1958-; People's Artist of the R.S.F.S.R. 1969; Lenin Prize 1970, Leninist Komsomol Prize 1968, Nijinsky Prize 1964, Grand Prix at Varna Int. Competition 1964, People's Artist of U.S.S.R. 1973. *Principal roles:* The Prince (Nutcracker), Pan (Valpurgis Night), The Poet (Chopiniana), Danila (Stone Flower), Prince Charming (Cinderella), Batyr (Shurale), Andrei (A Page of Life), Basil (Don Quixote), Albert (Giselle), Frondoso (Laurencia), Medjnun (Leili and Medjnun); also appeared in The Humpbacked Horse, Spartacus, Petrushka and Icarus 1978; dir. Anna Karenina (ballet) 1978, Così fan Tutte (with N. Kasatkina) 1978. *Address:* State Academic Bolshoi Theatre of the U.S.S.R., 1 Ploshchad Sverdlova, Moscow, U.S.S.R.

VASILIYEVA, Larisa; Soviet poet and writer; b. 1935, Kharkov, Ukraine; d. of Nikolai Alekseyevich and Yekaterina Vasilievna Kucherenko; m. Oleg Vasiliyev 1957; one s.; ed. Moscow Univ.; started publishing 1957; first collection of verse 1966; Sec. of Moscow Br. of R.S.F.S.R. Union of Writers; Moscow Komsomol Prize 1971. *Publications include: Poetry:* Fire-fly 1969, The Swan 1970, Blue Twilight 1970, Encounter 1974, A Rainbow of Snow 1974, Meadows 1975, Fire in the Window 1978, Russian Names 1980, Foliage 1980, Fireflower 1981, Selected Poetry 1981, Grove 1984, Mirror 1985, Moskovorechie 1985, Lantern 1985, Waiting For You In The Sky 1986. *Stories, prose works:* Albion and the Secret of Time 1978, Novel About My Father 1983, Cloud of Fire 1988, Selected Works (2 vols.) 1989. *Address:* ul. Usievicha 8, kv. 86; U.S.S.R. Union of Writers, ulitsa Vorovskogo 52, Moscow, U.S.S.R.

VASILYEV, Nikolay Fyodorovich; Soviet official; ed. Tadzhik Agricultural Inst.; with finance dept. of regional CP Cttee. 1932-40; mem. CPSU 1942-; served in Soviet Army 1940-46; dir. of a machine and tractor station, First Sec. of Regional Cttee. of Ukrainian CP 1946-58; First Sec. of Pavlograd City Cttee. Ukrainian CP 1958-60; Dept. head with Dnepropetrovsk Dist. Cttee. of Ukrainian CP 1960-61; Deputy 1959-64, mem. Presidium Supreme Soviet of Ukrainian S.S.R. 1963-64; Chair. of Exec. Cttee. of Dnepropetrovsk Dist. Soviet of Workers' Depts. 1961-64; First Sec. of Belgorod Dist. Cttee. CPSU 1964-71; mem. Cen. Cttee. CPSU 1966-; Deputy Chair. of Council of Ministers of R.S.F.S.R. 1971-; Minister of Land Improvement and Water Conservancy of U.S.S.R. 1979-89; Order of Lenin 1976. *Address:* c/o Ministry of Land Improvement and Water Conservancy, Moscow, Novobasmannaya ul. 10, U.S.S.R.

VASSALLI, Giuliano; Italian politician and fmr. lawyer; b. 25 April 1915, Perugia; m.; six c.; Prof. of Penal Law, Univ. of Rome 1960-; fmr. Prof., Law Faculties of Univs. of Urbino, Pavia, Padua, Genoa and Naples; practised as lawyer 1944-81; co-founder clandestine Unità Popolare during Fascist regime; mem. Partisan Mil. Command, Rome; subsequently active in various socialist groups and parties; joined Partito Socialista Italiano 1959; City Councillor, Rome 1962-66; M.P. 1968-83, Senator 1983-; Minister of Justice 1987-; Vice-Pres. Int. Asscn. of Penal Law; Co-Ed. La Giustizia Penale and other legal journals, and Enciclopedia del Diritto; mem. Accademia dei Lincei. *Publications:* over 100 publs. on penal law and criminology. *Address:* Ministry of Justice, Via Avenula 70, 00186 Rome, Italy.

VASSILIOU, George Vassos, D.ECON.; Cypriot politician; b. 20 May 1931, Famagusta; s. of Vasos Vassiliou and Fofo Vassiliou; m. Androulla Vassiliou 1966; one s. two d.; ed. Univs. of Geneva, Vienna, Budapest; Market Researcher Read Paper Group -1962; f., Chair., Man. Dir. Middle E. Marketing Research Bureau 1962-; f. Middle E. Centres for Man. and Computing Studies 1984; f. Inst. of Dirs. (Cyprus Br.), also Hon. Sec.; Pres. of Cyprus 1988-; fmr. Vice-Pres. Nicosia Chamber of Commerce; fmr. mem. Exec. Cttee. Cyprus Chamber of Commerce, Special Cttee. on Cost of Living Allowance, Bd. Cyprus Fair Authority; mem. Bd. and Exec. Cttee. Bank of Cyprus, Econ. Advisory Council of Church of Cyprus, Educ. Advisory Council; Visiting Prof. Cranfield School of Man., U.K.

Publications: Marketing in the Middle East 1980, Marketing Handbook. *Address:* Office of the President, Nicosia, Cyprus.

VASSILIOU, Simos G., B.SC.(ECON.), F.I.S.; Cypriot economist; b. 11 Jan. 1919, Cyprus; ed. Nicosia Agric. Coll., Univ. of London, Harvard Univ., U.S.A.; Produce Insp., Dept. of Agric. 1935–40; Customs and Excise Officer 1940–54; Statistics and Research Officer, Labour Dept. 1954–55; Asst. Govt. Statistician Financial Sec.'s Office 1955–57, Govt. Statistician 1957–62; Econ. Affairs Officer, UN 1962–64, Head of Tech. Co-operation Section 1964–65, Officer-in-Charge, Devt. Planning Advisory Services 1965–69, Asst. Dir. 1969–77, Dir. 1977–80, Interregional Adviser on Devt. Planning 1980–81; Minister of Finance 1982–85. *Publications:* The Economy of Cyprus (with A. J. Mayer) 1963. *Address:* 7 Chalcedon Street, Nicosia 133, Cyprus (Home).

VASSOGNE, Jean Georges, D. EN D.; French judge; b. 22 Feb. 1919, Dommartin-lès-Toul; s. of Georges Vassogne and Marie Redouté; m. Nicole Richer 1948; two s., one d.; ed. Douai and Poitiers lycées, Univ. of Poitiers; trainee barrister, Poitiers Court of Appeal 1941–43; Deputy Public Prosecutor, Evreux 1943, Paris 1944; Judge, Versailles 1954, Paris 1955; Examining Magistrate, Paris 1956; Vice-Chair. Tribunal de la Seine 1962; Judge of Appeal, Paris Court of Appeal, First Chair. 1976–85; First Vice-Chair. Tribunal de Paris 1968; Judge of Appeal, Cour de cassation 1971; Chair. Tribunal de grande instance, Paris 1972, Paris Court of Appeal 1976; Commandeur, Légion d'honneur, Ordre nat. du mérite. *Publications:* La responsabilité des agences de renseignements commerciaux (thesis) 1943; contrib. to La semaine juridique and Encyclopédie Dalloz. *Address:* 9 rue de la Bienfaisance, 75008 Paris, France (Home). *Telephone:* (1) 43-87-81-47.

VASTAGH, Pal; Hungarian academic and politician; b. 23 Sept. 1946, Nagyszenas; m.; two c.; ed. Jozsef Attila Univ. of Sciences, Szeged; lecturer, later Prin. Asst., Asst. Prof. and Dean, Faculty of State Law and Jurisprudence, Joszef Attila Univ. of Sciences; Pres. Univ. and Coll. Council, KISZ Cen. Cttee. 1973, mem. Exec. Cttee. 1976–81; mem. HWSP 1966–; First Sec. HWSP Co. Csongrad Cttee. Dec. 1988–; mem. HSWP Political Cttee. April 1989–. *Address:* Hungarian Socialist Workers Party Central Committee, Szechenyi rakpart 19, 1387 Budapest, Hungary.

VASYAGIN, Gen. Semyon Petrovich; Soviet army officer; b. 14 Feb. 1910, Belyayevo, Tver (now Kalinin) oblast; ed. Communist Univ. and Lenin Mil. Political Acad.; mem. CPSU 1932–; joined Soviet Army 1932; various mil. political posts during Second World War; Head of Political Admin. of Far Eastern Forces 1950–53; mem. Mil. Council and Head of Political Admin. of Far Eastern Mil. Dist. 1953–57, Odessa Mil. Dist. 1957–58, of Soviet Forces in Germany 1958–67; mem. Mil. Council and Head of Political Admin. Land Forces Nov. 1967–; mem. Cen. Auditing Comm. 1966–81; Deputy to U.S.S.R. Supreme Soviet 1958 and 1966–; Order of Red Banner (four times), Order of October Revolution and other decorations. *Address:* U.S.S.R. Ministry of Defence, The Kremlin, Moscow, U.S.S.R.

VATIKIOTIS, Panayiotis (J.) Jerasimos, PH.D.; American (Greek-born) university professor; b. 5 Feb. 1928, Jerusalem; s. of Jerasimos Vatikiotis and Paraskevi Vatikiotis (née Meimarachi); m. Patricia Mary Theresa Mumford 1956; one s. two d.; ed. Greek and English pvt. schools in Palestine, American Univ. in Cairo, Johns Hopkins Univ., U.S.A.; Instructor, American Univ. in Cairo 1948–49; Instructor in Arabic, Johns Hopkins Univ. 1952–53; Dept. of Govt., Indiana Univ., to Prof. of Govt. 1953–65; Prof. of Politics with reference to Near and Middle E., S.O.A.S., Univ. of London, England 1965–; Guggenheim Fellow 1961–62; Rockefeller Fellow 1959–60; mem. Editorial Advisory Bd. Middle Eastern Studies 1964–; Chair. Centre for Middle Eastern Studies, S.O.A.S. 1966–69; Visiting Prof., Univ. of Calif. at L.A. 1969, 1983; Sr. Visiting Fellow and Visiting Prof., Princeton Univ. 1973–74; Acad. Dir., Greek Mediterranean Centre for Arab and Islamic Studies, Athens 1977–80; Co-ordinator, Mediterranean Project, Aspen Inst. Italia, Rome 1985–86; Distinguished Visiting Prof., American Univ. in Cairo 1986; Hon. Dir. The Aegean Foundation. *Publications:* The Fatimid Theory of the State 1957, The Egyptian Army in Politics 1961, Politics and the Military in Jordan 1967, The Modern History of Egypt 1969, 1980, 1985, Greece, A Political Essay 1975, Nasser and his Generation 1978, Arab and Regional Politics in the Middle East 1984, Islam and the State 1987; major entries in Encyclopedia of Islam. *Leisure interests:* travel, swimming, music. *Address:* School of Oriental and African Studies, University of London, Malet Street, London, WC1E 7HP, England. *Telephone:* 01-637 2388.

VATOLIN, Nikolay Anatolevich; Soviet metallurgist; b. 1926; ed. Urals Polytech. Inst.; on staff of U.S.S.R. Acad. of Sciences Inst. of Metallurgy (Urals Br.) 1950–; mem. CPSU 1952–; Dir. 1967–; Prof. 1969, then Prof. at Sverdlovsk Mining Inst. 1973–; Corresp. mem. of U.S.S.R. Acad. of Sciences 1970–81, mem. 1981–. *Publications:* (co-author): Physico-chemical Foundations of Steel Hot Leading 1977, Oxidation of Vanadium Slags 1978, Interparticle Interaction in Molten Metals 1979, Diffraction Studies of High Temperature Melts 1980, Computerization of Thermodynamic Calculations of Metallurgical Processes 1982, Electrical Properties of Oxide Melts 1984, Hydrometallurgy of Ferropowders 1984, Computer Simulation

of Amorphous Metals 1985. *Address:* Institute of Metallurgy, U.S.S.R. Academy of Sciences, 101 Amundsen Street, Sverdlovsk, U.S.S.R.

VAUGHAN, Sir (George) Edgar, K.B.E.; British former professor and diplomatist; b. 24 Feb. 1907, Cardiff; s. of William John and Emma Kate (Caudle) Vaughan; m. 1st Elsie Winifred Deubert (died 1982), one s. two d.; m. 2nd Caroleen Mary Sayers 1987; ed. Cheltenham Grammar School and Jesus Coll., Oxford; Vice-Consul, Hamburg 1931; Second Sec. and Vice-Consul, La Paz 1932–35; Vice-Consul, Barcelona 1935–38, Buenos Aires 1938–44; Chargé d'affaires and Consul-Gen., Monrovia 1945–46; Consul, Seattle 1946–49; Consul-Gen., Lourenço Marques 1949–53, Amsterdam 1953–56; Minister and Consul-Gen., Buenos Aires 1956–60; Amb. to Panama 1960–63, to Colombia 1964–66; Special Lecturer in History, Univ. of Sask. (Regina Campus) 1966–67, Prof. of History 1967–74 (retd. 1974), Dean of Arts and Science 1969–73; Fellow, Royal Historical Soc. 1965; Hon. Fellow Jesus Coll., Oxford 1966–. *Address:* 9 The Glade, off Sandy Lane, Cheam, Surrey, SM2 7NZ, England. *Telephone:* 01-643 1958.

VAUGHAN, Dame Janet Maria, D.B.E., D.M., F.R.C.P., M.A., F.R.S.; British doctor and university official; b. 18 Oct. 1899, Clifton, Bristol; d. of William Wyana Vaughan and Margaret (née Symonds) Vaughan; m. David Gourlay 1930; two d.; ed. Univ. Coll. Hospital and Somerville Coll., Oxford; Asst. Clinical Pathologist, Univ. Coll. Hosp. 1927–29; Rockefeller Travelling Fellow 1929–30; Beit Memorial Fellow 1931–34; Leverhulme Fellow, Royal Coll. of Physicians 1934–35; Clinical Pathologist British Post-Graduate Medical School 1935–39; Dir. N.W. London Blood Supply Depot 1939–45; Prin. Somerville Coll. 1945–67, Hon. Fellow 1967–; Chair. Oxford Regional Hosp. Bd. 1950–51; Dir. Medical Research Unit for Research on Bone-Seeking Isotopes 1950–; mem. Royal Comm. for Equal Pay 1944–45, Phillips Cttee. on Econs. and Problems of the Provision for Old Age 1953, Commonwealth Scholarship Comm. 1964–, Cttee. on Libraries of Univ. Grants Cttee. 1965–67; Trustee Nuffield Foundation; Hon. Fellow, Wolfson Coll., Oxford 1981, Girton Coll., Cambridge 1986; Hon. D.SC. (Wales) 1960, (Leeds) 1973, Hon. D.C.L. (Oxford) 1967, (London) 1968, (Bristol) 1971. *Publications:* The Anaemias 1934, The Physiology of Bone 1970, 1975, 1981, The Effects of Irradiation on the Skeleton 1973, and numerous scientific papers. *Leisure interests:* gardening, travel. *Address:* 5 Fairlawn Flats, First Turn, Wolvercote, Oxford, England. *Telephone:* Oxford 514069.

VAUGHAN, Sarah; American jazz singer; b. 27 March 1924, Newark, N.J.; d. of Asbury and Ada (née Baylor) Vaughan; m. 3rd Marshall Fisher; one d.; began singing career 1942; has sung with bands of Earl Hines, Billy Eckstine and John Kirby Combo; Vocalist Award, Downbeat 1946–52, Playboy Vocalist Award 1975, Grammy Award 1983. *Recordings include:* I'll Wait and Pray, It's Magic, Tenderly, Misty, Broken Hearted Melody, My Funny Valentine, A Foggy Day, The Lamp is Low, Sweet Gingerbread Man, Alone Again (Naturally), Lord's Prayer, The Summer Knows, Rainy Days and Mondays, Over the Rainbow. *Leisure interests:* sewing, golf. *Address:* c/o De Vine One Corn., 9309B Burton Way, B.H., Calif. 90210, U.S.A.

VÁVRA, Otakar; Czechoslovak scriptwriter and film director; b. 28 Feb. 1911, Hradec Králové; s. of Alois and Marie Vávra; m. Helena Vávrová 1946; one s.; ed. Czech Tech. Coll.; scriptwriter, dir. Moldavia-film, Elekta-film, Lucernafilm companies 1931–45; scriptwriter, dir. Barrandov Film Studios, Prague 1945–; art team man. Barrandov Film Studios, Prague 1947–51; teacher, Film Faculty, Acad. of Music and Dramatic Arts, Prague 1949–51, Head, Film and Television direction dept. 1956–70, Prof. 1963–; mem. collective man. bd., Barrandov Film Studios, Prague 1951–54; art team man. Barrandov Film Studios, Prague 1954–56; Chair. feature film section, Union of Czechoslovak Film and Television Artists 1965; mem. Cen. Cttee., Union of Czechoslovak Film and Television Artists 1966–70; Pro-Rector Acad. of Music and Dramatic Arts, Prague 1967–70; scriptwriter and dir. of short films Light Penetrates Darkness 1931, We Live in Prague 1934, November 1935; *author and co-author of films:* The Eleventh Commandment, Maryša 1935, The Lane in Paradise, A Camel through a Needle's Eye 1936, Guard No. 47, Morality above All 1937; Dir.: Gaudeamus igitur, Virginity 1937, The Guild of the Maids of Kutná Hora 1938, Humoresque 1939, The House of Magic 1939, The Enchanted Masqued Lover, The Girl in Blue, The Mistress in Disguise, Dr. Hegl's Patient, The May Tale 1940, The Turbine 1941, Come Right Back 1942, Happy Journey 1942, Rozina the Bastard 1945, The Mischievous Bachelor 1946, Presentiment 1947, Krakatit 1948, The Silent Barricade 1949, Deployment 1952, Jan Hus 1955, A Hussite Warrior 1956, Against All 1957, Citizen Brych 1958, The First Rescue Party 1959, The Curfew 1960, August Sunday 1960, The Night Guest 1961, The Burning Heart 1962, The Golden Queening 1965, Romance for a Bugle 1966, 13 Chamber 1968, Witch-Hunt 1969, The Days of Betrayal 1973, Sokolovo 1974, The Liberation of Prague 1977, A Story of Love and Honour 1977, The Dark Sun 1980, Jan Amos Commenius 1982, Comedian 1983, Oldřich a Božena 1984, Veronika 1985, Europe was Waltzing, Temptation Catherine, Chief Witness 1985–87, Till 1987; written 89 film scripts and dir. 46 films; Czechoslovak Film Prize 1937, 1938, Nat. Prize 1941, Czech Land Prize 1948, State Prize 1949, Artist of Merit 1955, Order of Labour 1960, State Prize of Klement Gottwald 1968, Nat. Artist 1968, Prize of Antonín Zápotocký 1973, State Prize of Klement Gottwald 1977, Order of Repub. 1981 and various other awards. *Address:* Faculty of Cinema, Academy of Music and Dramatic Arts, Prague (Office); Mladé Gardy 7, Prague, Czechoslovakia (Home).

VÄYRYNEN, Paavo Matti, M.POL.SC.; Finnish politician; b. 2 Sept. 1946, Keminmoa; s. of Juho Eemeli and Anna Liisa (Kaijankoski) Väyrynen; m. Vuokko Kaarina Tervonen 1968; one s. two d.; M.P. 1970–; Political Sec. to Prime Minister 1970–71; Vice-Chair. Centre Party 1972–80, Chair. 1980–; mem. Nordic Council 1972–75; Minister of Educ. 1975–76, of Labour 1976–77; Minister for Foreign Affairs 1977–82. *Publications:* Köyhän asialla (Speaking for the Poor) 1971, On muutoksen aika (This is a Time of Change) 1974, Kaupallisia Kysymyksiä 1981. *Address:* Keskustapuolue (KP), Pursi-miehenkatu 15, Helsinki 17, Finland.

VAZ, Douglas Crompton; Jamaican politician and business executive; b. 20 May 1937, Kingston; s. of the late Harold W. Vaz and Lillian Emlyn; m. Sonia M. Lugo 1959; three s.; ed. Jamaica Coll. and Fashion Inst. of Tech.; Production Man. Formfit Int. Ltd. 1958; later Man. Dir. H. W. Vaz and L. F. Vaz Ltd., Bindings and Accessories Ltd. and Jamaica Brassiere Enterprise Ltd.; Pres. Jamaica Mfrs. Asscn. 1973–76; M.P. 1976–; Minister of Industry and Commerce 1980–86. *Leisure interests:* reading, tennis, table-tennis, golf. *Address:* c/o Ministry of Foreign Affairs and Industry, Kingston, Jamaica.

VDOVIN, Valentin Petrovich; Soviet diplomatist (retd.); b. 1927; diplomatic service 1959–; Counsellor at Embassy in France 1959–65; Amb. to Chad. 1965–69; with Ministry of Foreign Affairs 1969–72; Amb. to Laos 1972–76, to Mozambique 1980–82, to Portugal 1983–87.

VEALE, Sir Alan John Ralph, Kt., F.ENG.; British engineer; b. 2 Feb. 1920, Exeter; s. of Leslie Henry Veale and Eleanor Veale; m. Muriel Edwards 1946; two s.; ed. Exeter School, Manchester Coll. of Tech. (now UMIST), London Business School; Dir. and Gen. Man. A.E.I. Motor and Control Group 1966–68; Man. Dir. G.E.C. Diesels Ltd. 1968–70, G.E.C. Power Eng. Ltd. 1970–85, Dir. G.E.C. PLC 1973–85; Chair. Rossmore Warwick Ltd. 1987–, R.F.S. Industries Ltd. 1987–; Dir. The Throgmorton Trust 1986–; Hon. D.Sc. (Salford) 1984. *Leisure interests:* sailing, walking. *Address:* 41 Northumberland Road, Leamington Spa, Warwicks., CV32 6HF, England. *Telephone:* (0926) 424349.

VEASEY, Josephine, C.B.E.; British (mezzo-soprano) opera singer (retd.) and teacher; b. 10 July 1930, London; m. Ande Anderson 1951 (divorced 1969); one s. one d.; ed. singing studies with Audrey Langford, A.R.C.M.; mem. chorus Covent Garden Opera Company 1948–50, returned as soloist 1955; prin. mezzo-soprano, Royal Opera House, Covent Garden; has sung every major mezzo-soprano role in repertory; many foreign engagements have included Salzburg Festival, La Scala, Milan, Metropolitan Opera House, New York, and Paris opera; has made recordings with Karajan, Solti, Bernstein and Colin Davis; Prof. Royal Acad. of Music 1982–83; Vocal consultant, English Nat. Opera; Hon. R.A.M. *Address:* Pound Cottage, St. Mary Bourne, Andover, Hants., England.

VEDEL, Georges, D. EN D.; French lawyer; b. 5 July 1910, Auch; s. of Henri Vedel and Marie-Laure Rouanet; m. Lucienne Deveille; three d.; ed. Lycée français, Mainz and Faculté de Droit and Faculté des Lettres, Univ. of Toulouse; Prof. of Law, Poitiers 1937–38, Toulouse 1939–48, Paris 1948–79; Dean, Faculté de Droit, Paris 1962–67; Prof. Emer. Univ. of Paris II 1980–; political adviser to French del. at Common Market negotiations 1956–57; Pres. Conseil Supérieur de L'Educ. Nat. 1971–79; mem. Conseil Econ. et Social 1969–79, Conseil Constitutionnel 1980–; Pres. Int. Asscn. of Comparative Law 1978–; Pres. Nat. Bar Asscn. 1979–, Asscn. française de science politique 1983–; mem. Acad. of Morocco 1980–; Hon. degree (Brussels, Lausanne, Athens); Grand Officier, Légion d'honneur, Ordre nat. du Mérite, Croix de guerre, Commdr. des Palmes académiques. *Publications:* Droit constitutionnel 1940, Droit administratif 1958 and numerous articles in legal journals. *Leisure interest:* bridge. *Address:* 201 boulevard Saint-Germain, 75007 Paris; Le Palombier, 64210 Bidart, France. *Telephone:* 222.10.15 (Paris).

VEDERNIKOV, Gennadiy Georgiyevich; Soviet politician; b. 1937; ed. Siberian Metallurgical Inst., CPSU Cen. Cttee. School; technician at Chelyabinsk Metallurgical Works 1960–70; mem. CPSU 1965–; Second Sec. of Chelyabinsk Regional Cttee. of CPSU 1970–73; deputy, chief engineer of Chelyabinsk Metallurgical Works 1973–78; Second, First Sec. of Chelyabinsk City Cttee. of CPSU 1978–80; Sec. of Chelyabinsk Dist. Cttee. of CPSU 1980–83, First Sec. 1984–86; Deputy Pres. of U.S.S.R. Council of Ministers 1986–; Deputy to U.S.S.R. Supreme Soviet; mem. of Cen. Cttee. of CPSU 1986–. *Address:* The Kremlin, Moscow, U.S.S.R.

VEEN, Christian van, DR.JUR.SC.; Netherlands politician; b. 19 Dec. 1922, Barneveld; m. Petronilla G. de Korte; one s. one d.; Official Office of the Town Clerk, Rijswijk 1950–60; Town Clerk, Hoogeveen 1960–64, Groningen 1964–67; Parl. Under-Sec. for the Interior 1967–71; Minister of Educ. and Science 1971–73; Pres. Fed. of Netherlands Industry 1974–84.

VEGA DE SEOANE AZPILICUETA, Javier; Spanish mining engineer; b. 13 Sept. 1947, San Sebastian; s. of Joaquin Vega de Seoane and Rosa Azpilicueta; m. Mercedes Pérez de Villaamil Lapiedra 1970; two s. one d.; ed. Escuela Técnica Superior de Ingenieros de Minas, Madrid and Glasgow Business School, Scotland; Asst. Production Dir., Fundiciones del Estanda S.A. 1972–75; Asst. to C.E.O., Leyland Iberica S.A. 1975–77; Gen. Man. SKF Española S.A. 1977–83, Pres. and C.E.O. 1983–84; Gen. Man. Instituto Nacional de Industria 1984–. *Leisure interests:* golf, squash, scuba diving. *Address:* Plaza Salamanca 8, 28006 Madrid, Spain (Office).

VÉGH VILLEGAS, Alejandro; Uruguayan industrial engineer and politician; b. 22 Sept. 1928; ed. Escuela de Ingeniería de Montevideo, Univ. of Harvard; Prof. Escuela de Ingeniería, Montevideo; Prof. Univ. Nacional de Buenos Aires; consultant in power economy in Venezuela; Planning Adviser, Hidronor S.A., Argentina; Adviser, Planning Ministry of Brazil; Consultant of IDB, OAS, ECLA and IBRD; Under-Sec. of State, Ministry of Industry and Trade 1967; Dir. Planning and Budget Office 1968; Minister of Finance 1974–76, of Econ. and Finance 1983–85; mem. Council of State 1976–83; Amb. to U.S.A. 1982–83. *Address:* c/o Ministry of Finance, Montevideo, Uruguay.

VEIL, Simone, L.EN.D.; French politician and fmr. lawyer; b. 13 July 1927, Nice; d. of André Jacob and Yvonne Steinmetz; m. Antoine Veil 1946; three s.; ed. Inst. d'Etudes Politiques de Paris; Attaché Ministry of Justice 1957–59; Tech. Adviser to Office of René Pleven, Keeper of the Seals 1969; Sec.-Gen. Conseil Supérieur de la Magistrature 1970–74; mem. ORTF Admin. Council 1972–74; Minister of Health 1974–78, of Health and Family Affairs 1978–79; mem. European Parl. 1979–, (Pres. 1979–82, Chair. of Legal Affairs Cttee. 1982–), Chair. Liberal and Democratic Group June 1984–; Leader Centre-Right List for European elections 1989; Dr. h.c. (Princeton) 1975, (Weizmann Inst.) 1976, (Bar Ilan) 1980, (Yale) 1980, (Cambridge) 1980, (Edinburgh) 1980, (Georgetown) 1981, (Urbino) 1981, (Sussex) 1982, (Yeshiva) 1982, (Free Univ., Brussels) 1984, (Yale) 1988, Chevalier Ordre nat. du Mérite, Médaille pénitentiaire, Médaille de l'Education surveillée; numerous foreign decorations including Grand Officer, National Order of the Lion (Senegal), Order of Merit of the Repub. (Ivory Coast), Isabel la Católica (Spain), Grand Cross Order of Merit (Fed. Repub. of Germany), Order of Rio Branco (Brazil), Order of Merit (Luxembourg), Order of the Phoenix (Greece); Onassis Foundation Prize 1980, Charlemagne Prize 1981, Louise Weiss Foundation Prize 1981, Louise Michel Prize 1983, European Merit Prize 1983, Jabotinsky Prize (U.S.A.) 1983, Prize for Everyday Courage 1984, Special Freedom Prize 1984, Fiera di Messina 1984. *Publication:* Les données psycho-sociologiques de l'adoption (with Prof. Launay and Dr. Soule) 1969. *Address:* 1 rue Bixio, 75007 Paris (Office); 11 Place Vauban, 75007 Paris, France (Home). *Telephone:* (1) 45-51-09-68.

VELASQUEZ-GÁZTELU RUIZ, Cándido; Spanish business executive; b. 1937, Jerez de la Frontera; ed. Univ. of Granada; Dir. Coca-Cola and other cos.; Head of sales and Commercial Dir. Tabalcera S.A. 1973, Gen. Dir. 1981, Chair. 1982–89; Pres. Compañía Telefónica Nacional de España 1989–. *Address:* Barquillo 5, 28004 Madrid, Spain. *Telephone:* (91) 2327600.

VELAYATI, Dr. Ali Akbar; Iranian politician; b. 1945, Teheran; s. of Ali Asghar and Zobeideh Asgah; m. Skina Khosshnevissan; three c.; ed. Teheran Univ.; joined Nat. Front (of Mossadegh) 1961; a founder of the Islamic Asscn. of Faculty of Medicine, Teheran Univ. 1963; underground political activities in support of Ayatollah Khomeini 1979; Vice-Minister, Ministry of Health 1979–80; proposed for Prime Minister by Ayatollah Khomeini Oct. 1981 (candidature rejected by the Majlis); Minister of Foreign Affairs Dec. 1981–. *Publications:* Infectious Diseases (3 vols.) 1979, numerous articles. *Address:* Ministry of Foreign Affairs, Teheran, Iran.

VELICHKO, Vladimir Makarovich; Soviet politician; b. 1937; trained as mechanical engineer; mem. of CPSU 1962; started career as foreman and rose to dir. of machine bldg. plant; First Deputy Minister, Ministry of Power Eng. of U.S.S.R. 1975–83, Minister 1983–87; Minister for Heavy Power and Transport Construction 1987–; elected to Congress of People's Deputies of the U.S.S.R. 1989; awarded State Prize. *Address:* Ministry of Power Engineering, Moscow, Nizhny Kislovsky per. 5, U.S.S.R. *Telephone:* (095) 203-04-37.

VELIKHOV, Yevgeniy Pavlovich; Soviet physicist; b. 2 Feb. 1935, Moscow; s. of Pavel Pavlovich Velikhov and Natalia Vsevolodoma Velikhova; m. Natalia Alekseevna Arseniyeva 1959; two s. one d.; mem. of staff, Inst. of Atomic Energy 1958–, Head of Lab. 1962–70, Deputy Dir., then Dir. of branch of Inst. 1971–; Prof., Moscow Univ. 1973–; mem. CPSU Cen. Cttee. April 1989–; Academician and fmr. Vice-Pres. U.S.S.R Acad. of Sciences; mem. Supreme Soviet of U.S.S.R.; elected to Congress of People's Deputies of the U.S.S.R. 1989; Chair. Cttee. of Soviet Scientists for Peace against Nuclear Threat; del. to numerous scientific and peace confs.; Order of Lenin (three times) and other awards *Publications:* numerous, related both to science and the problems of prevention of nuclear war. *Leisure interests:* mountain skiing, underwater swimming, windsurfing. *Address:* Moscow V-71, Leninski prospect 14, Moscow, U.S.S.R.

VELLA, Karmenu, B.A., B.ARCH. (HONS); Maltese politician; b. 19 June 1950, Zurrieq; ed. Lyceum, Univ. of Malta; Pres. Zurrieq section Labour League of Youth; Dir. Mid-Med Bank 1974, Bank of Valletta 1975; M.P. for Fifth Dist. 1976–; Minister of Works 1981–83, of Industry 1983–87; Man. Dir. Libyan-Arab Maltese Holding Co. 1976–81. *Address:* c/o Ministry of Industry, Auberge d'Aragon, Valletta, Malta.

VELLU, Dato S. Samy; Malaysian politician; b. 8 March 1936, Kluang, Johore; m. R. Indrani; two c.; ed. Royal Inst. of British Architects; mem. Parl. for Sungei Siput 1974; Deputy Minister of Housing and Local Govt. 1978; Minister of Works and Utilities 1979–; Deputy Pres. Malaysian

Indian Congress (MIC) 1977–79, Acting Pres. 1979–81, Pres. March 1981–. *Address:* Ministry of Works and Utilities, Jalan Mahameru, Kuala Lumpur, Malaysia.

VENDLER, Helen Hennessy, PH.D.; American professor and literary critic; b. 30 April 1933, Boston, Mass.; d. of George Hennessy and Helen Conway; one s.; ed. Emmanuel Coll. and Harvard Univ.; Instructor Cornell Univ. 1960–63; lecturer, Swarthmore Coll., Pa. and Haverford Coll., Pa. 1963–64; Asst. Prof. Smith Coll. Northampton, Mass. 1964–66; Assoc. Prof. Boston Univ. 1966–68, Prof. 1968–85; Visiting Prof. Harvard Univ. 1981–85, Kenan Prof. 1985–, Assoc. Acad. Dean 1987–, Sr. Fellow, Harvard Soc. of Fellows 1981–; poetry critic, New Yorker 1978–; mem. American Acad. of Arts and Sciences, Norwegian Acad.; Fulbright Fellow 1954; A.A.U.W. Fellow 1959; Guggenheim Fellow 1971–72; American Council of Learned Socs. Fellow 1971–72; N.E.H. Fellow 1980, 1985; Fulbright Lecturer, Univ. of Bordeaux 1968–69; Overseas Fellow, Churchill Coll. Cambridge 1980; Lowell Prize 1969; Explicator Prize 1969; Nat. Inst. of Arts and Letters Award 1975; Nat. Book Critics Award 1980; several hon. degrees. *Publications include:* Yeat's Vision and the Later Plays 1963, On Extended Wings: Wallace Stevens' Longer Poems 1969, The Poetry of George Herbert 1975, Part of Nature, Part of Us 1980, The Odes of John Keats 1983, Wallace Stevens: Words Chosen Out of Desire 1985, Harvard Book of Contemporary American Poetry 1985. *Address:* Warren House, Harvard University, Cambridge, Mass. 02138; 16a Still Street, Brookline, Mass. 02146, U.S.A.

VENIAMIN, Christodoulos; Cypriot government official; b. Sept. 1922; ed. in Nicosia and Middle Temple, London; junior officer in govt. service 1942, admin. officer 1949; served as Asst. Sec. in Depts. of Local Govt. and Admin., Personnel, Finance, Commerce and Industry, Social Services, Communications and Works, Agric. and Natural Resources; Asst. Dist. Commr., Larnaca; Asst. Sec. Ministry of Interior during transitional period; Dist. Officer, Limassol Dist. 1960–68; Dir.-Gen. Ministry of Foreign Affairs 1968; Minister of Interior and Defence 1975–84, of Interior Feb. 1988–. *Address:* Ministry of Interior, Nicosia, Cyprus. *Telephone:* (02) 402423.

VENKATARAMAN, Ramaswamy, M.A., B.L.; Indian politician; b. 4 Dec. 1910; s. of Ramaswami Iyer; m. Janaki Venkataraman; three d.; ed. Madras Univ.; Advocate, Madras High Court and Supreme Court; detained during Quit India Movt. 1942–44; mem. Provisional Parl. 1950–52; mem. Lok Sabha 1952–57, 1977–; Sec. Congress Party 1952–54; mem. Standing Finance Cttee., Estimates Cttee., Public Accounts Cttee., Privileges Cttee.; Minister for Industry and Labour and leader of the House, Govt. of Madras 1957–67, mem. Planning Comm. 1967–71; Chair. Nat. Research and Devt. Corpn.; Man. Ed. Labour Law Journal 1971–; Minister of Finance and Industry 1980–82, of Defence 1982–84; Vice-Pres. of India 1984–87, Pres. of India July 1987–; del. to ILO 1958, UN Gen. Ass. 1953–61. *Leisure interests:* arts, music, tennis. *Address:* Rashtrapti Bhavan, New Delhi 110004, India.

VENKATASUBBAIAH, Pendekanti; Indian politician; b. 18 June 1921, Sanjamala, Kurnool Dist., Andhra Pradesh; m. Kanakamma Venkatasubbaiah; three s. two d.; ed. high school and Theosophical Coll.; active participant in underground 'Quit India' Movt.; f. Banaganapalli State Congress which eventually led to the merging of the State in Indian Union 1948; mem. Madras State Assembly 1948; Pres. Dist. Congress Cttee. Kurnool, Pres. Andhra Pradesh Congress Cttee. and subsequently Gen. Sec. All India Congress Cttee.; mem. Lok Sabha for Nandyal 1957–84; Minister of State for Home and Parl. Affairs 1980–84; Gov. of Bihar 1985–87, of Karnataka Feb. 1988–. *Address:* c/o Office of the Governor, Raj. Bhavan, Bangalore, India.

VENNAMO, Pekka Veikko; Finnish politician; b. 1944, Helsinki; ed. Helsinki Univ. of Tech.; Asst. Helsinki Inst. of Tech. 1964–65; mem. Parl. 1972–75, 1979–; Chair. Finnish Rural Party 1979–; reporter Suomen Uutiset (party newspaper) 1970–71, Man. Dir. 1976–; Minister, Ministry of Finance 1983–87; Minister of Transport and Communications 1987–. *Address:* Ministry of Transport and Communications, Eteläesplanadi 16, 00130 Helsinki, Finland.

VENNAMO, Veikko Emil Alexsander, LL.L.; Finnish politician; b. 11 June 1913, Jaakkima; s. of Emil Fennander and Sivi Haikala; m. Sirkka Tuominen 1944; one s. two d.; Barrister-at-Law 1939; Sec.-Gen. Emergency Resettlement Bd. 1940–41; Chief, Bureau for Reconstruction of the Rural Districts of Ceded Karelia 1942–43; Acting Chief Resettlement Dept., Ministry of Agric. 1943, Chief 1944–59; M.P. 1945–62, 1966–; accounting and econ. dept. Bd. of Customs 1960–80; mem. Bd. of Dirs. Treasury Office, and of Programme Council of Finnish Broadcasting Corpn. 1946–47; Chair. Finnish Small Farmers Party (later Rural Party) 1959–79; Presidential cand. 1968, 1978, 1981; Supervisor, Bank of Finland; mem. Helsinki Town Council 1968–72, 1981–84, Int. Parl. Union, Finland Section. *Leisure interests:* foreign policy, historical interests, travelling. *Address:* Ritokalliontie 1, 00330 Helsinki 33, Finland. *Telephone:* 48-2915, 86-8076 (summer).

VENTURI, Franco; Italian professor of modern history; b. 16 May 1914, Rome; s. of Lionello Venturi; m. Gigliola Spinelli 1945; one s.; ed. Univ. of Paris; Partisan in the Alps 1943–45; Cultural Attaché, Moscow 1947–50; Prof. of Modern History in Cagliari and Genoa from 1952, now in Turin; Visiting Prof. in Cambridge (Mass.), Oxford, Chicago; Corresp. Fellow of British Acad.; Hon. Degree of Univs. of London, Geneva, Chicago and Cambridge. *Publications:* Il Populismo Russo 1952, Settecento Riformatore, Vol. I Da Muratori a Beccaria 1969, Vol. II. La Chiesa e la Repubblica entro i loro Limiti 1976, Vol. III. La Prima Crisi dell'Antico Regime (1768–1776) 1979, Vol. IV, La Caduta dell' Antico Regime 1984, Vol. V.1, L'Italia dei lumi 1987, Utopia and Reform in the Enlightenment 1971. *Leisure interests:* skiing, mountaineering. *Address:* Piazza Amedeo Peyron 7, Turin, Italy. *Telephone:* 771 0380.

VENTURI, Robert, A.B., M.F.A.; American architect; b. 25 June 1925, Philadelphia, Pa.; s. of Robert C. Venturi and Vanna Lanzetta; m. Denise (Lakofski) Scott Brown 1967; one s.; ed. Princeton Univ.; Designer, Oskar Stonorov 1950, Eero Saarinen & Assoc. 1950–53; Rome Prize Fellow, American Acad. in Rome 1954–56; Designer, Louis I. Khan 1957; Assoc. Prof., School of Fine Arts, Univ. of Pennsylvania 1957–65; Charlotte Shepherd Davenport Prof., Yale Univ. 1966–70; Prin., Venturi, Cope & Lippincott 1958–61, Venturi and Short 1961–64, Venturi and Rauch 1964–80, Venturi, Rauch and Scott Brown (architects and planners) 1980–; *works include:* Vanna Venturi House, Phila., Pa. 1961, Guild House, Phila. 1961, Franklin Court, Phila. 1972, Allen Memorial Art Museum Addition, Oberlin, Ohio 1973, Inst. for Scientific Information Corpn. HQ, Phila. 1978, Gordon Wu Hall, Princeton Univ., N.J. 1980, Seattle Art Museum, Seattle, Wash. 1984, Nat. Gallery, Sainsbury Wing, London, U.K. 1986, Orchestra Hall, Philadelphia, Pa. 1987; Fellow American Inst. of Architects, American Acad. in Rome, Accademia Nazionale di San Luca, American Acad. of Arts and Sciences; Hon. Fellow Royal Incorporation of Architects in Scotland; Hon. D.F.A. (Oberlin, Yale, Penn., Princeton, Phila. Coll of Art), Hon. L.H.D. (N.J. Inst. of Tech.), and numerous awards. *Publications:* Complexity and Contradiction in Architecture 1966, Learning from Las Vegas (with Denise Scott Brown and Steven Izenour) 1972, A View from the Campidoglio: Selected Essays, 1953–1984 (with Denise Scott Brown) 1984; numerous articles in professional journals. *Leisure interest:* travel. *Address:* Venturi, Rauch and Scott Brown, 4236 Main Street, Philadelphia, Pa. 19127, U.S.A. *Telephone:* (215) 487-0400 (Office).

VENZO, Mario, S.J.; Italian painter; b. 14 Feb. 1900; ed. Accademia di Belle Arti, Venice; painter in Paris 1926–39; entered Soc. of Jesus 1940; exhbns. in Milan 1951–53, Rio de Janeiro 1955, Turin 1958, Trieste 61, Zürich 1964, Munich and Berne 1965, Monte Carlo and Padua 1966, Turin and Milan 1967, Zürich 1968, Rome 1970; First Prize Ucai, Vicenza 1950, Monte Carlo 1966, Nat. Exhbn. Prize, Milan, Turin 1972. *Major works:* Via Crucis (Lonigo) 1960, Crocefissione (Coll. Pio-Latino-Americano, Rome) 1962, Via Crucis (Villa Cavalletti, Frascati) 1964, Crocefissione (Alte, Vicenza) 1965, Via Crucis (Prospiano) 1967, paintings in Galleria d'Arte di Venezia, Museo Civico di Vicenza, Museo di Brescia, Galleria d'arte Moderna di Milano. *Address:* Aloysianum, 1-20013 Gallarate, Varese, Italy. *Telephone:* 796167.

VERBA, Sidney, PH.D.; American academic; b. 26 May 1932, Brooklyn, New York; s. of Morris Verba and Recci Salman; m. E. Cynthia Winston 1955; three d.; ed. Harvard Coll. and Princeton Univ.; Asst., then Assoc. Prof. of Politics Princeton Univ. 1960–64; Prof. of Political Science Stanford Univ. 1964–68; Sr. Study Dir. Nat. Opinion Research Center 1968–72; Prof. of Political Science Univ. of Chicago 1968–72; Prof. of Govt. Harvard Univ. 1972–, Clarence Dillon Prof. of Int. Affairs 1983–84, Carl H. Pforzheimer Univ. Prof. 1984–, Assoc. Dean for Undergraduate Educ., Faculty of Arts and Sciences 1981–84, Dir. Harvard Univ. Library 1984–; mem. N.A.S., American Acad. of Arts and Sciences; Guggenheim Fellow; Woodrow Wilson and Kammerer Book Awards. *Publications:* Small Groups and Political Behavior 1961, The Civic Culture 1963, Participation in America 1972, Participation and Political Equality 1978, The Changing American Voter 1979, Injury to Insult 1979, Equality in America 1985, Elites and the Idea of Equality. *Address:* Wadsworth House, Harvard University, Cambridge, Mass. 02138 (Office); 142 Summit Avenue, Brookline, Mass. 02146, U.S.A. (Home). *Telephone:* (617) 495-3650 (Office); (617) 232-4987 (Home).

VERBEEK, Paul, D.IUR.; German diplomatist; b. 1 June 1925, Cologne; s. of Heinrich Verbeek and Paula Heidermanns; m. Gisela Lehmann 1966; two d.; ed. Cologne Univ.; lawyer in Cologne 1955–57; entered Foreign Service 1957; Counsellor in Fed. Chancellery 1967–70; Counsellor, Fed. Press Office 1970–73; Amb. to Ivory Coast 1973–76; Deputy Head of Legal Dept., Foreign Ministry, Bonn 1976–80; Amb. to Argentina 1980–84, to Holy See 1987–; Chief Insp. German Foreign Service 1984–87; various decorations from France, Netherlands, Brazil, Ivory Coast, Argentina, Order of Merit (Fed. Repub. of Germany). *Leisure interest:* golf. *Address:* Via di Villa Sacchetti 4–6, 00197 Rome, Italy.

VERBURGT, Paul Adriaan; Netherlands banker; b. 23 Jan. 1935, Bussum; s. of Dr. G. Verburgt and A. C. (née Koole) Verburgt; m. 1958; one s. one d.; ed. Econ. High School and Private Banking School; Dutch Banking Group, South Africa 1955–57, Belgium 1957–65; joined Bank of America, Antwerp Branch 1965, Man. Rotterdam br. until 1972, Regional Vice-Pres. for Scandinavia and Benelux countries 1972–73; Sr. Vice-Pres., Head of Int. Financial Centre, London 1973–, Cashier, Europe, Middle East and Africa Div. 1973–, Head of Middle East Area 1979–, Head of Africa Area 1981–, Exec. Vice-Pres. Europe, Middle East and Africa

Div. March 1982-. *Leisure interests:* photography, vintage cars. *Address:* Hillside, St. George's Hill, Weybridge, Surrey, England. *Telephone:* 51669.

VERCORS (pseudonym of Jean Bruller); French writer, graphic artist and engraver; b. 26 Feb. 1902, Paris; s. of Louis Bruller and Ernestine (née Bourbon) Bruller; m. 1st Jeanne Barusseau (divorced), 2nd Rita Barisse 1956; three s.; ed. Ecole alsacienne, Paris; early career as graphic artist and engraver; f. Editions de Minuit with Pierre de Lescure 1941; many lecturing tours throughout the world since 1945; retrospective exhbn., Saint-Nazaire 1989; mem. PEN Club; Hon. Pres. Nat. Cttee. of Writers; Médaille de la Résistance, Prix du Conseil de l'Europe 1981, Prix de l'Union rationaliste 1982; Officier, Légion d'honneur, Commdr. des Arts et des Lettres. *Major works* (graphic art and engraving): 21 recettes de mort violente 1926, 1977. Hypothèses sur les amateurs de peinture 1927, Un homme coupé en tranches 1929, Nouvelle clé des songes 1934, L'enfer 1935, Images rassurantes de la guerre 1936, Silence 1937, La danse des vivants (160 prints) 1938, Hamlet (French adaptation, with aqua-forte illustrations) 1965. *Publications:* Le silence de la mer 1941, La marche à l'etoile 1943, Le sable du temps 1945, Les armes de la nuit 1946, Les yeux et la lumière 1948, Plus ou moins homme 1950, La puissance du jour 1951, Les animaux dénaturés 1952, Les pas dans le sable, Portrait d'une amitié 1954, Divagations d'un Français en Chine 1956, Colères 1956, P.P.C. 1957, Sur ce rivage Vol. 1 1958, Vol. 2 1958, Vol. 3 1960, Sylva 1961, Zoo ou l'assassin philanthrope (play) 1963, Les chemins de l'être (with P. Misraki) 1965, Quota ou les pléthoriens (with P. Coronel) 1966, La bataille du silence 1967, Le radeau de la Méduse 1969, Le fer et le velours (play) 1969, Oedipe (play) 1970, Hamlet et Oedipe 1970, Contes des cataplasmes (children) 1971, Sillages (novel) 1972, Sept sentiers du désert (short stories) 1972, Questions sur la vie 1973, Comme un frère (novel) 1973, Tendre naufrage (novel) 1974, Ce que je crois (essay) 1975, Je cuisine comme un chef (cookery book) 1976, Les chevaux du temps (novel) 1977, 21 recettes de Mort violente (satirical album) 1977, Macbeth (play) 1977, Sens et non-sens de l'histoire (essay) 1978, Théâtre (2 vols.) 1978, Camille ou l'enfant double (for children) 1978, Le piège à loup (novel) 1979, Cent ans d'histoire de France (1862-1962) 3 vols. 1981, Moi, Aristide Briand 1981, Les occasions perdues 1982, Les nouveaux jours 1984, Anne Boleyn 1985, Le Tigre d'Anvers 1986. *Address:* 58 quai des Orfèvres, 75001 Paris, France.

VERDAN, Claude-Edouard; Swiss hand surgeon (retd.); b. 21 Sept. 1909, Yverdon; s. of Edouard and Adeline (née Henrioud) Verdan; m. Sylva Malan 1934; one s. (deceased) one d.; ed. Faculty of Medicine, Univ. of Lausanne; Graduate in Medicine, Conféd. helvétique (Lausanne); Doctor of Medicine, Univ. of Zürich; specialist in surgery, Foederatio Medicorum Helveticorum (FMH); Chief surgeon, Clinique chirurgicale et Permanence de Longeraie, Lausanne; Prof. Univ. of Lausanne; Sr. Dean Faculty of Medicine 1972-74; Pres. Soc. suisse de médecine des accidents et des maladies professionnelles 1961-66; Pres. Soc. française de chirurgie plastique et reconstructive 1964; Sec.-Gen. and Founder, Groupe suisse d'étude de chirurgie de la main 1966-72; Pres. Comm. for war surgery, Fed. Mil. (Defence) Dept. (médecin-Col.) 1965-69; retd. from medical practice 1980; f. Museum of the Human Hand (Foundation Claude Verdan), Lausanne 1981; first exhbn. "The Man's Hand" 1983; Hon. mem. British Soc. for Surgery of the Hand 1959; Corresp. mem. Belgian Soc. for Forensic Traumatology 1963, Italian Soc. for Hand Surgery 1970; Assoc. mem. Acad. of Surgery, Paris 1974; Hon. mem. American Soc. for Surgery of the Hand 1960, Swiss Soc. for Medicine in Casualty 1966, Swiss Soc. for Orthopedics 1967, German-speaking Assen. for Hand Surgery 1971, Soc. vaudoise de médecine 1975, Spanish Soc. for Hand Surgery, French Soc. for Orthopedics and Traumatology 1979, French Soc. of Hand Surgery 1979; Hon. mem. de l'Assen. française du chirurgie 1981; Specialist FMH in plastic and reconstructive surgery 1977; Ed. Annales de chirurgie de la main 1982-, Ed.-in-Chief Emer. 1985; Hon. Prof., Univ. of Lausanne 1979; Gold Medal Prix César Roux (Faculty of Medicine, Lausanne) 1933; nominated Pioneer of Hand Surgery, 3rd Congress IFSS, Tokyo 1986; Chevalier Légion d'honneur. *Publications:* numerous books and articles on hand surgery. *Leisure interests:* sculpting, collecting articles concerning the hand, objets d'art. *Address:* 9 avenue de la Gare, CH-1003 Lausanne, Switzerland. *Telephone:* (021) 312.22.10.

VERDEȚ, Ilie; Romanian politician; b. 10 May 1925, Comănești, Bacău County; m. Regina Manescu (sister of Nicolae Ceausescu, q.v.); ed. Acad. of Econ. Studies, Bucharest; mem. Romanian CP (RCP) 1945-; worked in the Party local organs of Banat Region 1948-54; Head of Section in Central Cttee. RCP 1954-; First Sec. Hunedoara Regional Party Cttee. 1954-65; mem. Cen. Cttee. RCP 1960-; mem. Grand Nat. Ass. 1961-; Alt. mem. Exec. Cttee. of Cen. Cttee. of RCP 1965-66, mem. 1966-86; mem. Perm. Presidium of Cen. Cttee. 1966-74, 1984-86; mem. Standing Bureau Exec. Political Cttee. 1977-86, Chair. Cen. Auditing Cttee. 1986-; Sec. Cen. Cttee. 1974-78, 1982-85; Deputy Chair. Council of Ministers 1965-66, First Deputy Chair. 1966-74, First Vice Prime Minister 1978-79, Prime Minister 1979-82; Minister of Mines 1985-86; Chair. Cen. Council of Workers' Control over Econ. and Social Activity 1974-78, 1982-; Vice Chair. Supreme Council on Social and Econ. Devt. 1973-86; Chair. State Planning Cttee. 1978-79; mem. Nat. Council Front of Socialist Democracy and Unity 1980-; Hero of Socialist Labour 1971. *Address:* c/o Comitetul Central al PCR, Str. Academiei 34, Bucharest, Romania.

VERDON-SMITH, Sir (William) Reginald, Kt. D.L.; British business executive; b. 5 Nov. 1912, London; s. of late Sir William George Verdon-Smith, C.B.E., and Florence Jane (Anders) Verdon-Smith; m. Jane Margaret Hobbs 1946; one s. one d.; ed. Repton School and Brasenose Coll., Oxford; Pres. Soc. of British Aircraft Constructors 1946-48; Chair. British Aircraft Corpn. (Holdings) Ltd. 1968-72; Deputy Chair. Lloyds Bank Ltd. 1967-79, Dir. 1952-83; Pro-Chancellor, Bristol Univ. 1965-86; Chair. Lloyds Bank Int. Ltd. 1973-79, Dir 1973-83; Chair. Bristol Regional Bd. 1976-82; Deputy Lieut. County of Avon 1980-88. *Leisure interests:* golf, sailing. *Address:* Flat 3, Spring Leigh Church Road, Leigh Woods, Bristol, BS8 3PG, England. *Telephone:* (0272) 738319 (Home).

VERE-JONES, David, M.SC., D.PHIL., F.R.S.N.Z.; British professor of mathematics; b. 17 April 1936, London; s. of Noel W. Vere-Jones and Isabel M. I. Wyllie; m. Mary To Kei Chung 1965; two s. one d.; ed. Cheadle Hulme School, Cheshire, Hutt Valley High School, N.Z., Vic. Univ. of Wellington and Univ. of Oxford; emigrated to New Zealand 1949; Rhodes Scholar 1958-61; sr. scientist, Applied Math. Div. Dept. of Scientific & Industrial Research, N.Z. 1961-65; Fellow, Sr. Fellow, Dept. of Statistics, A.N.U. 1965-69; Prof. of Math. Vic. Univ. of Wellington 1970-; Founding Pres. N.Z. Math Soc. 1975; other professional affiliations. *Publications:* An Introduction to the Theory of Point Processes (with D. J. Daley) 1988; about 60 papers on probability theory, seismology, mathematical educ. *Leisure interests:* tennis, walking, languages. *Address:* Department of Mathematics, Victoria University of Wellington, Private Bag, Wellington (Office); 15 Farm Road, Northland, Wellington 5, New Zealand (Home). *Telephone:* (04) 721-000 (Office); (04) 757-249 (Home).

VERESS, Péter; Hungarian economist and politician; b. 1928, Gyimesközéplak (Romania); ed. Acad. for Foreign Trade; Commercial Counsellor; Leader, Hungarian Trade Mission in Damascus 1958, Tel-Aviv 1963; Deputy Dir.-Gen., then Dir.-Gen. Int. Dept. for Non-Socialist Countries Overseas, Ministry of Foreign Trade 1963-71; Deputy Minister of Foreign Trade 1971-74; Amb. to Paris 1974-79; Minister of Foreign Trade March 1979-87; Labour Order of Merit, Golden Degree, Order for Socialist Hungary 1983. *Address:* Kereskedelmi Minisztérium, Budapest V, Honvéd-utca 13/15. *Telephone:* 530-000.

VEREY, Michael John, T.D., M.A.; British merchant banker; b. 12 Oct. 1912, London; s. of late Henry Edward Verey and late Lucy Alice Verey; m. Sylvia Mary Wilson 1947; two s. one d.; ed. Eton Coll., Trinity Coll., Cambridge; joined Helbert Wagg and Co. Ltd. 1934; served in Warwickshire Yeomanry, Middle East and Italy becoming Lieut.-Col. 1939-45; Chair. Brixton Estate Ltd. 1971-83, Schroders Ltd. 1973-77, Accepting Houses Cttee. 1974-77, Broadstone Investment Trust Ltd. 1963-83, Charities Official Investment Fund 1974-83, London American Energy Investments Ltd. 1981-84; Vice-Chair. Commercial Union Assurance Co. Ltd. 1975-78, Deputy Chair. 1978-82; Dir. Boots Co. Ltd. (Vice-Chair. 1978-83), Invest. SpA (Italy) 1970-85, British Petroleum Co. 1974-82, Invest International Holdings; mem. Covent Garden Market Authority 1961-66; High Sheriff of Berks. 1971; Pres. Royal Worcs. and Warwicks. Yeomanry Regimental Assen. 1971-86; Gov. Pangbourne Coll. 1972-82. *Leisure interests:* gardening and travel. *Address:* Little Bowden, Pangbourne, Berks., England. *Telephone:* (073 57) 2210.

VEREYSKY, Orest Georgievich; Soviet graphic artist and illustrator; b. 20 July 1915, Anosovo, Smolensk Dist.; s. of Georgi Vereysky and Elena Vereskaja; m. Ludmila Rusanova; one d.; ed. Inst. of Painting, Sculpture and Architecture, Leningrad; Corresp. mem. of U.S.S.R. Acad. of Arts 1958-83, mem. 1983-; People's Artist of R.S.F.S.R. 1970, People's Artist of U.S.S.R. 1983, Orders of Red Star, Labour Red Banner, Fatherland, and various medals. *Works include:* illustrations to Tvardovsky's Vasily Tyorkin 1942-48, and House By the Road 1957, Fadeyev's Defeat 1949, Sholokhov's Quiet Flows the Don 1951-52, Fate of a Man 1958 and Virgin Soil Upturned 1967, the 200-volume Library of World Literature (U.S.S.R. State Prize 1978), Anna Karenina 1977-81, Lyric Book (A. Tvardovskys) 1983, Son of Regiment (V. Kataevs) 1986, and a whole series of drawings, watercolours and lithographs of his journeys abroad to Czechoslovakia, Finland, the Middle East, U.S.A., China, Iceland and Italy. *Address:* c/o U.S.S.R. Academy of Arts, Ul. Kropotkinskaya 21, Moscow, U.S.S.R.

VERGE, Pierre, M.A., LL.L., LL.M., LL.D., F.R.S.C.; Canadian professor of law; b. 9 Jan. 1936, Quebec City; m. Colette Habel 1963; two s. one d.; ed. Univ. Laval, McGill Univ. and Univ. of Toronto; mem. Quebec Bar 1961; Q.C. 1976; Prof. of Law, Univ. Laval 1961-, Dean, Faculty of Law 1973-77; Commonwealth Fellowship, St. John's Coll. Cambridge 1977; mem. Canadian Assen. of Law Teachers (Pres. 1972-73), Royal Soc. of Canada. *Publications:* Le droit de grèves, fondement et limites, Droit du travail (co-author). *Address:* Faculté de droit, Université Laval, Québec, G1K 7P4, Canada. *Telephone:* 418-656-559.

VERGÈS, Jacques; French lawyer; b. 1925, Thailand; of Vietnamese-French parentage; m. Djamila Bouhired; two c.; ed. legal studies in Paris; served with Free French in World War II in N. Africa, Italy, France and Germany; joined French CP 1945; Sec. Int. Union of Students, Prague 1951-55; joined Paris Bar 1955; defended many Algerian FLN militants; pvt. legal practice in Algeria 1965-70; activities unknown 1970-78; returned to Paris Bar 1978; appeared for defence at trial of Nazi war criminal Klaus

Barbie gaoled for atrocities in Lyons in World War II 1987. *Publication:* Beauté du Crime 1988.

VERGHESE, Rev. Thadikkal Paul (see Gregorios, Bishop Paul).

VERHOOGEN, John, PH.D.; American professor of geophysics; b. 1 Feb. 1912, Brussels, Belgium; s. of Dr. René Verhoogen and Lucy Vinçotte; m. Ilse Goldschmidt 1939 (died 1981); two s. two d.; ed. Univs. of Brussels and Liège and Stanford Univ.; Asst. Univ. of Brussels 1936–39, Fonds Nat. de la Recherche 1939–40; with Mines d'Or de Kilo-Moto 1940–43; Gov.-Gen. Belgian Congo 1943–46; Prof. of Geophysics, Univ. of Calif. at Berkeley 1947–77, Prof. Emer. 1977–; mem. N.A.S.; Day Medal, Geological Soc. of America. *Publications:* Igneous and Metamorphic Petrology (with F. J. Turner) 1951, Metamorphic Reactions (with F. J. Turner and W. S. Fyfe) 1958, The Earth 1970. *Leisure interest:* doing nothing. *Address:* Department of Geology and Geophysics, University of California, Berkeley, Calif. 94720; 2100 Marin Avenue, Berkeley, Calif. 94707, U.S.A. (Home). *Telephone:* (415) 642-2575 (Office); (415) 526-8061 (Home).

VERITY, Calvin William, Jr., B.A.; American steel executive; b. 26 Jan. 1917, Middletown, Ohio; s. of C. William Verity, Sr. and Elizabeth O'Brien Verity; m. Margaret Burnley Wymond 1941; two s. one d.; ed. Phillips Exeter Acad. and Yale Univ.; with Armco Inc., Middletown, Ohio 1940–42, 1946–, Dir. Org. Planning and Devt. 1957–61, Dir. of Public Relations 1961–62, Asst. to Pres. 1962–63, Vice-Pres. and Gen. Man. 1963–65, Exec. Vice-Pres. 1965–66, Pres. 1965–71, C.E.O. 1971–79, Chair. 1979–83; Sec. of Commerce 1987–89; Dir. First Nat. Bank, Middletown, Mead Corpn., Dayton, Ohio, Business Int., New York, Taft Broadcasting Co., Cincinnati, Chase Manhattan Bank, New York; mem. Pres. Export Council; Co-Chair, U.S.-U.S.S.R. Trade and Econ. Council, New York, U.S. Chamber of Commerce 1980, Bd. of Trustees Ford's Theatre Soc., Washington D.C.; Hon. D.H., (Univ. of Dayton); Hon. B.A. (S. Dak. School of Mines and Tech., Ohio Northern Univ.), Hon. LL.D. (Xavier and Wright State Univs.), Hon. D.Hum. Litt. (Ohio Univ.). *Leisure interests:* golf, hunting, tennis. *Address:* 600 Thorn Hill Lane, Middletown, Ohio, U.S.A. (Home).

VERIVAKIS, Elevtherios; Greek politician; b. 21 Jan. 1935, Crete; m. Lila Christoforidou 1981; Pres. Centre Youth org., then Pres. League of Young Scientists and Intellectuals, also Sec.-Gen. Democratic Leagues until 1967; political prisoner 1967, 1968–73; M.P. 1977–; Minister for Educ. and Culture 1981–82, for Social Security 1982–84, for Energy and National Resources 1984–85, for Industry, Energy and Tech. 1985–86, of Justice 1986–87; mem. Panhellenic Socialist Movement. *Address:* c/o Ministry of Justice, Odos Zinonos 12, Athens, Greece.

VERKAUF-VERLON, Willy André; Austrian artist; b. 6 March 1917, Zurich; s. of Bernard and Bertha Verkauf; m. 1st Hanna Verkauf-Verlon 1936, 2nd Helga Verkauf-Verlon 1975; Gen.-Sec. Free Austria Movt. in Middle East 1942–45; with Psychological Dept. British 8th Army, Jerusalem 1945; Publr. in Vienna and Switzerland 1945–54; visual artist, writer, publicist in Paris and Vienna 1955–; Pres. Asscn. of Austrian Artists, Friends of the Künstlerhaus, Vienna, etc.; Prof. h.c., Ehrenkreuz für Kunst und Wissenschaft, Ehrenzeichen für Verdienste zur Befreiung Osterreichs, Goldene Ehrenmedaille der Stadt Wien 1987, etc. *Publications:* Dada: Monography of a Movement 1957, Montage and Collage 1983, Situationen. Eine autobiographische Wort-Collage 1984, Paintings (with Catalogue of works) 1986, Mit Scharfer Optik 1989, etc. *Address:* A-1120, Arndtstrasse 90, Austria. *Telephone:* 87 23 48, 87 38 77, 02666-3296.

VERKIN, Boris Yeremievich; DR. OF PHYSICAL-MATH. SC.; Soviet physicist; b. 8 Aug. 1919, Kharkov; s. of Yeremia Stepanovich Verkin and Maria Konstantinovna Verkina; m. Galina Vasil'evna; one s. two d.; ed. Kharkov Univ.; Prof., Academician, Ukrainian Acad. of Sciences; Deputy, Supreme Soviet of Ukrainian S.S.R.; numerous medals and State prizes. *Publications:* over 400 publs. on electronic properties of normal metals and alloys, fundamental and applied superconductivity, preparation and study of quantum liquids and crystals at superlow temperatures, application of cryoeng. and nitrogen technologies. *Leisure interests:* history, art, literature. *Address:* Institute for Low Temperature Physics and Engineering, Ukrainian S.S.R. Academy of Sciences, 47 Lenin Avenue, 310164 Kharkov, U.S.S.R. *Telephone:* 32-10-41.

VERLINDEN, (Jean) Charles (Alphonse), M.A., PH.D.; Belgian historian; b. 3 Feb. 1907, St. Gilles, Brussels; s. of Emile Verlinden; m. Nelly Noulard 1931; no c.; ed. Univ. of Ghent, Sorbonne, Ecole des Hautes Etudes, Paris, Ecole des Chartes, Paris and Centro de Estudios Historicos, Madrid; Studies and research Paris 1933, Madrid 1934, Italy 1938; Asst. Prof. of Econ. History, Business Univ., Antwerp 1940; Asst. Prof. of History, Univ. of Ghent 1944, Prof. 1944–74, Emer. 1974–; Dir. Belgian Acad., Rome 1959–77; Dir. Belgian Historical Inst., Rome 1955–86; Pres. Int. Comm. of Maritime History (Int. Comm. of Historical Sciences) 1980–85; mem. Royal Belgian Acad. (Flemish Section), Acad. de la Historia, Madrid, Royal Historical Soc., Medieval Acad. of America, Accademia dei Lincei, Rome, Società Nazionale di Scienze, Lettere ed Arti, Naples, Acad. da Historia, Lisbon, Acad. das Ciencias, Lisbon, Inst. Coimbra, Soc. de Historia, Lima, Comisión Panamericana de Historia, Caracas, Acad. Siciliana Lettere ed Arti, Palermo; has taught and lectured in 46 univs. in Europe and America; Dr. h.c. (Seville) 1968, (Coimbra) 1988; Int. Prize Galileo Galilei 1970. *Publications:* L'esclavage dans l'Europe médiévale,

Vol. I Péninsule Ibérique, France 1955, Vol. II Italie, Colonies italiennes du Levant. Levant latin, Empire byzantin 1977, Documents sur l'histoire des prix et salaires en Flandre et en Brabant (XIII-XIXe siecle), 5 vols. 1959–73, Les origines de la civilisation atlantique, De la renaissance à l'âge des lumières 1966, Cristóbal Colón 1967, The beginnings of modern colonization 1970, De Koloniale expansie in de XVe en XVIe eeuw 1975, Die mittelalterlichen Urspeiinge der grossen Entdeckungen 1986. *Leisure interests:* classical music, travel. *Address:* 3 avenue du Derby, 1050 Brussels, Belgium. *Telephone:* 02/6492381.

VERNEJOUL, Robert, Baron de, D. EN MED.; French professor of clinical surgery; b. 19 March 1890, Montcaret, Dordogne; s. of Edgard de Vernejoul and Lucie Laurens; m. Madeleine Hotz 1926 (deceased); two s. one d.; ed. Lycée Blaise Pascal, Clermont-Ferrand and Facultés de Médecine, Paris and Marseilles; founder and Head, Centre for Cardiac Surgery, Marseilles 1955–63 and Prof. of Clinical and Experimental Surgery, Faculté de Médecine, Marseilles, Hon. Prof. 1963–; Pres. Conseil nat. de l'Ordre des Médecins 1956–70, Hon. Pres. 1970–; mem. Nat. Council for Higher Educ. and Research 1973–; mem. Inst. Français (Acad. des Sciences) 1970–, Acad. nat. de Médecine 1962– (Hon. mem. 1986), Acad. de Chirurgie 1957–; Pres. haut-comité médical de la Sécurité Sociale 1959–; Grand-Croix de la Légion d'honneur, Croix de guerre, Médaille de la Résistance. *Leisure interest:* golf. *Address:* 96 rue Sylvabelle, 13006 Marseille, France. *Telephone:* 37-56-47.

VERNEUIL, Henri; French film director; b. 15 Oct. 1920, Rodosto, Turkey; s. of Agop Malakian and Araxi Kirazian; m. Françoise Bonnot (divorced); one s. one d.; journalist and critic 1944–48; made 30 short films 1948–50, 29 long films 1950–78; Best Foreign Language Film (U.S.A.) 1963, Victoire du Cinéma Français 1963, Mystery Writers' Award (U.S.A.) 1964, Prix Saint-Simon for Mayrig 1986; Officier, Légion d'honneur, des Arts et des Lettres. *Films include:* La vache et le prisonnier 1959, Le Président 1960, Un singe en hiver 1962, Melodie en sous-sol (Any Number Can Win) 1963, Weekend à Zuydcoote 1964, La 25ème heure 1966, Le clan des siciliens 1969, Le casse 1970, Le serpent 1972, Peur sur la ville 1975, Le corps de mon ennemi 1976, I comme Icare 1979, Mille milliards de dollars 1981, Les Morfalous 1983. *Publication:* Mayrig 1985. *Leisure interest:* magic. *Address:* 21 rue du Bois de Boulogne, 92200 Neuilly-sur-Seine, France.

VERNIER-PALLIEZ, Bernard Maurice Alexandre, L. EN D.; French business executive and diplomatist; b. 2 March 1918; m. Denise Silet-Pathe 1952; one s. three d.; ed. Ecole Libre des Sciences Politiques, Ecole des Hautes Etudes Commerciales; Head of Welfare, Régie Nat. des Usines Renault 1945–47, Sec. to Sec.-Gen. 1947–48, Sec.-Gen. 1948–67, Deputy Man. Dir. 1967–71, Chair. and Man. Dir. 1975–81; Chair. and Man. Dir. SAVIEM 1967–74; Del.-Gen. for commercial vehicles, coaches and buses, Régie Renault; Pres. Berliet 1975–76; Vice-Pres. Supervisory Bd. of SAVIEM 1975; Amb. to U.S.A. 1982–84; mem. European Advisory Council TENNECO, Int. Advisory Bd. A.I.G., Int. Bd. James F. Byrne Inst., Bd. I.D.V. Europe; Chair. Supervisory Bd. Case-Poclain; Chair. Bd. French Inst. of Int. Relations; Ambassadeur de France 1984; Commdr., Légion d'honneur, Croix de guerre, Médaille de la Résistance. *Address:* 25 Grande Rue, 78170 La Celle St.-Cloud, France. *Telephone:* (1) 39.69.30.11.

VERNON, Sir James, A.C., C.B.E., PH.D., F.R.A.C.I., F.A.I.M., F.T.S.; Australian business executive; b. 13 June 1910, Tamworth; s. of Donald Vernon; m. Mavis Lonsdale-Smith (deceased); two d.; ed. Sydney Univ., Univ. Coll. London; Chief Chemist, Colonial Sugar Refining Co. Ltd. (C.S.R.) 1938–51, Sr. Exec. Officer 1951–56, Asst. G. Man. 1956–57, Gen. Man. 1958–72; Dir. C.S.R. Ltd. 1958–82, Chair. 1978–80; Dir. Westham Dredging Co. Pty. Ltd.; Chair. CIBC N.Z. Ltd., Volvo Australia Pty. Ltd.; Chair. Commonwealth Cttee. of Econ. Inquiry 1963–65, Australian Post Office Comm. of Inquiry 1973–74; Int. Pres. Pacific Basin Econ. Council 1980–82; Fellow, Australian Inst. of Man., Australian Acad. of Tech. Sciences; Royal Australian Chemical Inst.; Hon. D.Sc. (Univs. of Sydney and Newcastle); Order of the Sacred Treasure, 1st class (Japan); Leighton Memorial Medal, Royal Australian Chemical Inst. 1965; John Storey Medal, Australian Inst. of Management 1971. *Leisure interests:* fishing, music. *Address:* 27 Manning Road, Double Bay, N.S.W. 2028, Australia.

VERNON, (William) Michael; British business executive; b. 17 April 1926, Cheshire; s. of late Sir Wilfred Vernon; m. 1st Rosheen O'Meara 1952 (dissolved 1977), one s.; m. 2nd Jane Kilham-Roberts 1977; ed. Marlborough Coll. and Trinity Coll., Cambridge; joined Spillers (millers and animal food manufacturers) as trainee 1948, Dir. 1960–80, Joint Man. Dir. 1962–67, Deputy Chair. 1967–68, Chair. 1968–80; Chair. Famous Names Ltd. 1981–85, Granville Meat Co. Ltd. 1981–; Dir. Electrical and Musical Industries Ltd. 1973–80, Strong and Fisher (Holdings) PLC 1980–; Pres. British Food Export Council 1977–79; Vice-Pres. and Deputy Chair. Royal Nat. Lifeboat Inst. 1980–. *Leisure interests:* sailing, shooting, skiing. *Address:* Fyfield Manor, Andover, Hants., England (Home).

VERONESE, Vittorino, D.IUR.; Italian administrator; b. 1 March 1910, Vicenza; m. Maria Petrarca; four s. three d.; fmr. Gen. Sec. Catholic Movement of Univ. Graduates, Prof. Inst. of Social Sciences, Athenaeum Angelicum, Rome, Pres. Catholic Action, Pius XII Foundation, Cen. Inst.

of Credit, Consorzio di Credito per le Opere Publiche; Sec. Perm. Int. Congress of Lay Apostolate, Rome; mem. Italian Del. to UNESCO 1948–58; mem. Italian Nat. UNESCO Comm.; mem. UNESCO Exec. Bd. 1952–56, Pres. 1956–58; Dir.-Gen. UNESCO 1958–61; Chair. Bd. of Dirs. of Banco di Roma 1961–76; Vice-Chair. Banco di Roma (France), Paris, Banco di Roma (Belgium), Brussels; Vice-Chair. Banco di Roma (Ethiopia), Addis Ababa; Dir. and mem. Exec. Cttee. of Fondazione Cini, Venice; Dir. Soc. Italiana per l'Organizzazione Internazionale; Pres. Italian Cttee. for Human Rights 1965; mem. Pontifical Comm. for Justice and Peace, Vatican City 1967; Vice-Pres. Int. Consultative Liaison Cttee. for Literacy, UNESCO. *Address:* c/o Banco di Roma, 307 Via del Corso, Rome, Italy.

VEROSTA, Stephan Eduard, LL.D.; Austrian lawyer and diplomatist; b. 16 Oct. 1909, Vienna; s. of Rudolf Verosta and Elisabeth (née Szalay) Verosta; m. Maria Stuehler 1942; two s. one d.; ed. Gymnasium, Vienna, Univ. of Vienna and studied in Paris, Geneva and Acad. of Int. Law, The Hague; legal practice 1932–35, Judge 1936; Legal Dept., Austrian Foreign Office 1935–38, Deputy Legal Adviser 1945–48, 1949–51; Counsellor, Austrian Legation, Rome, Minister, Budapest 1951–52; Head of Legal Dept., Foreign Office 1953–56; Amb. to Poland 1956–61; Austrian Del. to various int. confs. and UN; mem. Perm. Court of Arbitration, The Hague 1957–; Consultant to Foreign Office 1962–; Dozent in Int. Law, Univ. of Vienna 1946, Prof. of Int. Law, Jurisprudence and Int. Relations 1962–80; Chair. U.S.-Finnish Comm. of Conciliation 1964–; mem. Dutch-Fed. German Comm. of Conciliation, Inst. de Droit Int. 1961; mem. Founding Cttee. UN Univ. 1972; mem. Appeals Board, Council of Europe 1974; mem. Int. Law Comm. of UN 1977–82, Council, UN Univ. 1977–83; mem. Austrian Acad. of Science 1964; numerous decorations. *Publications:* Les avis consultatifs de la Cour Permanente de Justice Internationale, etc. 1932, Jean Dumont und seine Bedeutung für das Völkerrecht 1934, Liberale und planwirtschaftliche Handelspolitik (with Gottfried Haberler) 1934, Richterliches Gewohnheitsrecht in Österreich 1942, Die Satzung der Vereinten Nationen 1946, Die internationale Stellung Österreichs von 1938–1947 1947, Die geschichtliche Kontinuität des österreichischen Staates und seine europäische Funktion 1954, Johannes Chrysostomus, Staatsphilosoph 1960, Geschichte des Völkerrechts 1964, International Law in Europe and Western Asia between 100-650 A.D. 1966, Dauernde Neutralität 1967, Theorie und Realität von Bündnissen Heinrich Lammasch, Karl Renner und der Zweibund 1897-1914 1971, L'histoire de l'Académie de Droit International de la Haye 1973, History of the Law of Nations 1648 to 1815 1984, Kollektivaktionen der Mächte des Europäischen Konzerts bis 1914 1988. *Leisure interests:* collecting old books, stamps. *Address:* 1180 Vienna, Hockegasse 15, Austria. *Telephone:* 47-13-48.

VERRETT, Shirley; American soprano singer; b. 31 May 1931, New Orleans; d. of Leon Verrett and Elvira Verrett; m. Louis Lomonaco 1963; one d.; ed. Juilliard School of Music, New York; operatic début as mezzo-soprano taking title role of Carmen, Spoleto Festival 1962; same role for début at Bolshoi Opera, Moscow 1963, New York City Opera 1966, Florence 1968, Metropolitan Opera, New York 1968; sang at Covent Garden, London in roles of Ulrica (Un Ballo in Maschera) 1966, Amneris (Aida) 1967, Eboli (Don Carlos) 1968, Azucena (Il Trovatore) 1970; début at San Carlo, Naples as Elisabetta (Maria Stuarda) 1969, at La Scala, Milan as Delilah (Samson et Dalila) 1970, at Vienna Staatsoper as Eboli 1970, at Teatro Liceo, Barcelona as Eboli 1971, at Paris Opera as Azucena 1972; other mezzo-soprano roles in Orfeo (Gluck), as Dido (Les Troyens), Judith (Bluebeard's Castle), Neocle (Siege of Corinth), Adalgisa (Norma, first performance at Metropolitan, New York 1976); made début as soprano in title role of La Favorita, Dallas Civic Opera 1971; début at San Francisco Opera in title role of L'Africaine 1972; first artist to sing roles of both Dido and Cassandra in one single full-length production of Les Troyens, Metropolitan 1973; other soprano roles: Lady Macbeth, La Scala 1975, and with La Scala at Kennedy Center, Washington, D.C. 1976, also with Opera Co. of Boston 1976; title role of Norma, Metropolitan Opera 1976 (in the same season took mezzo-soprano role of Adalgisa, being the first singer since Grisi to sing both roles); New Prioress in Dialogues of the Carmelites, Metropolitan 1977; now sings only soprano roles; Amellia, La Scala 1978, title role in Favorita, Metropolitan 1978; in Tosca at Metropolitan, New York 1978; frequent appearances with U.S. and European opera houses, with U.S. symphony orchestras; has appeared as soloist on Milan's RAI; was subject of BBC TV feature Profiles in Music 1971. *Leisure interests:* cooking, musical biographies, collecting English and American antiques, collecting engravings of famous singers. *Address:* c/o Columbia Artists Management Inc., 165 West 57th Street, New York, N.Y. 10019, U.S.A.

VERRI, Carlo; Italian businessman; b. 26 June 1939, Bari; m.; two c.; ed. Bari Univ.; Sales Forecasts and Planning, RIV-Officine di Villar Perosa S.p.A., Turin 1963–65; Export Area Man. for Africa, Belgium, Portugal, Sales Man. for Belgium, INDESIT S.p.A., Turin 1965–67; Dir.-Gen., Cometane S.A. 1967–71; Export Man., RIV-SKF Officine di Villar Perosa S.p.A. 1972–74, Deputy Dir. Milan Branch Offices 1974–75, Commercial Man. 1975–77, Man. Dir. and Dir.-Gen. 1978–84; Man. Dir. and Dir.-Gen., Industries Zanussi S.p.A., Pordenone 1985–; Chair. Electrolux Components Group 1987–; mem. Exec. Cttee. Electrolux Group 1988–; Chair. Alitalia, Linee Aeree Italiane S.p.A. 1988–; mem. Bd. Industrial Junta, Turin, AMAA, Turin; Pres. Asscn. of Financiers, School of Business Admin.,

Turin Univ. *Address:* Alitalia, Palazzo Alitalia, Piazzale Guilio Pastoré, 00144 Rome, Italy.

VERSACE, Gianni; Italian couturier; b. 2 Dec. 1946, Reggio Calabria; s. of Antonio Versace and Francesca Versace; ed. high school Reggio Calabria; began career in mother's dressmaking atelier Reggio Calabria 1964, became travelling buyer for atelier 1968; moved to Milan and designed for various fashion houses including Complice, Genny and Callaghan 1972; designed first women's wear collection 1978; presented menswear collection and inaugurated first (of 80) boutiques 1979; costume designer for ballets Josephlegend and Lieb und Leid, La Scala 1983, Dyonisos 1984, for opera Don Pasquale, La Scala 1984; launched Balneum Romanum range of bath products 1983, mens' fragrance 'Versace l'homme' 1984; Golden Eye Award 1982, 1984, Cutty Sark Award 1983. *Leisure interests:* music, art, theatre. *Address:* Via della Spiga 25, 20121 Milan, Italy. *Telephone:* 5456201.

VERSTRAETE, Marc, M.D., PH.D., F.R.C.P., F.A.C.P.; Belgian professor of medicine; b. 1 April 1925, Bruges; s. of Louis Verstraete and Jeanne Coppin; m. Bernadette Moyersoen 1955; one s. four d.; ed. Leuven and Oxford Univs. and Cornell Univ. Medical Coll., New York; Lecturer, Univ. of Leuven 1957, Asst. Prof. 1961, Assoc. Prof. 1963, Prof. 1968–, Dir. Centre for Thrombosis and Vascular Research; Dr. h.c. (Cordoba, Argentina); mem. Acad. of Medicine of Belgium, South Africa and Argentina. *Publications:* Arterial Hypertension 1966, 1972, Haemostatic Drugs 1977, Methods in Angiology 1980, Haemostasis 1980, Thrombosis 1982, Thrombolysis 1985; numerous articles in scientific journals. *Leisure interests:* reading, skiing, swimming, tennis. *Address:* Minderbroedersstraat 29, 3000 Leuven (Home); Center for Thrombosis and Vascular Research, Campus Gasthuisberg, University of Leuven, Heresbraat 49, 3000 Leuven, Belgium. *Telephone:* (016) 21 57 75 (Office); (016) 22 66 74. (Home).

VESELSKY, Dr. Ernst Eugen; Austrian politician; b. 2 Dec. 1932, Vienna; s. of Maria and Rudolf Veselsky; m. Franziska Raser 1956; one s. one d.; joined Econ. Section, Vienna Chamber of Labour 1956; Head, Econ. Section, Vorarlberg Chamber of Labour 1959; Sec. Vienna Chamber of Labour 1963; Exec. Sec., Econ. and Social Advisory Bd. (subsidiary body of Joint Council for Wages and Prices) 1965; mem. Bd. of Dirs., Austrian Nat. Bank 1969–70; mem. Nationalrat 1970–; Sec. of State to Fed. Chancellery (Nationalized Industries) 1970–77. *Leisure interests:* modern arts, books, music, sport. *Address:* Aslangasse 51, A-1190 Vienna, Austria. *Telephone:* 32-42-61.

VESSEY, Gen. John W., Jr., D.S.C., D.S.M.; American army officer; b. 22 June 1922, Minneapolis, Minn.; s. of John William and Emily (née Roche) Vessey; m. Avis C. Funk; two s. one d.; enlisted in Minn. Nat. Guard 1939; commissioned 2nd Lieut., Field Artillery, Anzio May 1944; served successively with 34th Infantry Div., N. Africa and Italy, 4th Infantry and 3rd Armoured Div., Germany, 25th Infantry Div., S. Viet-Nam; promoted Gen. 1976; Commdr. U.S. Forces, S. Korea 1976–79; Army Vice-Chief of Staff 1979–82; Chair. Joint Chiefs of Staff 1982–85; Legion of Merit, Bronze Star, Air Medal, Jt. Services Commendation Medal, Purple Heart and other decorations. *Address:* c/o The Pentagon, Room 3E666, Washington, D.C. 20301, U.S.A.

VEST, George S., M.A.; American diplomatist; b. 25 Dec. 1918, Columbia, Va.; s. of late George S. Vest and Nancy Robertson Vest; m. Emily B. Clemons 1947; two s. one d.; ed. Univ. of Virginia; served in U.S. Army 1941–46; entered Foreign Service 1947, at embassies in Ecuador, Canada, France, Belgium; Deputy Chief of U.S. Mission to the European Communities 1967–69, to NATO 1969–72; Head of U.S. Del. at negotiations for Conf. on Security and Co-operation in Europe, Helsinki and Geneva 1972–73; Special Asst. to Sec. of State for Press Relations 1973–74; Dir. Bureau of Political and Mil. Affairs 1974–76; Asst. Sec. of State for European Affairs 1977–81; U.S. Rep. to the European Communities 1981–85; Dir.-Gen. of Foreign Service, Washington 1985–89. *Leisure interests:* gardening, music, walking. *Address:* c/o Department of State, 2201 C Street, N.W., Washington, D.C. 20520, U.S.A.

VESTEY, Edmund Hoyle, D.L., F.R.S.A., F.C.I.T.; British business executive; b. 19 June 1932; s. of Ronald Arthur Vestey; m. Anne Moubray Scoones 1960; four s.; ed. Eton; 2nd Lieut. Queens Bays 1951; Lieut. City of London Yeomanry; Chair. Union Int. PLC, Blue Star Line Ltd.; Pres. Essex County Scout Council 1979–87, Gen. Council of British Shipping 1981–82; High Sheriff, Essex 1977, Hon.D.L. (Essex) 1978. *Leisure interest:* foxhunting. *Address:* Little Thurlow Hall, Haverhill, Suffolk, England.

VETLESEN, Vesla; Norwegian politician; b. 19 Oct. 1939, Farsund; m.; worked in Uganda 1968–70; fmr. leader Norwegian Save the Children Fund, Norwegian People's Relief Assen; fmr. Sec. Devt. Co-operation for LO's (Norwegian TU Fed.); Minister of Devt. Co-operation 1986–88. *Address:* c/o Ministry of Development Co-operation, P.O. Box 8142, Dep., Oslo 1, Norway.

VÉZINA, Monique; Canadian politician; b. July 1935, Rimouski; m.; four c.; Dir. and Chair. Fédération des caisses populaires Desjardins du Bas Saint-Laurent; Chair. Gérardin-Vaillancourt Foundation; Sec. and Dir. Confédération des caisses populaires Desjardins du Québec; Minister for External Relations 1984–86, of Supply and Services 1986–87, of State (Transport) 1987–88, of State for Employment and Immigration 1988–, for

Sr. Citizens Jan. 1989–; mem. Bd. of Dirs., Rimouski Chamber of Commerce, Soc. immobilière du Québec; fmr. Chair. Comm. on Secondary Educ.; fmr. Vice-Pres. Régie de l'assurance automobile du Québec; fmr. mem. Superior Council of Educ.; Progressive Conservative. *Address:* House of Commons, Parliament Buildings, Ottawa, Ont. K1A, Canada.

VIALAR, Paul; French writer; b. 18 Sept. 1898, Saint-Denis; s. of Eugène Vialar and Geneviève Nabielak; m. 3rd Antoinette Wielowiejska 1969; one s. one d. (from a previous marriage); ed. Lycée Janson-de-Sailly, Paris; fmr. Pres. Soc. des Gens de Lettres; Hon. Pres. Syndicat des Ecrivains Français; Hon. Pres. Fed. Nat. des Socs. d'Auteurs: Assen. des Ecrivains Sportifs; Pres. Int. Writers' Guild 1969; Hon. Pres. Syndicat Nat. des Auteurs et Compositeurs 1974; mem. Council of Alliance Française; mem. Conseil supérieur des Lettres 1974–; Commdr., Légion d'honneur, Ordre des Arts et Lettres; Croix de guerre; numerous foreign awards. *Publications:* 15 plays and 100 novels including La rose de la mer (Prix Femina) 1939, La mort est un commencement (8 vols.) (Grand Prix de la Ville de Paris) 1948, Chronique française du XXème siècle (10 vols. completed), Les invités de la chasse 1969, Les députés, Ceux du cirque, Safari vérité 1970, Mon seul amour, la caille et le butor 1972, La croule 1974, Le triangle de fer 1976, Lettre aux chasseurs 1977, La chasse de décembre 1979, Rien que la vérité 1980, L'homme du fleuve 1981. *Address:* 5 rue de Conseiller Collignon, 75016 Paris, France.

VIBE, Kjeld, LL.D.; Norwegian diplomatist; b. 5 Oct 1927, Stavanger; s. of Christopher Andreas Vibe and Thordis Amundsen; m. Beate Meyer 1953; one s. three d.; ed. Univ. of Oslo; entered foreign service 1954; Sec., Del. to NATO and OEEC, Paris 1956–59; First Sec. Ministry of Foreign Affairs 1959–62; Temp. Head, Norwegian Mil. Mission, Berlin 1961; Personal Sec. to Minister of Foreign Affairs 1962–65; Counsellor, Norwegian Embassy, Wash. 1965–69; Deputy Dir.-Gen. for Political Affairs, Ministry of Foreign Affairs 1969–72, Dir.-Gen. 1972–77; Amb., Perm. Rep. to NATO 1977–84; Sec.-Gen. Ministry of Foreign Affairs 1984–. *Leisure interests:* skiing, history, music. *Address:* c/o Ministry of Foreign Affairs, 7 juni pl. 1, P.O. Box 8114, Dep., 0030, Oslo 1, Norway.

VICHIT-VADAKAN, Vinyu; Thai economist and educationist; b. 21 July 1937; s. of Luang and Prapapan Vichit-Vadakan; m. Chantima Vichit-Vadakan 1967; two s. one d.; ed. Univ. of Fribourg; Economist, Nat. Econ. Devt. Bd. 1962–71; Acting Dean Faculty of Econs., Thammasat Univ. 1971–72, Dean 1972–73; Dir. UN Asian and Pacific Devt. Inst. Jan. 1974–. *Leisure interests:* electronics, photography. *Address:* United Nations Asian and Pacific Development Institute, P.O. Box 2-136, Sri Ayudhya Road, Bangkok, Thailand. *Telephone:* 2815400.

VICK, Sir (Francis) Arthur, Kt., O.B.E., D.SC., PH.D., LL.D., D.C.L., F.INST.P., F.I.E.E., M.R.I.A.; British physicist; b. 5 June 1911, Solihull, Warwicks.; s. of Wallace Devenport Vick; m. Elizabeth Dorothy Story 1943; one d.; ed. Waverley Grammar School and Birmingham Univ.; Asst. lecturer in Physics, Univ. Coll., London 1936, Lecturer 1939–44; Asst. Dir. of Scientific Research, Ministry of Supply 1944–47; lecturer in Physics, Manchester Univ. 1944–47, Sr. Lecturer 1947–50; Prof. of Physics, Univ. Coll. of N. Staffordshire (now Univ. of Keele) 1950–59, Vice-Prin. 1950–54; Deputy Dir. Atomic Energy Research Est., Harwell 1959–60, Dir. 1960–64, Dir. Research Group 1961–64, mem. for Research U.K. Atomic Energy Authority 1964–66; mem. Advisory Council on Research and Devt., Ministry of Power 1960–63; mem. Governing body, Nat. Inst. for Research in Nuclear Science 1964–65; mem. Nuclear Safety Advisory Cttee., Ministry of Power 1960–66, Univ. Grants Cttee. 1959–66; Pres. Assen. of Teachers in Colls. and Depts. of Educ. 1964–72, Hon. mem. 1972; Pres. and Vice-Chancellor, Queen's Univ., Belfast Oct. 1966–76; Pro-Chancellor and Chair. of Council, Univ. of Warwick 1977–; Hon. mem. Assen. for Science Educ. 1969; Chair. Acad. Advisory Council, Ministry of Defence 1969–76; Knight Commdr., Humane Order of African Redemption (Liberia) 1962. *Publications:* papers on solid-state physics, contributions to books on science and education. *Leisure interests:* music, gardening, the countryside. *Address:* Fieldhead Cottage, Fieldhead Lane, Myton Road, Warwick, CV34 6QF, England. *Telephone:* (0926) 491822.

VICKERS, Jon, O.C., C.C.; Canadian tenor; 29 Oct. 1926, Prince Albert, Saskatchewan; s. of William Vickers and Myrle Mossip; m. Henrietta Outerbridge 1953; three s. two d.; began career as concert and opera singer in Canada; joined Royal Opera House, Covent Garden (London) 1957; sang at Bayreuth Festival, Vienna State Opera, San Francisco, Chicago Lyric Opera, Metropolitan Opera, La Scala, Milan, Paris Opera, Boston, Buenos Aires, Athens, Ottawa, Houston, Dallas, Hamburg, Berlin, Munich, Athens Festival, Salzburg Festival, Festival of Orange, Tanglewood Festival, Rio de Janeiro; mem. Royal Acad. Music, London; Hon. LL.D. (Sask.); Hon. C.L.D. (Bishop's Univ.); Mus.D. (Brandon Univ., Univ. of Western Ont.), LL.D. (Univ. of Guelph), Civ. L.D. (Univ. of Laval), D.Mus. (Univ. of Ill.); Critics Award, London 1978, Grammy Award 1979. *Films include:* Carmen, Pagliacci, Norma, Otello, Peter Grimes. *Recordings:* Messiah, Otello, Aida, Die Walküre, Samson and Delilah, Fidelio, Italian Arias, Verdi Requiem, Peter Grimes, Das Lied von der Erde, Les Troyens, Tristan und Isolde. *Address:* c/o Metropolitan Opera, New York, N.Y. 10018, U.S.A.; c/o John Coast Agency, 1 Park Close, London, SW1X 7PQ, England.

VICTOR, Paul-Emile, L. ÉS SC., DIPL. D'ETHNOLOGIE; French explorer and civil engineer; b. 28 June 1907, Geneva, Switzerland; s. of Eric-Henry Victor and M.-L. Baume; m. 1st Eliane Decrais 1946 (divorced), two s. one d.; m. 2nd Colette Faure de la Vaulx 1965, one s.; ed. Lycée Rouget de Lisle (Lons-le-Saulnier), Ecole Cen. de Lyon, Faculty of Science and Letters and Inst. of Ethnology, Paris; Greenland Expedition 1934–35; crossed Greenland by dog sleigh 1936; wintered on east coast of Greenland 1936–37; trans-Alpine crossing by dog sleigh Nice-Chamonix 1938; expedition to Lapland 1939; Second Naval Attaché for France in Scandinavia 1939–40; U.S.A.F. (parachutist commanding Nome flight of Alaska search and rescue squadron) 1942–46; has organized and directed the Expéditions Polaires Françaises (missions Paul-Emile Victor—Arctic and Antarctic expeditions) since 1947; Pres. French Antarctic Cttee. Int. Geophysical Year; Pres. Groupe Paul-Emile Victor for the Protection of Man and his Environment 1973–; Head of Int. Glaciological Expedition to Greenland; Chair. Int. Logistics Group of Scientific Cttee. on Antarctic Research; resident in Bora-Bora, French Polynesia 1977–; Commdr., Légion d'honneur, Grand Croix, Etoile d'Anjouan, Officer of the Orders of Vasa and Dannebrog, Gold Medal of the Royal Geographical Soc. (London), Vega Gold Medal (Sweden), Médaille spéciale de l'Administration des Monnaies. *Publications:* Boréal 1938, Banquise 1939, Apoutsiak 1947, Aventure Esquimau 1948, La grande faim 1958, Pôle Sud 1960, La voie lactée 1961, L'homme à la conquête des Pôles 1962, Pôle Nord 1963, Poèmes Eskimo 1965, Tahiti 1966, Pôle Nord-Pôle Sud 1967, Terres polaires, Terres tragiques 1971, Eskimos, nomades de glaces 1972, La prodigieuse histoire des pôles 1974, Chiens de traîneaux compagnons du risque 1975, Mes aventures polaires 1975, La vie des Eskimos 1975, A l'assaut du pôle nord 1976, Du Groenland à Tahiti 1977, Les Survivants du Groenland 1977, Protégeons l'eau 1978, Nanouk l'eskimo 1979, Jusqu'au au cou . . . et comment s'en sortir 1979, Les Loups 1980, La Mansarde 1981, Blizzards 1982, Doumidia 1982, Les Pôles et leurs secrets 1982. *Leisure interests:* skiing, swimming, deep sea diving, painting, engraving. *Address:* Expéditions Polaires Françaises, 47 avenue du Maréchal-Fayolle, 75116 Paris, France. *Telephone:* 45-04-17-71.

VIDAL, Gore; American writer; b. 3 Oct. 1925; s. of Eugene L. and Nina (Gore) Vidal; ed. Phillips Acad., Exeter, N.H.; served in U.S. Army 1943–46; Edgar Allen Poe award for Television 1955; Drama Critic Reporter (magazine) 1959, Democratic-Liberal Cand. for U.S. Congress from New York 1960; Pres. Kennedy's Advisory Council on the Arts 1961–63; Co-Chair. People's Party 1970–72; Hon. Citizen, Ravello, Italy 1983. *Publications: Novels:* Williwaw 1946, In a Yellow Wood 1947, The City and the Pillar 1948, The Season of Comfort 1949, A Search for the King 1950, Dark Green, Bright Red 1950, The Judgment of Paris 1952, Messiah 1954, Julian 1964, Washington, D.C. 1967, Myra Breckinridge 1968, Two Sisters 1970, Burr 1972, Myron 1974, 1876 1976, Kalki 1978, Creation 1980, Duluth 1983, Lincoln 1984, Empire 1987; *Short stories:* A Thirsty Evil 1956; *Plays:* Visit to a Small Planet 1956, The Best Man 1960, Romulus 1962, Weekend 1968, An Evening with Richard Nixon 1972; *Travel:* Vidal in Venice 1986. *Film scripts and adaptations:* Wedding Breakfast, I Accuse, Ben Hur, Suddenly Last Summer, The Best Man, Caligula, Dress Gray; *Essays:* Rocking the Boat 1963, Reflections upon a Sinking Ship 1969, Homage to Daniel Shays 1972, Matters of Fact and Fiction: Essays 1973–76, 1977, The Second American Revolution 1982, Armageddon? 1987, At Home: Essays 1982–88 1988; criticism in Partisan Review, The Nation, New York Review of Books, Esquire, etc. *Address:* c/o Random House, 201 East 50th Street, New York, N.Y. 10022, U.S.A.

VIDAL, H.E. Cardinal Ricardo; Philippine ecclesiastic; b. 6 Feb. 1931, Mogpog, Marinduque; s. of Fructuoso Vidal and Natividad Jamin; ordained 1956; consecrated Bishop (Titular Church of Claterna) 1971; Archbishop of Lipa 1973–82, of Cebu 1982–; cr. Cardinal 1985; Chair. Episcopal Comm. on Clergy; Convenor Fed. of Asian Bishops' Conf.; mem. Council of Perm. Synod Secr., Vatican. *Leisure interest:* walking. *Address:* Chancery, P.O. Box 52, Cebu City 6401, Philippines. *Telephone:* 7-22-32.

VIDELA, Lt.-Gen. Jorge Rafael; Argentine army officer and politician; b. 2 Aug. 1925, Mercedes, Prov. of Buenos Aires; m. Alicia Hartridge; six c.; ed. Nat. Mil. Coll. and War School; commissioned in Infantry 1944; Lieut. in Vigilance Co., Ministry of War 1946; with Motorized Army Regt. 1947–48; Nat. Mil. Coll. 1948; Student, War School, with rank of Army Capt. 1951–54; Staff Officer, Nat. Mil. Coll. 1954–56; Adviser to Office of Mil. Attaché, Washington, D.C. 1956–58; Staff Officer, Army Gen. Command 1962–65, 1966–68; Col. 1965; engaged on course in Strategy, Army Centre of Higher Studies 1965–66; Lieut.-Col., Chief of Cadet Corps 1968; Second in Command and Chief of Staff, Fifth Infantry Brigade 1968–70; Chief of Operations, Third Army Corps 1970–71; Brig., Head of Nat. Mil. Coll. 1971–73; Chief of Army Gen. Staff 1973–75, of Joint High Command 1975; C.-in-C. of Army 1975–78; led coup to depose Pres. María Perón March 1976; Pres. of Argentina 1976–81; fmr. mem. Inter-American Defence Bd., Washington, D.C.; arrested Aug. 1984, on trial for human rights offences 1985, sentenced to life imprisonment Dec. 1985.

VIEILLARD, Roger; French artist; b. 9 Feb. 1907, Le Mans, Sarthe; s. of Edmond Vieillard and Madeleine Magimel; m. Anita de Caro, painter, 1939; ed. Univ. of Paris; took part in exhbns. by Jeune Gravure Contemporaine, Soc. des Peintres Graveurs, Salon de Mai, Biennales of Venice, and

São Paulo; works exhibited in Paris (Bibliothèque Nat., Galerie de France, la Hune, Adrien Maeght, Galerie Coard, Galerie Sagot le Garrec), London (Hanover Gallery), Rotterdam (Boymans Museum), Berne (Musée de Berne), Galerie d'Art Moderne, Basel, Galerie le Garrec Sagot, Musée des Arts Décoratifs, Bordeaux; has specialized in line engraving; prints in French and foreign museums and private collections; works at Manufacture Nat. de Sèvres, Musée Nat. de Monnaies et Médailles; Pres. Soc. des Peintres Graveurs 1979-; Vice-Pres. Comité Nat. de la Gravure Française 1949-, Comité Nat. du Livre Illustré française 1966-; Chevalier, Légion d'honneur, Officier des Arts et des Lettres. *Principal works:* Illustrations for: La Fable de Phaeton d'Ovide 1939, Hommage à Rimbaud 1944, Poèmes de Jean Tardieu 1945, Discours de la Méthode 1948, L'Ecclésiaste 1951, Le Banquet de Platon 1952, Poèmes d'André Frenaud 1956, Eléments 1956, Retour du Pays d'Ombre 1972, Voyage en Pays Circulaire 1973, Amers de Saint John Perse 1979, La Princesse de Clèves 1979. *Address:* 7 rue de l'Estrapade, 75005 Paris, France. *Telephone:* 43-54-40-78.

VIEIRA, Commdt. João Bernardo; Guinean politician; b. 1939, Bissau; joined Partido Africano da Independência da Guiné e Cabo Verde (PAIGC) 1960; Political and Mil. Chief of Catió 1961-64; Mil. Chief of the Southern Front and mem. Political Bureau 1964-65; Vice-Pres. Council of War 1965-67; Rep. of the Political Bureau for the Southern Front 1967-70; mem. Council of War, responsible for mil. operations 1970-71; mem. Exec. Cttee. and Council of War 1971-73; mem. Perm. Secr. of PAIGC 1973-; Pres. of People's Nat. Ass. 1973-78; State Commr. for the Armed Forces Sept. 1973-78; Chief State Commr. 1978-84; Pres. 1980-, C.-in-C. of Armed Forces 1982-, Minister of Defence and of Interior 1982-; led coup to depose Pres. Luiz Cabral (q.v.); Sec. Gen. Revolutionary Council Nov. 1980-. *Address:* Conselho de Estado, Bissau, Guinea-Bissau.

VIENOT, Marc, L.ÈS.L.; French banker; b. 1 Nov. 1928, Paris; m. Christiane Regnault 1953; two s. two d.; ed. Nat. Inst. of Politicial Studies and Ecole Nat. d'Admin.; Inspector of Finance 1955; special envoy to Cabinet of Minister of Econ. and Finance April-June 1957, to Cabinet of Minister of Finance, Econ. and Planning June-Nov. 1957; special envoy to cabinet of Pres. of French Parl. 1957-58; special envoy to Treasury Div. July 1958; Chair. Study Cttee. OECD 1961-65; Sec. to Bd. of Econ. and Social Devt. Fund 1963-65; Under-Sec. Treasury Div. 1965; Head, Financial Activities Service, Treasury Div. 1967; Minister (Financial Counsellor), French embassies in U.S.A. and Canada and Dir. IBRD and IMF 1970-73; Deputy Gen. Man. Société Générale 1973, Gen. Man. 1977, Chair. and C.E.O. 1986-; Officier, Légion d'honneur; Officier, Ordre Nat. du Mérite. *Address:* 4 avenue Raymond Poincaré, 75116 Paris, France.

VIERECK, Peter, B.S., M.A., PH.D.; American poet, historian and dramatist; b. 5 Aug. 1916, New York; s. of George S. and Margaret (Hein) Viereck; m. 1st Anya de Markov 1945 (divorced 1970); one s. one d.; m. 2nd Betty Martin Falkenberg 1972; ed. Harvard Univ. and Christ Church, Oxford; Teaching Asst., Harvard Univ. 1941-42, Instructor in German Literature and tutor 1946-47; History Instructor, U.S. Army, Univ. of Florence, Italy 1945; Asst. Prof. History, Smith Coll. 1947-48; Assoc. Prof. Mount Holyoke Coll. 1948-55, Prof. of European and Russian History 1955-, Distinguished William R. Kenan Prof. 1979-; U.S. State Dept. mission of cultural exchange to U.S.S.R. 1961; awarded Tietjens Prize for Poetry 1948, Pulitzer Prize for Poetry 1949, Sadin Poetry Prize New York Quarterly 1977, Varouja Prize 1983; Guggenheim Fellow, Rome 1949-50; Visiting Lecturer Univ. of Paris, American Univ., Beirut, and American Univ. Cairo 1966; L.H.D. (Olivet Coll.) 1959. *Publications:* Metapolitics—From the Romantics to Hitler 1941, Terror and Decorum (poems) 1948, Who Killed the Universe? 1948, Conservation Revisited—The Revolt Against Revolt—1815-1849 1949, Strike Through the Mask: New Lyrical Poems 1950, The First Morning: New Poems 1952, Shame and Glory of the Intellectuals 1953, Dream and Responsibility: The Tension Between Poetry and Society 1953, The Unadjusted Man: a New Hero for Americans 1956, Conservatism: From John Adams to Churchill 1956, The Persimmon Tree (poems) 1956, The Tree Witch: A Poem and Play 1961, Metapolitics: The Roots of the Nazi Mind 1961, Conservatism Revisited and the New Conservatism: What Went Wrong? 1962, New and Selected Poems 1967, Soviet Policy Making 1967, Outside Looking In 1972, A Question of Quality 1976, Archer in the Marrow (poems) 1986; numerous articles and poems. *Address:* Mount Holyoke College, South Hadley, Mass. 01075 (Office); 12 Silver Street, South Hadley, Mass., 01075, U.S.A. (Home). *Telephone:* (413) 534-5504 (Home).

VIERU, Anatol; Romanian composer; b. 8 June 1926, Iaşi; s. of Leon Vieru and Eti Vieru; m. 1954; one s. one d.; Prof. of composition, Bucharest Conservatory; Visiting Prof. Jerusalem 1982, 1983, Darmstadt 1984; Enescu Prize of the Romanian Acad. 1967; Queen Marie José Prize, Geneva 1963, Prize Herder 1986, D.Mus. 1978. *Major works include:* Concerto for Orchestra 1954, Six String Quartets 1955-86, Struggle Against Inertia (for voices and instruments) 1959, Cello Concerto (Geneva, Suisse Romande Orchestra) 1962, Games for Piano and Orchestra 1963, Night Scenes (a dramatic madrigal on verse by Federigo García Lorca) 1965, Violin Concerto 1965, Ode to Silence 1966, Steps of Silence (Koussevitzky Foundation, Washington) 1968, Clepsydre (commissioned by H. H. Strobel, Donaueschingen) 1969, Clarinet Concerto 1975, Eratosthene's Sieve (Mayence) 1969, Mosaic for three Percussions (Zagreb) 1972, Four Angles to Contem-

plate Florence (Champigny, France) 1974, The Birth of a Language 1970, Stone Land 1970, Screen (performed by Bruno Maderna and the Philharmonic Orchestra ORTF in Royan) 1971, Museum Music, harpsichord and 12 strings (Modern Art Museum, Paris) 1968, Jonas, a tragic opera 1976, Joseph and his Brothers (Metz Festival) 1979, Five Symphonies 1966-85, Double Concerto 1980, The Feast of the Beggars 1981. *Publications:* The Book of Modes 1980. *Address:* Uniunea Compozitorilor, Str. Constantin Exarhul 2, Bucharest (Office); Str. Stirbei-Vodă 68, ap. 3, Bucharest 70734, Romania (Home). *Telephone:* 13-34-06 (Home).

VIGNAL, Renaud; French diplomatist; b. 1943, Valence; s. of Jean Vignal and Reine Mouet; m. 1st Monique Tuffelli 1966, 2nd Anne de Villiers de la Noue 1983; two d.; ed. Lycées Montaigne and Louis-le-Grand, Paris, Facultés de Droit et des Lettres, Paris, Inst. d'Etudes Politiques and Ecole Nat. d'Admin.; Second Sec. Embassy Cairo 1971-74; mem. policy planning staff, Ministry of Foreign Affairs 1974-75; Press Officer, Washington 1975-77; Deputy Spokesman, Ministry of Foreign Affairs 1980-81; Prin. Sec. to Minister for Co-operation and Devt. 1981-82; Consul-Gen. Quebec 1983-87; Amb. to Seychelles 1987-. *Leisure interest:* horses. *Address:* 15 rue Moncex, 75009 Paris, France.

VIGUERIE, Richard Art, B.S.; American business executive and publisher; b. 23 Sept. 1933, Golden Acres, Tex.; s. of Arthur C. Viguerie and Elizabeth Mary Stoufflet Viguerie; m. Elaine Adele O'Leary 1962; one s. two d.; ed. Texas A & I, Kingsville and Univ. of Houston, Texas; Exec. Dir. Young Americans for Freedom, New York 1961-63; Founder and Pres. The Viguerie Co., Falls Church, Va. 1965-; Publr. Conservative Digest 1975-85; Chair. of Bd. Diversified Mail Marketing Inc., Waldorf, Md. 1971-, American Mailing List Corpn., Falls Church, Va. 1972-. *Publications:* The New Right—We're Ready To Lead 1980, The Establishment vs The People 1983. *Leisure interests:* golf, tennis, travel, reading. *Address:* The Viguerie Company, 7777 Leesburg Pike, Falls Church, Va. 22043 (Office); Box 210, Washington, Va. 22747, U.S.A. (Home). *Telephone:* 703-356-9440 (Office).

VIKSTRÖM, John Edvin, D.THEOL.; Finnish ecclesiastic; b. 1 Oct. 1931, Kronoby; s. of Edvin and Hilma (née Lindström) Vikström; m. Birgitta Hellberg 1957; two s. one d.; ordained 1956; Pastor for Porvoo (Borgå) Diocese 1957-61; Asst. in Theological Faculty of Åbo Akademi, Turku 1963-65, Instructor 1966-70, Assoc. Prof. 1970; Bishop of Porvoo (Borgå) Diocese 1970-82; Archbishop of the Evangelical-Lutheran Church of Finland 1982-; mem. Cen. Cttee. World Council of Churches 1983-; Dr. h.c. (Theological Acad. of Leningrad) 1985, (Theological Acad. of Budapest) 1987; Great Award of the Swedish Culture Foundation 1981. *Publications:* Religion och kultur 1966, Effekten av religiös fostran 1970, Tro i kris 1972, Fråga biskopen om tro 1980, Herdestaven 1982, Ihmisen usko 1982, Kuitenkin 1983, Uusi rohkeus elää 1985, Kirjeen Kääntöpiiri 1987. *Leisure interests:* history of ideas and culture, sports. *Address:* Agricolankatu 2, SF-20500 Turku 50, Finland. *Telephone:* 921-516-500 (Office); 921-516-568.

VIKULOV, Vladimir Ivanovich; Soviet ice-hockey player; b. 20 July 1946, Moscow; Honoured Master of Sport 1967; mem. CPSU 1971; champion of U.S.S.R. 1966, 1968, 1970; champion of Winter Olympic Games 1968 and holder of Cup of European Champions for ice-hockey 1969-70.

VILARDELL, Francisco, M.D., D.SC.(MED.); Spanish physician; b. 1 April 1926, Barcelona; s. of Jacinto Vilardell and Mercedes Viñas; m. Leonor Vilardell 1958; one s. two d.; ed. Univs. of Barcelona and Pennsylvania; Dir. Gastroenterology Service, Hospital Santa Cruz y San Pablo, Barcelona 1963-; Dir. Postgrad. School of Gastroenterology, Autonomous Univ. of Barcelona 1969-; Pres. European Assen. for Digestive Endoscopy 1970-74, European Asscn. for Study of the Liver 1975-76, World Org. of Gastroenterology 1982- (Sec.-Gen. 1974-82), Council of Int. Orgs. in Medical Science 1987-; Dir.-Gen. Health Planning, Ministry of Health 1981-82; Gold Medal, Barcelona Acad. of Medicine; Gold Medal, Spanish Soc. of Gastroenterology; Chevalier, Légion d'honneur. *Publications:* ed. of six books; 170 papers in medical journals. *Leisure interests:* music, philology. *Address:* Escuela de Patología Digestiva, Hospital de la Santa Cruz y San Pablo, 08025 Barcelona (Office); CIOMS, c/o World Health Organization, 1211 Geneva 27, Switzerland; Juan Sebastian Bach 11, 08021 Barcelona, Spain (Home). *Telephone:* 256.07.05 (Office); 91.34.06 (CIOMS); 201.45.11 (Home).

VILARIÑO PINTOS, Daría; Spanish librarian; b. 26 Jan. 1928, Santiago de Compostela; d. of José Vilariño de Andrés and Daría Pintos Castro; mem. staff, state library, museum and archives depts. 1957-70; Deputy Dir. Library of Univ. of Santiago 1970-73, Dir. 1973-. *Publications:* Ó Libro Galego onte e hoxe (with Virtudes Pardo) 1981, Hechos de D. Berenguel de Landoria (Co-author) 1983, Vasco de Aponte. Recuento de las Casas Antiguas del Reino de Galicia. Edición crítica (co-author) 1986; articles in professional journals, bibliographical catalogues. *Leisure interest:* reading. *Address:* Calle San Miguel No. 5, 2°, 15705 Santiago de Compostela, La Coruña, Spain. *Telephone:* 58 36 58.

VÎLCU, Vasile; Romanian politician; b. 26 Sept. 1910, Ciamurlia de Jos, Constanţa County; m. Inda Vîlcu; one s. one d.; ed Party High School, "Stefan Gheorghiu" Acad., Bucharest; Mem. Romanian Communist Party (RCP) 1929-; imprisoned for political activities 1941-44; Sec. Dolj Dist. Cttee. of RCP 1944-46, Tulcea Dist. Cttee. of RCP 1946-47; Vice-Chair. Party Control Comm. 1947-52; First Sec. Dobrogea Regional Cttee. of RCP 1956-65; Alt. mem. Cen. Cttee. of RCP 1958-60, mem. 1960-76; Alt.

mem. Exec. Political Cttee. of Cen. Cttee. of RCP 1965–66, mem. 1966–76; mem. Grand Nat. Ass. 1948–52, 1957–; Chair. Council of Nat. Union of Agricultural Production Co-operatives 1966–69; mem. Exec. Bureau of Nat. Cttee. of Socialist Unity Front 1968–76; First Vice-Pres. Nat. Council, Front of Socialist Democracy and Unity 1976–80; Vice-Pres. State Council 1969–75, mem. 1977–; First Sec. Constanţa County Cttee. of RCP 1971–76, Chair. Exec. Cttee. 1971–76; Chair. Cen. Auditing Comm. of RCP 1976–; Hero of Socialist Labour 1971. *Address:* Central Committee of the Romanian Communist Party, Str. Academiei 34, Bucharest, Romania. *Telephone:* 15-02-000.

VILHJALMSSON, Thor; Icelandic lawyer; b. 9 June 1930, Reykjavík; s. of Vilhjalmur Th. Gislason and Inga Arnadottir Gislason; m. Ragnhildur Helgadottir Vilhjalmsson 1950; one s. three d.; ed. Reykjavík Grammar School, St. Andrews Univ., Scotland, Univ. of Iceland, New York Univ. and Univ. of Copenhagen; Asst. lecturer, Univ. of Iceland 1959–62, part-time lecturer 1962–67, Prof. 1967–76, and Dean, Faculty of Law 1968–70, Dir. Inst. of Law 1974–76; Deputy Judge Reykjavík Civil Court 1960–62, Judge 1962–67; Judge European Court of Human Rights 1971–; Assoc. Justice of the Supreme Court of Iceland 1976–, Pres. 1983–84; mem. Icelandic Del. to UN Gen. Ass. 1963, UN Sea-Bed Cttee. 1972, 1973 to Law of the Sea Conf. 1974, 1975, and other int. confs.; Pres. Asscn. of Icelandic Lawyers 1971–74; Ed. Icelandic Law Review 1973–83. *Publications:* Civil Procedure I–IV and studies on human rights and legal history. *Address:* The Supreme Court, Reykjavík, Iceland.

VILJOEN, Gerrit van Niekerk, D.LITT. ET PHIL., M.A.; South African politician; b. 11 Sept. 1926, Cape Town; s. of late Hendrik Geldenhuys Viljoen; m. Magdalena Maria van der Merwe 1951; seven c.; ed. Afrikaanse Hoër Seunskool, Pretoria, Univ. of Pretoria, King's Coll., Cambridge, Ryksuniversiteit, Leiden, Sorbonne; Sr. Lecturer in Classics, Univ. of S.A. 1955–57, Prof. 1957–67; Admin.-Gen. Namibia (S.W. Africa) 1979–80; Minister of Nat. Educ. 1980–84, of Co-operation and Devt. and (Black) Educ. (renamed Devt. Aid and Educ.) 1984–86, of Devt. Aid and Educ. Nov. 1986–; Rector, Rand Afrikaans Univ. 1967–79; Corresp. mem. Royal Netherlands Acad. of Sciences; mem. Suid-Afrikaanse Akad.; Hon. Pres. Classical Asscn. of S.A.; Hon. LL.D. (Rand Afrikaans) 1980, Hon. D.Ed. (Orange Free State Univ.). *Address:* Ministry of National Education, Private Bag X122, Pretoria, South Africa.

VILJOEN, Henri Pieter, S.C., B.A., LL.B.; South African lawyer; b. 29 Nov. 1932, Bloemfontein; s. of Henri P. Viljoen and Francis de Villiers; m. Maureen M. Fleischer 1955; two s. one d.; ed. Grey Coll. Bloemfontein, St. Andrew's Coll. Grahamstown and Univ. of O.F.S.; newspaper reporter 1951–52; man. family men's clothing business (while studying extra-murally); admitted to Bar 1958; practised at bar of O.F.S. Provincial Div. of Supreme Court 1961–81; Sr. Counsel 1976; Leader of Bar of O.F.S. 1979–81; moved to Cape Town to practise at Bar of Cape Province 1982; Vice-Chair. Gen. Council of Bar of S.A. 1981–84, Chair. 1984–88; mem. Council, Int. Bar Asscn. 1984–88. *Leisure interests:* bird-watching, photography, hiking, motor-cycling. *Address:* 607 Huguenot Chambers, 40 Queen Victoria Street, Cape Town 8001 (Office); 9 Sun Valley Avenue, Constantia, 7800 Cape, South Africa (Home). *Telephone:* (21) 249371 (Office); (21) 742591 (Home).

VILJOEN, Marais, D.M.S.; South African politician (retd.); b. 2 Dec. 1915, Robertson; s. of Gabriël and Magdalena (née de Villiers) Viljoen; m. Dorothea Maria Brink 1940; one d.; ed. Jan van Riebeeck High School, Cape Town, and Univ. of Cape Town; Man., Die Transvaler Boekhandel 1940–43; Co-founder Nat. Youth League 1940–45; Organizer, Transvaal Nat. Party 1945–49; mem. Transvaal Prov. Council for Pretoria 1949–53; Sec. for Information of Nat. Party, Transvaal 1957–59; M.P. for Alberton, Transvaal 1953–76; Deputy Minister of Labour and of Mines 1958–61, of Labour and Immigration 1961–62, of the Interior, Educ., Arts, Science, Labour and Immigration 1962–66; Minister of Labour and of Coloured Affairs 1966–70, also Minister of Rehoboth Affairs 1969–70; Minister of Labour and of the Interior 1970, of Labour and of Posts and Telecommunications 1970–76; Chair. Information Cttee., Fed. Council until 1976; Deputy Chair. Nat. Party until 1976; Pres. of Senate 1976–79; State Pres. of S.A. 1979–84. *Leisure interests:* golf, bowls, reading. *Address:* P.O. Box 5555, Pretoria 0001, Republic of South Africa.

VILLA, José García, A.B.; Philippine poet and critic; b. 5 Aug. 1914, Manila; s. of Dr. Simeon Villa and Maria García; two s.; ed. Univs. of the Philippines, of New Mexico and Columbia Univ.; Assoc. Ed. New Directions Books 1949; Cultural Attaché Philippine Mission to UN 1953–63; Dir. N.Y. City Coll. Poetry Workshop 1952–63, Prof. of Poetry, New School for Social Research 1964–73; Philippines Presidential Adviser on Cultural Affairs 1968–; Guggenheim Fellowship 1943, Bollingen Fellowship 1951, Rockefeller Grant 1964; American Acad. of Arts and Letters Award 1942, Shelley Memorial Award 1959, Pro Patria Award 1961, Philippines Cultural Heritage Award 1962, Nat. Artist in Literature 1973; Hon. D.Litt. (Far Eastern Univ.) 1959, Hon. L.H.D. (Philippines) 1973. *Publications:* Footnote to Youth (stories) 1933, Many Voices 1939, Poems by Doveglion 1941, Have Come, Am Here 1942, Volume Two 1949, Selected Poems and New 1958, Poems Fifty-five 1962, Poems in Praise of Love 1962, Selected Stories 1962, The Portable Villa 1963, The Essential Villa 1965, Appassionata 1979; Ed.: A Celebration for Edith Sitwell 1948, Doveglion Book of Philippine

Poetry 1975, Bravo: the Poet's Magazine 1981. *Leisure interests:* dogs, plants, cooking. *Address:* 780 Greenwich Street, New York, N.Y. 10014, U.S.A.

VILLA-VICENCIO, Rev. Charles, S.T.M., PH.D.; South African professor of religious studies; b. 7 Nov. 1942, Johannesburg; m. Eileen van Sittert 1968; two d.; ed. Rhodes Univ. Grahamstown, and Natal, Yale and Drew Univs.; with Standard Bank of S.A. 1961–64; Probationer Minister, Methodist Church of Southern Africa 1965–70; ordained Minister 1970; Minister of varous congregations in S. Africa and U.S.A.; Teaching Fellow, Drew Univ. 1974–75; part-time lecturer, Univ. of Cape Town 1976–77; Sr. Lecturer, Univ. of S. Africa 1978–81, Assoc. Prof. 1981–82; Sr. Lecturer, Univ. of Cape Town 1982–, Assoc Prof. 1984–, Head, Dept of Religious Studies 1986–; mem. S.A. Theological Soc.; del. to numerous confs. etc. *Publications include:* Between Christ and Caesar: Classical and Contemporary Texts 1986; ed. or co-ed. of and contrib. to several vols. of essays; numerous articles including many on the church and politics in South Africa. *Address:* Department of Religious Studies, University of Cape Town, Rondebosch 7700, Cape Town (Office); 14 Annerley Road, Rosebank, Cape Town 7700, South Africa (Home). *Telephone:* 021-6503454 (Office); 021-6868643 (Home).

VILLAIN, Claude Edouard Louis Etienne, L. EN D.; French international civil servant; b. 4 Jan. 1935, Paris; s. of Etienne and Marie Louise (Caudron) Villain; m. Bernadette Olivier 1962; two s.; ed. Lycée Voltaire, Lycée Louis-le-Grand, Univ. of Paris; Trainee in French Overseas Admin. 1956–59, Officer in Dept. of Algerian Affairs 1959–61; Officer for Econ. Studies in Agricultural Devt. Bureau 1962–64; Officer in Ministry of Econ. and Finance 1964, Head of Dept. 1969, Deputy Dir. of Ministry 1973; Tech. Adviser in Office of Valéry Giscard d'Estaing (then Minister of Econ. and Finance) 1973–74; Dir.-Gen. of Competition and Prices in Ministry of Econ. and Finance 1974–78; Administrateur Soc. Nat. des Chemins de fer Français (SNCF) 1974–78; Administrateur Soc. Nat. Elf Aquitaine 1974–79; Dir.-Gen. of Agric., Comm. of EEC 1979–85; Dir.-Gen. Socopa Int., Vice-Pres. Socopa France 1985–; Special Adviser to Minister of Econ. and Finance 1986–88; Chevalier, Légion d'honneur; Chevalier, Ordre nat. du Mérite; Croix de Valeur Mil.; Commandeur du Mérite Agricole. *Address:* c/o Ministère de l'Economie, des Finances et de la Privatisation, 246 boulevard Saint-Germain, 75700 Paris, France.

VILLALBA, Jovito; Venezuelan politician; b. 1908; ed. Liceo Caracas, Univ. Cen. de Venezuela and Univ. Libre, Colombia; fmr. Prof. of Constitutional Rights and Political Theory, Univ. Cen. de Venezuela; Sec., Fed. of Venezuelan Students 1928; imprisoned 1928–34; Sec.-Gen. Nat. Democratic Party 1936; exile in Colombia 1936–38; f. Unión Republicana Democrática 1946, now leader; exiled 1952–57; Leader, Junta Patriótica 1958; Presidential Cand. 1963, 1973. *Address:* Unión Republicana Democrática, Caracas, Venezuela.

VILLÁNYI, Miklós; Hungarian economist and politician; b. 1931, Gyürüs; ed. Karl Marx Univ. of Economy, Budapest; joined the HSWP 1953; research studies in political economy and finance under Hungarian Acad. of Sciences project 1953–55; with Ministry of Finance, head of dept., main dept. head, then Deputy Minister 1955–82; Sec. of State for Ministry of Agric. and Food 1982–88; Minister of Finance 1988–89. *Address:* c/o Ministry of Finance, Budapest V. József nádor tér 2/4, Hungary.

VILLAR, Francisco, B.L.; Spanish diplomatist; b. 8 Jan. 1945, Salamanca; m.; two c.; ed. Univ. of Salamanca; entered diplomatic service 1971; Sec. of Embassy, Perm. Mission of Spain at UN 1973–78; lecturer and Dir. of Studies, Escuela Diplomatica, Madrid 1978–81; Ministry of Foreign Affairs 1981–83; with Perm. Mission at UN, New York and mem. Spanish Del. to UN Security Council 1982–83; Dir.-Gen. of Int. Orgs. and Confs. Ministry of Foreign Affairs 1983–87; Perm. Rep. to UN 1987–; del. to numerous int. confs. *Publications:* El Proceso de Autodeterminacion del Sahara Occidental 1982, numerous articles on politics and int. relations. *Address:* Permanent Mission of Spain to the United Nations, 809 United Nations Plaza, 6th Floor, New York, N.Y. 10017, U.S.A.

VILLAS BÔAS, Claudio; Brazilian anthropologist and explorer; b. 1916, Botucatu, São Paulo; s. of Agnelo and Arlinda Villas Bôas; brother of Orlando Villas Bôas (q.v.); has lived in the Brazilian jungle around the River Xingu and worked among the Indians since 1945; f. aid posts for Indians and opened airstrips in the jungle; worked in the Indian Protection Service; mem. Fundação Nacional do Indio 1967–; Gold Medal, Royal Geographical Soc. *Leisure interests:* reading, philosophy, ethnology, classical music. *Address:* Parque Nacional do Xingu, Praça Franklin Roosevelt 278, Apto 123, São Paulo, SP, Brazil.

VILLAS-BOAS, José Manuel P. de; Portuguese diplomatist; b. 23 Feb. 1931, Oporto; s. of João and Maria Margarida de Villas-Boas; m. Maria do Patrocinio de Almeida Braga 1956; ed. Lisbon Univ.; Attaché, Ministry of Foreign Affairs 1954; Embassies, Pretoria 1959, London 1963; Counsellor 1969; Head of African Dept., Ministry of Foreign Affairs 1970–72; Consul-Gen., Milan 1972–74; Minister Plenipotentiary, Asst. Dir.-Gen. of Political Affairs, Ministry of Foreign Affairs 1974–77, Dir.-Gen. of Political Affairs 1977–79; Amb. and Perm. Rep. to NATO 1979–84, Amb. to South Africa 1984–; Hon. K.C.M.G.; Grand Cross of St. Olav (Norway), of Merit (Spain), Cruzeiro do Sul (Brazil); Grand Officer of the Order of Merit (Fed. Repub. of Germany), Rio Branco (Brazil), Lion (Senegal), Commdr., Légion d'honneur, Merit (Italy), etc. *Leisure interests:* music, travelling. *Address:* Portuguese Embassy, 599 Leyds Street, Muckleneuk, 0002 Pretoria, South Africa.

VILLAS BÔAS, Orlando; Brazilian anthropologist and explorer; b. 1914, Botucatu, São Paulo; s. of Agnelo and Arlinda Villas Bôas; m. Marina Lopes de Lima Villas Bôas; one s.; brother of Claudio Villas Bôas (q.v.); has lived in the Brazilian jungle around the River Xingu and worked among the Indians with his brother since 1945; co-founder (with his brother) of the Parque Nacional do Xingu (Brazil's most important reservation for Indians), Dir. 1961–; Gold Medal, Royal Geographical Soc. *Leisure interests:* theatre, reading, travel. *Address:* Parque Nacional do Xingu, Rua Capital Federal 309, 01259 São Paulo, SP, Brazil.

VILLEGAS DE CLERCAMP, Eric Auguste Marc Ghislain de, D.IUR., CAND. IN PHIL. AND LETTERS; Belgian business executive and lawyer; b. 19 June 1924, Brussels; s. of late Count de Villegas de Clercamp and of Elisabeth de Lantsheere; m. Béatrice Met den Ancxt 1981; three s.; joined Soc. Gen. de Banque (now Gen. Bank) 1947, Head of Service, Turnhout 1953, Sub-Man. Louvain 1956, Asst. Man. 1958, Man. Ghent 1959, Gen. Man. and mem. Local Man. Cttee., Ghent 1959, Exec. Mem. Local Cttee., Brussels 1963, Dir. 1967, Man. Dir. 1968, Chair. Bd. of Man. Dirs. Jan. 1980–; Officier de l'Ordre de la Couronne. *Leisure interests:* riding, gardening, antiques. *Address:* Kasteel von Bever, Hof te Beverlaan, 150, 1820 Grimbergen (Strombeer-Bever), Belgium. *Telephone:* 02/269.27.90.

VILLELLA, Edward, B.S.; American ballet dancer; b. 1 Jan. 1936, New York; s. of Joseph and Mildred (De Giovanni) Villella; m. 1st Janet Greschler 1962 (divorced 1970), one s.; m. 2nd Linda Carbonetto 1980, one d.; ed. N.Y. State Maritime Coll.; joined N.Y. City Ballet 1957, becoming soloist within a year, now Premier Dancer; originated leading roles in George Balanchine's Bugaku, Tarantella, Stars and Stripes, Harlequinade, Jewels, Glinkaiana, A Midsummer Night's Dream; first danced his famous role of Prodigal Son 1960; has also danced leading roles in Allegro Brillante, Jeux, Pas de Deux, Raymonda Variations, Scotch Symphony, Swan Lake; choreographed Narkissos; has appeared at Bolshoi Theatre, with Royal Danish Ballet and in London, and made numerous guest appearances; choreographed and starred in revivals of Brigadoon, Carousel; Dance magazine award 1965; Chair. N.Y. City Comm. of Cultural Affairs 1978–; Artistic Co-ordinator Eglersky Ballet Co. (now André Eglersky State Ballet of New York) 1979–84, Choreographer 1980–84; Choreographer N.J. Ballet 1980–; Artistic Dir. Ballet Okla. 1983–86, Miami City Ballet 1986–; mem. Nat. Council on the Arts 1968–74; Golden Plate Award (American Acad. of Achievement) 1971, Emmy Award 1975. *Address:* Prodigal Productions, 129 West 69th Street, New York, N.Y. 10023, U.S.A.

VILLEMÉJANE, Bernard de; French business executive; b. 10 March 1930, Marseille; s. of Pierre and Marie-Thérèse (née Gettes) de Villeméjane; m. Françoise Boucheronde 1965; two s.; ed. Ecole Polytechnique and Ecole des Mines, Paris; with Direction des Mines et de la Géologie, French W. Africa 1955–60; Ministry of Industry 1960–61; Eng. Adviser, Banque Rothschild 1961–62; Deputy Man. Dir. Société Penarroya 1963, Man Dir. 1967, Chair. of Bd. and Man. Dir. 1971–86, Dir. 1986–; Man Dir. Société Le Nickel 1971–74, Imetal 1974 (Chair. 1979); Chair. of Bd. and Man. Dir. S.M. le Nickel S.L.N. 1974–83, Dir. 1984–; Dir. Copperweld Corpn., U.S.A. 1976–; Cookson PLC UK; Dir. of various other European and American cos.; Chevalier, Légion d'honneur, Officier, Ordre nat. du Mérite, Grand Cross, Orden del Mérito (Spain). *Address:* 102 rue d'Assas, 75006 Paris, France (Home). *Telephone:* 45-38-48-48.

VILLIERS, Sir Charles Hyde, Kt., M.C.; British business executive; b. 14 Aug. 1912, London; s. of late Algernon Hyde Villiers and of Beatrix Elinor (née Paul) Villiers (Dowager Lady Aldenham); m. 1st Pamela Constance Flower (died 1943), one s.; m. 2nd Marie José de la Barre d'Erquelinnes 1946, two d.; ed. Eton, New Coll., Oxford; joined Glyn Mills and Co. (bankers) 1931; Grenadier Guards (Supplementary Reserve of Officers) 1936, served at Dunkirk 1940 (wounded 1942), Special Operations Exec., London, Italy, Yugoslavia 1943–45, Lt.-Col. and Commdr. 6 Special Force Staff Section 1945; Partner in Helbert Wagg 1948; Man. Dir. Schroder Wagg 1960–68; Man. Dir. Industrial Reorg. Corpn. 1968–71; Chair. Guinness Mahon and Co. Ltd. 1971–76; Exec. Deputy Chair. Guinness Peat Group 1973–76; Chair. British Steel Corpn. 1976–80; Chair. British Steel Corpn. (Industry) Ltd. 1977–; Dir. Bass Charrington, Courtaulds, Sun Life Assurance, Banque Belge, Financor SA, Darling & Co. Pty. Ltd.; fmr. Chair. Ashdown Trans-Europe and Trans-Australian Investment Trusts; Chair. Fed. Trust Group on European Monetary Integration 1972, Northern Ireland Finance Corpn. 1972–73; Co-Chair. Europalia Festival 1973; Trustee, Royal Opera House Trust 1974–; mem. Inst. Int. d'Etudes Bancaires 1959–76 (Pres. 1964), Minister of Labour's Resettlement Cttee. for London and S.E. 1958 (Chair. 1961–68); Review Body for N. Ireland Econ. Devt. 1971, NEDC 1976–80; Chelsea Borough Council 1950–53; Lubbock Memorial Lecturer, Oxford 1971; Order of the People (Yugoslavia) 1970; Grand Officer of Order of Léopold II 1974; Gold Medal of IRI (Italy) 1975. *Publications:* Tomorrow's Management (Lubbock Memorial Lecture) 1971, We All Live Here 1976, People Not Paper 1976, Start Again, Britain 1984. *Leisure interests:* gardening, writing. *Address:* 65 Eaton Square, London, S.W.1, England. *Telephone:* 01-235 7634.

VIMOND, Paul Marcel; French architect; b. 20 June 1922, La Meurdraquière; s. of Ernest Vimond and Marie Lehuby; m. Jacqueline Lefèvre 1945; two s. two d.; ed. Lycée de Coutances, Ecole préparatoire des beaux-arts de Rennes and Ecole nat. supérieure des beaux-arts, Paris; Acad. de France at Rome 1950–52; Chief architect, public buildings & national monuments 1954–; mem. Jury of Nat. School of Fine Arts; mem. Diocesan Comm. on Sacred Art, Paris; Expert for Tribunals and Cour d'Appel, Paris; Chevalier, Légion d'honneur, des Palmes académiques, des Arts et des Lettres and of Pontifical Order of Merit; Premier Grand Prix de Rome 1949, Officier, Ordre nat. du Mérite. *Major architectural works include:* Architect in charge of Int. Exhbn. of Sacred Art, Rome 1953; responsible for films and architectural reconstructions of tomb of Saint Peter, Rome; Buildings in Paris for: Assemblée de l'Union française, Conseil économique et social, Union de l'Europe occidentale, Org. de co-opération et de développement économiques; planner and architect for Palais d'Iéna, Paris; town planner for Cherbourg; Atomic Power Station, The Hague; two theatres, three churches in Paris, hotels, restaurants, hospitals, and numerous lycées in France; 800 pvt. houses; 15,000 flats in six new towns; technical insts. at Besançon, Montpellier, Paris, Orsay, Nice, Toulon, Troyes; Faculty of medicine, Nice; many telephone exchanges and 14 large postal sorting offices in Paris region and provinces; sorting offices in Riyadh, Jeddah and Dammam and project for television centre in Saudi Arabia, project for town in Zaire. *Leisure interests:* painting, golf. *Address:* 91 avenue Niel, 75017 Paris, France. *Telephone:* 47-63-87-84.

VIMONT, Jacques Pierre, L. EN D.; French diplomatist; b. 17 July 1911, Paris; s. of Marcel and Alice (née Durantet) Vimont; m. Anne Brun 1942; one s. two d.; ed. Lycée de Nice, Faculté de Droit, Paris and Ecole Libre des Sciences Politiques; Attaché, Belgrade 1938; Asst. Dir. Office of Resident-Gen., Tunis 1939–42; Ministry of Foreign Affairs 1944–46; Counsellor to Sherifian Govt. 1946–49; Counsellor, Berne 1949–50; Sec.-Gen. Tunisian Govt. 1950–51; Counsellor, Rio de Janeiro 1951–53; Asst. Dir. Office of Minister of Foreign Affairs 1953–54; Minister-Counsellor, Washington 1954–57; Dir. of Personnel, Ministry of Foreign Affairs 1958–65; Amb. to Mexico 1965–69, to Czechoslovakia 1969–73, to U.S.S.R. 1973–76; mem. Admin. Council Air France 1976–80; mem. Council Légion d'honneur 1977–81; Ambassadeur de France 1975; Grand Officier, Ordre nat. du Mérite, Commdr. Légion d'honneur, des Arts et des Lettres, des Palmes académiques. *Address:* 42 avenue Bosquet, 75007 Paris, France.

VINAY, Jean-Paul, O.C., M.A., D. EN L., D. EN D., F.R.S.C.; Canadian/French professor of linguistics; b. 18 Oct. 1910, Paris; s. of Maurice A. Vinay and Blanche Leconte; m. Marie-Paule Amidieu du Clos 1940; two s. two d.; ed. Lycée du Havre, Univ. Coll., London and advanced studies in Paris; various posts at Univ. Coll., London and in Paris 1930–40; Prof. later Dean, Faculté des Lettres, Univ. de Montréal 1946–66; Prof. then Dean, Univ. of Victoria 1966–76, Prof. Emer. 1976–; fmr. Pres. Canadian Linguistic Assocn.; other professional affiliations; Chevalier, Légion d'honneur; Centennial Medal; Queen's Jubilee Medal; Officier de l'Acad. (Paris). *Publications include:* The Basis and Essentials of Welsh 1947, The Canadian Bilingual Dictionary (ed.) 1962, Le Français international; book chapters and articles on linguistics. *Leisure interests:* painting, music (oboe, English horn). *Address:* 2620 Margate Avenue, Victoria, B.C. V8S 3A5, Canada.

VINCENT, Daniel, D. ÈS SC., M.D., PHARM.D.; French doctor and pharmacologist; b. 12 Oct. 1907, Dortan, Ain; s. of Albert Vincent and Marie-Thérèse Blanc; m. Marie-Louise Doucet-Bon 1933; one s. three d.; ed. Univ. of Lyon; Head medical chemist, Faculty of Medicine and Pharmacy, Univ. of Lyon, and Head of Medical Clinic 1938–39; Prof. Faculty of Medicine and Pharmacy, Toulouse 1943–78, and Lyon 1965–78; Biologist of Hospitals in Lyon 1969–78; Regional Insp. of Pharmacy 1942–45 and Prin. Insp. 1955; mem. Regional Council Ordre des Pharmaciens, Toulouse 1950–65, New York Acad. of Sciences 1961; Lauréat de l'Inst. de France, Prix Pourat 1939; Lauréat de l'Acad. de Médecine, Prix Marc Sée 1945, Prix Jansen 1961; Chevalier, Légion d'honneur. *Address:* Les Crètes, 54 avenue Valioud, 69110 Sainte Foy-Les-Lyon, France. *Telephone:* (7) 836-00-56.

VINCENT, Jean-Pierre, L. ÈS L.; French theatre director; b. 26 Aug. 1942, Juvisy-sur-Orge, Essonne; s. of André Vincent and Paulette Loyot; one s.; ed. Lycées Montaigne, Louis-le-Grand, Paris, Univ. de Paris (Sorbonne); amateur actor Univ. theatre Lycée Louis-le-Grand 1958–64; mem. Patrice Chéreau theatre co. 1965–68, Dir. 1968–72; Dir., Admin. Dir. Espérance Theatre 1972–74; Dir. at Théâtre Nat. and Ecole Supérieure d'art dramatique, Strasbourg 1975–83; Gen. Admin. Comédie-Française 1983–86; Lecturer Inst. d'études théâtrales de Paris 1969–70; Studio Dir. Conservatoire Nat. Supérieur d'art dramatique 1969–70, Prof. 1986–89; Pres. Syndicat Nat. de Dirs. d'entreprises artistiques et culturelles (Syndeac) 1978–82; numerous critics' prizes, including Molière Prize for Best Dir. 1987, Prix de la Critique 1988. *Address:* CNSAD, 2 bis rue du Conservatoire, 75009 Paris, France.

VINCENT, Olatunde Olabode; Nigerian banker; b. 16 May 1925, Lagos; s. of Josiah O. and Comfort A. Vincent; m. Edith Adenike Gooding 1958; three s. one d.; ed. C.M.S. Grammar School, Lagos, Chartered Inst. of Secs., London, Univ. of Manchester, and Admin. Staff Coll., Henley, England; Nigerian Army 1942–46; Financial Sec.'s Office 1947–56; Fed. Ministry of Finance 1956–61; Asst. Gen. Man. Central Bank of Nigeria 1961–62, Deputy Gen. Man. 1962, Gen. Man. 1963–66, Adviser 1973–75,

Deputy Gov. 1975–77, Gov. 1977–82; co-f., then Vice-Pres. African Devt. Bank, Abidjan, Ivory Coast 1966–73; Part-time Lecturer in Econs., Extra-Mural Dept., Univ. Coll. of Ibadan 1957–60; mem. Lagos Exec. Devt. Bd. 1960–61; Dir. Nigerian Industrial Devt. Bank 1964–66, Nigerian Security Printing and Minting Co. Ltd., Lagos, 1975–77; Chair. Sona Dairies Ltd. 1985–, City Business Computers Ltd. 1985–, Equity and Trust Finance Co. Ltd. 1986–; Chair. Capital Issues Comm., Lagos, 1975–77, Southern Africa Relief Fund 1977–82, Cttee. on Motor Vehicle Advances and Basic Allowance 1978–; Fellow Nigerian Inst. of Bankers; mem. Nat. Econ. Council 1979–82, Soc. for Int. Devt., Nigerian Econ. Soc., Nigerian Inst. of Man., Nigerian Stock Exchange, Nigeria-Britain Asscn., Nigerian Conservation Foundation, Int. Airline Passengers Asscn., London, Trustee, African Church Cathedral (Bethel); African Church Primatial Honours Award 1981, Distinguished Nigerian Community Leader Award 1983; Commdr. Order of Fed. Repub. 1982. *Leisure interests:* reading, listening to African and light classical music, gardening. *Address:* Plot 884 Balarabe Musa Crescent, Victoria Island, P.O. Box 8780, Lagos, Nigeria. *Telephone:* 615687.

VINDE, Pierre L. V., JUR.CAND., PHIL.CAND.; Swedish international civil servant; b. 15 Aug. 1931, Paris, France; s. of Victor Vinde and Rita Wilson; ed. schools in France, Sweden and U.K., Univs. of Uppsala and Stockholm; in Prime Minister's Office 1957–58; Ministry of Trade 1958–60; Ministry of Finance 1961–76, Budget Dir. 1970–74, Under-Sec. 1974–76; mem. Bd. Devt. Assistance Agency 1962–65, Inst. of Defence Org. and Man. 1968–70, Nat. Audit Office 1969–74, Agency for Admin. Devt. 1974–76; Deputy Group of Ten 1974–76; Chair. Bd. of Dirs. Bank of Sweden 1974–76; mem. Police Comm. 1962–64, Defence Comm. 1965–68; Chair. Relocation of Gov. Admin. Comm. 1970–72; Sr. Vice-Pres. PKbanken 1977–80; Asst. Admin. (Finance and Admin.), UN Devt. Program 1980–85, Deputy Sec.-Gen. OECD 1985–. *Publications:* Frankr av i dag o i morgon 1960, Hur Sverige styres (The Government of Sweden) 1968, Den sv. statsförvaltningen 1969, Swedish Government Administration 1971. *Address:* Organization for Economic Co-operation and Development, 2 rue André Pascal, 75775 Paris Cedex 16, France.

VINES, Sir William Joshua, Kt., C.M.G.; Australian business executive and farmer; b. 27 May 1916, Terang; s. of Percy V. and Isabella Vines; m. Thelma J. Ogden 1939; one s. two d.; ed. Haileybury Coll., Victoria; army service, Middle East, New Guinea and Borneo 1939–45; Sec. Alexander Fergusson Pty. Ltd. 1938–40, 1945–47; Dir. Goodlass Wall and Co. Pty. Ltd. 1947–49, Lewis Berger and Sons (Australia) Pty. Ltd. and Sherwin Williams Co. (Aust.) Pty. Ltd. 1952–55; Man. Dir. Lewis Berger and Sons (Victoria) Pty. Ltd. 1949–55, Lewis Berger & Sons Ltd. 1955–60, Berger, Jensen & Nicholson Ltd. 1960–61, Int. Wool Secr. 1961–69, mem. Bd. 1969–79; Chair. Dalgety Australia Ltd. 1969–80, Carbonless Papers (Wiggins Teape) Pty. Ltd. 1970–78, Assoc. Pulp & Paper Mills Ltd. 1978–82; Deputy Chair. and Dir. Tubemakers of Australia Ltd. 1970–86; Dir. Commercial Union Assurance Co. of Australia Ltd. 1969–78, Port Phillip Mills Pty. Ltd., Conzinc Riotinto of Australia Ltd. 1976–84, Dalgety Australia Holdings Ltd. 1980–, A.N.Z. Banking Group Ltd. (Deputy Chair. 1980–82, Chair. 1982–89), Grindlays Holdings (now A.N.Z. U.K. Holdings PLC) 1985–, Grindlays Bank 1987–; Chair. Sir Robert Menzies Memorial Trust; Chair. Council, Hawkesbury Agricultural Coll. 1975–85. *Address:* 38 Bridge Street, Sydney, N.S.W. 2000 (Office); Cliffdale, Currabubula, N.S.W., 2342, Australia (Home). *Telephone:* (067) 689 109 (Home).

VINOGRADOV, Oleg Mikhailovich; Soviet ballet master; b. 1937; ed. Vaganov Choreographic School, Leningrad; danced with Novosibirsk Acad. Theatre and dir. Cinderella 1964, Romeo and Juliet 1965; ballet master at Kirov Ballet, Leningrad 1968–; R.S.F.S.R. State Prize 1970 for Kazhlaev's Goryanka; Chief Ballet Master of Maly Dance Co. 1973–77; People's Artist of U.S.S.R. 1977; chief ballet master of Kirov, Leningrad 1977–. *Productions include:* Useless Precaution (Hérold) 1971, Coppélia 1973, Yaroslavna (by Tishchenko) 1974, The Ballad of a Hussar (Khrennikov), The Government Inspector, The Battleship Potemkin (A. Chaikovsky). *Address:* Kirov Theatre, Theatre Square, Leningrad, U.S.S.R.

VINOGRADOV, Vladimir Alekseyevich; Soviet economist; b. 2 July 1921, Kazan; mem. CPSU 1943–; ed. Inst. of Int. Relations, Moscow; mem. of staff of Presidium of U.S.S.R. Acad. of Sciences 1948–; lecturer at Dept. of Political Econ., Moscow Univ. 1954–60; Deputy Scientific Sec. of Presidium of U.S.S.R. Acad. of Sciences 1961–; mem. of Soviet UNESCO Comm. 1965–; Head of Section of Inst. of World Econ. and Int. Relations 1967–; Vice-Pres. of Int. Asscn. for Econ. History 1968–; Dir. of Inst. of Scientific Information of Social Sciences 1979–; mem. Acad. of Sciences; Order of the Red Banner of Labour, other medals. *Address:* U.S.S.R. Academy of Sciences, Leninsky Pr. 14, Moscow V-71, U.S.S.R.

VINOGRADOV, Vladimir Mikhailovich; Soviet diplomatist; b. 1921, Moscow; ed. Moscow Mendeleyev Inst. of Chemistry and Tech., Union Acad. of Foreign Trade; served in Soviet Army 1939–43; mem. CPSU 1942–; Dept. Head at Trade Mission in U.K. 1950–52; mem. staff, Ministry of Foreign Trade 1952–62; Amb. to Japan 1962–67, to United Arab Repub. (Egypt) 1970–74, to Iran 1978–82; Deputy Minister of Foreign Affairs 1967–70; Minister of Foreign Affairs of R.S.F.S.R. May 1982–; cand. mem. Cen. Cttee. of CPSU 1971–76; Rep. at Geneva Middle East Conf. 1974–77.

Address: c/o Ministry of Foreign Affairs, Moscow, Smolenskaya-Sennaya pl. 32/34, U.S.S.R.

VINOKUROV, Evgeny Mikhailovich; Soviet poet and essayist; b. 1925, Bryansk; ed. Artillery Officers' School, Moscow, Gorky Inst. of Literature; commdr. of artillery unit in World War II 1942–45; first works published 1948; mem. CPSU 1952–; Teacher at Gorky Inst. 1965–; U.S.S.R. State Prize 1987. *Publications include:* Poems on Duty 1951, War Lyrics, Sky Blue 1956, Admissions 1958, Human Face 1960, Word 1962, Music 1964, Characters 1964, The Bounds of the Earth 1965, Poetry and Thought (Collected Essays) 1966, Gesture 1969, Metaphors 1972, Per Force of Things 1973, Contrasts 1975, Space 1976, Home and World 1977, She 1977, The Lot 1978, Reverence 1981, Being 1985, Hypostasis 1986. *Address:* Gorky Institute of Literature, Ul. Vorovskogo 25a, Moscow, U.S.S.R.

VIOLA, Field-Marshal Roberto Eduardo; Argentine army officer and politician; b. 13 Oct. 1924, Buenos Aires; m. Nelida Giorgio; two s.; ed. Argentine Mil. Coll. 1942, rank of Second Lieut. 1944, Lieut. 1946, First Lieut. 1948, Capt. 1951, Maj. 1956, Lieut.-Col. 1960, Brig. 1965, Lieut.-Gen. 1971, Gen. 1975, Field-Marshal 1978 (retd. 1979); attended Gen. Staff Coll. 1952-54; served in 27th Infantry Regt. 1944, War Office 1957, Secr. of War 1962, Army Chief Command 1967; Mil. Adviser of del. to Interamerican Council of Defence 1967–68; Deputy Dir. of Mil. Coll. 1969; Commdr. 3rd Infantry Brigade 1972, Deputy Commdr. and Chief of Staff, 2nd Army Corps 1973, Commdr. 1975, Pres. Sr. Officers' Qualifying Bd. 1976–78, C.-in-C. of Army and mem. Governing Junta 1978–79; Pres. of Argentina March–Dec. 1981; on trial for alleged violations of human rights 1982, sentenced to 17 years' imprisonment Dec. 1985; decorations from Bolivia, Colombia, Paraguay, Peru, Spain and Venezuela.

VIOLLET, Paul; French engineer; b. 10 Nov. 1919, Paris; s. of Louis Viollet and Paule Mornard; m. Laetitia de Royer-Dupré 1944; one s. two d.; ed. Coll. Stanislas, Paris, Ecole Polytechnique de Paris and C.P.A. de Paris; Man. Cie. de Saint-Gobain 1956–61; Vice-Chair. and Gen. Man. Produits Chimiques Pechiney-Saint-Gobain 1961–72; Dir.-Gen. Man. of Rhône-Progil 1972–75; Gen. Man. Rhône-Poulenc-Polymères 1975–77; Chair. Syndicat Professionel des Fabricants de Matières Plastiques 1975; Dir. Rhône-Poulenc-Industries, Générale des Engrais S.A. 1977–82; Chevalier, Légion d'honneur. *Address:* 125 avenue de Versailles, 75016 Paris, France.

VIOT, Jacques Edmond, L. ÈS L.; French diplomatist; b. 25 Aug. 1921, Bordeaux; m. Jeanne de Martimprey de Romecourt 1950; ed. Bordeaux and Paris lycées and Ecole Normale Supérieure and Ecole nat. d'Admin.; Lecturer in French, Univ. of Dublin 1945–47, Ecole Nat. d'Admin. 1948–50; Foreign Office 1951–53, Second Sec., London 1953–57; First Sec., Rabat 1957–61; held various posts in cen. admin. 1961–72; Amb. to Canada 1972–77; Gen. Insp. for Foreign Affairs 1977–78; Dir. de Cabinet, Ministry of Foreign Affairs 1978–81; Gen. Insp. for Foreign Affairs 1981–84; Amb. to U.K. 1984–86; Chair. Review Cttee. on Foreign Affairs, Paris 1986–87; Chair. France-Grande Bretagne 1987; Ambassadeur de France; Officier, Légion d'honneur, Commdr., Ordre Nat. du Mérite. *Address:* 19 rue de Civry, 75016 Paris, France. *Telephone:* (1) 46-51-73-79.

VIOT, Pierre, L. ÈS L.; French barrister; b. 9 April 1925, Bordeaux; s. of Edmund Viot and Irma Viot; m. Monique Fruchier 1952; two s. two d.; ed. Faculté de droit de Bordeaux, Inst. d'études politiques de Paris, Ecole nat. d'admin.; Jr. Official Cour des Comptes 1953, Chief Counsel; Asst. Bureau des Commrs. aux Comptes, NATO 1957–61; Regional and Urban Dept. Head, Planning Office 1961; Spokesman Nat. and Regional Devt. Cttee. 1961; Sec.-Gen. Conseil des Impots 1971; Dir.-Gen. Centre nat. de la Cinématographie 1973–1984; Pres. Cannes Film Festival 1984–; Pres. Bd. of Dirs., Etablissement public de l'Opéra de la Bastille 1985–; Croix de guerre, Officier légion d'honneur, Commdr. ordre nat. du Mérite, Arts et Lettres. *Leisure interests:* tennis, gardening. *Address:* 13 rue Cambon, 75001 Paris (Office); 38 avenue Emile Zola, 75015 Paris, France (Home).

VIPLER, Vladimír, PH.DR., C.SC.; Czechoslovak publicist and historian; b. 18 Jan. 1927, Krompachy, Spišská Nová Ves Dist.; s. of Josef Vipler and Irena Viplerová (née Puchová); m. Marie Blažková 1954; one s.; ed. Coll. of Political and Social Sciences 1948–52; Ed. Czechoslovak Radio 1949–53, Assoc. Prof. at insts. of higher learning 1953–65, Ed.-in-Chief Czechoslovak Radio External Services 1965–69, Dir. External Services and Deputy Dir.-Gen. Czechoslovak Radio 1969–77; Dir.-Gen. Orbis Press Agency 1977–; Award for Outstanding Work 1969, Award for Merits in Construction 1977, Order of Labour 1982, Order of Victorious February 1987. *Address:* Orbis Press Agency, Vinohradská 46, 120 41 Prague 2, Czechoslovakia.

VIRATA, Cesar Enrique, B.S.BUS.ADM., B.S.MECH.ENG., M.B.A.; Philippine management consultant; b. 12 Dec. 1930, Manila; s. of Enrique Virata and Leonor Aguinaldo; m. Joy Gamboa 1956; two s. one d.; ed. Univ. of Pennsylvania, U.S.A. and Univ. of the Philippines; Dean, Coll. of Business Admin., Univ. of the Philippines 1961–69; Chair. and Dir. Philippine Nat. Bank 1967–69; Deputy Dir.-Gen. Presidential Econ. Staff 1967–68; Under-Sec. of Industry 1967–69; Chair. Bd. of Investments 1968–; Minister of Finance 1970–86; Prime Minister of the Philippines 1981–86; Chair. Land Bank of the Philippines 1973–86; mem. Monetary Bd.; mem. Nat. Econ. and Devt. Authority 1972–86; Adviser to the Co-ordinating Council for the Philippines Aid Plan Feb. 1989–; Chair. IMF and IBRD Devt. Cttee.

1976–80; mem. Nat. Ass. 1978–86; Prin. C. Virata & Assocs. (Man. Consultants) 1986–; Chair. Bd. of Govs., Asian Devt. Bank 1979–80; L.H.D. h.c., D.P.A. h.c., Dr. h.c. (Philippines). *Leisure interests:* tennis, reading. *Address:* 63 East Maya Drive, Quezon City, Philippines (Home). *Telephone:* 673 5711/12 (Office); 99-74-19 (Home).

VIREN, Lasse; Finnish athlete; b. 22 July 1949, Myrskylä; m. Päivi Kajander 1976; two s.; competed Olympic Games, Munich 1972, won gold medal at 5,000 m. and 10,000 m.; Montreal 1976, won gold medal at 5,000 m. and 10,000 m., 5th in marathon; Moscow 1980, 5th in 10,000 m.; only athlete to retain 5,000 m. and 10,000 m. titles at successive Olympics; has held World records at 2 miles, 5,000 m. and 10,000 m.; recreation officer. *Address:* Suomen Urheilulitto ry, Box 25202, 00250, Helsinki 25, Finland.

VIROLAINEN, Johannes, PH.D.; Finnish politician and farmer; b. 31 Jan. 1914, Viipuri; s. of Paavo Virolainen and Anna-Lydia Skyttä; m. Eeva Kyllikki Salojärvi 1981; ed. Helsinki Univ. (Agric. and Forestry); M.P. 1945–; Vice-Chair. Agrarian Party 1946–64, Chair. 1965–80 (name of party changed to Centre Party 1965); Second Minister of Interior 1950–51; Second Minister of Prime Minister's Office 1951; Minister of Educ. 1953–54, 1968–70, of Foreign Affairs 1954–56, 1957, 1958, of Agric. 1961–63, of Agric. and Forestry 1976–78; Deputy Prime Minister 1958, 1962–63, 1968–70, 1977–79; Prime Minister 1964–66; Speaker of Parl. 1966–69, 1979–83; First Minister of Finance 1972–75; Chair. Nat. Planning Council 1956–66; Centre Party Cand. for Pres. of Finland 1982; Pres. IPU 1982–83; Grand Crosses Orders of Merit (Argentina), Leopold (Belgium), Dannebrog (Denmark), Hawk (Iceland), North Star (Sweden), Sankt Olav (Norway), White Rose (Finland), Hungary, Colombia; Grand Officer Order of Polonia Restituta (Poland). *Publications:* Pöytäkirjat puhuvat 1948, Maaseutuhekinen elämänkatsomus 1949, Maatalousmaan arvioimisesta ja arvosta Suomessa vuosina 1934–38 1950, Karjalainen kotikylä 1955, Maalaisliiton johtavat aatfeet 1961, Pääministerinä Suomessa 1969, Ainoa vaihtoehto, poliittinen kestusta 1971, Kuka ottaa vastuun? 1978, Onko valta kansalla? 1981, Yöpakkasista juhannuspommiin 1982, Sanoi Paasikivi 1983, Muistiinpanoja ja myllykirjeitä 1984, Yhden äänen presidentti 1985, Vallankäyttö Kekkosen aikana 1986, Karjalaiset Suomen Kohtaloissa 1988. *Address:* Kirkniemi, Lohja, Finland.

VIRSALADZE, Eliso; Soviet-Georgian pianist; b. 14 Sept. 1942, Tbilisi; studied under grandmother, Prof. Anastasia Virsaladze; then at Tbilisi Conservatory; won first prize at Soviet Competition of Performing Musicians, Moscow 1961; Bronze Medal at Tchaikovsky Competition 1962, Prize at Schumann Competition; Asst. Prof., Moscow Conservatory 1962–; played as a soloist all over the world and on tour in Europe and U.S.A. with Leningrad Philharmonic; soloist with U.S.S.R. Symphony Orchestra in U.K. 1983–84, Germany 1984–85. *Address:* Moscow Conservatory of Music, Moscow, U.S.S.R.

VIRTA, Nikolay Yevgeniyevich; Soviet writer; b. 19 Dec. 1906, Lazovka, Tambov Region; journalist 1923–35; State prizewinner (four times). *Publications:* plays: Earth 1937, Slander 1939, Our Daily Bread 1947, Plot of the Doomed 1948, Endless Horizons 1957, In Summer the Sky is High 1960, Three Stones of Faith 1960, Operation Czech Forest 1961, Thirst 1961, Golgotha 1961, Winds Blew and Blew 1962, Niagara Falls 1962, Secret of Clemance and Son 1964; novels: Loneliness 1935, The Adventurer 1937, Evening Bells 1951, Steep Hills 1955, Soil Returned 1960, The One We don't Know 1960, Our Bertha 1960, Field Marshal 1961, Aksushka 1962, Two Days of their Life 1962, Fast Running Days 1965, Novels of Last Years 1965, Cat with a Long, Long Tail 1966, The End of a Career 1967, How it used to be and how it is 1973, Selected Works (2 vols.) 1973. *Address:* c/o U.S.S.R. Union of Writers, 52 Vorovskogo ulitsa, Moscow, U.S.S.R.

VISENTINI, Bruno, D.IUR.; Italian lawyer, politician and business executive; b. 1 Aug. 1914, Treviso; s. of Gustavo Visentini and Margherita (née Tosello) Visenti; m. Ernesta Caccianiga 1941; two s. two d.; ed. Univ. of Padua; Mem. Consultative Ass.; Under-Sec. of Finance, Govt. of Alcide de Gasperi; Vice-Chair. Istituto per la Ricostruzione Industriale (I.R.I.) 1950–72; Chair. and Pres. Olivetti C., S.p.A. 1964–74, Vice-Chair. 1976–78, Chair. 1978–83 (C.E.O. 1978–82); Vice-Chair. Confindustria until 1974; Dir. Montecatini-Edison; fmr. Prof. of Commercial Law, Univ. of Urbino; lecturer in Business Law, Univ. of Rome; Pres. Italian Venice Cttee.; M.P. 1972–; Minister of Finance 1974–76, 1983–87; Pres. Partito Repubblicano Italiano (PRI) 1980–. *Address:* Partito Repubblicano Italiano, Piazza dei Caprettari 70, 00186 Rome, Italy.

VISHNEVSKAYA, Galina Pavlovna; Russian singer; b. 25 Oct. 1926, Leningrad; m. Mstislav Rostropovich (q.v.); studied with Vera Garina 1942–52; Leningrad Musical Theatres 1944–52; joined Bolshoi Theatre 1952–; retd. from operatic stage as Tatiana (Eugene Onegin) Paris 1982, continues to give recitals; numerous parts in operas, notably Leonora in Fidelio, and Tatiana in Eugene Onegin (also in the film), Aida (Aida), Kupava (Snow Maiden), Liza (Queen of Spades), Chio-Chio-San (Madame Butterfly), Margaret (Faust), Natasha (War and Peace), Cherubino (Marriage of Figaro). *Publication:* Galina (autobiog.) 1985.

VISSEUR, Pierre, LL.D.; Swiss international administrator; b. 10 June 1920, Bré; s. of Pierre L. Visseur and Charlotte van Aken; m. Suzy Butikoffer 1947; one s. two d.; ed. Univs. of Basel, Geneva and Berne, and

Inst. of Int. Studies, Geneva; Sec.-Gen., European Div., World Brotherhood 1950–62; Dir. World Fed. for Mental Health 1963–68; Dir. Pharmaceutical Proprietary Asscn. of Europe (AESGP) 1969–80; fmr. Pres. Fed. of Private and Semi-Official Int. Orgs. in Geneva. *Publication:* Evolution of Control of International Labour Legislation 1946. *Leisure interests:* mountaineering, gardening, history. *Address:* Casa Angelina, CH-6925 Gentilino, Switzerland. *Telephone:* 091-544492.

VITALI, Felice Antonio; Swiss radio and television official; b. 24 March 1907, Bellano; s. of Battista and Leonie Vitali; m. Hilda Schlatter 1930; ed. St. Gall Gymnasium and Commercial Coll.; Ed. Die Presse 1928; Radio Berne 1929; Ed. Schweizer Radio Zeitung 1930; Dir. Radio Svizzera Italiana 1931–47; corresp. Swiss Radio in Berlin 1948–57; Project-leader UNESCO Radio advisory Mission to Libya 1957–58; Head of Information Services, Swiss Television (Zürich) 1958–67; Programme Liaison of Swiss Television, Lugano 1967–85; Prix Pisa of the Prix Italia 1962 (for TV documentary). *Radio plays:* I tre amici, La capanna del Bertuli, Idol und Masse, Kraftwerk Mittelmeer, Flut ohne Ebbe, Kampf um die öffentliche Meinung 1955, Atome für die Politik 1956, Die sieben Kiesel 1961. *Television documentaries:* Der alte Mensch, Was war der Generalstreik? Kranke Menschen, halbe Hilfe, Urteil ohne Richter, Testfall Celerina, Die Polizei des Bürgers, Frau Grossrätin, Hauptmann Grüninger, Die Barriere, Das Wagnis, Partner im Rollstuhl, Betrifft Friedrich Glauser. *Publications:* Reporter erleben England, Confidenze del Microfono, Radiohörer das geht dich an, Der alte Mensch und das Fernsehen, Altersprogramme—Ghetto oder Treffpunkt?, Zwischen den Grenzen, Lebensbericht eines Medienmachers: 1907–83, Die Matusa: Tessiner Dorfgeschichten (1983–89). *Leisure interests:* walking, gardening. *Address:* Ronco Nuovo, 6949 Comano-Lugano, Switzerland. *Telephone:* (091)-51-12-50.

VITSAXIS, Vassilios, PH.D.; Greek diplomatist; b. 22 Oct. 1920, Athens; s. of George and Iphigenia Vitsaxis; m. Zoe-Ketty Ioannidou 1946; no c.; ed. Univ. of Athens; entered diplomatic service 1946; Liaison Officer of Greek Govt. to Balkan Cttee. of UN 1947; later Sec., Paris; mem. del. to Council of Europe; Consul, Counsellor and Chargé d'affaires, Perm. Mission of Greece at UN and Consul-Gen., New York; Counsellor, Ankara 1964, Minister-Counsellor and Chargé d'affaires 1965–66; Amb. and Perm. Del. to Council of Europe 1966–69; Amb. to U.S.A. 1969–72; Amb. to India, Nepal, Sri Lanka, Bangladesh, Burma, Malaysia, Singapore, Thailand 1973–78 (fmrly. accred. to Indonesia and Repub. of Viet-Nam); mem. Inst. of Int. and Private Law, PEN Clubs of Greece, India, Argentina, Dean Asscn. of Greek Writers; Pres. Hellenic Soc. of Translators of Literature; mem. Asscn. of Literary Critics (Paris); Silver Pen Award of PEN Clubs; Poet Laureate of Int. Congress of Poetry; Grand Commdr. Royal Order of George I, Grand Commdr. of Phoenix, Commdr. of the Holy Sepulchre (Jerusalem) and Golden Cross of the Crown (Belgium), Grand Cross of Thailand, Poetry Award of Acad. Française. *Publications:* Plato and the Upanishads, Hindu Epics, Myths and Legends, Monopatia, Pantoteina Kai Proskaira (poetry), The Influence of Greek Philosophy in the Evolution of Roman Law, Studies in Hellenic Labour Law; Reflets (collection of poetry); translations into Greek of 82 contemporary Indian poets, and four contemporary poets laureate of Argentina. *Leisure interests:* photography, poetry, ham radio. *Address:* Tsakona 7, Pal. Psychico, Athens 154-52, Greece.

VITTI, Monica (Monica Luisa Ceciarelli); Italian actress; b. 3 Nov. 1931, Rome; films include L'Avventura 1959, La Notte 1960, L'Eclisse 1962, Dragées au Poivre 1963, The Red Desert 1964, Modesty Blaise 1966, The Chastity Belt 1967, Girl With a Pistol 1969, Le Coppie 1971, La Pacifiste 1971, La Tosca 1971, Teresa la larda 1973, A mezzanotte va la ronda de piacere 1975, Duck in Orange Sauce 1975, An Almost Perfect Affair 1979, Teresa the Thief 1979, Le Coppie 1980, The Oberwald Mystery 1981, Broadway Danny Rose 1984.

VIZZINI, Carlo; Italian politician and university teacher; b. 28 April 1947, Palermo; elected Social Democrat M.P. for Palermo-Trapani-Agrigento-Caltanisetta 1976–; Nat. Deputy Sec. Italian Social Democrat Party and head of Econ. Dept. 1980–88; Under-Sec. of State in Ministry of Budget and Econ. Planning; Minister for Regional Affairs 1986–87, of Cultural Heritage 1987–88; Prof. of History of Econs., Univ. of Palermo. *Address:* Camera dei Deputati, Rome, Italy.

VLAAR, Nicolaas Jacob; Netherlands professor of geophysics; b. 17 March 1933, Mijnsheerenland; m. 1st Joanna Lambermont 1956 (died 1976), 2nd Everdina den Hartog 1980; three s. one d.; ed. Bisschoppelijk Coll., Tech. Univ., Delft and Utrecht Univ.; Asst. Calif. Inst. of Tech. 1965–66, St. Louis Univ. 1966–67, Utrecht Univ. 1963–, Prof. of Theoretical Geophysics 1973–; Prof. of Theoretical Geophysics, Free Univ. 1983–; mem. Royal Netherlands Acad. of Science 1984–; Royal Dutch/Shell Prize 1982. *Publications:* numerous works on seismology and geodynamics. *Leisure interests:* nature, esoterics. *Address:* Mauritslaan 5, 3818 GJ Amersfoort, Netherlands.

VLADIMIROV, Igor Petrovich; Soviet actor and film director; b. 1 Jan. 1919; ed. Leningrad Theatre Inst.; worked with both Lenin Komsomol Theatre, Leningrad and Gorky Theatre 1948–60; prin. dir. of Lensoviet Theatre, Leningrad 1960–; worked in films 1957–; U.S.S.R. People's Artist 1978. *Films include:* Your Contemporary 1968, People on the Nile 1972,

Taming of Fire 1972, The Hottest Month 1974, An Ordinary Month 1976, Tales of Old Arbat 1982, An Extra Ticket 1983 etc. *Address:* c/o Gosudarstvenny Teatr Lensoviета, Leningrad, U.S.S.R.

VLADIMIROV, Vasiliy Sergeyevich, D.SC.; Soviet mathematician; b. 9 Jan. 1923, Djaglevo, Petrograd (now Leningrad) Region; s. of Sergey Ivanovich Vladimirov and Maria Semyonovna Vladimirova; m. Nina Yakovlevna Ovsyannikova 1948; two s.; ed. Leningrad State Univ.; Jr. Research Worker, Leningrad Red Banner 1947; V. A. Steklov Inst. of Math., U.S.S.R. Acad. of Sciences 1948-56; Sr. Research Worker, Steklov Inst. of Maths., Moscow 1956-69, Head, Dept. of Math. Physics 1969; Prof. Physico-tech. Inst. 1965-86; Vice-Dir. Stekhov Inst. 1986-; mem. CPSU 1944-; corresp. mem. U.S.S.R. Acad. of Sciences 1968-70, mem. 1970-; mem. Saxony Akademie der Wissenschaften 1985, Acad. of Sciences and Arts Voievodina (Yugoslavia) 1987; State Prize 1953, 1987 (twice); Gold Medal of A. N. Liapounov 1971; Gold Medal Bernarda Bolzana CSR Acad. of Science 1982; Orders of the Labour Red Banner 1967, 1973; Order of Lenin (twice) 1975, 1983; Order of the Great Patriotic War 1941-45 'of 2nd degree 1985; Hero of Socialist Labour, Hammer and Sickle Gold Medal and other decorations. *Publications:* Methods of the Theory of Functions of Several Complex Variables 1964, Equations of Mathematical Physics 1967, Distributions in Mathematical Physics 1976, Many Dimensional Theorems for Distributions (with others) 1986 and works in the field of numerical methods of problems solution of mathematical physics; analysis of transfer equation; theory of holomorphic functions of several complex variables and distribution theory, and their applications in mathematical physics. *Leisure interests:* skiing, fishing. *Address:* c/o Steklov Institute of Mathematics, Vavilova Street 42, B-333 Moscow, U.S.S.R.

VLADIMOV, Georgiy Nikolayevich (pseudonym of G. N. Volosevich); Soviet writer and literary critic; b. 1931, Kharkov; ed. Leningrad State Univ.; started literary activity as critic 1954, and as prose-writer 1960; expelled from U.S.S.R. Writers' Union 1982, and refused visa to emigrate. *Publications include:* Faithful Ruslan 1965, Letter to the IVth Presidium of U.S.S.R. Writers' Union (samizdat) 1967, Three Minutes of Silence 1982.

VLADYCHENKO, Ivan Maximovich; Soviet politician; b. 1924; ed. Donetsk Industrial Inst.; served in Soviet Army 1941-45; mem. of CPSU 1943; worked in mines of Chistyakovantracit trust in Donbas (asst. chief, then chief of mine sector) 1951-52; Second Sec. of Chistyakov City Cttee. of CP of Ukraine (Donetsk Region) 1952-59; Chair. of Cen. Cttee. of Coal Industry Workers Union 1959-64; Sec. of U.S.S.R. Cen. Council of Trade Unions 1964-81; Chair. of U.S.S.R. State Cttee. for Industrial Safety and the Supervision of Mines July 1981-; mem. of Cen. Auditing Comm. of CPSU 1961-66; alt. mem. of CPSU Cen. Cttee. 1966-. *Address:* The Kremlin, Moscow, U.S.S.R.

VLAJKOVIĆ, Radovan; Yugoslav politician; b. 18 Nov. 1922, Budjanovci, Vojvodina; s. of Sava Vlajkovic and Draginja Vlajkovic; m. 1948; one s. one d.; with Workers' Movt. 1940, Nat. Liberation Struggle 1941; mem. Communist Party of Yugoslavia 1943-; fmr. Sec. of Dist. and Regional Cttees. of League of Communist Youth of Yugoslavia, mem. of Regional Cttee. of CP; fmr. Sec. of Regional and City Cttee. of CP in Pančevo and Novi Sad; fmr. Pres. Prov. Council of Fed. Trade Unions for Vojvodina 1958, mem. Cen. Council; mem. Cen. Cttee. of League of Communists of Serbia 1959-68, mem. of Presidency of Cen. Cttee. 1966-; fmr. Pres. of Ass. of Vojvodina 1963; fmr. Pres. of Council for Agric. of Fed. Chamber of Ass. of Yugoslavia 1967-69; fmr. Deputy, Chamber of Nationalities of Fed. Ass. 1969-74; mem. Prov. Cttee. of Vojvodina 1949-69; fmr. Pres. of Presidency of Vojvodina and ex-officio mem. of Presidency of Serbia 1974-81; mem. for Vojvodina of Presidency of Yugoslavia 1981-, Pres. Collective Presidency 1985-86, mem. Presidency of Yugoslavia 1986-; Partisan Memorial Medal and numerous others. *Leisure interests:* hunting, gardening. *Address:* c/o Presidency of the Socialist Federal Republic of Yugoslavia, Novi Beograd, B. Lenjina 2, Yugoslavia.

VLASOV, Lieut.-Gen. Alexander Vladimirovich; Soviet politician; b. 1933; ed. Irkutsk Inst. of Mining and Metallurgy; fmr. mining engineer involved in supervising econ. expansion of Siberia; fmr. mem. North Caucasus Mil. Council; mem. CPSU 1956-; Komsomol and Party work 1954-65; Sec. then Second Sec. Yakutsk Dist. Cttee. 1965-72; work with CPSU Cen. Cttee. 1972-75; First Sec. Checheno-Ingush Dist. Cttee. 1975-84; Dir. Rostov Industrial Zone 1984-86; Minister of Interior and Head of Civilian Police 1986-88; Chair. R.S.F.S.R. Council of Ministers Oct. 1988-; Gen.-Lieut. 1986; candidate mem. Politburo 1988-; elected to Congress of People's Deputies of the U.S.S.R. 1988-89. *Address:* The Kremlin, Moscow, U.S.S.R.

VLATKOVIĆ, Dušan; Yugoslav (Serbian) central banker; b. 1938, Bačka Topola, Vojvodina; m. Tatjana Kneževič 1968; one s. one d.; ed. Faculty of Econs.; Man. Planning and Research Inst. Ass. of Bačka Topola Commune 1963-65; Vice-Pres. Bačka Topola Commune 1965-69; Sec. for Finance, Autonomous Prov. of Vojvodina and mem. Exec. Council of Ass. of Autonomous Prov. of Vojvodina 1969; Gen. Man. Vojvodjanska Banka-Udružena Banka, Novi Sad 1974-78, Chair. of Business Bd. 1978; del. to Socio-political Chamber of Ass. of Autonomous Prov. of Vojvodina; mem. Ass. of Autonomous Prov. of Vojvodina del. in Chamber of Repubs. and Provs. of Fed. Ass. 1982; mem. Presidency of Autonomous Prov. of

Vojvodina 1974-78; fmr. Pres. Yugoslav Banking Assen., mem. Exec. Bd. of Yugoslav Chamber of Economy; mem. Fed. Econ. Council; Gov. Nat. Bank of Yugoslavia 1986-. *Address:* National Bank of Yugoslavia, Bulavar Revolucije 15, 11000 Belgrade, Yugoslavia. *Telephone:* 340-652.

VLOK, Adriaan; South African politician; b. Sutherland; joined Dept. of Justice 1957; became prosecutor and sr. magistrate; Asst. Pvt. Sec. to Prime Minister John Vorster 1967; subsequently entered pvt. business; later Deputy Sheriff, E. Pretoria; mem. Parl. 1974-; fmr. Deputy Speaker of House of Ass.; Deputy Minister of Defence and Deputy Minister of Law and Order 1985-86; Minister of Law and Order 1986-. *Leisure interests:* rugby (referee in Northern Transvaal), military history, chewing biltong. *Address:* Ministry of Law and Order, Civitas Bldg., Pretoria, South Africa.

VO CHI CONG: Vietnamese politician; b. 1914, Central Viet-Nam; fmr. mem. Vietcong force; fmr. Sec. Southern People's Party, a main element in Nat. Liberation Front (NLF); mem. Cen. Cttee. of Lao Dong party for many years; Minister for Fisheries, Socialist Repub. of Viet-Nam 1976-77; Vice-Premier, Council of Ministers 1976-82, now mem.; Minister for Agric. 1977-78; mem. Politburo of CP of Viet-Nam Dec. 1976-; Pres. of Vietnam June 1987-. *Address:* c/o Council of Ministers, Bac Thao, Hanoi, Viet-Nam.

VO NGUYEN GIAP, Gen.; Vietnamese army officer; b. 1912, Quangbinh Province; ed. French Lycée in Hué, and law studies at Univ. of Hanoi; History teacher, Thang Long School, Hanoi; joined Viet-Nam CP in early 1930s; fled to China 1939, helped organize Vietminh Front, Viet-Nam 1941; Minister of Interior 1945, became Commdr.-in-Chief of Vietminh Army 1946; defeated French at Dien Bien Phu 1954; Vice-Chair. Council of Ministers July 1976-, Minister of Defence, C.-in-C., Democratic Repub. of Viet-Nam to 1976, Socialist Repub. of Viet-Nam 1976-80; mem. Politburo Lao-Dong Party until 1976, CP of Viet-Nam 1976-82. *Publications:* People's War, People's Army, Big Victory, Great Task 1968. *Address:* Dang Cong san Viet-Nam, 1C boulevard Hoang Van Thu, Hanoi, Viet-Nam.

VO VAN KIET; Vietnamese politician; b. 1922, S. Viet-Nam; joined CP of Indo-China in 1930s; mem. Lao Dong Party (renamed Communist Party of Viet-Nam Dec. 1976), mem. Cen. Cttee. 1958-; mem. Cen. Office for S. Viet-Nam during war; alt. mem. Politburo, CP of Viet-Nam 1976, now mem.; Vice-Chair. Council of Ministers April 1982-; Chair. State Planning Cttee. 1982-88; Chair. party Cttee. in Ho Chi Minh City. *Address:* Council of Ministers, Hanoi, Viet-Nam.

VOGEL, Bernhard, D.PHIL.; German politician; b. 19 Dec. 1932, Göttingen; s. of Prof. Dr. Hermann Vogel and Caroline (née Brinz) Vogel; unmarried; ed. Univs. of Heidelberg and Munich; Lecturer, Inst. für Politische Wissenschaft, Heidelberg 1961; mem. Bundestag 1965-67; Minister of Educ. and Culture, Rhineland-Palatinate 1967-76; mem. Rhineland-Palatinate State Parl. 1971; Chair. CDU Rhineland-Palatinate 1974-; Minister-President, Rhineland-Palatinate 1976-88; Pres. Bundesrat 1976-77; Chair. Advisory Bd., Zweites Deutsches Fernsehen 1979-; Pres. Bundesverband "Schutzgemeinschaft Deutscher Wald" 1980-; Pres. Maximilian-Kolbe Works 1984-; Senator Max-Planck Assen. 1984-; mem. Fed. Bd. of CDU; Grosses Bundesverdienstkreuz mit Stern und Schulterband; decorations from France, Luxembourg, U.K., Senegal and Vatican; Grosskreuz St. Gregorius; Gold Medal of Strasbourg; Christian Democrat. *Publications:* Wahlen und Wahlsysteme 1961, Kontrolliert der Bundestag die Regierung? 1964, Wahlkampf und Wählertradition 1965; numerous essays and speeches. *Leisure interests:* mountaineering, literature. *Address:* Landauer Warte 16, D6720 Speyer, Federal Republic of Germany (Home).

VOGEL, Hans-Jochen, DR.JUR.; German politician; b. 3 Feb. 1926, Göttingen; m. 1st Ilse Leisnering 1951' (divorced 1972), one s. two d.; m. 2nd Liselotte Sonnenholzer (née Biersack) 1972; ed. Univs. of Munich and Marburg; Asst., Bavarian Justice Ministry 1952-54; lawyer, Traunstein Dist. Court 1954-55; Bavarian State Chancellery 1955-58; mem. Munich City Council 1958-60; Chief Burgomaster of Munich 1960-72; mem. Bundestag 1972-; Minister for Regional Planning, Building and Urban Devt. 1972-81, of Justice 1974; Mayor, West Berlin Jan.-June 1981; Chair. SPD Parl. Party 1984-; Deputy Chair. SPD 1984-87, Chair. March 1987-; Vice-Pres. Org. Cttee. for Munich Olympic Games 1972; numerous decorations including Grosses Bundesverdienstkreuz, Bayerischer Verdienstorden, Hon. C.B.E. (U.K.) and honours from France, Italy, etc. *Address:* Erich-Ollenhauer-Haus, 5300 Bonn 1, Federal Republic of Germany.

VOGEL, Rudolf, DR.ING.; German business executive; b. 10 Feb. 1918, Hamburg; s. of Paul and Meta (née Liebetrau) Vogel; m. Marianne Ahlers 1950; one s. one d.; ed. Staatslehranstalt and Univ. of Hamburg and Technische Hochschulen, Brunswick and Aachen; Head clerk Gutehoffnungshütte Sterkrade AG 1954-64; Man. Ottensener Eisenwerke GmbH, Hamburg 1964-68; mem. Exec. Bd., Salzgitter Maschinen AG and Eisenhütte Prinz Rudolph AG 1968-75; fmr. mem. Supervisory Bd., Kermansha Sugar Corpn., Teheran, Zippel Corpn., U.S.A.; Consulting Engineer Devt., Innovation, Licenser 1975- (ERNO Raumfahrttechnik GmbH, etc.). *Leisure interests:* reading, music, hiking, travel. *Address:* 2000 Hamburg 55 (Blankenese), Pikartenkamp 42a, Federal Republic of Germany. *Telephone:* 040-868424.

VOGELS, Dr. Hanns Arnt; German business executive; b. 22 Jan. 1926, Berlin-Charlottenburg; s. of Heinz Vogels and Josephine Rohden; m.; two c.; ed. Berlin Technische Hochschule, Aachen Technische Hochschule; labour service, mil. service, prisoner of war 1944–45; with Gebrüder Böhler and Co. 1949–55, section Head and Deputy Head 1954–55; Head of Plant Eng. Dept., Mannesmann-Forschungsinstitut GmbH 1955–57; Sr. Engineer and Head Quality Office Mannesmann AG 1957–63; Man. Rheinische Stahlwerke AG 1963; Corporate Man. Rheinstahl Hüttenwerke AG 1963–66; Gen. Man. Friedrich Flick KG 1967–78, Man.-shareholder 1978–83; Pres. and Gen. Man. Messerschmitt-Bölkow-Blohm GmbH Feb. 1983–; Chair. and mem. supervisory bds. of numerous cos.; mem. Advisory Bd. Bayerische Landesbank, STEAG; mem. nat. cttee., World Energy Conf.; Chair. Vereinigung Industrielle Kraftwirtschaft. *Address:* Messerschmitt-Bölkow-Blohm GmbH, Postfach 80 11 09, 8000 München 80, Federal Republic of Germany. *Telephone:* (089) 60 00 25 90.

VOGELSANG, Günter; German business executive; b. 20 Jan. 1920, Krefeld; s. of Robert Vogelsang; m. Ingelinde Halbach; fmr. mem. Man. Bd. Mannesmann AG; Chair. Man. Bd. Fried. Krupp GmbH 1968–72; Chair. Bd. Dirs. Veba AG, Düsseldorf, Blohm & Voss AG, Hamburg, Gerling-Konzern Versicherungs-Beteiligungs-AG, Cologne, Gerling-Konzern Allgemeine Versicherungs-AG, Cologne, Thyssen AG, Duisburg; mem. Bd. Dirs. Daimler-Benz AG, Stuttgart, Deutsche Bank AG, Frankfurt ARBED Saarstahl GmbH, Völklingen/Saar, Hapag-Lloyd AG, Hamburg; Dep. Chair. Admin. Council, Kommanditgesellschaft Diehl, Nürnberg. *Address:* Kaiser-Friedrich-Ring 84, 4000 Düsseldorf-Oberkassel, Federal Republic of Germany.

VOGT, Hersleb; Norwegian diplomatist; b. 20 May 1912, Oslo; s. of Lorentz Vogt and Ida Fabricius; m. Inger Hansen 1947; one d.; ed. Univ. of Oslo; entered Diplomatic Service and served Ministry of Foreign Affairs 1936, Paris and Luxembourg 1937, Rome 1938; Ministry of Foreign Affairs London 1944, Oslo 1945, Brussels and Luxembourg 1948, London and Dublin 1949; Minister to Japan 1953–58, Amb. 1958; Amb. to Fed. Repub. of Germany 1958–63, to Denmark 1963–67, to France 1967–73, 1977–80, to Sweden 1973–77; Commdr. Order of St. Olav; Hon. C.V.O.; Commdr. Order of Phoenix (Greece); Grand Cross Order of Rising Sun (Japan); Grand Cross (First Class), Order of Merit (Fed. Repub. of Germany); Grand Cross, Order of Dannebrog (Denmark); Grand Commdr. Légion d'honneur; Grand Cross, Order of Nordstjarnen (Sweden). *Address:* 25 rue du Docteur Finlay, 75015 Paris, France. *Telephone:* 45-77-85-33.

VOGT, Marthe Louise, DR.MED., DR. PHIL., PH.D., F.R.S.; British scientist; b. 1903; d. of Oskar Vogt and Cécile Mugnier; ed. Univ. of Berlin; Research Asst., Dept. of Pharmacology, Univ. of Berlin 1930; Research Asst. and Head, Chemical Div., Kaiser Wilhelm Inst. für Hirnforschung, Berlin 1931–35; Rockefeller Travelling Fellow 1935–36; Research Worker, Dept. of Pharmacology, Univ. of Cambridge 1935–40; Alfred Yarrow Research Fellow, Girton Coll., Cambridge 1937–40; mem. Staff, Coll. of Pharmaceutical Soc., London 1941–46; Lecturer, later Reader in Pharmacology, Univ. of Edinburgh 1947–60; Head, Pharmacology Unit, Agricultural Research Council, Inst. of Animal Physiology 1960–68; Visiting Assoc. Prof. in Pharmacology, Columbia Univ., New York 1949; Visiting Prof., Sydney Univ. 1965, Montreal 1968; Hon. mem. Physiological Soc. 1974, British Pharmacological Soc. 1974, Hungarian Acad. of Sciences 1981, British Asscn. for Psychopharmacology 1983; Foreign Hon. mem. American Acad. of Arts and Sciences 1977; Life Fellow, Girton Coll., Cambridge 1970; Hon. F.R.S.M.; Hon. D.Sc. (Edinburgh) 1974, (Cambridge) 1983; Schmiedeberg Plakette 1974; Royal Medal, Royal Soc. 1981. *Publications:* papers in neurological, physiological and pharmacological journals. *Leisure interests:* gardening, travel. *Address:* c/o Agricultural and Food Research Council, Institute of Animal Physiology, Babraham, Cambridge, CB2 4AT, England. *Telephone:* (0223) 832312.

VOGT, Peter K., PH.D.; American (b. German) professor of microbiology; b. 3 Oct. 1932; s. of Josef and Else (née Thiemann) Vogt; ed. Univ. of Tubingen; Asst. Prof. of Pathology, Univ. of Colorado 1962–66, Assoc. Prof. 1966–67; Assoc. Prof. of Microbiology, Univ. of Washington 1967–69, Prof. 1969–71; Hastings Prof. of Microbiology, Univ. of Southern Calif. 1971–78, Hastings Distinguished Prof. of Microbiology 1978–80, Chair. Dept. of Microbiology 1980–; Calif. Scientist of the Year 1975, Award of Nat. Acad. of Sciences 1980, Alexander von Humboldt Prize 1983, Ernst Jung Prize for Medicine 1985. *Publications:* Genetics of RNA Tumor Viruses 1977, The Genetic Structure of RNA Tumor Viruses 1977, Class II Defective Avian Sarcoma Viruses: Comparative Analysis of Genome Structure 1982. *Leisure interest:* painting. *Address:* Department of Microbiology, University of Southern California School of Medicine, 2011 Zonal Avenue, HMR-401, Los Angeles, Calif. 90033, U.S.A. *Telephone:* (213) 224-7139.

VOGÜÉ, Comte Arnaud de; French businessman; b. 11 June 1904; Hon. Pres. Cie. de Saint-Gobain 1970–; Officier, Légion d'honneur, Croix de guerre, Commdr. Palmes académiques. *Address:* 48 rue du Docteur-Blanche, Paris 75016; le Peseau, 18 Boulleret, France (Homes).

VOHS, James Arthur, B.A.; American business executive; b. 26 Sept. 1928, Idaho Falls, Ida.; s. of John D. Vohs and Lucille Packer; m. Janice Hughes 1953; four d.; ed. Univ. of Calif. Berkeley and Harvard School of Business; joined Kaiser org. 1952; Exec. Vice-Pres. Kaiser Foundation Health Plan,

Inc. and Kaiser Foundation Hosps. 1969, mem. Bd. of Dirs. 1970, Pres. 1975–, C.E.O. 1977–, Chair. 1980–. *Address:* Kaiser Foundation Health Plan Inc., 1 Kaiser Plaza, Oakland, Calif. 94612 (Office); 17 Westminster Drive, Oakland, Calif. 94618, U.S.A. (Home). *Telephone:* 415-271-2656 (Office); 415-653-5858 (Home).

VOIGHT, Jon, American actor; b. 29 Dec. 1938, Yonkers, New York; s. of Elmer Voight and Barbara (née Camp) Voight; m. 1st Lauri Peters 1962 (divorced 1967); m. 2nd Marcheline Bertrand 1971 (divorced); one s. one d.; ed. Catholic Univ.; Acad. Award (Best Actor) for Coming Home 1979, Best Actor Awards for Midnight Cowboy 1969, Coming Home 1979, Cannes Int. Film Festival, Golden Globe Award for Best Actor for Coming Home. *Theatre includes:* A View From the Bridge (New York); That Summer That Fall (New York) 1966; played Romeo at the San Diego Shakespeare Festival; Stanley Kowalski in A Streetcar Named Desire, Los Angeles 1973; *Films include:* Hour of the Gun 1967, Fearless Frank 1968, Out of It 1969, Midnight Cowboy 1969, The Revolutionary 1970, The All-American Boy 1970, Catch 22 1970, Deliverance 1972, Conrack 1974, The Odessa File 1974, Coming Home 1978, The Champ 1979, Lookin' to get out (also wrote screenplay) 1982, Table for Five 1983, Runaway Train 1985, Desert Bloom 1986. *Television includes:* End of the Game 1976, Gunsmoke and Cimmaron Strip. *Address:* c/o Screen Actors Guild, 7095 Hollywood Boulevard, Hollywood, Calif. 90028, U.S.A.

VOIGT, Hans-Heinrich, DR.RER.NAT.; German professor of astronomy and astrophysics; b. 18 April 1921, Eitzendorf; s. of Pastor Wilhelm and Thea (née Zietz) Voigt; m. Margaret Moericke 1949 (died 1979); two d.; ed. Univs. of Göttingen and Kiel; Research Assoc., Lick Observatory, Mt. Hamilton, Calif. 1951–52; Asst., Univ. Observatory, Göttingen 1952–58; Chief Observer, Hamburger Sternwarte 1958–63; Prof. of Astronomy and Astrophysics, Univ. of Göttingen 1963–86, Rector 1969–70, Dir. of Observatory 1963–86, now Prof. Emer.; Chair. Astronomische Gesellschaft 1972–77; Pres. Acad. of Science of Göttingen 1978–86. *Publications:* Abriss der Astronomie 1980, Astronomy and Astrophysics (ed.); several articles in scientific journals. *Address:* Universitäts-Sternwarte, Geismarlandstr. 11, 3400 Göttingen; Nikolausberger Weg 74, 3400 Göttingen, Federal Republic of Germany (Home). *Telephone:* 0551-395041 (Office); 0551-55879 (Home).

VOINEA, Radu, PH.D.; Romanian civil engineer and scientist; b. 24 May 1923, Craiova; s. of Policarp Voinea and Gabriela Voinea; m. 1st Maria Marta Gorgos 1951 (divorced 1957), one s. one d.; m. 2nd Aurica Daghie 1959; ed. Polytech. School, Bucharest; Asst. Prof. 1947; Sr. lecturer, Inst. of Civil Eng., Bucharest 1951; Prof., Polytech. Inst., Bucharest 1962, Pro-Rector 1964–67, Rector 1972–81; Corresp. mem. Romanian Acad. 1962, Gen. Sec. 1967–74, mem. 1974, Pres. 1984–; mem. European Acad. of Arts, Sciences and Humanities 1985. *Publications:* Curs de rezistenţa materialelor (Lectures on the Strength of Materials), with A. Beles 1958, Mecanica teoretică (Theoretical Mechanics), with V. Vâlcovici and Ş. Bălan 1959, 1963, 1968, Metode analitice în teoria mecanismelor (Analytical Methods in the Theory of Mechanisms), with M. C. Atanasiu 1964, Mecanica (Mechanics), with D. Voiculescu and V. Ceausu 1975, 1983, Contributions to the Improvement of Motor-car Suspension with Mariana Fraţilă, Int. Symposium COPISEE-Bruit, Varna 1975, Elasticitate şi Plasticitate (Elasticity and Plasticity), with D. Voiculescu and V. Ceauşu 1976, Vibratii mecanice (Mechanical Vibrations) with D. Voiculescu 1979, Positional and Kinematic Analysis of Mechanisms (with Z. Atanasiu), 7th World Congress on Theory of Machines and Mechanisms, Seville 1987, Introducere în Mecanica Solidului pentru ingineri (Introduction to mechanics of solids for engineers) with D. Voiculescu and F. Simion 1989. *Address:* c/o Institutul Politechnic, Splaiul Independenţei 313, Bucharest, Romania.

VOINOVICH, Vladimir Nikolayevich; Soviet author, playwright and film script-writer; b. 1932, Stalinabad (now Dushanbe), Tadzhikistan; s. of Nikolai Pavlovich Voinovich and Rosa (née Goikhman) Voinovich; m. 1st Valentina Voinovich; one s. one d.; m. 2nd Irina Braude 1970; one d.; served in Soviet Army 1951–55; worked as carpenter 1956–57; studied Moscow Pedagogical Inst. 1958–59; settled in Kazakhstan 1960; started literary activity (and song-writing for Moscow Radio) 1960; various dissident activities 1966–74; expelled from U.S.S.R. Writers' Union 1974; admitted to Int. PEN Club 1974 and elected mem. French PEN Centre 1975; emigrated from U.S.S.R. 1979; mem. Bavarian Acad. of Fine Arts. *Publications include:* The Life and Unusual Adventures of Private Ivan Chonkin (samizdat 1967) 1975 (English trans. 1977), By Way of Mutual Correspondence 1979, Pretender to the Throne 1981, Moscow-2042 1987. *Address:* Hans Carossa Strasse 5, 8035 Stockdorf, Federal Republic of Germany.

VOLCKER, Paul A., M.A.; American banker and government official; b. 5 Sept. 1927, Cape May, N.J.; s. of Paul A. and Alma Klippel Volcker; m. Barbara Marie Bahnson 1954; one s. one d.; ed. Princeton Univ., Harvard Univ. Graduate School of Public Admin., and L.S.E.; Special Asst. Securities Dept., Fed. Reserve Bank of N.Y. 1953–57; Financial Economist, Chase Manhattan Bank, N.Y.C. 1957–62, Dir. of Forward Planning 1965–69; Dir. Office of Financial Analysis, U.S. Treasury Dept. 1962–63, Deputy Under-Sec. for Monetary Affairs 1963–65, Under-Sec. Monetary Affairs 1969–74; Sr. Fellow, Woodrow Wilson School of Public and Int. Affairs, Princeton Univ. 1974–75; Pres. N.Y. Fed. Reserve Bank 1975–79; Chair.

Bd. of Govs., Fed. Reserve System 1979-87; Chair. James D. Wolfensohn Co. 1988-; Freiderick H. Schultz Prof. of Inst. Econ. Policy, Princeton Univ. 1988-; Consultant IBRD on Debts; Dir. (non-exec.) ICI 1988-; Hon. LL.D. (Adelphi Univ., Notre Dame Univ.) 1980, (Farleigh Dickinson Univ.) 1981, (Princeton Univ., Univ. of N.H.) 1982, (New York Univ., Lamar Univ., Dartmouth Coll.) 1983; Admin. Fellowship (Harvard), Rotary Foundation Fellow (L.S.E.), Arthur S. Flemming Award (Fed. Govt.), U.S. Treasury Dept. Exceptional Service Award, Alexander Hamilton Award, Fred Hirsch Memorial Lecture 1978, Public Service Award (Tax Foundation) 1981, Courage Award 1989. *Address:* 153 East 79th Street, New York, N.Y. 10021, U.S.A.

VOLKENSTEIN, Mikhail Vladimirovich; Soviet physicist; b. 23 Oct. 1912, St. Petersburg (now Leningrad); s. of Vladimir Mikhailovich Volkenshtein and Maria Mikhailovna Volkenshtein; m. Stella Iosifovna Alenikova 1947; one s. one d.; ed. Moscow Univ.; specialist in molecular physics, polymers, biophysics and spectroscopy; Research Assoc. Karpov Physico-Chemical Inst. 1933-41, Optical Inst. 1942-48; Prof. Leningrad Univ. 1945-53, 1962-67; Prof. Inst. of High Molecular Compounds, Acad. of Sciences 1948-67, Inst. of Molecular Biology 1967-; Corresp. mem. U.S.S.R. Acad. of Sciences 1966-; State Prize 1950. *Publications:* Vibrations of Molecules 1949 (2nd edn. 1974), Molecular Optics 1951, Structure of Molecules 1955, Configurational Statistics of Polymeric Chains 1958 (English edn. 1963), Molecules and Life 1965 (English edns. 1970, 1974), Enzyme Physics 1967 (English edn. 1970), Molecular Biophysics 1975 (English edn. 1976), General Biophysics 1978, Biophysics 1981, Entropy and Information 1986. *Leisure interests:* painting, literature. *Address:* c/o Institute of Molecular Biology, U.S.S.R. Academy of Sciences, Ul. Vavilova 32, Moscow, U.S.S.R.

VOLODIN, Boris Mikhailovich, CAND.ECON.SC.; Soviet politician; b. 1931; Pres. of collective farm, Stavropol Dist. 1953-68; mem. CPSU 1955-; agric. man. of Karachevo-Cherkessky collective farm dist. exec. cttee. 1968-71; Dir. of experimental farm in Stavropol dist. and Dir. of Agric. Inst. 1971-74; First Sec. of Predgorny Regional Cttee. of CPSU (Stavropol) 1974-75; Head of Section of Stavropol Dist. Cttee. of CPSU 1975-82; Sec. of Stavropol Dist. Cttee. 1982-84; Pres. of Rostov-on-Don Dist Cttee. 1984-86, First Sec. 1986-; mem. of U.S.S.R. Cen. Cttee. 1986-; Hero of Socialist Labour 1966. *Address:* Communist Party of Soviet Union District Committee, Rostov-on-Don, U.S.S.R.

VOLONTIR, Mikhail Yermolaevich; Soviet actor; b. 1934; ed. Actors' Training School; actor with Alecsandri Beltski Music and Drama Theatre 1957-; recent work in TV and films; U.S.S.R. People's Artist 1984. *Roles include:* Ion (Caragiale's Attack), The Old Man (Gorky's Old Man), Despot Vode (V. Alecsandri), Vasil', (Dudarev's Twilight). *Films include:* Dmitri Kantemir (U.S.S.R. State Prize 1976), This Sweet Word Freedom, Special Attention (R.S.F.S.R. Bros. Vasiliev State Prize 1980), From the Bug to the Vistula (TV film The Gypsies), The Attack, Twilight.

VOLPE, John Anthony; American engineer and politician; b. 8 Dec. 1908, Wakefield, Mass.; s. of Vito and Filomena Volpe; m. Jennie Benedetto 1934; one s. one d.; ed. Wentworth Inst., Boston, Mass.; Pres., John A. Volpe Construction Co. 1933-69; Comm. of Public Works, Mass. 1953-56; Fed. Highway Admin. 1956-57; Gov. of Mass. 1960-62, 1964-69; U.S. Sec. of Transportation 1969-73; Amb. to Italy 1973-77; mem. President's Urban Affairs Council 1969; Past Chair. Nat. Govs. Conf.; Republican; Grand Officer, Order of Merit (Italy) 1957, Kt. of Malta 1960. *Leisure interests:* golf, family activities. *Address:* c/o Department of State, 2201 C Street, N.W., Washington, D.C. 20520, U.S.A.

VOLPIN, Aleksandr Sergeyevich (Esenin-); Russian mathematician, philosopher, poet, dissident and mentor of Human Rights Movt.; b. 1924, Leningrad; s. of poet Sergey Esenin (1895-1925) and N. D. Volpina; m. 1st V. B. Volpina; m. 2nd I. G. Kristi; studied at Faculty of Mathematics, Moscow Univ. 1941-46; arrested for poetry and committed to mental asylum 1949; forced labour camp 1950; amnestied 1953; wrote numerous articles on logic and mathematics and translated extensively; at U.S.S.R. Acad. of Sciences Inst. of Scientific and Tech. Information 1961-72; dissident activity 1959-; emigrated to Israel 1972. *Publications include:* A Free Philosophical Treatise 1959, A Leaf of Spring 1959, 1961, Open Letter to Solzhenitsyn 1970, Report on Committee on Rights of Man 1971.

VOLSKY, Arkadiy Ivanovich; Soviet official and economic adviser; b. 15 May 1932; Sec., Party Cttee. of Likhachev Automobile Plant, Moscow 1966-70; mem. of editorial staff of Agitator 1972-; Deputy Head, Dept. of Machine Bldg., Cen. Cttee. CPSU 1978-81; First Deputy Head of Dept. of Machine Bldg., Cen. Cttee. CPSU 1981-83, Head 1985-; Aide to Gen. Sec., Cen. Cttee. CPSU 1983-85; Deputy to R.S.F.S.R. Supreme Soviet 1983-85; Deputy to Council of Nationalities 1984-; mem. Comm. on Industry 1984-; mem. Cen. Cttee. CPSU 1986-. *Address:* The Kremlin, Moscow, U.S.S.R.

VOLSKY, Yuriy Ivanovich; Soviet diplomat; b. 1922; mem. diplomatic service 1959-; Counsellor at Embassy, U.S.A. 1959-62; Deputy Minister of Foreign Affairs for R.S.F.S.R. 1962-66; Amb. to Argentina 1966-72, to Mexico 1976-86, and fmrly. to Jamaica. *Address:* c/o Ministry of Foreign Affairs, Smolenskaya-Sennaya pl. 32-34, Moscow, U.S.S.R.

VON BAUDISSIN, Wolf, Graf; German army officer (retd.) and university professor; b. 8 May 1907, Trier; s. of Theodor, Graf von Baudissin, and

Lily von Borcke; m. Dagmar, Burggrafin zu Dohna-Schlodien 1947; ed. Marienwerder, Univ. of Berlin; General staff officer, German Armed Forces 1926-45; artistic pottery 1947-51; with Dienststelle Blank, becoming Chief of Sub-Dept. 1951-58; Brigade Commdr., Göttingen 1958-61; Rep., Chief of Gen. Staff, NATO HQ, Fontainbleau 1961-63; Commdr. NATO Defence Coll., Paris 1963-65; Head, Office of Planning, SHAPE, Paris and Mons 1965-67; lecturer Univ. of Hamburg 1968, then Prof. of Social Sciences; Dir. Inst. of Peace Research and Security Policy, Univ. of Hamburg 1971-84; lecturer, Hochschule der Bundeswehr, Hamburg; Frhr. v. Stein Medail, Theodor-Heuss-Preis, Bundesverdienstkreuz. *Publications:* Soldat für den Frieden-Entwürfe für eine zeitgemässe Bundeswehr 1970, Nie wieder Sieg! Programmatische Schriften 1951-1981 1982. *Leisure interest:* modern arts. *Address:* Hemmingstedter Weg 51, 2000 Hamburg 52, Federal Republic of Germany. *Telephone:* (040) 82 52 82.

VON BECKH, Harald J., M.D.; Argentine medical scientist; b. 17 Nov. 1917, Vienna, Austria; s. of Johannes A. and Elisabeth von Beckh (née Flach-Hillé); ed. Theresianum High School, Vienna and Vienna Univ.; career devoted to aviation and later to space medicine, and in particular to weightlessness and its effects on living organisms; Lecturer Aeromedical Acad. Berlin 1941, Buenos Aires Nat. Inst. of Aviation Medicine 1947; joined staff of U.S.Air Force Aeromedical Field Laboratory, Holloman Air Force Base, N.M. 1956, Scientific Dir. Oct. 1958-64; Chief Scientist 1964-70; Dir. of Research Aerospace Medical Research Dept., Naval Air Devt. Center 1970-; Prof. of Human Physiology, New Mexico State Univ. 1959-70; mem. Armed Forces/Nat. Research Council Cttee. on Bio-Astronautics 1958-61; mem. Space Medicine Cttee. of Int. Astronautical Fed. 1961-, Int. Acad. of Astronautics; hon. mem. German Rocket Soc., Medical Assscn. of Armed Forces of Argentina, Portuguese Centre of Astronautical Studies, Spanish Soc. of Aerospace Medicine, Austrian Astronautical Soc.; Fellow, British Interplanetary Soc., Aerospace Medical Assscn. (Pres. Space Medicine Branch 1978-79); Assoc. Fellow, A.I.A.A.; Sr. member. American Rocket Soc. (Pres. Holloman Section 1959-61); mem. Int. Acad. of Aviation Medicine; Arnold D. Tuttle Award of the Aerospace Medical Assscn. 1972, Melbourne W. Boynton Award of the American Astronautical Soc. 1972, Hermann Oberth Honor Ring, Hermann Oberth Soc. 1975, Hubertus Strughold Award of Aerospace Medical Assscn. 1976, Jeffries Medical Research Award of A.I.A.A. 1977, Fellow Award, NADC 1988. *Publications:* Fisiología del Vuelo 1955, Basic Principles of Aerospace Medicine 1960; numerous papers in Journal of Aviation Medicine and Journal of the British Interplanetary Society and other aeronautical and aeromedical journals in U.S.A., Great Britain, Germany, Argentina and Spain. *Leisure interests:* French and Spanish literature, flying. *Address:* P.O. Box 421, Warminster, Pa. 18974, U.S.A. *Telephone:* (215) 441-2741 (Office): (215) 672-4455 (Home).

VON BÜLOW, Andreas, DR.JUR.; German politician and lawyer; b. 17 July 1937, Dresden; s. of Georg-Ulrich and Susanne (née Haym) von Bülow; m. Anna Barbara Duden 1961; two s. two d.; law studies in Heidelberg, Berlin and Munich, studied in France and U.S.A.; entered higher admin. service of State of Baden-Württemberg 1966, on staff of Rural Dist. Offices of Heidelberg and Balingen, Pres. Admin. Dist. of Süd-Württemberg Hohenzollern at Tübingen; mem. Bundestag (Parl.) 1969-; Parl. State Sec. Fed. Ministry of Defence 1976-80; Fed. Minister for Research and Tech. 1980-82; mem. Social Democratic Party 1960-, Public Services and Transport Workers' Union. *Publications:* Die Überwachung der Erdgasindustrie durch die Federal Power Commission als Beispiel der Funktionen der unabhängigen wirtschaftskommissionen der amerikanischen Bundesverwaltung 1967 (dissertation), Gedanken zur weiterentwicklung der Verteidigungsstrategien in west und ost 1984, Alpträume west gegen Alpträume Ost—ein Beitrag zur Bedrohungsanalyse 1984, Skizzen einer Bundeswehrstruktur der 90er Jahre 1985, Die eingebildete Unterlegenheit—das Kräfteverhältnis west-ost, wie es wirklich ist 1985. *Leisure interests:* music, geology, history, swimming, hiking, skiing. *Address:* Hesselbergstrasse 15, 7460 Balingen 14, Federal Republic of Germany.

VON DER DUNK, Hermann Walther; Netherlands professor of history; b. 9 Oct. 1928, Bonn, Germany; s. of Heinrich M. von der Dunk and Ilse Löb; m. Goverdina S. Stekhoven 1958; two s. one d.; ed. Univ. of Utrecht and Inst. für Europäische Geschichte, Mainz; school teacher, Bilthoven 1961-63; Asst. Prof. Dept. of History, Univ. of Utrecht 1963-67, Prof. of Contemporary History and Head of Dept. 1967-88, Prof. and Head, Dept. of Cultural History 1988-; mem. Royal Netherlands Acad. *Publications:* Kleio heeft 1000 ogen (essays) 1974, Conservatisme 1976, De organisatie van het verleden 1982; articles and contribs. to textbooks, journals and newspapers. *Leisure interests:* music (plays piano), drawing and painting, writing. *Address:* Lucas Bolwerk 5, 3512 EG Utrecht (Office); Nicolailaan 20, 7 23 HS Bilthoven, Netherlands (Home). *Telephone:* 30/392451 (Office); 30/785401 (Home).

VON DOHNÁNYI, Christoph; German musician; b. 8 Sept. 1929, Berlin; s. of Johann-Georg and Christine (née Bonhoeffer) von Dohnányi; brother of Klaus von Dohnányi (q.v.); m. 1st Renate Zillessen, one s. one d.; m. 2nd Anja Silja (q.v.) 1979, one s. two d.; abandoned legal training to study music 1948; studied in U.S.A. under grandfather, Ernst von Dohnányi 1951; chorus master and leader under Georg Solti (q.v.), Frankfurt 1952; Gen. Music Dir. Lübeck 1957-63, Kassel 1963-66, conductor of Cologne

Broadcasting Symphony Orchestra 1964–68, Gen. Music Dir. and Opera Dir., Frankfurt 1968–77, Dir. and Gen. Music Dir., Hamburg State Opera 1977–84; Music Dir. Desig. Cleveland Orchestra 1982–84, Music Dir. 1984–; Guest Conductor at Munich Festivals, Vienna Festivals, Salzburg Festivals, Metropolitan Opera (New York), San Francisco Opera, Vienna, London, Berlin, Chicago; recipient Richard Strauss Prize, Bartok Prize, and numerous other awards. *Address:* The Cleveland Orchestra, Severance Hall, Cleveland, Ohio 44106, U.S.A. *Telephone:* 2317300.

VON DOHNÁNYI, Klaus, DR.JUR.; German politician; b. 23 June 1928, Hamburg; s. of Johann-Georg and Christine (née Bonhoeffer) von Dohnányi; brother of Christoph von Dohnányi (q.v.); m. 2nd Christa Gross 1966; two s. one d.; ed. Munich, Columbia, Stanford and Yale Univs.; frmly. with Ford Motor Co., Detroit, Mich. and Cologne; Dir. Planning Div. Ford-Werke, Cologne 1956-60; Dir. Inst. für Marktforschung und Unternehmensberatung, Munich 1960-67; Sec. of State, Fed. Ministry of Economy 1968-69; mem. Bundestag 1969-81; Parl. Sec. of State, Ministry of Educ. and Science 1969-72; Minister of Educ. and Science 1972-74; Minister of State and Parl. Sec. of State, Fed. Foreign Office 1976-81, First Burgomaster and Pres. Senate, Hamburg 1981-88; Social Democrat. *Address:* Leinpfad 22, 2 Hamburg 60, Federal Republic of Germany.

VON HIRSCHBERG, C. F. G.; South African diplomatist; b. 13 Jan. 1926, Jamestown; two s. one d.; ed. Univ. of Cape Town; entered foreign service 1948; served in London 1952-57, Vienna 1957-62; served in Dept. of Foreign Affairs, Pretoria 1962-67, Head UN and Int. Orgs. Div 1966-67; mem. S.A. del. to gen. confs. of IAEA 1957-61, alt. Gov. 1957-62; Del. to UN Gen. Ass. 1967-74; Minister to Perm. Mission to UN 1968-70; Amb. and Perm. Rep. to UN 1970-74; Consul-Gen., Tokyo 1975-78; Deputy Sec. Dept. of Foreign Affairs, Pretoria 1979-81, Deputy Dir.-Gen. 1981-. *Leisure interests:* golf, boating. *Address:* c/o Department of Foreign Affairs, Union Buildings, Pretoria, South Africa. *Telephone:* 012-28-6912.

VON KLITZING, Klaus; German physicist; b. 28 June 1943, Schroda; s. of Bogislav von Klitzing and Anny (née Ulbrich) von Klitzing; m. Renate Falkenberg 1971; two s. one d.; ed. Technische Universität, Brunswick, Universität Würzburg; Prof., Technische Universität, Munich 1980-84; Dir. Max-Planck Inst. for Solid State Research, Stuttgart 1985-; awarded Schottky Prize, Hewlett-Packard Prize, Nobel Prize for Physics 1985. *Address:* Max-Planck Institut für Festkörperforschung, Heisenbergstr. 1, Postfach 800665, 7000 Stuttgart 80, Federal Republic of Germany. *Telephone:* 6860-1.

VON OTTER, Anne Sofie; Swedish singer; b. 9 May 1955, Stockholm; ed. Conservatorium, Stockholm, studied interpretation with Erik Werba (Vienna) and Geoffrey Parsons (London) and vocal studies since 1981 with Vera Rozsa; mem. Basel Opera, Switzerland 1982-85; début France at Opéra de Marseille (Nozze di Figaro-Cherubino) and Aix-en-Provence Festival (La Finta Giardiniera) 1984, Rome, Accad. di Santa Cecilia 1984, Geneva (Così fan tutte-Dorabella) 1985, Berlin (Così fan tutte) 1985, U.S.A. in Chicago (Mozart's C minor Mass) and Philadelphia (Bach's B minor Mass) 1985, London at Royal Opera, Covent Garden (Nozze di Figaro) 1985, Lyon (La Finta Giardiniera) 1986, La Scala, Milan (Alceste) 1987, Munich (Le Nozze di Figaro) 1987, Stockholm (Der Rosenkavalier) 1988, The Metropolitan Opera, New York (Le Nozze di Figaro) 1988; numerous recordings for Philips, EMI and Decca; has given recitals in Lyon, Brussels, Geneva, Stockholm and London. *Address:* c/o Lies Askonas Ltd., 186 Drury Lane, London, WC2B 5RY, England.

VON SCHLABRENDORFF, Fabian Gotthard Herbert, M.A., D.IUR.; German lawyer; b. 23 Dec. 1944, Berlin; s. of Fabian von Schlabrendorff and Luitarde (née von Bismarck) von Schlabrendorff; m. Maria de la Cruz Caballero Palamero 1977; two c.; ed. Univs. of Tubingen, Berlin, Geneva, Frankfurt and Chicago; service in Bundeswehr 1964-68; Research coordinator, Inst. of Int. and Foreign Trade and Business Law, Frankfurt 1975-82; lawyer with Pünder, Volhard and Weber, Frankfurt 1982, partner 1984; CEPES award 1987. *Publications:* (co-author) Mining Ventures in Developing Countries, (parts 1 and 2) 1979/81, The Legal Structure of Transnational Forest-Based Investments in Developing Countries 1987, (co-author) European Banking and Securities Law 1988. *Leisure interests:* classical music, literature. *Address:* Pünder, Volhard und Weber, Mainzer Landstrasse 46, 6000 Frankfurt am Main, Federal Republic of Germany. *Telephone:* 069-719901.

VON STADE, Frederica; American mezzo-soprano; b. 1 June 1945, Somerville, N.J.; m. Peter Elkus 1973; two d.; ed. Mannes Coll. of Music, New York; opera début with Metropolitan Opera, New York (in Die Zauberflöte) 1970; has also sung Paris Opera, San Francisco Opera, Salzburg Festival, Covent Garden, London, Spoleto Festival, Boston Opera Co., Santa Fe Opera, Houston Grand Opera, La Scala, Milan; recital and concert artist; recordings include Frederica von Stade Sings Mozart and Rossini Opera Arias, French Opera Arias. *Address:* c/o Columbia Artists Management, 165 West 57th Street, New York, N.Y. 10019, U.S.A.

VON WILPERT, Gero, PH.D., F.A.H.A.; Australian professor of German; b. 13 March 1933, Dorpat, Estonia; s. of Arno von Wilpert and Gerda Baumann; m. Margrit Laskowski 1953; three s.; ed. Univs. of Heidelberg and N.S.W.; publrs. reader and literary dir. Stuttgart 1957-72; Sr. Lecturer in German, Univ. of N.S.W. 1973-78, Assoc. Prof. 1978-81; McCaughey

Prof. of German, Univ. of Sydney 1982-. *Publications include:* Sachwörterbuch der Literatur 1955, Deutsche Literatur in Bildern 1957, Schiller-Chronik 1958, Deutsches Dichterlexicon 1963, Der verlorene Schatten 1978. *Leisure interests:* 18th century French art and antiques. *Address:* Werrington House, Werrington, N.S.W. 2760, Australia. *Telephone:* 6922380 (Office); 6231026 (Home).

VONGSAY, Kithong, DR.RER.POL.; Laotian diplomatist; b. 17 May 1937, Vientiane; m.; three c.; ed. Toulouse Univ.; Counsellor, Paris 1970-73; Deputy Minister for Foreign Affairs of Prov. Govt. 1975; Head Press and Information Dept., Ministry of Foreign Affairs 1975-78; Amb. to India, Burma, Sri Lanka and Nepal 1978-83; Perm. Rep. to UN, New York 1983-88.

VONNEGUT, Kurt, Jr.; American author; b. 11 Nov. 1922, Indianapolis; s. of Kurt Vonnegut and Edith Lieber; m. 1st Jane Marie Cox 1945 (deceased), one s. two d.; m. 2nd Jill Krementz 1979; ed. Cornell Univ., Carnegie Inst. of Tech. and Univ. of Chicago; served with U.S. Army as Infantry Combat Scout, World War II; P.O.W., Dresden 1945; police reporter, Chicago City News Bureau 1945-47; P.R.O., G.E.C. Schenectady 1947-50; contrib. Saturday Evening Post, Collier's, Galaxy, etc. *Publications:* novels: Player Piano 1952, The Sirens of Titan 1959, Mother Night 1961, Cat's Cradle 1963, God Bless you, Mr. Rosewater 1965, Slaughterhouse-Five 1969, Between Time and Timbuktu 1972, Breakfast of Champions 1973, Wampeters, Foma and Granfalloons 1974, Slapstick 1976, Jail Bird 1979, Palm Sunday 1981, Dead-Eye Dick 1982, Galápagos 1985, Bluebeard 1987; play: Happy Birthday, Wanda June 1971; short stories: Welcome to the Monkey House 1968. *Address:* c/o Donald C. Farber Tanner, Gilbert, Propp & Sterner, 99 Park Avenue, 25th Floor, New York, N.Y. 10016, U.S.A.

VONSOVSKIY, Sergey Vasiliyevich; Soviet physicist; b. 2 Sept. 1910, Tashkent; s. of Vasiliy Semenovich Vonsovskiy and Sophia I. Vonsovskiy; m. A. Shubina Lubov 1939 (died 1982); one s. two d.; ed. Leningrad State Univ.; Engineer, Chief Engineer, Ural Physical-Tech. Inst. 1932-39; Junior Scientific Worker, Sr. Scientific Worker, Inst. for Investigation of Metals, for Metallophysics and Metallurgy, Urals Branch of U.S.S.R. Acad. of Sciences 1939-47; Chief Dept., Deputy Dir. Inst. of Physics of Metals, Urals Branch of U.S.S.R. Acad. of Sciences 1947-; Corresp. mem. U.S.S.R. Acad. of Sciences 1953-66, mem. 1966-, mem. Presidium 1971-; fmr. Chair. Presidium Urals Scientific Centre, Hon. Chair. 1986-; Foreign mem. Acad. of Science of G.D.R. 1971-, Poland 1977-; Hero of Socialist Labour 1969, Order of Lenin (thrice) and other decorations. *Leisure interests:* literature, music, painting. *Address:* Institute of Metal Physics, Urals Scientific Centre of the U.S.S.R., Academy of Sciences, Ulitsa S. Kovalevskoi 18, 620219 GSP-170 Sverdlovsk, U.S.S.R.

VORA, Motilal; Indian politician; b. 29 Dec. 1928, Nagor, Rajasthan; fmr. journalist; elected Councillor, Durg Municipality 1968, Congress Party mem. Madhya Pradesh Vidhan Sabha 1972; Minister of State for Educ. and Minister for Local Govt. 1981-82; Minister of Transport, Science and Tech. 1982-83, of Higher Educ. 1983-84, of Health and Family Welfare and Civil Aviation 1988-89; Pres. Madhya Pradesh Congress (I) Cttee. 1984-85; elected Leader Congress (I) Legis. Party 1985; Chief Minister, Madhya Pradesh 1985-88, Jan. 1989-. *Address:* Raj Bhawan, Bhopal 462003, India.

VOROBYOV, Ivan Alekseyevich; Soviet military official; b. 26 Aug. 1921, Gorbachevo, Tula Dist.; entered Soviet army 1940; ed. Tambov Mil. Aviation School for Pilots and Red Banner Air Force Acad.; mem. CPSU 1944-; flew about 400 missions in World War II; command posts -1958; instructor 1958-; Order of Lenin, Order of Red Banner (twice), Order of Patriotic War (twice), Hero of Soviet Union (twice), Order of Alexander Nevsky, Order of Red Star (twice), various medals. *Address:* c/o Ministry of Defence, Moscow, U.S.S.R.

VORONIN, Lev Alekseyevich; Soviet politician; b. 22 Feb. 1928, Perm; ed. Ural Polytechnic Inst., Sverdlovsk; mine foreman, then political work in machine-bldg. plant, Sverdlovsk 1949-59; mem. CPSU 1953-; chief engineer at armaments plant in Kamensk-Uralsk and Sverdlovsk 1959-63; Head of Admin., Cen. Ural Sovnarkhoz 1963-65; Dir. eng. plant, Krasnogorsk, Moscow 1965-68; Head of Planning and Production Admin., U.S.S.R. Ministry of Defence Industry 1968-72; Deputy Minister of U.S.S.R. Defence Industry 1979-80; First Deputy Chair. of U.S.S.R. State Planning Cttee. (Gosplan) 1980-85; Deputy to Council of Nationalities U.S.S.R. Supreme Soviet; mem. Cen. Cttee. CPSU 1981-; mem. Comm. for Power 1982-85; Chair. of U.S.S.R. State Comm. for Material and Technical Supply (Gossnab); Vice-Chair. Council of Ministers 1985-; Lenin Prize, Order of Lenin, Order of Red Banner, Badge of Honour, other medals. *Address:* The Kremlin, Moscow, U.S.S.R.

VORONKOV, Mikhail Grigorevich; DR. OF CHEM. SC.; Soviet chemical scientist; b. 6 Dec 1921, Orel; s. of Grigorii Vasilievich and Raisa Mikhailovna Voronkova; m. Lilia Iliinichna Makhnina 1943; one s. one d.; ed. Sverdlovsk Univ.; Sr. Scientist, Chemical Dept., Leningrad Univ. 1944-54; Head of Lab., Inst. of Chem. of Silicates, U.S.S.R. Acad. of Sciences 1954-61; Head of Lab. of Inst. of Organic Synthesis, Latvian Acad. of Sciences 1961-70; Dir. of Inst. of Organic Chemistry, Siberian br. of

U.S.S.R. Acad. of Sciences, Irkutsk 1970-; corresp. mem. of Latvian Acad. of Sciences 1966-, U.S.S.R. Acad. of Sciences 1970-, Braunschweig Scientific Soc., Fed. Repub. of Germany 1976. *Leisure interests:* numismatics, humour in chemistry. *Address:* U.S.S.R. Academy of Sciences, Leninsky Pr. 14, Moscow V-71, U.S.S.R.

VORONOV, Avenir Arkadyevich, D.SC.; Soviet automation specialist; b. 28 Nov. 1910, Lomonosov, St. Petersburg (now Leningrad) Region; s. of Arkadiy Vasilyevich Voronov and Vera Dmitriyevna Bystrova; m. Nina Petrovna Aleksandrova 1938; one s. one d.; ed. Leningrad Polytechnic Inst.; Engineer, Gorky electrical power plant 1938-39; army service 1939-46; mem. CPSU 1943-; Lecturer Moscow Bauman Higher School 1946-48; Research Assoc., Inst. of Automation and Telemechanics, U.S.S.R. Acad. of Sciences 1948-55; lecturer, Moscow Power Inst. 1948-55; Head of Lab., Vice-Dir. Inst. of Electromechanics 1955-64, Inst. of Control Problems 1964-70; lecturer, Leningrad Polytech. Inst. 1955-64, Moscow Inst. of Radioeng., Electronics and Automation 1964-70, 1982-; Deputy Chair. Presidium, Far Eastern Scientific Centre, U.S.S.R. Acad. of Sciences 1971-; Dir. Inst. of Automation and Control Processes 1971-; Academician, U.S.S.R. Acad. of Sciences 1970-; Head of Dept. Inst. of System Studies, U.S.S.R. Acad. of Sciences, Moscow. *Publications:* (in Russian) The Elements of Automatic Regulation Theory 1950, Digital Analogues for Automatic Control Systems 1960, Fundamentals of Automatic Control Theory Part I 1965, Part II 1966, Part III 1970, Operations Research and Control 1970, Stability, Controlability, Observability 1979, Introduction to Complex System Dynamics 1985, Basic Principles of Automatic Control Theory: Special and Nonlinear Systems 1985, Management and Control in Large Systems (ed.) 1986. *Address:* VNIISI, 117312 prospect 60th Anniversary of October, 9, Moscow, U.S.S.R. *Telephone:* 135-40-22.

VORONTSOV, Yuliy Mikhailovich; Soviet diplomatist; b. 1929; ed. Moscow Inst. of Int. Relations; various posts in Ministry of Foreign Affairs 1952-54; mem. CPSU 1956-; U.S.S.R. rep. at UN 1954-58, 1963-65; Embassy Counsellor 1966-70, Counsellor-Envoy, Washington Embassy 1970-77; Amb. to India 1977-83, to France 1983-86, to Afghanistan 1988-; First Deputy Minister of Foreign Affairs 1986-88. *Address:* Embassy of the U.S.S.R., Dar-ul-Aman Wat, Kabul, Afghanistan.

VOROPAYEV, Mikhail Gavrilovich; Soviet politician; b. 1919; ed. Rostov-on-Don Inst. of Railway Engineering; mem. CPSU 1945; Sec. of Young Communist League (YCL) cttee. at Locomotive depot, Sec. of YCL city cttee. and raion cttee., Chelyabinsk; Second Sec. Chelyabinsk region cttee. CPSU 1944-49, 1960-63, First Sec. 1970-; Engineer at metallurgical enterprises in Chelyabinsk, Sec. of Chelyabinsk region cttee. CPSU 1949-60; First Sec. Chelyabinsk City Cttee.; Deputy Chair. CPSU Cen. Cttee. for Party Control 1984-; Head Soviet Del. Soviet-U.S. Arms Talks, Geneva 1987-; Deputy to Supreme Soviet U.S.S.R. 1966-; mem. Cen. Cttee. CPSU 1971-; various decorations. *Address:* Chelyabinsk Region Committee of the CPSU, Chelyabinsk, U.S.S.R.

VOROTNIKOV, Vitaliy Ivanovich; Soviet official and diplomat; b. 1926; ed. Kuibyshev Aviation Inst.; technologist, later sec. party cttee. and chief controller of a plant 1942-44, 1947-60; Sec. Kuibyshev Dist. Cttee. 1961-67; Chair. Kuibyshev Exec. Cttee. of Dist. Soviet of Workers' Deputies 1967-71; Deputy to U.S.S.R. Supreme Soviet 1970-; First Sec. Voronezh Dist. Cttee. of CPSU 1971-75; mem. Cen. Cttee. of CPSU 1971-; First Deputy Chair. Council of Ministers of R.S.F.S.R. 1975-76; Chair. U.S.S.R.-Angola Friendship Soc. 1976-79; Amb. to Cuba 1980-82; Cand. mem. Politburo June 1983, mem. Dec. 1983-; Chair. Council of Ministers of R.S.F.S.R. 1983-88; Pres. of Supreme Soviet of R.S.F.S.R. 1988-; a Deputy Chair. Presidium of the Supreme Soviet of the U.S.S.R. 1988-; elected to Congress of People's Deputies of the U.S.S.R. 1989; Hero of Socialist Labour 1986. *Address:* R.S.F.S.R. Council of Ministers, 3 Delegatskaya ulitsa, Moscow, U.S.S.R.

VOSKANYAN, Grant Mushegovich; Soviet party official and politician; b. 1924, Armenia; Red Army 1943-46; work for Kirovakan regional cttee. 1946-52; Dir. of Kirovakan Komsomol and Abelyan Theatre 1952-54; head of a boarding school 1954-57; Sec., First Sec. of Kirovakan City Cttee. of CPSU 1959-67; post in Cen. Cttee. of CPSU 1967-73; head of section of Cen. Cttee. of Armenian CP 1973-75; Sec. of Cen. Cttee. of Armenian CP 1975-85; Chair. Presidium U.S.S.R. Supreme Soviet 1985-, Deputy Pres. 1986-; Deputy to Supreme Soviet. *Address:* Central Committee of Armenian Communist Party, Yerevan, Armenia, U.S.S.R.

VOSS, August Eduardovich; Soviet politician; b. 30 Oct. 1916, Saltykovo, Omsk Region; ed. Teacher-Training Inst., CPSU Higher Party School and CPSU Acad. of Social Sciences; Soviet Army service 1940-45; Party Official in Latvia 1945-49; Head of Dept. of Science and Culture, Cen. Cttee. CP of Latvia 1953-54; Party Official at Cen. Cttee., CP of Latvia 1954-60; Sec. Cen. Cttee., CP of Latvia 1960-66, First Sec. 1966-84; Chair. Soviet of Nationalities, U.S.S.R. Supreme Soviet April 1984-; Deputy to U.S.S.R. Supreme Soviet 1966-; Chair. Comm. for Public Educ., Science and Culture, Soviet of Union, and Latvian Supreme Soviet; mem. CPSU Cen. Cttee. 1971-, Order of Lenin and other decorations. *Address:* The Kremlin, Moscow, U.S.S.R.

VOUEL, Raymond; Luxembourg politician and international official; b. 1923; m.; three c.; began career as a journalist on Tageblatt socialist daily newspaper; Admin. Dir. Esch Hospital 1954-64; Town Councillor, Esch 1963, Chair. Buildings Cttee.; mem. Chamber of Deputies 1964-76; State Sec. for Public Health, for Employment, for Social Security and for the Mining Industry 1964-69; Chair. Parl. Socialist Group 1970-74; Gen. Sec. Parti Ouvrier Socialiste Luxembourgeois (Socialist Party) 1970; Deputy Prime Minister, Minister for Finance and Land Devt. 1974-76; mem. Comm. of European Communities with responsibility for Competition, Personnel and Admin. 1976, for Competition Policy Jan. 1977-80. *Address:* c/o Ministry of Foreign Affairs, Luxembourg.

VOYENUSHKIN, S. F.; Soviet politician; b. 26 Nov. 1929; m.; one s. one d.; ed. Karelo Finnish State Univ.; fmr. head of several geological prospecting groups; work in construction materials industry 1958-; fmr. Head of Directorates of construction materials industry, Karelian and North-West Nat. Econ. Councils; various posts at U.S.S.R. Ministry of Construction Materials Industry 1965-70; First Deputy Minister, R.S.F.S.R. 1975; Minister of Construction Materials Industry, R.S.F.S.R. 1979; Deputy, R.S.F.S.R. Supreme Soviet; mem. CPSU 1951-; Minister of Construction Materials Industry 1985-; Order of Red Banner of Labour, Badge of Honour, medals etc. *Address:* Ministry of Construction Materials Industry, Moscow, U.S.S.R.

VOZNESENSKY, Andrey Andreyevich; Soviet poet; b. 12 May 1933, Moscow; s. of Andrey N. and Antonina S. Voznesensky; m. Zoya Boguslavskaya 1965; one s.; ed. Moscow Architectural Inst.; mem. Union of Soviet Writers, mem. Bd. 1967-; Hon. mem. American Acad. of Arts and Letters 1972, Bayerischen Kunst Akad., French Acad. Merime; Int. Award for Distinguished Achievement in Poetry 1978, State Prize 1978, Order of the Red Banner of Labour. *Publications:* poems: The Masters 1959, Forty Lyrical Digressions from a Triangular Pear 1962, Longjumeau 1963, Oza 1964, Story Under Full Sail 1970, Ice-69 1970, Queen of Clubs 1974, The Eternal Flesh 1978, Andrey Polisadov 1980, Unaccountable 1981; collections: Parabola 1960, Mosaic 1960, Anti-Worlds 1964, Heart of Achilles 1966, Verses 1967, The Shadow of a Sound 1970, The Glance 1972, Let The Bird Free 1974, Violoncello Oak Leaf 1975, The Master of Stained Glass 1976, Temptation 1978, Metropol (poetry and prose, co-author with 22 others) 1979, Selected Poems 1979; *In English:* Selected Poems 1964, Anti-worlds 1966, Anti-worlds and the Fifth Ace 1967, Dogalypse 1972, Story under Full Sail 1974, Nostalgia for the Present 1978. *Address:* Kotelnicheskaya nab. 1/15, bl.W, Apt. 62, Moscow 109240, U.S.S.R. *Telephone:* 443-08-93.

VRAALSEN, Tom Eric, M.ECON.; Norwegian diplomatist; b. 26 Jan. 1936, Oslo; m.; Århus School of Econs. and Business Admin., Denmark; joined Norwegian Foreign Service 1960; various diplomatic positions, Beijing 1962-64, 1969-70, Cairo 1964-67, Manila 1970-71; in charge of Norwegian relations with Africa, Asia and Latin America, Political Dept., Ministry of Foreign Affairs 1971-73, in charge of UN and int. org. affairs 1973-75, Dir.-Gen. Political Dept. 1981-82; mem. Norwegian dels. to UN Gen. Ass. 1971-, to Governing Council, UNDP 1975-76; Deputy Perm. Rep. of Norway to the UN 1975-79, Perm. Rep. March 1982-. *Address:* Permanent Mission of Norway to the United Nations, 825 Third Avenue, 18th Floor, New York, N.Y. 10022, U.S.A.

VRANITZKY, Franz, D.COMM.; Austrian banker and politician; b. 4 Oct. 1937, Vienna; s. of Franz Vranitsky and Rosa Vernitsky; m. Christine Kristen; one s. one d.; ed. Vienna XVII High School, Coll. (now Univ.) of Commerce, Vienna; joined Siemens-Schuckert Gesellschaft m.b.H., Vienna 1961; Dept. of Nat. Econs., Austrian Nat. Bank 1961-69, seconded to the Office of the First Vice-Pres. 1969-70; Advisor on Econ. and Financial Policy to Minister of Finance 1970-76; Deputy-Chair. Bd. of Dirs. Creditanstalt-Bankverein 1976-81, Österreichische Länderbank 1981, Chair. Bd. of Dirs. 1981-84; Fed. Minister of Finance 1984-86; Fed. Chancellor June 1986-; Chair. Austrian Socialist Party May 1988-. *Address:* Federal Chancellery, Vienna, Austria.

VRATUŠA, Dr. Anton; Yugoslav diplomatist and politician; b. 21 Feb. 1915, Doljnja Slaveča; ed. Univ. of Ljubljana; Col. in Yugoslav People's Army 1941-45; various appointments in Ministry of Foreign Affairs and Fed. Exec. Council 1945-78; mem. Fed. Ass. 1965-67, 1982-86, Speaker Fed. Chamber 1982-83; mem. numerous dels. to UN; Pres. Yugoslav Nat. Comm. for UNESCO; Dir. Inst. for Social Sciences; Perm. Rep. to UN 1967-69; Prof. of Political Sciences, Belgrade Univ. 1969-, Ljubljana Univ. 1975-; Deputy Minister of Foreign Affairs 1969-71; Vice-Pres. Fed. Exec. Council 1971-78; Pres. Fed. Council for Socio-Political System 1973-78; mem. of Council SFR Yugoslavia 1986-; Pres. Exec. Council, S.R. of Slovenia 1978-80; mem. Presidency of Cen. Cttee. of League of Communists of Slovenia 1978-82; mem. Cen. Cttee. League of Communists of Yugoslavia 1982-86; Pres. Council, Int. Center for Public Enterprises in Developing Countries Oct. 1978-82; Hon. Pres. Nov. 1982-; mem. Bd. of UNITAR 1980-86; mem. Slovenian Acad. of Sciences and Arts 1986. *Publications:* numerous works on self-management system in Yugoslavia and international relations. *Address:* c/o ICPE, Titova 104, Ljubljana, Yugoslavia.

VREDELING, Henk; Netherlands politician; b. 20 Nov. 1924, Amersfoort; m. Jola Schouten 1948; three s. one d.; ed. Agricultural Univ., Wageningen; mem. Second Chamber of States-Gen. (Parl.) 1956-73; mem. European Parl. 1958-73; Socio-econ. Adviser to Agricultural Workers' Union 1950-73;

Minister of Defence 1973–76; Commr. for Employment and Social Affairs and for Tripartite Conf., Comm. of European Communities 1977–81; mem. Equal Opportunities Council 1981–85, Advisory Council on Peace and Security 1987–. *Address:* Rembrandtlaan 13A, 3712 A J Huis ter Heide, Netherlands. *Telephone:* 03404-31633.

VREDENBURGH, Dorothy McElroy (see Bush, Dorothy McElroy Vredenburgh).

VREEKEN, Johannes, M.D.; Netherlands professor of medicine; b. 7 Dec. 1929, Amsterdam; m. M. A. J. van Brink 1956; one s. one d.; ed. Univ. of Amsterdam; Head, blood-clotting lab., Central Lab. Blood Transfusion Service 1963; Prof. of Medicine, Univ. of Amsterdam 1969–. *Publications:* articles in professional journals. *Leisure interests:* long distance skating. *Address:* Academic Medical Center, Meibergdreef 9, 1105 AZ Amsterdam, Netherlands. *Telephone:* 020-5669111.

VREVEN, Alfred, LL.M.; Belgian lawyer and politician; b. 24 March 1937, Sint-Truiden; s. of Raoul Vreven; m. Betty Bollaerts; two s. one d.; ed. Free Univ. of Brussels; notary, Sint-Truiden 1962; mem. House of Reps. 1970–; mem. Exec. Party for Liberty and Progress (PVV) 1980; Minister of Nat. Defence 1981–85. *Address:* Terbiestwegg 95, 3800 Sint-Truiden, Belgium (Home). *Telephone:* 011/68.24.33 (Home).

VRHOVEC, Josip; Yugoslav (Croatian) politician; b. 1926, Zagreb, Croatia; ed. Faculty of Econs., Inst. of Social Services, Zagreb; with Nat. Liberation Movt. 1941; mem. of League of Communist Youth 1941; with Nat. Liberation Army of Yugoslavia 1943, Reserve Officer in Yugoslav Army; mem. League of Communists 1943–; fmr. ed., foreign affairs Corresp., Ed.-in-Chief of daily newspaper 'Vjesnik' and weekly 'Vjesnik u Srijedu'; mem. of Exec. Cttee. of Cen. Cttee. of League of Communists of Croatia 1969–71, Sec. 1972–74; mem. of Presidency of Cen. Cttee. of League of Communists of Yugoslavia and Chair. Cttee. for Ideological and Theoretical Questions 1974–78; mem. of Collective State Presidency for Croatia; Federal Sec. for Foreign Affairs 1978–82; fmr. Pres. of Presidency of Cen. Cttee. of Croatia and mem. Cen. Cttee. of Yugoslavia; numerous Yugoslav and foreign awards. *Publications:* numerous works on social sciences and international relations. *Address:* c/o Savez komunista Jugoslavije, Novi Beograd, bul. Lenjina 6, Yugoslavia.

VRIES, Egbert de, DR. AGR.; Netherlands economist; b. 29 Jan. 1901, Grypskerke; s. of Jan de Vries and Johanna Willemina Luuring; m. 1st Tine Berg 1924 (died 1945), 2nd Alexandrine Duvekot 1947; five s. two d.; ed. Univ. of Wageningen; Govt. service in Netherlands E. Indies 1924–41; Head of Div. for Gen. Econ. Affairs in Dept. of Econ. Affairs 1938–41; Prof. of Agricultural Econs. and Dean of Agricultural Faculty, Univ. of Indonesia 1941–46; returned to Netherlands 1946; Prof. of Tropical Agricultural Econs., Univ. of Wageningen, and adviser to Netherlands Ministry of Overseas Affairs 1947–50; Chief of Econ. Resources Div. of Econ. Dept. of IBRD 1950–52; Chief of Econ. Div. of Tech. Operations Dept. 1952–53, Agricultural Div. 1953–56; Chair. Working Cttee. of Dept. of Studies, Div. Church and Soc., World Council of Churches 1954–61; mem. of Cttee. on Developing Countries, World Council of Churches 1962–66; Rector Inst. of Social Studies, The Hague 1956–66, Fellow 1966–; Dir. Netherlands Univs. Foundation for Int. Co-operation 1956–66; Chair. Nat. Org. for Int. Co-operation 1956–61, Vice-Chair. 1961–66, Fellow 1966–; Prof. of Int. Devt., Univ. of Pittsburgh 1966–73, Prof. Emer. Public and Int. Affairs 1973–; Vice-Chair. Bd. of Council for Study of Mankind 1968–70, mem. 1970–78; partner with D.C. Stone in consultancy on econ. and public admin. 1973–; Trustee Obor Foundation 1971–, Chair. Bd. of Trustees 1975–; Trustee Interfuture 1971–81; Chair. Bd. Int. Devt. Services 1981–; Visiting Prof. Univ. of Suriname 1982–; Egbert de Vries Chair, Agricultural Univ., Wageningen 1985; Chair. Council Academic Advisors 1981; Kt. Order of Netherlands Lion 1950; Commdr. Order of Orange-Nassau 1966. *Leisure interests:* gardening, stamps. *Address:* 3955 Bigelow Boulevard, Apt. 601, Pittsburgh, Pa. 15213, U.S.A. *Telephone:* (412) 683-5645.

VRIGNY, Roger, L. ÈS L.; French writer; b. 19 May 1920, Paris; s. of Georges Vrigny and Suzanne Benoist; unmarried; ed. Collège oratorien de Rocroy-Saint-Léon Paris, Lycée Condorcet, Paris, and Univ. of Paris; Prof. of Literature, Coll. Rocroy-Saint-Léon; founder of Le Miroir Theatre Co. 1950; broadcaster and radio producer; mem. Renaudot prize jury; Prix Femina for La Nuit de Mougins 1963, Prix Dumas-Miller (Académie française) for Sentiments distingués 1984; Chevalier des Arts et des Lettres. *Publications:* novels: Arban, Lauréna, Barbegal, La nuit de Mougins 1963; essay: Fin de journée 1968; diaries: La vie brève 1972, Pourquoi cette joie? 1974; Les Irascibles (TV) 1964, Le serment d'Amboise (TV) 1966, Un ange passe 1979, Sentiments distingués 1983, Accident de

parcours 1985; farce: Marute; sketches: L'enlèvement d'Arabelle, L'impromptu du réverbère; mystery: La dame d'Onfrède. *Address:* Radio-France, 116 avenue du Président-Kennedy, 75016 Paris (Office); 4 rue Jean-Ferrandi, 75006 Paris, France (Home).

VU VAN MAU, LL.D.; Vietnamese lawyer, diplomatist and politician; b. 25 July 1914; ed. Univ. of Hanoi and Univ. of Paris; Lawyer, Hanoi 1949; Dean, Faculty of Law, Univ. of Saigon 1955–58, Prof. of Law 1965; First Pres. Vietnamese Supreme Court of Appeal 1955; Minister of Foreign Affairs 1955; Sec. of State for Foreign Affairs 1956–63 (resgnd.); Pres. Vietnamese Nat. Asscn. of Comparative Law; Amb. to U.K., Belgium and Netherlands 1964–65; Senator 1970–75; Prime Minister 28–30 April 1975. *Publications:* legal works in French and Vietnamese. *Address:* 132 Suong Nguyet Anh, Ho Chi Minh City, Viet-Nam.

VUNIBOBO, Berenado, C.B.E., B.AGR.SC.; Fijian agronomist and government official; b. 24 Sept. 1932, Nukutubu, Rewa; s. of Mateo Vunibobo and Maria Kelekeletabua; m. Luisa Marama Tabumoce 1953; two s. three d.; ed. St. Joseph's Catholic Mission School, Rewa, Marist Brothers High School, Suva, Queensland State Agric. Coll., Queensland Univ. Imperial Coll. of Tropical Agric., Trinidad; Govt. Service 1951–, Dist. Agric. Officer 1962–67, Sr. Agric. Officer and later Chief Agric. Officer 1968–69; Deputy Dir. of Agric. 1969–70, Dir. of Agric. 1970–71; Perm. Sec. for Agric., Fisheries and Forests 1971–72, for Works 1973–76; Perm. Rep. to UN, Amb. to U.S.A., High Commr. in Canada 1976–80; Perm. Sec. for Tourism, Transport and Civil Aviation 1980–81; Resident Rep. UNDP, Repub. of Korea 1981–86; Resident Rep. UNDP, Pakistan 1986–87; Minister of Trade and Commerce Dec. 1987–; Chair. UN Visiting Mission to Cayman Islands and U.S. Virgin Islands 1978; Vice-Pres. UN Gen. Ass.; Pres. UN Pledging Conf., Governing Council, UNDP; Chair. UN Observer Mission to New Hebrides (Vanuatu); Chair. Coconut Pests and Diseases Bd., Banana Marketing Bd., Nat. Marketing Authority 1970–72; Chair. Civil Aviation Authority, Fiji, Air Terminal Services, Fiji; mem. Bd., Fiji Devt. Bank 1970–72; mem. Native Lands Trust Bd. 1968–75, Fijian Affairs Bd. 1968–76, Great Council of Chiefs 1968–76, Cen. Whitley Council 1970–76, Jt. Industrial Council 1970–76, Fiji Electricity Authority 1975–76. Gold Medal (Queensland Agric. Coll.) 1986. *Leisure interests:* reading, debating, walking, gardening, swimming, golf. *Address:* c/o Ministry of Trade and Commerce, P.O. Box 2118, Government Buildings, Suva, Fiji. *Telephone:* 211-327.

VUONG VAN BAC; Vietnamese diplomatist; b. 1927, Bac Ninh, N. Viet-Nam; ed. Hanoi Univ., Michigan State Univ., Vanderbilt Univ., U.S.A.; admitted to Hanoi Bar Asscn. 1952, Saigon Bar Asscn. 1954; Prof. of Constitutional and Political Science, Nat. Inst. of Admin. 1955; Chair. Dalat Univ. 1965; Sec.-Gen. Viet-Nam Lawyers' Fed. 1961; mem. Council of Lawyers, Saigon High Court 1962–68, Bd. of Dirs. Viet-Nam Council on Foreign Relations 1968; Legal Adviser to Repub. of Viet-Nam Liaison and Observation Del. at Paris talks 1968; Amb. to U.K. 1972–73; Minister of Foreign Affairs 1973–75; has attended numerous int. confs. on legal and econ. affairs.

VUORISTO, Osmo Jalmari, PH.D.; Finnish museum director; b. 13 Feb. 1929, Helsinki; m. Helena Korpinen 1954; two s.; ed. Univ. of Helsinki; Dir. Northern Karelia Museum, Joensuu 1955–58; Curator, Nat. Museum of Finland, Helsinki 1958–72, Head of Museology Section 1972–78, Museum Dir. 1979–; Docent in Ethnology, Univ. of Helsinki 1979–. *Publications:* Suomalaiset haarikka-astiat/ Die Trinkgefässe vom haarikka-Typ in Finnland 1978, ethnological and museological articles, author of 13 ethnological short films. *Address:* Mannerheimintie 34, P.O. Box 913, SF-00101 Helsinki 10 (Office); Kontulankaari 3 G 161, SF-00940 Helsinki 94, Finland (Home).

VUROBARAVU, Nikenike, B.A.; Vanuatu diplomatist; b. 3 Dec. 1951; m.; one s.; ed. Univ. of the South Pacific, Fiji; Ed. Vanua-Aku Viewpoints 1978–79; Public Relations Officer, New Hebrides Govt. 1979–80; Foreign Affairs Officer, Dept. of Foreign Affairs, Govt. of Vanuatu 1981–83; Sec. for Foreign Affairs 1983–85; Perm. Rep. of Vanuatu to UN 1985–. *Address:* Permanent Mission of the Republic of Vanuatu to the United Nations, 411 West 148th Street, New York, N.Y. 10031, U.S.A. *Telephone:* 926-5762.

VYALYAS, Vaino Iosipovich; Soviet official and diplomatist; b. 1931, Estonia; ed. Tartu Univ.; joined Komsomol 1948; Sec. Tartu City Cttee. of Estonian Komsomol 1952–55; First Sec. Estonian Komsomol 1955–61; mem. Cen. Cttee. of Estonian CP 1956–; cand. mem. Politburo 1960–61, mem. 1961–; Sec. 1971–76; First Sec. Tallinn City Cttee. of Estonian CP 1961–71; First Sec. of Gen. Cttee. of Estonian S.S.R. June 1988–; Amb. to Jamaica 1975–80, to Venezuela 1980–86. *Address:* c/o Ministry of Foreign Affairs, Smolenskaya-Sennaya pl. 32-34, Moscow, U.S.S.R.

W

WAALER, Bjarne Arentz, DR.MED.; Norwegian professor of medicine; b. 18 April 1925, Bergen; s. of Prof. Rolf and Gudrun Waaler; m. Gudrun Arentz 1950; two s. one d.; ed. Univ. of Oslo; various positions in Norwegian hospitals 1950–56; research fellow in haematology and physiology, Univ. of Oslo 1956–58; research fellow in physiology, Univ. of Oxford 1958–61; Prof. of Medicine (Physiology), Univ. of Oslo 1962–, Dean, Faculty of Medicine 1974–77; Rector, Univ. of Oslo 1977–84; Vice-Pres. Norwegian Acad. of Science and Letters, mem. U.K. Physiological Soc.; Commdr. Royal Norwegian Order of St. Olav. *Publications:* about 120 publications in the fields of blood coagulation, blood circulation, and university matters. *Leisure interests:* fly fishing, literature. *Address:* University of Oslo, Karl Johans gt. 47, Oslo 1; Kaptein Oppegaards vei 36B, Oslo 11, Norway (Home). *Telephone:* 02 42 90 10 (Office); 02 28 23 65 (Home).

WÄCHTER, Eberhard; Austrian opera-singer; b. 8 July 1929, Vienna; m. 1954; three s. three d.; studied with Elisabeth Rado, Vienna; début with Volksoper, Vienna; mem. State Opera, Vienna 1955–; has sung in Germany, France, Holland, England, Spain, U.S.A. and Italy, Bayreuth Festival, Salzburg Festival, etc. *Address:* Vienna XIX, 46 Felix-Mottlstrasse, Austria. *Telephone:* 3417-212.

WACHTMEISTER, Count Wilhelm Hans Frederik; Swedish diplomatist; b. 29 April 1923, Wanås; s. of Count Gustaf Wachtmeister and Countess Margaretha Wachtmeister (née Trolle); m. Countess Ulla Wachtmeister (née Leuhusen); one s. two d.; ed. Stockholm Univ.; Attaché, Foreign Office 1946–47, Embassy in Vienna 1947–49, in Madrid Feb.-May 1949, in Lisbon 1949–50, Foreign Office 1950–52; Second Sec. Foreign Office 1952–55; Second Sec. Embassy in Moscow 1955–56, First Sec. 1956–58; Special Asst. to Sec.-Gen. of UN 1958–62; Head of Div. for UN Affairs, Foreign Office 1962–63, Head of Div. 1963–65, Head of Dept. July-Oct. 1965, Asst. Under-Sec. of State 1965–66; Amb. to Algeria 1966–68; Deputy Under-Sec. of State and Head of Political Div. 1968–74; Amb. to U.S.A. 1974–89; Hon. LL.D. *Address:* c/o Ministry of Foreign Affairs, 10335 Stockholm, Sweden; 3900 Nebraska Avenue, N.W., Washington, D.C. 20016, U.S.A. (Residence). *Telephone:* (202) 362-3270 (Residence).

WADATI, Kiyoo; Japanese geophysicist; b. 8 Sept. 1902, Nagoya; s. of Yotaro and Kin Wadati; m. Kuniko Wadati 1928; three s. four d.; ed. Tokyo Univ.; entered Meteorological Observatory; has conducted research into earthquakes, tidal waves etc.; Dir.-Gen. Japan Meteorological Agency 1956–63; fmr. Pres. Science Council of Japan; Pres. Saitama Univ. 1966–72; mem. Japan Acad. (Pres. 1974–80). *Publications:* Earthquakes, Kisyo No Jiten (Encyclopaedia of Meteorology), Kaiyo No Jiten (Encyclopaedia of Oceanography). *Address:* Japan Academy, 7-32, Ueno Park, Taito-ku, Tokyo 110 (Office); 1-8 Naitomachi, Shinjiku-ku, Tokyo, Japan (Home). *Telephone:* 03-341-3503.

WADDELL, Gordon Herbert, M.B.A., B.A.; South African business executive; b. 12 April 1937, Glasgow; s. of Mr. and Mrs. Herbert Waddell; m. 2nd Kathy May Gallagher 1974; one s. four d.; ed. Fettes Coll., Edinburgh, Univ. of Cambridge and Stanford Univ., U.S.A.; Dir. E. Oppenheimer and Son 1965–87; Dir. Anglo American Corpn. of S.A. Ltd. 1969–71, Exec. Dir. 1971–87; Dir. Johannesburg Consolidated Investment Co. Ltd. 1978–, Deputy Chair. 1980–81, Chair. 1981–87; Dir. Rustenburg Platinum Holdings Ltd. 1978–, Deputy Chair. 1980–81, Chair. 1981–87; M.P. for Johannesburg North (Progressive Fed. Party) 1974–77; Chair. S.A. Breweries Ltd. 1984–87. *Address:* Cloud End, West Road South, Morningside, Sandton, Transvaal, South Africa.

WADDS, Jean Casselman, O.C., B.A.; Canadian diplomatist; b. 16 Sept. 1920, Newton Robinson, Ont.; d. of William Earl Rowe and Treva (Lennox) Rowe; m. 1st. A. Clair Casselman 1946 (deceased), one s. one d.; m. 2nd Robert Wadds 1964 (divorced); ed. Univ. of Toronto, Weller Business Coll.; mem. House of Commons 1958–68; mem. Canadian Del. to UN 1961; Parl. Sec. to Minister of Health and Welfare 1962; Dir Bell Canada, Canadian Pacific, Celanese Canada Inc., Royal Trust Co. Ltd., Royal Winnipeg Ballet; mem. of Agric., Broadcasting, Civil Service and External Affairs Cttees.; Nat. Sec. Progressive Conservative Party 1971–75; mem. Ont. Municipal Bd. 1975–79; Canadian High Commr. in U.K. 1980–83; mem. Royal Comm. on Econ. Union and Devt. Prospects for Canada 1983–85; mem. Bd. of Trustees Royal Winnipeg Ballet; Hon. Fellowship, Breton Hall Coll., Yorks., England 1982; Hon. Patron, mem. Bd. Advisors, Grenville Christian Coll.; Commdr., Mil. and Hospitaller Order of St. Lazarus 1983; Freeman City of London 1981; Hon. D.C.L. (Acadia Univ.) 1981, (Univ. of Toronto) 1985, (Dalhousie Univ.) 1985, Hon. LL.D. (St. Thomas Univ.) 1983. *Leisure interests:* golf, skiing, swimming. *Address:* P.O. Box 579, Prescott, Ont. K1E 1T0, Canada. *Telephone:* (613) 996 1166.

WADE, Sir (Henry) William Rawson, Kt., Q.C., LL.D., D.C.L., F.B.A.; British professor of law (retd.); b. 16 Jan. 1918, London; s. of Col. H. O. and E. L. Wade; m. 1st Marie Osland-Hill 1943 (died 1980), 2nd Marjorie Grace Hope Browne 1982; two s.; ed. Shrewsbury School, Gonville and Caius Coll. Cambridge and Harvard Law School, U.S.A.; Temporary Officer, H.M. Treasury 1940–45; Barrister, Lincoln's Inn 1946; Fellow, Trinity Coll. Cambridge and Univ. Lecturer/Reader 1946–61; Prof. of English Law, Oxford Univ., and Fellow of St. John's Coll. 1961–76; Master of Gonville and Caius Coll. Cambridge 1976–88; Prof. of English Law, Cambridge Univ. 1978–82; Guest Lecturer in many countries; mem. Council on Tribunals 1958–71, Relationships Comm.; Uganda 1961, Royal Comm. on Tribunals of Inquiry 1966; Vice-Pres. British Acad. 1981–83; Hon. Bencher, Lincoln's Inn 1964; Hon. Fellow, St. John's Coll. 1976. *Publications:* The Law of Real Property (with Sir Robert Megarry), 5th edn. 1984, Administrative Law, 6th edn. 1988, Towards Administrative Justice 1963, Legal Control of Government (with B. Schwartz) 1972, Constitutional Fundamentals (Hamlyn Lectures) 1980; articles in legal journals. *Leisure interests:* climbing, gardening and music. *Address:* Gonville and Caius College, Cambridge, CB2 1TA (Office); The Green, 1A Ludlow Lane, Fulbourn, Cambridge, CB1 5BL, England (Home). *Telephone:* (0223) 332400 (Office); (0223) 881745 (Home).

WADE, (Sarah) Virginia, O.B.E.; British tennis player; b. 10 July 1945, Bournemouth, Hants. (now Dorset); d. of Canon Eustace Wade (fmr. Archdeacon of Durban, S.A.); ed. Univ. of Sussex; amateur player 1962–68, professional 1968–; British Hard Court Champion 1967, 1968, 1973, 1974; U.S.A. Champion 1968 (singles), 1973, 1975 (doubles); Italian Champion 1971; Australian Champion 1972; Wimbledon Ladies Champion 1977; played Wightman Cup for G.B. 1965–81, Capt. 1973–80; played Fed. Cup for G.B. 1967–81, Capt. 1973–81; mem. Cttee. All England Lawn Tennis Club 1983–; Hon. LL.D. (Sussex) 1985; Int. Tennis Hall of Fame 1989. *Publications:* Courting Triumph (with Mary Lou Mellace) 1978, Ladies of the Court 1984. *Leisure interest:* reading. *Address:* c/o International Management Group, 1 Erieview Plaza, Cleveland, Ohio 44199, U.S.A.; Sharsted Court, Nr. Sittingbourne, Kent, England.

WADE-GERY, Sir Robert (Lucian), K.C.M.G., K.C.V.O., M.A.; British banker and fmr. diplomatist; b. 22 April 1929, Oxford; s. of Prof. H. T. and V. Wade-Gery; m. Sarah Marris 1962; one s. one d.; ed. Winchester Coll. and New Coll., Oxford; Fellow, All Souls Coll., Oxford 1951–73, 1987–; joined Foreign (now Diplomatic) Service 1951; in Foreign Office (FO) Econ. Relations Dept. 1951–54; at Embassy in Bonn 1954–57, Tel-Aviv 1961–64, Saigon (now Ho Chi Min City) 1967–68; FO 1957–60, 1964–67; Cabinet Office 1968–69; Counsellor 1969; on loan to Bank of England 1969; Head of Financial Policy and Aid Dept., FCO 1970; Under-Sec., Cen. Policy Review Staff, Cabinet Office 1971–73; Minister at Embassy, Madrid 1973–77, Moscow 1977–79; Deputy Sec. of Cabinet 1979–82; High Commr. in India 1982–87; Exec. Dir. Barclays de Zoete Wedd 1987–. *Leisure interests:* walking, sailing, travel. *Address:* 7 Rothwell Street, London, NW1 8YH, England. *Telephone:* 01-623 2323 (Office); 01-722 4754 (Home).

WADLEIGH, Cecil Herbert, PH.D.; American plant physiologist (retd.); b. 1 Oct. 1907, Gilbertville, Mass.; s. of Hazen Carl and Lucy (née Whitehead) Wadleigh; m. Clarice Lucile Bean 1930; one s. three d.; ed. Univ. of Massachusetts, Ohio State Univ., Rutgers Univ.; Research Asst. Plant Physiology, Rutgers Univ. 1933–36; Asst. Research Prof. Plant Physiology, Univ. of Arkansas 1936–41; Sr. Chemist U.S. Regional Salinity Lab., Riverside, Calif. 1941–48, Prin. Physiologist 1948–51; Head Physiologist-in-Charge Div. Sugar Plant Investigations, Bureau Plant Industry, U.S. Dept. of Agric., Beltsville, Md. 1951–54, Head Soils and Plant Relationships 1954–55, Dir. Soil and Water Conservation 1955–70; Science Advisor U.S. Dept. of Agric. 1971–72; retd. 1972; Fellow A.A.A.S. 1947–; Pres. American Soc. of Plant Physiology 1951–52; mem. White House Panel on Indus Basin of Pakistan 1961–63, of White House Cttee. on Water Resources Research 1963–69; has represented U.S. Dept. of Agric. at numerous confs. internationally and nationally; mem. N.A.S. 1973–; Distinguished Visiting Prof. Mich. Univ. 1969; Lectures on Environmental Protection, Hungary, Romania, Bulgaria 1973; Distinguished Service Award U.S. Dept. of Agric. 1967; Hugh Hammond Bennett Award Soil Conservation Soc. of America 1976; Hon. D.Sc. (Mass.) 1974. *Publications:* numerous articles in specialist journals. *Leisure interests:* maintaining a large collection of recently introduced cultivars of the tall bearded iris, American Civil War history. *Address:* 5621 Whitefield Chapel Road, Lanham, Md. 20706, U.S.A. (Home). *Telephone:* (301) 577-6199.

WAELBROECK, Jean Louis, PH.D.; Belgian professor of economics; b. 2 May 1927, Petit Saconnet (Sw.); s. of Pierre G. Waelbroeck and Elisabeth M. Varlez; m. Isabelle Gogneaux 1954; two s. three d.; ed. Strathcona High School, McGill Univ. and Free Univ. of Brussels; Research Dept., Nat. Bank of Belgium 1952–55; Econ. Office, NATO 1955–59, Head, Soviet Section 1958; Chargé de cours, Free Univ. of Brussels 1959–63, Prof. 1963–; Fellow, Econometric Soc. *Publication:* Activity Analysis and General Equilibrium Modelling (with V. Ginsburgh). *Leisure interests:* fruit growing, music. *Address:* 29 rue d'Heuval, 1490 Court-St.-Etienne, Belgium. *Telephone:* 010/612326.

WAELSCH, Salome G., PH.D.; American (b. German) geneticist; b. 6 Oct. 1907, Danzig, Germany (now Gdańsk, Poland; d. of Ilyia and Nadia Gluecksohn; m. Heinrich B. Waelsch 1943; one s. one d.; ed. Univs. of Königsberg, Berlin, Freiburg; Research Assoc. in Genetics, Columbia Univ., New York 1936-55; Assoc. Prof. of Anatomy (Genetics), Albert Einstein Coll. of Medicine, Bronx, New York 1955-58, Prof. of Anatomy (Genetics) 1958-63, Chair. of Dept. of Genetics 1963-76, Prof. of Genetics 1963-; mem. N.A.S.; Fellow, American Acad. of Arts and Sciences. *Publications:* more than 100 articles in the field of developmental genetics in various scientific journals. *Address:* Department of Genetics, Albert Einstein College of Medicine, 1300 Morris Park Avenue, Bronx, N.Y. 10461 (Office); 90 Morningside Drive, New York, N.Y. 10027, U.S.A. (Home). *Telephone:* (212) 430-3185 (Office); (212) 662-5331 (Home).

WAGGONER, Paul Edward, PH.D.; American scientist; b. 29 March 1923, Appanoose County, Ia.; s. of Walter Loyal Waggoner and Kathryn Maring Waggoner; m. Barbara Ann Lockerbie 1945; two s.; ed. Univ. of Chicago and Iowa State Coll., Ames; Asst., then Assoc., then Chief Scientist, The Connecticut Agricultural Experiment Station, New Haven, Conn. 1951-71, Vice-Dir. 1969-71, Dir. 1972-87, Distinguished Scientist 1987-; Guggenheim Fellow 1963; mem. N.A.S.; Fellow A.A.A.S., American Soc. of Agronomy, American Phytopathological Soc. *Publications:* Agricultural Meteorology (Ed.) 1965 and articles on phytopathology. *Leisure interest:* gardening. *Address:* The Connecticut Agricultural Experiment Station, 123 Huntington Street, Box 1106, New Haven, Conn. 06504 (Office); 314 Vineyard Road, Guilford, Conn. 06437, U.S.A. (Home). *Telephone:* (203) 789-7214 (Office); (203) 453-2816 (Home).

WAGNER, Sir Anthony Richard, K.C.B., K.C.V.O., D.LITT., F.S.A.; British herald; b. 6 Sept. 1908, London; s. of late Orlando H. Wagner and Monica Bell; m. Gillian M. M. Graham 1953; two s. one d.; ed. Eton and Balliol Coll., Oxford; Portcullis Pursuivant 1931-43; Richmond Herald 1943-61; War Office 1939-43; Private Sec. to Minister of Town and Country Planning 1944-45; mem. Advisory Cttee. on Historic Buildings 1947-66; Registrar, Coll. of Arms 1953-60; Sec. of Order of the Garter 1952-61; Jt. Registrar of Court of Chivalry 1954-; Garter Principal King of Arms 1961-78, Clarenceux King of Arms 1978-; Insp. of Regimental Colours 1961-77; Kt. Prin., Imperial Soc. of Kts. Bachelor 1962-82; Genealogist of the Order of the Bath 1961-72, of the Order of St. John 1961-75; Trustee, Nat. Portrait Gallery 1963-80; Chair. of Trustees, Marc Fitch Fund 1971-77; Dir. Heralds' Museum, Tower of London 1978-83; Master of Vintners' Co. 1973-74; Hon. Fellow, Heraldry Soc. of Canada 1976, Balliol Coll., Oxford 1980; Kt. St. J. *Publications:* Catalogue of the Heralds Commemorative Exhibition 1934, Historic Heraldry of Britain 1939, Heralds and Heraldry in the Middle Ages 1939, Heraldry in England 1946, Catalogue of English Mediaeval Rolls of Arms 1950, The Records and Collections of the College of Arms 1952, English Genealogy 1960, English Ancestry 1961, Heralds of England 1967, Pedigree and Progress 1975, Heralds and Ancestors 1978, Leakes' Heraldo Memoriale 1981, The Wagners of Brighton 1983, How Lord Birkenhead Saved the Heralds 1987, A Herald's World 1988; Ed. Society of Antiquaries Dictionary of British Arms 1940-; author of numerous articles and encyclopedia contributions on heraldry and genealogy. *Address:* College of Arms, Queen Victoria Street, London, E.C.4 (Office); 68A Chelsea Square, London, S.W.3; Wyndham Cottage, Aldeburgh, Suffolk, England (Homes). *Telephone:* 01-248 4300 (Office); 01-352 0934, (072885) 2596 (Homes).

WAGNER, Aubrey Joseph; American engineer and government official; b. 12 Jan. 1912, Hillsboro, Wis.; s. of Joseph M. and Wilhelmina F. Wagner; m. Dorothea J. Huber 1933; three s. one d.; ed. Univ. of Wisconsin; joined Tennessee Valley Authority 1934, successively Jr. Hydraulic Engineer, Asst. Hydraulic Engineer, Assoc. Navigation Engineer, Asst. Chief, River Transportation Branch, Act. Chief. later Chief Navigation and Transportation Branch, Asst. Gen. Man. 1951-54, Gen. Man. 1954-61, Dir. 1961-62, Chair. 1962-78; mem. Advisory Cttee. UN Conf. on Human Environment 1971-72, Nat. Advisory Council 1974, World Energy Conf. 1971-74, Exec. Cttee. Fed. Energy Admin. 1975-; Vice-Chair. Nat. Div. World Energy Conf. 1976-; Consultant, energy and resource use Knoxville 1978-; mem. Bd. Dirs. Electric Power Research Inst. 1977-; mem. Nat. Acad. of Eng. 1973; Hon. LL.B. (Newberry Coll.), Hon. degree in Public Admin. (Lenoir Rhyne Coll., N.C.); N. W. Dougherty Award (Univ. of Tenn.) 1969, Lambda Chi Alpha Order of Achievement 1970. *Publications:* Articles in various journals and magazines. *Leisure interests:* fishing, woodworking. *Address:* 201 Whittington Drive, Knoxville, Tennessee 37919, U.S.A. (Home). *Telephone:* (615) 693-4779 (Home).

WAGNER, Falk (Oskar Paul Alfred), DR.THEOL.; German professor of theology; b. 25 Feb. 1939, Vienna, Austria; s. of Robert Wagner and Friedel Wagner; m. Inamaria Winnefeld 1968; two d.; ed. Gymnasium Wiesbaden and Univs. of Frankfurt and Mainz; Research Fellow for Economic Ethics and Adult Educ., Karlsruhe 1968-69; Research Fellow, Deutsches Inst. für Int. Pädagogische Forschung, Frankfurt-am-Main 1969-72; Asst. Univ. of Munich 1970-72, lecturer in Systematic Theology 1972, Prof. 1978-. *Publications include:* Über die Legitimität der Mission 1968, Der Gedanke der Persönlichkeit Gottes bei Fichte und Hegel 1972, Schleiermachers Dialektik 1974, Geld oder Gott? 1985, Was ist Religion? 1986, Die vergessene spekulative Theologie 1987; numerous articles on theological, philosophical and ethical questions. *Address:* Universität

München, Institut für Systematische Theologie, Schellingstrasse 3, 8000 Munich 22 (Office); Niblerstrasse 13a, 8031 Eichenau, Federal Republic of Germany (Home). *Telephone:* 089-2180/2834 (Office); 08141-71915 (Home).

WAGNER, Gerhard; Austrian banker; b. 4 Oct. 1933, Grafenschlag; s. of Johann Wagner; m.; one d.; ed. High School, Horn, Lower Austria and Univ. of Man. and Business Admin.; joined Zentralsparkasse, Vienna 1956, Asst. Departmental Man. (Mortgage Loans) 1965, Departmental Man. (Mortgage Loans—Public Sector lending) 1968, Deputy Gen. Man. 1973; First Depty Gov. Postsparkasse (Postal Saving Bank) 1977-79; Sr. Gen. Man. Zentralsparkasse responsible for Corp. lending and Branch Offices (outside Vienna), Man. Z-Bank G.m.b.H., Vienna 1979-81; mem. Bd. of Man. Dirs., Österreichische Länderbank AG 1981-, Chair. 1984-; Chair. Wiener Borselkammer. *Address:* Österreichische Länderbank AG, Generaldirektion, Am Hof 2, 1010 Vienna, Austria. *Telephone:* 531-24-3131; 531-24-3132.

WAGNER, Gerrit Abram, LL.M.; Netherlands oil executive; b. 21 Oct. 1916, Maassluis; s. of Adrianus and Antonia Jacoba (Van der Hout) Wagner; one s. three d.; ed. Leiden Univ.; Royal Dutch/Shell Group 1946-77, working in various parts of world; Vice-Pres. Compania Shell de Venezuela 1959-61, Pres. 1961-64; Man. Dir. N.V. Koninklijke Nederlandsche Petroleum Maatschappij, Shell Petroleum Co. 1964-71, Pres. 1971-77, Chair. Supervisory Bd. 1977-; Dir. Shell Oil Co. 1971-77, Chair. 1972-77; Dir. Shell Canada Ltd. 1971-77; Chair. Supervisory Bd. De Nederlandsche Bank N.V., Amsterdam, KLM, Amsterdam, Gist-Brocades N.V., Delft; Vice-Chair. Supervisory Bd. Hoogovens Gp. B.V.; mem. Int. Advisory Cttee. Chase Manhattan Bank, New York, Robert Bosch Stuttgart/Zurich; Chair. Foundation Praemium Erasmianum, Amsterdam; mem. European Advisory Council; mem. Cttee. Carnegie Foundation, The Hague; Order of Francisco de Miranda, Second Class (Venezuela), Kt. Order of the Netherlands Lion; Hon. K.B.E. (U.K.) 1977; Officier Légion d'honneur, Grand Officer, Order of Orange Nassau 1983. *Address:* c/o N.V. Koninklijke Nederlandsche Petroleum Maatschappij, 30 Carel van Bylandtlaan, 2596 HR, The Hague, Netherlands.

WAGNER, Heinz Georg, DR.RER.NAT.; German professor of physical chemistry; b. 20 Sept. 1928, Hof, Bavaria; s. of Georg Wagner and Frida Spiess; m. Renate C. Heuer 1974; ed. Tech. Hochschule, Darmstadt and Univ .of Göttingen; lecturer, Univ. of Göttingen 1960-65, Prof. of Physical Chem. 1971-; Prof. Ruhr Univ. Bochum 1965-70; Dir. Max-Planck-Inst. für Strömungsforschung, Göttingen 1971-; Vice-Pres. Deutsche Forschungsgemeinschaft 1983-; scientific mem. Max-Planck-Gesellschaft; mem. Göttingen Acad., Acad. Leopoldina, Int. Acad. of Astronautics, American Physical Soc., Royal Soc. of Chem. etc.; Bundesverdienstkreuz; Fritz-Haber Prize, Bernard Lewis Gold Medal, Numa Manson Medal 1987 and other awards. *Publications:* articles on combustion, reaction kinetics, thermodynamics of liquid mixtures. *Address:* Institut für Physikalische Chemie, Universität Göttingen, Tammannstr. 6, 3400 Göttingen, Federal Republic of Germany. *Telephone:* 0051/393111.

WAGNER, Philip Marshall; American newspaper columnist and viticulturist; b. 18 Feb. 1904, New Haven, Conn.; m. 1st Helen Crocker 1925, 2nd Jocelyn McDonough 1940; two c.; ed. Kent School and Univ. of Michigan; with General Electric Co. 1925-30; Editorial Writer, Baltimore Evening Sun 1930-36, London Corresp. Baltimore Sun 1936-37, Ed. Evening Sun 1938-43, Ed. Baltimore Sun 1943-64; writer of syndicated newspaper column on public affairs 1964-; with wife has introduced new grape varieties into American viticulture; American Del. Fédération Nat. de la Viticulture Nouvelle; Officier du Mérite Agricole, France. *Publications:* American Wines and How to Make Them 1933, Wine Grapes and How to Grow Them 1937, The Wine-Grower's Guide 1945, American Wines and Wine Making 1956, H. L. Mencken (American Writers Series) 1966; Edited (with Dr. Stanford V. Larkey) Turner on Wines 1941, Grapes into Wine 1976. *Address:* Boordy Vineyard, Box 38, Riderwood, Md., U.S.A. *Telephone:* (301) 823-4624.

WAGNER, Wolfgang; German opera director; b. 30 Aug. 1919, Bayreuth; s. of Siegfried and Winifred (née Williams) Wagner; m. 1st Ellen Drexel 1943; one s. two d.; m. 2nd Gudrun Arman 1976; one d; mil. service 1938-40; stage man. at Bayreuth Festival 1940; Asst. with Preussischer Staatsoper, Berlin 1940-44; returned to Bayreuth after war, worked with brother (the late Wieland Wagner) as dir. of annual Wagner operatic festival 1951-66, on his own 1967-; directed 346 performances 1953-88; numerous guest appearances and int. tours; Bayerischer Maximiliansorden 1984; Bayerische Akademie der Schönen Künste 1986; Ehrensenator Graz 1987, Munich 1988, Tübingen 1988. *Productions include:* Andreasnach (Berlin 1944), The Rhinegold (Naples 1952), The Valkyrie (Naples 1952, 1953, Barcelona 1955, Venice 1957, Palermo 1962, Osaka 1967), Lohengrin (Bayreuth 1953, 1967, Siegfried (Naples 1953, Brussels 1954, Venice 1957, Bologna 1957), The Flying Dutchman (Bayreuth 1955), Tristan and Isolde (Barcelona 1955, Bayreuth 1957, Venice 1958, Palermo 1960, Osaka 1967, Milan 1978), Parsifal (Barcelona 1955, Bayreuth 1975), Don Giovanni (Brunswick 1955), The Mastersingers of Nuremberg (Rome 1956, Bayreuth 1968, 1981), The Nibelung's Ring (Venice 1957, Bayreuth 1960, 1970), Götterdämmerung (Venice 1957), Tannhäuser (Bayreuth 1985). *Address:* Festspielhügel Nr. 3, 8580 Bayreuth, Federal Republic of Germany. *Telephone:* 0049-921-20221.

WAGNER TIZON, Allan; Peruvian politician and diplomatist; b. 7 Feb. 1942, Lima; ed. Universidad Católica and Universidad de San Marcos; joined Ministry of Foreign Affairs 1963; joined Diplomatic Service 1968; Minister of Foreign Affairs 1985–89. *Address:* c/o Ministry of Foreign Affairs, Ucayali 363, Lima, Peru.

WAHI, Prem Nath, M.D., F.R.C.P.; Indian physician; b. 10 April 1908; ed. K.G. Medical Coll., Lucknow, London Hospital Medical School, London, and New England Deaconess Hospital, Boston, U.S.A.; Prof. of Pathology, S.N. Medical Coll., Agra 1941–; Prin., S.N. Medical Coll., Agra 1960–; Dean, Faculty of Medicine, Agra Univ. 1961–64; Dir. WHO Int. Reference Centre and Cancer Registry 1963–; mem. Expert Panel of WHO on Cancer, Lyon, France 1965–; has attended numerous int. conferences on cancer; Lady Brahamachari Readership, Calcutta Univ. 1965; Fellow, Nat. Inst. of Sciences, India; Founder Fellow, Coll. of Pathologists, London 1963; Founder Fellow, Indian Acad. of Medical Sciences 1964. *Address:* S.N. Medical College, Agra (U.P.), India.

WAHL, Jacques Henri; French administrator; b. 18 Jan. 1932, Lille; s. of Abraham Wahl and Simone Kornbluth; m. Inna Cytrin 1969; two s. one d.; ed. Inst. d'Etudes Politiques, Paris, Univs. of Lille and Paris, Ecole Nat. d'Admin.; Insp. des Finances 1961–; Treasury Dept. 1965–68; Special Asst. to Ministers of Econ. and Finance, François Ortoli 1968–69, Valéry Giscard d'Estaing 1969–71; Asst. Dir. of the Treasury for Int. Affairs 1971–73; Chair. Invisible Transactions Cttee., OECD 1971–73; lecturer, Inst. d'Etudes Politiques and Ecole Nat. d'Admin., Paris 1969–73; Financial Minister, French Embassies, U.S.A. and Canada 1973–78; Exec. Dir. IMF, IBRD 1973–78; Sec.-Gen. to the Presidency of the French Repub. 1978–81; Insp.-Gen. des Finances 1981; Dir.-Gen. Banque Nat. de Paris 1982–; Officier, Légion d'honneur, Ordre Nat. du Mérite, Commdr. Ordre Nat. de Côte d'Ivoire, Officier Ordre du Mérite de la République Centrafricaine, Chevalier, Ordre du Mérite de Haute Volta. *Address:* Banque Nationale de Paris, 16 boulevard des Italiens, 75450 Paris; 15 avenue de la Bourdonnais, 75007 Paris, France (Home).

WAHLGREN, Olof Gustaf Christerson, PH.D.; Swedish newspaper editor; b. 21 Sept. 1927, Stockholm; s. of Christer and Jeanne (Nyblaeus) Wahlgren; m. Ulla Andersson 1955; one s. two d.; Mem. staff Sydsvenska Dagbladet, Malmö 1953–87, Deputy Dir. 1963–67, Man. Dir. 1967–78, Chief Ed. 1967–87; Man. Dir. Kvällsposten, Malmö 1963–78; mem. Bd. of Dirs. Sydsvenska Dagbladets AB and Kvällspostens AB 1949–87, Chair. 1978–87; Pres. S. Sweden Div., Swedish Newspaper Publishers Assen. 1967–87 (Hon. Chair. 1987–); Chair. Swedish Nat. Cttee., Int. Press Inst. 1972–82; Vice-Pres. Int. Press Inst., Zürich-London 1974–76, Pres. 1976–78; Vice-Pres. World Press Freedom Cttee., Miami, Fla., U.S.A. 1976–78; mem. Exec. Cttee. Int. Newspaper Publrs.' Assen. (FIEJ), Paris 1974, Sec.-Gen. 1978–84; Founder and Chair. United Liberal Parties Movement, Sweden 1964–69; Vice-Pres. Malmö Municipal Art Cttee. 1967–76; Officier, Légion d'honneur, Officer Italian Order of Merit 1969, Commdr. Finnish Order of the Lion 1971, Kt. Danish Order of the Dannebrog 1972, Commdr. Icelandic Order of the Falcon 1974, Kt. Polish Order of Polonia Restituta 1974, Kt. Order of Vasa (First Class) 1975, Commdr., Order of Merit (Fed. Repub. of Germany) 1981. *Publications:* Motsols genom Frankrike 1962. *Leisure interest:* modern art. *Address:* Nicoloviusgatan 5 b, S-217 57 Malmö, Sweden. *Telephone:* 40/91-51-46.

WAHLSTRÖM, Jarl Holger; Finnish Salvation Army officer (retd.); b. 9 July 1918, Helsinki; s. of Rafael Alexander and Aina Maria (née Dahlberg) Wahlström; m. Maire Helfrid Nyberg 1944; two s. one d.; ed. Salvation Army Int. Training Coll., Denmark Hill, London; Salvation Army Field Officer, Finland 1939–45, Youth Officer 1945–52, 1954–60, Private Sec. to Territorial Commdr. 1952–54, Div. Commdr. 1960–63, Training Coll. Prin. 1963–68; Chief Sec., Finland 1968–72, Canada and Bermuda 1972–76; Territorial Commdr., Finland 1976–80, Sweden 1981; Int. Leader of the Salvation Army 1981–86; Hon. D.Hum.Litt. (Western Illinois Univ.); Kt., Order of Lion of Finland, Finnish Liberty Cross (Fourth Class), Order of Civil Merit, Mugungkwa Medal (Repub. of Korea). *Publication:* autobiography: Matkalaulu (Finnish), En Vallfartssäng (Swedish) 1989. *Leisure interest:* music. *Address:* Borgströminkuja 1A10, 00840 Helsinki 84, Finland. *Telephone:* 698-2413.

WAIDELICH, Charles J., B.S., C.E.; American business executive; b. 2 May 1929, Columbus, O.; s. of Bernard H. Waidelich and Alberta L. Poth; m. Margaret E. Finley 1950; one s. one d.; ed. Purdue Univ.; Engineer, Cities Service Oil Co. 1951–53; Asst. to Pres. Cities Service Pipeline Co. 1956–59; Pipeline Co-ordinator, Cities Service Co. 1959–65; Transport Co-ordinator 1965–66; Staff Vice-Pres. Operations Co-ordination 1966–68; Vice-Pres., Operations, Tenn. Corpn. 1968–69; Exec. Vice-Pres. Cities Service Co. 1970–71, Dir. 1970–83, Pres. 1971–81, Chair. 1982–83; Dir. Bank of Okla. 1974–84; Vice-Chair., Dir. Occidental Petroleum 1982–83. *Leisure interests:* reading, hunting, fishing, travel. *Address:* P.O. Box 898, Rancho Santa Fe, Calif. 92067, U.S.A.

WAIGEL, Theodor, DR.IUR.; German politician; b. 22 April 1939, Oberrohr; s. of August Waigel and Genoveva Konrad; m. Karin Hönig 1966; one s. one d.; ed. Univs. of Munich and Würzburg; Bavarian Ministries of Finance and of Econ. and Transport 1969–72; mem. Bundestag 1972–; Chair. CSU Land (Bavarian) Group in Bundestag 1982–; Pres. Land (Bavarian) Council

of CSU 1987–; Minister of Finance April 1989–; Bayerischer Verdienstorden. *Leisure interests:* climbing, theatre. *Address:* Ministry of Finance, Graurheindorfstrasse 108, 5300 Bonn 1; Oberrohr, 8909 Ursberg, Federal Republic of Germany.

WAIHEE, John David, III, B.A., J.D.; American state governor; b. 19 May 1946, Honokaa, Hawaii; m. Lynne Kobashigawa; one s. one d.; ed. Andrews Univ., Central Mich. Univ. and Univ. of Hawaii; admitted to Hawaii Bar 1976; Community Educ. Co-ordinator, Benton Harbor (Mich.) area schools 1968–70; Asst. Dir. Community Educ. 1970–71; Program Evaluator, Admin. Asst. to Dirs., Planner, Honolulu Model Cities Program 1971–73; Sr. Planner, Office of Human Resources, City and Co. of Honolulu 1973–74, Program Man. 1974–75; Assoc. Shim, Sigal, Tam & Naito, Honolulu 1975–79; partner, Waihee, Manuia, Yap, Pablo & Hoe, Honolulu 1979–82; mem. Hawaiian House of Reps. 1980–882; Lieut. Gov. of Hawaii 1982–86, Gov. 1986–; Democrat. *Address:* Office of the Governor, 5th Floor, State Capitol, Honolulu, Hawaii 96813, U.S.A.

WAIN, John Barrington, C.B.E., M.A.; British writer; b. 14 March 1925, Stoke-on-Trent, Staffs.; s. of Arnold A. and Anne Wain; m. Eirian James 1960; three s.; ed. High School, Newcastle-under-Lyme and St. John's Coll., Oxford; Lecturer in English Literature, Univ. of Reading 1947–55; resgnd. 1955 to become free-lance writer and literary critic; occasional academic assignments incl. Churchill Visiting Prof., Univ. of Bristol 1967, Visiting Prof., Centre Univ. Expérimental, Vincennes, France and George Elliston Lecturer on Poetry, Univ. of Cincinnati, U.S.A.; 1st holder, Fellowship in Creative Arts, Brasenose Coll., Oxford Univ. 1971–72; Prof. of Poetry, Oxford Univ. 1973–78; Supernumerary Fellow Brasenose Coll. 1973–; Dir. 1st "Poetry at the Mermaid" Festival London 1961; Somerset Maugham Award 1958, James Tait Black Memorial Prize 1974, Heinemann Award 1975 for Samuel Johnson, Whitbread Award (for Young Shoulders) 1982, Hon. D.L.H. (Keele) 1985; Hon. D.Litt. (Loughborough) 1985; F.R.S.L. 1960 (resgnd. 1961). *Publications:* poetry: Mixed Feelings 1951, A Word Carved on a Sill 1956, Weep Before God 1961, Wildtrack 1965, Letters to Five Artists 1969, The Shape of Feng 1972, Feng 1975, Poems 1949–1979 1981; novels: Hurry on Down 1953, Living in the Present 1955, The Contenders 1958, A Travelling Woman 1959, Strike the Father Dead 1962, The Young Visitors 1965, The Smaller Sky 1967, A Winter in the Hills 1970, The Pardoner's Tale 1978, Lizzie's Floating Shop 1981, Young Shoulders 1982, Where the Rivers Meet 1988; stories: Nuncle and other Stories 1960, Death of the Hind Legs 1966, The Life Guard 1971; plays: Harry in the Night 1975, Frank 1982; non-fiction: Preliminary Essays 1957, Sprightly Running (autobiog.) 1962, Essays on Literature and Ideas 1963, The Living World of Shakespeare 1964, A House for the Truth 1972, Samuel Johnson 1974, Professing Poetry 1977, Dear Shadows, portraits from Memory (memoirs) 1986; edited: Johnson as Critic 1974, Johnson on Johnson 1976, An Edmund Wilson Celebration 1978, Everyman's Book of English Verse 1981, Open Country (poems) 1987. *Leisure interests:* walking, canoeing. *Address:* c/o Century Hutchinson Ltd., 62–65 Chandos Place, London, W.C.2, England.

WAIN, Ralph Louis, C.B.E., D.SC., F.R.S.; British professor of chemistry; b. 29 May 1911, Hyde; s. of Mr. and Mrs. G. Wain; m. Joan Bowker 1940; one s. one d.; ed. County Grammar School, Hyde and Univ. of Sheffield and Manchester; postdoctorate research, Univ. of Manchester 1935–37; lecturer in Chemistry, Wye Coll., Univ. of London 1937–39, Univ. of Bristol 1939–45; Head, Dept. of Chem. Wye Coll. 1945–50; Prof. of Agricultural Chem. Univ. of London 1950–78, Prof. Emer. 1978–; Dir. Agricultural Research Council Unit on Plant Growth Regulation 1953–78; Hon. Prof. of Chem. Univ. of Kent 1978–; Fellow, Wye Coll. 1981–; several awards, including Mullard Medal, Royal Soc. 1988; Hon. D.Sc. (Kent, Sheffield, Lausanne); Hon. D. Agric. (Ghent). *Publications:* some 250 papers in professional journals. *Leisure interests:* painting, travel. *Address:* Crown Point, Scotton Street, Wye, Kent, TN25 5BZ, England. *Telephone:* (0233) 812157.

WAITE, Terence Hardy, M.B.E.; British religious adviser; b. 31 May 1939, Bollington; s. of Thomas William Waite and Lena (née Hardy) Waite; m. Helen Frances Watters 1964; one s. three d.; ed. Wilmslow School, Stockton Heath, Cheshire, Church Army Coll., London, pvtly. in U.S.A. and Europe; Lay Training Adviser to Bishop and Diocese of Bristol 1964–68; Adviser to Archbishop of Uganda, Rwanda and Burundi 1968–71; int. consultant working with Roman Catholic Church 1972–79; Adviser to Archbishop of Canterbury on Anglican Communion Affairs 1980–, Libyan hostages mission 1985; disappeared in Beirut Jan. 1987; mem. Church of England Nat. Ass. 1966–68; Co-ordinator Southern Sudan Relief Project 1969–71; mem. Royal Inst. of Int. Affairs 1980–, Butler Trust (Prison Officers Award Programme), Council of Worldlife Fund, Council of Uganda Soc. for Disabled Children; Chair. YMCA Int. Relief and Devt. Cttee.; Patron Strode Park Foundation for the Disabled, Hearne, Kent; U.K. 'Man of the Year' 1985 (Radar Award); Hon. D.C.L. (Kent) 1986, (City of London); Hon. D.LL. (Liverpool). *Leisure interests:* music, walking, travel, Jungian studies, int. affairs and politics. *Address:* c/o Lambeth Palace, London, SE1 7JU, England.

WAIYAKI, Dr. Munyua; Kenyan doctor and politician; b. 1926, Kikuyu, Kiambu Dist.; ed. Alliance High School, Kikuyu, Adams Coll., South Africa, Fort Hare Univ. Coll., South Africa, St. Andrews Univ., Scotland, and

Lund Univ., Sweden; Medical House Officer, Stracathro Gen. and Montrose Mental Hospitals 1957–58; Medical Officer, Kenya Medical Dept. 1958–59; pvt. practice 1959; Chair. Nairobi Branch, Kenya African Nat. Union (KANU); mem. Legis. (now Nat.) Ass. 1961–83; Parl. Sec. Ministry of Health and Housing 1963–64, Ministry of Defence in Office of Prime Minister 1964–66; later Asst. Minister of Health and Housing; later Deputy Speaker, Nat. Ass.; Minister of Foreign Affairs 1974–79, of Energy 1979–80, of Industry 1980–82, of Agric. 1982–83; Vice-Pres. Inter-African Coffee Org. 1983; Dr. h.c. (American Univ., Washington, D.C.) 1981.

WAJDA, Andrzej; Polish film and theatrical director; b. 6 March 1926, Suwałki; s. of Jakub Wajda and Aniela Wajda; m. 1st Beata Tyszkiewicz 1967 (divorced), one d.; m. 2nd Krystyna Zachwatowicz 1975; ed. Acad. of Fine Arts, Cracow and Film Acad., Łódź; Asst. Stage Man. 1953; Film Dir. 1954–; Stage Man. Teatr Stary, Cracow 1973; Pres. Polish Film Asscn. 1978–83; Hon. mem. Union of Polish Artists and Designers (ZPAP) 1977; Dr. h.c. (American Univ., Washington) 1981; Polish State Prize for Film Generation, Silver Palm for Kanal, Cannes 1957, Fipresci Prize for Ashes and Diamonds, Venice 1957, for the Birch Wood, Milan 1970, for Landscape after Battle, Milan 1971, for Man of Marble, Cannes 1978, Silver Prize for The Wedding, San Sebastian 1973, Grand Prize for Landscape After Battle, Colombo 1973, State First Class Prize 1974, Grand Prix, Moscow Film Festival 1975, Int. Prize for The Promised Land, Chicago Festival 1975, K. Swinarski Prize 1976, Valladolid Prize 1976, Grand Prix Gdańsk Lions for Without Anaesthetic 1978, First Prize and Best Dir. for the Promised Land, XVIII Film Festival, Cartagena-Colombia 1978, Premie David di Donatelle 'Luchino Visconti' 1978, Prize of Cttee. for Polish Radio and TV 1980, Palme d'Or for Man of Iron, Cannes 1981, Cesar Award 1981, 1982, British Acad. Award for Services to Film 1982, BAFTA Fellowship 1982, Onassis Prize 1982, Luis Delluc Prize for Danton 1982, Pirandello Artistic Award, Italy 1986, Kyoto Prize, Japan 1987; Order of the Banner of Labour (Second Class) 1975, Officer's Cross of Order of Polonia Restituta, Officier, Légion d'honneur 1982, Order of Kirill and Methodius (First Class), Bulgaria. *Films:* Pokolenie (Generation) 1954, Idę do słońca (I'm Going to the Sun) 1955, Kanal 1956, Popiół i diament (Ashes and Diamonds) 1957, Lotna 1959, Niewinni czarodzieje (Innocent Sorcerers) 1959, Samson 1960, Serbian Lady Macbeth 1961, Miłość dwudziestolatków (Love at Twenty) 1961, Popioły (Ashes) 1965, Bramy Raju (Gates of Paradise) 1967, Wszystko na sprzedaż (Everything for Sale) 1968, Przekładaniec (Jigsaw Puzzle)—for TV, Polowanie na muchy (Hunting Flies) 1969, Macbeth (TV) 1969, Krajobraz po bitwie (Landscape After Battle) 1970, Brzezina (The Birch Wood) 1970, Piłat (Pilatus)—for TV 1971, Mistrze i Małgorzata (Master and Margaret)—for TV 1972, Wesele (The Wedding) 1972, Ziemia obiecana (The Promised Land) 1974, Smuga cienia (The Shadow Line) 1976, Umarła klasa (A Dead Class)—for TV 1976, Człowiek z marmuru (Man of Marble) 1977 (Fipresci Prize, Cannes 1978, Jury Special Prize, Cartagena 1980), Bez znieczulenia (Without Anaesthetic) 1978, (OCIC Prize, Cannes 1979), Dyrygent (The Orchestral Conductor) 1979, Panny z Wilka (The Maids of Wilko) 1979 (Oscar Nomination 1980), Człowiek z żelaza (Man of Iron) 1981, Danton 1982, Miłość w Niemczech (Love in Germany) 1985, Kronika wypadków miłosnych (Chronicle of Love Affairs) 1986, Biesy (The Possessed) 1987. *Plays:* Kapelusz pełen deszczu (Hatful of Rain) 1959, Hamlet 1960, 1980, Dwoje na huśtawce (Two on the Seesaw) 1960, The Wedding 1962, The Possessed 1963, 1971, 1975, Play Strindberg 1969, Sticks and Bones, Moscow 1972, Der Mittmacher 1973, Noc listopadowa (November Night) 1974, Sprawa Dantona (The Danton Case) 1975, 1978, Idiota (Idiot) 1971, 1975, Kiedy rozum śpi (When Reason is Asleep) 1976, Emigranci (Emigres) 1976, Nastasia Philipovna (improvisation based on Dostoyevsky's The Idiot) 1977, Rozmowy z katem (Conversation with the Executioner) 1977, Z biegiem lat z biegiem dni . . . (Gone with the Years, Gone with the Days . . .) 1978, Antygone 1984, Zbrodnia i kara (Crime and Punishment) 1984, 1986, 1987, Nastasya (adapted from The Idiot) 1989, scenography for several productions. *Publication:* My Life in Film (autobiog.) 1989. *Address:* Film Polski, ul. Mazowiecka 6/8, Warsaw (Office); ul. Jozefa Hauke Bosaka 14, 01-540 Warsaw, Poland (Home).

WAKEFIELD, Sir Peter George Arthur, K.B.E., C.M.G.; British diplomatist; b. 13 May 1922; s. of John Bunting and Dorothy Ina (née Stace) Wakefield; m. Felicity Maurice-Jones 1951; four s. one d.; ed. Cranleigh School and Corpus Christi Coll., Oxford; served in Army 1942–47; Mil. Govt., Eritrea 1946–47; Hulton Press 1947–49; entered Diplomatic Service 1949; Middle East Centre for Arab Studies 1950; Second Sec., British Embassy, Jordan 1950–52; Foreign Office 1953–55, 1964–66; First Sec., British Middle East Office, Nicosia 1955–56; First Sec. (Commercial), Egypt 1956, Austria 1957–60, Japan 1960–63; Admin. Staff Coll., Henley 1957; Consul-Gen. and Counsellor, Benghazi 1966–69; Econ. and Commercial Counsellor, Tokyo 1970–72, Econ. and Commercial Minister 1973; seconded as Special Adviser on the Japanese Market, British Overseas Trade Bd. 1973–75; Amb. to Lebanon 1975–78, to Belgium 1979–81; Dir. Nat. Art Collections Fund London 1982–. *Leisure interests:* ceramics, restoring ruins, tennis, swimming. *Address:* Lincoln House, Montpelier Row, Twickenham, Middx., England; La Molineta, Frigiliana, nr. Malaga, Spain. *Telephone:* 01-892 6390 (England).

WAKEHAM, Rt. Hon. John, J.P., F.C.A.; British politician; b. 22 June 1932, Godalming, Surrey; s. of late Major W. J. Wakeham and Mrs. E. R.

Wakeham; m. 1st Anne Roberta Bailey 1965 (died 1984), 2nd Alison Bridget Ward 1985; three s.; ed. Charterhouse School; J.P. Inner London 1972–; M.P. for Maldon 1974–83, for Colchester S. and Maldon 1983–; Asst. Govt. Whip 1979–81, Govt. Whip 1981, Govt. Chief Whip 1983–87; Lord Commr. of H.M. Treasury 1981, Minister of State 1982–83, Parl. Sec. 1983–87; Parl. Under-Sec. of State, Dept. of Industry 1981–82; Lord Privy Seal 1987–88; Leader of House of Commons 1987–; Lord Pres. of Council Jan. 1988–. *Publications:* The Case Against Wealth Tax 1968, A Personal View 1969. *Leisure interests:* farming, sailing, racing and reading. *Address:* House of Commons, London, SW1A 0AA, England.

WAKIL, Abdul; Afghan politician; b. 1945, Kabul province; ed. Kabul Univ.; fmr. Sec. Gen. of Afghan Foreign Ministry, Minister of Finance, Amb. to U.K. and to Vietnam; mem. People's Democratic Party of Afghanistan (PDPA) 1964, mem. Cen. Cttee. 1977; mem. of Revolutionary Council of Afghanistan; Minister of Foreign Affairs 1986–89. *Address:* c/o Ministry of Foreign Affairs, Kabul, Afghanistan.

WALCHA, Helmut; German organist and harpsichordist; b. 27 Oct. 1907, Leipzig; s. of Emil Walcha and Anna Ficker; m. Ursula Koch 1939; ed. Leipzig Inst. of Music; Organist and teacher Musikhochschule, Frankfurt/Main 1929, Prof. of Music 1946–72; Organist, Dreikönigskirche, Frankfurt/Main 1946–81. *Compositions:* Choral Preludes (4 vols.). *Recordings:* incl. complete works of Bach for organ solo and for harpsichord solo. *Leisure interest:* literature. *Address:* Hasselhorstweg 27, 6000 Frankfurt/Main, Federal Republic of Germany. *Telephone:* 68-44-49.

WALD, George, PH.D.; American university professor; b. 18 Nov. 1906, New York; s. of Isaac W. and Ernestine Rosenmann; m. 1st Frances Kingsley 1931 (divorced), two s.; m. 2nd Dr. Ruth Hubbard 1958; one s. one d.; ed. New York Univ. and Columbia Univ., New York; Nat. Research Council Fellow, Kaiser Wilhelm Inst., Berlin and Heidelberg, Univ. of Zurich and Univ. of Chicago 1932–34; Tutor in Biochemical Sciences Harvard Univ. 1934–35, Instructor in Biology 1935–39, Faculty Instructor 1939–44, Assoc. Prof. of Biology 1944–48, Prof. 1948–77, Prof. Emer. 1977–, Higgins Prof. of Biology 1968–80; Visiting Prof. of Biochem., Univ. of Calif., Berkeley 1956; Vice-Pres. Perm. People's Tribunal, Rome 1980–; Chair. Div. Cttee. on Biology and Medical Sciences, Nat. Science Foundation 1954–56; Guggenheim Fellow 1963–64; Overseas Fellow, Churchill Coll., Cambridge 1963–64; mem. N.A.S.; Eli Lilly Prize, American Chemical Soc. 1939; Lasker Award, Public Health Asscn. 1953; Proctor Award, Asscn. for Research in Ophthalmology 1955; Rumford Medal, American Acad. of Arts and Sciences 1959; Ives Medal, Optical Soc. of America 1966; Paul Karrer Medal in Chem., Univ. of Zürich 1967; co-recipient Nobel Prize for Medicine 1967; T. Duckett Jones Memorial Award 1967, Bradford Washburn Medal 1968, Max Berg Award 1969, Joseph Priestley Award 1970. *Address:* 21 Lakeview Avenue, Cambridge, Mass. 02138, or 67 Gardiner Road, Woods Hole, Mass. 02543, U.S.A. (Home). *Telephone:* (617) 868-7748 (Cambridge), (617) 548-1748.

WALD, Patricia McGowan, LL.B.; American circuit judge; b. 16 Sept. 1928, Torrington, Conn.; d. of Joseph and Margaret (née O'Keefe) McGowan; m. Robert L. Wald 1952; two s. three d.; ed. Connecticut Coll. for Women, Yale Law School; Law Clerk, U.S. Court of Appeals for the Second Circuit 1951–52; Assoc. Arnold, Fortas and Porter, Washington, D.C. 1952–53; mem. Nat. Conf. on Bail and Criminal Justice 1963–64; Consultant, Nat. Conf. on Law and Poverty 1965; mem. President's Comm. on Crime in the Dist. of Columbia 1965–66, on Law Enforcement and Admin. of Criminal Justice 1966–67; Attorney, Office of Criminal Justice, Dept. of Justice 1967–68, Neighborhood Legal Services Program 1968–70; Co-Dir., Ford Foundation Drug Abuse Research Project 1970; Attorney, Center for Law and Social Policy 1971–72, Mental Health Law Project 1972–77; Asst. Attorney for Legis. Affairs, Dept. of Justice 1977–79; Circuit Judge, U.S. Court of Appeals for the Dist. of Columbia Circuit 1979–, now Chief Judge; August Voelmer Award, American Soc. of Criminology 1976, Woman Lawyer of the Year, Women's Bar Asscn. 1984; LL.D. (Hon.) George Washington Univ. Law School 1983, John Jay School of Criminal Justice 1985, Mt. Holyoke Coll. 1985. *Publications:* Bail in the United States (with Daniel J. Freed) 1964, Bail Reform: A Decade of Promise Without Fulfillment, Vol. 1 1972, Juvenile Detention in 'Pursuing Justice for the Child' 1977, The Rights of Children and the Rites of Passage in 'Child Psychiatry and the Law' 1980, Dealing with Drug Abuse: A Report to the Ford Foundation (with Peter Barton Hutt) 1972, Law and Poverty: Report to the Nat. Conf. on Law and Poverty 1965, and numerous learned articles. *Address:* 3832 United States Courthouse, 3rd Street and Constitution Ave., N.W., Washington, D.C. 20001 (Office); 2101 Connecticut Ave., N.W., Apt. 38, Washington, D.C. 20008, U.S.A. (Home). *Telephone:* (202) 535 3366 (Office); (202) 232 1158 (Home).

WALD, Richard C., M.A.; American journalist; b. New York; s. of Joseph S. and Lily (Forstate) Wald; m. Edith May Leslie 1953; two s. one d.; ed. Columbia Univ. and Clare Coll., Cambridge; reporter, later Man. Ed. Herald Tribune 1955–66; Asst. Man. Ed. Washington Post 1967; Exec. Vice-Pres. Whitney Communications Corpn. New York 1968–; Vice-Pres. News NBC, Pres. 1968–78; Sr. Vice-Pres. ABC News 1978–; Chair. of Bd. Columbia Spectator; mem. Bd. of Dirs. The Associated Press, Worldwide TV News. *Address:* 7 West 66th Street, New York, N.Y. 10023, U.S.A. (Office).

WÄLDE, Thomas, DR.IUR., LL.M.; German lawyer; b. 9 Jan. 1949, Pluderhausen; s. of Dr Ernst Wälde; m. Gabriele Wälde-Sinigoj 1981; one s.; ed. Univs. of Heidelberg, Lausanne, Berlin and Frankfurt and Harvard Law School; Research Fellow, Inst. for Foreign and Int. Econ. Law, Frankfurt 1973–77; Legal Officer, UN Centre on Transnational Corporations New York 1976–77; Resident Investment Adviser, UNIDO, Vienna 1978–79; Interregional Adviser on Mineral Devt. Legislation, Dept. of Tech. Co-operation for Devt., UN, New York 1980–85, Interregional Adviser on Petroleum and Mineral Legislation 1986–; Maier Leibnitz Award 1978; American Inst. of Mining Engineers Award 1985. *Publications:* Decision Analysis and Economic Legislation 1976, Transnational Investment Agreements 1978, Renegotiation of Transnational Agreements 1978, Methods and Mechanisms of International Industrial Enterprise Cooperation 1979, International Economic Development Law 1982, Permanent Sovereignty over Natural Resources 1985, Petroleum Investment in Developing Countries 1988. *Leisure interests:* history, anthropology. *Address:* DC1-846, NRED/DTCD, United Nations, One UN Plaza, New York, N.Y. 10017, U.S.A. *Telephone:* 212-963-8783.

WALDEN, (Alastair) Brian; British broadcaster and journalist; b. 8 July 1932; s. of W. F. Walden; m. Hazel Downes; one s., and three s. from fmr. marriages; ed. West Bromwich Grammar School, Queen's Coll. and Nuffield Coll., Oxford; univ. lecturer; M.P. for Birmingham All Saints 1964–74, Birmingham Ladywood 1974–77, Labour; TV presenter, Weekend World (London Weekend TV) 1977–86; mem. W. Midland Bd., Cen. Ind. TV 1982–84; Columnist London Standard 1983–86, Thomson Regional Newspapers 1983–86; Shell Int. Award 1982, BAFTA Richard Dimbleby Award 1985; columnist, The Sunday Times. *Leisure interests:* chess, gardening. *Address:* Landfall, Fort Road, St. Peter Port, Guernsey.

WALDENSTRÖM, Erland, F.R.S.A.; Swedish civil engineer and company director; b. 4 June 1911, Malmö; s. of Martin Waldenström and Hedvig Lion; m. Dorothy Ethel Boleyn Drewry 1945; one s. two d.; ed. Royal Inst. of Technology; Engineer, Korsnäs Sågwerks AB, Gävle 1934, 1936–40; Expert, Tech. Research and Devt. Swedish Fed. of Industries 1940–42; Official Expert and Sec. State Cttee. on Tech. Research 1941–42; Chief, Tech. Office, Svenska Cellulosa AB, Sundsvall 1942–46, Chief Engineer 1947–49; Industrial Counsellor UN Econ. Comm. for Europe (ECE), Geneva 1948; Dir. Luossavaara-Kiirunavaara AB 1950–81, Pres. 1950–57; Pres. Gränges AB 1950–71, Chair. Bd. 1971–77; Dir. Fed. of Swedish Industries 1951–84, Chair. 1971–73; Dir.-Gen. Export Asscn. of Sweden 1951–59, 1973–74, Chair. 1971–73; Dir. Swedish Employers' Confed. 1951–72; Dir. Liberian American-Swedish Minerals Co. (LAMCO) (Monrovia) 1955–75, Chair. 1975–76; Dir. Ironmasters Fed. 1955–62; Dir. Liberian Iron Ore Ltd. (Toronto) 1958–70, Chair. and Pres. 1970–77; Chair. Swedish Mining Asscn. 1957–59; Dir. Skandinaviska Banken 1957–71, 1st Vice-Chair. 1968–71, Dir. and 1st Vice-Chair. Skandinaviska Enskilda Banken 1972–82; Chair. LAMCO Joint Venture 1960–75; Chair. Swedish LAMCO Syndicate 1963–78; Dir. AB Bofors (Bofors) 1960–82; Chair. Thiel Art Gallery 1961–84; Dir. Stockholm School of Econs. 1961–77; Dir. S.A. Cockerill-Ougrée-Providence et Espérance-Longdoz (Seraing) 1970–78 (Espérance-Longdoz 1964–70); Dir. Bethlehem Copper Corpn. (Vancouver) 1970–73; Dir. Royal Swedish Opera 1961–72; Chair. Concert Asscn. of Stockholm 1973–83 (mem. Bd. 1956–83); mem. Royal Swedish Acad. of Eng. Sciences 1948–, Pres. 1977–79; Hon. mem. Royal Swedish Acad. of Music 1985–; mem. Centre d'Etudes Industrielles Foundation Bd. (Geneva) 1970–78. *Publications:* On Industrial Progress in Sweden 1942, Waste and Residual Products in Forestry 1942, Development Trends in Forestry 1946, The Wage Earner's Fund Game 1982; also several essays on tech. and econ. questions. *Address:* Linnégatan 86, S-115 23, Stockholm, Sweden (Home). *Telephone:* (0) 8-625066.

WALDENSTRÖM, Jan Gosta, M.D.; Swedish professor of medicine; b. 17 April 1906, Stockholm; s. of Prof. Henning Waldenström and Elsa Laurin; m. 1st Elisabet Waldenström 1932, 2nd Karin Nordsjö 1957; five s. two d.; ed. Univs. of Uppsala and Cambridge, Tech. Hochschule, Munich; various positions at Academic Hosp., Uppsala; Prof. of Theoretical Medicine, Uppsala 1947; Prof. of Practical Medicine, Univ. of Lund 1950–72; Physician-in-Chief, Dept. of Gen. Medicine, Gen. Hospital, Malmö 1950–72; foreign mem. N.A.S., U.S.A., French Acad. of Sciences; Hon. mem. Royal Soc. of Medicine, London and other foreign acads.; Jahre Scandinavian Prize in Medicine 1962, Gairdner Award 1966, Paul Ehrlich Prize 1972; hon. degrees from Univs. of Oslo, Dublin, Mainz, Oxford, Paris, London, Innsbruck and Poitiers, Freiburg im Breisgau. *Publications:* Studien über Porphyrie, 1937, Monoclonal and polyclonal hypergammaglobulinemia 1968, Diagnosis and Treatment of Multiple Myeloma 1970, Paraneoplasia 1978; numerous publs. on metabolic, hematologic and other subjects of internal medicine; chapters in many textbooks. *Leisure interests:* history, botany, travelling, art. *Address:* Department of Medicine, Malmö General Hospital, S 214 01 Malmö (Office); Roskildevägen 11A, 217 46 Malmö, Sweden (Home). *Telephone:* 040/91-62-02.

WALDHEIM, Kurt, LL.D.; Austrian diplomatist and United Nations official; b. 21 Dec. 1918; m. Elisabeth Ritschel Waldheim 1944; one s. two d.; ed. Consular Acad. of Vienna, Univ. of Vienna; entered foreign service 1945; served Ministry of Foreign Affairs; mem. Austrian Del. to Paris, London and Moscow for negotiation on Austrian State Treaty; 1st Sec.

1945–47; served Paris 1948–51; Counsellor and Head of Personnel Div., Ministry of Foreign Affairs 1951–55; Perm. Austrian Observer to UN 1955–56; Minister to Canada 1956–58, Amb. to Canada 1958–60; Dir.-Gen. for Political Affairs, Ministry for Foreign Affairs 1960–64; Perm. Rep. to UN 1964–68; Chair. Outer Space Cttee. of UN 1965–68, 1970–71; Fed. Minister for Foreign Affairs 1968–70; Perm. Rep. to UN 1970–71; Cand. for Pres. of Austria 1971, Pres. of Austria July 1986–; Sec.-Gen. of UN 1972–82; Guest Prof. of Diplomacy, Georgetown Univ., Washington, D.C. 1982–84; numerous hon. degrees; several decorations; Hussein bin Ali Medal 1987. *Publications:* Der österreichische Weg (The Austrian Example), Un metier unique au monde, Der schwierigste Job der Welt, The Challenge of Peace 1980, Building The Future Order 1980, In the Eye of the Storm 1985. *Address:* Ballhausplatz 2, 1010 Vienna, Austria.

WALES, H.R.H. The Prince of, and Earl of Chester (cr. 1958); **Prince Charles Philip Arthur George**, K.G., K.T., P.C., G.C.B., M.A., Duke of Cornwall and Rothesay, Earl of Carrick, Baron of Renfrew, Lord of the Isles and Great Steward of Scotland (cr. 1952); b. 14 Nov. 1948, London; eldest son of Princess Elizabeth (now H.M. Queen Elizabeth II, q.v.) and Prince Philip, Duke of Edinburgh (q.v.); m. Lady Diana Spencer (now H.R.H. The Princess of Wales, q.v.) 29 July 1981; two s., H.R.H. Prince William Arthur Philip Louis, b. 21 June 1982, H.R.H. Prince Henry Charles Albert David, b. 15 Sept. 1984; ed. Cheam School, Gordonstoun School, Geelong Grammar School, Trinity Coll., Cambridge, and Univ. Coll. of Wales, Aberystwyth; Barrister, Gray's Inn 1974, Hon. Bencher 1975; Personal A.D.C. to H.M. the Queen 1973–; Capt. R.N. 1988–; Col.-in-Chief The Royal Regt. of Wales (24th/41st Foot) 1969–; Col. Welsh Guards 1974–; Col.-in-Chief The Cheshire Regt. 1977–, The Gordon Highlanders 1977–, Lord Strathcona's Horse (Royal Canadian) Regt. 1977–, The Parachute Regt. 1977–, The Royal Australian Armoured Corps 1977–, The Royal Regt. of Canada 1977–, 2nd King Edward VII Own Gurkhas 1977–, The Royal Winnipeg Rifles 1977–, Pacific Islands Regt. 1984–, Royal Canadian Dragoon 1985–; Group Capt. 1988–; Hon. Air Cdre. R.A.F. Brawdy 1977–; Air Cdre. in Chief R.N.Z.A.F. 1977–; Col.-in-Chief Air Reserves Group of Air Command in Canada 1977–; Pres. Soc. of St. George's and Descendants of Knights of the Garter 1975–; Dr. h.c. (Royal Coll. of Music) 1981; Cdre. Royal Thames Yacht Club 1974–; High Steward, Royal Borough of Windsor and Maidenhead 1974–; Chair. Queen's Silver Jubilee Trust 1978–, The Mountbatten Memorial Trust 1979–; Pres. United World Colls. 1978–; Chair. The Prince of Wales' Cttee. for Wales 1971–; Pres. The Prince's Trust 1975–, Royal Forestry Soc. 1982–, Royal Acad. of Music 1985–, Young Business Trust 1986–; Chancellor, Univ. of Wales 1976–; mem. Bd. Commonwealth Devt. Corpn. 1979; Trustee, Nat. Gallery 1986–; represented H.M. the Queen at Independence Celebrations in Fiji 1970, at Requiem Mass for Gen. Charles de Gaulle 1970, at Bahamas Independence Celebrations 1973, at Papua New Guinea Independence Celebrations 1975, at Coronation of King of Nepal 1975, at funeral of Sir Robert Menzies 1978, at funeral of Jomo Kenyatta 1978; Coronation Medal 1953, The Queen's Silver Jubilee Medal 1977, Grand Cross of The Southern Cross of Brazil 1978, Grand Cross of The White Rose of Finland 1969, Grand Cordon of the Supreme of the Chrysanthemum of Japan 1971, Grand Cross of The House of Orange of the Netherlands 1972, Grand Cross Order of Oak Crown of Luxembourg 1972, Kt. of The Order of Elephant of Denmark 1974, Grand Cross of The Order of Ojasvi Rajanya of Nepal 1975, Order of the Repub. of Egypt (First Class) 1981; cr. Prince of Wales and Earl of Chester (invested July 1969); K.G. 1958 (invested and installed 1968), K.T. 1977, P.C. 1977, G.C.B. and Great Master of Order of the Bath 1975; Royal Fellowship of the Australian Acad. of Science 1979; Hon. Fellowship of Royal Coll. of Surgeons 1978, Royal Aeronautical Soc. 1978, Inst. of Mechanical Engineers 1979; received Freedom of City of Cardiff 1969, of Royal Borough of New Windsor 1970, of City of London 1971, of Chester 1973, of City of Canterbury 1978, City of Portsmouth 1979; Hon. Fellow, Trinity Coll., Cambridge 1988; Liveryman of Fishmongers' Co. 1971; Freeman of Drapers' Co. 1971; Freeman of Shipwrights' Co. 1978; Hon. Freeman and Liveryman of Goldsmiths Co. 1979; Hon. mem. of Hon. Co. of Master Mariners 1977 (Master 1988), of Merchants of City of Edinburgh 1979; Hon. Life mem. Incorporation of Gardeners of Glasgow 1989. *Publication:* The Old Man of Lochnagar 1980. *Address:* Kensington Palace, London, W.8; Highgrove House, Doughton, Nr. Tetbury, Gloucs., England.

WALES, H.R.H. The Princess of; b. (as Diana Frances Spencer) 1 July 1961, Sandringham, Norfolk; d. of 8th Earl Spencer and Countess Spencer (née Frances Roche, now Hon. Mrs. Peter Shand Kydd); m. H.R.H. The Prince of Wales (q.v.) 29 July 1981; two s., H.R.H. Prince William Arthur Philip Louis, b. 21 June 1982, H.R.H. Prince Henry Charles Albert David, b. 15 Sept. 1984; ed. Riddlesworth Hall Preparatory School, Diss, West Heath School, Sevenoaks; Teacher Young England Kindergarten School, Pimlico, London 1979–81; Patron, Welsh Nat. Opera 1982–, Royal School for the Blind, Leatherhead 1982–, The Malcolm Sargent Cancer Fund for Children 1982–, Pre-school Playgroups Assocn. 1982–, Swansea Festival of Music and the Arts 1983–, Royal Coll. of Physicians and Surgeons of Glasgow 1983–, British Deaf Assocn. 1983–, Nat. Children's Orchestra 1983–, The British Red Cross Youth Div. 1983–, London City Ballet 1983–, Nat. Rubella Council 1983–, Birthright 1984–, Help The Aged 1985–, The Commonwealth Soc. for the Deaf 1985–; British Lung Foundation 1986, British Sports Assocn. for the Disabled 1986, Nat. Hosps. for Nervous

Diseases, English Nat. Ballet 1989-, Relate 1989-; Pres. The Albany (a community centre in the East End of London) 1982-, Wales Craft Council 1983-, Dr. Barnardo's 1984-, Royal Acad. of Music 1985-, R.A.D.A. 1989-; Hon. Col.-in-Chief 13th-18th Hussars. *Address:* Kensington Palace, London, W.8; Highgrove House, Doughton, Nr. Tetbury, Gloucs., England.

WAŁĘSA, Lech; Polish trade union activist; b. 29 Sept. 1943, Popowo; s. of the late Bolesław and of Feliksa Wałęsa; m. Mirosława Wałęsa 1969; four s. four d.; ed. primary and tech. schools; electrician, Lenin Shipyard, Gdańsk 1966-76, 1980-; Chair. Strike Cttee. in Lenin Shipyard 1970; employed Zremb and Elektromontaż 1976-80; Chair. Inter-institutional Strike Cttee., Gdańsk Aug.-Sept. 1980; fmr. Chair. Nat. Co-ordinating Comm. of Independent Autonomous Trade Union "Solidarity" (NSZZ Solidarność), Chair. All-Poland Understanding Comm. NSZZ Solidarnoć 1980-82; fmr. mem. State Comm. for Formulation of Trade Union Activity; interned 1981-82; Dr. h.c. (Alliance Coll., Cambridge, Mass.) 1981, (Providence Coll.) 1981, (Univ. of Columbia) 1981, (Catholic Univ., Louvain) 1981, (MacMurry Coll., Jacksonville) 1982, (St. Denis Univ., Paris) 1982; Hon. citizen of Buffalo, N.Y. 1981, Osaka 1981; Man of the Year, Financial Times 1980, The Observer 1980, Die Welt 1980, Die Zeit 1981, L'Express 1981, Le Soir 1981, Time 1981, Le Point 1981; Awarded "Let us Live" peace prize of Swedish journal Arbetet 1981, Love International Award (Athens) 1981, Freedom Medal (Philadelphia) 1981, Medal of Merit, (Congress of Polish Community in U.S.A.) 1981, Free World Prize (Norway) 1982, Social Justice Award 1983, Nobel Peace Prize 1983, Human Rights Prize, Council of Europe 1989, and other awards and prizes; Dr. h.c. (Harvard) 1983, (Fordham) 1984. *Publication:* Le Chemin d'espoir (autobiography) 1987. *Leisure interest:* fishing. *Address:* ul. Polanki 54, Gdańsk-Oliwa, Poland (Home).

WALHAIN, Michel Octave Marie Louis, L. EN D.; French business executive; b. 25 Sept. 1915, Neuilly-sur-Seine; s. of Charles and Marie (Fritz de Graw) Walhain; m. Ketty Eloy 1943; one s. one d.; ed. Collège Sainte Croix de Neuilly, Lycée Pasteur, Faculté de Droit, Paris; Asst. Gen. Man. Thomson-Houston-Hotchkiss-Brandt (now Thomson S.A.) 1972-76, Pres. Thomson-Brandt 1976-81, Hon. Pres. 1981-87; Vice-Pres. Thomson-CSF 1976-; Officier, Légion d'honneur; Commdr., Ordre nat. du Mérite; Croix de guerre. *Address:* 148 boulevard Bineau, 92200 Neuilly-sur-Seine, France (Home). *Telephone:* 722-87-47 (Home).

WALKER, Rev. Sir Alan, Kt., O.B.E., M.A., D.D.; Australian ecclesiastic; b. 4 June 1911, Sydney; s. of Rev. Alfred E. and Violet L. Walker; m. Winifred G. Channon 1938; three s. one d.; ed. Fort Street Boys' High School, Sydney, Leigh Theological Coll., Enfield, Sydney and Univ. of Sydney; ordained Minister of Methodist Church of Australia 1934; Assoc. Dir. Methodist Young People's Dept., N.S.W. Conf. 1936-38; Minister, Cessnock, N.S.W. 1939-44; Supt. Waverley Methodist Mission, Sydney 1944-54; Dir. Mission to the Nation, Methodist Church of Australia 1953-56; Mission to America, Mission to Canada 1956-57; Visiting Prof. of Evangelism, Boston School of Theology, U.S.A. 1957-58; Supt. Cen. Methodist Mission, Sydney 1958-78; Dir. of World Evangelism, World Methodist Council 1978-88; Prin. Pacific Coll. for Evangelism 1989-; Chair. Australian Nat. Goals and Directions Inc.; has undertaken many lecturing and preaching engagements in U.S.A. and elsewhere; received (jtly. with Lady Winifred Walker) World Methodist Peace Award 1986. *Publications:* more than 20 books including: Life Begins at Christ 1980, Standing up to Preach 1983, Life in the Holy Spirit 1986. *Leisure interests:* swimming, gardening, amateur movies. *Address:* 14 Owen Stanley Avenue, Beacon Hill 2100, N.S.W., Australia. *Telephone:* (02) 4513923.

WALKER, Alice Malsenior; American author; b. 9 Feb. 1944, Eatonton, Ga.; d. of Willie L. Walker and Minnie (Grant) Walker; m. Melvyn R. Leventhal 1967 (divorced 1977); one d.; ed. Sarah Lawrence Coll.; Lillian Smith Award 1974, Rosenthal Award, Nat. Inst. of Arts and Letters 1973, Guggenheim Foundation Award 1979, American Book Award 1983, Pulitzer Prize 1983; Hon. Ph.D. (Russell Sage Univ.) 1972 Hon. D.H.L. (Univ. of Mass.) 1983. *Publications:* Once 1968, The Third Life of George Copeland 1970, In Love and Trouble 1973, Langston Hughes, American Poet 1973, Revolutionary Petunias 1974, Meridian 1976, I Love Myself When I am Laughing 1979, You Can't Keep a Good Woman Down 1981, Good Night Willi Lee, I'll See You in the Morning 1979, The Colour Purple 1982, In Search of Our Mothers' Gardens 1983, Horses Make a Landscape Look More Beautiful 1984, To Hell with Dying 1988, Living By the Word 1988, The Temple of My Familiar 1989. *Address:* c/o Harcourt Brace Jovanovitch Inc., 111 Fifth Avenue, New York, N.Y. 10003, U.S.A.

WALKER, Ardis Manly, B.S.; American engineer, poet and writer; b. 9 April 1901, Keysville, Calif.; s. of William Brannon Walker and Etta May Bole; m. Gayle Mendelssohn 1937; ed. Univ. of California, and Univ. of Southern California; mem. Tech. Staff Bell Telephone Labs. New York City 1927-32; poet and writer on American-Indian lore and early Californian history; also lecturer. *Publications:* Quatrains (verse), Muse, American Lyric Poetry, Sierra Prologue, Poets on Parade, Poetry Digest, The Winged Word, Mission Sonnets, Francisco Garces, Man and Missionary, Pioneer Padre, The Manly Story, Judas on the Kern, Sierra Sonnets, Last Gunmen, Freeman Junction, Walker Pass, Borax Smith: an Evaluation, Kern River Vignettes, The Rough and the Righteous, High Choice (verse), Vigor (verse), Haiku and Camera, West From Manhattan, The Prospectors

(verse), The Pageant (verse), Buena Vista (Haiku), West from Manhattan (prose poems); biographical study of artist Philip R. Goodwin 1977, Boreal Wilderness (verse and prose poems) 1977, From Wild Rootage (verse and prose poems) 1979, Greetings and Broadsides (poems) 1980, Rose Sequence (sonnets) 1982, Further Venturings (verse) 1982, Wild Wonder 1984, Love Harvest 1987. *Leisure interests:* collecting and researching Western Americana, conservation, exploring High Sierra Nevada. *Address:* P.O. Box 37, Kernville, Calif. 93238, U.S.A. *Telephone:* 376-6296.

WALKER, Charls Edward, M.B.A., PH.D.; American economist; b. 24 Dec. 1923, Graham, Tex.; s. of Pinkney Clay Walker and Sammye McCombs Walker; m. Harmolyn Hart 1949; one s. one d.; ed. Univ. of Texas and Univ. of Philadelphia; Pilot, U.S.A.F. World War II; Instructor in Finance and later Asst. and Assoc. Prof., Univ. of Tex. 1947-54; Instructor in Finance, Wharton School 1948-50; Assoc. Economist, Fed. Reserve Bank of Philadelphia 1953-54; Economist and Special Asst. to Pres. of the Repub. Nat. Bank of Dallas 1955-56; Vice-Pres. and Financial Economist, Fed. Reserve Bank of Dallas 1958-61; Asst. to the Sec. of the Treasury 1959-61; Exec. Vice-Pres., American Bankers' Asscn. 1961-69; Under-Sec. of the Treasury 1969-72; Deputy Sec. of the Treasury 1972-73; Chair. Charls E. Walker Assocs., Inc., Washington 1973-, American Council for Capital Formation; Co-Chair. Presidential Debates 1976; Chair., Pres.-Elect Reagan's Task Force on Tax Policy 1980; Co-founder Cttee. on the Present Danger; Co-Chair. Bretton Woods Cttee.; Hon. LL.D. (Ashland Coll.) 1970. *Publications:* The Banker's Handbook 1978 (co-Ed.), New Directions in Federal Tax Policy 1983 (co-Ed.), The Consumption Tax: A Better Alternative (co-Ed.) 1987, Intellectual Property Rights and Capital Formation in the Next Decade 1988; numerous articles in economic and other journals. *Leisure interests:* golf, music. *Address:* 1730 Pennsylvania Avenue, N.W., Washington, D.C. 20006 (Office); 10120 Chapel Road, Potomac, Md. 20854, U.S.A. *Telephone:* (202) 393-4760 (Office); (301) 299-5414 (Home).

WALKER, Daniel, J.D.; American lawyer and politician; b. 6 Aug. 1922, San Diego, Calif.; m. Roberta Dowse 1947; three s. four d.; ed. U.S. Naval Acad. of Northwestern Univ.; Admin. Aide to Gov. Adlai E. Stevenson II (Illinois) 1952; with Hopkins, Sutter, Owen, Mulroy, Wentz and Davis (law firm) 1953-66; Vice-Pres. and Gen. Counsel, Marcor and Vice-Pres., Gen. Counsel and Dir. Montgomery Ward & Co. 1966-71; Pres. Chicago Crime Comm. 1968-69; Gov. of Illinois 1973-77; Hon D.Hum.Litt. (Carroll Coll.) and several awards for distinguished service. *Publications:* Spotlights on Organized Crime, Rights in Conflict, Military Law (Textbook). *Leisure interests:* hunting, tennis. *Address:* 1152 Norman Lane, Deerfield, Ill. 60015, U.S.A.

WALKER, David Alan, PH.D., D.SC., F.R.S., F.I.BIOL.; British professor of photosynthesis; b. 18 Aug. 1928, Hull; s. of Cyril and Dorothy Walker; m. Shirley Wynne Mason 1956; one s. one d.; ed. Univ. of Newcastle; Royal Naval Air Service 1946-48; at Univ. of Newcastle 1948-58, Purdue Univ., Indiana 1953-54; Reader in Botany, Queen Mary Coll., Univ. of London 1963; Reader in Enzymology, Imperial Coll., Univ. of London 1964-70; Prof. of Biology, Univ. of Sheffield 1970-84, Dir. Research Inst. for Photosynthesis 1984-88, Prof. of Photosynthesis 1988-; Visiting Fellow, Connecticut Agricultural Experimental Station 1965; Corresp. mem. American Soc. of Plant Physiology 1979. *Publications:* C_3C_4 (with Gerry Edwards) 1983; over 200 publications on photosynthetic carbon assimilation. *Leisure interest:* singing the Sheffield carols. *Address:* Robert Hill Research Institute for Photosynthesis, University of Sheffield, Sheffield, S10 2TN, England. *Telephone:* (0742) 768555.

WALKER, David Alan, M.A.; British financial executive; b. 31 Dec. 1939; s. of Harold Walker and Marian Walker; m. Isobel Cooper 1963; one s. two d.; ed. Chesterfield School and Queens' Coll., Cambridge; joined H.M. Treasury 1961, Pvt. Sec. to Jt. Perm. Sec. 1964-66, Asst. Sec. 1973-77; seconded to staff IMF, Washington 1970-73; joined Bank of England as Chief Adviser, then Chief Econ. Intelligence Dept. 1977, Asst. Dir. 1980, Dir. 1982-88 (non-Exec. 1988-); Chair. Securities and Investment Bd. June 1988-; part-time Bd. mem. Cen. Electricity Generating Bd. 1987. *Leisure interests:* music, long-distance walking. *Address:* Securities and Investment Board, 3 Royal Exchange Bldgs, London, EC3V 3NL, England.

WALKER, David Bruce, M.SC.; Australian business executive; b. 30 Aug. 1934; s. of Noel B. Walker and June R. Walker; m. Leonora C. Freeman 1961; two s.; ed. Knox Grammar School, Wahroonga, N.S.W. and Univ. of Sydney; Demonstrator in Geology, Univ. of Sydney 1956-58, Bristol Univ., England 1958-59; Geologist with British Petroleum Co. in U.K., Gambia, Algeria, Libya, Colombia, Kuwait, Iran and U.S.A. 1959-74, Vice-Pres. Production Planning, U.S.A. 1974-77, Regional Co-ordinator Western Hemisphere 1977-79, Controller BP Exploration 1979-80, Chief Exec. BP Petroleum Devt. (U.K.) 1980-82, Dir. Resources Devt., BP Australia 1982-85; Chief Exec. Britoil PLC 1985-88; Chair. Sun Int. Exploration and Production Co., Sun Oil Britain Ltd. 1988-; Part-time Bd. mem. British Coal Corpn. 1988-; mem. Scottish Econ. Council, Gen. Cttee. of Lloyd's Register, British Olympic Asscn. Scottish Appeal Council; CBIM. *Leisure interests:* cricket, music, gardening. *Address:* Whippletrees, Chetnole, Sherborne, Dorset, England. *Telephone:* (0935) 872604.

WALKER, David Maxwell, C.B.E., Q.C., PH.D., LL.D., F.B.A., F.R.S.E.; British university professor and barrister; b. 9 April 1920, Glasgow, Scotland; s.

of James Mitchell Walker and Mary Paton Colquhoun Irvine; m. Margaret Knox 1954; ed. High School of Glasgow, Univs. of Glasgow, Edinburgh and London; army service in India, N. Africa and Italy, Capt., Indian Army 1939–46; practised at Scottish Bar 1948–53; Prof. of Jurisprudence, Glasgow Univ. 1954–58, Regius Prof. of Law 1958–, Dean of Faculty of Law 1956–59, Convener of School of Law 1984–88; Chair. Hamlyn Trust; Hon. LL.D. (Edin.) 1974. *Publications:* Law of Damages in Scotland 1955, The Scottish Legal System (5th edn.) 1981, Law of Delict in Scotland (2nd edn.) 1981, Law of Civil Remedies in Scotland 1974, Law of Contracts in Scotland (2nd edn.) 1981, Principles of Scottish Private Law (4th edn.) 1988, The Oxford Companion to Law 1980, The Scottish Jurists 1985, Stair's Institutions (Ed.; 6th edn.) 1981, Legal History of Scotland, Vol. I 1988. *Leisure interest:* book collecting. *Address:* Department of Private Law, University of Glasgow, Glasgow, G12 8QQ (Office); 1 Beaumont Gate, Glasgow, G12 9EE, Scotland (Home). *Telephone:* (041) 339 8855 (Office); (041) 339 2802 (Home).

WALKER, Edward Bullock, III, M.S.; American geologist and business executive; b. 10 Jan. 1922, Norfolk, Va.; s. of Edward Bullock Walker, Jr., and Mary (Ray) Walker; m. Katherine Miller 1953; two s.; ed. Boston Latin High School and Mass. Inst. of Tech.; joined Gulf Oil Corpn. 1947, Exploration Man., Mene Grande Oil Co., Venezuela 1947–62, Vice-Pres. 1967–68, Exploration Co-ordinator, Gulf Eastern, London 1962–67, Dir. Exploration Div., Gulf Research and Devt. Co., Harmarville, Pa. 1967; Pres. Gulf Mineral Resources Co., Denver, Colo. 1968–71, Vice-Pres. Gulf Oil Corpn., Pittsburgh, Pa. 1971, Exec. Vice-Pres. 1971–75, Pres. Gulf Energy and Minerals Co., Houston, Tex. 1975–78, Exec. Vice-Pres. Gulf Oil Corpn., Houston, Tex. 1978–81, Pres. and C.O.O. 1981–84, mem. Bd. of Dirs. 1974–84; Pres., C.E.O. San Tomé Venture Corpn., Houston 1984–. *Address:* San Tomé Venture Corporation, 3355 W. Alabama Suite, 840 Houston, Tex. 77098, U.S.A.

WALKER, Sir (Edward) Ronald, C.B.E., M.A., PH.D., LITT.D., D.SC.(ECON.); Australian economist and diplomatist; b. 26 Jan. 1907, Cobar; s. of Frederick T. Walker; m. Louise Donckers 1933; one s. one d.; ed. Univ. of Sydney and Cambridge Univ.; Lecturer in Econs., Univ. of Sydney 1927–38; Prof. of Econs., Univ. of Tasmania 1939–46; Econ. Adviser, N.S.W. Treasury 1938–39, Govt. of Tasmania 1939–42; Deputy Dir.-Gen. Australian Dept. of War Org. of Industry 1942–45; Econ. Counsellor for Europe and Counsellor, Australian Embassy, Paris 1945–50; Exec. mem. Australian Nat. Security Resources Bd. 1950–52; Amb. to Japan 1952–55, to U.N. 1956–59, and Australian Rep. on the Security Council 1956–57; Amb. to France 1959–68, to Fed. Repub. of Germany 1968–71, to OECD 1971–73; Chair. UNESCO Exec. Bd. 1947–48, Pres. UNESCO Gen. Conf. 1949; Chair. UN Experts on Full Employment 1949; Australian Rep. on Disarmament Comm. 1956–58, on Econ. and Social Council 1948–50, 1962–64 (Pres. 1964), Advisory Cttee. on Application of Science and Tech. 1964–74; Adviser to Govt. on Multinat. Corpns. 1973–74. *Publications:* An Outline of Australian Economics 1931, Australia in the World Depression 1933, Money (co-author) 1935, Unemployment Policy 1936, War-time Economics 1939, From Economic Theory to Policy 1943, The Australian Economy in War and Reconstruction 1947, National and International Measures for Full Employment (in collab.) 1950. *Address:* 1 rue de Longchamp, 75116 Paris, France. *Telephone:* 553-0300.

WALKER, George P. L., PH.D., F.R.S.; British geologist and volcanologist; b. 2 March 1926, London; s. of L. R. T. Walker and E. F. Walker (née McConkey; m. Hazel R. Smith 1958; one s. one d.; ed. Wallace High School, Lisburn, Northern Ireland, Queen's Univ. of Belfast and Univ. of Leeds; Asst. Lecturer, Imperial Coll. of Science and Tech., Univ. of London 1951–54, Lecturer 1954–64, Reader in Geology 1964–80; Capt. James Cook Research Fellow of Royal Soc. of N.Z., based at Univ. of Auckland 1978–80; Gordon A. Macdonald Prof. of Volcanology, Univ. of Hawaii, Manoa 1981–; Fellow Geological Soc. of America 1987, American Geophysical Union 1988; Hon. mem. Visindafelag Islendinga (Iceland), Royal Soc. of N.Z.; Hon. D.Sc. (Univ. of Iceland) 1988; Moiety of Lyell Fund, and Lyell Medal, Geological Soc. of London 1963, 1982; McKay Hammer Award, Geological Soc. of N.Z. 1982; Excellence in Research Award, Univ. of Hawaii 1985; Icelandic Order of the Falcon, Kt.'s Class 1980. *Publications:* scientific papers on the geology and mineralogy of Iceland, and processes in volcanology. *Address:* Hawaii Institute of Geophysics, 2525 Correa Road, Honolulu, Hawaii 96822, U.S.A. *Telephone:* (808) 948-7826.

WALKER, Herbert John, C.M.G., J.P.; New Zealand chartered accountant and politician; b. 2 June 1919, Rangiora; s. of Robert J. Walker and Margaret J. Johnston; m. 1st Phyllis Tregurtha 1942 (died 1980), three s.; m. 2nd Dame Susannah McLean 1981, two step-s. two step-d.; Accountant, Lincoln Agricultural Coll. 1954–60; Lincoln Coll. Bd. of Govs. 1960–70; Pres. Canterbury Trustee Savings Bank 1969; mem. Parl. 1960–78; Minister of Tourism, Minister of Broadcasting 1969–72, also Postmaster-Gen. Feb.–Dec. 1972; Minister of Social Welfare 1975–78, also Minister in charge of State Insurance Office, Govt. Life Insurance, Earthquake and War Damage; Accident Compensation Commr. 1979–80, Accident Compensation Corpn. 1981–; Pres. S. Island (NZ) Promotion Asscn. 1981–; Exec. mem. Returned Servicemen's Asscn. 1981–; Kt. of Grace, Military and Hospitaller, Order of St. Lazarus of Jerusalem 1979, Kt. Commdr. 1982. *Leisure interest:* community activities. *Address:* 21 Witbrock Crescent, Christchurch 5, New Zealand.

WALKER, John, B.A.; American art museum director; b. 24 Dec. 1906, Pittsburgh, Pa.; s. of Hay and Rebekah (Friend) Walker; m. Lady Margaret Gwendolen Mary Drummond 1937 (died 1987); one d. (and one s. deceased); ed. Harvard Univ., and with Berenson in Florence; Assoc. in charge of Fine Arts, American Acad. in Rome 1935–39; Chief Curator, Nat. Gallery of Art, Washington 1939–69, and Dir. 1956–69 (now Dir. Emer.); Trustee, American Fed. of Arts, Nat. Trust for Historic Preservation, A. W. Mellon Educational & Charitable Trust, Wallace Foundation; mem. Advisory Council, Inst. of Fine Arts of New York Univ.; mem. Bd. of Advisers of Dumbarton Oaks, Art Advisory Panel, British Nat. Trust, White House Historical Asscn.; Hon. D.F.A. (Tufts, Brown Univs., La Salle Coll.); Hon. D.Litt. (Notre Dame, Washington and Jefferson, and other hon. degrees); Officier Légion d'honneur. *Publications:* A Guide to the Gardens and Villas of Italy (with Amey Aldrich) 1938; edited: Great American Paintings from Smibert to Bellows 1729-1924 (with Macgill James) 1943, Masterpieces of Painting from the National Gallery of Art (with Huntington Cairns) 1944, Great Paintings from the National Gallery of Art (with Huntington Cairns) 1952; Paintings from America 1951, Bellini and Titian at Ferrara 1956, The National Gallery of Art, Washington 1956, Treasures from the National Gallery of Art (with Huntington Cairns) 1962, The National Gallery of Art, Washington, D.C. 1963, 1976, 1978, Pageant of Painting 1966, Self-Portrait with Donors 1974, Turner 1976, Constable 1978. *Leisure interests:* chess, bridge. *Address:* 4th Floor, 1729 H Street, N.W., Washington, D.C. 20006, U.S.A. *Telephone:* 298-8064.

WALKER, John Charles, M.S., PH.D.; American plant pathologist; b. 6 July 1893, Racine, Wis.; s. of Samuel B. and Alice D. Walker; m. 1st 1920 (died 1966), 2nd 1966 (died 1982); one s.; ed. Univ. of Wisconsin; Asst. in Plant Pathology, Univ. of Wisconsin 1914–17, Instr. 1919, Asst. Prof. 1919–25, Assoc. Prof. 1925–28, Prof. 1928–64, Prof. Emer. 1964–; Scientific Asst. U.S. Dept. of Agric. 1917–19, Asst. Pathologist 1919–25, Agent 1925–45, Collaborator 1945–; mem. N.A.S., American Phytopathological Soc., Botanical Soc. of America, American Soc. of Naturalists; Hon. mem. Asscn. Applied Phytopathological Soc., British Mycological Soc. 1980; E. C. Stakman Award (Univ of Minn.) 1972, Wolf Prize in Agric. 1978. *Publications:* Diseases of Vegetable Crops 1952, Plant Pathology 1950. *Leisure interests:* bowling, travel. *Address:* 10045 Royal Oak Road, Apt. 45, Sun City, Arizona 85351, U.S.A. *Telephone:* (602) 977-3788.

WALKER, Miles Rawstron; British politician; b. 13 Nov. 1940, Isle of Man; s. of George D. Walker and Alice Rawstron; m. Mary L. Cowell 1966; one s. one d.; ed. Castle Rushen High School and Shropshire Agric. Coll.; co. dir. farming and retail trade; mem. and past Chair. Arbory Parish Commrs. 1970–76; mem. House of Keys (Ind.) 1976–; mem. Bd. of Agric. Local Govt. Bd., Manx Museum 1976–81; Chair. Broadcasting Comm. 1979, Local Govt. Bd. 1981–86; mem. Exec. Council 1981–; mem. Assessment Bd. 1983–86; Vice-Chair. Post Office Authority 1984–86; Chief Minister, Isle of Man Govt. 1986–. *Address:* Magher Feailley, Main Road, Colby, Isle of Man. *Telephone:* Port Erin 833728.

WALKER, Rt. Hon. Peter Edward, P.C., M.B.E., M.P.; British businessman and politician; b. 25 March 1932; s. of Sydney and Rose Walker; m. Tessa Joan Pout 1969; three s. two d.; ed. Latymer Upper School; Chair. Rose, Thomson, Young and Co. Ltd. (Lloyd's Brokers) 1956–70; Deputy Chair. Slater Walker Securities Ltd. 1964–70; Dir. Adwest Ltd. 1963–70; mem. Lloyd's 1969–75; Parl. cand. for Dartford 1955 and 1959, M.P. for Worcester 1961–; mem. Nat. Exec. of Conservative Party 1956–; Nat. Chair. Young Conservatives 1958–60; mem. Conservative Commonwealth Council Gen. Cttee. 1960; Parl. Pvt. Sec. to Leader of House of Commons 1963–64; Opposition Spokesman Finance and Econs. 1964–66, Transport 1966–68, Housing and Local Govt. 1968–70; Minister of Housing and Local Govt. 1970; Sec. of State for the Environment 1970–72, for Trade and Industry 1972–74; Opposition Spokesman on Trade and Industry 1974, Defence 1974–75; Sec. of State for Agric., Fisheries and Food 1979–83, for Energy 1983–87, for Wales June 1987–; Conservative. *Publications:* The Ascent of Britain 1977, Trust the People 1987. *Address:* House of Commons, London, S.W.1; Abbots Morton Manor, Grooms Hill, Abbots Morton, Worcester, WR7 4LT, England (Home).

WALKER, Robert Mowbray, PH.D.; American physicist; b. 6 Feb. 1929, Philadelphia; s. of Robert Walker and Margaret Seivwright; m. 2nd Ghislaine Crozaz 1973; two s. by previous marriage; ed. Union Coll., Schenectady, New York, Yale Univ.; Research Physicist, Gen. Electric Lab., Schenectady 1954–66; Adjunct Prof. Metallurgy Dept. Rennslaer Polytechnic Inst., Troy 1958, Physics Dept. 1965–66; Nat. Science Foundation Senior post-doctoral Fellow and Visiting Prof. Univ. of Paris 1962–63; McDonnell Prof. of Physics and Dir. Lab. for Space Physics, Washington Univ. 1966–75; Visiting Prof. of Physics and Geology, Calif. Inst. of Tech. Jan.–June 1972; Visiting Scientist, Laboratoire Rene Bernas, Univ. of Paris, France May–Aug. 1975; McDonnell Prof. of Physics and Dir. McDonnell Center for the Space Sciences, Washington Univ. 1975–; Visiting Scientist Physical Research Lab., Ahmedabad, India 1981; Visiting Scientist, Institut d'Astrophysique, Paris and Laboratoire Rene Bernas, France March–Aug. 1981; Founder Vols. in Tech Assistance (VITA) 1960, Pres. 1960–62, 1965–66, mem. Bd. of Dirs. 1961–; numerous honours and awards. *Publications:* 185 scientific papers and book: Nuclear Tracks in Solids. *Address:* McDonnell Center for the Space Sciences, Box 1105, Washington University, St. Louis, Mo. 63130, U.S.A. *Telephone:* (314) 889-6225.

WALKER, Sir Ronald (see Walker, Sir Edward Ronald).

WALKER, Sarah Elizabeth Royle, L.R.A.M., F.R.C.M., F.G.S.M.; British mezzo-soprano; b. Cheltenham; d. of Elizabeth Brownrigg and Alan Royle Walker; m. Graham Allum 1972; ed. Pate's Grammar School for Girls, Cheltenham, R.C.M. and privately with Vera Rozsa; studied violin and cello and then voice (with Ruth Packer and Cuthbert Smith) at R.C.M.; Martin Musical Trust Scholarship to begin vocal studies with Vera Rozsa 1967; operatic débuts: Kent Opera, Ottavia in Coronation of Poppea 1969, Glyndebourne Festival, Diana/Giove in La Calisto 1970, Scottish Opera, Didon in Les Troyens 1971, English Nat. Opera, Wellgunde in The Ring 1971; Prin. singer with English Nat. Opera 1972-76; début Royal Opera House, Covent Garden as Charlotte in Werther 1979; début Metropolitan Opera, New York, as Micha in Handel's Samson 1986; has sung opera in Chicago, San Francisco, Göttingen, Geneva, Vienna and Brussels; concert repertoire includes, in addition to standard works, contemporary and avant-garde works by Berio, Boulez, Cage, Ligeti, Xenakis and others; sang Rule Britannia at last night of 1985 BBC Promenade concerts, London; recital début, Wigmore Hall, London with regular recital partner, Roger Vignoles, 1979; recital tours Australia, N. America, Europe; numerous recordings including Handel's Hercules and Julius Caesar and Stravinsky's Rake's Progress; video recordings of Gloriana (title role), Julius Caesar (Cornelia) and King Priam (Andromache); Pres. Cheltenham Bach Choir. *Leisure interests:* interior design, gardening, battling against incipient laziness. *Address:* c/o Robert Rattray, Lies Askonas Ltd., 186 Drury Lane, London, WC2B 5RY, England. *Telephone:* 01-405 1808.

WALL, Brian; American sculptor; b. 5 Sept. 1931, London, England; s. of Arthur F. Wall and Dorothy Seymour; m. Sylvia Brown 1973; two s.; ed. Luton Coll. of Art, England; numerous one-man exhbns. in London, Bristol, San Francisco, New York, Houston, etc. 1957-; has participated in numerous group exhbns. in U.K., Europe, N. America, Australia and N.Z.; works in many public collections including Tate Gallery, London, Art Gallery of N.S.W., Sydney, Museum of Art, Dublin and Seattle Art Museum; Asst. Prof. of Art, Univ. of Calif., Berkeley 1975-77, Assoc. Prof. 1977-81, Prof. 1981-. *Address:* 306 Lombard Street, San Francisco, Calif. 94133, U.S.A. *Telephone:* (415) 652-6042.

WALL, Charles Terence Clegg, PH.D., F.R.S.; British professor of mathematics; b. 14 Dec. 1936, Bristol; s. of Charles Wall and Ruth (née Clegg); m. Alexandra Joy Hearnshaw 1959; two s. two d.; ed. Marlborough Coll. and Trinity Coll. Cambridge; Fellow of Trinity Coll. 1959-64; Harkness Fellow at Inst. for Advanced Study, Princeton, U.S.A. 1960-61; Reader in Mathematics and Fellow of St. Catherine's Coll. Oxford 1964-65; Prof. of Pure Mathematics Univ. of Liverpool 1965-; Royal Soc. Leverhulme Visiting Prof., CIEA, Mexico 1967; Science and Engineering Research Council (SERC) Sr. Research Fellow 1983-88; mem. Council of Royal Soc. 1974-76, Council of London Mathematical Soc. 1972-80, Pres. 1978-80; Treas. Wirral Area SDP 1985-88, Wirral West SLD 1988-; Jr. Berwick Prize, Whitehead Prize, Polya Prize (London Mathematical Soc.), Sylvester Medal (Royal Soc.). *Publications:* Surgery on Compact Manifolds 1971, A Geometric Introduction to Topology 1971; over 100 research publs. in mathematical journals. *Leisure interests:* gardening, home winemaking. *Address:* Department of Pure Mathematics, The University, Liverpool, L69 3BX (Office); 5 Kirby Park, West Kirby, Wirral, Merseyside, L48 2HA, England (Home). *Telephone:* 051-794 4062 (Office); 051-625 5063 (Home).

WALL, Frank A., LL.M.; Irish politician and solicitor; b. 10 Oct. 1949, Limerick; s. of Frank M. Wall and Eileen Pierse; m. Margot Hourigan 1977; three s. one d.; ed. Mungret Coll., Limerick, Univ. Coll., Cork Inc. Law Soc., Dublin and Free Univ. of Brussels; Adviser Group of European Progressive Democrats, European Parl. 1974-79; Adviser to Minister for Agric., Dublin 1980; Nat. Dir. of Elections 1982; Senator 1982-83; mem. Exec. Cttee., Irish Council of the European Movt. 1980-; Gen. Sec. Fianna Fail 1981-; mem. Bd., Friends of Fianna Fail Inc., U.S.A. 1986-. *Publications:* European Regional Policy (with Sean Brosnan) 1978. *Leisure interests:* politics, gaelic football, golf, rugby, gardening. *Address:* Aras de Valera, 13 Upper Mount Street, Dublin 2, Ireland. *Telephone:* (01) 761551.

WALL, Frederick Theodore, B.CHEM., PH.D.; American physical chemist; b. 14 Dec. 1912, Chisholm, Minn.; s. of Peter Wall and Fanny Rauhala Wall; m. Clara Vivian 1940; two d.; ed. Univ. of Minnesota; Instructor to Prof. of Chem., Univ. of Ill. 1937-64, Dean of Graduate Coll. 1955-63; Prof. of Chem., Univ. of Calif. at Santa Barbara 1964-66, Vice-Chancellor Research 1965-66; Vice-Chancellor Graduate Studies and Research, and Prof. of Chem., Univ. of Calif. at San Diego 1966-69; Ed. Journal of Physical Chemistry 1965-69; Exec. Dir. of American Chem. Soc. 1969-72; Prof. of Chem., Rice Univ. 1972-78, San Diego State Univ. 1979-81; Adjunct Prof. Univ. of Calif., San Diego 1982-; Fellow American Acad. of Arts and Sciences; mem. N.A.S.; Corresp. mem. Finnish Chemical Soc.; American Chemical Soc. Award in Pure Chem. 1945, Univ. of Minn. Outstanding Achievement Award 1959. *Publications:* Chemical Thermodynamics 1958; numerous scientific articles on statistics of macromolecular configurations and discrete quantum mechanics. *Address:* 2468 Via Viesta, La Jolla, Calif. 92037, U.S.A. *Telephone:* (619) 459-8570.

WALL, Patrick David, M.A., B.M., B.CH., D.M., F.R.C.P., F.R.S.; British professor of anatomy; b. 5 April 1925, Nottingham; s. of T. Wall and R. Cresswell; ed. St. Paul's School and Christchurch, Oxford; Instructor of Physiology, Yale Univ. 1948-50; Asst. Prof. of Anatomy, Chicago Univ. 1950-53; Instructor of Physiology, Harvard Univ. 1953-55; Assoc. Prof. of Biology, M.I.T. 1957-59, Prof. 1959-67; Prof. of Anatomy, Univ. Coll., London 1967-; Visiting Prof., Hebrew Univ., Jerusalem 1972-; Dr. h.c. (Siena); Sherrington Medal (Royal Soc. of Medicine), Bonica Medal. *Address:* Cerebral Functions Research Group, Department of Anatomy, University College, London, Gower Street, London, WC1E 6BT, England. *Telephone:* 01-380 7376.

WALLACE, Anthony F. C., PH.D.; American anthropologist; b. 15 April 1923, Toronto, Canada; s. of Paul A. W. Wallace and Dorothy E. Clarke; m. Betty Shillot 1942; four s. two d.; ed. Annville High School, Lebanon Valley Coll. and Univ. of Pennsylvania; Medical Research Scientist, Eastern Pa. Psychiatric Inst. 1955-80; Prof. Dept. of Anthropology, Univ. of Pa. 1961-83, Univ. Prof. 1983-, Chair. 1961-71; mem. N.A.S., American Philosophical Soc.; Bancroft Prize in American History 1979, Guggenheim Fellow 1978-79; L.H.D. (Chicago) 1983. *Publications:* Culture and Personality 1961, Religion 1966, The Death and Rebirth of the Seneca 1970, Rockdale 1978, The Social Context of Innovation 1982, St. Clair 1987. *Leisure interest:* photography. *Address:* Department of Anthropology, University of Pennsylvania, Philadelphia, Pa. 19014-6398, U.S.A. *Telephone:* (215) 898-5208.

WALLACE, Bruce, PH.D.; American professor of genetics; b. 18 May 1920, McKean, Pa.; s. of George E. and Rose Paterson Wallace; m. Miriam Covalla 1945; one s. one d.; ed. Columbia Coll. and Columbia Univ.; Research Assoc., Dept. of Genetics, Carnegie Inst. of Washington 1947-49; Geneticist, later Asst. Dir., Biological Lab., Cold Spring Harbour, N.Y. 1949-58; Assoc. Prof., Cornell Univ. 1958-61, Prof. of Genetics 1961-81; Univ. Distinguished Prof. of Biology, Virginia Polytech. Inst. and State Univ. 1981-; mem. N.A.S., American Acad. of Arts and Sciences. *Publications:* Radiation, Genes, and Man (with Th. Dobzhansky) 1959, Adaptation (with A. M. Srb) 1961, Chromosomes, Giant Molecules and Evolution 1966, Topics in Population Genetics 1968, Genetic Load 1970, Essays in Social Biology (3 vols.) 1972, Basic Population Genetics 1981, Dobzhansky's Genetics of Natural Populations I-XLIII (with others) 1982, Human Culture: A Moment in Evolution (with others) 1983, Biology for Living (with G. M. Simmons, Jr.) 1987. *Address:* 940 McBryde Drive, Blacksburg, Va. 24060, U.S.A. *Telephone:* (703) 951-2464.

WALLACE, David James, PH.D., F.R.S.E., F.R.S.; British professor of mathematical physics; b. 7 Oct. 1945, Hawick, Scotland; s. of Robert Elder Wallace and Jane McConnell Wallace (née Elliot); m. Elizabeth Anne Yeats 1970; one d.; ed. Hawick High School and Edinburgh Univ.; Harkness Fellow, Princeton Univ., U.S.A. 1970-72; Lecturer in Physics, Univ. of Southampton 1972-78, Reader 1978-79; Tait Prof. of Math. Physics, Univ. of Edin. 1979-; Dir Edin. Concurrent Supercomputer Project 1987-; Chair. Physics Cttee., Science and Eng. Research Council 1987-; Maxwell Medal, Inst. of Physics 1980. *Publications:* articles in research and review journals on theoretical and computational physics, including neural network models. *Leisure interests:* eating at la Potinière, running. *Address:* Physics Department, University of Edinburgh, Mayfield Road, Edin., EH9 3JZ, Scotland. *Telephone:* 031-667 1081 (Ext. 2850).

WALLACE, Doreen (Mrs. D. E. A. Rash), M.A.; British writer; b. 18 June 1897, Lorton, Cumberland; d. of R. B. A. Wallace and Mary Elizabeth Peebles; m. Rowland H. Rash 1922; one s. two d.; ed. Malvern Girl's Coll., and Somerville Coll., Oxford; fmr. teacher; anti-tithe publicist; novelist and reviewer. *Publications:* Esques (with E. F. A. Geach) 1918, A Little Learning, The Gentle Heart, The Portion of the Levites, Creatures of an Hour, Even Such is Time, The Tithe War 1933, Barnham Rectory 1934, Latter Howe 1935, Going to Sea 1936, Old Father Antic 1937, The Faithful Compass 1937, The Time of Wild Roses 1938, A Handful of Silver 1939, East Anglia 1939, English Lakeland 1940, The Spring Returns 1940, Green Acres 1941, Land from the Waters 1944, Carlotta Green 1944, The Noble Savage 1945, Billy Potter 1946, Willow Farm 1948, How Little We Know 1949, Only One Life 1950, In a Green Shade 1950, Root of Evil 1952, Sons of Gentlemen 1953, The Younger Son 1954, Daughters 1955, The Interloper 1956, The Money Field 1957, Forty Years On 1958, Richard and Lucy 1959, Mayland Hall 1960, Lindsay Langton and Wives 1961, Woman with a Mirror 1963, The Mill Pond 1966, Ashbury People 1968, The Turtle 1969, Elegy 1970, An Earthly Paradise 1971, A Thinking Reed 1973, Changes and Chances 1975, Landscape with Figures 1976. *Leisure interests:* painting, gardening, stirring up politics. *Address:* 2 Manor Gardens, Diss, Norfolk, England. *Telephone:* (0379) 643479.

WALLACE, George Corley; American lawyer and politician; b. 25 April 1919, Clio, Ala.; s. of George C. and Mozell (Smith) Wallace; m. 1st Lurleen Wallace (died 1968), 2nd Cornelia Ellis Snively 1971 (divorced 1978), 3rd Liza Taylor 1981 (divorced 1987); one s. three d.; ed. Univ. of Alabama; fmr. state judge, Alabama; fmr. mem. Alabama State Legislature; Gov. of Alabama 1963-67, 1971-79, 1983-87; Dir. of Devt. for Rehabilitation Resources, Univ. of Alabama School System 1978-83; Counsellor to Gov.; cand. for Pres. American Ind. Party 1968; shot and wounded in assassination attempt May 1972; Chair. Dept. of Public Admin., Troy Univ. 1987-; Order of Lafayette Freedom Award 1973; Democrat. *Address:* Troy State

University, P.O. Box 4419, Montgomery, Ala. 36195-5701; 3140 Fitzgerald Road, Montgomery, Ala. 36106, U.S.A.

WALLACE, Ian, O.B.E., M.A.; British singer, actor and broadcaster; b. 10 July 1919, London; s. of Sir John Wallace and Mary Temple; m. Patricia G. Black 1948; one s. one d.; ed. Charterhouse School and Trinity Hall, Cambridge; appeared in buffo roles at Glyndebourne 1948 and continued to appear in opera in Britain and briefly in Italy until 1970s; later appeared on concert platforms and also in straight plays, reviews, musicals and pantomimes as well as in many television and radio shows notably My Music; has now returned to acting both in films and TV; Pres. Incorporated Soc. of Musicians 1979-80; Hon. mem. Royal Acad. of Music, Royal Coll. of Music. *Film appearances include:* Plenty, Porterhouse Blue. *Publications:* autobiography: Vol. I Promise Me You'll Sing Mud 1975, Vol. II Nothing Quite Like It 1982. *Leisure interests:* walking, photography, birdwatching, sport, reading. *Address:* c/o Fraser & Dunlop Ltd., 91 Regent Street, London, W1R 8RU, England. *Telephone:* 01-734 7311.

WALLACE, Walter Wilkinson, C.V.O., C.B.E., D.S.C.; British overseas administrator; b. 23 Sept. 1923, Edinburgh; s. of late Walter W. Wallace and of Helen M. Douglas; m. Susan Blanche Parry 1955; one s. one d.; ed. George Heriot's School, Edinburgh; Capt. Royal Marines 1942-46; Asst. District Commr., Sierra Leone 1948-54; Prin., Colonial Office 1955-57; Dist. Commr., Sierra Leone 1957-61, Prov. Commr. 1961, Devt. Sec. 1962-64; Establishment Sec., Bahamas 1964-67; Sec. to the Cabinet, Bermuda 1968-73; H.M. Commr., Anguilla 1973; Gov. of British Virgin Islands 1974-78; Foreign and Commonwealth Office 1980-. *Leisure interest:* golf. *Address:* Becketts, Itchenor, W. Sussex, England (Home). *Telephone:* (0243) 512438.

WALLACE-CRABBE, Christopher Keith, M.A., F.A.H.A.; Australian poet and critic; b. 6 May 1934, Melbourne; s. of Kenneth Eyre Inverell Wallace-Crabbe and Phyllis Vera May Wallace-Crabbe (née Cock); m. 1st Helen Margaret Wiltshire 1957, 2nd Marianne Sophie Feil 1978; three s. one d.; ed. Melbourne Univ., Yale Univ., U.S.A.; cadet metallurgist 1951-52; then journalist clerk, schoolteacher; Lockie Fellow in Australian Literature, Univ. of Melbourne 1962; Harkness Fellow, Yale Univ. 1965-67; Sr. Lecturer in English, Univ. of Melbourne 1967, Reader 1976, Personal Chair. 1987-; Visiting Chair. in Australian Studies, Harvard Univ., U.S.A. 1987-88; Masefield Prize for Poetry 1957, Farmer's Poetry Prize 1964, Grace Leven Prize 1986, Dublin Prize 1987. *Publications:* The Music of Division 1959, Selected Poems 1974, Melbourne or the Bush 1974, The Emotions are not Skilled Workers 1980, Toil and Spin: Two Directions in Modern Poetry 1980, Splinters (novel) 1981, The Amorous Cannibal 1985, I'm Deadly Serious 1988. *Leisure interests:* drawing, tennis, surfing. *Address:* 910 Drummond Street, North Carlton, Vic., 3054 Australia. *Telephone:* (03) 344-5504.

WALLACH, Eli, M.S. IN ED.; American actor; b. 7 Dec. 1915, Brooklyn, N.Y.; m. Anne Jackson 1948; one s. two d.; ed. Univ. of Texas, City Coll. of New York, Neighbourhood Playhouse School of Theatre; started theatre career 1946, film career 1955; Donaldson Award, Tony Award, British Film Acad. Award 1956; acted in plays: The Rose Tattoo, The Teahouse of the August Moon 1954-55, Camino Real, Luv, Typists and Tiger 1964, Promenade All 1973, Waltz of the Toreadors 1974, The Diary of Anne Frank 1978, Opera Comique 1987, The Flowering Peach in Florida 1987. *Films include:* Baby Doll 1956, The Line-Up 1958, Seven Thieves 1959, The Magnificent Seven 1960, The Misfits 1961, How the West Was Won 1962, The Victors 1963, The Moonspinners 1964, Lord Jim 1965, Genghis Khan 1965, How to Steal a Million 1966, The Good, the Bad and the Ugly 1967, The Tiger Makes Out 1967, Mackenna's Gold 1968, Cinderella Liberty 1973, Domino Principle 1975, The Sentinel 1975, The Deep 1975, Winter Kills 1975, The Silent Flute 1978, Movie Movie 1978, The Hunter 1979, The Wall 1980, The Executioner's Song 1982, Sam's Son 1985, Tough Guys 1986, Rocket to the Moon 1986, Nuts 1987. *Leisure interest:* photography.

WALLENBERG, Peter, LL.M.; Swedish business executive; b. 29 May 1926, Stockholm; s. of Dr. Marcus Wallenberg and Dorothy Mackay; m. (divorced); two s. one d.; ed. Univ. of Stockholm; various positions with Atlas Copco Group in U.S.A., Rhodesia, Congo and U.K. 1953-67; Deputy Man. Dir. Atlas Copco AB 1970, Chair. 1974; Skandinaviska Enskilda Banken 1974-, Vice-Chair. 1980, First Vice-Chair. 1984-; Chair. STORA, Investor, Providentia, Wallenberg Foundation, Enskilda Securities, London; Vice-Chair. ASEA, Electrolux, Telefon AB, L. M. Ericsson, SKF; Chair. Fed. of Swedish Industries; Pres. ICC, Paris; Dr. h.c. (Stockholm School of Econs., Augustana Coll., U.S.A.). *Leisure interests:* hunting, tennis, sailing. *Address:* Skandinaviska Enskilda Banken, S-106 40 Stockholm, Sweden. *Telephone:* 8 22 19 00.

WALLERSTEIN, Ralph O., M.D.; American professor of medicine; b. 7 March 1922, Düsseldorf, Germany; s. of O. R. Wallerstein; m. Betty A. Christensen 1952; two s. one d.; ed. Univ. of California Medical School, San Francisco; Chief of Clinical Hematology, San Francisco Gen. Hosp. 1953-81, Clinical Dir. of Blood Bank 1955-80; Chief of Staff, Children's Hosp. 1968-72; Clinical Prof., Univ. of Calif. 1969-; mem. Exec. Cttee. American Soc. of Hematology 1971-78, Pres. 1978; Chair. Bd. of Govs. American Bd. of Internal Medicine 1982-83, Chair. Cttee. on Hematology 1974-77; Gov., N. Calif., American Coll. of Physicians 1977-81, Chair. Bd.

of Govs. 1980-81, Regent 1981-87, Pres. 1987-88; mem. Residency Review Cttee. for Internal Medicine 1985-; Fellow A.A.A.S., A.C.P.; mem. American Medical Asscn., American Fed. for Clinical Research, American Asscn. of Blood Banks, American Soc. of Hematology, Inst. of Medicine, American Soc. of Clinical Oncology. *Publications:* Iron in Clinical Medicine (with S. R. Mettier) 1958, 27 articles in specialized journals. *Leisure interest:* photography. *Address:* Suite 707, 3838 California Street, San Francisco, Calif. 94118, U.S.A. *Telephone:* (415) 668-0160.

WALLING, Cheves (Thomson), PH.D.; American professor of chemistry; b. 28 Feb. 1916, Evanston, Illinois; s. of Willoughby George Walling and Frederika Christina Haskell; m. Jane Ann Wilson 1940; two s. four d.; ed. Harvard Univ. and Univ. of Chicago; Research chemist, E. I. Du Pont de Nemours and Co. 1939-43, U.S. Rubber Co. 1943-49; Tech. Aide, Office of Scientific Research and Devt. 1945; Research Supervisor, Lever Bros. Co. 1949-52; Prof. of Chem., Columbia Univ. 1952-70; Chair. Dept. of Chem., 1963-66; Distinguished Prof. of Chem., Univ. of Utah 1970-; Ed. Journal of the American Soc. 1975-81; mem. N.A.S., American Acad. of Arts and Sciences. *Publications:* numerous research publications; Free Radicals in Solution 1957. *Leisure interests:* skiing, sailing, photography, hiking. *Address:* Department of Chemistry, Univ. of Utah, Salt Lake City, Utah 84112 (Office); 2784 Blue Spruce Drive, Salt Lake City, Utah 84117, U.S.A. (Home). *Telephone:* (801) 581-8336 (Office); (801) 277-7565 (Home).

WALLMAN, Walter, DR. JUR.; German politician; b. 24 Sept. 1932, Uelzen; m.; one s.; ed. Univ. of Marburg; Judge at Rotenburg, Kassel and Giessen; mem. Hessischer Landtag 1966; mem. Bundestag 1970; Oberbürgermeister, City of Frankfurt-am-Main 1977; Chair. Christlich-Demokratische Union (CDU) in State of Hesse 1982-; Prime Minister of Hesse 1987-; Deputy Chair. CDU 1985; Fed. Minister for Environment, Nature Conservation and Nuclear Safety 1986-87; Minister-Pres., Hesse 1987-; Bundesverdienstkreuz. *Publication:* Der Preis des Fortschritts. *Address:* Bierstadter Strasse 2, 6200 Wiesbaden, Federal Republic of Germany.

WALLOP, Malcolm, B.A.; American politician; b. 27 Feb. 1933, New York; s. of Oliver M. Wallop and Jean Moore; m. French Wallop; three s. one d.; ed. Yale Univ.; owner, operator, Canyon Ranch, Big Horn, Wyo.; service U.S. army 1955-57; mem. Wyo. House of Reps. 1969-73, Wyo. Senate 1973-77; Senator from Wyoming 1976-; official observer from Senate on arms control negotiations; mem. Comm. on Security and Co-operation in Europe; Republican. *Address:* 237 Russell Senate Building, Washington, D.C. 20510, U.S.A.

WALLOT, Jean-Pierre, L. ÈS L., PH.D.; Canadian archivist; b. 22 May 1935, Valleyfield, Québec; s. of late Albert Wallot and of Adrienne Thibodeau; m. Rita Girard; two s. one d.; ed. Univ. de Montréal; Prof. and Dir. History Dept. Univ. de Montréal 1961-66, 1973-85; Historian Museum of Man of Canada 1966-69; Prof. Univ. of Toronto 1969-71, Concordia Univ. 1971-73; Nat. Archivist of Canada April 1985-; Dir. d'études associé, Ecole des Hautes Etudes en Sciences Sociales, Paris 1975, 1979, 1981, 1983, 1985, 1987; Dr. h.c. (Rennes) 1987; Marie Tremaine Medal (Canadian Bibliographic Soc.) 1973, Tyrrell Medal (Royal Soc. of Canada) 1983; Officier Ordre des Arts et Lettres. *Publications:* Intrigues françaises et américaines au Canada 1965, Les Imprimés dans le Bas-Canada (with John Hare) 1967, Un Québec qui bougeait 1973, Patronage et Pouvoir dans le Bas-Canada (with G. Paquet) 1973. *Leisure interest:* music, especially jazz—plays drums. *Address:* 395 Wellington Street, Ottawa, Ont., Canada K1A 0N3. *Telephone:* (613) 992-2473.

WALLS, Daniel Frank, PH.D., F.R.S.N.Z.; New Zealand professor of physics; b. 13 Sept. 1942, Napier; s. of James R. Walls and Barbara G. Walls; m. Fari Khoy 1968; one s.; ed. Auckland Grammar School and Auckland and Harvard Univs.; Asst. Prof. Univ. of Stuttgart 1970; Postdoctoral Fellow, Univ. of Auckland 1971; Sr. Lecturer, Univ. of Waikato 1972-76, Reader 1976-80, Prof. 1980-87; Prof. Univ. of Auckland 1987-; Adjunct Prof. Univ. of Arizona 1986-; Fellow, American Physical Soc., Optical Soc. of America; Frank Knox Memorial Fellow, Fulbright Fellow. *Publications:* 160 publs. in scientific journals; ed. of 4 books. *Leisure interests:* tennis, jogging, skiing. *Address:* 19A Holgate Road, Kohimarama, Auckland, New Zealand. *Telephone:* 64 9 585 212.

WALLS, Gen. (George) Peter, M.B.E.; Zimbabwean fmr. army officer; b. 28 July 1926, Salisbury; ed. Plumtree School, Royal Mil. Acad., Sandhurst, and Camberley Staff Coll., U.K.; enlisted in Southern Rhodesian Army 1944; commissioned into the Black Watch (Royal Highland Regt.), British Army 1946; attested back to Southern Rhodesian Perm. Staff Corps 1948, commissioned 1949; Commdr. C. Squadron, 22nd Special Air Service in Malaya 1951-53; Officer Commdg. Tactical Wing, later Chief Instructor, School of Infantry 1954-56; Co. Commdr. Northern Rhodesian Regt. 1956-59; Brigade Maj. Copperbelt Area and later N. Rhodesia District 1961-62; Adjutant-Gen. Rhodesian Army 1962-64; C.O. 1st Bn. Rhodesian Light Infantry 1964-67; Commdr. 2nd Brigade 1967-68; Chief of Staff, Rhodesian Army 1968-72, Commdr. 1972-77; Commdr. Combined Operations 1977-80, of Jt. Operations 1980; barred from Zimbabwe 1980; Grand Officer of the Legion of Merit, Defence Cross for Distinguished Service.

WALSER, Martin, DR. PHIL.; German writer; b. 24 March 1927, Wasserburg/Bodensee; s. of Martin Walser and Augusta Schmid; m. Käthe Jehle 1950; four d.; ed. Theologisch-Philosophische Hochschule, Regensburg, and

Univ. of Tübingen; writer 1951–; Group 47 Prize 1955, Hermann-Hesse Prize 1957, Gerhart-Hauptmann Prize 1962, Schiller Prize 1980, Büchner Prize 1981. *Publications:* short stories: Ein Flugzeug über dem Haus 1955, Lügengeschichten 1964; novels: Ehen in Philippsburg 1957, Halbzeit 1960, Das Einhorn 1966, Fiction 1970, Die Gallistl'sche Krankheit 1972, Der Sturz 1973, Jenseits der Liebe 1976, Ein fliehendes Pferd 1978, Seelenarbeit 1979, Das Schwanenhaus 1980, Brief an Lord Liszt 1982, Brandung 1985, Dorle und Wolf 1987, Jagd 1988; plays: Der Abstecher 1961, Eiche und Angora 1962, Überlebensgross Herr Krott 1963, Der schwarze Schwan 1964, Die Zimmerschlacht 1967, Ein Kinderspiel 1970, Das Sauspiel 1975, In Goethe's Hand 1982, Die Ohrfeige 1986; essays: Beschreibung einer Form, Versuch über Franz Kafka 1961, Erfahrungen und Leseerfahrungen 1965, Heimatkunde 1968, Wie und wovon handelt Literatur 1973 Wer ist ein Schriftsteller 1978, Selbstbewusstsein und Ironie 1981, Messmers Gedanken 1985, Uber Deutschland reden 1988; poems: Der Grund zur Freude 1978. *Address:* 777 Überlingen-Nussdorf, Zum Hecht 36, Federal Republic of Germany. *Telephone:* (07551) 4131.

WALSH, Sir Alan, Kt., M.SC.TECH., D.SC., F.INST.P., F.A.I.P., F.A.A., F.R.S., F.T.S.; British research physicist; b. 19 Dec. 1916, Darwen, Lancs.; s. of late Thomas Haworth Walsh and Betsy Alice Robinson; m. Audrey Dale Hutchinson 1949; two s.; ed. Darwen Grammar School and Manchester Univ.; at British Non-Ferrous Metals Research Asscn. 1939–46; seconded to Ministry of Aircraft Production 1943; joined Commonwealth Scientific and Industrial Research Org. (CSIRO), Australia 1946, Asst. Chief of Div. of Chemical Physics, CSIRO 1961–76; Consultant, Perkin-Elmer Corpn., Norwalk, U.S.A. 1977–; Hon. mem. Soc. for Analytical Chem., Royal Soc. of N.Z., Japan Soc. for Analytical Chem.; Foreign mem. Royal Acad. of Sciences, Stockholm; Pres. Australian Inst. of Physics 1968–69; Hon. Research Fellow, Monash Univ.; Hon. Fellow, Chemical Soc., London 1972, Australian Inst. of Physics 1979; Torbern Bergman Memorial Lecturer, Swedish Chem. Soc. 1976; Hon. D.Sc. (Manchester) 1984, (Monash); Britannica Australia Science Award 1966; Royal Soc. of Victoria Medal 1969, Talanta Gold Medal 1969, Kronland Medal, Czechoslovak Spectroscopic Soc. 1975, Matthew Flinders Medal, Australian Acad. of Science 1980, Robert Boyle Medal (Royal Soc. of Chem.) 1982; Maurice Hasler Award, Soc. for Applied Spectroscopy (U.S.A.) 1972; James Cook Medal, Royal Soc. of N.S.W. 1976; Royal Medal of Royal Soc. 1976; John Scott Award (City of Philadelphia) 1978; K. L. Sutherland Medal, Australian Acad. of Technological Sciences 1982. *Publications:* numerous papers in scientific journals. *Leisure interests:* gardening, golf. *Address:* 11 Norwood Avenue, Brighton, Vic. 3186, Australia (Home). *Telephone:* 03-592 4897.

WALSH, Arthur Stephen, C.B.E., M.A., F.ENG., F.I.E.E.; British business executive; b. 16 Aug. 1926, Wigan; s. of Wilfrid Walsh and Doris Walsh; m. 2nd Judith Martha Westenborg; one s. one d.; ed. Selwyn Coll., Cambridge; joined G.E.C. 1952, various sr. appointments, including Tech. Dir. of G.E.C./A.E.L. 1952–79; Man. Dir. Marconi Space and Defence Systems 1979–82; Man. Dir. The Marconi Co. 1982–85; Chief Exec., STC PLC 1985–. *Leisure interests:* sailing, skiing. *Address:* Aiglemont, Trout Rise, Loudwater, Rickmansworth, Herts., England. *Telephone:* (0923) 770883.

WALSH, Prof. Don, PH.D., M.S., M.A., B.S.; American business executive, fmr. university administrator and fmr. naval officer; b. 1931; Berkeley, Calif.; s. of J. Don and Marta G. Walsh; m. Joan A. Betzmer 1962; one s. one d.; ed. San Diego State Coll., Texas A. & M. Univ. and U.S. Naval Acad.; entered navy 1950, submarine service 1956; became Officer-in-Charge Submersible Test Group and Bathyscaph Trieste 1959, made record dive to 35,780 ft., Jan. 1960; Submarine service 1962–64; at Dept. of Oceanography, Texas A. & M. Univ. 1965–68; commanded submarine Bashaw 1968–69; Scientific Liaison Officer Submarine Devt. Group One 1969–70; Special Asst. to Asst. Sec. of the Navy for Research and Devt., Washington, D.C. 1970–73; Research Fellow, Woodrow Wilson Int. Center for Scholars 1973–74; Deputy Dir. Naval Labs. 1974–75; retd. from navy with rank of Capt. 1975; Dir. Inst. for Marine and Coastal Studies and Prof. of Ocean Eng., Univ. of Southern Calif. 1975–83; Pres. Int. Maritime Inc. 1976–; Vice-Pres. Parker Diving Service 1985–; mem. American Geophysical Union, American Asscn. for Advancement of Science, U.S. Naval Inst., Nat. Advisory Cttee. on Oceans and Atmosphere 1979–86, Law of the Sea Advisory Cttee. (U.S. State Dept.) 1979–83, Soc. of Naval Architects and Marine Engineers, American Soc. for Naval Engineers, Bd. of Govs., Calif. Maritime Acad. 1985–, etc.; Ed. Marine Tech. Soc. Journal 1976–80; Fellow Explorers Club, Marine Tech. Soc. 1980; Legion of Merit; Gold Medals from City of Trieste and Chicago Geographic Socs., U.S. Coast Guard Meritorious Public Service Medal 1980 (two awards), Meritorious Service Medal (two awards), Lowell Thomas Award from Explorers' Club 1987 and other awards. *Publications:* author of about 100 papers, articles, etc. on marine subjects; ed. and contrib Law of the Sea: Issues in Ocean Resources Management; Energy and Resource Development of the Continental Margins (co-ed.) 1980, Energy from the Sea: Challenge for the Decade (ed.) 1982, Waste Disposal in the Oceans: Minimum Impact, Maximize Benefits (co-Ed.) 1983. *Leisure interests:* writing, travel, sailing, flying. *Address:* International Maritime Inc., 839 South Beacon Street, Suite 217, San Pedro, Calif. 90731 (Office); 1337 Via Zumaya, Palos Verdes Estates, Calif. 90274, U.S.A. (Home). *Telephone:* (213) 514-8304 (Office); (213) 541-8397 (Home).

WALSH, Lawrence Edward, LL.D.; American lawyer; b. 8 Jan. 1912, Port Maitland, N.S., Canada; s. of Dr. Cornelius E. Walsh and Lila M. Sanders; m. Mary A. Porter; one s. four d.; ed. Columbia Univ.; mem. Bar, New York State 1936, Dist. of Columbia 1981, Oklahoma 1981, U.S. Supreme Court 1951; Special Asst. Attorney-Gen. Drukman Investigation 1936–38; Deputy Asst. Dist. Attorney, New York County 1938–41; Assoc. Davis Polk, Wardwell, Sunderland, and Kiendl 1941–43; Asst. Counsel to Gov. of New York 1943–49, Counsel to Gov. 1950–51; Counsel, Public Service Comm. 1951–53; Gen. Counsel, Exec. Dir. Waterfront Comm. of New York Harbor 1953–54; U.S. Judge, South Dist. New York 1954–57; U.S. Deputy Attorney-Gen. 1957–60; Partner, Davis, Polk & Wardwell 1961–81; Counsel, Crowe & Dunlevy, Oklahoma City 1981–; Special Prosecutor, "Iran-Contra affair" 1987–; many public appts. and mem. numerous bar and lawyers' assens.; five hon. degrees. *Address:* 1800 Mid-America Tower, Oklahoma City, Okla. 73102, (Office); 1902 Bedford Street, Oklahoma City, Okla. 73116, U.S.A. (Home).

WALSH, Peter Alexander; Australian politician; b. 11 March 1935, Kellerberrin, W. Australia; m.; four c.; fmrly. farmed family farm in Kellerberrin Shire for 25 years and held exec. positions in W. Australian Farmers' Union; mem. Senate 1974–; mem. Shadow Ministry 1977–83; Minister for Resources and Energy 1983–84, for Finance (and Minister assisting the Prime Minister for Public Service Matters) 1984–87, for Finance 1987–; Australian Labor Party. *Address:* Parliament House, Canberra, A.C.T. 2600, Australia.

WALSTON, Baron (Life Peer), cr. 1961, of Newton, Cambridge; **Henry David Leonard George Walston,** C.V.O., J.P., D.C.L., M.A.; British farmer and politician; b. 16 June 1912, Cambridge; s. of Sir Charles Walston and Florence Einstein; m. 1st Catherine Macdonald 1935 (died 1978); m. 2nd Elizabeth Scott 1979; three s. two d.; ed. Eton and King's Coll., Cambridge; Research Fellow in Bacteriology, Harvard Univ. 1934–35; mem. Hunts. War Agricultural Cttee. 1939–45, Cambs. Agricultural Cttee. 1948–50; Dir. of Agric. British Zone of Germany 1946–47; Agricultural Adviser for Germany to Foreign Office 1947–48; Counsellor of Duchy of Lancaster 1948–54; Trustee Rural Industries Bureau; mem. Home Office Cttee. on Experiments on Living Animals 1963–64; Deputy Chair. Council of Royal Commonwealth Soc. April 1963–64; Parl. Under-Sec. of State for Foreign Affairs 1964–67; Special Amb. of British Govt. at Presidential Inaugurations in Mexico 1964, Colombia 1966, Liberia 1967; Parl. Sec., Bd. of Trade Jan.-Aug. 1967; Crown Estate Commr. 1967–75; Chair. Inst. of Race Relations 1968–71; Chair. E. Anglia Regional Econ. Planning Council 1970–79, Great Britain/East Europe Centre 1974–86, Centre of East Anglian Studies, Univ. of East Anglia 1975–79, Harwich Harbour Conservancy Bd. 1976–79; Del. to Council of Europe 1971–74; mem. European Parl. 1975–76, Commonwealth Devt. Corpn. 1975–83, Deputy Chair. 1981–83; Vice-Pres. Voluntary Service Overseas 1982–; Hon. D.C.L.; S.D.P. *Publications:* From Forces to Farming 1944, Our Daily Bread 1952, No More Bread 1954, Life on the Land (with John Mackie) 1954, Land Nationalisation, For and Against 1958, Agriculture under Communism 1961, The Farmer and Europe 1962, The Farm Gate to Brussels 1970, Dealing with Hunger 1976. *Leisure interests:* shooting, sailing. *Address:* Town's End Springs, Thriplow, Royston, Herts., England; Marquis Estates, St. Lucia, West Indies. *Telephone:* (076 382) 388.

WALTER, The Hon. Sir Harold Edward, Kt., Q.C.; Mauritian lawyer and politician; b. 17 April 1920, Quartier Militaire, Moka; s. of Rev. Edward Walter and Marie Augusta Donat; m. Yvette Nidza Toolsy 1942; no c.; ed. Royal Coll., Curepipe; called to the Bar, Lincoln's Inn, London 1951; practised at Bar, Mauritius 1951–59; Village Councillor 1952, Municipal Councillor 1956, mem. Legis. Council (now Legis. Ass.) for Mahebourg 1959–82; Minister of Works and Communications 1959–65, of Health 1965–67, of Labour 1967–71, of Health 1971–76, of External Affairs, Tourism and Emigration 1976–82 (resgnd.); Chair. Commonwealth Medical Conf. 1972–74; Pres. World Health Org. 1976–77; Chair. Council of Ministers, Org. of African Unity 1976–77; Expert Consultant UNCTAD 1982–; Vice-Pres. Int. Cttee. for Communities of Democracy 1985; army service 1940–48, Staff Capt. M.E. Land Forces; Pres. YMCA 1955; Commdr., Ordre nat. des Palmes académiques (France) 1974, Commdr., Légion d'honneur (France) 1979, Grand Officier de l'Ordre diplomatique de la Corée 1980; Hon. D.C.L. (Mauritius) 1986; mem. Mauritius Labour Party. *Address:* La Rocca, Eau Coulée, Mauritius. *Telephone:* 860300.

WALTERS, Sir Alan Arthur, Kt., B.SC.; British economist; b. 17 June 1926, Leicester; s. of James Arthur and Clarabel Walters; m. 2nd Margaret Patricia Wilson 1975; one d. by previous marriage; ed. Alderman Newton's Secondary School, Leicester, Univ. Coll., Leicester, and Nuffield Coll., Oxford; Prof. of Econometrics and Social Statistics, Univ. of Birmingham 1961–68; Sir Ernest Cassel Prof. of Econs., L.S.E. 1968–75; Prof. of Econs., Johns Hopkins Univ., Baltimore, Md. 1976–; Visiting Fellow, Nuffield Coll., Oxford 1982–83; Econ. Adviser to World Bank, Washington, D.C. 1976–80; Econ. Adviser to Margaret Thatcher (q.v.) Jan. 1981– (part-time 1983–89); Dir. (non-exec.) Olympic Holidays 1983–; Hon. D.Litt. (Edinburgh, Leicester) 1981, Hon. D.Soc.Sci. (Birmingham) 1984. *Publications:* Economics of Road User Charges 1968, Money in Boom and Slump 1968, Noise and Prices 1975, Port Pricing and Investment for Developing Countries 1979, Microeconomic Theory (with Richard Layard) 1978, Britian's Economic

Renaissance: Margaret Thatcher's reforms 1979-1984 1986. *Leisure interests:* theatre, opera, music. *Address:* 2820 P Street N.W., Washington, D.C. 20007, U.S.A.

WALTERS, Barbara, B.A.; American television broadcaster; b. 25 Sept. 1931, Brookline, Mass.; d. of Lou Walters and Dena (Selett) Walters; m. 1st Lee Guber 1963 (divorced 1976), one adopted d.; m. 2nd Merv Adelson 1986; ed. Sarah Lawrence Coll., Bronxville, N.Y.; fmr. writer and producer with WNBC TV, then with Station WPIX and CBS TV morning broadcasts; Producer, NBC TV; joined Today programme, NBC TV 1961 as a writer, then gen. reporter, regular panel mem. 1963-74, Co-Host 1974-76; Moderator, Not for Women Only (syndicated TV programme) for five years; Corresp., ABC News, Co-Anchor of evening news programme 1976-78, Co-Host 20/20 1979-; Barbara Walters Specials 1976-; Hon. L.H.D. (Ohio State Univ., Marymount Coll., New York Temple Univ., etc.); Broadcaster of the Year, Int. Radio and TV Soc. 1975, Emmy Award of Nat. Acad. of TV Arts and Sciences 1975. *Publications:* How to Talk with Practically Anybody about Practically Anything 1970; contributions to Good Housekeeping, Family Weekly, Reader's Digest. *Address:* c/o ABC News, 7 West 66 Street, New York, N.Y. 10023, U.S.A.

WALTERS, Sir Peter Ingram, Kt., B.COM.; British oil executive; b. 11 March 1931, Birmingham; s. of Stephen and Edna F. (née Redgate) Walters; m. Patricia Anne Tulloch 1960; two s. one. d.; ed. King Edward's School, Birmingham and Univ. of Birmingham; served R.A.S.C. 1952-54; joined BP 1954, Vice-Pres. BP North America 1965-67, Gen. Man. Supply and Devt. 1969-70, Regional Dir. Western Hemisphere 1971-72; Dir. BP Trading Ltd. 1971-73, BP Chemicals Int. 1972, Chair. 1978-; Deputy Chair. The British Petroleum Co. Ltd. 1980-81, Chair. Nov. 1981-; Vice-Pres. Gen. Council of British Shipping 1974-76, Pres. 1977-78; Pres. Soc. of Chemical Industry 1978-79, Inst. of Manpower Studies 1980-; Dir. Post Office 1978-79, Nat. Westminster Bank 1981- (Deputy Chair. 1987-89); mem. of Council, Industrial Soc.; Gov. London Business School 1981-; Pres. Inst. of Dirs. 1986-; Trustee, mem. Foundation Bd. Nat. Maritime Museum 1982-83; Chair. Int. Man. Inst., Geneva 1984-; Hon. D. Univ. (Stirling) 1987. *Leisure interests:* golf, gardening. *Address:* The British Petroleum Company Ltd., Britannic House, London, E.C.2, England.

WALTERS, Sir Roger Talbot, K.B.E., F.R.I.B.A., F.I.STRUCT.E.; British architect; b. 31 March 1917, Chorley Wood, Herts.; s. of Alfred Bernard Walters; ed. Oundle School, Architectural Assocn. School of Architecture, Liverpool Univ. and Birbeck Coll.; entered office of Sir. E. Owen Williams 1936; Directorate of Constructional Design, Ministry of Works 1941-43; served in Royal Engineers 1943-46; Architect, Timber Devt. Assocn. 1946-49; Prin. Asst. Architect, E. Region, British Railways 1949-59; Chief Architect (Devt.), Directorate of Works, War Office 1959-62; Deputy Dir.-Gen. Research and Devt., Ministry of Public Bldgs. and Works 1962-67, Dir.-Gen. for Production 1967-69, Controller Gen. 1969-71; Architect and Controller of Construction Services, Greater London Council 1971-78; Prin. The Self-Employed Agency 1981-83; private practice 1984-87; Hon. F.A.I.A. *Address:* 46 Princess Road, London, N.W.1, England (Home). *Telephone:* 01-722 3740.

WALTERS, Lieut.-Gen. Vernon Anthony; American army officer and diplomatist; b. 3 Jan. 1917, New York City; s. of Frederick J. and Laura (O'Connor) Walters; ed. St. Louis Gonzaga School, Paris, Stonyhurst Coll., England; Second Lieut. U.S. Army 1941, rising to rank of Lieut.-Gen., served N. Africa, Italy; Mil. Attaché, Brazil 1945-48; Mil. Attaché at large, Paris 1948-50; Asst. to Deputy Chief of Staff, SHAPE, Paris 1951-56; staff asst. to Pres. Eisenhower 1956-60; mem. NATO Standing group 1956-60; Army Attaché, U.S. Embassy, Rome 1960-62; Defence Attaché, U.S. Embassy, Rio de Janeiro 1962-67; served Viet-Nam 1967; Defence Attaché, U.S. Embassy, Paris 1967-72; Deputy Dir. CIA 1972-76; Roving U.S. Amb. for Special Missions 1981-85; Perm. Rep. to UN 1985-89; Amb. (desig.) to Fed. Repub. of Germany Jan. 1989; interpreter to Pres. Truman, Eisenhower, Nixon; Distinguished Service Medal with oak leaf cluster, Distinguished Intelligence Medal, Legion of Merit with oak leaf cluster, Bronze Star, Air Medal (U.S.), Army Commendation, Nat. Security Medal 1976, Commdr., Légion d'honneur, Croix de guerre with palms, War Cross (Brazil), Bronze Medal Valor (Italy). *Publication:* Silent Missions 1978. *Address:* American Embassy, 5300 Bonn 2, Deichmanns Aue 29, Federal Republic of Germany; 2295 S. Ocean Boulevard, Palm Beach, Fla. 33480, U.S.A.

WALTERSPIEL, Otto Heinrich, PH.D.; German businessman; b. 7 Sept. 1927, Munich; m. Almuth Schaetz 1957; two s. two d.; ed. Tech. Univ., Munich and Purdue Univ., W. Lafayette, Ind., U.S.A.; worked in Export and Agrochemical Sales in BASF AG 1954-73, Man. Far Eastern Div. 1973-74; Chair. Exec. Bd. Kali und Salz AG, Kassel 1975-, Wintershall AG, Kassel 1976-80. *Address:* Friedrich-Ebert-Strasse 160, D3500 Kassel, Federal Republic of Germany. *Telephone:* (0) 561-3010.

WALTHER, Herbert, DR.RER.NAT.; German professor of physics; b. 19 Jan. 1935, Ludwigshafen; s. of Philipp Walther and Anna Lorenz; m. Margot Gröschel 1962; one s. one d.; ed. Univ. of Heidelberg and Tech. Univ. of Hannover; Asst. Univ. of Hannover 1963-68, lecturer in Physics 1968-69; Prof. of Physics, Univ. of Bonn 1971, Univ. of Cologne 1971-75, Univ. of Munich 1975-; Dir. Max-Planck-Inst. für Quantenoptik 1981-; mem. Bav-

arian Acad. of Sciences, Acad. Leopoldina; Max Born Prize, Inst. of Physics 1978. *Publications:* 4 books on laser spectroscopy and high power lasers and applications; 180 articles in professional journals. *Address:* Sektion Physik, Universität München, Am Coulombwall 1, 8046 Garching; Max-Planck-Institut für Quantenoptik, 8046 Garching (Office); Egenhoferstrasse 7a, 8000 Munich 60, Federal Republic of Germany (Home). *Telephone:* (089) 3209-5142; (089) 32905-704 (Office); (089) 8349859 (Home).

WALTHER, Rosel (née Fischer); German politician; b. 12 Jan. 1928, Landsberg; m.; two c.; Deputy to People's Chamber (Volkskammer), G.D.R. 1950-58, 1967-, Deputy Chair. 1967-71, First Deputy Chair. Constitutional and Legal Cttee. 1971-; mem. Council of State 1971-; Sec. Main Cttee. Nat. Democratic Party of Germany (NDPD) 1972-, Deputy Leader in Volkskammer 1976-; mem. World Peace Council 1974-. *Address:* Staatsrat, 1020 Berlin, German Democratic Republic.

WALTON, Ernest Thomas Sinton, M.A., M.SC., PH.D.; Irish university professor; b. 6 Oct. 1903, Dungarvan, Co. Waterford; s. of Rev. John Arthur Walton and Anne Elizabeth Walton (née Sinton); m. Winifred I. Wilson 1934; two s. two d. (and one deceased); ed. Methodist Coll., Belfast, Trinity Coll., Dublin, and Cambridge Univ.; Fellow Trinity Coll. Dublin 1934-74, Fellow Emer. 1974-, Erasmus Smith's Prof. of Natural and Experimental Philosophy 1946-74; awarded Hughes Medal, Royal Soc. (jointly with Sir John Cockcroft) 1938; Nobel Prize in Physics (jointly with Sir John Cockcroft) 1951, for pioneer work in the field of nuclear physics: Hon. D.Sc. (Belfast) 1959, (Gustavus Adolphus Coll.) 1975, (Ulster) 1988; Hon. Life mem. Royal Dublin Soc. 1981, Hon. Fellow Inst. of Engineers of Ireland. *Leisure interests:* gardening, woodwork and metal work. *Address:* 26 St. Kevin's Park, Dartry Road, Dublin 6, Ireland. *Telephone:* 971 328.

WALTON, Henry John, M.D., PH.D., F.R.C.P.(E), F.R.C.PSYCH., D.P.M.; British physician, psychiatrist and medical educator; b. 15 Feb. 1924, Kuruman; ed. Univs. of Cape Town, London and Edinburgh and Columbia Univ., New York; Registrar in Neurology and Psychiatry, Univ. of Cape Town 1946-54, Head, Dept. of Psychiatry 1957-60; Sr. Registrar, Maudsley Hosp. London 1955-57; Sr. Lecturer in Psychiatry, Univ. of Edin. 1962-70, Prof. of Psychiatry 1970-85, Prof. of Int. Medical Educ. 1986-; Ed. Medical Educ. 1976-; Pres. Asscn. for Medical Educ. in Europe 1972-86, Hon. Life Pres. 1986-; Pres. World Fed. for Medical Educ. 1983-; frequent consultant to WHO and mem. Advisory Panel on Health Manpower; led worldwide inquiry into training of doctors since 1983; Pres. World Conf. on Medical Educ., Edin. 1988; mem. Soc. of Medical Studies of Greece; Academician, Acad. of Medical Sciences of Buenos Aires; Foundation mem. Nat. Asscn. for Medical Educ. of Czechoslovakia; Hermann Sahili Medal, Univ. of Berne 1976; Thureus Prize, Swedish Acad. of Medical Sciences 1982; De Lancey Prize, Royal Soc. of Medicine 1984; Joffre Medal, Spanish Soc. for Advancement of Psychiatry 1985, WHO Medal 1988. *Publications:* Alcoholism (with N. Kessel) 1966, 1988, Small Group Psychotherapy (Ed.) 1974, Dictionary of Psychiatry (Ed.) 1985, Newer Developments in Assessing Clinical Competence (Ed. with others), Problem-based Learning (Ed. with M. B. Matthews) 1988. *Leisure interests:* literature, visual arts, particularly Western painting, Chinese and Japanese Art. *Address:* International Medical Education, The Medical School, University of Edinburgh, Teviot Place, Edinburgh, EH8 2AG (Office); 38 Blackett Place, Edinburgh, EH9 1RL, Scotland (Home). *Telephone:* 031-226 3125 (Office); 031-667 7811 (Home).

WALTON, Sir John Nicholas, Kt., T.D., M.D., D.SC., F.R.C.P.; British neurologist; b. 16 Sept. 1922, Rowlands Gill; s. of Herbert and Eleanor Watson (née Ward) Walton; m. Mary Elizabeth Harrison 1946; one s. two d.; ed. Alderman Wraith Grammar School, Spennymoor, Co. Durham, King's Coll., Medical School, Univ. of Durham; served Royal Army Medical Corps 1947-49; Medical Registrar, Royal Victoria Infirmary, Newcastle upon Tyne 1949-51; Nuffield Foundation Travelling Fellow, Mass. Gen. Hosp., Harvard Medical School, Boston, U.S.A., King's Coll. Travelling Fellow, MRC Neurology Unit, Nat. Hosp., Queen Sq., London 1954-55; First Asst. in Neurology, Univ. of Durham (Newcastle upon Tyne) 1955-58; Consultant Neurologist, Newcastle Hosps. 1958-83; Prof. of Neurology, Univ. of Newcastle upon Tyne 1968-83, Dean of Medicine 1971-81; Warden, Green Coll., Oxford Oct. 1983-; mem. MRC 1974-78, Gen. Medical Council (Chair. Educ. Cttee.) 1971-, Pres. 1982-; Chair. Muscular Dystrophy Group of G.B. 1971-; Pres. British Medical Asscn. 1980-82; Pres. Royal Soc. of Medicine 1984-86; First Vice-Pres. World Fed. of Neurology 1981-; Hon. F.A.C.P. 1980; Hon. F.R.C.P. (Edinburgh) 1981, etc.; Hon. Dr. de l'Univ. (Aix-Marseille) 1975; Hon. D.Sc. (Leeds) 1979, (Leicester) 1980; Hon. M.D. (Sheffield) 1987; Hon. D.C.L. (Newcastle) 1988. *Publications:* Subarachnoid Haemorrhage 1956, Polymyositis (with R. D. Adams) 1958, Essentials of Neurology 1961, Disorders of Voluntary Muscle (Ed.) 1964, Brain's Diseases of the Nervous System 1985 (9th edition), Skeletal Muscle Pathology (with F. L. Mastaglia) 1982, Oxford Companion to Medicine (Ed.) 1986, and numerous articles in scientific journals. *Leisure interests:* music, golf, reading, cricket. *Address:* Green College, Radcliffe Observatory, Oxford, OX2 6HG, England.

WALY, Youssef, PH.D.; Egyptian politician; b. 1930; ed. Faculty of Agric., Cairo Univ. and in U.S.A.; Reader, later Prof. Faculty of Agric., Cairo Univ.; Consultant, Ministry of Scientific Research and Ministry of Agric. and Land Reform; fmr. Agric. Planning Consultant in Libya; Deputy Prime

Minister Sept. 1985–; Minister of State for Agric. and Food Security 1982–87, of Agric. and Land Reclamation 1987–. *Address:* Ministry of Agriculture, Sharia Wizaret Al Ziraa, Dokki, Giza, Egypt. *Telephone:* 702677.

WAMBAUGH, Joseph, M.A.; American author; b. 22 Jan. 1937, East Pittsburgh, Pa.; s. of Joseph A. Wambaugh and Anne Malloy; ed. Calif. State Coll. Los. Angeles; served U.S. Marine Corps. 1954–57; police officer, Los Angeles 1960–74; creator, TV series, Police Story 1973. *Publications:* The New Centurions 1971, The Blue Knight 1972, The Onion Field 1973, The Choirboys 1975, The Black Marble 1978, The Glitter Dome 1981, The Delta Star 1983, Lines and Shadows 1984, The Secrets of Harry Bright 1985, Echoes in the Darkness 1987, The Brooding 1989.

WAN DA; Chinese party official; Deputy Sec. Yiyang Dist. CP, Hunan 1952; Dir. Rural Work Dept., CCP Cttee., Hunan 1957; Sec. Secr., CCP Cttee., Hunan 1966; mem. Standing Cttee., Prov. Revolutionary Cttee., Hunan 1970; Vice-Chair. Prov. Revolutionary Cttee. 1970–79; Sec. CCP Cttee., Hunan 1973–79; mem. 11th Cen. Cttee., CCP 1977; Second Sec., CCP Cttee., Hunan 1979; Chair. Prov. People's Congress, Hunan 1979–83; mem. 12th Cen. Cttee., CCP 1982–87; Chair. Advisory Cttee., CCP Cttee., Hunan 1985–. *Address:* People's Congress, Hunan Province, People's Republic of China.

WAN FANG; Chinese playwright; b. 1952; fmr. mem. Opera Troupe of Shenyang Mil. Command of the PLA; mem. Cen. Opera Troupe, Beijing; *Works include:* adaptation of Prarie for 1987 Chinese Arts Festival. *Address:* Central Opera Troupe, Beijing, People's Republic of China.

WAN HAIFENG; Chinese army officer; Deputy Commdr. Beijing Mil. Region 1972–74, Deputy Political Commissar 1975–82; mem. 12th Cen. Cttee. CCP 1982–87; Political Commissar Chengdu Mil. Region 1982–, Party Cttee. Sec. 1985–. *Address:* People's Liberation Army, Chengdu Units, Sichuan, People's Republic of China.

WAN LI; Chinese government official; b. Dec. 1916, Dongping County, Shandong Prov.; joined CCP 1936; trained as teacher; various posts in Dongping County CCP Cttee.; served on Hebei-Shangdong CCP Cttee., Deputy Dir. Financial and Econ. Cttee., Nanjing Mil. Control Comm.; Head Econ. Dept. and Dir. Construction Bureau 1947–49; Deputy Head, then Head Industrial Dept., Southwest China Mil. and Admin. Cttee.; Vice-Minister of Bldg., Minister of Urban Construction 1949–58; subsequently Sec. Beijing Municipal CCP Cttee., Deputy Mayor of Beijing, Asst. to Premier Zhou Enlai in planning and organizing work of Ten Major Projects of the Capital (including Great Hall of the People) and other important construction projects; persecuted during Cultural Revolution 1966–73; Vice-Chair. Municipal Revolutionary Cttee.; fmr. Minister of Railways, Head Provisional Leading Party mems.' group in Ministry; closely allied with Deng Xiaoping's policies; dismissed as Minister when latter fell from favour 1976; First Vice-Minister of Light Industry 1977; First Sec. Anhui Prov. CCP Cttee., Chair. Anhui Prov. Revolutionary Cttee., First Political Commissar, Anhui Mil. Area 1977–80; Vice-Premier, State Council and Chair. State Agricultural Comm., Sec. Leading Party Group, Chair. Cen. Afforestation Comm., State People's Air Defence Comm. 1980–; Deputy to 2nd, 3rd, 4th, 5th and 7th NPC, Chair. Standing Cttee. 7th NPC; elected mem. CCP 11th Cen. Cttee., mem. Secr. CCP 11th Cen. Cttee.; elected mem. Politburo CCP Cen. Cttee. and mem. Secr. 1982, 1987; Hon. Chair. Chinese Tennis Asscn. 1982–; Hon. Pres. Bridge Asscn. 1980–. *Leisure interests:* tennis, bridge. *Address:* c/o State Council, Beijing, People's Republic of China.

WAN SHAOFEN; Chinese party official, economist and lawyer; Leading Sec. CCP Cttee., Jiangxi 1985–; mem. CCP Cen. Cttee. 1985–; Chair. Prov. Women's Fed., Jiangxi 1983–. *Address:* Jiangxi Provincial Chinese Communist Party, Nanchang, Jiangxi, People's Republic of China.

WANAMAKER, Sam; American actor and film and theatre director; b. 14 June 1919, Chicago, Ill.; s. of Maurice Wanamaker and Molly Bobele; m. Charlotte Holland 1940; three d.; ed. Drake Univ., Iowa, and Goodman Theatre, Chicago; Dir. Jewish People's Inst., Chicago 1930–40; radio acting New York 1940–41; acted in Cafe Crown 1941 and Counterattack 1942, Broadway; U.S. Army 1942–45; actor and dir. 1946–; Artistic Dir. New Shakespeare Theatre, Liverpool 1957–59; three-picture contract with M.G.M. 1968; acted in and directed Joan of Lorraine (Broadway) 1946; acted in My Girl Tisa 1947, Christ in Concrete 1949, Denning Drives North 1951; directed Gentlemen from Athens 1948, Goodbye my Fancy 1949, Caesar and Cleopatra, Revival of Gardsman; acted in and/or directed Winter Journey, The Shrike, The Rainmaker, Threepenny Opera, The Big Knife, A Hatful of Rain, A View from the Bridge, Reclining Figure, Othello, The Rose Tattoo 1959, A Far Country 1961; acted in film Taras Bulba 1962; directed on Broadway plays Children from Their Games (Irwin Shaw) 1962, Case of Libel (Louis Nizer) 1963, A Murderer Among Us (Louis Nizer) 1963; directed at Covent Garden opera King Priam (Tippett) 1963, Forza del Destino (Verdi) 1963; acted in film Those Magnificent Men in their Flying Machines 1964; directed and acted in Macbeth, Goodman Theatre, Chicago 1964; acted in film The Spy Who Came in From the Cold 1965; directed or acted in TV films The Defenders, For the People, Gunsmoke, The Baron 1962–66; acted in and/or directed (TV) The Day the Fish Came Out 1966, Warning Shot 1966, and TV films Custer, Hawk,

Lassiter, Cimmarron Strip, Court Martial, The Champions, Lancer 1966–67; director The Chinese Visitor 1968, The File of the Golden Goose 1968, The Executioner 1969, Catlow 1969–70; founder Globe Playhouse Trust and World Centre for Shakespeare Studies 1970–71; producer War and Peace (opening production Sydney Opera House) 1973, John Player Season at Bankside Globe Playhouse 1972–73, Shakespeare Birthday Celebrations Southwark Cathedral 1972–73; acted in films The Law, The Spiral Staircase, produced Dickens, Shakespeare and Bankside Summer Festivals 1974, acted in film The Sell Out, directed film Sinbad and the Eye of the Tiger 1975, acted in film The Voyage of the Damned 1975; Billy Jack Goes to Washington, Billion Dollar Bubble, Impossible Dream (BBC), Blind Love (Granada TV) 1976; directed film Colombo (NBC), opera Ice Break (Tippett), Covent Garden, acted in TV films Blind Love 1976, The Holocaust (also dir.) 1977, The Return of the Saint (also dir.) 1978, Charlie Muffin 1979, The Family Business 1981; acted in films Death on the Nile 1978, From Hell to Victory 1978; dir. Chicago Lyric Opera Gala 1979; acted in films Private Benjamin 1980, The Competition 1980, The Ghost Writer (BBC) 1982, The Aviator 1983, Irreconcilable Differences 1984, The Berrengers (TV series NBC) 1984; directed opera Aida, San Francisco 1981, King Priam, Covent Garden, London 1985, acted in Elegy for a Lady (BBC) 1985, Stravinsky's Oedipus Rex (narrator, BBC) 1985, film Raw Deal 1985, TV films Embassy (NBC) 1985, Deceptions (CBS) 1985, Two Mrs Granvilles (NBC TV) 1986, Superman IV (film) 1986, Baby Boom (film) 1986, Tosca (opera) 1986, Sadie and Son (NBC TV) 1987, Judgment in Berlin (MGM) 1987, Secret Ingredient (Columbia) 1987, Baby Boom (NBC TV series) 1988–89. *Leisure interest:* art. *Address:* Shakespeare Globe Trust, Bear Gardens, London, SE1, England.

WANG ANYI; Chinese writer; b. 6 March 1954, Nanjing; d. of Wang Xiaoping and Ru Zijuan; m. Li Zhang 1981. *Publications:* short stories: Life in a Small Courtyard, The Newly Arrived Coach, Black and White; novels: The 1969 Junior Middle School Graduates, Man at the Old Course of the Huanghe River; novelettes: Elapse, Epilogue, The Xiaobaozhuang Village; also collected stories and novels. *Leisure interests:* films, TV, music. *Address:* 675 Ju Lu Road, Shanghai, People's Republic of China. *Telephone:* 377175.

WANG BINGQIAN; Chinese politician; b. 1925, Li Co., Hebei Prov.; Deputy Section Chief, Auditing Div., Dept. of Finance 1948–49; Section Chief, later Dir., Vice-Minister, Minister of Finance, Cen. Govt.; Dir. Budget Dept. 1963; Deputy Minister of Finance 1973–80, Minister of Finance Aug. 1980–; mem. 12th Cen. Cttee. CCP 1982, 13th Cen. Cttee. 1987–; Pres. Accounting Soc. 1980–; Chinese Gov., World Bank 1986–; Hon. Chair. Bd. of Dirs., China Investment Bank 1981–; State Councillor June 1983–; Chair. Cen. Treasury Bond Sales Promotion Cttee. 1984–; mem. State Planning Comm. 1988–; Hon. Pres. Auditing Soc. 1984–. *Address:* State Council, Beijing, People's Republic of China.

WANG CHANG-CHING, M.SC.; Chinese politician; b. 22 Sept. 1920, Chingshan County, Hupeh; m. Lin Hsueh-chen; one s. one d.; ed. Nat. Chiaotung Univ. and Johns Hopkins Univ.; Sr. Eng. and concurrently Div. Chief, Dept. of Communications, Taiwan Provincial Govt. 1949–58; Dir. Public Works Bureau, Taiwan Provincial Govt. 1958–69; Dir. Dept. of Public Works, Taipei City Govt. 1967–69; Vice-Minister, Ministry of Communications 1969–77; Vice-Chair. Council for Econ. Planning and Devt. 1977–84; Sec.-Gen. Exec. Yuan 1984–. *Address:* 1, Chunghsiao E. Road, Sect. 1, Taipei, Taiwan.

WANG CHAOWEN; Chinese politician; Sec. Guizhou Communist Youth League 1973; Vice-Chair. Prov. Revolutionary Cttee., Guizhou 1977–79; Sec. CCP Cttee., Guizhou 1980–83, Deputy Sec. 1981–; Vice-Gov. of Guizhou 1980–83, Gov. 1983–; mem. Cen. Cttee. CCP 1982–. *Address:* Office of the Governor, Guiyang, Guizhou Province, People's Republic of China.

WANG CHENGBIN; Chinese party and military official; Deputy Commdr. Nanjing Mil. Region 1985–; mem. CCP Cen. Cttee. 1987–. *Address:* Central Committee of the Chinese Communist Party, Zhongnanhai, Beijing, People's Republic of China.

WANG CHENGHAN; Chinese party and military official; b. Hubei; Battalion Commdr. 25th Army 1936; Battalion Commdr. 386th Brigade, 129th Div., 8th Route Army 1937; Commdr. of Shanyin Regiment (Daiyue) Mil. Dist. 1945; Commdr. 39th Brigade, N. China Field Army 1948; Commdr. 181st Div. 2nd Field Army 1949; Commdr. 181st Div., Chinese People's Volunteers in the Korean War 1957; Chief of Staff 60th Army, Chinese People's Volunteers 1952; made Maj.-Gen., PLA 1955; Commdr. 60th Army 1958; Deputy Commdr. PLA Tibet Mil. Region 1964; Deputy Commdr. PLA Chengdu Mil. Region 1973–82; Deputy for PLA, 5th NPC 1978; Vice-Chair. People's Air Defence Cttee., PLA Chengdu Mil. Region; mem. 12th Cen. Cttee. CCP 1982–87, mem. Cen. Advisory Comm. 1987–; Commdr. PLA Chengdu Mil. Region 1982–85; Leading Comrade, Chengdu Mil. Region 1985–; Political Commissar Acad. of Med. Science Oct. 1986–; mem. Standing Cttee., CCP Prov. Cttee., Sichuan 1983–. *Address:* People's Liberation Army Headquarters, Chengdu Military Region, People's Republic of China.

WANG CHONGLUN; Chinese model worker and union official; b. July 1927, Liaoning Prov.; started as worker in Anshan Iron and Steel Co. 1949, successively held posts Workshop Dir., Factory Deputy Dir. and

Deputy Man. etc.; invented Universal Fixture 1958; Vice-Chair. Anshan Municipal Trade Union Council 1977, China Asscn. of Inventions 1978; Chair. Nat. Cttee. of Tech. Coordination for Workers and Staff 1978; elected Deputy to NPC 1954, 1959, 1965, 1975, 1978; mem. 12th CCP Cen. Cttee. 1982–87; Nat. Model Worker 1956, 1959, 1977; Vice-Chair. All-China Fed. of Trade Unions 1978–. *Leisure interests:* table tennis, calligraphy. *Address:* All-China Federation of Trade Unions, 10 Fuxingmenwai Street, Beijing, People's Republic of China.

WANG CHUANBIN; Chinese diplomatist; mem. Cen. Cttee. China Youth League 1957, Sec.-Gen. 1960–64; Consul-Gen. San Marino 1973; Counsellor, Embassy, Italy 1974–79; Amb. to Niger 1979–82, to Pakistan 1982–. *Address:* Embassy of People's Republic of China, 23-24 Shalimar 6/4, Islamabad, Pakistan.

WANG CONGWU; Chinese party official; b. 1905, Henan; ed. Sun Yat-sen Univ., Moscow; joined CCP 1927; Alt. mem. 7th Cen. Cttee., CCP 1945; Sec. Party School Cen. Bureau, Shanxi-Hebei-Shandong-Henan border region; Dir. Rural Work Dept. and Org. Bureau, N. China Bureau 1950; Chair. Cttee. for Inspecting Discipline 1951–54; mem. N. China Admin. Council 1952–54; First Deputy Sec., N. China Bureau 1953–54; mem. Standing Cttee., CPPCC 1954–64; mem. 8th Cen. Cttee., CCP, also mem. and Deputy Sec. Cen. Control Comm. 1956; Pres. CCP Higher Party School 1961–63; Deputy Dir. Org. Dept., CCP Cen. Cttee. 1961; mem. Standing Cttee., Cen. Control Comm., CCP Cen. Cttee. 1963; disappeared during Cultural Revolution; mem. Standing Cttee., 5th CPPCC 1978; Deputy Sec. Cen. Comm. for Inspecting Discipline, Cen. Cttee. 1978; Sec. 1982–85; mem. Cen. Advisory Comm. 1985–. *Address:* Central Committee, Chinese Communist Party, Beijing, People's Republic of China.

WANG DAOHAN; Chinese politician; b. 1915, Anhui; Minister of E. China Industry Dept. 1949–52; Deputy Minister, First Ministry of Machine Bldg. 1952–65; Dir.-Gen. Mech. Eng. Soc. of China 1955–81; Vice-Chair. Comm. for Econ. Relations with Foreign Countries 1965–79, then Deputy Minister, Ministry of Econ. Relations with Foreign Countries; Vice-Chair. Import and Export Admin. Comm. and Foreign Investment Comm. 1979–80; Mayor of Shanghai 1980–85; Pres. Urban Econ. Soc. of China 1986–; Dir. Planning Office of Shanghai Econ. Zone under the State Council 1986; part-time Prof. Dept. of Econs., Beijing Univ.; Prof. Fudan Univ., Prof. Tong Ji Univ.; Hon. Dir.-Gen. Mechanical Eng. Soc. of China; Dr. h.c. Tufts Univ.; Adviser to Shanghai Municipal People's Govt. 1985–; mem. Cen. Advisory Comm. 1987–. *Address:* Shanghai Municipal Offices, Shanghai, People's Republic of China.

WANG DEYAN; Chinese banker; b. 1931; with Bank of China 1953, Vice-Pres. 1984, Pres. June 1985–, Chair. Aug. 1986–. *Address:* Bank of China, 410 Fuchengmennei Dajie, Beijing, People's Republic of China.

WANG DEZHAO, PH.D.; Chinese academic; b. 1902; Dir. Inst. of Electronics 1961–64; Dir. Inst. of Acoustics 1964–66, 1979–; in political disgrace 1966–73; mem. Presidium CPPCC 1983–; Hon. Chair. Fed. of Returned Overseas Chinese 1985, Acoustical Soc. 1985; Pres. Soc. of Instruments and Meters 1979–87, Hon. Pres. April 1987–. *Address:* Chinese Academy of Science, Beijing, People's Republic of China.

WANG DONGHAI; Chinese woodcut artist; b. 7 Dec. 1938, Qinhuangdao, Hebei; s. of the late Wang Yuchen and Li Yunlan; m. 1st Chen Shumin 1966 (divorced 1983); m. 2nd Feng Lisha 1985; one s. one d.; mem. and Deputy Sec.-Gen. Standing Cttee. of China Ex Libris Inst., China Asscn. of Graphic Artists; Art Ed. Beijing Review; his woodcuts have been shown at many exhbns. at home and abroad and published in many newspapers and periodicals. *Leisure interest:* photography. *Address:* 24 Baiwanzhuang Road, Beijing, People's Republic of China. *Telephone:* 8315599.

WANG DONGLING; Chinese calligrapher; b. 1945; lecturer Zhejiang Coll. of Art; Dir. Chinese Calligraphy Asscn. *Address:* Zhejiang College of Art, Hangzhou, Zhejiang Province, People's Republic of China.

WANG DONGXING; Chinese party official; bodyguard of Mao Tse-tung 1947; Capt. of Guards of Cen. Cttee., CCP 1947–49; Capt. of Guards, Gen. Admin. Council 1949–54; Vice-Minister of Public Security 1955–58, 1962–80; Vice-Gov. of Jiangxi 1958–60; Sec. CCP Jiangxi 1958–60; mem. Cen. Cultural Revolution Group 1967; Dir. Admin. Office of Cen. Cttee., CCP 1969; Alt. mem. Politburo, 9th Cen. Cttee. of CCP 1969; mem. Politburo, 10th Cen. Cttee. of CCP 1973, Politburo 11th Cen. Cttee. CCP 1977; mem. Standing Cttee. 1977; Vice-Chair. CCP 1977; Exec. Chair. Pres. 5th Nat. People's Congress 1978; lost all posts 1980; deputy admin., Jiangxi Prov. 1980–; alt. mem. 12th Cen. Cttee. CCP 1982–85, mem. Cen. Advisory Comm. 1987–. *Address:* Jiangxi Province, People's Republic of China.

WANG ENMAO, Lieut.-Gen.; Chinese army officer and politician; b. 1912, Jiangxi Prov.; mem. Xinjiang Bureau, Cen. Cttee. 1949–50; Political Commissar, 1st Field Army 1949–50; mem. People's Govt. Xinjiang 1949–50; mem. N.W. China Mil. and Admin. Council 1950–53; Sec. Xinjiang Prov. CP Cttee. 1952–55; Political Commissar, Xinjiang Mil. Region 1952; First Sec. Xinjiang Autonomous Region CP Cttee. 1955; alt. mem. 8th CCP Cen. Cttee. 1956–58, mem. 1958–69; Commdr. Xinjiang Mil. Region 1956; mem. Nat. Defence Council 1965; Sec. N.W. China Bureau 1965; First Sec. CP Cttee., PLA Xinjiang Construction Corps 1966; severely criticized 1968; alt. mem. 9th CCP Cen. Cttee. 1969–73; Deputy Political Commissar, Nanjing Mil. Region 1975–; First Sec. CP Cttee., Jilin Prov. 1977–82; CCP Xinjiang 1982–; Chair. Prov. Revolutionary Cttee., Jilin 1977–79; First Political Commissar, Jilin Mil. Dist.; Deputy Commdr. Shenyang Mil. Region 1977; mem. 11th CCP Cen. Cttee. 1977–82; Deputy Political Commissar, Shenyang Mil. Region 1978; Dir. Jilin Party School 1978; First Sec. CP Cttee., Jilin Mil. Dist. 1977–85; First Political Commissar Xinjiang Mil. Region 1982–85; First Sec. Xinjiang CCP Cttee. 1981–85; mem. 12th Cen. Cttee. CCP 1982–85; Deputy for Xinjiang Autonomous Region to 6th NPC 1983; mem. CPPCC Nat. Cttee. 1986–, Presidium CPPCC 1986–; Chair. Advisory Cttee., CCP Cttee., Xinjiang 1985–; Vice-Chair. CCP 1988–. *Address:* Communist Party Committee, Jilin Military District, People's Republic of China.

WANG FANG; Chinese party official; m. Liu Xin; Political Commissar 94th Div., 32nd Army, 3rd Field Army 1949; Deputy Commdr. Hangzhou Air Defence Command 1950; Deputy Dir. Public Security Dept., People's Govt., Zhejiang 1951; Political Commissar Public Security Forces, Zhejiang 1954; Dir. Public Security Dept., People's Govt., Zhejiang 1955; Vice-Gov. Zhejiang 1964–Cultural Revolution; branded as a counter-revolutionary and purged 1967; Vice-Chair. Prov. Revolutionary Cttee., Zhejiang 1977–79; Deputy Sec. CCP Cttee., Zhejiang 1978–83; Vice-Chair. Prov. People's Congress Zhejiang 1979–83; mem. 12th Cen. Cttee. CCP 1982–87, mem. Cen. Advisory Comm. 1987–; First Sec. CCP Cttee., Zhejiang 1983–87; Minister of Public Security April 1987–; First Political Commissar, Chinese People's Armed Police Force 1987–; State Councillor April 1988–. *Address:* Ministry of Public Security, East Changan Street, Beijing, People's Republic of China.

WANG FENG; Chinese government official; b. 1907, Shaanxi Province; Commdr. Security Force, Shaanxi-Gansu-Ningxia Border Region and concurrently Commdr., Lushan Mil. Region; Political Commissar 38th Army PLA 1946; Dir. United Front Dept. N.W. Bureau CCP Cen. Cttee. 1949–52; Chair. Nationalities Affairs Cttee. N.W. Mil and Admin. Cttee. 1950–52; mem. Land Reform Cttee. N.W. Mil. and Admin. Cttee. 1951; Pres. N.W. Nationalities Coll. 1952; mem. Political and Legal Cttee. N.W. Mil. and Admin. Cttee. 1952; Vice-Chair. Nat. Affairs Cttee., Govt. Admin. Council 1952–54; Vice-Chair. Nat. Affairs Cttee., State Council 1954; mem. N.W. Admin. Cttee. 1953–54; Deputy for Qinghai 1st NPC 1954; Deputy Dir., United Front Dept. CCP Cen. Cttee. 1955; mem. Standing Cttee. 1st NPC 1958–59; Alt. mem. CCP 8th Cen. Cttee. 1958; First Sec. CCP Ningxia Provincial Cttee. 1958–61; mem. Nationalities Cttee. 2nd NPC 1959–64; First Sec. CCP Gansu Provincial Cttee. 1961–66; mem. Standing Cttee. 3rd NPC 1965; Sec. CCP N.W. Bureau 1965–68; mem. Pres., 11th Nat. Congress CCP 1977–; mem. CCP 11th Cen. Cttee. 1977, mem. Cen. Advisory Comm. 1987–; mem. Standing Cttee. CPPCC 1987–, Vice-Chair. Nat. Cttee. 1987–; First Sec. Xinjiang Prov. CCP Cttee. 1978–82; Chair. Xinjiang CCP Revolutionary Cttee. 1978–80; First Political Commissar PLA Xinjiang Mil. Region 1978–82. *Address:* People's Republic of China.

WANG FUZHI; Chinese army officer; mil. leader in Beijing 1971; Commdr., Shanxi Mil. Dist. 1976–80; alt. mem. 11th CCP Cen. Cttee. 1977, 12th Cen. Cttee. 1982–87; Sec. CCP Cttee., Shanxi Prov. 1977–80; Deputy Commdr., Xinjiang Mil. Region 1981–85 (now Lanzhou Mil. Region). *Address:* Lanzhou Military Region Headquarters, Lanzhou, Gansu, People's Republic of China.

WANG GANCHANG; Chinese nuclear physicist; b. 28 May 1907, Changshu, Jiangsu Prov.; m.; two s. three d.; ed. Qinhua Univ. and Berlin Univ.; Research Prof. of Nuclear Physics, Shandong and Zhejiang Univs. 1934–50, and suggested first detecting the neutrino by 7Be in 1942; Vice-Dir. Inst. of Modern Physics, Acad. of Sciences of China 1950–56; Vice-Dir. Jt. Inst. of Nuclear Research, Dubna, U.S.S.R. 1959–60, led research team and discovered anti-sigma negative hyperon 1960; working in nuclear bases in north-western deserts in 1960s, was one of group of leading scientists guiding devt. of China's first atomic bomb in 1964 and first hydrogen bomb in 1967; independently suggested the concept on inertia confine fusion by strong laser 1964; Dir. Inst. of Atomic Energy, Beijing 1978–; Vice-Chair. China Asscn. for Science and Tech. 1980–86; Hon. Pres. Soc. of Nuclear Physics 1980–; Pres. Chinese Nuclear Soc. 1980–83, Hon. Pres. 1985–; Vice-Pres. Commn of Science and Tech., Minister of Nuclear Industry 1983; mem. Standing Cttee. 6th NPC 1983; mem. Educ., Science, Culture and Public Health Cttee., NPC 1983; Deputy Head China-Turkey Friendship Group 1985; Hon. Pres. Inst. of Atomic Energy 1986–; Vice-Pres. China Asscn. for Int. Exchange of Personnel 1986–; Leading mem. China Nuclear Instruments Asscn. 1987–; Natural Science Award (First Class) 1982. *Address:* Chinese Nuclear Society, P.O. Box 2125, Beijing, People's Republic of China.

WANG GUANGYING; Chinese business executive; b. 1919, Beijing; m. 1943; ed. Catholic Fudan Univ.; set up own business in Tianjin 1943; Vice-Chair. China Democratic Nat. Construction Asscn. 1954; gaoled for eight years during cultural revolution 1967–75; Vice-Chair. All China Fed. of Industry and Commerce 1982–; f. and Chair. China Everbright Co. (China's first trans-nat. corpn.), Hong Kong 1983–; Exec. Chair. Presidium CPPCC 1983–; Vice-Chair. CPPCC Nat. Cttee. 1983–. *Address:* All China Federation of Industry and Commerce, 93 Beiheyan Dajie, Beijing, People's Republic of China.

WANG GUANGYU; Chinese party official; b. Nov. 1919, Anhui Prov.; m. Sun Shu 1941; four s. one d.; mem. Land Reform Cttee., North Anhui Admin. Office; Dir. Rural Work Dept., Anhui Prov. CCP; mem. People's Council, Anhui 1955; Dir. Agricultural Coll., Anhui 1956; Vice-Gov. Anhui 1956–67; Sec. to Secr. of CCP Cttee., Anhui 1958–67; disappeared during Cultural Revolution 1967–73; Sec. to Secr. of CCP Cttee., Anhui 1973–83, Deputy Sec. 1983–; Vice-Chair. Revolutionary Cttee., Anhui 1973–79; mem. 11th CCP Cen. Cttee. 1977; Chair. Anhui Prov. Armed Forces Cttee. 1981; mem. 12th CCP Cen. Cttee. 1982–87; Chair. Standing Cttee., People's Congress Anhui 1985–; mem. 6th Nat. People's Congress. *Address:* Anhui Provincial Chinese Communist Party, Hefei, Anhui, People's Republic of China.

WANG GUANGZHONG; Chinese party official and provincial administrator; Vice-Chair. Revolutionary Cttee., Liaoning Prov. 1977–79; Vice-Gov. of Liaoning 1980–85; mem. 12th CCP Cen. Cttee. 1982–87; Vice-Chair. standing Cttee., Liaoning Prov. People's Congress 1985 Jan. 1988–. *Address:* Liaoning Provincial People's Government, Shenyang, Liaoning, People's Republic of China.

WANG HAI, Gen; Chinese army officer; b. 1925, Weihai City, Shandong Prov.; ed. China's North-East Aviation Acad.; joined PLA 1945; Group Commdr., air force brigade and sent to Korean battlefield 1950; promoted Col. PLA 1964; Commdr., Air Force of Guangzhou Mil. Region 1975–83; Deputy Commdr., PLA Air Force 1983–85; Commdr., PLA Air Force 1985–; mem., CCP 12th Cen. Cttee. 1985–; promoted Gen. PLA 1988. *Address:* Ministry of Defence, Beijing, People's Republic of China.

WANG HANBIN; Chinese state and party official; b. 28 Aug. 1925; m. Peng Peiyun; two s. two d.; Deputy Sec.-Gen. NPC Legal Comm. 1979–80; Vice-Chair. and Sec.-Gen. NPC Legal Comm. 1980–83; Deputy Sec.-Gen., Political and Legal Comm. of CCP Cen. Cttee. 1980–82, Constitution Revision Cttee. of P.R.C. 1980–82; Vice-Pres. Chinese Law Soc. 1982–86; mem. 12th CCP Cen. Cttee. 1982–86, 13th Cen. Cttee. 1987–; Deputy Sec.-Gen. 5th NPC Standing Cttee. 1982–83; Deputy for Beijing to 6th NPC 1983–87; Exec. Chair. Presidium of 6th NPC 1986, 1987; Deputy Sec.-Gen. of Presidium of NPC 1982–87; Sec.-Gen. NPC Standing Cttee. 1983–87, Chair. Legis. Affairs Comm. 1983–; Vice-Chair. Cttee. for Drafting Basic Law of Hong Kong Special Admin. Zone of People's Republic of China 1985–. *Leisure interest:* bridge. *Address:* c/o National People's Congress Standing Committee, Beijing, People's Republic of China.

WANG HESHOU; Chinese party official; b. 1908, Hebei; ed. Sun Yat-sen Univ., Moscow; joined CCP late 1920s; Dir. Propaganda Dept., CCP Cttee., Manchuria 1930; mem. Org. Dept., CCP Cen. Cttee. 1940; Political Commissar, Heilongjiang Mil. Region 1946; Minister of Industry, People's Govt. of N.E. China 1949; Minister of Heavy Industry 1952–56; mem. 2nd CPPCC 1954–59; Chair. State Construction Comm., State Council 1956–58; Minister of Metallurgical Industry 1956–64; Alt. mem. 8th Cen. Cttee., CCP 1956; Deputy for Hebei, 2nd NPC 1956–64, for Liaoning 3rd NPC 1964; First Sec. CCP Cttee., Anshan Municipality 1965; disappeared during Cultural Revolution; Deputy Sec. Cen. Comm. for Inspecting Discipline, Cen. Cttee., CCP 1978, Perm. Sec. 1982–; mem. 11th Cen. Cttee., CCP, 12th Cen. Cttee. 1982–85, mem. Cen. Advisory Comm. 1987–; Second Sec. Cen. Comm. for Political Inspection 1985–. *Address:* Communist Party Central Committee, Beijing, People's Republic of China.

WANG HONGWEN; Chinese fmr. party offical; b. 1937; Worker Shanghai No. 17 Cotton Textile Mill; Founded Shanghai Workers Revolutionary Rebel Gen. H.Q. during Cultural Revolution 1967; Vice-Chair. Shanghai Revolutionary Cttee. 1968; Sec. CCP Shanghai 1971; Political Commissar Shanghai Garrison District, PLA 1972; Vice-Chair. CCP 1973–76; mem. Standing Cttee. of Politburo, CCP 1973–76; Vice-Chair. CCP Military Affairs Comm. 1975–76; arrested as mem. of "gang of four" Oct 1976; on trial Nov. 1980–Jan. 1981; sentenced to life imprisonment 1981. *Address:* People's Republic of China.

WANG JIALIU; Chinese party official; mem. Cen. Cttee., Communist Youth League 1957; Deputy Sec. Beijing Branch Communist Youth League 1960; purged 1966; alt. mem. 12th CCP Cen. Cttee. 1982, 13th Cen. Cttee. 1987; Head Educ. Work Dept., CCP Beijing Municipal Cttee. 1984–. *Address:* c/o Chinese Communist Party Central Committee, Beijing, People's Republic of China.

WANG JIANGONG; Chinese party official and youth leader; Sec. Communist Youth League 1981–82; alt. mem. 12th CCP Cen. Cttee. 1982–87; Deputy Sec. CCP Prov. Cttee., Shanxi 1985–. *Address:* c/o Chinese Communist Party Central Committee, Beijing, People's Republic of China.

WANG JIANSHUANG; Chinese party official; b. 1937, Tongan County, Fujian Prov.; fmr. Head of Dept. of Light Industry, Fujian Prov.; Sec. Xiamen Municipal CCP Cttee. 1987–. *Address:* Xiamen Municipal Chinese Communist Party Committee, Xiamen City, Fujian Province, People's Republic of China.

WANG JIDA; Chinese sculptor; b. 27 Oct. 1935, Beijing; s. of Wang Sho Yi and Chiu Chen Shin; m. Jin Gao 1971; two c.; ed. Cen. Inst. of Fine Arts, Beijing; worked for Inner Mongolia Artists' Assocn.; Prof. Teacher's Coll. Inner Mongolia 1981–; Asst. Dir. Standing Council, Inner Mongolia Sculptors' Asscn.; mem. Chinese Artists Asscn.; sculptures reflect life of

Mongolian herdsmen; mem. American Sculpture Asscn. 1988. *Leisure interests:* athletics, music, literature. *Address:* Inner Mongolia Artists' Association, 33 W Street, Hu Hua Hao Te, Inner Mongolia, People's Republic of China; 76-12 35th Avenue, Apartment 3E, Jackson Heights, N.Y. 11372, U.S.A. *Telephone:* 25775 (China); (718) 651-3944 (U.S.A.).

WANG JINXU; Chinese artist; b. 1939, Henan. *Address:* People's Liberation Army Units, Canton, Guangdong, People's Republic of China.

WANG JINYUAN; Chinese artist; b. 1940, Leting Co., Hubei; ed. Cen. Acad. of Fine Arts, Beijing. *Works include:* Cactus in Bloom. *Address:* People's Republic of China.

WANG JUN; Chinese trade unionist and party official; Chair. Harbin Municipal Fed. of Trades Unions 1959–64; mem. of Del. to Congress on Int. Problems of Women's Work, Bucharest 1963; mem. Beijing CCP Municipal Cttee. 1986–, Chair. Planning Comm. 1984–; Vice-Pres. China Int. Trust and Investment Corpn. 1986–. *Address:* China International Trust and Investment Corporation, 2 Qianmen Street East, Beijing, People's Republic of China.

WANG KEFEN; Chinese dance historian; b. 1 April 1927, Yunyang, Sichian; s. of Wang Baifan and Liao Huiqing; m. Zhang Wengang 1949; one s. one d.; Research Fellow, Inst. of Dance, Chinese Acad. of Arts 1977–. *Publications:* The History of Chinese Dance 1980, The Stories of Ancient Chinese Dancer 1983, The History of Chinese Dance: Ming Dynasty, Qing Dynasty 1984, Sui Dynasty and Tang Dynasty 1987, The History of Chinese Dance Development; contrib. to the Dictionary of Chinese Dance. *Leisure interests:* choreography and dance. *Address:* Institute of Dance, Chinese Academy of Arts, 17 Qianhai Xi Jie, Beijing, People's Republic of China. *Telephone:* 6015551-35.

WANG KEWEN; Chinese party and state official; b. Nov. 1917, Shanxi Prov.; m. Hu Qi 1953; two s. two d.; mem. Financial and Econ. Council and Dir. Finance Dept., People's Govt., Hubei Prov. 1950; Sec.-Gen. People's Council, Wuhan Municipality 1952–54; Deputy Mayor, Wuhan 1955–57, Acting Mayor 1957; Sec. CCP Cttee., Wuhan 1959; disappeared during Cultural Revolution 1966–71; Sec. CCP Cttee., Wuhan 1971–73; First Sec. 1973–78; Sec. CCP Cttee., Hubei Prov. 1973–78; Sec. CCP Cttee., Shanxi Prov. 1978–83, Deputy Sec. 1983–85; Hon. Pres. Shanxi Prov. Capital Construction Econ. Research Asscn. 1981–86; mem. 12th CCP Cen. Cttee. 1982–87; Chair. Advisory Cttee., CCP Cttee., Shanxi 1985–; Hon. Pres. Hubei Prov. Political Science Research Asscn. 1986–; Vice-Chair. Advisory Cttee. CCP Cttee., Hubei 1986–. *Address:* Hubei Provincial Advisory Committee, Wuhan, Hubei, People's Republic of China.

WANG KUI; Chinese athlete; b. 15 Aug. 1931, Xin Min County, Liaoning; s. of Wang Haiqing and Wang Qiuping; m. Wang Qinghua 1961; one s.; ed. Shenyang Physical Culture Inst.; Coach at Sports School, Fuxin, Liaoning 1973–77; Walking Team Coach, Liaoning Prov. 1978–; Prin. Walking School, Liaoning Prov. 1986–. *Leisure interest:* billiards. *Address:* Liaoning Walking Team, Shenyang, People's Republic of China. *Telephone:* 33460.

WANG LEI; Chinese politician; Cadre in S.W. China 1950; Vice-Minister of Commerce 1953; Vice-Minister of First Ministry of Commerce 1958; Deputy Sec.-Gen. Beijing Revolutionary Cttee. 1973; Minister of Commerce 1977–78, 1979–82; Vice-Minister of State Econ. Comm. 1982–85; Chair. Bd. of Dirs. Nat. Silk Corpn. 1982–; mem. Cen. Advisory Cttee. 1985–. *Address:* c/o State Council, Beijing, People's Republic of China.

WANG LIN; Chinese party and government official; political instructor on Long March 1934–35; worked on Liu Shaoqi in Shaanxi-Gansu-Ningxia Border Area 1938; mem. Tangshan Municipal CCP Cttee., Hebei Prov. 1949–50; Dir., Gen. Office of Ministry of Fuel Industry 1950–54, Vice-Minister 1954–55; Del. to 10th Anniversary celebrations of Czechoslovakian Liberation, Prague, May 1955; Vice-Minister of Electric Power 1955–58; signatory, China-Czechoslovak Scientific and Tech. Co-operation Protocol, Sept. 1956; mem. Yellow River Project Cttee. 1957–58; mem. Sungari River Project 1958; alt. Sec. N.W. Region CCP Cttee. 1963–65, Sec. 1965–66; Vice-Chair. Beijing Municipal Construction Cttee. 1965; purged 1966, rehabilitated 1976; Sec. Shaanxi Prov. CCP Cttee. 1977–79; mem. Cen. Advisory Cttee. of CCP Cen. Cttee. 1987–. *Address:* Central Advisory Committee of the Central Committee of the Chinese Communist Party, Zhongnanhai, Beijing, People's Republic of China.

WANG LING, M.A., PH.D.; Chinese historian (retd.); b. 23 Dec. 1918, Nandong, Jiangsu Province; s. of C. C. Wang; m. Ruth Burkitt 1961; two s.; ed. National Central Univ., China, and Trinity Coll., Cambridge; Junior Research Fellow, Inst. of History and Philology, Acad. Sinica 1941–44; Senior Lecturer, Nat. Fu-tan Univ. 1944–45, Assoc. Prof. 1945–46; Asst. to J. Needham, F.R.S., Cambridge Univ. 1946–57; Visiting Lecturer, Cambridge Univ. 1953; Sr. Lecturer Canberra Univ. Coll., Melbourne Univ. 1957–59; Assoc. Fellow, Nat. Acad. of Science, Acad. Sinica 1955–57; Senior Lecturer Univ. Coll., Australian Nat. Univ., Canberra 1960–61, Assoc. Prof. 1961–63; Professorial Fellow, Inst. of Advanced Studies, Australian Nat. Univ. 1963–; Visiting Prof. of Chinese Literature, Cornell Univ. 1965; Visiting Prof. of Chinese Classics, Wisconsin Univ. 1965–66, Univ. of Washington 1967–70; mem. Comm. for the History of the Social Relations of Science of the Int. Union for the History of Science 1948–56; Corresp.

mem. Int. Acad. of History of Science, Paris 1964–; Wei-kung Prize (jtly.) 1989. *Publications:* Science and Civilisation in China (asst. to Dr. J. Needham, F.R.S.) Vol. I 1954, Vol. II 1956, Vol. III 1959, Vol. IVa 1962, Vol. IVb 1964, Vol. IVc 1971, Heavenly Clockwork (asst.to Dr. J. Needham) 1960, A Study on the Chiu Chang Suan Shu 1962. *Address:* 16 Fergusson Crescent, Canberra, 2600, Australia. *Telephone:* (062) 733827.

WANG LIUSHENG; Chinese army officer and party official; b. 1912, Sichuan; Maj. Gen. PLA, Shanghai 1964; Deputy Political Commissar Nanjing Mil. Region, PLA 1966; Alt. mem. 9th Cen. Cttee. of CCP 1969; First Political Commissar Wuhan Mil. Region, PLA 1972; Second Sec. CCP Hubei 1972; Alt. mem. 10th Cen. Cttee. of CCP 1973, 11th Cen. Cttee. CCP 1977; Political Commissar PLA Eng. Corps 1976–; Alt. mem. 12th Cen. Cttee. CCP 1982–85, mem. Cen. Advisory Comm. 1987–. *Address:* People's Republic of China.

WANG MAOLIN; Chinese party and government official; Vice-Chair. Shanxi Prov. Revolutionary Cttee. 1977–78; Vice-Gov. Shanxi Prov. 1979–88; Vice-Chair. Shanxi Prov. People's Congress 1981–88; Deputy Sec. Shanxi Prov. Jan. 1988–; mem. CCP Cen. Cttee. 1987–. *Address:* Central Committee of the Chinese Communist Party, Zhongnanhai, Beijing, People's Republic of China.

WANG MENG; Chinese writer and party official; b. 15 Oct. 1934, Beijing; s. of Wang Jindi and Tong Min; m. Cui Ruifang 1957; two s. one d.; criticized 1957–76; rehabilitated 1979; Alt. mem. 12th Cen. Cttee. CCP 1982, mem. 12th Cen. Cttee. CCP 1985, mem. 13th Cen. Cttee. 1987–; Minister of Culture June 1986–; mem. Secr. Chinese Writers' Assen. 1981–, Vice-Chair. 1985–; Vice-Pres. China PEN Centre 1982–; Vice-Pres. Assen. for Int. Understanding 1985–; Chief Ed. People's Literature 1985–86. *Publications include:* The Young Newcomer in the Organization Department 1956, Long Live the Youth 1957, The Barber's Tale 1979, A Spate of Visitors 1980, A Night in the City 1980, The Butterfly 1980, The Metamorphosis of Human Nature 1986. *Leisure interests:* swimming, drinking. *Address:* c/o China PEN, Shatan Beijie 2, Beijing; Ministry of Culture, Donganmen Street, Beijing, People's Republic of China.

WANG MINGYUAN; Chinese calligrapher; b. 1951, Zhaoyuan Co., Heilongjiang Prov.; mem. Chinese Calligraphy Assen. *Address:* Special Art Company, Ministry of Aviation Industry, Beijing, People's Republic of China.

WANG NAILIN; Chinese artist; ed. Beijing Cen. Acad. of Arts and Design; exhibitor at Nat. Arts and Crafts Works Exhbn. *Address:* Chinese Artist's Association, Beijing, People's Republic of China.

WANG PING; Chinese government official; b. 1911, Jiangxi; Dir. Political Dept. 3rd Red Army Corps 1935; Chair. Mobilization Cttee. N. China Bureau 1937; Acting Chief, 29th Group CCP Section, Mil. Mediation Dept. 1946; Chair. Tadong Mil. Control Comm. 1949; Vice-Chair. Zhahar 1949–52; Deputy Chief, Shansi-Hebei-Zhahar Sub-Del. to visit bases in N. China 1951; Dir., Cadres Dept., N. China Mil. Region 1953; attained rank of Gen. 1955; Deputy Political Commissar, Chinese People's Volunteers 1957, Political Commissar 1957–58; Deputy for PLA to 2nd NPC 1959, (re-elected to 3rd NPC 1964); Political Commissar Nanjing Mil. Region 1959; mem. Nat. Defence Council, 1959 (re-appointed 1965); mem. Pres. CCP 11th Cen. Cttee. 1977–; mem. CCP 11th Cen. Cttee. 1977–82; Political Commissar PLA Gen. Logistics Dept. 1978–; mem. Standing Cttee. Mil. Comm., Cen. Cttee. 1980–; Vice-Chair. PLA All-Army Sports Guidance Comm. 1978–; Vice-Chair. Cen. Patriotic Sanitation Campaign Cttee., Cen. Cttee., CCP 1981; mem. Standing Cttee., Cen. Advisory Comm. 1987–. *Address:* People's Republic of China.

WANG QIAN; Chinese party official; b. 1917; Sec.-Gen. and Dir. Civil Affairs Dept. Guomindang Prov. Govt., Shanxi; Sec. Changzhi Dist. Communist Party, Sichuan 1951; Deputy Dir. Rural Work Dept. North China Bureau CCP Cen. Cttee. 1953–55; Sec. CCP Prov. Cttee. Shanxi 1955–66, Second Sec. 1966, Sec. 1974–75, Sec. 1975–80; Gov. of Shanxi 1960–66; Deputy for Shanxi to 2nd NPC 1960, 5th NPC 1978; disappeared during the Cultural Revolution 1967–73; alt. mem. 10th Cen. Cttee. 1973, 11th Cen. Cttee. 1977, 12th Cen. Cttee. 1982–; Vice-Chair. Shanxi Prov. Revolutionary Cttee. 1974–75, Chair. 1975–79; First Political Commissar Shanxi Mil. Dist. 1979; mem. Presidium 5th NPC 1979–82; Sec. CCP Prov. Cttee. Sichuan 1981–83; First Sec. CCP Chongqing Municipal Cttee. 1981–85; Deputy for Sichuan to 6th NPC 1983–; mem. Cen. Advisory Comm. 1985–; Vice-Chair. Financial and Econ. Cttee. NPC 1986. *Address:* Chinese National People's Congress, Beijing, People's Republic of China.

WANG QUN; Chinese party official; Sec. Hubei Branch Communist Youth League 1978; Deputy Sec. CCP Cttee., Hubei Prov. 1978–82, Sec. 1982–83, Deputy Sec. 1983; First Sec. CCP Cttee., Wuhan Municipality 1982–; alt. mem. 12th CCP Cen. Cttee. 1982–87, mem. 13th Cen. Cttee. 1987–; Sec. Inner Mongolian Autonomous Regional Cttee. 1987–. *Address:* Inner Mongolia Autonomous Regional Cttee., People's Republic of China.

WANG RENZHI; Chinese journalist and party official; Deputy Ed.-in-Chief, Hong Qi 1982; alt. mem. 12th CCP Cen. Cttee. 1982, mem. 1985, mem. 13th Cen. Cttee. 1987–; Head, Propaganda Dept. CCP 1987–. *Address:* Editorial Committee, Hong Qi, Beijing, People's Republic of China.

WANG RENZHONG; Chinese government official; b. 1917, Jingxian Co., Hebei Prov.; joined CCP 1933; Deputy Dir. Propaganda Dept. Hebei-Shandong-Henan Area CCP Cttee., mem. Standing Cttee. of Southern Hebei Area CCP Cttee. and Dir. Propaganda Dept. and other party posts 1937–45; Dir. Admin. Office, Southern Hebei Area, Deputy Sec. CCP Cttee. 1946–49; Vice-Chair. Hubei Prov. People's Govt., First Sec. Wuhan Municipal CCP Cttee., Acting Mayor of Wuhan, First Sec. Hubei Prov. CCP Cttee., First Political Commissar of Wuhan Units of PLA, Chair. Hubei Prov. Cttee. of CPPCC, First Sec. Cen.-South China Bureau of CCP Cen. Cttee. 1949–78; First Sec. Shaanxi Prov. CCP Cttee., Chair. Shaanxi Prov. Revolutionary Cttee., Vice-Premier of State Council, Chair. State Agricultural Comm., Sec. of Comm.'s leading group, Chair. Cen. Cttee. for Patriotic Sanitation Campaign, mem. Secr. of CCP Cen. Cttee. and Dir. of Propaganda Dept., alt. mem. 8th CCP Cen. Cttee., mem. 11th, 12th, 13th Cen. Cttees.; Vice-Chair. Standing Cttee. 6th NPC 1983, Financial and Econ. Cttee. NPC 1983; Hon. Chair. China Consumers' Assen. 1984–, Urban Econs. Soc. 1986–. *Address:* c/o State Council, Beijing, People's Republic of China.

WANG SENHAO; Chinese government official; Deputy to 6th NPC 1983; mem. CPC 4th Prov. Cttee., Shaanxi 1983–; Deputy Sec. CCP Cttee., Shaanxi Prov. 1983–; Gov. of Shaanxi Prov. 1983–; mem. CCP Cen. Cttee. 1985–. *Address:* Office of the Governor, Provincial People's Government, Shaanxi Province, People's Republic of China.

WANG SHANGRONG; Chinese army officer; b. 1906, Shanxi; ed. Sun Yat-sen Univ., Moscow; on Long March 1934; Div. Commdr., Red Army 1936; Vice-Commdr. 359th Brigade, 120th Div. and concurrently Commdr. 4th Sub-Mil. Region, 1940; Commdr. 5th Sub-Region, Shanxi-Suiyan Mil. Region 1940; Commdr. 3rd Army, 1st Field Army 1949; mem. Qinghai Mil. Region 1949; mem. Qinghai People's Govt. 1949–51; Vice-Chair. Financial and Economic Cttee., Qinghai People's Govt. 1950–51; Dir., War Strategy Dept., People's Revolutionary Mil. Council 1952–54; Lieut.-Gen. 1955; Alt. mem. CCP 8th Cen. Cttee. 1958; Dir., War Strategy Dept., Gen. Office of Chiefs of Staff PLA 1959–66; branded an anti-party element 1966; resumed activities as Deputy Chief of Gen. Staff, PLA 1974, 1978–; Alt. mem. CCP 11th Cen. Cttee. 1977–82. *Address:* People's Republic of China.

WANG SHITAI; Chinese party official; b. 1909, Luochuan Co., Shaanxi; ed. Middle School, Yan'an; Deputy Commdr. Shaanxi-Gansu-Ningxia Border Region HQ 1934, Commdr. 1946; Acting Commdr. Joint Defence HQ, Shanxi-Suiyuan-Shaanxi-Gansu-Ningxia 1941; Commdr. 4th Corps, 1st Field Army 1947; Political Commissar 2nd Army Corps, 1st Field Army 1949; mem. Nat. Cttee., CPPCC 1949; mem. N.W. China Mil. and Admin. Council (NWMAC) 1949–52; Vice-Chair. Prov. People's Govt., Gansu 1949–52; Chair. Financial and Econ. Cttee., NWMAC 1950–52; Dir. and Political Commissar N.W. Bureau of Railway Tech. 1951; mem. N.W. Bureau, CCP Cen. Cttee. 1951; Vice-Minister of Railways 1952–54; Deputy for Jiangsu, 1st NPC 1954–59; mem. Nat. Defence Council 1954–Cultural Revolution; Vice-Chair. State Construction Comm., State Council 1954–58; Alt. mem. 8th Cen. Cttee., CCP 1956; Sec. Secr., CCP Gansu 1962–Cultural Revolution; Deputy for Gansu, 3rd NPC 1964; mem. Standing Cttee., 3rd NPC, and of N.W. China Bureau, CCP Cen. Cttee. 1965; disappeared during Cultural Revolution; mem. Standing Cttee., 4th NPC 1975; mem. 11th Cen. Cttee., CCP 1977; Vice-Chair. Prov. Revolutionary Cttee., Gansu 1977–79; Deputy for Gansu, 5th NPC 1978; Chair. Prov. People's Congress, Gansu 1979–83; mem. Cen. Advisory Comm., CCP Cen. Cttee. 1982. *Address:* People's Congress, Gansu Province, People's Republic of China.

WANG SHOUDAO; Chinese party official; b. 1907, Hunan; joined CCP 1925; Gov. Hunan 1950–52; Vice-Minister of Communications 1952–58, Minister 1958–64; Sec. Cen.-South Bureau CCP 1964–67; Vice-Chair. Guangdong Revolutionary Cttee. 1968–78; Sec. Guangdong CCP 1970–78; Chair. Family Planning Assen. 1980; mem. Standing Cttee. Cen. Advisory Cttee. 1982–; mem. Party Cttee. of Special Orgs. under Cen. Advisory Cttee. 1983–; Pres. China Assen. for Int. Friendly Contacts 1984–, China Population Welfare Foundation 1987–; Hon. Dir. Nat. Welfare Fund for Aged 1986–. *Address:* Advisory Commission, Central Committee of Chinese Communist Party, Beijing, People's Republic of China.

WANG SHOUGUAN; Chinese astronomer and university professor; b. 15 Jan. 1925, Fuzhou; s. of B. L. Wang and S. Y. Gao; m. Lin Zhihuan 1955; one s. one d.; Dir. Beijing Astronomical Observatory 1978–; Deputy Head, Div. of Math. and Physics, Chinese Acad. of Sciences 1981–; Visiting Prof., Beijing Normal Univ. 1987–; Pres. Chinese Astronomical Soc. 1985–; Chief Ed. Vol. Astronomy, Chinese Encyclopaedia 1980; Nat. Science Congress Award 1978, Nat. Science and Tech. Progress Award 1985. *Leisure interest:* poetry. *Address:* No. 404, Block 808, Zhong-Guan-Cun, Beijing, People's Republic of China. *Telephone:* 28-5228.

WANG SHUMING; Chinese government official; Deputy Sec.-Gen. State Council Jan. 1986–; Deputy Head Co-ordination Group for Tourist Industry 1986–. *Address:* State Council, Zhong Nan Hai, Beijing, People's Republic of China.

WANG TAO; Chinese geologist and state official; b. 1932, Leting, Hebei; Chief Geologist, Dagang Oil Field; Chief Geologist, Liaohe Petroleum Prospecting Bureau; Gen. Man., South China Sea, Eastern District, China Nat. Offshore Oil Corpn.; Minister of Petroleum Industry 1985–88; Pres.

State Petroleum and Natural Gas Corpn. May 1988–; mem. CCP Cen. Cttee. 1985–. *Address:* State Petroleum and Natural Gas Corpn., Liupukang Deshengmenwai, Beijing, People's Republic of China.

WANG TIAN-REN; Chinese sculptor; b. 26 July 1939, Henan. *Address:* Shaanxi Sculptor Studio, Longshoucun, Xian, People's Republic of China.

WANG WEI; Chinese government official; b. 1915, Henan; Chair. Youth Work Cttee. CCP 1952–67; in political disgrace 1967–78; Vice-Minister of Public Health 1978–83; fmr. Minister, State Family Planning Comm.; Vice-Chair. Educ., Science, Culture and Public Health Cttee. *Address:* State Council, Beijing, People's Republic of China.

WANG WENJIAO; Chinese sports coach; led Chinese badminton team in World Badminton Championships 1986; Pres. Badminton Asscn. April 1988–. *Address:* China Sports Federation, Beijing, People's Republic of China.

WANG WENSHI; Chinese writer; b. 21 Nov. 1921, Shaanxi Prov.; s. of Wang Zhitong and Cui Jinxiu; m. Gao Bin 1949; two s. one d. *Publications:* Comrade-in-Arms (opera libretto), The Night of Wind and Snow, Hei Feng (novel), The Dunes, New Acquaintance, Yiyun Ji (Echo the Views of Others: essay). *Leisure interests:* playing Mahjong, calligraphy. *Address:* Union of Chinese Writers, Shaanxi Branch Xi'an, Shaanxi Province, People's Republic of China.

WANG XIAODONG; Chinese violinist; b. 1970; winner, junior Section, Yehudi Menuhin Int. Violin Competition, U.K. 1983.

WANG XIAOGUANG; Chinese jurist; Deputy Procurator-Gen. 1983–; mem. CCP Discipline Inspection Comm. 1982–; Sec. Party Cttee. Beijing Univ. 1985–. *Address:* Supreme People's Procuratorate, Beijing, People's Republic of China.

WANG XIULI; Chinese speed skater; 1,000 metre gold medalist, 1,500 metre silver medalist, Asian Winter Games 1986. *Address:* China Sports Federation, Beijing, People's Republic of China.

WANG XUEZHEN; Chinese academic; b. 31 Aug. 1926, Zhejiang; s. of Wang Hai Shan and Xu Cui Feng; m. Gu Zhi Ying 1954; two d.; ed. Peking Univ.; Vice-Pres. Peking Univ. 1981, Sec. Univ. CCP Cttee., Chair. Univ. Council 1984–; alt. mem. 12th CCP Cen. Cttee. 1982, 13th Cen. Cttee. 1987. *Leisure interest:* literature. *Address:* Peking University, Beijing, People's Republic of China. *Telephone:* 28-2471-3955.

WANG YOU-TSAO, M.SC., PH.D.; Chinese government official; b. 2 July 1925, Chinchiang County, Fukien; s. of Wang Hsiao-kwei and Wang-Huang Pei-feng; m. Wang Jean Eng-ling 1954; two s. one d.; ed. Nat. Taiwan Univ. and Iowa State Univ.; Asst., Instr., Assoc. Prof. Dept. of Agric. Econs. Nat. Taiwan Univ. 1954–60, Prof. 1965–66; Specialist, Rural Econs. Div., Jt. Comm. on Rural Reconstruction 1960–63, Sr. Specialist 1965–66, Chief, Rural Econs. Div. 1966–71, Chief, Office of Planning and Programming 1971–72, Deputy Sec.-Gen. Jt. Comm. on Rural Reconstruction 1972–73, Sec.-Gen. 1973–79; Sec.-Gen. Council for Agric. Planning and Devt., Exec. Yuan 1979, Vice-Chair. 1979–84, Chair. 1984–88. *Address:* 14-6 Alley 1, Lane 194, Chunghsiao E. Road, Sect. 4, Taipei, Taiwan.

WANG YUANJIAN; Chinese writer; b. 1929, Shandong; s. of Nang Zhengian and Qion Zhihua; m. Wong Yani 1952; three d.; war correspondent 1944; ed. of A Single Spark Can Start a Prairie Fire 1952. *Publications:* Party Membership Dues, An Ordinary Labourer, An Invaluable Memento. *Leisure interests:* calligraphy, swimming. *Address:* August 1st Film Studios, Beijing, People's Republic of China.

WANG YUEFENG; Chinese party and state official; Deputy for Guangdong Prov. to 5th NPC 1978; mem. State Nationalities Comm. 1982–83; alt. mem. 12th CCP Cen. Cttee. 1982, 13th Cen. Cttee. 1987. *Address:* c/o Chinese Communist Party Central Committee, Beijing, People's Republic of China.

WANG YUNG-CHING; Taiwan business executive; b. 18 Jan. 1917, Taiwan; m. Yueh-lan Wang; two s. eight d.; founder/owner Formosa Plastics Group, a multinational petrochemical conglomerate consisting of over 20 cos. including Nan Ya Plastics Corpn., Formosa Plastics Corpn., Formosa Chemicals & Fibre Corpn. and three cos. in U.S.A. *Address:* 201, Tunhua N. Road, Taipei, Taiwan.

WANG YUZHAO; Chinese government official; b. 9 Feb. 1926, Shandong; s. of Wang Qiming and Yu Shi; m. Jia Suihua 1954; one s. one d.; Deputy Sec. CPC 3rd and 4th Prov. Cttee., Anhui Prov. 1983, 1984; Gov. of Anhui 1983–87; mem. Rural Policy Research Centre, Secr. of CCP Cen. Cttee. 1987–; alt. mem. 12th CCP Cen. Cttee. 1985–87. *Leisure interest:* photography. *Address:* 85 Changjiang Road, Hefei, People's Republic of China. *Telephone:* 74751.

WANG ZE; Chinese diplomatist; b. 1923; Consul-Gen. Burma 1955–61; Consul-Gen. Embassy, Pakistan 1965–67; Amb. to Nepal 1969–72, to Mauritius 1972–77, to Peru 1977–81, to Mexico 1981–83, to Sweden 1983.

WANG ZENGQI; Chinese writer; b. 5 March 1920, Gaoyou County, Jiangsu Prov.; s. of Wang Jusheng; m. Shi Songqing 1950; one s. two d.; ed. Southwest Associated Univ.; teacher 1943–47; office worker, Museum of History 1948–49; Ed. Peking Literature and Art, Peking Ballads, Folk

Literature 1950–58; playwright, Beijing Opera Troupe 1962; Council mem. China Fed. of Art and Literature. *Publications:* Fang Jin Passes Examination (Peking Opera), Shajiapang (Peking Opera), A Selection from Wang Zengqi's Short Stories 1982, Wild Jasmine Short Stories 1985. *Leisure interests:* Chinese calligraphy, painting, cooking. *Address:* Beijing Opera Troupe, Hufangchiao, Beijing, People's Republic of China.

WANG ZHAOGUO; Chinese party official; b. 1941; First Sec. China Youth League 1982–; mem. 12th Cen. Cttee. CCP 1982; Deputy for Hubei to 6th NPC 1983; Dir.-Gen. Office Cen. Cttee. CCP 1984–86; Chief Rep. 21st Century Cttee. for Chinese-Japanese Friendship 1984–; Vice-Gov. and Acting Gov. of Fujian 1987–88, Gov. Jan. 1988–; mem. Secretariat, CCP Central Cttee. 1985; mem. Cen. Party Consolidation Guidance Comm. 1983–; Deputy Head, Leading Group for Rectification of Party Style within Cen. Depts., CCP Cen. Cttee. 1986–; mem. Presidium 6th NPC 1986–, Standing Cttee. 6th NPC 1986–; mem. 13th CCP Cen. Cttee. 1987–. *Address:* Central Committee of Chinese Communist Party, Beijing, People's Republic of China.

WANG ZHEN; Chinese government official; b. 1909, Liuyang, Hunan; Regimental Political Commissar 1930; Alt. mem. 7th Cen. Cttee. of CCP 1945; Commdr. of 1st Army Corps, 1st Field Army, PLA 1949; Commdr. Xinjiang Mil. Region, PLA 1950; Minister of State Farms and Land Reclamation 1956; mem. 8th Cen. Cttee. of CCP 1956, 9th Cen. Cttee. 1969, 10th Cen. Cttee. 1973; Vice-Premier of State Council 1975–80; Vice-Pres. of China April 1988–; mem. 11th Cen. Cttee. CCP 1977, mem. 12th Cen. Cttee. CCP 1982; Deputy for Shensi 5th NPC 1978; mem. Presidium NPC 1978; mem. Politburo of Cen. Cttee. of CCP 1978, 1982–85; Dir. Cen. Cttee. of CCP Party School 1982–; Chair. Admin. Cttee., Fudan Univ. 1979; Deputy for Hubei to 6th NPC 1983; Adviser Cen. Party Consolidation Guidance Comm. 1983–; Chair. Chinese Cttee. Council of Chinese and Japanese Non-Governmental Personages 1983–; Hon. Pres. China-Japan Friendship Asscn. 1983–; China Asscn. for Int. Friendly Contacts 1984–; Hon. Dir.-in-Chief China Welfare Fund for the Handicapped 1984–; Vice-Chair. Cen. Advisory Cttee. 1985–87; Hon. Chair. China Inst. of Agricultural Tech. 1987–. *Address:* Office of the Vice-President, State Council, Beijing, People's Republic of China.

WANG ZHONGSHU; Chinese archaeologist; Dir. Inst. of Archaeology 1982–. *Address:* Chinese Academy of Social Sciences, Beijing, People's Republic of China.

WANG ZHONGYU; Chinese party official; Sec. Gen. Jilin Prov. CCP Cttee. 1984, Deputy Sec. 1985–; alt. mem. CCP Cen. Cttee. 1987–. *Address:* Central Committee of the Chinese Communist Party, Zhongnanhai, Beijing, People's Republic of China.

WANG ZIGANG; Chinese politician; Minister of Posts and Telecommunications 1978–79; Pres. Inst. of Communications 1980–; Adviser, Ministry of Posts and Telecommunications 1981; mem. Cen. Advisory Comm. 1982. *Address:* c/o State Council, Beijing, People's Republic of China.

WANG ZIKUN, D.SC.; Chinese professor and university administrator; b. 21 April 1929, Jiangxi Prov.; s. of Wang Zhao-ji and Guo Xiang-e; m. Tain Der-Lin 1958; two s.; ed. Wuhan Univ. and Moscow Univ.; Asst. Prof., then Prof. Nankai Univ. 1952–84; Pres. and Prof. Beijing Normal Univ. 1984–; Dir. of China Math. Soc.; mem. of Standing Bd. China Probalistical-Statistics Soc., China Higher Educational Soc.; mem. of editorial bd. Society, Scientia Sinica, Science Bulletin of China; China Science Conference Award 1978, China Natural Science Prize 1982, China Excellent Popular Science Works Award 1981, and numerous other awards. *Publications:* Foundations of Probability Theory and Their Applications 1976, Theory of Stochastic Processes 1965, Birth-Death Processes and Markov Chains 1980, Brownian Motion and Potentials 1982, Probability Theory and Statistical Prediction 1978, Talks on Scientific Discovery 1978, and many other math. articles and popular scientific publs. *Leisure interest:* literature. *Address:* President's Office, Beijing Normal University, Beijing, People's Republic of China. *Telephone:* 2011674.

WANGCHUK, Jigme Singye; King (Druk Gyalpo) of Bhutan; b. 11 Nov. 1955; s. of late Druk Gyalpo Jigme Dorji Wangchuk and of Queen Ashi Kesang; ed. North Point, Darjeeling, Ugyuen Wangchuk Acad., Paro, also in England; Crown Prince March 1972; succeeded to throne 24 July 1972, crowned 2 June 1974; Chair. Planning Comm. of Bhutan March 1972–; C.-in-C. of Armed Forces. *Address:* Royal Palace, Thimphu, Bhutan.

WAPENYI, Eldad Kanyanya, B.A.; Ugandan diplomatist; b. 15 Aug. 1936, Gulu; s. of William M. Wapenyi and Sera Elizabeth Woniaye; m. Freda Nanziri Kase 1964; four s. one d.; ed. Busugo Coll., Mwiri, Makerere and Harvard Univs.; New Zealand Foreign Office; Asst. District Commr., Kigezi March-Oct. 1962; Asst. Sec. (Protocol, Political and Econ.), Ministry of Foreign Affairs, Entebbe 1962–64; Second Sec. and Head of Chancery, Uganda Embassy, Moscow 1964–65; Second Sec., Uganda Embassy, Bonn 1965–66; Exec. Asst. to Chair., Uganda Devt. Corpn., Kampala 1966–68; Senior Asst. Sec. (Econ.), Ministry of Foreign Affairs, Kampala 1968–69; First Sec. and Head of Chancery, Uganda High Comm., India 1970–71; Counsellor and Head of Chancery, Perm. Mission of Uganda to the UN 1971–78, 1971–75; Consultant UN Conf. on the Law of the Sea 1975; Special Asst. to the Under-Sec. Gen. on the Law of the Sea 1975–79; Prin.

Pvt. Sec. to the Pres. of Uganda 1979; Amb. and Perm. Rep. of Uganda to UN 1979–80; Amb. to France 1980–82; Dir. Ministry of Foreign Affairs, Kampala 1986–; mem. Uganda Export Promotion Council 1966–67, Uganda Industrial Licensing Bd. 1967. *Leisure interests:* music, golf, farming. *Address:* c/o Ministry of Foreign Affairs, P.O. Box 7048, Kampala, Uganda.

WAPNEWSKI, Peter, DR.PHIL.; German professor of medieval literature; b. 7 Sept. 1922, Kiel; s. of Harald and Gertrud (née Hennings) Wapnewski; m. 1st Caroline Gräfin Finckenstein 1950 (divorced 1959), 2nd Monica Plange 1971; ed. Univs. of Berlin, Freiburg, Jena and Hamburg; Prof. of Medieval German Literature, Heidelberg 1959, Free Univ. of Berlin 1966, Univ. of Karlsruhe 1969, Tech. Univ. of Berlin 1982–; Rector, Wissenschaftskolleg, Berlin 1980–86, Perm. mem. 1986–; Vice-Pres. Goethe Inst. 1977–; mem. Deutsche Akademie für Sprache und Dichtung, PEN Club, American Medieval Acad.; Grosses Bundesverdienstkreuz 1986. *Publications:* Wolframs Parzival 1955, Deutsche Literatur des Mittelalters 1960, Walther von der Vogelweide (ed.), Hartmann von Aue 1962, Die Lyrik Wolframs von Eschenbach 1972, Richard Wagner—Die Szene und ihr Meister 1978, Der Traurige Gott 1978, Zumutungen 1979, Tristan der Held Richard Wagners 1981, Minnesang des Codex Manesse 1982, Eduard Hanslick, Ausmeinem Leben (Ed.) 1987, Götternot und Göttertrauer 1988, Die unerhörten Künste (Ed.) 1989; about 200 articles on medieval and modern German literature. *Address:* Wallotstrasse 19, D-1000 Berlin 33, Federal Republic of Germany. *Telephone:* (030) 89001-0.

WARBURTON, Dame Anne Marion, D.C.V.O., C.M.G., M.A.; British diplomatist; b. 8 June 1927; d. of Capt. Eliot and Mary Louise (née Thompson) Warburton; ed. Barnard Coll., Columbia Univ., Somerville Coll., Oxford; with Econ. Co-operation Admin., London 1949–52;· NATO Secr., Paris 1952–54; Lazard Bros., London 1955–57; entered Diplomatic Service 1957; Second Sec., Foreign Office 1957–59; Second, then First Sec., U.K. Mission to UN, New York 1959–62; First Sec., Bonn 1962–65; Diplomatic Service Admin. Office, London 1965–67, Foreign Office, then FCO 1967–70; Counsellor, U.K. Mission to UN, Geneva 1970–75; Head of Guidance and Information Policy Dept., FCO 1975–76; Amb. to Denmark 1976–83, to UN at Geneva 1983–85; Pres. Lucy Cavendish Coll., Cambridge 1985–; Equal Opportunities Commr. 1986–87; Verdienstkreuz (First Class), Fed. Repub. of Germany 1965; Grand Cross, Order of Dannebrog, Denmark 1979. *Leisure interests:* performing arts, walking, travel. *Address:* Lucy Cavendish College, Cambridge, England.

WARD, Ian Macmillan, M.A., D.PHIL., F.R.S.; British professor of physics; b. 9 April 1928, Stockton-on-Tees; s. of Harry Ward and Joan Moodie (née Burt); m. Margaret Linley 1960; two s. one d.; ed. Royal Grammar School, Newcastle-upon-Tyne and Magdalen Coll., Oxford; Tech. Officer, ICI Fibres 1954–61; seconded to Div. of Applied Math. Brown Univ., U.S.A. 1961–62; Head, Basic Physics Section, ICI Fibres 1962–65; Sr. lecturer in Physics of Materials, Univ. of Bristol 1965–69; Prof. of Physics, Univ. of Leeds 1970– (Chair. of Dept. 1975–78, 1987–); Pres., British Soc. of Rheology 1984–86; A. A. Griffith Medal 1982, S. G. Smith Memorial Medal 1984, Swinburne Award 1988. *Publications:* Mechanical Properties of Solid Polymers 1971, ed. Structure and Properties of Oriented Polymers 1975, Ultra High Modulus Polymers 1979. *Leisure interests:* music, walking. *Address:* Department of Physics, University of Leeds, Leeds, LS2 9JT (Office); Kirkstill, 2 Creskeld Drive, Bramhope, Leeds, LS16 9EL, England. *Telephone:* (0532) 431751 (Office); (0532) 673637 (Home).

WARD, Most Rev. John Aloysius; British ecclesiastic; b. 24 Jan. 1929, Leeds; s. of Eugene Ward and Hannah Cheetham; ed. Prior Park Coll., Bath and Theological Seminaries of Franciscan Order, Olton, Crawley; entered Capuchin Franciscan Order 1945, Friar 1950–53, Priest 1953–; Travelling Missioner of Diocese of Menevia, Wales 1954–60; Superior (Guardian) and Parish Priest of Franciscan Friary, Peckham, London 1960–66; Provincial Definitor (Councillor) of British Prov. of Order 1963–69, Minister Provincial 1969–70; General Definitor (Councillor) of Order in Rome 1970–80; Coadjutor Bishop of Menevia July 1980, Bishop Oct. 1980, succeeded to See 1981; Archbishop of Cardiff and Metropolitan of Welsh Prov. 1983–; Order of Friars Minor Capuchin. *Address:* Archbishop's House, 41-43 Cathedral Road, Cardiff, CF1 9HD, Wales. *Telephone:* 0222-220411.

WARD, John Manning, A.O., M.A., LL.B.; Australian university vice-chancellor; b. 6 July 1919, Sydney; s. of Alexander T. and Mildred B. (Davis) Ward; m. Patricia B. Webb 1951; two d.; ed. Univ. of Sydney; Challis Prof. of History, Univ. of Sydney 1949–82, Dean, Faculty of Arts 1962, Pro-Dean, Faculty of Arts 1970–71, Deputy Vice-Chancellor 1979–81, Vice-Chancellor and Prin. 1981–89; Dominion Fellow, St. John's Coll., Cambridge 1951; Visiting Prof., Yale Univ. 1963; Visiting Fellow, All Souls Coll., Oxford 1968; Smuts Visiting Fellow, Cambridge 1972. *Publications:* British Policy in the South Pacific 1948, Earl Grey and the Australian Colonies 1946–57 1958, Empire in the Antipodes c. 1840–1860 1966, Changes in Britain 1919–1957 1968, Colonial Self-Government, The British Experience 1759–1856 1976, James Macarthur, Colonial Conservative 1798–1887 1981 and contributions to other historical works. *Leisure interests:* music, railways. *Address:* c/o Vice-Chancellor's Office, University of Sydney, N.S.W. 2006, Australia.

WARD, Michael Phelps, C.B.E., M.D., F.R.C.S.; British consultant surgeon; b. 26 March 1925, London; m. Felicity Jane Ewbank 1957; one s.; ed.

Marlborough Coll., Peterhouse, Cambridge, London Hosp.; House Surgeon, Registrar, Sr. Registrar, London Hosp. 1950–64; lecturer in Surgery, London Hosp. Medical Coll. 1964–; Consultant Surgeon, City and East London Area Hosp. Authority (Teaching) 1964–; took part in Everest Reconnaissance 1951, First Ascent 1953, Himalayan Scientific Expedition 1960–61; Leader scientific expeditions N. Bhutan 1964, 1965, Southern Xinjiang (First Ascent Mount Kongur) 1980, 1981; Royal Soc./Chinese Acad. of Sciences Tibet Geotraverse 1985–86; Chair. Mount Everest Foundation 1978–80; Hunterian Prof., Royal Coll. of Surgeons 1954; Cuthbert Peek Award, Royal Geographical Soc. 1973, Founders (Royal) Medal, Royal Geographical Soc. 1982, Cullum Medal, American Geographical Soc. 1954. *Publications:* Mountaineer's Companion 1966, In This Short Span 1972, Mountain Medicine 1975, High Altitude Medicine and Physiology (Co-Author) 1989; articles and medical papers on the effects of great altitude, exposure to cold and on exercise; also on exploratory journeys in Nepal, Bhutan, Chinese Cen. Asia and Tibet. *Leisure interests:* mountaineering, skiing. *Address:* St. Andrew's Hospital, Bow, London, E3 3NT, England. *Telephone:* 01-987 2030.

WARD, Simon; British actor; b. 19 Oct. 1941, Beckenham; s. of Leonard Fox Ward and Winifred Ward; m. Alexandra Malcolm; ed. Alleyn's School, Dulwich, and Royal Acad. of Dramatic Art; mem. Nat. Youth Theatre from its foundation (as Youth Theatre) 1956; first professional stage appearance in Hobson's Choice, Northampton Repertory Theatre 1963; London debut in The Fourth of June, St. Martin's Theatre 1964; film debut in Frankenstein Must Be Destroyed 1969. *Stage roles include:* Konstantin in The Seagull, Birmingham Repertory 1964; Abel Drugger in The Alchemist and Hippolytus in Phèdre, Playhouse, Oxford 1965–66; Dennis in Loot, Jeannetta Cochrane and Criterion 1966; the Unknown Soldier in The Unknown Soldier and His Wife, Ferdinand in The Tempest and Henry in The Skin of Our Teeth, Chichester Festival 1968; Donald in Spoiled, Haymarket 1971; Romeo in Romeo and Juliet, Shaw 1972; Troilus in Troilus and Cressida, Young Vic 1976, House Guest 1982, Whose Life is it Anyway?, Birmingham 1982, Heartbreak House 1983, Dial M for Murder 1983, Ross 1986, Paris Match 1988. *Films include:* I Start Counting 1970, Young Winston 1971, Hitler—The Last Ten Days 1972, The Three Musketeers 1973, The Four Musketeers, Deadly Strangers, All Creatures Great and Small 1974–75, Aces High 1975, Battle Flag 1976, The Four Feathers 1978, Zulu Dawn 1979. *TV includes:* The Black Tulip, The Roads to Freedom, Holocaust (serials). *Leisure interests:* music, gardening, reading, badminton. *Address:* c/o IFA Ltd., 11–12 Hanover Street, London, W.1, England.

WARDEBERG, George E., B.A.; American business executive; b. 1935, Barnesville, Minn.; m.; ed. Michigan State Univ.; joined Whirlpool Corpn., Benton Harbor, Mich. 1957, Man. Trainee, St. Joseph Div. 1957–61, Man. Quality Control, Clyde Div. 1961–66, Dir. Personnel, parent co. 1966–67, Dir. Floor-care Products and Sales to Sears, St. Paul Div., Dir. Mfg. Material Control, parent co. 1970–78, Man. St. Paul Div. 1978–80, Div. Vice-Pres., St. Paul 1980–81, Vice-Pres. Sales to Sears 1981–83, Exec. Vice-Pres. Sales to Sears 1983–84, Exec. Vice-Pres. Int. Div. 1984–85, Vice-Chair. and C.O.O. 1985–, mem. Bd. of Dirs.; mem. Bd. of Dirs. Inglis Ltd.; mem. GMI Eng. and Man. Inst. *Address:* Whirlpool Corpn., Administrative Center, Benton Harbor, Mich. 49022, U.S.A.

WARDHANA, Ali, M.A., PH.D.; Indonesian economist and politician; b. 6 May 1928, Surakarta, Central Java; m. Renny Wardhana 1953; one s. three d.; ed. Univ. of Indonesia, Jakarta and Univ. of California (Berkeley) U.S.A.; Dir., Research Inst. of Econ. and Social Studies 1962–67; Prof. of Econs., Univ. of Indonesia 1967–, Dean Faculty of Econs. 1967–78; Adviser to Gov. of Cen. Bank 1964–68; mem. team of experts of Presidential Staff 1966–68; Minister of Finance 1968–83; Co-ordinating Minister for Econ., Finance, Industry and Devt. Control 1983–88; Chair. Cttee. of Bd. of Governors of the IMF on Reform of the Int. Monetary System and Related Issues 1972–74; Grand Cross Order of Léopold II (Belgium) 1970, Grand Cross Order of Orange Nassau (Netherlands) 1971, Mahaputra Adipradhna II Award (Indonesia) 1973. *Leisure interests:* reading, tennis, bowling, swimming. *Address:* 5, Jalan Brawijaya III, Kebayoran Baru, Jakarta, Indonesia.

WARIOBA, Joseph Sinde, LL.B.; Tanzanian politician; b. 1940; m. Evelyn Grace 1969; three s. one d.; ed. Univ. of Dar es Salaam; fmr. Dir. of Legal Affairs, Ministry of Foreign Affairs; Attorney-Gen. and Minister of Justice 1977; Prime Minister and First Vice-Pres. 1985–; mem. Cen. Cttee., Nat. Exec. Cttee. (NEC) of ruling party Chama Cha Mapinduzi (CCM); Sec. CCM's Nat. Defence and Security Council; Chair. Preparatory Comm. for the Int. Sea-Bed Authority for the Law of the Sea 1983–87. *Address:* Office of the Prime Minister, P.O.B. 980, Dodoma, Tanzania. *Telephone:* 20511.

WARIS, Klaus, PH.D.; Finnish economist; b. 17 March 1914, Helsinki; s. of Dr. Erkki Warén and Katri Cannelin; m. Elina Leppänen 1939; two s. one d.; ed. Turku, Helsinki Univ.; Chief, Econ. Affairs Div., Ministry of Finance 1946–49; Prof. Econs. Finnish Inst. of Tech. 1949–52; mem. Man. Bd. Bank of Finland 1952–57; Gov. Bank of Finland 1957–67; Gov. for Finland, IMF 1958–68; Chancellor, Helsinki School of Econs. 1967–80; Chancellor, Order of the White Rose and of the Lion of Finland 1983–87. *Address:* Kartanontie 12, Helsinki 33, Finland. *Telephone:* 482-979.

WARNER, Bishop Bennie D., M.SC., TH.M., D.D.; Liberian ecclesiastic; b. 30 April 1935, Caresburg District; ed. Monrovia Gbargna United Methodist Mission School, Booker Washington Inst., Kakata, Cuttington Univ. Coll., Suakoto, Syracuse Univ. and Boston Univ. School of Theology (U.S.A.); ordained Deacon 1961; acting Dir. Pastors' Inst. of the United Methodist Church 1961; educ. counsellor and maths. and social studies teacher, W.V.S. Tubman Elementary School 1962–68; fmr. Chair. Nat. Student Christian Council of Liberia; later ordained Elder; fmr. Pastor, St. John's United Methodist Church, Gbarnga, and Reeves Memorial United Methodist Church, Crozierville; fmr. Chair. Interim Cttee. for the Admin. of the Coll. of W. Africa, Bd. of Ministry, Liberia Annual Conference of United Methodist Church; ordained Bishop 1973; later Chair. Bd. of Trustees of the Coll. of W. Africa; Vice-Pres. of Liberia 1977–80; mem. Bd. of Trustees, Cuttington Coll. and Divinity School, Bd. of the Booker Washington Inst., Nat. Disaster Comm., Council of Bishops, World Methodist Council; Grand Band, Order of the Star of Africa; in exile in U.S.A.

WARNER, Brian, PH.D., M.A., D.SC., F.R.A.S., F.R.S. (S.A.); British astronomer; b. 25 May 1939, Sussex; s. of Leslie and Edith M. (née Bashford) Warner; m. 1st Carole Christian 1965 (divorced 1973), one s. one d.; m. 2nd Nancy Russell 1976 (divorced 1987); ed. Univ. of London and Univ. of Oxford; Research Asst., Univ. of London Observatory 1964–65; Radcliffe-Henry Skynner Sr. Research Fellow, Balliol Coll., Oxford 1965–67; Asst. Prof., Univ. of Texas at Austin 1967–69, Assoc. Prof. 1969–72; Prof. and Head, Dept. of Astronomy, Univ. of Cape Town 1972–, Fellow 1978; Alfred P. Sloan Fellow 1969–71; Visiting Fellow, Univ. of Colo. 1977; Visiting Sr. Fellow, Dept. of Astrophysics Univ. of Oxford 1985; Visiting Prof. Dartmouth Coll. and Univ. of Texas 1986–87; Fellow, Royal Astronomical Soc.; Pres. Royal Soc. of South Africa 1981–83; Pres. Comm. 42 of Int. Astronomical Union 1978–82; Pres. Astronomical Soc. of Southern Africa 1977–78, The Owl Club 1985–86; mem. Bd. of Trustees, South African Museum 1981–, Deputy Chair. 1988–; Boyden Premium, Franklin Inst. 1980; McIntyre Award, Astronomical Soc. of Southern Africa 1983, John F. W. Herschel Medal, Royal Soc. of S.A.. Publications: Astronomers at the Royal Observatory, Cape of Good Hope 1979, Charles Piazzi Smyth 1983, Maclear and Herschel 1984, The Journal of Lady Jane Franklin 1985, High Speed Astronomical Photometry 1988, William Mann 1989; over 200 scientific research papers. Leisure interests: golf, 19th-century science and exploration, baroque music. Address: Department of Astronomy, University of Cape Town, Rondebosch, 7700 Cape; 14 Argyle Road, Newlands, 7700 Cape, South Africa (Home). Telephone: 6863443 (Office); 6851443 (Home).

WARNER, David; British actor; b. 29 July 1941, Manchester; s. of Herbert Simon Warner; ed. Feldon School, Leamington Spa, and Royal Acad. of Dramatic Art; worked as bookseller; stage début as Snout in A Midsummer Night's Dream, Royal Court 1962; film debut in Tom Jones 1963; joined Royal Shakespeare Co. (RSC) 1963 and appeared as Trinculo in The Tempest, Cinna in Julius Caesar, title role in Henry VI, Edward IV in adaptation of Henry VI (Parts I, II and III) comprising first two parts of trilogy The Wars of the Roses (Stratford). Other roles include: Henry VI in The Wars of the Roses, Aldwych 1964; Richard II, Mouldy in Henry IV (Part II) and Henry VI in The Wars of the Roses, RSC, Stratford 1964; Valentine Brose in Eh?, Aldwych 1964, Hamlet, Stratford and Aldwych 1965; the Postmaster in The Government Inspector, Aldwych 1965; Hamlet, Sir Andrew Aguecheek in Twelfth Night, Stratford 1966; Claudius in I, Claudius, Hampstead 1972. Films include: Morgan—A Suitable Case for Treatment 1966, Work is a Four Letter Word 1967, The Bofors Gun, The Fixer, The Seagull 1968–69, The Ballad of Cable Hogue 1970, Straw Dogs 1971, A Doll's House 1972, The Omen 1975, Cross of Iron, Providence, Silver Bears 1976, The Disappearance 1977, The Thirty Nine Steps 1978, Nightwing, Time After Time 1979, The Island 1980. TV includes: Clouds of Glory 1977, Holocaust 1977, Charlie 1984.

WARNER, Denis Ashton, C.M.G., O.B.E.; Australian journalist and author; b. 12 December 1917, Tasmania; s. of Hugh Ashton Warner and Nelly Callan; m. Peggy Strafford Hick 1945; one s. two d.; ed. Hutchins School, Hobart, Harvard Univ.; war corresp. Australian Publications 1944–45; Reuter-AAP Editorial Man., Tokyo 1947–49; Roving Far Eastern Corresp. Melbourne Herald and Daily Telegraph (London) 1949–55; Far Eastern Corresp. Reporter Magazine 1957–68; Asian Corresp. Look Magazine 1968–72; Author of syndicated column on Far Eastern Affairs 1957–; Ed. Pacific Defence Reporter 1981–; Australian Corresp. London Daily Telegraph 1958–86; mem. Editorial Bd., Conflict, Int. Advisory Bd., Political Communication and Persuasion; Pres. Australian Defence Correspondents' Asscn. 1985–87; Citations Overseas Press Club of New York for Best Magazine Reporting 1956, 1958. Publications: Out of the Gun 1956, The Last Confucian 1963, Not with Guns Alone 1977; with Peggy Warner: The Tide at Sunrise: A History of the Russo-Japanese War 1904–05 1974, Japan's Highway to the 20th Century 1980, The Sacred Warriors 1982. Leisure interest: dry fly fishing. Address: Ramslade, Nepean Highway, Mt. Eliza, Vic., Australia 3930. Telephone: 059-752706.

WARNER, Sir Fred. Archibald, G.C.V.O., K.C.M.G., M.A.; British businessman, farmer and politician; b. 2 May 1918, Bournemouth; s. of Frederick A. Warner and Marjorie M. Winants; m. Simone Georgina de Ferranti 1971; two s.; ed. Royal Naval Coll., Dartmouth and Magdalen Coll., Oxford; served Royal Navy 1932–37, 1939–46; joined Foreign Office 1946; served in Moscow 1950–51, Rangoon 1956–58, Athens 1958–59; Amb. to Laos 1965–67; Minister, NATO 1967–68; Deputy Perm. Rep. to UN 1969–70; Amb. to Japan 1972–75; mem. of European Parl. for Somerset and South Avon 1979–84; Dir. Loral Int.; Chair. Overseas Cttee. CBI 1985–88. Address: 3 Kelvin Court, Kensington Park Road, London, W.11; Inkpen House, Newbury, Berks., England. Telephone: 01-727 2016 (London); (048 84) 266 (Berks.).

WARNER, Sir Frederick Edward, Kt., F.ENG., F.R.S.; British engineer and university professor; b. 31 March 1910, London; s. of Frederick Warner; m. 1st Margaret Anderson McCrea, two s. two d.; m. 2nd Barbara Ivy Reynolds; ed. Bancrofts School, Univ. Coll., London; chemical engineer with various cos. 1934–56; partner in firm of consulting chemical engineers working in U.K., Ireland, U.S.S.R., India, Iran, Jordan, Africa 1956–80; Senior Partner, Cremer and Warner 1963–80, now Emer.; Visiting Prof. Bartlett School of Arch., Univ. Coll., London 1970–; Visiting Prof. of Chem. Eng., Imperial Coll., London 1970–78; Visiting Prof. Univ. of Essex 1983–; Pro-Chancellor, Open Univ. 1974–79; mem. Advisory Council on Energy Conservation, Dept. of Energy 1974–80; Pres. British Standards Inst. 1980–83, Vice-Pres. 1976–80, 1983–; Pres. British Asscn. for Commercial and Industrial Educ. 1977–, Inst. of Quality Assurance 1987–; Chair. British Nat. Cttee. on Problems of Environment, Royal Soc. 1973–80, Council of Science and Tech. Insts. 1987–; Treas. SCOPE 1982; Pres. Fédération Européene d'Associations Nationales d'Ingénieurs 1968–71; Hon. mem. Royal Inst. of Engineers, Netherlands 1972; Fellow, Univ. Coll., London 1967; Hon. Fellow, School of Pharmacy, London 1979, UMIST 1986; Hon. D.Tech. (Bradford) 1969, Hon. D.Sc. (Aston) 1970, (Cranfield) 1978, (Heriot-Watt) 1978, (Newcastle) 1979, Hon. D.Univ. (Open) 1980; Gold Medal, Czechoslovak Soc. for Int. Relations 1969; Medal, Insinöö riliitto, Finland 1969, Bronze Medal, Associazione Nationale Ingegneri e Architetti d'Italia 1971, Leverhulme Medal (Royal Soc.) 1978, Buchanan Medal 1982; Tuev Rheinland Prize 1984; Académico Correspondiente la Academia de Ingenieria, Mexico. Publications: Problem in Chemical Engineering Design (with J. M. Coulson) 1949; papers on nitric acid, heat transfer, underground gasification of coal, air and water pollution, contracts, planning, safety, risk, technology transfer, professional and continuous educ., nuclear winter, Chernobyl. Leisure interests: monumental brasses, ceramics, gardens. Address: Essex University, Colchester, CO4 3JQ, England. Telephone: (0206) 873370.

WARNER, John W., B.S., LL.B.; American government official; b. 18 Feb. 1927, Washington, D.C.; s. of late Dr. John W. Warner and of Martha (Budd) Warner; m. 1st Catherine Conover Mellon (divorced 1973), one s. two d.; m. 2nd Elizabeth Taylor (q.v.) 1976 (divorced 1982); ed. public schools in Washington, D.C., school of Naval Research Laboratory, Washington, D.C., Washington and Lee Univ. and Univ. of Virginia Law School; in U.S. Navy attained rank of Electronic Technician 3rd Class 1944–46; subsequently enlisted in U.S. Marine Corps Reserve, active duty as Communications Officer 1950–52, Captain in Marine Corps Reserve 1952–61; admitted to the Bar 1954; pvt. practice 1954–56; in U.S. Attorney's office as Special Asst. 1956, Asst. 1957, trial lawyer 1960–; joined campaign staff of then Vice-Pres. Richard Nixon 1960; associated with law firm Hogan & Hartson 1960, gen. partner 1964; Dir. of Ocean Affairs as rep. of Dept. of Defense 1971; Under-Sec. of U.S. Navy 1969–72, Sec. 1972–74; Dir. American Revolution Bicentennial Admin. 1974–76; Senator from Virginia 1979–; head of U.S. Del. to Moscow on Naval Affairs; Republican. Address: 421 Russell Senate Office Building, Washington, D.C. 20510 (Office); Atoka Farm, P.O. Box 1320, Middleburg, Va. 22117; 700 New Hampshire Avenue, N.W., Washington, D.C. 20037, U.S.A. (Homes).

WARNER, Rawleigh, Jr., A.B.; American business executive; b. 13 Feb. 1921, Chicago, Ill.; s. of late Rawleigh Warner and Dorothy Haskins Warner; m. Mary Ann de Clairmont 1946; two d.; ed. Lawrenceville School and Princeton Univ.; Mobil Oil and Assocs. 1953–; Asst. to Financial Dir. Socony Vacuum Overseas Supply Co. 1953–56; Man. Econs. Dept., Mobil Oil Corpn. 1956–58, Man. Middle East Affairs Dept. 1958–59, Regional Vice-Pres. for Middle East 1959–60; Exec. Vice-Pres. Mobil Int. Oil Co. 1960–63, Pres. 1963; Dir. Exec. Vice-Pres. and mem. Exec. Cttee. Mobil Oil Corpn., with responsibility for Mobil Int. and Mobil Petroleum Corpn. Inc. 1964–65, Pres. Mobil Oil Corpn. 1965–69, Chair. and C.E.O. 1969–82; Chair. and C.E.O. Mobil Corpn. 1976–86; Dir. American Petroleum Inst., American Telephone and Telegraph Co., American Express Co. and American Express Int. Banking Co., Caterpillar Tractor Co., Chemical New York Corpn. and Chemical Bank, Nat. Council for U.S.-China Trade, Wheelabrator-Frye Inc.; Trustee Mayo Foundation Bd. of Trustees; Chair. Princeton Univ. Council for Univ. Resources; mem. The Business Council, White House Labor-Man. Cttee.; Purple Heart, Bronze Star, Silver Star. Leisure interests: golf, walking, reading (mystery and adventure). Address: c/o Mobil Oil Corporation, 150 East 42nd Street, New York, N.Y. 10017, U.S.A.

WARNKE, Paul Culliton, B.A., LL.B.; American government official and lawyer; b. 31 Jan. 1920, Webster, Mass.; s. of Paul Martin and Lillian (née Culliton) Warnke; m. Jean Farjeon Rowe 1948; three s. two d.; ed. Yale Univ., Columbia Univ., New York; served U.S. Coast Guard, to Lieut. 1942–46; admitted to D.C. Bar 1948; Assoc., Covington and Burling,

Washington, D.C. 1948-57, Partner 1957-66; Gen. Counsel, Dept. of Defense 1966-67; Asst. Sec. of Defense for Int. Security Affairs 1967-69; Partner, Clifford, Warnke, Glass, McIlwain and Finney 1969-77; Dir. U.S. Arms Control and Disarmament Agency (ACDA) 1977-78; Chief Negotiator for Strategic Arms Limitation Talks (SALT) 1977-78; part-time Consultant to State Dept. 1978-80; Partner Clifford and Warnke 1978-; mem. Md. and D.C. Advisory Comms. to U.S. Comm. on Civil Rights 1962-66; Dir. Exec. Cttee. of Int. Voluntary Services 1972; mem. Exec. Cttee. of Trilateral Comm.; mem. Bd. of Govs., D.C. Bar 1976; Trustee, Potomac School 1958-66, Chair. Bd. 1965-66; mem. Bd. of Dirs., Health and Welfare Council of Nat. Capital Area 1966-67; Trustee, Northland Coll. 1970-76, Columbia Univ. 1984-; Chair. Bd. of Visitors, Georgetown School of Foreign Service 1971-76; mem. Bd. of Visitors, Columbia Univ. School of Law 1971-; mem. Bd. of Dirs. Georgetown Univ. 1979-; mem. American Soc. of Int. Law, Council on Foreign Relations, of Bd. of Canadian Inst. for Int. Peace and Security 1985-, American Bar Asscn. Standing Cttee. on World Order under Law 1986-; Alumni Trustee, Columbia Univ. 1985-; Chair. Cttee. for Nat. Security; Democrat. *Address:* 815 Connecticut Avenue, Washington, D.C. 20006; 5037 Garfield Street, N.W., Washington, D.C. 20016, U.S.A. (Home). *Telephone:* (202) 828-4246 (Office); (202) 966-0397 (Home).

WARNOCK, Baroness (Life Peer), cr. 1985, of Weeke in the City of Westminster; **(Helen) Mary Warnock**, D.B.E., F.C.P.; British philosopher and university administrator; b. 14 April 1924; d. of the late Archibald Edward Wilson; m. Geoffrey J. Warnock (q.v.) 1949; two s. three d.; ed. St. Swithun's, Winchester and Lady Margaret Hall, Oxford; Tutor in Philosophy, St. Hugh's Coll., Oxford 1949-66; Headmistress, Oxford High School 1966-72; Talbot Research Fellow, Lady Margaret Hall 1972-76; Sr. Research Fellow, St. Hugh's Coll. 1976-84; Mistress of Girton Coll., Cambridge 1985-; Chair. Cttee. of Inquiry into Special Educ. 1974-78, Advisory Cttee. on Animal Experiments 1979-86, Cttee. of Inquiry into Human Fertilization 1982-84; mem. Independent Broadcasting Authority (IBA) 1973-81, Royal Comm. on Environmental Pollution 1979-84, Social Science Research Council 1981-, U.K. Nat. Comm. for UNESCO 1981-85; Hon. Master of the Bench, Gray's Inn 1986; Hon. F.I.C. 1986; Hon. D.Univ. (Open Univ.) 1980, Hon. LL.D. (Manchester) 1987, Hon. D.Litt. (Glasgow) 1988. *Publications:* Ethics since 1900 1960, J.-P. Sartre 1963, Existentialist Ethics 1966, Existentialism 1970, Imagination 1976, Schools of Thought 1977, What Must We Teach? (with T. Devlin) 1977, Education: A Way Forward 1979, A Question of Life 1985, Teacher Teach Thyself (Dimbleby Lecture) 1985, Memory 1987, A Common Policy for Education 1989. *Leisure interests:* music, gardening. *Address:* Girton College, Cambridge; Brick House, Axford, England. *Telephone:* (0672) 54686.

WARNOCK, Sir Geoffrey James, Kt., M.A.; British philosopher and university administrator (retd.); b. 16 Aug. 1923, Leeds; s. of James Warnock; m. Mary Wilson (Baroness Warnock, q.v.) 1949; two s. three d.; ed. Winchester Coll. and New Coll., Oxford; Fellow, Magdalen Coll., Oxford 1949, 1953-71, Brasenose Coll. 1950-53; Prin., Hertford Coll., Oxford 1972-88; Vice-Chancellor, Oxford Univ. 1981-85; Visiting Lecturer, Univs. of Ill. and Wis. and Princeton Univ.; Hon. Fellow, New Coll., Magdalen Coll., Hertford Coll., Oxford. *Publications:* Berkeley 1953, English Philosophy since 1900 1958, Contemporary Moral Philosophy 1967, The Object of Morality 1971, Morality and Language 1983. *Leisure interest:* golf. *Address:* Brick House, Axford, Marlsborough, Wilts., SN8 2EX, England. *Telephone:* (0672) 54686.

WARRELL, David Alan, M.A., D.M., F.R.C.P.; British physician; b. 6 Oct. 1939, Singapore; s. of Mr and Mrs A. T. Warrell; m. Dr. Mary J. Prentice 1975; two d.; ed. Portsmouth Grammar School, Christ Church, Oxford and St. Thomas's Hosp. Medical School, London; Oxford Univ. Radcliffe Travelling Fellow, Univ. of Calif. San Diego 1969; Sr. Lecturer, Ahmadu Bello Univ., Nigeria and Lecturer and Consultant Physician, Royal Post-grad. Medical School, London and Hammersmith Hosp. 1970-75; Dir. Wellcome-Mahidol Univ., Oxford Tropical Medicine Research Programme, Bangkok and Wellcome Reader in Tropical Medicine, Univ. of Oxford 1979-86; Prof. of Tropical Medicine and Infectious Diseases, Nuffield Dept. of Clinical Medicine, Univ. of Oxford 1987-; Hon. Consultant in Malariology to British Army 1989-; WHO Consultant 1979-; Fellow St. Cross Coll. 1975-; Chair. AIDS Therapeutic Trials Cttee., MRC; Marc Daniels and Bradshaw Lecturer, Royal Coll. of Physicians; Chalmer's Medal, Royal Soc. of Tropical Medicine and Hygiene 1981. *Publications:* scientific papers and book chapters; Ed. Oxford Textbook of Medicine. *Leisure interests:* book-collecting, music, bird-watching, mountain-walking. *Address:* Nuffield Department of Clinical Medicine, University of Oxford, John Radcliffe Hospital, Headington, Oxford, OX3 9DU (Office); 4 Larkins Lane, Old Headington, Oxford, OX3 9DW, England (Home). *Telephone:* (0865) 817398 (Office); (0865) 66865 (Home).

WARREN, Sir Frederick Miles, K.B.E., F.N.Z.I.A., A.R.I.B.A., DIP.ARCH.; New Zealand architect; b. 10 May 1929, Christchurch; s. of M. B. and J. Warren (née Hay); ed. Christ's Coll., Auckland Univ. School of Architecture; worked for late C. W. Wood, 1946-47, for late R. C. Munroe, A.N.Z.I.A. 1948; joined partnership with late G. T. Lucas 1956; started firm Warren and Mahoney 1958, Sr. Partner; Fellow, New Zealand Inst. of Architects 1965; Pres. Canterbury Soc. of Arts 1972-76; Warren and Mahoney

awarded N.Z.I.A. Gold Medal for Dental Nurses' Training School 1960, for Christchurch Memorial Garden Crematorium 1964, for Christchurch Coll. Halls of Residence 1969, for Christchurch Town Hall and Civic Centre 1973; won Architectural Competition for design of Condominium Offices, New Hebrides 1966; Gold Medal N.Z.I.A. 1980, 1981, 1983, 1984, 1985. *Leisure interests:* yachting, water-colouring, sketching. *Address:* 65 Cambridge Terrace, Christchurch 1, New Zealand. *Telephone:* 799.640.

WARREN, Jack Hamilton, O.C.; Canadian banker and business executive; b. 10 April 1921; m. Hilary J. Titterington; four c.; ed. Queen's Univ., Kingston, Ont.; Royal Canadian Navy 1941-45; joined Dept. of External Affairs 1945; served in London 1948-51; transferred to Dept. of Finance and served as Financial Counsellor, Washington, D.C. and as Alt. Dir. for Canada, IMF and IBRD 1954-57; Canadian Del. to OECD and NATO 1957-58; Asst. Deputy Minister of Trade and Commerce 1958-64; Chair. GATT Contracting Parties 1962-65; Deputy Minister of Trade and Commerce 1964-68, of Industry, Trade and Commerce 1968-71; High Commr. to U.K. 1971-74; Amb. to U.S.A. 1975-77; Canadian Coordinator for the Multilateral Trade Negotiations 1977-79; Vice-Chair. Bank of Montreal 1979-86; Chair. Bank of Montreal Int. Ltd. 1983-; Prin. Adviser on Trade Liberalization, Govt. of Quebec 1986-; Deputy N. American Chair. Trilateral Comm. 1986-; Hon. LL.D. (Queen's Univ.) 1974; Outstanding Achievement Award, Public Service of Canada 1975. *Address:* Box 282, R.R.I, Chelsea, Quebec JOX 1NO, Canada (Home).

WARREN, Kenneth S., A.B., M.D.; American professor of medicine; b. 11 June 1929, New York; m. Sylvia M. Rothwell 1959; one s. one d.; ed. Harvard Univ., Harvard Medical School and London School of Hygiene and Tropical Medicine, England; Intern, Harvard Service Boston City Hosp. 1955-56; Research Assoc., Lab. of Tropical Diseases, Nat. Insts. of Health, Bethesda, Md. 1956-62; Asst. Prof. of Medicine, Case Western Reserve Univ. 1963-68, Assoc. Prof. 1968-75, Prof. 1975-77, Prof. of Library Sciences 1974-77; Dir. Health Sciences Div., Rockefeller Foundation, New York 1977-88, Assoc. Vice-Pres. 1988-; Prof. of Medicine, New York Univ. 1977-; Fellow, American Coll. of Physicians; Bailey K. Ashford Award (American Soc. of Tropical Medicine and Hygiene) 1974, Squibb Award 1975. *Publications:* Schistosomiasis: The Evolution of a Medical Literature: Selected Abstracts and Citations 1852-1972, Geographic Medicine for the Practitioner 1985, Scientific Information Systems and the Principle of Selectivity 1980, Coping with the Biomedical Literature 1981, Immunology of Parasitic Diseases 1983, Tropical and Geographical Medicine 1984, Strategies in Primary Health Care 1986. *Leisure interests:* bicycling, reading and snorkelling. *Address:* The Rockefeller Foundation, Division of Health Sciences, 1133 Avenue of the Americas, New York, N.Y. 10036; 125 Southlawn Avenue, Dobbs Ferry, N.Y. 10522, U.S.A. (Home). *Telephone:* (212) 869-8500, Ext. 320 (Office) (914) 693-8082 (Home).

WARREN, Robert Penn, B.A., B.LITT.; American university professor and writer; b. 24 April 1905, Guthrie, Ky.; s. of Robert Franklin Warren and Anna Ruth Penn; m. 1st Emma Brescia 1930 (divorced 1951), 2nd Eleanor Clark 1952; one s. one d.; ed. Vanderbilt, Oxford and Yale Univs. and Univ. of California; Asst. Prof., Southwestern Coll. 1930-31, Vanderbilt Univ. 1931-34; Asst. Prof. Louisiana State Univ. 1934-36, Assoc. Prof. 1936-42; Prof. Univ. of Minnesota 1942-50; Lecturer Yale Univ. 1950-51, Prof. of Playwriting 1951-56, of English 1961-73, Prof. Emer. 1973-; Consultant in Poetry, Library of Congress, and Poet Laureate of U.S.A. 1986-87; Poetry, Library of Congress 1944-45; a Founder and Ed. Southern Review 1935-42; mem. American Acad. of Poets (and Chancellor), American Acad. of Arts and Letters, American Acad. of Arts and Sciences, American Philosophical Soc.; Hon. Fellow; Modern Language Asscn.; Rhodes Scholarship, Houghton Mifflin Literary Fellowship 1936, Guggenheim Fellowship 1939-40 and 1947-48; Levinson Prize 1936, Caroline Sinker Prize 1936, 1937, 1938, Shelley Memorial Award 1942, Pulitzer Prize for Fiction 1947, Southern Prize 1947, Robert Melzer Award (Screen Writer's Guild) 1949, Millay Award (American Poetry Soc.), Nat. Book Award, Pulitzer Prize for Poetry 1958, 1979, Sidney Hillman Award for Journalism 1959, Irita Van Doren Award (New York Herald Tribune) 1965; Bollingen Prize in Poetry 1967; Nat. Medal for Literature 1970; Hon. Litt.D. (from 17 univs.), Hon. LL.D. (Univ. of Bridgeport) 1965, Hon. L.H.D. (Kenyon Coll.); Van Wyck Brooks Poetry Award 1970, Bellaman Award 1970, Jefferson Lecturer, Nat. Endowment for the Humanities 1974, Thoreau-Emerson Medal, American Acad. of Arts and Sciences 1975, Copernicus Prize, American Acad. of Poets 1976, Roswell Messing Jr. Award 1977, Harriet Monroe Award 1977, Connecticut Arts Award 1980, Pres. Freedom Medal 1980, Commonwealth Award 1980, Hubbell Medallion Award, Modern Language Asscn. 1980, Fellow, MacArthur Foundation 1981, Nat. Medal of Arts Award 1989. *Publications:* John Brown: The Making of a Martyr 1929, XXXVI Poems 1936, An Approach to Literature (with Cleanth Brooks and John Purser) 1937, Understanding Poetry (with Cleanth Brooks) 1938, Night Rider (novel) 1939, At Heaven's Gate (novel) 1943, Eleven Poems on the Same Theme 1942, Selected Poems 1944, All the King's Men (novel) 1946, Circus in the Attic (stories) 1948, World Enough and Time (novel) 1950, Brother to Dragons (verse) 1953, Band of Angels (novel) 1955, Segregation: The Inner Conflict of the South 1956, Promises (verse) 1957, Selected Essays 1958, The Cave (novel) 1959, You, Emperors and Others (verse) 1960, The Legacy of the Civil War 1961, Wilderness (novel) 1961, Flood (novel) 1964, Who Speaks for the Negro? 1965, Selected

Poems, New and Old 1966, Incarnations: Poems 1966–68 1968, Audubon: A Vision (a poem) 1969, Meet Me in the Green Glen (novel) 1972, American Literature: the Makers and the Making (with Cleanth Brooks and R. W. B. Lewis) 1973, Or Else: Poem/Poems 1968–74 1974, Now and Then: Poems 1978, Democracy and Poetry 1975, Selected Poems 1923–75 1977, A Place to Come To (novel) 1977, Being Here (poems) 1980, Jefferson Davis Gets His Citizenship Back, Rumor Verified (poems) 1977–81, 1981, Chief Joseph (poem) 1983, New and Selected Poems 1923–1985 1985, Portrait of a Father 1988. *Leisure interests:* gardening, walking, swimming. *Address:* 2495 Redding Road, Fairfield, Conn. 03460, U.S.A.

WARRINGTON, Elizabeth Kerr, PH.D., D.SC., F.R.S.; British professor of clinical neuropsychology; d. of the late Prof. John A. V. Butler, F.R.S. and Margaret L. Butler; m.; one d.; ed. Univ. Coll. London; Research Fellow, Inst. of Neurology 1956; Sr. Clinical Psychologist, Nat. Hosp. 1960, Prin. Psychologist 1962, Top Grade Clinical Psychologist 1972–82, Prof. of Clinical Neuropsychology 1982–. *Publications:* numerous papers in professional journals. *Address:* National Hospital, Queen Square, London, WC1N 3BG, England. *Telephone:* 01-837 3611.

WASER, Peter Gaudenz, M.D., D.PHIL.; Swiss professor of pharmacology; b. 21 July 1918, Zürich; s. of Ernst Waser and Margerit Ruttiman; m. Marion Edmée Bodmer 1946; one s. two d.; ed. Univ. of Zürich, Basle Univ. Hospital, California Inst. of Tech.; Prof. of Medicine, Univ. of Zürich 1959, Dir. Inst. of Pharmacology 1963–87, Prof. of Pharmacy 1965–87, Dean of Faculty of Medicine 1970–72, Rector 1978–80; Pres. Engadine Collegium in Philosophy 1967–, Int. Union of Pharmacology 1978–81, Int. Council of Scientific Unions 1981–84. *Publications:* Mechanisms of Synaptic Transmission 1969 (with Akert), Cholinergic Mechanisms 1975, Praktische Pharmakotherapie 1987 (with C. Steinbach). *Leisure interests:* mountaineering, skiing, gardening, painting. *Address:* Institute of Pharmacology, Gloriastrasse 32, 8006 Zürich; Research Department of Psychiatry, University Clinic, Lenggstrasse 31, 8029 Zürich; Ob. Heuelsteig 12, 8032 Zürich; Switzerland (Home). *Telephone:* 01-257-2660 (Pharmacology); 01-257 5011 (Psychiatry); 01-251-2814 (Home).

WASHINGTON, Walter E., LL.B.; American government official; b. 15 April 1915, Dawson, Georgia; s. of William L. and Willie Mae (Thornton) Washington; m. Bennetta Bullock; one d.; ed. Howard Univ. and Howard Law School; with Nat. Capital Housing Authority, Washington, D.C. 1941–66, Exec. Dir. 1961–66; Chair. New York City Housing Authority 1966–67; Commr. of Dist. of Columbia and Mayor of Washington 1967–74; Mayor D.C. 1975–79; partner law firm Burns, Jackson, Miller, Summit 1979–; Dir. Woodward and Lothrop Inc., Nat. Perm. Fed. Savings and Loan Assen., Dist. Realty Title Insurance Corpn.; mem. Advisory Bd. U.S. Confed. of Mayors, Insurance Panel Nat. Advisory Comm. on Civil Disorders; 14 hon. degrees. *Address:* 1025 15th Street, N.W., Washington, D.C. 20015, U.S.A.

WASILEWSKI, Andrzej, M.A.; Polish publisher, literary critic and politician; b. 22 Sept. 1928, Radom; m.; one d.; ed. Polish Philology Faculty of Warsaw Univ.; during Nazi occupation mem. Szare Szeregi (Grey Ranks) of underground Polish Pathfinders' Union; mem. Polish Youth Union 1948–52; Head, Culture Section of journal Po Prostu 1949–51; scientific worker, Literary Research Inst. of Polish Acad. of Sciences 1951–54; Head, criticism section of Nowa Kultura (weekly) 1954–58; Ed.-in-Chief, Antena (weekly) 1958; Sub-Ed. Nowa Kultura (weekly) 1958–60; First Sec., Polish Embassy Rome 1961–64; journalist of Kultura 1964–70; Deputy Ed.-in-Chief of TV Cultural Programmes 1966–67; Ed.-in-Chief PIW State Publishing Inst., Warsaw 1967–86, Dir. 1971–86; Pres. Polish Soc. of Book Publrs. 1972–80; mem. Polish United Workers' Party (PZPR) 1952–, alt. mem. PZPR Cen. Cttee. 1971–80 and 1984–86, mem. 1980–81, July 1986–, Sec. 1986–88; Head, Culture Comm. 1986–; mem. Nat. Culture Council 1983–; Minister of Culture and Art Award 1974, Trybuna Ludo Prize 1980; Order of Banner of Labour (1st and 2nd Class); Commdr's Cross of Order of Polonia Restituta and other decorations. *Publications:* Paszport do Włoch 1966, Cywilizacja i literatura 1969, Jacy jesteśmy 1979, Wschód, Zachód i Polska 1985; contribs. to Kultura, Polityka, Zycie Literackie, Twórczość, Miesięcznik Literacki and other journals. *Leisure interests:* long walks, swimming, car-driving, classical music. *Address:* Komitet Centralny PZPR, ul. Nowy Swiat 6, 00-497 Warsaw; ul. Bonifraterska 6 m. 35, 00-213 Warsaw, Poland (Home). *Telephone:* 28-41-12 (Office).

WASS, Sir Douglas William Gretton, G.C.B., M.A.; British business executive and fmr. civil servant; b. 15 April 1923, Wallasey, Cheshire; s. of late Arthur W. and Elsie W. Wass; m. Dr. Milica Pavicić 1954; one s. one d.; ed. Nottingham High School, St. John's Coll., Cambridge; Scientific Research with Admiralty 1943–46; Asst. Prin., Treasury 1946, Prin. 1951; Commonwealth Fund Fellow, U.S.A. 1958–59; Fellow, Brookings Inst., Washington 1959; Pvt. Sec. to Chancellor 1959–61; Pvt. Sec. to Chief Sec. 1961–62; Alt. Exec. Dir. to IMF and Financial Counsellor, British Embassy, Washington 1965–67; Under-Sec. of Treasury 1968, Deputy Sec. 1970, Second Perm. Sec. 1973, Perm. Sec. 1974–83; Jt. Head, Home Civil Service 1981–83; Reith Lecturer, BBC 1983; Chair. British Selection Cttee., Harkness Fellowships 1981–84; Governing Body of the Ditchley Foundation, Council of the Policy Studies Inst.; Chair. Econ. Policy Cttee., OECD 1982; Chair. Nomura Int. Ltd. 1986–, Equity and Law Life Assurance Soc. PLC 1986- (Dir. 1984–); Gov. Centre for Econ. Policy Research; Adviser

to Campaign for Freedom of Information; Dir. De La Rue Co. PLC 1983–, Coopers and Lybrand 1984–86, Barclays Bank PLC 1984–87; Administrateur, Compagnie du Midi S.A. 1987–; Vice-Pres. Constitutional Reform Centre 1984–; mem. of Council of Univ. of Bath; Pres. Market Research Soc. 1987–; Hon. D.Litt. (Bath); Hon. Fellow, St. John's Coll., Cambridge. *Publications:* The Changing Problems of Economic Management 1978, The Public Service in Modern Society 1982, Government and the Governed 1984, The Civil Service at the Crossroads 1985, What Sort of Industrial Policy? 1986, Checks and Balances in Public Policy Making 1987. *Leisure interest:* golf. *Address:* 6 Dora Road, Wimbledon, London, S.W.19, England. *Telephone:* 01-946 5556.

WASSERBURG, Gerald Joseph, M.SC., PH.D.; American professor of geology and geophysics; b. 25 March 1927, New Brunswick, N.J.; s. of Charles Wasserburg and Sarah Levine Wasserburg; m.; two s.; ed. Univ. of Chicago; Rifleman, U.S. Army Second Infantry Div. 1943–46; with Resurrection Mining Co. 1947; Juneau Ice Field Research Project, Alaska 1950; Consultant Argonne Nat. Laboratory, Lamont, Ill. 1952–55; Research Assoc., Inst. for Nuclear Studies, Chicago 1954–55; Asst. Prof. of Geology, Calif. Inst. of Tech. 1955–59, Assoc. Prof. of Geology 1959–62, Prof. of Geology and Geophysics 1962–; Adviser to NASA 1968–; Vice-Chair. Lunar Sample Analysis Planning Team, MSC, NASA 1970; mem. Lunar Sample Review Bd. 1970–72, Science Working Panel 1971–73, Physical Sciences Cttee. 1971–75; Ed. Earth and Planetary Science Letters 1967–74; Chair. Comm. for Planetary and Lunar Exploration, Space Science Bd. 1975–78; Vinton Hayes Sr. Fellow, Harvard 1980; Jaeger-Hales Lecture, Australian Nat. Univ. 1980; Harold Jeffreys Lecture, Royal Astronomical Soc. 1981; John D. MacArthur Prof. of Geology and Geophysics, Calif. Inst. of Tech. 1982–, Chair. Div. of Geological and Planetary Sciences 1987–; Pres. Meteoritical Soc. 1987–88; mem. N.A.S.; Fellow, American Acad. of Arts and Sciences, American Geophysical Union, Geological Soc. of America; Regents Fellow, Smithsonian Inst. 1982; mem. American Philosophical Soc. 1982; Foreign mem. Norwegian Acad. of Science and Letters 1988; Hon. Foreign Fellow European Union of Geosciences (EUG) 1983; Dr. h.c. (Brussels) 1985, Hon. D.Sc. (Ariz.) 1987; Combat Infantryman's Badge, Purple Heart; Exceptional Scientific Achievement Medal, NASA 1970; Arthur L. Day Medal, Geological Soc. of America 1970; Distinguished Public Service Medal, NASA 1972, and with cluster 1978; James Furman Kemp Medal, Columbia Univ. 1973, Leonard Medal, Meteoritical Soc. 1975; V. M. Goldschmidt Medal, Geochemical Soc. 1978, Univ. of Chicago Alumni Assen. Professional Achievement Award 1978; Arthur L. Day Prize, N.A.S. 1981, J. Lawrence Smith Medal, N.A.S. 1985, Wollaston Medal, Geological Soc. of London 1985, Sr. U.S. Scientist Award, Alexander von Humboldt-Stiftung 1985, Harry H. Hess Medal, American Geophysical Union, Crafoord Prize, Swedish Royal Acad. 1986, Holmes Medal, EUG 1987. *Publications:* research papers in several scientific journals, in the fields of geochemistry, geophysics and astrophysics, and the application of the methods of chemical physics to problems in the earth and planetary sciences; major researches: determination of the time scale of the solar system, chronology of the moon, establishment of dating methods using long-lived natural radioactivities, study of geological processes using nuclear and isotopic effects as a tracer in nature and the application of thermodynamic methods to geological systems. *Leisure interests:* hiking, music, art. *Address:* California Institute of Technology, Division of Geological and Planetary Sciences, Pasadena, Calif. 91125; Home: 2100 Pinecrest Drive, Altadena, Calif. 91001, U.S.A. *Telephone:* (818) 356-6139 (Office); (818) 798-8171 (Home).

WASSERMAN, Lew R.; American film and record company executive; b. 15 March 1913, Cleveland, Ohio; m. Edith T. Beckerman 1936; one d.; Nat. Dir. Advertising and Publicity, Music Corpn. of America (MCA) 1936–38, Vice-Pres. 1938–39, apptd. Vice-Pres. Motion Picture Div. 1940, now Chair. Bd. of Dirs., C.E.O. and mem. Exec. Cttee. MCA Inc.; also Chair. Bd., C.E.O. and Dir. subsidiary corpns.; Dir. American Airlines; Chair. Emer. Assen. of Motion Picture and TV Producers; Trustee John F. Kennedy Library, John F. Kennedy Center for the Performing Arts, Calif. Inst. of Tech., Jules Stein Eye Inst., Carter Presidential Center, Lyndon Baines Johnson Foundation; Pres. Hollywood Canteen Foundation; Chair. Research to Prevent Blindness Foundation; Hon. Chair. Bd. Center Theatre Group L.A. Music Center; mem. Bd. of Dirs. Amateur Athletic Foundation of L.A., L.A. Music Center Foundation; mem. Bd. of Govs. Ronald Reagan Presidential Foundation; Dr. h.c. (Brandeis Univ., New York Univ.); Jean Hersholt Humanitarian Award, Acad. of Motion Picture Arts and Sciences 1973. *Address:* MCA Inc., 100 Universal City Plaza, Universal City, Calif. 91608, U.S.A.

WASSERMAN, Robert Harold, PH.D.; American professor of sciences; b. 11 Feb. 1926, Schenectady, New York; s. of Joseph Wasserman and Sylvia Rosenburg; m. Marilyn M. Wasserman 1950; three d.; ed. Mount Pleasant High School, N.Y., Cornell Univ., Michigan State Univ.; Research Assoc. and Assoc. Prof. of Biochem. Univ. of Tenn. Atomic Energy Comm. Agricultural Research Program, Oak Ridge 1953–55; Sr. Scientist Medical Div., Oak Ridge Inst. of Nuclear Studies 1955–57; Research Assoc. in Radiation Biology N.Y. State Veterinary Coll., Cornell Univ. 1957–59; Assoc. Prof. of Radiation Biology, Dept. of Physical Biology 1959–63, Prof. of Radiation Biology 1963–80, Prof. of Physiology, Coll. of Veterinary

Medicine 1980–83, Prof. and Chair. of Dept. and Section 1983–87; Chair. Common Meat and Poultry Inspection, Nat. Research Council 1983–85, mem. Food and Nutrition Bd. 1984–87; Visiting Scientist Inst. of Biological Chem., Copenhagen, Denmark 1964–65; Guggenheim Fellowship 1964, 1972; mem. N.A.S. 1980–; Mead-Johnson Award in Nutrition 1969; Wise and Helen Burroughs Lectureship 1974; A. Lichtwitz Prize (INSERM) 1982. *Publications:* numerous articles in specialist journals. *Leisure interests:* sailing, reading, sports, computers, cards. *Address:* Department and Section of Physiology—717VRT, New York State College of Veterinary Medicine, Cornell University, Ithaca, N.Y. 14853, U.S.A. *Telephone:* (607) 253-3430.

WATANABE, Bunzo, B.A.; Japanese company executive; b. 20 May 1907, Tokyo; s. of Tomekichi and Shisa Watanabe; m. Yoko Hikosaka 1933; two d.; ed. Hitotsubashi Univ.; Vice-Pres., Ajinomoto Co. Inc. 1965, Pres. 1973–82, Hon. Chair. June 1981–; Chair. Bd. Knorr Foods Co. Ltd., Japan 1973–88, Sr. Adviser to the Bd. 1988–; mem. Bd. Morishita Pharmaceutical Co. Ltd. 1963–, Ajinomoto Gen. Foods Inc. 1973–, Eurolysine S.A., France 1974–, Ajinomoto U.S.A. Inc. 1974–, Union Chemicals Inc., Philippines 1975–, Keizai Doyukai (Japan Cttee. for Industrial Devt.) 1972–, Keidanren (Fed. of Econ. Orgs.) 1973–; Trustee, Int. Christian Univ., Tokyo 1973–; Blue Ribbon Medal 1975. *Leisure interests:* golf, Japanese classical music. *Address:* Ajinomoto Co. Inc., 5-8 Kyobashi, 1-Chome, Chuo-ku, Tokyo 104, Japan.

WATANABE, Michio; Japanese politician; b. 28 July 1923, Tochigi Pref.; m.; two s. one d.; ed. Tokyo Commercial Coll. (now Hitotsubashi Univ.); mil. service; engaged as salesman 1945–50; practice as tax lawyer; mem. Prefectural Legislature of Tochigi; elected nine times to House of Reps. 1963–; Parl. Vice Minister of Agric. and Forestry; Deputy Sec.-Gen. of Liberal Democratic Party (LDP); Chair. of Cabinet Cttee. of House of Reps.; Minister of Health and Welfare 1976–77, of Agric., Forestry and Fisheries 1978–79, of Finance 1980–82, of Int. Trade and Industry 1985–86; Acting Sec.-Gen. LDP 1984; Chair. LDP Policy Research Council 1987–; mem. of Seirankai (conservative group) in LDP. *Leisure interests:* reading, golf, photography. *Address:* Giin Kaikan, 2-2-1 Nagata-cho, Chiyoda-ku, Tokyo 100, Japan.

WATANABE, Takeji; Japanese journalist; b. 12 July 1913, Taegu, Korea; s. of Kesaji and Kin Watanabe; m. Chiyo Matsuoka 1953; one s. one d.; ed. Foreign Language Inst., Nihon Univ.; joined Domei News Agency 1936, with Kyodo News Service following disbandment of Domei 1945–, Econ. News Ed. 1952–58, New York Bureau Man. 1958–60, Washington Bureau Man. and Chief Rep. for N. America 1960–68, Exec. Dir. 1968–70, Man. Dir. (ex officio) 1970–72, Ed.-in-Chief (ex officio) 1972–74, Man. Dir. 1974–78, Pres. 1978–86; Exec. Dir. (ex officio) Matsushita Graphic Communication Systems 1968–, Dentsu Inc. 1971–; Order of the Sacred Treasure (First Class) 1984. *Publications:* History of Japanese News Agencies 1958, How to Read Economic Reports 1961. *Leisure interests:* skating, reading. *Address:* 1-14-5 Nakadai, Itabashi-ku, Tokyo, Japan. *Telephone:* (03) 935-8881.

WATANABE, Takeshi; Japanese banker and financial consultant; b. 15 Feb. 1906, Tokyo; s. of Chifuyu Watanabe (fmr. Minister of Justice) and Yoshiko Watanabe; m. Fusako Yamakawa 1933; three s. two d.; ed. Law School of Tokyo Imperial Univ.; Ministry of Finance, Japan 1930, serving as Chief Liaison Officer, Chief of the Ministers' Secr. and Financial Commr.; Minister, Japanese Embassy, Washington 1952–56; Exec. Dir. for Japan, IBRD (World Bank) and IMF 1956–60; Int. Financial Consultant 1960–65; Adviser to Minister of Finance, Japan, in charge of preparatory work for the establishment of the Asian Devt. Bank 1965; Pres. Asian Devt. Bank, Manila 1966–72, Japan Credit Rating Agency 1985–; Chair. Trident Int. Finance Ltd., Hong Kong 1972–77, Revlon K.K., Japan 1977–85, Japan Silver Volunteers Inc. 1980–; Adviser to Bank of Tokyo 1973–79; Japanese Chair. Trilateral Comm. 1973–85; Chair. AFS Japan 1980–, Foster Parents Plan of Japan 1983–, Asia Community Trust 1979–; Dir. Asia Productivity Org. 1980–82 (resgnd.); Hon. Fellow L.S.E.; Order of Sacred Treasures (1st Class). *Publications:* Japanese Finance in Early Post-War Years (in Japanese) 1966, Towards a New Asia 1977. *Leisure interests:* photography, watercolour painting, gardening. *Address:* Japan Credit Rating Agency, B-14 Shuwa Shiba Park Bldg., 2-4-1 Shibakoen, Minato-ku, Tokyo; 35-19 Oyama-cho, Shibuya-ku, Tokyo, Japan. *Telephone:* 03 (466) 0610.

WATANABE, Youji; Japanese architect; b. 14 June 1923, Naoetsu City; ed. Waseda Univ.; Asst. to Prof. Takamasa Yosizaka (q.v.), Architectural Inst., Waseda Univ. 1955–58; lecturer in Architecture, Waseda Univ. 1959–, Special Postgraduate Student of City Planning 1968–73; Visiting Lecturer, Montana State Univ. 1983; Oceanic Architectural Students' Congress, Auckland Univ. 1983; prizes in architectural competitions; exhbns. at VIII Salone Internazionale della Industrializzazione Edilizia, Bologna 1972, Georges Pompidou Centre, Paris 1977, Centro Edile, Milan 1977, Museum of Modern Art, New York 1978, The Peak Competition, Hong Kong 1982, Paris Opera Bastille Competition 1982. *Publication:* Approach to Architecture 1974. *Address:* 1-6-13 Hirakawa-cho, Chiyoda-ku, Tokyo, Japan. *Telephone:* 03-262-5629.

WATANUKI, Tamisuke; Japanese politician; b. 1927; previous posts include: Parl. Vice-Minister of Int. Trade and Industry and of Posts and Telecommunications; Chair. Cttees. on Finance, on Justice and on Rules and Admin., House of Reps.; Deputy Chair. Liberal Democratic Party (LDP) Diet Affairs Cttee. (LDP); Minister of State (Dir.-Gen. Nat. Land Agency, Hokkaido Devt. Agency and Okinawa Devt. Agency) 1986–87; Liberal Democratic Party. *Address:* c/o House of Representatives, Tokyo, Japan.

WATARI, Sugiichiro, B.A.; Japanese business executive; b. 28 March 1925, Yamagata Pref.; s. of Yoshihiro Watari and Aki Watari; m. Katsuko Inatome 1954; one s.; ed. Tokyo Univ.; Sr. Vice-Pres. Toshiba Corpn. 1980–82, Exec. Vice-Pres. 1982–84, Sr. Exec. Vice-Pres. 1984–86, Pres. 1986–87, Adviser to Bd. 1987–. *Address:* Toshibo Corporation, 1-1, Shibaura 1-chome, Minato-ku, Tokyo 105; Kamigoya Town Home, Room 310, 18 16 Kamigoya 3-chome, Setagaya-ku, Tokyo 105, Japan (Home).

WATERHOUSE, Douglas Frew, A.O., C.M.G., D.SC., F.A.A., F.R.S.; Australian entomologist; b. 3 June 1916, Sydney; s. of Prof. E. G. and Mrs. J. F. (née Kellie) Waterhouse; m. Allison D. Calthorpe 1944; three s. one d.; ed. Univs. of Sydney and Cambridge; Research Officer, CSIR Div. of Econ. Entomology 1938; Asst. Chief, CSIRO Div. of Entomology until 1960, Chief 1960–81, Hon. Research Fellow 1981–; Consultant, Australian Centre for Int. Agricultural Research 1983–; Pres. Nat. Trust of Australia (ACT) 1983–88; many other professional appts.; Foreign Assoc. N.A.S.; Foreign mem. U.S.S.R. Acad. of Sciences, etc.; Hon. D.Sc. (Australian Nat. Univ.). *Publications:* Butterflies of Australia (jtly.), Biological Control: Pacific Prospects (jtly.) 1987; over 100 articles in scientific journals. *Leisure interests:* gardening, fishing, Gyotaku (ancient Japanese art of fish painting). *Address:* Division of Entomology, CSIRO Box 1700 City, Canberra 2601 (Office); 60 National Circuit, Canberra, A.C.T. 2600, Australia (Home). *Telephone:* (062) 465-833 (Office); (062) 731-772 (Home).

WATERHOUSE, Keith Spencer; British writer; b. 6 Feb. 1929; s. of Ernest Waterhouse and Elsie Edith Waterhouse; m. 2nd Stella Bingham 1984; one s. two d. by previous marriage; journalist 1950–, columnist, Daily Mirror 1970–86, Daily Mail 1986–, contrib., Punch 1966–; mem. Punch Table 1979; mem. Kingman Cttee. on Teaching of the English Language 1987–88; Granada Columnist of the Year Award 1970; IPC Descriptive Writer of the Year Award 1970; IPC Columnist of the Year Award 1973; British Press Awards Columnist of the Year 1978; Granada Special Quarter Century Award 1982. *Films (with Willis Hall) include:* Billy Liar, Whistle Down the Wind, A Kind of Loving, Lock Up Your Daughters. *Play:* Mr. and Mrs. Nobody 1986. *Plays (with Willis Hall) include:* Billy Liar 1960, Celebration 1961, All Things Bright and Beautiful 1963, Say Who You Are 1965, Whoops-a-Daisy 1968, Children's Day 1969, Who's Who 1972, The Card (musical) 1973, Saturday, Sunday, Monday (adapted from play by de Filippo) 1973, Filumena (adapted from de Filippo) 1977, Worzel Gummidge 1981, Jeffrey Bernard is Unwell 1989. *TV series:* Budgie, Queenie's Castle, The Upper Crusts, Billy Liar, The Upchat Line, The Upchat Connection, Worzel Gummidge, West End Tales, The Happy Apple, Charters and Caldicott. *TV films:* Charlie Muffin 1983, This Office Life 1985, Slip-Up 1986. *Publications:* (novels) There is a Happy Land 1957, Billy Liar 1959, Jubb 1963, The Bucket Shop 1968, Billy Liar on the Moon 1975, Office Life 1978, Maggie Muggins 1981, In the Mood 1983, Thinks 1984; *Others:* Café Royal (with Guy Deghy) 1956, Writers' Theatre (Ed.) 1967, The Passing of the Third-floor Buck 1974, Mondays, Thursdays 1976, Rhubarb, Rhubarb 1979, Daily Mirror Style 1980, Fanny Peculiar 1983, Mrs Pooter's Diary 1983, Waterhouse At Large 1985, Collected Letters of a Nobody 1986, The Theory and Practice of Lunch 1986, Our Song, The Theory and Practice of Travel 1988. *Address:* 29 Kenway Road, London, S.W.5, England.

WATERLOW, John Conrad, C.M.G., M.D., SC.D., F.R.S.; British professor of human nutrition; b. 14 June 1916, London; s. of Sir Sydney Waterlow, K.C.M.G., C.B.E. and Margery H. Eckhard; m. Angela P. Gray 1939; two s. one d.; ed. Eton, Trinity Coll., Cambridge and London Hosp. Medical Coll.; Persia/Iraq force 1943; mem. scientific staff, MRC 1942–70; Dir. Tropical Metabolism Research Unit, Univ. of the West Indies 1954–70; Prof. of Human Nutrition, London School of Hygiene and Tropical Medicine 1970–82, Prof. Emer. 1982–; Murgatroyd Prize for Tropical Medicine; Bristol-Myers Prize for Nutrition. *Publications:* Protein Turnover in the Whole Body and in Mammalian Tissues 1978; many papers and reviews on malnutrition and protein metabolism. *Leisure interest:* mountain walking. *Address:* 15 Hillgate Street, London, W8 7SP, England. *Telephone:* 01-727 7456.

WATERS, Aaron Clement, PH.D.; American geologist; b. 6 May 1905, Waterville, Wash.; s. of Richard J. Waters and Hattie Lovina Clement Waters; m. Elizabeth P. von Hoene 1940; two d.; ed. Univ. of Wash. and Yale Univ.; Instructor in Geology, Yale Univ. 1928–30, Asst. Prof., Stanford Univ. 1930–33, Assoc. Prof. 1933–38, Prof. 1938–42, 1945–51; Staff Geologist and Research geologist, U.S. Geological Survey 1942–45; Prof. of Geology, Johns Hopkins Univ. 1952–63, Univ. of Calif. at Santa Barbara 1963–67; Prof. of Earth Sciences, Univ. of Calif. at Santa Cruz 1967–72, Prof. Emer. 1972–; Visiting Prof., Oregon State Univ. 1974, Univ. of Texas at El Paso 1978–80; Distinguished Visiting Prof., Calif. State Univs. (L.A.) 1979; Consultant Los Alamos Scientific Labs., New Mexico 1980–; Guggenheim Fellow, Nat. Science Foundation Senior Postdoctoral Fellow; mem. N.A.S., American Acad. of Arts and Sciences. *Publications:*

Textbooks (co-author) 1951; over 100 articles in professional journals. *Leisure interests:* varied and changeable.

WATHELET, Melchior, L. EN D., LL.M.; Belgian politician; b. 6 March 1949, Petit-Rechain; m.; one c.; ed. Univ. of Liège, Harvard Univ., U.S.A.; researcher, Univ. of Liège 1973-77; Sec. of State for Regional Economy (French Sector) and for Housing 1980-81, Minister of New Tech., Planning and Foresty (French sector) 1981-85; Minister and Chair. French Regional Exec. responsible for New Tech., Foreign Affairs, Gen. Afffairs and Personnel 1985-88; Deputy Prime Minister and Minister of Justice and of the Middle Classes 1988-. *Address:* Ministry of Justice, 4 place Poelaert, 1000 Brussels, Belgium. *Telephone:* (02) 511-42-00.

WATKINS, Adm. James David, M.S.; American naval officer; b. 7 March 1927, Alhambra, Calif.; s. of Edward Francis and Louise Whipple (née Ward) Watkins; m. Sheila Jo Kinney 1950; three s. three d.; ed. U.S. Naval Acad., Naval Postgraduate School; Ensign, U.S. Navy 1949, rose to Vice-Adm. 1975; Commdr. U.S.S. Snook 1964-66; Exec. Officer U.S.S. Long Beach 1967-69; Head Submarine/Nuclear Distribution Control Branch, Naval Personnel Bureau, Navy Dept., Washington, D.C. 1961-71, Dir. Enlisted Personnel Div. 1971-72, Asst. Chief of Naval Personnel for Enlisted Personnel Control 1972-73; Commdr. Cruiser-Destroyer Group 1 1973-75; Deputy Chief of Naval Operations (Manpower), Chief of Naval Personnel 1975-76, Commdr. Sixth Fleet 1978-79, Vice-Chief of Naval Operations 1980-81, Commdr.-in-Chief U.S. Pacific Fleet 1981-82, Chief of Naval Operations 1982-86; Sec. of Energy Feb. 1989-; Distinguished Service Medal; Legion of Merit with two gold stars; Bronze Star Medal, Navy Commendation Medal; numerous hon. degrees, decorations from many countries. *Address:* Secretary of Energy, James Forrestal Bldg., 1000 Independence Avenue, S.W., Washington, D.C. 20585, U.S.A. (Office). *Telephone:* (202) 252-5000.

WATKINS, Winifred May, D.SC., F.R.C.PATH., F.R.S.; British scientist; b. 6 Aug. 1924, London; d. of Albert E. Watkins and Annie B. Watkins; ed. Godolphin and Latymer School, London, Univ. of London; Research Student, St. Bartholomew's Hosp. Medical School, London 1948-50; MRC Grantee, Lister Inst. Preventive Medicine, London 1950-52, Beit Memorial Research Fellow 1952-55, mem. scientific staff 1955-75, Prof. of Biochem. and Head, Dept. of Biochem. 1968-75; Wellcome Travelling Fellow, Univ. of Calif., Berkeley 1960-61; Reader in Biochem., Univ. of London 1965-68; Head of Div. of Immunochemical Genetics, MRC Clinical Research Centre 1976-; Hon. mem. Int. Soc. of Blood Transfusion; Foreign mem. Polish Acad. of Sciences; Award of Oliver Memorial Fund for outstanding contribs. in blood transfusion 1965; Karl Landsteiner Award, American Asscn. of Blood Banks (jtly.) 1967; Paul Erhlich-Ludwig Darmstädter Medal and Prize (jtly.) 1969; William Julius Mickle Fellowship Award, Univ. of London 1970; Kenneth Goldsmith Award of British Blood Transfusion Soc. 1986; Royal Medal of Royal Soc. *Publications:* numerous papers in scientific journals. *Leisure interests:* reading. *Address:* Division of Immunochemical Genetics, Medical Research Council Clinical Research Centre, Watford Road, Harrow, Middx., HA1 3UJ, England (Office). *Telephone:* 01-864 5311, Ext. 2674.

WATKINSON, 1st Viscount (cr. 1964), of Woking in the County of Surrey; Harold Arthur Watkinson, P.C., C.H.; British politician and business executive; b. 25 Jan. 1910, Walton-on-Thames; s. of Arthur Gill Watkinson and Mary Casey; m. Vera Langmead 1939; two d.; ed. King's Coll., London; Conservative M.P. 1950-64; Parl. Sec. Ministry of Labour 1952-55; Minister of Transport and Civil Aviation 1955-59, Minister of Defence 1959-62; mem. Cttee. of Inquiry into events leading to Argentine invasion of the Falkland Islands 1982; Dir. Midland Bank 1964-83, Deputy Chair. 1969-76, British Insulated Callender Cables Ltd. 1968-77; Group Man. Dir. Schweppes Ltd. 1963-69, Exec. Chair. Cadbury Schweppes Ltd. 1969-74; Chair. Cttee. for Exports to U.S.A. 1964-67; Council British Inst. of Man. 1968-70; Pres. Inst. of Grocery Distribution 1970-72, World Travel Market Advisory Council 1979-80; Chair. CBI Cttee. on Company Responsibility 1972-, Deputy Pres. CBI 1975-76, Pres. 1976-77. *Publications:* Blueprint for Industrial Survival 1976, Turning Points 1986, The Mountain 1988. *Leisure interests:* sailing, mountaineering, walking.

WATSON, Alexander Fletcher, M.A.; American diplomatist; b. 8 Aug. 1939, Boston, Mass.; s. of Fletcher G. Watson and Alice Victoria Hodson Watson; m. Judith Dawson Tuttle 1962; one s. one d.; ed. Harvard Coll., Boston and Univ. of Wisconsin, Madison; Consular Officer, Santo Domingo, Dominican Repub. 1962-64, Madrid 1964-66; Int. Relations Officer, Dept. of State, Washington, D.C. 1966-68; Political Officer, Brasilia, Brazil 1969-70; Prin. Officer, Consulate, Salvador, Bahia 1970-73; Int. Relations Officer, Dept. of State, Washington, D.C. 1973-75, Special Asst. 1975-77, Dir., Office of Devt. Finance 1978-79; Deputy Chief of Mission, La Paz, Bolivia 1979-81, Bogotá, Colombia 1981-84, Brasilia 1984-86; Amb. to Peru 1986-; Order of the Condor, Bolivia, Order of San Carlos, Colombia. *Leisure interests:* golf, tennis, music, literature. *Address:* American Embassy (Lima), APO Miami 34031, U.S.A.; American Embassy, Avenida Garcilazo de la Vega No. 1400, Lima, Peru.

WATSON, Arthur Christopher, C.M.G., M.A.; British diplomatist (retd.); b. 2 Jan. 1927, Kunming, China; s. of the late Dr. Alexander J. Watson and

of Dr. Mary L. Watson; m. Mary Cecil Candler (née Earl) 1956; one d. one step-s. one step-d.; ed. Norwich School, St. Catharine's Coll., Cambridge; Royal Naval Service 1945-48; Colonial Admin. Service (later H.M. Overseas Civil Service), Uganda 1951, Dist. Commr. 1959, Principal Asst. Sec. 1960; Prin., Commonwealth Relations Office, London 1963; First Sec., Karachi 1964-67; H.M. Diplomatic Service 1965-; Acting Deputy High Commr., Karachi 1967; FCO 1967-71; H.M. Commr. in Anguilla 1971-74; Gov. Turks and Caicos Islands 1975-78; High Commr. in Brunei 1978-83; Gov. Montserrat 1985-87. *Address:* Holmesdale, Oval Way, Gerrards Cross, Bucks., SL9 8QB, England.

WATSON, Sir Bruce, Kt., B.E., B.COM.; Australian electrical engineer and business executive; b. 1 Aug. 1928, Stanthorpe, Queensland; s. of Harvey and Edith Watson; m. June Kilgour 1952; one s. two d.; ed. Univ. of Queensland; Engineer, Tasmanian Hydro-electricity Comm. 1950-54, Townsville Regional Electricity Bd. 1954-56; with Mount Isa Mines (M.I.M. Holdings) Group of Cos. 1956-, Engineer, Copper Refineries Pty. Ltd., Townsville 1956-69, Mount Isa Mines Ltd. 1970-73; Group Industrial Relations Man., M.I.M. Group, Brisbane 1974-75, First Gen. Man. Agnew Mining Co., W. Australia 1975-77, Dir. M.I.M. Holdings Ltd., Brisbane 1977, Man. Dir. 1980-83, Chair. and C.E.O. 1983-; Dir. Asarco Inc. 1985-. *Leisure interest:* golf. *Address:* M.I.M. Holdings Limited, 410 Ann Street, Brisbane, Queensland 4001, Australia. *Telephone:* (07) 833 88000.

WATSON, Sir Francis John Bagott, K.C.V.O., B.A., F.B.A., F.S.A.; British museum director and civil servant; b. 24 Aug. 1907, Dudley, Worcs.; s. of Hugh Watson and Ellen Marian (née Bagott); m. Mary Rosalie Gray Strong 1941 (died 1969); one s. (adopted); ed. Shrewsbury School, and St. John's Coll., Cambridge; Registrar Courtauld Inst. of Art 1934-38; Asst. Keeper, later Asst. Dir. Wallace Collection 1938-63, Dir. 1963-74; Asst. Surveyor of the King's (later the Queen's) Works of Art 1946-63, Surveyor 1963-72, Adviser for The Queen's Works of Art 1972-; Trustee, Whitechapel Art Gallery 1949-74; Chair. Furniture History Soc. 1966-74; Slade Prof. of Fine Art, Oxford Univ. 1969-70; Kress Prof., Washington 1975-76; Chair. Walpole Soc. 1970-77; Ben Sonnenberg Prof. of the History of Art, New York Univ. 1979-80 (Wrightsman Prof. 1970-71); Sr. Resident Scholar J. Paul Getty Museum 1980-83; Smithsonian Regent Fellow 1982-84; Hon. M.A. (Oxford) 1970; Ufficiale dell'Ordine al Merito della Repubblica Italiana; New York Univ. Gold Medal. *Publications:* Canaletto 1949, Southill, A Regency House (with others) 1951, Catalogue of the Furniture in the Wallace Collection 1956, Louis XVI Furniture 1959 (revised French edn. 1963), The Choiseul Gold Box 1963, Wrightsman Catalogue (vols. I, II) 1966 (vols. III, IV) 1970 (vol. V) 1974, Eighteenth Century Gold Boxes of Europe (with others), The Guardi Family of Painters 1966, Tiepolo 1966, Fragonard 1967, The French Bronze 1500-1800 1968, Catalogue of Pictures and Drawings in the Wallace Collection (16th edn.) 1968, Chinese Porcelains in European Mounts 1980, Catalogue of Mounted Porcelain in J. Paul Getty Museum 1983, Oriental Porcelains in European Mounts 1986, Systematic Catalogue of Seventeenth and Eighteenth Century French Furniture, Nat. Gallery, Washington 1989. *Leisure interests:* chinoiserie, collecting Western Americana. *Address:* West Farm House, Corton, Wilts, BA12 0SY, England.

WATSON, James Dewey, B.S., PH.D.; American biologist; b. 6 April 1928, Chicago, Ill.; s. of James D. and Jean Mitchell Watson; m. Elizabeth Lewis 1968; two s.; ed. Univ. of Chicago, and Univ. of Indiana; Research Fellow, U.S. Nat. Research Council, Univ. of Copenhagen 1950-51; Fellow U.S. Nat. Foundation, Cavendish Lab., Univ. of Cambridge, England 1951-53, 1955-56; Sr. Research Fellow in Biology, Calif. Inst. of Tech. 1953-55; Asst. Prof. of Biology, Harvard Univ. 1956-58, Assoc. Prof. 1958-61, Prof. 1961-76; Dir. Cold Spring Harbor Lab. 1968-; mem. N.A.S., Danish Acad. of Arts and Sciences, American Acad. of Arts and Sciences, American Soc. of Biological Chemists; Sr. Fellow, Soc. of Fellows, Harvard Univ. 1964-70; Hon. Fellow of Clare Coll., Univ. of Cambridge 1967; mem. American Philosophical Soc. 1978; Eli Lilly Award in Biochem. 1959, Lasker Prize (American Public Health Asscn.) 1960, Nobel Prize for Medicine (with F. H. C. Crick and M. F. H. Wilkins) 1962, John J. Carty Gold Medal (Nat. Acad. of Sciences) 1971, Medal of Freedom 1977, and other awards; Hon. D.Sc. (Chicago, Indiana, Long Island, Adelphi, Brandeis, Hofstra, Harvard, Rockefeller, State Univ. of New York, Albert Einstein Coll. of Medicine, Clarkson Coll.), Hon. LL.D. (Notre Dame) 1965; Hon. M.D. (Buenos Aires) 1986; Foreign mem. Royal Soc. 1981; Hon. Fellow, Clarkson Coll. 1982, Gold Medal Award, Nat. Inst. of Social Sciences 1984. *Publications:* Molecular Biology of the Gene 1965 (2nd edn. 1970, 3rd edn. 1976), The Double Helix 1968, The DNA Story 1981 (with John Tooze), Recombinant DNA: A Short Course (with others), The Molecular Biology of the Cell (with others) 1986, papers on structure of deoxyribonucleic acid (DNA), on protein synthesis and on the induction of cancer by viruses. *Address:* Cold Spring Harbor Laboratory, Cold Spring Harbor, Long Island, New York, N.Y. 11724 (Office); Bungtown Road, Cold Spring Harbor, New York, N.Y. 11724, U.S.A. (Home). *Telephone:* (516) 367-8310.

WATSON, James Kay Graham, PH.D., F.R.S.; British research scientist; b. 20 April 1936, Denny High School, Scotland; s. of Thomas Watson and Mary C. Miller; m. Carolyn M. L. Kerr 1981; ed. Denny High School of Stirling and Univ. of Glasgow; Carnegie Sr. Scholar, Dept. of Chem., Univ. Coll. London 1961-63; Postdoctorate Fellow, Nat. Research Council,

Ottawa 1963-65; ICI Research Fellow, Univ. of Reading 1965-66, Lecturer in Chemical Physics 1966-71; Visiting Assoc. Prof. in Physics, Ohio State Univ. 1971-75; S. R. C. Sr. Research Fellow in Chem. Univ. of Southampton 1975-79, 1980-82; Visiting Scientist, Nat. Research Council, Ottawa 1979-80, Sr. and now Principal Research Officer 1982-; Chem. Soc. Award 1974; Plyler Prize, American Physical Soc. 1986. *Publications:* 80 articles on molecular physics in learned journals. *Leisure interests:* music, golf, tree-watching. *Address:* 183 Stanley Avenue, Ottawa, Ontario, K1M 1P2, Canada. *Telephone:* 613-990-0739 (Office); 613-745-7928 (Home).

WATSON, Kenneth Marshall, PH.D.; American physicist and professor of oceanography; b. 7 Sept. 1921, Des Moines, Ia.; s. of Louis Erwin Watson and Irene Watson; m. Elaine C. Miller 1946; two s.; ed. Iowa State Coll., Univ. of Iowa; Asst. Prof. Indiana Univ. 1951-54; Assoc. Prof. Univ. of Wis. 1954-57; Prof. of Physics Univ. of Calif., Berkeley 1957-81; Dir. Marine Physical Lab. and Prof. Univ. of Calif., San Diego 1981-; mem. N.A.S.; Dr. h.c. (Indiana Univ.). *Publications:* Collision Theory (with Goldberger John Wiley) 1964, Atomic Theory of Gas Dynamics (with Welch and Bond) 1965, Topics in Several Particle Dynamics (with Nuttall) 1967. *Leisure interest:* sailing. *Address:* Marine Physical Laboratory, Scripps Institution of Oceanography, University of California A-013, La Jolla, Calif. 92093, U.S.A. *Telephone:* (619) 534-6620.

WATSON, Lyall, PH.D., F.Z.S., F.L.S.; British biologist and author; b. 12 April 1939, South Africa; m. Vivienne Mawson 1961 (divorced 1966); ed. Rondebosch Boys High School, Witwatersrand Univ. and Univs. of Natal and London; Dir. Johannesburg Zoo 1964-65; Producer and Reporter, BBC Television 1966-67; Founder and Dir. Biologic of London (Consultancy) 1968-; organizer and leader of numerous expeditions 1970-; Commr. for Seychelles on Int. Whaling Comm. 1978-82; Kt. Order of Golden Ark, Netherlands 1983. *Publications:* Omnivore 1970, Supernature 1972, The Romeo Error 1974, Gifts of Unknown Things 1976, Lifetide 1978, Lightning Bird 1980, Whales of the World 1982, Heavens Breath 1984, Earthworks 1986, Beyond Supernature 1986, Supernature II 1986, The Water Planet 1987, Sumo 1988, Neophilia 1988, The Secret Life of Machines 1988. *Leisure interests:* bird-watching, ethnobotany, archaeology, tribal art, conchology. *Address:* BCM-Biologic, London, WC1N 3XX, England (Office); Ballydehob, Co. Cork, Ireland (Home).

WATSON, Richard Burges, C.M.G., M.A.; British diplomatist; b. 23 Sept. 1930, London; s. of Harold Watson and Marjorie Burges Watson; m. Ann Rosamund Clarke 1966; two s. three d.; ed. King Edward VI School, Bury St. Edmunds, St. John's Coll., Cambridge; joined Foreign Office 1954, Third then Second Sec., Tokyo 1954-60, Foreign Office, London 1960-63, First Sec., Bamako 1963-66, First Sec., OECD, Paris 1966-69, FCO, London 1969-71, Princeton Univ., U.S.A. 1971-72, Econ. Counsellor, Tokyo 1972-76, Commercial Counsellor, Brussels 1976-78, Head of Trade Relations and Exports Dept., FCO 1978-81, Sabbatical, Florence 1981-82, temporary duties, FCO 1982-83, Minister Commercial and Consul-Gen., Milan 1983-86, Amb. to Nepal 1987-. *Leisure interests:* hill walking, skiing, tennis. *Address:* British Embassy, P.O. Box 106, Lainchaur, Kathmandu, Nepal.

WATSON, Thomas J., Jr., B.A.; American business executive and diplomatist; b. 8 Jan. 1914, Dayton, Ohio; s. of Thomas J. and Jeanette (née Kittredge) Watson; m. Olive Field Cawley 1941; one s. five d.; ed. Brown Univ.; rank of Lieut.-Col. U.S.A.F. 1940-45; with Int. Business Machines (IBM) Corpn. 1937-40, 1946-79, Pres. 1952-61, C.E.O. 1961-71, Chair. of Bd. 1961-71, C.E.O. 1971-79, Dir. and Chair. Emer. 1981-84, Chair. Emer. 1981-; Amb. to U.S.S.R. 1978-79; Chair. Gen. Advisory Cttee., Arms Control and Disarmament 1970-79; fmr. Pres. Greater N.Y. Councils, Boy Scouts of America (BSA), Nat. Council BSA; fmr. Dir. numerous cos., Citizen Regent Smithsonian Inst. 1981-; fmr. mem. numerous cttees., mem. Council on Foreign Relations 1961-, Grad. mem. the Business Council 1951-; fmr. Pres.'s Comm. on Nat. Goals, Advisory Cttee. on Troop Information and Educ., Defense Dept., Task Force on War against Poverty, Nat. Comm. on Tech., Govt., Automation and Econ. Progress, Advisory Cttee. on Labor Man. Policy, Pres.'s Comm. on Income Maintenance Programs; Sr. Fellow, Wilson Nat. Fellowship Found. 1973-79; Vice-Chancellor, Brown Univ. 1979-85, Trustee 1947-85; Trustee, American Museum of Natural History 1955-78, Hon. Trustee 1978-, Trustee, George C. Marshall Research Found. 1958-, Calif. Inst. of Tech. 1960-79, 1981-84, Life Trustee 1984-, John F. Kennedy Library 1964-, M.I.T. 1957-62, Mystic Seaport Inc. 1967-69, 1981-, Mayo Foundation 1975-79, 1981-85, Trustee Emer. 1985-, Inst. for Advanced Study, Princeton 1968-75, World Wildlife Fund 1974-78, U.S. Council of Int. Chamber of Commerce (Chair. 1955-57), Rockefeller Foundation 1963-71; numerous hon. degrees; Army Commendation Ribbon, U.S. Air Medal, Presidential Medal of Freedom, Légion d'honneur, many other foreign awards. *Address:* c/o IBM, Old Orchard Road, Armonk, New York, N.Y. 10504, U.S.A. (Office).

WATSON, Thomas Sturges (Tom); American golfer; b. 4 Sept. 1949, Kansas City, Mo.; s. of Raymond Etheridge Watson and Sarah Elizabeth Ridge; m. Linda Tova Rubin 1973; one s. one d.; ed. Stanford Univ.; professional 1971-; British Open Champion 1975, 1977, 1980, 1982, 1983; record low aggregate for British Open of 268, record two single round scores of 65, lowest final 36-hole score of 130, Turnberry 1977; won U.S. Masters title 1977, 1981; won U.S Open 1982; won World Series 1975,

1977, 1980; winner numerous other open championships 1974-; top money winner on U.S. P.G.A. circuit 1977, 1978, 1979, 1980; U.S. P.G.A. Player of the Year 1977, 1978, 1979, 1980, 1982; first player ever to win in excess of $500,000 in prize money in one season 1980; Ryder Cup Player 1977, 1979. *Address:* 1313 Commerce Tower, Kansas City, Mo. 64105, U.S.A. *Telephone:* 816-421-4770.

WATSON, William, C.B.E., F.B.A.; British professor of Chinese and Japanese Art History; b. 9 Dec. 1917, Darley Abbey; s. of Robert Scouler Watson and Lily Waterfield; m. Katherine Sylvia Mary Watson 1940; four s.; ed. Glasgow High School, Herbert Strutt School and Gonville and Caius Coll., Cambridge; Asst. Keeper, British Museum, first in Dept. of British and Medieval Antiquities, then in Dept. of Oriental Antiquities 1947-66; Slade Prof. of Fine Art, Cambridge Univ. 1975-76; Prof. of Chinese Art and Archaeology, Univ. of London (S.O.A.S.) 1966-83, Prof. Emer. 1983-; Pres. of Oriental Ceramic Soc. 1981-84; Hon. D. Litt. (Chinese Univ. of Hong Kong) 1973; Trustee of the British Museum. *Publications:* The Sculpture of Japan 1959, Archaeology in China 1960, China before the Han Dynasty 1961, Ancient Chinese Bronzes 1961, Jade Books in the Chester Beatty Library 1963, Cultural Frontiers in Ancient East Asia 1971, The Genius of China 1973, Style in the Arts of China 1974, L'Art de l'Ancienne Chine 1980; Ed. Catalogue of the Great Japan Exhibition 1981-82, Tang and Liao Ceramics 1984. *Leisure interests:* Iberia and claret. *Address:* Cefn y Maes, Parc, Bala, Gwynedd, LL23 7YS, Wales. *Telephone:* (06784) 302.

WATT, James Gaius, B.S., J.D.; American lawyer and politician; b. 31 Jan. 1938, Lusk, Wyo.; s. of William G. and Lois M. (Williams) Watt; m. Leilani Bomgardner 1957; one s. one d.; ed. Univ. of Wyoming; admitted to Wyo. bar 1962, U.S. Supreme Court bar 1966; Sec. Natural Resources Comm. and Environmental Pollution Advisory Panel, U.S. Chamber of Commerce 1966-69; Legis. Asst., Counsel to Senator Simpson of Wyo. 1962-66; Deputy Asst. Sec. for Water and Power, Dept. of the Interior 1969-72; Dir. Bureau of Outdoor Recreation, U.S. Dept. of the Interior 1972-75; U.S. Sec. of the Interior 1981-83; practising law, Washington 1983-86, Jackson Hole, Wyo. 1986-; Vice-Chair. Fed. Power Comm. 1975-77; Pres., Chief Legal Officer, Mountain States Legal Foundation, Denver 1977-80; Instructor, Coll. of Commerce and Industry, Univ. of Wyoming; Chair. of Bd. Environmental Diagnostics Inc. 1984-87, Disease Detection Int. 1987-. *Publication:* The Courage of a Conservative (with Doug Wead) 1985. *Address:* 1800 N. Spirit Dance Road, Jackson Hole, Wyoming 83001, U.S.A.

WATT, James Park, M.B.E.; Scottish boxer (retd.); b. 18 July 1948, Glasgow; s. of James and Ina Watt; m. Margaret Black; two s. one d.; ed. Glasgow Grammar School; rep. Scotland, amateur boxing; Amateur Boxing Asscn. (ABA) lightweight champion 1968; declined invitation to join British Olympic team 1968; turned professional Oct. 1968; beaten in British lightweight championship fight v. Willie Reilly Feb. 1972; won title, beating Tony Riley after Willie Reilly relinquished it May 1972; lost title to Ken Buchanan Jan. 1973; won vacant title v. Johnny Cheshire Jan. 1975; won Lonsdale Belt outright by retaining British title v. Johnny Claydon Feb. 1977; beaten by Jonathan Dele for vacant Commonwealth lightweight title May 1975; won vacant European title, beating André Holyk in first round Aug. 1977; relinquished British title July 1977; retained European title twice in 1978; won vacant World Boxing Council (WBC) version of world lightweight championship April 1979, beating Alfredo Pitalua; defended it v. Roberto Vasquez Nov. 1979, Charlie Nash March 1980, Howard Davis June 1980 and Sean O'Grady Nov. 1980; 45 fights, 38 wins; now works as TV commentator. *Leisure interests:* football and music. *Address:* c/o British Boxing Board of Control, 2 Ramilles Buildings, Hills Place, London W.1, England.

WATTS, Arthur Desmond, C.M.G., K.C.M.G., Q.C., LL.B.; British diplomatist; b. 14 Nov. 1931, Wimbledon; s. of the late Col. A. E. Watts and Eileen May (née Challons) Watts; m Iris Ann Collier 1957; one s. one d.; ed. Haileybury, Royal Mil. Acad. and Downing Coll., Cambridge; called to Bar, Gray's Inn 1957; Legal Asst. Foreign Office 1957-59, Asst. Legal Adviser 1962-67; Legal Adviser British Property Comm. (now British Embassy), Cairo 1959-62, Embassy, Bonn 1967-69; Asst. Solicitor Law Officer's Dept. 1969-70; Legal Counsellor FCO 1970-73, 1977-82, Deputy Legal Adviser 1982-87, Legal Adviser 1987-; Legal Counsellor, Perm. Rep. to the EEC, Brussels 1973-77. *Publications:* Legal Effects of War (with Lord McNair) 1966, Encyclopaedic Dictionary of International Law (with Parry, Grant) 1986. *Address:* c/o Foreign and Commonwealth Office, Whitehall, London, SW1, England. *Telephone:* 01-270 3048.

WATTS, Helen Josephine, C.B.E.; British contralto; b. 7 Dec. 1927, Milford Haven, Wales; d. of Thomas Watts and Winifred Morgan; m. Michael Mitchell 1980; ed. St. Mary and St. Anne's School, Abbot Bromley; singer in Glyndebourne and BBC choruses; toured Russia with English Opera Group 1964; Concert tours in U.S.A. 1967-85 (retd.); has appeared with all major European and American orchestras; numerous recordings; has sung at the Salzburg Festival, Covent Garden and the Hong Kong Festival; major appearances include: The Ring at Covent Garden; Mozart Opera at Salzburg Festival; four Promenade concerts 1974; Hon. F.R.A.M. *Recordings include:* Handel Arias, Orfeo, B Minor Mass, Beethoven's Mass in C Minor, The Dream of Gerontius, The Apostles, Götterdämmerung. *Leisure interest:* gardening. *Address:* Rock House, Wallis, Ambleston, Haverfordwest, Dyfed, SA62 5RA, Wales.

WATTS, Roy, C.B.E., M.A.; British business executive; b. 17 Aug. 1925, Doncaster; m. Jean Roseline Watts 1951; one s. two d.; ed. Doncaster Grammar School and Edinburgh Univ.; commissioned Sandhurst, served in Royal Tank Regt. 1943-47; Accountant in local govt. 1950-55; joined BEA 1955, Org. and Methods Officer, Chief Internal Auditor, Man. Sweden and Finland, Fleet Planning Man., Route Gen. Man., N. and E. Europe Dir. S1-11 Div., Chief Exec. 1972-74, Chair. Jan.-March 1974; Dir. Commercial Operations, B.A. 1974, Dir. Finance and Planning, Chief Exec. 1979-83, also Deputy Chair. 1980-83; Chair. Thames Water Authority 1983-, Cabletime Installations Ltd. 1984-, Armstrong Equipment PLC 1986-, Lowndes Lambert Holdings 1988-; Deputy Chair. Brymon Airways 1983-; mem. Chartered Inst. of Public Finance and Accountancy; Fellow, Royal Aeronautical Soc., Chartered Inst. of Transport. *Leisure interests:* squash, cricket, walking. *Address:* Baywell House, Fawler Road, Charlbury, Oxford, England. *Telephone:* Charlbury 810385.

WAUGH, Auberon Alexander; British writer; b. 17 Nov. 1939, Dulverton, Somerset; s. of late Evelyn Waugh and Laura Waugh; m. Teresa Onslow 1961; two s. two d.; ed. Downside School, Christ Church, Oxford; editorial staff, Daily Telegraph 1960-63; special writer, IPC Publications 1964-67; political corresp., Spectator 1967-70, Chief Fiction Reviewer 1970-73, weekly columnist 1976-; political corresp. and columnist, Private Eye 1970-86; Chief Book Reviewer, The Independent 1986-; columnist The Times 1970-71, The Sunday Telegraph 1981-; weekly columnist, New Statesman 1973-76; Chief Fiction Reviewer, Evening Standard 1973-80; monthly columnist, Books and Bookmen 1973-80; Chief Fiction Reviewer, Daily Mail 1980-86; Ed. The Literary Review Jan. 1986-; British Press Award, "Critic of the Year" commendations 1977 and 1978, Granada TV "What the Papers Say", Columnist of the Year 1979. *Publications:* The Foxglove Saga 1960, Consider the Lilies 1968, Biafra: Britain's Shame (with S. Cronje) 1969, Country Topics 1974, Four Crowded Years 1976, In the Lion's Den 1979, The Last Word: The Trial of Jeremy Thorpe 1980, Auberon Waugh's Yearbook 1981, The Diaries of Auberon Waugh, A Turbulent Decade 1976-85 1985, Waugh on Wine 1986, Another Voice (essays) 1986, Women 1987. *Leisure interest:* gossip. *Address:* Combe Florey House, Combe Florey, Taunton, Somerset, England; La Pesegado, 11320 Montmaur, Labastide d'Anjou, France. *Telephone:* (0823) 432297 (Somerset).

WAUGH, John Stewart, PH.D.; American professor of chemistry; b. 25 April 1929, Willimantic, Conn.; s. of Albert E. Waugh and Edith S. Waugh; m. Susan M. Walsh 1983; one s. one d.; ed. Windham High School, Dartmouth Coll. and Calif. Inst. of Tech.; mem. Faculty, M.I.T. 1953-, A. A. Noyes Prof. of Chem. 1973-; Visiting Scientist, U.S.S.R. Acad. of Sciences 1962, Univ. of Calif. 1963, Harvard Univ. 1975; Visiting Prof. Max Planck Inst. for Medical Research 1971, East China Normal Univ., Shanghai 1984, Texas A & M Univ. 1986; Joliot-Curie Prof. Ecole Supérieure de Physique et Chimie, Paris 1985; Chair. Div. of Chem. Physics, American Physical Soc. 1984-85; von Humboldt Award 1971, Langmuir Award 1974, Pittsburgh Spectroscopy Award 1978; Wolf Laureate 1984; Pauling Medal 1985. *Publications:* many scientific research papers. *Leisure interest:* sailing. *Address:* Department of Chemistry, Massachusetts Institute of Technology, Cambridge, Mass. 02139, U.S.A. *Telephone:* 617-253-1901.

WAY, Alva Otis, A.B.; American business executive; b. 27 April 1929, Schenectady; s. of Alva Otis and Margaret L. (née Sigsbee) Way; m. Eleonore Maurer; one s. two d.; ed. Brown Univ.; served with U.S. Army 1952-54; with Gen. Electric Co. (G.E.C.) 1951-70, various domestic and foreign managerial positions in Venezuela, Brazil, France; Vice-Pres. of Finance, Chief Financial Officer G.E.C., Fairfield, Conn. 1973-79; mem. corporate policy Bd. 1974; Dir. Gen. Electric Credit Corpn., Canadian G.E.C. Ltd., Utah Int. Inc.; Vice-Pres. Honeywell Information Systems Inc. 1970-73, Sr. Vice-Pres. of Finance 1977-79, Vice-Chair., Dir., Chair. Finance Cttee. American Express Co. 1979, Pres. 1981-83; Chair. and C.E.O. American Express Int. Banking Corpn. 1980-82; Pres., Travelers Insurance Co., Hartford, Conn. 1983-85, Dir. 1983-85, Consultant 1985-; Chair. Schroeder Bank and Trust Co., New York 1986-; Dir. Dayton Hudson Corpn., Eli Lilly and Co., Schroders PLC 1985-; Trustee Brown Univ. *Address:* Schroeder Bank and Trust Company, 1 State Street, New York, N.Y. 10004, U.S.A.

WAY, Sir Richard, K.C.B., C.B.E.; British civil servant and university administrator; b. 15 Sept. 1914, London; s. of Frederick Way and Clara Way (née Willetts); m. Ursula Joan Starr 1947; one s. two d.; ed. Polytechnic Secondary School, London; joined Civil Service 1933; Perm. Under-Sec. of State for War 1960-63; Perm. Sec. Ministry of Aviation 1963-66; Chair. Lansing Bagnall Ltd. 1967-69; Chair. London Transport 1970-74; Prin., King's Coll., London 1975-80; mem. Council London Zoological Soc. 1977-82, 1984-87, Vice-Pres. 1979-82, 1984-87; American Medal of Freedom (with bronze palm) 1946; Commdr. Order of St. John of Jerusalem 1974; Hon. D.Sc. (Loughborough) 1986. *Address:* The Old Forge, Shalden, Alton, Hants., England. *Telephone:* (0420) 82383.

WAYMAN, Patrick Arthur, PH.D., M.A.; British astronomer; b. 8 Oct. 1927, Bromley; s. of Lieut.-Col. L. J. Wayman, O.B.E., T.D., and Mary (née Palmer) Wayman; m. Mavis McIntyre Smith Gibson 1954; one s. two d.; ed. City of London School, Emmanuel Coll., Cambridge; with Royal Greenwich

Observatory 1951-64, Head of Solar Dept. 1956-57, Meridian Dept. 1962-64; Sr. Prof., Astronomy Section, School of Cosmic Physics, Dublin Inst. for Advanced Studies 1964-; Gen. Sec. Int. Astronomical Union 1979-82; Assoc. Royal Astronomical Soc.; mem. Royal Irish Acad.; Chair. Editorial Bd., Irish Astronomical Journal 1979-; Hon. Andrews Prof. of Astronomy, Trinity Coll., Dublin 1984-. *Publications:* Ed.: Highlights of Astronomy (vol. 5) 1980, Transactions of the International Astronomical Union (vol. 17B) 1980, Dunsinh Observatory 1785-1985 1987. *Leisure interests:* church music, open air, architecture. *Address:* Dunsinh Observatory, Dublin 15, Ireland.

WAZZAN, Chafiq al-, LL.B.; Lebanese politician and lawyer; b. 1925, Beirut; m.; two s.; ed. al-Makassed Coll., St. Joseph's Univ., Beirut; law practice 1947-; Deputy for Beirut, Nat. Ass. 1968; Minister of Justice Jan.-Oct. 1969; Pres. Higher Islamic Council 1963-, Lebanese Muslim Congress; fmr. mem. Presidium al-Hayat al-Wataniya party; Prime Minister 1980-84. *Address:* Rue Haroun el-Rashid, Immeuble Wazzan, Beirut, Lebanon (Home).

WEATHERALL, Sir David John, Kt., M.D., F.R.S., F.R.C.P., F.R.C.PATH.; British professor of clinical medicine; b. 9 March 1933, Liverpool; s. of Harry and Gwendoline Weatherall; m. Stella Nestler 1962; one s.; ed. Calday Grammar School and Univ. of Liverpool; various resident posts in medicine 1956-58; jr. medical specialist, Royal Army Corps, Singapore 1959-60; Research Fellow, Johns Hopkins Hosp. 1961-65; Reader in Haematology, Univ. of Liverpool 1969-71, Prof. 1971-74; consultant to WHO 1967-82; Nuffield Prof. of Clinical Medicine, Univ. of Oxford 1974-, Hon. Dir. MRC Molecular Haematology Unit 1979-, Inst. of Molecular Medicine 1988-; Fellow, Magdalen Coll., Oxford 1974-; mem. American Acad. of Arts and Sciences; Watson-Smith Lecture 1974, Croonian Lecture 1984, Foundation Lecture (F.R.C. Path.) 1979, Darwin Lecture (Eugenics Soc.) 1979; Sims Visiting Prof. 1982; Hon. F.R.C.O.G.; Hon. M.D. (Leeds) 1988, (Sheffield, Manchester) 1989; Hon. D.Sc. (Edin.) 1989; Stratton Award and Medal (Int. Haematology Soc.) 1982; Ballantyne Prize (R.C.P. Edinburgh) 1983; Feldberg Foundation Award 1984. *Publications:* The New Genetics and Clinical Practice 1982, The Thalassaemia Syndrome (with J. B. Clegg) 1982, Oxford Textbook of Medicine (with others) 1983. *Leisure interest:* music. *Address:* Nuffield Department of Clinical Medicine, John Radcliffe Hospital, Headington, Oxford, OX3 9DU (Office); 8 Cumnor Rise Road, Cumnor Hill, Oxford, England (Home). *Telephone:* (0865) 862467.

WEATHERHEAD, Rev. James Leslie, M.A., LL.B.; British ecclesiastic in Church of Scotland; b. 29 March 1931, Dundee; s. of Leslie Binnie Weatherhead and Janet Hood Arnot Smith; m. Anne Elizabeth Shepherd 1962; two s.; ed. High School, Dundee and Univ. of Edinburgh; nat. service in R.N. 1955-56; ordained 1960; Parish Minister Trinity Church, Rothesay 1962-69; The Old Church, Montrose 1969-85; Prin. Clerk of Gen. Ass. of Church of Scotland 1985-. *Leisure interests:* music and sailing. *Address:* 28 Castle Terrace, Edinburgh, EH1 2EL (Home); Church of Scotland Offices, 121 George Street, Edinburgh, EH2 4YN, Scotland (Office). *Telephone:* 031-228 6460 (Home); 031-225 5722 (Office).

WEATHERILL, Rt. Hon. (Bruce) Bernard; British politician and master tailor; b. 25 Nov. 1920, Sunningdale, Surrey; s. of the late Bernard Weatherill and of Gertrude Creak; m. Lyn Eatwell 1949; two s. one d.; ed. Malvern Coll.; served Royal Dragoon Guards, Indian Army, 19th King George V's Own Lancers 1939-45; Man. Dir. Bernard Weatherill Ltd. 1957-70; M.P. for Croydon North East 1964-; Opposition Whip 1967-70; Lord Commr. of H.M. Treasury 1970-71; Vice-Chamberlain of the Royal Household 1971-72, Comptroller 1972-73; Treasurer of the Household and Deputy Chief Whip 1974-79; Chair. Ways and Means and Deputy Speaker 1979-83; Speaker of the House of Commons 1983-; Chair. Commonwealth Speakers and Presiding Officers 1986-88. *Publication:* Acorns to Oaks. *Leisure interests:* golf, tennis. *Address:* Speaker's House, Westminster, London, S.W.1, England.

WEATHERLEY, Paul Egerton, D.PHIL., F.R.S.; British professor of botany; b. 6 May 1917, Leicester; s. of Leonard Weatherley and Ethel (née Collin); m. Margaret Logan Pirie 1942; one s. three d.; ed. Wyggeston School, Leicester and Keble Coll. Oxford; Colonial Office Scholarship, course in Tropical Agric. at Imperial Coll. of Tropical Agric., Trinidad 1940-42; Botanist in Uganda, Colonial Service 1942-47; Asst. Lecturer, Botany Dept., Manchester Univ. 1947-49; Lecturer, then Sr. Lecturer, Botany Dept., Nottingham Univ. 1949-59; Regius Prof. of Botany, Univ. of Aberdeen 1959-81, Prof. Emer. 1981-. *Publications:* scientific papers. *Leisure interest:* sketching. *Address:* Greystones, Torphins, Banchory, Kincardineshire, AB3 4HP, Scotland. *Telephone:* (033 982) 379.

WEATHERSTONE, Dennis, F.I.B.; British banker; b. 29 Nov. 1930, London; s. of Henry Philip Weatherstone and Gladys Hart; m. Marion Blunsum 1959; one s. three d.; ed. Acland High School, Northwestern Polytechnic, London; Vice-Pres. Morgan Guaranty Trust Co. 1965-72, Sr. Vice-Pres. 1972-77, Exec. Vice-Pres. and Treas. 1977-79; Vice-Chair. Morgan Guaranty Trust Co. (now J. P. Morgan & Co. Inc.) 1979-80, Chair. Exec. Cttee. 1980-86, Pres. 1987-. *Leisure interest:* tennis. *Address:* J. P. Morgan & Co. Inc. of New York, 23 Wall Street, New York N.Y. 10015 (Office); 28 Beach Drive, Darien, Conn. 06820, U.S.A. (Home). *Telephone:* (212) 483-4789 (Office); (203) 655-4432 (Home).

WEAVER, Michael; American boxer; b. 7 July 1952, Gatesville, Tex.; m. three d.; ed. High School; joined U.S. Marines 1969; began amateur boxing 1971; served in Viet-Nam; American Services heavyweight champion; professional Sept. 1972-; sparring partner for leading heavyweights Ken Norton and Bernardo Mercado; knocked out Mercado Oct. 1978; won U.S heavyweight title Jan. 1979; lost in 12 rounds to Larry Holmes for World Boxing Council (WBC) version of world heavyweight title June 1979; won World Boxing Assen. version of title by knocking out John Tate in 15th round, Knoxville, U.S.A. March 1980; retained title, knocking out Gerrie Coetzee, Bophuthatswana, S.A. Oct. 1980; 31 fights, 22 wins. *Address:* Marina del Rey, Calif. 90291, U.S.A.

WEAVER, Robert C., B.S., M.A., PH.D.; American economist and government official; b. 29 Dec. 1907, Washington, D.C.; s. of Mortimer G. Weaver and Florence Freeman Weaver; m. Ella Haith Weaver 1935; one s. (deceased); ed. Harvard Univ.; Adviser on Negro Affairs (Dept. of the Interior) 1933-37; Consultant (Housing Div., Public Works Admin.) 1934-37; Special Asst. to Admin., U.S. Housing Authority 1937-40; Chief, Negro Employment and Training (Office of Production Man. and later War Production Bd.) 1940-44; Visiting Prof. New York Univ. 1948-50; Dir. Opportunity Fellowships (J. H. Whitney Foundation) 1950-55; Deputy Commr. of Housing, N.Y. State 1955, Rent Admin. 1955-59; Consultant, Ford Foundation 1959-60; Vice-Chair. Housing and Redevt. Bd., N.Y. City 1960-61; Admin. Housing and Home Finance Agency 1961-66; fmr. Chair. Nat. Assen. for the Advancement of Colored People; mem. Advisory Comm. U.S. Housing Census for 1960, Nat. Comm. for Selection (Fulbright Fellowships), Exec. Cttee. of Action; Dir. Lavenburg Foundation; Sec. Dept. of Housing and Urban Devt. 1966-68; Pres. Bernard-Baruch Coll., City Univ. of New York (C.U.N.Y.) 1969-70; Distinguished Prof. of Urban Affairs, Hunter Coll., C.U.N.Y. 1970-78, Prof. Emer. 1978-; Dir. of Urban Programs, Brookdale Cen. on Aging, Hunter Coll. 1978-79; Chair. of Bd. FNMA 1961-68; Pres. Nat. Comm. against Discrimination in Housing 1973-87; mem. Bd. Municipal Assistance Corpn., New York 1975-; numerous hon. degrees. *Publications:* Negro Labor: A National Problem 1946, The Negro Ghetto 1948, The Urban Complex 1964, Dilemmas of Urban America 1965. *Address:* 215 East 68th Street, New York, N.Y. 10021, U.S.A. (Home). *Telephone:* (212) 288 0124.

WEAVER, Sigourney; American actress; b. 1949, New York; d. of Pat Weaver and Elizabeth Inglis; m. James Simpson 1984. *Films include:* Annie Hall 1977, Tribute to a Madman 1977, Camp 708 1978, Alien 1979, Eyewitness 1981, The Year of Living Dangerously 1982, Deal of the Century 1983, Ghostbusters 1984, Une Femme ou Deux 1985, Half Moon Street 1986, Aliens 1986, Gorillas in the Mist (Best Supporting Actress Award Golden Globe) 1988, Working Girl (Golden Globe Best Actress Award) 1988, Ghostbusters II 1989. *Address:* c/o Sam Cohn, 40 West 57th Street, New York, N.Y. 10012, U.S.A.

WEBB, James H., Jr., J.D.; American government official; b. 9 Feb. 1946, Arlington, Va.; m.; three c.; ed. U.S. Naval Acad. and Georgetown Univ.; Asst. Minority Counsel, House Cttee. on Veterans Affairs, Washington 1977-78, Chief Minority Counsel 1979-81; Visiting Writer, U.S. Naval Acad. 1979; Asst. Sec. for Reserve Affairs, Dept. of Defense 1984-87; Sec. of the Navy 1987-88. *Publications include:* A Country Such As This. *Address:* c/o The Pentagon, Washington, D.C. 20301, U.S.A.

WEBB DUARTE, Richard Charles, PH.D.; Peruvian economist; b. 8 July 1937, Bellavista, Callao; s. of Philip Webb and Graciela Duarte; m. Josefina Caminatti 1982; two s. three d. by previous marriage; ed. St. Andrew's Coll., Ont., Univ. of St. Andrews, Scotland, and Harvard Univ.; fmr. Pres. Banco Central de Reserva del Perú. *Leisure interests:* tennis, squash, frontón. *Address:* Edif. Las Gaviotas, dpt. 110, La Herradura, Chorrillos, Lima, Peru (Home).

WEBER, Ernst, D.SC., D.PHIL., D.ENG.; Austrian engineer; b. 6 Sept. 1901, Vienna; s. of Hermann Rudolf Weber and Josefine Pauline Swoboda; m. 1st Irma Lintner (divorced 1933), 2nd Charlotte Sonya Escherich 1936; two step-d.; ed. Vienna Tech. Univ.; Research Engineer Oesterreichische Siemens-Schuckert Co. Vienna 1924-29; Design Engineer Siemens-Schuckert Co. Berlin 1929-30; Visiting Prof. Polytechnic Inst. of Brooklyn, N.Y. 1930-31, Research Prof. of Electrical Eng. 1931-41, Head Research and Graduate Study in Electrical Eng. 1942-45; Head Dept. of Electrical Eng. and Dir. of Microwave Research Inst. 1945-57, Vice-Pres. for Research 1957-63; Pres. Polytechnic Inst. of Brooklyn 1957-69, Pres. Emer.; Consultant PRD Electronics Inc.; Founding mem. Nat. Acad. of Eng.; mem. N.A.S., Nat. Research Council 1969-79; Pres. Inst. Radio Engineers 1959; Pres. Inst. of Electrical and Electronics Engineers 1963; Nat. Medal of Science 1987. *Leisure interests:* mountain climbing, music. *Address:* P.O. Box 1619, Tryon, N.C. 28782, U.S.A. (Home). *Telephone:* (704) 859-6224 (Home).

WEBER, Maria; German trade unionist; b. 27 Dec. 1919, Gelsenkirchen-Horst; seamstress, telephonist, raw material tester, Gelsenberg-Benzin (Deputy Chair. Works Council to 1945); Works Acad. 1947-48; Union Sec. German Fed. of Trade Unions 1950-, mem. Man. Bd. with responsibility for training, professional educ. and wages policy 1956-, Deputy Chair. 1972-83; Chair. Study Group, Christian Democratic Fed. of Trade Unions 1973-, Admin. Bd. CEDEFOP 1979-; mem. several supervisory bds.;

Grosse Bundesverdienstkreuz 1979. *Address:* Hans-Böckler-Strasse 39, 4000 Düsseldorf, Federal Republic of Germany (Office). *Telephone:* 4-30 12 86.

WEBSTER, Charles, D.SC., F.B.A.; British academic; b. 23 Oct. 1936, Lowdham; Fellow Corpus Christi Coll., Oxford 1972-88; Dir. Wellcome Unit for the History of Medicine, Oxford 1972-88; Reader in Medicine, Univ. of Oxford 1972-88; Sr. Research Fellow All Souls Coll., Oxford 1988-. *Publications:* Samuel Hartlib and the Advancement of Learning 1972, The Great Instauration 1975, From Paracelsus to Newton 1982, Problems of Health Care, The British National Health Service Before 1957 1988. *Address:* 45-47 Banbury Road, Oxford, OX2 6PE, England.

WEBSTER, William Hedgcock, LL.B.; American judge and government official; b. 6 March 1924, St. Louis, Mo.; s. of Thomas M. and Katherine (Hedgcock) Webster; m. Drusilla Lane 1950 (deceased); one s. two d.; ed. Amherst Coll., Washington Univ. Law School; admitted to Mo. Bar 1949; attorney with Armstrong, Teasdale, Kramer and Vaughan, and predecessors, St. Louis 1949-50, 1952-59, partner 1956-59, 1961-70; U.S. Attorney, Eastern Dist., Mo. 1960-61; Judge U.S. Dist. Court, Eastern Mo. 1971-73, U.S. Court of Appeals 1973-78; Dir. FBI 1978-87; Dir. of Cen. Intelligence Agency (CIA) 1987-; Trustee, Washington Univ. 1974-; served as Lieut. U.S.N.R. 1943-46, 1951-52; mem. American, Fed., Mo., and St. Louis Bar assens., American Law Inst., Council 1978-, Inst. of Judicial Admin. Inc. (Pres.-elect 1982); Fellow, American Bar Foundation; Hon. LL.D. (Amherst Coll. 1975, DePauw Univ. 1978, Washington Univ. 1978, William Woods Coll. 1979 and numerous others); Wash. Univ. Distinguished Alumnus Award 1977; American Legion Distinguished Service Award 1979; Order of the Coif; St. Louis Globe-Democrat Man of the Year 1980; Washington Univ. William Greenleaf Elliot Award 1981; Riot Relief Fund of N.Y. Award 1981, Young Lawyers of the American Bar Assen. Award 1982, Fordham-Stein Award 1982, William Moss Inst.-American Univ. Award 1983. *Leisure interest:* tennis. *Address:* Central Intelligence Agency, Washington, D.C. 20505; 9409 Brooke Drive, Bethesda, Md. 20817, U.S.A. (Home).

WECHMAR, Rüdiger Baron Von; German diplomatist and journalist; b. 15 Nov. 1923, Berlin; s. of Irnfried Baron von Wechmar and Ilse Baroness von Wechmar (née von Binzer); m. 1st Rosemarie Warlimont 1947 (divorced), one s. one d.; m. 2nd Susanne Woldenga 1961, one d.; with German News Service (DPD); joined United Press 1948, Head of Bonn Bureau 1954-58; Press Attaché, German Consulate-Gen., N.Y. 1958; Head of E. European Bureau, Zweites Deutsches Fernsehen, Vienna 1963; Dir. German Information Center, New York 1968; Deputy Head of Govt. Press and Information Office 1969-, State Sec., Head of Govt. Press and Information Office, Chief Govt. Spokesman 1972-74; Perm. Rep. to UN 1974-81, Pres. UN Gen. Ass. 1980-81; Amb. to Italy 1981-83, Amb. to U.K. 1984-88; mem. Deutsche Gesellschaft für Auswärtige Politik, N.S. Round Table, Advisory Council Friedrich Naumann Foundation; Sr. Fellow Aspen Inst., mem. Exec. Council Aspen Italy; Paul Klinger Prize 1973, Dag Hammarskjöld Gold Medal 1981, UN Gold Medal 1981 and other decorations. *Publications:* numerous works and articles on foreign and UN affairs.

WECKMANN-MUÑOZ, Luis, PH.D., LL.D., M.A.; Mexican diplomatist and historian; b. 7 April 1923, Ciudad Lerdo, Durango; s. of José Bernardo Weckmann and Ana Muñoz; ed. Univ. Nacional Autónoma de México, Univs. of Paris and Calif., Inst. des Hautes Etudes Int. and Ecole des Chartes, Paris; successively Sec. of Legation and Chargé d'affaires, Czechoslovakia, Sec. of Embassy and Chargé d'affaires, France 1952-59; Dir.-Gen. for Int. Educ. Affairs and Exec. Sec.-Gen. Mexican Nat. Council for UNESCO 1959-64; Minister Plenipotentiary and Chargé d'affaires, France 1965-66; Amb. to Israel 1967-69, to Austria 1969-72, to Fed. Repub. of Germany 1973-74; Special Rep. of UN Sec.-Gen. to Iran and Iraq 1974; Special Rep. of UN Sec.-Gen. in Cyprus 1974-75; Amb. to Iran 1976-79, to UN 1979-80, to Italy 1981-86, to Belgium and the EEC 1986-88; Consul-Gen. in Rio de Janeiro 1988-; Vice-Pres. 1st Interamerican Meeting on Science and Tech., Washington; UNESCO's expert for Latin America on Cultural Exchanges. *Publications:* La Sociedad Feudal 1944, Las Bulas Alejandrinas de 1943 y la Teoría Política del Papado Medieval 1949, El Pensamiento Político Medieval y una nueva base para el Derecho Internacional 1950, Les origines des Missions Diplomatiques Permanentes 1953, Panorama de la Cultura Medieval 1962, Las Relaciones Franco-Mexicanas (1823-1885) vol. I 1961, vol. II 1963, vol. III 1972, La Herencia Medieval de México, vols. I and II 1984, Carlota de Bélgica: Correspondencia y Escritos sobre México en los archivos Europeos, 1861-1868 1989. *Leisure interest:* reading. *Address:* Consulate-General of Mexico, Praia de Bokafogo 28/301, 22.250 Rio de Janeiro, Brazil.

WEDDERBURN OF CHARLTON, Baron (Life Peer), cr. 1977; **Kenneth William Wedderburn,** M.A., LL.B., F.B.A.; British professor of law; b. 13 April 1927, London; s. of Herbert John and Mabel Ethel Wedderburn; m. 1st Nina Salaman 1951 (divorced 1961), one s. two d.; m. 2nd Dorothy Cole 1962 (divorced 1969); m. 3rd Frances Ann Knight 1969, one s.; ed. Aske's (Hatcham) Grammar School, Whitgift School, Queen's Coll., Cambridge; Lecturer in Law, Cambridge Univ. 1952-64; Fellow, Clare Coll., Cambridge; Cassel Prof. of Commercial Law, L.S.E. 1964-; Visiting Prof., Harvard Law School 1969-70, Univ. of Calif., Los Angeles 1969; Gen. Ed. Modern Law Review 1970-; mem. Civil Service Arbitration Tribunal 1973-;

Chair. Trades Union Congress Ind. Review Cttee. 1975-; Barrister at Law (Middle Temple) 1953-; Fellow, British Acad. 1981; Hon. D. Giur. (Pavìa); Chancellor's Medal for English Law (Cambridge) 1949. *Publications:* Employment Grievances and Disputes Procedures in Britain (with P. L. Davies) 1969, Cases and Materials on Labour Law 1967, The Worker and the Law 1971, 1986, Industrial Conflict—A Comparative Legal Survey (co-ed. with B. Aaron) 1972, Democrazia Politica e Democrazia Industriale 1978, co-ed. Modern Company Law (with L. C. B. Gower) 1979, Discrimination in Employment 1978, Labour Law and the Community (with W. T. Murphy) 1983, Labour Law and Industrial Relations (with R. Lewis and J. Clark) 1983, numerous articles on legal subjects. *Leisure interest:* Charlton Athletic Football Club. *Address:* London School of Economics, Aldwych, London, W.C.2 (Office); 29 Woodside Avenue, Highgate, London, N.6, England (Home). *Telephone:* 01-405 7686 (Office); 01-444 8472 (Home).

WEDGWOOD, Dame (Cicely) Veronica, O.M., D.B.E., M.A., F.R.HIST.S., F.R.S.L., F.B.A.; British author and historian; b. 20 July 1910, Stocksfield, Northumberland; d. of the late Sir Ralph Wedgwood and Iris Veronica (née Pawson); sister of Sir John Wedgwood (q.v.); ed. Lady Margaret Hall, Oxford; Pres. English Centre Int. PEN Club 1951-57; Pres. English Asscn. 1955-56; Clark Lecturer, Cambridge Univ. 1957-58; Northcliffe Lecturer, Univ. of London 1959; mem. Arts Council 1958-61, 1966-67; mem. Royal Comm. on Historical MSS 1953-77, Inst. of Advanced Study, Princeton 1952-68; Trustee Nat. Gallery, London 1963-68, 1970-76; Officer, Order of Orange-Nassau, Goethe Medal 1959; mem. American Acad.; Fellow, British Acad. 1975; Hon. D.Litt. (Univs. of Oxford, Sheffield, Keele, Sussex, Smith Coll., Liverpool and Harvard Univ.), Hon. LL.D. (Glasgow). *Publications:* Strafford 1935, The Thirty Years' War 1938, Oliver Cromwell 1939, William the Silent 1944, Velvet Studies 1946, Richelieu 1949, English Literature in the Seventeenth Century 1950, The Last of the Radicals 1951, Montrose 1952, The King's Peace 1955, The King's War 1958, Truth and Opinion 1960, Poetry and Politics Under the Stuarts 1960, Thomas Wentworth: A Revaluation 1961, The Trial of Charles I 1964, Milton and his World 1969, The Political Career of Rubens 1975, The Spoils of Time 1984, History and Hope 1987. *Leisure interests:* poetry, opera, theatre, the arts, seeing my friends. *Address:* Whitegate, Alciston, nr. Polegate, Sussex, England.

WEDGWOOD, Sir John Hamilton, Bt., T.D., F.R.S.A., F.R.G.S.; British master potter; b. 16 Nov. 1907, Newcastle upon Tyne; s. of the late Sir Ralph L. Wedgwood and Iris Veronica (née Pawson); brother of Dame Veronica Wedgwood (q.v.); m. 1st Diana Hawkshaw 1933 (died 1976), three s. (one deceased) one d.; m. 2nd Pamela Tudor Craig 1982; one step d.; ed. Winchester Coll., Trinity Coll., Cambridge, and in France, Germany, etc.; joined Josiah Wedgwood and Sons Ltd. 1931, Dir. 1935 and Deputy Chair. 1955-66; Pres. United Commercial Travellers' Asscn.; mem. British Nat. Export Council 1964-66; Chair. Anglo-American Relations Cttee., Lakenheath Airbase 1972-76; Liveryman, Worshipful Co. of Painter-Stainers; Hon. LL.D. (Birmingham), Hon. D.Litt. (William Jewell Coll., Liberty) 1983. *Leisure interests:* mountaineering (mem. Alpine Club), walking, spelaeology, foreign travel (mem. Travelers Century Club). *Address:* c/o English Speaking Union, 37 Charles Street, London, W.1; Little Gidding, Huntingdon, Cambs., England. *Telephone:* (083 23) 393 (Home).

WEE CHONG JIN, M.A.; Singapore judge; b. 28 Sept. 1917, Penang, Malaya; s. of late Wee Gim Puay and Lim Paik Yew; m. Cecilia Mary Henderson 1955; three s. one d.; ed. Penang Free School, St. John's Coll., Cambridge; called to Bar, Middle Temple, London 1938, admitted Advocate and Solicitor of Straits Settlements 1940; practised in Penang and Singapore 1940-57; Puisne Judge, Singapore 1957; Chief Justice 1963-; Acting Pres. of Singapore March-Aug. 1985; Hon. D.C.L. (Oxford) 1987. *Leisure interest:* golf. *Address:* Chief Justice's Chambers, Supreme Court, Singapore 0617, Singapore. *Telephone:* 3309901.

WEE KIM WEE; Singapore politician and diplomatist; b. 4 Nov. 1915; m. Koh Sok Hiong 1936; one s. six d.; ed. Raffles Inst.; clerk Circulation Dept. Straits Times, then Advertising Dept. then reporter, rejoined as Deputy Ed. (Singapore) 1959, covered civil war in Belgian Congo (now Zaire) and was first Singapore journalist to enter Jakarta during Confrontation 1966; joined United Press Asscn. 1941, rejoined 1945-59; served in Air Raid Precautions during attack on Malaya and Singapore; worked as clerk in Japanese mil. establishments during occupation; High Commr. to Malaysia 1973-80; Dean Diplomatic Corps, Kuala Lumpur 1978-80; mem. Singapore Del. to UN Gen. Ass. 1977; Amb. to Japan 1980-84, to Repub. of Korea 1981-84; Chair. Singapore Broadcasting Corpn. 1984-85; Pres. Repub. of Singapore Aug. 1985-; fmr. Pres. Singapore Badminton Asscn., Chair. Singapore Anti-Tuberculosis Asscn.; fmr. mem. Rent Control Bd., Film Appeal Cttee., Land Acquisition Bd., Bd. of Visiting Justices, Nat. Theatre Trust; J.P. 1966; Public Service Star 1963, Meritorious Service Medal 1979; Jr. Singles Badminton Champion of Singapore 1937. *Address:* Office of the President, Istana, Singapore 0923, Singapore.

WEEDON, Basil Charles Leicester, C.B.E., F.R.S., D.SC., F.R.I.C.; British chemist and university administrator; b. 18 July 1923, London; s. of the late Charles William Weedon; m. Barbara Mary Dawe 1959; one s. one d.; ed. Wandsworth School, Imperial Coll. of Science and Tech., Univ. of London; Research Chemist, ICI Ltd. (Dyestuffs Div.) 1945-47; Lecturer in Organic Chem., Imperial Coll. of Science and Tech. 1947-55, Reader 1955-60; Prof. of Organic Chem., Queen Mary Coll., Univ. of London

1960-75; Vice-Chancellor, Univ. of Nottingham 1976-88; Chair. Food Additives and Contaminants Cttee. 1968-83, Nat. Stone Centre 1985-; Scientific Ed., Pure and Applied Chemistry 1960-75; mem. EEC Scientific Cttee. for Food 1974-81; Fellow Queen Mary Coll. 1984; Hon. D.Tech. (Brunel) 1975; Hon. LL.D. (Nottingham) 1988; Meldola Medal, Royal Inst. of Chem.; Tilden Lecturer of Chem. Soc. *Publications:* numerous papers in scientific journals, mainly in Journal of the Chemical Society. *Address:* (from Sept. 1988) Sheepwash Grange, Heighington Road, Canwick, Lincoln, LN4 2RJ, England. *Telephone:* (0522) 22488.

WEESE, Harry M.; American architect; b. 30 June 1915, Evanston, Ill.; s. of Harry Ernest Weese and Marjorie Mohr Weese; m. Kate Baldwin 1945; three d.; ed. Yale Univ. School of Architecture, M.I.T., Cranbrook Acad. of Art; Research Asst. Bemis Housing Foundation, M.I.T. (prefabricated and low-cost housing) 1939; Principal, Baldwin & Weese (architects) 1940-42; U.S. Navy 1942-46; Sr. Designer, Chicago office Skidmore, Owings & Merrill 1946-47; ind. practice 1947-; Fellow, A.I.A. and Pres. Chicago Chapter 1975; Co-Chair. Mayor Byrne's Architects' Advisory Cttee., Chicago 1979-; mem. Nat. Acad. of Design, Nat. Council on the Arts, Advisory Bd., Nat. Asscn. of Housing and Redevt. Officials 1985-, Urban Design Review Bd., San José Redevt. Agency 1984-, Design Arts Cttee., Nat. Council on Arts 1984-; Publr. Inland Architect Magazine; fmr. mem. Pres.'s Citizens' Advisory Cttee. on Environmental Quality; Total Design Award, Ill. Chapter, A.I.A. 1975, Firm of the Year Award, A.I.A. 1978, Distinguished Chapter Award, Chicago Chapter, A.I.A. 1981, Diplôme de Lauréat, Biennale Mondiale de l'Architecture, Union of Architects, Bulgaria 1983, Chicago Architecture Award, Architectural Magazine and Ill. Council A.I.A. 1987. *Principal projects:* U.S. Embassy, Accra, Ghana, Hyde Park Redevelopment Project, Chicago, Arena Stage, Washington D.C., Elvehjem Art Center, Univ. of Wis., Milwaukee Center for the Performing Arts, Wis., Metro Rapid Rail Transit System, Washington D.C., IBM Building, Milwaukee, Time & Life Building, Chicago, Technical Center, Cummins Engine Co., Columbus, Ind., Staff Housing Air India, Bombay, First Baptist Church, Columbus, Ind., Crown Center Hotel, Kansas City, Physical Education Building, Educ. and Communications Building, Univ. of Ill. Chicago Circle Campus, U.S. Courthouse Annex, Chicago, Fine Arts Center, Carleton Coll., Social Sciences Campus, New York State Univ., Buffalo-Amherst Campus, Student and Fine Arts Centers, Drake Univ., Terman Eng. Center, Stanford Univ., Calif.; Loop Subway System Study, CTA Determination of System and Design Elements (with American Bechtel) for Chicago Central Transportation District; Dade County Transit System, Miami, Fla. (with Kaiser Eng); Performing Arts Center; Grand Rapids, Mich.; New Town, Riyadh Int. Airport, Saudi Arabia; restoration of Adler-Sullivan Auditorium Theater, Chicago; U.S. Embassy Staff Housing, Tokyo, Wolf Point Landings, Chicago; 200 Wacker Drive, Chicago; Buffalo, N.Y. Rapid Transit System, Metro Rail Project, Los Angeles; Master Plan and Architectural Design, Chinatown, Chicago; Renovation and Master Plan, Field Museum of Natural History, Chicago; Master Plan, Fed. Triangle, Washington, D.C.; Dallas Area Rapid Transit Project, Tex.; Renovation and Master Plan, Henry Ives Cobb Bldg., Newberry Library, Chicago; Printing House Row, Chicago; Oak Park Village Hall, Ill.; First Nat. Bank in Albuquerque, N.M.; Corp. HQ, Union Underwear Co., Bowling Green, Ky.; Navy Pier Marina, Chicago; St. Louis Customs House and Post Office Renovation, Mo.; Harwick Bldg., Mayo Clinic, Rochester, Minn.; Chicago and Northwestern Railroad Station Trainshed, Chicago; 411 E. Wis. Office Bldg., Milwaukee; S. Cove Marina and Condominiums, New Buffalo, Mich.; Swiss Grand Hotel, Chicago *Leisure interests:* sailing, skiing, tennis. *Address:* 10 West Hubbard Street, Chicago, Ill. 60610 (Office); 314 West Willow Street, Chicago, Ill. 60610, U.S.A. (Home). *Telephone:* 467-7030 (Office); MI-2-1498 (Home).

WĘGRZYN, Stefan, D.ENG.; Polish scientist; b. 20 May 1925, Cracow; s. of Jan Węgrzyn and Maria Wilgocka; ed. Silesian Technical Univ., Gliwice; Asst. Electrical Dept. Silesian Tech. Univ. 1949, Asst. Prof. 1954-61, Prof. 1961-; Dir. Inst. of Complex Control Systems, Silesian Tech. Univ. 1968-72, Dir. Inst. of Informatics 1972-; Deputy Dir. for Scientific Affairs, Inst. of Automation, Polish Acad. of Sciences 1953-69, then Head Inst. of Complex Automation Systems, Gliwice 1968-; corresp. mem. Polish Acad. of Sciences 1964-73, mem. 1973-, mem. Presidium 1974-81, 1983-, fmr. Deputy Dir. Centre of Scientific Research, Polish Acad. of Sciences, Katowice Voivodship; mem. Consultative Council attached to Chair. of State Council 1986-; Commdr.'s, Officer's and Kt.'s Cross of Order Polonia Restituta; State Prize 1966, 1976 (collective 1st class); Order of Labour Ensign 1985, Dr. h.c. (Lille) 1973, (Univ. of Sherbrooke, Canada) 1977; Chevalier, Ordre des Palmes académiques 1978, Officier 1984. *Publications:* Rachunek operatorowy 1955, Podstawy automatyki 1963, Calcul opérationel en électrotechnique 1967, Introduction à l'étude de la stabilité dans les espaces métriques 1971, Podstawy informatyki 1981. *Address:* Politechnika Śląska, 44-100 Gliwice, Pstrowskiego 16 (Office); Konarskiego 11 m. 3, 44-100 Gliwice, Poland (Home). *Telephone:* 314673 (Office); 310110 (Home).

WEHNER, Herbert; German journalist and politician; b. 11 July 1906, Dresden; s. of Richard and Antonie (née Diener) Wehner; m. 1st Charlotte Clausen (died 1979); m. 2nd 1983; ed. Realschule; business apprenticeship and student of economics; mem. Saxony Prov. Parl. 1930-32; resistance movement 1933; emigrated to various countries including U.S.S.R. and Sweden 1935-46; later Ed., Hamburg; Chair. Hamburg Union Sozialdemokratische Partei Deutschlands (SPD), Deputy Chair. Federal SPD 1958-73, Chair. Parl. Party 1969-83; mem. Bundestag 1949-83; Minister of All-German Affairs 1966-69; mem. SPD 1923-27, German Communist Party (KPD) 1927-46, SPD 1946-; Grosskreuz VO 1973, Wenzel Jaksch Memorial Prize 1979, Polish Distinguished Service Cross 1984, Hon. Citizen of Hamburg 1986. *Publications:* Sozialdemokratie in Europa 1965, Wandel und Bewährung 1968, Zeugnis 1982. *Leisure interests:* books, music, gardening, pipe collecting. *Address:* c/o Sozialdemokratische Partei Deutschlands, 5300 Bonn, 12 Deutscher Bundestag Görrestrasse, Federal Republic of Germany.

WEI BAOSHAN; Chinese diplomatist; counsellor Embassy, Mongolia 1964-66; Chargé d'affaires a.i. Algeria 1971, Kenya 1972; Amb. to Togo 1973-74, to Cameroon 1974-81, to Argentina 1982.

WEI CHUNSHU; Chinese party and government official; b. 3 March 1922, Xang Zhou County, Guangxi; m. Yao Shaoying; two s. two d.; Sec. CCP Cttee., Nanning City, Mayor of Nanning 1980; Deputy, 6th NPC 1983; Deputy Sec. CPC 4th Autonomous Regional Cttee., Guangxi 1983-; Chair. People's Govt. of Guangxi Zhuang Autonomous Region 1983-; mem. Presidium 6th NPC 1986-; mem. CCP Cen. Advisory Comm. 1987-. *Leisure interests:* running, swimming. *Address:* Office of the Chairman of Guangxi People's Government, Nanning, People's Republic of China. *Telephone:* 27778.

WEI GUOQING, Gen.; Chinese army officer and party official; b. 1913, Donglan, Guangxi; Regimental Commdr. 1933; on Long March 1934-35; served successively in Red Army as Co., Battalian and Regt. Commdr., then Deputy Head, 1st Branch, Chinese People's Anti-Japanese Mil. and Political Coll., Political Commissar then Commdr. 9th Brigade of New Fourth Army, Deputy Commdr. 4th Div. 1929-45; served as Commdr. and Political Commissar of 2nd Column, E. China Field Army and Commdr. Northern Jiangsu Army 1946-49; Political Commissar 10th Army Corps, 3rd Field Army, PLA 1949; Head, Mil. Advisory Group to Viet-Nam; First Sec. CCP Guangxi Zhuang Cttee. 1961-68; Chair. Guangxi People's Govt. 1958-68; Second Sec. Cen.-South Bureau, CCP Cen. Cttee. 1966; Political Commissar Guangzhou Mil. Region, PLA 1967-74, First Political Commissar 1974-78; Dir. Gen. Political Dept., PLA; mem. Standing Cttee. of Mil. Comm. of CCP Cen. Cttee. and Deputy Sec.-Gen. of Comm.; mem. Standing Cttee. 1st NPC, Vice-Chair. 4th, 5th Nat. Cttee. of CPPCC; alt. mem., then mem. 8th CCP Cen. Cttee., mem. 9th Cen. Cttee., mem. Political Bureau of 10th, 11th and 12th Cen. Cttees. *Address:* c/o Standing Committee, National People's Congress, Beijing, People's Republic of China.

WEI JIANXING; Chinese state official; alt. mem. CCP Cen. Cttee. 1982-85, mem. 1985-; Deputy Sec. CCP Cttee., Harbin Municipality 1982-85; Mayor of Harbin 1983-85; Minister of Supervision July 1987-; Head, Org. Dept., CCP Cen. Cttee. 1985. *Address:* Office of the Mayor, Harbin, Heilongjiang, People's Republic of China.

WEI JINSHAN; Chinese army officer; Deputy for PLA to 5th NPC 1978, 6th NPC 1983; alt. mem. 12th CCP Cen. Cttee. 1982, mem. 1985, mem. 13th Cen. Cttee. 1987-; Dir. Political Dept., Nanjing Mil. Region 1983-85; Deputy Political Commissar, PLA Navy 1985-. *Address:* Nanjing Military Region Headquarters, Nanjing, Jiangsu, People's Republic of China.

WEI MINGYI; Chinese state official; Vice-Minister of Electronics Industry 1982-; alt. mem. 12th CCP Cen. Cttee. 1982; Vice-Pres. China Int. Trust and Investment Corpn. 1985-; Chair. Bd. of Dirs., China Nat. Electronics Import and Export Corpn. 1984-. *Address:* Ministry of Electronics Industry, Beijing, People's Republic of China. *Telephone:* 810731.

WEI XINGJIAN; Chinese party and trade union official; b. 1931; ed. Dalien Coll. of Eng. and in U.S.S.R.; factory head and Sr. Engineer, Manchuria Light Alloy Processing Factory 1978-80; mem. 12th Nat. Party Congress 1980; Deputy Party Sec. Harbin 1981; alt. mem. CCP 12th Cen. Cttee. 1982, mem. 1985-; Mayor of Harbin 1983-; Deputy Chair. and Secr. Sec. of All-China Fed. of Trade Unions; Dept. Deputy Head of CCP Cen. Organizational Dept. 1984-85, Head 1985. *Address:* All-China Federation of Trade Unions, Beijing, People's Republic of China.

WEI WEI; Chinese author; b. 1920, Zhengzhou, Henan; joined CCP 1937; fought in Sino-Japanese War; mem. Chinese People's Volunteers in Korea 1950; Leading mem. Soc. for Study of Int. Reportage Writing 1980-; Vice-Pres. China-Korea Friendship Assen. 1984-. *Works include:* Those Most to be Loved 1951, The East (Mao Dun Literature Prize 1982).

WEI WENE; Chinese papercut artist; b. 1963, Fengning, Hebei. *Address:* Fengning Recreation Centre, Fengning Co. Hebei, People's Republic of China.

WEI YONGQING; Chinese diplomatist; b. 11 Jan. 1923, Beijing; m. Wang Zhan 1949; two s. one d.; Amb. to Kenya 1984-86; Permanent Rep. to UN Environment Programme 1985-87. *Address:* Ministry of Foreign Affairs, Beijing, People's Republic of China.

WEI YUNG, PH.D.; Chinese politician; b. 5 May 1937, Hupeh; m. Serena Ning Sun; two d.; ed. Nat. Chengchi Univ., Taipei, Univ. of Oregon U.S.A.; Instructor to Asst. Prof., Dept. of Political Science, Univ. of Nevada 1966-68; Asst. Prof., Dept of Political Science, Memphis State Univ. 1968-69; Visiting Scholar, Survey Research Centre, Univ. of Mich. 1969;

Assoc. Prof. of Political Science, Memphis State Univ. 1969-74; Visiting Assoc. Prof., Nat. Chengchi Univ. 1970-71; Prof. and Chair. of Graduate Program in Political Science, Memphis State Univ. 1974; Nat. Fellowship, Hoover Inst., Stanford Univ. 1974-75; Deputy Dir. Inst. of Int. Relations 1975-76; Eisenhower Exchange Fellow 1977; Chair. Research, Devt. and Evaluation Comm., Exec. Yuan, Taiwan 1976; Adjunct Prof., Dept. of Political Science, Nat. Taiwan Univ. and Nat. Chengchi Univ.; mem. Cen. Planning Cttee., Kuomintang. *Publications:* The Nature and Methods of the Social Sciences, Taiwan: A Modernizing Chinese Society, Communist China; A System-Functional Reader; Political Development in the Republic of China on Taiwan; Analysis and Projections; A Methodological Critique of Current Studies on Chinese Political Culture; Republic of China in 1970s; Striving for A Future of Growth, Equity, and Security, Policy Planning of the Republic of China in the 1980s. *Address:* 9, Alley 14, Lane 283, Roosevelt Road, Sect. 3, Taipei; Apartment 5B 1-1, Lane 21, Lishui Street, Taipei 106, Taiwan.

WEICKER, Lowell Palmer, Jr., LL.B.; American senator; b. 16 May 1931, Paris, France; s. of Lowell Palmer Weicker and Mary (Bickford) Paulsen; m. 1st Camille Di Lorenzo Butler; five s. three d.; m. 2nd Claudia Testa Ingram 1984; ed. Lawrenceville School, Yale Univ. and Univ. of Virginia; State Rep. in Conn. Gen. Assembly 1963-69; U.S. Rep., Fourth Congressional District, Conn. 1969-71; Senator from Conn. 1971-89; 1st Selectman of Greenwich 1964-68; mem. Select Cttee. for Investigation of the Watergate Case 1973; Senate Appropriations Cttee., Senate Labor and Human Resources Cttee., Chair. Senate Small Business Cttee., Sub-cttee. on State, Justice, Commerce, the Judiciary and related agencies, Senate Energy and Natural Resources Cttee.; Republican. *Leisure interests:* tennis, scuba, history.

WEIDENBAUM, Murray Lew, M.A., PH.D.; American economist and government official; b. 10 Feb. 1927, Bronx, New York; s. of David and Rose (Warshaw) Weidenbaum; m. Phyllis Green 1954; one s. two d.; ed. City Coll. New York, Columbia Univ., New York, and Princeton Univ.; Fiscal Economist, Budget Bureau, Washington 1949-57; Corpn. Economist, Boeing Co., Seattle 1958-62; Sr. Economist, Stanford Research Inst., Palo Alto, Calif. 1962-63; mem. Faculty, Washington Univ., St. Louis, Mo. 1964-; Dir. of Center for Study of American Business at Washington Univ. 1975-81, 1982-; Prof. and Chair. Dept. of Econs. 1966-69, Mallinckrodt Prof. 1971-; Asst. Sec. for Econ. Policy, Treasury Dept., Washington 1969-71; Head, Council of Econ. Advisers, U.S. Govt. 1981-82; Chair. Research Advisory Cttee., St. Louis Regional Industrial Devt. Corpn. 1965-69; Exec. Sec. Pres.'s Cttee. on Econ. Impact of Defense and Disarmament 1964; mem. U.S. Financial Investment Advisory Panel 1970-72; mem. Pres.'s Econ. Policy Advisory Bd. 1982-, Bd. of Dirs. Contel Corpn. 1986-, Harbour Group Ltd., May Dept. Stores Co. 1982; consultant to various firms and insts.; Fellow, Nat. Asscn. of Business Economists; Treasury Dept. Alexander Hamilton Medal 1971; Distinguished Writer Award, Georgetown Univ. 1975, Free Market Hall of Fame 1983. *Publications:* Federal Budgeting 1964, Economic Impact of the Vietnam War 1967, Modern Public Sector 1969, Economics of Peacetime Defense 1974, Government-Mandated Price Increases 1975, The Future of Business Regulation 1979, Business, Government, and the Public 1986; articles in economic journals. *Address:* Center for the Study of American Business, Washington University, St. Louis, Mo. 63130; 6231 Rosebury Avenue, St. Louis, Mo. 63105, U.S.A. (Home). *Telephone:* (314) 889-5662.

WEIDENFELD, Baron (Life Peer), cr. 1976, of Chelsea in Greater London; **Arthur George Weidenfeld,** Kt; British publisher; b. 13 Sept. 1919, Vienna, Austria; s. of the late Max Weidenfeld and Rosa (née Eisenstein-ish Horowitz) Weidenfeld; m. 1st Jane Sieff 1952, one d.; m. 2nd Barbara Skelton Connolly 1956 (divorced 1961); m. 3rd Sandra Payson Meyer 1966 (divorced 1976); ed. Piaristen Gymnasium, Vienna, Univ. of Vienna and Konsular Akademie; came to England 1938; BBC Monitoring Service 1939-42; BBC News Commentator on European Affairs on BBC Empire and N. American service 1942-46; Foreign Affairs columnist, News Chronicle 1943-44; Political Adviser and Chief of Cabinet of Pres. Weizmann of Israel 1949-50; founder of Contact Magazine 1945, Weidenfeld & Nicolson Ltd 1948; Chair. Weidenfeld & Nicolson Ltd. 1948-, Wheatland Corpn., N.Y. 1985-, Grove Press, N.Y. 1985-, Wheatland Foundation, San Francisco and New York 1985-, J.M. Dent and Everyman Library 1987-; Vice-Chair. Bd. of Govs., Ben Gurion Univ. of the Negev, Israel; Gov. of Tel-Aviv Univ., Weizmann Inst., Bezalel Art Acad., Jerusalem; Pres. British-Israel Public Affairs Cttee.; Vice-Chair. Zionist Fed. of G.B.; Dir., South Bank Bd. 1986-, English Nat. Opera 1988-, and holder of many other public posts; Trustee Nat. Portrait Gallery 1988-; Hon. Ph.D. (Ben Gurion Univ.). *Publication:* The Goebbels Experiment 1943. *Leisure interests:* opera, travel. *Address:* 9 Chelsea Embankment, London, S.W.3, England.

WEIDENFELD, Werner, DR.PHIL.; German professor of political science; b. 2 July 1947, Cochem; s. of Dr. Josef and Maria (née Walther) Weidenfeld; m. Gabriele Kokott-Weidenfeld 1976; ed. Univ. of Bonn; Prof. of Political Science, Univ. of Mainz 1976-; Assoc. Prof., Sorbonne, Paris 1986-88; Co-ordinator for German-American Co-operation 1987-. *Publications:* Die England politik Gustav Stresemanns 1972, Konrad Adenauer und Europa 1976, Europa 2000 1980, Die Frage nach der Einheit der deutschen Nation 1981, Die Identität der Deutschen 1983, Die Bilanz der Europäischer

Integration 1984, Nachdenken über Deutschland 1985, 30 Jahre EG 1987, Geschichtsbewusstsein der Deutschen 1987, Jahrbuch der Europäischen Integration (Ed.). *Address:* Institut für Politikwissenschaft, Universität Mainz, Saarstrasse 21, D-6500 Mainz (Office); D-5400 Koblenz, Layer Strasse 42, Federal Republic of Germany (Home). *Telephone:* 06131/392150 (Office); 0261/43291 (Home).

WEIDLINGER, Paul, M.S.; American engineer; b. 22 Dec. 1914, Budapest, Hungary; s. of Andrew and Juliette Weidlinger; m. Solveig Højberg 1964; two s. one d.; ed. Tech. Inst., Brno, Czechoslovakia, Swiss Polytechnic Inst., Zürich; Chief Engineer, Bureau of Reclamation, La Paz, Bolivia 1939–42; Prof. of Eng., San Andrés Univ. La Paz 1939–42; went to U.S.A. 1944, naturalized 1949; Chief Engineer, Atlas Aircraft, New York 1944–46; Dir. of Div., Nat. Housing Agency, Washington, D.C. 1946–47; Engineer, private practice 1947–; Sr. partner Weidlinger Assocs., New York 1949–; Visiting Lecturer, Harvard Univ., M.I.T.; mem. Scientific Advisory Bd., U.S.A.F.; Consultant to Rand Corpn.; Fellow of Hudson Inst., American Soc. of Civil Engineers (A.S.C.E.), American Concrete Inst., Int. Assen. of Bridge and Structural Engineers, New York Acad. of Sciences, A.I.A.A., Nat. Acad. of Eng.; J. R. Croes Medal 1963, Moisseiff Award 1975 (both A.S.C.E.), Ernest E. Howard Award (A.S.C.E.) 1985. *Publications:* articles in journals. *Address:* 333 Seventh Avenue, New York, N.Y. 10001 (Office); 301 East 47th Street, New York, N.Y. 10017, U.S.A. (Home). *Telephone:* (212) 563 5200.

WEIGHT, Carel Victor Morlais, C.B.E., R.A.; British artist; b. 10 Sept. 1908, London; s. of Sidney L. Weight and Blanche H. C. Weight; ed. Sloane School and Goldsmiths' Coll. Univ. of London; first exhibited Royal Acad. 1931; first one-man show, Cooling Galleries 1934; Retrospective Exhbn. Royal Acad. 1982; many other one-man and retrospective exhbns.; has contributed to many group exhbns. of contemporary British art in Britain and abroad including U.S.S.R. 1957; works in many public and pvt. collections including Tate Gallery, Victoria & Albert Museum, Melbourne Art Gallery, Nat. Gallery, Adelaide etc.; official war artist 1945; teacher of painting, Royal Coll. of Art 1947, Fellow 1956, Prof. of Painting 1957–73, Prof. Emer. 1973–, Sr. Fellow 1984–; mem. London Group 1950, Fine Arts Panel, Arts Council 1951–57, Rome Faculty of Art 1960; Trustee, Royal Acad. 1975–84; Hon. D. Univ. (Heriot-Watt) 1983; Hon. mem. Royal Soc. of British Artists 1972, Royal Soc. of Painters in Water Colours 1985. *Leisure interests:* music, reading. *Address:* 33 Spencer Road, London, S.W.18, England. *Telephone:* 01-228 6928.

WEIKL, Bernd; Austrian baritone; b. 29 July 1942, Vienna; ed. Mainz Conservatoire and Hochschule für Musik, Hanover; mem. Hamburg State Opera 1973–; guest artist, Bayreuth Festivals 1973–75. *Address:* c/o Lies Askonas Ltd., 186 Drury Lane, London, WC2B 5QD, England. *Telephone:* 01-405 1808.

WEIL, Raymond; French professor; b. 29 Oct. 1923, Biarritz; s. of Andre Weil and Lucie Chimenes; m. Dr Marise Heimann 1952; one s. two d.; ed. Lycée de Toulouse and Univs. of Toulouse and Paris; Prof., Univ. of Montpellier 1959, Univ. of Dijon 1961, Univ. of Paris 1967, Univ. of Paris-Sorbonne 1973–; Dir. Inst. de grec de la Sorbonne 1981–85; mem. Acad. des inscriptions et belles lettres. *Publications:* books on art and on Ancient Greek and Latin language and literature. *Leisure interest:* walking. *Address:* 15, rue Michel-Ange, 75016 Paris, France.

WEILL, Sanford I., B.A.; American banker; b. 16 March 1933, New York; s. of Max and Etta (née Kalika) Weill; m. Joan Mosher 1955; one s., one d., ed. Peekskill Mil. Acad., Cornell Univ., School Business and Public Admin.; C.E.O. Carter, Berlind and Weill (now Shearson/American Express Inc.) New York 1960–, Pres. and C.E.O. 1978–85; Dir. Arlen Realty and Devt. Corpn.; Terra Nova Insurance Co. 1984–; mem. Midwest Stock Exchange Bd.; Assoc. mem. New York Stock Exchange. *Address:* Andrew Carnegie Society, 767 Fifth Avenue, New York, N.Y. 10022, U.S.A.

WEILLER, Paul-Louis; French engineer; b. 29 Sept. 1893, Paris; s. of Lazare and Alice (née Javal) Weiller; m. 1st Princess Alexandra Ghika (deceased), one d.; m. 2nd Aliki Diplarakos 1932, one s.; ed. Lycée Carnot, Paris, Ecole centrale des arts et manufactures; Asst. Dir. Soc. des moteurs Gnome et Rhône 1922–40, Cie. Int. de navigation aérienne (Cidna); fmr. Dir. Air France; Free mem. Inst. de France (Acad. des Beaux-Arts) 1965–, Pres. 1980, Pres. Acad. des Beaux-Arts 1980; Grand Officier, Légion d'honneur, Croix de guerre, Médaille de la Résistance, Commdr. des Arts et des Lettres, Grand Cross of Order of Malta, Military Cross, Kt. of the Crown of Italy, Commdr. de Saint-Maurice et Lazare, of Christ (Portugal), of St. Sava (Yugoslavia), Kt. of the White Eagle (Yugoslavia), Officier de Saint-Alexandre (Bulgaria). *Leisure interests:* tennis, swimming, skiing, water-skiing. *Address:* 14 rue du Bois-de-Boulogne, 92200 Neuilly-sur-Seine, France; 19 quai des Bergues, CH 1201 Geneva, Switzerland (Home).

WEINBERG, Alvin M., S.M., PH.D.; American physicist and scientific administrator; b. 20 April 1915, Chicago, Ill.; s. of Jacob and Emma Levinson Weinberg; m. 1st Margaret Despres 1940 (died 1969), two s.; m. 2nd Gene Kellerman 1974; ed. Univ. of Chicago; Biophysics research Univ. of Chicago 1939–42; Hanford reactor design Univ. of Chicago Metallurgical Laboratory 1942–45; Section Chief Physics Div., Oak Ridge Nat. Laboratory 1945–47; Dir. Physics Div. 1947–48; Research Dir. 1948–55; Dir. Oak Ridge Nat.

Lab. 1955–73; Dir. Office of Energy Research and Devt., Fed. Energy Office 1974, Inst. for Energy Analysis 1975–85 (Distinguished Fellow 1985–); mem. Scientific Advisory Bd. to the Air Force 1955–59; mem. President's Science Advisory Cttee. 1960–63; Chair. Advisory Cttee. on Carbon Dioxide, Dept. of Energy 1978–80; Fellow, American Nuclear Soc., American Physical Soc.; mem. American Acad. of Arts and Sciences, Nat. Acad. of Eng., N.A.S., Cttee. on Science and Public Policy of Nat. Acad. of Sciences 1963–66, Council of N.A.S. 1967–70, American Philosophical Soc.; Foreign mem. Royal Netherlands Acad. of Sciences; mem. Pres. Nixon's Task Force on Science Policy 1969, Nat. Cancer Plan Evaluation Cttee. 1972; Regents' Lecturer Univ. of Calif., San Diego 1980; co-recipient Atoms for Peace Award 1960, Ernest O. Lawrence Memorial Award of Atomic Energy Comm. 1960, Univ. of Chicago Alumni Medal 1966, Heinrich Hertz Energy Prize 1975, New York Acad. of Sciences Award 1976, Enrico Fermi Award 1980, Harvey Prize 1982; contributions to nuclear tech. in reactor theory, reactor design, breeder reactor systems, implications of nuclear energy; formulation of science policy; energy supply and demand. *Publications:* The Physical Theory of Neutron Chain Reactors (with Eugene P. Wigner) 1958, Reflections on Big Science 1967, Continuing the Nuclear Dialogue 1985, The Nuclear Connection (Co-Ed.) 1985, Strategic Defenses and Arms Control (Co-Ed.) 1987. *Leisure interests:* piano, tennis, swimming. *Address:* Institute for Energy Analysis, Oak Ridge Associated Universities, P.O. Box 117, Oak Ridge, Tenn. 37830 (Office); 111 Moylan Lane, Oak Ridge, Tenn. 37830, U.S.A. (Home). *Telephone:* (615) 576-3171 (Office); (615) 483-6045 (Home).

WEINBERG, Felix Jiri, D.SC., PH.D., F.R.S.; British professor of combustion physics; b. 2 April 1928; s. of Victor Weinberg and Nelly Marie (née Altschul); m. Jill Nesta Piggott 1954; three s.; ed. Univ. of London; Lecturer, Dept. of Chemical Eng. and Chemical Tech., Imperial Coll., London 1956–60, Sr. Lecturer 1960–64, Reader in Combustion 1964–67, Prof. of Combustion Physics 1967–; Dir. Combustion Inst. 1978–88, Chair. British Section 1975–80; Founder and 1st Chair. Combustion Physics Group, Inst. of Physics 1974–77, Rep. on Watt Cttee. on Energy 1979–84; mem. Council, Inst. of Energy 1976–79; M.R.I.; C.Eng.; F.Inst.P.; F.I.E.; Combustion Inst. Silver Combustion Medal 1972, Bernard Lewis Gold Medal 1980, Royal Soc. Rumford Medal 1988. *Publications:* Optics of Flames 1963, Electrical Aspects of Combustion 1969, Combustion Inst. European Symposium (ed.) 1973, Advanced Combustion Methods 1986; over 150 scientific papers. *Leisure interests:* eastern philosophies, travel. *Address:* Imperial College, London, SW7 2BY (Office); 59 Vicarage Road, London, SW14 8RY, England (Home). *Telephone:* 01-589 5111 (Office); 01-876 1540 (Home).

WEINBERG, Robert A., PH.D.; American professor of biochemistry; b. 11 Nov. 1942, Pittsburgh, Pa.; s. of Dr. Fritz E. and Lore W. (née Reichhardt) Weinberg; m. Amy Shulman 1976; two c.; ed. M.I.T.; Instructor in Biology, Stillman Coll., Ala. 1965–66; Fellow Weizmann Inst., Israel 1969–70; Fellow Salk Inst., Calif. 1970–72; Research Assoc. Fellow M.I.T. 1972–73, Asst. Prof., Dept. of Biology and Center for Cancer Research 1973–76, Assoc. Prof. 1976–82, Prof. and mem. Whitehead Inst. for Biomedical Research 1982–; mem. N.A.S.; numerous awards including Hon. Sc.D. (Northwestern Univ., Ill.) 1984. *Leisure interests:* house building, gardening, genealogy. *Address:* Whitehead Institute, 9 Cambridge Center, Cambridge, Mass. 02142, U.S.A. *Telephone:* (617) 258 5159.

WEINBERG, Steven, PH.D.; American physicist; b. 3 May 1933, New York; s. of Fred and Eva Weinberg; m. Louise Goldwasser 1954; one d.; ed. Cornell Univ., Univ. of Copenhagen and Princeton Univ.; Columbia Univ. 1957–59; Lawrence Radiation Lab. 1959–60; Univ. of Calif. (Berkeley) 1960–69; Prof. of Physics, Mass. Inst. of Technology 1969–73; Higgins Prof. of Physics, Harvard Univ. 1973–83; Sr. Scientist, Smithsonian Astrophysical Observatory 1973–83; Josey Regental Prof. of Science, Univ. of Texas, Austin 1982–; Co-Ed. Cambridge Univ. Press Monographs on Mathematical Physics 1978; Dir. Jerusalem Winter School of Theoretical Physics 1983–; mem. A.P. Sloan Foundation Science Book Cttee. 1985–, Einstein Archives Int. Advisory Bd. 1988–, American Acad. of Arts and Sciences 1968–, N.A.S. 1972–, Council for Foreign Relations, President's Cttee. on the Nat. Medal of Science 1979–80, Royal Soc. 1982–, American Philosophical Soc. 1983–; fmr. mem. Council, American Physical Soc., Int. Astronomical Union, Philosophical Soc. of Tex.; Loeb Lecturer, Harvard Univ. and Visiting Lecturer M.I.T. 1966–69, Richtmeyer Lecturer of American Assen. of Physics Teachers 1974, Scott Lecturer, Cavendish Lab. 1975, Silliman Lecturer, Yale 1977, Lauritsen Lecturer, Calif. Inst. of Tech. 1979, Bethe Lecturer, Cornell Univ. 1979, Harris Lecturer, Northwestern Univ. 1982, Cherwell-Simon Lecturer, Oxford Univ. 1983, Bampton Lecturer, Columbia Univ. 1983, Hilldale Lecturer, Univ. of Wisconsin 1985, Brickweede Lecturer, Johns Hopkins Univ. 1986, Dirac Lecturer, Univ. of Cambridge 1986; Hon. D.Sc. (Knox Coll.) 1978, (Chicago, Yale, Rochester) 1979, (City Univ., New York) 1980, (Clark Univ.) 1982, (Dartmouth) 1984, (Weizmann Inst.) 1985; Hon. D.Litt. (Washington Coll.) 1985; J. R. Oppenheimer Prize 1973, Dannie Heinemann Mathematical Physics Prize 1977, American Inst. of Physics-U.S. Steel Foundation Science Writing Award 1977, Elliott Cresson Medal, Franklin Inst. 1979, Joint Winner, Nobel Prize for Physics 1979. *Publications:* Gravitation and Cosmology 1972, The First Three Minutes 1977, The Discovery of Subatomic Particles 1982, Elementary Particles and the Laws of Physics (with R. P. Feynman) 1987, and over

200 articles. *Leisure interest:* medieval history. *Address:* Department of Physics, University of Texas, Austin, Tex. 78712, U.S.A. *Telephone:* (512) 4714394.

WEINBERGER, Caspar Willard, A.B., M.C.L.; American government official; b. 18 Aug. 1917, San Francisco; s. of Herman and Cerise Carpenter (Hampson) Weinberger; m. Jane Dalton 1942; one s. one d.; ed. Harvard Coll. and Law School; served with AUS 1941–45; with Heller, Ehrman, White and McAuliffe 1947–69, partner 1959–69; mem. Calif. State Legislature 1952–58; Vice-Chair. Calif. Republican Central Cttee. 1960–62, Chair. 1962–64; Chair. Calif. Govt. Cttee. on Org. and Econ. 1967–68; Dir. of Finance, Calif. 1968–69; Chair. Fed. Trade Comm. 1970; Deputy Dir. Office of Man. and Budget 1970–72, Dir. 1972–73; Counsellor to Pres. 1973; Sec. of Health, Educ. and Welfare 1973–75; Sec. of Defense 1981–87; specialist in int. law and finance, Rogers & Wells, Washington 1988–; Publr. Forbes Magazine 1988–; Distinguished Visiting Prof. Inst. for Advanced Studies in the Humanities, Edin. Univ. 1988; Gen. Counsel for the Bechtel Group of Cos. including Bechtel Power Corpn. and Bechtel Inc. 1975–80; Chair. Pres.'s Cttee. on Mental Retardation 1973–75; fmr. Dir. Pepsico Corpn., Quaker Oats Corpn., American Ditchley Foundation, Yosemite Inst.; fmr. Treas. Episcopal Diocese; fmr. Pres. Nat. Trustees of the Nat. Symphony, Washington, D.C.; fmr. mem. American Assembly Bd. of Trustees, Trilateral Comm.; American Bar Asscn., State Bar Calif.; Harvard Univ. John F. Kennedy School of Govt. Medal 1982, 1986; Hon. G.B.E 1988; Grand Cordon of the Order of the Rising Sun 1988. *Address:* Roger and Wells, 1737 H Street, N.W., Washington, D.C. 20006, U.S.A.

WEINER, Gerry, B.A., B.SC.; Canadian politician; b. 26 June 1933, Montreal; m. Judith Weiner; one s. one d.; ed. Univ. of Montreal and McGill Univ.; pharmacist; fmr. Mayor Dollard-des-Ormeaux; fmr. Pres. North Shore Youth Services; exec. mem. B'nai Brith Univ. Lodge, Lakeshore Gen. Hosps. Foundation and Beechwood Home and Scholastic Asscn.; M.P. 1984–; Parl. Sec. to Sec. of State for External Affairs, then Parl. Sec. to Minister of Employment 1985–86; Minister of State for Immigration 1986–88, for Multiculturalism and Citizenship 1988–; Progressive Conservative. *Address:* House of Commons, Ottawa, Ont. K1A Canada.

WEINER, Mervyn Lester, M.PHIL.; Canadian development finance official; b. 30 Oct. 1922, Montreal; s. of Louis Weiner and Beatrice Feinstein; m. Shirley R. Hurwitz 1951; one s. one d.; ed. McGill Univ., Balliol Coll., Oxford, Univ. of Pennsylvania and Johns Hopkins Univ.; Instructor, Wharton School of Commerce and Finance, Univ. of Pennsylvania 1948–49; Instructor Johns Hopkins Univ. 1949–51; Econ. Affairs Officer UN 1950; IBRD officer 1951–84, Research Economist 1951–55, Country Economist 1955–61, Loan Officer 1961–63, Div. Chief 1963–65, Econ. Adviser, later Chief Economist, Western Hemisphere Dept. 1965–69, Dir. Public Utilities Projects Dept. 1969–72, Dir. Asia Region Projects Dept. 1972–74, Regional Vice-Pres. S. Asia 1974–75, Dir.-Gen. Operations Evaluation 1975–84; Int. Consultant 1984–. *Address:* 3206 Cummings Lane, Chevy Chase, Md. 20815, U.S.A. (Home). *Telephone:* (301) 656-5675 (Home).

WEINSTEIN, Irwin M., M.D.; American professor of medicine; b. 5 March 1926, Denver, Colo.; m. Judith Braun 1951; two s.; ed. Dartmouth Coll., Hanover, N.H., Williams Coll., Williamstown, Mass. and Univ. of Colo.; Intern, Montefiore Hosp. New York 1949–50, Jr. Asst. Res. 1950–51; Sr. Asst. Res. in Medicine, Univ. of Chicago 1951–52, Res. 1952–53, Instructor in Medicine 1953–54, Asst. Prof. 1954–55; Visiting Assoc. Prof. of Medicine, Univ. of Calif., L.A. 1955–56; Section Chief in Medicine, Hematology Section, Wadsworth Gen. Hosp. Veterans Admin. Center, L.A. 1956–59; Assoc. Clinical Prof. of Medicine, Center for the Health Sciences, Univ. of Calif., L.A. 1957–70, Clinical Prof. of Medicine, 1970–; numerous acad. affiliations; mem. American Asscn. for Advancement of Science, American Medical Asscn., Royal Soc. of Medicine etc.; numerous awards and distinctions. *Publications:* seven books and 33 articles in professional journals. *Address:* 8635 West 3rd Street, 1165-W, Los Angeles, Calif. 90048 (Office); 9509 Heather Road, Beverly Hills, Calif. 90210, U.S.A. (Home). *Telephone:* 213-659-6080 (Office); 213-275-3047 (Home).

WEINSTOCK, Baron (Life Peer), cr. 1980, of Bowden in the County of Wiltshire; **Arnold Weinstock,** Kt., B.SC.(ECON.), F.S.S.; British business executive; b. 29 July 1924, s. of Simon Weinstock and Golda Weinstock; m. Netta Sobell 1949; one s. one d.; ed. Univ. of London; Jr. Admin. Officer, Admiralty 1944–47; with pvt. group of cos. engaged in finance and property devt. 1947–54; Man. Dir. Radio and Allied Industries Ltd. (now Radio and Allied Holdings Ltd.) 1954–63; Dir. General Electric Co. Ltd. 1961–, Man. Dir. 1963–; Dir. Rolls-Royce (1971) Ltd. 1971–73; mem. Advisory Council Merrill Lynch Oct. 1985–; Hon. Fellow, Peterhouse, Cambridge, L.S.E.; Hon. Master of the Bench, Gray's Inn 1982; Trustee, British Museum 1985–; Hon. F.R.C.R., Hon. D.Sc. (Salford) 1975, (Aston) 1976, (Bath) 1978, (Reading) 1978, Hon. LL.D. (Leeds) 1978, (Wales) 1985, Hon. D.Tech. (Loughborough) 1981, Dr. h.c. (Ulster) 1986. *Leisure interests:* racing and bloodstock, music. *Address:* 7 Grosvenor Square, London, W.1, England.

WEIR, Gillian Constance; British (N.Z.-born) concert organist and harpsichordist; b. 17 Jan. 1941, Martinborough, New Zealand; d. of Cecil Alexander Weir and Clarice Mildred Foy Weir (née Bignell); ed. Wanganui Girls' Coll., N.Z. and Royal Coll. of Music, London; winner St. Albans Int.

Organ Festival Competition 1964; débuts Royal Festival Hall and Royal Albert Hall, London 1965; world wide career since 1965 as organist and latterly as harpsichordist also; has appeared with all leading British orchestras and with many abroad, under leading conductors; many radio and TV appearances; adjudicator in int. competitions and artist-in-residence at major univs.; gives lectures and master classes in many countries; many premières including first British performance of Messiaen's *Méditations* of 1972; many works written for her including concertos by William Mathias and Peter Racine Fricker; recordings include major series of French baroque music for Argo; Pres. Incorporated Asscn. of Organists (first woman Pres.) 1981–83; mem. Exec. Council, Royal Coll. of Organists (first woman mem.) 1981–85, Council (first woman mem.) 1977–; Hon. F.R.C.O.; Hon. D.Mus. (Victoria, Univ. of Wellington, N.Z.) 1983; Int. Performer of Year Award, American Guild of Organists 1983; Turnovsky Prize for Outstanding Achievement in the Arts 1985. *Leisure interests:* theatre, reading. *Address:* c/o Rawstron-Still International Management, 113 Church Road, London, SE19 2PR, England.

WEIR, Peter Lindsay; Australian film director; b. 21 Aug. 1944, Sydney; s. of Lindsay Weir and Peggy Barnsley; m. Wendy Stites 1966; one s. one d.; ed. Scots Coll., Sydney, Vaucluse Boys' High School, Sydney Univ.; worked in real estate until 1965; worked as stagehand in television, Sydney 1967; dir. film sequences in variety show 1968; dir. amateur univ. reviews 1967–69; dir. for Film Australia 1969–73; made own short films 1969–73, independent feature-film dir. and writer 1973–; various film awards. *Films:* Cars that Ate Paris 1973, Picnic at Hanging Rock 1975, The Last Wave 1977, The Plumber (television) 1978, Gallipoli 1980, The Year of Living Dangerously 1982, Witness 1985, The Mosquito Coast 1986, The Dead Poets Society 1989. *Address:* 56 Sunrise Road, Palm Beach, N.S.W. 2108, Australia (Home).

WEIR, Stuart Peter, B.A.; British journalist; b. 13 Oct. 1938, Frimley, Surrey; s. of Robert H. Weir and Edna F. Lewis; m. 1st Doffy Burnham 1963, 2nd Elizabeth E. Bisset 1987; two s. two d.; ed. Peter Symonds School, Winchester and Brasenose Coll. Oxford; Feature Writer, Oxford Mail 1964–67; Diarist, the Times 1967–71; Dir. Citizens Rights Office 1971–75; Founding Ed. Roof Magazine (Shelter) 1975–77; Deputy Ed. New Society 1977–84; Ed. New Socialist 1984–87; Political Columnist, London Daily News 1987; Ed. New Statesman 1987–88, New Statesman & Soc. 1988–. *Publications:* Manifesto 1981; contributor to: The Other Britain 1982, Consuming Secrets 1982. *Leisure interests:* children, cooking, gardening. *Address:* NSS, Foundation House, Perseverance Works, 38 Kingsland Road, London, E.2. (Office); 15 Grazebrook Road, London, N.16, England (Home). *Telephone:* 01-739-3211 (Office).

WEIS, Eberhard, DR.PHIL.; German professor of history; b. 31 Oct. 1925, Schmalkalden; m. Ingeborg Koeniger 1953; two s.; ed. Univs. of Munich, Dijon and Paris; Archivist, Bavarian State Archives 1953–69; Prof. of Modern History, Freie Univ. Berlin 1969–70, Univ. of Münster 1970–74, Univ. of Munich 1974–; Pres. Historical Comm., Bavarian Acad. of Sciences 1987–; mem. several scientific socs. and insts. *Publications:* several books inc. Geschichtsschreibung und Staatsauffassung in der französischen Enzyklopädie 1956, Montgelas 1759–1799 1971, and more than 100 other publs. *Address:* Ammerseestrasse 32, 8035 Gauting, Federal Republic of Germany. *Telephone:* 089 8505408.

WEISBROD, Burton A., M.A., PH.D.; American professor of economics; b. 13 Feb. 1931, Chicago, Ill.; s. of Leon H. Weisbrod and Idelle Chernoff; m. Shirley L. Weisbrod 1951; one s. one d.; ed. Northwestern Univ. and Univ. of Illinois; Sr. Staff mem. Council of Econ. Advisers to the Pres. 1963–64; Prof. of Econs., Univ. of Wis., Madison 1966–, Evjue-Bascom Prof. 1985–; Dir. Nat Inst. of Mental Health Training Program in Health and Mental Health Econs. 1983–, Center for Health Econs. and Law 1983–; Visiting Prof. Princeton Univ. 1962–63, Yale Univ. 1975–76, Harvard Univ. 1982–83, Brandeis Univ. 1982–83; Fellow A.A.A.S. *Publications:* numerous books and more than 100 articles and book chapters. *Address:* University of Wisconsin (Madison), Department of Economics, 1180 Observatory Drive, Madison, Wis. 53706, U.S.A. *Telephone:* 608-262-6196.

WEISKRANTZ, Lawrence, PH.D., F.R.S.; American professor of psychology; b. 28 March 1926, Philadelphia; s. of Benjamin Weiskrantz and Rose Weiskrantz (née Rifkin); m. Barbara Collins 1954; one s. one d.; ed. Girard Coll. of Philadelphia, Swarthmore and Univs. of Oxford and Harvard; parttime Lecturer, Tufts Univ. 1952; Research Assoc., Inst. of Living 1952–55; Sr. Postdoctoral Fellow, N.A.S. 1955–56; Research Assoc., Cambridge Univ., England 1956–61, Asst. Dir. of Research 1961–66, Fellow, Churchill Coll. 1964–67, Reader in Physiological Psychology 1966–67; Prof. of Psychology and Head of Dept. of Experimental Psychology, Oxford Univ. 1967–; Fellow of Magdalen Coll. Oxford; Kenneth Craik Research Award, St. John's Coll. Cambridge 1975–76; Sir Frederick Bartlett Memorial Lecturer 1980; Ferrier Lecturer, Royal Soc. 1989; Deputy Ed. Brain 1981–; mem. N.A.S. *Publications:* Analysis of Behavioral Change (Ed.) 1967, Animal Intelligence (Ed.) 1985, Neuropsychology of Cognitive Function (Ed.) 1986, Blindsight 1986, Thought Without Language (Ed.) 1988, and articles in Science, Nature, Quarterly Journal of Experimental Psychology, Journal of Comparative Physiological Psychology, Animal Behaviour and Brain. *Leisure interests:* music, walking. *Address:* Department of Experimental

Psychology, University of Oxford, South Parks Road, Oxford, OX1 3UD, England. *Telephone:* (0865) 271 444.

WEISS, Paul Alfred, PH.D.; American biologist; b. 21 March 1898, Vienna, Austria; s. of Carl S. and Rosalia Weiss; m. Maria Helene Blaschka 1926; ed. Univ. of Vienna; Asst. Dir. Biology Research Inst., Acad. of Sciences, Vienna 1922–29; Sterling Fellow, Yale Univ. 1930–32; Prof. of Zoology, Univ. of Chicago 1933–54; Prof., Rockefeller Inst., New York 1954–64; Prof. and Dean Graduate School of Biomedical Sciences, Univ. of Texas 1964–66; Prof. Emer. Rockefeller Univ. 1966–; Visiting Prof. at many Univs.; mem. Science Advisory Cttee. of Pres. of U.S.A. 1958–60; Chair. Div. Biology and Agric., Nat. Research Council 1951–55, Biology Council, Nat. Acad. Sciences 1953–58, U.S.A. Nat. Comm., Int. Union Biological Sciences 1953–64; Consultant, U.S. Dept. of State; mem. Nat. Acad. Sciences, mem. Council 1964–67; mem. Royal Swedish Acad. Science, Serbian Acad. Science, German Acad. of Science, Leopoldina, American Philosophical Soc., A.A.A.S. (Vice-Pres. 1952–53), Max-Planck Soc.; Pres. Growth Soc. 1941, Harvey Soc. 1962–63, Int. Soc. Cell Biology 1965–68; Hon. M.D., Hon. Dr. med., Hon. Sc.D., Hon. Dr. med. and surg., Hon. Dr. rer. nat., Hon. Dr. (Notre Dame and Rockefeller Univ.); U.S. Army-Navy Citation for Outstanding Merit, Leitz Award, Weinstein Award of UN Cerebral Palsy Asscn., John F. Lewis Prize and Lashley Prize of American Philosophical Soc., Wakeman Award for Research in Neuro Sciences, The Nat. Science Medal 1980 and other awards. *Publications:* Entwicklungsphysiologie der Tiere 1930, Aus den Werkstätten der Lebensforschung 1931, Principles of Development 1939, Dynamics of Development: Experiments and Inferences 1968, Life, Order and Understanding 1970, Biomedical Excursions 1971, Within the Gates of Science and Beyond 1971, Hierarchically Organized Systems 1971, The Science of Life: The Living System—a System of Living 1973, Knowledge in Search of Understanding 1975, From Cell Research to Nerve Repair 1976, over 350 scientific papers on growth, development, nerve function, theoretical biology, etc. *Leisure interests:* art, writing, music. *Address:* 450 East 63rd Street, New York, N.Y. 10021, U.S.A.

WEISS, Ulrich; German banker; b. 3 June 1936; mem. Bd. of Man. Dirs., Deutsche Bank AG, Frankfurt; Chair. Supervisory Bd., Schmalbach-Lubeca AG, Brunswick; Deputy Chair. Supervisory Bd., Frankfurter Hypothekenbank AG, Frankfurt, Schiffshypothekenbank zu Lübeck AG, Kiel; mem. Supervisory Bd., Bank Européene de Crédit S.A., Brussels, Brown, Boveri and Cie. AG, Mannheim, Klein, Schanzlin & Becker AG, Frankenthal, Orenstein and Koppel AG, Berlin/Dortmund, G. M. Pfaff AG, Kaiserslautern, Rheinelektra AG, Mannheim, Standard Elektrik Lorenz AG, Stuttgart, Süddeutsche Zucker AG, Mannheim; mem. Admin. Council Deutsche Bank Luxembourg, Luxembourg, Banca d'America e d'Italia, Mailand; mem. of Advisory Bd. Privatdiskont AG, Frankfurt. *Address:* Taunusanlage 12, 6000 Frankfurt am Main, Federal Republic of Germany.

WEISSENBERG, Alexis; Bulgarian pianist; b. 26 July 1929, Sofia; studied piano and composition with Pancho Vladigerov, also with Olga Samaroff at Juilliard School, New York; debut at age 14; numerous appearances in Europe, South America, U.S.A., Japan; American debut with New York Philharmonic; soloist with Berlin, Vienna, Japan, Czechoslovak Philharmonics, Philadelphia, Cleveland, Minnesota, Royal Danish, and Salzburg Festival orchestras, Boston, Chicago, Pittsburgh Symphony orchestras, Orchestre de Paris and others; recording artist with RCA, Angel; first prize Int. Leventritt competition and Philadelphia Youth competition 1946. *Address:* c/o Columbia Artists Management Inc., 165 West 57th Street, New York, N.Y. 10019, U.S.A.

WEISSKOPF, Victor Frederick, PH.D.; American (b. Austrian) physicist; b. 19 Sept. 1908, Vienna; s. of Emil Weisskopf and Martha Gut; m. Ellen Tvede 1934; one s. one d.; ed. Vienna and Göttingen Univs.; Research Assoc., Berlin 1931–32; Zürich Inst. of Tech. 1932–36, Rockefeller Foundation Fellow, Copenhagen and Cambridge 1936–37; Instructor of Physics, Univ. of Rochester 1937–40, Asst. Prof. 1940–43; Group Leader, Los Alamos Scientific Laboratory 1943–47; Prof. of Physics, M.I.T. 1946–60, Inst. Prof. 1965–; mem. Directorate, European Org. for Nuclear Research 1960–61, Dir. Gen. 1961–65; Pres. American Physical Soc. 1960, American Acad. of Arts and Sciences 1975–79; mem. N.A.S., Acad. dei Lincei Pontifical Acad., Rome; corresp. mem. French, Austrian and Bavarian Acads. of Sciences; foreign mem. Danish Soc. of Sciences, Soviet, Spanish and Scottish Acads. of Science; Hon. Fellow, French Soc. of Physics, Royal Soc. of Edinburgh, Weizmann Inst., Israel; Max Planck Medal 1950; Bors Pregel Award (U.S.A.) 1971, Cino del Duca Award (France) 1972, Nat. Medal of Science (U.S.A.); several hon. degrees. *Publications:* Theoretical Nuclear Physics (with J. Blatt) 1952, Knowledge and Wonder 1962, Physics in the Twentieth Century 1972, The Privilege of Being a Physicist 1989. *Address:* 36 Arlington Street, Cambridge, Mass. 02140, U.S.A. *Telephone:* (617) 868-2390.

WEISSMANN, N. Charles; M.D.; PH.D.; Swiss molecular biologist; b. 14 Oct. 1931, Budapest; m.; three c.; ed. Kantonales Gymnasium, Zürich and Univ. of Zürich; Asst. to Prof. P. Karrer, Univ. of Zürich 1960–61; Fellow, Stiftung für Stipendien auf dem Gebiete der Chemie 1961–63; Instr. in Biochem. New York Univ. School of Medicine 1963–64, Asst. Prof. of Biochem. 1965–67, Prof. extraordinarius in Molecular Biol. 1967–70, Prof. ordinarius 1970–; Dir. Inst. of Molecular Biol. Univ. of Zürich 1967–; Pres.

Roche Research Foundation 1971–77; mem. scientific Bd. of Biogen 1978–; mem. several editorial bds.; Pres. Schweizerische Gesellschaft für Zell-und Molekularbiologie 1970–72; Pres. Ernst Hadom-Stiftung, Zurich 1986–; Hon. mem. American Soc. of Biol. Chem.; Foreign mem. Royal Soc., Deutsche Akad. der Naturforscher Leopoldina; Ruzicka Prize in Chem. 1966, Marcel Benoist Prize 1970, Sir Hans Krebs Medaille 1974, Otto Warburg Prize 1980, Dr H.P. Heineken Prize 1982, Scheele Medal 1982, Jung-Preis Für Medizin 1988. *Address:* Institute of Molecular Biology, University of Zürich, Ramistrasse 71, 8093 Zürich, Switzerland.

WEITZ, Raanan; Israeli rural development planner; b. 27 July 1913, Rehovoth, Israel; s. of Joseph and Ruchama Weitz; m. Rivka Schechtman; one s. one d.; ed. Hebrew Gymnasia, Jerusalem, Hebrew Univ., and Univ. of Florence; Agricultural Settlement Dept., Jewish Agency 1937-, fmr. Village Instructor Head of Dept. 1963–84; Chair. Nat. and Univ. Inst. of Agric. 1960–66; Head Settlement Study Centre 1963–; service with Intelligence Corps. British 8th Army, Second World War; fmr. mem. Hagana; mem. Exec., Zionist Org. 1963–84; Prof. Rural Devt. Planning, Univ. of Haifa 1973–78, of Rural Devt. Theory Bar-Ilan Univ. 1978–82. *Publications:* Agriculture and Rural Development in Israel: Projection and Planning 1963, Rural Planning in Development Countries (editor) 1965, Agricultural Development—Planning and Implementation 1968, Rural Development in a Changing World (editor) 1971, From Peasant to Farmer: a Revolutionary Strategy for Development 1971, Urbanization and the Developing Countries: Report on the Sixth Rehovot Conference (editor) 1973, Employment and Income Generation in New Settlement Projects 1978, Integrated Rural Development: The Rehovot Approach 1979, Growth and Values in Development: An Alternative Direction, New Roads to Development, a Twentieth Century Fund essay; and papers on problems of comprehensive planning. *Address:* Settlement Study Centre, Rehovot, P.O. Box 2355 (Office); 15 Diskin Street, Kiriyat Wolfson, Israel (Home). *Telephone:* 08-474111 (Office); 02-668764 (Home).

WEIZ, Herbert, DR.RER.OEC.; German politician; b. 27 June 1924, Cumbach; ed. Univs. of Jena and Berlin and Technische Hochschule, Dresden; fmr. employee, VEB Optima Büromaschinenwerk, Erfurt and VEB Carl Zeiss, Jena 1952–55; mem. Communist Party 1945, Socialist Unity Party (SED) 1946–; mem. SED Cen. Cttee. 1958–; State Sec. for Research and Tech., G.D.R. 1962–67; a Deputy Chair. Council of Ministers July 1967–, also Minister for Science and Tech. Feb. 1974–; Vaterländischer Verdienstorden in Bronze and Silver, and other decorations. *Address:* c/o Ministerrat, Berlin, German Democratic Republic.

WEIZMAN, Gen. Ezer; Israeli air force officer and politician; b. 15 June 1924, Tel-Aviv; nephew of Chaim Weizmann (1st Pres. of Israel); m.; two c.; ed. R.A.F. Staff Coll.; Officer, Israel Air Force 1948–66 and fmr. C.O., I.A.F.; Chief General Staff Branch 1966–69; Minister of Transport 1969–70, of Defence 1977–80, of Communications 1984–88, of Science Dec. 1988–; Chair. Exec. Cttee. Herut Party 1971–73; mem. Likud front 1973–80; in pvt. business 1980–84; Minister without Portfolio in Cabinet, Head of Yahad Party in Nat. Unity Govt. 1984–. *Publications:* On Eagles Wings 1978, The Battle for Peace 1981. *Address:* 2 Hadekel Street, Caesarea, Israel.

WEIZSÄCKER, Carl Friedrich, Freiherr von, PH.D.; German professor of philosophy and director of research; b. 28 June 1912, Kiel; s. of Ernst von Weizsäcker and Marianne Graevenitz; m. Gundalena Wille 1937; four c.; ed. Univs. of Berlin, Göttingen and Leipzig; lecturer Kaiser-Wilhelm-Institut, Berlin 1936–42; Assoc. Prof. Univ. of Strasbourg 1942–44; Head Dept. Max-Planck-Inst. for Physics, Göttingen 1946–57; Hon. Prof. Univ. of Göttingen 1946–57; Prof. of Philosophy Univ. of Hamburg 1957–69; Dir. Max-Planck-Inst. for Research on Preconditions of Human Life in the Modern World, Starnberg 1970–80; Emer. Scientific mem. Max-Planck-Gesellschaft, Munich 1980–; mem. Deutsche Akademie der Naturforscher, Leopoldina, Göttinger Akademie der Wissenschaften, Sächsische Akademie der Wissenschaften, Leipzig, Österreichische Akademie der Wissenschaften, Bayerische Akademie der Wissenschaften, Bayerische Akademie der Schonen Kunste, Deutsche Physikalische Gesellschaft, American Physical Soc., Orden Pour le Mérite, Académie des Sciences Morales et Politiques, Institut de France; Hon. Dr. Iur. (Vrije Universiteit, Amsterdam) 1975, (Alberta) 1981; Hon. Dr. Theol. (Catholic Theol. Faculty, Tubingen) 1977; Hon. Dr. rer. nat. (Karl-Marx-Universitat, Leipzig) 1987; Hon. Dr. Phil. (Freie Universität, Berlin) 1987; numerous prizes and medals including Bundesverdienstkreuz, John M. Templeton Prize for Progress in Religion (jtly.) 1989. *Publications:* Die Atomkerne 1937, Zum Weltbild der Physik 1943, Die Geschichte der Natur 1948, Bedingungen des Friedens 1963, Die Tragweite der Wissenschaft 1964, Gedanken über unsere Zukunft 1966, Der ungesicherte Friede 1969, Die Einheit der Natur 1971, Wege in der Gefahr 1977, Der Garten des Menschlichen 1978, Deutlichkeit 1978, Der bedrohte Friede 1981, Wahrnehmung der Neuzeit 1983, Aufbau der Physik 1985, Die Zeit drängt 1986, Bewusstseinswandel 1988. *Address:* Alpenstrasse 15, 8131 Starnberg-Söcking, Federal Republic of Germany. *Telephone:* 08151 7091.

WEIZSÄCKER, Richard von, DR.JUR.; German lawyer and politician; b. 15 April 1920, Stuttgart; s. of late Baron Ernst von Weizsäcker; m. Marianne von Kretschmann 1953; three s. one d.; ed. Berlin, law studies at Oxford, Grenoble, Göttingen; army service 1938–45; prof. lawyer 1955–;

fmr. mem. Bd. Allianz Lebensversicherung-AG, Stuttgart, Robeco-Gruppe, Amsterdam; mem. Robert Bosch Foundation, Stuttgart; mem. Synod and Council of German Protestant Church 1969-84, Pres. Protestant Church Congress 1964-70-; mem. Fed. Bd. CDU, Deputy Chair. CDU/CSU Party 1972-79; mem. Bundestag 1969-81, Vice-Pres. 1979-81; Governing Mayor of West Berlin 1981-84; Pres. Fed. Repub. of Germany July 1984-; Theodor Heuss Prize 1983; Hon. D.C.L. (Oxford) 1988. *Publications:* Die deutsche Geschichte geht weiter 1983, Von Deutschland aus 1985. *Address:* Office of the President, 5300 Bonn, Adenauer-Allee 135, Federal Republic of Germany. *Telephone:* (0228) 2001.

WEKWERTH, Manfred, PH.D.; German theatre director; b. 3 Dec. 1929, Köthen; s. of Karl and Helene Wekwerth; m. 1st Renate Meiners 1953, 2nd Renate Richter 1963; one d.; ed. Humboldt Univ., Berlin; worked as teacher, Köthen 1949; area sec. DSF regional cttee. 1950; Production Asst. Berliner Ensemble, G.D.R. 1955, Producer 1955, Chief Dir. 1963, Theatre Man. 1977-; Dir. Deutsches Theater 1971, Guest Dir. 1971; Dir. Berlin Inst. for Theatre Direction 1974, Prof. 1975; Pres. Akademie der Künste der DDR 1982-; Ericht Weinert Medal 1957; Nat. Prize (3rd Class 1959, 2nd Class 1961); Vaterländischer Verdienstorden (Bronze 1969, Gold 1979); Artur Becker Medal in Gold 1973; Heinrich Greif Prize (2nd Class) 1976. *Publications:* Der Biberpelz: Wir arbeiten an Gerhart Hauptmanns Komödie 1953, Auffinden einer ästhetischen Kategorie 1957, Stellungen, Gruppierungen, Gänge auf der Bühne 1957, Über Regiearbeit mit Laienkünstlern 1958, Theater in Veränderung 1960, Notate: Zur Arbeit des Berliner Ensembles 1956-66 1967, Das Theater Brechts 1968, Theater und Wissenschaft 1970, Schriften: Arbeit mit Brecht 1973, Brecht? 1976, Er hat Vorschläge gemacht 1977, Brecht-Theater in der Gegenwart 1980, Theater in der Diskussion 1982. *Address:* Akademie der Künste der DDR, 1040 Berlin, Hermann-Matern-Strasse 58-60; 1180 Berlin, Rabindran-anth-Tagore-Strasse 13, German Democratic Republic (Home). *Telephone:* 287 83 11 (Office), 681 32 97 (Home)

WELCH, John Francis, Jr., PH.D.; American business executive; b. 19 Nov. 1935, Peabody, Mass.; s. of John Francis and Grace (née Andrews) Welch; m. Carolyn B. Osburn 1959; two s. two d.; ed. Univ. of Mass.; joined Gen. Electric Co., Fairfield, Conn. 1960-, Vice-Pres. 1972, Vice-Pres. Exec. Components and Materials Group 1973-77, Sr. Vice-Pres. Sector Exec., Consumer Products and Services Sector 1977-79, Vice-Chair, C.E.O. 1979-81, Chair. 1981-86, C.E.O. and Chair. 1988-; Pres. and C.E.O. Nat. Broadcasting Co. Aug. 1986-, Dir.-Gen. Electric Credit Corpn. *Address:* General Electric Co., 3135 Eastern Turnpike, Fairfield, Conn. 06431, U.S.A.

WELCH, Raquel; American actress; b. 5 Sept. 1940, Chicago, Ill.; d. of Armand and Josepha (née Hall) Tejada; m. 1st James Westley Welch 1959 (divorced), two c.; m. 2nd Patrick Curtis (divorced); m. 3rd Andre Weinfeld 1980; fmr. model for Neiman-Marcus stores. *Films include:* Fantastic Voyage 1966, One Million Years B.C. 1967, Fathom 1967, The Biggest Bundle of Them All 1968, Magic Christian 1970, Myra Breckinridge 1970, Fuzz 1972, Bluebeard 1972, Hannie Caulder 1972, Kansas City Bomber 1972, The Last of Sheila 1973, The Three Musketeers 1974, The Wild Party 1975, The Four Musketeers 1975, Mother, Jugs and Speed 1976, Crossed Swords 1978, L'Animal 1979, Walks for Women 1981; acted in play: Woman of the Year (Broadway) 1982. *Videos:* Raquel: Total Beauty and Fitness 1984, A Week with Raquel 1987, Raquel: Lose 10lbs in 3 Weeks 1989. *Publication:* The Raquel Welch Total Beauty and Fitness Program 1984. *Address:* 200 Central Park South, New York, N.Y. 10019, U.S.A.

WELDON, Fay, M.A.; British author; b. 22 Sept. 1931, Alvechurch, Worcs.; d. of Frank T. and Margaret J. Birkinshaw; m. Ronald Weldon 1960; four s.; ed. Girls' High School, Christchurch, New Zealand, and Univ. of St. Andrews; Chair. of Judges, Booker McConnell Prize 1983. *Publications:* novels: The Fat Woman's Joke 1967 (republished as . . . And the Wife Ran Away 1968), Down Among the Women 1971, Words of Advice 1974, Female Friends 1975, Remember Me 1976, Praxis 1978, Puffball 1980, The President's Child 1982, The Life and Loves of a She-Devil 1984, Letters to Alice—On First Reading Jane Austen 1984, Rebecca West 1985, The Shrapnel Academy 1986, The Heart of the Country 1987, The Hearts and Lives of Men 1987, Leader of the Band 1988, The Cloning of Joanna May 1989; plays: Permanence 1969, Words of Advice 1974, Moving House 1976, Mr Director 1978, Action Replay 1979, After the Prize 1981, I Love My Love 1981, Love Among the Women 1982, Woodworm 1983, Short stories: Polaris and Other Stories, Watching Me, Watching You; novella: The Rules of Life 1986; more than 50 television plays, dramatisations and radio plays. *Address:* c/o Anthony Sheil Associates, 43 Doughty Street, London, WC1N 2LF, England.

WELDON, Virginia Verral, A.B., M.D.; American professor of paediatrics; b. 8 Sept. 1935, Toronto, Canada; d. of John Edward Verral and Carolyn Edith Swift; m. (divorced); two c.; ed. Smith Coll., State Univ. of New York at Buffalo, Johns Hopkins Univ. School of Medicine, U.S.A.; Instructor in Paediatrics, Johns Hopkins Hosp. 1967-68; Washington Univ. School of Medicine 1968-69, Asst. Prof. of Paediatrics 1973-79, Prof. 1979-89, Asst. Vice-Chancellor for Medical Affairs 1975-81, Assoc. Vice-Chancellor 1981-83, Deputy Vice-Chancellor 1983-89, Vice-Pres. Washington Univ. Medical Center 1980-89; Vice-Pres. Scientific Affairs, Monsanto Co. '1989-; Fellow

A.A.A.S.; Smith Coll. Medal 1984. *Publications:* numerous articles in scientific journals. *Leisure interest:* civic affairs. *Address:* Monsanto Company, 800 North Lindbergh Boulevard, St. Louis, Mo. 63110, U.S.A. *Telephone:* (314) 694 3901.

WELENSKY, Rt. Hon. Sir Roy (Roland), Kt., P.C., K.C.M.G.; Rhodesian politician (retd.); b. 20 Jan. 1907, Salisbury (now Harare); s. of Polish Jewish father and South African Dutch mother; m. 1st Elizabeth Henderson 1928 (died 1969), one s. one d.; m. 2nd M. Valerie Scott, two d.; ed. Primary School, Salisbury; worked for Rhodesia Railways (beginning as fireman and engine driver) 1924-53; M.L.C. Northern Rhodesia 1938-53; mem. Exec. Council 1940-53; Dir. of Manpower 1941-46; Leader of the Unofficial Mems. 1946-53; Deputy Prime Minister Fed. Govt. of Rhodesia and Nyasaland 1953-56, Min. of Transport 1953-56, of Posts 1953-56, Prime Minister and Minister of External Affairs 1956-63, of Defence 1956-59; Pres. United Fed. Party 1956-63; Leader New Rhodesia Party Aug.-Dec. 1964. *Leisure interests:* fishing, reading, light and grand opera, music. *Address:* Shaftesbury House, Milldown Road, Blandford Forum, Dorset, DT11 7DE, England.

WELFORD, Walter Thompson, PH.D., F.R.S.; British professor of physics; b. 31 Aug. 1916, London; s. of Abraham and Sonia Weinstein; m. Jacqueline Thompson 1948; two s.; lecturer in Physics, Imperial Coll., London 1951, Reader 1959, Prof. 1973, Prof. Emer. 1983-; consultant in applied optics to industry.; Thomas Young Award 1973, Sir Charles Parsons Medal 1983. *Publications:* Geometrical Optics 1962, Aberrations of the Symmetrical Optical System 1974, Optics 1976, Optics of Nonimaging Concentrators (with R. Winston) 1978, Aberrations of Optical Systems 1986. *Leisure interest:* surviving. *Address:* Physics Department, Imperial College, London, SW7 2BZ (Office); 8 Chiswick Road, London, W4 5RB, England (Home). *Telephone:* 01-589 5111 Ext. 6847 (Office); 01-995 2340 (Home).

WELL, Günther Wilhelm van; German diplomatist (retd.); b. 15 Oct. 1922, Osterath; s. of Friedrich and Magda (née Hülser) van Well; m. Carolyn Bradley 1957; one s. one d.; ed. Bonn and Harvard Univs.; Office of Perm. Observer of Fed. Repub. of Germany at UN, New York 1954-59; Foreign Office, Bonn 1959-62; Fellow, Center for Int. Affairs, Harvard Univ. 1962-63; Counsellor for Political Affairs, Tokyo 1963-67; Head of Section, Foreign Office, Bonn 1967-71, Deputy Dir. of Political Affairs 1971-72, Dir. of Political Affairs 1972-77, State Sec. 1977-81; Amb. and Perm. Rep. to UN 1981-84, Amb to U.S.A. 1984-87; Grosses Bundesverdienstkreuz mit Stern. *Publications:* several publications on foreign policy questions in German and other European periodicals. *Address:* c/o Ministry of Foreign Affairs, 5300 Bonn, Adenauerallee 99-103, Federal Republic of Germany.

WELLAND, Colin (b. Williams); British playwright and actor; b. 4 July 1934, Liverpool; s. of John Arthur Williams and Norah Williams; m. Patricia Sweeney 1962; one s. three d.; ed. Newton-le-Willows Grammar School, Goldsmiths' Coll., London; art teacher 1958-62; entered theatre 1962-, Library Theatre, Manchester 1962-64; Dir. Radio Aire 1981-; *acted in films:* Kes, Villain, Straw Dogs, Sweeney; wrote screenplay for Yanks 1978, Chariots of Fire 1980, Twice in a Lifetime 1986; *acted in plays:* Waiting for Godot 1987, The Churchill; *wrote plays:* Say Goodnight to Grandma 1973, Roll on Four O'Clock 1981; *TV plays include* Kisses at 50, Leeds United, Your Man from Six Counties. *Publications:* plays Roomful of Holes 1972, Say Goodnight to Grandma 1973. *Leisure interests:* cricket, watching rugby and soccer, films, dining out. *Address:* c/o Anthony Jones, A.D. Peters Ltd., 10 Buckingham Street, London, WC2N 6BU, England.

WELLEK, René, LITT.D., PH.D., D. ÈS L.; American professor of comparative literature; b. 22 Aug. 1903, Vienna, Austria; s. of Bronislav Wellek and Gabriele von Zelewski; m. 1st Olga Brodská 1932 (died 1967), one s.; m. 2nd Nonna Dolodarenko 1968; ed. Gymnasium and Charles Univ., Prague and Princeton Univ.; Instructor, Smith Coll. 1928-29, Princeton Univ. 1929-30; Docent, Charles Univ. 1931-35; Lecturer of Czech Language and Literature, School of Slavonic Studies, Univ. of London 1935-39; Prof. of English, Univ. of Iowa 1939-46; Prof. of Slavic and Comparative Literature, Yale Univ. 1946-52, Sterling Prof. of Comparative Literature 1952-72, Emer. Prof. 1972-; Fellow Silliman Coll. 1950-; mem. American Acad. of Arts and Sciences, Bavarian Acad., British Acad., Int. Asscn. Comparative Lit.; Foreign mem. Royal Netherlands Acad., Italian Nat. Acad.; 14 hon. degrees, three Guggenheim awards. *Publications:* Immanuel Kant in England 1931, The Rise of English Literary History 1941, Theory of Literature (with Austin Warren) 1948, A History of Modern Criticism (six vols.) 1955-86, Dostoevsky 1962, Essays on Czech Literature 1963, Concepts of Criticism 1963, Confrontations 1965, Discriminations 1970, Four Critics: Croce, Valéry, Lukács, Ingardon 1981, The Attack on Literature and Other Essays 1982, Chekhov: New Perspectives 1984. *Address:* 45 Fairgrounds Road, Woodbridge, Conn. 06525, U.S.A. *Telephone:* (203) 397-2437.

WELLER, Albert Hermann, DR. RER. NAT.; German professor of chemistry; b. 5 April 1922, Welzheim; s. of Albert Weller and Elisabeth Scharwächter; m. Brigitte von der Chevallerie 1951; one s. two d.; ed. Univs. of Leipzig and Tübingen; Research Assoc. Univ. of Minnesota 1951-52, Univ. of Stuttgart 1952-57; lecturer and Assoc. Prof. Univ. of Stuttgart 1957-62; Prof. of Physical Chemistry, Free Univ. Amsterdam 1962-65; Dir. Max-

Planck-Inst. für Spektroskopie 1965–71; Hon. Prof. Univ. of Göttingen 1968–; Scientific Mem. and Dir. Max-Planck-Inst. für biophysikalische Chemie, Göttingen 1971–; Visiting professorships at univs. in Belgium, U.S.S.R., U.S.A., Canada; mem. Deutsche Akad. der Naturforscher Leopoldina, Akad. der Wissenschaften, Göttingen; Foreign mem. Finnish Acad.; Bodenstein Award 1962; Hon. Dr. Sc. (Leuven) 1983; Hon. Dr. rer. nat. (Bayreuth) 1987. *Publications:* numerous articles on physical chemistry in professional journals. *Leisure interests:* theology and natural philosophy, limericks, spoonerisms and palindromes. *Address:* Max-Planck-Institut für physikalische Chemie, P.O.B., 3400 Göttingen (Office); Am Weinberg 18a, 3406 Bovenden, Federal Republic of Germany (Home). *Telephone:* 0551-201 261 (Office); 0551-201 426 (Home).

WELLER, Thomas Huckle, A.B., M.S., M.D.; American scientist and university professor; b. 1915, Ann Arbor, Mich.; s. of Carl V. and Elsie H. Weller; m. Kathleen R. Fahey 1945; two s. two d.; ed. Harvard Univ. and Univ. of Michigan; Teaching Fellow, Harvard Medical School 1940–42; served Medical Corps, U.S. Army 1942–45; Asst. Resident, Children's Hospital, Boston 1946–47; Research Fellow, Harvard Medical School 1947–48, Instructor 1948–49; Asst. Prof. Tropical Public Health, Harvard School of Public Health 1949, Assoc. Prof. 1950–54, Richard Pearson Strong Prof. 1954–85, Emer. 1985, and Head of Dept. 1954–81; Asst. Dir. Research Div. of Infectious Diseases, Children's Medical Center, Boston 1949–55; Dir. Comm. on Parasitic Diseases, Armed Forces Epidemiological Bd. 1953–59; Consultant on Tropical Diseases, U.S. Public Health Service; Dir. Center for Prevention of Infectious Diseases, Harvard School of Public Health 1966–81; Consultant practice: viral and parasitic diseases, int. health 1985–; mem. N.A.S.; winner (jointly) of E. Mead Johnson Award 1953, Kimble Methodology Award 1954, Nobel Prize in Medicine and Physiology 1954, Weinstein Cerebral Palsy Award 1973; Ledlie Prize 1963; Bristol Award, Infectious Diseases Soc. of America 1980; Gold Medal and Diploma of Honor, Univ. Costa Rica, 1984; Hon. LL.D., Sc.D., L.H.D., Sc.D. *Publications:* Papers on infectious diseases, tropical medicine, virus cultivation (especially poliomyelitis and mumps), the etiology of varicella, cytomegalic inclusion disease and rubella, herpes zoster, laboratory diagnosis of schistosomiasis. *Leisure interests:* gardening, ornithology, photography. *Address:* 56 Winding River Road, Needham, Mass. 02192, U.S.A. (Home).

WELLER, Walter; Austrian conductor; b. 30 Nov. 1939; s. of Walter and Anna Weller; m. Elisabeth Samohyl; 1966; one s.; ed. Realgymnasium, Vienna, Akademie für Musik, Vienna; f. Weller Quartet 1958–69; mem. Vienna Philharmonic 1958–60, First Leader 1960–69; Conductor, Vienna State Opera 1969–75; Guest Conductor with all main European, American and Japan Broadcasting Corpn. orchestras 1973–; Chief Conductor, Tonkünstler Orchestra, Vienna 1974–77; Principal Conductor and Artistic Adviser, Royal Liverpool Philharmonic Orchestra 1977–80, Guest Conductor Laureate 1980; Prin. Conductor, Royal Philharmonic Orchestra 1980–85, Chief Guest Conductor 1985–; Chief Guest Conductor, Nat. Orchestra of Spain 1987–; Medal of Arts and Sciences (Austria) 1968, Grand Prix du Disque, Charles Cross for Duke's symphony in C. *Leisure interests:* magic, model railways, sailing, swimming, stamp-collecting, skiing. *Address:* Döblinger Hauptstrasse 40, 1190 Vienna, Austria. *Telephone:* 34 01 64.

WELLERSHOFF, Dieter, D.PHIL.; German writer; b. 3 Nov. 1925, Neuss/Rhein; s. of Walter Wellershoff and Kläre Weber; m. Dr. Maria von Thadden 1952; one s. two d.; ed. Gymnasium in Grevenbroich and Univ. Bonn; Ed. 1952–55; freelance writer 1956–59, 1981–; Reader Kiepenheuer and Witsch Publishing House, Cologne 1959–81; Hörspielpreis der Kriegsblinden 1961; Literaturpreis Verband der deutschen Kritiker 1970, Heinrich Böll Prize, Cologne 1988. *Publications:* Gottfried Benn, Phänotyp dieser Stunde 1958, Der Gleichgültige 1963, Ein schöner Tag 1966, Literatur und Veränderung 1969, Einladung an alle 1972, Die Schönheit der Schimpansen 1977, Die Sirene 1980, Der Sieger nimmt alles 1983, Die Arbeit des Lebens 1985, Die Körper und die Träume 1986, Der Roman und die Ehfahrbarkeit der Welt 1988, (ed.) Gottfried Benn, Gesammelte Werke 1958, works translated into 15 languages. *Address:* Mainzer Strasse 45, 5000 Köln 1, Federal Republic of Germany. *Telephone:* (0221) 388565.

WELLERSHOFF, Adm. Dieter; German naval officer; b. 16 March 1933, Dortmund; s. of Kurt W. Wellershoff and Maria Wellershoff; m. Emma Johanna Wefer 1958; two s. one d.; joined navy 1957; specialization mine warfare and communications; C.O. minesweeper 1962–63; Armed Forces Command and Staff Coll. 1967–69; C.O. destroyer 1971–73; Commdr. Mine Warfare Forces, Capt. 1975–77; Deputy Chief of Staff (Armaments), Naval Staff Ministry of Defence, rank of Rear Adm. 1977–81; Commandant, Fed. Armed Forces Command and Staff Coll. 1981–84; Chief of Staff, Navy, rank of Vice Adm. 1985–86; Chief of Staff, Fed. Armed Forces, rank of Adm. 1986–; Commdr.'s Cross, Order of Merit; Gold Cross of Honour, Fed. Armed Forces; Commdr.'s Cross, Légion d'honneur. *Publication:* Freiheit, Was ist Das? 1984. *Leisure interests:* music (traditional/swing jazz), hiking. *Address:* Ministry of Defence, P.O. Box 1328, D-5300 Bonn 1, Federal Republic of Germany.

WELLS, Herman B, B.S., A.M., LL.D.; American educationist; b. 7 June 1902, Jamestown, Indiana; s. of Joseph Granville and Anna Bernice (née Harting) Wells; ed. Univs. of Illinois and Wisconsin, and Indiana Univ.; Asst. Cashier, First Nat. Bank, Lebanon, Ind. 1924–26; Asst., Dept. of Econs., Univ. of Wisconsin 1927–28; Field Sec. Indiana Bankers' Asscn. 1928–31;

Sec. and Research Dir. Study Comm. for Indiana Financial Insts. 1931–33; Instructor in Econs. Indiana Univ. 1930–33, Asst. Prof. 1933–35; Supervisor Div. of Banks and Trust Cos. and Div. of Research and Statistics, Dept. of Financial Insts. State of Indiana 1933–35, Sec. Comm. for Financial Insts. 1933–36; Dean and Prof. School of Business Admin. Indiana Univ. 1935–37, Acting Pres. of Univ. 1937–38, Pres. of Univ. 1938–62, Chancellor 1962–; Pres. Indiana Univ. Foundation 1962–69, Chair. of Bd. 1937–62, 1969–72, Chair. Exec. Cttee. 1969–, Vice-Pres. 1975–; Chair. American Council on Educ. 1944–45; Trustee, Carnegie Foundation for Advancement of Teaching 1941–62; Special Advisor Liberated Areas, U.S. Dept. of State 1944; Consultant, American Council on Educ. to U.S. Del. at San Francisco Conf. 1945; mem. Allied Missions for Observation of Greek Elections 1946; adviser cultural affairs Mil. Govt., U.S. Zone, Germany 1947–48; mem. UNESCO Comm. of Experts on German Questions 1949–50; U.S. mem. Governing Bd. UNESCO Inst. for Educ., Hamburg 1951–57; U.S. Nat. Comm. for UNESCO 1951–55, Vice-Chair. 1953–54; mem. U.S. Del. to UN 1957; adviser to Pakistan Ministry of Educ. 1959; Vice-Pres. Int. Asscn. of Univs. 1955–60; Head U.S. Del. SEATO Preparatory Comm. on Univ. Problems 1960; mem. U.S. Cttee. reviewing activities and org. of UN Secr. 1960–61; Chair. Bd. American Research Inst. for the Arts 1975–78; Chair. Bd. of Trustees, Educ. and World Affairs 1963–70; mem. President's Cttee. on U.S.-Soviet Trade Relations 1965, on Overseas Voluntary Activities 1967; mem. Review Cttee. on Haile Sellassie I Univ. 1966–74; mem. Nat. Cttee. on U.S.-China Relations 1969, numerous Cttees.; mem. Bd. Lilly Endowment; mem. Bd. Chemed Corpn. 1970–85, Hon. mem. 1985–, Lilly Endowment Inc. 1973–; mem. Visiting Cttee., Tulane Univ.; hon. degrees from 25 univs. and colls.; Commdr's Cross of Order of Merit, Fed. Repub. of Germany and numerous other orders. *Leisure interest:* travelling. *Address:* Office of the Chancellor, Owen Hall, Indiana University, Bloomington, Ind. 47405; 1321 East 10th Street, Bloomington, Ind. 47401, U.S.A. (Home). *Telephone:* (812) 855-6647 (Office); (812) 336-6275 (Home).

WELLS, John West, PH.D.; American geologist; b. 15 July 1907, Philadelphia, Pa.; s. of Raymond Wells and Maida West; m. Elizabeth Baker 1932; one d.; ed. Univ. of Pittsburgh and Cornell Univ.; Instructor in Geology Univ. of Texas 1929–31; Instructor-Prof. of Geology Ohio State Univ. 1938–48; Geologist U.S. Geological Survey 1946–; Prof. of Geology Cornell Univ., N.Y. 1948–73, Prof. Emer. 1973–; Bikini Scientific Resurvey 1947; Arno Atoll Expedition for Pacific Science Bd. 1950; Fulbright Lecturer Univ. of Queensland, Australia 1954; Fellow, Geological Soc. of America; mem. Paleontological Soc. (Pres. 1961–62), Paleontological Research Inst. (Pres. 1961–64), N.A.S.; Paleontologist Soc. Medal 1987, James Hall Medal 1987. *Leisure interests:* history of geology, prize books. *Address:* 104 Brook Lane, Ithaca, New York 14850, U.S.A. *Telephone:* (607) 257-7854.

WELLS, Rufus Michael Grant, PH.D., F.R.S.N.Z.; New Zealand professor of zoology; b. 3 July 1947, Cardiff, Wales; s. of Peter F. Wells and Jean Chiles; m. Jane Nelson 1969; one s. one d.; ed. Hamilton Boys' High School, Univ. of Auckland, Bedford Coll., Univ. of London, U.K.; researcher in molecular physiology of haemoglobin and respiration (medical, animal, and fisheries science), Antarctic biology; Asst. Lecturer in Statistics, Univ. of Auckland 1970–71; Research Asst. and Ph.D. student Bedford Coll., London 1971–74; Biochemist and MRC Fellow, Univ. Coll. Hosp., London 1974–75; lecturer, then Sr. Lecturer in Zoology, then Prof., Univ. of Auckland 1975–; biological and editorial consultant, specializing in Antarctic Science and Science Educ.; mem. Nat. Comm. for Antarctic Research 1987–; Physiological Soc. of N.Z. Medal 1983. *Publications:* 130 scientific papers. *Leisure interests:* cross-country and marathon running. *Address:* Department of Zoology, University of Auckland, Auckland (Office); 5A Landscape Road, Epsom, Auckland, New Zealand (Home). *Telephone:* (09) 737-999 (Office); (09) 689-031 (Home).

WELSH, Moray Meston, B.A., L.R.A.M., A.R.C.M.; British 'cellist; b. 1 March 1947, Haddington; s. of D. A. Welsh and C. (née Meston) Welsh; m. Melissa Phelps 1984; ed. York Univ. and Moscow Conservatoire; 'cello solo appearances in U.K., U.S.A., U.S.S.R., Europe and Scandinavia; appeared in concertos and chamber music with major U.K. orchestras, radio, TV; also festivals at Bath, Edinburgh, Aldeburgh, Bergen and Helsinki; records include concertos by Boccherini, Vivaldi, Goehr, Hoddinott, Hugh Wood (record of the year); recorded with James Galway, Kyung-Wha Chung, Allegri Quartet, Alberni Quartet; Lecturer, Royal Northern Coll. of Music, Manchester 1977–; British Council Award, Gulbenkian Fellowship. *Address:* 28 Summerfield Avenue, Queens Park, London, NW6 6JY, England. *Telephone:* 01-960 9122.

WELTING, Ruth Lynn; American opera singer (coloratura soprano); b. 5 Nov. 1948, Memphis, Tenn.; d. of W. E. Welting; ed. Memphis State Univ., Juilliard School of Music and under Jani Strasser (Glyndebourne), Daniel Ferro and Luigi Ricci (Rome Opera); début, New York City Opera in Die Entführung 1971, Metropolitan Opera as Zerbinetta in Ariadne auf Naxos 1975, Chicago Lyric Opera as Olympia in Tales of Hoffmann 1975, Royal Opera House, Covent Garden as Rosina in Il Barbiere di Siviglia 1976, Paris Opera 1983; has appeared at many int. music festivals. *Leisure interests:* Christian ministries, sport, cooking. *Address:* c/o Bob Lombardo Associates, One Harkness Plaza, 61 West 62nd Street, New York, N.Y. 10023, U.S.A. *Telephone:* (212) 586-4453.

WELTY, Eudora, B.A.; American writer; b. 1909, Jackson, Miss.; d. of Christian Webb and Chestina (Andrews) Welty; ed. Mississippi State Coll. for Women, Univ. of Wisconsin and Columbia Univ.; mem. American Acad. of Arts and Letters 1969; Gold Medal, Nat. Inst. Arts and Letters 1972; Pulitzer Prize for Fiction for The Optimist's Daughter 1973; Nat. Medal for Literature 1980; Presidential Medal of Freedom 1980. Commonwealth Award for Distinguished Service in Literature (Modern Language Asscn. of America) 1984. *Publications:* A Curtain of Green 1941, Robber Bridegroom 1942, The Wide Net 1943, Delta Wedding 1946, The Golden Apples 1949, The Ponder Heart 1954, The Bride of Innisfallen 1955, The Shoe Bird 1964, Losing Battles 1970, One Time, One Place 1971, The Optimist's Daughter 1972, The Eye of the Story 1978, The Collected Stories of Eudora Welty 1980, One Writer's Beginnings 1984. *Address:* 1119 Pinehurst Street, Jackson, Miss. 39202, U.S.A.

WEN JIABAO; Chinese party and state official; b. 1942; geological research worker in Gansu Prov. 1968–1982; Dir. Reform Research Office of the Geological and Mining Bureau of the State Council 1982–83; Deputy Minister of Geology and Mining 1983–85; Vice-Dir. of the Cen. Gen. Office of the CCP Cen. Cttee. 1985; Alternate mem. Secr. of Cen. Cttee. *Address:* Central General Office of the Chinese Communist Party Central Committee, Beijing, People's Republic of China.

WEN MINSHENG; Chinese politician; b. 1910, Henan Prov.; ed. Beijing Univ.; Sec., Jianglin (Jingzhou) County CP Cttee., Hubei Prov. 1950; Deputy Sec.-Gen. Cen.-S. China Mil. and Admin. Council 1950–52, mem. of its Political and Legal Affairs Cttee. 1951–54; Deputy Dir. of its Public Security Dept. 1952–53; Dir. Political Dept., Public Security Forces, Cen.-S. China Mil. Region 1954; Vice-Chair. Guangdong Prov. People's Govt. 1954–55; Sec. Guangdong Prov. CP Cttee. 1955–62; Dir. Social Affairs Dept., S. China Sub-bureau, Cen.-S. China Bureau, CCP Cen. Cttee. 1955; Vice-Gov. Guangdong Prov. 1955–56; Deputy to 2nd NPC 1958–64; Sec. Henan Prov. CP Cttee. 1962–65; Gov. Henan Prov. 1963; Deputy to 3rd NPC 1964; Second Sec. Henan Prov. CP Cttee. 1965; purged during Cultural Revolution; Sec. Heilongjiang Prov. CP Cttee. 1979–81; First Sec. Harbin Municipality CP 1979–81; Minister of Posts and Telecommunications 1981–84, Adviser 1984–; mem. Cen. Advisory Comm. 1985–. *Address:* c/o State Council, Beijing, People's Republic of China.

WENDERS, Wim; German film director; b. 1945, Düsseldorf; *Films include:* Summer in the City 1970, The Goalies Anxiety at the Penalty Kick 1972, The Scarlet Letter 1973, Alice in the Cities 1974, The Wrong Move 1975, Kings of the Road 1976, The American Friend 1977, Lightning Over Water 1980, The State of Things 1982, Hammett 1982, Paris, Texas 1984, Wings of Desire 1987 (Cannes Film Festival Award). *Address:* c/o Jess S. Morgan & Co., 6420 Wilshire Boulevard, Los Angeles, Calif. 90048, U.S.A.

WENGER, Antoine, Rév. Père; French theologian, journalist and historian; b. 2 Sept. 1919, Rohrwiller (Bas-Rhin); s. of Charles and Philomène Gambel; ed. Sorbonne, Strasbourg Univ.; Dir. of Oriental Theology, Univ. Catholique de Lyon 1948–56, Prof. 1956; Chief Ed. La Croix 1957–69; Pres. Fédération Internationale des Directeurs de Journaux Catholiques 1957–65; mem. Pontifical Marian Acad., Rome 1959; Prof. of Ancient Christian Literature Strasbourg Univ. 1969–73; Ecclesiastical Counsellor to the French Amb. to the Holy See 1973–83; Advisor to Council for Church (Vatican) and Public Affairs 1983–, to Pontifical Council for non-believers 1987–. *Publications:* L'Assomption dans la tradition orientale 1955, Homélies Baptismales inédites de St. Jean Chrysostome 1957, La Russie de Khrouchtchev 1959, Vatican II, Première Session 1963, Vatican II, Deuxième Session 1964, Vatican II, Troisième Session 1966, Quatrième Session 1966, Upsal, le Défi du Siècle aux Eglises 1968, Rome et Moscou, 1900–1950 1987, Le cardinal Jean Villot, Secrétaire d'Etat de trois Papes 1988. *Leisure interests:* old books, stamps. *Address:* Via San Pio V, 55, 00165 Rome, Italy. *Telephone:* 46-38-41 (Office); 6223998 (Home).

WENTZEL, Jacob Johannes Greyling; South African farmer and politician; b. 23 July 1925, Potchefstroom; m. Margaretha Hugo; four d.; ed. Hoogenhout High School and Glen Coll. of Agric.; farmer at Trichardtsfontein, Bethal Dist.; Chair. Eastern Transvaal Co-operative Ltd., Trichardt Farm Labourers' Co-operative, Trichardt Farmers' Asscn.; mem. Advisory Council, Transvaal Livestock Co-operative; mem. House of Ass. 1966–; has served on numerous comms. of inquiry into agric.; Deputy Minister of Devt. 1979, of Devt. and Land Affairs 1980; Minister of Agric. 1982–84, of Agric. Nov. 1986–, of Agricultural Econs. and Water Affairs 1984–86; National Party. *Address:* House of Assembly, Cape Town 8000, South Africa.

WEPENER, Willem Jacobus, B.A.; South African journalist; b. 11 Jan. 1927, Vrede, O.F.S.; s. of Daniël Johannes Wepener and Elsie Caroline (née De Villiers) Wepener; m. Ita Duvenage 1955; three d.; ed. Univ. of Orange Free State; Reporter, Die Burger Cape Town 1949–54, Chief Sub-Ed. 1954–60, News Ed. 1961–68, Ed. 1970; Asst. Ed. Die Beeld (Sunday) Johannesburg 1968–70; Ed. and Man. Rapport Johannesburg 1970–78; Gen. Man. (Marketing) Nasionale Tydskrifte Cape Town 1979–83; Ed.-in-Chief Beeld and Dir. Nasionale Media 1983–. *Publications:* contribs. to manuals, textbooks and other works on journalsism. *Leisure interests:* fishing, snooker, sea diving. *Address:* Beeld, P.O. Box 5425, Johannesburg 2000

(Office); 46 Greenway, Greenside 2194, South Africa (Home). *Telephone:* (011) 402-1460 (Office).

WERNER, Ernest George Germain; Netherlands oil company executive; b. 23 Dec. 1920, The Hague; m. Elly Agnese J. Asmussen 1945; two s.; ed. Technological Univ. of Delft; joined Royal Dutch/Shell Group as research chemist at Amsterdam lab. 1945; subsequent appointments in chemical eng. and research at Amsterdam, London and the Pernis refinery; Head of Plastics, Resins and Elastomers Div. 1961–63, of Industrial and Agricultural Chemicals Div. 1963–64; Mfg. Co-ordinator for Chemicals 1964–67, Dir. for Chemicals 1967–70; Man. Dir. N.V. Koninklijke Nederlandsche Petroleum Maatschappij (Royal Dutch) 1970–81, mem. Supervisory Bd. 1981–; Man. Dir. The Shell Petroleum Co. Ltd. 1970–81, mem. Bd. Dirs. 1981–; Prin. Dir. Shell Petroleum N.V. 1970–; Kt. Order of Dutch Lion, Officier, Légion d'Honneur. *Address:* N.V. Koninklijke Nederlandsche Petroleum Maatschappij, 30 Carel van Bylandtlaan, The Hague, Netherlands (Office). *Telephone:* 771435 (Office).

WERNER, Helmut; German business executive; b. 2 Sept. 1936, Cologne; m. Erika Werner; one s. one d.; ed. business studies in Cologne; various man. posts with Englebert & Co. GmbH, Aachen 1961–78, Man. Dir. for marketing, mfg. and devt., Europe 1978; mem. Exec. Bd. Continental Gummi-Werke AG 1979, Chair. 1983–87; mem. Exec. Bd. Daimler Benz 1987–. *Address:* Daimler Benz AG, Stuttgart 60, Undertürkheim, Federal Republic of Germany. *Telephone:* 0511/765-1.

WERNER, Pierre; Luxembourg lawyer and politician; b. 29 Dec. 1913, Saint André, Lille, France; m. Henriette Pescatore 1939; three s. two d.; ed. Univ. of Paris and Luxembourg; practising lawyer 1938–39 and 1944–45; with Banque Générale du Luxembourg 1939–44; with Ministry of Finance 1945; Commr. of Bank Control 1946–53 and of Nat. Savings 1948–53; Sec. to the Council of Govt. 1949–53; Minister of Finance and of the Armed Forces 1953–58; Prime Minister and Minister of Finance 1959–64; Prime Minister, Min. of Foreign Affairs, of Treasury, and of Justice 1964–66; Prime Minister, Minister of Treasury and of Civil Service 1967–69; Prime Minister, Minister of Finance and Minister of Cultural Affairs 1969–74, Prime Minister and Minister of Cultural Affairs 1979–84; Gov. EIB 1958–74, 1979–84; Chair. EEC Cttee. on Monetary Union 1970–71; Chair. Parl. Christian Social group 1974–79; mem. European Parl. 1979; Chair. Compagnie Luxembourg de Télédiffusion 1985–87; Christian Social Party; numerous European and foreign decorations. *Publications:* various publs. on European and monetary matters. *Address:* 2, Rond-Point Robert Schuman, Luxembourg (Home). *Telephone:* 225-74 (Home).

WERTHÉN, Hans Lennart Oscar, D.TECH.; Swedish business executive; b. 15 June 1919, Ludvika; s. of Oscar F. and Mabel (née Evans) Werthén; m. Britta Ekström 1950; three d.; ed. Falu Läroverk, Falun, Royal Inst. of Tech., Stockholm; Asst. Prof., Royal Inst. of Tech., Stockholm 1942–46, Chief of Television Research 1947–51; Chief of Television Research Lab., AGA AB 1952–56; Vice-Pres. (Eng.) Norrköpings Elektrotekniska Fabrikers AB (NEFA) (Philips) 1956–59; Vice-Pres. L. M. Ericsson Telephone Co., Stockholm 1960, Sr. Vice-Pres. 1963–67, Chair. June 1981–; Pres. AB Electrolux 1967–74, Group Exec. Chair. 1974–81, Chair. 1981–; Chair. Gränges AB 1977–; mem. Bd. Dirs. Fed. of Swedish Industries 1980–; numerous other public positions and appointments; Kt. Commdr., Royal Order of Vasa 1973, Kt. Commdr., Order of the White Rose (Finland) 1975, John Ericson Medal 1982. *Leisure interests:* history, music, mountain climbing. *Address:* AB Electrolux, 105 45 Stockholm; Karlavägen 67VI, 114 49 Stockholm, Sweden. *Telephone:* (08) 7386000 (Office); (08) 661-08-00, 662-24-67 (Home).

WESCHKE, Karl Martin; German artist; b. 7 June 1925, Gera, Thüringen; m. 1st Alison de Vere 1948, (divorced 1957), 2nd Liese Dennis 1963 (divorced 1968); two s. two d.; ed. elementary school and self-taught as painter; has lived in England since 1948; Visiting Lecturer at several art colls.; one-man exhbns. in London and other cities in U.K. 1958–; has participated in numerous group exhbns. in U.K., U.S.A., Germany and Austria 1959–; works in several public galleries in U.K., U.S.A. and Australia including Tate Gallery and Museum of Modern Art, New York; Arts Council of G.B. Major Award 1976, etc. *Address:* Ruston, Cape Cornwall, St. Just, Penzance, Cornwall, England.

WESKER, Arnold, F.R.S.L.; British playwright; b. 24 May 1932, Stepney, London; s. of Joseph Wesker and Leah Wesker (née Perlmutter); m. Doreen (Dusty) Cecile Bicker 1958; two s. two d.; ed. mixed elementary schools and Upton House Central School, Hackney, London; left school 1948, worked as furniture maker's apprentice, carpenter's mate, bookseller's asst. R.A.F. 1950–52 (ran drama group); plumber's mate, road labourer, farm labourer, seed sorter, kitchen porter and pastry-cook; studied 9 months, London School of Film Technique; Chair. British Cen. of Int. Theatre Inst. 1978–82; Pres. Perm. Cttee. of Playwrights 1979–83; Arts Council Bursary 1959; Dir. Centre 42, 1961–70; Encyclopaedia Britannica Competition, 1st Prize (for Chicken Soup with Barley), 3rd Prize 1961 (for The Kitchen); Premio Marzotto Drama Prize (for Their Very Own Golden City) 1964; Gold Medal, Premios el Espectador y la Critica (for The Kitchen) 1973, (for Chicken Soup with Barley) 1979; The Goldie Award (for Roots) 1986; Hon. D.Litt. (Univ. of E. Anglia) 1989; began directing his own plays: The Four Seasons, Cuba 1968, world première of his own play The Friends at Stadsteatern, Stockholm 1970, London 1970, The Old Ones, Munich, Their Very Own and Golden City, Aarhus 1974, Love Letters on Blue Paper, Nat. Theatre 1978, Oslo 1980, Annie Wobbler, Birmingham 1983, London 1984; dir. Osborne's The Entertainer, Theatre Clwyd 1983, Yardsale and Whatever Happened to Betty Lemon, London 1987. *Publications:* Plays: The Kitchen 1957, The trilogy—Chicken Soup with Barley 1958, Roots 1959, I'm Talking about Jerusalem 1960, Chips with Everything 1962, Menace 1963, Their Very Own and Golden City 1964, The Four Seasons 1965, The Friends 1970, The Old Ones 1972, The Journalists 1972, The Wedding Feast 1973, The Merchant 1975, Love Letters on Blue Paper 1978, Caritas 1981, One More Ride on the Merry-Go-Round 1984; also: Fear of Fragmentation (essays and lectures), Six Sundays in January (miscellaneous), Love Letters on Blue Paper (short stories) 1974, Say Goodbye You May Never See Them Again (text to accompany book of paintings by John Allin) 1974, Words as Definitions of Experience (essay), Journey Into Journalism (non-fiction) 1977, Said The Old Man To The Young Man (stories) 1978, Fatlips (children's book) 1978, The Journalists (triptych) 1979, Collected Plays and Stories (5 vols.) 1979, Annie Wobbler 1983, Four Portraits and Sullied Hand (2 one-act plays) 1983, Lady O (filmscript) 1983, Breakfast (TV play) 1983, Bluey (radio-play) 1983, Yardsale (one-act play) 1984, Distinctions (collected lectures and essays) 1985, Thieves in the Night (4-part adaption for TV of Arthur Koestler's novel) 1984-85, When God Wanted a Son 1985, Whatever Happened to Betty Lemon (one-act play) 1987, Badenheim 1939 (adaptation of Aharon Applefeld's novel) 1987, Little Old Lady and Shoeshine (two one-act plays for young people) 1987, Lady Othello (adapted from his original film script) 1987, Beorhtel's Hill 1989, The Mistress 1989. *Leisure interest:* listening to gramophone records. *Address:* 37 Ashley Road, London, N19 3AG, England.

WESSELMANN, Tom, B.A.; American artist; b. 23 Feb. 1931, Cincinnati, Ohio; s. of Edwin W. and Grace D. Wesselmann; m. 2nd Claire Selley 1963; one s. two d.; ed. Univ. of Cincinnati, Art Acad. of Cincinnati and Cooper Union, N.Y; taught art New York City Junior and Senior High Schools 1959-62; one-man exhbns. 1961-, incl. Tanager Gallery, New York 1961, Green Gallery, New York 1962, 1964, 1965, Museum of Contemporary Art, Chicago 1968, Newport Harbor Art Museum, Calif. 1970, Jack Glenn Gallery, Calif. 1971, Calif. State Univ. 1974, Sidney Janis Gallery 1966, 1968, 1970, 1972, 1974, 1976, 1979, 1980, 1982, 1983, 1985, 1988, Inst. of Contemporary Art, Boston 1978, Ehrlich Gallery, New York 1979, Margo Leavin Gallery, Hokin Gallery, Fla. 1981, 1984, 1986, Los Angeles 1982, Carl Solway Gallery, Cincinnati 1982, Delahunty Gallery, Dallas 1983. Hokin Gallery, Fla. 1984, McIntosh Drysdale Gallery, Houston 1984, Jeff Hoffeld Gallery, New York 1985, Carl Solway Gallery 1986, Galerie Denise Rene Hans Mayer, Düsseldorf 1986, Galerie de France, Paris 1987, Galerie Esperanza, Montreal 1984, 1987, The Queen's Museum, New York 1987, Joachim Becker, Cannes 1986, 1987, Galeria Fernando Quintana, Bogotá, Colombia 1986, Blum Helman Gallery, L.A. 1989, Waddington Gallery, London 1989. *Leisure interest:* writing country music. *Address:* 231 Bowery, New York, N.Y. 10012, U.S.A. *Telephone:* (212) 228-3930.

WEST, Edward Mark, C.M.G., M.A.; British administrator; b. 11 March 1923, London; m. Lydia Hollander 1948; three s.; ed. Hendon County School, Univ. Coll., Oxford; Lieut., R.A. 1942-44; Capt., Dept. of Political and Psychological Warfare 1944-45; Home Civil Service 1947-58; Head of Chancery, U.K. Comm., Singapore 1958-61; Pvt. Sec. to Sec. of State for Commonwealth and Colonial Affairs 1962-64; Head of Natural Resources Dept., Ministry of Overseas Devt. 1964-70; Dir. Programme Formulation, FAO of the UN 1970, Asst. Dir.-Gen. for Admin. and Finance 1974-76, Asst. Dir.-Gen. for Programme Budget and Evaluation 1976-81, Deputy Dir.-Gen. 1982-85, Sr. Consultant 1985-. *Address:* 10 Warwick Mansions, Cromwell Crescent, London. S.W.5, England.

WEST, Francis James, PH.D., F.B.A., F.R.HIST.S., F.A.H.A.; British/Australian professor of history; b. 26 June 1927, E. Yorks.; s. of George H. West and Florence C. Selby; m. Katharine White 1963 (divorced 1976); one d.; ed. Hymers Coll. E. Yorks, Univ. of Leeds and Trinity Coll. Cambridge; Fellow, A.N.U. 1952-55; Sr. Lecturer, Victoria Univ. of Wellington 1955-59; Professorial Fellow, Inst. of Advanced Studies, A.N.U. 1960-73; Dean of Arts and Social Studies, Univ. of Buckingham 1973-75; Prof. of History and Govt. and Dean of Social Sciences, Deakin Univ. Geelong 1976-, Pro Vice-Chancellor (Research) 1986-; Overseas Fellow, Churchill Coll. Cambridge 1981-82, 1984-85; mem. Australian Humanities Research Council 1966. *Publications:* Political Advancement in the South Pacific 1961, The Justiciarship in England 1966, Hubert Murray: Australian Pro Consul 1968, Biography as History 1973, University House 1979, Gilbert Murray: A Life 1984. *Leisure interests:* music, occasional journalism and broadcasting. *Address:* Pro Vice-Chancellor's Office, Deakin University, Vic. 3217 (Office); 6 Sylvan Court, Newtown, Vic. 3220, Australia (Home). *Telephone:* 052-471213 (Office); 052-212375 (Home).

WEST, John C., LL.B.; American lawyer, fmr. state governor and diplomatist; b. 27 Aug. 1922, Camden, S.C.; s. of late Shelton J. West and of Mattie (Ratterree) West; m. Lois Rhame 1942; two s. one d.; ed. Univ. of S. Carolina; U.S. Army 1942-46; elected to S. Carolina Senate 1954, re-elected 1958, 1962; Lieut.-Gov. of S. Carolina 1966-70; Gov. of S. Carolina 1971-75; Amb. to Saudi Arabia 1977-81; with law firm John C. West 1981-;

of Counsel, McNair Law Firm 1988-; Distinguished Prof. of Middle East Studies, Univ. of South Carolina 1981-; mem. Bd. Trustees Southern Centre for Int. Studies; Army Commendation Medal, Knight Commdr. Order of Merit, Fed. Repub. of Germany; Democrat. *Address:* P.O. Box Drawer 13, Hilton Head Island, S.C. 29938, U.S.A.

WEST, Martin Litchfield, D.PHIL, F.B.A.; British scholar; b. 23 Sept. 1937, London; s. of Maurice Charles West and Catherine Baker West (née Stainthorpe); m. Stephanie Roberta Pickard 1960; one s. one d; ed. St. Paul's School, London and Balliol Coll., Oxford; Woodhouse Jr. Research Fellow, St. John's Coll., Oxford 1960-63; Fellow and Praelector in Classics, Univ. Coll., Oxford 1963-74; Prof. of Greek, Univ. of London (Bedford Coll., since 1985 Royal Holloway and Bedford New Coll.) 1974-. *Publications:* Hesiod, Theogony (ed.) 1966, Fragmenta Hesiodea (ed. with R. Merkelbach) 1967, Early Greek Philosophy and the Orient 1971, Sing Me, Goddess 1971, Iambi et Elegi Graeci (ed.) 1971-72, Textual Criticism and Editorial Technique 1973, Studies in Greek Elegy and Iambus 1974, Hesiod, Works and Days (ed.) 1978, Theognidis et Phocylidis fragmenta 1978, Delectus ex Iambis et Elegis Graecis 1980, Greek Metre 1982, The Orphic Poems 1983, Carmina Anacreontea 1984, The Hesiodic Catalogue of Women 1985, Introduction to Greek Metre 1987, Euripides Orestes (ed.) 1987, Hesiod (trans.) 1988. *Leisure interest:* music. *Address:* Department of Classics, Royal Holloway and Bedford New College, Egham Hill, Egham, Surrey, TW20 0EX; 42 Portland Road, Oxford, OX2 7EY, England (Home). *Telephone:* (0784) 34455 (College).

WEST, Morris (Langlo), A.M., B.A.; Australian author; b. 26 April 1916, Melbourne; s. of Charles Langlo West and Florence Guilfoyle (Hanlon); m. Joyce Lawford 1953; three s. one d.; ed. Univ. of Melbourne; teacher of Modern Languages and Mathematics, New South Wales and Tasmania 1933-39; Army service 1939-43; Sec. to William Morris Hughes, fmr. Prime Minister of Australia 1943; Fellow, Royal Soc. of Literature, World Acad. of Arts and Science; Nat. Brotherhood Award, Nat. Council of Christians and Jews 1960, James Tait Black Memorial Prize 1960, Royal Soc. of Literature Heinemann Award 1960 (All prizes for The Devil's Advocate); Hon. D.Litt. (Santa Clara Univ., Calif.) 1969, (Mercy Coll., New York) 1982; Int. Dag Hammarskjold Prize (Grand Collar of Merit) 1978. *Publications:* Gallows on the Sand 1955, Kundu 1956, Children of the Sun 1957, The Crooked Road (English title The Big Story) 1957, The Concubine 1958, Backlash (English title Second Victory) 1958, The Devil's Advocate 1959 (filmed 1977), The Naked Country 1960, Daughter of Silence (novel and play) 1961, The Shoes of the Fisherman 1963, The Ambassador 1965, The Tower of Babel 1968, The Heretic, a Play in Three Acts 1970, Scandal in the Assembly (with Robert Francis) 1970, Summer of the Red Wolf 1971, The Salamander 1973, Harlequin 1974, The Navigator 1976, Proteus 1979, The Clowns of God 1981, The World is Made of Glass 1983 (play 1984), Cassidy 1986, Masterclass 1988. *Address:* c/o Maurice Greenbaum, Rosenman Colin, Freund Lewis & Cohen, 587 Madison Avenue, New York, N.Y. 10022, U.S.A.; 310 Hudson Parade, Clareville, N.S.W. 2107, Australia.

WEST, Richard G., M.A., SC.D., F.R.S.; British professor of botany; b. 31 May 1926, Hendon, Middx.; m. 1st Janet Abram 1958, one s.; m. 2nd Hazel Gristwood 1973, two d.; ed. King's School, Canterbury and Univ. of Cambridge; Fellow, Clare Coll., Cambridge 1954-; Lecturer in Botany, Univ. of Cambridge 1960-68, Reader in Quaternary Research 1968-74, Prof. of Palaeoecology 1974-77; Prof. of Botany and Head, Dept. of Botany 1977-, Dir. Sub-dept. of Quaternary Research 1966-87; hon. mem. Royal Belgian Acad.; Hon. M.R.I.A.; Bigsby Medal, Geological Soc. 1968, Lyell Medal, Geological Soc. 1988. *Publications:* Pleistocene Geology and Biology 1968, The Ice Age in Britain (jtly.) 1972, The Pre-glacial Pleistocene of the Norfolk and Suffolk Coasts 1980. *Leisure interest:* sailing. *Address:* Clare College, Cambridge; 3A Woollards Lane, Great Shelford, Cambridge, CB2 5LZ, England (Home). *Telephone:* Cambridge 842578 (Home).

WEST, Stewart John; Australian politician; b. 31 March 1934, Forbes, N.S.W.; ed. Wollongong High School; worked as bank officer and steel worker before becoming a waterside worker; Pres., S. Coast Branch, Waterside Workers' Fed. 1972-77; M.P. for Cunningham, N.S.W., House of Reps. Oct. 1977-; Minister for Immigration and Ethnic Affairs 1983-84, for Housing and Construction 1984-87, of Admin. Services Aug. 1987-; Labor Party. *Leisure interests:* reading, particularly on economics, ancient history, archaeology and international affairs. *Address:* Department of Administrative Services, P.O. Box 1920, Canberra, A.C.T. 2601, Australia. *Telephone:* (062) 753000.

WEST, Timothy Lancaster, C.B.E.; British actor and director; b. 20 Oct. 1934, Bradford, Yorks.; s. of H. Lockwood West and the late Olive Carleton-Crowe; m. 1st Jacqueline Boyer 1956 (dissolved), one d.; m. 2nd Prunella Scales 1963, two s.; ed. John Lyon School, Harrow and Regent Street Polytechnic; repertory seasons, Wimbledon, Hull, Salisbury, Northampton 1956-60; *London stage appearances in* Caught Napping 1959, Galileo 1960, Gentle Jack 1963, The Trigon 1963, The Italian Girl 1968, Abelard and Heloise 1970, Exiles 1970, The Critic as Artist 1971, The Houseboy 1973, A Month in the Country 1974, A Room with a View 1975, Laughter 1978, The Homecoming 1978, Beecham 1980, Master Class 1984, The War at Home 1984, When We are Married 1986, The Sneeze 1988; numerous appearances with Prospect Theatre Co., Royal Shakespeare Co. and regional theatres; recent TV appearances include: The Monocled

Mutineer, The Good Doctor Bodkin Adams, Harry's Kingdom, When We Are Married, Breakthrough at Reykjavik, Strife, A Shadow on the Sun, The Contractor; *films include:* The Looking Glass War, Nicholas and Alexandra, The Day of the Jackal, The Devil's Advocate, The Thirty-Nine Steps, Oliver Twist and Cry Freedom; Artistic Dir. Old Vic 1980–81; Dir.-in-residence, Univ. of W. Australia 1982. *Leisure interests:* music, travel, inland waterways, old railways. *Address:* c/o James Sharkey Associates, 15 Golden Square, London, W1R 3AG, England; c/o Smith Freedman Associates, 123 N. San Vicente Boulevard, Beverly Hills, Calif. 90211, U.S.A. *Telephone:* 01-434 3801 (London); 213-852-4777 (California).

WESTBROOK, Roger, M.A.; British diplomatist; b. 26 May 1941; s. of Edward George Westbrook and Beatrice Minnie Marshall; ed. Dulwich Coll. and Hertford Coll., Oxford; Foreign Office 1964; Asst. Pvt. Sec. to the Chancellery of the Duchy of Lancaster 1965; held posts in Yaoundé 1967, Rio de Janeiro 1971, Brasilia 1972; Private Sec. to Minister of State, FCO 1975; Head of Chancery, Lisbon 1977; Deputy Head, News Dept., FCO 1980, Deputy Head, Falkland Islands Dept. 1982, Overseas Inspectorate 1984; British High Commr., Brunei Darussalam 1986–. *Leisure interests:* doodling, sightseeing, theatre. *Address:* British High Commission, Bandar Seri Begawan, Negara Brunei Darussalam. *Telephone:* 22231.

WESTCOTT, John Hugh, D.SC., F.ENG., F.R.S.; British university professor; b. 3 Nov. 1920, London; m. Helen Fay Morgan 1950; two s. one d.; ed. City and Guilds Coll., London, Imperial Coll. London and M.I.T., U.S.A.; Lecturer in Electrical Eng., Imperial Coll. 1950–56, Reader 1956–61, Prof. of Control Systems 1961–, Head of Dept. of Computing and Control 1970–79, Sr. Research Fellow 1984–; Chair. Feedback PLC, Churchill Controls Ltd.; Sr. Studentship, Royal Comm. for Exhbn. of 1851. *Publications:* An Exposition of Adaptive Control 1962, monographs and papers on topics related to control systems. *Address:* Electrical Engineering Department, Imperial College, London, SW7 2BT (Office); 8 Fernhill, Oxshott, Surrey, KT22 0JH, England (Home). *Telephone:* 01-589 5111 (Ext. 5106) (Office); (037 284) 3245 (Home).

WESTENDORF, Wolfhart, D.PHIL.; German egyptologist; b. 18 Sept. 1924, Schwiebus; s. of Otto Westendorf and Charlotte Mechler; m. Marianne Harder 1952; two c.; ed. Humboldt Univ. Berlin; Research Fellow, Inst. für Orientforschung, Akad. der Wissenschaften, Berlin 1952–61; Lecturer, Univ. of Munich 1961–65; Extraordinary Prof. Univ. of Munich 1965–66, Prof. and Head of Dept. 1966–67; Prof. Univ. of Göttingen 1967–; mem. Göttingen Acad., German Archaeological Inst.; Deutscher Nationalpreis. *Publications:* Gebrauch des Passivs 1953, Grammatik der mediz. Texte 1962, Darstellungen des Sonnenlaufs 1962, Das alte Ägypten 1968, Koptisches Handwörterbuch 1977. *Address:* Über den Höfen 15, 34 Göttingen, Federal Republic of Germany.

WESTERFIELD, Putney, B.A.; American business executive; b. 9 Feb. 1930, New Haven, Conn.; s. of Ray Bert Westerfield and Beatrice Putney; m. Anne Montgomery 1954; two s. one d.; ed. Choate School and Yale Univ.; Vice-Pres. and Co-founder, Careers Inc. 1950–52; Man. S.E. Asia Operations, Swen Publs.; service with Dept. of State in Korea, Washington, Saigon 1953–59; Asst. to Publr. of Time 1957–59, Asst. to Circulation Dir. 1959–61, Circulation Dir. 1961–66, Asst. Publr. 1966–68; Asst. Publr. of Life 1968–69; Publr. of Fortune 1969–73; Pres. Chase World Information Corpn. 1973–75; Vice-Pres. Boyden Assocs. Int. 1976–80, Sr. Vice-Pres., Western Man. 1980–84, Pres. and C.E.O. 1984–. *Leisure interests:* reading, music, tennis, swimming. *Address:* c/o Boyden Associates International, 1 Maritime Plaza, Suite 1760, San Francisco, Calif. 94111 (Office); 360 Robinwood Lane, Hillsborough, Calif. 94010, U.S.A. (Home). *Telephone:* (203) 869-8884.

WESTERMAN, Sir (Wilfred) Alan, Kt., C.B.E., M.A.ECON., B.ED., ED.D.; Australian business executive; b. 25 March 1913, New Zealand; m. Margaret de B. H. White; two s. (from previous m.); ed. Knox Grammar School, Univs. of Tasmania, Melbourne and Columbia; fmr. Lecturer in Rural Sociology, Columbia Univ.; Trade Commr. Service 1946–49; Dir. Trade Promotion and Int. Trade Relations 1949–53; First Asst. Sec., Dept. of Commerce and Agric. 1953–58; Chair. Commonwealth Tariff Bd. 1958–60; Sec. Dept. of Trade and Industry 1960–71; Exec. Chair. Australian Industry Devt. Corpn. 1971–77; Chair. Australian Industry Devt. Corpn. 1971–83; Dir. Philips Industries Ltd. 1977–, Ampol Ltd. 1977–; Chair. Australian Stevedoring Industry Consultative Council 1978–. *Address:* P.O. Box 1483, Canberra, A.C.T. 2601, Australia.

WESTERTERP, Theodorus Engelbertus (Tjerk); Netherlands politician; b. 2 Dec. 1930, Rotterdam; m. 1954; ed. High School Breda, Univ. of Nijmegen; journalist 1949–53; civil servant European Parl. 1953–63; M.P. 1963–71; State Sec. for Foreign Affairs 1971–73; Minister of Transport, Water Control and Public Works 1973–77; Gen. Man. European Options Exchange 1978–; Grand Officer Order of Bernado O'Higgins (Chile); Grand Cross Order of the Lion (Finland); Grand Cross (Italy); Catholic People's Party. *Address:* Damrak 40a, Amsterdam, Netherlands.

WESTHEIMER, Frank Henry, M.A., PH.D.; American professor of chemistry; b. 15 Jan. 1912, Baltimore, Md.; s. of Henry F. and Carrie (Burgunder) Westheimer; m. Jeanne Friedman 1937; two d.; ed. Dartmouth Coll. and Harvard Univ.; Nat. Research Fellow, Columbia Univ. 1935–36; Research Assoc., Instr., Asst. Prof. of Chem., Univ. of Chicago 1936–44; Research

Supervisor, NDRC Explosives Research Lab. 1944–45; Assoc. Prof. Dept. of Chem., Univ. of Chicago 1946–48, Prof. 1948–54; Visiting Prof. of Chem. Harvard Univ. 1953–54, Prof. 1954–83, Morris Loeb Prof. of Chem. Emer. 1983–; Visiting Prof., Boston Univ. 1984, Ohio State Univ. 1985, Univ. of Calif. (San Diego) 1986, 1988; mem. Pres.'s Science Advisory Cttee. 1967–70; mem. American Acad. of Arts and Sciences, N.A.S., American Philosophical Soc.; Foreign mem. Royal Soc.; numerous awards and prizes including Willard Gibbs Medal, Ingold Medal, N.A.S. Award in the Chemical Sciences, Nichols Medal, James Flack Norris Award, Richards Medal, Welch Award, Nat. Medal of Science, Paracelsus Medal (Swiss Chemical Soc.), Priestley Award (American Chemical Soc.); recipient of seven hon. degrees. *Publications:* Chemistry, Opportunities and Needs 1965; about 200 articles in scientific journals. *Address:* Department of Chemistry, Harvard University, 12 Oxford Street, Cambridge, Mass. 02138 (Office); 3 Berkeley Street, Cambridge, Mass. 02138, U.S.A. (Home). *Telephone:* (617) 495-4096 (Office); (617) 661-8177.

WESTMORELAND, Gen. William Childs; American retd. army officer; b. 26 March 1914, Spartanburg County, S. Carolina; s. of James R. and Eugenia Childs Westmoreland; m. Katherine S. Van Deusen 1947; one s. two d.; ed. U.S. Mil. Acad.; U.S. Army 1936–72; Maj.Gen. 1956, Lieut.-Gen. 1963, Gen. 1964; Battery Officer, Oklahoma and Hawaii 1936–41; Commdg. Officer, 34th Field Artillery Battalion 1942–44; Exec. Officer 9th Infantry Div. Artillery 1944, Chief of Staff 1944–45, Commdr. 60th Infantry Regt., Germany 1945, 504th Parachute Infantry Regt., Fort Bragg 1946–47; Chief of Staff, 82nd Airborne Div. 1947–50; Instructor, Command and Gen. Staff Coll., and Army War Coll. 1950–52; Commdr. 187th Airborne Regimental Combat Team, Korea and Japan 1952–53; Deputy Asst. Chief of Staff G1, for Manpower Control, Dept. of Army 1953–54, Sec. Gen. Staff 1955–58; Commdg. Gen. 101st Airborne Div. and Fort Campbell, Kentucky 1958–60; Supt. U.S. Mil. Acad., West Point 1960–63; Commdr. 18th Airborne Corps, Fort Bragg 1963–64; Deputy Commdr. U.S. Mil. Assistance Command Viet-Nam 1964, Commdr. 1964–68; Chief of Staff, U.S. Army, The Pentagon 1968–72; retd. from army 1972. *Publications:* Report on the War in Vietnam, A Soldier Reports and numerous articles in military publications and the press. *Address:* P.O. Box 1059, Charleston, S.C. 29402, U.S.A.

WESTMORLAND, 15th Earl of (cr. 1624); David Anthony Thomas Fane, K.C.V.O.; b. 31 March 1924; s. of the late 14th Earl of Westmorland and Hon. Diana Lister; m. Jane Lewis Findlay 1950; two s. one d.; served in World War II 1939–45; Capt. (Hon.) Royal Horse Guards 1950; A Lord in Waiting to H.M. Queen Elizabeth II 1955–78; Master of the Horse 1978–; Dir. Sotheby's Holdings Inc. 1983, Deputy-Chair. 1979, Chair. 1980–82; Dir. Sotheby Advisory Bd. 1987–. *Address:* Kingsmead, Didmarton, Glos.; 23 Chester Row, London, S.W.1, England.

WESTPHAL, Heinz; German politician; b. 4 June 1924, Berlin; s. of Max and Alice (née Dusedau) Westphal; m. Ingeborg Riemann 1950; one d.; trainee aircraft mechanic, Daimler-Benz 1939–42, instructor 1942–43; war service 1943–45; mem. SPD 1945–; mem. staff, Int. Union of Socialist Youth 1948–57; Chair. Die Falken (Socialist youth movt.) 1953–57, German Youth Council 1955–56, Chief Exec. 1958–65; mem. Advisory Council, Zweites Deutsches Fernsehen 1965–74; Chair. Admin. Council, German Volunteer Service 1974–82; mem. Bundestag 1965–, Vice-Pres. 1983–; Parl. Sec. of State, Ministry of Youth and Family 1969–74; Minister of Labour and Social Affairs April-Oct. 1982. *Leisure interests:* reading, walking, swimming. *Address:* Droste-Hülshoffstrasse 2, 5300 Bonn, Federal Republic of Germany.

WETERE, Koro Tainui, M.P.; New Zealand politician; b. 1935; m.; five c.; ed. Te Kuiti High School, Massey Univ. Agricultural Coll.; M.P. for Western Maori 1969–; Opposition Shadow Minister for Maori Affairs and Lands 1981–84; mem. Maori Policy Cttee. 1984–; Minister of Maori Affairs, of Lands, Forests and in charge of Valuation Dept. 1984–87, of Maori Affairs 1987–89; Chair. Bd. of Maori Affairs, Maori Purposes Fund; Pres. New Zealand Maori Rugby League. *Address:* Parliament Buildings, Wellington, New Zealand.

WETHERILL, George West, PH.D.; American geophysicist; b. 12 Aug. 1925, Philadelphia, Pa.; s. of George W. Wetherill and Leah Hardwick Wetherill; m. Phyllis May Steiss 1950; three c.; ed. Univ. of Chicago; Prof. of Geophysics and Geology, Univ. of Calif., Los Angeles 1960–75, Chair. Dept. of Planetary and Space Science 1968–72; Dir. Dept. of Terrestrial Magnetism, Carnegie Inst. of Washington 1975–; Pres. Geochemical Soc. 1975–76, Int. Asscn. of Geochemistry and Cosmochemistry 1977–80, Meteoritical Soc. 1983–85; Fellow American Acad. of Arts and Sciences; mem. N.A.S.; Leonard Medal (Meteoritical Soc.), G. K. Gilbert Award (Geological Soc. of America), G. P. Kuiper Prize 1986. *Publications:* about 150 papers in scientific journals. *Address:* Department of Terrestrial Magnetism, Carnegie Institution of Washington, 5241 Broad Branch Road, N.W., Washington, D.C. 20015, U.S.A.

WETTER, H.E. Cardinal Friedrich; German ecclesiastic; b. 20 Feb. 1928, Landau, Speyer; ordained 1953; consecrated Bishop of Speyer 1968; Archbishop of Munich and Freising 1982–; cr. Cardinal 1985. *Address:* Postfach 360, 8000 München 33, Federal Republic of Germany. *Telephone:* (089) 21371.

WETTSTEIN, Diter von, DR.RER.NAT.; Danish professor of genetics; b. 20 Sept. 1929, Göttingen, Germany; s. of Fritz von Wettstein and Elsa Jesser; m. Penny von Wettstein-Knowles 1967; two d.; ed. school in Innsbruck, Austria, Univ. of Tübingen, Germany, Univ. of Stockholm, Sweden; Research Asst., Genetics Dept., Forest Research Inst., Stockholm 1951-54; Asst. and Assoc. Prof. in Genetics, Univ. of Stockholm 1954-62; Prof. of Genetics and Head, Inst. of Genetics, Univ. of Copenhagen, Denmark 1962-75; Acting Head, Dept. of Physiology, Carlsberg Lab., Copenhagen 1972-75, Prof. of Physiology and Head of Dept. 1975-; Rockefeller Fellow 1958; Visiting Prof., Univ. of Calif., Davis 1966, 1972, 1973, 1974, Washington State Univ. 1969. *Publications:* 200 scientific papers on mutation research, developmental physiology and cell research. *Address:* Department of Physiology, Carlsberg Laboratory, Gamle Carlsberg Vej 10, DK-2500 Copenhagen Valby (Office); Aasevej 13, 3500 Vaerløse, Denmark (Home). *Telephone:* (01) 22 10 22, ext. 5225 (Office); (02) 48 19 98 (Home).

WEYAND, Gen. Frederick Carlton; American army officer (retd.); b. 15 Sept. 1916, Calif.; s. of Frederick C. and Velma Semans Weyand; m. L. Arline Langhart 1940; one s. two d.; Univ. of Calif., Berkeley, Nat. War Coll., Washington, and Infantry School, Fort Benning; commissioned 1938; mem. Berkeley Police Dept. 1939-40; active service 1940; served in India, Burma, China 1944-45; Intelligence duties 1946-49; Bn. Commdr. and 3rd Div. Operations Officer, Korea 1950-51; Exec. Officer, Sec. of Army 1954-57; Brigade Commdr., Berlin 1958-60; Legis. Liaison with Congress 1960-64; Commdr. U.S. 25th Infantry Div. 1964-67; Field Force Commdr., Viet-Nam 1967-68; Mil. Rep. to Paris Peace Talks 1969-70; Deputy Commdr. and Commdr. U.S. Mil. Assistance Command, Viet-Nam 1970-73; Vice-Chief of Staff of the Army 1973-74; Chief of Staff 1974-76; Sr. Vice-Pres. First Hawaiian Bank 1976-82, Consultant 1982-; Dir. Pacific Guardian Life Insurance Co. 1982-86; Trustee Estate of S. M. Damon, Honolulu 1982-; Distinguished Service Cross, Silver Star, Distinguished Service Medal, Legion of Merit. *Leisure interests:* sport (golf and tennis), music (guitar and saxophone), reading (history). *Address:* First Hawaiian Bank, 165 South King Street, Honolulu, 96813; 2121 Ala Wai Boulevard, Honolulu, Hawaii 96815.

WEYERHAEUSER, George Hunt, B.S.; American timber executive; b. 8 July 1926, Seattle; s. of late J. P. Weyerhaeuser and Helen Walker Weyerhaeuser; m. Wendy Wagner 1948; two s. four d.; ed. Yale Univ.; served in U.S. Navy 1944-46; Weyerhaeuser Co. 1947-, serving respectively as: Shift Supt. 1949-51, Wood Products Man. 1954, Asst. to Exec. Vice-Pres. 1957-58, Man. Wood Products Group, later Vice-Pres. 1958; elected to Bd. of Dirs. 1960; Exec. Vice-Pres. for Wood Products, Timber and Lands 1961-64, Exec. Vice-Pres. for Operations 1964-66, Pres. and C.E.O. 1966-88, Chair. 1988-; Pres. and Dir. Weyerhaeuser Int. Inc., Weyerhaeuser Int. S.A., Weyerhaeuser American Corpn., Weyerhaeuser Co.; Dir. Standard Oil Corpn., Safeco Insurance Co., Rand Corpn., Boeing Co., Puget Sound Nat. Bank, Equitable Life Assurance Soc. of the U.S., Barlow Weyerhaeuser Packaging Investments (Pty.) Ltd., R-W Paper Co., Weyerhaeuser Canada Ltd., and and others; mem. Bd. of Trustees, Charles Wright Acad., Weyerhaeuser Co. Foundation; mem. Business Council, Japan-Calif. Asscn., Advisory Council Stanford Research Inst., Yale School of Forestry and Natural Environment, etc. *Leisure interest:* tennis. *Address:* 2525 South 36th Street, Federal Way, Wash. 98002 (Office); 11801 Gravelly Lake Drive, S.W., Tacoma, Wash. 98499, U.S.A. (Home)

WEYMANN, Gert; German theatre director and playwright; b. 31 March 1919, Berlin; s. of Hans Weymann and Gertrud Israel; ed. Grammar School, Berlin, and Berlin Univ.; Asst. Dir., later Dir. Berlin theatre 1947-; worked as Dir. in several W. German cities and New York; lecturer in Drama Dept., American univs. 1963, 1966; lecturer at Goethe Inst., Berlin 1970-; perm. ind. mem. SFB (radio and television plays); Gerhart Hauptmann Prize for Generationen 1954. *Plays:* Generationen, Eh' die Brücken verbrennen, Der Ehrentag; TV Plays: Das Liebesmahl eines Wucherers, Familie; Radio Plays: Der Anhalter, Die Übergabe. *Address:* 1000 Berlin 31, Karlsruherstrasse 7, Federal Republic of Germany. *Telephone:* 891 1861.

WEYNEN, Wolfgang, LL.D.; German press agency executive; b. 5 July 1913, Nilvingen, Alsace Lorraine; s. of Wilhelm Weynen and Maria Weynen (née Bremer); m. Lieselotte Hoffmann 1964; one d.; ed. Univs. of Bonn, Paris, Königsberg and Leipzig; Legal adviser and Deputy Gen. Man. Chamber of Industries and Commerce, Wiesbaden 1946-48, Gen. Man. 1948-55; Gen. Man. and Chief Exec. Deutsche Press-Agentur 1955-81; Hon. Pres. of Alliance Européenne des Agences de Presse 1956, Chair. Satellite Sub-Cttee. of Int. Press Telecommunications Cttee. (IPTC) 1965, mem. Presidency Cultural Cttee. of German-Korean Friendship Asscn., Vice-Pres. IPTC 1967-68; Chair. IPTC 1968; Bd. of Vereinigte Wirtschaftsdienste, Frankfurt; Grosses Verdienstkreuz der Republik Österreich, Chevalier, Légion d'honneur, Grosses Silbernes Ehrenzeichen der Republik Österreich, Commdr., Cross of Italian Repub., Bundesverdienstkreuz 1st Class, Fed. Repub. of Germany, Knight, Royal Order of Vasa, Sweden, Commdr. de l'Ordre de la Couronne Belge, Grosses Verdienstkreuz der Bundesrepublik Deutschland, Commdr. Royal Order of Oranje-Nassau 1979, Komturkreuz des Ordens des Finnischen Löwens 1979. *Publications:* Die Arbeitszeitregelung in kontinuierlichen Betrieben 1938, Nachrichten im Zeitalter der Satelliten 1969. *Address:* Gaedechensweg 4, 2000 Hamburg 20, Federal Republic of Germany (Home). *Telephone:* 475899 (Home).

WHARTON, Clifton R., Jr., PH.D.; American educator and insurance executive; b. 13 Sept. 1926, Boston, Mass.; s. of Hon. Clifton R. Wharton Sr. and Harriette B. Wharton; m. Dolores Duncan 1950; two s.; ed. Boston Latin School, Harvard Univ., Johns Hopkins Univ. School of Advanced Int. Studies and Univ. of Chicago; Head of Reports and Analysis Dept., American Int. Assen. for Econ. and Social Devt. 1948-53; Research Assoc., Univ. of Chicago 1953-57; Assoc., Agricultural Devt. Council 1957-58, stationed in S.E. Asia 1958-64, Dir. of the Council's American Univs. Research Program 1964-66, Vice-Pres. 1967-69, mem. Bd. of Dirs. 1973-80, Pres. Mich. State Univ. and Prof. of Econs. 1970-78; Chancellor, State Univ. of N.Y. System 1978-87; Chair. and C.E.O. TIAA-CREF 1987-; Visiting Prof., Univ. of Malaya 1958-64, Stanford Univ. 1964-65; fmr. Chair. Bd. for Int. Food and Agric. Devt. (AID), U.S. Dept. of State; mem. Presidential Comm. on World Hunger, Presidential Mission to Latin America; Chair. Bd. Rockefeller Foundation 1982-; Dir. or Trustee of numerous orgs. including Overseas Devt. Council 1969-, Ford Motor Co., Aspen Inst. for Humanistic Studies, Time Inc., Federated Dept. Stores; Deputy Chair. Fed. Reserve Bank, New York 1985-86. *Publications:* Subsistence Agriculture and Economic Development (ed.) 1969, Patterns for Lifelong Learning (co-author) 1973. *Address:* TIAA/CREF, 730 Third Avenue, New York, N.Y. 10017, U.S.A. *Telephone:* (212) 490-9000.

WHATLEY, Frederick Robert, PH.D., F.R.S.; British plant biochemist; b. 26 Jan. 1924, Wilton, Wilts.; s. of Frederick Norman Whatley and Maud Louise (née Hare); m. Jean Margaret Smith Bowie 1951; two d.; ed. Bishop Wordsworth's School, Salisbury and Selwyn Coll., Cambridge; Research Assoc., Univ. of Calif., Berkeley, U.S.A. 1948-50; Sr. Lecturer in Biochemistry, Univ. of Sydney, Australia 1951-53; Asst. Plant Physiologist, Univ. of Calif., Berkeley 1953-59; Guggenheim Fellow at Univ. of Oxford and Nobel Inst., Stockholm 1959-60; Assoc. Plant Physiologist, Univ. of Calif., Berkeley 1960-62, Assoc. Biochemist 1962-64; Prof. of Botany, King's Coll., Univ. of London 1964-71; Sherardian Prof. of Botany, Head of Dept. of Plant Sciences, Oxford Univ. 1971-. *Publications:* articles and reviews in scientific journals. *Address:* Department of Plant Sciences, South Parks Road, Oxford, OX1 3RA; 50 Church Road, Sandford on Thames, Oxford, OX4 4XZ, England (Home). *Telephone:* (0865) 275000; (0865) 771602 (Home).

WHEELDON, John Murray, B.A.; Australian lawyer, politician and journalist; b. 9 August 1929, Subiaco, W. Australia; s. of Murray Walter and Marjorie Lillian Wheeldon; m. Judith Tanya Shaw; two s. one d.; ed. Perth Modern School, Univ. of Western Australia; Australian Labor Party Senator for W.A. 1965-81; Chair. Australian Parl. Cttee. on Foreign Affairs and Defence 1973-75; Minister for Repatriation and Compensation 1974-75, for Social Security June-Nov. 1975; Chair. Australian Parl. Sub-Cttee. on Human Rights in Soviet Union 1978-79; mem. Australian del. to 35th UN Gen. Ass. 1980; Assoc. Ed. The Australian 1981-; Chair. Australian Cttee. for a Community of the Democracies; Convenor, Australian Cttee. for Lebanon. *Address:* 11 Wellesley Road, Pymble, N.S.W. 2073, Australia. *Telephone:* (02) 4499717.

WHEELER, John Archibald, D.SC., PH.D.; American physicist; b. 9 July 1911, Jacksonville, Fla.; s. of Dr. Joseph Lewis Wheeler and Mabel Archibald; m. Janette Latourette Zabriskie Hegner 1935; one s. two d.; ed. Johns Hopkins Univ.; Nat. Research Council Fellow, New York and Copenhagen 1933-35; Asst. Prof. of Physics, Univ. of N.C. 1935-38; Asst. Prof. of Physics, Princeton Univ. 1938-42, Assoc. Prof. 1945-47, Prof. 1947-66, Joseph Henry Prof. of Physics 1966-76, Emer. 1976-; Prof. of Physics, Univ. of Texas at Austin 1976-; Ashbel Smith Prof. of Physics 1979-86; Blumberg Prof. of Physics 1981-86, Prof. Emer. 1986-; Physicist, Manhattan project of U.S. Govt., Chicago, Wilmington, Hanford 1942-45; Dir. Project Matterhorn, Princeton 1951-53; Lorentz Prof., Univ. of Leiden 1956; Fulbright Prof., Univ. of Kyoto 1962; Guggenheim Fellow, Paris and Copenhagen 1949-50; visiting Fellow, Clare Coll., Cambridge 1964; mem. Editorial Bd., Physical Review, Review of Modern Physics; Chair. Jt. Cttee. of American Physical Soc. and American Philosophical Soc. on History of Theoretical Physics; mem. U.S. Gen. Advisory Cttee. on Arms Control and Disarmament 1969-76; Fellow, American Physical Soc. (Pres. 1966, mem. Council), American Philosophical Soc., A.A.A.S. (mem. Bd. of Dirs. 1963-68); mem. American Acad. of Arts and Sciences, N.A.S.; Trustee Battelle Memorial Inst.; Hon. Sc.D. (Western Reserve, Yeshiva, Rutgers and Yale Univs., Univs. of N.C. and Pa., Middlebury Coll., Catholic Univ. of America, Univ. of Conn. and Gustavus Adolphus Univ.); Hon. D.Sc. (Newcastle Univ., England) 1983; Hon. LL.D. (Johns Hopkins) 1976; Hon. Ph.D. (Uppsala, Maryland) 1976; A. Cressy Morrison Prize, N.Y. Acad. of Sciences 1947, Albert Einstein Prize, Strauss Foundation 1965, Enrico Fermi Award, U.S. Atomic Energy Comm. 1968, Franklin Medal of Franklin Inst. 1969, Nat. Medal of Science 1971, Herzfeld Award 1975, Outstanding Graduate Teaching Award (Univ. of Texas at Austin) 1981, Niels Bohr Int. Gold Medal 1982, Oersted Medal 1983, J. Robert Oppenheimer Memorial Prize 1984. *Publications:* Geometrodynamics 1962, Gravitation Theory and Gravitational Collapse 1965, Spacetime Physics 1966, Einstein's Vision 1968, Black Holes, Gravitational Waves and Cosmology (with Rees and Ruffini) 1974, Gravitation (with Thorne and Misner) 1973, Frontiers of Time 1979, Quantum Theory and Measurement (with Zurek) 1983. *Leisure interests:* swimming, sculpture in nature. *Address:* Department of Physics, Princeton University, Princeton, N.J. 08544; 1904 Meadow Lakes,

Hightstown, N.J. 08520, U.S.A. (Home). *Telephone:* (609) 452-5824 (Princeton Univ.); (609) 426-6239 (Home).

WHELAN, Eugene; Canadian farmer and politician; b. 11 July 1924, Amherstburg, Ont.; s. of Charles B. and Frances L. (Kelly) Whelan; m. Elizabeth Pollinger 1960; three d.; ed. Windsor, Ont., vocational and tech. school; fmr. mem. Ont. Fed. of Agric.; fmr. Dir. United Co-operatives, Ont.; fmr. Pres. Essex Co. Fed. of Agric.; mem. House of Commons 1962-85; Parl. Sec. to the Minister of Fisheries and Forestry 1968-70; Minister of Agric. 1972-79, 1980-84; Pres. World Food Council 1984; mem. of numerous farming orgs.; Canadian Rep. to World Food Council; Kt. of Columbus; Liberal. *Address:* 727 Front Road North, Amhestburg, Ont. N9V 2V6, Canada (Home).

WHELAN, Michael John, PH.D., F.R.S.; British university reader; b. 2 Nov. 1931, Leeds; s. of William Whelan and Ellen Whelan (née Pound); ed. Gonville and Caius Coll., Cambridge; Royal Soc. Mr. and Mrs. John Jaffe Donation Research Fellow 1959-61; Demonstrator in Physics, Univ. of Cambridge 1961-65, Asst. Dir. of Research 1965-66, Fellow of Gonville and Caius Coll. 1958-66; Reader, Dept. of Metallurgy and Science of Materials, Univ. of Oxford 1966-; Fellow, Linacre Coll., Univ. of Oxford 1968-; C. V. Boys Prize, Inst. of Physics 1965, Hughes Medal, Royal Soc. 1988. *Publications:* Electron Microscopy of Thin Crystals (co-author) 1965, numerous papers and articles in scientific journals. *Leisure interests:* gardening, tinkering, Japanese language. *Address:* 18 Salford Road, Old Marston, Oxford, OX3 0RX, England. *Telephone:* (0865) 244556 (Home).

WHELAN, Noel, B.COMM., M.ECON.SC., PH.D., D.P.A.; Irish civil servant and banker; b. 28 Dec. 1940, Cork; s. of Richard Whelan and Ann (née Crowley) Whelan; m. Joan Gaughan 1970; two s. two d.; ed. Nat. School, Buttevant, Co. Cork, Sacred Heart Coll., Buttevant, Univ. Coll., Dublin; Nat. Univ. of Ireland; Exec. Officer, Irish Civil Service 1960-62; Sr. Admin. Officer and Head of Research Evaluation, an Foras Taluntais (Agricultural Research Inst. of Ireland) 1962-69; Asst. Gen. Man. Córas Iompair Éireann (Irish Transport Authority) 1969-74; Deputy Sec. Dept. of Public Service 1974-77; Special Consultant (part-time), OECD 1975-80; Sec. Dept. of Econ. Planning and Devt. 1977-80; Second Sec. Dept. of the Taoiseach (Prime Minister) 1980, Sec. 1980-82; Chair. Irish Sectoral Devt. Cttee., Irish Govt. 1980-82; Vice-Pres. and Vice-Chair., Bd. of Dirs. European Investment Bank, Luxembourg 1982-88, Hon. Vice-Pres. 1988-; Sec., Dept. of the Tadiseach 1988-; Chair. Nat. Econ. and Social Council of Ireland 1978-84; Pres. and Chair. Inst. of Public Admin. (part-time); Vice-Pres. Inst. of Public Admin.; Council mem. and mem. Exec. Cttee., Econ. and Social Research Inst.; Council mem. Statistical and Social Enquiry Soc.; Council mem. and Fellow Irish Man. Inst. *Publications:* miscellaneous papers and reports in various academic and research journals. *Leisure interests:* reading, photography, music. *Address:* 74 Northbrook Avenue, Ranelagh, Dublin 6, Ireland (Home). *Telephone:* 332249 (Home); 960646 (Ireland).

WHELAN, William Joseph, B.SC., PH.D., D.SC.; British biochemist; b. 14 Nov. 1924, Salford; s. of William Joseph Whelan and Jane Antoinette Bertram; m. Margaret Miller Birnie 1951; ed. Univ. of Birmingham. Asst. Lecturer, Univ. of Birmingham 1947-48; Asst. Lecturer, Lecturer and Sr. Lecturer, Univ. Coll. of N. Wales 1948-55; Sr. mem. Lister Inst. of Preventive Medicine 1956-64; Prof. and Head of Biochem. Dept., Royal Free Hosp. Medical School, Univ. of London 1964-67; Prof. and Chair. of Biochem. and Molecular Biology, Dept., Univ. of Miami, U.S.A. 1967-; Chair. Physiological, Chem. Study Section, Nat. Inst. of Health 1973-75, Cttee. on Genetic Experimentation 1977-81; Sec.-Gen. Fed. of European Biochemical Socs. 1965-67, Pan-American Asscn. of Biochemical Socs. 1970-71; Gen. Sec. Int. Union of Biochem. 1973-83; Chair. The ICSU Press 1983-; Alsberg Award, American Asscn. of Cereal Chemists 1967, CIBA Medal of the British Biochemical Soc. 1969, Diplôme d'honneur, Fed. of European Biochemical Socs. 1974, Award of Merit, Japanese Soc. of Starch Science 1975, Saare Medal, Asscn. of Cereal Research 1979; Wood-Whelan Fellowships Int. Union of Biochem. 1985; Hon. mem. Royal Coll. of Physicians, London 1986. *Publications:* (ed.) Control of Glycogen Metabolism 1964, 1968, Carbohydrate Metabolism and its Disorders 1968, 1981, Biochemistry of Carbohydrates 1975, Trends in Biochemical Sciences 1976-78, Recombinant DNA and Genetic Experimentation 1979, From Genetic Experimentation to Biotechnology 1982, Bioessays 1984. *Address:* Department of Biochemistry and Molecular Biology, University of Miami, P.O. Box 016129 Miami, Fla. 33101 (Office); Apt. 1003, 1420 South Bayshore Drive, Miami, Fla. 33131, U.S.A. (Home). *Telephone:* (305) 547-6265 (Office); (305) 373-8039 (Home).

WHICKER, Alan Donald, F.R.S.A.; British television broadcaster and journalist; b. 2 Aug. 1925; s. of late Charles Henry Whicker and Anne Jane Cross; ed. Haberdashers' Aske's School; Dir. Army Film and Photo Section, with 8th Army and U.S. 5th Army; War Corresp., Korea; joined BBC TV 1957; regular appearances on "Tonight" programme, then series Whicker's World 1959-60, Whicker Down Under 1961, Whicker in Sweden 1963, Whicker's World 1965-67; joined Yorkshire TV 1968, made 16 documentaries including Whicker's New World Series, Whicker in Europe, World of Whicker; returned to BBC TV 1982; programmes include: India 1978, Indonesia 1979, California 1980, Whicker's World—The First Million Miles! 1982, Whicker's World, A Fast Boat to China 1983, Whicker (series

talk shows) 1984, Whicker's World Down Under—Living with Uncle Sam (10 programmes) 1985, Whicker's World—Living with Waltzing Matilda (10 programmes) 1988; Whicker's Wireless World (BBC Radio series) 1983; various awards, including Guild of TV Producers and Dirs., Personality of the Year 1964, Silver Medal, Royal TV Soc., Dimbleby Award, BAFTA 1978, TV Times Special Award 1978. *Publications:* Some Rise by Sin 1949, Away—With Alan Whicker 1963, Best of Everything 1980, Within Whicker's World (autobiog.) 1982, Whicker's Business Travellers Guide 1983, Whicker's New World 1985, Whicker's World Down Under 1988, Whicker's World—Hong Kong 1989. *Address:* Le Gallais Chambers, St. Helier, Jersey.

WHIFFEN, David Hardy, D.PHIL., D.SC., F.R.S., F.R.S.C.; British university teacher and civil servant (retd.); b. 15 Jan. 1922, Esher, Surrey; s. of Noel H. Whiffen and Mary W. Whiffen (née Foot); m. Jean Percival Bell 1949; four s.; ed. Oundle School and St John's Coll. Oxford; Harkness Fellow (Bell Telephone Labs.) 1946-47; Sr. Student for the Exhbn. of 1851 (held at Oxford) 1947-49; Lecturer in Chem., Birmingham Univ. 1949-59; Scientific Civil Servant, Nat. Physical Lab., Basic Physics Div., Div. of Molecular Science (Supt. 1966-68) 1959-68; Prof. of Physical Chem., Univ. of Newcastle upon Tyne 1968-85, Dean of Science 1974-77, Pro-Vice-Chancellor 1980-83; Hon. Sec. Chemical Soc. 1966-71; Pres. Faraday Div. Royal Soc. of Chem. 1981-83; mem. Newcastle Health Authority 1978-85, Vice-Chair. 1983-85. *Publications:* Spectroscopy 1966 and over 170 scientific publs. *Address:* 16 St Andrew's Road, Stogursey, Somerset, TA5 1TE, England.

WHINNERY, John Roy, PH.D.; American professor of electrical engineering; b. 26 July 1916; s. of Ralph Vincent and Edith Bent Whinnery; m. Patricia Barry 1944; three d.; ed. Modesto Junior Coll. Calif., Univ. of Calif., Berkeley; Student Engineer to Research Engineer, Gen. Electric Co. 1937-46; Lecturer, Union Coll., Schenectady, N.Y., 1945-46; Univ. of Calif., Berkeley, Lecturer, Assoc. Prof., Prof., Chair. of Dept., Dean of Coll. 1959-63, Univ. Prof. 1980-; Guggenheim Fellow E.T.H., Zurich, Switzerland 1959; Head of Microwave Tube Research at Hughes Aircraft Co., Culver City, Calif. 1952-53; visiting mem. of Tech. Staff, Bell Telephone Labs. 1963-64; Visiting Prof. Stanford Univ. 1969-70; Research Professorship in Miller Inst. for Basic Research in Science 1973-74; mem. Visiting Review Bd., Dept. of Electrical Eng., M.I.T. 1968, Div. of Applied Science, Harvard Univ. 1974, 1979, 1980, 1981, 1982, 1983, Dept. of Eng. and Applied Science, Calif. Inst. of Tech. 1977, 1979, 1980; Hon. Prof. of Chengdu Inst. of Tech., Sichuan, Chengdu, People's Repub. of China 1986; mem. Nat. Acad. of Eng. 1965, Pres.'s Cttee. Nat. Medal of Science 1970-72, 1979-81, N.A.S. 1973, Optical Soc. of America, American Acad. of Arts and Sciences; life mem. Inst. of Electronics and Electrical Eng.; Educ. Medal Inst. Electronics and Electrical Engineers, Outstanding Educators of America Award (Univ. of Calif., Berkeley) 1974, Lamme Award of American Soc. on Eng. Educ. 1975, Microwave Career Award of Inst. Electronics and Electrical Eng. 1976, Distinguished Eng. Alumnus Award, Univ. of Calif., Berkeley 1980, Inst. of Electronics and Electrical Eng. Centennial Medallist 1984, Medal of Honor Award from Inst. of Electronics and Electrical Eng. 1985, Founder's Award, Nat. Acad. of Eng. 1986, Berkeley Citation, Univ. of Calif., Berkeley 1987. *Publications:* Fields and Waves in Modern Radio (with Simon Ramo) 1944, 1952, World of Engineering 1965, Fields and Waves in Communication Electronics (with Simon Ramo and T. Van Duzer) 1965, Introduction to Electronic Systems Circuits and Devices (with D. O. Pederson and J. J. Studer) 1966, 140 tech. articles and patents on microwaves and lasers. *Leisure interests:* hiking, skiing, golf, writing poetry and children's stories. *Address:* Department of Electrical Engineering and Computer Sciences, Univ. of Calif., Berkeley, Calif. 94720 (Office); 1 Daphne Court, Orinda, Calif. 94563, U.S.A. (Home). *Telephone:* (415) 642-1030 (Office); (415) 254-3098 (Home).

WHIPPLE, Fred Lawrence, PH.D.; American astronomer; b. 5 Nov. 1906, Red Oak, Iowa; s. of Harry Lawrence Whipple and Celestia (MacFarland) Whipple; m. 1st Dorothy Woods 1928 (divorced 1935), one s.; m. 2nd Babette Samelson 1946, two d.; ed. Univ. of Calif.; mem. Staff Harvard Coll. Observatory 1931-77; in charge of Oak Ridge Station 1932-37; Instructor 1932-38, Lecturer 1938-45, Assoc. Prof. 1945-50, Prof. of Astronomy 1950-, Chair. Dept. of Astronomy 1949-56, Phillips Prof. of Astronomy 1968-77; Chair. Cttee. on Concentration in the Physical Sciences 1947-49; Research Associate Radio Research Lab. 1942-45, in charge of Confusion Reflectors "Window" (radar countermeasure); Dir. Smithsonian Inst. Astrophysical Observatory 1955-73, Sr. Scientist 1973-; mem. Rocket and Satellite Research Panel 1946-58, U.S. Nat. Advisory Cttee. on Aeronautics Sub-Cttee. 1946-52, U.S. Research and Devt. Bd. Panel 1947-52, U.S. Nat. Cttee. I.G.Y. 1955-59, Advisory Panel on Astronomy to the Nat. Science Foundation 1952-55 and Chair. 1954-55, mem. Div. Cttee. for Mathematical and Physical Sciences 1964-70, many other scientific cttees., etc.; Project Leader, Harvard Radio Meteor Project 1958-65; mem. NASA Optical Astronomy Panel, Astronomy Missions Bd. 1968; mem. NASA Science and Tech. Advisory Cttee. 1969; mem. NASA Comet and Asteroid Working Group 1971-72, Chair. 1972; Voting Rep. of U.S.A. in Int. Astronomical Union 1952 and 1955; Assoc. Ed. Astrophysical Journal 1952-54, Astronomical Journal 1954-56, 1964-; Ed. Planetary and Space Science 1958-, Harvard's Announcement Cards 1952-60, Smithsonian Contributions to Astrophysics 1956-73; Lowell Lecturer, Lowell Inst. Boston 1947; Vice-

Pres. American Astronomical Soc. 1948-50, 1960-67, Cttee. on Space Research (COSPAR) 1960; Editorial Bd. Space Science Reviews 1961-70; Editorial Cttee. Annual Review of Astronomy and Astrophysics 1965-69; mem. R.S.A., Benjamin Franklin Fellow 1968-; Assoc. Royal Astronomical Soc. 1970; numerous hon. degrees, Donohue Medals, Pres. Certificate of Merit, J. Lawrence Smith Medal of Nat. Acad. of Sciences, Exceptional Service Award (U.S.A.F.), Liège Univ. Medal, Space Flight Award, Commr. of Order of Merit for Research and Invention; Distinguished Federal Civilian Service Award from President Kennedy, Alumnus of the Year Achievement Award (Univ. of Calif.), Leonard Medal, Meteoritical Soc. 1970, Nat. Civil Service League's Career Service Award for Sustained Excellence 1972, Kepler Medal, A.A.A.S., Gold Medal, Royal Astronomical Soc., London and Astronomical Soc. of the Pacific, Kuiper Award, American Astronomical Soc. *Publications:* Earth, Moon and Planets 1942, Orbiting the Sun 1981, The Mystery of Comets 1985 and many scientific papers. *Leisure interests:* scuba diving, stochastic painting, cycling. *Address:* Smithsonian Astrophysical Observatory, 60 Garden Street, Cambridge, Mass. 02138; 35 Elizabeth Road, Belmont, Mass. 02178, U.S.A. (Home).

WHISTLER, Laurence, C.B.E., M.A., F.R.S.L.; British writer and glass engraver; b. 21 Jan. 1912, Eltham, Kent; s. of Henry Whistler and Helen Ward; brother of the late Rex Whistler; m. 1st Jill Furse 1939 (died 1944), one s. one d.; m. 2nd Theresa Furse (younger sister of Jill Furse) 1950 (divorced 1985), one s. one d.; m. 3rd Carol Dawson (née Groves) 1987; ed. Stowe School, Balliol Coll., Oxford; served World War II, commissioned 1941; Hon. Fellow, Balliol Coll.; First Pres. Guild of Glass Engravers 1975-80; King's Gold Medal for poetry 1935, Atlantic Award for Literature 1945; work on glass includes: goblets in point-engraving and drill, engraved church windows and panels at Sherborne Abbey, Moreton, Dorset, Checkendon, Oxon., Ilton, Somerset, Eastbury, Berks., Guards' Chapel, London, Ashmansworth, Berks., Steep, Hants., Yalding, Kent; exhbns.: Agnews, Bond Street 1969, Marble Hill, Twickenham 1972, Corning Museum, U.S.A. 1974, Ashmolean, Oxford 1976, 1985, Kenwood, Hampstead 1985. *Publications:* Sir John Vanbrugh (biog.) 1938, The English Festivals 1947, Rex Whistler, His Life and His Drawings 1948, The World's Room (Collected Poems) 1949, The Engraved Glass of Laurence Whistler 1952, Rex Whistler: the Königsmark Drawings 1952, The Imagination of Vanbrugh and His Fellow Artists 1954, The View From This Window (poems) 1956, Engraved Glass 1952-58, The Work of Rex Whistler (co-author) 1960, Audible Silence (poems) 1961, The Initials in the Heart: the story of a marriage 1964, To Celebrate Her Living (poems) 1967, Pictures on Glass 1972, The Image on the Glass 1975, Scenes and Signs of Glass 1985, The Laughter and the Urn: The Life of Rex Whistler 1985, Enter (poems) 1987. *Address:* c/o Lloyds Bank, 6 Pall Mall, London, SW1Y 5NH, England.

WHITAKER, Thomas Kenneth, M.SC.(ECON.); Irish financial administrator; b. 8 Dec. 1916, Rostrevor, Co. Down; s. of Edward Whitaker and Jane O'Connor; m. Nora Fogarty 1941; five s. one d.; ed. Christian Brothers' School, Drogheda; entered Irish Civil Service 1934; Sec. Dept. of Finance 1956-69; Dir. Cen. Bank of Ireland 1958-69, Gov. 1969-76; Dir. Bank of Ireland 1976-85; mem. Senate 1977-82; Jt. Chair. Anglo-Irish Encounter 1983-; Pres. Econ. and Social Research Inst.; Dir. Arthur Guinness and Sons 1976-84; Chancellor, Nat. Univ. of Ireland 1976-; Chair. Dublin Inst. for Advanced Studies 1980-; Pres. Royal Irish Acad. 1985-87; Hon. D.Econ.Sc. (Nat. Univ. of Ireland), Hon. LL.D. (Univ. of Dublin, Queen's Univ. of Belfast, Univ. of Ulster); Commdr., Légion d'honneur. *Publications:* Financing by Credit Creation, Economic Development 1958, Interests 1983. *Leisure interests:* angling, golf, music. *Address:* 148 Stillorgan Road, Donnybrook, Dublin 4, Ireland. *Telephone:* Dublin 69 3474.

WHITBREAD, Fatima, M.B.E.; British athlete; b. 1 March 1961, Stoke Newington; unmarried; UK int. debut as javelin thrower 1977; European Jr. Champion 1979; European Cup Champion 1983; European Cup Silver Medallist 1985; European Champion 1986; Commonwealth Games Bronze Medallist 1982, Silver Medallist 1986; Olympic Games Bronze Medallist 1984, Silver Medallist 1988; World Championships Silver Medallist 1983; World Champion 1987; World Record Holder 1987; mem. British Olympic Cttee.; BBC Sports Personality of the Year 1987; British Sports Writers Sportswoman of the Year 1986, 1987; British Athletic Writers Woman Athlete of the Year, 1986, 1987. *Leisure interests:* interior design,theatre. *Address:* 116 Godman Road, Chadwell St. Mary, Grays, Essex, England.

WHITBREAD, Samuel Charles, D.L.; British business executive; b. 22 Feb. 1937, London; s. of Major Simon Whitbread and H. B. M. Trefusis; m. Jane M. Hayter 1961; three s. one d.; ed. Eton Coll.; served Beds. and Herts. Regt. 1955-57; Dir. Whitbread & Co. 1972, Deputy Chair. Jan. 1984, Chair. Whitbread & Co. PLC Aug. 1984-. *Leisure interests:* shooting, travel, photography, music. *Address:* Brewery, Chiswell Street, London, EC1Y 4SD (Office); Southill Park, Biggleswade, Beds., SG18 9LL, England (Home). *Telephone:* 01-606 4455 (Office); (0462) 813272 (Home).

WHITE, Baroness (Life Peer), cr. 1970, of Rhymney in the county of Monmouth; **Eirene Lloyd White;** British politician; b. 7 Nov. 1909, Belfast; d. of late Dr. Thomas Jones; m. John Cameron White 1948 (died 1968); ed. St. Paul's Girls' School, and Somerville Coll., Oxford; Ministry of Labour 1941-45; Political Corresp. Manchester Evening News 1945-49; Labour M.P. for E. Flintshire 1950-70; Parl. Under-Sec. of State, Colonial Office 1964-66; Minister of State, Foreign Office 1966-67; Minister of State for

Wales 1967-70; mem. Nat. Exec. Cttee., Labour Party 1947-53, 1958-72, Chair. 1968-69; Deputy Chair. Metrication Bd. 1972-76; Chair. Land Authority for Wales 1975-80; mem. Royal Comm. on Environmental Pollution 1974-81, British Waterways Bd. 1974-80, Univ. Grants Cttee. 1977-79; Deputy Speaker House of Lords 1979-; Prin. Deputy Chair. of Cttees., House of Lords 1980-82, Chair. Select Cttee. on European Communities 1980-82; Gov. Nat. Library of Wales, British Film Inst. and Nat. Film Theatre 1959-64; Chair. Advisory Cttee. on Pollution at Sea 1974-78; Pres. Council for the Protection of Rural Wales; Vice-Pres. Commonwealth Countries' League, Council for Nat. Parks; Hon. Fellow, Somerville Coll., Oxford 1966; Chair. Univ. of Wales Inst. of Science and Tech. 1983-88, Vice-Pres. 1988-; Hon. LL.D. (Wales) 1979, (Queen's Univ., Belfast) 1981, (Bath Univ.) 1983. *Publication:* The Ladies of Gregynog 1985. *Address:* 64 Vandon Court, Petty France, London, SW1H 9HF, England. *Telephone:* 01-222 5107.

WHITE, Christopher John, PH.D.; British arts administrator; b. 19 Sept. 1930; s. of Gabriel Ernest E. F. White; m. Rosemary Katharine Desages 1957; one s. two d.; ed. Downside School, Courtauld Inst. of Art, London Univ.; army service 1949-50; Asst. Keeper, Dept. of Prints and Drawings, British Museum 1954-65; Dir. P. and D. Colnaghi 1965-71; Curator of Graphic Arts, Nat. Gallery of Art, Washington 1971-73; Dir. of Studies, Paul Mellon Centre for Studies in British Art 1973-85; Assoc. Dir. Yale Centre for British Art, New Haven 1976-85; Adjunct Prof. of History of Art, Yale Univ. 1977-85; Dir. Ashmolean Museum, Oxford Oct. 1985-; Fellow, Worcester Coll., Oxford 1985-; Hermione Lecturer, Alexandra Coll., Dublin 1959; Adjunct Prof., Inst. of Fine Arts, New York Univ. 1973, 1976; Visiting Prof., Yale Univ. 1976; Conf. Dir., European-American Ass. on Art Museums 1975; Reviews Ed., Master Drawings 1967-80. *Publications:* Rembrandt and His World 1964, The Flower Drawings of Jan van Huysum 1965, Rubens and His World 1968, Rembrandt as an Etcher 1969, Rembrandt's Etchings: a catalogue raisonné (jtly.) 1970, Dürer: the Artist and His Drawings 1972, English Landscape 1630-1850 1977, The Dutch Paintings in the Collection of H.M. The Queen 1982, Rembrandt in Eighteenth Century England (Ed.) 1983, Peter Paul Rubens: Man and Artist 1987, Drawing in England from Hilliard to Hogarth (jtly.) 1987. *Address:* 135 Walton Street, Oxford, OX1 2HQ; 14 South Villas, London, NW1 9BS, England.

WHITE, Frank; American politician; b. 28 Oct. 1932, Prescott, Ark.; s. of Herman and Ruth House White; m. Patricia Ann Bolt 1951; four s.; ed. Henderson State Univ., Univ. of Ark.; served U.S.A.F. 1951-53; Supervisor Reynolds Metals Co. 1956-79; Co. Treas., Clark Co. Republican Party, Ark. 1971-74, Chair. 1977-; Gov. of Ark. 1980-83. *Address:* c/o Office of the Governor, 250 State Capitol, Little Rock, Ark. 72201, U.S.A.

WHITE, Sir Frederick William George, K.B.E., PH.D., F.A.A., F.R.S.; Australian physicist; b. 26 May 1905, Wellington, New Zealand; s. of late W. H. White; m. Elizabeth Cooper 1932; one s. one d.; ed. Wellington Coll., Victoria Univ. Coll., New Zealand, and Cambridge Univ.; post-graduate work at Cavendish Lab., Cambridge 1929-31; Demonstrator in Physics, Lecturer in Physics, King's Coll., London 1931-37; Prof. of Physics, Canterbury Univ. Coll., New Zealand 1937; seconded to Council for Scientific and Industrial Research as Chair. Radiophysics Advisory Bd. 1941; Chief Div. of Radiophysics 1942; Exec. Officer C.S.I.R. 1945, mem. Exec. Cttee. 1946, C.E.O. CSIRO 1949-56, Deputy Chair. CSIRO 1957-59, Chair. 1959-70; Chair. Australian and N.Z. Assen. for Advancement of Science; Hon. D.Sc. (Monash Univ., Melbourne, Australian Nat. Univ., Canberra, Univ. of Papua New Guinea). *Publications:* Electromagnetic Waves 1934 and numerous scientific papers. *Leisure interests:* fishing, walking. *Address:* 57 Investigator Street, Red Hill, Canberra, A.C.T. 2603, Australia. *Telephone:* 957424.

WHITE, Gilbert F(owler), PH.D.; American geographer; b. 26 Nov. 1911, Chicago; s. of Arthur E. White and Mary (Guthrie) White; m. Anne E. Underwood 1944; one s. two d.; ed. Univ. of Chicago; Geographer, Miss. Valley Comm. of P.W.A. 1934, Nat. Resources Bd. 1934-35; Sec. Land and Water Comm., Nat. Resources Comm. and Nat. Resources Planning Bd. 1935-40; Bureau of Budget, Exec. Office of Pres. 1941-42; Relief Admin. in France 1942-43; interned Baden-Baden; Sec. American Relief for India 1945-46; Pres. Haverford Coll. 1946-55; Prof. of Geography Univ. of Chicago 1956-69; Prof. of Geography and Dir. Inst. of Behavioral Sciences, Univ. of Colorado 1970-78, Gustavson Distinguished Prof. Emer. 1979-; mem. numerous nat. and int. advisory comms. etc.; Exec. Ed. Environment 1983-; Visiting Prof. Univ. of Oxford 1962-63; mem. N.A.S., Assen. of American Geographers; hon. mem. Royal Geographical Soc., Soviet Soc.; Foreign mem. U.S.S.R. Acad. of Sciences; recipient of numerous awards and hon. degrees. *Publications:* author, co-author and ed. of books on flood management and other environmental issues. *Address:* Campus Box 482, University of Colorado, Boulder, Colo. 80309 (Office); 624 Pearl Street, Boulder, Colo. 80302, U.S.A.

WHITE, Guy Kendall, M.SC., D.PHIL., F.A.A.; Australian physicist; b. 31 May 1925, Sydney; s. of Percival George White and Eugenie White (née Kendall); m. Judith Kelly McAuliffe 1955; one s. two d.; ed. The Scots Coll., Sydney, Univ. of Sydney, Magdalen Coll., Oxford, U.K.; Research Officer CSIRO Div. of Physics 1950-54; Assoc. Research Officer, Nat. Research Council of Canada 1955-58; Prin. Research Scientist, CSIRO

1958–62, Sr. Research Scientist 1962–69, Chief Research Scientist 1969–; Syme Medal (Melbourne Univ.) 1966, Armco Iron Award, U.S.A. 1983. *Publication:* Experimental Techniques in Low Temperature Physics 1958. *Leisure interests:* golf, bush-walking, swimming. *Address:* CSIRO Division of Applied Physics, National Measurement Laboratory, P.O. Box 218, Lindfield, N.S.W. 2070, Australia. *Telephone:* (02) 467-6318.

WHITE, Sir Harold Leslie, Kt., C.B.E., M.A., F.L.A.A., F.A.S.S.A.; Australian librarian (retd.); b. 14 June 1905, Numurkah, Vic.; s. of James White and Beatrice Hodge; m. Elizabeth Wilson, M.B.E. 1930; two s. two d.; ed. Wesley Coll., Melbourne, and Queen's Coll. of Melbourne Univ.; Commonwealth Parl. Library 1923–67, Parl. Librarian 1947–67; Nat. Librarian, Nat. Library of Australia 1947–70; Chair. Standing Cttee. Australian Advisory Council on Bibliographical Services 1960–70; Gov. Australian Film Inst. 1958–77; Chair. Advisory Cttee. Australian Encyclopaedia 1970–87; mem. Nat. Memorials Cttee. 1975–, Australian Cttees. for UNESCO, Australian Nat. Film Bd. 1947–70; mem. UNESCO Int. Cttee. Bibliography, Documentation and Terminology 1961–65; Hon. Vice-Pres. Library Asscn. U.K. 1970–; Fellow, Univ. of Melbourne 1988; H. C. L. Anderson Award, Library Asscn. of Australia 1983; Hon. F.A.H.A. *Publication:* (Ed.) Canberra: A Nation's Capital. *Address:* 27 Mugga Way, Red Hill, Canberra, A.C.T. 2603, Australia (Home).

WHITE, Mark Wells, Jr., J.D.; American state governor; b. 17 March 1940, Henderson, Tex.; s. of Mark Wells White and Sarah E. White; m. Linda G. Thompson 1966; two s. one d.; ed. Baylor Univ., Waco, Tex.; admitted to Texas Bar 1965; Asst. Attorney-Gen. Insurance, Banking and Securities Div., State of Texas 1966–69; Assoc. Reynolds, White, Allen & Cook, Houston 1969–71, Partner 1971–73; Sec. of State, State of Tex. 1973–79, Attorney-Gen. 1979–83; Gov. of Texas 1983–87; Democrat. *Address:* c/o Governor's Mansion, 1010 Colorado, Austin, Tex. 78701, U.S.A.

WHITE, Michael Simon; British theatrical and film producer and impresario; b. 16 Jan. 1936; s. of Victor White and Doris White; m. 1st Sarah Hillsdon 1965 (divorced 1973), two s. one d.; m. 2nd Louise Moores 1985, one s.; ed. Lyceum Alpinum, Zuoz, Switzerland, Pisa Univ. and Sorbonne, Paris; began career by bringing Cambridge Footlights to London's West End; Asst. to Sir Peter Daubeny 1956–61; *stage productions include:* Rocky Horror Show, Jabberwocky, Sleuth, America Hurrah, Oh, Calcutta!, The Connection, Joseph and the Amazing Technicolour Dreamcoat, Loot, The Blood Knot, A Chorus Line, Deathtrap, Annie, Pirates of Penzance, On Your Toes, The Mystery of Edwin Drood, Metropolis; *films include:* Monty Python and the Holy Grail, Rocky Horror Picture Show, My Dinner with André, Ploughman's Lunch, Moonlighting, Strangers' Kiss, The Comic Strip Presents, The Supergrass, High Season, Eat the Rich, White Mischief. *Publication:* Empty Seats 1984. *Leisure interests:* art, skiing, racing. *Address:* 13 Duke Street, St. James's, London, S.W.1, England. *Telephone:* 01-839 3971.

WHITE, Norman A., PH.D., F.I.MECH.E., F.R.S.A.,C.ENG.; British company executive and university professor; b. 11 April 1922, Hetton-le-Hole, Durham; m. 1st Joyce Marjorie Rogers 1944 (died 1982), one s. one d.; m. 2nd Marjorie Iris Rushton 1983; ed. Manchester Inst. of Science and Technology, Univ. of London, Univ. of Philippines, London Polytechnic, Harvard Business School, London School of Econs.; apprenticeship with George Kent Ltd. and D. Napier and Sons Ltd. 1936–43; Flight Test Engineer, Mil. Aircraft Devt. 1943–45; with Royal Dutch Shell Group 1945–72, numerous posts, including Chair. and Dir. of Shell Oil and int. mining cos. 1963–72; f. Norman White Assocs. 1972, Chair. 1972–; tech. consultant to numerous cos. 1972–; Chair. and Dir. numerous eng. and oil cos. 1972–; mem. Council and Chair. Eng.-Man. Div., Inst. Mechanical Engineers 1980–85, 1987–; mem. Council and Vice-Pres. Inst. of Petroleum 1975–81; Visiting Prof. Univ. of Manchester and Henley Man. Coll.; mem. numerous academic and educational cttees. including Senate and Advisory Bd. in Eng., Univ. of London; mem. House of Commons Parl. and Scientific Cttee. 1977–83, 1987–; Chair. British Nat. Cttee. of World Petroleum Congresses (WPC) 1977–, U.K. Rep. WPC Int. Exec. Bd. and Perm. Council 1979, Treas. 1983; mem. Conservative Comm. for World Energy 1979–; Chair. Int. Task Force on Oil Substitution 1979–84; mem. int. energy/petroleum dels. to U.S.S.R, People's Repub. of China, Romania, G.D.R., Japan, Korea, India, Mexico, Argentina, Brazil 1979–; Freeman of the City of London; Liveryman, Worshipful Co. of Engineers, Worshipful Co. of Spectacle Makers; mem. numerous professional eng. insts.; f. mem. British Inst. of Energy Econs.; mem. American Soc. of Petroleum Engineers; Canadian Inst. of Mining and Metallurgy; numerous honours. *Publications:* Financing the International Petroleum Industry 1978, The International Outlook for Oil Substitution to 2020 1983, Handbook of Engineering Management 1989, articles in professional journals in U.K. and Canada. *Leisure interests:* family, walking, international affairs, comparative religions, odd-jobbing. *Address:* 123/125 Harley Street, London, W1N 1HE (Office); Green Ridges, Downside Road, Guildford, Surrey, GU4 8PH, England (Home). *Telephone:* 01-935 7387; (0483) 67523.

WHITE, Padraic, B.COMM.; Irish public administrator; b. 25 June 1942, Leitrim; m. Mary Casey; one d.; ed. De La Salle Coll., Ballyshannon, Co. Donegal, Univ. Coll. Dublin; Exec. Officer, Dept. of Defence 1960–64; Admin. Officer Dept. of Health 1964–70; Regional Planning Officer, Indus-

trial Devt. Authority 1971–73, Man. Press and Public Relations 1973–75, Man. Planning and Devt. 1975–79, Exec. Dir. and Bd. mem. 1979–80, Man. Dir. 1980; mem. Bd., Industrial Credit Corpn., Irish Man., Inst., Econ. and Social Research Inst., Irish American Cultural Inst.; Chair., Irish American Partnership, Consultative Group of Chief Execs. of Semi-State Bodies; Eisenhower Fellowship Award for Ireland 1980. *Leisure interests:* running, opera. *Address:* 6 Wyckham Park Road, Dundrum, Dublin 16, Ireland.

WHITE, Patrick, B.A.; Australian writer; b. 28 May 1912, London, England; s. of Victor White and Ruth Withycombe; ed. Cheltenham Coll., and King's Coll., Cambridge; Intelligence officer, R.A.F., World War II; W. H. Smith & Son Award 1959; Nobel Prize for Literature 1973; Companion, Order of Australia 1975; resgnd. from Order of Australia June 1976. *Publications:* Happy Valley 1939, The Living and the Dead 1941, The Aunt's Story 1948, The Tree of Man 1955, Voss 1957, Riders in the Chariot 1961, The Burnt Ones 1964, Four Plays 1965, The Solid Mandala 1966, The Vivisector 1970, The Eye of the Storm 1973, The Cockatoos 1974, A Fringe of Leaves 1976, The Twyborn Affair 1979, Big Toys (play) 1977, The Night The Prowler (screenplay) 1977, Signal Driver (play) 1982, A Self-Portrait: Flaws in the Glass (autobiog.) 1981, Netherwood (play) 1983, Memoirs of Many in One (novel) 1986, Shepherd on the Rocks (play) 1986, Three Uneasy Pieces (stories) 1987. *Address:* 20 Martin Road, Centennial Park, Sydney, N.S.W. 2021, Australia.

WHITE, Raymond P., D.D.S., PH.D.; American oral and maxillofacial surgeon; b. 13 Feb. 1937, New York; s. of Raymond P. and Mabel S. White; m. Betty P. White 1961; one s. one d.; ed. Medical Coll. of Virginia and Washington & Lee Univ.; Asst. Prof. of Oral Surgery, Univ. of Kentucky 1967–70, Assoc. Prof. 1970–71, Chair. Oral Surgery Dept. 1969–71; Prof. of Oral Surgery, Virginia Commonwealth Univ. 1971–74; Prof. of Oral and Maxillofacial Surgery, Univ. of N.C. School of Dentistry 1974–, Dean 1974–81; Assoc. Dean. Univ. of N.C. School of Medicine 1981–; Research Assoc. Univ. of N.C. Health Services Research Center 1982–; mem. Inst. of Medicine, N.A.S. *Publications:* co-author, Fundamentals of Oral Surgery 1971, Surgical Correction of Dentofacial Deformities 1980. *Leisure interests:* tennis, sailing. *Address:* 188 Dental Office Building 209H, CB 7450, University of North Carolina, Chapel Hill, N.C. 27514 (Office); 1506 Velma Road, Chapel Hill, N.C. 27514, U.S.A. (Home). *Telephone:* 919-966-1126 (Office); 919-967-4064 (Home).

WHITE, Raymond Walter Ralph, C.M.G., F.C.A., F.C.I.S.; New Zealand company director; b. 23 June 1923 Feilding; s. of Henry Underhill White and Ethel Annie White; m. Nola Colleen Adin 1946; one s. two d.; ed. Queen Elizabeth Coll., Palmerston North; Deputy Gov. Reserve Bank of N.Z. 1967, Gov. 1977–82; Chair. BP N.Z. 1984–; Westpac Life N.Z. 1986–; Dir. Alcan Australia Ltd. 1988–; Dir. N.Z. Advisory Bd., Westpac Banking Corpn. 1982–, N.Z. Guardian Trust Co. Ltd. 1983–, Mair Astley Ltd. 1984–, I.C.I. N.Z. Ltd. 1984–; Chair. N.Z. Inst. of Econ. Research 1984–. *Leisure interests:* tennis, gardening, golf. *Address:* 63 Chatsworth Road, Silverstream, New Zealand. *Telephone:* Wellington 282084.

WHITE, Robert James, A.O., F.A.I.B., F.A.I.M.; Australian banker; b. 18 Oct. 1923, Deniliquin, N.S.W.; s. of late A. W. White and S. J. White; m. Molly McKinnon 1950; ed. War Memorial High School, Hay, N.S.W.; joined Bank of N.S.W. 1940, Asst. Chief Man., New Zealand 1965–66, Deputy Chief Accountant 1967–69, Man., Sydney 1970–71, Chief Man., U.K. and Europe 1972–74, Gen. Man. 1974–77, Dir. and Chief Gen. Man. Bank of N.S.W. 1977–82, Man. Dir. Westpac Banking Corpn. (merger of Bank of N.S.W. with Commercial Bank of Australia) 1982–87, Dir. 1988–; Dir. ICI Australia Ltd. 1987–, Australia Guarantee Group 1977–; Pres. Australian Inst. of Bankers 1980–86; Chair. Australian Bankers' Asscn. 1978–79, 1983–84, 1987; Dir. Int. Monetary Conf. 1982–85; Pres. Asian Pacific Bankers' Club 1983–84; mem. Trade Devt. Council 1981–84; Pres. Business Council of Australia 1984–86; mem. Nat. Pacific Co-operation Cttee. 1984–; mem. Exec. Bd. ICC 1987–; Storey Medal, Australian Inst. of Man. 1987. *Address:* Westpac Banking Corporation, 60 Martin Place, Sydney, N.S.W. 2000, Australia. *Telephone:* (02) 226.3311.

WHITE, Robert M., II; American journalist; b. 6 April 1915, Mexico, Mo.; s. of L. Mitchell White and Maude (née See) White; m. 1st Barbara Spurgeon 1948 (died 1983); one s. three d.; m. 2nd Peggy Lee Crolius 1983; ed. Missouri Military Acad., and Washington and Lee Univ.; with United Press 1939; Army service 1940–45; Pres., Ed. and Publr. Mexico (Missouri) Ledger 1945–87, Ed. 1987–; Ed. and Pres. New York Herald Tribune 1959–61; Dir. American Newspaper Publishers' Asscn. 1955–63, Treas. 1962–63; Dir. New York World's Fair 1964–65; fmr. Chair. Associated Press Nominating Cttee.; fmr. Chair. and Pres., Inland Daily Press Asscn.; Dir. Stephen's Coll.; Pres. See TV Co. 1965–81; American Cttee. Int. Press. Inst., Vice-Chair. 1968–71, 1981–, Chair. 1982–86; Dir. American Soc. of Newspaper Eds. 1968–70; Dir. Missouri Mil. Acad.; Visiting Prof., Univ. of Missouri 1968–69; mem. Pulitzer Prize Jury for Journalism 1964–66; Chair. American Soc. of Newspaper Eds. Freedom of Information Cttee. 1970–72; Chair. Missouri Free Press-Fair Trial Cttee.1970–74; Pres. Missouri Press Asscn.; Vice-Pres. Mo. Inst. for Justice 1978–82, Bd. of Dirs. 1982–87; Vice-Pres. MacArthur Memorial Foundation 1979–81, Pres. 1981–; mem. Bd. of Dirs. Associated Press 1971–80, Bd. of Dirs. Washington Journalism Center 1972–84, State Historical Soc. of Missouri, Missouri

Public Expenditure Survey 1980-85, Pres. 1981-83, Bd. of Dirs. Washington and Lee Univ. Alumni Inc. 1976-80, World Press Freedom Comm. 1984-; Dir. Commerce Bank of Mexico 1971-85, Commerce Bancshares Inc. 1971-85; mem. Bd. of Dirs. Int. Eye Foundation 1987-; Distinguished Service to Journalism Award, Univ. of Missouri 1967, Nat. Newspapers Assen. Pres. Award of Merit 1967. *Publications:* A study of the Printing and Publishing Business in the Soviet Union (co-author), China Journey 1972, Second Journey To China 1977. *Leisure interests:* hunting, fishing. *Address:* Box 8, Ledger Plaza, Mexico, Mo. 65265 (Office); 8 Melody Lane, Mexico, Mo. 65265, U.S.A. *Telephone:* (314) 581-1111 (Office); (314) 581-4372 (Home).

WHITE, Robert Mayer, SC.D.; American meteorologist; b. 13 Feb. 1923, Boston, Mass.; s. of David and Mary (Winkeller) White; m. Mavis Seagle 1948; one s. one d.; ed. Harvard Univ. and M.I.T.; war service with U.S.A.F., exec. at Atmospheric Analysis Lab., Geophysics Research Directorate, Air Force Cambridge Research Center 1952-58, Chief of Meteorological Devt. Lab. 1958; Research Assoc. M.I.T. 1959; Travelers Insurance Cos. 1959-60, Pres. Travelers Research Center, Hartford 1960-63; Chief of Weather Bureau, U.S. Dept. of Commerce 1963-65; Admin. Environmental Science Services Admin., U.S. Dept. of Commerce 1965-70; Perm. Rep. and mem. Exec. Cttee. of World Meteorological Org. 1963-77; Administrator Nat. Oceanic and Atmospheric Admin. 1971-77; Chair. Joint Oceanographic Inst., Inc., 1977-79; Chair. Climate Research Bd. of N.A.S. 1977-79; Admin. Nat. Research Council, Exec. Officer 1979-80; Pres. Univ. Corpn. Atmospheric Research 1979-83; mem. Exec. Cttee. American Geophysical Union, Council Nat. Acad. of Eng., (Pres. 1983-), Marine Tech. Soc., Royal Meteorological Soc., Nat. Advisory Cttee. on Oceans and Atmosphere 1979-84, Nat. Advisory Cttee. on Govt. and Public Affairs, Univ. of Ill. 1987-; Bd. of Overseers Harvard Univ. 1977-79; mem. of numerous weather research cttees., Commr. Int. Whaling Comm. 1973-77; Cleveland Abbe award, American Meteorological Soc. 1969, Rockefeller Public Service award 1974, David B. Stone award, New England Aquarium 1975, Matthew Fontaine Maury award Smithsonian Inst., Int. Conservation award Nat. Wildlife Fed. 1976, Neptune Award American Oceanic Org. 1977, Charles Franklin Brooks award 1978, Int. Meteorological Assen. Prize 1980. *Leisure interests:* gardening, reading. *Address:* 2101 Constitution Avenue, N.W., Washington, D.C., 20418 (Office); 8306 Melody Court, Bethesda, Md. 20817, U.S.A. (Home). *Telephone:* (202) 334-3200 (Office); (301) 365-3927 (Home).

WHITE, William James, B.S., M.B.A.; American business executive; b. 30 May 1938, Kenosha, Wis.; s. of William H. White and Dorothy Caroline White; m. Jane Schulte 1960; one s. one d.; ed. Northwestern and Harvard Univs.; Mechanical Planning Engineer, Procter & Gamble Corpn. 1961-62; Corp. Vice-Pres. Hartmarx Corpn., Chicago 1963-74; Group Vice-Pres. Mead Corpn., Dayton, Ohio 1974-81; Pres., C.O.O. and Dir. Masonite Corpn., Chicago 1981-85; Exec. Vice-Pres. and Dir. USG Corpn. 1985-; Dir. Material Sciences Corpn., Elk Grove Village, Ill., Midwest Stock Exchange, Chicago; mem. The Chicago Cttee., Advisory Council Tech. Inst., Northwestern Univ.; Chair. Business Advisory Council, Univ. of Ill., Chicago 1981-. *Publication:* Creative Collective Bargaining (Co-author) 1965. *Address:* USG Corporation, 101 South Wacker Drive, Chicago, Ill. 60606, U.S.A.

WHITE, William Smith; American journalist; b. 20 May 1907; ed. Univ. of Texas; held various posts with Associated Press (News Ed., War Ed. and War Corresp.); mem. Washington staff, The New York Times 1945-57; Chief Congressional corresp. 1957-58; nationally syndicated Political Columnist 1958-74; Regents Prof. Univ. of Calif. (Berkeley) 1957-58; contrib. ed. Harper's Magazine 1960-62; Pulitzer Prize in Letters, etc. *Publications:* The Taft Story 1954, Citadel: The Story of the U.S. Senate 1957, Majesty and Mischief: A Mixed Tribute to F.D.R. 1961, The Professional; Lyndon B. Johnson 1964, Home Place: The Story of the U.S. House of Representatives 1965, The Responsibles 1972. *Address:* 800 S. Fourth Street, 1606 Louisville, Ky. 40203, U.S.A.

WHITEHEAD, George William, PH.D.; American mathematician; b. 2 Aug. 1918, Bloomington, Ill.; s. of George William Whitehead and Mary Gutschlag Whitehead; m. Kathleen Ethelwyn Butcher 1947; ed. Univ. of Chicago; Instructor in Math. Purdue Univ. 1941-45, Princeton Univ. 1945-47; Asst. Prof. of Math. Brown Univ. 1947-48, Assoc. Prof. 1948-49; Asst. Prof. of Math. M.I.T. 1949-51, Assoc. Prof. 1951-57, Prof. 1957-85, Prof. Emer. 1985-; Fellow, American Acad. of Arts and Sciences 1954; mem. N.A.S. 1972-. *Publications:* Homotopy Theory 1966, Recent Advances in Homotopy Theory 1970, Elements of Homotopy Theory 1978, and articles in scientific journals. *Leisure interests:* bridge, archaeology, genealogy. *Address:* Room 2-247, Department of Mathematics, Massachusetts Institute of Technology, Cambridge, Mass. 02139; 25 Bellevue Road, Arlington, Mass. 02174, U.S.A. (Home). *Telephone:* (617) 253-4350 (Office); (617) 643-0911 (Home).

WHITEHEAD, John Ernest Michael, M.A., M.B., B.CHIR., F.R.C.PATH.; British microbiologist (retd.); b. 7 Aug. 1920, London; s. of Dr. C. E. Whitehead and Mrs. Whitehead; m. Elizabeth B. Cochran 1946; one s. one d.; ed. Merchant Taylors' School, Northwood, Gonville and Caius Coll., Cambridge and St. Thomas's Hosp. Medical School, London; lecturer in Bacteriology St. Thomas's Hosp. Medical School 1948-51; Deputy Dir. Public Health Lab., Sheffield 1953-58; Coventry 1958-75; Deputy Dir. Public Health Lab.

Service 1975-81, Dir. 1981-85; Temp. Adviser WHO 1976-81; Consultant Adviser in Microbiology Dept. of Health and Social Security 1981-83; Specialist Adviser to Parl. Select Cttee. on Agric. 1988-89; Vice-Pres. Royal Coll. of Pathologists 1983-86; Chair. Assen. of Medical Microbiologists 1983-85; Hon. Lecturer Univ. of Sheffield 1954-58, Birmingham 1962-75; Travelling Fellowship British Postgraduate Medical Fed. *Publications:* various papers and reviews on microbiological subjects. *Leisure interests:* skiing, modern languages and house and garden maintenance. *Address:* Martins, Lee Common, Great Missenden, Bucks., HP16 9JP, England. *Telephone:* (024020) 492.

WHITEHEAD, Sir John Stainton, K.C.M.G., C.V.O., M.A. British diplomatist; b. 20 Sept. 1932; s. of John William Whitehead and Kathleen Whitehead; m. Mary Carolyn Hilton 1964; two s. two d.; ed. Christ's Hosp. and Hertford Coll., Oxford; served H.M. Forces 1950-52; Foreign Office 1955-56, Third Sec., later Second Sec., Tokyo 1956-61, Foreign Office 1961-64, First Sec. Washington 1964-67, First Sec. Econ., Tokyo 1968-71, FCO 1971-76, Head of Personnel Services Dept. 1973-76, Counsellor and Head of Chancery, Bonn 1976-80, Minster, Tokyo 1980-84, FCO, Deputy Under-Sec. of State (Chief Clerk) 1984-86; Amb. to Japan 1986-. *Leisure interests:* music, travel, tree-felling, walking, golf, chess. *Address:* British Embassy, 1 Ichiban-cho, Chiyoda-Ku, Tokyo 102, Japan; Bracken Edge, High Pitfold, Hindhead, Surrey, England (Home). *Telephone:* (03) 265-5511 (Embassy, Tokyo); (042 873) 4162 (Home, England).

WHITEHOUSE, Alton Winslow, Jr., LL.B.; American oil executive; b. 1 Aug. 1927, Albany, N.Y.; s. of Alton Winslow and Catherine L. Whitehouse; m. Helen MacDonald 1953; two s. one d.; ed. Univ. of Virginia; Assoc. Partner, McAfee, Hanning, Newcomber, Hazlett & Wheeler 1952-68; Vice-Pres. and General Counsel, Standard Oil Co. of Ohio 1968-69, Sr. Vice-Pres. and Gen. Counsel 1969, Pres. and C.O.O. 1970-76, Vice-Chair. 1977-78, Chair. and C.E.O. 1978-86; Dir. (non-exec.) British Petroleum Feb. 1980-. *Leisure interests:* hunting, fishing, golf. *Address:* 200 Public Square, Cleveland, Ohio 44114, U.S.A.

WHITELAW, Billie; British actress; b. 6 June 1932; d. of Perceval and Frances Whitelaw; m. 1st Peter Vaughan (divorced); m. 2nd Robert Muller; one s.; ed. Thornton Grammar School, Bradford. *Plays include:* Hotel Paradiso, Winter Garden 1954 and Oxford Playhouse 1956, Progress to the Park, Theatre Workshop and Saville 1961, England our England, Prince's 1962, Touch of the Poet, Venice and Dublin 1962; with Nat. Theatre 1963-65, Othello, London and Moscow, Hobson's Choice, Play (Beckett), Trelawny of the Wells, The Dutch Courtesan, After Haggerty, Criterion 1971, Not I, Royal Court 1973 and 1975, Alphabetical Order, Mayfair 1975, Footfalls, Royal Court 1976, Molly, Comedy 1978, Happy Days, Royal Court 1979, The Greeks, Aldwych 1980, Passion Play, Aldwych 1981, Rockaby, Nat. Theatre 1982, New York 1982, 1984, Riverside Studios 1986, world tour 1985/86, Tales from Hollywood, Nat. Theatre 1983, Who's Afraid of Virginia Woolf?, Young Vic 1987. *Films include:* No Love For Johnnie 1961, Charlie Bubbles 1968, Twisted Nerve 1968, The Adding Machine 1969, Start the Revolution Without Me, Leo the Last, Eagle in a Cage 1971, Gumshoe 1971, Frenzy 1972, Night Watch 1973, The Omen 1976, Leopard in the Snow, The Water Babies 1977, An Unsuitable Job for a Woman 1981, Slayground 1983, The Chain 1984, Shadey 1985, Maurice 1986, The Dressmaker 1988, Joyriders 1989. *Television includes:* No Trams to Lime Street, Lena Oh My Lena, Resurrection, The Skin Game, Beyond the Horizon, Anna Christie, Lady of the Camelias, The Pity of it all, Love on the Dole, A World of Time, You and I, Poet Game, Sextet (8 plays), Napoleon and Love (9 plays, as Josephine), The Fifty Pound Note (Ten From the Twenties), The Withered Arm (Wessex Tales), The Werewolf Reunion (2 plays), Two Plays by Samuel Beckett, Not I, Eustace and Hilda (2 plays), The Serpent Son, Happy Days (dir. by Beckett), A Tale of Two Cities, Jamaica Inn, Private Schultz, Camille, Old Girlfriends, The Picnic 1989. *Plays for radio:* The Master Builder, Hindle Wakes, Jane Eyre, The Female Messiah, Alpha Beta, Marching Song, The Cherry Orchard, Vassa; Hon. D. Litt. (Bradford) 1981; Variety Club Silver Heart Award 1961; TV Actress of Year 1961, 1972; British Acad. Award 1968; U.S. Film Critics' Award 1977; Evening News Film Award as Best Actress 1977; Sony Best Radio Actress award 1987, Evening Standard Best Actress Award 1988. *Leisure interest:* pottering about the house. *Address:* c/o Duncan Heath Associates, Paramount House, 162 Wardour Street, London, W.1; Rose Cottage, Plum Street, Glemsford, England. *Telephone:* 0787-280219.

WHITELAW OF PENRITH, 1st Viscount (cr. 1983) of Penrith in the County of Cumbria; **William (Stephen Ian) Whitelaw,** C.H., M.C., D.L.; British politician; b. 28 June 1918, Edinburgh; s. of Mr. and Mrs. W. A. Whitelaw; m. Cecilia Doriel Sprot; four d.; ed. Winchester Coll. and Trinity Coll., Cambridge; M.P. for Penrith and Border Div. of Cumberland 1955-83; Parl. Pvt. Sec. to Chancellor of Exchequer 1957-58; Asst. Govt. Whip 1959-61; a Lord Commr. of the Treasury 1961-62; Parl. Sec. Ministry of Labour 1962-64; Opposition Chief Whip 1964-70; Lord Pres. of Council and Leader of House of Commons 1970-72; Sec. of State for N. Ireland 1972-73, for Employment 1973-74; Chair. Conservative Party 1974-75; Deputy Leader of the Conservative Party 1975-88; Opposition Spokesman on Home Affairs 1975-79; Home Sec. 1979-83; Lord Pres. of the Council and Leader of the House of Lords 1983-87; Chair. Carlton Club 1986-; Pres. Penrith Agricultural Soc. 1988-; Chair. St. Bees School, Cumbria

1984–. *Publication:* The Whitelaw Memoirs (autobiog.) 1989. *Leisure interests:* golf, shooting. *Address:* House of Lords, London, S.W.1, England.

WHITHAM, Gerald Beresford, PH.D., F.A.A.A.S., F.R.S.; British professor of applied mathematics; b. 13 Dec. 1927, Halifax; s. of Harry and Elizabeth E. Whitham; m. Nancy Lord 1951; one s. two d.; ed. Elland Grammar School and Univ. of Manchester; Research Assoc. New York Univ. 1951–53; Lecturer in Applied Math. Manchester Univ. 1953–56; Assoc. Prof. of Applied Math., Inst. of Mathematical Sciences, New York 1956–59; Prof. of Math. M.I.T. 1959–62; Prof. of Aeronautics and Math. Calif. Inst. of Tech. 1962–67, of Applied Math. 1967–83, Charles Lee Powell Prof. of Applied Math. 1983–; Wiener Prize 1980. *Publications:* Linear and Non-linear Waves 1974, Lectures on Wave Propagation 1980. *Address:* Applied Mathematics 217-50, California Institute of Technology, Pasadena, Calif. 91125, U.S.A. *Telephone:* (818) 356-4561.

WHITLAM, (Edward) Gough, A.C., Q.C., B.A., LL.B.; Australian diplomatist and politician; b. 11 July 1916, Melbourne; s. of late H. F. E. Whitlam; m. Margaret Dovey 1942; three s. one d.; ed. Knox Grammar School, Sydney, Canberra High School, Canberra Grammar School and Univ. of Sydney; R.A.A.F. 1941–45; admitted to N.S.W. Bar 1947; mem. House of Reps. 1952–78; mem. Parl. Cttee. on Constitutional Review 1956–59; mem. Federal Parl. Exec. of Australian Labor Party 1959–77; Deputy Leader of Australian Labor Party in Fed. Parl. 1960–67, Leader 1967–77; Leader of the Opposition 1967–72, 1975–77; Prime Minister 1972–75, concurrently Minister of Foreign Affairs 1972–73; Rep. to UNESCO, Paris 1983–86, mem. Exec. Bd. 1985–89; mem. Australian Constitutional Convention 1973–76, Independent Comm. on Int. Humanitarian Issues 1983–, Constitutional Comm. 1986–; Chair. Australia-China Council 1986–, Australian Nat. Gallery 1987–; Visiting Fellow (lecturing in Political Science and Int. Relations) Australian Nat. Univ. 1978–80, Nat. Fellow 1980–81; Fellow Univ. of Sydney Senate 1981–83, 1986–; Pres. Int. Comm. of Jurists (Australian Section) 1982–83; Visiting Prof. Harvard Univ. 1979; Hon. LL.D. (The Philippines) 1974; Hon. D.Litt. (Sydney) 1981; Socialist Int. Silver Plate of Honour 1976, Vice-Pres. 1976–77, Hon. Pres. 1983–; Hon. mem. Int. Union for Nature Conservation. *Publications:* Australian Foreign Policy 1963, Australia—Base or Bridge (Evatt Memorial Lecture) 1966, Beyond Vietnam—Australia's Regional Responsibilities 1968, An Urban Nation 1969, The New Federalism 1971, Towards a New Australia—Australia and Her Region 1972, Labor in Power 1972, Australian Public Administration and the Labor Government (Sir Robert Garran Oration) 1973, Australia's Foreign Policy: New Directions, New Definitions (Roy Milne Memorial Lecture) 1973, Road to Reform: Labor in Government 1975, Government of the People, for the People by the People's House 1975, The Labor Government and the Constitution 1976, On Australia's Constitution (articles and lectures 1957–77) 1977, Reform During Recession 1978, The Truth of the Matter 1979, Labor Essays 1980, The Italian Inspiration in English Literature 1980, A Pacific Community (Harvard lectures) 1981, The Cost of Federalism 1983, The Whitlam Government 1985. *Address:* 100 William Street, Sydney, N.S.W. 2011, Australia. *Telephone:* 3582022.

WHITMAN, Marina von Neumann, PH.D.; American economist; b. 6 March 1935, New York; d. of John von Neumann and Mariette Kovesi (Mrs. J. B. H. Kuper); m. Robert F. Whitman 1956; one s. one d.; ed. Radcliffe Coll. and Columbia Univ.; Lecturer in Econs., Univ. of Pittsburgh 1962–64, Asst. Prof. 1964–66, Assoc. Prof. 1966–71, Prof. of Econs. 1971–73, Distinguished Public Service Prof. 1973–79; Sr. Staff Economist, Council of Econ. Advisers 1970–71; mem. President's Price Comm. 1971–72; mem. President's Council of Econ. Advisers (with special responsibility for int. monetary and trade problems) 1972–73; Vice-Pres., Chief Econ. Gen. Motors Corpn., New York 1979–, now Group Vice-Pres. for Public Affairs; mem. Trilateral Comm. 1973–, Bd. of Dirs. Council on Foreign Relations 1977–; Mfrs. Hanover Trust Co. 1973–, Proctor and Gamble Co. 1976–; Bd. of Trustees, Princeton Univ. 1980–; mem. Consultative Group on Int. Econ. and Monetary Affairs 1979–. *Publications:* various books and articles on economic topics. *Address:* General Motors Corporation, 3044 West Grand Boulevard, Detroit, Mich. 48202, U.S.A.

WHITMORE, Kay Rex, M.S.; American business executive; b. 24 July 1932, Salt Lake City, Utah; s. of Rex Grange and Ferrol Terry, m. Yvonne E. Schofield 1956; two s. four d.; ed. Univ. of Utah and M.I.T.; joined Kodak 1957, Gen. Man. Latin-American Region, Int. Photographic Div. 1975, Vice-Pres. and Asst. Gen. Man. U.S. and Canadian Photographic Div. 1978, Exec. Vice-Pres. and Gen. Man. Photographic Div. 1981, mem. Bd. of Dirs. 1982, Pres. Kodak 1983–; mem. Soc. of Photographic Scientists and Engineers. *Leisure interest:* skiing. *Address:* Eastman Kodak Co., 343 State Street, Rochester, N.Y. 14650, U.S.A. *Telephone:* (716) 724-5150.

WHITNEY, Hassler, MUS.B., PH.D.; American educator; b. 23 March 1907, New York; s. of Edward B. Whitney and A. Josepha Whitney (née Newcomb); ed. Yale and Harvard Univs.; Nat. Research Fellow 1931–33, Instructor in Math., Harvard Univ. 1933–35, Asst. Prof. 1935–40, Assoc. Prof. 1940–46, Prof. 1946–52, Prof. Inst. for Advanced Study 1952–77, Emer. 1977–; Pres. Int. Comm. Math. Instruction 1979–82; Research Mathematician, Nat. Defense Research Cttee. 1943–45; mem. N.A.S., American Philosophical Society; Nat. Medal of Science 1976, Wolf Foundation Prize 1982, Steele Prize 1985.
[*Died 10 May 1989.*]

WHITNEY, John Norton Braithwaite, F.R.S.A.; British broadcasting official; b. 20 Dec. 1930, Burnham, Bucks.; s. of Willis Bevan Whitney and Dorothy Anne Whitney; m. Roma Elizabeth Hodgson 1956; one s. one d.; ed. Leighton Park Friends' School, Reading; radio producer 1951–64; set up Ross Radio Productions Ltd. 1951, Autocue Ltd. 1955; f. Radio Antilles 1963; Man. Dir. Capital Radio 1973–82; Dir.-Gen. Ind. Broadcasting Authority 1982–89; Man. Dir. Really Useful Group April 1989–; wrote, edited and devised numerous TV series 1952–82; Dir. Duke of York's Theatre 1979–82; Satellite TV PLC March–May 1982; co-founder and Chair. Local Radio Asscn. 1964; Chair. Asscn. of Ind. Local Radio Contractors 1973–75, 1980, Events and Media Cttee. of the Royal Coll. of Music Centenary Appeal, Artsline 1983–; Chair. and Trustee Soundaround (Nat. Sound Magazine for the Blind); Pres. London Marriage Guidance Council (now known as Relate); Vice-Pres. Commonwealth Youth Exchange Council; Trustee, The Venture Trust, Artsline; mem. Admin. Council, Royal Jubilee Trusts, Appeal Cttee., Nat. Council for Voluntary Orgs., Council Operation Drake Fellowship, Films, TV and Video Advisory Cttee. of the British Council, Intermediate Tech. Devt. Group; mem. Bd. Nat. Theatre 1982–, Dir. Friends' Provident Life Office 1982–, Chair. Friends' Provident Stewardship Trust 1985–; mem. Council, Royal London Aid Soc. 1966–, Drake Fellowship 1981– (Trustee 1987–), Intermediate Tech. Group 1982–85; Bd. mem. Open Coll. 1987–. *Leisure interests:* chess, photography, sculpture, looking at sunrises. *Address:* Really Useful Group PLC, 20 Greek Street, London, W1, England. *Telephone:* 01-734-2114.

WHITTAM, Ronald, F.R.S.; British physiologist and university professor; b. 21 March 1925, Oldham, Lancs.; s. of Edward Whittam and May Whittam; m. Christine Patricia Margaret Lamb 1957; one s. one d.; ed. Council and Tech. School, Oldham, Univs. of Manchester, Sheffield, King's Coll., Univ. of Cambridge; served R.A.F. 1943–47; Beit Memorial Research Fellow, Physiological Lab., Univ. of Cambridge 1955–58; Lecturer in Biochem., Univ. of Oxford 1960–66; Prof. of Physiology, Univ. of Leicester 1966–83, Prof. Emer. 1983–, Research Worker 1983–86; Dean of Science Faculty 1979–82; Hon. Sec. Physiological Soc. 1969–74, Hon. mem. 1986–; mem. cttees. Univ. Grants Council and MRC 1970–83; mem. Royal Soc. Educ. Cttee. 1974–83. *Publications:* numerous articles and reviews in scientific journals. *Leisure interests:* walking, theology. *Address:* 9 Guilford Road, Stoneygate, Leicester, LE2 2RD, England (Home). *Telephone:* (0533) 707132 (Home).

WHITTAM SMITH, Andreas; British journalist; b. 13 June 1937; s. of Canon J. S. Smith; m. Valerie Catherine Sherry 1964; two s.; ed. Keble Coll., Oxford; with N. M. Rothschild 1960–62, Stock Exchange Gazette 1962–63, Financial Times 1963–64, The Times 1964–66; Deputy City Ed. The Telegraph 1966–69; City Ed. The Guardian 1969–70; Ed. Investors Chronicle, Stock Exchange Gazette and Dir. Throgmorton Publs. 1970–77; City Ed. Daily Telegraph 1977–85; Ed. The Independent 1986–, C.E.O. 1987–; Dir. Newspaper Publishing PLC 1986–; Vice-Pres. Nat. Council for One Parent Families 1982–; Wincott Award 1975; Journalist of the Year 1987; Hon. Fellow Keble Coll., Oxford; Hon. D.Litt. (St. Andrews, Salford) 1989. *Leisure interests:* music, history. *Address:* 31 Brunswick Gardens, London, W.8., England.

WHITTERIDGE, David, D.M., F.R.C.P., F.R.S.; British physiologist; b. 22 June 1912, London; s. of W. R. and Jeanne (née Carouge) Whitteridge; m. Gweneth Hutchings, Hon. F.R.C.P. 1938; three d.; ed. Whitgift School, Croydon, Magdalen Coll., Oxford and King's Coll. Hosp.; Fellow, by special election, Magdalen Coll., Oxford 1945–50; Prof. of Physiology, Univ. of Edin. 1950–68; Waynflete Prof. of Physiology Univ. of Oxford 1968–79; research worker on MRC grants 1979–; Hon. Fellow, Magdalen Coll., Oxford 1980–; hon. mem. Physiological Soc., Assoc. of British Neurologists; Feldberg Prize. *Publications:* articles in scientific journals. *Leisure interests:* gardening, Indology. *Address:* Winterslow, Lincombe Lane, Boars Hill, Oxford, OX1 5DZ, England. *Telephone:* (0865) 735211 (Home).

WHITTLE, Eric Yvon, M.A.; British banker; b. 9 Dec. 1925, London; s. of the late Horace Edwin Whittle and Winifred Edith Whittle; m. Magali Ritter 1955; one s. one d.; ed. Wyggeston Grammar School, Leicester, Christ Church, Oxford; Chair., Bank of London and S. America Ltd. 1968; Dir. Lloyds Bank Int. 1974, Chief Exec. 1978; Dir. Lloyds Bank PLC 1979. *Leisure interest:* walking. *Address:* c/o Lloyds Bank International PLC, 40-66 Queen Victoria Street, London, EC4P 4EL; 42 Addison Avenue, London, W.11, England (Home). *Telephone:* 01-248 9822 (Office); 01-603 3557 (Home).

WHITTLE, Air Commodore Sir Frank, O.M., K.B.E., C.B., M.A., F.R.S., F.ENG., R.A.F. (retd.); British aeronautical expert; b. 1 June 1907, Coventry; s. of Moses and Sarah Alice Whittle; m. 1st Dorothy Lee 1930 (divorced 1976), two s.; m. 2nd Hazel Ardyce Hall (née Steenberg) 1976; ed. Leamington Coll., Royal Air Force Coll., Cranwell, and Cambridge Univ.; posted to 111 Fighter Squadron as Pilot Officer 1928, attended Flying Instructors' Course 1929; Flying Instructor at No. 2 Flying Training School, Digby 1930; Test Pilot, Marine Aircraft Experimental Est., Felixstowe 1931–32; attended Officers' School of Eng. at Henlow 1932–34; Cambridge Univ. 1934–37; posted to Special Duty List to continue work on Whittle jet-propulsion gas turbine 1937-46; Tech. Adviser on Engine Design and Production to the Controller of Supplies (Air), Ministry of Supply 1946-48; retd. R.A.F. 1948; Tech. Adviser to BOAC 1948-52; consultant to Power Jets (Research and Devt.) Ltd 1950-53; Bataafsche Petroleum Maatschappij, The Hague 1953-57; Tech. Adviser on Devt. of Whittle Turb-Drill by Bristol Siddeley Engines 1961-66 and Rolls-Royce 1966-70; Navair Research Prof., U.S. Naval Acad. 1977-78, Research Prof. 1978-; mem. Livery, Guild of Air Pilots and Air Navigators; Hon. mem. Eng. Inst. of Canada, Soc. Royale Belge des Ingénieurs; Foreign Assoc. U.S. Nat. Acad. of Eng. 1979; Hon. Foreign mem. American Acad. of Arts and Sciences; Founder Fellow, Fellowship of Eng. 1976; Hon. Fellow, Aeronautical Soc. of India, Soc. of Experimental Test Pilots (U.S.A.) 1966, American Inst. Aeronautics and Astronautics 1968, Peterhouse, Cambridge; Hon. F.I.Mech.E.; Hon. F.R.Ae.S.; Gold Medal (Royal Aeronautical Soc.); Hon. D.Sc. (Oxford, Manchester, Bath, Warwick, Leicester, Exeter, Cranfield Inst. of Tech.), Hon. Sc.D. (Cambridge), Hon. LL.D. (Edinburgh), Hon. D.Tech. (Technical Univ. of Norway), (Loughborough Inst. of Tech.) 1987; James Alfred Ewing Medal; Daniel Guggenheim Medal 1946; Kelvin Gold Medal 1947; Melchett Medal 1949; Rumford Medal of Royal Soc. 1950; Gold Medal of Fed. Aéronautique Internationale 1951; Churchill Medal of Soc. of Engineers; Albert Medal of Royal Soc. of Arts 1952; Franklin Medal, U.S.A. 1956; John Scott Award, City of Philadelphia 1957; U.S. Legion of Merit; first recipient Goddard Award of American Inst. of Aeronautics and Astronautics 1965; Award of Merit City of Coventry 1966; Int. Communications Prize (Genoa) 1966; Int. Hall of Fame, San Diego 1968; Tony Jannus Award 1969; James Watt Int. Gold Medal 1977; Dept. of Transportation (F.A.A.) Award for Extraordinary Service 1978; R. Tom Sawyer Award (A.S.M.E.) 1978; W. E. Downes Memorial Award 1979; Nat. Air and Space Museum Trophy 1986; Hon. Freeman Royal Leamington Spa. *Publications:* The Early History of the Whittle Jet-Propulsion Gas Turbine (First James Clayton Lecture) 1945, Jet: The Story of a Pioneer 1953, Gas Turbine Aero-thermodynamics 1981. *Leisure interests:* walking, tennis, reading.

WHITTLE, Peter, PH.D., F.R.S.; New Zealand academic; b. 27 Feb. 1927, Wellington; s. of Percy Whittle and Elsie (née Tregurtha) Whittle; m. Kathe Hildegard Blomquist 1951; three s. three d.; ed. Wellington Boys' Coll., Victoria Univ. Coll., N.Z., Uppsala Univ., Sweden; N.Z. Sr. Prin. Scientific Officer 1953-59; Lecturer in Mathematics Univ. of Cambridge 1959-61, Churchill Prof. of the Mathematics of Operational Research 1967-; Prof. of Mathematical Statistics, Univ. of Manchester 1961-67; mem. Royal Soc. of N.Z. 1981; Hon. D. Sc. (Victoria Univ. of Wellington) 1987. *Publications:* Hypothesis Testing in Time Series Analysis 1951, Prediction and Regulation 1963, Probability 1970, Optimisation under Constraints 1971, Optimisation over Time 1982, Systems in Stochastic Equilibrium 1986. *Leisure interests:* guitar playing, jogging, cultivation of an ash coppice. *Address:* Statistical Laboratory, 16 Mill Lane, Cambridge, CB2 1SB (Office); 268 Queen Edith's Way, Cambridge, CB1 4NL, England (Home). *Telephone:* (0223) 65621 (Office); (0223) 245422 (Home).

WHYTE, Sir William Erskine Hamilton, K.C.M.G., B.A.; British diplomatist (retd.); b. 28 May 1927, Bristol; s. of Prof. W. Hamilton Whyte and Janet née Williamson; m. Sheila A. Duck 1953; three d. (one deceased); ed. King's School, Bruton and Queen's Coll., Oxford; served R.N. 1945-48; Civil Asst. War Office 1952-55; joined diplomatic service 1955; served Vienna 1956, Bangkok 1959, U.K. Mission to UN, New York 1963, Foreign Office 1966; Counsellor, Kinshasa, Zaire 1970-71; Dir.-Gen. British Inf. Services and Deputy Consul-Gen. (Information), New York 1972-76; Head, News Dept., FCO 1976-79; Minister (Econ. and Social Affairs), U.K. Mission to UN, New York 1979-81, Amb. and Deputy Perm. Rep. to UN 1981-83; High Commr. to Nigeria 1983-84, to Singapore 1984-87; Chair. U.K. Trident Shipping Agencies Ltd. 1988-; Dir. Irvin Group Britain Ltd. 1988-; Consultant Booke and Co. Inc., New York. *Leisure interests:* gardening, photography. *Address:* Apt. 14K 120 East 34th Street, New York, N.Y. 10016, U.S.A.; The Lodge, Ford Lane, Ford, Sussex, BN18 ODE, England. *Telephone:* (212) 779-4539; (0243) 551-377.

WHYTE, William Hollingsworth; American writer; b. 1 Oct. 1917, West Chester, Pa.; s. of William Hollingsworth Whyte and Louise Price; m. Jenny Bell Bechtel 1964; one d.; ed. Princeton Univ.; worked for Vick Chemical Co. 1939-41; served with U.S. Marine Corps 1941-45; joined Fortune Magazine 1946, Asst. Man. Ed. 1951-58; Dir. Street Life Project 1970-, Municipal Art Soc. of Landmarks Conservancy; Trustee Conservation Foundation; mem. American Conservation Assen.; LL.D. h.c., Grinnell Coll.; Benjamin Franklin Award 1955, Doris Freedman Award 1983. *Publications:* Is Anybody Listening 1952, The Organisation Man 1956, The Exploding Metropolis 1959, Cluster Development 1964, The Last Landscape 1968, The Social Life of Small Urban Spaces 1980, City: Rediscovering The Center 1989. *Leisure interests:* conservation, urban planning, photography. *Address:* 175 East 94th Street, New York, N.Y. 10128, U.S.A. *Telephone:* 369-0014.

WIBAUX, Fernand, D. EN D.; French diplomatist; b. 21 July 1921, Paris; s. of René Wibaux and Marcelle Caudrelier; m. 1st Jaqueline Piezel (deceased); m. 2nd Jeanine Petrequin; one s. two d.; ed. Lycée de Lille and Faculté de Droit, Paris; Civil Service admin., Algeria 1944; Attaché to Sec. of State for Overseas Territories 1949, to Minister of Merchant

Marine 1950-51, to High Commr., French W. Africa 1952-55; Chief Asst. to Ministers for Overseas Territories 1956-58; Dir.-Gen. Niger Office 1956; Consul-Gen. Bamako 1960-61; Amb. to Mali 1961-64; Dir. Office de Coopération et d'Accueil Universitaire 1964-68; Amb. to Chad 1968-74; Dir. of Cultural and Social Affairs, Ministry of Co-operation 1974-77; Amb. to Senegal (also to Cape Verde and the Gambia) 1977-83, to Lebanon 1983-85; High Commr. in New Caledonia 1985-86; Diplomatic Adviser to Govt. 1986; Croix de guerre; Commdr., Légion d'honneur, Ordre nat. du Mérite. *Address:* 6 rue du Hêtre, 94170 Le Perreux-sur-Marne, France.

WIBERG, Kenneth Berle, PH.D.; American professor of chemistry; b. 22 Sept. 1927, New York; s. of Halfdan Wiberg and Solveig Berle; m. Marguerite Louise Koch 1951; two s. one d.; ed. Mass. Inst. of Technology and Columbia Univ.; Instructor, Univ. of Washington 1950-52, Asst. Prof. 1952-55, Assoc. Prof. 1955-57, Prof. 1958-62; Prof., Yale Univ. 1962-68, Chair. Dept. of Chem. 1968-71, Whitehead Prof. of Chem. 1968-; Visiting Prof., Harvard Univ. 1957-58; A. P. Sloan Foundation Fellow 1958-62, J. S. Guggenheim Fellow 1961-62; mem. N.A.S., A.A.A.S.; California Section Award of American Chemical Soc. 1962, J. F. Norris Award of American Chemical Soc. 1973. *Publications:* Laboratory Technique in Organic Chemistry 1960, Interpretation of NMR Spectra 1964, Physical Organic Chemistry 1964, Oxidation in Organic Chemistry (Ed.) 1965, Computer Programming for Chemists 1966, Sigma Molecular Orbital Theory (with Sinanoglu) 1970; approx. 150 articles in scientific journals. *Address:* Department of Chemistry, Yale University, 225 Prospect Street, New Haven, Conn. 06520 (Office); 160 Carmalt Road, Hamden, Conn. 06517, U.S.A. (Home). *Telephone:* (203) 436-2443 (Office).

WICHTERLE, Otto, RNDR., DR.SC.; Czechoslovak chemist; b. 27 Oct. 1913, Prostějov; s. of Karel Wichterle and Slávka Podivínská; m. Ludmila Zahradníková 1938; two s.; ed. Czech Technical Univ., Prague, and Medical Faculty, Charles Univ., Prague; Asst. Lecturer, Inst. of Experimental Organic Chem., Czech Tech. Univ., Prague 1935-39; Head of Polymer Dept., Bata-Zlín 1940-42, 1944-45; Gestapo prisoner 1942-43; Asst. Prof. Faculty of Chem., Czech Tech. Univ., Prague 1945, later Prof.; Prof. Coll. Macromolecular Chem., Tech. Univ., Prague 1949-69; Academician, Czechoslovak Acad. of Sciences; Head of Dept. of Macromolecular Chem., Inst. of Chem. 1955-59; Dir. Inst. of Macromolecular Chem. 1959-70, Sr. Scientific Worker 1970-; Chair. Comm. for Macromolecular Chem.; mem. Bureau Int. Union of Pure and Applied Chem. 1962-; Deputy Chair. Scientific Collegium for Chem. and Chemical Tech., Czechoslovak Acad. of Sciences, Prague 1963; mem. Exec. Cttee. Int. Union of Pure and Applied Chem. 1967; Deputy to Czech Nat. Council 1968-69; Deputy to House of Nations, Fed. Ass. 1969; Pres. Union of Czech Scientific Workers 1969-70; Centennial Foreign Fellow American Chem. Soc. 1976; Patron Int. Soc. for Contact Lens Research 1980; Chair. Organizing Cttee., Soc. for Human Rights 1968; State Prize 1954; Order of Labour 1966; Klement Gottwald State Prize 1967; Javal Medal, Tokyo 1979, Founders Award, American Acad. of Optometry 1981, Dallos Award Asscn. of Contact Lens Industry 1982, Jaroslav Heyrovský Golden Plaque, Czechoslovak Acad. of Sciences 1983, Clemson Award, Soc. for Biomaterials 1984, Wood Prize, American Optical Soc. 1984, H. F. Mark Medal Österreichisches Kunststoffinstitut 1987, Services to Mankind Award, Soc. of Plastic Engineers 1989; inventor of soft contact lenses 1961. *Publications:* numerous papers and Foundations of Preparative Organic Chemistry (with others) 1951, Organic Chemistry 1952, 1955, Inorganic Chemistry (with Petrǎu) 1953, 1956, Macromolecular Chemistry 1957. *Leisure interests:* mechanical and optical workshop, gardening. *Address:* Institute of Macromolecular Chemistry, 162 06 Prague 6, Na Petřinách 1888 (Office); U. Andelky 27, 162 00 Prague 6, Czechoslovakia (Home). *Telephone:* Prague 36-0340 (Office); Prague 355070 (Home).

WICK, Charles Z., B.M.; American government official; b. 12 Oct. 1917, Cleveland, Ohio; m.; five c.; ed. Univ. of Michigan, W. Reserve Law School; f., Pres., C.E.O., Wick Financial Corpn. and Mapleton Enterprises, Los Angeles; Dir. United States Information Agency, Washington, D.C. 1981-; Co.-Chair. Presidential Inaugural Comm. 1981; mem. Calif. Bar Asscn. *Address:* Office of the Director, United States Information Agency, 400 C. Street, S.W., Washington, D.C. 20547, U.S.A. *Telephone:* (202) 485-7860.

WICKBERG, Erik E.; Swedish Salvation Army officer; b. 6 July 1904; s. of David Wickberg and Betty Lundblad; m. 1st Frieda de Groot 1929 (died 1930); m. 2nd Margarete Dietrich 1932 (died 1976); two s. two d.; m. 3rd Eivor Lindberg 1977; ed. Uppsala, Berlin, Stockholm, The Salvation Army Int. Training Coll., and Staff Coll.; Salvation Army 1925-; appointments in Scotland, Berlin, London; Div. Commdr., Uppsala 1946-48; Chief Sec. Switzerland 1948-53, Sweden 1953-57; Territorial Commdr., Germany 1957-61; Chief of Staff, Int. HQ London 1961-69; Gen. of The Salvation Army 1969-74; Hon. LL.D. (Korea) 1970; Commdr., Order of Vasa 1970, Order of Moo Koong-Wha (Korea) 1970, Grand Cross of Merit (Fed. Rep. of Germany) 1971, King's Medal in Gold (Sweden) 1980. *Publications:* In Darkest England Now 1974, Inkallad (memoirs) 1978 and articles in Salvation Army periodicals and year book. *Leisure interests:* reading, fishing, chess.

WICKBOM, Sten, LL.B.; Swedish politician; b. 14 March 1931, Stockholm; two s. two d.; trainee legal asst. 1955-57; reporting clerk, Svea Court of Appeal 1958-62, asst. judge 1962-64, Assoc. Judge of Appeal 1964, Judge of Appeal 1969; legal adviser, Ministry of Labour and Housing 1964-67;

Deputy Asst. Under-Sec., Ministry of Transport and Communications 1967–69, Under-Sec. for Legal Affairs, Ministry of Physical Planning and Local Govt. 1969–73, Ministry of Housing 1974; Dir.-Gen. and Head of Nat. Land Survey 1974–83; Minister of Justice 1983–87; chair. of various govt. cttees. *Address:* c/o Ministry of Justice, 103 33 Stockholm, Sweden. *Telephone:* 08/763 4728.

WICKERT, Erwin, PH.D.; German diplomatist (retd.) and author; b. 7 Jan. 1915, Bralitz; s. of Erwin and Hanna (née Dornbusch) Wickert; m. Ingeborg Weides 1939; two s. one d.; ed. Friedrich-Wilhelm Univ., Berlin, Dickinson Coll., Carlisle, Pa., and Heidelberg Univ.; attaché, German Foreign Office 1939; attaché, Shanghai 1940–41, Tokyo 1941–45; repatriated to Germany 1947 and lived as writer in Heidelberg; re-entered foreign service, Fed. Repub. of Germany 1955; Counsellor, German Embassy NATO, Paris 1955–60; Ministry of Foreign Affairs, Bonn 1960–68; Minister Plenipotentiary, London 1968–71; Amb. to Romania 1971–76, to People's Repub. of China 1976–80; mem. Mainz Acad. of Sciences and Literature; Grosses Bundesverdienstkreuz; German Radio Play Award of War Blind 1952. *Publications:* Fata Morgana über den Strassen 1938, Du musst dein Leben ändern, 1949, Dramatische Tage in Hitlers Reich 1952, Der Auftrag des Himmels (novel) 1961, Der Purpur (novel) 1966, China von innen gesehen 1982, The Middle Kingdom 1983, Der verlassene Tempel (novel) 1985, Der Kaiser und der Grosshistoriker (seven radio plays) 1987, Der fremde Osten 1988. *Address:* Rheinhoehenweg 22, Oberwinter, D-5480 Remagen 2, Federal Republic of Germany. *Telephone:* (022 28) 1726.

WICKMAN, Krister, LL.B., PH.D.; Swedish bank governor and former politician; b. 13 April 1924, Stockholm; s. of Johannes Wickman; at Nat. Swedish Inst. of Econ. Research 1951; Under-Sec. of State at Ministry of Finance 1959; M.P. 1967–73; mem. Cabinet and Minister without Portfolio for Econ. Policy 1967; Minister for Industry 1969–71, for Foreign Affairs 1971–73; Sec. of Parl. Standing Cttee. on Banking and Currency 1953–58; Vice-Chair. of Bd. LKAB Mining Co. 1962–67; Chair. of Bd. Swedish Film Inst. 1963–67; Chair. of Bd. and mem. Bd. of Govs. Bank of Sweden 1964–67, Gov. 1973–76; Chair. Econ. Policy Council 1968–71; Dir. BIS 1973–, SAS 1974–; Social Democrat. *Address:* Haga Trädgård, 17153 Solna, Sweden.

WICKRAMASINGHE, Nalin Chandra, M.A., PH.D., SC.D.; British professor of astronomy; b. 20 Jan. 1939, Colombo, Sri Lanka; s. of Percival H. and Theresa E. Wickramasinghe; m. Nelum Priyadarshini Pereira 1966; one s. two d.; ed. Royal Coll., Colombo, and Univs. of Colombo and Cambridge; Research Fellow, Jesus Coll., Cambridge 1963–66, Fellow 1967–73, Tutor 1970–73; Staff mem. Inst. of Theoretical Astronomy, Univ. of Cambridge 1968–73; Prof. and Head of Dept. of Applied Math. and Astronomy, Univ. Coll., Cardiff 1973–88; Prof. of Applied Math. and Astronomy, Univ. of Wales Coll. of Cardiff 1988–; Dir. Inst. of Fundamental Studies, Sri Lanka 1982–83; UNDP Consultant and Scientific Adviser to Pres. of Sri Lanka 1970–81; Visiting Prof., Univs. of Ceylon, Maryland, Arizona and Kyoto 1966–70, Univ. of W. Ontario 1974–76; Dag Hammarskjöld laureate in science 1986. *Publications:* Interstellar Grains 1967, Light Scattering Functions for Small Particles with Applications in Astronomy 1973, The Cosmic Laboratory 1975; with Sir Fred Hoyle (q.v.): Life Cloud: The Origin of Life in the Universe 1978, Diseases from Space 1979, The Origin of Life 1980, Evolution from Space 1981, Space Travellers, The Bringers of Life, Is Life an Astronomical Phenomenon? 1982, Why Neo-Darwinism doesn't work 1982, Proofs that Life is Cosmic 1982, Fundamental Studies and the Future of Science 1984, From Grains to Bacteria 1984, Living Comets 1985, Archaeopteryx, the Primordial Bird: a case of fossil forgery 1986, Cosmic Life Force 1987; with F. D. Kahn and P. G. Mezger: Interstellar Matter 1972; with D. J. Morgan: Solid State Astrophysics 1976. *Leisure interests:* photography, poetry. *Address:* School of Mathematics, University of Wales College of Cardiff, Senghenydd Road, Cardiff, CF2 4AG, Wales. *Telephone:* (0222) 874811.

WIDDRINGTON, Peter Nigel Tinling, M.B.A.; Canadian business executive; b. 2 June 1930, Toronto; s. of Gerard Widdrington and Margery (MacDonald) Widdrington; m. Betty Ann Lawrence 1956; two d.; ed. Pickering Coll., Newmarket, Ont., Queen's Univ. and Harvard Business School; Asst. Regional Man. Labatt's Ontario Breweries Ltd. 1957, Regional Man. 1958; Gen. Man. Kiewel and Pelissiers, Winnipeg 1961; Gen. Man. Labatt's Manitoba Breweries Ltd. 1962, Labatt's B.C. Breweries Ltd. 1965; Pres. Lucky Breweries Inc., San Francisco 1968; Vice-Pres. Corporate Devt., John Labatt Ltd. 1971, Sr. Vice-Pres. 1973, Pres. and C.E.O. 1973–, Chair. Sept. 1987–; Dir. Brascan -1977, BP Canada -1977, Toronto Blue Jays Baseball Club 1981–, Canadian Imperial Bank of Canada, Laidlaw Transportation Ltd., Grocery Mfrs. of America; mem. Bd. Ellis Don Ltd. *Address:* John Labatt Ltd., 451 Ridout Street North, London, Ont., N6A 5L3, Canada.

WIDERBERG, Bo; Swedish film director; b. 8 June 1930, Malmö; s. of Arvid Widerberg and Margaretha Gustafsson; m. 1st Ann-Mari Björklund 1953; m. 2nd Vanja Nettelbladt 1957; had 12 different jobs before military service; fmr. literary critic. *Films:* Barnvagnen (The Pram) 1962, Kvarteret Korpne (Raven's End) 1963, Kärlek 65 (Love 65) 1965, Elvira Madigan 1967, Adalen '31 1969 (Award for Best Foreign Film, U.S. Film Critics Guild), The Ballad of Joe Hill 1971, Fimpen (Stubby) 1974, Man on the Roof 1977, Victoria 1979. *Publications:* Kyssas (short story) 1952, Erotikon

(novel) 1957, En stuhl, Madame (autobiographical short story) 1961, Den gröna draken (novel), Visionen i svensk film (essays). *Address:* c/o Svenska Filminstitutet, Kungsgatan 48, Stockholm C, Sweden.

WIDMARK, Richard, B.A.; American actor; b. 26 Dec. 1914, Sunrise, Minn.; s. of Carl H. Widmark and Ethel Barr; m. Ora Jean Hazlewood 1942; one d.; ed. Lake Forest Coll.; Drama instructor at Lake Forest Coll. 1936–38; radio actor for New York networks 1938–47; Broadway appearances include Kiss and Tell 1943, Get Away Old Man 1943, Trio 1944, Kiss Them For Me 1944, Dunnigan's Daughter 1945, Dream Girl 1946. *Films include:* Kiss of Death 1947, Road House 1948, Yellow Sky 1949, Slattery's Hurricane 1949, Night and the City 1950, No Way Out 1950, Halls of Montezuma 1950, Red Skies of Montana 1950, Full House 1952, Destination Gobi 1953, Hell and High Water 1954, Garden of Evil 1954, Broken Lance 1954, Backlash 1956, St. Joan 1957, Tunnel of Love 1958, The Alamo 1960, Secret Ways 1961, Judgement at Nuremberg 1961, How the West Was Won 1963, Madigan 1969, The Moonshine War 1970, When Legends Die 1972, Murder on the Orient Express 1974, To the Devil a Daughter 1975, The Sellout 1976, The Domino Principle 1976, Roller Coaster 1976, The Swarm 1977, Coma 1978, Bear Island 1979, All God's Children 1980, Who Dares Wins 1982, The Final Option 1983, Against All Odds 1984; television includes Vanished 1970, and the series Madigan 1972. *Address:* c/o ICM, 8899 Beverley Boulevard, Los Angeles, Calif. 90048, U.S.A.

WIDOM, Benjamin, PH.D.; American professor of chemistry; b. 13 Oct. 1927, Newark, N.J.; s. of Morris Widom and Rebecca Hertz Widom; m. Joanne McCurdy 1953; two s. one d.; ed. Stuyvesant High School, New York and Columbia and Cornell Univs.; Research Assoc., Univ. of N.C. 1952–54; Instructor in Chem., Cornell Univ. 1954–55, Asst. Prof. 1955–59, Assoc. Prof. 1959–63, Prof. 1963–, Goldwin Smith Prof. 1983–; van der Waals Prof., Univ. of Amsterdam 1972; Visiting Prof. of Chem., Harvard Univ. 1975; IBM Visiting Prof. of Theoretical Chem., Oxford Univ. 1978; Lorentz Prof., Leiden Univ. 1985; Visiting Prof., Katholieke Univ., Leuven 1988; Fellow American Acad. of Arts and Sciences; mem. N.A.S.; Boris Pregel Award (New York Acad. of Sciences); Langmuir Award (American Chemical Soc.); Dickson Prize for Science (Carnegie-Mellon Univ.). *Publication:* Molecular Theory of Capillarity (with J. S. Rowlinson) 1982. *Address:* Department of Chemistry, Baker Laboratory, Cornell University, Ithaca, N.Y. 14853, U.S.A. *Telephone:* (607) 255-3363.

WIECK, Hans-Georg, D.PHIL.; German diplomatist; b. 28 March 1928, Hamburg; s. of John and Elisabeth (née Hall) Wieck; m. Anneliese Dietz 1958 (died 1977); three s. one d.; ed. Univ. of Hamburg; entered Foreign Service, Fed. Repub. of Germany 1954, assignments in Bonn (Soviet Affairs), New York (Fed. German Observer Mission to UN), Washington, D.C. (Fed. German Embassy), Bonn (Berlin Affairs); Chef de Cabinet to Foreign Minister Schroeder 1966, to Defence Minister Schroeder 1966–69; Dir. Policy Planning Staff, Fed. Ministry of Defence, Bonn 1970–74; Amb. to Iran 1974–77, to U.S.S.R. 1977–80; Amb. and Perm. Rep. to NATO 1980–85; Pres. Fed. German Intelligence System Aug. 1985–. *Publications:* The Establishment of the Christian Democratic Union in Germany 1953, The Christian Democrats and the Liberals in Southern Germany 1958. *Leisure interests:* sports, hunting, history, architecture. *Address:* Bundesnachrichtendienst, 8023 Pullach im Isartal, Heilmannstrasse, Federal Republic of Germany. *Telephone:* (089) 793-1567.

WIECZOREK, Marek, M.ECON.SCI.; Polish politician and economist; b. 4 Dec. 1929, Częstochowa; ed. Higher School of Econs., Częstochowa; Admin. Man., Plant of Craft Co-operative of Weavers and Knitters, Częstochowa 1948–54; Head of Częstochowa Gastronomic Plants 1954–58; Sec., Town Cttee. of Democratic Party (SD), Częstochowa 1958–60; Dir., Municipal Retail Trade Establishment, Częstochowa 1960–61; Deputy Chair., Pres. of Municipal Nat. Council, Częstochowa 1961–73, Deputy Mayor of Częstochowa 1973–78; Under-Sec. of State, Ministry of Internal Trade and Services 1978–81; mem. SD 1946–, including Deputy Chair. and Chair. Town and Dist. Cttee., Częstochowa 1965–76, Chair. Voivodship Cttee., Częstochowa 1976–77, mem. SD Cen. Cttee. 1969–, mem. Presidium 1981–, Sec. 1981–83, Deputy Chair. 1983–; Deputy to Seym (Parl.) 1985–, Vice-Marshal of Seym 1985–; Deputy Chair. All-Poland Peace Cttee. 1983–; Commdr.'s Cross of Order of Polonia Restituta, Gold Cross of Merit and others. *Address:* Centralny Komitet SD, ul. Rutkowskiego 9, 00-021 Warsaw, Poland. *Telephone:* 27-29-37.

WIEDEMANN, Josef; German architect; b. 15 Oct. 1910, Munich; s. of Thomas and Maria (née Anwald) Wiedemann; m. Hilma Bittorf 1939; one d.; ed. Tech. Univ., Munich; worked with Prof. Roderich Fick 1935–42; freelance architect 1946–; Prof. of Design, Conservation and Sacred Bldg., Dept. of Architecture, Tech. Univ., Munich 1955–76, now Prof. Emer.; mem. Bayerische Akad. der Schönen Künste; corresp. mem. Acad. d'Architecture, Paris; Komturkreuz, St.-Sylvester Orden; BDA Prize 1975; work includes reconstruction work and new shops, offices, homes, churches in Munich and other towns and cities, including Glyptothek, Munich, Karmel Hlg. Blut, Dachau, Allianz Head Office, Munich, Verbandsschule and Maria am Wege church, Windach, St. Ignatius, Munich, St. Stephan, Diessen/A. *Publications:* Der Friedhof m.O. Valentien 1963, Ornament heute? 1974, Antoni Gaudi 1974, Sakralbau in "München und seine Bauten" 1983, Musik und Architektur 1986, Neuer Kirchenbau in 'Wörterbuch der Kurst'.

Leisure interests: theory and philosophy of architecture, sculpture. *Address:* Im Eichgehölz 11, D-8000 Munich 50, Federal Republic of Germany. *Telephone:* 089/811 41 53.

WIEHAHN, Nicholas E., LL.D.; South African university professor and consultant; b. 29 April 1929, Mafeking (now Mafikeng); s. of Johannes and Anna C. Wiehahn; m. Huiberdina J. Verhage 1956; two s.; ed. Univ. of O.F.S., Univ. of S. Africa; research work in Univs. of Hamburg, Cologne, Heidelberg, Munich and London; research visits to labour insts. and univs. in Europe, Israel, Canada, U.S.A. and Japan; Advocate, Supreme Court of S.A. and High Court of Lesotho; Prof. in Labour and Industrial Law at various univs.; Prof. Extra-Ordinarius, Univ. of S.A. 1980–, Dir. Inst. of Labour Relations 1976–77; fmr. Prof. Siemens Chair of Industrial Relations, School of Business Leadership, Univ. of S.A., Pretoria, Dir. Oct. 1984–; mem. Council, Univ. of Port Elizabeth 1973–75, Free State Univ. 1980–; Chair. Council, Univ. of Zululand 1981–; Dir. Bureau for Int. Labour Affairs, Dept. of Manpower 1977–78, Ed.-in-Chief EMPACT 1977–78, Labour Adviser to Minister of Manpower 1977–79; mem. Prime Minister's Econ. Advisory Council 1977–; Pres. Industrial Court of S.A. 1979–80; Chair. Comm. of Inquiry into Labour Legis. (Wiehahn Comm.) 1977–80, into Labour Matters (Namibia) 1987–88; Chair. Labour Council, S.A. Transport Services 1988–; mem. various govt. comms., advisory cttees., etc.; other public and educational appointments; dir. of several cos. 1981–; recipient of several awards and bursaries. *Publications:* articles on labour law and industrial relations in periodicals, commentaries and other publs.; Change in South Africa 1983. *Leisure interests:* reading, gardening. *Address:* School of Business Leadership, University of South Africa, P.O. Box 392, Pretoria-0001, South Africa. *Telephone:* 26-4014, 28-1771 (Office); 47-4438 (Home).

WIEJACZ, Józef, M.A.; Polish diplomatist; b. 8 March 1933, Jędrzejów; m.; one s.; ed. Main School of Foreign Service, Warsaw; with Ministry of Foreign Affairs 1954–; attaché, Embassy, Ankara 1957–58, Teheran 1958–60; First Sec., Embassy, Oslo 1962–68, Deputy Dir. of Dept., Ministry of Foreign Affairs 1971–73, Counsellor-Minister Plenipotentiary, Embassy in Washington 1973–77; Dir. of Dept. of Studies and Programming, Ministry of Foreign Affairs 1977–80, Under-Sec. of State, Ministry of Foreign Affairs 1980–84, Amb. to Italy, also accred. to Malta 1984–; mem. Polish del. to some sessions of UN Gen. Ass., Deputy Chair. Polish del. 1981, 1982; mem. Polish del. Conf. on Security and Co-operation in Europe, Helsinki 1973, Geneva 1973, Belgrade 1978–79, Chair. Madrid 1982–; mem. Scientific Council of Polish Inst. of Foreign Affairs; mem. Polish United Workers' Party (PZPR); Kt.'s Cross of Order of Polonia Restituta, Gold Cross of Merit, others. *Leisure interests:* sightseeing, mountaineering. *Address:* Polish Embassy, via Peter Paul Rubens 20, Monti Parioli, Rome, Italy. *Telephone:* 360-96-95.

WIELAND, Joyce, O.C.; Canadian artist and film maker; b. 30 June 1931, Toronto; ed. Cen. Tech. School; one-man exhbns. at Isaacs Gallery Toronto 1960, 1963, 1967, 1972, 1974, 1981, 1983, 1987, Vancouver Art Gallery 1968, Museum of Modern Art, New York 1971, Cannes Film Festival 1976, Canadian Film Arts Centre, Hong Kong 1981, Nat. Gallery of Canada 1978, Yajima Gallery, Montreal 1982; has participated in several group exhbns. including Canadian Pavilion at Expo 67, Montreal 1967; maj. travelling retrospective, Art Gallery of Ont., Toronto 1981–82, 1987–88, Canada House, London 1988–89; film The Far Shore received three Canadian awards 1977; Retrospective Films of Joyce Wieland, Whitney Museum, New York 1973, San Francisco Art Inst. 1985, Art Gallery of Ontario (touring) 1987–88, Nat. Film Theatre, London 1988, Georges Pompidou Centre 1989; selection of films screened at Ciné-Club de Saint-Charles, Univ. of Paris, Sorbonne 1986; Artists on Fire film documentary 1987; two awards for Rat Life and Diet in N. America, Third Ind. Filmakers Festival, New York 1969, Award for A and B in Ontario, Ann Arbor Film Festival 1986, YWCA Woman of Distinction Award 1987. *Publications:* True Patriot Love 1971, Joyce Wieland 1987, Joyce Wieland: Quilts, Paintings and Works of Paper 1988. *Address:* 497 Queen Street East, Toronto, Ont., Canada. *Telephone:* (416) 366-2986.

WIERZBICKI, Eugeniusz; Polish architect; b. 31 March 1909, Chanżenkowo; s. of Ryszard and Maria Wierzbicki; m. Zofia Szemińska 1945; one c.; ed. Warsaw Tech. Univ.; mem. Polish Assen. of Architects (SARP) 1936–, Pres. Warsaw Branch 1951–53, of Cen. Bd. 1953–57, mem. Council and Collective Judge 1953–80; Sr. Designer, Warsaw Design Office of Gen. Architecture; retd. 1974; First Prizes in collaboration with W. Kłyszewski (q.v.) and J. Mokrzyński (q.v.) 1940; State Prize, 3rd Class 1951, 2nd Class 1955, 1st Class 1974, Kt.'s Cross, Order of Polonia Restituta 1957, Gold Award of Rebuilding of Warsaw 1958, Hon. Prize of SARP 1968, of Katowice Branch of SARP 1972, Order of Banner of Labour, 2nd Class 1969, Prize of Minister of Construction, 1st Class 1973. *Buildings include:* Polish United Workers' Party Building, Warsaw; hotels and museum in Białystok; Sailors' Home, Szczecin; Museum of Modern Art, Skopje, Yugoslavia; Railway Station, Katowice (all in collaboration with W. Kłyszewski and J. Mokrzyński). *Publications:* numerous articles in newspapers. *Leisure interests:* motor cars, books, nature. *Address:* Al. Wyzwolenia 2 m. 54, 00-570 Warsaw, Poland.

WIESEL, Elie; American author; b. 30 Sept. 1928, Sighet, Romania; s. of Shlomo Wiesel and Sarah (Feig) Wiesel; m. Marion E. Rose 1969; one s.; ed. Sorbonne, Paris; Distinguished Prof. Coll. of City of New York 1972–76; Andrew Mellon Prof. in Humanities, Boston Univ. 1976–; Prix Rivarol 1964, Jewish Heritage Award 1965, Remembrance Award 1965, Prix Medicis 1968, Prix Bordin (Acad. Française) 1972, Eleanor Roosevelt Memorial Award 1972, American Liberties Medallion, American Jewish Comm. 1972, Martin Luther King Jr. Award (Coll. of City of New York) 1973, Faculty Distinguished Scholar Award, Hofstra Univ. 1973–74, Nobel Peace Prize 1986; recipient of numerous hon. degrees. *Publications:* Night 1960, Dawn 1961, The Accident 1962, The Town Beyond the Wall 1964, The Gates of the Forest 1966, The Jews of Silence 1966, Legends of Our Time 1968, A Beggar in Jerusalem 1970, One Generation After 1971, Souls on Fire 1972, The Oath 1973, Ani Maamin, Cantata 1973, Zalmen or the Madness of God (play) 1975, Messengers of God 1966, A Jew Today 1978, Four Hasidic Masters 1978, The Trial of God 1979, Le Testament d'un Poète Juif Assassine 1980 (Prix Livre-Inter 1980, Prix des Bibliothèquaires 1981), Five Biblical Portraits 1981, Somewhere a Master: Further Tales of the Hasidic Master 1982, Paroles d'étranger 1982, The Golem 1983, The Fifth Son (Grand Prix de la Littérature, Paris) 1985, Signes d'exode 1985, Against Silence 1985, A Song for Hope 1987, Twilight (novel) 1988, The Six Days of Destruction (with Albert Friedlander) 1988. *Address:* Boston University, 745 Commonwealth Avenue, Boston, Mass. 02215, U.S.A.

WIESENTHAL, Simon; Austrian war crimes investigator and former architect; b. 31 Dec. 1908, Buczacz, Poland (now Buchach, U.S.S.R.); s. of Hans Wiesenthal; m. Cyla Müller 1936; one d.; ed. architectural studies in Prague and Lvov (Lemberg); practised architecture until World War II; prisoner in Nazi concentration camps 1941–43, 1944–45; active since the war in searching for Nazi criminals, assisting Jewish victims of Nazi regime and in Jewish civic affairs; Head of Jewish Historical Documentation Centre, Linz, Austria 1947–54; Dir. Jewish Documentation Centre, Vienna 1961–; Chair. Asscn. of Jews Persecuted by the Nazi Regime; Diploma of Honour, Int. Fed. of Resistance Movements, Vienna; Dr. h.c. (Hebrew Union Coll., N.Y.) 1974, (Hebrew Theological Coll., Skokie, Ill.) 1976, (Washington Univ.) 1981; Dr. h.c. of Criminal Justice (Colby Coll., John Jay Coll.); many awards and honours, including Medal of Freedom (Netherlands), Congressional Gold Medal (U.S.A.) 1980, Dutch Medal for Freedom, Medal for Freedom of Luxembourg, Jean-Moulin-Médaille of the French Resistance, Kaj-Munk-Medal, Denmark, Hon. mem. Dutch Resistance, Hon. mem. Danish Asscn. of Freedom Fighters, Justice Louis Brandeis Award of Zionist Org. in U.S.A., Jerusalem Medal, Great Medal of Merit, Fed. Repub. of Germany, Chevalier, Légion d'honneur, Commdr. of Oranje-Nassau (Netherlands), Commendatore della Repubblica Italiana. *Publications:* KZ Mauthausen 1946, Head Mufti, Agent of the Axis 1947, I Hunted Eichmann 1961, Limitation 1964, The Murderers Among Us 1967, Sunflower 1969, Sails of Hope 1973, The Case of Krystyna Jaworska 1975, Max and Helen 1982, Every Day Remembrance Day—A chronicle of Jewish martyrdom 1986, Justice not Revenge 1989. *Leisure interest:* philately. *Address:* Jewish Documentation Centre, Salztorgasse 6, 1010 Vienna; Mestrozigasse 5, 1190 Vienna, Austria (Home). *Telephone:* 63 91 31 and 63 98 05 (Office).

WIESNER-DURAN, Eduardo, M.A.; Colombian economist; b. 1934; ed. University of the Andes, Colombia, and Stanford Univ., Calif.; held several teaching posts in univs. and advisory posts on comms. in Colombia; with staff of OAS and Inter-American Devt. Bank; Pres. Bankers' Asscn. of Colombia 1976, Nat. Professional Econ. Council of Colombia 1977; Head of Nat. Planning Dept.; Minister of Finance 1978–82; Dir. Western Hemisphere Dept., IMF 1982–87, Special Trade Rep. of IMF July 1987–, Dir. IMF Office, Geneva 1987–. *Address:* IMF, 700 19th Street, N.W., Washington, D.C. 20431, U.S.A.

WIESNER, Jerome Bert, PH.D.; American professor and communications engineer; b. 30 May 1915, Detroit; s. of Joseph Wiesner and Ida Friedman; m. Laya Wainger 1940; three s. one d.; ed. Univ. of Michigan; Chief Engineer Library of Congress, Washington 1940–42; mem. staff M.I.T. Radiation Lab., Cambridge, Mass. 1942–45; mem. staff Univ. of Calif., Los Alamos Lab. 1945–46; Prof. of Electrical Eng., Assoc. Dir. and Dir. Research Lab. of Electronics, Chair. Dept. of Electrical Eng., M.I.T. 1948–61, Dean of Science 1964–66, Provost 1966–71, Pres. 1971–80, Pres. Emer. and Inst. Prof. 1980–; Special Asst. to Pres. for Science and Tech., Dir. Office of Science and Tech., White House 1961–64; mem. Pres.'s Science Advisory Cttee. 1958–68; Chair. Tech. Assessment Advisory Council, U.S. Congress 1976–79; Dir. Automatix, Damon Biotech, Cons. for Man. Inc., The Faxon Co., MacArthur Foundation; Fellow I.E.E.E., American Acad. of Arts and Sciences; mem. Inst. of Radio Engineers, Acoustical Soc. of America, Fed. of American Scientists, A.A.A.S., N.A.S., Nat. Acad. of Eng., American Asscn. of Univ. Professors, Geophysical Union, American Philosophical Soc. *Publications:* Where Science and Politics Meet 1964, ABM, An Evaluation of the Decision to Deploy an Antiballistic Missile System 1969. *Leisure interests:* politics, writing, sailing, skiing. *Address:* Massachusetts Institute of Technology, 20 Ames Street, Room E15-207, Cambridge, Mass. 02139; 61 Shattuck Road, Watertown, Mass. 02172, U.S.A. (Home).

WIETHÜCHTER, Horst, D.ECON.; German tobacco industry executive; b. 5 July 1928, Bielefeld; s. of Heinrich and Ida (née Bottemöller) Wiethüchter; m. Ilse Kochsiek 1957; one s. one d.; ed. Bonn and Cologne Univs.; Head of Central Admin. Rheinische Schmirgelwerke GmbH and Nicco-Werke GmbH 1954–63; Vice-Pres., Finance, Dr. Kurt Herberts & Co. GmbH 1963–71; mem. for Finance, Bd. of Dirs. Reemtsma Cigarettenfabriken GmbH 1971-, Spokesman of the Bd. 1975-, Chair. 1976–84; Chair. Supervisory Bd. Henninger Bräu KGaA; Chair. Supervisory Bd., Brau AG, Nuremberg, Beirat Hannen GmbH, Willich; mem. Supervisory Bd. Possehl GmbH, Lübeck. *Address:* Kreetkamp 13, 2000 Hamburg 52, Federal Republic of Germany. *Telephone:* 82 36 16.

WIGGINS, David, M.A., F.B.A.; British university teacher; b. 8 March 1933, London; s. of Norman Wiggins and Diana (née Priestley) Wiggins; ed. St. Paul's School and Brasenose Coll., Oxford; Asst. Prin. Colonial Office 1957–58; Jane Eliza Procter Visiting Fellow, Princeton Univ. 1958–59; Lecturer, New Coll., Oxford 1959, Fellow and Lecturer 1960–67; Prof. of Philosophy, Bedford Coll., London 1967–78; Fellow and Praelector in Philosophy, Univ. Coll., Oxford 1981–89; Chair. and Prof. Dept. of Philosophy, Birkbeck Coll., London Jan. 1989-; visiting appts. Stanford Univ. 1964, 1965, Harvard Univ. 1968, 1972, All Souls Coll., Oxford 1973, Princeton Univ. 1980; Fellow, Center for Advanced Study in Behavioral Sciences, Stanford 1985–86; mem. Independent Comm. on Transport 1973–74, Cen. Transport Consultative Cttee.; Chair. Transport Users' Consultative Cttee. for South-East 1977–79. *Publications:* Identity and Spatio Temporal Continuity 1967, Truth, Invention and the Meaning of Life 1978, Sameness and Substance 1980, Needs, Values, Truth 1987; articles in learned journals. *Address:* Birkbeck College, Malet Street, London, WC1, England.

WIGGINS, James Russell; American newspaperman; b. 4 Dec. 1903, Luverne, Minn.; s. of James Wiggins and Edith Binford; m. Mabel E. Preston 1923; two s. two d.; ed. Luverne High School, and USAF Air Intelligence School; with Rock County Star 1922–30; Editorial Writer St. Paul Dispatch and St. Paul Pioneer Press 1930–33, Washington Corresp. 1933–38, Man. Ed. 1938–42, 1945–46; U.S. Army Air Force 1942–45; Asst. Publr. New York Times 1946–47; Man. Ed. The Washington Post 1947–55, Vice-Pres. 1953–60, Exec. Ed. 1955–60, Ed. and Exec. Vice-Pres. 1960–68; Perm. Rep. to UN 1968–69; Ed., Publr. Ellsworth American 1969-; Eliza Lovejoy Award 1954, John Zenger Award 1957, Golden Key Award 1960. *Publication:* Freedom or Secrecy 1956. *Address:* Water Street, Ellsworth, Me. 04605 (Office); Carlton Cove, Brooklin, Me. 04616, U.S.A. (Home).

WIGGLESWORTH, Sir Vincent (Brian), Kt., C.B.E., F.R.S., M.A., M.D., B.CH., F.R.E.S.; British entomologist; b. 17 April 1899; s. of the late Sidney Wigglesworth; m. Mabel Katherine Semple 1928 (died 1986); three s. one d.; ed. Repton, Caius Coll., Cambridge; St. Thomas 2nd Lieut. Royal Field Artillery 1917–18, served in France; Frank Smart student Caius Coll. 1922–24; lecturer in medical entomology, London School of Hygiene and Tropical Medicine 1926, Reader in Entomology, Univ. of London 1936–44, Univ. of Cambridge 1945–52; Quick Prof. of Biology, Cambridge 1952–66; Dir. Agricultural Research Council, Unit of Insect Physiology 1943–67; Fellow, Gonville and Caius Coll., Cambridge, Imperial Coll., London 1977; mem. many nat. and int. socs.; many awards and medals; several hon. degrees. *Publications:* Insect Physiology 1934, The Principles of Insect Physiology 1939, The Physiology of Insect Metamorphosis 1954, The Life of Insects 1964, Insect Hormones 1970, Insects and the Life of Man 1976; numerous scientific papers. *Address:* 14 Shilling Street, Lavenham, Suffolk, England. *Telephone:* (0787) 247293.

WIGHTMAN, Arthur Strong, PH.D.; American professor of mathematics and physics; b. 30 March 1922, Rochester, N.Y.; s. of Eugene Pinckney and Edith Stephenson Wightman; m. 1st Anna-Greta Larsson 1945 (died 1976), one d.; m. 2nd Ludmila Popova 1977; ed. Yale Coll. and Princeton Univ.; Instructor in Physics, Yale Univ. 1943–44; U.S. Navy 1944–46; Instructor in Physics, Princeton Univ. 1949, Asst. Prof., Assoc. Prof., Prof. of Math. Physics, 1960-, Thomas D. Jones Prof. of Math. Physics 1971-; Visiting Prof. Sorbonne, Paris 1957; Fellow American Acad. of Arts and Sciences, Royal Society of Arts; mem. N.A.S., American Math. Soc., American Physical Soc.; Dannie Heinemann Prize in Mathematical Physics 1969; D.Sc. h.c. (ETH, Zürich) 1969. *Publication:* PCT, Spin and Statistics and All That (with R. F. Streater) 1964. *Leisure interests:* art, music, tennis. *Address:* Joseph Henry Laboratories of Physics, Princeton University, Box 708, Princeton, N.J. 08544; 16 Balsam Lane, Princeton, N.J. 08540, U.S.A. (Home). *Telephone:* (609) 452-5835 (Office).

WIGLEY, Dafydd, B.SC.; British (Welsh) politician; b. 1 April 1943, Derby; s. of Elfyn Edward Wigley and Myfanwy (née Batterbee) Wigley; m. Elinor Bennett Owen 1967; three s. (two deceased) one d.; ed. Sir Hugh Owen School, Caernarfon, Rydal School, Colwyn Bay, Victoria Univ. of Manchester; Econ. Analyst, Ford Motor Co. 1964–67; Chief Cost Accountant, Mars Ltd. 1967–71; Financial Controller, Hoover Ltd. 1971–74; Co. Borough Councillor, Merthyr Tydfil 1972–74; Vice-Chair. Plaid Cymru 1972–74, Pres. 1981–84; M.P. for Caernarfon 1974-; Chair. All Party House of Commons Reform Group 1983-; Vice-Chair. Parl. Social Services Group 1985-; Pres. Spastic Soc. of Wales 1985-; Vice-Pres. Welsh Asscn. of Community Councils 1978-, Fed. of Industrial Devt. Assens. 1980-; Sponsor, Disabled Persons Act 1981; Pres. Caernarfon Town FC 1987-; Hon. mem. Gorsedd of Welsh Bards; Grimshaw Memorial Award, Nat. Fed. of the Blind 1982. *Publication:* An Economic Plan for Wales 1970. *Leisure interests:* football, tennis, swimming, chess. *Address:* House of Commons, London, S.W.1, England; 21 Penllyn, Caernarfon, Gwynedd,

Wales (Constituency Office). *Telephone:* 01-219 4182 or 5021 (London); (0286) 2076 (Caernarfon).

WIGNER, Eugene Paul, DR.ING.; American physicist; b. 17 Nov. 1902, Budapest, Hungary; s. of Antal and Elisabeth (née Einhorn) Wigner; m. 1st Amelia Z. Frank 1936 (died 1937); m. 2nd Mary A. Wheeler 1941 (died 1977); one s. one d.; m. 3rd Eileen C. P. Hamilton 1979; ed. Müegyetem, Budapest and Technische Hochschule, Berlin; Asst. Technische Hochschule, Berlin 1926–27, Univ. of Göttingen 1927–28; Lecturer, Technische Hochschule, Berlin 1928–33; Prof. of Math. Physics, Princeton Univ., on part-time basis 1930–36; Prof. of Physics, Univ. of Wisconsin 1936–38; Thomas D. Jones Prof. of Math. Physics, Princeton Univ. 1938–71; Visiting Lecturer, Univ. of Mass. 1971, 1972; Consulting Prof. Louisiana State Univ. 1972–85, also at Ettore Majorana Center 1972, 1976, 1981, 1982, 1983, 1984, 1985, Technion, Haifa 1973, 1981, Rockefeller Univ. 1974, Princeton Univ. 1975, 1976, Univ. of Utrecht 1975, Inst. des Hautes Etudes scientifiques 1977, Univ. of Texas at Austin 1978, Free Univ. of Mexico and Univ. of B.C. 1979, Univ. of Delaware 1980, Max Planck Inst. 1981, State Univ. of N.Y., Plattsburg 1982; mem. of Visiting Cttee., Nat. Bureau of Standards 1947–51, Bd. of Dirs., Oak Ridge Inst. of Nuclear Studies 1947–50; mem. Gen. Advisory Cttee. to U.S. Atomic Energy Comm. 1952–57, 1959–64; on leave of absence at the Metallurgical Lab., Univ. of Chicago (Plutonium Project) 1942–45; on leave of absence as Dir. of Research and Devt. of the Clinton Labs., Oak Ridge, Tenn. 1946–47, as Lorentz Lecturer, Inst. Lorentz, Leyden, Neths. 1957; mem. American Physical Soc., American Mathematical Soc., American Philosophical Soc., N.A.S., American Acad. of Arts and Sciences, Franklin Soc. (Franklin Medal 1950), Royal Netherlands Acad., Austrian Acad. of Sciences, American Nuclear Soc. (Dir. 1960–61); foreign mem. Royal Society 1970; corresp. mem. Akad. der Wissenschaften, Göttingen; Hon. mem. Eötvös Lorand Physical Soc. 1977; Vice-Pres. American Physical Society 1955, Pres. 1956; Dir. Int. School of Physics, Enrico Fermi Course 1959, Varenna 1963, Nat. Acad. Sciences Harbour Project 1963; Dir. (on leave of absence) Civil Defense Project, Oak Ridge Nat. Lab. 1964–65; numerous honorary degrees; Medal for Merit 1946; Franklin Medal 1950; Fermi Award 1958; Atoms for Peace Award 1960, Max Planck Medal of German Physical Soc. 1961, Nobel Prize for Physics 1963, George Washington Award of the American Hungarian Studies Foundation, Semmelweiss Medal of American Hungarian Medical Assen. 1965, U.S. Nat. Medal of Science 1969, Pfizer Award of Merit 1971, Albert Einstein Award 1972, Wigner Medal 1978, Founders Medal, Int. Cultural Foundation 1982, Medal of the Hungarian Cen. Research Inst., etc. *Publications:* Gruppentheorie und ihre Anwendungen auf die Quantenmechanik der Atomspektren 1931, Nuclear Structure (with L. Eisenbud) 1958, Physical Theory of Neutron Chain Reactors (with A. M. Weinberg) 1958, Project Harbour Summary Report (with R. Park) 1964, Symmetries and Reflections 1967, Who Speaks for Civil Defense (editor) 1968, Survival and the Bomb 1969. *Leisure interests:* walking, swimming. *Address:* Jadwin Hall, Princeton Univ., P.O. Box 708, Princeton, N.J. 08544; 8 Ober Road, Princeton, N.J. 08540, U.S.A. *Telephone:* (609) 924-1189.

WIIN-NIELSEN, Aksel Christopher, DR.SC.; Danish professor of physics; b. 17 Dec. 1929, Klakring; s. of Aage Nielsen and Marie Petre (née Kristoffersen) Nielsen; m. Bente Havsteen (née Zimsen) Wiin-Nielsen 1953; three d.; ed. Univs. of Copenhagen and Stockholm; staff mem. Danish Meteorological Inst. 1952–55, Int. Meteorological Inst. 1955–58, Jt. Numerical Weather Prediction 1959–61, Nat. Centre for Atmospheric Research 1961–63; Prof. (Chair.), Univ. of Mich., U.S.A. 1963–73; Dir. European Centre for Medium-Range Weather Forecasts 1979–84; Sec.-Gen. WMO 1979–84; Dir. Danish Meteorological Inst. 1984–87; Prof. of Physics, Univ. of Copenhagen 1988-; Hon. D.Sc. (Reading, Copenhagen); Ohridsky Medal, Univ. of Sofia, Bulgaria; Buys-Ballot Medal, Royal Netherlands Acad. of Science; Wihuri Int. Science Prize, Wihuri Foundation, Helsinki, Finland; Rossby Prize, Swedish Geophysical Soc.; Silver Medal, Univ. of Helsinki; Palmen Medal, Finnish Geophysical Soc. *Publications:* Problems in Dynamic Meteorology 1970, Dynamic Meteorology 1973, Predictability (in Danish) 1987; about 100 articles on dynamic meteorology, numerical weather prediction and atmospheric energetics. *Address:* Geophysical Institute, University of Copenhagen, 6 Haraldsgade, 2200 Copenhagen N, Denmark. *Telephone:* (1) 818166.

WIJESEKERA, Nandadeva, D.LITT., PH.D.; Sri Lankan anthropologist, archaeologist and government official (retd.); b. 11 Dec. 1908, Moonamalwatta, Sri Lanka; s. of Muhandiram N. G. de S. Wijesekera and Dona Emaliya de Alwis Gunatilaka; m. Leila Jayatilaka 1941; one d.; ed. Ananda Coll., Colombo, Univ. Coll. Colombo, Trinity Coll. Cambridge, England, Univ. Coll. London, Vienna Univ. and Calcutta Univ.; Asst. in Ethnology, Colombo Museum 1937–44; war service in civilian duties 1940–44; Deputy Supt. of Census 1945–50; Dir. Census and Statistics 1950–54; mem. UNESCO Nat. Comm. 1950; Asst. Sec., Ministry of Finance 1951; Sec. Royal Comm. on Languages 1951; Acting Dir. Census and Statistics 1954, Dir. 1955; Dir. Official Language Dept. 1956; Deputy Commr. Official Language Affairs 1959–60, Commr. 1960–67; Amb. 1967–70; Leader Ceylon Del. to Colombo Plan Conf. 1967; Adviser to Dept. of Archaeology 1983-; mem. Bd. of Man. Inst. of Indigenous Medicine 1983-; has been mem. of numerous govt. dels. and has held many official appointments; represented All-Ceylon cricket team 1932; Pres. Nondescripts Cricket Club 1952; Pres. Royal Asiatic Soc. 1966–67, 1971–74, All-Ceylon Football Assen. 1963, Nat.

Acad. of Sciences 1986; Founder Pres. Archaeological Soc. 1966; Ed.-in-Chief Mahavamsa (in Pali and Sinhala); Gold Medal, Royal Asiatic Soc. 1973; Purā vidyā Chakravarti 1986. *Publications:* many books, including (Sinhala) Lanka Janatawa 1955, Perani Bitusituvam 1964, Perani Murti Kalawa 1970, Proper Names in Sinhala Literature 1988; (English) People of Ceylon 1949, Early Sinhalese Painting 1959, Veddas in Transition 1964, Biography of Sir D. B. Jayatilaka 1973, Selected Writings 1983, Heritage of Sri Lanka 1984, Anthropological Gleanings from Sinhala Literature 1985, Contacts and Conflicts with Sri Lanka 1986. *Leisure interests:* reading and writing. *Address:* No. 34 Dudley Senanayake Mawatha, Borella, Colombo 8, Sri Lanka. *Telephone:* Colombo 94089.

WIJETUNGE, D.B.; Sri Lankan politician; b. 1922; Minister of Information and Broadcasting 1978-79, of Power and Highways 1979-80, of Power, Energy, Posts and Telecommunications 1980-82, of Posts and Telecommunications 1982-87, of Agricultural Devt. and Research 1987, of Finance and Planning Feb. 1989-; Gov. Northwestern Prov. 1988; Prime Minister of Sri Lanka March 1989-. *Address:* Office of the Prime Minister, 58 Sir Ernest de Silva Mawatha, Colombo 7, Sri Lanka. *Telephone:* (1) 36281.

WIJEWARDANE, Nissanka; Sri Lankan civil servant and diplomatist; b. 1926; ed. Univ. of Ceylon; joined Ceylon Civil Service 1949; among posts held were Sec. to the Gov.-Gen., Commr., Local Govt., Chair. Local Govt. Service Comm., Admin. Officer, WHO, Colombo; Chair. Bank of Ceylon 1977-84; Perm. Rep. to UN 1984-88. *Address:* c/o Ministry of Foreign Affairs, Republic Bldg., Colombo 1, Sri Lanka.

WIKSTRÖM, Jan-Erik, B.A.; Swedish politician and publisher; b. 11 Sept. 1932, St. Skedvi, Dalarna; s. of Börje Wikström and Essy (Lilja) Wikström; m. Inger Wikström; two s. one d.; ed. Gothenberg Univ.; Man. Dir. Gummessons Bokförlag Publishing House 1961-76; mem. Municipal Council, Stockholm 1962-70; mem. Riksdag (Parl.) 1971-73, 1976-; Minister of Educ. and Cultural Affairs 1976-82; mem. Folkpartiet (Liberal Party). *Publications:* Röd och gul och vit och svart 1950, Skall kyrkan skiljas från staten 1958, Storm över Kongo 1961, Indien vid korsvägen 1962, Inför Herrens ansikte 1962, Politik och kristen tro 1964, Skall samhället utbilda präster? 1966, Liberala positioner 1969, Med frisinnat förtecken 1970, En bättre skola 1973, Möten med Mästaren 1975, I väntan på befrielsen 1977, Friket Mångfald Kvalitet 1978, Liberalism med frisinnat förtecken 1981. *Leisure interests:* literary history, biographies, political literature, tennis. *Address:* Rikshagen 100 12, Stockholm; Tegnérgatan 4, 11358 Stockholm, Sweden (Home). *Telephone:* 08/786 45 96 (Office); 08/30 20 18 (Home).

WILANDER, Mats; Swedish tennis player; m. Sonja Mulholland 1987; Australian Open Champion 1984, 1985, 1988 (finalist 1986), French Open Champion 1982, 1985, 1988 (finalist 1983, 1987), U.S. Open Champion 1988; winner Wimbledon Men's Doubles Championship (with Joakin Nystrom) 1986; mem. victorious Swedish Davis Cup Team 1984, 1987, 1988; ranked World Number 1 1988; voted official World Champion 1988.

WILBERFORCE, Baron (Life Peer), cr. 1964; **Richard Orme Wilberforce,** C.M.G., O.B.E., F.R.C.M., Q.C., M.A.; British judge; b. 11 March 1907, Jullundur; s. of Samuel Wilberforce and Katherine Sheepshanks; m. Yvette Lenoan 1947; one s. one d.; ed. Winchester Coll. and Oxford Univ.; called to Bar 1932; Fellow, All Souls Coll., Oxford 1932-; Chief, Legal Div., Control Comm., Germany 1945; U.K. Rep. Legal Cttee. ICAO 1949-; Judge, High Court 1961-64; Lord of Appeal in Ordinary 1964-82; mem. Perm. Court of Arbitration 1964-; Chair. Exec. Council, Int. Law Asscn. 1965-87; Pres. Appeals Tribunal of Lloyds of London 1983-87; Pres. U.K. Assc n. of European Law; Pres. Int. Fed. for European Law 1978-80; High Steward, Oxford Univ. 1967-; Chancellor, Hull Univ. 1978-; Chair. Court of Inquiry into Electricity Workers' Dispute 1970-71, Mineworkers' Dispute 1972; Hon. mem. Faculty of Advocates, Scotland, Canadian Bar Assc n., American Soc. of Int. Law; Hon. D.C.L. (Oxford) 1968, LL.D. (London) 1972, (Hull) 1973, (Bristol) 1983. *Publication:* The Law of Restrictive Practices and Monopolies (joint author) 1957. *Leisure interests:* music, golf, philately, the turf. *Address:* 8 Cambridge Place, London, W.8, England.

WILBERFORCE, William John Antony, C.M.G., M.A.; British diplomatist (retd.); b. 3 Jan. 1930, Camberley; m. Laura Sykes 1953; one s. two d.; ed. Ampleforth Coll. and Christ Church, Oxford; joined Foreign Office 1953; served Oslo 1955-57, Berlin 1957-59, Ankara 1962-64, Abidjan 1964-67, Washington, D.C. 1972-75; Head of Defence Dept., FCO 1975-78; Asst. Under-Sec., Royal Coll. of Defence Studies 1979; Amb. and leader of U.K. del. to Madrid CSCE Review Meeting 1980-82; High Commr. to Cyprus 1982-88; Hon. D. Hum. (Wilberforce Univ.). *Address:* Markington Hall, Harrogate, N. Yorks., England. *Telephone:* (0765) 87356 (Home).

WILBRAHAM, John Harry George, F.R.A.M., L.R.A.M., A.R.C.M.; British musician; b. 15 April 1944, Bournemouth; s. of Harry Plunkett Wilbraham and Doreen Edith Mather; m. Susan Drake 1970; ed. Raynes Park Country Grammar School and R.A.M., London; mem. Philharmonia Orchestra 1967-69; Prin. Trumpet, Royal Philharmonic Orchestra 1967-72, BBC Symphony Orchestra 1972-80; Prof. of Cornet and Trumpet, Royal Mil. School of Music, Kneller Hall 1982-85; Prof. of Trumpet, Birmingham School of Music 1983-, R.A.M. 1985-, Nat. Youth Orchestra of G.B. 1983-; Silver Medal, Worshipful Co. of Musicians. *Leisure interests:* cricket, theatre,

cooking, jazz. *Address:* 16 Ravensmede Way, London, W4 1TD, England. *Telephone:* 01-747 0652.

WILBUR, Richard (Purdy), M.A.; American poet and fmr. university professor; b. 1 March 1921, New York City; s. of Lawrence L. Wilbur and Helen Purdy Wilbur; m. Charlotte Ward 1942; three s. one d.; ed. Amherst Coll., and Harvard Univ.; Asst. Prof. of English, Harvard Univ. 1950-54; Assoc. Prof. Wellesley Coll. 1954-57; Prof. Wesleyan Univ. 1957-77; Writer in Residence, Smith Coll., Northampton, Mass. 1977-86; mem. Nat. Inst. of Arts and Letters, American Acad. of Arts and Sciences, Soc. of Fellows of Harvard Univ. 1947-50; Guggenheim Fellow 1952-53, Ford Fellow 1961, Guggenheim Fellow 1963; Chancellor, Acad. of American Poets 1961; Poet Laureate of U.S.A. 1987-88; mem. PEN; Pres. American Acad. of Arts and Letters 1974-76, Chancellor 1977-78; mem. Dramatists Guild; Hon. Fellow, Modern Language Asscn. 1986; Harriet Monroe Prize 1948; Oscar Blumenthal Prize 1950; Prix de Rome from American Acad. of Arts and Letters 1954-55; Edna St. Vincent Millay Memorial Award 1956; Nat. Book Award Pulitzer Prize 1957, co-recipient Bollingen Translation Prize 1963; co-recipient Bollingen Prize in Poetry 1971; Prix Henri Desfeuilles 1971; Brandeis Creative Arts Award 1971; Shelley Memorial Prize 1973, Harriet Monroe Poetry Award 1978, Drama Desk Award 1983, PEN Translation Prize 1983, St. Botolph's Foundation Award 1983, Aiken Taylor Award 1988, L. A. Times Book Award 1988, Pulitzer Prize 1989; Chevalier, Ordre des Palmes Académiques 1984. *Publications:* The Beautiful Changes and other poems 1947, Ceremony and other poems 1950, A Bestiary (anthology, with Alexander Calder) 1955, The Misanthrope (trans. from Molière) 1955, Things of this World (poems) 1956, Poems 1943-1956 1957, Candide (comic opera, with Lillian Hellman and others) 1957, Poe (edition of his poems with introduction and notes) 1959, Advice to a Prophet (poems) 1961, Tartuffe (trans. from Molière) 1963, The Poems of Richard Wilbur 1963, Loudmouse (for children) 1963, Poems of Shakespeare (with Alfred Harbage) 1966, Walking to Sleep (new poems and translations) 1969, School for Wives (trans. from Molière) 1971, Opposites (Children's Verse, illustrated by the author) 1973, The Mind-Reader 1976, Responses: Prose Pieces 1953-1976 1976, The Learned Ladies (trans. from Molière) 1978, Selected Poems of Witter Bynner (editor) 1978, Seven Poems 1981, Andromache (trans. from Racine)˙1982, The Whale (translations) 1982, Molière: Four Comedies (contains 4 plays translated previously listed) 1982, Phaedra (trans. from Racine) 1986, Lying and Other Poems 1987, New and Collected Poems 1988. *Leisure interests:* tennis, walking, herb gardening. *Address:* Dodwells Road, Cummington, Mass. 01026, U.S.A. *Telephone:* (413) 634-2275.

WILBUR, Richard Sloan, M.D.; American physician and association executive; b. 8 April 1924, Boston; s. of Blake Colburn Wilbur and Mary Caldwell Sloan; m. Betty Lou Fannin 1951; three s.; ed. Stanford Univ.; Intern, San Francisco County Hosp. 1946-47; Resident, Stanford Hosp. 1949-51, Univ. of Pa. Hosp. 1951-52; mem. of Staff, Palo Alto Medical Clinic, Calif. 1952-69; Deputy Exec. Vice-Pres., American Medical Asscn., Chicago 1969-71, 1973-74; Asst. Sec., Health and Environment Dept. 1971-73; Sr. Vice-Pres., Baxter Labs Inc., Deerfield, Ill. 1974-76; Exec. Vice-Pres. Council Medical Speciality Socs. 1976-; Sec., Accreditation Council for Continuing Medical Educ. 1979-; Assoc. Prof. of Medicine, Georgetown Univ. Medical School 1971-, Stanford Medical School 1952-69; Vice-Pres. Nat. Resident Matching Plan 1980-; Chair. Bd. Calif. Medical Asscn. 1968-69; Chair. Calif. Blue Shield 1966-68; Pres. American Coll. of Physician Executives 1988-89; mem. numerous other medical asscns. *Publications:* contribs. to medical journals. *Address:* 985 North Hawthorne Place, Lake Forest, Ill. 60045 (Home); P.O. Box 70, Lake Forest, Ill. 60045, U.S.A. (Office).

WILCKENS, Ulrich; German ecclesiastic; b. 5 Aug. 1928, Hamburg; s. of Dr. Hans Wilckens and Annemarie (née Arning) Wilckens; m. Inge Westermann 1954; three d.; ed. Univs. of Heidelberg and Tübingen; Vicar, Hinterzarten, Black Forest 1953-55; Asst., Ökumenisches Inst., Univ. of Heidelberg 1955-58; Docent, Marburg 1958-60; Prof. of New Testament, Kirchliche Hochschule, Berlin 1960-68, Theological Faculty, Univ. of Hamburg 1968-81; Bishop of Holstein-Lübeck 1981-. *Publications:* Weisheit und Torheit 1959, Die Missionsreden der Apostelgeschichte 1961, Das Neue Testament übersetzt und kommentiert 1970, Rechtfertigung als Freiheit, Paulusstudien 1974, Der Brief an die Römer, (Vol. I) 1978, (Vol. II) 1980, (Vol. III) 1982. *Address:* Bäckerstrasse 3-5, 2400 Lübeck 1, Federal Republic of Germany. *Telephone:* 0451-79 71 76.

WILCZEK, Mieczysław, M.ENG., M.A.; Polish chemist, lawyer and politician; b. 25 January 1932, Komorowice Bielskie; m.; one d.; ed. Silesian Tech. Univ., Warsaw Univ. 1965; scientific worker, Silesian Tech. Univ., Gliwice 1954-57; Dir. VIOLA Cosmetics Plant 1957-61; Deputy Dir. AROMA Warsaw Aromatic Synthetics Plant 1961-64; Deputy Dir. POLLENA Household Chemistry Industrial Union, Warsaw 1965-69; Dir. Cen. Research and Developmental Centre, Bldg. Joinery Industry 1971-74; private businessman, joint owner of feed concentrates mill 1974-85; jt. owner LAVIL Enterprise, Stanisławów, Siedlce Voivodship 1985-88; Minister of Industry 1988-; mem. Econ. Cttee. of Council of Ministers 1988-; mem. Social-Econ. Council attached to Seym (Parl.); Deputy Pres. Soc. for Econ. Initiatives Supporting; mem. Polish United workers' Party (PZPR); Knight's Cross of Polonia Restituta Order. *Publications:* author or co-author of 20 Polish and foreign patents in chemical and feed industry.

Leisure interests: tennis, horsemanship, belle-lettres. *Address:* Ministerstwo Przemysłu, ul. Wspólna 4, 00-921 Warsaw, Poland. *Telephone:* 28 01 82 (Office).

WILD, Earl; American pianist and composer; b. 26 Nov. 1915, Pittsburgh, Pa.; s. of Royland and Lillian G. Wild; ed. Carnegie Technical Coll., Pittsburgh; studied with Selmar Jansen, Egon Petri, Helene Barrere, Volya Cossack and Paul Doguereau; first American soloist to perform with NBC Orchestra conducted by Toscanini 1942, has performed with symphony orchestras and given recitals in many countries; has appeared with Sir Malcolm Sargent, Jascha Horenstein, Sir Georg Solti, Arthur Fiedler; played first TV piano recital 1939; has played for 7 Presidents of U.S., incl. inauguration of Pres. J. F. Kennedy; numerous recordings for RCA, EMI, Columbia, Nonesuch, Readers Digest and Vanguard Records. *Compositions include:* Piano Concerto, The Turquoise Horse (choral work) and ballet music, oratorios, solo piano music, choral work and popular songs. *Leisure interests:* writing poetry, playing piano.

WILD, John Paul, A.C., C.B.E., F.R.S., F.A.A., F.T.S., M.A., SC.D.; Australian radio astronomer; b. 1923, Sheffield, England; s. of late Bessie (née Arnold), and late Alwyn H. Wild; m. Elaine Poole Hull 1948; two s. one d.; ed. Whitgift School, Croydon, England and Peterhouse, Cambridge; Radar Officer, Royal Navy 1943–47; Research Scientist, Div. of Radiophysics, Commonwealth Scientific and Industrial Research Org. (CSIRO), N.S.W., Australia 1947–71, Chief of Div. 1971–77, Assoc. mem. 1977–78, full-time mem. of CSIRO Exec. 1978–85, Chair Sept. 1978–85; Chair. Very Fast Train (VFT) Jt. Venture 1986–; Pres. Radio Astronomy Comm. of Int. Astronomical Union 1967–70; mem. Anglo-Australian Telescope Bd. 1973–82, Chair. 1975–80; Foreign mem. American Philosophical Soc.; Foreign Hon. mem. American Acad. of Arts and Sciences; Corresp. mem. Royal Soc. of Sciences, Liège; Hon. D.Sc. (Aust. Nat. Univ.) 1979, (Newcastle Univ.) 1982; Hale Prize for Solar Astronomy, American Astronomical Soc. 1980; Edgeworth David Medal, Hendryk Arctowski Gold Medal of N.A.S. U.S., Balthasar van der Pol Gold Medal of Int. Union of Radio Science, Herschel Medal of Royal Astronomical Soc., Thomas Rankin Lyle Medal of Australian Acad. of Science, Royal Medal, Royal Soc. of London 1980, ANZAAS Medal 1984. *Publications:* various papers on radio astronomy in scientific journals. *Address:* VFT, GPO Box 2188, Canberra, A.C.T. (Office); RMB 338, Sutton Road, Via Queanbeyan, N.S.W. 2620, Australia (Home).

WILDENSTEIN, Daniel Leopold, L. ÈS L.; French art historian; b. 11 Sept. 1917, Verrières-le-Buisson; s. of Georges and Jane (Lévi) Wildenstein; m. 1st Martine Kapferer 1939 (divorced 1968); two s.; m. 2nd Sylvia Roth 1978; ed. Cours Hattemer, Sorbonne; joined Wildenstein and Co. Inc., New York 1940, Vice-Pres. 1943–59, Pres. 1959–68, Chair. 1968–; Pres. Wildenstein Foundation Inc., New York 1964–; Dir. Wildenstein and Co. Ltd., London, and Wildenstein Arte, Buenos Aires 1963–; Founder and mem. American Inst. of France, New York 1947–; Dir. of Activities, Musée Jacquemart-André, and of Musée Chaalis (Institut de France), Paris, 1956–62; Dir. Gazette des Beaux-Arts 1963–; mem. French Chamber of Commerce in U.S. (Counsellor) 1942–, Haut Comité du Musée de Monaco 1973–; organizer of art competitions (Hallmark art award); mem. Inst. de France (Académie des Beaux-Arts), Commdr. des Arts et des Lettres, Commdr. de l'ordre de Léopold II (Belgium). *Publications:* Claude Monet (Vol. I) 1975, (Vol. II, III) 1979, (Vol. IV) 1985, Edouard Manet (Vol. I) 1976, (Vol. II) 1977, Gustave Courbet (Vol. I) 1977, (Vol. II) 1978. *Leisure interest:* horse racing. *Address:* 57 rue la Boétie, 75008 Paris, France (Office); 48 avenue de Rumine, 1007 Lausanne, Switzerland (Home).

WILDER, Billy; American film writer, producer and director; b. 22 June 1906, Austria; m. Audrey Young; fmr. reporter, Berlin; film scriptwriter 1930–; wrote People on Sunday, Emil and the Detectives, Germany; writer and dir. Mauvaise Graine, Paris 1933; went to U.S. 1934; writer in collaboration Bluebeard's Eighth Wife 1938, Midnight 1939, Ninotchka 1939, What A Life 1939, Arise, My Love 1940, Hold Back the Dawn 1941, Ball of Fire 1941. *Films directed* (also co-scripted): The Major and the Minor 1942, Five Graves to Cairo 1943, Double Indemnity 1944, The Lost Weekend (Acad. Award) 1945, The Emperor Waltz 1947, A Foreign Affair 1948, Sunset Boulevard (Acad. Award) 1950; Producer, dir. and writer (in collaboration): The Big Carnival (or Ace in the Hole) 1951, Stalag 17 1953, Sabrina 1954, The Spirit of St. Louis 1957, Love in the Afternoon 1957, Witness for the Prosecution 1958, Some Like It Hot 1959, The Apartment (Acad. Award) 1960, One, Two, Three 1961, Irma La Douce 1963, Kiss Me, Stupid 1964, The Fortune Cookie (British title Meet Whiplash Willie) 1966, The Private Life of Sherlock Holmes 1970, Avanti 1972, Fedora 1978; co-producer, dir. and writer (in collaboration) The Seven Year Itch 1955; dir. and writer Buddy Buddy 1981; six Academy Awards (for Lost Weekend, Sunset Boulevard and The Apartment), American Film Inst. Life Achievement Award 1985, Irving G. Thalberg Award 1988. *Address:* c/o Equitable Investment Corporation, P.O. Box 93877, Hollywood, Calif. 90093, U.S.A.

WILEY, W. Bradford, B.A.; American book publisher; b. 17 Nov. 1910, Orange, N.J.; s. of William Carroll Wiley and Isabelle LeCato; m. Esther Terry Booth 1936; two s. one d.; ed. Colgate Univ., Harvard Business School; Chair. John Wiley & Sons Inc., New York City, John Wiley & Sons Ltd., London, John Wiley & Sons Canada Ltd., Jacaranda Wiley; Dir. Wiley Eastern Ltd.; Chair. Franklin Book Programs 1964–66, Assen.

of American Publishers 1970–72, U.S. Govt. Advisory Cttee. for Int. Book and Library Programs 1967–70 (mem. 1962–70), IPA and STM Copyright Cttees., Int. Publishers' Assen. 1981–84, Copyright Clearance Center 1986–; U.S. Rep. to Int. Publishers' Assen. 1962–76; mem. Man. Bd. M.I.T. Press; Trustee Colgate Univ. 1968–74, 1979–81, Drew Univ. 1979–81; Hon. LL.D. (Colgate) 1966; Andrew Wellington Cordier Fellow 1978, Curtis G. Benjamin Award 1983, Publishing Hall of Fame 1985. *Leisure interests:* golf, sailing, fishing. *Address:* John Wiley & Sons Inc., 605 Third Avenue, New York, N.Y. 10158 (Office); 57 Prospect Hill Avenue, Summit, N.J. 07901 (Home). *Telephone:* (212) 850-6101 (Office); (401) 635-4283 (Home, Little Compton).

WILFORD, Sir (Kenneth) Michael, G.C.M.G.; British diplomatist (retd.); b. 31 Jan. 1922, Wellington, New Zealand; s. of late George McLean Wilford and Dorothy Veronica (née Wilson); m. Joan Mary Law 1944; three d.; ed. Wrekin Coll. and Cambridge Univ.; Army service 1940–46 (mentioned in despatches); Foreign (later Diplomatic) Service 1947–81, Third Sec. Berlin 1947; Asst. Pvt. Sec. to Sec. of State, FO 1949; served France 1952, Singapore 1955; Asst. Pvt. Sec. to Sec. of State, FO 1959; Pvt. Sec. to Lord Privy Seal 1960; served Morocco 1962; Counsellor, Office of British Chargé d'Affaires, also Consul-Gen., People's Repub. of China 1964–66; Visiting Fellow, All Souls Coll., Oxford 1966–67; Counsellor, U.S.A. 1967–69; Asst. Under-Sec. of State, FCO 1969–73, Deputy Under-Sec. of State 1973–75; Amb. to Japan 1975–80; Pres. Japan Assen. 1981–; Dir. Lloyds Bank Int. Ltd. 1982–85, Lloyds Merchant Bank 1986–87; Adviser Barings Int. Investment Man. Ltd. 1982–; Chair. Royal Soc. for Asian Affairs 1984–. *Leisure interests:* golf, gardening. *Address:* Brook Cottage, Abbotts Ann, Andover, Hants., England (Home). *Telephone:* (0264) 710509.

WILHJELM, Nils; Danish politician; b. 17 June 1936, Copenhagen; s. of Erik Wilhjelm; Forestry Researcher, Royal Veterinary and Agricultural Univ., Copenhagen 1963–68; Exec. Sec. A/S Junckers Saværk, Køge 1968–70; fmr. Man. Dir. Junckers Industrier A/S, Incentive holding co.; fmr. Pres. Fed. of Danish Industries (Industrirådet); Minister of Industry 1986–. *Address:* Ministry of Industry, Slotsholmsgade 12, 1216 Copenhagen K, Denmark. *Telephone:* (01) 92-33-50.

WILKES, Maurice Vincent, PH.D., F.R.S., F.ENG., F.I.E.E., F.B.C.S.; British computer engineer; b. 26 June 1913, Dudley; s. of Vincent J. Wilkes, O.B.E.; m. Nina Twyman 1947; one s. two d.; ed. King Edward VI School, Stourbridge, and St. John's Coll., Cambridge; University Demonstrator 1937; Radar and Operational Research, Second World War; Univ. Lecturer and Acting Dir. of Mathematical Lab., Cambridge 1945, Dir 1946–70; Head of Computer Lab. 1970; Prof. of Computer Technology, Univ. of Cambridge 1965–80; Staff Consultant, Digital Equipment Corpn. 1980–86; Adjunct Prof. M.I.T. 1981–85; mem. for Research Strategy, Olivetti Research Bd. 1986–; mem. Measurement and Control Section Cttee., Inst. of Electrical Engineers 1956–59; First Pres. British Computer Soc. 1957–60; mem. Council Int. Fed. for Information Processing 1960–63, Council of the Inst. of Electrical Engineers 1973–76; Turing Lecturer Assen. for Computing Machinery 1967; Distinguished Fellow, British Computer Soc. 1973; Foreign Hon. mem. American Acad. Arts and Sciences 1974; Foreign Assoc. U.S. Nat. Acad. of Engineering 1977, N.A.S. 1980; Dr. h.c. (Amsterdam) 1978, (Newcastle-on-Tyne, Hull, Kent, City Univ. (London), Linköping, Munich, Bath); Harry Goode Memorial Award, American Fed. of Information Processing Socs. 1968, Eckert-Mauchly Award, American Fed. of Information Processing Socs. 1980, McDowell Award, I.E.E.E. 1981, Faraday Medal, I.E.E. 1981, Pender Award, Univ. of Pa. 1982, C and C Prize, Tokyo 1988. *Publications:* Oscillations of the Earth's Atmosphere 1949, Preparation of Programs for an Electronic Digital Computer 1951, 1957, Automatic Digital Computers 1956, A Short Introduction to Numerical Analysis 1966, Time-Sharing Computer Systems 1968, The Cambridge CAP Computer and its Operating System 1979, Memoirs of a Computer Pioneer 1985. *Address:* Olivetti Research Ltd., 24A Trumpington Street, Cambridge, CB2 1QA, England. *Telephone:* (0223) 343 300.

WILKIE, Douglas Robert, M.D., F.R.C.P., F.R.S.; British professor of physiology; b. 2 Oct. 1922, London; s. of Robert M. Wilkie and Lilian Creed; m. Dr. June Hill 1948 (divorced 1982); one s.; ed. Bec School, Univ. Coll. London and Univ. Coll. Hosp.; Lecturer Dept. of Physiology Univ. Coll., London 1948, Locke Research Fellow (Royal Soc.) 1951–54, Reader in Experimental Physiology 1954–65, Prof. of Experimental Physiology 1965–69, Jodrell Research Prof. and Head Physiology Dept. 1969–79, Jodrell Research Prof. of Physiology 1979–88, Prof. Emer. 1988–; Inst. of Aviation Medicine, Farnborough 1948–50, later Researcher, Physiological Consultant; Fellow Univ. Coll. London; lifelong research into mechanism by which muscles convert chemical energy into mechanical work. *Publications:* 125 scientific papers and two books concerned with muscle biology, dimensional analysis, manpowered flight, thermodynamics and the application of nuclear magnetic resonance methods. *Leisure interests:* sailing small cruising boats, photography. *Address:* Department of Physiology, University College London, Gower Street, London, WC1E 6BT (Office); 2 Wychwood End, Stanhope Road, London, N6 5DE, England (Home). *Telephone:* 01-387 7050 (Office); 01-272 4024 (Home).

WILKINS, Sir Graham John, Kt.; British business executive; b. 22 Jan. 1924, Mudford, Somerset; s. of George W. and Ann May Wilkins (née Clarke); m. Daphne Mildred Haynes 1945; ed. Yeovil School, Univ. Coll.

of South West, Exeter; Man. Dir. Beecham Research Laboratories 1961; Chair. Beecham Pharmaceutical Div., Dir. Beecham Group PLC 1964, Man. Dir. (Pharmaceuticals) 1973; Exec. Vice-Chair. Beecham Group PLC 1974-75, Chair. 1975-84, Pres. 1984-; Vice-Chair. Proprietary Asscn. of Great Britain 1966-68, ICC (U.K.); Pres. Asscn. of British Pharmaceutical Industry 1969-71, European Fed. of Pharmaceutical Industries Asscns. 1978-82, Advertising Asscn.; Chair. Medico-Pharmaceutical Forum 1972, 1973, ICC United Kingdom 1985-, Review Body for Doctors' and Dentists' Remuneration 1986-, Chair. 1987-; mem. Council, London School of Pharmacy 1986-, Chair. 1987-. *Leisure interests:* golf, travel. *Address:* 'Alceda', Walton Lane, Shepperton-on-Thames, Middlesex, England.

WILKINS, Maurice Hugh Frederick, C.B.E., PH.D., F.R.S.; British molecular biologist; b. 15 Dec. 1916, Pongaroa, New Zealand; s. of late E. H. Wilkins and of Eveline Whittaker; m. Patricia Chidgey 1959; two s. two d.; ed. St. John's Coll., Cambridge; Research on luminescence of solids, Physics Dept. Birmingham Univ.; Ministry of Home Security and Aircraft Production 1938; Manhattan Project (Ministry of Supply), Univ. of Calif. 1944; Lecturer in Physics, St. Andrews Univ. 1945; Medical Research Council, Biophysics Unit, King's Coll., London 1946, Deputy Dir. 1955-70, Dir. 1970-72, Dir. Neurobiology Unit (Cell Biophysics Unit 1974-80), MRC 1972; Prof. of Biophysics and Head of Dept., King's Coll. 1970-82, Emer. Prof. 1981-, Fellow 1973-; mem. Russell Cttee. against Chemical Weapons 1981-; Pres. British Soc. for Social Responsibility in Science 1969-, Food and Disarmament Int. 1984-; Hon. mem. American Soc. of Biological Chemists 1964; Foreign Hon. mem. American Acad. of Arts and Sciences 1970; Hon. LL.D.; Albert Lasker Award, American Public Health Asscn. 1960; Joint Nobel Prize for Physiology or Medicine 1962. *Publications:* Papers on luminescence and topics in biophysics, e.g. molecular structure of nucleic acids and structure of nerve membranes. *Address:* King's College, Strand, London, W.C.2; 30 St. John's Park, London, S.E.3, England. *Telephone:* 01-836 5454.

WILKINS Roger C.; American insurance executive (retd.); b. 6 June 1906, Houlton, Me.; s. of George and Amanda Wilkins (née Carson); m. Evelyn McFadden, 1933; one d.; ed. Univ. of Maine; joined Travelers Corpn. 1929, Vice-Pres. 1953, Sr. Vice-Pres. 1965, Dir. and Chair. of Finance Cttee. 1968, Pres. and Chief Exec. Officer 1969-71, Chair. 1971-74, Chair. Exec. Cttee. 1974; Chair. Broadcast Plaza Inc.; Dir. Prospect Co., Conn. Bank and Trust Co., Conn. Natural Gas Co., Chemical Express Co., United Aircraft Corpn., Allis-Chalmers Corpn.; Dir./Trustee U.S. Chamber of Commerce, American Life Insurance Asscn. of America, Nat. Telephone Co., Wells Fargo Mortgage Investors and of numerous other business and philanthropic concerns; Hon. LL.D. (Univ. of Hartford) 1966, (Ricker Coll.) 1970, (Trinity Coll.) 1973. *Leisure interests:* golf, fishing, horticulture. *Address:* 791 Prospect Avenue, West Hartford, Conn. 06105, U.S.A.

WILKINSON, Sir Denys Haigh, Kt., D.SC., PH.D., SC.D., F.R.S.; British physicist and university professor; b. 5 Sept. 1922, Leeds; s. of Charles and Hilda Wilkinson; m. 1st Christiane Clavier 1947, three d.; m. 2nd Helen Sellschop 1967; ed. Jesus Coll., Cambridge; worked on British Atomic Energy Project 1943-46, on Canadian Atomic Energy Project 1945-46; Demonstrator 1947-51, Lecturer 1951-56 and Reader 1950-57 Cavendish Laboratory of Univ. of Cambridge; Fellow, Jesus Coll., Cambridge 1944-59, Hon. Fellow 1961-; Student of Christ Church, Oxford 1957-76, Emer. 1976-79, Hon. 1979-; Prof. of Nuclear Physics Clarendon Laboratory of Univ. of Oxford 1957-59, Prof. of Experimental Physics 1959-76, Head of Dept. of Nuclear Physics 1962-76; Vice-Chancellor Sussex Univ. 1976-87, Emer. Prof. 1987-; Pres. Inst. of Physics 1980-82; Rutherford Memorial Lecturer of British Physical Soc. 1962; mem. Governing Bd. Nat. Inst. for Research in Nuclear Science 1958-64; Queen's Lecturer Berlin 1966; Cherwell-Simon Memorial Lecturer, Oxford 1970; Tizard Memorial Lecturer 1975, Lauritsen Memorial Lecturer Calif. Inst. of Tech. 1976, Schiff Memorial Lecturer Stanford Univ. 1977, Racah Memorial Lecturer Univ. of Jerusalem 1977, Solly Cohen Memorial Lecturer, Hebrew Univ. of Jerusalem 1985, Axel Memorial Lecturer, Univ. of Ill. 1985, Breit Memorial Lecturer, Yale Univ. 1987; mem. Science Research Council 1967-70; Chair. S.R.C. Nuclear Physics Bd. 1968-70, Physics III Cttee. CERN, Geneva 1971-75, Radioactive Waste Man. Advisory Cttee. 1978-83; Vice-Pres. IUPAP 1985-; mem. Council of the Asscn. of Commonwealth Univs. 1981-87; Foreign mem. Royal Swedish Acad. of Sciences; Hon. D.Sc. (Univ. of Saskatchewan, Utah State Univ., Univ. of Guelph, Queen's Univ., Ont.); Hon. Fil.Dr. (Univ. of Uppsala); Hon. LL.D. (Sussex) 1987; Holweck Medallist of French and British Physical Socs. 1957, Hughes Medal of the Royal Soc. 1965, Bruce-Preller Prize of Royal Soc. of Edinburgh 1969; Battelle Distinguished Prof., Univ. of Washington 1970; Tom W. Bonner Prize of American Physical Soc. 1974, Royal Medal, Royal Soc. 1980; Guthrie Medal of Inst. of Physics 1986, CCSEM Gold Medal 1988. *Publications:* Ionization Chambers and Counters 1950, Editor: Isospin in Nuclear Physics 1969, Progress in Particle and Nuclear Physics 1977, Mesons in Nuclei (joint ed.) 1979 and many articles in learned journals. *Leisure interests:* early music and art, ornithology. *Address:* University of Sussex, Falmer, Brighton, Sussex, BN1 9QH, England. *Telephone:* (0273) 678081.

WILKINSON, Sir Geoffrey, Kt., PH.D., F.R.S.; British professor of inorganic chemistry; b. 14 July 1921, Todmorden; s. of Henry and Ruth Wilkinson; m. Lise Sølver Schou 1953; two d.; ed. Todmorden Secondary School,

Imperial Coll., London; Junior Scientific Officer, Nat. Research Council of Canada 1943-46; Research Assoc., Radiation Lab., Univ. of Calif. 1946-50, Mass. Inst. of Technology 1950-51; Asst. Prof. Harvard Univ. 1951-55; Prof. Inorganic Chem., Imperial Coll., London 1956, Sir Edward Frankland Prof. 1956-88, Prof. Emer. 1988-; Sr. Research Fellow, Imperial Coll. 1988-; Dwyer Memorial Lecturer, Univ. N.S.W. 1977; First Mond Lecturer, Chem. Soc. 1980; First Chini Lecturer, Italian Chem. Soc.; First Sir Edward Frankland Lecturer, Royal Soc. of Chemistry 1983; Foreign mem. Royal Danish Acad. of Science, American Acad. of Arts and Sciences, Nat. Acad. of Sciences; Hon. Counsellor Spanish Research Council; Centennial Foreign Fellow, American Chemical Soc. 1976; Hon. D.Sc. (Edinburgh, Granada) 1976, (Columbia) 1978, (Bath) 1980; Lavoisier Medal 1959, Nobel Prize for Chem. 1973, Royal Medal 1981; Hiroshima Univ. Medal; Galileo Medal, Univ. of Pisa 1983, Longstaff Medal, Royal Soc. of Chem. 1987. *Publications:* Advanced Inorganic Chemistry (with F. A. Cotton), Basic Inorganic Chemistry (with F. A. Cotton) 1976, and over 400 scientific papers. *Leisure interest:* organic chemistry. *Address:* Chemistry Department, Imperial College, London, SW7 2AY, England. *Telephone:* 01-589 5111, Ext. 1203.

WILKINSON, John Frederick, PH.D., M.D., F.R.C.P., C.CHEM., F.R.S.C.; British physician; b. 10 June 1897, Oldham; s. of John Frederick and Ann (Wareham) Wilkinson; m. Marion Crossfield 1964; ed. Arnold School, Blackpool, Univ. of Manchester, Manchester Royal Infirmary School of Medicine; service with Royal Naval Air Service, Royal Navy and Tank Corps 1915-19; Hon. Demonstrator and Lecturer, Manchester Univ. 1920-26, 1929-47; Head of Science Dept. Hyde Tech. Coll., Cheshire 1924-28; Dir. Dept. of Clinical Investigations and Medical Research, Manchester Royal Infirmary 1929-47, Hon. Physician 1932-47; Hon. Consulting Physician Christie Cancer Hosp., Holt Radium Inst., Duchess of York Babies' Hosp., Manchester 1934-48; Dir. N.W. Regional Blood Transfusion Service and Resuscitation Service 1938-46; Consultant Physician, Dir. Dept. of Haematology and Reader in Medicine, Manchester Univ. and United Manchester Hosps. 1947-62; mem. numerous foreign haematological and medico-legal socs.; fmr. Pres. Int. and European Haematological Socs.; Pres. Manchester Pathological Soc. 1948-49; fmr. Pres. Manchester Medical Soc., Life mem. and Hon. Ed. 1956-; Consulting Physician, Haematologist and Chartered Chemist in private practice 1962-; Liveryman Worshipful Soc. of Apothecaries 1948; Freeman City of London 1949; Hon. D.Sc. (Bradford) 1976. *Publications:* author, editor, contributor various medical and scientific works; The Land of the Midnight Sun (travel) 1963; Antique English Apothecaries' Drug Jars 1969; The Tools of the English Apothecary 1977, articles in medical and art journals 1929-84. *Leisure interests:* antiques, aquariums, travel, zoos, motoring, lecturing. *Address:* Consulting Rooms, Mobberley Old Hall, Mobberley, via Knutsford, Cheshire, WA16 7AB, England. *Telephone:* 056-587 2111.

WILKINSON, Kenneth Grahame, C.B.E., B.SC., F.C.G.I., D.I.C., F.ENG., F.C.I.T., F.R.S.A., C.B.I.M.; British aviation consultant; b. 14 July 1917, London; s. of Bertie and Dorothy Wilkinson; m. Mary Holman Victory 1941; one s. one d.; ed. Shooters Hill School, London, Coll. of Aeronautical Engineering, Chelsea and Imperial Coll., London; Aerodynamics Dept., Royal Aircraft Establishment, Farnborough 1938-46, Sr. Scientific Officer 1945; Supt. Performance and Analysis, British European Airways 1946-52, Schedules Planning Man. 1952-59, Fleet Planning Man. 1960-61, Asst. to Chief Maintenance Engineer 1961-62, Asst. Chief Engineer 1962-64, Chief Engineer 1964-70, mem. Bd. 1968-72, Deputy Chief Exec. and Man. Dir. Mainline BEA 1971-72, Chair. and Chief Exec. Sept.-Nov. 1972, mem. Bd. British Airways 1971-72, 1976-82, Eng. Dir. 1976-79, Deputy Chair. 1979-80; Chair. Air Transport and Travel Industry Training Bd. 1981-82; Dir. British Rail Eng. Ltd. 1982-89; Visiting Prof., Cranfield Inst. of Tech. 1981-, Deputy Chair. of Council 1983-; Dir. Airways Aero Asscns. Ltd.; Man. Dir. Rolls-Royce (1971) Ltd. 1972-74, Vice-Chair. and mem. Bd. 1974-76; Chair. BGA Tech. Cttee. 1946-48, BGA 1970, Vice-Pres. 1972; Chair. New Media Productions Ltd. 1989-; Pres. Royal Aeronautical Soc. 1972 (Hon. Fellow 1986); mem. Cranwell Advisory Bd. 1970-, Council Cranfield Inst. of Tech. 1971-; Hon. F.R.A.eS.; Hon. D.Sc.; British Gold Medal 1979. *Publications:* Sailplanes of the World (with B. S. Shenstone) (Vol. I) 1960 (Vol. II) 1963, articles and papers in Journal of Royal Aeronautical Soc. on aircraft engineering. *Leisure interests:* flying, sailing, gardening, travel. *Address:* Pheasants, Mill End, Hambleden, Henley on Thames, Oxon., RG9 3BL, England. *Telephone:* (0491) 571368.

WILKINSON, Sir Martin (see Wilkinson, Sir Robert Francis Martin).

WILKINSON, Paul; British professor of international relations; b. 9 May 1937, Harrow, Middx.; s. of Walter Ross Wilkinson and Joan Rosemary Paul; m. Susan Wilkinson 1960; two s. one d.; ed. Lower School of John Lyon, Harrow, Univ. Coll., Swansea and Univ. of Wales; regular officer R.A.F. 1959-65; Asst. Lecturer in Politics, Univ. Coll., Cardiff 1966-68, lecturer 1968-75, Sr. Lecturer 1975-68; Reader in Politics, Univ. of Wales 1978-79; Chair. in Int. Relations, Aberdeen Univ. 1979-, Head Dept. of Politics and Int. Relations 1985-; Dir Inst. for the Study of Conflict, London 1989-; Hon. Fellow Univ. Coll., Swansea 1986. *Publications:* Social Movement 1971, Political Terrorism 1974, Terrorism versus Liberal Democracy 1976, Terrorism and the Liberal State (revised edn.) 1986, British Perspectives on Terrorism 1981, Terrorism: Theory and Practice (jtly.) 1978, The New Fascists (revised edn.) 1983, Contemporary Research on Terrorism 1987, and numerous articles in specialist journals. *Leisure interests:* modern art, poetry, walking. *Address:* Department of Politics and International Relations, University of Aberdeen, Edward Wright Building, Dunbar Street, Old Aberdeen, Aberdeen, AB9 2YT, Scotland. *Telephone:* (0224) 272717/4.

WILKINSON, Peter Ian, B.A.(HONS.), LL.B.; New Zealand politician; b. 12 Nov. 1934; s. of Rev. G. L. B. and Joyce Wilkinson (now McLay); m. Cunitia Evelyn Tattersfield 1969; ed. Auckland Grammar School, Durham Univ., Univ. of Auckland; M.P. for Rodney 1969–78, for Kaipara 1978–84; Attorney-Gen. and Minister of Customs 1975–78, later also Postmaster-Gen.; Chair. Parl. Foreign Affairs Cttee. 1979–; Leader N.Z. Election Observer Mission to Rhodesia 1980. *Leisure interests:* gardening, motoring, boating. *Address:* P.O. Box 66, Warkworth, North Auckland, New Zealand. *Telephone:* Warkworth 55 800.

WILKINSON, Sir Philip William, Kt., F.C.I.B.; English business executive; b. 8 May 1927; m. Eileen Patricia (née Malkin) Wilkinson 1951; one s. two d.; ed. Leyton County High School; joined Westminster Bank (later Nat. Westminster Bank) 1943, Dir. 1979–, Deputy Chair. 1987–; Chief Exec. Lombard North Cen. Ltd. 1975; Gen. Man. Related Banking Services Div. 1978, Deputy Group Chief Exec. 1980, Group Chief Exec. 1983–87. *Leisure interests:* golf, watching sport. *Address:* 41 Lothbury, London, EC2P 2BP, England. *Telephone:* 01-726 1266.

WILKINSON, Sir (Robert Francis) Martin, Kt.; British stockbroker; b. 4 June 1911, Blackheath, London; s. of the late Sir Robert Pelham Wilkinson and the late Phyllis Marian Wilkinson; m. Dora Esme Arendt 1936; three d.; ed. Repton School; served with R.A.F. 1940–45; Partner, de Zoete and Gorton 1936–70, de Zoete and Bevan 1970–76; mem. London Stock Exchange 1933–, mem. Council 1959–73, Deputy Chair. 1963–65, Chair. 1965–73, Chair. March–June 1973; Chair. Altifund 1976–81; fmr. Dir. City of London Brewery Trust (Chair. 1977–78) (resgnd. 1981); apptd. one of H.M. Lieutenants for City of London 1973; became Freeman, City of London in Co. of Needlemakers 1946. *Leisure interests:* cricket, gardening. *Address:* Hurst-an-Clays, Ship Street, East Grinstead, W. Sussex, RH19 4EE, England.

WILKINSON, Wallace G.; American business executive and politician; b. 12 Dec. 1941, Casey Co., Ky.; m. Martha Stafford Wilkinson; two s.; ed. Univ. of Kentucky; f. Kentucky Paperback Gallery, Lexington, now part of nationwide Wallace's Coll. Book Co.; involved in commerce, real estate, farming, etc. and developed Capital Plaza Hotel, Frankfort, Ky. and Quality Place, Lexington; Gov. of Kentucky 1987–; mem. fmr. mem., or Dir. Lexington Econ. Devt. Comm., Lexington Area Chamber of Commerce, Kentucky River Task Force, Kentucky Educ. Foundation, Kentucky Opera Bd.; Democrat. *Address:* Governor's Office, Capitol Building, Room 100, Frankfort, Kentucky 40601 (Office); Governor's Mansion, Frankfort, Kentucky 40601, U.S.A. (Home). *Telephone:* (502) 564-2611 (Office); (502) 564-8004 (Home).

WIŁKOMIRSKA, Wanda; Polish violinist; b. 11 Jan. 1929, Warsaw; d. of Alfred Wiłkomirski and Dorota Temkin; m.; two s.; ed. Łódź Conservatory and in Budapest and France; public debut at age of 7 years; first appearance with orchestra aged 15, in Cracow; studied under Irena Dubiska (Łódź), Ede Zathureczky (Budapest) and Henryk Szeryng (Paris); Polish State Prize 1952, 1964; several foreign prizes, including Bach Competition award of Dem. German radio; Officer's Cross of Polonia Restituta 1953; Order of Banner of Labour 2nd Class 1959, 1st Class 1964; Culture and Arts Prize, 1st Class 1975, Orpheus Prize, Polish Musicians' Asscn. 1979; numerous recordings; now appears frequently with most of the major orchestras throughout the world; defected whilst on tour of Fed. Repub. of Germany March 1982. *Leisure interests:* theatre, literature, sports.

WILLATS, Stephen; British artist; b. 17 Aug. 1943, London; m. Stephanie Craven 1983; three s.; ed. Drayton School and Ealing School of Art; Lecturer, Ipswich School of Art 1965–67; Lecturer, Nottingham Coll. of Art 1968–72; Organiser, Centre for Behavioural Art, Gallery House, London 1972–73; numerous one-person exhbns. including Concerning Our Present Way of Living, Whitechapel Art Gallery, London 1979, Four Islands in Berlin, National Gallery, Berlin 1980, Meta Filter and Related Works, Tate Gallery, London 1982, Another City, Riverside Studios, London 1984, Doppelgänger, Lisson Gallery, Double Crossing, Ralph Wernicke Gallery, Stuttgart 1985, City of Concrete, Ikon Gallery, Birmingham, Fragments of Modern Living, in Regensburg and Cologne, Fed. Repub. of Germany, and Utrecht, Netherlands, Concepts and Models, ICA Gallery, London, Vier Huizen in Den Haag, Netherlands, Striking Back, Mappin Art Gallery, Sheffield 1986, Between Objects and People, Leeds City Art Gallery 1987, Transformers, People's Lives in the Modern World, Laing Art Gallery, Newcastle 1988, Gallery Torch, Amsterdam 1988; numerous group exhbns. in the U.K., Netherlands, Italy and Fed. Repub. of Germany, including Venice Biennale 1982, The Sculpture Show, Hayward Gallery 1983, The New Art, Tate Gallery, London 1983, Sculptural Alternatives, Tate Gallery, London 1985, The British Art Show, Nat. Art Gallery N.Z. 1985, The British Show, Art Gallery of N.S.W, then touring Australia 1985, The Art of Peace Biennale, Kunstverein Hamburg 1986; numerous project works, including Inside an Ocean, Mile End, London 1979, Two Worlds Apart,

Hayes 1981 and Blocks, Avondale Estate, London 1982, Brentford Towers, W. London 1985; D.A.A.D. Fellowship, Berlin 1979–81. *Publications:* several books, including The Artist as an Instigator of Changes in Social Cognition and Behaviour 1973, Art and Social Function 1976, The Lurky Place 1978, Doppelgänger 1985, Intervention and Audience 1986, Concepts and Projects, Bookworks by Stephen Willats; numerous articles in art magazines, including Control Magazine which he f. 1965. *Address:* 5 London Mews, London, W.2, England.

WILLATT, Sir Hugh, Kt., M.A., F.R.S.A.; British fmr. solicitor and arts administrator; b. 25 April 1909, Nottingham; s. of Robert John Willatt and Marguerite Gardner; m. Evelyn Gibbs, R.E., A.R.C.A. 1945; ed. Repton and Pembroke Coll., Oxford; qualified as Solicitor 1934, practised in family firm in Nottingham until 1960, Partner in Lewis Silkin & Partners, Westminster 1960–68; mem. Arts Council Drama Panel 1955–58, Chair. 1960–68; Sec.-Gen. of Arts Council of Great Britain 1968–75; mem. Bd. Nottingham Playhouse, Mercury Trust Ltd. (Ballet Rambert) and Nat. Theatre, Chair. Riverside Studios, Visiting Arts at various times; mem. Council English Stage Co. (Royal Court Theatre) 1976–; Chair. Nat. Opera Studio. *Leisure interests:* reading, travel, sport. *Address:* 4 St. Peter's Wharf, Hammersmith Terrace, London, W.6, England. *Telephone:* 01-741 2707.

WILLCOCKS, Sir David (Valentine), Kt., C.B.E., M.C., M.A., MUS.B., F.R.C.O., F.R.C.M.; British musician; b. 30 Dec. 1919, Newquay, Cornwall; s. of T. H. Willcocks; m. Rachel Blyth 1947; two s. two d.; ed. Clifton Coll. and King's Coll., Cambridge; Fellow, King's Coll., Cambridge 1947–51; Organist Salisbury Cathedral 1947–50, Worcester Cathedral 1950–57; Conductor, Worcester Three Choirs Festival and City of Birmingham Choir 1950–57; Fellow and Dir. of Music, King's Coll., Cambridge 1957–73; Lecturer in Music, Cambridge Univ. and Cambridge Univ. Organist 1957–74; Conductor Cambridge Univ. Music Soc. 1958–73; Musical Dir. Bach Choir, London 1960–; Pres. Royal Coll. of Organists 1966–68; Pres. Incorporated Soc. of Musicians 1978–79; Pres. Nat. Fed. of Music Soc. 1980–89; Dir. Royal Coll. of Music, London 1974–84; Hon. D.Mus. (Exeter, Bristol and Leicester Univs., Westminster Choir Coll., Princeton), Hon. D.Litt. (Sussex Univ.), Hon. D.S.L. (Trinity Coll., Toronto), Hon. M.A. (Bradford Univ.), Hon. R.A.M., Hon. G.S.M., Hon. Fellow, Royal Canadian Coll. of Organists, King's Coll., Cambridge; F.R.N.C.M., F.R.S.A.M.D., F.R.S.C.M., F.T.C.L. *Address:* 13 Grange Road, Cambridge, CB3 9AS, England. *Telephone:* (0223) 359559.

WILLEBRANDS, H.E. Cardinal Johannes Gerardus Maria, DR. PHIL.; Netherlands ecclesiastic; b. 4 Sept. 1909, Bovenkarspel; s. of Herman Willebrands and Afra Kok; ed. Warmond Seminary, Holland, Angelicum, Rome; ordained 1934; Chaplain, Begijnhof Church, Amsterdam 1937–40; Prof. of Philosophy, Warmond 1940, Dir. 1945; Pres. St. Williborord Asscn. 1946; organized Catholic Conf. on Ecumenical Questions 1951; Sec. Vatican Secretariat for Promoting Christian Unity 1960, Pres. 1969–; created Bishop 1964; created Cardinal 1969; appointed Archbishop of Utrecht 1975 (retd. 1983); Hon. D.D. (Oxford) 1987. *Publications:* La Liberté religieuse et l'oecuménisme; Ecumenismo e problemi attuali, Oecuménisme et problèmes actuels; Bibel, ekumenik och sekularisering; Christus, Zeichen und Ursprung der Einheit in einer geteilten Welt. *Address:* Segretariato per l'unione dei cristiani, Via dell'Erba I, Rome 00193, Italy. *Telephone:* Rome 698-4181.

WILLESEE, Donald Robert; Australian politician; b. 14 April 1916, Derby, W. Australia; m.; four s. two d.; ed. state schools; mem. Senate 1949–75; Leader of Opposition in Senate 1966–67, Deputy Leader 1969–72; Deputy Leader of Govt. in Senate 1972–75; Special Minister of State, Minister Assisting the Prime Minister 1972–73; Minister for Foreign Affairs 1973–75, Leader of Australian Del. to UN Gen. Ass. 1973, 1974, 1975; mem. Jt. Cttee. on Foreign Affairs 1967, Privileges Cttee. 1969; mem. several Parl. dels. abroad. *Address:* 5 Walton Place, Quinns Rock, W.A. 6030, Australia.

WILLETTS, Bernard Frederick, PH.D., C.ENG., F.I.MECH.E., C.B.I.M.; British engineer; b. 24 March 1927; s. of James Frederick and Effie (née Hurst) Willetts; m. Norah Elizabeth Law 1952; two s.; ed. Birmingham and Durham Univs.; Section Leader, Vickers Armstrong (Eng.) Ltd. 1954–56, Asst. to Works Dir. 1956–58; Chief Eng. Massey-Ferguson (U.K.) Ltd., then Dir. of Eng., Mfg. Dir., Deputy Dir. 1958–68; Group Man. Dir. (Telecommunications), The Plessey Co. Ltd., joined Main Bd., Deputy Chief Exec. 1968–78; Asst. Man. Dir., then Man. Dir. Vickers Ltd. 1978–80; Non-Exec. Dir. Massey-Ferguson Holdings 1980–, Liverpool Daily Post and Echo 1976–, Telephone Rentals Ltd. 1981–; Deputy Chief Exec., Dubai Aluminium Co. Ltd. 1981–; Fellow, Inst. of Production Engineers (Vice-Pres. 1979–82). *Leisure interests:* gardening, sport and stamp collecting. *Address:* Suna Court, Pearson Road, Sonning-on-Thames, Berkshire, England. *Telephone:* (0734) 695050.

WILLEY, Gordon Randolph, PH.D.; American archaeologist; b. 7 March 1913, Chariton, Ia.; s. of Frank Willey and Agnes Caroline Wilson; m. Katharine Winston Whaley 1938; two d.; ed. Univ. of Arizona and Columbia Univ.; Instructor in Anthropology, Columbia Univ. 1942–43; Anthropologist, Bureau of American Ethnology, Smithsonian Inst. 1943–50; Bowditch Prof. of Mexican and Cen. American Archaeology, Harvard Univ. 1950–83,

Sr. Prof. in Anthropology 1983–87, Chair. Dept. Anthropology 1954–57; mem. N.A.S.; Hon. D.Litt. (Cambridge) 1977, (Univ. of Arizona) 1981, (Univ. of New Mexico) 1984; Wenner-Gren Medal for Archaeology 1953, Order of Quetzal, Republic of Guatemala 1968, Archaeological Inst. of America Gold Medal 1973, A. V. Kidder Medal for Archaeology (American Anthropological Asscn.) 1974; Huxley Medal, Royal Anthropological Inst. of Great Britain 1979; Walker Prize, Boston Museum of Science 1981, Drexel Medal (Univ. Museum, Philadelphia) 1982, Golden Plate Award, American Acad. of Achievement 1987. *Publications:* Archaeology of the Florida Gulf Coast 1949, Prehistoric Settlement Patterns of the Viru Valley, Peru 1953, Method and Theory in American Archaeology 1958, Prehistoric Maya Settlements in the Belize Valley 1965, An Introduction to American Archaeology Vol. I 1966, Vol. II 1971, Excavations at Altar de Sacrificios, Guatemala 1973, A History of American Archaeology (co-author) 1974, Excavations at Seibal, Guatemala 1975, The Origins of Maya Civilization 1977, Lowland Maya Settlement Patterns: A Summary View 1981, Essays in Maya Archaeology 1987. *Leisure interests:* tennis, swimming, English literature and literary criticism. *Address:* 25 Gray Gardens E., Cambridge, Mass., U.S.A. (Home). *Telephone:* EL4-1287 (Home).

WILLIAMS, Sir Alwyn, Kt., PH.D., F.R.S., F.R.S.E., M.R.I.A.; British geologist and academic; b. 8 June 1921, Aberdare; s. of D. Daniel Williams and E. May (née Rogers); m. Edith Joan Bevan 1949; one s. one d.; ed. Aberdare Boys' Grammar School and Univ. Coll. of Wales, Aberystwyth; Fellow of Univ. of Wales, Sedgwick Museum, Cambridge 1947–48; Commonwealth Fund (Harkness) Fellow, U.S. Nat. Museum 1948–50; Lecturer in Geology, Univ. of Glasgow 1950–54; Prof. of Geology Queen's Univ., Belfast 1954–74; Lapworth Prof. of Geology Univ. of Birmingham 1974–76; Prin. and Vice-Chancellor, Univ. of Glasgow 1976–88; Pres. Royal Soc., Edin. 1985–88; Hon. D.Sc. (Wales) 1973, (Queen's Univ. Belfast) 1975, (Edin.) 1979, (Strathclyde) 1982; Hon. D.C.L. (Oxford) 1987, Hon. LL.D. (Glasgow) 1988; Hon. F.R.C.P.S., F.D.S., R.C.P.S.; Hon. Fellow, Geological Soc. of America; Foreign mem. Polish Acad. of Sciences. *Publications:* monographs in professional journals. *Leisure interests:* music, art. *Address:* 25 Sutherland Avenue, Pollokshields, Glasgow, G4I 4HG, Scotland.

WILLIAMS, Bernard Arthur Owen, M.A., F.B.A.; British philosopher; b. 21 Sept. 1929, Westcliff; s. of Owen Williams and Hilda Williams; m. 1st Shirley Catlin (q.v.) 1955 (divorced 1974), one d.; m. 2nd Patricia Skinner, two s.; ed. Chigwell School, Essex, Balliol Coll., Oxford; Fellow, All Souls Coll., Oxford 1951–54, New Coll., Oxford 1954–59; Lecturer, Univ. Coll., London 1959–64; Prof. Bedford Coll., London 1964–67; Knightsbridge Prof. of Philosophy, Cambridge 1967–79; Provost, King's Coll., Cambridge 1979–87; Monroe Deutsch Prof. of Philosophy, Univ. of Calif. 1987–; visiting appointments, Univ. Coll. of Ghana 1958–59, Princeton 1963, A.N.U. 1969, Harvard 1973, Univ. of California, Berkeley 1986; Dir. English Nat. Opera 1968–86; Hon. Litt.D. (Dublin) 1981, Hon. Litt. (Aberdeen) 1987, Hon. Fellow Balliol Coll., Oxford 1984. *Publications:* Morality 1972, Problems of The Self 1973, A Critique of Utilitarianism 1973, Descartes: The Project of Pure Enquiry 1978, Moral Luck 1981, Ethics and the Limits of Philosophy 1985. *Leisure interest:* music. *Address:* Department of Philosophy, University of California, Berkeley, Calif. 94720, U.S.A.

WILLIAMS, Betty; British peace campaigner; b. 22 May 1943, Belfast; m. 1st Ralph Williams 1961 (divorced); one s. one d.; m. 2nd James T. Perkins 1982; ed. St. Teresa's Primary School, Belfast; works as office receptionist; joint winner of Nobel Peace Prize for launching the Northern Ireland Peace Movement (later renamed Community of the Peace People) 1976, Joint Leader 1976–78; Carl von Ossietzky Medal for Courage (Berlin Section, Int. League of Human Rights); Hon. LL.D. (Yale Univ.); Hon. D.Hum.Litt. (Coll. of Sienna Heights, Mich.) 1977. *Leisure interest:* gardening. *Address:* c/o Peace People, 224 Lisburn Road, Belfast, BT9 6GE, Northern Ireland.

WILLIAMS, Sir Bruce (Rodda), K.B.E., M.A.; economist and research director; b. 10 Jan. 1919, Warragul, Vic.; s. of the late Rev. W. J. Williams and of Helen Maud Baud; m. Roma Olive Hotten 1942; five d.; ed. Wesley Coll., Melbourne, Queen's Coll., Univ. of Melbourne; Prof. of Econs., Univ. Coll., North Staffordshire 1950–59; Robert Otley Prof., Stanley Jevons Prof., Univ. of Manchester 1959–67; Sec. and Jt. Dir. of Research, Science and Industry Cttee. 1952–59; mem. U.K. Nat. Bd. for Prices and Incomes 1966–67; Econ. Adviser to U.K. Ministry of Tech. 1966–67; mem. U.K. Cen. Advisory Council on Science and Tech. 1967; Vice-Chancellor and Principal, Univ. of Sydney 1967–81; Dir. Tech. Change Centre 1981–86; Chair. Australian Inquiry into the Eng. Disciplines 1987–88; Chair. N.S.W. State Cancer Council 1967–81; mem. Bd. of Reserve Bank of Australia 1969–81; Chair. Australian Vice-Chancellors' Cttee. 1972–74, Nat. Cttee. of Inquiry into Educ. and Training 1976–79; Dir. Parramatta Hospitals Bd. 1978–81; mem. Commonwealth Working Group on the Man. of Technological Change 1984–85, on Distance Teaching and Open Learning 1986–87; Hon. D.Litt. (Univ. of Keele) 1973, (Univ. of Sydney) 1982, Hon. D.Econ. (Univ. of Queensland) 1980, Hon. LL.D. (Univ. of Melbourne) 1981, (Univ. of Manchester) 1982, Hon. D.Sc. (Univ. of Aston) 1982. *Publications:* The Socialist Order and Freedom 1942, Industry and Technical Progress (with C. F. Carter) 1957, Investment in Innovation (with C. F. Carter) 1958, Science in Industry (with C. F. Carter) 1959, Technology, Investment and Growth 1967, Science and Technology in Economic Growth 1973, Systems

of Higher Education: Australia 1978, Education Training and Employment 1979, Disappointed Expectations 1981, Living with Technology 1982, Knowns and Unknowns in Technical Change 1985, Technological Change: Enhancing the Benefits (co-author) 1985, The Influence of Attitudes to New Technology on National Growth Rates 1986, Towards a Commonwealth of Learning (co-author) 1987. *Leisure interests:* music, theatre. *Address:* 106 Grange Road, Ealing Common, London, W5 3PJ, England. *Telephone:* 01-567 1526.

WILLIAMS, Carroll Milton, PH.D., M.D.; American professor of biology; b. 2 Dec. 1916, Richmond, Va.; s. of George Leslie and Jessie Hendricks Williams; m. Muriel Voter 1941; four s. (two deceased); ed. Univ. of Richmond and Harvard Univ.; Asst. Prof., Harvard Univ. 1946–48, Assoc. Prof. 1948–53, Prof. 1953–66, Bussey Prof. of Biology 1966–87, Bussey Prof. Emer. 1987–; Jr. Prize Fellow of Harvard Soc. of Fellows 1941–45, Guggenheim Fellow 1955–56; Fellow, American Acad. of Arts and Sciences; Chair. Zoology Section N.A.S. 1970–72, mem. Council N.A.S. 1973–76, 1985–88; American Philosophical Soc., Inst. of Medicine of N.A.S.; Hon. D.Sc.; Annual Research Prize of A.A.A.S. 1950, Boylston Prize and Gold Medal of Harvard Medical School 1961, George Ledlie Prize of Harvard Univ. 1967, H. T. Ricketts Award of Univ. of Chicago 1969. *Publications:* over 200 scientific articles on biology with special reference to insects. *Leisure interests:* music, entomology. *Address:* The Biological Laboratories, Harvard University, 16 Divinity Avenue, Cambridge, Mass. 02138; 27 Eliot Road, Lexington, Mass. 02173, U.S.A. (Home).

WILLIAMS, Daniel Charles, LL.B.; Grenada lawyer and politician; b. 4 Nov. 1935, Grenada; m.; five c.; ed. St. David's Roman Catholic School, Chiswick Polytechnic, London, and Holborn Coll. of Law & Languages, London; schoolteacher, Grenada 1952–58; civil servant, London 1960–65; magistrate, St. Lucia 1970–74; Barrister-at-law in pvt. practice, Grenada 1974–84; Minister of Health, Housing and Women's Affairs 1984–88, of Health, Housing and Legal Affairs March 1988–, of Community Devt. 1984–87, of Physical Planning 1987–; Attorney-Gen. March 1988–. *Publications:* Index of the Laws of Grenada 1959–79, The Laws of Grenada; newspaper articles. *Address:* Ministry of Physical Planning, St. George's, Grenada.

WILLIAMS, Adm. Sir David, G.C.B., F.R.S.A.; British naval officer; b. 22 Oct. 1921; s. of A. E. Williams; m. Philippa Beatrice Stevens 1947; two s.; ed. Yardley Court School, Tonbridge, R.N. Coll., Dartmouth, U.S. Naval War Coll., Newport, R.I.; served in World War II 1939–45 at sea in R.N.; rank of Commdr. 1952; Capt. 1960; Naval Asst. to First Sea Lord 1961–64; H.M.S. Devonshire 1964–66; Dir. of Naval Plans 1966–68; Capt. R.N. Coll., Dartmouth 1968–70; Rear-Adm. 1970; Flag Officer, Second-in-Command Far East Fleet 1970–72; Vice-Adm. 1973; Dir.-Gen. Naval Manpower and Training 1972–74; Adm. 1974; Chief of Naval Personnel and Second Sea Lord 1974–77; C.-in-C. Naval Home Command and ADC to the Queen 1977–79; Gov. and C.-in-C., Gibraltar 1982–85; a Gentleman Usher to the Queen 1979–82, an Extra Gentleman Usher 1982–; mem. Commonwealth War Graves Comm. 1979–89, Vice-Chair. 1985–89; Chair. Council, Missions to Seamen 1989–; Pres. Ex-Services Mental Welfare Soc. 1979–; mem. Museum and Galleries Comm. 1987–; Hon. Liveryman, Fruiterers' Co.; K.St.J. 1982; D.L. Devon 1981. *Leisure interests:* sailing, tennis, gardening. *Address:* Brockholt, Strete, Dartmouth, Devon, England.

WILLIAMS, Denys Ambrose, M.A.; Barbados barrister; b. 12 Oct. 1929; s. of George Cuthbert Williams and Violet Irene Gilkes; m. Carmel Mary Coleman 1954; two s. four d.; ed. Combermere School, Harrison Coll., Worcester Coll., Oxford and Middle Temple, London; Asst. Legal Draftsman, Asst. to Attorney Gen., Barbados; Asst. Legal Draftsman, Fed. of West Indies; Sr. Parl. Counsel, Barbados 1963–67, Supreme Court Judge 1967–86, Chief Justice 1987–; Kt. Bachelor Gold Crown of Merit. *Leisure interests:* horse-racing, tennis, gardening, walking. *Address:* 9 Garrison, St. Michael, Barbados, West indies. *Telephone:* 42 7 11 64.

WILLIAMS, Dudley Howard, PH.D., SC.D., F.R.S.; British scientist; b. 25 May 1937, Leeds; s. of Lawrence Williams and Evelyn Williams; m. Lorna Patricia Phyllis Bedford 1963; two s.; ed. Univ. of Leeds, Stanford Univ., Calif.; Asst. Dir. Research, Univ. Chem. Lab., Univ. of Cambridge 1966–74, Fellow Churchill Coll. 1964–, Reader in Organic Chem. 1974–; Visiting Prof. and Lecturer, Univs. of Calif. 1967, Cape Town 1972, Sydney 1972, Fla. 1973, Wis. 1975, Copenhagen 1976, Australian Nat. Univ., Canberra 1980; Meldola Medal, Royal Inst. of Chem. 1966; Corday-Morgan Medal, Chemical Soc. 1968, Tilden Lecturer, Royal Soc. of Chem. 1983. *Publications:* 10 books, including Spectroscopic Methods in Organic Chemistry (with I. Fleming), about 300 scientific publications dealing with the devt. of mass spectrometry and nuclear magnetic resonance, and the structure elucidation of complex molecules. *Leisure interests:* music, skiing, squash. *Address:* University Chemical Laboratory, Lensfield Road, Cambridge, CB2 1EW (Office); 7 Balsham Road, Fulbourn, Cambridge, CB1 5BZ, England (Home). *Telephone:* (0223) 336368 (Office); (0223) 880592 (Home).

WILLIAMS, Elizabeth (see Williams, Betty).

WILLIAMS, Glanmor, C.B.E., M.A., D.LITT., F.B.A., F.S.A., F.R.HIST.S.; British professor of history (retd.); b. 5 May 1920, Dowlais, Glam.; s. of Daniel Williams and Ceinwen Williams; m. Margaret F. Davies 1946; one s. one d.; ed. Cyfarthfa Secondary School, Merthyr Tydfil and Univ. Coll. of

Wales, Aberystwyth; Lecturer and Sr. Lecturer in History, Univ. Coll. of Swansea 1945–57, Prof. of History 1957–82, Vice-Prin. 1975–78; Vice-Pres. Univ. Coll. of Wales 1986–; mem. Bd. of Govs. BBC 1965–71, British Library Bd. 1973–80; Chair. Ancient Monuments Bd. (Wales) 1983–, Royal Comm. on Ancient and Historical Monuments (Wales) 1986–; Chair. British Library, Advisory Council 1981–86. *Publications:* The Welsh Church 1962, Welsh Reformation Essays 1966, Religion, Language and Nationality in Wales 1979, Henry Tudor 1985, Recovery, Reorientation and Reformation: Wales, 1415–1642 1987, Glamorgan County History, Vols. I–VI 1971–88 (Ed.). *Leisure interests:* gramophone, cine-photography. *Address:* 11 Grosvenor Road, Sketty, Swansea, SA2 0SP, Wales. *Telephone:* (0792) 204113.

WILLIAMS, Glanville Llewelyn, Q.C., LL.D., PH.D., F.B.A.; British professor of law and author; b. 15 Feb. 1911, Bridgend, Mid-Glam.; s. of late B. E. and Gwladys Williams; m. Lorna M. Lawfield 1939; one s.; ed. Cowbridge and Univ. Coll. of Wales, Aberystwyth; Prof. of Public Law and later Quain Prof. of Jurisprudence, Univ. of London 1945–55; Prof. of English Law, Univ. of Cambridge 1966–78; Pres. Abortion Law Reform Assen. 1962–; Vice-Pres. Voluntary Euthanasia 1985–; mem. Home Office Criminal Law Revision Cttee. 1959–80, Cttee. on Mentally Abnormal Offenders 1972; Hon. Fellow, Jesus Coll., Cambridge; Hon. Bencher of the Middle Temple; several awards and hon. degrees, including Hon. LL.D. (Sussex) 1987, (Cambridge) 1987. *Publications:* Liability for Animals 1939, Learning the Law 1945, Crown Proceedings 1948, Joint Torts of Contributory Negligence 1950, Criminal Law: The General Part 1953, The Proof of Guilt 1955, The Sanctity of Life and the Criminal Law 1958, Textbook of Criminal Law 1978. *Leisure interest:* walking. *Address:* Merrion Gate, Gazeley Road, Cambridge, CB2 2HB, England. *Telephone:* (0223) 841175.

WILLIAMS, Harrison Arlington, Jr., B.A., LL.D.; American lawyer and politician; b. 10 Dec. 1919; ed. Oberlin Coll., Ohio, Columbia Univ. Law School, and Georgetown Univ. Foreign Service School; seaman on a minesweeper and Navy pilot during Second World War; admitted to N.H. Bar 1948, N.J. Bar 1951, practice in N.J. 1951–; mem. U.S. House of Reps. 1953–56; U.S. Senator from New Jersey 1959–82; Chair. U.S. Senate Labor and Human Resources Cttee. 1971–81; sentenced to three years' imprisonment for bribery and conspiracy Jan. 1984; Democrat. *Address:* P.O. Box 02, Holland Road, Bedminster, N.J. 07921, U.S.A. (Home).

WILLIAMS, Ian George Keith, B.SC.ECON.; British international civil servant; b. 19 Nov. 1921, Southsea, Hants.; s. of George James and Dorothy Gertrude (née Hollier) Williams; m. Florence Davies 1946; one d.; ed. Purbrook Park County High School and privately; Royal Artillery (Field) 1941–46; mem. Bd. of Trade and Ministry of Supply 1946–55; Sr. Staff UKAEA 1955–66; Deputy Dir.-Gen., OECD Nuclear Energy Agency 1966–77, Dir.-Gen. 1977–82. *Leisure interests:* golf, opera. *Address:* Falcon, La Couture, St. Peter Port, Guernsey. *Telephone:* (0481) 71-04-96.

WILLIAMS, Jack Kenny, M.A., PH.D.; American medical centre administrator; b. 5 April 1920, Galax, Va.; s. of Floyd W. and Mary J. (Vass) Williams; m. Margaret Pierce 1943; two d. and one foster d.; ed. Emory and Henry Coll. and Emory Univ.; high school teacher, Va. 1940–42; mem. Clemson Univ. Faculty 1947–66; Dean, Graduate School, Clemson Univ. 1957–60, Dean of Faculties 1960–63, Vice-Pres. for Acad. Affairs 1963–66; Commr. Co-ordinating Bd., Texas Coll. and Univ. System 1966–68; Vice-Pres. for Academic Affairs, The Univ. of Tennessee System 1968–70; Pres. Texas A & M Univ. and the Texas A & M System 1970–77, Chancellor 1977–79; Exec. Vice-Pres. and Dir. Texas Medical Center Inc. 1980–; Chair. Comm. on Colls., Southern Assen. of Colls. and Schools 1968–76; mem. Bd. of Trustees, Nat. Coll. Entrance Examination Bd. 1974–76; mem. Bd. of Dirs. Anderson-Clayton Co., Diamond-Shamrock Corpn., Campbell Taggart Inc., Gifford-Hill Co.; Nat. Merit Scholarship Corpn.; mem. Philosophical Soc., Texas; Hon. LL.D. (Univ. of Fla. and Austin Coll.); Hon. Litt.D. (Emory and Henry Coll.). *Publications:* Vogues in Villainy 1959, Duelling in the Old South 1980. *Address:* Texas Medical Center Inc., 1133 M. D. Anderson Boulevard, Houston, Texas 77030, U.S.A. *Telephone:* 713/797-0100 (Office).

WILLIAMS, John, A.O., O.B.E.; British guitarist; b. 24 April 1941, Melbourne, Australia; s. of Len Williams and Melaan Ket; m. 1st Linda Susan Kendall 1964 (divorced), one d.; m. 2nd Sue Cook 1981 (divorced), one s.; ed. Friern Barnet Grammar School, and Royal Coll. of Music, London; studied guitar with father and Segovia at Accad. Chigiana, Siena); has toured widely and appears frequently on TV and radio; numerous transcriptions and gramophone recordings as solo guitarist and with leading orchestras; founded The Height Below (ensemble) with Brian Gascoigne 1974, John Williams and Friends (ensemble) and founder mem. group Sky 1979–83; Artistic Dir. South Bank Summer Music Festival 1984–85, Melbourne Summer Music 1987. *Leisure interests:* people, living, chess, table tennis, music. *Address:* c/o Harold Holt Ltd., 31 Sinclair Road, London, W14, England.

WILLIAMS, John Ellis Caerwyn, M.A., B.D., D.LITT., F.B.A.; British university professor (retd.); b. 17 Jan. 1912, Glam. Wales; s. of John Williams and Maria Williams; m. Gwenifed Watkins 1946; no c.; ed. Univ. Coll. of N. Wales, Bangor, Nat. Univ. of Ireland, Dublin, Trinity Coll., Dublin, United Theological Coll., Aberystwyth and Bala Theological Coll.; Research Lecturer, Univ. Coll. of N. Wales 1937–39; Fellow, Univ. of Wales 1939–41;

Lecturer, Univ. Coll. of N. Wales 1945–51, Sr. Lecturer 1951–53, Prof. of Welsh 1953–65; Prof. of Irish, Univ. Coll. of Wales, Aberystwyth 1965–79, Prof. Emer. 1979–; Hon. Dir. Centre for Advanced Studies in Welsh and Celtic 1979–85; Leverhulme Fellow 1963–64; Visiting Prof. U.C.L.A. 1968, Harvard Summer School 1968; Chair. Welsh Acad. 1965–75; Derek Allen Prize (British Acad.) 1983; Hon. D.Litt. Celt. (Ireland) 1967, (Wales) 1983. *Publications:* several books. *Leisure interest:* walking. *Address:* 6 Pant-y-Rhos, Waunfawr, Aberystwyth, Dyfed, Wales. *Telephone:* 612959.

WILLIAMS, (John) Kyffin, O.B.E., R.A.; Welsh artist; s. of Henry Inglis Wynne Williams and Essyllt Mary Williams (née Williams); ed. Shrewsbury School, Slade School of Art; Sr. Art Master, Highgate School 1944–73; one-man shows Leicester Galleries 1951, 1953, 1956, 1960, 1966, 1970; Colnaghi Galleries 1948, 1949, 1965, 1970; Thackeray Galleries 1975, 1977, 1979, 1981, 1983, 1985, 1987; Pres. Royal Cambrian Acad. 1969–76; Winston Churchill Fellow 1968; D.L. Gwynedd 1985; Hon. M.A. (Wales) 1973. *Publication:* Across The Straits (autobiog.) 1973. *Leisure interests:* the countryside, sport. *Address:* Pwllfanogl, Llanfairpwll, Gwynedd, LL61 6PD, Wales. *Telephone:* (0248) 714693.

WILLIAMS, John Peter Rhys, M.B.E., M.R.C.S., L.R.C.P., M.B., B.S., F.R.C.S.(E.); Welsh orthopaedic surgeon and rugby player; b. 2 March 1949, Cardiff; s. of Peter and Margaret Williams; m. Priscilla Williams 1973; three d.; ed. Bridgend Grammar School, Millfield, St. Mary's Hosp. Medical School; British Junior Tennis Champion, Wimbledon 1966; Welsh int. rugby player 1969–79, 1980–81; 55 caps for Wales; on tour with British Lions to New Zealand 1971, South Africa 1974; 8 test matches for British Lions, winning both series; qualified as medical doctor 1973; surgical Registrar, Cardiff Hosp. 1977–80, Orthopaedic Registrar 1980–82; Orthopaedic Sr. Registrar, St. Mary's Hosp., London 1982–85; Consultant Orthopaedic Surgeon, Princess of Wales Hosp., Bridgend Jan. 1986–; Captain of Welsh rugby team 1978–79; Primary F.R.C.S. 1976. *Publications:* Irish Conference on Sporting Injuries, Dublin (ed.) 1975, JPR (autobiography) 1979, Cervical neck injuries in Rugby Football, British Medical Journal 1978, Trans-Oral Fusion of the Cervical Spine, Journal of Bone and Joint Surgery 1985. *Leisure interests:* sport, music. *Address:* Llansannor Lodge, Llansannor, near Cowbridge, South Glamorgan, Wales.

WILLIAMS, Sir John Robert, K.C.M.G., M.A.; British diplomatist; b. 15 Sept. 1922, London; s. of S. J. Williams; m. Helga Elizabeth Konow Lund 1958; two s. two d.; ed. Sheen Co. School, Univ. of Cambridge; War Service 1941–46; Colonial Office 1949–56; First Sec., High Comm., New Delhi 1956–58; Commonwealth Relations Office 1958–59; Deputy High Commr., North Malaya 1959–62; Counsellor, New Delhi 1963–66; Prin. Private Sec., Commonwealth Office 1966–68; Diplomatic Service Insp. 1968–70; High Commr. in Fiji 1970–74; FCO 1974; Officer, Lagos 1974–79; F.C.O. Asst. Under-Sec. of State, Africa 1979; High Commr. in Kenya 1979–82; U.K. Perm. Rep. to UNEP and UN Centre for Human Settlements 1979–82; Chair. Commonwealth Inst. 1984–87; Hon. Fellow Fitzwilliam Coll., Cambridge 1983. *Leisure interests:* tennis, croquet, music. *Address:* Eton House, Hanging Langford, Salisbury, SP3 4NN, England. *Telephone:* (0722) 790562.

WILLIAMS, John T.; American composer of film music; b. 8 Feb. 1932, Flushing, N.Y.; ed. Juilliard School; Conductor Boston Pops Orchestra 1980–84; numerous hon. degrees; Oscars for Fiddler on the Roof, Jaws, Star Wars, E.T.; 14 Grammys; two Emmys; Golden Globe Award 1978. *Filmscores:* The Secret Ways 1961, Diamond Head 1962, None But the Brave 1965, How to Steal a Million 1966, Valley of the Dolls 1967, The Cowboys 1972, The Poseidon Adventure 1972, Tom Sawyer 1973, Earthquake 1974, The Towering Inferno 1974, Jaws 1975, The Eiger Sanction 1975, Family Plot 1976, Midway 1976, The Missouri Breaks 1976, Raggedy Ann and Andy 1977, Black Sunday 1977, Star Wars 1977, Close Encounters of the Third Kind 1977, The Fury 1978, Jaws II 1976, Superman 1978, Dracula 1979, The Empire Strikes Back 1980, Raiders of the Lost Ark 1981, E.T.: The Extra Terrestrial 1982, Return of the Jedi 1983, Indiana Jones and the Temple of Doom 1984, The River 1985, Space Camp 1986, The Witches of Eastwick 1987, Empire of the Sun (BAPTA Best Score Award) 1988. *Address:* c/o Triad Artistic Inc., 10100 Santa Monica Boulevard, 16th Floor, Los Angeles, Calif. 90067, U.S.A.

WILLIAMS, Joseph Dalton, B.SC.; American business executive; b. 15 Aug. 1926, Washington, Pa.; s. of Joseph Dalton Williams and Jane Day; m. Millie E. Bellaire 1973; one s. one d.; ed. Univ. of Nebraska; Sales Rep., Parke-Davis, Kan. City 1950, Field Man. 1956, Asst. Man. Market Research 1958, Asst. to Dir. Sales Research and Devt. 1962, Dir. Medical-Surgical Market Devt. 1967, Dir. U.S. Marketing 1968, Group Vice-Pres., Marketing and Sales 1970; following merger of cos., Vice-Pres., Warner-Lambert, mem. Bd., Parke-Davis; Exec. Vice-Pres. and C.E.O. Parke-Davis 1971, Pres. and C.E.O. 1973; mem. Bd of Dirs. Warner-Lambert 1973–, Sr Vice-Pres. 1973, Exec. Vice-Pres. and Pres. Pharmaceutical Group 1976, Sr. Exec. Vice-Pres., mem. Office of Chair. and Pres. Int. Group 1977, Pres. Warner-Lambert 1979, Pres. and C.O.O. 1980, Pres., C.E.O. and C.O.O. 1985, Chair. of Bd. and C.E.O. 1985–; Hon. Dr. of Pharmacy (Nebraska), Hon. D.Hum.Litt. (Union Univ.); Remington Honor Medal, American Pharmaceutical Assen., Rutgers Univ. Award 1982. *Leisure interest:* golf. *Address:* Warner-Lambert Company, 201 Tabor Road,

Morris Plains, N.J. 07950 (Office); P.O. Box 836, Bernardsville, N.J. 07924, U.S.A. (Home). *Telephone:* (201) 540-3404 (Office).

WILLIAMS, Kenneth Rigby, F.I.C.A.; British chartered accountant; b. 25 Aug. 1936, Stockport; m.; one s. one d.; ed. Haywood Grammar School, Manchester and Inst. of Chartered Accountants; articled clerk, Rhodesian audit firm 1959-62; Head Office Accountant, Rhodesian Breweries Ltd. 1962-63, Branch Accountant 1963-65, Chief Accountant 1965-67; Financial Controller, Beer Div., S.A. Breweries 1967-68, subsequently apptd. Group Financial Controller and later Group Commercial Man.; Group Gen. Man. and Dir. S.A. Breweries 1972-80, Chair. Beverage Div. 1980-, Man. Dir. Int. Interests 1986-. *Leisure interests:* golf, tennis, reading, sailing. *Address:* The South African Breweries Ltd., P.O. Box 1099, 2 Jan Smuts Avenue, Braamfontein, Johannesburg 2001, South Africa.

WILLIAMS, Leslie Henry, B.SC.; British company director; b. 26 Jan. 1903, London; s. of late Edward Henry and of Jessie Williams; m. Alice Helen Harrison 1930; one s.; ed. Highbury County School, and London Univ.; ICI Ltd., Paints Div. 1929, Dir. 1943-46, Man. Dir. 1946-48, Chair. 1949-56, Dir. ICI Main Bd. 1957-60, Deputy Chair. ICI Ltd. 1960-67; Dir. British Nylon Spinners Ltd. 1957-64, Ilford Ltd. 1958-67; Chair. ICI Fibres Ltd. 1965-66; Pres. Royal Inst. of Chemistry 1967-70; mem. Monopolies Comm. 1967-73; Hon. F.R.S.C., Hon. D.Sc. (Salford). *Leisure interests:* garden, music. *Address:* Apartment 18, Albury Park, Albury, Guildford, Surrey, GU5 9BB, England. *Telephone:* (048 641) 3373.

WILLIAMS, Lynn Russell; American union official; b. 21 July 1924, Springfield, Ont., Canada; s. of Waldemar Williams and Emma Elizabeth (née Fisher) Williams; m. Audrey Hansuld 1946; two s. two d.; ed. McMaster Univ.; organiser Canadian Labour Congress 1947-55; joined United Steelworkers of America, Toronto, Ont. 1947, Staff Rep. 1956-57, Asst. Dir. Dist. 6 1963-73, Dir. Dist. 6 1973-77; Int. Sec. United Steelworkers of America, Pittsburgh 1977-83, Int. Pres. 1983-; mem. Exec. Cttee. AFL-CIO, Washington 1983; Dir. American Arbitration Assen. 1983; mem. Bd. of Dirs., African-American Labor Center, Cttee. for Nat. Health Insurance, Work in America Inst.; mem. Panel, Econ. Policy Council; Vice-Pres. Americans for Democratic Action; mem. UN Econ. Policy Council, Canada-America Comm. *Leisure interests:* running, jogging, reading, skiing. *Address:* United Steelworkers of America, Five Gateway Center, Pittsburgh, Pa. 15222, U.S.A.

WILLIAMS, Maurice Jacoutot, M.A.; American international civil servant; b. 13 Nov. 1920, Moncton, N.B., Canada; s. of Alfred Jacoutot Williams and Yvonne Theberge; m. Betty Jane Bath 1943; three s.; ed. Northwestern Univ., Evanston, Ill., Victoria Univ. of Manchester, England, Univ. of Chicago, Ill., London School of Econs.; Capt. Mil. Intelligence, U.S. Army 1942-46; Dir. Reynolds Club, Univ. of Chicago 1946-48; Prin. Examiner, Chicago Civil Service Comm. 1948-49; Economist, Int. Trade Policy, Dept. of State, Washington 1950-53; Foreign Service Officer, London Embassy, 1953-55; Chief of Econ. Defense Co-ordination, Washington 1955-58; Deputy Dir. U.S. Agency for Int. Devt. (AID), Pakistan 1963-66; Asst. Admin. Near East-South Asia Bureau, AID, Washington 1967-69, Deputy Admin. AID 1970-74; U.S. Pres. Co-ordinator, Foreign Disaster Relief, Bangladesh, Peru, African Sahel 1971-74; Co-Chair. U.S.-N. Viet-Nam Jt. Econ. Comm. 1974; Chair. Devt. Assistance Cttee., OECD 1975-78; Exec. Dir. UN World Food Council, Rome 1978-86; Sec.-Gen. Soc. of Int. Devt. 1986-; U.S. Civil Service Award 1971, AID Distinguished Honor Award 1974, Rockefeller Public Service Award 1974. *Publications:* Development Cooperation in Reviews 1974-78, and over 20 articles on econ. devt. and food policy. *Address:* c/o Society for International Development, Palazzo Civilta del Lavoro, 00144 Rome, Italy. *Telephone:* (06) 591-7897.

WILLIAMS, Nicholas James Donald; British solicitor and business executive; b. 21 Oct. 1925, Calcutta, India; s. of the late Nicholas T. and Daisy (Hollow) Williams; m. 1st Dawn Hill 1947 (dissolved); one s. one d.; m. 2nd Sheila M. Dalgety 1955; two s. one d.; ed. Rugby School; Partner, Nicholas Williams and Co., London 1950-61; Sr. Partner, Surridge and Beecheno, Karachi, Pakistan 1955-61; Legal Adviser, The Burmah Oil Co., London 1961-63, Co-ordinator, Eastern Operations 1963-65, Exec. Dir. 1965-67; Asst. Man. Dir. 1967-69, Man. Dir. 1969-75, also Chief Exec. 1971-75; Dir. Flarebay Ltd. 1978-85, EBC Group PLC 1986-, Ranvet Ltd. 1986-. *Leisure interest:* sailing. *Address:* Purlieus Farmhouse, Ewen, Cirencester, Gloucestershire, England.

WILLIAMS, Nick B.; American newspaper editor; b. 23 Aug. 1906, Onancock, Va.; s. of John Frederick and Anne M. Williams; m. 1st Elizabeth Rickenbaker 1933 (died 1973), one s. three d.; m. 2nd Barbara Steele 1973; ed. Univ. of the South and Univ. of Texas; Editorial worker, Texas, Tennessee and California 1927-58; Man. Ed. Los Angeles Times 1958, Ed. 1959-71; D.C.L. (Univ. of the South); Kt., Order of Leopold, Freedoms Foundation Award; Nat. Press Club's Fourth Estate Award 1981. *Leisure interests:* reviewing mystery novels for the L.A. Times, gardening. *Address:* 3 Bay Drive, South Laguna, Calif. 92677, U.S.A. *Telephone:* (714) 499-4707.

WILLIAMS, Nigel Christopher Ransome, C.M.G.; British diplomatist; b. 29 April 1937, Norwich; s. of Cecil Gwynne Ransome Williams and Corinne Belden (née Rudd) Williams; ed. Merchant Taylors' School and St. John's Coll., Oxford; entered Foreign Service 1961; third, later second Sec. to

British Embassy, Tokyo 1961-66; Foreign Office 1966-70; first Sec. UK Mission to UN 1970-73; Foreign Office 1973-75; Econ. Counsellor, Tokyo 1976-79; Head UN Dept., FCO 1980-85; Minister Embassy, Bonn 1985-88; Amb. to Denmark 1989-. *Address:* c/o Foreign and Commonwealth Office, London SW1, England.

WILLIAMS, Peter Orchard, M.B., F.R.C.P.; British doctor and medical director; b. 23 Sept. 1925, Trinidad; s. of Robert O. Williams and Agnes A. Birkinshaw; m. Billie I. Brown 1949; two d.; ed. Caterham School, Queen's Royal Coll., Trinidad, St. John's Coll., Cambridge and St. Mary's Hosp. Medical School; House Physician, St. Mary's Hosp., London 1950-51; Registrar, Royal Free Hosp. 1951-52; Medical Specialist, R.A.M.C. 1954; Medical Officer, Medical Research Council H.Q. 1955-60; Asst. and Deputy Scientific Sec. Wellcome Trust 1960-64, Scientific Sec. 1964-65, Dir. 1965-; Hon. Fellow, London School of Hygiene and Tropical Medicine. *Publication:* Careers in Medicine 1952. *Leisure interests:* gardening, travel, golf. *Address:* The Wellcome Trust, 1 Park Square West, London, NW1 4LJ; Symonds House, Symonds Street, Winchester, SO23 9JS, England. *Telephone:* 01-486 4902 (London); (0962) 52650 (Winchester).

WILLIAMS, Robert Joseph Paton, D.PHIL., F.R.S., F.R.C.S.; British professor of chemistry; b. 25 Feb. 1926, Wallasey; s. of Ernest Ivor Williams and Alice Roberts; m. Jelly Klara Buchli 1952; two s.; ed. Oxford Univ.; Rotary Int. Fellow 1951-52; Research Fellow, Merton Coll., Oxford Univ. 1952-55; Fellow, Wadham Coll., Oxford Univ. 1955-; Lecturer, Oxford Univ. 1955-70, Reader 1970-72, Napier Royal Soc. Research Prof. 1972-; Hon. Fellow, Merton Coll., Oxford; Foreign mem. Royal Swedish Acad. of Science, Lisbon Acad. of Science, Czechoslovak Acad. of Science, Royal Soc. of Science, Liège; Hon. D.Sc. (Univ. of Louvain, Univ. of Leicester); Tilden Medal (Chem. Soc. of England); Liversidge Medal (Chem. Soc. of England); Keilen Medal (Biochem. Soc.); Hughes Medal (Royal Soc.); Sir Hans Krebs Medal (European Biochem. Soc.); Linderstrøm-Lang Medal (Denmark), Sigillum Magna (Univ. of Bologna), Heyrovsky Medal (Int. Union of Biochem.), Sir Frederick Gowland Hopkins Medal (Biochem. Soc.). *Publications:* Inorganic Chemistry (with C. S. G. Phillips), NMR in Biology, Recent Trends in Bioinorganic Chemistry. *Leisure interest:* walking in the country. *Address:* Wadham College, Oxford (Office); 115 Victoria Road, Oxford, OX2 7QG, England (Home). *Telephone:* (0865) 58926 (Home).

WILLIAMS, Robert Martin, C.B., C.B.E., PH.D.; New Zealand mathematician; b. 30 March 1919, Christchurch; s. of the late Canon Henry Williams; m. Mary Constance Thorpe 1944; one s. two d.; ed. Christ's Coll., Canterbury Univ., N.Z., St. John's Coll., Cambridge; Mathematician, Radar Devt. Laboratory, D.S.I.R., N.Z. 1941-44; mem. U.K. Atomic Group in U.S.A. 1944-45; mem. Applied Math. Laboratory, D.S.I.R. 1949-53, Dir. 1953-62; Commr. State Services Comm. N.Z. 1963-66; Vice-Chancellor Univ. of Otago 1967-73, A.N.U. 1973-75; Chair. State Services Comm. 1975-81; mem. Int. Statistical Inst. 1961-; Hon. LL.D. (Otago). *Publications:* papers on mathematical statistics. *Address:* 21 Wadestown Road, Wellington, New Zealand (Home). *Telephone:* 726698 (Home).

WILLIAMS, Robin Murphy, Jr., PH.D.; American professor of social sciences; b. 11 Oct. 1914, North Carolina; m. Marguerite York 1939; one s. (deceased) two d.; ed. North Carolina State Coll. and Harvard Univ.; Instructor and Research Asst., Univ. of Ky. 1939-42; Statistical Analyst, U.S. War Dept. 1942-46; Assoc. Prof., Cornell Univ. 1946-48, Prof. 1948-67, Dir. Social Science Research Center 1949-54, Chair. Dept. of Sociology and Anthropology 1956-61, Henry Scarborough Prof. of Social Science 1967-85, Prof. Emer. 1985-; Ed. Sociological Forum 1984; Chair. Cttee. on Status of Black Americans, Nat. Research Council; mem. American Philosophical Soc., American Acad. of Arts and Sciences, N.A.S. *Publications:* Strangers Next Door 1964, American Society 1951, Mutual Accommodation 1977. *Leisure interest:* work. *Address:* 342 Uris Hall, Cornell University, Ithaca, N.Y. 14853; 414 Oak Avenue, Ithaca, N.Y. 14850, U.S.A. (Home). *Telephone:* (607) 256-4266 (Univ.); (607) 273-9119 (Home).

WILLIAMS, Roger Stanley, M.D., F.R.C.S., F.R.C.P.; British consultant physician; b. 28 Aug. 1931; s. of Stanley George Williams and Doris Dagmar Clatworthy; m. 1st Lindsay Mary Elliott 1954 (divorced 1977), two s. three d.; m. 2nd Stephanie Gay de Laszlo 1978, one s. two d.; ed. St Mary's Coll., Southampton, London Hosp. Medical School, Univ. of London; House Doctor London Hosp. 1953-56; Jr. Medical Specialist, Queen Alexandra Hosp. 1956-58; Medical Registrar and Tutor, Royal Postgraduate Medical School 1958-59; Lecturer in Medicine Royal Free Hosp. 1959-65; Consultant Physician Royal S. Hants. and Southampton Gen. Hosp. 1965-66; Consultant Physician and Dir., Liver Unit, King's Coll. Hosp., London; mem. WHO Scientific Group on Viral Hepatitis, Geneva 1972, Transplant Advisory Panel DHSS 1974-83, Advisory Group on Hepatitis DHSS 1980-, European Assen. for the Study of the Liver (Pres. 1983) 1966-, Harveian Soc. of London (Pres. 1974-75), British Assen. for the Study of the Liver (Pres. 1984), Royal Soc. of Medicine, British Soc. of Gastroenterology (Pres.-elect 1988); Hon. Consultant in Medicine to the Army; Rep. to Select Cttee. of Experts on Organisational Aspects of Co-operation in Organ Transplantation, Congress of Europe; Sir Ernest Finch Visiting Prof. Univ. of Sheffield 1974. *Publications:* Fifth Symposium on Advanced Medicine (Ed.) 1969, Immunology of the Liver 1971, Artificial Liver Support 1975, Immune Reactions in Liver Disease 1978, Drug Reactions and the Liver 1981, Clinics in Critical Care Medicine—Liver Failure 1986;

author of over 800 papers, reviews and book chapters. *Leisure interests:* tennis, sailing, opera. *Address:* King's College Hospital, Denmark Hill, London, SE5 9RS, England. *Telephone:* 01-274 6222.

WILLIAMS, Rt. Hon. Shirley, P.C., M.A.; British politician; b. 27 July 1930, London; d. of the late Sir George Catlin and Vera Brittain; m. 1st Bernard Williams 1955 (divorced 1974), one d.; m. 2nd Richard Neustadt (q.v.) 1987; ed. Summit School, Minn., U.S.A., St. Paul's Girls' School, Somerville Coll., Oxford, and Columbia Univ.; Gen. Sec. Fabian Soc. 1960–64; Labour M.P. for Hitchin 1964–74, fo. Hertford and Stevenage 1974–79; Social Democratic Party M.P. for Crosby 1981–83; Parl. Pvt. Sec., Minister of Health 1964–66; Parl. Sec. Minister of Labour 1966–67; Minister of State, Dept. of Education and Science 1967–69; Minister of State, Home Office 1969–70; Opposition Spokesman on Health and Social Security 1970–71, on Home Affairs 1971–73, on Prices and Consumer Affairs 1973–74; Sec. of State for Prices and Consumer Protection 1974–76, for Educ. and Science 1976–79; Paymaster-Gen. April 1976–79; Sr. Research Fellow (part-time) Policy Research Inst. 1979–85; mem. Labour Party Nat. Exec. Cttee. 1970–81; mem. Council for Social Democracy Jan.–March 1981; left Labour Party March 1981; co-founder Social Democratic Party March 1981, Pres. 1982–88; mem. Social and Liberal Democratic Party 1988, The Democrats 1988–; TV series: Shirley Williams in Conversation 1980; Visiting Fellow, Nuffield Coll., Oxford 1967–75; Trustee Twentieth Century Fund, U.S.A.; Hon. D.Ed., C.N.A.A.; Hon. Dr.Pol.Econ., Univ. of Leuven, Belgium, Radcliffe Coll., U.S.A.; Hon. LL.D. (Leeds Univ.) 1979, (Southampton) 1981. *Publications:* Politics is for People 1981, A Job to Live 1985, pamphlets on European Community, and economics of Central Africa; articles and broadcasts. *Leisure interests:* riding, rough walking, music. *Address:* c/o SDP, 4 Cowley Street, London, SW1P 3NB, England. *Telephone:* 01-222 7999.

WILLIAMS, Stephen, PH.D.; American professor of anthropology and archaeologist; b. 28 Aug. 1926, Minneapolis, Minn.; s. of Clyde G. and Lois M. (Simmons) Williams; m. Eunice Ford 1962; two s.; ed. Univ. of Michigan and Yale Univ.; Historical and Archaeological Research on Caddo Indians for U.S. Dept. of Justice 1954–55; Research Fellow in N. American Archaeology, Peabody Museum of Archaeology and Ethnology, Harvard Univ. 1955–58; Lecturer in Anthropology, Harvard Univ. 1956–58, Asst. Prof. of Anthropology 1958–62, Assoc. Prof. 1962–67, Prof. of Anthropology 1967–72, Peabody Prof. 1972–, Chair. Dept. of Anthropology 1967–69; mem. of Bd. of Freshmen Advisers, Harvard Univ. 1959–60, 1961–65; Asst. Curator of N. American Archaeology, Peabody Museum 1957–58, Curator of N. American Archaeology 1962–; Dir. Peabody Museum 1967–77, Dir. Peabody Museum Lower Mississippi Survey 1958–; Distinguished Fellow School of American Research, Santa Fé 1977–78; Hon. M.A. (Harvard Univ.). *Publications:* Five monographs incl. Excavations at the Lake George Site, Yazoo County, Miss. 1958–60 (with Jeffrey P. Brain); numerous articles in journals. *Address:* Peabody Museum of Archaeology and Ethnology, Harvard University, 11 Divinity Avenue, Cambridge, Mass. 02138; 103 Old Colony Road, Wellesley, Mass. 02181, U.S.A. (Home). *Telephone:* (617) 495-2250 (Office); (617) 235-7588 (Home).

WILLIAMS, H.E. Cardinal Thomas Stafford, S.T.L., B.SOC.SC.; New Zealand ecclesiastic; b. 20 March 1930, Wellington; s. of Thomas S. and Lillian M. (née Kelly) Williams; ed. St. Patrick's Coll., Wellington, Victoria Univ., Wellington, St. Kevin's Coll., Oamaru, Holy Cross Coll., Mosgiel, Pontifical Urban Coll. de Propaganda Fide, Rome and Univ. Coll., Dublin; ordained priest, Rome 1959; Asst. St. Patrick's Parish, Palmerston North 1963; Dir. of Studies, Catholic Enquiry Centre, Wellington 1965; parish priest, St. Anne's, Leulumoega, Western Samoa 1971, Holy Family Parish, Porirua East, Wellington 1976; Archbishop of Wellington and Metropolitan of N.Z. 1979–; cr. Cardinal 1983. *Address:* Viard, 21 Eccleston Hill, P.O. Box 198, Wellington 1, New Zealand. *Telephone:* 728-576.

WILLIAMS, Walter Fred; American business executive; b. 7 Feb. 1929, Upland, Pa.; s. of Walter James and Florence (née Stott) Williams; m. Joan Bernice Carey 1950; three s.; ed. Univs. of Delaware and Harvard; joined Bethlehem Steel Corpn. (Pa.) 1951; an asst. chief engineer on staff of Vice-Pres. (Operations) 1965–66; Chief Engineer (Construction), Burns Harbor, Ind., plant 1966–67; Chief Engineer, Projects Group Eng. Dept., Bethlehem, then Man. Eng. in charge of Projects, Design and Construction 1967–68; Asst. to Vice-Pres. (Eng.) 1968, to Vice-Pres. (Shipbuilding) 1968–70; Vice-Pres. (Shipbuilding) 1970–75, (Steel Operations) 1975–77, Sr. Vice-Pres. (Steel Operations) 1978–80; Pres. and C.O.O. 1980–86, Chair., Pres. and C.E.O. 1986–, also Dir.; Vice-Chair. American Iron and Steel Inst.; mem. Business Council, Business Roundtable and Conf. Bd.; Dir. Iacocca Inst., Lehigh Valley Partnership, Nat. Assen. of Mfrs; Trustee Moravian Coll. *Leisure interest:* golf. *Address:* Bethlehem Steel Corpn., Bethlehem, Pa. 18016 (Office); Saucon Valley, RD4, Bethlehem, Pa. 18015, U.S.A. (Home).

WILLIAMS, William John, J.D.; American business executive; b. 8 Oct. 1928, Penn Yan, N.Y.; s. of Freeborn Williams and Josephine O'Keefe; m. Sara Jane Washeim 1950; three s. one d.; ed. Penn Yan Acad. and Univ. of Richmond, Va.; attorney, Hunton, Williams, Gay, Powell & Gibson, Richmond, Va. 1957–63; Asst. Counsel, Republic Steel Corpn. (now LTV Steel), Cleveland, Ohio 1963, Asst. Gen. Counsel 1966, Gen. Counsel 1971, Vice-Pres., Gen. Counsel and Sec. 1973, Exec. Vice-Pres. 1976, mem. Bd. of Dirs. 1978, Vice-Chair. 1980, Pres. and C.O.O. 1982–. *Leisure interests:*

flying, boating, golf. *Address:* 1707 Republic Building, P.O. Box 6778, Cleveland, Ohio (Office); 7640 Waterfall Trail, Chagrin Falls, Ohio 44022, U.S.A. (Home). *Telephone:* (213) 622-5700.

WILLIAMS OF ELVEL, Baron (Life Peer), cr. 1985, of Llansantffraed in Elvel in the county of Powys; **Charles Cuthbert Powell Williams**, C.B.E., M.A., F.R.S.A.; British business executive and politician; b. 9 Feb. 1933; s. of late Norman P. Williams and Muriel Cazenove; m. Jane G. Portal 1975; one step-s.; ed. Westminster School, Christ Church, Oxford and London School of Econs.; British Petroleum Co. Ltd. 1958–64; Bank of London and Montreal 1964–66; Eurofinance SA, Paris 1966–70; Baring Brothers & Co. Ltd. 1970–77, Man. Dir. 1971–77; Chair. Price Comm. 1977–79; Man. Dir. Henry Ansbacher & Co. Ltd. 1980–82, Chair. 1982–85; Chief Exec. Henry Ansbacher Holdings PLC 1982–85; Chair. Berkeley Exploration and Production PLC 1982–; Chair. Acad. of St. Martin in the Fields 1988–; parliamentary candidate (Labour) 1964; Opposition Spokesman for Trade and Industry, House of Lords. *Leisure interests:* cricket, music, real tennis. *Address:* 48 Thurloe Square, London, SW7 2SX, England.

WILLIAMSON, David F., C.B., M.A.; British government official; b. 8 May 1934; m.; two s.; ed. Tonbridge School and Exeter Coll. Oxford; Army service 1956–58; entered Ministry of Agric., Fisheries and Food 1958; seconded to H.M. Diplomatic Service as First Sec. (Agric. and Food), Geneva, for Kennedy Round Trade Negotiation 1965–67; Prin. Pvt. Sec. to successive Ministers, Ministry of Agric., Fisheries and Food 1967–70; Head of Milk and Milk Products Div. 1970–74; Under-Sec. 1974; Deputy Dir.-Gen. (Agric.), Comm. of European Communities 1977–83; Deputy Sec. and Head of European Secr. Cabinet Office 1983–87; Sec.-Gen. Comm. of European Communities 1987–. *Address:* Commission of the European Communities, 200 rue de la Loi, 1049 Brussels, Belgium.

WILLIAMSON, David Keith, A.O., B.E.; Australian playwright and screenwriter; b. 24 Feb. 1942, Melbourne; s. of Edwin Keith David Williamson and Elvie May (née Armstrong) Williamson; m. Kristin Ingrid Green 1974; two s. one d.; ed. Monash Univ.; Design Engineer Gen. Motors-Holden's 1965; lecturer Swinbourne Tech. Coll. 1966–72; freelance writer 1972–. *Plays:* The Removalists 1972, Don's Party 1973, Three Plays 1974, The Department 1975, A Handful of Friends 1976, The Club 1977, Travelling North 1979, The Perfectionist 1981, Sons of Cain 1985, Emerald City 1987. *Sceenplays:* Gallipoli 1981, Phar Lap 1983, The Year of Living Dangerously 1983, Travelling North 1986, Emerald City 1988, The Four Minute Mile (2-part TV series) 1988, The Four Day Revolution (6-hour TV series) 1988. *Address:* c/o Anthony Williams Management Pty. Ltd., The Basement, 55 Victoria Street, Potts Point, N.S.W. 2011, Australia.

WILLIAMSON, David Theodore Nelson, F.R.S.; British research engineer (retd.); b. 15 Feb. 1923, Edinburgh; s. of David Williamson and Ellie Nelson; m. Alexandra Janet Smith Neilson 1951; two s. two d.; ed. George Heriot's School, Edin. and Univ. of Edinburgh; on staff of M.O. Valve Co. Ltd. 1943–46, of Ferranti Ltd., Edin. 1946–61, devt. of industrial uses of wartime tech., especially computer-controlled machine tools 1951–61, Man. Machine Tool Control Dept. 1959–61, contributions to devt. of sound reproduction included contrast expansion 1943, Williamson amplifier 1947, Ferranti ribbon pickup 1949, record "click" suppression 1953, first full range electrostatic loudspeaker (with P. J. Walker) 1951–56; Dir. of Research and Devt., Molins Ltd., London 1961–74 (devts. included high-speed cigarette-making machinery and first flexible mfg. system, SYSTEM 24); Dir. of Eng., Rank Xerox 1974–75, Group Dir. (Eng.) 1975–76; Hon. D.Sc. (Heriot-Watt) 1973, (Edin.) 1985. *Publications:* papers and articles on eng. subjects, including James Clayton Lecture, Inst. of Mechanical Eng. 1968. *Leisure interests:* music, photography, electronics. *Address:* Villa Belvedere, La Cima, Tuoro-sul-Trasimeno, 06069 (Pg), Umbria, Italy. *Telephone:* (075) 826285.

WILLIAMSON, Air Chief Marshal Sir Keith (Alec), G.C.B., A.F.C.; British air force officer; b. 25 Feb. 1928; s. of Percy and Gertrude Williamson; m. Patricia Ann Watts 1953; two s. two d.; ed. Bancrofts' School, Woodford Green, Market Harborough Grammar School, R.A.F. Coll. Cranwell; commissioned 1950; with R.A.A.F. in Korea 1953; C.O. 23 Squadron 1966–68; C.O., R.A.F. Gütersloh 1968–70; Royal Coll. Defence Studies 1971; Dir., Air Staff Plans 1972–75; Commdt. R.A.F. Staff Coll. 1975–77; Asst. Chief of Staff (Plans and Policy) S.H.A.P.E. 1977–78; Air Officer Commdr. in Chief, R.A.F. Support Command 1978–80; R.A.F. Strike Command and C.-in-C. U.K. Air Forces 1980–82; Chief of Air Staff 1982–85; Air A.D.C. to the Queen 1982–85. *Leisure interest:* golf. *Address:* c/o Midland Bank, 25 Notting Hill Gate, London, W.11, England.

WILLIAMSON, Malcolm Benjamin Graham, C.B.E.; British composer, pianist and organist; b. 21 Nov. 1931, Sydney, N.S.W., Australia; s. of George and Bessie Williamson; m. Dolores Daniel 1960; one s. two d.; ed. Barker Coll., Hornsby, N.S.W., and Sydney Conservatorium of Music; Asst. organist, Farm Street, London 1955–58; Organist, St. Peter's, Limehouse 1958–60; lecturer in Music, Cen. School of Speech and Drama, London 1961–62; Exec. Cttee., Composers' Guild of Great Britain 1964; Composer-in-Residence Westminster Choir Coll., Princeton, N.J. 1970–71; Master of the Queen's Music 1975–; Pres. Beauchamp Sinfonietta 1972–, Birmingham Chamber Music Soc. 1975–, Royal Philharmonic Orchestra

1977-82, Univ. of London Choir 1976-, Sing for Pleasure 1977-, British Soc. for Music Therapy 1977-; Ramasciotti Medical Research Fellow, Univ. of N.S.W. 1982; Visiting Prof., Univ. of Strathclyde 1983-86; Hon. Dr.Mus. (Westminster Choir Coll.) 1970, (Univ. of Melbourne) 1982, (Univ. of Sydney) 1982, (The Open Univ.) 1983; Sir Arnold Bax Memorial Prize 1963; Hon. A.O. 1987. *Compositions include:* Operas: Our Man in Havana 1963, English Eccentrics 1964, The Happy Prince 1964, Julius Caesar Jones 1965, The Violins of St. Jacques 1966, Dunstan and the Devil 1967, The Growing Castle 1968, Lucky-Peter's Journey 1969, The Red Sea 1972; Cassations: The Moonrakers 1967, The Snow Wolf, Knights in Shining Armour 1968, Genesis, The Stone Wall 1971, The Winter Star 1973, The Glitter Gang 1974, The Terrain of the Kings 1975, The Valley and the Hill 1977, Le Pont du Diable 1982; Ballets: The Display 1964, Sun into Darkness 1966, Perisynthyon; Orchestral: Piano Concertos 1958, 1960, 1961, Organ Concerto 1961, Violin Concerto 1965, Elevamini (Symphony) 1956, Santiago de Espada (Overture) 1956, Sinfonia Concertante 1961, Sinfonietta 1965, Symphonic Variations 1965, Concerto Grosso 1965, Symphony No. 2 1969, Symphony No. 3 (The Icy Mirror) 1972, Symphony No. 4 1977, Symphony No. 5 1980, Symphony No. 6 1982, Symphony No. 7 1984, Mass of Christ the King 1977, A Pilgrim Liturgy (Cantata) 1984; Chamber: Variations for Cello and Piano 1964, Concerto for Wind Quintet and Two Pianos, Eight Hands 1965, Pas de Quatre (Piano and woodwind) 1967; Organ: Fons Amoris 1957, Symphony 1960, Vision of Christ Phoenix 1961, Elegy JFK 1964, Peace Pieces 1971, The Lion of Suffolk; The Brilliant and the Dark (operatic sequence) 1966, Two piano sonatas 1967, From a Child's Garden (tenor and piano) 1968, Little Carols of the Saints, Hammarskjöld Portrait 1974, also choral and piano music. *Leisure interest:* literature. *Address:* c/o Campion Press, Sandon, Buntingford, Herts. SG9 0QW, England.

WILLIAMSON, Nicol; British actor; b. 14 Sept. 1938, Hamilton, Scotland; m. Jill Townsend 1971 (divorced 1977); one s.; began career with Dundee Repertory Theatre 1960-61; London début at Royal Court, That's Us 1961; joined R.S.C. 1962; *theatre appearances include:* Satin in The Lower Depths 1962, Leantio in Women Beware Women 1962, Kelly's Eye 1963, The Ginger Man 1963, Vladimir in Waiting for Godot 1964, Bill Maitland in Inadmissible Evidence 1964, 1965, 1978, Diary of A Madman 1968, Hamlet 1969, Uncle Vanya 1973, Coriolanus 1973, Malvolio in Twelfth Night 1974, Macbeth 1974, Rex 1975, Inadmissible Evidence 1981, Macbeth 1982, The Entertainer 1983, The Lark 1983, The Real Thing 1985; *films include:* Inadmissible Evidence 1967, Laughter in the Dark 1968, Bofors Gun 1968, The Reckoning 1969, Hamlet 1969, The Jerusalem File 1972, The Wilby Conspiracy 1974, Robin and Marian 1976, The Seven Per Cent Solution 1976, The Human Factor 1980, Knights 1980, Excalibur 1980, Venom 1980, I'm Dancing as Fast as I Can 1981, Return to Oz 1984, Black Widow 1986; *television includes:* Terrible Jim Fitch, Arturo Ui, I Know What I Meant, The Word 1977, Macbeth 1982, Mountbatten—the Last Viceroy 1985, Passion Flower 1985; New York Drama Critics Award for Inadmissible Evidence 1965-66; Evening Standard Award for Best Actor, for Inadmissible Evidence 1964, for Hamlet 1969. *Address:* c/o ICM, 388-396 Oxford Street, London, W.1, England.

WILLICH, (Walter) Martin (Philipp), DR.JUR.; German business executive and politician; b. 24 April 1945, Erfurt; s. of Philipp and Helene (née Schatz) Willich; m. Angela Willich 1972; two d.; with firm of chartered accountants 1975-77; in cigarette industry 1978-80; Man. Studio Hamburg Atelier GmbH 1980-84, Pres. 1984-; mem. CDU 1965-; mem. Hamburg City Council 1974, Pres. 1982-83, 1986-87. *Address:* Bekwisch 6, 2000 Hamburg 65, Federal Republic of Germany.

WILLIS, Baron (Life Peer), cr. 1963, of Chislehurst; **Edward (Ted) Willis;** British author; b. 13 Jan. 1918, London; s. of Alfred John and Maria Harriet Willis; m. Audrey Hale 1944; one s. one d.; ed. Tottenham Cen. School; Royal Fusiliers 1940-44; professional writer 1945-; Chair. Screenwriters' Guild 1958-68, Channel Theatre Co.; Dir. World Wide Pictures 1967-, Duke of York's Theatre, Capital Radio Ltd. 1974-, Leisure Technics Ltd. 1983-, Vitalcall Ltd. 1983-; Labour. *Works include:* plays: Woman in a Dressing Gown 1956, Hot Summer Night 1959, Doctor in the House 1960, Mother 1961, Slow Roll of Drums 1964, Knock on any Door 1964, Queenie 1967, Dead on Saturday 1970, Mr. Polly 1977, Doctor on the Boil 1978, Stardust 1983, Cat and Mouse 1985, Old Flames 1986, Tommy Boy 1988; Whatever Happened to Tom Mix (autobiog.) 1970; novels: Death May Surprise Us 1974, The Left-Handed Sleeper 1975, Man-Eater 1976, The Churchill Commando 1977, The Buckingham Palace Connection 1978, The Lions of Judah 1979, The Naked Sun 1980, The Most Beautiful Girl in the World 1982, Spring at the Winged Horse 1982, The Green Leaves of Summer 1987. *Films include:* Blue Lamp, Bitter Harvest, A Long Way to Shiloh 1969, No Trees in the Street, Woman in a Dressing Gown 1973, Mrs Harris M.P. 1985, Mrs Harris Goes to New York 1986, Mrs Harris Goes to Moscow 1987, Mrs Harris Goes to Monte Carlo 1987. *TV series include:* Dixon of Dock Green, Sergeant Cork, Crime of Passion, Hunter's Walk, A Home for Animals 1985, Racecourse 1986. *Publication:* A Problem for Mother Christmas (children's book) 1986. *Leisure interests:* tennis, Association Football. *Address:* 5 Shepherds Green, Chislehurst, Kent, BR7 6PB, England.

WILLIS, Sir Eric Archibald, K.B.E., C.M.G.; Australian fmr. politician; b. 15 Jan. 1922, Murwillumbah, N.S.W.; s. of the late Archibald Clarence

Willis and of Vida Mabel Willis (née Buttenshaw); m. 1st Norma Dorothy Knight 1951, two s. one d.; m. 2nd Lynn Anitra (Roberts) Ward 1982; ed. Murwillumbah High School, Univ. of Sydney; mem. N.S.W. Legis. Ass. 1950-78, Deputy Leader of Opposition 1959-65; Minister for Labour and Industry 1965-71, Chief Sec. 1965-72, Minister for Tourism 1965-72, for Sport 1971-72, for Educ. 1972-76, Premier and Treas. Jan.-May 1976; Leader of Opposition 1976-77; Exec. Sec. Royal Australian Coll. of Ophthalmologists 1978-83; Exec. Dir. Arthritis Foundation of Australia (N.S.W.) 1984-. *Leisure interests:* reading, swimming. *Address:* 5/94 Kurraba Road, Neutral Bay, N.S.W. 2089, Australia. *Telephone:* (02) 9093432.

WILLIS, James Alfred, PH.D., F.A.H.A.; British professor of classics; b. 11 Jan. 1925, London; s. of Arthur James Willis and Hilda Quick; m. Anna Suzanna Sölner 1964; one s. two d.; ed. Sir Anthony Browne's School, Brentwood, Univ. Coll. London; Asst. Lecturer, then lecturer Univ. Coll. London 1949-62; Reader, Univ. of Western Australia 1962-73, Prof. of Classics 1973-88; Visiting Prof., Univ. of Calif., Berkeley 1983, 1987. *Publications:* Critical Edn. of Macrobius, 2 vols., 1963, 1970, Critical Edn. of Martianus Capella 1983, Latin Textual Criticism 1972. *Leisure interest:* maintenance and restoration of decrepit motor cars. *Address:* Department of Classics, University of Western Australia, Nedlands, W.A. 6009 (Office); 96 Mundaring Weir Road, Kalamunda, W.A. 6076, Australia (Home). *Telephone:* 380 2189 (Office); 293 4882 (Home).

WILLIS, Norman David; British trade union official; b. 21 Jan. 1933; s. of Victor J. M. and Kate E. Willis; m. Maureen Kenning 1963; one s. one d.; ed. Ashford County Grammar School, Ruskin and Oriel Colls., Oxford; Personal Research Asst. to Gen. Sec. Transport & General Workers' Union (TGWU) 1959-70; Nat. Sec. Research and Educ. TGWU 1970-74; Asst. Gen. Sec. Trades Union Congress 1974-77, Deputy Gen. Sec. 1977-84, Gen. Sec. 1984-; Councillor (Labour), Staines Urban Dist. Council 1971-74; Chair. Nat. Pensioners Convention Steering Cttee. 1979-; Vice-Pres. European TUC 1984-, ICFTU 1984-, Inst. of Manpower Studies 1985-; Trustee Anglo-German Foundation for Study of Industrial Soc. 1986-, Duke of Edin.'s Commonwealth Study Conf. 1986-; Patron West Indian Welfare (U.K.) Trust 1986; mem. NEDC 1984-, Council, Overseas Devt. Inst. 1985-, Council, Motability 1985-, Exec. Bd. UNICEF 1986-, Trade Union Advisory Cttee. to OECD 1986-, Council of Prince of Wales Youth Business Trust 1986-; Vice-Pres. Poetry Soc.; Hon. Fellow Oriel Coll., Oxford. *Leisure interests:* painting, poetry, natural history, architecture, canals. *Address:* Trades Union Congress, Congress House, Great Russell Street, London, WC1B 3LS, England.

WILLIS, Ralph; Australian politician; b. 14 April 1938, Melbourne; s. of Stanley Willis and Doris Willis; m. Carol Joyce Dawson 1970; one s. two d.; ed. Univ. High School and Melbourne Univ.; research officer, Australian Council of Trade Unions (ACTU) 1960, industrial advocate 1970; mem. House of Reps. 1972-; Minister for Employment and Industrial Relations and Minister assisting Prime Minister in Public Service Industrial Matters 1983-87, Minister for Industrial Relations and Minister assisting Prime Minister in Public Service Matters 1987-88, for Transport and Communications Sept. 1988-; Australian Labor Party. *Leisure interests:* squash, reading, watching football. *Address:* Department of Transport and Communications, Cnr Northbourne Avenue and Cooyong Street, Canberra, A.C.T. 2600; 70 Victoria Street, Williamstown, Vic. 3016, Australia.

WILLOCH, Kåre Isaachsen, CAND. OECON.; Norwegian politician; b. 3 Oct. 1928, Oslo; s. of Haakon Willoch and Agnes Saure; m. Anne Marie Jørgensen 1954; one s. two d.; ed. Ullern Gymnasium and Univ. of Oslo; Sec. Fed. of Norwegian Shipowners 1951-53, Counsellor Fed. of Norwegian Industries 1954-63; mem. Nat. Cttee. Conservative Party 1961-; Sec.-Gen. Conservative Party 1963-65; Minister of Trade and Shipping 1963, 1965-70; mem. Storting 1958-; Chair. World Bank Group 1967; Chair. Conservative Party 1970-74; Chair. Conservative Party Parl. Group 1970-81; mem. Nordic Council 1970-86, Pres. 1973; Prime Minister 1981-86; Chair. Int. Democratic Union 1987-; Chair. Foreign Affairs Cttee. of Parl. 1986-. *Publications:* Personal Savings 1955, Price Policy in Norway (with L. B. Bachke) 1958. *Leisure interests:* skiing, touring. *Address:* Stortinget, 0026 Oslo 1, Norway.

WILLOTT, (William) Brian, PH.D.; British business executive; b. 14 May 1940; s. of William Harford and Beryl P. M. Willott; m. Alison Leyland Pyke-Lees 1970; two s. two d.; ed. Trinity Coll., Cambridge; Research Assoc., Univ. of Md. 1965-67; Asst. Prin. Bd. of Trade 1967-69, Prin. 1969-73; H.M. Treasury 1973-75; Asst. Sec. Dept. of Industry 1975-78, Sec. Ind. Devt. Unit 1978-80; Sec. Nat. Enterprise Bd. 1980-81; C.E.O. British Tech. Group (Nat. Enterprise Bd. and Nat. Research and Devt. Corpn.) 1981-84; Head, Information Tech. Div., Dept. of Trade and Industry 1984-87, Head, Financial Services Div. 1987-. *Leisure interests:* music, reading, ancient history, gardening. *Address:* Department of Trade and Industry, 10-18 Victoria Street, SW1H 0NN, England. *Telephone:* 01-215 3160.

WILLOUGHBY, Christopher R., M.A.; British economist; b. 24 Feb. 1938, Guildford; s. of Ronald James Edward Willoughby and Constance Louisa (née Sherbrooke) Willoughby; m. Marie-Anne Isabelle Normand 1972; ed. Lambroke School, Marlborough Coll., Univ. of Grenoble, Jt. Services School for Linguists, Balliol Coll., Oxford, Univ. of California, Berkeley;

R.N. 1956-58, Lieut., R.N. Reserve 1958; New York Times Wash. Bureau 1962-63; economist World Bank 1963-, Dir. of Operations, Evaluation Dept. 1973-76, Transport, Water and Telecommunications Dept. 1976-83, Econ. Devt. Inst. 1983-. *Leisure interests:* running, swimming, house remodelling. *Address:* Economic Development Institute, World Bank, 1818 H Street, N.W., Washington D.C. 20433 (Office); 5340 Falmouth Road, Bethesda, Maryland 20816, U.S.A. (Home). *Telephone:* (202) 334-8527 (Office); (301) 320-5582 (Home).

WILLS, Dean Robert, A.M.; Australian business executive; b. 10 July 1933, Australia; s. of Walter W. Wills; m. Margaret F. Wills 1955; one s. two d.; ed. Sacred Heart Coll., S. Australia and S. Australian Inst. of Tech.; Dir. W. D. & H. O. Wills (Australia) 1974-86, Man. Dir. 1977-86, Chair. 1983-86; Dir. AMATIL Ltd. 1975, Deputy Chair. 1983-84, Chair. and Man. Dir. 1984-; Chair. Australian Eagle Insurance Co. 1986-; mem. Business Council of Australia 1984-, Vice-Pres. 1987-88, Pres. 1988-. *Leisure interests:* tennis, vintage cars. *Address:* AMATIL Ltd., 71 Macquarie Street, Sydney, N.S.W. 2000; 44 Warrangi Street, Turramurra, N.S.W. 2075, Australia. *Telephone:* 449.5154.

WILLS, Sir John Spencer, Kt., F.C.I.T.; British business executive; b. 10 Aug. 1904, London; s. of Cedric Spencer Wills and Cécile Charlotte; m. Elizabeth Garcke 1936; two s.; ed. Cleobury Mortimer Coll., Shropshire, and Merchant Taylors' School, London; Dir. and Chair. E. Yorkshire Motor Services Ltd. 1931-65, Dir. and Chair. Birmingham & Midland Motor Omnibus Co. Ltd. 1946-68; Man. Dir. British Electric Traction Co. Ltd. 1946-73, Deputy Chair. 1951-66, Chair. 1966-82; Chair. Nat. Electric Construction Co. Ltd. 1945-, Electrical and Industrial Investment Co. Ltd. 1946-, The Birmingham and Dist. Investment Trust Ltd. 1946-, Rediffusion Ltd. 1947-78, Rediffusion Television Ltd. 1954-78, Wembley Stadium Ltd. 1960-82; Dir. Monotype Corpn. Ltd. 1947- (Deputy Chair. 1953-71); Gov. Royal Shakespeare Theatre, Stratford on Avon 1946-74; Fellow, Chartered Inst. of Transport (Pres. 1950-51), mem. Council of Public Road Transport Assen. (Chair. 1945-46); mem. of Council, Royal Opera House Soc. 1962-74; Vice-Patron, Theatre Royal Windsor Trust 1965-; also occupied in forestry and farming. *Leisure interests:* complete idleness, formerly: flying, swimming, skiing, tennis, riding, shooting. *Address:* 1 Campden House Terrace, Kensington Church Street, London, W8 4BQ; Beech Farm, Battle, Sussex, England. *Telephone:* 01-727 5981; (042 46) 2950.

WILLSON, Francis Michael Glenn, M.A., D.PHIL.; British professor and university administrator; b. 29 Sept. 1924, Carlisle; s. of the late Christopher Glenn Willson and Katherine Mattick; m. Jean Carlyle 1945; two d.; ed. Carlisle Grammar School, Univ. of Manchester, Balliol and Nuffield Colls., Oxford; war service in Merchant Navy 1941-42 and R.A.F. 1943-47; seconded to BOAC 1946-47; Research Officer, Royal Inst. of Public Admin. 1953-60; Research Fellow, Nuffield Coll., Oxford 1955-60; Lecturer in Politics, St. Edmund Hall, Oxford 1958-60; Prof. of Govt., Univ. Coll. of Rhodesia and Nyasaland 1961-64, Dean of Social Studies 1962-64; Prof. of Govt. and Politics, Univ. of Calif., Santa Cruz 1965-74, Provost of Stevenson Coll. 1967-74, Vice-Chancellor Coll. and Student Affairs 1973-74; Visiting Prof. 1985-; Warden of Goldsmith's Coll., London 1974-75; Prin. of London Univ. 1975-78; Vice-Chancellor Murdoch Univ., W. Australia 1978-84. *Publications:* Organization of British Central Government 1914-1956 (with D. N. Chester) 1957, 2nd edn. 1914-1964 1968, Administrators in Action 1961. *Leisure interests:* listening to music, reading. *Address:* 32 Digby Mansions, Hammersmith Bridge Road, London, W6 9DF, England.

WILMOT, Robert William, C.B.E., B.SC., C.B.I.M.; British business executive; b. 2 Jan. 1945, Malvern, Worcs.; s. of Thomas A. W. Wilmot and Frances M. Hull; m. Mary J. Sharkey 1969; two s.; ed. Royal Grammar School, Worcester and Univ. of Nottingham; Micro-electronics Design Eng., Texas Instruments, Bedford 1966, Dept. Man. Advanced Tech. Products 1970, Technical Dir. European Calculator Div., Nice 1974, Man. Professional Calculator Div., Dallas 1975, Man. Dir. Texas Instruments, Bedford 1978-81; Man. Dir. Int. Computers (ICL) 1981, Chief Exec. 1984, Chair. 1984-85; Chair. Wilmot Enterprises Ltd. 1984-; f. and Co-Chair. European Silicon Structures 1985-; Dir. Octagon Industries Ltd. 1986-, Competitive Man. Initiative C.M.I. 1986-, Comproft Holdings PLC 1987-; f. and Dir. MOVID Tech. Inc. 1987-, POQET Inc. 1988-; Partner Euroventurer U.K. and Ireland Programme 1987-; mem. Council, Centre for Business Strategy, London Business School 1987-; f. and Chair. OASIS 1986-; Hon. D.Sc. (Nottingham and City Univs.). *Address:* The White House, Bolney Road, Lower Shiplake, Henley-on-Thames, Oxon., RG9 3PA, England. *Telephone:* (073 522) 4252.

WILMS, Dorothee, DR.RER.POL.; German politician; b. 11 Oct. 1929, Grevenbroich; d. of Lorenz Wilms and Lieselotte Wilms; scientific adviser, Deputy Dir. Dept. of Educ. and Social Research and mem. Admin. Bd., Inst. der Deutschen Wirtschaft 1955-73, Dir. of Research, Inst. for Educational and Socio-political Devt. 1977-82; Part-time lecturer in econs., adult educ. coll. 1960-67; mem. CDU 1961-; mem. Bundestag 1976-; Minister of Educ. and Science 1982-87, of Intra-German Relations March 1987-. *Publications:* numerous articles on politics of education, the family and women. *Leisure interests:* walking, classical music, historical books. *Address:* Ministry for Intra-German Relations, Godesberger Allee 140, 5300 Bonn 2, Federal Republic of Germany. *Telephone:* (0228) 3060.

WILSON, Sir Alan Herries, F.R.S.; British industrial executive; b. 2 July 1906; m. Margaret Monks 1934 (died 1961); two s.; ed. Wallasey Grammar School and Emmanuel Coll., Cambridge; Fellow, Emmanuel Coll., Cambridge 1929-33, Hon. Fellow 1959; Fellow and lecturer, Trinity Coll., Cambridge 1933-45; Univ. lecturer in Mathematics, Cambridge 1933-45; joined Courtaulds Ltd. 1945, Man. Dir. 1954, Deputy Chair. 1957-62; Dir. Int. Computers Holdings Ltd. 1962-72; Chair. Cttee. on Coal Derivatives 1959-60, on Problem of Noise 1960-63; Chair. and Dir. Glaxo Group Ltd. 1963-73; Deputy Chair. Electricity Council 1966-76; mem. Iron and Steel Bd. 1960-67; Hon. Fellow, Inst. of Math., Inst. of Physics; Hon. D.Sc. (Oxford and Edinburgh), Gold Medal of the Inst. of Math. 1984. *Publications:* The Theory of Metals 1936, 1953, Semi-Conductors and Metals 1939, Thermodynamics and Statistical Mechanics 1957. *Address:* 65 Oakleigh Park South, Whetstone, London, N20 9JL, England. *Telephone:* 01-445 3030.

WILSON, Alexander, C.B.E., F.L.A.; British librarian; b. 12 Feb. 1921, Greenock, Scotland; s. of late William Wilson and Amelia Wilson; m. Mary Catherin Traynor 1949; two s.; ed. Bolton Co. Grammar School; Dir. Libraries, Museums and Arts with Dudley Co. Borough 1952-68, with Coventry City Council 1968-72, with Cheshire Co. Council 1972-80; Consultant to Nat. Library of Malaysia 1978, Nat. Library of Pakistan 1983; Dir.-Gen. British Library Reference Div. 1980-86; Pres. Library Assen. 1986, Harold Macmillan Trust 1986-; Fellow, Birmingham Polytechnic; Hon. D.Lit. (Sheffield). *Leisure interests:* music, walking. *Address:* 1 Brockway West, Tattenhall, Chester, CH3 9EZ, England (Home). *Telephone:* (0829) 70179 (Home).

WILSON, Alexander (Sandy) Galbraith; British writer and composer; b. 19 May 1924, Sale, Cheshire; s. of George Wilson and Caroline Humphrey; ed. Harrow School, Oxford Univ. and Old Vic Theatre School; contributed to revues Slings and Arrows, Oranges and Lemons 1948; wrote revues for Watergate Theatre, London, See You Later, See You Again 1951-52; wrote musical The Boy Friend for Players Club Theatre 1953, transferred to Wyndhams Theatre and on Broadway 1954 (London revival 1984), The Buccaneer 1955, Valmouth London 1958, U.S.A. 1960, Chichester 1982, Divorce me Darling 1965; Dir. London revival of The Boy Friend 1967; Composed music for As Dorothy Parker Once Said London 1969; songs for BBC television Charley's Aunt 1969; wrote and performed Sandy Wilson Thanks the Ladies (one man show) London 1971; wrote His Monkey Wife London 1971, The Clapham Wonder 1978, Aladdin (London) 1979. *Publications:* This is Sylvia 1954, The Poodle from Rome 1962, I Could be Happy (autobiog.) 1975, Ivor 1975, The Roaring Twenties 1977. *Leisure interests:* cinema, cookery, travel. *Address:* 2 Southwell Gardens, London, S.W.7, England. *Telephone:* 01-373 6172.

WILSON, Andrew N., M.A., F.R.S.L.; British author; b. 27 Oct. 1950; s. of late N. Wilson and of Jean Dorothy (née Crowder) Wilson; m. Katherine Duncan-Jones 1971; two d.; ed. Rugby School and New Coll., Oxford; Asst. Master Merchant Taylors' School 1975-76; lecturer St. Hugh's Coll. and New Coll., Oxford 1976-81; Literary Ed. Spectator 1981-83; Chancellor's Essay Prize 1975, Ellerton Theological Prize 1975. *Publications:* fiction: The Sweets of Pimlico 1977, Unguarded Hours 1978, Kindly Light 1979, The Healing Art (Somerset Maugham Award) 1980, Who Was Oswald Fish? 1981, Wise Virgin (W. H. Smiths Award) 1982, Scandal 1983, Gentleman in England 1985, Love Unknown 1986, Stray 1987, Incline Our Hearts 1988; non-fiction: The Laird of Abbotsford 1980, A Life of John Milton 1983, Hilaire Belloc 1984, How Can We Know? An Essay on the Christian Religion 1985, The Church in Crisis (jtly.) 1986, The Lion and the Honeycomb 1987, Penfriends from Porlock 1988, Tolstoy (Whitbread Award for Biography and Autobiography) 1988. *Address:* 16 Richmond Road, Oxford, OX1 2JL, England.

WILSON, Sir Angus (Frank Johnstone), Kt., C.B.E., B.A., F.R.S.L.; British writer; b. 11 Aug. 1913, Sussex; s. of William Johnstone-Wilson and Maud (née Caney); ed. Westminster School, and Merton Coll., Oxford; Asst. Keeper, Dept. of Printed Books, British Museum 1936-55; full-time writer 1955-; lecturer, School of English Studies, Univ. of E. Anglia 1963-, Prof. 1966-78, Emer. 1978-; Ewing Lecturer Univ. of Calif 1960, Northcliffe Lecturer Univ. of London 1961, Leslie Stephen lecturer Cambridge 1963, Beckman Prof. Univ. of Calif. 1967, John Hinkley Prof. Johns Hopkins Univ. 1974, Distinguished Visiting Prof. Univ. of Delaware 1977, Georgia State Univ. 1979, Univ. of Mich. 1979, Univ. of Minnesota 1980, Ida Beam Prof. Univ. of Ia. 1978, Univ. Pittsburgh 1981, St. Louis Univ. 1982; mem. Arts Council 1967-69; Chair. Nat. Book League 1971-74; Pres. Dickens Fellowship 1974-75; Pres. Kipling Soc. 1981-87; Pres. Royal Soc. of Literature 1982-87; Foreign Hon. mem. American Acad. and Inst. of Arts and Letters 1980; C.Lit. 1972; Hon. D.Litt. (Univ. of Leicester), (Univs. of E. Anglia and Liverpool) 1979, (Univ. of Sussex) 1981, (Sorbonne) 1983; Chevalier de l'Ordre des Arts et des Lettres 1972. *Publications:* The Wrong Set 1949, Such Darling Dodos 1950, Hemlock and After 1952, For Whom the Cloche Tolls 1953, Emile Zola 1954, The Mulberry Bush (a play, produced Bristol Old Vic 1955, Royal Court Theatre 1956, published 1956), Anglo-Saxon Attitudes 1956, A Bit off the Map 1957, The Middle Age of Mrs. Eliot 1958, The Old Men at the Zoo 1961, The Wild Garden 1963, Late Call 1964, No Laughing Matter 1967, The World of Charles Dickens 1970, As if by Magic 1973, The Naughty Nineties 1976, The Strange Ride of Rudyard Kipling: His Life and Works 1977, Setting the World on Fire 1980, Diversity and Depth in Fiction (literary essays) 1982, Dickens' Portable Viking (ed.) 1982, East Anglia Verse Anthology, Reflections in a Writer's Eye 1986, The Collected Stories of Angus Wilson 1987; also several (unpublished) plays for television. *Leisure interests:* travel, architecture, gardening. *Address:* P.O. Box 95, 13533 San Remy, Provence, France.

WILSON, Sir Anthony, Kt., F.C.A., F.R.S.A.; British accountant; b. 17 Feb. 1928, Leeds; s. of late Charles E. and Martha C. (née Mee) Wilson; m. Margaret J. Hudson 1955; two s. one d.; ed. Giggleswick School, Yorks.; service in R.N. 1946–49; joined John Gordon Walton & Co. 1945–46, 1949–52; mem. staff, Price Waterhouse 1952–61, Partner 1961–84; mem. Govt. Production Statistics Advisory Cttee. 1972–84; Head, Govt. Accountancy Service and Accountancy Adviser to Treasury 1984–88; mem. Council, Inst. of Chartered Accountants in England and Wales 1985–88, Accounting Standards Cttee. 1985–, Auditing Practices Cttee. 1987–88; S.W. Regional Arts Assen. 1983–, Chair. 1988–, Top Salaries Review Body 1989–; Dir. Opera 80 1989–; Chair. Dorset Opera 1988–; Pres. Chandos Chamber Choir 1986–88. *Leisure interests:* fishing, gardening, collecting pottery, opera, golf. *Address:* The Barn House, 89 Newland, Sherborne, Dorset, DT9 3AG, England (Home). *Telephone:* (0935) 815674 (Home).

WILSON, Prof. Arthur James Cochran, F.I.M., F.INST.P., F.R.S.; British professor of crystallography (retd.); b. 28 Nov. 1914, Springhill, Canada; m. Harriett Charlotte Friedeberg 1946; two s. one d.; ed. Dalhousie Univ., Halifax, M.I.T., Univ. of Cambridge; lecturer, then Sr. Lecturer, then Prof. of Physics and Head Dept., Univ. Coll., Cardiff Univ. 1945–65; Prof. of Crystallography Dept. of Physics, Univ. of Birmingham 1965–82, now Prof. Emer.; Emer. Fellow Crystallographic Data Centre, Univ. Chemical Lab., Cambridge 1982–; Ed. Int. Tables for Crystallography 1982–. *Publications:* X-Ray Optics 1949, Mathematical Theory of X-Ray Powder Diffractometry 1963, Elements of X-Ray Crystallography 1970, numerous papers, collaborative books, ed. various books, including Structure and Statistics in Crystallography 1985, Direct Methods, Macromolecular Methods and Crystallographic Statistics 1987. *Address:* Crystallographic Data Centre, University Chemical Laboratory, Lensfield Road, Cambridge, CB2 1EW, England.

WILSON, Brian G., PH.D.; Australian academic; b. 9 April 1930, Belfast, N. Ireland; s. of Charles W. and Isobel C. (née Ferguson) Wilson; m. 1st Barbara Wilkie 1959 (divorced 1975); two s. one d.; m. 2nd Jeanne Henry 1978; ed. Methodist Coll., Belfast, Queens Univ. Belfast and Nat. Univ. of Ireland; Postdoctoral Fellow, Nat. Research Council of Canada 1955–57; Officer-in-charge, Sulphur Mount Lab., Banff, Alberta 1957–60; Assoc. Prof. of Physics, Univ. of Calgary 1960–65, Prof. 1965–70, Dean of Arts and Science 1967–70; Vice-Pres. Simon Fraser Univ., Burnaby, N.C. 1970–78; Vice-Chancellor, Univ. of Queensland 1979–; Hon. LL.D. (Calgary) 1984. *Publications:* over 50 scientific articles in int. journals. *Address:* University of Queensland, St. Lucia, Queensland, Australia 4067 (Office); 55 Walcott Street, St. Lucia, Queensland, Australia 4067 (Home). *Telephone:* 61-7-3772200 (Office); 61-7-8708757 (Home).

WILSON, Charles; British journalist; b. Aug. 1935, Glasgow, Scotland; m. 1st Anne Robinson 1968, one d.; m. 2nd Sally O'Sullivan 1980, one s. one d.; ed. Eastbank School, Glasgow and Kingston Grammar School, Surrey; copy boy, The People 1951; later reporter with Bristol Evening World, News Chronicle and Daily Mail; Ed., Evening Times, Glasgow 1976; later Ed., Glasgow Herald; Ed. Sunday Standard, Glasgow 1981–82; Exec. Ed., The Times 1982, Jt. Deputy Ed. 1984–85, Ed. 1985–. *Leisure interests:* National Hunt racing, collecting Victorian cheese dishes. *Address:* The Times, 1 Pennington Street, London, E1 9DD, England. *Telephone:* 01-782-5000.

WILSON, Sir Charles Haynes, Kt., M.A., LL.D., D.C.L., D.LITT.; British university officer; b. 16 May 1909, Glasgow, Scotland; s. of George Wilson and Florence Hannay; m. Jessie Wilson 1935; one s. two d.; ed. Glasgow Univ. and Oxford Univ.; Fellow and Tutor in Modern History, Corpus Christi Coll., Oxford 1939–52, Jr. Proctor 1945; Prin. Univ. Coll. of Leicester 1952–57; Vice-Chancellor, Univ. of Leicester 1957–61; Prin. and Vice-Chancellor, Univ. of Glasgow 1961–76; Hon. Fellow, Corpus Christi Coll., Oxford 1963. *Address:* Whinnymuir Dalry, Castle Douglas, DG7 3TT, Scotland. *Telephone:* 064-43-218.

WILSON, Charles Henry, C.B.E., LITT.D.; British professor of history; b. 16 April 1916, Market Rasen; s., of Joseph Wilson and Louisa Wilson; one d.; ed. De Aston Grammar School, Market Rasen, Jesus Coll., Cambridge; undertook historical research in Holland and Germany 1937–39; service with R.N.V.R. and Admiralty 1940–45; Fellow, Bursar, Dir. of Studies in History, Jesus Coll., Cambridge 1945–64; Reader in Econ. History, Univ. of Cambridge 1964–65, Prof. 1965–79, Prof. Emer. 1979–; First Prof. of History European Univ. Inst., Florence 1975–80; Visiting Chairs, Harvard and North Western Univs. 1954–55; Ford's Lecturer, Univ. of Oxford 1968–69; Ed. (Jt.) Economic History Review 1960–67; Fellow Royal Danish Acad., Royal Belgian Acad., Litt. Dr. h.c. (Groningen and Louvain), Commdr. Order of Orange-Nassau (Netherlands). *Publications:* Anglo-Dutch Commerce and Finance 1941, History of Unilever 1954, England's Apprenticeship 1965, The Dutch Republic 1968, Queen Elizabeth and Revolt of Netherlands 1970, Cambridge Economic History of Europe, Vols. IV &

V, Ed., 1967–77, First with the News, A History of W. H. Smith 1792–1972 1985. *Leisure interests:* music, talking. *Address:* Jesus College, Cambridge; 23 Storey's Way, Cambridge, CB3 0DP, England (Home).

WILSON, Colin Henry; British writer; b. 26 June 1931, Leicester; s. of Arthur Wilson and Annetta Jones; m. 1st Dorothy Troop 1951, one s.; m. 2nd Joy Stewart 1960, two s. one d.; ed. Gateway Secondary Technical School, Leicester; laboratory asst. 1948–49, civil servant (taxes) 1949–50; R.A.F. 1950, discharged on medical grounds 1950; then navvy, boot and shoe operative, dish washer, plastic moulder; lived Strasbourg 1950, Paris 1953; later factory hand and dish washer; writer 1956–; Writer in Residence, Hollins Coll., Virginia, U.S.A. 1966–67; Visiting Prof., Univ. of Washington 1967–68, Dowling Coll., Majorca 1969, Rutgers Univ., N.J. 1974. *Publications include:* philosophy: The Outsider 1956, Religion and the Rebel 1957, The Age of Defeat 1958, The Strength to Dream 1961, Origins of the Sexual Impulse 1963, Beyond the Outsider 1965, Introduction to the New Existentialism 1966; other non-fiction: Encyclopaedia of Murder 1960, Rasputin and the Fall of of the Romanovs 1964, Brandy of the Damned (music essays) 1965, Eagle and Earwig (literary essays) 1965, Sex and the Intelligent Teenager 1966, Voyage to a Beginning (autobiography) 1968, Shaw: A Reassessment 1969, A Casebook of Murder 1969, Poetry and Mysticism 1970, The Strange Genius of David Lindsay (with E. H. Visiak) 1970, The Occult 1971, New Pathways in Psychology 1972, Strange Powers 1973, A Book of Booze 1974, The Craft of the Novel 1975, The Geller Phenomenon 1977, Mysteries 1978, Beyond The Occult 1988; novels: Ritual in the Dark 1960, Adrift in Soho 1961, The World of Violence 1963, Man Without a Shadow 1963, Necessary Doubt 1964, The Glass Cage 1966, The Mind Parasites 1967, The Philosopher's Stone 1969, The Killer 1970, The God of the Labyrinth 1970, The Black Room 1970, The Schoolgirl Murder Case 1974, The Space Vampires 1976, Men of Strange Powers 1976, Enigmas and Mysteries 1977; *other works include:* The Quest for Wilhelm Reich 1979, The War Against Sleep: the Philosophy of Gurdjieff 1980, Starseekers 1980, Frankenstein's Castle 1980, The Directory of Possibilities (ed. with John Grant) 1981, Poltergeist! 1981, Access to Inner Worlds 1983, Encyclopaedia of Modern Murder (with Donald Seaman) 1983, The Psychic Detectives 1984, The Janus Murder Case 1984, The Personality Surgeon 1984, A Criminal History of Mankind 1984, Encyclopaedia of Scandal (with Donald Seaman) 1985, Afterlife 1985, Rudolf Steiner 1985, Strindberg (play) 1970, Spiderworld—the tower 1987, Encyclopaedia of Unsolved Mysteries (with Damon Wilson) 1987, Aleister Crowley: the nature of the beast 1987, The Misfits 1988. *Leisure interests:* music, mathematics, wine. *Address:* Tetherdown, Trewallock Lane, Gorran Haven, Cornwall, England.

WILSON, Sir David Clive, K.C.M.G., PH.D.; British diplomatist; b. 14 Feb. 1935; s. of Rev. William Skinner Wilson and Enid Wilson; m. Natasha Helen Mary Alexander 1967; two s.; ed. Keble Coll., Oxford; nat. service, The Black Watch 1953–55; entered Foreign Service 1958, Third Sec., Vientiane 1959–60, Second then First Sec., Peking 1963–65, FCO 1965–68, Cabinet Office 1974–77, Political Adviser, Hong Kong 1977–81, Head S. European Dept., FCO 1981–84, Asst. Under-Sec. of State 1984–87; Gov. and Commdr.-in-Chief of Hong Kong April 1987–; Language Student, Hong Kong 1960–62; Ed. China Quarterly 1968–74; Visiting Scholar, Columbia Univ., New York 1972; Hon. LL.D. (Aberdeen) 1988. *Leisure interests:* mountaineering, reading. *Address:* c/o Foreign and Commonwealth Office, London, S.W.1, England.

WILSON, Sir David Mackenzie, Kt., LITT.D., F.B.A., F.S.A.; British Museum director; b. 30 Oct. 1931, Dacre Banks; s. of Rev. J. Wilson; m. Eva Sjögren 1955; one s. one d.; ed. Kingswood School, St. John's Coll., Cambridge, Lund Univ., Sweden; Asst. Keeper, The British Museum 1955–64; Reader in Archaeology, Univ. of London 1964–71, Prof. of Medieval Archaeology 1971–76; Dir. British Museum 1977–; Hon. Fellow Univ. Coll., London. *Publications:* The Anglo-Saxons 1960, Catalogue of Anglo-Saxon Metalwork 700–1100 in the British Museum 1964, Anglo-Saxon Art 1964, The Bayeux Tapestry 1985, Viking Art (with O. Klindt-Jensen) 1966, Three Viking Graves in the Isle of Man (with G. Bersu) 1966, The Vikings and their Origins 1970, The Viking Achievement (with P. Foote) 1970, St. Ninian's Isle and its Treasure (with A. Small and A. C. Thomas) 1973, The Viking Age in the Isle of Man 1974; Editor: The Archaeology of the Anglo-Saxons 1976, The Northern World 1980, The Art of the Anglo-Saxons 1984, The Bayeux Tapestry 1985; many articles and pamphlets. *Address:* c/o The British Museum, London, WC1B 3DG, England.

WILSON, Donald M.; American journalist and publishing executive; b. 27 June 1925; m. Susan M. Neuberger 1957; one s. two d.; ed. Yale Univ.; Air Corps Navigator, Second World War; magazine assignments in 35 countries 1951–61; fmr. Far Eastern Corresp., Life magazine, Chief Washington Correspondent 1957–61; Deputy Dir. U.S. Information Agency 1961–65; Gen. Man. Time-Life Int. 1965–68; Assoc. Publisher Life magazine 1968–69; Vice-Pres. Corp. and Public Affairs, Time Inc. 1969–81, Corp. Vice-Pres. Public Affairs Time Inc. 1981–. *Address:* Time Inc., Time-Life Building, Rockefeller Center, New York, N.Y. 10020 (Office); 4574 Province Line Road, Princeton, N.J. 08540, U.S.A. (Home).

WILSON, E(dgar) Bright, PH.D.; American professor of chemistry; b. 18 Dec. 1908, Gallatin, Tenn.; s. of E. Bright Wilson and Alma Lackey; m. 1st Emily Buckingham 1935, 2nd Therese Bremer 1955; four s. two d.; ed.

Princeton Univ. and Calif. Inst. of Technology; Teaching Fellow in Chem., Calif. Inst. of Technology 1931-33, Fellow 1933-34; Jr. Fellow, Harvard Univ. 1934-36, Asst. Prof. of Chem. 1936-39, Assoc. Prof. 1939-46, Prof. 1946-47, Theodore William Richards Prof. 1947-79, Emer. 1979-; Research Dir. Underwater Explosives Research Laboratory, Woods Hole 1942-44; Chief Div. 2, Nat. Defense Research Cttee. 1944-46; Research Dir. Weapons System Evaluation Group 1952-53; Hon. Trustee, Oceanographic Inst., Woods Hole; Chair. Cttee. on Radioactive Waste Man., N.A.S. 1979-81; Fulbright Grantee and Guggenheim Fellow, Oxford 1949-50; Dr. h.c. (Univ. of Brussels) 1975, (Univ. of Bologna) 1976, D.Sc. (Dickinson Coll.) 1976, (Columbia Univ.) 1979, (Princeton Univ.) 1981, (Harvard and Clarkson Univs.) 1983; American Chemical Soc. Award in Pure Chem., Debye Award, Norris Award in Teaching of Chem., G. N. Lewis Award, Pauling Award, Rumford Medal; Nat. Medal of Science 1975, Antonio Feltrinelli Award 1976, Ferst Award 1977, Pittsburgh Spectroscopy Award 1978, Plyler Award 1978, Richards Medal 1978, Welch Award 1978, Gibbs Award 1979, Lippincott Award 1979, Elliott Cresson Medal Franklin Inst. 1982. *Publications:* Introduction to Quantum Mechanics with Applications to Chemistry (with Linus Pauling) 1935, An Introduction to Scientific Research 1952, Molecular Vibrations: The Theory of Infra-red and Raman Vibrational Spectra (with P. C. Cross and J. C. Decius) 1955. *Address:* 12 Oxford Street, Cambridge, Mass. 02138 (Office); 993 Memorial Drive, Cambridge, Mass. 02138, U.S.A. (Home). *Telephone:* (617) 495-4085 (Office); (617) 354-3088 (Home).

WILSON, Edward Osborne, PH.D.; American university professor and author; b. 10 June 1929, Birmingham, Ala.; s. of the late Edward Osborne Wilson Sr. and of Inez Freeman Huddleston; m. Irene Kelley 1955; one d.; ed. Univ. of Ala. and Harvard Univ.; Jr. Fellow, Soc. of Fellows, Harvard Univ. 1953-56, Prof. of Zoology 1964-76, F. B. Baird Prof. of Science 1976-, Curator of Entomology, Museum of Comparative Zoology, 1972-; Fellow, Guggenheim Foundation 1977-78, Advisory Bd. 1979-, mem. Selection Cttee. 1982-; mem. Bd. of Dirs., World Wildlife Fund 1983-; Org. for Tropical Studies 1984-; Cleveland Prize, A.A.A.S. 1968, Pulitzer Prize in gen. non-fiction 1979; Mercer Award, Ecological Soc. of America 1971, Founders' Memorial Award, Entomological Soc. of America 1972, Distinguished Service Award, American Inst. of Biological Science 1976, Carr Medal, Univ. of Fla. 1978, Leidy Medal, Acad. of Natural Sciences (Philadelphia) 1978, Distinguished Service Award, American Humanist Soc. 1982, Nat. Medal of Science 1977 (U.S.A.), Tyler Prize for Environmental Achievement 1984, L.O. Howard Award, Entomological Soc. of America 1985, Nat. Zoological Park Medal 1987, Ecology Inst. Prize (Fed. Repub. of Germany) 1987. *Publications:* The Theory of Island Biogeography (with R. H. MacArthur) 1967, The Insect Societies 1971, Sociobiology: The New Synthesis 1975, On Human Nature 1978, Caste and Ecology in the Social Insects (with G. F. Oster) 1978, Genes, Mind and Culture (with C. J. Lumsden) 1981, Promethean Fire (with C. J. Lumsden) 1983, Biophilia 1984, Biodiversity (Ed.) 1988; numerous articles on evolutionary biology, entomology and conservation. *Address:* Harvard University, Cambridge, Mass. 02138 (Office); 9 Foster Road, Lexington, Mass. 02173, U.S.A. (Home).

WILSON, Hon. Geoffrey Hazlitt, B.A., F.C.A.; British accountant and business executive; b. 28 Dec. 1929, London; s. of Lord Moran; m. Barbara Jane Hebblethwaite 1955; two s. two d.; ed. Eton Coll. and King's Coll., Cambridge; with English Electric Co. Ltd. 1956-68, Deputy Comptroller 1967-68; Financial Controller (Overseas), General Electric Co. Ltd. 1968-69; Financial Dir., Cables Div., Delta PLC 1969, Group Financial Dir. 1972, Jt. Man. Dir. 1977, Dir. 1977, Deputy Chief Exec. 1980, Chief Exec. 1981-88, Chair. 1982-; Dir. Blue Circle Industries PLC 1981-, English & Int. Trust PLC 1977-; Nat. Westminster Bank PLC (W. Midlands and Wales Regional Bd.) 1985-; Hon. Treasurer, mem. Admin. Council The Royal Jubilee Trusts; Deputy Pres. Eng. Employers' Fed.; Pres. British Fed. of Electrotechnical and Allied Mfrs'. Asscns. 1987-88; Hon. mem. The Hundred Group of Chartered Accountants (Chair. 1979-81); mem. Court of Appeal, Worshipful Co. of Chartered Accountants in England and Wales. *Leisure interests:* family, reading, vintage cars. *Address:* Delta PLC, 1 Kingsway, London, WC2B 6XF, England. *Telephone:* 01-836 3535.

WILSON, Sir Geoffrey Masterman, K.C.B., C.M.G.; British international civil servant; b. 7 April 1910; s. of late Alexander Cowan Wilson and Edith Jane Brayshaw; m. Julie Stafford Trowbridge 1946 (divorced 1979); two s. two d.; ed. Manchester Grammar School, Oriel Coll., Oxford, and Middle Temple; practised law as barrister 1935-39; served in British Embassy, Moscow and Russian Dept. of Foreign Office 1940-45; in H.M. Treasury 1947-51, 1953-58; Dir. Colombo Plan Technical Co-operation Bureau 1951-53; Under-Sec. Overseas Finance Div., H.M. Treasury and mem. Man. Bd. of European Payments Union 1956-58; Financial Attaché, British Embassy, Washington and Alt. Exec. Dir. for U.K., World Bank, Int. Finance Corpn. and Int. Devt. Assen. 1958-61; Consultant, World Bank Sept.-Dec. 1961; Dir. of Operations for S. Asia and the Middle East 1961-62; Vice-Pres. World Bank 1962-66; Deputy Sec. Ministry of Overseas Devt. 1966-68, Perm. Sec. 1968-71; Deputy Sec.-Gen., Commonwealth Secr. 1971; Chair. Race Relations Bd. 1971-77, Oxfam 1977-83; Hon. Fellow, Wolfson Coll., Cambridge 1971. *Address:* 4 Polstead Road, Oxford, OX2 6TN, Oxon., England.

WILSON, Georges; French theatre and film director; b. 16 Oct. 1921, Champigny-sur-Marne; m. Nicole Mulon 1956; two s.; ed. Centre dramatique de la rue Blanche, Paris; acted in two plays in Grenier-Hussenot Company 1947; entered Comédie de l'Ouest 1950; entered Théâtre Nat. Populaire (T.N.P.) 1952, played important roles in almost all the plays; Dir. L'école des femmes, Le client du matin (Théâtre de l'Oeuvre), Un otage (Théâtre de France), La vie de Galilée, Lumières de Bohème, La folle de Chaillot, Le diable et le bon Dieu, Chêne et lapins angora, Les prodiges 1971, Turandot 1971, Long voyage vers la nuit 1973, Othello 1975, Un habit pour l'hiver 1979, Huis clos, K2 1983, l'Escalier 1985; Dir. T.N.P. 1963-72; Chair. Interim Action Cttee. British Film Authority 1979; Chevalier, Légion d'honneur, Officier, Ordre nat. du Mérite, Chevalier, Ordre des Arts et Lettres. *Films directed include:* Une aussi longue absence, La jument verte, Le Caïd, Terrain vague, Lucky Joe, Dragées au poivre, Chair de poule, Max et les ferrailleurs 1970, Blanche 1971, Nous sommes tous en liberté provisoire 1973, Asphalte 1981, L'honneur d'un capitaine 1982, Itinéaires bis 1983, Tango, l'exil de Gardel 1985; several TV appearances. *Address:* Moulin de Vilegris, Clairefontaine-en-Yvelines, 78120 Rambouillet, France (Home).

WILSON, Gordon (see Wilson, (Robert) Gordon).

WILSON, Sir (James) Harold (see Wilson of Rievaulx, Baron).

WILSON, James Tylee; American company director; b. 18 June 1931, Teaneck, N.J.; s. of the late Eric J. and Florence Q. Wilson; m. Patricia F. Harrington 1970; two s. one d.; ed. Lafayette Coll.; Scott Paper Co. 1953-54; mil. service 1954-56; Zone Sales Man. Procter & Gamble 1956-60; Regional Sales Man. Chesebrough-Pond's Inc. 1960-63, Vice-Pres. Sales 1963-69, Pres. Chesebrough-Ponds (Canada) Ltd. 1969-71, Corp. Vice-Pres. and Gen. Man. Health and Beauty Products Div. of Chesebrough-Ponds Inc. 1971-72, Group Vice-Pres., Dir. and mem. Exec. Cttee. 1972-74; Pres., C.E.O. and Dir. RJR Foods Inc. 1974-76; Pres. and C.E.O. R. J. Reynolds Tobacco Int. Inc. 1976, Chair. and C.E.O. 1976-78; Exec. Vice-Pres. and Dir. R. J. Reynolds Industries Inc. 1976-79, Pres. and Dir. 1979-84, Pres. and C.E.O. 1983-84, Chair. and C.E.O. 1984-86, C.E.O. R.J.R. Nabisco (after merger of Reynolds with Nabisco) 1985-86, Chair. 1985-87; Pres. J. Tylee Assocs. 1987-; Dir. numerous cos. *Leisure interests:* tennis, fishing and boating. *Address:* J. Tylee Associates, 301 W. Bay Street, Suite 2706, Jacksonville, Fla. 32202-4425, U.S.A.

WILSON, Jean Donald, M.D.; American professor of internal medicine; b. 26 Aug. 1932, Wellington, Tex.; s. of J. D. Wilson and Maggie E. (Hill) Wilson; ed. Hillsboro Coll., Univ. of Texas at Austin and Univ. of Texas Southwestern Medical School, Dallas; Medical Intern and Asst. Resident in Internal Medicine, Parkland Memorial Hosp. Dallas 1955-58; Clinical Assoc. Nat. Heart Inst. Bethesda, Md. 1958-60; Instr. Univ. of Texas Health Science Center 1960-, Prof. of Internal Medicine 1968-; Established Investigator, American Heart Assen. 1960-65; Travelling Fellow, Royal Soc. of Medicine, Strangeways Research Lab. Cambridge 1970; mem. N.A.S., American Acad. of Arts and Sciences etc.; several honours and awards. *Publications:* 200 scientific articles in various medical journals. *Leisure interests:* gardening, opera. *Address:* Division of Endocrinology, Department of Internal Medicine, University of Texas Southwestern Medical Center at Dallas, 5323 Harry Hines Boulevard, Dallas, Tex. 75235, U.S.A. *Telephone:* (214) 688-3494.

WILSON, Sir John Foster, Kt., C.B.E., M.A.; British international health administrator; b. 20 Jan. 1919, Nottingham; s. of Rev. George and Leonore Carrick Wilson; m. Chloe J. McDermid 1944; two d.; ed. Worcester Coll. for the Blind and St. Catherine's Coll., Oxford; founded Royal Commonwealth Soc. for the Blind 1950, Dir. 1950-84, Vice-Pres. 1983; First Pres. Int. Agency for Prevention of Blindness 1975, Hon. Life Pres. 1982; initiated IMPACT (Int. Initiative against Avoidable Disablement) 1982; Sr. Consultant to UNDP 1983-. *Publications:* Travelling Blind 1964, Preventable Disablement: The Global Challenge 1983, World Blindness and its Prevention (Vol. I) 1979, (Vol. II) 1984. *Leisure interests:* music, radio, gardening, wine making. *Address:* 22, The Cliff, Roedean, Brighton, East Sussex, BN2 5RE, England. *Telephone:* (0273) 607667.

WILSON, John P., M.A., T.D.; Irish politician and university lecturer; b. 8 July 1923, Co. Cavan; s. of John and Brigid Wilson; m. Ita M. Ward 1953; one s. four d.; ed. St. Mel's Coll., Longford, Nat. Univ. of Ireland, Univ. of London and Zaragoza Univ.; taught in England and Ireland 1947-73; mem. of the Dáil 1973-; Opposition Spokesman on Educ. and the Arts 1973-77, Jan.-Dec. 1982; Minister for Educ. 1977-81, for Transport and for Posts and Telegraphs 1982; Opposition Spokesman on Transport 1983-87; Minister for Tourism and Transport 1987-; Pres. Perm. Comm., Eurocontrol 1989-. *Leisure interests:* theatre, reading, fishing, Gaelic football and hurling, cruising. *Address:* Kilgolagh, Co. Cavan; 13 Braemor Avenue, Churchtown, Dublin 14, Ireland. *Telephone:* 01-789181 (Office); (043) 81130.

WILSON, John Tuzo, C.C., O.B.E., PH.D., SC.D., LL.D., F.R.S., F.R.S.C.; Canadian geologist; b. 24 Oct. 1908, Ottawa; s. of John Armitstead Wilson, C.B.E., and Henrietta Loetitia (née Tuzo); m. Isabel Jean Dickson 1938; two d.; ed. Ashbury Coll. School, Ottawa, Univs. of Toronto and Cambridge, and Princeton Univ.; summer field parties 1924-35; Asst. Geologist, Geological Survey of Canada 1936-39; Field Service and Staff (Col.), Canadian Army 1939-46; Prof. of Geophysics, Univ. of Toronto 1946-74, Emer. 1977-,

Fellow, Massey Coll., Univ. of Toronto 1962-, Prin. Erindale Coll., Univ. of Toronto 1967-74; Dir.-Gen. Ontario Science Centre 1974-85; Chancellor, York Univ., Toronto 1983-87; Pres. Int. Union of Geodesy and Geophysics 1957-60; Pres. American Geophysical Union 1980-82; Trustee, Nat. Museums of Canada 1967-74; Foreign Assoc., U.S. Nat. Acad. of Sciences; Bucher Medal, American Geophysical Union; Wollaston Medal, Geological Soc. of London; Penrose Medal, Geological Soc. of America; Carty Medal, U.S. N.A.S.; Civic Award of Merit, City of Toronto, Vetlesen Prize, Columbia Univ. Encyclopaedia Britannica Award 1986, Wegener Medal, European Union of Geosciences 1989, Killam Award, Canada Council 1989; Hon. F.R.S.E. 1986. *Publications:* Physics and Geology (with J. A. Jacobs and R. D. Russell) 1959, 2nd edn. 1973, One Chinese Moon 1959, IGY: Year of the New Moons 1961, Continents Adrift (Ed.) 1973, Unglazed China 1973, Continents Adrift and Continents Aground (Ed.) 1976; more than 100 scientific papers. *Leisure interests:* visits to 200 univs. and 100 countries, North Pole to Antarctica, walking and sailing the Great Lakes in a Hong Kong junk. *Address:* 27 Pricefield Road, Toronto, Ont., M4W IZ8, Canada. *Telephone:* (416) 923-4244.

WILSON, Linda S., PH.D.; American university administrator and chemist; b. 10 Nov. 1936, Washington D.C.; d. of Fred M. Smith and Virginia D. (Thompson) Smith; m. 1st Malcolm C. Whatley 1957 (divorced); one d.; m. 2nd Paul A. Wilson 1970; one step-d.; ed. Tulane Univ. and Univ. of Wisconsin (Madison); Asst. Vice-Chancellor for Research, Washington, Univ., St Louis, Mo. 1968-74, Assoc. Vice-Chancellor 1974-75; Assoc. Vice-Chancellor for Research, Univ. of Ill., Urbana, Ill. 1975-85, Assoc. Dean, Graduate Coll. 1978-85; Vice-Pres. for Research, Univ. of Mich., Ann Arbor, Mich. 1985-; mem. Inst. of Medicine (N.A.S.); Fellow A.A.A.S.; Distinguished Contribution to Research Admin. Award, Soc. of Research Admins. *Publications:* 7 book chapters, 10 journal articles, 6 maj. reports, 4 commissioned studies, 12 papers on chem., science policy and research policy. *Address:* University of Michigan, 4080 Fleming Administration Building, Ann Arbor, Mich. 48109; 2524 Blueberry Lane, Ann Arbor, Mich. 48103, U.S.A. (Home). *Telephone:* (313) 764-1185 (Office).

WILSON, Very Rev. Lois Miriam, O.C., D.MIN.; Canadian ecclesiastic; b. 8 April 1927, Winnipeg, Manitoba; d. of Rev. Dr. E. G. D. Freeman and Ada M. Davis; m. Rev. Dr. Roy F. Wilson 1950; two s. two d.; ordained United Church of Canada 1965; Minister, First Church United, Thunder Bay, Ont. 1965-69, Hamilton, Ont. 1969-78, Chalmers United Church, Kingston, Ont. 1978-80; Pres. Canadian Council of Churches 1976-79; Moderator, United Church of Canada 1980-82; Dir. Ecumenical Forum of Canada 1983-89; Pres. World Council of Churches 1983-; The United Church of Canada McGeachy Sr. Scholar 1989-91; mem. Bd. Canadian Inst. for Int. Peace and Security, Amnesty Int. 1978-, Refugee Status Advisory Bd. 1985-, Canadian Assen. of Adult Educ. 1987-, Civil Liberties Assen. of Canada 1987-, Co-op Program in Int. Devt., Univ. of Toronto 1987-, Public Review Bd., Canada 1989-; 11 hon. degrees; Pearson Peace Prize 1985; World Federalist Peace Prize 1985; Queen's Jubilee Medal; 7 hon. degrees. *Publication:* Like a Mighty River 1981. *Leisure interests:* skiing, sailing, canoeing, reading. *Address:* 11 Madison Avenue, Toronto, Ont., M5R 2S2 (Office); 482 Markham Street, Toronto, Ont., M6G 2L3, Canada (Home). *Telephone:* 416-924-9351 (Office); 416-531-1732 (Home).

WILSON, Gen. Louis Hugh, B.A.; American marine corps officer; b. 11 Feb. 1920, Brandon, Miss.; s. of Louis and Bertha (née Buchann) Wilson; m. Jane Clark 1944; one d.; ed. Millsaps Coll.; enlisted in Marine Corps Reserve 1941, Second Lieut. 1941, 9th Marine Regt., San Diego, Guadalcanal, Efate, Bougainville; Capt. 1943; participated in assault on Guam 1944; Company C.O., Camp Pendleton 1944; Detachment Commdr., Washington, D.C. 1944-46; Dean, later Asst. Dir. Marine Corps Inst., later ADC to Commdg: Gen. of Fleet Marine Force, Pacific; Recruiting Officer, N.Y.; Lieut.-Col. 1951; exec. posts at Basic School, Quantico, Va.; C.O., Camp Barrett 1951-54; with 1st Marine Div. as Asst. G-3 in Korea 1954-55; Head of Operations, HQ Marine Corps 1956-68; C.O., Test and Training Regt., then of Basic School, Quantico 1958-61; Deputy Chief of Staff, HQ Marine Corps 1962-65; Asst. Chief of Staff, G-3 1st Marine Div., Repub. of Viet-Nam 1965; Command, 6th Marine Corps District, Atlanta, Ga. 1966; Brig.-Gen. 1966; Legis. Asst. to Commdt. of Marine Corps 1967-68; Chief of Staff, HQ Fleet Marine Force, Pacific 1968-70; Maj.-Gen. 1970; Command, 1st Marine Amphibious Force, 3rd Marine Div., Okinawa 1970; Dir. of Educ., Quantico 1971-72; Lieut.-Gen. 1972; Command, Fleet Marine Force, Pacific 1972-75; 26th Commdt. Marine Corps 1975-79; designated mem. Jt. Chiefs of Staff Oct. 1978-; mem. Bd. Dirs. Merrill Lynch and Co., Fluor Corpn., La. Lands Exploration Co., Unifirst Savings and Loan Assen.; Hon. LL.D. 1976; Hon. D.Hum. 1978; Medal of Honor 1944, Legion of Merit with Combat V and 2 Gold Stars, Purple Heart with 2 Stars, Cross of Gallantry with Gold Star (Repub. of Viet-Nam) 1965, Order of Nat. Security Merit (Repub. of Korea), GUK-SEON Medal, Commdr., Legion of Honour (Philippines), Outstanding American Award 1975, Int. Order of Merit 1976, Spanish Grand Cross of Naval Merit 1977, Order of Nat. Security Merit, Tong-Il Medal (Korea) 1977, Distinguished American Award 1977, Def. D.S.M. *Leisure interests:* hunting, golf. *Address:* The Barrington, Box 19, 1200 Meadowbrook Road, Jackson, Miss. 39206, U.S.A.

WILSON, Michael Holcombe; Canadian politician; b. 4 Nov. 1937, Toronto; s. of Harry Holcombe Wilson and Constance (née Lloyd) Wilson; m. Margaret Smellie 1964; two s. one d.; ed. Upper Canada Coll., Univ. of

Toronto; fmr. Exec. Vice-Pres. Dominion Securities investment firm; M.P. 1979-, Minister of State for Int. Trade 1979; fmr. mem. Fed. Progressive Conservative Party Priorities and Planning Cttee., fmr. Chair. Caucus Cttee. for Econ. Devt. and Job Creation, fmr. Adviser on Prime Minister's Econ. Council; Minister of Finance Sept. 1984-; Progressive Conservative Party (cand. for leadership 1983). *Address:* Department of Finance, Place Bell Canada, 160 Elgin Street, Ottawa, Ont., K1A OG5, Canada. *Telephone:* (613) 992-1573.

WILSON, Nigel Guy, M.A., F.B.A.; British academic; b. 23 July 1935, London; s. of Noel Wilson and Joan L. Wilson; ed. Univ. Coll. School and Corpus Christi Coll., Oxford; Lecturer, Merton Coll., Oxford 1957-62; Fellow and Tutor in Classics, Lincoln Coll., Oxford 1962-; Gordon Duff Prize 1968. *Publications:* Scribes and Scholars (with L. D. Reynolds) (2nd edn.) 1974, An Anthology of Byzantine Prose 1971, Medieval Greek Bookhands 1973, St. Basil on the Value of Greek Literature 1975, Scholia in Aristophanis Acharnenses 1975, Menander Rhetor (with D. A. Russell) 1981, Scholars of Byzantium 1983. *Leisure interests:* bridge, squash, real tennis. *Address:* Lincoln College, Oxford, OX1 3DR, England. *Telephone:* (0865) 279794.

WILSON, Olin C., PH.D.; American astronomer; b. 13 Jan. 1909, San Francisco, Calif.; s. of Olin and Sophie Wilson; m. Katherine E. Johnson 1943; one s. one d.; ed. Univ. of California (Berkeley), and Calif. Inst. of Tech.; Asst. Mount Wilson Observatory 1931-36, Asst. Astronomer 1936-50, Astronomer, Mount Wilson and Palomar Observatories 1950-75 (retd.); Russell Lecture American Astronomical Soc. 1977; mem. N.A.S.; Bruce Medal, Astronomical Soc. of the Pacific 1984. *Publications:* numerous research papers, chiefly in stellar and nebular spectroscopy. *Leisure interests:* reading, hiking. *Address:* 1754 Locust Street, Pasadena, Calif. 91106, U.S.A. (Home). *Telephone:* 577-1122 (Office); 796-6436 (Home).

WILSON, Pete, LL.B.; American lawyer and politician; b. 23 Aug. 1933, Lake Forest, Ill.; s. of James Boone and Margaret (Callahan) Wilson; m. 1st Betty Robertson (divorced); m. 2nd Gayle Edlund Graham 1983; admitted to Calif. Bar; Asst. Exec. Dir. Republican Assen., San Diego Co. 1963-64; Exec. Dir. San Diego Co. Republican Cen. Comm. 1964-65; legal service officer, Calif. State Republican Cen. Comm. 1965; mem. Calif. Ass. 1967-71; Mayor of San Diego 1971-83; Senator from Calif. Jan. 1983-; mem. Presidential Advisory Cttee. on Environmental Quality, Task Force Land Use and Urban Growth Policy. *Address:* Hart Senate Office Building, 720, Washington, D.C. 20510, U.S.A.

WILSON, Robert, C.B.E., PH.D., F.INST.P., F.R.S.; British astrophysicist; b. 16 April 1927; s. of Robert G. Wilson and Anne Riddle; m. Fiona Nicholson; ed. South Shields High School and Univs. of Durham and Edinburgh; astronomer, Royal Observatory, Edinburgh 1952-57; NRC Research Fellow, Dominion Astrophysical Observatory, B.C., Canada 1957-58; Leader, Plasma Spectroscopy Group, Atomic Energy Research Establishment, Harwell 1958-62; Head, Spectroscopy Div. Culham Lab., Oxon. 1962-68; Dir. SRC Astrophysics Research Unit, Culham 1968-72; Perren Prof. of Astronomy, Univ. Coll. London 1972-, Dean of Science 1982-85, Head, Dept. of Physics and Astronomy 1987-; Chair. Anglo-Australian Telescope Bd. 1986-, James Clerk Maxwell Telescope Bd. 1987-; mem. Cospar Bureau; Science Award, Int. Acad. of Astronautics; Herschel Medal, Royal Astronomical Soc, U.S. Design Award for Int. Ultraviolet Explorer Satellite 1988, Pres. Award for Design Excellence (U.S.A.) 1988. *Publications:* nearly 200 papers in optical astronomy, plasma spectroscopy, solar physics and ultraviolet astronomy. *Address:* Department of Physics and Astronomy, University College, Gower Street, London, WC1E 6BT, England.

WILSON, (Robert) Gordon, LL.D.; British (Scottish) politician and solicitor; b. 16 April 1938, Glasgow, Scotland; s. of Robert George Wilson and Robina Wilson; m. Edith Hassall 1965; two d.; ed. Douglas High School and Edinburgh Univ.; Asst. Nat. Sec. Scottish Nat. Party 1963-64, Nat. Sec. 1964-71, Exec. Vice-Chair. 1972-73, Sr. Vice-Chair. 1973-74, Chair. 1979-; M.P. for Dundee E. 1974-87; Party Spokesman on Oil and Energy 1974-87, Jt. Spokesman on Devolution 1976-79; Rector of Univ. of Dundee 1983-86. *Leisure interests:* photography, sailing. *Address:* 48 Monifieth Road, Dundee, DD5 2RX, Scotland (Home).

WILSON, Robert McLachlan, PH.D., B.D., F.B.A.; British professor of biblical criticism; b. 13 Feb. 1916, Gourock, Scotland; s. of Hugh McLachlan Wilson and Janet N. Struthers; m. Enid Mary Bomford 1945; two s.; ed. Greenock Acad., Royal High School, Edin., Edin. and Cambridge Univs.; Minister of Rankin Church, Strathaven 1946-54; Lecturer in New Testament Language and Literature, St Mary's Coll., Univ. of St. Andrews 1954-64, Sr. Lecturer 1964-69, Prof. (personal chair) 1969-78, Prof. of Biblical Criticism 1978-83; Assoc. Ed. New Testament Studies 1967-77, Ed. 1977-83; Hon. D.D. (Aberdeen) 1982; Hon. mem. Soc. of Biblical Literature. *Publications:* The Gnostic Problem 1958, Studies in the Gospel of Thomas 1960, The Gospel of Philip 1962, Gnosis and the New Testament 1968, Nag Hammadi and Gnosis (Ed.) 1978; Translation Ed. of: Hennecke-Schneemelcher Vol. 1 1963, Vol. 2 1965, New Testament Apocrypha 1963, Foerster, Gnosis Vol. 1 1972, Vol. 2 1974, Haenchen, Acts 1971, The Future of Coptic Studies 1978, Rudolph, Gnosis 1983, Commentary on Hebrews 1987. *Leisure interest:* golf. *Address:* 10 Murrayfield Road, St. Andrews, Fife, KY16 9NB, Scotland. *Telephone:* (0334) 74331.

WILSON, Robert Rathbun, PH.D.; American professor of physics; b. 4 March 1914, Frontier, Wyo.; s. of Platt E. Wilson and Edith Rathbun; m.

Jane Inez Scheyer 1940; three s.; ed. Univ. of California at Berkeley; Instructor, Princeton Univ. 1940–42, Asst. Prof. and Head of Isotron Devt. Project 1942–45; Leader Cyclotron Group, then Head of Experimental Research Div., Manhattan Project, Los Alamos, N.M. 1944–46; Assoc. Prof. of Physics Harvard Univ. 1946–47; Prof. of Physics and Dir. Lab. of Nuclear Studies, Cornell Univ. 1947–67; Guggenheim Fellowship 1955–56, 1961–62; Exchange Prof. Univ. of Paris 1954–55; Fulbright Fellowship, Rome 1961–62; Dir. Fermi Nat. Accelerator Lab., Batavia, Ill. 1967–78; Prof. of Physics, Univ. of Chicago 1967–78, Peter B. Ritzma Prof. 1978–80; Michael Pupin Prof. Colombia Univ. 1980–83; mem. Fed. of American Scientists (first Chair.), N.A.S., American Physical Soc., A.A.A.S., American Philosophical Soc.; Hon. Sc.D. (Univ. of Bonn) 1978; Elliot Cresson Medal 1964, Nat. Medal of Science 1973, Enrico Fermi Award 1984. *Address:* Department of Physics, Columbia University, Broadway and W. 116th, New York, N.Y. 10027, U.S.A.

WILSON, Robert Woodrow, PH.D.; American radio astronomer; b. 10 Jan. 1936, Houston; s. of Ralph Woodrow Wilson, and Fannie May (née Willis) Wilson; m. Elizabeth Rhoads Sawin 1958; two s. one d.; ed. Rice Univ., Calif. Inst. of Tech.; mem. of Technical Staff, AT & T Bell Labs., Holmdel, N.J. 1963–76, Head of Radio Physics Research Dept. 1976–; mem. N.A.S., American Astronomical Soc., American Physical Soc., Int. Astronomical Union; Henry Draper Award 1977; Herschel Award 1977; Nobel Prize For Physics 1978. *Publications:* numerous articles in scientific journals. *Leisure interests:* running, skiing, playing piano. *Address:* 9 Valley Point Drive, Holmdel, N.J. 07733, U.S.A. *Telephone:* (201) 671-7807.

WILSON, Rt. Rev. Roger Plumpton, K.C.V.O., M.A., D.D.; British ecclesiastic; b. 3 Aug. 1905, Manchester; s. of Canon Clifford Plumpton and Hester Marion (Wansey) Wilson; m. Mabel Joyce Avery 1935; two s. one d.; ed. Winchester Coll., and Keble Coll., Oxford; Classical Master Shrewsbury School 1928–30 and 1932–34, St. Andrew's, Grahamstown, S. Africa 1930–32; ordained Deacon 1935; Curate St. Paul's Liverpool 1935–38; Curate St. John's, Westminster 1938–39; Vicar of South Shore, Blackpool 1939–45, Radcliffe-on-Trent, Notts. 1945–49; Archdeacon of Nottingham 1945–49; Bishop of Wakefield 1949–58; Bishop of Chichester 1958–74; Clerk of the Closet to the Queen 1963–75; mem. of Presidium of the Conf. of European Churches 1967–74. *Address:* Kingsett, Wrington, Bristol, BS18 7NH, England.

WILSON, Sir Roland, K.B.E., D.PHIL., PH.D.; Australian economist; b. 7 April 1904, Ulverstone, Tasmania; s. of Thomas and Mabel (née Inglis) Wilson; m. 1st Valeska Thompson 1930 (died 1971), 2nd Joyce Clarice Chivers 1975; ed. Univs. of Tasmania, Oxford and Chicago; Lecturer in Econs., Tasmania Univ. 1930–32; Economist in Commonwealth Statistician's Office 1932–35, Commonwealth Statistician and Econ. Adviser to Treasury 1936–40, 1946–51; Sec. Commonwealth Dept. of Labour and Nat. Service 1941–46; Chair. UN Economic and Employment Comm. 1948–51; Sec. to the Treasury 1951–66; Chair. Commonwealth Banking Corpn. 1966–75, Qantas Airways, Qantas-Wentworth Hotel 1966–73; fmr. Dir. MCC Ltd., ICI Australia; Hon. Fellow, The Acad. of Social Sciences in Australia 1972; Hon. LL.D. (Univ. of Tasmania). *Publications:* Capital Imports and the Terms of Trade 1931, Public and Private Investment in Australia 1939, Facts and Fancies of Productivity 1946. *Leisure interests:* cabinet-making, engineering. *Address:* 64 Empire Circuit, Forrest, Canberra, A.C.T. 2603, Australia. *Telephone:* (062) 95-2560.

WILSON, Stanley John, C.B.E., C.A.(S.A.), F.R.S.A., F.C.I.S., A.S.A.A., A.C.M.A.; South African oil executive; b. 23 Oct. 1921, Johannesburg; s. of Joseph Wilson and Jessie Cormack; m. Molly Ann Clarkson 1952; two step s.; ed. King Edward VII School, Johannesburg, Witwatersrand Univ.; posts held 1945–73; Chartered Accountant, Savory & Dickinson; Sec. and Sales Man., Rhodesian Timber Holdings; Chair. and Chief Exec. for S. Africa, Vacuum Oil Co.; Regional Vice-Pres. for S. and E. Africa, Mobil Petroleum; Pres. Mobil Sekiyu; Pres. Mobil Europe Inc. 1973–75; Pres. Mobil East Inc. 1975–; Chief Exec. and Man. Dir. The Burmah Oil Co. Ltd.; Man. Dir. and Chief Exec. Burmah Group 1980–82; Chair. Burmah Oil Trading 1980–82; Underwriting mem. Lloyds, Fellow, Inst. of Petroleum, B.I.M., R.S.A.; Assoc., Inst. of Cost and Man. Accountants, Soc. of Inc. Accountants and Auditors; Freeman of the City of London; mem. Guild Freeman; Liveryman of Worshipful Co. of Basketmakers; Companion (B.I.M.); Wallace Memorial Prize, England. *Leisure interests:* golf, shooting, fishing. *Address:* The Jetty, P.O. Box 751, Plettenberg Bay 6600, Cape Province, South Africa. *Telephone:* Plettenberg Bay 9624.

WILSON, Thomas, O.B.E., PH.D., F.B.A., F.R.S.E.; British university professor; b. 23 June 1916, Belfast; s. of John B. Wilson and Margaret E. Wilson; m. Dorothy Joan Parry, MVO 1943; one s. two d.; ed. Queen's Univ., Belfast and L.S.E.; Mynors Fellowship in Econ., Univ. Coll., Oxford 1946–58; Ed. Oxford Econ. Papers 1948–58; Adam Smith Prof. of Political Econ., Glasgow Univ. 1958–82; Prof. Emer. with hon. appointments at Glasgow and Bristol Univs. *Publications:* Fluctuations in Income and Employment 1942, Oxford Studies in the Price of Mechanism 1952, Inflation 1961, Planning and Growth 1964, The Political Economy of the Welfare State 1982, Inflation, Unemployment and the Market 1984, Unemployment and the Labour Market 1987, Ulster: Conflict or Consent 1989. *Leisure interests:* walking, photography. *Address:* 1 Chatford House, The Promenade, Clifton, BS8 3NG, England. *Telephone:* (0272) 730741.

WILSON, T(hornton Arnold), M.SC.; American aircraft company executive; b. 8 Feb. 1921, Sikeston, Mo.; s. of Thornton Arnold and Daffodil (née Allen) Wilson; m. Grace Miller 1944; three c.; ed. Iowa State Coll. and Calif. Inst. of Tech.; joined Boeing Co., Seattle 1943, Draughtsman on mil. transport version of B-29, The Boeing Co. 1943, worked on B-47 bomber programme, then became Project Engineer for B-52, Asst. Chief Tech. Staff, Project Eng. Man. 1957–58, leader of Boeing's contribution to Int. Continental Ballistic Missile Program 1960, Vice-Pres., Man. Minuteman Branch, Aerospace Div. 1962–64, Vice-Pres. and Head of Corp. HQ's Operations and Planning 1964–66, Exec. Vice-Pres. 1966–68, Pres. and C.E.O. 1969–72, Pres. 1972–86, Chair. 1972–87, C.E.O. 1972–86, Hon. Chair. Jan. 1988–; Sloan Fellow M.I.T. 1952; mem. Corpn. of M.I.T., Bd. of Govs. of Iowa State Univ.; Bd. of Govs. Aerospace Industries Assen.; Bd. of Dirs. of Seattle-First Nat. Bank, U.S. Steel and Paccar Inc.; Hon. Fellow, A.I.A.A. *Leisure interests:* shoot pool, bee-keeping, swimming, golf. *Address:* The Boeing Company, P.O. Box 3707, Seattle, Wash. 98124, U.S.A. *Telephone:* (206) 655-6707.

WILSON, Trevor Gordon, M.A., D.PHIL., F.R.HIST.S., F.A.H.A.; New Zealand professor of history; b. 24 Dec. 1928, Auckland; s. of late Gordon Wilson and of Winifred Wilson; m. Jane Verney 1957; two d.; ed. Mount Albert Grammar School, Univs. of Auckland and Oxford; Asst. Lecturer in History Canterbury Univ. 1952, Auckland Univ. 1953–55; Research Asst. in Govt. Univ. of Manchester 1956–59; lecturer then Sr. Lecturer in History Univ. of Adelaide 1960–67, Prof. 1968–; Commonwealth Fellow St. John's Coll., Cambridge 1972; Visiting Fellow Magdalen Coll., Oxford 1987; Nuffield Dominion Travelling Fellowship 1964–65; Univ. of N.Z. Overseas Travelling Scholarship 1953; Gilbert Campion Prize (jt. winner) 1960, Higby Prize 1965. *Publications:* The Downfall of the Liberal Party (1914–35) 1966, The Political Diaries of C. P. Scott 1911–28 1970, The Myriad Faces of War: Britain and the Great War 1914-18 1986. *Leisure interests:* collecting jazz records, swimming and orienteering. *Address:* Department of History, University of Adelaide, North Terrace, S. Australia 5001.

WILSON, William Douglas, B.A., LL.B., F.R.S.A.; South African lawyer and business executive; b. 13 July 1915, Johannesburg; s. of Douglas and Jessie Frances Wilson; m. Beatrice Helen Buchanan 1947; one s. two d.; ed. St. John's Coll., Johannesburg, Michaelhouse, Natal, Cambridge Univ.; called to the Bar (Middle Temple), London; Advocate, Supreme Court of S.A. 1938–; served World War II with 1st S.A. Div. and British Mil. Mission to Yugoslavia 1940-45, Lieut.-Col., despatches; practised at S.A. Bar 1938–40, 1945–46; joined Anglo-American Corpn., Johannesburg 1946, Dir. 1954–57, Man. Dir. 1957–64; Deputy Chair. and Man. Dir. Charter Consolidated, London 1965–68; Deputy Chair. Anglo-American Corpn. of S.A. 1970–75; Dir. Anglo-American 1975–87; Hon. LL.D. (Witwatersrand Univ.). *Address:* 34 Palmboom Road, Newlands 7700, Cape Town, South Africa. *Telephone:* 685621.

WILSON OF RIEVAULX, Baron (Life Peer), cr. 1983, of Kirklees in the County of West Yorkshire; **(James) Harold Wilson,** K.G., P.C., O.B.E., F.R.S.A., F.R.S.; British politician; b. 11 March 1916; s. of James Herbert Wilson and late Ethel Wilson; m. Gladys Mary Baldwin 1940; two s.; ed. Milnsbridge Council School, Royds Hall School, Huddersfield, Wirral Grammar School, Cheshire, and Jesus Coll., Oxford; lecturer in Econs., New Coll., Oxford 1938; Fellow of Univ. Coll., Oxford and research asst. to Sir William (later Lord) Beveridge 1938–39; Econ. Asst. to War Cabinet Secr. 1940–41; Mines Dept. (later a part of Ministry of Labour) 1941–43; Dir. Econs. and Statistics, Ministry of Fuel and Power 1943–44; M.P. 1945–83; Parl. Sec. Ministry of Works 1945–47; Sec. for Overseas Trade March–Oct. 1947; Pres. of Bd. of Trade Oct. 1947–51 (resgnd.); mem. Nat. Exec. of Labour Party 1952–76 (Chair. 1961–62), and of Parl. Cttee. 1954–63; Chair. Public Accounts Cttee. of House of Commons 1959–63; Leader of Parl. Labour Party 1963–76; Prime Minister 1964–70; Leader of the Opposition 1970–74; Prime Minister 1974–76; Chair. Cttee. to Review Functioning of Financial Institutions 1976–80, British Screen Advisory Council 1985–87; Chancellor, Univ. of Bradford 1966–85; Pres. Royal Statistical Soc. 1972–73, Royal Shakespeare Theatre Co. 1976–85, Market Research Soc. 1978–; Trustee, Theatres Trust 1977–; Freeman, City of London 1975; Hon. D.Iur. (Bridgeport, U.S.A.) 1964; Hon. LL.D. (Lancaster) 1964, (Liverpool) 1965, (Nottingham) 1966; Hon. D.C.L. (Oxford) 1965; Hon. D.Tech. (Bradford) 1966; D.Univ. (Essex) 1967; Hon. D.Phil. (Weizman Inst. of Science); Henrietta Szold Award 1976. *Publications:* New Deal for Coal 1945, In Place of Dollars 1952, War on Want, The War on World Poverty 1953, Purpose in Politics 1964, The Relevance of British Socialism 1964, The New Britain (speeches) 1964, Purpose in Power 1966, The Labour Government 1964-70 1971, The Governance of Britain 1976, A Prime Minister on Prime Ministers 1977, The Final Term: The Labour Government 1974–76 1979, The Chariot of Israel 1981, Harold Wilson Memoirs 1916–1964, The Making of a Prime Minister 1986. *Leisure interest:* golf. *Address:* House of Lords, London, S.W.1, England.

WILSON-JOHNSON, David Robert, B.A., F.R.A.M.; British baritone; b. 16 Nov. 1950, Northampton; s. of Harry K. Johnson and Sylvia C. Wilson; ed. Wellingborough School, Northants., British Inst. of Florence, St. Catharine's Coll., Cambridge and Royal Acad. of Music; debut at Royal Opera House, Covent Garden in We Come to the River 1976; has since appeared in Billy Budd, L'Enfant et les Sortilèges, Le Rossignol, Les

Noces, Boris Godunov, Die Zauberflöte, Turandot, Werther, Madam Butterfly; Wigmore Hall recital debut 1977; BBC Promenade Concert debut 1981; appeared at Edin. Festival 1976, Glyndebourne Festival 1980 and at festivals in Bath, Bergen, Berlin, Geneva, Graz, Netherlands, Hong Kong, Jerusalem, Orange, Paris and Vienna; Paris Opéra debut in Die Meistersinger 1989. *Films include:* A Midsummer Marriage 1988; Nat. Fed. of Music Soc. Award 1977; Gulbenkian Fellowship 1978-81. *Recordings include:* Schubert's Winterreise, Mozart Masses from King's College, Cambridge, Haydn's Nelson Mass, Schoenberg's Ode to Napoleon, King Priam, Punch and Judy, La Traviata, Lucrezia Borgia and Michael Berkeley's Or Shall We Die? *Leisure interests:* swimming, slimming, gardening and growing walnuts in the Dordogne. *Address:* 28 Englefield Road, London, N1 4ET, England. *Telephone:* 01-254 0941 (London); 65.38.43.22 (France).

WILTON, Sir (Arthur) John, K.C.M.G., K.C.V.O., M.C., M.A., F.R.S.A.; British diplomatist (retd.); b. 21 Oct. 1921, London; s. of the late Walter Wilton and of Annetta Irene (née Perman) Wilton; m. Maureen Elizabeth Alison Meaker 1950; four s. one d.; ed. Wanstead High School and St. John's Coll., Oxford; commissioned Royal Ulster Rifles 1942, served with Irish Brigade in N. Africa, Italy and Austria 1943-46 (mentioned in despatches 1945); H.M. Diplomatic Service 1947-79; served Lebanon, Egypt, Gulf Sheikhdoms, Romania, Aden, Yugoslavia; Dir. Middle East Centre for Arab Studies 1960-65; Amb. to Kuwait 1970-74; Asst. Under-Sec., FCO 1974-76; Amb. to Saudi Arabia 1976-79; Dir. London House for Overseas Graduates 1979-86; Chair. Arab-British Centre 1981-86; Hon. LL.D. (New England Coll., N.H.) 1986. *Address:* Legassick House, 69 Fore Street, Plympton St. Maurice, Plymouth, PL7 3NA, England.

WIMALASENA, Nanediri; Sri Lankan diplomatist; b. 22 March 1914, Kandy; m. Prema Wijesekera (Fernando) 1938; one s. two d.; ed. Ananda Coll., Colombo, Ceylon Univ. Coll., Ceylon Law Coll.; mem. Kandy Municipal Council 1946-67, Deputy Mayor of Kandy 1946, Mayor 1963; M.P. for Senkadagala 1960-77, Deputy Minister of Finance 1965-70; Gov. Asian Devt. Bank 1966-70, Pres. 1968-69; High Commr. in U.K. 1977-81; Deputy Dir.-Gen. Greater Colombo Econ. Comm. 1981-; mem. del. to IPU Conf. Ottawa 1965; mem. Sri Lanka Branch of Exec. Cttee., of IPU 1965-77. *Leisure interests:* social service, hiking, tennis. *Address:* No. 3 Greenlands Avenue, Havelock Town, Colombo 5, Sri Lanka.

WIMMER, Hans; German sculptor; b. 19 March 1907, Pfarrkirchen; s. of Johann Wimmer and Amalie Huber; m. 1939; one s. one d.; ed. Humanistisches Gymnasium, Landshut, Tech. Hochschule, Munich and Akad. der Bildenden Künste, Munich; Prof. Akad. der Bildenden Künste, Nuremberg 1943-44, 1949; mem. Bayerische Akad. der Schönen Künste; Hon. mem. Nuremberg and Munich Acads.; mem. Royal Belgian Acad.; Hon. Senator, Dresden Acad.; Orden pour le Mérite; Grosses Verdienstkreuz mit Stern; Bayrischer Verdienstorden; Papal Order of St. Gregory. *Publications:* Bildnisse unser Zeit 1958, Über die Bildhauerei 1961, Niederbayerische Kindheit und Jugend 1981, Zeichnungen 1982, Hans-Wimmer Sammlung 1987. *Leisure interest:* riding. *Address:* Kunigundenstrasse 42, 8000 Munich 40, Federal Republic of Germany. *Telephone:* 36 12 767.

WIMMER, Maria; German actress; b. Dresden; d. of Max Wimmer and Helene Friedrich; m. Otto Seemüller 1950; stage appearances in works by Schiller, Goethe, Lessing, Kleist, Grillparzer etc. in Stettin, Frankfurt-am-Main, Hamburg, Munich, Düsseldorf, Berlin, Zürich, Vienna; also appears on television; mem. Akad. der Künste, Berlin; Kulturpreis of Fed. Republic of Germany 1971; Orden Pour le Mérite; Grosses Bundesverdienstkrkreuz mit Stern; Bayerischer Maximiliansorden. *Films include:* Der fallende Stern, Der gr. Zapfenstreich, Sauerbruch, Ein Engel mit dem Flammenschwert. *Address:* 8000 Munich 80, Osserstrasse 16, Federal Republic of Germany.

WIN MAUNG, U, B.A.; Burmese politician; b. 1916; ed. Judson Coll., Rangoon; joined Burmah Oil Co. after leaving coll.; then entered govt. dept.; joined Army as 2nd Lieut. 1940; during Second World War took active part in resistance movement of Anti-Fascist Organization; went to India, where he received training in tactics of mil. and guerrilla warfare at Mil. Coll., Calcutta and Mil. Camp, Colombo 1944; rejoined guerrilla forces in Burma 1945; Vice-Pres. Karen Youth Org. and Ed. Taing Yin Tha 1945; mem. Constituent Ass. 1947; Minister for Industry and Labour 1947, of Transport and Communications 1949; later Minister for Port, Marine, Civil Aviation and Coastal Shipping; M.P. for Maubin South (Karen) 1951-55 and 1956-57; Pres. of the Union of Burma 1957-62; detained after coup d'état 1962-67. *Address:* Rangoon, Burma.

WINBERG, (Sven) Håkan, LL.B.; Swedish lawyer and politician; b. 30 July 1931, Ånge; s. of Sven Winberg and Sally Angman; m. Ulla Greta Petersson; Justice, Court of Appeal; mem. Exec. Swedish Moderate Party 1972-, mem. Steering Cttee. 1975-; mem. Press Assistance Bd. 1971-79, Bd. of Council for Prevention of Crime 1974-79, Co. Boundaries Cttee. 1970-74, Cttee. of Inquiry into the Press 1972-75, New Labour Laws Cttee. 1976-78, Nat. Police Bd. 1977-79, Nordic Council 1977-82; M.P. 1971-82; County Councillor 1974-79; Minister of Justice 1979-81; Pres. Court of Appeal 1982-; mem. Election Review Cttee. of the Riksdag 1983-; mem. Parl. Comm. for Investigation into the murder of Prime Minister Olof Palme 1987-88. *Leisure interest:* skiing. *Address:* Bleckslagaregatan 14, S-85239 Sundsvall, Sweden (Home).

WINCH, Donald Norman, PH.D., F.B.A., F.R.HIST.S.; British professor of economics; b. 15 April 1935, London; s. of Sidney Winch and Iris Winch; m. Doreen Lidster 1983; ed. Sutton Grammar School, London School of Econs., Princeton Univ.; Visiting Lecturer Univ. of Calif. 1959-60; Lecturer in Econs. Univ. of Edinburgh 1960-63; Univ. of Sussex 1963-66, Reader 1966-69, Prof. History of Econs. 1969-, Dean School of Social Studies 1968-74, Pro-Vice-Chancellor (Arts and Social Studies) 1986-; Visiting Fellow, School of Social Science, Inst. of Advanced Study, Princeton 1974-75, King's Coll., Cambridge 1983, History of Ideas Unit, Australian Nat. Univ. 1983; Visiting Prof. Tulane Univ. 1984; Review Ed. The Economic Journal 1976-83. *Publications:* Classical Political Economy & Colonies 1965, James Mill, Selected Economic Writings 1966, Economics and Policy 1969, The Economic Advisory Council 1930-39 (with S. K. Howson) 1976, Adam Smith's Politics 1978, That Noble Science of Politics (with S. Collini and J. W. Burrow) 1983, Malthus 1987. *Leisure interest:* gardening. *Address:* The University of Sussex, Brighton, BN1 9QN, England. *Telephone:* (0273) 678028.

WINDELEN, Heinrich; German politician and businessman; b. 25 June 1921, Bolkenhain, Silesia (now part of Poland); s. of Engelbert and Anna (née von den Driesch) Windelen; m. Ingeborg Kreutzer 1954; one s. three d.; ed. in Striegau and Univ. of Breslau; served in war 1941-45; mem. Christian Democratic Union (CDU) 1946-; mem. Bundestag 1957-, Vice-Pres. 1981-83; Pres. Deutsche Stiftung für europäische Friedensfragen 1966-74; Minister for Refugees, Expellees and War Veterans 1969; Deputy Chair. CDU/CSU Parl. Group 1969-80; Chair. CDU, Westphalia 1970-77, Budget-Comm. Bundestag 1977-81; mem. Advisory Council, Westdeutscher Rundfunk 1971-85, Advisory Council Deutsche Bundespost 1977-83 (Chair. 1987); Minister for Inter-German Relations 1983-87; Dr. h.c. rer. pol. (Hanyang, S. Korea) 1983; Grosses Verdienstkreuz mit Stern 1977, Grosses Goldenes Ehrenzeichen mit Stern (Austria) 1983. *Address:* 441 Warendorf, Hermanstrasse 1, Federal Republic of Germany. *Telephone:* 02581-3522.

WINDEYER, Sir Brian Wellingham, Kt., F.R.C.P., F.R.C.S., F.R.C.R., F.R.S.M.; British university administrator; b. 7 Feb. 1904, Sydney, Australia; s. of Richard Windeyer, K.C. and Mabel Fuller Windeyer; m. 1st Joyce Ziele Russell 1928, one s. one d.; m. 2nd Elspeth Anne Bowrey 1948, one s. two d.; ed. Sydney Church of England Grammar School and Univ. of Sydney; Middlesex Hosp. and Medical School 1931-69; Prof. of Radiology, Univ. of London 1942-69, Vice-Chancellor 1969-72; Consultant Advisor in Radiotherapy, Min. of Health 1948-72; mem. Clinical Research Bd. 1954-62, Chair. 1968-72; mem. Medical Research Council 1958-62, 1968-72; Chair. Nat. Radiological Protection Bd. 1970-78; Dean, Middx. Hosp. Medical School 1954-67; Dean, Faculty of Medicine, Univ. of London 1964-68; Chair., Academic Bd. 1968-69, Dir. Radiotherapy Dept. Mount Vernon Hosp. 1945-69; Chair. Inst. of Educ., Univ. of London 1973-82, Kennedy Inst. of Rheumatism 1970-77, Royal Surgical Aid Soc. Council, R.S.A. 1973-78, Council, Westfield Coll., London Univ. 1972-79; Skinner Lecturer, Knox Lecturer, Faculty of Radiologists; Pres. Faculty of Radiologists 1949-52; Pres. Section of Radiology, Royal Soc. of Medicine 1967-68, of Section of Medical Educ.; mem. Royal Comm. on Medical Educ.; Soc. of Apothecaries of London, mem. of Court 1963-78, Jr. Warden 1970-71, Sr. Warden 1971-72, Master 1972-73; Hon. F.R.A.C.S., F.R.A.C.R., F.A.C.R.; Hon. D.Sc. (British Columbia, Wales, Cambridge), LL.D. (Glasgow); Hon. M.D. (Sydney). *Publications:* British Practice in Radiotherapy (co-editor) 1955; articles on cancer and radiotherapy. *Leisure interests:* gardening, golf. *Address:* 9 Dale Close, St. Ebbe's, Oxford, OX1 1TU, England. *Telephone:* (0865) 242816

WINDLESHAM, 3rd Baron; David James George Hennessy, P.C., C.V.O., M.A.; British politician; b. 28 Jan. 1932; s. of 2nd Baron Windlesham and Angela Mary (Duggan); m. Prudence Glynn 1965 (died 1986); one s. one d.; ed. Ampleforth, Trinity Coll., Oxford; Chair. of Bow Group 1959-60, 1962-63; mem. Westminster City Council 1958-62; Dir. Rediffusion Television 1965-67; Man. Dir. Grampian Television 1967-70; Minister of State Home Office 1970-72; Minister of State Northern Ireland 1972-73; Lord Privy Seal, Leader House of Lords 1973-74; Opposition Leader, House of Lords March-Oct. 1974; Jt. Man. Dir. ATV Network 1974-75, Man. Dir. 1975-81, Chair. 1981; Chair. Independent Television Cos. Asscn. 1976-78; Deputy Chair. Queen's Silver Jubilee Appeal 1976-77, and Trust 1977-80; Dir. W. H. Smith, The Observer; Trustee, Charities Aid Foundation 1977-81, Int. Inst. of Communications 1981-83, Community Service Volunteers 1981-; Chair. Oxford Preservation Trust 1979-, Parole Bd. 1982-88, Oxford Soc. 1985-88; Prin. Brasenose Coll., Oxford Aug. 1989-; Trustee, British Museum 1981-, Chair. 1986-; mem. Museums and Galleries Comm. 1984-86; Hon. Fellow Trinity Coll., Oxford 1982; Visiting Fellow All Souls Coll., Oxford 1986. *Publications:* Communication and Political Power 1966, Politics in Practice 1975, Broadcasting in a Free Society 1980, Responses to Crime 1987, Windlesham/Rampton Report on Death on the Rock 1989. *Address:* House of Lords, London, S.W.1, England.

WINGTI, Rt. Hon. Paias, P.C.; Papua New Guinea politician; b. 1951; ed. Univ. of Port Moresby; mem. Parl.; fmr. Minister of Transport and then of Planning in Govts. of Michael Somare; formed People's Democratic Movt. March 1985; Prime Minister of Papua New Guinea 1985-88. *Address:* c/o Office of the Prime Minister, Port Moresby, Papua New Guinea.

WINKELMANN, Günter Heinz Willi, DR. RER. POL.; German business executive; b. 18 Aug. 1919, Stargard; s. of Willi and Margarete (née Unger) Winkelmann; m. Erika Gies 1947; one s. one d.; ed. Univ. of Hamburg; Asst. Hamburg firm of chartered accountants 1948–49; Dir. of Accounting, Hamburg Import-Exportfirma 1949–53; Asst. to Herr Berthold Beitz, Iduna-Germania, Hamburg 1953; Asst. to Chief. Exec. Beitz, Krupp, Essen 1953–54; Head, Dept. of Procurement and Distribution, Krupp, Essen 1954–57, Dir. 1956; Man. Krupp Reederei und Brenstoffhandel GmbH 1953–62; mem. Man. Bd. Hugo Stinnes AG, Mülheim/Ruhr 1963, Chair. 1969–; mem. Man. Bd. VEBA AG, Düsseldorf 1969. *Leisure interests:* art and music. *Address:* Bockumerstrasse 331, 4000 Wittlaer, Federal Republic of Germany (Home). *Telephone:* 0211-40 17 23.

WINKLER, Hans Günter; German showjumper and company executive; b. 24 July 1926, Barmen; s. of Paul Winkler; m. 1st Inge Fellgiebel 1957 (divorced); m. 2nd Comtesse Marianne Moltke 1962, two c.; m. 3rd Astrid Nunez 1976; mem. Exec., German Riding and Motoring Assen. 1958–, German Olympic Riding Cttee. 1981–; winner of about 1,000 events, incl. over 500 int. events, up to 1964; took part in six Olympiads 1956–76, winning 106 nat. prizes, five Gold Medals, one Bronze Medal (Mexico City) 1968, one Silver Medal (Montreal) 1976; World Riding Champion 1954, 1955; European Champion 1957; Winner, King George V Cup 1965, 1968; Needle of Honour, Senate of West Berlin 1954; Sportsman of the Year 1955, 1956; Gold Band, German Sports Press Assen. 1956; Best Sportsman of the Decade 1960; Needle of Honour, Int. Riding Assen. 1964; Grand Cross of Honour of Fed. Repub. of Germany 1974; FN Award in Gold with Olympic Rings, Laurel Wreath and Diamonds 1976; Hon. mem. Riding and Motoring Assens. of Warendorf, Ludwigsburg, Herborn, Darmstadt, Bayreuth, Salzburg, Frankfurt am Main, Mitterfels, Kassel, Hünfeld; Hon. Citizen of Warendorf; world's most successful Olympic showjumping rider. *Publications:* Meine Pferde und ich (My Horses and I), Pferde und Reiter in aller Welt (Horses and Riders of the World) 1956, Halla D., Geschichte ihrer Laufbahn (Halla D., A History of her Career) 1961, Springreiten (Jumping) 1979, Halla die Olympiadiva: Olympiareiter in Warendorf 1981. *Leisure interests:* skiing, hunting. *Address:* Dr. Rau Allee 48, 4410 Warendorf, Federal Republic of Germany. *Telephone:* 2361.

WINNACKER, Karl, DR. ING; German chemist; b. 21 Sept. 1903, Wuppertal; s. of Ernst Winnacker and Martha Wallis; m. Gertrud Deitenbeck 1936; two s. one d.; ed. Brunswick and Darmstadt Technical Univs.; Hon. Prof. Frankfurt-am-Main Univ. 1953–71; Pres. (Gen. Man.) Hoechst AG until 1969, Pres. Advisory Bd., Hoechst AG 1969–80, now Hon. Pres.; Hon. Pres. Wacker-Chemie GmbH, Munich; mem. industrial and scientific orgs.; Hon. Pres. Dechema; Dr. rer. Nat. h.c. (Technische Hochschule, Brunswick, and Mainz Univ.), Dr. Phil. h.c. (Marburg Univ.); Dr. ciencias quim h.c. (Madrid); Dr. techn. h.c. (Lund). *Publications:* Chemische Technologie (Co-Ed.) 1969–75 (7 vols.), Nie den Mut verlieren 1971, Challenging Years 1972, Das unverstandene Wunder (with K. Wirtz) 1975, Schicksalsfrage Kernenergie 1978. *Leisure interests:* music, aquatic activities. *Address:* Ölmühlweg 31A, 6240 Königstein, Federal Republic of Germany.

WINNER, Michael Robert, M.A.; British film producer and director; b. 30 Oct. 1935, London; s. of late George Joseph Winner and Helen Winner; ed. Cambridge Univ.; Ed. and film critic of Cambridge Univ. paper; entered film industry as film critic and columnist for nat. newspapers and magazines 1951; wrote, produced and directed many documentary, TV and feature films for the Film Producers Guild, Anglo Amalgamated, United Artists 1955–61; Chair. Scimitar Films Ltd., Michael Winner Ltd., Motion Picture and Theatrical Investments Ltd. 1957–; Chief Censorship Officer, Dirs. Guild of G.B. 1983–; f. Council of Dirs. Guild of G.B. 1983–; f. Police Memorial Trust, Chair. 1984–. *Films:* Play It Cool (Dir.) 1962, The Cool Mikado (Dir., writer) 1962, West 11 (Dir.) 1963, The System (Co-producer and Dir.) 1963–64, You Must Be Joking (original story, Dir.) 1964–65, The Jokers (Writer, Dir.) 1966, I'll Never Forget What's 'is Name (Producer, Dir.) 1967, Hannibal Brooks (Producer, Dir., original story) 1968, The Games (Dir.) 1969, Lawman (Producer, Dir.) 1970, The Nightcomers (Producer, Dir.) 1971, Chato's Land (Producer, Dir.) 1971, The Mechanic (Dir.) 1972, Scorpio (Dir.) 1972, The Stone Killer (Producer, Dir.) 1973, Death Wish (Dir.) 1974, Won Ton Ton—The Dog Who Saved Hollywood (Producer, Dir.) 1975, The Sentinel (Producer, Dir., Screenplay) 1976, The Big Sleep (Producer, Dir., Writer) 1977, Firepower (Producer, Dir., Writer) 1978, Death Wish II (Producer, Dir., Writer) 1981, The Wicked Lady (Dir., Writer) 1982, Scream For Help (Producer, Dir.) 1983, Death Wish III 1985, Appointment with Death (Producer, Dir., Writer) 1987, A Chorus of Disapproval (Dir., co-writer) 1989. *Theatre:* A Day in Hollywood, A Night in the Ukraine (Producer) (Evening Standard Award for Best Comedy of the Year 1979). *Leisure interest:* art. *Address:* Scimitar Films Ltd., 6-8 Sackville Street, London, W1X 1DD, England. *Telephone:* 01-734 8385.

WINNING, Most Rev. Thomas Joseph, S.T.L., D.C.L., D.D.; British ecclesiastic; b. 3 June 1925, Wishaw, Lanarkshire; s. of Thomas and Agnes (née Canning) Winning; ed. St. Mary's Coll., Blairs, Aberdeen, St. Peter's Coll., Bearsden, Pontifical Scots Coll. and Pontifical Gregorian Univ.; ordained priest, Rome 1949; asst. priest, Chapelhall 1949-50, St. Mary, Hamilton 1953-57; Cathedral, Motherwell 1957-58; Chaplain, Franciscans of the Immaculate Conception, Bothwell 1958-61; Diocesan Sec., Motherwell 1956-61; Spiritual Dir. Pontifical Scots Coll., Rome 1961-66; parish priest,

St. Luke's, Motherwell 1966-70; Officialis and Vicar Episcopal, Motherwell 1966-70; Pres. Scottish Catholic Marriage Tribunal 1970; Auxiliary Bishop and Vicar Gen., Glasgow 1971-74; parish priest, Our Holy Redeemer's Clydebank 1972-74; Archbishop of Glasgow 1974-; Pres. Scottish Bishops' Conf. 1985-; mem. Sacred Congregation for the Doctrine of the Faith, Rome 1978-85; Hon. D.D. (Glasgow Univ.); Hon. F.E.I.S. 1986. *Leisure interests:* golf, watching Glasgow Celtic, listening to good music (not necessarily classical). *Address:* 18 Park Circus, Glasgow, G3 6BE (Office); 40 Newlands Road, Glasgow, G4 2JD, Scotland (Home). *Telephone:* 041-332 9473 (Office).

WINNINGTON-INGRAM, Reginald Pepys, F.B.A.; British professor of Greek language and literature; b. 22 Jan. 1904, Sherborne, Dorset; s. of the late Rear-Adm. C. W. Winnington-Ingram and I. V. M. Winnington-Ingram; m. Edith Mary Cousins 1938; ed. Clifton Coll. and Trinity Coll., Cambridge; Asst. Lecturer in Classics, Manchester Univ. 1928-29, Lecturer 1930-31; Reader in Classics, London Univ. (Birkbeck Coll.) 1934-48; Ministry of Labour and Nat. Service 1940-45; Prof. of Classics London Univ. (Westfield Coll.) 1948-53, Prof. of Greek (King's Coll.) 1953-71, Emer. Prof. 1971-, Fellow 1969-; Fellow Trinity Coll. 1928-32; Hon. D.Litt. (Glasgow) 1969, (London) 1985. *Publications:* Mode in Ancient Greek Music 1936, Euripides and Dionysus 1948, Aristides Quintilianus, De musica (Ed.) 1963, Sophocles, an Interpretation 1980, Studies in Aeschylus 1983. *Leisure interest:* music. *Address:* 12 Greenhill, London, NW3 5UB, England. *Telephone:* 01-435 6843.

WINOGRAD, Shmuel, PH.D.; American mathematician and computer scientist; b. 4 Jan. 1936, Tel Aviv, Israel; s. of Pinchas Mordecai and Rachel Winograd; m. Elaine R. Tates 1958; one s. one d.; ed. Massachusetts Inst. of Technology and New York Univ.; research staff mem. IBM Thomas J. Watson Research Center 1961-70; MacKay Lecturer, Univ. of Calif., Berkeley 1967-68; Adjunct Prof. New York Univ. Courant Inst. of Math. Sciences 1968; Dir. Mathematical Sciences Dept. IBM Research Center 1970-74, 1981-, Computing Tech. Dept. 1984-; IBM Fellow 1972; Perm. Visiting Prof. Technion, Israel 1972-; Hitchcock Prof. Univ. of Calif. 1970. *Publications:* Reliable Computations in the Presence of Noise (with J. D. Cowan) 1963; articles in professional journals. *Address:* IBM Thomas J. Watson Research Center, P.O. Box 218, Yorktown Heights, N.Y. 10598 (Office); 235 Glendale Road, Scarsdale, N.Y. 10598, U.S.A. (Home). *Telephone:* (914) 945-2443 (Office).

WINQWIST, Carl-Henrik; Swedish lawyer; b. 4 Nov. 1932, Menton, France; s. of Folke and Annajo Winqwist; m. Caroline Crafoord 1959; two s. three d.; ed. Sigtunastifelsens Humanistiska Läroverk, and Univ. of Stockholm; Chair. Swedish Conservative Student Union 1959-62; Sec.-Gen. Inst. Christian Democratic and Conservative Student Union 1962-65; Man. Dir. of an econ. research bureau 1962-68; Int. Sec. Conservative Party 1965-71; Dir.-Gen. Swedish Moderate party 1968-71; with Skandinaviska Enskilda Banken 1971-72; Sec.-Gen. Int. Chamber of Commerce 1973-82; mem. Royal Comm. of Advertising 1966-74. *Publications:* Sweden and Nuclear Missiles 1959, One Europe 1962. *Leisure interests:* classical music, Richard Wagner, cooking, squash. *Address:* 1 avenue Silvestre de Sacy, 75007 Paris, France (Home). *Telephone:* 551-70-96 (Home).

WINTER, Charles Milne, F.I.B. (SCOT.); British banker; b. 21 July 1933; s. of David Winter and Annie Winter; m. Audrey Hynd 1957; one s. one d.; ed. Harris Acad., Dundee; served R.A.F. 1951-53; joined The Royal Bank of Scotland 1949, Exec. Dir. 1981-86, Man. Dir. 1982-85, Group Chief Exec. 1985-; Dir. William & Glyn's Bank 1982-85 (Man. Dir. March-Oct. 1985); Vice-Pres. Edin. Chamber of Commerce and Mfrs. 1987-. *Leisure interests:* golf, choral music. *Address:* 4 Charteris Park, Longniddry, East Lothian, EH32 ONY, Scotland.

WINTER, Frederick Thomas, C.B.E.; British racehorse trainer; b. 20 Sept. 1926, Andover, Hants.; s. of late Frederick N. Winter and of Anne Winter; m. Diana Ruth Pearson 1956; three d.; ed. Ewell Castle School; served with 6 Bn. Parachute Regt. 1944-47; Nat. Hunt Jockey (four times Champion) 1947-64, Trainer (seven times Champion) 1964-. *Leisure interests:* golf, gardening. *Address:* Uplands, Lambourn, Berkshire, England. *Telephone:* (0488) 71438.

WINTER, Richard; Romanian politician; b. 15 May 1934, Sighişoara; ed. Stefan Gheorghiu Acad., Bucharest; joined Romanian Communist Party (RCP) 1954; Sec. County Cttee., Sibiu 1968, First Sec. County Cttee., Sibiu, and Chair. Exec. Cttee. of People's Council, Sibiu County 1968-78, Alt. mem. Exec. Political Cttee. of RCP Cen. Cttee. 1972-; mem. Nat. Council of Socialist Unity and Democracy Front 1968-; mem. Grand Nat. Ass. 1966-; Vice-Pres. Council of Working People of German Nationality 1968-; Minister-State Sec., Ministry for Tech. Material Supply and Fixed Assets Man. Control 1978-85, of Woodworking and Construction Materials 1985-87. *Address:* c/o Ministerul industrializării lemnului şi materilebr de constructii, Calea Grivitei 21, Bucharest, Romania. *Telephone:* 50-64-30.

WINTERBOTTOM, Michael, D.PHIL.; British university teacher; b. 22 Sept. 1934, Sale, Cheshire; s. of Allan Winterbottom and Kathleen Mary Winterbottom (née Wallis); m. 1st Helen Spencer 1963 (divorced 1983), two s.; m. 2nd Nicolette Janet Streatfeild Bergel 1986; ed. Dulwich Coll., London and Pembroke Coll. Oxford; Domus Sr. Scholar, Merton Coll. Oxford 1958-59; Research Lecturer, Christ Church Oxford 1959-62; Lecturer in Latin and Greek, Univ. Coll. London 1962-67; Fellow and Tutor in Classics, Worcester Coll. Oxford 1967-; Craven Scholar 1954; Derby Scholar 1956; Dr. h.c. (Besançon) 1985. *Publications:* Quintilian (Ed.) 1970, Ancient Literary Criticism (with D. A. Russell) 1972, Three Lives of English Saints 1972, The Elder Seneca (Ed. and Trans.) 1974, Tacitus, Opera Minora (with R. M. Ogilvie) 1975, Gildas (Ed. and Trans.) 1978, Roman Declamation 1980, The Minor Declamations Ascribed to Quintilian (Ed., with commentary) 1984, Sopatros the Rhetor (with D. C. Innes) 1988. *Leisure interests:* travel and hill walking. *Address:* 172 Walton Street, Oxford, England. *Telephone:* (0865) 515727.

WINTERFELDT, Ekkehard, DR.RER.NAT.; German professor of organic chemistry; b. 13 May 1932, Danzig; s. of Herbert and Herta Winterfeldt; m. Marianne Heinemann 1958; one s. one d.; ed. Tech. Hoschschule Braunschweig, Tech. Univ. of Berlin; Asst. Prof., Tech. Univ. of Berlin 1959, Assoc. Prof. 1967; Prof. and Head of Dept. of Organic Chem., Hannover Univ. 1970-; Dozentenstipendium des Fonds der Chemischen Industrie 1969. *Publications:* 130 publs. in scientific journals. *Address:* Sieversdamm 34, 3004 Isernhagen 2, Federal Republic of Germany. *Telephone:* 0511/77 84 99.

WINTERS, Robert Cushing, B.A., M.B.A.; American insurance company executive; b. 8 Dec. 1931, Hartford, Conn.; s. of George Warren and Hazel Keith (Cushing) Winters; m. Patricia Ann Martini 1962; two d.; ed. Yale and Boston Univs.; with Prudential Insurance Co. of America 1953-, Vice-Pres., Actuary 1969-75, Sr. Vice-Pres. Cen. Atlantic Home Office 1975-78, Exec. Vice-Pres., Newark 1978-84, Vice-Chair. 1984-86, Chair. and C.E.O. 1987-; Fellow Soc. of Actuaries; mem. and fmr. Pres. American Acad. of Actuaries; mem. Business Council, Business Roundtable. *Address:* Prudential Insurance Company, 745 Broad Street, Prudential Plaza, Newark, N.J. 07101, U.S.A.

WINTERS, Shelley; American actress; b. 18 Aug. 1922, St. Louis, Mo.; m. 1st Vittorio Gassmann (divorced); one d.; m. 2nd Anthony Franciosa 1957; ed. Wayne Univ; *films include:* A Thousand and One Nights, A Place in the Sun, Playgirl, Executive Suite, The Diary of Anne Frank 1958, Odds Against Tomorrow, Let No Man Write My Epitaph, Lolita 1962, Wives and Lovers 1963, The Balcony 1964, A House is not a Home 1964, A Patch of Blue, Time of Indifference 1965, Alfie 1965, The Moving Target 1965, The Poseidon Adventure 1972, Cleopatra Jones 1973, Blume in Love 1974, Whoever Slew Auntie Roo 1974, Heaven Save Us from Our Friends 1975, Diamonds 1975, That Lucky Touch 1975, Next Stop Greenwich Village 1976, The Tenant 1976, Pete's Dragon 1977, The Magician 1979, The Visitor 1980, Over the Brooklyn Bridge 1983, The Delta Force 1985; *stage appearances include:* A Hatful of Rain 1955, Girls of Summer 1957, The Night of the Iguana, Cages, Who's Afraid of Virginia Woolf?; *TV appearances include:* The Vamp 1972-73; Acad. Awards for best supporting actress in The Diary of Anne Frank 1959, A Patch of Blue 1964, Emmy Award for Best Actress 1964, Monte Carlo Golden Nymph Award 1964, Int. Television Award, Cannes Festival 1965. *Publications:* Shelley also Known as Shirley (autobiog.), One Night Stands of a Noisy Passenger (play) 1971. *Address:* c/o International Creative Management, 8899 Beverly Boulevard, Los Angeles, Calif. 90048, U.S.A.

WINTHER, Eva; Swedish politician; b. 3 Aug. 1921, Stockholm; m. Arne Winther 1946; three c.; qualified as children's nurse 1945; mem. of Exec. of Liberal Party 1971-81; mem. Kiruna Municipal Council and mem. Kiruna Cen. Social Welfare Cttee. 1967-76; mem. Norrbotten Co. Council 1976-78, Chair. Norrbotten Constituency Assen. until 1978; mem. Riksdag 1976-82; Chair. Standing Cttee. on Labour Market affairs 1978; Minister in Labour Ministry responsible for Immigrant Affairs and Questions concerning Equality between Men and Women 1978-79; mem. Standing Cttee. on Labour Market Affairs 1979-82; mem. Halland County Council 1985-. *Leisure interests:* art, fiction, poetry, outdoor life. *Address:* Box 101, 43041 Kullavik, Sweden.

WINTOUR, Charles Vere, M.A., C.B.E.; British journalist; b. 18 May 1917, Wimborne, Dorset; s. of F. Wintour and Blanche Foster; m. Eleanor Baker 1940 (dissolved), two s. two d.; m. 2nd Audrey Slaughter 1979; ed. Oundle School, and Peterhouse, Cambridge Univ.; Royal Norfolk Regiment 1940, G.S.O. Headquarters, Chief of Staff to Supreme Allied Commdr. (designate) and SHAEF (despatches); Evening Standard 1946, political Ed. 1952, Deputy Ed. 1954-57, Ed. 1959-76, 1978-80; Asst. Ed. Sunday Express 1952-54, Ed. Sunday Express Magazine 1981-82; Man. Ed. Daily Express 1957-59, Man. Dir. 1977-78; Chair. Evening Standard Co. 1968-80; Gov. L.S.E.; Dir. Beaverbrook Newspapers 1964-82; Dir. (non-exec.) TV-am News 1982-84; Dir. Wintour Publs. 1984-86; Ed. U.K. Press Gazette 1985-86; Editorial Consultant to Robert Maxwell 1986-87; Pres. Media Soc. 1989-; Croix de guerre 1945; Bronze Star (U.S.) 1945, S.W.E.T. Special Award 1982. *Publication:* Pressures on the Press 1972. *Leisure interests:* theatre, travel. *Address:* 5 Alwyne Road, London, N1 2HH, England. *Telephone:* 01-359 4590.

WIRAHADIKUSUMAH, Gen. Umar; Indonesian politician and retd. army officer; b. 10 Oct. 1924, Sumedang, West Java; platoon commdr. Tasikmalaya 1942; mem. PETA (Self-Defence Forces) 1944; Commdr. TKR (People's Security Army), Cicalengka, West Java 1945; Chief of Staff of Gen. Div., Siliwangi 1949; Commdr. of Mil. Command of Greater City of Djakarta 1959; Commdr. of Mil. Command of Territory V/Jaya and played key role in crushing abortive communist coup 1965; Commdr. of Kostrad 1966; Army Chief of Staff 1969; Chair. Audit Bd. (BPK) 1973-83; Vice-Pres. of Indonesia 1983-88; twelve Indonesian mil. decorations and decorations from U.S.A., Fed. Repub. of Germany, Netherlands, Yugoslavia, Repub. of Korea, Belgium and Malaysia. *Address:* Office of the Vice-President, Djakarta, Indonesia.

WIROWSKI, Maciej, M.ENG.; Polish politician; b. 2 March 1929, Katowice; s. of Bolesław Wirowski and Anna Wirowski; m. Danuta Budna 1951; one s.; ed. Silesian Tech. Univ., Gliwice, Warsaw Tech. Univ.; Asst., then Sr. Asst., Inorganic Chemistry Dept. of Silesian Tech. Univ., Gliwice 1950-54; master, then Chief of Dept. and Chief Eng., Chemical Reagents Factory, Gliwice 1955-60; Deputy Dir., Inorganic Chemistry Inst., Warsaw 1961-63; Deputy Dir. of Dept., Ministry of Chemical Industry 1963-66, Dir. of Dept. 1966-69, Under-Sec. of State 1969-71; Deputy Chair. Planning Comm. attached to Council of Ministers 1971-74; Minister of Chemical Industry 1974-76; First Deputy Chair. Planning Comm. attached to Council of Ministers; mem. Council of Ministers 1976-80; Amb. to G.D.R. 1981-86; Chief of Parl. Chancellery May 1986-; Pres. Assen. of Engs. and Technicians of Chemical Industry 1971-81; Deputy Pres., Polish Fed. of Eng. Assens. (NOT) 1976-81; Treas. Polish Club of Int. Relations 1988-; mem. Polish United Workers' Party (PZPR), alt. mem. PZPR Cen. Cttee. 1972-81; Order of Banner of Labour (1st and 2nd Class), Kt.'s Cross of Order of Polonia Restituta and other decorations. *Leisure interests:* graphic arts, medal engraving, tourism. *Address:* Kancelaria Sejmu PRL, ul. Wiejska 4/6/8, 00-902 Warsaw, Poland. *Telephone:* 28.32.97.

WIRTÉN, Rolf; Swedish politician and businessman; b. 4 May 1931, Eskilstuna; s. of Karl-Gustav and Ebba (née Sandgren) Wirtén; m. Gunvor Wirtén; two s. one d.; ed. secondary school in Flen; elementary school teacher in Jönköping 1954; Headmaster, Taberg 1959; Sec. Jönköping Educ. Council 1960; Headmaster Jönköping Vocational Schools 1964; Deputy Chief Educ. Officer Jönköping 1965; Liberal mem. Jönköping Finance Dept. 1963-70, mem. Jönköping Co. Council 1971-76, Chair. 1974-76; mem. Riksdag (Parl.) 1966-83, Vice-Chair. Liberal Party 1974, Chair. 1976-78; Chair. Standing Cttee. on Labour Market Affairs 1976; mem. Advisory Council on Foreign Affairs and on Nordic Council; mem. Exec. of Liberal Party 1969-84; mem. Working Cttee. of Exec. 1969-83, Chair. Working Cttee. 1977-; Minister of Labour 1978-80, of Budget 1980-82, of Econ. Affairs 1981-82. *Leisure interests:* fitness training, sport and nature study. *Address:* Ansvar, Mutual General Insurance for Total Abstainers, Box 5071, S-102 42 Stockholm, Sweden.

WIRTH, Timothy Endicott, PH.D.; American politician; b. 22 Sept. 1939, Santa Fé; s. of Cecil Wirth and Virginia Maude Davis; m. Wren Winslow 1965; one s. one d.; ed. Harvard and Stanford Univs.; Special Asst. to Sec. Dept. of Health, Educ. and Welfare 1967, Deputy Asst. Sec. for Educ. 1969; Asst. to Chair., Nat. Urban Coalition 1968; Vice-Pres. Great Western United Corpn., Denver 1970; Man. Arthur D. Little Inc. 1971-73; mem. 94th-99th Congresses from 2nd Dist. Colo.; Senator from Colorado Jan. 1987-; Ford Foundation Fellow 1964-66; Pres. White House Fellows Assen. 1968-69; mem. Exec. Cttee. Denver Council Foreign Relations 1974-75; mem. Bd. of Visitors, U.S.A.F. Acad. 1978-; Advisor, Pres. Comm. on the 80s 1979-80; Democrat. *Address:* U.S. Senate, Washington, D.C. 20510, U.S.A.

WIRTZ, William Willard, A.B., LL.B.; American lawyer and government official; b. 14 March 1912, DeKalb, Ill.; s. of William Wilbur and Alpha Belle (née White) Wirtz; m. Mary Jan Quisenberry 1936; two s.; ed. Univ. of California (Berkeley), Beloit Coll., and Harvard Law School; teacher 1933-39; Asst. Prof. School of Law, Northwestern Univ. 1939-42; Asst. Gen. Counsel, Bd. of Econ. Warfare 1942-43; served War Labor Bd. 1943-45; Chair. Nat. Wage Stabilization Bd. 1946; Prof. of Law, Northwestern Univ. 1946-54; law practice 1955-61; Under-Sec. of Labor 1961-62, Sec. of Labor 1962-69; now Partner, Wirtz and Lapointe, Washington; Trustee, Penn Cen. 1970; Hon. degrees from Michigan, Rhode Island, Northwestern, Yeshiva, and Roosevelt Univs. and Amherst, Monmouth Colls.; Democrat. *Address:* 1211 Connecticut Avenue, N.W., Washington, D.C. 20036, U.S.A. (Office).

WISCHNEWSKI, Hans-Jürgen; German politican; b. 24 July 1922, Allenstein; m. 2nd Katharina de Kiff 1978; three c.; ed. Berlin Gymnasium; served German Forces 1940-45; worked in metal industry after war; mem. Social Democrat party 1946; (Exec. Sec. 1968-72; Sec. Metal Workers' Union, Cologne 1952; mem. Bundestag 1957-; Chair. Young Socialists 1960; mem. European Parl. 1961-65; Fed. Minister for Econ. Co-operation 1966-68; Chair. Stiftung für Entwicklungsländer (Foundation for Developing Countries) 1970-72; Minister of State in Federal Foreign Office 1974-82, in Chancellery April-Oct. 1982; Nat. Vice-Chair. SPD 1979-82, Treas. 1984-85. *Publication:* The North-South Conflict 1969. *Leisure interest:* stamp-collecting. *Address:* Hermann-Ehlers Strasse 10, 5300 Bonn 1, Federal Republic of Germany.

WISE, John, M.P.; Canadian politician; b. 12 Dec. 1935, St. Thomas, Ont.; s. of Clayton Wesley Wise and Mary White; m. Ann Dimora Richardson; two d.; ed. Univ. of Guelph; mem. House of Commons 1972-; Minister of Agric. 1979, 1984-88; fmr. Caucus Spokesperson for Ministry of State for

Youth; Reeve of Yarmouth Township 1968–69, Warden of Elgin Co. 1969, Chair. of Elgin Planning Bd. 1971–72; Progressive Conservative Party. *Address:* R.R.4, St. Thomas, Ont., N5P 3S8, Canada.

WISE, Michael John, C.B.E., M.C., PH.D., F.R.G.S., F.R.S.A.; British geographer; b. 17 Aug. 1918, Stafford; s. of Harry Cuthbert and Sarah Evelyn Wise; m. Barbara Mary Hodgetts 1942; one s. one d.; ed. Saltley Grammar School, Birmingham and Birmingham Univ.; served with R.A. and Northamptonshire Regt. in Middle East and Italy 1941–46; Lecturer in Geography, Univ. of Birmingham 1946–51, L.S.E. 1951–54; Cassel Reader in Econ. Geography, L.S.E. 1954–58, Prof. of Geography 1958–83; Pro-Dir. L.S.E. 1983–85, (Hon. Fellow 1988); Erskine Fellow, Univ. of Canterbury, N.Z. 1970; Chair. Ministry of Agric. Cttee. of Inquiry into Statutory Smallholdings 1963–67; Chair. Dept. of Transport Landscape Advisory Cttee. 1981–, Court of Govs., Birkbeck Coll. 1983–89; Pres. Inst. of British Geographers 1974, Int. Geographical Union 1976–80, Geographical Asscn. 1976–77; Pres. Royal Geographical Soc. 1980–82; mem. Univ. Grants Cttee., Hong Kong 1966–73, Social Science Research Council 1976–82; Hon. mem. Geographical Soc., U.S.S.R. 1975, Paris 1984, Mexico 1984, Poland 1986, Asscn. Japanese Geographers 1980, British Inst. of Geographers 1989; Hon. D.Univ. (Open Univ.) 1978, Hon. D.Sc. (Birmingham) 1982; Gill Memorial Award of Royal Geographical Soc. 1958, Founder's Medal 1977; Alexander Csoma Körös Medal of Hungarian Geographical Soc. 1980, Tokyo Geographical Soc.'s Medal 1981, Lauréat d' Honneur Int. Geographical Union 1984. *Publications:* Hon. Ed., Birmingham and its Regional Setting 1950, A Pictorial Geography of the West Midlands 1958, Ed. (with E. M. Rawstron), R. O. Buchanan and Economic Geography 1973, General Consultant, An Atlas of Earth Resources 1979, The Ordnance Survey Atlas of Great Britain 1982, numerous papers on economic and urban geography. *Leisure interests:* music, gardening. *Address:* London School of Economics, Houghton Street, Aldwych, London, W.C.2; 45 Oakleigh Avenue, Whetstone, London, N.20, England. *Telephone:* 01-405 7686 (Office); 01-445 6057.

WISE, Robert Earl; American film producer and director; b. 10 Sept. 1914, Winchester, Ind.; s. of Earl W. Wise and Olive Longenecker; m. Patricia Doyle 1942; one s.; ed. Franklin Coll., Ind.; joined RKO 1933, apprentice sound effects cutter, then Asst. Ed. and later Film Ed.; films edited include Citizen Kane and The Magnificent Ambersons; Film Dir. 1943–, partner in independent film co. 1970–; Vice-Pres. The Filmakers Group; mem. Bd. of Govs., Acad. of Motion Picture Arts and Sciences, Pres. 1985–87; mem. Dirs. Guild of America; mem. Nat. Council on the Arts; four Acad. Awards (Best Film and Best Dir. West Side Story and The Sound of Music), Irving Thalberg Award, Acad. of Motion Picture Arts and Sciences, D. W. Griffith Award 1988. *Films include:* Curse of the Cat People 1944, The Body Snatcher 1945, The Set Up 1949, The Day the Earth Stood Still 1951, The Desert Rats 1953, Executive Suite 1954, Helen of Troy 1955, Tribute to a Bad Man 1956, Somebody Up There Likes Me 1956, Until They Sail 1957, Run Silent, Run Deep 1958, I Want to Live 1958, Odds Against Tomorrow 1959, West Side Story 1961, Two for the Seesaw 1962, The Haunting 1963, The Sound of Music 1965. The Sand Pebbles 1966, Star! 1968, The Andromeda Strain 1971, Two People 1973, The Hindenberg 1975, Audrey Rose 1977, Star Trek 1979. *Address:* Robert Wise Productions, 315 S. Beverly Drive, Suite 214, Beverly Hills, Calif. 90212-4301, U.S.A.

WISEMAN, Donald John, M.A., D.LIT., O.B.E., F.B.A.; British academic (retd.); b. 25 Oct. 1918, Emsworth; s. of Percy Wiseman and Gertrude Savage; m. Mary Ruoff 1948; three d.; ed. Dulwich Coll., Kings Coll., London, Wadham Coll., Oxford; during war mem. R.A.F.V.R. 1939–41, rank of Group Capt.; Intelligence Officer 1942–45; Asst. Keeper, The British Museum (Egyptian and Assyrian, Western Asiatic Antiquities) 1948–61; Prof. of Assyriology, Univ. of London 1961–82, Emer. Prof. 1982–; Jt. Dir. British School of Archaeology in Iraq 1964–65, Chair. 1971–; Ed. of Iraq 1953–78; Chair. Tyndale House for Biblical Research, Cambridge 1957–86; Pres. Soc. for Old Testament Studies 1980; Vice-Pres. British Acad. 1977; Schweich Lecturer 1983; U.S.A. Bronze Star; Hon. Fellow Kings Coll., London 1982. *Publications:* The Alalakh Tablets 1953, Babylonian Chronicles of Chaldaean Kings 1956, Vassal-Treaties of Esarhaddon 1958, Cylinder Seals of Western Asia 1959, Peoples of Old Testament Times 1973, Nebuchadrezzar and Babylon 1985. *Leisure interests:* philately, horticulture, grandchildren. *Address:* Low Barn, 26 Downs Way, Tadworth, Surrey, KT20 5DZ, England.

WISNER, Frank George, B.A.; American diplomatist; b. 2 July 1938, New York; s. of Frank G. Wisner and Mary E. Knowles; m. 2nd Christine Wisner 1976; two s. two d.; ed. Woodberry Forest School, Rugby School and Princeton Univ.; joined U.S. Foreign Service 1961; various posts 1961–75; Special Asst. to Under-Sec. for Political Affairs 1975–76; Dir. Office of Southern African Affairs 1976–77; Deputy Exec. Sec. 1977–79; Amb. to Zambia 1979–82; Deputy Asst. Sec. for African Affairs 1982–86; Amb. to Egypt 1986–; Presidential Meritorious Service Award, Dept. of State Meritorious Honor, Vietnam Service Award, Repub. of Vietnam Mil. Medal of Honour. *Leisure interests:* hunting, squash, horseback riding. *Address:* American Embassy, 5 Sharia Latin America, Cairo, Egypt. *Telephone:* 355-7371.

WITHERS, Rt. Hon. Reginald Greive, P.C., LL.B.; Australian politician; b. 26 Oct. 1924, Bunbury, W.A.; s. of late F.J. Withers; m. Shirley Lloyd-Jones 1953; two s. one d.; ed. Bunbury and Univ. of Western Australia; served in Royal Australian Navy 1942–46; mem. Bunbury Municipal Council 1954–56, Bunbury Diocesan Council 1958–59, Treas. 1961–68; State Vice-Pres., Liberal and Country League of W.A. 1958–61, State Pres. 1961–65; mem. Fed. Exec. of Liberal Party 1961–65, Fed. Vice-Pres. 1962–65; mem. Senate for W.A. Feb.-Nov. 1966, 1967–87, Govt. Whip in Senate 1969–71, Leader of Opposition in Senate 1972–75; Special Minister of State, Minister for A.C.T., Minister for the Media and Minister for Tourism and Recreation Nov.-Dec. 1975, Leader of Govt. in Senate and Minister for Admin. Services 1975–78, Vice-Pres. Exec. Council 1975–78. *Leisure interests:* swimming, reading, painting. *Address:* 23 Malcolm Street, West Perth, W.A. 6005, Australia. *Telephone:* (09) 3214608.

WITKOP, Bernhard, PH.D., SC.D.; American chemist; b. 9 May 1917, Freiburg (Baden), Germany; s. of Prof. Philipp W. Witkop and Hedwig M. Hirschhorn; m. Marlene Prinz 1945; one s. two d.; ed. Univ. of Munich; Dozent Univ. of Munich 1946; Matthew T. Mellon Fellow Harvard Univ., U.S.A. 1947; Instructor and Lecturer 1948–50; Special Fellow U.S. Public Health Service 1950–53; Research Fellow Nat. Heart Inst. 1950; Special Fellow, Nat. Inst. of Arthritis and Metabolic Diseases, Nat. Insts. of Health 1952, Chief of Section on Metabolites 1955–, Chief of Lab. of Chem., Nat. Inst. of Arthritis, Metabolic and Digestive Diseases 1957–87; N.I.H. Inst. Scholar 1987–; Visiting Prof., Kyoto Univ. 1961, Univ. of Freiburg 1962; Lecturer, Univ. of Zürich 1972; Ed. (U.S.A.) FEBS Letters 1979–; mem. N.A.S., Acad. Leopoldina-Carolina 1972, Comm. on Int. Relations, Nat. Acad. of Sciences 1978, American Acad. of Arts and Sciences 1978, Paul Ehrlich Foundation, Frankfurt 1979–; Hon. mem. Pharmaceutical Soc. of Japan 1978, Chemical Soc. 1982–, Japanese Biochemical Soc. 1983–; Hillebrand Award of American Chemical Soc. 1959; Paul Karrer Medallist; Order of the Sacred Treasure, Japan 1975; U.S. Sr. A. von Humboldt Award (Univ. of Hamburg) 1979. *Publications:* Mushroom Poisons 1940, Curare Arrow Poisons 1942, Yohimbine 1943, Kynurenine 1944, Indole Alkaloids 1947–50, Oxidation Mechanisms, Ozonization, Peroxides 1952, Hydroxyaminoacids, Metabolites, Building Stones and Biosynthesis of Collagen 1955, Mescalin and LSD Metabolism 1958, Pharmacodynamic Amines 1960, Nonenzymatic Cleavage and Modification of Enzymes 1961, Gramicidin A 1964, Rufomycin 1964, Photo-Reductions, -Additions, -Cyclizations 1966, Microsomal Hydroxylations, Arenoxide Metabolites, "NIH-Shift" 1967, Amphibian Venoms, Batrachotoxin, Pumiliotoxin 1968, Norepinephrine Release, Inactivation, False transmitters 1968, Histrionicotoxin, a selective inhibitor of cholinergic receptors 1970–72, Interaction of Polynucleotides Stimulators of Interferon 1973–74, Gephyrotoxin, a Muscarinic Antagonist 1978, Anatoxin-a: The most potent Agonist at the nicotinic receptor 1980–82, Paul Ehrlich: His Ideas and his Legacy, Nobel Symposium 1981, Amphibian Alkaloids 1983, Forty Years of "Trypto-Fun" 1984, Mind over Matter (lecture at Israel Acad. of Sciences, Jerusalem) 1987. *Leisure interests:* languages, etymology, literature, piano, chamber music, hiking, skating, mountaineering. *Address:* National Institute of Diabetes, Digestive and Kidney Diseases, National Institutes of Health, Bethesda, Md. 20892; 3807 Montrose Driveway, Chevy Chase, Md. 20815, U.S.A. (Home). *Telephone:* (301) 496-5455.

WITTEVEEN, Hendrikus Johannes; Netherlands economist, politician and international administrator; b. 12 June 1921, Zeist; m. Liesbeth De Vries Feyens 1949; two s. one d.; ed. Netherlands School of Econs., Rotterdam; Netherlands Cen. Planning Office 1947–48, Prof. of Business Cycles and Econs., Univ. of Rotterdam 1948–63; mem. First Chamber, States-Gen. 1959–63, 1971–73, Second Chamber 1965–67; Minister of Finance 1963–65, 1967–71, also First Deputy Prime Minister 1967–71; mem. Advisory Bd. Unilever N.V. 1972–73, Robeco 1972–73; Man. Dir. Int. Monetary Fund 1973–78; Adviser to Bd. of Man. Amsterdam-Rotterdam Bank N.V. 1979–; Chair. Consultative Group on Int. Econ. and Monetary Affairs 1979–85, Hon. Chair. 1985–; mem. Bd. Robeco 1979–, Royal Dutch Shell, Thyssen-Bornemisza 1978–86, Nationale-Nederlanden 1979–; mem. European Advisory Council Gen. Motors, Int. Council Morgan Guaranty Trust Co. 1978–85; Commdr., Order of Netherlands Lion, Commdr., Order of Orange Nassau; Liberal. *Publications:* Loonshoogte en Werkgelegenheid 1947, Growth and Business Cycles 1954. *Leisure interests:* classical music, English and French literature. *Address:* Amsterdam-Rotterdam Bank N.V.; Herengracht 595, Amsterdam; Waldeck Pyrmontlaan 15, Wassenaar, Netherlands (Home). *Telephone:* (020) 284600 (Office); 01751-79824 (Home).

WOELFLE, Arthur W.; American business executive; b. 8 March 1920, Dunkirk, N.Y.; s. of Arthur Woelfle Sr. and Agnes Johnson; m. Ruth Godden; three d.; ed. Univ. of Buffalo; served in U.S. Marine Corps 1940–45; Sec.-Treas. Bedford Products until 1955; Sr. Vice-Pres. Bedford Products Division, Kraft Inc. 1959; Div. Product Man. Kraft's Eastern Div. 1959; later various positions with Kraft Foods Div.; C.E.O. Kraft Foods, Fed. Repub. of Germany 1966–69; Chair. and Man. Dir. Kraft Foods Ltd., U.K. and Scandinavia 1969–73; Dir. Kraft Inc. 1973–, Vice-Chair. 1982–; Pres. and C.O.O. 1973–82, Chair. 1982–; Dir. Dart and Kraft Inc. 1980–, Vice-Chair. 1982–; Dir. First Nat. Bank of Chicago, First Chicago Corpn., Santa Fe Southern Pacific Corpn., Atchison, Tokeka & Santa Fe Railway. *Address:* Dart and Kraft Inc., Glenview, Ill. 60025, U.S.A.

WOESSNER, Mark Matthias, DR.ING.; German business executive; b. 14 Oct. 1938, Berlin; m. Lieselotte Woessner; two c.; ed. Studium TH, Karlsruhe, then apprenticeship; Asst. to Man. Bertelsmann AG 1968-72; Tech. Man. Mohndruck Printing Co. 1972-74, C.E.O. 1974-76; mem. Exec. Bd. Bertelsmann AG, Pres. Printing and Mfg. Div. 1976-83, Pres. and C.E.O. 1983-. *Publications:* several technical publs. at the Univ. of Stuttgart. *Leisure interest:* sport. *Address:* Bertelsmann AG, Car-Bertelsmann-Strasse 270, 4830 Gütersloh, Federal Republic of Germany.

WOGAN, Gerald Norman, PH.D.; American educator; b. 11 Jan. 1930, Altoona, Pa.; s. of Thomas B. Wogan and Florence E. (Corl) Wogan; m. Henrietta E. Hoenicke 1957; one s. one d.; ed. Juniata Coll. and Univ. of Illinois; Asst. Prof. of Physiology, Rutgers Univ., New Brunswick, N.J. 1957-61; Asst. Prof. of Toxicology, M.I.T., Cambridge, Mass. 1962-65, Assoc. Prof. 1965-69, Prof. 1969-, Head of Dept. of Applied Biological Sciences 1979-; Consultant to nat. and int. govt. agencies and industries; mem. N.A.S. *Publications:* articles and reviews in professional journals. *Address:* Department of Applied Biological Sciences, Massachusetts Institute of Technology, Cambridge, Mass. 02139, U.S.A. *Telephone:* (617) 253-3188.

WOHLIN, Lars Magnus, PH.D.; Swedish economist and banker; b. 24 June 1933, Stockholm; m. Karin Almqvist 1966; two s. one d.; ed. Stockholm School of Econs., Harvard Univ., Berkeley Univ., Calif.; Sec. Industrial Council for Social and Econ. Studies 1959-70; with Industrial Inst. for Econ. and Social Research (two years in U.S.A.) 1960-76, Sec. 1967-70, Dir. 1973-76; Under-Sec. of State at Ministry of Econ. Affairs 1976-79; Gov. Bank of Sweden 1979-82; Man. Dir. The Urban Mortgage Bank of Sweden 1982-. *Publications:* Employment, Price Level and Developments 1962, Forest-Based Industries: Structural Change and Growth Potentials 1970, Development of a Forecasting Model for the Pulp and Paper Industry 1971, The Use of a Capital-Vintage Model in Long-Term Forecasting of Technical Progress and Structural Change. *Address:* Gudmundudgen 6, S-182 61 Djursholm, Sweden. *Telephone:* 08/753 10 48.

WOJCIECHOWSKI, Mirosław Jan; Polish journalist and diplomatist; b. 23 Aug. 1931, Dąbrowa Górnicza; m.; one d.; ed. Warsaw Tech. Univ., Mil. Tech. Acad., Main School of Foreign Service, Warsaw; on Gen. Staff of Polish Army, Warsaw 1951-71, posts in Mil. Attache Office, Polish Embassy Washington 1960-62, London 1962-64, Mil., Air and Naval Attache in Stockholm 1967-71; Head Section of Analysis and Information Foreign Dept., PZPR Cen. Cttee. 1971-76; Dir., Ed.-in-Chief Polish Interpress Agency, Warsaw 1976-83; Pres. Radio and TV Cttee., Polish Radio and TV 1983-86; Amb. to Morocco 1986-, to Mauritania 1988-; mem. PZPR 1953-; Pres. Polish Skiing Union 1980-84; Hon. mem. Polish Translator's Assen. 1985; Kt.'s Cross, Order of Polonia Restituta. *Publications:* numerous magazines. *Leisure interest:* skiing. *Address:* Polish Embassy, 23 Zankat Oqbah, Rabat, Morocco; ul. Laserowa 4, 01-490 Warsaw, Poland (Home).*Telephone:* 36-02-00.

WÓJCIK, Andrzej, M.A.; Polish politician; b. 1 Jan. 1932, Włocławek; ed. Warsaw Univ. and Main School of Planning and Statistics, Warsaw; worked at Varimex Polish Soc. of Foreign Trade 1950-54; Interpreter, Control and Supervision Comm., Cambodia 1954-55; Head of Dept. Cen. Bd. of Eng. Ministry of Foreign Trade 1955-64; Commercial Consul, Bombay, India 1964-68; Deputy Gen. Dir., then Gen. Dir., Universal Foreign Trade Enterprise 1968-73; Commercial Counsellor of Polish Embassy, Paris 1973-76; Dir. of Dept., Ministry of Foreign Trade and Maritime Economy 1976-81; Commercial Counsellor, Minister Plenipotentiary of Polish Embassy, Washington, D.C. 1981-85; Minister of Foreign Trade 1985-87; Sec. of State, Ministry of Foreign Trade. Relations 1987-; mem. Polish United Workers' Party (PZPR) 1960-; Kt.'s Cross of Order of Polonia Restituta and other decorations. *Address:* Ministerstwo Współpracy Gospodarczej z Zagranicą, ul. Wiejska 10, P.O. Box P-22, 00 950 Warsaw, Poland. *Telephone:* 29-68-95.

WOJNA, Ryszard; Polish journalist; b. 2 July 1920, Sanok; m. Elżbieta Wojna; two c.; ed. Jagiellonian Univ., Cracow and Univ. of Grenoble; Ed., Echo Krakowa 1948-49; Foreign Ed., Głos Pracy, Warsaw 1951-56, Perm. corresp. in Middle East 1957-61, in Bonn 1963-67; Deputy Ed. Życie Warszawy 1968-71, Ed. 1971-72; Journalist Trybuna Ludu 1972-81; political commentator of "Rzeczpospolita" 1983-; Deputy mem. Cen. Cttee. Polish United Workers' Party 1971-76, mem. 1976-81; Deputy to Seym April 1976-; Chair. Seym Comm. for Foreign Affairs 1981-; mem. Consultative Council attached to Chair. of State Council 1986-; mem. Presidium All-Polish Peace Cttee.; Officer's Cross of Order Polonia Restituta 1972, State Prize for Literature and Journalism 1974, Order of Banner of Labour (1st and 2nd Class), Cross of Valour. *Publications:* Szkice arabskie 1964, Spokojnie płynie Ren 1971, Rozmowa z ojcem 1978, Dojrzewanie 1980, Komentarz do współczesności 1988. *Leisure interest:* skiing. *Address:* Rzeczpospolita, ul. Mysia 2, 00-955 Warsaw, Poland.

WOJTECKI, Jerzy, AGRIC.ENG.; Polish agriculturalist and politician; b. 25 Oct. 1929, Wągrowiec; s. of Stanisław and Anna Wojtecki; m. Irena Hekiert 1953; two s.; ed. Higher School of Agric., Wrocław; activist in Youth Org. of Workers' Univ. Soc. and Polish Youth Union 1948-56; employee, Voivodship Station for Quarantine and Protection of Plants, Poznań 1954-64; Head of Poznań Branch, Agrochem Fertilizer Sales Enterprise 1964-66;

Head of Agric., Forestry and Procurement Dept., Voivodship Nat. Council, Poznań 1966-72; Agric. Sec. of Voivodship Cttee. of Polish United Workers' Party (PZPR), Poznań 1972-74; Head of Agric. and Food Economy Dept., PZPR Cen. Cttee. 1974-81; Minister of Agric. and Food Economy 1981-83, mem. Govt. Presidium 1981-83; Amb. to the Netherlands 1983-88; mem. Seym 1976-85; mem. PZPR 1960-, deputy mem. PZPR Cen. Cttee. 1976-80, mem. 1980-86, Sec. 1980-81; Officer's Cross of Order of Polonia Restituta and other decorations. *Address:* c/o Ministry of Foreign Affairs, ul. I Armii WP 23, 00-918 Warsaw, Poland.

WOJTYŁA, H.E. Cardinal Karol (see John Paul II, His Holiness Pope).

WOLF, Markus, Col.-Gen.; East German intelligence official; b. Stuttgart; went to U.S.S.R. with parents when Nazi party took power; ed. Moscow Univ.and Comitern Training School; returned to G.D.R., joined diplomatic service 1949; served two years in Moscow, then joined Ministry of State Security, Deputy Minister of State Security and Head of foreign intelligence operations 1958-87; awarded Order of Karl Marx 1987. *Publication:* Troika. *Address:* Ministry of State Security, Berlin, German Democratic Republic.

WOLFBEIN, Seymour Louis, PH.D.; American government official and educator; b. 8 Nov. 1915, New York; s. of Samuel Wolfbein and Fannie Katz; m. Mae Lachterman 1941; two d.; ed. Brooklyn Coll., and Columbia Univ.; Research Assoc. U.S. Senate Comm. on Unemployment and Relief 1938; Economist, Research Div., Works Project Admin. 1939-42; Economist, Bureau of Labor Statistics, Dept. of Labor 1942-45, Head, Occupational Outlook Div. 1946-49, Head, Manpower and Productivity Div. 1949-50, Manpower and Employment Div. 1950-59, Deputy Asst. Sec. of Labor 1959-62, Dir. Office of Manpower, Automation and Training 1962-65, Econ. Adviser to Sec. of Labor 1965-67; Visiting Prof. Univ. of Mich. 1950-; Adjunct Prof. American Univ. 1951-; Dean School of Business Admin., Temple Univ. 1967-78, J.A. Boettner Prof. of Business Admin 1978-; Dean Temple Univ., Japan 1983-; Pres. T.W.O. Man. Consultants 1986-; Comm. on Human Resources, N.A.S. 1976-; Vice-Pres. World Trade Council 1980-; Fellow, American Statistical Assen., A.A.A.S.; Distinguished Service Award, Dept. of Labor 1955 and 1961; Eminent Man of Guidance Award 1970. *Publications:* Decline of a Cotton Textile City 1942, The World of Work 1951, Employment and Unemployment in the U.S. 1964, Employment, Unemployment and Public Policy 1965, Education and Training for Full Employment 1967, Occupational Information 1968, Emerging Sectors of Collective Bargaining 1970, Work in the American Society 1971, Manpower Policy: Perspectives and Prospects 1973, Labor Market Information for Youths 1975, The Pre-Retirement Years 1977, Establishment Reporting in the U.S.A. 1978, The Demography of the Disabled 1988, The Temporary Help Supply Industry 1989. *Leisure interest:* painting. *Address:* East 706 Parktowne, 2200 Benjamin Franklin Parkway, Pa. 19130, U.S.A. (Home).

WOLFE, Thomas Kennerly, Jr., A.B., PH.D.; American author and journalist; b. 2 March 1931, Richmond, Va.; s. of Thomas Kennerly and Helen Hughes; m. Sheila Wolfe; one s. one d.; ed. Washington and Lee Univ., and Yale; reporter Springfield (Mass.) Union 1956-59; reporter, Latin American Corresp. Washington Post 1959-62; reporter, magazine writer New York Herald Tribune 1962-66; magazine writer New York World Journal Tribune 1966-67; Contributing Ed. New York magazine 1968-76, Esquire Magazine 1977-; Contributing Artist Harper's magazine 1978-81; exhibited one-man show of drawings, Maynard Walker Gallery, New York 1965, Tunnel Gallery, New York 1974; Hon. D.F.A. (Minneapolis Coll. of Art) 1971, Hon. Litt. D. (Washington and Lee) 1974, Hon. L.H.D. (Va. Commonwealth Univ.) 1983, (Southampton Coll., N.Y.) 1984; Front Page Awards for Humour and Foreign News Reporting, Washington Newspaper Guild 1961, Award of Excellence, Soc. of Magazine Writers 1970, Frank Luther Mott Research Award 1973, Va. Laureate for Literature 1977, Harold D. Vursell Memorial Award, American Acad. and Inst. of Arts and Letters 1980, American Book Award for Gen. Non-Fiction 1980, Columbia Journalism Award 1980, Citation for Art History, Nat. Sculpture Soc. 1980, John Dos Passos Award 1984. *Publications:* The Kandy-Kolored Tangerine-Flake Streamline Baby 1965, The Electric Kool-Aid Acid Test 1968, The Pump House Gang 1968, Radical Chic and Mau-mauing the Flak Catchers 1970, The New Journalism 1973, The Painted Word 1975, Mauve Gloves and Madmen, Clutter and Vine 1976, The Right Stuff 1979, In Our Time 1980, From Bauhaus to Our House 1981, Bonfire of the Vanities 1987, The New America 1989. *Address:* c/o Farrar, Straus and Giroux Inc., 19 Union Square, W., New York, N.Y. 10003, U.S.A.

WOLFENDALE, Arnold Whittaker, PH.D., F.R.S., F.R.A.S., F.INST.P.; British professor of physics; b. 25 June 1927; s. of Arnold Wolfendale and Doris Wolfendale; m. Audrey Darby 1951; two s.; ed. Manchester Univ.; Asst. Lecturer, Manchester Univ. 1951-54, Lecturer 1954-56; Lecturer, Univ. of Durham 1956-59, Sr. Lecturer 1959-63, Reader in Physics 1963-65, Prof. 1965-, Head of Dept. 1973-77, 1980-83, 1986-; Chair., Northern Region Action Cttee., Manpower Services Comm. Job Creation Programme 1975-78; Pres. Royal Astronomical Soc. 1981-83; mem. Science and Eng. Research Council 1988-; Silver Jubilee Medal 1977, Univ. of Turku Medal 1987. *Publications:* Cosmic Rays 1963; Ed. Cosmic Rays at Ground Level 1973, Origin of Cosmic Rays 1974, Gamma Ray Astronomy 1981, Progress in Cosmology 1982, Gamma Ray Astronomy (with P. V. Ramana Murthy) 1986; Co-Ed. Origin of Cosmic Rays 1981; numerous papers on cosmic radiation. *Leisure interests:* walking, gardening, foreign travel. *Address:* Ansford, Potters Bank, Durham, England. *Telephone:* (0385) 45642.

WOLFENSOHN, James David, B.A., LL.B., M.B.A.; American banker; b. 1 Dec. 1933, Sydney, Australia; s. of Hyman Wolfensohn and Dora Weinbaum; m. Elaine R. Botwinick 1961; one s. two d.; ed. Sydney Boys' High School, Univ. of Sydney, Harvard Univ.; Attorney, Supreme Court, Australia 1957; Dir. Growth and Devt., Rheem Int., New York 1960-62; Partner, Ord Minnett (brokers), Australia 1963-65; Man. Dir. Darling & Co. (investment bankers), Australia 1965-67, J. Henry Schroder Wagg and Co., London 1967-70; Pres. and C.E.O. J. Henry Schroder Banking Corpn., New York 1970-76; Exec. Deputy Chair. and Prin. Exec. Officer, Schroders Ltd., London 1974-77; Exec. Partner, Salomon Bros., New York 1977-81; Pres. James D. Wolfensohn Inc., New York Oct. 1981-. *Publications:* articles in professional journals. *Address:* 425 Park Avenue, New York, N.Y. 10022, U.S.A.

WOLFENSTEIN, Lincoln, PH.D.; American physics professor; b. 10 Feb. 1923, Cleveland, Ohio; s. of Leo Wolfenstein and Anna Koppel; m. Wilma C. Miller 1957; three c.; ed. Univ. of Chicago; Physicist, Nat. Advisory Comm. for Aeronautics 1944-46; Asst. Prof., Carnegie-Mellon Univ. 1948-57, Assoc. Prof. 1957-60, Prof. 1960-78, Univ. Prof. 1978-; Guggenheim Fellow 1973-74, 1983-84; mem. N.A.S. *Publications:* over 100 papers on theoretical particle and nuclear physics, weak interactions, c.p. violation, neutrino physics. *Address:* Physics Department, Carnegie-Mellon University, Pittsburgh, Pa. 15213, U.S.A. *Telephone:* (412) 578-2740.

WOLFF, Etienne Charles, PH.D.; French embryologist; b. 12 Feb. 1904, Auxerre; s. of Armand and Gabrielle (née Cahen) Wolff; m. Emilienne Hennig 1927 (deceased); ed. Univ. de Strasbourg; Asst. at Biological Laboratory of Wimereux, Univ. of Paris 1927-28; Asst. at Medical Faculty, Univ. of Strasbourg 1933-37; Assoc. Prof. of Biology, Univ. of Strasbourg 1937-42, Prof. of Zoology and Embryology 1942-55; Prof., then Hon. Prof. Coll. de France 1955-, Administrateur, Coll. de France 1965-75; Pres. Inst. Int. d'Embryologie 1960-68; Dir. Inst. of Embryology and Teratology, C.N.R.S. 1947-75; Dir. Lab. of Embryology, Ecole Pratique des Hautes Etudes, Paris; Pres. Ligue française des droits de l'animal 1984-; mem. Acad. Française, Acad. des Sciences, Acad. nat. de Médecine, Conseil supérieur des Lettres; Assoc. mem. Acad. Royale de Belgique; Foreign mem. Royal Swedish Acad. of Sciences; Commdr., Légion d'honneur; Commdr. de l'Ordre nat. du Mérite; Commdr. des Palmes académiques; Commdr. des Arts et des Lettres; Prix de l'Institut de France; Dr. h.c. (Univs. of Ghent, Louvain and Geneva). *Publications:* Les changements de sexe 1946, La science des monstres 1948, Les chemins de la vie 1964, Les pancrates, nos nouveaux maîtres 1975, Dialogues avec mes animaux familiers 1979. *Address:* 23-25 rue de l'Estrapade 75005 Paris, France (Home).

WOLFF, Otto Herbert, C.B.E., M.D.; British professor of child health; b. 10 Jan. 1920, Hamburg, Germany; s. of the late Dr. and Mrs. H. A. Wolff; m. Jill Freeborough 1952; one s. one d.; ed. Peterhouse, Cambridge, Univ. Coll. Hosp., London; Lieut. and Capt. R.A.M.C. 1944-47; Resident Medical Officer, Registrar and Sr. Medical Registrar, Birmingham Children's Hosp. 1948-51; Lecturer, Sr. Lecturer, Reader Dept. of Pediatrics and Child Health, Univ. of Birmingham 1951-64; Nuffield Prof. of Child Health, Univ. of London 1964-85; Dean Inst. of Child Health until 1985; Consulting Physician Hosp. for Sick Children London until 1985; fmr. Senator London Univ.; fmr. Pres. of British Pediatric Asscn.; fmr. mem. Gen. Medical Council; mem. Royal Soc. of Medicine and British Medical Asscn.; corresp. mem. Société Française de Pediatrie, Société Suisse de Pediatrie, and numerous others; Dawson Williams Memorial Prize, Medal of Asscn. Française pour le Dépistage et la Prévention des Maladies Métaboliques et des Handicaps de l'Enfant 1986, Harding Award of Action for the Crippled Child 1987, James Spence Medal of the British Pediatric Asscn. 1988. *Publications:* articles in the Lancet and British Medical Journal. *Leisure interest:* music. *Address:* 53 Danbury Street, London, N1 8LE, England. *Telephone:* 01-226 0748.

WOLFF, Philippe, D. ÈS L.; French professor of history; b. 2 Sept. 1913, Montmorency; s. of Lucien Wolff and Gabrielle Dubois; m. Odette Desgrées 1944; two s. two d.; ed. Lycée de Rennes, Univs. of Rennes and Paris; Liaison Officer, 51st Div. (Highland Div.) 1940; Lecturer, Univ. of Paris (Sorbonne) 1943-45; Prof., Univ. of Toulouse 1945-74, Emer. Prof. 1974-; Visiting Prof., Univs. of São Paulo, Houston, Cambridge (Mass.), Calif. at Berkeley, Mich. at Ann Arbour, Washington at Seattle, Bonn, St. Paul's (Tokyo); mem. Institut de France; Silver Medal (C.N.R.S.); Chevalier, Légion d'honneur, Commdr. Ordre des Arts et des Lettres. *Publications:* Commerces et marchands de Toulouse c. 1350-c. 1450 1954, Histoire de Toulouse 1958, The Awakening of Europe 1968, Les origines linguistiques de l'Europe 1971, Ongles bleus, Jacques et Ciompi, Les révolutions populaires en Europe aux XIVe et XVe siècles (with Michel Mollat) 1970, Automne du Moyen Age ou printemps des Temps Nouveaux? 1986, gen. edition of historical works (with Privat and Éché), Les Toulousains dans l'histoire 1984. *Leisure interest:* music. *Address:* El Cedre, Edif. Roureda Tapada 2a 7, Santa Coloma, Andorra; 3 rue Espinasse, 31000 Toulouse, France. *Telephone:* 28858.

WOLFF, Torben, D.SC.; Danish curator; b. 21 July 1919, Copenhagen; s. of Jorgen Frederik de Lichtenberg Wolff and Karen Margrethe Lunn; m.

Lisbeth Christensen; two d.; ed. Copenhagen Univ.; Curator Zoological Museum, Univ. of Copenhagen 1953-66, Chief Curator 1966-80, 1983-89; Dir. Denmark's Aquarium 1983; Deputy Leader Danish Galathea Expedition Round the World 1950-52; mem. Danish Atlantide Expedition to West Africa 1945-46, numerous other expeditions; Hon. mem. R.S.N.Z., 1977; Royal Galathea Medal 1955, G.E.C. Gad's Grant of Honour 1964, Popular Science Prize, Danish Assen. of Authors 1983. *Publications:* A Year in Nature 1944, The Systematics and Biology of Isopoda Asellota 1961, Danish Expeditions on the Seven Seas 1967, The History of Danish Zoology 1979, The History of the Danish Natural History Society 1933-83, 1983. *Leisure interest:* guiding tours abroad to places off the beaten track. *Address:* Zoological Museum, Univ. of Copenhagen, Universitetsparken 15, 2100 Copenhagen O (Office); Hesseltoften 12, 2900 Hellerup, Denmark (Home). *Telephone:* (45) 31 35 41 11 (Office); (45) 31 62 89 71 (Home).

WOLFF VON AMERONGEN, Otto; German industrialist; b. 6 Aug. 1918; Chair. Supervisory Bd. Otto Wolff A.G.; mem. Bd. of Dirs. Exxon Corpn., New York; Chair., Deputy Chair. and mem. Supervisory Bds. various nat. and int. corpns.; Chair. Assen. of German Chambers of Commerce and Industry; Chair. Cologne Chamber of Commerce and Industry; Chair. Ostausschuss der Deutschen Wirtschaft; mem. Bd. of Dirs., The Germany Fund, New York; mem. Advisory Council United Technologies Corpn., Creditanstalt Bankverein Wien; Hon. Chair. Assen. of German Chambers of Commerce and Industry. *Address:* Zeughausstrasse 2, Cologne, Federal Republic of Germany. *Telephone:* (02221) 16410.

WOLFOWITZ, Paul Dundes, PH.D.; American diplomatist; b. 22 Dec. 1943, New York City; s. of Jacob Wolfowitz and Lillian (née Dundes) Wolfowitz; m. Clare Selgin 1968; one s. two d.; ed. Cornell Univ. and Univ. of Chicago; Lecturer, later Asst. Prof. Yale Univ. 1970-73; U.S. Arms Control and Disarmament Agency 1973-77, Special Asst. to Dir. 1974-75, Deputy Asst. Dir. 1976; Special Asst. SALT 1976-77; Deputy Asst. Sec. of Defense, Defense Dept. 1977-80; Visiting Assoc. Prof. School of Advanced Int. Studies, Johns Hopkins Univ. 1980-81; Dir. Policy Planning Staff, State Dept. 1981-82; Asst. Sec. of State East Asian and Pacific Affairs 1982-86; Amb. to Indonesia 1986-89; D.S.M. (Civilian), Distinguished Honor Award. *Address:* c/o American Embassy, Box 1, APO San Francisco 96356, U.S.A.

WOLFRAM, Herwig, D.PHIL.; Austrian professor; b. 14 Feb. 1934, Vienna; s. of Dr Fritz Wolfram and Rosa Wolfram; m. Adelheid Schorghofer 1958; three s. one d.; ed. Univ. of Vienna; Lecturer 1959-68, Univ. of Vienna 1967; Assoc. Prof., Los Angeles 1968; Assoc. Prof. of Medieval History, Univ. of Vienna 1969, Prof. 1971-; Dean Faculty of Arts 1981-83; Dir. Inst. für osterr. Geschichtsforschung, Vienna 1983-; Fellow Austrian Acad. of Sciences 1985-. *Publications include:* Splendor Imperii 1963, Intitulatio I 1967, II 1973, III 1988, History of the Goths, die Geburt Mitteleuropas 1987, over 70 articles. *Leisure interest:* sport. *Address:* Wilheminenstrasse 173, 1160 Vienna, Austria. *Telephone:* 4300/2180.

WOLFSON, Baron (Life Peer), cr. 1985, of Marylebone in the City of Westminster; **Leonard Gordon,** Kt.; British retail executive; b. 11 Nov. 1927; s. of Sir Isaac Wolfson (q.v.); m. Ruth Sterling 1949; four d.; ed. King's School, Worcester; Dir. Great Universal Stores Ltd. 1952-; Man. Dir. 1962-84, Jt. Chair. and Man. Dir. 1984-87, Chair. and Man. Dir. Jan. 1987-; Chair. Great Universal Stores Merchandise Corpn. Ltd. 1966-; Chair. Burberrys Ltd. 1978-; Chair. and Founder Trustee Wolfson Foundation; Patron Royal Coll. of Surgeons; Hon. Fellow Wolfson Coll., Cambridge, Wolfson Coll., St. Catherine's Coll. and Worcester Coll., Oxford, Univ. Coll. London, Queen Mary Coll., London Univ.; Hon. F.R.C.P.; Hon. F.B.A.; Hon. D.C.L. (Oxon, E. Anglia), Hon. Ph.D. (Tel Aviv and Hebrew Univ.), Hon. LL.D. (Strathclyde, Dundee, Cambridge, London), Hon. D.Sc. (Hull, Univ. of Wales), Hon. D.H.L. (Bar Ilan, Israel). *Leisure interests:* history, economics, golf. *Address:* Universal House, 251 Tottenham Court Road, London, W1A 1BZ, England (Office).

WOLFSON, Sir Isaac, Bt., F.R.S.; British businessman; b. 17 Sept 1897; m. Edith Specterman 1926 (died 1981); father of Lord Wolfson (q.v.); ed. Queen's Park School, Glasgow; joined the Great Universal Stores Ltd. 1932, Man. Dir. 1934, Jt. Chair. 1946-86, Hon. Life Pres. 1987-; mem. Grand Council British Empire Cancer Campaign; Hon. Pres. Weizmann Inst. of Science Foundation; Trustee Religious Centre, Jerusalem; Founder and Trustee the Wolfson Foundation, created 1955, mainly for the advancement of health, education and youth activities in the U.K. and British Commonwealth, Pres. (fmrly. Chair.) 1975-; Hon. Fellow Weizmann Inst. of Science, Israel, St. Edmund Hall, Oxford, Jews' Coll., Lady Margaret Hall, Oxford, Hon. F.R.C.P., Hon. F.R.C.S.; Hon. LL.D. (London, Glasgow, Cambridge, Manchester, Brandeis Univ., Nottingham and Strathclyde); Hon. Ph.D. (Jerusalem Univ.); Hon. D.C.L. (Oxford); Einstein Award for Philanthropy 1967, Lehmann Award 1968; Freeman, City of Glasgow. *Address:* Universal House, 251 Tottenham Court Road, London, W1A 1BZ, England. *Telephone:* 01-580 6441.

WOLPER, David Lloyd; American film and television producer; b. 11 Jan. 1928, New York; s. of Irving S. Wolper and Anna (née Fass) Wolper; m. 1st Margaret Dawn Richard 1958, two s. one d.; m. 2nd Gloria Diane Hill 1974; ed. Drake Univ. and Univ. of Southern California; Vice-Pres.

and Treasurer Flamingo Films TV Sales Co. 1948-50, Vice-Pres. W. Coast Operations 1954-58; Chair. Bd. and Pres. Wolper Productions 1958-, Wolper Pictures Ltd. 1968-, The Wolper Org. Inc. 1971-; Pres. Fountainhead Int. 1960-, Wolper TV Sales Co. 1964-, Wolper Productions Inc. 1970-; Vice-Pres. Metromedia Inc. 1965-68; Consultant and Exec. Producer Warner Brothers Inc. 1976-; Chair. Bd. Dirs. Amateur Athletic Foundation of Los Angeles; mem. Bd. of Dirs. Acad. of TV Arts and Sciences Foundation, S. Calif. Cttee. for Olympic Games, Univ. of S. Calif. Cinema/TV Dept.; mem. Acad. of Motion Picture Arts and Sciences, Acad. of TV Arts and Sciences, Producers' Guild of America, Caucus for Producers, Writers and Dirs.; mem. Bd. of Govs. Cedars Sinai Medical Center; mem. Bd. of Trustees, American Film Inst., Museum of Broadcasting, Los Angeles Country Museum of Art and numerous other bds. of trustees; seven Golden Globe Awards, five George Foster Peabody Awards, Distinguished Service Award, U.S. Jr. Chamber of Commerce, 46 Emmy Awards, Academy of TV Arts and Sciences, Monte Carlo Int. Film Festival Award 1964, Cannes Film Festival Grand Prix for TV Programmes 1964, two Acad. Awards: Best Documentary Film 1972, Jean Hersholt Humanitarian Award 1985. *TV productions include*: The Race for Space, The Making of the President, Hollywood and the Stars, March of Time Specials, The Rise and Fall of the Third Reich, The Undersea World of Jacques Cousteau, China: Roots of Madness, Primal Man, Welcome Back, Kotter, Roots, Victory at Entebbe, Roots: The Next Generations, The Thorn Birds, North and South—Books I and II, The Morning After; has produced numerous feature films and several live special events, including Opening and Closing Ceremonies of 1984 Olympic Games, L.A., 100th Anniversary and Unveiling of the Statue of Liberty 1986 *Address:* Warner Brothers Inc., 4000 Warner Boulevard, Burbank, Calif. 91522 (Office); 10847 Bellagio Road, Los Angeles, Calif. 90077, U.S.A.

WOLPERT, Julian, PH.D.; American geographer; b. 26 Dec. 1932, New York, N.Y.; s. of Harry Wolpert and Rose Wolpert; m. Eileen Selig 1955; three s. one d.; ed. Erasmus Hall High School, Columbia Coll. and Univ. of Wisconsin; U.S.N. service 1955-59; Asst. Prof. of Regional Science and Geography, Univ. of Pa. 1963-65, Assoc. Prof. 1966-68, Prof. 1969-73; Henry G. Bryant Prof. of Geography, Public Affairs and Urban Planning, Woodrow Wilson School, Princeton Univ. 1973-; Pres. Asscn. of American Geographers 1973-74; Fellow A.A.A.S., Woodrow Wilson Center 1987-88, Guggenheim Fellow 1987-88; mem. N.A.S. *Publications:* numerous articles on migration, location theory, human services and the siting of public facilities. *Address:* Woodrow Wilson School, Princeton University, Princeton, N.J. 08544; 4588 Provinceline Road, Princeton, N.J. 08540, U.S.A. (Home). *Telephone:* (609) 452-5931 (Office).

WONDER, Stevie; American singer, musician and composer; b. (as Steveland Judkins Morris) 13 May 1950, Saginaw, Mich.; step-s. of Paul Hardaway; m. 1st Syreeta Wright 1971 (divorced 1972); m. 2nd Yolanda Simmons, three s.; ed. Michigan School for the Blind; first appeared as solo singer at Whitestone Baptist Church, Detroit 1959; recording artist with Motown, Detroit 1961-; f. and Pres. Black Bull Music Inc. 1970; owner KJLH, Los Angeles; named Best Selling Male Soul Artist of Year (Nat. Assen. of Record Merchandisers) 1974; Grammy Awards (You Are the Sunshine of My Life, Innervisions, Superstition) 1974, (Fulfillingness' First Finale, Boogie on Reggae Woman, Living for the City) 1975, (Songs in the Key of Life, I Wish) 1977, Acad. and Golden Globe Awards for song I Just Called to Say I Love You 1985. *Numerous recordings:* singles include Fingertips 1963, Uptight/Purple Raindrops 1965, Someday At Christmas/The Miracles of Christmas, I'm Wondering/Everytime I See You I Go Wild 1966, I Was Made to Love Her/Hold Me 1967, Shoo-Be-Doo-Be-Doo-Da-Day/Why Don't You Lead Me To Love, You Met Your Match/My Girl 1968, For Once in My Life, I Don't Know Why, My Cherie Amour, Yester-Me, Yester-You, Yesterday, Never Had a Dream Come True, Signed, Sealed, Delivered, I'm Yours, Heaven Help Us All, Superstition, You are the Sunshine of My Life, Higher Ground, Living For the City, Boogie on Reggae Women, Don't You Worry About a Thing, I Wish, Sir Duke, Another Star, Lately, Jammin', We Are the World (with others), I Just Called to Say I Love You; albums include: Little Stevie Wonder: The Twelve-Year-Old Genius, Tribute To Uncle Ray, Jazz Soul, With A Song In My Heart, At The Beach, Uptight 1966, Down To Earth 1966, I Was Made To Love Her 1967, Someday At Christmas 1967, Stevie Wonder: Greatest Hits 1968, Music Of My Mind 1972, Innervisions 1973, Fulfillingness' First Finale 1975, Songs in the Key of Life 1976, Journey Through the Secret Life of Plants 1979, Hotter than July 1980, Original Musiquarium 1981, Woman in Red 1984, In Square Circle 1986, Characters 1987. *Address:* c/o Black Bull Music, 4616 Magnolia Boulevard, Burbank, Calif. 91505, U.S.A.

WONG KAN SENG, B.A., M.SC.; Singapore politician; b. 8 Sept. 1946; m. Lee Hong Geok; two s.; ed. Univ. of Singapore, Univ. of London, U.K.; Teacher, Ministry of Educ. 1964-67; various posts in Admin. Service 1970-81; Personnel Man., Hewlett Packard Singapore 1981-85; elected M.P. for Kuo Chuan 1984; apptd. Minister of State, Home Affairs and Community Devt. Feb. 1985, Community Devt. and Communications and Information May 1985, Acting Minister for Community Devt. and Minister of State (Communications and Information) 1986, Minister and Second Minister for Foreign Affairs 1987; Minister for Community Devt. and Minister for Foreign Affairs 1988-. *Leisure interests:* swimming, golf.

Address: Ministry of Foreign Affairs, 250 North Bridge Road, City Tower, Singapore 0617. *Telephone:* 3361177.

WONTNER, Sir Hugh Walter Kingwell, G.B.E., C.V.O.; British hotelier; b. 22 Oct. 1908; s. of late Arthur Wontner; m. Catherine Irvin 1936; two s. one d.; ed. Oundle, and in France.; mem. Secretarial Staff of London Chamber of Commerce 1927-33; Gen. Sec. Hotels and Restaurants Assen. of Great Britain 1933-38; Sec. Coronation Accommodation Cttee. 1936-37; Asst. to Sir George Reeves-Smith at the Savoy Hotel 1938-41; Dir. of the Savoy, Claridge's and Berkeley Hotels, London 1940, Man. Dir. 1941-81, Chair. 1948-84; Chair. Savoy Theatre Ltd. 1948-, Eurocard Int., S.A. 1965-78, Lancaster Hotel, Paris 1973-; Trustee D'Oyly Carte Opera Trust, Coll. of Arms Trust, Southwark Cathedral Devt. Trust, Morden Coll., Temple Bar Trust, Heritage of London Trust 1980-; Chair. Exec. Cttee. British Hotels and Restaurants Assen. 1957-59, Council 1969-73; Pres. Int. Hotel Assen. 1962-65; Chair. Nutrition Cttee., Univ. Coll. Hosp. 1945-52; mem. Lloyds 1937-; mem. of Bd. British Travel Assen. 1950-69; mem. Historic Buildings Council for England 1968-73; Chair. Coronation Accommodation Cttee. 1952-53, Historic Houses Cttee. (British Tourist Authority) 1965-77; mem. Barbican Centre Cttee. 1970-84; Master Worshipful Co. of Feltmakers 1962, 1973, of Clockmakers 1976; Clerk of Royal Kitchens 1953-; Freeman of the City of London 1934, Alderman 1963-79, Sheriff 1970-71, Lord Mayor 1973-74; Lieut. of the City and J.P. 1963-79; Hon. D.Litt. 1973; numerous awards and decorations. *Address:* 1 Savoy Hill, London, W.C.2; and Hedsor Priory, Hedsor, Buckinghamshire, England. *Telephone:* 01-836 1533.

WOOD, Arthur M., B.L.; American business executive; b. 27 Jan. 1913, Chicago; s. of R. Arthur Wood and Emily (née Smith) Wood; m. Pauline Palmer 1945; one s. one d.; ed. Princeton Univ., Harvard Law School; service in Second World War; joined Sears, Roebuck and Co. 1946, Co. Sec. 1952-61, Vice-Pres. 1956, mem. Bd. of Dirs. 1959-, Vice-Pres. and Comptroller 1960-62, Vice-Pres. in charge of Far West Territory 1962-67, of Midwest Territory 1967, Pres. 1968-73; Chair. Bd. of Dirs. and Chief Exec. Sears Roebuck Foundation 1973-78; Chair. U.S. Industrial Payroll Savings Cttee. for Chicago 1974-, U.S. Public Oversight Bd. 1984-; Dir. Allstate Insurance Co., Continental Illinois Corpn., Simpsons-Sears Ltd., Homart Devt. Co., Quaker Oats Co., Council for Financial Aid to Educ., United Way of America, Community Fund of Chicago; Trustee Tax Foundation Inc., Cttee. for Econ. Devt., Art Inst. of Chicago, Rush Presbyterian St. Luke's Medical Center; mem. President's Advisory Cttee. on Labor Man., Business Council, Nat. Industrial Energy Conservation Council. *Address:* Sears Tower, Suite 9800, Chicago, Ill. 60684, U.S.A.

WOOD, Charles Gerald, F.R.S.L.; British scriptwriter and playwright; b. 6 Aug. 1932; s. of John Edward Wood and Catherine Mae (née Harris) Wood; m. Valerie Elizabeth Newman 1954; one s. one d.; ed. King Charles I School, Kidderminister and Birmingham Coll. of Art; corporal 17/21st Lancers 1950-55; factory worker 1955-57; Stage Man., scenic artist, cartoonist, advertising artist 1957-59; Bristol Evening Post 1959-62; mem. Drama Advisory Panel, South Western Arts 1972-73; consultant to Nat. Film Devt. Fund 1980-82. *Plays include:* Prisoner and Escort, Spare, John Thomas 1963, Meals on Wheels 1965, Don't Make Me Laugh 1966, Fill the Stage with Happy Hours 1967, Dingo 1967, H 1969, Welfare 1971, Veterans 1972, Jingo 1975, Has 'Washington' Legs? 1978, Red Star 1984, Across from the Garden of Allah 1986. *TV Plays include:* Prisoner and Escort, Drill Pig, A Bit of a Holiday, A Bit of an Adventure, Love Lies Bleeding, Dust to Dust. *Screenplays include:* The Knack 1965, Help! 1965, How I Won the War 1967, The Charge of the Light Brigade 1968, The Long Day's Dying 1969, Cuba 1980, Wagner 1983, Red Monarch 1983, Puccini 1984, Tumbledown 1985. *TV Series:* Company of Adventurers 1986, My Family and Other Animals 1987. *Publications:* (Plays) Cockade 1965, Fill the Stage with Happy Hours 1967, Dingo 1967, H 1970, Veterans 1972, Has 'Washington' Legs? 1978. *Leisure interests:* mil. and theatrical studies, gardening. *Address:* c/o Fraser and Dunlop Scripts Ltd., 91 Regent Street, London, W1R 8RU, England.

WOOD, D. Joseph, B.PHIL.; American international finance official; b. 13 May 1941, Indianapolis, Ind.; s. of Donald E. and Agnes Davis Wood; m. Kathleen Sinclair 1964; two d.; ed. Yale and Oxford Univs.; joined IBRD (World Bank) 1967; Economist, Nairobi office 1968-71; Sr. Economist, Devt. Finance Cos. 1971-73; Div. Chief, Financial Analysis and Projections 1973-75; Asst. Dir. Financial Policy 1975-79; Dir. Financial Policy and Analysis Dept. 1980-82; Vice-Pres. Financial Policy, Planning and Budgeting 1982-; Rhodes Scholar 1963. *Leisure interests:* tennis, skiing, trekking. *Address:* 2938 Macomb Street, N.W., Washington, D.C. 20008, U.S.A. *Telephone:* (202) 477-2784 (Office); (202) 244-1276 (Home).

WOOD, Sir Frederick (Ambrose Stuart), Kt.; British business executive; b. 30 May 1926; s. of Alfred Phillip and Charlotte (née Barnes) Wood; m. J. R. (née Su) King 1947; two s. one d.; ed. Felsted School, Essex; Clare Coll., Cambridge; Sub-Lieut. (A) Observer, Fleet Air Arm 1944-47; Trainee Man. Croda Ltd. 1947-50, Pres. Croda Inc., New York 1950-53; Man. Dir. Croda Int. Ltd. 1953-85, Chair. 1960-86, Hon. Life Pres. 1987-; Chair. Nat. Bus Co. 1972-78; mem. Nat. Research and Devt. Corpn. 1973-78, Chair. 1979-83; Chair. Nat. Enterprise Bd. 1981-83; Chair. British Tech. Group 1981-83; mem. Nationalised Industries Chairs. Group 1975-78; Hon.

LL.D. (Hull) 1983. *Address:* Plaster Hill Farm, Churt, Surrey, England. *Telephone:* (0428) 712134.

WOOD, Harland G., A.B., PH.D.; American university professor of biochemistry; b. 2 Sept. 1907, Delavan, Minn.; s. of William C. and Inez (Goff) Wood; m. Mildred Lenora Davis 1929; three d. (one deceased); ed. Macalester and Iowa State Colls.; Fellow, Nat. Research Council, Bacteriology Dept., Univ. of Wis. 1935-36; Asst. Prof., Bacteriology Dept., Iowa State Coll. 1936-43; Assoc. Prof., Physiological Chem. Dept., Univ. of Minn. 1943-46; Prof. and Dir. Dept. of Biochem., Western Reserve Univ. 1946-65, Prof. of Biochem., Case Western Reserve Univ. 1965-78, Dean of Sciences 1967-69, Univ. Prof. 1970-78, Prof. Emer. 1978-; Pres. American Soc. of Biological Chemists 1959-60; Sec.-Gen. Int. Union of Biochemistry 1970-73, Pres. 1979-85; mem. Presidential Science Advisory Cttee., Washington D.C. 1968-72; Sr. Fulbright Research Scholar, New Zealand 1955; Guggenheim Fellow 1962; mem. N.A.S., American Acad. of Arts and Sciences, Bayerische Akad., Germany; Hon. mem. Biochemical Soc. of Japan; Hon. Sc.D. (Malcalester Coll.) 1946; Hon. D.Sc. (Northwestern Univ.) 1972, (Univ. of Cincinnati) 1982; Eli Lilly Award in Bacteriology 1942, Carl Neuberg Medal 1952, Glycerine Award 1954, Modern Medicine Award for Distinguished Achievement 1968, Lynen Lecture and Medal 1972; Senior Scholar Award to Australia 1976, Sr. Scientist Humboldt Award, Germany 1979, Selman A. Waksman Award in Microbiology 1986, Rosenstiel Medical Research Award 1987, Michelson-Morley Achievement Award 1987. *Publications:* over 200 scientific papers; Editorial Cttee., Journal of Biological Chemistry 1949-54, and of Biochemistry 1964-69, 1975-78, Trends in Biochemical Science 1976-78. *Leisure interests:* skiing, hunting, fishing. *Address:* Department of Biochemistry, Case Western Reserve University, School of Medicine, 2109 Adelbert Road, Cleveland, Ohio 44106, U.S.A.

WOOD, Sir Martin (Francis), Kt., O.B.E., M.A., F.R.S., D.L.; British scientist and business executive; b. 1927; s. of Arthur Henry Wood and Katharine Mary Altham (née Cumberlege) Wood; m. Audrey Buxton (née Stanfield) Wood 1955; one s. one d. one step-s. one step-d.; ed. Gresham's, Trinity Coll. Cambridge, Imperial Coll. London, Christ Church Oxford; with Nat. Coal Bd. 1953-55; Sr. Research Officer, Clarendon Lab., Oxford Univ. 1956-69; f. Oxford Instruments Group PLC 1959, Chair. 1959-83, Deputy Chair. 1983-; Chair. Nat. Comm. for Superconductivity 1987-; mem. Advisory Bd. for Research Councils 1983-; Dir. Celltech Ltd. and other cos.; Tech. Consultant African Medical and Research Foundation; f. Northmoor Trust (for nature conservation), Oxford Trust (for encouragement of study and application of science and tech.); Hon. D.Sc. (Cranfield Inst. of Tech.) 1983; Hon. D.Tech. (Loughborough Univ. of Tech.) 1985; Mullard Medal, Royal Soc. 1982. *Address:* c/o Oxford Instruments Group PLD, Eynsham, Oxford, OX8 1TL, England.

WOOD, Maurice, M.B., B.S., F.R.C.G.P., F.A.A.F.P.; American physician; b. 28 June 1922, Pelton, Co. Durham, England; s. of Joseph Wood and Eugenie (Lumley) Wood; m. Erica J. Noble 1948; two s. one d.; ed. Chester Le-Street Grammar School and Univ. of Durham; various hosp. appts. 1945-46, 1949-50; Maj, R.A.M.C. 1946-49; Sr. Partner, Medical Practice, South Shields 1950-71; Gen. Practice Teaching Group, Univ. of Newcastle-upon-Tyne 1969-71; Clinical Asst. Dept. of Psychological Medicine, South Shields Gen. Hosp. 1966-71; Assoc. Prof., Dir. of Research, Dept. of Family Practice, Medical Coll. of Va., Va. Commonwealth Univ., Richmond, Va. 1971-73, Prof. and Dir. of Research 1973-87, Prof. Emer. 1987-; Exec. Dir. N. American Primary Care Research Group 1983-; Consultant Adviser, WHO 1979-; other professional appts. and memberships; mem. Inst. of Medicine, N.A.S. and other awards and distinctions. *Publications:* International Class of Primary Care 1987, numerous articles in professional journals and book chapters. *Leisure interests:* sailing, gliding, skiing. *Address:* Department of Family Practice, Medical College of Virginia, Medical College of Virginia Station, Box 251, Richmond, Va. 23298-001; Route 1, Box 672, Roseland, Va. 22967, U.S.A. *Telephone:* (804) 786-9625; (804) 325-1383.

WOOD, Rt. Rev. Maurice Arthur Ponsonby, D.S.C., M.A.; British ecclesiastic; b. 26 Aug. 1916, London; s. of the late Arthur S. Wood and of Jane Elspeth (née Piper) Wood; m. 1st Marjorie Pennell 1947 (died 1954), two s. one d.; m. 2nd M. Margaret Sandford 1955, two s. one d.; ed. Monkton Combe School, Queens' Coll., Cambridge and Ridley Hall, Cambridge; ordained 1940; Curate, St. Paul's Portman Square, London 1940-43; Royal Naval Chaplain 1943-47; Rector, St. Ebbe's Oxford 1947-52; Vicar and Rural Dean of Islington 1952-61; Prin., Oak Hill Theological Coll., Southgate, London 1961-71; Bishop of Norwich 1971-85; Hon. Chaplain, R.N.R. 1971-, Hon. Asst. Bishop, Diocese of London 1985-; Resident Priest of Englefield 1987-; entered House of Lords 1975; Chaplain, Commando Asscn., Worshipful Co. of Weavers; Chair. Order of Christian Unity 1986-; Gov. Monkton Combe School, Bath, Gresham's School, Norfolk. *Publications:* Like a Mighty Army 1956, Your Suffering 1959, Christian Stability 1968, To Everyman's Door 1968, Into the Way of Peace 1982, This is our Faith 1985. *Leisure interests:* painting, sailing, supporting Dr Billy Graham (q.v.) and Norwich City Football Club. *Address:* St. Mark's House, Englefield, Nr. Reading, RG7 5EN, England. *Telephone:* (0734) 302 227.

WOOD, Rt. Hon. Richard Frederick (see Holderness, Baron).

WOOD, Ronald Karslake Starr, F.R.S.; British professor of plant pathology; b. 8 April 1919, Ferndale; s. of Percival T. E. Wood and Florence Dix Starr; m. Marjorie Schofield 1947; one s. one d.; ed. Ferndale Grammar School and Imperial Coll., London; Ministry of Aircraft Production 1942; Lecturer Imperial Coll. 1947, Reader in Plant Pathology 1955, Prof. of Plant Pathology 1964-, mem. Governing Body, Head Dept. of Pure and Applied Biology 1981-84; Dean Royal Coll. of Science 1975; Dir. NATO Advanced Study Insts. 1970, 1975, 1980; Sir C. V. Raman Prof. Univ. of Madras 1980; Regent's Lecturer Univ. of Calif. 1981; Otto-Appel Denkmünster 1978; Sec.-Gen. First Int. Congress of Plant Pathology 1968; Founder Pres. Int. Soc. for Plant Pathology 1968, now Hon. mem.; Commonwealth Fund Fellow 1950, Research Fellow Conn. Agricultural Experimental Station 1957, American Phytopathological Soc. 1976, Thurburn Fellow Univ. of Sydney 1979; Vice-Chair. Governing Body E. Malling Research Station; Gov. Inst. of Horticultural Research; Corresp. mem. Deutsche Phytomedizinische Gesellschaft 1973. *Publications:* Physiological Plant Pathology 1967, Phytotoxins in Plant Diseases (Ed. with A. Ballio and A. Graniti) 1972, Specificity in Plant Diseases (Ed. with A. Graniti) 1976, Active Defence Mechanisms in Plants (Ed.) 1981, Plant Diseases: infection, damage and loss (Ed.) 1984; numerous papers in scientific journals. *Leisure interest:* gardening. *Address:* Imperial College, London, SW7 2BB (Office); Pyrford Woods, Pyrford, nr. Woking, Surrey, England (Home). *Telephone:* 01-589 5111 (Office); (093 23) 43827 (Home).

WOOD, William B., III, PH.D.; American professor of biology; b. 19 Feb. 1938, Baltimore, Md.; s. of Dr. W. Barry Wood, Jr. and Mary L. Hutchins; m. Renate Marie-Elisabeth Hartisch 1961; two s.; ed. Harvard Coll., Stanford Univ. and Univ. of Geneva; Nat. Acad. of Sciences—Nat. Research Council Postdoctoral Fellow, Univ. of Geneva 1964; Asst. Prof. of Biology, Calif. Inst. of Tech. 1965-68, Assoc. Prof. 1968-70, Prof. 1970-77; Prof. of Molecular Biology, Univ. of Colo., Boulder 1977-, Chair. of Dept. 1978-83; mem. N.A.S., American Acad. of Arts and Sciences, A.A.A.S., American Soc. of Biological Chemists, Soc. for Developmental Biology. *Publications:* Biochemistry, A Problems Approach (with J. H. Wilson, R. M. Benbow and L. E. Hood) 1974, 1981, Molecular Design in Living Systems 1974, The Molecular Basis of Metabolism 1974, Molecular Biology of Eucaryotic Cells (with L. E. Hood and J. H. Wilson) 1975, Immunology (with L. E. Hood and I. Weissman) 1978, 1984, The Nematode Caenorhaboitis Elegans (Ed.) 1988, articles in professional journals. *Leisure interests:* music, tennis, camping. *Address:* Department of Molecular, Cellular and Developmental Biology, Box 347, University of Colorado, Boulder, Colo. 80309, U.S.A.

WOODCOCK, George, D. LITT., LL.D. F.R.G.S.; Canadian writer, b. 8 May 1912, Winnipeg, Man. s. of Samuel Arthur and Margaret Gertrude (Lewis) Woodcock; m. Ingeborg Hedwig Linzer 1949; ed. Sir William Borlase's School, Marlow, England, and Morley Coll., London; Eng. Dept. Great Western Railway, England 1929-40; has been a writer since then, with interruptions of farming and univ. teaching; lived in Canada 1949-, with periods of travel in Asia, N. and S. America, Oceania and most European countries; Ed., Now 1940-47; Asst. Prof. of English, Univ. of Washington 1954-56; Assoc. Prof. of English., Univ. of British Columbia 1956-63; Ed. Canadian Literature 1959-77; Hon. LL.D., Hon. D. Litt.; Gov.-Gen.'s Award for Literature 1967; Molson Prize 1973. *Publications:* The White Island (poems) 1940, William Godwin 1946, The Writer and Politics 1948, The Anarchist Prince 1950, Pierre-Joseph Proudhon 1956, Incas and Other Men 1959, Anarchism 1962, Faces of India 1964, The Crystal Spirit 1966, The Doukhobors 1968, Odysseus Ever Returning 1970, Canada and the Canadians 1970, Herbert Read 1972, The Rejection of Politics 1972, Who Killed the British Empire? 1974, Notes on Visitations (poems) 1975, Gabrial Dumont 1975, Peoples of the Coast 1977, Thomas Merton, Monk and Poet 1978, Faces from History 1978, The Kestrel and Other Poems 1978, The Canadians 1979, The World of Canadian Writing 1980, The George Woodcock Reader 1980, The Mountain Road (poems) 1980, Taking It to the Letter 1981, Ivan Eyre 1981, Confederation Betrayed 1981, The Benefactor 1982, Letter to the Past 1982, Collected Poems 1983, British Columbia: A Celebration 1983, Orwell's Message 1984, Strange Bedfellows: The State and the Arts in Canada 1985, Walls of India 1985; The University of British Columbia: A Souvenir 1986, Letters from Sooke 1986, Northern Spring 1987, Beyond the Blue Mountains 1987, Social History of Canada 1988, The Purdy-Woodcock Letters 1988, Caves in the Desert 1988, The Marvelous Century 1989, Power of Observation 1989, The Century that Made Us 1989; articles in many British, U.S. and Canadian journals; many plays, documentaries and talks for Canadian Broadcasting Corpn.; scripts for films on South Pacific Islands and various Canadian themes. *Leisure interests:* travel, reading. *Address:* 6429 McCleery Street, Vancouver, B.C. V6N 1G5. Canada. *Telephone:* (604) 266-9393.

WOODCOCK, Leonard; American labour leader and diplomatist; b. 15 Feb. 1911, Providence, R.I.; s. of Ernest and Margaret (née Freel) Woodcock; m. 1st Loula Martin 1941, one s. two d.; m. 2nd Sharon Lee Tuohy 1978; ed. St. Wilfred's Coll. Oakmore, Northampton Town and Country School (England) and intermittent courses at Wayne State Univ.; Regional Dir., UAW 1947-55; Vice-Pres. UAW 1955-70; Pres. Int. Union, United Automobile, Aerospace and Agricultural Implement Workers of America (UAW) 1970-77, Pres. Emer. 1977-; Chief U.S. Liaison Office, Peking 1977-78; Amb. to People's Repub. of China 1979-81; Adjunct Prof., Univ. of Mich. 1981-. *Leisure interests:* music and literature. *Address:* 2404

Vinewood Boulevard, Ann Arbor, Mich. 48104, U.S.A. *Telephone:* (313) 662-8963.

WOODHOUSE, Rt. Hon. Sir (Arthur) Owen, K.B.E., D.S.C., P.C., LL.B.; New Zealand judge; b. 18 July 1916, Napier; s. of A. J. Woodhouse; m. Margaret Leah Thorp 1940; four s. two d.; ed. Napier Boys' High School and Auckland Univ.; military and naval service 1939–45; joined Lusk, Willis & Sproule, barristers and solicitors 1946; Crown Solicitor, Napier 1953; Judge of Supreme Court 1961–; a Judge of Court of Appeal 1974–86; Pres. Court of Appeal 1981–86; Pres. Law Comm. 1986–; Chair. Royal Comm. on Compensation and Rehabilitation in respect of Personal Injury in New Zealand 1966–67, Chair. inquiry into similar questions in Australia 1973–74; Hon. LL.D. (Victoria Univ. of Wellington) 1978, (Univ. of York, Toronto, Canada) 1981. *Leisure interests:* music, golf. *Address:* Law Commission, P.O. Box 2590, Wellington, New Zealand.

WOODHOUSE, Hon. (Christopher) Montague, D.S.O., O.B.E., M.A., F.R.S.L.; British politician; b. 11 May 1917, London; s. of Lord and Lady Terrington; m. Lady Davina Lytton (Countess of Erne) 1945; two s. one d; ed. Winchester Coll., and New Coll., Oxford; commissioned R.A. 1940; commanded Allied Mil. Mission in German occupied Greece 1943–44; Asst. Sec. Nuffield Foundation 1947; served Foreign Office in Athens 1945 and Teheran 1951; Fellow Trinity Hall, Cambridge 1949; Dir.-Gen. Royal Inst. of Int. Affairs 1955–59; M.P. for Oxford 1959–66, 1970–74; Parl. Sec. Ministry of Aviation 1961–62, Jt. Under-Sec. of State Home Office 1962–64; Chief Ed. Penguin Books 1960; Dir. of Educ. and Training, CBI 1966–70; Chair. Council Royal Soc. of Literature 1977–86; Visiting Prof., King's Coll. London; Special mem. Acad. of Athens 1980; Visiting Fellow Nuffield Coll. 1956; Fellow New Coll., Oxford 1982; Legion of Merit (U.S.A.); Order of Phoenix with Swords (Greece); Conservative. *Publications:* Apple of Discord 1948, One Omen 1950, Dostoievsky 1951, The Greek War of Independence 1952, Britain and the Middle East 1959, British Foreign Policy since the Second World War 1961, Rhodes (with J. G. Lockhart) 1963, The New Concert of Nations 1964, The Battle of Navarino 1965, Postwar Britain 1966, The Story of Modern Greece 1968, The Philhellenes 1969, Capodistria 1973, The Struggle for Greece (1941–1949) 1976, Something Ventured 1982, Karamanlis: The Restorer of Greek Democracy 1982, The Rise and Fall of the Greek Colonels 1985, Gemistos Plethon: the last of the Hellenes 1986. *Leisure interests:* fishing, music. *Address:* Willow Cottage, Latimer, Bucks., England. *Telephone:* (024 04) 2627.

WOODROOFE, Sir Ernest George, Kt., PH.D., F.INST.P., F.I.CHEM.E.; British business executive; b. 6 Jan. 1912, Liverpool; s. of Ernest George and Ada (Dickinson) Woodroofe; m. 1st Margaret Downes 1938, 2nd Enid Grace Hutchinson Arnold 1962; one d.; ed. Leeds Univ.; Dir. British Oil and Cake Mills Ltd. 1951–56; Dir. Unilever Ltd. and Unilever N.V., in charge of Research 1956–61, Vice-Chair. Unilever Ltd. 1961–70, Chair. 1970–74; Vice-Chair. Unilever N.V. 1970–74; Dir. Commonwealth Devt. Finance Co. Ltd. 1970–75, Schroders Ltd. 1974–, Burton Group 1974–83, British Gas Corpn. 1972–81, Guthrie Corpn. 1975–82; Chair. Review Body on Doctors' and Dentists' Remuneration 1975–79; Chair. Leverhulme Trust 1975–82; Vice-Chair. Atlantic Salmon Trust 1984–; Visiting Fellow, Nuffield Coll., Oxford 1972–80; Hon. LL.D., Hon. D.Sc. (from two univs.), Hon. D. Univ.; Commdr. Order of Orange-Nassau 1972. *Leisure interests:* fishing, golf. *Address:* 44 The Street, Puttenham, Guildford, Surrey, England. *Telephone:* (0483) 810977.

WOODROW, Bill (William Robert), D.F.A.; British artist and sculptor; b. 1 Nov. 1948, Henley-on-Thames, Oxon.; s. of Geoffrey W. Woodrow and Doreen M. Fasken; m. Pauline Rowley 1970; one s. one d.; ed. Barton Peveril Grammar School, and Winchester, St. Martin's and Chelsea Schools of Art; 40 one-man exhbns. in U.K., Fed. Repub. of Germany, France, Australia, Netherlands, Belgium, Italy, U.S.A., Canada, Switzerland, Sweden, Ireland and Yugoslavia since 1979; has participated in many group exhbns. around the world including British Sculpture in the 20th Century (Whitechapel Gallery), An Int. Survey of Recent Painting and Sculpture (Museum of Modern Art, N.Y.) and Skulptur im 20. Jahrhundert (Basle), Carnegie Int. (Pittsburgh) 1985; represented Britain at Biennales of Sydney 1982, Paris 1982, São Paulo 1983, Paris 1985; works in many public collections in U.K. and abroad; finalist in Turner Prize 1986, winner Anne Gerber Award, Seattle Museum of Art, U.S.A. 1988. *Publications include:* Bill Woodrow, Sculpture 1980–86, A Quiet Revolution—Recent British Sculpture. *Address:* c/o Lisson Gallery, 67 Lisson Street, London, NW1 5DA; 44 Camberwell Grove, London, S.E.5, England.

WOODRUFF, Alan Waller, C.M.G., M.D., F.R.C.P., F.R.C.P.E.; British professor of medicine; b. 27 June 1916, Sunderland; s. of William Henry Woodruff and Mary Margaret (née Thomson) Woodruff; m. Mercia Helen Arnold 1946; two s. one d.; ed. Bede Collegiate School, Univ. of Durham; squadron leader, medical specialist with R.A.F. 1940–46; Prof. of Clinical Tropical Medicine, London School of Medicine and Tropical Hygiene, Univ. of London, and the Hosp. for Tropical Diseases, London 1952–81; Hon. Consultant in Tropical Medicine, British Army 1956–81, British Airways 1962–; mem. Expert Panel on Parasitic Diseases WHO 1963–; Prof. of Medicine Univ. of Juba, Sudan 1981–; Pres. Royal Soc. of Tropical Medicine and Hygiene 1973–75, Medical Soc. of London 1975–76, History Section, Royal Soc. of Medicine 1977–79, Durham Univ. Soc. 1963–73; Hon. R.E. 1979; Katherine Bishop Harman Prize of British Medical Asscn. 1951;

Cullen Prize, Royal Coll. of Physicians, Edin. 1982. *Publications:* numerous scientific papers on tropical diseases, jt. author A Synopsis of Infectious Tropical Diseases 1987, Ed. Medicine in the Tropics 1984. *Leisure interests:* sketching and engraving, astronomy, fishing. *Address:* University of Juba, P.O. Box 82, Juba, Sudan (Office); 122 Ferndene Road, London, SE24 OBA, England (Home). *Telephone:* Juba 2114 (Office); 01-274 3578 (Home).

WOODRUFF, Judy Carline, B.A.; American broadcast journalist; b. 20 Nov. 1946, Tulsa, Okla.; d. of William Henry and Anna Lee (Payne) Woodruff; m. Albert R. Hunt, Jr. 1980; ed. Meredith Coll., Duke Univ.; News Announcer, Reporter WAGA-TV, Atlanta 1970–75; News Corresp. NBC News, Atlanta 1975–76; White House Corresp., NBC News, Washington 1977–83; Corresp. MacNeil-Lehrer News Hour, PBS, Washington 1983–; Anchor for Frontline (PBS documentary series) 1983–; mem. Bd. of Advisers Henry Grady School of Journalism, Univ. of Ga. 1979–82, Bd. of Visitors Wake Fores Univ. 1982–, Bd. of Advisers Benton Fellowship in Broadcast Journalism, Univ. of Chicago 1984–; Trustee Duke Univ. 1985–; Knight Fellowship in broadcast journalism Stanford Univ. 1985–; mem. Nat. Acad. of TV Arts and Sciences, White House Corresps. Asscn. *Publication:* This is Judy Woodruff at the White House 1982. *Address:* c/o PBS, 1320 Braddock Place, Alexandria, Va. 22314, U.S.A.

WOODRUFF, Sir Michael Francis Addison, Kt., F.R.S., F.R.C.S., D.SC.; British surgeon; b. 3. April 1911, London; s. of the late Prof. Harold Addison Woodruff and Margaret Ada Cooper; m. Hazel Gwenyth Ashby 1946; two s. one d.; ed. Wesley Coll., Melbourne, Queen's Coll., Univ. of Melbourne, Australia; served as Captain, Australian Army Medical Corps, Malaya 1940–46; Tutor in Surgery, Univ. of Sheffield 1946–48; Lecturer in Surgery, Univ. of Aberdeen 1948–52; Prof. of Surgery, Univ. of Otago, New Zealand 1953–56; Prof. of Surgery, Univ. of Edinburgh 1957–77, Emer. 1977–; Surgeon, Edinburgh Royal Infirmary 1957–77; fmr. Dir. Nuffield Transplantation Surgery Unit, Edinburgh; Foreign Assoc., Acad. de Chirurgie (France) 1964; Hon. mem. American Surgical Asscn. 1965; Corresp. mem. Deutsche Gesellschaft für Chirurgie 1968; Hon. Fellow, American Coll. of Surgeons 1975, Royal Coll. of Physicians, Edin. 1981; Lister Medal 1969. *Publications:* Deficiency Diseases in Japanese Prison Camps (with A. Dean Smith) 1951, Transplantation of Tissues and Organs 1960, On Science and Surgery 1976, The Interaction of Cancer and Host 1980, Surgery for Dental Students (4th Edn.) (with Hedley Berry) 1984; articles on surgical topics and transplantation and tumour immunology. *Leisure interests:* music, sailing. *Address:* The Bield, 506 Lanark Road, Juniper Green, Midlothian, EH14 5DH, Scotland. *Telephone:* 031-453-3653.

WOODRUFF, Philip (see Mason, Philip).

WOODS, The Most Rev. Frank, K.B.E., M.A., D.D.; British ecclesiastic; b. 6 April 1907, Switzerland; s. of late Edward Sydney Woods and Clemence Rachel Woods; m. Jean M. Sprules 1936; two s. two d.; ed. Marlborough Coll., Trinity Coll., Cambridge, and Westcott House Theological Coll., Cambridge; Curate of St. Mary, Portsea 1931–33; Chaplain Trinity Coll., Cambridge and Examining Chaplain to Bishop of Bristol 1933–36; Vice-Prin. Wells Theological Coll. 1936–45; Chaplain to the Forces 1939–45; Vicar of Huddersfield 1945–52; Rural Dean of Huddersfield 1945–52; Hon. Canon of Wakefield and Proctor in Convocation Wakefield 1947–52; Chaplain to H.M. The King 1951–52; Bishop Suffragan of Middleton and Canon Residentiary of Manchester Cathedral 1952–57; Archbishop of Melbourne 1957–77; Chaplain, (Victoria) Order of St. John of Jerusalem 1962–71; Primate of the Church of England in Australia 1971–77; Hon. Fellow, Trinity Coll., Melbourne 1981; Hon. D.D. (Lambeth) 1957; Hon. LL.D. (Monash) 1979. *Leisure interests:* music, walking. *Address:* 18 Victoria Road, Camberwell, Vic. 3124, Australia.

WOODS, Michael, PH.D.; Irish politician; b. 8 Dec. 1935, Bray, Co. Wicklow; m. Margaret Maher; three s. two d.; ed. Univ. Coll. Dublin and Harvard Business School; fmr. horticulturalist and business exec.; mem Dail 1977–; Minister of State, Depts. of Taoiseach and Defence 1979; Minister for Health and Social Welfare 1979–81, March-Dec. 1982, for Social Welfare 1987–; Fianna Fail. *Address:* 13 Kilbarrack Grove, Raheny, Dublin 5, Republic of Ireland. *Telephone:* (01) 323357.

WOODSIDE, William Stewart, B.S., M.A.; American business executive; b. 31 Jan. 1922, Columbus, Ohio; s. of William S. Woodside and Harriet Frances (née Moorman) Woodside; m. Margaret-Sue Bernard 1975; ed. Lehigh Univ., Harvard Univ.; joined American Can Co. (now Primerica Corpn.) 1950, Asst. to Vice-Pres., Gen. Man. Dixie Cup Div., Easton, Pa. 1962–64, Admin. Asst. to Chair. Bd. 1964–66, to Vice-Pres. 1966–69, Sr. Vice-Pres. and Group Exec. World Wide Packaging 1969–74, Exec. Vice-Pres. Operations 1974–75, Pres. and C.O.O. 1975–80, Pres. and C.E.O. 1980, Chair. 1980–87 (C.E.O. 1980–84), Chair. Exec. Cttee. 1987–. *Address:* Primerica Corpn., 9 West 57th Street, New York, N.Y. 10019, U.S.A. (Office).

WOODWARD, C(omer) Vann, PH.D.; American historian; b. 13 Nov. 1908, Vanndale, Ark.; s. of Hugh Allison Woodward and Bess Vann Woodward; m. Glenn MacLeod 1937 (deceased); one s. (deceased); ed. Emory Univ., Columbia Univ. and Univ. of N. Carolina; Asst. Prof. Univ. of Fla. 1937–39, Univ. of Va. 1939–40; Assoc. Prof. Scripps Coll., Claremont Colls. 1940–43; Lieut. U.S.N.R. 1943–46; Prof. Johns Hopkins Univ. 1947–61; Sterling Prof. of History, Yale Univ. 1962–77, Prof. Emer. 1977–; Pres. American

Historical Asscn. 1968–69, Org. of American Historians 1968–69, Southern Historical Asscn. 1952–53; mem. American Philosophical Soc., Nat. Inst. of Arts and Letters, American Acad. of Arts and Sciences (Vice-Pres. 1987–88); Hon. LL.D. (Mich.) 1971, Hon. L.H.D. (Columbia) 1972, (Northwestern) 1977, (Brandeis) 1983, Hon. D.Litt. (Princeton) 1971, Hon. Litt.D. (Cambridge) 1975; Bancroft Prize for History 1952, Writing Award, American Acad. of Arts and Letters 1953, Pulitzer Prize for History 1982, Talcott Parsons Prize, American Acad. of Arts and Sciences. *Publications:* Tom Watson: Agrarian Rebel 1938, The Battle for Leyte Gulf 1947, Reunion and Reaction 1951, Origins of the New South 1951, The Strange Career of Jim Crow 1955, The Burden of Southern History 1960, American Counterpoint 1971, Thinking Back: The Perils of Writing History 1986; Ed.: The Comparative Approach to American History 1968, Responses of the President to Charges of Misconduct 1973, Mary Chesnut's Civil War 1981, The Private Mary Chestnut (co-ed.) 1984. *Leisure interests:* gardening, tennis. *Address:* 83 Rogers Road, Hamden, Conn. 06517, U.S.A. *Telephone:* (203) 624-4534.

WOODWARD, Edward, O.B.E.; British actor and singer; b. 1 June 1930; s. of Edward Oliver Woodward and Violet Edith Woodward; m. 1st Venetia Mary Collett 1952; two s. one d.; m. 2nd Michele Dotrice 1987; one d.; ed. Kingston Coll. and Royal Acad. of Dramatic Art; stage debut Castle Theatre, Farnham 1946; in repertory cos. in England and Scotland; London debut, Where There's a Will, Garrick Theatre 1955. *Other stage appearances include:* Mercutio in Romeo and Juliet, Laertes in Hamlet, Stratford 1958, Rattle of a Simple Man, Garrick 1962, Two Cities (musical) 1968, Cyrano in Cyrano de Bergerac, Flamineo in The White Devil, Nat. Theatre Co. 1971, The Wolf, Apollo 1973, Male of the Species, Piccadilly 1975, On Approval, Theatre Royal Haymarket 1976, The Dark Horse, Comedy 1978, Beggar's Opera (also dir.) 1980, The Assassin 1982, Richard III 1982; three productions, New York. *Films include:* Becket 1966, The File on the Golden Goose 1968, Hunted 1973, Sitting Target, Young Winston, The Wicker Man 1974, Stand Up Virgin Soldiers 1977, Breaker Morant 1980, The Appointment 1981, Comeback, Merlin and the Sword 1982, Champions 1983, A Christmas Carol, King David 1984, Uncle Tom's Cabin; over 2000 TV productions; title role in TV serials Callan 1966–71, The Equalizer 1985–89; 11 LP records as singer and three of poetry; numerous int. and nat. acting awards. *Leisure interests:* boating, geology. *Address:* c/o Eric Glass Ltd., 28 Berkeley Square, London, W1X 6HD, England. *Telephone:* 01-629 7162.

WOODWARD, Joanne Gignilliat; American actress; b. 27 Feb. 1930, Thomasville, Ga.; d. of Wade Woodward and Elinor Trimmier; m. Paul Newman (q.v.) 1958; three d.; ed. Louisiana State Univ.; numerous awards including Foreign Press Award for Best Actress 1957, Acad. Award 1957, Nat. Bd. Review Award 1957, Best Actress Award, Soc. of Film and TV Arts 1974. *Films include:* Count Three and Pray 1955, A Kiss Before Dying 1956, The Three Faces of Eve 1957, The Long Hot Summer 1958, Rally Round the Flag Boys 1958, The Sound and the Fury 1959, The Fugitive Kind 1959, From the Terrace 1960, Paris Blues 1961, The Stripper 1963, A New Kind of Love 1963, Signpost to Murder 1964, A Big Hand for the Little Lady 1966, A Fine Madness 1966, Rachel Rachel 1968, Winning 1969, W.U.S.A. 1970, They Might Be Giants 1971, The Effects of Gamma Rays on Man-in-the-Moon Marigolds 1972, The Death of a Snow Queen 1973, Summer Wishes, Winter Dreams 1973, The Drowning Pool 1975, The End 1978, The Shadow Box 1980, Candida (Play) 1981, Harry and Son 1984, The Glass Menagerie 1987. *TV includes:* All the Way Home, See How She Runs 1978, Streets of L.A. 1979, Crisis at Central High 1981, Do You Remember Love? 1985. *Address:* c/o Toni Howard, William Morris Agency, 151 El Camino, Beverly Hills, Calif. 90212, U.S.A.

WOODWARD, Adm. Sir John Forster, K.C.B.; British naval officer (retd.); b. 1 May 1932, Marazion, Cornwall; s. of late Tom Woodward and Mabel B. M. Woodward; m. Charlotte M. McMurtrie 1960; one s. one d.; ed. Britannia Royal Naval Coll., Dartmouth; Commanding Officer, H.M.S. Tireless 1961–62, H.M.S. Grampus 1964–65; Exec. Officer, H.M.S. Valiant 1965–67; Commdg. Officer, H.M.S. Warspite 1969; at Royal Coll. of Defence Studies, then in Directorate of Naval Plans, Ministry of Defence; Commdg. Officer, H.M.S. Sheffield 1976–78; Dir. of Naval Plans, Ministry of Defence 1978–81; Flag Officer, First Flotilla 1981–83; commanded British naval task force during Falkland Islands campaign 1982; Flag Officer, Submarines, and Commdr. Submarines, Eastern Atlantic, NATO May 1983–84; Deputy Chief of Defence Staff (Commitments) 1985–87; C.-in-C. Naval Home Command 1987–89, rank of Adm.; Flag Aide-de-Camp to H.M. the Queen 1987–. *Publication:* Strategy by Matrix 1980. *Leisure interests:* sailing, philately, skiing. *Address:* c/o The Naval Secretary, Ministry of Defence, Old Admiralty Building, Whitehall, London, SW1A 2BE, England.

WOODWARD, Kirsten; British couturier; b. 15 Nov. 1959, London; d. of Prof. Woodward and J. B. Woodward; ed. London Coll. of Fashion; stall at Hyper Hyper while still a student 1983; Designer Karl Lagerfeld 1984–; f. Kirsten Woodward Hats 1985–; also designed for Lanvin, Victor Edelstein, Betty Jackson, Alistair Blair, The Emanuels, Belleville Sassoon, Katharine Hammnet. *Leisure interests:* boats, horses, geography and ancient history, anthropology, writing. *Address:* c/o Kirsten Woodward Hats, 26 Portobello Green Arcade, London, W.10.

WOODWARD, Roger Robert, O.B.E.; Australian pianist, conductor and composer; b. 20 Dec. 1942, Sydney; s. of Francis W. and Gladys A. Woodward; one s. one d.; ed. Conservatorium of Music, Sydney and PWSH, Warsaw; début at Royal Festival Hall, London 1970; subsequently appeared with the five London orchestras; has performed throughout Eastern and Western Europe, Japan and the U.S.A.; has appeared at int. festivals and with the major orchestras throughout world; extensive repertoire and is noted for interpretation of Chopin, Beethoven, Bach and Twentieth Century Music; Artistic Dir. Nat. Chamber Orchestra for Contemporary Music in Australia 'Alpha Centaure' 1989 and festivals in London; performs each season at leading int. festivals works by contemporary composers; Fellow Chopin Inst., Warsaw; Kt. (Breffini). *Leisure interests:* cooking, chess, swimming, gardening, painting, design. *Address:* c/o Norman Lawrence Artists Management, 35 Britannia Row, London, N.1, England. *Telephone:* 01-226 3377, 01-359 0579.

WOOLARD, Edgar Smith, Jr., B.SC.; American business executive; b. 15 April 1934, Washington, N.C.; s. of Edgar Smith and Mamie Rowena (née Boone) Woolard; m. Peggy Lou Harrell 1956; two d.; ed. North Carolina State Univ.; Gen. Man. Textile Fibres, E.I. du Pont de Nemours & Co. Inc., Wilmington, Del. 1978–81, Vice-Pres. Textile Fibres 1981–83, Exec. Vice-Pres. 1983–85, Vice-Chair. 1985–87, Pres. and C.O.O. 1987–; mem. Bd. of Dirs. Diamond State Telephone Co., Wilmington, N.C. Textile Foundation, Raleigh, Citicorp. *Address:* E.I. du Pont de Nemours & Co., 1007 Market Street, Wilmington, Del. 19898, U.S.A.

WOOLCOTT, Richard, A.O., B.A.; Australian diplomatist; b. 11 June 1928, Sydney; s. of Dr. and Mrs. A. R. Woolcott; m. Birgit Christensen 1952; two s. one d.; ed. Frankston High School, Geelong Grammar School, Univ. of Melbourne and London Univ. School of Slavonic and E. European Studies; joined Australian Foreign Service 1951; served in Australian missions in London, Moscow (twice), S. Africa, Malaya, Singapore and Ghana; attended UN Gen. Ass. 1962; Acting High Commr. to Singapore 1963–64; High Commr. to Ghana 1967–70; accompanied Prime Ministers Menzies 1965, Holt 1966, McMahon 1971, 1972 and Whitlam 1973, 1974 on visits to Asia, Europe, the Americas and the Pacific; Adviser at Commonwealth Heads of Govt. Confs. London 1965, Ottawa 1973; Pacific Forum 1972, 1973; Australia-Japan Ministerial Cttee. 1972, 1973; Head, S. Asia Div., Dept. of Foreign Affairs 1973; Deputy Sec. Dept. of Foreign Affairs 1974; Amb. to Indonesia 1975–78, to Philippines 1978–82; Perm. Rep. to UN July 1982–; Australian Rep. on UN Security Council 1985–86; attended confs. UNCTAD V (Manila) 1979, ESCAP (Manila) 1979, South-East Asian Ministers of Educ. Cttee. (Manila) 1980; rep. of Australia at Non-aligned Summit meeting, Harare 1986. *Publication:* Australian Foreign Policy 1973. *Address:* Permanent Mission of Australia to the United Nations, 1 Dag Hammarskjöld Plaza, 885 Second Avenue, 16th Floor, New York, N.Y. 10017, U.S.A.

WOOLDRIDGE, Dean E., M.S., PH.D.; American engineer; b. May 1913, Chickasha, Okla.; s. of Auttie Noonan and Irene Amanda (née Kerr) Wooldridge; m. M. Helene Detweiler 1936; two s. one d.; ed. Univ. of Okla. and Calif. Inst. of Tech.; mem. tech. staff, Bell Telephone Labs. 1936–46; Dir. of Electronic Research and Devt., Hughes Aircraft Co. 1946, subsequently Vice-Pres. for Research and Devt.; Co-founder & Pres. Ramo-Wooldridge Corpn. 1953–58, Pres. Thompson Ramo Wooldridge Inc. (TRW Inc.) 1958–62, Dir. until 1969; Research Assoc. in Eng., Calif. Inst. of Tech. 1962–; Chair. Nat. Inst. of Health Study Cttee. 1964, 1965; Fellow, American Acad. of Arts and Sciences, American Physical Soc., A.A.A.S., Inst. of Electrical and Electronic Engineers, A.I.A.A.; mem. N.A.S., Nat. Acad. of Eng.; Citation of Honor, Air Force Asscn.; E. E. Hackett Award 1955; Distinguished Service Citation, Univ. of Okla. 1960, A.A.A.S.—Westinghouse Award for Science Writing, Distinguished Alumni Award, Calif. Inst. of Tech. 1983. *Publications:* The Machinery of the Brain 1963, The Machinery of Life 1966, Mechanical Man: The Physical Basis of Intelligent Life 1968, Sensory Processing in the Brain 1979; several articles in journals and magazines. *Address:* 4545 Via Esperanza, Santa Barbara, Calif. 93110, U.S.A.

WOOLFORD, Harry Russell Halkerston, O.B.E. ; British art gallery director; b. 23 May 1905; s. of H. Woolford; m. Nancy Philip 1932; one d.; ed. Edinburgh Coll. of Art; studied art in London, Paris and Italy; Chief, now Consultant Restorer, Nat. Gallery of Scotland; Fellow Museums Asscn., Inst. of Conservation, Int. Inst. for Conservation of Historic and Artistic works; Hon. mem. Asscn. of British Picture Restorers; Hon. M.A. (Dundee Univ.) 1976. *Address:* 7A Bartongate Avenue, Edinburgh, EH4 8BD, Scotland. *Telephone:* 031-339 6861.

WOOLLCOMBE, Rt. Rev. Kenneth John, M.A., S.T.D.; British ecclesiastic; b. 2 Jan. 1924, Sutton, Surrey; s. of Rev. Edward P. Woollcombe O.B.E., and Elsie O. Wood; m. 1st Gwendoline R. V. Hodges 1950 (died 1976); m. 2nd Juliet Dearmer 1980; four d.; ed. Haileybury Coll., Technical Coll., Wednesbury, St. John's Coll., Oxford and Westcott House, Cambridge; Sub-Lieut., R.N.V.R. 1945–46; Curate, Grimsby Parish Church 1951–53; Fellow, Chaplain and Tutor, St. John's Coll., Oxford 1953–60; Prof. of Dogmatic Theology, Gen. Theological Seminary, New York 1960–63, Prin. of Episcopal Theological Coll., Edinburgh and Canon of St. Mary's Cathedral, Edinburgh 1963–71; Bishop of Oxford 1971–78; Asst. Bishop of London 1978–81, Diocese of Worcester March 1989–; Canon Residentiary,

St. Paul's Cathedral 1981-, Precentor 1982-; Chair. Soc. for Promotion of Christian Knowledge (S.P.C.K.) 1973-79; Chair. Churches' Council for Covenanting 1978-82; Chair. Cttee. for Roman Catholic Relations 1985-88; mem. Court of Ecclesiastical Causes Reserved 1984; Hon. Fellow St. John's Coll., Oxford 1971; Hon. S.T.D. (Univ. of the South, Sewanee, Tennessee) 1963; Hon. D.D. (Hartford, Conn.) 1975. *Publications:* Essays on Typology (joint author) 1957, and contributions to other theological publications. *Leisure interests:* reading, music. *Address:* 5 Amen Court, London, EC4M 7BU, England.

WOOLLEY, Kenneth Frank, B.ARCH., L.F.R.A.I.A.; Australian architect; b. 29 May 1933, Sydney; s. of Frank and Doris May (Mudear) Woolley; m. 1st Cynthia Stuart (divorced 1979); m. 2nd Virginia Braden 1980; two s. one d.; ed. Sydney Boys' High School, Univ. of Sydney; Design Architect, Govt. Architect's Office, Sydney 1955-56, 1957-63; Asst. Architect, Chamberlin, Powell and Bon, London 1956-57; Partner, Ancher, Mortlock, Murray & Woolley, Sydney 1964-69, Dir. 1969-75; Dir. Ancher, Mortlock & Woolley Pty. Ltd., Sydney 1975-; mem. Quality Review Cttee. Darung Harbour Redevt. Authority 1985; Visiting Prof., Univ. of N.S.W. School of Architecture 1983; Visiting Tutor and Critic, Univ. of Sydney, Univ. of N.S.W., N.S.W. Inst. of Tech., Sydney; mem. N.S.W. Bd. of Architects 1960-72, N.S.W. Bldg. Regulations Advisory Cttee. 1960-74, N.S.W. Bd. of Architectural Educ. 1969-72, Royal Australian Inst. of Architects Aboriginal Housing Panel 1972-76; Life F.R.A.I.A. 1976; Sulman Award 1962, Bronze Medal 1962, Wilkinson Award 1962, 1968, 1983, Blacket Award 1964, 1969, Civic Design Award 1983, numerous other architectural awards. *Major works include:* Australian Embassy, Bangkok, Sydney Town Hall renovations, new offices and city sq., three student union bldgs., Univs. in N.S.W., numerous urban housing devts., radio stations, Vanuatu, Solomon Islands, over 4,000 production houses, State Govt. offices, Sydney, Fisher Library, Sydney Univ. *Publications:* numerous papers and articles in architectural journals. *Leisure interests:* golf, sailing, music, drawing. *Address:* 40 Collins Street, Surrey Hills, N.S.W. 2010 (Office); 8A Cooper Street, Paddington, N.S.W. 2021, Australia 2010 (Home). *Telephone:* 332 1255 (Office); 357 6658 (Home).

WOOLSEY. Clinton Nathan, M.D.; American professor of neurophysiology; b. 30 Nov. 1904, Brooklyn, New York; s. of Joseph Woodhull Woolsey and Lillian Matilda Aichholz; m. Harriet Runion 1942; three s.; ed. public schools, N.Y. State, Union Coll., Schenectady, N.Y., and Johns Hopkins School of Medicine; Asst. in Physiology, subsequently Assoc. Prof. of Physiology, Johns Hopkins Univ. School of Medicine 1933-48; Charles Sumner Slichter Prof. of Neurophysiology Univ.of Wis. 1948-75, Emer. 1975-; Dir. Lab. of Neurophysiology 1960-73, Biomedical Unit Co-ordinator Waisman Center on Mental Retardation and Human Devt. 1973-78; Organizer IBRO-Workshops for Western Hemisphere and Asia 1979-82; mem. N.A.S.; Fellow, A.A.A.S., American Physiological Soc. and mem. several other professional orgs.; mem. Div. of Medical Science, Nat. Research Council 1952-58; consultant or mem. many nat. cttees; various awards and hon. lectureships; Ralph Gerard Award, Soc. for Neuroscience (with Jerzy E. Rose) 1982. *Publication:* Ed. Multiple Cortical Somatic, Visual and Auditory Areas 1981. *Address:* 106 Virginia Terrace, Madison, Wis. 53705, U.S.A. (Home). *Telephone:* (608) 233-6094.

WOOTTON, Charles Greenwood, M.A., N.D.C.; American diplomatist and oil company executive; b. 8 Aug. 1924, Elizabethtown, Ill.; s. of Estel C. Wootton and Sarah B. Greenwood; m. Elizabeth Grechko 1944; one s. five d.; ed. Columbia and Stanford Univs., Nat. Defence Coll. of Canada; Vice-Consul, Stuttgart 1949; Second Sec., American Embassy, Manila 1951; Consul, Vice-Consul, Bordeaux 1954; Int. Economist, Dept. of Commerce 1956; First Sec., Second Sec., Mission to European Communities 1959; Counsellor for Econ. and Commercial Affairs, American Embassy, Ottawa 1965; Counsellor for Econ. and Commercial Affairs, American Embassy, Bonn 1970, Minister 1971; Deputy Sec.-Gen. OECD 1974-80; with Gulf Oil Corpn. 1980-85; Co-ordinator Int. Public Affairs, Chevron Corpn., San Francisco 1985-; Chair. Standing Group of Secs. Gen. of Co-ordinated Int. Orgs. 1974-78, OECD Ad Hoc Group on Steel Industry 1977-78; Trustee, Nat. Planning Asscn., Washington, D.C., mem. State Dept. Advisory Cttee., Canadian-American Cttee.; mem. Advisory Bd., Inst. for Int. Educ., W. Coast Region; mem. Bd. of Dirs., Int. Visitors Center of the Bay Area; Superior Honor Medal, Dept. of State 1964, Golden Sports Medal (Fed. Germany) 1973. *Leisure interests:* jogging, squash, other sports, reading. *Address:* Chevron Corporation, 225 Bush Street, San Francisco, Calif. 94104, U.S.A. *Telephone:* (412) 284-4260 (Home).

WORCESTER, Robert Milton, B.SC., M.B.I.M.; American opinion researcher; b. 21 Dec. 1933, Kansas City; s. of late C. M. and Violet Worcester; m. 1st Joann Ransdell 1958; m. 2nd Margaret Noel Smallbone 1982; two s.; ed. Univ. of Kansas; Consultant with McKinsey & Co. 1962-65; Controller and Asst. to Chair. Opinion Research Corpn. 1965-69; Man. Dir. Market & Opinion Research Int. Ltd. (MORI) 1969-, Chair. 1973-; Consultant to The Times, Sunday Times, The Economist; Vice-Pres. Int. Soc. Science Council UNESCO 1989-; Trustee World Wildlife Fund (U.K.), British Museum Devt. Trust; mem. Pilgrims Soc.; F.R.S.A.; Co-Ed. Int. Journal of Public Opinion Research. *Publications:* Political Communications (with Martin Harrop) 1982, Political Opinion Polling: An International Review 1983, Consumer Market Research Handbook (3rd. edn., Ed. with John

Downham) 1986, Private Opinions, Public Polls (with Lesley Watkins) 1986. *Leisure interests:* choral music, scuba diving, skiing. *Address:* 32 Old Queen Street, London, SW1H 9HP, England. *Telephone:* 01-222 0232.

WORLOCK, Most Rev. Archbishop Derek John Harford; British ecclesiastic; b. 4 Feb. 1920; s. of Capt. Harford and Dora (Hoblyn) Worlock; ed. St. Edmund's Coll., Ware; ordained Roman Catholic priest 1944; Curate, Our Lady of Victories, Kensington 1944-45; Pvt. Sec. to Archbishop of Westminster 1945-64; Rector and Rural Dean, Church of St. Mary and St. Michael, London, E.1 1964-65; Bishop of Portsmouth 1965-76; Privy Chamberlain to Pope Pius XII 1949-53; Domestic Prelate of the Pope 1953-65; Peritus at Vatican Council II 1963-65; Consultor to Council of Laity 1967-76; Episcopal Sec. to Roman Catholic Bishops' Conf. 1967-76, Vice-Pres. 1979-; Archbishop of Liverpool and Metropolitan of the Northern Province 1976-; mem. Synod Council 1976-77, Holy See's Laity Council 1977-; Cttee. for the Family 1977-81; English del. to Int. Synod of Bishops 1974, 1977, 1980, 1983, 1987; Hon. Fellowship Portsmouth Polytechnic 1988; Hon. LL.D. (Liverpool) 1981; Hon. D. Tech. (Liverpool Polytechnic) 1987; Kt. Commdr. of the Holy Sepulchre of Jerusalem 1966. *Publications:* (Compiler) Seek Ye First 1949, Take One at Bedtime (anthology) 1962, English Bishops at the Council 1965, Turn and Turn Again 1971, Give Me Your Hand 1977, Better Together (with David Sheppard, q.v.) 1987. *Address:* Archbishop's House, 87 Green Lane, Liverpool, L18 2EP, England. *Telephone:* 051-722 2379.

WORMS, Gérard Etienne; French company director; b. 1 Aug. 1936, Paris; s. of André Worms and Thérèse Dreyfus; m. Michèle Rousseau 1960; one s. one d.; ed. Lycées Carnot, Saint-Louis, and Ecole Nat. Supérieure des Mines, Paris; Engineer, Org. commune des régions sahariennes 1960-62; Head of Dept., Délégation à l'Aménagement du Territoire et à l'Action Régionale 1963-67; Tech. Adviser, Office of Olivier Guichard (Minister of Industry, later of Planning) 1967-69, Office of Jacques Chaban-Delmas (Prime Minister) 1969-71; Asst. Man. Dir., Librairie Hachette 1972-75, Man. Dir. 1975-81, Dir. 1978-81; Prof., Ecole des Hautes Etudes Commerciales 1962-69, Supervisor of complementary courses, Faculty of Letters and Human Sciences, Paris 1963-69; Prof. Ecole Polytechnique 1974-; Vice-Pres. Syndicat nat. de l'édition 1974-81; Exec. Vice-Pres. Rhône-Poulenc S.A. 1981-83; Exec. Vice-Pres. Compagnie Financière de Suez 1983; Chevalier, Ordre nat. du Mérite, Chevalier, Ordre du Mérite maritime, Chevalier, Légion d'honneur. *Publications:* Les méthodes modernes de l'économie appliquée 1965; various articles on economic methods in specialized journals. *Address:* 61 bis avenue de la Motte Picquet, 75015 Paris, France. *Telephone:* 47.83.99.43.

WORNER, Howard Knox, C.B.E., D.SC., F.A.A., F.T.S., F.R.A.C.I., F.I.M., F.I.M.M., F.A.I.E., M.A.I.M.E.; Australian metallurgist and scientific consultant; b. 3 Aug. 1913; s. of late John and Ida Worner; m. Rilda B. Muller 1937; two s. (one deceased) one d.; ed. Bendigo School of Mines and Univ. of Melbourne; Lecturer in Metallography, Univ. of Melbourne 1935-38; Research Fellow, Nat. Health and Medical Research Council of Australia 1939-46; Consultant, Defence Forces, on Dental and Surgical Materials 1940-46; tropical scientific service, Australian army 1944-45; Prof. of Metallurgy, Univ. of Melbourne 1947-55, Dean, Faculty of Eng. 1953-55; Dir. of Research, The Broken Hill Pty. Co. Ltd. 1956-62; int. consultant 1963; Dir. of New Process Devt., CRA Ltd. 1964-75; Chair. Nat. Energy Advisory Cttee. 1976-77; Chair. Victoria Brown Coal Cttee. (later Council) and mem. Nat. Energy Research and Devt. Cttee. 1976-81; scientific consultant 1981-; Hon. Sec. Australian Acad. of Tech. Sciences 1975-86; Hon. Prof., Univ. of Wollongong 1987-; Dir. Microwave Applications Research Centre 1987-; seven medals from professional socs. and univs. and numerous other awards; Hon. D.Sc. (Newcastle) 1966, Hon. D.Eng. (Melbourne) 1983. *Publications:* 145 scientific papers and monographs. *Leisure interests:* mineral collecting, oil painting. *Address:* 4/3 Georges Place, Wollongong, N.S.W. 2500, Australia. *Telephone:* (042) 270375 (Office); (042) 273578 (Home).

WÖRNER, Manfred, DR.JUR.; German politician; b. 24 Sept. 1934, Stuttgart; s. of Carl Wörner; m. 2nd Elfriede Reinsch 1982; one s. by previous marriage; ed. Univs. of Heidelberg, Paris, and Munich; CDU State Parl. Adviser, Baden-Württemberg 1962-64; mem. Bundestag 1965-88, Deputy Chair. CDU/CSU Parl. Party; Minister of Defence 1982-88; Sec.-Gen. of NATO July 1988-. *Address:* Office of the Secretary-General, NATO, 1110 Brussels, Belgium.

WORRALL, Denis John, PH.D.; South African lawyer and politician; b. 29 May 1935, Benoni; s. of Cecil John and Hazel Worrall; m. Anita Denise Ianco 1965; three s.; ed. Univ. of Cape Town, Univ. of S.A. and Cornell Univ., U.S.A.; taught political science, Cornell Univ., Univ. of Calif. at Los Angeles, Univ. of Natal, Univ. of S.A. and Univ. of Witwatersrand; Cornell Research Fellow, Univ. of Ibadan, Nigeria 1962-63; f. and Ed. New Nation 1967-74; Research Prof. and Dir. Inst. for Social and Econ. Research, Rhodes Univ. -1974; Senator for Cape 1974-77; Amb. to Australia 1983-84, to U.K. 1984-87; Advocate, Supreme Court of S.A.; M.P. for Cape Town-Gardens 1977-83; independent cand. for Helderberg in 1987 Election; mem. Pres's. Council 1980-83; mem. Nat. Democratic Movt. 1987-88; f. Ind. Movt. 1988; Leader Ind. Party 1988-89; co-founder Democratic Party 1989. *Publications:* South Africa: Government and Politics; numerous articles. *Leisure interests:* reading, tennis. *Address:* 42 Rhodes

Avenue, Newlands, Cape, 8001, South Africa. *Telephone:* 024 222 10 (Office).

WORSTHORNE, Peregrine Gerard, M.A.; British journalist; b. 22 Dec. 1923, London; s. of Col. A. Koch de Gooreynd, and Baroness Norman; m. Claudia Bertrand de Colasse 1950; one d.; ed. Stowe School, Peterhouse, Cambridge and Magdalen Coll., Oxford; editorial staff, Glasgow Herald 1946–48; editorial staff, The Times 1948–50, Washington corresp. 1950–52, Leader writer 1952–55; Leader writer, Daily Telegraph 1955–61; Assoc. Ed. Sunday Telegraph 1961–86, Ed. 1986–; Granada Television Journalist of the Year 1981. *Publications:* The Socialist Myth 1972, Peregrinations 1980, By The Right 1987. *Leisure interests:* walking, tennis. *Address:* 6 Kempson Road, London, SW6 4PU; Westerlies, Anchor Hill, Wivenhoe, Essex, England. *Telephone:* (020622) 2886.

WORSWICK (George) David (Norman), C.B.E., M.A., F.B.A.; British economist; b. 18 Aug. 1916, London; s. of Thomas Worswick and Eveline (née Green) Worswick; m. Sylvia E. Walsh 1940; one s. two d.; ed. St. Paul's School, London and New Coll., Oxford; research staff, Oxford Univ. Inst. of Statistics 1940–60; Fellow and Tutor in Econs. Magdalen Coll., Oxford 1945–65; Dir. Nat. Inst. of Econ. and Social Research 1965–82, Consultant 1985–; Visiting Prof. M.I.T. 1962–63; Pres. Royal Econ. Soc. 1982–84; Hon. D.Sc. (City Univ.) 1975. *Publications:* ed. and contrib. to books on econs. and articles in journals. *Leisure interest:* walking. *Address:* 25 Beech Croft Road, Oxford, OX2 7AY, England. *Telephone:* (0865) 52486.

WORTH, Irene; American actress; b. 23 June 1916; ed. Univ. of Calif. at Los Angeles; Daily Mail Nat. Television Award 1953–54; British Film Acad. Award for Orders to Kill 1958; Page One Award, Newspaper Guild of New York, for Toys in the Attic 1960; American Theatre Wing "Tony" Award for Tiny Alice 1965; Evening Standard Award for Noel Coward Trilogy 1966; Whitbread Anglo-American Theatre Award 1967; Variety Club of Great Britain Award 1967; Tony Award and Jefferson Award for Sweet Bird of Youth 1975; Drama Desk Award for The Cherry Orchard 1977; Whitbread Anglo-American Award 1967; Hon. C.B.E. 1975; first appeared as Fenella in Escape Me Never, New York 1942; debut on Broadway as Cecily Hardern in The Two Mrs. Carrolls 1948; London appearances in Love Goes to Press 1946, The Play's the Thing 1947, Edward My Son 1948, Home is Tomorrow 1948, Champagne for Delilah 1949, The Cocktail Party 1950, Othello 1951, A Midsummer Night's Dream 1952, The Other Heart 1952, The Merchant of Venice 1953, A Day by the Sea 1953–54, The Queen and the Rebels 1955, Hotel Paradiso 1956, Maria Stuart 1958, The Potting Shed 1958, King Lear 1962, The Physicists 1963, The Ides of March 1963, A Song at Twilight 1966, Shadows of the Evening 1966, Come into the Garden Maud 1966, Heartbreak House 1967, Oedipus 1968, Notes on a Love Affair, Lyric Theatre, other appearances include: The Cocktail Party, New York 1950, Old Vic tour of S. Africa 1952, Shakespeare Festival, Stratford, Ont. 1953, 1959, A Life in the Sun, Edinburgh Festival 1955, Maria Stuart, New York 1957, Toys in the Attic, New York 1960, Royal Shakespeare Theatre, Stratford 1962, World tour of King Lear 1964, Tiny Alice, New York 1965, worked with Peter Brook's Int. Theatre Research Centre, Paris and Iran 1970, 1971, Hedda in Hedda Gabler, Stratford, Ont. 1970, The Seagull, Chichester Festival Theatre 1973, Ghosts, The Seagull, Hamlet, Greenwich Theatre 1974, Sweet Bird of Youth, Kennedy Center, Washington D.C., Brooklyn Acad. of Music, and Harkness Theatre, New York, Drake Theatre, Ill. 1975, Misalliance, Drake Theatre, Lake Forest, Ill. 1976, The Cherry Orchard, Lincoln Center 1977, Old Times, Ill. 1977, After the Season 1978, Happy Days, New York 1979, The Lady from Dubuque, New York 1980, L'Olimpiade, Edin. Festival 1982, The Chalk Garden, New York 1982, The Physicists, Washington 1983, The Golden Age, New York 1984, Coriolanus, Nat. Theatre 1984, The Bay at Nice, London 1986, The Mask of the Red Death, New York 1987, You Never Can Tell, London 1987–88, Coriolanus, New York 1988; films include: Orders to Kill 1957, The Scapegoat 1958, King Lear, Nicholas and Alexandra 1971, Eye Witness 1981; television: Coriolanus 1984. *Address:* c/o ICM Sixth Floor, Milton Goldman, 6th Floor, 40 West 57th Street, New York, N.Y. 10019, U.S.A.

WORTHINGTON, Edgar Barton, C.B.E., F.L.S., F.R.G.S., PH.D.; British biologist; b. 13 Jan. 1905, London; s. of Edgar Worthington and Amy Beale; m. 1st Stella Johnson 1930 (died 1978), three d.; m. 2nd Harriett Stockton 1980; ed. Rugby School, and Gonville and Caius Coll., Cambridge; Frank Smart Student Gonville and Caius Coll. during Fishing Surveys of African Lakes 1927–30; Balfour Student Cambridge Univ. 1930–33, Leader Expedition to E. African Lakes; Demonstrator in Zoology Cambridge Univ. 1933–37; Scientist for African Research Survey 1934–37; Dir. Freshwater Biological Assen. of British Empire 1937–46; Scientific Adviser Middle East Supply Council 1943–45; Devt. Adviser, Uganda 1946; Scientific Sec. Colonial Research Council 1946–49; Seconded as Scientific Sec. E. Africa High Comm. 1947–51; Sec.-Gen. Scientific Council for Africa South of the Sahara 1951–55; Deputy Dir.-Gen. (Scientific) Nature Conservancy, London 1956–65; Scientific Dir. of Int. Biological Programme 1965–75; Hon. mem. Int. Union for Conservation of Nature 1978; Mungo Park Medal of Royal Scottish Geographical Soc. 1938; Knight of the Golden Ark (Netherlands) 1976. *Publications:* Fishing Survey of Lakes Albert and Kioga 1929, Fisheries of Uganda 1932, Inland Waters of Africa (with Stella Worthington) 1933, Science in Africa 1938, Middle East Science 1946, Development

Plan for Uganda 1947, Life in Lakes and Rivers (with T. T. Macan) 1951, Survey of Research and Scientific Services in East Africa 1952, Science in the Development of Africa 1958, Man-made Lakes: Problems and Environmental Effects (Editor) 1973, The Evolution of IBP 1975, Arid-land Irrigation: Environmental Problems (Editor) 1977, The Nile 1978, The Ecological Century 1983, and over 100 scientific papers and articles in journals. *Leisure interests:* field sports, farming. *Address:* Colin Godmans, Furner's Green, nr. Uckfield, Sussex TN22 3RR, England. *Telephone:* (082 574) 322.

WOUK, Herman, A.B.; American writer; b. 27 May 1915, New York; s. of Abraham Isaac Wouk and Esther Levine; m. Betty Sarah Brown 1945; three s. (one deceased); ed. Columbia Univ.; radio script-writer for leading comedians, New York 1935–41; presidential consultant to U.S. Treasury 1941; served U.S.N.R. 1942–46; Visiting Prof. of English, Yeshiva Univ., N.Y. 1952–57; Trustee, Coll. of the Virgin Islands 1961–69; mem. Authors' Guild, U.S.A., Author's League, Center for Book Nat. Advisory Bd., Library of Congress, Advisory Council, Center for U.S.–China Arts Exchange; Hon. L.H.D. (Yeshiva Univ.); Hon. D.Litt. (Clark Univ.), Hon. D.Lit. (American Int. Coll.) 1979; Pulitzer Prize for Fiction 1952, Columbia Univ. Medal for Excellence, Alexander Hamilton Medal, Columbia Univ. 1980, Ralph Waldo Emerson Award, Int. Platform Assen. 1981, Univ. of Calif., Berkeley Medal 1984. *Publications:* Aurora Dawn 1947, The City Boy 1948, Slattery's Hurricane 1949, The Traitor (play) 1949, The Caine Mutiny (novel) 1951, The Caine Mutiny Court-Martial (play) 1953, Marjorie Morningstar 1955, Nature's Way (play) 1957, This is my God 1959, Youngblood Hawke (novel) 1962, Don't Stop the Carnival (novel) 1965, The Winds of War (novel) 1971, War and Remembrance 1978 (screenplay for TV serial 1986), The Winds of War (TV screenplay) 1983, Inside, Outside 1985. *Leisure interests:* Hebraic studies, travel. *Address:* c/o BSW Literary Agency, 3255 N Street, N.W., Washington, D.C. 20007, U.S.A.

WOYTOWICZ-RUDNICKA, Stefania; Polish concert singer; b. 8 Oct. 1922, Orynin; d. of Michał and Domicela Zwolakowska Woytowicz; m. 1952; ed. State Higher School of Music; concerts in Europe, U.S.A., China, Japan; tour of Singapore, Hong Kong, New Zealand, India with Australian Broadcasting Comm.; contract with Deutsche Grammophon; also recorded with RCA Victor, Supraphon, Polskie Nagrania and others; participates in Vienna Festival, Edinburgh Festival, Warsaw Autumn and others; Pres. Gen. Bd., Warsaw Music Assen.; First Prize in Prague Spring Int. Singing Competition 1954, State Prize (2nd Class) 1964, Officer's Cross, Order of Polonia Restituta 1968, Orpheus Prize, Polish Musicians' Assen. 1967, Diploma of Ministry of Foreign Affairs 1970, Medal of 30th Anniversary of People's Poland 1974, Prize of Minister of Culture and Arts (1st Class) 1975, Prize of Union of Polish Composers 1978, Prize of daily "Trybuna Ludu" 1978. *Address:* Al. Przyjaciół 3 m. 13, 00-565 Warsaw, Poland.

WOŹNIAK, Jerzy; Polish economist and politician; b. 13 Dec. 1932, Jaworznik; ed. Acad. of Mining and Metallurgy, Cracow; foreman, then man. of steel plant Ironworks "Batory", Chorzów 1957–66; man. of steel plant, then Deputy Dir. for Production Feliks Dzierżyński Ironworks, Dąbrowa Górnicza 1966–72; Vice-Dir. for Metallurgy, Union of Iron and Steel Metallurgy 1972–73; Dir. Ironworks Baildon, Katowice 1973–76; Under-Sec. of State, Ministry of Metallurgy 1976–81, First Deputy Minister 1978–81; Under-Sec. of State, Deputy Minister, Ministry of Metallurgy and Machine Industry 1981–83; Minister of Economy of Materials 1983–85, of Economy of Materials and Fuels 1985–87; Amb. to Romania 1988–; mem. PZPR 1953–; Kt.'s and Commdr.'s Cross, Order of Polonia Restituta, Order of Banner of Labour (2nd Class) and other distinctions. *Address:* Embassy of the Polish People's Republic, Al Alexandru 23, Bucharest, Romania.

WOŹNIAK, Marian, M.ECON.; Polish politician; b. 2 March 1936, Dąbrowica; ed. Higher School of Econs., Poznań; employee, Voivodship Econ. Planning Comm., Zielona Góra 1957–61; Head of Investment Planning Section, Mazovian Refining and Petrochemical Plant, Płock 1961–65; Vice-Dir. Petrobudowa Enterprise, Płock 1965–67; Chair. Town Nat. Council, Płock 1967–70; Deputy Chair. Voivodship Nat. Council, Warsaw 1970–72; Vice-Dir., later Dir. of Team for Local Economy in Planning Comm. attached to Council of Ministers 1973–78; Voivode of Siedlce 1979–81; mem. Comm. for Econ. Reform, Chair. Team for admin. and local economy 1980–88; mem. Polish United Workers' Party (PZPR) 1960–, First Sec. PZPR Voivodship Cttee., Siedlce 1981, mem. PZPR Cen. Cttee. 1981–, Sec. PZPR Cen. Cttee. 1981–82, 1985–88, alt. mem. Political Bureau of PZPR Cen. Cttee. Feb.–July 1982, mem. 1982–88; First Sec. PZPR Warsaw Cttee. 1982–85; Head of Comm. of Econ. Policy, Econ. Reform and Workers self-govt. of PZPR Cen. Cttee. 1986–88; Chair. Party Govt. Comm. for Inspection and Modernization of Organization Structures of Econ. and the State 1986–88; Amb. to People's Repub. of China 1988–; Deputy to Seym 1985–; Kt.'s and Commdr.'s Cross, Order of Polonia Restituta and other decorations. *Address:* Embassy of the People's Polish Republic, 1, Ri Tan Lu, Beijing, People's Republic of China.

WRAN, Hon. Neville Kenneth, Q.C., LL.B.; Australian barrister and politician; b. Sydney; m. Jill Hickson 1976; one s. one d. by previous marriage; ed. Fort Street Boys' High School, Sydney Univ.; solicitor, then admitted to Bar 1957; apptd. Q.C. 1986; mem. N.S.W. Legis. Council 1970–73; Deputy Leader of Opposition 1971–72; Leader of Legis. Council 1972–73; mem. N.S.W. Legis. Assembly for Bass Hill 1973–86; Leader of Opposition 1973–76; Premier of N.S.W. 1976–84, Premier and Minister for the Arts

1984–85, Premier, Minister for the Arts and Minister for Ethnic Affairs 1985–86 (resgnd.); Nat. Pres. Australian Labor Party 1980–86; Chair. CSIRO 1986–; Exec. Dir. Whitlam, Turnbull and Co. 1987–; mem. Australian Bicentennial Authority 1986–88; Branch and Electorate Council positions; mem. Cen. Exec. N.S.W. Branch, Labor Party; fmr. mem. Health Cttee; Nat. Pres. Labor Party 1980–82. *Leisure interests:* reading, walking, swimming, cycling, tennis. *Address:* 9th Floor, 60 Park Street, Sydney, N.S.W. 200; GPO Box 4545, Sydney, N.S.W. 2001, Australia. *Telephone:* 267-8500.

WRAY, Gordon Richard, EUR.ING., PH.D., D.SC., F.ENG., F.R.S.; British professor of engineering design; b. 30 Jan. 1928, Farnworth, Lancs.; s. of Joseph Wray and Letitia Wray (née Jones); m. Kathleen Senior 1954; one s. one d.; ed. Bolton Tech. Coll. and Univ. of Manchester; Eng. Apprentice, Bennis Combustion, Bolton 1943; Design Draughtsman, Dobson and Barlow, Bolton 1946; Sir Walter Preston Scholar, Univ. of Manchester 1949; Devt. Eng., Platts (Barton) 1952; Lecturer in Mechanical Eng., Bolton Tech. Coll. 1953; Lecturer in Textile Eng., UMIST 1955; Reader in Mechanical Eng., Loughborough Univ. 1966–70, Prof. and Head of Dept. 1970–88; Fellowship of Eng. Prof. in the Principles of Eng. Design and Dir. Eng. Design Inst., Loughborough Univ. of Tech. 1988–; mem. Dept. of Industry Chief Scientist's Requirements Bd. 1974–75, SEFI Cttee. on Innovation, Brussels 1980–82, Royal Soc. Working Group on Agricultural Eng. 1981–82, Royal Soc. Sectional Cttee. 4(1) 1985, Cttee. of the Eng. Profs. Conf. 1985, Council, I.Mech.E. 1964–67; I.Mech.E., Viscount Weir Prize 1959, Water Arbitration Prize 1972, James Clayton Prize 1975; Warner Medal, Textile Inst. 1976, S. G. Brown Award and Medal, Royal Soc. 1978; First recipient of title 'European Engineer' (Eur. Ing.), Paris 1987. *Publications:* Textile Engineering Processes (contrib.) 1959, Modern Yarn Production from Man-made Fibres 1960, Modern Developments in Weaving Machinery 1961, An Introduction to the Study of Spinning 1962, Contemporary Textile Engineering (contrib.) 1982; numerous papers in learned journals. *Leisure interests:* fell-walking, photography, theatre, music, gardening, DIY. *Address:* Engineering Design Institute, Loughborough University of Technology, Ashby Road, Loughborough, Leics., LE11 3TU; Stonestack, Rempstone, Loughborough, Leics., LE12 6RH, England. *Telephone:* (0509) 223175 (Office); (0509) 880043 (Home).

WRIEDT, Kenneth Shaw; Australian politician; b. 11 July 1927; s. of Frederick and Ivy Ethleen (Renfrey) Wriedt; m. Helga Anne-Rose Burger 1959; two d.; ed. Univ. High School, Melbourne; served in the Merchant Navy 1944–58; State Insurance Office, Tasmania 1958–67; mem. Senate 1967–80; Minister of Primary Industry 1972–75; Minister for Minerals and Energy 1975; Leader of Govt. in Senate Feb.–Nov. 1975; Leader of Opposition in Senate 1976–80; Shadow Minister for Foreign Affairs 1976–80; M.P. for Franklin (Tasmanian Parl.) 1982–; Leader of the Opposition 1982–86; Shadow Minister for Transport; Labor Party. *Leisure interests:* classical music, collecting historical nautical publications. *Address:* Parliament House, Hobart, Tasmania 7000; 25 Corinth Street, Howrah, Hobart, Tasmania 7018, Australia (Home). *Telephone:* 302385 (Office).

WRIGHT, Georg Henrik von, M.A., DR. PHIL.; Finnish philosopher; b. 14 June 1916, Helsinki; s. of Tor von Wright and Ragni Elisabeth Alfthan; m. Baroness Maria Elisabeth von Troil 1941; one s. one d.; ed. Helsinki and Cambridge Univs.; Lecturer in Philosophy, Univ. of Helsinki 1943–46; Prof. of Philosophy, Univ. of Helsinki 1946–61; Prof. of Philosophy, Univ. of Cambridge 1948–51; sometime Fellow, Trinity Coll., Cambridge, Hon. Fellow 1983; Visiting Prof., Cornell Univ. 1954, 1958, Univ. of Calif. 1963, Univ. of Pittsburgh 1966, Univ. of Karlsruhe 1975; Research Fellow, Acad. of Finland 1961–86; Andrew D. White Prof.-at-Large, Cornell Univ. 1965–77; Chancellor of Åbo Acad. 1968–77; Gifford Lecturer Univ. of St. Andrews 1959–60; Tarner Lecturer, Trinity Coll., Cambridge 1969; Woodbridge Lecturer, Columbia Univ. 1972; Nellie Wallace Lecturer, Univ. of Oxford 1978; Tanner Lecturer, Univ. of Helsinki 1984; Pres. Philosophical Soc. of Finland 1962–73; Pres. Int. Union of History and Philosophy of Science 1963–65, Inst. Int. de Philosophie, Paris 1975–78; Fellow, Finnish Soc. of Sciences, Royal Swedish Acad. of Sciences, British Acad., Royal Danish Acad. of Sciences, Norwegian Acad. of Sciences and Letters, European Acad. of Arts, Sciences and Humanities, World Acad. of Arts and Sciences, Serbian Acad. of Arts and Sciences; Hon. Foreign mem. American Acad. of Arts and Sciences; Dr. h.c. (Helsinki, Liverpool, Lund, Turku, Tampere, St. Olaf Coll., U.S.A., Buenos Aires, Salta), Wihuri Foundation Int. Prize 1976, Alexander von Humboldt Foundation Research Award 1986. *Publications:* The Logical Problem of Induction 1941, A Treatise on Induction and Probability 1951, An Essay in Modal Logic 1951, Logical Studies 1957, The Varieties of Goodness 1963, Norm and Action 1963, The Logic of Preference 1963, An Essay in Deontic Logic 1968, Explanation and Understanding 1971, Causality and Determinism 1974, Freedom and Determination 1980, Wittgenstein 1982, Philosophical Papers I–III 1983–84. *Address:* 4 Skepparegatan, Helsinki, Finland. *Telephone:* 655-192.

WRIGHT, James Claude, Jr.; American politician; b. 22 Dec. 1922, Fort Worth, Tex.; s. of James C. Wright and Marie (née Lyster) Wright; m. Betty Hay 1972; one s. three d. (by previous marriage); ed. Weatherford Coll. and Univ. of Texas; army service 1942–45, D.F.C., Legion of Merit; Partner, advertising and trade extension firm; mem. Texas Legislature 1947–49; Mayor of Weatherford, Tex. 1950–54; mem. League of Texas Municipalities, Pres. 1953; fmr. Lay Minister in Presbyterian Church; mem. for Fort Worth (12th District of Tex.), U.S. House of Reps. 1954–, Deputy Democratic Whip until 1976, Majority Leader in House of Reps. 1976–87; Chair. Democratic Steering and Policy Cttee. in House, Vice-Chair. 1976–87, Speaker, House of Reps. Jan. 1987–; mem. Budget Cttee. 1974–87; fmr. ranking mem. Public Works and Transportation Cttee.; fmr. mem. Govt. Operations Cttee.; fmr. Chair. Comm. on Highway Beautification; Cand. for U.S. Senate 1961. *Publications:* You and Your Congressman 1965, The Coming Water Famine 1966, Of Swords and Plowshares 1968; co-author: Congress and Conscience 1970, Reflections of a Public Man 1984. *Address:* 1236 Longworth House Office Building, Washington, D.C. 20515, U.S.A.

WRIGHT, Sir (John) Oliver, G.C.M.G., G.C.V.O., D.S.C.; British diplomatist; b. 6 March 1921, London; m. Marjory Osborne 1942; three s.; ed. Solihull School, and Christ's Coll., Cambridge; Royal Navy 1941–45; joined Foreign Office Nov. 1945; served New York 1946–47, Bucharest 1948–50, Singapore 1950–54, Berlin 1954–56, Pretoria 1957–58; Imperial Defence Coll. 1959; Asst. Pvt. Sec. to Foreign Sec. 1960–63, Pvt. Sec. Jan.-Nov. 1963; Pvt. Sec. to Prime Minister 1963–66; Amb. to Denmark 1966–69; U.K. Rep. to Northern Ireland Govt. Aug. 1969–March 1970; Deputy Under-Sec. of State and Chief Clerk, FCO 1970–72; Deputy Under-Sec. for EEC and Econ. Affairs 1972–75; Amb. to Fed. Repub. of Germany 1975–81, to U.S.A. 1982–86; Clark Fellow, Cornell Univ. 1987; Lewin Prof., Wash. Univ., St. Louis, Mo.; Trustee British Museum Bd., British Council, British Shakespeare Globe Centre; Co-Chair. Anglo-Irish Encounter; Chair. British Königswinter Steering Cttee.; Vice-Pres. German Chamber of Commerce and Industry in London; Gov. Reigate Grammar School; Hon. Fellow, Christ's Coll., Cambridge 1981. *Leisure interests:* theatre, gardening. *Address:* Burstow Hall, Horley, Surrey, RH6 9SR, England. *Telephone:* (0293) 783494.

WRIGHT, Judith Arundell; Australian writer; b. 31 May 1915; Armidale, N.S.W.; d. of late Phillip Arundell Wright and Ethel Mabel Bigg; m. J. P. McKinney; one d.; ed. New England Girls' School, Armidale, N.S.W., and Sydney Univ.; Commonwealth Literary Fund Scholarship 1949, 1962; Lecturer in Australian literature at various Australian univs.; Fellow, Australian Acad. of Humanities; Hon. D.Litt. (Queensland 1962, New England 1963, Sydney 1976, Monash 1977, Australian Nat. Univ. 1981, Melbourne 1988); Robert Frost Memorial Medal 1976; Sr. Writers' Fellowship, Australia Council 1977–79; Encyclopaedia Britannica Writers' Award 1964, The Alice Award 1980, Asan World Prize 1984. *Publications:* Poetry: The Moving Image 1946, Woman to Man 1949, The Gateway 1953, The Two Fires 1955, A Book of Birds 1962, Five Senses 1963, The Other Half 1966, Collected Poems 1971, Alive 1972, Fourth Quarter 1976, The Double Tree 1978, Phantom Dwelling 1985; criticism: Charles Harpur 1963, Preoccupations in Australian Poetry 1964, Because I Was Invited 1975; anthologies: A Book of Australian Verse 1956, New Land, New Language 1957, The Oxford Book of Australian Verse 1968; biography: The Generations of Men 1958, The Cry for the Dead 1981; short stories: The Nature of Love 1966; The Coral Battleground (documentary) 1977, We Call for a Treaty (documentary) 1985; also books for children. *Leisure interests:* gardening, walking. *Address:* "Edge", Half Moon Flat, Mongarlowe, N.S.W. 2622, P.O. Box 93, Braidwood, Australia. *Telephone:* (048) 42 8051.

WRIGHT, Sir Oliver (see Wright, Sir John Oliver).

WRIGHT, Sir Patrick (Richard Henry), K.C.M.G.; British diplomatist; b. 28 June 1931, Reading; s. of the late Herbert H. S. Wright and of Rachel Wright (née Green); m. Virginia Anne Gaffney 1958; two s. one d.; ed. Marlborough Coll., Merton Coll., Univ. of Oxford; served R.A. 1950–51; joined Diplomatic Service 1955, Middle East Centre for Arabic Studies 1956–57, Third Sec., British Embassy, Beirut 1958–60, Private Sec. to Amb., later First Sec., British Embassy, Washington 1960–65, Private Sec. to Perm. Under-Sec., FCO 1965–67, First Sec. and Head of Chancery, Cairo 1967–70, Deputy Political Resident, Bahrain 1971–72, Head of Middle East Dept., FCO 1972–74, Private Sec. (Overseas Affairs) to Prime Minister 1974–77, Amb. to Luxembourg 1977–79, to Syria 1979–81, to Saudi Arabia 1984–86; Deputy Under-Sec. FCO 1982–84; Perm. Under-Sec. of State, FCO and Head Diplomatic Service 1986–. *Leisure interests:* music, philately, walking. *Address:* Foreign and Commonwealth Office, King Charles' Street, London, S.W.1, England.

WRIGHT, Very Rev. (Ronald W. V.) Selby, C.V.O., M.A., D.D., F.S.A. (SCOTLAND), F.R.S.E.; British ecclesiastic; b. 12 June 1908, Scotland; s. of Vernon O. Wright and Anna G. Selby; unmarried; ed. Melville Coll., Edinburgh Acad., Edinburgh Univ. and New Coll., Edinburgh; Minister of the Canongate, Edinburgh 1937–77, Emer. Minister 1977–; Moderator of the Church of Scotland 1972–73; Chaplain to H.M. Forces 1942–47; Chaplain to the Royal Co. (H.M. The Queen's Bodyguard for Scotland) 1973–; Chaplain to H.M. The Queen 1961–77, Extra Chaplain 1977–; Chaplain to Edinburgh Castle 1937–, to Gov. of Edinburgh Castle 1959–; Extraordinary Dir. Edinburgh Acad. 1973–. *Publications:* Asking them Questions (6 vols.), Take Up God's Armour, Seven Sevens, Another Home; various vols. of radio and other talks. *Address:* The Queen's House, 36 Moray Place, Edinburgh, EH3 6BX, Scotland. *Telephone:* 031-226 5566.

WRIGHT, Sir Rowland Sydney, Kt., C.B.E., B.SC., C.CHEM., F.R.S.C.; British business executive; b. 4 Oct. 1915, Northampton; s. of late Sydney H.

Wright and Elsie M. Wright; m. Kathleen Mary Hodgkinson; two s. one d.; ed. High Pavement School, Nottingham and Univ. Coll. Nottingham; joined ICI Ltd. (Dyestuffs Div.) 1937; Production Dir. Imperial Chemical (Pharmaceuticals) Ltd. 1955–57; Production Dir. Dyestuffs Div. 1957–58; Research Dir. 1958–61; Jt. Man. Dir. ICI Ltd., Agricultural Div. 1961–63, Chair. Agricultural Div. 1964–65; Dir. ICI Ltd. 1966; Personnel Dir. 1966–70; Dir. AE & CI Ltd. 1970–75, Deputy Chair. 1971–75; Deputy Chair. ICI Ltd. 1971–75; Chair. 1975–78; Chair. Blue Circle Industries Ltd. 1978–83; Chair. Reorganization Cttee. for Eggs 1967–68; mem. Council, Foundation for Management Educ. 1967–70, Council of Chemical Industries Asscn. 1968–73, British Shippers' Council 1975–78; Dir. Royal Insurance Co. Ltd. 1973–79, Barclays Bank Ltd. 1977–84, Shell Transport and Trading Co. 1981–86; Dir. Hawker-Siddeley Group 1979–; Gov. London Graduate School of Business Studies 1975–78; Chancellor, Queen's Univ. Belfast 1985–; Pres. Inst. of Manpower Studies 1971–77, Hon. Pres. 1977–; Vice-Pres. Soc. of Chemical Industry 1971–74; B.I.M.; Hon. F.I.Chem.E.; mem. Ford European Advisory Council 1976–83, Trustee Civic Trust 1975–78, Westminster Abbey Trust 1984–; Companion B.I.M.; Hon. LL.D. (St. Andrews) 1977, (Queen's Univ., Belfast) 1978, (Nottingham) 1978; Hon. D.Sc. (Queen's Univ., Belfast) 1985. *Leisure interests:* gardening, photography. *Address:* Newick Lodge, Church Road, Newick, Lewes, East Sussex, BN8 4JZ, England. *Telephone:* 082-5723848.

WRIGHT, Sir (Roy) Douglas, A.K., M.B., M.S., D.SC.; Australian university teacher and medical research scientist; b. 7 Aug. 1907, Tasmania; s. of John and Emma Wright; m. 1st Julia V. Bell 1932; m. 2nd Meriel A. Wilmot 1964; one s. one d.; ed. Devonport High School and Univs. of Tasmania and Melbourne; Sr. Lecturer, Pathology, Univ. of Melbourne 1933–38, Prof. of Physiology 1939–71, Prof. Emer. 1971–, mem. Council 1963–, Deputy Chancellor 1971–80, Chancellor 1980–, Research Consultant, Howard Florey Inst. 1975–; Surgeon, Royal Melbourne Hosp. and Austin Hosp. 1935–38; mem. Council, Australian Nat. Univ. 1946–76; Chair. of Exec., Cancer Inst. of Vic. 1948–71, Medical Dir. 1971–75; Hon. LL.D. (Australian Nat. Univ.) 1977. *Publications:* Primer in Clinical Science 1947; articles in scientific journals. *Leisure interest:* gardening. *Address:* Howard Florey Institute, University of Melbourne, Parkville, Vic. 3052, Australia.

WRIGHT, Roy W., C.B.E.; British mining executive; b. 10 Sept. 1914; s. of the late Arthur William Wright; m. Mary Letitia Davies 1939; two d.; ed. King Edward VI School, Chelmsford, Faraday House Coll., London; fmr. Dir. Brush Eng. Co.; joined Rio Tinto Zinc Corpn. 1952; Man. Dir. Rio Tinto Mining Co. of Canada 1956; Deputy Chair., Deputy Chief Exec. Rio Tinto Zinc Corpn. 1965–75, non-exec. Dir. 1975–85; Chair. Electronics Industry Econ. Devt. Cttee. of Nat. Econ. Devt. Office 1971–76; non-exec. Dir. Palabora Mining Co. 1963–80, Rio Algom Ltd. 1960–80, Davy Corpn. Ltd. 1976–85, A.P.V. Holdings Ltd. 1976–85, Transportation Systems and Market Research 1978–85. *Address:* Cobbers, Forest Row, Sussex, England. *Telephone:* (034 282) 2009.

WRIGHT, Verna, M.D., F.R.C.P.; British professor of rheumatology; b. 31 Dec. 1928, Devonport; s. of Thomas William Wright and Nancy Eleanor Knight; m. Esther Margaret Wright 1953; five s. four d.; ed. Bedford School and Liverpool Univ.; House Physician, Broadgreen Hosp., Liverpool 1954; Sr. House Officer, Stoke Mandeville Hosp. 1954–56; Research Asst., Dept. of Clinical Medicine, Gen. Infirmary, Leeds 1956–58; Research Fellow, Div. of Applied Physiology, Johns Hopkins Hosp., Baltimore 1958–59; Lecturer, Dept. of Clinical Medicine, Leeds Univ. 1960–64, Sr. Lecturer, Dept. of Medicine 1964–70, Prof. of Rheumatology 1970–; mem. Johns Hopkins Soc. for Scholars 1978; Hon. mem. American Rheumatism Asscn. 1985; Elizabeth Fink Award, Nat. Ankylosing Spondylitis Soc. 1987. *Publications:* The Relevance of Christianity in a Scientific Age 1981, Osteoarthritis; Clinics in Rheumatic Diseases 1982, Bone and Joint Disease in the Elderly 1983, Personal Peace in a Nuclear Age 1985, Pain, Clinical Rheumatology, Int. Practice and Research 1987; (Co-Author) Seronegative Polyarthritis 1976, Introduction to the Biomechanics of Joints and Joint Replacement 1981, Applied Drug Therapy of the Rheumatic Diseases 1982, Integrated Clinical Science: musculo-skeletal disease 1984. *Leisure interest:* Leader of Harrogate Young Life Group. *Address:* Rheumatology and Rehabilitation Research Unit, 36 Clarendon Road, Leeds, LS2 9PJ; Inglehurst, Park Drive, Harrogate, HG2 9AX, England. *Telephone:* (0532) 441199 (ext. 280) (Office); (0423) 502326 (Home).

WRIGLEY, Edward Anthony, M.A., PH.D., F.B.A.; British academic; b. 17 Aug. 1931, Manchester; s. of Edward and Jessie Wrigley; m. Maria Laura Spelberg 1960; one s. three d.; ed. King's School, Macclesfield and Peterhouse, Cambridge; William Volker Research Fellow, Univ. of Chicago 1953–54; Fellow, Peterhouse 1958–, Sr. Bursar 1964–74; Lecturer in Geography, Cambridge 1958–74; Assoc. Dir. Cambridge Group for the History of Population and Social Structure 1964–; mem. Inst. of Advanced Study, Princeton 1970–71; Hinkley Visiting Prof., Johns Hopkins Univ. 1975; Tinbergen Visiting Prof., Erasmus Univ., Rotterdam 1979; Prof. of Population Studies, L.S.E. 1979–88; James Ford Special Lecturer, Oxford 1986; Ellen Macarthur Lecturer, Cambridge 1987; Pres. British Soc. for Population Studies 1977–79; Chair. Population Investigation Cttee. 1984–; Sr. Research Fellow All Souls Coll., Oxford 1988–; Ed. Econ. History Review 1985–. *Publications:* several works on econ. and demographic history. *Leisure interest:* gardening. *Address:* 13 Sedley Taylor Road, Cambridge, CB2 2PW, England. *Telephone:* (0223) 247 614.

WRISTON, Walter B., B.A., M.A.; American banker; b. 3 Aug. 1919, Middleton, Conn.; s. of late Henry Merritt Wriston and late Ruth Bigelow; m. 1st Barbara Brengle 1942 (deceased); one d.; m. 2nd Kathryn A. Dineen 1968; ed. Wesleyan Univ., The Fletcher School of Law and Diplomacy, Ecole Française and American Inst. of Banking; Jr. Insp., Comptrollers Div., First Nat. City Bank 1946–48, Sr. Insp. 1948–49, Domestic Div. 1949–50, Asst. Cashier 1950–52, Asst. Vice-Pres. 1952–54, Vice-Pres. 1954–58, European Div. 1956–58, Sr. Vice-Pres. 1958–59, in charge of Overseas Div. 1959–67, Exec. Vice-Pres. 1960–67, Pres. and Dir. Citibank N.A. 1967–70; Chair. and Dir. Citibank N.A. and CITICORP 1970–84 and other cos.; Chair., Pres. Econ. Policy Advisory Bd.; Dir. Gen. Electric Co., J. C. Penney Co. Inc., Chubb Corpn., Bechtel Investments, Inc., Sequoia Ventures Inc., Pfizer Inc., Pan Am Corpn., Reuter's Holdings PLC, Tandem Computers Inc., Brintec Corpn., United Meridian Corpn.; mem. Nat. Comm. for Industrial Peace 1973–74, Council on Foreign Relations 1981–; Consultant to State Dept. 1984–; fmr. Chair. Business Council; Hon. LL.D. (Lawrence Coll., Brown, Tufts, Fordham, Wesleyan and Columbia Univs., Morehouse Coll.), D.C.S. (Pace, New York and St. John's Univs.), D.H.L. (Lafayette Coll.). *Publication:* Risk and Other Four-Letter Words. *Address:* Citicorp Center, 153 East 53rd Street, Suite 4000, New York, N.Y. 10043, U.S.A.

WRÓBLEWSKI, Andrzej, M.ECON.; Polish economist and politician; b. 22 Nov. 1950, Smogóry, Gorzów Wielkopolski Voivodship; m.; one d.; ed. Cen. School of Planning and Statistics, Warsaw; economist, STOMIL Rubber Industry Plant, Piastów 1972–74; Chief, Mining Dept. at Ministry of Finance 1974–80; political worker, Trade and Finance Dept. of PZPR Cen. Cttee. 1980–81; mem. Comm. for Econ. Reform 1980–, Sec. 1987–; mem. Secr. 1980–86; Adviser to Govt. Plenipotentiary for Econ. Reform 1981–85; Dir., Team of Methodology of Planning and Regulating Systems, Planning Comm. attached to Council of Ministers 1985–88; Under-Sec. of State, Ministry of Industry 1987–88; Minister of Finance 1988–; mem. Econ. Cttee. of Council of Ministers 1988–, Polish Econ. Soc. 1974–, Presidium of Gen. Bd. 1982–; mem. Polish United Workers' Party (PZPR) 1971–; Knight's Cross of Polonia Restituta Order and other decorations. *Publications:* numerous works on economy, econ. reform, finance system of enterprises and tax system. *Address:* Ministerstwo Finansów, ul. Świętokrzyska 12, 00-044 Warsaw, Poland.

WROŃSKI, Stanisław, M.A.; Polish politician; b. 17 June 1916, Sielec, Jędrzejów district; ed. Warsaw Univ. and Inst. of Social Sciences, Cen. Cttee. of Polish United Workers' Party, Warsaw; mem. Communist Union of Polish Youth 1930–36, Polish Workers' Party 1945–48, Polish United Workers' Party (PUWP) 1948–; Deputy mem. Cen. Cttee., PUWP 1964–68, mem. 1968–81; Lecturer, Inst. of Social Sciences 1950–56; Scientific Worker, Polish Acad. of Sciences and Mil. Historical Inst. 1957–62; Pres. and Editor-in-Chief, Publishing Co-operative "Książka i Wiedza" 1963–71; Deputy to Seym 1969–85; Vice-Chair. Seym Comm. of Culture and Art 1969–72; Minister of Culture and Art 1971–74, without Portfolio Feb.–June 1974; mem. Council of State 1974–85; Chair. Gen. Bd. ZBoWiD (Union of Fighters for Freedom and Democracy) 1972–80; Editor-in-Chief Nowe Drogi 1974–87; mem. scientific councils of Polish Inst. of Int. Affairs, Int. of History of Polish-Soviet Friendship, Polish Acad. of Sciences, Chair. Cen. Bd. Soc. for Polish-Soviet Friendship 1980–87, Deputy Pres. FIR May 1978–; mem. other scientific councils, etc.; Order of Banner of Labour (1st and 2nd class), Grunwald Cross (Order 2nd class), Order of Builders of People's Poland 1979. *Publications:* numerous papers on modern history.

WU, Gordon; Hong Kong businessman; Chair. Hopewell Holdings, Hong Kong; responsible for bldg. of colony's tallest bldg., Hopewell Holdings H.Q.; built China Hotel, Canton, China; built new coal-fired power station for Prov. of Guangdong, China; new motorway linking Hong Kong to Shenzen and Canton now under construction; is responsible for design of many of his own bldgs. *Leisure interest:* classical music. *Address:* Hopewell Holdings, Hong Kong.

WU, H.E. Cardinal John Baptist, D.C.L.; Chinese ecclesiastic; b. 26 March 1925, Kwangtung; s. of Wu Shing Sing and Mary Chow; ed. Ka-Ying Seminary, South China Regional Seminary, Hong Kong, and Pontifical Univ. Urbaniani, Rome; ordained priest 1952; pastoral ministry, Refugee Centre, Tung-tao-tsuen, Kowloon 1952–53; worked at Chancery of Archdiocese of New York, Boston and Chicago 1956–57; pastoral ministry, Taiwan 1957–75; Bishop of Hong Kong 1975–; cr. Cardinal 1988. *Address:* Catholic Diocese Centre, 16 Caine Road, Hong Kong.

WU BANGGUO; Chinese engineer and party official; b. 1932, Shanghai; engineer and Deputy Sec. CCP Cttee. Shanghai Municipal Meters Bureau; mem. Standing Cttee. Shanghai Municipal CCP Cttee. 1983–, Deputy Sec. 1985–; alt. mem. CCP Cen. Cttee. 1985–; Vice-Pres. Asscn. for Int. Understanding 1986–. *Address:* Shanghai Municipal Meters Bureau, Shanghai, People's Republic of China.

WU BOSHAN; Chinese government official; Chair. Board of Dirs. China Investment Bank 1981–; mem. Council People's Bank of China 1984–; Vice-Chair. China Investment Consultants 1986–. *Address:* China Investment Bank, Wanshou Road, Beijing, People's Republic of China.

WU CHI-FANG, B.SC.; Chinese politician; b. 14 Dec. 1919, Ichang Co., Hupeh; m. J. J. Char; two s. two d.; ed. Nat. Chungking Univ.; Fellow,

E.D.I., World Bank 1968–69; Dir. Dept. of Commerce, Ministry of Econ. Affairs 1972–77; Dir.-Gen. Nat. Bureau of Standards, Ministry of Econ. Affairs 1977–79; Vice-Chair. Research, Devt. and Evaluation Comm., Exec. Yuan 1979–80; Deputy Sec.-Gen. Exec. Yuan 1980–. *Publications:* World Economic Thought, The Economic Development of the Republic of China, The Financial and Monetary Situation of Communist China. *Address:* Executive Yuan, Taipei; 1-108, Hsinyi Road, Sect. 4, Taipei, Taiwan.

WU CHILIAN; Chinese agronomist and local government leader of Miao nationality; first woman and nat. minority cadre to become Co. Head, Head Guzhang Co, Hunan 1983–. *Address:* Guzhang Branch, Chinese Communist Party, Guzhang, Hunan, People's Republic of China.

WU DE; Chinese party official; b. 1914, Fengrun, Hebei; ed. China Univ., Beijing; workers leader in Tangshan 1935; Regimental Political Commissar 1942; Vice-Minister of Fuel Industry 1949–50; Sec. CCP Pingyuan 1950–52; Deputy Sec. CCP Tianjin 1952–55; Deputy Mayor of Tianjin 1952–53, Mayor 1953–55; Pres. Tianjin Univ. 1952–57; Alt. mem. 8th Cen. Cttee. of CCP 1956; First Sec. CCP Jilin 1956–66; Political Commissar Jilin Mil. District, People's Liberation Army 1958; Sec. N.E. Bureau, CCP 1961; Second Sec. CCP Beijing 1966; Acting Mayor of Beijing 1966–78; Vice-Chair. Beijing Revolutionary Cttee. 1967–72, Chair. 1972–78; mem. 9th Cen. Cttee. of CCP 1969; Head of Cultural Group, State Council 1971; Second Sec. CCP Beijing 1971, First Sec. 1972–78; mem. Politburo, 10th Cen. Cttee. CCP 1973, and 11th Cen. Cttee. 1977–82; Second Political Commissar Beijing Mil. Region, PLA; a Vice-Chair. Standing Cttee., Nat. People's Congress 1978; Exec. Chair. Presidium 5th Nat. People's Congress 1978; Deputy Dir. Acad. of Social Sciences 1980; dismissed from Politburo, lost all posts Feb. 1980; mem. Cen. Advisory Comm. 1982–. *Address:* People's Republic of China.

WU FUSHAN, Lieut.-Gen.; Chinese soldier and party official; b. 1911, Ji'an Co., Jiangxi Prov.; ed. Chinese Worker-Peasant Red Army Coll.; joined CCP and Red Army 1930; Political Cttee. 8th Route Army 1938; Political Cttee. W. Liaoning Mil. Dist. 1947; N.E. Field Army 1948; 4th Field Army 1949; PLA del. to Canton All-Circles People's Conf. 1949; mem. Canton Prov. People's Govt. 1950; Deputy, Political Cttee. PLA A.F. Command Cen. S. China 1951–; A.F. Political Cttee. Canton Mil. Region 1954–; Lieut. Gen. PLA 1955–; Commdr. PLA A.F., Canton Mil. Region 1958–; purged 1967, rehabilitated 1973; Deputy Commdr. Canton Mil. Region 1974–; Deputy Commdr. PLA A.F. 1977–; PLA Deputy to 5th NPC 1978; mem Cen. Advisory Cttee. of CCP Cen. Cttee. 1987–. *Address:* Central Advisory Committee of the Central Committee of the Chinese Communist Party, Zhongnanhai, Beijing, People's Republic of China.

WU GUANZHENG; Chinese party and government official; b. 1938, Yugan Co., Jiangxi Prov.; ed. Qinghua Univ., Beijing; fmr. Sec. CCP Cttee. and Mayor of Wuhan City, Hubei; alt. mem. 12th CCP Cen. Cttee. 1982; Deputy Sec. Jiangxi Prov. CCP Cttee. and Gov. Jiangxi Prov. 1986–. *Address:* Office of the Governor, Nanchang, Jiangxi Province, People's Republic of China.

WU GUANZHONG; Chinese artist; b. 1919, Yixing Co., Jiangsu; ed. Nat. Inst. of Fine Arts, Huangzhou, Ecole Nat. Supérieure des Beaux Arts, Paris, France; teacher Cen. Acad. of Fine Arts and Qinghua Univ. 1950; Prof. Cen. Inst. of Applied Arts. *Address:* Central Institute of Applied Arts, Beijing, People's Republic of China.

WU HUALUN; Chinese artist; b. June 1942, Tianjin; s. of Wu Bing-Zheng and Wang Ya-Xin; m. Zeng Wan 1985; one d.; ed. Cen. Acad. of Arts and Crafts; mem. China Artists' Assen. 1982–, China Calligraphists' Assen. 1986–; Sr. Art Ed., China People's Fine Art Publishing House; works have been exhibited many times in Japan, Hong Kong and U.S.A.; First Prize, Chinese Paintings Competition 1988. *Leisure interests:* travelling, playing badminton. *Address:* People's Fine Arts Publishing House, 32 Bei Zong Zu Hu tong, Beijing 100735, People's Republic of China. *Telephone:* 553405.

WU JINGHUA; Chinese state official; b. 1931, Mianning Co., Sichuan Prov.; Deputy to 4th NPC 1975; Vice-Minister, State Nationalities' Affairs Comm. 1979; Vice-Chair. Sichuan Prov. People's Congress 1979–83; Pres. Sichuan Prov. Soc. for Agricultural Modernization in Areas Inhabited by Minorities 1981–; mem. 12th CCP Cen. Cttee. 1982, 13th Cen. Cttee. 1987–; Sec. CCP Cttee., Tibet 1985–88; Political Commissar, PLA Tibet Mil. Dist. 1985–88. *Address:* Society for Agricultural Modernization in Areas Inhabited by Minorities, Chengdu, Sichuan, People's Republic of China.

WU LANYING; Chinese shooting champion; gold medallist, 6th Asian Shooting Championships. *Address:* Chinese Sports Federation, Beijing, People's Republic of China.

WU LENGXI; Chinese party official and journalist; b. 1909, Jiangzi; ed. Wuhan Univ., Lu Xun Acad. of Arts; worked for Mass Daily, Henan 1937; Man. Ed. 7 July Daily, Cen. Plain Mil. Region 1937; Deputy Dir. Propaganda Dept., Cen. Plain Mil. Region 1948; Prin. Cadre New China News Agency (NCNA), trained in Pingshanxian, Hebei 1949; Man. Ed. NCNA 1949–50, Deputy Dir. 1950–52, Dir. 1952–Cultural Revolution; Deputy for Tianjin, 1st NPC 1954–59; mem. Comm. for Cultural Relations with Foreign Countries 1954; Man. Ed. Renmin Ribao (People's Daily) 1958–Cultural Revolution; Deputy for Guangdong, 2nd NPC 1958, 3rd NPC 1964; Deputy Dir. Propaganda Dept., CCP Cen. Cttee. 1964–Cultural Revolution; mem.

Standing Cttee., 3rd NPC 1965-Cultural Revolution; disappeared 1966–72; leading mem. People's Daily 1972; mem. Standing Cttee., 4th NPC 1975; Alt. mem. 11th Cen. Cttee., CCP 1977, 12th Cen. Cttee. 1982; Deputy for Shanghai, 5th NPC 1978; mem. Standing Cttee., 5th NPC 1978; Deputy Dir. Propaganda Dept., Cen. Cttee. 1978; mem. Standing Cttee., Nat. Cttee., 5th CPPCC 1978; fmr. Sec. CCP Cttee., Guangdong; Adviser Beijing Journalism Studies Soc. 1980; Alt. mem. 12th Cen. Cttee. CCP 1982–87; Minister of Radio and TV 1982–86; Chair. Journalists' Assen. 1983–; Vice-Pres. China Int. Cultural Exchange Centre 1984–; Pres. Soc. of Radio and TV Oct. 1986–, Soc. for Studies of Radio and TV Oct. 1986–. *Address:* State Council, Beijing, People's Republic of China.

WU MINDA; Chinese academic and government official; b. 1929; Dir.-Gen. of experimental factory, Zhejiang Univ.; Chair. Zhejiang Prov. Planning and Econ. Cttee. 1987–; Vice-Chair. Zhejiang Prov. People's Congress Feb. 1988–. *Address:* Zhejiang University, Hangzhou City, Zhejiang Province, People's Republic of China.

WU MINGYU; Chinese government official; b. Aug. 1931, Zhe Jiang; m. 1954; one s. one d.; Deputy Dir.-Gen. Research Centre for Econ., Tech. and Social Devt. of State Council 1986–; Chair. China Nat. Research Centre for Science and Tech. for Devt. 1982–; Vice-Pres. China Soc. of Scientology and Science and Tech. Policy 1980–; Council mem. Chinese People's Assen. of Foreign Affairs 1984–; Dir. Song Qinglin Foundation 1983–. *Leisure interests:* bridge, Go. *Address:* Research Centre for Economic, Technical and Social Development of the State Council, 22 Xianmen Street, Beijing, People's Republic of China.

WU MINQIAN; Chinese chess player; b. 8 Jan. 1961, Hangzhou, Zhejiang; m.; Int. Grand Master 1985. *Address:* Chinese Chess Association, 9 Tiyuguan Road, Beijing, People's Republic of China. *Telephone:* 753110.

WU POH-HSIUNG, B.SC.; Chinese politician; b. 19 June 1939, Taoyuan County; m. Mei-yu Dai; two s. one d.; ed. Nat. Cheng Kung Univ. and Advanced Research Inst., Kuomintang; school-teacher 1963–65; mem. Taiwan Provincial Ass. 1968–72; Assoc. Prof. Nan Ya Jr. Coll. of Tech. 1971–73; Magistrate, Taoyuan County 1973–76; Dir. Taiwan Tobacco and Wine Monopoly Bureau 1976–80; Dir. Inst. of Industrial and Vocational Training for Workmen 1976–80; Dir. Friends of Labor Assen. 1976–80; Chair. Repub. of China Amateur Boxing Assen. 1981–82; Dir. Secr., Cen. Cttee., Kuomintang 1982–84; Minister of Interior 1984–88; Mayor of Taipei 1988–. *Address:* 39 Chang An West Road, Taipei; 4th Floor, 35, Lane 37, Yungkany Street, Taipei, Taiwan. *Telephone:* 5115890.

WU QUANQING; Chinese oil worker; mem. 11th CCP Cen. Cttee. 1977, 12th Cen. Cttee. 1982–87; Chair. Revolutionary Cttee., Daqing Oil Field 1978. *Address:* Daqing Oil Field, Daqing, Heilongjiang, People's Republic of China.

WU SHENGRONG; Chinese government official; Sec., CCP Henan Prov. Cttee.; Deputy Commdr. PLA Lanzhou Mil. Region 1971–; Commdr. Qinghai Prov. Mil. Dist. 1978–; Vice-Chair. Prov. People's Congress, Qinghai 1979–83. *Address:* People's Republic of China.

WU SHI; Chinese party and government official; Vice-Gov. of Guizhou 1955–57; Deputy for Guizhou, 3rd NPC 1964; branded "a big renegade" by Radio Guizhou 1968; Vice-Chair. Prov. Revolutionary Cttee., Guizhou 1977–79; Deputy for Guizhou, 5th NPC, 1978; Deputy Sec. CCP Cttee., Guizhou Prov. 1980; Chair. Prov. People's Congress 1983–85. *Address:* c/o Guizhou Province, People's Republic of China.

WU TIANMING; Chinese film director; b. Oct. 1939, Shaanxi Prov.; m. Mu Shulan; ed. Xi'an Drama School; Head of Xian Film Studio 1983–. *Films:* Kith and Kin 1981, River Without Buoys 1983, Life 1984, The Old Well 1987. *Address:* Xian Film Studio, Xian, Shaanxi Province, People's Republic of China.

WU WEIRAN; Chinese surgeon; b. 14 Oct. 1920, Changzhou, Jiangsu Prov.; s. of Wu Jingyi and Zheng Zhixia; m. Huang Wuchiung 1951; three d.; Deputy Dir. Surgery Soc., attached to the Medical Soc. 1972; Deputy Dir. Surgery Dept., Beijing Hosp., Chinese Acad. of Medical Sciences 1972; now Prof. of Surgery, Surgical Dept., Peking Union Medical Coll. Hosp., Chinese Acad. of Medical Sciences; Hon. Dir. Beijing Hosp.; alt. mem. 12th CCP Cen. Cttee. 1982, mem. 1985, mem. 13th Cen. Cttee. 1987–. *Leisure interest:* gardening. *Address:* Surgery Department, Beijing Hospital, 1 Dahualu, Dondan, Beijing, People's Republic of China. *Telephone:* 556031.

WU WENJUN; Chinese mathematician; b. 12 May 1919, Jiansu Prov.; ed. in U.S.A.; returned to China in 1950; Deputy Dir., Math. Inst. Acad. Sinica 1964; mem. Standing Cttee. of 5th CPPCC 1978; Deputy Dir., Inst. of Systems Science, Acad. Sinica 1980; mem., Standing Cttee. of 6th CPPCC 1983; Pres., Math. Soc. of China 1984; mem., Dept. of Math. and Physics, Acad. Sinica 1985; mem. Standing Cttee. of 7th CPPCC 1988. *Address:* Rm. 303, Bldg. 809, Huangzhuang, Haidian, Beijing 100080, People's Republic of China. *Telephone:* 285128 (Beijing).

WU WENYING; Chinese politician and cotton spinner; b. 1932, Changzhou City, Jiangsu Prov.; ed. E. China Textile Eng. Inst., Shanghai; began work as cotton spinner in a textile mill, Changzhou 1947; held various leading posts in textile mills, Changzhou Municipal Party Cttee. and City

Govt.; Alt. mem. 12th Cen. Cttee. CCP 1982–85, mem. 1985–; Minister of Textile Industry March 1983–. *Address:* c/o State Council, Beijing, People's Republic of China.

WU XIANGBI; Chinese party official; b. 1 Jan. 1926, Songtao Co., Guizhou Prov.; s. of Wu Hechun and Long Annü; m. 1st Long Runnü 1943; m. 2nd Lo Tinglan 1980; six c.; mem. CCP 1952–; clerical worker; Vice-Head Dist. Govt.; Vice-Sec., then Sec. Dist. CCP Cttee.; mem., Vice-Sec. then Sec. and First Sec. CCP Co. Cttee.; Commissar of Co. mil. service; Chair. Co. People's Political Consultative Conf.; Deputy for Songtao Co. to 1st, 2nd and 3rd NPC; Deputy for Tongren Co. to 1st NPC; mem. of CCP Pref. Cttee.; mem. and Sec. CCP Cttee., Guizhou Prov.; Deputy for Guizhou Prov. to 5th NPC; Vice-Pres. Cen. Inst. for Nationalities; Deputy to 6th NPC; Vice-Chair. Nationalities Cttee., 5th and 6th NPC; mem. Chinese United Front Theory Soc.; Vice-Chair. Chinese Nationalities Theory Soc., Chinese Nationalities Theory Researching Union; Vice-Group Leader Nationalities Philosophy Researching Programme Group; Deputy for Haidian Dist., Beijing to 7th NPC; Deputy for Beijing to 5th NPC; Deputy to 10th, 11th and 12th Congresses of CCP; alt. mem. 10th, 11th and 12th CCP Cen. Cttee. *Publications:* Glory to all Nationalities Forming the People's Republic of China, and other articles. *Leisure interest:* painting. *Address:* 5–28 Building 24, Fuwai Street, Beijing, People's Republic of China. *Telephone:* 367920.

WU XIAOBANG; Chinese dancer; b. 18 Dec. 1906; Chair. Chinese Dancers' Asscn. Nov. 1979–. *Address:* China Federation of Literature and Art, Beijing, People's Republic of China.

WU XIUQUAN; Chinese military official; b. 1909, Wuchang, Hubei; ed. Middle school, Wuchang, Hubei; Sec.-Gen. Shaanxi-Gansu-Ninxia (Shaan-Gan-Ning) Border Regional Govt. 1938–39; Chief-of-Staff N.E. Democratic Allied Army 1946; Chief-of-Staff N.E. Mil. Region 1948; Commdr. Shenyang Garrison 1948; Deputy Dir. for Soviet Union and E. European Affairs, Ministry of Foreign Affairs 1949–52; Vice-Minister of Foreign Affairs 1951–55; Deputy for Sichuan, 1st NPC 1954; Amb. to Yugoslavia 1955–58; mem. 8th Cen. Cttee. CCP 1956; Deputy Dir. Int. Liaison Dept., Cen. Cttee. CCP 1964–67; Vice-Minister of Foreign Affairs 1966; mem. Standing Cttee., 4th NPC 1975–78; Deputy Chief of Gen. Staff, PLA 1975–; mem. 11th Cen. Cttee. CCP 1977; mem. Standing Cttee., Cen. Advisory Cttee. 1982–; mem. Party Cttee. of Special Orgs. under Cen. Advisory Cttee. 1983–; Pres. Chinese Army Men's Asscn. 1979–; Dir. Beijing Inst. for Int. Strategic Studies 1980–; Pres. Soc. of Soviet and E. European Studies 1986–. *Address:* Office of the Director, Beijing Institute for International Strategic Studies, Beijing, People's Republic of China.

WU XUEQIAN; Chinese politician; b. 1908, Wuchang, Hubei; m. Bi Ling; ed. Sun Yat-sen Univ., U.S.S.R.; Lecturer in Political Science, Fudan Univ., Shanghai 1931; Staff mem. Red Army HQ and Lecturer Red Army Univ. 1932; Deputy Chief of Staff 3rd Army Corps (in which he served during Long March) 1934; Head Foreign Affairs Dept., CCP Cen. Cttee. 1936; one of cadres transferred to Manchuria with Lin Biao 1945; Chair. Shenyang Mil. Control Comm. Nov. 1948; mem. People's Govt. of North East 1949; Dir. U.S.S.R. and Eastern Europe Dept., Ministry of Foreign Affairs 1949–52; Vice-Minister of Foreign Affairs 1951–55; Deputy Sichuan Prov., 1st NPC 1954–59; Amb. to Yugoslavia 1955–58; mem. CCP Cen. Cttee., 8th Party Congress 1956–Cultural Revolution; Dir. Int. Liaison Dept., CCP Cen. Cttee. 1959; mem. Standing Cttee. CPPCC 1965–Cultural Revolution; disappeared during Cultural Revolution 1967–74; mem. Standing Cttee., 4th NPC 1975–78; mem. CCP Cen. Cttee., 11th Party Congress 1977–; Vice-Minister of Foreign Affairs May–Nov. 1982; Minister of Foreign Affairs 1982–88; State Councillor 1983–88, Vice-Premier State Council April 1988–; mem. 12th Cen. Cttee. CCP 1982, 13th Cen. Cttee. 1987; mem. Political Bureau of Cen. Cttee. 1985–; Pres. Armymen's Asscn. 1979; Dir. Comm. for Commemorating 40th Anniversary of UN 1985; Chair. State Tourism Cttee. April 1988–; mem. and head numerous dels. abroad. *Address:* State Council, Beijing, People's Republic of China.

WU YIGONG; Chinese film director; b. 1 Dec. 1938, Zhongqing; s. of Wu Tiesan and Yu Minhua; m. Zhang Wen Rong 1967; one s.; Head Shanghai Film Bureau, Gen. Man. Shanghai Film Corpn., Vice-Pres. China Film Artists' Asscn. 1985–; Golden Rooster Award 1984 for best Dir. of film My Memories of Old Beijing, Magnolia Prize for A Man Aged 18 1988; other films include University in Exile, The Tribulations of a Chinese Gentleman, Bitter Sea. *Leisure interests:* music, sports. *Address:* 796 Huaihailu, Shanghai, People's Republic of China. *Telephone:* 336710, 388100.

WU ZEYAN; Chinese etymologist; b. 4 April 1913, Changshu City, Jiangsu; s. of Wu He; m. Wang Jiazhen 1937; two s. one d.; ed. Daxia Univ., Shanghai; Ed. and Deputy Ed.-in-Chief, Commercial Press 1934–86, Adviser 1986–; Ed.-in-Chief Dictionary of Etymology (of Chinese Language); mem. CPPCC 1978–. *Address:* 016 Building 4, Dongdaqiao, Chaoyang District, Beijing, People's Republic of China. *Telephone:* 5003086.

WU ZHEN; Chinese party and government official; b. 1949; Vice-Minister of Agric. 1964; mem. del. to Tibet Autonomous Region 1965; Chair. Tianjin People's Congress May 1988–. *Address:* Tianjin People's Congress, Tianjin, People's Republic of China.

WU ZHONGHUA; Chinese traditional medical practitioner; b. 1951; ed. Jiaozuo Mining Coll., Henan Prov.; based at Coal Mining Bureau of

Pingdingshan 1976–77; Dir. Inst. of Eng. Thermo-Physics 1981–; Pres. Soc. of Eng. Thermo-Physics 1986–. *Address:* Health Section, Luoyang Military Sub-Area, Henan Province, People's Republic of China.

WU ZHONGUAN; Chinese government official; b. 26 Dec. 1926, Shanghai; s. of Wu Juenong and Chen Xuanzhao; m. Xu Mo 1953; one s. one d.; Dir. Information Dept., State Physical Culture and Sports Comm. 1983–, Spokesman for Comm. 1983–; Exec. mem. Int. Sports Press Asscn. 1985–; Vice-Pres. Asian Sports Press Asscn. 1986; Dir. Press Comm. of Chinese Olympic Cttee. 1979. *Leisure interests:* writing, playing tennis. *Address:* 9 Tiyuguan Road, Beijing, People's Republic of China.

WU ZUOREN; Chinese artist; b. 1908, Jingxian Co., Anhui Prov.; ed. Ecole nat. supérieure des Beaux-Arts, Paris, France, Académie royale de Belgique, Brussels, Belgium; studied under Xu Beihong and Alfred Bastien; returned to China 1935; teacher, Cen. Univ., Nanjing; travelled in Tibet 1940s; leading exponent of "yijing" (idea and situation) school of landscape painters; in disgrace during Cultural Revolution; Deputy for Shanghai Municipality, 4th and 5th NPCs 1975–; mem. Presidium and mem. Standing Cttee., 6th NPC 1986–; Pres. Cen. Acad. of Fine Arts; Vice-Chair. China Fed. of Literary and Art Circles 1979–; Chair. Chinese Artists' Asscn. 1983–; Deputy Head China–European Parl. Friendship Group 1985–. *Works include:* The Karakorum Mountains, A Stream in the Gobi, Serfs, Women carrying Water, Galloping Yaks, A Portrait of the Painter Qi Baishi. *Address:* c/o Central Academy of Fine Arts, Beijing, People's Republic of China.

WU ZUQIANG; Chinese musician; Vice-Pres. Cen. Conservatory of Music 1981–82, Pres. 1982–; Vice-Pres. China Musicians' Asscn. 1985–; alt. mem. 12th CCP Cen. Cttee. 1982. *Address:* Chinese Central Conservatory of Music, Beijing, People's Republic of China.

WUNSCH, Carl Isaac, PH.D.; American physical oceanographer and university professor; b. 5 May 1941, Brooklyn, New York; s. of Harry Wunsch and Helen (Gellis) Wunsch; m. Marjory Markel 1980; one s. one d.; ed. Massachusetts Inst. of Technology; Lecturer in Oceanography, M.I.T. 1966–67, Asst. Prof. 1967–70, Assoc. Prof. 1970–75, Prof. of Physical Oceanography 1975–76, Cecil and Ida Green Prof. 1976–, Sec. of Navy Research Prof. 1985–89; Sr. Visiting Fellow, Dept. of Applied Math. and Theoretical Physics, Cambridge Univ., England 1969, 1974–75, 1981–82; Fulbright Scholar 1981–82; John Simon Guggenheim Foundation Fellow 1981–82; Fellow American Acad. of Arts and Sciences, American Geophysical Union; mem. N.A.S., Royal Astronomical Soc., American Meteorological Soc.; James R. Macelwane Award, American Geophysical Union 1971, Founders Prize, Texas Instrument Foundation 1975. *Publications:* many tech. papers; Co-Ed. Evolution of Physical Oceanography. *Leisure interest:* sailing. *Address:* Room 54-1324, Center for Meteorology and Physical Oceanography, Department of Earth, Atmospheric and Planetary Science, Massachusetts Institute of Technology, Cambridge, Mass. 02139, U.S.A. *Telephone:* (617) 253-5937.

WÜNSCHE, Kurt Hermann, PROF. DR.IUR., DR.SC.; German lawyer and politician; b. 14 Dec. 1929, Obernigk; s. of Dr. Phil. Hermann and Hilde (née Wagner) Wünsche; m. Ursula Kreutzer 1952 (divorced 1972); one s.; m. 2nd Dr. Phil. Maria Dikowa 1972; one d.; ed. Schillerschule, Dresden, and Deutsche Akademie für Staats- und Rechtswissenschaft, Potsdam-Babelsberg; mem. Liberal Democratic Party (L.D.P.D.) 1946–, mem. Cen. Cttee. 1954–, Sec. of Cen. Man. Cttee. 1954–60, Deputy Sec.-Gen. 1960–65, Deputy Chair. 1967–72, mem. Presidium of Cen. Cttee. 1987–; Vice-Chair. of Council of Ministers of G.D.R. 1965–72; Minister of Justice 1967–72; mem. Volkskammer 1954–76, Presidium of League for People's Friendship 1961–71; Nat. Council of Nat. Front 1970–; Vice-Pres. G.D.R.-Latin-America Soc. 1976–; Prof. of Judicature Law, Humboldt Univ., Berlin 1972–; Vaterländischer Verdienstorden in Bronze and Silver, and other decorations. *Publications:* Funktion und Entwicklung der Liberal-Demokratischen Partei Deutschlands im Mehrparteiensystem der Deutschen Demokratischen Republik 1964, Zur Geschichte des Gerichtsverfassungsrechts der DDR 1978, Grundlagen der Rechtspflege 1983. *Address:* 108 Berlin, Unter den Linden 6, German Democratic Republic.

WURMSER, René Bernard; French professor of biochemistry; b. 24 Sept. 1890, Paris; m. Sabine Filitti 1936; ed. Univ. of Paris; Dir. of Biophysical Lab. of Ecole des Hautes Etudes 1927–45; Prof. Faculté des Sciences, Univ. of Paris 1945–60, Hon. Prof. 1960–; mem. Acad. des Sciences. *Publications:* Recherches sur l'assimilation chlorophyllienne 1921, Oxydations et reductions 1930, Thermodynamique des réactions immunologiques 1954. *Address:* 36 rue de l'Université, 75007 Paris, France. *Telephone:* 42.61.02.55.

WURTH, Pierre, D. EN D.; Luxembourg diplomatist; b. 6 June 1926, Luxembourg; s. of Edouard Wurth and Marie-Thérèse Lambert; m. Jeanine Rentier 1968; ed. Lycée de Garçons, Luxembourg, and Univ. of Paris; Lawyer 1951–52; Ministry of Foreign Affairs, Luxembourg 1953–54; Luxembourg Embassy, Paris 1954–59; Deputy Chief, Political Section, Ministry of Foreign Affairs, Luxembourg, and Perm. Rep. to Council of Europe 1959–64; Perm. Rep. of Luxembourg to UN 1964–68; Amb. to U.S.S.R. and Poland 1968–71; Sec.-Gen., Ministry of Foreign Affairs 1971–77; Amb. to Belgium and Perm. Del. to NATO 1977–84; Amb. to France 1984–87.

Address: c/o Ministry of Foreign Affairs, Foreign Trade and Co-operation, 5 rue Notre Dame, 2240 Luxembourg-Ville, Luxembourg.

WUTTKE, Hans A., DR.JUR.; German banker; b. 23 Oct. 1923, Hamburg; m. 1st Marina M. Schorsch 1957 (divorced 1976), two s. two d.; m. 2nd Jagoda M. Buić 1982; ed. Univs. of Cologne and Salamanca; with Dresdner Bank AG 1949-54, Daimler-Benz AG 1954-61; Partner M. M. Warburg-Brinckmann, Wirtz and Co., Hamburg 1961-75; Exec. Dir. S. G. Warburg and Co. Ltd., London; Man. Dir. Dresdner Bank AG, Frankfurt 1975-80; Chair. Deutsch-Südamerikanische Bank AG 1980-81; mem. Bd. several European cos.; Chair. E. Asia Asscn. 1963-73; Chair. Comité Européen pour le Progrès Economique et Social (CEPES) 1976-; mem. Bd., German Devt. Co., Cologne; Exec. Vice-Pres. IFC (World Bank Group), Washington 1981-84; mem. Bd. and Adviser to several European cos.; Personal Adviser to Chair. of China Int. Trust and Investment Corpn., Beijing 1985-. *Address:* 77 Cadogan Square, London, S.W.1, England (Home); 38 quai d'Orléans, Paris, France.

WYART, Jean, D. ÈS SC.; French university professor; b. 16 Oct. 1902, Avion; m. Madeleine Bourdon 1943; one s.; ed. Ecole Normale Supérieure; Asst. Univ. of Paris 1928, Deputy Prof. 1933-46; Prof. of Mineralogy, Sorbonne and Ecole de Physique et Chimie 1946-73; Sec. French Society of Mineralogy 1931-40, Pres. 1945; Dir. of Documentation Service, C.N.R.S. 1941-73; Pres. Int. Union of Crystallography 1957; mem. Acad. des Sciences 1959, Deutsche Akademie der Naturforscher Leopoldina 1966; Hon. mem. Royal Inst. 1960. *Leisure interests:* sport, travel. *Address:* Université de Paris, Tour 16, 4 Place Jussieu, 75230 Paris; 18 rue Pierre-Curie, Paris 75005, France (Home). *Telephone:* 43.26.94.29.

WYATT, Arthur Hope, C.M.G.; British diplomatist; b. 12 Oct. 1929, Adlington; s. of Frank Wyatt and Maggie Wyatt; m. Barbara Yvonne Flynn 1957; two d.; ed. Bolton School; nat. service, H.M. Forces 1948-50; overseas diplomatic appointments in Istanbul, Ankara and Phnom Penh 1952-61, First Sec. H.M. Diplomatic Service in London and Bonn 1962-72, Counsellor in Lagos, Malta, FCO, Teheran and Ankara 1972-84; Minister, British High Comm., Lagos 1984-86; High Commr. in Ghana, (also accred. to Togo) 1986-. *Leisure interests:* golf, bridge. *Address:* c/o Foreign and Commonwealth Office, King Charles Street, London, SW1A 2AH, England.

WYATT, Christopher Terrel, F.ENG., F.I.C.E.; British business executive; b. 17 July 1927, Ewell, Surrey; s. of Lional H. Wyatt and Audrey Vere Wyatt; m. Geertruida Willer 1970; four s.; ed. Kingston Grammar School, Battersea Polytechnic and Imperial Coll., London; Charles Brand & Son, Ltd., 1948-54; joined Richard Costain Ltd., 1955, Dir. 1970-87, Group Chief Exec. 1975-80, Deputy Chair. 1979-80, Chair. Costain Group PLC 1980-87; Chair., C.E.O. W. S. Atkins Ltd. 1987-. *Leisure interest:* sailing. *Address:* Lower Hawksfold, Fernhurst, Nr. Haslemere, Surrey, GU27 3NR, England. *Telephone:* (0428) 54538.

WYCKOFF, Ralph Walter Graystone, B.S., PH.D.; American scientist; b. 9 Aug. 1897, Geneva, N.Y.; s. of Abram Ralph Wyckoff and Ethel Agnes Catchpole; m. Laura Kissam Laidlaw 1927; one s. two d.; ed. Hobart Coll., and Cornell Univ.; Instructor, analytical chemistry, Cornell Univ. 1917-19; Physical Chemist, Geophysical Lab., Carnegie Inst. of Washington 1919-27; Research Assoc., Calif. Inst. of Tech. 1921-22; Assoc. mem. Rockefeller Inst. for Medical Research 1927-37; with Lederle Labs. Inc. as scientist 1937-40, as Assoc. Dir. in charge of virus research 1940-42; Technical Dir., Reichel Labs. Inc. 1942-43; Lecturer in epidemiology, Univ. of Mich. 1943-45; Sr. Scientist, U.S. Public Health Service 1945; Scientist Dir. 1946-52; Foreign Service Reserve Officer (Science Office), American Embassy, London 1952-54; Biophysicist, P.H.S. Nat. Inst. of Health 1954-59; Prof. of Physics Univs. of Ariz. 1959-81; Consultant, Duval Corpn. 1978-84; Dir. de Recherches, C.N.R.S., France 1958-62, 1969; Exchange Prof., Univ. of Paris 1965; mem. N.A.S., American Acad. of Arts and Sciences; Foreign mem. Royal Netherlands Acad. of Sciences and Literature, Royal Society, London; foreign mem. Acad. des Sciences, Paris; hon. mem. Société Française de Minéralogie et de Crystallographie, Société Française de Microbiologie, Royal Microscopical Society, London; Hon. Fellow Indian Acad. of Sciences; Hon. M.D. (Masaryk Univ.); Hon. Sc.D. (Univ. of Strasbourg, Hobart Coll.). *Publications:* An Analytical Expression of the Results of the Theory of Space Groups 1922, 1930, The Structure of Crystals 1924, 1930, 1934, Crystal Structures 1948, 1951, 1953, 1957, 1958, 1959, 1960, 1963, 1964, 1965, 1966, 1968, 1969, 1971, Electron Microscopy 1949, The World of the Electron Microscope 1958, The Biochemistry of Animal Fossils 1972. *Address:* 4741 East Cherry Hills Drive, Tucson, Ariz. 85718, U.S.A. *Telephone:* (602) 299-6029.

WYETH, Andrew N.; American artist; b. 12 July 1917, Chadds Ford, Pa.; s. of Newell Converse and Caroline (née Bockius) Wyeth; m. Betsy Merle James 1940; two s.; ed. privately; artist, landscape painter 1936-; first one-man exhbn. William Macbeth Gallery, New York 1937; one-man exhbns. at Doll and Richard, Boston 1938, 1940, 1942, 1944, 1946, 1950; Macbeth Gallery 1937, 1939, 1941, 1943, 1945, 1948, 1950, 1952; M. Knoedler and Co., New York 1953, 1958, Leferre Gallery 1974, Art Emporium, Vancouver 1977, Galerie Claude Bernard, Paris 1980, Funabashi Gallery, Tokyo 1984, Gallery Iida 1984; Group and other one-man exhbns. at M.I.T., Cambridge 1960; Dunn Int. Exhbn., London 1963; The White House, Washington, D.C. 1970, Nat. Museum of Modern Art, Tokyo 1974; retrospective exhbns., Tokyo 1974, 1979, Metropolitan Museum, New York

1976, R.A. (first by living American artist) 1980; An American Vision: Three Generations of Wyeth Art, Leningrad, Moscow, Washington, D.C., Dallas 1977, Chicago, Tokyo, Milan, Cambridge, U.K., Chaddsford, Pa. 1988; Andrew Wyeth: The Helga Pictures, Washington, D.C. 1987, Boston, Houston, Los Angeles, San Francisco, Detroit 1988; mem. Nat. Inst. of Arts and Letters, American Acad. of Arts and Sciences; Hon. mem. Soviet Acad. of the Arts 1978; U.S. Presidential Medal of Freedom 1963; Einstein Award 1967; Hon. D.F.A. (Maine, Harvard, Dickinson, Swarthmore, Temple Univ., Delaware, Northeastern Univ., Md.); Hon. L.H.D. (Tufts Univ.) 1963. *Address:* c/o Frank E. Fowler, P.O. Box 247, Lookout Mountain, Tenn. 37350, U.S.A.

WYLIE, Sir Campbell, Kt., LL.M., E.D., Q.C.; British Commonwealth judge; b. 14 May 1905, New Zealand; s. of William James Wylie and Edith Grace Stagg; m. Leita Caroline Clark 1933 (deceased); no c.; ed. Dannevirke High School, Auckland Grammar School and Victoria Univ. of Wellington; Barrister and solicitor, New Zealand 1928; Barrister-at-law, Inner Temple, London 1950; pvt. legal practice, New Zealand until 1940; New Zealand Expeditionary Force 1940-46 (despatches); legal adviser, various Malay States 1945-51; Attorney-Gen. Barbados 1952-55, British Guiana 1955-56; Attorney-Gen. of W. Indies 1956-59; Federal Justice, W. Indies 1959-63; Chief Justice, Unified Judiciary of Sarawak, N. Borneo and Brunei 1962-63; Chief Justice, High Court, Eastern Malaysia (Sarawak and Sabah) 1963-66; Law Revision Commr., Tonga 1966-67; Chief Justice of the Seychelles 1967-69; Commr. for Law Reform and Revision, Seychelles 1970-72. *Address:* Unit 80, Heron Court, 98 Bayview Street, Runaway Bay, Queensland 4216, Australia. *Telephone:* 075-372398.

WYLIE, Laurence William; American university professor; b. 19 Nov. 1909, Indianapolis; s. of William H. and Maude Stout Wylie; m. 1st Anne Stiles 1940 (divorced 1986), two s.; m. 2nd Joan Dreyfus 1988; ed. Indiana Univ., Institut des Etudes Politiques, Paris, and Brown Univ.; Instructor, Simmons College 1936-40, Asst. Prof. 1940-43; Asst. Prof. Haverford Coll. 1943-48, Assoc. Prof. 1948-57, Prof. 1957-58, Chair. Dept. of Romance Languages 1948-59; C. Douglas Dillon Prof. of French Civilization, Harvard Univ. 1959-80, Prof. Emer. 1981-; Visiting Prof. New York Univ. 1979, Stanford Univ. 1979, Hampshire Coll. 1980; Cultural Attaché, American Embassy, Paris 1965-67; mem. Modern Languages Asscn., Soc. d'ethnographie française, American Acad. of Arts and Sciences, Int. Sociological Asscn.; Fellow, Kirkland House; Officier, Légion d'honneur. *Publications:* Saint-Marc Girardin Bourgeois 1947, Village in the Vaucluse 1957, Deux villages 1966, Les français 1970, Beaux Gestes: A Guide to French Body Talk 1977; co-author: In Search of France 1962, Youth: Change and Challenge 1963, Chanzeaux, A Village in Anjou 1967, France: The Events of May–June 1968: A critical bibliography 1972, The Image of the United States in French Textbooks 1980; films: Répertoire des gestes-signes français 1973, Quand les gestes prennent la parole 1976, The French Family 1980, Roussillon—Forty Years Later 1988. *Leisure interests:* swimming, running. *Address:* 1010 Memorial Drive 5-F, Cambridge, Mass. 02138, U.S.A. *Telephone:* (617) 876-3227.

WYLLIE, Peter John, PH.D., F.R.S.; British geologist; b. 8 Feb. 1930, London; s. of George W. Wyllie and Beatrice G. Weaver; m. F. Rosemary Blair 1956; two s. one d. (and one d. deceased); glaciologist, British West Greenland Expedition 1950; British North Greenland Expedition 1952-54; Asst. Lecturer in Geology, Univ. of St. Andrews 1955-56; Research Asst. to O. F. Tuttle (q.v.), Pa. State Univ. 1956-58, Asst. Prof. of Geochem. 1959-60; Research Fellow in Chem., Univ. Leeds 1959-60, lecturer in Experimental Petrology 1960-61; Assoc. Prof. of Petrology, Pa. State Univ. 1961-65; Prof. of Petrology and Geochem., Univ. of Chicago 1965-83, Homer J. Livingston Prof. 1978-83; Chair. Dept. of Geophysical Sciences 1979-82; Chair. Div. of Geological and Planetary Sciences, Calif. Inst. of Tech. 1983-87, Prof. of Geology 1987-; Foreign Assoc. N.A.S.; Fellow, American Acad. of Arts and Sciences 1982, Royal Soc., London 1984; Corresp. Fellow, Edin. Geological Soc. 1985-; Hon. mem. Mineralogical Soc. of G.B. and Ireland 1986; Pres. Int. Mineralogical Asscn. 1986-; Hon. D.Sc. (St. Andrews) 1974; Polar Medal 1954, Mineralogical Soc. of America Award 1965, Quantrell Award 1979, Wollaston Medal (Geological Soc., London) 1982, Abraham-Gottlob-Werner-Medaille, German Mineralogical Soc. 1987. *Publications:* Ultramafic and Related Rocks (ed.) 1967, The Dynamic Earth 1971, The Way the Earth Works 1976; numerous articles in scientific journals. *Leisure interests:* concerts, theatre. *Address:* Division of Geological and Planetary Sciences, California Institute of Technology, Pasadena, Calif. 91125; 2150 Kinclair Drive, Pasadena, Calif. 91107, U.S.A. *Telephone:* (213) 356-6461 (Office); (818) 791-9164 (Home).

WYMAN, Thomas Hunt, B.A.; American business executive; b. 30 Nov. 1929, St. Louis, Mo.; s. of Edmund Allan and Nancy (née Hunt) Wyman; m. Elizabeth Minnerly 1960; three s. one d.; ed. Amherst Coll., Mass.; Sr. Vice-Pres., Gen. Man. and Chair. Mann. Exec. Cttee. Polaroid Corpn. 1965-75; Pres. and C.E.O. Green Giant Co. 1975-79; Vice-Chair. The Pillsbury Co. 1979-80; Pres. 1980-86, C.E.O. CBS Inc. 1980-83, Chair. 1983-86; Dir. AT & T, General Motors Corpn., Lincoln Center for the Performing Arts; mem. Council on Foreign Relations, Business Council, Business Roundtable; Trustee, Ford Foundation, Amherst Coll., Museum of Broadcasting, Phillips Acad., Andover. *Address:* c/o CBS Inc., 51 West 52nd Street, New York, N.Y. 10019, U.S.A. (Office).

WYNGAARDEN, James Barnes, M.D., F.R.C.P.; American physician; b. 19 Oct. 1924, East Grand Rapids, Mich.; s. of Martin J. Wyngaarden and Johanna Kempers Wyngaarden; m. Ethel D. Vredevoogd 1946 (divorced 1976); one s. four d.; ed. Calvin Coll. Grand Rapids, Western Mich. Univ. and Univ. of Mich. Medical School; Research and Clinical Assoc. Nat. Inst. of Health 1953–56; Assoc. Prof. of Medicine, Duke Univ. Medical Center 1956–61, Prof. of Medicine 1961–65, 1967–82; Chair. Dept. of Medicine, Univ. of Penn. Medical School 1965–67; Dir. N.I.H. 1982–; mem. various cttees. etc.; mem. N.A.S., American Acad. of Arts and Sciences; Dr. h.c. (Michigan) 1980, (Ohio) 1984, (Univ. of Ill. at Chicago) 1985, (George Washington Univ.) 1986; Hon. Ph.D. (Tel Aviv) 1987; numerous awards. *Publication:* Textbook of Medicine (18th edn.) (co-ed. with L. H. Smith, Jr.) 1988. *Leisure interests:* tennis, skiing, painting. *Address:* Building 1, Room 124, Bethesda, Md. 20892, U.S.A. *Telephone:* (301) 496-2433.

WYNNE, Charles Gorrie, B.A., PH.D., F.R.S.; British scientist; b. 18 May 1911; s. of C. H. and A. E. Wynne; m. Jean Richardson 1937; one s. one d.; ed. Wyggeston Grammar School, Leicester, Exeter Coll., Oxford; optical designer, Taylor, Taylor & Hobson Ltd. 1935–43, Wray (Optical Works) Ltd. 1943–60, latterly Dir.; Prof. of Optical Design, Univ. of London 1969–78, now Prof. Emer.; Dir. Optical Design Group, Imperial Coll., London 1960–78; Sr. Visiting Fellow, Inst. of Astronomy, Cambridge 1988–; Visiting Prof. Univ. of Durham; Ed. Optica Acta 1954–65; Hon. Sec. (Business), Physical Soc. 1947–56, Inst. of Physics and Physical Soc. 1960–66; Thomas Young Medal, Inst. of Physics 1971; Gold Medal, Royal Astronomical Soc. 1979, Rumford Medal of the Royal Soc. 1982. *Publications:* papers on aberration theory and optical instruments in scientific journals. *Address:* 4 Holben Close, Barton, Cambs., CB3 7AQ, England. *Telephone:* (0223) 263098.

WYNNE-EDWARDS, Vero Copner, C.B.E., M.A., D.SC., F.R.S.C., F.R.S.E., F.R.S.; British zoologist; b. 4 July 1906, Leeds, Yorks.; s. of Rev. Canon J. R. Wynne-Edwards and Lilian Streatfeild; m. Jeannie Campbell Morris 1929; one s. one d.; ed. Leeds Grammar School, Rugby School and New Coll., Oxford; Student Probationer Marine Biological Laboratory Plymouth 1927–29; Asst. Lecturer Bristol Univ. 1929–30; Asst. Prof. Zoology McGill Univ. Montreal 1930–44, Assoc. Prof. 1944–46; Regius Prof. of Natural History Aberdeen Univ. 1946–74; Visiting Prof. of Conservation Univ. of Louisville, Kentucky 1959; Commonwealth Interchange Fellow, New Zealand 1962; Ed. Journal of Applied Ecology 1964–68; Pres. British Ornithologists' Union 1965–70, Scottish Marine Biological Assen. 1967–73; Chair. Nat. Environmental Research Council 1968–71; mem. Royal Comm. on Environmental Pollution 1970–74; foreign mem. Societas Scientiarum, Finland; Hon. D.Univ. (Stirling), LL.D. (Aberdeen). *Publications:* Animal Dispersion in Relation to Social Behaviour 1962, Evolution through Group Selection 1986; and scientific articles, mainly on marine and Arctic birds and population ecology. *Leisure interests:* skiing, hill-walking, natural history. *Address:* Zoology Department, Tillydrone Avenue, Aberdeen AB9 2TN, Scotland; Ravelston, Torphins, Aberdeenshire AB3 4JR, Scotland (Home). *Telephone:* (0224) 272000 (Univ.); (033 982) 434 (Home).

WYNTER, Hector Lincoln, M.A., J.P.; Jamaican educationist, journalist and diplomatist; b. 27 July 1926, Cuba; s. of late Percival and Lola (Parkinson) Wynter; m. 1st Jacqueline Antrobus 1956 (dissolved), 2nd Diana Ayee 1970; four s. two d.; ed. Havana, Oxford, and London Univs.; Teacher of Spanish 1945–49; Resident Tutor, Dept. of Extra-mural Studies, Univ. of W. Indies 1953–55, Deputy Registrar 1955–60, Dir. Extra-mural Studies 1960–63; Senator 1962–72; High Commr., Trinidad and Tobago 1963–64;

Registrar, Univ. of W. Indies 1964–65; Parl. Sec. to Prime Minister on External Affairs 1965–67; Minister of State for Educ. 1967–69, for Youth and Devt. 1969–72; mem. Exec. Bd. UNESCO 1970–76, 1981–85, Chair. 1975–76, Chair. Finance Cttee. 1972–74, Rep. UNESCO Int. Prog. for Devt. of Communication 1986–; Exec. Ed. Daily Gleaner 1974–76, Ed. 1976–85; Dir. Gleaner Co. 1979–88; Chair. Bustamante Inst. of Public and Int. Affairs 1984–; Dir. Projects Assen. of Caribbean Univs. 1973; mem. Exec. Bd. Int. Press Inst. 1986–; Chair. New Radio Co. of Jamaica 1989–; Chair. and mem. several statutory bds. and voluntary assens.; Rhodes Scholarship 1949, Commonwealth Scholarship 1949, UN Fellow 1952, Journalist of the Year 1973, Commonwealth Finance Journalism Scholarship 1975; Order of Jamaica 1981. *Publications:* numerous articles on education and politics. *Leisure interests:* cricket, horse-racing, reading law. *Address:* Bustamante Institute of Public and International Affairs, 11 Worthington Avenue, Kingston 5 (Office); 5 Monterey Drive, Kingston 6, Jamaica (Home). *Telephone:* 92-77110 (Home).

WYSCHOFSKY, Günther; German chemist and politician; b. 8 May 1929, Bischofswerda, Saxony; mem. Communist Party 1945, Socialist Unity Party (SED) 1946–; Head, Raw Materials Industry section of Secr. Cen. Cttee. SED 1960–62; Deputy Chair. G.D.R. State Planning Comm. 1962–65; Minister of the Chemical Industry May 1966–; Cand. mem. SED Cen. Cttee. 1963–64, mem. 1964–; Vaterländischer Verdienstorden in Bronze and other decorations. *Address:* Ministerrat, Berlin, German Democratic Republic.

WYTRZENS, Günther, PH.D.; Austrian professor of Slavistics (retd.); b. 21 July 1922, Orlova, Czechoslovakia; m. Anna Ott 1957; one s. one d.; ed. Gymnasia Oderberg and Freiwaldau and Univ. of Vienna; Visiting Asst. Prof. Univ. of Kansas 1962; Assoc. Prof. Univ. of Vienna 1963, Prof. 1965–87, Dean Faculty of Humanities 1977–79; mem. Austrian Acad. of Sciences, Chair. Cttee. of Literary Sciences 1983–; mem. Int. Cttee. of Slavists 1965–89. *Publications:* Slavische Geisteswelt (co-author) 1959, Pjotr A. Vjazemskij 1961, Marina Cvetaeva, Nesobrannye proizvedenija x 1971, Die Slavica der Wiener Mechitharisten-Druckerei 1985; four vols. of Slavistic literary bibliographies; translation. *Leisure interest:* stamp collecting. *Address:* Am Modenpark 13/7, 1030 Vienna, Austria. *Telephone:* 71 36 738.

WYZNER, Eugeniusz, M.A.; Polish diplomatist; b. 31 Oct. 1931, Chełmno; s. of Henryk Wyzner and Janina (Czaplicka) Wyzner; m. Elzbieta Laudanska 1961; one s.; ed. Jagellonian Univ., Cracow, Warsaw Univ. and Acad. of Int. Law, The Hague; official, Ministry of Foreign Affairs 1952–; Sec. Neutral States Supervisory Comm. in Korea 1954–55; Deputy Perm. Rep. to UN 1961–68; Deputy Dir. of Dept. at Ministry of Foreign Affairs 1968–71, Dir. of Dept. 1971–73, Amb., Perm. Rep. to UN, Geneva 1973–78; Dir. of Dept., Ministry of Foreign Affairs 1978–81; Perm. Rep. to UN 1981–82; UN Under-Sec.-Gen. 1982–; Chair. UN Publs. Bd.; mem. Bd. of Dirs. Int. Inst. of Space Law, Paris, Int. Peace Acad., New York, Int. Congress Inst. 1987–; mem. Polish United Workers' Party (PZPR) 1951–, UN Programme Planning and Budgetary Bd.; rank of Amb. 1984–; Gold Cross of Merit 1964, Officer's Cross of Order of Polonia Restituta and other decorations. *Publications:* Wybrane zagadnienia z działalności ONZ w dziedzinie kodyfikacji i postepowego rozwoju prawa międzynarodowego 1962, Niektóre aspekty prawne finansowania operacji ONZ w Kongo i na Bliskim Wschodzie 1963. *Leisure interests:* cross-country skiing, mountain walking. *Address:* United Nations Secretariat, New York, N.Y. 10017, U.S.A.

X

XENAKIS, Iannis; French (b. Greek) composer, architect and engineer; b. 29 May 1922, Athens, Greece; s. of Clearchos Xenakis and Fotini Pavlou; m. Françoise Gargouïl; one d.; ed. Athens Polytechnic Inst., Ecole Normale de Musique, Paris (with Milhaud), Gravesano (with Scherchen) and Paris Conservatoire (under Messiaen); studied engineering in Athens; fought in Greek Resistance, World War II, condemned to death; went into exile in France 1947; collaborated as engineer and architect with Le Corbusier 1947–60; innovator of mass concept of music, Stochastic Music and Symbolic Music through probability calculus and set theory into instrumental, electro-acoustic and computerized musical composition; designer, Philips Pavilion, Brussels World Fair 1958, sonic, sculptural and light composition Polytope for French Pavilion, Expo 1967 Montreal, music and light spectacle Persepolis on ruins and mountain, Persepolis, Iran, Polytope de Cluny, Paris 1972; founder and Dir. Equipe de Mathématique et Automatique Musicales, Paris, Center for Mathematical and Automated Music, Indiana Univ.; Assoc. Prof. Indiana Univ. 1967–72; Prof. Univ. of Paris I; Gresham Prof. in Music, City Univ., London; mem. Centre Nat. de Recherche Scientifique, France; Hon. mem. American Acad. of Arts and Letters, Acad. des Beaux Arts, France, Nat. Inst. of Arts and Letters; Maurice Ravel Gold Medal 1974; Beethoven Prize (Fed. Repub. of Germany) 1977; Officier de l'Ordre des Arts et Lettres, Officier Ordre nat. du Mérite, Chevalier, Légion d'honneur; Hon. D. Mus. (Edin.) 1989. *Works include:* Metastasis (for orchestra) 1954, Pithoprakta (for string orchestra) 1956, Achorripsis (for 21 instruments) 1957, Symos (for 18 string instruments) 1959, Analogiques (for 9 string instruments and magnetic tape) 1959, ST/10-1,080262 (for 10 instruments) 1957–62, Atrées (for 10 instruments) 1962, Amorsima-Morsima (for 4 instruments) 1962, Stratégie (for 84 instruments and 2 conductors) 1963, ST/4-2 (for string quartet) 1962, Eonta (for piano and brass) 1963, Akrat 1965, Terretektorh 1966, Nuits 1968, Nomos Gamma 1968, Persephassa 1969, Antikhthon 1971, Aroura 1971, Linaia-Agon 1972, Eridanos 1973, Cendrées 1974, Erikhthon 1974, Gmeeoorh 1974, Noomena 1974, Empreintes 1975, Phlegra 1975, Psappha 1975, N'Shima 1975, Khoaï 1976, Retours—Windungen 1976, Epeï 1976, Dmaathen 1976, Akanthos 1977, Kottos 1977, Jonchaies 1977, Le Diatope (Actions of Laser Beams, Electron, Flashes, 7-Track Tape music, computer controlled show in portable structure) 1978, Polytope at Mycenae 1978, Pleiades 1978, Aïs 1980, Nekuïa 1981, Komboï 1981, For the Whales 1982, Shaar 1983, Tetras 1983, Lichens 1984, Naama 1984, Thalein 1984, Keqrops 1986, Horos 1986, A l'île de Gorée 1986, Akea 1986 and other works for magnetic tape. *Publications:* Musiques formelles 1963, Formalized Music 1970, Musique Architecture 1970, Xenakis—les Polytopes 1975, Arts/Sciences: Alloys 1979, and many articles. *Leisure interests:* camping and kayaks. *Address:* 9 rue Chaptal, 75009 Paris, France.

XI AXING; Chinese woodcut artist; b. 8 Feb. 1944, Shanghai; depictions of everyday life in the style of traditional Chinese folk art; Art Ed. Shanghai Children's Publishing House. *Address:* Shanghai Children's Publishing House, Shanghai, People's Republic of China.

XI ZHONGXUN; Chinese party official; b. 1912, Fuping, Shaanxi; joined CCP 1927; Alt. mem. 7th Cen. Cttee., CCP 1945, Dir. Org. Dept., Cen. Cttee. 1945; Deputy Sec. N.W. Bureau, Cen. Cttee. 1945–48, Sec. 1948; Political Commissar 1st Field Army 1949; Vice-Chair. N.W. Mil. and Admin. Council 1949; Political Commissar N.W. Mil. Region 1949–54; Vice-Chair. Cultural and Educational Cttee., Govt. Admin. Council 1952–54; mem. State Planning Comm. 1952; Vice-Chair. N.W. Admin. Council 1953; Dir. Propaganda Dept., CCP Cen. Cttee. 1953–54; Sec.-Gen. Govt. Admin. Council 1953–54; Deputy for Xi'an, 1st NPC 1954; Sec.-Gen. State Council 1954; mem. 8th Cen. Cttee. CCP 1956; Vice-Chair. Cen. Relief Comm. 1957; Deputy for Shaanxi, 2nd NPC 1958; Vice-Premier State Council 1959; disappeared 1962–66; purged 1967; mem. Standing Cttee., 5th CPPCC 1978; Second Sec. CCP Cttee., Guangdong 1978, First Sec. 1979; Vice-Chair. Prov. Revolutionary Cttee., Guangdong 1978–79, Chair. 1979; mem. 11th Cen. Cttee., CCP 1979; First Political Commissar, Guangdong Mil. Region 1979–80; Vice-Chair. Standing Cttee., 5th NPC 1980–83, Vice-Chair. 7th NPC April 1988–; Chair. Comm. on Legis. Affairs, NPC 1981–, Bills Cttee. 5th NPC 1981–83; mem. Secr., Cen. Cttee. 1981–85; mem. Politburo, Cen. Cttee. 1982–87; Deputy Sec.-Gen. CCP 12th Nat. Congress 1982; Gov. of Guangdong 1982–83; Adviser, Cen. Party Consolidation Guidance Comm. 1983–; Hon. Pres. Beijing Social Welfare Foundation 1984–, Badminton Asscn. 1985–. *Address:* Office of the Governor, Guangdong Province, People's Republic of China.

XIA JUHUA: Chinese acrobat; Gold Medallist, 6th Circus of Tomorrow Festival, Paris 1983; Chair. Chinese Acrobatic Assocn. 1981–. *Address:* Beijing Academy of Performing Arts, Beijing, People's Republic of China.

XIA SHIHOU; Chinese party and government official; mem. Hubei Prov. People's Congress 1955–68; Vice-Gov. Hubei Prov. 1962–67; Vice-Commdr. Hubei Resist Drought HQ 1966; mem. special squad responsible for agric. production, finance and trade 1966; Vice-Chair. Hubei Prov. Revolutionary Cttee. 1973–78; mem. Standing Cttee. Hubei Prov. CCP Cttee. 1978–;

Vice-Chair. Hubei Prov. People's Congress 1980–81; mem. Cen. Advisory Cttee. of CCP Cen. Cttee. 1982–. *Address:* Central Advisory Committee of the Central Committee of the Chinese Communist Party, Zhongnanhai, Beijing, People's Republic of China.

XIA YAN (pen name of Shen Duanxian); Chinese writer, journalist and politician; b. 30 Oct. 1900, Hangzhou, Zhejiang Prov.; m. Cai Shuxin 1930; one s. one d.; ed. Hangzhou Tech. Coll., Kyushu Tech. Inst., Japan; affiliated to left wing of Kuomintang 1925–27; mem. CCP 1927–; founded drama club Yishu (Art) in Shanghai 1929; Ed. newspapers and journals, Shanghai and Hong Kong 1937–48; Deputy Dir. Propaganda Dept., E. China Bureau of CCP Cen. Cttee. 1949; mem. E. China Mil. and Admin. Council 1949–54; Dir. Asia Dept., Ministry of Foreign Affairs 1949–52; Dir. Shanghai Culture Bureau 1950–53; mem. Shanghai People's Govt. 1950–55; Vice-Minister of Culture 1954–65; Deputy for Shandong, 2nd NPC 1958; Vice-Chair. Assn. for Cultural Relations with Foreign Countries 1963–66; disappeared during Cultural Revolution; Vice-Chair. Assn. for Friendship with Foreign Countries 1975–86; mem. Standing Cttee., 5th CPPCC 1978–81; Vice-Chair. China Fed. of Literary and Art Circles 1978–88, China Pen Centre 1982–; Chair. China Film Artists' Assn. 1979, Sino-Japanese Friendship Assn. 1983–86; Adviser to Chinese Writers' Assn. 1984–. *Publications:* Lanxun Jiumeng Lu (Recollections) 1985, Xiayan Wenji (Selected Works), 4 vols. 1988. *Leisure interests:* philately, keeping pet cats. *Address:* 14 Daliubukoujie Street, Beijing 100031, People's Republic of China. *Telephone:* 65 7129.

XIANG NAN; Chinese party official; b. 1916, Liancheng Co., Fujian Prov.; Second Deputy Sec. E. China Work Cttee. (NDYL); concurrently mem. Standing Cttee. and Sec. Secr., E. China Work Cttee., NDYL 1953; Deputy for Anhui, 1st NPC 1954; Dir. Propaganda Dept., NDYL 1955; concurrently mem. Cen. Cttee., Standing Cttee. and Sec. Secr., NDYL 1957; Exec. Sec. CCP Cttee., Fujian 1981; First Sec. 1982–85; First Political Commissar, Fujian Mil. Dist. 1982–85; mem. 12th Cen. Cttee. CCP 1982–87, mem. CCP Cen. Advisory Comm. 1987–; mem. Presidium 6th NPC 1982; Chair. Prov. People's Congress, Fujian 1982–83. *Address:* First Political Commissar, Fujian Military District, People's Republic of China.

XIANG SHOUZHI, Gen.; Chinese soldier; b. 1917, Xuanhan Co., Sichuan Prov.; joined Red Army 1934, CCP 1936; Commdr., Second Artillery Corps, PLA 1976–81, Nanjing Mil. Unit 1982–; Deputy Commdr. PLA Nanjing Mil. Region 1977–82, Commdr. 1982–; mem. 12th Cen. Cttee. CCP 1982–87, mem. CCP Cen. Advisory Comm. 1987–.

XIAO HAN; Chinese government and party official; Vice Minister of the Coal Industry, then Minister 1977–80; Deputy Minister, State Econ. Comm. 1980–82; Alt. mem. 11th Cen. Cttee. of CCP 1977; mem. 12th Cen. Cttee. CCP 1982–87; Vice-Chair. Shandong Prov. People's Congress 1985–. *Address:* People's Republic of China.

XIAO KE, Col.-Gen.; Chinese politician; b. 1908, Jiahe Cty., Hunan; joined CCP 1927; on Long March; then Deputy Commdr. Second Front Army, Commdr. 31st army of Fourth Front Army, Commdr. Hebei-Rhe-Chahar advance army (successively); Dir. mil. training dept. under Mil. Comm. CCP Cen. Cttee. and Vice-Minister Nat. Defence after 1949; Pres. Mil. and Political Acad. 1972; Commandant PLA Mil. Acad. 1978, First Political Commissar 1979; Vice-Minister Nat. Defence 1980; Vice-Chair. CPPCC Nat. Cttee. 1980; mem. Standing Cttee., Cen. Advisory Cttee. 1983–.

XIAO QUANFU, Maj.-Gen.; Chinese politician; b. 1916, Jinzhai Co., Anhui Prov.; joined Red Army 1930, CCP 1932; Maj.-Gen., PLA Units, Jilin 1960; Responsible Person, PLA Forces, Tumen, Jilin 1960; Responsible Person, PLA Shenyang Units 1965; Deputy Commdr. PLA Shenyang Units 1972–80; Commdr. PLA Xinjiang Mil. Region 1980–85; mem. 12th Cen. Cttee. CCP 1982–85; mem. Cen. Advisory Cttee. 1985–. *Address:* People's Liberation Army Headquarters, Urumqi, People's Republic of China.

XIAO WANGDONG, Lieut.-Gen.; Chinese government official; b. 1910, Ji'an Co., Jiangxi Prov.; m. Xin Ping; three s. three d.; Leader Guerrilla Detachment, New 4th Army 1938; mem. E. China Mil. and Admin. Cttee. 1949–53; Sec. CCP N. Jiangsu Dist. Cttee. 1949; mem. Northern Admin. Council 1950–52; mem. Jiangsu People's Prov. Govt. 1952; mem. E. China Admin. Cttee. 1953; Deputy Political Commissar, PLA Nanjing Mil. Region 1957; Deputy Sec. CCP Cttee. PLA Nanjing Units 1958; Lieut.-Gen. PLA 1958; Deputy for Nanjing Units to 2nd NPC 1958, re-elected 3rd NPC 1964; mem. Nat. Defence Council 1965–67; Vice-Minister of Culture 1965–67; Sec., Cultural Dept., CCP Cen. Cttee. 1966; Acting Dir., Cultural Dept., CCP Cen. Cttee. 1966; branded Capitalist roader and a counter-revolutionary revisionist July 1967; Political Commissar Jinan PLA Mil. Region 1978, First Political Commr. PLA, Jinan Mil. Region 1980–82; mem. Cen. Advisory Comm. 1982–. *Address:* People's Republic of China.

XIE BINGXIN; Chinese writer; b. 5 Oct. 1900, Fu Zhou, Fujian (as Xie Wanying); d. of Xie Boazhang and Yang Fuci; m. Wu Wenzao 1929; one s.

two d.; ed. Bridgeman Acad. for Girls, Women's Union Coll., Yanjing Univ, Wellesley Coll., U.S.A.; participated in May 4th Movt.; lecturer, Yanjing Univ., Qinghua Univ. and Women's Coll. of Science and Arts 1926-37; studied Tokyo Univ., Japan 1949-50; mem. NPC 1954-59, 1959-64, 1964-69; May 7th Cadres' School, Hubei 1970-72; Cen. Inst. of Nationalities, Beijing 1972-76; Vice-Chair. Assen. for Promoting Democracy 1979-88, China Fed. of Literature and Art 1979-88; mem. Standing Cttee. CPPCC 1978-; Hon. Pres. Prose Soc. 1984-; Adviser China Literary Foundation 1983-, China Writers' Asscn. 1984-. *Publications:* poetry: Spring Water 1922, A Maze of Stars 1922; prose: Letters to Young Readers 1923-26, Returning South 1931, We Have Awoken Spring 1959, More Letters to Young Readers 1958-60, Ode to Cherry Blossoms 1961; stories: Superman 1923, Parting of the Ways 1931, Empty Nest 1980; novella: Tao Qi's Diary 1952; translations: Gibran's The Prophet 1931, Sand and Foam 1963, Tagore's Gitanjali, The Gardener 1955. *Address:* Flat 4, Unit 34, Residential Quarters, Central Institute of Nationalities, Beijing, People's Republic of China. *Telephone:* 89.8046.

XIE FEI; Chinese party official; b. 1932, Lufeng, Guangdong Prov.; m. Peng Yuzhen 1957; two s.; alt. mem. 12th CCP Cen. Cttee. 1982-87, mem. 13th Cen. Cttee. 1987; Deputy Sec. CCP Cttee., Guangdong 1983-87, Vice-Chair. 1987-88; Sec. CCP Cttee., Guangzhou 1986-. *Leisure interest:* reading. *Address:* Guangdong Provincial Chinese Communist Party, Guangzhou, Guangdong, People's Republic of China.

XIE FENG; Chinese party official; b. 7 Dec. 1922, East Dugang Village, Yexian, Hebei Prov.; s. of Wu Mei-wu and Wu Hao-shi; m. Jiang De-pei; five c.; successively held posts of Dist. and Co. Mil. Cttees., Dept. of People's Armed Force and Public Security Bureau Dir.; Sec.-Gen. Chahar Prov. Procurational Office; Commr., Zhangjiakou Admin. Office; Second Sec., CCP Zhangjiakou Pref. Cttee.; First Sec., CCP Shijiazhuang Pref. Cttee.; Deputy Sec. and Organizing Dept. Dir., CCP Cttee., Hebei Prov.; Sec. CCP Cttee., Hebei Prov., Deputy Sec. 1983-; Gov. Hebei Prov.; mem. 12th CCP Cen. Cttee. *Leisure interests:* reading, enjoying operas, watching sports, films and TV. *Address:* 10 Weiming Street, Shijiazhuang, Hebei Province, People's Republic of China. *Telephone:* 25951.

XIE HENG; Chinese government official; b. 5 Oct. 1921, Ha Er Bin; s. of Xie Ru Qing and Xie Yan Shi; m. Guo Da Reno 1987; one d.; Adviser Ministry of Public Security Aug. 1983-; Pres. Chinese Asscn. of Fire Protection 1984-. *Leisure interest:* going for walks. *Address:* Ministry of Public Security, Beijing; 14 Dong Chang An Street, Beijing, People's Republic of China. *Telephone:* 5122702.

XIE JIN; Chinese film director; b. 1923, Shangyu Co., Zhejiang Prov.; ed. Sichuan Nat. Drama School; Film Dir., Datong Film Studio, Shanghai 1948-50; Film Dir., Shanghai Film Studio 1953-. *Films include:* Red Girl's Army (Hundred Flavers Award) 1960, Legend of Tian Yun (1st Golden Rooster Best Film Award) 1981, Lotus Town (Golden Rooster Best Film Dir. Award) 1987. *Address:* Shanghai Film Studio, 595 Caoxi Beilu, Shanghai, People's Republic of China. *Telephone:* 388100 (Shanghai).

XIE XIDE, PH.D.; Chinese physicist; b. 19 March 1921, Jinjiang, Fujian Prov.; d. of Xie Yuming (Yu Ming Hsieh) and Zhang Shunying; m. Cao Tianqin (Tian Chin Tsao) 1952; one s.; ed. Smith Coll. and Massachusetts Inst. of Tech., U.S.A.; taught in Physics Dept., Fudan Univ. 1952-77, Vice-Pres. Physics Soc. 1978, Vice-Pres. Fudan Univ. 1978-83, Pres. 1983-; Chair. Shanghai Municipal Cttee. April 1988-; mem. Presidium, mem. Scientific Council and Vice-Chair., Vice-Pres. Chinese Physical Soc.; Pres. Shanghai Asscn. of Science and Tech., Science Fund Cttee., Acad. of Sciences 1981; mem. 12th CCP Cen. Cttee. 1982, mem. 13th Cen. Cttee. 1987-; Hon. D.S. (Smith Coll., Mass.) 1981, (CCNY of Columbia Univ., New York) 1981, (Leeds Univ., U.K.) 1985, (Mount Holyoke Coll., U.S.A.) 1986, (Kansai Univ., Japan) 1986, (Beloit Coll., Wis., U.S.A.) 1987, (State Univ. of N.Y., Albany, U.S.A.) 1987, (Tokyo Univ., Japan) 1987. *Publications:* Semiconductor Physics (with Huang Kun) 1958, Solid Physics (with Fang Junxin) 1962, chapter on Non-crystalline Material, Solid State Physics, Vol. II (by Fang Junxin and Lu Dong) 1982, Group Theory and its Applications (maj. author) 1986; many papers in int. scientific journals. *Leisure interests:* reading, music appreciation, stamp collecting. *Address:* Fudan University, Shanghai, People's Republic of China. *Telephone:* 484906-2644.

XIE ZHENHUA; Chinese army officer and party official; Chief of Staff, 3rd Army, Chinese People's Volunteers in Korea 1952; rank of Maj.-Gen. 1955; Deputy Commdr. 3rd Army 1957; Commdr. Jilin City Garrison 1958-67; Mil. leader in Shanxi 1967; Vice-Chair. Revolutionary Cttee., Shanxi 1967-69; Commdr. Shanxi Mil. Dist. 1969-74; First Sec. CCP Cttee. Shanxi 1971-75; Chair. Revolutionary Cttee., Shanxi 1971-74; alt. mem. 10th CCP Cen. Cttee. 1973; Deputy Commdr. Shenyang Mil. Region 1979-82, Deputy Political Commissar 1979; mem. 12th CCP Cen. Cttee. 1982; Political Commissar, Kunming Mil. Region 1982-85 (now Chengdu Mil. Region); mem. Cen. Advisory Comm. 1985-; Deputy Sec. Chengdu Mil. Region 1986-. *Address:* Chengdu Military Region Headquarters, Chengdu, Sichuan, People's Republic of China.

XING BENSI; Chinese philosopher and university professor; b. 7 Oct. 1929, Hangzhou; s. of Xing Tinxu and Guei Yuyin; m. Zhou Bangyuan 1953; two d.; ed. Nantong Coll., Beijing Coll. of Foreign Languages; Asst.

and Lecturer Beijing Coll. of Foreign Languages 1952-56; Asst. Research Fellow and Research Prof. Inst. of Philosophy 1957-85, Deputy Dir. 1978-82, Dir. 1983-; Prof. Grad. School of Chinese Acad. of Social Sciences 1984-; Prof. Qinghua Univ. 1984-; mem. of Cttee. Chinese Acad. of Social Sciences 1982-; Trustee, Center for Int. Cultural Exchange 1984-; Deputy Gen. Ed. Philosophy vol. of Chinese Encyclopaedia 1982-; Visiting Scholar Columbia Univ. 1981. *Publications:* The Dualism of Ludwig Feurbach's Anthropology 1963, The Social Theory and Historical Viewpoint of Saint-Simon 1964, Humanism in the History of European Philosophy 1978, Philosophy and Enlightenment 1979, The Anthropology of Ludwig Feurbach 1981, Philosophy and Time 1984, Philosophy (Introduction to Philosophy vol. of Chinese Encyclopaedia) 1987, The Past, Present and Future of Philosophy (Introduction, Little Encyclopaedia of Philosophy) 1987, and many other essays. *Leisure interests:* music, literature, Peking Opera, Chinese calligraphy. *Address:* Institute of Philosophy, Chinese Academy of Social Sciences, Beijing, People's Republic of China. *Telephone:* 500.7744-2219.

XING CHONGZHI; Chinese party official; mem. Cen. Cttee., Communist Youth League 1964; Vice-Chair. Preparatory Cttee., 10th Congress of Communist Youth League 1978; Vice-Minister of Agric. 1979-82; alt. mem. 12th CCP Cen. Cttee. 1982, mem. 1985; Sec. CCP Cttee., Hebei 1985-. *Address:* Hebei Provincial Chinese Communist Party, Shijiazhung, Hebei, People's Republic of China.

XING YANZI; Chinese party official; b. 1940, Tianjin; ed. Dazhongzhuang People's Commune; joined CCP 1960; Deputy for H•bei to 3rd NPC 1964; mem. Revolutionary Cttee., Hebei Prov. 1968; Vice-Chair. Communist Youth League, Hebei 1973; mem. 10th CCP Cen. Cttee. 1973, 11th 1977, 12th 1982; Sec. CCP Cttee., Tianjin Municipality 1974-77; Vice-Chair. Revolutionary Cttee., Tianjin 1975-77. *Address:* Tianjin Municipal Chinese Communist Party, Tianjin, People's Republic of China.

XING ZHIKANG; Chinese party official; b. 1930; ed. Shanghai Normal Coll.; joined CCP 1946; Prin. of a Shanghai High School 1964; criticized during Cultural Revolution 1967; Deputy Dir. Propaganda Dept., Xuhui Dist. CCP, Shanghai 1978; alt. mem. 12th CCP Cen. Cttee. 1982, 13th Cen. Cttee. 1987. *Address:* Xuhui District Chinese Communist Party, Shanghai, People's Republic of China.

XIONG FU; Chinese newspaper executive and party official; b. 1916, Sichuan; Deputy Dir. Propaganda Dept., Central-South Bureau of CCP 1949; Dir. Changjiang Daily, Wuhan 1950; Chief of Information and Publs. Bureau, Cen.-South Mil. and Admin. Cttee. 1950-67, mem. Cultural and Educational Cttee. 1950, mem. Cttee. for Simplification and Practising Economy 1951; Sec.-Gen. Propaganda Dept. and other posts, CCP Cen. Cttee. 1956-67; criticized and removed from office during Cultural Revolution 1967; Head of Dept. in CCP Cen. Cttee. 1977; del. to 4th CPPCC and mem. Nat. Cttee. 1964, mem. Standing Cttee. 1978; Ed.-in-Chief Hong qi (Red Flag) 1978-; Vice-Pres. Beijing Journalism Studies Soc. 1980; Deputy Sec.-Gen. Secr. Cttee. for the Revision of CPPCC Constitution Standing Cttee., 5th CPPCC 1980-. *Address:* Red Flag, Beijing, People's Republic of China.

XIONG QINGQUAN; Chinese party and state official; Mayor of Changsha 1982; alt. mem. 12th CCP Cen. Cttee. 1982, mem. 1985-; Sec. CCP Cttee., Hunan Prov. 1983-85, Deputy Sec. 1985-88, Sec. April 1988-; Gov. of Hunan 1985-. *Address:* Office of the Governor, Hunan Provincial People's Government, Changsha, Hunan, People's Republic of China.

XU BING, M.A.; Chinese artist; b. 8 Feb. 1955, Chongqing; s. of Hua-min Xu and Shi-ying Yang; ed. Cen. Acad. of Fine Arts, Beijing; Teacher Engraving Dept., Cen. Acad. of Fine Arts 1981-84, 1987-; Post-graduate Dept. 1984-87; exhbns. in France, U.S.A., Switzerland, U.K., Italy, Japan, G.D.R., China 1979-; mem. Chinese Engraving Artists' Asscn. 1981-, Chinese Artists' Asscn. 1982-, Dir. 1985-; Dir. Chinese Engraving Artists' Asscn. 1986-; prizes from Art Exhbns. of Chinese Young Artists' Works 1980, 1985, 8th Exhbn. of China's Wooden Paintings 1983, Medal, 9th Chinese Engraving Exhbn. 1986. *Publications:* Wooden Painting Sketches of Xu Bing 1986, Engravings of Xu Bing; numerous articles in magazines and newspapers. *Leisure interest:* hiking. *Address:* Engraving Department, Central Academy of Fine Arts, Beijing, People's Republic of China. *Telephone:* 554731.

XU DEHENG; Chinese politician and university professor; b. Sept. 1890, Jiou Jiang, Jiangxi Prov.; two s. one d.; ed. English Dept., Beijing Univ., Sociology Dept., Univ. of Paris, France; returned to China 1927; Political Instructor, Huang Pu Mil. Acad.; Prof., Zhong Shan Univ.; Gen. Sec. and Acting Dir., Gen. Political Dept., Nat. People's Revolutionary Army 1927; Prof., Jinan Univ., Beijing Univ., Beijing Legal and Commercial Acad., Beijing Normal Univ. 1928-52; mem. People's Political Council under Nationalist Govt. 1947; mem. Nat. Cttee., 1st CPPCC 1949; Chief of Political and Legal Section, CPPCC 1949-54; mem. Political and Legal Cttee., Gen. Advisory Council (GAC) 1949-54; Chair. Cen. Cttee. Jiu San Soc. (JSS); mem. Cttee. for Checking up on Austerity Programme, GAC 1951; mem. CPPCC Standing Cttee. 1953; Vice-Chief and Acting Chief of Legality Cttee. GAC 1952-55; mem. Bills Cttee., 1st NPC 1954; mem. Standing Cttee., 1st NPC 1954-56; mem. Standing Cttee., 2nd CPPCC 1954; Chief of Educ. Section, CPPCC 1954; Vice-Chair. Study Cttee.,

CPPCC 1956; Minister of Aquatic Products 1956-69; Chair. 2nd Cen. Cttee., JSS 1958; mem. Standing Cttee., 3rd CPPCC 1959; Vice-Chair. Standing Cttee., 4th CPPCC 1965-78; Vice-Chair. Standing Cttee., 4th NPC 1975-78; Vice-Chair. Standing Cttee., 5th CPPCC 1978; Vice-Chair. Standing Cttee., 5th NPC 1978; Vice-Chair. Standing Cttee., NPC 1978; Chair. Jiusan Soc. Cen. Cttee. 1979, Hon. Chair. Jan. 1988-; Exec. Chair. Presidium, 6th NPC 1986. *Leisure intersts:* Chinese clasical poetry, Chinese calligraphy. *Address:* Standing Committee, Quanguo Renmin Daibiao Dahui, Beijing, People's Republic of China.

XU HAIFENG; Chinese pistol champion; won Gold Medal, 1984 Olympic Games. *Address:* Chinese Sports Federation, Beijing, People's Republic of China.

XU HOUZE; Chinese geodesist and geophysicist; b. 4 May 1934, Anhui; s. of Xu Zuoren and Jiang Xinghua; m. Yang Huiji 1967; one s. one d.; ed. Tongji Univ., Shanghai, Dept. of Geodesy; Asst. Researcher Inst. of Geodesy and Geophysics, Chinese Acad. of Sciences 1963, Assoc. Prof. 1978, Prof. 1982-, Dir. 1983-; mem. Chinese Geophysics Soc. 1978-; Vice-Pres. Int. Gravimetry Cttee. and mem. Perm. Cttee. of Earth Tides, Int. Asscn. of Geodesy (IAG) 1983-; Vice-Pres. Science-Tech. Soc. of Hubei Prov. 1984-, Chinese Survey and Mapping Soc. 1985-; Prof. Tongji Univ. 1985-, Wuhan Tech. Univ. of Survey and Mapping 1986-. *Publications:* The Approximation of Stokes' Function and the Estimation of Trunction Error 1981, The Effect of Oceanic Tides on Gravity Tide Observations 1982, The Tidal Correction in Astrometry 1982, Accuracy Estimation of Loading Correction in Gravity Observation 1984, The Effect of Different Earth Models on Load Tide Correction 1985, Representation of Gravity Field outside the Earth using Fictitious Single Layer Density 1984. *Address:* Xu Dong Road 54, Building 2-7, Wuhan, People's Republic of China. *Telephone:* 813805.

XU HUAIZHONG; Chinese writer; b. 1929, Hebei Prov.; s. of Xu Hongchang and Xin Zhuoliang; m. Yu Zengxiang; one s. two d.; mem. Presidium and Dir. Bd. of Dirs., Chinese Writers' Asscn. 1983-; Deputy Cultural Dir., Gen. Political Dept. of PLA 1985-88, Dir. Sept. 1988-. *Publications:* Rainbow over the Earth, On the Tibetan Highlands, Anecdotes from the Western Front, The Wingless Angel (collection of medium-length novels and short stories). *Leisure interests:* playing table tennis and traditional Chinese shadow boxing. *Address:* 21 North Street Andeli, East District, Beijing, People's Republic of China.

XU JIANSHENG; Chinese party official; fmr. Sec.-Gen. New China News Agency before 1949; Sec.-Gen. Prov. People's Govt., Guizhou 1950; Dir. Dept. of United Front Work, Guizhou 1954; Deputy for Guizhou, 1st NPC 1954, 2nd NPC 1958, 3rd NPC 1964; Vice-Gov. of Guizhou 1955-Cultural Revolution; mem. Standing Cttee., CCP Cttee., Guizhou 1956; Sec. Secr., CCP Cttee., Guizhou 1961, 1966, Alt. Sec. 1962; disappeared 1967-72; cadre CCP Cen. Cttee. 1973; Deputy Sec. CCP Cttee., Guizhou 1977; First Sec. Municipal CCP Cttee., Guiyang 1977; Chair. Prov. People's Congress, Guizhou 1979-83; Deputy Head People's Air Defence Leading Group, Guizhou Mil. Dist. 1981. *Address:* People's Congress, Guizhou Province, People's Republic of China.

XU JIATUN; Chinese politician; b. 1916, Jiangsu; mem. of CCP, Deputy Sec., Sec., Fuzhou Municipal Cttee. in Fujian 1950; Sec. Nanjing Municipal Cttee. CCP in Jiangsu 1954; Sec. Secr. and mem. Standing Cttee. Jiangsu Provincial Cttee. CCP; Deputy Gov. of Jiangsu 1956; Vice-Chair. Jiangsu Prov. Revolutionary Cttee. 1970, 1974, Chair. 1977-79; Sec., then First Sec. Jiangsu Prov. Cttee. CCP; Chair. Standing Cttee. of Fifth People's Congress of Jiangsu; First Political Commissar of PLA of Jiangsu Prov. Mil. Dist. 1977-; Chair. Jiangsu Prov. People's Congress 1979-83; First Sec. of Party Cttee. 1977-83, mem. 11th Cen. Cttee. of CCP 1977-82, 12th Cen. Cttee. CCP 1982-85; mem. Cen. Advisory Comm. 1985-; mem. Presidium 6th NPC 1986-; Vice-Chair. Cttee. for Drafting Basic Law of Hong Kong Special Admin. Region 1985-; Dir. Xinhua News Agency, Hong Kong July 1983-; mem. Standing Cttee., CCP 1988-. *Address:* Xinhua News Agency, 387 Queen's Road, East, Hong Kong. *Telephone:* 5-8314333.

XU LINLU; Chinese artist; b. 23 Sept. 1916, Penglai Co., Shandong; s. of late Shuting Xu and Gaoshi Xu; m. Wang Lingwen 1936; four s. four d.; ed. commercial school, Tianjin; studied under Qi Baishi 1938; Deputy Dir. Beijing Municipal Traditional Chinese Painting Research Inst.; mem. Beijing Municipal People's Political Consultative Conf.; Deputy Dir., Sec. Gen. Sun Yat-sen Painting Asscn.; Chair. Flower and Bird Painting Research Inst. *Works include:* Grapevine and Sparrows, White Plum, Crabapple and Dragonfly, Lychees, Clay Figurines, Lotus and Mandarin Fish, Folk toys, Landscape, Eagle, Panda. *Leisure interest:* collecting antiques. *Address:* Room 302, Apt. 1, Bldg. 8, East Street, Chongwenmen, Beijing, People's Republic of China.

XU QIN; Chinese party and state official; Deputy for Jiangxi to 5th NPC 1978; Vice-Gov. Jiangxi 1979-83; Deputy Sec. CCP Cttee., Jiangxi 1981; Vice-Chair. Jiangxi People's Congress 1981, Chair. Feb. 1988-; alt. mem. 12th CCP Cen. Cttee. 1982-87. *Address:* Jiangxi Provincial Chinese Communist Party, Nanchang, Jiangxi, People's Republic of China.

XU SHAOFU; Chinese party official; Sec. CCP Cttee., Shenyang Municipality 1956; alt. Sec. CCP Cttee., Liaoning Prov. 1962-68; disappeared

during Cultural Revolution 1968-78; mem. Comm. for Inspecting Discipline, CCP Cen. Cttee. 1978-82; Sec. CCP Cttee., Liaoning 1979-83; mem. 12th CCP Cen. Cttee. 1982-87; Chair. CPCC Liaoning Prov. Cttee. 1985-. *Address:* Liaoning Provincial Chinese Communist Party, Shenyang, Liaoning, People's Republic of China.

XU SHUYANG; Chinese sculptor; b. March 1927, Shanghai; ed. Suzhou Art Coll., Cen. Acad. of Fine Arts, Hangzhou and Cen. Acad. of Fine Arts, Beijing; squad leader, Art Troupe, Party Cttee. N. Jiangsu Pref. 1948-50; artist and mem. staff, Art Dept. East China Culture Bd. Shanghai 1950-51; lecturer, Dept. of Sculpture, Zhejiang Acad. of Fine Arts 1961-83, Assoc. Prof. 1983-; works include numerous public monuments and sculptures; recipient of several prizes including Nat. Urban Sculpture Award 1987. *Publications:* articles in fine arts journals. *Address:* P.O. Box 169, Zhejiang Academy of Fine Arts, Hangzhou, China.

XU XIANGQIAN; Chinese politician; b. 1902, Wutai Co., Shanxi; ed. elementary school; Dir. Political Dept. Student Army; Chief-of-Staff and Commdr. Red Div. 1927; Commdr. 31st Div., Workers-Peasants Red Army 1929; C.-in-C. 4th Front Army 1931; Vice-Commdr. 129th Division, 8th Route Army 1937; Vice-Commdr. Jt. Defence Forces 1941; mem. 7th Cen. Cttee. CCP 1945; Vice-Commdr. Shanxi-Hebei-Shandong-Henan Mil. Region 1947; Commdr. and Political Commissar 1st Army Corps, N. China Field Army 1948; Commdr. Taiyuan Front 1948; Commdr. 18th Army Group 1948; Chair. Taiyuan Mil. Control Comm. 1949; Vice-Commdr. PLA N. China Mil. Region 1949-54; mem. People's Revolutionary Mil. Council 1949; Chief of Gen. Staff PLA 1949-54; mem. Cen. People's Govt. Council 1949-54; Vice-Chair. People's Revolutionary Mil. Council, 1954; Deputy for PLA, 1st NPC 1954; mem. Standing Cttee., 1st NPC 1954-58; Vice-Chair. Nat. Defence Council 1954-75; rank of Marshal PLA 1955; mem. 8th Cen. Cttee. CCP 1956; Deputy for PLA, 2nd NPC 1958; Deputy for PLA, 3rd NPC 1964; Vice-Chair. Standing Cttee., 3rd NPC 1965-75; mem. Standing Cttee., CCP Mil. Affairs Comm. 1966; Dir. Cultural Revolution Group, CCP Mil. Affairs Comm. 1967; Vice-Chair. CCP Mil. Affairs Comm. 1967; mem. Politburo 8th Cen. Cttee. CCP 1967; mem. 9th Cen. Cttee. CCP 1969; Deputy for PLA, 4th NPC 1975; Vice-Chair. Standing Cttee., 4th NPC 1975-78; mem. Politburo, 11th Cen. Cttee. CCP 1977; Vice-Premier, State Council 1978-80; Minister of Nat. Defence 1978-81; Deputy for PLA, 5th NPC 1978; mem. Politburo 12th Cen. Cttee. CCP 1982-85; Vice-Chair. Cen. Mil. Comm. 1983-87, Chair. People's Armament Cttee. 1984-. *Address:* CCP Military Affairs Commission, Beijing, People's Republic of China.

XU XIN; Chinese party and military official; Chief of Staff, Beijing Units 1970-80; Political Commissar, Tianjin Garrison 1974; Sec. CCP Cttee., Tianjin 1975; Deputy for PLA, 5th NPC 1978; Deputy Dir. Beijing Inst. for Int. Strategic Studies 1981-87, Dir. Dec. 1987-; Asst. to Chief of Gen. Staff, PLA 1980-82; alt. mem. 12th Cen. Cttee. CCP 1982-87; Deputy Chief of Gen. Staff, PLA 1982-; Chair. Nat. Advertising Asscn. for Foreign Econ. Relations and Trade 1985-; mem. Cen. Advisory Comm. 1987-. *Address:* c/o Beijing Institute for International Strategic Studies, Beijing, People's Republic of China.

XU YINSHENG; Chinese government official; b. 12 June 1938; m. Chen Liwen; one s.; World table tennis champion three times; Vice-Minister for Physical Educ. and Sport 1977-; Pres. Table Tennis Asscn. 1979-, Boxing Asscn. 1987-; Exec. Vice-Chair. Preparatory Cttee. for 6th Nat. games 1985; Vice-Pres. All-China Sports Fed. 1986-; Vice-Pres. Chinese Olympic Cttee. 1986-. *Publication:* How to Play Table Tennis by Dialectics. *Leisure interests:* tennis, fishing. *Address:* 9 Tiyuguan Road, Beijing, People's Republic of China. *Telephone:* 5112233.

XU YOUFANG; Chinese government official; Dir. Forestry Industry Bureau 1985; Vice-Minister for Forestry 1986-. *Address:* Ministry of Forestry, Beijing, People's Republic of China.

XU ZHENSHI; Chinese artist and photographer; b. 1937; ed. Zhejiang Fine Arts Coll.; Dir. Picture Ed. Dept. of People's Fine Arts Publishing House. *Address:* People's Fine Arts Publishing House, Beijing, People's Republic of China.

XU ZI; Chinese fashion designer; b. Tianjin; fmr. singer in Song and Dance Troupe of All-China Fed. of Trades Unions, Beijing; European Exhbn. of designs 1986. *Address:* China International Cultural Exchange Centre, Beijing, People's Republic of China.

XUE JU; Chinese party and government official; b. 1922; Deputy Sec. CCP Cttee., Zhejiang 1978-79; Vice-Chair. Prov. CPPCC Cttee., Zhejiang 1979-83; mem. 12th Cen. Cttee. 1982-; mem. Presidium 6th NPC 1986-; Gov. of Zhejiang 1983-; Sec. Zhejiang CCP Cttee. 1987-. *Address:* Zhejiang Provincial People's Government, Hangzhou, Zhejiang Province, People's Republic of China.

XUE MUQIAO; Chinese economist and politician; b. 25 Oct. 1904, Wuxi Co., Jiangsu Prov.; largely self-taught, ed. later high school; worked in Inst. of Social Sciences attached to Cen. Research Acad. conducting surveys of rural economy 1920s; Prof. of Rural Econs., normal school, Guangxi Prov. 1933; with other organized Soc. for Research in China's Rural Economy and Ed. Rural China monthly, Shanghai; First Dir. of Dept. of Training, Anti-Japanese Mil. and Political Acad. of Cen. China, Sec.-

Gen. Anti-Japanese Democratic Govt. of Shandong Prov., war with Japan 1937–45; successively Sec.-Gen. of Financial and Econ. Comm. of Govt. Admin. Council, Vice-Minister in Charge of State Planning Comm., Dir. of State Statistical Bureau, Dir. Nat. Price Comm., mem. Council of Social Sciences, Academia Sinica; del. to First, Second and Third Nat. People's Congresses; mem. Nat. Cttee. Fifth CPPCC; adviser to State Planning Comm. 1979–, Dir. of its Econ. Inst., Prof., Peking Univ., Pres. Statistical Soc. 1979–, Nat. Statistical Soc.; Hon. Pres. Soc. of Systems Eng. 1980–; Pres. Planning Soc. 1984–; Adviser, Fed. of Econs. Socs. 1981–, State Comm. for Restructuring of Econ. System 1984–85; Hon. Dir.-Gen. Econ., Tech. and Social Devt. Research Center 1985–; Hon. Pres. Industrial Co-operative Assen. 1983–; mem. Academic Cttees. of the Econ. Inst. and Inst. of the World Economy, Chinese Acad. of Social Sciences. *Publications:* The Elementary Knowledge of China's Rural Economy, The ABC of Rural Economy, The Socialist Transformation of China's National Economy, Some Theoretical Problems Concerning the Socialist Economy, Research on Problems Concerning China's Socialist Economy. *Address:* State Planning Commission, Beijing, People's Republic of China.

XUEREB, Paul; Maltese politician; b. 21 July 1923, Rabat; m. Mary Edwige Muscat; one d.; ed. St. Aloysius Coll. and Flores Coll., Malta, and City Literary Inst. and Regent Street Polytechnic, London; M.P. 1962–83; fmr. Parl. Sec. in office of Prime Minister; Minister of Trade and Industry 1971–76; Speaker House of Reps. 1986–87; Acting Pres. of Repub. of Malta 1987–89; Labour. *Publications:* numerous short stories, novels and historical guide books. *Address:* c/o Office of the President, The Palace, Valletta, Malta.

Y

YAACOBI, Gad, M.SC.; Israeli politician b. 18 Jan. 1935, Moshav Kfar Vitkin; s. of Alexander and Sara Yaacobi; m. Nela Yaacobi; three s. one d.; ed. Tel Aviv Univ., School of Law and Econs.; mem. Moshavim Movt. 1960-67; Asst. to Minister of Agric., Head of Agric. and Settlement Planning and Devt. Centre 1960-66; mem. Cen. Cttee. Histadrut, Labour Union, Rafi Faction 1966-69; Chair. Econ. Council Rafi Faction 1966-67; mem. Cen. Cttee., Secr. Labour Party; Asst. to Sec. Labour Party 1966-70; M.P. (Knesset) 1969-, Parl. Finance Cttee. 1969-70, Parl. Defence and Foreign Affairs Cttee. 1974; Deputy Minister of Transport 1970-74, Minister 1974-77, of Econs. and Planning 1984-88, of Communications Dec. 1988-; Chair. Parl. Econ. Cttee. 1977-; Chair. Labour Party Econ. Council. *Publications:* The Quality of Power 1971, The Freedom to Choose 1975, The Government 1980, A Call for Change 1983, and many articles on economics and politics. *Leisure interests:* theatre, reading, writing poetry. *Address:* c/o Israel Labour Party, P.O. Box 36, Tel-Aviv.

YACÉ, Philippe Grégoire; Côte d'Ivoire politician; b. 23 Jan. 1920, Jacqueville; ed. William Ponty School, Dakar, and Univ. of Dakar; French Army 1940-45; mem. Democratic Party of Côte d'Ivoire (PDCI) 1946-, Sec.-Gen. 1959-80, mem. Political Bureau 1985-; mem. Territorial Ass., Ivory Coast 1952-58; Deputy to Ivory Coast Constituent Ass. 1958-59; Senator of the French Community 1959-61; Pres. Nat. Ass., Ivory Coast 1960-80; Pres., High Court of Justice 1963-83; Pres. Parl. Conference of EEC and African States 1969-; Chair. Union of African Parls.; Grand Officier, Légion d'honneur, Grand Officier, Ordre National de la République de la Côte d'Ivoire. *Address:* c/o Palais de l'Assemblée, B.P. 1381, Abidjan, Côte d'Ivoire.

YACOUB, Magdi Habib, F.R.C.S.; cardiac surgeon; b. 16 Nov. 1935, Cairo; m.; one s. two d.; ed. Univ. of Cairo; Consultant cardiac surgeon, Harefield Hospital and Nat. Heart Hospital; Prof. of Cardio-Thoracic Surgery, Brompton Hosp. Cardio-Thoracic Inst., London 1986-; pioneered techniques of heart-lung transplants; Hon. M.Ch. (Wales) 1986. *Publications:* numerous medical papers. *Leisure interest:* orchid growing. *Address:* 21 Wimpole Street, London, W.1, England.

YADLIN, Aharon; Israeli politician; b. 17 April 1926, Tel-Aviv; s. of Haim and Zipora Yadlin; m. Ada Hacohen 1950; three s.; ed. Hebrew Univ.; Co-founder Kibbutz Hatzerim; fmr. mem. Presidium, Israel Scouts Movement; mem. Exec. Council Histadrut (Israel Fed. of Labour) 1950-52; Prin. Beit Berl (Labour Party's centre for Educ.) 1956-58; mem. Knesset (Parl.) 1959-79; Deputy Minister of Educ. and Culture 1964-72; Gen. Sec. Israel Labour Party 1972-74, mem. Bureau; Minister of Educ. and Culture 1974-77; Chair. Educational and Cultural Cttee., Knesset 1977-79; Chair. Beit Berl Coll. of Educ. 1977-; Sec.-Gen. United Kibbutz Movt. (TAKAM) July 1985-; Chair. Beer-Sheva Theatre, Janush Korczak Asscn. in Israel; Chair. Scientific Cttee. Ben Gurion Research Inst. and Archives 1979-; lecturer and researcher in EFAL (educ. centre of United Kibutzin movt.). *Publications:* Introduction to Sociology 1957, The Aim and The Movement 1969 and articles on sociology, education and youth. *Leisure interests:* stamps, gardening. *Address:* Kibbutz Hatzerim, Mobile Post, Hanegev II, Israel. *Telephone:* 057-433608.

YAFI, Abdullah Aref al-; Lebanese lawyer and politician; b. 1901; ed. Collège des Pères Jésuites, Beirut, and Univ. de Paris à la Sorbonne; admitted to Beirut Bar 1926; Prime Minister and Minister of Justice 1938-39; Lebanese del. to preparatory conf. for founding League of Arab States 1944, to San Francisco Conf. 1945; Minister of Justice Dec. 1946-April 1947; Prime Minister 1951-52, 1953-54, March-Nov. 1956, April-Dec. 1966, 1968-69, concurrently Minister of the Interior 1951-52, 1953-54, March-Nov. 1956, July-Oct. 1968, of Defence 1953-54, Feb.-Oct. 1968, of Information 1953-54, April-Dec. 1966, 1968-69, of Finance March-Sept. 1954, of Planning June-Nov. 1956, April-Dec. 1966, Feb.-July 1968, 1968-69, of Social Affairs 1968-69, of Education 1968-69.

YAGI, Yasuhiro; Japanese engineer; b. 15 Feb. 1920; m.; one s. two d.; ed. Imperial Univ., Tokyo; joined Kawasaki Heavy Industries Ltd. 1943; Dir. and Asst. Gen. Supt. Mizushima Works 1971-74, Man. Dir. 1974-77, Sr. Man. Dir. Corporate Tech., Engineering and Tubarao Project 1977-79, Exec. Vice-Pres. Corporate Tech. and Tubarao Project 1979-82; Pres. Kawasaki Steel Corpn. June 1982-. *Leisure interests:* golf, "Go". *Address:* Kawasaki Steel Corporation, Hibiya Kokusai Building, 2-3, Uchisaiwaicho 2-chome, Chiyoda-ku, Tokyo 100, Japan.

YAGO, H.E. Cardinal Bernard; Côte d'Ivoire ecclesiastic; b. July 1916, Abidjan; ordained priest 1947; Archbishop of Abidjan 1960-; cr. Cardinal 1983; Pres. Episcopal Conference of Côte d'Ivoire; mem. Secr. for Christian Unity. *Address:* BP 1287, Abidjan, Côte d'Ivoire. *Telephone:* 332256.

YAGODIN, Gennadiy Alekseyevich; Soviet physical chemist; b. 3 June 1927; ed. Mendeleyev Chemical Tech. Inst., Moscow; Deputy Dean, Mendeleyev Chemical Tech. Inst., Moscow 1956-59, Dean, Dept. of Physical Chemistry 1959-63, Prof. of Chemical Tech. 1959-63, 1966-; Deputy Dir.-

Gen. (Head of Dept. of Training and Technical Information 1963-64, Head of Dept. of Technical Operations 1964-66), IAEA Vienna 1963-66, Dean Dept. of Physical Chem., Mendeleyev Chemical Tech. Inst. 1966-73, Rector Inst. 1973-85; Minister of Higher and Secondary Specialized Educ. 1984-88; Chair. State Cttee. for Nat. Educ. March 1988-; mem. Cen. Cttee. CPSU 1986-; Corresp. mem. U.S.S.R. Acad. of Sciences 1976-; Order of Lenin, Order of Red Banner of Labour, State Prize 1985 and other decorations. *Address:* State Committee for National Education, Lusinovskaya str. 51, Moscow 113833, U.S.S.R.

YAGUDIN, Shamil Khairulovich; Soviet ballet dancer; b. 1932; ed. Moscow Ballet School of Bolshoi Theatre; joined Bolshoi Theatre Ballet 1952; with Bolshoi Ballet has toured U.K., Bulgaria, German Democratic Repub., Denmark, India, Canada, Norway, Egypt, France, U.S.A. and Czechoslovakia; Honoured Art Worker of R.S.F.S.R. 1962. *Main roles:* The Jester (Romeo and Juliet, Prokofiev), Karen (Gayane, Khachaturian), Nurali (Fountain of Bakhchisarai, Afasyev), The Wicked Witch (Swan Lake, Tchaikovsky), Jester (Cinderella, Prokofiev), Petrushka (Petrushka, Stravinsky), Ibn Salom (Leili and Medjnun, Balasanyan). *Address:* State Academic Bolshoi Theatre of the U.S.S.R., Ploshchad Sverdlova 1, Moscow, U.S.S.R.

YAHYAWI, Muhammad Saleh; Algerian politician; b. 1932, Barika; worked as a teacher before start of Algerian war for nat. independence; joined Maquisards 1956; promoted Capt., then Commdt. 1962-64; elected to Cen. Cttee. of Nat. Liberation Front (FLN) 1964, Revolutionary Council July 1965; Regional Mil. Commdr. 1965; Head Mil. Acad. at Cherchill 1969-77; Exec. Sec. of FLN 1977-86. *Address:* Front de libération nationale, place Emir Abdelkader, Algiers, Algeria.

YAKAS, Orestes, M.SC., PH.D.; Greek architect and politician; b. 14 Sept. 1920, Thessaloniki; s. of Athanase and Helene (née Xanthopoulou) Yakas; m. Eugenia Kerameos 1959; two s.; ed. Athens Nat. Polytechnic and Melbourne Univ.; in pvt. practice in Melbourne 1955; Head, Town Planning Section, Doxiades Assocs. 1957; Chief Rep. of Doxiades Assocs., Islamabad, Pakistan 1959; Vice-Pres. Doxiades Assocs. 1963; in pvt. practice in Athens 1966, also Adviser to Sec.-Gen. for Sport; Adviser to Gov. of Investment Bank 1971; Minister of Mercantile Marine, Transport and Communications Aug. 1971-July 1972, May-Nov. 1973; Alt. Minister of Interior 1972-73; Man. Dir. Yakas Consulting Group 1974-76; Man. Dir. Société d'Etudes Techniques et Economiques S.A., Geneva 1977-87; Dir.-Gen. Société Générale pour l'Industrie-Ingénieurs Conseils, Geneva 1982, Exec. Vice-Pres. 1985-87. *Publications:* Town Planning Elements Influencing Urban Economics 1971; many lectures, radio talks, etc. *Leisure interest:* sport. *Address:* 41 Voriou Epirou Str., Philothei, Athens, Greece; 22 chemin du Pommier, 1218 Geneva, Switzerland. *Telephone:* 6822685; 6819240 (Greece); (022) 981534, 981520 (Switzerland).

YAKOVLEV, Aleksandr Nikolayevich; Soviet politician; b. 2 Dec. 1923; ed. Yaroslavl Pedagogical Inst. 1946; served in Soviet Army 1941-43; mem. CPSU 1944-; mem. of Yaroslavl Dist. Cttee. CPSU 1946-48; chief lecturer at Yaroslavl Party School and worked on dist. newspaper 1948-50; Deputy Head of Dept. of Science and Culture, Cen. Cttee. of CPSU 1953-56; in apparatus of Cen. Cttee. CPSU 1960-62; Instructor with Dept. of Propaganda and Agitation of Cen. Cttee. CPSU 1962-64; Cand. mem. Politburo 1987, now full mem.; Head of Radio and TV Broadcasting Propaganda Dept. of Cen. Cttee. CPSU 1964-65; mem. of editorial staff of journal Kommunist; First Deputy Head, Acting Head of Cen. Cttee., Propaganda Dept. 1965-73; mem. of Cen. Auditing Comm. of Cen. Cttee. CPSU 1971-76; Amb. to Canada 1973-83; Dir. Inst. of World Econs. and Int. Relations, U.S.S.R. Acad. Sciences 1983-85; mem. of Council of Nationalities, U.S.S.R. Supreme Soviet, mem. of U.S.S.R. Parl. Group Cttee. 1984-; Corresp. mem. Acad. of Sciences (Econs. Dept.) 1984-; Head of Cen. Cttee. CPSU Propaganda Dept. 1985-; mem. Cen. Cttee. CPSU 1986-; Sec. responsible for Propaganda of Cen. Cttee. CPSU 1986-; mem. Political Bureau June 1987-; Head. Int. Policy Comm. Dec. 1988-; elected to Congress of People's Deputies 1989; Order of Red Banner 1962, Order of Friendship of Peoples 1983. *Address:* The Kremlin, Moscow, U.S.S.R.

YAKOVLEV, Aleksandr Sergeyevich; Soviet aircraft designer; b. 1 April 1906, Moscow; ed. Zhukovsky Air Force Engineering Acad.; mem. CPSU 1938; Deputy Minister of the Aircraft Industry of U.S.S.R. 1940-56; Chief Designer to Ministry of Aircraft Industry 1956-; Col.-Gen. of Air Force Engineering Service 1946; Deputy to U.S.S.R. Supreme Soviet 1946-; designed sport, training, passenger, and combat aeroplanes, founded aircraft design school; Corresp. mem. U.S.S.R. Acad. of Sciences 1943-76, mem. 1976-; State Prize 1941, 1943, 1944, 1946, 1947, 1948, 1977, Hero of Socialist Labour 1940, 1957, Order of Lenin (nine times), Hammer and Sickle Gold Medal (twice), Lenin Prize 1972, Croix de la Légion d'honneur, and many other U.S.S.R. and foreign awards. *Publications:* Aim of a Lifetime, Soviet Aeroplanes, Notes of an Aircraft Designer. *Address:* Ministry of the Aircraft Industry, Moscow, U.S.S.R.

YALOW, Rosalyn Sussman, PH.D.; American medical physicist; b. 19 July 1921, New York; d. of Simon and Clara (Zipper) Sussman; m. Aaron Yalow 1943; one s. one d.; ed. Hunter Coll., New York, Univ. of Illinois; Asst. in Physics, Univ. of Ill. 1941–43, Instructor 1944–45; Lecturer and temp. Asst. Prof. in Physics, Hunter Coll., New York 1946–50; Physicist and Asst. Chief, Radioisotope Service, Veterans Admin. Hosp., Bronx 1950–70, Acting Chief 1968–70, Chief Radioimmunoassay Reference Lab. 1969, Chief Nuclear Medicine Service 1970–80, Sr. Medical Investigator 1972–; Dir. Solomon A. Berson Research Lab. Veterans Admin. Medical Centre 1973–; Research Prof., Dept. of Medicine, Mount Sinai School of Medicine, New York 1968–74, Distinguished Service Prof. 1974–79; Distinguished Prof.-at-Large, Albert Einstein Coll. of Medicine, Yeshiva 1979–85, Prof. Emer. 1985–; Chair. Dept. of Clinical Sciences, Montefiore Hosp., Bronx, N.Y. 1980–85; Harvey Lecturer 1966, American Gastroenterology Asscn. Memorial Lecturer 1972, Joslyn Lecturer, New England Diabetes Asscn. 1972, Franklin I. Harris Memorial Lecturer 1973, 1st Hagedorn Memorial Lecturer, Acta Endocrinologica Congress 1973; Pres. Endocrine Soc. 1978–79; mem. Nat. Acad. of Sciences 1975–, American Physics Soc., Radiation Research Soc., American Asscn. Physicists in Medicine, Biophysics Soc., American Acad. of Arts and Sciences, American Physiology Soc.; Foreign Assoc. French Acad. of Medicine 1981; Fellow New York Acad. of Science, Radiation Research Soc., American Asscn. of Physicists in Medicine; Assoc. Fellow in Physics, American Coll. of Radiology, American Diabetes Asscn., Endocrine Soc., Soc. of Nuclear Medicine; Dr. h.c. (Univ. Claude Bernard, Lyons and Univ. of Rosario, Argentina, Univ. of Ghent); Hon. D.Sc. from 49 univs., including Ill., New York Medical Coll., Princeton, Rutgers, Alberta (Canada), Tel. Aviv; Hon. D.Hum.Lett. (Hunter Coll., New York, St. Michael's Coll., Winooski Park, Vt., Sacred Heart Univ., Johns Hopkins Univ., Columbia Univ.); Hon. D.Med.Sc. (Medical Univ. of S.C.); Hon. LL.D. (Beaver Coll., Glenside, Pa.); also D. Hum. Lett. (5 times); D. Phil. h.c. (Bar-Ilan) 1987; First William S. Middleton Medical Research Award 1960; Fed. Woman's Award, Eli Lilly Award (American Diabetes Asscn.) 1961; Van Slyke Award (American Asscn. of Clinical Chem.) 1968; American Coll. of Physicians Award 1971, Howard Taylor Ricketts Award (Univ. of Chicago) 1971, Dickson Prize (Univ. of Pittsburgh) 1971, Gairdner Foundation Int. Award 1971, Koch Award (Endocrine Soc.) 1972, Commemorative Medallion (American Diabetes Asscn.) 1972; Anachem Award (Detroit Asscn. of Analytical Chemists) 1973; Albion O. Bernstein M.D. Award (Medical Soc., N.Y.) 1974; American Asscn. of Clinical Chemists Award 1975, Scientific Achievement Award (American Medical Asscn.) 1975, Veterans Administration Exceptional Service Award 1975, 1978, A. Cressy Morrison Award in Natural Sciences (New York Acad. of Sciences) 1975, Sustaining Membership Award (Asscn. of Mil. Surgeons) 1975; Lasker Award 1976; jt. Nobel Prize Winner for Physiology or Medicine for discoveries concerning peptide hormones 1977, "La Madonnina" International Prize of Milan 1977, Gratum Genus Humanum Gold Medal, World Fed. of Nuclear Medicine and Biology 1978, G. Von Hevesy Medal 1978, Citation of Esteem, St. John's Univ., New York 1979, Sarasota Medical Award for Achievement and Excellence 1979, Annual Gold Medal Award, Achievement in Life Award, Encyclopaedia Britannica 1980, First Joseph Handleman Award, Jewish Acad. of Arts and Sciences 1981, Theobald Smith Award 1982, Pres.'s Cabinet Award, Univ. of Detroit 1982, John and Samuel Bard Award in Medicine and Science, Bard Coll., New York 1982, Georg Charles de Hevesy Nuclear Medicine Pioneer Award 1986, Enshrinement by the Eng. and Science Hall of Fame, Dayton, Ohio 1987, Dorothy S. Levine Humanitarian Award, Bnai Zion 1987, Special Award, Clinical Ligand Assay Soc. 1988. *Address:* Veterans Administration Medical Centre, 130 West Kingsbridge Road, Bronx, New York, N.Y. 10468; 3242 Tibbett Avenue, Bronx, New York, N.Y. 10463, U.S.A. (Office). *Telephone:* 212-579-1644; KI3-7792 (Home).

YAMAGUCHI, Kenji, M.A. (ECON.); Japanese government official; b. 19 July 1933, Yamagata; s. of Futao and Yoshi Yamaguchi; m. Momoe Matsumoto 1962; one s. one d.; ed. Univ. of Tokyo; entered Budget Bureau, Ministry of Finance 1956; Nat. Tax Admin. Agency 1963; Ministry of Interior 1966; Econ. Planning Agency 1968; First Sec. Okinawa Reversion Preparatory Cttee., Foreign Minister's Office and Counsellor, Okinawa Bureau, Prime Minister's Office 1969; Int. Finance Bureau, Ministry of Finance 1971; Consul for Japan, Sydney 1972; Counsellor, Personnel Bureau, Prime Minister's Office 1975; Finance Bureau, Ministry of Finance 1977; Dir.-Gen. North East Japan Finance Bureau, Ministry of Finance 1981; Special Asst. to Minister of Foreign Affairs 1982–; Exec. Dir. for Japan, IBRD and affiliates 1982–, Dean IBRD Bd. 1985–87; Sr. Exec. Dir. Water Resources Devt. Public Corpn. 1988–; mem. Org. for Industry, Science and Cultural Advancement 1987–. *Publications:* The World Bank and It's Role in the World Economy 1988, and several books on financial matters, foreign affairs, etc. *Leisure interests:* reading, swimming, golf. *Address:* 3-16-43 Utsukushiga-Oka, Midori-ku, Yokohama City, 227, Japan. *Telephone:* 045 901 7309.

YAMAGUCHI, Toshio; Japanese politician; b. 29 Aug. 1940; ed. Meiji Univ.; mem. House of Reps. 1967–; Parl. Vice-Minister for Health and Welfare 1973; f. and Sec.-Gen. New Liberal Club 1976–; Minister of Labour 1984–85. *Leisure interest:* golf. *Address:* c/o Ministry of Labour, 1-3, Ote-Machi, Chiyoda-ku, Tokyo 100, Japan.

YAMAMOTO, Kenichi; Japanese business executive; b. 16 Sept. 1922, Kumamoto; s. of Yoshio and Keiko Yamamoto; m. Sumiko Fukazawa 1948; one s. one d.; ed. Tokyo Univ.; joined Toyo Kogyo Co. (now Mazda Motor Corpn.) 1946, Man. Rotary Engine Research and Devt. Div. 1963, Man. Dir. 1978, Sr. Man. Dir. 1982, Pres. 1984–87, Chair. Dec. 1987–; mem. Soc. of Automotive Engineers of Japan; Purple Ribbon Medal 1971. *Leisure interests:* "go" game, music, painting, watching baseball. *Address:* 4-6-19 Funairi-Minami, Minami-ku, Hiroshima, Japan. *Telephone:* (082) 231-8446.

YAMAMOTO, Sachio; Japanese politician; b. 1911; ed. Univ. of Tokyo; fmr. Chief of Prefectural Police, Osaka, Head of Secr. Ministry of Construction, Vice-Minister of Construction; held posts of Vice-Chair. Police Affairs Research Council and Parl. Vice-Minister of Finance; Minister of Home Affairs 1982–83; elected to House of Reps. five times from Mie Pref. *Leisure interests:* photography, driving, art. *Address:* Liberal-Democratic Party, 7, 2-chome, Hirakawacho, Chiyoda-ku, Tokyo, Japan.

YAMANAKA, Sadanori; Japanese politician; b. 1921; Dir.-Gen. Prime Minister's Office under Prime Minister Sato; fmr. Chair. Liberal-Democratic Party Research Comm. on Taxation System; elected to House of Reps. eleven times from Kagoshima Pref.; Minister of Int. Trade and Industry 1982–83; Leader LDP Tax Council. *Address:* Liberal-Democratic Party, 7, 2-chome, Hirakawacho, Chiyoda-ku, Tokyo, Japan.

YAMANI, Shaikh Ahmed Zaki; Saudi Arabian politician; b. 1930, Mecca; ed. Cairo Univ., New York Univ. and Harvard Univ.; Saudi Arabian Govt. Service; private law practice; Legal Adviser to Council of Ministers 1958–60; mem. Council of Ministers 1960–86; Minister of State 1960–62; Minister of Petroleum and Mineral Resources 1962–86; Dir. Arabian American Oil Company 1962–86; Chair. of Bd. of Dirs. General Petroleum and Mineral Org., (PETROMIN) 1963–86, Coll. of Petroleum and Minerals, Dhahran 1963–86, Saudi Arabian Fertilizer Co. (SAFCO) 1966–86; Sec.-Gen. Org. of Arab Petroleum Exporting Countries (OAPEC) 1968–69, Chair. 1974–75; mem. several Int. Law Asscns. *Publication:* Islamic Law and Contemporary Issues. *Address:* c/o Ministry of Petroleum and Mineral Resources, Riyadh, Saudi Arabia.

YAMANOUCHI, Ichiro; Japanese politician; b. 15 Feb. 1913, Fukui Pref.; ed. Tokyo Univ.; joined Home Affairs Ministry 1936; Vice-Minister of Construction 1963–65; mem. House of Councillors 1965–; Chair. Standing Cttee. on Local Admin., House of Councillors 1970–71; Parl. Vice-Minister of Nat. Land Agency 1974–76; Vice-Chair. Liberal-Democratic Party Policy Affairs Research Council 1977; Chair. Standing Cttee. on Budget, House of Councillors 1979–80; Minister of Posts and Telecommunications 1980–81. *Publications include:* Mitekita Soren, Chukinto 1967. *Address:* c/o Liberal-Democratic Party, 7, 2-chome, Hirakawacho, Chiyoda-ku, Tokyo, Japan.

YAMASAKI, Hiro, D.ENG.; Japanese professor of mathematical engineering and information physics; b. 21 July 1932, Tokyo; s. of Taro Yamasaki and Sumiko Yamasaki; m. Takako Hori 1961; one s. one d.; ed. Univ. of Tokyo; Research Physicist, Man. of Research and Devt., Yokogawa Electric Corpn., Tokyo 1956–74; Part-time Lecturer, Univ. of Tokyo 1971–74, Prof. Dept. of Math. Eng. and Information Physics 1975–, Dir. Univ. of Tokyo Library System 1985–88; Pres. Soc. of Instrument and Control Engineers 1989–; Okochi Memorial Prize 1965, 1981, SICE Paper Awards 1968, 1985. *Publications:* Automatic Control Engineering Handbook (Co-Ed.) 1983, Fundamentals of Sensor Technology 1985. *Leisure interests:* classical music (Mozart), travel. *Address:* 2-47-9, Den-en-chofu, Ota-ku, Tokyo 145, Japan. *Telephone:* 03-721-4358.

YAMASAKI, Yoshiki, M.ME.; Japanese business executive; b. 8 April 1914, Hiroshima; m. Hisae Sugihara 1942; two s. (one deceased); ed. Hiroshima Univ.; joined Toyo Kogyo Co. Ltd. 1938, Dir. and Gen. Man. Automobile Manufacturing 1970, Man. Dir. 1973, Sr. Man. Dir. 1975, Pres. 1977–; Man. Dir. Keidanren (Fed. of Econ. Orgs.) 1978–, Kansai Fed. of Econ. Orgs. 1978–; Dir. Japan Automobile Mfrs. Asscn. Inc. 1978, Japan Automobile Fed. 1978, Japan Motor Industrial Fed. 1978; Chair. and Rep. Dir. Japan Automatic Transmission Co. Ltd. 1978; Purple Ribbon Medal 1979. *Leisure interest:* golf. *Address:* 11-23, Kitaoko-cho, Hiroshima, Japan. *Telephone:* (0822) 51-4850.

YAMASHIRO, Yoshinari; Japanese steel company executive; b. 7 Feb. 1923, Tokyo; one s. one d.; ed. Faculty of Law, Tokyo Univ.; joined N.K.K. Corpn. 1947, mem. Bd. of Dirs. 1976–, Man. Dir. 1978–80, Sr. Man. Dir. 1980–82, Exec. Vice-Pres. 1982–85, Pres. 1985–; Dir. and mem. Exec. Cttee. Int. Iron and Steel Inst.; Dir. Japan Iron and Steel Fed.; Exec. mem. Bd. of Dirs. Fed. of Econ. Orgs. (Keidanren); Exec. Dir. Japan Fed. of Employers' Asscns; Medal of Honour with Blue Ribbon 1986. *Leisure interest:* golf. *Address:* N.K.K. Corporation, 1-1-2 Marunouchi, Chiyoda-ku, Tokyo 100 (Office); 3-19-32 Kitaterao, Tsurumi-ku, Yokohama, Kanagawa 230, Japan (Home). *Telephone:* 03-212-7111 (Office); (045) 571-3609 (Home).

YAMASHITA, Isamu; Japanese business executive; b. 15 Feb. 1911, Tokyo; m. Aiko Yamashita 1938; three s. one d.; ed. Tokyo Imperial Univ.; joined shipbuilding dept., Mitsui & Co. 1933; entered Tamano Shipyard Ltd. (predecessor of Mitsui Eng. & Shipbuilding Co. Ltd.) 1937; Man. Dir. Mitsui Eng. & Shipbuilding Co. Ltd. 1962, Senior Man. Dir. 1966, Vice-Pres. 1968, Pres. 1970–79, Chair. 1979–85, Sr. Adviser 1985–; Chair. East Japan Railway Co. 1987–. *Leisure interests:* golf, reading. *Address:* Mitsui

Engineering & Shipbuilding Co. Ltd., 6-4, Tsukiji 5-chome, Chuo-ku, Tokyo (Office); 401 Meguro Royal Heights, 4-16, Meguro 3-chome, Meguro-ku, Tokyo, Japan (Home). *Telephone:* 544-3001 (Office); 711-9300 (Home).

YAMASHITA, Takuo; Japanese politician; b. 7 Oct. 1919; ed. Meiji and Senshu Univs.; joined Yamashita Timber Co. later Pres.; mem. Saga Pref. Ass. later Chair.; mem. House of Reps. 1969–; Parl. Vice-Minister for Health and Welfare 1974; Chair. House of Reps. Social Labour Cttee. 1980; Parl. Vice-Minister for Int. Trade and Industry; Vice-Chair. Liberal Democratic Party Policy Affairs Research Council; Minister of Transport 1984–85; Minister of State and Dir.-Gen., Man. Co-ordination Agency Jan.–Nov. 1987. *Leisure interests:* travelling, reading, kendo, judo. *Address:* c/o House of Representatives, Tokyo, Japan.

YAMASHITA, Toshihiko; Japanese business executive; b. 18 July 1919, Osaka; ed. Osaka Prefectural Izuo Tech. School; joined Matsushita Electric Industrial Co. Ltd. 1938, Asst. Gen. Man. Electron Tube Div. and Plant Man. Electronic Component Factory 1956; Man. Dir. West Electric Co. Ltd. 1962–65; Gen. Man. Air Conditioner Dept., Matsushita Electric Industrial Co. Ltd. 1965, mem. Advisory Council 1971–74, Dir. 1974–, Pres. 1977–86, Exec. Adviser 1986–; Chevalier de l'Ordre Nat. (Malagasy Dem. Repub.) 1979. *Address:* Matsushita Electric Industrial Co. Ltd., 1006 Kadoma, Kadoma, Osaka 571 (Office); 4-11-10 Aoyama-dai, Suita City, Osaka 571, Japan (Home).

YAMAZAKI, Koji, PH.D.; Japanese economist and public official; b. 10 Aug. 1933; s. of Yosuke Yamazaki and Yae Yamazaki; m. Atsuo Yamazaki 1973; one s. two d.; ed. Tokyo Univ. and Univ. of Edinburgh, Scotland; Chief, Koishikawa Taxation Office 1964; Deputy Dir. Int. Tax Div., Tax Bureau 1965, Govt. Bond Div., Finance Bureau 1967; Special Asst. to Vice-Minister for Int. Affairs 1974; Dir. Treasury Div., Finance Bureau 1978; Financial Minister, Embassy of Japan, London 1981–84; Deputy Dir.-Gen. Minister's Secr., in charge of Customs and Tariff Bureau 1984; Snr. Research Fellow, Inst. of Fiscal and Monetary Policy 1986; Exec. Dir. for Japan, IMF 1986–; Chair. Econ. Reps. in London 1983–84; Acting Head of Del. to Customs Co-operation Council, Brussels 1984–86. *Publications:* trans. of The Path to Leadership by Field-Marshal Montgomery 1972; several essays. *Leisure interests:* literature, classical music. *Address:* International Monetary Fund, 700 19th Street, N.W., Washington, D.C. 20431 (Office); 7002 Heatherhill Road, Bethesda, Md. 20817, U.S.A. (Home). *Telephone:* (202) 623-7208 (Office); (301) 229-4527 (Home).

YAMAZAKI, Toshio; Japanese diplomatist (retd.); b. 13 Aug. 1922, Tokyo; m. Yasuko Arakawa 1955; one s. one d.; ed. Faculty of Law, Tokyo Univ.; Second Sec. Embassy U.K. 1955–59, Dir. British Commonwealth Div. European and Oceanic Affairs Bureau, Ministry of Foreign Affairs 1962–64, Counsellor Perm. Mission to UN, New York 1964–67, Dir. Financial Affairs Div. Minister's Sec., Ministry of Foreign Affairs, Japan 1967–70, Deputy Dir.-Gen. Treaties Bureau 1970, Minister, Embassy, Washington, D.C. 1971–74; Dir.-Gen. American Affairs Bureau, Ministry of Foreign Affairs 1974–77; Deputy Vice-Minister for Admin. 1978–80, Amb. to Egypt 1980–82, to Indonesia 1982–84, to U.K. 1985–88; Corp. Adviser, Mitsubishi Corpn., Tokyo 1988–. *Leisure interest:* golf. *Address:* 3-14-6 Zempukuji, Suginami-ku, Tokyo, Japan.

YAMÉOGO, Maurice; Burkinabê politician; b. 31 Dec. 1921; ed. High School, mem. of Grand Council French W. Africa 1947, Minister of Agric. 1955, of Interior 1956, Premier 1958–60; Pres. Council of Ministers 1960–66, Minister of Defence 1965–66; Pres. of the Repub. of Upper Volta (now Burkina Faso) 1960–66; deposed by mil. coup Jan. 1966; fmr. mem. Rassemblement Démocratique Africain (RDA); on trial for embezzlement April 1969; sentenced to 5 years' hard labour May 1969, sentence reduced to 2 years Aug. 1969, released Aug. 1970; under restriction order 1983–84, released Sept. 1984. *Address:* Ouagadougou, Burkina Faso.

YAMEY, Basil Selig, C.B.E., B.COMM., F.B.A.; British economist; b. 4 May 1919, Cape Town, South Africa; s. of Solomon Yamey and Leah Yamey; m. Helen Bloch 1948 (died 1980); one s. one d.; ed. Tulbagh High School and Univ. of Cape Town; Prof. of Econs. London School of Econs. 1960–84, Prof. Emer. 1984–; mem. Monopolies and Mergers Comm. 1966–78; Trustee Nat. Gallery, London 1974–81, Tate Gallery, London 1977–81, Inst. of Econ. Affairs 1987–; Hon. Fellow L.S.E. 1988. *Publications:* Economics of Resale Price Maintenance 1951, Economics of Underdeveloped Countries (with P. T. Bauer) 1956, Economics of Futures Trading (with B. A. Goss) 1976, Essays on the History of Accounting 1978, Arte e Contabilità 1986, Art and Accounting 1989. *Address:* 36 Hampstead Way, London, N.W.11, England. *Telephone:* 01-455 5810; 01-405 7686.

YAN DAKAI; Chinese party official; b. c. 1915, Hebei; ed. Party School of CCP Cttee., Yan'an; Head 3rd Dept., Party School of CCP Cttee., Yan'an 1943; Vice-Gov. of Hebei and Deputy Sec. CCP Cttee. 1954; Sec. CCP Cttee. 1958; Acting Second Sec. CCP Cttee., Tianjin 1967; Vice-Dir. Revolutionary Cttee., Tianjin 1972; Sec. CCP Cttee., Tianjin 1977; Chair. Standing Cttee. of Municipal People's Congress, Tianjin 1979–83; mem. Standing Cttee. of Advisory Comm., Cen. Cttee. 1982–87. *Address:* Standing Committee of People's Congress, Tianjin, People's Republic of China.

YAN DONGSHENG, PH.D.; Chinese academic; b. Feb. 1918, Shanghai; m. Bi-Rou Sun 1943; one s. one d.; ed. Yanjing Univ., Beijing, Univ. of Illinois,

U.S.A.; Deputy Dir. Inst. of Chem. Eng., Kailuan Mining Admin. 1950–54; Research Prof., Inst. of Metallurgy and Ceramics, Acad. of Sciences 1955–62; Vice-Pres. Silicates Soc. 1959, Pres. 1963; Deputy Dir. Silicate Inst., Acad. of Sciences 1961, Dir. 1980; mem. ed. Bd., Chinese Science Bulletin 1961; Dir. Shanghai Inst. of Ceramic Chem. and Tech. 1960; mem. Comm. for Inspecting Discipline under CCP Cen. Cttee. 1978–82; Vice-Pres. Shanghai Univ. of Science and Tech. 1980; mem. Chinese Acad. of Sciences (Vice-Pres. 1980–87); mem. Acad. Degrees Cttee. 1981, Dir. Dept. of Chem. 1981, Vice-Chair. Fund Cttee. 1981; mem. 12th CCP Cen. Cttee. 1982; mem. Standing Cttee. CPPCC 1987–; Pres. Chinese Chemical Soc. 1982–86; mem. Scientific Advisory Comm. to the Cabinet 1982; Ed.-in-Chief Ceramics Int.; Ed. Mat. Letters (Int.), Int. Solid State Chem., High Tech Ceramics (Intel); mem. Leading Group for Scientific Work, State Council 1983–; Party Sec. Chinese Acad. of Sciences 1984–88, Special Adviser Jan. 1988–; Pres. Silicate Soc. 1983–; Vice-Pres. China-U.S. People's Friendship Assn. 1986–; Vice-Chair. Shanghai Municipal Cttee. 1987–; Hon. D.Sc. (Ill., Bordeaux) 1986. *Leisure interest:* tennis, classical music, bridge. *Address:* Chinese Academy of Sciences, 52 San Li He Road, Beijing, People's Republic of China.

YAN GELING; Chinese writer; b. 1958, Sichuan Prov.; dancer in Sichuan PLA Troupe 1971–83. *Publications include:* A Women Soldier's Monologue, Green Blood. *Address:* China Writers' Association, Beijing, People's Republic of China.

YAN HAN; Chinese artist; b. 29 July 1916, Lianyungang, Jiangsu; m. Bai Yan 1940; two s.; ed. Huangzhou Coll. of Arts; teacher, Lu Xun Acad. of Arts; teacher, North China Univ., Yan'an 1939–43; Prof. Cen. Acad. of Fine Arts, Beijing 1949–; mem. Nat. Cttee. of China Fed. of Literary and Art Circles; Sec. Secretariat of the Chinese Artists Assn. and Dir. of Graphic Arts Cttee.; Vice-Chair. Chinese Graphic Artists' Assn. *Publications:* collections of woodcuts, illustrations and paintings. *Leisure interests:* literature, history and sight-seeing. *Address:* Central Academy of Fine Arts, Beijing, People's Republic of China.

YAN HONG; Chinese athlete; b. 1965 Liaoning Prov.; World Women's 5,000 metres Walk record holder 1984. *Address:* Chinese Sports Federation, Beijing, People's Republic of China.

YAN JICI, PH.D.; Chinese academic; b. 1900, Dongyang Co., Zhejiang Prov.; ed. Paris; Dir. Physics Research Inst., Beijing 1930; Dir. Gen. Office, Chinese Acad. of Sciences 1949; Vice-Pres. Univ. of Science and Tech. 1961, Hon. Pres. 1985–; Vice-Chair. Jiusan Soc. 1979–; Pres. Zhejiang Univ. of Science and Tech. 1980–84; Vice-Chair. Standing Cttee. 6th NPC 1983; Exec. Chair. Presidium 1986–; Hon. Chair. China Assn. of Science and Tech. 1986–; Hon. Pres. Optical Soc. 1979–, Soc. of Physics 1983–. *Address:* China Association of Science and Technology, Beijing, People's Republic of China.

YAN MING; Chinese swimmer; b. 1969, Qiqihar, Heilongjian Prov.; Nat. Freestyle Champion 1985. *Address:* National Swimming Team, Wuhan, People's Republic of China.

YAN WENJING; Chinese writer; b. 15 Oct. 1915, Wuchang, Hubei; m. 1st Li Shuhua 1939 (died 1976); m. 2nd Kang Zhichiang 1976; one s. five d.; joined CCP 1938; worked in literature dept. of Lu Xun Art Acad., Yan'an; Asst. Ed.-in-Chief North East Daily 1945; worked in Propaganda Dept., Cen. Cttee., CCP after 1949; Chief Ed. People's Literature; Dir. People's Literature Publishing House, Head 1973–83; mem. Presidium Chinese Writers' Assn. 1985–; Vice-Pres. China Pen Centre 1982–; writes children's stories. *Publications include:* A Man's Troubles (novel), Nannan and Uncle Whiskers, The Echo, The Little Stream Sings, Next Time Port, Fables of Yan Wenjing, Selected Prose Poems of Yan Wenjing. *Address:* People's Literature Publishing House, Beijing, People's Republic of China. *Telephone:* 500 3312.

YAN YING; Chinese government official; Deputy Sec.-Gen. State Council 1985–; mem. Council, People's Bank of China 1984–. *Address:* State Council, Zhong Nan Hai, Beijing, People's Republic of China.

YAN ZHENG; Chinese army officer; Political Commissar Wuhan Mil. Region 1977–; alt. mem. 12th Central Cttee. CCP 1982–87. *Address:* People's Liberation Army Wuhan Units, Hubei, People's Republic of China.

YANAGIYA, Kensuke; Japanese diplomatist; b. 19 June 1924, Tokyo; s. of Yuzo Yanagiya and Teiko Yanagiya; m. Tomako Yanai 1954; two s.; ed. Tokyo Univ.; entered Ministry of Foreign Affairs 1948; Minister Japanese Embassy, Beijing 1973–76; Dir.-Gen. Public Information and Cultural Affairs Bureau, Ministry of Foreign Affairs 1976–78, Dir.-Gen. Asian Affairs Bureau 1978–80, Deputy Vice-Minister for Admin. 1980–81, Deputy Minister for Foreign Affairs 1981; Amb. to Australia 1982–85; Vice-Minister for Foreign Affairs 1985–87, Adviser to the Foreign Minister 1987–88; Pres. Japan Int. Co-operation Agency 1988–. *Address:* 4, Goban-cho, Chiyoda-ku, Tokyo, Japan.

YANENKO, Nikolay Nikolayevich; Soviet mechanical engineer and mathematician; b. 22 May 1921, Kuibyshev, Novosibirsk oblast; s. of Nikolay Pavlovich Yanenko and Natalya Borisovna Tchernenkaya; m. Irina Konstantinovna Yanenko 1947; two d.; ed. Tomsk State Univ.; Senior

Lecturer, Moscow State Univ. 1949–56; Scientific Assoc., Geophysical Inst., U.S.S.R. Acad. of Sciences 1948–53; Head of Lab., Computing Centre, Siberian Branch, U.S.S.R. Acad. of Sciences 1963–; Prof. 1960–, Chair. of Dept., Novosibirsk State Univ. 1964–; Corresp. mem. U.S.S.R. Acad. of Sciences 1966–70, mem. 1970–; mem. CPSU 1952–; U.S.S.R. State Prize 1953, 1972, Order of Lenin, Order of October Revolution and other decorations. *Publications:* The Method of Fractional Steps 1971, and other books (in collaboration) on Gas Dynamics. *Address:* Institute of Theoretical and Applied Mechanics, U.S.S.R. Academy of Sciences, Novosibirsk 630090, U.S.S.R. *Telephone:* 65-42-70.

YANG, Sir Ti Liang, Kt., LL.B.; British judge; b. 30 June 1929, Shanghai, China; s. of Shao-nan Yang and Elsie Chun; m. Eileen Barbara Tam; two s.; ed. The Comparative Law School of China, Soochow Univ., Shanghai, Univ. Coll. London, U.K.; called to Bar (with hons.), Gray's Inn 1954; Rockefeller Fellow, London Univ. 1963–64; Magistrate, Hong Kong 1956, Sr. Magistrate 1963, Dist. Judge, Dist. Court 1968, Justice of High Court 1975, Justice of Appeal 1980, Vice-Pres. Court of Appeal 1987, Chief Justice of Hong Kong 1988–; Chair. Kowloon Disturbances Claims Assessment Bd. 1966, Compensation Bd. 1967, Comm. of Inquiry into the Rainstorm Disasters 1972, into Lelung Wing-sang Case 1976, into McLennan Case 1980; mem. Law Reform Comm. (Chair. Sub-Cttee. on law relating to homosexuality) 1980; Chair. Chief Justice Working Party on Voir Dire Procs. and Judges' Rules 1979, Univ. and Polytechnic Grants Cttee. 1981–84; mem. Chinese Language Cttee. (Chair. Legal sub-cttee.) 1970; Chair. Hong Kong Univ. Council 1985; Vice-Chair. Hong Kong Sea Cadet Corps; Patron The Soc. for the Rehabilitation of Offenders, Hong Kong; Hon. Pres. Scouts Asscn., Against Child Abuse; Adviser Hong Kong Juvenile Care Centre; Hon. LL.D. (Chinese Univ. of Hong Kong). *Leisure interests:* philately, reading, walking, oriental ceramics, travelling, music. *Address:* Supreme Court, Hong Kong; Flat 45 Grove Hall Court, 6th Floor, 2-4 Hall Road, St. John's Wood, London, N.W.8, England. *Telephone:* 5-821 4601 (Hong Kong); 01-289 9480 (London).

YANG BAIBING; Chinese army officer; Deputy Political Commissar, Beijing Mil. Region, PLA 1983–85, Political Commissar 1985–; Deputy Dir., Bureau under Int. Liaison Dept., State Council 1985–87; Dir. Gen. Political Dept. Nov. 1987–; mem. Cen. Mil. Comm., PRC April 1988–; mem. 13th CCP Cen. Cttee. 1987–. *Address:* Beijing Military Region Headquarters, Beijing, People's Republic of China.

YANG BO; Chinese party and government official; b. 1921, Shandong; concurrently Dir. Research Office and Comprehensive Dept., State Statistics Bureau, State Council; Deputy Dir. then Dir. Shandong Prov. Statistics Comm.; Vice-Chair. Prov. Revolutionary Cttee., Shandong 1977; Vice-Minister State Planning Comm., State Council 1979; Deputy Man. 7th Dept., China Nat. Tech. Import Corpn. (TECHIMPORT) 1980; Vice-Minister State Energy Comm., State Council 1981; Minister of Light Industry 1982–87; Sec. Party Group 1983–; mem. 12th Cen. Cttee., CCP 1982–87; Adviser, China-Japan Personnel Exchange Cttee. 1985–. *Address:* State Council, Beijing, People's Republic of China.

YANG CHEN; Chinese government official; Vice-Minister for Civil Affairs 1982–87; Dir. Gen. Office Leading Group for Resettlement of Demobilized Soldiers and Officers, State Council 1983–. *Address:* Ministry of Civil Affairs, Beijing, People's Republic of China.

YANG CHENGWU, Col.-Gen.; Chinese army officer; b. 1912, Yangting, Fujian Prov.; Deputy Commdr. Beijing-Tianjin Mil. Region 1949–50, Commdr. 1950; Commdr. Tianjin Garrison 1949; Chief of Staff, N. China Mil. Region 1949; mem. Nat. Cttee. (Communist) Democratic Youth Fed. 1949, 1st CCP Cen. Cttee. 1949, People's Govt. Council, Tianjin 1950, N. China Admin. Council 1951; Commdr. 66th, 67th and 68th Armies, Chinese People's Volunteers, Korean War 1951; Chief of Staff, N. China Mil. Region 1953; mem. Nat. Defence Council 1954–Cultural Revolution; Commdr. Air Defence, PLA 1956; alt. mem. 8th CCP Cen. Cttee. 1956–Cultural Revolution; served as common soldier 1958; Deputy Chief of Staff, PLA 1959–68, Acting Chief of Staff 1966–68; Deputy Head, PLA Cultural Revolution Group 1967; Vice-Chair. Mil. Council, CCP Cen. Cttee. 1967; relieved of all posts 1968; Deputy Chief of Staff, PLA 1974–77; mem. 11th CCP Cen. Cttee. 1977; Commdr. Fuzhou Mil. Region 1978–80; mem. Standing Cttee., CCP Secr., Fuzhou Mil. Region 1978–80; First Sec. CCP Cttee. Fuzhou Mil. Region 1978–80; mem. 12th Cen. Cttee. CCP 1982–87; Exec. Chair. Presidium CPPCC 1983–; Vice-Chair. CPPCC Nat. Cttee. 1983–; Chair. Cultural and Historical Data Research Cttee. 1983–; Hon. Pres. Soc. for Study of Painting and Calligraphy of the Aged 1984–. *Address:* People's Republic of China.

YANG CHEN NING, PH.D.; American (b. Chinese) professor of physics; b. 22 Sept. 1922, Hofei Co., Anwei Prov.; s. of Ke Chen Yung and Meng Hwa Lo; m. Chih Li Tu 1950; two s. one d.; ed. Nat. Southwest Associated Univ., Kunming, and Univ. of Chicago; Instructor, Univ. of Chicago 1948–49; mem. Inst. for Advanced Study, Princeton, N.J. 1949–55, and Prof. 1955–65; Albert E. Einstein Prof. of Science and Dir. Inst. for Theoretical Physics, New York State Univ. 1965–; Visiting Prof. Univ. of Paris 1957; Hon. D.Sc. (Princeton Univ., Brooklyn Polytechnical Inst., Univ. of Wrocław); Nobel Prize in Physics 1957; A. Einstein Commemorative Award 1957, Nat. Medal of Science 1986, Liberty Award 1986; mem.

N.A.S., American Physical Soc., A.A.A.S., and numerous other Acads. and socs. *Address:* Department of Physics, State University of New York, Stony Brook, N.Y. 11790 (Office); 14 Woodhull Cove, Setauket, New York, N.Y. 11733, U.S.A. (Home).

YANG CHUNSHENG; Chinese amateur artist; b. 5 April 1939, Beijing; s. of Yang Wenhai and Zhao Fu; m. Li Xueqin 1972; one d.; self-taught artist; worker in Beijing Foreign Languages Printing House 1956–86; Art Ed., Social Security Newspaper 1986–; published in Beijing Review, Beijing Literature, All-China Trade Union publ. *Leisure interests:* painting and photography. *Address:* No. 301, Gate 11, Building 4, Living Quarter of Foreign Languages Printing House, Huayuancun, Beijing, People's Republic of China. *Telephone:* 8653901, Ext. 274 (work unit).

YANG DAYI; Chinese army officer; b. 1919, Cangxi Co., Sichuan Prov.; joined Red Army 1933, CCP 1934; Regimental Commander 1949; Deputy Commdr. Hunan Mil. District PLA 1967, Commdr. 1969–75; Commdr. Liaoning Mil. District PLA 1976–; Vice-Chair. Hunan Revolutionary Cttee. 1968; Deputy Sec. CCP Hunan 1970, Sec. 1973; Alt. mem. 10th Cen. Cttee. CCP 1973, 11th Cen. Cttee. 1977. *Address:* People's Liberation Army Headquarters, Liaoning Military District, People's Republic of China.

YANG DEZHI, Col.-Gen.; Chinese army officer; b. 1910, Liling, Hunan; ed. Red Army Acad. and Nanjing Mil. Acad.; joined CCP 1927; on Long March 1934–35; Regimental Commdr., Red Army 1935; Commdr. Ningxia Mil. Region, People's Liberation Army 1949; Chief of Staff Chinese People's Volunteers in Korea 1951, Deputy Commdr. Chinese People's Volunteers 1953–54, Commdr. 1954–55; mem. Nat. Defence Council 1954; Gen. 1955; Alt. mem. 8th Cen. Cttee. of CCP 1956; Commdr. Jinan Mil. Region, PLA 1958–73; First Vice-Chair. Shandong Revolutionary Cttee. 1967, Chair. 1971–76; mem. 9th Cen. Cttee. of CCP 1969; First Sec. CCP Shandong 1971–76; Vice-Chair. Liaoning Revolutionary Cttee. 1972; mem. 10th Cen. Cttee. of CCP 1973; Commdr. Wuhan Mil. Region, PLA 1972–79; Commdr. PLA Kunming Mil. Region 1979–80; Chief of Staff, PLA 1980–81; First Sec. Party Cttee. 1981–; Vice-Minister of Nat. Defence 1980; mem. 11th Cen. Cttee. CCP 1977, mem. Politburo 12th Cen. Cttee. 1982–87; Sec., Secr., Cen. Cttee. 1980–82; Deputy Sec. Mil. Comm. under CCP Cen. Cttee. 1983–; mem. Presidium 6th NPC 1986–; mem. Standing Cttee. Cen. Advisory Comm. 1987–; Deputy Sec.-Gen., Cen. Mil. Comm. of PRC 1983–; Hon. Pres. Mountaineers Soc. 1984–. *Address:* People's Republic of China.

YANG DEZHONG; Chinese state official; Dir. of a Dept. under Ministry of Public Security 1964; Chair. Revolutionary Cttee., Beijing Univ. 1969; Deputy Dir. Gen. Office under CCP Cen. Cttee. 1980; mem. 12th CCP Cen. Cttee. 1982–; First Deputy Dir., Gen. Office, Party Cttee. of Depts. under Cen. Cttee. 1983–. *Address:* Chinese Communist Party Central Committee General Office, Beijing, People's Republic of China.

YANG DI; Chinese party official; b. 1924, Qingpu Co., Shanghai; joined New 4th Army 1938; joined CCP 1939; Section Chief, Shanghai Public Security Bureau 1952; Dir. Shanghai Post and Telecommunications Bureau, Dir. Shanghai Public Security Bureau, Vice-Mayor, Shanghai 1977–83; mem. 12th CCP Cen. Cttee. 1982–87; Sec. CCP Cttee., Shanghai 1983, Deputy Sec. March 1983–. *Address:* Shanghai Municipal Chinese Communist Party, Shanghai, People's Republic of China.

YANG HAIBO; Chinese party official; b. 1912, Jiangsu Prov.; mem. of Liaodong Prov. People's Govt. 1950–54; Sec. Youth Work Cttee., Liaodong CCP 1950–54; mem. Northeast Admin. Council 1953–54; Deputy Sec. Northeast Regional Work Cttee., New Democratic Youth League 1953–54; mem. Cen. Cttee., New Democratic Youth League 1953–57; Deputy for Fushun Municipality to 1st NPC 1954; mem. Communist Youth League Standing Cttee. 1957; Deputy for Liaoning Prov. to 2nd NPC 1958, 3rd NPC 1964; mem. State Physical Culture and Sports Comm. 1959; Sec. Communist Youth League 1960; Vice-Chair. China Afro-Asian Solidarity Cttee. 1965; Vice-Pres. Science and Tech. Univ., Beijing 1980–82; alt. mem. 12th CCP Cen. Cttee. 1982–87; Deputy Sec. CCP Cttee., Anhui Prov. 1983–85; Vice-Minister, State Educ. Comm. 1985; Deputy Sec., Party Group, State Educ. Comm. 1985; Chair. PRC Nat. Comm. for UNESCO 1986–; Sec. Party Cttee., Univ. of Science and Tech. 1984–. *Address:* Anhui Provincial Chinese Communist Party, Hefei, Anhui, People's Republic of China.

YANG JING; Chinese artist; b.1952; specialises in clay sculpture; sent to Inner Mongolia during Cultural Revolution. *Address:* Restoration Section, Palace Museum, Chang An Avenue, Beijing, People's Republic of China.

YANG JINGREN; Chinese politician; b. 1905, Gansu; former High Iman of Islam; First Sec. Ningxia Hui, CCP 1961–67; criticized and removed from office during Cultural Revolution 1967; mem. 11th Cen. Cttee. 1977; Minister in charge of the Comm. for Minority Nationalities 1978–86; Vice-Premier, State Council 1980–82; Dir. United Front Work Dept., Cen. Cttee. CCP 1982–; mem. 12th Cen. Cttee. CCP 1982–; Vice-Chair. Credentials Cttee. 5th NPC 1979–83; Deputy from Gansu to 6th NPC 1983; Exec.-Chair. Presidium 6th NPC 1986–; Vice-Chair. NPC Nat. Cttee. 1983–; Chair. Nationalities Cttee. 1988–. *Address:* State Council, Beijing, People's Republic of China.

YANG LIGONG; Chinese politician; Vice-Minister of Agric. Machinery 1962, of 8th Ministry of Machine Bldg. 1965, of Agric. and Forestry

1970–79, of Agric. Machinery 1979–82; Adviser to Minister of Machine-Building Industry 1982–84; mem. NPC Standing Cttee. 1983–; mem. Overseas Chinese Cttee., NPC 1986–; Deputy Head China-Italy Friendship Group 1985–. *Address:* c/o San Li He, Beijing, People's Republic of China. *Telephone:* 861843.

YANG LIUZONG; Chinese government official; Gov. Sichuan 1983–86; Sec. CCP. Henan Prov. 1986. *Address:* Henan Provincial Chinese Communist Party, Henan, People's Republic of China.

YANG RUDAI; Chinese party official; b. 1926; cadre in Sichuan 1977–79; Vice-Gov. of Sichuan 1979–84; mem. 12th Cen. Cttee. CCP 1982–, Politburo 1987–; Political Commissar Sichuan Mil. Dist. 1983–86; First Sec. Party Cttee. 1985–; Sec. CCP Sichuan 1983–; Chair. Armament Cttee., CCP Sichuan 1984–. *Address:* Chinese Communist Party of Sichuan, Chengdu, Sichuan, People's Republic of China.

YANG SHANGKUN; Chinese politician; b. 1907, Sichuan; m. Li Bozhao (died 1985); joined CCP 1926; Dir. Propaganda Dept., Jiangsu Prov. Cttee., CCP 1931; Sec. CCP and Chinese Youth League Sec., Jiangsu Fed. of Trade Unions 1931; mem. Cen. Exec. Cttee., Second Cen. Soviet Govt. 1932; Dir. Political Dept., Red 1st Army 1931; Political Commissar, 3rd Army Corps. 1933, 1934; Dir. Political Dept., 1st Front Army 1933; mem. Cen. Exec. Cttee., 2nd Soviet Congress 1934; on Long March 1934–35; Acting Dir., Gen. Political Dept. 1935; Political Commissar, Shensi-Hansu Detachment, Chinese Worker-Peasant Red Army 1935; Sec. N. Bureau 1937; Sec., CCP, N. China Bureau 1943, Dir. United Front Work Dept. 1943; Dir. Staff Office, CCP Cen. Cttee. 1945–66, Deputy Sec. Gen. 1955, Alt. Sec., Secr. 1956–66, 1st Sec. (organs directly under Cen. Cttee.) 1958–66; mem. Standing Cttee., 2nd CPPCC 1954; mem. CCP 8th Cen. Cttee. 1956–66; mem. Standing Cttee., 3rd NPC 1965–66; removed from office during Cultural Revolution 1966; mem. CCP 11th Cen. Cttee. 1979; Vice-Chair. 5th NPC Standing Cttee. 1980–83, Sec.-Gen. 1980; Sec.-Gen. CCP Mil. Comm. 1981; Pres. of People's Republic of China April 1988–; Perm. Vice-Chair., PLA Mil. Comm. Sept. 1982–; mem. Politburo 12th Cen. Cttee. CCP 1982, Politburo 13th Cen. Cttee. 1987–; Deputy Sec.-Gen. 1982; mem. Cen. Mil. Comm. 1983–; Adviser, Cen. Party Consolidation Guidance Comm. 1983–; mem. Leading Group for Party History, CCP Cen. Cttee. 1984–; Hon. Pres. Table Tennis Asscn. 1983–. *Address:* Office of the President, Beijing, People's Republic of China.

YANG SHOUZHENG; Chinese diplomatist; m. Gong Runbing; Amb. to Somalia 1964–67, to Sudan 1970–74, to Ethiopia 1974–77, to Mozambique 1977–80, to U.S.S.R. 1980–86; Vice-Pres. China-U.S.S.R. Friendship Group 1986–; Vice-Pres. Huanxia Acad. April 1987–. *Address:* c/o Ministry of Foreign Affairs, Beijing, People's Republic of China.

YANG TAIFANG; Chinese politician; b. 30 April 1927, Mei Co., Guangdong Prov.; s. of Yang Shukum and Wen Xinyun; m. Wu Youhong 1957; one s. two d.; mem. 12th Cen. Cttee. CCP 1982, 13th Cen. Cttee. 1987; Vice-Minister of Posts and Telecommunications 1982–84, Minister 1984–. *Leisure interests:* music, bridge, Taiji boxing. *Address:* Ministry of Posts and Telecommunications, 13 West Changan Avenue, Beijing, People's Republic of China.

YANG XINGHUA; Chinese ballet dancer; b. 2 Sept. 1963, Shanghai; won men's individual performance 4th Osaka Int. Ballet Contest 1984; performed at 11th Festival of Asian Arts, Hong Kong 1986, *Leisure interests:* classical music, soccer, volleyball, cinema. *Address:* Beijing Dance School, Beijing, People's Republic of China.

YANG XIZONG; Chinese government official; b. 27 Sept. 1928, Dayi Co., Sichuan Prov.; s. of Yang Qunling and Yang Chunbing; m. Zhou Feng; one s. two d.; alt. mem. CPC Cen. Cttee. 1983; Deputy to 6th NPC 1983; Deputy Sec. CPC 4th Prov. Cttee., Sichuan 1983–85; Gov. of Sichuan 1983–85; Sec. CPC Prov. Cttee. Henan May 1985–; mem. 12th CCP Cen. Cttee. 1985–, 13th CCP Cen. Cttee. Oct. 1987. *Leisure interest:* reading. *Address:* Provincial Communist Party Committee, Zhengzhou, Henan Province, People's Republic of China.

YANG YANG; Chinese badminton player; b. 1958; Men's Singles Champion, 1987 World Championships. *Address:* China Sports Federation, Beijing, People's Republic of China.

YANG YI; Chinese sculptor; b. 1939, Zhongshan Co., Guangdong Prov.; Sec. Secr., All China Journalist's Asscn. Nov. 1985–. *Address:* Tianjin Art Studio, Tianjin, People's Republic of China.

YANG YICHEN; Chinese party official; b. 1911, Liaoning; Vice-Gov. Heilongjiang 1958–60, Sec. CCP 1961–67, First Sec. Prov. CCP Cttee. 1977–83; mem. 11th Cen. Cttee. CCP 1977; First Political Commissar, PLA Heilongjiang Mil. Dist. 1979–; mem. 12th Cen. Cttee. CCP 1982–85; mem. Cen. Advisory Comm. 1987–; Procurator-Gen., Supreme People's Procuratorate 1983. *Address:* Foreign Affairs Office, People's Government of Heilongjiang Province, People's Republic of China.

YANG YINGXIU; Chinese traditional artist; b. 1912, Hunan. *Address:* Changsha Peasants Artists' Institute, Changsha, Hunan, People's Republic of China.

YANG YONGLIANG; Chinese party official; b. 1944; alt. mem. 11th CCP Cen. Cttee. 1977, 12th Cen. Cttee. 1982, 13th Cen. Cttee. 1987; Deputy Sec. CCP Cttee., Hefei Municipality 1982–86, Sec. 1986–; mem. Standing Cttee., Anhui Prov. 1986–. *Address:* Hefei Municipal Chinese Communist Party, Hefei, Anhui, People's Republic of China.

YANG ZENYU; Chinese artist; b. 1938, Linqu Co., Shandong Prov.; art lecturer at Shandong Fine Arts Inst. *Address:* Shandong Fine Arts Institute, Shandong Province, People's Republic of China.

YANG ZHENGWU; Chinese state official; alt. mem. 12th CCP Cen. Cttee. 1982, mem. 1985, mem. 13th CCP Cen. Cttee. 1987–; Vice-Chair. West Hunan Tujia and Miao Autonomous Pref. 1982–. *Address:* West Hunan Tujia and Miao Autonomous Prefecture People's Government, Hunan, People's Republic of China.

YANG ZHENHUAI; Chinese government official; Vice-Minister for Water Resources and Electric Power 1983–88, Minister April 1988–; Sec.-Gen. Cen. Flood Control H.Q. 1986–88, Deputy Head April 1988–. *Address:* Ministry of Water Resources and Electric Power, Beijing, People's Republic of China.

YANG ZHENYA; Chinese government official; Curator, Museum of Chinese History 1973–; Deputy Dir. Asian Affairs Dept., Ministry of Foreign Affairs 1982–. *Address:* Ministry of Foreign Affairs, Beijing, People's Republic of China.

YANG ZHIGUANG; Chinese artist; b. 11 Oct. 1930, Shanghai; s. of Yang Miaocheng and Shi Qinxian; m. Ou Yang 1958; two d.; ed. Cen. Acad. of Fine Art; Vice-Pres. and Prof., Guangzhou Inst. of Fine Arts; Exec. mem. Bd. of Chinese Artists' Asscn.; does traditional Chinese figure painting, calligraphy and seal-making; Gold Medal winner, 7th Vienna World Youth Festival, for picture Sending Food in Heavy Snow 1959. *Publications:* Skill of Chinese Traditional Figure Painting, Selections of Portraits, Chinese Water Colours, Yang Zhiguang's Sketches in China's North-west, Portraits of Modern Chinese Artists, Painting Selections of Mr. and Mrs. Yang Zhiguang. *Leisure interests:* calligraphy, seal-making, poetry. *Address:* Guangzhou Institute of Fine Art, No. 257, Chang Gang Dong Lu Street, Haizhu District, Guangzhou, People's Republic of China. *Telephone:* 449883 (Office); 417598 (Home).

YANG ZHONG; Chinese government official; b. 1932, Sichuan; fmr. Sec. Guangan Co. CCP Cttee., Acting First Sec., Wushong Co. CCP Cttee., First Political Commissar People's Arms Dept., Wushong Co., Sec. Guangan Co. CCP Cttee., First Political Commissar People's Arms Dept., Guangan Co. Vice-Gov. of Sichuan 1979; Minister of Forestry 1982–87; Vice-Chair. Cen. Greening Cttee. 1983–; Pres. China Worldlife Conservation Asscn. 1983–. *Address:* State Council, Beijing, People's Republic of China.

YANG-KANG LIN (alias Chih-Hung), B.A.; Chinese politician; b. 10 June 1927, Nantou Co., Taiwan Prov.; s. of Chih-Chang Lin and Chen Ruan; m. Chen Ho 1945; one s. three d.; ed. Dept. of Political Science, Nat. Taiwan Univ.; Chief Admin. Civil Affairs Section, Nantou Co. Govt. 1952–61, Sec. 1962–64; Sec. Taiwan Prov. Govt. 1964; Chair. Yunlin Co. HQ, Kuomintang 1964–67; Magistrate, Nantou Co. 1967–72; Commr., Dept. of Reconstruction 1972–76; Mayor, Taipei Special Municipality 1976–78; Gov. of Taiwan Prov. Govt. 1978–81; Minister of Interior 1981–84; Vice-Premier of Exec. Yuan 1984–87; Pres. of Judicial Yuan 1987; Order of Diplomatic Service Merit, Korea 1977. *Leisure interests:* hiking, reading and studying, music. *Address:* 124 Chung Ching South Road, Section 1, Taipei, Taiwan 10036 (Home).

YANGLING DUOJI; Chinese (Tibetan) party and state official; Vice-Gov. Sichuan Prov. 1979–81; Sec. CCP Cttee., Tibet Autonomous Region 1981–86; Vice-Chair. Tibet 1982–83; alt. mem. 12th CCP Cen. Cttee. 1982–87; Chair. Tibet Branch, CPPCC 1983; Vice-Chair. CPPCC Prov. Cttee., Sichuan 1986–. *Address:* Office of the Vice Chairman of the Chinese People's Consultative Council, Sichuan, People's Republic of China.

YANKELEVSKY, Vladimir; Soviet artist; ed. Moscow Secondary Art School, ed. Acad. of Design and Moscow Polygraphic Inst.; took part in famous Manège Exhbn. of 1962 and thereafter worked closely with sculptor Ernst Neizvestny (q.v.). *Exhibitions:* Moscow 1962, 1965, 1975, Italy 1965, Poland, Czechoslovakia 1965, Rome 1967, Florence 1969, Lugano 1970, Zurich, Cologne 1970, Paris 1973, Vienna 1975, France, Fed. Germany, U.S.A. 1976.

YANO, Jun'ya; Japanese politician; b. 27 April 1932, Osaka; m. Mitsuko Yano 1961; one s.; ed. Kyoto Univ.; with Ohbayashi-gumi Ltd. 1956–; mem. Osaka Prefectural Assembly 1963; mem. House of Reps. 1967–; Sec.-Gen. Komeito (Clean Govt.) Party 1967–89; Party Chair. 1986–89. *Leisure interests:* reading, listening to music. *Address:* Komeito, 17 Minamimotomachi, Shinjuku-ku, Tokyo.

YANOFSKY, Charles, PH.D.; American professor of biology; b. 17 April 1925, New York, N.Y.; s. of Frank Yanofsky and Jennie Kopatz Yanofsky; m. Carol Cohen 1949; three s.; ed. City Coll. of New York and Yale Univ.; Research Asst. in Microbiology, Yale Univ. 1951–53; Asst. Prof. of Microbiology Western Reserve Univ. 1954–58; Assoc. Prof., Dept. of Biological Sciences, Stanford Univ., Prof., Dept. of Biological Sciences

1961–; Herzstein Prof. of Biology 1967; Pres. Genetics Soc. of America 1969, American Soc. of Biological Chemists 1984; Career Investigator American Heart Asscn. 1969; mem. N.A.S., American Acad. of Arts and Sciences; Foreign mem. Royal Soc. 1985–; Hon. mem. Japanese Biochemical Soc. 1985–; Hon. D.Sc. (Univ. of Chicago) 1980, (Yale Univ.) 1981; Louisa Gross Horwitz Prize 1976; Eli Lilly Award in Bacteriology 1959, U.S. Steel Award in Molecular Biology 1964, Howard Taylor Ricketts Award 1966, Albert Lasker Award for Basic Medical Research 1971, Selman A. Waksman Award 1972, Townsend Harris Medal, City Coll. of New York, Mattia Award, Roche Inst. 1982, Genetics Soc. of America Medal 1983, Gairdner Foundation Award 1985. *Publications:* Scientific articles in Proceedings of Nat. Acad. of Sciences, etc. *Leisure interests:* tennis, sports. *Address:* 725 Mayfield Avenue, Stanford, Calif. 94305, U.S.A. *Telephone:* 415-725-1835 (Office); 415-857-9057.

YANSANE, Sékou; Guinean diplomatist; b. 1934, Forecariah; s. of Elhadj Fodé and Hadja M. Touré; m. Nana Fofana 1958; three s. four d.; ed. Lycée VanVollen Hoven, Dakar and Faculté des Lettres et des Sciences Humaines, Dakar, Poitiers, Paris; Coll. Prin., Conakry 1960; Headmaster Lycée Classique de Donka 1964; Prof. Inst. Nat. de Recherche et de Documentation 1965–76; Amb. to People's Repub. of China, also accred. to Viet-Nam, Cambodia (now People's Repub. of Kampuchea), Democratic People's Repub. of Korea, and Pakistan 1976–78; Perm. Rep. to UN, also accred. to Argentina, Brazil, Venezuela, Haiti, Jamaica and Canada 1978–80; Amb. to Algeria, also accred. to Tunisia 1980; Gov. of Dabola 1981–83, of Dinguiraye 1983–84; Perm. Del. to UNESCO 1984–87. *Publications:* numerous articles on African Literature and politics. *Address:* B.P. 62, Conakry, Republic of Guinea.

YAO GUANG; Chinese diplomatist; Dir. Foreign Affairs Office, Hubei Prov. People's Govt. 1954; Deputy Dir. W. Europe and Africa Dept., Ministry of Foreign Affairs 1956; Counsellor, Embassy in Poland 1957–63; Deputy Dir. Second Asia Dept., Ministry of Foreign Affairs 1964, Dir. 1964–69; Amb. to Poland 1970–71, to Canada 1972–73, to Mexico 1973–77, to Egypt 1977–80 (also to Djibouti 1979–80), to France 1980–82, First Vice-Minister of Foreign Affairs 1982–86, Adviser 1986–; mem. 12th Cen. Cttee. CCP 1982. *Address:* Ministry of Foreign Affairs, Beijing, People's Republic of China.

YAO SHUN, LL.B., M.A.; Chinese government official; b. 4 Sept. 1919, Yuyua County, Chekiang; m.; one s. one d.; ed. Nat. Wuhan Univ., Univ. of Tennessee; Dist. Judge Liaoning 1946–47; Section Chief, Taiwan Provincial HQ, Kuomintang Youth Corps 1947–48; Section Chief, Ministry of Educ. 1949–51, Fifth Dept., Cen. Cttee. Kuomintang 1952–58; Sec.-Gen. China Youth Corps 1958–68; Dir. Bureau of Int. Cultural and Educ. Relations, Ministry of Educ. 1970–72; Sec.-Gen. Nat. Youth Comm. Exec. Yuan 1972–83, Vice-Chair. 1983–84, Chair. 1984–, Hon. Ph.D. (Konkuk) 1978. *Address:* National Youth Commission, Executive Yuan, Taipei, Taiwan.

YAO WENYUAN; Chinese journalist; b. 1924; journalist and youth activist before Cultural Revolution; leading pro-Maoist journalist during Cultural Revolution 1965–66; Ed. Wen Hui Bao 1966, Liberation Daily 1966; mem. Cen. Cultural Revolution Group, CCP 1966; Vice-Chair. Shanghai Revolutionary Cttee. 1967–76; Ed. People's Daily 1967–76; mem. Politburo, CCP Cen. Cttee. 1969–76; Second Sec. CCP Shanghai 1971; arrested as mem. of "Gang of Four" Oct. 1976; expelled from CCP July 1977; in detention; on trial Nov. 1980–Jan. 1981; sentenced to 20 years imprisonment.

YAO XUEYIN; Chinese novelist; b. 1911, Dengxian, Henan; Prof., Daxia Univ., Shanghai 1946; mem. Henan Fed. of Literary and Art Circles 1951; mem. Wuhan Writers' Asscn. 1953; *works include:* Niu Quande and the Reddish Turnips, When Flowers Blossom in Spring, A Love Story on The Battlefield, Li Zicheng (three vols.). *Address:* c/o Wuhan Writers' Association, Wuhan, Hubei Province, People's Republic of China.

YAO YILIN; Chinese government official; b. 1915, Jiangsi Province; Sec.-Gen. CCP N. China Bureau Cen. Cttee. 1937–46; mem. Financial and Econ. Cttee. N. China People's Govt. 1948–49; Dir., Dept. of Industry and Commerce, N. China People's Govt. 1948–49; Vice-Minister of Trade 1949–52; mem. Provisional Bd. of Dirs., All-China Fed. of Co-operatives 1950; mem. Cen. Cttee. to check Austerity Program 1951; Vice-Minister of Commerce 1952–58; mem. Nat. Cttee. All China Federation of Supply and Marketing Co-operatives 1954; Deputy for Jiangsi to 1st NPC 1954; Vice-Minister, First Minister of Commerce 1958; alt. mem. CCP 8th Cen. Cttee. 1958; Deputy Dir., Finance and Trade Admin. Office, State Council, 1959; mem., Pres., All-China Conf. of Advanced Producers, 1959; mem., Standing Cttee. 3rd CPPCC 1959; Deputy Dir. Finance and Trade Work Dept. CCP Cen. Cttee. 1959–67; Minister of Commerce 1960–67; Dir., Political Dept. Financial and Trade Dept. CCP Cen. Cttee. 1964–67; accused of being a counter-revolutionary revisionist 1967; alt. mem. CCP 10th Cen. Cttee. 1973; Vice-Minister of Foreign Trade 1973–78; mem. Presidium CCP 11th Nat. Congress 1977–; a Vice-Premier 1979–; Minister of Commerce 1978–79, of Fourth Ministry of Machine Building 1979–80, in charge of State Planning Comm. June 1987–; Sec.-Gen. State Finance and Econ. Comm. 1979; Dir., Gen. Office, CCP 1979; Sec., Secr. and Deputy Sec.-Gen. Cen. Cttee. 1980–; Minister in Charge of State Planning Comm. 1980–83; Alt. mem. 11th Cen. Cttee. of CCP 1977, mem. 12th Cen. Cttee.

1982, 13th Cen. Cttee. 1987; mem. Politburo CCP Cen. Cttee. 1982–87, Standing Cttee. of Politburo 1987–; Sec. Secr. CCP 1982–85. *Address:* State Council, Beijing, People's Republic of China.

YAO YONGMAO; Chinese artist; b. 17 Aug. 1935, Bo-xi village, Dayao County, Yunnan (Yi nationality); s. of Yao Fengchao and Yao Fenglan; m. Han Jufang 1965; two d. one s.; ed. Dept. of Oils, Yunnan Coll. of Arts; fmr. soldier and worker; head, oil-painting teaching Group, Yunnan Coll. of Arts 1981–; Vice-Pres. Yunnan Provincial Artists Asscn.; mem. Chinese Artists Asscn. *Works include:* Chinese paintings: A Yi man, Willows in a Spring Breeze, Mother, Defying Frost and Snow, Images in the Long Couplet of Da Gung Pavilion, On the Way to Liain Wang Mountain, Bang Na Gardenyard; paintings: Mountain Villages, Pastoral. *Leisure interests:* dealing with young people, making friends. *Address:* College of Arts, 101 Mayuan, West Outskirts Kunming, Yunnan, People's Republic of China. *Telephone:* 82026.

YAO ZHONGHUA; Chinese artist; b. 17 July 1939, Kunming, Yunnan; s. of late Yao Penxien and late Wang Huiyuan; m. Ma Huixian 1969; two s.; ed. Cen. Acad. of Fine Arts; one-man show, Beijing 1980, Cité Int. Arts, Paris 1985 and exhbns. in Paris and E. Europe; four oil paintings including The Dream of Clay Forest exhibited Beijing and Kunming 1986; oil painting Red Plateau included in China Oil Paintings of Present Age exhbn., New York, U.S.A. 1987; six oil paintings exhibited Melbourne, Sydney, Australia 1987; mem. Council China Artists' Asscn.; Vice-Pres. Yunnan Painting Inst. *Works include:* Oh, the Land!, Sani Minority's Festival, The Yellow River, Zhenghe's Voyage, The Jinsha Jiang Flowing beside the Jade Dragon Mountain, Chinese Ink and Water. *Leisure interests:* music, literature. *Address:* Yunnan Painting Institute, Qin Nian Road, Kunming, Yunnan Province (Office); No. 4 Shu Guang Hang, Wen Miao Street, Kunming, Yunnan Province, People's Republic of China (Home). *Telephone:* 23665, 28811.

YAO ZHONGMING; Chinese government official; b. 1912, Weixian Co., Shandong Prov.; fmr. Vice-Chair. PRC Nat. Cttee. for UNESCO; Vice-Chair. Cttee. for Cultural Exchange with Foreign Countries 1983–; Vice-Pres. China Int. Cultural Exchange Centre 1984–; mem. Nat. Cttee. Chinese People's Political Consultative Conf. 1984–; Sr. Consultant Beijing Inst. for Int. Strategic Studies 1985–; Vice-Chair. China Asscn. of Cultural Exchange with Foreign Countries 1986. *Address:* Ministry of Culture, Dongamen North Street, Beijing, People's Republic of China. *Telephone:* 446571-259.

YAR'ADUA, Major-Gen. Shehu; Nigerian army officer; b. 5 March 1943, Katsina, Kaduna State; m.; three d.; ed. Govt. Secondary School, Katsina, Nigerian Mil. Training Coll., Zaria, Royal Mil. Coll., Sandhurst, U.K., Command and Staff Coll., U.K.; Platoon Commdr. 1964–65, Battalion Adjutant 1965–67, Co. Commdr. 1967, Asst. Adjutant Gen., 2nd Div. 1967; Commanded 6th Infantry Brigade in Second Infantry Div. with service in Onitsha Sector 1968; Commanded 9th Infantry Brigade (based at Warri during civil war) 1969–72; Commr. for Transport 1975–76; Chief of Staff, Supreme HQ (Chief of Army Staff) 1976–79; Vice-Pres. Supreme Mil. Council 1976–79. *Address:* c/o Ministry of Defence, Lagos, Nigeria.

YARMOLINSKY, Adam, LL.B., A.B.; American university professor, lawyer, and fmr. government official; b. 17 Nov. 1922, New York; s. of Avrahm Yarmolinsky and Babette Deutsch Yarmolinsky; m. 1st Harriet Rypins 1945 (divorced 1980); m. 2nd Jane C. Vonnegut 1984 (died 1986); three s. one d.; ed. Harvard Univ. and Yale Law School; practised as lawyer 1949–55; Law Clerk, Supreme Court 1950–51; Sec. Fund for the Repub. 1955–57; consultant to philanthropic foundations 1959–60; Kennedy Presidential Campaign and talent hunt 1960; Special Asst. to Sec. of Defense 1961–64; Deputy Dir. Pres.'s Anti-Poverty Task Force 1964; Prin. Deputy Asst. Sec. of Defense (Int. Security Affairs) 1965–66; Prof. of Law, Harvard Law School, mem. Inst. of Politics, John Fitzgerald Kennedy School of Govt. 1966–72, C.E.O. Welfare Island Devt. Corpn., New York City 1971–72; Ralph Waldo Emerson Univ. Prof., Univ. of Mass. 1972–79; Counsellor, U.S. Arms Control and Disarmament Agency 1977–79; pvt. law practice, Kominers, Fort Schlefer & Boyer 1979–85, counsel 1985–; Prof. of Policy Sciences, Graduate Program in Policy Sciences, Univ. of Md., Baltimore County 1985–, Provost 1986–; Trustee Robert F. Kennedy Memorial 1968–, Bennington Coll. 1984– (Chair. 1986–); mem. Bd. Center for Nat. Policy 1981–; Cttee. on Nat. Security 1983– (Chair. 1985–), Inst. for Nat. Strategy (Advisory Bd.) 1983–, New Directions 1976–77, 1979–81; Fellow American Acad. of Arts and Sciences; mem. American Bar Asscn., American Law Inst. (life), Council on Foreign Relations, Int. Inst. for Strategic Studies, Hudson Inst., Cttee. on East-West Relations. *Publications:* Recognition of Excellence 1960, The Military Establishment 1971, Paradoxes of Power 1983; (Ed.) Case Studies in Personnel Security 1955, Race and Schooling in the City 1981. *Leisure interests:* reading, conversation, walking. *Address:* Office of the Provost, University of Maryland, Baltimore County, Baltimore, Md. 21228; 3307 Highland Place, N.W., Washington, D.C. 20008, U.S.A. (Home). *Telephone:* (301) 455-2300 (Office); (202) 363-7642 (Home).

YARROW, Sir Eric Grant, 3rd Bt. (cr. 1916), M.B.E., D.L.; British business executive; b. 23 April 1920, Glasgow; s. of late Sir Harold Yarrow, 2nd Bt., and late Eleanor Etheldreda; m. 1st Rosemary Ann Young 1951 (died

1957), one s. (deceased); m. 2nd Annette Elizabeth Françoise Steven 1959 (divorced 1975), three s.; m. 3rd Joan Botting 1982; ed. Marlborough Coll., Glasgow Univ.; served apprenticeship with G. and J. Weir Ltd.; army service in Burma 1939–45, Major Royal Engineers 1945; trained with English Electric Co. 1945–46; Asst. Man., Yarrow and Co. Ltd. 1946, Dir. 1948, Man. Dir. 1958–67, Chair. 1962–85, Pres. 1985–86; Chair. Yarrow (Shipbuilders) Ltd. 1962–79, Clydesdale Bank PLC 1985–; mem. Council, Royal Inst. Naval Architects 1957–, Vice-Pres. 1965, Hon. Vice-Pres. 1972; mem. Gen. Cttee. Lloyd's Register of Shipping 1960–87, Hon. Pres. 1986–; Prime Warden, Worshipful Co. of Shipwrights 1970–71; Deacon, Incorpn. of Hammermen of Glasgow 1961–62; fmr. mem. Council of Inst. Engineers and Shipbuilders in Scotland; Chair. Exec. Cttee. Princess Louise Scottish Hosp., Erskine 1980–86, Hon. Pres. 1986–; Pres. Scottish Convalescent Home for Children 1958–70; Fellow of Royal Soc. of Edin. 1975; Officer of Order of St. John. *Leisure interests:* golf, shooting. *Address:* Cloak, Kilmacolm, Renfrewshire, PA13 4SD, Scotland. *Telephone:* 041-248-7070 (Office); 041-549-2067 (Home).

YASSUKOVICH, Stanislas Michael; American banker; b. 5 Feb. 1935, Paris, France; s. of Dimitri Yassukovich and Denise Yassukovich; m. Diana Townsend 1961; two s. one d.; ed. Deerfield Acad., Mass. and Harvard Univ.; U.S. Marine Corps. 1957–61; joined White, Weld and Co. 1961, London Office 1962, Br. Man. 1967–69, Gen. Partner, New York 1969–73, Man. Dir., London 1969–73; Man. Dir. European Banking Co. S.A. Brussels 1983–85, Chief Exec. European Banking Group 1983–85; Chair. Merrill Lynch Europe Ltd. 1985–; Jt. Deputy Chair. London Stock Exchange 1986–; Chair. Securities Asscn. 1988–. *Leisure interests:* hunting, shooting and polo. *Address:* Merrill Lynch Europe Ltd., 25 Ropemaker Street, London, EC2Y 9LY, England. *Telephone:* 01-897 2953.

YASTREBOV, Ivan Pavlovich; Soviet official; b. 20 Jan. 1911; ed. Urals Polytech. Inst., Sverdlovsk; head of tech. dept. of a metallurgical plant 1936–46; mem. CPSU 1941; party work 1946–50; head of a dept., Perm Dist. Cttee. CPSU 1951–53; First Sec., Perm City Cttee. CPSU 1953–54; Deputy Head, then First Deputy Head of Dept. for Heavy Industry, Cen. Cttee. CPSU 1954–62, 1962–84, Head of Dept. 1984–; mem. Cen. Auditing Comm., Cen. Cttee. CPSU 1971–81; Deputy to R.S.F.S.R. Supreme Soviet 1980– ; cand. mem. Cen. Cttee. CPSU 1981–86, mem. 1986–89; Head of Dept. for Heavy Industry and Power 1984–89. U.S.S.R. State Prize 1943. *Address:* The Kremlin, Moscow, U.S.S.R.

YASUI, Kaoru, LL.D.; Japanese jurist and poet; b. 25 April 1907, Osaka; s. of Harumoto and Harue Yasuri; m. Tazuko Kuki 1936; one s. one d.; ed. Tokyo Univ.; Asst. Prof. Tokyo Univ. 1932–42, Prof. 1942–48; Prof. Hosei Univ. 1952, Dean Faculty of Jurisprudence 1957–63, Dir. 1963–66, Prof. Emer. 1978–; Leader (Chair. etc.) Japan Council Against Atomic and Hydrogen Bombs 1954–65; Pres. Japanese Inst. for World Peace 1965–; Dir. Maruki Gallery for Hiroshima Panels 1968–; Chair. Japan-Korea (Democratic People's Repub.) Solidarity Cttee. of Social Scientists 1972–; Dir-Gen. Int. Inst. of the Juche Idea 1978–; Hon. mem. Japanese Asscn. of Int. Law 1976–; Hon. D.Jur. (San Gabriel Coll., U.S.A.); mem. Lenin Peace Prize Cttee.; Lenin Peace Prize 1958; Gold Medal (Czechoslovakia) 1965. *Publications:* Outline of International Law 1939, Banning Weapons of Mass Destruction 1955, People and Peace 1955, Collection of Treaties 1960, My Way 1967, The Dialectical Method and the Science of International Law 1970, A Piece of Eternity (Poems) 1977. *Address:* Minami-Ogikubo 3-13-11, Suginami-ku, Tokyo, Japan. *Telephone:* Tokyo 03-332-3580.

YATES, Frank, C.B.E., SC.D., F.R.S.; British research scientist; b. 1902; ed. Clifton Coll., and St. John's Coll., Cambridge; Research Officer and Mathematical Adviser, Gold Coast Geodetic Survey 1927–31; at Rothamsted Experimental Station 1931–; Head of Dept. of Statistics 1933–68, Deputy Dir. 1958–68, Hon. Scientist 1980–; Scientific Adviser to various Ministries 1939–; Hon. Wing-Commdr., R.A.F. 1943–45; Head of Agricultural Research Statistical Service 1947–68; mem. UN Sub-Comm. on Statistical Sampling 1947–51; mem. Governing Body Grassland Research Station 1948–69; mem. Int. Statistical Inst. 1947–; Pres. of British Computer Soc. 1961–62; Pres. Royal Statistical Soc. 1967–68; Sr. Research Fellow, Imperial Coll., London 1969–74; Sr. Visiting Fellow 1974–77; Royal Medal, Royal Soc. 1966; Hon. D.Sc. (Univ. of London) 1982. *Publications:* Design and Analysis of Factorial Experiments 1937, Statistical Tables for Biological, Medical and Agricultural Research (with R. A. Fisher) 1938–63, Sampling Methods for Censuses and Surveys 1949–81, Experimental Design: Selected Papers 1970. *Address:* Rothamsted Experimental Station, Harpenden, Hertfordshire, AL5 2JQ, England. *Telephone:* (058 27) 63133.

YATES, Peter; British film and theatre producer and director; b. 24 July 1929; s. of Col. Robert Yates and Constance Yates; m. Virginia Pope 1960, two s. two d. (one deceased); ed. Charterhouse, R.A.D.A.; entered film industry as studio man. and dubbing asst. with De Lane Lea; Asst. Dir. The Entertainer, The Guns of Navarone, A Taste of Honey, etc.; *Films directed include:* Summer Holiday 1962, Danger Man, Saint (TV series) 1963–65, Bullitt 1968, John and Mary 1969, Murphy's War, Mother, Jugs and Speed 1975, The Deep 1976, Breaking Away (also produced) 1979, The Janitor (Eyewitness in U.S.A.; also produced) 1980, Krull 1982, The Dresser (also produced) 1983, Eleni 1984, The House on Carroll Street (also produced) 1986, Suspect 1987. *Plays directed:* The American Dream 1961, The

Death of Bessie Smith 1961, Passing Game 1977, Interpreters 1985. *Leisure interests:* tennis, sailing, skiing. *Address:* c/o Sam Cohn, ICM Inc., 40 West 57th Street, New York, N.Y. 10019, U.S.A.

YATIM, Dato Rais, M.A., LL.B.; Malaysian politician; b. 1942, Jelebu, Negeri Sembilan; m. Datin Masnah Mohamat; two c.; ed. Univ. of Northern Illinois and Univ. of Singapore; lecturer at ITM, School of Law and also managed own law firm in Kuala Lumpur 1973; mem. Bar Council 1973; mem. Parl. 1974; Parl. Sec. Ministry of Youth, Sport and Culture 1974; Deputy Minister of Law 1976, of Home Affairs 1978; elected to State Ass., Negeri Sembilan 1978; Menteri Besar, Negeri Sembilan 1978; Minister of Land and Regional Devt. 1982, of Information 1984–86, of Foreign Affairs 1986–87; Advocate and Solicitor, High Court of Malaysia 1988–; returned to Law practice, Kuala Lumpur 1988–; mem. United Malays' Nat. Org. (UMNO) Supreme Council of Malaysia 1982-. *Address:* 41 Road 12, Taman Grandview, Ampang Jaya, 68000 Ampang, Selangor Darul Ehsan, Malaysia (Home). *Telephone:* (03) 456921.

YAVUZTÜRK, Zeki; Turkish politician; b. 1935, Kemaliye; m.; two c.; ed. Michigan Univ.; mining and metallurgy engineer in Turkish Coal Enterprises and Gen. Dir. of Etibank, Keban Holding 1972–83; Minister of Defence 1983–87. *Address:* Savunma Bakanliği, Ankara, Turkey.

YAZDI, Dr. Ibrahim; Iranian politician; b. c. 1933; m.; two s. four d.; studied and worked as physician in U.S.A. for sixteen years; close assoc. of Ayatollah Khomeini (q.v.) during exile in Neauphlé-le-Château, France Oct. 1978–Feb. 1979; Deputy Prime Minister with responsibility for Revolutionary Affairs Feb.-April 1979; Minister of Foreign Affairs April-Nov. 1979; Special Emissary of Ayatollah Khomeini on Provincial Problems 1979; Supervisor Keyhan Org. 1980–; Deputy in Parl. for Tehran 1980–84; mem. Foreign Affairs, Health and Welfare Parl. Comms. *Publications:* Final Efforts in Terminal Days: Some Untold Stories of the Islamic Revolution of Iran 1984, Principles of Molecular Genetics 1985, other publs. on carcinogenics, the nucleic acid of cancer cells, and Islamic and social topics. *Address:* 35 Masjid Alley, Ekhtiary-Yeh, Teheran, Iran.

YAZOV, Dmitri Timofeevich; Soviet military official; b. 1923; ed. Frunze Mil. Acad. and Mil. Acad. of Gen. Staff; entered Soviet army 1941–; active service 1941–45; command posts 1945–76; Deputy Commdr. of Far Eastern Mil. Dist. 1976–79; Commdr. of Cen. Group Forces in Czechoslovakia 1979–80; Deputy to U.S.S.R. Supreme Soviet 1979–; Commdr. of Cen. Asian Mil. Dist. 1980; Deputy Minister of Defence Feb.-June 1987, Minister of Defence and Head of Armed Forces June 1987–; mem. of Cen. Cttee. of Kazakh CP 1981–; Cand. mem. of Cen. Cttee. of CPSU 1981-. *Address:* Soviet Army Headquarters, Central Asian Military District, U.S.S.R.

YE FEI; Chinese party official; b. 1909, Fuan, Fujian; Guerilla leader in Fujian 1926–29; joined CCP 1927; Div. Commdr. New 4th Army 1941; Corps Commdr. 3rd Field Army 1949; Vice-Gov. of Fujian 1954–59, Gov. 1955–59; Mayor of Xiamen 1949; First Sec. CCP Fujian 1955–68; Gen. 1955; Alt. mem. 8th Cen. Cttee. of CCP 1956; Political Commissar Fuzhou Mil. Region, PLA 1957–67; Sec. E. China Bureau, CCP 1963–68; criticized and removed from office during Cultural Revolution 1967; Alt. mem. 10th Cen. Cttee. of CCP 1973; Minister of Communications 1975–79; mem. 11th Cen. Cttee. CCP 1977; First Political Commissar PLA Naval Units 1979–80; First Sec. CCP Cttee. PLA Navy 1979–82; Commdr. Navy 1980–82; mem. 12th Cen. Cttee. CCP 1982–87; Vice-Chair. Standing Cttee. and Chair. Overseas Cttee. 6th NPC 1983–; Exec. Chair., Presidium 6th NPC 1986–, Vice-Chair. Standing Cttee. 1983–; Hon. Pres. All-China Fed. of Returned Overseas Chinese 1984–, Soc. on History of Overseas Chinese 1986–; Pres. Overseas Chinese Univ. 1983-. *Address:* People's Republic of China.

YE JUNJIAN; Chinese writer and translator; b. 1915, Hupei Prov.; Founder Chinese Literature (monthly, English and French); Vice-Pres. China PEN Centre 1982–; Chair. Comm. for Chinese-Foreign Literary Exchange 1985; mem. All-China Fed. of Literary and Art Circles Council, Chinese Writers Asscn. Council. *Publications:* (in English as Chun-Chan Yeh) The Mountain Village, They Fly South, The Ignorant and the Forgotten, Three Seasons and Other Stories; (in Chinese) New Schoolmates, The Emperor Real and False, Sketches of Two Capitals, Pioneers of the Virgin Soil, On the Steppe, Flames, Freedom, Dawn, Essays from Western Studio, Selected Writings, Selected Stories, Old Souvenirs and New Friends, Cambridge Revisited, The Leaves are Red, The Art of Reading, etc.; trans.: Complete Hans Andersen, Agamemnon, etc. *Address:* 6 Gongjian Hutong, Di An Men, Beijing, People's Republic of China.

YE LIANSONG; Chinese engineer, party and government official; b. 1935, Shanghai; ed. Jiaotong Univ., Shanghai; engineer, Shijiazhuang Municipal Diesel Plant 1960–80; Vice-Mayor Shijiazhuang 1982–; mem. Standing Cttee. Hebei Prov. CCP Cttee. 1983–; Vice-Gov. Hebei Prov. 1985–; alt. mem. CCP Cen. Cttee. 1987-. *Address:* Central Committee of the Chinese Communist Party, Zhongnanhai, Beijing, People's Republic of China.

YE RUTANG; Chinese government official; b. 1940; Minister of Urban and Rural Construction 1985–88, Vice-Minister May 1988–; Minister of Environmental Protection 1987; Vice-Chair. Environmental Protection Cttee., State Council 1986. *Address:* Ministry of Urban and Rural Construction, Beijing, People's Republic of China.

YE RUZHANG; Chinese sculptor; b. 1933, Shanghai; currently an engineer. *Address:* Beijing Architectural Sculpture Factory, Beijing, People's Republic of China.

YE XIAOGANG; Chinese musical composer; b. 23 Sept. 1955, Shanghai, China; s. of Ye Chunzi and Ho Ying; m. Xu Jing 1987; ed. Eastman School of Music, U.S.A. (post-graduate); lecturer Cen. Conservatory of Music, Beijing. *Compositions:* Xi Jiang Yue Symphony 1984, Horizon Symphony 1985, Piano Ballade 1987, Dance Drama: The Love Story of Da Lai VI 1988. *Address:* 115 Summit Drive, Rochester, New York 14620, U.S.A. *Telephone:* (716) 244 3835.

YE XUANPING; Chinese state official; b. 1925, Guangdong Prov.; s. of late Ye Jianying and Zeng Xianzhi; ed. Yan'an Coll. of Natural Sciences, specialist in machinery, studies in U.S.S.R. 1950-54; Dir. Beijing No. 1 Machine-tool Factory 1963; Vice-Gov. Guangdong Prov. 1980-83; Chair. Guangdong Prov. Scientific and Tech. Cttee. 1981; alt. mem. 12th CCP Cen. Cttee. 1982, mem. 13th CCP Cen. Cttee. 1987-; Deputy Sec. CCP Cttee., Guangzhou Municipality 1983-; Acting Mayor Guangzhou 1983, Mayor 1983-85; Deputy for Guangdong Prov. to 6th NPC 1983; Exec. Chair. Preparatory Cttee. for 6th NPC Games 1985-; Gov. of Guangdong 1985-. *Address:* Office of the Governor, Guangdong, People's Republic of China.

YEATES, W(illiam) Keith, M.D., M.S., F.R.C.S., F.R.C.S.(E.); British urological surgeon; b. 10 March 1920, Helensburgh, Scotland; s. of William R. Yeates and Winifred (Scott) Yeates; m. Jozy McIntyre Fairweather 1946; one s. one d.; ed. Univ. of Newcastle upon Tyne, Royal Vic. Infirmary, Newcastle upon Tyne, St. Paul's Hosp., London and Dept. of Urology, Newcastle Gen. Hosp.; Consultant Urologist, Newcastle Health Authority 1952-85, Hon. Consultant Urologist 1985-; Consultant Adviser, Dept. of Health 1978-84; Chair. Intercollegiate Bd. in Urology 1984-88; Pres. British Asscn. of Urological Surgeons 1980-82; Visiting Prof. Univs. of Baghdad, Calif. (Los Angeles), Texas (Dallas), Delhi, Cairo, Kuwait 1974-80 and several other guest lectureships etc.; mem. various cttees., editorial bds. etc.; Hon. mem. Urological Soc. of Australia, Canadian Urological Asscn. St Peter's Medal, British Asscn. of Urological Surgeons 1983. *Publications:* articles in various textbooks on urology and papers in professional journals. *Leisure interest:* education in urology. *Address:* 22 Castleton Grove, Newcastle upon Tyne, NE2 2HD; 71 King Henry's Road, London, NW3 3QU, England. *Telephone:* 091 2814030; 01-586 7633.

YEEND, Sir Geoffrey John, Kt., A.C., C.B.E., B.COMM., F.A.I.M.; Australian civil servant; b. 1 May 1927, Melbourne, Vic.; s. of late Herbert John Yeend and Ellen Yeend; m. Laurel Dawn Mahoney 1952; one s. one d.; ed. Canberra High School, Canberra Coll., Univ. of Melbourne; served R.A.E. 1945-46; with Dept. of Post War Reconstruction 1944-49; Prime Minister's Dept. 1950, Pvt. Sec. to Prime Minister 1952-55; Asst. Sec., High Comm., London 1958-61; Dept. of Prime Minister and Cabinet 1961-86, Deputy Sec. 1973-75, Under-Sec. 1976-77, Sec. 1978-86; Dir. AMATIL Ltd. 1986-, Alcan Australia Ltd. 1986-, Civic Advance Bank Ltd. 1987-, Menzies Memorial Trust; mem. Advisory Council on Australian Archives 1985-87; Pro-Chancellor A.N.U. 1988-; Australian Eisenhower Fellow 1971, Fellow, Australian Inst. of Man.; Vice-Pres. Australian Inst. of Public Admin. 1979-86; Vice-Pres. Int. Hockey Fed. 1967-76 (mem. of Honour 1979); Trustee Australian Youth Cricket Foundation. *Leisure interests:* golf, fishing. *Address:* 1 Loftus Street, Yarralumla, A.C.T. 2600, Australia (Home). *Telephone:* 062-813266.

YEFIMOV, Air Marshal Aleksandr Nikolayevich, M.SC.; Soviet air force officer; b. 6 Feb. 1923, Kantemirovka, Voronezh Oblast; ed. Voroshilovograd Mil. Air Acad., Mil. Acad. of Gen. Staff; joined CPSU 1943; served in Soviet army 1941; fought on the Western and on 2nd Byelorussian Fronts at Vyazma, Smolensk, in Byelorussia, Poland and Germany 1942-45; by July 1944 had flown about 100 missions and was made Hero of the Soviet Union; completed his 222nd mission on 8 May 1945; awarded second Gold Star; held various command posts 1945-69; First Deputy C.-in-C., Soviet Air Defence Forces March 1969-; Deputy to Supreme Soviet 1946-50, 1974-; rank of Marshal 1975; Hero of the Soviet Union (twice), Order of Lenin (twice), Order of the Red Banner (five times), Aleksandr Nevsky Order, Merited Mil. Pilot of U.S.S.R. 1970 and other decorations. *Publication:* Over the Field of Battle 1976. *Address:* c/o Ministry of Defence, Moscow, U.S.S.R.

YEFIMOV, Anatoliy Stepanovich; Soviet politician; b. 1939; ed. Leningrad Mechanical Inst.; constructor in Leningrad 1962-65; mem. CPSU 1966-; Second, First Sec. of Kalinin Regional Komsomol Cttee. (Leningrad) 1965-70; Sec., First Sec. of Leningrad Dist. Komsomol Cttee. 1970-73; Sec. of Party Cttee. at Kirov Works 1973-76; Second, First Sec. of Tikhvin City Cttee. of CPSU 1976-82; First Sec. of Vyborg Regional Cttee. of CPSU (Leningrad) 1982-86; First Sec. of Navoy Dist. Cttee. of Uzbek CP, 1986-; cand. mem. of CPSU Cen. Cttee. 1986-. *Address:* Navoy District Committee of Communist Party, Tashkent, Uzbek S.S.R., U.S.S.R.

YEFIMOV, Nikolai Nikolayevich; Soviet physicist; b. 1928; ed. Yakutsk Inst.; teacher 1949-52; chief ed. of Scientific Publishing House, Yakutsk 1952-56; mem. of Staff of Inst. for Research into Space Physics, Yakutsk Br. of U.S.S.R. Acad. of Sciences 1956-, head of lab. 1969; Lenin Prize 1982. *Publications include:* numerous works on space research 1947-80.

Address: U.S.S.R. Academy of Sciences, Leninsky Prospekt 14, Moscow V-71, U.S.S.R.

YEFREMOV, Mikhail Timofeyevich; Soviet politician; b. 22 May 1911; ed. Industrial Inst., Kuibyshev; mem. CPSU 1932-; party work 1943-; Second Sec. then Sec. Kuibyshev District Cttee. CPSU 1951-59; Head of section of party organ of Cen. Cttee. of CPSU for R.S.F.S.R. and mem. Bureau 1959-61; mem. Cen. Cttee. CPSU 1956-76; First Sec. Cheliabinsk District Cttee., CPSU 1961-62; First Sec. Gorsky District Cttee., CPSU and mem. Bureau of Cen. Cttee. of CPSU for R.S.F.S.R. 1962-65; Deputy Chair. U.S.S.R. Council of Ministers 1965-71; Amb. to German Democratic Repub. 1971-75; Deputy to U.S.S.R. Supreme Soviet 1954-; Amb. to Austria 1975-86; Order of Lenin (three times) and other decorations. *Address:* Embassy of the U.S.S.R., Reisnerstrasse 45-47, Vienna, Austria.

YEFREMOV, Olyeg Nikolayevich; Soviet actor and director; b. 1 Oct. 1927, Moscow; ed. Moscow Arts Theatre Studio; Studio School of Moscow Art Theatres 1945-49; Actor and producer at Cen. Children's Theatre 1949-56; Chief Producer Sovremennik Theatre 1956-70; Chief Stage Man. Moscow Art Theatre 1970-; has produced many plays at Sovremennik Theatre; film work 1955-; Merited Art Worker of R.S.F.S.R. 1957, R.S.F.S.R. People's Actor 1969, U.S.S.R. State Prize 1969. *Address:* Moscow Art Theatre, Proezd Khudozhestvennogò Teatra 3, Moscow, U.S.S.R.

YEGOROV, Anatoliy Grigoryevich, DR. PHIL. SC.; Soviet academic and political scientist; b. 1920; ed. Moscow Pedagogical Inst.; active service in Soviet Army 1942-46; mem. CPSU 1944-; teacher, Vladivostok Teachers' Training Coll. 1946-52; consultant, Deputy Ed., Chief Ed. Kommunist 1952-56; Ed.-in-Chief of journal Political Self-Education 1956-61; work with CPSU Cen. Cttee. 1961-65; corresp. mem. of U.S.S.R. Acad. of Sciences 1962, mem. 1974-; Ed.-in-Chief of Kommunist 1965-74; Dir. of Inst. of World Literature, CPSU Cen. Cttee. 1974-87; Academic Sec. of Philosophy and Law Div. of U.S.S.R. Acad. of Sciences 1987-; mem. of CPSU Cen. Cttee. 1986-89. *Address:* U.S.S.R. Academy of Sciences, Leninsky Prospekt 49, Moscow, U.S.S.R.

YEGOROV, Adm. Georgiy Mikhailovich; Soviet naval officer; b. 30 Oct. 1918, Mestnovo, Leningrad Oblast; joined CPSU 1942; served in navy 1936-; graduated from Frunze Naval Coll. 1940, Naval Acad. 1959; Navigation officer, aide to Commdr. 1941-44; submarine commdr. Baltic Fleet 1944, Pacific Fleet 1950-59; Commdr. of submarine unit, Northern Fleet 1959-63; Chief of Staff of Fleet 1963-67; Deputy C.-in-C. of Navy Jan. 1967-; Commdr. of Northern Fleet 1972-77; rank of Adm. 1973; First Deputy C.-in-C., Soviet Navy July 1977-; Cand. mem. CPSU Cen. Cttee. 1976-89; Deputy to Supreme Soviet 1974-; mem. Pres. of Supreme Soviet of U.S.S.R. 1984-; Order of Lenin, Order of the October Revolution, Order of Red Flag (three times) and other decorations. *Address:* c/o Ministry of Defence, Moscow, U.S.S.R.

YEGOROV, Mikhail Vasilevich; Soviet politician; b. 17 Jan. 1907, Gatchina, Leningrad Oblast; ed. Dzerzhinsky Higher School for Naval Engineering; mem. CPSU 1938-, mem. Cen. Cttee. 1981-; ship mechanic until 1939; Head and Chief Engineer in several administrative posts, Ministry of Shipbuilding, Deputy Minister 1939-58, First Deputy Chairman, State Cttee. for Shipbuilding, Council of Ministers, 1958-1976; Deputy U.S.S.R. Supreme Soviet 1974-; Minister of Shipbuilding 1976-84; Order of Lenin (five times), Hero of Socialist Labour 1963, Order of October Revolution and other decorations. *Address:* c/o Ministry of Shipbuilding, Moscow, U.S.S.R.

YELCHENKO, Yuri Nikiforovich; Soviet politician; b. 1929; ed. Kiev Polytechnic Inst.; technician sec. of party cttee. at machine-construction plant 1952-55; mem. CPSU 1953-; Head of Section of Zhovtnevo Regional Cttee. of Ukrainian CP 1955-57; Sec., Second Sec. of Kiev City Cttee. Komsomol 1957-58; Sec., Second, First Sec. of Cen. Cttee. of Ukrainian Komsomol 1958-68; work for Cen. Cttee. of Ukrainian CP 1968-69; Second Sec. of Lvov Dist. Cttee. of Ukrainian CP 1969-71; Minister of Culture for Ukraine 1971-73; Head of Section of Cen. Cttee. of Ukrainian CP 1973-80; First Sec. of Kiev City Cttee. 1980-87; mem. of CPSU Cen. Cttee. 1986-; Sec. of Cen. Cttee. of Ukrainian CP 1987-; Deputy to U.S.S.R. Supreme Soviet. *Address:* Kiev City Committee of Ukrainian Communist Party, Kiev, Ukrainian S.S.R., U.S.S.R.

YELISEYEV, Georgiy Ivanovich; Soviet sports administrator; b. 1913; ed. Leningrad Builders' School and Leningrad Inst. of Physical Culture; Technician, then building engineer 1935-37; Chief Training Sports Dept., then Asst. Chair. Regional Council Sporting Soc. Burevestnik, Leningrad 1937-39; mem. CPSU 1944; engineer for sporting constructions, Regional Council Sporting Soc. Burevestnik, Leningrad 1947-49; Chair. Central Council Sporting Soc. Burevestnik 1949-53, 1955-56, 1962-; Section Chief of Physical Culture and Sports Dept. of U.S.S.R. Central Council of Trade Unions 1953-55, Chief 1956-61; Pres. U.S.S.R. Council Voluntary Sporting Socs. of Trade Unions 1961-; Deputy Pres. Central Council U.S.S.R. Union of Sporting Socs. and Orgs. 1965-; U.S.S.R. Cttee. for Sports and Physical Culture 1968-; Order of Red Banner (twice), Alexander Nevsky, Great Patriotic War, Red Star, Red Banner of Labour. *Address:* 4 Skatertny pereulok, Moscow, U.S.S.R.

YELTSIN, Boris Nikolayevich; Soviet politician; b. 1 Feb. 1931, Sverdlovsk; ed. Urals Polytech. Inst.; construction-worker with various orgs. in Sverdlovsk Dist. 1955-68; mem. CPSU 1961; party work 1968-; First Sec. Sverdlovsk Dist. Cen. Cttee. CPSU 1976-; Deputy to Supreme Soviet of U.S.S.R.; Sec. of Cen. Cttee. CPSU 1985-86; First Sec. of Moscow City Party Cttee. 1985-87; First Deputy Chair. State Cttee. for Construction Nov. 1987-; elected to Congress of People's Deputies of the U.S.S.R. 1989. *Address:* The Kremlin, Moscow, U.S.S.R.

YEMEN, former King of (see Saif al-Islam, Mohammed al-Badr).

YEMOKHONOV, Nikolay Pavlovich, Gen., DR. TECH. SC.; Soviet politician and army officer; b. 1921; ed. Mil. Acad.; active service with Soviet Army 1939-45; mem. CPSU 1947-; engineer, sr. engineer, Dir. of Inst. 1952-68; man., Deputy Pres., First Deputy Pres. 1968-84; Chief of KGB 1984-88; Army Gen. 1985; Deputy to U.S.S.R. Supreme Soviet; mem. of CPSU Cen. Cttee. 1986; U.S.S.R. State Prize 1972, Lenin Prize 1976. *Address:* The Kremlin, Moscow, U.S.S.R.

YEN CHEN-HSING, PH.D.; Chinese government official; b. 10 July 1912, Junan Co., Honan; m. Sou-lien Yen; two s. one d.; ed. Nat. Tsinghua Univ. and Univ. of Iowa; Prof. Nat. Tsinghua Univ. 1941-46; Dean, Coll. of Eng., Nat. Honan Univ. 1947-48; Chief Eng. Kaohsiung Habor Bureau 1949-57; Dean, Coll. of Eng. Nat. Taiwan Univ. 1953-55; Commr. Dept. of Educ. Taiwan Provincial Govt. 1962-63; Pres. Nat. Chengkung Univ. 1957-65; Minister of Educ. 1965-69; Chair. Nat. Youth Comm., Exec. Yuan 1966-70; Pres. Chungshan Inst. 1969-75, Nat. Tsinghua Univ. 1969-70, Nat. Taiwan Univ. 1970-81, Hon. Prof. 1981-; Chair. Atomic Energy Council, Exec. Yuan 1981-; mem. Acad. Sinica 1982-. *Publications:* numerous publs. on construction. *Address:* Atomic Energy Council, 67 Lane 144, Keelung Road, Sec. 4, Taipei; 3, Lane 11, Chingtien Street, Taipei, Taiwan.

YEN CHIA-KAN, B.SC.; Chinese politician; b. 23 Oct. 1905; s. of Yen Yang-ho and Yen Wan Hsiang-ying; m. C. S. Liu 1924; five s. four d.; ed. St. John's Univ., Shanghai; various govt. posts including Commr. of Reconstruction, Fukien (now Fujian) Prov. Govt. 1938-39, Finance Commr. Fukien (now Fujian) Prov., Chair. Fukien Prov. Bank 1939-45; Dir. of Procurement, War Production Bd. 1945; Communications Commr., Taiwan Prov. Govt. 1945-46, Finance Commr. 1946-49; Chair. Bank of Taiwan 1946-49; Minister of Econ. Affairs, Republic of China (Taiwan) 1950, of Finance 1950-54, 1958-63; Vice-Chair. Council for U.S. Aid 1950; Gov. of Taiwan 1954-57; Minister without Portfolio 1957-58; Chair. Council for U.S. Aid 1957-58; Pres. Exec. Yuan (Prime Minister) 1963-72; Chair. Council for Int. Econ. Co-operation and Devt. 1963-69; Vice-Pres. of Taiwan 1966-75, Pres. 1975-78; Hon. LL.D. (Nat. Seoul Univ., Korea, Chinese Culture Univ., Taiwan), Hon. D.Pol. (Nat. Chulalongkorn Univ., Thailand) 1968, Hon. Litt.D. (Soochow Univ., Taiwan) 1980; numerous foreign decorations. *Leisure interests:* music, photography. *Address:* 4 Chungking South Road, Sect. 2, Taipei, Taiwan (Home).

YENDO, Masayoshi, B.SC.(ARCH); Japanese architect; b. 30 Nov. 1920, Yokohama; s. of Masanao Yendo and Ima Nakamura; m. Fumi Matsuzaki 1956; two s.; ed. Waseda Univ.; Murano Architect Office 1946-49; Pres. M. Yendo Associated Architects and Engineers 1952-; Dir. Bd., Japan Architects Asscn. 1971-, Pres. 1981-86; Hon. Fellow American Inst. of Architects 1987; Geijutsu Sensyo (Art Commendation Award) 1965; Architectural Inst. of Japan Award 1965; *Buildings include:* Keio Terminal and Dept. Store Building 1960, Resort Hotel Kasyóen 1962, Yamaguchi Bank Head Office 1962, Coca-Cola (Japan) Head Office 1968, Yakult Co. Ltd. Head Office 1970, Tokyo American Club 1971, Heibon-sha Co. Head Office 1972, Taiyo Fishery Co. Ltd. Head Office 1973, Seiyu Store Kasugai Shopping Centre 1975. *Leisure interest:* golf. *Address:* M. Yendo Associated Architects and Engineers, Nakajima Building, 5-6, Ginza 8-chome, Chuo-ku, Tokyo 104, Japan.

YENNIMATAS, Georgios; Greek civil engineer and politician; b. 1939, Athens; m.; two d.; ed. Nat. Tech. Univ., Athens; active in Liberal youth orgs. and ONEK from 1956; mem. Council, Athens Soc. of Civil Engs. 1966-67; Pres. Greek Soc. of Civil Engs. 1974-78; Head, Dept. of Industrial Studies, Agric. Bank of Greece; mem. Cen. Cttee. and Exec. Office, Panhellenic Socialist Movement 1977-; Minister of the Interior 1981-83, of Health, Welfare and Social Services -1987, of Labour June 1988-. *Address:* Ministry of Labour, Odos Pireos 40, Athens, Greece. *Telephone:* (01) 5233110.

YENTOB, Alan, LL.B.; British television administrator; b. 11 March 1947; s. of Isaac Yentob and Flora Yentob (née Khazam); ed. King's School, Ely, Univ. of Grenoble, France, Univ. of Leeds; BBC gen. trainee 1968, Producer/Dir. 1970-, Head of Music and Arts, BBC-TV 1985-88, Controller, BBC2 1988-; mem. Bd. of Dirs. Riverside Studios 1984-, British Film Inst. Production Bd. 1985-. *Leisure interests:* swimming, books. *Address:* 99 Blenheim Crescent, London, W.11, England.

YEO CHEOW TONG, B.ENG.; Singapore politician; b. 1947; m.; two d.; ed. Anglo-Chinese School, Univ. of Western Australia; worked in Econ. Devt. Bd. 1972-75; joined LeBlond Makino Asia Pte. Ltd. (LMA) as Staff Engineer 1975, subsequently promoted to Eng. Man., then Operations Dir.; Man. Dir. LMA and subsidiary co., Pacific Precision Castings (Pte.) Ltd. (PPC) 1981-85; elected M.P. for Hong Kah 1984; Minister of State

for Health and Foreign Affairs 1985-87; Acting Minister for Health, Sr. Minister of State for Foreign Affairs 1987-. *Address:* Ministry of Health, College of Medicine Building, 16 College Road, Singapore 0316. *Telephone:* 2237777.

YEO NING HONG, C.CHEM. F.R.S.C., PH.D.; Singapore politician and scientist; b. 3 Nov 1943, Singapore; m.; two d.; ed. Univs. of Singapore, Stanford, U.S.A., Cambridge, London Business School, England; Research Assoc. Stanford Univ. 1970-71; Fellow Christ's Coll., Univ. of Cambridge 1970-73; Lecturer Univ. (now Nat. Univ.) of Singapore 1971-74; various managerial positions with pharmaceutical cos. 1974-81; M.P. for Kim Seng 1980-; Minister of State for Defence 1981-85, Acting Minister for Communications 1983-85, Minister of Communications and Information (and Second Minister of Defence) May 1985-; mem. British Inst. of Man. 1977; Fellow Singapore Nat. Inst. of Chem. 1978; Memorial Medal Royal Inst. of Chem. 1966; Charles Darwin Memorial Prize for Natural Sciences 1970. *Publications:* over 25 research papers in int. scientific journals; founding Ed. Singapore Nat. Inst. of Chem. Bulletin 1972-74. *Leisure interests:* sailing, golf, jogging. *Address:* Ministry of Communications, PSA Building, No 39-00, 460 Alexandra Road, Singapore 0511. *Telephone:* 2799700.

YERBY, Frank Garvin; American novelist; b. 5 Sept. 1916, Augusta, Ga.; s. of Rufus and Wilhelmina Yerby; m. 2nd Blanca Calle Pérez 1956; two s. two d. (from previous m.); ed. Paine Coll., Fisk Univ. and Univ. of Chicago; Teacher, Florida Agricultural and Mechanical Coll. 1939, Southern Univ. 1940-41; Lab. Technician, Ford Motor Co., Detroit 1941-44, Ranger Aircraft, New York 1944-45; writer 1944-; O. Henry Award for Short Story 1944. *Publications:* The Foxes of Harrow 1946, The Vixens 1947, The Golden Hawk 1948, Pride's Castle 1949, Flood Tide 1950, A Woman Called Fancy 1951, The Saracen Blade 1952, The Devil's Laughter 1953, Benton's Row 1954, The Treasure of Pleasant Valley 1955, Captain Rebel 1956, Fairoaks 1957, The Serpent and the Staff 1958, Jarrett's Jade 1959, Gillian 1960, The Garfield Honor 1961, Griffin's Way 1962, The Old Gods Laugh 1964, An Odour of Sanctity 1966, Goat Song 1967, Judas, My Brother 1968, Speak Now 1969, The Dahomean 1971, The Girl from Storyville 1972, The Voyage Unplanned 1974, Tobias and the Angel 1975, A Rose for Ana Maria 1976, Hail the Conquering Hero 1978, A Darkness at Ingraham's Crest 1979, Western, A Saga of the Great Plains 1982, Devilseed 1984, McKenzie's Hundred 1985. *Leisure interests:* photography, electronics, painting. *Address:* c/o William Morris Agency, 1350 Avenue of the Americas, New York, N.Y. 10019, U.S.A.; Edificio Torres Blancas, Avenida de América 37, Madrid 2, Spain.

YERMAKOVA, Valentina Aleksandrovna; Soviet actress; b. 1924, Saratov; mem. CPSU 1971-; studied drama studio of Saratov TYUZ (Youth Theatre); worked with Gorky Theatre, Tashkent 1955-56; with Gorky Theatre Volgograd 1956-60; with Karl Marx Theatre, Saratov 1960-; People's Artist of R.S.F.S.R. 1973, People's Artist of U.S.S.R. 1981. *Address:* Karl Marx Theatre, Saratov, U.S.S.R.

YERMIN, Lev Borisovich, CAND.ECON.SC.; Soviet politician; b. 1923; ed. Azov-Black Sea Agric. Inst.; mem. CPSU 1943-; Soviet Army 1941-47; chief agronomist, Sec. of Veselovsky Regional Cttee., First Sec. of Razdorsky Regional Cttee. (Rostov Dist.) 1952-59; work for CPSU Cen. Cttee. 1959-61; First Sec. of Penza Dist. Cttee. 1961-79; First Deputy Pres. of R.S.F.S.R. Council of Mins., concurrently Pres. of R.S.F.S.R. State Agro-Industrial Cttee. 1979-85; mem. of CPSU Cen. Cttee. 1971-89; Deputy to U.S.S.R. Supreme Soviet. *Address:* The Kremlin, Moscow, U.S.S.R.

YEROFEYEV, Benedikt; Russian writer; b. 1938, Vladimir; ed. Moscow Univ., Vladimir Pedagogical Inst.; various jobs, including manual work, since 1965. *Works (mainly samizdat) include:* Notes of a Psychopath 1956-57, Moskva-Petushki (Moscow to the End of the Road) 1969 (French trans. 1976, German 1978, English 1980), Vasilii Rozanov through the Eyes of an Eccentric 1973.

YEUTTER, Clayton K.; American government official; b. 10 Dec. 1930, Eustis, Neb.; m. Jeanne Vierk; two s. two d.; ed. Univ. of Nebraska; served U.S.A.F. 1952-57; ran family farm from 1957; law degree, Univ. of Neb. 1963, agricultural econs. degree 1966, subsequently Prof., Dir. Agricultural and Tech. Assistance Programme in Bogotá, Colombia 1968-70; Asst. Sec. of Agric. in charge of Int. Affairs and Commodity Programs, U.S. Govt. 1970-75; Deputy Special Trade Rep. 1975-77, U.S. Trade Rep. 1985-88; Sec. of State for Agric. 1989-; Pres. Chicago Mercantile Exchange 1978-85. *Address:* Department of Agriculture, 14th St and Independence Avenue, S.W., Washington, D.C. 20250, U.S.A. *Telephone:* (202) 655-4000.

YEVSTIGNEYEV, Yevgeny Aleksandrovich; Soviet theatre and film actor; b. 1926, Gorky; ed. Gorky Theatre School, Nemirovich-Danchenko Studio School of Moscow Arts Theatre, Moscow (under Massalsky); mem. CPSU 1960-; started work as actor with the Lunacharsky Theatre, Vladimir 1951-57; actor with Sovremennik Theatre, Moscow (major roles: Satin in Gorky's Lower Depths, the King in Shvarts's Naked King) 1957-70; with Moscow Arts Theatre 1970-; State Prize 1974; acted in films since 1957; teacher at Moscow Arts Theatre 1975, Prof. 1983-; People's Artist of U.S.S.R. 1983. *Address:* c/o Moscow Arts Theatre, Moscow, U.S.S.R.

YEVTUSHENKO, Yevgeniy Aleksandrovich; Soviet poet; b. 18 July 1933, Zima, Irkutsk Region; m. 1st Bella Akhmadulina 1954; m. 2nd Galina

Semionova; m. 3rd Jan Butler 1978; one s.; m. 4th Maria Novikova 1986; ed. Moscow Literary Inst.; Geological expeditions with father to Kazakhstan 1948, the Altai 1950; literary work 1949-; visits to France, Africa, U.S.A., Cuba, U.K., Germany; mem. Editorial Bd. of Yunost magazine; elected to Congress of People's Deputies of the U.S.S.R. May 1989; U.S.S.R. Cttee. for Defence of Peace Award 1965, Order of Red Banner of Labour (twice), U.S.S.R. State Prize 1984. *Publications:* verse: Scouts of the Future (collected verse) 1952, The Third Snow (lyric verse) 1955, The Highway of Enthusiasts 1956, Zima Junction 1956, The Promise (collected verse) 1959, Conversation with a Count, Moscow Goods Station, At the Skorokhod Plant, The Nihilist, The Apple 1960-61, A Sweep of the Arm 1962, Tenderness 1962, A Precocious Autobiography 1963, Cashier, Woman, Mother, On the Banks of the Dnieper River, A Woman and A Girl, Do the Russians Want War?, Bratskaya Hydro-Electric Power Station 1965, A Boat of Communication 1966, Poems Chosen by the Author 1966, Collection of Verses 1967, That's What Is Happening to Me 1968, It's Snowing White 1969, Kazan University 1971, I am of Siberian Stock 1971, The Singing Domba 1972, Stolen Apples 1972, Under the Skin of the Statue of Liberty (play) 1972, Intimate Lyrics 1973, A Father's Hearing 1976, From Desire to Desire 1976, Love Poems 1977, People of the Morning 1978, Heavy Soils 1978, Winter Station 1978, Selected Works 1979, The Face Behind the Face 1979, Ivan the Terrible and Ivan the Fool 1979, Berries (novel) 1981, Ardabiola (short story) 1981, Almost At the End (prose and verse) 1987, A Wind of Tomorrow (essays) 1987; acted in Ascent (film on Tsiolkovsky) 1979; dir. Kindergarten 1984. *Address:* Union of U.S.S.R. Writers, ul. Vorovskogo 52, Moscow; Moskovskaya Oblast, Gogolia 1, 142783 Moscow, U.S.S.R.

YEXI DANZENG; Chinese writer; b. 1943, Tibet (now Xizang Autonomous Region); ed. Cen. Inst. for Nationalities, Beijing. *Publication:* Survival. *Address:* People's Republic of China.

YEZHEVSKY, Aleksandr Aleksandrovich; Soviet party official; b. 1915, Tulun, Irkutsk Province; ed. Workers' Faculty and Faculty for Mechanization of Agric., Irkutsk Agricultural Inst.; engaged in teaching and research there 1939-42; Dir. various factories in Siberia 1942-54; U.S.S.R. Deputy Minister of Tractor and Agricultural Machine Building 1954-56, First Deputy 1956-62, Minister 1983-; Chair. Automobile, Tractors and Machine Dept., State Planning Cttee. 1954-62; Chair. Agricultural Machinery Trust 1962-78; mem. U.S.S.R. Supreme Soviet 1966-; cand. mem. Cen. Cttee. of CPSU 1966-71, mem. 1971-; Order of Lenin and other awards. *Address:* The Kremlin, Moscow, U.S.S.R.

YEZHOV, Valentin Ivanovich; Soviet screenplay writer; b. 21 Jan. 1921, Kuibyshev; m.; one s.; ed. All-Union State Inst. of Cinematography; mem. CPSU 1951-; Lenin Prize 1961 for script of Ballad of a Soldier 1959; co-author scripts for Our Champions 1954, World Champion 1955, Liana 1956, A Man from the Planet Earth 1958, The House of Gold 1959, The Volga Flows 1962, Wings 1966, Thirty Three 1967, White Sun of the Desert 1969, A Nest of Gentry 1969, The Legend 1971, This Sweet Word Liberty 1973, Eleven Hopefuls 1974, Siberiade 1977, Meadow Flowers 1981, The Girl and the Grand 1982, Alexander the Small 1982. *Address:* U.S.S.R. State Cinema Committee, Maly Gnezdnikovsky st., 7, Moscow, U.S.S.R.

YHAP, Laetitia, D.F.A.; British artist; b. 1 May 1941, St. Albans; d. of Leslie Neville and Elizabeth (née Kogler) Yhap; one s.; ed. Camberwell School of Arts and Crafts, Slade School of Fine Art, Univ. Coll. London; Artist-in-Residence Chatham House Grammar School, Ramsgate 1981; numerous one-woman exhbns. 1965-; works in public collections in U.K.; John Moores Prize 1973. *Leisure interests:* music, attending concerts, playing badminton. *Address:* 12 The Croft, Hastings, Sussex, TN34 3HH, England. *Telephone:* (0424) 426222.

YHOMBI-OPANGO, Brig.-Gen. Joachim; Congolese army officer and Head of State; b. 1939; trained in French army; fmr. military attaché at Congolese Embassy, Moscow; Chief of Staff, People's National Army 1968-73, Insp.-Gen. 1973-74; Sec.-Gen. of Council of State with rank of Minister 1974-75, Council of State Delegate responsible for Defence and Security 1974-75; Pres. of Republic, Pres. Council of Ministers, Pres. Mil. Council of Congolese Labour Party 1977-79; arrested 1979, detained 1979-84, released from detention Nov. 1984, rearrested Sept. 1987; Order of Nat. Flag (North Korea) 1978. *Address:* c/o Comité Militaire du Parti Congolais du Travail, Brazzaville, Congo.

YI MEIHOU; Chinese government official; b. 1910, Chenghai Co., Guangdong Prov.; Vice-Chair. Chinese Overseas Welfare Soc., Thailand 1945; Overseas Chinese Del. to CPPCC 1945-49; Chair. Guangdong Fed. of Returned Overseas Chinese 1952-68; Exec. Commr. All-China Fed. of Industry and Commerce 1953-56; Vice-Pres. S. China Region Overseas Chinese Investment Co. 1955; Pres. 3rd Guangdong People's Congress 1963; purged 1967; rehabilitated 1972; Guangdong Deputy to 5th NPC 1978; mem. Standing Cttee. CPPCC 1987-; Vice-Chair. Standing Cttee., Guangdong Prov. People's Congress 1979-; Vice-Chair. All-China Fed. of Returned Overseas Chinese 1978-. *Address:* Chinese People's Political Consultative Conference, Beijing, People's Republic of China.

YIANNOPOULOS, Evangelos; Greek politician; b. 1918, Gortynia, Peloponnese; m. Konstantina Yiannopoulou 1954; one s. one d.; served as officer in Albanian war (wounded) and later in Greek resistance movement in

World War II as bn. commdr. in Greek Popular Liberation Army; mem. Nat. Progressive Centre Union; joined Centre Union youth org., Centre Union Party 1960; arrested and deported to remote area 1969, rearrested and imprisoned for political activities 1970; founding mem. Panhellenic Socialist Movement (PASOK); also mem. Cen. Cttee.; Pres. Athens Lawyer's Assen. 1976-81; mem. Gov. Council, Inst. of Int. and Alien Law; Minister of Labour 1981-85, 1985-86, of Merchant Marine 1987-89, of the Aegean March 1989-. *Address:* c/o Ministry of Merchant Marine, Odos Vassilissis Sophias 150, Piraeus; Panepistimiou 34, Athens, Greece (Home). *Telephone:* 361 7779 (Home).

YILMAZ, A. Mesut; Turkish politician; b. 6 Nov. 1947, Istanbul; s. of Hasan Yilmaz and Güzide Yilmaz; m. Berna Müren; two s.; ed. Istanbul High School for Boys, Faculty of Political Studies, Ankara and in London and Cologne; fmr. company dir. in pvt. business sector; Deputy for Rize 1983-; fmr. Minister of State; Minister of Culture and Tourism 1986-87, of Foreign Affairs Dec. 1987-; mem. Motherland Party. *Address:* Ministry of Foreign Affairs, Disisleri Bakanliği, Bakanliklar, Ankara, Turkey. *Telephone:* (4) 134 2920.

YIN CHANGMIN; Chinese party and state official; b. Sept. 1923, Nanchang, Jiangxi Prov.; d. of Yin Renqing; m. Bei Xiaoliang; two s.; alt. mem. 12th CCP Cen. Cttee. 1982, mem. 1986; alt. mem. 13th CCP Cen. Cttee. 1987; Prof. Hunan Normal Univ. 1979, Vice-Pres. 1973, Pres. 1981, Consultant 1985; Vice-Chair. CPPCC Prov. Cttee., Hunan 1985-; mem. CCP Cttee., Hunan 1983-85; Vice-Chair. Hunan Branch Assen. for Science and Tech. 1980-86, Hon. Chair. 1986; mem. Bd. of Dirs., Chinese Zoological Soc. 1984; Chair. Bd. of Dirs. Biology Soc. and Zoological Soc. 1981-. *Leisure interest:* literature. *Address:* Hunan Committee of Chinese People's Political Consultative Conference, Changsha, Hunan Province, People's Republic of China. *Telephone:* 26523.

YIN FATANG; Chinese politician; b. 1922, Shandong; Head Political Dept., PLA Jinan Units 1975-80; Acting First Sec., CCP Xizang Autonomous Regional Cttee. 1980, Chair. 1981-83; First Political Commissar, PLA Xizang Mil. Area Command 1980-85; Acting First Sec. Xizang CCP, First Sec. 1982-85; Deputy Political Commissar PLA Chengdu Mil. Region 1982-85; mem. 12th Cen. CCP Cttee. 1982-87; Deputy from Tibet to 6th NPC 1983; Deputy Political Commissar, Air Force Hosp., Fuzhou 1985. *Address:* Air Force Hospital, Fuzhou, People's Republic of China.

YIN JUN; Chinese party official; b. Sept. 1932; alt. mem. 12th CCP Cen. Cttee. 1982; Chair. and Gov., Dali Bai Autonomous Pref., Yunnan Prov. 1982-; Sec. Discipline Inspection Cttee., Yunnan CCP Prov. Cttee. 1985-; alt. mem. 13th CCP Cen. Cttee. 1987-. *Address:* Dali Bai Autonomous Prefectural People's Government, Yunnan, People's Republic of China.

YIN KESHENG; Chinese party official; b. 1932; ed. Beijing Petroleum Inst.; Vice-Gov., Qinghai 1983; Sec. CCP Cttee., Qinghai 1985-; mem. 12th CCP Cen. Cttee. 1985-. *Address:* Qinghai Provincial Chinese Communist Party, Xining, Qinghai, People's Republic of China.

YIN YUAN; Chinese party official; Man. Anshan Iron and Steel Co.; mem. 12th CCP Cen. Cttee. 1982-87; Sec. CCP Cttee., Anshan City 1983-. *Address:* Anshan Municipal Chinese Communist Party, Anshan, Liaoning, People's Republic of China.

YING RUOCHENG; Chinese actor and politician; b. 21 June 1929, Beijing; s. of Chienli Ignatius Ying and Baozhen Ying; m. Wu Shiliang 1950 (deceased); two c.; Man. People's Art Theatre, Peking; Vice-Minister of Culture July 1986-; has appeared in numerous plays including Chinese version of Death of a Salesman; *films include:* Dr Bethune, Measure for Measure, Intimate Friends, Teahouse, The Last Emperor 1987. *Address:* Ministry of Culture, Donganmen North Street, Beijing; 10 Qianchang Hutong, East City, Beijing, People's Republic of China (Home).

YODER, Hatten Schuyler, Jr., PH.D.; American petrologist; b. 20 March 1921, Cleveland, Ohio; s. of Hatten Schuyler Yoder and Elizabeth Katherine (née Knieling); m. Elizabeth Marie Bruffey 1959; one s. one d.; ed. Univs. of Chicago and Minnesota and M.I.T.; active duty, U.S. Naval Reserve 1942-46, MOKO expedition to Siberia 1945-46, Lieut.-Commdr., retd.; Petrologist, Geophysical Lab., Carnegie Inst. of Washington 1948-, Dir. 1971-86, Dir. Emer. 1986-; mem. Editorial Bd. Geochimica et Cosmochimica 1958-68; N. American Ed., Journal of Petrology 1959-68, Hon. mem. Advisory Bd. 1968-79; Assoc. Ed. American Journal of Science 1972-; Consultant Los Alamos Nat. Lab. 1971-; Visiting Prof. of Geochemistry, Calif. Inst. of Tech. 1958, Visiting Prof. of Petrology, Univ. of Tex. 1964, Univ. of Colo. 1966, Univ. of Cape Town 1967; new mineral, Yoderite named in his honour; Participant, Nobel Symposium, Royal Swedish Acad. of Sciences 1979; Fellow, Mineralogical Soc. of America (mem. Council 1962-64, Vice-Pres. 1970-71, Pres. 1971-72), Geological Soc. of America (mem. Council 1966-68), American Geophysical Union (Pres. Volcanology, Geochemistry and Petrology Section 1961-64, mem. Council 1965-68); mem. N.A.S. 1958- (Geology Section Chair. 1973-76); mem. U.S. Nat. Cttee. for Geology 1973-76, for Geochemistry 1973-76, on the history of Geology 1982-(90), American Philosophical Soc. 1979, (Council 1983-85), Geochemical Soc. (Organizing and Founding mem., Council 1956-58); Hon. mem. Mineralogical Soc. of Great Britain 1983-; Hon. mem. All-Union Mineralogical Soc. of U.S.S.R. 1977-, Soc. Française de Minéralogie et de Cristallographie

1986–; Fellow, American Acad. of Arts and Sciences 1979, Geological Soc. of S.A. 1988–; Corresp. Fellow, Edinburgh Geological Soc.; Fellow, Explorers Club, New York 1979; Dr. h.c. (Univ. of Paris VI) 1981; Mineralogical Soc. of America Award 1954, Columbia Univ. Bicentennial Medal 1954, Arthur L. Day Medal of Geological Soc. of America 1962, A. L. Day Prize and Lectureship of Nat. Acad. of Sciences 1972, A. G. Werner Medal of German Mineralogical Soc. 1972, Golden Plate, American Acad. of Achievement 1976, Wollaston Medal, Geological Soc. of London 1979. *Publications:* Principal papers: The Jadeite Problem (American Journal of Science Vol. 248) 1950, High-low Quartz Inversion up to 10,000 Bars (Transactions of American Geophysical Union Vol. 31) 1950, The MgO—Al_2O_3—SiO_2—H_2O System and Related Metamorphic Facies (American Journal of Science Bowen Volume) 1952, Role of Water in Metamorphism (Geological Soc. of America Special Paper No. 62) 1955, Experimental and Theoretical Studies of the Mica Polymorphs (with J. V. Smith, Mineral Magazine Vol. 31) 1956, Origin of Basalt Magmas: an Experimental Study of Natural and Synthetic Rock Systems (with C. E. Tilley, Journal of Petrology Vol. 3 1962), Contemporaneous Basaltic and Rhyolitic Magmas (American Mineralogist, Vol. 58) 1973–, Basic Magma Generation and Aggregation (Bulletin volcanologique, Vol. 41) 1978; Book: Generation of Basaltic Magma 1976, The Evolution of the Igneous Rocks: Fiftieth Anniversary Perspectives (editor) 1979. *Leisure interests:* camping, trombone, rifle and pistol marksmanship, gardening, philately, genealogy. *Address:* Geophysical Laboratory, Carnegie Institution of Washington, Washington, D.C. 20008, U.S.A. *Telephone:* (202) 966-0334.

YOKOTE, Kohsuke; Japanese banker; b. 24 March 1931, Akita Pref.; m. Takako Sato 1962; one s. two d.; ed. Tohoku Univ.; joined The Kyowa Bank Ltd. 1953, Chief Man. Nara Branch 1969, Gen. Man. L.A. Agency 1974, Planning Div. 1976, Personnel Div. 1979, Dir. and Gen. Man. Personnel Div. 1981, Man. Dir. Int. Banking HQ 1982, Sr. Man. Dir. Branch Banking HQ 1984, Deputy Pres. Branch Banking HQ 1985; Pres. The Kyowa Bank Ltd. 1986–. *Leisure interests:* appreciation of pictures, golf, reading. *Address:* Kyowa Bank Ltd., 1-2, Ohtemachi 1-chome, Chiyoda-ku, Tokyo 100; 6-31-11 Misaki, Funabashi-shi, Chiba Prefecture, Japan. *Telephone:* 0474-49-2813.

YON, Hyong Muk; Korean politician; b. c. 1923; Vice-Premier and Minister of Metals and Machinery 1985–86; Prime Minister of Democratic People's Repub. of Korea Dec. 1988–; Sec. Korean Workers Party 1986; mem. Political Bureau, Cen. Cttee. of Korean Workers' Party Dec. 1986–. *Address:* Office of the Prime Minister, Pyongyang, Democratic Republic of Korea.

YONDON, Daramyn; Mongolian diplomatist; b. 10 Feb. 1927; ed. Mongolian State Univ.; Cen. Cttee. official, Mongolian People's Revolutionary Party (MPRP) 1949–59; Asst. of First Sec. of MPRP Cen. Cttee.; Asst. to Chair. Council of Ministers 1959–69; Deputy Minister of Foreign Affairs 1970–72, First Deputy Minister 1972–; mem. Cen. Cttee. of MPRP 1976–. *Address:* c/o Minister of Foreign Affairs, Ulan Bator, Mongolia.

YONG KUET TZE, Datuk Amar Stephen, LL.B.; Malaysian politician; b. 2 June 1921, Simunjan First Div. Sarawak; ed. St. Thomas' School, Kuching, Univ. of Nottingham and Lincoln's Inn, London; schoolteacher 1941; river motor launch man. 1942–45; insurance agent, shipping agent, snakeskin dealer and clerk in law firm 1946–50; called to the Bar 1953; Asst. Mark Morrison & Co. (law firm), Kuching 1954–55; Proprietor and Sr. Partner, Yong & Co. Kuching 1956–82; mem. Parl. 1963–; Deputy Chief Minister of Sarawak and State Minister of Communication and Works 1970–74; Fed. Minister of Science, Tech. and the Environment May 1982–; Chair. Sarawak United People's Party, Panlima Negara Bintang Sarawak, Datuk Amar. *Address:* Ministry of Science, Technology and the Environment, 14th Floor, MUI Plaza, Jalan P. Ramlee, Kuala Lumpur, Malaysia.

YONG NYUK LIN; Singapore politician and diplomatist; b. 24 June 1918, Seremban, Malaya; s. of the late Yong Thean Yong and Chen Shak Moi; m. Kwa Geok Lan 1939; two d.; ed. Raffles Coll.; Science master, King George V School, Seremban, Malaya 1938–41; Overseas Assurance Corpn., Singapore, rising to Gen. Man. 1941–58, resigned; Minister for Educ. 1959–63; Chair. Singapore Harbour Bd. 1961–62; Minister for Health 1963–68, for Communications 1968–75, without Portfolio 1975–76; High Commr. in U.K. 1975–76; mem. Presidential Council for Minority Rights, Singapore. *Leisure interests:* swimming, stereo music. *Address:* 50 Oei Tiong Ham Park, Singapore 1026.

YONG WENTAO; Chinese politician; b. Guizhou Prov.; Chair. Gen. Office of Econ. Planning Cttee. North-East People's Govt. (NEPG) 1949; mem. Standing Cttee. NEPG 1950–54; Sec.-Gen. NEPG 1950; Dir. Forestry Dept. NEPG 1952; mem. North-East Admin. Cttee., Vice-Chair. of its Financial and Econ. Cttee. 1953–54; Vice-Minister of Forestry 1954–56, 1958–61; Vice-Minister of Timber Industry 1956–58; Sec.-Gen. Central-South Bureau of CCP 1961–66; mem. Standing Cttee. Central-South Bureau of CCP 1963–66; Sec. Secr., CCP Guangdong Provincial Cttee. 1965–66; 1st Sec. CCP Canton Municipal Cttee. 1965–66; Sec. Secr. CCP Beijing Municipal Cttee. 1966–67; Vice-Chair. Standing Cttee. Office of Culture and Educ., State Council 1967; Dir. Cultural and Educational Political Dept. CCP Cen. Cttee. 1967; Deputy Dir. Propaganda Dept. CCP Cen. Cttee. 1966–67; criticized and removed from office during Cultural Revolu-

tion 1967; Vice-Minister of Forestry 1979–80, Minister 1980–82, Adviser 1983–; mem. Cen. Advisory Comm. 1982–; mem. Cen. Party Consolidation Guidance Comm. 1983; Pres. Forestry Economics Soc. 1980, Greening Foundation 1985–; Vice-Chair. Cen. Greening Cttee. 1983–. *Address:* c/o The State Council, Beijing, People's Republic of China.

YOO CHANG-SOON; Korean businessman and politician; b. 6 Aug. 1918, Anju, Pyongan namdo; m.; five s. one d.; ed. Hastings Coll., U.S.A.; Branch Dir. Bank of Korea, Tokyo; Head of U.S. Operations, Bank of Korea, New York 1953; Gov. Bank of Korea 1961–62; Minister of Commerce and Industry 1962–63; Chair. Econ. Planning Bd. Feb.–Dec. 1963; Chair. Lotte Confectionary Co. 1967, Counsellor 1985; Chair. Korean Traders' Asscn. 1981–82; Prime Minister, Republic of Korea Jan.–June 1982; Pres. Repub. of Korea Nat. Red Cross 1982–; Chair. UN Korean Asscn. 1981–; mem. Advisory Council on State Affairs; mem. Seoul Olympics Organizing Cttee. 1981. *Leisure interests:* golf, gardening. *Address:* 98-6 Kalwol-dong, Yongsan-ku, Seoul, Republic of Korea.

YOON SUNG MIN, Gen.; Korean army officer and politician; b. 15 Oct. 1926, Muan-kun, Cholla-namdo Prov.; m. Chung Hae Woo; two d.; ed. Korea Mil. Acad., Korea Army Coll., Nat. Defence Coll., Grad. School of Public Admin., Seoul Nat. Univ.; Regimental Commdr. 20th Infantry Div. 1964, Asst. Div. Commdr. 8th Infantry Div. 1966, apptd. Brig. Gen. and Asst. Chief of Staff for Personnel, Korea Army 1967; Chief of Staff in Viet-Nam 1968; Commanding Gen. First Field Army 1979; Chair. Jt. Chiefs of Staff 1981; Minister of Nat. Defence 1982–86; awarded Order of Nat. Security Merit, Tongil Medal; Order of Mil. Service Merit, Ulchi Medal, Chung-Mu Medal, etc. *Leisure interests:* reading, golf and tennis. *Address:* Hyundae APT 106-606, 298 Apkujong-dong, Kangnam-ku, Seoul 135, Republic of Korea. *Telephone;* 543-5100.

YORK, Herbert Frank, PH.D.; American physicist; b. 24 Nov. 1921, Rochester, N.Y.; s. of Herbert and Nellie York; m. Sybil Dunford 1947; one s. two d.; ed. Rochester and California Univs.; joined staff of Calif. Univ. Radiation Lab. 1943; attached to Y-12 Plant, Oak Ridge, Tenn. 1944–45; Univ. of Calif. Graduate School 1945–49; undertook, with Dr. Hugh Bradner, design and execution of major experiment in "Operation Greenhouse" (Eniwetok) 1950; Asst. Prof. of Physics, Univ. of Calif. 1951; headed programme, Livermore weapon devt. lab. 1952–54, Dir. 1954–58; Assoc. Dir. Univ. of Calif. Radiation Lab. 1954–58; Dir. of Research, Advanced Research Projects Div., Inst. for Defense Analyses, Chief Scientist, Dept. of Defense Advanced Research and Devt. Agency 1958; Dir. of Defence Research and Eng. 1958–61; Chancellor, Univ. of Calif. at San Diego 1961–64, 1970–72, Dean of Graduate Studies 1969–70, Dir. Program in Science, Tech. and Public Affairs 1973–88, Prof. of Physics, Univ. of Calif. 1961–; Consultant in Office of Secretary of Defense 1977–81, 1987–, in Exec. Office of Pres. 1977–81; mem. Defense Science Bd. 1978–82; Dir. Inst. on Global Conflict and Co-operation 1982–88; Amb. to Comprehensive Test Ban Negotiations 1979–81; fmr. mem. Army and Air Force Scientific Advisory Bd.; Vice-Chair. President's Science Advisory Cttee. 1965–67, mem. 1957–58, 1964–68; mem. Gen. Advisory Cttee. for Arms Control and Disarmament 1962–69; mem. President's Comm. on Mil. Compensation 1977–78; mem. Bd. of Trustees, Aerospace Corpn. 1961–, Bd. of Trustees, Inst. for Defense Analyses 1964–; mem. Bd. of Dirs., Educ. Foundation for Nuclear Science; mem. Exec. Cttee. Fed. of American Scientists 1970–75, Int. Council, Pugwash Movement 1972–76; Personal Rep. of Sec. of Defense at Anti-Satellite Arms Negotiations, Helsinki 1977, Berne 1978; mem. American Acad. of Arts and Sciences. *Publications:* Race to Oblivion 1970, Arms Control Readings 1973, The Advisors 1976, A Shield in the Sky (with David Shakoff) 1989, and various articles on physics and arms control problems. *Address:* University of California, San Diego, Q-060, La Jolla, Calif. 92093 (Office); 6110 Camino de la Costa, La Jolla, Calif., U.S.A. (Home). *Telephone:* (619) 534-3357 (Office); (619) 459-1776 (Home).

YORK, Michael (Michael York-Johnson), B.A.; British actor; b. 27 March 1942, Fulmer; s. of Joseph Gwynne and Florence Edith (neé Chown) Johnson; m. Patricia McCallum 1968; ed. Univ. Coll., Oxford; with Dundee Repertory Co. 1964, Nat. Theatre Co. 1965. *TV appearances include:* The Forsyte Saga, Rebel in the Grave, True Patriot, Much Ado About Nothing, Jesus of Nazareth, A Man Called Intrepid, For Those I Loved, The Weather in The Streets, The Master of Ballantrae, Space, The Far Country, Are You My Mother 1986, Ponce de Leon 1987, Knot's Landing 1987, The Four Minute Mile 1988, The Lady and the Highwayman 1988, The Heat of the Day 1988. *Stage appearances include:* Any Just Cause 1967, Hamlet 1970, Outcry (Broadway) 1973, Ring Round the Moon 1975, Outcry, Bent, Cyrano de Bergerac. *Films include:* The Taming of the Shrew 1966, Accident 1966, Red and Blue 1967, Smashing Time 1967, Romeo and Juliet 1967, The Strange Affair 1967, The Guru 1968, Alfred the Great 1968, Justine 1969, Something for Everyone 1969, Zeppelin 1970, La Poudre D'Escampette 1971, Cabaret 1971, England Made Me 1971, Lost Horizon 1972, The Three Musketeers 1973, Murder on the Orient Express 1974, Great Expectations 1974, Conduct Unbecoming 1974, The Four Musketeers 1975, Logan's Run 1976, Seven Nights in Japan, The Last Remake of Beau Geste 1977, The Island of Dr. Moreau 1977, Fedora 1977, The Riddle of the Sands 1978, Final Assignment 1979, Success is The Best Revenge 1984, Dawn 1985, Vengence 1986, The Secret of the Sahara 1987, Imbalances 1987, Lethal Obsession 1987, The Return of the

Musketeers 1988. *Publications:* The Courage of Conviction (contrib.) 1986, Voices of Survival (contrib.) 1987. *Address:* c/o Duncan Heath Associates, Paramount House, Wardour Street, London, W1V 3AS, England. *Telephone:* 01-439 1471.

YORK, Susannah; British actress; b. 9 Jan. 1941, London; m. Michael Wells (divorced); one s. one d.; ed. Royal Acad. of Dramatic Art; acted in films: Tunes of Glory 1960, There Was A Crooked Man 1960, The Greengage Summer 1961, Freud 1962, Tom Jones 1963, The Seventh Dawn 1964, Scene Nun—Take One 1964, Sands of the Kalahari 1965, Scruggs 1966, Kaleidoscope 1966, A Man for All Seasons 1966, Sebastian 1967, The Killing of Sister George 1968, Duffy 1968, Oh What a Lovely War 1968, The Battle of Britain, Lock up Your Daughters 1969, They Shoot Horses, Don't They? 1969, Country Dance 1970, Jane Eyre 1970, Zee and Co. 1971, Happy Birthday Wanda June 1971, Images 1972, The Maids, Gold 1974, Conduct Unbecoming 1974, That Lucky Touch 1975, Skyriders 1976, Eliza Fraser 1976, The Shout 1977, The Silent Partner, Superman II 1980, Yellowbeard, Fatal Attraction 1985, Just Ask for Diamond 1988, The Glass Menagerie 1989, Melancholia 1989; plays: Wings of a Dove, A Singular Man, A Cheap Bunch of Nice Flowers, The Maids, The Great Ban, Peter Pan 1977, Appearances 1980, The Awakening 1980, Hedda Gabler (New York) 1981, Cinderella, Agnes of God 1983, Penthisilea, The Human Voice 1984, The Apple Cart 1986, The Women 1986, Lyric for a Tango 1988, television: The Crucible, The Creditors, La Grande Breteche, Fallen Angels, Second Chance, We'll Meet Again, The Other Side of Me, Macho; producer: The Big One 1983. *Publications:* children's books: In Search of Unicorns, Lark's Castle. *Leisure interests:* reading, writing, gardening, travelling, riding, films. *Address:* c/o Jeremy Conway, 109 Jermyn Street, London, SW1Y 6HB, England.

YOSHIDA, Taroichi; Japanese international banker; b. 24 Dec. 1919, Kyoto; s. of S. and M. Yoshida; m. Mutsuko Yoshida 1946; two s.; ed. Tokyo Imperial Univ.; served Ministry of Finance, Dir. of Banking Bureau, later Vice-Minister for Int. Affairs and Special Adviser to Minister 1944–76; Chair. and Pres. Asian Devt. Bank 1976–81, Adviser, Industrial Bank of Japan 1982–; Pres. Foundation for Advanced Information and Research 1985. *Leisure interests:* painting, horticulture, wood carving. *Address:* Industrial Bank of Japan, 3-3 Marunouchi 1-chome, Chiyoda-ku, Tokyo 100, Japan.

YOSHIKI, Masao, DR. ENG.; Japanese engineer; b. 20 Jan. 1908, Nagasaki; s. of Tei and Kuni Yoshiki; m. Miyoko Kuwabara 1933; two s. four d.; ed. Univ. of Tokyo; Lecturer, School of Eng., Univ. of Tokyo 1930–32, Asst. Prof. 1932–44, Prof. of Naval Architecture 1944–68, Prof. Emer. 1968–, Dean, School of Eng. 1962–64; Chief Dir. Japan Soc. for the Promotion of Science 1968–76; Commr. Space Activities Comm. 1968–74, 1974–85; Pres. Science Univ. of Tokyo 1982–; Pres. Soc. of Naval Architects of Japan 1961–63, Japan Fed. of Eng. Socs. 1975–84, Ocean Developing Council 1980–, Council for Transportation Tech. 1983–; Vice-Pres. Science Council of Japan 1969–72, Japan Nat. Comm. for UNESCO 1976–80 (Pres. 1980–83); Chair. Int. Ship Structures Congress 1967–70; mem. Council for Science and Tech. 1974–77, Japan Acad. 1982–; Prize of Japan Acad. 1966, Purple Ribbon Decoration 1968, Fujiwara Prize 1968, Chevalier, Légion d'honneur 1977, Order of the Sacred Treasure (1st Rank), Order of Culture 1982. *Publications:* articles in journals. *Leisure interests:* golf, Japanese chess. *Address:* Science University of Tokyo, 1-3 Kagurazaka, Shinjuku-ku, 162 Tokyo; 43-14, Izumi 2-chome, Suginami-ku, Tokyo, Japan. *Telephone:* 03-581-1559 (Office); 03-328-0210 (Home).

YOSHIMURA, Junzo; Japanese architect; b. 7 Sept. 1908, Tokyo; s. of Shinzo and Tama Yoshimura; m. Takiko Ohmura 1944; one d.; ed. Tokyo Acad. of Fine Arts; at Architectural Office of Antonin Raymond 1931–42; own architectural practice 1943–; Asst. Prof. in Architecture, Tokyo Univ. of Arts 1945–61, Prof. 1962–70, Prof. Emer. 1970–; mem. Architectural Inst. of Japan, Japan Architects' Assch., Soc. de Arquitectos Mexicanos; Hon. Fellow American Inst. of Architects 1975–; Architectural Inst. Prize 1956, Parsons Medal (New York) 1956, Japanese Acad. of Arts Award 1975. *Works include:* International House of Japan, Tokyo 1955, Public Kambara Hospital 1956, The Motel on the Mountain, New York 1956, Hotel Kowakien, Hakone 1959, Mountain House for Yawata Iron and Steel Co., Kujyu 1960, N.C.R. H.Q., Tokyo 1962, Americana Building, Osaka 1965, Prefectural Aichi Univ. of Arts, Aichi 1965–71, Aoyama Tower Building, Tokyo 1969, Hotel Fujita, Kyoto 1970, Japan House, New York 1971, Nara Nat. Museum 1973, Norwegian Embassy, Tokyo 1978, and many residences. *Leisure interests:* music, travel. *Address:* 8-6, Mejiro 3-chome, Toshima-ku, Tokyo (Office); 30-24 Minamidai 5-chome Nakano-ku, Tokyo, Japan (Home). *Telephone:* 954-0991 (Office) and 381-1282 (Home).

YOSHINAGA, Sayuri; Japanese film actress; b. 1945, m. Tado Okada; ed. Waseda Univ.; film debut in Town with a Cupola 1962; has since appeared in nearly 100 films including The Sound of Waves, The Makioka Sisters, The Diary of Yumechiyo, Ohan, Heaven Station, Killing Time by the Shores of a Mysterious Sea, Joyu; Japan Acad. Award for Best Actress 1985.

YOSHINO, Bunroku; Japanese diplomatist; b. 8 Aug. 1918, Matsumoto; m.; one s. one d.; entered Foreign Ministry 1941; Attaché, Berlin 1941; Sec., Washington, D.C. 1953; Econ. Dept. of Ministry 1956; Counsellor,

Bonn 1961; Deputy Dir.-Gen. Econ. Co-operation Dept. of Ministry 1964; Deputy Head of Mission, Washington, D.C. 1968; Dir.-Gen. U.S. Dept. of Ministry 1971; Amb. to OECD, Paris 1972; Sec. of State, Foreign Ministry 1975; Amb. to Fed. Repub. of Germany 1978–82; Sr. Adviser to the Pres. of Keidanren 1983, Chair. Inst. for Int. Econ. Studies 1983–. *Leisure interests:* books, golf. *Address:* Institute for International Economic Studies, No. 3-18, Kudan-Minami, 2-chome, Chiyoda-ku, Tokyo, Japan.

YOSHIYAMA, Hirokichi; Japanese business executive; b. 1 Dec. 1911, Hyogo Pref.; s. of Kyosuke and Rei Yoshiyama; m. Michi Samejima; two d.; ed. Electrical Engineering Dept., Univ. of Tokyo; joined Hitachi, Ltd. 1935, Dir. 1961, Exec. Man. Dir. 1964, Senior Exec. Man. Dir. 1968, Exec. Vice-Pres. 1969, Pres. and Rep. Dir. 1971–81, Chair. and Rep. Dir. 1981–87, Consultant to the Bd. of Dirs. 1987–; Commr. Space Activities Comm., Science and Tech. Agency 1985–; Vice-Pres. Assch. for Promotion of Int. Trade 1978–, Japan Machinery Fed. 1978–; Adviser Fed. of Econ. Org. 1986–. *Leisure interests:* golf, Go. *Address:* 6, Kanda-Surugadai 4-chome, Chiyoda-ku, Tokyo 101 (Office); 17-15-103, 3-chome Uehara, Shibuya-ku, Tokyo, Japan (Home). *Telephone:* 03-258-1111 (Office).

YOSIZAKA, Takamasa; Japanese architect and town planner; b. 13 Feb. 1917, Tokyo; s. of Syunzô Yosizaka; m. Kôno-Hukoko 1945; two s. one d.; ed. Waseda Univ., Tokyo; lecturer, Japan Women's Coll. 1942–50, Tokyo Agricultural School 1945–48, Yamanasi Univ. 1956–57, Tucumán Nat. Univ. Argentina 1961–62; Asst. Prof. Waseda Univ. 1950, Prof. 1959, Head of Dept. of Architecture 1964–65, Dean of School of Science and Eng. 1969–72; Man. Waseda Univ. Expedition to Equatorial Africa 1958, and Leader of its MacKinley Alaska Expedition 1960; Vice-Pres. Architectural Inst. of Japan 1967–68, Pres. 1973–74; Pres. Inst. of Studies on Living, Building Survey Inst.; mem. Japanese Assch. of Architects; Dir. Capital Region Comprehensive Planning Inst.; Pres. Waseda Univ. Coll. 1978–; G.S.D. (Harvard Univ.) 1978. *Principal works:* Japanese Pavilion, Venice Biennale 1956, Maison Franco-Japonaise 1959, Athénée Français 1962, Gotu City Hall 1962, Univ. Seminar House 1965, Ikoma Space Museum 1969; Projects: Redevelopment Plans for Tokada-no Baba District and Izu, Oosima, Hirosaki, Sendai. *Publications:* Form and Environment 1955, Primitive Country to Civilized Country 1961, Study on Dwelling 1965, Directive Proclamations 1972, Moi, j'aime pas la mer (trans. into Japanese) 1973, Le Corbusier Oeuvres complètes (8 vols., trans. into Japanese) 1977–79, Primitive Architecture, Enrico Guidoni (trans. into Japanese) 1980. *Leisure interests:* mountaineering, skiing. *Address:* 2-17-24 Hyakunintyô, Sinziku-ku, Tokyo 160, Japan. *Telephone:* 03-361-1083.

YOSSELIANI, Otar; Soviet film director; b. 1935, Georgia; ed. Tbilisi Conservatoire and Moscow Film Inst.; also studied mechanics and mathematics in Moscow; films include April, When Leaves Fall, There was a Singing Blackbird, Pastorale, Euskadi—Summer of '82 and Les Favoris de la lune (filmed in Paris); has also worked as a sailor and a miner and univ. lecturer; teacher of film at Tbilisi Acad. of Fine Arts. *Address:* Tbilisi Academy of Fine Arts, Tbilisi, Georgian S.S.R., U.S.S.R.

YOU TAIZHONG, Gen.; Chinese party official; b. 1914, Sichuan; Commdr. People's Liberation Army Unit 6410, Jiangsu 1968; Alt. mem. 9th Cen. Cttee. of CCP 1969; Chair. Nei Monggol Revolutionary Cttee. 1970; First Sec. CCP Nei Monggol 1971–78; mem. 10th Cen. Cttee. of CCP 1973; Commdr. Nei Monggol Mil. District; mem. 11th Cen. Cttee. CCP 1977; Deputy Commdr. Beijing PLA Mil. Units 1978; mem. 12th Cen. Cttee. CCP 1982–87; mem. Cen. Advisory Comm. 1987–; Commdr. Chengdu Units 1980–82, Guangzhou Units 1982, Chair. People's Air Defence Cttee. PLA Chengdu Mil. Dist. 1982, Commdr. Chengdu Mil. Dist. 1982.

YOUN, Kong-Hi (Victorinus), S.T.D., D.D.; Korean ecclesiastic; b. 8 Nov. 1924, Jinnampo City, N. Korea; s. of (Peter) Sang Youn and (Victoria) Sang Sook Choi; ed. St. Willibrord's Maj. Seminary, Dok-Won, Urban Coll., Rome, Gregorian Univ., Rome; ordained priest 1950; Asst. Priest, Cathedral of Seoul (Myong-Dong) 1950; Chaplain, Pusan UN P.O.W. Camp 1952, Vice-Pres. Catholic Library, Pusan 1954; teacher, Song-Shin (Holy Ghost) Middle and High School 1956; Sec. Catholic Conf. of Korea 1960; ordained Bishop 1963; Ordinary of Su-Won Diocese 1963; Admin. Seoul Archdiocese 1967; Archbishop and Ordinary of Kwangju Archdiocese 1973; Rep. Kwangju Catholic Coll. Foundation 1974–; Chair. Episcopal Conf. of Korea 1975; Rep. of Episcopal Cttee. of Bicentennial of Catholic Church in Korea 1980; Episcopal Moderator, Justice and Peace Cttee. 1979–; Second Sec., Comm. for Discipline Inspection, CPC Cen. Mil. Comm. Sept. 1988–. *Publication:* Radio Message 1963. *Leisure interest:* mountain climbing. *Address:* Archdiocese of Kwangju, 5-32 Im Dong, Puk-Ku, Kwangju City 500-010; P.O. Box 28, Puk-(North) Kwangju City 500-600, Republic of Korea (Postal address). *Telephone:* (062) 525-9004/6, 9504.

YOUNES, Mahmoud; Egyptian engineer; b. 3 April 1912, Cairo; m. 1941; two s. one d.; ed. Royal Coll. of Engineers, Cairo Univ. and Staff Officers' Coll.; Engineer with Mechanical and Electrical Dept., Ministry of Public Works, Cairo 1937; army engineer 1937; with Mil. Operations Directorate 1943; lecturer, Staff Officers' Coll. 1944 and 1947; Dir. Technical Affairs Office, G.H.Q. 1952; mem. Permanent Bd. for Development of Nat. Production 1953; Man. Dir. and Chair. Gen. Petroleum Authority 1954; Pres. Engineers' Syndicate 1954–65; Dir. and Chair. Cie. Orientale des Pétroles d'Egypte et Soc. Coopérative des Pétroles 1958-65; Counsellor, Ministry of Commerce and Industry and Mineral Wealth; Man. Dir. and Deputy Chair. Suez Canal Authority 1956, Chair. 1957-65; mem. Nat. Assembly 1964; Deputy Prime Minister for Transport and Communications 1965-67; Minister of Oil and Transport 1967; now in private consulting office in Beirut, Lebanon; Order of Merit (Class I), Order of the Nile (Class III), Military Star, Liberation Medal, Palestine Medal, Grand Cordon of the Order of the Yugoslav Standard, Grand Officer of the Panamanian Nat. Order of Vasco Nuñez de Balboa, Republic Medal (Class III), Mil. Service Medal (Class I), Order of The Republic (Class I), and other decorations. *Leisure interests:* swimming, reading. *Address:* 26 July Street 21, Cairo, Egypt. *Telephone:* 750714.

YOUNG, Baroness (Life Peer), cr. 1971, of Farnworth in the County Palatine of Lancaster; **Janet Mary Young**, P.C., M.A.; British politician; b. 23 Oct. 1926, Widnes; d. of John N. L. Baker; m. Dr. Geoffrey Tyndale Young 1950; three d.; ed. Dragon School, Oxford, Headington School, St. Anne's Coll., Oxford, and New Haven, Conn., U.S.A.; Councillor, Oxford City Council 1957, Alderman and leader of Conservative Group 1967; Baroness in Waiting (Govt. Whip in House of Lords) 1972-73; Parl. Under-Sec. of State, Dept. of Environment 1973-74; Minister of State, Dept. of Educ. and Science 1979-81; Chancellor of Duchy of Lancaster and Leader of House of Lords 1981-82; Minister in charge of Civil Service Dept. 1981; Lord Privy Seal and Leader of House of Lords 1982-83; Minister in charge of Management and Personnel Office 1981-83; Minister of State, FCO 1983-87; a Vice-Chair. Conservative Party Org. 1975-83, Deputy Chair. 1977-79, Co-Chair. Women's Nat. Comm. 1979-83; Dir. Nat. Westminster Bank PLC 1987-, Marks and Spencer PLC 1987-; Hon. Fellow, Inst. of Civil Engineers, St. Anne's Coll., Oxford; Hon. D.C.L. (Mt. Holyoake Coll.). *Leisure interest:* music. *Address:* House of Lords, London, SW1A 0PW, England.

YOUNG, Alec David, O.B.E., F.ENG., F.R.S.; British professor of aeronautical engineering (retd.); b. 15 Aug. 1913, London; s. of Isaac and Katherine (née Freeman) Young; m. 1st Dora Caplan 1937 (died 1970); m. 2nd Rena Waldmann 1971; two s. one d.; ed. Central Foundation School, London and Gonville & Caius Coll., Cambridge; mem. scientific Staff, Royal Aircraft Establishment 1936-46; Sr. Lecturer, Coll. of Aeronautics, Cranfield 1946-50, Prof. of Aerodynamics 1950-54; Prof. and Head, Dept. of Aeronautical Eng. Queen Mary Coll., London 1954-78; Dean. Faculty of Eng., Univ. of London 1962-66; Vice-Prin., Queen Mary Coll. 1966-78; Prof. Emer. Univ. of London 1978-; Chair. Aeronautical Research Council 1968-71, Bd. of Direction of Von Karman Inst. for Fluid Dynamics, Belgium 1964-; Exec. Sec. Int. Council of the Aeronautical Sciences 1986-; Gold Medal, Royal Aeronautical Soc. 1972; Commdr. Ordre de Léopold; Prandtl Ring 1976, Von Karman Medal 1979; Hon. F.R.Ae.S., etc. *Publications:* The Mechanics of Fluids (with W. J. Duncan and A. S. Thom), Aircraft Excrescence Drag (with J. H. Paterson), Boundary Layers 1989, articles in professional journals. *Leisure interests:* sketching, etching, drama. *Address:* 70 Gilbert Road, Cambridge, CB4 3PD, England. *Telephone:* (0223) 354625.

YOUNG, Andrew; American clergyman, politician and diplomatist; b. 12 March 1932, New Orleans, La.; s. of Andrew J. Young and Daisy Fuller; m. Jean Childs 1954; one s. three d.; ed. Howard Univ. and Hartford Theological Seminary; ordained to ministry, Congregational Church 1955, pastor in Thomasville, Ga. 1955-57; Assoc. Dir. for Youth Work, Nat. Council of Churches 1957-61; Admin. Citizenship Educ. Program, United Church of Christ 1961-64; on staff Southern Christian Leadership Conf. 1961-70, Exec. Dir. 1964-70, Exec. Vice-Pres. 1967-70, now Dir.; mem. House of Reps. 1972, re-elected 1974, 1976; Perm. Rep. to U.N. 1977-79; Mayor of Atlanta 1982-; Chair. Atlanta Community Relations Comm. 1970-72; Chair. Democratic voter registration drive 1976; organizer of voter registration and community devt. programmes for civil rights movement in 1960s; Medal of Freedom 1980, Légion d'honneur 1982, numerous awards and hon. degrees. *Address:* The Office of the Mayor, 68 Mitchell Street, S.W., Atlanta, Georgia 30303, U.S.A.

YOUNG, Sir Brian (Walter Mark), Kt.; British administrator; b. 23 Aug. 1922, Ceylon (now Sri Lanka); s. of late Sir Mark Young and Josephine Price; m. Fiona Marjorie Young 1947; one s. two d.; ed. Eton Coll., and King's Coll., Cambridge; Asst. Master, Eton Coll., 1947-52; Headmaster of Charterhouse 1952-64; Dir. of Nuffield Foundation 1964-70, Trustee 1978-; mem. Central Advisory Council for Educ. 1956-59; fmr. mem. U.K. Nat. Comm. for UNESCO; Dir.-Gen. IBA 1970-82; Chair. Christian Aid 1983-, Associated Bd. Royal Schools of Music 1984-87; mem. Arts Council of Great Britain 1983-88, Exec. Cttee. British Council of Churches 1983-; Trustee, Imperial War Museum 1985-. *Publications:* Via Vertendi 1952, Intelligent Reading 1964. *Leisure interests:* watching television, reading, music, travel, Romanesque sculpture. *Address:* Hill End, Woodhill Avenue, Gerrards Cross, Bucks., England.

YOUNG, (David) Junor; British diplomatist; b. 23 April 1934, Aberdeen; s. of David Young; m. Kathleen Brooks 1954; two s. two d.; ed. Robert Gordon's Coll.; joined Foreign Office 1951; Consul, Stuttgart 1978-81; First Sec., Kampala 1981-84; Consul Gen., Hamburg 1984-86; Commercial Counsellor, Bonn 1986-88; High Commr. in Solomon Islands 1988-. *Leisure interests:* fishing, shooting, golf. *Address:* Pine Cottage, Hintlesham, Suffolk, England (Home).

YOUNG, Freddie, O.B.E.; British cinematographer; b. 9 Oct. 1902, London; s. of Henry and Anne Young; m. 1st Marjorie Gaffney (died 1963), one s. one d.; m. 2nd Joan Morduch 1964, one s.; ed. privately; joined film industry 1917; Gaumont Film Studios 1917-27; Dir. of Photography 1927-; British and Dominions Film Corpn. with Herbert Wilcox 1929-39; freelance 1939-40; Capt. in Army (Training Films) 1940-43, invalided out; Chief Cameraman, MGM 1944-59; freelance 1959-; three Acad. Awards (Oscars), three Golden Cameras, one Golden Globe, Prix d'Honneur, Emmy Award from NBC. *Films:* Bitter Sweet 1933, Nell Gwyn 1934, When Knights Were Bold 1936, Victoria the Great 1937, Sixty Glorious Years 1938, Goodbye Mr. Chips 1939, Nurse Edith Cavell 1939, The Man in the Iron Mask 1939, 49th Parallel 1941, The Young Mr. Pitt 1941, Caesar and Cleopatra 1945, Bedelia 1946, So Well Remembered 1947, The Winslow Boy 1948, Edward My Son 1949, Treasure Island 1950, Calling Bulldog Drummond 1951, Ivanhoe 1952, Bhowani Junction 1956, Invitation to the Dance 1956, Island in the Sun 1956, Indiscreet 1958, Lawrence of Arabia (Acad. Award) 1962, The Seventh Dawn 1964, Dr. Zhivago (Acad. Award) 1965, Rotten to the Core 1965, Lord Jim 1965, The Deadly Affair 1967, You Only Live Twice 1967, Battle of Britain 1969, Ryan's Daughter (Acad. Award) 1970, Nicholas and Alexandra 1971, Blue Bird (U.S.S.R.), Permission to Kill, Stevie, Ike, the War Years, Bloodline, Roughcut, Richard's Things. *Publication:* The Work of the Motion Picture Cameraman 1972. *Leisure interests:* gardening, painting. *Address:* 3 Roehampton Close, London, SW15 5LU, England. *Telephone:* 01-878 1802.

YOUNG, John Atherton, D.SC., M.D., F.A.A., F.R.A.C.P.; Australian professor of physiology; b. Brisbane, Queensland; s. of William Young and Betty Young (née Atherton); ed. Brisbane Church of England Grammar School, Univ. of Queensland; Jr. Registrar, Royal Brisbane Hosp. 1961; Sr. Research Officer, Kanematsu Inst., Sydney Hosp. 1962-64; Research Scientist, Physiology Inst., Free Univ. of Berlin 1965-66; Sr. Lecturer, then Assoc. Prof., Univ. of Sydney 1967-76, Prof. of Physiology and Head of Dept. 1976-; Fellow Senate Univ., Sydney 1988. *Publications:* Morphology of Salivary Glands 1978, Centenary Book of the University of Sydney Medical School 1983, Across the Years 1987; four other scientific books, 120 articles in scientific journals and three articles in historical journals. *Leisure interests:* history, music. *Address:* Department of Physiology, University of Sydney, Sydney, N.S.W. 2006, Australia. *Telephone:* 692 3478.

YOUNG, Hon. Sir John (McIntosh), K.C.M.G., M.A., LL.B.; Australian judge; b. 17 Dec. 1919, Melbourne; s. of George D. Young and Kathleen M. Young; m. Elisabeth M. Twining 1951; one s. two d.; ed. Geelong Grammar School, Brasenose Coll. Oxford, Inner Temple and Univ. of Melbourne; served Scots Guards 1940-46; admitted Victoria Bar 1948; Assoc. to Mr. Justice Dixon, High Court of Australia 1948; practising barrister 1949-74; lecturer in Company Law, Univ. of Melbourne 1957-61; admitted Tasmanian Bar 1964, Q.C. 1964; N.S.W. Bar 1968, Q.C. 1968; consultant, Faculty of Law, Monash Univ. 1968-74; Lieut.-Gov. of Victoria and Chief Justice, Supreme Court of Victoria 1974-; Chancellor, Order of St. John in Australia 1982-; holder of many other public and charitable offices; Hon. LL.D. (Monash). *Publications:* Australian Company Law and Practice (co-author); articles in legal journals. *Leisure interests:* riding, golf. *Address:* 17 Sorrett Avenue, Malvern, Vic. 3144, Australia.

YOUNG, John Zachary, M.A., F.R.S., F.B.A.; British zoologist; b. 18 March 1907, Bristol; s. of Philip and Constance M. Lloyd; m. 1st Phyllis Heaney 1931; one s. two d.; m. 2nd Raymonde Parsons 1987; one d.; ed. Marlborough Coll. and Magdalen Coll., Oxford; Fellow, Magdalen Coll., Oxford 1931-45, Hon. Fellow 1976; Univ. Demonstrator in Zoology and Comparative Anatomy, Oxford 1933-45; Prof. of Anatomy, Univ. Coll., London 1945-74, Emer. 1974-; Rockefeller Fellow 1936; BBC Reith Lecturer 1950; Pres. Marine Biol. Asscn. 1976-86; Chair. Zoology Section, British Assen. for Advancement of Science 1957; Foreign Hon. mem. American Acad. of Arts and Sciences 1957, Philosophical Soc.; Hon. Fellow Acad. Lincei; Hon. mem. Alpha Omega Medical Soc., Calif. 1978; Hon. D.Sc. (Bristol 1956, McGill 1966, Durham 1969, Bath 1974, Oxford 1979, Aberdeen 1980), LL.D. (Glasgow 1974, Duke Univ.); Royal Medal, Royal Soc. 1967, Linnean Soc. Gold Medal 1973, Zoological Soc. Medal 1974, Swammerdam Medal, Amsterdam 1980. *Publications:* The Life of Vertebrates 1950, Doubt and Certainty in Science 1951, The Life of Mammals 1957, A Model of the Brain 1964, The Memory System of the Brain 1966, Introduction to the Study of Man 1971, The Anatomy of the Nervous System of Octopus vulgaris 1971, Programs of the Brain 1978, Philosophy and the Brain 1987. *Leisure interests:* work and walking. *Address:* Department of Experimental Psychology, University of Oxford, Oxford, OX1 3UD (Office); 1 The Crossroads, Brill, Bucks., HP18 9TL, England (Home). *Telephone:* (0865) 271-361 (Office); (0844) 237-412 (Home).

YOUNG, Michael Jerome; Australian politician; b. 9 Oct. 1936; m. Mary Dollard 1960; one s. one d.; ed. Marist Bros. Coll., N.S.W.; S. Australian State Sec. Australian Labor Party 1968-74, Fed. Sec. 1969-73, mem. Parl. for Port Adelaide, S. Australia 1974-, Special Minister of State Commonwealth Parl., Vice-Pres. Exec. Council, Leader of House of Reps. 1983 (resgnd. July 1983), Minister of State Jan. 1984, Minister for Immigration, Local Govt. and Ethnic Affairs, Vice-Pres. of the Exec. Council and Minister Assisting the Prime Minister on Multicultural Affairs 1987, resgnd. all posts 1988; Leader of House of Reps. Jan. 1984–88; Pres. Labor Party. *Leisure interests:* tennis, swimming. *Address:* 6 Sunlake Place, Tennyson, South Australia 5022.

YOUNG, Wayland (see Kennet, 2nd Baron).

YOUNG, William Lambert; New Zealand diplomatist; b. 13 Nov. 1913, Kawakawa; s. of James Young and Alice G. A. Young; m. Isobel J. Luke 1949; one s. four d.; commenced work 1930 and spent first 16 years with farm servicing co.; served in N. Africa with Eighth Army 1940–43; took over man. of wholesale distributing co. handling N.Z. and manufactured goods; Gen. Man. of co. manufacturing radios, records, electronic equipment and owning 32 retail stores 1956; J.P. 1962; M.P. (Nat. Party) for Miramar 1966–81; Minister of Works and Devt. 1975–81; Trustee Wellington Savings Bank 1967–75; Chair. N.Z. Fisheries Licensing Authority 1982; rep. of N.Z. at various official visits abroad and UN World Water Conf. 1977; High. Commr. in U.K. (also accred. to Ireland and Nigeria) 1982–85; Pres. Starboating Club 1980–. *Leisure interests:* rowing, rugby. *Address:* 31 Moana Road, Kelburn, Wellington, New Zealand. *Telephone:* (04) 759164.

YOUNG OF DARTINGTON, Baron (Life Peer), cr. 1977, of Dartington in the County of Devon; **Michael Young,** PH.D.; British sociologist; b. 9 Aug. 1915, Manchester; ed. Dartington Hall School, London Univ. and Gray's Inn, London; Dir. of Political and Econ. Planning 1941–45; Sec. Research Dept., Labour Party 1945–51; Dir. Inst. of Community Studies 1953–; Chair. Consumers' Assn. 1956–65, Pres. 1965–; Chair. Advisory Centre for Educ. 1959–76, Pres. 1977–; Lecturer in Sociology, Cambridge Univ. 1961–63, Trustee, Dartington Hall 1942–; Chair. Social Science Research Council 1965–68, Chair. Nat. Extension Coll. 1962–; Chair. Int. Extension Coll. 1970–; Dir. Mauritius Coll. of the Air 1972; Visiting Prof. Ahmadu Bello Univ., Nigeria 1974; Chair. Nat. Consumer Council 1975–77; Chair. Mutual Aid Centre 1977–; Chair. Dartington Inst. of Community Studies 1980–; Chair. Tawney Soc. (SDP) 1982–85, College of Health 1983–, Open Coll. of the Arts 1986–, Open School 1988–. *Publications:* Family and Kinship in East London (with Peter Willmott) 1957, The Rise of the Meritocracy 1959, Family and Class in a London Suburb (with Peter Willmott) 1961, Innovation and Research in Education 1965, Learning Begins at Home 1967, Forecasting and the Social Sciences 1968, The Symmetrical Family (with Peter Willmott) 1973, Poverty Report (Ed.) 1974, Distance Teaching for the Third World 1980 (with others), The Elmhirsts of Dartington 1982, Revolution from Within 1983, The Metronomous Society—Natural Rhythm and Home Timetables. *Address:* 18 Victoria Park Square, London, E.2, England.

YOUNG OF GRAFFHAM, Baron (Life Peer), cr. 1984, of Graffham in the County of West Sussex; **David Ivor Young,** P.C., LL.B.; British politician; b. 27 Feb. 1932; s. of Joseph and Rebecca Young; m. Lita Marianne Shaw 1956; two d.; ed. Christ's Coll., Finchley and Univ. Coll., London; admitted solicitor 1956; Exec. Great Universal Stores 1956–61; Chair. Eldonwall Ltd. 1961–75, Mfrs. Hanover Property Services Ltd. 1974–84; Dir. Centre for Policy Studies 1979–82; Chair. Manpower Services Comm. 1982–84; Minister without Portfolio 1984–85, Sec. of State for Employment 1985–87, for Trade and Industry June 1987–; Chair. British Org. for Rehabilitation by Training 1975–80, Pres. 1980–82; mem. English Industrial Estates Corpn. 1980–82, Industrial Adviser 1979–80, Special Adviser 1980–82; mem. NEDC 1982–; Chair. Int. Council of Jewish Social and Welfare Services 1981–84; Hon. F.R.P.S. 1981; Hon. Fellow Univ. Coll., London 1988. *Address:* 88 Brook Street, London, W.1, England.

YOUNGER, Rt. Hon. George (Kenneth Hotson), P.C., T.D., D.L., M.P.; British politician; b. 22 Sept. 1931; s. of 3rd Viscount Younger of Leckie; m. Diana Rhona Tuck 1954, three s. one d.; ed. Winchester Coll., New Coll., Oxford; commissioned in Argyll and Sutherland Highlanders 1950, served BAOR and Korea 1951, with 7th Bn. Argyll and Sutherland Highlanders, T.A. 1951–65; M.P. for Ayr 1964–; Parl. Under-Sec. of State for Devt., Scottish Office 1970–74; Minister of State for Defence 1974; Sec. of State for Scotland 1979–86, for Defence Jan. 1986–; fmr. Dir. George Younger and Son Ltd., Maclachlans Ltd., J. G. Thomson and Co. Ltd.; Dir. Tennant Caledonian Breweries Ltd. 1977–79; fmr. Chair. Conservative Party in Scotland; Pres. Nat. Union of Conservative and Unionist Assens. 1987–88; Scottish Conservative Whip 1965–67. *Leisure interests:* music, tennis, sailing, golf. *Address:* House of Commons, Westminster, London, S.W.1; Easter Leckie, Gargunnock, Stirlingshire, Scotland.

YU BEN; Chinese artist; b. 1905, Taishan Cty., Guangdong; ed. Winnipeg School of Art and Ont. Coll. of Art, Canada; worked as professional painter, Hong Kong 1936. *Works include:* Before the Typhoon, Harvest Time, A Girl with Lychees, Waterfall at Lake Jingbo, Transportation Beyond the Great Wall, The Three Gorges, Picking Mulberry Leaves, The Land of Fish and Rice. *Address:* nr. Yuexiu Hill, Guangzhou, People's Republic of China.

YU GUANGYUAN; Chinese academic; b. 1915, Shanghai; ed. Qinghua Univ., Beijing; taught in Physics Dept., Lingnan Univ., Guangzhou 1936–37; engaged in youth movement, land reform, propaganda, culture, journalism, higher educ. and social research 1940s; in CCP Cen. Dept. of Propaganda, in charge of social and natural sciences research 1949–75; mem. Academic Cttee., Acad. of Sciences of China 1955–; Deputy Dir. State Comm. of Science and Tech. 1964; Vice-Pres. Acad. of Social Sciences

of China 1978–82, Adviser 1982–; Pres. Soc. for Study of the Works of Marx, Engels, Lenin, and Stalin 1980–, Soc. of Production Power Economics 1980, Soc. of Research in Dialetics of Nature 1980, Soc. of Territorial Econs. 1981; Adviser Environmental Protection Cttee., State Council 1985; Pres. China Environmental Strategy Research Centre 1985; Vice-Pres. China Int. Cultural Centre 1984–; mem. Cen. Advisory Comm. CCP 1987–. *Publications:* Study of Land Problems in Sui Mi County in China, Exploration of Political Economy of the Socialist Period, On the Objective Nature of Law, and numerous other books on economics and philosophy. *Address:* 5 Jianguomen Nei Da Jie, Beijing, People's Republic of China. *Telephone:* 554631.

YU HONGEN; Chinese state official; b. 1928, Shandong Prov.; ed. Beijing Coll. of Mining; Sr. Engineer transferred to Ministry of Coal Industry 1981; Vice-Minister of Coal Industry 1982, Minister 1985–88; Pres. State Coal Corpn. May 1988–; Sec. Party Group Ministry of Coal Industry 1986–88; mem. 12th CCP Cen. Cttee. 1982, 13th Cen. Cttee. 1987. *Address:* State Coal Corporation, Beijing, People's Republic of China.

YU HONGLI; Chinese party official; alt. mem. 12th CCP Cttee. 1982–87; Commdr. PLA Shanxi Prov. Command March 1988–. *Address:* c/o Chinese Communist Party Central Committee, Beijing, People's Republic of China.

YU KUO-HWA, B.A.; Chinese politician and banker; b. 10 Jan. 1914, Chekiang; s. of Choping Yu and Eirying Hu; m. Yu Toong Metsung 1946; two s.; ed. Tsinghua Univ., Harvard Univ. Graduate School, L.S.E.; Sec. to Pres. of Nat. Mil. Council 1936–44; Alt. Exec. Dir. Int. Bank for Reconstruction and Devt. 1947–50, IMF 1951–55; Pres. Cen. Trust of China 1955–61; Chair. Bd. of Dirs. Bank of China 1961–67; Alt. Gov. IBRD 1964–67, Gov. for Repub. of China 1967–69; Minister of Finance 1967–69; Gov. Cen. Bank of China 1969–84; Minister of State 1969–84; Gov. IMF 1969–80, Asian Devt. Bank 1969–84; Prime Minister of Taiwan 1984–89; mem. Cen. Standing Cttee., Kuomintang 1969–; Chair. Council for Econ. Planning and Devt. 1977–84; Hon. Dr. (St. John's Univ., Jamaica, New York). *Address:* c/o Office of the Prime Minister, 1 Chung Hsiao East Road, Section 1, Taipei, 10023 Taiwan.

YU MINGTAO; Chinese politician; b. Nov. 1917, Shen County, Hebei Prov.; m. Wang Rongying; one s. one d.; Cadre, Lingling Special Dist., Hunan Prov. 1951; Dir. Industry Dept., Hunan Prov. CP 1953, Sec. Hunan Prov. CP 1959; mem. Standing Cttee., Cen. S. China Bureau, CCP Cen. Cttee. 1961; disappeared during Cultural Revolution; Vice-Chair. Hunan Prov. Revolutionary Cttee. 1971; mem. Standing Cttee., Hunan Prov. CP 1972–73, Sec. Hunan Prov. CP 1973–77; First Sec. Changsha Municipality CP 1973–77; mem. 11th CCP Cen. Cttee. 1977; Vice-Chair. Shaanxi Prov. Revolutionary Cttee. 1977–79, Chair. May–Dec. 1979; Sec. Shaanxi Prov. CP 1977–82; Deputy for Shaanxi Prov., 5th NPC 1978; Auditor Gen. of Auditing Admin. 1983–85, Pres. 1984; mem. Credentials Cttee., Second Session of NPC 1979; Gov. Shaanxi 1979–82; mem. 11th, 12th Cen. CCP Cttee. 1982–; del. to the 4th, 5th Nat. People's Congress; mem. 4th Nat. Political Consultative Conference; Vice-Chair. People's Arms Cttee., PLA Shaanxi Mil. Dist. 1981–. *Leisure interests:* sport, chess. *Address:* Audit Administration, 12 Caishi Road, Haidian District, Beijing, People's Republic of China. *Telephone:* 815631.

YU PEIWEN; Chinese diplomatist; Deputy Dir. Foreign Office, People's Council of Shanghai 1950, Acting Dir. 1954; mem. Inst. of Foreign Affairs 1955; Dir. Protocol Dept., Ministry of Foreign Affairs 1958; Amb. to Sudan 1966–Cultural Revolution; Amb. to Ethiopia 1971–74, to Austria 1974–80; Perm. Rep. to Geneva office of UN 1980–85; Leader, Del. to UNIDO Confs., New York 1978, Vienna 1979; Vice-Pres. China Assen. for Promotion of Int. Friendship May 1985–. *Address:* China Association for Advancement of International Friendship, Beijing, People's Republic of China.

YU PENG; Chinese artist; b. 1921, Dalian, Liaoning. *Address:* Beijing Art Institute, Beijing, People's Republic of China.

YU QIULI, Lieut-Gen.; Chinese politician; b. 1914, Ji'an Co., Sichuan Prov.; Political Commissar of Detachment, 120th Div. 1934; Deputy Political Commissar Qinghai Mil. District, People's Liberation Army 1949; Lieut.-Gen. PLA 1955; Dir. Finance Dept., PLA 1956–57; Political Commissar Gen. Logistics Dept., PLA 1957–58; Minister of Petroleum Industry 1958; Vice-Chair. State Planning Comm. 1965, Chair. 1972–80, Minister in Charge 1980; mem. 9th Cen. Cttee. of CCP 1969, 10th Cen. Cttee. 1973; Vice-Premier, State Council 1975–82, State Councillor 1982–84; Dir. Gen. Political Dept. PLA 1982–87; mem. Politburo, 11th Cen. Cttee. CCP 1977; mem. Politburo 12th Cen. CCP Cttee. 1982–87; Deputy for Kiangsu, 5th NPC 1978; mem. Presidium 5th NPC 1978; Sec., Secr., Cen. Cttee. 1980–82; mem. 1982–; Minister in Charge of State Energy Comm. 1980–82; State Councillor, State Council 1982–83; Deputy Sec.-Gen. Mil. Comm. under CCP Cen. Cttee. 1982–87; Deputy for PLA to 6th NPC 1983; Vice-Chair. Cen. Party Consolidation Guidance Comm. 1983–; mem. Presidium 6th NPC 1986; mem. Standing Cttee. Cen. Advisory Comm. 1987; Chair. PLA Literary Awards Examination Cttee. 1986–; Hon. Pres. Basketball Assen. 1984–. *Address:* c/o PLA Political Department, Beijing, People's Republic of China.

YU REN; Chinese artist; b. 1931, Tieling, Liaoning; ed. Lu Xun Acad. of Art and Literature, N.E. China; Art Ed. Gongren Ribao (Workers' Daily). *Address:* People's Republic of China.

YU WEN; Chinese party official; b. 1917, Shanxi Prov.; m. Liao Bing; two s. two d.; Deputy Sec.-Gen. Chinese Academy of Sciences 1959; in political disgrace 1967–73; Sec.-Gen. Chinese Acad. of Sciences 1978–83; Perm. Deputy Head, Propaganda Dept. CCP 1983–85; Deputy Sec.-Gen. Presidium 6th NPC 1986–; Deputy to 6th NPC for Qinghai Prov. 1986; mem. Standing Cttee. NPC 1986–; Vice-Chair. Nationalities Cttee. 1986; Head Nat. Examination Cttee. for Higher Posts of Journalists 1983. *Address:* Central Committee of Chinese Communist Party, Beijing, People's Republic of China.

YU YI; Chinese government official; b. 1925, Shandong; fmr. Deputy Dir. Jiangbei Machine-Building Factory, Jilin; concurrently Chief Engineer, Dir. and Sec. Jianhua Machine-Building Factory, Qiqiha; fmr. Deputy Dir. Dept. of Nat. Defence Industry, Heilongjiang; fmr. Vice-Minister 5th Ministry of Machine-Building; Minister of Ordnance Industry 1982; Chair. Bd. of Dirs., China Northern Industrial Corpn. Sept. 1986–. *Address:* c/o State Council, Beijing, People's Republic of China.

YU ZHAN; Chinese diplomatist; m. Zuo Yi; with Embassy, Poland 1955–57; in Socialist Countries Dept., Ministry of Foreign Affairs 1958–72; Vice-Minister of Foreign Affairs 1972–83; Amb. to Canada 1983–87; mem. Presidium 7th NPC 1988–. *Address:* Central Committee of Chinese Communist Party, Beijing, Peoples Republic of China.

YU ZHEN; Chinese government official; Vice-Minister of Light Industry 1985–; Pres. China Nat. Light Industrial Machinery Corpn. 1985–. *Address:* China National Light Industrial Machinery Corporation, 59 Youanmen Street, Beijing, People's Republic of China. *Telephone:* 336878.

YU ZHENWU; Chinese air force officer; b. 1931, Kuandian, Liaoning Prov.; joined Red Army 1947; alt. mem. 12th CCP Cen. Cttee. 1982, 13th Cen. Cttee. 1987; Commdr. of a corps of the PLA Air Force, Deputy Commdr. PLA Air Force 1985–. *Address:* c/o Chinese Communist Party Central Committee, Beijing, People's Republic of China.

YU ZHIXUE; Chinese artist; b. 27 Feb. 1935, Zhaodong Co., Heilongjiang; s. of Yu Tinanxi and Li Wenying; m. Zhao Sujing 1957; two s. one d.; ed. Harbin Chun Hua Art School; Art Ed. Heilongjiang Pictorial 1960–62, Heilongjiang People's Publishing House 1963–79; Deputy Sec.-Gen. Inst. of Chinese Painting, Heilongjiang; Chair. Inst. of Ice and Snow Painting; Dir. Heilongjiang br., China Int. Cultural Exchange Center 1984–; Chair. Dept. of Art Creation, Heilongjiang Inst. of Calligraphy and Painting; Guest Lecturer Calgary, Alberta 1984; exhbns. of paintings in Japan, Canada, U.S.A., Fed. Repub. of Germany and Singapore. *Publications include:* On Landscape Painting of Ice and Snow 1982, On the Founder of Ice and Snow Painting 1986. *Leisure interests:* reading, literature, travelling. *Address:* Institute of Calligraphy and Painting, Heilongjiang, Harbin, People's Republic of China. *Telephone:* 35666.

YU ZHIZHEN; Chinese artist; b. 28 Nov. 1915, Beijing; d. of Yu Liangchen and Shen Mingruo; m. Liu Lishang 1952, one s.; studied traditional Chinese painting under Yu Feian, Huang Binhong and Zhang Daqian, engaged in research on ancient Chinese paintings at Chinese Painting Research Studio of Palace Museum; Prof., Cen Acad. of Applied Arts; and China Correspondence Coll. of Calligraphy and Painting; famous for her illustrations of Guo Moruo's A Hundred Flowers 1959. *Publications include:* Paintings by Yu Zhizhen 1980, Brush techniques in Meticulous Style Paintings 1981, A Book on the Art of Flower and Plant Paintings 1987, Selected Paintings (with Liu Lishang) 1987. *Leisure interests:* drama, dance. *Address:* Central Academy of Applied Arts, Guanghua Road, Beijing, People's Republic of China.

YUAN BAOHUA; Chinese politician; b. 1916, Henan Prov.; Sec.-Gen. People's Govt. of Pingyuan Prov. 1950, mem. Finance and Commerce Cttee. 1950; Asst. to Minister of Metallurgical Industry 1957–59; Vice-Minister of Metallurgical Industry 1959; Vice-Chair. State Econ. Comm., State Council 1960; Dir., Gen. Bureau for State Material Control 1963–64; Deputy for Henan Prov., 3rd NPC 1964; Minister of Material Allocation 1964–Cultural Revolution; Vice-Chair. State Planning Comm., State Council 1974–78; alt. mem. 11th CCP Cen. Cttee. 1977–82, mem. 12th CCP Cen. Cttee. 1982–85; mem. Cen. Advisory Comm. CCP 1987–; Vice-Chair. State Econ. Comm., State Council 1978–81, Chair. 1981–82; Pres. Enterprise Man. Asscn. 1979–; Vice-Chair. Patriotic Sanitation Campaign Cttee. 1981–; Hon. Pres. Nat. Food Processing Industry Asscn. 1981–; Vice-Minister of State, Economic Comm. State Council 1982–; Chair. Nat. Workers' In Service Educ. Man. Cttee. 1983–; Head, All-China Enterprise Consolidation Leading Group 1984–; Adviser China-Japan Personnel Exchange Cttee. 1985–; Pres. People's Univ. 1985–. *Leisure interests:* drama and dances. *Address:* c/o State Council, Beijing, People's Republic of China.

YUAN ENFENG; Chinese folk singer; b. 22 Jan. 1940, Shaanxi Prov.; d. of Yuan Zaiming and Li Dexian; m. Sun Shao, composer; three d.; participated in over 3,000 performances, including numerous solo concerts and 1,000 radio and TV programmes; appearances abroad include Romania, Bulgaria, Czechoslovakia, U.S.S.R., Japan, Thailand, Philippines and U.S.A.; Chair. Folk Music Section, Shaanxi Broadcasting Station; Vice-Chair. Shaanxi TV Station; mem. Chinese Musicians' Asscn.; mem. of Bd., Shaanxi Br., Chinese Cultural Exchange Centre; mem. of many other official orgs. *Compositions (with Sun Shao) include:* Millet is Delicious and

Caves are Warm, Nowhere is Better than Our North Shaanxi; many recordings and song books. *Address:* Folk Music Section, Provincial Broadcasting and Television Station, Xian, Shaanxi, People's Republic of China. *Telephone:* 24741.

YUAN FANGLIE; Chinese party official; b. Dec. 1929, Yinan, Shandong Prov.; m. Xu Suzheng; one s. three d.; Vice-Chair. Revolutionary Cttee., Zhejiang Prov. 1977–79; mem. CCP Cttee., Zhejiang 1978; Vice-Gov. of Zhejiang 1979–81; alt. mem. 12th CCP Cen. Cttee. 1982; First Sec. CCP Cttee., Wenchou Pref. 1981–85; Sec. Politics and Law Cttee. of CCP Cttee., Zhejiang 1986–; Pres. Prov. Higher People's Court, Zhejiang Feb. 1988–. *Address:* Zhejiang Prov. People's Congress, Zhejiang, People's Republic of China.

YUAN JUN; Chinese army officer; mem. CCP Cttee., Heilongjiang Prov. 1977; Deputy Commdr. Shenyang Mil. Region 1982–; alt. mem. 12th CCP Cen. Cttee. 1982, 13th Cen. Cttee. 1987. *Address:* Shenyang Military Region Headquarters, Shenyang, Liaoning, People's Republic of China.

YUAN SHENGPING; Chinese soldier and party official; b. 1912, Ji'an Co., Jiangxi Prov.; joined CCP 1930; served with 1st Front Army on Long March 1934–35; 8th Route Army 1937; Political Cttee. Shanxi-Chahar-Hebei Mil. Region 1939; 3rd Div. Shandong Liberation Army 1945; 4th Field Army, Hainan Mil. Admin. Cttee. 1949–50; Korean People's Volunteers 1950–53; Dir. Political Dept. Beijing-Tianjin Garrison 1955; Lieut.-Gen.; mem. Shandong Prov. People's Congress 1960; Head PLA units in Jinan 1963–; mem 9th CCP Cen. Cttee. 1969; First Sec. Political Cttee. Jinan Mil. Region 1970–73; First Vice-Chair. Shandong Prov. Revolutionary Cttee. 1970–73; Second Sec. Shandong Prov. CCP Cttee. 1971–73; presidium 9th CCP Nat. Congress 1969; purged as follower of Lin Biao 1973, cleared of charges and rehabilitated 1978; mem. Political Cttee. Beijing Mil. Region 1980–81; mem. Cen. Advisory Cttee. of CCP Cen. Cttee. 1987–; Order of Liberation 1st Class. *Address:* Central Advisory Committee of the Central Committee of the Chinese Communist Party, Zhongnanhai, Beijing, People's Republic of China.

YUAN TSEH LEE, M.S., PH.D.; American professor of chemistry; b. 19 Nov. 1936, Hsinchu, Taiwan; m. Bernice Wu; two s. one d.; ed. Nat. Taiwan Univ., Nat. Tsinghua Univ. and Univ. of Calif. (Berkeley); postgraduate work in Prof. Bruce Mahan's group, Univ. of Calif. (Berkeley) 1962–67; Post-doctoral Fellow, Harvard Univ. 1967–68; Asst. Prof. Dept. of Chemistry and James Franck Inst. Univ. of Chicago 1968, Assoc. Prof. 1971, Prof. 1973–74; Prof. of Chemistry and Prin. Investigator, Lawrence Berkeley Lab. Univ. of Calif. (Berkeley) 1974–; mem. N.A.S., Academia Sinica, Taiwan; Fellow, American Acad. of Arts and Science, American Physical Soc.; Nat. Medal of Science 1986; shared Nobel Prize for Chemistry 1986; Dr. h.c. (Waterloo) 1986; other awards and distinctions. *Address:* Department of Chemistry, University of California, Berkeley, Calif. 94720, U.S.A.

YUAN WEIMIN; Chinese sportsman and politician; b. 1939, Suzhou City, Jiangsu Prov.; ed. Nanjing Inst. of Physical Culture; mem. Nat. Men's Volleyball Team 1962; Asst. Instr. to Nat. Volleyball Team 1974; Head Coach, Nat. Women's Volleyball Team 1976; Vice-Minister in charge of Comm. for Physical Culture and Sports of PRC 1984–; alt. mem. 12th Cen. Cttee. of C.C.P. 1985–87; Pres. Chinese Football Asscn. 1986; Vice-Pres. All-China Sports Fed. 1986–; Pres. Volleyball Asscn. April 1988–; mem. 13th Cen. Cttee. of C.P. of China 1987. *Address:* 9 Tiyuguan Road, Beijing, People's Republic of China.

YUAN YUNSHENG; Chinese artist; b. 1937, Nantong, Jiangsu; teacher Dept. of Mural Painting, Cen. Acad. of Fine Arts, Beijing. *Address:* Central Academy of Fine Arts, Beijing, People's Republic of China.

YUE HONG; Chinese film actress; b. 1962, Chendu, Sichun Prov.; ed. Cen. Drama Inst., winner of the Golden Rooster Best Actress Award for In the Wild Mountains; winner of 1st Bronze Chariot Best Actress Award for In the Wild Mountains; winner of the Chinese Performing Asscn. Best Actress Award for In the Wild Mountains. *Films include:* Island, They Are Still Young, Eight Women Soldiers, Assassination of Sun. *Address:* August First Film Studio, Beijing, People's Republic of China.

YUKAWA, Morio, G.C.V.O.; Japanese diplomatist (retd.); b. 23 Feb. 1908, Morioka City; m. Teiko Kohiyama 1940; two s.; ed. Tokyo Univ.; entered Foreign Service 1933; served U.K., Geneva; Dir. Trade Bureau Econ. Stabilization Board, Cabinet 1950–51; Dir. Gen. Econ. Affairs Bureau, Foreign Office 1951–52; Minister Counsellor to France 1952–54; Dir. Gen. Int. Co-operation Bureau, Foreign Office 1954–55; Dir. Gen. Econ. Affairs Bureau, Foreign Office 1955–57; Amb. to Philippines 1957–61; Deputy Vice-Minister, Foreign Office 1961–63; Amb. to Belgium, Luxembourg and European Econ. Community 1963–68, to U.K. 1968–72; Grand Master of the Ceremonies, Imperial Household 1973–79. *Leisure interests:* historical or biographical works, theatre, golf. *Address:* Sanbancho Hilltop 5-10 Sanbancho, Chiyoda-ku, Tokyo 102, Japan.

YUN, Isang; German composer and professor of composition; b. 17 Sept. 1917, Tong Yong, S. Korea; s. of Ki-Hyun Yun and Pu-Ku Yun-Chu; m. Soo Ya Lee 1950; one s. one d.; ed. Paris Conservatoire and Hochschule für Musik, Berlin; underground resistance fighter in Korea 1943–45; teacher of music in schools and univs. 1946–55; music studies in Europe 1956–59;

successful composer in Europe 1959–67; political prisoner in S. Korea 1967–69; Prof. of Composition, Hochschule der Künste, Berlin 1970–85; now freelance composer; Kulturpreis der Stadt Kiel; Koussevitzky Music Award; Grosses Bundesverdienstkreuz; Dr. h.c. (Tübingen). *Compositions:* about 90 works. *Leisure interest:* fishing. *Address:* Sakrower Kirchweg 47, 1000 Berlin 22, Germany. *Telephone:* (030) 3652805.

YUNICH, David Lawrence; American consumer companies consultant; b. 21 May 1917, Albany, N.Y.; s. of Max A. and Bessie (Feldman) Yunich; m. Beverly F. Blickman 1941; two s.; ed. Union Coll. and Harvard Graduate School of Business Admin.; L. Bamberger and Co., Newark 1947–48, Pres. and Dir. 1955–62; Vice-Pres. Macy's, New York 1941–51, Sr. Vice-Pres. 1951–62, Pres. 1962–71; Vice-Chair. Bd. R. H. Macy and Co. Inc. 1971–73, Dir. 1958–73 (retd.); Chair. Metropolitan Transportation Authority 1974–77; Dir. Prudential Insurance Co., N.Y. Telephone Co., U.S. Industries Inc., East River Savings Bank, Diners Club Inc., Harwood Mfg. Co. Inc., W. R. Grace and Co., J. Walter Thompson Co.; mem. N.Y. State Banking Bd.; Chair. of Bd. N.Y. Chamber of Commerce and Industry; Chair. Mayor's Council (New York) Econ. and Business Advisors; Dir. Educational Broadcasting Corpn., Nat. Jewish Hospital, Denver; Trustee Carnegie Hall Corpn., Albany Med. Coll., St. Vincent's Hospital, Rutgers Univ., Union Coll., Skidmore Coll.; Pres. Retail Dry Goods Asscn.; Dir. Nat. Retail Merchants Asscn., American Management Asscn. *Address:* 1114 Avenue of the Americas, New York, N.Y. 10036 (Office); Five Birches, 26 Cooper Road, Scarsdale, N.Y. 10583, U.S.A. (Home). *Telephone:* (914) 723-6509/3959.

YURSKY, Sergey Yurevich; Soviet actor; b. 16 March 1935; ed. Leningrad Theatre Inst. 1959; worked for Gorky Theatre, Leningrad 1957–, Mossoviet Theatre 1979–; acted in films 1960–; R.S.F.S.R. Artist of Merit 1968. *Roles include:* Vikniksor (The SHKID Republic 1966), Oppenheimer (Choosing a Purpose 1976), M. Jourdain (A Dervish Blows Up Paris 1978), Improvvisatore (The Little Tragedies 1980); work for TV; A Little Dacha for One Family 1979, You Can't Change the Meeting Place 1979, Cherchez la Femme 1982. *Films include:* The Serf Actress 1963, Time, Foreward March! 1966, The Golden Calf 1968. *Address:* c/o Gosudarstvenny; Teatr Mossovieta, Moscow, U.S.S.R.

YUSIF-ZADE, Ziya Mamediya ogly; Soviet official; b. 1929, Azerbaidzhan; cand. mem. of Cen. Cttee. of Azerbaidzhan CP 1971–80, mem. 1980–; Deputy Chair. of Cttee. for State Security of Azerbaidzhan S.S.R. 1975–77, First Deputy Chair. 1977–80, Chair. 1980–88; cand. mem. Politburo Cen. Cttee. of Azerbaidzhan CP 1980–81, mem. 1981–. *Address:* Central Committee of Azerbaidzhan CP, Baku Azerbaidzhan S.S.R., U.S.S.R.

YUSSOF, Dr. Mohammed; Afghan politician; b. 21 Jan. 1917, Kabul; one s. one d.; fmr. Minister of Mines and Industries; Prime Minister and Minister of Foreign Affairs 1963–65; Amb. to Fed. Repub. of Germany, also accred. to Denmark, Sweden and Switzerland 1966–73.

Z

ZABALETA, Nicanor; Spanish harpist; b. 7 Jan. 1907, San Sebastian; m. Graciela Torres 1952; one s. one d.; ed. Madrid Conservatory of Music, studied in Paris; harp soloist with the Berlin Philharmonic, Vienna Philharmonic, Israel Philharmonic, Orchestre de Paris, NHK Symphony, Tokyo, New York Philharmonic, Philadelphia Orchestra, BBC Symphony, Philharmonia Orchestra, L.A. and San Francisco Symphony Orchestras; has played at numerous music festivals; many solo pieces and concertos have been composed for him; most of his repertoire has been recorded; awards include Grand Prix du Disque (France), Grand Prix Edison (Holland), Medallo d'oro de Bellas Artes (Spain) 1981. *Leisure interests:* nature, arts. *Address:* Villa Izar, Aldapeta, 20009 San Sebastian, Spain. *Telephone:* (43) 466349.

ZACHAU, Hans G., DR. RER. NAT.; German molecular biologist; b. 16 May 1930, Berlin; s. of Drs. Erich Zachau and Gertrud Zachau; m. Elisabeth Vorster 1960; three s.; ed. Univs. of Frankfurt/Main and Tübingen; Postdoctoral Fellow, Mass. Inst. of Tech. and Rockefeller Univ. 1956-58; Max-Planck-Inst. für Biochemie, Munich 1958-61; Inst. für Genetik, Cologne 1961-66; Prof. of Physiological Chemistry and Head of Inst., Univ. of Munich 1967-; mem. Deutsche Akad. der Naturforscher Leopoldina; mem. Austrian and Bavarian Acads.; hon. mem. American Soc. of Biological Chemists; Orden pour le merite; Grosses Bundesverdienstkreuz mit Stern; Richard Kuhn Medaille. *Publications:* numerous publs. in professional journals. *Address:* Institut für Physiologische Chemie der Universität München, Goethestrasse 33, 8000 Munich 2, Federal Republic of Germany. *Telephone:* (089) 5996 429.

ZADOK, Haim J.; Israeli politician; b. 2 Oct. 1913, Poland; s. of Abraham Zadok and Malka Zadok; m. Esther Berger; two d.; ed. Warsaw Univ. and Jerusalem Law School; joined Labour Zionist Movt. 1930; emigrated to Palestine 1935; with Haganah and Jewish Settlement Police until 1948; with Israel Defence Forces in War of Independence 1948; Deputy Attorney-Gen. 1949-52; pvt. law practice 1952-65, 1967-74, 1978-; Lecturer in Commercial Law, Tel Aviv Law School 1953-61; mem. Knesset (Parl.) 1959-78; Minister of Commerce and Industry 1965-66, concurrently of Devt., of Justice 1974-77, of Religious Affairs June-Nov. 1974, Jan.-June 1977; Chair. Exec. Cttee. Hebrew Univ., Jerusalem 1969-74, Knesset Foreign Affairs and Defence Cttee. 1970-74; mem. Advisory Council, Bank of Israel 1963-74; Lecturer in Govt., Hebrew Univ. 1978-80; Chair. Exec. Cttee. Ben-Gurion Univ. of the Negev 1982-; mem. Leadership Bureau and Political Cttee. Labour Party. *Address:* 31 Hamitnadev Street, Afeka, Tel-Aviv, Israel. *Telephone:* (3) 412482.

ZADORNOV, Nikolai Pavlovich; Soviet writer; b. 5 Dec. 1909, Penza; began publishing 1941; State Prize 1952, Cultural Worker of the Latvian S.S.R. 1969, three orders, other medals. *Publications include:* Amur the Father 1941-46, The Distant Land 1946-49, Toward the Ocean 1949, Captain Nevel'skoi 1956-58, Yellow, Green, Blue... 1967, The Blue Hour (essays) 1968, The First Discovery 1969, War for the Ocean 1960-62, Gold Fever 1969, Tsunami 1971.

ZAGLADIN, Vadim Valentinovich; Soviet official; b. 23 June 1927, Moscow; m. Janetta Rogacheva; one s. three d.; ed. Moscow Inst. of Int. Relations; taught at Moscow Inst. of Int. Relations 1949-54; mem. CPSU 1955-; editorial work on various journals 1954-64; editorial post in Prague 1960-64; mem. Int. Dept., Cen. Cttee. of CPSU 1964-67; Deputy Head of Int. Dept., Cen. Cttee. of CPSU 1967-82, First Deputy Head 1982-; mem. Cen. Auditing Cttee. 1971-76; cand. mem. Cen. Cttee. of CPSU 1976-81, mem. 1981-; Deputy, Supreme Soviet of U.S.S.R. and Sec. Foreign Affairs Cttee. 1981-; Chair. Section of Global Problems of Scientific Council of Pres., Acad. of Sciences of U.S.S.R. 1981-; Deputy Chair. Parl. Group of U.S.S.R. 1981-88; Adviser to Pres. Gorbachev (q.v.) Oct. 1988-; Order of Lenin, Order of October Revolution, Order of Red Banner of Labour (thrice), and other awards. *Address:* Starokonuchenny 26, Moscow, U.S.S.R.

ZAHEDI, Ardeshir, LL.B.; Iranian diplomatist; b. 16 Oct. 1928, Teheran; s. of Gen. Fazlollah and Khadijeh Zahedi; m. Princess Shahnaz Pahlavi 1957 (dissolved 1964); one d.; ed. in Teheran, American Univ. of Beirut and Utah State Univ., U.S.A.; Civil Adjutant to His Imperial Majesty the Shah of Iran 1954-79; Amb. to U.S.A. 1959-61, to U.K. 1962-67; Minister of Foreign Affairs 1967-71; Amb. to U.S.A. 1973-79 and to Mexico 1973-76; Hon. LL.D. (Utah State 1960, Chungang Univ. of Seoul 1969, East Texas State 1973, Kent State 1974, St. Louis 1975); sentenced to death (in absentia) by Islamic Revolutionary Court; numerous decorations including Crown with Grand Cordon, Order of Taj (First Class) 1975.

ZAHID, Anwar, M.A.; Bangladesh politician; b. 12 June 1938, Jhenidah; s. of the late A. M. Dilwar Hossain; m.; five c.; ed. Rajshahi and Dhaka Univs.; imprisoned for political activities 1955, 1960, 1964, 1970; Asst. Ed., then Ed. with several East Pakistan and Bangladesh newspapers 1957-86; fmr. Pres. Union of Journalists; Sec. East Pakistan Youth League 1958; mem. Cen. Cttee. Nat. Awami Party 1965, Jt. Sec. 1968-77, Gen. Sec.

1977; mem. 11-man Steering Cttee. Nationalist Front 1978, of Jatiyo Front 1985-86, mem. Sec. Jatiyo Party 1986; M.P. 1986-, Minister of Information 1986-88. *Address:* c/o Ministry of Information, Bangladesh Secretariat, 2nd 9-Storey Bldg., 8th Floor, Dhaka, Bangladesh. *Telephone:* (2) 235111.

ZAHIR, Abdul; Afghan politician; b. 3 May 1910, Lagham; ed. Habibia High School, Kabul and Columbia and Johns Hopkins Univs., U.S.A.; practised medicine in U.S.A. before returning to Kabul 1943; Chief Doctor, Municipal Hosp., Kabul 1943-50; Deputy Minister of Health 1950-55, Minister 1955-58; Amb. to Pakistan 1958-61; Chair. House of the People 1961-64, 1965-69; Deputy Prime Minister and Minister of Health 1964-65; Amb. to Italy 1969-71; Prime Minister 1971-72.

ZAHIR SHAH (see Mohammed Zahir Shah).

ZAHN, Joachim, DR.JUR.; German business executive; b. 24 Jan. 1914, Wuppertal; s. of Hans Zahn; Man. Bd. Deutsche Treuhandgesellschaft 1945-54, Aschaffenburger Zellstoffwerke 1955-58; Dir. Daimler-Benz AG 1958-79, Spokesman, Bd. of Man. 1965-71, Chair. 1971-79; mem. supervisory Bds. of Daimler-Benz AG subsidiary and assoc. cos. Hanomag-Henschel Fahrzeugwerke GmbH, Motoren- und Turbinen-Union, Friedrichshafen and Munich, Mercedes-Benz of N. America, Argentina, Australia, Canada, U.K. and assocs. in Brazil, France, Italy, Spain, South Africa, Switzerland and India; Dir. Fried. Krupp GmbH, Portland Zementwerke, Heidelberg, Frankfurter Versicherung AG, Frankfurter Hypothekenbank, Hannoversche Messe AG, Obermain Schuhfabrik AG; Hon. Vice-Pres. and Treas. Bundesverband der Deutschen Industrie; mem. Bd. Verband der Deutschen Automobilindustrie; Senator Max-Planck-Soc.; Chair. Baden-Württemberg Landeskuratorium des Stifterverbands für die deutsche Wissenschaft; Grosses Bundesverdienstkreuz. *Address:* Gerokstrasse 13B, 7000 Stuttgart 1, Federal Republic of Germany.

ZAHN, Johannes, D.JUR.; German banker; b. 21 Jan. 1907, Aachen; s. of Hans Zahn and Käthe (née Cossel) Zahn; m. Victoria Brandeis 1938, one s. three d.; ed. Tübingen, Bonn and Harvard Univs.; Dept. Man. Reichskreditgesellschaft, Berlin 1937-45; Partner, C. G. Trinkaus, Düsseldorf 1946-71; Exec. Dir. World Bank, Washington 1952-54; Pres. Stock Exchange 1967-77; mem. Bd. Trinkaus and Burkhardt 1972- (Chair 1972-82); Grosses Bundesverdienstkreuz (Germany), Commdr., Ordre Léopold II (Belgium), Ordre de Mérite (Luxembourg), St. Olaf (Norway), Merito Civil (Spain). *Publications:* Der Privatbankier, Zahlung und Zahlungssicherung im Aussenhandel 6 ed. 1985, Banktechnik des Aussenhandeles 8 ed. 1987. *Leisure interests:* violin, golf. *Address:* 3 Malkastenstrasse, 4000 Düsseldorf 1, Federal Republic of Germany. *Telephone:* (0211) 35 98 37.

ZAHN, Rudolf Karl; German university professor; b. 6 Feb. 1920, Bad Orb; s. of Maria Margarethe Noll and Jakob Zahn; m. Dr Gertrud Daimler 1942; one d.; studied chem., physics, medicine; Physician, Scientific Asst. in Biochemistry, Univ. Hosp. Frankfurt 1948-51; High Temperature Engineer, Debus-Werke, Frankfurt, Head Kidney Lab., Univ. of Frankfurt 1951-53; Instructor in Biochemistry, Univ. of Frankfurt 1953-56, Assoc. Prof. of Biochem. and Physiology 1956-61, Asst. Prof. 1961-67; Full Prof., Chair. and Dir. Inst. of Physiological Chem., Univ. of Mainz 1967-88, Prof. Emer. 1988-; Head Group Research in Programmed Biosynthesis; Chair. Comm. for Molelcular Biology 1971; mem. Inst. of Physiological Chem., Univ. of Mainz 1967; mem. and Prof. of Medicinal Biochem. Kurume Univ., Japan 1981; Co-Chief Lab. for Marine Molecular Biology, Rudjer Boskovic Inst., Rovinj; Yugoslavia and Mainz; European Co-Ed. Mechanisms of Ageing and Development (journal); Ed. Research in Molecular Biology (Acad. series); Rockefeller Fellow 1948; mem. Acad. of Science and Literature; Dr. h.c. (Zagreb) 1988; Hon. Prof. (Kurume Univ.) 1988; Distinguished mem. Award, Rudjer Boskovic Inst. 1981, Golden Medal 1985. *Publications:* 450 publs. in int. scientific journals, on ageing, molecular biology and morphology of deoxyribonucleic acid (DNA), DNA damage under physiological conditions and under pollution. *Leisure interests:* botany, diving, travelling. *Address:* Oderstrasse 12, 6200 Wiesbaden-Schierstein, Federal Republic of Germany. *Telephone:* 2 29 84.

ZAIKOV, Lev Nikolayevich; Soviet official; b. 1923; ed. Leningrad Econ. Eng. Inst.; mem. CPSU 1957-; metal worker, shop-supt., production chief at a plant 1941-61; dir. a plant in Leningrad 1961-71; Gen. Dir. of a scientific production asscn. 1971-76; Chair. Exec. Cttee., Leningrad City Soviet 1976-; Deputy to U.S.S.R. Supreme Soviet 1979-; mem. Cen. Cttee. of CPSU 1981-, Sec. 1985-; First Sec. of Moscow City Party Cttee. 1985-; mem. Politburo CPSU March 1986-, also mem. Secr.; elected to Congress of People's Deputies of the U.S.S.R. 1989; First Sec. Leningrad Dist. Party Org. 1984; Hero of Socialist Labour 1971. *Address:* Leningrad City Soviet, Leningrad, U.S.S.R.

ZAIL SINGH, Giani (see Singh, Giani Zail).

ZAIN AZRAAI, Datuk; Malaysian diplomatist; b. 1936; m. Dawn Zain 1967; two d.; ed. Univ. of Oxford and L.S.E.; Asst. Sec., Political Div., Ministry of Foreign Affairs 1959-62; engaged in work connected with formation of Malaysia, High Comm., London 1962; Perm. Mission to UN 1962-66; Prin. Asst. Sec., later Under-Sec. for Political Affairs, Ministry of Foreign Affairs 1966-71; Prin. Private Sec. to Tun Abdul Razak, Prime Minister of Malaysia 1971-76; Amb. to U.S.A., also accred. to Mexico 1976-84; Perm. Rep. to the UN 1984-86; Exec. Dir. IBRD 1978-84; del. to numerous int. confs. inc. Non-Aligned Summit, Algiers 1973, ASEAN Summit, Bali 1976; Chair. Bd. of Trustees, Malaysian Nat. Art Gallery. *Address:* c/o Ministry of Foreign Affairs, Kuala Lumpur, Malaysia.

ZAINUDDIN, Daim, LL.B.; Malaysian lawyer, business executive and politician; b. 1938, Alor Star, Kedah State; ed. London, Univ. of Calif.; called to the Bar Lincoln's Inn; magistrate, then Deputy Public Prosecutor; later set up own law firm; Head Peremba 1979-; mem. Dewan Negara (Senate) 1980-82; mem. Dewan Rakat (House of Reps.) 1982-; Minister of Finance July 1984-; Chair. Fleet Group; Chair. and Dir. numerous cos. *Address:* Ministry of Finance, Block 9, Jalan Duta, Kuala Lumpur, Malaysia. *Telephone:* 948111.

ZAITSEV, Mikhail Mitrofanovich; Soviet military official; b. 1923; ed. Mil. Acad. of Tank Troops, Mil. Acad. of Gen. Staff; served in Soviet Army 1941-; mem. CPSU 1943-; fought on various fronts in World War II 1942-45; rank of Gen., Commdr. of various units 1957-69; Deputy Dist. Commdr., Dist. Commdr. 1969-80; mem. Cen. Cttee. of Byelorussian CP 1976-81; mem. Cen. Cttee. CPSU 1981-89; Commdr. of Troops in Germany 1980-85, in Afghanistan 1985; Deputy to Supreme Soviet of U.S.S.R. *Address:* Kommunisticheskaya Partiya Sovetskovo Soyuza, Staraya pl. 4, Moscow, U.S.S.R.

ZAKARIA, Datuk Haji Mohamed Ali; Malaysian diplomatist; b. 8 Oct. 1929, Kuala Lumpur; m. Razimah Zakaria 1957, one d.; ed. Univ. of Malaya, Singapore, and L.S.E.; served in various capacities in Malayan Civil Service; entered foreign service 1956; Second Sec., later Information Officer, London 1957-59; First Sec., later Counsellor, Perm. Mission of Malaya at UN 1959-65; Deputy Sec. (Gen. Affairs), Ministry of Foreign Affairs 1965-67; Deputy High Commr. to U.K. 1967-70; High Commr. to Canada 1970-75 and concurrently Perm. Rep. to UN 1970-74; Sec.-Gen. Ministry of Foreign Affairs 1976-; Panglima Selia Di Raja, Johan Mangku Negara, Ahli Mangku Negara. *Address:* c/o Ministry of Foreign Affairs, Wisma Putra, Jalan Wisma Putra, 50602 Kuala Lumpur, Malaysia.

ZAKHAROV, Vasiliv Georgiyevich, DR.ECON.SCI.; Soviet politician; b. 1934; ed. Leningrad Univ.; asst. lecturer in political econs., Tomsk Polytechnic Inst.; asst. lecturer, head of dept. of political econs., Lensoviet Leningrad Tech. Inst. 1963-73; mem. CPSU 1964-; work for Leningrad Dist. Cttee. of CPSU 1973-78; Prof. 1975; Sec. of Leningrad Dist. Cttee. of CPSU 1978-83; first deputy head of section of CPSU Cen. Cttee. 1983-86; Second Sec. of Moscow City Cttee. of CPSU Cen. Cttee. Jan.-Aug. 1986; mem. of CPSU Cen. Cttee. 1986; U.S.S.R. Minister of Culture Aug. 1986-. *Address:* Ministry of Culture, Moscow, U.S.S.R.

ZAKIS, Juris, DR.SC.; Soviet solid-state physicist; ed. Riga Univ.; Prof., Pro-Rector of Science Dept., and Rector of Riga Univ.; corresp. mem. of Latvian Acad. of Sciences. *Address:* Peter Stuchka Latvian State University, 19 Rainis Boulevard, Riga 226098, Latvian S.S.R., U.S.S.R.

ZALDIVAR LARRAIN, Andrés; Chilean politician; b. 18 March 1936, Santiago; s. of Alberto Zaldívar Errázuriz and Josefina Larraín Tejada; m. Inés Hurtado Ruiz-Tagle 1959; four d.; ed. Inst. Alonso de Ercilla de los Hermanos Maristas and Univ. de Chile; Sec. to Ministers of Supreme Court 1956-59; Lawyer-Sec. to Municipality of Colina 1959-63; also practised in company law and taxation; Under-Sec. of Finance 1964-68; Minister of Economy, Devt. and Reconstruction Jan.-May 1968, also Minister of Finance 1968-70; Gov. of Inter-American Devt. Bank for Chile 1969; Pres. Sociedad Celulosa Aranco 1971; Senator for Atacama and Coquimbo Provs. 1973; Pres. Partido Demócrata-Cristiano de Chile 1977, Vice-Pres. Aug. 1987-; expelled from Chile Oct. 1980; Pres. Christian Democratic Int. 1982-85. *Address:* c/o Christian Democratic World Union, Via del Plebiscito 107, 00186 Rome, Italy.

ZALM, Hon. William N. Vander; Canadian politician; b. 29 May 1934, Noordwykerhout, Netherlands; s. of Wilhelmus Nicholaas van der Zalm and Agatha C. Warmerdam; m. Lillian Vander Zalm; two s. two d.; ed. Phillip Sheffield High School, B.C.; emigrated to Canada 1947; owner and Co. Pres. Art Knapp Nurseries Ltd. 1956-; Alderman Surrey Municipal Council 1965-69, Mayor 1969-75; elected to Prov. Legis. for Social Credit Party 1969; Minister of Human Resources 1975-78, Municipal Affairs and responsible for Urban Transit Authority 1978-82, of Educ. and responsible for B.C. Transit 1982-86; established Fantasy Garden World, Richmond 1983; Leader of B.C. Social Credit Party 1986-; Premier of B.C. 1986-. *Address:* Office of the Premier, Parliament Buildings, Vic., B.C., V8V 4R3, Canada.

ZALYGIN, Sergey Pavlovich; Soviet writer; b. 6 Dec. 1913, Durasovka, Bashkir A.S.S.R.; ed. Omsk Agricultural Inst.; worked as engineer-hydrologist with Siberian branch of U.S.S.R. Acad. of Sciences; first works published 1936; State Prize 1968; Order of Red Banner of Labour, various medals. *Publications include:* Stories 1941, Spring of 1954 1955, Red Clover 1955, Altai Paths 1962, The Salty Ravine 1967-68, My Poet 1969,

Traits of the Profession 1970, and many others. *Address:* U.S.S.R. Union of Writers, Moscow, U.S.S.R.

ZAMECNIK, Paul Charles, M.D.; American physician; b. 22 Nov. 1912, Cleveland, Ohio; s. of John Zamecnik and Mary McCarthy; m. Mary Connor 1936; one s. two d.; ed. Dartmouth Coll. and Harvard Medical School; Resident, Huntington Memorial Hosp., Boston, Mass. 1936-37; Intern, Univ. Hosps., Cleveland, Ohio 1938-39; Moseley Travelling Fellow of Harvard Univ. at Carlsberg Labs., Copenhagen 1939-40; Fellow Rockefeller Inst., New York 1941-42; Physician, Harvard Univ. at Mass. Gen. Hosp. 1956-79, Hon. Physician 1983-, Exec. Sec. of Cttee. on Research 1948-50, Chair. Cttee. on Research 1954-56; Chair. Exec. Cttee. of Depts. of Medicine, Harvard Medical School 1956-61, 1968-71; Collis P. Huntington Prof. of Oncologic Medicine, Harvard Medical School 1956-79; Prin. Scientist Worcester Foundation of Experimental Biology, Shrewsbury, Mass. 1979-; Dir. John Collins Warren Laboratories of Harvard Univ. at Mass. Gen. Hosp. 1956-79; Pres. American Asscn. for Cancer Research 1964-65; Jubilee Lecturer, Biochemical Soc., London 1962; Fogarty Scholar 1975, 1978; Foreign mem. Royal Danish Acad. of Sciences; mem. N.A.S., American Acad. of Arts and Sciences, Asscn. American Physicians, American Asscn. of Biological Chemists, American Asscn. of Cancer Research (Pres. 1964-65); Hon. D.Sc. (Utrecht) 1966, (Columbia) 1971, (Harvard) 1982, (Roger Williams) 1983; John Collins Warren Triennial Prize 1946, 1950, James Ewing Award 1963, Borden Award in Medical Sciences 1965, Passano Award 1970. *Publications:* Historical and Current Aspects of the Problem of Protein Synthesis (Harvey Lectures Series 54) 1960, Unsettled Questions in the Field of Protein Synthesis (Bio-chemical Journal 85) 1962, The Mechanics of Protein Synthesis and its Possible Alterations in the Presence of Oncogenic RNA Viruses (Cancer Research 26) 1966. *Leisure interests:* skiing, tennis, pre-Columbian and ancient art. *Address:* Worcester Foundation for Experimental Biology, 222 Maple Street, Shrewsbury, Mass. 01545 (Office); 29 LeBeaux Drive, Shrewsbury, Mass. 01545, U.S.A. (Home).

ZAMFIR, Gheorghe; Romanian musician; b. 6 April 1941, Găeşti, nr. Bucharest; ed. self-taught and Bucharest Acad. of Music (studied under Fănică Luca); graduated in conducting at Ciprian Porumbescu Conservatory, Bucharest 1968; toured numerous countries in Europe as student and won first prize in many int. competitions; conductor of 'Ciocirlia' Folk Ensemble in Bucharest 1969-; Prof. of Pan-Pipes 1970; formed own orchestra 1970; numerous trips to Europe, Australia, S. America, Canada and U.S.A. and recordings. *Address:* 4 rue Tronchet, Paris, France; Dr. Teohari str. 10, Bucharest, Romania.

ZAMYATIN, Leonid Mitrofanovich; Soviet diplomatist and journalist; b. 9 March 1922, Nizhni Devitsk, Voronezh Region; m. 1946; one d.; ed. Moscow Aviation Inst. and Higher Diplomatic School; mem. CPSU 1944-, mem. Cen. Cttee. 1981-; at Ministry of Foreign Affairs 1946-50; First Sec., Secr. of Minister of Foreign Affairs 1950-52; Asst. Head, Third European Dept., Ministry of Foreign Affairs 1952-53; First Sec., Counsellor on Political Questions of U.S.S.R. Mission to UN 1953-57; Soviet Deputy Rep. on Preparatory Cttee., and later on Bd. of Govs., Int. Atomic Energy Agency (IAEA) 1957-59, Soviet Rep. on IAEA 1959-60; Deputy Head, American Countries Dept., Ministry of Foreign Affairs 1960-62, Head of Press Dept. 1962-70, mem. of Collegium of Ministry 1962-70; Dir.-Gen. TASS News Agency 1970-78, Govt. Minister 1972; Deputy to U.S.S.R. Supreme Soviet 1970-; Chief, Dept. of Int. Information, Cen. Cttee. CPSU 1978-85, Amb. to U.K. 1986-; mem. Comm. for Foreign Relations, Soviet of Nationalities 1974-; Lenin Prize 1978; Orders and medals of U.S.S.R. including Order of Lenin (twice). *Address:* Soviet Embassy, 13 Kensington Palace Gardens, London, W8 4QX, England. *Telephone:* 01-229 3628.

ŽANDAROWSKI, Zdzisław, M.PH.; Polish politician; b. 23 Aug. 1929, Warsaw; ed. Univs. of Łódź and Warsaw; mem. of Fighting Youth Union (ZMW) 1948, of Polish Workers' Party (PPR) 1948, now of Polish United Workers' Party (PZPR), expelled 1981; First Sec. of Univ. Cttee., PZPR 1954-56, Deputy Head and later Head of Propaganda Dept., later of Science and Educ. Dept., of Warsaw Cttee. 1956-60, Sec. of Warsaw Cttee. 1960-69, mem. Cen. Cttee. 1968-80, Deputy Head of Cen. Cttee. Org. Dept. and Editor-in-Chief Życie Partii 1969-70, Head of Org. Dept. 1970-77, mem. Secr. of Cen. Cttee. 1972-75, Sec. of Cen. Cttee. 1975-80; Deputy mem. Political Bureau, Cen. Cttee. PZPR Feb.-Aug. 1980; mem. Council of State April-Oct. 1980; deputy to Seym 1976-80; fmr. Chair. Seym Mandates-Statutory Comm.; Order of Banner of Labour (2nd Class), Kt.'s Cross, Order of Polonia Restituta.

ZANG ZHUBIN; Chinese zoologist; b. 1935, Shandong Prov.; leading expert on Siberian tigers. *Address:* Dalien Zoo, Dalien, Liaoning Province, People's Republic of China.

ZANKER, Paul, DR.PHIL.; German professor of archaeology; b. 7 Feb. 1937, Konstanz; ed. Univs. of Munich, Freiburg and Rome; Deutsches Archäologisches Inst. Rome 1963; Asst. Bonn 1964; lecturer, Freiburg 1967; Prof. Göttingen 1972; Prof. of Classical Archaeology, Univ. of Munich 1976-; mem. Inst. of Advanced Study, Princeton, N.J.; mem. Bayerische Akad. der Wissenschaften, Deutsches Archäologisches Inst. *Publications:* Wandel der Hermesgestalt 1965, Forum Augusta 1968, Forum Romanum 1972, Porträts 1973, Klassizistische Statuen 1974, Provinzielle Kaiserbildnisse 1983, Augustus und die Macht der Bilder 1987. *Address:* Meiserstrasse 10, 8000 Munich 2, Federal Republic of Germany.

ZANONE, Valerio; Italian politician; b. 22 Jan. 1936, Turin; ed. Univ. of Turin; worked as journalist; mem. Italian Liberal Party 1955-, mem. Nat. Council 1969-, mem. Nat. Exec. 1971-; Regional Councillor, Piedmont 1970-76; M.P. for Turin 1976-; Gen. Sec. Italian Liberal Party 1976-85; Minister for Industry 1986-87, for Defence July 1987-. *Address:* Ministry of Defence, Palazzo Baracchini, Via XX Settembre, 00187 Rome, Italy.

ZANUCK, Richard Darryl, B.A.; American film company executive; b. 13 Dec. 1934, Beverly Hills, Calif.; s. of Darryl F. and Virginia (Fox) Zanuck; m. 1st Lili Gentle; two d.; m. 2nd Linda Harrison 1969; two step-s.; m. 3rd Lili Fini 1978; ed. Harvard Mil. Acad. and Stanford Univ.; Story, Production Asst. Darryl F. Zanuck Productions 1956, Vice-Pres. 1956-62; President's Production Rep. 20th Century-Fox Studios, Beverly Hills 1962-63, Vice-Pres. in charge of Production 1963-69, Pres. 1969-71, Dir. 1966-; Chair. 20th Century-Fox TV Inc.; Sr. Vice-Pres. Warner Bros. Inc. 1971-72; Co-founder, Pres. Zanuck/Brown Co. 1972-; mem. Acad. of Motion Picture Arts and Sciences. *Producer:* The Sting 1973 (Acad. Award), Jaws 1975, Jaws II 1978, The Island 1980, Neighbors 1982, The Verdict 1983, Cocoon 1985, Target 1985; Nat. Chair. Fibrosis Asscn. 1966-; mem. Organizing Cttee. 1984 Olympics; Trustee, Harvard School; mem. Bd. of Govs. Acad. Motion Picture Arts and Sciences, and Screen Producers' Guild. *Address:* 202 N. Canon Drive, Beverly Hills, Calif. 90210, U.S.A.

ZANUSO, Marco; Italian architect; b. 14 May 1916; ed. Politecnico de Milano; architectural practice 1945-; mem. C.I.A.M. 1956-, Istituto Naz. Urbanistica 1956-; Dir. Inst. of Tech. and Faculty of Architecture, Milan Polytechnic 1970; Visiting Prof. of Industrial Design 1976; City Councillor, Milan 1956-60; mem. Building Comm., Milan Corpn. 1961-63, 1967-69; mem. City Devt. Comm., Milan 1969; lecturer, Faculty of Architecture, Milan Polytechnic; Pres. Asscn. for Industrial Design 1966-; numerous gold medals; Int. Plastic Exhbn. Prize, London 1966; Gold Medal, Ministry of Industry and Commerce 1966, etc. *Buildings include:* H.Q. for American Co. 1948; Olivetti buildings, Buenos Aires 1954; Olivetti buildings, São Paulo 1965; Brinnel buildings, Casella d'Asolo 1966; Int. H.Q., S.G.S. Fairchild, Agrate 1967; Olivetti buildings, Scarmagno (Ivrea) 1968; Olivetti factories, Crema and Marcianise 1971; regional H.Q. for Edgars Stores Ltd., Johannesburg 1972; Conference Centre, Grado 1974-75, IBM Bldg. Segrate, Acad. of San Luca 1980, IBM Bldg., San Palomba, Rome 1979-83, restoration Teatro Fossati, Milan 1980-86, Piccolo Theatre project, Milan, 1980-86. *Address:* Piazza Castello 20, Milan, Italy (Home). *Telephone:* 866127 (Home).

ZANUSSI, Krzysztof; Polish film director and scriptwriter; b. 17 June 1939, Warsaw; s. of Jerzy and Jadwiga Zanussi; ed. Warsaw and Cracow Univs. and Łódź Higher Film School; Dir. TOR Film Unit of Zespoty Filmowe Film Enterprise 1967-; Vice-Chair., Polish Film Asscn. 1971-81; has directed numerous short feature films; Prize for Illumination, Locarno Film Festival 1973, Special Prize, VII Polish Film Festival 1980, Special Jury Prize, Venice Film Festival 1982, State Prize 1st Class 1984, Kt's Cross of Order of Polonia Restituta, Gold Cross of Merit 1981, Chevalier de l'Ordre des Sciences et Lettres 1986; films include: Death of Provincial 1966 (awards in Venice, Mannheim, Valladolid and Moscow), Structure of Crystals 1969 (award in Mar del Plata), Family Life 1971 (awards in Chicago, Valladolid and Colombo), Illumination 1972 (Grand prize in Locarno), The Catamount Killing (U.S.A.) 1973, Quarterly Balance 1975 (OCIC Prize, West Berlin Int. Film Festival 1975) 1974, Camouflage 1977 (special prize, Teheran Int. Film Festival 1977, Grand Prix, Polish Film Festival 1977), Spiral 1978 (Prize of Journalists, V Polish Film Festival 1978, Cannes 1978, OCIC Prize), Wege in der Nacht 1979 (Fed. Repub. of Germany), Constant Factor (Best Dir. Cannes, OCIC Prize) 1980, Contract (Distribution Prize, Venice Film Festival) 1980, From a Far Country 1980 (Donatello Prize, Florence), Versuchung 1981, Imperative, The Unapproachable 1982, Year of the Quiet Sun 1984 (Grand Prix Golden Lion, Pasinetti Award, Venice), The Power of Evil 1985 (OCIC Prize, Montreal); TV films: Portrait of the Composer (prizes in Cracow, Leipzig), Face to Face 1967, Credit 1968, Pass Mark 1969, Mountains at Dark 1970, Role (Fed. Repub. of Germany) 1971, Behind the Wall 1971, (Grand Prix, San Remo Int. Film Festival 1972), Hipotese (Fed. Repub. of Germany) 1972, Nachtdienst (Fed. Repub. of Germany) 1975, Penderecki Lutosławski Baird (documentary) 1976, Anatomiestunde (Fed. Repub. of Germany) 1977, Haus der Frauen (Fed. Repub. of Germany) 1978, Mein Krakau (documentary) 1979, Paradigme ou le Pouvoir du Mal 1983 (Prix Oecumenic, Montreal), Blaubard (Fed. Repub. of Germany) 1984 (Prize, Venice Film Festival), Mia Varsavia 1987, Erloeschene Zeiten 1987, Wherever You Are 1988; stage plays: One Flew Over the Cuckoo's Nest 1979, Der König stirbt 1980, Mattatoiò 1982, Day and Night, Duo for One 1983, Hiòb, Les Joeux des Fammes 1985, Alle Meine Sonne 1986, Giulio Cesare 1986, Alte Zeiten 1988, Koenig Roger 1988, Geburstag der Infantin 1989, Regina dei Insort 1989. *Publications:* Nowele Filmowe (short feature films) 1976, Scenariusze Filmowe (film scripts) 1978, Un rigorista nella fortezza assediata 1982. *Leisure interest:* travel. *Address:* Kaniowska 114, 01-529 Warsaw, Poland; 8 Rue Richepance, Paris 75001, France. *Telephone:* 39-25-56 (Warsaw); 4297 5900 (Paris).

ZAPATERO GOMEZ, Virgilio; Spanish politician; b. 26 June 1946, Palencia, Cisneros de Campos; m.; two s.; ed. Strasbourg and Hamburg Univs.; worked as teacher, then Lecturer in Philosophy of Law; mem. Socialist Party (PSOE) 1970-; M.P. for Cuenca 1977-; Asst. Sec.-Gen. Parl. Socialist Group; fmr. Sec. of State for Parl. Relations; Minister for Parl. Relations and Sec. to Govt. 1986-. *Publications:* Marxismo y teoria del derecho, Marxismo y filosofia en la II Internacional. *Address:* Edificio Inia, Complejo de la Moncloa, 28003 Madrid, Spain.

ZAPFE, Helmuth, DR.PHIL.; Austrian professor of palaeontology; b. 16 Sept. 1913, Vienna; s. of Bruno Zapfe and Anna Schlimm; m. Ruth Clair 1959; ed. Univ. of Vienna; Univ. Asst. 1935-45; pvt. employment, geologist at Austrian state coalmines 1945-51; scientific official Natural History Museum of Vienna 1951-65, Dir. Geological-Palaeontological Dept.; Prof. of Palaeontology, Univ. of Vienna 1965-82, Prof. Emer. 1982-; mem. Austrian Acad.; corresp. mem. Bavarian and Yugoslav Acads. *Publications:* more than 200 publs. on fossil mammals of the Miocene and invertebrates of the Alpine Traissic. *Leisure interests:* prehistory, roman numismatics. *Address:* Laimgrubengasse 4, 1060 Vienna, Austria. *Telephone:* 587 53 40.

ZAPOTOCKY, Evzen, DR.SOC.SC.; Czechoslovak diplomatist; b. 1929, Prague; m.; two s.; ed. Coll. of Politics and Social Sciences, Prague; Asst. Prof. Prague School of Econs. 1952-58, Head Dept. Devt. Econs. 1961-66, Dean Faculty of Trade 1966-70; Second Sec. Perm. Mission to UN, New York 1958-61, Perm. Rep. 1987-; Deputy Perm. Rep. to UN Office, Geneva 1976-82; Head Dept. of Int. Econ. Relations Ministry of Foreign Affairs 1982-87; mem. expert group that published report on A New Structure for Global Econ. Co-operation 1974. *Address:* Permanent Mission of Romania to the United Nations, 573-577 Third Avenue, New York, N.Y. 10016, U.S.A. *Telephone:* (212) 682-3273.

ZAPP, Dr. Herbert; German banker; b. 15 March 1928; mem. Bd. of Man. Dirs. Deutsche Bank AG, Frankfurt; Chair. of Supervisory Bd. Deutsche Beteiligungs AG Unternehmensbeteiligungsgesellschaft, Königstein; Hoesch AG, Dortmund; NINO AG, Nordhorn; Schubert & Salzer Maschinenfabrik AG, Ingolstadt; Carl Spaeter GmbH, Düsseldorf; WFG Deutsche Gesellschaft für Wagniskapital mbH, Königstein; Wieland-Werke AG Ulm; Deputy Chair. of Supervisory Bd.: Deutsche Bank Berlin AG, Berlin; mem. of Supervisory Bd. Feldmühle Nobel AG, Düsseldorf; Horten AG, Düsseldorf; Nixdorf Computer AG, Paderborn; Phoenix AG, Hamburg; Stinnes AG, Mülheim/Ruhr; VEBA OEL AG, Gelsenkirchen; Chair. of Advisory Bd.: Bekleidungswerk Erwin Hucke OHG, Lübbecke; Deutsche Beteiligungsgesellschaft mbH, Frankfurt; Industrie-Assekuranz GmbH, Frankfurt; Reinz-Dichtungs-Gesellschaft mbH, Neu-Ulm; Deputy Chair. of Advisory Bd.: GEFA Gesellschaft für Absatzfinanzierung mbH, Wuppertal; GEFA-LEASING GmbH, Wuppertal. *Address:* Königsallee 51, 4000 Düsseldorf, Federal Republic of Germany.

ZAPPA, Frank; American musician, composer and record producer; b. 21 Dec. 1940, Baltimore; s. of Francis Vincent Zappa Sr.; m. Gail Sloatman 1967; two s. two d.; Pres. Pumpko Industries Ltd., Los Angeles; f. musical group Mothers of Invention 1964. *Films/videos:* 200 Motels 1971, Baby Snakes 1979, Dub Room Special 1982, Does Humour Belong in Music? 1985. *Recordings include:* Freak Out 1965, Apostrophe 1974, Ship Arriving Too Late to Save a Drowning Witch 1982, London Symphony Orchestra, Vol. I 1982 & Vol. II 1987, Boulez Conducts Zappa/The Perfect Stranger 1984, FZ Meets the Mothers of Prevention 1985, Jazz From Hell 1986, You Can't Do That Onstage Anymore 1987, The Old Masters series 1985-. *Publication:* Z/Pac re: First Amendment to the Constitution of the United States of America. *Address:* c/o Barking Pumpkin Records, Box 5265, North Hollywood, Calif. 91616-5265, U.S.A. *Telephone:* (818) 786-7546.

ZARB, Frank Gustav, M.B.A.; American government official; b. 17 Feb. 1935, New York; s. of Gustave and Rosemary (née Antinora) Zarb; m. Patricia Koster 1957; one s. one d.; ed. Hofstra Univ.; Graduate trainee, Cities Service Oil Co. 1957-62; Gen. Partner, Goodbody & Co. 1962-69; Exec. Vice-Pres., CBWL-Hayden Stone 1969-71; Asst. Sec., U.S. Dept. of Labor 1971-72; Exec. Vice-Pres. Hayden Stone 1972-73, 1977; Assoc. Dir. Exec. Office of the Pres., Office of Man. and Budget 1973-74; Admin., Fed. Energy Admin. 1974-77; Asst. to the Pres. for Energy Affairs 1976; Gen. Partner Lazard Frères 1977-88; Chair. and C.E.O. Smith Barney, Harris Upham 1988-; Dir. Securities Investor Protection Corpn. 1988-; Chair. Bd. of Trustees, Hofstra Univ.; mem. U.S. Presidential Advisory Cttee. on Fed. Pay, U.S. Investment Policy Advisory Cttee.; mem. Bd. of Trustees Gerald R. Ford Foundation; Distinguished Scholar Award, Hofstra Univ. *Publications:* The Stockmarket Handbook 1969, Handbook of Financial Markets 1981. *Address:* Smith Barney, Harris Upham & Co., 1345 Avenue of the Americas, New York, N.Y. 10105, U.S.A.

ZARE, Richard Neil, B.A., PH.D.; American professor of chemistry; b. 19 Nov. 1939, Cleveland, Ohio; s. of Milton Zare and Dorothy Sylvia (Amdur) Zare; m. Susan Leigh Shively 1963; three d.; ed. Harvard Univ., of California, Berkeley; Postdoctoral Research Assoc., Jt. Inst. for Lab. Astrophysics, Univ. of Colo. 1964-65; Asst. Prof., Dept. of Chem. M.I.T. 1964-65; Asst. Prof., Dept. of Physics and Astrophysics, Univ. of Colo. 1965-68, Assoc. Prof. 1968-69; Prof. of Chem., Columbia Univ. 1969-77, Higgins Prof. of Natural Science 1975-77; Prof. of Chem., Stanford Univ.

1977– (Marguerite Blake Wilbur Prof. 1987–), Shell Distinguished Prof. of Chem. 1980–85, Fellow 1984–86; Christensen Fellow, St. Catherine's Coll., Oxford 1982; Chair. Nat. Science Foundation Advisory Panel (Chem. Div.) 1980–82; Chair., Div. of Chemical Physics, American Physical Soc. 1982–85; Ed. Chemical Physics Letters; mem. Bd. of Eds. Chemical Physics, Journal of Molecular Spectroscopy, Applied Physics; mem. N.A.S. 1976–, A.A.A.S., American Chemical Soc., American Acad. of Arts and Sciences, etc.; numerous honours and awards, including Nat. Medal of Science 1983, Irving Langmuir Prize of the American Physical Soc. 1985, Kirkwood Award Medal (Yale Univ.) 1986. *Publications:* over 300 research articles. *Address:* Department of Chemistry, Stanford University, Stanford, Calif. 94305, U.S.A. *Telephone:* (415) 723-3062.

ZARIF, Mohammad Farid; Afghan diplomatist; b. 9 Jan. 1951, Kabul; s. of Mohammed and Safia Zarif; m. Alia Zarif 1973; two s.; ed. Kabul Univ., Oxford Univ.; Acting Dir. First Political Div., Ministry of Foreign Affairs 1978; First Sec. (later Chargé d'affaires), Embassy, Cuba 1979–80; Counsellor (later Chargé d'affaires), Perm. Mission of Afghanistan to the UN 1980–81, Perm. Rep. 1981–87; Vice-Chair. Cttee. on the Exercise of the Inalienable Rights of the Palestinian People 1980–; Deputy Head of Afghanistan del. to UN Gen. Ass. 1980–, Head of Afghan del. to Confs. of Non-Aligned Movt. 1978–. *Leisure interest:* reading. *Address:* c/o Ministry of Foreign Affairs, Shah Mahmoud Ghazi Street, Shar-i-Nau, Kabul, Afghanistan.

ZARKHY, Aleksandr Grigoriyevich; Soviet film producer; b. 18 Feb. 1908, St. Petersburg (now Leningrad); ed. Leningrad Technicum of Dramatic Art; Asst. Producer 1928, Producer for Lenfilm 1929–49, for Byelorusfilm 1950–55, for Mosfilm 1957–; mem. CPSU 1948–; State Prize Winner 1941, 1946; Honoured Art Worker of Byelorussian S.S.R., People's Artist of R.S.F.S.R. 1965, of the U.S.S.R. 1969; Hero of Socialist Labour 1978. *Films include:* The Wind into the Face 1929, Hot Days 1933, The Deputy of the Baltic 1937, The Member of the Government 1939, His Name is Suhi Bator 1943, Malahov Kurgan 1944, In the Name of Life 1946, Nesterko 1953, The Height 1957, The People on the Bridge 1959, Hallo Life 1962, Anna Karenina 1968, Cities and Years 1973, Twenty-six Days in the Life of Dostoevsky 1980. *Address:* Mosfilm Studio, 1 Mosfilmovskaya ulitsa, Moscow, U.S.S.R.

ŽARKOVIĆ, Vidoje; Yugoslav (Montenegrin) politician; b. 10 June 1927, Nedajno; s. of Milovan Žarković and Ljubica Žarković-Dakić; m. Ljiljana Mihovilović; two d.; ed. Higher Mil. Naval Acad., Djuro Djaković Higher School of Politics, Faculty of Political Sciences; took part in war of liberation 1941–45, holding responsible positions; staff posts in the Army after the war; Sec. Cen. Cttee., League of Communists of Montenegro; Pres. Exec. Council of Montenegro, Ass. of Montenegro; mem. Presidency of League of Communists of Yugoslavia 1974–89; mem. Presidency of Socialist Fed. Repub. of Yugoslavia 1974–84; Vice-Pres. 1976–77, 1983–84; 1941 Partisan Memorial Medal and other higher orders of war and peacetime. *Leisure interests:* hunting and fishing. *Address:* c/o Predsedništvo SFRJ, Belgrade (Office); Strumička 88c, Belgrade, Yugoslavia (Home). *Telephone:* 415-330 (Home).

ZASLAVSKAYA, Tatiana Ivanovna; Soviet economist; b. 1927, Kiev; ed. Moscow Univ.; research at Inst. of Econs. of Acad. of Sciences; mem. CPSU 1954–; mem. of Inst. of Econs. and Org. of Industrial Production in Siberian Div. of U.S.S.R. Acad. of Sciences 1963–; Corresp. mem. of U.S.S.R. Acad. of Sciences 1968–81, mem. 1981–; Dir. Public Opinion Research Centre, Moscow March 1988–. *Publications include:* The Principle of Material Interest and Wage-Earning on Soviet Kolkhozes 1958, Contemporary Economics of Kolkhozes 1960, Labour Division on the Kolkhoz 1966, The Migration of the Rural Population in the U.S.S.R. *Address:* U.S.S.R. Academy of Sciences, Institute of the Economics and Organisation of Industrial Production, Pr. Nauky 17, Novosibirsk, U.S.S.R.

ZÁTOPEK, Emil; Czechoslovak athlete; b. 19 Sept. 1922, Kopřivnice, Nový Jičín dist.; s. of František Zatopek and Anežka Zátopková; m. Dana Zátopková (Olympic javelin champion, 1952) 1948; ed. Mil. Acad. Hranice; mem. Czechoslovak People's Army 1945–70; with Czechoslovak Physical Training Assn. 1970; 10,000 metres gold medal, 5,000 metres silver medal, Olympic Games, London 1948; 5,000 metres, 10,000 metres and marathon gold medals, Olympic Games, Helsinki 1952; first in 5,000 and 10,000 metres, European Championships 1950; first in 10,000 metres, European Championships 1954; set 18 world records at 5,000 and 10,000 metres, 20, 25 and 30 km., 6, 10 and 15 miles and the one-hour race 1949–55; Meritorious Master of Sports 1948, Order of the Republic 1953, Miroslav Tyrš Medal 1982. *Publications:* My Training and Races 1955, As Told by Dana and Emil 1962. *Leisure interests:* garden, philosophy. *Address:* Nad Kázankou 3, 17100 Prague 7, Czechoslovakia. *Telephone:* 840 898.

ZATSEPIN, Georgiy Timofeyevich; Soviet nuclear physicist; b. 1927; ed. Moscow Univ.; on staff of U.S.S.R. Acad. of Sciences Inst. of Physics 1944–71; mem. CPSU 1954; Prof. 1958, corresp. mem. of U.S.S.R. Acad. of Sciences 1968; Prof. Moscow Univ. 1958–; Head of Lab. of U.S.S.R. Acad. of Sciences Inst. of Nuclear Research 1971–; main work has been on the physics of cosmic rays and neutrino astrophysics; U.S.S.R. State Prize 1951. *Address:* U.S.S.R. Academy of Sciences Institute of Nuclear Physics, Profsoyuznaya 7a, Moscow, U.S.S.R.

ZAVADIL, Miroslav; Czechoslovak politician; b. 9 Jan. 1932, Prerov, N. Moravia; fmr. mineworker; joined CP of Czechoslovakia (CPCZ) 1948; studied at CPCZ Political Coll. 1957–60; Chair. Czechoslovak Youth Union 1963; leading Sec. and Deputy Chair. Nat. Front, Czech Repub. 1970–72; Dir.-Gen. Cedok 1972–75; Cen. Sec. Czechoslovak-Soviet Friendship Union 1975; Amb. to U.S.S.R. 1984–86; Chair. Cen. Council of Trade Unions 1987; cand. mem. CPCZ Cen. Cttee. 1971, mem. 1976, mem. Secr. 1987–88; mem. Presidium of CPCZ Cen. Cttee. 1988–; Deputy to House of Nations; mem. Cen. Cttee. Czechoslovak Nat. Front; Vice-Pres. WFTU. *Address:* Central Committee of the Communist Party of Czechoslovakia, Nábř. Ludvíka Svobody 12, 125 11 Prague 1, Czechoslovakia.

ZAVALA, Silvio, D. EN D.; Mexican historian; b. 1909, Mérida, Yucatán; s. of Arturo Zavala and Mercedes Vallado; m. Huguette Joris 1951; one s. three d.; ed. Univ. del Sureste, Univ. Nacional Autónoma de México and Univ. Central de Madrid, Spain; Centre of Historical Studies, Madrid 1933–36; Sec. Nat. Museum of Mexico 1937–38; founder and dir. Revista de Historia de América (review of Pan-American Inst. of Geography and History) 1938–65; Pres. Historical Comm. of Pan-American Inst. of Geography and History 1946–65; mem. Colegio de México 1940, Emer. Prof. 1981–; life mem. El Colegio Nacional 1947; Visiting Prof. Univ. de Puerto Rico 1945, Univ. de la Habana 1946; Prof. of History of Social Insts. of America, Univ. Nacional Autónoma de México; Visiting Prof. Mexico City Coll.; Prof. Smith Coll., Mexico; Dir. Nat. Museum of History, Chapultepec 1946–54; Chief, Section of Educ., Science and Culture of UN 1947; Visiting Lecturer Harvard 1953, Visiting Prof. Washington (Seattle) and Ghent 1956; Perm. mem. UNESCO 1956–62, mem. Exec. Council 1960–66, Vice-Pres. 1962–64; Vice-Pres. Int. Council of Human Sciences and Philosophy 1959–65, Pres. 1965–71; Amb. to France 1966–75; Pres. Colegio de México 1963–66; mem. Exec. Council, Int. Cttee for Historical Sciences; mem. Nat. Acad. of History and Geography, Mexican Acad. of History, Mexican Acad. of Language 1976; corresp. mem. numerous Acads. of History, etc.; hon. mem. Historical Assen. England 1956, Royal Historical Soc., London 1957, American Historical Assen., Washington, D.C. 1959, Academia Portuguesa da Historia 1987; Prof. h.c. Colegio de San Nicolás, Morelia, Inst. of Latin American Studies Univ. of Texas; Hon. D.Litt. (Columbia Univ.) 1954, (Ghent Univ.) 1956, (Toulouse Univ.) 1965, (Montpellier Univ.) 1967; Nat. Literary Prize, History Div., Mexico 1969, History Prize, Acad. du Monde Latin, Paris 1974, Arch. C. Gerlach Prize, Panamerican Inst. of Geography and History 1986; Grand Officier, Légion d'honneur 1973, Grand-Croix, Ordre nat. du Mérite 1975, Gran Cruz Orden Civil Alfonso X el Sabio 1983. *Publications:* many works on the Spanish colonization of America, Latin American history, New World history. *Address:* Montes Urales 310, Lomas de Chapultepec, Deleg. M. Hidalgo, 11000, México, D.F., Mexico.

ZAVALA BAQUERIZO, Jorge Enrique; Ecuadorean lawyer and politician; b. 13 May 1922, Guayaquil; s. of Oswaldo Zavala Arbaiza and Ana C. Baquerizo Germán de Zavala; m. Carolina Egas Núñez de Zavala; four s.; ed. Univ. de Guayaquil; Public Prosecutor, 2nd Criminal Tribunal of Guayas 1947; Prof. of Law, Univ. de Guayaquil; Provincial Counsellor Guayas 1956–58; Vice-Deputy of Guayas 1958–60; Pres. Guayaquil Coll. of Lawyers (twice); Constitutional Vice-Pres. of Republic of Ecuador 1968–72; Pres. Acad. de Abogados de Guayaquil 1973–74, 1st Nat. Congress of Lawyers 1960, Nat. Comm. of Human Rights, XXV Curso Int. de Criminología; Vice-Pres. various legal confs.; Del. of Sociedad Int. de Criminología; mem. Int. Lawyers' Comm., Int. Lawyers' Assen., American Bar Assen., American Judicature Soc., Int. Assen. of Penal Law, Exec. Cttee. of World Habeas Corpus; Premio Código Civil 1940, Premio Código Penal 1944; Cotenta Prize for university work, Premio al Mérito Científico of Municipality of Guayaquil 1966, 1976. *Publication:* El Proceso Penal Ecuatoriano, Los Delitos contra la Propiedad. *Address:* Aguirre No. 324 y Chile, Guayaquil, Ecuador. *Telephone:* 512517, 516925, 512433.

ZAWADZKI, Sylwester, D.JUR.; Polish lawyer and politician; b. 19 Oct. 1921, Warsaw; m. Barbara Zawadzka 1954; two s.; ed. Warsaw Univ.; researcher Legal Sciences Inst. of Polish Acad. of Sciences, Warsaw 1957–63; Asst. Prof. in Higher School of Social Sciences of Polish United Workers' Party (PZPR) Cen. Cttee., Warsaw 1955–63, Extraordinary Prof. 1963–67; Prof. Warsaw Univ. 1968–, in Inst. of Political Science 1968–69; Dir. State and Law Sciences Inst. 1969–77, Ordinary Prof. 1972–; Deputy Sec. Social Sciences Dept. of Polish Acad. of Sciences 1963–68; Ed.-in-Chief monthly Państwo i Prawo (State and Law) 1967–81; mem. advisers' team of PZPR First Sec. 1977–80; Pres. Chief Admin. Court 1980–81; Minister of Justice 1981–83; mem. Seym 1972–, Chair. Legis. Comm. 1980–81; mem. Legis. Council of Chair. of Council of Ministers 1973–, Chair. 1981–86; mem. Council of State 1985–; Corresp. mem. Polish Acad. of Sciences 1976–, Foreign mem. Serbian Acad. of Sciences 1981–; Vice-Pres. Int. Assen. of Constitutional Law 1987; Dr. h.c. (Wrocław Univ.) 1981, (Ritsumeikan Univ.) 1986; mem. Polish Socialist Party 1946–48, PZPR 1948–; numerous prizes; Commdr.'s, Officer's and Knight's Cross of Order of Polonia Restituta, Order of Banner of Labour (1st Class) and many other decorations. *Publications:* numerous works on the theory of state and law and on constitutional law. *Leisure interest:* travel. *Address:* ul. Wiejska 18 m. 6, 00-490 Warsaw, Poland. *Telephone:* 28-56-19.

ZAWINUL, Josef; Austrian jazz musician; b. 7 July 1932, Vienna; s. of Josef and Maria Zawinul; m. Maxine Byars 1964; three s.; ed. Grammar

School, Real Gymnasium, Vienna Conservatoire, studied piano under Prof. Valerie Zschörner in Vienna, under Raymond Lewental in New York; studied and played classical, folk and jazz music since early childhood; started as professional musician playing with leading Austrian bands and orchestras throughout Europe 1947–59; moved to U.S.A. 1959; pianist for Dinah Washington (blues singer) and Joe Williams 1959–61; joined Julian Cannonball Adderley's band, writing songs including Mercy, Mercy, Mercy, and playing in numerous recordings 1961–69; wrote and played on 5 albums of Miles Davis (q.v.) including album in electric jazz In a Silent Way, and Bitches Brew; teamed with Wayne Shorter to form own band "Weather Report", working as producer, main composer, and keyboard instrumentalist 1970; Grammy Awards for composition of Mercy, Mercy Mercy 1967, In a Silent Way 1967, Birdland (Best Instrumental Composition) 1977; "Weather Report" named No. 1 Jazz Band 1972–78, 5 of the 8 "Weather Report" albums named Jazz Albums of the Year (Downbeat Magazine), No. 1. Synthesizer Player 4 consecutive years, No. 1 Composer, "Weather Report" No. 1 Group, (Jazz Forum). *Recordings include:* The Rise and Fall of the Third Stream, Zawinul 1969, Weather Report 1971, I Sing the Body Electric 1972, Sweetnighter 1973, Mysterious Traveller 1974, Tale Spinning 1975, Black Market 1976, Heavy Weather 1977, Mr. Gone 1978, Night Passage 1980. *Leisure interests:* boxing, soccer, swimming, philosophy. *Address:* Columbia/CBS, 51 W. 52nd Street, New York, N.Y. 10019; 1 Richland Place, Pasadena, Calif., U.S.A. (Home). *Telephone:* (213) 681-7766 (Home).

ZAWISTOWSKI, Zbigniew; Polish architect; b. 2 Feb. 1944, Warsaw; s. of Tadeusz and Zofia Zawistowski; m. Elżbieta Bauer 1967; one d.; ed. Faculty of Arch., Warsaw Tech. Univ. 1967; Asst. designer, Design Office of Investment Service "Inwestprojekt", Warsaw 1967–72; designer, then sr. designer, then studio head Design Office of Town Bldg. Plant, Warsaw 1972–76; studio head, Planning Office of Warsaw Devt. 1976–79; Gen. Designer Research and Design Office of Gen. Bldg. Miastoprojekt, Warsaw 1979–; mem. Polish Architects' Asscn. (SARP) 1967–, Pres. Young Architects' Section (SARP) Warsaw Branch 1970–71, Vice-Pres. 1976–77, Vice-Pres. Gen. Bd. SARP, Pres. Gen. Bd. SARP 1981–85; own design practice 1984–; mem. Int. Union of Architects Council 1985–; Pres. Architectural Creativity Comm., Ministry of Culture 1982–; mem. Nat. Council of Culture; numerous major group architectural and town-planning designs including housing estate in Ostrowiec Świętokrzyski 1969–73, conceptional design of dist. Ursynów North, Warsaw 1972–74; dwelling houses, Stokłosy estate, Ursynów North, Warsaw 1974–76 (head of group), design of detailed plan of the town of Zakroczym 1977; Interior designs: Faculty, Białystok Tech. Univ. 1978–79, Inn in Jurowce 1980–81. *Leisure interest:* photography. *Address:* ul. Złotych Piasków 1 m. 40, 02-759 Warsaw, Poland. *Telephone:* 42-71.91.

ZAYYEN, Dr. Yusuf (see Zeayen).

ZEA AGUILAR, Leopoldo, PH.D.; Mexican university professor and writer; b. 30 June 1912, Mexico; s. of Leopoldo Zea and Luz Aguilar; m. 1st Elena Prado Vertiz 1943 (divorced), two s. four d.; m. 2nd María Elena Rodríguez Ozan 1982; Ed. review Tierra Nueva 1940; Prof. Escuela Nacional Preparatoria 1942–47; Prof. Escuela Normal de Maestros 1944–45; Prof. Faculty of Philosophy and Letters, Univ. Nacional Autónoma de México 1944; mem. El Colegio de México 1940; Pres., Cttee. for the History of Ideas, Panamerican Inst. of Geography and History; Chief of Dept. of Univ. Studies, Sec. of Public Educ. 1953–54; research work, 1954–; mem. Soc. Européenne de Culture 1953–; Dir.-Gen. of Cultural Relations Foreign Office; Vice-Pres. Historical Comm. of Pan American Inst. of Geography and History 1961–; Dir. of Faculty of Philosophy and Letters 1966–70, Prof. Emer. 1971; Dir.-Gen. of Cultural Broadcasting 1970–; Co-ordinator, Co-ordination and Diffusion Cen. for Latin American Studies; Dir. h.c. (Univ. of Paris X) 1984, (Moscow) 1984, (Univ. de la Repub., Uruguay) 1985, (Univ. Nacional Autónoma, Mexico) 1985; Nat. Prize for Sciences and Arts 1980, decorations from Italy, France, Peru, Yugoslavia, Venezuela and Spain. *Publications:* El Positivismo en México 1943, Apogeo y Decadencia del Positivismo en México 1944, Ensayos sobre Filosofía en la Historia 1948, Dos Etapas del Pensamiento en Hispanoamérica 1949, La Filosofía como Compromiso 1952, América como Conciencia 1952, Conciencia y posibilidad del Mexicano 1952, El Occidente y la Conciencia de México 1953, La Conciencia del Hombre en la Filosofía 1952, América en la conciencia de Europa 1955, La Filosofía en México 1955, Esquema para una Historia de las ideas en América 1956, Del Liberalismo a la Revolución en la Educación Mexicana 1956, América en la Historia 1957, La Cultura y el Hombre de nuestros Días 1959, Latinoamérica y el Mundo 1960, Ensayos sobre México y Latinoamérica 1960, Democracias y Dictaduras en Latinoamérica 1960, Amerique Latina e la Culture Occidentalie 1961, El Pensamiento Latino-americano 1963, Latinamérica en la Formación de nuestro tiempo 1965, Antología de la Filosofía Americana Contemporánea 1968, Latin America and the World 1969, Dependencia y Liberación en la Cultura Latinoamericana 1974, Cultura y Filosofía en Latino-América 1976, Dialéctica de la Conciencia Americana 1976, Latinamérica Tercer Mundo 1977, Filosofía de la Historia Americana 1978, Simon Bolivar 1980, Latinoamerica en la Encrucijada de la Historia 1980, Sentido de la Difusion Cultural Latinoamerica 1981, Premio Interamericano de Cultura "Gabriela Mistral" 1987, otorgado por la Organización de los Estados Americanos 1988. *Leisure interests:* music, art. *Address:* Planta Baja de la Torre I de

Humanidades, Ciudad Universitaria, 04510, Mexico D.F. (Office); Cerrada de las Margaritas 25, Col. Florida, 01030 Mexico D.F., Mexico (Home). *Telephone:* 548-96-62 (Office); 524-31-26 (Home).

ZEA HERNÁNDEZ, Germán; Colombian lawyer, politician and diplomatist; b. 15 April 1905; s. of Luis Zea Uribe and Clorinda Hernández; m. Beatriz Gutiérrez 1937; two s. one d.; ed. Colegio de Araújo and Univ. Libre, Bogotá; mem. Congress and Senate of Colombia at various times; Mayor of Bogotá 1938–41; Comptroller-Gen. of Colombia 1941; Gov. of Cundinamarca 1943–44; Minister of Justice 1960–62; Pres. Dirección Nacional Liberal 1960; Colombian Rep. at Int. Confs. and Chief of Perm. Colombian del. to UN 1962–65, Perm. Rep. to UN 1976–78; Minister of Foreign Affairs 1966–68; Minister of Interior 1978–81; Prof. of Constitutional and Admin. Law, Univ. Libre, Bogotá, Pres. of Univ.; mem. Acad. Colombiana de Jurisprudencia; decorations from Colombia, Venezuela, Brazil, Chile, Mexico, Panama, Argentina, Peru, China, Paraguay and Bolivia. *Leisure interests:* music, reading. *Address:* Universidad Libre de Colombia, Carrera 6, No. 8-06, Bogotá, Colombia.

ZEAYEN, Dr. Yusuf; Syrian physician and politician; b. 1931; ed. Univ. of Damascus; Minister of Agrarian Reform 1963; mem. Presidential Council 1964–65; Prime Minister Sept.-Dec. 1965, 1966–68; Baath Party. *Address:* c/o Baath Party, Damascus, Syrian Arab Republic.

ZECCHINI, Salvatore, M.B.A.; Italian international finance official; b. 1943; ed. Univ. of Palermo, Columbia Univ. and Univ. of Pennsylvania; attorney-at-law until 1968; economist, Research Dept., Banca d'Italia 1972–81, Dir. Research Dept. 1981–84; econ. adviser to Prime Minister, Ministers of Treasury, Agric. and Co-ordination of (European) Community Policies; rep. Banca d'Italia at financial and econ. cttees. of several regional econ. orgs.; Exec. Dir. IMF 1984–. *Publications:* studies on econ. and financial subjects. *Address:* International Monetary Fund, 700 19th Street, N.W., Washington, D.C. 20431, U.S.A.

ZECH, Walther; German publisher; b. 12 Nov. 1918; m. Christine Herbst; two s.; ed. Düsseldorf Realgymnasium (Hindenburgschule); pupil in private bank of B. Simons & Co. (now Poensgen, Marx & Co.) Düsseldorf 1937–39; war service 1940–45, P.O.W. 1945–46; Dept. Man. Essen branch, "Die Welt" Verlags GmbH 1947–49; Ed. Düsseldorfer Zeitschriftenverlag 1950–52; Ed. and Man. Dir. VDI-Verlag GmbH, Düsseldorf 1952–62; Ed., Man. Dir. Mainzer Verlagsanstalt und Drückerei 1962–81; Man. Dir. Verlag von Hase und Koehler, Mainz; mem. Kuratorium Stifterverband für die Deutsche Wissenschaft, Kuratorium Deutsche Sporthilfe, Treas. Int. Gutenberg Ges; Grosses Bundesverdienstkreuz, Officier, Ordre nat. du Mérite (France), Ring of Honour (Mainz). *Address:* Bahnhofstrasse 4-6, 6500 Mainz, Federal Republic of Germany. *Telephone:* 06131-1441.

ZEFFIRELLI, G. Franco (Corsi); Italian theatrical, opera and film producer and designer; b. 12 Feb. 1923; ed. Liceo Artistico, Florence and School of Agriculture, Florence; designer Univ. Productions, Florence; actor Morelli Stoppa Co.; collaborated with Salvador Dali on sets for As You Like It 1948; designed sets for A Streetcar Named Desire, Troilus and Cressida, Three Sisters; producer and designer of numerous operas at La Scala, Milan 1952–, and worldwide; *operas include:* Lucia di Lammermoor, Cavalleria Rusticana, Pagliacci (Covent Garden) 1959, 1973, Falstaff (Covent Garden) 1961, L'elisir d'amore (Glyndebourne) 1961, Don Giovanni, Alcina (Covent Garden) 1962, Tosca, Rigoletto (Covent Garden) 1964, 1966, 1973, (Metropolitan, New York) 1985, Don Giovanni (Staatsoper-Wien) 1972, Otello (Metropolitan, New York) 1972, Antony and Cleopatra (Metropolitan, New York) 1973, Otello (La Scala) 1976, La Bohème (Metropolitan, New York) 1981, Turandot (La Scala) 1983, 1985, (Metropolitan, New York) 1987; *theatre:* Romeo and Juliet (Old Vic, London) 1960, Othello (Stratford) 1961, Amleto (Nat. Theatre, London) 1964, After the Fall (Rome) 1964, Who's Afraid of Virginia Woolf (Paris) 1964, (Milan) 1965, La Lupa (Rome) 1965, Much Ado About Nothing (Nat. Theatre, London) 1966, Black Comedy (Rome) 1967, A Delicate Balance (Rome) 1967, Saturday, Sunday, Monday (Nat. Theatre, London) 1973, Filumena (Lyric, London) 1977; *films:* The Taming of the Shrew 1966, Florence, Days of Destruction 1966, Romeo and Juliet 1967, Brother Sun and Sister Moon 1973, Jesus of Nazareth 1977, The Champ 1979, Endless Love 1981, La Traviata 1983, Cavalleria Rusticana 1983, Otello 1986, The Young Toscanini 1987; *ballet:* Swan Lake 1985; produced Beethoven's Missa Solemnis, San Pietro, Rome 1971; Prix des Nations 1964. *Publication:* Zeffirelli by Zeffirelli (autobiog.) 1986. *Address:* Via due Macelli 31, Rome, Italy.

ZEHRFUSS, Bernard; French architect; b. 20 Oct. 1911, Angers; s. of Henri Zehrfuss and Jeanne Hottois; m. Simone Samama, 1950; one d., one step-d.; ed. Collège Stanislas, and Ecole nationale supérieure des beaux-arts; Head, Architecture and Town Planning Services, Tunisia 1943–48; mem. Conseil Nat. de la Construction 1950–53; Consulting Architect, Ministry of Construction, Chief Architect of Public Buildings and Nat. Palaces 1953–65; Gen. Insp. of Public Buildings and Nat. Palaces 1965–68; mem. Acad. des beaux-arts 1983–, Acad. d'architecture, Acad. Int. d'architecture; Officier, Légion d'honneur, Officier, Ordre nat. du Mérite, Commdr. des Arts et des Lettres, and several foreign decorations. *Projects:* buildings in Tunisia, Algeria and in France including UNESCO Building, Paris, Palais du Centre National des Industries et des Techniques, Paris, Renault factory at Flins, Hôtel du Mont d'Arbois, Megève, Danish

Embassy in Paris, Super-Montparnasse in Paris, Science Faculty in Tunis, Société Siemens in Paris, Société Jeumont-Schneider in Puteaux, Société Sandoz in Rueil-Malmaison, French Embassy in Warsaw, Musée Gallo-Romain, Lyon, Société Spie-Batignolles in Puteaux. *Address:* 55 rue du Rocher, 75008 Paris (Office); 52 rue Saint-Georges, 75009 Paris, France (Home). *Telephone:* 42.93.61.75.

ZEIDLER, Sir David Ronald, Kt., C.B.E.; Australian business executive; b. 18 March 1918, Melbourne; s. of O. W. Zeidler; m. June Broadhurst 1943; four d.; ed. Scotch Coll., Univ. Melbourne; with CSIRO 1941-51; joined ICI Australia Research Dept. 1952, Research Man. 1953-59, Devt. Man. 1959-62, Controller Dyes and Fabrics Group 1962-63, Dir. 1963-71, Man. Dir. 1963-80, Deputy Chair. 1972-73; Chair. ICI Australia 1973-80; Chair. Metal Mfrs. Ltd. 1980-88; Dir. Amatil Ltd. 1979-89, BHP Co. Ltd. 1978-88, Westpac Banking Corpn. 1982- (Deputy Chair. 1989-), Australian Foundation Investment Co. Ltd. 1982-; Pres. Australian Acad. of Tech. Sciences and Eng. 1983-88; Vice-Pres. Walter and Eliza Hall Inst. of Medical Research 1978-; mem. of the Bd. of various insts.; Fellow, Australian Acad. of Science, Royal Australian Chemical Inst.; mem. Inst. of Chemical Engs. *Leisure interests:* skiing, tennis, sailing, fishing. *Address:* 22nd Floor, Collins Wales House, 360 Collins Street, Melbourne, Victoria 3000 (Office); 45/238 The Avenue, Parkville, Victoria 3052, Australia.

ZELADA DE ANDRES MORENO, Fermín; Spanish lawyer and banker; b. 27 Nov. 1912, La Coruña; m. María del Carmen Jurado y Herrera; six s. three d.; ed. Univs. of Santiago de Compostela, Paris and Milan; Prof. Univ. of Santiago de Compostela, Int. Univ. of Santander; joined Banco Exterior de España as Head of Legal Advisory Office 1948, Gen. Sec. 1958, Chair. Banco Exterior de España 1977-83, Hon. Chair. 1983-; nominated mem. Senate 1977-78. *Address:* Hermanos Becquer 4, Madrid, Spain (Home). *Telephone:* 232 1052 (Office).

ZELBSTEIN, Uri; French (b. Lithuanian) scientist; b. 10 Jan. 1912, Vilnius; s. of Philippe Zelbstein and Fryda Milikowski; m. Paule Pougnet 1946; one s.; ed. Univ. of Bordeaux and of Paris; successively Head of Lab. and Dir. Radio-Electronic Labs., fmr. Vitus Ests. 1933-39; Head, Electronic Dept., D.F. Factories 1940-46; Head of Electronic Research Dept., Nat. Soc. for Research and Construction of Aircraft Engines (S.N.E.C.M.A.) 1946-51; Tech. Dir. and Dir.-Gen. Sexta Soc. 1951-58; Head of Physics and Electronics Labs., later Asst. to Pres. of Atomic Div., S.N.E.C.M.A. 1960-69; Asst. to Dir. Hispano-Suiza Div. of S.N.E.C.M.A. 1969-73, Scientific Counsellor 1974-; Hon. Expert, Appeal Court of Versailles; Fellow, Asscn. des Ecrivains Scientifiques de France; mem. Accademia Teatina for Sciences (Italy), Accademia Tiberina (Italy), Soc. Française d'Histoire des Sciences et des Techniques, Soc. des Electriciens (S.E.E.), Soc. Française d'Histoire de la Médecine, laureate Acad. Int. de Lutèce, Soc. des Ecrivains des Provinces Françaises, foundation Michel-Ange (Prix du Conte); Officer of the Order of Merit for Research and Invention, Chevalier de l'Ordre nat. du Mérite; mem. Unione della Legion d'Oro (Italy). *Publications:* Les bâtisseurs du progrès (Histoire des Inventions), Le monde étrange des énergies, Laboratoires de Métrologie, Les capteurs en instrumentation industrielle, Machines, automates et robots, Les certitudes de l' à-peu-près. *Leisure interests:* history and philosophy of science. *Address:* 1 Villa des Iris, 92220 Bagneux, France. *Telephone:* (1) 46636933.

ZELENKA, Jan, PH.DR., C.SC.; Czechoslovak journalist and broadcasting executive; b. 5 Dec. 1923, Ústí nad Orlicí; m.; one s. three d.; ed. Charles Univ., Prague; Dir-Gen. Czechoslovak Television Aug. 1969-; Deputy to House of the People, Fed. Ass. 1971-; Chair. Admin. Council Int. Radio and TV Org. 1971-73; mem. CPC Cttee. 1981-; Gold Dove First Prize of Int. Leipzig TV Festival for TV Film Great Concert 1971; Order of 25th February 1948, 1949, Order of Labour 1973, Czechoslovak Prize for Journalism 1979, Order of Victorious February 1983. *Publications:* articles in journals and theoretical works on journalism. *Address:* Československá televíze, Prague 4, Kavčí hory, Czechoslovakia.

ZELLERBACH, William Joseph; American forest products industry executive (retd.); b. 15 Sept. 1920, San Francisco; s. of Harold Lionel and Doris J. Zellerbach; m. Margery Haber 1946; three s. one d.; ed. Univ. of Pennsylvania; Crown Zellerbach Corpn. 1946-85, Dir. 1960-85, Sr. Vice-Pres. 1971-85; Dir. Lloyds Bank, Calif. 1963-86; Pres. Zellerbach Family Fund; mem. Nat. Paper Trade Asscn. (Pres. 1970). *Leisure interest:* golf. *Address:* Suite 600, 98 Battery Street, San Francisco, Calif. 94111, U.S.A.

ZEMAN, Zbyněk Anthony Bohuslav, M.A., D.PHIL.; British historian and writer; b. 18 Oct. 1928, Prague, Czechoslovakia; s. of Jaroslav Zeman and Růžena Zeman; m. Sarah Anthea Collins 1956 (separated); two s. one d.; ed. London and Oxford Univs.; Asst. Ed. Foreign Office (Documents on German Foreign Policy) 1957-58; Research Fellow St. Antony's Coll., Oxford 1958-61; mem. ed. staff The Economist 1959-62; Lecturer in Modern History Univ. of St. Andrews 1963-70; Head of Research Amnesty Int. 1970-73; Dir. European Co-operation Research Group and East-West SPRL 1974-76; Prof. of Cen. and S.E. European Studies Lancaster Univ. 1976-82, Dir. Comenius Centre 1976-82, School of European Studies 1976-82; Research Prof. in European History, Oxford Univ. 1982-; Professorial Fellow St. Edmund Hall, Oxford 1983-. *Publications:* The Break-up of the Habsburg Empire 1914-1918 1961, Nazi Propaganda 1964, (co-author) The Merchant of Revolution, A Life of Alexander Helphand

(Parvus) 1965, Prague Spring 1969, A Diplomatic History of the First World War 1971, (jt. ed.) International Yearbook of East-West Trade 1975, The Masaryks 1976, (co-author) Comecon Oil and Gas 1977, Selling the War: Art and Propaganda in the Second World War 1978, Heckling Hitler: caricatures of the Third Reich 1984, Pursued by a Bear, The Making of Eastern Europe 1989. *Leisure interests:* skiing, tennis and cooking. *Address:* St. Edmund Hall, Oxford, England.

ZEMANEK, Heinz, D.TECH., DIPL.ENG.; Austrian computer scientist; b. 1 Jan. 1920, Vienna; s. of Ferdinand Zemanek and Theresia Renner; m. Maria Assumpta Lindebner 1950; one s. one d.; ed. Tech. Univ. of Vienna; telecommunications researcher, German Air Force 1943-45; in business 1945-47; mem. Faculty, Univ. of Tech., Vienna 1947-61; Dir. IBM Lab., Vienna 1961-75, IBM Fellow 1975-85; Guest Prof., Univ. of Tech., Munich 1985-86; lecturer, Univ. of Stuttgart, 1988-89; Chair. TC2 Int. Fed. of Information Processing (IFIP) 1961-68, Vice-Pres. 1968-71, Pres. 1971-74, Hon. mem. 1977-; Founding Pres. Austrian Computer Soc. 1975; mem. Acad. of Sciences (Austria), Acad. of Fine Arts (W. Berlin), Catholic Acad. (Vienna); Corresp. mem. Royal Acad. of Spain; Hon. mem. IFIP, Computer Socs. of Austria, Japan, S. Africa; Heinz Zemanek Prize 1985; Grosses Gold Ehrenzeichen (Austria) 1974, Gold. Ehrenzeichen (Vienna) 1986. *Publications:* Information Theory 1959, Calendar and Chronology, (4th edn.) 1987, Collected Papers 1988; Co-author: Computers 1971; Ed.: IFIP 10 Years 1972, IFIP 25 Years 1986; more than 400 scientific papers. *Leisure interests:* automata and their history, music. *Address:* P.O. Box 251, A-1011 Vienna, Austria.

ZEN, E-An, PH.D.; American (b. Chinese) geologist; b. 31 May 1928, Beijing; s. of Hung-chun Zen and Sophia Heng-chih Chen Zen; ed. Cornell Univ., Harvard Univ.; went to U.S.A. 1946, naturalized U.S. Citizen 1963; Research Assoc. Fellow Woods Hole Oceanographic Inst. 1955-56, Research Assoc. 1956-58; Asst. Prof. Univ. of N.C. 1958-59; Geologist U.S. Geological Survey 1959-80, Research Geologist 1980-; Visiting Assoc. Prof. Calif. Inst. of Technology 1962; Crosby Visiting Prof. M.I.T. 1973; Harry H. Hess Sr. Visiting Fellow Princeton Univ. 1981; Fellow Geological Soc. of America (mem. Council 1985-88), American Acad. of Arts and Sciences, A.A.A.S., Mineral Soc. of America, Council 1975-77, Pres. 1975-76; mem. Geological Soc. Washington (Pres. 1973); mem. N.A.S., Mineral Assscn. of Canada; Arthur L. Day Medal, Geological Soc. of America 1986. *Publications:* about 150 scientific articles and monographs in professional journals. *Address:* 959 National Center, U.S. Geological Survey, Reston, Va. 22092, U.S.A. *Telephone:* (703) 648-6166.

ZENDER, Hans; German composer and conductor; b. 22 Nov. 1936, Wiesbaden; s. of Dr. Franz and Marianne (née Fromm) Zender; m. Gertrud-Maria Achenbach 1962; studied composition and piano; conductor, Freiburg im Breisgau 1959-63; Chief Conductor, Bonn City Theatre 1964-68; Gen. Dir. of Music, Kiel 1969-72; Chief Conductor, Radio Symphony and Chamber Orchestras, Saarbrücken 1972-82; Gen. Dir. of Music (Philharmonia and City Opera), Hamburg 1984-87; Chief Conductor Radio Chamber Orchestra, Netherlands Broadcasting Corpn.; Prin. Guest Conductor Opéra Nat., Brussels 1987-; *major works include:* Canto I-V 1965-74, Zeitströme 1974, Mujinokyo 1975, Litanei 1976, Lo-Shu I-V 1977-82, Hölderlin Lesen (string quartet) 1979, Dialog mit Haydn 1982, Stephen Climax (opera) 1983-86. *Leisure interests:* literature, art. *Address:* Am Rosenbeck, 6232 Bad Soden, Federal Republic of Germany.

ZENG SHENG, Maj.-Gen.: Chinese politician; b. 1910, Bao'an Co., Guangdong Prov.; joined CCP 1936; Minister of Communications 1979-82; Adviser to State Council 1981; mem. Cen. Advisory Comm. 1987-. *Address:* People's Republic of China.

ZENG TAO; Chinese journalist, politician and diplomatist; b. 1 May 1914, Taixing County, Tiangsu; s. of Zeng Baiqin and Zhang Xiuying; m. Zhu Liqing 1939; three s. five d.; Deputy Sec. Zhenjiang Prefectural CP Cttee., Jiangsu Prov. 1949-51; Sec.-Gen. S. Jiangsu Region CP Cttee. 1951-52; Deputy Sec.-Gen. Shanghai CP Cttee. 1952-56; Sec.-Gen. People's Council, Shanghai 1956-60; Head Havana Bureau, Xinhua News Agency and Rep. of Govt. 1960-61; Adviser and Spokesman to Chinese del., Geneva Conf. on Laos 1961; Sec.-Gen. Foreign Affairs Office, State Council 1961-62; Amb. to Algeria 1962-67, to Yugoslavia 1970-73, to France 1973-77; Deputy Dir.-Gen. Xinhua News Agency March-Nov. 1977, Dir.-Gen. 1977-82; mem. Patriotic Health Campaign Cttee., CCP Cen. Cttee. 1978; Deputy Sec.-Gen. Standing Cttee., 5th NPC 1979-83; Exec. Chair. All-China Journalists Assscn. 1980-83; Deputy, mem. Standing Cttee., Vice-Chair. Foreign Affairs Comm.; Chair. NPC-European Parl. Friendship Group, 6th NPC 1983; Deputy Sec.-Gen. Presidium 6th NPC 1986-88, 7th NPC March 1988-. *Address:* Xinhua News Agency, 57 Xuanwumen Xidajie, Beijing, People's Republic of China. *Telephone:* 666957.

ZENG XIANLIN; Chinese government official; Vice-Minister for State Planning Comm. 1986-; Vice-Minister for Science and Tech. 1985-87, for State Planning Comm. 1986-87; Minister for Light Industry April 1987-; alt. mem. 13th CCP Cen. Cttee. 1987-. *Address:* State Planning Commission, Beijing, People's Republic of China.

ZENG YI; Chinese virologist and cancer research specialist; b. 1929, Guangdong Prov.; ed. Shanghai No. 1 Medical Coll.; Vice-Pres. Chinese

Acad. of Preventative Medicine Jan. 1988–. *Address:* Chinese Academy of Preventative Medicine, Beijing, People's Republic of China.

ZENG ZHI; Chinese party official; b. Yizhang Co., Hunan Prov.; m. Tao Zhu (deceased); one d.; Deputy Head Organization Dept. CCP Cen. Cttee. 1978; mem. Cen. Advisory Comm. 1982–. *Address:* Central Committee of the Chinese Communist Party, Beijing, People's Republic of China.

ZENTAR, Mehdi M'rani; Moroccan diplomatist; b. 6 Sept. 1929, Meknès; m. Milouda Zentar 1959; one d.; ed. Lycée de Meknès, Faculté de Droit, Univ. of Paris; Chef de Cabinet of Moroccan Minister of State responsible for independence negotiations with France and Spain 1956; Dir. of Gen. Admin. (with rank of Minister Plenipotentiary), Ministry of Foreign Affairs 1956–58, Dir. African Div. 1958; Dir. Nat. Tourist Office 1958; Consul-Gen., Paris 1959; Legal Adviser to Ministry of Foreign Affairs 1960–61, Dir. of Political Affairs (with rank of Amb.) 1961–63; Head of Moroccan del. to Constitutional Conf. of OAU 1962; Amb. to Yugoslavia 1964–66, to U.A.R. (now Egypt) 1966–70, to Italy (also accred. to Greece) 1974–78; Perm. Rep. to UN 1971–74, 1981–85; Amb. to U.S.S.R. 1986–. *Leisure interests:* yachting, swimming, touring. *Address:* Embassy of Morocco, per. Ostrovskovo 8, Moscow, U.S.S.R.; 3 rue Taddert, Boulevard Panoramic, Casablanca, Morocco.

ZENTMYER, George Aubrey, Jr., A.B., PH.D.; American professor of plant pathology; b. 9 Aug. 1913, Nebraska; s. of George Aubrey and Mary Strahorn Zentmyer; m. Dorothy Anne Dudley 1941; three d.; ed. Univ. of California; Asst. Forest Pathologist, U.S. Dept. of Agric., San Francisco 1937–40; Asst. Plant Pathologist Conn. Agric. Experimental Station, New Haven 1940–44; Asst. Plant Pathologist to Plant Pathologist Univ. of California 1944–62, Plant Pathologist and Prof. of Plant Pathology 1962–81, Prof. Emer. 1981–, Chair. Dept. of Plant Pathology 1968–73; Pres. American Phytopathological Soc. 1966, Fellow 1968; Fellow A.A.A.S., mem. Int. Soc. for Plant Pathology, N.A.S., and numerous socs. and cttees.; Award of Honor Calif. Avocado Soc. 1954, Special Award 1981, Award of Distinction, American Phytopathological Soc. 1983. *Publications:* Recent Advances in Pest Control 1957, Plant Disease Development and Control 1968, Plant Pathology: An Advanced Treatise 1977, Soil-Root Interface 1979, Phytophthora: Its Biology, Taxonomy, Ecology, Pathology 1983, Ecology and Management of Soilborne Plant Pathogens 1985, and numerous papers in scientific journals. *Leisure interests:* fishing, sports, stamp collecting, photography. *Address:* Department of Plant Pathology, University of California, Riverside, Calif. 92521, U.S.A. *Telephone:* (714) 787-4126.

ZEPOS, Constantine; Greek diplomatist; b. 1931, Athens; m.; two c.;ed. Athens Univ.; served in Greek Embassy, Nicosia 1960, London 1964; Alt. Rep. of Greece to the EEC and to the Conf. on Security and Co-operation in Europe 1974; Amb. to Ireland 1977; Apptd. to Ministry of Foreign Affairs 1981; Minister Plenipotentiary, First Class 1984; Perm. Rep. to the UN Aug. 1987–. *Address:* Permanent Mission of Greece to the United Nations, 733 Third Avenue, 23rd Floor, New York, N.Y. 10017, U.S.A. *Telephone:* (212) 490-6060.

ZERBO, Col. Saye; Burkinabê army officer and politician; b. Aug. 1932, Tougan; joined French army 1950, Upper Voltan army 1961; fmr. paratrooper; served Indo-China and Algeria; studied Mil. Coll., Fréjus; courses at Artillery School and Staff Coll. 1966; graduated from Ecole supérieure de guerre 1973; Minister of Foreign Affairs 1974–76; Commdr. Combined Regt., Ouagadougou, and Dir. Bureau of Studies, Armed Forces Staff; led coup to depose Pres. Lamizana Nov. 1980; Pres. of Upper Volta (now Burkina Faso) 1980–82 (overthrown in coup Nov. 1982, arrested Sept. 1983, sentenced to 15 years' imprisonment, May 1984).

ZERMATTEN, Maurice; Swiss writer; b. 22 Oct. 1910, Saint Martin; s. of Antoine Zermatten; m. Hélène Kaiser, 1941, two s. four d.; ed. Fribourg Univ.; teacher of French literature; fmr. Pres. Soc. Suisse des écrivains; Dr. h.c. (Univ. of Fribourg); awarded Prix Fondation Schiller 1938, Prix Bodmer 1940, Prix d'honneur Schiller 1946, Grand Prix catholique de littérature, Paris 1959, Grand Prix Gottfried Keller 1960, French Acad. Prize 1961, Prix Monceau 1968, Grand Prix de l'Acad. Française pour le Rayonnement de la langue française, Prix Alpes et Jura, mem. de l'Acad. europeénne des Sciences, des Lettres et des Arts. *Publications:* Le Cœur Inutile, Le Chemin difficile, Contes des Hauts-Pays du Rhône, Les Chapelles Valaisannes, La Colère de Dieu, Le Sang des Morts, Christine, Le Pain Noir, L'Esprit des Tempêtes, Connaissance de Ramuz, Traversée d'un Paradis, Les Mains Pures, Isabelle de Chevron, La Montagne sans Etoiles, Le Lierre et le Figuier, La Fontaine d'Aréthuse, Un Lys de Savoie, Le Bouclier d'Or, Le Cancer des Solitudes, La Rose noire de Marignan, La Louve, Pays sans Chemin, Visages, Les Sèves d'Enfance, Une Soutane aux Orties, La Porte Blanche, Les dernières années de Rainer Maria Rilke, Pour prolonger l'Adieu, Un Amour à Grenchen-Nord, L'Homme aux Herbes, Gonzague de Reynold l'Homme et l'Oeuvre, A l'Est du Grand Couloir, Contes et Légendes de la Montagne valaisanne, L'Epée au Bois dormant, Georges Borgeaud, Théodore Stravinsky, Terre de fer, Ciel d'airain, Vous que je n'ai pas assez aimée. *Address:* Gravelone, Sion, Valais, Switzerland. *Telephone:* 027 22 20 84.

ZETTERLING, Mai Elisabeth; Swedish film director, actress and writer; b. 24 May 1925; d. of Joel Zetterling and Linnea Thörnblom; m. 1st Tutte Lemkow 1944 (divorced 1953), one s. one d.; m. 2nd David Hughes 1958

(divorced 1977); ed. Royal Theatre School of Drama, Stockholm; Staff of Nat. Theatre, Stockholm 1943–45; first prize Venice Film Festival (The War Game) 1963; under contract film director to Sandrews of Sweden. *Swedish stage appearances include:* St. Mark's Eve, The Beautiful People, Shadow and Substance, Twelfth Night, Merchant of Venice, Les Mouches, House of Bernada; *London stage appearances include:* The Wild Duck and The Doll's House (Ibsen), Point of Departure and Restless Heart (Anouilh), The Seagull (Chekhov), Creditors (Strindberg): acted in films: Frenzy 1944, Frieda 1947, The Bad Lord Byron 1948, Quartet 1948, Knock on Wood 1954, A Prize of Gold 1955, Seven Waves Away 1956, Only Two Can Play 1962, The Main Attraction 1962, The Bay of St. Michael 1963, The Witches 1988; film dir. BBC Television Documentaries; Dir. and Co-writer films: The War Game 1963, Loving Couples 1965, Night Games 1966, Dr. Glas 1968, The Girls 1968, Flickorna 1968, Visions of Eight (co-dir.) 1973, Vincent the Dutchman, We Have Many Names 1975, The Moon Is a Green Cheese 1976, The Native Squatter 1977, Lady Policeman 1979, Of Seals and Men 1979, Scrubbers 1983, Amorosa 1986. *Publications:* The Cat's Tale (with David Hughes) 1965, Night Games (novel, also film), In the Shadow of the Sun (short stories) 1975, Bird of Passage (novel) 1976, Rains Hat (children's book) 1979, Ice Island (novel) 1979, All those Tomorrows (autobiog.) 1985, The Crystal Castle 1985. *Address:* c/o Douglas Rae Management Ltd., 28 Charing Cross Road, London, W.1, England.

ZEVI, Bruno; Italian architect; b. 22 Jan. 1918, Rome; s. of Guido Zevi and Ada Bondí; m. Tullia Calabi 1940; one s. one d.; ed. Graduate School of Design, Harvard Univ. and Faculty of Architecture, Univ. of Rome; left Italy for political reasons 1939–44; Ed. Quaderni Italiani (anti-Fascist magazine smuggled into Italy from U.S.A.) 1941–43; Dir. tech. magazines of U.S. Information Service in Italy 1944–46; co-founder Asscn. for an Organic Architecture in Italy 1946; co-Ed. Metron, an architectural magazine 1945–55; Prof. History of Architecture, Univ. of Venice 1948–63; Prof. History of Architecture, Univ. of Rome 1963–79; Gen. Sec. Italian Town Planning Inst. 1952–68; Vice-Pres. Italian Inst. of Architecture; Ed. L'architettura—cronache e storia 1955–; architectural critic of the weekly L'Espresso 1955–; Pres. Int. Cttee. of Architectural Critics; Academician Venice Acad. of Art 1953, Accad. di San Luca, Rome 1960–; Hon. mem. Royal Inst. of British Architects, Italian Parl. 1987–; Hon. Fellow American Inst. of Architects. *Publications:* Towards an Organic Architecture 1945, Saper Vedere l'Architettura 1948 (Architecture as Space), Poetica dell'Architettura Neoplastica 1953, Architecture (in International Encyclopaedia of the Arts) 1958, Biagio Rossetti, architetto ferrarese—il primo urbanista moderno europeo 1960, Architectura in nuce 1960, Michelangelo architetto 1964, Erich Mendelsohn: opera completa 1970, Cronache d'architettura 1970–80, Saper vedere l'urbanistica 1971, Spazi dell' architettura moderna 1973, Il linguaggio moderno dell' architettura (The Modern Language of Architecture) 1973, Architettura e Storiografia 1974, Storia dell' architettura moderna 1975, Editoriali di architettura 1979, Frank Lloyd Wright 1979, Giuseppe Terragni 1980, Pretesti di critica architettonica 1983. *Leisure interests:* tennis, swimming. *Address:* Via Nomentana 150, 00162-Rome, Italy. *Telephone:* 8320684.

ZHAN WU; Chinese economic official; Asst. Gen. Man., Bank of China 1957; Dir. Agricultural Econs. Inst. 1979–; mem. State Comm. for Restructuring Econ. System 1984–; leading mem. Research Soc. of Animal Husbandry Econ. Theory 1978; Leading mem. Research Soc. of Forestry Econ. Theory 1978. *Address:* State Council, Beijing, People's Republic of China.

ZHANG AIPING, Gen.; Chinese army officer and politician; b. 1910, Daxian Co., Sichuan Prov.; joined CCP 1926; veteran army and party cadre; mil. cadre in East China 1949–54; Deputy Chief of Gen. Staff PLA 1954–67; alt. mem. 8th Cen. Cttee. CCP 1958; criticized and removed from office during Cultural Revolution 1967; Chair. Science and Tech. Comm. for Nat. Defence 1975–77; Deputy Chief of Gen. Staff PLA 1977; mem. 11th Cen. Cttee. CCP 1977; a Vice-Premier 1980–82; Minister of Defence 1982–88; mem. 12th Cen. Cttee. CCP 1982–85; State Councillor 1982–88; Deputy Sec.-Gen. Mil. Comm. under CCP Cen. Cttee. 1982–88; mem. Cen. Mil. Comm. 1983–88; mem. Standing Cttee. of Cen. Advisory Comm. 1987–. *Address:* State Council, Beijing, People's Republic of China.

ZHANG BANGYING; Chinese party and government official; b. 1907, Yao Co., Shaanxi Prov.; joined CCP 1935; mem. Council All-Circles Asscn. for Promoting Constitutional Govt., Yenan 1940; org. dept. official 1940–49; mem. Finance and Econ. Cttee., Dir. Public Security Dept., Shaanxi Prov. People's Govt. 1950; Vice-Gov. Shaanxi Prov. 1950–53; mem. N.W. Mil. Admin. Cttee. 1950–53; Third Sec. Xinjiang Prov. CCP Cttee. 1951–54; Dir. Political Dept., PLA, Xinjiang Mil. Dist. 1953; mem. 1st NPC 1954, del. to Finland Aug. 1957; Deputy Dir. Communications Work Dept. of CCP Cen. Cttee. 1958; mem. 3rd CPPCC 1958–60; alt. Sec., Secr. CCP Cen. Cttee. N. China Bureau 1963; purged 1967, rehabilitated 1973; mem. Standing Cttee. 5th CPPCC 1978; mem. Cen. Advisory Cttee. of CCP Cen. Cttee. 1982. *Address:* Central Advisory Committee of the Central Committee of the Chinese Communist Party, Zhongnanhai, Beijing, People's Republic of China.

ZHANG BOXIANG, Maj.-Gen.; Chinese army officer; b. 1918 Laiwu Co., Shandong Prov.; PLA Maj.-Gen. stationed in Beijing 1964; Dir. Org. Dept., PLA Gen. Political Dept. 1981–; alt. mem. 12th CCP Cen. Cttee. 1982–87.

Address: Organization Department, People's Liberation Army General Political Department, Beijing, People's Republic of China.

ZHANG CAIQIAN; Chinese army officer; b. 1912, Anhui; guerilla leader in Hubei, Henan, Anhui and Hunan 1946; Chief of Staff Hubei Mil. District, PLA 1950; Lieut.-Gen. PLA 1958; Deputy Commdr. Nanjing Mil. Region, PLA 1958–70; mem. 9th Cen. Cttee. of CCP 1969, 10th Cen. Cttee. 1973, 11th Cen. Cttee. 1977; Deputy Chief of Staff PLA 1971; Commdr. PLA Wuhan Units 1980–82; mem. Cen. Advisory Comm. 1982–87. *Address:* People's Liberation Army Headquarters, Wuhan, People's Republic of China.

ZHANG CHEN; Chinese government official; b. 1918, Henan; fmr. Dir. Org. Dept., Wuhan Municipal Enterprise CCP Cttee., Deputy Dir. Tianjin No. 2 Cotton Mill, Vice-Chair. Shenyang Municipal Planning Comm., Deputy Dir. 13th Bureau and Dir. 1st Bureau, 2nd Ministry of Machine-Building; Minister of Nuclear Industry 1982–83, Adviser Ministry of Nuclear Industry 1984; Adviser Finance and Econ. Cttee. NPC 1986. *Address:* State Council, Beijing, People's Republic of China.

ZHANG CHENGZHI; Chinese writer; b. 1948, Beijing; ed. Beijing Univ.; mem. Inst. of Nationalities, Chinese Acad. of Social Sciences; mem. Chinese Writers' Assocn. *Publications include:* The Black Steed, Rivers of the North, Golden Pastureland. *Address:* Chinese Writers' Association, Beijing, People's Republic of China.

ZHANG CHUNQIAO; Chinese party official; b. circa 1911; Dir. East China Gen. Branch, New China News Agency 1950; Dir. Liberation Daily, Shanghai 1954; Alt. Sec. CCP Shanghai 1964, Sec. 1965; Chair. Shanghai Revolutionary Cttee. 1967; Deputy Head Cen. Cultural Revolution Group 1967; First Political Commissar Nanjing Mil. Region, PLA 1967; mem. Politburo, 9th Cen. Cttee., CCP 1969; First Sec. CCP Shanghai 1971–76; mem. Standing Cttee., Politburo, 10th Cen. Cttee. of CCP 1973, 1975–76; Vice-Premier State Council 1975–76; Dir.-Gen. Political Dept., PLA 1975–76; arrested as mem. of "Gang of Four" Oct. 1976, expelled from CCP July 1977; in detention; on trial Nov. 1980–Jan. 1981; sentenced to death Jan. 1981 (sentence suspended), life imprisonment Jan. 1983. *Address:* People's Republic of China.

ZHANG DEDI; Chinese sculptor; b. 1933, Heze, Shandong; ed. Cen. Inst. of Fine Arts, Beijing. *Works include:* Tibetan Boy, The Poet Ai Qing, Debut, Rowing. *Address:* People's Republic of China.

ZHANG DEHUA; Chinese sculptress; b. 1931, Qingdao, Shandong; awarded Gold Medal, Paris Salon of Arts 1982, for "Yearning for . . ."

ZHANG DEWEI; Chinese diplomatist; Amb. to Democratic Kampuchea, concurrently Perm. Rep. to ESCAP 1985–. *Address:* Embassy of the People's Republic of China, Phnom Penh, Kampuchea.

ZHANG FENGBO, PH.D.; Chinese economist; b. 1957; ed. Shanghai Foreign Languages Inst., Kyoto Univ., Japan; first Chinese liberal arts student to gain Japanese Doctorate; Sr. Research Fellow at State Council Research Cen. on Econ., Tech. and Social Devt. *Publications include:* On the Developing Trend of Chinese Communications and Transportations, On the Reasons for the Japanese State-Owned Railway's Deficit. *Address:* Research Centre on Economic, Technological and Social Development, The State Council, Beijing, People's Republic of China.

ZHANG GENSHENG; Chinese party official b. April 1923, Hebei; m. Du Qingyan 1945; three s. one d.; Sec. CCP Cttee., Zhujiang Co., Guangdong 1951, Beijiang Dist., Guangdong 1952, Second Sec., Beijiang Dist. 1952; Sec. CCP Cttee., N. Guangdong Dist. 1955; mem. CCP Cttee., Guangdong 1957, Sec.-Gen. 1958, mem. Standing Cttee. 1959, Alt. Sec. Secr. 1962; stood trial during Cultural Revolution; Vice-Chair. Prov. Revolutionary Cttee. 1973–77; mem. Standing Cttee., CCP Cttee., Guangdong 1973–75, Sec. CCP Cttee. 1975–77; Vice-Minister of Agric. and Forestry 1978, of Agric. 1979; Sec. CCP Cttee., Jilin 1980; Acting Gov. of Jilin 1982, Gov. 1982–83; 12th Cen. Cttee., CCP 1982; Deputy Dir.Gen. of Research Centre for Econ., Tech. and Social Devt. of State Council 1985; Deputy Dir. Research Centre for Rural Devt. of State Council 1986–. *Address:* Office of Research Centre of State Council, No. 9 Xihuanggenanjie, Beijing, People's Republic of China. *Telephone:* 652578.

ZHANG GUOSHENG; Chinese politician; Sec. Qinghai Prov. CP 1959; disappeared 1960; Sec. Qinghai Prov. CP 1979–85; Chair. Qinghai Prov. Revolutionary Cttee. 1979; Gov. Qinghai Prov. 1979–82; mem. Presidium CPPCC 1983, Standing Cttee. CPPCC 1983.

ZHANG JIANMIN; Chinese party official; Dir. Org. Dept., Guizhou Prov. CCP 1958; Sec. CCP Cttee., Guizhou 1966; dismissed from all posts Jan. 1967; Vice-Chair. Revolutionary Cttee., Guizhou 1975; Vice-Gov. Shanxi Prov. 1979–83, Vice-Chair. 1985–; alt. mem. 12th CCP Cen. Cttee. 1982–87; mem. CCP Cttee., Shanxi 1983; Vice-Mayor of Beijing 1984–; mem. Standing Cttee., Beijing 1987–. *Address:* Beijing Municipal People's Government, Beijing, People's Republic of China.

ZHANG JIANZHANG; Chinese artist; b. 1938, Kunming, Yunnan; ed. Yunnan Coll. of Arts. *Works include:* Yi Women.

ZHANG JIARUI; Chinese artist; b. 1934, Dalien, Liaoning Prov.; specialises in traditional style prints. *Address:* Dalien Daily, Dalien, Liaoning Province, People's Republic of China.

ZHANG JIE; Chinese writer; b. 27 April 1937, Beijing; d. of Zhang Shuan Zi; m. Sun You Yu 1986; one d.; ed. People's Univ., Beijing; Council mem. Chinese Asscn. of Writers; mem. Int. PEN (China br.); mem. Beijing Political Consultative Conf.; Nat. Awards for Short Story, Novelette and Novel (first writer to win all three kinds of awards). *Publications:* Love Must Not Be Forgotten 1979, Leaden Wings 1981, The Ark (in German, French, Swedish and English) 1982. *Leisure interest:* music. *Address:* Beijing Writers' Association, Beijing, People's Republic of China.

ZHANG JINGFU; Chinese politician; b. 1901, Beijing; mem. CCP 1934–; fmr. Vice-Minister of Local Industry and Vice-Pres. Scientific and Tech. Comm.; alt. mem. 8th Cen. Cttee. of CCP 1956; Vice-Minister of Forestry 1956–58; criticized and removed from office during Cultural Revolution 1967; Minister of Finance 1975–79; Gov. and First Sec. Anhui Prov. Cttee. 1980–81; First Political Comm. Anhui Mil. Div. 1980–82; State Councillor 1982–88; Minister in Charge of State Econ. Comm. 1982–84; mem. State Finance and Econ. Comm.; mem. 12th Cen. CCP Cttee. 1982–87; mem. Standing Comm. of Cen. Advisory Comm. 1987–; Chair. Guidance Cttee. for State Examinations for Econ. Man. Personnel 1983–; Hon. Pres. Soc. for Study of Workers' Educ. 1984; Chair. Nat. Industrial Safety Cttee. 1985–; Pres. Chinese Asscn. for Int. Exchange of Personnel 1986–. *Address:* c/o State Economic Commission, Sanlihe, Fuxingmenwai, Beijing, People's Republic of China.

ZHANG JINGLI; Chinese industrialist and party official; Jiangsu Del. to NPC 1959–68; Dir. China Int. Trust and Investment Corpn. 1979; Vice-Chair. All China Fed. of Industry and Commerce 1979–; Vice-Chair. Jiangsu Prov. CPPCC; Vice-Chair. China Industry, Commerce and Econ. Devt. Corpn. 1987–. *Address:* China Industry, Commerce and Economy Development Corporation, Beijing, People's Republic of China.

ZHANG JUN; Chinese government official; b. 1919, Shandong; Second Political Commissar Public Security Corps, PLA Kunming Units, Deputy Political Commissar Yunnan Mil. Dist. (dates unknown); mem. Standing Cttee., 3rd NPC 1965; Vice-Minister 7th Ministry of Machine-Building 1976; Sec. CCP Cttee., No. 1 Compound, 7th Ministry of Machine-Building 1976; Minister of Spaceflight Industry 1982. *Address:* State Council, Beijing, People's Republic of China.

ZHANG KERANG; Chinese artist; b. 1937, Liaoning; ed. Graphic Art Dept., Lu Xun Inst. of Arts; Vice-Chair. Hebei Prov. People's Congress 1985–. *Address:* People's Republic of China.

ZHANG LICHANG; Chinese party and government official; b. 1939, Tianjin; Dir. Tianjin Bureau of Metallurgy, Chair. Tianjin Municipal Econ. Cttee. 1985–; Vice-Mayor Tianjin 1985–; alt. mem. CCP Cen. Cttee. 1985–. *Address:* Central Committee of the Chinese Communist Party, Zhongnanhai, Beijing, People's Republic of China.

ZHANG QINZU; Chinese woodcut artist; b. 1927, Hebei; Deputy Curator Xu Beihang Museum. *Leisure interests:* Chinese national folk arts and Chinese painting. *Address:* c/o Xu Beihang Museum, Beijing, People's Republic of China. *Telephone:* 65.3540.

ZHANG RENZHI; Chinese landscape artist; b. 7 Dec. 1935, Hebei Prov.; s. of Zhang Pu and Zhang Chen; m. Lang Mei 1966; two s.; ed. Cen. Art Inst.; joined Beijing Art Acad. as professional artist; jt. exhbn. Xinxiang, Henan Prov., solo exhbn. Tianjin, exhbns. Algiers, Germany, Guyana, U.S.A.; prize for 'Lasting Forever' (burnt pine tree). *Publication:* Zhang Renzhi's Album of Paintings. *Leisure interest:* travel. *Address:* Art Academy, Beijing, People's Republic of China. *Telephone:* 581993.

ZHANG SHOU; Chinese academic and government official; b. 19 July 1930, Changshu Co., Jiangsu Prov.; ed. Jiaotong Univ.; joined CCP 1949; taught at Jiaotong Univ. 1953–80, Deputy Dir. Dept. of Eng. and Physics 1958–62, Dept. of Naval Architecture 1962–72, Dir. 1972–78; Vice-Pres. Jiaotong Univ. 1979, First Vice-Pres. 1980–82; Visiting Scholar at Univ. of Pennsylvania 1981–82; mem. 12th CCP Cen. Cttee. 1982; mem. 13th CCP Cen. Cttee. 1987; Vice Minister State Planning Comm. 1983–; Chair. State Econ. Information Centre 1987–; Dir. Data for Int. Devt. Asscn. 1987–; Consultant System Eng. Asscn. of China 1985–; Hon. Dir. Computer Asscn. of China 1987–; Consultant State Natural Science Foundation of China 1987–. *Publications:* Hydrostatics of Naval Architecture 1964, A Concise English-Chinese Naval Architecture Dictionary 1973, Econometrics 1984, Scientific Progress and Economic Development 1988, Reform and Development 1988. *Address:* State Planning Commission, 38 Sanlihe, Fuxingmenwai, Beijing, People's Republic of China. *Telephone:* 868521.

ZHANG SHUBIN; Chinese ice skater; b. 1966, Heilongjiang; winner Men's Figure Skating Contest, 12th World Univ. Games, Belluno, Italy 1985. *Address:* Chinese Sports Federation, Harbin, Heilongjiang, People's Republic of China.

ZHANG SHUGUANG; Chinese party and government official; mem. 12th Cen. Cttee. CCP 1982; Sec. CPC 2nd Prov. Cttee., Hebei; Gov. of Hebei 1983–86; Sec. CCP Cttee. Nei Monggol 1986; mem. Cen. Advisory Comm.

1987–. *Address:* Office of the Governor, Provincial People's Government, Hebei Province, People's Republic of China.

ZHANG TANGMIN; Chinese chemist and traditional medical practitioner; b. 1940; Asst. Researcher, Chem. Research Inst. 1962–81; self-taught in traditional Chinese medicine 1964–; assigned to Beijing Xuanwu Hosp. 1981–; opened own clinic 1981. *Address:* Chemistry Research Institute, Chinese Academy of Sciences, Beijing, People's Republic of China.

ZHANG TING; Chinese government official; b. 1923, Shanxi; fmr. Deputy Dir. Planning Dept., 1st Ministry of Machine-Building, later of 3rd Ministry; fmr. Dir. Planning Bureau, 4th Ministry of Machine-Building and concurrently Vice-Minister 4th Ministry of Machine-Building; Minister of Electronics Industry 1982–83, Adviser 1984; Vice-Chair. China Nat. Electronic Tech. Import and Export Corpn. 1981; Dir. Political Dept., Beijing Mil. Region 1985–. *Address:* State Council, Beijing, People's Republic of China.

ZHANG TINGFA; Chinese air force officer and party official; b. 1917, Hubei; Deputy Chief of Staff, PLA Air Force 1958, Deputy Commdr. 1964; criticized and removed from office during Cultural Revolution 1967; Deputy Commdr. Air Force 1973; Political Commissar 1976; mem. Politburo, 11th Cen. Cttee. of CCP 1977; mem. Politburo 12th Cen. CCP Cttee. 1982–85; Commdr. PLA Air Force 1978–85; Pres. Spare-time Univ. for Cadres of Air Force Orgs. 1983–; Chair. Air Force Academic Research Cttee. 1983–; mem. Cen. Advisory Comm. 1985–. *Address:* People's Liberation Army Air Force Headquarters, Beijing, People's Republic of China.

ZHANG TONG, Col.; Chinese army officer and diplomatist; b. 1919; m. Fang Yanzhuan; Mil. attaché, Embassy in India 1956–60; Chargé d'affaires (a.i.), accred. to pro-Lumumba regime in Stanleyville, Congo (now Kisangani, Zaire) 1961; Deputy Dir. First Asian Affairs Dept., Ministry of Foreign Affairs 1962–64, Dir. 1964–67; Amb. to Pakistan 1969–74, to Egypt 1974–77, to Fed. Repub. of Germany 1977–82. *Address:* c/o Ministry of Foreign Affairs, Beijing, People's Republic of China.

ZHANG WANNIAN; Chinese army officer; b. 1 Aug. 1928, Huangxian Co., Sangdong Prov.; s. of Jin Man Zhang and Li Shi Zhang; m. Pei Zhao Zhong 1954; four d.; alt. mem. 12th CCP Cen. Cttee. 1982, 13th Cen. Cttee. 1987; Deputy Commdr. Wuhan Mil. Region (now Canton Mil. Region) 1982–87, Commdr. 1987–; Deputy Sec. Party Cttee., Guangzhou Mil. Region 1987–; Standing mem. Party Cttee., Guangzhou Mil. Region 1985–. *Address:* Canton Military Region Headquarters, Guangzhou, Guangdong, People's Republic of China. *Telephone:* 777585.

ZHANG WANXIN; Chinese party official; b. 5 May 1930, Harbin; m. Den Yinin 1958; one s. one d.; Vice-Pres. China Petrochemical Corpn. 1983–; alt. mem. 12th CCP Cen. Cttee. 1982; alt. mem. 13th CCP Cen. Cttee. 1987; Vice-Chair. China Chemical Eng. and Industry Soc.; Prof. Shenzhen Univ.; mem. CCP Cttee., Beijing Municipality 1982–; Deputy Dir.-Gen. Econ., Tech. and Social Devt. Research Center April 1988–. *Leisure interest:* liberal arts. *Address:* China Petro-Chemical Corporation, P.O. Box 1429, Beijing, People's Republic of China. *Telephone:* 4216402.

ZHANG WEIXUN; Chinese civil servant and United Nations official; fmrly. in Foreign Relations Dept., Ministry of Health, Peking; Asst. Dir.-Gen. World Health Org. (WHO), in charge of family health and health services divs. 1973–. *Address:* c/o Ministry of Foreign Affairs, Beijing, People's Republic of China.

ZHANG WENJIN; Chinese diplomatist; b. 13 June 1914, Beijing; m. Zhang Ying 1946; three s. one d.; ed. Qinghua Univ.; Deputy Chief (later Chief), Office of Foreign Affairs, Tianjin Municipality 1949–54; Deputy Dir. (later Dir.), Dept. of Asian Affairs, Ministry of Foreign Affairs 1954–64; attended Geneva Conf. 1954; Amb. of People's Repub. of China to Pakistan 1965–66; mem., Chinese Del., Sino-Soviet Border Talks 1969–70; Dir., Dept. of European and American Affairs and Asst. Minister, Ministry of Foreign Affairs 1971–73, Vice-Minister 1978–83; Amb. to Canada 1973–76; Chair., Chinese Del., 37th UN Gen. Ass. 1982; Amb. to U.S.A. 1983–85; Dir. Inst. of Foreign Relations, Beijing Univ. 1985–; Pres. Chinese People's Asscn. for Friendship with Foreign Countries 1986–; Vice-Chair. Organizing Cttee. for Int. Peace Year 1986; Vice-Chair. Foreign Affairs Cttee., Nat. People's Congress 1988, mem. Standing Cttee., NPC 1988–. *Address:* Chinese People's Association for Friendship with Foreign Countries, 1 Tai Ji Chang, Beijing, People's Republic of China. *Telephone:* 544463.

ZHANG WENSHOU; Chinese government official; Deputy Sec.-Gen. State Council 1985–; Sec. CCP Cttee. of State Council Organs 1985–. *Address:* State Council, Zhong Nan Hai, Beijing, People's Republic of China.

ZHANG WENYU; Chinese physicist; b. 1910; ed. Cambridge Univ.; Prof. Princeton Univ. 1938–45; Dir. Inst. of High Energy Physics 1977–; Pres. Soc. High Energy Physics 1981–; mem. Presidium 6th NPC 1986, Standing Cttee. NPC 1983–; Hon. Pres. Nuclear Soc. 1984–. *Address:* Chinese Academy of Science, Beijing, People's Republic of China.

ZHANG XIAN; Chinese writer; b. 22 June 1934, Shanghai; s. of Zhang Zuyin and Li Dezhen; m. Zhang Ling 1967; one s. one d.; ed. Qinghua Univ. (Mechanical Eng.) 1953; began publishing when working at Iron and Steel Industry, Inst. of Eng.; then labourer; became professional writer of Jiangsu Br. of Chinese Writers' Asscn. 1983. *Publications:* Memories, A Corner Forsaken by Love, Widow, An Unbreakable Red Silk Thread,

Ginkgo Tree (stories), Selected Film Scenarios, The Collection of New Film Scenarios, The Selection of New Film Scenarios. *Leisure interests:* music, travel. *Address:* Jiangsu Branch of Chinese Writers' Association, Nanjing, People's Republic of China.

ZHANG XIANG; Chinese army medical officer; b. 16 Feb. 1919, Da Wu County, Hubei Prov.; s. of Chang Zi Yu and Chang Li Shi; m. Yao Di 1946; two s. two d.; Deputy Dir. Public Health Dept. under PLA Gen. Logistics Dept. 1976–79, Dir. Public Health Dept. 1979–82; Deputy Dir. PLA Gen. Logistics Dept. 1982. *Leisure interests:* hunting and fishing. *Address:* People's Liberation Army General Logistics Department, Beijing, People's Republic of China.

ZHANG XIANGSHAN; Chinese journalist and politician; b. 1914, Zhejiang Prov; ed. partly in Japan; Dir. Inst. of Marxism-Leninism, Beijing 1950; Cadre, Dept. in CCP Cen. Cttee. 1959; Sec.-Gen. del. to 3rd Conf. for Afro-Asian Solidarity, Tanganyika 1963; mem. del. to 10th and 11th World Confs. Against Atomic and Hydrogen Bombs, Japan 1964, 1965; Cadre, Int. Liaison Dept., CCP Cen. Cttee. 1971, Deputy Dir. 1973–76; Dir. Cen. Broadcasting Admin. 1977–; Deputy Dir. Propaganda Dept., CCP Cen. Cttee. 1977–82; mem. Standing Cttee., 5th CPPCC 1978; Adviser, Ministry of Foreign Affairs 1972; Vice-Pres. China-Japan Friendship Asscn. 1973–; Adviser Ministry of Radio and T.V. 1982, Int. Liaison Dept., Cen. Cttee. CCP 1982–; Vice-Pres. Asscn. for Int. Understanding March 1988–; mem. Presidium CPPCC 1983, Standing Cttee. CPPCC 1983. *Address:* c/o Central Committee, Chinese Communist Party, Beijing, People's Republic of China.

ZHANG XIANLIANG; Chinese writer; b. 1936, Jiangsu; fmr. teacher in Beijing and Ningxia; in political disgrace 1957–79. *Publications:* Soul and Flesh, Half of Man is Woman 1988. *Address:* Editorial Staff, Shoufang, Shanghai, People's Republic of China.

ZHANG XIAODONG; Chinese windsurfer; b. 1965, Zhanjiang, Guangdong; won Marathon and Triangle Race, 11th World Windsurfing Championships, Australia 1985. *Address:* China Windsurfing Association, Beijing, People's Republic of China.

ZHANG XINTAI; Chinese party official; alt. mem. 12th CCP Cen. Cttee. 1982–87; Vice-Minister of Railways 1983–. *Address:* c/o Chinese Communist Party Central Committee, Beijing, People's Republic of China.

ZHANG XINXIN; Chinese drama director; b. 1953; d. of Zhang Lin and Ning Fan; first woman to cycle the length of the Grand Canal from Beijing to Hangzhou; Dir. Beijing People's Art Theatre 1984–; hostess on China Cen. TV Station and China Cen. People's Broadcasting Station. *Publications:* Chinese Profiles, On the Same Horizon, Dreams of Those of Our Age, On the Road 1987. *Address:* Beijing People's Art Theatre, Beijing, People's Republic of China.

ZHANG XINYU; Chinese artist; b. 20 Oct. 1932, Jiangsu; s. of Zhang Qingping and Chen Suxin; m. Zhu Qinbao 1958; one s. two d.; famed for watercolours and woodcuts; Vice-Pres. Jiangsu Woodcut Asscn.; Dir. Nat. Art Asscn.; numerous exhbns. in China, Japan and France. *Publications:* Creative Reading Notes of Woodcut, Creative Reading Notes of Watercolour Woodcut. *Address:* Jiangsu Art Gallery, Nanjing, Jiangsu, People's Republic of China.

ZHANG XIULONG; Chinese soldier; Deputy Commdr. Zhejiang Mil. District, PLA 1966–72; Deputy Commdr. PLA Wuhan Mil. Region 1978–83; Vice-Chair. Prov. People's Congress, Hubei 1980–83; Commdr. Hubei Mil. District, PLA 1972–82. *Address:* People's Liberation Army Headquarters, Hubei Military District, Wuhan, People's Republic of China.

ZHANG XIUSHAN; Chinese party and government official; Deputy Dir. State Agric. Comm., Chair. N.E. People's Govt. Control Cttee., Dir. Org. Dept. 1950–; Deputy Sec. N.E. Region CCP Cttee. 1952–53; mem. N.E. Admin. Cttee. 1953–; mem. Cen. Advisory Cttee. CCP Cen. Cttee. 1982–. *Address:* Central Advisory Committee of the Central Committee of the Chinese Communist Party, Zhongnanhai, Beijing, People's Republic of China.

ZHANG XUDENG; Chinese army officer; Commdr. Guangxi Mil. District 1980–85; Alt. mem. 12th Cen. CCP Cttee. 1982–87; Deputy Commdr. Guangzhou Mil. Region 1982–85, Sec. Discipline Inspection Cttee. 1987–. *Address:* People's Liberation Army Headquarters, Guangxi Military District, Nanning, People's Republic of China.

ZHANG YANNING; Chinese government official; Vice-Minister for State Econ. Comm. 1983–88 for Restructuring the Economy May 1988–; mem. State Educ. Comm. 1985–; Vice-Chair. Guidance Cttee. for State Examinations for Econ. Managerial Personnel 1983; Chair. China-Japan Personnel Exchange Cttee. 1985–. *Address:* State Economic Commission, Beijing, People's Republic of China.

ZHANG YIMOU; Chinese film actor and director; b. 1951, Xi'an, Shanxi Prov.; m. Xiao Hua 1982; ed. Xi'an Middle School, Beijing Film Acad.; 8th Golden Rooster Best Actor Award for Old Well 1988. *Address:* Xi'an Film Studio, Xi'an City, Shaanxi Province, Peoples Republic of China.

ZHANG YOUFU; Chinese hydrologist; b. 21 May 1940; research into prevention of mudflow damage in Sichuan Prov. *Address:* Chengdu Institute of Geography, Chengdu, Sichuan Province, People's Republic of China.

ZHANG YOUYU; Chinese jurist; b. 1899, Shanxi; m. Han Youtong 1933; one s. one d.; Prof. of Law, Peiping Univ. 1937; Vice-Mayor of Beijing 1949–58; Vice-Chair. Politics and Law Asscn.; Pres. Chinese Asscn. of Political Science 1981; Dir. Inst. of Law, Chinese Acad. of Science 1981–83; Pres. China Law Soc.; Deputy NPC; mem. of Standing Cttee. of NPC; Chair. Law Advisory Cttee. 1982–. *Address:* Chinese Academy of Social Sciences, Jianguomen Nei, Beijing, People's Republic of China.

ZHANG YU; Chinese film actress; Hundred Flowers Best Actress Award for Evening Rain 1981; Golden Rooster Best Actress Award for Love at Lushan 1981; Dir. Inst. of Foreign Literature, Acad. of Social Sciences 1986–. *Address:* Institute of Foreign Literature, Acad. of Social Sciences, 5 Jianguomen Nei Da Jie 5, Hao, Beijing, People's Republic of China.

ZHANG YUE; Chinese diplomatist; Deputy Dir. W. European and African Affairs Dept., Ministry of Foreign Affairs 1952–56; Council mem. Inst. of Foreign Affairs 1955; Deputy Head, Office of Chinese Trade Rep., Cairo, Egypt 1956; Counsellor at Embassy, Kingdom of Yemen (now Yemen Arab Repub.) 1956–61; Amb. to Somalia 1961–64, to Sudan 1974–78, to Italy 1979–81; Vice-Pres. China U.S.S.R. Friendship Asscn. 1984–. *Address:* c/o Ministry of Foreign Affairs, Beijing, People's Republic of China.

ZHANG ZAIWANG; Chinese party and government official; b. Aug. 1918, Nanjing, Jiangsu Prov.; s. of Zhang Fajia and Zhang Yuqing; m. Luo Ying 1945; five s.; mem. 12th Cen. Cttee. CCP 1982–87; Sec. CCP Cttee., Tianjin 1982; Chair. Municipal People's Congress, Tianjin 1983–. *Leisure interests:* tennis and billiards. *Address:* Municipal People's Congress, Tianjin, People's Republic of China.

ZHANG ZHEN; Chinese army officer and politician; b. Oct. 1914, Ping Jian Co., Hunan; joined Red Army 1930, rising to rank of Regimental Chief of Staff; participated in the Long March; Column Chief of Staff Eighth Route Army, Div. Chief of Staff and Brigade Commdr. in New Fourth Army in War against Japan 1937–45; during War of Liberation served as Column Commdr., Political Commissar in Cen. China Field Army, Corps Chief of Staff, Chief of Staff East China Mil. Command and Chief of Staff of Third Field Army 1946–49; Dir. of Operation Dept., HQ of PLA Gen. Staff, Acting Corps Commdr. and Political Commissar, Deputy Commandant and Commandant of the Mil. Coll. of PLA; Deputy Commdr. Wuhan Mil. Command, Deputy Dir. and Dir. of PLA Gen. Logistics Dept., Deputy Chief of PLA Gen. Staff, Lieut.-Gen. 1955; Pres. Nat. Defence Univ., PLA, 1985–; alt. mem. 11th Cen. Cttee. CCP; mem. 12th Cen. Cttee. CCP; mem. Cen. Advisory Comm. CCP. *Address:* c/o State Council, Beijing, People's Republic of China.

ZHANG ZHIXIU; Chinese army officer; Head (Maj.-Gen) PLA Yentai Units, Shandong 1957; Deputy Commdr. Jinan Mil. Region, post-Cultural Revolution; Sec., CCP Shandong Prov. Cttee. and Vice-Chair. Shandong Revolutionary Cttee. Pre-1975; Deputy Commdr. Kunming Mil. Region 1976–80; Sec. CCP Yunnan Prov. Cttee. 1977; Vice-Chair. Yunnan Prov. Revolutionary Cttee. 1977; mem. Presidium CCP 11th NPC; mem. 11th Cen. Cttee. 1977–82; Commdr. Kunming Mil. Region 1980–85; Vice-Chair. Prov. People's Congress, Yunnan 1979–83; mem. 12th Cen. CCP Cttee. 1982–85; mem. Cen. Advisory Comm. 1985–. *Address:* People's Liberation Army Headquarters, Kunming Military Region, People's Republic of China.

ZHANG ZHONG; Chinese air force officer; Deputy Chief-of-Staff PLA Air Force 1974–85; Dir. Cen. Archives Bureau CCP Cen. Cttee. 1982. *Address:* People's Liberation Army Air Force Headquarters, Beijing, People's Republic of China.

ZHANG ZHONGXIAN; Chinese army officer; b. Jan. 1926; Political Commissar, Canton Mil. Region, PLA 1985; alt. mem. 12th CCP Cen. Cttee. 1985–87; mem. 13th Cen. Cttee. 1987–; Standing mem. Party Cttee., Canton Mil. Region 1986–, Political Commissar 1986–. *Address:* Canton Military Region Headquarters, Guangzhou, Guangdong, People's Republic of China.

ZHANG ZHU; Chinese government official; Vice-Minister for Nationatities Affairs Comm. 1986–; Pres. Advertising Society, Acad. of Social Sciences 1982–. *Address:* State Nationalities Affairs Commission, Beijing, People's Republic of China.

ZHANG ZICUN, PH.D.; Chinese economist; b. 5 April 1918; m. Zhang Wenya 1944; one s. one d.; ed. Qinghua Univ., Beijing, Univ. of Cambridge; Instructor, Dept. of Econs., Qinghua Univ. 1940–43; Economist, Statistics Div., Research Dept., IMF 1947–48; Sr. Econ. Affairs Officer, Econ. Stability Section, UN 1948, Chief, Developing Areas Section 1955, Deputy Dir. Centre for Devt. Planning, Projections and Policies 1963, Dir. Div. of Public Admin. and Finance 1973, Sr. Adviser, Dept. of Tech. Co-operation for Devt. 1980; Deputy Dir. Financial Research Inst., People's Bank of China 1980; Exec. Dir. for China, IMF 1980–85. *Publications:* Cyclical Movements in the Balance of Payments 1949 and articles in various professional journals. *Address:* 36 Kilmer Road, Larchmont, N.Y. 10538, U.S.A. *Telephone:* (914) 834-7257.

ZHAO CANGBI; Chinese government official; b. 1909, Shaanxi; Cadre in S.W. China in early 1950s, Vice-Gov. Sichuan 1958, Sec. CCP Sichuan 1960, 1976; removed from office during Cultural Revolution 1967; mem 11th Cen. Cttee., CCP 1977; Minister of Public Security 1977–83; Deputy leader Political and Legal Affairs Group, Cen. Cttee, CCP 1978–; mem. 12th Cen. CCP Cttee. 1982–85; mem. Cen. Advisory Comm. 1985–. *Address:* State Council, Beijing, People's Republic of China.

ZHAO DEZUN; Chinese party official (retd.); b. 30 April 1913, Laoning; Vice-Gov., Prov. Govt., Heilongjiang 1979; Sec. CCP Cttee., Heilongjiang 1979; Chair. Prov. People's Congress, Heilongjiang 1979–85. *Address:* c/o People's Congress, Heilongjiang Province, People's Republic of China.

ZHAO DI; Chinese party and government official; Vice-Mayor Kaifeng; mem. Standing Cttee. Henan Prov. CCP Cttee. 1983–, Deputy Sec. 1984–86; alt. mem. CCP Cen. Cttee. 1985–. *Address:* Central Committee of the Chinese Communist Party, Zhongnanhai, Beijing, People's Republic of China.

ZHAO DONGWAN; Chinese mechanical engineer and state official; b. 1926, Henan Prov.; m. Zhang Leiyan 1951; two s. one d.; Vice-Chair. Science and Tech. Comm. 1977; Dir. Cttee. for the Promotion of Int. Measurements 1979; Chinese Chair. PRC-U.S.A. Joint Cttee. on High Energy Physics 1979; Vice-Chair. State Planning Comm. 1982; alt. mem. 12th CCP Cen. Cttee. 1982–87; mem. 13th CCP Cen. Cttee. 1987; Minister of Labour and Personnel 1985–. *Leisure interest:* swimming. *Address:* Ministry of Labour and Personnel, 12 Hepingli Zhongjie, Beijing, People's Republic of China. *Telephone:* 462209.

ZHAO FENG; Chinese musicologist; b. 26 Oct. 1916, Kaifeng, Henan Prov.; s. of Zhao Xiangchen and Qi-yuqing; m. Wu Xilin 1947; two s. and two d.; ed. Jianhua Art School; Ed.-in-Chief New Music Magazine 1939–49; music teacher Fujiang State Music School and Liangjiang Women's Sports School 1940; Vice-Pres. China Conservatory of Music, Hong Kong 1946; music teacher Guangdong Art School 1947; Pres. Chinese Arts Specialized School, Singapore 1948; mem. Culture and Educ. Comm. of Govt. Council 1949; Dir.-Gen. Office of Culture Ministry 1952–57; Head of Bureau of Art, Finance, and Foreign Liaison; Acting Sec.-Gen. All-China Fed. of Literary and Art Circles; Sec.-Gen. Nat. Musicians' Asscn.; mem. Academic Terms Unifying Comm., Acad. of Sciences 1952–57; Vice-Pres., then Pres. Cen. Conservatory of Music 1957–84, Hon. Pres. 1985–; Deputy Dir. Art Comm. of Culture Ministry; Ed.-in-Chief Music Research (quarterly); Deputy of Third Nat. People's Congress; mem. All-China Illiteracy Reducing Comm.; mem. Fifth Chinese People's Political Consultative Conf.; Vice-Pres. Chinese Musicians' Asscn. 1979–; Prof. Xiamen Univ. and Nankai Univ.; Bd. Chair. China Culture and Art Travel Service 1987–. *Address:* 47 Xin Wenhua Street, Beijing, People's Republic of China. *Telephone:* 660356.

ZHAO FULIN; Chinese party official; Deputy Sec. Hubei Prov. CCP Cttee. 1986–, Sec. Discipline Inspection Cttee. 1986–; mem. CCP Cen. Cttee. 1987–. *Address:* Central Committee of the Chinese Communist Party, Zhongnanhai, Beijing, People's Republic of China.

ZHAO FUSAN; Chinese government official; mem. Exec. Bureau UNESCO 1985–; mem. Presidium 6th CPPCC 1983–; mem. Standing Cttee. CPPCC Nat. Cttee. 1983–; mem. Exec. Bureau, Chinese Del. to UNESCO 1985–; Vice-Pres. Acad. of Social Sciences 1985–; Vice-Pres. China Asscn. for Advancement of Int. Friendship 1985–, Taiwan Studies Soc. Aug. 1988–. *Address:* Chinese Academy of Social Sciences, Beijing, People's Republic of China.

ZHAO HAIFENG; Chinese party official; Vice-Chair. Prov. Revolutionary Cttee., Qinghai 1977–78; Deputy Sec. CCP Cttee., Qinghai 1978–81; Vice-Gov. of Qinghai 1979–81; Perm. Sec. CCP Cttee., Qinghai 1981–83; Chair. Prov. CPPCC Cttee., Qinghai 1981–83; mem. 12th Cen. Cttee. CCP 1982; First Sec. CCP Cttee., Qinghai 1983–85; Chair. Advisory Cttee., CCP Cttee., Qinghai 1985–. *Address:* Provincial Government, Xining, Qinghai Province, People's Republic of China.

ZHAO JIANMIN; Chinese soldier, party and government official; b. 1910, Shandong Prov.; Deputy Dir. Mil. Control Comm., Guiyang 1949; Political Cttee. 4th Field Army 1950; Dir. Communications Dept. S.W. Mil. Admin. Cttee. 1951–52, Financial and Econ. Cttee. 1952–57; Vice-Minister of Railroads 1953–58; Gov. Shandong Prov. 1955–58; 3rd Sec. Shandong Prov. CCP Cttee. 1956, Sec. 1956–60; alt. mem. 8th CCP Cen. Cttee. Sept. 1958; criticised at 2nd Shandong Prov. People's Congress Oct.-Nov. 1958; Sec. Yunnan Prov. CCP Cttee. 1963–67; purged 1968, rehabilitated 1978; Adviser, Ministry of Aviation Industry 1982–; mem. CCP Cen. Cttee. 1982–; mem. Cen. Advisory Cttee. of CCP Cen. Cttee. 1987–. *Address:* Central Advisory Committee of the Central Committee of the Chinese Communist Party, Zhongnanhai, Beijing, People's Republic of China.

ZHAO LIN; Chinese party official; Sec. Municipal CCP Cttee., Taiyuan 1937; served 1st Field Army; Deputy Sec. CCP N. Sichuan Dist. Cttee. 1950–52; mem. S.W. China Mil. and Admin. Council 1950–52; mem. S.W. Admin. Cttee. 1953–54; Deputy Sec. CCP Cttee., Sichuan 1954; Sec. Jilin 1956, Second Sec. 1960, Acting First Sec. 1966; disappeared during Cultural Revolution; Sec. CCP Cttee., Shandong 1978; Chair. Prov. People's Congress, Shandong 1979–83; mem. Cen. Advisory Comm., CCP Cen. Cttee. 1982–87. *Address:* People's Congress, Shandong Province, People's Republic of China.

ZHAO PENGFEI; Chinese party and government official; b. 1920, Shanxi; Dir. Industry Dept. Prov. People's Govt., Chahar 1946; Deputy Dir. Beijing Construction Bureau 1949-52; Procurator, Supreme People's Procuracy 1954; Deputy Dir. Gen. Office, 1st NPC 1956; Deputy Mayor, Beijing 1960-64; Dir. State Housing Admin. Bureau 1962; Deputy Sec.-Gen. State Council 1963-66; Deputy for Hebei, 3rd NPC; denounced by Red Guards as "a counter-revolutionary revisionist"; Vice-Chair. Municipal Revolutionary Cttee., Beijing 1977-79; Deputy for Beijing, 5th NPC; Chair. Municipal CPPCC Cttee., Beijing 1979-83; Sec. CCP Cttee., Beijing 1980-84; Vice Mayor Beijing 1981-83; Chair. Municipal People's Congress, Beijing 1983-; mem. Presidium 6th NPC 1986-, Nationalities Cttee. 1986-. *Address:* Municipal People's Congress, Beijing, People's Republic of China.

ZHAO PUCHU; Chinese Buddhist leader and poet; b. 1907, Taihu Co., Anhui Prov.; mem., as a Buddhist rep., 1st CPPCC, Beijing 1949; Vice-Pres. and Sec.-Gen. China's Buddhist Asscn. 1953-79; Vice-Chair. Sino-Japanese Friendship Asscn. 1963-66; mem. Presidium 4th NPC 1975; Pres., Chinese Buddhist Asscn. 1979-; Vice-Chair., 6th CPPCC 1983-88; Pres., Soc. for Study Sino-Japanese Relations 1984-; Vice-Chair. 7th CPPCC 1988-; Buddhist Evangelist Prize 1982, Niwano Peace Prize 1985. *Publications:* Selected Poetry Dishuiji 1964, Collection of Poems Pianshiji 1978. *Address:* Standing Committee of Chinese People's Political Consultative Conference, Taiping Qiao Road, Beijing, Peoples Republic of China.

ZHAO RUICHUN; Chinese artist; b. Nov. 1935, Wenzhou, Zhejiang; s. of Zhao Loshu and Huang Shenghong; m. 1st 1956; one d.; m. 2nd Yun Xiuying; one d.; ed. Chinese Cen. Fine Arts Inst.; lecturer Guangzhou Inst. of Fine Arts 1959-71; teacher Chinese Cen. Fine Arts Inst. 1980-82; painter Guangzhou Art Acad. 1984-; first one-man exhbn. 1962; mem. Chinese Artists' Asscn., Chinese Engraving Asscn.; Sec.-Gen. Chinese Asscn. of Copper-Plate, Lithographic and Silkscreen Engraving; Ed.-in-Chief Modern Engraving; works exhibited in U.S.A., Japan, England, Australia, New Zealand, Ireland, Singapore, Denmark, Switzerland, Korea, Sweden, Thailand, Canada, U.S.S.R., Algeria and Taiwan. *Publications:* On Engraving Education 1981, Woodcut Techniques 1983, Practice and Theory of Sketching 1986, Silk-screen Plate Techniques 1987. *Leisure interest:* Chinese cooking. *Address:* 210 Yuexiubei Road, Guangzhou; 29 Tian Jin Lane, Wenzhou, Zhejiang, People's Republic of China. *Telephone:* Guangzhou 332261.

ZHAO RUIYING; Chinese sculptor; b. Qiqihar, Heilongjiang Prov. *Address:* Central Academy of Fine Arts, Beijing, People's Republic of China.

ZHAO SHIYING; Chinese artist; b. Yantai, Shandong; ed. Beijing Teachers' Coll.; teacher in middle schools; Art Ed. Wudao (Dance). *Address:* People's Republic of China.

ZHAO SHOUYI; Chinese government official; b. 1917, Weinan Co., Shaanxi Prov.; fmr. Deputy Dir. Propaganda Dept., N.W. China Bureau; mem. Cultural and Educational Cttee., N.W. Mil. and Admin. Council 1950; Dir. Propaganda Dept., CCP Cttee., Shaanxi, mem. Standing Cttee., Alt. Sec. Secr. 1958, Sec. 1964; identified as judge, Anhui 1958; disappeared during Cultural Revolution; sent by special directive of Hua Guofeng (q.v.) and CCP Cen. Cttee. to deal with difficulties within Anhui leadership 1977; Vice-Chair. Prov. Revolutionary Cttee., Anhui 1978-79; Sec. CCP Cttee., Anhui 1978; Deputy for Anhui, 5th NPC 1978; Dir. CCP Party School, Anhui 1978; Deputy Dir. Propaganda Dept., CCP Cen. Cttee. 1982; Minister of Labour and Personnel 1982-85; mem. 12th Cen. Cttee., CCP 1982-85; mem. Cen. Advisory Comm. 1985-87, Leading Group for Scientific Work, State Council 1983-. *Address:* State Council, Beijing, People's Republic of China.

ZHAO WEICHEN; Chinese government official; Vice-Minister of State Econ. Comm. 1983; Vice-Chair. Environmental Protection Cttee., State Council 1984; Deputy Head Leading Group in charge of Sea, Land and Air Ports, State Council 1985; Head Leading Group for Cen. China Power Network, State Council 1984; Head Nat. Leading Group for Packaging Inspection, State Council 1984; Head Leading Group for Import and Export of Grain and Cotton, State Council 1985; Vice-Chair. Guangxi Zhuang Autonomous Regional People's Govt. July 1987-. *Address:* Guangxi Zhuang Autonomous Region People's Government, Guangxi Zhuang Provincial, People's Republic of China.

ZHAO WENFU; Chinese party and government official; Deputy Dir. Org. Dept. CCP Cttee, Henan CPPCC; Dir. Personnel Dept., Prov. People's Govt., Henan 1952; Deputy for Henan, 1st NPC 1954; Vice-Gov. of Henan 1955-Cultural Revolution; Sec. CCP Cttee., Henan 1956-Cultural Revolution; Deputy for Henan, 2nd NPC 1958; Deputy for Henan, 3rd NPC; branded as "a capitalist roader" and purged 1967; Sec. CCP Cttee., Henan 1979-85; Vice-Chair. Prov. Revolutionary Cttee., Henan 1979; Chair. Prov. CPPCC Cttee., Henan 1979-83; Chair. Prov. People's Congress, Henan 1983-88. *Address:* c/o Provincial People's Congress, Zhenghou, Henan Province, People's Republic of China.

ZHAO WENJIN Maj.-Gen.; Chinese army officer; b. 1913 Dawu Co., Hubei Prov.; joined Red Army 1929, CCP 1932; Vice-Commdr. 9th Regiment Pingxi Advance Army, 8th Route Army 1938; Vice- Commdr. PLA Tibet Mil. Region 1962; Deputy for PLA, 5th NPC 1978; Deputy. Commdr.

PLA Chengdu Units 1978-; Commdr. Sichuan Mil. Dist. PLA 1978-; Vice-Chair. People's Air Defence Cttee., PLA Sichuan Mil. Dist. 1982-. *Address:* People's Liberation Army Headquarters, Sichuan Military District, Chengdu, People's Republic of China.

ZHAO WUCHENG; Chinese party and government official; Council mem. Zhengzhou Municipal People's Govt., Deputy Sec. Zhengzhou Municipal CCP Cttee. 1950-; Second Sec., Secr. Canton Municipal CCP Cttee. 1955-57, 1960-64, Acting First Sec. 1961-64; Second Sec. Tianjin Municipal CCP Cttee. 1964-66, First Sec. 1966-67; First Vice-Chair. Tianjin Municipal Revolutionary Cttee. 1970-74, 1977-78; head of Tianjin Friendship Del. to Japan April 1974; Third Sec. Tianjin Municipal CCP Cttee. 1977-80; alt. mem. 11th CCP Cen. Cttee. 1977; Vice-Minister State Capital Construction Comm. 1980; mem. Cen. Advisory Cttee. of CCP Cen. Cttee. 1982-. *Address:* Central Advisory Committee of the Central Committee of the Chinese Communist Party, Zhongnanhai, Beijing, People's Republic of China.

ZHAO XINCHU; Chinese party official; b. 1915, Hubei; Sec., CCP Hubei 1957-65; Vice-Gov. Hubei 1958-64; Vice-Minister of Culture 1965; criticized and removed from office during Cultural Revolution 1966; rehabilitated as a "leading cadre" in Nei Monggol A.R. 1972; Vice-Chair. Provincial Revolutionary Cttee. and Sec. CCP, Hubei 1973, Chair. Revolutionary Cttee. and First Sec., Hubei 1975-78; mem. 11th Cen. Cttee. of CCP 1977-82; Minister of Food 1980-82; mem. Cen. Advisory Comm. 1982-87; mem. 13th CCP Cen. Cttee. 1987-. *Address:* c/o State Council, Beijing, People's Republic of China.

ZHAO XINGYUAN; Chinese army officer; b. 1926, Shandong Prov.; 'War Hero' of civil war period; participant in Korean War; Commdr. 353rd Regiment of 118th Div., 4th Field Army 1958; Deputy for PLA units of Shenyang Mil. Region to 2nd NPC 1959, and 3rd NPC 1964; Chief of Staff, 118th Div. 1962, Deputy Commdr. 1965, Commdr. 1967; alt. mem. 9th CCP Cen. Cttee. 1969; Political Commissar, Heilongjiang Mil. Dist. 1975-(88); mem. 12th CCP Cen. Cttee. 1982; mem. Cen. Comm. for Discipline Inspection 1987-. *Address:* Heilongjiang Military District Headquarters, Harbin, Heilongjiang, People's Republic of China.

ZHAO XIU; Chinese party and government official; First Sec. CCP Hsiongyang Dist. Work Cttee.; Vice-Gov. Hubei 1964-67; Sec. CCP Cttee. Hubei 1973-77; Dir. Animal Husbandry Bureau, Ministry of Agric. 1979; Vice-Minister of Agric. 1979-82; Pres. Seed Asscn. 1980-; Sec. CCP Cttee., Jilin 1982-85; Gov. of Jilin 1983-85; Chair. Prov. People's Congress, Jilin 1985-88; mem. Presidium 6th NPC 1986-87; mem. Standing Cttee., CCP April 1988-. *Address:* Provincial People's Congress, Fuzhou, Jilin Province, People's Republic of China.

ZHAO YANNIAN; Chinese woodcut artist and professor; b. 11 April 1924, Suzhou, Jiansu; s. of Zhao Zhiyuan and Yao Demei; m. Hua Ling 1943; two s. one d.; ed. Shanghai School of Fine Arts, Arts Acad. of Guangdong Prov.; teacher and ed. in field of fine arts; Head of Woodcut Art, Vice-Chair. and Prof., Zhejiang Acad. of Fine Arts 1957-86; Dir. All-China Nat. Woodcut Asscn. 1946-49; Dir. Artists Asscn. of China 1960; Standing Dir. Woodcut Artists Asscn. of China 1986-; works exhibited in China and overseas; prizes for Shanghai Fine Arts Exhbn. 1950, Zhejiang Prov. 1980, Nat. Woodcut Print Exhbn. 1986, Nat. Arts Exhbn. 1987, numerous other awards and prizes. *Publications:* Selected Works of Zhao Yannian's Woodcut Prints 1979, The Woodcut Plates of Zhao Yannian 1979, On Woodcut Art 1986, many articles. *Leisure intérests:* reading, films, theatre, art, music. *Address:* Zhejiang Academy of Fine Arts, Hangzhou, People's Republic of China.

ZHAO YANXIA; Chinese opera star; b. 1930, Beijing; m. Liu Xinyuan; one d.; Head First Troupe, Beijing Opera Theatre of Beijing. *Address:* c/o Beijing Opera Theatre, Beijing, People's Republic of China. *Telephone:* 660425.

ZHAO ZENGUI; Chinese party and government official; b. Jan. 1920; m. Li Jian 1949; four c.; Sec. CCP Cttee., Kunming 1956; mem. Standing Cttee., Yunnan 1965; Deputy Sec. CCP Cttee., Yunnan 1977-78; Vice-Chair. Prov. Revolutionary Cttee., Vice-Gov.; Sec. CCP Cttee., Jiangxi Prov., Governor of Jiangxi 1982-85; Chair. Jiangxi Advisory Cttee. 1985-; Deputy for Yunnan, 5th NPC 1978, 6th NPC 1983. *Address:* Nanchang, Jiangxi Province, People's Republic of China.

ZHAO ZIYANG; Chinese party official; b. 1919, Huaxian Co., Henan Prov.; m. Liang Boqi; four s. one d.; joined CCP 1938; Sec.-Gen. S. China Sub-Bureau, CCP 1950-54, Third Sec. 1954-55; Third Deputy Sec. CCP Guangdong 1955, Sec. 1962, First Sec. 1965-67; Political Commissar Guangdong Mil. District, PLA 1964; Sec. Cen.-South Bureau, CCP 1965-67; criticized and removed from office during Cultural Revolution 1967; Vice-Chair. Nei Monggol Revolutionary Cttee. 1971; Sec. CCP Nei Monggol 1971, CCP Guangdong 1972; Vice-Chair. Guangdong Revolutionary Cttee. 1972; mem. 10th Cen. Cttee. of CCP 1973; Alt. mem. Politburo, 11th Cen. Cttee. of CCP 1977-79, mem. 1979-; mem. Politburo 12th Cen. Cttee. 1982; First Sec. CCP Guangdong 1974; Chair. Guangdong Revolutionary Cttee. 1974; First Sec. Sichuan CCP Cttee. 1975-80; Chair. Sichuan Revolutionary Cttee. 1975-80; Exec. Chair. 5th CPPCC Nat. Cttee., Vice-Chair. 1978-; First Political Commissar Chengdu Mil. District, PLA

1980-87; Minister of State Comm. for Econ. Reconstruction 1982-87; Acting Gen. Sec. CCP Jan.-Oct. 1987, Gen. Sec. Nov. 1987-; Sec.-Gen. CCP Nat. Congress 1982; Head, Leading Group for Co-ordinating Nat. Scientific Work 1983-; First Vice-Chair. Mil. Comm. CCP Cen. Cttee. 1987-; Vice-Chair. State Cen. Mil. Comm. April 1988-; Hon. Pres. Golf Asscn. Jan. 1988-; Deputy for Beijing to 6th NPC 1983; visited U.S.A. 1984; Gold Mercury Int. Emblem for Peace 1984. *Leisure interests:* jogging, arguing. *Address:* State Council, Beijing, People's Republic of China.

ZHAO ZIYUE; Chinese film actor; b. 15 June 1909, Gu Co., Shanxi Prov.; s. of Zhao Weiding and Zhao Shishi; m. 1st Zhang Jian (died 1966); m. 2nd Cao Mengzhen 1970; one s.; *films include:* An Epic of Sons and Daughters, After the Truce, Song of Youth, Add Flowers to the Brocade, Get Rich the Proper Way, The Storm, An Epic of Red Flag, The Rickshaw Boy. *TV drama:* The Family Head Jing Shouben. *Address:* Beijing Film Studios, Beijing, People's Republic of China. *Telephone:* 201-3377, Ext. 382.

ZHAO ZONGNAI; Chinese state official; b. 1927, Beijing; ed. Qinghua Univ.; Deputy Man. Yumen oil field 1960; Dir. Yumen Petroleum Bureau 1978; Dir. Oceanic Petroleum Exploration Bureau under Ministry of Petroleum Industry 1981; alt. mem. 12th CCP Cen. Cttee. 1982-87, mem. 13th Cen. Cttee. 1987-; Vice-Minister of Petroleum Industry 1983-88; Exec. Deputy Sec. Party Cttee. of Depts. under Cen. Cttee. 1986-88; Deputy Head Org. Dept. March 1988-. *Address:* c/o Ministry of Petroleum Industry, Liupukang, Deshengmenwai, Beijing, People's Republic of China.

ZHAVORONKOV, Nikolay Mikhailovich; Soviet chemist; b. 7 Aug. 1907, Streletskie Vyselki, Ryazan Region; ed. Mendeleev Chemical Technological Inst.; scientific worker State Inst. of Nitrogen Industry 1930-32, Asst. Prof. Mendeleev Chemical Tech. Inst. 1933-42, Prof. 1942-65; Dir. Karpov Physicochemical Inst. 1944-48; Rector Mendeleev Chemical Tech. Inst. 1948-62; Dir. Inst. of General and Inorganic Chem., U.S.S.R. Acad. of Sciences 1962-; mem. Scientific and Tech. Bd. of Ministry of Chemical Industry 1946-; mem. State Cttee. of U.S.S.R. for Science and Tech. 1966-; Corresp. mem. U.S.S.R. Acad. of Sciences 1953-62, mem. 1962-; mem. Presidium Acad. of Sciences of U.S.S.R., Academician Sec. Dept. of Physical Chem. and Tech. of Inorganic Compounds 1963-; Foreign mem. Hungarian Acad. of Sciences 1970-, G.D.R. Acad. of Sciences 1977-, Czechoslovak Acad. of Sciences 1977-, Polish Acad. of Sciences 1977-, mem. Communist Party 1939-; Hero of Socialist Labour 1969, State Prize 1950, Order of Lenin (three times), Mendeleev Prize 1950, Mendeleev Gold Medal 1969, Tchugaev Prize 1979, Kurnakov Prize 1982 and other decorations. *Publications include:* Hydraulic Principles of the Scrubber Process and Heat Transfer in Scrubbers 1944, Nitrogen in Nature and Engineering 1951, Sources of Industrial Bonded Nitrogen 1951, Mass Transfer in the Film or Thin Film Absorption Process 1951, Determining the Separation Factor of Boron Isotopes with Equilibrium Evaporation of BCl_3 1956, Chemical Industry and Research in the Soviet Union 1956, K. A. Timiryazev and the Nitrogen Problem 1956, Separating Stable Boron Isotopes 1960, Investigations of Film or Thin Film Absorption Process with High Speed of Gas 1961, High Temperature Gas-Liquid Chromatography 1962, Investigation of Hydrogen Isotopic Exchange between Water and Thiolates 1962, Principal Directions in Development of Separation Methods of Stable Isotopes 1963, Phase Equilibria for Mixtures Acrilonitrile—Acetonitrile 1964, Dissolution of Solid Particles Suspended in Agitated Vessels 1983. *Address:* Institute of General and Inorganic Chemistry of Academy of Sciences of U.S.S.R., Leninsky prospekt 31, Moscow 117071, U.S.S.R.

ZHAXI WANGQUG; Chinese (Tibetan) party official; b. 1913, Ganzi State, Si Chuan Prov.; m. Zhou Shu-fen 1948; three s. two d.; ed. Yan'an Nationalities Inst.; mem. Nationalities Cttee., N.W. China Mil. and Admin. Council 1950; Council mem. Prov. People's Govt., Qinghai 1951; Chair. Guoluo Tibetan Autonomous Zhou People's Govt., Qinghai 1953; Deputy for Qinghai, 1st NPC 1954, 2nd NPC 1958, 3rd NPC 1964, 4th NPC 1975; mem. Nationalities Cttee., 1st NPC 1954, 2nd NPC, 3rd NPC; Vice-Gov. of Qinghai Prov. 1955; mem. State Nationalities Affairs Comm., State Council 1956; Sec. Secr., CCP Cttee., Qinghai 1957; disappeared during Cultural Revolution; mem. State Nationalities Affairs Comm., State Council 1979; Sec. CCP Cttee., Qinghai 1979; Chair. Prov. People's Congress, Qinghai 1981-83; mem. Standing Cttee. NPC 1983-, Nationalities Cttee. NPC 1983-, Credentials Cttee. NPC April 1988-. *Address:* No. 44B, Fu Sui Jing Lane, West District, Beijing, People's Republic of China. *Telephone:* Beijing 653050.

ZHDANOV, Viktor Mikhailovich; Soviet virologist; b. 1 Feb. 1914, Shtepino, Donetsk Dist.; ed. Kharkov Medical Inst.; mem. CPSU 1941-; Head of Lab. and Dir. of Inst. of Microbiology and Epidemiology, Kharkov 1946-50; Head of Lab. D. I. Ivanovsky Inst. of Virology, U.S.S.R. Acad. of Medical Sciences 1951-61, Dir. 1961-; mem. Acad. of Medical Sciences of U.S.S.R. *Address:* D. I. Ivanovsky Institute of Virology, Ul. Gamalei 16, Moscow 123098, U.S.S.R.

ZHELUDEV, Ivan Stepanovich, D.SC.; Soviet scientist; b. 7 March 1921, Pskov Region; s. of Stepan Zheludev and Ekaterina Sapozhnikova; m. Galina Antonovna Krasnikova 1947; two s. one d.; ed. Moscow State Univ.; Senior Lecturer, Moscow State Univ. 1955-62, Prof. 1965; Head of Lab.

of Electrical Properties of Crystals, Inst. of Crystallography, U.S.S.R. Acad. of Sciences, Moscow 1961-66, 1971-75, 1981-; Deputy Dir.-Gen. (Dept. of Tech. Operations), Int. Atomic Energy Agency, Vienna 1966-71, 1975-81; Visiting Prof., Indian Inst. of Science, Bangalore 1962-63; U.S.S.R. State Award for Science 1975, Diploma for discovery of Electrogiration 1980. *Leisure interests:* fishing and hunting. *Address:* Institute of Crystallography, Academy of Sciences, 59 Leninsky Prospekt, 117333 Moscow, U.S.S.R.

ZHENG GUANGDI; Chinese state official; b. 1935; alt. mem. 12th CCP Cen. Cttee. 1982; Vice-Minister of Communications 1982-; Deputy Head, Co-ordination Group of Water Resources, State Council 1985-, Leading Group for Import and Export of Grain and Cotton 1983-. *Address:* Ministry of Communications, 10 Fuxing Road, Beijing, People's Republic of China. *Telephone:* 864021.

ZHENG TIANXIANG; Chinese politician; b. Sept. 1914, Inner Mongolia; Rep. 7th Party Congress 1945; Commr. CCP Party Cttee., Suinan Pref. 1945-47; Sec. CCP Party Cttee., Mayor Baotou City 1949-52; Sec.-Gen., Vice-Sec. CCP Party Cttee., Beijing Municipality 1953-66; Minister of the Seventh Ministry of Machine Building 1978-82; mem. Cen. Advisory Cttee. of CCP 1982-; Pres. Supreme People's Court 1983-88; Dir. Cttee., Training Centre for Sr. Judges Feb. 1988-. *Address:* Supreme People's Court, Beijing, People's Republic of China.

ZHENG TUOBIN; Chinese politician; Trade Counsellor, Embassy in Moscow 1960-64; disappeared during Cultural Revolution; Deputy Dir. Dept. in Ministry of Foreign Trade 1972; Dir. Third Dept., Ministry of Foreign trade 1973-77; Leader, Trade Dels. to Europe, N. America and Asia; Vice-Minister of Foreign Trade 1978-81, Minister 1981-82; Vice-Minister of Foreign Econ. Relations and Trade 1982-85, Minister March 1985-; mem. 12th Cen. CCP Cttee. 1982, 13th CCP Cen. Cttee. 1987-; Deputy Sec. Party Group Ministry of Foreign Econ. Relations and Trade 1983-; Deputy Dir. Comm. for Commemorating 40th Anniversary of UN 1985. *Address:* c/o State Council, Beijing, People's Republic of China.

ZHENG WEISHAN; Chinese army officer; b. 1914, Hubei; Commdr. Lanzhou Mil. Region 1983-85; mem. Cen. Advisory Comm. 1987-. *Address:* People's Liberation Army Lanzhou Units, Gansu, People's Republic of China.

ZHENG WEIZHI; Chinese diplomatist; b. 1912, Guangdong; Counsellor, Embassy, Pakistan 1951-55; Amb. to Denmark 1956-61; Dir. America and Australia Dept., Ministry of Foreign Affairs 1961-64; Amb. to Argentina 1972-77, to Venezuela 1978-81, to Belgium 1981-83 (also accred. to EEC 1981-83); Dir. Inst. of Int. Studies 1984-; Adviser Foreign Affairs Cttee. 1983. *Address:* 3 Toutiao, Taijichang, Beijing, People's Republic of China. *Telephone:* 556383.

ZHIGALIN, Vladimir Fedorovich; Soviet engineer and politician; b. 3 March 1907; ed. Leningrad Mechanical Inst.; Leningrad and Moscow factories 1931-40; Chief of Dept. People's Commissariat of Heavy Machine-Building 1940-45; Deputy People's Commissar, Deputy, later First Deputy Minister, of Heavy Machine-Building 1945-57; Deputy later First Deputy Chair., Moscow City Econ. Council 1957-61, Chair. 1961-63; First Deputy Chair. U.S.S.R. Council of National Economy 1963-65; Minister of Heavy Power and Transport Eng. 1965-75, Minister of Heavy and Transport Eng. 1975-83; Cand. mem. Cen. Cttee. of CPSU 1961-64, mem. Cen. Cttee. of CPSU 1964-; Deputy to U.S.S.R. Supreme Soviet 1962-; Order of Lenin (three). *Address:* c/o Ministry of Heavy and Transport Engineering, Moscow, U.S.S.R.

ZHILIN, Pavel Andreyevich; Soviet official, military historian and academic; b. 1913, Vorobyovka, Voronezh Dist.; ed. Frunze Mil. Acad.; mem. CPSU 1942-; Deputy Ed.-in-Chief of The Military-Historical Journal 1958-64; Pro-rector of Acad. of Social Sciences of Cen. Cttee. CPSU 1964-66; Corresp. mem. of U.S.S.R. Acad. of Sciences 1968-; Lieut.-Gen. 1968; U.S.S.R. State Prize 1952, Order of Red Banner of Labour, Order of Red Star (twice) etc. *Publications include:* The Defeat of the Turkish Army in 1811 1952, The Counter-Offensive of the Russian Army in 1812 1953, How Fascist Germany Prepared the Attack on the Soviet Union 1965, The Defeat of the Napoleonic Army in Russia 1968. *Address:* U.S.S.R. Academy of Sciences, Leninsky Pr. 14, Moscow V-71, U.S.S.R.

ZHIVKOV, Todor; Bulgarian politician; b. 7 Sept. 1911, Pravets Village, Sofia Dist.; m. Mara Maleyeva (deceased); one s. one d. (deceased); ed. Secondary School of Printing and Graphic Arts; printing worker; joined Bulgarian Young Communist League 1929, CP 1932; mem. Resistance against Nazis 1941-44; cand. mem., Cen. Cttee., Communist Party 1945, full mem. 1948-; First Sec., Sofia City Cttee. 1948-49 also Chair. Sofia City People's Council; cand. mem. Political Bureau and Cen. Cttee. 1950 also First Sec. Sofia City Cttee. and Sofia County Cttee. of CP; mem. Political Bureau 1951, First Sec. Cen. Cttee. 1954-81, Gen. Sec. 1981-; deputy Nat. Ass. 1945-, of Presidium 1946-62; Prime Minister 1962-71; Pres. of State Council (Head of State) July 1971-; People's Rep. to Nat. Ass. 1945-; mem. Council of People's Repub. 1971-; Hero of People's Repub. of Bulgaria 1971, 1981, Hero of Socialist Labour 1961, Order of Lenin (three times), numerous awards and decorations. *Publications:* Rural Co-operation 1957, Report to Seventh Congress 1958, Developing the

Economy 1959, UN General Assembly 1960, Agricultural Production 1961, The XXII Congress of the Communist Party of the Soviet Union and its Lessons for the Bulgarian Communist Party 1961 and works on the arts, science, econs., int. relations and culture. *Address:* Durzhaven Suvet, Sofia, Bulgaria.

ZHIVKOV, Zhivko; Bulgarian politician; b. 1915, Toshevtsi, Vidin; ed. Sofia Univ.; Young Communist League 1931-, CP 1935-; imprisoned 1942-44; mem. Cen. Cttee., later Sec., Young Communist League; fmr. Deputy to Foreign Minister; Minister of Foreign Trade 1952-57, of Educ. and Culture 1958-59, Deputy Prime Minister 1959-62, First Deputy Chair. Council of Ministers 1962-71, Deputy Chair. 1971-76; Chair. Cttee. for Econ. Co-ordination 1969-; mem. Cen. Cttee. of Bulgarian Communist Party 1954-, mem. Political Bureau 1962-76; mem. State Council June 1976-; mem. Nat. Ass. *Address:* Durzhaven Suvet, Sofia, Bulgaria.

ZHONG HONGLIAN; Chinese footballer; b. 1960, Dalian; Capt. of the Chinese Nat. Women's Football Team. *Address:* State Physical Culture and Sports Commission, Beijing, People's Republic of China.

ZHOU CHANGXING; Chinese artist; b. 1930; specialises in stonecarving in the Yixing pottery style of Jiangsu Prov. *Address:* Shanghai Exhibition Centre, Shanghai, People's Republic of China.

ZHOU GUANGZHAO; Chinese physicist; b. 15 May 1929, Chang Sha, Hunan; m. Zheng Aiqin 1955; one d.; Prof. of Physics, Beijing Univ.; Dean Science Coll., Qinghua Univ.; Dir. Inst. of Theoretical Physics 1983-; Vice-Pres. Soc. of Physics 1983; Vice-Pres. Chinese Acad. of Sciences 1984-, Pres. 1987-; mem. 12th CCP Cen. Cttee. 1985; 13th CCP Cen. Cttee. 1987-; Vice-Pres. Assen. for Int. Understanding 1985-, Chinese People's Assen. for Peace and Disarmament 1985-. *Address:* Chinese Academy of Sciences, 52 San Li He Road, Beijing, People's Republic of China. *Telephone:* 868361.

ZHOU GUCHENG; Chinese professor and government official; b. 28 July 1898, Yiyang, Hunan; ed. Beijing Normal Univ.; Prof. and Dir., Sociology Dept., Sun Yat-sen Univ., Guangzhou; from 1934 Prof. of History, Jinan Univ., Shanghai, Fudan Univ., Shanghai, Deputy for Hunan, 1st NPC 1954; Deputy for Hunan, 2nd NPC 1958; Deputy for Hunan, 3rd NPC 1964; denounced as "a counter-revolutionary revisionist" 1966; Deputy for Shanghai, 5th NPC 1979-83; Vice-Chair. Chinese Peasants' and Workers' Democratic Party 1979-; Vice-Chair. People's Congress, Shanghai 1979-83; Vice-Chair. Standing Cttee., 6th NPC 1983; Exec. Chair. Presidium 6th NPC 1986-; Chair. Educ., Science, Culture and Public Health Cttee. NPC 1983-; Chair. Chinese Peasants' and Workers' Democratic Party 1987-; Adviser Higher Educ. Soc. 1987-. *Publications include:* A System of Living, Political History of China, Comprehensive World History. *Address:* Office of the Vice-Chairman, Chinese Peasants' and Workers' Democratic Party, Beijing, People's Republic of China.

ZHOU GUOZHEN; Chinese sculptor and ceramic artist; b. July 1931, Anren Co., Hunan; s. of Zhou Wanlong and He Zhaoxiu; m. Hu Zhenxian 1955; one s. one d.; ed. Cen. China Art High School, Suzhou Art School, Cen. Fine Arts Inst., Beijing; at Jingdezhen Ceramic Research Inst. -1966; denounced as 'reactionary' 1966; returned to Jingdezhen Ceramic Research Inst. 1971, teacher 1976-83, Prof. 1982-; Pres. Jiangxi Sculptors Assen. 1984-, Jingdezhen Sculptors Assen. 1983-; Dir. Nat. Artists' Assen. 1985-; one-man shows at Shanghai, Beijing, Jingdezhen, Hong Kong; numerous prizes and awards for his works. *Works include:* Slingshooter 1956, Dawn, Leopard on the Snow, Black and White Cats, An Old Yellow Bull, Tiger on the Road, Dark-leaf Monkey. *Publications:* Anthology of Animal Sketches 1983, The Drawing and Shape of Animal Sculpture 1983, The Characteristics of Zhou Guozhen's Ceramic Art 1985. *Address:* Jingdezhen Ceramic Institute, Jingdezhen, Jiangxi Province, People's Republic of China. *Telephone:* 3845.

ZHOU HUI; Chinese government official; mem. Hunan Provincial People's Council 1955; Deputy Sec. CCP Hunan Provincial Cttee. 1956; Sec. CCP Hunan Prov. 1957; Head 2nd sub-group, large delegation to inspect Hunan's Campaign for Increasing Production and Practising Austerity 1959; First Sec. Nei Monggol CCP Cttee. 1978-83; First Political Commissar PLA Inner Mongolia 1979-83; mem. 11th Cen. Cttee. 1978-; mem. 12th Cen. CCP Cttee. 1982-87; mem. Cen. Advisory Comm. 1987-; Head of Co-operation Group for North China Econ. Tech. 1983-. *Address:* Zhongguo Gongchan Dang, Beijing, People's Republic of China.

ZHOU JIANFU; Chinese artist; b. 1937, Shanxi; Prof. and Dean of Studies, Cen. Acad. of Fine Arts; mem. Chinese Artists' Assen.; mem. Chinese Printmakers' Assen. *Publication:* Artistry of Woodcut. *Address:* Central Academy of Fine Arts, Beijing, People's Republic of China.

ZHOU JIANJUN; Chinese philatelist and stamp designer; b. 1943, Changsha, Hunan Prov. *Address:* All-China Philatelic Federation, Beijing, People's Republic of China.

ZHOU JIANNAN; Chinese government official; b. 1917, Yixing Co., Jiangsu Prov.; Dir. Electric Instrument Admin. Bureau, 1st Ministry of Machine-Building 1954; Asst. to Minister of 1st Ministry of Machine-Building 1956-57, to Minister of Electrical Equipment Industry 1957; Deputy Dir. Bureau for Econ. Relations with Foreign Countries, State

Council 1961-64; Vice-Minister 1st Ministry of Machine-Building 1961-Cultural Revolution and 1978; disappeared during Cultural Revolution; Vice-Minister State Comm. for Regulating Foreign Investments, State Council 1979; Minister of Machine-Building Industry 1982-85; Chair. Promotion Cttee. for Int. System of Measurements 1979-; mem. 12th Cen. Cttee.. CCP 1982-87; Adviser Financial and Econ. Leading Group CCP Cen. Cttee. 1985; mem. Cen. Advisory Comm. 1987-. *Address:* State Council, Beijing, People's Republic of China.

ZHOU KEQIN; Chinese novelist; b. 1937, Jianyang Co., Sichuan; ed. Chengdu Agro-tech. school 1958; started writing 1960; joined Sichuan Branch, Chinese Writers' Assoc. 1979; Prize winner, National Short Story Competition for Forget-Me-Not 1980 and The Moon Does Not Know My Heart 1981; awarded Mao Dun Literature Prize, for Xu Mao and His Daughters 1982. *Address:* Chinese Writers Association, Sichuan Province, People's Republic of China.

ZHOU LIN; Chinese party and government official; b. 1905, Guizhou Prov.; ed. Guizhou Univ.; Mayor of Xuzhou, mem. Xuzhou Mil. Control Comm. 1948; Sec.-Gen. Shanghai Municipal People's Govt. 1949-51; mem. S.W. Mil. Admin. Cttee. 1951-54; First Sec. Guizhou CCP Cttee. 1954-65; Vice-Gov. Guizhou 1951-55, Acting Gov. 1954-55, Gov. 1955-65; First Sec. Political Cttee. Guizhou Mil. Dist. 1958-65; Council mem. Chinese-African People's Friendship Assen. 1960-; purged Feb. 1968, rehabilitated Oct. 1975; Vice-Minister Educ. 1977-82; Sec. Beijing Univ. CCP Cttee. 1978; mem. Cen. Advisory Cttee. of CCP Cen. Cttee. 1982-. *Address:* Central Advisory Committee of the Central Committee of the Chinese Communist Party, Zhongnanhai, Beijing, People's Republic of China.

ZHOU MINGZHEN, PH.D.; Chinese academic; b. 9 Nov. 1918; s. of Henry Zhou and Zhou Chingru; m. Maychen Chay 1940; two s. one d.; Prof. Inst. Vertebrate Palaeontology 1956-; Dir. Beijing Natural History Museum; mem. Chinese Acad. of Sciences. *Leisure interests:* photography, music, reading. *Address:* P.O. Box 643, Beijing, People's Republic of China. *Telephone:* 28-2246.

ZHOU NAN; Chinese government official; Vice-Foreign Minister 1984-; Head of del. to Sino-Portuguese Talks on Macao Question 1986. *Address:* Ministry of Foreign Affairs, 225 Chaonei Street, Dongsi, Beijing, People's Republic of China.

ZHOU PEIYUAN; Chinese scientist and politician; b. 1902, Yixing Cty., Jiangsu; m. Wang Dicheng; ed. Qinghua Univ.; research on theoretical physics, U.S.A., Germany and Switzerland; Dean and Prof. of Physics, Qinghua Univ. 1947-52; Chair. Physics Soc. 1948-58; mem. Council, Fed. of Scientific Socs. 1950, Dir. Org. Dept. 1952; mem. Cen. Cttee., Jiusan Soc. 1953-, Vice-Chair. 1958-88, Chair. Jan. 1988-; on staff of Beijing Univ. 1953-, Vice-Chair. Revolutionary Cttee. 1970, Pres. Beijing Univ. 1978-; Deputy to NPC 1954-, mem. Standing Cttee. 1978; mem. Council, World Fed. of Scientific Workers March 1956, Hon. Sec. April 1956; mem. Council, Dynamics Soc. 1957-58, Vice-Chair. 1958; mem. Scientific Planning Comm., State Council 1957-58; mem. World Peace Council 1957-65; Sec. Scientific and Tech. Assen. 1958, Vice-Chair. 1963-77, Chair. 1977-; joined CCP 1959; mem. Standing Cttee., CPPCC 1959-78; Deputy Dir. Inst. of Foreign Affairs 1972-; Vice-Pres. Acad. of Sciences 1978-; Pres. Physics Soc. 1978-; Deputy Dir. for Promotion of Int. Measurement 1979; Vice-Chair. Nat. Cttee. 5th CPPCC 1980-83; Pres. China-Poland Friendship Assen. 1984-, Chinese People's Assen. for Peace and Disarmament 1985-; Exec. Chair. 6th CPPCC 1983-; Chair. China Assen. for Science and Tech. 1980-86, Hon. Chair. 1986-; Pres. China Int. Science and Tech. Conf. Centre 1986-; Hon. Pres. Soc. of Nuclear Physics 1986-; Vice-Chair. Organizing Cttee. for Int. Peace Year 1985-. *Address:* Office of the President, Beijing University, Beijing, People's Republic of China.

ZHOU SHIZHONG; Chinese army officer; Chief-of-Staff, Fuzhou Mil. Region 1960-67; Deputy Commdr. Wuhan Mil. Region 1976-82; Commdr. Wuhan Mil. Region 1982-; mem. CCP Cen. Advisory Comm. 1987-. *Address:* People's Liberation Army Wuhan Units, Hubei, People's Republic of China.

ZHOU WEIZHI; Chinese composer, writer and politician; b. 13 June 1916, Jiangsu; m. Wang Kun 1943; two s.; Vice-Chair. Dancers' and Artists' Union, 1960-Cultural Revolution; Deputy Dir. Art Bureau, Ministry of Culture 1960-Cultural Revolution; Deputy for Jiangsu, 3rd NPC 1964; disappeared during Cultural Revolution; Vice-Minister of Culture 1978-81, Acting Minister 1981-82; mem. Exec. Cttee., Welfare Inst. 1978; First Vice-Minister of Culture 1981-86; Vice-Chair. Chinese Musicians' Assen. 1979; Head Nat. Leading Group of Artistic Courses, Ministry of Culture 1984; Pres. Chinese Assen. for Mass Culture 1985; Deputy Pres. Chinese Assen. for Cultural Exchange with Foreign Countries 1986-. *Publication:* Works on Art 1985. *Leisure interest:* bridge. *Address:* c/o State Council, Beijing, People's Republic of China. *Telephone:* 447700.

ZHOU WENYUAN; Chinese army officer; b. 1945; Deputy Dir. Gen. Political Dept. PLA 1985-; alt. mem. 13th CCP Cen. Cttee. 1987-. *Address:* People's Liberation Army General Political Department, Beijing, People's Republic of China.

ZHOU YANG (b. Zhou Qiying); Chinese journalist and politician; b. 1907, Hunan Prov.; ed. Shanghai Univ. and Japan; Sec. League of Left-wing

Writers, Shanghai 1930; joined CCP 1932; Dir. Lu Xun Art Inst., Yanan 1940; in U.S.A. 1946–48; Dir. Propaganda Dept., N. China Bureau, CCP Cen. Cttee., and Deputy Dir. Propaganda Dept., CCP Cen. Cttee. 1949–54; Ed. Wen Xue Bao (Literary Journal) 1949; Vice-Chair. Union of Chinese Writers 1953–Cultural Revolution, 1977–; Deputy for Guangdong, 1st NPC 1954; mem. Scientific Planning Comm. 1956; alt. mem. 8th CCP Cen. Cttee. 1956; Prof., Cen. Theatrical Inst. 1958; mem. Standing Cttee., CPPCC 1959; removed from posts during Cultural Revolution; Adviser, Acad. of Social Sciences 1978; mem. Standing Cttee., 5th CPPCC 1978, Head, Cultural Group 1979; Dir. Postgraduate Inst. of Acad. of Social Sciences 1978; Vice-Pres. Acad. of Social Sciences 1978; mem. 11th CCP Cen. Cttee. 1979; Chair. Fed. of Literary and Art Circles 1979–; Chair. China Soc. for Study of Folk Literature and Art 1979–; Vice-Chair. Nat. Acad. Degrees Cttee., State Council 1980; Adviser Propaganda Dept., CCP Cen. Cttee. 1982–; Hon. Pres. Soc. of Aesthetics 1980. *Address:* Academy of Social Sciences, Beijing, People's Republic of China.

ZHOU YOUGUANG; Chinese economist and linguist; b. 13 Jan. 1906, Changzhou City, Jiangsu Prov.; s. of Zhou Qixian and Xu Wen; m. Zhang Yunhe 1933; one s.; ed. Changzhou High School, St. John's Univ. and Guanghua Univ. 1927; teaching in Guanghua Univ., Shanghai and other univs. 1927–37; Sinhua Bank, Shanghai and Hong Kong 1937–45; Rep. of Sinhua Bank, to New York and London 1946–48; Prof., Fudan Univ. and Shanghai Coll. of Finance and Econs. 1949–55; Research Prof., Cttee. for Written Languages Reform of China 1956–87, Research Prof. State Language Comm. and Chinese Social Sciences Acad., Beijing 1987–. *Publications include:* Language Reform of China 1961. *Address:* Chaonei Hou-Guaibang Hutong A-2, 1-301, Beijing, Peoples Republic of China. *Telephone:* 554765 (Beijing).

ZHOU ZHIHANG; Chinese amateur painter; b. 16 June 1963, Shunde County, Guangdong; s. of Zhou Zirun and Liang Sumei; worker, Garment Factory, Rongqi township, Shunde. *Works include:* Fragrances of Litchi, Tea Garden, The Song of Morning. *Address:* Rongqi, Shunde County, Guangdong Province, People's Republic of China.

ZHOU ZHILONG; Chinese actor; b. 1940, Guangxi; Deputy Dir. Chinese Inst. of Traditional Opera 1984–. *Address:* Chinese Institute of Traditional Opera, Beijing, People's Republic of China.

ZHOU ZIJIAN; Chinese politician; b. 1913; Chief, Secr., United Front Work Dept., CCP Cen. Cttee. 1949; Deputy Chief, Sec., Gen. Advisory Council (GAC) and concurrently Chief Gen. Office (GAC) 1949–50; Dep. Dir. Govt. Offices Bureau, 1951–54; Asst. to Minister, First Ministry of Machine-Building 1956–59; Dir. Third Bureau, First Ministry of Machine-Building 1959, Vice-Minister 1960–73, Minister 1973–79; Alt. mem. 11th Cen. Cttee. 1977; Minister, First Ministry of Machine-Building 1980–81, of Machine Building Industry 1982; Gov. and First Sec. Anhui Prov. Cttee. 1981–83, mem. 12th Cen. CCP Cttee. 1982–85; mem. Cen. Advisory Comm. CCP 1987–; Deputy for Shaanxi to 6th NPC 1983; mem. Law Cttee. NPC 1986; Deputy Head China France Friendship Group 1985. *Address:* State Council, Beijing, People's Republic of China.

ZHU GUANG; Chinese government and military official; b. 1911, Bobai Co., Guangxi Prov.; ed. Arts Univ. Shanghai; active in left-wing artists' socs. 1928–31; on Long March 1934; Dir. Propaganda Dept., Cen. Bureau, Yenan 1937; Chief of CCP Del. to Beijing to supervise truce with Kuomintang 1946–47; Pres. Canton People's Court 1949, Chief Justice 1951; Vice-Mayor Canton 1949–54; Vice-Chair. Canton 5-Anti Movt. Cttee. 1952; Mil. Attache Chinese Embassy, N. Korea 1953; Mayor of Canton 1955–60; Sec., Secr. Canton Municipal CCP Cttee. 1957–60; Vice-Chair. State Council Comm. for Cultural Relations with Foreign Countries 1961–65; mem. Standing Cttee. Anhui Prov. CCP Cttee. 1966–; Sec. Political Cttee. PLA A.F. 1985–; mem. 13th CCP Cen. Cttee. *Address:* Central Committee of the Chinese Communist Party, Zhongnanhai, Beijing, People's Republic of China.

ZHU GUANGYA, PH.D.; Chinese physicist and state official; b. 1913, Hubei Prov.; Prof. in Tech. Faculty, Beijing Univ. 1940; mem. Youth League Cen. Cttee. 1953; Deputy for Hubei to 32nd NPC 1964; alt. mem. 9th CCP Cen. Cttee. 1969; mem. 11th CCP Cen. Cttee. 1977; Deputy for PLA to 5th NPC 1978; Vice-Pres. Nuclear Physics Soc. 1980; Vice-Minister, State Scientific and Tech. Comm. 1981–82; Vice-Chair. Science and Tech. Cttee. for Nat. Defense of the PLA 1982–86, Chair. Jan. 1986–; mem. 12th CCP Cttee. 1982, 13th Cen. Cttee. 1987–; Vice-Chair. China Asscn. for Science and Tech. 1986–. *Address:* State Scientific and Technical Commission, 52 Sanlihe, Fuxingmenwai, Beijing, People's Republic of China. *Telephone:* 868361.

ZHU HOUZE; Chinese party official; b. 16th Jan. 1931, Guiyang Municipality, Guizhou Prov.; s. of Zhu Mei-lu and Xiong Lan-Xian; m. Xiong Zhen-gun; one s. two d.; alt. mem. 12th CCP Cen. Cttee. 1982, mem. 1985; Sec. CCP Cttee. Guiyang Municipality 1982; Sec. CCP Cttee., Guizhou Prov. 1983–85; Head, Propaganda Dept. CCP 1985; Deputy Dir. Research Centre for Rural Devt. of the State Council 1987–. *Leisure interests:* swimming, music. *Address:* Research Centre for Rural Development of the State Council, Beijing, People's Republic of China. *Telephone:* 662732.

ZHU JIANHUA; Chinese athlete; b. 1962, Shanghai; improved Asian high jump record three times in 1982; set world record in high jump (2.33

metres), 1982; set world record for high jumps, 2.36 metres, 2.37 metres, 1983.

ZHU JING; Chinese academic and literary translator; b. 1945; ed. Beijing Foreign Language Inst. and Paris; lecturer at Fudan Univ., Shanghai; introduced modern French literature to China. *Address:* Foreign Language Department, Fudan University, Shanghai, People's Republic of China.

ZHU JUNXIAN; Chinese artist; b. 1943, Zhejiang Prov.; specialises in watercolours. *Address:* Beijing College of Industry, Beijing, People's Republic of China.

ZHU KAIXUAN; Chinese government official; Vice-Minister, State Educ. Comm. 1985–; alt. mem. 13th CCP Cen. Cttee. 1987–. *Address:* State Education Commission, Beijing, People's Republic of China.

ZHU LILAN; Chinese government official; Dir. Inst. of Chemistry, Chinese Acad. of Sciences 1985–86; Vice-Minister for Science and Tech. 1986–. *Address:* State Science and Technology Commission, Beijing, People's Republic of China.

ZHU MINGSHAN; Chinese jurist; b. May 1937, Jilin Prov.; Judge Criminal Court, Supreme People's Court 1978–82, Vice-Pres. 1982–83, Vice-Pres. Supreme People's Court 1983–. *Address:* Supreme People's Court, Beijing, People's Republic of China.

ZHU MUZHI; Chinese government official; b. 25 Dec. 1916, Jiangyin City, Jiangsu; s. of Zhu Zushou and He Jiazhen; m. Zhou Luo 1945; one s. two d.; joined CCP 1938; Deputy Ed.-in-Chief Xinhua News Agency 1950, Deputy Dir. 1952; Deputy Dir. New China News Agency (NCNA), State Council 1952–72; Deputy for Jiangsu, 2nd NPC 1958, 3rd NPC 1964; disappeared during Cultural Revolution; Dir. NCNA 1972–77; mem. 10th Cen. Cttee., CCP 1973, 11th Cen. Cttee. 1977; Deputy Dir. Propaganda Dept., CCP Cen. Cttee. 1977; mem. Standing Cttee., Nat. Cttee., 5th CPPCC 1978; mem. Comm. for Inspecting Discipline, CCP Cen. Cttee. 1978; Minister of Culture 1982–86; Adviser, Beijing Journalism Studies Soc. 1980; mem. 12th Cen. Cttee., CCP 1982–85; mem. Advisory Cen. Cttee. CCP 1985, 13th Cen. Cttee. 1987; mem. Fed. of Literature and Art Circles 1982–; Pres. Asscn. for Cultural Exchanges with Foreign Countries 1986–. *Address:* State Council, Beijing, People's Republic of China.

ZHU QINBAO; Chinese artist; b. 19 Feb. 1934, Wuxi, Jiangsu; d. of Zhu Wenchuan and Gou Yalin; m. Zhang Singyu 1958; one s. two d.; ed. Zhejiang Prov. Art Inst.; worked at Jiangsu Art Gallery 1961–; specialist in watercolour woodcuts and copper plate engravings; best-known works include Spring 1959, Morning in a Fishing Village 1962 and Mountain Stream 1980; exhbns. in China, Japan, Norway and Italy; mem. Chinese Nat. Art Asscn. and Chinese Nat. Woodcut Asscn.; Luxun Prize 1987. *Leisure interests:* penmanship, traditional Chinese painting. *Address:* Jiangsu Art Gallery, 266 Changjiang Road, Nanjing, Jiangsu, People's Republic of China.

ZHU QIZHAN; Chinese artist; b. 1891, Taicang, Jiangsu; ed. Sr. Industrial School attached to Post Ministry, Shanghai Acad. of Fine Arts; taught Sr. Industrial School 1913, later Xinhua Inst. of Fine Arts, Shanghai Acad. of Chinese Painting; Prof. Fine Art Dept., E. China Normal Univ. *Works include:* Plum Flowers and Bamboos, Autumn Day, Mountains Obscured by Rain, Setting Sun After Rainfall. *Publication:* Principles of Painting Life in Oils. *Address:* People's Republic of China.

ZHU QIZHEN; Chinese government official; Vice-Minister of Foreign Affairs 1984–. *Address:* Ministry of Foreign Affairs, Beijing, People's Republic of China.

ZHU RONGJI; Chinese government official; Vice-Minister of State Economic Comm. 1983–88; Perm. Dir. China Int. Trust and Investment Corpn. Aug. 1988–; Deputy Sec. Shanghai Municipal Cttee. 1987–; Mayor Shanghai Municipal People's Govt. April 1988–; alt. mem. 13th CCP Cen. Cttee. 1987–. *Address:* Shanghai Municipal People's Government, Shanghai, People's Republic of China.

ZHU SONGFA; Chinese artist; b. Dec. 1942, Anhui; s. of the late Zhu Wei-yu and Bi Gen-zhi; m. Yang Chun-fen 1968; one s. one d.; ed. Anhui Art Inst.; Prof. Chinese Painting, Dean of Art Dept., Anhui Art Inst.; mem. Chinese Artists' Asscn.; paintings include: Song of a Prisoner 1977, After Rainfall 1980, The Golden Years 1984, Jade Universe (plum blossom); exhbns: Nat. Art Works Exhbn., Nanjiang Museum. *Publication:* All Over China (album) 1987. *Leisure interests:* travel, visiting historical sites. *Address:* Anhui Art Institute, Hefei, Anhui, People's Republic of China. *Telephone:* 54338, 52401.

ZHU XIANSONG; Chinese diplomatist; Amb. to Benin 1985–. *Address:* Embassy of the People's Republic of China, B.P. 196, Cotonou, Benin.

ZHU XUEFAN; Chinese state official; b. 1905, Jiashan Zhejiang (now in Jiangsu); ed. Shanghai Inst. of Law; mem. Guomindang (Kuomintang) Legis. Yuan 1932; Minister of Posts and Telecommunications 1949–Cultural Revolution; mem. Financial and Econ. Affairs Cttee., Govt. Admin. Council 1949; mem. Standing Cttee., Cen. Cttee., Guomindang Revolutionary Cttee. 1949; Deputy for Guangdong, 1st NPC 1954, 2nd NPC 1958, 3rd NPC 1964; mem. Standing Cttee., 2nd CPPCC 1954; mem. Gen. Council, WFTU 1960; disappeared during Cultural Revolution; Deputy for Shandong, 5th NPC 1978; mem. Standing Cttee., 5th NPC 1978, Vice-Chair. 1981–83, Vice-Chair. Credentials Cttee. 1981–83; Vice-Pres. Asscn. for Int. Understanding 1981–; Children's Foundation of China 1981–; Vice-Chair. Standing Cttee., 6th NPC 1983–; Vice-Chair. Cen. Cttee., Guomindang Revolutionary Cttee. 1979; Exec. Chair. Presidium 6th NPC 1986–; Chair. China Asscn. for the Advancement of Int. Friendship 1987–; Chair. Revolutionary Cttee. of the Chinese Kuomingtang Jan. 1988–; Hon. Chair. Chinese Workers' Centre for Int. Exchange 1984–; Hon. Pres. China Red Cross Soc. 1985–. *Address:* Guomindang Revolutionary Committee, Beijing, People's Republic of China.

ZHU XUN; Chinese state official; b. 1937; Vice-Minister of Geology and Minerals 1982–85, Minister 1985–; alt. mem. 12th CCP Cen. Cttee. 1982, mem. 1985–87. *Address:* Ministry of Geology and Minerals, 64 Fuxingmenwai Street, Beijing, People's Republic of China. *Telephone:* 668571.

ZI HUAYIN; Chinese choreographer; b. 1936; China Cen. Dance Ensemble 1950; won Berlin folk dance competition 1951; bronze medal, Warsaw 1955; mem. Chinese Dance Asscn.; Dir. Dance Research Inst. of Chinese Art Research Acad. *Address:* Dance Research Institute, Chinese Art Research Academy, Beijing, People's Republic of China.

ZICHICHI, Antonino; Italian physicist; b. 15 Oct. 1929, Trapani; s. of Salvatore Zichichi and Maria Coccellato; m. Maria Ludovica Bernardini 1958; three s.; ed. Univs. of Palermo and Rome; fmr. Dir. Postgraduate School of Physics, Univ. of Bologna, now Prof. of Advanced Physics (on leave of absence); fmr. Dir. Bologna Section, Nat. Inst. for Nuclear Physics; fmr. Pres. European Physical Soc., Instituto Nazionale di Fisica Nucleare; Pres. World Lab., Galileo Galilei Foundation, Science for Peace Int. Cttee.; Dir. Ettore Majorana Interdisciplinary Centre for Scientific Culture; Sr. Physicist, CERN, Geneva; mem. Council, Fondation Jean Monnet pour l'Europe; recipient of numerous awards, medals and prizes. *Publications:* over 200 scientific research papers. *Address:* CERN, 1211 Geneva 23, Switzerland. *Telephone:* 0044-1-580 8236.

ZIĘBA, Stanisław, PH.D.; Polish politician; b. 22 Nov. 1934, Cracow; ed. Coll. of Agric., Cracow, Main School of Farming, Warsaw; agrotechnician, then Deputy Dir. Sugar-Factory, Leśmierz 1955–63; Deputy Head Dept. of Agric. and Forestry Provincial Voivodship National Council, Łódź 1963–69; Dir. Voivodship Experimental Agricultural Plant, Bratoszewice 1969–71; Head Dept. of Agric. and Forestry, Presidium Voivodship Nat. Council, Łódź 1971–73; Vice-Voivode of Łódź 1973–75; Agricultural Sec. PZPR Voivodship Cttee., Piotrków Trybunalski 1975–76; Deputy Head Dept. of Agric. and Food Economy PZPR Cen. Cttee. 1976–81, Head 1981–83; Minister of Agric. and Food Economy 1983–85, of Agric., Forestry and Food Economy 1985–88; Chair. Polish FAO/UN Nat. Cttee. 1987; mem. PZPR 1966–; Kt.'s and Commdr.'s Cross Order of Polonia Restituta. *Publications:* many scientific works on agric. chemistry and fertilization. *Address:* c/o Ministerstwo Rolnictwa, Leśnictwa i Gospodarki Żywnościowej, ul. Wspólna 30, 00-930 Warsaw, Poland.

ZIEGLER, Henri Alexandre Léonard; French aviation executive (retd.); b. 18 Nov. 1906, Limoges; s. of Charles Ziegler and Marguerite Mousnier-Buisson; m. Gillette Rizzi 1932; three s. one d.; ed. Collège Stanislas, Paris; Officer-pilot in air-force 1928; engineer, Corps aéronautique 1929; Deputy Dir. Centre d'essais en vol 1938; Col.-in-Chief Forces françaises de l'Intérieur (London) 1944; Dir.-Gen. Air France 1946–54; Dir. of Cabinet of J. Chaban-Delmas (Min. of Public Works, Transport and Tourism) 1954, and of Gen. Corniglion-Molinier (Min. of Public Works) 1955–56; Admin. Dir.-Gen. Soc. des Ateliers d'Aviation Louis Bréguet 1957–67; Admin. Soc. des Engins Matra, Soc. France-Couleur; fmr. Pres. and mem. of Council, Asscn. Technique pour l'Energie Nucléaire (A.T.E.N.); fmr. Pres. Forum Atomique Européen (FORATOM); Pres. Dir.-Gen. Soc. AIR-Alpes; Pres. Dir.-Gen. Sud-Aviation 1968–70; Pres. Dir.-Gen. Soc. Nat. Industrielle Aérospatiale (co. formed following merger of Sud-Aviation with Nord Aviation and Soc. d'Etudes et Réalisations d'Engins Ballistiques-SEREB) 1970–73, Hon. Pres. 1974–; Admin. Gérant Airbus Industrie 1970–75; Pres. Union Syndicale des Industries Aérospatiales 1971–73, Hon. Pres. 1974–; Hon. mem. l'institut du transport aérien 1977–; Grand Officier Légion d'honneur, Croix de guerre, Rosette de la Résistance, Legion of Merit, C.B.E., C.V.O., and other French and foreign decorations. *Leisure interest:* mountaineering. *Address:* 55 boulevard Lannes, 75116 Paris, France (Home). *Telephone:* 4504-6153.

ZIEGLER, Hubert, DR. RER. NAT.; German professor of botany; b. 28 Sept. 1924, Regensburg; s. of Dr. Max Ziegler and Laura Sohler; m. Dr. Irmgard Guender 1955; one s.; ed. Univ. of Munich; Asst. Univ. of Munich 1950–56, lecturer 1956–58; Assoc. Prof. Tech. Univ. Darmstadt 1959–62, Prof. and Dir. Dept. of Botany and Botanical Gardens 1962–70; Prof. and Dir. Dept. of Botany and Microbiology, Tech. Univ. Munich 1970–; Pres. Int. Asscn. of Plant Physiology 1984–; mem. Senate, Deutsche Forschungsgemeinschaft 1985–; mem. Deutsche Akad. der Naturforscher Leopoldina, Bayerische Akad. der Wissenschaften. *Publications:* about 280 scientific publs. *Address:* Richildenstrasse 74, 8000 Munich 19, Federal Republic of Germany.

ZIEGLER, Martin Arthur Erich; German ecclesiastic; b. 1 Oct. 1931, Berlin; s. of Max Ziegler and Margarete Kohn; m. Gertrude Paehold 1956; three s. one d.; ed. Humboldt Univ. Berlin; priest in Grosskayna/Kr.

Merseburg 1957–62, Kötzschen/Kr. Merseburg 1962–68; cathedral priest and Supt. Merseburg 1968–74; Dir. of Internal Mission and Welfare of Evangelical Church in Berlin-Brandenburg 1974–83; Gen. Sec. Union of Evangelical Churches in G.D.R. 1983–. *Leisure interests:* gardening, literature. *Address:* Tieckstrasse 17, Berlin 1040, Germany. *Telephone:* 282 9368.

ZIEGLER, Peter Alfred, PH.D.; Swiss geologist; b. 2 Nov. 1928, Winterthur; s. of Eugen Ziegler and Adelheid Riggenbach; m. Yvonne M. Bohrer 1960; two s.; ed. Univ. of Zürich; joined petroleum industry 1955; field geologist in Israel, Madagascar, Algeria; joined Shell Canada 1958; transferred to Shell Int. Petroleum Maatschappij BV, The Hague 1977; tech. adviser, North Sea Exploration 1970–77; exploration consultant Europe, South America; Deputy Head, new ventures and exploration advice with worldwide responsibility 1982; Sr. exploration consultant 1984–88, ind. petroleum exploration consultant 1988–; lecturer, Geological Inst., Univ. of Basle; mem. Royal Netherlands Acad.; Hon. Fellow, Geological Soc. London; Fourmarier Medal (Geological Soc. Belgium); Van Waterschot van der Gracht Medal; William Smith Medal (Geological Soc. London). *Publications include:* Geological Atlas of Western and Central Europe 1982. *Leisure interests:* gardening, hiking. *Address:* Kirchweg 41, CH 4102 Binningen, Switzerland. *Telephone:* 41-61-475535.

ZIELENKIEWICZ, Wojciech, D.CHEM.; Polish physical chemist; b. 6 June 1933, Warsaw; s. of Edward Zielenkiewicz and Barbara Zielenkiewicz; m. Anna Zielenkiewicz; one s.; ed. Chemistry Faculty of Warsaw Univ.; researcher, Physical Chemistry Inst. of Polish Acad. of Sciences, Warsaw 1955–, Asst., Lecturer 1955–65, Head, Microcalorimetry Lab. 1965–68, Calorimetry Inst. 1968–, Asst. Prof. 1966–71, Extraordinary Prof. 1971–87, Ordinary Prof. 1987–, Dir. of Inst. 1973–; Gen.-Dir., Polish Acad. of Sciences (PAN) 1968–69, Deputy Gen. Sec. PAN 1969–72, Deputy Sec. PAN Mathematical, Physical and Chemical Sciences Dept. 1972–80, Sec. of Dept. 1984–; corresp. mem. Real Academia de Ciencias y Artes de Barcelona 1975–, Polish Acad. of Sciences 1977–; titular mem. of Thermochemistry and Thermodynamics Comm. of Int. Union of Pure and Applied Chemistry (IUPAC) 1976–85; Chair., Comm. of Metrology and Scientific Apparatus of Polish Acad. of Sciences; mem. Polish United Workers' Party (PZPR) 1954–; Ed.-in-Chief Bulletin of the Polish Acad. of Sciences, Int. Journal Scientific Instrumentation 1972–85; awards of Science and Tech. Cttee. and of PAN; Commdr.'s Cross of Order of Polonia Restituta, Order of Banner of Labour 2nd Class, Gold Cross of Merit, Medal of 30th Anniversary of People's Poland and other decorations. *Publications:* over 100 original scientific works in Polish and foreign journals. *Address:* Instytut Chemii Fizycznej PAN, ul. Kasprzaka 44/52, 01-224 Warsaw (Office); Schillera 8m. 30, 00-248 Warsaw, Poland (Home). *Telephone:* 32-32-21 (Office).

ZIENKIEWICZ, Olgierd Cecil, C.B.E., PH.D., DIP.ENG., F.I.C.E., F.A.S.C.E., F.R.S., F.ENG.; British professor of engineering; b. 18 May 1921, Caterham; s. of Casimir Zienkiewicz and Edith V. Penny; m. Helen J. Fleming 1952; two s. one d.; ed. Katowice, Poland and Imperial Coll., London; consulting eng. 1945–49; Lecturer, Univ. of Edin. 1949–57; Prof. of Structural Mechanics, Northwestern Univ. 1957–61; Prof. and Head Civil Eng. Dept. and Dir. Inst. for Numerical Methods in Eng., Univ. of Wales, Swansea 1961–; Naval Sea Systems Command Research Prof. Monterey, Calif. 1979–80; Hon. founder mem. GAMNI, France; Foreign Assoc. U.S. Nat. Acad. of Eng.; Foreign mem. Polish Acad. of Science 1985; J. A. Ewing Research Medal (Inst. of Civil Engs.) 1980, Newmark Medal (A.S.C.E.) 1980, Gauss Medal, Acad. of Science, Braunschwieg 1987, recipient of 7 hon. doctorates and other awards and prizes; Assoc. City of Guilds and London Inst.; Diploma The Imperial Coll.; four hon. degrees. *Publications:* seven books and numerous articles in professional journals. *Leisure interests:* sailing, skin-diving. *Address:* 29 Somerset Road, Langland, Swansea, SA3 4PG, Wales. *Telephone:* (0792) 295-250 (Office); (0792) 368-776 (Home).

ZIJLSTRA, Jelle, DR. ECON.SC.; Netherlands university professor, politician and banker; b. 27 Aug. 1918, Barradeel; s. of A. J. Zijlstra and Pietje Postuma; m. Hetty Bloksma 1946; two s. three d.; ed. Netherlands School of Econs.; Asst. Netherlands School of Econs. 1945–46, lecturer 1947; Prof. of Econ. Sciences, Free Univ. of Amsterdam 1948–52; Minister of Econ. Affairs 1952–59, of Finance 1959–63; Prof. of Econ. Sciences, Free Univ. of Amsterdam 1963–67; Pres. Bd. of Govs., European Investment Bank 1962–63; Prime Minister 1966–67; Pres. Netherlands Bank 1967–81; Pres. Bank for Int. Settlements and Chair. of Bd. of Dirs. 1967–81; Gov. IMF, Washington 1967–81; mem. Supervisory Bd. Royal Dutch Petroleum 1982–; Anti-Revolutionary Party. *Publication:* The Velocity of Circulation of Money and its Significance for the Value of Money and Monetary Equilibrium 1948. *Address:* Achtergracht 14, 1017 WP Amsterdam, Netherlands.

ZIMAN, John Michael, F.R.S.; British physicist; b. 16 May 1925; s. of the late Solomon Netheim Ziman and of Nellie Francis (née Gaster) Ziman; m. Rosemary Milnes Dixon 1951; two adopted s. two adopted d.; ed. Hamilton High School, New Zealand, Victoria Coll., Wellington, Balliol Coll., Oxford; Junior Lecturer in Mathematics, Oxford Univ. 1951–53, Pressed Steel Ltd. Research Fellow 1953–54; Lecturer in Physics, Cambridge Univ. 1954–64, Fellow of King's Coll. 1957–64, Ed. Cambridge Review 1958–59, Tutor for Advanced Students, King's Coll. 1959–63; Prof. of Theoretical Physics, Univ. of Bristol 1964–69, Melville Wills Prof. 1969–76, Henry Overton Wills Prof. and Dir. H. H. Wills Physics Lab. 1976–81, Prof. Emer. 1989–; Visiting Prof. in Depts. of Social and Econ.

Studies and Humanities, Imperial Coll. of Science and Tech. 1982-; Chair. Science Policy Support Group 1986-; Jt. Ed., Science Progress 1965-; Hon. Ed. Reports on Progress in Physics 1968-76; Gen. Ed. Cambridge Monographs on Physics; Chair. Council for Science and Society; Rutherford Memorial Lecturer in India and Pakistan 1968; Airey Neave Memorial Award 1981. *Publications:* Electrons and Phonons 1960, Electrons in Metals 1963, Camford Observed (with Jasper Rose) 1964, Principles of the Theory of Solids 1965, Public Knowledge 1968, Elements of Advanced Quantum Theory 1969, The Force of Knowledge 1976, Reliable Knowledge 1979, Models of Disorder 1979, Teaching and Learning about Science and Society 1980, Puzzles, Problems and Enigmas 1981, An Introduction to Science Studies 1984, The World of Science and the Rule of Law (with Paul Sieghart and John Humphrey) 1986, Knowing Everything about Nothing 1987; numerous articles in scientific journals. *Address:* 23 Henrietta Street, London, WC2E 8NA, England. *Telephone:* 01-836-6515.

ZIMERMAN, Krystian; Polish pianist; b. 5 Dec. 1956, Zabrze; ed. Acad. of Music, Katowice; won 1st Prize, Chopin Competition, Warsaw 1975; soloist, appearences in many countries in Europe and U.S.A. *Address:* c/o Harrison/Parrott Ltd., 12 Penzance Place, London, W11 4PA, England. *Telephone:* 01-229 9166.

ZIMIN, Aleksandr Aleksandrovich, DR.HIST.SC.; Soviet historian; b. 22 Feb. 1920; ed. Univ. of Cen. Asia, then sr. research assoc. Inst. of History, U.S.S.R. Acad. of Sciences; Prof. of Historical Science 1970. *Publications:* author of numerous works on history of Russia from 11th to 18th centuries, including I. S. Peresvetov and His Contemporaries 1958, Methods of Publication of Medieval Russian Deeds 1959, Russian Chronicles and Chronographs of the end of the 15th and 16th Centuries 1960, The Reforms of Ivan the Terrible 1960, The Oprichniki of Ivan the Terrible 1964, Russia on the Threshold of a New Age 1972. *Address:* Institute of History, U.S.S.R. Academy of Sciences, Leninsky Pr. 14, Moscow V-71, U.S.S.R.

ZIMM, Bruno Hasbrouck, PH.D.; American research chemist and professor; b. 31 Oct. 1920, Woodstock, N.Y.; s. of Bruno L. Zimm and Louise Hasbrouck Zimm; m. Georgianna Grevatt 1944; two s.; ed. Columbia Univ.; teaching Asst. Columbia Univ., New York 1941-44; Civilian Staff mem., Atomic Energy Comm., New York, N.Y. 1942-43; with Office of Scientific Research and Devt. New York, N.Y.; Research Assoc. and Instructor Polytechnic Inst. of Brooklyn 1944-46; Instructor, Univ. of Calif. at Berkeley 1946-47, Asst. Prof. 1947-49, Assoc. Prof. 1950-52; Research Assoc., Gen. Electric Research Lab., Schenectady, N.Y. 1951-60; Prof. of Chem., Univ. of Calif. at San Diego 1960-; Visiting Lecturer in Chem. Harvard Univ. 1950-51; Visiting Prof. Yale Univ. 1960-; mem. N.A.S. (Chemical Science Award 1981); Leo Hendrik Baekeland Award, N. Jersey Section of American Chemical Soc. 1957, Bingham Medal, Soc. of Rheology 1960, High Polymer Physics Prize, American Physical Soc. 1963. *Publications:* over 100 articles in scientific journals. *Leisure interests:* playing clarinet, tennis, sailing. *Address:* Department of Chemistry, University of California, Box 017, San Diego, Calif. 92093; 2522 Horizon Way, La Jolla, Calif. 92037, U.S.A. (Home). *Telephone:* (619) 452-4416 (Office).

ZIMMERMAN, Charles J., B.S., M.B.A.; American insurance executive; b. 9 Jan. 1902; m. Opal Marie Smith 1942 (died 1985); ed. Dartmouth Coll., The Amos Tuck School of Business Admin.; Exec. Man. New York Life Underwriters' Asscn. 1924-26; Gen. Agent, The Conn. Mutual Life Insurance Co. 1926-46; Capt. U.S.N. 1942-46; Man. Dir. Life Insurance Agency Man. Asscn. 1946-56; Pres. The Conn. Mutual Life Insurance Co. 1956-67, Chair. 1967-68, Chair. of Bd. 1968-72; Founder Univ. of Hartford 1957; Trustee, Dartmouth Coll. 1952-72 (Chair. 1970-72), Lawrence Acad. 1963-70, Nat. Conf. of Christians and Jews 1961-; Chair. American Coll. of Life Underwriters 1965-69, Life Trustee 1969-; S. S. Huebner Foundation for Insurance and Educ., Chair. 1968; Dir. Inst. of Living 1964-77 (Pres. 1968-72, Nat. Bd. of Govs. 1977-), Life Insurance Medical Research Fund (Chair. 1963-69), Nat. Asscn. for Mental Health Inc. 1962-68; Conn. Bank and Trust Co. 1960-72, Connecticut Natural Gas Corpn. 1960-72, State Dime Savings Bank 1956-70, Jr. Achievement of Hartford Inc. 1957-74 (Pres. 1966-68); mem. Exec. Cttee. American Life Convention, Pres. Exec. Cttee. 1969-70; John Newton Russell Memorial Award 1951, Insurance Hall of Fame 1969. *Address:* 140 Garden Street, Hartford, Conn. 06154; 70 Mohawk Drive, West Hartford, Conn. 06117, U.S.A. *Telephone:* 203-727-6500 (Office); 203-232-1533 (Home).

ZIMMERMAN, Howard Elliot, PH.D.; American professor of chemistry; b. 5 July 1926, New York; m. 1st Jane Kirschenheiter 1950 (deceased); m. 2nd Martha L. Bailey Kaufman 1975; three s. one step-s. one step-d.; ed. Yale and Harvard Univs.; Instructor Northwestern Univ. 1954-55, Asst. Prof. 1955-60; Assoc. Prof. Univ. of Wisconsin 1960-61, Prof. 1961-, Arthur C. Cope Prof. of Chem. 1975-; mem. several editorial bds. etc.; mem. N.A.S.; Alfred P. Sloan Fellow 1956-60; James Flack Norris Award (American Chem. Soc.) 1976; Halpern Award 1979, Pioneer Award, Nat. Inst. of Chemists 1986. *Publications:* Quantum Mechanics for Organic Chemists 1975; 4 book chapters and more than 200 scientific articles. *Address:* Department of Chemistry, University of Wisconsin, 1101 University Avenue, Madison, Wis. 53706; 1 Oconto Court, Madison, Wis. 53705, U.S.A. *Telephone:* 608-262-1502 (Office); 608-233-0140 (Home).

ZIMMERMANN, Friedrich, DR.JUR.; German politician; b. 18 July 1925, Munich; s. of Josef and Luise (née Wenger) Zimmermann; m. 2nd Birgit

Kemmler 1988; two d. by previous marriage; ed. Univ. of Munich; asst. legal officer, Bavarian State Ministry of Justice 1951-54, legal adviser, Bavarian State Chancellery 1954; called to the Bar, Munich 1963; mem. Supervisory Bd., Adler Feuerversicherung AG, Berlin 1955-82, Versicherung für den öffentlichen Dienst AG im Adler-Iduna-Verbund, Berlin 1978-82, Fernsehstudios München Atelierbetriebsgesellschaft mbH 1974-82, Chair. July-Sept. 1982; Deputy Chair. Advisory Council, Zweites Deutsches Fernsehen 1964-; mem. CSU 1948-, now mem. Presidium; mem. Bundestag 1957-; Fed. Minister of the Interior 1982-89, of Transport April 1989-. *Publications:* Anspruch und Leistung: Widmungen für Franz Josef Strauss 1980, Ausgewählte Bundestagsreden. *Leisure interests:* tennis, skiing, hunting. *Address:* Kennedyallee 72, 5300 Bonn 2 (Office). *Telephone:* 0228/3001 (Office).

ZIMMERMANN, Heinz, DIPL.ING.; German town planner, academic and training college instructor; b. 6 March 1921, Zülpich; s. of Josef and Helene (née Esser) Zimmermann; m. Maria Frings 1955; one s. one d.; ed. Technische Hochschule, Aachen; Asst. to Prof. Dr. Roloff 1950-56; architect and town planner 1956-; town planner for various towns and cities including Cologne, Porz, Neuss, Kleve, Berg-Gladbach, Bergheim, Zülpich, Deutsche Akademie für Städte Bau und Landesplanung, etc.; recipient of numerous first prizes in competitions. *Publication:* Xanten, Europäische Beispielstadt. *Address:* August-Macke-Strasse 20, 5000 Cologne 41, Federal Republic of Germany. *Telephone:* 0221/411011.

ZIMYANIN, Mikhail Vasiliyevich; Soviet journalist and diplomatist; b. 21 Nov. 1914, Vitebsk, Byelorussia; ed. Mogilev Pedagogical Inst.; mem. CPSU 1939-; First Sec. Cen. Cttee., Komsomol Byelorussia 1940-46; Second Sec. Gomel Regional Cttee. CP of Byelorussia 1946; Minister of Educ., Byelorussia 1946-47; Sec., Second Sec. Cen. Cttee. CP Byelorussia 1947-53; Ministry of Foreign Affairs 1953-56, Far Eastern Dept. 1957-60; Amb. to Democratic Repub. of Viet-Nam 1956-57, to Czechoslovakia 1960-65; Deputy Minister for Foreign Affairs, U.S.S.R. 1965-87; Ed. of Pravda 1965-76; mem. Cen. Cttee. CPSU 1952-56, 1966-89, Secr. 1976-86; Head of Dept. of Agitation and Propaganda Cen. Cttee. 1978; mem. Cen. Auditing Comm. CPSU 1956-66; Vice-Chair. Council of Nationalities of USSR Supreme Soviet 1950-54; Deputy to U.S.S.R. Supreme Soviet 1946-54, 1966-; Order of Lenin (three times), Red Banner, Red Banner of Labour (twice), Sixty Years of Armed Forces of U.S.S.R. Medal. *Address:* c/o Central Committee of the CPSU, Moscow, U.S.S.R.

ZINDER, Norton David, PH.D.; American professor and geneticist; b. 7 Nov. 1928, New York, N.Y.; s. of Harry Zinder and Jean Gottesman Zinder; m. Marilyn Esteicher 1949; two s.; ed. Columbia Univ. and Univ. of Wisconsin; Wisconsin Alumni Fund Fellow, Univ. of Wis. 1948-50, Research Assoc. 1950-56; Asst., Rockefeller Univ. (then Rockefeller Inst.) 1952-56, Assoc. 1956-58, Assoc. Prof. 1958-64, Prof. 1964-, John D. Rockefeller Jr. Prof. 1976-; mem. of following cttees.: Int. Inst. of Cellular and Molecular Pathology (ICP), Brussels 1985-, Science and Law sub-cttee. New York City Bar Asscn. 1985-, Council on Foreign Relations 1986-, NAS/NRC (BAST) Panel on Chemical Weapons Research and Devt. Defense 1986-, NAS/NRC Chair. to Review the Army Chemical Weapons Stockpile Disposal Program 1987-, Alliance Int. Health Care Trust 1984-; mem. N.A.S., American Acad. of Arts and Sciences, American Soc. of Microbiology, American Soc. of Biological Chemists, Genetics Soc. of America, American Asscn. for the Advancement of Science, American Soc. of Virology; Scholar of American Cancer Soc. 1955-58, Eli Lilly Award in Microbiology 1962, United State Steel Foundation Award of N.A.S. in Molecular Biology 1966, Medal of Excellence from Columbia Univ. 1969, AAAS Award in Scientific Freedom and Responsibility 1982. *Publications:* Infective Heredity in Bacteria, Cold Spring Harbor Symposium on Quantitative Biology XVIII 1953; and scientific articles in learned journals. *Address:* Rockefeller University, 66th Street and York Avenue, New York, N.Y. 10021 (Office); 450 East 63rd Street, New York City, N.Y. 10021, U.S.A. (Home). *Telephone:* 421-3777.

ZINMAN, David Joel; American conductor; b. 9 July 1936, New York; s. of Samuel Zinman and Rachel Ilo (Samuels) Zinman; m. 1st Leslie Heyman (deceased); two s. one d.; m. 2nd Mary Ingham 1974; ed. Oberlin Conservatory, Ohio and Univ. of Minnesota; studied conducting Berks. Music Center, Tanglewood and with Pierre Monteux; Asst. to Monteux 1961-64; Guest Conductor Nederlands Kamerorkest 1964-77; Music Dir. Rochester Philharmonic Orchestra, New York 1974-85, Baltimore Symphony Orchestra 1985-; Prin. Guest Conductor Rotterdam Philharmonic Orchestra 1977-79, Chief Conductor 1979-; numerous recordings; Grand Prix du Disque; Edison Award. *Address:* Baltimore Symphony Orchestra, 1212 Cathedral Street, Baltimore, Md. 21201, U.S.A.

ZINNEMANN, Fred; American (b. Austrian) film director; b. 29 April 1907; s. of Dr. Oskar Zinnemann and Anna F. Zinnemann; m. Renée Bartlett 1936; one s.; ed. Univ. of Vienna, Law School and School of Cinematography, Paris; studied techniques of camera, lighting and mechanics, Paris; went to U.S.A. 1929; directed documentaries and short films until 1941, major films 1941-; initiated, with others, school of neo-realism in American Cinema; awards include 4 Academy Awards, 4 New York Film Critics Awards, 2 Directors' Guild of America Annual Awards; Golden Thistle Award, Edinburgh Film Festival 1965; Gold Medal, City of Vienna 1967; Hon. Award for A Man for All Seasons, Moscow Film Festival 1967,

D. W. Griffith Award 1969; David di Donatello Award (Florence) 1978; Contributor to Encyclopaedia Britannica (Film Directing); Hon. Fellow, British Acad. of Film and Television Arts (BAFTA) 1978, Officer of Order of Arts and Sciences (France) 1982; U.S. Congressional Lifetime Achievement Award 1987. *Films include:* The Wave (documentary for Mexican Govt.) 1934, Crime Does Not Pay (series of shorts) 1937–41, The Seventh Cross 1944, The Search 1948, Act of Violence 1949, The Men 1950, Teresa 1951, Benjy (Acad. Award Documentary) 1951, High Noon 1952, The Member of the Wedding 1953, From Here to Eternity (Acad. Award) 1953, Oklahoma! 1955, A Hatful of Rain 1957, The Nun's Story 1958, The Sundowners 1960, Behold a Pale Horse 1964, A Man for all Seasons (Acad. Award) 1966, The Day of the Jackal 1973, Julia 1977 (British Acad. Award 1979), Five Days in Summer 1982. *Leisure interests:* chamber music, mountain climbing. *Address:* 128 Mount Street, London, W.1, England. *Telephone:* 01-499 8810.

ZINOVIEV, Aleksandr Aleksandrovich, D.S.; Soviet philosopher; b. 1922; Prof. of Logic & Methodology of Science, Moscow Univ. 1970–78; actively campaigned against and discredited in 1970s, expelled 1978; Research post at Univ. of Munich 1978–; mem. Finnish Acad. of Sciences; Prix Tocqueville 1982. *Publications include:* Philosophical Problems of Polyvalent Logic (Russian 1960, English 1963), Principles of the Logical Theory of Scientific Knowledge 1967 (trans. Eng. 1973), An Essay on Polyvalent Logic 1968 (trans. German 1968); Complex Logic 1970 (trans. German Komplexe Logik 1970), Logical Physics 1972, Logische Sprachregeln (with A. N. Wessel) 1975; non-philosophic works: Ziyayushchiye vysoty (Yawning Heights) 1976 (fiction), A Radiant Future 1978, The Yellow House (2 vols.) 1980, The Reality of Communism 1983, Homo Soveticus 1985, The Madhouse 1986, Para Bellum 1987.

ZINSOU, Emile Derlin; Benin doctor and politician; b. 23 March 1918; ed. Ecole Primaire Supérieure, Ecole Africaine de Médecine, Dakar and Faculté de Médecine, Paris; Represented Dahomey in French Nat. Assembly; fmr. Vice-Pres. Assemblée de l'Union française, Senator, Territorial Council; fmr. Minister of Economy and of The Plan; fmr. Amb. to France; Pres. Supreme Court of Dahomey; Minister of Foreign Affairs 1961–63, 1965–67; Pres. of Dahomey (now Benin) 1968–69; sentenced to death in absentia 1975; numerous decorations include Grand Croix Ordre Nat., Dahomey, Grand Officier Légion d'honneur. *Address:* Paris, France.

ZIPPELIUS, Reinhold, DR. JUR.; German professor of law; b. 19 May 1928, Ansbach; s. of Hans Zippelius and Marie Zippelius; m. Annelore Fricke 1959; one s. one d.; ed. Univs. of Würzburg, Erlangen and Munich; Govt. official 1956–63; Privatdozent, Univ. of Munich 1961–63; Prof. and Dir. Inst. für Rechtsphilosophie und Allgemeine Staatslehre, Univ. of Erlangen-Nuremberg 1963–; mem. Akad. der Wissenschaften und Literatur in Mainz. *Publications:* numerous works on legal subjects. *Address:* Kochstrasse 2, 8520 Erlangen, Federal Republic of Germany. *Telephone:* 09131/85-2238.

ZITTOUNI, Messaoud; Algerian politician; b. 10 March 1940, Azzaba; m.; three c.; Head Surgeon, C.H.U., Algiers; Dir. Inst. des Sciences Medicales, Algiers 1975–80; Dir. Inst. Nat. d'Enseignement Supérieur en Sciences Medicales, Algiers 1985–86; Minister of Health 1988–. *Address:* 25 blvd Laala Abd ar-Rahmane, El-Madania, Algiers, Algeria. *Telephone:* (2) 66-33-15.

ZIV-AV, Itzhak; Israeli administrative official and journalist; b. 4 June 1907, Russia; s. of Abraham and Miriam Ziv-Av; m. Debora Kobrinsky 1934; two s.; ed. Inst. of Pedagogy, Smolensk; Farmer and Man. Local Council of Magdiel settlement, Israel 1926–34; Man. Ed. Haboker (daily) 1935–48; Dir. Public Relations Div., Ministry of Defence and GHQ, Israel Defence Forces 1948–52; Dir.-Gen. Israel Farmers' Union 1952–75, Chair. Council 1975–86, Pres. Hon. Court 1986–; Chair. Exec. Cttee., Co-ordinating Bureau, Israeli Econ. Orgs. 1967–86; Ed. Farmers of Israel monthly 1962–; mem. Bd. of Dirs. Jewish Nat. Fund; Chair. Bd., Land Devt. Authority 1960–; mem. Council, State Land Authority 1962–, Exec. Bd., Int. Fed. Agricultural Producers (IFAP) 1960–80. *Publications:* The Unknown Land, I Seek My Brethren, The Price of Freedom, Forever Ours, From Frontier to Frontier, A World to Live in, Another World, There is a Land, All the Hopes are Reborn, Beautiful Are the Nights in Canaan, The People of 1948, and poetry for children. *Leisure interests:* reading, gardening, travel. *Address:* Israel Farmers' Federation, Kaplan Street 8, Tel-Aviv 64734 (Office); Ramat-Qan 52587, Sh'mueli Street 3, Israel (Home). *Telephone:* 03-25-22-27 (Office); 03-7510227 (Home).

ZOITAKIS, Gen. George; Greek army officer; b. 1910; Nafpaktos, Aitolo-Akarnania; m. Sophia D. Vouranzeris 1949; one d.; ed. Cadet School, Higher War Coll. of Greece School of Nat. Defence, and American School of Special Arms, Germany; Infantry 2nd Lieut. 1932; 1st Lieut. 1935; Captain 1938; Maj. 1946; Lieut.-Col. 1949; Col. 1955; Brig. 1960; Maj.-Gen. 1963; Lieut.-Gen. 1965; Under-Sec. of State for Nat. Defence April 1967; Regent of Greece 1967–72; Gen. 1970; arrested Feb 1975, charged with high treason and insurrection, sentenced to life imprisonment Aug. 1975; mem. Mixed Greco-Bulgarian Cttee. for settling frontier incidents, then Pres. of corresp. Greek-Yugoslav Cttee.; numerous medals.

ZOLLINGER, Heinrich Fritz, PH.D., D.SC.; Swiss professor and university administrator; b. 29 Nov. 1919, Aarau; s. of Dr. Fritz Zollinger and Helene

Prior; m. Heidi Frick 1948; three s.; ed. Fed. Inst. of Tech. (ETH), Univ. of Basel, M.I.T.; Chemist, Dyestuff Research Dept., CIBA Ltd. 1945–60; Lecturer in Dyestuff Chem., Univ. of Basel 1952–60; Prof. of Textile Chem., Fed. Inst. of Tech. 1960–; Rector 1973–77; Pres. Organic Chem. Div. of IUPAC 1975–77, Pres. IUPAC 1979–81; Pres. Council Swiss Science Foundation 1979–82; Hon. Ph.D. (Stuttgart) 1976, (Tokyo Inst. Tech.) 1983; Foreign Fellow, Royal Swedish Acad. of Eng. 1979, Hon. Fellow, Soc. of Dyers and Colourists (U.K.) 1981, Chem. Soc. of Japan 1985, Swiss Soc. of Dyers and Colourists (SVCC) 1987; Foreign Fellow, Acad. of Sciences, Göttingen 1984; Werner Prize 1959, Ruzicka Award 1960, Lewinstein Award 1964, Conrad Prize 1970, O. N. Witt Gold Medal 1980, M. Kehren Gold Medal 1984. *Publications:* Chemie der Azofarbstoffe 1958 (Russian 1960), Diazo and Azo Chemistry 1961, Leitfaden der Farbstoffchemie 1970, 1976, 1982 (English 1972, Japanese 1972), Chemie und Hochschule 1978, Colour Chemistry 1987; volumes on aromatic chemistry in Int. Review of Science 1973, 1976; 310 scientific papers. *Leisure interests:* clarinet, climbing, skiing, sailing, colour studies. *Address:* Technisch-Chemisches Laboratorium, Eidgenössische Technische Hochschule, Universitätsstrasse 6, CH-8092, Zürich (Office); Boglerenstrasse 45, CH-8700 Küsnacht, Switzerland (Home). *Telephone:* 01-256-41-68 (Laboratory); 01-910-53-08 (Home).

ZOLOTAS, Xenophon, DR.ECON.; Greek university professor; b. 26 March 1904, Athens; s. of the late Efthymios Zolotas; m. Kallirhoe Ritsos 1958; ed. Univs. of Athens, Leipzig and Paris; Prof. of Econs. Univ. of Thessaloniki 1928, of Athens 1931–68; mem. of Supreme Council of Greece 1932, of Greek del. to the Econ. Council of the Entente Balkanique 1934–39; Chair. Bd. of Dirs., Agricultural Bank of Greece 1936–40; Joint Gov. Bank of Greece (after Liberation) Oct. 1944–45; mem. UNRRA Council 1946; Gov. of IMF for Greece 1946–67, 1974–81, mem. Greek Del. to UN Gen. Ass. 1948–53; Del. to Econ. Comm. for Europe 1949–53; mem. Currency Cttee. 1950, 1974–81; Vice-Chair. ECE 1952; Minister of Co-ordination Oct. 1952; Gov. Bank of Greece 1955–67, 1974–81, Hon. Gov. 1981–; Minister of Econ. Co-ordination July-Nov. 1974; mem. "Group of Four" for remodelling of OEEC 1960; mem. Acad. of Athens 1952–; Hon. Pres. Int. Econ. Asscn. 1980; Grand Cross of Royal Order of the Phoenix, of the Ordre nat. du Mérite (France), Grand Officier, Légion d'honneur (France) and others. *Publications:* Griechenland auf dem Wege zur Industrialisierung 1926, Wirtschaftsstruktur und Wirtschaftsbeziehungen Griechenlands 1931, L'étalon-or en théorie et en pratique 1933, La question de l'or et le problème monétaire 1938, La théorie économique traverse-t-elle une crise? 1938, La transformation du capitalisme 1953, Monetary Stability and Economic Development 1958, Economic Development and Technical Education 1960, The Problem of the International Monetary Liquidity 1961, Towards a Reinforced Gold Exchange Standard 1961, Economic Development and Private Enterprise 1962, International Monetary Order, Problems and Policies 1962, The Role of the Banks in a Developing Country 1963, The Multicurrency Standard and the International Monetary Fund 1963, Monetary Equilibrium and Economic Development 1965, Remodelling the International Monetary System 1965, Alternative Systems for International Monetary Reform, A Comparative Appraisal 1965, Current Monetary and Economic Developments in Greece 1966, International Labor Migration and Economic Development 1966, Monetary Planning 1967, The Gold Trap and the Dollar 1968, Speculocracy and the International Monetary System 1969, The International Money Mess 1973, From Anarchy to International Monetary Order 1973, The Energy Problem in Greece 1975, Recession and Reflation in the Greek Economy 1975, Developments and Prospects of the Greek Economy 1975, Guidelines for Industrial Development in Greece 1976, Greece in the European Community 1976, International Monetary Vacillations 1976, International Monetary Issues and Development Policies 1977, Inflation and the Monetary Target in Greece 1978, An International Loan Insurance Scheme 1978, The Positive Contribution of Greece to the European Community 1978, The Dollar Crisis and Other Papers 1979, On the Issue of a Stable Monetary Standard 1981, Economic Growth and Declining Social Welfare 1981, The Unruly International Monetary System 1985, The Dollar and the New Form of International Co-operation 1986, The Enigma of the U.S. Trade Deficit 1986, The European Monetary System, the Dollar and the Need for Reform 1987, Co-operation and Disco-ordination in International Monetary Policies, the Need for Rules of Conduct 1988, The European Monetary System and the Challenge of 1992 1988; in Greek: Monetary Stabilization 1929, Economics 1942, Creative Socialism 1944, The Monetary Problem and the Greek Economy 1950, Inflationary Pressures in the Greek Economy 1951, Regional Planning and Economic Development 1961, Human Capital and Economic Development 1968, The Contribution of Exports to Economic Development 1976, Social Welfare and Economic Organization 1976, Consumption, Investment and Monetary Equilibrium 1977, Economic and Monetary Problems in Greece 1979. *Address:* Bank of Greece, 21 Panepistimou Street, Athens 102 50 (Office); 25 Dionissiou Areopagitou Street, Athens 117 42, Greece (Home). *Telephone:* 3230-317 (Office); 9214-780 (Home).

ZOLTÁN, Imre, M.D.; Hungarian obstetrician and gynaecologist; b. 12 Dec. 1909, Budapest; s. of E. Zoltan; m. Edith Rokay 1953; one d.; ed. Pazmany Peter Univ. (now Semmelweis Univ. of Medical Sciences); Asst. in Dept. of Obstetrics and Gynaecology, Univ. Clinic, Pazmany Peter Univ. 1933–46, Assoc. Prof. 1946–50, Prof. and Dir. of Dept. 1950–79; Sec. Gen. Fed. of Hungarian Medical Socs. 1966–70, Pres. 1974–85; Vice-Pres. Int. Fed. of

Gynaecology and Obstetrics 1970-73; Dir. Nat. Inst. of Obstetrics and Gynaecology 1973-79, Consulting Prof. 1979-; mem. Presidency of Fed. Hungarian Medical Socs. 1985-. *Publications:* Textbooks of Obstetrics and Gynaecology 1951-70; Co-author: Semmelweis. His Life and Work. *Leisure interests:* sport, tennis, gastronomy. *Address:* Bartók Béla ut. 31, 1114 Budapest, Hungary. *Telephone:* 667-149.

ZONG KEWEN; Chinese diplomatist; Amb. to Czechoslovakia 1971-75, to Sierra Leone 1975-78, to Senegal 1978-82, to Democratic People's Republic of Korea 1982-87; Vice-Chair. Heilongjiang Prov. Cttee. March 1987-. *Address:* Heilongjiang Provincial Committee, Heilongjiang, of People's Republic of China.

ZONG PU; Chinese writer; b. (as Feng Zhong Pu) 26 July 1928, Beijing; d. of Feng Yuolan and Ren Zai Kun; m. Cai Zhong De; one d.; ed. Qinghua Univ.; mem. editorial bds. Literary Gazette and World Literature. *Publications:* The Red Beans 1957, Melody in Dreams (Nat. Prize for Short Stories) 1978, Who Am I? 1979, Lu Lu 1980, The Everlasting Rock 1980, Fairy Tales from a Wind Cottage 1984, Bear Palm (short stories) 1985, Lilac Knot (essays) 1986, Retreat to the South (Vol. I of Ordeal) 1988. *Leisure interests:* music, travel. *Address:* Beijing University, 57 Yan Nan Yuan, Beijing, People's Republic of China.

ZORRILLA, China; Uruguayan actress, director and producer; b. 1922; d. of Jose Luis Zorrilla de San Martin; unmarried; ed. Royal Acad. of Dramatic Art, London; worked with Ars Pulchra group, Uruguayan Independent Theatre; later worked as journalist and as actress and dir. Nat. Theatre of Uruguay; f. with Antonio Larreta and Enrique Guarnero, Theatre of City of Montevideo 1961; directed show Canciones para mirar, New York 1965 and later in Buenos Aires; staged Jacobo Langsner's El Tobogán and Neil Simon's Plaza Suite, Montevideo 1969; has made several films in Argentina; director, Como en casa (television show); newscaster, Radio Belgrano; noted theatrical appearances including one-woman show Hola, hola, un, dos, tres (toured Argentina, Venezuela and U.S.A.) and as Emily in Spanish-language version of William Luce's The Belle of Amherst throughout Latin America and in U.S.A. since 1981.

ZOU JIAHUA; Chinese engineer and state official; b. 1926, Shanghai; s. of Zou Caofen, elder brother of Zou Jingmeng (q.v.); fmr. Dir. Shenyang No. 2 Machine Tool Plant; Dir. Machine Tool Inst., First Ministry of Machine Bldg.; Deputy Dir. Communication of Science, Tech. and Industry for Nat. Defence; alt. mem. 12th CCP Cen. Cttee. 1982, mem. 1985; Minister of Ordnance Industry 1985-86, of State Machine-Bldg. Industry Comm. 1986-88, of Machine Bldg. and Electronics Industry April 1988-; State Councillor April 1988-; mem. 13th CCP Cen. Cttee. 1987-. *Address:* Ministry of State Machine-Building Industry Commission, Beijing, People's Republic of China.

ZOU JINGMENG; Chinese meteorologist; b. 1929, Shanghai; s. of Zou Caofen, younger brother of Zou Jiahua (q.v.); meteorological observer in 8th Route Army 1944; studied meteorology at Harbin Inst. of Eng. 1949-; cadre of Cen. Meteorological Bureau 1974; Vice-Pres. Soc. of Meteorology 1975; Deputy Dir. Cen. Meteorological Bureau 1980-82, Dir. 1982-; Perm. Rep. World Meteorological Org. 1984-; alt. mem. 12th CCP Cen. Cttee. 1982, 13th Cen. Cttee. 1987. *Address:* Beijing, People's Republic of China.

ZOU YU; Chinese government official; b. 3 Oct. 1920, Guangdong Prov.; m. Xue Xia Liang 1953; three s. two d.; ed. Inst. of Shaan Bei; Deputy Dir. Public Security Dept. Jilin City 1938-49; First Deputy Dir. Guangdong Prov. Public Security Dept., Commr. Shantou Dist., Leader Guangdong Prov. Govt. 1950-77; Dir. State Seismological Bureau, State Council 1978-80; Deputy Dir. Legis. Affairs Comm., Standing Cttee., NPC 1980; Vice-Minister of Justice 1982-83, Minister 1983-88; Pres. Nat. Lawyers Asscn. 1986-; Pres. China Univ. of Political Science and Law 1985-88; mem. Standing Cttee., NPC 1988. *Publications:* The Strategic Meaning of Spreading Basic Legal Knowledge among the People 1986, The Social Position and Meaning on Civil Conciliation 1987. *Leisure interests:* music, painting, calligraphy. *Address:* 1 Qiang Zhao Jia Lou, Dong Cheng District, Beijing, People's Republic of China. *Telephone:* 55 83 61.

ZOUBI, Mahmoud; Syrian politician; b. 1938, Khirbet Ghazaleh, Dar'a governate; m.; three c.; fmr. Chair. Agric. Centre, al-Ghab; Chair. Agricultural Produce Dept. 1963-64; Dir. of Agric. and Agrarian Reform, al-Ghab Dist. 1964-68, Hama 1969-71; mem. al-Ghab Dist. Baath Party leadership; mem. Admin. Council, Agronomists' Union; mem. People's Ass. 1971; Sec. Bath Party Peasants' Bureau 1972-73; Gen. Dir. Euphrates Basin Investment Establishment 1973-76; reserve mem. Baath Party's Regional Leadership 1975-80, mem. 1980; Speaker, People's Ass. 1981-87; Prime Minister of Syria 1987-. *Address:* Office of the Prime Minister, Damascus, Syria.

ZOUNGRANA, H.E. Cardinal Paul; Burkinabê ecclesiastic; b. 3 Sept. 1917, Ouagadougou; ed. l'Institut Catholique de Paris, and Univ. Pontificale Grégorienne; ordained priest 1942; mem. Missionary Soc. of Africa; Archbishop of Ouagadougou 1960-; cr. Cardinal 1965. *Address:* Archevêché, B.P. 1472, Ouagadougou, Burkina Faso.

ZUCKERMAN, Baron (Life Peer), cr. 1971, of Burnham Thorpe in the County of Norfolk; **Solly Zuckerman,** O.M., K.C.B., M.A., M.D., D.SC., LL.D., M.R.C.S., F.R.C.P., F.R.S.; British anatomist; b. 1904, Cape Town; s. of late Moses Zuckerman; m. Lady Joan Rufus Isaacs; one s. one d.; ed. South African Coll. School, Cape Town Univ., and Univ. Coll. Hospital London; Demonstrator of Anatomy Cape Town Univ. 1923-25; Union Research Scholar 1925; Research Anatomist to London Zoological Soc. and Demonstrator of Anatomy, Univ. Coll., London 1928-32; Research Assoc. and Rockefeller Research Fellow, Yale Univ. 1933-34; William Julius Mickle Fellow, London Univ. 1935; Beit Memorial Research Fellow 1934-37; Univ. Demonstrator Human Anatomy Dept. Oxford 1934-45; Hunterian Prof. Royal Coll. of Surgeons 1937; Sands Cox Prof. of Anatomy, Birmingham Univ. 1943-68; Prof. Emer. Univs. of E. Anglia, Birmingham; Scientific Adviser British Mil. Orgs. 1939-46; Group Capt. (Hon.) R.A.F. 1943-46; Deputy Chair. Advisory Council on Scientific Policy 1948-64; Chair. Nat. Resources (Tech.) Cttee. 1951-64; mem. Agricultural Research Council 1949-59; Hon. Sec. Zoological Soc., London 1955-77; Chair. Cen. Advisory Cttee. for Science and Tech. 1965-70; Trustee, British Museum (Natural History) 1967-77; Fellow, Univ. Coll., London; Fellow Commoner, Christ's Coll., Cambridge; Pres. Parl. and Scientific Cttee. 1973-76, Asscn. Learned and Professional Society Publishers 1973-77, Fauna Preservation Soc. 1974-81, British Industrial Biol. Research Assscn. 1974-, Zoological Soc., London 1977-84; Gregynog Lecturer, Univ. of Wales 1956; Mason Lecturer, Univ. of Birmingham 1957, Lees Knowles Lecturer, Cambridge Univ. 1965, Romanes Lecturer, Oxford Univ. 1975; Rhodes Lecturer, S. Africa 1975; Chief Scientific Adviser to Sec. of State for Defence 1960-66; Chief Scientific Adviser to the Govt. 1964-71; Hon. Fellow, Royal Coll. of Surgeons, Pharmaceutical Soc. of Great Britain 1975; Hon. mem. American Acad. of Arts and Sciences; Foreign mem. American Philosophical Soc. *Publications:* The Social Life of Monkeys and Apes 1932, 1981, Functional Affinities of Man, Monkeys and Apes 1933, A New System of Anatomy 1961, 1981, Scientists and War 1966, Beyond the Ivory Tower 1970, The Ovary (editor) 1962, 1977, From Apes to Warlords 1904-46 (autobiog. Vol. I) 1978, Great Zoos of the World (ed.) 1980, Nuclear Illusion and Reality 1982, Star Wars in a Nuclear World 1986, Monkeys, Men and Missiles 1946-88 (autobiog. Vol. II) 1988. *Address:* University of East Anglia, Norwich NR4 7TJ, England. *Telephone:* (0603) 56161.

ZUIDEMA, George Dale, M.D.; American physician; b. 8 March 1928, Holland, Mich.; s. of Jacob Zuidema and Reka Zuidema; m. Joan K. Houtman 1953; one s. three d.; ed. Hope Coll., Johns Hopkins Univ.; Intern Mass. Gen. Hosp. 1953-54, Asst. Resident Surgeon, then Chief Resident Surgeon 1954-59; Asst. Prof. Surgery, then Assoc. Prof. Univ. of Mich. School of Medicine 1960-64; Prof. Surgery and Dir. of Dept. Johns Hopkins School of Medicine and Surgeon-in-Chief Johns Hopkins Hosp. 1964-84; Vice-Provost Medical Affairs Univ. Mich. 1984-, Prof. of Surgery 1984-; mem. Council on Graduate Medical Educ. 1989-(94); Trustee Hope Coll., Holland, Mich.; mem. Bd. of Dirs., William Beaumont Hosp. 1986-; Consultant Walter Reed Army Medical Center, Sinai Hosp., Baltimore, Baltimore City Hosp., Clinical Center of N.I.H.; Chair. Study on Surgical Services for U.S.A. 1970-75; John and Mary R. Markle Scholar academic medicine 1961-66, recipient Henry Russell Award Univ. of Michigan 1963; Hon. Fellow, Royal Coll. of Surgeons Ireland; mem. Assn. American Medical Colls., Central Soc. Clinical Research, Assn. of Academic Surgeons (Pres. 1967-69), Hon. D.Sc. (Hope Coll.) 1969. *Publications:* Jt. Ed. Gravitational Stress in Aerospace Medicine 1961, Jt. author Surgery—A Concise Guide to Clinical Practice 1961, Jt. author Physical Diagnosis, Jt. author Management of Trauma 1968, Jt. author Atlas of Human Functional Anatomy 1977, Ed. Journal of Surgical Research 1966-72, Co-Ed. Surgery 1975-, Surgery of the Alimentary Tract (Ed. with W. B. Saunders) 1989. *Address:* Office of the Vice-Provost for Medical Affairs, University of Michigan, Ann Arbor, Mich. 48109 (Office); 443 Huntington Place, Ann Arbor, Mich. 48104, U.S.A. (Home). *Telephone:* 313-764 2104 (Office); 313-668 0206 (Home).

ZUKERMAN, Pinchas; Israeli violinist; b. 16 July 1948, Tel Aviv; s. of Jehuda Zukerman and Miriam Zukerman; m. 1st Eugenia Rich 1968; two d.; m. 2nd Tuesday Weld 1985; ed. Israel Conservatory, Acad. of Music, Tel-Aviv, Juilliard School of Music, New York; studied with Ivan Galamian; début in New York with New York Philharmonic 1969, in U.K. at Brighton Festival 1969; concert and recital performances throughout U.S.A. and Europe; directs, tours and plays with English Chamber Orchestra; has performed at Spoleto, Pablo Casals and Edinburgh Festivals; Dir. S. Bank Summer Music 1978-80; Musical Dir. St. Paul Chamber Orchestra 1980-81, 1981-87; Leventritt Award 1967. *Address:* c/o Shirley Kirshbaum and Associates, 711 West End Avenue, New York, N.Y. 10025, U.S.A. *Telephone:* (212) 222-4843.

ZUKROWSKI, Wojciech; Polish writer; b. 14 April 1916, Cracow; s. of Zygmunt Żukrowski and Jadwiga Wojtowicz; m. Maria Woltersdorf 1945; one d.; ed. Wrocław Univ. and Jagiellonian Univ., Cracow; War Corresp., North Viet-Nam 1954; Counsellor, Polish Embassy, New Delhi 1956-58; Deputy to Seym 1972- Co-Ed. Widnokręgi (monthly) and Nowe Książki; mem. All-Poland Peace Cttee., Chief Council of Union of Fighters for Freedom and Democracy (Z BoWiD); Chair. Soc. for Polish-Spanish Friendship 1978-85; State Prize 1953, 1978 (1st Class), Ludwik Waryński Prize 1986, Maxim Gorky IBBY Prize 1986, Kt.'s and Officer's Cross, Order Polonia Restituta 1953, 1954, Award of Minister of Nat. Defence 1961, Order of Banner of Labour (1st, 2nd and 3rd, Class), Prize of Minister of Culture and Art 1963, 1965, 1969, Pietrzak Prize 1967, Order of Builders of People's Poland 1976, Prize of Prime Minister for literary production for children and youth 1977, Meritous Activist of Culture 1978, and others; mem. Polish Union of Writers, Gen. Bd. ZLP, and PEN Club. *Publications:* Short stories: Z kraju milczenia (From the Land of Silence), Piórkiem flaminga (With a Flamingo's Quill), Córeczka (Little Daughter), Okruchy weselnego tortu (Crumbs from the Wedding Cake), Ręka ojca (Father's Hand); Novels: Dni klęski (Days of Defeat), Skąpani w ogniu, Bathed in Fire (Ministry of Defence Prize 1961), Kamienne Tablice (The Stone Tables) 1966, Szczęściarz (The Lucky Devil), Plaża nad Styksem (Styx Beach) 1976, Zapach psiej sierści 1979; Travel: Dom bez ścian (House without Walls), Wędrówki z moim guru (Wanderings with my Guru: India), W królestwie miliona słoni (In the Kingdom of a Million Elephants: Laos), Nieśmiały narzeczony (Chinese legends); Fairy-tales for children: Porwanie w Tiutiurlistanie, Na tronie w Blabonie 1986; Essays: W głębi zwierciadła (Inside Mirror) 1973, Karambole (Collisions) 1973; Films: Bathed in Fire, Direction Berlin, The Last Days, Lotna, Potop, The Stone Tables. *Leisure interest:* travel. *Address:* 00-324 Warsaw, Karowa 14/16 m. 22, Poland. *Telephone:* 26 16 18.

ZULEEG, Manfred (Friedrich), DR.JUR.; German professor and international judge; b. 21 March 1935, Creglingen; s. of Ludwig Zuleeg and Thea (née Ohr) Zuleeg; m. Sigrid Feuerhahn 1965; three s. one d.; ed. Univs. of Erlangen and Hamburg, Bologna Center of Johns Hopkins Univ. in Int. Relations; Research Asst., Inst. for Law of the European Communities, Univ. of Cologne 1962-68, Sr. Lecturer 1968-71; Prof. of Public Law and Law of the European Communities, Univ. of Bonn 1971-78; Prof. of Public Law, including European and Public Int. Law, Univ. of Frankfurt 1978-88; Judge, Court of Justice, European Communities 1988-; Research Fellow Univ. of California, Berkeley 1969-70. *Publications:* Die Rechtsform der Subventionen 1965, Das Recht der Europäischen Gemeinschaften im innerstaatlichen Bereich 1969, Subventionskontrolle durch Konkurrentenklage 1974; contrib. to other works. *Leisure interests:* jogging, mountaineering, literature. *Address:* Court of Justice of the European Communities, L-2925, Luxembourg (Office); Kaiser-Sigmund-Strasse 32, 6000 Frankfurt 1, Federal Republic of Germany (Home). *Telephone:* 00 352/ 43 03 22 30 (Office); 06 11/ 56 43 93 (Home).

ZULU, Alexander Grey; Zambian politician; b. 3 Sept. 1924, Chipata, Eastern Province; s. of Agrippa and Tionenji Zulu; m. 1952; four s. four d.; ed. Mafuta Lower Primary School and Munali Secondary School; Water Devt. Asst., Northern Rhodesia 1950-53; Bookkeeper/Man. Kabwe Co-operative Soc. 1953-62; Parl. Sec., Northern Rhodesia 1963; Minister of Commerce and Industry 1964, of Transport and Works 1964, of Mines and Co-operatives 1965-67, of Home Affairs 1967-70, of Defence 1970-73; Sec. of State (subsequently Chair. of Sub-Cttee.) for Defence and Security 1979-85; Sec.-Gen. United Nat. Independence Party (UNIP) 1973-79, 1985-; M.P. 1979-. *Address:* Private Bag RW 17X, Lusaka, Zambia.

ZULU, Justin B., PH.D.; Zambian international finance official; b. 15 Aug. 1934; m. Gertrude K. Kazunga 1965; three s. one d.; ed. Univ. of Colorado; Gov. of Bank of Zambia 1967-70; Special Asst. to Pres. of Zambia 1970-71; Adviser to an Exec. Dir. of IMF 1971-74, Alt. Exec. Dir. 1974-76, Deputy Dir. 1976, Dir. African Dept. 1976-84, Dir. Cen. Banking Dept. IMF 1984-. *Leisure interests:* reading, soccer, table tennis. *Address:* International Monetary Fund, 700 19th Street, N.W., Washington, D.C. 20431, U.S.A. *Telephone:* 623-8560.

ZUMWALT, Admiral Elmo Russell, Jr., B.SC.; American naval officer; b. 29 Nov. 1920, San Francisco, Calif.; s. of Dr. Elmo Russell Zumwalt and Dr. Frances Z. Frank; m. Mouza Coutelais-du-Roche 1945; two s. two d.; ed. U.S. Naval Acad., Naval War Coll., Nat. War Coll.; commissioned Ensign, U.S. Navy 1942, advanced through ranks to Adm. 1970; service on USS Phelps 1942-43, USS Robinson 1943-45, USS Saufley 1945-46, USS Zellars 1946-48; Asst. Prof. Naval Science 1948-50; Commdg. Officer USS Tills 1950-51; Navigator USS Wisconsin 1951-52; Head Shore and Overseas Bases Section, Naval Personnel, Washington 1953-55; Commdg. Officer USS Arnold J. Isbell 1955-57; LT Detailer, Naval Personnel 1957; Special Asst. for Naval Personnel, Officer of Asst. Sec. of the Navy, Washington 1957-58, Exec. Asst., Sr. Aide 1958-59; Commdg. Officer USS Dewey 1959-61; Desk Officer for France, Spain and Portugal, Office of Asst. Sec. of Defense for Int. Security Affairs 1962-63; Dir. Arms Control and Contingency Planning for Cuba 1963; Exec. Asst., Sr. Aide, Sec. of Navy 1963-65; Commdg. Officer Cruiser-Destroyer Flotilla Seven 1965-66; Dir. Chief Naval Operations Systems Analysis Group, Washington 1966-68; Commdr. U.S. Naval Forces, Vietnam, Chief, Naval Advisory Group Vietnam 1968-70; Chief of Naval Operations 1970-74; Pres. Adm. Zumwalt and Assocs. Inc. 1978-85, Pres. Adm. Zumwalt Consultants 1986-; Chair. and C.E.O., American Medical Bldg. 1983-85, Chair. 1985-; Gov. American Stock Exchange 1979-85; Dir. American Bldg. Maintenance Industries, Esmark, Inc. 1975-84, Gifford-Hill & Co., Inc., 1980-86, Navistar Int. Co., Transway Int. Corpn. 1976-85, Unicorp American Corpn., Langley Corpn., NL Industries Inc., Fleet Aerospace Corpn., Aeronea Inc., Airship Industries Inc., AP Industries, Fathom Oceanology Ltd.; Chair. Phelps-Stokes Fund; Chair. Ethics and Public Policy Center; Distinguished Service Medal with Gold Star, Legion of Merit with Gold Star, Bronze Star Medal with Combat V, Navy Commendation Medal with Combat V, and many other national and foreign decorations; Hon. LL.D. (Villanova, Univ. of N.C.,

Nat Univ.), Hon. D. Hum. Litt. (U.S. Int. Univ.), Hon. Dr. Public Service (Central Mich. Univ.). *Publications:* On Watch 1976, My Father, My Son 1986, syndicated columns. *Leisure interests:* jogging, tennis. *Address:* Admiral Zumwalt Consultants, 1500 Wilson Boulevard, Arlington, Va. 22209, U.S.A. (Office). *Telephone:* (703) 841 8960 (Office).

ZUNINO REGGIO, Pio; Italian business executive; b. 8 March 1920, Venice; s. of Mario Zunino Reggio and Isabella Rosso di Cerami; m. Beatrice Zileri Dal Verme 1944; five c.; ed. Univ. of Padua; joined staff of Petrocaltex (later known as Caltex Italiana and from 1967 as Chevron Oil Italiana S.p.A.) 1951; Dir. Bologna Sales Area Office, Caltex 1969, Dir. N. Italy Div. 1964; assigned to Chevron Oil Europe, New York, U.S.A. 1968-69; Sales Man. and mem. Bd. of Dirs. Chevron Oil Italiana S.p.A. 1970, Vice-Pres. and Gen. Man. 1977, Pres. and Man. Dir. 1981-; mem. Bd. of Dirs. of VECAL S.p.A. 1967-70, of CAPO S.p.A. 1969-70; Pres. SERAM S.p.A. 1977-79, 1985-; Vice-Pres. Raffineria di Roma S.p.A. 1981-; Bd. mem. SARPOM S.p.A. 1981-; mem. Exec. Cttee. Italian Petroleum Fed. 1981-; Commendatore dell'Ordine al Merito della Repubblica Italiana 1974. *Leisure interests:* sailing, skiing. *Address:* Chevron Oil Italiana S.p.A., via V. Brancati 60, 00144 Rome (Office); via di Villa Patrizi 4, 00161 Rome, Italy (Home). *Telephone:* (06) 500921 (Office).

ZUNTZ, Günther, D.PHIL., F.B.A.; British (b. German) academic; b. 28 Jan. 1902, Berlin; s. of Leo Zuntz and Edith Bähring; m. Mary Alyson Garratt 1947; two s. one d.; ed. Bismark-Gymnasium, Berlin-Wilmersdorf Univs. of Berlin, Marburg, Göttingen and Graz; teacher at Odenwaldschule 1924-26, at Marburg Gymnasium and Kassel Gymnasium 1926-32; worked for Monumenta Musicae Byzantinae, Copenhagen 1935-39, Oxford 1939-47; Librarian, Mansfield Coll., Oxford 1944-47; Sr. Lecturer Manchester Univ. 1947-55, Reader 1955-63, Prof. of Hellenistic Greek 1963-69, currently Prof. Emer.; Corresp. mem. Austrian Akademie der Wissenschaften 1974, Heidelberger Akademie der Wissenschaften 1984; D.Phil. h.c. Tübingen 1983. *Publications:* Hölderlins Pindar-Übersetzung 1928, Prophetologium I-V (with C. Höeg) 1939-78, The Ancestry of the Harklean New Testament 1945, The Text of the Epistles 1953, The Political Plays of Euripides 1955, The Transmission of Plays of Euripides 1965, Persephone 1971, Opuscula Selecta 1972, Ein griechischer Lehrgang 1983, Drei Kapitel zur Griechischen Metrik 1984, and articles in many learned journals. *Leisure interest:* music. *Address:* 1 Humberstone Road, Cambridge, England. *Telephone:* 357789.

ZUO GUANGRUI; Chinese space technologist; b. 1934, Liaoning; ed. Harbin Industrial Univ. 1960; Leader of China's rocket programme. *Address:* Beijing Institute of Control Engineering, Beijing, People's Republic of China.

ZURAYK, Constantine Kaysar, M.A., PH.D.; Lebanese educationist; b. 18 April 1909; s. of Kaysar Zurayk and Afifeh Khoury; m. Najla Cortas 1940; four d.; ed. American Univ. of Beirut, Univ. of Chicago and Princeton Univ.; Asst. Prof. of History, American Univ. of Beirut 1930-42, Assoc. Prof. 1942-45; First Counsellor, Syrian Legation, Washington 1945-46; Syrian Minister to U.S.A. 1946-47; Vice-Pres. and Prof. of History, American Univ. of Beirut 1947-49; Rector, Syrian Univ., Damascus 1949-52; Vice-Pres. American Univ. of Beirut 1952-54, Acting Pres. 1954-57, Distinguished Prof. of History 1956-77, Prof. Emer. 1977-; del. UN Gen. Ass. and Alt. Rep. of Syria on Security Council 1946-47; Pres. Inst. Asscn. of Univs. 1965-70, Hon. Pres. 1970-; Chair. Bd. of Trustees, Inst. for Palestine Studies 1965-; mem. Iraq Acad., Arab Acad., Damascus, American Historical Asscn.; Order of Merit (distinguished class) (Syria); Educ. Medal (First Class), Commdr., Order of Cedar (Lebanon). *Publications:* Al-Wa'y al Qawmi (National Consciousness), Ma'na al-Nakbah (The Meaning of the Disaster), Ayyu Ghadin (Whither Tomorrow?), Nahnu wa-l-Tarikh (Facing History), Hadha al-' Asr al-Mutafajjir (This Explosive Age), Fi Ma'rakat al-Hadarah (In the Battle for Culture), Ma'na al-Nakbah Mujaddadan (The Meaning of the Disaster Again); Nahnu wa-l-Mustaqbal (Facing the Future), Matalib al-Mustaqbal (The Demands of the Future); Ed. Isma'il Beg Chol's Al-Yazidiyyah qadiman wa hadithan (Yazidis past and present), Ibn al-Furat's History Vols. VII-IX (with Najla Izzedin); Ed. and Trans. Miskawayh's Tahdhib al-Akhlaq (The Refinement of Character). *Leisure interests:* reading, walking, social activities. *Address:* c/o American University of Beirut, Beirut, Lebanon (Office); Artois Street, Beirut, Lebanon (Home). *Telephone:* Beirut 343174 (Home).

ZUYDTWYCK, Baron Constantin Bonifatius Hermann Josef Maria Heereman von; German farmer; b. 17 Dec. 1931, Münster; s. of Baron Theodor Heereman and Elisabeth (née von Bongart) von Zuydtwyck; m. Margarethe von Wrede 1956; one s. four d.; farmer in Surenberg 1955-; Pres. Westphalia regional Farmers' Asscn. 1968-; Pres. German Farmers' Asscn. 1969-; Pres. Cttee. of Agricultural Orgs. in the European Community 1979-81; Pres. Int. Fed. of Agricultural Producers 1982; Bundesverdienstkreuz; Prize of the Italian Agricultural Press. *Publication:* Not Only With A Green View of Everything (in German) 1982. *Leisure interests:* hunting, horses, skiing. *Address:* Schloss Surenberg, 4441 Hörstel Riesenbeck, Federal Republic of Germany. *Telephone:* (0) 5454-377.

ZUYEV, Vladimir Yvseyevich; Soviet physicist; b. 1925, Malye gory, Irkutsk Dist.; s. of late Evsei F. and Paulina I. Zuyev; m. Nina I. Zueva 1946; one s. two d.; ed. Univ. of Tomsk; mem. CPSU 1945-; served in

Soviet Army 1943–46; post-graduate, Asst. Prof. Tomsk Univ. 1951–55; on staff of Siberian Physico-Tech. Inst. of Tomsk Univ., Sr. Researcher, then Head of Lab., then Deputy Dir. 1955–69; Prof. Tomsk Univ. 1966–; Dir. of Siberian Div. of U.S.S.R. Acad. of Sciences Inst. of Atmospheric Optics 1969–; Corresp. mem. of U.S.S.R. Acad. of Sciences 1970, mem. 1981–; Pres. of Presidium of Tomsk Br. of Siberian Div. of Acad. of Sciences 1979–; Deputy to U.S.S.R. Supreme Soviet 1970–84; Hero of Socialist Labour 1985, Order of Lenin, Order of Patriotic War, Order of Red Banner of Labour (twice), Order of Badge of Honour and various medals. *Leisure interests:* skiing, long-distance running, classical and folk music. *Address:* U.S.S.R. Academy of Sciences Institute of Atmospheric Optics, Ul. Gertsena 8, Tomsk, 634055, U.S.S.R.

ZUZE, Peter Dingiswayo; Zambian diplomatist; b. 18 Dec. 1942; m.; four c.; ed. Munali Secondary School; joined Zambian Air Force 1965, Commdr., Operations Squadron 1968, Commdr., Helicopter Squadron 1970, Chief of Staff (Air) 1971, Air Commdr. 1972; Deputy Commdr., Chief of Gen. Staff, Zambia Nat. Defence 1976–77, Commdr., Chief of Gen. Staff 1977; High Comm. in Canada 1979–82, in U.K. 1982–86; Perm. Rep. of Zambia to UN 1986–. *Address:* Permanent Mission of Zambia to the United Nations, 237 East 52nd Street, New York, N.Y. 10022, U.S.A. *Telephone:* 758-1110.

ZVEREV, Aleksey Ilyich; Soviet politician; b. 1929; ed. Byelorlussian Agric. Acad.; chief agronomist, Inst. of Agronomy, Moscow 1951–56; mem. CPSU 1951–; Sec., Second, First Sec. of Regional Cttee. of CPSU in Novossibirsk Dist. 1956–62; Sec., Second Sec. of Novossibirsk Dist. Cttee. of CPSU 1962–64, Pres. 1964–73; R.S.F.S.R. Minister of Forestry 1973–84; Pres. of U.S.S.R. State Comm. on Forestry 1984–88; mem. of CPSU Cen. Auditing Comm. 1986–89. *Address:* c/o U.S.S.R. State Commission on Forestry, The Kremlin, Moscow, U.S.S.R.

ZVIAK, Charles, L.ès SC.; French business executive; b. 8 Feb. 1922, Paris; s. of Adolphe Zviak and Sora Schitzgal; m. Bernardette Krouck 1950; two d.; ed. Lycée Arago, Coll. Chaptal, Faculté des Sciences and Ecole Nat. Supérieure de Chimie, Paris; Chemical Eng. Monsavon-L'Oreal 1945–53; Man. Research Labs. L'Oreal 1953–73, Vice-Pres. 1965, Vice-Pres. and Gen. Man. 1973–84, Pres., Dir. Gen. 1984–; Pres. Int. Fed. of Socs. of Cosmetic Chemists 1969–70; Chevalier, Légion d'honneur. *Publications:* Problèmes capillaires 1966, Recherche industrielle et Marketing 1973, The Science of Hair Care 1986. *Address:* L'Oreal, 41 rue Martre, 92110 Clichy (Office); 1 rue Soldini, 95130 Franconville, France (Home). *Telephone:* 4759.88.19 (Office); 34.13.12.13 (Home).

ZWANE, Ambrose Phesheya, M.B., B.CH.; Swazi medical practitioner and politician; b. 30 April 1924, Manzini, Swaziland; ed. St. Joseph's Catholic Mission, Manzini, Inkamana R.C.S., Vryheid, Natal, S. African Native Coll., Fort Hare, and Univ. of Witwatersrand; as a child, looked after cattle at Bulunga, Manzini, Swaziland; House physician, Charles Johnson Memorial Hosp. 1952; Medical Officer, Anglican Mission Hosp. 1953–59, Swaziland Colonial Admin. 1959–60; Gen. Sec. Swaziland Progressive Party (S.P.P.) 1960–61, split with S.P.P. 1961; Pres. Ngwane Nat. Liberatory Congress; M.P. 1972–73; under detention May–July 1973, July–Sept. 1973, Jan.–March 1974, Oct.–Dec. 1975, 1978; escaped to Mozambique, repatriated to Swaziland from Tanzania under amnesty from King Sobhuza 1979; publ. two newspapers Kusile Ngwane (monthly) and Ngwane Forum (monthly). *Address:* Manzini, Swaziland.

ZWANZIG, Robert Walter, M.S., PH.D.; American professor of chemical physics; b. 9 April 1928, Brooklyn, N.Y.; s. of Walter Zwanzig and Bertha Weil Zwanzig; m. Francis Ryder Zwanzig 1953; one s. one d.; ed. Polytechnic Inst. of Brooklyn, Univ. of Southern Calif. and Calif. Inst. of Techn.; Research Fellow, Yale Univ. 1951–54; Asst. Prof. Chem., Johns Hopkins Univ. 1954–58; Physical Chemist Nat. Bureau of Standards, Washington, D.C. 1958–66; Research Prof., Inst. for Physical Science and Tech., Univ. of Md. 1966–80, Distinguished Prof. of Physical Science 1980–88, Research Chemist N.I.H. 1988–; Fellow, American Acad. of Arts and Sciences; mem. of Nat. Acad. of Sciences; Silver Medal, U.S. Dept. of Commerce; Peter Debye Award in Physical Chem. (A.C.S.) 1976, Irving Langmuir Award in Chemical Physics 1984. *Publications:* about 110 articles in scientific periodicals. *Address:* Laboratory of Chemical Physics, National Institutes of Health, Bethesda, Md. 20892 (Office); 5314 Sangamore Road, Bethesda, Md. 20816, U.S.A. (Home). *Telephone:* 301-496-8048 (Office).

ZWAVELING, Albert, M.D., PH.D.; Netherlands professor of surgery; b. 21 July 1927, Schoonebeek; s. of Jan H. Zwaveling and Engeline F. (née Hinnen) Zwaveling; m. 1st Susanna M. van Soest 1952 (died 1966); one s.; m. 2nd Anna M. F. Bloem 1969; two d.; ed. State Univ. of Utrecht, University Hosp., Leiden; Mil. doctor (rank of maj.) 1954–57; Gen. Practioner in Indonesia 1957–58; surgical trainee, Leiden 1958–63; Fellow in Oncology, Univ. of Wis., U.S.A. 1963–64; Jr. Consultant 1964–68; Assoc. Prof. of Surgical Oncology, Leiden Univ. 1968–72, Prof. of Surgery 1972–; Head, Dept. of Surgery, Univ. Hosp., Leiden 1981–; Chair. Concilium Chirurgicum Utrecht 1985, Medical Staff Univ. Hosp., Leiden 1986; mem. Royal Netherlands Acad. of Sciences 1979; Hon. mem. Dutch Soc. of Oncology, Dutch Assen. of Surgery 1987; awarded Rotgans Medal of Nat. Cancer Inst. 1963, Zwanenberg Award 1969. *Publications:* Dutch Textbook of Oncology (3rd edition) 1986, Dutch Textbook of Surgery (3rd edition) 1988; 6 monographs on oncology, mainly cancer; more than 120 scientific

papers. *Leisure interests:* collecting modern plastic art, gardening. *Address:* University Hospital, Leiden (Office); Vlietpark 4, 2355 CT Hoogmade, Netherlands (Home). *Telephone:* 071-264005 (Office); 01712-8622 (Home).

ZWEIGERT, Konrad Erdmann, DR.JUR.; German lawyer; b. 22 Jan. 1911, Posen; s. of Erich Zweigert and E. Nagel; m. Irmgard Koenigs 1946; nine c.; ed. Univs. of Grenoble, London, Barcelona, Berlin, Göttingen; Research Assoc. Kaiser-Wilhelm (later Max Planck) Inst. of Private Int. Law and Comparative Law 1937; Prof. of Law, Univ. of Tübingen 1948; Justice, Fed. Constitutional Court, Karlsruhe 1951–56; Prof. of Law, Univ. of Hamburg 1956; Dir. Max Planck Inst. of Private Int. and Foreign Law 1963–79; mem. of Bd. Int. Cttee. on Comparative Law 1955; Pres. Int. Assen. of Legal Science 1964; Vice-Pres. Max-Planck-Gesellschaft zur Förderung der Wissenschaften 1967–78; Dr. h.c. (Uppsala 1974, Paris 1975, Southampton 1979). *Publications:* numerous books and articles on Comparative Law including: Die Einwirkung des Krieges auf Verträge 1941, Einführung in die Rechtsvergleichung 2 vols. 1969–71; Gen. Ed. International Encyclopedia of Comparative Law 1971. *Address:* Baron-Voght-Strasse 63, 2000 Hamburg 52, Federal Republic of Germany. *Telephone:* 040-41-27-1.

ZWERENZ, Gerhard; German writer; b. 3 June 1925, Gablenz; s. of Rudolf and Liesbeth Zwerenz; m. Ingrid Hoffman 1957; one d.; ed. Univ. of Leipzig; worked as coppersmith 1939–42; army service 1942–44, deserted to join Red Army 1944; P.O.W. in Minsk, U.S.S.R. 1944–48; obliged to serve with G.D.R. police 1948–50; studied at Leipzig Univ. 1952–56; first publication 1956; expelled from CP, fled to W. Berlin 1957; Ernst Reuter Prize 1975, Carl-von-Ossietžky-preis 1986. *Publications:* 65 books including Aufs Rad geflochten 1959, Die Liebe der toten Männer 1959, Heldengedenktag 1964, Rasputin 1970, Der Widerspruch 1974, Die Westdeutschen 1977, Die Ehe der Maria Braun 1979, Der lange Tod des Rainer-Werner Fassbinder 1982.

ZWICK, Charles John, B.S., PH.D.; American economist and banker; b. 17 July 1926, Plantsville; s. of Louis C. Zwick and Mabel (née Rich) Zwick; m. Joan Cameron 1952; one s. one d.; ed. Univ. of Connecticut and Harvard Univ.; Instructor, Univ. of Conn. 1951; Harvard Univ. 1954–56; Head, Logistics Dept. the RAND Corpn. 1956–63, mem. Research Council 1963–65; Asst. Dir. U.S. Bureau of the Budget 1965–68, Dir. 1968–69; Pres. Southeast Banking Corpn., Miami July 1969–; Chair. and C.E.O. 1982–; Chair. Bd. and C.E.O. Southeast Bank 1982–; Dir. Manville Corpn. and numerous other companies; Chair. Pres.'s Comm. on Mil. Compensation; Trustee, Carnegie Endowment for Int. Peace; mem. Reserve City Bankers Assen., The Conference Bd., Council of the Int. Exec. Service Corps, Econ. Soc. of S. Fla., Council of 100. *Address:* P.O. Box 2500, Miami, Florida 33101; 4210 Santa Maria Street, Coral Gables, Fla. 33146 U.S.A. (Home). *Telephone:* 305-577-4015 (Office); 305-666-9208 (Home).

ZYGMUND, Antoni, PH.D.; American university professor; b. 26 Dec. 1900, Warsaw, Poland; s. of Wincenty and Antonina (Perkowska) Zygmund; m. Irena Parnowska 1925; one s.; ed. Univ. of Warsaw; Instructor, Polytechnical School, Warsaw 1922–29; Docent, Univ. of Warsaw 1926–30; Prof. Univ. of Wilno, Poland 1930–39; Prof. Mount Holyoke Coll., South Hadley, Mass. 1940–45; Prof., Univ. of Pa. 1945–47; Prof. Univ. of Chicago 1947–, now Emer.; mem. N.A.S., Polish, Italian, Spanish and Argentine Acads.; Dr. h.c. (Washington, St. Louis, Torun (Poland), Uppsala, Paris-Sud); Distinguished Service Prof. Univ. of Chicago; Hon. mem. London Math. Soc. *Publications:* Trigonometric Series 1935, 1959, Analytic Functions (with S. Saks) 1938, 1965, Measure and Integral (with R. Wheeden) 1977. *Address:* Department of Mathematics, University of Chicago, Chicago, Ill. 60637 (Office); 5420 East View Park, Chicago, Ill. 60615 U.S.A. (Home). *Telephone:* (312) 643-6913 (Home).

ZYGULSKI, Kazimierz, H.H.D.; Polish professor and politician; b. 8 Dec. 1919, Wolanka; s. of Zdzisław and Maria Żygulski; m. Helena Gutkowa 1955; one s.; ed. Univ. of Lwów (now Lvov, U.S.S.R.); in resistance movement in Lwów Voivodship during Nazi occupation; imprisoned in U.S.S.R. 1944–56; researcher, Sociology and History of Culture Research Centre of Polish Acad. of Sciences, Łódź 1956–59; scientific worker, Philosophy and Sociology Inst. of Polish Acad. of Sciences, Warsaw 1959–, Extraordinary Prof. 1973–83, Ordinary Prof. 1983–; Pro-Rector, State Film, TV and Theatrical Higher School, Łódź 1970–71; counsellor to Deputy Chair. of Council of Ministers 1971–72; Minister of Culture and Art 1982–86; mem. Polish Cttee. ICOM 1972–, mem. Presidium State Prizes Cttee. 1975–, mem. Presidium Nat. Council for Culture 1983–; Chair. Polish Nat. Comm. for UNESCO 1987–; mem. UNESCO Exec. Bd. 1987–; Officer's Cross Order of Polonia Restituta. *Publications:* numerous research works and monographs on sociology of culture. *Leisure interest:* history of art. *Address:* Polski Komitet ds. UNESCO, Patac Kultury i Nauki, 17 piętro, 00-901 Warsaw (Office); ul. Madalińskiego 50/52, 02-581 Warsaw, Poland (Home).

ZYKINA, Lyudmila Georgiyevna; Soviet singer; b. 1929; ed. Ippolitov-Ivanov Music School; soloist with Pyatnitsky Choir 1947–50; soloist with Choir for Russian Vocal Music of Union Radio and TV Station 1959; soloist with Moskontsert 1960–; People's Artist of the R.S.F.S.R. 1968; Lenin Prize 1970; People's Artist of the U.S.S.R. 1973.

ZYKOV, Spartak Sergeyevich; Soviet diplomatist; b. 1925; Counsellor, Embassy in Somalia 1960–63, in Ethiopia 1964–71; Counsellor-Envoy,

with Moskontsert 1960–; People's Artist of the R.S.F.S.R. 1968; Lenin Prize 1970; People's Artist of the U.S.S.R. 1973.

ZYKOV, Spartak Sergeyevich; Soviet diplomatist; b. 1925; Counsellor, Embassy in Somalia 1960–63, in Ethiopia 1964–71; Counsellor-Envoy, Embassy in Mali 1971–74, in Algeria 1974–78; Amb. to Chad 1979, to Cameroon 1980–87. *Address:* c/o Ministry of Foreign Affairs, Moscow, U.S.S.R.

ZYLIS-GARA, Teresa; Polish artist and singer; b. 23 Jan. 1935, Vilnius; m., one c.; ed. State Higher School of Music, Łódź 1954; soloist, Cracow Philharmonic 1954–58 and Cracow Opera 1958–59; foreign contracts in operas: Oberhausen 1961–63, Städtische Bühnen, Dortmund 1963–65, Deutsche Oper am Rhein, Düsseldorf 1965–70; *debuts abroad:* Paris Opera 1966, San Francisco Opera 1968, Metropolitan Opera, New York 1968, Royal Opera House, Covent Garden 1968, Vienna Opera 1970, Nat. Theatre, Prague 1974, Nat. Theatre, Budapest 1976, Great Theatre, Warsaw 1976, La Scala, Milan 1977, Bolshoi Theatre, Moscow 1978, Teatro Colon, Buenos Aires 1981; *participation in festivals include:* Glyndbourne Festival 1965, Salzburg Festival 1968, Festival Aix-en-Provence 1972, Festival in Ancient Theatre, Orange 1975; performances in many countries; regular performances in Metropolitan Opera in New York in various opera parts 1968–; Prime Minister's Prize (1st Class) 1979; Kt.'s Cross Order of Polonia Restituta. *Address:* 16A Boulevard de Belgique, Principality of Monaco.

ZYMIERSKI, Marshal Michał (pseudonym Rola); Polish army officer; b. 4 September 1890, Cracow; s. of Wojciech and Maria Zymierski; m. Sofia Zymierski 1933; one d.; ed. Jagiellonian Univ., Cracow 1910–14, Commercial Acad., Cracow 1912–13, École Superieure de Guerre, Paris 1921–24; participant of struggle for independence in Polish Rifle Brigades 1910–14, to rank of battalion commdr. heavily wounded in the battle of Laski, rank of Lieut.-Col., regt. commdr. of Polish Legions 1914–17, Col., Chief of Staff 2nd Polish Corps in the East 1918; Polish Army 1919–; Chief of Headquarters Agy., Sosnowiec, organizer of assistance for the first Silesian Rising 1919, brigade commdr., divisional commdr. 1919–20, Brig-Gen. 1924, Deputy Chief of Army Admin. for Armament 1924–26; political prisoner 1926–31; émigre in France 1931–38; participant of Resistance Movement during German occupation, mil. adviser in Headquarters of People's Guard 1943, mem. Presidium Nat. People's Council and Commdr.-in-Chief People's Army 1944; General-in-Arms 1944; Head Dept. of Nat. Defence Polish Cttee. of Nat. Liberation, co-organizer Polish People's Army 1944–45; Marshal of Poland 1945–; C.-in-C. Polish People's Army, Minister of Nat. Defence 1945–49; mem. State Council 1949–52; imprisoned 1952–55; Vice-Pres. Polish Nat. Bank and Pres. Council of Commercial Bank Co. Ltd., Warsaw 1956–68; Emer. 1968–; Deputy to Legis. Seym 1947–52; Hon. Pres. Union of Fighters for Freedom and Democracy (ZBoWiD); mem. Polish Workers' Party 1943–48, PZPR 1948–; mem. PZPR Cen. Cttee 1981–; Grand Cross of Polonia Restituta Order, Order of Banner of Labour (1st Class), and numerous other Polish and foreign decorations, Hon. Citizen of Cracow, Lublin, Chełm and 17 other towns. *Leisure interests:* riding, hunting, theatres and museums. *Address:* ul. Narbutta 7 m. 10, 02-564 Warsaw, Poland. *Telephone:* 49-25-09.

ŻYTA, Józef, LL.M.; Polish lawyer and state official; b. 1927, Żytniów, Częstochowa Voivodship; ed. Faculty of Law, Wrocław Univ.; worker in Staff Schooling Inst. –1956; official in organizational units of Prosecutor's Office 1956–, including posts of Dist. Prosecutor, Deputy Voivodship Prosecutor, Voivodship Prosecutor in Gdańsk and recently Deputy Prosecutor-Gen. of Poland; Prosecutor-Gen. of Poland May 1984–; mem. Polish United Workers' Party (PZPR); mem. PZPR Cen. Control and Revisional Comm. 1986–; Order of Banner of Labour (2nd Class), Officer's and Kt.'s Crosses of Order of Polonia Restituta and other decorations. *Address:* Prokuratura Generalna PRL, ul. Krakowskie Przedmieście 25, 00-071 Warsaw, Poland.